R COLUMBIA UNIVERSITY PRESS PUBLICATIONS

umbia Granger's® World of Poetry Online at www.columbiagrangers.org

Classic Writings on Poetry.

William Harmon, ed. (2003)

THE COLU

GRANGE

INDEX TO P

IN ANTHOL

OTH

The C

THE COLUMBIA GRANGER'S® INDEX TO POETRY IN ANTHOLOGIES

THIRTEENTH EDITION, COMPLETELY REVISED
INDEXING ANTHOLOGIES
PUBLISHED THROUGH MAY 31, 2006

EDITED BY

TESSA KALE

COLUMBIA UNIVERSITY PRESS
NEW YORK

THE COLUMBIA GRANGER'S® INDEX TO POETRY
IN ANTHOLOGIES

COPYRIGHT © 1904, 1918, 1929, 1940, 1945, 1953, 1957, 1962,
1973, 1978, 1982, 1986, 1990, 1994, 1996, 1997, 2002, 2007
BY COLUMBIA UNIVERSITY PRESS

THIRTEENTH EDITION COMPLETELY REVISED

LIBRARY OF CONGRESS CATALOGING-IN-PUBLICATION DATA

Kale, Tessa.
The Columbia Granger's index to poetry in
Anthologies. 13th ed., completely rev., indexing anthologies published through May
31, 2006 / edited by Tessa Kale.
p. cm.
ISBN 978–0–231–13988–5
    1. Poetry—Indexes. 2. English poetry—Indexes.
I. Kale, Tessa. Index to poetry.
PN1022.H39   2007
016.80881—dc22   2006014853
                                                             CIP

CASEBOUND EDITIONS OF COLUMBIA UNIVERSITY PRESS BOOKS
ARE PRINTED ON PERMANENT AND DURABLE ACID-FREE PAPER.
THIS BOOK WAS PRINTED ON PAPER WITH RECYCLED CONTENT.

PRINTED IN THE UNITED STATES OF AMERICA
c   10   9   8   7   6   5   4   3   2   1

CONTENTS

PREFACE ix

HOW TO USE THE INDEXES xi

LIST OF ANTHOLOGIES xv

ABBREVIATIONS xxix

TITLE, FIRST LINE, AND LAST LINE INDEX 1

AUTHOR INDEX 1437

SUBJECT INDEX 1757

The Columbia Granger's® Index to Poetry in Anthologies

THIRTEENTH EDITION

PUBLISHER
Jim Jordan

REFERENCE PUBLISHER
Karen Casey

DIRECTOR OF DESIGN AND PRODUCTION
Linda Secondari

EDITOR
Tessa Kale

MANAGING EDITOR FOR REFERENCE AND ELECTRONIC PUBLISHING
Stephen Sterns

ASSISTANT EDITOR
Alexander Samsky

STAFF

MK Babcock	Dan Glauber
Alyson Berman	Elizabeth Jardine
Nick Bredie	Rita Sanchez

PREFACE

Granger's is one of the oldest continuously published reference works in the United States. Since the fourth edition in 1953, the book has been in fact, if not in name, The Columbia Granger's® Index to Poetry in Anthologies.

The words "in Anthologies" are new since the eleventh edition. They distinguish this volume from its companion, *The Columbia Granger's® Index to Poetry in Collected and Selected Works,* which was first published in 1996. With the publication of that volume, Granger's effectively became a two-volume work indexing the two types of poetry book most frequently shelved by libraries—anthologies and collections of the work of individual authors.

In this volume we return to anthologies. The thirteenth edition locates 70,000 poems, by title, first line, author, and subject, all the poetry in anthologies that the Press, together with the members of our Board of Consultants, identified as those whose high editorial and design standards mark them as likely to be found on library shelves. Of these anthologies, 150 are new. This is the first volume to include some poetry from other languages: Spanish, Vietnamese, and French. Anthologies of translations are here too.

This edition indexes 12,257 authors writing from all parts of the world, and from remotest antiquity to present. They write on more than 4,500 subjects, ranging from acrobats to zoos. In the subject index we have arranged citations alphabetically by authors' names.

We provide last-line indexing for 10,000 of the most frequently anthologized poems.

HOW TO USE THE INDEXES

This volume is divided into three sections:
 —Title, First Line, and Last Line Index
 —Author Index
 —Subject Index

Each section is arranged alphabetically.

Every poem covered here is cited at least once in each of the three sections (except for those not in the Author Index because their author is unknown, or not in the Subject Index because they are too abstract to be assigned to any heading there). Every poem cited here appears in at least one anthology listed on pages xiii–xxvi.

See also the explanatory notes at the beginning of each of the three sections, pages 1, 1437, and 1757.

Title, First Line, and Last Line Index

The clearest way to explain the Title, First Line, and Last Line Index is to begin by showing how it answers specific questions brought to it.

Where can I find a poem called "A Bad Time for the Sublime"? Go to the Title, First Line, and Last Line Index. The citation for "A Bad Time for the Sublime" is followed by the name of the poem's author, Kay Ryan, and by the letter code OxBoAm. (The articles "a" and "the" are transposed, so you would look under "B" for "Bad.") Look up OxBoAm in the List of Anthologies, where the codes, not the titles of anthologies, are arranged alphabetically. There you learn that you can read "A Bad Time for the Sublime" in *The Oxford Book of American Poetry* edited by David Lehman and published by Oxford University Press in 2006.

What is the title of the poem that begins "I struck the board and cried, No more"? The first-line citation is followed by the title, "The Collar," and then by the author, George Herbert, and 62 letter codes, including NOP5 and BASC, which stand for anthologies. The List of Anthologies shows that they are *The Norton Anthology of Poetry, 5th Edition* (W. W. Norton, 2005) and *The Broadview Anthology of Seventeenth Century Poetry* (Broadview Press, 2000).

What poem ends with the line "We have become beautiful without even knowing it"? The last-line citation is followed by the title, "Nightclub," and then by the author, Billy Collins, and three letter codes, FaoP, GoPo, and SUP. The List of Anthologies indicates that the title of the anthology coded FaoP is *The Face of Poetry* (University of California Press, 2005), *Good Poetry* (edited by Garrison Keillor, Viking, 2002), and *Stand up Poetry* (University of Iowa Press, 2002).

First Lines and Last Lines.   First-line and last-line citations are followed by the title (except where the poem has no title). The sign (LL) following last-line citations distinguishes them from first lines.

You know, for example, that "They also serve who only stand and wait" is not a title because the title, "On His Blindness," follows it, and because the initial letters of all the words (except the first one) are lowercase. You know that the citation is a last line and not a first line because it is followed by (LL).

When the first line or the last line of a poem is the same as or slightly longer than the title, most often only one of them is listed. The poem with the first line "And did those feet in ancient time," has no listing for title because the title is the same.

Brackets. Brackets usually show variant spellings. For example, see the first-line citation "Whan that Aprille [or April or Aprill] with his[e] shoures [or showres] sote [or soote]." In the several anthologies in which that first line appears, the spelling may vary as indicated in brackets.

Capitalization. The first letter of the first word in every citation is capitalized, even when in its published form it appears as lowercase.

Initial Articles. An article—"a," "an," or "the"—that begins a title or a line is transposed to the end of the citation. "A boy who played and talked and read with me" by Donald Hall, for example, is listed as "Boy who played and talked and read with me, The."

Titles. Initial capitals in the important words usually indicate that the citation is the title of the poem. "I Take Back Everything I've Said," by Nicano Parra, for example, is a title.

Parentheses. When an entire citation is enclosed by parentheses, it usually means that it is a variant title, variant first line, or variant last line. Parentheses are used instead of brackets when it is necessary to indicate a version that varies widely from the standard version, with the result that, in this alphabetized index, it can also be found in a place far from where the standard version is listed.

See, for example, "The Terrorist, He Watches" by Wislawa Szymborska.

> Bomb will explode in the bar at twenty past one, The. Terrorist, He Watches, The.
>   Wislawa Szymborska. PoSu
> (Bomb will go off in the bar at one twenty p.m., The.) AF

In the anthology indicated by the code AF the poem can be found with the first line, "The Bomb will go off in the bar at one twenty p.m." This information is especially useful when looking for a poem in the table of contents or the first line index of the anthology being indicated.

Indentation. Indentation of a citation indicates that it is a selection. See, for example, "The Countess of Pembroke's Arcadia."

> Countess of Pembroke's Arcadia, The. Sir Philip Sidney.
>   Delight of Solitariness, The. NoSic

"The Delight of Solitariness" is indented because it is a selection from "the Countess of Pembroke's Arcadia."

Author Index

Under each author's name, poems are listed alphabetically by title or, where the poem has no title, by first line.

What poems can I find by Richard Wilbur? The Author Index lists 92 poems.

HOW TO USE THE INDEXES

Subject Index

Under each subject heading, poems are listed alphabetically by author's name.

What poems can I find about 9/11? The subject index shows that there are 54 poems under September 11, 2001, by 49 different poets, including Jane Hirschfield and Galway Kinnell. Citations for all these poems can be found in the Title, First Line, and Last Line Index, where the letter codes, which refer to the List of Anthologies, indicate in which books the poems are published.

Did Anne Sexton write poems about Sylvia Plath? Go to the heading for "Plath, Sylvia" and locate "Sexton" in the list of poems alphabetized by author.

LIST OF ANTHOLOGIES

The anthologies in this list are arranged alphabetically by their codes, not by their titles. Anthologies marked with two asterisks (**) are recommended for priority acquisition by small libraries, one asterisk (*) for further acquisition.

ACAMVP   A Cappella: Mennonite Voices in Poetry. *Ann Hostetler, ed.* (1st ed., 2003) University of Iowa Press. 199p.

AEP   An Anthology of Elizabethan Poetry. *Sukanta Chaudhuri, ed.* (1992) Oxford University Press. 170p.

AF   *Against Forgetting; Twentieth-Century Poetry of Witness. *Carolyn Forché, ed.* (1993) W.W. Norton and Company. 81p.

AFaM   Appetite: Food as Metaphor, an Anthology of Women Poets. *Phyllis Stowell and Jeanne Foster, eds.* (1st ed., 2002) BOA Editions. 151p.

AfrBLW   Afrekete; an Anthology of Black Lesbian Writing. *L. Joyce DeLaney and Catherine E. McKinley, eds.* (1995) Anchor Books. 317p.

AHA   The Angel Hair Anthology. *Anne Waldman and Lewis Warsh, eds.* (1st ed., 2001) Granary Books. 619p.

AllShUp   All Shook Up; Collected Poems about Elvis. *Will Clemens, ed.* (1st ed., 2001) University of Arkansas Press. 131p.

AmAlph   American Alphabets. *David Walker, ed.* (1st ed., 2006) Oberlin College Press. 425p.

AmFaPo   *Americans' Favorite Poems; The Favorite Poem Project Anthology. *Robert Pinsky and Maggie Dietz, eds.* (1st ed., 2000) W.W. Norton. 327p.

AmPoNex   American Poetry; The Next Generation. *Gerald Costanzo and Jim Daniels, eds.* (1st ed., 2000) Carnegie Mellon Univ. Press. 480p.

AmWaPo   **American War Poetry. *Lorrie Goldensohn, ed.* (1st ed., 2006) Columbia University Press. 413p.

AmWit   American Wits: an Anthology of Light Verse. *John Hollander, ed.* (1st ed., 2003) The Library of America. 194p.

AmZen   America Zen: A Gathering of Poets. *Ray McNiece and Larry Smith, eds.* (1st ed., 2004) Bottom Dog Press. 224p.

AngWePo   Anglo-Welsh Poetry, 1480–1990. *Raymond Garlick and Roland Mathias, eds.* (1993) Poetry Wales Press. 377p., pap.

AnSo   Another South: Experimental Writing in the South. *Bill Lavender, ed.* (1st ed., 2003) University of Alabama Press. 277p.

AnVo   Angry Voices: An Anthology of the Off-Beat New Egyptian Poets. *Mohamed Metwalli, ed.* (1st ed., 2003) University of Arkansas Press. 109p.

APN-1   **American Poetry; The Nineteenth Century. Vol. 1. *John Hollander, ed.* (1993) The Library of America. 1,099p.

APN-2   **American Poetry; The Nineteenth Century. Vol. 2. *John Hollander, ed.* (1993) The Library of America. 1,050p.

APSN   American Poetry since 1950; Innovators and Outsiders. *Eliot Weinberger, ed.* (1993) Marsilio Publishers. 433p.

APT-1   **American Poetry; The Twentieth Century, Vol. 1. *Robert Hass, John Hollander, Carolyn Kizer, Nathaniel Mackey, and Marjorie Perloff, eds.* (1st ed., 2000) Library of America. 986p.

APT-2   **American Poetry; The Twentieth Century. Vol. 2. *Robert Hass, John Hollander, Carolyn Kizer, Nathaniel Mackey, and Marjorie Perloff, eds.* (2000) The Library of America. 1,009p.

ArBi   The Art of Bicycling: A Treasury of Poems. *Justin Daniel Belmont, ed.* (1st ed., 2005) Breakaway Books. 348p.

ArkPo   Ariake; Poems of Love and Longing by the Women Courtiers of Ancient Japan. *Liza Dalby and Rae Grant, eds.* (2000) Chronicle Books. 79p.

ARWW   An Anthology of Russian Women's Writing, 1777–1992. *Catriona Kelly, ed.* (1994) Oxford University Press. 535p.

ASA   The Addison Street Anthology: Berkeley's Poetry Walk. *Robert Hass and Jessica Fisher, eds.* (1st ed., 2004) Heyday Books. 284p.

AtGh   Atomic Ghost: Poets Respond to the Nuclear Age. *John Bradley, ed.* (1st ed., 1995) Coffee House Press. 330p.

ATSWP   The Adulterer's Tongue, Six Welsh Poets: A Facing-Text Anthology. *Robert Minhinnick, ed.* (1st ed., 2003) Carcanet. 125p.

AWPTFC   American Women Poets in the 21st Century. *Claudia Rankine and Juliana Spahr, eds.* (1st ed., 2002) Wesleyan University Press. 439p.

AWTN   Acquainted with the Night; Insomnia Poems. *Lisa Russ Spaar, ed.* (1999) Columbia University Press. 183p.

BAP-01   The Best American Poetry, 2001. *Robert Hass, ed.* (2001) Scribner. 287p.

BAP-04   The Best American Poetry, 2004. *Lyn Hejinian and David Lehman, eds.* (1st ed., 2004) Scribner. 278p.

BAP-97   The Best American Poetry, 1997. *James Tate, ed.* (1997) Scribner. 269p.

BASC   *The Broadview Anthology of Seventeenth Century Verse and Prose. *Alan Rudrum, Joseph Black, and Holly Faith Nelson, eds.* (1st ed., 2000) Broadview Press. 1,303p.

BB   The Beat Book; Poems and Fiction of the Beat Generation. *Anne Waldman, ed.* (1996) Shambhala. 351p., pap.

BBASP   Burning Bright; an Anthology of Sacred Poetry. *Patricia Hampl, ed.* (1995) Ballantine Books. 178p.

BBMWP   The Bloodaxe Book of Modern Welsh Poetry. *Menna Elfyn and John Rowlands, eds.* (1st ed., 2003) Bloodaxe Books. 448p.

BeAl   Being Alive. *Neil Astley, ed.* (1st ed., 2004) Bloodaxe Books. 512p.

BecRai   Because of the Rain: Korean Zen Poems. *Daljin Kim, ed.* (1st ed., 2005) White Pine Press. 93p.

BeDoSh   Bend, Don't Shatter: Poets on the Beginning of Desire. *T. Cole Rachel and Rita D. Costello, eds.* (1st ed., 2004) Red Rattle Books. 111p.

BloBone   Blood and Bone; Poems by Physicians. *Angela Belli and Jack Coulehan, eds.* (1st ed., 1998) University of Iowa Press. 160p.

BLPJKO   The Best-Loved Poems of Jacqueline Kennedy Onassis. *Caroline Kennedy, ed.* (1st ed., 2001) Hyperion. 180p.

BLPSL   The Best 100 Love Poems of the Spanish Language. *Rigas Kappatos and Pedro Lastra, eds.* (1998) Seaburn Publishing. 275p.

BLT   A Book of Luminous Things; an International Anthology of Poetry. *Czeslaw Milosz, ed.* (1996) Harcourt Brace and Company. 320p.

BMAP   The Bloodaxe Book of Modern Australian Poetry. *John Tranter and Philip Mead, eds.* (1991, 1994) Bloodaxe Books. 474p., pap.

BodElec   The Body Electric; America's Best Poetry from The American Poetry Review. *Stephen Berg, David Bonanno, and Arthur Vogelsang, eds.* (1st ed., 2000) W.W. Norton and Company. 820p.

BrAP   The Broadview Anthology of Poetry. *Herbert Rosengarten and Amanda Goldrick-Jones, eds.* (1st ed., 1993) Broadview Press. 964p.

BRP   Best Remembered Poems. *Martin Gardner, ed.* (1992) Dover Publications. 210p.

BRtP   Bum Rush the Page. *Tony Medina, ed.* (1st ed., 2001) Three Rivers Press. 282p.

BtF   Beyond the Frontier: African American Poetry for the 21st Century. *E. Ethelbert Miller, ed.* (1st ed., 2002) Black Classic Press. 572p.

CA   Celebrating America; a Collection of Poems and Images of the American Spirit. *Laura Whipple, ed.* (1994) Philomel Books. 79p.

CABP   *The Columbia Anthology of British Poetry. *Woodring, Carl and James Shapiro, eds.* (1995) Columbia University Press. 891p.

CaDao   Ca Dao Vietnam; a Bilingual Anthology of Vietnamese Folk Poetry. *John Balaban, ed.* (3rd ed., 1980) Mosaic Press. 87p.

CAGL   The Columbia Anthology of Gay Literature. *Byrne R. S. Fone, ed.* (1998) Columbia University Press. 829p.

LIST OF ANTHOLOGIES

CalPo	California Poetry: From the Gold Rush to the Present. *Dana Gioia, Chryss Yost, and Jack Hicks, eds.* (1st ed., 2004) Heyday Books. 376p.
CAMKP	The Columbia Anthology of Modern Korean Poetry. *David R. McCann, ed.* (2004) Columbia University Press. 269p.
CAoMJL1	The Columbia Anthology of Modern Japanese Literature, Volume 1: From Restoration to Occupation, 1868–1945. *J. Thomas Rimer and Van C. Gessel, eds.* (1st ed., 2005) Columbia University Press. 863p.
CAP-8	**Contemporary American Poetry. *A. Poulin, Jr. and Michael Waters, eds.* (8th ed., 2006) Houghton Mifflin. 690p.
CATKP	The Columbia Anthology of Traditional Korean Poetry. *Peter H. Lee, ed.* (2002) Columbia University Press. 358p.
CavPo	The Cavalier Poets; an Anthology. *Thomas Crofts, ed.* (1995) Dover Publications, Inc. 92p.
CBCWP	The Columbia Book of Civil War Poetry. *Richard Marius, ed.* (1994) Columbia University Press. 543p.
CBWP-1	Collected Black Women's Poetry. Vol. I. *Joan R. Sherman, ed.* (1988) Oxford University Press.
CBWP-2	Collected Black Women's Poetry. Vol. II. *Joan R. Sherman, ed.* (1988) Oxford University Press.
CBWP-3	Collected Black Women's Poetry. Vol. III. *Joan R. Sherman, ed.* (1988) Oxford University Press.
CBWP-4	Collected Black Women's Poetry. Vol. IV. *Joan R. Sherman, ed.* (1988) Oxford University Press.
CCL1	Classical Chinese Literature, Volume 1: From Antiquity to the Tang Dynasty. *John Minford and Joseph S. M. Lau, eds.* (2000) Columbia University Press. 1,176p.
CenSon	A Century of Sonnets; The Romantic-Era Revival, 1750–1850. *Paula R. Feldman and Daniel Robinson, eds.* (1st ed., 1999) Oxford University Press. 279p.
CFP	A Chorus for Peace: A Global Anthology of Poetry by Women. *Marilyn Arnold and Bonnie Ballif-Spanvill, eds.* (1st ed., 2002) University of Iowa Press. 202p.
ChAP	A Child's Anthology of Poetry. *Elizabeth Hauge Sword and Victoria Flournoy McCarthy, eds.* (1995) Ecco Press. 323p.
ChinPo	Chinese Poetry; an Anthology of Major Modes and Genres. *Wai-Lim Yip, ed.* (3rd ed., 2000) Duke University Press. 357p.
ChIV-1	Chapters into Verse. Vol. I: Genesis to Malachi. *Robert Atwan and Laurance Wieder, eds.* (1993) Oxford University Press. 481p.
ChIV-2	Chapters into Verse. Vol. II: Gospels to Revelation. *Robert Atwan and Laurance Wieder, eds.* (1993) Oxford University Press. 391p.
ChrPo	Christmas Poems. *John Hollander and J. D. McClatchy, eds.* (1999) Alfred A. Knopf. 254p.
CItWP	Contemporary Italian Women Poets; a Bilingual Anthology. *Cinzia Sartini Blum and Lara Trubowitz, eds.* (1st ed., 2001) Italica Press. 308p.
ClHu	*The Classic Hundred; All-Time Favorite Poems. *William Harmon, ed.* (1990) Columbia University Press. 250p.
CLPP	City Lights Pocket Poets Anthology. *Lawrence Ferlinghetti, ed.* (1995) City Lights Books. 259p.
Coast	Coastlines: The Poetry of Atlantic Canada. *Anne Compton, Laurence Hutchman, and Ross Leckie, eds.* (1st ed., 2002) Goose Lane Editions. 311p.
ColAnChi	The Columbia Anthology of Traditional Chinese Literature. *Victor Mair, ed.* (1st ed., 1994) Columbia University Press. 1,335p.
ColAP	*The Columbia Anthology of American Poetry. *Jay Parini, ed.* (1995) Columbia University Press. 757p.
ConPit	Conductors of the Pit. *Clayton Eshleman, ed.* (2005) Soft Skull Press. 242p.
CRWP	An Anthology of Contemporary Russian Women Poets. *Valentina Polukhina and Daniel Weissbort, eds.* (1st ed., 2005) University of Iowa Press. 266p.
CrYelRi	Crossing the Yellow River; Three Hundred Poems from the Chinese. *Sam Hamill, ed.* (1st ed., 2000) Boa Editions. 280p.
CSCBP	Clay and Star: Contemporary Bulgarian Poets. *Lisa Sapinkopf and Georgi Belev, eds.* (1st ed., 1992) Milkweed Editions. 227p.
CSKM	The Clouds Should Know Me by Now: Buddhist Poet Monks of China. *Red Pine and Mike O'Connor, eds.* (1st ed., 1998) Wisdom Publications. 211p.

CtM   Committed to Memory: 100 Best Poems to Memorize. *John Hollander, ed.* (1st ed., 1996) Books & Co. and Turtle Point Press. 196p.

CuPo   The Cubist Poets in Paris. *L. C. Breunig, ed.* (1st ed., 1995) University of Nebraska Press. 326p.

DiBP   The Dog in British Poetry. *R. Maynard Leonard, ed.* (2nd, 2005) Chronicle Books. 350p.

DTA   Dreaming the Actual; Contemporary Fiction and Poetry by Israeli Women Writers. *Miriyam Glazer, ed.* (2000) State University of New York. 396p.

EaWin   East Window; The Asian Translations. *W. S. Merwin, ed.* (1st ed., 1998) Copper Canyon Press. 337p.

EcSo   Echoing Song: Contemporary Korean Women Poets. *Peter H. Lee, ed.* (1st ed., 2005) White Pine Press. 304p.

EdScPo   The Edinburgh Book of Twentieth-Century Scottish Poetry. *Maurice Lindsay and Lesley Duncan, eds.* (1st ed., 2005) Edinburgh University Press. 420p.

EGAG   Every Goodbye Ain't Gone: An Anthology of Innovative Poetry by African Americans. *Aldon Lynn Nielsen and Lauri Ramey, eds.* (1st ed., 2006) University of Alabama Press. 305p.

EH   The Essential Haiku; Versions of Bashō, Buson, and Issa. *Robert Hass, ed.* (1994) Ecco Press. 329p.

EmeKit   Emergency Kit; Poems for Strange Times. *Jo Shapcott and Matthew Sweeney, eds.* (1st ed., 1996) Faber and Faber. 306p.

EMJL   Early Modern Japanese Literature: An Anthology, 1600–1900. *Haruo Shirane, ed.* (2002) Columbia University Press. 1,027p.

EMP   **100 Essential Modern Poems. *Joseph Parisi, ed.* (1st ed., 2005) Ivan R. Dee. 305p.

EMWP   **Early Modern Women Poets (1520–1700). *Jane Stevenson and Peter Davidson, eds.* (2001) Oxford University Press. 585p.

Eno   Enough. *Rick London and Leslie Scalapino, eds.* (1st ed., 2003) O Books. 159p.

EroLit   Erotic Literature; Twenty-four Centuries of Sensual Writing. *Jane Mills, ed.* (1st ed., 1993) HarperCollins. 375p.

ErotSp   The Erotic Spirit. *Sam Hamill, ed.* (1st ed., 1996) Shambhala Press. 200p.

ESEAA   Every Shut Eye Ain't Asleep; an Anthology of Poetry by African Americans since 1945. *Michael S. Harper and Anthony Walton, eds.* (1994) Little, Brown. 327p.

ExTi   The Extraordinary Tide; New Poetry by American Women. *Susan Aizenberg and Erin Belieu, eds.* (1st ed., 2001) Columbia University Press. 464p.

FaBoA   The Faber Book of America. *Christopher Ricks and William L. Vance, eds.* (1992) Faber and Faber. 467p.

FaBoTC   The Faber Book of Twentieth-Century Scottish Poetry. *Douglas Dunn, ed.* (1992) Faber and Faber. 424p.

FaBoVe   The Faber Book of Vernacular Verse. *Tom Paulin, ed.* (1990) Faber and Faber. 407p.

FaBoWar   The Faber Book of War Poetry. *Kenneth Baker, ed.* (1996) Faber and Faber. 598p.

FaoP   The Face of Poetry. *Zack Rogow, ed.* (1st ed., 2005) Uinversity of California Press. 354p.

FFC   A Formal Feeling Comes; Poems in Form by Contemporary Women. *Annie Finch, ed.* (1994) Story Line Press. 308p., pap.

FiBr   **A Fierce Brightness: Twenty-five Years of Women's Poetry. *Margarita Donnelly, Beverly McFarland, and Micki Reaman, eds.* (1st ed., 2002) CALYX Books. 217p.

FIT   Found in Translation; a Hundred Years of Modern Hebrew Poetry. *Gabriel Levin, ed.* (1999) Menard Press. 126p.

FreRad   Free Radicals: American Poets Before Their First Books. *Jordan Davis and Sarah Manguso, eds.* (1st ed., 2004) Subpress. 136p.

FSCP   Five Seventeenth-Century Poets; Donne, Herbert, Crashaw, Marvell, Vaughan. *Brijraj Singh, ed.* (1992) Oxford University Press. 297p.

FTOS   From the Other Side of the Century; a New American Poetry 1960–1990. *Douglas Messerli, ed.* (1994) Sun & Moon Press. 1,136p.

FTtHH   From Totems to Hip-Hop. *Ishmael Reed, ed.* (1st ed., 2003) Ishmael Reed. 523p.

FuFl   Furious Flower: African American Poetry from the Black Arts Movement to the Present. *Joanne V. Gabbin, ed.* (1st ed., 2004) University of Virginia Press. 286p.

FuPo   The Fugitive Poets: Modern Southern Poetry in Perspective. *William Pratt, ed.* (1991) J. S.
            Sanders & Company. 159p., pap.

GeoH   The Geography of Hope; Poets of Colorado's Western Slope. *David J. Rothman, ed.* (2nd ed.,
            2000) Conundrum Press. 146p.

GeoHom   The Geography of Home; California's Poetry of Place. *Christopher Buckley and Gary Young, eds.*
            (1st ed., 1999) Heyday Books. 444p.

GePo   German Poetry; from the Beginnings to 1750. *Ingrid Walsøe–Engel, ed.* (1992) Continuum.
            338p., pap.

GI   The Gospels in Our Image; an Anthology of Twentieth-Century Poetry Based on Biblical Texts.
            David Curzon, ed. (1995) Harcourt Brace. 279p.

GifTon   The Gift of Tongues; Twenty-five Years of Poetry from Copper Canyon Press. *Sam Hamill, ed.*
            (1st ed., 1996) Copper Canyon Press. 356p.

GM   The Great Machines; Poems and Songs of the American Railroad. *Robert Hedin, ed.* (1996)
            University of Iowa Press. 251p

GoPo   *Good Poems. *Garrison Keillor, ed.* (1st ed., 2002) Viking. 476p.

GPPA   The Griffin Poetry Prize Anthology: A Selection of the 2003 Shortlist. *Sharon Thesen, ed.* (1st
            ed., 2003) Anansi. 93p.

GPTC   100 Great Poems of the Twentieth Century. *Mark Strand, ed.* (1st ed., 2005) W.W. Norton and
            Company. 320p.

GS   The Gazer's Spirit: Poems Speaking to Silent Works of Art. *John Hollander, ed.* (1995) The
            University of Chicago Press. 380p.

GSo   Great Sonnets. *Paul Negri, ed.* (1994) Dover. 96p., pap.

GT   The Garden Thrives; Twentieth-Century African-American Poetry. *Clarence Major, ed.* (1996)
            HarperCollins. 470p., pap.

GTCP   German 20th Century Poetry. *Reinhold Grimm and Irmgard Hunt, eds.* (1st ed., 2001) Contin-
            uum. 270p.

HarvBoo   The Harvill Book of Twentieth-Century Poetry in English. *Michael Schmidt, ed.* (1st ed., 1999)
            The Harvill Press. 728p.

HATNAP   *Harper's Anthology of 20th Century Native American Poetry. *Duane Niatum, ed.* (1988)
            Harper & Row. 396p., o.p.

HAWP   The Heinemann Book of African Women's Poetry. *Stella Chipasula and Frank Chipasula, eds.*
            (1995) Heinemann Publishers. 227p.

HBAPE   The Heinemann Book of African Poetry in English. *Adewale Maja-Pearce, ed.* (1990) Heine-
            mann. 224p., pap.

HeIP-4   The Heath Introduction to Poetry. *Joseph DeRoche, ed.* (4th ed., 1992) D. C. Heath. 561p.,
            pap.

HeMarv   Heights of the Marvelous; a New York Anthology. *Todd Colby, ed.* (1st ed., 2000) St. Martin's
            Griffin. 224p.

HePo   Hellenistic Poetry; an Anthology. *Barbara Hughes Fowler, ed.* (1990) University of Wisconsin
            Press. 357p.

HHAm   Hand in Hand; an American History through Poetry. *Lee Bennett Hopkins, ed.* (1994) Simon
            and Schuster. 144p.

HiArP   Hispano-Arabic Poetry: A Student Anthology. *James T. Monroe, ed.* Gorgias Press. 402p.

HotL   Hibiscus on the Lake: Twentieth-Century Teluga Poetry from India. *Velcheru Narayana Rao, ed.*
            (1st ed., 2003) University of Wisconsin Press. 330p.

HP   Holocaust Poetry. *Hilda Schiff, ed.* 1995 HarperCollins. 234p.

HW   Her Words; an Anthology of Poetry about the Great Goddess. *Burleigh Muté, ed.* (1999) Sham-
            bhala. 249p.

IaFF   In a Fine Frenzy: Poets Respond to Shakespeare. *David Starkey and Paul J. Willis, eds.* (1st ed.,
            2005) University of Iowa Press. 192p.

IAoNAP   The Iowa Anthology of New American Poetries. *Reginald Shepherd, ed.* (1st ed., 2004) Uni-
            versity of Iowa Press. 310p.

IBB   The Illustrated Border Ballads. *John Marden, ed.* (1990) University of Texas Press. 192p.

ICANM   In Company: An Anthology of New Mexico Poets after 1960. *Lee Bartlett, V. B. Price, and Dianne
            Edwards, eds.* (1st ed., 2004) University of New Mexico Press. 542p.

IFF In Fine Form: The Canadian Book of Form Poetry. *Kate Braid and Sandy Shreve, eds.* (1st ed., 2005) Polestar. 303p.

IIR Isn't It Romantic: 100 Love Poems by Younger American Poets. *Brett Fletcher Lauer and Aimee Kelley, eds.* (1st ed., 2004) Verse Press. 184p.

IJHIL I Just Hope It's Lethal. *Liz Rosenberg and Deena November, eds.* (1st ed., 2005) Graphia. 190p.

IllVoic Illinois Voices. *Kevin Stein and G. E. Murray, eds.* (1st ed., 2001) University of Illinois Press. 366p.

InGu Invited Guest: An Anthology of Twentieth-Century Southern Poetry. *David Rigsbee and Steven Ford Brown, eds.* (1st ed., 2001) University Press of Virginia. 296p.

InoFa Inventions of Farewell: A Book of Elegies. *Sandra M. Gilbert, ed.* (1st ed., 2001) W.W. Norton and Company. 478p.

INSAB I never saw another butterfly; Children's Drawings and Poems from Terezin Concentration Camp, 1942–1944. *Hana Volavková, ed.* (2nd ed., 1993) Schocken Books. 106p.

InTrad In the Tradition; an Anthology of Young Black Writers. *Kevin Powell and Ras Baraka, eds.* (1st ed., 1992) Harlem River Press. 398p.

InvLad The Invisible Ladder; an Anthology of Contemporary American Poems for Young Readers. *Liz Rosenberg, ed.* (1st ed., 1996) Henry Holt and Co. 209p.

InvLi Invisible Light; Poems about God. *Diana Culbertson, ed.* (2000) Columbia University Press. 174p.

IPoFL In Praise of Fertile Land. *Claudia Mauro, ed.* (1st ed., 2003) Whit Press. 175p.

IQMS In Quest of the Miracle Stag; The Poetry of Hungary. *Adam Makkai, ed.* (1996) Atlantic-Centaur, Inc; Corvina Publishers; and M. Szivárvány. 964p.

IrLP Ireland's Love Poems. *A. Norman Jeffares, ed.* (1st ed., 2002) W.W. Norton and Company. 353p.

IrPoTo *Iraqi Poetry Today. *Saadi Simawe and Daniel Weissbort, eds.* (1st ed., 2003) King's College London. 288p.

IrV Irish Verse: An Anthology. *Bob Blaisdell, ed.* (1st ed., 2002) Dover Publications. 134p.

ISC In Search of Color Everywhere: A Collection of African–American Poetry. *E. Ethelbert Miller, ed.* (1994) Stewart, Tabori & Chang. 256p., pap.

ITBLP The Ideals Treasury of Best Loved Poems. *Patricia A. Pingry, ed.* (1997) Ideals Publications. 160p.

ItGoST In the Grip of Strange Thoughts; Russian Poetry in a New Era. *J. Kates, ed.* (1999) Zephyr Press. 444p.

ItP **An Invitation to Poetry: A New Favorite Poem Project Anthology. *Robert Pinsky and Maggie Dietz, eds.* (1st ed., 2004) W.W. Norton and Company. 308p.

ItPo Italian Poetry, 1950–1990. *Gayle Ridinger and Gian Paulo Renello, eds.* (1996) Dante University of America. 407p.

ItWoWo It's a Woman's World; a Century of Women's Voices in Poetry. *Neil Philip, ed.* (1st ed., 2000) Dutton Children's Books. 93p.

KGB The KGB Bar Book of Poems. *David Lehman and Star Black, eds.* (2000) HarperCollins. 256p.

LaCa Last Call: Poems on Alcoholism, Addiction, & Deliverance. *Sarah Gorham and Jeffrey Skinner, eds.* (1st ed., 1997) Sarabande Books. 191p.

LegDan Legitimate Dangers: American Poets of the New Century. *Michael Dumanis and Cate Marvin, eds.* (1st ed., 2006) Sarabande Books. 491p.

LiTh Like Thunder: Poets Respond to Violence in America. *Virgil Suárez and Ryan G. Van Cleave, eds.* (1st ed., 2002) University of Iowa Press. 222p.

LoL The Language of Life; a Festival of Poets. *Bill Moyers, ed.* (1995) Doubleday. 450p., pap.

LPSFW Locales: Poems from the Fellowship of Southern Writers. *Fred Chappell, ed.* (1st ed., 2003) Louisiana State Univ. Press. 134p.

LTA Letters to America: Contemporary American Poetry on Race. *Jim Daniels, ed.* (1995) Wayne State University Press. 230p., pap.

LW Love's Witness; Five Centuries of Love Poetry by Women. *Jill Hollis, ed.* (1993) Carroll and Graf Publishers. 334p., pap.

LWR Landscape with Rowers: Poetry from the Netherlands. *Nicholas Jenkins, ed.* (1st ed., 2004) Princeton University Press. 105p.

LIST OF ANTHOLOGIES

MAAN — Manthology: Poems on the Male Experience. *C. Crist-Evans, K. Fetherston, and R. Weingarten, eds.* (1st ed., 2006) University of Iowa Press. 186p.

MakPoe — **The Making of a Poem; a Norton Anthology of Poetic Forms. *Mark Strand and Eavan Boland, eds.* (1st ed., 2000) W.W. Norton and Company. 366p.

MFP — Modern French Poetry. *Martin Sorrell, ed.* (1992) Forest Books. 242p., pap.

MFPA — Making for Planet Alice; New Women Poets. *Maura Dooley, ed.* (1997) Bloodaxe Books. 173p.

MirDau — Miriam's Daughters; Jewish Latin American Women Poets. *Marjorie Agosin, ed.* (1st ed., 2001) Sherman Asher Publishing. 240p.

MiVo — Mixed Voices; Contemporary Poems about Music. *Emilie Buchwald and Ruth Roston, eds.* (1st ed., 1991) Milkweed Editions. 185p.

MoAmPo — Modern American Poetry. *Louis Untermeyer, ed.* (8th rev. ed., 1962) Harcourt Brace. 701p., o.p.

MoASP — Motion; American Sports Poems. *Noah Blaustein, ed.* (2001) University of Iowa Press. 250p.

MoBrPo — Modern British Poetry. *Louis Untermeyer, ed.* (7th rev. ed., 1962) Harcourt Brace. 500p., o.p.

ModIr — Modern Irish Poetry. *Patrick Crotty, ed.* (1st ed., 1995) The Blackstaff Press. 436p.

MotU — Models of the Universe: an Anthology of the Prose Poem. *Stuart Friebert and David Young, eds.* (1st ed., 1995) Oberlin College Press. 320p.

MoW — A Mind of Winter: Poems for a Snowy Season. *Robert Atwan, ed.* (1st ed., 2002) Beacon Press. 84p.

MoWP — Modern Women Poets. *Deryn Rees-Jones, ed.* (1st ed., 2005) Bloodaxe Books. 416p.

MPUn — A More Perfect Union; Poems and Stories About the Modern Wedding. *Virginia Hartman and Barbara Esstman, eds.* (1st ed., 1998) St. Martin's Press. 295p.

NAAL-3 — The Norton Anthology of American Literature. *Nina Baym, ed.* (3rd ed., 1989) W.W. Norton and Company. 2,459p., pap.

NAAL-5 — **The Norton Anthology of American Literature. *Nina Baym, ed.* (5th ed., 1999) W.W. Norton and Company. 2,879p., pap.

NAAPv.1 — The New Anthology of American Poetry, Volume I: Traditions and Revolutions, Beginnings to 1900. *Steven Gould Axelrod, Camille Roman, and Thomas Travisano, eds.* (1st ed., 2003) Rutgers University Press. 736p.

NAAPv.2 — The New Anthology of American Poetry, Volume II: Modernisms 1900-1950. *Steven Gould Axelrod, Camille Roman, and Thomas Travisano, eds.* (1st ed., 2005) Rutgers University Press. 819p.

NAEL-6v1 — The Norton Anthology of English Literature. 6th ed. Vol.1. *M. H. Abrams, ed.* (6th ed., 1993) W.W. Norton and Company. 2,586p.

NAEL-6v2 — The Norton Anthology of English Literature. 6th ed. Vol. 2. *M. H. Abrams, ed.* (6th ed., 1993) W.W. Norton and Company. 2,543p.

NAEL-7v1 — **The Norton Anthology of English Literature. 7th ed. Vol. 1. *M. H. Abrams, ed.* (7th ed., 2000) W.W. Norton and Company. 2,974p.

NAEL-7v2 — **The Norton Anthology of English Literature. 7th ed. Vol. 2. *M. H. Abrams , ed.* (7th ed., 2000) W.W. Norton and Company. 2,963p.

NAfrP — *The New African Poetry: an Anthology. *Tanure Ojaide and Tijan M. Sallah, eds.* (1999) Lynne Rienner Publishers. 233p.

NALW — The Norton Anthology of Literature by Women: the Tradition in English. *Sandra M. Gilber and Susan Guber, eds.* (1985) W.W. Norton and Company. 2,457p.

NAMCP V.1 — **The Norton Anthology of Modern and Contemporary Poetry, V. 1: Modern Poetry. *Jahan Ramazani, Richard Ellmann, and Robert O'Clair, eds.* (1st ed., 2003) W.W. Norton and Company. 1,062p.

NAMCP V.2 — **The Norton Anthology of Modern and Contemporary Poetry, V. 2: Contemporary Poetry. *Jahan Ramazani, Richard Ellmann, and Robert O'Clair, eds.* (1st ed., 2003) W.W. Norton and Company. 1,210p.

NAPBL — The New American Poets: a Bread Loaf Anthology. *Michael Collier, ed.* (2000) Univ. Press of New England. 280p.

NaPG — Nightingales & Pleasure Gardens. *Talat S. Halman and Jayne L. Warner, eds.* (1st ed., 2005) Syracuse University Press. 159p.

NAWM-5v1   The Norton Anthology of World Masterpieces. Vol. 1. *Maynard Mack, ed.* (5th ed., 1985) W.W. Norton and Company. 2,052p.

NAWM-7v1   The Norton Anthology of World Masterpieces. Vol. 1. *Sarah Lawall and Maynard Mack, eds.* (7th ed., 1999) W.W. Norton and Company. 2,270p.

NAWM-7v2   The Norton Anthology of World Masterpieces. Vol. 2. *Sarah Lawall and Maynard Mack, eds.* (7th ed., 1999) W.W. Norton and Company. 2,194p.

NBLV   The Norton Book of Light Verse. *Russell Baker, ed.* (1986) W.W. Norton and Company. 447p.

NCAP   Nineteenth Century American Poetry. *William C. Spengemann and Jessica F. Roberts, eds.* (1996) Penguin Books. 447p., pap.

NDACCP   *The New Directions Anthology of Classical Chinese Poetry. *Eliot Weinberger, ed.* (2003) New Directions. 242p.

NeAmPo   The New Young American Poets. *Kevin Prufer, ed.* (1st ed., 2000) Southern Illinois University P. 243p.

NeBl   New Blood. *Neil Astley, ed.* (1st ed., 1999) Bloodaxe Books. 240p.

NeBrP   *New British Poetry. *Don Paterson and Charles Simic, eds.* (1st ed., 2004) Graywolf Press. 191p.

NeIt   New Italian Poets. *Dana Gioia and Michael Palma, eds.* (1991) Story Line Press. 385p., pap.

NeNiPo   25 New Nigerian Poets. *Toyin Adewale, ed.* (1st ed., 2000) Ishmael Reed Publishing. 67p.

NePenScot   The New Penguin Book of Scottish Verse. *Robert Crawford and Mick Imlah, eds.* (1st ed., 2000) Penguin Press. 554p.

NevBe   Never Before: Poems about First Experiences. *Laure-Anne Bosselaar, ed.* (1st ed., 2005) Four Way Book. 211p., pap.

NewEx   The New Exeter Book of Riddles. *Kevin Crossley-Holland and Lawrence Sail, eds.* (1st ed., 1999) Enitharmon Press. 66p.

NIL-7   The Norton Introduction to Literature. *Jerome Beaty and J. Paul Hunter, eds.* (7th ed., 1998) W.W. Norton and Company. 2,278p., cloth

NIP-4   *The Norton Introduction to Poetry. *J. Paul Hunter, ed.* (4th ed., 1991) W.W. Norton and Company. 578p.

NIrP   The New Irish Poets. *Selina Guinness, ed.* (1st ed., 2004) Bloodaxe Books. 336p.

NLP   The New Lake Poets. *William Scammell, ed.* (1991) Bloodaxe Books. 160p.

NLPA   The New Long Poem Anthology. *Sharon Thesen, ed.* (2nd ed., 2001) Talonbooks. 496p.

NoAM   The Norton Anthology of Modern Poetry. *Richard Ellmann and Robert O'Clair, eds.* (2nd ed., 1988) W.W. Norton and Company. 1,863p.

NOBAu   The New Oxford Book of Australian Verse. *Les A. Murray, ed.* (Enl. ed., 1991) Oxford University Press. 399p.

NOBRP   The New Oxford Book of Romantic Period Verse. *Jerome J. McGann, ed.* (1993) Oxford University Press. 832p.

NoP-4   The Norton Anthology of Poetry. *Margaret Ferguson, Mary Jo Salter, and Jon Stallworthy, eds.* (1996) W.W. Norton and Company. 1,998p., pap.

NoP-5   **The Norton Anthology of Poetry. *Margaret Ferguson, Mary Jo Salter, and Jon Stallworthy, eds.* (5th ed., 2005) W.W. Norton and Company. 2,182p.

NOSC   The New Oxford Book of Seventeenth Century Verse. *Alistair Fowler, ed.* (1991) Oxford University Press. 831p.

NoSic   The New Oxford Book of Sixteenth Century Verse. *Emrys Jones, ed.* (1991) Oxford University Press. 769p.

NOxBChV   The New Oxford Book of Children's Verse. *Neil Philip, ed.* (1996) Oxford University Press. 371p.

NPBRoP   **The New Penguin Book of Romantic Poetry. *Jonathan Wordsworth and Jessica Wordsworth, eds.* (3rd ed., 2003) Penguin Books. 1,005p.

NPeEn   **The New Penguin Book of English Verse. *Paul Keegan, ed.* (1st ed., 2000) Penguin Press. 1,139p.

NRoS   No Rattling of Sabers: An Anthology of Israeli War Poetry. *Annes McCann-Baker, ed.* (1st ed., 1995) University of Texas at Austin. 179p.

NTCP   A New Treasury of Children's Poetry: Old Favorites and New Discoveries. *Joanna Cole, ed.* (1984) Doubleday. 224p., pap.

LIST OF ANTHOLOGIES

NYP2   The New York Poets II: An Anthology. *Mark Ford and Trevor Winkfield, eds.* (1st ed., 2006) Carcanet. 216p.

OBCoV   The Oxford Book of Comic Verse. *John Gross, ed.* (1994) Oxford University Press. 512p.

OBCP   The Oxford Book of Christmas Poems. *Michael Harrison and Christopher Stuart-Clark, eds.* (1983) Oxford University Press. 160p.

OBEV   The Oxford Book of English Verse, 1250–1918. *Sir Arthur Quiller-Couch, ed.* (New ed., rev. and enl., 1939) Oxford University Press. 1,083p.

OBGa   The Oxford Book of Garden Verse. *John Dixon Hunt, ed.* (1993) Oxford University Press. 341p.

OBMV   The Oxford Book of Modern Verse, 1892–1935. *William Butler Yeats, ed.* (1936) Oxford University Press. 454p.

OBNV   The Oxford Book of Narrative Verse. *Iona Opie and Peter Opie, eds.* (1983) Oxford University Press. 407p.

OBSP   The Oxford Book of Story Poems. *Michael Harrison and Christopher Stuart-Clark, eds.* (1990) Oxford University Press. 175p.

OBSV   The Oxford Book of Satirical Verse. *Geoffrey Grigson, ed.* (1980) Oxford University Press. 454p.

OBVE   The Oxford Book of Verse in English Translation. *Charles Tomlinson, ed.* (1980) Oxford University Press. 608p.

OBWP   *The Oxford Book of War Poetry. *Jon Stallworthy, ed.* (1984) Oxford University Press. 358p.

OBWVE   The Oxford Book of Welsh Verse in English. *Gwyn Jones, ed.* (1977) Oxford University Press, 313p.

OGAHCP   Open Gate: An Anthology of Haitian Creole Poetry. *Paul Laraque and Jack Hirschman, eds.* (1st ed., 2001) Curbstone Press. 235p.

OHMEL   One Hundred Middle English Lyrics. *Robert D. Stevick, ed.* (2nd ed., 1994) University of Illinois Press. 194p.

OLP   Ottoman Lyric Poetry. *Walter G. Andrews, Najaat Black, and Mehmet Kalpakli, eds.* (1st ed., 1997) University of Texas Press. 312p.

OnScMo   One Score More: The Second 20 Years of Burning Deck 1982–2002. *Alison Bundy, Keith Waldrop, and Rosmarie Waldrop, eds.* (1st ed., 2002) Burning Deck. 240p.

OpBo   *The Open Boat: Poems from Asian America. *Garrett Hongo, ed.* (1993) Doubleday. 303p.

OpeFie   *Open Field: 30 Contemporary Canadian Poets. *Sina Queyras, ed.* (1st ed., 2005) Persea Books. 249p.

OPOU   100 Poems on the Underground. *Gerald Benson, Judith Cherniak, and Cicely Herbert, eds.* (1991) Cassell Publishers. 144p., pap.

OPRER   Outsiders: Poems about Rebels, Exiles, and Renegades. *Laure-Anne Bosselaar, ed.* (1999) Milkweed Editions. 323p.

Oth   Other: British and Irish Poetry since 1970. *Richard Caddel and Peter Quartermain, eds.* (1st ed., 1999) Wesleyan University Press. 280p.

OtW   On the Wing: American Poems of Air and Space Flight. *Karen Yelena Olsen, ed.* (1st ed., 2005) University of Iowa Press. 236p.

OWABP   Of Words: An Anthology of Belizean Poetry. *Michael D. Phillips, ed.* (1st ed., 1997) Cubola Productions. 104p.

OWoS   On Wings of Song: Poems about Birds. *J. D. McClatchy, ed.* (2000) Alfred A. Knopf. 256p.

OxAAAP   **The Oxford Anthology of African American Poetry. *Arnold Rampersad and Hilary Herbold, eds.* (1st ed., 2006) Oxford University Press. 424p.

OxAEP-1   The Oxford Anthology of English Poetry. Vol. I: Spenser to Crabbe. *John Wain, ed.* (1990) Oxford University Press. 659p.

OxAEP-2   The Oxford Anthology of English Poetry. Vol. II: Blake to Heaney. *John Wain, ed.* (1990) Oxford University Press. 770p.

OxBEV   The Oxford Book of English Verse. *Christopher Ricks, ed.* (1999) Oxford University Press. 690p.

OxBoAm   The Oxford Book of American Poetry. *David Lehman, ed.* (2006) Oxford University Press. 1,132p.

OxBSo   The Oxford Book of Sonnets. *John Fuller, ed.* (2000) Oxford University Press. 362p.

OxWW   The Oxford Book of Women's Writing in the United States.   *Linda Wagner-Martin and Cathy N. Davidson, eds.*   (1995)   Oxford University Press. 596p.

P180   Poetry 180: A Turning Back to Poetry.   *Billy Collins, ed.*   (1st ed., 2003)   Random House. 323p.

PA9/11   Poetry After 9/11: An Anthology of New York Poets.   *Dennis Loy Johnson and Valerie Merians, eds.*   (2002)   Melville House. 112p.

PasH   Passionate Hearts: the Poetry of Sexual Love.   *Wendy Maltz, ed.*   (1996)   New World Library. 209p.

PBCAP   The Pittsburgh Book of Contemporary American Poetry.   *Ed Ochester and Peter Oresick, eds.*   (1993)   University of Pittsburgh Press. 397p.

PBCIP   The Penguin Book of Contemporary Irish Poetry.   *Peter Fallon and Derek Mahon, eds.*   (1990)   Penguin Books. 462p., pap.

PBRV   The Penguin Book of Renaissance Verse 1509–1659.   *David Norbrook, ed.*   (1992)   Penguin Books. 920p., pap.

PCW   **Poets of the Civil War.   *J. D. McClatchy, ed.*   (1st ed., 2005)   Library of America

PEW   Poetry by English Women: Elizabethan to Victorian.   *R. E. Pritchard, ed.*   (1990)   Continuum. 272p., pap.

PfS   Poetry from Sojourner: A Feminist Anthology.   *Ruth Lepson and Lynne Yamaguchi, eds.*   (1st ed., 2004)   University of Illinois Press. 236p.

PfSP   Poems for a Small Planet: Contemporary American Nature Poetry.   *Robert Pack and Jay Parini, eds.*   (1st ed., 1993)   Middlebury College Press. 301p.

PFTM-1   Poems for the Millennium: the University of California Book of Modern & Postmodern Poetry. Vol. 1.   *Jerome Rothenberg and Pierre Joris, eds.*   (1995)   University of California Press. 811p.

PFTM-2   Poems for the Millennium: the University of California Book of Modern & Postmodern Poetry. Vol. 2.   *Jerome Rothenberg and Pierre Joris, eds.*   (1998)   University of California Press. 871p.

PLBUT   Poems to Live By in Uncertain Times.   *Joan Murray, ed.*   (1st ed., 2001)   Beacon Press. 125p.

PmAP   Postmodern American Poetry: a Norton Anthology.   *Paul Hoover, ed.*   (1994)   W.W. Norton and Company. 701p.

PML   The Poetry of Men's Lives: An International Anthology.   *Fred Moramarco and Al Zolynas, eds.*   (1st ed., 2004)   University of Georgia Press. 417p.

PNI   Poets from the North of Ireland.   *Frank Ormsby, ed.*   (New ed., 1990)   The Blackstaff Press. 336p.

PoA 2002   *The Poetry Anthology, 1912–2002.   *Joseph Parisi and Stephen Young, eds.*   (1st ed., 2002)   Ivan R. Dee. 509p.

PoAgWa   101 Poems Against War.   *Matthew Hollis and Paul Keegan, eds.*   (1st ed., 2003)   Faber and Faber. 147p.

PoArWo   The Poetry of Arab Women: a Contemporary Anthology.   *Nathalie Handal, ed.*   (1st ed., 2001)   Interlink Books. 355p.

PoBW   Poems Between Women: Four Centuries of Love, Romantic Friendship, and Desire.   *Emma Donoghue, ed.*   (1997)   Columbia University Press. 209p.

PoChi   The Poet's Child.   *Michael Wiegers, ed.*   (1st ed., 2002)   Copper Canyon Press. 139p.

PoCho   **Poet's Choice.   *Edward Hirsch, ed.*   (1st ed., 2006)   Harcourt. 432p.

PoCoUp   Poetry Comes Up Where It Can; an Anthology: Poems from the Amicus Journal, 1990–2000.   *Brian Swann, ed.*   (1st ed., 2000)   University of Utah Press. 168p.

PoCu   The Poetry Cure.   *Julia Darling and Cynthia Fuller, eds.*   (1st ed., 2005)   Bloodaxe Books. 112p.

PoDa   Poetry Daily: 366 Poems from the World's Most Popular Poetry Website.   *Diane Boller, Don Selby, and Chryss Yost, eds.*   (1st ed., 2003)   Sourcebooks, Inc. 470p.

PoetW   The Poetry of Our World: an International Anthology of Contemporary Poetry.   *Jeffrey Paine, ed.*   (2000)   HarperCollins. 511p., cloth

PoPoPo   Poems, Poets, Poetry: an Introduction and Anthology.   *Helen Vendler, ed.*   (1996)   Bedford Books. 656p., pap.

PoPra   Post-Prairie: An Anthology of New Poetry.   *Jon Paul Fiorentino and Robert Kroetsch, eds.*   (1st ed., 2005)   Talonbooks. 151p.

PoSl   The Poetry of Slavery: An Anglo-American Anthology 1764–1865.   *Marcus Wood, ed.*   (2nd ed., 2003)   Oxford University Press. 704p.

PoSol   The Poetry of Solitude: a Tribute to Edward Hopper. *Gail Levin, ed.* (1995) Universe Publishing. 80p.

PoSu   The Poetry of Survival: Post-War Poets of Central and Eastern Europe. *Daniel Weissbort, ed.* (1991) Anvil Press Poetry. 384p.

PoWW   Poetry of the World Wars. *Michael Foss, ed.* (1990) Peter Bedrick Books. 192p.

PriapPo   The Priapus Poems: Erotic Epigrams from Ancient Rome. *Richard W. Hooper, ed.* (1st ed., 1999) University of Illinois Press. 147p.

Prnts   Parents: an Anthology of Poems by Women Writers. *Myra Schneider and Dilys Wood, eds.* (2000) Enitharmon Press. 218p.

Prolet   Proletpen: America's Rebel Yiddish Poets. *Amelia Glaser and David Weintraub, eds.* (2nd ed., 2005) University of Wisconsin Press. 409p.

PrTe   Present/Tense: Poets in the World. *Mark Pawlak, ed.* (1st ed., 2004) Hanging Loose Press. 212p.

PtR   *Poems to Read: A New Favorite Poem Project Anthology. *Robert Pinsky and Maggie Dietz, eds.* (1st ed., 2002) W.W. Norton and Company. 352p.

PueRic   Puerto Rican Writers at Home. *Faythe Turner, ed.* (1991) Open Hand Publishing. 349p.

PuP-23   The Pushcart Prize XXIII Best of the Small Presses. *Bill Henderson, ed.* (1st ed., 1999) Pushcart Press. 606p.

PWW2   *Poets of World War II. *Harvey Shapiro, ed.* (1st ed., 2003) The Library of America. 262p.

RA   Rebel Angels: 25 Poets of the New Formalism. *Mark Jarman and David Mason, eds.* (1996) Story Line Press. 259p., pap.

RaBo   The Rag and Bone Shop of the Heart: Poems for Men. *Robert Bly, James Hillman, and Michael Meade, eds.* (1992) HarperCollins. 536p.

RACG   The Routledge Anthology of Cross-Gendered Verse. *Alan Michael Parker and Mark Willhardt, eds.* (1996) Routledge. 216p., pap.

RaF   Revenge and Forgiveness: An Anthology of Poems. *Patrice Vecchione, ed.* (1st ed., 2004) Henry Holt and Company. 148p.

RaW   Roots & Wings: Poetry From Spain 1900–1975. *Hardie St. Martin, ed.* (2nd ed., 2005) White Pine Press. 525p.

RD   Rainbow Darkness: An Anthology of African American Poetry. *Keith Tuma, ed.* (1st ed., 2003) Miami University Press. 226p.

ReBoTo   Returning a Borrowed Tongue: an Anthology of Filipino and Filipino American Poetry. *Nick Carbo, ed.* (1st ed., 1995) Coffee House Press. 238p.

ReEnLa   Reinventing the Enemy's Language: Contemporary Native Women's Writings of North America. *Joy Harjo and Gloria Bird, eds.* (1st ed., 1997) W.W. Norton and Company. 573p.

ReLy   Reading Lyrics. *Robert Gottlieb and Robert Kimball, eds.* (1st ed., 2000) Pantheon Books. 705p.

ReTh   Real Things: an Anthology of Popular Culture in American Poetry. *Jim Elledge, ed.* (1st ed., 1999) Indiana University Press. 336p.

RMCMP   **Reversible Monuments: Contemporary Mexican Poetry. *Mónica de la Torre and Michael Wiegers, eds.* (1st ed., 2002) Copper Canyon Press. 674p.

RomPo   Roman Poets of the Early Empire. *A.J. Boyle and J.P. Sullivan, eds.* (1st ed., 1991) Penguin Books. 450p.

RoV   Range of Voices. *Tod Marshall, ed.* (1st ed., 2005) Eastern Washington Univ. Press. 197p.

RSaN   Red Sky at Night: Socialist Poetry. *Andy Croft and Adrian Mitchell, eds.* (1st ed., 2003) Five Leaves Publications. 304p.

RSR   Run, Shepherds, Run. *L. William Countryman, ed.* (1st ed., 2005) Morehouse. 100p.

RusPo   Russian Poetry. *R. A. D. Ford, ed.* (3rd ed., 2000) Mosaic Press. 93p.

RWB   Red, White, and Blues: Poets on the Promise of America. *Virgil Suárez and Ryan G. Van Cleave, eds.* (1st ed., 2004) University of Iowa Press. 233p.

RWP   Romantic Women Poets: an Anthology. *Duncan Wu, ed.* (1997) Blackwell Publishers. 629p.

RWPCtW   Radio Waves: Poems Celebrating the Wireless. *Seán Street, ed.* (1st ed., 2004) Enitharmon Press. 96p.

SacPr   A Sacrifice of Praise: an Anthology of Christian Poetry in English from Caedmon to the Mid-Twentieth Century. *James H. Trott, ed.* (1999) Cumberland House Publishing. 797p.

SaLy — Sappho's Lyre: Archaic Lyric and Women Poets of Ancient Greece. *Diane J. Rayor, ed.* (1991) University of California Press. 207p.

SAmP — Six American Poets: an Anthology. *Joel Conarroe, ed.* (1991) Random House. 281p.

SCFWP — Six Contemporary French Women Poets. *Serge Gavronsky, ed.* (1st ed., 1997) Southern Illinois University P. 113p.

SeSe — The Second Set: the Jazz Poetry Anthology, Volume 2. *Sascha Feinstein and Yusef Komunyakaa, eds.* (1996) Indiana University Press. 250p

SinGod — Singing to the Goddess: Poems to Kālī and Umā from Bengal. *Rachel Fell McDermott, ed.* (1st ed., 2001) Oxford University Press. 189p.

SLW — Songs of Love and War: Afghan Women's Poetry. *Sayd Bahodine Majrouh, ed.* (1st ed., 2003) Other Press. 105p.

SonAtl — The Song Atlas: A Book of World Poetry. *John Gallas, ed.* (1st ed., 2002) Carcanet. 240p.

SoOfWa — The Sound of Water: Haiku by Bashō, Buson, Issa, and Other Poets. *Sam Hamill, ed.* (1st ed., 2000) Shambala. 125p.

SoSe-8 — Sound and Sense: an Introduction to Poetry. *Laurence Perrine and Thomas R. Arp, eds.* (8th ed., 1992) Harcourt Brace Jovanovich. 342p.

SpanPo — Spanish Poetry: a Dual-Language Anthology. *Angel Flores, ed.* (1st ed., 1998) Dover Publications. 401p.

SpirFl — Spirit and Flame: an Anthology of Contemporary African American Poetry. *Keith Gilyard, ed.* (1st ed., 1997) Syracuse University Press. 304p.

SPl — Secret Places. *Charlotte Huck, ed.* (1993) Greenwillow Books. 32p.

Spl — Splinters: a Book of Very Short Poems. *Michael Harrison, ed.* (1989) Oxford University Press. 121 p

SPV — Sin Puertas Visibles: An Anthology of Contemporary Poetry by Mexican Women. *Jen Hofer, ed.* (1st ed., 2003) University of Pittsburgh Press. 241p.

SSCS — Sky Scrape / City Scape. *Jane Yolen, ed.* (1996) Boyds Mills Press. 32p.

SSLK — Shimmy Shimmy Shimmy like My Sister Kate. *Nikki Giovanni, ed.* (1996) Henry Holt and Company. 188p.

SSUS — Slave Songs of the United States. *William Francis Allen, Charles Pickard Ware, and Lucy McKim Garrison, eds.* (1st ed., 1867) Applewood Books. 115p.

StAl — Staying Alive: Real Poems for Unreal Times. *Neil Astley, ed.* (1st ed., 2003) Miramax Books, Hyperion. 496p.

STuOW — The Stuffed Owl, an Anthology of Bad Verse. *D. B. Wyndham Lewis and Charles Lee, eds.* (2003) New York Review Books. 264p.

STV — Sappho to Valéry: Poems in Translation. *John Frederick Nims, ed.* (Rev. and enl., 1990) University of Arkansas Press. 415p.

SUP — Stand Up Poetry: An Expanded Anthology. *Charles Harper Webb, ed.* (1st ed., 2002) University of Iowa Press. 322p.

SurPaPo — Surrealist Painters and Poets. *Mary Ann Caws, ed.* (1st ed., 2001) MIT Press. 525p.

SurWo — Surrealist Women: an International Anthology. *Penelope Rosemont, ed.* (1998) University of Texas Press. 516p.

SWaP — She Wields a Pen: American Women Poets of the Nineteenth Century. *Janet Gray, ed.* (1997) University of Iowa Press. 374p.

SweBea — Sweeping Beauty: Contemporary Women Poets do Housework. *Pamela Gemin, ed.* (1st ed., 2005) University of Iowa Press. 180p.

SwNoth — Sweet Nothings: an Anthology of Rock and Roll in American Poetry. *Jim Elledge, ed.* (1st ed., 1994) Indiana University Press. 283p.

SxFrPo — *Six French Poets of the Nineteenth Century: Lamartine, Hugo, Baudelaire, Verlaine, Rimbaud, Mallarmé. *A. M. Blackmore and E. H. Blackmore, eds.* (2000) Oxford University Press. 334p.

TAL — A Treasury of Asian Literature. *John D. Yohannon, ed.* (1984) Mentor Books. 432p., pap.

TANSG — These Are Not Sweet Girls: Poetry by Latin American Women. *Marjorie Agosin, ed.* (1994) White Pine Press. 368p., pap.

TAPaP — This Art: Poems About Poetry. *Michael Wiegers, ed.* (1st ed., 2003) Copper Canyon Press. 165p.

TaR   Telling and Remembering: a Century of American Jewish Poetry. *Steven J. Rubin, ed.* (1997) Beacon Press. 499p.

TCAPo   Three Centuries of American Poetry. *Allen Mandelbaum and Robert D. Richardson, Jr., eds.* (1st ed., 1999) Bantam Books. 733p.

TCAWP   Twentieth Century Anglo-Welsh Poetry. *Dannie Abse, ed.* (1997) Seren Books/Dufour Editions. 273p.

TCLAP   Twentieth-Century Latin American Poetry. *Stephen Tapscott, ed.* (1996) University of Texas Press. 418p.

TCRusP   Twentieth-Century Russian Poetry. *John Glad and Daniel Weissbort, eds.* (1992) University of Iowa Press. 384p.

TFi   **The Top 500 Poems. *William Harmon, ed.* (1992) Columbia University Press. 113p.

TiP2   Texas in Poetry 2. *Billy Bob Hill, ed.* (1st ed., 2002) TCU Press. 497p.

TLR   Talking like the Rain: a First Book of Poems. *X. J. Kennedy and Dorothy M. Kennedy, eds.* (1992) Little Brown and Company. 96p.

TouFir   Touching the Fire: Fifteen Poets of Today's Latino Renaissance. *Ray González, ed.* (1st ed., 1998) Anchor Books. 304p.

TreFP   Treasury of Favorite Poems. *Joseph H. Head, ed.* (3rd ed., 2000) Gramercy Books. 336p.

TriCat   The Triumphant Cat. *Walter Payne, ed.* (1993) Carrol and Graf Publishers. 160p.

TRP   To Read a Poem. *Donald Hall, ed.* (2nd ed., 1992) Harcourt Brace Jovanovich. 411p.

TSAP   Ten South African Poets. *Adam Schwartzman, ed.* (1st ed., 1999) Carcanet. 226p.

TuT   Turning Tides: Modern Dutch and Flemish Verse in English Versions by Irish Poets. *Peter van de Kamp, ed.* (1994) Story Line Press. 432p.

TWF   Teaching with Fire: Poetry that Sustains the Courage to Teach. *Sam M. Intrator and Megan Scribner, eds.* (1st ed., 2003) Jossey-Bass. 225p.

TWW   Two Worlds Walking: Short Stories, Essays, and Poetry by Writers with Mixed Heritages. *Diane Glancy and C. W. Truesdale, eds.* (1st ed., 1994) New Rivers Press. 308p.

UnSA   Unsettling America: an Anthology of Contemporary Multicultural Poetry. *Maria Mazziotti Gillan and Jennifer Gillan, eds.* (1994) Penguin Books. 406p., pap.

UpMys   Upholding Mystery: An Anthology of Contemporary Christian Poetry. *David Impastato, ed.* (1st ed., 1997) Oxford University Press. 369p.

UrbNat   Urban Nature: Poems about Wildlife in the City. *Laure-Anne Bosselaar, ed.* (1st ed., 2000) Milkweed Editions. 265p.

UV   Unauthorized Versions: Poems and Their Parodies. *Kenneth Baker, ed.* (1990) Faber and Faber. 446p.

VaPo   Vanishing Points: New Modernist Poems. *Rod Mengham, ed.* (1st ed., 2004) Salt Publishing. 311p.

VCAP   The Vintage Book of Contemporary American Poetry. *J. D. McClatchy, ed.* (1990) Vintage Books. 560p.

VCWP   The Vintage Book of Contemporary World Poetry. *J. D. McClatchy, ed.* (1996) Vintage Books. 655p., pap.

VerBaPo   Very Bad Poetry. *Kathryn Petras and Ross Petras, eds.* (1st ed., 1997) Vintage Books. 126p.

Vesp   Vespers: Contemporary American Poems of Religion and Spirituality. *Virgil Suárez and Ryan G. Van Cleave, eds.* (1st ed., 2003) University of Iowa Press. 160p.

VisFro   Visiting Frost: Poems Inspired by the Life and Work of Robert Frost. *Sheila Coghill and Thom Tammaro, eds.* (1st ed., 2005) University of Iowa Press. 180p.

ViWalt   Visiting Walt: Poems Inspired by the Life & Work of Walt Whitman. *Sheila Coghill and Thom Tammaro, eds.* (1st ed., 2003) University of Iowa Press. 234p.

ViWPN   Victorian Women Poets: a New Annotated Anthology. *Virginia Blain, ed.* (2001) Longman. 382p.

VWP   Victorian Women Poets: an Anthology. *Angela Leighton and Margaret Reynolds, eds.* (1991) Blackwell. 691p., pap.

WaAnP   **The Wadsworth Anthology of Poetry. *Jay Parini, ed.* (1st ed., 2006) Thomson Wadsworth. 1,712p.

WaCA   Wheel and Come Again: an Anthology of Reggae Poetry. *Kwame Dawes, ed.* (1st ed., 1998) Goose Lane Editions. 218p.

WANABP	The Wisdom Anthology of North American Buddhist Poetry. *Andrew Schelling, ed.* (1st ed., 2005) Wisdom Publications. 397p.
WED	The Winged Energy of Delight: Selected Translations. *Robert Bly, ed.* (1st ed., 2005) Perennial. 405p.
WeW-3	Western Wind: an Introduction to Poetry. *John Frederick Nims, ed.* (3d ed., 1992) Random House. 639p., pap.
WhBo	What Book!?: Buddha Poems from Beat to HipHop. *Gary Gach, ed.* (2nd ed., 1998) Parallax Press. 248p.
WHSW	Who Has Seen the Wind? an Illustrated Collection of Poetry for Young People. *Kathryn Sky-Peck, ed.* (1991) Museum of Fine Arts, Boston. 63p.
WiU	The World in Us: Lesbian and Gay Poetry of the Next Wave. *Elena Georgiou and Michael Lassell, eds.* (2000) St. Martin's Press. 392p.
WoBe	World Beat. *Eliot Weinberger, ed.* (1st ed., 2006) New Directions. 258p.
WoPoe	*World Poetry: an Anthology of Verse from Antiquity to Our Time. *Katharine Washburn and John S. Major, eds.* (1st ed., 1998) W.W. Norton and Company. 1,338p.
WoRP	Women Romantic Poets, 1785-1832: an Anthology. *Jennifer Breen, ed.* (1992) J. M. Dent & Sons. 182p.
WPoS	Women in Praise of the Sacred: 43 Centuries of Spiritual Poetry by Women. *Jane Hirshfield, ed.* (1994) HarperCollins. 259p
YaTCFP	**The Yale Anthology of Twentieth-Century French Poetry. *Mary Ann Caws, ed.* (1st ed., 2004) Yale University Press. 646p.
YaYoPo	The Yale Younger Poets Anthology. *George Bradley, ed.* (1st ed., 1998) Yale University Press. 306p.
ZenPo	Zen Poetry. *Lucien Stryk and Takashi Ikemoto, eds.* (1st ed., 1995) Grove Press. 124p.

ABBREVIATIONS

abr.	abridged	*mod.*	modernized or modern
ad.	adapted	*N.T.*	New Testament
add.	additional	*O.T.*	Old Testament
arr.	arranged	*orig.*	original
at.	attributed	*par.*	paraphrase or paraphrased
Bk.	book	*pr.*	prose
br.	brief	*Pt.*	part
ch.	chapter	*rev.*	revised
comp.	compiled or compiler	*sc.*	scene
comps.	compilers	*Sec.*	section
cond.	condensed	*sel.*	selection
diff.	different	*sels.*	selections
fr.	from	*sl.*	slightly
frag.	fragment	*st.*	stanza
incl.	included or including	*sts.*	stanzas
introd.	introduction or introductory	*tr.*	translator, translation, or translated
ll.	lines	*trs.*	translators or translations
LL.	last line	*var.*	various
med.	medieval	*vers.*	version or versions
misc.	miscellaneous	*wr.*	wrong or wrongly

TITLE, FIRST LINE, AND LAST LINE INDEX

Titles, first lines, and last lines are arranged in one alphabetical listing in the Title, First Line, and Last Line Index. Titles are distinguished by initial capital letters on the important words. All first-line entries are followed by the title of the poem, if there is a title. When the title and the first line of a poem are identical, or nearly so, only one of them is listed, although occasionally, for purposes of clarity, the first line has been added in quotation marks and in parenthesis to the title entry.

Anthology codes are listed after titles, first lines, and last lines. Last lines are distinguished from first lines by the symbol (LL). However, more complete information as to translators, acts and scenes, abridgements, and variant titles is given in the title entry.

An indented citation indicates that the poem is a selection from the work listed one level above. A citation indented and inside parenthesis indicates a variant title, variant first line, or variant last line as used in the anthologies that follow.

Generic title entries, such as Ode, Song, Sonnet, are followed by the first line in quotation marks for easy identification. Such entries, of course, may also be located by first-line listing.

Numerals in citations of poems by Horace refer to the Odes; *in citations of poems by Ovid, to the* Elegies; *and in citations of poems by Tennyson, to* In Memoriam A. H. H.

Titles and lines beginning with "O" and "Oh" are alphabetized separately, with cross-references where necessary. Names beginning with "Mac," "Mc," and "M" are placed in alphabetical order.

A. Louis Zukofsky.
"A" 11. APSN; APT-2; ColAP; GPTC; NAAPv.2; OxBoAm
"A" 12.
   "In peace." APT-2
   "Like Grandpa Paul / The water is all of my mind." ChIV-1
   "Red horse, A." PFTM-2
"A" 15.
   "Hinny / by / stallion, An." APSN
"A" 18.
   "*He* has become as / talkative as Bottom a weaver and says for." APSN
   "Unearthing / my valentine, An." APSN
   "Weeping: the food he eats." APSN
   "When they use elbow or arm boards to." APSN
A, a, a, Domine Deus. David Jones. HarvBoo
A / ABA. Richard Kostelanetz. WhBo
A. / Acacia. flowering and an archway. Vines. Pamela Alexander. AmAlph
A B C. Charles Stuart Calverley. OBCoV
A B C D. *Unknown.* SonAtl, *tr. by* Mounther Alogaily and Cee Kassen
A B C D E F G H. I've Got a Gal in Kalamazoo. Mack Gordon. ReLy
A, B, C's, The. Imamu Amiri Baraka. EGAG
A Bas la Gloire! Edward Wyndham Tennant. FaBoWar
A begat B begat C. BE-. Sharon Bryan. PoDa
A-bide a- a-. Monk. John Taggart. FTOS; PFTM-2
A black, E white, I red, U green, O blue, vowels. Voyelles. Arthur Rimbaud. WoPoe, *tr. by* F. Scott Fitzgerald
A black, E white, I red, U green, O blue: vowels. Vowels. Arthur Rimbaud. SxFrPo, *tr. by* Martin Sorrell
A / blake. Little song, A. B. P. Nichol. OpeFie
A call ya brudda. Ring da till. Wopko Jensma. TSAP
A cannae hear his name an' hide. Wee Lassie's First Luve, The. George Francis Savage-Armstrong. IrV
A Capella. Robert Patrick Dana. Vesp
A Cappella. Shari Miller Wagner. ACAMVP
A. D. Blood. Edgar Lee Masters. APT-1 *Fr.* Spoon River Anthology.
A / different / tongue. Gyno-Text. Lola Lemire Tostevin. NLPA
A doesn't know. A B C D. *Unknown.* SonAtl, *tr. by* Mounther Alogaily and Cee Kassen
A Don Francisco Giner de los Ríos. Antonio Machado Ruiz. RaW
A. E. F. Carl Sandburg. MoAmPo
A. E. Housman. W. H. Auden. OxAEP-2
A. E. Housman and a Few Friends. Humbert Wolfe. UV
A esta mujer la sangre se le fuga. Mónica Nepote. SPV
Á fin all was strange. Gravity and Grace. Claudia Keelan. BodElec
A fuerza de inventar un riachuelo sobre la azotea y de ir forcejeando con las baldosas quemantes. Diluvio. Laura Solórzano. SPV
A. G. / present as a gift. Gate Gate Paragate Parasmgate Bodhi Svaha. C. Robert Lloyd. ICANM
A in I as was Blackening Read (Mandala). Ken Harris. AnSo

A is an Apple, as everyone knows. Abecedarie. Thomas M. Disch. OBCoV
A is for apron in plastic or cloth. Edna's Alphabet. Barry Humphries. OBCoV
A la Bourbon. Richard Lovelace. CavPo
A la fin tu es las de ce monde ancien. Zone. Guillaume Apollinaire. YaTCFP
A La Recherche. Miklós Radnóti. IQMS, *tr. by* Peter Zollman
A La Une. Marie Ponsot. CLPP
À la voix de Kathleen Ferrier. Yves Bonnefoy. YaTCFP
A Larra con Unas Violetas. Luis Cernuda. RaW
À l'ombre du tapis chatoyant, ah! Poème Amoureux. Gisèle Prassinos. YaTCFP
A l'unisson crient les mouettes. *Unknown.* CCL1 *Fr.* Guan-ju.
À mes carreaux nul n'a dansé. À mes carreaux. Valentine Penrose. YaTCFP
A mid the non com mit t e d / com pound s of t he m in d. Metagnomy. Norman Henry, II Pritchard. EGAG
A. N. Marquis has erased. To Paul Robeson, Opus no. 3. Percy Johnston. EGAG
A nadie debe alarmar que el horizonte acumule detrás de los follajes volutas y nubes como del Greco: una tarde tan barroca no pasa del ensayo general. Meditar. Gerardo Deniz. RMCMP
A / Niece / Comes, dripping. Ancutsa, Ancutsa. Cathal McCabe. NIrP
À Noël. Emmanuel Hocquard. YaTCFP
   1. YaTCFP
   2. YaTCFP
   3. YaTCFP
   25. YaTCFP
À Noël, Cyrille a introduit les loups dans la. Emmanuel Hocquard. YaTCFP *Fr.* À Noël.
A Nos Glorieux Morts. Jan Eijkelboom. TuT, *tr. by* Michael O'Loughlin
A Paris la tour Saint-Jacques chancelante. Vigilance. André Breton. YaTCFP
A Punto de Caer. Blas de Otero. RaW
A qué te tiras. Rancho. Cecilio Garcia-Camarillo. ICANM
À Quoi Bon Dire. Charlotte Mew. MakPoe; NPeEn; OxBEV; VWP
A Si Wha New Belize. Philip Lewis. OWABP
A. Smith, I. Brown and my own self. Dear Stars, Rock Me to Sleep. István Sinka. IQMS, *tr. by* Adam Makkai
A! Sone, tak hede to me whos sone thou wast. *Unknown.* OHMEL
A. Stands for Absolutely Anything. Noël Coward. NBLV *Fr.* Little Ones' A. B. C, The.
A, stands for Americans, who scorn to be slaves. Alphabet. *Unknown.* NAAPv.1
A stands for Archibald who told no lies. Joseph Hilaire Pierre Belloc. NoAM *Fr.* Moral Alphabet, A.
A Terre. Wilfred Owen. FaBoWar; PoWW
A ti, manzana. Oda a la Manzana. Pablo Neruda. IPoFL

A tink a si wha new Belize weh. A Si Wha New Belize. Philip Lewis. OWABP

A todo se le ve la cara, blanca. Aurora de Trasmuros. Juan Ramón Jiménez. RaW

A un Desconocido. Lorna Dee Cervantes. TouFir

A un voyageur. Mohammed Dib. YaTCFP

A veces prefiero la llama de la hornilla en la estufa a un resplandor de fuego. Tímidos, Los. Antonio Deltoro. RMCMP

A veces te muestras. Epifanía. Elsa Cross. RMCMP

Aa this while, Peter wis doun ablò i the yaird. Bible, *N.T.* FaBoVe *Fr.* St. Mark.

Aaannghh! Aaannghh! Counting Breaths. Denise Lassaw-Paljor. WhBo

Aambl. Seitlhamo Motsapi. TSAP

Aan de vaas. Hans Faverey. LWR

Aarde; uit aardewerk bestaande, De. Hans Faverey. LWR

Aaron. George Herbert. BASC; ChIV-1; FSCP; NOSC; SacPr

Aaron had a passion for the lost chord. Aaron. Edwin Denby. NYP2

Aaron Stark. Edwin Arlington Robinson. APN-2; MoAmPo

Aa's a broken-hairted keelman and Aa's ower heid in love. Cushie Butterfield. George Ridley. FaBoVe

Aasvogel brolga colibri dickcissel. Bird Bee. Bob Cobbing. Oth

A—B—on the Learned Bartholo Sylva. Anne Cooke Bacon. EMWP

Abandoning All Pretense, the Vandals. Alan Michael Parker. NAPBL

Abandon. Li Po. CCL1, *tr. by* Arthur Cooper

Abandon'd Day, why dost thou now appear? On My Wedding Day. Sarah Fyge Egerton. EMWP

Abandoned by my words I'm left alone. Jonah's Prayer. Mihály Babits. IQMS, *tr. by* Peter Zollman

Abandoned Conversation with the Senses. Matthea Harvey. LegDan

Abandoned corpses. Evidence. Toki Zenmaro. CAoMJL1, *tr. by* Makoto Ueda

Abandoned Farmhouse. Ted Kooser. WeW-3

Abandoned House, The. César Dávila Andrade. SonAtl, *tr. by* Jenny Boarder, Thomas Boarder, Lisa Martin and Lisandro Pena

Abandoned in the grass. Southwest. Viktor Krivulin. TCRusP, *tr. by* Anna Barker and Daniel Weissbort

Abandoned Outport. Tom Dawe. Coast

Abandoned Princess, The. *Korean Oral Tradition.* CATKP, *tr. by* Peter H. Lee

Abandoned, The. Zbigniew Herbert. PoSu, *tr. by* Michael March *and* Jaroslaw Anders

Abandoning Your Car in a Snowstorm: Rosslyn, Virginia. Michael C. Blumenthal. NoAM

Abandonment. Al-Zahra Al-Mansouri. PoArWo, *tr. by* Richard McKane and Tahia Abdel Nasser

Abandonment, since it is what I have. (LL) Geoffrey Hill. NAMCP V.2; NoAM; UpMys *Fr.* Funeral Music.

Abattoir, The. Ania Walwicz. BMAP

Abba Jacob and St. Francis. Marilyn Nelson Waniek. PfSP

Abba Jacob with his invention. Abba Jacob and St. Francis. Marilyn Nelson Waniek. PfSP

Abbé rambles—Marquis, I think you'll find, The. On the Grass. Paul Verlaine. SxFrPo, *tr. by* Martin Sorrell

Abbey Cwmhir. Harri Webb. AngWePo

Abt Vogler. Robert Browning. NAEL-6v2; NAEL-7v2

Abbott's Lagoon. Dennis Schmitz. GeoHom

(Abbr.) W. / (accus.) You little wretch. Definition of Weather. Matthea Harvey. LegDan

Abbreviated serpent among crystal rocks. Capture of Larache, The. Luis de Góngora y Argote. SpanPo, *tr. by* Frances Fletcher

ABC. Robert Pinsky. BeAl; FaoP; NAMCP V.2; NoP-5

Abd El-Hadi Fights a Superpower. Taha Muhammad Ali. PoCho, *tr. by* Peter Cole

Abdiel. Lord Byron. DiBP *Fr.* Darkness.

Abduction, The. Stanley Kunitz. CAP-8; WeW-3

Abecedary. Thomas M. Disch. OBCoV

Abecedary of slaughter. Europa. Anatol Stern. PFTM-1

Abel. John Wheelwright. ChIV-1

Abel and Abel. Silvio Giussani. ItPo, *tr. by* Gayle Ridinger

Abelard to Eloisa. Judith Madan. RACG

Abel's Blood. Henry Vaughan. OBWVE

Abel's Bride. Denise Levertov. NALW; OxBoAm

Abel's Brothers. Ferial J. Ghazoul. IrPoTo

Aberdarcy: The Main Square. Kingsley Amis. NoAM *Fr.* Evans Country, The.

Aberdare, Llanwynno through. Glyn Cynon Wood. *Unknown.* OBWVE, *tr. by* Gwyn Williams

Aberdeen. Robin Robertson. NePenScot

Aberfan. Kirkpatrick Dobie. EdScPo

Abeulo, why are there flies? Abuelo, Answers and Questions. Maurice Kilwein Guevara. TouFir

Abhor[re], and spew out all neutralities. (LL) Neutrality Loathsome. Robert Herrick. ChIV-1; NoP-4; NoP-5

Abhorring a Vacuum. Chris Wallace-Crabbe. BMAP

Abide With Me. Henry Francis Lyte. InvLi

Abide with me me me. (LL) Monk. John Taggart. FTOS; PFTM-2

Abiding Mountain. Muso Soseki. EaWin, *tr. by* W. S. Merwin

Abiku. John Pepper Clark Bekedermo. HBAPE

Abiku. Wole Soyinka. PoetW

Abiku-child, The. Lunching. Lori Tsang. BtF

Abilene, TX: We Pull Out For New England. Robert A. Fink. TiP2

Ability to Make a Face Like a Spider While Singing Blues: Junior Wells, The. Sandra McPherson. SeSe

Abiquiu. Luis Lopez. GeoH

Able at last to give with an open hand. (LL) New Zealand. James Keir Baxter. NoP-4; NoP-5

Able Baker Charlie Dog. Jethro Somes' Apostrophe to His Former Comrades. John Pauker. PWW2

Able to see in the dark. (LL) Doll. Josephine Miles. FTtHH; NALW

Ablution. Angelina Muñiz Huberman. MirDau, *tr. by* Aurora Camacho

Abnormal Is Not Courage, The. Jack Gilbert. YaYoPo

Aboard at a Ship's Helm. Walt Whitman. APN-1; PtR

Aboard, at home again, this book closes. Lamp, The. Paul Farley. NeBrP

Abode of Arrival. Ahmed Taha. NAfrP, *tr. by* Clarissa C. Burt

Abode of the Unplanned Effect. Chia Tao. CSKM, *tr. by* Mike O'Connor

Abolished, and its weeks spent walking aimlessly. Where When Was. Reginald Shepherd. GT

Abomination. Mary Crockett Hill. AmPoNex

Abomination Of Evil, The. "Angelus Silesius." GePo *Fr.* Cherubical Wanderer, The.

Ab*original* Elegy: The Once and Future Queen. Askia Muhammad Touré. FuFl

Aborigine Sound Poem. *Unknown.* PFTM-1

Abortion. Iman Mirsal. NAfrP, *tr. by* Clarissa C. Burt

Abortion, An. Frank O'Hara. AHA

Abortion, The. Anne Sexton. CAP-8

Abortions will not let you forget. Gwendolyn Brooks. CAP-8; ESEAA; IllVoic; ISC; MoWP; NAAL-5; NALW; OxAAAP; OxBoAm; PoPoPo *Fr.* Street in Bronzeville, A.

Abou Ben Adhem (may his tribe increase!). Abou Ben Adhem. Leigh Hunt. BRP; ChAP; ITBLP; NPBRoP; OBEV; OxAEP-2; TFi

About a Transdanurban Almond Tree. Janus Pannonius. IQMS, *tr. by* Adam Makkai

About a year has passed. I've returned to the place of battle. Elegy. Joseph Brodsky. AF, *tr. by* the author

About all these I write freely. Other Life, the. Nina Cassian. PoSu, *tr. by* Cristian Andrei and Daniel Weissbort

About Atlanta. Ntozake Shange. ISC

About beef, for instance? Christmas. Leigh Hunt. OBCP

About Benwell. Gillian Allnutt. RSaN

About cruelty yet. (LL) W. C. W. Watching Presley's Second Appearance on The Ed Sullivan Show: Mercy Hospital, Newark, 1956. David Wojahn. AllShUp; SwNoth

About Death. Patricia K. Page. StAl

About eight of us were nailing up forts. Words for My Daughter. John Balaban. PoChi; RaBo; SUP

About Eyes. Edwin Rolfe. OtW

About Face. Alice Fulton. AllShUp

About four, a few flakes. Six Winter Privacy Poems. Robert Bly. CAP-8

About him, and lies down to pleasant dreams. (LL) Thanatopsis. William Cullen Bryant. APN-1; BRP; ColAP; NAAL-3; NAAL-5; NAAPv.1; NCAP; NoP-5; OBEV; OxBoAm; TCAPo; TFi

About his chair there wenten white alauns. Geoffrey Chaucer. DiBP *Fr.* Canterbury Tales, The.

About Ice. Malcolm Lowry. OxBSo

About inspiration the Old Masters. Inspiration. Stephen Stepanchev. PoA 2002

About Limits. Tatiana Shcherbina. CRWP, *tr. by* Derek Walcott

About Love. Evgeniya Lavut. CRWP, *tr. by* Yury Drobyshev and Carol Rumens

About Marriage. Denise Levertov. NALW

About me the night, moonless, wimples the mountains. Vancouver Lights. Earle Birney. BrAP

About Mount Uludağ. Nazim Hikmet. WoPoe, *tr. by* Randy Blasing and Mutlu Konuk

About my angry lines, burn them, do. Anger Poem, The (1.16). Horace. WED, *tr. by* Robert Bly

About my crevice and burrow. (LL) Drumlin Woodchuck, A. Robert Frost.
     APT-1; NoAM

About My Grandfather. József Kiss. *tr. by* Anthony Edkins
     "Make haste slowly, my friend, make haste slowly." IQMS, *tr. by* Anthony
     Edkins

About My Poems. Donald Justice. PoA 2002
     (Early Poems.) CAP-8

About noon on Avenue C yesterday, I was stopped by a boy who looked about 7
     or 8. Seeds. Katie Degentesh. FreRad

About our hips. Harriet Jacobs. SpirFl

About pigs and trees, stars and horses. (LL) Lunch with Pancho Villa. Paul
     Muldoon. ModIr; NAMCP V.2

About Poems. Evan X. Hyde. OWABP

About Scotland, &C. Ruthven Todd. EdScPo

About suffering they were never wrong. Musée des Beaux Arts. W. H.
     Auden. BeAl; BrAP; CABP; ClHu; EMP; GS; HeIP-4; NAEL-6v2;
     NAEL-7v2; NAMCP V.1; NIL-7; NoAM; NoP-4; NoP-5; NPeEn; OxAEP-
     2; OxBEV; OxBoAm; PoPoPo; RaBo; RSaN; SoSe-8; TFi; TRP; WaAnP

About suffering we are always wrong. Brief To Butterick. Stephen Rodefer.
     VaPo

About ten days or so. Reassurance, The. Thom Gunn. NPeEn; StAl

About ten million years ago. Speck Speaks, A. Adrian Mitchell. OBSP

About the Cool Water. Sappho. OBVE, *tr. by* Kenneth Rexroth

About the Extinction of. A. Di Michele. AnSo

About the field / Crow moves. Issa. ZenPo, *tr. by* Takashi Ikemoto and
     Lucien Stryk

About the grave / Waves of spring mist. Naito Joso. ZenPo, *tr. by* Takashi
     Ikemoto and Lucien Stryk

About the little chambers of my heart. Gone. Mary Elizabeth Coleridge.
     OBEV; PoBW; VWP

About the Men. Adele Ne Jame. PoArWo

About the pain the folk. Your Name is Gift. Stella P. Chipasula. HAWP

About the Phoenix. James Merrill. NoAM

About the Princes. András Szkhárosi Horvát. *tr. by* Adam Makkai
     "You live in dishonor grave, Dukes and Mighty Princes." IQMS, *tr. by*
     Adam Makkai

About the Shark, phlegmatical one. Maldive Shark, The. Herman Melville.
     APN-2; BrAP; ColAP; NAAL-3; NAAPv.1; NCAP; NoP-4; NoP-5;
     OxBoAm; TCAPo; WaAnP

About the Shipwrecked Frandus. Janus Pannonius. IQMS, *tr. by* Iain
     MacLeod

About the size of an old-style dollar bill. Poem. Elizabeth Bishop. Coast;
     NAMCP V.2; NoAM; PoetW; PoPoPo; VCAP

About These Things. Elizabeth Jennings. MoWP

About these things I always shall be dumb. About These Things. Elizabeth
     Jennings. MoWP

About this snow I'd say. Kind of Catastrophe, A. Rachel Zucker. IIR

About this time streetlamps flicker up like. Ken Edwards. Oth *Fr.* Five
     Nocturnes, after Derek Jarman.

About this Woman. Judith Rodriguez. BMAP

About Time ("At dusk the silence by the sea.") Laurens Vancrevel. TuT, *tr.
     by* Greg Delanty

About Time ("This silence at the sea's edge, so late in the afternoon.") Laurens
     Vancrevel. TuT, *tr. by* Anne Kennedy

About to Fall. Blas de Otero. RaW, *tr. by* Hardie St. Martin

About Tu Fu. Li Po. CrYelRi, *tr. by* Sam Hamill

About twilight we came to the whitewashed pub. East Coast Journey. James
     Keir Baxter. NoP-4; NoP-5

About Two Kinds of Faith: That of Christ and That of the Pope's Ragged
     Patchwork. András Szkhárosi Horvát. *tr. by* Adam Makkai
     "Hurry up, Christendom, think about salvation." IQMS, *tr. by* Adam Makkai

About two miles east of here. King Cobra as Political Assassin, The. Ray A.
     Young Bear. HATNAP

About us. Rest shall we. (LL) Impercipient, The. Thomas Hardy. NAEL-
     6v2; NAEL-7v2

About where my funeral might be going next. (LL) Detour. Michael Longley.
     BeAl; NAMCP V.2

About Women. Ch'oe Sûngja. EcSo, *tr. by* Mickey Hong

About women no one can know. There are some. Mary Magdalene. Saunders
     Lewis. OBWVE, *tr. by* Gwyn Morgan

About writing a poem. It occurs to me. Ars Poetica. John Gilgun. SUP

Above a ceiling of emerald junipers. Dry Spell of Faith, A. Timothy Geiger.
     AmPoNex

Above a stretch of still unravaged weald. Garden Party, The. Donald Davie.
     OxBEV

Above, above. Behold. *Unknown.* WoPoe, *tr. by* Alfons L. Korn and Mary
     Kawena Pukui

Above / above. *Wintu Oral Tradition.* NAAPv.1 *Fr.* Six Dream Songs.

Above all guard yourself against bitterness, black child. Black City, The.
     Breyten Breytenbach. PoetW, *tr. by* Leon de Kock and Sonia van
     Schalwyk

Above all, in droves, they simply leave. We Have Some Urgent Messages.
     Kate Clanchy. EdScPo

Above all rivers thy river hath renown. William Dunbar. OPOU *Fr.* To [*or* In
     Honour of] the City of London.

Above All That? James Merrill. AmWit

Above an empty heart. (LL) He Resigns. John Berryman. HarvBoo; WeW-3

Above, below, in sky and sod. Over-Heart, The. John Greenleaf Whittier.
     ChIV-2

Above everything, I make a jagged, blue edge. Easter Revolt Painted on a
     Tablespoon, The. Maurice Kilwein Guevara. TouFir

Above her face. 1815. Jeffrey Wainwright. NPeEn

Above high-tide mark on the long beach. Half Measures. Thomas McGrath.
     BodElec

Above his dreamy abstract stare. (LL) Ex-Queen Among the Astronomers,
     The. Fleur Adcock. MoWP; NAEL-6v2; NAEL-7v2; NALW; NoP-4;
     NoP-5

Above / in the west, in the flat of the flowers. *Wintu Oral Tradition.*
     NAAPv.1 *Fr.* Six Dream Songs.

Above, it's spring, I think. Poem for R. Kim Ly Bui-Burton. PasH

Above me hangs the dry firmament of the Urarts. Nina Gabrielian. CRWP *Fr.*
     Erebuni.

Above me no seraphim or nymphs. On Being Kicked Out of the Harold
     Washington Library Center for Napping on the Floor. Thom Ward.
     OPRER

Above my desk / the Rabbi of Auschwitz. On a Drawing by Flavio. Philip
     Levine. BodElec

Above my desk, whirring and self-important. Angel. James Merrill. BrAP

Above our cupped world no tall stack opens. Depression, The. David
     Gwenallt Jones. BBMWP, *tr. by* Anthony Conran

Above Pate Valley. Gary Snyder. GeoHom; NAMCP V.2; NoP-4; NoP-5;
     OxBoAm; StAl; TRP

Above / rise / will. *Wintu Oral Tradition.* NAAPv.1 *Fr.* Six Dream Songs.

Above the baby powder clouds. Spring Evening. Frederick Turner. RA

Above the banks of fog the muffled thud. White Paintings IV (Independence
     Day). Laura Mullen. RoV

Above the boat. Kikaku. BLT; ZenPo, *tr. by* Takashi Ikemoto and Lucien
     Stryk

Above the Boca del Arno the sky. Outside Pisa. Chitra Divakaruni. OpBo

Above the brink. Lethe. Mary Barnard. APT-2

Above the cinderblocks. Dawn in El Paso. Carol Coffee Reposa. TiP2

Above the Circus of the World she sat. Rome. Madison Cawein. APN-2

Above the City. James Laughlin. OtW

Above the corner of Water and Seventeenth, when pigeons. Rooftop. James
     Kimbrell. AmPoNex

Above the deli in Hell's Kitchen where the fire erupted. Mayan Astronomer in
     Hell's Kitchen, A. Martín Espada. PoDa

Above the forest of the parakeets. Bird with the Coppery, Keen Claws, The.
     Wallace Stevens. OxBoAm

Above the Fray Is Only Thin Air. A. R. Ammons. BodElec

Above the freeway, over the music. Jazz Station. Michael S. Harper. NoAM

Above the fresh ruffles of the surf. Voyages. Hart Crane. APT-2; CAGL;
     NAAPv.2; NAMCP V.1; NoAM; NoP-5

Above the hood of an illegally parked red Toyota Corolla. I Found Orpheus
     Levitating. Nick Carbó. NAPBL; ReBoTo

Above the lake the sun is high. On The Reedy Lake. János Vajda. IQMS, *tr.
     by* Jean Overton Fuller

Above the Rio Grande. Charles Tomlinson. ICANM

Above the spleen of the landscape. July. Julio Herrera y Reissig. TCLAP, *tr.
     by* Andrew Rosing

Above the Timberline. Alan Michael Parker. AmPoNex

Above the tower—a lone, twice-sized moon. Full Moon. Tu Fu [*or* Du Fu].
     NDACCP, *tr. by* David Hinton

Above the Tree. Elizabeth Stoddard. SWaP

Above the walls the west light hangs, until. Walled Garden. Dorothy,
     Duchess of Wellington Wellesley. OBGa

Above the waste allotments the dawn halts. (LL) Light Breaks Where No Sun
     Shines. Dylan Thomas. MoBrPo; OxAEP-2; OxBEV

Above the whispering sea. Air Raid Across the Bay at Plymouth. Stephen
     Spender. AF

Above the white pond. Decline. Georg Trakl. WoPoe, *tr. by* Robert Firmage

Above the white pond. Downfall. Georg Trakl. AF, *tr. by* Daniel Simko

Above the window a gray obelisk hangs. Sterile Dish, The. Lenka Valachová.
     SurWo, *tr. by* Katerina Pinosová

Above their narrow beds. (LL) Migration. Jane Griffiths. BeAl; NeBl

Above them spread a stranger sky. Indian's Welcome to the Pilgrim Fathers,
     The. Lydia Huntley Sigourney. TCAPo

Above, through lunar woods a goddess flees. Lovers, The. William Jay Smith. MoAmPo

Above Us. Julia Hartwig. BLT

Above us, stars. Beneath us, constellations. Flying at Night. Ted Kooser. OtW; PBCAP

Above us, where the clouds'. Emyr Lewis. ATSWP *Fr.* Revolution.

Above Vitebsk. Shirley Kaufman. TaR

Above yon sombre swell of land. Plough, The. Richard Henry Horne. OBEV

Above, you paint the sky. How to Paint a Perfect Christmas. Miroslav Holub. OBCP, *tr. by* Ian Milner and George Theiner

Abracadabra. Oskar Pastior. OnScMo, *tr. by* Harry Mathews

Abracadabra as was. Abracadabra. Oskar Pastior. OnScMo, *tr. by* Harry Mathews

Abraham. Edwin Muir. ChIV-1

Abraham. Delmore Schwartz. ChIV-1; TaR

Abraham Davenport. John Greenleaf Whittier. NoP-4; TCAPo

Abraham Got All the Stars n the Sand. Ruth Forman. AmPoNex; OxAAAP

Abraham Lincoln. William Cullen Bryant. *See* Death of Lincoln, The.

Abraham Lincoln. Mildred Plew Meigs. CA

Abraham Lincoln Walks at Midnight. Vachel Lindsay. APT-1; CBCWP; IllVoic; MoAmPo; NAAPv.2; TCAPo; TFi

Abraham to kill him. Emily Dickinson. ChIV-1; SoSe-8

Abraham's God appeared to me. Disease That Arrives at Death. No Hyegyông. EcSo, *tr. by* Ann Y. Choi

Abraham's Madness. Bink Noll. ChIV-1

Abraham's Sacrifice of Isaac. Sir John Stradling. NOSC

Abrazada a una Lágrima. Luis Rosales. RaW

Abrupt and charming mover. Stephen Spender. CAGL

Abrupt and charming mover. Abrupt and charming mover. Stephen Spender. CAGL

Absalom. Muriel Rukeyser. NAMCP V.2

Absalom and Achitophel. John Dryden. BASC; NAEL-6v1; NAEL-7v1; NOSC

"In pious times ere [*or* e'r] priest-craft did begin." MakPoe; NoP-5; NOSC (Monmouth.) NPeEn

"Of these the false Achitophel was first." OxBEV

Popish Plot, The. BrAP

Shaftesbury. NPeEn: NOSC

"Some by their friends, more by themselves thought wise." ChIV-1; OBSV

"Some of their chiefs were princes of the land." OxBEV

Zimri: The Duke of Buckingham. OBSV

Abschied des Freundes, Der. Wang Wei. CCL1, *tr. by* Hans Bethge

Absence. Elizabeth Cobbold. CenSon *Fr.* Sonnets of Laura.

Absence. Jaime Jacinto. ReBoTo

Absence. Richard Jago. OBEV

Absence. Luljeta Lleshanaku. WoBe, *tr. by* Henry Israeli

Absence. Charlotte Mew. MoBrPo

Absence. Gabriela Mistral. SpanPo, *tr. by* Kate Flores

Absence. Takahashi Shinkichi. ZenPo, *tr. by* Takashi Ikemoto and Lucien Stryk

Absence / Can you imagine. Can You Imagine. Artur Miedzyrzecki. PoSu

Absence is paine. (LL) Fulke, 1st Baron Brooke Greville. NPeEn; PBRV *Fr.* Caelica.

Absence, Luminescent. Valerie Martínez. TouFir

Absence, my angel, presence at my side. James Vincent Cunningham. APT-2

Absence of Joaquín. Pablo Neruda. ItP, *tr. by* W. S. Merwin

Absence of the Soul. Federico García Lorca. WoPoe *Fr.* Lament for Ignacio Sanchez Mejias.

Absence, The. Sylvia Townsend Warner. MoBrPo

Absence, the noble truce. Fulke, 1st Baron Brooke Greville. NPeEn; PBRV *Fr.* Caelica.

Absence: "There are men and women huddled in rooms tonight." Bob Hicok. PoDa

Absences. Donald Justice. CAP-8

Absences. Philip Larkin. OxBEV

Absent from Dances 1925. Stephanie Strickland. ExTi

Absent from thee, I languish still. Song. John Wilmot, 2d Earl of Rochester. NPeEn; OxBEV

Absent ones whisper and the night is dense, The. Night is the. Deaf Lantern. Alejandra Pizarnik. MirDau, *tr. by* Celeste Kostopulos-Cooperman

Absent so often, you leave open a rough way back—to enjoy, to decide. Out of Bounds. Harry Mathews. OnScMo

Absent, The. Edwin Muir. GPTC; NAMCP V.1; NoAM

Absent, The. May Muzaffar. PoArWo, *tr. by* Tahia Abdel Nasser

Absented from felicity a year. Horatio's Philosophy. R. S. Gwynn. IaFF

Absentia Animi. Gunnar Ekelof. PFTM-1

Absent-Minded Beggar, The. Rudyard Kipling. FaBoWar

Absentmindedly. 529 1983. Gerda Mayer. Spl

Absinthe, green, bewitching moon. Good Friday. João da Cruz e Sousa. TCLAP, *tr. by* Flavia Vidal

Absalom and Achitophel, Part 2. John Dryden and Nahum Tate. "To make quick way I'll leap o'er heavy blocks." OBSV

Absolute cold; absence of things. Fall on Me. Kate Schmitt. IJHIL

Absolute dark; and if you say, A cloud—, The. Mutations. Robert Fitzgerald. APT-2

Absolute / Reality, namely. Philip Whalen. WhBo

Absolute September. Mary Jo Salter. ExTi

Absolute zero: the locust sings. Summer. Conrad Potter Aiken. NoAM

Absolutely everyone is wild about. Xena, Warrior Princess. Campbell McGrath. MAAN

Absolutely Ordinary Rainbow, An. Les A. Murray. HarvBoo; StAl

Absolution. Diane Ward. FTOS

Absorbing a taste of magic. Oaktown CA. Reginald Lockett. FTtHH

Absorption of Rock. Maxine Hong Kingston. OpBo

Abstaining from the congregation. Yom Kippur, 5726. Cynthia Ozick. TaR

Abstinence Sows Sand All Over. William Blake. OxBEV *Fr.* Gnomic Verses.

Abstract. Sam Hamill. BodElec

Abstracted by silence from the age of seven. On Himself. David Wright. OPOU

Abstraction. Sikong Tu. CCL1 *Fr.* Twenty-Four Modes of Poetry.

Abstraction. Eleanor Wilner. ExTi

Abstracts hover like dull angels, The. Magi. Sylvia Plath. GI

Absurd to speculate; but then—the woman saw *something*. (LL) Robert Pinsky. NoP-4; NoP-5 *Fr.* Essay on Psychiatrists.

Abu Salim, Healer. Rachel Tzvia Back. DTA

Abuela Rufa. Oysters and Zarzuelas. Maria Ercilla. FiBr

Abuelo, Answers and Questions. Maurice Kilwein Guevara. TouFir

Abundance. John Cage. APSN *Fr.* Diary: How to Improve the World (You Will Only Make Matters Worse).

Abundance. Carl Phillips. PuP-23

Abundance of Grey, An. Ogaga Ifowodo. NeNiPo

Abundant Catch (Luke 5:4–10). Czeslaw Milosz. GI

Abundantly. In His Name / Phillis. (LL) Letter from Phillis Wheatley, A. Robert Earl Hayden. ESEAA; NoAM

Abundantly in honor of the ritual celebration, meant twined twirled aperiodic dance. Eleusis. Jim Leftwich. AnSo

Abuse Poems: For Kodzo and Others. Komi Ekpe. PFTM-2, *tr. by* Kofi Awoonor

Abused Child. Michael O'Reilly. BloBone

Abusive! that's the word! Mark Prejsnar. AnSo

Abysmal circle is in the sky, An. At the moment we are an infinite line. Sabah Al-Kharrat Zwein. PoArWo *Fr.* As If in Flaw, or in the Flaw of Space.

Abyss. Diane Di Prima. BB

AC. Geraldine Monk. Oth

Academia; or The Humours of the University of Oxford. Alicia D'Anvers. To the University. NOSC

Academic. John Skoyles. PoA 2002

Academic Graffiti. W. H. Auden.

"John Milton." AmWit

"My First Name, Wystan." AmWit

"Oscar Wilde." AmWit

Academy of the future is opening its doors, The. Ted Berrigan. NYP2; PFTM-2 *Fr.* Sonnets, The.

Acanthus. Arthur Sze. AmAlph; BAP-04

Acanthus. Lawrence L. White. IAoNAP

Accelerando. José Hierro. RaW, *tr. by* Rachel Benson

Accelerated leaf fall October looks like. It Is Difficult to Exaggerate the Importance of Mushrooms as Food. Chris Torrance. Oth

Accentuate the Positive. Johnny Mercer. ReLy

Accept, Boscawen, these unpolished lays. Sensibility: A Poetical Epistle to the Hon. Mrs. Boscawen. Hannah More. RWP

Accept, O Priapus, the moister. Catullus. PriapPo, *tr. by* Richard W. Hooper

Accept thou Shrine of my Dead Saint! Exequy, The. Henry King, Bishop of Chichester. NAEL-6v1

Acceptance. Robert Frost. GSo

Acceptance. John Wieners. FTOS

Acceptance Speech. Elizabeth Kerlikowske. SUP

Accepting. Motion of the Cypher. Ray DiPalma. FTOS

Accessible Heaven. Thylias Moss. OxAAAP

Accessories shop, The. Pierre McOrlan. MFP, *tr. by* Martin Sorrell

Accident, An. Gjertrud Schnackenberg. ArBi

Accident, The. Tatamkulu Afrika. TSAP

Accident, The. Liz Rosenberg. PBCAP

Accident in a naked place. Kim Hunter. RD

Accident in Art. Richard Hovey. APN-2

Accidental far into the longer light. San Juan. June Jordan. EGAG

Accidentally / having broken a teacup. Tanka. Ishikawa Takuboku. CAoMJL1, *tr. by* Makoto Ueda

Accidents will happen by land and by sea. William McGonagall. VerBaPo *Fr.* Clepington Catastrophe, The.

Acclamation, An. John Davies. SacPr

Accompani'd with thine. (LL) Soldier Going to the Field, The. Sir William Davenant. FaBoWar; OBWP

Accompanist, The. William Matthews. P180

Accomplice. Peter Johnson. LiTh

Accomplice, The. David Clewell. PoDa

Accomplices. Thomas Bailey Aldrich. *See* By the Potomac.

Accomplices. Bei Dao. AF, *tr. by* Bonnie S. McDougall

Accomplices. Zhao Zhenkai. VCWP

According to Brueghel. William Carlos Williams. BrAP; NAAL-5; NAAPv.2; NAMCP V.1; NoAM; NoP-5; OtW; OxBoAm; PoPoPo *Fr.* Pictures from Brueghel.

According to *Culture Shock.* Yes. Denise Duhamel. AmPoNex

According to Dineen, a Gael unsurpassed. From the Irish. Ian Duhig. NeBl

According to my Mood. Benjamin Zephaniah. NOxBChV

According to my Teachers. Gwendolyn Brooks. ESEAA *Fr.* Children Going Home.

According to our Code of Honor. From a Revolutionary to J. L. Borges. Roque Dalton. TCLAP, *tr. by* Julie Schumacher

According to Ovid. Bin Ramke. PoA 2002

According to the chef. Chittlin's. Cornelius Eady. BtF

According to the classification born a woman. Femmemasochism. Alicia Galaz Vivar. TANSG, *tr. by* Dave Oliphant

According to the director. Happy and Unhappy Families 2. Lisel Mueller. ExTi

According to the geological version. Hula Dancers Dance the Hula, Kilauea the Caldera, The. John Tarrant. WhBo

According to the silence, winter has arrived. Shepherd. William Stafford. PoA 2002

According to the theory. Night of the Hunter. Paul Hoover. LiTh

According to the *Times.* All the News—September 23, 2001. Mark Pawlak. PrTe

Accordion considers the tunes it knows best, The. Another Night in Crawley's Cove. Al Pittman. Coast

Account, An. Mick North. NLP

Account of the Marvels Whispered in a Mannequin's Ear. Jorge Fernández Granados. RMCMP, *tr. by* John Oliver Simon

Accountability. Paul Laurence Dunbar. APN-2; NAAPv.1

Accountant, The. Michael C. Blumenthal. PoDa

Accounted our commodities. Quiet Neighbour, A. John Heywood. NoSic

Accounting. Claribel Alegría. TANSG, *tr. by* Darwin Flakoll

Accounting Cat, The. John Clarke. UV

Accoutrement. 'Marnia. LW

Accra. Alexander Gerov. CSCBP, *tr. by* Georgi Belev and Lisa Sapinkopf

Accretion / dispossession. Object of Burial Is Intent, The. Rebecca Reynolds. AmPoNex

Accross the fallow clods at early morn. Pewits Nest. John Clare. FaBoVe

Accumulation of Small Acts of Kindness, The. Selima Hill. Masters. MoWP

Accuracy of the Scale, The. Alberto Blanco. RMCMP, *tr. by* Joan Lindgren

Accursed power which stands on Privilege, The. On a General Election. Joseph Hilaire Pierre Belloc. NPeEn; OBSV; OxBEV

Accursed. The curse which with its curving unsheathed letter will never. Nigger in a Photograph, The. Ece Ayhan. PFTM-2, *tr. by* Murat Nemet-Nejat

Accursed the man, whom fate ordains, in spite. Author, The. Charles Churchill.

Accurst [*or* accursed], and in a cursed [*or* cursed] hour he hies. (LL) John Milton. NAEL-6v1; OxAEP-1 *Fr.* Paradise Lost.

Accuse me not, beseech thee, that I wear. Elizabeth Barrett Browning. CenSon *Fr.* Sonnets from the Portuguese.

Accuser, The. Shirley Kaufman. GifTon

Ace. Mark Pawlak. PrTe

Ace of spades. Poem. Paul Dermée. CuPo

Acelerando. José Hierro. RaW

Acer. Peter Finch. AngWePo

Acetylene, all manner of racks, pins the 7 poisons known only to emperors. Men Together. Richard Murray Vaughan. Coast

Ache of it, The. (LL) Ache of Marriage, The. Denise Levertov. BeAl; ColAP; NALW; NAMCP V.2; NoAM; OxBoAm; PmAP; PoPoPo; VCAP; WaAnP

Ache of love! (LL) On the Beach at Fontana. James Joyce. MoBrPo; OBMV; RaBo

Ache of Marriage, The. Denise Levertov. BeAl; ColAP; NALW; NAMCP V.2; NoAM; OxBoAm; PmAP; PoPoPo; VCAP; WaAnP

Achill. Derek Mahon. PBCIP; PNI

Achill Woman, The. Eavan Boland. HarvBoo

Achille looked up at the hole the laurel had left. Derek Walcott. WaAnP *Fr.* Omeros.

Achille peed in the dark, then bolted the half-door shut. Derek Walcott. WaAnP *Fr.* Omeros.

Achilles and Priam. Homer. NAWM-7v1 *Fr.* Iliad, The.

Achilles and the Tortoise. Miroslav Holub. PoSu, *tr. by* Stuart Friebert *and* Dana Hábová

Achilles' baneful wrath resound, O goddess, that imposed. Homer. NOSC *Fr.* Iliad, The.

Achilles' Dream. Homer. CAGL *Fr.* Iliad, The.

Achilles' Lament and the Funeral of Patroclus. Homer. CAGL *Fr.* Iliad, The.

Achilles Over the Trench. Homer. OBVE *Fr.* Iliad, The.

Achilles' Song. Robert Duncan. FTOS

Achilles with wild fury in his heart. Homer. OBWP *Fr.* Iliad, The.

Achilleus to Odysseus. Gig Ryan. VaPo

Aching. Speech / is a mouth. (LL) Language, The. Robert Creeley. CAP-8; PmAP

Acid for the whorls of the fingertips; for the face, a surgeon's knife; oblivion to the name. Escape. Kenneth Fearing. APT-2

Acid today / is trendy entertainment. Why I Choose Black Men for My Lovers. La Loca. CLPP

Acis and Galatea: An English Pastoral Opera. John Gay.
    Air. NAEL-6v1
    "I rage, I melt, I burn." NAEL-6v1

Ack-ack, aye-aye. Blah-Blah. Harryette Mullen. OxAAAP

Ackermann Steppe, The. Adam Mickiewicz. WoPoe, *tr. by* Vyt Bakaitis

Acknowledgement. Keorapetse Kgositsile. SeSe

A-clank to my stride. (LL) Angry Samson. Robert Graves. ChIV-1; OxBEV

Acolyte, The. Denise Levertov. CAP-8

Acoma. William Oandasan. HATNAP

Acorn Song, The. *Unknown.* APN-2 *Fr.* Sacred Songs of the Konkau.

Acorn Speaks, The. Theo Sontrop. TuT, *tr. by* Theo Dorgan

Acorn, The. Gail Mazur. ExTi

Acorns come down from heaven, The. *Unknown.* APN-2 *Fr.* Sacred Songs of the Konkau.

Acorns scatter the ground. Winter burn. Miriam Sagan. WhBo

Acotamiento. Pedro Serrano. RMCMP

Acoustics. William H. New. IFF

Acquaintance of mine, an old-timer veteran, An. Unpleasantness During a Memorial Service. Arye Sivan. NRoS, *tr. by* Esther Raizen

Acquaintance with Time in Early Autumn. Robert Penn Warren. NAAL-5

Acquaintances. Alvaro Cardona-Hine. ICANM

Acquainted with the Night. Robert Frost. AmFaPo; APT-1; AWTN; BLPJKO; BrAP; GSo; HarvBoo; MoAmPo; NAAPv.2; NAMCP V.1; NoAM; NoP-4; NoP-5; OxBoAm; SAmP; TFi; TRP; WeW-3

Acre of Grass, An. William Butler Yeats. HarvBoo; NAMCP V.1; NoAM

Acres of power within me lie. Acres of Power. Randall Swingler. RSaN

Acrimony hangs at the curtain. Conclusion Is Not Drawn, The. Nicole Espagnol. SurWo, *tr. by* Myrna Bell Rochester

Acrobat of Pain. João da Cruz e Sousa. TCLAP, *tr. by* Flavia Vidal

Acrobats were out in Washington Square Park, The. Meeting the Animal in Washington Square Park. Luis J. Rodriguez. FaoP

Aromatic Dawn. Yi Hyangji. EcSo, *tr. by* Catherine J. Kim

Acrophobia. Nancy Means Wright. PfS

Acropolis. Lawrence Durrell. OxAEP-2

Acrospirical Meanderings in a Tongue of the Time. Chris Torrance. Oth

Across a purple west the ship is swimming. Death of Pan, The. Gyula Reviczky. IQMS, *tr. by* Watson Kirkconnell

Across a red west of great mesas. Desert Wisdom. Reg Saner. PoCoUp

Across a room. Blood or Color. Marjorie Welish. FTOS; OnScMo

Across a windowsill a smell of toasted bread. Ah, Nadya, Nadyenka. Bulat Shalvovich Okudzhava. ItGoST, *tr. by* Ronnie Apter and Mark Herman

Across and rain of away, The. I took shred of an umbrella. Furious'd Garb. Russell Atkins. EGAG

Across, beyond, moving toward the soon other coast. Transcircularities. Quincy Troupe. PrTe

Across Black Combe's black sky? (LL) Halley's Comet. Norman Nicholson. NoP-4; NoP-5

Across daubed rock evacuates its dead. (LL) Requiem for the Plantagenet Kings. Geoffrey Hill. CABP; NAEL-6v2; NAEL-7v2; NoAM

Across eternity, across its snows. Dogs and Wolves. Sorley MacLean. EdScPo

Across from glorious Erytheia. Stesichoros. SaLy, *tr. by* Diane Rayor

Across from the gas station. Through the Window of the All-Night Restaurant. Nicholas Christopher. P180

Across from the tract of cinderblock houses. By All Lights: 1959. B. H. Boston. GeoHom

Across Majestic Boulevard, *Steam Bath*. Adagio. Lynda Hull. LaCa

Across muscles and through seizure. Newton's Descent. Irene Plazewska. SurWo

Across My Face the Nights Fall. Patrizia Cavalli. CItWP, *tr.* by Cinzia Sartini Blum and Lara Trubowitz

Across North Wales. Dafydd ap Gwilym Resents the Winter. Rolfe Humphries. WoPoe

Across old peach cans and old jelly jars. (LL) Birth in a narrow room, The. Gwendolyn Brooks. NoP-4; NoP-5

Across Roblin Lake, two shores away. Wilderness Gothic. Alfred Wellington Purdy. BrAP; HeIP-4; NoP-4

Across the Bay. Donald Davie. CABP; NAMCP V.2; NoAM

Across the Bay. Naomi Shihab Nye. ExTi

Across the blank blue of my study window. Visit of the Hawk. David Huddle. PfSP

Across the bridge, where in the morning blow. Sunday Chimes in the City. Louise Imogen Guiney. APN-2

Across the dark fields the family is spread. Wild Radishes. John Kinsella. NeBl

Across the dim frozen fields of night. Night Train. Robert Francis. GM

Across the ditch by the graveyard fence. Lupines. Al Pittman. Coast

Across the Eastern sky has glowed. Crowing of the Red Cock, The. Emma Lazarus. TaR

Across the expedient and wicked stones. (LL) Auto Wreck. Karl Shapiro. APT-2; NIL-7; NIP-4

Across the ferry. Wayfarer, The. Pak Mogwŏl [*or* Mokwŏl]. CAMKP, *tr.* by Kevin O'Rourke

Across the field from a warehouse. Staff Sgt. Edward A. Carter, Jr.: There and Back. Jabari Asim. BtF

Across the Field of the Old Corporal. *Vietnamese Oral Tradition*. CaDao, *tr.* by John Balaban

Across the field the great willow rocking its head. Chosen to Be Water. Christopher Gilbert. SwNoth

Across the footpath (tidy). Mercy. Andrew Lansdown. NOBAu

Across the high plateau. (LL) Green Beret. Ho Thien. FaBoWar; PoAgWa, *tr.* by Unknown

Across the huddled lamplight window glass. Sunt Lacrimae Rerum et Mentem Mortalia Tangunt. R. P. Blackmur. APT-2

Across the Jarbok. Gerrit Achterberg. TuT, *tr.* by Dennis O'Driscoll

Across the lake the small houses appear. For Two Children. David Malouf. BMAP

Across the marketplace. Deserted Village. Johannes Bobrowski. GTCP, *tr.* by Reinhold Grimm

Across the meadow, sea smoke. Seal Island. Tom Sexton. PoCoUp

Across the millstream below the bridge. Blue Swallows, The. Howard Nemerov. MakPoe; NoP-4; NoP-5; OWoS

Across the narrow street from the old hotel that now. Affect of Elms, The. Reginald Gibbons. UrbNat

Across the newly-plastered wall. In Time of War. Amy Lowell. NAAPv.2

Across the night a crimson comet lies. Comet, The. János Vajda. IQMS, *tr.* by Watson Kirkconnell

Across the open countryside. Unsettled Motorcyclist's Vision of His Death, The. Thom Gunn. PoA 2002

Across the Place du Marché Ste-Catherine. Squares and Courtyards. Marilyn Hacker. WiU

Across the Prairie's silent waste I stray. Richard Henry Wilde. APN-1 *Fr.* Hesperia.

Across the red cliff, dotted in, stand the apparent colonnades. Apparent Colonnades, The. Jeffrey Wainwright. HarvBoo

Across the River. Brian Henry. PoDa

Across the sandy dry plains. Apocalypse. Charlie R. Braxton. InTrad

Across the Sea, Along the Shore. Arthur Hugh Clough. ChIV-2

Across the sky run streaks of white light, aching. Before Olympus. John Gould Fletcher. MoAmPo

Across the snout. Ars Poetica. Robert Desnos. AF, *tr.* by Carolyn Forché

Across the street: closed shops. Sunday A.M. Not in Manhattan. John Hollander. PoSol

Across the street, two large cottonwoods, a tree I've never. Joining the Circus. David Keller. NevBe

Across the street—the freeway. Beneath the Shadow of the Freeway. Lorna Dee Cervantes. PBCAP

Across the Swamp. Olav H. Hauge. RaBo; WED; WoPoe, *tr.* by Robert Bly

Across the ward green biros of monitors. Monitors. Geoffrey Holloway. NLP

Across the waves that vague, moss-covered knell. Surf Motel, The. Stephen Knight. NeBl

Across the wide green water. (LL) Poem of Attrition, A. Etheridge Knight. GT; OxAAAP

Across those plains where once there roamed the Indian and the Scout. Mid-West, The. *Unknown*. OBCoV

Across upon this undulated board of verdure chequered bright. David Jones. NAMCP V.1; NoAM *Fr.* In Parenthesis.

Acrostic on Wharton, An. *Unknown*. OBSV

Acrostick Eligie on the Death of the No Less Prudent than Victorious Prince Oliver Lord Protector, An. Elianour Havey. EMWP

Acrostiteliostichon. Joshua Sylvester. OxBSo *Fr.* Du Bartas: His Divine Weeks and Works.

Act. Gerardo Deniz. RMCMP, *tr.* by Mónica de la Torre

Act, The. William Scammell. RSaN

Act, The. William Carlos Williams. PtR; SAmP

Act 1: The Citadel of Antiochus at Jerusalem. Henry Wadsworth Longfellow. AWPTFC *Fr.* Judas Maccabaeus.

Act #2. John Weiners. BB

Act II - Crossing At the Tracks. Fiona Templeton. FTOS *Fr.* You: The City.

Act like a crazy dog. Wear sashes & other fine clothes, carry a. Crazy Dog Events. Jerome Rothenberg. RaBo

Act of Caution, An. Mahe Jabeen. HotL, *tr.* by V. Narayana Rao

Act of Love, The. Robert Creeley. CAP-8

Act of Mercy. Sarah Klassen. ACAMVP

Act One. Chana Bloch. ExTi

Act One. Danusha Laméris de Garza. IaFF

Act Six. Peter Goldsworthy. NOBAu

Act so that there is no use in a centre. Gertrude Stein. NAMCP V.1 *Fr.* Tender Buttons.

Actaeon. Ovid. WaAnP *Fr.* Metamorphoses [Hughes Translation].

Actaeon and His Hounds. Ovid. DiBP *Fr.* Metamorphoses.

Acteon. Ovid. *Fr.* Metamorphoses.

Acteur on le voit comme à travers des cristaux, Un. Antonin Artaud. YaTCFP *Fr.* Pèse-nerfs, Le.

Acting: "I most remember the class where we lie." Suzanne Cleary. BeAl; P180

Action Would Kill It / A Gamble. Robert Adamson. BMAP

Action-Packed Sonnet. Prageeta Sharma. HeMarv

Actions in my brain: these verbs, whose celerity. Amelia Rosselli. ItPo, *tr.* by Gayle Ridinger

Actions of Buddha. Philip Whalen. WANABP *Fr.* Epigrams & Imitations.

Actions to save the world. For Sho the New Head Priest of Erin-ji. Muso Soseki. EaWin, *tr.* by W. S. Merwin

Actis and Deidis of the Illustere and Vailyeand Campioun Schir William Wallace, Knicht of Ellerslie, The. Henry the Minstrel (Blind Harry). Sevint Buik, Lines 1029–92, The. NePenScot

Active in 's brain, and passive in his bones. (LL) On Playwright ("Playwright convict of public wrongs to men.") Ben Jonson. NoP-4; NoP-5

Active Reader, The. Bob Hicok. AmAlph

Acto. Gerardo Deniz. RMCMP

Actor, The. Tom Mandel. OnScMo

Actor occupies himself perfectly, The. Role. John Redmond. NIrP

Actor Speaks, An. Ben Scammell. NLP

Actress, The. Dorothy Parker. AmWit *Fr.* Tombstones in the Starlight.

Acts 8; On the Baptized Æthiopian. Richard Crashaw. *See* On the Baptized Ethiopian.

Acts of Love. Edgar Silex. NAPBL

Acts of Power. Sharan Strange. InTrad

Acts of Youth, The. John Weiners. BB

Actual killing actual death the hanging the beating the running into fire. Violence of the mind is the violence of god, The. Imamu Amiri Baraka. EGAG

Actual Vision of Morning's Extrusion. Alan Dugan. YaYoPo

Actualities. Sikong Tu. CCL1 *Fr.* Twenty-Four Modes of Poetry.

Actually, at the turn of the stair.. (LL) "H. D." NALW; NAMCP V.1 *Fr.* Tribute to the Angels.

Actually: it's the balls I look for, always. Balls. Anne McNaughton. RaBo

Actually Swallowed. Douglas Messerli. FTOS

Actually the idea of representing. Detail. Charles North. NYP2

Acum / minature minat minet. Acer. Peter Finch. AngWePo

Acupuncture and Cleansing at 48. Len Roberts. BodElec

Ad. Clark Coolidge. AHA *Fr.* Ing.

AD. Kenneth Fearing. NAAPv.2

AD 1905 Pablo / Picasso how old. Embrace, The. Louis Aragon. YaTCFP, *tr.* by Edward Lucie-Smith

Ad Infinitum. Joan Aronsten. NOBAu

Ad Miró. Pierre Alechinsky. PFTM-2, *tr.* by Michael Fineberg

Ad Quintilianum. Martial. RomPo, *tr.* by Robert Louis Stevenson

Adage: "Gardener's rule applies to youth and age, The." Henry James Byron. NBLV

Adagio. Gerald William Barrax. GT

Adagio. Lynda Hull. LaCa

Adagio at Twilight. John Carter. PasH

Adam. Honor Arundel. RSaN

Adam. Anthony Hecht. TaR

Adam. Yevgeny Mikhailovich Vinokurov. TCRusP, *tr. by* Daniel Weissbort

Adam, a brown old vulture in the rain. Ancient History. Siegfried Sassoon. ChIV-1

Adam and Eve. Jaime Sabines.
   4: The Animals. MotU, *tr. by* Ameen Alwan
   13: Eve No Longer Exists. MotU, *tr. by* Ameen Alwan
   1: I'm Naked, Bruised, and I Smell of You. MotU, *tr. by* Ameen Alwan

Adam and Eve. Karl Shapiro.
   Recognition of Eve, The. ChIV-1

Adam and Eve led out of Paradise. John Milton. NPeEn *Fr.* Paradise Lost.

Adam and Eve on the Hollywood Tread Mill. David Trinidad. PA9/11

Adam Describes His Own Creation and That of Eve; Having Repeated His Warning, the Angel Departs. John Milton. NAWM-7v1 *Fr.* Paradise Lost.

Adam / Had 'em. On the Antiquity of Microbes. Strickland W. Gillilan. NBLV

Adam / Had 'em. Poem to Answer the Question: How Old Are Fleas? *Unknown*. Spl

Adam, I think I'm going to be a mother. Imre Madách. IQMS *Fr.* Tragedy of Man.

Adam, indignant, would not eat with Eve. Paradise Saved. Alec Derwent Hope. OxBSo

Adam Lay Bound. *Unknown. See* Adam Lay Ybounden [*or* I-bounden].

Adam lay i-bounde. *Unknown. See* Adam lay ybounden [*or* i-bounden], bounded in a bond.

Adam lay ibowndyn, bowndyn in a bond. *Unknown. See* Adam lay ybounden [*or* i-bounden], bounded in a bond.

Adam Lay Ybounden [*or* I-bounden]. *Unknown*. ChIV-2; NoP-5; TFi; TRP; WeW-3
   (Adam Lay Bound.) NAEL-6v1; NAEL-7v1

Adam lay ybounden [*or* i-bounden], bounded in a bond. Adam Lay Ybounden [*or* I-bounden]. *Unknown*. ChIV-2; NoP-5; TFi; TRP; WeW-3
   (Adam lay i-bounde.) OHMEL
   (Adam lay ibowndyn, bowndyn in a bond.) OxBEV
   (Adam lay y-bownden bownden in a bond.) NPeEn

Adam lay y-bownden bownden in a bond. *Unknown. See* Adam lay ybounden [*or* i-bounden], bounded in a bond.

Adam, my child, my son. Adam. Anthony Hecht. TaR

Adam Pos'd. Anne Finch, Countess of Winchilsea. *See* Adam Posed.

Adam Posed. Anne Finch, Countess of Winchilsea. ChIV-1; NoP-4; NoP-5
   (Adam Pos'd.) NPeEn

Adam, quoth He, the beauties manifold. Guillaume de Salluste Du Bartas. InvLi *Fr.* Divine Weeks and Works, The.

Adam scriveyn [*or* scrivain *or* scrivein], if ever[e] it thee bifalle. Chaucer's Wordes unto Adam, his Owne Scriveyn. Geoffrey Chaucer. NAEL-6v1; NAEL-7v1

Adam went to her and took her. Jaime Sabines. MotU *Fr.* Adam and Eve.

Adam, Where Art Thou? Endre Ady. IQMS, *tr. by* Anton N. Nyerges

Adam will never change. I. Eve. Julio Marzán. PueRic

Adam, your namesake lives. Namesake. Imtiaz Dharker. NeBl

Adamantine Perfection of Desire, The. Jane Hirshfield. WhBo

Adams and Liberty. Robert Treat Paine. NAAPv.1

Adam's Cry. Nengi Ilagha. NeNiPo

Adam's Curse. William Butler Yeats. NAEL-6v2; NAEL-7v2; NAMCP V.1; NoAM; NoP-4; NoP-5; WeW-3

Adam's Dream. Edwin Muir. NoP-4; NoP-5

Adam's Task. John Hollander. NAMCP V.2; NIL-7; NIP-4; NoP-4; NoP-5; OxBoAm; WoPoe

Adaptation. Konstantin Pavlov. CSCBP, *tr. by* Georgi Belev and Lisa Sapinkopf

Add up without me. (LL) Roll-Call in the Concentration Camp. Dan Pagis. FIT; PoSu, *tr. by* Robert Friend

Adde Merum Vinoque. Tibullus. *tr. by* Rachel Hadas
   "Fill up my glass again! The anodyne." WoPoe, *tr. by* Rachel Hadas

Added cups and plates. My Uncruel April, My Totally Equal Unfortold April Unfolded. Lee Ann Brown. VaPo

Added to a Letter Sent to a Traveler. Pao Ling-hui. ColAnChi, *tr. by* Anne Birrell and Jeanne Larsen

Added to / making a Republic. Charles Olson. PFTM-2 *Fr.* Maximus Poems, The.

Addiction. Cindy Goff. LaCa

Addiction. Sheryl St. Germain. IllVoic

Addison Street. David Wright. ACAMVP

Addition to Kipling's "The Dead King (Edward VII), 1910." Max Beerbohm. OBCoV

Address. Leonard Nolens. TuT, *tr. by* Michael O'Loughlin

Address. Adrienne Su. AmPoNex

Address by an Ex-Confederate Soldier to the Grand Army of the Republic, An. Maurice Thompson. CBCWP

Address of my house has changed, The. Prison. Mahmoud Darwish. AF, *tr. by* Denys Johnson-Davies

Address to a Child during a Boisterous Winter Evening. Dorothy Wordsworth. WoRP

Address to a Haggis. Robert Burns. *See* To a Haggis.

Address to Ethiopia. Priscilla Jane Thompson. CBWP-2

Address to My Harp. Mary Tighe. NPBRoP

Address to My Infant Daughter, Dora on Being Reminded That She Was a Month Old That Day, September 16. William Wordsworth.
   Asked and Answered. STuOW

Address to Nature on its Cruelty, An. Ellen Johnston. VWP

Address to Poetry, An. Helen Maria Williams.
   "Blest Poesy! Oh sent to calm." NOBRP

Address to Poets. John Keble. SacPr

Address to the Deil. Robert Burns. NePenScot

Address to the King, An. John Gower.
   Peace. SacPr

Address to the Lord. John Berryman. GoPo

Address to the Muses, An. Joanna Baillie.
   "Youthful poet, pen in hand, The." NPBRoP

Address to the New Tay Bridge, An. William McGonagall.
   "Beautiful new railway bridge of the Silvery Tay." VerBaPo

Address to the Ocean. Lord Byron. ITBLP

Address to the Ocean. Barry Cornwall and Adelaide Anne Procter. TreFP

Address to the Unco Guid, or the Rigidly Righteous. Robert Burns. ChIV-1; OxBEV

Address to the Woodlark. Robert Burns. OWoS

Addressed to Haydon. John Keats. CenSon

Addressed to Sensibility. Ann Yearsley. RWP

Addressing the readers of a well-run newspaper, that is, one abounding. Silent World Is Our Only Homeland, The. Francis Ponge. AF, *tr. by* Beth Archer

Adds the cool head, and the unblemish'd [*or* unblemished] heart! (LL) To the Naiad of the Arun. Charlotte Smith. CenSon; RWP

Add-Water Instant Blues. Robin Morgan. PoA 2002

Adela, Adela, Adela Chart. To Henry James. Robert Louis Stevenson. OBCoV

Adelaide Crapsey. Carl Sandburg. APT-1

Adelaide's Lament. Frank Loesser. ReLy

Adelina Patti. Adah Isaacs Menken. CBWP-1

Aden. J. D. McClatchy. WaAnP

Adequate of Hell, The. (LL) Remorse—is Memory—awake. Emily Dickinson. NAAL-3; NoP-4; NoP-5; SAmP

Adhesion to this body. Squeeze. Abigail Child. FTOS

Adieu. Pierre Reverdy. CuPo

Adieu. Mary E. Tucker. CBWP-1

Adieu À Charlot [*see also* Ferlinghetti, "Poets, come out of your closets"]. Lawrence Ferlinghetti. FTtHH

Adieu, Adieu, Forever. Priscilla Jane Thompson. CBWP-2

"Adieu, adieu," forevermore. (LL) Alfred Tennyson. NAEL-6v2; NAEL-7v2 *Fr.* In Memoriam A. H. H.

Adieu and Recall to Love, The. Robert Merry. NOBRP

Adieu, dear name which birth and nature gave. Elegy on a Maiden Name, An. Jane Cave. CABP

Adieu, dear object of my love's excess. Orinda to Lucasia Parting, October, 1661, at London. Katherine Philips. BASC

Adieu; fare-well earth's bliss. Thomas Nashe. *See* Adieu, farewell, earth's bliss[e].

Adieu, Farewell, Earth's Bliss[e]. Thomas Nashe. HeIP-4; NoP-4; NoP-5; NoSic; NPeEn; OxBEV; TFi; TRP *Fr.* Summer's Last Will and Testament.

Adieu, L'. Guillaume Apollinaire. YaTCFP

Adieu, my flocks! he said, my wonted care. William Shenstone. STuOW *Fr.* He Repeats the Song of Colin, a Discerning Shepherd [*or* Elegy 18].

Adieu, New-England's smiling meads. Farewel[l] to America, A. To Mrs. S. W. Phillis Wheatley. NoP-4; NoP-5

Adieu, the years are a broken song. *Unknown*. NOBAu

Adieu to Belashanny [*or* Ballyshannon]! where I was bred and born. Winding Banks of Erne, The[: Or, The Emigrant's Adieu to His Birthplace]. William Allingham. IrV

Adieu, you haughty maiden! Adieu, Adieu, Forever. Priscilla Jane Thompson. CBWP-2

Adios, Carnage. Derek Walcott. NoP-5 *Fr.* Schooner Flight, The.

Adirondack Moosehead. Jeffrey Harrison. PoA 2002

Adirondack Return. Jean Nordhaus. PfSP

Adjectives all ganged up on the nouns, The. Student Theme, The. Ronald Wallace. P180

Adjunctant in the life. Spread. Leandro Katz. AHA

Adjustan Mysel tae the Situation. William J. Tait. EdScPo

Adler. Gerald Stern. TaR

Adlestrop. Edward Thomas. CtM; HarvBoo; NAEL-6v2; NAEL-7v2; NAMCP V.1; NoP-4; NoP-5; OBEV; UV; WaAnP

Ad-men bandy slogans, like Pupils Guaranteed. Eyeball Works, The. Stephen Knight. NeBl

Admiralls Being Slaine, They Likewise, The. Anne Dowriche. EMWP

Admiral's Caravan, The. Charles Edward Carryl.
　(Camel's Complaint, The.) NOxBChV

Admirals (Columbus). Suzanne Gardinier. NeAmPo

Admiration. Josephine D. Henderson Heard. CBWP-4

Admirations—and Contempts—of time, The. Emily Dickinson. APN-2

Admire Cranmer! Stevie Smith. NoAM

Admire the old man, admire him, admire him. Admire Cranmer! Stevie Smith. NoAM

Admiring it and adding noughts in vain. (LL) Star-Gazer. Louis MacNeice. ModIr; NAEL-6v2; NAEL-7v2; NoP-4; NoP-5

Admiring stranger, that with ling'ring feet. Written in Tintern Abbey, Monmouthshire. CenSon

Admit them, admit them. (LL) Song of a Man Who Has Come Through. D. H. Lawrence. HarvBoo; RaBo; TRP

Admit them, admit them. (LL) D. H. Lawrence. RaBo; TRP *Fr.* Song of a Man Who Has Come Through.

Admit then and be glad. Poem for an Anniversary. Cecil Day Lewis. CABP

Admit us—we would deem it shame. Plea of Texas, The. Mary Austin Holley. TiP2

Admonishing a Younger Teacher. Ch'i-chi. CSKM, *tr. by* Burton Watson

Admonition. Tzu Yeh. CrYelRi, *tr. by* Sam Hamill

Admonition by the Auctor to all yong Gentilwomen: And to al other Maids being in Love, The. Isabella Whitney.
　"Ye virgins that from Cupid's tents." PEW

Admonition to Myself, An. Chao Meng-fu. WoPoe, *tr. by* Jonathan Chaves

Admonitions. Lucille Clifton. NALW

Admonitions. Sylvia Plath. WaAnP

Admonitions of the Boudoir. Anne Waldman. AmZen

Adolescence. W. H. Auden. *See* Adolescence.

Adolescence. W. H. Auden. OxBEV; NoAM

Adolescence. Rebecca Gordon. FiBr

Adolescence. Allison Joseph. AmPoNex

Adolescence—2. Rita Dove. AmAlph; AWTN; ISC; NAAL-5; NAMCP V.2; NoAM; PoPoPo; VCAP

Adolescence—1. Rita Dove. ISC; NAAL-5; NoAM

Adolescence—3. Rita Dove. ISC; NAAL-5; NoAM

Adolescence: "We were alone together." Juan Ramón Jiménez. WED, *tr. by* Robert Bly

Adolescent Experiences. Sion Eirian. BBMWP, *tr. by* Robert Minhinnick
Conquest. BBMWP, *tr. by* Robert Minhinnick
Endsong. BBMWP, *tr. by* Robert Minhinnick
Englishwoman, An. BBMWP, *tr. by* Robert Minhinnick
Learning. BBMWP, *tr. by* Robert Minhinnick

Adolescent Suicide, The. Jill Bialosky. LiTh

Adolf Hitler ———1 April, 1945. W. D. Snodgrass. BodElec *Fr.* Führer Bunker, The.

Adolf Hitler ———20 April, 1934; 1900 hours. W. D. Snodgrass. BodElec *Fr.* Führer Bunker, The.

Adonais; An Elegy on the Death of John Keats. Percy Bysshe Shelley. CABP; InoFa; NAEL-6v2; NAEL-7v2; NOBRP; NoP-4; NoP-5; OxAEP-2; TFi; WaAnP
　"Go thou to Rome,—at once the paradise." CtM
　"One remains, the many change and pass, The." NPeEn

Adonis. Theocritus. NoSic; NPeEn, *tr. by* Theocritus and *Unknown*

Adoption Papers, The. Jackie Kay.
　Chapter 7: Black Bottom. MoWP

Adoration of the Kings, The. William Carlos Williams. ChrPo

Adoration of the Magi, The. Andrew Hudgins. UpMys

Adoration of the Magi, The. Christopher Pilling. OBCP

Adore November's sacred seventeenth day. Morris Kyffin. AngWePo *Fr.* Blessednes of Brytaine, The.

Adore the Roses; nor delay. Rosary Beads. Herman Melville. NCAP

Adown the Heights of Ages. Priscilla Jane Thompson. CBWP-2

Adreint al with shennesse, y-drawe down with shame. (LL) Who is This that Cometh from Edom? William Herebert. ChIV-1; SacPr

Adriani Morientis ad Animam Suam. Emperor Hadrian. OBVE, *tr. by* Matthew Prior

Adriatic was no sailor's sea, The. Battle Report. Harvey Shapiro. PWW2

Adrift. David Gwenallt Jones. BBMWP, *tr. by* Joseph P. Clancy

Adult. Linda Gregg. BLT

Adult Joy. Brenda Hillman. RoV

Adulterer, The. Scott Cairns. UpMys

Adultery. James Dickey. CAP-8

Adultery. Carol Ann Duffy. EmeKit

Adults Only. William Stafford. CAP-8

Adupe. Jayne Cortez. ESEAA

Advance of Education, The [*with music*]. Josephine D. Henderson Heard. CBWP-4

Advance of the Grizzly, The. Barbara Guest. BodElec

Advance to Hamburg broke with all the plans, The. England Nil. Anne Rouse. MFPA; NeBl

Advanced out toward the external from. Charles Olson. NAAL-5 *Fr.* Maximus Poems, The.

Advantages of Being a World Class Athlete, The. Anthony Lacavaro. MoASP

8. Advent. William Everson. CalPo *Fr.* Falling of the Grain, The.

Advent. Christina Georgina Rossetti. ChrPo

Advent; a Carol. Patric Dickinson. OBCP

Advent Calendar. Gjertrud Schnackenberg. ChrPo

Advent: "Come, thou dost say to Angels." Christina Georgina Rossetti. RSR

Advent Meditation. Alice Thompson Meynell. RSR

Advent 1955. Sir John Betjeman. OBCP

Advent 1966. Denise Levertov. APSN

Advent of our God With eager hearts we greet, The. Charles Coffin. SacPr

Advent of the new habit, The. Breakfast with Cats. Molly Peacock. KGB

Advent Sequence. David Brendon Hopes.
　"When the wolf moon howls, when the juncos." UpMys

Advent ("This Advent moon shines cold and clear.") Christina Georgina Rossetti. RSR

Advent wind begins to stir, The. Advent 1955. Sir John Betjeman. OBCP

Adventure. Betty Comden and Adolph Green. ReLy

Adventure. Bill Griffiths. Oth *Fr.* Building: The New London Hospital.

Adventure is all in a three-wheel pushchair. It lives in, The. Produce from the colonies. Pierre McOrlan. MFP, *tr. by* Martin Sorrell

Adventure of the Quartz Pebble, The. Vasco [*or Vasko*] Popa. PoSu *Fr.* Quartz Pebble, The.

Adventure somehow decides to bypass all the already. Ideas Gray Suits Bowler Hats Baal. Ed Roberson. BAP-04

Adventures of Grandmaster Flash, The. DJ Renegade. BRtP

Adventures of Huckleberry Finn, The. Mark Twain.
　Emmeline Grangerford's Ode to Stephen Dowling Bots, Dec'd. NBLV
　(Ode to Stephen Dowling Bots, Dec'd.) APN-2; TCAPo

Adventures of Id, The. Morris Gilbert Bishop. OBCoV

Adventures of Isabel. Ogden Nash. ChAP; MoAmPo; NOxBChV; NTCP; PtR

Adventures of Master F. I, The. George Gascoigne.
　(And If I Did What Then?) NoP-4; NoP-5; WaAnP

Adventures with Nick & Cindy. Peter Schjeldahl. AHA

Adventurous baron the bright locks admired, The. Alexander Pope. EroLit *Fr.* Rape of the Lock, The: An Heroi-Comical Poem in Five Cantos.

Adventurous mariner! in whose gray skiff. Sonnet 18. Amos Bronson Alcott. APN-1

Adversary, The. Phyllis McGinley. SoSe-8

Advertisement. Tedi López Mills. RMCMP, *tr. by* C. M. Mayo

Advertisement for a Scottish Servant. Ron Butlin. EdScPo

Advertisement for the Waldorf-Astoria. Langston Hughes. FTtHH

Advertisement of a Lost Day. Lydia Huntley Sigourney. TreFP

Advertisements. Thomas McGrath. BodElec

Advertising Agency Song, The [*with music*]. *Unknown*. NBLV

Advertising Rhymes. *Unknown*.
　Burma-Shave Roadside Signs. OBCoV
　Force. OBCoV
　"There was a little man." OBCoV
　Waverly Pen, The. OBCoV

Advice. Lee Cataldi. BMAP

Advice. Bill Holm. RaBo

Advice. Langston Hughes. NBLV; SAmP

Advice. Suzanne Wise. LegDan

Advice for a Journey. Sidney Keyes. PoWW

Advice from Poor Robin's Almanack. *Unknown*. OBCP

Advice from the Experts. Bill Knott. P180

Advice Gratis to Certain Women. Phoebe Cary. APN-2

Advice Like That. Eloise Klein Healy. SUP

Advice of Housewives. Thomas Tusser. NoSic *Fr.* Five Hundred Points of Good Husbandry.

Advice on Adultery. Gwyneth Lewis. MFPA; NeBrP *Fr.* Welsh Espionage.

Advice to a Clam-Digger. Wilbert Snow. APT-1

Advice to a Coming Child. Benjamin Scott Grossberg. LiTh

Advice to a Discarded Lover [*with music*]. Fleur Adcock. StAl

Advice to a Dog Painter. Jonathan Swift. DiBP

Advice to a First Cousin. Alberto A. Ríos. NAAL-5; NIL-7

Advice to a Lover. S. Charles Jellicoe. IrLP

Advice to a Man Who Lost a Dog. Howard Baker. APT-2

Advice to a Prophet. Richard Wilbur. AtGh; GPTC; HarvBoo; MoAmPo; NoP-4; NoP-5; OBWP; OxBoAm; UpMys; VCAP

Advice to a Raven in Russia. Joel Barlow. *See* Advice to a Raven in Russia [December, 1812].

Advice to a Raven in Russia [December, 1812]. Joel Barlow. AmWaPo; APN-1; NAAL-3; OBWP; ColAP

   (Advice to a Raven in Russia.)

Advice to a Reckless Youth. Ben Johnson. TreFP

Advice to a Young Man. *Unknown.* CAGL, *tr.* by James J. Wilhelm

Advice to a Young Philosopher. Anselm Berrigan. HeMarv

Advice to Her Son on Marriage. Mary Barber. IrLP *Fr.* Conclusion of a Letter to the Rev. Mr C———, The.

Advice to His Grace. "Ephelia." EMWP

Advice to Paulinus. Pacifico Massimi. CAGL *Fr.* Hecateleguim.

Advice to Pilgrims. Robinson Jeffers. APT-1

Advice to Slave-Owners. James Grainger. STuOW *Fr.* Sugar Cane, The.

Advice to the Orchestra [*with music*]. David Wagoner. NoAM

Advice to the Stout. John Armstrong. STuOW *Fr.* Art of Preserving Health, The.

Advice to the Young. Miriam Waddington. NIP-4

Advice to Travelers. Walker Gibson. NBLV

Advice to Virgins. Katherine Philips. EMWP

Advice to Young Ladies. Alec Derwent Hope. NAMCP V.1; NoAM; NoP-4; NoP-5

Advice to Young Ladies. Ann Plato. SWaP

Ae boat anerlie nou. Largo. Sydney Goodsir Smith. EdScPo

Ae Fond Kiss, and Then. Erasmus Darwin. STuOW *Fr.* Temple of Nature; or, The Origin of Society, The.

Ae fond kiss, and then we sever. Ae Fond Kiss. Robert Burns. NAEL-6v2; NePenScot; NPBRoP; OBEV

Ae weet forenicht i' the yow-trummle. Watergaw, The. Hugh MacDiarmid. FaBoVe; HarvBoo; NAEL-6v2; NePenScot; NPeEn

Aedh Tells of the Rose in His Heart. William Butler Yeats. MoBrPo

A-eee! Shee-yew! Sheeeeee! So dangerous! So high! Road to Shu Is Hard, The. Li Po. CCL1; WoPoe, *tr.* by Elling O. Eide

Aegean Melancholy [*with music*]. Odysseus Elytis. VCWP

Aegean Sea. Manuel Ulacia. RMCMP, *tr.* by Indran Amirthanayagam

Aegean, The. Maria Luisa Spaziani. NeIt, *tr.* by Beverly Allen

Aella; a Tragycal Enterlude. Thomas Chatterton.

   (Mynstrelle's Songe.) OxAEP-1; CABP

   (Song: "O sing into my roundelay.") OBEV

   There Lackethe Somethynge Stylle. OxAEP-1

Aeneas Arrives in Carthage. Virgil. NAWM-5v1; NAWM-7v1 *Fr.* Aeneid [*or* Eneados *or* Aeneis], The.

Aeneas at Washington. Allen Tate. APT-2; FuPo; NoAM

Aeneas' Image of War. Virgil. OBVE *Fr.* Aeneid [*or* Eneados *or* Aeneis], The.

Aeneas in the Underworld. Virgil. NAWM-5v1; NAWM-7v1 *Fr.* Aeneid [*or* Eneados *or* Aeneis], The.

Aeneas Searches for his Wife. Virgil. NPeEn *Fr.* Aeneid [*or* Eneados *or* Aeneis], The.

Aeneas (with Achates) Meets His Mother, Venus. Virgil. OBVE *Fr.* Aeneid [*or* Eneados *or* Aeneis], The.

Aeneid (Dryden translation). Virgil. *tr.* by John Dryden

   Book 2. *tr.* by John Dryden

   "By destiny compell'd, and in despair." FaBoWar, *tr.* by John Dryden

   Book 3. *tr.* by John Dryden

   Harpies, The. OWoS, *tr.* by John Dryden

Aeneid [*or* Eneados *or* Aeneis], The. Virgil.

   Aeneas Arrives in Carthage. NAWM-5v1; NAWM-7v1, *tr.* by Robert Fitzgerald

   Aeneas' Image of War. OBVE

   Aeneas in the Underworld. NAWM-5v1; NAWM-7v1, *tr.* by Robert Fitzgerald

   Aeneas Searches for his Wife. NPeEn, *tr.* by Henry Howard, Earl of Surrey

   Aeneas (with Achates) Meets His Mother, Venus. OBVE

   Aeolus Looses the Winds. NPeEn, *tr.* by Gawin Douglas

"And now Aeneas charges straight at Turnus." OBWP

"Arms, and the Man I sing, who, forc'd by Fate." FaBoWar; OBVE; OxBEV; WoPoe, *tr.* by John Dryden

"As bryght Phebus, scheyn soverane hevynnys e." NPeEn, *tr.* by Gawin Douglas

   Book 2. *tr.* by Henry Howard, Earl of Surrey

   Laocoön. OBVE

   "Then indeed into all our fluttering hearts." FaBoWar, *tr.* by Charles Hubert Sisson

   Building of Carthage, The. OBVE

   "By a bold people's stubborn arms oppressed." BASC, *tr.* by Abraham Cowley

   Charon. NPeEn, *tr.* by John Dryden

   Charon. OBVE *tr.* by Gawin Douglas

   Creusa. NoSic

   "Dawn leaves the bed of Dark and climbs the sky." EroLit, *tr.* by Kenneth McLeish

   "Dear Sister, my resentment had not been." OBVE

   Death of Priam, The. NPeEn, *tr.* by John Dryden

   Death of Priam, The. OBVE

   Death of Turnus, The. NAWM-5v1; NAWM-7v1, *tr.* by Robert Fitzgerald

   Defeat of Turnus, The. OBVE

   Dido by Night. OBVE

   Dido to Her Sister Anna. OBVE

   Dido's Suicide. OBVE

   Diomede Mourns His Fate and That of His Friends to the Latian Ambassador Who Seeks His Alliance against Aeneas. OBVE

   Euryalus and Nisus Meet Their Deaths. NoSic

   Fame. NPeEn; OBVE, *tr.* by John Dryden

   "Heaven, the earth, and all the liquid main [*or* mayne], The." OBVE

   How They Took the City. NAWM-5v1; NAWM-7v1, *tr.* by Robert Fitzgerald

   "In Heaven, Queen Juno saw. She's trapped." EroLit, *tr.* by Kenneth McLeish

   Jilted Queen, The. NAEL-7v1, *tr.* by Henry Howard, Earl of Surrey

   Night-Piece, The. MakPoe, *tr.* by Henry Howard, Earl of Surrey

   "Now manhood and garbroyls I chaunt, and martial horror." OBVE

   Passion of the Queen, The. NAWM-5v1; NAWM-7v1, *tr.* by Robert Fitzgerald

   Polyphemus. NoSic

   "Priests, prophets, helpless. She's beside herself." EroLit, *tr.* by Kenneth McLeish

   Prologue. NAWM-5v1; NAWM-7v1, *tr.* by Robert Fitzgerald

   Pyres, The. WoPoe, *tr.* by Robert Fitzgerald

   Rubric, The. OBVE

   Shield of Aeneas, The. NAWM-5v1; NAWM-7v1, *tr.* by Robert Fitzgerald

   "Sky rumbles. Gathers. Rain." EroLit, *tr.* by Kenneth McLeish

   Sleep of Palinurus, The. WoPoe, *tr.* by Cecil Day Lewis

   Sybil, The. OBVE

   "Thir riveris and thir watteris kepit war." OxBEV, *tr.* by Gawin Douglas

   Turnus and the Courser. OBVE

   Turnus and the Stone. OBVE

   Turnus and the Wanton Courser. OBVE

   Turnus Summons His Allies, Aeneas Is "Perturbit wyth Gret Thochtis." OBVE

   "Wee leave Creete Country; and our sayls unwrapped uphoysing." OBVE

   Wooden Horse Is Brought into Troy, The. OBVE

Aeolian Harp, The. Herman Melville. NCAP

Aeolian [*or* Eolian] Harp, The. Samuel Taylor Coleridge. NAEL-6v2; NAEL-7v2; NOBRP; NoP-4; NoP-5; NPBRoP; NPeEn *Fr.* Effusions.

Aeolus Looses the Winds. Virgil. NPeEn *Fr.* Aeneid [*or* Eneados *or* Aeneis], The.

Aéreas / nacidas en la altura. Baniano. Elsa Cross. RMCMP

Aerial, / born in the heights. Banyan. Elsa Cross. TANSG, *tr.* by Patricia Dubrava

Aerial Photograph, An. Thomas Carper. OtW

Aerial, The. Reiner Kunze. PoSu, *tr.* by Ewald Osers

Aerial, The. Robert Minhinnick. TCAWP

Aerogramme 1–5: Los Angeles. Russell Leong. FTtHH *Fr.* Aerogrammes.

Aerogrammes. Russell Leong. OpBo

   Aerogramme 1–5: Los Angeles. FTtHH

Aerolingual Poet of Prey. Eugene B. Redmond. SpirFl

Aeronauts, The. Rhoda Hero Dunn. OtW

Aeroplane. Pudjipangu. NOBAu, *tr.* by George von Brandenstein

Aeroplane is shaped like a bird, The. Chinese Quatrains (The Woman in Tomb 44). Marilyn Chin. NAMCP V.2

Aeschyleans, The. Bernadette Mayer. FTOS

Aesop, mine author, makis mention. Robert Henryson. *See* Esope, myne Authour, makis mentioun.

Aesop Revised by Archy. Don Marquis. APT-1

Aesop's Fable of the Frogs. Jean de La Fontaine. OBVE, *tr. by* John Hookham Frere

Aestas. Joshua Sylvester. NOSC

Aesthete [*or* Esthete] in Harlem. Langston Hughes. ColAP; WaAnP

Aesthetic Point of View, The. W. H. Auden. NBLV; OBCoV

Aesthetics. Joel Brouwer. LegDan

Aesthetics after War. Richard Eberhart. "There are many intricate pieces of workmanship." PWW2

Aesthetics of the Bases Loaded Walk. Joe Wenderoth. AmPoNex

Aestivation [an Unpublished Poem, by My Late Latin Tutor]. Oliver Wendell Holmes. TCAPo *Fr.* Autocrat of the Breakfast Table, The.

Aestuary, An. George Croly. NOBRP

Af, Af, Af, Af, Af, Af. Public Stammer, The. Ron Schreiber. PrTe

Af it part of a shlocky. Sham Jew. Matt Morris. MAAN

Afakem! Afakem! Lalla Taouchamt! Praise to the Tattoo Mistress. Mririda n'Ait Attik. WoPoe, *tr. by* Daniel Halpern and Paula Paley

Afar though near the silence waxes. Cloak, The. Norman Henry, II Pritchard. GT

Afdaling op klaarlichte dag. Rutger Kopland. LWR

Affable Irregular, An. William Butler Yeats. NPeEn *Fr.* Meditations in Time of Civil War.

Affair of Kites. Robin Robertson. EdScPo

Affair of the Heart. Peter Porter. BMAP

Affair With a Chair, An. Christopher Pilling. NLP

Affairs of Memory. Teresa Calderón. TANSG, *tr. by* Celeste Kostopulos-Cooperman

Affairs of the world, The. To the Emperor's Messenger. Muso Soseki. EaWin, *tr. by* W. S. Merwin

Affect of Elms, The. Reginald Gibbons. UrbNat

Affectionate. Else Von Freytag-Loringhoven. PFTM-1

Affectionate Heart, The. Joseph Cottle. STuOW

Affectionate Shepherd [*or* Shephearde], The. Richard Barnfield. (Affectionate Shepherd, The.) OBGa
"But if thou wilt not pittie my complaint." CAGL
Daphnis to Ganymede. CAGL
"Oh would to God he would but pitty mee." CAGL
"Scarce had the morning starre hid from the light." CAGL; NoSic
"When will my May come, that I may embrace thee?" CAGL

Affectionate Shepherd, The. Richard Barnfield. *See* Daphnis to Ganymede.

Affections, instincts, principles, and powers. Written in Butler's Sermons. Matthew Arnold. OxBSo

Affections Must Not. Denise Riley. MoWP

Affinity, The. Anna Wickham. NALW

Affirmative Action Blues (1993). Elizabeth Alexander. ExTi; FaoP

Affirming it a Soul. (LL) Props assist the House, The. Emily Dickinson. APN-2; GoPo; WPoS

Affliction (1). Sir John Davies. WoPoe *Fr.* Nosce Teipsum.

Affliction (1). George Herbert. BASC; FSCP; NAEL-6v1; NAEL-7v1; NoP-4; NoP-5; NOSC

Affliction (2). George Herbert. NOSC

Affliction (3). George Herbert. NOSC

Affliction (4). George Herbert. CABP; NOSC

Affliction of Margaret, The. William Wordsworth. RACG

Affliction shall advance the flight in me. (LL) Easter Wings. George Herbert. AngWePo; BASC; BrAP; CABP; ChIV-1; FSCP; HeIP-4; MakPoe; NAEL-6v1; NAEL-7v1; NIL-7; NIP-4; NoP-4; NoP-5; NOSC; PBRV; PoPoPo; SacPr; TFi; TRP; WaAnP; WeW-3; WoPoe

Affluence—define it as. Hezutsu Tosaku. EMJL, *tr. by* Burton Watson

Affrayit, I glistnyt of sleip, and stert on feit. Virgil. OBVE *Fr.* Aeneid [*or* Eneados *or* Aeneis], The.

Afloat between lives and stale truths. Guardian Angel, The. Stephen Dunn. OPRER

Afreeka Brass. Mwatabu Okantah. SeSe

Afresh'd with paint the shop had glare. New Storefront. Russell Atkins. GT

Africa. Maya Angelou. NIL-7; NIP-4

Africa. Maria White Lowell. NAAPv.1

Africa. Claude McKay. APT-1; FTtHH; NAAL-5

Africa. Joaquin Miller. APN-2

Africa. Lizelia Augusta Jenkins Moorer. CBWP-3

Africa. Rosario Morales. PueRic

Africa cannot be wounded. Angel in the Temple of Luxor, An. Rodney M. McNeil. InTrad

Africa: "I looked out toward the pasture at the cows." Michael Heffernan. VisFro

Africa of the Statue, The. Amina Saïd. HAWP; NAfrP, *tr. by* Eric Sellin

Africa Says. Carl Phillips. PoPoPo

Africa Sky. Kojo Laing. HBAPE

Africa waters the roots of my tree. Africa. Rosario Morales. PueRic

African Beneath the American, The. Wanda Coleman. RD

African Boog. Allen Fisher. Oth

African Burial Ground called Tribeca, The. David Henderson. BRtP

African Chief, The. William Cullen Bryant. ColAP

African China. Melvin B. Tolson. ColAP

African Christmas. John Press. OBCP

African Desert. Samuel Greenberg. APT-1

African Dream. Bob Kaufman. GT; OxAAAP

African drumbeat. Lost. Corinth Morter-Lewis. OWABP

African Elegy, An. Robert Duncan. NoAM

African Image Is Not An Image by Equation, The. Léopold Sédar Senghor. PFTM-1

African Lion, The. A. E. Housman. NOxBChV

African Morning. Mwatabu Okantah. BtF

African of the statue, The. Africa of the Statue, The. Amina Saïd. HAWP; NAfrP, *tr. by* Eric Sellin

African Poem. Agostinho Neto. PoetW, *tr. by* W. S. Merwin

African Queen. Willem M. Roggeman. TuT, *tr. by* Gabriel Rosenstock

African Sculpture. Christopher Gilbert. ESEAA

African sister, standing there in her radiant beauty. Poetry for the Goddess. William T. Crawley III. InTrad

African Sleeping Sickness. Wanda Coleman. PmAP; WaAnP

African Sunday. Maureen Owen. PmAP

African Sunrunner. Wanda Winbush-David. BtF

Afro-American. Henry Dumas. OxAAAP

Afro-American Fragment. Langston Hughes. OxAAAP

After. Ralph Hodgson. MoBrPo

After. Shirley Kaufman. InoFa

After. May Probyn. VWP

After Eighteen Years of This Sort of Thing. Mark Robinson. RSaN

After a bear ransacked their hive, strewing wood, wax. Bees, The. Christopher Merrill. PfSP

After a black day, I play Haydn. Allegro. Tomas Tranströmer. WED, *tr. by* Robert Bly

After a Death. Roo Borson. NIL-7

After a Death. Charles Tomlinson. HarvBoo

After a Death. Tomas Tranströmer. VCWP, *tr. by* Robert Bly

After a Friendship. Robert Minhinnick. AngWePo

After a hundred years. Emily Dickinson. APN-2

After a Journey. Thomas Hardy. HarvBoo; NPeEn; OxAEP-2; OxBEV

After a June sun licked afternoon onto the infield. Sestina Halted in a Rain Delay. Miles Garett Watson. RWB

After a lifetime of leaning over his guitar. Hacedor. Joseph Stroud. TAPaP

After a long day of cracking Red Skull's. Captain America at Home. Jarret Keene. RWB

After a Long Illness. Robert Duncan. PFTM-2

After a long nap. Issa. SoOfWa, *tr. by* Sam Hamill

After a long night of love. (LL) Kenneth Rexroth. APSN; APT-2; NAAPv.2; NAMCP V.1 *Fr.* Love Poems of Marichiko, The.

After a moment, the driver, a salesman. Hitchhiker. Galway Kinnell. OxBoAm

After a month and a half without rain, at last, in late August. August Rain. Robert Bly. MotU

After a Movie. Henry Taylor. GoPo

After a Native Poem from the Solomon Islands that Begins: "Your Shameful Parts Are the White Man's Gramophone." Gabriel Celaya. RaW, *tr. by* Robert Mezey

After a night of boozing and praying. Primo Levi. Emrys Roberts. BBMWP, *tr. by* Richard Poole

After a night of languor without rest. Sea-Breeze at Matanzas, The. Epes Sargent. APN-1

After a night of rage. Love Poem for a Wife, 2. A. K. Ramanujan. WoPoe

After a night of rain. In a Japanese Moss Garden. Brad Leithauser. OBGa

After a Phrase Abandoned by Wallace Stevens. Donald Justice. NAMCP V.2

After a pretty amorous discourse. Imperfect Enjoyment, The. Sir George Etherege. NOSC

After a rain, ah, comes a thick snow. Threading Frost. *Unknown*. CATKP, *tr. by* Peter H. Lee

After a rain on the long dike, grasses are thick. Parting. Chŏng Chisang. CATKP, *tr. by* Peter H. Lee

After a Reading at a Black College. Toi Derricotte. FuFl

After a restless night, dreams. Enough. Lucien Stryk. Vesp

After a ship had been wrecked. Parrot at Sea, A. Yelena Shwarts. ItGoST, *tr. by* Catriona Kelly

After a slow day of repose. Old Dog. Michael L. Johnson. UrbNat

After a Spring meeting in their nineteenth-century fastness at. Irish Hierarchy Bans Colour Photography. Paul Durcan. PBCIP

After a Storm, Going a Hawking. George Daniel. NOSC

After a supper of roasted lamb and eggplant. World Is a Wedding, The. Adele Ne Jame. PoArWo

After a Tempest. William Cullen Bryant. APN-1

After a thousand days. Marriage Patois. Megan Sexton. PoDa

After a thousand years of grief / at their hearts. (LL) Way of Tet, The. Bruce Weigl. AF; AmAlph

After a Time. Elizabeth Jennings. HarvBoo

After a time, Hoss, it makes such little difference. Relics. Charles Wright. CAP-8

After a time the grave got up and went away. (LL) As He Came Near Death. Roy Fisher. HarvBoo; InoFa; NPeEn

After a Train Journey. May Sarton. GM

After a war come the memorials. Men. William Stafford. PWW2

After a week of physical anguish. Evening Lull, An. Walt Whitman. NAAL-3

After a while you'd stop talking. Homesteaders. Debra Nystrom. RWB

After / a winding walk. Flower from Robert Kennedy's Grave, A. Edward Sanders. FTtHH

After a Winter of Grieving. Sam Hamill. AmZen

After Aesop. Malinda Markham. IAoNAP

After: "After chopping off all the arms that reached out to me." Octavio Paz. TWF, tr. by Eliot Weinberger

After All. Juan Felipe Herrera. PfSP

After All. Theodore Weiss. VisFro

After: "All long labors, whether for hunger, for duty, for." Jeanne Marie Beaumont. PoDa

After all the breath, we were altered of heart. Ian Patterson. VaPo Fr. Hardihood.

After all the drive-in theaters have closed. Translated from the American. Sherman Alexie. UnSA

After all the hard noise. After All. Juan Felipe Herrera. PfSP

After all the wit. Oscar Wilde. Ulick O'Connor. IrLP

After all, there's no need. Flirtation. Rita Dove. PoA 2002

After All These Years. May Sarton. PoBW

After all this time without you. I Wish I Didn't Love You So. Frank Loesser. ReLy

After all those months of slowed heartbeat. Meeting Up with the Picaro. Patricia Smith. ICANM

After all those years. Accomplices. Zhao Zhenkai. VCWP

After all, you are my rather tedious hero. To Myself. Kenneth Slessor. BMAP

After an All Day Skirmish with the Clouds. Eli Goodwin. BtF

After an early breakfast we hoisted sail, preferring to confront the falls in better weather. For Dorothy Wordsworth. Charles North. NYP2

After an hour's climb, I am no closer. Little Blessing, A. Nancy Willard. PfSP

After Annunciation. Anna Wickham. MoBrPo

After Apple-Picking. Robert Frost. APT-1; BrAP; IPoFL; ItP; MoAmPo; NAAL-5; NAAPv.2; NAMCP V.1; NoAM; NoP-5; OxBoAm; SAmP; SoSe-8; TCAPo; TFi; TRP; WaAnP

After Arguing against the Contention That Art Must Come from Discontent. William Stafford. NoAM

After Aughrim. Emily Lawless. OBEV

After Auschwitz, it's been said, it's no longer possible. Cherries. Michael C. Blumenthal. PfSP

After autumn's fever and its vivid trees. Six Poems on Nothing. Gwyneth Lewis. HarvBoo

After Babel. Peter Goldsworthy. NOBAu

After Barranquillo, before Belize. Matthew Kearney. MAAN

After Bird Watching near the Mexican Border. Robert Burlingame. TiP2

After Blenheim. Robert Southey. See Battle of Blenheim, The.

After Burying Her Son, A Mother Speaks. Mark Pawlak. GifTon

After C (3): Tayloriana. John Keene. FuFl

After Carnival. Peter Rafferty. NLP

After cheating each other for eighteen years. On the Island. Gerald Stern. WaAnP

After chopping off all the arms that reached out to me. After. Octavio Paz. TWF, tr. by Eliot Weinberger

After Christmas. W. H. Auden. ChrPo; MoBrPo; OBCP Fr. For the Time Being; a Christmas Oratorio.

After Christmas. Michael Richards. OBCP

After Ch'u Yuan. Ch'u Yüan. NDACCP

After church meeting. Tanka. Lenard D. Moore. SpirFl

After church spires and city chimneys have sunk below the horizon. In England. Duo Duo. PoetW, tr. by Maghiel van Crevel

After cities full of flashbacks and bad debts. Post-Revolutionary Letter. Carolyne Wright. RoV

After Collecting the Autumn Taxes. Po Chü-i. BLT, tr. by Arthur Waley

After Communion. Christina Georgina Rossetti. SacPr; WPoS

After: "Composition was shy, The." Gillian Conoley. RoV

After Culloden. Alasdair Maclean. EdScPo

After Cycling. Gary Young. ArBi

After Dark Vapours Have Oppressed Our Plains. John Keats. CenSon; NPeEn

After days of putting down my poem. January. Ellen Bryant Voigt. CAP-8

After Death. Christina Georgina Rossetti. NAEL-6v2; NAEL-7v2; NALW

After death, and clean as a finishing line. (LL) Crafty Butcher, The. Susan Hampton. BMAP; NOBAu

After Death Nothing Is. Seneca. OBVE Fr. Troades.

After death, suppose we were judged by animals. Tribunal, The. Chris Wallace-Crabbe. ChIV-2

After diana died. Asha Bandele. BRtP

After dinner Erasmus. Edmund Clerihew Bentley. OBCoV Fr. Clerihews.

After dream / How real. Ome Shushiki. ZenPo, tr. by Takashi Ikemoto and Lucien Stryk

After each drop of rain. Ivan Metodiev. CSCBP Fr. Songs for Orphans Big and Small.

After each war. End and Beginning. Wisława Szymborska. PLBUT, tr. by Joseph Brodsky

After Eden. Rachel Tzvia Back. DTA

After Eden. James Simmons. PNI

After Edward Hopper. Lawrence Raab. PoSol

After eight dry months of dirt. Everywhere the Earth Is Opening. Jennifer Richter. FiBr

After Eight Years of Marriage. Mamta Kalia. ItWoWo

After Endless Discussions. Ishikawa Takuboku. CAoMJL1, tr. by Leith Morton

After Esenin. David St. John. RoV

After Estrangement. Molly Bendall. AmPoNex

After evening sitting. Soliloquy of the Danish Cloister. Mike O'Connor. WANABP

After Ever Happily [or , The Princess and the Woodcutter]. Ian Serraillier. OBSP

After every war. End and the Beginning, The. Wisława Szymborska. CFP; StAl; VCWP, tr. by Stanisław Barańczak and Clare Cavanagh

After every war. End and the Beginning, The. Wisława Szymborska. GPTC, tr. by Joanna Trzeciak

After experience taught me that all the ordinary. After Experience Taught Me. W. D. Snodgrass. CAP-8; OBWP

After explanations and regulations, he. WASP Woman Visits a Black Junkie in Prison, A. Etheridge Knight. LaCa

After Fall, 1956. Devorah Amir. DTA, tr. by Miriyam Glazer

After father died. Jill Bialosky. InoFa Fr. Fathers in the Snow.

After Fighting for Hours. Kate Gleason. BAP-97

After Finding a One Hundred Dollar Bill. David Chapman Berry. PoA 2002

After five years maternity leave. Gap, The. Annie Foster. NLP

After forty minutes. Flesh and Fluids. Rupert M. Loydell. PoCu

After Forty Years of Marriage, She Tries a New Recipe for Hamburger Hot Dish. Leo Dangel. GoPo

After freedom struck my country. Fear freedom. Wopko Jensma. TSAP

After Friedan and the flare. Wildsisters Bar. Judith Vollmer. SwNoth

After fruition ne're to be concern'd. (LL) To Alexis in Answer to His Poem Against Fruition. Ode. Aphra Behn. BrAP; NOSC

After Galen. Oliver St. John Gogarty. OBMV

After gazing fixedly upon expression and substance. Sikong Tu. CCL1 Fr. Twenty-Four Modes of Poetry.

After Getting Drunk, Becoming Sober in the Night. Po Chü-i. BLT, tr. by Arthur Waley

After Getting Drunk in a Hermitage on Chiri Mountain. Suk Mumyong. BecRai, tr. by Kim Daljin, Kim Won-Chung and Christopher Merrill

After Grave Deliberation. Elizabeth Flynn. NBLV

After great pain a formal feeling comes. Emily Dickinson. APN-2; BrAP; HeIP-4; MoAmPo; NAAL-3; NAAL-5; NAAPv.1; NALW; NAMCP V.1; NAWM-7v2; NIL-7; NIP-4; NoAM; NoP-4; NoP-5; OxBoAm; OxWW; PoPoPo; PtR; SAmP; TCAPo; TFi; TRP

After Greece. James Merrill. BrAP; ColAP; TRP

After hangin' Danny Deever in the mornin'! (LL) Danny Deever. Rudyard Kipling. BRP; FaBoWar; InoFa; MoBrPo; NAEL-6v2; NAEL-7v2; NAMCP V.1; NoAM; NPeEn; OxBEV; TFi

After having loved we lie close together. Sailing. Henrik Nordbrandt. VCWP, tr. by Henrik Norbrandt and Alexander Taylor

After he buttered his bread with that old bread knife that he passed down to you. (LL) No Sorry. Catherine Bowman. BAP-97; RaF; SUP

After he did what he did, and was ashamed. Shame Place, The. Stephen Dunn. SUP

After he died. She Lived. Lucille Clifton. LoL

After He Had Gone. Sylvia Townsend Warner. MoBrPo

After he told us that being blown. Problem, The. Len Roberts. PML

After hearing about the death of Melvin. Return to Temptation. Mary Weems. SpirFl

After Hearing Heterosexual Poets in October 1974: What It Seems Like To Write a Male Homosexual Love Poem Now. Joseph Cady. CAGL

After hearing on the radio news. Inquiry into Gifts, or the Indigo Bunting. Jeff Gundy. ACAMVP

After Heart-Bypass Surgery, Another Ritual for Continuing Struggle. Ralph Salisbury. RWB

After he'd consumed tons of lipstick. Don Juan (After He'd Consumed Tons of Lipstick). Martin Sorescu. PML; PoDa, *tr. by* Adam J. Sorkin and Irina Grigorescu Pan

After he'd crossed seven borders. Appointment, The. Matthew Sweeney. BeAl

After her father died they found nine guns in the house. 7 or 8 Things I Know About Her—A Stolen Biography. Michael Ondaatje. MotU

After her husband died, Zita decided to get the face-lift. Distance from Loved Ones. James Tate. MotU; OxBoAm

After Her Man Had Left Her for the Sixth Time That Year (An Uncommon Occurrence). Haki R. Madhubuti. GT

After her pills the girl slept and counted. Tally. Josephine Miles. NoAM

After her wedding-night, the nymph. Martial. RomPo, *tr. by* Peter Whigham

After high school Latin class. Preparing the Dead. Paulette Roeske. IllVoic

After Hilaire Belloc. Max Beerbohm. UV

After Hilaire Belloc. Max Beerbohm. OBCoV

After his ham & cheese in the drape factory cafeteria. Torque. David Rivard. PBCAP

After his shower he reaches for. Robe, The. Martha Rhodes. ExTi

After his stroke, he would walk into the woods. Walt Whitman Bathing. David Wagoner. ViWalt

After his third operation, his heart. Dead, The. Miroslav Holub. StAl, *tr. by* Ewald Osers

After his tryst. Fujiwara noTeika. WoPoe, *tr. by* Steven D. Carter

After hot loveless nights, when cold winds stream. Sisters, The. Roy Campbell. NoP-4; NoP-5; OBMV

After Hours. Robert Trammell. TiP2

After I did it with her, the day I first did it with my wife. Sex. Kim Suyŏng. CAMKP, *tr. by* Young-Jun Lee

After I got religion and steadied down. Edgar Lee Masters. APT-1 *Fr.* Spoon River Anthology.

After I had cut off my hands. Intrusion. Denise Levertov. VCAP

After I Seized the Pentagon. Robert Hass. YaYoPo

After I Was Dead. Laura Mullen. ExTi

After I was separated from my mother. Looking Back at My Shadow. Chunghur Hyujung. BecRai, *tr. by* Kim Daljin, Kim Won-Chung and Christopher Merrill

After I write *My face burned and I wanted to cry*. Courage, or One of Gene Horner's Fiddles. Lisa Coffman. AmPoNex

After it rains you should sigh a little for the spongy world. Sounds, The. Gerald Stern. BodElec

After it was over, though still gusting balefully. Eternity. Hart Crane. NAAPv.2

After its caw. Ray McNiece. AmZen

After Jesus raised him from the dead. Lazarus. Ron Koertge. OPRER

After Jill died they remembered how she liked this chair. Jill's Death. George Buchanan. PNI

After knowledge extinguished the last of the beautiful. New Intelligence, The. Timothy Donnelly. LegDan

After Kuo Chu-Pu's Poems. T'ao Ch'ien. PoChi, *tr. by* David Hinton

After Laforgue. Sean O'Brien. NeBrP

After Lalon. Allen Ginsberg. BB

After late spring rain the falling petals swirl. Han-shan Te-ch'ing. CSKM, *tr. by* Red Pine

After Li Ch'ing-Chao. John Brandi. ICANM

After Liberation. J. C. Bloem. TuT, *tr. by* Seamus Heaney

After Life. Anna Hajnal. IQMS, *tr. by* Jeannette Nichols

After Listening to Jack Teagarden . . . . James McKean. SeSe

After living here for 12 years. New Mexico Time. Mary McGinnis. ICANM

After Long Busyness. Robert Bly. CAP-8; OxBoAm

After Long Rain. Wang Wei. TAL

After Long Silence. Jane Hirshfield. WANABP

After Long Silence [*fr.* Words for Music Perhaps]. William Butler Yeats. HeIP-4; NAEL-6v2; NAEL-7v2; OBMV

After long wars when comes release. Herba Santa. Herman Melville. NCAP

After Lorca [(*For M. Marti*)]. Robert Creeley. CAP-8; OxBoAm; PmAP

After Lorca. Ted Hughes. PoA 2002

After Love. Sara Teasdale. APT-1

After Mahler. Ann Lauterbach. BAP-04

After Making Love. Stephen Dunn. EMP; PoA 2002

After making love. Midnight. Alison Kolodinsky. PasH

After Making Love We Hear Footsteps. Galway Kinnell. BeAl; CAP-8; ColAP; EMP; NAAL-5; NAMCP V.2; NIL-7; NIP-4; NoAM; NoP-4; NoP-5; PasH; RaBo; VCAP; WaAnP

After many scorns [*or* scornes] like these. Ben Jonson. NAEL-7v1 *Fr.* Celebration of Charis in Ten Lyric[k] Pieces [*or* Peeces], A.

After mass, became drunk, fell down, and made violent love to nobody. My Life in Yonago. Sharon Mesmer. HeMarv

After Mayakovsky. Sotère Torregian. AHA

After Midnight. Louis Simpson. BLT; NoAM

After midnight. Drunk. Pink Triangles. Larry Wayne Johns. LiTh

After midnight I heard a scream. By Night. Robert Francis. APT-2

After midnight the blizzard howls itself out. Blizzard. Bill Holm. MiVo

After midnight they load up. Boat People. Yusef Komunyakaa. AF; PoPoPo

After "Mindwalk." Denise Levertov. UpMys

After Minor Surgery. Linda Pastan. EMP; PoA 2002

After MLK: the marksman marked leftover kill. Lloyd Addison. EGAG

After months abroad. Basel Square. Aharon Shabtai. WoBe, *tr. by* Peter Cole

After months of sitting. Diane Di Prima. WhBo

After much biologic research. Original Summer Girl, The. Carolyn Wells. SWaP

After Music. Josephine Preston Peabody. TCAPo

After my daughter Katherine was born. To the Roman Forum. Kenneth Koch. NAMCP V.2

After My Death. David Young. InoFa

After my determined calendar of checkups. Emergency. Julio Marzán. PueRic

After my grandfather died I went back home. Spooning. David Mason. WaAnP

After my reading. Exile. Danton R. Remoto. ReBoTo

After Nam he lost himself. Losses. Yusef Komunyakaa. OxAAAP

After night in. Issa. IllVoic *Fr.* Issa: A Suite of Haiku.

After night's thunder far away had rolled. Haymaking. Edward Thomas. MoBrPo

After noon I lie down. Josephine Miles. APT-2

After: "Once upon a time." Wendy Wilder Larsen. NevBe

After one moment when I bowed my head. Convert, The. G. K. Chesterton. ChIV-2; SacPr

After one whole quart of brandy. Bewitched, Bothered and Bewildered. Lorenz Hart. APT-2

(He's a fool, and don't I know it.) ReLy

After others had said their say. When Helen Keller Spoke. George Jay Smith. ViWalt

After our war, how will love speak? (LL) After Our War. John Balaban. GifTon; TAPaP

After our war, the dismembered bits. After Our War. John Balaban. GifTon; TAPaP

After Ovid, Tristia. Peter Scupham. HarvBoo

After Parade the little American girl left the theater. Fairy Scene. Jean Cocteau. CuPo

After Paradise. Czeslaw Milosz. PML, *tr. by* the author and Robert Hass

After Paul Durcan left his wife. Levite and His Concubine at Gibeah, The. Paul Durcan. ModIr

After Picasso. Franz Wright.

Depiction of Childhood. BLT

After picking herbs, I rest on the bank of a stream. On the Bank of a Stream by Taedun Temple. Choeui Eusoon. BecRai, *tr. by* Kim Daljin, Kim Won-Chung and Christopher Merrill

After pissing around his gut-level. Homo Erectus. Yusef Komunyakaa. PML

After practice: right foot. Boy Juggling a Soccer Ball, A. Christopher Merrill. MoASP; PML

After Prayers, Lie Cold. Clive Staples Lewis. SacPr

After Rain. Allan Cooper. Coast

After Rain. Patricia K. Page. BrAP

After Rain. Tu Fu [*or* Du Fu]. CrYelRi, *tr. by* Sam Hamill

After rain, flowers bloom in the night. Flowers in the Garden. Pyungyang Ungee. BecRai, *tr. by* Kim Daljin, Kim Won-Chung and Christopher Merrill

After rain, in the darkened room, the body. Body in Youth, The. Ellen Hinsey. YaYoPo

After rain, mushrooms. Washington Etude. Elizabeth Alexander. NAPBL

After rain, through afterglow, the unfolding fan. Train Ride. John Wheelwright. OxBoAm

After Reading Han-Shan. Thomas Rain Crowe. AmZen

After Reading in a Letter Proposals for Building a Cottage. John Clare. OxAEP-2

After Reading Lao Tzu. Po Chü-i. CrYelRi, *tr. by* Sam Hamill

After Reading *Mickey in the Night Kitchen* for the Third Time Before Bed. Rita Dove. CAP-8; LoL; NAMCP V.2; OxAAAP; ReTh

After Reading *Poems to Einhir*. Gwyn Williams. TCAWP

After Reading Reznikoff. Kate Daniels. ExTi

After Reading Shakspere. Edwin Markham. APN-2

After Reading the Book of Splendor. Emily Warn. GifTon

After Reading "The Country of the Pointed Firs." Jean Garrigue. VCAP

After Reading the Poems of Master Han Shan. Wang Chiu-ssu. *tr. by* Jonathan Chaves

   "Floating, floating, the river waters." WoPoe, *tr. by* Jonathan Chaves

   "This crazy man has escaped the world." WoPoe, *tr. by* Jonathan Chaves

After Reading Tu Fu, I Go Outside to the Dwarf Orchard. Charles Wright. ItP

After Rishikesh / the Ganges is still green. Key of Water, The. Octavio Paz. VCWP; WoPoe, *tr. by* Elizabeth Bishop

After Sappho. Lee Ann Brown. IIR

After School Commute with My Girl. L. B. BeDoSh

After School, Street Football, Eighth Grade. Dennis Cooper. WiU

After Seeing Paintings in a Small Book by T. C. Cannon (1946-1978). Alice Sadongei. HATNAP

After separating from Penelope, Ulysses. Dawn, with Cardinals. Jeffrey Levine. PoDa

After seven years and as the wine. Ourselves or Nothing. Carolyn Forché. BodElec; GifTon

After seven years the dyes have surrendered. After Seven Years. Anne Valley Fox. ICANM

After shaking paws with his dog. W. H. Auden. GI *Fr.* Horae Canonicae.

After she rose from the dark throat. Undine. Nicole Cooley. AmPoNex

After she said it. Emperor Has No Clothes!, The. Kathleen Norris. UpMys

After Shih-te ("I climb these hills as if walking on air.") Shih Shu. CSKM, *tr. by* James H. Sanford

After Shih-te ("My ragged cloak is streaked with mountain shadows.") Shih Shu. CSKM, *tr. by* James H. Sanford

After Shih-te ("Perfumed springs ripple over skeletal outcrops.") Shih Shu. CSKM, *tr. by* James H. Sanford

After shutting the door on the rest of the party. Strip-Tease. Gwyneth Lewis. BBMWP, *tr. by* Joseph P. Clancy

After singing the final page. Unacknowledged Legislator. Harryette Mullen. RD

After six little spaces of chill, and six of burning. (LL) John Crowe Ransom. APT-1; MoAmPo; NAAPv.2; NAMCP V.1; NoAM *Fr.* Sixteen Poems in Eight Pairings.

After six months of wandering Whitman found himself. Whitman Pinch Hits, 1861. Floyd Skloot. ViWalt

After 65. Richard Howard. BAP-01; OxBoAm

After Snow, Longing for Elder Brother Hsi-ch'iao. Wang Shih-chieng. ColAnChi

After Snow-Mobiling. Alec Bond. VisFro

After so long. Diaspora. S. V. Atalla. PoArWo

After so long a race as I have run. Edmund Spenser. CABP *Fr.* Amoretti.

After so many years. Hand Mirror. Daisy Zamora. LoL, *tr. by* Barbara Paschke

After solstice, the sunlight slowly lengthens. From. After Solstice. Tu Fu [*or* Du Fu]. CrYelRi, *tr. by* Sam Hamill

After Soufrière. Michael Field. VWP

After Source of the Peach Blossom Stream. Wang Wei. ChinPo, *tr. by* Ye Weilian [*or* Yeh Wei-lien *or* Wai-lim Yip]

After spring has come. *Unknown*. ArkPo, *tr. by* Edwin A. Cranston

After spring leaves, the mountain is empty. Arriving at Yongmun Temple. Choeui Eusoon. BecRai, *tr. by* Kim Daljin, Kim Won-Chung and Christopher Merrill

After spring snow, the capital's a city of mud. Working for the Government. Wang An-shih. CrYelRi, *tr. by* Sam Hamill

After Stalin's death, strangers often stopped Akhmatova on the. Patrick Friesen. NLPA *Fr.* Anna.

After such painstaking study of empty-gate dharma. Idle Song. Po Chü-i. NDACCP, *tr. by* David Hinton

After such years of dissension and strife. Dust to Dust. Thomas Hood. NBLV

After sundown the clouds start to burn. Thunderstorm. Sam Mitchell. NOBAu, *tr. by* George von Brandenstein

After Supper. David Keller. SwNoth

After supper in the big room. Broken Sonnets. Kim Addonizio. OPRER

After Symond's *Venice*. John Wieners. AHA

After ten thousand years I will repeat my claim. Back to the First Bar. Emmy Bridgwater. SurWo

After ten years in the red-light district. Ikkyu Sojun. ZenPo, *tr. by* Takashi Ikemoto and Lucien Stryk

After that first birth. Newborn Found Alive in Shallow Grave. David Citino. LiTh

After the abduction by the eagle, after the lovely indiscretion with the boy. Hebe and Ganymede. *Unknown*. CAGL, *tr. by* John Boswell

After the abortion. What does a man do. Tyehimba Jess. BtF

After the act of stabbing and. Stone Wall and Celebration. János Pilinszky. PoSu, *tr. by* Peter Jay

After the air of summer. (LL) Roman Fountain. Louise Bogan. APT-2; NoP-4; NoP-5

After the all been done and i. Island Mary. Lucille Clifton. NALW

After the Alphabets. W. S. Merwin. PoA 2002

After the American Wake. Vincent Woods. NIrP

After the Anti-Semitic Calls on a Local Talk Station. Lyn Lifshin. UnSA

After the Argument. Stephen Dunn. GoPo

After the Argument. Joyce Peseroff. PfS

After the autumn wind sweeps the garden. Song for Late Autumn. Master Naong. BecRai, *tr. by* Kim Daljin, Kim Won-Chung and Christopher Merrill

After the baths and bowel-work, he was dead. Gwendolyn Brooks. ColAP *Fr.* Notes from the Childhood and the Girlhood.

After the Battle. Victor Hugo. SxFrPo, *tr. by* A. M. and E. H. Blackmore

After the Battle. Anton Malczewski. WoPoe, *tr. by* Jerzy Peterkiewicz and Burns Singer

After the Big Flood, we elected. Transposition of Clermont, The. Les A. Murray. EmeKit

After the bird has flown. (LL) Refusal to Mourn, A. Derek Mahon. ModIr; PNI

After the bitter mood had gone again. (LL) Glass of Water, A: "Here is a glass of water from my well." May Sarton. IJHIL; StAl

After the bitter weather. Spring. R. Williams Parry. BBMWP, *tr. by* Joseph P. Clancy

After the blast of lightning from the east. End, The. Wilfred Owen. ChIV-1

After the Bomb Tests. Jane Cooper.

   "Atom bellies like a cauliflower, The." MakPoe

After the border, it was trees all the way to. British Columbia. William Stafford. GifTon

After the boy threw the pregnant turtle. Turtle Blessing. Penny Harter. TWW

After the break-in. Unnatural Light. Peter Meinke. UrbNat

After the brief bivouac of Sunday. Stenographers, The. Patricia K. Page. BrAP; HeIP-4; NALW; NAMCP V.2; NoAM

After the burial-parties leave. Hyaenas [*or* Hyenas], The. Rudyard Kipling. BrAP; NAEL-6v2; NAEL-7v2; OBSV

After the cancer, the kidneys. Dialysis. Lucille Clifton. FuFl

After the Children Have Gone to Bed. Nicholas Samaras. TWW

After the cloud came to a dead stop. Genoa. Dino Campana. PFTM-1

After the cloud embankments. Reconnaissance. Arna Bontemps. APT-2

After the Colombian Earthquake. Maurice Kilwein Guevara. NAPBL

After the Convention. Robert Lowell. NoAM

After the Country Tavern & all the bars in Gregg County. After Hours. Robert Trammell. TiP2

After the cries of gulls and the fogbound island. Homecoming. Thomas McGrath. PWW2

After the Dance. Reuben Jackson. GT

After the Dance for the Dead. Sogetsuni. SoOfWa, *tr. by* Sam Hamill

After the dancing ended, and the Russians. Slow Night on Texas Street, A. James Kimbrell. NAPBL

After the deaths I've seen in Eastanalle Valley. Hymn for the Sound of Hymns. George Scarbrough. LPSFW

After the Defeat. Yannis Ritsos. AF, *tr. by* Edmund Keeley

After the Deluge. Pierre Jean Jouve. YaTCFP, *tr. by* Lee Fahnestock

After the Deluge. Wole Soyinka. HBAPE

After the dew fell silently last night. Untitled 2. Ch'oe Sûngja. EcSo, *tr. by* Mickey Hong

After the Dinner Party. Robert Penn Warren. NAAL-5; PoCho

After the dread tales and red yarns of the Line. First Time In. Ivor Gurney. FaBoVe; NAMCP V.1; NoP-4; NoP-5

After the drink, after dinner, after the half-hour idiot kids' cartoon special on the TV. Mistress, The. C. K. Williams. StAl

After the eating, the drinking, the singing. Song. Liu Yung. CrYelRi, *tr. by* Sam Hamill

After the End. Ann Townsend. AmPoNex

After the End of It. Anne Stevenson. StAl

After the End of the World. David Jauss. SeSe

After the end of the world. In the Middle of Life. Tadeusz Rózewicz. GPTC, *tr. by* Joanna Trzeciak

After the Exam. Gwyn Williams. BBMWP, *tr. by* Christopher Meredith

After the exhilaration of jazz at Sweet Basil. Two Stories. Ron Overton. PrTe

After the explosion and the hail. Women of Lockerbie, The. Richard Robbins. OtW

After the eyes that looked, the lips that spake. Gettysburg Ode. Bayard Taylor. CBCWP

After the Fact: To Ted Bundy. Robert Phillips. LiTh

After the fair, I'd still a light heart. Lammas Hireling, The. Ian Duhig. NeBrP

After the Fall [of Saigon]. Yusef Komunyakaa. AF

After the fallen sun the wind was sad. Moonrise Over Battlefield. Edgell Rickword. PoWW

After the fervor. Waiting. Shirley Kaufman. TAPaP

After the fierce midsummer all ablaze. Friendship After Love. Ella Wheeler Wilcox. APN-2; LW

After the final heave, house collapsing. Gaza, Undated. Rachel Tzvia Back. DTA

After the first death, there is no other. (LL) Refusal to Mourn the Death, by Fire, of a Child in London, A. Dylan Thomas. AF; BrAP; FaBoWar; HarvBoo; HeIP-4; MoBrPo; NAMCP V.2; NoAM; NoP-4; NoP-5; OBWVE; OxAEP-2; PoAgWa; PoWW; TFi; WaAnP

After the first powerful plain manifesto. Express, The. Stephen Spender. BrAP; HeIP-4; MoBrPo; NAMCP V.1; NIL-7; NoAM

After the First Snow. David Keller. NevBe

After the first terror. Nuclear Winter. Thomas McGrath. AtGh; GifTon

After the Flood. John Foulcher. NOBAu

After the Flood. Maurice Kilwein Guevara. NAPBL

After the Flood. Sir David Lyndsay. ChIV-1 Fr. Monarche, The.

After the Flood. Arthur Rimbaud. SxFrPo, tr. by Martin Sorrell

After the full-day's westward drive you find. Always. Roddy Lumsden. NeBrP

After the Funeral. Meg Bateman. BeAl, tr. by the author

After the Funeral. Paulette Roeske. Vesp

After the funeral, mule praises, brays. After the Funeral. Dylan Thomas. AngWePo; BrAP; NAEL-6v2; NAEL-7v2; NoP-4; NoP-5; OBWVE; OxAEP-2; TCAWP

After the Funeral of Assam Hamady. Sam Hamod. UnSA

After the general had broken the blockade at Hsüan-chou. Ballad of the Maiden of Lan-ling. Chin Ho. ColAnChi, tr. by Victor H. Mair

After the gods left, the trucks of evening. Atlantis. Joanna Fuhrman. AmPoNex

After the green storm / True color. Mukai Kyorai. ZenPo, tr. by Takashi Ikemoto and Lucien Stryk

After the Harvest. Tu Fu [or Du Fu]. CrYelRi, tr. by Sam Hamill

After the heart attack, prodigious events. Concordiam in Populo. Bernard O'Donoghue. BeAl

After the heavy losses that the Athenians suffered at Aegospotami, / and a little later. After the Defeat. Yannis Ritsos. AF, tr. by Edmund Keeley

After the hours that Sarajevans pass. Bright Lights of Sarajevo, The. Tony Harrison. EmeKit

After the Hurricane. Sinéad Morrissey. MFPA

After the Industrial Revolution, All Things Happen at Once. Robert Bly. OxBoAm

After the Irish of Egan O'Rahilly. Egan O'Rahilly. PBCIP,

After the last breath, eyelids must be closed. Souls. Dannie Abse. PLBUT

After the Last Bulletins. Richard Wilbur. MoAmPo

After the Last Dynasty. Stanley Kunitz. InvLad

After the last exhausted horse. Pat Taffe and Arkle. Tracey Herd. MFPA

After the Last Words. Scott Cairns. UpMys

After the leaves have fallen, we return. Plain Sense of Things, The. Wallace Stevens. APT-1; EmeKit; NAAL-5; NAMCP V.1; NoAM; OxBoAm

After the Leningrad trials, after solitary confinement. Bread and Water. Shirley Kaufman. CFP

After *The Little Mariner*. Olga Broumas. BodElec

After the long season of tending and growth, the harvest comes. (LL) Marge Piercy. IPoFL; TWF Fr. Laying Down the Tower.

After the Lord. New Nephilim, A. Afaa Michael Weaver. OxAAAP

After the midnight unfolding of the White Rose. Feast of Stephen, The. Kevin Nichols. OBCP

After the midwinter marriages—the bride of snow. John Hollander. VCAP Fr. Powers of Thirteen.

After the Miscarriage. Diane Gilliam Fisher. SweBea

After the Missionaries. Michael Chitwood. PoA 2002

After / the Moratorium Reading. Nigel Roberts. NOBAu

After the murder. Last Quatrain of the Ballad of Emmett Till, The. Gwendolyn Brooks. ESEAA; NAEL-5; NAMCP V.2

After the Mute Centuries. Waldo Williams. BBMWP, tr. by Rowan Williams

After the Neutron. Terrance Keenan. AtGh

After the Newport Bridge, the interior of the boat is broken. Block Island Ferry. Catherine Imbriglio. IAoNAP

After the night's black veil. Separation from Clorila, The. José Manuel Martínez de Navarrete. BLPSL, tr. by Rene de Costa, Rigas Kappatos and Eleni Paidoussi

After the Noise of Saigon ("If where we hunt defines us."). Walter McDonald. OPRER

After the noose, and the black diary deeds. Richard Murphy. ModIr; PBCIP Fr. Battle of Aughrim, The.

After the nuclear strike. War Games. Connie Bensley. FaBoWar

After the Obsession. Helon Habila. NeNiPo

After the Opera. D. H. Lawrence. BrAP

After the pantomime, carrying you back to the car. Cinders. Roger McGough. StAl

After the paradiso and the milky way and the kosmos, seeming. Yolanda Meets the Wild Boys. Jessica Tarahata Hagedorn. OpBo

After the Party. Luigi Fontanella. Neft, tr. by W. S. Di Piero

After the Persian. Louise Bogan. PoA 2002

After the pilgrimage. Shiny Aluminum of God, The. Martín Espada. Vesp

After the planes unloaded, we fell down. Dead in Europe, The. Robert Lowell. WoPoe

After the Pleasure Party [Lines Traced under an Image of Amor Threatening]. Herman Melville. APN-2; NAAL-3; OxBoAm

After the ploughshare and the stumbling team. (LL) As the Team's Head-Brass. Edward Thomas. CABP; HarvBoo; NAEL-6v2; NAEL-7v2; NoP-4; NoP-5; OBWP; OxAEP-2; StAl

After the Poem Who Knows. Alan Michael Parker. NAPBL

After the police left, having told me of your death. Amor Diving. Marion Lomax. NeBl

After the Prom. Lisa D. Chavez. AmPoNex

After the promise has been kept, or. Afterward. Robert Penn Warren. BodElec

After the Quarrel. Priscilla Jane Thompson. CBWP-2

After the quarrelling at recess. Learning to Sing in Parts. Jean Janzen. ACAMVP

After the Raiders Have Gone: To Clerks and Officials. Yüan Chieh. CCL1, tr. by Stephen Owen

After the Rain. Joseph Ceravolo. NYP2

After the Rain. Anne Marie Macari. MotU

After the Rain. Kristina Rungano. HAWP

After the rain of stars. At the Gate of the Valley. Zbigniew Herbert. PoSu, tr. by Czeslaw Milosz

After the rain, when the earth releases. Eating Wild Mushrooms. Gary Young. GeoHom

After the Rains of Saigon ("I put back the rifle on a steel rack."). Walter McDonald. TiP2

After the Random Tornado. Walter McDonald. TiP2

After the ranks of stubble have lain bare. Autumn Ploughing. John Masefield. OxBEV

After the Rebellion, Visiting West Mountain Temple. Ch'i-chi. CSKM, tr. by Burton Watson

After the red-rose-bordered hem. (LL) To Ireland in the Coming Times. William Butler Yeats. IrV; NAMCP V.1; NoAM

After the Report from Iron Mountain. Jerry W., Jr. Ward. FuFl

After the revolution came the Fuehrer. Traditional Tune. Muriel Rukeyser. TaR

After the rushing waters had subsided the Lenape of the turtle were close together, in hollow houses, living together there. Unknown. APN-2 Fr. Walam Olum; or, Red Score [of the Lenâpé], The [or The Wallam Olum; The Red Score or Painted History of the Lenni Lenape].

After the sadness of apples in August. Aubade. Robin Behn. AmAlph

After the sea-ship, after the whistling winds. After the Sea-Ship. Walt Whitman. APN-1

After the second book. Poet at Work. Richard Tipping. BMAP

After the Seizer there were ten chiefs, and there was much warfare south and east. Unknown. OBVE Fr. Walam Olum; or, Red Score [of the Lenâpé], The [or The Wallam Olum; The Red Score or Painted History of the Lenni Lenape].

After the Separation, Dad Takes Me to the Dance for the Dead. Mira Chieko Shimabukuro. FiBr

After the Shipwreck. Corey Marks. LegDan

After the Shipwreck. Alicia Ostriker. PLBUT

After the silence of the centuries? (LL) Man with the Hoe, The. Edwin Markham. APN-2; BRP; CalPo; GS; MoAmPo; NAAPv.1; OxBoAm; TCAPo; TFi

After the Small Pox. Mary Jones. PEW

After the Snow. Rayne Mackinnon. EdScPo

After the Snow in the Mountains. Yi Chehyŏn. CATKP, tr. by Chi-gyu Kim [or Kim Chonggil]

After the Solstice. Daryl Hine. PoA 2002

After the spring song, "Vast emptiness, no holiness." Shunoku. ZenPo, tr. by Takashi Ikemoto and Lucien Stryk

After the stars were all hung separately. Book of How, The. Merrill Moore. MoAmPo

    (After the stars were all hung separately out.) FuPo

After the sticky steam of plums. Chicken Guts. Jean Janzen. ACAMVP

After the Storm. Edmond Yi-teh Chang. OpBo

After the Storm. Henri Faust. YaYoPo

After the Storm. Henrietta Cordelia Ray. CBWP-3

After the Storm, August. Gail Mazur. ExTi

After the sudden rain. Old Currawong. Jennifer Rankin. BMAP

After the sun's eclipse. Teresa. Richard Wilbur. NoAM; UpMys

After the supper and talk—after the day is done. After the Supper and Talk. Walt Whitman. MoAmPo; NAAL-3

After the Surprising Conversions. Robert Lowell. NAMCP V.2; NoAM; TRP

After the Survivors Are Gone. Peter Balakian. WaAnP

After the sweat of swathes and the sinking madder sun. Drink of Spring, A. John Ennis. PBCIP

After the Symbols. Gus Blaisdell. ICANM

After the Terror. Jay Parini. WaAnP

After the terror I. What I Said. Norman Stock. PA9/11

After the third evening roud. Vasco [or Vasko] Popa. PoSu Fr. Raw Flesh.

After the third evening round. Vasco [or Vasko] Popa. See After the third evening roud.

After the thorns I came to the first page. Sleeping Beauty, The: Variation of the Prince. Randall Jarrell. PoA 2002

After the tiff there was stiff silence, till. Lovers, The. William Robert Rodgers. IrLP; PNI

After the torchlight red on sweaty faces. T. S. Eliot. Fr. Waste Land, The.

After the Trial. Weldon Kees. MakPoe

After the Trial of Hamlet, Chicago. Sherman Alexie. PrTe

After the tumult and the blood. At Vshchizh. Fyodor Ivanovich Tyutchev. OBWP; OxBEV; WoPoe, tr. by Henry Gifford and Charles Tomlinson

After the 200th White Person Locks Her Car Door at Me. Bruce A. Jacobs. BtF

After the uprising of the 17th June. Solution, The. Bertolt Brecht. PoSu, tr. by Dereck Bowman

After the Verdict. Tony Medina. SpirFl

After the Voices. Victor Hugo. SxFrPo, tr. by A. M. and E. H. Blackmore

After the wailing had already begun. On Reading a Recent Greek Poet. Bertolt Brecht. WoPoe, tr. by John Peck

After the wake and speeches, when the guests in black. Lazarus. James Keir Baxter. HarvBoo

After the war she could live. Tattoo. Liliane Welch. Coast

After the war, she painted her walls. Aunt Lily and Frederick the Great. Jean Nordhaus. PoDa

After the war, the terror people underwent produced profound if not irrevocable. Hazardous Waste. James Sherry. FTOS

After the War; When Coltrane Only Wanted to Play Dance Tunes. Matthew Graham. SeSe

After the wars were over, the ones people sang about. Industrial Teflon Comes Into Domestic Use. Fleda Brown Jackson. PoA 2002

After the Wedding. David Biespiel. NAPBL

After the Wedding Party. Matthew Rohrer. ReTh

After the whey-faced anonymity. South Country. Kenneth Slessor. BMAP

After the whoosh of doors slid shut. At Lansdowne Bridge. Arthur Nortje. HBAPE; TSAP

After the Wilderness. Andrew Hudgins. CBCWP

After the wolves and before the elms. My Country in Darkness. Eavan Boland. PoCho

After the Word Love Was Spoken. Anthony Caleshu. NIrP

After the worst part of four years. Sick Man, The. E. du Perron. TuT, tr. by Pat Boran

After the Zhivago of it all, the terrible sleeve. Housekeeping. Lucie Brock-Broido. ExTi

After Theresienstadt. Myra Sklarew. TaR

After these things should be. (LL) New House, The. Edward Thomas. MoBrPo; OBEV; OBWVE

After these words, the prince of the Weather-Geats. Unknown. WaAnP Fr. Beowulf [Heaney Translation].

After they all leave. Surely You Remember. Dahlia Ravikovitch. VCWP

After they had not made love. Happy Ending. Fleur Adcock. LW

After they sawed through the bone. Daughter, That Picture of You. Keith Gilyard. SpirFl

After they threw me in a cell and locked the door. Song of the Slave Girl, The. Fadil Azzawi. IrPoTo, tr. by Ralph Saverese and Saadi A. Simawe

After thinking this fortnight of Whig and of Tory. My Opinion. Charles, 6th Earl of Dorset Sackville. BASC

After this graveyard shift, the escape I want. For Michaela. David Rivard. MAAN

After this life here, we're to be awakened one day. Vladimir Holan. See Is it true that after this life of ours we shall one day be awakened.

After this much time, it's still impossible. The SS man with his stiff hair and his uniform. Spit. C. K. Williams. TaR

After this oracle there will be no more oracles. Last Statement for a Last Oracle. Alan Dugan. NoAM

After three days of summer rain. Kerouac Creek Work Tune. Hoa Nguyen. WANABP

After Tomasito's Departure. Thomas McGrath. PoChi

After Tonight. Gary Soto. NAMCP V.2; NoAM

After Treblinka. How We See. Edward Bond. HP

After Twenty Years. Adrienne Rich. TRP

After Twenty Years. Fadwa Tuqan. AF, tr. by Unknown

After twenty years in France. After Twenty Years. Eleanor Ross Taylor. AmWaPo

After two sittings, now our Lady State. Andrew Marvell. OBSV Fr. Last Instructions to a Painter, The.

After two snips her pantycelyn came off. Oedipus to the Third Power. Gerardo Deniz. RMCMP, tr. by Mónica de la Torre

After Two Years. Richard Aldington. MoBrPo

After Us. Connie Wanek. P180

After us there will be. Scrap. Tomasz Jastrun. AF, tr. by Daniel Bourne

After Visiting Hours. U. A. Fanthorpe. PoCu

After wandering for so many hours up and down. Reminiscence. Vladimir Holan. PoSu, tr. by George Theiner

After War. Ivor Gurney. HarvBoo

After washing Paddington loos. Return, The. Moeen Faruqi. PML

After watching your appeal from ev'ry angle. All of You. Cole Porter. ReLy

After we flew across the country we. Topography. Sharon Olds. GoPo; OxBoAm; WaAnP

After we had crossed the long illness. Further Arrivals. Margaret Atwood. BrAP

After we had loved each other intently. Listening to the Köln Concert. Robert Bly. RaBo

After we make love, I teach you. In Language. Eugene Gloria. OpBo

After we / ovulate. Overworked. Lucy Partlow. BRtP

After west when every bit of it. After West. James Harms. RWB

After Winter. Sterling Allen Brown. GT

After winter '76. Lionel Abrahams. TSAP

After Wiriyamu Village Massacre by Portuguese. Jack A. Mapanje. AF

After Work. Richard Jones. GoPo

After working the midtown ambulance night slot. One Too Many Mornings. David Rivard. PBCAP

After writing. Past Midnight. Edmund Wilson. PoA 2002

After Years of Feasting and No Sacrifice. Linda Zisquit. DTA

After years the reunion. Brushed the dogs. Party. Eddy Van Vliet. VCWP, tr. by John Van Tiel

After Yeats. Allen Ginsberg. FTOS

After Yes. James Harms. AmPoNex

After you brought her home with your first child. Richard Murphy. ModIr Fr. Price of Stone, The.

After you died I dreamed you were at my apartment. For Suzuki Roshi. Diane Di Prima. WANABP

After you finish your work. Ballad of Orange and Grape. Muriel Rukeyser. ChAP; NoAM; NoP-4; NoP-5; WaAnP

After you have gone. Song of Parting. Wang Po-ch'eng. CrYelRi, tr. by Sam Hamill

After You Left. Mark Ivey. ICANM

After You Left. Heather McHugh. BodElec

After you left me forever. Semele Recycled. Carolyn Kizer. CAP-8; NALW

After you left me, I was so lonely and sad, I became but an apparition, a ghost of who I had been. Nirvana. Nin Andrews. AmZen

After your death, the fortune teller. Dad-Baby, The. Amanda Dalton. NeBl

After your letter arrived I left the oven on. Still Life. Madeline DeFrees. VisFro

After You've Gone. Henry Creamer. ReLy

After you've shown me the bedraggled cockatoo. Cockatoo. Pam Bridgeman. Prnts

After-Dinner Poem (Terpsichore), An. Oliver Wendell Holmes. TCAPo

Aftereffects of a mother's neglects, The. Mother, Mother, Are You All There? Felicia Lamport. NBLV

Afterglow. Amy Lowell. NAAPv.2

After-Glow of Pain, The. Clara Ann Thompson. CBWP-2

Afterglow, The. Henrietta Cordelia Ray. CBWP-3

After-Image. Linda Bierds. ExTi

Afterimages. Audre Lorde. LTA; VCAP

Afterimages. Takahashi Shinkichi. ZenPo, tr. by Takashi Ikemoto and Lucien Stryk

After-Life, The. Anne Waldman. AHA

Afterlife of Trees, The. Brian Bartlett. Coast

Afterlives. Derek Mahon. NAMCP V.2

Aftermath. Henry Wadsworth Longfellow. APN-1; NAAL-3; NAAPv.1; PoPoPo

Aftermath. Paul Muldoon. NAMCP V.2

Aftermath. Siegfried Sassoon. BLPJKO; MoBrPo; PoWW

Aftermath (1945). Henriette de Saussure Blanding. ASA

Afternoon. Louisa Sarah Bevington. PEW

Afternoon. Yannis Ritsos. AF, tr. by Edmund Keeley

Afternoon. Takahashi Shinkichi. ZenPo,

Afternoon. Across the garden, in Green Hall. Love in the Classroom. Al Zolynas. BLT; LTA; TWF

Afternoon: Amagansett Beach. John Hall Wheelock. APT-1

Afternoon and two men. In the Woods. Heinz Piontek. CLPP, tr. by Jerome Rothenberg

Afternoon / and your eyes walk. Whispers, Secrets, and Promises. E. Ethelbert Miller. FuFl

Afternoon arrived, The. Water Wheel, The. Antonio Machado Ruiz. WED, tr. by Robert Bly

Afternoon at the Beach, An. Edgar Bowers. CalPo; VCAP

8. Afternoon Bus to Toronto. David McFadden. NLPA

Afternoon cooking in the fall sun. Song. Robert Hass. ASA; LoL; NAMCP V.2

Afternoon falls, The. Water Wheel, The. Antonio Machado Ruiz. SpanPo, tr. by James Duffy

Afternoon Gossip, An. Priscilla Jane Thompson. CBWP-2

Afternoon Happiness. Carolyn Kizer. GeoHom

Afternoon I was killed, The. Close. Andrew Motion. HarvBoo; StAl

Afternoon in Austin. Betsy Berry. TiP2

Afternoon in February. Henry Wadsworth Longfellow. APN-1; ColAP

Afternoon in Pangasinan with No Electricity, An. Regie Cabico. ReBoTo

Afternoon in sultry summer, An. Amores (after Ovid). Ovid. WaAnP

Afternoon in the Garden. Ethel Louisa Mason Anderson. NOBAu

Afternoon is absorbed in your silence, The. Ivy. Elsa Cross. RMCMP, tr. by Margaret Sayers Peden

Afternoon is all fallen plaster, black stones, dry thorns, The. Afternoon. Yannis Ritsos. AF, tr. by Edmund Keeley

Afternoon is offered to us, The. Love. Oscar Cerruto. BLPSL, tr. by Rene de Costa, Rigas Kappatos and Eleni Paidoussi

Afternoon is sad and gray, The. Tropical Afternoon. Rubén Darío. TCLAP, tr. by Lysander Kemp

Afternoon it changes. Place, The. Robert Creeley. BodElec

Afternoon, its lazy ways, The. Girl. Octavio Paz. STV, tr. by John Frederick Nims

Afternoon light like pollen. In Berkeley. Robert Pinsky. PfSP

Afternoon of a Faun, The. Stéphane Mallarmé. NAWM-7v2, tr. by Henry Weinfield

Afternoon of a Faun, The. Stéphane Mallarmé. WoPoe, tr. by Louis Simpson

Afternoon of the Sheep, The. Kazuko Shiraishi. WoBe, tr. by Samuel Grolmes and Yumiko Tsumura

Afternoon on a Hill. Edna St. Vincent Millay. APT-1; ChAP; NTCP

Afternoon Sleep. Robert Bly. WoPoe

Afternoon storm has hit, An. After the Fall [of Saigon]. Yusef Komunyakaa. AF

Afternoon sun is on their faces, The. Women in Dutch Painting. Eunice De Souza. NAMCP V.2

Afternoon sun/ somewhere in the South, The. Landscapes. Duriel Harris. SpirFl

Afternoon the neighborhood boys tied me and Mary Lou Mahar, The. Sixth Grade. Marie Howe. KGB

Afternoon Train. Afaa Michael Weaver. BRtP

Afternoon Walk: The Sea Ranch. Sandra M. Gilbert. ASA

Afternoon with a light brush stroke, The. Slow Delight. Leopoldo Lugones. BLPSL, tr. by Rene de Costa, Rigas Kappatos and Eleni Paidoussi

Afternoon, with light strokes, The. Indulgence. Leopoldo Lugones. TCLAP, tr. by Julie Schumacher

Afternoons. Philip Larkin. NPeEn; OxBEV; PoetW

Afternoons of dove-slurred languor. Ford Castle: The Borders. Geoffrey Holloway. NLP

After-State. Frederick William Faber. CenSon

Afterthought. Caroline Finkelstein. PfS

Afterthought. Elizabeth Jennings. NOxBChV; OBCP

After-Thought. William Wordsworth. CenSon; NPBRoP Fr. River Duddon [A Series of Sonnets], The.

After-Thought, The. Stevie Smith. MoWP

After-twelve darkly comes back full stop. At Night Keep Still. Russell Atkins. EGAG

Afterward. Herman Melville. APN-2 Fr. Clarel: A Poem and Pilgrimage in the Holy Land.

Afterward. Robert Penn Warren. BodElec

Afterward, There Will Be a Hallway. Arielle Greenberg. LegDan

Afterwards. Tristan Corbière. tr. by Randall Jarrell

"It's getting dark, little thief of starlight!" WoPoe, tr. by Randall Jarrell

Afterwards. Günter Grass. GTCP, tr. by Irmgard Hunt

Afterwards. Thomas Hardy. HarvBoo; ItP; MoBrPo; NAMCP V.1; NoP-4; NoP-5; OxAEP-2; OxBEV; PoPoPo; TFi; WoPoe

Afterwards. Frances Ridley Havergal. SacPr

Afterwards: Caliban. Ansel Talvikki. AmPoNex

Afterwards: "Earth will flame and glow, The." Moishe Nadir. Prolet, tr. by Amelia Glaser

Afterwards he sleeps. Reading in Bed. Magi Gibson. EdScPo

Afterwards, in the shower. Dolce. Kennette Wilkes. PasH

Afterwards she blamed it on the wind, cold. Meteorology. Linda France. MFPA

Afterwards, when we have slept, paradise. Knowing, The. Sharon Olds. PasH

Afterwards you had that drunk, drugged look. First Kiss. Kim Addonizio. NevBe

After-Word. Ras Baraka. InTrad

Afterword. Dan Beachy-Quick. LegDan

Afterwords. Dan Gerber. WhBo

Aftir þat heruest had his sheues. My Compleinte. Thomas Hoccleve.

Aftir that hervest inned had hise sheves. Thomas Hoccleve. NPeEn Fr. My Compleinte.

Afton Water. Robert Burns. CtM; NAEL-6v2; NAEL-7v2

Again. Robert Creeley. NAMCP V.2; VCAP

Again. / Midtown is blasted out and silent. Worked Late on a Tuesday Night. Deborah Garrison. GoPo

Again. Glyn Jones. OBWVE; TCAWP

Again. Charlotte Mew. MoBrPo

Again. Lenard D. Moore. GT

Again. Deanna Ortiz. ICANM

Again a Drab Khaki Light is Coming Down. Meir Wieseltier. NRoS, tr. by Esther Raizen

Again: Air in the Tops—Of Birches. Gennady Aygi. WoBe, tr. by Peter France

Again and again it sounds, / Thonah! Thonah! (LL) Unknown. APN-2; TCAPo Fr. Mountain Chant, The.

Again and again that scene, enthralling in ordinariness. Swept Away. László Kálnoky. IQMS, tr. by Kenneth McRobbie and Zita McRobbie

Again and again, / while History is unforgiven. (LL) In the Naked Bed, in Plato's Cave. Delmore Schwartz. APT-2; MoAmPo; NAMCP V.2; NoAM; PoA 2002; WaAnP

Again and then again . . . the year is born. New Year's Day. Robert Lowell. ChrPo; TRP

Again at Christmas did we weave. Alfred Tennyson. NAEL-6v2; NAEL-7v2; NAWM-7v2 Fr. In Memoriam A. H. H.

Again at the Crossroads. Im Hwa. CAMKP, tr. by Jiwon Shin

Again he made his way through bloody hell. Non Piu Leggevano. Árpád Tóth. IQMS, tr. by Jess Perlman

Again, here it comes, the nothing. Salamanders. A. K. Ramanujan. PoetW

Again I am summoned to the eternal field. First Love. Edwin Rolfe. AmWaPo; APT-2

Again I find myself alone. Charlotte Brontë. PEW (My Dreams.) VWP

Again I find myself alone, and ever. Again I find myself alone. Charlotte Brontë. PEW

Again I reply to the triple winds. January. William Carlos Williams. MoAmPo

Again I'm caught staring. Pleasures of the Imagination. Peter McDonald. PNI

Again I'm on the Tisza's banks as the sun climbs. Morning Splendour of the Tisza, The. György Bessenyei. IQMS, tr. by Gavin Ewart

Again, in the Book of Books, to-day. Prodigals. Phoebe Cary. SacPr

Again. Is this happening again? Once Again Another Century Ahead. Joanne Kyger. WANABP

Again it's love that sweeps me in. Aambl. Seitlhamo Motsapi. TSAP

Again I've returned to this country. Country Without a Post Office, The. Agha Shahid Ali. AmAlph; NAMCP V.2

Again last night. Road, The. Kim Sowŏl. CAMKP, tr. by David R. McCann

Again last night I dreamed the dream called Laundry. Mad Scene, The. James Merrill. CAP-8; ItP; PoA 2002

Again Love, glancing meltingly. Ibycus. SaLy, tr. by Diane Rayor

Again Love struck me like a smith with a giant. Anacreon. SaLy, tr. by Diane Rayor

Again, mother, I turn to you. From a New Height. Andrea Zanzotto. PML, *tr. by* Ruth Feldman and Brian Swann

Again retreated—and a second time faced the screen. (LL) Ivor Gurney. HarvBoo; NAEL-6v2; NAEL-7v2; NAMCP V.1; NoP-4; NoP-5; NPeEn; OBWP; PoWW *Fr.* Silent One, The.

Again sick. / Just now somehow paler. Aleksandra Petrova. CRWP, *tr. by* Dennis Silk

Again stands superb as a temple. (LL) Incident, An. Douglas Le Pan. BrAP; NoP-4

Again the cab slips west down 14th almost. Overheard in the Love Hotel. Robert Polito. KGB

Again the Cousin's whistle! Go, my Love. (LL) Andrea del Sarto. Robert Browning. NAEL-6v2; NAEL-7v2; NoP-4; NoP-5

Again the glory of the days! Battle Summers, The. Herman Melville. APN-2

Again the golden month, still. In September. John Ormond. TCAWP

Again the lake is a pretty catchphrase. Skater, The. Hester Knibbe. TuT, *tr. by* Micheal O'Siadhail

Again the last ebb. Dieppe. Samuel Beckett. YaTCFP, *tr. by* the author

Again the morning is wet. On High Street. Andrea Hollander Budy. UrbNat

Again, the same dream. Nightmare. Matilde Salganicoff. MirDau, *tr. by* Celeste Kostopulos-Cooperman

Again the shells were falling. Fresco Come to Life. Boris Leonidovich Pasternak. AF

Again the Summoning. Lawrence S. Cumberbatch. EGAG

Again. The. Time. Carla Harryman. BAP-04 *Fr.* Baby.

Again the violet of our early days. Spring. Ebenezer Elliott. OxAEP-2

Again the wood, and long-withdrawing vale. To Spring. Charlotte Smith. RWP

Again the world opens up like a girl's room. February Sun. Paul Rodenko. TuT, *tr. by* Mary E. O'Donnell

Again they come, and muttered [*or* mutter'd] as he died. (LL) George Crabbe. NPBRoP; OBNV *Fr.* Borough, The.

Again, this time from the chorus. (LL) Larry Neal. ISC; SeSe

Again thou reignest in thy golden hall. To the Harvest Moon. William Stanley Roscoe. CenSon

Again today it is. Self-Portrait Approaching Promontory, Utah. Michael Pettit. GM

Again, traveller, you have come a long way led by that star. Epitaph. Thomas McGrath. RaBo

Again very queer but I'll go on looking. (LL) Wodwo. Ted Hughes. BrAP; HarvBoo; NAMCP V.2; NoAM; WoPoe

Again we went out, O one who bore me, to the forced march in summer. Forced March in Summer. Yehoshua Zafrir. NRoS, *tr. by* Esther Raizen

Again when all the radiant sons of light. Bible, *O.T.* NOSC *Fr.* Paraphrase Upon Job, A.

Again when all the radiant sons of light. Bible, *O.T. Fr.* Paraphrase Upon Job, A.

Again with Music. Kay Smith. Coast

Against a backdrop of Pennsylvania hills. Such a Boat of Land. Lamont B. Steptoe. UnSA

Against a feathery sky. (LL) Adolescence—1. Rita Dove. ISC; NAAL-5; NoAM

Against a Rich Man Despising Poverty. Phineas Fletcher. NOSC (To a Rich Man.) SacPr

Against a Sickness: To the Female Double Principle God. Alan Dugan. NoAM

Against Absence. Sir John Suckling. CavPo

Against an elm a sheep was tied [*or* ty'd]. John Gay. NPeEn *Fr.* Fables.

Against both bar and tower the black sea runs. (LL) Point Shirley. Sylvia Plath. NIL-7; NIP-4

Against Botticelli. Robert Hass. OxBoAm

Against Broccoli. Roy Blount, Jr. . NBLV

Against brown walls, the servant bends. Vuillard Interior. Elise Partridge. IFF

Against Certainty. Jane Hirshfield. WANABP

Against Cinderella. Julia Alvarez. FiBr

Against compulsory military service: a *"deferment"* of each limb. Deferment. Marcel Duchamp. PFTM-1

Against Conscription. Wei Chuang. CrYelRi, *tr. by* Sam Hamill

Against Constancy. John Wilmot, 2d Earl of Rochester. NOSC; OxAEP-1

Against Coupling. Fleur Adcock. EmeKit; MoWP; NALW

Against downed trees. Festal Song. *Unknown.* CrYelRi, *tr. by* Sam Hamill

Against Extremity. Charles Tomlinson. HarvBoo

Against Fruition. Abraham Cowley. NOSC *Fr.* Mistress, The.

Against Fruition ("Stay here, fond youth, and ask no more.") Sir John Suckling. CavPo; NOSC

Against him, die, and find death good. (LL) Love On the Farm. D. H. Lawrence. CABP; MoBrPo; NAEL-6v2; NAEL-7v2; NAMCP V.1; NoAM; NoP-4; NoP-5

Against his forearm, leaning up against the barn. (LL) Land of Little Sticks, 1945. James Tate. AtGh; BodElec

Against his lip, whose service has been tendered. Lover Release Agreement. J. Allyn Rosser. PoA 2002

Against Hope. NOSC *Fr.* Mistress, The.

Against Horace. Mihály Babits. IQMS, *tr. by* Adam Makkai and J. G. Nichols

Against Ibn Arabi. Abdel Kader El Janabi. Eno, *tr. by* Pierre Joris

Against Idleness and Mischief. Isaac Watts. *See* How Doth the Little Busy Bee.

Against Indifference. Charles Webbe. OBEV

Against its own best time. (LL) Sex without Love. Sharon Olds. HeIP-4; NIL-7; NIP-4; TRP

Against Meaning. Andrei Codrescu. PmAP

Against Minoan sunlight. Wishes for Her. Denis Devlin. IrLP

Against my will. Footprints. Dan Pagis. VCWP, *tr. by* Stephen Mitchell

Against Nature. Timothy Liu. LiTh

Against Numerology. Richard Caddel. Oth

Against Parting. Natan Zach. HP; PoSu

Against Poetry. Sandra M. Gilbert. PoA 2002

Against red bark trunk. Allen Ginsberg. WhBo

Against Romanticism. Kingsley Amis. NAMCP V.2; NoAM

Against Silence. Pamela Stewart. ExTi

Against Surrealism. James Wright. MotU

Against that time, if ever that time come. William Shakespeare. OxAEP-1 *Fr.* Sonnets.

Against the burly air I strode. Genesis. Geoffrey Hill. ChIV-1; HarvBoo

Against the Current. Luciana Frezza. CItWP, *tr. by* Cinzia Sartini Blum and Lara Trubowitz

Against the Fear of Death (The Latter Part of the Third Book). Lucretius. *Fr.* De Rerum Natura (On the Nature of Things).

Against the gently flowing spring morning. 134. Shih Shu. CSKM, *tr. by* James H. Sanford

Against the Grain. Michael Brownstein. AHA

Against the invisible antagonist. Celestial Emperor, The. Howard Nemerov. BodElec

Against the iron fence surrounding pools. Uncle Harry at the La Brea Tar Pits. Ruth Whitman. TaR

Against the king, sir, now why would ye fight? Against the King. William Drummond of Hawthornden. NOSC

Against the lamp I sit by the south window. Sitting at Night. Po Chü-i. TAL

Against the Laws. Friedrich Wilhelm Nietzsche. WoPoe, *tr. by* W. S. Merwin

Against the pink-brown fence with the sprucelet. Ballad of the Pink-Brown Fence, The. Milton Acorn. IFF

Against the potent poison of your hate. (LL) White House, The. Claude McKay. ISC; NIP-4

Against the rigours of a damp cold heaven. John Armstrong. STuOW *Fr.* Art of Preserving Health, The.

Against the rubber tongues of cows and the hoeing hands of men. Thistles. Ted Hughes. FaBoVe; NAMCP V.2; NoAM; NPeEn; SoSe-8; WaAnP

Against the snow a tall Being of Beauty. Being Beauteous. Arthur Rimbaud. SxFrPo, *tr. by* Martin Sorrell

Against the wall, the firing squad ready. Dostoevsky. Charles Bukowski. GoPo

Against the War in Vietnam. Wendell Berry. WaAnP

Against the war, the shutter opens only. Interior with a Violin. Marianne Boruch. AmAlph

Against time and the damages of the brain. To Walker Evans. James Agee. APT-2

Against what light. Black Dada Nihilismus. Imamu Amiri Baraka. PFTM-2

Against Whatever It Is That's Encroaching. Charles Simic. ColAP

Against Whitman. Ira Sadoff. ViWalt

Against Women. *Unknown.*

"Woman is by aptitude." OBWVE

Against Writing about Children. Erin Belieu. PoChi

Against your black I set the dainty deer. Contrasts. Iain Crichton Smith. NePenScot

Agamemnon. Aeschylus. NAWM-5v1, *tr. by* Robert Fagles

Agamemnon. Aeschylus. *tr. by* Robert Browning, Dallam Simpson, Gilbert Murray and Louis MacNeice

"For Ares, gold-exchanger for the dead." FaBoWar, *tr. by* Robert Browning

"God, whose law it is that he who learns must suffer." BLPJKO, *tr. by* Edith Hamilton

Agamemnon. Aeschylus. *tr. by* Louis MacNeice

"If I were to tell of our labours, our hard lodging." FaBoWar, *tr. by* Louis MacNeice

Agamemnon's Tomb.   Sacheverell Sitwell.   OBMV
  "One by one, as harvesters, all heavy laden."   MoBrPo
Agapé.   Stephanie Brown.   SUP
Agape.   César Vallejo.   TCLAP, *tr. by* Gordon Brotherston and Edward Dorn
Agatha.   David Citino.   UpMys
Agatha Christie Books by the Window, The.   Michael Ondaatje.   BrAP
Agatha Christie to.   Said.   George Starbuck.   AmWit; OBCoV
Age ("Most explicit— / the sense of trap.")   Robert Creeley.   FTOS; PmAP
Age.   Walter Savage Landor.   OxBEV
Age.   Philip Larkin.   OxBEV
Age / is a way of feeling cold that takes me by surprise.   Easter.   Adelia Prado.   TANSG, *tr. by* Ellen Doré Watson
Age after age, the uninstructing dead. (LL)   Gulf, The.   Derek Walcott.   NoP-4; NoP-5; PoetW; PoPoPo
Age, and the deaths, and the ghosts.   He Resigns.   John Berryman.   HarvBoo; WeW-3
Age and the Secretary.   Diana Fitzgerald Bryden.   OpeFie
Age demanded an image, The.   Ezra Pound.   HarvBoo; MoAmPo; NPeEn *Fr.* Hugh Selwyn Mauberley (Life and Contacts).
Age Demanded, The.   Ernest Hemingway.   IllVoic
Age Demanded, The.   Ezra Pound.   TCAPo *Fr.* Hugh Selwyn Mauberley (Life and Contacts).
Age in her embraces passed [*or* pass'd, *or* past], An.   Mistress, The: A Song.   John Wilmot, 2d Earl of Rochester.   NOSC; NPeEn
Age in Prospect.   Robinson Jeffers.   MoAmPo
Age in Youth.   Trumbull Stickney.   ColAP
Age is dull and mean, The.   Men creep.   For Righteousness' Sake.   John Greenleaf Whittier.   OxBoAm
Age is wheat chaff.   Boat on the Pacific, A.   Najaat Al-Udwany.   PoArWo, *tr. by* Moulouk Berry and Ali Farghaly
Age is when to a man.   Samuel Beckett.   ModIr *Fr.* Words and Music.
Age Looks Back at Youth.   Thomas, 2d Baron Vaux of Harrowden Vaux.   NoSic
Age of a Dream, The.   Lionel Pigot Johnson.   OBMV
Age of aquarius mineral water taking a bath, The.   Aleksandr Shatalov.   PML, *tr. by* Vitaly Chernetsky
Age of Benevolence, The.   Carlos Wilcox.
  "Sultry noon, not in the summer's prime, A."   APN-1
Age of Bronze, The.   Lord Byron.
  "Alas, the country! how shall tongue or pen."   OBSV
Age of Correggio and the Carracci, The.   Charles Bernstein.   BodElec
Age of earth and us all chattering.   Susan Howe.   PFTM-2 *Fr.* Pythagorean Silence.
Age of mass consent: go global with her.   Geoffrey Hill.   RWPCtW *Fr.* Speech! Speech!
Age of Plastic, The.   John Forbes.   BMAP
Age of Terror.   Denise Levertov.   PFTM-2
Age of the Great Symphonies, The.   Rolf Jacobsen.   WED, *tr. by* Robert Bly
Age of unhappiness has arrived, or is it, The.   Antonio Porta.   CLPP
Age of War, The.   *Unknown.*   NOBRP
Age three.   Growth.   Shuntaro Tanikawa.   PoetW, *tr. by* Harold Wright
Age 3: I cry in tub as mob of older brother and sisters wearing cheap Halloween masks.   Odd Years, The.   Jeffery Conway.   BeDoSh
Aged, Aged Man, The.   William Wordsworth.   STuOW *Fr.* Resolution and Independence.
Aged Bard's Wish, The.   *Unknown.*   RWP, *tr. by* Anne Grant
Aged Lover Discourses in the Flat Style, The.   James Vincent Cunningham.   NoAM
Aged Lover Renounceth Love, The.   Thomas, 2d Baron Vaux of Harrowden Vaux.   NoSic
Aged man, that mowes [*or* mows] these fields.   Dialogue betwixt Time and a Pilgrim[e], A.   Aurelian Townshend.   NPeEn; OxBEV
Aged nightingale / How sweet.   Masaoka Shiki.   ZenPo, *tr. by* Takashi Ikemoto and Lucien Stryk
Ageing woman combs her hair, The.   Medusa.   Ann Turner.   EdScPo
Ages, The.   William Cullen Bryant.   APN-1
Ages ago, clouds brought them near.   Our Lost Angels.   Scott Cairns.   UpMys
Ages have passed since the stately Odes flourished.   Li Po.   ColAnChi *Fr.* Poems in an Old Style.
Ages like wine.   My Loneliness.   Thérèse 'Awwad.   PoArWo, *tr. by* Kamal Boullata
Ages of the world will not turn back, The.   Fourth Ecologue: Pollio, The.   Virgil.   WoPoe, *tr. by* David R. Slavitt
Agincourt.   Michael Drayton.   OBEV; OxAEP-1
Agincourt, Agincourt!   Song of the English Bowmen.   *Unknown.*   FaBoWar
Aging.   Randall Jarrell.   PoA 2002
Aging is an agony.   Aging.   *Unknown.*   WoPoe, *tr. by* Graeme Wilson

Aging pilgrim on a, An.   On Flower Wreath Hill.   Kenneth Rexroth.   APT-2; BodElec
Aging Poet, on a Reading Trip to Dayton, Visits the Air Force Museum and Discovers There a Plane He Once Flew, The.   Richard Snyder.   OtW
Agitation of the air, An.   End of Summer.   Stanley Kunitz.   LoL; MoAmPo
Aglaura.   Sir John Suckling.
  Song.   BASC; CavPo; ClHu; HeIP-4; ITBLP; NAEL-6v1; NAEL-7v1; NBLV; NIL-7; NIP-4; NoP-4; NoP-5; NPeEn; OBEV; OxAEP-1; OxBEV; TFi; WaAnP
Aglow in Nowhere.   James Richard Broughton.   CalPo
Agnes Moorehead, Hedy Lamarr.   Think Back.   Gerry Gomez Pearlberg.   WiU
Agnostic's funeral prayer.   Lionel Abrahams.   TSAP
Agnosto Theo [To an Unknown God].   Thomas Hardy.   InvLi
Agon.   Branko Miljkovic.   WoPoe, *tr. by* Charles Simic
Agonia Christiana.   János Pilinszky.   IQMS, *tr. by* Adam Makkai
Agonizing pincer-jaws of Heaven, The. (LL)   Sanctity.   Patrick Kavanagh.   NoP-4; NoP-5; StAl
Agony . . . A Resurrection, An.   Assumpta Acam-Oturu.   HAWP; NAfrP
Agony, An. As Now.   Imamu Amiri Baraka.   NAAL-5; NAMCP V.2; NoP-4; NoP-5; UnSA
Agony, The: I say their agony.   Peasants.   Syl Cheney-Coker.   NAfrP
Agony [*or* Agonie], The.   George Herbert.   CABP; FSCP
Agoraphobia.   Linda Pastan.   ExTi
Agosta the Winged Man and Rasha the Black Dove.   Rita Dove.   NAMCP V.2
Agosto.   Federico García Lorca.   RaW *Fr.* Teorías.
Agosu if you go tell them.   Kofi Awoonor.   HBAPE
Agreed, Shozi.   Waste land at Station 14, The.   Douglas Livingstone.   TSAP
Agreeing with that Latin writer, Great is Truth and will prevail in a bit. (LL)   Magna Est Veritas.   Stevie Smith.   NPeEn; OxBEV
Agreement of Predicate Pronouns, The.   Thomas M. Disch.   KGB
Agricola.   Natalia Toledo.   RMCMP, *tr. by* Alberto A. Ríos
Agrícola.   Natalia Toledo.   RMCMP
Agricultural labourer, who has, An.   Alan Brownjohn.   NoP-5; NOxBChV *Fr.* Pitman's Common Sense Arithmetic, 1917.
Agriculture.   Martial.   WoPoe, *tr. by* Fred Chappell
Agrippa's Pug.   Samuel Butler.   DiBP *Fr.* Hudibras.
Agrippina, well aware of Claudius' greed.   Of Moulds and Mushrooms.   Ruthven Todd.   NePenScot
Agua Desatándose.   Luis Rosales.   RaW
Agua desdichada, El.   Efraín Bartolomé.   RMCMP
Agua en su silencio de raíz, El.   Gloria Gervitz.   RMCMP *Fr.* Migraciones.
Aguacero.   Virgil Suarez.   PoDa
Ah.   Robin Blaser.   FTOS
Ah.   Robert Greene.   NoSic; RACG *Fr.* Greene's Mourning Garment.
Ah.   Felix White Sr.'s Introduction to Wakjankaga.   *Winnebago Oral Tradition.*   NAAL-5
Ah, ah, ah.   Moses and the Princess.   Peter Dickinson.   NOxBChV
Ah Ajaak Ajaak.   Loveshock.   *Unknown.*   SonAtl, *tr. by* Alan Brierly
Ah and woe!   Hell.   Andreas Gryphius.   WoPoe, *tr. by* Michael Hamburger
Ah, Are You Digging on My Grave?   Thomas Hardy.   MoBrPo; NAEL-6v2; NAEL-7v2
Ah Ben! / Say how, or when.   Ode for Him [*or* Ben Jonson], An.   Robert Herrick.   BASC; NoP-5; NOSC; WaAnP
Ah, blackbird, thou art satisfied.   Blackbird, The.   *Unknown.*   IrV, *tr. by* Kuno Meyer
Ah blessed absence of God.   God's Absence.   Mechthild von Magdeburg.   WPoS, *tr. by* Oliver Davies
Ah blow! thou art the last, the last!   Broken Heart.   Henrietta Cordelia Ray.   CBWP-3
Ah, breathe on it softly—it dies in an hour. (LL)   Riddle, A: "'Twas in heaven pronounced, and 'twas muttered in hell."   Catherine Maria Fanshawe.   NOBRP; OxBEV
Ah, broken is the golden bowl!—the spirit flown forever!   Lenore.   Edgar Allan Poe.   APN-1; TCAPo
Ah, but when I was young there was this hiss.   99.9 FM Radio Nostalgia.   Keith Bennett.   RWPCtW
Ah certainty of love in the hand.   [Ah certainty of love in the hand].   Janine Pommy-Vega.   CLPP
Ah! changed and cold, how changed and very cold!   Dead before Death.   Christina Georgina Rossetti.   NAEL-6v2; NAEL-7v2; NALW
Ah, Christ, I love you rings to the wild sky.   Allen Tate.   ChrPo *Fr.* Sonnets at Christmas.
Ah, could I lay me down in this long grass.   Journey.   Edna St. Vincent Millay.   BrAP
Ah! could I read Schemhammphorasch.   Schemhammphorasch.   Rose Terry Cooke.   NAAPv.1; SWaP
Ah, could you now with thinking tongue.   To My Infant Daughter.   Yvor Winters.   IllVoic

Ah, Dangerous Swain, tell me no more. Song. LW

Ah dear associate of youth's tender days. To Love. CenSon

Ah Dearest, let us haste us. Martin Opitz. GePo

Ah dearest limbs, my life's best joy and stay. Robert Sidney. NoSic

Ah, death is like the long cool night. Ah, Death is Like the Long Cool Night. Heinrich Heine. NAWM-7v2, tr. by Hal Draper

Ah, did you once see Shelley plain. Memorabilia. Robert Browning. NAEL-6v2; NAEL-7v2; NoP-4; NoP-5; NPeEn; OxBEV; PoPoPo

Ah, Douglass, we have fall'n on evil days. Douglass. Paul Laurence Dunbar. CBCWP; GSo; NAAPv.1; WaAnP

Ah, Eros doth not always smite. Michael Field. VWP

Ah face, young face, sweet with unpassionate joy. Faded. Augusta Davies Webster. VWP

Ah, Faustus, / Now hast thou but one bare hour[e] [or hower] to live. Christopher Marlowe. FaBoVe; HeIP-4 Fr. Doctor Faustus.

Ah, flowers that we wear! And Yet the Earth Remains Unchanged. *Unknown.* CA

A[h]! fredome [or freedom] is a noble thing! John Barbour. NePenScot; OBEV; TreFP Fr. Bruce, The.

Ah, friend you have changed; neckless. Friend, Ah You Have Changed! Frank Mkalawile Chipasula. HBAPE

Ah, from this Temperance army. Julia A. Moore. STuOW Fr. Temperance Army, The.

Ah, gaze not on those eyes! forbear. Vain Advice, The. Catherine Cockburn. LW

Ah, God, the way your little finger moved. Stephen Crane. APN-2

Ah, good morning, '*Pare. Kumusta naman?*. Manong Chito Tells Manong Ben about His Dream over Breakfast at the Manilatown Cafe. Vince Gotera. ReBoTo

Ah, good-evening. It's the two of them again. His Lamp Near Daybreak. Yannis Ritsos. AWTN, tr. by Martin McKinsey

Ah! habit, how unmusical and shy. Habit. Natalie Clifford Barney. PoBW

Ah, had you seen the Coolun. Coolun, The. Maurice Dugan. IrV, tr. by Sir Samuel Ferguson

Ah! Hannah, why should'st thou despair. Christopher Smart. ChIV-1 Fr. Hymns for the Amusement of Children.

Ah hapless sex! who bear no charms. To Alexis in Answer to His Poem Against Fruition. Ode. Aphra Behn. BrAP; NOSC

Ah, he was a grand man. Tullynoe: Tête-à-Tête in the Parish Priest's Parlour. Paul Durcan. BeAl; ModIr; NPeEn; OBCoV

Ah heart, heart, look! I throw myself at your feet. (LL) Stormy Night. William Robert Rodgers. ModIr; PNI

Ah heaven!—what *truth* to him. (LL) College Colonel, The. Herman Melville. AmWaPo; CBCWP; FaBoWar; NAAPv.1; NCAP; OBWP; PCW; WaAnP

Ah! hills belov'd!—where once a happy child. To the South Downs. Charlotte Smith. CenSon; NPBRoP

(Ah, hills beloved!)—where once, an happy child.) RWP

Ah, hills beloved!—where once, an happy child. Charlotte Smith. *See* Ah! hills belov'd!—where once a happy child.

Ah, holy Jesus, how hast thou offended. F. Heermann. SacPr, tr. by Robert Bridges

Ah! Hoyland, empress of my heart. Ode to Miss Hoyland. Thomas Chatterton. STuOW

Ah! I could curse them in my woe. Revenge. Mary E. Tucker. CBWP-1

Ah If at Least I Could. Alda Merini. CItWP, tr. by Cinzia Sartini Blum and Lara Trubowitz

Ah, if only the village were so small. Poem of the Girl from Velázquez. Ricardo Molinari. TCLAP, tr. by Inés Probert

Ah in the thunder air. Trees in the Garden. D. H. Lawrence. MoBrPo; NoP-4; NoP-5; WaAnP

Ah, is there no, no place on earth. Weariness. Mary E. Tucker. CBWP-1

Ah, it is so! Women's Rondo. *Unknown.* NOBAu

Ah! it's chic to be the Dauphin. Anne Portugal. SCFWP Fr. Bath, The.

Ah, Jesu Kri. María Sabina. PFTM-2 Fr. Midnight Velada, The.

Ah Julia! ask a Christmas rhyme. Irregular Verses. Dorothy Wordsworth. PoBW

Ah! knew he but his happiness, of men. Country Pastor, The. Timothy Dwight. SacPr

Ah, Lenin, you were richt. But I'm a poet. Second Hymn to Lenin. Hugh MacDiarmid. RSaN

Ah! let not hope fallacious, airy, wild. Mary Hays. CenSon

Ah life! Does no one answer? Response and Reconciliation. Octavio Paz. WoBe, tr. by Eliot Weinberger

Ah! light lovely lady with delicate lips aglow. At Mass. *Unknown.* IrLP, tr. by Robin Flower

Ah! little cause has Petrarch to complain. Elizabeth Cobbold. CenSon Fr. Sonnets of Laura.

Ah little recks the laborer. Song of the Exposition. Walt Whitman.

Ah, look, / How sucking their last sweetness from the air. Divers, The. Peter Quennell. MoBrPo

Ah love, the skies were always raining. Blind Country. Katharine Tynan Hinkson. IrLP

Ah, love, the teacher we decried. Pure Hypothesis, A. May Kendall. VWP

Ah, love, you smell of petroleum. Ah, Love, You Smell of Petroleum. Judy Grahn. PoBW

Ah, lute, how well I know each tone of thee. George Henry Boker. APN-2 Fr. Sonnets: A Sequence on Profane Love.

Ah Mater, quo te deplorem fonte? Dolores. George Herbert. PBRV Fr. Memoriae Matris Sacrum.

Ah me, if I grew sweet to man. Tragic Mary Queen of Scots, The. Michael Field. LW; OBMV

Ah me! it is the loon alone—the loon upon the lake. (LL) Loon upon the Lake, The. *Ojibwa Oral Tradition.* APN-2; OWoS, tr. by Charles Fenno Hoffman

Ah Miss Claire. Work's end. *Unknown.* SonAtl, tr. by Lester Browne, Cleveland Thompson and Janet Williams

Ah, Mr Businessman! Nothing but a heart-bank. Ah, Mr Businessman! Ahmad ibn Abd al-Latif Barbir. SonAtl, tr. by Nezahat Iplici and Michael Maguire

Ah, my brother, I weep for you. Beloved, You Must Not Die. Yosano Akiko. CAoMJL1, tr. by Janine Beichman

Ah my daughter, my grandchild! All You Others, Eat. Djurberaui. NOBAu, tr. by Catherine H. Berndt

Ah! my Dear. Full and True Account of a Dreaded Fire, that Lately Broke out in the Pope's Breeches, A. *Unknown.* EroLit

Ah my dear angry Lord. George Herbert. NoP-4

Ah my Perilla! do'st thou grieve to see. To Perilla. Robert Herrick. NOSC

Ah, my subject, the rose, I know. In A Queen's Domain. Sarah Morgan Bryan Piatt. NCAP

Ah, Nadya, Nadyenka. Bulat Shalvovich Okudzhava. ItGoST, tr. by Ronnie Apter and Mark Herman

Ah, Nature . . . Sure, Nature . . . And how about us? Newspapers on the Plateau. Irina Mashinskaya. CRWP, tr. by the author

Ah no, ah no, they weren't all gross and slow. Michael Foley. PNI Fr. True Life Love Stories.

Ah! no, not these! Parentage. Alice Thompson Meynell. InoFa; NALW; NPeEn; VWP

Ah no! / We have not fallen so. William Vaughn Moody. AmWaPo Fr. Ode in the Time of Hesitation.

Ah, now the puszta is indeed a waste! Puszta in Winter, The. Sándor Petőfi. IQMS, tr. by Watson Kirkconnell

Ah nuts! It's boring reading French newspapers. Les Luths. Frank O'Hara. NAMCP V.2; NoAM

Ah, pirates, pirates, pirates! Fernando Pessoa. PFTM-1 Fr. Maritime Ode.

Ah, poor negro Sadi, what sorrows, what anguish. Poor Negro Sadi, The. Charlotte Dacre. RWP

Ah poor repair for th'loss of such a Friend. (LL) On the Death of My Dear Friend and Play-Fellow Mrs. E. D. Having Dream'd the Night Before I Heard Thereof that I Had Lost a Pearl. Jane Barker. EMWP; PoBW

Ah rosie. H. C. Artmann. PFTM-2, tr. by Jerome Rothenberg

Ah! sad wer we as we did peace. Turnstile, The. William Barnes. NPeEn; OxBEV

Ah secret voice of dark love! Ah bleating without wool! Ah wound! Ah prick of gall, sunken camellia! Federico García Lorca. CAGL Fr. Sonetos del Amor Oscuro [Sonnets of Dark Love].

Ah, see the fair chivalry come, the companions of Christ! Te Martyrum Candidatus. Lionel Pigot Johnson. OBMV

Ah silly pug wert thou so sore afraid. Queen of England Elizabeth I. NoP-4; NoP-5

Ah, silly pug, wert thou so sore afraid? *Unknown.* NoSic

Ah! silly soul, what wilt thou say. Madrigal. William Drummond of Hawthornden. SacPr

Ah simple poet, ill-judged prayer! Answer by the Lady's Maid [to a Poem Left in a Lady's Toilet]. James Eyre Weeks. IrLP

Ah, Sleep, to me thou com'st not in the guise. To Sleep. Lord Alfred Bruce Douglas. GSo

Ah, so, yes. Ah, so, yes. Larry Eigner. PFTM-2

Ah! Sorrows known too soon! and felt too long! (LL) Reaches Sicily. Mary Robinson. CenSon; RWP

Ah Sun-flower! weary of time. William Blake. NAEL-6v2; NAEL-7v2; NIP-4; NOBRP; NoP-4; NoP-5; NPBRP; NPeEn; PoPoPo; TFi; WaAnP; WeW-3 Fr. Songs of Experience.

Ah! tell me why, deluded Sex, thus we. Emulation, The: A Pindarick Ode. *Unknown.* EMWP

Ah, thankless! canst thou envy him who gains. To a Friend, Who Thinks Sensibility a Misfortune. Anna Seward. CenSon

Ah! that once more I were a careless child! (LL) Sonnet to the River Otter. Samuel Taylor Coleridge. CenSon; OxBSo

Ah! that shady crab!   *Unknown*.   CCL1 *Fr.* Gan-tang [Translations].

Ah that the Tiger.   Cristina Campo.   CItWP *Fr.* Tiger's Absence.

Ah, That You Escape.   José Lezama Lima.   TCLAP, *tr. by* Willis Barnstone

Ah, that you escape in the flash.   Ah, That You Escape.   José Lezama Lima. TCLAP, *tr. by* Willis Barnstone

Ah, the blowfly is whining there, its maggots are eating the flesh.   Blowflies Buzz, The.   *Unknown*.   NOBAu, *tr. by* Catherine H. Berndt

Ah, the cold, cold days.   Grandmother Remembers, A.   Janet Lewis.   IllVoic

Ah, the day is waning, in the western sky, over the lonely river, the even pinkish flow is fading.   Fireworks.   Chu Yohan.   CAMKP, *tr. by* Kyung-Ja Chun

Ah, the glory that was Greece! . . . excrement in the street and houses without windows.   Peter Johnson.   PoDa *Fr.* Travels with Oedipus.

Ah, the sometime pain of being abandoned the sometime delight of singing. Butterfly, The.   Hô Sugyông.   EcSo, *tr. by* Youngju Ryu

Ah, the woods, the woods.   Indians in the Woods, The.   Janet Lewis.   IllVoic

Ah! the year is slowly dying.   Passing of the Old Year.   Mary Weston Fordham.   CBWP-2

Ah! / These under-formings in the mind.   Herman Melville.   TCAPo *Fr.* Clarel: A Poem and Pilgrimage in the Holy Land.

Ah! think'st thou, Laura, then, that wealth.   Stanzas.   Charlotte Smith.   NoP-4; NoP-5

Ah! Thomas, wherefore wouldst thou doubt.   Christopher Smart.   ChIV-2 *Fr.* Hymns and Spiritual Songs for the Fasts and Festivals of the Church of England.

Ah, those lips, kissed by so many.   Mikhail Alekseievich Kuzmin.   CAGL, *tr. by* Simon Karlinsky

Ah, through the open door.   Spring Morning.   D. H. Lawrence.   MoBrPo

Ah! thus man spoils Heaven's glorious works with Blood! (LL)   Sea View, The. Charlotte Smith.   CenSon; NAEL-7v2

Ah tink it's time.   New Dub, A.   "Mbala."   WaCA

Ah to be in Rarotonga, 'neath the languor-laden breeze.   Ah, To Be In.   Morris Gilbert Bishop.   AmWit

Ah, too, it has a wing. (LL)   Fame is a bee.   Emily Dickinson.   NoP-4; NoP-5; OxBoAm

Ah! what a weary race my feet have run.   Sonnet: To the River Lodon. Thomas, the Younger Warton.   CenSon; OxBSo

Ah what avails the scept[e]red race.   Rose Aylmer.   Walter Savage Landor. CABP; NAEL-6v2; NAEL-7v2; NOBRP; NoP-4; NoP-5; OBEV; OxAEP-2; TFi; WeW-3

Ah! what avails, when sinking down to sleep.   Written in Ill Health.   Anna Maria Smallpiece.   CenSon

Ah, what have I done?   Hwang Chini.   CATKP, *tr. by* Kevin O'Rourke

Ah, what of life! Does no one answer me?   Ah, What of Life! Does No One Answer Me?   Francisco de Quevedo y Villegas.   SpanPo, *tr. by* William M. Davis

Ah! what pleasant visions haunt me.   Galley of Count Arnaldos, The.   Henry Wadsworth Longfellow.   OBEV

Ah, what sagacity perished here! (LL)   Emily Dickinson. *See* Soundless as dots—on a Disc of Snow.

Ah, what shall I be at fifty.   Alfred Tennyson.   NAEL-6v2 *Fr.* Maud [A Monodrama].

Ah, wherefore, lonely, to and fro.   To———.   Herman Melville.   NCAP

Ah! whither art thou gone, poor Tray?   To Tray—Stolen.   Mary Russell Mitford.   DiBP

Ah who can guess the rest? (LL)   Aphra Behn.   LW; PEW

Ah, who can look on that celestial face.   On the Statue of an Angel, by Bienaimé, in the Possession of J.S. Copley Greene, Esq.   Washington Allston.   APN-1

Ah! who would wish to feel, or learn to love? (LL)   Sappho's Address to the Stars.   Mary Robinson.   CenSon; RWP

Ah! Why, Because the Dazzling Sun.   Emily Jane Brontë. *See* Stars.

Ah! why has happiness—no second Spring? (LL)   Sonnet Written at the Close of Spring [*or* Elegiac Sonnet].   Charlotte Smith.   CenSon; RWP

Ah! why is rapture so allied to pain? (LL)   To Phaon ("Why art thou changed? O Phaon! tell me why?")   Mary Robinson.   CenSon; RWP

Ah! why will Mem'ry with officious care.   To Mrs. G.   Charlotte Smith. RWP

Ah, wicked King! Accursed Gaveston!   Christopher Marlowe.   CAGL *Fr.* Edward the Second.

Ah, will no soul give ear unto my moan?   Echo, An.   Sir William Alexander, Earl of Stirling.   NOSC

Ah! with no careless pen would I report.   Bessie Rayner Parkes.   VWP *Fr.* Summer Sketches.

Ah! Woman Still.   Frances Sargent Osgood.   ColAP

Ah, yes, I wrote the "Purple Cow."   Cinq Ans Après.   Frank Gelett Burgess. OBCoV; TFi

Ah, yes, I wrote the "Purple Cow."   Purple Cow, The: Suite.   Frank Gelett Burgess.   CalPo

Ah, yes, to your misfortune.   Patrizia Cavalli.   NeIt; VCWP, *tr. by* Judith Baumel

Ah, you rare old devil, you fine fellow Finney.   Finney's Bar.   Deborah Randall.   StAl

Ah (you say), this is Holy Wisdom.   "H. D."   NAAPv.2; NALW; NAMCP V.1; NoAM *Fr.* Tribute to the Angels.

Ah, you should see Cynddylan on a tractor.   Cynddylan on a Tractor.   Ronald Stuart Thomas.   AngWePo; TCAWP

Ahead I bear; the Eagle of Gál.   *Unknown*.   OBMV *Fr.* Red Book of Hergest, The.

Ahead of me some owl feathers are lying.   Tohono O'odham.   NAAPv.1 *Fr.* Songs for Treating Sickness, Sung durring the Four Parts of the Night.

Ahead / of the center.   Stone or Water.   André Du Bouchet.   YaTCFP, *tr. by* Hoyt Rogers

Ahead, the sun's face in a flaring hood.   First Walk on the Moon.   May Swenson.   RACG

Ahem!   Application.   Paul Gallico.   TriCat

AHH! A TINY.   Michael McClure.   WANABP *Fr.* Haiku Rows.

Ahí Donde Duermes.   Francisco Segovia.   RMCMP

Ahí en el fondo, en una casa de muñecas, están ya mayores.   Anestesia. Antonio Deltoro.   RMCMP

Ah'm a skyscraper wean, Ah live on the nineteenth flair.   Jeelie Piece Song, The.   Adam McNaughton.   EdScPo

Aholibah.   Algernon Charles Swinburne.   ChIV-1

Ahonde en el lugar con recelo, el tacto torpe—como si desprendiera la espina. Lugar, El.   Mónica Nepote.   SPV

Ahora.   Sandra Maria Esteves.   PueRic

Ahora es cuando puedes empezar a morirte.   Escrito con Lluvia.   Blas de Otero.   RaW

Ahora que no hay yo, vamos al yo general.   Eduardo Milán.   RMCMP *Fr.* Cinco.

Ahora tengo estufa de gas.   Vida de una mujer cucapá, La.   Heriberto Yépez. RMCMP

Ahoy! Electronic nightmare.   Watching TV.   Joanne Kyger.   WANABP

Ahuehuetes are spinning airborne, The.   Tepozán.   Josué Ramírez.   RMCMP, *tr. by* Joan Lindgren

Ahuehuetes hilan en el aire, Los.   Tepozán.   Josué Ramírez.   RMCMP

Ahv drank.   Jist Ti Let Yi No.   Tom Leonard.   NePenScot

Aid el Kebir hajj via.   Bayou Arabic Argot.   Jessica Freeman.   AnSo

Aïda.   Alaa Khalid.   AnVo, *tr. by* Mohamed Enani

Aidel wore her nightshirt inside out.   At Five.   Oktavi.   BtF

Aider, why aider why whow.   Gertrude Stein.   NAAPv.2 *Fr.* Tender Buttons.

AIDS, Among Other Things.   Peter Kocan.   ChIV-2

AIDS Education, Seventh Grade.   Ruth L. Schwartz.   NeAmPo

Aïeul, L'.   Jean Grosjean.   YaTCFP

Aigles ou roitelets, dispersés en étincelles ou rassemblés en candélabres. Volière, La.   Saint-Pol Roux.   YaTCFP

Ailing.   Sennur Sezer.   NaPG, *tr. by* Talat Sait Halman

Ailing child, An.   Kitahara Hakushū.   CAoMJL1, *tr. by* Makoto Ueda

Ailing Woman Felt Her Forces Ebb, The.   Rosalía de Castro.   NAWM-7v2, *tr. by* S. Griswold Morley

Ailing woman felt her forces ebb, The.   Ailing Woman Felt Her Forces Ebb, The.   Rosalía de Castro.   NAWM-7v2, *tr. by* S. Griswold Morley

Ailsa Craig.   Gerald Mangan.   EdScPo

Aim.   Bruce Bond.   LiTh

Aim get your sights and its sound.   Canto 7: First Thesis.   Tom Weatherly. EGAG

Aim Was Song, The.   Robert Frost.   SoSe-8

Aimless caress slips through my fingers, The.   Lost Caress, The.   Alfonsina Storni.   BLPSL, *tr. by* Rene de Costa, Rigas Kappatos and Eleni Paidoussi

Ain' committed no federal crime.   Ezra Pound. *Fr.* Cantos.

Ainadamar.   Nigel Jenkins.   TCAWP

Aine, dé, trois, Caroline, ça ça yé comme ça ma chère.   Caroline.   *Unknown*. SSUS

Ainsi que la porno délibérée du vent.   Je veux revoir cette séquence.   Nicole Brossard.   YaTCFP

Ain't got the change of a nickel.   I ain't Got Nothin' But the Blues.   Don George.   ReLy

Ain't It a Shame About Mame.   Johnny Burke.   ReLy

Ain't Misbehavin'.   Andy Razaf.   ReLy

Ain't She Sweet?   Jack Yellen.   ReLy

Ain't That the Way It Goes?   Roy Turk.   ReLy

Ain't too many poets saw a bebop riff.   Bebop Trumpet.   Layding Lumumba Kaliba.   BRtP

Ain't We Got Fun.   Raymond B. Egan and Gustave Kahn.   ReLy

Ain't your fancy.   Harryette Mullen.   FaoP *Fr.* Muse and Drudge.

Air: "The Love of a Woman."   Robert Creeley.   VCAP

Air.   Charlotte Gardelle.   CuPo

Air: "O ruddier than the cherry!"   John Gay.   NAEL-6v1 *Fr.* Acis and Galatea: An English Pastoral Opera.

Air. John Godfrey. FTOS

Air: "Naturally it is night." W. S. Merwin. CAP-8

Air. Jennifer Maiden. BMAP

Air. Kathleen Jessie Raine. MoBrPo

Air: "Forgetting." Pierre Reverdy. CuPo

Air. Ann Taylor. NOxBChV

Air a-gittin' cool an' coolah. Signs of the Times. Paul Laurence Dunbar. APN-2

Air and Angels. Charles North. FTOS

Air and Angels. Kenneth Rexroth.
    Aspen Meadows. CalPo
    Coming. GoPo

Air and cement here are stained, The. No like place. Kim Hunter. RD

Air and Fire. Wendell Berry. LPSFW

Air commented in a whisper, The. (LL) Gallantry. Keith Douglas. NAEL-6v2; NAEL-7v2; NAMCP V.1; NoAM; NoP-4; NoP-5; OBWP; WaAnP

Air Dagger. Jack Marshall. GeoHom

Air Field. Robert Siegel. OtW

Air force jet set down like a god, The. Jackie in Cambodia. Catherine Bowman. ReTh

Air grows calm and clear, The. Ode to Francisco Salinas. Luís De León. SpanPo, tr. by Edwin Morgan

Air hazed by seed and bug, arms heavy. Eye Blade. George Evans. AF

Air is a smoke-tree, the wind, The. Reviewing Past Lives while Leaf-Burning. Anita Endrezze. HATNAP

Air is foul in the room, The. On a Dying Planet. Fadil Azzawi. IrPoTo, tr. by Ralph Saverese and Saadi A. Simawe

Air is good in here, The. Eros, Ethos, Economuos. Aaron McCollough. IIR

Air is mild and winter at an end, The. To the Stork. Mihály Tompa. IQMS, tr. by Yakov Hornstein

Air Is Motionless with Heat, The. Maria Petrovykh. TCRusP, tr. by Sharon Leiter

Air is motionless with heat, The. Air Is Motionless with Heat, The. Maria Petrovykh. TCRusP, tr. by Sharon Leiter

Air is quiet, The. Coming of Teddy Bears, The. Dennis Lee. TLR

Air is suffocating, the. Ironing Goatskin. Víctor Hernández Cruz. PueRic

Air is swimming with the bugs' forlorn Morse code on a hellish mid-morning, The. Divorced. Don Share. OPRER

Air like stained glass cuts me, The. Marge Piercy. FiBr

Air Plant, The. Hart Crane. MoAmPo

Air Raid. Sachiko Yoshihara. CFP; GifTon, tr. by Naoshi Koriyama and Edward Lueders and Edward Lueders

Air Raid Across the Bay at Plymouth. Stephen Spender. AF

Air Show. John Updike. OtW

Air Show: F-16s above Cleveland. Mary Quade. OtW

Air shrill with life. Below White Cliffs. Abigail Albrecht. GeoHom

Air smells of rhubarb, occasional, The. Blank Sonnet. George Elliott Clarke. Coast; OpeFie

Air stiffens to a crust, The. Wound, The. Louise Glück. NoAM

Air Street. David Morley. NLP

Air, The. Andrew Hudgins. InvLad

Air, the dream-inspiring air, The. Idyl of Spring, An. Henrietta Cordelia Ray. CBWP-3

Air War, The. Geoffrey Nutter. IAoNAP

Air was full of Gitane Filtre, her reflection, The. My Mother's Clothes. Pascale Petit. Prnts

Air was soft, the ground still cold, The. April 5, 1974. Richard Wilbur. StAl

Air without has taken fever, The. July. Alexander L. Posey. APN-2

Airborne. Elizabeth Garrett. MFPA

Air-borne ants attacked softer parts of the cyclist, measuring. Race on Gathering Bites. Kojo Laing. HBAPE

Aircraft is approaching, An. As You Say. Dennis Joseph Enright. PoAgWa

Air[e] and Angels. John Donne. BASC; NAEL-6v1; NAEL-7v1

Aire for the sweet cad. Joy Island. Marianne Vitale. HeMarv

Airey Force. Letitia Elizabeth Landon. RWP

Airing the Chapel. Sylvia Kantaris. LW

Airlift. Karen Chamberlain. GeoH

Airliner. Francis Webb. NOBAu

Airly Beacon, Airly Beacon. Airly Beacon. Charles Kingsley. OBEV

Airman. Stephen Spender. UV

Airman. Mariya Stepanova. CRWP, tr. by Richard McKane

Airman must be Irish, slightly mad, An. Lonely Impulse of Delight, A—W.B. Yeats. David Kirk Vaughan. OtW

Airman, The. Aleksandr Semionovich Kushner. TCRusP, tr. by Daniel Weissbort

Airman, The. Unknown. OtW

Airman Who Flew over Shakespeare's England, The. Hyam Plutzik. APT-2; PWW2

Airman's Virtue. William Meredith. WaAnP

Airplane. Sherman Alexie. OtW

Airplane Betty in Holland. Kenneth Koch. AHA

Airplane Betty sat down in Holland, she felt the cool breezes blowing. Airplane Betty in Holland. Kenneth Koch. AHA

Airport. W. S. Merwin. OtW

Airport. Lenard D. Moore. FuFl

Airport coffee tastes less of America, The. Gulf, The. Derek Walcott. NoP-4; NoP-5; PoetW; PoPoPo

Airports of the World. Eugene Richie. KGB

Airs and Graces. Peter Fallon. PBCIP

Air's cruel whip which deafened me, The. After Cycling. Gary Young. ArBi

Air's enveloping capacious sleeves, The. Between. Ágnes Nemes Nagy. IQMS, tr. by Alan Dixon

Air's heaviness in the dark room, as if a vague bloodlike, The. Dark Room, The. Enrique Lihn. TCLAP; VCWP, tr. by David Unger

Airs of Palestine. John Pierpont.
    "Here let us pause:—the opening prospect view." APN-1
    "In what rich harmony, what polished lays." APN-1; TreFP
    "Now, he recalls the lamentable wail." APN-1
    "On Arno's bosom, as he calmly flows." APN-1

Airstrip is soggy with humidity, The. Aubade: Macedonia. Nicholas Samaras. YaYoPo

Airstrip St Athan. Iorwerth Cyfeilog Peate. BBMWP, tr. by Nigel Jenkins

Air-Waves. Martyn Crucefix. RWPCtW

Airy, / born high overhead. Banyan. Elsa Cross. RMCMP, tr. by Margaret Sayers Peden

Airy Christ, The. Stevie Smith. ChIV-2

Airy Hall Icongraphy. Frederick D'Aguiar. Oth

Airy Hall Nightmare. Frederick D'Aguiar. NeBrP

Airy spirits, you who love. Inscription in a Beautiful Retreat Called Fairy Bower. Hannah More. NoP-4; NoP-5

Aisle of a Temple, The. William Congreve. OxAEP-1

Aisle of Dogs. Chase Twichell. EmeKit

Aisles and abysses; leagues no man explores. Caverns. Madison Cawein. APN-2

Aisling. Paul Muldoon. PNI

Aisne, The (1914–15). Alan Seeger. AmWaPo

Aix-La-Chappelle, 1945. Edgar Bowers. InGu

Aja, I am joyful; this is good! Utitia' q's Song. Unknown. APN-2, tr. by Franz Boas

A—JA—BU. Her. Stephen Chambers. EGAG

Ajanta. Muriel Rukeyser. APT-2; MoAmPo

Ajax. David Osborne Hamilton. YaYoPo

Ajax and his Brother. Homer. OBVE Fr. Iliad, The.

Ajax, / lion-coloured stallion from Sealey's stable. Derek Walcott. PoetW Fr. Divided Child, The.

Ajax, the bull-dog, on his cushioned place. Ajax. David Osborne Hamilton. YaYoPo

Ajax the swift swerv'd never from the side. Homer. OBVE Fr. Iliad, The.

Ajo Lily. Peggy Shumaker. PoCoUp

AKA. Bruce Andrews. PFTM-2

Ak'a ta majtanal te lotil. Pedro Pérez Conde. RMCMP

Ak'a-on jich bit'il marka-il ta wo/tan, jich bit'il senya-il ta k'a/b. Ta te/ak'etik yorail ya x-ajk'otajik. Pedro Pérez Conde. RMCMP

Akat'ani / x'aax'. Tlingit Concrete Poem. Nora Dauenhauer. NIP-4

Akbar. John Kinsella. VaPo

Akhmatova. Deborah Digges. ExTi

Akhmatova and Nedobrovo. Evening at Tsarskoe Selo. Polina Barskova. CRWP, tr. by Peter France

Akiba. Muriel Rukeyser. TaR

Akidáá jini, in the beginning, Áshiñih. Old Salt Woman. Luci Tapahonso. ICANM

Al Aaraaf. Edgar Allan Poe. APN-1

Al abrigo fatal de la cogulla. En Casa Ya. Miguel de Unamuno.

Al caer la tarde, absorto. Niño Tras un Cristal. Luis Cernuda. RaW

Al Capone's coins had a very good luster, good enough to use as a medal. Two People : 2. Yi Sang. CAMKP, tr. by Edward Mack

Al dar / At three. Viernes Santo / Good Friday. Francisco X. Alarcón. GeoHom

Al it is fantam that we mid fare. All Is Phantom. Unknown. SacPr

Al nyght by the rose, rose. Unknown. See All night by the rose, rose.

Al otro día, cuando abrí los ojos, había una avispa golpeando en el cristal de la ventana. Relación de maravillas susurradas al oído de un maniquí. Jorge Fernández Granados. RMCMP

Al Sol de la Guerra. Rafael Alberti. RaW

Al that I may swynke or swete. Unknown. OHMEL

Al Wat Kind Is. Ingrid de Kok. HAWP

Al worldly welthe passed me fro. *Unknown*. OHMEL

Al Zarpar. Gerardo Diego. RaW

Alabama Bus. William Hairston. WaAnP

Alabama Poem. Nikki Giovanni. OxAAAP

Alabama Song. Bertolt Brecht. PFTM-1

Alabanza: In Praise of Local 100. Martín Espada. PrTe

Alabanza. Praise the cook with a shaven head. Alabanza: In Praise of Local 100. Martín Espada. PrTe

Aladdin. James Russell Lowell. TCAPo

Alakanak Break-Up. Mei-Mei Berssenbrugge. PmAP

Alamo Plaza at Night. Carol Coffee Reposa. TiP2

Alamo, The: An Epic. Michael Lind.

   "Now Crockett said, 'You gentlemen are free.'" TiP2

Alan Turing's Imitation Game. Intimations. Howard Nemerov. BodElec

Alarm clocks tick in a thousand furnished rooms, The. North Infinity Street. Conrad Potter Aiken. InGu

Alarm of a lighter morning breathes before your eyes, The. All You Want. Bill Berkson. NYP2

Alarm rings: it's 2 PM, The. I get up, dress and go. Halloween 1967. Lewis Warsh. AHA

Alarm waiting a battery, An. Counsel of Birds, The. Ed Robeson. Eno

Alarmed Skipper, The. James Thomas Fields. NBLV

Alarum, The. Sylvia Townsend Warner. MoBrPo

Alas a dirty word, alas a dirty third alas a dirty third, alas a dirty bird. Gertrude Stein. NAAPv.2; NAMCP V.1 *Fr.* Tender Buttons.

Alas a doubt in case of more go to say what it is cress. What is it. Mean. Potato. Loaves. Gertrude Stein. NAMCP V.1 *Fr.* Tender Buttons.

Alas, Alack! Walter De la Mare. OPOU

Alas, alas, quo' bonny Heck. Bonny Heck. William Hamilton. DiBP

Alas! Alas! the father said. Cornelius Whur. STuOW; VerBaPo *Fr.* Armless Artist, The.

Alas, all my years, where have they disappeared? Walther von der Vogelweide. GePo

Alas! and am I born for this. On Liberty and Slavery. George Moses Horton. APN-1; NAAPv.1

Alas! Carolina! J. Gordon Coogler. VerBaPo

Alas, dear mother, fairest queen and best. Dialogue between Old England and New, A. Anne Bradstreet. BASC; EMWP

Alas, eheu, one question that sorely vexes. Ezra Pound. OBSV *Fr.* Homme Moyen Sensuel, L'.

Alas! for all the pretty women who marry dull men. Meditation at Kew. Anna Wickham. MoBrPo; NALW

Alas for Juan and Haidee! They were. Lord Byron. NePenScot *Fr.* Don Juan.

Alas! for Peter not an helping Hand. George Crabbe. NoP-4; NoP-5; NPeEn; OxBEV *Fr.* Borough, The.

Alas, for the blight of my fancies! Love Versus Learning. Constance Naden. ViWPN; VWP

Alas, for us, who need beware. On Worldly Prelates. Charles Wesley. ChIV-2

Alas, have I not pain enough, my friend. Sir Philip Sidney. NoP-4; NoP-5; NoSic *Fr.* Astrophil and Stella.

Alas how barbarous are we. Upon the graving of her Name upon a Tree in Barnelmes Walks. Katherine Philips. PBRV

Alas, how easily things go wrong! Sweet Peril. George Macdonald. ITBLP

Alas, how many years have flown. Beard and Bicycle. Guy Boas. ArBi

Alas, how soon the hours are over. Plays. Walter Savage Landor. NBLV

Alas! in every aspiration bold. Richard Polwhele. NOBRP *Fr.* Unsex'd Females, The.

Alas, is wiser far[re] than I. (LL) Bait[e], The. John Donne. NAEL-6v1; NAEL-7v1; NOSC; WaAnP

Alas! Lord and Lady Dalhousie are dead, and buried at last. William McGonagall. VerBaPo *Fr.* Death of Lord and Lady Dalhousie, The.

Alas! Lord and Lady Dalhousie are dead, and buried at last. Death of Lord and Lady Dalhousie, The. William McGonagall.

Alas, my love thy knocked you down. Breach in the Wall, The. *Unknown*. EMWP

Alas! my Purse! how lean and low! Mary Jones. PEW

Alas our good kaspar is dead. Kaspar Is Dead. Hans Arp. PFTM-1, *tr. by* Jerome Rothenberg

Alas our good kaspar is dead. Kaspar Is Dead. Hans Arp. GTCP, *tr. by* Christopher Middleton

Alas! our pleasant moments fly. On Parting. Edward Coote Pinkney. APN-1; TCAPo

Alas! Poor luckless nation, thou art dead. Dead Nation, The. DeWitt Clinton Duncan [Too-qua-stee]. NAAPv.1

Alas! Poor Queen. Marion Angus. EdScPo; NePenScot; NPeEn

Alas, poor Werter! to himself a prey. Elegy Written after Reading the "Sorrows of Werter." Robert Merry. STuOW

Alas poore Scholler, whither wilt thou goe. Robert Wild.
   "In a melancholly studdy." PBRV

Alas, shall I not see again. Heinrich von Morungen. GePo

Alas! Sir John Ogilvy is dead, aged eighty-seven. Late Sir John Ogilvy, The. William McGonagall. VerBaPo

Alas! so all thing[e]s now[e] do[e] hold[e] their peace. Henry Howard, Earl of Surrey. NAEL-6v1; NAEL-7v1; NoSic; NPeEn; OxBEV

Alas, successive sorrows crowd the space! (LL) To the Strawberry. Helen Maria Williams. CenSon; OxBSo; RWP

Alas, that I should be. Yvor Winters. WoPoe *Fr.* To My Infant Daughter.

Alas, That Is the Name of Our Town; I Have Been Concealing It All This Time. Joshua Clover. NeAmPo

Alas! that such a soul should taste of death. In Memory of Arthur Clement Williams. Eloise Bibb. CBWP-4

Alas, that wisdom, and youth. Walther von der Vogelweide. GePo

Alas, the country! how shall tongue or pen. Lord Byron. OBSV *Fr.* Age of Bronze, The.

Alas! the duck was doom'd not to succeed! (LL) Thomas Baker. STuOW; VerBaPo *Fr.* Steam Engine; or, The Power of the Flame, The.

Alas! the state of things tonight. Conversation with Death, A. Sileas Na Ceapaich. EMWP

Alas! the time has come, old dress. Lines to an Old Dress. Mary E. Tucker. CBWP-1

Alas! they were so young, so beautiful. Lord Byron. OxBEV EroLit; *Fr.* Don to Juan.

Alas, 'tis true, I have gone here and there. William Shakespeare. AEP; NAEL-6v1; NAEL-7v1; NoSic; OxAEP-1 *Fr.* Sonnets.

Alas! 'Tis Very Sad to Hear. Walter Savage Landor. WeW-3

Alas, to be / Mortal, and know our sad mortality! Echo. George Santayana. APN-2

Alas! When the instinct rules. Wrestling. "Rachel." FIT, *tr. by* Robert Friend

Alas! whom to should I complain. Bagsche's Complaint. Sir David Lyndsay. DiBP

Alas, why say you I am rich? when I. Robert Sidney. NoSic

Alas! young men, come, make lament. Dirge of St. Malo, The. George Washington Cable. APN-2

Alasdair, O calf of my senses. Song to Alasdair Mac Colla, A. Dorothy Brown. EMWP

Alasdair of Glengarry. Sileas Na Ceapaich. NePenScot *Fr.* Alasdair of Glengarry.

Alasdair of Glengarry. Sileas Na Ceapaich. *tr. by* Derick Thomson
   "Alasdair of Glengarry." NePenScot, *tr. by* Derick Thomson

Alaska. Mary Weston Fordham. CBWP-2

Alaskan Fragments June 1981—Summer Solstice. Wendy Rose. HATNAP

Alastair Buchan (1917). John, 1st Baron Tweedsmuir Buchan. EdScPo

Alastor; or, The Spirit of Solitude. Percy Bysshe Shelley. NAEL-6v2; NAEL-7v2
   "Poet wandering on, through Araby, The." NPBRoP

Alatus. Richard Wilbur. UpMys

Alba. Imamu Amiri Baraka. FTOS

Alba. Durs Grünbein. GTCP, *tr. by* Reinhold Grimm and Irmgard Hunt

Alba. Laura Mullen. IAoNAP

Alba ("When the nightingale to his mate"). *Unknown*. APT-1; OBVE; OxBoAm; WeW-3 *Fr.* Langue d'Oc.

Alba: Aberdeen. Cate Marvin. IIR

Alba Einstein. Robert Crawford. NeBrP

Alba, With a Refrain from the Provençal. *Unknown*. WoPoe, *tr. by* Tim Reynolds

Albacete knives, magnificent, The. Quarrel, The. Federico García Lorca. AF; WED, *tr. by* Robert Bly

Albania and the Death of Enver Hoxha. Will Alexander. PFTM-2

Albany in a time of khaki. Gathering Place, The. Alan Alexander. NOBAu

Albatross, The. Charles Baudelaire. OWoS, *tr. by* Richard Wilbur

Albatross, The. Charles Baudelaire. SxFrPo, *tr. by* James McGowan

Albert james was black long before me. Albert James. Reuben Jackson. UnSA

Albert Sidney Johnston. Kate Brownlee Sherwood. CBCWP

Albert Speer. W. D. Snodgrass. NoAM

Albert Victor loved his mother. Joseph Gwyer. VerBaPo *Fr.* On the Death of the Duke of Clarence.

Alberta. Priscilla Jane Thompson. CBWP-2

Alberto Giacometti. René Char. MotU, *tr. by* Charles Guenther

Albion Queens, The. John Banks.
   Wonder, The. STuOW

Albion, teach me (and not with loud, unsubtle). László Arany. IQMS *Fr.* Hero of the Mirages, The.

Albion's England. William Warner.
   Tale of the Beginning of Friars and Cloisterers, A. NoSic

Albion's Triumph. Aurelian Townshend.
  Song. OxBEV
Albuera. Thomas Hardy. FaBoWar *Fr.* Dynasts, The.
Album: "This is a hard life you are living." Josephine Miles. APT-2; CalPo; ColAP
Album is a banquet: from the store, An. To Dora W[ordsworth]; On Being Asked By Her Father to Write in Her Album. Charles Lamb. OxBSo
Album Leaf. Stéphane Mallarmé. OBVE, *tr. by* Keith Bosley
Album—A Runthru. Clark Coolidge. AHA; FTOS; NYP2
Albuquerque Graveyard, The. Jay Wright. ESEAA
Alcaics; to H. F. B. Robert Louis Stevenson. OBEV
Alcander's Flower Garden. William Mason. OBGa *Fr.* English Garden, The.
Alceste in the Wilderness [*Non, je ne puis souffrir cette lâche méthode / Qu'affectent la plupart de vos gens à la mode . . .*]. Anthony Hecht. PoA 2002
Alcestis on the Poetry Circuit. Erica Jong. NALW
Alcestis to Admetus. Mary Elizabeth Coleridge. ViWPN
Alchemical. Paul Celan. VCWP, *tr. by* Michael Hamburger
Alchemist, The. Louise Bogan. APT-2; MoAmPo; NAAPv.2; NAMCP V.1
Alchemist, The. Ben Jonson.
  "I will have all my beds blown[e] up, not stuft." OxBEV
Alchemists say the Stone turns lead to gold. David Foster. NOBAu *Fr.* Fleeing Atalanta, The.
Alchemist sleeps in the brain, An. Uranium Ore. Thomas Meyer. AnSo
Alchemy. Alan Michael Parker. AmPoNex
Alcheringa [Arunta of Australia, *alcheringa*], *n.* 1. The Eternal Dream Time. Alcheringa Definitions. Orpingalik. PFTM-1
Alcheringa Definitions. Orpingalik. PFTM-1
Alciphron and Leucippe. Walter Savage Landor. OBEV
Alcohol. Raymond Carver. LaCa
Alcohol. Franz Wright. AmAlph
Alcohol Question, The. Thomas Whitbread. TiP2
Alcoholic. John Berryman. BodElec
Alcoholic in the 3rd Week of the 3rd Treatment, The. John Berryman. BodElec
Alcoholic's Son at Ten, The. Kathleen Peirce. PBCAP
Alcott. James Russell Lowell. TCAPo *Fr.* Fable for Critics, A.
Alcyna met them at the outer gate. Ludovico Ariosto. OBVE *Fr.* Orlando Furioso.
Aldebaran at Dusk. George Sterling. TCAPo
Alderman. Marilyn Nelson Waniek. LTA
Ale they drink in Giggleswick, The. Dominic Bevan Wyndham Lewis. UV *Fr.* Downland Crisis, A.
Aleatory. Mary Zeppa. MiVo
Aleng Maria. Eugene Gloria. ReBoTo
Aleph Poem. Jerome Rothenberg. FTOS
Aleutian Islands. Blaise Cendrars. BLT, *tr. by* Monique Chefdor
Alex Katz Paints His North Window. Edwin Denby. OxBoAm
Alex, my son, with blackberry jam. Poem Against the First Grade. George Venn. TWF
Alex, Tiffany, Meg. Eva Salzman. MoWP
Alexander and Campaspe. John Lyly.
  (Cards and Kisses.) OBEV
  (Cupid and Campaspe.) OxAEP-1
  (Cupid and My Campaspe.) NoP-4; NoP-5
  Cupid and My Campaspe Played. NoSic
  (Oh, For a Bowl of Fat Canary.) NoP-4; NoP-5; WaAnP
  Serving Men's Song, A. NoSic
  (Spring's Welcome.) OBEV
  Trico's Song. NoSic
Alexander at Thebes. Anna Andreyevna Akhmatova. FaBoWar, *tr. by* Max Hayward and Stanley Kunitz
Alexander's Feast; or, The Power of Music [*or* Musique]. John Dryden. NAEL-6v1; NAEL-7v1; TFi; WaAnP
Alexander's Ragtime Band. Irving Berlin. NAAPv.2; ReLy; TCAPo
Alexandra. Mongane Wally Serote. *See* Alexandria.
Alexandreis. Anne Killigrew. NoP-4; NoP-5
Alexandria. Mongane Wally Serote. NAfrP
  (Alexandra.) TSAP
Alexis, here she stayed; among these pines. Sonnet. William Drummond of Hawthornden. NOSC
Alfonzo Prepares to Go Over the Top. Rita Dove. LoL
Alfred: A Masque. David Mallet and James Thomson.
  (Ode: Rule, Brittania!) NAEL-6v1; NAEL-7v1
  Rule, Britannia! OBWP; TreFP; WaAnP
Alfred de Musset. Maurice Evan Hare. OBCoV
A E Housman. R. Williams Parry. BBMWP, *tr. by* Joseph P. Clancy

Alfred Lord Tennyson. Dorothy Parker. NALW *Fr.* Pig's-Eye View of Literature, A.
Algernon Charles Swinburne. William Cole. AmWit *Fr.* Uncoupled Couplets.
Algren. Donny O'Rourke. PML
Ali, Bomaye. Hayes Davis. BRtP
Alibi of a Dead Man. Giovanni Raboni. ItPo, *tr. by* Gayle Ridinger
Alicante Lullaby. Sylvia Plath. PtR
Alice. Isa Blagden. PoBW
Alice. Michael S. Harper. ISC
Alice. Gale Jackson. SpirFl
Alice Blue Gown. Joseph McCarthy. ReLy
Alice, dear, what ails you. Frosty Night, A. Robert Graves. MoBrPo
Alice Fell; or, Poverty. William Wordsworth. OBNV
Alice grown lazy, mammoth but not fat. Last Days of Alice. Allen Tate. APT-2; FuPo
Alice is tall and upright as a pine. Resolution in Four Sonnets, of a Poetical Question Put to Me by a Friend, Concerning Four Rural Sisters. Charles Cotton. OxBSo
Alice is uglier now by several years. Alice Uglier. Elma Mitchell. MoWP
Alice of Daphne, 1799. John Ennis. PBCIP
Alice Uglier. Elma Mitchell. MoWP
Alice's Adventures in Wonderland. Lewis Carroll.
  Alice's Recitation. OBCoV; UV
  Crocodile, The. BLPJKO; ChAP; NBLV; OxBEV; TFi; UV
  Duchess's Lullaby, The. NBLV; UV
  Evidence Read at the Trial of the Knave of Hearts. NPeEn
  Father William. ChAP; NPeEn; OBCoV; OxBEV; TFi
    "You are old, Father William, the young man said." IJHIL
  Lobster Quadrille, A. NoAM; OxAEP-2; UV
  (Lullaby, A.) NOxBChV
  Mad Hatter's Song, The. UV
  Mouse's Tale, The. NoAM; OBCoV; NOxBChV
  Song of the Mock Turtle, The. UV
Alice's Cat, New Year's Eve 1990. Anne Grimes. Prnts
Alice's Recitation. Lewis Carroll. OBCoV; UV *Fr.* Alice's Adventures in Wonderland.
Alien. A. K. Ramanujan. NAMCP V.2
Alien parasites. Mars Needs Terrorists. K. Silem Mohammad. BAP-04
Alien, The. Greg Delanty. WaAnP
Alienation. Howard Phillips Lovecraft. APT-1
Aliens. John Peale Bishop. InGu
Alighting from my horse to drink with you. Wang Wei. NDACCP, *tr. by* William Carlos Williams
Alive. Hayden Carruth. BeAl
Alive for an Instant. Kenneth Koch. PmAP
Alive, I flourish. Edna Eglinton. NewEx
Alive, ne'er parted be. (LL) Song: "Sweetest love, I do not go[e]." John Donne. HeIP-4; NAEL-7v1; NoP-4; NoP-5; NoSic; TFi
Alive or Not. Alfred Wellington Purdy. BeAl
Alive, ridiculous, and dead, forgot! (LL) Alexander Pope. NPeEn; OBSV; OxBEV *Fr.* Epistle [II,] to a Lady[: Of the Characters of Women].
Alive Together. Lisel Mueller. IllVoic
Alive with surplus love. (LL) John Berryman. BeAl; NoP-4 *Fr.* Dream Songs.
Al-Khamasin. Michael Murphy. NIrP
All 21st century artists maintaining below status quo levels of mass intelligence. Wake Up, My Little Pretties. Liza Jessie Peterson. BRtP
All a January day, in the house above the cliff. Winter at Gurnard's Head. David Wright. NLP
All about. All about all with a word seeming across the world. Time Travel. Nick Piombino. FTOS
All about Boys and Girls. John Ciardi. NOxBChV
All about Carrowmore the lambs. Carrowmore. Lucie Brock-Broido. AWPTFC; PoPoPo
All after pleasures as I rid one day. Christmas. George Herbert. ChrPo; NOSC
All afternoon alterities advanced. Bricolage: Versicolor. Anna Rabinowitz. PA9/11
All afternoon cutting bramble blackberries off a tottering brown fence. Strange New Cottage in Berkeley, A. Allen Ginsberg. ASA
All afternoon I have been struggling. By a Swimming Pool Outside Siracusa. Billy Collins. CAP-8
All afternoon I hope. Gillian Clarke. NewEx
All afternoon I thought the decision must fall. Sleeping Man Must Be Awakened to Be Killed, A. Erin Belieu. NeAmPo
All afternoon it rained, then. Rain. Mary Oliver. OxBoAm
All afternoon my brothers and I have worked in the orchard. Planting a Sequoia. Dana Gioia. CalPo; GeoHom

All afternoon my father drove the country roads. Return, The. Philip Levine. OxBoAm

All afternoon: the rain, monotonous, my prison bars. For Hamlet. Peter Cooley. IaFF

All afternoon the town readied for storm. Letter from the Coast, A. Mark Doty. HarvBoo

All, all are gone, the old familiar faces. (LL) Old Familiar Faces, The. Charles Lamb. OBEV; OxAEP-2; OxBEV

All Alone. Mary E. Tucker. CBWP-1

All along the backwater. Kenneth Grahame. NOxBChV; NTCP; WHSW Fr. Wind in the Willows, The.

All along the railroad. Quincy Troupe. UnSA

All along the valley, stream that flashest white. In the Valley of Cauteretz. Alfred Tennyson. NAEL-6v2

All along this road. Basho. SoOfWa, tr. by Sam Hamill

All Apologies to L. Cohen. Simon Thompson. PML

All are ghosts beside. (LL) Voluntaries. Ralph Waldo Emerson. APN-1; CBCWP

All arms combined magnificently together. (LL) Persian Version, The. Robert Graves. EMP; NAMCP V.1; NoAM; NoP-4; NoP-5; OBWP; StAl; WeW-3

All Around My New House at Stone Gate. Hsieh Ling-yün. CCL1, tr. by John Frodsham

All around old Chattanooga. Freedom at McNealy's. Priscilla Jane Thompson. CBWP-2; SWaP

All around, shards of a lost tradition. John Montague. PBCIP Fr. Rough Field, The.

All around the altar, huge lianas. Reading the Bible Backwards. Eleanor Wilner. NoP-4; NoP-5

All around the apt. swimming pool. Swimming Pool, The. Thomas Lux. GoPo

All around the Town. Phyllis McGinley.
  J's the Jumping Jay-Walker. SSCS

All Around the Town. Genevieve Taggard. APT-2

All Around Us. Constance Urdang. PBCAP

All ashes, all ashes again. (LL) On Neal's Ashes. Allen Ginsberg. BB; PmAP

All asleep: mountain peaks and chasms. Alcman. SaLy, tr. by Diane Rayor

All at once something. Before Summer Rain. Rainer Maria Rilke. WoPoe, tr. by Mark Rudman

All attempts to remove. Mr. Cogito Meditates on Suffering. Zbigniew Herbert. VCWP, tr. by John Carpenter and Bogdana Carpenter

All balderdash and beauty, total trope and tremendousness. Darren Wershler-Henry. PoPra Fr. Ten Out of Ten, or, Why Poetry Criticism Sucks in 2003.

All blessings ask a blessed mood. Rods and Kisses. Coventry Patmore. SacPr

All busy punching tickets. Crickets. David McCord. NTCP

All but Blind. Walter De la Mare. MoBrPo; WeW-3

All but Lost. Mark Bibbins. LegDan

All but unutterable Name! Divine Presence, The. Adelaide Anne Procter. SacPr

All by itself. Ransetsu. SoOfWa, tr. by Sam Hamill

All Changeth. William Drummond of Hawthornden. NePenScot

All Circumstances are the Frame. Emily Dickinson. InvLi

All clocks are clouds. Autobiography. Michael Palmer. CalPo

All clowns are masked and all personae. Delmore Schwartz. OxBoAm Fr. Repetitive Heart, The.

All colors come from the sun. And it does not have. Czeslaw Milosz. ChAP Fr. World, The.

All creation and say, You can have it. (LL) You Can Have It. Philip Levine. AmFaPo; CAP-8; EMP; NAMCP V.2; NoP-4; NoP-5; OxBoAm; VCAP

All dat English you used to know. Don't Know No English. Nicolás Guillén. PFTM-1

All day, all night, I worry. Tu Fu [or Du Fu]. CrYelRi Fr. Random Pleasures.

All day all over the city every person. City Elegies. Robert Pinsky.

All day and every day the sea shone, steeped in its blueness. When I Was Young. Alun Llywelyn-Williams. OBWVE, tr. by Gwyn Williams

All day and night, save winter, every weather. Aspens. Edward Thomas. FaBoVe; NPeEn; OxBEV

All Day at Work. Deborah Abbott. PasH

All day beside the shattered tank he'd lain. Reconciliation. Cecil Day Lewis. PoWW

All day, day after day, they're bringing them home. Homecoming. Bruce Dawe. BMAP; EmeKit

All day desire. Nine Sentiments, The. Michael Ondaatje. NLPA; OpeFie

All day he roams the garden. Lessons. Graham Thomas. AngWePo

All day he's shoveled green pine sawdust. Chores. Maxine W. Kumin. IPoFL

All day I always want to know. When I Am 19 I Was a Medic. D. F. Brown. AmWaPo

All day I have been closed up. Of Rain and Air. Wayne Dodd. BLT

All day i have wandered in these southern reaches. B. P. Nichol. PFTM-2 Fr. Martyrology 7, The.

All day I search for you without success. To Peace. Suzanne Gardinier. AmPoNex

All day I think about it, then at night I say it. Who Says Words with My Mouth. Jelaluddin Rumi. AmFaPo, tr. by Coleman Barks and John Moyne

All day I tried to distinguish. Elms. Louise Glück. NoAM

All day it has rained, and we on the edge of the moors. All Day It Has Rained. Alun Lewis. AngWePo; NAEL-6v2; NoP-4; NoP-5; OBWP; OBWVE; RSaN; TCAWP; WaAnP

All day I've been searching for omens, flimsy as they are, and the cat. Aubade. Mark Wunderlich. WiU

All day I've listened to the industry. Limen. Natasha Trethewey. FuFl

All day long. (LL) Counting the Mad. Donald Justice. InGu; NIP-4; NoP-4; NoP-5; TRP

All day long. Ozaki Hosai. CAoMJL1, tr. by Donald Keene

All day long, at Scott's or Menzies', I await the gorging crowd. Wail of the Waiter, The. Marcus Clarke. NOBAu

All day long I have been working. Madonna of the Evening Flowers. Amy Lowell. NAAL-5; NALW

All day long on the long and narrow rails. All Day Long. Léopold Sédar Senghor. PoetW, tr. by Melvin Dixon

All day long she works to not feel fat. She culls. Weight. Jay Schneiders. OPRER

All day long to the judgement-seat. Gallio's Song. Rudyard Kipling. ChIV-2

All day long you're asking me. I Don't Know Why (I Just Do). Roy Turk. ReLy

All day roaming the flooded fields for food. Hard to find a thing. Checkmark. Stratis Haviaras. MotU

All day she studies her new. Bihari. ErotSp, tr. by Sam Hamill

All day the bicycles come and go. Nicholas Hasluck. NOBAu Fr. Rottnest Island.

All day, the cooper's hoops squeal and nibble. Van Leeuwenhoek: 1675. Linda Bierds. AmAlph

All day the doctrine of the dove. In Porthcawl. Will Ifan. BBMWP, tr. by Robert Minhinnick

All day, the drone of a saw. Salopian. Peter Reading. NeBrP

All day the fever tells lies. Allegory: Attic and Fever. David Wojahn. YaYoPo

All day the fitful rain. Vermont Ballad: Change of Season. Robert Penn Warren. ColAP

All day the great guns barked and roared. Molly Pitcher. Laura Elizabeth Richards. HHAm

All day the great planes gingerly descend. Air Field. Robert Siegel. OtW

All day the jets have rifled through the air. Jets. Christopher Meredith. AngWePo

All day the narrow shaft. Inside the Great Pyramid. Gwendolyn MacEwen. BrAP

All day the red spit of the chain-shot tore. Arthur Rimbaud. OBWP Fr. Eighteen-Seventy.

All day the wagons have gone by. Pioneer: The Vignette of an Oil-Field. Lexie Dean Robertson. TiP2

All day the wood is open, with the maples. Hemlocks in Autumn. Edward Weismiller. YaYoPo

All day there has been no peace. Meditation on Politics at the Quabbin Reservoir. Michael C. Blumenthal. PfSP

All day they will not surface, shy. Justin Quinn. NIrP Fr. Days of the New Republic.

All day we travel from bed to bed, our children. Visiting the Graves. Ellen Bryant Voigt. LPSFW

All day without he hears the roar of trade. Quiet Revery, A. Unknown. ArBi

All day you walk with a nap. Secret Brain, The. Dave Brinks. AnSo

All day—the wind's reception. Beginning from the Field. Gennady Aygi. WoBe, tr. by Peter France

All Death, All Love. Conrad Potter Aiken. InGu

All dem Mount Zion member, dey have many ups and downs. Hold Out to the End. Unknown. SSUS

All Do Not All Things Well. Thom Gunn. NoP-5

All Dreams Are Sexual. Hwang Insuk. EcSo, tr. by Peter H. Lee

All dripping in tangles green. Tuft of Kelp, The. Herman Melville. APN-2

All Dull, my Lord, my Spirits flat, and dead. Edward Taylor. NOSC; TCAPo Fr. Preparatory Meditations Before My Approach to the Lord's Supper.

All early, when the day. Spouse of Jesus Laments Her Heart's Flame, The. Friedrich Spee. GePo, tr. by George C. Schoolfield

All ears, nose, tongue and gut. Ellen Bryant Voigt. ExTi Fr. Kyrie.

All earthly pomp or beauty to express.   Old Song Ended, An.   J. D. McClatchy.   ChrPo

All Earth's Things.   Anne Perrier.   YaTCFP, *tr. by* Mary Ann Caws and Jean-Pierre Cauvin

All else for use, One only for desire.   Deo Optimo Maximo.   Louise Imogen Guiney.   SacPr

All er Nothin'.   Oscar Hammerstein, II.   ReLy

All evening, below a sprig of yarrow.   Heading Out West.   John Balaban.   OPRER

All evening I have watched the lightning.   Lightning.   Haniel Long.   APT-1

All evening the autumn thickets.   Grodek.   Georg Trakl.   SonAtl, *tr. by* Kurt Ganzl and Markus Jaigirder

All Except Hannibal.   Robert Graves.   EmeKit

All fathers in Western civilization must have.   Father of My Country, The.   Diane Wakoski.   NoAM

All feeling hearts must feel for him.   Coming Storm, The.   Herman Melville.   APN-2

All filthy facts, and secret acts.   Michael Wigglesworth.   NAAL-3 *Fr.* Day of Doom, The [First Section].

All flesh waxeth old as a garment.   Bible, Apocrypha.   OBVE *Fr.* Ecclesiasticus.

All folks who pretend to religion and grace.   Place of the Damned [*or* Damn'd], The.   Jonathan Swift.   ChIV-2; OBSV

All for her sake must the maiden die! (LL)   Marriage.   Mary Elizabeth Coleridge.   LW; NALW; PEW; PoBW; ViWPN; VWP

All for Nothing.   Lőrinc Szabó.   IQMS, *tr. by* Edwin Morgan

All freight, the sudden trains that uncouple my passage home.   Freight Train, Freight Train.   Alvin Greenberg.   GM

All Friends Together.   Ronald Albert Simpson.   NOBAu

All God's Chillun Got Rhythm.   Gustave Kahn.   ReLy

All grave old men, and souldiers they had bene, but for age.   Homer.   OBVE *Fr.* Iliad, The.

All great things crush themselves; such end the gods.   Lucan.   NoSic *Fr.* Civil War [Bellum Civile] *or* Pharsalia.

All Greece hates.   Helen.   "H. D."   APT-1; BrAP; ColAP; EMP; FTtHH; MoAmPo; NAAL-5; NAAPv.2; NALW; NAMCP V.1; NIL-7; NoAM; NoP-4; NoP-5; OxBoAm; PoPoPo

All Grows Old.   Yevgeny Mikhailovich Vinokurov.   TCRusP, *tr. by* Daniel Weissbort

All grows old. And what has aged.   All Grows Old.   Yevgeny Mikhailovich Vinokurov.   TCRusP, *tr. by* Daniel Weissbort

All Hail the Power of Jesus' Name.   Edward Perronet.   SacPr

All hail! thou gorgeous sunset.   Sunset.   Mary Weston Fordham.   CBWP-2

All hail! thou noble Land.   America to Great Britain.   Washington Allston.   APN-1

All hail to the Empress of India, Great Britain's Queen.   William McGonagall.   VerBaPo *Fr.* Royal Review, The.

All Hallow.   Josephine Miles.   APT-2

All Hallows.   Louise Glück.   PoPoPo

All halted elegance, you make a paper wolf for me.   H. Antecessor.   Joan Houlihan.   IAoNAP

All hazards of the field.   Militaris Cantio.   *Unknown.*   IQMS, *tr. by* Matthew Mead *and* Ruth Mead

All he does at work.   Karai Senryū.   EMJL, *tr. by* Makoto Ueda

All he wanted.   Blood Is the Argument.   Gary Johnston.   BRtP

All his children in the same house.   Job the Father.   Richard Shelton.   PBCAP

All his life Ruan Ji was lazy.   Farmers.   Wang Ji.   CCL1, *tr. by* Stephen Owen

All holy influences dwell within.   Children Band, The.   Sir Aubrey De Vere.   OBEV

All holyroadz home.   Mark S. Kuhar.   AmZen

All horizons are round.   Fragment 3.   Helmut Heissenbüttel.   GTCP, *tr. by* Christopher Middleton

All houses wherein men have lived and died.   Haunted Houses.   Henry Wadsworth Longfellow.   TCAPo

All how silent and how still.   Noon.   John Clare.   OxAEP-2

All human kind on earth.   Boethius.   NoSic *Fr.* Consolation of Philosophy, The ("De Consolacione Philosophie").

All human race would fain be wits.   On Poetry: a Rhapsody.   Jonathan Swift.   OBSV

All human things are subject to decay.   Mac Flecknoe [or, A Satire upon the True-Blue Protestant Poet T. S.].   John Dryden.   BASC; CABP; NAEL-6v1; NAEL-7v1; NoP-4; NoP-5; OBSV; OxAEP-1; TFi; NOSC; OBCoV; OxBEV

All human things are subject to decay.   Approaching a Significant Birthday, He Peruses The Norton Anthology of Poetry.   R. S. Gwynn.   RA

(All hung with stars!), there still would be no bear. (LL)   Great Bear, The.   John Hollander.   ColAP; NoAM

All hungers pass away.   Arthur Nortje.   TSAP

All hushed and still within the house.   Emily Jane Brontë.   NPeEn

All I can give you is broken-face gargoyles.   Broken-Face Gargoyles.   Carl Sandburg.   MoAmPo; TCAPo

All I could see from where I stood.   Renascence.   Edna St. Vincent Millay.   BRP; ColAP; MoAmPo; TCAPo

All I Did For Him.   Paul Muldoon and Gerald Stern.   GPPA

All I Do Is Dream of You.   Arthur Freed.   ReLy

All I know is a door into the dark.   Forge, The.   Seamus Heaney.   NAEL-6v2; NAEL-7v2; NoP-4; NoP-5; OxAEP-2; WaAnP

All I Need Is the Girl.   Stephen Sondheim.   ReLy

All I remember is she drives a red.   Yvette Mimieux in *Hit Lady*.   David Trinidad.   SUP

All I Want.   Luci Tapahonso.   ItWoWo; UnSA

All I want from this life.   Necessities.   Mei Yao Ch'en.   CrYelRi, *tr. by* Sam Hamill

All I want is a room somewhere.   Wouldn't It Be Luverly?   Alan Jay Lerner.   ReLy

All I want is the bread to turn out like hers just once.   All I Want.   Luci Tapahonso.   ItWoWo; UnSA

All I want now is a small dirt patio beneath two or three pines.   20 Years of Grant Applications and State College Jobs.   Christopher Buckley.   GeoHom

All I want to say is that I do not know.   Valediction—To My Father.   Eddy Van Vliet.   VCWP, *tr. by* John Van Tiel

All I Was Doing Was Breathing.   Mirabai.   WED; WoPoe; WPoS, *tr. by* Robert Bly

All ideas escape me.   Awakening of the Eremite, The.   Luljeta Lleshanaku.   WoBe, *tr. by* Henry Israeli

All Illusion Is a Form of Hope.   Aida Gelbtrunk.   MirDau, *tr. by* Roberta Gordenstein

All Impelled Onward Alike.   Robert Blair.   OxAEP-1 *Fr.* Grave, The.

All in a moment, through the gloom were seen.   John Milton.   TreFP *Fr.* Paradise Lost.

All in Due Time: love will emerge from hate.   All in Due Time.   James Vincent Cunningham.   NIP-4

All in green went my love riding.   E. E. Cummings.   HeIP-4; NAAPv.2; NoAM; NoP-4; NoP-5; OxBoAm; WaAnP

All in the April evening [morning].   Sheep and Lambs.   Katharine Tynan Hinkson.   OBEV; SacPr

All in the diffidence that faltered. (LL)   Ezra Pound.   APT-1; HarvBoo; NAMCP V.1; NoAM; RaBo *Fr.* Cantos.

All is best, though we oft doubt.   John Milton.   NOSC; OBEV; OxBEV *Fr.* Samson Agonistes.

All Is Cool and Boundless As A Rolling.   For Monk.   Michael McClure.   SeSe

All is Emptiness, And I Must Spin.   Thomas Kinsella.   PBCIP

All is gone—I have nothing to eat. (LL)   *Arapaho Oral Tradition.*   NAAL-5; NAAPv.2 *Fr.* Ghost-Dance Songs.

All is lithogenesis – or lochia.   Hugh MacDiarmid.   NPeEn *Fr.* On a Raised Beach.

All is One for Monk.   Imamu Amiri Baraka.   ISC

All Is Phantom.   *Unknown.*   SacPr

All is transformed and is sacred.   Octavio Paz.   BLPSL *Fr.* Sunstone.

All Is Vanity.   Andreas Gryphius.   GePo, *tr. by* George C. Schoolfield

All Is Vanity.   Anne Finch, Countess of Winchilsea.

   "*Bolder Youth*, grown of capable arms, A."   FaBoWar

'All Is Vanity, Saith the Preacher'.   Lord Byron.   ChIV-1

All jegged and tie.   Missa joe.   Seitlhamo Motsapi.   TSAP

All kinds of lines can be traced on a map.   Requiem for the Left Hand.   Nancy Morejón.   TANSG, *tr. by* Joy Renjilian-Burgy

All kinds of things happen, some of them better than this.   Without Heat.   Alexei Remizov.   MotU, *tr. by* Nancy Condee

All kings, and all their favourites [*or* favorites].   Anniversary [*or* Anniversarie], The.   John Donne.   BASC; FSCP; NoP-4; NoP-5; NoSic; TFi; WeW-3

All losses are restored [*or* restor'd] and sorrows end. (LL)   William Shakespeare.   BrAP; CABP; ClHu; GSo; HeIP-4; NAEL-6v1; NAEL-7v1; NoP-5; NoSic; OBEV; OxAEP-1; PoPoPo; TFi; WaAnP *Fr.* Sonnets.

All last night I kept speaking in this.   Mysteries.   Terence Winch.   OxBoAm

All Legendary Obstacles.   John Montague.

   "All legendary obstacles lay between."   NoP-4; NoP-5; PBCIP; PNI

   Trout, The.   ModIr; NoP-4; NoP-5; PBCIP; PNI; StAl

All legendary obstacles lay between.   John Montague.   NoP-4; NoP-5; PBCIP; PNI *Fr.* All Legendary Obstacles.

All light has left the yard.   My Brothers Make a Lantern.   David Scott Ward.   AmPoNex

All light is fossil light. It says the earliest moments of a star.   All Light.   John Smith.   Coast

All living beings sorrow and lament.   Ode to Knight Chukchi.   Tŭgo [*or* Tŭgogok].   CATKP, *tr. by* Peter H. Lee

All long labors, whether for hunger, for duty, for. After. Jeanne Marie Beaumont. PoDa

All look or [or and] likeness caught from earth. Phantom. Samuel Taylor Coleridge. NAEL-6v2

All married men desire to have good wives. Lady Anne Harris Southwell. EMWP

All meet here with us, finally: the. Ostriches & Grandmothers! Imamu Amiri Baraka. BrAP

All men are bad, and in their badness reign. (LL) William Shakespeare. CAGL; NoSic; OxAEP-1; PBRV Fr. Sonnets.

All Men have Follies, which they blindly trace. Cameleon's Defence, The. *Unknown*. TCAPo

All men in the world live. To You, My Beloved Ssuma Ch'ien. Mun Chônghui. EcSo, *tr. by* Catherine J. Kim

All men may hasty-gone happiness find. Shepherd-Song. Sigmund von Birken. GePo, *tr. by* George C. Schoolfield

All men wait for battle and when it comes. Apple Tree and a Pig, An. Emyr Humphreys. OBWVE

All Messages Have Been Played. John Ashbery. VaPo

All moose. (LL) Poetry, a Natural Thing. Robert Duncan. CalPo; NAMCP V.2; NoAM; OxBoAm; PmAP; TRP

All Morning. Gregory Orr. TRP

All morning, as I sit thinking of you. Monarchs. Sharon Olds. CAP-8

All morning, food full of sugar, as if he were a hummingbird or a fly. Blue Hat. Connie Voisine. FiBr

All morning, I nurse some fretful sorrow. Household Muse. Joyce Sutphen. SweBea

All morning, I watch him. Sunday. Carl Phillips. GT

All morning in the February light. Telephone Repairman. Joseph Millar. P180

All morning I've passed from window to window, shadowing. Doing Good. Nancy Esposito. PfS

All morning the dream lingers. All Morning. Gregory Orr. TRP

All morning, the man roofs the house. Hammer Falls, Is Falling, The. Marianne Boruch. AmAlph

All morning we saw flames in the distance. Last Still Days in a Bunker, The. Walter McDonald. AF

All my bones want to comfort each other. Contortionist. Lee Upton. AmAlph

All my dreams. East. Johannes Bobrowski. GTCP, *tr. by* Michael Hamburger

All my future plans, dear. Blue Room, The. Lorenz Hart. ReLy

All my hotheaded lovers will be pleased with me. *Unknown*. SLW, *tr. by* Marjolijn De Jager, Sayd Bahodin Majrouh and André Velter

All my life I have struggled from gentleness. Finale. Sue Lenier. LW

All my life I waited for an angel. I'll String Along with You. Al Dubin. ReLy

All my life, I've dreamed of lakes and rivers. Broken Boat, A. Tu Fu [*or* Du Fu]. CrYelRi, *tr. by* Sam Hamill

All my life I've had no interest in worldly success. Ryokan. EMJL, *tr. by* Haruo Shirane

All my life through. Retrospective. Ogata Kenzon. WoPoe, *tr. by* Richard L. Wilson

All my other lives. (LL) Waxwings. Robert Francis. APT-2; BLT; RaBo

All my past life is mine no more. Love And Life. John Wilmot, 2d Earl of Rochester. NPeEn; OBEV; OxBEV

All my past life is mine no more. Love and Life. Grace Buchanan Sherwood. NoP-4

All My Pretty Ones. Anne Sexton. NAMCP V.2; NoAM; OxBoAm

All my senses, like Beacons flame. Fulke, 1st Baron Brooke Greville. CABP; NOSC; NoSic Fr. Caelica.

All my sheep / Gather in a heap. Last Words before Winter. Louis Untermeyer. MoAmPo

All my shortcomings, in this year of grace. Dear Uncle Stranger. Conrad Potter Aiken. ColAP; NoAM

All my thoughts of you are good ones. Holy Ghost. Larissa Szporluk. LegDan; NeAmPo

All Nature felt a reverential shock. Bible, *O.T.* STuOW *Fr.* Paraphrase on the Book of Job, A.

All nature Her wealth. Sound of owls Her pillow. (LL) Flower No More Than Itself, A. Linda Gregg. BBASP; WaAnP

All nature ministers to Hope. The snow. Hartley Coleridge. CenSon

All Nature seems at work. Slugs leave their lair. Work without Hope. Samuel Taylor Coleridge. CenSon; GSo; NAEL-6v2; NAEL-7v2; NPBRoP; OBEV; OxAEP-2; OxBSo; WoPoe

All nature's incense rise! (LL) Universal Prayer, The [Deo Opt. Max.]. Alexander Pope. InvLi; NoP-4; NoP-5

All nearness pauses,while a star can grow. E. E. Cummings. NoAM

All Night. Tzu Yeh. CrYelRi, *tr. by* Sam Hamill

All night, all day, in dizzy, downward flight. Winter Landscape, A. Mathilde Blind. ViWPN

All night, all night. Interrogations of the Sparrow. Elizabeth Spires. FFC

All night and all day the wind roared in the trees. Mid-Country Blow. Theodore Roethke. HarvBoo

All night, and as the wind lieth among. Speech for Psyche in the Golden Book of Apuleius. Ezra Pound. HarvBoo

All night and day through summer the peat field. Moss Burning. Marianne Boruch. AmAlph

All night Brazil approached you through the dark. Brazil. Bill Manhire. HarvBoo

All Night by the Rose. *Unknown*. HeIP-4, *tr. by* Michael Rosen

All night by the rose, rose. All Night by the Rose. *Unknown*. HeIP-4, *tr. by* Michael Rosen

(Al nyght by the rose, rose.) OHMEL

(Alnight by the rose, rose.) NPeEn

All night had shout of men and cry. Easter Night. Alice Thompson Meynell. ChIV-2; SacPr

All night I am the doe, breathing. Strange People, The. Louise Erdrich. PoPoPo

All night I could not sleep. Ye Zi. WPoS

All night I dream of lips. Lumpectomy Eve. Lucille Clifton. CAP-8

All night / I float / in the shallow ponds. White Night. Mary Oliver. AWTN

All night I quarrel with you in my dreams. Reading Chiyo-Ni, 1703-1775, Japanese Woman Haikuist. Miriam Sagan. WANABP

All night I sat reading a book. Reader, The. Wallace Stevens. SAmP

All night I weep[e], all day I cry, Ay me[e]. Mary Sidney Wroth, Countess of Montgomery. NOSC *Fr.* Pamphilia to Amphilanthus.

All night it humps the air. Cannery Town in August. Lorna Dee Cervantes. NAMCP V.2; NoAM

All night long. Wake. Giuseppe Ungaretti. WoPoe, *tr. by* George Garrett

All night long I think of life's labyrinth. Betsugen. ZenPo, *tr. by* Takashi Ikemoto and Lucien Stryk

All night long the drinking fountains gurgled. Monastery. Ivan Davidkov. CSCBP, *tr. by* Georgi Belev and Lisa Sapinkopf

All night long the hockey pictures. To a Sad Daughter. Michael Ondaatje. NoAM

All night she dreams. All Night She Dreams. Cheryl Savageau. TWW

All night the booming minute-gun. Wreck, The. Felicia Dorothea Hemans. TreFP

All night the cocks crew, under a moon like day. Tears in Sleep. Louise Bogan. MakPoe

All night the dreadless Angel unpursu'd. John Milton. *Fr.* Paradise Lost.

All night the pimp's cars slide past the burning mill. Homage to Elvis, Homage to the Fathers. Bruce Weigl. ReTh

All night the priestesses of wisdom have been practicing. Poem on the First Day of School. Peter Cooley. NevBe; PoA 2002

All night the snowstorm raged, by morning it had cleared. Music. Vladislav Felitsianovich Khodasevich. TCRusP, *tr. by* Daniel Weissbort

All night the sound had. Rain, The. Robert Creeley. AmFaPo; BeAl; BrAP; ColAP; ErotSp; ICANM; InvLad; PmAP; RaBo; TRP; WaAnP

All night the sprockets have fallen from the sky. Rain of Bicycles, A. Jonathan Harrington. ArBi

All night the tall young man. Merlin and the Snake's Egg. Leslie Norris. OBSP

All night they marched, the infantrymen under pack. 1935. Stephen Vincent Benét. MoAmPo

All night they whine upon their ropes and boom. Nocturne of the Wharves. Arna Bontemps. ColAP; GT

All night, this headland. Sleepless at Crown Point. Richard Wilbur. WeW-3

All night vigil. Always Running. Luis J. Rodriguez. UnSA

All night waiting, in an empty house. Malcolm Cowley. PoA 2002 *Fr.* Blue Juniata.

All Nite Long. Kalamu ya Salaam. SpirFl *Fr.* New Orleans Haiku.

All no's become yes's under the law. Commandments, The. Lamea Abbas Amara. PoArWo, *tr. by* Mike Maggio

All of a sudden I see him standing there, just like that, like he dropped out of the sky. Little Man, The. David Connolly. AmWaPo

All of a sudden my delight in sightseeing wanes. Tune: "Pure Serene Music." Chang Yen. ColAnChi, *tr. by* Jiaosheng Wang

(All of a Sudden) My Heart Sings. Jean-Marie Blanvillain and Harold Rome. ReLy

All of a Summer. Jakov Steinberg. FIT, *tr. by* Robert Friend

All of a summer's day. (LL) Milton by Firelight. Gary Snyder. BB; NAMCP V.2

All of it, all of it, under one roof. (LL) Feminist Poem Number One. Elizabeth Alexander. FaoP; NAPBL

All of It, The. Chase Twichell. AmZen

All of Me. Gerald Marks and Seymour Simons. ReLy

All of my life.   All of My Life.   Betty Comden and Adolph Green.   ReLy

All of our lives. (LL)   Phantasia for Elvira Shatayev.   Adrienne Rich.   ItP; NALW

All of the Indians must have tragic features: tragic noses, eyes, and arms.   How to Write the Great American Indian Novel.   Sherman Alexie.   NAMCP V.2

All of the night on this earth.   Shore of Night.   José Luis Hidalgo.   RaW, tr. by Hardie St. Martin

All of the pens leaked.   Assignment, The.   Len Roberts.   OPRER

All of them are six.   For Beautiful Mary Brown: Chicago Rent Strike Leader.   June Jordan.   OxAAAP

All of These People.   Michael Longley.   StAl

All of those sensuous bodies.   Landscape with Nymphs and Satyrs.   Norman Henry, II Pritchard.   GT

All of us are sick, Sir.   Nissim Ezekiel.   OBCoV Fr. Songs for Nandu Bhende.

All of Us Here.   Irving Feldman.

  Of Course, We Would Wish.   VCAP

  Simple Outlines, Human Shapes.   VCAP

  Surely They're Just So Large.   VCAP

All of us on the sofa in a line, kneeling.   Sofa in the Forties, A.   Seamus Heaney.   EmeKit

All of us receive.   Get Blind Drunk.   Wang the Zealot.   CCL1, tr. by C. H. Kwock and Vincent McHugh and Vincent McHugh

All of Us So Close to Buddha.   Taigen Dan Leighton.   WhBo

All of us take our clothes to Carver.   Washboard Wizard.   Marilyn Nelson.   BtF

All of us were there.   Kaleidoscope.   Maria Elena Cruz Varela.   VCWP, tr. by Mairym Cruz-Bernal and Deborah Digges

All of what I feel—and for all I know.   Circumstance.   Butch Hancock.   WhBo

All of You.   Cole Porter.   ReLy

All of you hammered golden against the anvil. (LL)   October, Yellowstone Park.   Maxine W. Kumin.   ExTi; PfSP

All of you that desire to hear a jest.   Unknown.   EroLit

All of you that pour the bath for Pallas.   Callimachus.   HePo Fr. Hymns.

All old women sometimes come to this.   Old Women of Toronto.   Miriam Waddington.   IFF

All on a sudden, there rose on the stairs.   Leigh Hunt.   NPBRoP Fr. Feast of the Poets, The.

All on my own I'm happy.   Muso Soseki.   EaWin, tr. by W. S. Merwin

All on the mountains, as on tapestries.   For Robert Frost, in the Autumn, in Vermont.   Howard Nemerov.   VisFro

All on the threshold, yet all short of life. (LL)   Triad, A.   Christina Georgina Rossetti.   NAEL-6v2; NAEL-7v2; NALW

All One in Christ.   John Oxenham.   SacPr

All or nothing at all!   All or Nothing at All.   Jack Lawrence.   ReLy

All other fair, like flowers, untimely fade. (LL)   Edmund Spenser.   NoP-4; NoP-5 Fr. Amoretti.

All Other Love Is Like the Moon.   Unknown.   SacPr

All others talked as if.   Caedmon.   Denise Levertov.   BrAP; ItP; NAMCP V.2; NoAM; NoP-4; NoP-5; PoCho

  (All the others talked as if.)   UpMys

All our desire is a grain of wheat.   Mill, the Stone, and the Water, The.   Jelaluddin Rumi.   WED, tr. by Robert Bly

All our dreams are possible.   Illicit Passion.   Abena Busia.   NAfrP

"All our French poets can turn an inspired line."   Nihilist as Hero, The.   Robert Lowell.   VCAP

All our friends keep knocking at the door.   I Don't Want to Walk Without You.   Frank Loesser.   ReLy

All our jams are up.   Labor Day.   David Cope.   ViWalt

All Our Joy Is Enough.   Geoffrey Scott.   OBMV

All our life long.   Impermanence.   Ko Ŭn.   CAMKP, tr. by Anthony, Brother of Taizé

All our lives.   Both Yesterday and Today.   Georges Castera.   OGAHCP, tr. by Boadiba and Jack Hirschman

All our lives we've been told how things work.   Paso Robles, San Luis Obispo, San Luis Obispo.   David Oliveira.   CalPo; GeoHom

All our roads go nowhere.   On Inhabiting an Orange.   Josephine Miles.   NoAM; PoA 2002; WaAnP

All our stones like as much sun as possible.   Forecast.   Josephine Miles.   NoAM

All out of doors [or out-of-doors] looked darkly in at him.   Old Man's Winter Night, An.   Robert Frost.   APT-1; GPTC; ItP; MoAmPo; NAMCP V.1; NoAM; OxBoAm

All Over Again.   Ataol BehramoĞlu.   NaPG, tr. by Talat Sait Halman

All over America women are burning dinners.   What's That Smell in the Kitchen?   Marge Piercy.   NBLV; NIL-7; NIP-4

All over Chicago, Jim, the angels are making love.   Ode to the Angels Who Move Perpetually toward the Dayspring of Their Youth.   Paul Carroll.   IllVoic

All over the place. (LL)   At last we killed the roaches.   Lucille Clifton.   CAP-8; PtR

All paths lead.   Winter.   John Davies.   AngWePo

All power is saved, having no end.   Muriel Rukeyser.   PFTM-1

All problems being.   Forced Retirement.   Nikki Giovanni.   PfS

All projects failed, in the August afternoon.   Henry's Fate.   John Berryman.   ColAP

All Purpose Country and Western Self Pity Song, The.   Kit Wright.   StAl

All quail to the wallowing.   Lynne McMahon.   ExTi

All Quiet [For Robert Bly; Written at the start of one of our bombing pauses over North Vietnam].   David Ignatow.   PoCho

All quiet along the Potomac, they say.   All Quiet Along the Potomac.   Ethel Lynn Beers.   CBCWP; PCW

"All ready?" cried the captain.   Slave-Ships, The.   John Greenleaf Whittier.   TCAPo

All Religions Are One.   William Blake.   NAEL-6v2; NAEL-7v2

All Revelation.   Robert Frost.   APT-1

All right, gentlemen who cry blue murder as always.   Draft of a Reparations Agreement.   Dan Pagis.   HP; PoSu; WoPoe, tr. by Stephen Mitchell

All right, I admit it.   Talking to Vladimir Mayakovsky.   Ron Padgett.   NYP2

All right, I may have lied to you, and about you.   Love, 20c the First Quarter Mile.   Kenneth Fearing.   WoPoe

All right, I was Welsh. Does it matter?   Welsh Testament, A.   Ronald Stuart Thomas.   TCAWP

All right. Try this.   Northern Pike.   James Wright.   PLBUT

All rites pertaining to his maried state. (LL)   George Chapman.   NoSic; PBRV Fr. Hero and Leander.

All roocoogirls.   Song.   Hans Andreus.   TuT, tr. by Peter van de Kamp

All ruins, the empire; mountains and rivers in view.   Spring Scene.   Tu Fu [or Du Fu].   ChinPo, tr. by Ye Weilian [or Yeh Wei-lien or Wai-lim Yip]

All Saints' Day.   John Keble.   SacPr

All Saints Day, 2001.   Patricia Spears Jones.   PA9/11

All Saints' Day, Nov. 1.   Christopher Wordsworth.   SacPr

All saints revile her, and all sober men.   White Goddess, The.   Robert Graves.   HarvBoo; MoBrPo; NAEL-6v2; NAEL-7v2; NoP-4; NoP-5

All says a glass doorknow Parabola ghost.   Seth Young.   AnSo Fr. River we are caried by.

All Seasons in One.   Unknown.   HeIP-4

All shiny in your mind! (LL)   Some People.   Rachel Lyman Field.   ChAP; NTCP

All Shook Up.   Don Bogen.   AllShUp

All Shook Up.   Dan Sicoli.   AllShUp; SwNoth

All shrouded in the winter snow.   Storm-Beat Maid, The.   Joanna Baillie.   NPBRoP

All silence keep, both goats and sheep.   Michael Wigglesworth.   NAAL-3 Fr. Day of Doom, The [First Section].

All silence says music will follow.   Onion Bucket.   Lorenzo Thomas.   GT

All silent stood; at last stood forth one dolon, that did dare.   Homer.   FaBoWar Fr. Iliad, The.

All songs / are tattoos.   Singer, The.   Diane Wakoski.   HeIP-4

All sorts of men through various labours press[e].   Verses Written by Mrs. Hutchinson.   Lucy Hutchinson.   BASC; NOSC

All sorts of plants were beautiful.   Quick Sell the Pig.   Matthew Rohrer.   AmPoNex

All Souls'.   Ruth Bidgood.   AngWePo

All Souls'.   Rita Dove.   BAP-04

All Souls'.   Dana Gioia.   StAl

All Soul's Day.   Willem Jan Otten.   TuT, tr. by Micheal O'Siadhail

All Soul's Day.   Maurya Simon.   ExTi

All Souls' Night.   William Butler Yeats.   OxAEP-2 Fr. Vision, A.

All Souls' over, the roast seeds eaten, I set.   Totem.   Eamon Grennan.   ModIr

All spring, my sorrows grew like lotus leaves.   Alone by the Autumn River.   Li Shang-yin.   ColAnChi, tr. by Sam Hamill

All Suffering Comes from Attachment.   Ron Koertge.   SUP

All suiteth me! so that's enough, / My Mary. (LL)   My Mary.   John Clare.   NOBRP; NPBRoP

All sullen and obscene, they toiled in pain.   Epitaphs.   Edmund Wilson.   APT-2

All summer I heard them.   Snakes of September, The.   Stanley Kunitz.   ColAP; WaAnP

All summer I've watered your maple sapling.   Ritual.   Sue Chenette.   IFF

All summer listening for the crack.   Chopping Wood.   Geoffrey Cook.   Coast

All summer long hurricanes.   Tourist Weather.   Silvia Curbelo.   TouFir

All summer the sheep were strewn like crumbs.   Flanking Sheep in Mosedale.   David Scott.   NLP

All summer under klieg lights. Digs in Escondido Canyon, The. Walter McDonald. PoA 2002

All Sweet Things, Like Forgiveness, Are a Falling. Juanita Brunk. ACAMVP

All sweetness all irony gathered. To the Voice of Kathleen Ferrier. Yves Bonnefoy. YaTCFP, tr. by Mary Ann Caws and Jean-Pierre Cauvin

All swoln with chasing, down Adonis sits. William Shakespeare. EroLit Fr. Venus and Adonis.

All tempest. Witter Bynner. APT-1

All Ten Commandments I Have Broken. Unknown. SacPr

All that a dog could have. Melampus' Epitaph. William Drummond of Hawthornden. DiBP

All that ever was dismembered. Lay of the Rover. Aimé Césaire. WoPoe, tr. by Gregson Davis

All that Friday. Ulster Unionist Walks the Streets of London, An. Tom Paulin. PNI

All That Glitters. Maureen Owen. PmAP

All that I am hangs by a thread tonight. Muse, The. Anna Andreyevna Akhmatova. PoetW, tr. by Max Hayward and Stanley Kunitz

All that I had I brought. Exchanges. Ernest Dowson. OBMV

All That in the Voice I Have Adopted for This Lie. Michele Glazer. IAoNAP

All that is cold. (LL) Lamium. Louise Glück. HarvBoo; StAl

All That Is Lovely in Men. Robert Creeley. RaBo

All that is moulded of iron. Woodworker's Ballad. Herbert Edward Palmer. OBEV

All that is past of us. Johann Wolfgang von Goethe. WoPoe Fr. Faust.

All that I've never thought of—think of me! (LL) Sick Child, A. Randall Jarrell. NoP-4; OxBoAm

All that juniper west of. Priorities at Friday Ranch. William Stafford. BodElec

All that matters is to be at one with the living God. Pax. D. H. Lawrence. PLBUT

All That My Soul Possessed. Nikolai Alekseievich Zabolotsky. TCRusP, tr. by Kathy Lewis and Bob Perelman

All that my soul possessed, it seemed that again I had lost it all. All That My Soul Possessed. Nikolai Alekseievich Zabolotsky. TCRusP, tr. by Kathy Lewis and Bob Perelman

All That Really Happens. Joe Wenderoth. BodElec

All that the night. Nocturne. Xavier Villaurrutia. TCLAP, tr. by Xavier Leroux

All that winter you were gone. Solitaire. George Hitchcock. GifTon

All that year, the fronts of houses. 1919. Donald Revell. BodElec

All that you have lost, they told me, is yours. Boundaries. José Emilio Pacheco. PoetW; STV; TCLAP, tr. by John Frederick Nims

All that you've danced they take from you. Last Waltz in Santiago. Ariel Dorfman. AF, tr. by Ariel Dorfman and Edith Grossman

All that's left is the red ochre, and it's spreading. Burial Mound. Anne Marie Macari. MotU

All That's Past. Walter De la Mare. OBMV

All the above were friends. And then the foe. (LL) IFF. Howard Nemerov. AmWaPo; BodElec; PWW2

All the afternoon there has been a chirping of birds. Free Fantasia on Japanese Themes. Amy Lowell. MoAmPo

All the air quivers, and the east sky glows. (LL) Front, A. Randall Jarrell. NoP-4; NoP-5; OBWP; PoWW

All the boys always wanted her, so. Leda's Sister and the Geese. Katharyn Machan Aal. SoSe-8

All the bright day I rode my bike along the river. River, The. Patti Tana. PasH

All the children on this ward are dying of AIDS. Sacrament of Poverty, The. Marilyn Nelson Waniek. ExTi; GT

All the Cold Mechanicals. Joan Houlihan. IAoNAP

All the day long and each day the sea would gleam, stepped in blueness. When I Was a Boy. Alun Llywelyn-Williams. BBMWP, tr. by Joseph P. Clancy

All the Earth, All the Air. Theodore Roethke. HarvBoo

All the earth where she could open at it. XX. P. Inman. FTOS

All the exposure. Larissa Lai. PoPra

All the family dogs are dead. Transfer. Ingrid de Kok. TSAP

All the field hands. Basho. SoOfWa, tr. by Sam Hamill

All the flowers by the lake. Day and Night. Haniel Long. APT-1

All the flowers of the spring. John Webster. NOSC Fr. Devil's Law Case, The.

All the flutterlings gone. Del Ray Cross. FreRad

All the food critics hate iceberg lettuce. Iceberg Theory, The. Gerald Locklin. BeAl; GoPo

All the fruit is ripe, plunged in fire, cooked. Friedrich Hölderlin. WoPoe, tr. by Robert Bly

All the Generations Before Me. Yehuda Amichai. FIT, tr. by Robert Friend

All the Generations Before Me. Yehuda Amichai. PoSu, tr. by Harold Schimmel

All the generations that preceded me contributed me. All the Generations Before Me. Yehuda Amichai. FIT, tr. by Robert Friend

All the great jockeys were born premature. To the Man Saying "Come on Seis" at Hollywood Park. David Hayward. MoASP

All the green garden, flower-bed, shade, and plot. Leigh Hunt. NPBRoP Fr. Story of Rimini, The.

All the guys are there. Foreign Game, A. Joseph Somoza. ICANM

All the hills and vales along. Charles Hamilton Sorley. MoBrPo; OBWP; OxAEP-2; PoWW

All the houses are white. Virtue. Cynthia Huntington. PoDa

All the huskies are eaten. There is no space. Polar Explorer, A. Joseph Brodsky. WaAnP, tr. by the author

All the ladies feeling lucky at love. Autobiography of a Black Man. G. E. Patterson. AmPoNex

All the laughing girls wait for the hands. Your Face Here. Robin S. Chapman. PoCoUp

All the lies in our town ran to the river one summer night and jumped in. Right Time, The. William Stafford. MotU

All the light was north, snow on skylights. Lightfall. Pamela Alexander. AmAlph

All the lizards are asleep. Nature Study. Craig Raine. NoAM

All the mill-horses of Europe. Discovery of America, The. James Logie Robertson. NePenScot

All the money I lied about, the makeshift. Groupie. Mark Bibbins. LegDan

All the monsters live here. Army of Draculas. Patrick Sylvain. OGAHCP, tr. by Boadiba and Jack Hirschman

All the names I know from nurse. Flowers, The. Robert Louis Stevenson. BLPJKO

All the Natural Movements of the Soul. Olena Kalytiak Davis. LegDan

All the new thinking is about loss. Meditation at Lagunitas. Robert Hass. AmFaPo; CalPo; CAP-8; ColAP; FaoP; GeoHom; MakPoe; NAMCP V.2; NoP-4; NoP-5; OxBoAm; StAl; VCAP; WaAnP

All the News—September 23, 2001. Mark Pawlak. PrTe

All the night in woe. William Blake. NOBRP Fr. Songs of Experience.

All the night in woe. William Blake. NOBRP Fr. Songs of Innocence.

All the night sleep came not upon my eyelids. Sapphics. Sappho. NPeEn, tr. by Algernon Charles Swinburne

All, the Nothing, The. Yves Bonnefoy. VCWP, tr. by Lisa Sapinkopf

All the Old Songs. Walter McDonald. TiP2

All the opportunities we miss by being born too soon! Born Too Soon. James Fenton and John Fuller. OBCoV

All the others talked as if. Denise Levertov. See All others talked as if.

All the People Who Are Now Red Trees. Martín Espada. TouFir

All the perversions of the soul. Small Farm, A. Michael Hartnett. PBCIP

All the photographs are faded. In This House. Veronica Forrest-Thomson. EdScPo

All / the places. To the Father of Me. Lamont B. Steptoe. OxAAAP

All the poems of love are one. Poems of Love, The. Padraic Fallon. IrLP

All the Pools in Queens. Erika Meitner. NevBe

All the preachers claimed it was Satan. TV. Rodney Jones. BeAl; IllVoic; ReTh

All the Radios. Conrad Potter Aiken. InGu

All the Same. Clarence Major. BodElec

All the same she is not so beautiful as she was. (LL) Celts, The. Stevie Smith. NoP-4; NoP-5

All the sexually active people in Westport. Chaste Stranger, The. James Tate. NoAM

All the shoes are shined and the cotton is picked. Sharrif Simmons. BRtP

All the Sioux were defeated. Our clan. Report to Crazy Horse. William Stafford. NoAM

All the sleepless night. All Night. Tzu Yeh. CrYelRi, tr. by Sam Hamill

All the soups I've made in my life. All the Soups. Martha Rhodes. AFaM; ExTi; LaCa; SweBea

All the Stars Are Foxfire. Van K. Brock. AllShUp

All the teeth ever I had are worn down and fallen out. Rudaki. WoPoe, tr. by Basil Bunting

All the things I've written about us are untrue. Nazim Hikmet. NaPG, tr. by Talat Sait Halman

All the things of which there are none. Lloyd Addison. EGAG

All the things we hide in water. Landing under Water, I See Roots. Annie Finch. PoDa

All the Things You Are. Oscar Hammerstein, II. ReLy

All the time. And some punk. They Kill Us. Ron Schreiber. PrTe

All the time I pray to Buddha. Issa. EH, tr. by Robert Hass

All the time I was talking as if you listened. Words. Carlos A. Angeles. ReBoTo

All the time the teacher. Fights After School. Norman J. Loftis. SpirFl

All the time they were praying. Death Bed, The. Waring Cuney. APT-2

All the time we knew his corpse was rotting. Bones of Lazarus. John Bensko. YaYoPo

All the tongues are wagging. Ernst Mirville. OGAHCP, tr. by Boadiba and Jack Hirschman

All the toys of the world would break. (LL) Love Poem: "My clumsiest dear, whose hands shipwreck vases." John Frederick Nims. IllVoic; PoA 2002

All the Trees. Ellen Bass. PfS

All the truth you'll ever be able to cull. Spring. Carl Dennis. PfSP

All / the voices in the universe. History, Hollers, and Horn. Sterling Plumpp. FuFl

All the voices of the wood called "Muriel!" Then I Saw What the Calling Was. Muriel Rukeyser. ColAP

All the Way. Sammy Cahn. ReLy

All the way clear to Aliquippa. Mac Wellman. HeMarv Fr. Rat Minaret: Miniaturist-Divan, The.

All the way driving in. End of the Row. Anne Born. Prnts

All the Way Home. Primus St. John. EGAG

All the way to the hospital. Almond Tree, The. Jon Stallworthy. NoAM

All the while among. Fragrance of Life, Odor of Death. Denise Levertov. AF

All the while I was quite happy. (LL) Nikki-Rosa. Nikki Giovanni. FaBoA; FuFl; GT; HeIP-4; InGu; ISC; OxAAAP; SSLK; UnSA

All the white boxes. Yerba Buena, Nick & Jerry. Reed Bye. AHA

All the Wide Grin of Him. Eleanor Wilner. ExTi

All the women who leave tell me they're happy. Streamers. Sandra McPherson. VCAP

All the words that I utter. Where My Books Go. William Butler Yeats. OBEV

All the world for love may die. (LL) Ben Jonson. NAEL-7v1; NOSC; PtR Fr. Celebration of Charis in Ten Lyric[k] Pieces [or Peeces], A.

All the world is so sweet, dear. To Alice Dunbar. Paul Laurence Dunbar. NAAPv.1

All the world moved next to me strange. All the World Moved. June Jordan. EGAG; GT

"All the World's a Stage" [ballad, with music]. Victor Gray. NBLV

All the world's a stage. William Shakespeare. CtM; ITBLP; UV Fr. As You Like It.

All the year where cherries grow. (LL) Cherry-ripe [or Cherrie-ripe]. Robert Herrick. BASC; OBEV

All the young men I know. Tanka. Toki Zenmaro. CAoMJL1, tr. by Makoto Ueda

All their lights went out. In the Dark Word, Khurbn. Jerome Rothenberg. TaR

All their nails were painted scarlet. (LL) Slender Fingers. Chao Luan-luan. CCL1; NDACCP, tr. by Chung Ling and Kenneth Rexroth

All their pipes were still. Praise of Spenser. William Browne. OxAEP-1

All these and more came flocking; but with looks. John Milton. BrAP Fr. Paradise Lost.

All These Are Vile. John Keats. OBCoV

All these dead. In the Country of the Dead. Habib Tengour. YaTCFP, tr. by Marilyn Hacker

All these dormant fields are held beneath the fog. Muscat Pruning. William Everson. APT-2

All these fair sounds and sights I made my own. (LL) Long Island Sound. Emma Lazarus. APN-2; NAAPv.1; OxBoAm; SWaP

All these fellows were there inside. Fable of the Mermaid and the Drunks. Pablo Neruda. StAl, tr. by Alastair Reid

All these girls licking & sucking. Leaving Syracuse. Al Young. ESEAA

All these hang-ups, all this time wasted when. Manic: A Conversation with Jimi Hendrix. Tim Seibles. OPRER

All these journeys. Ferry Me Across. B. P. Nichol. FTOS

All these labors night and day. (LL) Epiphany: "Sometimes you show yourself." Elsa Cross. RMCMP; TAPaP, tr. by Margaret Sayers Peden

All these undertakings! Xenophon's Song. István Vas. IQMS, tr. by Geroge Gömöri and Clive Wilmer

All these years. Begin with the Heron and the Bat. Mary Sue Koeppel. AmZen

All these years behind windows. Animals, The. W. S. Merwin. VCAP; WaAnP

All these years I overlooked them in the. Springtime in the Rockies, Lichen. Lew Welch. WhBo

All these years to forgive? (LL) Up. Margaret Atwood. NoP-4; NoP-5

All they said was true. Edgar Lee Masters. APT-1 Fr. Spoon River Anthology.

All thing is contrivéd by mannes reasón. Magnificence. John Skelton.

All things. Hadewijch II. WPoS

All Things. Laura Riding Jackson. ColAP

All things. Comment on this: in the real scheme of things, poetry is marginal. Richard Jones. TAPaP

All things are cool in themselves and complete. (LL) Men and Women Have Meaning Only as Man and Woman. Joan Murray. OxBoAm; YaYoPo

All things are current found. Henry David Thoreau. TCAPo

All things are real. Letter to a Friend: Who Is Nancy Daum? James Schuyler. PmAP

All things are words of some strange tongue, in thrall. Compass. Jorge Luis Borges. PoetW, tr. by Richard Wilbur

All things bright and beauteous. Cecil Frances Alexander. See All Things Bright and Beautiful.

All Things Bright and Beautiful. Cecil Frances Alexander. SacPr; UV (All things bright and beauteous.) VWP (Creation, The.) ChAP

All things come apart. Daisen. ZenPo, tr. by Takashi Ikemoto and Lucien Stryk

All things come to an end. Train Ride. Ruth Stone. OxBoAm

All things come to one hideous Charybdis. Simonides. SaLy, tr. by Diane Rayor

All things die and all things live forever. Antonio Machado Ruiz. WED Fr. Moral Proverbs and Folk Songs.

All Things dull and Ugly. "Monty Python." UV

All things felt sweet were felt sweet overmuch. Two Dreams, The. Giovanni Boccaccio. OBGa, tr. by Algernon Charles Swinburne

All things I can endure, save one. Magdalen. Amy Levy. ViWPN; VWP

All things in nature are beautiful types to the soul that can read them. Correspondences. Christopher Pearse Cranch. APN-1

All things in this life that he could. (LL) Performance, The. James Dickey. FaBoWar; InGu

All things innocent, hapless, forsaken. (LL) Meadow Mouse, The. Theodore Roethke. ChAP; HeIP-4; TRP

All things must have an end; the world itself. Henry Wadsworth Longfellow. TCAPo Fr. Michael Angelo: A Fragment.

All things save Beauty alone. (LL) Ezra Pound. NAAPv.2; TCAPo Fr. Hugh Selwyn Mauberley (Life and Contacts).

All things that live. Writing What I've Seen. Yuan Mei. GifTon, tr. by Jerome P. Seaton

All things within this fading world hath [or have] end. Before the Birth of One of Her Children. Anne Bradstreet. AmFaPo; ColAP; EMWP; NAAL-3; NAAL-5; NAAPv.1; NoP-4; NoP-5; OxBoAm; PEW; SacPr

All this dead wood. Advertisements. Thomas McGrath. BodElec

All this did not happen in Budapest. Cart With Four Oxen,The. Sándor Petőfi. IQMS, tr. by Ila Egon

All this fall. Baudelaire's Spleen. Jaime Manrique. WiU

All this foolishness. Basho. EH, tr. by Robert Hass

All this imaging is only the subliminal daily cache because of your first. Fred Wah. NLPA Fr. This Dendrite Map: Father / Mother Haibun.

All this is ended now. It is over and done. Aftermath (1945). Henriette de Saussure Blanding. ASA

All this night long and longer. All this night long. Robert J. Gibbs. Coast

All this summer fun. / The big waves, and waiting. Lighthouse. Joseph Ceravolo. NYP2

All this time is spent around paper. Liberation. Vegunta Mohana Prasad. HotL, tr. by V. Narayana Rao

All this will never be again. (LL) Wheel Revolves, The. Kenneth Rexroth. NAMCP V.1; NoAM

All those evenings cradled in the sway. Getting over Robert Frost. Peter Davison. VisFro

All those / Liquid love affairs. Psychoalphadiscobetabioaquadoloop, A. Thomas Sayers Ellis. BRtP

All Those People. Marianne Boruch. AmAlph

All those plans for fame and fortune, honor and glory. Like Smoke from Our Campfire. David Budbill. AmZen

All those seen from behind who were moving away singing. Endless Journeys. Pierre Reverdy. WoPoe, tr. by John Ashbery

All those ships that never sailed. All those ships that never sailed. Bob Kaufman. PFTM-2

All those sleep shapes, crystalline. All those sleep shapes. Paul Celan. VCWP, tr. by Michael Hamburger

All those women working. Working. Maxine Scates. PBCAP

All those words we once used for things but have now discarded in order to come to know things. Michael Palmer. CalPo

All those years, alone. You Taught Me. Thomas McGrath. PoChi

All thoughts, all passions, all delights. Love. Samuel Taylor Coleridge. NPBRoP; OBEV

All three girls were in love with their music teacher. He Said Discipline Is the Highest Form of Love. Beckian Fritz Goldberg. AmAlph

All Through the Night. Unknown. ITBLP

All through the valley, the people are whispering. Return of the Wolves. Anita Endrezze. HATNAP

All through those final, fitful weeks we walked off the restlessness. Spring Comes to Chicago. Campbell McGrath. NeAmPo

All to be said goes on every morning in this yard. In the Backyard. Julio Marzán. PueRic

All today I lie in the bottom of the wardrobe. Yoko. Thom Gunn. NoAM; PtR

All tongues tell their monsters, shapes. Gypsy Teaches Her Grandchild Wolfen Ways, The. Susan Swartwout. ReTh

All Too Soon. Sergey Aleksandrovich Yesenin. RusPo, *tr. by* Robert Arthur Douglas Ford

All too soon, I fear. *Unknown.* ArkPo, *tr. by* Helen Craig McCullough

All too soon we will depart. All Too Soon. Sergey Aleksandrovich Yesenin. RusPo, *tr. by* Robert Arthur Douglas Ford

All travellers [*or* travelers] at first incline. Stella's Birthday [1721]. Jonathan Swift. NAEL-6v1; OxAEP-1

All trembling in my arms Aminta lay. Aphra Behn. RACG *Fr.* Voyage to the Isle of Love, A.

All truths wait in all things. Walt Whitman. ColAP *Fr.* Song of Myself.

All under the leaves, the leaves of life. Seven Virgins, The. *Unknown.* OBEV

All Up in There. Derrin Maxwell. BRtP

All up very very slowly. (LL) Misgivings. William Matthews. BeAL; PoDa

All veiled in black, with faces hid from sight. Mourning Women. Mathilde Blind. ViWPN

All very simple: a mouse—rubbish quivering. House in the Field. Gennady Aygi. WoBe, *tr. by* Peter France

All wars are holy. Year from Monday, A. Tom Clark and Lewis Warsh. AHA

All was as it is, before the beginning began, before. Jacob. Delmore Schwartz. ChIV-1; TaR

All was taken away from you: white dresses. On Angels. Czeslaw Milosz. AF; BBASP; WaAnP, *tr. by* the author

All Watched Over by Machines of Loving Grace. Richard Brautigan. CalPo

All waters as the shore. (LL) Ave atque Vale. Algernon Charles Swinburne. NAEL-6v2; NAEL-7v2; OBEV

All We Ask Is Justice. Mrs. Henry Linden. CBWP-4

All we can expect are. Sartor Resartus. Art Goodtimes. GeoH

All we can hope to leave them now is money. (LL) Homage to a Government. Philip Larkin. NAMCP V.2; NoAM; OxBEV

All we do—how old are we? I must be twelve, she a little older; thirteen, fourteen—is hold hands. Still Life. C. K. Williams. PtR

All we have willed or hoped or dreamed of good shall exist. Eternity Affirms the Hour. Robert Browning. SacPr

All we make is enough. All Our Joy Is Enough. Geoffrey Scott. OBMV

All we need is fourteen lines, well, thirteen now. Sonnet. Billy Collins. CAP-8; PoA 2002

All week she's cleaned. Domestic Work, 1937. Natasha Trethewey. PoDa; SpirFl; SweBea

All week, the explosions have increased. Feast of San Silvestro, The. V. Penelope Pelizzon. AmPoNex

All were attentive to the God-like Man. Virgil. *Fr.* Aeneid (Dryden translation).

All who come into being as flesh. Harper's Song for Inherkhawy, The. *Unknown.* WoPoe, *tr. by* John L. Foster

All whom I love, all neighbors. Ultima Thule. Thomas Lux. AmAlph

All wilie sleights, that subtile women know. Torquato Tasso. OxBEV *Fr.* Godfrey of Bulloigne; or, The Recoverie of Jerusalem [Gerusalemme Liberata].

All winter long you listened for the boom. Stoic, The: For Laura Von Courten. Edgar Bowers. CalPo; PWW2

All winter through I bow my head. Scarecrow, The. Walter De la Mare. MoBrPo

All winter we've been wheezing. Estuary. Julie Fay. PoDa

All winter you went to bed early, drugging yourself on *War and Peace*. Novel, The. Adrienne Rich. CAP-8

All winter your brute shoulders strained against collars, padding. Names of Horses. Donald Hall. AmFaPo; BeAL; GoPo; IPoFL; SoSe-8; TRP; TWF

All women are beautiful as they rise. Poem for Easter. Robert Kelly. ErotSp

All worldly shapes shall melt in gloom. Last Man, The. Thomas Campbell. NOBRP; NPBRoP

All worries and troubles. Muso Soseki. EaWin, *tr. by* W. S. Merwin

All Writing Is Garbage. Antonin Artaud. PFTM-1

All / wrong. Charles Olson. NoAM *Fr.* Maximus Poems, The.

All ye nations, pause a moment! listen to the Negro's voice. Voice of the Negro, The. Lizelia Augusta Jenkins Moorer. CBWP-3

All ye poets of the age. Namby-Pamby. A Panegyric on the New Versification, Address'd to A——— P———, Esq. Henry Carey. NPeEn; OBSV; UV

All ye who, far from town, in rural hall. On a Wet Summer. John Codrington Bampfylde. OxBSo

All Year Long. *Unknown.* NDACCP, *tr. by* Kenneth Rexroth

All year long, he never visits his home town. Merchant's Joy, The. Chang Yü. ColAnChi, *tr. by* Jonathan Chaves

All year, Mozart went under. To a Daughter at Fourteen Forsaking the Violin. Carole Oles. WeW-3

All year the flax-dam festered in the heart. Death of a Naturalist. Seamus Heaney. NAMCP V.2; NoAM; OxBEV; WaAnP; WeW-3

All you are doing and saying is to America dangled mirages. To a President. Walt Whitman. NAAL-3

All you can about animals as persons. What You Should Know to Be a Poet. Gary Snyder. APSN; OxBoAm; PFTM-2

All you have to do is listen to the way a man. Man in Space. Billy Collins. BeAl; CAP-8

All you need know is: you must not be bitter. (LL) Bitter Fruit of the Tree. Sterling Allen Brown. NoP-4; NoP-5; OxBoAm

(But my brother is bitter, and he does not hear.) (LL) PtR; RaF

All You Others, Eat. Djurberaui. NOBAu, *tr. by* Catherine H. Berndt

All you preachers. Stairway to Paradise. B. G. DeSylva and Arthur Francis. TCAPo

All you that are to mirth Inclin'd. Anna Alcox. EMWP

All you that have indulgent Parents been. Upon the Death of My Deare and Lovely Daughter J. P. Jane Pulter, Baptized May 1 1625 and Died Oct 8 1646 Aet. 20. Hester Lee Pulter. EMWP

All you violated ones with gentle hearts. For Malcolm X. Margaret Abigail Walker. FTtHH; OxAAAP

All You Want. Bill Berkson. NYP2

All you young men, I pray attend to these few lines I write. Irish Sailor, The. *Irish Oral Tradition.* IrV

All your carefully cultivated notions of realism. Night Ferry to Naxos 1. Monica Youn. LegDan

All your days are holy days. Lullaby for Rachael. James Simmons. PNI

All your life you wait around for some damn man! (LL) Chant for Dark Hours. Dorothy Parker. AmWit; ItWoWo

Allá, en las tierras altas. Antonio Machado Ruiz. RaW

All-Accomplished Rover. William Somervile. DiBP

Allansford Pursuit, The. *Unknown.* WoPoe, *tr. by* Robert Graves

Allas, departyng is ground of wo,—. *Unknown.* OHMEL

"Allas," sche seide, "how that this manis mynde." Boethius. OBMV *Fr.* Consolation of Philosophy, The ("De Consolacione Philosophie").

Allegheny Happiness. Dave Jeddie Smith. CAP-8

Allegiance. Forrest Hamer. MoASP

Allegiance. Sheenagh Pugh. TCAWP

Allegorical Matters. Stephen Dobyns. BodElec

Allegory. Rafael Campo. RA

Allegory. Carla Harryman. FTOS

Allegory: Attic and Fever. David Wojahn. YaYoPo

Allegory of Good Government. Rod Mengham. VaPo

Allegory of the Brevity of Things Human. Luis de Góngora y Argote. SpanPo; WoPoe *Fr.* Spectre of the Rose, The.

Allegory of the Supermarket. Stephanie Brown. AFaM; SUP

Allegory of the Wolf Boy, The. Thom Gunn. HarvBoo

Allegro. Tomas Tranströmer. WED, *tr. by* Robert Bly

Allegro! / Suddenly lifted out of the chair. Free Speech. Tom Clark and Lewis Warsh. AHA

Alleluia! light. Alleluia-verse for the Virgin. Hildegard von Bingen. WPoS, *tr. by* Barbara Newman

Alleluia-verse for the Virgin. Hildegard von Bingen. WPoS, *tr. by* Barbara Newman

Allen. Joe Lothamer. GeoH

Allen Gingsberg came to me in a dream. One Inch of Love Is an Inch of Ashes. Anne Waldman. AmZen

Allen Ginsberg. Toi Derricotte. PBCAP

Allen Ginsberg. Howl. Beau Sia. HeMarv

Allen Newport, famous in the first . . . Allen, forever. First Grade. Liam Rector. LiTh

Alley Blues. Wayde Compton. IFF

Alley Cat. Esther Valck Georges. Spl

Alley Cat Love Song. Dana Gioia. P180

Alley Games 6 / The Ascension. Ira B. Jones. BtF

Alley of Flowers, The. Chitra Divakaruni. FiBr

Alley, The. Lola Ridge.
"Because you are four years old." TCAPo

Alley Violinist. Robert Lax. GoPo

All-feeling God, hear in the war-night. Battle Hymn, The. Stephen Crane. AmWaPo

Allí Por La Calle San Luis. Carmen Tafolla. TiP2

Alligator, hippopotamus, fox, rhinoceros. Ruler, The. Robin Blaser. FTOS

Alligator Holes Down Along About Old Dock. A. R. Ammons. LPSFW

Alligators have left their home, The. Poem Of Adulthood, A. Stephen Harrigan. TiP2

All-meaning circle, The. Shoichi. ZenPo, *tr. by* Takashi Ikemoto and Lucien Stryk

All-Night Diner, The. Markham Johnson. ReTh

All-Night Issue, The. Jackie Warren-Moore. SpirFl

All-night stations—Tremayne pictures them, The. Insomnia of Tremayne, The. Donald Justice. AWTN

All-night Taxi Stand, The. Kenneth Slessor. BMAP

Allo. Benjamin Péret. YaTCFP

Allo allo encore une nuit pas la peine de chercher c'est moi l'homme des cavernes. Cristal Automatique. Aimé Césaire. YaTCFP

Allone, allone, allone, allone, allone / Heer I sitte allone, alas! allone. *Unknown.* OHMEL

Allow that the sea is pink, rich lobster pink. You and You, In the Pink. Christopher Pilling. NLP

Alloy. Muriel Rukeyser. NAMCP V.2; NoAM

All-Purpose Apology Poem. Austin Straus. SUP

All's All. A. R. Ammons. NoP-5

All's over, then: does truth sound bitter. Lost Mistress, The. Robert Browning. OBEV

All's right with the world! (LL) Robert Browning. BRP; ITBLP; NTCP; OBEV *Fr.* Pippa Passes.

All's Vast. Francis Thompson. MoBrPo; OBMV *Fr.* Heart, The.

All's Well That Ends Well. William Shakespeare.
  "O Lord, sir, let me live, or let me see my death!" OxAEP-1

All's well—a crush of stars. December Pastures. Andrey Andreievich Voznesensky. RusPo, *tr. by* Robert Arthur Douglas Ford

Allure of Forms, The. Coral Bracho. RMCMP; TAPaP, *tr. by* Mónica de la Torre

ALL-YOU-CAN-EAT / catfish houses. Keith Cartwright. AmPoNex

Alma. Tom Lehrer. NBLV

Alma Tenías, El. Pedro Salinas. RaW

Almagest, Last Letter to Zakarias. Siv Cedering Fox. PBCAP

Almanac. May Swenson. APT-2

Almanac, 1939, An. Kevin Young. AmPoNex

Almendares. Sandra M. Castillo. TouFir

Almería. Pablo Neruda. FaBoWar, *tr. by* Donald D. Walsh

Almighty God, Whose Justice Like a Sun. Joseph Hilaire Pierre Belloc. SacPr

Almighty on High! Almighty on High! *Unknown.* CCL1, *tr. by* Anne Birrell

Almighty Power! who rul'st this world of storms! Ode, An. Anne Batten Cristall. RWP

Almohadas. Antonio Deltoro. RMCMP

Almond flourisheth, the birch trees flow, The. Signs of Spring. Sir Thomas Browne. NOSC

Almond has trapped herself in a cage of bone, The. Spell to Soften the Hard Heart of a Woman. Jeni Couzyn. BrAP

Almond Tree, The. Jon Stallworthy. NoAM

Almoner, An. Michael Field. VWP

Almost. Rae Armantrout. BAP-04

Almost a child again. In the Formal Garden. Peter Jones. OBGa

Almost a God. Emanuel Carnevali. APT-2

Almost a Love Poem. Yehuda Amichai. HP, *tr. by* Glenda Abramson

Almost all the words we've said to one another are gone. Almost. Rae Armantrout. BAP-04

Almost as strange as they will someday be. (LL) Afternoon at the Beach, An. Edgar Bowers. CalPo; VCAP

Almost as though the eggs run and leap back into their shells. Remembering Fire. Rodney Jones. InGu

Almost at the end of the century. Feast Day. W. S. Merwin. BodElec

Almost at the Horizon. Alan Williamson. FaoP

Almost Aubade. Marilyn Hacker. NAMCP V.2; NoAM

Almost Bashfully. Walter Helmut Fritz. GTCP, *tr. by* Reinhold Grimm

Almost before the princess had grown cold. True Story of Snow White, The. Bruce Bennett. ReTh

Almost Bird. Amanda Dalton. NeBl *Fr.* Room of Leaves.

Almost Blue. Mark Doty. SeSe

Almost Casanova despite the phlebitis with everything else. Almost Casanova Electricity. Jackson Mac Low. FTOS

Almost Casanova Electricity. Jackson Mac Low. FTOS

Almost Communication. Rita Ann Higgins. ArBi

Almost dark, the rain begins. Bringing the Geranium in for Winter. Gillian Allnutt. MoWP

Almost everyone I know is sick, including me. It. Sick. Anne Waldman. AHA

Almost everything I know is glad. Opus from Space. Pattiann Rogers. PoCoUp

Almost four years, and, though I merely guess. Elegy, An: December, 1970. Edgar Bowers. InGu

Almost Going. David Huddle. PBCAP

Almost Human. Cecil Day Lewis. NAMCP V.1; NoAM

Almost Like Being in Love. Alan Jay Lerner. ReLy

Almost Midwinter. Kitasono Katsue. CAoMJL1, *tr. by* John Solt

Almost molecular: it is ridiculous, i know. Winter's affection, A; radiomimetic. Matt Robinson. Coast

Almost naked like the children of the sea. (LL) Portrait ("My childhood is memories of a patio in Seville.") Antonio Machado Ruiz. ItP; RaBo; WED; WoPoe, *tr. by* Robert Bly

Almost none. Ghazal 15. Mirza Asadullah Khan Ghalib. EaWin, *tr. by* Aijaz Ahmad and W. S. Merwin

Almost Over. *Unknown.* SSUS

Almost Spring, Driving Home, Reciting Hopkins. Maxine W. Kumin. ExTi

Almost Winter, snow in the air. Cold Landscape. Augusta Peaux. TuT, *tr. by* Tony Curtis

Alms. Stanley Plumly. BodElec

Almswomen. Edmund Charles Blunden. OBMV

Almyghty god, fadir of heuene. Petition to Father and Son and Holy Ghost, A. *Unknown.* SacPr

Alnight by the rose, rose. *Unknown. See* All night by the rose, rose.

Alnwick Castle. Fitz-Greene Halleck. APN-1

Aloe, agave, portulaca, prickly pear. Life of Ideas, The. Chris Wallace-Crabbe. OBGa

Aloft in Heavenly Mansions, Doubleyou One. Playboy of the Demi-World[: 1938], The. William Plomer. UV

Aloha'oe. Queen Lili'u-o-ka-lani. SWaP
  (Farewell to Thee.) NAAPv.1

Alone. Anna Andreyevna Akhmatova. GifTon, *tr. by* Stephen Berg

Alone. Ambrose Bierce. APN-2 *Fr.* Devil's Dictionary, The.

Alone. (LL) Conjured. Sterling Allen Brown. NoP-4; NoP-5

Alone. Aled Lewis Evans. BBMWP, *tr. by* Peter Finch

Alone. Michael S. Harper. ISC

Alone. Edgar Allan Poe. APN-1; ItP; NAAL-3; NAAPv.1

Alone. Celia Laighton Thaxter. TCAPo

Alone. Tomas Tranströmer. StAl; WoPoe, *tr. by* Robin Fulton

Alone, a young woman wept. That Day. Shin Kyŏngnim. CAMKP, *tr. by* David R. McCann

Alone after the news on a bitter. Hearth, The. C. K. Williams. BeAl; WaAnP

Alone, all alone, by the wave-washed strand. Slievenamon. Charles Joseph Kickham. IrLP

Alone, aloof. (LL) Elizabeth Barrett Browning. CenSon; OxAEP-2; VWP *Fr.* Sonnets from the Portuguese.

Alone, and spun in spills of sunshine. In the Sevan Mountains. Silva Kaputikyan. SonAtl, *tr. by* Dorli Meek

Alone and strong in my peace, I look upon you in yours. (LL) Sleeping Fury, The. Louise Bogan. NAAPv.2; NALW

Alone at home one afternoon. Love Letters. Lotte Kramer. Prnts

Alone at last in my room. By the Looking-Glass. Augusta Davies Webster. VWP

Alone at Night. Kwŏn P'il. GifTon, *tr. by* Sung-Il Lee

Alone Beside the Autumn River. Li Shang-yin. *See* Alone by the Autumn River.

Alone by the Autumn River. Li Shang-yin. ColAnChi, *tr. by* Sam Hamill
  (Alone Beside the Autumn River.) CrYelRi

Alone far in the wilds and mountains I hunt. Walt Whitman. SAmP; WaAnP *Fr.* Song of Myself.

Alone fishing chill river snow. (LL) River Snow ("These thousand peaks cut off the flight of birds.") Liu Tsung-yüan. ColAnChi; NDACCP, *tr. by* Gary Snyder

Alone for a Week. Dolores Kendrick. FFC

Alone / I listened to night birds serenading. After the Obsession. Helon Habila. NeNiPo

Alone I pine. Where is the one I desire? Homeward. P'an Yüeh. CCL1, *tr. by* Anne Birrell

Alone, I pour out spring wine. Tower by the Yangtze River, A. Tu Mu. CCL1, *tr. by* R. F. Burton

Alone I sat; the summer day. Emily Jane Brontë. NALW

Alone in a room Pope Gregory whispered his name. W. H. Auden. SacPr *Fr.* Memorial for the City.

Alone in Belize. Shonda Buchanan. BRtP

Alone in his room, the man eats what remains of the sauce and congealing fat at the bottom of the pot. Man Who Devoured Himself, The. Nasri Hajjaj. Eno, *tr. by* Ibrahim Muhawi

Alone in Martyrdom. Christine de Pisan. NAWM-7v1, *tr. by* Muriel Kittel

Alone in martyrdom I have been left. Alone in Martyrdom. Christine de Pisan. NAWM-7v1, *tr. by* Muriel Kittel

Alone, in mourning, wearing an archaic black gown. Sonnet. J. V. Foix. WoPoe, *tr. by* M. L. Rosenthal

Alone in my secluded hut. To Li Po on a Winter Day. Tu Fu [or Du Fu]. CrYelRi, tr. by Sam Hamill

Alone in the field, I touch. Against Silence. Pamela Stewart. ExTi

Alone in the house. Steve Sanfield. WhBo

Alone in the quiet night. Gunnar Ekelof. WoPoe Fr. Guide to the Underworld.

Alone in Your House. Kim Addonizio. PasH

Alone / is better. Spring Thaw. Yosano Akiko. CAoMJL1, tr. by Janine Beichman

Alone it stands in Poesy's fair land. Sonnet, The. Ella Wheeler Wilcox. APN-2

Alone, lonely, working at my loom. (LL) Busy in the Spring. Tzu Yeh. CrYelRi; ErotSp, tr. by Sam Hamill

Alone on Lykaion since man hath been. Trumbull Stickney. NAAPv.2 Fr. Sonnets from Greece.

Alone on the beach this morning. Daedalus. Tom Dawe. Coast

Alone, on the deserted dock, this Summer morning. Maritime Ode. Fernando Pessoa. tr. by Susan M. Brown and Edwin Honig

Alone on the hill of storms. Battle of the Stars. Adah Isaacs Menken. CBWP-1

Alone on the railroad track. Chemin de Fer. Elizabeth Bishop. StAl

Alone, quite alone now. Missing — Believed Drowned. Michael Greening. FaBoWar

Alone retired in my native cell. Unknown. EMWP

Alone than thou, their loneliness. (LL) Matthew Arnold. BrAP; NAEL-6v2; NAEL-7v2 Fr. Switzerland.

Alone, the wild goose refuses food and drink. Lone Wild Goose. Tu Fu [or Du Fu]. CrYelRi, tr. by Sam Hamill

Alone Together. Howard Dietz. ReLy

Alone together / Beyond the crowd. Alone Together. Howard Dietz. ReLy

Alone, unfriended, on a foreign shore. Indian, The. Eliza Kirkham Mathews. CenSon

Alone, with harsh marine aloneness. Elegy. José Gorostiza. TCLAP, tr. by Rachel Benson

Alone / with only. Claude Anshin Thomas. WhBo

Alone with our madness and favorite flower. Late Echo. John Ashbery. PoA 2002; WaAnP

Alone with the desert and / the metaphysical cigarette. (LL) Grow. Joseph Ceravolo. BodElec; NYP2

Along a Cliff. David Wheatley. NIrP

Along a luminous riverbank. Primitiveness of a Cup, The. Nishiwaki Junzaburo. CAoMJL1, tr. by Hosea Hirata

Along a tarn a delator entangled a dragline. Antic Quatrains. Jackson Mac Low. PmAP

Along Fall River, gibbons cry all night. Fall River Song. Li Po. CrYelRi, tr. by Sam Hamill

Along Galeana Street. Octavio Paz. VCWP, tr. by Elizabeth Bishop

Along History. Muriel Rukeyser. NALW

Along Lenox Avenue folk said. Old Pettigrew. Melvin B. Tolson. GT

Along my journey. Basho. SoOfWa, tr. by Sam Hamill

Along Overgrown Paths. James Schuyler. BAP-01

Along railroad tracks. Temple City Blvd. and Ellis Ln. Carol Lem. GeoHom

Along that ward men died each winter night. Ward, The. George MacBeth. EdScPo

Along the amazing road drawn from the throat of recent dates. Path of Affection, The. Laila 'Allush. PoArWo, tr. by Abdelwahab M. Elmessiri

Along the Banks of the Charles. Adelina da Silva. NAfrP, tr. by Don Burness

Along the banks where Babel's current flows. Psalm 137. Bible, O.T. ChIV-1, tr. by Joel Barlow

Along the bridge Lord Marmion rode. Sir Walter Scott. FaBoWar Fr. Marmion.

Along the Charles. Kenneth Rosen. UrbNat

Along the cracked seams of Wall Street, the poor. Homestead, USA. D. L. Crockett-Smith. OxAAAP

Along the East River and the Bronx. Ode to Walt Whitman. Federico García Lorca. ViWalt, tr. by Betty Jean Craige

Along the endless avenue stand poles. Rondeau Redoublé. Margaret Avison. IFF

Along the field as we came by. A. E. Housman. MoBrP; WeW-3 Fr. Shropshire Lad, A.

Along the flat roofs beneath our window. [Winter Sketches IV]. Charles Reznikoff. PoA 2002

Along the flat sand the cupped torsos of trash fish. Black Silhouettes of Shrimpers. Dave Jeddie Smith. NAMCP V.2

Along the Grand Canal. Ch'in Kuan. BLT, tr. by Kenneth Rexroth

Along the great coast south of Bordeaux. Michael O'Loughlin. PBCIP Fr. Shards, The.

Along the lake the bugle rings. Echo Reverie. Henrietta Cordelia Ray. CBWP-3

Along the narrow streets. (LL) Captured Goddess, The. Amy Lowell. NAAL-5; NAAPv.2

Along the north-south street, glass birds. Tsuneko—Psychiatric Medications Clinic. Susan Kolodny. OPRER

Along the path of ghosts, the ashen path. Package for Another World. Jemal Sharah. NOBAu

Along the promenade? (LL) To Evoke Posterity. Robert Graves. HarvBoo; NPeEn

Along the ramparts which surround the town. In the Defences. Elizabeth Akers Allen. SWaP

Along the river. At Nootka Sound. Susan Musgrave. BrAP

Along the River. Ad Zuiderent. ArBi, tr. by James S. Holmes

Along the river where fish with redpetal gills. End of Civilization as We Know It, The. Colleen J. McElroy. UrbNat

Along the river where the ice has melted and gone out. Spring's Path. Pak Chaesam. CAMKP, tr. by David R. McCann and Jiwon Shin

Along the road, the bright painted crosses. Ansel Talvikki. YaYoPo Fr. In Fragments, In Streams.

Along the roadside. Buson. SoOfWa, tr. by Sam Hamill

Along the roadside, like the flowers of gold. John Greenleaf Whittier. APN-1 Fr. Among the Hills.

Along the shore. Basho. EH, tr. by Robert Hass

Along the shore the tall, thin grass. In Memory of Colonel Charles Young. Countee Cullen. WaAnP

Along the side. Another Day. Belinda Zubicueta Carmona. TANSG, tr. by Celeste Kostopulos-Cooperman

Along the sprawled body of the derailed Great Northern freight car. James Wright. GM

Along the starlit Seine went music swelling. Pauline. Felicia Dorothea Hemans. RWP

Along the thread of veins. Rea Nikonova. CRWP, tr. by Gerald Janecek

Along the Tölös River. Song of the Tölös. Hulü Chin. ColAnChi, tr. by Victor H. Mair

Along this road where tiny frost-crabs edged. Vermont: Spring Rains. Edward Weismiller. YaYoPo

Along this spot where Jean Lafitte once paced. Galveston. Stanley E. Babb. TiP2

Along those roads we cannot hear him bark. (LL) Maltese Dog, A. Tymnes. Spl; WoPoe, tr. by Edmund Charles Blunden

Along thy dead indifference of walls. (LL) Berg, The. Herman Melville. ColAP; NCAP; NoP-4; NoP-5; PoPoPo; TCAPo

Along Without: A Fiction in Film for Poetry. Douglas Messerli.
  "NARRATOR: Suddenly someone wakes me. Still half-asleep, I see standing in front." FTOS

Along Yew's banks. Ru-fen: Along Yew's Banks. Unknown. CCL1, tr. by V. W. X.

Alongside the train I labor. Snow on a Southern State. James Dickey. LPSFW

Alongthehorizongrewanunbrokenlineoftrees. Landscape: 1. B. P. Nichol. OpeFie

Alonzo the Brave and the Fair Imogine. Matthew Gregory Lewis. NOBRP; NPBRoP

Aloof. Christina Georgina Rossetti. OBEV Fr. Thread of Life, The.

Aloof as aged kings. Day's Ending. Sara Teasdale. NAAPv.2

Aloof upon the day's immeasured dome. Black Vulture, The. George Sterling. APT-1; ASA; CalPo

(Aloof within the day's enormous dome.) TCAPo

Aloof within the day's enormous dome. George Sterling. See Aloof upon the day's immeasured dome.

Aloofe, aloofe, and come no neare. Sea Marke. John Smith. TCAPo

Alp at the end of the street, The. After a Phrase Abandoned by Wallace Stevens. Donald Justice. NAMCP V.2

Alpha. Melvin B. Tolson. APT-2 Fr. Harlem Gallery.

Alpha and Omega, God alone. Father, The. Joshua Sylvester. InvLi; SacPr

Alpha You, The. The omega You. I Am Like a Desert Owl, an Owl Among the Ruins. Noelle Kocot. LegDan

αιαι, ay, ay! . . . stutterer Demosthenes. Them & [uz]. Tony Harrison. NoP-4; NoP-5

Alphabet. Unknown. NAAPv.1

Alphabet Murders, The. John Tranter. BMAP Fr. Alphabet Murders, The.

Alphabet of Ahtt. Nathaniel Mackey. FTOS

Alphabet of, The. Botticellian Trees, The. William Carlos Williams. NAMCP V.1

Alphabet. Inger Christensen.
  "Apricot trees exist, apricot trees exist." WoBe, tr. by Susanna Nied
  9–10. PFTM-2, tr. by Pierre Joris

Alphabet Soup. Fatima Lim-Wilson. ReBoTo

Alphabet, The. Karl Shapiro. APT-2; EMP; NoAM; PoA 2002; TaR

Alphabet war-makers. Zangezi: R, K, L, G—. Velemir Khlebnikov. PFTM-1

Alphabet wonders, The.   Out of a Sudden.   Tom Raworth.   Oth
Alphabetical.   Patricia K. Page.
  "Curious concept—*afterwards*, A."   GPPA
Alphabetizer Speaks, The.   Patty Seyburn.   LegDan
Alphabets.   Seamus Heaney.   NAMCP V.2; NoAM
Alphonso of Castile.   Ralph Waldo Emerson.
  Efficiency.   STuOW
  Get-Together Song.   STuOW
Alpine is a fresh lust.   Alpine, Texas.   Thomas Whitbread.   TiP2
Alpine, Texas.   Thomas Whitbread.   TiP2
Already at a thousand feet.   Blackberries.   Maurina Sherman.   GeoHom
Already Embraced by the Arm of Heavenly Solace.   Nelly Sachs.   HP; PoSu,
  tr. by Michael Roloff
Already fallen plum-bloom stars the green.   Poor Man's Pig, The.   Edmund
  Charles Blunden.   MoBrPo
Already forfeit, now forever lost. (LL)   Dad.   Elaine Feinstein.   InoFa; Prnts
Already forgiving. (LL)   Letter: "Dear Antigone."   Leonard Nathan.   CalPo;
  PBCAP
Already her body is no more.   Breast.   Julia Copus.   PoCu
Already my temples are grey.   Anacreon.   SaLy, *tr. by* Diane Rayor
Already Night, Already Day.   Hedva Harechavi.   DTA, *tr. by* Miriyam Glazer
Already, no more suffering, no.   Svetlana Kekova.   CRWP, *tr. by* Ruth
  Fainlight
Already old, and still without a name.   Song of T'ung-ku.   Tu Fu [*or* Du Fu].
  CrYelRi, *tr. by* Sam Hamill
Already one day has detached itself from all the rest up ahead.   Reunion.
  Charles Wright.   CAP-8; OxBoAm
Already past mid-June.   Out of Work, Out of Touch, Out of Sorts.   Catherine
  Davis.   FFC
Already something of a stranger now.   Epil y Filiast.   Harri Webb.   AngWePo;
  TCAWP
Already subject to rebuke, instead.   Sonnet 20: Remembering, from a Nazi
  Prison, a Teacher Years Before.   William Pitt Root.   MiVo
Already the accursed rooster and his sad departure song.   *Unknown.*   SLW, *tr.*
  by Marjolijn De Jager, Sayd Bahodin Majrouh and André Velter
Already the air smells of snow, my beloved.   Already the Air Smells of Snow.
  Sarah Kirsch.   GTCP, *tr. by* Reinhold Grimm
Already the creamy Volkswagen rocks back.   American Roadside Elegy, An.
  Dave Jeddie Smith.   EmeKit
Already there was wanting to be simpler, wanting when they called you, never
  to go back. (LL)   Dress, The.   C. K. Williams.   BeAl; StAl
Already this tremor in my hands.   Black Irish Blues.   Joe-Anne McLaughlin-
  Carruth.   OPRER
Already to mine eyelids' shore.   Michael Field.   VWP
Already waiting. (LL)   You who want.   Hadewijch II.   HW; WPoS
Already you are moving down.   Ninth Month.   Victoria Redel.   BeAl
Already your flowering youth is gently evaporating.   To Il y a.   Hélène
  d'Oettingen.   CuPo
Als I me rode this endre day.   Singing Maid, The.   *Unknown.*   WaAnP
  (As I me rod this endre day.)   OHMEL
Alsatian.   George MacBeth.   EdScPo
Also I love him: me he's done no wrong.   John Berryman.   NAMCP V.2; NoP-
  4; NoP-5 *Fr.* Dream Songs.
Also Love You.   Reginald Shepherd.   IIR
Also survive its meanings, and my own. (LL)   After Greece.   James Merrill.
  BrAP; ColAP; TRP
Also ther was a disciple of Plato.   Geoffrey Chaucer.   SacPr *Fr.* Canterbury
  Tales, The.
Also Ulysses once—that other war.   Kilroy.   Peter Viereck.   MoAmPo;
  PWW2
Alstonefield V.   Peter Riley.
  "Another damp Sunday morning up and walk over."   Oth
Altamira: What She Remembered.   Linda Bierds.   AmAlph
Altar.   Marilyn Chin.   NAMCP V.2; PoPoPo
Altar, The.   George Herbert.   AngWePo; BASC; CABP; ChIV-1; NAEL-6v1;
  NAEL-7v1; NoP-4; NoP-5; NOSC; WaAnP
Altar boy marches up the altar steps, The.   Soldiers.   Padraic Fiacc.   PNI
Altar of glasses behind the bar, The.   Drinking Art, The.   Robert Minhinnick.
  AngWePo; TCAWP
Altar, 'tis of death, The! for there are laid.   Marriage Vow, The.   Letitia
  Elizabeth Landon.   VWP
Altazor.   Vincente Huidobro.   *tr. by* Rene de Costa, Stephen Fredman, Rigas
  Kappatos and Eleni Paidoussi
  Canto 2 (excerpts).   BLPSL, *tr. by* Rene de Costa, Rigas Kappatos and Eleni
    Paidoussi
  Canto I (excerpt).   PFTM-1
  "Here and now I have to dilute myself into many things."   TCLAP, *tr. by*
    Stephen Fredman
  "I am king."   TCLAP, *tr. by* Stephen Fredman

  "So you're a windmill."   TCLAP, *tr. by* Stephen Fredman
Altazor how did you lose your first serenity?   Vincente Huidobro.   PFTM-1 *Fr.*
  Altazor.
Alter! When the Hills do—.   Emily Dickinson.   SoSe-8; TCAPo
Altered look about the hills, An.   Emily Dickinson.   SoSe-8
Altermann, sipping wine, reads with a look.   Dom Moraes.   NoP-4; NoP-5 *Fr.*
  Two from Israel.
Alternately in Anecdotes go on.   "Peter Pindar."   OBCoV *Fr.* Bozzy and
  Piozzi.
Alternating tiles of white and black.   Archeology.   Yasser Abdullatif.   AnVo,
  tr. by Mohamed Enani
Alternative Endings to an Unwritten Ballad.   Paul Dehn.   OBCoV
Alternative to Speech, An.   David Lehman.   WaAnP
Altho' we mourn for one now gone.   Lisp in Numbers, A.   Edward Edwin
  Foot.   STuOW; VerBaPo
Although a temple.   Underneath Our Skirts.   Katie Donovan.   NeBl
Although art is autonomous.   On This Day I Complete My Fortieth Year.
  Peter Porter.   BMAP
Although art is, in the end, anonymous.   Having Completed My Fortieth Year.
  John Tranter.   BMAP
Although George Burroughs often used a knife.   George Burroughs.   Fred
  Cogswell.   Coast
Although, great Queen, thou now in silence lie.   In Honour of that High and
  Mighty Princess Queen Elizabeth of Happy Memory.   Anne Bradstreet.
  NAAL-5; NALW
Although he can not admit it even to himself.   Long Woman Bathing, The.
  Maurice Kilwein Guevara.   TouFir
Although hindsight accords a degree of humored.   Battle of Valcour Island,
  The.   Richard Kenney.   YaYoPo
Although I can see him still.   Fisherman, The.   William Butler Yeats.
  NAMCP V.1; NoAM
Although I do not / love flowers. (LL)   White Fish in Reeds.   Joseph Ceravolo.
  BodElec; NYP2
Although I mean it, and project the meaning.   Ice-Cream Wars, The.   John
  Ashbery.   PoA 2002
Although I put away his life.   Emily Dickinson.   MoAmPo
Although I shelter from the rain.   Lamentation of the Old Pensioner, The (1925
  version).   William Butler Yeats.   TRP; WeW-3
Although I try.   In the Autumn, on Retreat at a Mountain Temple.   Lady Izumi.
  WPoS
Although is is forever.   Hans Faverey.   WoBe *Fr.* Eighteen Poems.
Although it is a cold evening.   At the Fishhouses.   Elizabeth Bishop.
  AmFaPo; APT-2; BeAl; CAP-8; Coast; ItP; NAAL-5; NALW; NAMCP
  V.2; OxBoAm; PoetW; PoPoPo; VCAP
Although it is night, I sit in the bathroom, waiting.   Adolescence—2.   Rita
  Dove.   AmAlph; AWTN; ISC; NAAL-5; NAMCP V.2; NoAM; PoPoPo;
  VCAP
Although it is not yet evening.   Persistence of Song, The.   Howard Moss.
  GoPo; NoP-4; NoP-5
Although it never rivaled wheat, soybean.   Commercial Leech Farming Today.
  Thomas Lux.   BodElec
Although my feet.   Ono no Komachi.   ArkPo, *tr. by* Robert H. Brower and
  Earl Miner
Although my life, which thou hast scarred and shaken.   I Shall Forget.
  Laurence Hope.   OxBSo
Although only a fool would mock.   Queen Mother to New Queen.   Robert
  Graves.   OBSV
Although P'yŏngyang is my capital.   Song of P'yŏngyang without Refrain.
  Unknown.   CATKP, *tr. by* Peter H. Lee
Although she feeds me bread of bitterness.   America.   Claude McKay.
  NAAL-5; NAAPv.2; NAMCP V.1; NIL-7; NIP-4; NoAM; OxBoAm;
  PLBUT; WaAnP
Although she had lain. (LL)   Africa.   Maya Angelou.   NIL-7; NIP-4
Although some are afraid that to speak of a spade as a spade is a social mistake.
  Rigoletto.   Newman Levy.   AmWit
Although the aepyornis.   He "Digesteth Harde Yron."   Marianne Moore.
  APT-1; NAAPv.2; NAMCP V.1; NoAM; OWoS
Although the field lay cut in swaths.   Timothy.   Timothy Steele.   RA
Although the journey of the stars.   Tonight You Being From Me.   Aonghas
  MacNeacail.   EdScPo
Although the lamp was out, above its darkness.   Wedding Ring, The.   Zinaida
  Nikolayevna Gippius.   ARWW, *tr. by* Catriona Kelly
Although the paths lead into the forest, we are bitter with the bodies of days that
  end too early.   Karen Volkman.   IAoNAP
Although the Sky.   Elmaz Abinader.   PoArWo
Although the trumpet blew so loud. (LL)   Alfred Tennyson.   NAEL-6v2;
  NAEL-7v2 *Fr.* In Memoriam A. H. H.
Although the wind.   Lady Izumi.   WoPoe; WPoS, *tr. by* Mariko Aratani and
  Jane Hirshfield

Although their hair is turning gray. Meeting of Friends, A. Phillis Levin. RA

Although they may be. Dairy Cows of Maria Cristina Cortes. Sherod Santos. PfSP

Although you be, as I am, one of those. For Christopher Isherwood and Chester Kallman. W. H. Auden. SacPr

Although you have given me a stomach upset. Symptoms. Sophie Hannah. MFPA

Although you never asked to come with me. Peter Scupham. NewEx

Although you're far away. We'll Gather Lilacs. Ivor Novello. ReLy

Altitude. Stanley Plumly. OtW

Altocumulus. AC. Geraldine Monk. Oth

Altogether Singing. John Beecher. InGu

Altruism. Dionisio D. Martinez. TouFir

Aluminium shed the grab-hook. Impatient Man Kills with his Piano-playing, The. John Wilkinson. VaPo

Aluminum Oxide. Gu Cheng. WoBe *Fr.* Liquid Mercury.

Aluqa, the demon who swims underwater in streams. Meadow Bug. Rossana Ombres. NeIt

Alvargonzález, being single. House of Alvargonzález, The. Antonio Machado Ruiz. SpanPo, *tr. by* Denise Levertov

Alvin Cash/Keep on Dancin' [*to the children of intermediate school 55, ocean hill-brownsville*]. David Henderson. GT

Always. Guillaume Apollinaire. YaTCFP, *tr. by* Mary Ann Caws and Patricia Terry

Always. Brian Bartlett. Coast

Always. Irving Berlin. ReLy

Always. Roddy Lumsden. NeBrP

Always. Mark Strand. EmeKit; NoP-4; NoP-5; TRP

Always a nagging feeling, that I forgot something. When I look back a tnrasparent shadow chases me. Chasing Memory. Tripuraneni Srinivas. HotL, *tr. by* V. Narayana Rao

Always a third one's there. Uninvited, The. Dorothy Livesay. NoP-4

Always an angel rises from the figure. Masseuse, The. Olga Broumas. WiU

Always at dusk, the same tearless experience. Eyes of My Regret, The. Angelina Weld Grimké. IJHIL

Always at night I found them. Children of Saigon, The. Walter McDonald. AF

Always before your voice my soul. E. E. Cummings. MoAmPo

Always boys in my poems! Sandro Penna. CAGL, *tr. by* John McRae

Always evening. Always fall. Always, Not Always. Diana Fitzgerald Bryden. OpeFie

Always first to rise. In My Father's House. George Barlow. ESEAA; OxAAAP

Always for the First Time. André Breton. YaTCFP, *tr. by* Mary Ann Caws

Always for your never named sake. (LL) Lost baby poem, The. Lucille Clifton. AmFaPo; BeAl; CAP-8; ESEAA; InoFa; ISC; OxAAAP; WaAnP (My body breaking.) (LL) OxAAAP; WaAnP

Always Homing Now Soul Toward Light. Lorna Goodison. VCWP

Always homing now soul toward light. Always Homing Now Soul Toward Light. Lorna Goodison. VCWP

Always I am enjoying your company. (LL) Patriot, The. Nissim Ezekiel. EmeKit; FaBoVe

Always I have searched for the mislaid tin spoon. One Fine Day. János Pilinszky. PoSu, *tr. by* Peter Jay

Always I lay upon the brink of love. Judas. Vassar Miller. ChIV-2; MoAmPo

Always I thought they suffered, the way they huffed. On the Bearing of Waitresses. Rodney Jones. ReTh

Always in Anguish. Eli Alon. NRoS, *tr. by* Esther Raizen

Always in that clearing. Clearing, The. Richard Foerster. PoDa

Always, in the sun's eye. In India. Nissim Ezekiel. BrAP

Always, it shall be this way. Look to the Mountain. Simon J. Ortiz. PoCoUp

Always it's either. Al Young. OxAAAP *Fr.* Song Turning Back into Itself, The.

Always Know. Kalamu ya Salaam. SpirFl

Always, Not Always. Diana Fitzgerald Bryden. OpeFie

Always offshore, or already broken, gone. Wave. Mark Jarman. PfSP

Always on Monday, God's name is in the morning papers. Day After Sunday, The. Phyllis McGinley. AmWit; MoAmPo; OBSV

Always on the Train. Ruth Stone. TAPaP

Always passing bars has dulled. Panther, The. Rainer Maria Rilke. WoPoe, *tr. by* W. D. Snodgrass

Always pruning, always cropping? Matthew 9.12. Francis Quarles. ChIV-2

Always pyrotechnics. Leda 3. Lucille Clifton. NAMCP V.2

Always Returning: Holidays and Burials. Not Every Week. D. A. Powell. WiU

Always returning: holidays and burials. Not every week. Always Returning: Holidays and Burials. Not Every Week. D. A. Powell. WiU

Always Running. Luis J. Rodriguez. UnSA

Always Secondary. Deena November. IJHIL

Always so late in the day. Always. Mark Strand. EmeKit; NoP-4; NoP-5; TRP

Always that forgiving para- /noia. The Sisters of Charity. Radiance. Robert Patrick Dana. Vesp

Always the arriving winds of words. Words. William Robert Rodgers. PNI

Always the daughter. Ophelia. Elizabeth Burns. EdScPo

Always the Following Wind. W. H. Auden. MoBrPo

Always the same fine snow. Visitor, The. Anna Andreyevna Akhmatova. TCRusP, *tr. by* Daniel Weissbort

Always the same hills. Pietà. Ronald Stuart Thomas. NPeEn

Always the same, sweet hurt. Why Do So Few Blacks Study Creative Writing? Cornelius Eady. GT; LTA; OxAAAP

Always the same, when on a fated night. Onset, The. Robert Frost. APT-1; MoAmPo

Always the setting forth was the same. Odysseus. W. S. Merwin. NoP-4; NoP-5

Always the sound of choppers. Choppers. Dale Ritterbusch. AmWaPo

Always There Are the Children. Nikki Giovanni. WaAnP

Always think thinking inside myself no place. Music At The Heart Of Thinking 22. Fred Wah. OpeFie

Always this waking dream of palmtrees. Islands, The. Robert Earl Hayden. ESEAA

Always throughout his life. My Father's Irish Setters. James Merrill. StAl

Always Throw the First Punch. Miguel Algarin. PueRic

Always to be shrieked at people's estimation of undisturbed extinction. Loop, Fleck, Sound *and So On.* Marianne Vitale. HeMarv

Always to keep it in and never spare. Fear, A. Elizabeth Jennings. MoWP

Always to stand here by the old windows where she lay. Autumn Wind. Adriann Roland Holst. TuT, *tr. by* Desmond Egan

Always too eager for the future, we. Next, Please. Philip Larkin. CABP; GPTC; HarvBoo; MoBrPo

Always True to You in My Fashion. Cole Porter. ReLy "If a custom-tailored vet." NBLV

Always under your father's feet. Uascán. Ciaran Berry. PML

Always, / We hear at night approaching steps. Steps in the Night. Mahmoud Darwish. VCWP, *tr. by* Denys Johnson-Davies

Always / We'll go forward never getting anywhere. Always. Guillaume Apollinaire. YaTCFP, *tr. by* Mary Ann Caws and Patricia Terry

Always with love, with love. (LL) Letter, The. Elizabeth Riddell. LW; NOBAu

Alysoun. Geoffrey Chaucer. NPeEn *Fr.* Canterbury Tales, The.

Alzheimer's. Bob Hicok. AmPoNex; BeAl; P180; PoCu

Alzheimer's: The Wife. C. K. Williams. EMP; VCAP

A.M. Mark Strand. CAP-8

Am bodach-ròcais. Derick Thomson. EdScPo

Am, by being dead, immortal; Can ghosts die? (LL) Computation, The. John Donne. NoSic; SoSe-8

Am I. Lionel Fogarty. VaPo

Am I. Message Clear. Edwin Morgan. NePenScot

Am I a dead man? Am I a dead man? John Berryman Listening to Robert Johnson's "King of the Delta Blues," January 1972. David Wojahn. SeSe

Am I a french poet who writes poems twenty years too early? Carson Cistulli. FreRad *Fr.* Twenty-Six Friends, That's the Same as Your Age.

Am I a stone and not a sheep. Good Friday. Christina Georgina Rossetti. ChIV-2

Am I afraid of the tenth day? Kalyānkumār Mukhopādhyāy. SinGod, *tr. by* Rachel Fell McDermott

Am I alone. William Schwenck Gilbert. NAEL-6v2; NAEL-7v2; NBLV *Fr.* Patience.

Am I always to be a black man, the runaway slave. Douglass, a Last Letter. Tim Seibles. MAAN; RD

Am I Blue? Grant Clarke. ReLy

Am I mad, O noble Festus. Distracted Puritan, The. Richard Corbet. BASC; OBCoV

Am I really a sports fan, I ask myself. Boxing Match, The. David Ignatow. MoASP

Am I right to see myself introduced. Hand Further, The. Clark Coolidge. PmAP

Am I the Only One. Aydın HatipoĞlu. NaPG, *tr. by* Talat Sait Halman

Am I the same after we married as I was before? Inquisition, The: A Romance. Roger Weingarten. MAAN

Am I thirty two? That's nice. For My Birthday. Attila József. IQMS, *tr. by* Earl M. Herrick

Am I / this song. Lovers' Sestina, The. Bruce Meyer. IFF

Am I thus conquered [or conquer'd]? have I lost the powers. Mary Sidney Wroth, Countess of Montgomery. BASC; CABP; NAEL-6v1; NAEL-7v1; NOSC *Fr.* Pamphilia to Amphilanthus.

Am I thy gold? Or purse, Lord, for thy wealth. Edward Taylor. NOSC; TCAPo; WaAnP *Fr.* Preparatory Meditations Before My Approach to the Lord's Supper.

Am I to become profligate as if I were a blonde? Meditations in an Emergency. Frank O'Hara. PmAP; VCAP

Am I to go on. *Unknown.* ArkPo, *tr. by* Helen Craig McCullough

"Am I to lose you now?" The words were light. Am I to Lose You? Louisa Sarah Bevington. OxBSo

Am I your only love—in the whole world—now? Tell Me Again. Nigâr Hanim. ItWoWo; NaPG, *tr. by* Talat Sait Halman

Am lean against. Am Moor. Lucie Brock-Broido. AWPTFC

Am Moor. Lucie Brock-Broido. AWPTFC

A.M.: The Hopeful Monster. Alice Fulton. PfSP

Am, the world's my smilebutton. (LL) What the Motorcycle Said. Mona Van Duyn. NIL-7; NIP-4

Am we lonely these days. Am I. Lionel Fogarty. VaPo

Amadou. James E. Cherry. BRtP

Amadou Diallo. Psalm for Amadou Diallo. Jack Agüeros. PrTe

Amadou Diallo from Guinea to the Bronx Dead on Arrival. Carlos Raul Dufflar. BRtP

Amadou was always fascinated. Another Scream. Malkia M'Buzi Moore. BRtP

Amadu I live alone inside four walls of books. Letter to a Tormented Playwright. Syl Cheney-Coker. HBAPE

Amancer de Otoño. Antonio Machado Ruiz. RaW

Amanda. Lisa Glatt. AmPoNex

Amanda Barker. Edgar Lee Masters. APT-1; NAMCP V.1; NoAM; OxBoAm *Fr.* Spoon River Anthology.

Amanda, you'll be going. Thinking of Death and Dogfood. Maxine W. Kumin. ItP

Amanecer tiene, El. Aurora. Juan Ramón Jiménez. RaW

Amantium Irae. Richard Edwards. OBEV

Amantium irae amoris redintigratia est. Richard Edwards. OxBEV

Amanuensis. Mimi Khalvati. MoWP

Amarantha sweet and fair[e]. To Amarantha, That She Would Dishevel[l] Her Hair[e]. Richard Lovelace. CABP; CavPo; NIL-7; NoP-4; NoP-5; OBEV

Amaryllis. Ellen Bryant Voigt. AFaM

Amaryllis. Mark Wunderlich. LegDan; Vesp

Amaryllis Belladonna. Patricia Pogson. NLP

Amaryllis crowds its bowl with bulbs. (LL) Motion's Holdings. A. R. Ammons. NAMCP V.2; NoAM

Amateur Drummer. Roberta Gould. MiVo

Amateur God, The. Sean O'Brien. NeBrP

Amateur Night. Natasha Trethewey. OxAAAP

Amateurs of Heaven, The. Howard Nemerov. SoSe-8

Amaze. Adelaide Crapsey. APT-1; NAAPv.2; OxBoAm

Amazed, amazed, amazed, amazed, amazed. (LL) Rhyme for a Child Viewing a Naked Venus in a Painting [of "The Judgement of Paris"]. Robert Browning. NPeEn; OBCoV

Amazed by Chekhov. David Kirby. SUP

Amazing ability to forget, The. (LL) Roots. Bill Berkson. AHA; NYP2

Amazing Grace. John Newton. SacPr

Amazing Grace. Edward Smallfield. ASA

Amazing Grace in the Back Country. Robert Penn Warren. ColAP

Amazing, how the young man who empties. Wing Road. Eamon Grennan. PBCIP

Amazing monster! that, for aught I know. Leigh Hunt. NBLV; NPeEn *Fr.* Fish, the Man, and the Spirit, The.

Amazing to believe that nothingness. Mark Jarman. PoDa *Fr.* Unholy Sonnets.

Amazon Club. Kenward Elmslie. PmAP

Amazon Twins. Olga Broumas. FiBr

Amazone. Mary Jo Bona. UnSA

Ambassador Puser the ambassador. Memorial Rain. Archibald MacLeish. AmWaPo; MoAmPo; OBWP

Ambassador, The. Pablo Neruda. TAPaP, *tr. by* William O'Daly

Amber husk / fluted with gold. Sea Poppies. "H. D." APT-1; NALW

Ambiguity. Sir John Harington. DiBP *Fr.* Epigrams.

Ambiguity, an unsolved murder case from a hot August day in 1892. Sleeping Soundly Where Lizzie Borden Did. Vivian Shipley. LiTh

Ambition. Bruce Berger. GeoH

Ambition. W. H. Davies. MoBrPo

Ambition. Maggie Pogue Johnson. CBWP-4

Ambition. Henrietta Cordelia Ray. CBWP-3

Ambition—following down this far famed slope. William Wordsworth. OxBSo *Fr.* Memorials of a Tour of the Continent; 1820.

Ambition is that amber heron stretching its legs. January, Love, and the Galician. Jay Wright. ICANM

Ambition, The. Robert Harris. BMAP

Ambitious Ant, The. Amos Russel Wells. OBSP

Ambitious ant would a-travelling go, The. Ambitious Ant, The. Amos Russel Wells. OBSP

Ambivalent Nature of Healing, The. Ted Sexauer. WhBo

Amble. Maxine Chernoff. PmAP *Fr.* Japan.

Ambling across aeons to my backyard. Armadillo. Martin Staples Shockley. TiP2

Ambling within beech tree bouqet. Terrors of the In-Between. Paul Skyrm. AmZen

Amboyna; or, The Cruelties of the Dutch to the English Merchants. John Dryden.

   Prologue from Amboyna. OBSV

Ambrosia. Dorothy Marie Rice. FuFl

Ambulance men touched her cold, The. Death of Marilyn Monroe, The. Sharon Olds. HeIP-4; InoFa; ReTh

Ambulance stood in the bay downstairs, The. (LL) Twelfth Floor West. Marilyn Hacker. ExTi; NAMCP V.2

Ambulances. Philip Larkin. BrAP; NAEL-6v2; NAEL-7v2; NoP-4; NoP-5

Ambush. Yusef Komunyakaa. RoV

Amelia was just fourteen and out of the orphan asylum; at her first job—in the bindery, and yes sir, yes ma'am, oh, so anxious to please. Charles Reznikoff. ColAP; NAAPv.2 *Fr.* Testimony.

Amen. "H. D." WPoS *Fr.* Walls Do Not Fall, The.

Amen. Alvaro Mutis. TCLAP, *tr. by* Sophie Cabot Black and Maria Negroni

Amen. Jacques Réda. YaTCFP, *tr. by* Stephen Romer

Amen. Jacques Réda. YaTCFP

Amen. Christina Georgina Rossetti. WPoS

Amen, Amen, Amen. (LL) "H. D." APT-1; NAAL-5 *Fr.* Walls Do Not Fall, The.

Amen. The casket like a spaceship bears her. Annie Hill's Grave. James Merrill. WeW-3

Amen, who scared off my girl. (LL) Rattle Bag, The. Dafydd ap Gwilym. NBLV; WoPoe, *tr. by* Joseph P. Clancy

Amendis [or Amends] to the Telyouris [or Tailors] and Sowtaris [or Soutaris or Soutars or Shoemakers]. William Dunbar. OBSV

Amendment. Thomas Traherne. InvLi

Amends. Adrienne Rich. HarvBoo *Fr.* Not Somewhere Else, But Here.

Amergin. Susan Langstaff Mitchell. IrV

America. Kofi Awoonor. HBAPE

America. Lucretia Davidson. ColAP

America. Henry Dumas. ChAP; OxAAAP

America. Tony Hoagland. FaoP; StAl

America. Herman Melville. APN-2

America. Samuel Francis Smith. TCAPo

America. Stephen Sondheim. ReLy

America. Berysh Vaynshteyn. Prolet

   "But when one stops to think back a moment." Prolet, *tr. by* Amelia Glaser

America. Phillis Wheatley. TCAPo

America. James M. Whitfield. APN-2

America. Walt Whitman. FaBoA

America . . . then. *Unknown.* NAAPv.2

America: A Prophecy. William Blake.

   "Morning comes, the night decays, the watchmen leave their stations, The." NAEL-7v2

America: "Although she feeds me bread of bitterness." Claude McKay. NAAL-5; NAAPv.2; NAMCP V.1; NIL-7; NIP-4; NoAM; OxBoAm; PLBUT; WaAnP

America, America. Sa'di Yusuf. *tr. by* Khaled Mattawa

   "I too love jeans and jazz and *Treasure Island.*" PoAgWa; PoCho, *tr. by* Khaled Mattawa

America: "America I've given you all and now I'm nothing." Allen Ginsberg. CAP-8; MakPoe; NAMCP V.2; NoAM; OxBoAm; PFTM-2; PmAP; PoPoPo; TRP; WaAnP

America: "As for me, when I saw you." Bernadette Mayer. NYP2

America Eats Its Young. Jemeni. BRtP

America for Me. Henry Van Dyke. ChAP

America has a climate. Sound Check. Ted Pearson. Eno

America, I Do Not Call Your Name Without Hope. Pablo Neruda. AF; TCLAP, *tr. by* Robert Bly

America I'm putting my queer shoulder to the wheel. (LL) America: "America I've given you all and now I'm nothing." Allen Ginsberg. CAP-8; MakPoe; NAMCP V.2; NoAM; OxBoAm; PFTM-2; PmAP; PoPoPo; TRP; WaAnP

America in 1918. John Reed.
  "I have watched the summer day come up from the top of a pier of the
  Williamsburgh Bridge." APT-1; FTtHH
America Is Hard to See. Robert Frost. FaBoA
America, it is to thee. America. James M. Whitfield. APN-2
America I've given you all and now I'm nothing. America. Allen Ginsberg.
  CAP-8; MakPoe; NAMCP V.2; NoAM; OxBoAm; PFTM-2; PmAP;
  PoPoPo; TRP; WaAnP
America: "Please don't ask me, America." Dunya Mikhail. IrPoTo; WoBe, tr.
  by Liz Winslow
America that was supposed to be, The. (LL) Indian Movie, New Jersey.
  Chitra Divakaruni. NIL-7; UnSA
America the Beautiful. Katharine Lee Bates. APN-2; BLPJKO; FaBoA;
  HHAm; OxBoAm
America / The tongues of your rivers burn with thirst. Lackawanna Elegy.
  Iwan Goll. AF, tr. by Galway Kinnell
America to Great Britain. Washington Allston. APN-1
America, tom sawyer, is bigger. Water USA. Clarence Major. EGAG
America, you are luckier. United States, The. Johann Wolfgang von Goethe.
  FaBoA, tr. by Robert Bly
America, you ode for reality! America. Robert Creeley. MakPoe; UnSA;
  WaAnP
American Airlines to Chicago. Funeral. Clarence Major. BodElec
American, An. Rudyard Kipling. FaBoA
American Apocalypse. Edward Hirsch. IllVoic
American Avalon. Connie Deanovich. AmPoNex
American Bandstand. Michael Waters. SwNoth
American Beauty, An. Carolyn Kizer. GeoHom
American Century, The. Kenneth Rexroth. PoChi
American Cheese. G. E. Murray. IllVoic
American Classic. Louis Simpson. StAl
American culture is the pot. Ed Roberson. EGAG
American Dream, An. Mary Ruefle. AmAlph
American Dream: First Report. Joseph Papaleo. UnSA
American Dreams. "Sapphire." AfrBLW
American Exercises. Patricia Goedicke. RWB
American Express. Ted Berrigan. NYP2
American Flag. Jack Anderson. AHA
American Flag, The. Joseph Rodman Drake. APN-1; BRP
American Football (A Reflection upon the Gulf War). Harold Pinter. PoAgWa
American Forest Girl, The. Felicia Dorothea Hemans. RWP
American Gothic. Samuel Allen. See To Satch.
American Heartbreak. Langston Hughes. APT-2
American Heaven. Paul Hoover. Vesp
American hero must triumph over, The. Eisenhower's Visit to Franco, 1959.
  James Wright. PoAgWa
American History. Michael S. Harper. ESEAA; NAAL-5; NAMCP V.2;
  NoAM; PoPoPo
American History in Context. Antler. WhBo
American Indian Art: Form and Tradition. Diane Di Prima. BB
American Indian, The. Unknown. NBLV
[American Journal]. Robert Earl Hayden. ESEAA; ISC
American Lights, Seen from Off Abroad. John Berryman. OBCoV
American Literature. Lisel Mueller. PoSol
American Lit. is beside you. Studying. Primus St. John. EGAG
American Living Room, The: A Tract. William Meredith. BodElec
American Manhood. Robert Wrigley. PoDa
American Memory of Africa, An. Kofi Awoonor. HBAPE
American muse, whose strong and diverse heart. Stephen Vincent Benét.
  APT-2 Fr. John Brown's Body.
American Names. Stephen Vincent Benét. APT-2; FaBoA; OxBoAm
American Odalisque. Jane Miller. GifTon
American Peace, An. Peter Oresick.
  "In this third year of Reagan, my 27th year." AtGh
American Poem, An. Eileen Myles. WiU
American Poetry. Ras Baraka. BRtP
American Poetry. Louis Simpson. FaBoA; NAMCP V.2; NoAM; WaAnP
American Pragmatist Fell in Love, The. Tom Devaney. AmPoNex
American Pragmatist fell in love, the. American Pragmatist Fell in Love, The.
  Tom Devaney. AmPoNex
American Primitive. William Jay Smith. MoAmPo; RaBo
American Pylons. Kevin Durkin. PoDa
American Rain. Marilyn Chin. OpBo
American Rhapsody. Kenneth Fearing. APT-2; MoAmPo
American River Sky Alcohol Father. Jean Valentine. CAP-8; ExTi; LaCa
American Roadside Elegy, An. Dave Jeddie Smith. EmeKit

American Sketches (for William Carlos Williams). Donald Justice. StAl
  Crossing Kansas by Train. StAl
  Poem To Be Read at 3 a.m.. GoPo; StAl
American Smooth. Rita Dove. CAP-8
American Soldier, The. Philip Freneau. AmWaPo
American Solitude. Grace Schulman. PoSol
American Son. Mitsuye Yamada. UnSA
American Sonnet (10). Wanda Coleman. WaAnP
American Sonnet (46). Wanda Coleman. BtF
American Sonnets for My Father. Daniela Gioseffi. UnSA
American Spring Song. Sherwood Anderson. APT-1
American Standard. David Baratier. AmPoNex
American Sublime, The. Wallace Stevens. FaBoA; OxBoAm
American Tradition. William Wordsworth. CenSon Fr. River Duddon [A
  Series of Sonnets], The.
American Tragedy. Joe Bolton. AmPoNex
American Trains. Reginald Gibbons. GM
American Variation on How Rilke Loved a Princess and Got to Stay in Her
  Castle. Alan Dugan. BodElec
American who would have preferred / to be merely an Indian. (LL) Mr.
  Brodsky. Charles Tomlinson. NAMCP V.2; NoAM; NoP-4; NoP-5
Americana. Paisley Rekdal. RWB
Americana. Sam Witt. NeAmPo
Americana 3. Carl Rakosi. APT-2
American's Apostrophe to Boz, The. William Edmonstoune Aytoun.
  "We received thee warmly—kindly—though we knew thou wert a quiz."
  OBCoV
Americans in 1933–4–5–6–7–8–, Etc. Merrill Moore. FaBoA
America's still eating its young. America Eats Its Young. Jemeni. BRtP
America™. Forrest Cole. RWB
Amerigo has his finger on the pulse of China. Composed Near the Bay Bridge
  (after a wild party). Marilyn Chin. ExTi
Amethyst. Vibora breve. Alfonso D'Aquino. RMCMP
Amethyst. Brief Viper. Alfonso D'Aquino. RMCMP, tr. by Rebecca Seiferle
Amherst never had a witch. On a Theme by Frost. Robert Francis. VisFro
Amhrán na mBréag. Pearse Hutchinson. PBCIP
Ami sans coeur ou théâtre, L'. Pièce à grand spectacle. Louis Aragon.
  YaTCFP
Amid a jumble of. Masaoka Shiki. CAoMJL1, tr. by Burton Watson
Amid dancing and. Kalamu ya Salaam. SpirFl Fr. New Orleans Haiku.
Amid the holy weather of winter, one speaks. Snow. George Dillon. IllVoic
Amid the hush of the distant hills which house. Gettysburg. Edgar Lee
  Masters. CBCWP
Amid the iris and the rose. Much in Little. Yvor Winters. OxBoAm
Amid the medley of ironic things. Cage, The. Rosamund Marriott Watson.
  VWP
Amid the turbulent waters. Turbulent Water, The. Unknown. TAL
Amid these clear and windy hills. In Praise of California Wines. Yvor
  Winters. APT-2
Amid these fragments of heroic days. Sonnet. James Russell Lowell. NCAP
Amid this hot green glowing gloom. Interlude. Dame Edith Sitwell.
  MoBrPo
Amid white plum blossoms. Buson. EMJL, tr. by Haruo Shirane
Amidst high weeds that in rank plenty grew. (LL) Philip Freneau. NAAL-3;
  TCAPo Fr. House of Night, The.
Amidst our troubles, a sudden blessing. Ghazal: Comet. Jacqueline Osherow.
  ExTi
Amidst the too much that we buy and throw. Bear at the Dump, The. William
  Matthews. PfSP
Amiel's Leg. Thomas Lux. LaCa
Amiens' Song. William Shakespeare. NoSic; OBEV Fr. As You Like It.
Aminta. Torquato Tasso. tr. by Aphra Behn, Samuel Daniel and Leigh Hunt
  Golden Age, The. OBVE, tr. by Leigh Hunt
  Golden Age, The. A Paraphrase on a Translation out of French. BASC, tr.
  by Aphra Behn
Amish Rug, An. Michael Longley. PNI
Amiti´ Amoureuse. Gregorio Scalise. ItPo, tr. by Gayle Ridinger
Ammo. Liz Ahl. LiTh
Amnesty. Ivan Venediktovich Elagin. TCRusP, tr. by Bertram D. Wolfe
Amo, Amas, I Love a Lass. John O'Keefe. IrLP
Among. William Carlos Williams. See Among / of / green.
Among a race high-handed, strong of heart. Non-Combatant, The. Sir Henry
  John Newbolt. FaBoWar
Among all the things of which there are none. All the things of which there are
  none. Lloyd Addison. EGAG
Among bitterns one is blind. 2 Blinds & a Bittern. Michele Glazer. IAoNAP
Among black trees. Olga Popova. ItGoST, tr. by J. Kates

Among Goldfinches. Bill Morgan. ArBi

Among green shades and flowering ghosts, the remembrances of love. Two Fires, The. Judith Wright. MoBrPo

Among His Books. Robert Southey. OxAEP-2

Among mechanics. (LL) No Interval of Manner. George Oppen. APT-2; HarvBoo; PFTM-1

Among moon gazers. Basho. SoOfWa, tr. by Sam Hamill

Among mortal petals-and-leaves / light. (LL) Iris. Muriel Rukeyser. APSN; ColAP

Among mosquitoes. Mary Kinzie. FFC

Among My Friends. Robert Duncan. CLPP; HarvBoo

Among my friends love is a great sorrow. Among My Friends. Robert Duncan. CLPP; HarvBoo

Among my people. (LL) Prologue: "I have come down." Odia Ofeimun. HBAPE; NAfrP

Among My Souvenirs. Edgar Leslie. ReLy

Among Myths and Specters of the Future. Gabriella Leto. CItWP, tr. by Cinzia Sartini Blum and Lara Trubowitz

Among / of / green. Locust Tree in Flower, The. William Carlos Williams. NAAPv.2; OxBoAm; Spl

(Among.) PFTM-1

Among pelagian travelers. W. H. Auden. FaBoA

Among Philistines. R. S. Gwynn. RA

Among rocks and valleys. Muso Soseki. EaWin, tr. by W. S. Merwin

Among Royalists: Blois, Spring 1792. William Wordsworth. NPBRoP Fr. Prelude, The; Growth of a Poet's Mind [1805 version].

Among Saga's / Tall weeds. Masaoka Shiki. ZenPo, tr. by Takashi Ikemoto and Lucien Stryk

Among School Children. William Butler Yeats. BrAP; CABP; HarvBoo; MoBrPo; NAEL-6v2; NAEL-7v2; NAMCP V.1; NAWM-7v2; NIL-7; NIP-4; NoAM; NoP-4; NoP-5; NPeEn; OxBEV; PoPoPo; TFi; TRP; WaAnP

Among some hills there dwelt in parody. Song of Absinthe Granny, The. Ruth Stone. NALW

Among squat toad-leaves sprinkling the unborn / Erechtheion marbles. (LL) Sicilian Cyclamens. D. H. Lawrence. NAMCP V.1; NoAM

Among Strangers. Silvia Curbelo. OPRER

Among streetlights and unsuccessful neon. (LL) Poetics. August Kleinzahler. PmAP; WaAnP

Among that band of officers was one. William Wordsworth. NPBRoP Fr. Prelude, The; Growth of a Poet's Mind [1805 version].

Among the ancient tombs both high and low. On an Ancient Tomb East of the Village. Po Chü-i. TAL

Among the Berkshire Hills. Henrietta Cordelia Ray. CBWP-3

Among the blight-killed eucalypts, among. In California During the Gulf War. Denise Levertov. PrTe

Among the bumblebees in red-top hay, a freckled field of brown-eyed. Adelaide Crapsey. Carl Sandburg. APT-1

Among the clamor the single shout. Song. Blanca Wiethüchter. TANSG, tr. by Shaun Griffin and Emma Sepúlveda-Pulvirenti

Among the crevices of the rocks. (LL) Mid-day. "H. D." APT-1; NAAL-5; NAAPv.2; NAMCP V.1

Among the crooked lanes, on every hedge. James Thomson. NPeEn Fr. Seasons, The.

Among the deepening shades. (LL) Tower, The. William Butler Yeats. NAMCP V.1; NoAM

Among the favorites whom it pleased me well. William Wordsworth. NAEL-6v2; NAEL-7v2 Fr. Prelude, The; Growth of a Poet's Mind [1850 version].

Among the first to go are always a few. Only the Beards Are Different. Bruce Dawe. RSR

Among the first to wake. What wakes with me? Study, A. Alice Thompson Meynell. VWP

Among the friends my mother found it mete. Keeping. Richard Howard. MAAN

Among the grains how small you were. Anasphere: Le torse antique. Christopher Middleton. HarvBoo

Among the halleluyas of the triumphant dead? (LL) U. A. Fanthorpe. MoWP; Prnts Fr. Stations Underground.

Among the heaps of brick and plaster lies. Charles Reznikoff. APT-2

Among the Hebrides. Emily Jane Pfeiffer. ViWPN

Among the Hills. John Greenleaf Whittier.

Prelude. APN-1; NAAL-3

Among the iodoform, in twilight-sleep. Leg, The. Karl Shapiro. MoAmPo; WeW-3

Among the later dinosaurs. Pachycephalosaurus. Richard Armour. ChAP

Among the leaves the small birds sing. W. H. Auden. BBASP Fr. Horae Canonicae.

Among the Luminals. Walter Lowenfels. APT-2 Fr. Elegy in the Manner of a Requiem in Memory of D.H. Lawrence.

Among the men and women the multitude. Among the Multitude. Walt Whitman. APN-1; CAGL

Among the men some carved-bone dice are thrown. Mara Malanova. CRWP, tr. by Nika Skandiaka

Among the Missing. Richard Howard. OxBoAm

Among the Multitude. Walt Whitman. APN-1; CAGL

Among the oxen (like an ox I'm slow). Nativity, The. Clive Staples Lewis. ChIV-2

Among the pickled foetuses and bottled bones. Ezra Pound. MoAmPo; NAAPv.2 Fr. Hugh Selwyn Mauberley (Life and Contacts).

Among the pitiful dicotyledons. Ants, The. Svetlana Kekova. ItGoST, tr. by Judith Hemschemeyer

Among the primary rocks. Forest, The. Miroslav Holub. PoSu, tr. by George Theiner

Among the rain. Great Figure, The. William Carlos Williams. HeIP-4; NAAPv.2; NAMCP V.1; NoAM; SAmP

Among the Red Guns. Carl Sandburg. NAAPv.2

Among the red words that drink his voice. (LL) Yuba City School. Chitra Divakaruni. GeoHom; LTA; OpBo

Among the rocks. At the Cemetery, Walnut Grove Plantation, South Carolina, 1989. Lucille Clifton. CAP-8; LoL; NAMCP V.2

Among the shades I heard my father's father. Horace Gregory. APT-2 Fr. Chorus for Survival.

Among the smoke and fog [or fog and smoke] of a December afternoon. Portrait of a Lady. T. S. Eliot. APT-1; OxBoAm

Among the splendour of torches of darkness, shedding darkness on the lost bride and her groom. (LL) Bavarian Gentians. D. H. Lawrence. BrAP; CABP; HarvBoo; NAEL-6v2; NAEL-7v2; NAMCP V.1; NoAM; NoP-4; NoP-5; NPeEn; OxBEV; PoPoPo; TFi; TRP; WaAnP

Among the Springs which flow from Ida's Head. Unknown. OBVE Fr. Homeric Hymns.

Among the swells, the storm past, surfers sit. At Will Robers Beach. Timothy Steele. WeW-3

Among the tall reeds I am hiding. I Want the Words Back. Margaret Randall. FiBr

Among the Vertues Intellectual. Lady Diana Primrose. EMWP Fr. Chain of Pearl, A.

Among the yeomen's sons on my estate. Unknown. CAGL Fr. Don Leon.

Among them too are the Muses. Pindar. WoPoe Fr. Pythian Odes.

Among these arthritic contours. Cae Iago: May Day. Roland Mathias. TCAWP

Among these summer trees. Hut of the Phantom Dwelling, The. Basho. EMJL, tr. by Burton Watson

Among Those Killed in the Dawn Raid Was a Man Aged a Hundred. Dylan Thomas. OxBSo

Among tired men. Urban. Oliver Davies. AngWePo

Among twenty snowy mountains. Thirteen Ways of Looking at a Blackbird. Wallace Stevens. APT-1; BrAP; ChAP; ColAP; HeIP-4; NAAL-5; NAAPv.2; NAMCP V.1; NoAM; NoP-4; NoP-5; OWoS; OxBoAm; PoPoPo; PtR; SAmP; TCAPo; TFi

Among us are those who apply. Kiss Tomorrow Goodbye. Marjorie Welish. FTOS

Amongest many kings. Desire of Dominion. Timothy Kendall. NoSic

Amongst the highly placed. From a German War Primer. Bertolt Brecht. AF

Amongst the poets Dacus numbered is. Sir John Davies. NoSic Fr. Epigrams.

Amongst these graves where good men lie. In an Irish Churchyard. Violet Fane. VWP

Amor America (1400). Pablo Neruda. PoetW, tr. by Jack Schmitt

Amor Diving. Marion Lomax. NeBl

Amor, El. Seis variaciones acerca del amor. Víctor Terán. RMCMP

Amor fati / The love of fate. George Oppen. NAMCP V.1 Fr. Of Being Numerous.

Amor Mundi. Christina Georgina Rossetti. NoP-4; NoP-5; PEW; RACG

Amor Te Convierte, El. Gloria Fuertes. RaW

Amor te convierte en rosal, El. Amor Te Convierte, El. Gloria Fuertes. RaW

Amor Vincit Omnia. Edgar Bowers. VCAP

Amores. Ovid. tr. by Derek Mahon, Kenneth McLeish and Frederick Adam Wright

Ovid in Love. WoPoe, tr. by Derek Mahon

"She'd looks, she'd style." EroLit, tr. by Kenneth McLeish

Amores (after Ovid). Ovid. WaAnP

Amoret. Mark Akenside. OBEV

Amoretti. Edmund Spenser.

(Easter.) OBEV

("Fair is my love, when her fair golden hairs.") GSo

(Happy ye leaves! whenas those lily hands.) GSo

(Most glorious Lord of life, that on this day.) GSo

(One Day I Wrote Her Name Upon the Strand.) GSo

Sonnet 4. NoSic

Sonnet 8.　NoP-5; OxBSo

Sonnet 15.　HeIP-4; NIP-4; NoP-5

Sonnet 22.　WaAnP

Sonnet 26.　ItP

Sonnet 37.　BrAP; NAEL-6v1; NoP-4

Sonnet 54.　CABP; NAEL-7v1; NoP-4; NoP-5

Sonnet 61.　SacPr

Sonnet 64.　NAEL-6v1; OxBSo

Sonnet 65.　NAEL-6v1; NAEL-7v1

Sonnet 67.　HeIP-4; NoP-5

Sonnet 68.　ChIV-2; NoSic; SacPr; WaAnP

Sonnet 70.　NoP-5; OBEV

Sonnet 71.　NoP-4; NoP-5; PBRV; WaAnP

Sonnet 75.　BrAP; CABP; HeIP-4; NAEL-6v1; NAEL-7v1; NoP-4; NoP-5; NoSic; OxBSo; PoPoPo; TFi; WaAnP; WeW-3

Sonnet 77.　NIP-4; OxBSo

Sonnet 76.　NIP-4

Sonnet 78.　NoSic

Sonnet 79.　NoP-4; NoP-5

Sonnet 81.　NoP-5

Sonnet 82.　HeIP-4

Sonnet 23.　NoP-5

Sonnet 57.　OxBSo

(Sonnet 68: 'Most glorious Lord of Life'.)　AEP

Sonnet 80.　CABP

(Sonnet 65: 'The doubt which ye misdeem'.)　AEP

(Sonnet 10: 'Unrighteous Lord of Love'.)　AEP

(Sonnet 3: 'The sovereign beauty'.)　AEP

Amoroso.　Alfonso D'Aquino.　RMCMP

Amorous.　Alfonso D'Aquino.　RMCMP, tr. by Rebecca Seiferle

Amorous Leander, beautiful and young.　Christopher Marlowe.　CAGL Fr. Hero and Leander.

Amorous Neptune.　Christopher Marlowe.　WaAnP Fr. Hero and Leander.

Amorous Sonnet Defining Love.　Francisco de Quevedo y Villegas.　BLPSL, tr. by Rene de Costa, Rigas Kappatos and Eleni Paidoussi

Amour, L' / le bauch.　Chanson.　Ernst Jandl.　OnScMo; PFTM-2

Amour sans trêve, L'.　Antonin Artaud.　YaTCFP

Amour, Th'. (LL)　Chanson.　Ernst Jandl.　OnScMo; PFTM-2

Amoureuse, L'.　Paul Éluard.　YaTCFP

Amours de Voyage.　Arthur Hugh Clough.

　Claude to Eustace.　FaBoVe; NPeEn

　Claude to Eustace.　FaBoVe

　Claude to Eustace.　NPeEn; OxAEP-2

　Claude to Eustace—from Bellagio.　FaBoVe

　"Dear Eustatio, I write that you may write me an answer."　FaBoVe; NoP-5; OxAEP-2

　"Dulce it is, and decorum, no doubt, for the country to fall, to."　FaBoWar; OxAEP-2; PoAgWa; WaAnP

　Georgina Trevellyn to Luisa (At last, dearest Louisa . . .).　NoP-5

　Georgina Trevellyn to Luisa (Dearest Louisa, enquire . . .).　FaBoVe

　"It is most curious to see what a power a few calm words."　NPeEn

　"Luther, they say, was unwise; he didn't see how things were going."　FaBoVe

　Mary Trevellyn to Miss Roper.　FaBoVe

　"Only think, dearest Louisa, what fearful scenes we have witnessed!"　NPeEn

　"Over the great windy waters, and over the clear crested summits."　NoP-5

　Rome.　OxAEP-2

　"So, I have seen a man killed!"　NPeEn

　Spirit from Perfecter Ages.　OxAEP-2

　"When God makes a great Man he intends all others to crush him."　OBSV

Amparo.　Rafael Alberti.　RaW, tr. by Rachel Benson

Amparo.　Federico García Lorca.　SpanPo, tr. by Rachel Benson and Robert O'Brien

Amparo.　Amparo.　Federico García Lorca.　SpanPo, tr. by Rachel Benson and Robert O'Brien

Amparo. / I came to your sea of wheat and horses.　Amparo.　Rafael Alberti.　RaW, tr. by Rachel Benson

Amparo. / Vine a tu mar de trigos y caballos.　Amparo.　Rafael Alberti.　RaW

Ampersonata.　Andrew Zawacki.　IAoNAP

Amphibians.　Robert Fitzgerald.　PWW2

Amphibious Crocodile.　John Crowe Ransom.　FuPo

Amphitheatre, my scene, The.　Martial.　DiBP tr. by James Elphinston Fr. Epigrams.

Amphitryon.　John Dryden.

　(Mercury's Song [to Phaedra].)　NOSC

Ample make this Bed.　Emily Dickinson.　ItP; MoAmPo; NAAL-3; WoPoe

Amplified Dog.　Charles Harper Webb.　SUP

Amputated husband, The.　Downtown Sunday.　Robert Crawford.　OPRER

Amra: The Neuropharmacology of Nirvana.　Dale Pendell.　WANABP

Amsterdam Chronicle.　Rein Bloem.　TuT, tr. by John Hughes

Amsterdam Letter.　Jean Garrigue.　VCAP

Am/Trak.　Imamu Amiri Baraka.　PmAP

Amulet.　Ted Hughes.　NOxBChV

Amulet.　Carl Rakosi.　APT-2

Amusedly, among the ancient Dead. (LL)　Sonnet: "Oh! Death will find me, long before I tire."　Rupert Brooke.　NoP-4; NoP-5

Amusements.　George Crabbe.　Fr. Borough, The.

Amusing Our Daughters.　Carolyn Kizer.　VCAP

Amy was crooning and Linda was swooning the night I brought them here.　Postcard from Robert Frost's Grave.　Wyn Cooper.　VisFro

Amyd the wod his modir met thame tway.　Virgil.　OBVE Fr. Aeneid [or Eneados or Aeneis], The.

Amyir gaffirz Gaffir. Hark.　Feed Ma Lamz.　Tom Leonard.　EdScPo

Amyntor.　Antipater of Sidon.　PoCho, tr. by Burton Raffel

Amyntor, Philip's son, lies in this Lydian soil.　Amyntor.　Antipater of Sidon. PoCho, tr. by Burton Raffel

An 1905 Pablo, L'.　Étreinte, L'.　Louis Aragon.　YaTCFP

An dàrna eilean.　Derick Thomson.　EdScPo

An' fare 'ave yer bin to? A'n phat is it, Terrence?　Boycycle, The.　S. Conant Foster.　ArBi

An' him chucks on some riddim.　Riddim an' Hardtimes.　Lillian Allen. WaCA

An neuf.　Aimé Césaire.　YaTCFP

An nou ye staun transmogrified.　Cleikit.　David Purves.　EdScPo

An oidhch' ud,.　Am bodach-ròcais.　Derick Thomson.　EdScPo

An' so ole Tho'nton bounced you.　Turncoat, The.　Priscilla Jane Thompson. CBWP-2

An' thank en, I do veel a little shy. (LL)　False Friends-like.　William Barnes. NPeEn; OxBSo

An' the Crucified maun bleed. (LL)　Innumerable Christ, The.　Hugh MacDiarmid.　HarvBoo; OxAEP-2

An' the dawn comes up like thunder outer China 'crost the Bay! (LL) Mandalay.　Rudyard Kipling.　BRP; HarvBoo; MoBrPo; NPeEn; OxAEP-2

An' then she made the lasses, O. (LL)　Green Grow the Rashes [A Fragment]. Robert Burns.　NAEL-6v2; NAEL-7v2; NoP-4; NoP-5; OxAEP-2

An' there's no discharge in the war! (LL)　Boots.　Rudyard Kipling.　BRP; MoBrPo

An' Tommy ain't a bloomin' fool—you bet that Tommy sees! (LL)　Tommy. Rudyard Kipling.　CABP; FaBoWar; MoBrPo; NoP-4; NoP-5; OBWP; OxAEP-2; UV

An' tryin' to be good. (LL)　Favorite Slave's Story, The.　Priscilla Jane Thompson.　CBWP-2; RACG

Anabaptist, The.　Rowland Watkyns.　BASC

Anabasis.　"St.-John Perse."　OBVE Fr. Anabasis.

Anacapa.　Abigail Albrecht.　GeoHom

Anacona.　Danielle Legros Georges.　BtF

Anacreon.　Johann Wilhelm Ludwig Gleim.　GePo, tr. by George C. Schoolfield

Anacreon.　Friedrich von Hagedorn.　GePo, tr. by George C. Schoolfield

Anacreon, my teacher.　Anacreon.　Johann Wilhelm Ludwig Gleim.　GePo, tr. by George C. Schoolfield

Anacreon's Grave.　Johann Wolfgang von Goethe.　STV, tr. by John Frederick Nims

Anacreontic.　R. S. Gwynn.　RA

Anacreontic.　Robert Herrick.　CavPo

Anacreontic.　John Thelwall.　NOBRP

Anactoria.　Algernon Charles Swinburne.　RACG

Anaesthetist, The.　Anne Rouse.　NeBrP; PoCu

Anagram.　George Herbert.　ChIV-2

Anagram, An.　Unknown.　TCAPo

Anagram Born of Madness at Czernowitz, 12 November 1920.　Norman Dubie. BodElec

Anagrammic scramble. Scourge / of sound.　Alphabet of Ahtt.　Nathaniel Mackey.　FTOS

Anahorish.　Seamus Heaney.　HarvBoo; PBCIP

Anaktoria.　Sappho.　WoPoe, tr. by Guy Davenport

Analogies.　Arielle Greenberg.　LegDan

Analogue.　Marie Ponsot.　CLPP

Analogy.　János Székely.　IQMS, tr. by Geroge Gömöri

Analysis.　Syl Cheney-Coker.　NAfrP

Analysis, The.　David Citino.　UpMys

Analyst of birds, The.　Of Birds.　Tom Mandel.　OnScMo

Anam Street 1.　Yi Kyŏngnim.　EcSo, tr. by Peter H. Lee

Anam Street 2—Outside the Cinema.　Yi Kyŏngnim.　EcSo, tr. by Peter H. Lee

Anamorphosis Eisenhower. Sam Truitt.

  Kerf, The. AmPoNex

  Old World Monkeys. AmPoNex

Anarchy and grow your own. Durham. Tony Harrison. NoAM

Anarchy of the spirit no man is ascribed to be self-satisfying. Book 2: White Rose. Paul Skyrm. AmZen

Anasazi drink from underground rivers, The. David Ferry. FaBoA

Anascesis and Wreckage. Phillip Foss. ICANM

Anasphere: Le torse antique. Christopher Middleton. HarvBoo

Anastasia and Sandman. Larry Levis. BAP-97

Anastasia McLaughlin. Tom Paulin. PBCIP

Anastylosis. Carol Moldaw. ICANM

Anathema. Maranatha! John Wheelwright. APT-2

Anathemata, The. David Jones.

  Angle-Land. HarvBoo; NAMCP V.1; NoAM

  "Ship's master:/ before him, in the waist and before it." WoPoe

Anatomy. Harryette Mullen. OxAAAP

Anatomy. Kevin Young. OxAAAP

Anatomy Lesson. Jack Coulehan. BloBone

Anatomy of Departure. Elizabeth Garrett. NeBl

Anatomy of Humor, The. Morris Gilbert Bishop. NBLV

Anatomy of Melancholy, The. Robert Burton.

  Authors [or Author's] Abstract of Melancholy, The. NOSC

Anatomy [or Anatomie] of the World, An: The First Anniversary. John Donne.

  "And new philosophy calls all in doubt." NOSC

  "When that rich soul[e] which to her heaven is gone." NAEL-6v1; NAEL&nyhy;7v1

Ancapagari. Carolyn Forché. YaYoPo

Ancestor. Thomas Kinsella. ModIr; NPeEn; OxBEV; PBCIP

Ancestor, The. Jean Grosjean. YaTCFP, tr. by Mary Ann Caws and Jean-Pierre Cauvin and Patricia Terry

Ancestor, The. Paul Muldoon. GPPA

Ancestor dirt. Canto 2. Dionne Brand. BrAP

Ancestor Worship. Emyr Humphreys. AngWePo

Ancestored-Back Is the Overpresiding Spirit of This Poem. Albert Goldbarth. CAP-8; PoDa

Ancestors. Edward Kamau Brathwaite. NoP-4; NoP-5

Ancestors. Raymond Garlick. AngWePo

Ancestors. Karen Press. TSAP

Ancestral Burden. Alfonsina Storni. TCLAP, tr. by Andrew Rosing

Ancestral Echoes/Rap Music. Charles Lynch. SwNoth

Ancestral Houses. William Butler Yeats. OBGa Fr. Meditations in Time of Civil War.

Ancestral Messengers / Composition 13. Ntozake Shange. AFaM; GT; IPoFL

Anchor. John Montague. Fr. Great Cloak, The.

Anchor, The. John Blight. BMAP

Anchorage. Joy Harjo. HATNAP; LTA; OPRER

Anchorage, The. Mark Wunderlich. NeAmPo

Ancient Air. Li Po. BLT.

Ancient Airs. Li Po. CrYelRi, tr. by Sam Hamill

Ancient Autumn. Charles Simic. ColAP

Ancient borassus palms, masculine and feminine. Two Trees. Grace Schulman. ExTi

Ancient cedar. Cedar. David Tokuyu Reid-Marr. WhBo

Ancient chestnut's blossoms threw, An. Alciphron and Leucippe. Walter Savage Landor. OBEV

Ancient Custom, An. Anatoly Steiger. TCRusP, tr. by John Glad

Ancient Evenings. Michael Hofmann. EmeKit; NeBrP

Ancient exalted seed-scatterer whom time gave no progenitor. Maker on High, The. Saint Columba. NePenScot, tr. by Edwin Morgan

Ancient Gesture, An. Edna St. Vincent Millay. NALW; NIL-7

Ancient Greek Song of Exile. Felicia Dorothea Hemans. RWP

Ancient Gypsy, The. Mihály Vörösmarty. IQMS, tr. by Peter Zollman

Ancient History. Jamie McKendrick. NeBrP

Ancient History. Siegfried Sassoon. ChIV-1

Ancient "Kayán", The. Endre Ady. IQMS, tr. by Watson Kirkconnell

Ancient men with their hands forged this wondrous object. Song of the Old Sword. Ch'i-chi. CSKM, tr. by Burton Watson

Ancient Monuments. John Ormond. AngWePo; OBWVE

Ancient Music [par. of Sumer Is Icumen In]. Ezra Pound. AmWit; HeIP-4; NBLV; OBCoV; TCAPo; UV

Ancient New Parents. Robin Behn. AmAlph

Ancient of Days, old friend, no one believes you'll come back. Stone Canyon Nocturne. Charles Wright. ColAP; GeoHom; NAMCP V.2; VCAP

Ancient One, Wise One, Old Mother. Cicada. Eclipse. HW

Ancient Ones, The. Patricia Reis. HW

Ancient Ones, The: Betátakin. Janet Lewis. APT-2

Ancient Origin. Muso Soseki. EaWin, tr. by W. S. Merwin

Ancient person, for whom I. Song of a Young Lady to Her Ancient Lover, A. John Wilmot, 2d Earl of Rochester. BASC; NoP-4; NoP-5; NOSC; NPeEn; OxAEP-1; OxBEV; WaAnP

Ancient person of my heart. (LL) Song of a Young Lady to Her Ancient Lover, A. John Wilmot, 2d Earl of Rochester. BASC; NoP-4; NoP-5; NOSC; NPeEn; OxAEP-1; OxBEV; WaAnP

Ancient poets ne'er did dream, The. James McIntyre. VerBaPo Fr. Oxford Cheese Ode.

Ancient Revisits, An. Laura Riding Jackson. APT-2

Ancient Rites of the Condoling Council. Unknown.

  "TEHKARIHHOKEN! / Continue to listen!" APN-2

Ancient saga tells us how, An. Dead Cow Farm. Robert Graves. FaBoWar; PoWW

Ancient Sage, The. Alfred Tennyson. SacPr

Ancient Signs. Edward Hirsch. TaR

Ancient silent pond. Basho. WoPoe, tr. by John S. Major

Ancient Song, An. Marina Ivanovna Tsvetayeva. TCRusP, tr. by John Glad

Ancient songs, The. Choricos. Richard Aldington. PoA 2002

Ancient Temple. Cho Chihun. CAMKP, tr. by David R. McCann

Ancient terror burns in things, a deep and secret sigh, An. As the Great Days Flow. Enrique Molina. TCLAP, tr. by Naomi Lindstrom

Ancient Themes: The Night. Jeff Gundy. ACAMVP

Ancient tree. Lone Pine. Amy Uyematsu. WhBo

Ancients happily could sing, The. Our Naughty Time. Friedrich von Logau. GePo, tr. by George C. Schoolfield

Ancients of the World, The. Ronald Stuart Thomas. OPOU

Ancients were not able, save, The. Invention of Secrecy, The. David Citino. PoA 2002

Ancilla and servus. (LL) Geoffrey Hill. NAMCP V.2; NoAM; NoP-4 Fr. Mercian Hymns.

Ancutsa, Ancutsa. Cathal McCabe. NIrP

It was supposed to be Arts & Crafts for a week. At the Smithville Methodist Church. Stephen Dunn. SUP

And. Desire. Kurt Schwitters. PFTM-1

And . . . and so it goes. Coordinating Conjunction. John Hollander. PoA 2002

And a certaine Priest comming that way. Luke 10. Richard Crashaw. SacPr

And a cruel wind blows. (LL) End of Summer. Stanley Kunitz. LoL; MoAmPo

And a faggot of useless memories. (LL) Louis MacNeice. ModIr; PNI Fr. Autumn Journal.

And a father's love add up to silence. (LL) Story, A. Li-Young Lee. LoL; RaBo

And a fool, and a smart one, a miser. Bakhyt Kenjeev. ItGoST, tr. by Nina Kossman

And a housefly's panicked scribbling on the air. (LL) Signs. Gjertrud Schnackenberg. PoA 2002; StAl; VCAP

And a light sound. (LL) Knowledge. Louise Bogan. APT-2; NAMCP V.1; PoA 2002

And a man with his back to the East. (LL) Unwelcome. Mary Elizabeth Coleridge. OBEV; VWP

And a person for work that is real. (LL) To Be of Use. Marge Piercy. GoPo; IPoFL; TWF

And a pond edged with grayish [or greyish] leaves. (LL) Neutral Tones. Thomas Hardy. CABP; HeIP-4; MoBrPo; NAEL-6v2; NAEL-7v2; NAMCP V.1; NoAM; NoP-4; NoP-5; NPeEn; TFi; WaAnP

And a singe runs through lace and feather. (LL) Utilitarian View of the Monitor's Fight, A. Herman Melville. AmWaPo; APN-2; ColAP; NAAL-3; NAAPv.1; NCAP

And a stray face spins me back to the black-haired girl. Rain. Jeff Gundy. IllVoic

And a tall tree sprouted from his father's grave. (LL) Truisms, The. Louis MacNeice. OBSV; PNI

And a tenth part of Okeanos is given to dark night. Styx. Robert Duncan. VCAP

And a' the glory shall be thine, / Amen! Amen! (LL) Holy Willie's Prayer. Robert Burns. BrAP; CABP; NAEL-6v2; NAEL-7v2; NOBRP; NoP-5; NPBRoP; OBCoV; OBSV; TFi

And a thread too bright for the eye. (LL) Shroud. George Mackay Brown. NoP-4; NoP-5

And a wasted town. (LL) War Poet. Sidney Keyes. FaBoWar; NoP-4; NoP-5; PoWW; WaAnP

And abortions are hidden. (LL) Edgar Lee Masters. APT-1; OBSV; OxBoAm Fr. Spoon River Anthology.

And above all to gaze with innocence. As if nothing would happen. Paths of the Mirror. Alejandra Pizarnik. PFTM-2, tr. by Jason Weiss

And adjust, no one to drive the car. (LL) To Elsie. William Carlos Williams. AmFaPo; APT-1; NAAL-5; NAAPv.2; NAMCP V.1; OxBoAm; PoPoPo; StAl

And after a while he'd say his head was a rose. Blossom. Stanley Plumly. LiTh

And, after all, it is to them we return. Geoffrey Hill. NoAM *Fr.* Apology for the Revival of Christian Architecture in England, An.

And after all your trapesings, child, lie still! (LL) St. Helena Lullaby, A. Rudyard Kipling. FaBoWar; OBMV

And after fifty years of blindness. Corneal Graft. Anne Ridler. MoWP

And after Governor Faubus led his army against Little Rock and General Walker led his troops against the Supreme Court and Governor Wallace led his bombers against Birmingham. Execution, The. Walter Lowenfels. FTtHH

And after singing Psalm the Twelfth. Rochester Extempore. John Wilmot, 2d Earl of Rochester. ChIV-1

And after this it is hard to keep chewing away at our truth. (LL) Ox Looks at Man, An. Carlos Drummond de Andrade. IPoFL; PoetW; PtR; TCLAP, *tr. by* Mark Strand

And afterwards, here, in the dark bosom of the darkest river. Men of Dawn, The. Efraín Huerta. TCLAP, *tr. by* Todd Dampier

And afterwards? I do not know. Twenty Years in the Wadi. Dan Pagis. NRoS, *tr. by* Esther Raizen

And Again. Alison Fell. LW

And again, as always in the Land of Israel, the stones are steaming. Current Account. Haim Guri. NRoS, *tr. by* Esther Raizen

And again, being claimed. (LL) Thirty Years Rising. Olena Kalytiak Davis. AmPoNex; LegDan

And again Jesus spoke to them in parables, saying. Edwin Arlington Robinson. GI *Fr.* St. Matthew.

And ages drop in it like rain. (LL) Two Rivers. Ralph Waldo Emerson. APN-1; NCAP

And al is thorugh [*or;* thrugh *or* thurgh] thy negligence [*necligence*] and rape. (LL) Chaucer's Wordes unto Adam, his Owne Scriveyn. Geoffrey Chaucer. NAEL-6v1; NAEL-7v1

And all dishevelled wandering stars. (LL) Who Goes with Fergus? William Butler Yeats. NAEL-6v2; NAEL-7v2; NAMCP V.1; NoAM; TRP

And all her silken flanks with garlands drest. Vlamertinghe. Edmund Charles Blunden. NoP-4; OBWP

And all his fondest wishes, blend with mine. (LL) Previous to her Interview with Phaon. Mary Robinson. CenSon; RWP

And all his island shivered into flowers. (LL) Live Blindly. Trumbull Stickney. APN-2; OxBoAm; TCAPo; WoPoe

And all his magic books are drowned. (LL) Caliban's Books. Michael Donaghy. EmeKit; NeBrP

And all His marvels dead, His oceans rising, hell-bent to Heaven. (LL) Retro Creation. Aidan Rooney-Céspedes. BeAl; NIrP

And all is done as I have told. (LL) Mental Traveller, The. William Blake. ChIV-2; NAEL-6v2; WoPoe

And all is hushed at Shiloh. (LL) Shiloh (A Requiem). Herman Melville. AmWaPo; APN-2; CBCWP; ColAP; CtM; NAAPv.1; NoP-4; NoP-5; OBWP; OxBoAm; PCW; PoAgWa; TCAPo

And all is rolled back in the book of days. (LL) Alphabet, The. Karl Shapiro. APT-2; EMP; NoAM; PoA 2002; TaR

And all is undismayed. (LL) To My Mother. Wendell Berry. GoPo; PoA 2002

And all is well, though [*or* tho'] faith and form. Alfred Tennyson. NAEL-6v2; NAEL-7v2 *Fr.* In Memoriam A. H. H.

And all men are at home. (LL) House of Christmas, The. G. K. Chesterton. ChrPo; MoBrPo; SacPr

And all my hearts in unison strike twelve. (LL) Science of the Night, The. Stanley Kunitz. APT-2; ColAP; MoAmPo

And all my woe. (LL) Fantasy, A. Mathilde Blind. PoBW; ViWPN; VWP

And all night long we lie in sleep. Boyish sleep. Hamlin Garland. APN-2

And all of wood. Watch it closely. (LL) Monument, The. Elizabeth Bishop. NAMCP V.2; NoAM; TRP

And all our dead princes. (LL) Epil y Filiast. Harri Webb. AngWePo; TCAWP

And all poultry eaters are psychopaths. (LL) Annotations of Auschwitz. Peter Porter. BrAP; HP

And all that and then that having been blessed let us bless it. (LL) Valentine to Sherwood Anderson, A. Gertrude Stein. NoAM; PFTM-1

And All That Jazz. Fred Ebb. ReLy

And all that mighty heart is lying still! (LL) Composed upon Westminster Bridge, September 3, 1802. William Wordsworth. BrAP; CABP; CenSon; ChAP; ClHu; CtM; GSo; HeIP-4; ITBLP; MakPoe; NAEL-6v2; NAEL-7v2; NAWM-7v2; NOBRP; NoP-4; NoP-5; NPeEn; OPOU; OxBEV; OxBSo; TFi; WaAnP

And all that was taken away! (LL) How I Got That Name. Marilyn Chin. CalPo; GeoHom; LoL; NAMCP V.2

And all that we hope survives them. (LL) Elegy for Bob Marley, An. William Matthews. SwNoth; WaAnP

And all the hills echoed [*or* ecchoed]. (LL) William Blake. NAEL-6v2; NAEL-7v2; NPBRoP; RACG *Fr.* Songs of Innocence.

And all the old songs. And nothing to lose. (LL) Emigrant Irish, The. Eavan Boland. AmFaPo; EmeKit; MoWP

And All the Sisters Said. Janeya K. Hisle. BtF

And all the streets lie snug there, clean and regular. Morning. Alfred Lichtenstein. GTCP, *tr. by* Michael Hamburger

And all the streets were new. (LL) Exile. Donald Hall. NoP-4; NoP-5

And all the summer through the water saunter. (LL) On This Island. W. H. Auden. HarvBoo; NAEL-6v2; NAEL-7v2; NAMCP V.1; OxBEV

And all the while, he knew there was no river. (LL) Eli, Eli. Judith Wright. BMAP; GI

And all these through her eyes, have stopped her ears. (LL) My Picture Left in Scotland. Ben Jonson. NAEL-6v1; NAEL-7v1; NPeEn; PtR

And all they foul that thy complexion lack. (LL) William Shakespeare. OxAEP-1; WaAnP *Fr.* Sonnets.

And all this is folly to the world. (LL) Ezra Pound. MoAmPo; NOxBChV *Fr.* Ripostes of Ezra Pound.

And all this while I have been playing with toys. Window, at the Moment of Flame, The. Alicia Ostriker. PA9/11

And all thy sons, O Nature, learn my tale. (LL) Ode to Simplicity. William Collins. OBEV; OxAEP-1

And all we flow from, soul in soul. (LL) Alfred Tennyson. NAEL-6v2; NAEL-7v2 *Fr.* In Memoriam A. H. H.

And all we need of hell. (LL) My life closed twice before its close. Emily Dickinson. APN-2; ColAP; HeIP-4; LW; MoAmPo; NAAL-3; NAAL-5; NAAPv.1; NAMCP V.1; NIL-7; NIP-4; NoAM; NoP-5; OxBoAm; SacPr; SAmP; TCAPo; TFi

And almost gently asks: *Are you a Jew?*. (LL) First Time, The. Karl Shapiro. APT-2; NAMCP V.2

And already they are beginning to witness that Armageddon. Armageddon. István Vas. IQMS, *tr. by* William Jay Smith

And Also from the Son. Scott Cairns. UpMys

And also—the Minotaur, farmer, owner, respondent. Galina Ermoshina. CRWP, *tr. by* Gerald Janecek

And although it will be. Envoi. Caitríona O'Reilly. MoWP

And always not when absently enough and heard and said. Gertrude Stein. OxBoAm *Fr.* Book Concluding with As A Wife Has a Cow a Love Story, A.

And always, the damp blond curls. For the Taking. Linda Gregerson. AmAlph

And always there are the children. Always There Are the Children. Nikki Giovanni. WaAnP

And, always, there is desire. Beyond Having. Ray Gonzalez. TouFir

And am around, tenacious, acquisitive, tireless, and cannot be shaken away. (LL) Walt Whitman. ColAP; NAWM-7v2; WaAnP *Fr.* Song of Myself.

And anger moment by moment balanced. (LL) To Have without Holding. Marge Piercy. NIL-7; NIP-4

And Another Bloody Thing. Clare Pollard. BeAl

And another child. (LL) Once in a Lifetime, Snow. Les A. Murray. NoP-4; NoP-5

And another regrettable thing about death. Perfection Wasted. John Updike. GoPo

And another thing. Edwin Brock. BeAl

And answer, echoes, answer, dying, dying, dying. (LL) Alfred Tennyson. ClHu; CtM; HeIP-4; NAEL-6v1; NAEL-7v1; NoP-4; NoP-5; TFi *Fr.* Princess, The.

And answers my step, designates the branch, and picks the fruit. (LL) I Am Forbidden. Jacques Dupin. MotU; YaTCFP, *tr. by* Paul Auster

And anyhow: give up. Free Fall. Karl Krolow. GTCP, *tr. by* Reinhold Grimm

And are gone. (LL) Emplumada. Lorna Dee Cervantes. NoAM; PBCAP

And are we standing now, quietly, in the new life? (LL) Oceans. Juan Ramón Jiménez. RaW; WED, *tr. by* Robert Bly

And are ye sure the news is true? There's Nae Luck about the House. Jean Adams. NePenScot

And, as a boiling vessel cools once more. West, The. Alphonse Marie Louis de Lamartine. SxFrPo, *tr. by* A. M. and E. H. Blackmore

And as for Man. Loren C. Eiseley. GM

And as for me, though that I konne [*or* can] but [*or* my wit be] lyte. Geoffrey Chaucer. HeIP-4 *Fr.* Legend of Good Women, The.

And as he laboured, his mind ran o'er. Henry Wadsworth Longfellow. FaBoWar *Fr.* Building of the Ship, The.

And as her silver body downeward went. Christopher Marlowe. OxBEV *Fr.* Hero and Leander.

And As I Came Out from the Temples. Joan Murray. YaYoPo

And as I came out from the temples and stared. And As I Came Out from the Temples. Joan Murray. YaYoPo

And as I rock you. Freedom Child—Tilla's Lullaby. Eintou Pearl Springer. CFP

And as I talked, I swam. (LL) With Kit, Age 7, at the Beach. William Stafford. CAP-8; PoCho; RaBo

And, as in well-growne woods, on trees, cold spinie grashoppers. Homer. NPeEn *Fr.* Iliad, The.

And as in winter time when Jove his cold-sharpe javelines throwes. Homer. NPeEn; OBVE *Fr.* Iliad, The.

And as silently steal away. (LL)   Day Is Done, The. Henry Wadsworth Longfellow. APN-1; BRP; ChAP; ITBLP; NAAPv.1; NCAP; TreFP

And as the anatomist, with all his band. Robert Pollok. STuOW *Fr.* Course of Time, The.

And as the world turns, so turns the light. Bryan Ferry. B.D. Love. SwNoth

And as to the meaning, it's what you please. (LL)   Ballad: "Auld wife sat at her ivied door, The." Charles Stuart Calverley. CABP; NBLV; OBCoV; OxAEP-2; UV

And as to you Death, and you bitter hug of mortality, it is idle to try to alarm me. Walt Whitman. ColAP *Fr.* Song of Myself.

And as when with the West-wind's flawes the sea thrusts up her waves. Homer. OBVE *Fr.* Iliad, The.

And ash (not unlike flour) for one small loaf. (LL)   Tony Harrison. InoFa; NAEL-6v2; NAEL-7v2; NAMCP V.2 *Fr.* School of Eloquence, The.

And ask, once more, to enter that innocent first world. (LL)   Sunday Afternoon at Fulham Palace. Elizabeth Spires. AtGh; CAP-8

And ask the Gods to pardon this clear flame. (LL)   Light-winged smoke, Icarian bird. Henry David Thoreau. APN-1; ColAP; TCAPo

And ask them for your name again. (LL)   Mystery Boy Looks for Kin in Nashville. Robert Earl Hayden. NoAM; NoP-4; NoP-5

And at last I'm leaving the clinic. It Is August 24th. Cortney Davis. FiBr

And at night came to me. And at Night. Raiah Harnik. NRoS, *tr. by* Esther Raizen

And at noon I will fall in love. Brooklyn Anchorage. Lisa Jarnot. VaPo

And at the blue ice superior spot. Lorine Niedecker. FTOS *Fr.* Lake Superior.

And at the upper end of that faire rowme. Edmund Spenser. NPeEn *Fr.* Faerie Queene, The.

And at this I was mildly abashed. (LL)   Study in Aesthetics, The. Ezra Pound. APT-1; EMP

And awake, my heart, to be loved: awake, awake! (LL)   Awake, My Heart, to Be Loved. Robert Bridges. MoBrPo; OBEV

And away the vapo[u]r flew. (LL)   William Blake. NoP-4; NoP-5; WaAnP *Fr.* Songs of Innocence.

And aye she sat by the cheek of the grate. Wife of Crowle, The. James Hogg. NPBRoP

And barely can not hear them calling, "Here's one." (LL)   Memorial Service for the Invasion Beach Where the Vacation in the Flesh Is Over. Alan Dugan. AF; PWW2

And basked and battened in the woods. (LL)   Alfred Tennyson. NAEL-6v2; NAEL-7v2 *Fr.* In Memoriam A. H. H.

And be a friend to man. (LL)   House by the Side of the Road, The. Sam Walter Foss. BRP; ITBLP

And be among her cloudy trophies hung. (LL)   Ode on Melancholy. John Keats. BrAP; CABP; NAEL-6v2; NAEL-7v2; NAWM-7v2; NIL-7; NoP-4; NoP-5; NPBRoP; NPeEn; OxAEP-2; OxBEV; TFi; WaAnP

And anonymous? (LL)   Our Hunting Fathers. W. H. Auden. HarvBoo; NoAM

And be buried in the dust of marching feet. (LL)   For Black Poets Who Think of Suicide. Etheridge Knight. HeIP-4; LTA; OxAAAP; WaAnP

And be gone. (LL)   Robert Creeley. NAMCP V.2; WoBe *Fr.* Life and Death.

And be in his brave court a glorious light. Mary Sidney Wroth, Countess of Montgomery. BASC

And be like him and he will then love me. (LL)   William Blake. AmFaPo; CABP; ChAP; HeIP-4; NAEL-6v2; NAEL-7v2; NAWM-7v2; NOBRP; NoP-4; NoP-5; OBEV; PoPoPo; TFi *Fr.* Songs of Innocence.

And be the mistress of Mankind! (LL)   Upon [His] Leaving His Mistress. John Wilmot, 2d Earl of Rochester. BASC; NBLV; NOSC

And bear awhile—what Death alone can cure! (LL)   By the Same. To Solitude. Charlotte Smith. CenSon; RWP

And beat him today. (LL)   Jack. Charles Henry Ross. NOxBChV; Spl

And Beaumonts and Bens be his Kellys above. (LL)   Oliver Goldsmith. NPeEn; OxBEV *Fr.* Retaliation.

And beautiful as they. (LL)   Love-Charm Song. *Chippewa Oral Tradition.* NAAL-5; NAAPv.2

And because it is my heart. (LL)   In the desert. Stephen Crane. APN-2; ColAP; IJHIL; MoAmPo; NAAPv.1; NoP-4; NoP-5; OxBoAm; TCAPo

And Bees of Paradise. Hart Crane. OxBoAm

And before existing fade. (LL)   Post Card. Guillaume Apollinaire. AF; FaBoWar, *tr. by* Oliver Bernard

And before him you may all rejoyce. Epistle of Love and of Consolation unto Israel, An. Dorothy White. EMWP

And began to kill each other. (LL)   Nuclear Winter. Thomas McGrath. AtGh; GifTon

And being good for nothing else, be wise. (LL)   Disabled Debauchee, The. John Wilmot, 2d Earl of Rochester. BASC; NAEL-6v1; NAEL-7v1; NoP-4; NoP-5; NPeEn; OBSV

And beside the moon, a single star. (LL)   We started home, my son and I. Jaan Kaplinski. BLT; GifTon; PoChi; WoPoe, *tr. by* the author, Sam Hamill and Riina Tamm

And bid them seek the morn the hills and fields once more. (LL)   New Man, The. Jones Very. APN-1; TCAPo

And bide with her thou luvis best. (LL)   Hence, heart, with her that must depart. Alexander Scott. NePenScot; OBEV

And bids my hair stand up? (LL)   Mother of God, The. William Butler Yeats. BBASP; ChIV-2; ChrPo

And binding with briars my joys and desires. (LL)   William Blake. ItP; NAEL-6v2; NAEL-7v2; NoP-4; NoP-5; NPBRoP; NPeEn; OBGa; OxAEP-2; OxBEV; PoPoPo; TFi; TRP *Fr.* Songs of Experience.

And blacker. (LL)   Coffee. Wanda Coleman. BrAP; ISC

And blesses all creation with the sun. God Looks on Nature With a Glorious Eye. John Clare. BBASP

And blew. *"Childe Roland to the Dark Tower came".* (LL)   Childe Roland to the Dark Tower Came. Robert Browning. NAEL-6v2; NAEL-7v2; NAWM-7v2; NoP-4; NoP-5; OBNV; PoPoPo; WaAnP

And blights with plagues the Marriage hearse. (LL)   William Blake. BrAP; CABP; ClHu; HeIP-4; IJHIL; NAEL-6v2; NAEL-7v2; NAWM-7v2; NIL-7; NIP-4; NOBRP; NoP-4; NoP-5; NPBRoP; NPeEn; OxAEP-2; OxBEV; PoPoPo; TFi; TRP; WeW-3 *Fr.* Songs of Experience.

And blood hangs in the pine-soaked air. (LL)   Adolescence—3. Rita Dove. ISC; NoAM; NoAM

And blossom in purple and red. (LL)   Alfred Tennyson. OxAEP-2; OxBEV; UV; WoPoe *Fr.* Maud [A Monodrama].

And blow you all a kiss from the tomb. (LL)   New England Bachelor, A. Richard Eberhart. MoAmPo; NoAM

And blue-eyed bringer of truth, who will not easily be forgiven. (LL)   Body and Soul. B. H. Fairchild. MAAN; MoASP; SUP

And blueweed, blueweed. Tomas Tranströmer. WoBe *Fr.* Haiku.

And boars root safely along our circumference. (LL)   Sulpicia. Michael Longley. OxBSo; RACG

And bombs bursting in air, and at night the vari-color'd rockets. (LL)   Artilleryman's Vision, The. Walt Whitman. CBCWP; PCW

And both thy servants be. (LL)   Man. George Herbert. BASC; FSCP; NAEL-6v1; NAEL-7v1; NoP-4; NoP-5

And bowing not knowing to what. (LL)   For the Anniversary of My Death. W. S. Merwin. BeAl; CAP-8; ColAP; GoPo; NAMCP V.2; OxBoAm; PoPoPo; VCAP; WaAnP

And bring about the collapse of the whole empire. (LL)   Shame. Richard Wilbur. EmeKit; OBCoV; OxBoAm

And bring to my baby a fresh penny roll. (LL)   Mouse's Lullaby, The. Palmer Cox. NOxBChV; TLR

And bringe [*or* brynge] us to his heighe [*or* hye *or* highe] blisse [*or* blisss]! Amen. (LL)   Geoffrey Chaucer. NAEL-6v1; NAEL-7v1 *Fr.* Canterbury Tales, The.

And broad old cesspools glittered in the sun. (LL)   Mouse's Nest. John Clare. NAEL-6v2; NAEL-7v2; NPeEn

And broke on me generously as bread. (LL)   Moor, The. Ronald Stuart Thomas. OBWVE; WaAnP

And buds and blossoms like the rest. (LL)   Alfred Tennyson. NAEL-6v2; NAEL-7v2; NPeEn; WaAnP *Fr.* In Memoriam A. H. H.

And builds a Hell in Heaven's despite. (LL)   William Blake. NAEL-6v1; NAEL-7v1; NoP-4; NoP-5; NPBRoP; NPeEn; OxAEP-2; OxBEV; TFi *Fr.* Songs of Experience.

And built a braver Palace than before. (LL)   World, The. George Herbert. CtM; NOSC

And burgeoning words ascending. cosmos; starwort; the moon a tear. Sylvia Legris. PoPra *Fr.* Negative Garden.

And buried him where he fell. (LL)   Vigil Strange I Kept on the Field One Night. Walt Whitman. APN-1; BrAP; CAGL; CBCWP; ColAP; HeIP-4; MoAmPo; NAAL-3; NAAPv.1; NoP-4; NoP-5; OBWP; PCW; PoPoPo; TCAPo; WaAnP

And burn[e], yet[t] burning you will love the smart. Mary Sidney Wroth, Countess of Montgomery. BASC *Fr.* Pamphilia to Amphilanthus.

And burnt her on the Salem green? (LL)   Witch, The. Adelaide Crapsey. APT-1; NAAPv.2

And but a chair. (LL)   Pilgrimage, The. George Herbert. BASC; NAEL-6v1; NAEL-7v1; NOSC

And but in darkness is she visible. (LL)   To an Old Lady. William Empson. NoAM; OxAEP-2; OxBEV

And buzzings of the honied hours. (LL)   Alfred Tennyson. NAEL-6v2; NAEL-7v2; OBGa *Fr.* In Memoriam A. H. H.

And by a river forth I gan costey. John Lydgate. OBGa *Fr.* Complaint of the Black Knight, The.

And, by one o'clock, is gone. (LL)   V. B. Nimble, V. B. Quick. John Updike. NoP-4; NoP-5; OBCoV

And by that light around the dome appear'd. Philip Freneau. NAAL-3; TCAPo *Fr.* House of Night, The.

And call out your name across the great divide—Nessa. (LL)   She Mends an Ancient Wireless.   Paul Durcan.   IrLP; PBCIP

And call ye this to utter what is just.   Bible, *O.T.*   NoSic

And call ye[e] this to utter what is just.   Bible, *O.T.*   BASC; NoP-4; NoP-5; NPeEn; PEW *Fr.* Psalms.

And called each other "Dog." (LL)   Back in the Day.   Lorenzo Thomas.   AnSo; FuFl

And calm of mind all passion spent. (LL)   John Milton.   NOSC; OBEV; OxAEP-1; BASC; NAEL-6v1; OxBEV *Fr.* Samson Agonistes.

And calmly waits for more. (LL)   History Goes to Work.   Elizabeth Garrett.   MFPA; NeBl

And Camelot, and starlit Stonehenge. (LL)   Channel Firing.   Thomas Hardy.   BrAP; CABP; HarvBoo; HeIP-4; NAEL-6v2; NAEL-7v2; NAMCP V.1; NIL-7; NIP-4; NoAM; NoP-4; NoP-5; OxAEP-2; OxBEV; PoAgWa; PoPoPo; PoWW; SoSe-8; TFi; WaAnP

And can it be, that I should gain.   Free Grace.   Charles Wesley.   SacPr

And can return no more. (LL)   First Love.   John Clare.   GoPo; NoP-4; NoP-5; PoPoPo

And cannot change to grey. (LL)   I caught a little ladybird.   Christina Georgina Rossetti.   FaBoVe; NPeEn

And cannot come again. (LL)   Yon Far Country.   A. E. Housman.   HarvBoo; MoBrPo; NoAM; NPeEn; OPOU; OxAEP-2; OxBEV; TFi; WaAnP

And cannot come again. (LL)   A. E. Housman.   HarvBoo; MoBrPo; NoAM; NPeEn; OPOU; OxAEP-2; OxBEV; TFi; WaAnP *Fr.* Shropshire Lad, A.

& cannot end, not, at least, in the way.   Comma a Portrait, The.   Pamela Alexander.   AmAlph

And can't explode? (LL)   Sherbet.   Cornelius Eady.   GT; LTA

And, cast by conscience out, spendsavour salt? (LL)   Candle Indoors, The.   Gerard Manley Hopkins.   ChIV-2; OxAEP-2

And catch the heart off guard and blow it open. (LL)   Postscript.   Seamus Heaney.   ASA; GoPo; StAl

And Cause His Countenance to Shine upon You: *Corpus Christi, Texas*.   Cynthia MacDonald.   AFaM; TiP2

And celandines and white may and gorse flowers. (LL)   Gorse Fires.   Michael Longley.   NoP-4; NoP-5

And certainly they say, for fine behaving.   John Hookham Frere.   OBCoV *Fr.* Whistlecraft.

And change[,] with hurried hand, has swept these scenes.   Frederick Goddard Tuckerman.   APN-2; TCAPo *Fr.* Sonnets.

And charms the most concealed, are doubly graced. (LL)   She Endeavors to Fascinate Him.   Mary Robinson.   CenSon; RWP

And cheat the cruel day! (LL)   And on My Eyes Dark Sleep by Night.   Michael Field.   LW; OBMV

And cheroots upon the floor. (LL)   On Seeing an Old Poet in the Café Royal.   Sir John Betjeman.   OxBEV; UV

And children play in the street? (LL)   Cottage Hospital, The.   Sir John Betjeman.   BrAP; InoFa; NAMCP V.1

And children still grow up with longing eyes.   Twilight of the Outward Life.   Hugo von Hofmannsthal.   WoPoe, *tr. by* Peter Viereck

And children swarmed to him like settlers. He became a land. (LL)   Edward Lear.   W. H. Auden.   OxAEP-2; OxBSo

And Christe receive thy saule. (LL)   Lyke-Wake Dirge, The [*or* A].   *Unknown*.   EMWP; NPeEn; OBEV; OxBEV; TFi; WeW-3; WoPoe

And Churchill in a bowler.   Notes of a Cold War Veteran.   Natalya Gorbanevskaya.   CRWP, *tr. by* Daniel Weissbort

And closed her up, as in a tomb[e]. (LL)   Funeral[l] Rites of the Rose, The.   Robert Herrick.   NOSC; OBEV

And cluck my teeth. (LL)   Too Young to Know.   Cornelius Eady.   PfSP; WaAnP

And clung to a tall tree of snowy white. (LL)   One Who's in Love with Love, The.   Hagiwara Sakutaro.   CAoMJL1; PFTM-1, *tr. by* Hiroaki Sato

And cold as any icicle. (LL)   Parting, without a Sequel.   John Crowe Ransom.   MoAmPo; NoP-4; NoP-5; SoSe-8

And comes from a country far away as health. (LL)   Tulips.   Sylvia Plath.   NAMCP V.2; NoP-4; NoP-5; WeW-3

And common, and your flesh endure. (LL)   To Judge Faolain, Dead Long Enough: A Summons.   Linda McCarriston.   FaoP; LoL

And confident Thou'lt raise me with the just. (LL)   On Himself, upon Hearing What Was His Sentence.   James Graham, Marquess of Montrose.   NePenScot; NOSC; NPeEn

And Consciousness—is Noon. (LL)   There is a Zone whose even Years.   Emily Dickinson.   APN-2; NCAP

And consummation comes, and jars two hemispheres. (LL)   Convergence of the Twain, The.   Thomas Hardy.   BrAP; CABP; GPTC; HarvBoo; HeIP-4; MakPoe; MoBrPo; NAEL-6v2; NAEL-7v2; NAMCP V.1; NIL-7; NIP-4; NoAM; NoP-4; NoP-5; NPeEn; OxBEV; PoPoPo; TFi; WaAnP

And continue special friends. (LL)   Twelve Articles.   Jonathan Swift.   NBLV; OBCoV

And continued to knock him about. (LL)   Limerick: "There was an old man who screamed out."   Edward Lear.   NPeEn; OxAEP-2; OxBEV

And could no longer recollect my name. (LL)   Epigram: "Good Fortune, when I hailed her recently."   James Vincent Cunningham.   APT-2; VCAP

And courts the fatal fire by which it dies! (LL)   Supposed To Be Written by Werter.   Charlotte Smith.   CenSon; RWP

And covered up—our names. (LL)   I died for Beauty—but was scarce.   Emily Dickinson.   APN-2; BrAP; MakPoe; MoAmPo; NAAL-3; NAAL-5; NAAPv.1; NAWM-7v2; OxBoAm; SAmP

And crowd to Stella's at four score. (LL)   Stella's Birthday [1721].   Jonathan Swift.   NAEL-6v1; OxAEP-1

And crown with love my ever-during night. (LL)   My Sweetest Lesbia.   Catullus.   BrAP; NoP-5; WaAnP, *tr. by* Thomas Campion

And crown with love my ever-during night. (LL)   Catullus. *See* You of me & / I of you, / darling, have had.

And curl forever in some far-off farmyard flower. (LL)   Beehive.   Jean Toomer.   GT; OxBoAm

And custom for the spreading laurel tree. (LL)   Prayer for My Daughter, A.   William Butler Yeats.   BrAP; ItP; NAEL-6v2; NAEL-7v2; NAMCP V.1; NoAM; NoP-4; NoP-5; RaBo; TFi; WaAnP

And cut them and gave them to me / in my hand. (LL)   Act, The.   William Carlos Williams.   PtR; SAmP

And dance. (LL)   Soul, like the moon, The.   Lal Ded.   WoPoe; WPoS, *tr. by* Coleman Barks

And dance like a wave of the sea. (LL)   Fiddler of Dooney, The.   William Butler Yeats.   NBLV; OxAEP-2

And dances with the Daffodils. (LL)   I Wandered Lonely as a Cloud.   William Wordsworth.   BRP; CABP; ChAP; ClHu; NAEL-6v2; NAEL-7v2; NOBRP; NoP-4; NoP-5; PoPoPo; SoSe-8; TFi; WaAnP

And dandelion-seed under the ground. (LL)   "H. D."   APT-1; OxBoAm *Fr.* Sigil.

And day and night yield one delight once more? (LL)   Sudden Light.   Dante Gabriel Rossetti.   CABP; NoP-4; NoP-5; NPeEn; OxBEV

And day not breaking but already broken.   Ampersonata.   Andrew Zawacki.   IAoNAP

And day not long enough. (LL)   Skylark.   Basho.   WoPoe; ZenPo, *tr. by* Takashi Ikemoto and Lucien Stryk

And de moon will turn to blood.   Day of Judgment, The.   *Unknown*.   SSUS

And dead my life that wants such lively blis. (LL)   Edmund Spenser.   NoP-4; NoP-5

And death brooded over the pride of the Plain! (LL)   Cities of the Plain, The.   John Greenleaf Whittier.   ChIV-1; NCAP

And death i think is no parenthesis. (LL)   Since feeling is first.   E. E. Cummings.   GoPo; MoAmPo; NoP-4; NoP-5; WaAnP

And death is no evil. (LL)   Night.   Robinson Jeffers.   ColAP; MoAmPo

And Death must dig the level where these agree. (LL)   Elizabeth Barrett Browning.   CABP; CenSon; OBEV; OxAEP-2 *Fr.* Sonnets from the Portuguese.

And, Death once dead, there's no more dying then. (LL)   William Shakespeare.   BrAP; HeIP-4; NAEL-6v1; NAEL-7v1; NoP-4; NoP-5; OBEV; OxAEP-1; SacPr; TFi; WaAnP *Fr.* Sonnets.

And death shall be no more: Death, thou shalt die. (LL)   John Donne.   BASC; BLPJKO; BrAP; HeIP-4; InoFa; ITBLP; NAEL-6v1; NAEL-7v1; NAWM-5v1; NIL-7; NIP-4; NoP-5; NOSC; NPeEn; OPOU; OxAEP-1; OxBEV; OxBSo; PtR; RSR; SacPr; SoSe-8; TRP; WaAnP; WeW-3 *Fr.* Holy Sonnets.

And Death Shall Have No Dominion.   Dylan Thomas.   BrAP; ChIV-2; MoBrPo; NAMCP V.2; NoAM; PtR

And death this cold, black density of stone. (LL)   Rainy Mountain Cemetery.   N. Scott Momaday.   HATNAP; ICANM

And decides to snorkel in a cool mountain lake.   Man Gets Off Work Early, A.   Thomas Lux.   PoDa

& degrees of cousinage even misty like this. (LL)   Blue Collar Holiday.   Jeni Olin.   BAP-04; FreRad

And dense with happy blood, dark rainbow bliss in the sea. (LL)   Whales Weep Not!   D. H. Lawrence.   NAMCP V.1; NoAM

And despairs day, but for thy volume's light. (LL)   To the Memory of My Beloved, the Author Mr [*or* Master] William Shakespeare: And What He Hath Left Us.   Ben Jonson.   BASC; BrAP; HeIP-4; InoFa; NAEL-6v1; NAEL-7v1; NoP-4; NoP-5; NOSC; OxAEP-1; PoPoPo

And did these feet, in pre-war days.   New Jerusalem, The.   Allan M. Laing.   UV

And did those feet in ancient time.   Milton.   William Blake.   CABP; CHIV-1; ClHu; C & M; HeIP-4; NAEL-7v2; NAWM-7v2; NOBRP; NPeEn; OxBEV; TFi; WoPoe

And did you come there in summer, tobogganing in the slow sheets.   O Grandfather Dust.   Glenn Kletke.   IFF

And did you get what.   Late Fragment.   Raymond Carver.   IJHIL; StAl

And did you know.   Snowflakes.   Clive Sansom.   OBCP

And did you not hear of a jolly young waterman.   Jolly Young Waterman, The.   Charles Dibdin.   OxAEP-1

And did young Stephen sicken.   Mark Twain.   NBLV *Fr.* Adventures of Huckleberry Finn, The.

And didst thou love the race that loved not thee?   Jean Ingelow.   SacPr

And died, content. (LL) Youth in apparel that glittered, A. Stephen Crane. APN-2; MoAmPo; NAAPv.1

And died, there's nothing in it. (LL) Ezra Pound. MoAmPo; NAAPv.2 *Fr.* Hugh Selwyn Mauberley (Life and Contacts).

And dies! (LL) Already Embraced by the Arm of Heavenly Solace. Nelly Sachs. HP; PoSu, *tr. by* Michael Roloff

And dies between three cannibals. (LL) Fly, The. Karl Shapiro. NAMCP V.2; NoAM; SoSe-8

And dinner will be cold. (LL) A. E. Housman. HarvBoo; MoBrPo *Fr.* Shropshire Lad, A.

And disembodied bones. (LL) Eagle and the Mole, The. Elinor Wylie. CtM; MoAmPo; NAAPv.2; NALW

And dish water gives back no images. (LL) No Images. Waring Cuney. APT-2; NIP-4; SSLK

And dive and splash. (LL) Brimming Water. Tu Fu [*or* Du Fu]. CCL1; NDACCP, *tr. by* Kenneth Rexroth

And dive off in my grave like the old swimmin'-hole. (LL) Old Swimmin'-Hole, The. James Whitcomb Riley. APN-2; BRP

And do not even own clothing. (LL) Salutation. Ezra Pound. HeIP-4; MoAmPo; NAAPv.2; OxBoAm

And do not flow over like you or like me. (LL) Jugs, The. Paul Celan. HP; OBVE, *tr. by* Christopher Middleton

And do they so? have they a Sense. And do they so? Henry Vaughan. BASC; SacPr

And do they wear that lubricating lie. Alfred Austin. VerBaPo *Fr.* Human Tragedy, The.

And does another thousand start again? (LL) Mahratta Ghats, The. Alun Lewis. AngWePo; OBWVE; PoWW; TCAWP

And does not drift away. (LL) Medusa. Louise Bogan. APT-2; MoAmPo; NAAPv.2; NALW; NAMCP V.1; NoAM; NoP-4; NoP-5; PtR

And does the heart grow old? You know. To My Wife. James Vincent Cunningham. VCAP

And Don't Be Deaf to the Singing Beyond. Carter Revard. HATNAP

And don't blubber like lubbers when I turn up my keel. (LL) Tom Deadlight. Herman Melville. APN-2; NCAP

And don't have any kids yourself. (LL) This Be The Verse. Philip Larkin. NAMCP V.2; NoAM; NoP-5; NPeEn; PoetW; PoPoPo; StAl

And don't you budge the skin hasn't settled. Anne Portugal. SCFWP *Fr.* Bath, The.

And dost thou still, thou mass of breathing stone. To the Fragment of a Statue of Hercules, Commonly Called the Torso. Samuel Rogers. CenSon; GS

And draw me to her in the blessed place! (LL) Petrarch. NAWM-5v1; NAWM-7v1 *Fr.* Sonnets to Laura.

And dream my time away. (LL) Expostulation and Reply. William Wordsworth. NAEL-6v2; NAEL-7v2; NOBRP; NoP-5

And drew her backward home. (LL) Subverted Flower, The. Robert Frost. APT-1; ColAP; NoAM

And drink my cup of jade-white wine. (LL) Reading the Poetry of Meng Chiao: Two Poems. Su Tung-p'o. ColAnChi; WoPoe, *tr. by* Burton Watson

And drinks, and stares, diversified with boggles? (LL) Leigh Hunt. NBLV; NPeEn *Fr.* Fish, the Man, and the Spirit, The.

And drops all the spoons. (LL) Round the World with the Rumpus God. Meret Oppenheim. SurPaPo; SurWo, *tr. by* Catherine Schelbert

And drops dead into its own skeleton. (LL) Gyroscope. Howard Nemerov. NAMCP V.2; NoAM

And drunk the milk of Paradise. (LL) Kubla Khan: or, A Vision in a Dream. Samuel Taylor Coleridge. BLPJKO; BrAP; BRP; CABP; CtM; HeIP-4; NAEL-6v2; NAEL-7v2; NAWM-7v2; NIL-7; NIP-4; NOBRP; NoP-4; NoP-5; NPBRoP; NPeEn; OBEV; OBGa; OxAEP-2; OxBEV; PoPoPo; SoSe-8; TFi; TRP; WaAnP; WeW-3; WoPoe

And dulls to distance all we are. (LL) Ambulances. Philip Larkin. BrAP; NAEL-6v2; NAEL-7v2; NoP-4; NoP-5

And dust is for a time. (LL) In Distrust of Merits. Marianne Moore. AmWaPo; APT-1; ColAP; MoAmPo; NAAL-5; NAAPv.2; OBWP

And each anointed sense will see. (LL) Extreme Unction. Ernest Dowson. MoBrPo; OBMV

And each as silent as a man being shaved. (LL) Prolonged Sonnet: When the Troops were Returning from Milan. Niccolò degli Albizzi. FaBoWar; OBVE; PoAgWa, *tr. by* Dante Gabriel Rossetti

And each slow dusk a drawing-down of blinds. (LL) Anthem for Doomed Youth. Wilfred Owen. AF; BrAP; CABP; CAGL; ClHu; FaBoWar; GPTC; GSo; HarvBoo; HeIP-4; InoFa; MoBrPo; NAEL-6v2; NAEL-7v2; NAMCP V.1; NoAM; NoP-4; NoP-5; NPeEn; OBEV; OBWP; OxBEV; PoPoPo; SoSe-8; StAl; TCAWP; TFi; WaAnP; WeW-3

And Earth is but a star, that once had shone. (LL) James Elroy Flecker. OBMV; UV *Fr.* Golden Journey to Samarkand, The.

And eats the meadow flowers. (LL) Cow, The. Robert Louis Stevenson. NTCP; TLR; WHSW

And e'en for change of scene would seek the shades below. (LL) Lord Byron. NAEL-6v2; NAEL-7v2 *Fr.* Childe Harold's Pilgrimage.

And eke [*or* eek] men shal nat [*or* nought] make[n] ernest of game. (LL) Geoffrey Chaucer. NAEL-6v1; NAEL-7v1 *Fr.* Canterbury Tales, The.

And empty grows every bed. (LL) John Berryman. ColAP; EMP; NAMCP V.2; NoP-4; NoP-5; VCAP *Fr.* Dream Songs.

And ends that tiny, unearthly song. (LL) Poets in Late Winter. Mona Van Duyn. ExTi; PfSP

And ere she left with tottling steps. Elizabeth Oakes-Smith. STuOW *Fr.* Sinless Child, The.

And ere thou change all human song shall die! (LL) Cheyenne Mountain. Helen Hunt Jackson. APN-2; NAAPv.1

And Error loves and nourishes thy soul. (LL) Be still. The Hanging Gardens were a dream. Trumbull Stickney. APN-2; WoPoe

And escaped from the people of Basing. (LL) Limerick: "There was an Old Person of Basing." Edward Lear. NPeEn; OxAEP-2

And Eternity in an hour. (LL) William Blake. NPeEn; OxBEV; PtR *Fr.* Auguries of Innocence.

And Ettrick mourns with her their Poet [*or* Shepherd] dead. (LL) Extempore Effusion upon the Death of James Hogg. William Wordsworth. NAEL-6v2; NAEL-7v2; NPBRoP

And even here. Fields of this Summer. Gennady Aygi. WoBe, *tr. by* Peter France

And even there he didn't really come up to scratch. (LL) Poetry and Thought. René Daumal. MotU; YaTCFP, *tr. by* Michael Wood

And even this is only half a revenge. (LL) Autobiography. Dan Pagis. AF; VCWP, *tr. by* Stephen Mitchell. *See also* Though it's only a sour revenge.

And every memory you have—will begin / at Genesis. (LL) Temptation. Nina Cassian. AF; StAl, *tr. by* Brenda Walker and Andrea Deletant

And every Space that a Man views around his dwelling-place. William Blake. BLT *Fr.* Milton.

And every wave is charmed. (LL) Terminus ("It is time to be old.") Ralph Waldo Emerson. APN-1; BrAP; GoPo; NCAP; TCAPo

And everyone, everyone pointing up and shouting! (LL) Child on Top of a Greenhouse. Theodore Roethke. NoP-4; NoP-5; NOxBChV; PtR

And Everywhere Offering Human Sound. Joan Houlihan. IAoNAP

And ev'n Devotion! (LL) To a Louse [On Seeing One on a Lady's Bonnet at Church]. Robert Burns. FaBoVe; NAEL-6v2; NAEL-7v2; NePenScot; NOBRP

And exchange names and addresses. (LL) Truce. Paul Muldoon. FaBoWar; PBCIP; PNI

And excited the heart of Argive. Alcaeus. SaLy, *tr. by* Diane Rayor

And faded on the blowing of the horn. (LL) T. S. Eliot. NPeEn; OxBEV *Fr.* Four Quartets.

And faintly trust the larger hope. (LL) Alfred Tennyson. BrAP; NAEL-6v2; NAEL-7v2; NAWM-7v2; NoP-5; SacPr; WaAnP *Fr.* In Memoriam A. H. H.

And faith knows nothing of reasons. All Illusion Is a Form of Hope. Aida Gelbtrunk. MirDau, *tr. by* Roberta Gordenstein

And faith to Love—to our dead at rest. (LL) Augusta Davies Webster. ViWPN; VWP *Fr.* Mother and Daughter.

And fall. (LL) November Night. Adelaide Crapsey. APT-1; NAAPv.2; Spl; TCAPo

And fall in blood: we bring him even now. (LL) Six O'Clock. Trumbull Stickney. APN-2; OxBoAm

And falling all day. (LL) Spring sea rising, The. Buson. ASA; EH, *tr. by* Robert Hass

And fame of his descendants. (LL) Virgil. NAWM-5v1; NAWM-7v1 *Fr.* Aeneid [*or* Eneados *or* Aeneis], The.

& familiar. The dark watermark of your absence, a hush. (LL) Hush. David St. John. CalPo; FaoP

And fate change me to worms. (LL) Against Constancy. John Wilmot, 2d Earl of Rochester. NOSC; OxAEP-1

And fear lit by the breadth of such calmly turns to praise. (LL) City Limits, The. A. R. Ammons. EMP; GPTC; InGu; NAMCP V.2; NoAM; NoP-4; NoP-5; OxBoAm; PoPoPo; VCAP

And fears not portly Azcan nor his hoos. (LL) Bantams in Pine-Woods. Wallace Stevens. NAAPv.2; NAMCP V.1; NoAM; OxBoAm; SAmP

And feed me honey from the rock. (LL) Captivity. Louise Erdrich. AmWaPo; HATNAP; NAMCP V.2; NoAM

And feed my soul, with luxury of woe! (LL) Sappho Rejects Hope. Mary Robinson. CenSon; RWP

And feel I'm part of thee! (LL) My Childhood-Home I See Again. Abraham Lincoln. APN-1; NAAPv.1; PtR

And feel like flowers that fade. (LL) Sir Henry Taylor. OBEV; RACG *Fr.* Philip van Artevelde.

And fell it on the start. (LL) John Berryman. BrAP; CAP-8; InoFa; NAMCP V.2; PoPoPo; VCAP *Fr.* Dream Songs.

And felt the rock move beneath my hand. (LL) Butterfly on Rock. Irving Layton. BrAP; NoAM

And fiery tempered steel. (LL) Fragment 113: "Not honey, / not the plunder of the bee." "H. D." APT-1; NAAPv.2

And fill your heads with crotchets. (LL) Distracted Puritan, The. Richard Corbet. BASC; OBCoV

And find another lover. (LL) Song in Spite of Myself. Countee Cullen. ISC; ItP

And find th'effect, for I do burn in love. (LL) Sir Philip Sidney. NoP-4; NoP-5 *Fr.* Astrophil and Stella.

And Finished knowing—then. (LL) I Felt a Funeral in My Brain. Emily Dickinson. APN-2; HeIP-4; NAAL-3; NAAPv.1; NALW; NAMCP V.1; NoP-4; NoP-5; OxBoAm; RaBo; SoSe-8; TCAPo; TFi

And fire their only future. (LL) Asians Dying, The. W. S. Merwin. AmWaPo; NAMCP V.2; PoPoPo; VCAP; WaAnP

And firmly stands when Crowns and Scepters fall. (LL) On the 3 of September, 1651. Katherine Philips. BASC; EMWP; PBRV; WaAnP

And first the walles and dark entrie I sought. Virgil. NPeEn *Fr.* Aeneid [*or* Eneados *or* Aeneis], The.

And float with them about the summer waters. (LL) Happy Is England! I Could Be Content. John Keats. CenSon; OxAEP-2

And flood a fresher throat with song. (LL) Alfred Tennyson. NAEL-6v2; NAEL-7v2; WaAnP *Fr.* In Memoriam A. H. H.

And for all the adulation. Star, The. Clyde A. Wray. BtF

And for breakfast she said we have strawberries. (LL) Strawberries. W. S. Merwin. AmFaPo; NoP-4

And for her sake trip up Death. (LL) Little Elegy. X. J. Kennedy. InoFa; WaAnP

And for our little chat, it suited. (LL) Memo to Auden. Anne Rouse. MFPA; NeBrP

And, for our tongue, that still is so empayr'd. George Chapman. PBRV *Fr.* Homer's Iliad, To the Reader.

And for short time an endless[e] monument [*or* moniment]. (LL) Epithalamion: "Ye learned sisters which have oftentimes." Edmund Spenser. NAEL-6v1; NAEL-7v1; NoP-5; NoSic; OBEV; OxAEP-1; WaAnP

And for special things. Grim Sisters, The. Liz Lochhead. CABP; MoWP

And for the soul. Argonautica. George Seferis. PoetW, *tr. by* Rex Warner

And for what, except for you, do I feel love? Notes toward a Supreme Fiction. Wallace Stevens. APT-1

And forced the underbrush—and that was all. (LL) Most of It, The. Robert Frost. APT-1; BLT; NAMCP V.1; NoP-4; NoP-5; OxBoAm; TRP; WaAnP; WeW-3

And forget it, long before it is worn out. (LL) Present from the Emperor's New Concubine, A. Pan Chieh-yû. NDACCP; WoPoe, *tr. by* Kenneth Rexroth

And Forgive Us Our Traspasses. Sinéad Morrissey. MoWP; NIrP

And found Life—stepping on my feet! (LL) Aesthete [*or* Esthete] in Harlem. Langston Hughes. ColAP; WaAnP

And found to be not lawfully entitled to be or remain in the United States. (LL) Xenophobic Nightmare in a Foreign Language. Harryette Mullen. PrTe; WANABP

And frame from thinking and is realized. (LL) To an Old Philosopher in Rome. Wallace Stevens. APT-1; ColAP; NAMCP V.1; NoAM

And free land of the grave. (LL) Crossing Alone the Nighted Ferry. A. E. Housman. HarvBoo; NoP-4; NoP-5; NPeEn; OxBEV

And freed [*or* free'd] his soul the nearest way. (LL) On the Death of Dr [*or* Mr] Robert Levet [a Practiser in Physic]. Samuel Johnson. ChIV-2; NAEL-6v1; NAEL-7v1; NoP-4; NoP-5; NPeEn; OBEV; OxAEP-1; OxBEV; TFi; WaAnP

And Freedom's banner streaming o'er us. (LL) American Flag, The. Joseph Rodman Drake. APN-1; BRP

And from louts to run away. (LL) Sir Philip Sidney. NAEL-6v1; NAEL-7v1; NoSic; OxAEP-1 *Fr.* Astrophil and Stella.

And from the Citie Tegea there came the Paragone. Ovid. OBVE *Fr.* Metamorphoses.

And from the house his mother called his name. (LL) Childhood. Edwin Muir. HeIP-4; NePenScot; NoP-4; NoP-5; NPeEn

And from the red granite in the distance. Natural History. Giampiero Neri. ItPo, *tr. by* Gayle Ridinger

And from the woods the late resounding note. Philip Freneau. TCAPo *Fr.* House of Night, The.

And from within the howls of Death I heard. Philip Freneau. TCAPo *Fr.* House of Night, The.

And gained in service of our fair / And universal Queen. (LL) Pangloss's Song: A Comic-Opera Lyric. Richard Wilbur. NBLV; NoAM

And gallop terribly against each other's bodies. (LL) Autumn Begins in Martins Ferry, Ohio. James Wright. CAP-8; ColAP; EMP; HeIP-4; IJHIL; MoASP; NAAL-5; NAMCP V.2; NoAM; OxBoAm; StAl; VCAP; WaAnP; WeW-3

And gathering swallows twitter in the skies. (LL) To Autumn: "Season of mists and mellow fruitfulness!" John Keats. BrAP; CABP; ClHu; CtM; HeIP-4; ITBLP; MakPoe; NAEL-6v2; NAEL-7v2; NAWM-7v2; NIL-7; NIP-4; NOBRP; NoP-4; NoP-5; NPBRoP; NPeEn; OBEV; OxAEP-2; OxBEV; PoPoPo; PtR; RaBo; SoSe-8; TFi; TRP; WaAnP; WeW-3

And gave away her heart. (LL) Ballad of Aunt Geneva, The. Marilyn Nelson Waniek. FFC; GT

And gave me back my beauty. (LL) Fired Pot, The. Anna Wickham. LW; NPeEn

And gazing, died. (LL) White Women, The. Mary Elizabeth Coleridge. NALW; PEW; ViWPN; VWP

And give her no scouts doing their one good deed. Elderly Lady Crossing on Green. Wyatt Prunty. RA

And gliding forward, gaping wide. (LL) Staring at the Sea on the Day of the Death of Another. May Swenson. APT-2; NAMCP V.2; OxBoAm

And glittering eyelids of my soul's desire. (LL) Love And Sleep. Algernon Charles Swinburne. GSo; OxBSo

And Gloucester, today. The day you'll be sorry one day. (LL) Good Teachers, The. Carol Ann Duffy. ItWoWo; NAMCP V.2

And go down that river with the ivory, the copra and the gold. (LL) Somewhere in Africa. Anne Sexton. InoFa; NALW

And go to the moon. (LL) Bean Spasms. Ted Berrigan. AHA; PmAP

And God is all in all. (LL) Come on, my partners in distress. Charles Wesley. NoP-4; NoP-5; WaAnP

And God said, I will build a church here. Island, The. Ronald Stuart Thomas. InvLi

And God said, "Let the waters generate." John Milton. NOSC *Fr.* Paradise Lost.

And God said to the soul. God Speaks to the Soul. Mechthild von Magdeburg. WPoS, *tr. by* Oliver Davies

And God saw. Vera Pavlova. CRWP, *tr. by* Steven Seymour

And God saw that the wickedness of man was great. Bible, *O.T.* NAWM-5v1 *Fr.* Genesis.

And God shall bless you from above. (LL) To My Dear Children. Anne Bradstreet. BASC; NAAL-3; PtR

And God stepped out on space. Creation, The. James Weldon Johnson. AmFaPo; APT-1; ChIV-1; InGu; ISC; MoAmPo; NAMCP V.1; OxAAAP; OxBoAm; SacPr; SSLK

And God—at every Gate. (LL) Our journey had advanced. Emily Dickinson. APN-2; SoSe-8

And gods disgusting.—You and I, Cassandra. (LL) Cassandra. Robinson Jeffers. APT-1; HeIP-4

And going to the office in the train. (LL) Dreamers. Siegfried Sassoon. GSo; MoBrPo; NAMCP V.1; NoAM

And gold on my neck the sun. (LL) Collier, The. Vernon Watkins. OBWVE; TCAWP

And grackles by the shadow of a fountain. (LL) Dearest Reader. Michael Palmer. CAP-8; FTOS

And grant his reign over the entire building. (LL) Homage to the British Museum. William Empson. MoBrPo; NPeEn; OxBEV

And grave by grave we civilize the ground. (LL) To the Western World. Louis Simpson. OxBoAm; TRP

And great souls, at one stroke, may do and doat. (LL) Elizabeth Barrett Browning. CenSon; NAEL-6v2; NAEL-7v2 *Fr.* Sonnets from the Portuguese.

And green plaid shorts goes strolling. Eros in His Striped Blue Shirt. Reginald Shepherd. WiU

And grow incorporate into thee. (LL) Alfred Tennyson. NAEL-6v2; NAEL-7v2; NAWM-7v2; NoP-5; NPeEn; WaAnP *Fr.* In Memoriam A. H. H.

And guiltlessly watch the wrist-ropes fall? (LL) True Descenders. James Kimbrell. AmPoNex; NAPBL

And gulp from them the dailiness of life. (LL) Well Water. Randall Jarrell. NAAL-5; PoCho; VCAP

And Gwydion said to Math, when it was Spring. Wife of Llew, The. Francis Ledwidge. MakPoe

And half the seed of Europe, one by one. (LL) Parable of the Old Men and the Young, The. Wilfred Owen. ChIV-1; HarvBoo; RSaN

And handled with a Chain. (LL) Much Madness is divinest Sense. Emily Dickinson. APN-2; HeIP-4; IJHIL; NAAL-3; NAAL-5; NAAPv.1; NALW; NAMCP V.1; NAWM-7v2; NCAP; NoAM; NoP-4; NoP-5; OPOU; OxBoAm; PoPoPo; RaBo; SAmP; SoSe-8; TCAPo; TFi; TRP; WaAnP

And hang from implacable boughs. (LL) Chagrin. Isaac Rosenberg. HarvBoo; MoBrPo

And haply may forget. (LL) Song: "When I am dead, my dearest." Christina Georgina Rossetti. CABP; NAEL-6v2; NAEL-7v2; NoP-4; NoP-5; NPeEn; OBEV; OxAEP-2; ViWPN; VWP

And hardly safe from brother traitors there. (LL) To Sir Toby. Philip Freneau. NAAL-3; NAAPv.1; NoP-4; NoP-5; WaAnP

And has failed. (LL) Song at Midnight. Lucille Clifton. ErotSp; OxAAAP; UnSA

And has the nature of infinity. (LL) Instructions to the Player. Carl Rakosi. APT-2; MiVo

And has the remnant of my life. Thoughts on my sick-bed. Dorothy Wordsworth. NAEL-7v2; PEW

And have forgotten since their beauty passed. (LL) Tears. Edward Thomas. NAEL-6v2; NAEL-7v2

And have I strove in vain to move. To Anna Matilda. Robert Merry. NOBRP

And have one Titan at a time. (LL) Master, The. Edwin Arlington Robinson. CBCWP; MoAmPo

And have we lost another friend? John Close. STuOW *Fr.* In Respectful Memory of Mr. Yarker.

And having lost track, I walked. And Having Lost Track. Joanna Klink. LegDan

And having nothing, yet hath all. (LL) Character of a Happy Life, The. Sir Henry Wotton. BASC; NOSC; OBEV; OxBEV; SacPr

And, having started singing this melody. Natalya Gorbanevskaya. CFP, *tr. by* Gerald S. Smith

And haze and vista, and the far horizon fading away. (LL) Farm Picture, A. Walt Whitman. BLT; TRP

And He Answered Them Nothing. Richard Crashaw. ChIV-2; SacPr

And he called to him his twelve disciples. Philip Larkin. GI *Fr.* St. Matthew.

And he cast it down, down, on the green grass. New Ghost, The. Fredegond Maitland Shove. SacPr

And he drops, and turns, and goes. (LL) In the Servants' Quarters. Thomas Hardy. FaBoVe; MoBrPo

And he held me fast, and he said, At last. Ella Wheeler Wilcox. VerBaPo *Fr.* Drops of Water.

And he is Christ our Lord. (LL) Bible, *O.T.* NoP-4; NoP-5 *Fr.* Translation of the Psalms of David, A.

And he picked up a baseball. (LL) Origin of Baseball, The. Kenneth Patchen. APT-2; CLPP

And he pronounced it firm. (LL) How brittle are the Piers. Emily Dickinson. NCAP; SacPr

And he said, So is the kingdome of God. Bible, *N.T.* OBVE *Fr.* St. Mark.

And he said, So soule doth magnifie the Lord. Bible, *N.T.* OBVE *Fr.* St. Mark.

And he sees them, sees their faces. Remembering. László Kálnoky. IQMS, *tr. by* Kenneth McRobbie and Zita McRobbie

And he took a little weeping to my eyes. (LL) Heroes. Sorley MacLean. FaBoTC; FaBoWar

And he trembled like a heatwave and faded. (LL) Seamus Heaney. NPeEn; PBCIP *Fr.* Station Island.

And he was left lamenting. (LL) Lord Ullin's Daughter. Thomas Campbell. NOBRP; NPBRoP

And he was the evil spirit of my dreams, the most handsome. And He Was the Evil Spirit of My Dreams. Antonio Machado Ruiz. RaW, *tr. by* Robert Bly

And He Wept Aloud, So That the Egyptians Heard It. Alden Nowlan. Coast

And He Whispered Stolen Words. Toni Kan. NeNiPo

And he will make it plain. (LL) William Cowper. CABP; NoP-4; NoP-5; NPeEn; OxBEV; SacPr; TFi *Fr.* Olney Hymns.

And hear all day long the thrush repeat his song. (LL) Green Roads, The. Edward Thomas. NAMCP V.1; NoAM

And hear the household jar within. (LL) Alfred Tennyson. NAEL-6v2; NAEL-7v2 *Fr.* In Memoriam A. H. H.

And heard the sound of rushing wind. (LL) Coming of the Plague, The. Weldon Kees. ChIV-1; StAl

And hears an unintelligible prayer. (LL) Feast of Stephen, The. Anthony Hecht. NoAM; VCAP

And heartier loves; that lamp is from the tomb. (LL) Leaders of the Crowd, The. William Butler Yeats. MoBrPo; OxAEP-2

And hearts of olive-oil. (LL) Quarrel, The. Federico García Lorca. AF; WED, *tr. by* Robert Bly

And held her in my arms! (LL) Politics. William Butler Yeats. AmFaPo; GoPo; HeIP-4; ItP; NAMCP V.1; PLBUT

And her eyes lightnings and her shoulders wings. (LL) In Progress. Christina Georgina Rossetti. NAEL-6v2; NAEL-7v2

And her eyes that will die descend gently along my arms. (LL) Right Meaning, The. César Vallejo. MotU; PoDa; RaBo; WED, *tr. by* Robert Bly

And her face said to him. Between Two Lovers. Sonia Edwards. BBMWP, *tr. by* Sally Roberts Jones

And Her Mother Came Too. Dion Titherage. OBCoV; ReLy

And her quietus is to render thee. (LL) William Shakespeare. HeIP-4; NAEL-6v1; NAEL-7v1; NoP-5 *Fr.* Sonnets.

And her thorns were my only delight. (LL) William Blake. NAEL-6v2; NAEL-7v2; NOBRP; NPBRoP *Fr.* Songs of Experience.

And her welpointed wepons did about her dresse. (LL) Edmund Spenser. NAEL-6v1; NAEL-7v1 *Fr.* Faerie Queene, The.

And here and there, on trees by lightning scathed. James Thomson. NePenScot *Fr.* Castle of Indolence, The.

And here and there with laurel shrubs between. Philip Freneau. NAAL-3 *Fr.* House of Night, The.

And here are the famous colours. In Chartres. Euros Bowen. BBMWP, *tr. by the author*

And Here are the Poets in Their Sad Portraits. Belkis Cuza Malé. TANSG, *tr. by Pamela Carmell*

And here are the poets in their sad portraits. And Here are the Poets in Their Sad Portraits. Belkis Cuza Malé. TANSG, *tr. by Pamela Carmell*

And here face down beneath the sun. You, Andrew Marvell. Archibald MacLeish. APT-1; BeAl; BrAP; ColAP; HeIP-4; MoAmPo; NAMCP V.1; NoAM; NoP-4; SoSe-8; TFi; TRP

And here, forgetting human wisdom. At the Fishmonger's. Nikolai Alekseievich Zabolotsky. TCRusP, *tr. by* Alec Merivale

And here I wish my soul died with my breath. Ovid. OBVE *Fr.* Tristium.

And here let Memory turn her tearful glance. Robert Montgomery. STuOW *Fr.* Omnipresence of the Deity, The.

And here the cross on the window means myself. Louis MacNeice. ModIr *Fr.* Hand of Snapshots, A.

And here the dark infinitive to feel. A.M. Mark Strand. CAP-8

And here the precious dust is laid [*or* layd]. Maria Wentworth. Thomas Carew. NPeEn; CavPo

And here they are again, the duffel bags of sadness. My Brother's Anger. Patricia Goedicke. LiTh

And here we are back. Going Back Patiently. Frank Mkalawile Chipasula. HBAPE

And here we are, or rather, here am I. Marilyn Hacker. FaoP *Fr.* Separations Sequence.

And here you thought you were ineffectual. Why Life Is Worth Living. Suzanne Lummis. SUP

And hid his face amid a crowd of stars. (LL) When You Are Old. William Butler Yeats. AmFaPo; BrAP; ClHu; HeIP-4; MoBrPo; NAEL-6v2; NAEL-7v2; NAMCP V.1; NAWM-7v2; NoAM; NoP-4; NoP-5; OBEV; OxBEV; StAl; TFi; WoPoe

And hide its face / for shame. (LL) Death ("He's dead / the dog won't have to.") William Carlos Williams. InoFa; NAMCP V.1

And hide the shame! (LL) Ichabod[!]. John Greenleaf Whittier. APN-1; NAAL-3; NAAL-5; NAAPv.1; PoCho; TCAPo

And hide thy shame beneath the ground. (LL) Alfred Tennyson. NAEL-6v2; NAEL-7v2 *Fr.* In Memoriam A. H. H.

And Him. (LL) Clock stopped, A. Emily Dickinson. APN-2; NAAL-3; NAAL-5; NoP-4; NoP-5; TCAPo

And, Hinges. Ted Greenwald. FTOS

And his arm lay lightly around my breast—and that night I was happy. (LL) When I Heard At The Close Of The Day. Walt Whitman. APN-1; GoPo; NAAL-3; NoAM

And his black whiskers and his little dancing feet. (LL) Behaving Like a Jew. Gerald Stern. BodElec; InvLad; LoL; TaR

And his consort, the False Imogine! (LL) Alonzo the Brave and the Fair Imogine. Matthew Gregory Lewis. NOBRP; NPBRoP

And his first minute, after noon[e], is night. (LL) Lecture upon the Shadow, A. John Donne. NAEL-6v1; NAEL-7v1; NoSic

And His graver of frost. (LL) To a Snowflake. Francis Thompson. MoBrPo; SacPr

And his late kingdom, only from the road. (LL) *My house*, I say. But hark to the sunny doves. Robert Louis Stevenson. NPeEn; OxBEV

And his overthrow, our chorus. (LL) Thomas Love Peacock. CABP; FaBoWar; NAEL-6v2; NOBRP; NPeEn; OxAEP-2 *Fr.* Misfortunes of Elphin, The.

And His own face to see. (LL) Mystery, The. Ralph Hodgson. InvLi; MoBrPo

And his sepulchre shall not be whicted. (LL) Ambrose Bierce. APN-2; CalPo *Fr.* Devil's Dictionary, The.

And holy communion and work—the good life. (LL) My Belovèd Compares Herself to a Pint of Stout. Paul Durcan. EmeKit; StAl

And hope and history rhyme. (LL) Seamus Heaney. PLBUT; TWF *Fr.* Cure at Troy, The.

And Hope without an object cannot live. (LL) Work without Hope. Samuel Taylor Coleridge. CenSon; GSo; NAEL-6v2; NAEL-7v2; NPBRoP; OBEV; OxAEP-2; OxBSo; WoPoe

And hopes, almost misgivings! (LL) Farewell, The. Letitia Elizabeth Landon. RWP; VWP

And how do you react to exile? Politely. Mr Jones as the Transported Poet. T. Harri Jones. TCAWP

And how is it we think we make the world move. As If There were any Matter. Nathaniel Tarn. WANABP

And how terrific it is to write a radio poem. Poem Beginning with a Line by Frank Lima. Lisa Jarnot. LegDan; VaPo

And how they look—from the sea. Waterfront Bars. Keith Wilson. AmWaPo

And how were we able to sing. From the Willow Branches. Salvatore Quasimodo. WoPoe, *tr. by* Michael Egan

And hundreds of miles of water. (LL) Bodies of Water. Greg Williamson. NAPBL; NeAmPo

And hurl me to the shark, I shall not die! (LL) Leg, The. Karl Shapiro. MoAmPo; WeW-3

And hurls for him, O half hurls earth for him off under his feet. (LL) Hurrahing in Harvest. Gerard Manley Hopkins. MoBrPo; NAEL-6v2; NAEL-7v2; OxBSo; SacPr

And hurry along, Van Winkle—it's getting late! (LL) Hart Crane. MoAmPo; NAAPv.2 *Fr.* Bridge, The.

And hymn thy favo[u]rite name! (LL) Ode to Evening. William Collins. CABP; NAEL-6v1; NAEL-7v1; NoP-4; NoP-5; OBEV; OxAEP-1; TFi

And I a beginner. Answer to yo / question / of am I not yo / woman / even if you went on shit again. Sonia Sanchez. OxAAAP

And I am an unhappy stranger. Mexican Loneliness. Jack Kerouac. CLPP

And I am going without having received my inheritance. Now I Am Going. León Felipe. RaW, *tr. by* W. S. Merwin

And I am in the wilderness alone. (LL) Prairies, The. William Cullen Bryant. APN-1; ColAP; NAAL-3; NAAL-5; NCAP; TCAPo

And I am lonely and small in all this, goodnight. Dana Lisa Lustig. AnSo

And I am Marie of R[o]umania. (LL) Comment. Dorothy Parker. AmWit; LW; NBLV; NIL-7; NIP-4; OBCoV

And I am Nicholas. (LL) Czar's Last Christmas Letter, The: A Barn in the Urals. Norman Dubie. NoAM; PoChi

And I am not. (LL) They Say My Verse Is Sad: No Wonder. A. E. Housman. NAMCP V.1; NoAM

And I am safe and always have been. (LL) Kaddish. David Ignatow. GoPo; RaBo; TaR

And I am the final drop. (LL) Speaking About My Cracked Sump. Andrew Waterhouse. BeAl; PoCu

And I asked for directions from a bird who is myself. Paavo Haavikko. PFTM-2 *Fr.* Winter Palace, The.

And I became alone. (LL) Wind—tapped like a tired man, The. Emily Dickinson. FaBoVe; MoAmPo

And I came to, knowing I'd been bewitched. (LL) Tunnel, The. Nicanor Parra. GPTC; TCLAP, *tr. by* W. S. Merwin

And I can speak a little then. (LL) Alfred Tennyson. NAEL-6v2; NAEL-7v2; NAWM-7v2; NoP-5 *Fr.* In Memoriam A. H. H.

And I can walk through the woods. (LL) Snakes. A. K. Ramanujan. NoP-4; NoP-5; WaAnP

And I captive am again[e]. (LL) Mary Sidney Wroth, Countess of Montgomery. LW; PEW *Fr.* Urania.

And I choose—just a Crown. (LL) I'm ceded—I've stopped being Theirs. Emily Dickinson. APN-2; NAAPv.1; NALW; SacPr; TRP; WPoS

And I dance submerged. Dance, The. Marjorie Agosin. TCLAP, *tr. by* Cola Franzen

And I don't feel so well myself. (LL) On the Vanity of Earthly Greatness. Arthur Guiterman. AmWit; APT-1; HeIP-4

And I don't have to bother with Joan! (LL) Coming from Kansas. Myra Cohn Livingston. CalPo; NOxBChV

And I dream / of embroidering / new skin. (LL) Dreams in Harrison Railroad Park. Nellie Wong. CFP

And I eat men like air. (LL) Lady Lazarus. Sylvia Plath. AmFaPo; CAP-8; ChIV-2; ColAP; EMP; FTtHH; HarvBoo; IJHIL; MoWP; NAAL-5; NALW; NAMCP V.2; NIL-7; NIP-4; NoAM; NoP-4; NoP-5; OxBoAm; OxWW; PoetW; PoPoPo; TRP; VCAP; WaAnP

And I envied her the baby within. Man Impregnated. Moniza Alvi. NeBl

And I forget to age, through her sweet will. (LL) Augusta Davies Webster. OxBSo; ViWPN *Fr.* Mother and Daughter.

And I, forsooth, in love! I, that have been love's whip. William Shakespeare. *See* O! And I forsooth in love!

And I hadn't been. (LL) Come In. Robert Frost. APT-1; MoAmPo; NoP-4; NoP-5; OxBoAm; RaBo; TRP

And I hated myself. (LL) I, the Survivor. Bertolt Brecht. HP; PoSu

And I have broken down before the wind. (LL) Nocturne of the Wharves. Arna Bontemps. ColAP; GT

And I have never gone back. (LL) Night Thoughts. Lu Yu. NDACCP; WoPoe, *tr. by* Kenneth Rexroth

And I have stepped into the iceworld—at the snout. 66°7' N/22°17' W. Peter Rafferty. NLP

And I have told you this to make you grieve. (LL) Grief. William Matthews. BeAl; CAP-8; PoCho

And I have tried to keep them from falling. (LL) Ezra Pound. APT-1; NAAPv.2; OxBoAm; WaAnP *Fr.* Cantos.

And I implode from sheer emptiness. (LL) Houdini. Moniza Alvi. EmeKit; MFPA

And I in my bed again! (LL) Western Wind. *Unknown.* ClHu; HeIP-4; NAEL-6v1; NAEL-7v1; NIL-7; NoP-4; NoSic; OPOU; PoPoPo; SoSe-8; TFi; WeW-3; WoPoe

And I killed the Molione boys. Ibycus. SaLy, *tr. by* Diane Rayor

And I knew then that I had been away for a long time. (LL) Only Yak in Batesville, Virginia, The. Oni Buchanan. IIR; LegDan

And I know the amplitude of time. (LL) Walt Whitman. BrAP; CAGL; ColAP *Fr.* Song of Myself.

And I know the earth, and I am sad. (LL) Melancholy inside Families. Pablo Neruda. RaBo; WED, *tr. by* Robert Bly and James Wright

And I know where sleeps Holofernes. (LL) Judith. Adah Isaacs Menken. APN-2; CBWP-1; SWaP; ViWPN

And I lean toward mine. (LL) Beginning. James Wright. ColAP; VCAP

And I let the fish go. (LL) Fish, The. Elizabeth Bishop. APT-2; BeAl; BrAP; CAP-8; ChAP; HarvBoo; HeIP-4; MoAmPo; MoASP; NAAL-5; NALW; NAMCP V.2; NoAM; NoP-4; NoP-5; PoetW; PoPoPo; TFi; TRP; WaAnP

And I lie listening awake? (LL) Fragment 36 [*or* Thirty-Six]: "I know not what to do." "H. D." BrAP; NALW; PoBW

And I live at the back of beyond. (LL) Overheard in County Sligo. Gillian Clarke. HarvBoo; StAl; TCAWP

And I love my Daddy like he loves his Dollar. (LL) American Primitive. William Jay Smith. MoAmPo; RaBo

And I love the rain. (LL) April Rain Song. Langston Hughes. NOxBChV; NTCP

And I must tell you of this Octoroon. Albery Allson Whitman. NAAPv.1 *Fr.* Octoroon, The.

And I myself—am murmuring. Rustle of Birches. Gennady Aygi. TCRusP, *tr. by* Peter France

And I remain despairing of the port. (LL) Petrarch. OBVE; OxBEV; WeW-3 *Fr.* Sonnets to Laura.

And I remain despairing of the port. (LL) Sonnet: "My Galley Charged." Sir Thomas Wyatt. AEP; GSo

And I remember Spain. Louis MacNeice. OBWP; OxAEP-2 *Fr.* Autumn Journal.

And I remember the shade. River Girl. Keith Wilson. ICANM

And I remembered the cry of the peacocks. (LL) Domination of Black. Wallace Stevens. APT-1; MoAmPo; NAMCP V.1; OWoS; OxBoAm; TCAPo

And I replied, *My Lord.* (LL) Collar, The. George Herbert. BASC; BrAP; CABP; ClHu; FaBoVe; FSCP; HeIP-4; InvLi; ItP; NAEL-6v1; NAEL-7v1; NIL-7; NIP-4; NoP-4; NoP-5; NOSC; NPeEn; OBWVE; PBRV; PoPoPo; SacPr; TFi; WeW-3

And I rode the Greyhound down to Brooklyn. Wild Strawberry. Maurice Kenny. HATNAP

And I saw askant the armies. Walt Whitman. FaBoWar *Fr.* Memories of President Lincoln.

And I saw the midnight sun. Midnight Sun. Johnny Mercer. APT-2; ReLy

And I saw the more the fist pounded the more the mouth laughed. The fist is pounding and pounding, and the mouth answering. (LL) Gargoyle. Carl Sandburg. NAMCP V.1; NoAM

And I say, "Cousin Harriet, here is the *Boston Evening Transcript*." (LL) *Boston Evening Transcript*, The. T. S. Eliot. APT-1; TCAPo

And I shall be the mouth of copper. And I Shall Be the Mouth of Copper. Marianne van Hirtum. SurWo, *tr. by* Guy Flandre and Peter Wood

And I shall depart. And the birds will remain singing. Definitve Journey, The. Juan Ramón Jiménez. SpanPo, *tr. by* Angel Flores

And I shall not be here when you are gone. (LL) Why He Was There. Edwin Arlington Robinson. APT-1; OxBSo

And I shall place you living in your land. (LL) Emma Lazarus. ColAP; TCAPo

And I shall traverse old love's domain / Never again. (LL) At Castle Boterel. Thomas Hardy. NPeEn; OxAEP-2; OxBEV

And I shan't be home no more. (LL) Song of the Dying Gunner A.A.1. Charles Causley. FaBoWar; PoWW

And I shout at Iva, whine at you. Easily. Marilyn Hacker. VCAP *Fr.* Taking Notice.

And I sit here / for five days now. Changes—One. Norman J. Loftis. EGAG

And I Speak of Cosmic Things. Vsevolod Nekrasov. TCRusP, *tr. by* Daniel Weissbort

And I tasted the savour of their seed-bed. (LL) Origins. Eric Ormsby. NoP-4; NoP-5

And i' th' morning steal all to bed. (LL) John Lyly. NoSic; OBCoV *Fr.* Endimion.

And I Think it Yours. Gael Turnbull. EdScPo

And I thought over again. Song. *Eskimo Oral Tradition.* NAAPv.1

And I to my wife or mistress flee. (LL) Poet's Shuffle, The. Calvin Forbes. GT; LTA

And I too old to learn to love. (LL) Ballad: "Forgive me if I laugh." Sonia Sanchez. FuFl; PoDa

And I took her down by the river. Faithless Wife, The. Federico García Lorca. SpanPo, *tr. by* Robert O'Brien

And I took her to the river. Unfaithful Wife, The. Federico García Lorca. WoPoe, *tr. by* Michael Hartnett

And I touched your hand, and we kissed, without a word. (LL) Quarrel, The. Conrad Potter Aiken. MoAmPo; StAl

And I twist the dial a hairsbreadth into jazz. (LL) Short Wave. Hilary Llewellyn-Williams. RWPCtW; TCAWP

And I want to be wanted more than anything else in the world! (LL) Homosexuality. Frank O'Hara. CAGL; PFTM-2; PoA 2002; WaAnP

And / I was Born. Creation Is a Cycle. Empress. BRtP

And I was born with you, wasn't I, Blues? Blues Don't Change, The. Al Young. ESEAA; GT

And I was travelling lightly, barefoot. Dead Sea Poems, The. Simon Armitage. NeBrP

And I was unaware. (LL) Darkling Thrush, The. Thomas Hardy. AmFaPo; BrAP; CABP; ClHu; CtM; HarvBoo; MoBrPo; NAEL-6v2; NAEL-7v2; NAMCP V.1; NIL-7; NIP-4; NoAM; NoP-4; NoP-5; NPeEn; OBEV; OWoS; OxBEV; PoPoPo; SoSe-8; TFi; WaAnP; WoPoe

And I went up to that chandeliered place. Poem. Calvin C. Hernton. GT

And I when I meet you mean to discover you by the like in you. (LL) Among the Multitude. Walt Whitman. APN-1; CAGL

And I will [or shall] dwell in the house of the Lord for ever [or forever]. (LL) King James Version. BLPJKO; NAWM-5v1; NIL-7; NIP-4; TFi; WaAnP Fr. Psalms.

And I will sing a lullaby. Shannon Estuary 1988. Nuala Ni Dhomhnaill. IrLP

And I will venture, though I fall or tire. (LL) Francis Quarles. BASC; NOSC Fr. Emblems (Fragments).

And I with only a reed in my hands. Memory 1. George Seferis. PoetW, tr. by Edmund Keeley and Philip Sherrard

And I with thee will choose to live. (LL) Il Penseroso. John Milton. BASC; NAEL-6v1; NAEL-7v1; NoP-4; NoP-5; NOSC; OBEV; TFi

And I wonder if any good will come of either of them all the same. (LL) Circus, The ("I remember when I wrote The Circus.") Kenneth Koch. OxBoAm; PmAP

And if a juggler arrives in town. When Tomorrow Is Too Long. Tanure Ojaide. HBAPE

And If He Had Been Wrong for Me. Robert Duncan. RaBo

And if he's gone away, said she. Story. Dorothy Parker. AmWit

And if I devoted my life. Untitled. Cecilia Vicuña. WANABP, tr. by Eliot Weinberger

And If I Did What Then? George Gascoigne. NoP-4; NoP-5; WaAnP

And if I dye, who will saye: This was Immerito?. (LL) Iambicum Trimetrum. Edmund Spenser. NPeEn; OBEV

And if I feel like a woman looming over Lautrec. Blue Collar Holiday. Jeni Olin. BAP-04; FreRad

And if I lived in those olden times. Anonymous. Víctor Hernández Cruz. PueRic

And if I loved you Wednesday. Thursday. Edna St. Vincent Millay. AmWit; PoA 2002

And if it snowed and snow covered the drive. Poem. Simon Armitage. HarvBoo; NeBrP; StAl

And if it's not askin' too much, pleeease. B.B. Blues. Mary Weems. SpirFl

And if men ask you why you fled, and what. Refugees. Donald Davidson. FuPo

And if my light should. Elaine Randell. Oth Fr. Snoad Hill Poems, The.

And, if not shot or hang'd [or hanged], you'll get knighted. (LL) Stanzas: "When a man hath no freedom to fight for at home." Lord Byron. NBLV; NoP-4; NoP-5; OxAEP-2; TRP

And if the Shadows Weren't. Pedro Salinas. RaW, tr. by W. S. Merwin

And if ye stand in doubt. John Skelton. NAEL-6v1 Fr. Colin Clout.

And I'm afraid it's you. (LL) Valentine. Wendy Cope. NoP-4; NoP-5

And I'm afraid most of my friends are dead. (LL) In a Notebook. James Fenton. NeBrP; NPeEn

And I'm here, sizing the dark, saving my mother's seat. (LL) Sitting at Night on the Front Porch. Charles Wright. ColAP; GeoHom

And imagined her. She Had Known Brothers. Sherley Anne Williams. GT

And in a while you'll tell another tale. (LL) Dialogue between Old England and New, A. Anne Bradstreet. BASC; EMWP

And, in Africa, a carcass quick with flies. (LL) Black Tambourine. Hart Crane. NAMCP V.1; NoAM

And in August the barley grew up out of the grave. (LL) Requiem for the Croppies. Seamus Heaney. NAMCP V.2; OBWP

And in blue skies the Orb is manifest to sight. (LL) Epi-strauss-ium. Arthur Hugh Clough. NAEL-6v2; NAEL-7v2

And in God's house are many scansions. (LL) Poetry. Mary Elizabeth Fullerton. GI; NOBAu

And in immense perdition sinks the soul. (LL) To the University of Cambridge, in New-England. Phillis Wheatley. NAAL-3; NAAL-5; NAAPv.1; TCAPo

And, in its marriage robe, the heavy body wound. (LL) Lamia. John Keats. NAEL-6v2; NAEL-7v2; NoP-5

And in my joys for thee my only annoy. (LL) Sir Philip Sidney. NAEL-6v1; NAEL-7v1 Fr. Astrophil and Stella.

And in one another's blameless eyes go blind. (LL) Tally Stick, The. Jarold Ramsey. NIL-7; NIP-4

And in our faults by lies [or lyes] we flatter'd [or flattered] be. (LL) William Shakespeare. AmFaPo; CABP; HeIP-4; NAEL-6v1; NAEL-7v1; NoP-4; NoP-5; NoSic; NPeEn; OxAEP-1; OxBEV; PBRV; SoSe-8 Fr. Sonnets.

And in retirement, I can bless the shade. (LL) On Myself. Anne Finch, Countess of Winchilsea. NoP-4; NoP-5

And in that inner cinema saw. I had my eyes shut the whole time. Kate Clanchy. PoCu

And in that region there were shepherds out in the field. Bertolt Brecht. GI Fr. St. Luke.

And in that way, be known. (LL) So Much Happiness. Naomi Shihab Nye. BeAl; PLBUT

And in the Afternoons I Botanized. Elton Glaser. PoDa

And in the ear[e], not conscience ring. (LL) Windows, The. George Herbert. BASC; NAEL-6v1; NAEL-7v1; NoP-4; NoP-5

And in the end, the entire earth may answer to a single name. Franco Buffoni. ItPo, tr. by Gayle Ridinger

And in the evening the black river. Shadow Valley. Robert Morgan. AngWePo

And in the evening there was light. (LL) What the Birds Said. John Greenleaf Whittier. APN-1; OxBoAm

And in the frosty season, when the sun. William Wordsworth. WoPoe Fr. Prelude, The; Growth of a Poet's Mind [1805 version; Selections from Anthologies].

And in the Hanging Gardens. Conrad Potter Aiken. APT-1; MoAmPo

And in the light of truth thy Bondman let me live! (LL) Ode to Duty. William Wordsworth. NAEL-6v2; NAEL-7v2; NOBRP; OBEV

And in the midst of all, a fountaine stood. Edmund Spenser. EroLit Fr. Faerie Queene, The.

And in the mountains of Kiev, Sviatoslav. Unknown. WoPoe Fr. Song of Igor's Campaign, The.

And in the river the nameless body sifts. Solitaire. Conrad Potter Aiken. ColAP

And in the suburbs can't sat down and cried. (LL) Kilroy. Peter Viereck. MoAmPo; PWW2

And in the U.S.A. Miguel Algarin. FTtHH

And in their own heads. (LL) Louis Zukofsky. APT-2; NAMCP V.1; OxBoAm Fr. 29 Songs.

And in thy wisdom, make me wise. (LL) Alfred Tennyson. NAEL-6v2; NAEL-7v2; NAWM-7v2; SacPr Fr. In Memoriam A. H. H.

And in your fragrant bosom[e] dies [or dyes]. (LL) Song[, A]: "Ask[e] me no more where Jove bestow[e]s." Thomas Carew. BASC; CavPo; ClHu; NAEL-6v1; NAEL-7v1; NoP-4; NOSC; OBEV; OxBEV; TFi; CtM; NoP-5

And indeed I shall anchor, one day—some summer morning. Landfall. Randolph Stow. BMAP

And into his dead mouth slip the set of teeth. (LL) Michael Longley. ModIr; NPeEn Fr. Wreaths.

And invite the wind inside. (LL) Exaggeration of Despair, The. Sherman Alexie. BAP-97; NeAmPo; PrTe

And is all sense, all feeling gone. Manx. Mary Russell Mitford. DiBP

And is another, like the river with no end. (LL) Ars Poetica: "To look at the river made of time and water." Jorge Luis Borges. PtR; TCLAP, tr. by W. S. Merwin

And is fed upon, and is native, and maker. (LL) Sycamore, The. Wendell Berry. LPSFW; UpMys

And is it possible?—and must it be. Hic Jacet. Rosamund Marriott Watson. ViWPN

And is it true that I must go from Troy? William Shakespeare. OxAEP-1 Fr. Troilus and Cressida.

And is [or in] this life? and are we born for this? Unattained, The. Elizabeth Oakes-Smith. NAAPv.1

And is there care in heaven? and is there love. Edmund Spenser. NoSic Fr. Faerie Queene, The.

And is there glory from the heavens departed? Lost Pleiad. Felicia Dorothea Hemans. NOBRP

And is there honey still for tea? (LL) Old Vicarage, Grantchester, The. Rupert Brooke. MoBrPo; NoP-4; NoP-5

And is there sadness in thy dreams, my boy? Dreaming Child, The. Felicia Dorothea Hemans. NOBRP; NPBRoP

And is there then no earthly place. Thomas Moore. OBSV Fr. Rhymes on the Road.

And is thy glass run out? Is that oil spent. Upon the Poet of His Time, Ben Jonson: His Honoured Friend and Father. James Howell. NOSC

And Isabel calmly cured the doctor. (LL) Adventures of Isabel. Ogden Nash. ChAP; MoAmPo; NOxBChV; NTCP; PtR

And Ishmael crouch'd beside a crackling briar. Ishmael. Herbert Edward Palmer. OBEV

And Israel's body as smoke through the air! (LL) O the Chimneys. Nelly Sachs. AF; HP; PoetW, tr. by Michael Roloff

And it Came to Pass. C. D. Wright. TAPaP

And it came to pass in those days, that there went out a decree from Caesar Augustus. Bible, N.T. NAWM-5v1 Fr. St. Luke.

And it came to pass just as they had foretold. Adam Cornford. CLPP Fr. Rapture, The.

And it is cold here and a bit strange. Natalya Starodubtseva. CRWP, tr. by Daniel Weissbort

And it is hard to tell one. To a Friend Who Wouldn't Bother to Strain His Noodleboard Because Even So It Is Hard to Go Hunting When Your Rifle Is Blunt and Love Is Soft as an Old Blanket. Jacob Glatstein. PFTM-1

And It Is Still That Way. Hedva Harechavi. DTA, tr. by Miriyam Glazer

And it is yesterday again when I fell. Falling into Meditation. Gene Frumkin. ICANM

And it isn't for you. (LL) Several Voices Out of a Cloud. Louise Bogan. APT-2; NALW

And it seemed, while we waited, he began to walk to- / wards us. Geoffrey Hill. NAEL-7v2; NAMCP V.2; NoAM; NoP-4 Fr. Mercian Hymns.

And It Shall Come. Albert Young. RSaN

And it takes flight whitecaps typhoon thrum. Typhoon Thrum. Nicole Brossard. OpeFie, tr. by Robert Majzels and Erin Mouré

And it walks on knives, on knives. (LL) Almost Human. Cecil Day Lewis. NAMCP V.1; NoAM

And it was at that age . . . Poetry arrived. Poetry. Pablo Neruda. PoetW; VCWP, tr. by Alastair Reid

And it was first, after the mess and straining. First Things, Last Things. Peter Scupham. WaAnP

And it was then. Poem for the Father. Alejandra Pizarnik. TCLAP, tr. by Frank Graziano and María Rosa Fort

And it will be life to separate us, not death. Fragment. Alessandro Ceni. ItPo, tr. by Gayle Ridinger

And it will not affect your nostrils long. Odor of a Metal Is Not Strong, The. Merrill Moore. OxBSo

And it's been years. (LL) Anniversary: "When the world was created wasn't it like this?" Joy Harjo. CFP; PoDa

And its bleak sacrifice? (LL) Islands, The. "H. D." MoAmPo; TCAPo

And it's familiar. Flame. Jayne Cortez. OxAAAP

And it's for the ladies. This Is Just a Fairy Tale. Jane R. Ransom. PfS

And its hero the Conqueror Worm. (LL) Conqueror Worm, The. Edgar Allan Poe. APN-1; NCAP; TCAPo

And it's morning. Keita Fodeba. SonAtl, tr. by Gregory Beaven, Kurt Ganzl, Saul Goode and Jim Yarris

And it's the summer civil war. Eduard Veniaminovich Limonov. TCRusP Fr. Secret Notebook.

And its wavering image here. (LL) Bridge, The. Henry Wadsworth Longfellow. APN-1; ITBLP; NAAPv.1; OxBoAm

& I've always admired fiction but I've never admired the fiction. Various Multitudes Contained by the Loves of My Love, The. Anselm Berrigan. HeMarv; IIR

And Jesus said to him, "Foxes have holes." Karl Kirchwey. GI Fr. St. Matthew.

And Job from his mountain sees. David Brendon Hopes. UpMys Fr. Job from His Mountain.

And Joseph was brought down to Egypt. Bible, O.T. NAWM-5v1 Fr. Genesis.

And joy the poet's eye. (LL) Grave of a Poetess, The. Felicia Dorothea Hemans. NPBRoP; RWP; VWP

And Jude, now you're married, will stretch on the floor. (LL) On an Island. John Millington Synge. FaBoVe; MoBrPo; NPeEn; OxBEV

And just to show who's master I write the poem. (LL) Walking the Dog. Howard Nemerov. BeAl; GoPo

And just what color is blue? Thermometer. Giovanni Singleton. BtF

And just what the fuck else were we supposed to do. (LL) Rape. Jayne Cortez. GT; PmAP

And just when our maiden had got. Rapunzstiltskin. Liz Lochhead. BeAl; MoWP

And keep his ears glued to the big clock they keep winding. (LL) If Someone Tells You It's Not for Sure. Jaime Sabines. PoetW; TCLAP, tr. by Philip Levine

And keep on safely sleeping. (LL) Summary for Alastor. Laura Riding Jackson. FuPo; WoPoe

And kept my spirit with the free. (LL) Vision, A. John Clare. NAEL-6v2; NAEL-7v2; OxBEV

And kept on drinking. (LL) Miniver Cheevy. Edwin Arlington Robinson. AmWit; APT-1; ChAP; ClHu; ColAP; EMP; HeIP-4; MoAmPo; NAAL-5; NAAPv.1; NAMCP V.1; NBLV; NoAM; NoP-4; NoP-5; OBSV; OxBoAm; RaBo; SoSe-8; TCAPo; TFi; WaAnP

And kings rise eastward in the night. (LL) Epiphany: "Unearthly lightning of presage." Robert Fitzgerald. ChrPo; PoCho

And kiss Achilles' hand, the killer of my son. (LL) Ceasefire. Michael Longley. NAMCP V.2; StAl

And kneeling one day at the sea's edge God. Making of Eve, The. Julia Copus. NeBl

And knew no pain. (LL) Derek Mahon. See Somebody screams.

And knowledge past your agony and waste. (LL) Delia Rexroth ("Under your illkempt yellow roses.") Kenneth Rexroth. NAMCP V.1; OxBoAm

And knows herself in death. (LL) Great Breath, The. George Russell. MoBrPo; OBEV; OBMV

And laid them away in a box of gold. (LL) For a Poet. Countee Cullen. BLPJKO; ItP

And Langland told how heaven could not keep love. Beach, The. Peter Scupham. HarvBoo

And last but not least, my own brother. My Lost Brother. Ben Scammell. NLP

And later try hard to make them seem light. (LL) Under a Certain Little Star. Wisława Szymborska. PoetW; VCWP, tr. by Magnus J. Krynski and Robert A. Maguire

And, laterally / to Adam's pulsing eye. Cloud, The. Derek Walcott. ChIV-1

And laugh—but smile no more. (LL) Haunted Palace, The. Edgar Allan Poe. APN-1; BrAP; NAAL-3; NAAPv.1; OxBoAm; TCAPo; TFi

And laughing Ceres reassume the land. (LL) Alexander Pope. NPeEn; OxBEV Fr. Epistle IV to Richard Boyle, Earl of Burlington.

And laugh—No more have I. (LL) They shut me up in Prose. Emily Dickinson. APN-2; FaBoVe; NAAPv.1; NALW; NCAP; NoP-4; NoP-5; OxBoAm

And lay awake all night and suffered there. (LL) Bill Gets Burned. Howard Phelps Putnam. APT-2; OxBoAm

And leaf-shadow are lost. (LL) Evening. "H. D." APT-1; HarvBoo

And leans on the air that is hers and here. (LL) Hourglass. Josephine Jacobsen. NoP-4; NoP-5

And leaps from dreams to hail the coming day. (LL) South, The. Emma Lazarus. APN-2; ColAP; NAAPv.1

And learn a style from a despair. (LL) This Last Pain. William Empson. HarvBoo; MoBrPo; NoAM; NPeEn

And learn their languages. (LL) Kshemendra. EaWin; WoPoe Fr. Kavikanthabharana.

And leave her dreaming in the silent land. (LL) Old House, The. Amy Levy. PEW; ViWPN; VWP

And leave him then, being made a ready horse? (LL) John Donne. BASC; NoP-4; NoP-5; OxAEP-1 Fr. Elegies.

And leave our desert to its peace! (LL) Stanzas from the Grande Chartreuse. Matthew Arnold. NAEL-6v2; NAEL-7v2

And leave the old sheep alone. (LL) Rock O' My Soul. Unknown. SSUS; TCAPo

And leaves her too much alone. (LL) Beautiful Toilet, The. Mei Sheng. NDACCP; OBVE, tr. by Ezra Pound

And leaves his hold and c[r]ackles, groans, and dies. (LL) Badger. John Clare. NoP-4; NoP-5; NPeEn; PoPoPo; WaAnP

And led the flock away. (LL) I'll tell you how the Sun rose. Emily Dickinson. APN-2; ITBLP

And left me old, and cold, and grey. (LL) May: "I cannot tell you how it was." Christina Georgina Rossetti. NPeEn; OxBEV; WaAnP

And left the vivid air signed with their honour. (LL) I Think Continually of Those Who Were Truly Great. Stephen Spender. BLPJKO; HarvBoo; HeIP-4; MoBrPo; NoP-4; NoP-5; PLBUT; RaBo; TFi

And left with a debt to another white man. (LL) St. Peter Claver. Toi Derricotte. LTA; PBCAP

And Lena went,—to his dear arms she flew. Albery Allson Whitman. NAAPv.1 Fr. Octoroon, The.

And let go. (LL) Miscarriage. Jane Duran. PoCu; StAl

And let loose in a fearful roaming. (LL) Horses. Gwyn Thomas. BBMWP; OBWVE, tr. by Joseph P. Clancy

And let me die [or dye] before my death! (LL) Regeneration. Henry Vaughan. BASC; ChIV-1; FSCP; NAEL-6v1; NAEL-7v1; NoP-4; NoP-5

And let the ape and tiger die. (LL) Alfred Tennyson. BrAP; NAEL-6v2; NAEL-7v2; NAWM-7v2 Fr. In Memoriam A. H. H.

And let us say. Matthew Hollis. BeAl

And let your full lips laugh at Fate! (LL) To a Dark Girl. Gwendolyn B. Bennett. ColAP; WaAnP

And letting them out again. (LL) Gwendolyn Brooks. NAMCP V.2; NoAM; WaAnP Fr. Street in Bronzeville, A.

And life for me ain't been no crystal stair. (LL) Mother to Son. Langston Hughes. AmFaPo; BLPJKO; ChAP; ISC; NAAL-5; NTCP; SAmP; TWF; WaAnP; WoPoe

And Life steps almost straight. (LL) We grow accustomed to the Dark. Emily Dickinson. GoPo; SAmP

And lift off into the weather. (LL) Our Ground Time Here Will Be Brief. Maxine W. Kumin. NAMCP V.2; OtW

And light enough, to read it. (LL) Image from Beckett, An. Derek Mahon. ModIr; NPeEn

And lightly weight the air. (LL) Three Modes of History and Culture. Imamu Amiri Baraka. BrAP; ESEAA; OxAAAP; PmAP

And like a discarded statue, propped up in a cart. Man of 1794, A. Donald Justice. PoDa

And like a finer light in light. (LL) Alfred Tennyson. NAEL-6v2; NAEL-7v2 Fr. In Memoriam A. H. H.

And like a thunderbolt he falls. (LL) Eagle, The. Alfred Tennyson. ChAP; ClHu; HeIP-4; ITBLP; NAEL-6v2; NAEL-7v2; NoP-4; NoP-5; NTCP; OWoS; TFi; TRP; WaAnP

And little hunted hares. (LL) Bells of Heaven, The. Ralph Hodgson. MoBrPo; OBEV

And lived unburied / I thought. (LL) I married. Lorine Niedecker. APT-2; FTOS; NAAPv.2; OxBoAm

And lives to-day in Bread and Wine. (LL) Christmas. Sir John Betjeman. ChrPo; OBCP

And living selfishly when that too is exhaustible. (LL) Few Facts about Me, A. Charles North. NYP2; PmAP

And lo! Ben Adhem's name led all the rest! (LL) Abou Ben Adhem. Leigh Hunt. BRP; ChAP; ITBLP; NPBRoP; OBEV; OxAEP-2; TFi

And lo, there is descending, yea, a narrow footpath. I Chant of the Miracle Stag (Christian Version). *Hungarian Oral Tradition.* IQMS, *tr.* by Adam Makkai

And loftier passions, prompt the loftier theme! (LL) Her Reflections on the Leucadian Rock Before She Perishes. Mary Robinson. CenSon; RWP

And loneliness might bring a blessing upon us. (LL) Absent, The. Edwin Muir. GPTC; NAMCP V.1; NoAM

And Look for God. Else Lasker-Schüler. BBASP, *tr.* by Robert P. Newton

And looked and looked our infant sight away. (LL) Over 2000 Illustrations and a Complete Concordance. Elizabeth Bishop. APT-2; HarvBoo; NAMCP V.2; NoAM; OxBoAm; PoetW; VCAP

And, looking out, she might. Mariana. R. F. Langley. HarvBoo

And looking up devoutly as he went. Albery Allson Whitman. NAAPv.1 *Fr.* Octoroon, The.

And Loplop, Bird-Superior, has transformed himself into flesh. Max Ernst. PFTM-1 *Fr.* Hundred Headless Woman, The.

And lose my everlasting rest. (LL) Song: "Absent from thee, I languish still." John Wilmot, 2d Earl of Rochester. NPeEn; OxBEV

And lose the gift of prophecy. (LL) Helen's Burning. Laura Riding Jackson. ColAP; NAAPv.2

And love, and anguish, and war. (LL) Handbag. Ruth Fainlight. OPOU; StAl

And love, and man's unconquerable mind. (LL) To Toussaint L'Ouverture. William Wordsworth. CenSon; NPBRoP

And love arrived may find us somewhere else. (LL) Delay. Elizabeth Jennings. NIL-7; NIP-4; OPOU; StAl

And love as blight or the kind of drought. Rural Gothic. Shan Neilson. IFF

And Love be crowned, immortal as the Nine. (LL) Sappho's Prayer to Venus. Mary Robinson. CenSon; RWP

And Love doth hold my hand, and makes me write. (LL) Sir Philip Sidney. NoP-4; NoP-5; NoSic; WaAnP *Fr.* Astrophil and Stella.

And Love Hung Still. Louis MacNeice. MoBrPo *Fr.* Trilogy for X.

And love hung still as crystal over the bed. Louis MacNeice. MoBrPo *Fr.* Trilogy for X.

And love not strong enough. (LL) Vertigo. Andrew Zawacki. IIR; LegDan

And love will stay, al summer's day! Sea-Shell, The. Ina Coolbrith. NAAPv.1

And love with old familiar love. (LL) Convent Threshold, The. Christina Georgina Rossetti. NALW; NoP-4; NoP-5; VWP

And love you so much. (LL) Steps. Frank O'Hara. CAP-8; PmAP; PtR

And Lowells speak only to God. (LL) Boston. John Collins Bossidy. NBLV; OBCoV

And lulls, within its range, the great forest. (LL) Word from the Loki, A. Maurice Riordan. ModIr; NIrP

And lust is there, and nights not spent alone. (LL) I too beneath your moon, almighty Sex. Edna St. Vincent Millay. APT-1; NAAL-5; NALW

And made the kites to whet their beaks clack clack. (LL) Captain Carpenter. John Crowe Ransom. APT-1; FuPo; MoAmPo; NAAPv.2; NoAM; OxBoAm; TRP; WoPoe

And made their dove-wings tremble. On he flared. (LL) Fall of Hyperion, The; A Dream. John Keats. NAEL-6v2; NAEL-7v2

And magic wills that are more strong than ours. (LL) Anna Hempstead Branch. APT-1; NALW *Fr.* Sonnets from a Lock Box.

And mainly: the dawn symphony blazes sudden, reds. Angélica Tornero. SPV, *tr.* by Jen Hofer

And make America again! (LL) Let America Be America Again. Langston Hughes. AF; BLPJKO

And make us blest at last. (LL) Mistress, The: A Song. John Wilmot, 2d Earl of Rochester. NOSC; NPeEn

And makes a constant sacrament of praise. (LL) Peter Quince at the Clavier. Wallace Stevens. APT-1; HeIP-4; MoAmPo; NAAL-5; NAMCP V.1; NAWM-7v2; NoAM; NoP-4; NoP-5; OxBoAm; SAmP; TCAPo; TFi

And makes me end where I begun[ne]. (LL) Valediction, A: Forbidding Mourning. John Donne. AmFaPo; BASC; BrAP; CABP; FSCP; HeIP-4; NAEL-6v1; NAEL-7v1; NIL-7; NoP-4; NoP-5; NOSC; NPeEn; OxBEV; PBRV; PoPoPo; SoSe-8; TFi; WaAnP; WeW-3

And makes the happines she does not find. (LL) Vanity of Human Wishes, The; The Tenth Satire of Juvenal [Imitated]. Juvenal. CABP; MakPoe; NAEL-6v1; NAEL-7v1; NoP-4; NoP-5; OxAEP-1; OxBEV; TFi; UV; WaAnP; WoPoe, *tr.* by Samuel Johnson

And mama complains. Muddy Kid Comes Home. Sandra Cisneros. FFC

And Mama leads the yes chorus. (LL) Under the Oak Table. Colleen J. McElroy. GT; OxAAAP

And man became a living soul / Amen. Amen. (LL) Creation, The. James Weldon Johnson. AmFaPo; APT-1; ChIV-1; InGu; ISC; MoAmPo; NAMCP V.1; OxAAAP; OxBoAm; SacPr; SSLK

And manly hearts to guard the fair. (LL) David Mallet and James Thomson. OBWP; TreFP; WaAnP *Fr.* Alfred: A Masque.

And man's religion be complete. (LL) On the Religion of Nature. Philip Freneau. NAAL-3; NAAL-5

And many are amazed and many doubt. (LL) Divina Commedia. Henry Wadsworth Longfellow. APN-1; BrAP; TCAPo

And Marie Carmichael, and me. (LL) Mary Hamilton. *Unknown.* NePenScot; NoP-4; NoP-5

And Marie said, My soule doth magnifie the Lord. Bible, *N.T.* OBVE

And mark it with his name forevermore? (LL) Sonnet: "Oh for a poet—for a beacon bright." Edwin Arlington Robinson. APN-2; NCAP

And Maury clasped her, waving like a spray. Albery Allson Whitman. NAAPv.1 *Fr.* Octoroon, The.

And me happiest when I compose poems. Birth of Tragedy, The. Irving Layton. BrAP; NoAM; NoP-4; NoP-5

And mechanical America Montezuma still. (LL) Cypresses. D. H. Lawrence. NAEL-6v2; NAEL-7v2

And melt to pity the annalist's iron tongue. (LL) Scotland 1941. Edwin Muir. CABP; EdScPo; NePenScot

And men, coming and going on the earth. (LL) Clouds. Rupert Brooke. OBEV; OBMV

And men think I'm nothing. (LL) Birds Nest. Gloria Fuertes. RaBo; RaW, *tr.* by Philip Levine

And mend my rhyme [or ryme]. (LL) Denial[l]. George Herbert. BASC; FSCP; NAEL-6v1; NAEL-7v1; NoP-4; NoP-5; NPeEn; PBRV

And 'midst the stars inscribe Belinda's name. (LL) Rape of the Lock, The: An Heroi-Comical Poem in Five Cantos. Alexander Pope. CABP; NAEL-6v1; NAEL-7v1; NAWM-7v2; NoP-4; NoP-5; OBNV; WaAnP

And miles to go before I sleep. (LL) Stopping by Woods on a Snowy Evening. Robert Frost. APT-1; BLPJKO; BrAP; BRP; ChAP; ClHu; ColAP; EMP; HarvBoo; HeIP-4; ITBLP; MoAmPo; NAAL-5; NAAPv.2; NAMCP V.1; NIL-7; NIP-4; NoAM; NoP-4; NoP-5; NTCP; OxBoAm; PoPoPo; SAmP; SoSe-8; StAl; TFi; TRP; WaAnP

And mingle all the world with thee. (LL) Alfred Tennyson. CAGL; NAEL-6v2; NAEL-7v2 *Fr.* In Memoriam A. H. H.

And mirth was bounty with a humbler name. (LL) Prologue to Hugh Kelly's *A Word to the Wise.* Samuel Johnson. NPeEn; OxAEP-1

And mock you with me after I am gone. (LL) William Shakespeare. HeIP-4; InoFa; NAEL-6v1; NAEL-7v1; NoP-5; NoSic; OxAEP-1; TFi; WaAnP *Fr.* Sonnets.

And mocks my loss of liberty. (LL) How Sweet I Roamed [or Roam'd] from Field to Field. William Blake. BrAP; TFi

And Molina calls it his place of birth. (LL) Map, The. Gary Soto. NoAM; WaAnP

And mossy scabs of the worm fence, heaped stones, elder, mullein and poke-weed. (LL) Walt Whitman. CAGL; ColAP; NoP-5 *Fr.* Song of Myself.

And most mute is at last raised up into song. (LL) Enriching the Earth. Wendell Berry. InGu; WaAnP

And, Mother, if you are a beggar, sooner or later, / there is poison in your bread. (LL) Testimony. Charles Reznikoff. NAAPv.2; PFTM-1

And moulder in dust away! (LL) Children's Hour, The. Henry Wadsworth Longfellow. APN-1; BRP; ChAP; ITBLP; TCAPo; WHSW

And move to space beneath our sky. (LL) M., Singing. Louise Bogan. ColAP; NoAM; WaAnP

And moves like a hinge in the air above our bed. (LL) Japan. Billy Collins. CAP-8; FaoP; NoP-5

And Mr. Ferritt. Judith Wright. MoBrPo

And much more durable. (LL) Science Fiction. Kingsley Amis. NAMCP V.2; NoAM

And murmuring of innumerable bees. (LL) Alfred Tennyson. NAEL-6v2; NAEL-7v2; NPeEn; OBEV; OxBEV *Fr.* Princess, The.

And Music shall untune the Sky. (LL) Song for St Cecilia's Day, 1687, A. John Dryden. BASC; NAEL-6v1; NAEL-7v1; NoP-5; NOSC; OBEV; OxAEP-1; TFi; TreFP; WoPoe

And must I lose a soul's inheritance? (LL) Hélas! Oscar Wilde. CAGL; GSo; MoBrPo; NAEL-6v2; NAEL-7v2

And must I then, indeed, Pain, live with you. Edna St. Vincent Millay. NAAPv.2

And my beautiful daughter. Pittsburgh. Hayden Carruth. PoChi

And My Brother Was Silent. Amir Gilboa. NRoS, *tr.* by Esther Raizen

And my father saying things. (LL) My Father's Song. Simon J. Ortiz. HATNAP; NIL-7

And my lung full of budgerigars. (LL) Pneumoconiosis. Duncan Bush. AngWePo; TCAWP

And my mother's tunes are devoured of this music's ravaging glamour. (LL) Piano, The. D. H. Lawrence. PtR; WeW-3

And my name will be dropped. Anacona. Danielle Legros Georges. BtF

And my old body remembers the way you touched me. (LL) Resonance. Ruth Stone. BodElec; OxBoAm

And my opinion is that God sent the whale in time of need. William McGonagall. VerBaPo Fr. Famous Tay Whale, The.

And my rough feet shall thy smooth praises sing. (LL) Edward Taylor. NAAPv.1; TCAPo Fr. Preparatory Meditations Before My Approach to the Lord's Supper.

And myself. (LL) Lights Out. Edward Thomas. HarvBoo; OxAEP-2; PoWW; WoPoe

And nailed a small wing over the corn. (LL) Hawk, The. George Mackay Brown. BeAl; NoP-4; WaAnP

And naked was my pastime in between. (LL) James Vincent Cunningham. APT-2; TRP; WoPoe Fr. Five Epigrams.

And never can restore! (LL) To Mary. Charles Wolfe. IrLP; OBEV

And Never Did. Tedi López Mills. RMCMP, tr. by Esther Allen

And never for a moment suppose that they understand. (LL) Ram's Horn, The. John Hewitt. ModIr; PNI

And never get up at all? (LL) Skyscrapers. Rachel Lyman Field. ChAP; NOxBChV; SSCS

And never more will be. (LL) William Wordsworth. BrAP; NAEL-6v2; NAEL-7v2; NoP-5; NPBRoP Fr. Lucy.

And never see the chasms at your feet. (LL) Epithalamium: "So you are married, girl. It makes me sad." Roy McFadden. IrLP; PNI

And never wake to feel[e] the day[e]'s disdain [or disdayne]. (LL) Samuel Daniel. GSo; NAEL-6v1; NAEL-7v1; NIP-4; NoP-4; NoP-5; NoSic; NPeEn; OxAEP-1; OxBEV; OxBSo; TFi Fr. Sonnets to Delia.

And new philosophy calls all in doubt. John Donne. NOSC Fr. Anatomy [or Anatomie] of the World, An: The First Anniversary.

And Niamh calling Away, come away. (LL) Hosting of the Sidhe, The. William Butler Yeats. NAMCP V.1; NoAM

And night and distant travel; for the train. Last Evening. Rainer Maria Rilke. OBWP

And night came down over the solemn waste. Matthew Arnold. OxBEV Fr. Sohrab and Rustum.

And Night shall fold him in soft wings. (LL) Into Battle. Julian Grenfell. FaBoWar; OBEV; OBMV; OBWP

And no birds sing. (LL) Belle Dame sans Merci, La [A Ballad]. John Keats. BrAP; BRP; CABP; ClHu; CtM; HeIP-4; NAEL-6v2; NAEL-7v2; NAWM-7v2; NOBRP; NoP-4; NoP-5; NPBRoP; NPeEn; OBEV; OBSP; OxAEP-2; OxBEV; PoPoPo; SoSe-8; TFi; TRP; UV; WaAnP; WoPoe

And No Help Came. Peter Porter. BMAP

And no more elections. (LL) Election, The. Leonard Nathan. ASA; PBCAP

And no one has warned me that freedom. February 8, 1980: And No One Has Warned Me. Stanislaw Baranczak. AF, tr. by Magnus J. Krynski

And no one will worry a bit. (LL) Does It Matter? Siegfried Sassoon. MoBrPo; PoWW

And No Regrets. Lex Banning. NOBAu

And no verse illegitimate. (LL) Upon His Verses. Robert Herrick. NAEL-6v1; NAEL-7v1

And Noah was six hundred years old when the flood of waters. Bible, O.T. NAWM-5v1 Fr. Genesis.

And noble patriot! guard with love thy name. (LL) Toussaint L'Ouverture. Henrietta Cordelia Ray. CBWP-3; SWaP

And nobody shouts halt. Auschwitz, 1987. Adam Zych. HP, tr. by Hilda Schiff

And none has quite escaped my smile. (LL) Let No Charitable Hope. Elinor Wylie. APT-1; ColAP; IJHIL; MoAmPo; NAAPv.2; NALW; NAMCP V.1; OxBoAm

And none remain'd to give the rest. (LL) Cornelian, The. Lord Byron. CAGL; TreFP

And none shall speak his name. (LL) Poet. Karl Shapiro. MoAmPo; NoAM

And nor knows nor cares for Beeny, and will laugh there nevermore. (LL) Beeny Cliff. Thomas Hardy. CABP; OxAEP-2

And not a single regret. (LL) Edgar Lee Masters. IllVoic; NAMCP V.1; NoAM Fr. Spoon River Anthology.

And not be ashamed. (LL) April Fool Birthday Poem for Grandpa. Diane Di Prima. CLPP; FTtHH

And not be / one. (LL) From the House of Yemanjá. Audre Lorde. NALW; NAMCP V.2; NoAM; NoP-4; NoP-5

And, not crying in vain. And, Not crying in Vain. Marina Ivanovna Tsvetayeva. GI, tr. by Nancy Pollak

And not even when we ran over the badger. Between Hovers. Michael Longley. ModIr

And not kill you. (LL) Try Tropic. Genevieve Taggard. APT-2; MoAmPo

And not restore my life, but close my eyes. (LL) Orinda to Lucasia. Katherine Philips. BASC; NOSC

And not silence but to our grieving. Poppies of This Year. Gennady Aygi. TCRusP, tr. by Peter France

And not simply by the fact that this shading of. That the Science of Cartography Is Limited. Eavan Boland. EMP; HarvBoo; NAEL-7v2; NoP-4; NoP-5

And not the burthen that they bring. (LL) Alfred Tennyson. CAGL; NAEL-6v2; NAEL-7v2 Fr. In Memoriam A. H. H.

And not to feel bad about dying. Thoughts of a Solitary Farmhouse. Franz Wright. AmAlph

And not waving but drowning. (LL) Not Waving but Drowning. Stevie Smith. AmFaPo; BrAP; CABP; CtM; EmeKit; EMP; HarvBoo; HeIP-4; IJHIL; InoFa; MakPoe; MoWP; NAEL-6v2; NAEL-7v2; NALW; NAMCP V.1; NoAM; NoP-4; NoP-5; NPeEn; OxAEP-2; OxBEV; PoPoPo; StAl; TFi; UV; WaAnP; WeW-3

And not your yellow hair. (LL) For Anne Gregory. William Butler Yeats. NAEL-6v2; NAEL-7v2; OxAEP-2

And nothing but the sea-like sea beyond. (LL) Sea Sonnet. Alice Oswald. NeBrP; OxBSo

And nothing can stop me, no mother or father. (LL) My Life with Horses. Polly Clark. NeBl; StAl

And nothing I can keep from him. (LL) Guest, The. Anna Andreyevna Akhmatova. RaBo; WoPoe, tr. by Vera Dunham and Jane Kenyon

And nothing I had to do. (LL) Yesterday: "My friend says I was not a good son." W. S. Merwin. GoPo; OxBoAm; PML; PoChi; RaBo

And nothing permanent on earth. (LL) William Habington. BASC; NPeEn; OBEV; OxBEV Fr. Castara.

And nothing to say or do? (LL) Gloucester Moors. William Vaughn Moody. APN-2; TCAPo

And nought beyond, O earth! (LL) Graves of a Household, The. Felicia Dorothea Hemans. NOBRP; NPBRoP; RWP; TreFP

And now a few questions to end with. Edoardo Sanguineti. ItPo Fr. Scartabello.

And now a fig for the lower house. Fig for the Lower House, A. Patrick Carey. NOSC

And now a garden pland with nicest care. John Clare. OBGa Fr. Wish, The.

And now a little wind but little wind and stone and green. Held To. Gillian Allnutt. NeBrP

And now Aeneas charges straight at Turnus. Virgil. OBWP Fr. Aeneid [or Eneados or Aeneis], The.

And now all Nature seemed [or seem'd] in love. On a Bank [or Banck] as I Sat[e] [a-]Fishing; a Description of the Spring. Sir Henry Wotton. AmFaPo; BASC; NOSC

And now. An attempt. Behold the Lilies of the Field. Anthony Hecht. EmeKit

And now: And now: here begins Our Voyage, hunters and naturalists of indefatigable enthusiasm. Adolf Wölfli. PFTM-1 Fr. From The Cradle to the Graave, or, through working and sweating, suffering and hardship, even through prayyer into damnation.

And now as the iron rinds over. Skunk Cabbage. Mary Oliver. WaAnP

And now, at last, all proud deeds done. Old Mythologies. John Montague. NoP-4; NoP-5

And now behold your tender Nurse the Ayre. Sir John Davies. NPeEn Fr. Orchestra; or, A Poem[e] of Da[u]ncing.

And now Eurynome had bath'd the king. Homer. NOSC; OBVE Fr. Odyssey.

And now gentlemen. Base of All Metaphysics, The. Walt Whitman. APN-1

And now his well-known bow the Master bore. Homer. OBVE Fr. Odyssey.

And now I have a dog called Elderly. Dog Called Elderly, A. Adrian Mitchell. StAl

And now I have another lad! Danger of Writing Defiant Verse, The. Dorothy Parker. AmWit

And now i know. Always Know. Kalamu ya Salaam. SpirFl

And now I live, and now my life is done. (LL) Tichborne's Elegy. Chidiock Tichborne. AmFaPo; HeIP-4; InoFa; NIL-7; NoP-4; NoP-5; NoSic; PoPoPo; TFi; WeW-3

(And nowe I live, and nowe my life is donn.) (LL) NPeEn; PBRV

And now I too must wrestle with a brother. On the Pains of Translating Miklós Radnóti. Frederick Turner. RA

And now I will convey thee to thy world. Lord Byron. NOBRP Fr. Cain: A Mystery.

And now I'm engaged to Miss Joan Hunter Dunn. (LL) Subaltern's Love-Song, A. Sir John Betjeman. BrAP; NoAM; OxAEP-2

And now, in accents deep and low. Washington Allston. APN-1 Fr. Sylphs of the Seasons, The.

And now indeed it has come to pass. Zuni Oral Tradition. NAAPv.1 Fr. Shalako.

And now, it seems, you are fearful. Dark, The. Richard Poole. AngWePo

And now it's a boring fault too. (LL)   Antonio Machado Ruiz.   RaBo; WED *Fr.* Moral Proverbs and Folk Songs.

And now, kind friends, what I have wrote.   Julia A. Moore.   VerBaPo *Fr.* Author's Early Life, The.

And now, lash'd on by destiny severe.   William Falconer.   OxAEP-1 *Fr.* Shipwreck, The.

And now Love sang: but his was such a song.   Dante Gabriel Rossetti.   CABP; NAEL-6v2; OxBSo *Fr.* House of Life, The.

And now man-slaughtering Pallas took in hand.   Homer.   OBVE *Fr.* Odyssey.

And now, Mistress Mummy, since thus you've been found.   Child's Address to the Kentucky Mummy, The.   Hannah Flagg Gould.   SWaP

And now my work is done: no wrath of Jove.   Ovid.   WaAnP *Fr.* Metamorphoses.

And now one prayer.   *Unknown.*   OBVE *Fr.* Elder Edda, The.

And now th'art set wide ope, the Speare's sad art.   I Am the Door [*or* Doore].   Richard Crashaw.   NAEL-6v1; NAEL-7v1

And now the bus, on an elevated highway.   Bus Ride.   Harvey Shapiro.   PrTe

And now the dark comes on, all full of chitter noise.   Sound of Night, The.   Maxine W. Kumin.   SoSe-8

And now the dewy night had nearly come to its halfway.   Virgil.   WoPoe *Fr.* Aeneid [*or* Eneados *or* Aeneis], The.

And now the purple dusk of twilight time.   Star Dust.   Mitchell Parish.   NAAPv.2; ReLy

And now the Queene of women had intent.   Homer.   OBVE *Fr.* Odyssey.

And now the sea-scoured temptress, having failed.   Geoffrey Hill.   UpMys *Fr.* Metamorphoses.

And now the Storm-blast came, and he.   Samuel Taylor Coleridge.   OWoS *Fr.* Rime of the Ancient Mariner, The (1798 version).

"And now to God the Father," he ends.   Thomas Hardy.   MoBrPo *Fr.* Satires of Circumstance in Fifteen Glimpses.

And now to the ab[b]lyss I pass.   Andrew Marvell.   PBRV *Fr.* Upon Appleton House [To My Lord Fairfax].

And now, unveiled, the toilet stands displayed.   Alexander Pope.   OxAEP-1; OxBEV *Fr.* Rape of the Lock, The: An Heroi-Comical Poem in Five Cantos.

And now was Paris come / From his high towres.   Homer.   OBVE *Fr.* Iliad, The.

And now we gan draw near unto the gate.   Virgil.   NoSic *Fr.* Aeneid [*or* Eneados *or* Aeneis], The.

And now we walked along the solid mire.   Dante Alighieri.   OBVE *Fr.* Divina Commedia (Selections from Anthologies, in English).

And now what monarch would not gardener be.   To Amanda Walking in the Garden.   N. Hookes.   NOSC; OBGa

And now, with the reflected lights that glow.   Dante Alighieri.   NAWM-7v1 *Fr.* Divine Comedy, The (Mandelbaum Translation).

And now you ask.   My Message.   Cecil Rajendra.   PoetW

And Now You.   David S. Mills.   InTrad

And, O, pray too for me! (LL)   Walter Savage Landor.   OBEV; TreFP *Fr.* Citation and Examination of William Shakespeare, The.

And of the curveship lend a myth to God. (LL)   Hart Crane.   AmFaPo; ChIV-1; ClHu; ColAP; EMP; FaBoA; HarvBoo; MakPoe; MoAmPo; NAAL-5; NAAPv.2; NoP-4; OxBoAm; PoPoPo; TFi; TRP *Fr.* Bridge, The.

And of thir [*or* their] vain contest appeer'd [*or* appeared] no end. (LL)   John Milton.   NAEL-6v1; NAWM-5v1; NAWM-7v1; NoP-4; NoP-5 *Fr.* Paradise Lost.

And of what they did next there is no record. (LL)   Inspiration.   James Tate.   BodElec; OxBoAm

And oft the owle with rufull song complaine.   Virgil.   OBVE *Fr.* Aeneid [*or* Eneados *or* Aeneis], The.

And often swore my lips were sweet. (LL)   Mother, I Cannot Mind My Wheel.   Walter Savage Landor.   NAEL-6v2; NAEL-7v2; OBEV; OBVE

And, oh, may no other maiden know such reproach as I!   Cashel of Munster.   William English.   IrLP; IrV; OBEV, *tr. by* Sir Samuel Ferguson

And oh, 'tis true, 'tis true. (LL)   A. E. Housman.   ChAP; HeIP-4; ITBLP; ItP; MoBrPo; NAEL-6v2; NAEL-7v2; NAMCP V.1; NoAM; TFi; WaAnP *Fr.* Shropshire Lad, A.

And on hers / Though she doesn't know it.   Poem with Light on Its Shoulder.   Mary Ann Samyn.   AmPoNex

And on me.   Village, The.   Dafydd Rowlands.   BBMWP, *tr. by* Meic Stephens

And on My Eyes Dark Sleep by Night.   Michael Field.   LW; OBMV

And on, right onward towards the hills he shot.   Albery Allson Whitman.   NAAPv.1 *Fr.* Octoroon, The.

And on that day, upon the heavenly scarp.   Abraham Moses Klein.   PoA 2002 *Fr.* Psalter of Avram Haktani, The.

And on that final night I tore eye-holes.   Meditation on *The Consolation of Philosophy.*   Josh Bell.   LegDan

And on that holy day.   Word/Life.   Charlie R. Braxton.   BtF

And on the beach undid his corded bales. (LL)   Scholar Gypsy, The.   Matthew Arnold.   NAEL-6v2; NAEL-7v2; NoP-4; NoP-5; OBEV; OxAEP-1; TFi

And on the bridge, faces upturned to a roaring / Falcon. (LL)   Airman Who Flew over Shakespeare's England, The.   Hyam Plutzik.   APT-2; PWW2

And on the hillside.   Waiting at Cerbere.   Sylvia Townsend Warner.   MoWP

And on the mere the wailing died away. (LL)   Alfred Tennyson.   NIP-4; OBNV; OxAEP-2 *Fr.* Morte d'Arthur.

And on the porch, across the upturned chair.   Poet at Seven, The.   Donald Justice.   WeW-3

And on the right the slogan Born To Lose. (LL)   Black Jackets.   Thom Gunn.   HeIP-4; NAEL-6v2; NAEL-7v2; NoP-4; NoP-5

And on the seventh slept a deep Negro sleep. (LL)   To New York.   Léopold Sédar Senghor.   PoetW; WoPoe, *tr. by* Melvin Dixon

And on this day, which poets unto thee.   Ovid.   OBVE *Fr.* Tristium.

And once again Good Friday comes.   From My Diary, 3.   Vera Bulich.   ARWW, *tr. by* Catriona Kelly

And once again I was within that house.   Dream, The.   John Peale Bishop.   InGu

And once again the angel of Death came.   George MacBeth.   HP *Fr.* Rumanian of Maria Banus, The.

And one day Hughes said.   Changes—Eight.   Norman J. Loftis.   EGAG

And One for My Dame.   Anne Sexton.   NoP-4; NoP-5

And one is One, free in the tearing wind. (LL)   In a Dark Time.   Theodore Roethke.   APT-2; CAP-8; HeIP-4; ItP; MoAmPo; NAAL-5; NAMCP V.1; NoAM; NoP-4; NoP-5; OxBoAm; PLBUT; RaBo; TFi; VCAP

And one morning while in the woods I stumbled suddenly upon the /thing thing.   Between the World and Me.   Richard Wright.   FTtHH; ISC; SSLK

And one sweet smile o'erpaid an age of fears! (LL)   Describes the Fascinations of Love.   Mary Robinson.   CenSon; RWP

And one there was, a dreamer born.   John Greenleaf Whittier.   NCAP *Fr.* Tent on the Beach: [The Dreamer].

And one wants to know everything about everything.   Limited Liability.   John Ashbery.   BodElec

And one would stay home waiting for them in vain. (LL)   Henri Michaux.   GPTC; MotU *Fr.* I Am Writing to You from a Far-Off Country.

And only bitter land was washed away. (LL)   Childhood.   Margaret Abigail Walker.   NoP-4; NoP-5

And only: money.   My One.   Heather McHugh.   BAP-01

And only there, please highly for their sake. (LL)   William Cowper.   NAEL-6v1; NAEL-7v1 *Fr.* Task, The.

And only wake with you! (LL)   Stars.   Emily Jane Brontë.   AWTN; NAEL-6v2; NAEL-7v2; NALW

And ony sma'er thocht's impossible. (LL)   At My Father's Grave.   Hugh MacDiarmid.   HarvBoo; InoFa; NePenScot

And open unseen gates with key of gold? (LL)   City Visions.   Emma Lazarus.   APN-2; NAAPv.1; SWaP

And Opposition of the Stars. (LL)   Definition of Love, The.   Andrew Marvell.   BASC; BrAP; FSCP; ITBLP; NAEL-6v1; NAEL-7v1; NoP-4; NoP-5; NOSC; NPeEn; OBEV; PBRV; PtR; TFi; WaAnP

And our eternal home. (LL)   Man Frail, and God Eternal.   Isaac Watts.   InvLi; NPeEn; OBVE; OxBEV; SacPr

And our ordinary garments decent in the dead one's eyes. (LL)   Journey to the Place of Ghosts.   Jay Wright.   GT; VCAP

And our wheels grazed his dead face. (LL)   Dead Man's Dump.   Isaac Rosenberg.   NAEL-6v2; NAEL-7v2; NAMCP V.1; NoAM; NoP-5; OBWP; PoWW; WaAnP

And out into the winds her life withdrew. (LL)   Virgil.   NAWM-5v1; NAWM-7v1 *Fr.* Aeneid [*or* Eneados *or* Aeneis], The.

And out of dominion.   Drew Milne.   VaPo *Fr.* As It Were.

And out of the swing of the sea. (LL)   Heaven-Haven.   Gerard Manley Hopkins.   HeIP-4; MoBrPo; NoAM; OBEV; OxAEP-2; SoSe-8; TFi

And over all that is lost. (LL)   Wild Turkeys; The Dignity of the Damned.   Brigit Pegeen Kelly.   ExTi; IllVoic

And over all the sky—the sky! far, far out of reach, studded, breaking out, the eternal stars. (LL)   Bivouac on a Mountain Side.   Walt Whitman.   CBCWP; NAAPv.1; PCW

And over-read what I have writ. (LL)   Departure of the Good Daemon, The.   Robert Herrick.   BASC; NPeEn

And Pablo Neruda / that Chilean omnivore of poetry.   Lawrence Ferlinghetti.   BB *Fr.* Work-in-Progress.

And palms before my feet! (LL)   Donkey, The.   G. K. Chesterton.   ChIV-2; GI; MoBrPo; OBEV

And Paphos' son was Cinyras, a man.   Ovid.   NAWM-7v1 *Fr.* Metamorphoses.

And part, buried in itself, stays, forever, blinking into the glare, freezing. (LL)   Shade, The.   C. K. Williams.   BeAl; StAl

And part it, giving half to him. (LL)   Alfred Tennyson.   CAGL; NAEL-6v2; NAEL-7v2 *Fr.* In Memoriam A. H. H.

And passes into gloom again. (LL)   Alfred Tennyson.   NAEL-6v2; NAEL-7v2 *Fr.* In Memoriam A. H. H.

And passing away. (LL)   Kenneth Rexroth.   APSN; APT-2; NAAPv.2; NAMCP V.1 *Fr.* Love Poems of Marichiko, The.

And passionate as the dawn. (LL) Fisherman, The. William Butler Yeats. NAMCP V.1; NoAM

And pay thee with a grateful rhyme. (LL) Flaneur [or Flâneur], The. Oliver Wendell Holmes. APN-1; NAAPv.1

And peace on earth for men. (LL) Afterthought. Elizabeth Jennings. NOxBChV; OBCP

And pedal off, slightly displeased. (LL) Cyclist, The. Marge Piercy. NAMCP V.2; NoAM

And people aren't kind. (LL) Bus Driver, The. Hédi Kaddour. PML; YaTCFP, tr. by Marilyn Hacker

And Pergamos, / City of the Phrygians. Euripides. OBVE Fr. Iphigenia [or Iphigeneia] in Aulis.

And perhaps is ony needed once. (LL) I Will Live and Survive. Irina Ratushinskaya. CFP; ItGoST, tr. by David McDuff

And perish in our own.. (LL) Daisy. Francis Thompson. MoBrPo; OBEV

And Pilate Said. Joy Davidman. YaYoPo

And pity the poor planter, when the blast. James Grainger. STuOW Fr. Sugar Cane, The.

And plain old Margaret Fuller died as well. (LL) Ballad of Ladies Lost and Found. Marilyn Hacker. FFC; InoFa; VCAP

And plant it in their faces. (LL) Alex Comfort. MoBrPo; RSaN Fr. Song of Lazarus, The.

And plants our standard on QUEBEC. (LL) On the Conflagrations at Washington. Philip Freneau. AmWaPo; APN-1

And played it. (LL) Hope ("He rose up on his dying bed.") Langston Hughes. APSN; OxBoAm; PFTM-1

And please do not presume it was the way we planned it. And Please Do Not Presume. Deryn Rees-Jones. MFPA

And ploughs down palaces, and thrones, and towers. (LL) Serf, The. Roy Campbell. MoBrPo; OBMV

And pneumonia finished me. (LL) Edgar Lee Masters. APT-1; IllVoic Fr. Spoon River Anthology.

And Poe's house? What about Poe's house? Where's Poe's house? Poe's House. Juan Ramón Jiménez. MotU, tr. by Sandra Hoben

And point with taper spire to Heaven. (LL) Wish, A. Samuel Rogers. OBEV; OxAEP-2

And poplars stand there still as death. (LL) Southern Mansion. Arna Bontemps. APT-2; GT

And pray for Kharma under the holy mountain. (LL) Chard Whitlow. Henry Reed. MoBrPo; NBLV; NoP-4; NoP-5; OBCoV; UV

And pretty as a picture. (LL) Gallery. Albert Goldbarth. RWB; TaR

And prove that death but routs life into victory. (LL) Herman Melville. APN-2; NCAP; TCAPo Fr. Clarel: A Poem and Pilgrimage in the Holy Land.

And pull him close, stoned out of my gourd. (LL) David Cassidy Then. Dennis Cooper. ReTh; WiU

And put him into bed? Why don't they come? (LL) Disabled. Wilfred Owen. FaBoWar; NAEL-6v2; NAEL-7v2; NAMCP V.1; NIL-7; NoAM; OBWVE; PoPoPo

And put his gun to the back of her head. (LL) Praise of a Collie. Norman Alexander MacCaig. EdScPo; NePenScot; PoCho

And put in twa een o' tree. (LL) Tam Lin. Unknown. OBEV; OBNV

And quiet sleep and a sweet dream when the long trick's over. (LL) Sea Fever. John Masefield. BLPJKO; BRP; CABP; ChAP; ITBLP; MoBrPo; OxAEP-2; UV; WaAnP

And rain still falling. (LL) Nisei: Second Generation Japanese-American. James Masao Mitsui. GifTon; OpBo

And raising Charles his [or Charles's] chariot 'bove his wain[e]. (LL) Ben Jonson. BASC; NAEL-6v1; NAEL-7v1

And ran on. (LL) I saw a man pursuing the horizon. Stephen Crane. APN-2; ChAP; IJHIL; MoAmPo; NAAPv.1; NoP-4; OxBoAm; TCAPo

And rattles her crutch, which may put forth a small bloom, perhaps white. (LL) Pursuit. Robert Penn Warren. FuPo; MoAmPo

And read that moderate man Voltaire. (LL) Respectable Burgher, The. Thomas Hardy. ChIV-2; NoAM

And regardless / the heat. Ana Belén López Pulido. SPV, tr. by Jen Hofer

And remembers the water, white as their eyes. (LL) Landing of Rochambeau, The. Michael Davidson. FTOS; OnScMo

And renownèd be thy grave! (LL) William Shakespeare. ClHu; NoSic; OxAEP-1; SoSe-8; TFi Fr. Cymbeline.

And retreating, always retreating, behind it. (LL) Brazil, January 1, 1502. Elizabeth Bishop. BLT; NAMCP V.2; NoAM; PoetW; PoPoPo; VCAP

And returned to their homes by another way. (LL) Three Kings, The. Henry Wadsworth Longfellow. ChIV-2; ChrPo

And ride in triumph through Persepolis? Christopher Marlowe. FaBoWar Fr. Tamburlaine the Great.

And right before daybreak the little owl returned. Every Life. Brenda Hillman. BodElec

And rise, O moon, from yonder down. Alfred Tennyson. NAEL-6v2; NAEL-7v2 Fr. In Memoriam A. H. H.

And roaring then the ashen skies resound. On the Third Day. János Pilinszky. IQMS, tr. by Adam Makkai

And rode away horseless to the King's white hall. (LL) Riddle: "White bird featherless." Unknown. FaBoVe; OxBEV

And roll head over heels and tangle my hair full of wisps. (LL) Walt Whitman. ColAP; ITBLP; MoAmPo Fr. Song of Myself.

And rural mirth and manners are no more. (LL) Oliver Goldsmith. OBSV; UV Fr. Deserted Village, The.

And sae was pu'd or [or ere] noon! (LL) Banks o' Doon, The ("Ye flowery banks o' bon[n]ie Doon.") Robert Burns. NAEL-6v2; NoP-5; NPBRoP (But left the thorn wi' me.) (LL) TFi; WaAnP

And safe in heaven dead. (LL) Jack Kerouac. PFTM-2; PmAP Fr. Mexico City Blues.

And said: "Comrade! Brother!" (LL) I stood upon a high place. Stephen Crane. APN-2; NAAPv.1

And said: "He hadn't very far to fall." (LL) Ambrose Bierce. AmWit; APN-2 Fr. Devil's Dictionary, The.

And said I that my limbs were old. Sir Walter Scott. OxAEP-2 Fr. Lay of the Last Minstrel, The.

And said, "Nay, we are seven!" (LL) We Are Seven. William Wordsworth. NAEL-6v2; NAEL-7v2; NOBRP; NPBRoP

And said: "Why don't you get out of the rain?" (LL) I wrung my hands under my dark veil. Anna Andreyevna Akhmatova. PoetW; RaBo, tr. by Max Hayward and Stanley Kunitz

And sail from Beg-Innish. (LL) Beg-Innish. John Millington Synge. IrV; MoBrPo

And sanctify this ALTAR to be thine. (LL) Altar, The. George Herbert. AngWePo; BASC; CABP; ChIV-1; NAEL-6v1; NAEL-7v1; NoP-4; NoP-5; NOSC; WaAnP

And sank her in the sea. (LL) Demon Lover, The. Unknown. TFi; WeW-3

And save ourselves unaided. (LL) Storm Fear. Robert Frost. APT-1; ColAP; TCAPo

And save the serpent in their midst. (LL) In Memory of My Feelings. Frank O'Hara. APSN; ColAP; HarvBoo

And saved the sum of things for pay. (LL) Epitaph on an Army of Mercenaries. A. E. Housman. FaBoWar; NAEL-6v2; NAEL-7v2; NAMCP V.1; NoP-4; NoP-5; NPeEn; OxBEV; PoAgWa; SoSe-8; WaAnP

And say His name. (LL) Canticle to the Waterbirds, A. William Everson. APSN; APT-2; GeoHom

And schoolboys lag with satchels in their hands. (LL) Description of the Morning, A. Jonathan Swift. BrAP; HeIP-4; NIL-7; NoP-4; NoP-5; OxAEP-1; OxBEV; PoPoPo; SoSe-8; TFi

And scorning say,"See what it is to love." (LL) Sir Philip Sidney. NoP-4; NoP-5; OxAEP-1 Fr. Astrophil and Stella.

And seal the hushèd casket of my soul. (LL) To Sleep. John Keats. ItP; NIP-4; OBEV; OxBSo

And seasons, changeless since the day she died. (LL) Cross of Snow, The. Henry Wadsworth Longfellow. APN-1; AWTN; ColAP; GSo; HeIP-4; NAAPv.1; NoP-4; NoP-5; TCAPo

And see Plinlimmon! even the youthful sight. William Shenstone. STuOW Fr. Taking a View of the Country from His Retirement [or Elegy 21].

And see the storm ashore. (LL) Horace. NPeEn; OBVE Fr. Odes.

And see they blood warm when thou feel'st it cold. (LL) William Shakespeare. HeIP-4; ItP; NoP-5; NoSic Fr. Sonnets.

And see what kind of world comes out. (LL) Dead Water. Wen Yi-tuo [or Wen I-to]. PFTM-1; NoWPoe, tr. by Arthur Sze

And seeing the multitudes, he went up. Bible, N.T. NAWM-5v1 Fr. St. Matthew.

And seeing the multitudes, he went up into the mountain: and when he was set, his disciples came unto him. Bible, N.T. BLPJKO Fr. St. Matthew.

And seem the symbol of my present woe. (LL) To the Curlew. Helen Maria Williams. CenSon; WoRP

And sees within my eyes the tears of two. (LL) Elizabeth Barrett Browning. CenSon; LW; OBEV; OxAEP-2; PtR Fr. Sonnets from the Portuguese.

And send it a thousand miles, thinking. (LL) Exile's Letter. Li Po. APT-1; CCL1; NDACCP, tr. by Ezra Pound

And sends it sweeter on its way. (LL) Summer Commentary, A. Yvor Winters. CalPo; OxBoAm

And serious— / Water. (LL) My Life by Water. Lorine Niedecker. APT-2; NAAPv.2; NAMCP V.1; OxBoAm

And serve but Him alone. (LL) Nut-brown Maid, The. Unknown. NoSic; OBEV

And set off fireworks to praise a homemade day. (LL) Prison Song. Alan Dugan. PoA 2002; YaYoPo

And settled upon his eyes in a black soot. (LL) More Light! More Light! Anthony Hecht. AF; EmeKit; EMP; GPTC; HP; NoAM; NoP-4; OBWP; PWW2; TaR; VCAP

And shakes against the sea. (LL) Tiles. Witter Bynner. APT-1; TCAPo

And shall be evermore. (LL) Now Thank We All Our God. Martin Rinckhart. GePo; SacPr, tr. by Catherine Winkworth

And shall do so, until the world's last day. (LL)   Her Descending Down. Margaret Lucas Cavendish, Duchess of Newcastle.   BASC; NOSC

And shall I tell him that the thought of him.   Water and Marble.   Patricia K. Page.   IFF

And shall it ever be again—the joy.   Late.   Benjamin Paul Blood.   APN-2

And shall sing forth thy praise over this meat. (LL)   Edward Taylor.   ColAP; NAAPv.1 *Fr.* Preparatory Meditations Before My Approach to the Lord's Supper.

And Shall Trelawny Die?   Robert Stephen Hawker.   OxAEP-2

And shall we ever seek in vain.   All Alone.   Mary E. Tucker.   CBWP-1

And shall we view these miracles and more.   John Rollin Ridge.   APN-2; CalPo *Fr.* California.

And she, being old, fed from a mashed plate.   Old Woman.   Iain Crichton Smith.   EdScPo; HarvBoo; NePenScot; OxBEV

And she beside another lad. (LL)   A. E. Housman.   MoBrPo; WeW-3 *Fr.* Shropshire Lad, A.

And she carried a book. (LL)   "H. D."   NAAPv.2; NALW *Fr.* Tribute to the Angels.

And she didn't mean to do it. (LL)   She Didn't Mean to Do It.   Daisy Fried.   P180; PoDa

And she is gone. (LL)   Only a little shall we speak of thee.   Mary Elizabeth Coleridge.   PoBW; VWP

And she said I was quite fortunate.   My Mother and I Had a Discussion One Day.   Denise Sweet.   ReEnLa

And she saying, I cannot quite.   Heartland.   Trent Busch.   BAP-01

And She Washed His Feet with Her Tear[e]s, and Wiped Them with the Hairs of Her Head.   Sir Edward Sherburne.   NOSC

And she who flies the lover,—chains the soul! (LL)   To a Sigh.   Mary Robinson.   CenSon; RWP

And she who slays is she who bears, who bears. (LL)   Parentage.   Alice Thompson Meynell.   InoFa; NALW; NPeEn; VWP

And she will not cast me away. (LL)   Wisdom is / sweeter than honey.   Makeda (Queen of Sheba).   HW; WPoS

And shone that smile on us and sang. (LL)   Homage to the Empress of the Blues.   Robert Earl Hayden.   APT-2; ESEAA; NAAL-5; NAMCP V.2; OxAAAP; OxBoAm

And shook my head. (LL)   Moment Please, A.   Samuel Allen.   FuFl; SSLK

And shores and strands and naked piers.   Henry James at Newport.   Weldon Kees.   PoA 2002

And should I have the right to smile? (LL)   Portrait of a Lady.   T. S. Eliot.   APT-1; OxBoAm

And should remain empty. That was the idea. (LL)   Idea, The.   Mark Strand.   CAP-8; NAMCP V.2; OxBoAm

And shouts Munjoie! Munjoie! to hold the field. (LL)   *Unknown.*   NAWM-5v1; NAWM-7v1 *Fr.* Song of Roland, The.

And show his fainting soul,—a glimpse of Heaven. (LL)   Sonnet Introductory. Mary Robinson.   CenSon; RWP

And shut it up inside. (LL)   Red Cuckatoo, The.   Po Chü-i.   CCL1; WoPoe, *tr. by* Arthur Waley

And shuts his eyes. (LL)   Darwin in 1881.   Gjertrud Schnackenberg.   NoAM; NoP-4; NoP-5

And sighs of rapture, fan the blush of shame! (LL)   Her Passion Increases. Mary Robinson.   CenSon; RWP

And silence matched the silence under snow. (LL)   In the Theatre.   Dannie Abse.   BloBone; NoAM; TCAWP

And simplify me when I'm dead. (LL)   Simplify Me When I'm Dead.   Keith Douglas.   EdScPo; FaBoWar; NAMCP V.1; NoAM

And since thou own'st that praise, I spare thee mine. (LL)   To Mary Unwin. William Cowper.   CenSon; OBEV

And sing the centennial song. (LL)   Immigrant.   Arthur Nortje.   BrAP; TSAP

And sing the songs he loved to hear. (LL)   Alfred Tennyson.   NAEL-6v2; NAEL-7v2 *Fr.* In Memoriam A. H. H.

And sing / with you. (LL)   Where are those Songs?   Micere Githae Mugo. HAWP; PoetW

And singleness: we salute you / season of no bungling. (LL)   Variations Done for Gerald Van De Wiele.   Charles Olson.   APT-2; NoAM; NoP-4; NoP-5

And sink into the marsh near them. (LL)   Widow's Lament in Springtime, The. William Carlos Williams.   APT-1; CtM; FTtHH; NAAL-5; NAMCP V.1; NoAM; SAmP; SoSe-8; TCAPo

And sink me suddenly into bliss. (LL)   Night Journal.   Charles Wright.   CAP-8; InGu

And sit with me among the white clouds? (LL)   Cold Mountain Path, The. Han-shan (Cold Mountain).   CCL1; NDACCP, *tr. by* Gary Snyder

And sleeping in every muscle, every muzzle, every bone it has. (LL)   Studying Wu Wei, Muir Beach.   Jane Hirshfield.   AFaM; WANABP

And sleepy winter, like the sleep of death. (LL)   Wild Peaches.   Elinor Wylie. APT-1; ColAP; NAAPv.2; NALW; NAMCP V.1; OxBoAm; TCAPo

And slot me into his black car. That's all. (LL)   Deathplace, A.   Louis Edward Sissman.   NoP-4; NoP-5; PoDa

And smilest, knowing all is well. (LL)   Alfred Tennyson.   NAEL-6v2; NAEL-7v2 *Fr.* In Memoriam A. H. H.

And smoke and spit, no matter where.   I Love to See a Lady Nice and Natural at Any Price.   Amanda Ros.   VerBaPo

And smote himself, a shuddering heap of pain. (LL)   George Meredith. NAEL-6v2; NAEL-7v2 *Fr.* Modern Love.

And snapped my bitten fingers! (LL)   Thomas Kinsella.   NAMCP V.2; NoAM *Fr.* Songs of the Psyche.

And so an easier life our Cyclops drew.   Theocritus.   OBVE *Fr.* Idylls.

And so, as in the opening of a *quasida*.   Desert Song.   John Ash.   HarvBoo

And so, as this great sphere (now turning slow).   Sonnet.   Frederick Goddard Tuckerman.   ColAP; WaAnP

And so cold. (LL)   This Is Just to Say.   William Carlos Williams.   APT-1; BrAP; ChAP; GoPo; HarvBoo; HeIP-4; NAAL-5; NAAPv.2; NAMCP V.1; NIL-7; NIP-4; NoAM; NoP-4; NoP-5; OPOU; OxBoAm; PoPoPo; TRP; WaAnP

And so did I, and my three friends are dead. (LL)   Nights of 1964–66: The Old Reliable.   Marilyn Hacker.   OxBoAm; VCAP

And so do I. (LL)   Weathers [*or* Weather].   Thomas Hardy.   MoBrPo; OBMV

And so, Ernie, your laughing head floats.   Late Author: Snapshot in the Rain, The.   Dan Pagis.   FIT, *tr. by* Robert Friend

And so—for God's sake—hock and soda-water! (LL)   Lord Byron.   NAEL-6v2; NAEL-7v2; NoP-5; OxBEV *Fr.* Don Juan.

And so for nights.   Night-Blooming Cereus, The.   Robert Earl Hayden.   APT-2; ESEAA; ItP

And so from bridge to bridge we went, talking.   Dante Alighieri.   WoPoe *Fr.* Divina Commedia (Selections from Anthologies, in English).

And so going toward a dramatic center.   Andy Weaver.   PoPra *Fr.* Were the Bees.

And So Home.   Cornelius Whur.   STuOW *Fr.* Liberality of Sentiment.

And so I eat from a brown pot.   Brown Pot.   Ray Gonzalez.   TouFir

And so I led her down to the river.   Unfaithful Wife, The.   Federico García Lorca.   ErotSp, *tr. by* Sam Hamill

And so I went forth, exhilarated.   Exodus.   Robyn Selman.   WiU

And so I went, hands thrust in torn pockets.   My Bohemia (Fantasy).   Arthur Rimbaud.   SxFrPo, *tr. by* Martin Sorrell

And so I'm linked to you.   Watchers.   Robert Pack.   PfSP

And So It Begins Again.   Edward Hirsch.   RoV

And so it came about that there was no way.   Late Show, The.   Rachel Wetzsteon.   NeAmPo

And so it comes.   Train in the Desert—1916.   Christopher Buckley.   GM

And so it happens that late at night we come home after standing the livelong day.   Animal Has Drawn a Human, The.   Bert Schierbeek.   PFTM-2, *tr. by* Charles McGeehan

And so, Jesus, I see your feet again.   Pietà.   Rainer Maria Rilke.   GI

And so live ever—or else swoon to death. (LL)   Bright Star.   John Keats. AWTN; CABP; CenSon; GSo; MakPoe; NAEL-6v2; NAEL-7v2; NAWM-7v2; NIL-7; NIP-4; NoP-4; NoP-5; NPBRoP; NPeEn; OxBSo; TFi; WaAnP

And so make a *city* here. (LL)   Abraham Cowley.   BASC; NoP-4; NoP-5; NOSC; OBEV; OxAEP-1; PBRV *Fr.* Mistress, The.

And so, my dear, unheard, a single Santa Barbara sparrow.   Another Lo-Cal Elegy.   Stephen Yenser.   UrbNat

And so now, near the end of the game.   One Stick Song.   Sherman Alexie.   PrTe

And so, on my return, the terrapins.   Mercy.   Roddy Lumsden.   NeBl

And so our debt to Lionhood must never be forgotten. (LL)   Sunt Leones. Stevie Smith.   GoPo; NAMCP V.1; NoAM

And so stand stricken, so remembering him! (LL)   Sonnet 2: "Time does not bring relief; you all have lied."   Edna St. Vincent Millay.   HarvBoo; HeIP-4; LW; NAAPv.2; OxBSo; PLBUT; WaAnP

And so that all these ages, these years.   From the Domain of Arnheim.   Edwin Morgan.   EmeKit

And so, that was all of it.   Old Man's Monologue with Death, The.   Enrique Lihn.   GPTC, *tr. by* David Unger

And so the hogs streamed out of the theater crying, only hogs, only hogs. (LL) Performance at Hog Theater, A.   Russell Edson.   PmAP; PoCho

And so the others were the first to leave.   After the Party.   Luigi Fontanella. NeIt, *tr. by* W. S. Di Piero

And so the seed / Becomes a flower.   For Russell and Rowena Jelliffe. Langston Hughes.   OxAAAP

And so their spirits soared.   Homer.   NAWM-7v1 *Fr.* Iliad, The.

And so they came up over the reefs.   Visibility Trigger, The.   Edward Kamau Brathwaite.   WoBe

And so they found that the gold of the olive-root had dripped into the recesses of his heart.   Autopsy, The.   Odysseus Elytis.   AF, *tr. by* Edmund Keeley and Philip Sherrard

And so they liv'd; and so they died. (LL)   Epitaph, An: "Interr'd [*or* Interred] beneath this marble stone."   Matthew Prior.   NAEL-6v1; NAEL-7v1; OBCoV; OBSV

And so through the Jaffa Gate, the street. Western Wall, The. Shirley Kaufman. TaR

And so to bed. My heart is full of poems. Back Trouble. Emily Grosholz. RA

And so, when my core cried out. Man, A. Binyo Ivanov. CSCBP, *tr. by* Georgi Belev and Lisa Sapinkopf

And Socks of sullennes exce[e]ding[e] sweet[e]. (LL) Sir John Davies. NoSic; OxBSo; PBRV *Fr.* Gulling[e] Sonnets, The.

And softest silence broods o'er all the dale. (LL) By Derwent's Rapid Stream. Anna Seward. CenSon; NPBRoP

And some admired it for its form. Pyramid, The. Brian Henry. LegDan

And some there be which have no memorial. In Memoriam. M. R. Peacocke. NLP

And some time make the time to drive out west. Postscript. Seamus Heaney. ASA; GoPo; StAl

And sometimes I bring her a bottle of *Nuit d'Amour*. (LL) Dover Bitch, The. Anthony Hecht. AmWit; NBLV; NIL-7; NIP-4; NoP-5

And sometimes i hear this song in my head. Harriet Jacobs. SpirFl

And sometimes there were voices singing. (LL) I, Icarus. Alden Nowlan. BrAP; NOxBChV

And songs of love, the lover soothe to sleep! (LL) Describes her Bark. Mary Robinson. CenSon; RWP

And soon may give my dust their funeral shade. (LL) Awed I behold once more. Ralph Waldo Emerson. APN-1; ColAP

And soothe the pensive visionary mind! (LL) To Melancholy. Written on the Banks of the Arun, October 1785. Charlotte Smith. CenSon; RWP

And sorrow's cankering worm her heart devours! (LL) Suspects his Constancy. Mary Robinson. CenSon; RWP

And souls are candles, each lighting the other. People Are a Temple, The. Gennady Aygi. WoBe, *tr. by* Peter France

And sparrows sweep the ceiling of our day? (LL) Praise in Summer. Richard Wilbur. NoP-4; UpMys

And sped along without shadows. (LL) Iron Spike. Seamus Heaney. BodElec; TRP

And spin blithely into a crack in the kitchen table. (LL) Furious Cooking. Maureen Seaton. SUP; SweBea

And spin that chicken over my head, sprayin' blood like rain. (LL) Nobody Here But Us. Richard Garcia. OPRER; TouFir

And spit out the teeth. (LL) Watermelons. Charles Simic. OxBoAm; VCAP

And spoke the feeling for them, which was what they had lacked. (LL) Large Red Man Reading. Wallace Stevens. APT-1; NAAPv.2; NAMCP V.1

And spotless Pleasure builds her sacred bower. (LL) Edmund Spenser. NAEL-6v1; NAEL-7v1 *Fr.* Amoretti.

And squeezes through the blinds of the open window. Heat Sours, The. David Biespiel. AmPoNex

And stand icily about the bed looking worse and worse and worse. (LL) Things: "There are worse things than having behaved foolishly in public." Fleur Adcock. IJHIL; StAl

And stand like stone and cannot turn away. (LL) Bay, The. James Keir Baxter. BrAP; HarvBoo; StAl

And start to die together. (LL) My Son, My Executioner. Donald Hall. LoL; TRP

And still be dear to sorrow and to love! (LL) On the Departure of the Nightingale. Charlotte Smith. RWP; WoRP

And still Love sang, and what he sang was this. (LL) Dante Gabriel Rossetti. CABP; NAEL-6v2; OxBSo *Fr.* House of Life, The.

And still my feelings sprout richest. Uphold Me. Karen Gershon. LW

And still no stronger. Swathed in rugs he lingered. Day in August, A. Frank Ormsby. PBCIP; PNI

And still refusing to fit. (LL) Epith. Carol Muske-Dukes. MakPoe; PoDa

And still they die. And still the war goes on. (LL) Cambodia. James Fenton. AF; PoAgWa; StAl

And still upon my cheek I feel their breath. Evanescence. Hugo von Hofmannsthal. GTCP, *tr. by* Herman Salinger

And stood in his grandson's shape. (LL) James Dickey. *See* But saying, "Fathers! Fathers!"

And straight I called unto mind [*or* mynde] that it was Christmas Day[e]. (LL) Burning Babe, The. Robert Southwell. ChrPo; HeIP-4; NAEL-6v1; NAEL-7v1; NoP-4; NPeEn; NoSic; OBCP; OBEV; OxAEP-1; OxBEV; PBRV; SacPr; TFi; TRP; WaAnP; WoPoe

And straight I called unto minde, that it was Christmasse day. (LL) Robert Southwell. *See* And straight I called unto mind [*or* mynde] that it was Christmas Day[e].

And strange and loud was the dingoes' cry. (LL) Drought Year. Judith Wright. NAMCP V.2; NoAM

And stride out. (LL) Courage. Anne Sexton. GoPo; PLBUT; TWF

And strut down the streets with paint on my face. (LL) Gwendolyn Brooks. CAP-8; ESEAA; NAMCP V.2; NoAM; NOxBChV; OxBoAm *Fr.* Street in Bronzeville, A.

And such beginnings touch their END. (LL) Paradise. George Herbert. AngWePo; BASC; NOSC

And such exactly she would be: whatever is superfluous. Nike. Ernest Bryll. FaBoWar, *tr. by* Czeslaw Milosz

And suddenly, again. Of Gravity and Angels. Jane Hirshfield. PasH

And suddenly hears again the endless steps. (LL) Caesura. Kenneth Mackenzie. BeAl; BrAP; NOBAu; PoCu

And Suddenly It Is Evening. Salvatore Quasimodo. WoPoe, *tr. by* J. Ruth Gendler

And suffer vertigo. (LL) Building of the Skyscraper, The. George Oppen. CalPo; OxBoAm

And Summer mornings the mute child, rebellious. Eleven. Archibald MacLeish. WeW-3

And summer turns her head with its dark tangle. Ralegh's Prizes. Robert Pinsky. VCAP

And summons read, the great consult began. (LL) John Milton. NAEL-6v1; OxAEP-1 *Fr.* Paradise Lost.

And sunk [*or* sank] beneath thy chain to a lamented grave. (LL) Spleen, The: A Pindaric Poem. Anne Finch, Countess of Winchilsea. NALW; NoP-4; NoP-5; NOSC; WaAnP

And swears—Thy world, Columbus, shall be free. (LL) Eighteen Hundred and Eleven, a Poem. Anna Laetitia Barbauld. NOBRP; RWP

And sword upon parched veldt and fields of rain-swept gorse. (LL) Courtyards in Delft. Derek Mahon. ModIr; NPeEn; PBCIP; PNI

And Syllables Grow Wings There. Quincy Troupe. SpirFl

And take a lesson from this tale of the Spider and the Fly. (LL) Spider and the Fly, The. Mary Howitt. ITBLP; UV

And take a life immortal from my Verse. (LL) Robert Herrick. CavPo; PBRV

And take it like a man. (LL) Something of a Departure. Paul Muldoon. IrLP; PBCIP

And take majesty into the kitchen. (LL) Gods Are Here, The. Jean Toomer. APT-2; OxBoAm

And take short views. (LL) Under Which Lyre: A Reactionary Tract for the Times. W. H. Auden. AmWit; MoBrPo; OxBoAm

And take thy rest. (LL) On This Day I Complete My Thirty-sixth Year. Lord Byron. BrAP; CAGL; NAEL-6v2; NAEL-7v2; NoP-4; NoP-5; NPBRoP; NPeEn; OBWP

And take to thy cold arms, insensibly, thy prey. (LL) To Death. Anne Finch, Countess of Winchilsea. NoP-4; NoP-5

And take up his cold hands. (LL) Legend, The. Garrett Kaoru Hongo. LoL; MakPoe; OpBo; TRP

And taking stock of this and that. (LL) Brock. Paul Muldoon. NoAM; NoP-4

And taking the moon and leaving the paper dark. (LL) Prediction, The. Mark Strand. CAP-8; NAMCP V.2; NoP-4; NoP-5; VCAP

And tangled dry. It Sounded. Larry Eigner. FTOS

And taste the everlasting life. (LL) Fooling God. Louise Erdrich. ReEnLa; UpMys; WaAnP

And tell it as I saw it on the spot. (LL) My Dream. Christina Georgina Rossetti. ViWPN; VWP

And tell me not the secret that I ask. (LL) Mystery, The. Paul Laurence Dunbar. APN-2; NAAPv.1

And tell the ages what we are! (LL) Children of the Night, The. Edwin Arlington Robinson. APN-2; NAAPv.1

And tell th'unkinde, how dearely I have lov'd her. (LL) Samuel Daniel. NoP-4; NoP-5; WaAnP *Fr.* Sonnets to Delia.

And tell thy soul their roots are left in mine. (LL) Elizabeth Barrett Browning. CenSon; LW; OxBSo *Fr.* Sonnets from the Portuguese.

And thankfully, / For joy. (LL) Upon a Spider Catching a Fly. Edward Taylor. ColAP; NAAPv.1; NoP-4; NoP-5; OxBEV; OxBoAm; TCAPo; WaAnP

And that allows the poem to come. (LL) Jerome Rothenberg. FTOS; PFTM-2 *Fr.* Khurbn.

And that has made all the difference. (LL) Road Not Taken, The. Robert Frost. APT-1; BLPJKO; BrAP; ChAP; CtM; EMP; HarvBoo; HeIP-4; ITBLP; MoAmPo; NAAL-5; NAAPv.2; NAMCP V.1; NIL-7; NIP-4; NoAM; NoP-4; NoP-5; OxBoAm; PoPoPo; SAmP; SoSe-8; StAl; TCAPo; TFi; TRP; WaAnP

And that inverted Bowl they call the Sky. Omar Khayyám. CABP *Fr.* Rubáiyát of Omar Khayyám [of Naishápúr], The.

And that is how I came to know. (LL) Duel, The. Eugene Field. APN-2; ITBLP; NOxBChV; TFi

And that is how it is. (LL) Philanthropist and the Jelly-fish, The. May Kendall. ViWPN; VWP

And that is this, and this with thee remain[e]s. (LL) William Shakespeare. NAEL-6v1; NAEL-7v1; OxAEP-1; PBRV; WaAnP *Fr.* Sonnets.

And That Is Your Glory. Yehuda Amichai. BBASP, *tr. by* Stephen Mitchell

And that made up for all the rest. (LL) New-Born Baby's Song, The. Frances Darwin Cornford. MoWP; NIL-7

And that necessary. (LL) Variation on the Word *Sleep*. Margaret Atwood. AmFaPo; BeAl

And that night was as good as it's ever been. (LL) Chairmaker, The. Siobhan Campbell. IrLP; MFPA

And that pale Sustenance— / Despair. (LL) I cannot live with You. Emily Dickinson. APN-2; MoAmPo; NAAL-3; NAAL-5; NAAPv.1; NCAP; NoP-4; OxBoAm; TCAPo; TRP; WaAnP

And that simply couldn't be done. (LL) Roll Call of Bones, The. César Vallejo. AF; WED, tr. by Robert Bly

And that was all his travel's story. (LL) Idiot Boy, The. William Wordsworth. NOBRP; NPBRoP; OBNV

And that was the jolly part of it. Witter Bynner. ICANM

And that was the last one I have seen. (LL) Winged Snake Found on a Path. Matthew Rohrer. NevBe; PoDa

And that was the whole show. (LL) Country Fair. Charles Simic. EmeKit; OxBoAm; P180

And that water these words what can they do what can they do prince. (LL) Elegy of Fortinbras. Zbigniew Herbert. PoSu; VCWP; WoPoe, tr. by Czeslaw Milosz

And that would be Reznikoff. (LL) If I Were a Bird. Lorine Niedecker. FTOS; OxBoAm

And that's all that you'll be underground. (LL) God, A Poem. James Fenton. NAMCP V.2; NoAM; NoP-4; NoP-5; OBCoV

And that's what teaching is and was. (LL) History of Education. David McCord. AmWit; APT-2

And that's why I'm going to Tilbury Town. (LL) John Evereldown. Edwin Arlington Robinson. APN-2; NAAPv.1; NCAP

And the Americans put Pound in a cage. Cage, The. John Berryman. PoA 2002

And the ancestor dead long ago in Domingo or Guadaloupe. (LL) To Francis Jammes. Robert Bridges. NPeEn; OxBSo

And the Angel spoke, not without carefully hearing. Rainer Maria Rilke. WED Fr. Life of the Virgin Mary, The.

And the arrogance of fortunate races. (LL) Totem. Léopold Sédar Senghor. PML; PoetW, tr. by Melvin Dixon

And the banquet, the exile, the first crime. Octavio Paz. PoetW Fr. Sunstone.

And the Beatles' first LP. (LL) Annus Mirabilis. Philip Larkin. NBLV; NIP-4

And the bewildered [or bewilder'd] chimes. (LL) Fountain, The. William Wordsworth. NPBRoP; OxAEP-2

And the bicycle ticked, ticked, ticked. (LL) Seamus Heaney. ArBi; EmeKit Fr. Singing School.

And the birds declared my whereabouts all morning. (LL) Out of Hiding. Li-Young Lee. NoP-5; PoDa

And the Birds Sing of LIfe. Stephen Caldwell Wright. BtF

And the Bishop said: "The ways of God are strange!" (LL) "They." Siegfried Sassoon. NAEL-6v2; NAEL-7v2; NoP-4; NoP-5; OBSV; OBWP

And [or the] blackberries a-growing. (LL) What's the railroad to me? Henry David Thoreau. GM; HHAm

And the blind goddess, when we touched her. Blind Goddess, The. Fadhila Chabbi. PoArWo, tr. by Yaseen Noorani

And the blood was coming down all over her face and waist. (LL) Charles Reznikoff. ColAP; NAAPv.2 Fr. Testimony.

And the body underneath it says: I am. (LL) Knight, Death, and the Devil, The. Randall Jarrell. GS; WeW-3

And the Bordeaux plum. Camellia Sabina. Marianne Moore. AFaM

And the broad prairie melts in mist of tears. (LL) In Exile. Emma Lazarus. APN-2; NAAPv.1

And the carnival entered the last streets. Shak-shak. Seitlhamo Motsapi. TSAP

And the child draws another inscrutable house. (LL) Sestina: "September rain falls on the house." Elizabeth Bishop. APT-2; BrAP; NAAL-5; NAMCP V.2; NIL-7; NoP-4; NoP-5; OxBoAm; PoetW; PoPoPo; PtR; WaAnP

And the city is still! (LL) Solitaire. Amy Lowell. MoAmPo; TCAPo

And the Communists have nothing to offer but fat cheeks and eyeglasses and lying policemen. Kral Majales. Allen Ginsberg. BB; PFTM-2

And the condemned man ate a hearty meal. Runner, The. Louis Simpson. AF

And the Court awards. (LL) Death Sentence, The. Stevie Smith. NoP-4; NoP-5

And the Cow's dead, the old Cow's dead. (LL) Dead Cow Farm. Robert Graves. FaBoWar; PoWW

And the daughter of my father. Dissidents, The. Catherine Obianuju Acholonu. HAWP

And the Days Are Not Full Enough. Ezra Pound. Spl; StAl

And the dead nations never rise again. (LL) Jewish Cemetery at Newport, The. Henry Wadsworth Longfellow. APN-1; ChIV-1; ColAP; FaBoA; HeIP-4; NAAL-5; NAAPv.1; NCAP; NoP-4; NoP-5; OxBoAm; PoPoPo; TCAPo; WaAnP

And the deep river ran on. (LL) As I Walked Out One Evening. W. H. Auden. HeIP-4; NAMCP V.1; NIL-7; NoAM; NoP-4; NoP-5; OxAEP-2; OxBoAm; PoPoPo; PtR

And the deepened stillness as a calm, cast over us. David Jones. NPeEn Fr. In Parenthesis.

And the disconnected number I still call. (LL) Tony Harrison. NAEL-6v2; NAEL-7v2 Fr. School of Eloquence, The.

And the disconnected number I still call. (LL) Long Distance II. Tony Harrison. PoCu; StAl

And the dusk. (LL) Dusk. Angelina Weld Grimké. APT-1; NAAPv.2

And the dying Negro moan. (LL) Southern Cop. Sterling Allen Brown. OxBoAm; SoSe-8

And the Empress saying, 'And as for you' to the ones who did nothing. (LL) Twelve Bar Bessie. Jackie Kay. BeAl; NeBl

And the faint but perceptible scent of sweet clear water. (LL) Rosemary Dobson. ItWoWo; NOBAu Fr. Daily Living.

And the fatigue is flowing, and the grief without shore. (LL) Body of a Woman. Pablo Neruda. RaBo; WED, tr. by Robert Bly

And the fire and the rose are one. (LL) T. S. Eliot. CABP; NAAPv.2; NAEL-6v2; NAEL-7v2; NAMCP V.1; NAWM-7v2; NoAM; NoP-5; OxAEP-2; OxBoAm; TFi Fr. Four Quartets.

And the fire has a life of its own. (LL) Credo. Andrew Zawacki. IAoNAP; LegDan

And the first grey of morning filled the east. Sohrab and Rustum. Matthew Arnold. OBNV

And the first murderer lay upon the earth. (LL) Imperial Adam. Alec Derwent Hope. BMAP; BrAP; ChIV-1; HarvBoo; NIP-4; NoAM; NoP-4; NoP-5

And the fresh-severed head of it, my head. (LL) Show, The. Wilfred Owen. MoBrPo; OBWVE; OxBEV

And the fret lies on me. (LL) Lamentation of the Old Pensioner, The (1890 version). William Butler Yeats. NoAM; TRP; WeW-3

And the fumbling. Oh blessèd Lord the fumbling. Betty. Paul Mariani. SwNoth

And the gears notch and the engines wheel. (LL) Clear Night. Charles Wright. GeoHom; NAMCP V.2; StAl; VCAP

And the gentle light that strays and vanishes / and returns. (LL) Try to Praise the Mutilated World. Adam Zagajewski. BeAl; PLBUT; StAl, tr. by Clare Cavanagh

And the glass of windows. (LL) This land: / The hills, round under straw. George Oppen. APT-2; PFTM-1

And the glass shatters, and the iron sunders? (LL) Where Is the Angel? Denise Levertov. CAP-8; PmAP

And the glitter of jewels? (LL) On Her Decision to Stop Wearing Clothes. Mahadevi. ErotSp; WPoS, tr. by Jane Hirshfield

And the gods shook, they knew not why. (LL) Uriel. Ralph Waldo Emerson. APN-1; NAAL-3

And the graduates can't stand the college-trained staff. Lucky Eugene. Michael Foley. PNI

And the Grass Did Grow. Ralph Angel. PoA 2002

And the Great Mother said. Linda Reuther. HW Fr. Homecoming.

And the green grass growing over us. (LL) Basil Bunting. NPeEn; OxBEV Fr. Villon.

And the ground spinning beneath us / goes on talking. (LL) For Alva Benson, and for Those Who Have Learned to Speak. Joy Harjo. HATNAP; UnSA

And the ground spoke when she was born. For Alva Benson, and for Those Who Have Learned to Speak. Joy Harjo. HATNAP; UnSA

And the gulf enters the sea and so forth. Mississippi river empties into the gulf. Lucille Clifton. NAMCP V.2

And the Haggards Ride no more. (LL) To R. K. James Kenneth Stephen. NBLV; UV

And the harsh falcon its flightless young. (LL) Prayer: "Echo of the clocktower, footstep." Dana Gioia. NoP-4; NoP-5

And the heart. Rose of Silence. Gennady Aygi. ItGoST, tr. by Peter France

And the hills of Ise. (LL) Snow Party, The. Derek Mahon. HarvBoo; ModIr; NAMCP V.2; NPeEn; PBCIP; PNI; WaAnP

And the homogenous roar of the bleachers. Playing Fields. Michelle M. Maihiot. PfS

AND THE HORN may now paw the air howling goodbye . . . . Elegy for Alto. Christopher Okigbo. HBAPE; VCWP

And the houses, Egypt, the great houses, had an end. (LL) Icehouse in Summer, The. Howard Nemerov. NAMCP V.2; NoAM

And the hunter home from the hill. (LL) Requiem: "Under the wide and starry sky." Robert Louis Stevenson. BRP; MoBrPo; NBLV; NePenScot; OBEV; OxBEV; TFi; WaAnP

And the knob turns. (LL) Meditations in an Emergency. Frank O'Hara. PmAP; VCAP

And the lake is crystal-clear. (LL) At the end of a crazy-moon night. Lal Ded. AWTN; WPoS, tr. by Coleman Barks

And the lake was a dark spot. Night Without Stars, A. Nancy Eimers. ExTi

And the last bird fly into the last light. (LL) Dante Gabriel Rossetti. NoP-4; NoP-5 Fr. House of Life, The.

And the last day being come, Man stood alone. And, the last day being come, Man stood alone. Trumbull Stickney. APN-2; NoP-4; NoP-5

And the leaves of the Judgement / Book unfold! (LL) Bedouin Song. Bayard Taylor. APN-2; TCAPo

And the lightning laughs at the clouds. Lightning, The. Judah Al-Harizi. BLT, *tr.* by T. Carmi

And the lights go down. Cinema Verité. Dana Levin. LegDan

And the lips like pomegranate blossoms. (LL) Red Sandalwood Mouth. Chao Luan-luan. CCL1; NDACCP, *tr.* by Chung Ling and Kenneth Rexroth

And the little green cat is a bug in the grass. (LL) Rabbit Is King of the Ghosts, A. Wallace Stevens. NAMCP V.1; NoAM

And the long sorrow of the color red. (LL) Small Vases from Hebron, The. Naomi Shihab Nye. CAP-8; PoArWo

And the Lord God planted a garden eastward in Eden. Bible, *O.T.* OBGa *Fr.* Genesis.

And the lost delicate suitors who could sing. (LL) Geoffrey Hill. NPeEn; OxBEV *Fr.* Apology for the Revival of Christian Architecture in England, An.

And the love, whatever it was, an infection. (LL) Wanting to Die. Anne Sexton. ColAP; EMP; IJHIL; NoAM; OxBoAm; TRP; VCAP; WaAnP

And the luck of our husbands and lovers, who keep free women. (LL) Carolyn Kizer. BrAP; FThHH; NALW *Fr.* Pro Femina.

And the man said: I am hungry. Eternal Dialogue. Tasos Leivaditis. PML, *tr.* by Minas Savvas

And the me that was her with him in the past is still me. (LL) Being a Wife. Selima Hill. BeAl; EmeKit

And the midnight message of Paul Revere. (LL) Henry Wadsworth Longfellow. AmWaPo; BLPJKO; BRP; ChAP; ColAP; HHAm; ITBLP; NAAPv.1; NOxBChV; OBNV; OxBoAm; TCAPo; TFi; WaAnP *Fr.* Tales of a Wayside Inn.

And the minutes, the hours, the days. (LL) Bloody Men. Wendy Cope. BeAl; HarvBoo; NoP-4; NoP-5

And the miraculous hours of childhood wander in darkness. (LL) In Celebration. Mark Strand. NAMCP V.2; NoAM

And the mome raths outgrabe. (LL) Lewis Carroll. AmFaPo; BrAP; BRP; CABP; ChAP; ClHu; CtM; HeIP-4; ITBLP; NAEL-6v2; NAEL-7v2; NBLV; NoAM; NoP-4; NoP-5; NOxBChV; NTCP; OBSP; OxAEP-2; OxBEV; TFi; TRP; UV *Fr.* Through the Looking-Glass.

And the morning green, and the build-up of weather, and my brows. Morning, Noon and Night. Mark Strand. BAP-97

And the mountain: each day. Cézanne at Aix. Charles Tomlinson. NAMCP V.2

And the need of a world of men for me. (LL) Parting at Morning. Robert Browning. CABP; HeIP-4; NAEL-6v2; NAEL-7v2; OBEV; SoSe-8; TFi

And the neighbors wondered that she should die. (LL) Killed at the Ford. Henry Wadsworth Longfellow. CBCWP; PCW

And the new sun rose bringing the new year. (LL) Alfred Tennyson. NAEL-6v2; NAEL-7v2 *Fr.* Idylls of the King.

And the next day begins. Louis MacNeice. RWPCtW *Fr.* Autumn Journal.

And the notion I cannot endure! (LL) Lewis Carroll. NAEL-6v2; NAEL-7v2; OxAEP-2 *Fr.* Hunting of the Snark, The.

And the ocean smells like lilacs in late August—how is that. Walking to Martha's Vineyard. Franz Wright. AmAlph

And the old men, supervising grown grandsons, nephews. Charlene-N-Booker 4Ever. Forrest Hamer. GeoHom

And the Old Women Gathered. Mari E. Evans. OxAAAP

And the one that took this literally. Reflections after a Dry Spell. Charles Martin. PfSP

And the ones that got tough. Inheritors, The. William Peskett. PNI

And the only windows were the windows they drew. (LL) Ghetto. Michael Longley. EmeKit; NoP-4; NoP-5; PNI

And the path is born behind him. (LL) Vasco [or Vasko] Popa. PoSu; WoPoe *Fr.* St Sava's Spring.

And the peacock, once again, started to strut about the park, alone. Life of a Beetle, The. Frank André Jamme. YaTCFP, *tr.* by Michael Tweed

And the Percy led captive away. (LL) [Battle of Otterburn, The] [Version from Minstrelsy of the Scottish Border]. *Unknown.* IBB; NePenScot

And the picket's off duty forever! (LL) All Quiet Along the Potomac. Ethel Lynn Beers. CBCWP; PCW

And the pink's in us. (LL) After Reading *Mickey in the Night Kitchen* for the Third Time Before Bed. Rita Dove. CAP-8; LoL; NAMCP V.2; OxAAAP; ReTh

And the planet shifts imperceptibly. From a great distance she appears to be at peace. (LL) Fiddleheads. Maureen Seaton. BAP-97; SUP

And the point in the spectrum. "H. D." APT-1; NALW *Fr.* Tribute to the Angels.

And the poor stars. Federico García Lorca. PFTM-1 *Fr.* Night (Suite for Piano and Poet's Voice).

And the power over wild beasts. (LL) Ezra Pound. APT-1; PFTM-1 *Fr.* Cantos.

And the Queen Anne's lace! (LL) Portrait by a Neighbor. Edna St. Vincent Millay. BLPJKO; ItWoWo

And the quiet of love in her feet. (LL) Cap and Bells, The. William Butler Yeats. MoBrPo; NAMCP V.1; NoAM

And the rain washes them, and the winds lick them dry. (LL) Rhydcymerau. David Gwenallt Jones. BBMWP; OBWVE, *tr.* by Anthony Conran

And the reconstruction of the mind. (LL) Planetarium. Adrienne Rich. BrAP; CAP-8; EMP; NALW; NAMCP V.2; NIL-7; NIP-4; NoAM; VCAP

And the rich He hath sent empty away. (LL) Our Lady. Mary Elizabeth Coleridge. OBEV; OBMV; ViWPN

And the right one with its white foot. (LL) Truth Is, The. Linda Hogan. HATNAP; ItWoWo; LTA

And the roads deep in snow? (LL) First Death in Nova Scotia. Elizabeth Bishop. HarvBoo; InoFa

And the Saga Continues. Ted Wilson. BRtP

And the sea that bangs in my throat. (LL) Room of My Life, The. Anne Sexton. CAP-8; NAMCP V.2; VCAP

And the sea, the moving sea, the sea. / God is cold. (LL) Man adrift on a slim spar, A. Stephen Crane. APN-2; NAAPv.1; NoP-4; NoP-5

And the sea where it goes. (LL) Buried Life, The. Matthew Arnold. BrAP; NAEL-6v2; NAEL-7v2

And the Season Advances. Herménégilde Chiasson. IFF, *tr.* by Fred Cogswell and Jo-Anne Elder

And the secret names. I Learned That Her Name Was Proverb. Denise Levertov. UpMys

And the seeds of the senega root. (LL) Thomas Jefferson. Lorine Niedecker. HarvBoo; NAMCP V.1

And the shadow of a bird leaves its perch for a smaller twig. (LL) Lovers: "From somewhere over the houses, through the silence." Witter Bynner. APT-1; ASA

And the short quick quench of the sea. (LL) Raid, The. William Everson. NoAM; OtW; PWW2

And the silence off on the hills might be an echo. W. S. Merwin. GI *Fr.* "Prodigal Son," The.

And the silver age, unattainable. Viktor Krivulin. TCRusP, *tr.* by Anna Barker and Daniel Weissbort

And the single straight cord of the trumpets marine. Cantor. Guillaume Apollinaire. CuPo

And the skies are blear and grey. (LL) Ballad of the Bird-Bride. Rosamund Marriott Watson. ViWPN; VWP

And the smile on the face of the Tiger. (LL) There Was a Young Lady of Niger. Cosmo Monkhouse. NBLV; TLR

And the snake says to the toad. Niyi Osundare. NAfrP *Fr.* Waiting Laughters.

And the soldiers with their guns. (LL) Carrickfergus. Louis MacNeice. NAEL-6v2; NAMCP V.1; NoAM; PNI

And the spirit hissing away. (LL) Mississippi. Rita Dove. AmAlph; StAl

And the Squire, and Lady Susan, murmur mildly to me now. (LL) Friends Beyond. Thomas Hardy. FaBoVe; OBEV

And the stone word fell. Sentence, The. Anna Andreyevna Akhmatova. AmFaPo; ItP, *tr.* by Judith Hemschemeyer

And the storm has ceased to blow. (LL) Ye Mariners of England. Thomas Campbell. OBEV; OBWP; OxAEP-2; WaAnP

And the storm reestablished itself. Morning Jitters. John Ashbery. FTOS; PoA 2002

And the strutting fern lay seeds on the black sill. (LL) After the Funeral. Dylan Thomas. AngWePo; BrAP; NAEL-6v2; NAEL-7v2; NoP-4; NoP-5; OBWVE; OxAEP-2; TCAWP

And the sun was born. Heart of Time. Fanny Carrión de Fierro. TANSG, *tr.* by Sally Cheney Bell

And the telephone comes to mean. Lollies Noir. Dorothy Porter. BMAP

And the things we have seen and have known and have heard of fail us. (LL) On a Dead Child. Robert Bridges. NoAM; OBMV; OxAEP-2

And the thoughts of youth are long, long thoughts. (LL) My Lost Youth. Henry Wadsworth Longfellow. APN-1; BrAP; ITBLP; NAAL-3; NAAPv.1; OBEV; OxBoAm; TCAPo; TFi

And the tide rises, the tide falls. (LL) Tide Rises, the Tide Falls, The. Henry Wadsworth Longfellow. APN-1; BrAP; CtM; ITBLP; NAAPv.1; OxBoAm; PoPoPo

And the Trains Go On. Philip Levine. GM

And the trains that go from Rouen at the ending of the day. (LL) Rouen. May Wedderburn Cannan. NAEL-6v2; NAEL-7v2; OBWP

And the traveller hopes: let me be far from any. Journey to Iceland. W. H. Auden. PoA 2002

And the tree of death. (LL) Life Draws a Tree. Roberto Juarroz. GPTC; TCLAP, *tr.* by W. S. Merwin

And the true names of birds. (LL) True Names of Birds, The. Susan Goyette. Coast; OpeFie

And the vandals stomp inoutinoutinoutinout. (LL) Vandals, The. Alan Michael Parker. LegDan; NeAmPo

And the Vietnamese boat-people of Portadown. (LL) Home. Frank Ormsby. ModIr; PBCIP; PNI

And the warm weather is holding. Flame Ode. Barry MacSweeney. Oth

And the way goes on in the worn earth. Archibald MacLeish. NoAM *Fr.* Conquistador.

And the whole deck put on its leaves again. (LL) Old Ships, The. James Elroy Flecker. MoBrPo; OBMV

And the whole earth was of one language, and of one speech. Bible, *O.T.* NAWM-5v1 *Fr.* Genesis.

And the whole night she had told herself to be pleasant. Fury. Carol Frost. CAP-8

And the wild seed of Abraham is cold. (LL) Nicodemus. Howard Nemerov. GI; TaR

And the wind drove a cloud to seaward, and the sun began to shine. (LL) Revenge of Hamish, The. Sidney Lanier. APN-2; NCAP

And the woman calling. (LL) Voice, The. Thomas Hardy. HarvBoo; InoFa; NAEL-6v2; NAEL-7v2; NAMCP V.1; NoAM; NoP-4; NoP-5; NPeEn; OxAEP-2; OxBEV; TFi

And the women. (LL) Fragonard, / Your spiral women. George Oppen. APT-2; PFTM-1

And the Word became flesh and dwelt among us. Jorge Luis Borges. GI *Fr.* St. John.

And the word came—was it a god. Calling, The. Ronald Stuart Thomas. PoetW

And the world changed. Survival: Infantry. George Oppen. AmWaPo; FTOS; NAMCP V.1; PWW2

And the World was Calm. Chris Wallace-Crabbe. BMAP

And the world's danger. (LL) I saw a stable, low and very bare. Mary Elizabeth Coleridge. ChIV-2; OBCP; SacPr

And the worst friend and enemy is but Death. (LL) Rupert Brooke. NPeEn; OBWP; PoA 2002

And the Wright brothers said they thought they had invented. History of the Airplane. Lawrence Ferlinghetti. OtW

And thee returning on thy silver wheels. (LL) Tithonus. Alfred Tennyson. CABP; NAEL-6v2; NAEL-7v2; NAWM-7v2; NoP-4; NoP-5; NPeEn; OxBEV

And their eyes are burning. (LL) O What Is That Sound [Which So Thrills the Ear]. W. H. Auden. FaBoWar; PoAgWa

And their father, too, each name a net in his hands. (LL) Birth. Louise Erdrich. NoP-4; NoP-5

And their hands, the way. Song 9. Harry Gilonis. Oth

And their lives. (LL) Negro Hero. Gwendolyn Brooks. AmWaPo; ColAP; OxBoAm; PWW2; RACG; WaAnP

And their pain. (LL) Spirit is too Blunt an Instrument, The. Anne Stevenson. ColAP; StAl

And their snuff-laden breath blowing lightly over me in my first sleep. (LL) Frau Bauman, Frau Schmidt, and Frau Schwartze. Theodore Roethke. APT-2; NAMCP V.1; NoAM

And their tongues are teasing oil from whales. (LL) Lady in Kicking Horse Reservoir, The. Richard Hugo. CAP-8; NAMCP V.2; NoAM; NoP-4; NoP-5; VCAP

And Their Winter and Night in Disguise. George Oppen. APSN *Fr.* Some San Francisco Poems.

And then a desk. A newspaper. A window. English rain. (LL) In Your Mind. Carol Ann Duffy. EmeKit; StAl

And then a small song, a little mist, and then nothing? (LL) Miniature. Yannis Ritsos. GPTC; VCWP, *tr. by* Edmund Keeley

And then all of them heard the voice; It's enough to speak about words. Strategy. Gali-Danah Zinger. CRWP, *tr. by* the author and Ashraf Noor

And then (and only then) did Aaron laugh. (LL) Aaron Stark. Edwin Arlington Robinson. APN-2; MoAmPo

And then as regards the great wave. System. Tiziano Rossi. ItPo, *tr. by* Gayle Ridinger

And then down into the black soul. Helmut Heissenbüttel. PFTM-2 *Fr.* Textbook 10.

And then find out the rest. (LL) King Billy. Edwin Morgan. EdScPo; NePenScot; NoP-4; NoP-5

And then help me because and then and help and then i said i won you. Diary of a Rough Trade Angel. Lisa Jarnot. OnScMo

And then I / moved. (LL) Unconscious Came a Beauty. May Swenson. APT-2; NAMCP V.2; VCAP

And then I pressed the shell. Shell, The. James Stephens. IrV; MoBrPo

And then i see the cattle of my own town. My Dream About the Cows. Lucille Clifton. TRP

And then I smile and title it. If I Write a Poem. A. Van Jordan. SpirFl

And then I start getting this feeling of exaltation. (LL) Blessing in Disguise, A. John Ashbery. ColAP; ItP

And then I'm prey to panic again. (LL) Panic Bird, The. Robert Phillips. BeAl; P180; PoCu

And then in mid-May the first morning of steady heat. Late Spring. Robert Hass. BLT

And then it was. Poem for My Father. Alejandra Pizarnik. TANSG, *tr. by* Susan Bassnett

And then meet here. (LL) His Winding-Sheet. Robert Herrick. BASC; OBEV

And then moves on. (LL) Fog: "Fog comes, The." Carl Sandburg. APT-1; BLPJKO; BRP; ChAP; HeIP-4; ITBLP; MoAmPo; NAAL-5; NAAPv.2; Spl; TCAPo; TFi; WaAnP

And then night fell. *Unknown.* SonAtl, *tr. by* Albert Mahera, Ralph Regenvanu and Nick Thieberger

And then of course we argued about teachers. Tsitsa. Kofi Anyidoho. NAfrP

And then one morning. Yosano Akiko. CAoMJL1, *tr. by* Janine Beichman

And then one September evening, after these luminous days. Autumn Distance. Jacques Réda. YaTCFP, *tr. by* Stephen Romer

And then rides back to shave again. (LL) Commuter. Elwyn Brooks White. HHAm; NBLV

And then shines back through the white wings to be you again. (LL) How to Regain Your Soul. William Stafford. EMP; PoA 2002

And then start down! (LL) Afternoon on a Hill. Edna St. Vincent Millay. APT-1; ChAP; NTCP

And then the blue world daring onward. Handball Players at Brighton Beach, The. Irving Feldman. TaR

And Then the Water. Milo De Angelis. NeIt, *tr. by* Lawrence Venuti

And then there was a major exaggeration in the body count. On the Desire to Be Precise. Natan Zach. NRoS, *tr. by* Esther Raizen

And then they clearly flew instead of fell. (LL) Because You Asked about the Line between Prose and Poetry. Howard Nemerov. OxBoAm; VCAP; WeW-3

And then they have their answer home. (LL) Quip, The. George Herbert. BASC; NOSC; OxAEP-1; OxBEV

And then *vice versa,* without changing sides. (LL) Casting and Gathering. Seamus Heaney. NoP-4; NoP-5

And then went down to the ship. Homer. ColAP; MoAmPo; NAAL-5; NoAM; OBVE; PFTM-1 *Fr.* Odyssey.

And then went down to the ship. Ezra Pound. BrAP; NAAPv.2; NAMCP V.1; NoP-5; WaAnP *Fr.* Cantos.

And thEn with bronZe lance heads beaRing yet Arms. Writing through the Cantos. John Cage. PmAP

And then with patience bid me bear my fire. (LL) Sir Philip Sidney. NAEL-6v1; NAEL-7v1 *Fr.* Astrophil and Stella.

And then, without his knowing, sweet sleep descended down. William Williams. OBWVE *Fr.* View of Christ's Kingdom, A.

And then you suddenly cried, and turned away. (LL) Hill, The. Rupert Brooke. BLPJKO; MoBrPo; OxBSo

And there a clump of houses with a church. (LL) Onset, The. Robert Frost. APT-1; MoAmPo

And there, beyond the barbed wire, the view—. Natzweiler. Rutger Kopland. VCWP, *tr. by* James Brockway

"And there goes the bell for the third month." Fight of the Year, The. Robert McGough. OBCP

And there I found a gray and ancient ass. Pegasus Lost. Elinor Wylie. MoAmPo

And there I found myself more truly and more strange. (LL) Tea at the Palaz of Hoon. Wallace Stevens. AmFaPo; APT-1; NAMCP V.1; OxBoAm; PoA 2002; WoPoe

And there is dying in an hospital. (LL) Old Man Travelling [Animal Tranquillity and Decay, a Sketch]. William Wordsworth. NPeEn; OBWP

And there is no bottom to evil. (LL) Aleksander Wat. AF; WoPoe *Fr.* Persian Parables.

And there is no plot in that; it is devoid of poetry. (LL) Pantoum of the Great Depression. Donald Justice. InGu; MakPoe; NoP-5

And there is no sign of the wind. (LL) Fear: "Fear passes from man to man." Charles Simic. CAP-8; WaAnP; WeW-3

And there lay the lovers, lip-locked. Paulus Silentiarius. ErotSp, *tr. by* Sam Hamill

And there shall come forth a rod out of the stem of Jesse. Bible, *O.T.* OBVE *Fr.* Isaiah.

And there the island lay, the waves around. Enchanted Island, The. Letitia Elizabeth Landon. CABP; NOBRP

And there the mountains began to move. March of the Cordilleras, The. Raúl Zurita. TCLAP, *tr. by* Jack Schmitt

And there they got a Roundhead. (LL) Character of a Roundhead, The. *Unknown.* NOSC; WaAnP

And there was beauty. Irina Kovaleva. CRWP, *tr. by* Daniel Weissbort

And thereafter come...tears. Tears. Alena Synková. INSAB

And therefore if to love can be desert. Elizabeth Barrett Browning. CenSon *Fr.* Sonnets from the Portuguese.

And therefore I'm going to invite Patrick Kavanagh to join me. (LL) Oatmeal. Galway Kinnell. EmeKit; FaoP; StAl

And there's plenty to be unhappy about. Bad Modernism. Michael Davidson. BAP-04

And these about me die. Sandalphon. Ezra Pound. TCAPo

And these the last verses that I write for her. (LL)   Tonight I Can Write the Saddest Lines. Pablo Neruda. PoetW; TCLAP, tr. by W. S. Merwin

And these / these are scavengers birds. In the Zoo. A. K. Ramanujan. VCWP

And they always aske me "who do you." In the Tradition Too. Ras Baraka. InTrad

And they are cool as peonies and purple grapes. (LL) Creamy Breasts. Chao Luan-luan. CCL1; EroLit; NDACCP, tr. by Chung Ling and Kenneth Rexroth

And they are rich and ransom all ill deeds. (LL) William Shakespeare. HeIP-4; OxAEP-1 Fr. Sonnets.

And they are too many to bury. (LL) We Were Three. Claribel Alegría. AF; TCLAP, tr. by Carolyn Forché

And they both lived happily ever after. After Ever Happily [or , The Princess and the Woodcutter]. Ian Serraillier. OBSP

And they come in a smaller size. (LL) Fifteen Million Plastic Bags. Adrian Mitchell. EmeKit; OBSV

And they float out and are fixed. Day—Towards Evening. Gennady Aygi. WoBe, tr. by Peter France

And they have drowned thee then at last! poor Phillis! Canine Immortality. Robert Southey. DiBP

And they served the drink with one pearl, one real pearl. Chicago. Susan Marshall. FTtHH

And they stopped before that bad sculpture of a fisherman. Charles Olson. TRP Fr. Maximus Poems, The.

And they waved. (LL) No Tool or Rope or Pail. Bob Arnold. GoPo; IPoFL; OPRER

And they went to sea in a sieve. (LL) Jumblies, The. Edward Lear. CABP; NAEL-6v2; NAEL-7v2; NOxBChV; TFi; UV

And they were both right. Kapka Kassabova. StAl

And They were there in the City of Fire, enflamed. JuJu. Askia Muhammad Touré. SeSe

And they weren't even / sisters. (LL) For the Record. Audre Lorde. ESEAA; InoFa

And they'll all kowtow. (LL) Brush Up Your Shakespeare. Cole Porter. OBCoV; ReLy

And Thine Elect, rejectest never. (LL) Father, The. Joshua Sylvester. InvLi; SacPr

And thine immortal wine! (LL) Indian Summer. Emily Dickinson. APN-2; MoAmPo; NAAL-3; NAAL-5; TCAPo

And things just keep going, I guess. (LL) How Things Work. Gary Soto. NAMCP V.2; NoAM

And think how morning breaks. (LL) Mansion. A. R. Ammons. AmFaPo; OxBoAm

And think it's crazy. (LL) After Lorca. Robert Creeley. CAP-8; OxBoAm; PmAP

And thinks it unlikely. Though people have been shot for sprawl. (LL) Quality of Sprawl, The. Les A. Murray. EmeKit; HarvBoo; NoP-4; NoP-5

And this goes down for union. (LL) Frederick Douglass. NAAL-3; NAWM-7v2 Fr. Narrative of the Life of Frederick Douglass, an American Slave.

And This is a Beautiful Night That in the Heart. Patrizia Valduga. CItWP, tr. by Cinzia Sartini Blum and Lara Trubowitz

And this is Finlay's house. Finlay's House (in Rousay). Ian Hamilton Finlay. EdScPo

And This Is My Beloved. George Forrest and Robert Wright. ReLy

And This Is So. Joseph H. Ball. PasH

And this is the oppressor's language. (LL) Burning of Paper instead of Children, The. Adrienne Rich. HarvBoo; VCAP

And this, ladies and gentlemen, whom I am not in fact. Suicide, The. Louis MacNeice. ModIr

And this reft house is that the which he built. Samuel Taylor Coleridge. CenSon Fr. Sonnets Attempted in the Manner of Contemporary Writers.

And this, too, is love. Gwyneth Lewis. NeBl Fr. Parables & Faxes.

And this was once the realm of Nature, where. America. Lucretia Davidson. ColAP

And those level fingernails of theirs. Franco Buffoni. ItPo, tr. by Gayle Ridinger

And those things I could do that might cushion it. (LL) Bruise of This, The. Mark Wunderlich. NeAmPo; P180

And thou hast stolen a jewel, Death. Gerald Massey. TreFP Fr. Babe Christabel.

And thou like Adamant draw mine iron heart. (LL) John Donne. GSo; InvLi; NAEL-6v1; NAEL-7v1; NoP-4; NoP-5; NOSC; OxAEP-1 Fr. Holy Sonnets.

And thou, remembered Sagamore. Sagamore, The. B. P. Shillaber. TreFP

And thou shalt take a nobler leave. (LL) Alfred Tennyson. NAEL-6v2; NAEL-7v2 Fr. In Memoriam A. H. H.

And thou to be alone. (LL) Night Wind, The. Emily Jane Brontë. NAEL-6v2; NAEL-7v2; NALW; NIL-7

And thou wert sad—yet I was not with thee. Lines on Hearing That Lady Byron Was Ill. Lord Byron. NPeEn; OxAEP-2

And thou, who never yet of human wrong. Lord Byron. NAEL-6v2; NAEL-7v2 Fr. Childe Harold's Pilgrimage.

And though in demand without letup, you are not there. (LL) Astropastoral. Douglas Crase. KGB; OxBoAm

And though you have everything, you are lacking one thing: God! (LL) To Roosevelt. Rubén Darío. PFTM-1; TCLAP, tr. by Lysander Kemp

And thought on the Lamb of God. (LL) Sheep and Lambs. Katharine Tynan Hinkson. OBEV; SacPr

And thought them quite mysterious. She Called Them Stones. Robert Masterson. ICANM

And thunders up the bed. (LL) Insomnia. Homer. Taut Sails. Osip Emilevich Mandelstam. AWTN; PoCho, tr. by Clarence Brown and W. S. Merwin and W. S. Merwin

And thus as we wer[e] talking to and fro. Sir David Lyndsay. PBRV Fr. Dreme, The.

And thus continuing, she said. William Wordsworth. STuOW Fr. Sailor's Mother, The.

And thus declared that Arab lady. Solomon and the Witch. William Butler Yeats. ChIV-1; NoAM; WoPoe

And thus, forever driven towards new shores. Lake, The. Alphonse Marie Louis de Lamartine. NAWM-7v2, tr. by Andrea Moorhead

And thus I die. (LL) Four Ways of Dying. Steve Chimombo. HBAPE; NAfrP

And thus like slaves we sell our soules to sinne. Michael Drayton. CAGL Fr. Piers Gaveston [1619].

And thus she's dressed, till Death lays her in ground. (LL) Woman drest by Age, A. Margaret Lucas Cavendish, Duchess of Newcastle. BrAP; PEW

And thus the people every year. Attack of the Squash People. Marge Piercy. NBLV

& tie strings together. Ode Long Kesh. Barry MacSweeney. Oth

And Time locked in his tower? (LL) Merlin. Edwin Muir. EdScPo; NePenScot

And Time strews men like leaves upon the gale. (LL) John Rollin Ridge. APN-2; CalPo Fr. California.

And time to begin a new. (LL) Secular Masque, The. John Dryden. BASC; NAEL-6v1; NPeEn; OxAEP-1; OxBEV

And to Be Born Is Here an Unnameable Feast. Gonzalo Rojas. TCLAP, tr. by Christopher Maurer

And to die is different from what any one supposed, and luckier. (LL) Walt Whitman. ColAP; NoP-4; NoP-5; SAmP Fr. Song of Myself.

And to do that to birds was why she came. (LL) Never Again Would Birds' Song Be The Same. Robert Frost. APT-1; NAMCP V.1; NIP-4; NoAM; NoP-4; NoP-5; OWoS; OxBoAm; SoSe-8

And to forget Remembrance of Things Past. (LL) Bookmark, A. Thomas M. Disch. GoPo; RA

And to her lips. I will say nothing. (LL) Pomegranate, The. Eavan Boland. CABP; NAMCP V.2; NoP-4; NoP-5

And to Her-Without-Bounds I send. Robert Duncan. APSN Fr. Passages.

And to his joy he found an open door. Albery Allson Whitman. NAAPv.1 Fr. Octoroon, The.

And to liberty be true. (LL) Over There. George M. Cohan. FaBoA; ReLy

And to Private Ball it came as if a rigid beam of great weight. David Jones. OBWVE Fr. In Parenthesis.

And to render harmless a bomb or the like. Holding the Thought of Love. Bernadette Mayer. OxBoAm

And to see the city again and to see it again. Patrizia Cavalli. NeIt

And to the Young Men. Merrill Moore. MoAmPo

And to think I had just paid a cousin twenty dollars to shovel the walk. Another Attempt at Rescue. Mandy L. Smoker. PrTe

And tomorrow. Exile. Teresa Calderón. TANSG, tr. by Celeste Kostopulos-Cooperman

And tomorrow morning at 8 o'clock in Springfield, Massachusetts. Poem. Frank O'Hara. ItP

And tomorrow someone will say. I Am Not the Great Diver. León Felipe. RaW, tr. by Julio de la Torre

And tonight's headline news. Lydia's Phantasmagoria. Gloria Vando. TouFir

And tribal, intimate revenge. (LL) Punishment. Seamus Heaney. EmeKit; EMP; NAEL-6v2; NAEL-7v2; NAMCP V.2; NoAM; NoP-4; NoP-5; OxAEP-2; PBCIP; PoPoPo; WaAnP

And trodden out the Mills. (LL) Brain, within its Groove, The. Emily Dickinson. NCAP; NoAM; SAmP

And trotted home behind the lad. (LL) Recreation. Jane Taylor. OBCoV; PEW; WoRP

And trouble him; then Death's his Epilogue. (LL) De Morte. Sir Henry Wotton. BASC; NOSC

And Trouthe shal delivere, it is no drede. (LL) Geoffrey Chaucer. NoP-4; NoP-5; SacPr

And true savant of this dark nature be. (LL) Sun This March, The. Wallace Stevens. APT-1; HarvBoo

And Truth diffuse her Radiance from the Stage. (LL) Prologue Spoken by Mr[.] Garrick at the Opening of the Theatre in Drury Lane, 1747. Samuel Johnson. NAEL-6v1; NAEL-7v1; NoP-4; NoP-5; OxAEP-1

And Truth reveal herself to you! (LL) Insincere Wish Addressed to a Beggar, An. Mary Elizabeth Coleridge. NPeEn; PEW; VWP

And turned into a cluster of frogs. (LL) Gu Cheng. PFTM-2; VCWP *Fr.* Bulin File, The.

And turned my face toward the mountain range. (LL) Virgil. NAWM-5v1; NAWM-7v1 *Fr.* Aeneid [*or* Eneados *or* Aeneis], The.

And turns my sad black face to the light. (LL) On the Turning Up of Unidentified Black Female Corpses. Toi Derricotte. CFP; OxAAAP

And Turnus than, quhar he at erth dyd ly. Virgil. OBVE *Fr.* Aeneid [*or* Eneados *or* Aeneis], The.

And two blankets embroidered with smallpox. (LL) Meeting the British. Paul Muldoon. EmeKit; NAMCP V.2; NoAM; NoP-4; NoP-5; PNI

And two I knew, an old man and a boy. Frederick Goddard Tuckerman. APN-2 *Fr.* Sonnets.

And, undefeated, one of my songs survives. (LL) Song of the Juggler. Heberto Padilla. AF; BeAl, *tr. by* Andrew Hurley and Alastair Reid

And understand our wistful speech! (LL) Caged Bird, A. Sarah Orne Jewett. APN-2; ColAP; NAAPv.1

And Uniforms of Snow. (LL) To fight aloud, is very brave. Emily Dickinson. GoPo; ItP

And unsuckled. (LL) Coca-Cola and Coco Frío. Martín Espada. ReTh; UnSA

And unto me no second friend. (LL) Alfred Tennyson. NAEL-6v2; NAEL-7v2 *Fr.* In Memoriam A. H. H.

And unto miserly merchant hulks converted. (LL) Good Ships. John Crowe Ransom. OxBSo; WeW-3

And "Ut Pictura Poesis" Is Her Name. John Ashbery. EMP; VCAP

And vanishes along the level of the roofs. (LL) Morning at the Window. T. S. Eliot. OxBEV; PoA 2002; TCAPo

And verse is one of them—this most of all. (LL) Washing-Day. Anna Laetitia Barbauld. BrAP; NAEL-7v2; PEW; WoRP

And very softly, Criminal, I *damn* you for it. (LL) Badly-Chosen Lover. Rosemary Tonks. EmeKit; MoWP; StAl

And wait, and tend our agonizing seeds. (LL) From the Dark Tower. Countee Cullen. APT-2; BrAP; ColAP; MakPoe; NAAPv.2; WaAnP

And wake up to ourselves, nourished and surprised. (LL) For the Sleepwalkers. Edward Hirsch. IllVoic; SUP

And walk the rest of the way. (LL) Draft Horse, The. Robert Frost. APT-1; EmeKit; HeIP-4; SAmP; TRP; WoPoe

And walks on earth unseen forevermore. (LL) Henry Wadsworth Longfellow. NCAP; TCAPo *Fr.* Tales of a Wayside Inn.

And wanting to cry his hand beside me. Train Station Zoetrope. Geoffrey Nutter. IAoNAP

And warmth and chill of wedded life and death. (LL) Pontoosuce. Herman Melville. APN-2; NCAP; TCAPo

And was a povre Persoun of a Toun. Geoffrey Chaucer. SacPr *Fr.* Canterbury Tales, The.

And was helped to a hansom outside. (LL) Arrest of Oscar Wilde at the Cadogan Hotel, The. Sir John Betjeman. MoBrPo; NAMCP V.1; NoAM; NoP-4; NoP-5; NPeEn

And was hurled to the ground like a spear. Large Branch Splintering Off a Tree in a Storm, A. Thomas Lux. LaCa

And was it along this torpid muddy river. Mythical Founding of Buenos Aires, The. Jorge Luis Borges. TCLAP, *tr. by* Alastair Reid

And was it not a worthy sight. John Pickering. NoSic *Fr.* Horestes.

And was made man He was crucified. Et Homo Factus Est. Crucifixus. Saunders Lewis. BBMWP, *tr. by* Joseph P. Clancy

And was not afraid. / Mister? (LL) Music Swims Back to Me. Anne Sexton. ColAP; MiVo; VCAP

And was the day of my delight. Alfred Tennyson. NAEL-6v2; NAEL-7v2 *Fr.* In Memoriam A. H. H.

And wasnt there ever a time when flies. Flies. Jack Kerouac. CLPP

And watch the moon through the clear autumn. (LL) Jewel Stairs' Grievance, The. Li Po. NDACCP; OBVE, *tr. by* Ezra Pound

And watch the product coming up. (LL) Garden Song, A. George R. Sims. OBCoV; OBGa

And watches for the trout in the holy well. (LL) Gateposts. Medbh McGuckian. MakPoe; ModIr; PBCIP

And watching her undress across the room. Voyeur, The. Dana Gioia. MAAN

And Wayland's work / Is worn away. (LL) Junk. Richard Wilbur. NoP-4; NoP-5; WaAnP; WeW-3

And we are all. Herostratos and Herostratos. Sergey Stratanovsky. ItGoST, *tr. by* J. Kates

And we, are birds beak to beak. Wishful Thinking Is the Master of Reality. Duo Duo. AF, *tr. by* Gregory Lee *and* John Cayley

And we are going. (LL) We Are Going. Oodgeroo of the tribe Noonuccal. BMAP; NOBAu

And we call it wisdom. It is pain. (LL) 90 North. Randall Jarrell. HarvBoo; NAMCP V.2; NoAM; NoP-5; PtR; StAl; VCAP

And we don't know which, we are so close. (LL) This Dead Relationship. Katherine Pierpoint. EmeKit; StAl

And we emerged from the treeline. Blessing's Precision. Christopher Howell. RWB

And we fall, face forward, fighting, on the deck. (LL) Thirty Bob a Week. John Davidson. CABP; NePenScot; NPeEn; OxBEV

And we gave her all our money but our subway fares. (LL) Recuerdo. Edna St. Vincent Millay. APT-1; ChAP; EMP; ItP; NAAL-5; NAAPv.2; NAMCP V.1; NoAM; PoA 2002

And we guardsmen fed to the tigers. (LL) Lament of the Frontier Guard. Li Po. APT-1; NAMCP V.1; NDACCP; NPeEn; OBVE; OBWP; PoAgWa, *tr. by* Ezra Pound

And we had focused back on the furniture of the air. (LL) Melodic Trains. John Ashbery. FaoP; GM; NoP-4

And we join the line—back to back. Dream: Queue for Paraffin. Gennady Aygi. ItGoST, *tr. by* Peter France

And we missed it, lost it for ever. (LL) Youth and Art. Robert Browning. NAEL-6v2; NPeEn

And we, of the damned poor, trot our frost-furred horses. Thomas McGrath. GifTon *Fr.* Letter to an Imaginary Friend.

And we rebuild our cities, not dream of islands. (LL) Paysage Moralisé. W. H. Auden. HarvBoo; MoBrPo

And we shall remember 1926 until our blood is dry. (LL) Do You Remember 1926? Idris Davies. AngWePo; OBWVE

And we take him in. (LL) Snow in the Suburbs. Thomas Hardy. MoBrPo; OBMV

And we thought of wilderness. African Desert. Samuel Greenberg. APT-1

And we were born. And We Were Born. Amina Saïd. HAWP, *tr. by* Eric Sellin

And we were made afraid, and being afraid. Found in the Free Library. Eleanor Wilner. AmWaPo

And weariness follows, and the infinite ache. (LL) Body of a Woman. Pablo Neruda. ErotSp; PoCho; TCLAP, *tr. by* W. S. Merwin

And weep the more, because I weep in vain. (LL) Sonnet [on the Death of Mr. Richard West]. Thomas Gray. BrAP; CenSon; NoP-4; OxBSo

And weeping anarchic Aphrodite. (LL) In Memory of Sigmund Freud. W. H. Auden. NAMCP V.1; NoAM; OxBoAm

And we'll strive to please you every day. (LL) William Shakespeare. NoSic; OxAEP-1; TFi *Fr.* Twelfth Night.

And wept. (I heard her tears). (LL) Blessed Damozel, The. Dante Gabriel Rossetti. BrAP; CABP; NAEL-6v2; NAEL-7v2; NoP-4; NoP-5; OBEV; OxAEP-2; TFi; WaAnP

And were I not, as a man may say, cautious. Robert Browning. OBCoV *Fr.* Flight of the Duchess, The.

And whan this werk al brought was to an ende. Geoffrey Chaucer. OWoS *Fr.* Parlement of Foules, The.

And what a strange pain that traveler has given me! (LL) Spider, The. César Vallejo. RaBo; WED, *tr. by* Robert Bly

And what a time a reel of tape can play! (LL) I Was Fair Beat. Robert Garioch. EdScPo; OBCoV

And what can redeem them? What can redeem them? (LL) Watching "Dark Circle." Denise Levertov. AtGh; UpMys

And what did she get, the soldier's wife. What Did the Nazi Send His Wife? Bertolt Brecht. FaBoWar, *tr. by Unknown*

And what did the rubies say. Pablo Neruda. GifTon *Fr.* Book of Questions, The.

And what do I owe you, God, for my gifts. And What Do I Owe You, God. Jack Kerouac. InvLi

And what (extraordinary). In a Beautiful Glass. Dewi Stephen Jones. BBMWP, *tr. by* Joseph P. Clancy

And what if after so many words. And What If after So Many Words. César Vallejo. RaBo, *tr. by* Robert Bly and Douglas Lawder

And what if instead of going to the theater this evening I went off to Vietnam. Something Like A. Blas de Otero. RaW, *tr. by* Hardie St. Martin

And what if time were to stop? Birthplace. Nikolai Kanchev. CSCBP, *tr. by* Georgi Belev and Lisa Sapinkopf

And what is going on. (LL) Lullaby of the Onion. Miguel Hernández. AF; WED, *tr. by* Robert Bly

And what more do we know of it. Light Falls Obliquely. Eric Gamalinda. ReBoTo

And what of those. And What of Those Arbors of Vines. Vidya. WoPoe, *tr. by* Andrew Schelling

And What of Those Arbors of Vines. Vidya. WoPoe, *tr. by* Andrew Schelling

And what the *b* and *d* stood for. (LL) Body [*or* B o d y]. James Merrill. CAP-8; NAMCP V.2; OxBoAm

And what they dared, they dare. (LL) To the Veterans of the Abraham Lincoln Brigade. Genevieve Taggard. AmWaPo; NAAPv.2

And what thou art may never be destroyed. (LL) No Coward Soul is Mine. Emily Jane Brontë. CABP; InvLi; NAEL-6v2; NAEL-7v2; NALW; NoP-4; NoP-5; OxAEP-2; PEW; PoPoPo; TRP; VWP; WPoS

And what were you searching for, in that dream? Gloria Gervitz. MirDau *Fr.* Yiskor.

And what's your tune? Thomas Lovell Beddoes. NPeEn *Fr.* Death's Jest Book.

And whelm'd [*or* whelmed] in deeper gulphs [*or* gulfs] than he. (LL) Castaway, The. William Cowper. BrAP; NAEL-6v1; NAEL-7v1; NOBRP; NoP-4; NoP-5; NPeEn; OxBEV; PoPoPo; TRP

And when he cried the little children died in the streets. (LL) Epitaph on a Tyrant. W. H. Auden. AF; HeIP-4; NoAM; OxBEV; WaAnP

And when he was awakened by the cold, she was washing her hair. Dream Recalling a Temptation, A. Maysoun Saqr Al-Qasimi. PoArWo, *tr. by* Subhi Hadidi and Nathalie Handal

And when he was in heaven once again. Ovid. NAWM-7v1 *Fr.* Metamorphoses.

And when i die. Last Instructions. Garth Tate. ISC

And when I go up as a pilgrim in winter, to recover. Abraham Sutskever. HP *Fr.* Poems from a Diary.

And when I rose, I found myself in prayer. (LL) To William Wordsworth [1817 version]. Samuel Taylor Coleridge. NAEL-6v2; NAEL-7v2

And when I say eyes right I want to hear. Weapons Training. Bruce Dawe. OBCoV

And when I went to the woods. King Solomon's Magnetic Quiz. John Wieners. FTOS

And when, in the city in which I love you. City in Which I Love You, The. Li-Young Lee. ChIV-1

And when light was forged. Pablo Neruda. TAPaP *Fr.* Book of Questions, The.

And when like her, Oh Sáki, you shall pass. Omar Khayyám. TRP *Fr.* Rubáiyát of Omar Khayyám [of Naishápúr], The.

And when lincoln came here. Bath. John Knoepfle. IllVoic

And when she. so the novel. glistens in all its propriety. and then he. State of the Union. Alice Notley. BAP-04

And when she wakes she will not think it long. (LL) Rest. Christina Georgina Rossetti. GSo; OBEV

And when she'd finished—having smoothed out. Bishop Reading. J. D. McClatchy. KGB

And when that ballad lady went. Road in Kentucky, A. Robert Earl Hayden. ColAP

And when, that night, the unseasonable rain. Storm. Charles Wright. MotU

And when the Assyrians stopped waging war against the Chaldeans, they buried the dead. Stranger, Stranger. Jorge de Lima. TCLAP, *tr. by* Luiz Fernández García

And when the birds go. (LL) Forget What Did. Philip Larkin. NAMCP V.2; NoAM

And when the center opened. Ahora. Sandra Maria Esteves. PueRic

And when "the future" is uttered, swarms of mice. Joseph Brodsky. StAl *Fr.* Part of Speech, A.

And when the moment. Kiss. Susan Aizenberg. ExTi

And when the star that comes at the set of the sun. Mousetrap, The. Callimachus. HePo, *tr. by* Barbara Hughes Fowler

And, when the time comes to let it go, / to let it go. (LL) In Blackwater Woods. Mary Oliver. CAP-8; NAAL-5

And when the winter wind rushed straight into my heart. Georgi Borisov. CSCBP, *tr. by* Georgi Belev and Lisa Sapinkopf

And when they came together in one place. Homer. OBVE *Fr.* Iliad, The.

And when they drew near to Jerusalem. Boris Leonidovich Pasternak. GI *Fr.* St. Matthew.

And when they had sung a hymn, they went out to the Mount of Olives. Boris Leonidovich Pasternak. GI *Fr.* St. Mark.

And when they sat down in the morning. Sunday. Timothy Liu. NeAmPo

And when they would ask. Grocer's Dream, The. Giovanna Pollarolo. TANSG, *tr. by* Marjorie Agosin

And when thus the night availed. *Unknown.* IQMS *Fr.* Betrothal of Saint Catherine, The.

And when you are screaming. Passing Through This House. Brother Yao. BtF

And when you have forgotten the bright bedclothes on a Wednesday and a Saturday. When you have forgotten Sunday: the love story. Gwendolyn Brooks. ItP

And when you showed me Brooklyn Bridge. Hymn. Jack Kerouac. CLPP

And where. Sunday Brunch. Reuben Jackson. ISC

And Where Are the Graves. Moses ibn Ezra. WoPoe, *tr. by* Robert Mezey

And where are the graves, so many graves. And Where Are the Graves. Moses ibn Ezra. WoPoe, *tr. by* Robert Mezey

And where are they now? (LL) Adrienne Rich. NAAL-5; WaAnP *Fr.* Atlas of the Difficult World, An.

And where no snow had. Brian Coffey. ModIr *Fr.* For What For Whom Unwanted.

And Where Were You. Len Roberts. BodElec

And while stirring I saw. Year Passes in My Morning Teacup, The. Marilyn Chin. GeoHom

And while the song and tears of Ahkmatova. Lonely Masquerader. Velemir Khlebnikov. TCRusP, *tr. by* Kathy Lewis and Bob Perelman

And white owl's feather! (LL) Fairies, The. William Allingham. NOxBChV; OBEV; TFi

And white, still undeveloped. (LL) Postcard from Kashmir. Agha Shahid Ali. NAMCP V.2; NIL-7

And who can never forget you. (LL) Guardian Angel. Rolf Jacobsen. RaBo; WED, *tr. by* Robert Bly

And who is He that, sculptured in huge stone. "Moses" of Michael Angelo, The. Robert Browning. GS

And who really cares about the temperature. Anne Portugal. SCFWP *Fr.* Bath, The.

And who shall separate the dust. Common Dust. Georgia Douglas Johnson. NAAPv.2

And whom I love, I love indeed. (LL) Pains of Sleep, The. Samuel Taylor Coleridge. AWTN; NAEL-6v2; NAEL-7v2; NPBRoP

And why an honoured [*or* honour'd] ragged shirt, that shows. To a Lady with Child that Asked [*or* Ask'd] an Old Shirt. Richard Lovelace. BASC; NOSC

And why is it yet unfound? (LL) Facing West from California's Shores. Walt Whitman. MoAmPo; NAAL-3; NAAL-5; NAAPv.1; NIL-7

And why so coffin'd in this vile disguise. King's Disguise, The. John Cleveland. BASC

And why this vault and tomb? Alike we must. Wiston Vault. Katherine Philips. BASC; NOSC

And wilt for to hold though I seem tame. (LL) Whoso List to Hunt. Sir Thomas Wyatt. CABP; ItP; NAEL-6v1; NAEL-7v1; NoP-5; NoSic; OBVE; OxBSo; TFi; WoPoe

(And wylde for to hold though I seme tame.) (LL) BrAP; OxBEV; PBRV

And will be our bliss with saints above. (LL) Loving and Liking [Irregular Verses Addressed to A Child]. Dorothy Wordsworth. SacPr; WoRP

And will he [*or* a'] not come again? William Shakespeare. NoSic *Fr.* Hamlet.

And will not scare. (LL) Skunk Hour. Robert Lowell. BrAP; CAP-8; ColAP; EmeKit; HarvBoo; HeIP-4; IJHIL; MoAmPo; NAAL-5; NAMCP V.2; NIL-7; NIP-4; NoAM; NoP-4; NoP-5; OxBoAm; PoetW; PoPoPo; TFi; TRP; VCAP; WaAnP

And will not stop. (LL) Kenneth Rexroth. APSN; APT-2; NAAPv.2 *Fr.* Love Poems of Marichiko, The.

And will the flowers die? Poem from a Three Year Old. Brendan Kennelly. StAl

And will their sufferings well repay. (LL) Psalm 58: "Judges, who rule the world by laws." Bible, O.T. NoP-4; NoP-5, *tr. by* Isaac Watts

"And will you cut a stone for him." Stone, The. Wilfrid Wilson Gibson. MoBrPo

And willing nations knew their lawful lord. (LL) Absalom and Achitophel. John Dryden. BASC; NAEL-6v1; NAEL-7v1; NOSC

And willing nations knew their lawful lord. (LL) John Dryden. MakPoe; NoP-5; NOSC *Fr.* Absalom and Achitophel.

And willows could not hold more steady sound. (LL) Repose of Rivers. Hart Crane. APT-2; ColAP; MoAmPo; NAMCP V.1; OxBoAm

And wilt thou have me fashion into speech. Elizabeth Barrett Browning. CABP; CenSon; VWP; WaAnP *Fr.* Sonnets from the Portuguese.

And wilt [*or* wylt] thou le[a]ve me thus? Lover's Appeal, The. Sir Thomas Wyatt. NoSic

And wilt thou leave me thus? Sir Thomas Wyatt. *See* Lover's Appeal, The.

And win us both to May. (LL) Gardens of the Villa D'Este, The. Anthony Hecht. ColAP; OBGa

And wipes the floor with her. (LL) Lavatory Attendant, The. Wendy Cope. MoWP; UV

And with God be the rest! (LL) Prospice. Robert Browning. InoFa; ITBLP; NAEL-6v2; NAEL-7v2

And with great fear I inhabit the middle of the night. Acts of Youth, The. John Weiners. BB

And with him. Time Signature. Linda Andrews. MiVo

And with March a Decade in Bolinas. Joanne Kyger. BLT

And with memory I was there. (LL) Thoughts on my sick-bed. Dorothy Wordsworth. NAEL-7v2; PEW

And with new light salute our longing eyes. (LL) Sir Richard Fanshawe. NOSC; OBVE *Fr.* Il Pastor Fido.

And with no language but a cry. (LL) Alfred Tennyson. BrAP; CABP; ItP; NAEL-6v2; NAEL-7v2; NoP-5; WaAnP *Fr.* In Memoriam A. H. H.

And with red molecular eyes. Crow. Viktor Aleksandrovich Sosnora. ItGoST, *tr. by* Dinara Georgeoliani and Mark Halperin

And with that word he saide [or seyde] in this manere. (LL)   Geoffrey Chaucer. NAEL-6v1; NAEL-7v1 Fr. Canterbury Tales, The.

And with the explosion a rag slapped my face.   Piggy-back.   Ramy Ditzanny. NRoS, tr. by Esther Raizen

And with the left side of the face.   From Lines in a Dream.   Gennady Aygi. WoBe, tr. by Peter France

And within that time / develop. (LL)   I Have Tried Hard.   Zindzi Mandela. HAWP; NAfrP

And within the indestructable night I am alone. (LL)   Passage over Water. Robert Duncan.   NAMCP V.2; NoAM

And without a seam! (LL)   Cumberland, The.   Henry Wadsworth Longfellow. CBCWP; PCW

And women with small heads.   Men with Small Heads.   Thomas Lux.   SUP

And wonder, have I grown so thin? (LL)   Kenneth Rexroth.   APT-2; NAAPv.2; NAMCP V.1 Fr. Love Poems of Marichiko, The.

And work to do that never ends. (LL)   Han Yü.   CCL1; WoPoe Fr. Autumn Thoughts.

And would suffice. (LL)   Fire and Ice.   Robert Frost.   APT-1; BrAP; BRP; ColAP; HeIP-4; MoAmPo; NAAL-5; NAAPv.2; NAMCP V.1; NoAM; OxBoAm; RaBo; SoSe-8; TFi; WaAnP

And wring his bosom—is—to die. (LL)   Oliver Goldsmith.   CABP; NoP-4; NoP-5; NPeEn; OxBEV; TFi Fr. Vicar of Wakefield, The.

And wylde for to hold though I seme tame. (LL)   Sir Thomas Wyatt. See And wild for to hold though I seem tame.

And ye shall walk in silk attire.   Siller Croun, The.   Susanna Blamire.   LW; NPBRoP

And, yeah, brothers.   Dark Prophecy: I Sing of Shine.   Etheridge Knight. ESEAA; LTA; PBCAP

And, Yes, Those Spiritual Matters.   Christopher Gilbert.   ESEAA; InoFa

And Yet.   Patricia Goedicke.   ExTi

And yet abide the World! (LL)   There came a Wind like a Bugle.   Emily Dickinson.   APN-2; NAAL-3; NAWM-7v2; SAmP

And yet, and yet, these days are incomplete. (LL)   Friendship After Love.   Ella Wheeler Wilcox.   APN-2; LW

And yet, because thou overcomest so.   Elizabeth Barrett Browning.   CenSon Fr. Sonnets from the Portuguese.

And yet God has not said a word! (LL)   Porphyria's Lover.   Robert Browning. BrAP; NAEL-6v2; NAEL-7v2; NoP-5; OBEV

And yet I cannot reprehend the flight.   Samuel Daniel.   OBEV Fr. Sonnets to Delia.

And yet I have hated her all my life. (LL)   William Langland.   NAEL-6v1; NAEL-7v1 Fr. Vision of Piers Plowman, The.

And Yet I Know.   James Wright.   BodElec

And yet in some very subtle way,.   "H. D."   NALW; NAMCP V.1 Fr. Tribute to the Angels.

And yet (methinks) which I could well express between your sheets. (LL) Between Your Sheets.   Lady Mary Wortley Montagu.   LW; PEW

And yet she loves my master. (LL)   My Mistress.   Unknown.   NOSC; OBCoV

And yet the books will be there on the shelves, separate beings.   And Yet the Books.   Czeslaw Milosz.   OPOU, tr. by the author and Robert Hass

And Yet the Earth Remains Unchanged.   Unknown.   CA

And yet these are the faces I come from.   Walker Evans in Bridgeport.   Bill Zavatsky.   PrTe

And yet they repose me more than all my other poems. (LL)   Here the Frailest Leaves of Me.   Walt Whitman.   APN-1; CAGL; NAAL-3; NAAL-5; NAAPv.1

And yet this great wink of eternity.   Hart Crane.   ColAP; MoAmPo; OxBoAm; RaBo; TRP; WaAnP; WoPoe Fr. Voyages.

And yet, we have need as we tremble.   Say--So I'll Say.   Giancarlo Majorino. ItPo, tr. by Gayle Ridinger

And yet we should consider how we go forward.   Old Man on the River Bank, An.   George Seferis.   AmFaPo

And yet white.   Tadeusz Rózewicz.   VCWP

And yet whiteness.   Tadeusz Rózewicz.   BLT

And yet / without exactly the.   Alsatian.   George MacBeth.   EdScPo

And you above them, wounded and dominant. (LL)   Messengers.   Louise Glück.   ColAP; VCAP; WaAnP

And you / and / you. (LL)   Latin Music in New York.   Jessica Tarahata Hagedorn.   FTtHH; PmAP

And you can hide it behind your crocodile tie pin. (LL)   Neckties.   Liz Lochhead.   NePenScot; OBCoV

And you content that he be there. (LL)   Hunter Home from the Hill, The. Kerry Hardie.   BeAl; NIrP

And you could leave me now.   At Parting.   Edith Nesbit.   OBGa

And you, Dika, put lovely garlands round your hair.   Sappho.   SaLy, tr. by Diane Rayor

And you for ever clay. Have done! (LL)   Reader over My Shoulder, The. Robert Graves.   NAEL-6v2; NAEL-7v2

And you have failed, O Poet? Sad!   Failures.   May Kendall.   ViWPN; VWP

And You, Helen.   Edward Thomas.   OBWVE; TCAWP

And you, in the tree, waving and drowning.   Fourth World, The.   Vincent Woods.   NIrP

And you just know he knows he knows. (LL)   Sloth, The.   Theodore Roethke. ChAP; ItP; TRP

And you, kind and innocent accomplice, didn't give it to me. (LL)   To simulate the burning of the heart.   Patrizia Cavalli.   NeIt; VCWP, tr. by Judith Baumel

And you know, I believe him. (LL)   Creation.   Simon J. Ortiz.   ColAP; HATNAP

And you, Lucifer, standing there aloof.   Imre Madách.   IQMS Fr. Tragedy of Man.

And you must travel from place to place for food and shelter. (LL)   Internal Migration: On Being on Tour.   Alan Dugan.   NAMCP V.2; NoAM

And you my spent heart's treasure.   Félix Lope de Vega Carpio.   OxBEV; WoPoe Fr. Pentecost Castle, The.

And you once asked why.   Bonk'abajahile.   Mafika Pascal Gwala.   TSAP

And you remain. (LL)   Iris.   David St. John.   AmAlph; MakPoe

And you sang eloquently.   For Sappho/After Sappho.   Carolyn Kizer.   GifTon

And you smile up at us—eternally. (LL)   In Memory of My Mother.   Patrick Kavanagh.   NAMCP V.1; NoAM; RaBo

And you, smoke, dissonance, a psalm, a stairwell. (LL)   Elegy.   Carolyn Forché.   ExTi; LoL

And you stalwart loins. (LL)   From Pent-up Aching Rivers.   Walt Whitman. APN-1; EroLit; NAAL-3

And you will hear in every passing century.   Words of Departure.   Jorge de Lima.   TCLAP, tr. by Luiz Fernández García

And you, you . . . you, you utter / You wait! (LL)   Beyond Words.   Robert Frost.   Spl; WeW-3

And your little job is done. (LL)   Madam Life's A Piece in Bloom.   W. E. Henley.   NAEL-6v2; OxBEV

And your pulse separate doubly. (LL)   From this distance thinking toward you. George Oppen.   APT-2; PFTM-1

And your warm freshwater ripples, Horsey Mere. (LL)   East Anglian Bathe. Sir John Betjeman.   NoP-4; NoP-5

And your winter and night in disguise. (LL)   William Blake.   NPBRoP; PtR Fr. Songs of Experience.

And you—you are immortal after all. (LL)   After 65.   Richard Howard. BAP-01; OxBoAm

And Zero at the Bone. (LL)   Snake, The.   Emily Dickinson.   ClHu; HeIP-4; NAAL-3; NALW; NAMCP V.1; NIP-4; NoAM; NoP-4; NoP-5; SAmP; SoSe-8; TFi; TRP; WaAnP; WeW-3; WoPoe

Andalusian Exile, An.   Ahmad Shauqi.   BBASP, tr. by M. Mustafa Badawi and John Heath-Stubbs

Andalusian Landscape.   Aaron Kurtz.   Prolet, tr. by Amelia Glaser

Andante.   Gwen Harwood.   HarvBoo

Andif.   Seitlhamo Motsapi.   TSAP

Andirons were the dragons, The.   Castle in the Fire, The.   Mary Jane Carr. ChAP

And—more—is Nature's Roman, never to be scourged. (LL)   House-Top, The. Herman Melville.   APN-2; BrAP; CBCWP; NAAL-3; NAAPv.1; NCAP; OxBoAm; TCAPo

And—oh, heaven! 'twas her sister! (LL)   Masquerading.   May Probyn. NPeEn; VWP

Andraitx—Pomegranate Flowers.   D. H. Lawrence.   NAMCP V.1; NoP-4; NoP-5

Andre Gide, a like-minded but stupidly dead and French companion.   Business of Health, The.   Jennifer Timoner.   ICANM

André who was killed in Riga.   Constellation of Dead Brothers.   Victor Serge. AF, tr. by James Brook

Andrea del Sarto.   Robert Browning.   NAEL-6v2; NAEL-7v2; NoP-4; NoP-5

Andreas and Carl Larson were the thug twins.   Larson Arson.   Margaret Benbow.   PoDa

Andrée Rexroth ("Now once more gray mottled buckeye branches.")   Kenneth Rexroth.   APT-2; ASA; NAMCP V.1

Andrée Rexroth ("Years have gone, The. It is spring.")   Kenneth Rexroth. APSN

Mt. Tamalpais.   CalPo

Andrew Jackson & Martin Van Buren.   Jackson Mac Low.   APSN Fr. Presidents of the United States of America, The.

Andrew Jackson's last name's the same as my first.   Jackson Mac Low.   APSN Fr. Presidents of the United States of America, The.

Andrew Rykman's dead and gone.   Andrew Rykman's Prayer.   John Greenleaf Whittier.

Andrew Rykman's Prayer.   John Greenleaf Whittier. "Pardon, Lord, the lips that dare."   SacPr

Andreyevsky Church, The.   Nikolai Nikolaevich Morshen.   TCRusP, tr. by John Glad

Androgyny.   Steve Orlen.   OPRER

Andromache, I think of you. The Simois.   Swan, The.   Charles Baudelaire. WoPoe, tr. by Louis Simpson

Andromache, I think of you—this meagre stream. Swan, The. Charles Baudelaire. SxFrPo, *tr. by* James McGowan

Andromache's Lamentation. Homer. OBVE *Fr.* Iliad, The.

Andromeda. Gerard Manley Hopkins. OxAEP-2

Anduve por la cuesta de los días. Zacoalco o paisaje. Laura Solórzano. SPV, *tr. by* Jen Hofer

And—which is more—you'll be a Man, my son! (LL) If. Rudyard Kipling. BRP; ChAP; CtM; ITBLP; UV

Andy Hasselgard. Dave Etter. IllVoic

Andy Warhol Speaks to His Two Filipino Maids. Alfred A. Yuson. ReBoTo

Andy-the-German Servant of Two Masters. Andrew Duncan. VaPo

Ane Godly Dream. Elizabeth Melville, Lady Culross.
  "I luikit up unto that Castell fair." EMWP
  "Upon one day as I did mourn full sore." ChIV-1

Ane Satire [*or* Satyre] of the Three [*or* Thrie] Estaitis. Sir David Lyndsay.
  "My patent pardouns ye may see." OBSV

Anear the centre of that northern crest. James Thomson. GS; NePenScot *Fr.* City of Dreadful Night, The.

Anecdotal Evidence. Eliot Weinberger. WANABP

Anecdote: "So silent I when Love was by." Dorothy Parker. IJHIL

Anecdote for Fathers [Showing how the Art of Lying may be Taught]. William Wordsworth. NoP-5
  Baffled. STuOW

Anecdote of the Jar. Wallace Stevens. BrAP; ColAP; EMP; FaBoA; HeIP-4; MoAmPo; NAAL-5; NAAPv.2; NAMCP V.1; NAWM-7v2; NIL-7; NoAM; NoP-4; NoP-5; OxBoAm; PoA 2002; PoPoPo; SAmP; TCAPo; TFi; WaAnP

Anecdote of the Prince of Peacocks ("In the moonlight / I met Berserk.") Wallace Stevens. AWTN

Anecdotes of the Late War. Charles Olson. CBCWP

Anemia. Rosamond Zimmerman. PfS

Anemones. Marion Angus. EdScPo

Anemones, they say, are out. Anemones. Marion Angus. EdScPo

Anestesia. Antonio Deltoro. RMCMP

Anesthesia. Antonio Deltoro. RMCMP, *tr. by* Christian Viveros-Fauné

Anesthesia of Red Flowers. Kitahara Hakushū. CAoMJL1, *tr. by* Leith Morton

Anew 10. Louis Zukofsky. NAAPv.2

Anew 20. Louis Zukofsky. APT-2; NAAPv.2

Anew 21. Louis Zukofsky. APT-2; NAAPv.2

Angel. Andrew Elliott. PNI

Angel. John Forbes. NOBAu

Angel. James Merrill. BrAP

Angel. John Henry, Cardinal Newman. SacPr

Angel. Marisela Norte. GeoHom

Angel. Ruth Padel. MFPA; NeBrP

Angel. Benjamin Alire Sáenz. LiTh

Angel. Maxine Scates. PBCAP

Angel. Penelope Shuttle. MoWP

Angel, The. William Blake. RACG *Fr.* Songs of Experience.

Angel, The [*with music*]. Galway Kinnell. NoAM

Angel, The. James Wright. YaYoPo

Angel and the girl are met, the. Annunciation, The. Edwin Muir. ChIV-2

Angel Atrapado 7. John Yau. BodElec

Ángel Bueno, El. Rafael Alberti. RaW

Angel Butcher. Philip Levine. ColAP; WaAnP

Angel came to me, An. Madeleine L'Engle. OBCP *Fr.* Three Songs of Mary.

Ángel de Arena, El. Rafael Alberti. RaW

Angel Eyes. Earl Brent. ReLy

Angel Finally Admits What She Knows to Lou Binkler of Bethany, Missouri, An. Catie Rosemurgy. AmPoNex

Angel Hair sleeps with a boy in my head. He Dreams What Is Going On Inside His Head. Jonathan Cott. AHA

Angel has already said, *Be not afraid*, The. Cestello Annunciation, The. Andrew Hudgins. UpMys

Angel in Blythburgh Church, An. Peter Porter. NoP-4; NoP-5

Angel in the Deluge. Rosario Murillo. CLPP, *tr. by* Alejandro Murguía

Angel in the House, The. Coventry Patmore.
  Lover, The. OxAEP-2
  Married Lover, The. OBEV; OxAEP-2; SacPr
  Paragon, The. NAEL-6v2; NAEL-7v2
  "'Twas when the spousal time of May." OxAEP-2

Angel in the Temple of Luxor, An. Rodney M. McNeil. InTrad

Angel is coming down, The. Angel. Penelope Shuttle. MoWP

Angel island. Plum Blossom Poem, The. Gary Snyder. ASA

Angel Island—what a beautiful name. Karl Yoneda. NAAPv.2

Angel, king of streaming morn. Sun. Henry Rowe. OBEV

Angel kissed my alphabet, The. Poem. James Tate. NAMCP V.2

Angel of Death, The. *Unknown.* SacPr

Angel of Dread, The. Miklós Radnóti. ConPit; PFTM-1, *tr. by* Clayton Eshleman and Gyula Kodolanyi

Angel of letters, feed me. Alphabet Soup. Fatima Lim-Wilson. ReBoTo

Angel of moment is dust, The. Gavin Selerie. Oth *Fr.* Roxy.

Angel of Sand, The. Rafael Alberti. RaW, *tr. by* Rachel Benson

Angel of simple human affairs, The. Mother Sabbath. Nikolai Alekseievich Klyuyev. TCRusP, *tr. by* John Glad

Angel of the Rain. Harriet McEwen Kimball. TreFP

Angel on the Beach, An. Hamutal Bar Yosef. DTA, *tr. by* Shirley Kaufman

Angel on your shoulder, The. Bodhidharma Never Came to Hatboro. Tyler Doherty. WANABP

Angel, robed in spotless white, An. Dawn. Paul Laurence Dunbar. NAAPv.1; OxBoAm

Angel said to me: "Why are you laughing?", The. Sarah. Delmore Schwartz. ChIV-1; TaR

Angel Syphilis in the circle of Signators, The. Robert Duncan. PFTM-2 *Fr.* Passages.

Angel was tired of heaven, as he lounged in the golden street, An. Woman and the Angel, The. Robert W. Service. ChIV-1

Angel who divided us in remote times, The. Angel Who Separated Us with the Flame, The. Rossana Ombres. CItWP, *tr. by* Cinzia Sartini Blum and Lara Trubowitz

Angel Who Separated Us with the Flame, The. Rossana Ombres. CItWP, *tr. by* Cinzia Sartini Blum and Lara Trubowitz

Angel with a voice like summer show'rs, An. Repose. Henrietta Cordelia Ray. CBWP-3

Angela Davis, the Virgin Mary, and I. To Mainz! Ursula Krechel. GTCP, *tr. by* Irmgard Hunt

Angela Dominguez, Ever Present. Nancy Morejón. TANSG, *tr. by* Joy Renjilian-Burgy

Ángeles de la cal, Los. Baraja. David Huerta. RMCMP

Ángeles malos o buenos. Desahucio. Rafael Alberti. RaW

Angelica Rescued from the Sea-Monster, by Ingres; in the Luxembourg. Dante Gabriel Rossetti. CenSon

Angelita, do not run from the flame. (LL) Ten Million Flames of Los Angeles, The. Amy Uyematsu. CalPo; GeoHom

Angelitos Negros: A Salsa Ballet. Miguel Algarin.
  Prologue. PueRic

Angellica's Lament. Aphra Behn. LW

Angells' eyes, whome veyles cannot deceive, The. Robert Southwell. *See* Angels' eyes, whom veils cannot deceive, The.

Angels. Louise Erdrich. UpMys

Angels, The. Cleopatra Mathis. ExTi

Angels and ministers of grace defend us! William Shakespeare. OxAEP-1 *Fr.* Hamlet.

Angels are stooping, The. Cradle Song, A. William Butler Yeats. NOxBChV

Angels bad or good. Eviction. Rafael Alberti. RaW, *tr. by* Rachel Benson

Angels' eyes, whom veils cannot deceive, The. Of the Blessed Sacrament of the Altar. Robert Southwell. OBEV

(Angells' eyes, whome veyles cannot deceive, The.) SacPr

Angel's Flight. Maxine Scates. PBCAP

Angels in the House, The. *Unknown.* TreFP

Angels in Winter. Nancy Willard. ColAP

Angel's Message, The [*with music*]. Clara Ann Thompson. CBWP-2

Angels of Buena Vista, The. John Greenleaf Whittier. AmWaPo

Angels of Juárez, Mexico, The. Ray Gonzalez. TiP2; TouFir

Angels of lime, The. Deck of Cards. David Huerta. RMCMP, *tr. by* Mark Schafer

Angels of Mercy. Bob Hicok. AmAlph

Angels of the Ruins, The. Rafael Alberti. AF, *tr. by* Geoffrey Connell

Angels of Wine, The. Jonas Zdanys. PML

Angels rejoice in, The. Their Rectitude Their Beauty. Donald Davie. HarvBoo

Angel's Song. Charles Causley. OBCP

Angels stood, The. Blue Light, The. Kathleen Norris. UpMys

Angels' voices lost to air. Fugue. Shara McCallum. NAPBL

Angels walking under the palm trees. Little Carol of the Virgin, A. Félix Lope de Vega Carpio. SpanPo, *tr. by* Denise Levertov

Angels' Weather. Bruce Beaver. BMAP

Angelus. Kathleen Jessie Raine. BBASP

Anger. Robert Creeley. PFTM-2

Anger. Charles Lamb and Mary Lamb. NOxBChV

Anger. Anne Sexton. HP

Anger. César Vallejo. TCLAP, *tr. by* Thomas Merton

Anger Against Children. Robert Bly. LoL *Fr.* Anger Against Children.

Anger in its time and place. Anger. Charles Lamb and Mary Lamb. NOxBChV

Anger Poem, The (1.16). Horace. WED, tr. by Robert Bly

Anger Sweetened. Molly Peacock. FFC

Anger that Breaks a Man Down into Boys, The. César Vallejo. WED, tr. by Robert Bly

Anger that Breaks the Man into Children, The. César Vallejo. RaBo, tr. by Robert Bly and Clayton Eshleman

Anger the same thing as you behind my face, eyes, maybe. A larger than. Fred Wah. NLPA Fr. This Dendrite Map: Father / Mother Haibun.

Anger which breaks a man into children. Anger. César Vallejo. TCLAP, tr. by Thomas Merton

Angered, may I be near a glass of water. Sapphics Against Anger. Timothy Steele. CalPo

Angers. Bernard Noël. YaTCFP

Angers. Bernard Noël. YaTCFP, tr. by Rosemary Lloyd

Anghiari is medieval, a sleeve sloping down. Journey, The. James Wright. CAP-8; GPTC; NAAL-5; NoAM

Angina Pectoris. Nazim Hikmet. VCWP

Anglais Mort à Florence. Wallace Stevens. SAmP

Angle anatomy. Fragmento. Ulli Freer. VaPo

Angle of Geese. N. Scott Momaday. HATNAP

Angle of Vision. Robert Rendall. EdScPo

Angle-Land. David Jones. HarvBoo; NAMCP V.1; NoAM Fr. Anathemata, The.

Angler rose, he took his rod, The. Epitaph. Robert Louis Stevenson. OBCoV

Angler's Calendar, The. Yun Sŏndo. CATKP, tr. by Peter H. Lee
  Autumn. CATKP, tr. by Peter H. Lee
  "Autumn comes to a river village." CATKP, tr. by Peter H. Lee
  "Beyond where the wild geese fly." CATKP, tr. by Peter H. Lee
  "By the river a lone pine." CATKP, tr. by Peter H. Lee
  "Crows hastening to their nests, The." CATKP, tr. by Peter H. Lee
  "Day closes, / Time to feast and rest." CATKP, tr. by Peter H. Lee
  "Day is warm." CATKP, tr. by Peter H. Lee
  "Drunk I lie asleep." CATKP, tr. by Peter H. Lee
  "Fishes in the shallows." CATKP, tr. by Peter H. Lee
  "Frost falls on my clothes." CATKP, tr. by Peter H. Lee
  "Gently, the side wind blowing." CATKP, tr. by Peter H. Lee
  "How rare is a mossy jetty." CATKP, tr. by Peter H. Lee
  "I want to admire the dawn moon." CATKP, tr. by Peter H. Lee
  "Is it a cuckoo that cries?" CATKP; WoPoe, tr. by Peter H. Lee
  "I've forgotten the net and rod." CATKP, tr. by Peter H. Lee
  "Let's return to the shore." CATKP, tr. by Peter H. Lee
  "Let's spread our net out on the sand." CATKP, tr. by Peter H. Lee
  "Let's stop angling and see." CATKP, tr. by Peter H. Lee
  "Let's tread on fragrant grasses." CATKP, tr. by Peter H. Lee
  "Look! My snail-shell hut." CATKP, tr. by Peter H. Lee
  "Mend your fishing line and rod." CATKP, tr. by Peter H. Lee
  "People have praised my way of life." CATKP, tr. by Peter H. Lee
  "Puff of east wind ruffles, A." CATKP, tr. by Peter H. Lee
  "Red cliffs and emerald canyons." CATKP, tr. by Peter H. Lee
  "Scatter of silver dews, A." CATKP, tr. by Peter H. Lee
  "Setting sun is splendid, The." CATKP, tr. by Peter H. Lee
  "Silver scales and jade scales." CATKP, tr. by Peter H. Lee
  "Snow settles over the night, A." CATKP, tr. by Peter H. Lee
  Spring. CATKP, tr. by Peter H. Lee
  Summer. CATKP, tr. by Peter H. Lee
  "Sun's fair rays are shining, The." CATKP; WoPoe, tr. by Peter H. Lee
  "Tomorrow, tomorrow, we have tomorrow." CATKP, tr. by Peter H. Lee
  "What will the mood of the sky be?" CATKP, tr. by Peter H. Lee
  "Whelmed by my exalted moon." CATKP, tr. by Peter H. Lee
  "When the river is muddy." CATKP, tr. by Peter H. Lee
  "Where is it, where am I?" CATKP, tr. by Peter H. Lee
  "Where white clouds rise." CATKP, tr. by Peter H. Lee
  "Wind rises among the water chestnut, A." CATKP, tr. by Peter H. Lee
  Winter. CATKP, tr. by Peter H. Lee
  "Wrap the steamed rice in lotus leaves." CATKP, tr. by Peter H. Lee

Angler's Song, The. William Basse. NOSC Fr. Anglers Song, The.

Anglican curate in want, An. Ronald Arbuthnott Knox. OBCoV

Anglican firelight. Other Voice, The. Tom Paulin. PNI

Angling. Elise Paschen. PoA 2002

Angling. Unknown. WoPoe, tr. by Nguyen Ngoc Bich

Angling, a Day. Galway Kinnell. MoASP

Anglo Saxon Street. Earle Birney. HeIP-4; NIL-7; BrAP

Anglo-Mongrels and the Rose. Mina Loy.
  English Rose. NAMCP V.1

Anglorum Feriae. George Peele.
  "Write write yow Croniclers of Tyme and Fame." PBRV

Anglo-Saxon Comedy. Peter Rose. BMAP

Angola. Amélia Veiga. HAWP, tr. by Julia Kirst

Angry. Suki Wessling. ArBi

Angry boy takes out his realistic gun, The. Need for Attention, The. William Wadsworth. KGB

Angry Bride, The. Unknown. WoPoe, tr. by Kevin O'Rourke

Angry Dusk. Jack Lindsay. NOBAu

Angry Samson. Robert Graves. ChIV-1; OxBEV

Angry Summer 20, The. Idris Davies. TCAWP

Angry Summer 28, The. Idris Davies. TCAWP

Angry Summer, The ("From Abertillery and Aberdare.") Idris Davies. AngWePo

Angry Summer, The ("Mrs. Evans fach, you want butter again.") Idris Davies. AngWePo

(Mrs. Evans Fach, You Want Butter Again.) OBWVE

Angry Valentine, An. Myra Cohn Livingston. CalPo

Angry with China. Douglas Messerli. FTOS

Angrye winds not ay, The. All Changeth. William Drummond of Hawthornden. NePenScot

Anguish. Adelaide Crapsey. APT-1

Anguish. Henry Vaughan. OxAEP-1

Anguish. Andrey Andreievich Voznesensky. RusPo, tr. by Robert Arthur Douglas Ford

Anguish, a door, Le Portel, body bent over jagged rock. Placements I. Clayton Eshleman. PFTM-1

Anguish & Metaphor. Gustaf Sobin. WoBe

Anguish exists. Ars Poetica. Roque Dalton. TCLAP, tr. by Richard Schaaf

Anguish of Ants, The. David Campbell. BMAP

Angular discrimination, An. Locality. Claude Royet-Journoud. YaTCFP, tr. by Keith Waldrop

Ani Maamin, A Song Lost and Found Again. Elie Wiesel.
  "Behold, God of Abraham, God of mercy." HP

Anima 1. Takehisa Kosugi. WhBo

Animal bones and some mossy tent rings. Lament for the Dorsets. Alfred Wellington Purdy. BrAP; NoAM

Animal crackers, and cocoa to drink. Christopher Darlington Morley. ChAP

Animal Crackers in My Soup. Irving Caesar and Ted Koehler. ReLy

Animal Fair. Unknown. NTCP

Animal Has Drawn a Human, The. Bert Schierbeek. PFTM-2, tr. by Charles McGeehan

Animal House Shape of God. Christine Hume. IIR

Animal Languages. Chase Twichell. StAl

Animal Liberation. Genny Lim. FTtHH

Animal lives under the water, An. Hear children. After Aesop. Malinda Markham. IAoNAP

Animal Nativity. Les A. Murray. UpMys

Animal Song [with music]. Heather McHugh. WaAnP

Animal Spirits. Sikong Tu. CCL1 Fr. Twenty-Four Modes of Poetry.

Animal Spirits. John E. Smelcer. PoCoUp

Animal, the new, The. (LL) Mark Doty. InoFa; WiU Fr. Atlantis.

Animal Tranquillity and Decay. William Wordsworth. OxBEV
  (Old Man Travelling.) NPBRoP

Animal understands itself, The. Fable. Luiza Neto Jorge. SurWo, tr. by Jean R. Longland

Animal Weather-Forecasting. Thomas Lodge. NoSic

Animal Zen. Kathe Davis. AmZen

Animals. Robinson Jeffers. APT-1

Animals. Frank O'Hara. GoPo; HarvBoo; StAl

Animals. Sharon Thesen. BeAl

Animals. Miller Williams. BeAl; P180

Animals, The. W. S. Merwin. VCAP; WaAnP

Animals, The [with music]. Edwin Muir. ChIV-1; CtM; HeIP-4; MoBrPo

4: The Animals. Jaime Sabines. MotU Fr. Adam and Eve.

Animals Are Entering Our Lives. Lisel Mueller. ExTi

Animals are leaving, the. Privacy. C. D. Wright. AmAlph

Animals Are Passing from Our Lives. Philip Levine. CalPo; CAP-8; ColAP; RaBo; WaAnP

Animals are the latest decorating craze. Some Cool. Alice Fulton. AllShUp

Animals full of light. Meditation. William Stafford. WaAnP

Animals in That Country, The. Margaret Atwood. NALW; NoAM

Animals in the pastures. Landscape. Hendrik Marsman. TuT, tr. by Michael Longley

Animals never sleep. At night when it's dark. Face of a Horse, The. Nikolai Alekseievich Zabolotsky. TCRusP, tr. by Kathy Lewis and Bob Perelman

Animals of last year, The. (LL)   Temple of the Animals, The.   Robert Duncan.   CalPo; OxBoAm

Animals own a fur world.   Adults Only.   William Stafford.   CAP-8

Animals were, The.   Ode to the Cat.   Pablo Neruda.   VCWP, *tr. by* John Hollander

Ánimo vegetal.   Francisco Segovia.   RMCMP

Animula.   George Oppen.   FTOS

Animula vagula blandula.   Animula Vagula Blandula.   Conrad Potter Aiken.   OBCoV

Aniseed has a sinful taste.   Egypt.   Keith Douglas.   HarvBoo

Anita and Giovanni [*with music*].   Henrietta Cordelia Ray.   CBWP-3

Ank'hor Vat.   Denis Devlin.   ModIr

Ankle Bells.   Mirabai.   WED, *tr. by* Robert Bly

Ann, Ann! / Come! quick as you can!   Alas, Alack!   Walter De la Mare.   OPOU

Ann Griffiths.   Sally Roberts Jones.   AngWePo

Anna.   Patrick Friesen.   NLPA

   First dance.   NLPA

   Second dance.   NLPA

Anna Akhmatova Spends the Night on Miami Beach.   John Balaban.   GifTon

Anna Akhmatova's Funeral.   Martin Mooney.   ModIr

Anna Blossom Has Wheels.   Kurt Schwitters.   PFTM-1

Anna Blume.   Kurt Schwitters.   NAWM-7v2, *tr. by* David Britt

Anna Bullen.   John Banks.

   Short Curse.   STuOW

Anna Dering on Bartolomeo Silva, Doctor of Turin.   Anne Lok.   EMWP

Anna Liffey.   Eavan Boland.   BodElec; ModIr

Anna Magnani at the Castro.   Denise Nico Leto.   AFaM

Anna Magnani in *Mamma Roma*.   Anna Magnani at the Castro.   Denise Nico Leto.   AFaM

Anna: *Rose of Sharon*.   Rebecca Baggett.   FiBr *Fr.* Art of the Amish: A Quilt Exhibition.

Anna runs home under a dark beam of air coming near.   Geranium Flame.   Lucile Adler.   ICANM

Anna Speaks of the Childhood of Mary Her Daughter.   Lucille Clifton.   NALW

Annabel Lee.   Edgar Allan Poe.   BLPJKO; BRP; ChAP; HeIP-4; ITBLP; NAAL-3; NAAL-5; NAAPv.1; NCAP; NoP-5; OBSP; OxBoAm; TCAPo; TFi

Annabell and the Witches.   Mick Gowar.   OBSP

Annals say: when the monks of Clonmacnoise, The.   Seamus Heaney.   EmeKit; ModIr; NoP-5; NPeEn; StAl *Fr.* Squarings.

And, the last day being come, Man stood alone.   Trumbull Stickney.   APN-2; NoP-4

Anne.   Alice Derry.   FiBr

Anne and the Field-Mouse.   Ian Serraillier.   NOxBChV

Anne Boleyn.   Erica Bernheim.   LegDan

Anne Boleyn [*with music*].   Eloise Bibb.   CBWP-4

Anne Bradstreate.   Another.   Anne Bradstreet.   TCAPo

Anne Frank Huis.   Andrew Motion.   HarvBoo

Anne Hathaway.   Carol Ann Duffy.   NoP-5

Anne Hathaway Composes Her 18th Sonnet.   Neil Curry.   NLP

Anne Pauker.   Nokhem Vaysman.   Prolet, *tr. by* Amelia Glaser

Anne Rutledge.   Edgar Lee Masters.   CBCWP; MoAmPo; NAMCP V.1; NoAM; OxBoAm; TFi *Fr.* Spoon River Anthology.

Anne Steele.   Jean Balderston.   MPUn

Anne, who are dead—and whom I loved in a rather asinine fashion.   Wonderful Things.   Ron Padgett.   AHA; PmAP

Annette came through the meadows.   Pastoral.   Henrietta Cordelia Ray.   CBWP-3

Annette has MS, she needs Mickey's help.   Funicello at 50.   Klipschutz.   ReTh

Annie Hill's Grave.   James Merrill.   WeW-3

Annie, my first-born, gentle child.   To Annie.   Mary E. Tucker.   CBWP-1

Annie of Tharaw, my true love of old.   Annie of Tharaw.   *Unknown.*   GePo, *tr. by* Henry Wadsworth Longfellow

Annie Pearl Smith Discovers Moonlight.   Patricia Smith.   GT; OtW; OxAAAP

Annie Pengelly.   Lorna Goodison.   NAMCP V.2

Annihilation.   Conrad Potter Aiken.   MoAmPo

Annihilation.   Ko Un.   WhBo

Annihilation.   Elizabeth Oakes-Smith.   TCAPo *Fr.* Atheism.

Annihilation's Trio: Three Irrational Sonnets Begging the Question of Being and Act.   Jay Wright.   ICANM

Anniversaries.   Thomas Kinsella.

   1956.   ModIr

Anniversaries.   May Probyn.   VWP

Anniversaries of War.   Yehuda Amichai.   VCWP, *tr. by* Benjamin Harshav and Barbara Harshav

Anniversary.   Judith Ortiz Cofer.   PueRic; TouFir

Anniversary.   Lauris Edmond.   BeAl

Anniversary.   Odysseus Elytis.   AF, *tr. by* Edmund Keeley and Philip Sherrard

Anniversary.   William Greenway.   PoA 2002

Anniversary.   Dorothy Hewett.   BMAP

Anniversary.   Gary Metras.   PasH

Anniversary.   Davi Walders.   MPUn

Anniversary, An.   Wendell Berry.   UpMys

Anniversary, The.   Ai.   BodElec

Anniversary [*or* Anniversarie], The.   John Donne.   BASC; FSCP; NoP-4; NoP-5; NoSic; TFi; WeW-3

Anniversary Poem.   George Oppen.   APSN *Fr.* Some San Francisco Poems.

Anniversary Poem.   John Greenleaf Whittier.   PCW

Anniversary Soak.   Paul Groves.   TCAWP

Anniversary Trip.   James Hoggard.   TiP2

Anniversary: "When the world was created wasn't it like this?"   Joy Harjo.   CFP; PoDa

Anniversary with Agave Plants.   Margherita Guidacci.   CItWP, *tr. by* Cinzia Sartini Blum and Lara Trubowitz

Anno Domini MCMXLVII.   Salvatore Quasimodo.   GI, *tr. by* Jack Bevan

Anno 1829.   Heinrich Heine.   OBVE, *tr. by* Charles Stuart Calverley

Annotation in Her Last Court Diary.   Kimiko Hahn.   ExTi

Annotations of Auschwitz.   Peter Porter.   BrAP; HP

Annotations Tropes and Lacunae of the Itoku Master.   Ray DiPalma.   FTOS

Announced by all the trumpets of the sky.   Snow-Storm [*or* Snowstorm], The.   Ralph Waldo Emerson.   APN-1; BrAP; ITBLP; MoW; NAAL-3; NAAPv.1; NCAP; NoP-4; NoP-5; OxBoAm; PoPoPo; TCAPo; TFi; TreFP; WaAnP

Announcement: All pupils named Doug.   Community College in the Rain.   David Berman.   LegDan

Announcement, An.   Sri Sri.   HotL, *tr. by* V. Narayana Rao

Announcement of a New Grand Acceleration Company for the Promotion of the Speed of Literature.   Thomas Moore.   OBCoV

Annual Gaiety.   Wallace Stevens.   MoAmPo

Annual of the Dark Physics, An.   Norman Dubie.   BodElec

Annual Returns.   Greg Williamson.   RA

Annuals.   Daniel Halpern.   PfSP

Annuals and Perennials.   Janice W. Hodges.   BtF

Annunciation.   Ken Etheridge.   AngWePo

Annunciation.   Anna Kamienska.   GI, *tr. by* David Curzon and Grażyna Drabik

Annunciation.   Primo Levi.   AF; GI, *tr. by* Ruth Feldman

Annunciation.   Rainer Maria Rilke.   OBVE, *tr. by* James Blair Leishman

Annunciation.   Kay Smith.   NIL-7; NIP-4

Annunciation: "I saw my soul become flesh breaking open."   Jean Valentine.   118 CAP-8

Annunciation, The.   Elizabeth Jennings.   ChrPo

Annunciation, The.   Samuel Menashe.   GI

Annunciation, The.   Douglas Messerli.   FTOS

Annunciation, The.   Stephen Mitchell.   GI

Annunciation, The.   Edwin Muir.   ChIV-2

Annunciation, The: "Surely God thought this would be a moment."   David Starkey.   Vesp

Annunciation in an Initial R.   Angie Estes.   ExTi

Annunciation of time harrying time, The.   Spell.   Harry Mathews.   NYP2

Annunciations.   Nuala Ni Dhomhnaill.   ModIr, *tr. by* Michael Hartnett

Annus Mirabilis.   John Dryden.

   "By viewing nature, nature's handmaid, art."   BASC

   English Fleet Goes Out, The.   STuOW

   "Now on their coasts our conquering navy rides."   OxAEP-1

   "Now van to van the foremost squadrons meet."   OBWP

   "Our fleet divides, and straight the Dutch appear."   BASC; FaBoWar

   "Yet London, empress of the northern clime."   NAEL-6v1; NAEL-7v1

Annus Mirabilis.   Philip Larkin.   NBLV; NIP-4

Annus Mirabilis 1989.   Elaine Feinstein.   HP

Año, ya dormido, Un.   Ángel Bueno, El.   Rafael Alberti.   RaW

Anoch is tu bhuam.   Aonghas MacNeacail.   EdScPo

Anochecido, grandes nubes ahogan el pueblo.   Moguer.   Juan Ramón Jiménez.   RaW

Anodyne.   Yusef Komunyakaa.   AmAlph

Anoint the Ariston.   Odysseus Elytis.   *tr. by* Olga Broumas

   "I was late in understanding the meaning of humility."   GifTon, *tr. by* Olga Broumas

   "Whatever I was able to acquire in my life by way of acts visible to all, that is, to win my own transparency, I owe to a kind of special courage Poetry gave me: to be wind for the kite and kite for the wind, even when the sky is missing."   GifTon, *tr. by* Olga Broumas

Anointed stone, the coruscated crown, The. Circumstance, The. Hart Crane. PFTM-1

Anointing, An. Thylias Moss. GT; MotU; ReTh

Anon. Conor O'Callaghan. NIrP

Anon out of the earth a fabric huge. John Milton. MakPoe *Fr.* Paradise Lost.

Anonymous. Víctor Hernández Cruz. PueRic

Anonymous Drawing. Donald Justice. HeIP-4

Anonymous handsome, The. Rejoicing That Attend the Murder of Famous Men, The. Robley, Jr. Wilson. PBCAP

Anonymous Squad, An. Yekhi'el Mar. NRoS, *tr. by* Esther Raizen

Anonymous: "To the Department of Motor Vehicles." Susan Love Fitts. IJHIL

Anonymous Wedding Photo. Jennifer O'Grady. AmPoNex

An[o]on they kiste, and riden [*or* ryden] forth hir waye [*or* weye]. (LL) Geoffrey Chaucer. NAEL-6v1; NAEL-7v1; WaAnP *Fr.* Canterbury Tales, The.

Anorexia. Robert Budde. PoPra

Anorexia. Alice Jones. AFaM; BloBone

Anorexia. Jennifer Maiden. BMAP

Anorexic. Eavan Boland. NAMCP V.2

Anorexic, The. Ruth Anderson Barnett. OPRER

Another. Holley Blackwell. AnSo

Another. Thomas Carew. CavPo

Another. Skip Fox. AnSo

Another and another and another. James Henry. NPeEn; OxBEV

Another ("Anne Bradstreate.") Anne Bradstreet. TCAPo

Another April and another day. James Aitchison. EdScPo

Another armo[u]red animal—scale. Pangolin, The. Marianne Moore. APT-1; NAAPv.2; NAMCP V.1; NoAM; WaAnP

Another Artifact. Carla Harryman. BAP-04 *Fr.* Baby.

Another [*see also* "A Letter to Her Husband, Absent upon Public[k] Employment"]. Anne Bradstreet. EMWP; LW; NAAL-3

Another Attempt at Rescue. Mandy L. Smoker. PrTe

Another [Birthday Ode], 1743. Colley Cibber.

"Of fields, of forts, and floods, unknown to fame." STuOW

Another boat-load for the Further Shore. Charon's Song. Charles Murray. EdScPo

Another Canto. John Bingham Morton. UV

Another Century. David Keplinger. AmPoNex

Another chambered nautilus bequeathed me. Franchises in Flux. John Ashbery. VaPo

Another conference year has passed. To the Conference. Mrs. Henry Linden. CBWP-4

Another country, people act differently there. Past Is, The. Margaret Randall. ICANM

Another damp Sunday morning up and walk over. Peter Riley. Oth *Fr.* Alstonefield V.

Another dawn on the world! (LL) Northern Vigil, A. Bliss Carman. BrAP; OBEV

Another Day. Belinda Zubicueta Carmona. TANSG, *tr. by* Celeste Kostopulos-Cooperman

Another day. Morning Becomes Electric. Bruce Dawe. BMAP

Another day. Rosamond S. King. BtF

Another day has gone for keeps. Night in the Ghetto. *Unknown, fr. Terezin Concentration Camp.* INSAB

Another Day on the Pilgrimage. Peter Gizzi. VaPo

Another Duffer. Sam Hamill. BodElec

Another Easter Poem. Honorée Fanonne Jeffers. RD

Another Epitaph on an Army of Mercenaries [*see also* Housman, "Epitaph on an Army of Mercenaries"]. Hugh MacDiarmid. FaBoWar; NAEL-6v2; NAEL-7v2; NAMCP V.1; NoAM; NoP-4; NoP-5; OBWP; WaAnP

Another evening we sprawled about discussing. Charles on Fire. James Merrill. CAP-8; HeIP-4; OxBoAm

Another fire dying down, the view from here. Kindertotenlieder. Timothy Liu. NeAmPo

Another Fools' Day touches down, another homecoming. Another Fools' Day Touches Down: Shush. Jack A. Mapanje. HBAPE

Another Fools' Day Touches Down: Shush. Jack A. Mapanje. HBAPE

Another for Miss Pardo's Album. Mihály Vörösmarty. IQMS, *tr. by* Paul Tabori

Another for the Briar Rose [*with music*]. William Morris. OxBEV

Another funeral. White Paintings III. Laura Mullen. RoV

Another Genealogy. Luiza Neto Jorge. SurWo, *tr. by* Jean R. Longland

Another Grace for a Child. Robert Herrick. *See* Grace for a Child.

Another gray morning. Gray Poem. Peter Everwine. GeoHom

Another homicide, another trial. Prosecutor. William Baer. LiTh

Another hot afternoon upstairs after school. Killarney Clary. GeoHom

Another Hundred People. Stephen Sondheim. ReLy

Another hundred people just got off of the train. Another Hundred People. Stephen Sondheim. ReLy

Another Impostor. Bruce Jackson. AmPoNex

Another Insane Devotion. Gerald Stern. CAP-8

Another Kimono. Nancy Eimers. AtGh

Another Kind of Skin. Frances Sackett. Prnts

Another Lady's Exception, Present at the Hearing. Ben Jonson. NAEL-7v1 *Fr.* Celebration of Charis in Ten Lyric[k] Pieces [*or* Peeces], A.

Another Lazarus. Sally Roberts Jones. TCAWP

Another letter? Karai Senryū. EMJL, *tr. by* Haruo Shirane

Another Letter to a Friend. Mary Mollineux. PoBW

Another Life. Frank Bidart. OxBoAm; VCAP

Another Life. Taslima Nasrin. VCWP, *tr. by* Carolyne Wright

Another Little Boy. *Unknown.* NOxBChV

Another Lo-Cal Elegy. Stephen Yenser. UrbNat

Another Love Affair/Another Poem. E. Ethelbert Miller. ISC

Another [Madrigal]. Edward Herbert, 1st Baron Herbert of Cherbury. NOSC

Another maid there was, who also breathed. William Wordsworth. NPBRoP *Fr.* Prelude, The; Growth of a Poet's Mind [1805 version].

Another Meditation at the same Time. Edward Taylor. NOSC; TCAPo; WaAnP *Fr.* Preparatory Meditations Before My Approach to the Lord's Supper.

Another Merchant of Death. Merchant of Death. Ramabai Espinet. WaCA

Another Moment. Sim Kombem. NAfrP

Another Monday another mundane. Ordinary, The. Ray McNiece. AmZen

Another morn than ours! (LL) Death-Bed, The. Thomas Hood. InoFa; OBEV; TreFP

Another Mule. Sterling Plumpp. GT

Another mule kicking. Another Mule. Sterling Plumpp. GT

Another Name for the Cassiterides. Rod Mengham. VaPo

Another Nameless Prostitute Says the Man is Innocent. Martín Espada. ViWalt

Another Night in Crawley's Cove. Al Pittman. Coast

Another Night in the Ruins. Galway Kinnell. InvLad

Another Ode to Salt. Danielle Legros Georges. BtF

Another [On the Duke of Buckingham]. Thomas Carew. NOSC

Another on the Sun Shine. Lucy Hutchinson. EMWP

Another one, half-cracked: John Heydon. Ezra Pound. TCAPo *Fr.* Three Cantos of a Poem of Some Length.

Another one was coming toward me. So I Lost My Temper. Rose Romano. UnSA

Another [*see also* "A Letter to Her Husband, Absent upon Public[k] Employment"]. Anne Bradstreet. BASC

Another Place. Paul Zimmer. PfSP

Another Planet. Boris Iulianovich Poplavsky. TCRusP, *tr. by* Emmett Jarrett, Dick Lourie and Richard Lourie

Another pleasant book cover hides what I feel is the weightiest poetry collection of postmodern times. Darren Wershler-Henry. PoPra *Fr.* Ten Out of Ten, or, Why Poetry Criticism Sucks in 2003.

Another Poem about the Vandals. Alan Michael Parker. NeAmPo

Another Poem for Me (after Recovering from an O.D.). Etheridge Knight. LaCa; OxAAAP

Another Poem for Mothers. Erin Belieu. PoChi

Another Poem in English. Lorenzo Thomas. EGAG

Another Poem to My Mother. Clementina Suárez. TANSG, *tr. by* Janet N. Gold

Another Poetics. Octavio Armand. TCLAP, *tr. by* Carol Maier

Another Race. Delmira Agustini. TCLAP, *tr. by* Karl Kirchwey

Another Reason Why I Don't Keep a Gun in the House. Billy Collins. OxBoAm; SUP

Another Revenant. Denise Levertov. UpMys

Another Rhythm. Akasha (Gloria) Hull. ISC

Another round of *Dona Nobis Pacem.* Night Ferry to Naxos 2. Monica Youn. LegDan

Another Scream. Malkia M'Buzi Moore. BRtP

Another September. Thomas Kinsella. CABP; HarvBoo; NoP-4; NoP-5

Another Song. Scott Cairns. UpMys

Another Song. William Ross. NePenScot, *tr. by* Derick Thomson

Another Song About Paris. Dave Frishberg. ReLy

Another Song Exciting to Spirituall Mirth. Anne Collins.

Song. PEW

Another Sonnet to Black It Self [*or* Itself]. Edward Herbert, 1st Baron Herbert of Cherbury. NoP-5

Another Spring. Kenneth Rexroth. GoPo

Another Spring ("In all the country.") Tu Fu [*or* Du Fu]. CrYelRi, *tr. by* Sam Hamill

Another Spring on Olmstead Street. Len Roberts. UrbNat

Another Spring ("White birds over the grey river.") Tu Fu [*or* Du Fu]. BLT, *tr. by* Kenneth Rexroth

Another Stone in the Swamp. Rumen Leonidov. CSCBP, *tr. by* Georgi Belev and Lisa Sapinkopf

Another summer we must have blinked and missed. Back End. Peter Rafferty. NLP

Another Summit. Muso Soseki. EaWin, *tr. by* W. S. Merwin

Another Sunday morning comes. Wendell Berry. UpMys *Fr.* Sabbaths.

Another sunset of scrambled eggs. Ménage à Trois. Howard Moss. VCAP

Another [To His Booke]. Robert Herrick. NOSC

Another to the River Ankor. Michael Drayton. NOSC *Fr.* Idea.

Another to Urania. Benjamin Colman. ChIV-1

Another Version. Lisel Mueller. IllVoic

Another Version of an Ocean. Reginald Shepherd. NeAmPo

Another Vigil at San Quentin. Alison Luterman. RaF

Another village explodes. (LL) It Is Dangerous to Read Newspapers. Margaret Atwood. HeIP-4; ItP; OBWP

Another Voice. Victor Hugo. SxFrPo, *tr. by* A. M. and E. H. Blackmore

Another Voice. Richard Wilbur. UpMys

Another warning sound! The funeral bell. Stanzas to the Memory of the Late King. Felicia Dorothea Hemans. RWP

Another way of being. (LL) Meditation on the Threshold. Rosario Castellanos. CFP; TANSG, *tr. by* Magda Bogin

Another way—to see. (LL) Tint I cannot take—is best, The. Emily Dickinson. APN-2; MoAmPo

Another wedding & Aunt Cherry. Cherry. Stuart Dybek. PBCAP

Another Weeping Woman. Wallace Stevens. PoA 2002

Another winter. Old Age. Buland Al-Haidari. PML, *tr. by* Hamid Algar and Mounah Abdallah Khouri

Another Woman. Imtiaz Dharker. EmeKit

Another Woman. Nina Iskrenko. CRWP, *tr. by* Stephanie Sandler

Another word for *father* is *worry*. Words for Worry. Li-Young Lee. P180

Another World. Sándor Weöres. IQMS, *tr. by* Adam Makkai and Donald E. Morse

Another year! another deadly blow! November, 1806. William Wordsworth. OBWP

Another year gone. Basho. EH; NIL-7, *tr. by* Robert Hass

Another's gone, and who comes next. Pass of Death, The. George Darley. NOBRP

Anselmo in a fit of pique. Anselmo's Moment with God. Alberto A. Ríos. NAMCP V.2

Anselmo's Moment with God. Alberto A. Ríos. NAMCP V.2

Anseo. Paul Muldoon. ModIr; NAMCP V.2; NPeEn; PNI

Anster Fair. William Tennant.
   "My pulse beats fire—my pericranium glows." NePenScot
   "Upon a little dappled nag, whose mane." NOBRP

Anstruther. John Burnside. EdScPo

Answeare to my Lady Alice Edgertons Songe, Of I prethy send mee back my Hart, An. Lady Jane Cavendish. EMWP

Answer. Mildred Bowers. YaYoPo

Answer. Bei Dao. PoetW; VCWP, *tr. by* Donald Finkel

Answer, An. Robert Frost. OBCoV

Answer, The. Sir Robert Aytoun. NOSC

Answer, The. Bei Dao. AF; PFTM-2, *tr. by* Bonnie S. McDougall

Answer, The. George Herbert. FaBoVe; NPeEn

Answer, The. Sara Teasdale. PoA 2002

Answer, The [*To Pope's* Impromptu]. Anne Finch, Countess of Winchilsea. NAEL-7v1; NALW; NoP-4; NoP-5; WaAnP

Answer by the Lady's Maid [to a Poem Left in a Lady's Toilet]. James Eyre Weeks. IrLP

Answer Me. Adah Isaacs Menken. CBWP-1; PoBW; ViWPN

Answer Song. David Trinidad. WiU

Answer to a Child's Question. Samuel Taylor Coleridge. ITBLP; NOxBChV; NPBRoP

Answer to a Kind Enquiry. Mary Holtby. UV

Answer to a Love-Letter, An. Lady Mary Wortley Montagu. LW

Answer to Another Persuading a Lady to Marriage, An. Katherine Philips. WeW-3
   (Answer to another perswading a Lady to Marriage, An.) NPeEn; PBRV
   (To One Persuading a Lady to Marriage.) LW; OBEV

Answer to Cloe [*or* Chloe] Jealous. Matthew Prior. OxBEV
   (Better Answer, A.) NAEL-6v1; NAEL-7v1; OxAEP-1
   (Better Answer to Cloe [*or* Chloe] Jealous, A.) NPeEn

Answer to Herrick, An. Harry Gilonis. Oth

Answer to Master [*or* Mr.] Ben Jonson's Ode, to Persuade Him Not to Leave the Stage, An. Thomas Randolph. BASC

Answer to the Parson, An. William Blake. NBLV; WoPoe

Answer to Vice-Prefect Chang. Wang Wei. ChinPo, *tr. by* Ye Weilian [*or* Yeh Wei-lien *or* Wai-lim Yip]

Answer to yo / question / of am I not yo / woman / even if you went on shit again. Sonia Sanchez. OxAAAP

Answering A Child. Sarah Morgan Bryan Piatt. NCAP

Answering Robert Frost. Felix Stefanile. VisFro

Answers, The. Ed Robeson. Eno

Answers from the Elements. Jelaluddin Rumi. BBASP, *tr. by* Coleman Barks and John Moyne

Answers on a Postcard. David Morley. NLP

Answers to what comes next and how to like it. (LL) How To Like It. Stephen Dobyns. CAP-8; SUP

Ant, The. Richard Flecknoe. NOSC

Ant, The. Richard Lovelace. BASC

Ant climbs up a trunk, The. Short Story, A. David Escobar Galindo. ChAP, *tr. by* Jorge Piche

Ant Dodger. Bill Knott. PBCAP

Ant Farm. Thylias Moss. PoDa

Ant Hill, The. Cynthia Zarin. NoP-4; NoP-5

Ant nest. Jenny Joseph. MoWP

Ant on the tablecloth, An. Departmental. Robert Frost. HeIP-4; MoAmPo; NAAL-5; PtR; SoSe-8

Antarctica. Clive Holden. PoPra

Antarctica. Derek Mahon. NPeEn; PBCIP; StAl

Ante el Espejo. Vicente Aleixandre. RaW

Ante Mortem. Robinson Jeffers. MoAmPo

Ante-bellum Negro prayed, The. Must Be Freed. Lizelia Augusta Jenkins Moorer. CBWP-3

Ante-Bellum Sermon, An. Paul Laurence Dunbar. APN-2

Antelope white against the charred hills, The. Field. Dana Levin. AmPoNex

Antenor. Alan Riach. EdScPo

Anterooms keep nice and cool with you. To My Wife. Oktay Rifat. NaPG, *tr. by* Talat Sait Halman

Antes te fabulaba mi deseo. Fabulación. Elsa Cross. RMCMP

Anthelmintic. Chris O. Cook. FreRad

Anthem. Anthony Hecht. PoA 2002

Anthem, An. Sonia Sanchez. UnSA

Anthem for Doomed Youth. Raymond Garlick. AngWePo

Anthem for Doomed Youth. Wilfred Owen. AF; BrAP; CABP; CAGL; ClHu; FaBoWar; GPTC; GSo; HarvBoo; HeIP-4; InoFa; MoBrPo; NAEL-6v2; NAEL-7v2; NAMCP V.1; NoAM; NoP-4; NoP-5; NPeEn; OBEV; OBWP; OxBEV; PoPoPo; SoSe-8; StAl; TCAWP; TFi; WaAnP; WeW-3

Anthem for the Cathedral of Exeter. Joseph Hall. SacPr

Anthems. Irena Praitis. RWB

Anthills. Peter Meinke. Vesp

Anthologistics [*with music*]. Arthur Guiterman. NBLV

Anthropic Principle, The. Harryette Mullen. AWPTFC

Anthuriums, Pahoa. Joan Swift. PoCoUp

Anti-Bacchics 1. Julia A. Moore. STuOW *Fr.* Temperance Reform Clubs.

Anti-Bacchics 2. Julia A. Moore. STuOW *Fr.* Temperance Army, The.

Anti-aircraft seen from a certain distance. Dam Neck, Virginia. Richard Eberhart. NAAPv.2; PoWW

Antic Hay. Aldous Leonard Huxley.
   "Christlike is my behaviour." OBCoV

Antic Quatrains. Jackson Mac Low. PmAP

Antichrist, The. Stefan George. WoPoe, *tr. by* Peter Viereck

Antichrist in Arkansas, The. T. R. Hummer. LPSFW

Antichrist, or the Reunion of Christendom; an Ode. G. K. Chesterton. OBSV; OxAEP-2

Antichrist, playing his lissome flute and merry. Armageddon. John Crowe Ransom. ChIV-2

Antichromatic. Pamela Alexander. PfSW

Anticipation, The. Thomas Traherne. BASC

Antidepressant. Adrienne Su. AmPoNex

Anti-dithyrambics. John Peck. HarvBoo

Anti-Foucault Poem, The. Sandra Nelson. SUP

Antigone. Lajos Áprily. IQMS, *tr. by* Watson Kirkconnell

Antigone and Oedipus. Henrietta Cordelia Ray. CBWP-3

Antigone [Fagles Translation]. Sophocles. NAWM-5v1, *tr. by* Robert Fagles

Antigone. Sophocles.
   Ode 1. BLPJKO, *tr. by* Dudley Fitts and Robert Fitzgerald

Antigonish. Hughes Mearns. BRP; NBLV

Antigua. Gary Soto. PoA 2002

Anti-Lazarus, The. Nicanor Parra. GI, *tr. by* Edith Grossman

Anti-master-man, floribund ascetic, An. Landscape with Boat. Wallace Stevens. APT-1

Antimatter. Russell Edson. OxBoAm

Anti-Memoirs. Ted Berrigan.
"Mid-Friday morn, 10 o'clock, I go to India." AHA

Anti-mnemonic self-vaccination. Joyce Mansour. MFP, *tr. by* Martin Sorrell

Antinous. Mikhail Alekseievich Kuzmin. CAGL, *tr. by* Michael Green

Antiphon for Divine Wisdom. Hildegard von Bingen. WPoS, *tr. by* Barbara Newman

Antiphon for the Angels. Hildegard von Bingen. WPoS, *tr. by* Barbara Newman

Antiphon for the Holy Spirit. Hildegard von Bingen. WPoS, *tr. by* Barbara Newman

Antiphony. João da Cruz e Sousa. TCLAP, *tr. by* Nancy Vieira Couto

Antiplatonic[k], The. John Cleveland. NOSC
(Antiplatonick, The.) PBRV

Anti-Preening Poem. Anselm Berrigan. Eno

Antipsalm. Novica Tadic. VCWP, *tr. by* Charles Simic

Antiquary. John Donne. NOSC

Antique Harvesters. John Crowe Ransom. MoAmPo

Antiques. Walter De la Mare. PoA 2002

Antiquitez de Rome. Joachim Du Bellay. OBVE *Fr.* Ruins of Rome.

Anti-Semanticist, The. Everett Hoagland. OxAAAP

Antistrophe. "H. D." MotU

Antistrophe. Giacomo Leopardi. WoPoe, *tr. by* Robert Bringhurst

Anti-Suffragists, The. Charlotte Perkins Stetson Gilman. SWaP

Antlered forests, The. Ank'hor Vat. Denis Devlin. ModIr

Antlered scarab rolled a dungball, The. Near Damascus. W. S. Di Piero. ChIV-2

Antlia the Air Pump. Alan Robert Wilson. Coast

Anton Mikhailovich spat, said "Ugh," spat again, said "Ugh" again, spat. Symphony No. 2. Daniil Kharms. AF, *tr. by* George Gibian

Anton Steiner sits behind a rosewood desk. Chief of Medicine, The. Arthur Ginsberg. BloBone

Antonette's Boogie. Kendel Hippolyte. WaCA

Antonio Banderas in His Underwear. Regie Cabico. WiU

Antonio Ce De Baca. Mi Tío Baca el Poeta de Socorro. Jimmy Santiago Baca. PmAP

Antonio López and Emily. James Gregory Smith. TiP2

Antonio Torres Heredia. Arrest of Antoñito el Camborio. Federico García Lorca. SpanPo, *tr. by* Robert O'Brien

Antony and Cleopatra. William Shakespeare.
Death of Cleopatra. OxAEP-1
Drinking Song, A. NoSic
"Enobarbus, Antony." OxAEP-1
"Eros, thou yet behold'st me?" OxAEP-1
"How now! is he dead?" OxAEP-1
"I will tell you, / The barge she sat in, like a burnisht throne." OxBEV
"Most noble empress, you have heard of me?" OxAEP-1
"Noblest of men, woo't die?" OxAEP-1
"O! bear me witness, night." OxAEP-1
"Thou hast a sister by the mother's side." OxAEP-1

Antony's Oration [over Caesar's Body]. William Shakespeare. MakPoe; OxAEP-1; OxBEV; WaAnP *Fr.* Julius Caesar.

Ants. Alfred Kreymborg. APT-1

Ants. Ramón López Velarde. TCLAP, *tr. by* Samuel Beckett

Ants, The. John Clare. OxBSo

Ants, The. William Empson. OxBSo

Ants, The. Svetlana Kekova. ItGoST, *tr. by* Judith Hemschemeyer

Ants are walking under the ground, The. People, The. Elizabeth Madox Roberts. NOxBChV

Ants ate half its left wing. Crane in Reeds. William Heyen. PoCoUp

Ants look up as I trot by. Dog's Song. Robert Wallace. TLR

Ants on the Melon. Virginia Hamilton Adair. AFaM; StAl

Ant-seething city, city full of dreams. Seven Old Men, The. Charles Baudelaire. OBVE, *tr. by* Roy Campbell

Antwerp. Ford Madox Ford.
"For the white-limbed heroes of Hellas ride by upon their horses." FaBoWar
"This is Charing Cross." FaBoWar

Antwerp to Ghent. Dante Gabriel Rossetti. NPeEn *Fr.* Trip to Paris and Belgium, A.

Anulación de lo Peor. Jorge Guillén. RaW

Anuncio. Tedi López Mills. RMCMP

Anvil, The. Alfred Noyes. SacPr

Anwar Kamel Celebrates Le Quatorze Juillet. Ahmed Taha. AnVo, *tr. by* Mohamed Enani

Anxiety. Mary Julia Young. CenSon

Anxiety clears meat chunks out of the stew, carrots, takes. Anxiety's Prosody. A. R. Ammons. OxBoAm

Anxiety for the Future. Christian Morgenstern. WoPoe, *tr. by* W. D. Snodgrass

Anxiety's Prosody. A. R. Ammons. OxBoAm

Anxious at every moment of his life, without fail. Heart Stumbles in Darkness, The. Nathaniel Tarn. WANABP

Anxious only to fulfill the royal clause. *Various authors.* CATKP *Fr.* Songs of Flying Dragons.

Anxiously Autumn Arrives. Miklós Radnóti. ConPit, *tr. by* Clayton Eshleman and Gyula Kodolanyi

Any Afternoon. José Hierro. RaW, *tr. by* Robert Mezey

Any Blue Movie. Dave Brinks. AnSo

Any body can die, evidently. Few. ABC. Robert Pinsky. BeAl; FaoP; NAMCP V.2; NoP-5

Any Chippewa. Song of the Captive Sioux Woman. *Chippewa Oral Tradition.* NAAL-5; NAAPv.2

Any clear thing that blinds us with surprise. Fishnet. Robert Lowell. PoetW; VCAP

Any color, so long as it's red. Red. Eugene Field. CA

Any dogsbody can sit up all night. Power Cut. Seamus Deane. PBCIP

Any early morning talk about it. (LL) Happiness. Raymond Carver. GoPo; PoA 2002; StAl

Any fool can make a rule. Henry David Thoreau. TCAPo

Any girl who's reached the age. Boy Friend, The. Sandy Wilson. ReLy

Any Husband to Many a Wife. Emily Jane Pfeiffer. ViWPN; VWP

Any Lover to Any Beloved. Faiz Ahmad Faiz. RaF; WoPoe, *tr. by* Naomi Lazard

Any Man's Advice to His Son. Kenneth Fearing. IllVoic

Any moment (12/4/69 4:30 A.M. Chicago). Ed Roberson. EGAG

Any movement kills something. Roberto Juarroz. VCWP

Any Nest I Can't Sleep in Should Be Burned. Christopher Davis. AmPoNex

Any other time would have done. Witter Bynner. APT-1

Any Part of Piggy. Noël Coward. NBLV

Any poodle under ten inches high is a toy. How the Pope is Chosen. James Tate. OxBoAm; SUP

Any Saint. Francis Thompson. MoBrPo

Any Soul to Any Body. Cosmo Monkhouse. OxBEV

Any strong sensation is a welcome break. Radiator. Kimiko Hahn. ExTi

Any tale of spontaneous human combustion. Like a Face. Erica Bernheim. LegDan

Any Two Wheels. Jane Miller. BodElec

Any way you hold them, they hurt. Pine Cones. Dave Jeddie Smith. CAP-8

Any way you shuffle the cards. My Broad Back. Paul Laraque. OGAHCP, *tr. by* Boadiba and Jack Hirschman

Any Wife or Husband. Carol Haynes. ITBLP

Any Wife to Any Husband. Robert Browning. RACG

Any woman who can give birth to God deserves, I think, a pretty lively. So Let's Look at It Another Way. John Godfrey. PmAP

Anyemiyoo / do you remember *oshimashi*? Messages. Nanna Banyiwa Horne. NAfrP

Anyone can. Claude Anshin Thomas. WhBo

Anyone can get it wrong, laying low. Lies. Martha Collins. ExTi; PuP-23

Anyone here ever seen a white beetle? Dung-beetle. Breyten Breytenbach. PoetW, *tr. by* André Brink

Anyone lived in a pretty how town. E. E. Cummings. BrAP; ChAP; ColAP; CtM; EMP; MoAmPo; NAAL-5; NAMCP V.1; NoP-4; NoP-5; OxBoAm; PoA 2002; PoPoPo; TFi; WaAnP

Anyone of his birthplace—partner, The. Geraint Bowen. BBMWP *Fr.* Ode in Praise of the Farmer.

Anyone who has ever been hit. Sting, The. Tom Paulin. EmeKit

Anyone who has waded. Love's Constancy. Hadewijch. WPoS, *tr. by* Oliver Davies

Anyone who touched her would be sorry. Hairbrush. Selima Hill. BeAl

Anything. Brenda Brooks. PoBW

Anything above a primer would split my head today. Evangelical. Mary Ruefle. AmAlph

Anything but the space between. (LL) Annunciation. Kay Smith. NIL-7; NIP-4

Anything can be forgotten, become regular. Looping the Loop. Mark Ford. NeBrP

Anything Goes. Cole Porter. APT-1; ReLy

Anything I do will be an abuse of somebody's aesthetics. Warner Bros. Newest Thriller *Valentine*. Jeni Olin. FreRad

Anytime the thunder starts to rumble down. Sunny Disposish. Ira Gershwin. ReLy

Anyway. Ted Greenwald. BAP-04

Anyway. Barbara Jagger. Prnts

Anyway the time has come to explain. Poem. Jack Kerouac. CLPP

Aodh Ruadh O'Domhnaill. Thomas MacGreevy. OBMV

Aotromachd. Meg Bateman. EdScPo

Ap'ae Island 1—Diving Women. No Hyangnim. EcSo, *tr. by* Aimee N. Kwon

Apache, Omaha, Osage, Choctaw, Comanche, Cherokee, Oglala, Micmac. Parading with the Veterans of Foreign Wars. Carter Revard. OPRER

Apache Plume. Arthur Sze. AmAlph

Ap'ae Island 45—Once Upon a Time. No Hyangnim. EcSo, *tr. by* Aimee N. Kwon

Apagón, El. Sandra M. Castillo. TouFir

Aparecido, El. Rafael Alberti. RaW

Apart from being indebted to a practice. Message No. 32. Holley Blackwell. AnSo

Apart from the apparent values. Skating with Heather Grace. Thomas Lynch. BeAl

Apart from You. Daryl Hine. CAGL

Apart possibly from waving hello to the cliff-divers. Johnny Weissmuller Dead in Acapulco. Clive James. NOBAu

Apartment, The. Brady Street, San Francisco. Michael Lassell. WiU

Apartment is empty, The. My wife's slip hangs weighlessly, twisted over a chair. Farewell to Russia. Lev Mak. TCRusP, *tr. by* Daniel Weissbort

Apathy Is Ascribed to the Modest Man. Bhartrihari. WoPoe, *tr. by* Barbara Stoler Miller

Ape. Russell Edson. PmAP; RaBo; SUP

Apeherd. "Mang Ke." *tr. by* Nicholas Jose and Wu Baohe
  Section II. PFTM-2, *tr. by* Nicholas Jose and Wu Baohe

Apeneck Sweeney spreads his knees. Sweeney among the Nightingales. T. S. Eliot. APT-1; BrAP; HarvBoo; HeIP-4; NAEL-6v2; NAEL-7v2; NAMCP V.1; NoAM; NoP-4; NPeEn; OBMV; OxBEV; PoPoPo; TFi; WeW-3

Apes yawn and adore their fleas in the sun, The. Jaguar, The. Ted Hughes. BrAP

Apex. Nate Salsbury. NBLV

Aphelion. Joseph Sherman. Coast

Aphorisms. Francis Picabia. SurPaPo, *tr. by* Marcel Jean

Aphrodisiac, The. Medbh McGuckian. PBCIP

Aphrodite Adiposa. Leigh Hunt. STuOW *Fr.* Blue-Stocking Revels; or, The Feast of the Violets.

Aphrodite Metropolis (3). Kenneth Fearing. AmWit

Aphrodite of Economy. Mark McMorris. IAoNAP

Aphrodite Vrania. Charles Reznikoff. APT-2

Apiary. B. H. Boston. GeoHom

Apis Mellifica. Roger McDonald. NOBAu

Apocalypse. Charlie R. Braxton. InTrad

Apocalypse. Dennis Joseph Enright. OBSV

Apocalypse Dub. Dennis Scott. WaCA

Apocalyptic Yearnings. Michael Rothenberg. Eno

Apocolocyntosis. Seneca. *tr. by* J. P. Sullivan
  "This said, she twirled the thread on an ugly spool." RomPo, *tr. by* J. P. Sullivan

Apocrypha. János Pilinszky. PoSu, *tr. by* Ted Hughes

Apocrypha of Jacques Derrida, The. Norman Dubie. AmAlph

Apocryphal Gospel, An. Jorge Luis Borges. *tr. by* Norman Thomas Di Giovanni
  From an Apocryphal Gospel. GI

Apodyterium (dressing room). Matthea Harvey. IAoNAP *Fr.* Thermae.

Apolitical Intellectuals. Otto René Castillo. AF, *tr. by* Margaret Randall

APOLLINAIRE / NEVER KNEW ABOUT ROCK GUT CHARLIE. Unhistorical Events. Bob Kaufman. CLPP; EGAG

Apollo. Elizabeth Alexander. ExTi; PoA 2002

Apollo. Thomas Holley Chivers. APN-1

Apollo. James Dickey.
  2: The Moon Ground. OtW

Apollo and Daphne. Ovid. NAWM-7v1 *Fr.* Metamorphoses.

Apollo and Daphne. Yvor Winters. APT-2

Apollo and Hyacinthus. Ovid. CAGL *Fr.* Metamorphoses.

Apollo and Marsyas. Zbigniew Herbert. PoSu; WoPoe, *tr. by* Czeslaw Milosz and Peter Dale Scott

Apollo as lately a circuit he made. Circuit of Apollo, The. Anne Finch, Countess of Winchilsea. NALW

Apollo at Aberdeen. Herménégilde Chiasson. IFF, *tr. by* Fred Cogswell and Jo-Anne Elder

Apollo Belvidere was adorning, The. Miss Adair. Thomas Holley Chivers. STuOW

Apollo Defeats Patroclus. Homer. OBVE *Fr.* Iliad, The.

Apollo, having been given my desire. Lament for Evolution. Joy Davidman. YaYoPo

Apollo, if the sweet desire is still alive that inflamed you beside. Petrarch. NAWM-7v1 *Fr.* Sonnets to Laura.

Apollo pulls a cloud back like a foreskin. Supernal. Alice Fulton. MAAN

Apollo Strikes Patroclus. Homer. *See* Apollo Defeats Patroclus.

Apollo's first, at last, the true God's priest. (LL) Elegy upon the Death of the Dean of [St.] Paul's, Dr. John Donne, An. Thomas Carew. BASC; CABP; CavPo; NAEL-6v1; NAEL-7v1; NoP-4; NoP-5; WaAnP

Apologia (Nkomati). Wole Soyinka. HBAPE

Apologia Pro Poemate Meo. Wilfred Owen. MoBrPo; NAEL-6v2; NAEL-7v2; NAMCP V.1

Apologia Pro Vita Sua. Charles Wright.

Apologies. Gwendolyn MacEwen. StAl *Fr.* T. E. Lawrence Poems, The.

Apologist's Evening Prayer, The. Clive Staples Lewis. SacPr

Apologize for birth and. Embers. Claudia Keelan. RoV

Apology. Richard Cecil. BodElec

Apology: "Lately, too much disturbed, you stay breathing in me." Joanna Klink. IIR

Apology. Duane Niatum. HATNAP

Apology. Elizabeth Spires. FFC

Apology. William Carlos Williams. NAAPv.2; SAmP

Apology, An. William Morris. NAEL-6v2 *Fr.* Earthly Paradise, The.

Apology and Explanation. John Sparrow. OBCoV

Apology arouses father's curiosity, An. At the same time, it can also seem. Delaying Relevance. Ben Marcus. HeMarv

Apology, first: I did not guess, An. Beethoven: Op. 95. Karen Solie. OpeFie

Apology for Actors, An. Thomas Heywood.
  Author to His Book[e], The. NOSC; WaAnP

Apology for Bad Dreams. Robinson Jeffers. APT-1; MoAmPo

Apology for the Revival of Christian Architecture in England, An. Geoffrey Hill.
  Eve of St Mark, The. NPeEn; OxBEV
  Idylls of the King. NoAM
  Laurel Axe, The. NAEL-6v2; NAEL-7v2; NoAM; NoP-4; NoP-5; NPeEn
  Quaint Mazes. NoAM

Apology for Writing So Much upon This Book, An. Margaret Lucas Cavendish, Duchess of Newcastle. NoP-5

Apology of Genius. Mina Loy. APT-1

Apology to Andrew. Richard Jones. AWTN

Apology to Pangea. Tracie Morris. RD

Apophatic. Jocelyn Emerson. IAoNAP

Apostacy, The. Thomas Traherne. OxBEV; SacPr

Apostate, The. Alfred Edgar Coppard. OBMV

Apostle Qualities. Gisèle Prassinos. YaTCFP, *tr. by* Mary Ann Caws and Jean-Pierre Cauvin

Apostrophe to Man. Edna St. Vincent Millay. NAAL-5; NALW

Apostrophe to the Ocean. Lord Byron. OxAEP-2 *Fr.* Childe Harold's Pilgrimage.

Apotheosis. Wu Yun. ColAnChi, *tr. by* Edward H. Schafer

Apotheosis of Medusa. Pat Parnell. HW

Apotheosis of the Kitchen Goddess 2. Teresa Noelle Roberts. HW; IPoFL

Appalachia Novena. Kyle Thompson. RWB

Appalachian Book of the Dead 3, The. Charles Wright. AWTN

Appalachian Landscape. John Beecher. InGu

Appalachian Trees Encircled by Police Tape. Greg Williamson. NeAmPo

Appalling Heart. Else Von Freytag-Loringhoven. NAAPv.2

Appaloosa, The. Afaa Michael Weaver. GT

Appaloosa Hail Storm. Gerald Hausman. GifTon

Apparatus is right, The. Note to the Ophthalmologist. Dolores Kendrick. FFC

Apparent Colonnades, The. Jeffrey Wainwright. HarvBoo

Apparent Failure. Robert Browning. NAEL-6v2

Apparent gale, vaned in winding storms, The. Secrecy. Samuel Greenberg. APT-1

Apparently Someone in the Department. George Drew. VisFro

Apparently sudden appearance of, The. Exit Wound. Jorie Graham. AWPTFC

Apparently with no surprise. Emily Dickinson. NAAL-3; NAAL-5; SAmP; SoSe-8; TCAPo

Apparition: "I haven't." Sherwin Bitsui. LegDan

Apparition. Cho Chihun. CAMKP, *tr. by* Kyung-Ja Chun

Apparition (ca. 1896). Teresa Palma Acosta. TiP2

Apparition, The. Bade; FSCP; HeIP-4; NAEL-6v1; NAEL-7v1; NAWM-5v1; NoP-5; NoSic; OBEV; RaF; SoSe-8; TFi

Apparition, The. Bernard O'Donoghue. NoP-4

Apparition, The. Stephen Phillips. OBEV

Apparition, The. Carol J. Pierman. ReTh

Apparition, The—A Retrospect. Herman Melville. APN-2; NAAPv.1; NCAP; TCAPo

Apparition de la mer verte un soir. Viande de boucherie par Loti. Jude Stéfan. YaTCFP

Apparition of a salsa band, The. Latin Night at the Pawnshop. Martín Espada. TRP

Apparition of the green sea one evening. Butcher's Meat by Loti. Jude Stéfan. YaTCFP, *tr. by* Marilyn Hacker

Apparition of these faces in the crowd, The. In a Station of the Metro. Ezra Pound. APT-1; BrAP; ChAP; ColAP; HeIP-4; MoAmPo; NAAL-5; NAAPv.2; NAMCP V.1; NIL-7; NIP-4; NoAM; NoP-4; NoP-5; NPeEn; OxBoAm; PoA 2002; PoPoPo; TCAPo; TFi; WaAnP; WeW-3

Apparitions, The. William Butler Yeats. TRP

Appeal. Edith Nesbit. LW

Appeal. Mihály Vörösmarty. IQMS, *tr. by* Watson Kirkconnell

Appeal to Cats in the Business of Love, An. Thomas Flatman. OBCoV

Appeal to the Grammarians. Paul Violi. BAP-04; OxBoAm

Appeal to Women, An. "Ada." SWaP

Appeared to her in Massachusetts. Purple and green. Spots, The. Joel Brouwer. LegDan

Appellants, The. Alice Rahon. SurWo, *tr. by* Myrna Bell Rochester

Appendix to the Vision of Peace, An. Yehuda Amichai. PoSu, *tr. by* Glenda Abramson and Tudor Parfitt

Appetite, the Great Painting. Nance Van Winckel. RoV

Appetizers'. Bruce Andrews. FTOS *Fr.* Tizzy Boost.

Applauding youths laughed with young prostitutes. Harlem Dancer, The. Claude McKay. APT-1; ISC; NAAL-5; NAAPv.2; NAMCP V.1; NIL-7; NIP-4; NoAM; OxBoAm; TCAPo; WaAnP

Applause. Carol Muske-Dukes. AmAlph

Apple. Aleida Rodríguez. FaoP

Apple. Gertrude Stein. MotU *Fr.* Tender Buttons.

Apple. Susan Stewart. AmAlph; BAP-01

Apple, The. Radu Andriescu. PML, *tr. by* the author and Adam J. Sorkin

Apple, The. Bruce Guernsey. IllVoic

Apple, The. Plato. WeW-3

Apple, The. Vladimir Alekseievich Soloukhin. TCRusP, *tr. by* Daniel Weissbort

Apple alone in a bowl, and. Lines Written in the Dark Illegible Next Day. Franz Wright. AmAlph

Apple blossoms look like snow. Comparison, A. John Chipman Farrar. WHSW

Apple Core. Clarence Major. GT

Apple Dumplings. Mary E. Tucker. CBWP-1

Apple Dumplings and a King, The. "Peter Pindar." OBSV

Apple falls, falling in the quiet night, The. (LL) Robert Penn Warren. CBCWP; MoAmPo *Fr.* Kentucky Mountain Farm.

Apple Fools. David Craig. UpMys

Apple fools we are. Apple Fools. David Craig. UpMys

Apple from Walt Whitman, An. Eric Torgerson. ViWalt

Apple Gathering, An. Christina Georgina Rossetti. CtM; NAEL-6v2; NAEL-7v2

Apple is shot not. Lyn Hejinian. AWPTFC *Fr.* Writing Is an Aid to Memory.

Apple Island. Robert Graves. EmeKit

Apple of islands, Sirmio, & bright peninsulas, set. 31. Catullus. AmFaPo, *tr. by* Peter Whigam. *Fr.* Carmina.

Apple on its bough is her desire, The. Garden Abstract. Hart Crane. OBGa

Apple plum, carpet steak, seed clam, colored wine, calm seen, cold cream. Gertrude Stein. MotU *Fr.* Tender Buttons.

Apple Shrine, The. Linda Pastan. Vesp

Apple Tree and a Pig, An. Emyr Humphreys. OBWVE

Apple Trees in Sussex, The. Samuel Allen. FuFl

Apple-Culture. John Philips. OxAEP-1 *Fr.* Cyder.

Apple-green west and an orange bar. Frost To-night. Edith Matilda Thomas. TCAPo

Apple-raid, The. Vernon Scannell. NOxBChV

Apples. Shirley Kaufman. AFaM

Apples. Josée Lapeyrère. SCFWP, *tr. by* Serge Gavronsky
"At the moment the train passes throw." SCFWP, *tr. by* Serge Gavronsky
"Fracas of light falling on apples." SCFWP, *tr. by* Serge Gavronsky
"In the fruit bowl shutters half-closed." SCFWP, *tr. by* Serge Gavronsky
"It is already a murder mystery." SCFWP, *tr. by* Serge Gavronsky
"On the riverbanks farmers threw." SCFWP, *tr. by* Serge Gavronsky
"Or else orange red spiraling." SCFWP, *tr. by* Serge Gavronsky
"What bliss it would be to die." SCFWP, *tr. by* Serge Gavronsky
"With the pear perhaps they are." SCFWP, *tr. by* Serge Gavronsky

Apples. Patricia Pogson. NLP

Apples. Maurice Riordan. NIrP

Apples, Bill, the apples!, The. (LL) Sunday Morning Apples. Hart Crane. HarvBoo; ItP

Apples glow. Fall, The. Daniel David Moses. IFF

Apples, Normandy, 1944. Frank Ormsby. PNI *Fr.* Northern Spring, A.

Apples of gold, in silver pictures shrined. Edward Taylor. NAAL-3; NAAL-5; NAAPv.1 *Fr.* Preparatory Meditations Before My Approach to the Lord's Supper.

Apples of gold the Hero dropt. Good Luck. Oliver St. John Gogarty. IrLP

Apples on Champlain. Richard Kenney. NoP-4; NoP-5

Apples on the tree are full of wasps, The. Wasps, The. David Constantine. StAl

Apple-Tree Man, The. Charles Causley. OBSP

Applicant, The. Sylvia Plath. BeAl; EmeKit; NAMCP V.2; OxBoAm; PoPoPo

Application. Paul Gallico. TriCat

Applications of. Laura Mullen. IAoNAP

Appointed Rounds. Louis Jenkins. RaBo

Appointment, The. Louis Simpson. BodElec

Appointment, The. Matthew Sweeney. BeAl

Appointment in June. Claire Malroux. YaTCFP, *tr. by* Marilyn Hacker

Appointment on a rainy afternoon. Buttons. Tessa Rose Chester. MFPA

Appointments you did not make. Night Words. Isabel Meyrelles. SurWo, *tr. by* Jean R. Longland

Appomattox. Terese Svoboda. ExTi

Appraisal. Sara Teasdale. MoAmPo

Apprehension. Hannah Flagg Gould. SWaP

Apprehension. Jeremy Ingalls. YaYoPo

Apprentice Eats Glass, The. David Craig. UpMys

Apprentice Is Amazed, The. David Craig. UpMys

Apprentice Prophecies, The. David Craig. UpMys

Apprentice Sees Himself in the Sunset, The. David Craig. UpMys

Apprentice, The. Gerard Malanga. AHA

Apprentice's day off. Buson. EH, *tr. by* Robert Hass

Approach of the Storm, The. *Chippewa Oral Tradition.* NAAL-5; NAAPv.2; OBVE, *tr. by* Frances Densmore

Approach of War, The. Ellen Hinsey. AmPoNex

Approach, The. Daniel Halpern. PfSP

Approach the enigma. Dolores Dorantes. SPV, *tr. by* Jen Hofer

Approach to the bar, The. Pole Vaulter. David Allan Evans. MoASP

Approach to Thebes, The. Stanley Kunitz. PoA 2002

Approach us assertively, try not to. How to Behave with the Ill. Julia Darling. PoCu

Approach, vain man! and bid thy pride be mute. Deserted Died. Thomas Erskine, 1st Baron Erskine. DiBP

Approaching a Significant Birthday, He Peruses The Norton Anthology of Poetry. R. S. Gwynn. RA

Approaching August. Sandra Alcosser. PfSP

Approaching Dance, The. *Unknown.* APN-2 *Fr.* War Dance.

Approaching the Equinox. John Tritica. ICANM

Approaching Winter, The. Dániel Berzsenyi. IQMS, *tr. by* Peter Zollman

Appropriation of a host, The. Rust Eclogues, The: Radnoti, Poetry, and the Strains of Appropriation. John Kinsella. VaPo

Approximate and unfulfilled, a devilish nymph. Personals. Star Black. KGB

Approximate Man, The. Tristan Tzara.
  [Part One]. PFTM-1

Approximately. Diane Ward. FTOS

Aprendí / la interminable lista. In Memoriam. Manuel Vázquez Montalbán. RaW

Après le déluge. Pierre Jean Jouve. YaTCFP

Après-dîner we sip anisette. First Blood. Dorothy Molloy. NIrP

Apricot blossom opens to five petals, An. String Diamond, The. Arthur Sze. AmAlph

Apricot grows a long-lived tree, The. Stone Fruit. Lin Max. FiBr

Apricot Tree, The. Gyula Illyés. IQMS, *tr. by* Christine Brooke-Rose

Apricot trees exist, apricot trees exist. Inger Christensen. WoBe *Fr.* Alphabet.

Apricots Die Young. Meng Chiao.
  1. CCL1, *tr. by* Stephen Owen
  2. CCL1, *tr. by* Stephen Owen

April. Cornelius Eady. ESEAA

April. Amy Lowell. PoBW

April. Pak Mogwŏl [*or* Mokwŏl]. CAMKP, *tr. by* Kevin O'Rourke

April. Henrietta Cordelia Ray. CBWP-3

April. Charles Reznikoff. APT-2

April. Angela Shaw. NeAmPo

April. Charles Wright. GeoHom

April 5, 1974. Richard Wilbur. StAl

April 13, 1865. David Berman. LegDan

April 19, 19—: A Sonnet. George Elliott Clarke. BtF

April 19, 1999. Alex Rawls. AnSo *Fr.* What's Your Sign?

April 27, 1994. Donna Brook. PrTe

April 30, 1975. John Balaban. AmWaPo

April 30, 2001 (1). Tom Montag. AmZen *Fr.* Plain Poems: A Fairwater Daybook.

April '68. Elouise Loftin. EGAG

April 5th.   Vera Gheraducci.   CItWP, *tr. by* Cinzia Sartini Blum and Lara Trubowitz

April again, and it is a year again.   Elegy.   Sidney Keyes.   NoP-4; NoP-5

April and Elias.   The green month and my brother's son.   Pond and Peace.   Geoffrey Nutter.   IAoNAP

April and Silence.   Tomas Tranströmer.   WED, *tr. by* Robert Bly

April, and the last of the plum blossoms.   Sleepless Night, A.   Philip Levine.   BLT

April, April, / Laugh thy girlish laughter.   Song.   Sir William Watson.   OBEV

April Elegy (Sam Selvon d.1994).   Christopher Wiseman.   IFF

April Fool Birthday Poem for Grandpa.   Diane Di Prima.   CLPP; FTtHH

April Fools' Day.   Yusef Komunyakaa.   GT

47. April Fool's Day, or St. Mary Egypt.   John Berryman.   CAP-8; ChIV-2 *Fr.* Dream Songs.

April Gale.   Ivor Gurney.   Spl

April in Hollywood.   Wanda Coleman.   GeoHom

April in Houston.   Dolores de Iruretagoyena de Humphrey.   ReBoTo

April in Paris.   E. Y. Harburg.   ReLy

April in the Old Park.   Anna Hajnal.   IQMS, *tr. by* Daniel Gerard Hoffman

April in Town.   Lizette Woodworth Reese.   APN-2

April Inventory.   W. D. Snodgrass.   BrAP; ColAP; EMP; GPTC; NAMCP V.2; NoAM; NoP-4; OxBoAm; TRP; VCAP; WaAnP

April is in my mistress' face.   All Seasons in One.   *Unknown.*   HeIP-4

April is the cruellest month, breeding.   Waste Land, The.   T. S. Eliot.   APT-1; CABP; MoAmPo; NAAL-5; NAAPv.2; NAEL-6v2; NAEL-7v2; NAMCP V.1; NAWM-7v2; NoAM; NoP-4; NoP-5; OxAEP-2; OxBoAm; TCAPo; TFi; WaAnP

April is the month to bring the boats down.   For Boats Only.   Janine Pommy-Vega.   PrTe

April Mortality.   Léonie Adams.   APT-2; CtM; MoAmPo

April, New Hampshire.   Sharon Olds.   BodElec

April Not an Inventory but a Blizzard.   Alice Notley.   OxBoAm

April plunges the classroom into light.   Remembering the Ardèche.   Emily Grosholz.   RA

April Rain Song.   Langston Hughes.   NOxBChV; NTCP

April: "Sheer grip and the push of it—growth gets, The."   Alice Oswald.   NeBrP

April Showers.   B. G. DeSylva.   ReLy

April snow.   Anne Carson.   WoBe *Fr.* Truth About God, The.

April sun burned through the dirty glass, The.   Sorrow and Rapture.   Maura Stanton.   IllVoic

April Wind.   Frederick Turner.   RA

April wind travels the snow geese route.   Black Sunday, April 14, 1935.   Naomi Stroud Simmons.   TiP2

April winds rise, and the willow whips, The.   Spring Shade.   Robert Fitzgerald.   APT-2

April. You hearken, my fellow.   Earth's Lyric.   APN-2

Aprill.   Edmund Spenser.   NAEL-6v1; NoP-5; OBEV *Fr.* Shepherd's Calender, The.

April's in the air.   April in Paris.   E. Y. Harburg.   ReLy

Apropos of Garden Statuary: A Disquisition upon a Minor Genre.   Robert Druce.   OBGa

Apropos of garden statuary, sir.   Apropos of Garden Statuary: A Disquisition upon a Minor Genre.   Robert Druce.   OBGa

APROVECHE. Soneto 1962. Excelente estado de conservación. Ofertas.   Gerardo Deniz.   RMCMP

Apte the Mind or Fancie is to roave.   John Milton.   TWF *Fr.* Paradise Lost.

Aquarium du Trocadéro.   Duncan Bush.   AngWePo; TCAWP

Aquarium, The.   Thom Gunn.   NOxBChV *Fr.* Three for Children.

Aquellos que no pudieron ser ni siquiera estos.   Metempsicosis del perro.   Alfonso D'Aquino.   RMCMP

Aquí.   Carmen Tafolla.   TiP2

Aquí empieza la historia. Fue una tarde.   Aquí Empieza la Historia.   Carlos Sahagún.   RaW

Aquí, en este momento, termina todo.   Acelerando.   José Hierro.   RaW

Arab and His Donkey, An.   *Unknown.*   NBLV

Arab came to the river side, An.   Arab and His Donkey, An.   *Unknown.*   NBLV

Arab Love-Song, An.   Francis Thompson.   MoBrPo

Arabella Stuart.   Felicia Dorothea Hemans.   NPBRoP; RWP

Arabesque.   Ahmed Taha.   NAfrP, *tr. by* Clarissa C. Burt

Arabian Knight.   Manuel Ulacia.   RMCMP, *tr. by* Indran Amirthanayagam

Arabian Night.   James Merrill.   NoP-5

Arabic.   Agha Shahid Ali. *See* Ghazal: "Only language of loss left in the world is Arabic, The."

Arabic.   Naomi Shihab Nye.   CAP-8; PoArWo

Arabic Coffee.   Naomi Shihab Nye.   AFaM

Arabic tapestry embroidered.   Embroidered Memory.   Lorene Zarou-Zouzounis.   PoArWo

ArabInnocents.   Joanna Kadi.   PoArWo

Arachne.   Rose Terry Cooke.   APN-2; NAAPv.1

Arachne.   William Empson.   OBMV

Aragon Ballroom, The.   John Dickson.   IllVoic

Aransas was stormy.   Copano, 1834.   Bryce Milligan.   TiP2

Ararat.   Charles Tomlinson.   NoP-4; NoP-5

Árboles son una agitada melena amarillenta, Los.   Poza.   Pedro Serrano.   RMCMP

Arbor.   Carrie St. George Comer.   LegDan

Arbor, The.   Sappho.   WoPoe, *tr. by* Guy Davenport

Arbor 1937, The.   Susan Stewart.   ExTi

Arbor of Amorous Devises, The.   Nicholas Breton.
   (Cradle Song.)   OBEV
   Sweet lullabie, A.   RACG

Arbor Vitae.   Coventry Patmore.   OxBEV *Fr.* Unknown Eros, The.

Arboretum.   Alison Deming.   LiTh

Arbres se défont à l'intérieur d'une sphère de brouillard, Les.   Francis Ponge.   YaTCFP

Arbutus.   Adelaide Crapsey.   APT-1

Arc de Triomphe.   Bert Meyers.   CalPo

Arc des roses autour du gazon, leurs joues pâles, L'.   Rendez-vous en juin.   Claire Malroux.   YaTCFP

Arc Inside and Out, The.   A. R. Ammons.   NoAM; NoP-4; NoP-5

Arc of the pitching arm, The.   Pitching Coups.   Ron Wellburn.   MoASP

Arc Welder.   Martha Vertreace.   MAAN

Arca.   Gerardo Deniz.   RMCMP

Arca del día, El.   Dana Gelinas.   SPV

Arcades.   John Milton.
   Song.   OxBEV
   Song.   OBEV

Arcana 4: The Emperor.   Veronica Volkow.   RMCMP, *tr. by* Margaret Sayers Peden

Arcana 8: Justice.   Veronica Volkow.   RMCMP, *tr. by* Margaret Sayers Peden

Arcana 12: The Hanged Man.   Veronica Volkow.   RMCMP, *tr. by* Margaret Sayers Peden

Arcana 10: Fortune.   Veronica Volkow.   RMCMP, *tr. by* Margaret Sayers Peden

Arcano 4: El Emperador.   Veronica Volkow.   RMCMP

Arcano 8: La Justicia.   Veronica Volkow.   RMCMP

Arcano 10: La Fortuna.   Veronica Volkow.   RMCMP

Arcano 12: El Colgado.   Veronica Volkow.   RMCMP

Arch film duds.   Bee Elk.   Clark Coolidge.   NYP2

Arch inverted: white peony.   Absence, Luminescent.   Valerie Martínez.   TouFir

Arch of Sanctification, The.   Bob Hicok.   Vesp

Arch of Titus.   Barry Goldensohn.   PoA 2002

Arch, The.   Herman Melville.   NCAP

Archælogical Site, An.   Ivan Tsanev.   CSCBP, *tr. by* Georgi Belev and Lisa Sapinkopf

Archaeological Find.   Willem M. Roggeman.   TuT, *tr. by* Gabriel Rosenstock

Archæologist, The.   James Simmons.   PBCIP

Archaeologist recently, An.   Archaeological Find.   Willem M. Roggeman.   TuT, *tr. by* Gabriel Rosenstock

Archaeologists have determined.   High-Five for I-5, A.   Lawson Fusao Inada.   WANABP

Archaeology of Divorce, The.   Patricia Storace.   FFC

Archaic Torso of Apollo.   Rainer Maria Rilke.   WoPoe, *tr. by* Edward Snow

Archaic Torso of Apollo [*see also* "We have no idea what his fantastic head"].   Rainer Maria Rilke.   NAWM-7v2; PtR; RaBo; TWF, *tr. by* Stephen Mitchell

Archaic Torso of Kim.   Erin Mouré.   NLPA *Fr.* Wittgenstein Letters to Mel Gibson's Braveheart, The.

Archaic Torsos.   David Shapiro.   BodElec

Archangel.   Ai.   SeSe

Archangel bears down from his pinnacle, The.   Pearls.   Janet Fisher.   MFPA

Archangel Cathedral.   Olga Postnikova.   CRWP, *tr. by* Richard McKane

Archangel Open the Door.   *Unknown.*   SSUS

Archangel's silver panties glint as he flies, The.   Michael.   Sandra McPherson.   MotU

Archangel's Toilet, An.   Abraham Cowley.   STuOW *Fr.* Davideis.

Archbishop is away, The. The church is gray.   Gray Stones and Gray Pigeons.   Wallace Stevens.   SAmP

Archbishop, The.   Dana Gioia.   OxBoAm

Archeology.   Yasser Abdullatif.   AnVo, *tr. by* Mohamed Enani

Archeology.   Lorna Dee Cervantes.   TouFir

Archer.   "H. D."   OxBoAm

Archer, The. Arthur James Marshall Smith. BrAP

Archer with time, The. Evening. Ronald Stuart Thomas. HarvBoo

Archetypal Chillies. John Kinsella. NeBl

Archeus Terrae. John Peck. HarvBoo

Archibald Higbie. Edgar Lee Masters. APT-1; OxBoAm *Fr.* Spoon River Anthology.

Archibald MacLeish Suspends the Five Little Pigs. Louis Untermeyer. MoAmPo *Fr.* Mother Goose Up-to-Date.

Archipelago. Dafydd Rowlands. BBMWP, *tr. by* Meic Stephens

Archipelago, The. John Ashbery. BodElec

Archipelago, The. Herman Melville. APN-2

Archipelago (Interra Diocesan). A. Di Michele. AnSo

Archipelago of Kisses, The. Jeffrey McDaniel. LegDan

Architect. Adrienne Rich. BAP-01

Architect Monk, The. Laurence Lieberman. BodElec

Architect wanted to build a stairway, The. Stairway, The. Stephen Dunn. CAP-8

Architecture. Jocelyn Emerson. IAoNAP

Architecture (2). Jocelyn Emerson. IAoNAP

Architecture is when the sun shines on a facade daily. Frank Kuppner. NePenScot *Fr.* Old Guidebook to Prague, An.

Architecture of the Wings, The. Amy Newman. IAoNAP

Archival Print, An. William Stafford. OxBoAm

Archive Film Material. Ruth Fainlight. HP

Archive of Confessions, a Genealogy of Confessions, An. Joshua Clover. NeAmPo

Archives. Michael S. Harper. MoASP

Archivist in us shudders at such cold, The. Love-Letter-Burning. Daniel Hall. NoP-4; NoP-5

Archpoet's Confession, The. *Unknown.* WoPoe, *tr. by* Phillip Holland

Archwald Lee Wright, born age three. Old Mongoose, The—*for Mac.* Murray Jackson. OxAAAP

Archy and Mehitabel. Don Marquis.

   Archy at the Zoo. AmWit; NBLV

   Archy Confesses. APT-1

   Archy Interviews a Pharoah. OBCoV

   Song of Mehitabel, The. AmWit; APT-1; OBCoV

Archys Life of Mehitabel. Don Marquis.

   Ballade of the Under Side. AmWit

Arcs through the midwinter sky. (LL) Winter Sky. Sŏ Chŏngju. CAMKP; VCWP, *tr. by* David R. McCann

Arctic Convoy. James King Annand. EdScPo

Arctic honey blabbed over the report causing darkness, The. Leaving the Atocha Station. John Ashbery. PmAP

Arctic Spring. Denise Levertov. PfS

Arctic Sun. Christine Hume. IAoNAP

Arctic voyager with a room to cross, An. Arctic Voyager, An. Charles Simic. MotU

Arcturus, the bear driver. Night Sky. Louise Erdrich. HATNAP

Arde el horizonte. Ernesto Lumbreras. RMCMP

Ardelia to Flavia, an Epistle. Charlotte Lennox. PoBW

Arden la torcida, entre mis ojos, y la jerarquía intermedia de una imagen esta tarde. Angélica Tornero. SPV

Ardent in love and cold in charity. Man's [a] Sliding Mood, A. Mary Elizabeth Fullerton. NOBAu

Ardent work is a painkiller. Painkiller. Jane Mayhall. PoCho

Ardoise, L'. Francis Ponge. YaTCFP

Ardoise—à y bien réfléchir c'est-à-dire peu, L'. Ardoise, L'. Francis Ponge. YaTCFP

Ardor. Donald Hall. CAP-8

Ardor. Joan Houlihan. IAoNAP

Are a firm and lacquered black. (LL) John Montague. ModIr; NPeEn *Fr.* Chosen Light, A.

Are added unto them that have plenty of water. (LL) Green, Green Is El Aghir. Norman Cameron. NePenScot; NPeEn; OBWP

Are afraid to kiss. My heart, America, my heart. (LL) Dear America. Jeffrey McDaniel. LegDan; RWB

Are *all* the dragons fled? Concerning Dragons. H. D. C. Pepler. NOxBChV

Are all these stones. Close-up. A. R. Ammons. PoA 2002

Are always at home. (LL) Baby-Sermon, A. George Macdonald. NOxBChV; Spl

Are ashes under Uricon. (LL) A. E. Housman. BrAP; HarvBoo; MoBrPo; NAEL-6v2; NAEL-7v2; NAMCP V.1; NoP-4; NoP-5; OxAEP-2; TFi *Fr.* Shropshire Lad, A.

Are begging theory. Young, The. David Alpaugh. CalPo

Are by the sunbeams tickled by degrees. (LL) Coming of Good Luck, The. Robert Herrick. NPeEn; OxBEV; Spl

Are cat and dog, and rogue and whore. (LL) Phyllis [*or* Phillis] [*or* Progress of Love, The]. Jonathan Swift. OBCoV; OBSV

Are chestnuts falling. Hwang Hŭi. CATKP, *tr. by* Peter H. Lee

Are etched deep within. Archetypal Chillies. John Kinsella. NeBl

Are ever different. (LL) Ode to Language. Robert Kelly. PFTM-2; SeSe

Are freshening off schedule again. There is nothing to fear. (LL) There Is No Real Peace in the World. Douglas Crase. BodElec; OxBoAm

Are great imitators. Japs. Lawson Fusao Inada. FTtHH

Are heading south, pulled. Birds, The. Linda Pastan. PfSP

Are his company. (LL) Ballad of John Cable and Three Gentlemen. W. S. Merwin. MakPoe; YaYoPo

Are his life's eyes. (LL) Deaths everywhere. George Oppen. APT-2; PFTM-1

Are Holy-Land! (LL) To Helen ("Helen, thy beauty is to me.") Edgar Allan Poe. APN-1; BrAP; BRP; ClHu; ColAP; CtM; HeIP-4; NAAL-3; NAAL-5; NAAPv.1; NIP-4; NoP-4; NoP-5; OBEV; OxBoAm; PoPoPo; PtR; TCAPo; TFi; WaAnP; WeW-3

Are in the kitchen. Soldiers. Patricia Blanco. AFaM

Are ligneous, muscular, chemical. Lives of the Heart,The. Jane Hirshfield. ExTi; GoPo

Are not the Arabs cousins of the Jews? Nasser is dead. Arthur Nortje. TSAP

Are of bones. Pause of Joe, The. Imamu Amiri Baraka. FTOS

Are on your face. (LL) Troop ship, The. Isaac Rosenberg. OxBEV; PoWW

Are one. (LL) To Jane: The keen stars were twinkling. Percy Bysshe Shelley. NAEL-6v2; NAEL-7v2

ARE quiet unquiet between cap and nose. Murderers, The. Paul Van Ostaijen. PFTM-1

Are shaken with earth's old and weary cry. (LL) Sorrow of Love, The [1892 Version]. William Butler Yeats. MoBrPo; NAMCP V.1; NoAM; NPeEn; OxBEV

Are sisters under their skins! (LL) Ladies, The. Rudyard Kipling. FaBoWar; MoBrPo; NAEL-6v2; NAEL-7v2

Are so needy. (LL) Return, The. Rosario Castellanos. TANSG; TCLAP, *tr. by* Magda Bogin

Are sore. It's dusk. Your daughter's tall. (LL) Little Tooth, A. Thomas Lux. BodElec; GoPo

Are sung—but never more beautiful than there under the gun's noise. (LL) First Time In. Ivor Gurney. FaBoVe; NAMCP V.1; NoP-4; NoP-5

Are sweet like wanton loves because I hate. (LL) White City, The. Claude McKay. APT-1; NAMCP V.1; NoAM; OxBoAm; RaBo

Are taking me. (LL) Kenneth Rexroth. APSN; APT-2 *Fr.* Love Poems of Marichiko, The.

Are the cliffs of your dream the colour of dawn? Buried Birds, The. Ida G. M. Gerhardt. TuT, *tr. by* Medbh McGuckian

Are the dark seeds, and they end. (LL) It Is This Way with Men. C. K. Williams. RaBo; VCAP

Are the desolate, dark weeks. These. William Carlos Williams. APT-1; GPTC; MoAmPo; NAAPv.2; OxBoAm

Are the fallen stars. Yonejiro (Yone) Noguchi. CalPo, NAAPv.2 *Fr.* Japanese Hokkus.

Are there any american poets in here? American Poetry. Ras Baraka. BRtP

Are there / Short-cuts in the sky. Sute-Jo, Lady. ZenPo, *tr. by* Takashi Ikemoto and Lucien Stryk

Are these ashes in my hand. "H. D." APT-1 *Fr.* Sigil.

Are they blind, the lords of Gaza. False Report, A. Robert Graves. OxBEV

Are they blind, the lords of Gaza. Angry Samson. Robert Graves. ChVI-1; OxBEV

Are they clinging to their crosses. Antichrist, or the Reunion of Christendom; an Ode. G. K. Chesterton. OBSV; OxAEP-2

Are They Not All Ministering Spirits? Robert Stephen Hawker. OxAEP-2

Are They Shadows [That We See]? Samuel Daniel. NOSC *Fr.* Tethy's Festival.

Are they there in the daytime. Marfa Lights, The. W. S. Merwin. BodElec

Are those beets your dog's eating? Yellow Star Again, The. Max Jacob. PoCho, *tr. by* William Kulik

Are those fingers, the ones playing Bach just now. Porno-Bach. Shuntaro Tanikawa. PoetW, *tr. by* Harold Wright

Are too long, too many; and not enough. (LL) Elegy for David Beynon. Leslie Norris. AngWePo; TCAWP

Are we condemned to repeat, you and I. To the Muse. Caitríona O'Reilly. NIrP

Are we not all of race divine. English Bull Dog, Dutch Mastiff, and Quail, The. Christopher Smart. DiBP

Are we on the ground now? Ally cells and I said operations. Dropping Leaflets. Jena Osman. Eno

Are we rolling am I am I audible. Asleeping: a Kind of Rendezvous. John Lowther. AnSo

Are we there yet? are we there yet? Labour Pantoum. Kirsten Emmott. IFF

Are we to keep Christ writhing on the cross! (LL) Calvary. Edwin Arlington Robinson. GI; MoAmPo

Are what we have. (LL) Because You Mentioned the Spiritual Life. Stephen Dunn. BodElec; Vesp

Are writing poems about death and resurrection. My Students against the Cemetery Pines. Keith Ratzlaff. ACAMVP

Are you / a gentle ray of moonlight. In Search of Krishna. Devulapalli Krishna Sastri. HotL, tr. by V. Narayana Rao

Are you a glass of milk, rich and cold? Song for the Moon. Nazik al-Mala'ika. BBASP, tr. by Christopher Middleton and Matthew Sorenson

Are You a Star? Chŏng Hyŏnjong. CAMKP, tr. by John M. Frankl

Are you alive? Pool, The. "H. D." APT-1; HarvBoo; NAMCP V.1

Are you Alive, Dead or DeadAlive? Poem. Mohammed Iqbal. SonAtl, tr. by V. Allison, Harjeet Singh Gill and Nasreen Shaikh

Are you an ethnic poet? After the Dance. Reuben Jackson. GT

Are you angry at nature? said God to His woman. Anne Carson. OxBoAm; WoBe Fr. Truth About God, The.

"Are you awake, Gemelli." Star-Talk. Robert Graves. MoBrPo

Are you becoming enslaved. Chill Core. Dana Levin. LegDan

Are you bound for Boulder? the lady asked. If a Fish Fell in a Forest. John Nelson. GeoH

Are you feeling better now? "I'll be fine." "You're such a sweet heart, you know that Janine." After School Commute with My Girl. L. B. BeDoSh

Are you grown up now, John, now that it's over? John and Anne. William Meredith. BodElec

Are you, happy man, grandson of Kronos. Korinna [or Corinna]. SaLy, tr. by Diane Rayor

Are You Havin' Any Fun? Jack Yellen. ReLy

Are you healed or do you only think you're healed? Mutable Earth. Louise Glück. BodElec

Are You Lonesome Tonight? Roy Turk. ReLy

Are You Looking for Me? Kabir. WED; WoPoe,

Are you looking for me? Mathenge. Marjorie Oludhe Macgoye. HBAPE

Are You looking for us? We are here. 151st Psalm, The. Karl Shapiro. TaR

Are You Makin' Any Money? Herman Hupfeld. ReLy

Are you more than editions, or the grave's. Letter to Walt Whitman. Mark Doty. ViWalt

Are you ready? soul said again. Two Trinities. Kenneth Mackenzie. BrAP

Are you self of my self. Alice Fulton. AllShUp Fr. Wonder Stings Me More than the Bee.

Are you sleeping endlessly? You never did before, Korinna. Korinna [or Corinna]. SaLy, tr. by Diane Rayor

Are you still living, my darling? Letter to My Mother. Sergey Aleksandrovich Yesenin. RusPo, tr. by Robert Arthur Douglas Ford

Are you still longing. Yosano Akiko. ErotSp, tr. by Sam Hamill

Are You the New Person Drawn toward Me? Walt Whitman. APN-1

Are you the sole owner of a seedy night club? Club Midnight. Charles Simic. BodElec

Are You There, Mr Punch? William Neill. EdScPo

Are you washed in the blood of the Lamb? (LL) General William Booth Enters into Heaven. Vachel Lindsay. APT-1; ChIV-2; ColAP; MoAmPo; NAAPv.2; PoA 2002; TCAPo

Are you You or Me or It? Hello Up There. Marge Piercy. NBLV

Are your rocks shelter for ships. Shrine, The. "H. D." ColAP

Arena en blanco. Dolores Dorantes. SPV

Aren't lightning flashes the same shape in other countries too? 1914. Max Jacob. PFTM-1

Arere, Eiroworowin and Eomakan. *Unknown.* SonAtl, tr. by Ross Arthur, Solange Petit-Skinner and Steve Trussell

Ares at last has quit the field. Under Which Lyre: A Reactionary Tract for the Times. W. H. Auden. AmWit; MoBrPo; OxBoAm

Arethusa found. Ovid. WoPoe Fr. Metamorphoses.

Areyto. Víctor Hernández Cruz. PmAP

Argalus and Parthenia. Francis Quarles.
   Hos Ego Versiculos. NOSC

Argent, L'. Lorenzo Thomas. FuFl

Argentina in one swing of the bell skirt. Beautiful Train, The. William Empson. OxAEP-2

Argentinean Pampas grass slices the careless ankle easily. Desert Backyard. Rita Dove. AmAlph

Argia. Italo Calvino. MotU Fr. Invisible Cities.

Argoed. T. Gwynn Jones. BBMWP; OBWVE, tr. by Anthony Conran

Argonautica. George Seferis. PoetW, tr. by Rex Warner

Argonautica, The. Apollonius Rhodius. HePo, tr. by Barbara Hughes Fowler

Argonautica, The. Gaius Valerius Flaccus. tr. by Kenneth McLeish and Frederic Raphael
   Book 7. RomPo, tr. by Kenneth McLeish and Frederic Raphael

Argonauts, The. D. H. Lawrence. NoAM

Argos. Michael Collier. WaAnP

Argos. Homer. ModIr Fr. Odyssey.

Arguing Bartusiak. Albert Goldbarth. CAP-8

Arguing liberation theology. My Dada. Judith Kazantzis. Prnts

Arguing over its cost died to silence. Yellow Bike, The. John Lancaster. ArBi

Argument. René Char. AF

Argument. Jonathan Galassi. KGB

Argument, The. All Religions Are One. William Blake. NAEL-6v2; NAEL-7v2

Argument, The. Samuel Butler. BASC; NAEL-6v1; NAEL-7v1 Fr. Hudibras.

Argument, The. Christiane Jacox Kyle. YaYoPo

Argument, The. Sir Thomas Wyatt. SacPr

Argument for an Elemental Aesthetic. Andrew Zawacki. IAoNAP

Argument For Small Arms, An. Karen Solie. OpeFie

Argument. Man has no notion of moral fitness but from Education, The. There Is No Natural Religion. William Blake. NAEL-6v2; NAEL-7v2

Argument of His Book, The. Robert Herrick. BASC; CavPo; NAEL-6v1; NAEL-7v1; NoP-4; NoP-5; NOSC; NPeEn; OxAEP-1; PoPoPo; SacPr; TFi; WaAnP; WoPoe

Argument of the Third Booke, The. Lucy Hutchinson. EMWP

Argument: On 1942, An. David Mura. PoPoPo; LoL

Arguments. Lisa Suhair Majaj. PoArWo

Arguments against restraint, The. To His Dear Friend, Bones. Jay Parini. WaAnP

Arguments of Everlasting. Brigit Pegeen Kelly. PoDa

Argus. Alexander Pope. DiBP

Aria. Irène Hamoir. SurWo, tr. by Myrna Bell Rochester

Aria 1. Ingeborg Bachmann. See In the Storm of Roses.

Aria from X. Thulani Davis. WhBo

Ariadne lay, Theseus' ship sailing away. Ariadne Lay, Theseus' Ship Sailing Away. Propertius. WoPoe, tr. by Vincent Katz

Ariadne, waiting. Cynthia Cruz. IAoNAP

Arid fields / The only life—. Kagami Shiko. ZenPo, tr. by Takashi Ikemoto and Lucien Stryk

Arid that country and high, anger of sun on the mountains, but. Rattlesnake Country. Robert Penn Warren. VCAP

Aridity. Michael Field. OBMV

Aridness of Air, The. Silvio Giussani. ItPo, tr. by Gayle Ridinger

Ariel. Eva Hooker. IaFF

Ariel. Sylvia Plath. BrAP; ColAP; HeIP-4; NALW; NAMCP V.2; NoAM; NoP-4; NoP-5; VCAP

Ariel is a trawler. In Eyemouth Harbour. Gordon Meade. EdScPo

Ariel Singing. Timothy Liu. NeAmPo

Ariel was glad he had written his poems. Planet on the Table, The. Wallace Stevens. APT-1; NAMCP V.1; OxBoAm; PoPoPo; SAmP

Ariel's Song: "Come unto these yellow sands." William Shakespeare. NOSC; NoSic; NPeEn; OBEV; SoSe-8; TFi Fr. Tempest, The.

Arioso Dolente. Anne Stevenson. NoP-5; Prnts

Ariosto. Osip Emilevich Mandelstam. OBVE

Ariosto's Orlando Furioso Book 34. Sir John Harington.
   "Thus all that day, they spent in divers talke." PBRV

Ari-rang Ari-rang A-ra-ri-yo. *Unknown.* NAAPv.2

Arise, arise! (LL) William Shakespeare. ITBLP; NIL-7; NIP-4; NoSic; TFi; UV Fr. Cymbeline.

Arise earelie. Katherine Dowe. EMWP

Arise my body, my small body, we have striven. After Prayers, Lie Cold. Clive Staples Lewis. SacPr

Arise, my soul, arise, Shake off thy guilty fears. Charles Wesley. SacPr

Arise, my soul, on wings enraptured [or enraptur'd], rise. Thoughts on the Works of Providence. Phillis Wheatley. ColAP; InvLi; NAAL-3; NAAL-5

Arise, take up your bed and walk, O Wind. Wales 1937. R. Williams Parry. BBMWP, tr. by Joseph P. Clancy

Arise!—the Sea-god's groaning shell. Rebellion of the Waters, The. George Darley. NOBRP

"Arise! thrust in Thy sickle"? (LL) Corruption. Henry Vaughan. NAEL-6v1; NAEL-7v1; NOSC

Arise to the Day's Toil. Assumpta Acam-Oturu. HAWP

Aristeas 2. Peter Huchel. GTCP, tr. by Reinhold Grimm

Aristocrat, The. G. K. Chesterton. OBCoV

Aristocrats. Keith Douglas. FaBoWar; NAEL-6v2; NAEL-7v2; NAMCP V.1; NoAM; NoP-4; NoP-5; OBWP
   (Sportsmen.) OxBEV

Aristomenes. Lord Byron. NPeEn

Aristotle said. Greek History. Olga Nolla. TANSG, tr. by Paula Vega

Aristotle was a little man with / eyes like a lizard. Humanities Lecture. William Stafford. NoAM

Arithmetic of the Lips. *Unknown.* EroLit

Arithmetic on the Frontier. Rudyard Kipling. OBWP

Arithmetical Progression of the Verb "To Be." Walter Conrad Arensberg. APT-1

Arithmetique [or Arithmetic] nine digits, and no more. Upon the Loss[e] of His Little Finger. Thomas Randolph. NOSC

Arizona Desert. Charles Tomlinson. ICANM

Arizona Highways. James Welch. NoAM

Arizona Midnight. Robert Penn Warren. AmFaPo

Arizona Nature Myth. James Michie. FaBoA

Arizona Nocturne. Carlos Reyes. UrbNat

Arjuna, his war flag a rampant monkey. *Unknown*. WoPoe *Fr.* Bhagavad-Gita, The.

Arjuna sat dejected. *Unknown*. WoPoe *Fr.* Bhagavad-Gita, The.

Ark. Gerardo Deniz. RMCMP, *tr. by* Mónica de la Torre

Ark. Gu Cheng. VCWP

Ark. Ronald Johnson.
    Ark 34, Spire on the Death of L. Z. FTOS
    Ark 44, The Rod of Aaron. FTOS
    Ark 37, Prospero's Songs to Ariel (constructed in the form of a quilt snipped from Roger Tory Peterson's *A Field Guide to Western Birds*). APSN
    Beam 30, The Garden. FTOS
    Beam 7. APSN
    Beam 4. APSN
    Beam 25, A Bicentennial Hymn. APSN

Ark for Lawrence Durrell, An. Robert Duncan. RaBo

Ark of Day, The. Dana Gelinas. SPV, *tr. by* Jen Hofer

Arkansas Testament, The. Derek Walcott. CBCWP

Arkestra glitters in their Saturn gowns, The. After the End of the World. David Jauss. SeSe

Arm around the plexi with your head to the side. Zoo, The. Jordan Davis. HeMarv

Arm for a pillow, my happiness overflows. (LL) White Crane Hill. Su Tung-p'o. ColAnChi; GifTon, *tr. by* Burton Watson

Arm in arm in the Dutch dyke. Arm in Arm. Louis Simpson. PWW2

Arm in arm with you, I have touched the horizon. Nike. Nengi Ilagha. NeNiPo

Arm thee with thunder, heavenly muse. Law Given at Sinai, The. Isaac Watts. ChIV-1

Armada of Thirty Whales, An. Daniel Gerard Hoffman. YaYoPo

Armadillo. Martin Staples Shockley. TiP2

Armadillo, The. Elizabeth Bishop. APT-2; BrAP; ColAP; NAAL-5; NAMCP V.2; NIL-7; NoAM; NoP-4; NoP-5; VCAP; WaAnP

Armadillo Charm. Carlos Cumpian. IllVoic

Armadillos are flattened on roads every week. Armadillo Charm. Carlos Cumpian. IllVoic

Armageddon. William Dickey. AtGh

Armageddon. John Crowe Ransom. ChIV-2

Armageddon. István Vas. IQMS, *tr. by* William Jay Smith

Armageddon in Albyn. Sydney Goodsir Smith.
    War in Fife, The. NePenScot

Armchairs. Zbigniew Herbert. MotU, *tr. by* Czeslaw Milosz

Armed with his crutches, the thief, wolf-like. Outsider, The. Syl Cheney-Coker. HBAPE

Armed with the eyesight of slender wasps. Eyesight of Wasps. Osip Emilevich Mandelstam. StAl, *tr. by* Elizabeth McKane and Richard McKane

Armenian language is the home, The. Armenian Language Is the Home of the Armenian, The. Moushegh Ishkhan. BLT; WoPoe, *tr. by* Diana Der Hovanessian

Armenonville. Edna St. Vincent Millay. NoP-4; NoP-5

Armfull bedwork carbonized. Graph. Leroy McLucas. EGAG

Armgart, to many minds the first success. "George Eliot." VWP *Fr.* Armgart.

Armies and lemmings do not go. New from Ethiopia and the Sudan, The. John Pepper Clark Bekedermo. HBAPE

Armies of the Wilderness, The. Herman Melville. PCW

Armilla. Italo Calvino. MotU *Fr.* Invisible Cities.

armillaria mellea. Tony Baker. Oth

Arminius. Daniel Casper von Lohenstein.
    Sonnet. GePo
    Sonnet. GePo
    Sonnet. GePo

Armistice Day. Charles Causley. NAEL-6v2; NAEL-7v2; NoP-4; NoP-5; OBWP

Armistice Day '77, Honiton. John Tripp. TCAWP

Armitage Street. David Hernandez. UnSA

Armless Artist, The. Cornelius Whur.
    Catastrophe. STuOW; VerBaPo

Armor, dogs and horses. Sea Breeze. Mitch Highfill. HeMarv

Armor of the Petrograd oak is rusty, but, The. Yury Mikhailovich Kublanovsky. TCRusP *Fr.* In Petrograd.

Armored Hearts. David Bottoms. PoA 2002

Armored in oxygen. Astronauts. Robert Earl Hayden. ESEAA; OtW

Armored in red, her voice commands. Birth Day. Elise Paschen. P180

Armour. Aldous Leonard Huxley. OxBSo

Armour has foregathered, snuffling. Opening of an Offensive. Hamish Henderson. FaBoWar

Armpits smell of linden blossom. Vera Pavlova. CRWP, *tr. by* Steven Seymour

Arms and shoulders carved with serpents. Blōdmōnath. Jon Furberg. IFF

Arms and the Boy. Wilfred Owen. BrAP; MoBrPo; OxBEV; WeW-3

Arms and the girl I sing—O rare. Fearful Women. Carolyn Kizer. ExTi

Arms and the Man. Samuel Butler. NOSC *Fr.* Hudibras.

Arms, and the Man I sing, who, forc'd by Fate. Virgil. FaBoWar; OBVE; OxBEV; WoPoe *Fr.* Aeneid [or Eneados or Aeneis], The.

Arms, and the Man I sing, who forc'd by Fate. Aeneid (Dryden translation). Virgil. *tr. by* John Dryden

Arms and the Woman. Dorothy Livesay. PoBW

Arms and the Woman. Dorothea MacKellar. NOBAu

Arms reversed and banners craped. Dirge for McPherson, A. Herman Melville. CBCWP

Armstrong and Aldrin on the Moon. William Richard Philip George. BBMWP, *tr. by* Richard Poole

Army. Ciaran Carson. PBCIP

Army, The. Hagiwara Sakutaro. CAoMJL1, *tr. by* Hiroaki Sato

Army Ballad. Wang Wei. ColAnChi, *tr. by* Stephen Owen

Army Beach with Trumpets. Jack Spicer. APSN

Army Corps on the March, An. Walt Whitman. CBCWP

Army Dance, The. *Unknown*. FaBoWar

Army of Draculas. Patrick Sylvain. OGAHCP, *tr. by* Boadiba and Jack Hirschman

Army of Lovers, An. Alicia Ostriker. AtGh

Army of Occupation. Sarah Morgan Bryan Piatt. NCAP

Army of unalterable law, The. (LL) Lucifer in Starlight. George Meredith. CABP; ChIV-1; CtM; GSo; NAEL-6v2; NAEL-7v2; NoP-4; NoP-5; OBEV; OxBSo; TFi

Army-surplus tents baked. Campsite. Chris Willerton. TiP2

Aroma of fresh bread, The. Thing or Two about Childhood, A. Yury Iofe. TCRusP, *tr. by* John Glad

Around Amida's lake of bliss. What Is Hoped For. James Laughlin. WhBo

Around Costessey. Francis Webb.
    Art. BMAP

Around existence twine. Basho. TAL

Around five in the next garden, a rooster. Likelihood of Snow, The/ The Danger of Fire. Gerald Dawe. PNI

Around flowers. Fear of the Future. Gillian Ferguson. NeBl

Around her leg she wore a purple garter. Far Away. *Unknown*. FaBoWar

Around islands of jade and malachite. Arthur Davison Ficke. PoA 2002 *Fr.* Four Japanese Paintings.

Around my porch and lowly casement spread. Written at a Farm. John Codrington Bampfylde. CenSon

Around My Room. William Jay Smith. TLR

Around stones called precious. Black Meat. Jean Follain. BLT

Around the Campfire. Nathan Alterman. NRoS, *tr. by* Esther Raizen

Around the Campfire. Andrew Hudgins. CBCWP

Around the cold pool in the metal light. Hotel Normandie Pool, The. Derek Walcott. VCWP

Around the Corner from Francis Bacon. Paul Durcan. ModIr

Around the dried-up bay the road. Irish Sheep, The. Job Degenaar. TuT, *tr. by* Aidan Sharkey

Around / The / Ears. Michael McClure. WANABP *Fr.* Haiku Rows.

Around the fireplace, pointing at the fire. On Falling Asleep by Firelight. William Meredith. ChIV-1; NoAM

Around the gods, each seated on a throne. Haloes, Not Hats [or A Vision of the Gods]. John Close. STuOW

Around the house. (LL) Routine Things Around the House, The. Stephen Dunn. CAP-8; MAAN

Around the house stood an. Grandmothers Land. William Oandasan. HATNAP

Around the house the flakes fly faster. Birds at Winter Nightfall. Thomas Hardy. MoBrPo

Around the points. (LL) Emmanuel Hocquard. OnScMo; YaTCFP *Fr.* At Christmas.

Around the small house. Buson. EH, *tr. by* Robert Hass

Around the Star's Throne. Hans Arp. MotU, *tr. by* Bethany Schneider

Around the Water Near the Birds. Yair Hurvitz. NRoS, *tr. by* Esther Raizen

Around This Body of Mine. Amelia Rosselli. CItWP, *tr.* by Cinzia Sartini Blum and Lara Trubowitz

Around this rod my writhing self might twist. Anna Hempstead Branch. APT-1 *Fr.* Sonnets from a Lock Box.

Around Us, Dawning. Wole Soyinka. NAMCP V.2

Arousing the lands where dwell the five peoples. *Unknown.* WoPoe *Fr.* Rig Veda.

Arousing the lands where dwell the five peoples. *Unknown.* WoPoe *Fr.* Vedic Hymns.

Arp and the barbered arbor. Maison Aragon. Tristan Tzara. PFTM-1

Arp might have done a version in white marble. Walrus Tusk from Alaska, A. Alfred Corn. MakPoe

Arraheids. Kathleen Jamie. EdScPo; GPPA

Arraigned by silence, I recall. Brethren, The. Seamus Deane. PNI

Arraignment of Paris, The. George Peele. Fair and Fair. OBEV

Arran. *Unknown.* NePenScot, *tr.* by Thomas Owen Clancy

Arran of the many deer. Arran. *Unknown.* NePenScot, *tr.* by Thomas Owen Clancy

Arrange the scene with only a shade of difference. Incident, An. Douglas Le Pan. BrAP; NoP-4

Arranged Marriage, The. *Vietnamese Oral Tradition.* CaDao, *tr.* by John Balaban

Arrangement. Glenna Luschei. GeoHom

Arrangements. Alan Williamson. InoFa

Arrangements with Earth for Three Dead Friends. James Wright. NIL-7; NIP-4

Arrest of Antoñito el Camborio. Federico García Lorca. SpanPo, *tr.* by Robert O'Brien

Arrest of Oscar Wilde at the Cadogan Hotel, The. Sir John Betjeman. MoBrPo; NAMCP V.1; NoAM; NoP-4; NoP-5; NPeEn

Arrhythmia. Barry McKinnon. NLPA
    Part 1. NLPA
    Part 2. NLPA

Arria to Poetus. Mary E. Tucker. CBWP-1

Arrival. Debra Kang Dean. UrbNat

Arrival. Patricia Dienstfrey. ASA

Arrival: "Did you hear." Fedya Filkova. CSCBP, *tr.* by Georgi Belev and Lisa Sapinkopf

Arrival: "I will consider my son William." Jeffrey Harrison. NevBe

Arrival 1946. Moniza Alvi. BeAl

Arrival at terminal laxative. In and out with fries. Fox mauls hill. #6 Sepulveda. Harryette Mullen. RD

Arrival in Hades. Edith Södergran. WoPoe, *tr.* by David McDuff

Arrival of My Mother, The. Keith Wilson. ICANM

Arrival of the Bee Box, The. Sylvia Plath. NALW; NAMCP V.2; NPeEn; OxBoAm

Arrival of the Titanic, The. William Dickey. PoA 2002

Arrivals at a Watering-Place. Winthrop Mackworth Praed. NOBRP; NPeEn

Arrivals, Departures. Philip Larkin. MoBrPo

Arrivants. Musaemura Bonus Zimunya. HBAPE; NAfrP

Arrivants: A New World Trilogy, The. Edward Kamau Brathwaite.
    New World A-Comin'. NoP-4; NoP-5
    Wings of a Dove. BrAP; NAMCP V.2

Arrive. The Ladies from the Ladies' Betterment League. Lovers of the Poor, The. Gwendolyn Brooks. CAP-8; ESEAA; IllVoic; LTA; NoAM; SSLK

Arrived from scattered cities, several lands. Shipment to Maidanek. Ephim G. Fogel. OBWP; HP

Arrived now at our ship, we launched and set. Homer. NOSC *Fr.* Odyssey.

Arriving at Ba Gorge in the Morning. Wang Wei. WoPoe, *tr.* by Tony Barnstone, Willis Barnstone and Haixin Xu

Arriving at Yongmun Temple. Choeui Eusoon. BecRai, *tr.* by Kim Daljin, Kim Won-Chung and Christopher Merrill

Arriving, we walked down as if we were hill-born. First. Maurice Manning. LegDan

Arrow, The. Martin Sorescu. StAl, *tr.* by Hilde Ottschofski and John Hartley Williams

Arrow and the Song, The. Henry Wadsworth Longfellow. BRP; ColAP; TCAPo; UV

Arrow Flying Past, An. Gustavo Adolfo Bécquer. SpanPo, *tr.* by J.M. Cohen

Arrow in the Wall. Andrey Andreievich Voznesensky. RusPo, *tr.* by Robert Arthur Douglas Ford

Arrow of your glance pierces my wounded, The. Fevrî. OLP, *tr.* by Walter Andrews, Najaat Black and Mehmet Kalpakli

Arrow, so much sun, An. So much ammunition of rays crossing. Every point pricks. Splinter. Silvia Eugenia Castillero. SPV, *tr.* by Jen Hofer

Arrow Song. *Chippewa Oral Tradition.* NAAPv.2; TCAPo

Arrowhead Christian Center and No-Smoking Luncheonette. Janet Sylvester. ReTh

Arrowhead from the Ancient Battlefield of Ch'ang-p'ing, An. Li Ho. FaBoWar, *tr.* by A. C. Graham

Arrows striking all sides of the body and St. Sebastian smiling. Consent. Carol Frost. OPRER

Arroyo, The. Brenda Hillman. ExTi

Arrythmia (1–10). Dallas Angguish. BeDoSh

Ars Amoris. James Vincent Cunningham. WaAnP

Ars Poetica. Claribel Alegría. LoL; TANSG, *tr.* by Darwin Flakoll

Ars Poetica. Roque Dalton. TCLAP, *tr.* by Richard Schaaf

Ars Poetica. Robert Desnos. AF, *tr.* by Carolyn Forché

Ars Poetica. Blaga Dimitrova. PoCho, *tr.* by Ludmilla G. Popova

Ars Poetica. Jane Hirshfield. BodElec

Ars Poetica. Vincente Huidobro. PFTM-1; TCLAP, *tr.* by David Guss

Ars Poetica. Attila József. IQMS, *tr.* by Michael Beevor

Ars Poetica. Linda Pastan. NIP-4

Ars Poetica. Sándor Weöres. IQMS, *tr.* by Edwin Morgan

Ars Poetica: A Stone Soup. Norman Dubie. TAPaP

Ars Poetica: "About writing a poem. It occurs to me." John Gilgun. SUP

Ars Poetica: "At the edge of the forest." Primus St. John. TAPaP

Ars Poetica: "It is almost polio season. The girls." Norman Dubie. TAPaP

Ars Poetica: "I've written love notes all my life." Kevin Prufer. IIR

Ars Poetica: "Poem should be palpable and mute, A." Archibald MacLeish. APT-1; BrAP; ColAP; HeIP-4; IllVoic; ItP; MoAmPo; NAAPv.2; NAMCP V.1; NIL-7; NIP-4; NoP-4; NoP-5; OxBoAm; PoA 2002; PoPoPo; StAl; TFi; WaAnP; WeW-3

Ars Poetica: "Six monarch butterfly cocoons." Dana Levin. TAPaP

Ars Poetica: "They wanted from us." Eleanor Wilner. TAPaP

Ars Poetica: "This hush, my pollen—the ordinary grace in the buds." Dana Levin. TAPaP

Ars Poetica: "To look at the river made of time and water." Jorge Luis Borges. PtR; TCLAP, *tr.* by W. S. Merwin

Ars Poetica: "Write each of your poems." Blaga Dimitrova. PoCho, *tr.* by Ludmilla G. Popova

Ars Poetica at the Window. Marvin Bell. CAP-8

Ars Poetica Feminae. Sandra Kohler. Vessel. FiBr

Ars Poetica (the idea). Dana Levin. LegDan

Arsenal at Springfield, The. Henry Wadsworth Longfellow. AmWaPo

Arson. Nicole Cooley. LiTh

Arson. Charles Harper Webb. GeoHom

Arsonist Tells His Story to the Attorney, The. Charles Rafferty. AmPoNex

Art. Susan Aizenberg. ExTi

Art. Washington Allston. APN-1

Art. Denise Duhamel. AmPoNex

Art. Ralph Waldo Emerson. APN-1

Art. Théophile Gautier. WoPoe, *tr.* by Louis Simpson

Art: "In placid hours well-pleased we dream." Herman Melville. AmFaPo; APN-2; BrAP; ColAP; NAAL-3; NAAPv.1; NCAP

Art: "Poem is a holy glass— put, A." José Asunción Silva. SonAtl, *tr.* by Eleanor Davidson, Carole Gibson and Lisa Martin

Art. *Unknown.* NBLV

Art. Francis Webb. BMAP *Fr.* Around Costessey.

Art, I. Alfred Noyes. OBEV

Art, II. Alfred Noyes. OBEV

Art above Nature, to Julia. Robert Herrick. NOSC

Art and Extinction. Tony Harrison. HarvBoo

Art and Life. Agnes Mary Frances Robinson. OxBSo; VWP

Art Class. James Galvin. TAPaP

Art goes to sleep for the birth of a new world. Proclamation without Pretention. Tristan Tzara. NAWM-7v2, *tr.* by Mary Ann Caws and Jean-Pierre Cauvin

Art History (Sandro Botticelli). Alena Nádvorníková. SurWo

Art in Architecture. Regie Cabico. WiU

Art is the true and happy science of the soul. Robert Bridges. GS *Fr.* Testament of Beauty, The.

Art is / what has no opposite. Robert Kelly. WANABP *Fr.* Threads.

Art, Love, Geology. Bin Ramke. RoV

Art, my dears, is not cleaning up. Andy Warhol Speaks to His Two Filipino Maids. Alfred A. Yuson. ReBoTo

Art of a Cold Sun. G. E. Murray. IllVoic

Art of Benny Carter, The. Al Young. OxAAAP

Art of Clay, The. Duane Niatum. HATNAP

Art of Coquetry, The. Charlotte Lennox. LW *Fr.* Art of Coquetry, The.

Art of definition—is this, An. Ken Edwards. Oth *Fr.* Five Nocturnes, after Derek Jarman.

Art of Disappearing, The. Naomi Shihab Nye. LoL

Art of Getting Lost, The. Art Goodtimes. GeoH

Art of Giving, The (1850). Martin Farquhar Tupper. STuOW

Art of Hurricanes, The. Víctor Hernández Cruz. TouFir

Art of Interpretation, The. Julia Copus. NeBl

Art of joining, union, The. Five Notebooks for Exit Art. Cecilia Vicuña. PFTM-2

Art of Kissing, The. Mary Ann Samyn. AmPoNex

Art of losing isn't hard to master, The. One Art. Elizabeth Bishop. AmFaPo; APT-2; BLPJKO; BrAP; CAP-8; EMP; HarvBoo; IJHIL; MakPoe; NAAL-5; NALW; NAMCP V.2; NoAM; NoP-4; NoP-5; OxBoAm; PoetW; PoPoPo; SoSe-8; StAl; VCAP; WaAnP

Art of Love, The. Arnaut Daniel. NAWM-7v1, tr. by Frederick Goldin

Art of Measuring Light, The. Ellen Hinsey. AmPoNex; YaYoPo

Art of mowing's paltry craft, The. I prolong. May Mowing Clover. Lisa Lewis. SweBea

Art of Poetry, The. Jaime Gil de Biedma. RaW, tr. by Timothy Baland

Art of Poetry, The. Horace. tr. by John Oldham
  "As woods whose change appears." OBVE
  "Should some ill Painter in a wild design." OBVE

Art of Poetry, The ("Let's hear the music first and foremost.") Paul Verlaine. SxFrPo, tr. by Martin Sorrell

Art of Poetry, The ("You must have music first of all.") Paul Verlaine. NAWM-7v2, tr. by Carlyle Ferren MacIntyre

Art of Preserving Health, The. John Armstrong.
  Advice to the Stout. STuOW
  "But if through genuine tenderness of heart." OBGa
  Diet. VerBaPo
  Gastric Muse, The. STuOW
  On Feather Beds. STuOW
  On Washing. STuOW
  Rustic Interior. STuOW

Art of Reduction, The. Dan Pagis. MotU, tr. by Shirley Kaufman

Art of Response, The. Audre Lorde. BrAP

Art of Satire, The. Alexander Pope. OBSV Fr. Epilogue to the Satires, in Two Dialogues.

Art of the Amish: A Quilt Exhibition. Rebecca Baggett.
  Anna: *Rose of Sharon.* FiBr
  Rachel: *Crown of Thorns.* FiBr
  Rachel: *Queen Charlotte's Crown.* FiBr

Art of the Fugue, The: A Prayer. James Wright. BBASP

Art of the Nickname, The. Dominique Parker. SpirFl

Art of the Snake Story, The. Amy England. BAP-01

Art of Translation, The. Adrienne Rich. BodElec

Art of Writing, The. Lu Chi. tr. by Tony Barnstone, Willis Barnstone and Haixin Xu, Chou Ping and Sam Hamill
  Music of Words, The. WoPoe, tr. by Tony Barnstone, Willis Barnstone and Haixin Xu and Chou Ping
  Riding Crop, The. WoPoe, tr. by Tony Barnstone, Willis Barnstone and Haixin Xu and Chou Ping
  Satisfaction, The. WoPoe, tr. by Sam Hamill

Art Pepper. Edward Hirsch. SeSe

Art Review. Kenneth Fearing. APT-2; NAAPv.2

Art thou. To a Hermit Thrush. Adelaide Crapsey. APT-1

Art thou beguiled now? tut, a Lady can. Cyril Tourneur. OxBEV Fr. Revenger's Tragedy, The.

Art thou pale for weariness. To the Moon. Percy Bysshe Shelley. OxAEP-2

Art thou poor, yet hast thou golden slumbers? Thomas Dekker *and others.* NoSic, PBRV Fr. Pleasant Comedy of Patient Grissell [*or* Grissel *or* Grissill], The.

Art thou the thing I wanted? [vers. 1]. Emily Dickinson. AFaM

Art thou weary, art thou languid. Guide from St. Stephen the Sabaite, The. John Mason Neale. SacPr

Art was our bones. Emmett Williams. PFTM-2 Fr. Ultimate Poem, The.

Arte Poética. Jaime Gil de Biedma. RaW

Artemeias, surely when you from the nether world's bark. Antipater of Sidon. HePo, tr. by Barbara Hughes Fowler

Artemidorus sold his land to buy a boy. Martial. CAGL Fr. Epigrams.

Artemis. Olga Broumas. YaYoPo

Artemis: "Bear mother, supple." V. B. Price. ICANM

Artemis in Echo Park. Eloise Klein Healy. CalPo; GeoHom

Artemisia Village. *Unknown.* CCL1, tr. by Anne Birrell

Artemisia Village—whose is this land? Artemisia Village. *Unknown.* CCL1, tr. by Anne Birrell

Arthur. Geoffrey Adkins. FaBoWar

Arthur. Edward Robert Bulwer-Lytton.
  Bloodhounds on Arthur's Track. DiBP
  Gawaine and the Hound. DiBP

Arthur. Ogden Nash. AmWit; NoP-4

Arthur Mervyn; A Tale of Social Grievances. Samuel Carter.
  Passing of Arthur, The. STuOW

Arthur Murray Taught Me Dancing in a Hurry. Johnny Mercer. ReLy

Arthur Thinks on Kennedy. Myra Cohn Livingston. HHAm

Arthur was mortally wounded, grievously badly. Layamon. NAEL-7v1 Fr. Brut, The.

Arthur! whose path is in the quiet shade. To Arthur de Noé Walker. Walter Savage Landor. OxBSo

Arthur's Dream. Layamon. NAEL-7v1 Fr. Brut, The.

Artichoke. Robin Robertson. NeBrP

Artichokes. Georges Ribemont-Dessaignes. PFTM-1

Articulation. Rae Armantrout. OxBoAm

Artifice of Absorption. Charles Bernstein.
  "By absorption I mean engrossing, engulfing." PFTM-2
  "Intersection, The." PFTM-2

Artifice of War, The. Brandon D. Johnson. BtF

Artificial Terra-cotta Skin Mutagen Mask of Humbaba/Humwawa. Sandy Baldwin. AnSo

Artillery [*or* Artillerie]. George Herbert. NoP-4; NoP-5; WaAnP

Artilleryman's Vision, The. Walt Whitman. CBCWP; PCW

Artist, An. Seamus Heaney. PoetW Fr. Sweeney Redivivus.

Artist, An. Robinson Jeffers. HarvBoo

Artist, The. Han Yong'un [*or* Yongwun]. WoPoe, tr. by Bruce Taylor

Artist, The. Han Yong'un [*or* Yongwun]. CAMKP, tr. by Sammy Solberg

Artist, The. *Unknown.* WoPoe, tr. by Elvira Abascal and Denise Levertov

Artist, The. William Carlos Williams. SAmP

Artist and a Wailing Mother, An. Freddy Macha. NAfrP

Artist and Medium. Sarah Klassen. ACAMVP

Artist: disciple, abundant, multiple, restless, The. Artist, The. *Unknown.* WoPoe, tr. by Elvira Abascal and Denise Levertov

Artist painted the end of the world, The. Lost Masterpiece, The. Vincent Woods. NIrP

Artist's Daughter, The. Kimiko Hahn. CAP-8

Artists, The. Gearóid Mac Lochlainn. NIrP, tr. by the author

Arts Are Black, The. Charlie R. Braxton. InTrad

Arts are old, old as the stones, The. Vachel Lindsay. APT-1 Fr. Mae Marsh, Motion Picture Actress.

Arturo. Maria Gillan. UnSA

Arundel Tomb, An. Philip Larkin. BeAl; BrAP; ItP; NAMCP V.2; NoP-4; NoP-5; OxAEP-2; WaAnP

Arundhati, my all. Blindfold. Sunil Gangopadhyay. PML, tr. by Nandini Gupta

ARVN colonel smokes a cigarette, An. (LL) Assassination of Robert Goulet as Performed by Elvis Presley: Memphis, 1968, The. David Wojahn. AllShUp; IllVoic

As a bathtub lined with white porcelain. Bathtub [*or* Bath Tub], The. Ezra Pound. NIP-4; TRP; WeW-3

As a blind man. Lovers. Meirion Pennar. BBMWP, tr. by Martin Davis

As a Blow, from the West. Carl Phillips. FaoP

As a boat begins its life on the water. Floating. It Was a Boy. Tracy Philpot. IAoNAP

As a boy, I'd still have asked. Barbie Says Math is Hard. Kyoko Mori. InvLad; ReTh

As a boy, it was a scale-model Messerschmitt. First Lesson in Unpopular Mechanics. Ken Babstock. OpeFie

As a boy with a richness of needs I wandered. As a Boy With a Richness of Needs I Wandered. Clifford Dyment. TCAWP

As a brave man faces the foe. At Sea. Richard Hovey. APN-2

As a Child. Robert Bly. InvLad

As a child before she knew. Experiments with God. Karen Gershon. HP

As a child I could. Imagine a Revolution. Yasser Musa. OWABP

As a child, I could never sleep. For Karen. Elizabeth Robinson. AmPoNex

As a child, I hated licorice. Licorice. Laini Mataka. BtF

As a child, I knew the privilege. White Horse. Gwyneth Lewis. BBMWP, tr. by the author and Richard Poole

As a child I learned from the twisted necks. Airlift. Karen Chamberlain. GeoH

As a child I loved. Childhood. Nikolai Stepanovich Gumilyov. TCRusP, tr. by Joseph Kiegel

As a child, I was a fussy eater. Notes for a Poem on Being Asian American. Dwight Okita. NIL-7; UnSA

As a child, I would awaken dark mornings. Cameo. Natasha Trethewey. NeAmPo

As a child (in Australia). Strange Adventure. Rossana Ombres. NeIt

As a Child in the Temple. Andrew Hudgins. UpMys

As a Child, Sleepless. W. D. Snodgrass. PoA 2002

As a child, they could not keep me from wells. Personal Helicon. Seamus Heaney. BrAP; NPeEn; WaAnP

As a dare-gale skylark scanted in a dull cage.   Caged Skylark, The.   Gerard Manley Hopkins.   MoBrPo; OBMV; OWoS; SoSe-8

As a decrepit father takes delight.   William Shakespeare.   GoPo *Fr.* Sonnets.

As a devout Christian, my father.   Perhaps No Poem at All But All I Can Say and I Cannot Be Silent.   Denise Levertov.   SacPr

As a dove is spoken of, or the Bible.   After the Word Love Was Spoken.   Anthony Caleshu.   NIrP

As a Finn, this infuriates me.   (LL)   James Tate.   EmeKit; OxBoAm; SUP *Fr.* I Am A Finn.

As a fond mother, when the day is o'er.   Nature.   Henry Wadsworth Longfellow.   ITBLP; NAAPv.1

As a friend to the children commend me the Yak.   Yak, The.   Joseph Hilaire Pierre Belloc.   MoBrPo; NBLV; NoAM

As a full fruit, ripe.   Grenade.   Francis Scarfe.   FaBoWar

As a girl she body surfed on the tidal sandbars.   Swimming with Seiger.   Rick Agran.   AmPoNex

As a lad I never had any idea of the taste of sorrow.   Tune: "Picking Mulberry Seeds" Written on a Wall en route to Po-shan.   Hsin Ch'i-chi.   ColAnChi, *tr. by* Jiaosheng Wang

As a landscape in the far distance.   Fumi Saito.   WoPoe, *tr. by* Edith Marcombe Shiffert and Yuki Sawa

As a man and woman make.   White Lilies, The.   Louise Glück.   PoPoPo

As a man is able.   (LL)   Man's Requirements, A.   Elizabeth Barrett Browning.   RACG; ViWPN

As a naked man I go.   In Waste Places.   James Stephens.   MoBrPo

As a people favoured by the Almighty.   Eden Says No.   Robert Johnstone.   PNI

As a Plane Tree by the Water.   Robert Lowell.   BrAP; MoAmPo

As a precautionary measure, whether he did or not.   (LL)   News of the Phoenix.   Arthur James Marshall Smith.   BrAP; IFF

As a prodigal daughter I have gone back to my memories.   Prodigal Daughter.   Angelina Muñiz Huberman.   MirDau, *tr. by* Aurora Camacho

As a queen sits down, knowing that a chair will be there.   Walking to Sleep.   Richard Wilbur.   VCAP

As a rain-grey helicopter climbs the coastline.   Bead.   John Redmond.   NIrP

As a reed with the reeds in the river.   (LL)   Musical Instrument, A.   Elizabeth Barrett Browning.   BrAP; CABP; NAEL-6v2; NoP-4; NoP-5; NPeEn; OBEV; PEW; PoPoPo; ViWPN; VWP

As a responsible adult I must admit.   All-Purpose Apology Poem.   Austin Straus.   SUP

As a restless needle held by the constant north we always have in mind.   (LL)   Constant North, The.   J. F. Hendry.   EdScPo; GoPo

As a rule all servants dress in their masters' livery.   French Dress.   Friedrich von Logau.   GePo, *tr. by* George C. Schoolfield

As a rule, the patients I know do not pace.   Robert Pinsky.   NoAM *Fr.* Essay on Psychiatrists.

As a sad man, when evenings grayer grow.   Trumbull Stickney.   APN-2

As a servant earnestly desireth the shadow, and as an hireling looketh for the reward of his work.   Bible, *O.T.*   AWTN *Fr.* Job.

As a short before the main feature.   Experiment.   Wisława Szymborska.   PoSu, *tr. by* Magnus F. Krynski

As a sloop with a sweep of immaculate wing on her delicate spine.   Buick.   Karl Shapiro.   OxBoAm

As a small child I would accompany my uncle the levitator from town to town, plaza to plaza.   My Uncle the Levitator.   Rafael Pérez Estrada.   PML, *tr. by* Steven J. Stewart

As a soul from whom companionships subside.   Edgar Lee Masters.   GeoHom *Fr.* Spoon River Anthology.

As a source of information to the biologist I put my loves in the runninglike a stripe in the cake.   Just Dump Me on the Palace Steps.   Ange Mlinko.   IIR

As a starved little bird, who sees and hears.   Vittoria da, Marchesa di Pescara Colonna.   WPoS

As a stone has a sense of its hardness.   Utopian Melodies.   Stephen Dobyns.   PoA 2002

As a symbol.   Sabina Lampadius.   WPoS

As a teen-ager I was very shy.   Norma.   Sonia Sanchez.   UnSA

As a torn paper might seal up its side.   Pruned Tree, The.   Howard Moss.   BeAl; VCAP

As a tot.   How Long Has This Been Going On?   Ira Gershwin.   ReLy

As a voice in a vision that's vanished.   From Lines of Swinburne.   Charles Bernstein.   FTOS

As a warm gust strokes young poplars.   Requiescat.   Leo Ross.   TuT, *tr. by* Sean Dunne

As a white candle.   Old Woman, The.   Joseph Campbell.   IrV; MoBrPo

As a woman might.   Hans Faverey.   WoBe *Fr.* Eighteen Poems.

As a young girl.   Changeling, The.   Judith Ortiz Cofer.   NIL-7; TouFir

As a young girl attending Sunday mass.   Purpose of Nuns, The.   Judith Ortiz Cofer.   TouFir

As a young man I was headstrong, willfull, rash.   To Fortuna Parvulorum.   Anthony Hecht.   OxBoAm

As a youth I was obsessed with graves.   Memory of the Graves.   Ko Ŭn.   CAMKP, *tr. by* David R. McCann

As Adam Early in the Morning.   Walt Whitman.   APN-1; ChIV-1; ColAP; NAAPv.1; SAmP; WaAnP

As all the pigs have turned back into men.   W. H. Auden.   *Fr.* Sea and the Mirror, The.

As Always.   James Harms.   NAPBL

As always, the music was divided into two unequal.   Intermission.   Andrew Feld.   LegDan

As an American traveler I have.   Internal Migration: On Being on Tour.   Alan Dugan.   NAMCP V.2; NoAM

As an intruder I trudged with careful innocence.   Old Mansion.   John Crowe Ransom.   FuPo; HeIP-4

As an unperfect actor on the stage.   William Shakespeare.   CABP; ItP; NoSic *Fr.* Sonnets.

As Ann came in one summer's day.   Sleeper, The.   Walter De la Mare.   MoBrPo

As Anne, long barren, mother did become.   To St John Baptist.   Henry Constable.   ChIV-2; NoSic

As any she belied with false compare.   (LL)   William Shakespeare.   AEP; CABP; HeIP-4; NAEL-6v1; NAEL-7v1; NIL-7; NIP-4; NoP-5; NoSic; OxAEP-1; OxBEV; PoPoPo; SoSe-8; TFi; WaAnP; WeW-3 *Fr.* Sonnets.

As any words, or wagon, / can be made.   (LL)   In Cold Hell, in Thicket.   Charles Olson.   APT-2; PmAP

As apple tree among the trees of wood.   Bible, *O.T.*   EMWP *Fr.* Song of Solomon, The.

As autumn marched, the pond was drained.   From the Outland.   Peter Davison.   UrbNat

As Bad as a Mile.   Philip Larkin.   OxBEV

As bamboo chill drifts into the bedroom.   Restless Night.   Tu Fu [*or* Du Fu].   NDACCP, *tr. by* David Hinton

As beautiful Kitty one morning was tripping.   Kitty of Coleraine.   Edward Lysaght.   IrLP

As Befits a Man.   Langston Hughes.   GoPo

As best I can tell, most of our quilts here were inherited.   New Mennonite Replies to Julia Kasdorf, A.   David Wright.   ACAMVP

As Birds in Rain.   Kirsten Kaschock.   IaFF

As black as death, emitting a strange odor.   (LL)   Inner Part, The.   Louis Simpson.   PLBUT; RaBo

As black in the hollows of white.   Instructing Clarity in a Confusion.   Arkadii Dragomoschenko.   ItGoST, *tr. by* Elena Balashova and Lyn Hejinian

As boy, I thought myself a clever fellow.   Lord Byron.   NAEL-6v2; NAEL-7v2 *Fr.* Don Juan.

As bryght Phebus, scheyn soverane hevynnys e.   Virgil.   NPeEn *Fr.* Aeneid [*or* Eneados *or* Aeneis], The.

As by my own hand cupped around my breast.   (LL)   Lost Property.   Elizabeth Garrett.   MFPA; MoWP

As by the stream[e]s of Babylon [*or* Babilon].   Thomas Campion.   BASC

As by the wood drifts thistle-down.   Herman Melville.   APN-2 *Fr.* Clarel: A Poem and Pilgrimage in the Holy Land.

As Cabeza de Vaca was.   Charles Olson.   BodElec

As Catullus wrote, a man's voice deserts him.   Aleksandr Semionovich Kushner.   ItGoST, *tr. by* Paul Graves and Carol Ueland

As Children Together.   Carolyn Forché.   NoAM; OxWW

As children we dashed.   Pig Melons.   John Kinsella.   NeBl

As Christ intact before the infidel.   (LL)   Constancy.   Michael Field.   ViWPN; VWP

As Christ the Lord was passing by.   He Came unto His Own, and His Own Received Him Not.   Mary Elizabeth Coleridge.   ViWPN

As close as you your weding kept.   I. W. To her unconstant Lover.   Isabella Whitney.   EMWP; PBRV

As clouds think of her clothing, as blossoms think of her face.   Suite in the Ch'ing-p'ing Mode, A.   Li Po.   ColAnChi, *tr. by* Elling O. Eide

As Concerning Man.   Alexander Radcliffe.   NOSC; OBSV

As cool as the pale wet leaves.   Alba.   Ezra Pound.   TCAPo; WaAnP; WeW-3

As Corydon went shiv'ring by.   Fire Us with Ice, Burn Us with Snow.   Mary Monk.   LW

As Cynddylan passes proudly up the lane.   (LL)   Cynddylan on a Tractor.   Ronald Stuart Thomas.   AngWePo; TCAWP

As Dancers.   Lisa Teasley.   BtF

As darkness and ships ruffle the sky.   (LL)   Morning Jitters.   John Ashbery.   FTOS; PoA 2002

As day did darken on the dewless grass.   Wind at the Door, The.   William Barnes.   OxAEP-2

As day fades into dusk, the bell at a mountain temple sounds.   Returning Home to Deer-Gate Mountain at Night.   Meng Hao Jan.   NDACCP, *tr. by* David Hinton

As day new opening fills the hemisphere. Sir William Davenant. NOSC *Fr.* Gondibert.

As dew-drops freeze. As Dew-Drops Freeze. Juan Chi. CCL1, *tr. by* Michael Bullock and C. J. Chen

As Dick and I. Lines Left at Mr Theodore Hook's House in June, 1834. Thomas Ingoldsby. OBCoV

As Difference Blends into Identity. Josephine Miles. NoAM; OxBoAm

As doctors give physic by way of prevention. For My Own Monument. Matthew Prior. OBEV

As Dorothy Parker once said to her boyfriend. Just One of Those Things. Cole Porter. APT-1; ReLy

As dusk fell, nurse went in to stoke up the fire and heat the children's formulae. Nature Study. Trevor Winkfield. KGB

As each year might assign. (LL) He Never Expected Much. Thomas Hardy. NAEL-6v2; NAEL-7v2; NAMCP V.1; NoAM

As earthquakes happened far too frequently. Inquisition, The. Victor Hugo. SxFrPo, *tr. by* A. M. and E. H. Blackmore

As Easily As Trees. Robert Francis. APT-2

As easily as trees have dropped. As Easily As Trees. Robert Francis. APT-2

As Eileen unchains her bicycle. Moonstones. David Trinidad. WiU

As Endymion. Odysseus Elytis. GifTon, *tr. by* Olga Broumas

As, even today, the airman, feeling the plane sweat. Icarus. Valentin Iremonger. ModIr

As evening comes down, the boy. Boy Behind a Window. Luis Cernuda. RaW, *tr. by* Hardie St. Martin

As evening splendors fade. Nightfall. Alexander L. Posey. APN-2

As ever in my great task-ma[i]ster's eye. (LL) How soon hath Time the subtle [*or* suttle] thief [*or* theef] of youth. John Milton. HeIP-4; NAEL-6v1; NoP-4; NOSC

As falling dews to thirsty flowers. (LL) John Clare. NPBRoP; WaAnP *Fr.* Shepherd's [*or* Shepheards] Calendar, The.

As far as Cho-fu-Sa. (LL) River Merchant's Wife, The; A Letter. Li Po. AmFaPo; APT-1; BrAP; ClHu; ColAP; EMP; HarvBoo; HeIP-4; MoAmPo; NAAL-5; NAAPv.2; NAMCP V.1; NDACCP; NIL-7; NIP-4; NoAM; NoP-4; NoP-5; NPeEn; OBMV; OBVE; OxBoAm; PoPoPo; RaBo; RACG; TCAPo; TFi; TRP; WaAnP; WeW-3, *tr. by* Ezra Pound

As far as statues go, so far there's not. From Trollope's Journal. Elizabeth Bishop. AmWaPo; CBCWP; PoAgWa

As far as the poem was concerned. Poor Zelda. Cindy Day Roberts. LaCa

As fast as we have to. (LL) In Memory of the Utah Stars. William Matthews. CAP-8; MoASP

As F—at her Toilet sat. Song. Margaret, Lady Godolphin. EMWP

As, first, your pains in bearing me was such. To the Right Worshipful Lady Her Most Dear Mother, the Lady Prudentia Munda, the True Pattern of Piety and Virtue, C. M. Wisheth Increase of Happiness. Constantia Munda. EMWP

As flowing waters disappear into the mist. 70. Shih Shu. CSKM, *tr. by* James H. Sanford

As for Granata, the Siberian gulag, Ostia. Mario Luzi. ItPo *Fr.* Pieces from a Mortal Duet.

As for him who. Fragment. William Carlos Williams. Spl

As for me I am a child of the god of the mountains. Gary Snyder. PFTM-2 *Fr.* Myths and Texts.

As for me / I have seen Llywelyn. Day Which Endures Not, A. A. G. Prys-Jones. OBWVE, *tr. by* Anthony Conran

As for me, when I saw you. America. Bernadette Mayer. NYP2

As for my life, I've led it. Placid Man's Epitaph, A. Thomas Hardy. MoBrPo

As for Poets. Gary Snyder. BB; PmAP; WhBo

As for the hibiscus. Basho. EH, *tr. by* Robert Hass

As for the Quince. Nuala Ni Dhomhnaill. PBCIP, *tr. by* Paul Muldoon

As for the Quince. Nuala Ni Dhomhnaill. MoWP

As for the stars, they are always on. Joseph Brodsky. StAl *Fr.* Part of Speech, A.

As for you loud Greenock long ropeworking. Greenock at Night I Find You. William Sydney Graham. EdScPo

As Frazier one night at her Post in the Drawing Room stood. Katherine Colyear, Countess of Dorchester. EMWP

As free as anybody. Season of Paradise, A. José Luis Rivas. RMCMP, *tr. by* Reginald Gibbons

As from a Quiver of Arrows. Carl Phillips. AmAlph; BtF; WaAnP; WiU

As from a shell, a husk, I stripped you bare. IQMS *Fr.* Cricket Music. Lőrinc Szabó.

As from each fragrant sweet the honny Bee. Upon the Necessity and Benefite of Learning Written in the Beginning of a Common Place Booke Belonging to W. B. a Young Scholler. Anna Norman Ley. EMWP

As from the house your mother sees. Robert Louis Stevenson. NePenScot *Fr.* To Any Reader.

As from their ancestral oak. Percy Bysshe Shelley. NAEL-6v1; NAEL-7v2

As ghost I returned to them. Christ, the End. Gaylord Brewer. Vesp

As glad to have my body, as my mind. (LL) Blossom[e], The. John Donne. NAEL-6v1; NAEL-7v1

As Gold is better that's in fire tride. John Taylor. PBRV *Fr.* Sculler, The.

As gold nuggets contained in crystal. Sanctuary. Angelina Muñiz Huberman. MirDau, *tr. by* Aurora Camacho

As good there, as he[e]re to burn[e]. (LL) Mary Sidney Wroth, Countess of Montgomery. NAEL-6v1; NAEL-7v1 *Fr.* Pamphilia to Amphilanthus.

As good to write as for to lie and groan. Sir Philip Sidney. NoSic *Fr.* Astrophil and Stella.

As graceful as the Babylonian willow. To Isa Sleeping. Thomas Holley Chivers. APN-1

As happy as Cliff Klingenhagen is. (LL) Cliff Klingenhagen. Edwin Arlington Robinson. APN-2; MoAmPo; NCAP

As hath been, lo, these many generations. John Crowe Ransom. MoAmPo

As he becomes a father. For the Sake of Man. Mun Chŏnghui. EcSo, *tr. by* Catherine J. Kim

As he came near death things grew shallower for us. As He Came Near Death. Roy Fisher. HarvBoo; InoFa; NPeEn

As he climbs down our hill, my kestrel rises. Esyllt. Glyn Jones. AngWePo; OBWVE

As he knelt by the grave of his mother and father. Milkweed and Monarch. Paul Muldoon. NAEL-7v2; NoP-4; NoP-5; PoetW; WaAnP

As he lay dead. Dilemma. Phoebe Hesketh. Prnts

As he left them there, as he left them there. (LL) W. H. Auden. NoAM; OxBEV; UV *Fr.* Five Songs.

As he moves the mine-detector. Hunting Civil War Relics at Nimblewill Creek. James Dickey. LPSFW

As he passed us and vanished. (LL) Tao and Unfitness at Inistiogue on the River Nore. Thomas Kinsella. NPeEn; PBCIP

As he put me on the train to college, Father said, don't make any mistakes. Mistakes. Judith Taylor. SUP

As he read the reports. Mermaids Explained. Christopher Reid. NeBrP

As he rode back Yesugei came on a camp of the Tatar. *Unknown.* WoPoe *Fr.* Secret History of the Mongols, The.

As he said vanity, so vain say I. Vanity of All Worldly Things, The. Anne Bradstreet. ChIV-1

As he sang upon a tree! (LL) Rivals, The. James Stephens. OBEV; OBMV

As he sat eating by the fire one night. Fire and St. Francis. Andrew Hudgins. UpMys

As he sinks two into the chains. (LL) Makin' Jump Shots. Michael S. Harper. ISC; MoASP

As he smiles. Karai Senryū. EMJL, *tr. by* Makoto Ueda

As he stood against the fretted hedge, which was like white lace. (LL) To a Conscript of 1940. Sir Herbert Read. OBWP; PoWW

As He, the maker of this Song. (LL) Meditation for His Mistress[e], A. Robert Herrick. NOSC; OBEV

As he then staggered and dropped to the ground. In the Proximity of Andy Warhol. Jürgen Becker. GTCP, *tr. by* Reinhold Grimm

As he went on fishing his way. (LL) Lady and the Bear, The. Theodore Roethke. ChAP; NBLV

As he would burn or better far his book. (LL) To Elizabeth, Countess of Rutland. Ben Jonson. NoP-4; NoP-5

As Hector turned for home his helmet flashed. Homer. NAWM-7v1 *Fr.* Iliad, The.

As here on earth's soil God's Son Eternal. Cynewulf. SacPr *Fr.* Ascension, The.

As his hideous body grabs them. (LL) Bride of Frankenstein, The. Edward Field. HeIP-4; ReTh; SUP

As homeward with his maid young Maury went. Albery Allson Whitman. NAAPv.1 *Fr.* Octoroon, The.

As honest Jacob on a night. Patriarch, The. Robert Burns. ChIV-1

As Hour and Year Collapsed. Joe Wenderoth. LegDan; NAPBL

As I am mine, their sweating selves; but worse. (LL) I Wake and Feel the Fell of Dark, Not Day. Gerard Manley Hopkins. AWTN; BrAP; CABP; FaBoVe; NAEL-6v2; NAEL-7v2; NAMCP V.1; NoP-4; NoP-5; NPeEn; OxAEP-2; OxBSo; RSR; TRP; WaAnP

As I Am My Father's. Rose Drachler. TaR

As I beheld a winters evening air. Another. Richard Lovelace. OxBEV

As I Came Down from Lebanon. Clinton Scollard. APN-2

As I came from the. Kenneth Rexroth. APSN; NAMCP V.1 *Fr.* Love Poems of Marichiko, The.

As I Came Home from Labour. F. C. Boden. RSaN

As I came round the harbor buoy. Long White Seam, The. Jean Ingelow. OxBEV

As I came to the edge of the woods. Come In. Robert Frost. APT-1; MoAmPo; NoP-4; NoP-5; OxBoAm; RaBo; TRP

As I Composed This Little Book. Rosalía de Castro. NAWM-7v2, *tr. by* S. Griswold Morley

As I composed this little book, I thought. As I Composed This Little Book. Rosalía de Castro. NAWM-7v2, *tr. by* S. Griswold Morley

As I descended black, impassive Rivers. Drunken Boat, The. Arthur Rimbaud. NAWM-7v2, *tr.* by Stephen Stepanchev

As I develop the awakening mind. Bodhisattva Vow. Adam Yauch. WhBo

As I did the washing one day. Shirt of a Lad, The. *Unknown.* OBWVE, *tr.* by Anthony Conran

As I do now. (LL) July 4, 1984: For Buck. June Jordan. NAMCP V.2; NoAM

As I do zew, wi' nimble hand. Lwonesomeness. William Barnes. OxBEV

As I drive to the junction of lane and highway. At Castle Boterel. Thomas Hardy. NPeEn; OxAEP-2; OxBEV

As I Ebb'd with the Ocean of Life. Walt Whitman. APN-1; NAAL-3; NAAL-5; NAAPv.1; OxBoAm; TCAPo

As I fear the friends below. (LL) Dirge: "From a friend's friend I taste friendship." Stevie Smith. HarvBoo; NPeEn

As I gaed doon by the twa mill dams i' the mornin. Water-Hen, The. Violet Jacob. EdScPo

As I gaze upon. Tanka. Kanoko Okamoto. CAoMJL1, *tr.* by Makoto Ueda

As I give birth. Cords. Kiren Shoman. OWABP

As I glance through a few thin pages and switch off the light. (LL) Achill. Derek Mahon. PBCIP; PNI

As I grow older. Issa. NIL-7, *tr.* by Daniel C. Buchanan

As I guard o'er the fold. (LL) William Blake. ITBLP; OBEV *Fr.* Songs of Innocence.

As I have often said—If art is infancy and criticism the day of atonement. Roget, Papier, Schism! Michael Portnoy. HeMarv

As I have seen a child. High Adventure. A. W. Spalding. ITBLP

As I in hoary [*or* hoarie] Winter's night stood[e] shivering[e] in the snow[e]. Burning Babe, The. Robert Southwell. AEP; ChrPo; HeIP-4; NAEL-6v1; NAEL-7v1; NoP-4; NoP-5; NoSic; OBCP; OBEV; OxAEP-1; OxBEV; PoPoPo; PBRV; SacPr; TFi; TRP; WaAnP; WoPoe

As I lay asleep in Italy. Mask [*or* Masque] of Anarchy, The. Percy Bysshe Shelley. NPBRoP; NPeEn; OBSV; OxAEP-2; WoPoe

As I lay at your feet the other day. At Her Feet. Violet Fane. PoBW

As I lay, fullness of praise. Rattle Bag, The. Dafydd ap Gwilym. NBLV; WoPoe, *tr.* by Joseph P. Clancy

As I lay here alone. It Just Doesn't Matter. Rodney M. McNeil. InTrad

As I lay in bed naked. Eye Poem. Harris Schiff. AHA

As I Lay with My Head in Your Lap Camerado. Walt Whitman. CAGL; CBCWP; NAAL-3; NCAP

As I lean. Hearing the Gibbons Call in Pa Gorge. Wen Chao. CSKM, *tr.* by Paul Hansen

As I leaned at my window. Song of Samuel Sweet, The. Charles Causley. OBNV

As I Leave You. Chrystos. ReEnLa

As I lie beside my mother. Saitō Mokichi. CAoMJL1, *tr.* by Amy Vladek Heinrich

As I lie here in the sun. Jonah. Randall Jarrell. ChIV-1

As I lie next to you. Music. Natasha Josefowitz. PasH

As I lie now. (LL) Man Alone. Louise Bogan. NoP-4; NoP-5

As I listened from a beach-chair in the shade. Their Lonely Betters. W. H. Auden. NAEL-6v2; NAEL-7v2; NoAM; NoP-5; OBGa

As I me rod this endre day. *Unknown.* OHMEL

As I me rod this endre day. *Unknown. See* Als I me rode this endre day.

As I near my village, spring deepens. Buson. EMJL *Fr.* Spring Breeze on the Kema Embankment.

As I one evening [*or* ev'ning] sat before my cell. Artillery [*or* Artillerie]. George Herbert. NoP-4; NoP-5; WaAnP

As I open the mirror and enter. Remembering the Day I Gave Birth to a Daughter. Kim Hyesun. CAMKP, *tr.* by Jiwon Shin

As I pass through my incarnations in every age and race. Gods of the Copybook Headings, The. Rudyard Kipling. NoAM; OBSV

As I Play the Flute. Cho Chihun. CAMKP, *tr.* by Kyung-Ja Chun

As I raised it for the second bite, I saw a tiny man, waving his arms and cursing in French. Four About Apples. David Young. MotU

As I ride, as I ride. Through the Metidja to Abd-el-Kadr. Robert Browning. WoPoe

As I rise from my couch at the first dawn of day. Roll On, Shining Wheel! C.T. Mitchell. ArBi

As I rode in to Burrumbeet. Traveller, The. C. J. Dennis. NOBAu

As I roved out impatiently. In the Ringwood. Thomas Kinsella. PBCIP

As I Sat at the Café. Arthur Hugh Clough. NBLV; OBCoV *Fr.* Spectator ab Extra.

As I sat by my window last evening. Miss Foggerty's Cake. *Unknown.* NBLV

As I sat down by the bus window in the gate of Verona. Silent Angel, The. James Wright. BodElec

As I sat down to breakfast in state. Country Clergyman's Trip to Cambridge, The. Thomas Babington Macaulay, 1st Baron Macaulay. OBSV

As I saw. George Oppen. APT-2; PFTM-1

As I sd to my. I Know a Man. Robert Creeley. AmFaPo; CAP-8; ICANM; NAMCP V.2; NIP-4; NoP-4; NoP-5; OxBoAm; StAl; VCAP

As I sit by the ruddy oak fire. Nestle-down Cottage. Mary Weston Fordham. CBWP-2

As I sit looking out of a window of the building. Instruction Manual, The. John Ashbery. NAMCP V.2; NoAM; OxBoAm; YaYoPo

As I sit squeezing lemon juice on dacron shirt, beside. Lexington Avenue Express. Percy Johnston. EGAG

As I sit writing here, sick and grown old. As I Sit Writing Here. Walt Whitman. NAAL-3

As I slowed up and shifted down gear. Air-Waves. Martyn Crucefix. RWPCtW

As I stepped out the doorway it was ten o'clock. Peace, Horror. Miklós Radnóti. AF, *tr.* by Emery E. George

As I suddenly enter a side path. Masks. Kim Ch'unsu [*or* Chun-soo]. CAMKP, *tr.* by Anthony, Brother of Taizé

As I talked, I kept thinking. Murderer, The. Christopher Davis. OPRER

As I travel the Strath of Drumochter. Lament for the State of the Country, A. Iain Lom. NePenScot, *tr.* by Meg Bateman

As I walk in the cool of the autumn night. Autumn Night Message: To Qiu. Wei Ying-wu. CCL1, *tr.* by Witter Bynner

As I walked down the new cut road. Charleston Gals. *Unknown.* SSUS

As I walked out early. Thomas A. Clark. Oth *Fr.* Sixteen Sonnets.

As I walked out in the streets of Laredo. Cowboy's Lament, The. *Unknown.* APN-2; ChAP; FaBoA

As I Walked Out One Evening. W. H. Auden. HeIP-4; NAMCP V.1; NIL-7; NoAM; NoP-4; NoP-5; OxAEP-2; OxBoAm; PoPoPo; PtR

(Song: "As I walked out one evening.") BrAP; MoBrPo

As I walked out one morning for pleasure. *Unknown.* APN-2

As I wandered on the beach. Great Blue Heron, The. Carolyn Kizer. InoFa; InvLad; WaAnP

As I was a walking by yon green garding. As I Was A-walking by Yon Green Garden. *Unknown.* NePenScot

As I was a-gwine down the road. Turkey in the Straw. *Unknown.* TCAPo

As I Was A-walking by Yon Green Garden. *Unknown.* NePenScot

As I was by one brought forth, I would bring forth another. (LL) Fain Would I Wed. Thomas Campion. NAEL-6v1; NAEL-7v1

As I was going to St. Ives. Mother Goose. NTCP

As I was in my hut. Gray She-Wolf, The. *Unknown.* WoPoe, *tr.* by W. S. Merwin

As I was lodged at Shih-hao one night. Draft Board at Shih-hao, The. Tu Fu [*or* Du Fu]. CrYelRi, *tr.* by Sam Hamill

As I was lumb'ring down de street. Buffalo Gals. *Unknown.* APN-2

As I was passing by the ruins. Ranch on the Limpia, The. Dorys Crow Grover. TiP2

As I was ploughing in my field. Ballad of John Barleycorn, the Ploughman, and the Furrow, The. George Mackay Brown. BeAl

As I was putting away the groceries. Bali Hai Calls Mama. Marilyn Nelson Waniek. ISC

As I was sitting in my chair. Perfect Reactionary, The. Hughes Mearns. NTCP

As I Was Standing in the Street. *Unknown.* NTCP

As I was standing, not even at the window. At My Doorstep. Ekaterina Iosifova. CSCBP, *tr.* by Georgi Belev and Lisa Sapinkopf

As I was waiting for the bus. Sight Unseen. Kingsley Amis. NoAM

As I was walkin' the jungle round, a-killin' of tigers an' time. Ballad. Guy Wetmore Carryl. NBLV

As I was walking. Kore. Robert Creeley. NAAL-5; OxBoAm; RaBo

As I was walking all alane [*or* alone]. Twa Corbies, The. *Unknown.* NePenScot; NoP-5; NPeEn; OBEV; OWoS; OxBEV

As I was walking forth one day. Royal health to the Rising Sun, The. *Unknown.* BASC

As I was walking in the fields last Tuesday of all days. Slender Lad, The. *Unknown.* OBWVE, *tr.* by Kenneth Hurlstone Jackson

As I was walking towards the Café de Paris one morning around ten, lost in the dream of the previous night. Three Cows in Hamra Street. Nasri Hajjaj. Eno, *tr.* by Ibrahim Muhawi

As I was walking up the stair. Hughes Mearns. NOxBChV

As I Was Wandering with My Unhappy Thoughts. Charles Reznikoff. NAAPv.2

As I went by the harbour when folk were abed. Dead-Tryst, The. Katharine Tynan Hinkson. IrLP

As I went down in de valley to pray. Good Old Way, The. *Unknown.* SSUS

As I went down that yella bank. Riddle. *Unknown.* FaBoVe

As I went down the hill along the wall. Meeting and Passing. Robert Frost. OxBoAm; OxBSo

As I went out a Crow. Last Word of a Bluebird, The. Robert Frost. NOxBChV

As I went out one frosty morning. Frozen Stiff. Sean O Riordain. ModIr, *tr.* by Patrick Crotty

As I went through a guttery gap / I met a wee man with a red cap.   Riddle. *Unknown.*   FaBoVe

As I went through yon guttery gap / I met my Uncle Davy.   Riddle.   *Unknown.* FaBoVe

As I went up by Ovillers.   Ballad of the Three Spectres.   Ivor Gurney. OBWP

As I would free the white almond from the green husk.   Aubade.   Amy Lowell.   NAAPv.2; NIL-7

As ice on Mont Blanc's frozen crest.   Twenty Years After.   János Vajda. IQMS, *tr. by* Neville Masterman

As If.   Jim Peterson.   IaFF

As if a distinction might be drawn at the edge of a continuum.   Sinister. Forrest Gander.   PoDa

As if a few odd bombs were bouncing around.   Alan Bold.   EdScPo *Fr.* Edinburgh Castle.

As if a nest of hornets rose to sting.   János Arany.   IQMS *Fr.* Toldi.

As if a one-room schoolhouse were all we knew.   Amish Rug, An.   Michael Longley.   PNI

As If a Phantom Caress'd Me.   Walt Whitman.   SAmP

As if a quiet branch drew a line.   Eduard Veniaminovich Limonov.   TCRusP, *tr. by* Mary Jane White

As if a wood of oaks gave.   Suicide.   Menke Katz.   Prolet, *tr. by* Amelia Glaser

As if admonished from another world. (LL)   William Wordsworth.   NPBRoP; WaAnP *Fr.* Prelude, The; Growth of a Poet's Mind [1805 version].

As if, after High Street.   Freedom Ride.   Rita Dove.   FuFl

As if as if as if a hiss a swish of.   Golden Bough: The Feather Palm.   Susan Mitchell.   ExTi

As if because you lay.   Twelfth Birthday.   Rachel Hadas.   PoA 2002

As if brightness or sweetness could save us. (LL)   Zombies.   Lavinia Greenlaw.   BeAl; NeBrP

As if Cézanne had rendered it: a palimpsest.   Mountain View with Figures. Paul Mariani.   PfSP

As if dead the buried text.   III.   Danielle Collobert.   MFP, *tr. by* Martin Sorrell

As if God were an old man.   Task, The.   Denise Levertov.   InvLi; UpMys

As if gods wrestled here. (LL)   Work.   Yusef Komunyakaa.   CAP-8; LPSFW

As if happiness.   Inahata Teiko.   NAEL-7v1, *tr. by* Makoto Ueda

As if having a thought makes anything, and assuming.   Four Minute History of Getting It Together in Order to Be Fabulous, Briefly, A.   Anselm Berrigan. HeMarv

As if he had been poured.   Grauballe Man, The.   Seamus Heaney.   BrAP; NAMCP V.2; OxBEV; PoetW

As if I craved error, as if love were ahistorical.   Testimonial.   Claudia Rankine. ExTi; NeAmPo

As If I Knew.   Max Winter.   FreRad

As if I were given a reversed telescope instead of eyes, the world moves away. Poetic State, A.   Czeslaw Milosz.   MotU, *tr. by* the author and Robert Hass

As If in Flaw, or in the Flaw of Space.   Sabah Al-Kharrat Zwein.   *tr. by* Kaissar Afif

"Abysmal circle is in the sky, An. At the moment we are an infinite line,." PoArWo, *tr. by* Kaissar Afif

As if in water.   Tanka.   Ishikawa Takuboku.   CAoMJL1, *tr. by* Makoto Ueda

As if it had forgotten everything—hatred, vindictiveness, the meaning of pain. Custom.   Carol Frost.   MoASP

As if it had not been. (LL)   Moment, A.   Mary Elizabeth Coleridge.   LW; PEW

As if it were a scene made-up by the mind.   Often I Am Permitted to Return to a Meadow.   Robert Duncan.   ColAP; HarvBoo; NAMCP V.2; OxBoAm; PFTM-2; PmAP; WaAnP

As if it were crisp onion skin.   Balkan.   Gabriel Spera.   PoA 2002

As if it were his own! (LL)   Little Madness in the Spring, A.   Emily Dickinson.   AmFaPo; TCAPo

As if it were us the day were hauling.   Day's Labor, The.   Paul De Roux. YaTCFP, *tr. by* Stephen Romer

As if it's as if it's part of the whole endeavor to get back the finger beclouding what's.   Methodology.   Bruce Andrews.   FTOS

As if lyric.   Hermetic Diary.   Bruce Beasley.   AmAlph

As if our sneakers froze to the ground . . . .   Call of the Lake, The.   Andrey Andreievich Voznesensky.   VCWP

As if owned by someone unshakable.   To Isle of Wight.   Dave Jeddie Smith. InGu

As if regret were in it and were sacred.   Poem Beginning with a Line from Frost.   Dan Chiasson.   VisFro

As if some little Arctic flower.   Emily Dickinson.   APN-2

As if some monk bored.   Illumination.   R. T. Smith.   PoDa; Vesp

As if that fury of death itself were dying. (LL)   Then.   Edwin Muir.   OxBEV; PoA 2002

As if that night.   Troubling the Water.   Yusef Komunyakaa.   OxBoAm

As if the chart were given. (LL)   Emily Dickinson. *See* As if the Checks were given.

As if the Checks were given. (LL)   I never saw a Moor.   Emily Dickinson. AmFaPo; HeIP-4; ITBLP; MoAmPo; SAmP; TFi; WPoS

(As if the chart were given.) (LL)   BRP; ChAP

As if the flow of the waters.   Ka Waiapo Lani.   Queen Lili'u-o-ka-lani.   SWaP

As if the miracle were working, on the wrong balcony. (LL)   Miracle for Breakfast, A.   Elizabeth Bishop.   OxBoAm; PoA 2002

As if the sky broke up.   On the Origin of the Contrary.   Miroslav Holub. VCWP, *tr. by* Stuart Friebert *and* Dana Hábová

As if the snow itself were a country.   White, White.   David Morley.   NLP

As if the trees were not indifferent.   Gathered at the River.   Denise Levertov. AtGh

As If There were any Matter.   Nathaniel Tarn.   WANABP

As If There Were Only One.   Martha Serpas.   Vesp

As if they don't always remember that twining.   Steelhead in the Whitehorse Rearing Pond.   Joan Swift.   PoCoUp

As if they might start speaking. (LL)   Breasts.   Maxine Chernoff.   PmAP; ReTh

As if they were his ripe prize vegetables. (LL)   My Father's Garden.   David Wagoner.   NIL-7; NIP-1

As if they were not men.   Swamp Formalism.   Lisa Jarnot.   Eno

As if this were our honeymoon again, the man I've slept with.   First Night in the New House.   Andrea Hollander Budy.   NevBe

As if thou hadst sealed my pardon, with thy blood. (LL)   John Donne.   BASC; BrAP; ChIV-2; ClHu; CtM; HeIP-4; MakPoe; NAEL-6v1; NAEL-7v1; NAWM-5v1; NoP-5; NOSC; NPeEn; OxAEP-1; OxBEV; OxBSo; RSR; SacPr; TFi; WaAnP; WoPoe *Fr.* Holy Sonnets.

As if to draw the light to the body.   There Were No Deer in the Thicket. David Biespiel.   AmPoNex

As if to escape were part of what it meant to strip to nothing.   From the Book of Divine Consolation.   Andrew Zawacki.   IAoNAP

As if to lift my babe-in-arms.   Bihari.   ErotSp, *tr. by* Sam Hamill

As if under this wood a spirit could rise.   Trying To.   Wendy Barker.   InoFa

As if war made language and language.   Robert Kelly.   WANABP *Fr.* Threads.

As if with a straw you drink my soul.   As If with a Straw.   Anna Andreyevna Akhmatova.   FiBr, *tr. by* Judith Hemschemeyer

As if words could shed their skin.   Morning.   Pauline Kaldas.   PoArWo

As imperceptibly as Grief.   Emily Dickinson.   APN-2; NoP-4; NoP-5; SoSe-8

As in a duskie [*or* dusky] and tempestuous night.   Sonnet.   William Drummond of Hawthornden.   NOSC; OxAEP-1

As in a film by Godard: alone.   Pier Paolo Pasolini.   PFTM-2 *Fr.* Desperate Vitality, A.

As in a parable the truant father.   Pealing, The.   Olga Broumas.   BodElec

As in a Watteau fete of rose and silver blue.   Tempest, The.   Marya Alexandrovna Zaturenska.   MoAmPo

As in another life we were of the same blood. (LL)   Pond, The.   Louise Glück. ColAP; WaAnP

As in Frege's luminous counter-example.   Counter-Example, The.   David Shapiro.   PmAP

As in his burning throne he sits emparadised. (LL)   Giles Fletcher, the Younger. ChIV-2; NOSC; SacPr *Fr.* Christ's Victory and Triumph.

As in Sodom one day, our day.   Porfirio Barba-Jacob.   CAGL *Fr.* Song of an Impossible Blue.

As in that trance of wondrous thought I lay.   Percy Bysshe Shelley.   NPeEn *Fr.* Triumph of Life, The.

As in that twilight, superstitious age.   On Rembrant; Occasioned by His Picture of Jacob's Dream.   Washington Allston.   APN-1

As in the midst of battle there is room.   George Santayana.   APN-2 *Fr.* Sonnets.

As in the Small Gaps Between Minutes.   Gillian Conoley.   RoV

As in thee resteth my joye and confort.   *Unknown.*   OHMEL

As incense smoke thins, a stupendous.   God's Measurements.   Laurence Lieberman.   IllVoic

As incremental desire is counted out.   Impulse to Call & Spring Upo[...] Lee Ann Brown.   VaPo

As innocent as now thou art. (LL)   To His Son [*or* Sonne], Vince[...] Richard Corbet.   NOSC; OxAEP-1

As innocently as he had seen it first. (LL)   Someone.   Dennis [...] InoFa; StAl

As into the Garden Elizabeth Ran.   A. E. Housman.   NBI[...]

As inward love breeds outward talk.   William Basse.   N[...] The.

As iron from the mines.   Sikong Tu.   CCL1 *Fr.* Twe[...]

As is His Wont.   Nance Van Winckel.   RoV

As is the sand upon the ocean's shore.   One gene[...] another generation cometh: but the earth ab[...] Jones Very.   ChIV-1

As Is / you're bearing.   Written in My Drea[...] Ginsberg.   PoA 2002

As Israel's king kept his in shepherd's weed. (LL) To St John Baptist. Henry Constable. ChIV-2; NoSic

As it comes back, brick by smoky brick. In the Lost Province. Tom Paulin. PBCIP

As it does each day. (LL) Round, The. Stanley Kunitz. BeAl; BodElec; NAMCP V.1

As it fell out on a holy day [or upon a bright holiday or upon one day]. Bitter Withy, The. Unknown. NoP-4; NoP-5

As it fell upon a day. Richard Barnfield. OBEV Fr. Passionate Pilgrim, The.

As it has for so long. Morning in Norfolk. George Barker. HarvBoo

As it leaves the bell. (LL) Coolness. Buson. EH; NIL-7, tr. by Robert Hass

As It Should Be. Derek Mahon. EmeKit

As it turned out. Lawson Fusao Inada. AmWaPo Fr. Legends from Camp.

As it was in the beginning. Robin Morgan. HW Fr. Network of the Imaginary Mother, The.

As It Were. Drew Milne.
    "And out of dominion." VaPo

As Jupiter's all-seeing eye. John Gay. Fr. Fables: First Series.

As kerosene climbs through a wick. Transmigration. Bruce Berger. GeoH

As king I grow thin. Slice of Moon, A. Ko Ŭn. CAMKP, tr. by David R. McCann

As kingfishers catch fire, dragonflies dráw fláme. As Kingfishers Catch Fire. Gerard Manley Hopkins. MoBrPo; NAEL-6v2; NAEL-7v2; NAMCP V.1; NoP-4; NoP-5; NPeEn; OxAEP-2

As Lady Wei's star pupil, your calligraphy. Homage to the Painter General Ts'ao. Tu Fu [or Du Fu]. CrYelRi, tr. by Sam Hamill

As late I journeyed o'er the extensive plain. Samuel Taylor Coleridge. CenSon

As late I lay in slumber's shadowy vale. Samuel Taylor Coleridge. CenSon Fr. Effusions.

As late I rambled in the happy fields. To a Friend Who Sent Me Some Roses. John Keats. CenSon

As late we lived upon the gentle stream. Lines Written in Boston on a Beautiful Autumnal Day. Margaret Fuller. SWaP

As light as whatever you wish. Woodcock Feather. Peter Sanger. Coast

As light-shy owls stare into the sun. Old Houses on the Quays. Augusta Peaux. TuT, tr. by Tony Curtis

As Like As Not. Fanny Howe. AFaM

As long ago, my love, how long ago! (LL) Echo. Christina Georgina Rossetti. LW; NoP-4; NoP-5; PEW; PoBW; VWP

As long ago they raced. Dream of Trains, A. Mark Van Doren. GM

As long as Fame's imperious music rings. Three Quatrains. Edwin Arlington Robinson. NCAP

As Long As He Needs Me. Lionel Bart. ReLy

As Long As I Live. Ted Koehler. ReLy

As long as it was still noon and the earth. Callimachus. HePo Fr. Hecale.

As long as nothing can be known for sure. Ball, The. Wisława Szymborska. BeAl, tr. by Stanislaw Baranczak and Clare Cavanagh

    the corpses aren't carried off. (LL) Torture Chamber. Enrique PoetW; VCWP, tr. by Mary Crow

    he rain. Paper 33. Dominique Batraville. OGAHCP, tr. by   and Jack Hirschman

    Tatra breeze will. Lasting Things, The. Franz Werfel. GTCP,   Grimm

    ing whatever. (LL) Vasco [or Vasko] Popa. PoSu;

    ror. Kenneth Rexroth. OxBoAm

    e. Western Approaches, The.

    An. Alden Nowlan. StAl

    NoSic Fr. Idea.   dstreet.

As men that are with visions grac'd. To Rosania (now Mrs Montague) Being With Her, 25th September 1652. Katherine Philips. PoBW

As meteors pierce the sky's tin vault. Birdsong from Inside the Egg. Timothy Donnelly. LegDan

As 'mid moonbeams shifted through a cloud! (LL) Palimpsest, A. Michael Field. ViWPN; VWP

As 'mid these moldering walls I pensive stray. Written in a Ruinous Abbey. Susan Evance. CenSon

As motionless as possible in movement. Entirely You. Anton Korteweg. ArBi, tr. by the author

As much as pilots are happy when they are traversing the sea. Angelo Poliziano. CAGL Fr. Greek Epigrams.

As much as the image of you, I have seen. Astropastoral. Douglas Crase. KGB; OxBoAm

As musing pensive in my silent home. Written at Scarborough. Mary Tighe. CenSon; NPBRoP; WaAnP

As My Cat Eats the Head of a Field Mouse He Has Caught. M. Loncar. NAPBL

As my eyes. Chippewa Oral Tradition. APT-1 Fr. Chippewa Music.

As my eyes search the prairie. Chippewa Oral Tradition. See As my eyes.

As my father died of cancer of the asshole. For Euthanasia and Pain-Killing Drugs. Alan Dugan. NAMCP V.2

As my father turned the car into the drive. Winter, 1963. David Mason. VisFro

As my father's breathing. Stone at the Bottom, The. Manuel Ulacia. VCWP, tr. by Reginald Gibbons

As my mind in fancy wanders. Negro Has a Chance, The. Maggie Pogue Johnson. CBWP-4

As my mother ages and becomes. My Mother in Old Age. Eric Ormsby. NIP-4

As my shadow touches them. Crab. Angela Dove. Prnts

As My Will Concurred Not To My Being, It Were But Right and Equal to Reduce Me to My Dust. Yi Sanghŭi. EcSo, tr. by Jennifer M. Lee

As needy gallants in the scriv'ners' hands. John Dryden. OBSV Fr. Amboyna; or, The Cruelties of the Dutch to the English Merchants.

As night drew on, and, from the crest. John Greenleaf Whittier. CtM Fr. Snow-Bound [or Snow-Bound] [A Winter Idyl].

As night follows night. Unknown. ErotSp, tr. by Sam Hamill

As night succeeds night. Unknown. ArkPo, tr. by Helen Craig McCullough

As night was falling slowly on city, town and bush. Bastard from the Bush, The. Unknown. NOBAu

As Nilus' sudden ebbing here. Dream Broke, A. William Cartwright. NOSC

As none at all can perfect passage finde. (LL) Sir John Davies. See As none at all can perfect passage find.

As not yet come to our impiety. (LL) Fulke, 1st Baron Brooke Greville. NoSic; SacPr Fr. Caelica.

As now they do, to hear a boy's heart break. (LL) Incident in the Early Life of Ebenezer Jones, Poet, 1828, An. Sir John Betjeman. NAMCP V.1; NoAM

As o'er my latest book I pored. Printer's Error. P. G. Wodehouse. OBCoV

As o'er our heads, a place of bliss. (LL) Thomas Traherne. NAEL-6v1; NAEL-7v1

As o'er the dying embers oft I cower. On the Death of Priscilla Farmer. Charles Lloyd. NPBRoP

As o'er thy loved one now in grief ye bendeth. Solace. Josephine D. Henderson Heard. CBWP-4

As of late, the President. Executive Privilege. Danny Shot. BRtP

As oft I do record. Jinny. Unknown. NOSC

As oftentimes a river, it might seem. William Wordsworth. Fr. Prelude, The; Growth of a Poet's Mind [1805 version].

As oftentimes the too resplendent sun. Silentium Amoris. Oscar Wilde. IrLP

As old age weakens me, I grow lazy and foolish. Departing from Ch'in-chou. Tu Fu [or Du Fu]. CrYelRi, tr. by Sam Hamill

As Old As Then. Jan Eijkelboom. TuT, tr. by Michael O'Loughlin

As old salts know. Elena Suntsova. CRWP, tr. by Nika Skandiaka

As on all its sides a kitchen-match darts white. Spanish Dancer. Rainer Maria Rilke. NAWM-7v2, tr. by Stephen Mitchell

    n autumn night a herdman's fire. János Arany. IQMS Fr. Toldi.

    ble sorrow we attend. (LL) Lovers. Michael Field. PoBW;

    N

    Cross, the Saviour hung. Deep Spring. Unknown. SacPr

    , if not with light regard. Ode on the Poetical Character. William ollins. NAEL-6v1; NAEL-7v1; NoP-4; NoP-5; WaAnP

    nce in black I disrespected walked. Thomas Randolph. OBGa

    one, at midnight wakened by the call. Prelude. Wilfrid Wilson Gibson. MoBrPo

As one hears the cry. Lady Kasa. ArkPo, tr. by Edwin A. Cranston

As One Listens to the Rain. Octavio Paz. GPTC, tr. by Eliot Weinberger

As One Put Drunk into the Packet-Boat. John Ashbery. NAMCP V.2; VCAP

As one sees on the branch in the month of May the rose. Roses. Pierre de Ronsard. WoPoe, *tr. by* Vernon Watkins

As one that for a weary space has lain. Odyssey, The. Andrew Lang. OBEV

As one that strives, being sick, and sick to death. To Celia, upon Love's Ubiquity. Thomas Carew. CavPo

As One Who Bears beneath His Neighbor's Roof. Robert Silliman Hillyer. MoAmPo

As one who cons at evening o'er an album, all alone. James Whitcomb Riley. ITBLP *Fr.* Old Sweetheart of Mine, An.

As one who destined from his friends to part. On Being Forced to Part with his Library for the Benefit of his Creditors. William Stanley Roscoe. CenSon

As one who goes between high garden walls. Personality. Agnes Mary Frances Robinson. VWP

As one who goes from holding converse sweet. Lowlands. William Reed Huntington. APN-2

As one who hangs down-bending from the side. William Wordsworth. NAEL-6v2; NAEL-7v2 *Fr.* Prelude, The; Growth of a Poet's Mind [1850 version].

As one who in his journey bates at Noon. John Milton. *Fr.* Paradise Lost.

As one, who, journeying westward with the sun. Uncalled. Madison Cawein. TCAPo

As one who late hath lost a friend adored. Mary Tighe. CenSon

As one who, long in thickets and in brakes. William Cowper. *Fr.* Task, The.

As one who meditates at evening tide. Robert Pollok. *Fr.* Course of Time, The.

As one young guy screwed another young guy. David Trinidad. WiU *Fr.* Eighteen to Twenty-One.

As only a sort of They! (LL) Rudyard Kipling. NAMCP V.1; NoAM *Fr.* Debits and Credits.

As other men, so I myself do muse. Michael Drayton. NOSC; NoSic *Fr.* Idea.

As our bloods separate the clock resumes. As our bloods separate. David Constantine. StAl

As Our Bodies Rise, Our Names Turn into Light. Charles Wright. NoP-5

As our good manners required. (LL) Manners. Elizabeth Bishop. EMP; GoPo; NOxBChV

As our metal eyes wake. We Are Listening. Diane Ackerman. PoA 2002

As our plane droned south to Peoria. Atomic Ghost. John Balaban. AtGh

As our reward, she cut for the girls the nervous ribbon. Girls, The. Oni Buchanan. LegDan

As over muddy shores a dragon flock. Fear, The. Lascelles Abercrombie. OBMV

As Parmigianino did it, the right hand. Self-Portrait in a Convex Mirror. John Ashbery. CAP-8; NAMCP V.2; OxBoAm

As phoebus in his spheris hicht. Marie Maitland Lauder. EMWP

As Porcelain. (LL) Death is the supple Suitor. Emily Dickinson. NALW; NCAP

As puffed up. First Robin. Jane Yolen. NOxBChV

As quiet and chaste as the author's own life. (LL) James Russell Lowell. APN-1; OxBoAm; TCAPo *Fr.* Fable for Critics, A.

As real as melancholy, baldness, headache. Lovesickness: A Medieval Text. Jack Coulehan. BloBone

As reason's pow'rs by day our God disclose. Phillis Wheatley. SacPr *Fr.* Thoughts on the Works of Providence.

As red as her lips were she wasn't there. Milagrosa, La. Víctor Hernández Cruz. TouFir

As Rich as Solomon (21). Khwaja Shams-ad-din Muhammad Hafiz. WED, *tr. by* Robert Bly and Leonard Lewisohn

As riper years approach us. Glimpses of Infancy. Priscilla Jane Thompson. CBWP-2

As Rochefoucauld his maxims drew. Verses on the Death of Dr. Swift, D.S.P.D, Occasioned by Reading a Maxim in Rochefoucauld. Jonathan Swift. NAEL-6v1; NAEL-7v1; NoP-5

As rocks resist the billows and the sky. (LL) Deserted Village, The. Oliver Goldsmith. NAEL-6v1; NAEL-7v1; NoP-4; NoP-5; OxAEP-1; TFi

As round the rose's heart the golden threads. Soul Incense. Henrietta Cordelia Ray. CBWP-3

As Sam crumbles lumps of tofu on her tray. Gardens We Have Left. David Mura. OpBo

As sea.. rain. Takings. Gael Turnbull. Oth

As second wife, I never liked the first. Concubine, The. *Vietnamese Oral Tradition.* CaDao, *tr. by* John Balaban

As shakes the canvass of a thousand ships. Cornelius Mathews. APN-1 *Fr.* Poems on Man in His Various Aspects under the American Republic.

As she finally tore herself in two. (LL) Rapunzstiltskin. Liz Lochhead. BeAl; MoWP

As she goes out to sing this city home. (LL) Homecoming Singer, The. Jay Wright. OxBoAm; VCAP

As she is showering, I wake to see. Aubade, An. Timothy Steele. PasH; RA

As she is showering, I wake to see. Au Aubade. Timothy Steele. CalPo

As she laughed I was aware of becoming involved in her laughter. Hysteria. T. S. Eliot. IJHIL; OxBEV

As she liv'd peerless. William Shakespeare. OxAEP-1 *Fr.* Winter's Tale, The.

As she passes over them. (LL) Wind and Silver. Amy Lowell. HeIP-4; MoAmPo; Spl; TCAPo

As she reads, she rolls something around in her mouth, hard candy it must be, from how long it lasts. Reading: The Bus. C. K. Williams. PoCho

As she was lighting up her cigarette. Anne Portugal. SCFWP *Fr.* Bath, The.

As she would. Curling on the Bottom of My Mother's Bed. Lyn Lifshin. PfS

As shepherds in the red dusk went to hurry. Watteau, a Dream. Emile Nelligan. WoPoe, *tr. by* David Rattray

As shines the sunbeam through dark clouds. Hope. Mary E. Tucker. CBWP-1

As ships, becalmed at eve, that lay. Qua Cursum Ventus. Arthur Hugh Clough. OBEV

As simple as a drop of water. Hans Faverey. WoBe *Fr.* Eighteen Poems.

As simply as a self-effacing bar of soap. Man May Change, A. Marvin Bell. PoDa

As sincerely as possible. Steve Benson. FTOS *Fr.* Reverse Order.

As Sisyphus against the infernal steep. Lord Byron. OBSV *Fr.* English Bards and Scotch Reviewers [1812 version].

As slow our ship her foamy track. Journey Onwards, The. Thomas Moore. OxAEP-2

As slowly he sat up, near his left shoulder. Lazarus. Ágnes Nemes Nagy. IQMS, *tr. by* Adam Makkai

As slowly wanders thy sequestered stream. To the River Wenbeck. William Lisle Bowles. CenSon

As small-arms fire explodes outside the walls. (LL) Little Brown Brother. Nick Carbó. AmPoNex; ReBoTo

As soft and as pink as a nursery. Eleanor Wilner. PoChi

As solid-seeming as antiquity. Marriage in the Sixties, A. Adrienne Rich. OxBoAm

As some brave Admiral in former War. Disabled Debauchee, The. John Wilmot, 2d Earl of Rochester. BASC; NAEL-6v1; NAEL-7v1; NoP-4; NoP-5; NPeEn; OBSV

As some fond virgin, whom her mother's care. Epistle to Miss [*or* Miss Teresa] Blount, on Her Leaving the Town after the Coronation. Alexander Pope. NAEL-6v1; NAEL-7v1; NoP-4; NoP-5

As someone on his back for months of illness. Ausiàs March. STV

As Sometimes in a Grove. Frederick Goddard Tuckerman. NCAP

As soon as could this rod. Zhu-gan: This Rod. *Unknown.* CCL1, *tr. by* V. W. X.

As soon as he realized he was lost, that. Lifeline. Vijay Seshadri. BAP-97

As soon as I knew all the verses of the Shema. Samuel. Judith Baumel. TaR

As soon as I left. Mammals. Lesley Dauer. NAPBL

As soon as I open the door. Spring Snow. Chŏng Chiyong. CAMKP, *tr. by* Anthony, Brother of Taizé

As soon as I raise my eyes. Hans Faverey. WoBe *Fr.* Eighteen Poems.

As soon as I saw I was naked. Will the Real Me Please Stand Up? A. L. Hendriks. PML

As Soon As It's Here It's Gone But So What. Emilie Buchwald. MiVo

As soon as my sister and I got out of our. Sisters of Sexual Treasure, The. Sharon Olds. PBCAP

As soon as night descends, we meet. Mary Magdalene (I). Boris Leonidovich Pasternak. AF, *tr. by* Lydia Pasternak Slater

As soon as the idea of the Flood had subsided. After the Flood. Arthur Rimbaud. SxFrPo, *tr. by* Martin Sorrell

As stab it in the back with gentleness. (LL) Elizabethan and Nova Scotian Music. Charles North. NYP2; PmAP

As stands a statue on its pedestal. George Henry Boker. APN-2 *Fr.* So A Sequence on Profane Love.

As stated above, we were not expecting. We Were Not Expecting th To-day. Muriel Spark. EdScPo

As still he envied me, so fair she was! (LL) Bishop Orders His Praxed's Church, The. Robert Browning. BrAP; CABP; 6v2; NAEL-7v2; NAWM-7v2; NoP-4; NoP-5; NPeEn; TE

As structures go, it wasn't such a bad one. Old Complex, T FTOS

As sultry as the cruising hum. Muted Music. Robert P NAMCP V.1

As, sum tyme, dois the curser stert and ryn. Virgil. Eneados *or* Aeneis], The.

As sunbeams stream through liberal space. Woo stream through liberal space"). Ralph Wal

As surely as there are crumbs on the lips. Ke C. D. Wright. AmAlph

As sweet Polly Oliver lay musing in bed. FaBoWar

As Syllable from Sound. (LL) Brain—is wider than the Sky, The. Emily Dickinson. APN-2; MoAmPo; NAAL-3; NAAL-5; NAAPv.1; NAMCP V.1; NAWM-7v2; NCAP; NIL-7; OxBoAm; PoPoPo

As / the. Claude Anshin Thomas. WhBo

As the Allied tanks trod Germany to shard. May, 1945. Peter Porter. HP

As the basket comes in procession, greet it, women. Callimachus. HePo *Fr.* Hymns.

As the Beer Trucks Eclipse the Light of Morning. Anthony R. Vigil. AmPoNex

As the black curtain of the night. Reveille Matin, or Good Morrow to a Friend. Mildmay Fane, 2d Earl of Westmorland. NOSC

As the black storm upon the mountain top. William Wordsworth. NAEL-6v2; NAEL-7v2 *Fr.* Prelude, The; Growth of a Poet's Mind [1850 version; Selections from Anthologies].

As the blackbird in the spring, beneath the willow tree. Aura Lee. *Unknown.* NAAPv.1

As the blind Milton's memory of light. City Visions. Emma Lazarus. APN-2; NAAPv.1; SWaP

As the boat glides slowly. Pall Hanging over Manila. Mila D. Aguilar. ReBoTo

As the Breeze that cools the blood. As the Breeze that Cools the Blood. Gustavo Adolfo Bécquer. SpanPo, *tr. by* Edward F. Gahan

As the broad mountain where the shadows flit. Thomas Cole. APN-1 *Fr.* Voyage of Life, The.

As the Buck Lay Dead. Marsden Hartley. APT-1

As the bud bursts into the world's brightness. (LL) Muted Music. Robert Penn Warren. APT-2; NAMCP V.1

As the car alarms disconcertingly. Immaterial Nocturnes: Hudson and Worth. Tony Towle. PA9/11

As the cat. Poem. William Carlos Williams. ChAP; HarvBoo; NoP-4; NoP-5; OxBoAm; PoPoPo; SoSe-8

As the century. American Heaven. Paul Hoover. Vesp

As the Chameleon, who is known. Chameleon, The. Matthew Prior. OBSV

As the choir of stars begins. Dream of the Condor, The. José Santos Chocano. TCLAP, *tr. by* Andrew Rosing

As the companion is dead. Vigil. Cecília Meireles. TCLAP, *tr. by* James Merrill

As the Crow Flies, Let Him Fly. Samuel Hoffenstein.
"Early bird may catch the worm, The." NBLV

As the dawn was breaking the Sambhur belled. Rudyard Kipling. BLPJKO *Fr.* Jungle Book, The.

As the day, babbling, and dazzled by the light. (LL) Blindfold, The. Greta Stoddart. BeAl; MoWP

As the day stands when the Sun begins to glow. Dante Alighieri. NAWM-5v1 *Fr.* Divina Commedia (Selections from Anthologies, in English).

As the Dead Prey upon Us. Charles Olson. APT-2

As the dream a consciousness adored. Sonnet. Karen Volkman. IAoNAP

As the establishment of an ant citadel under the top-soil makes desert a considerable area. Ant nest. Jenny Joseph. MoWP

As the fire devours the grass. Explorer of Aromas. Toyin Adewale. NeNiPo

first trucks blundered past, chains pounding, the first delighted children out with sleds. (LL) Snow: II. C. K. Williams. NoP-4; NoP-5

the Grass. May Probyn. VWP

Poem. Kenneth Rexroth. GifTon

Memory of a Poet. Olga Sedakova. CRWP, *tr. by*

West. Bodhidharma Crossing the
McNulty. GifTon

AP, *tr. by* Naomi Lindstrom

APT-2

on the Hill.

As the needs of your new and childfree girl. (LL) On Not Being Your Lover. Medbh McGuckian. IrLP; PBCIP; PNI

As the ninth wave of the sea. (LL) Song of Blodeuwedd, The. *Unknown.* NoP-4; WoPoe, *tr. by* Robert Graves

As the observer wills. (LL) Study of Two Pears. Wallace Stevens. APT-1; BLT; NAMCP V.1; NoAM; OxBoAm

As the old woodland's legacy of song. (LL) Nightingale's Nest, The. John Clare. NAEL-7v2; NPeEn

As the ospreys woo. *Unknown.* CCL1 *Fr.* Guan-ju.

As the phobic said: it is torture. Suspension: Junior Wells on a Small Stage in a Converted Barn. Sandra McPherson. SeSe

As the prey-freighted eagle cleaves the storm. Free-booter, The. George Darley. OxBSo

As the primal spunk of the cosmos bellowed Out! (LL) Spunk Talking. Anne Rouse. BeAl; MFPA; NeBl

As the procession passes the palace the blinds are drawn. William McGonagall. VerBaPo *Fr.* Funeral of the German Emperor, The.

As the prophet says, / tarry. (LL) Anne Carson. BodElec; WoBe *Fr.* Truth About God, The.

As the queen upon her throne. (LL) Frances Ellen Watkins Harper. NAAPv.1; NALW *Fr.* Aunt Chloe.

As the rain falls. Rain. William Carlos Williams. ItP; OxBoAm; WaAnP

As the rain is lagging, wayward, in the river. On the Fragile Labyrinth. José Emilio Pacheco. STV, *tr. by* John Frederick Nims

As the rock and ocean that we were made from. (LL) Carmel Point. Robinson Jeffers. APT-1; ASA; BLT; CalPo; NAAL-5; NAMCP V.1; NoAM; NoP-4; WaAnP; WhBo

As the seasons have dealt with this ancient terrace. Climbing in Autumn for a View from the Temple on the Terrace of General Wu. Liu Ch'ang-ch'ing. CCL1, *tr. by* Witter Bynner

As the seed of a mole for. Perpetua. Olga Broumas. ErotSp

As the sepals of a bud signal. Field of Poppies, A. Barbara Baldwin. FiBr

As the sound fades. Basho. EH, *tr. by* Robert Hass

As the sound of a night fountain, under a bell of leaves, of a tree itself. Sage's Family, The. Francis Ponge. MotU, *tr. by* Cid Corman

As the spring. Kim Namjo. CAMKP *Fr.* Love's Cursive.

As the stars hide in the light before daybreak. Avoiding News by the River. W. S. Merwin. GifTon

As the stores close, a winter light. February Evening in New York. Denise Levertov. NoAM

As the stubborn ant carries its load counting on it to stay alive. Locked with a Tear. Luis Rosales. RaW, *tr. by* Ralph Nelson and Rita García Nelson

As the suffering hart confounded. Sándor Kisfaludy. IQMS *Fr.* Unhappy Love.

As the sun dancers, in their helmets of sage. Sacraments, The. Louise Erdrich. UpMys

As the sun sets in the western hills. Song of the Magic Strings. Li Ho. CCL1, *tr. by* John Frodsham

As the sun that lights creation. Africa. Lizelia Augusta Jenkins Moorer. CBWP-3

As the sweet sweat of roses in a still. John Donne. BASC *Fr.* Elegies.

As the team's head-brass flashed out on the turn. As the Team's Head-Brass. Edward Thomas. CABP; HarvBoo; NAEL-6v2; NAEL-7v2; NoP-4; NoP-5; OBWP; OxAEP-2; StAl

As the thread of my breath. *Unknown.* ArkPo, *tr. by* Edwin A. Cranston

As the thrushes do. (LL) I so liked Spring last year. Charlotte Mew. OxAEP-2; OxBEV

As the train approaches the tunnel, the kids. Children's Train, The. Dorianne Laux. GM

As the true stars at daybreak. (LL) Daybreak: "On the tidal mud, just before sunset." Galway Kinnell. BLT; ChAP

As the two ripe halves. Anatomy of Departure. Elizabeth Garrett. NeBl

As the wayward satellite believes its rescuers. Whoever You Are. Matthew Zapruder. LegDan

As the wheel follows the hoof. Kenneth Rexroth. APSN *Fr.* Love Poems of Marichiko, The.

ise men of old brought gifts. Gift, The. William Carlos Williams. GI

phoenix, duteous to his sire. Renewal. Michael Field. ViWPN

ful morning's light,. On S. John the Baptist. Thomas Stanley. -2

modesty now proved bothersome. Poem Without a Freight Train or a ocket Watch. Thom Ward. NevBe

eir names occurred. (LL) Anseo. Paul Muldoon. ModIr; NAMCP V.2; NPeEn; PNI

s These Letters—humid, sunless. The writing occurs on their walls. (LL) Sun ("Write this. We have burned all their villages.") Michael Palmer. APSN; CAP-8; FTOS; NAMCP V.2; PFTM-2

As they bury the dead. Bell Hooks. WhBo

As they made their turn into the empty highway. (LL) Waving Good-Bye. Gerald Stern. GoPo; PoA 2002

As they sat sipping their glasses in the courtyard. Dinner at the Hotel de la Tigresse Verte. Donald Evans. TCAPo

As they sit there, happily drinking. Yorkshiremen in Pub Gardens. Gavin Ewart. GoPo

As they were saying this. Alec Derwent Hope. GI *Fr.* St. Luke.

As this child rests upon my arm. Double Mirror. Ann Stanford. CalPo

As this convine and ordinance was mayd. Virgil. OBVE *Fr.* Aeneid [*or* Eneados *or* Aeneis], The.

As this in Kew thirst for the Red Dawn. (LL) Note on Local Flora. William Empson. OxAEP-2; OxBEV

As Thoreau might say. Three Poems 1989. Larry Eigner. PFTM-2

As those we love decay, we die in part. James Thomson. OBEV *Fr.* On the Death of Mr. William Aikman the Painter.

As those who are not athletic at breakfast day by day. Nature Morte. Louis MacNeice. NAMCP V.1; NoAM

As, thou being mine, mine is thy good report. (LL) William Shakespeare. HeIP-4; PBRV *Fr.* Sonnets.

As thou wouldst fly for very eagerness. (LL) Frost at Midnight [1798 version]. Samuel Taylor Coleridge. NOBRP; NPBRoP; WaAnP

As though. Chopin Preludes, Opus 28. J. R. Solonche. MiVo

As though a bare bulb hung. Billy. Linda McCarriston. LoL

As though all windows had been nailed shut. New Orpheus, The. Christopher Howell. RoV

As though explaining the idea of dancing. Explanation of America, An. Robert Pinsky.

As though good Doctor Botkin in his wisdom. In the Botkin Hospital. Bella Akhatovna Akhmadulina. CRWP, *tr. by* Catriona Kelly

As though his subject had decided to remain a prayer. (LL) Painter, The. John Ashbery. EmeKit; NoP-4; NoP-5; PoPoPo; YaYoPo

As though it knows exactly where we are going. (LL) Mind-Body Problem. Katha Pollitt. KGB; OxBoAm

As though it soared suchwise through heaven too. (LL) Royal Palm. Hart Crane. MoAmPo; NAMCP V.1; NoAM

As though it was meant to happen. (LL) Jack Johnson Does the Eagle Rock. Cornelius Eady. ESEAA; MoASP

As though recalling a moment in Creation. Palace of Fine Arts in San Francisco, The. Fidelito Cortes. ReBoTo

As though squeaks in the piano were not enough, a mouse. Summerhouse Piano. Sascha Feinstein. AmPoNex

As though you were near, you confessed. Wrought Figure. Linda McCarriston. FaoP

As through a neighb'ring grove, where ancient beech. William Mason. OBGa *Fr.* English Garden, The.

As through earth's garden once I strayed. Crushed Flower, The. Mary E. Tucker. CBWP-1

As through marble or the lining of. Blue. Carl Phillips. BtF; OxAAAP

As thumb is genius of the hand. Objects in Mirror are Closer Than They Appear. Jeffrey Skinner. PBCAP

As thus I bend me o'er thy babbling stream. To a Brook Near the Village of Corston. Robert Southey. NPBRoP

As Time Goes By. Herman Hupfeld. ReLy

As time will turn our bodies straight. Religion Is That I Love You. Kenneth Patchen. APT-2

As to an unknown lover I returned. Touro Synagogue. Ruth Whitman. TaR

As to Himself at last eternity changes him. Tomb of Edgar Poe, The. Stéphane Mallarmé. NAWM-7v2, *tr. by* Henry Weinfield

As To His Choice of Her. Wilfrid Scawen Blunt. GSo *Fr.* Love Sonnets of Proteus, The.

As to / "how do you write a poem." Book V. Steve Jonas. EGAG

As to How Much. Louis Zukofsky. APT-2

As to my heart, that may as well be forgotten. Personal Column. Basil Bunting. BrAP

As to my own concerns, it seems odd, given. Robert Pinsky. NoAM *Fr.* Essay on Psychiatrists.

As to the blooming prime. To Favonius. Edmund Bolton. NoSic

As to th'Eternall often in anguishes. Bible, *O.T.* BASC; OxBEV *Fr.* Psalms.

As Toilsome I Wander'd Virginia's Woods. Walt Whitman. APN-1; BLT; NAAL-3; PoAgWa

As travellours [*or* travellers] when the twilight's come. Pilgrimage, The. Henry Vaughan. ChIV-2

As twilight softly turns to sombre brown. Question at Night. Mihály Babits. IQMS, *tr. by* Peter Zollman

As two fair vessels side by side. Michael Field. VWP

As unpredictable as picnic weather, blue. Guide to the Perplexed. David Malouf. NOBAu

As usual, I had my zealous eye. God's Penis. Jeffrey Harrison. MAAN

As usual, I was desperate. Coming Home. Tess Gallagher. LaCa

As usual I'm up before the sun. John Berryman. WaAnP *Fr.* Sonnets to Chris.

As usual, the clock in The Clock Bar was a good few minutes. Hamlet. Ciaran Carson. FaBoVe; ModIr; PNI

As usual, the first gate is modest. It is dilapidated. She can't tell. Tan Tien. Mei-Mei Berssenbrugge. OpBo

As usual, the guard who worked. On the Last Day of the World. Sherod Santos. GeoHom

As usual, the seasons change too fast. To Eva. Jacqueline Osherow. TaR

As Venus wandered 'midst the Idalian bower. Camellia, The. William Stanley Roscoe. CenSon

As virtuous men pass[e] mildly away. Valediction, A: Forbidding Mourning. John Donne. AmFaPo; BASC; BrAP; CABP; FSCP; HeIP-4; NAEL-6v1; NAEL-7v1; NIL-7; NoP-4; NoP-5; NOSC; NPeEn; OxBEV; PBRV; PoPoPo; SoSe-8; TFi; WaAnP; WeW-3

As warm as bread or as a homecoming. (LL) Upstate. Derek Walcott. GT; OPRER

As was my duty, I oversaw the carting in of birds. Monologue of the Falconer's Wife. Colette Inez. PuP-23

As *water Rarified* doth make *Winds* blow. Of Cold Winds. Margaret Lucas Cavendish, Duchess of Newcastle. EMWP

As water, silk. On Sitting Down to Write, I Decide Instead to Go to Fred Herko's Concert. Diane Di Prima. PmAP

As *we crossed the field*, I told her. (LL) Centaur, The. May Swenson. APT-2; ItP; NAMCP V.2

As we drove back, crossing the hill. Locked House, A. W. D. Snodgrass. VCAP

As we ever got. (LL) My old man. Charles Bukowski. CalPo; OxBoAm; PmAP

As we eye the blue horizon's bend. I Can Dream, Can't I? Irving Kahal. ReLy

As we fall into step I ask a penny for your thoughts. Between. Micheal O'Siadhail. StAl

As We Forgive Those. Eric Pankey. GI

As we gasp between lines. A Cappella. Shari Miller Wagner. ACAMVP

As we get older we do not get any younger. Chard Whitlow. Henry Reed. MoBrPo; NBLV; NoP-4; NoP-5; OBCoV; UV

As we go about the toils of life. As We Sow We Shall Reap. Maggie Pogue Johnson. CBWP-4

As we grow old / What triumph. Issa. ZenPo, *tr. by* Takashi Ikemoto and Lucien Stryk

As we hold each other dull and loveless passersby sadly look away. David McFadden. NLPA

As we left the garden-party. Leaving. Richard Wilbur. HarvBoo

As we made love for the third day. Ecstasy. Sharon Olds. EmeKit; MoWP; StAl

As we raised our tent—in the winter firmament, it seemed. Prospect. Sydney Lea. PfSP

As We Sow We Shall Reap. Maggie Pogue Johnson. CBWP-4

As we strolled. Annuals and Perennials. Janice W. Hodges. BtF

As We Were Marching. Aharon Shabtai. WoBe, *tr. by* Peter Cole

As Weary Pilgrim, Now at Rest. Anne Bradstreet. NAAPv.1 (As Weary Pilgrim.) ColAP; NAAL-3

As weary-hearted as that hollow moon. (LL) Adam's Curse. William Butler Yeats. NAEL-6v2; NAEL-7v2; NAMCP V.1; NoAM; NoP-4; NoP-5; WeW-3

As well as any other, Erato. As Well As Any Other. Laura Riding Jackson. APT-2

As well as if a manor of thy friend's. (LL) Ruins of a Great House. Derek Walcott. BrAP; PoPoPo

As well as the wind's deliberate pornography. I Want to Revise This Sequence. Nicole Brossard. YaTCFP, *tr. by* Marilyn Hacker

As well as these poor poems. Black Box, The. Gavin Ewart. OBCoV

As well as things. (LL) Riprap. Gary Snyder. CalPo; NAAL-5; NAMCP V.2; NoAM; OxBoAm; PmAP; PoCho; PoPoPo; VCAP

As well, maybe, that you cannot read our minds. Enemy, The. Randolph Stow. NOBAu

As We're Told. Rae Armantrout. AWPTFC

As west behind Xian Mountain the setting sun would fall. Xiangyang Song. Li Po. CCL1, *tr. by* Elling O. Eide

As Western Culture Declined Without Its Knowing. Steve Healey. LegDan

As what he loves may never like too much. (LL) On My First Son. Ben Jonson. AmFaPo; BASC; BrAP; CABP; ClHu; InoFa; MakPoe; NAEL-6v1; NAEL-7v1; NIL-7; NIP-4; NoP-4; NoP-5; NOSC; NPeEn; OxBEV; PBRV; PoPoPo; RaBo; SUP; TFi; TRP; WaAnP; WeW-3; WoPoe

As, when a beauteous nymph decays. Stella's Birthday, 1725. Jonathan Swift. CABP; IrLP

As when a child on some long winter's night. Samuel Taylor Coleridge. CenSon *Fr.* Effusions.

As when a Conqu'rour does in Triumph come. To My Lady Morland at Tunbridge [*or* Tunbridge]. Aphra Behn. PoBW

As when a Fragment, from a Mountain torn. Virgil. OBVE *Fr.* Aeneid [*or* Eneados *or* Aeneis], The.

As when a heavy bomber in the cloud. Simile. William Meredith. PWW2

As when a traveller, forced to journey back. Parting. William Johnson Cory. CAGL

As when an architect some palace wall. Homer. OBVE *Fr.* Iliad, The.

As when at first primitive men were dwelling on the fruitful earth. Mildred Cecil, Lady Burleigh. EMWP

As when devouring flames some forest seize. Homer. OBVE *Fr.* Iliad, The.

As when down some broad river dropping, we. Frederick Goddard Tuckerman. APN-2 *Fr.* Sonnets: First Series, 1854–1860.

As when far off in the middle of the ocean. Wave, The. Virgil. PoDa, *tr. by* Robert Pinsky

As when far off the warbled strains are heard. Samuel Taylor Coleridge. CenSon *Fr.* Effusions.

As when it hapneth that some lovely Towne. Content and Resolute. William Drummond of Hawthornden. NPeEn; PBRV

As when of frequent bees. Homer. OBVE *Fr.* Iliad, The.

As when of old some orator renowed. John Milton. ChIV-1 *Fr.* Paradise Lost.

As when rooting in a bin. Dick, a Maggot. Jonathan Swift. NBLV

As when some mighty Hero first appears. To Mrs. Manley, upon Her Tragedy Call'd The Royal Mischief. Mary Pix. EMWP

As, when some treasurer lays down the stick. John Dryden. NOSC *Fr.* Love Triumphant.

As when the bright[e] Crulean firmament. Sir John Davies. NoSic *Fr.* Gulling[e] Sonnets, The.

As when the cheerfull Sunne, elamping wide. Giles Fletcher, the Younger. PBRV *Fr.* Christs Victorie, and Triumph in Heaven, and Earth, over, and after death.

As when the glorious Magazine of Light. On the 3 of September, 1651. Katherine Philips. BASC; EMWP; PBRV; WaAnP

As, when the squire and tinker, Wood. Prometheus. Jonathan Swift. WaAnP

As when the winds, ascending by degrees. Homer. OBVE *Fr.* Iliad, The.

As when, to one who long hath watched, the morn. John Codrington Bampfylde. CenSon

As when two men have loved a woman well. Dante Gabriel Rossetti. NoP-4 *Fr.* House of Life, The.

As when with downcast eyes we muse and brood. Alfred Tennyson. CenSon

As whenever. Simonides. SaLy, *tr. by* Diane Rayor

As where a wind blows. Guardian Angel of Not Feeling, The. Jorie Graham. ExTi

As white their bark, so white this lady's hours. (LL) Ezra Pound. ColAP; MoAmPo; NAAPv.2; NIL-7; NIP-4; TCAPo *Fr.* Ripostes of Ezra Pound.

As who by being poisoned doth poison know. (LL) Sir Philip Sidney. NAEL-6v1; NAEL-7v1 *Fr.* Astrophil and Stella.

As who was not, in laughter, pain, and love. (LL) Days of 1964. James Merrill. NAMCP V.2; OxBoAm; VCAP

As with any child, you find your own more beautiful. Failure. Dana Gioia. KGB

As with armor-plated tanks. (LL) Psalm 5: "Give ear to my words, O Lord." Ernesto Cardenal. PLBUT; TCLAP, *tr. by* Robert Marquez

As with sex, I did as instructed the first time. I let it. Sperm Count. Steven Huff. NevBe

As with tending a newborn, the days pass slowly, the months. Sewing Without Mother: A Zuihitsu. Kimiko Hahn. PuP-23

As with the dapper terns, or that sole cloud. Trolling for Blues. Richard Wilbur. PoA 2002

As With Them. Boris Leonidovich Pasternak. TCRusP, *tr. by* Bogdan Boychuk and Mark Rudman

As with your shadow I with these did play. (LL) William Shakespeare. NAEL-6v1; NAEL-7v1; NoSic; OBEV; OxAEP-1 *Fr.* Sonnets.

As withereth the primrose by the river. Palinode, A. Edmund Bolton. NoSic

As Women of Our Race. Mrs. Henry Linden. CBWP-4

As woods whose change appears. Horace. OBVE *Fr.* Art of Poetry, The.

As yawns an earthquake, when imprison'd air. Edward Young. STuOW *Fr.* Last Day, The.

As Yesterday's surprise. (LL) Riddle we can guess, The. Emily Dickinson. OxBoAm; SAmP

As yonder lamp in my vacated room. Lamp, The. Charles Whitehead. OBEV

As you and I stand long. Elena Suntsova. CRWP, *tr. by* Nika Skandiaka

As you bake in the oven, wafting sweet scent. Bread and I, The. Yi Yônju. EcSo, *tr. by* Yung-Hee Kim

As You Came from the Holy Land [of Walsingham]. *Unknown, sometimes at. to* Sir Walter Ralegh. NoSic; NPeEn; OBEV; OxAEP-2; OxBEV; PBRV; TFi

As you descend, slowly, falling faster past. Marine Snow at Mid-Depths and Down. Thomas Lux. AmAlph

As you described your mastectomy in calm detail. American Beauty, An. Carolyn Kizer. GeoHom

As you drank deep as Thor, did you think of milk or wine? Fish Food. John Wheelwright. APT-2

As you enter the room a door knob. Burning of Bustin's Island, The. Jim Carroll. AHA

As you have taught me, oh distant and brilliant and lonely. (LL) Dog, The. Gerald Stern. BeAl; WeW-3

As you lay in sleep. Cartography. Louise Bogan. TRP

As You Leave Me. Etheridge Knight. InGu

As You Like It. William Shakespeare.
    Amien's Song. NoSic
    Amiens's Song. NoSic; OBEV
    Amiens's Song. NoSic; OBEV
    (Blow, Blow, Thou Winter Wind.) CtM; NAEL-6v1; NoP-5; WaAnP
    Country Song. NoSic; OBEV; TFi
    (It Was a Lover and His Lass.) NAEL-6v1; NoP-5; WaAnP
    Motley's the Only Wear. OBCoV
    Seven Ages of Man, The. CtM; ITBLP; UV
    (Song.) OxAEP-1
    (Song.) OxAEP-1
    "Thou seest, we are not all alone unhappie." OxBEV
    (Under the Greenwood Tree.) NAEL-6v1; NoP-4; NoP-5; WaAnP
    "What would you have? Your gentleness shall force." OxAEP-1

As you might expect, my momentary vision barely. And Also from the Son. Scott Cairns. UpMys

As you plaited the harvest bow. Harvest Bow, The. Seamus Heaney. HarvBoo; ModIr; NoAM; PBCIP; PNI

As You Say. Dennis Joseph Enright. PoAgWa

As you see each of the stars has a voice. Glassy Sea. W. S. Merwin. BodElec

As you set out for Ithaka. Ithaka. Constantine P. Cavafy. BeAl; PtR, *tr. by* Edmund Keeley and Philip Sherrard

As you stand still in the hall thinking what. Purr, The. Molly Peacock. ExTi; PasH

As you would a faithful horse. (LL) Freedom at McNealy's. Priscilla Jane Thompson. CBWP-2; SWaP

As your bright leaf? (LL) Sea Poppies. "H. D." APT-1; NALW

As Your Eyes Are Blue. Lee Harwood. AHA

As your mind dissolves in God. (LL) On the way to God the difficulties. Lal Ded. WoPoe; WPoS, *tr. by* Coleman Barks

As Zeus. Ron Drummond. PA9/11

Asagumori. Kenneth Rexroth. GifTon

Asalteris. Norman Henry, II Pritchard. EGAG

Asante. Leticia R. Benson. InTrad

Ascend Lu-Shan. Pao Chao. ChinPo, *tr. by* Ye Weilian [*or* Yeh Wei-lien *or* Wai-lim Yip]

Ascend, my Muse, on sorrow's sable plume. Elegy on Mr. William Smith. Thomas Chatterton.

Ascend my shoulders, firmly keep thy seat. *Unknown, formerly at. to* Homer. OBVE *Fr.* Batrachomyomachia; The Battle of the Frogs and Mice.

Ascend the Heron Tower. Wang Chih-huan. ChinPo, *tr. by* Ye Weilian [*or* Yeh Wei-lien *or* Wai-lim Yip]

Ascend the Phoenix Terrace. Li Po. ChinPo, *tr. by* Ye Weilian [*or* Yeh Wei-lien *or* Wai-lim Yip]

Ascend the Three Mountains Toward the Evening: Looking Back at the Capital. Hsieh T'iao. ChinPo, *tr. by* Ye Weilian [*or* Yeh Wei-lien *or* Wai-lim Yip]

Ascending pile, The. John Milton. NOSC *Fr.* Paradise Lost.

Ascending Strathbraan. Tom Pow. EdScPo

Ascending the corner of the city wall—oh! Longing to Return: A Lament. Shi Chong. CCL1, *tr. by* Hellmut Wilhelm

Ascending the Mountain. Bernard Tetsugen Glassman. WhBo

Ascension. Denis Devlin. ChIV-2

Ascension Provisos. Andrew Zawacki. IAoNAP

Ascension, The. Cynewulf. *tr. by* Charles William Kennedy
    Redeemer, The.
        "As here on earth's soil God's Son Eternal." SacPr, *tr. by* Charles William Kennedy

Ascension Thursday. Saunders Lewis. OBWVE, *tr. by* Gwyn Morgan

Ascension Thursday. Saunders Lewis. BBMWP, *tr. by* Gwyn Williams

Ascensions, The. William Pillen. RaBo

Ascent. Anne Morrow Lindbergh. OtW

Ascent of F6, The. W. H. Auden and Christopher Isherwood.
    "Turn off the wireless." RWPCtW
    "Turn off the wireless; we are tired." RWPCtW

Ascent of Man, The. Mathilde Blind.
    Chaunts of Life. VWP
    Motherhood. ViWPN

Ascent of Species. John Milton. NOSC *Fr.* Paradise Lost.

Ascent, The. Max Winter. FreRad

Ascetic dyes his robes, The. Ascetic Dyes His Robes, The. Kabir. WoPoe, *tr. by* Pritish Nandy

Ascetic / He emerges from its belly into the grave. Chaldean Ruins, The. Dunya Mikhail. PoArWo, *tr. by* Samira Kawar

Ascot Waistcoat. David McCord. NBLV

(Sportif.) AmWit

Asdrubral Jiménez has not disappeared. Asdrubral Jiménez. Charles McDonald. NLP

Asenath. Diana Hume George. ChIV-1

AsforoursocalledVitalOrgansandViscerawilltheyeverbeDistinguishablefroma FloodedCattleShed? (LL) Yi Sang. CAMKP; PFTM-1 *Fr.* Crow's-Eye View.

Ash. Jayanta Mahapatra. PoA 2002; VCWP

Ash Keys. Michael Longley. PBCIP

Ash on an old man's sleeve. T. S. Eliot. NPeEn; OxBEV *Fr.* Four Quartets.

Ash Range, The. Laurie Duggan.

One. One. BMAP

Five. One. BMAP

Ash Wednesday, 2002. Andrea Carter Brown. PA9/11

Ash Wednesday [*or* Ash-Wednesday]. T. S. Eliot. APT-1; MoAmPo

1. SacPr

5. UV

Ashbery Explains. Clark Coolidge. NYP2

Ash-colored silence. Tomas Tranströmer. WoBe *Fr.* Haiku.

Ashes. Annie Foster. NLP

Ashes. Andrew Hudgins. CAP-8

Ashes. Malena Morling. InoFa

Ashes. Alejandra Pizarnik. TCLAP, *tr. by* Frank Graziano and María Rosa Fort

Ashes, The. Carolyn Kizer. BAP-01

Ashes have collected in the heart and in the memory. Only Choice, The. Jawad Yaqoob. IrPoTo, *tr. by* Chuck Miller and Saadi A. Simawe

Ashes head to toes. Canto 1. Dionne Brand. BrAP

Ashes Hill Mountain, toward it I am running. Tohono O'odham. NAAPv.1 *Fr.* Songs for Treating Sickness, Sung durring the Four Parts of the Night.

Ashes in Oxford. Francisco Brines. RaW, *tr. by* Hardie St. Martin

Ashes, Lord. Nat Turner in the Clearing. Alvin Aubert. FuFl

Ashes of me. Witch! Leonora Speyer. APT-1

Ashes of soldiers South or North. Ashes of Soldiers. Walt Whitman. FaBoWar

Ashes to ashes, dust to dust. Duties and Vocations. Jane Satterfield. SweBea

Ashikaga Tadayoshi's Palace. Muso Soseki. EaWin, *tr. by* W. S. Merwin

Ashkelon is not cut off with the remnant of a valley. Judith. Adah Isaacs Menken. APN-2; CBWP-1; SWaP; ViWPN

Ashtabula Disaster, The. Julia A. Moore. VerBaPo

(Steam: The Steamy Side.) STuOW

Ashtaroth: A Dramatic Lyric. Adam Lindsay Gordon.

Scene—A Castle in Normandy.

"What share have I at their festive board?" STuOW

Scene—The Same.

"Husband, that man is ill and weak." STuOW

Ashtray in the Snow. Robert Wrigley. RoV

Ashurbanipal fell in love with me. Transformations of Aisha: Aisha's Birth and Death in the Magical Rituals Inscribed in Cuneiform on the Nineveh Tablets. Abdul Wahab Al-Bayati. IrPoTo, *tr. by* Farouk Abdel Wahab

Ashy Gal. Baba Lukata. BtF

Así que el hombre ha hundido su barbilla en la mano. Mirándose. Francisco Brines. RaW

Asia. Will Alexander.

"Let us recall the illusion." WANABP

Asian Am Anthem, An. Thien-bao Thuc Phi. BRtP

Asian American. Making It Stick. Lawson Fusao Inada. BAP-97

Asian Century wasn't supposed to start like this, The. No Matter What Sign You Are. Jeni Olin. FreRad

Asian Desert. Dorothy, Duchess of Wellington Wellesley. OBMV

Asians Dying, The. W. S. Merwin. AmWaPo; NAMCP V.2; PoPoPo; VCAP; WaAnP

Aside from rain, the weather stays the same. Letter from Home. G. E. Patterson. AmPoNex

Asides on the Oboe. Wallace Stevens. MoAmPo

A-sitting on a gate. (LL) Lewis Carroll. BrAP; NAEL-6v2; NAEL-7v2; NoAM; NoP-4; NoP-5; TFi; UV *Fr.* Through the Looking-Glass.

Ask about my wailing from the prayers. Ahmed Pasha. OLP, *tr. by* Walter Andrews, Najaat Black and Mehmet Kalpakli

Ask, and let your words diminish your asking. Waiting. Jean Valentine. YaYoPo

Ask anyone up Harlem way. Bojangles of Harlem. Dorothy Fields. ReLy

Ask many women and they'll claim no knowledge, but some. Jennie Fontana. NewEx

Ask Me. William Stafford. CAP-8; LoL; OxBoAm

Ask me how do I feel. If I Were a Bell. Frank Loesser. ReLy

Ask me no more, my truth to prove. Winter Song. Elizabeth Tollet. WaAnP

Ask me no more: the moon may draw the sea. Alfred Tennyson. NAEL-6v2; NAEL-7v2 *Fr.* Princess, The.

Ask[e] me no more where Jove bestow[e]s. Song[, A]. Thomas Carew. BASC; CavPo; ClHu; NAEL-6v1; NAEL-7v1; NoP-4; NOSC; OBEV; OxBEV; TFi; CtM; NoP-5

(Aske me no more whither doe stray.) NPeEn

Ask No Return. Horace Gregory. MoAmPo *Fr.* Chorus for Survival.

Ask no return for love that's given. Horace Gregory. MoAmPo *Fr.* Chorus for Survival.

Ask not the cause why sullen Spring. Song to a Fair Young Lady, Going Out of the Town in the Spring. John Dryden. OBEV

Ask not why sorrow shades my brow. Song: Montrose. Charles Cotton. NOSC

Ask the old men in Chinatown. Not Translation, Not Poetry. Daryl Ngee Chinn. LTA

Ask you what provocation I have had? Alexander Pope. OBSV *Fr.* Epilogue to the Satires, in Two Dialogues.

Ask[e] me no more why I send you here. Primrose, The. Robert Herrick. OBEV

Asked and Answered. William Wordsworth. STuOW *Fr.* Address to My Infant Daughter, Dora on Being Reminded That She Was a Month Old That Day, September 16.

Asked, Don't you dream, do you ever. Erolog. Michael Palmer. FTOS

Asked for a Happy Memory of Her Father, She Recalls Wrigley Field. Beth Ann Fennelly. RWB

Asked how old he was. Issa. EH, *tr. by* Robert Hass

Asked me for a kiss. (LL) Suicide's Note. Langston Hughes. APT-2; NAMCP V.1; OxAAAP; PoPoPo; SAmP

Askest, 'How long thou shalt stay'. Visit, The. Ralph Waldo Emerson. APN-1

Asking Favors. Wilma Elizabeth McDaniel. GeoHom

Asking for it. Carmel Gahan. BBMWP, *tr. by* Robert Minhinnick

Asking the Second Nun. Yasui. EMJL *Fr.* Mad Verse.

Asking the Way. Ko Un. WhBo

Ask-Vubba: A Decalogue. Tyrone Williams. RD

Asleep / sleap / am welcome drifting. Bride's Day. Susan Howe. FTOS

Asleep at the wheel nearly. Driving Home to See the Folks. Anthony Sobin. MAAN

Asleep beneath the cold and virgin stars. Village Night. Gyula Juhász. IQMS, *tr. by* Anthony Edkins

Asleep he wheezes at his ease. Roger the Dog. Ted Hughes. ChAP

Asleep in spring unaware of dawn. Spring Dawn. Meng Hao Jan. ColAnChi, *tr. by* Elling O. Eide

Asleep in the City. Michael Smith. PBCIP

Asleep in the Valley. Paul Verlaine. SxFrPo, *tr. by* Martin Sorrell

Asleep upon a chair. (LL) Ballad of Father Gilligan, The. William Butler Yeats. IrV; MoBrPo

Asleeping: a kind of rendezvous. John Lowther. AnSo

Asomado a la olla de los fenómenos. Olla, La. David Huerta. RMCMP

Asómate al enigma. Dolores Dorantes. SPV

Asparagus is a lean in a lean to hot. Gertrude Stein. NAAPv.2 *Fr.* Tender Buttons.

Aspatia's Song. Francis Beaumont and John Fletcher. OBEV *Fr.* Maid's Tragedy, The.

Aspects of Love. Ruth Miller. LW *Fr.* Aspects of Love.

Aspects of Now. Gwyn Williams.

"Today has it all, sunshine." OBWVE

Aspects of Robinson. Weldon Kees. OxBoAm

Aspen Meadows. Kenneth Rexroth. CalPo *Fr.* Air and Angels.

Aspen meadows / the first day of November. Aspen Meadows. Ward Abbott. ICANM

Aspen tree, your leaves glance white into the dark. Aspen Tree. Paul Celan. PoetW, *tr. by* John Felstiner

Aspen tree, your leaves glance white into the dark. Aspen Tree. Paul Celan. PoSu, *tr. by* Michael Hamburger

Aspens. Edward Thomas. FaBoVe; NPeEn; OxBEV

Asperger Child. Tom French. NIrP

Asphalt. Chimalum Nwankwo. NAfrP

Asphalt Musings. Carl Hancock Rux. HeMarv

Asphyxiated Man, The. Victor Serge. AF, *tr. by* James Brook

Aspiration. Adah Isaacs Menken. CBWP-1; ViWPN

Aspiration. Emily Jane Pfeiffer. ViWPN

Aspiration. Henrietta Cordelia Ray. CBWP-3

Aspiration. Edward William Thomson. SacPr

Aspirin. Elizabeth Alexander. AmPoNex

Ass passed like an ass, The. Entry into Jerusalem. Dmitry Aleksandrovich Prigov. ItGoST, *tr. by* Robert Reid

Ass, that for her slowness, was forbid, The. On Balaam's Ass. Francis Quarles. ChIV-1

Assail the breast, when passion rages there! (LL) Phaon Forsakes Her. Mary Robinson. CenSon; RWP

Assassination. Haki R. Madhubuti. GT

Assassination, The. Robert Silliman Hillyer. MoAmPo

Assassination, The. Donald Justice. VCAP

Assassination of Charlie Parker, The. Arthur Brown. SeSe

Assassination of John Lennon as Depicted by the Madame Tussaud Wax Museum, Niagara Falls, Ontario, 1987, The. David Wojahn. P180; PBCAP *Fr.* Mystery Train: A Sequence.

Assassination of Robert Goulet as Performed by Elvis Presley: Memphis, 1968, The. David Wojahn. AllShUp; IllVoic

Assassination of the President, The. November 25, 1963. Thomas Whitbread. TiP2

Assault. Reinhold Grimm. GTCP, *tr. by* the author

Ass[e], The. Robert Herrick. ChIV-1

Assemble, all ye maidens, at the door. Elegy on a Lady, Whom Grief for the Death of Her Betrothed Killed. Robert Bridges. OBEV

Assembled sirs. The courtesies afforded us by the Dali Lama. Daniel Berrigan. UpMys *Fr.* Funeral Oration as Pronounced by the Compassionate Buddha, The.

Assembler. Debra Allbery. PBCAP

Assembling My Shepherd. Tessa Rumsey. LegDan

Assembly Line. "Shu Ting." VCWP

Assembly of Ladies, The. The Lady of the Assembly. OBGa *Fr.* Assembly of Ladies, The.

Assembly Point D. Tony Lopez.
    "Dauntless the slug-horn to my lips I set." Oth

Assembly tree and bowl of thorns. Blouse of Felt. Amina Calil. BAP-01

Asseverations. Arthur Nortje. HBAPE

Ass-Face. Dame Edith Sitwell. OBMV *Fr.* Façade.

Ass-Face drank / The asses' milk of the stars. Dame Edith Sitwell. OBMV *Fr.* Façade.

Assiette, The (The Plate). Francis Ponge. WED, *tr. by* Robert Bly

Assignment, The. Len Roberts. OPRER

Assimilation. Eugene Gloria. ReBoTo

Assimilation, The. Barry Spacks. RWB

Assise, la fileuse au bleu de la croisée. Fileuse, La. Paul Valéry. YaTCFP

Assist me while I wander here. Caroline Codling. FaBoVe

Assistant holds her on the table, The. Putting Down the Cat. Billy Collins. BeAl

Assorted needles and coloured threads. Sewing Lesson, The. Kate Lilley. BMAP

Assuage Bane. Mark Prejsnar. AnSo

Assuming rain, the exotic. "Night in the Tropics" (1858-59?). Michael Waters. MiVo

Assumption of Miriam from the Street in the Winter of 1942, The. Jerzy Ficowski. *tr. by* Keith Bosley
    Assumption of Miriam from the Street in the Winter of 1942, The. HP

Assurance. Josephine D. Henderson Heard. CBWP-4

Assurances—the way, in our absence, things repair themselves. Architecture (2). Jocelyn Emerson. IAoNAP

Assuredly, that fissured face. Eulogy to W.H. Auden. Derek Walcott. ESEAA

Assyrian came down like the wolf on the fold, The. Destruction of Sennacherib, The. Lord Byron. BRP; CABP; ChAP; ChIV-1; FaBoWar; HeIP-4; NoP-4; NoP-5; OBWP; OxAEP-2; TFi; WeW-3; WoPoe

Assyrian [*or* Assyrians'] King in peace, with foul desire, The [*or* Th']. Sardanapalus. Henry Howard, Earl of Surrey. NAEL-6v1; NAEL-7v1; NoSic
    (Thassyryans king, in peas with fowle desyre.) WaAnP

Aster. Plato. WoPoe, *tr. by* Peter Jay

Astig. Eric Fructuoso. ReBoTo

Astilla. Silvia Eugenia Castillero. SPV

Astolfo flies by Chariot to the Moon, where he collects Orlando's lost wits. Sir John Harington. NPeEn *Fr.* Orlando Furioso.

Astonished Muse finds thousands at her side, The. (LL) Ode, Inscribed to W. H. Channing. Ralph Waldo Emerson. AmWaPo; APN-1; ColAP; NAAL-3; NAAPv.1; NCAP; NoP-4; NoP-5; OxBoAm; TCAPo; WaAnP

Astonished stood Lucrece and Nara. Lucrece and Nara. Laura Riding Jackson. APT-2

Astonishing love, The. Oh, Astonishing Love. Javier Sologuren. BLPSL, *tr. by* Rene de Costa, Rigas Kappatos and Eleni Paidoussi

Astonishment. Daniel Berrigan. UpMys
    "Wonder / why illness." UpMys

Astræa. Ralph Waldo Emerson. APN-1

Astræa. John Greenleaf Whittier. APN-1

Astraea Redux. John Dryden.
    Return of Charles II, The. STuOW

Astragaloi. Mark Jarman. PoCho

Astrea in this time. William Drummond of Hawthornden. NOSC *Fr.* Urania, or Spiritual Poems.

Astrelegy. Andrew Zawacki. IAoNAP

Astrid brought an oxhorn. Show and Tell. Roddy Lumsden. NeBl

Astrid comes from upstate New York. Feminine Intuition. Stephanie Brown. AmPoNex; BAP-97

Astride my dual prayerwheel. Bhakti Yogi Buys a Bike, The. Gus Ferguson. ArBi

Astrologer Predicts at Mary's Birth, The. Lucille Clifton. NALW

Astrologer, The. Sir Thomas More. WoPoe, *tr. by* James Vincent Cunningham

Astrologer's Song, An. Rudyard Kipling. MoBrPo

Astrology? Jean Valerie. BtF

Astronauts. Robert Earl Hayden. ESEAA; OtW

Astronomer, / I strike my gong for you. Mirror of a Day Chiming Marigold, The. Diane Wakoski. NALW

Astronomer with patient, searching gaze, The. Slowness of Belief in a Spiritual World, The. Jones Very. NCAP

Astronomer Works Nights: A Parable of Science, The. Bin Ramke. YaYoPo

Astronomer's Journal, An. Jane Shore. PoA 2002

Astronomers of Mont Blanc, The. Edgar Bowers. PoA 2002

Astronomica, The. Marcus Manilius. *tr. by* Eugene O'Connor
    "Why do we in worries waste our lives, and torture." RomPo, *tr. by* Eugene O'Connor

Astronomies and slangs to find you, dear. John Berryman. AWTN *Fr.* Sonnets to Chris.

Astronomy. A. E. Housman. NoP-4; NoP-5; OBWP

Astronomy. David Walker. MotU

Astronomy. M. L. Williams. GeoHom

Astropastoral. Douglas Crase. KGB; OxBoAm

Astrophil and Stella. Sir Philip Sidney.
    (15.) CABP
    (31.) BrAP
    (47.) BrAP
    (54.) CABP
    (71.) BrAP
    (Highway, The.) OBEV; OxAEP-1
    (His Lady's Cruelty.) OBEV
    (Sleep.) OBEV
    First Song. OxAEP-1
    Second Song. NoSic
    Fourth Song. NAEL-6v1; NAEL-7v1; NoP-4; NoP-5; NoSic
    Eleventh Song. NAEL-6v1; NAEL-7v1; NoSic; OxAEP-1
    Eighth Song. NoSic; PBRV
    Ninth Song. NoSic
    Sonnet 1. BrAP; CABP; GSo; NAEL-6v1; NAEL-7v1; NoP-4; NoP-5; NoSic; NPeEn; OxAEP-1; OxBEV; OxBSo; PBRV; TFi
    Sonnet 2. NAEL-6v1; NAEL-7v1
    Sonnet 3. NoSic
    Sonnet 5. NAEL-6v1; NAEL-7v1; NoSic
    Sonnet 6. NAEL-6v1; NAEL-7v1; NoSic
    Sonnet 7. NAEL-6v1; NAEL-7v1; NIL-7; NIP-4
    Sonnet 9. NAEL-6v1; NAEL-7v1
    Sonnet 10. NAEL-6v1; NAEL-7v1
    Sonnet 11. OxBSo
    Sonnet 14. NoP-4; NoP-5; NoSic
    Sonnet 15. NoSic; OxAEP-1
    Sonnet 16. NAEL-6v1; NAEL-7v1
    Sonnet 18. NAEL-6v1; NAEL-7v1; NoSic
    Sonnet 19. NoSic
    Sonnet 20. NAEL-7v1; NoSic
    Sonnet 21. NAEL-7v1; NoP-5; NoSic
    Sonnet 25. NoP-4; NoP-5
    Sonnet 27. CABP; NoSic
    Sonnet 28. NAEL-7v1; NoSic
    Sonnet 30. NoSic
    Sonnet 31. AEP; CABP; GSo; HeIP-4; NAEL-6v1; NAEL-7v1; NoP-4; NoP-5; NoSic; NPeEn; OxAEP-1; OxBEV; OxBSo; TFi; TRP; WaAnP
    Sonnet 33. NPeEn
    Sonnet 37. NAEL-6v1; NAEL-7v1
    Sonnet 39. GSo; NAEL-6v1; NAEL-7v1; NoSic; OxAEP-1; OxBSo; TFi; WaAnP
    Sonnet 40. NoSic

Sonnet 41. NAEL-6v1; NAEL-7v1
Sonnet 45. NAEL-6v1; NAEL-7v1; NoSic
Sonnet 47. NAEL-6v1; NAEL-7v1; NoP-4; NoP-5
Sonnet 48. NoP-4; NoP-5
Sonnet 49. NAEL-6v1; NAEL-7v1; NoP-4; NoP-5
Sonnet 52. NAEL-6v1; NAEL-7v1; NoP-4; NoP-5
Sonnet 53. NAEL-6v1; NAEL-7v1; NoSic
Sonnet 54. NoSic
Sonnet 56. NAEL-6v1; NAEL-7v1
Sonnet 61. NAEL-6v1; NAEL-7v1
Sonnet 63. NoP-5
Sonnet 69. NAEL-6v1; NAEL-7v1; OxAEP-1
Sonnet 71. NAEL-6v1; NAEL-7v1; NoP-4; NoP-5; NoSic
Sonnet 72. NAEL-6v1; NAEL-7v1; NoP-5
Sonnet 74. NAEL-6v1; NAEL-7v1; NoSic
Sonnet 75. NoSic
Sonnet 81. NAEL-6v1; NAEL-7v1; OxBSo
Sonnet 87. NAEL-6v1; NAEL-7v1
Sonnet 89. NAEL-6v1; NAEL-7v1
Sonnet 90. NoP-4; NoP-5; NoSic; WaAnP
Sonnet 91. NAEL-6v1; NAEL-7v1
Sonnet 92. NoSic
Sonnet 99. NoSic
Sonnet 103. OxAEP-1
Sonnet 107. NoP-4; NoP-5; OxAEP-1
Sonnet 108. NAEL-6v1; NAEL-7v1
(Sonnet 41: 'Having this day my horse, my lance'.) AEP
(Sonnet 6: 'some lovers speak'.) AEP
(Sonnet 72: 'Desire, though thou my old companion art'.) AEP
(Sonnet 20: 'Fly, fly, my friends'.) AEP
(Stella's Kiss.) NoSic
(Voices at the Window.) OBEV
Astrophysics. Sylvia Townsend Warner.
  "To no believable blue I turn my eyes." OxBSo
A-swell within her billowed skirts. Mad Woman of Punnet's Town, The.
  Leonard Alfred George Strong. MoBrPo
Asylum. Quan Barry. PoDa
Asylum. Star Black. PA9/11
Asylum. Breyten Breytenbach. VCWP, tr. by Stephen Gray and A. J. Coetzee
Asylum. Rafael Campo. NeAmPo
Asylum. Ciaran Carson. PNI
Asylum. Herman Fong. BAP-97
Asylum. John Freeman. OBMV
Asylum is water and the sea is stone, The. Asylum is Water, The. Vincent
  Woods. NIrP
Asylum is Water, The. Vincent Woods. NIrP
Asylum of Gestures. Carl Hancock Rux. HeMarv
Asymmetry 205. Jackson Mac Low. PFTM-2
Asymmetry of the Universe. Fabio Doplicher. NeIt, tr. by Stephen Sartarelli
At 29. Speculations on the Present through the Prism of the Past. June
  Jordan. GT
At 4:00 A.M. Asleep. John Balaban. SUP
At 6 a.m. the ominous zooming, war-sound, of helicopters breaks into our sleep.
  Denise Levertov. ASA Fr. Staying Alive.
At 8 / The magnets of my fickle thoughts. Acts of Power. Sharan Strange.
  InTrad
At a Bach Concert. Adrienne Rich. NIL-7; NIP-4; YaYoPo
At a Calvary near the Ancre. Wilfred Owen. ChIV-2; GI
At a certain point I lost track of you. Farewell. Agha Shahid Ali. PoDa
At a city square. Envying the Children of San Francisco. Gary Soto. CAP-8
At a Concert of Music. Conrad Potter Aiken. MoAmPo
At a Country Funeral. Wendell Berry. UpMys
At a Dinner Party. Amy Levy. PoBW
At a Grave. Martinus Nijhoff. TuT, tr. by Desmond Egan
At a House in the Bamboo Grove. Wang Wei. CrYelRi, tr. by Sam Hamill
At a house no. 99. Bkln. Elouise Loftin. EGAG
At a little grass-hut in the valley of the river. From My Study at the Mouth of
  the Valley: A Message to Censor Yang. Ch'ien Ch'i. CCL1, tr. by Witter
  Bynner
At a lonely ranch 'neath a lonely sky. Ennui. Larry Chittendon. TiP2
At a meadow in Golden Gate Park. Aglow in Nowhere. James Richard
  Broughton. CalPo
At a Motel near O'Hare Airport. Jane Kenyon. OtW
At a party I spy a handsome psychiatrist. Afternoon Happiness. Carolyn
  Kizer. GeoHom
At a party in a Spanish kind of tiled house. Honor, The. Denis Johnson.
  LaCa

At a place in the mountains. Savior Is Abducted in Puerto Rico, The. Martín
  Espada. TRP
At a pleasant evening party I had taken down to supper. Ferdinando and
  Elvira; or, The Gentle Pieman. William Schwenck Gilbert. OBCoV
At a quarter of five in the morning a sparrow worries. Good Man's Fate, A.
  William Loran Smith. LaCa
At a quarter to eleven. Let Us Go and Find a Place of Worship. Carmelita
  McGrath. Coast
At a quarter to seven we sat down to dine. Shall We Join the Ladies?
  Marshall Barer. ReLy
At a Reception. Karen Gershon. LW
At a roadside shrine. Buson. SoOfWa, tr. by Sam Hamill
At a shout to a disco drum, the women dance. Uni-Gym, The. Anne Rouse.
  NeBl
At a Solemn Music[k]. John Milton. HeIP-4; OBEV; SacPr
At a summer home in Ningpo, near Shanghai. Picture of my Mother's Family,
  A. Wing Tek Lum. OpBo
At a Sunlit Window. Ondra Lysohorsky. AF, tr. by Ewald Osers
At a Symphony. Louise Imogen Guiney. APN-2
At a Time Like This. Alex Liban. NRoS, tr. by Esther Raizen
At a Village in Scotland. William Lisle Bowles. NPBRoP
At a wash place by the stream under a drooping willow. Yi Chehyŏn. CATKP
  Fr. Contemporary Folk Songs.
At a Wine House near Taegu. Sŏ Chŏngju. CAMKP, tr. by David R. McCann
At all times I see them. Harbach 1944. János Pilinszky. AF; HP; PoSu;
  WoPoe, tr. by Janos Csokits and Ted Hughes and Ted Hughes
At an English conference presentation. Dancing in the Dark. Demetrice A.
  Worley. SpirFl
At an Exhibition of Historical Paintings, Hobart. Vivian Smith. NOBAu
At an Island Farm. Brad Leithauser. PoA 2002
At anchor in Hampton Roads we lay. Cumberland, The. Henry Wadsworth
  Longfellow. CBCWP; PCW
At Annika's Place. Siv Widerberg. NTCP, tr. by Verne Moberg
At any turn. East Song. Alvaro Mutis. TCLAP, tr. by Sophie Cabot Black
  and Maria Negroni
At Apollinaire's Grave. Allen Ginsberg. BB
At April. Angelina Weld Grimké. GT
At Aspen Pavilion there are marvellous bamboos. Flute, The. Hsiao Yen [or
  Emperor Wu of Liang]. CCL1, tr. by Anne Birrell
At Asuka, the river of birds in flight. Mourning Princess Asuka. Kakinomoto
  no Hitomaro. WoPoe, tr. by Helen Craig McCullough
At Auke Bay the whales dance. Sheila Nickerson. GifTon
At Autumn Cove, so many white monkeys. Autumn Cove. Li Po.
  ColAnChi, tr. by Burton Watson
At Baia. "H. D." APT-1; ColAP; PoBW
At Barstow. Charles Tomlinson. NoAM
At behest of usura. (LL) Ezra Pound. APT-1; ColAP; HarvBoo; NAAL-5;
  NAAPv.2; NAMCP V.1; NoP-5; OxBoAm Fr. Cantos.
At Betharram. Robert Hedin. GifTon
At Bon Odori. James Masao Mitsui. OpBo
At Branwen's Grave. Dudley G. Davies. AngWePo
At break of dawn. W. H. Auden. CAGL Fr. Three Posthumous Poems.
At break of day from frightful dreams. Gottfried August Bürger. See At break
  of day, with frightful dreams.
At break of day my heart is still unquiet. Summoning the Recluse. Lu Chi.
  CCL1, tr. by John Frodsham
At break of day, with frightful dreams. Lenora. Gottfried August Bürger.
  NPBRoP, tr. by William Taylor
  (At break of day from frightful dreams.) NOBRP
At Breakfast. Giovanna Pollarolo. TANSG, tr. by Marjorie Agosin
At breakfast mother sipped her buttermilk. Magic Curtain, The. Stanley
  Kunitz. NAMCP V.1
At breakfast, my mother has a list of things. Her List. Sharon Olds.
  BodElec
At breakfast they are sober, subdued. Grenoble Café. Jean Garrigue. APT-2;
  OxBoAm
At Candlemas. Charles Causley. OBCP
At Carmel Highlands. Janet Lewis. PoA 2002
  (Carmel Highlands.) CalPo
At Casa Grande, only the names. Dry Rivers—Arizona. Ramona Wilson.
  ReEnLa
At Casterbridge Fair. Thomas Hardy.
  Former Beauties. NoAM; OBMV
At Castle Boterel. Thomas Hardy. NPeEn; OxAEP-2; OxBEV
At certain times, this could be the Twelve Nights of Haydn, our husbands.
  Pandora's Box. Saul Kirsch. PFTM-2, tr. by Wayne Kvam
At Chadwicks Bar and Grill. Lance Henson. HATNAP
At Chancellorsville. Andrew Hudgins. CBCWP

At Ch'ang-ku, Reading: To Show to My Man Pa. Li Ho. ColAnChi, *tr. by* Burton Watson

At Ch'ang-men Palace. Li Po. CrYelRi, *tr. by* Sam Hamill

At Ch'ang-men, the grass is green. To the Tune: In the Hills. Hsueh Chao-yun. CrYelRi, *tr. by* Sam Hamill

At Chien-nan, sudden news of retaking Chi-pei. Hearing of Imperial Forces Retaking Ho-Nan and Ho-Pei. Tu Fu [*or* Du Fu]. ChinPo, *tr. by* Ye Weilian [*or* Yeh Wei-lien *or* Wai-lim Yip]

At childhood's end, the houses petered out. Little Red-Cap. Carol Ann Duffy. MoWP; NeBrP; NoP-5

At Chonymyung Temple. Daegak Euchon. BecRai, *tr. by* Kim Daljin, Kim Won-Chung and Christopher Merrill

At Christmas. Emmanuel Hocquard. *tr. by* Rosmarie Waldrop
   1. OnScMo; YaTCFP, *tr. by* Rosmarie Waldrop
   2. OnScMo; YaTCFP, *tr. by* Rosmarie Waldrop
   3. OnScMo; YaTCFP, *tr. by* Rosmarie Waldrop
   25. OnScMo; YaTCFP, *tr. by* Rosmarie Waldrop

At Christmas, Cyrille brought the wolves into the. Emmanuel Hocquard. OnScMo; YaTCFP *Fr.* At Christmas.

At Christmas, when old friends are meeting. Good Will to Men—Christmas Greetings in Six Languages. Dorothy Brown Thompson. OBCP

At Christmas-Tide. Henrietta Cordelia Ray. CBWP-3

At Chuzhou on the Western Stream. Wei Ying-wu. CCL1, *tr. by* Witter Bynner

At Cockcrow. Lizette Woodworth Reese. SacPr

At confident moments, thinking on Death. Awe. Bob Kaufman. OxAAAP

At Cooloolah. Judith Wright. BMAP; BrAP; HarvBoo

At counters where I eat my lunch. Marble-Top. Elwyn Brooks White. AmWit

At court I met it, in clothes brave enough. On Something, that Walks Somewhere. Ben Jonson. BASC; NAEL-6v1; NAEL-7v1

At Cove at our camp in the open canyon. At Cove on the Crooked River. William Stafford. WaAnP

At Cow's Creek. Night Morring at Cow's Creek: I Think of the Old Man. Li Po. CCL1, *tr. by* C. H. Kwock and Vincent McHugh

At Daedun Temple. Jungkwan Ilson. BecRai, *tr. by* Kim Daljin, Kim Won-Chung and Christopher Merrill

At dangerous places. Three-Step Waterfall. Muso Soseki. EaWin, *tr. by* W. S. Merwin

At Darien Bridge. James Dickey. InGu; LPSFW

At dark, when the waves leapt. Water Man, The. Mary Dalton. OpeFie

At dawn. Acquaintances. Alvaro Cardona-Hine. ICANM

At Dawn. Michael Patrick Hearn. CA

At dawn a knot of sea-lions lies off the shore. Animals. Robinson Jeffers. APT-1

At dawn, falling asleep on the freeway. Fault, The. Carol Muske-Dukes. GeoHom

At dawn four-footed, at midday erect. Oedipus and the Riddle. Jorge Luis Borges. WoPoe, *tr. by* John Hollander

At dawn I rise to water. Episodes with unusables. Arthur Nortje. TSAP

At dawn I set out from the sunlit cliffs. On My Way from South Mountain to North Mountain, I Glance at the Scenery from the Lake. Hsieh Ling-yün. ColAnChi, *tr. by* Kang-i Sun Chang

At dawn I sighed to see my hairs fall. On his Baldness. Po Chü-i. CCL1, *tr. by* Arthur Waley

At dawn I took leave of the White Emperor. Early Departure from White Emperor Fortress. Li Po. CCL1, *tr. by* Elling O. Eide

At dawn / on the window sill. Poem on My Son's Birthday. Jim Carroll. AHA

At dawn she unmasked. Masquerading. May Probyn. NPeEn; VWP

At dawn slowly. Love Cycle. Chinua Achebe. PML

At dawn the dove croons. California Spring. Charles Wright. ColAP

At dawn, the liquid clatter of rain. Rented House in Maine, The. William Matthews. PfSP

At dawn the panther of the heavens peers over the edge of the world. Insomnia and the Seven Steps to Grace. Joy Harjo. NAMCP V.2

At dawn the ridge emerges massed and dun. Attack. Siegfried Sassoon. MoBrPo

At Dawn the Virgin Is Born. Félix Lope de Vega Carpio. SpanPo, *tr. by* W. S. Merwin

At dawn they came for you. Requiem. Anna Andreyevna Akhmatova. TCRusP, *tr. by* Daniel Weissbort

At dawn to-morrow. After Hilaire Belloc. Max Beerbohm. OBCoV

At dawn we buried Melanippus. At sunset. Callimachus. HePo, *tr. by* Barbara Hughes Fowler

At dawn with staff in hand I climbed the crags. On Climbing the Highest Peak of Stone Gate. Hsieh Ling-yün. CCL1, *tr. by* John Frodsham

At dawn, / with the shadows of solitude. Smoke upon Smoke. Mehmet Salihoǧlu. NaPG, *tr. by* Talat Sait Halman

At daybreak. Saitō Mokichi. CAoMJL1, *tr. by* Amy Vladek Heinrich

At Daybreak. Adam Zagajewski. VCWP, *tr. by* Renata Gorczynski, Benjamin Ivry and C. K. Williams

At daybreak I dropped in on a beauty. *Unknown.* NaPG, *tr. by* Talat Sait Halman

At daylight on St. John's, the day after Epiphany, we got our orders. March toward the Front, The. Odysseus Elytis. AF, *tr. by* Edmund Keeley and George Savidis

At day's end I look back and see the bridge that my breath has / abandoned. Enough Horses. Alvaro Cardona-Hine. ICANM

At dead low water. Signs of an Organised Hand. Paul Grattan. NIrP

At departure time the family came. I Rejoice. Kofi Awoonor. BrAP

At dinner, she is hostess, I am host. George Meredith. NAEL-6v2; NAEL-7v2; NoP-5; NPeEn; WaAnP *Fr.* Modern Love.

At dinner we discuss marriage. Good Company. William Matthews. BodElec

At distance far approaching to the tomb. Philip Freneau. NAAL-3; TCAPo *Fr.* House of Night, The.

At Dragon Gate Mountain stands a turpentine tree. Seven Exhortations to Rise, The. Mei Sheng. CCL1, *tr. by* John A. Scott

At Dryhope lived a lady hair. Dowie Dens of Yarrow, The [Version from Blackwood's Magazine]. *Unknown.* IBB

At Dunbar, Castle or Arcade. Double Feature. Robert Earl Hayden. NoAM

At dusk. EMJL *Fr.* Mad Verse.

At dusk, everything blurs and softens. Riding Out at Evening. Linda McCarriston. BBASP; WaAnP

At dusk / from the island in the river. If the Owl Calls Again. John Haines. GifTon; HeIP-3

At dusk I sought lodging at Shih-hao village. Recruiting Officer of Shih-hao. Tu Fu [*or* Du Fu]. ColAnChi, *tr. by* Irving Y. Lo

At dusk the silence by the sea. About Time. Laurens Vancrevel. TuT, *tr. by* Greg Delanty

At dusk, the sun-bleached fence. Winter Fruit. Juan Delgado. TouFir

At dusk the window panes grew grey. Forgiveness. George Russell. IrLP; IrV

At dusk / they come back from their parched fields. Peasants Waiting for Rain. G. S. Sharat Chandra. PoA 2002

At dusk we listened too much to the rats' cry. Rubbish Tip, The. Donald Evans. BBMWP, *tr. by* Gillian Clarke

At dusk you appear, a school-girl still. Boris Leonidovich Pasternak. WoPoe *Fr.* Illness.

At early dawn I once had been. Dawning of the Day, The. Edward Walsh. IrLP

At early morn the old platation stirred. Albery Allson Whitman. NAAPv.1 *Fr.* Octoroon, The.

At Ease. Elinor Benedict. MAAN

At Egypt. Clark Coolidge.
   "I came here. I don't know you here." PmAP
   "Morning muezzin in orange and a mosquito." FTOS
   "New hunt / the morning bent, A." APSN

At eight I was brilliant with my body. Black Hair. Gary Soto. CAP-8; MoASP; UnSA

At eight, she stole a look at herself in the mirror. Without Title. Li Shang-yin. CCL1, *tr. by* James J. Y. Liu

At eight, we strung rope across Oregon. After the Separation, Dad Takes Me to the Dance for the Dead. Mira Chieko Shimabukuro. FiBr

At eight years old, his cancer running rampage. Candor. John Graham-Pole. BloBone

At Eighty. Edwin Morgan. PoCu

At either's feet a trusty squire. Sir Walter Scott. DiBP *Fr.* Marmion.

At eleven he carried maps in his head. England, His Love. Maurice Riordan. NIrP

At end of day. (LL) Roundelay: "On all that strand." Samuel Beckett. ModIr; OxBEV

At Eton with Orwell, at Oxford with Waugh. On Himself. Cyril Connolly. OBCoV

At Evening. Anthony Thwaite. OxBEV

At evening the autumnal forests drone. Grodek (Second Version). Georg Trakl. GTCP, *tr. by* Robert Firmage

At evening the complaint of the cuckoo. Summer. Georg Trakl. WED, *tr. by* Robert Bly

At evening the musk of falling snow reaches the earth. Child of the Earth. Don Domanski. Coast

At evening the woods of autumn are full of the sound. Grodek. Georg Trakl. WED, *tr. by* Robert Bly

At evening too the dazzled light. Joseph Gwyer. VerBaPo *Fr.* On a Procession with the Prince of Wales.

At evening when the lamp is lit. Land of Story-Books, The. Robert Louis Stevenson. ChAP; ITBLP; NePenScot

At Eventide. James Clarence Harvey. ArBi

At fifteen I joined the army.   At Fifteen I Joined the Army.   *Unknown*.   CCL1, *tr. by* Anne Birrell

At fifteen I went to war.   At Fifteen I Went to War.   *Unknown*.   ChinPo, *tr. by* Ye Weilian [*or* Yeh Wei-lien *or* Wai-lim Yip]

At fifteen I'd buy bottles.   White Port and Lemon Juice.   Yusef Komunyakaa.   ISC

At fifteen, shaving by then, I passed.   At the Rainbow.   Robert Vasquez.   GeoHom

At fifteen she belonged to the Princess of Pingyang.   Dance, The.   HSü Ling.   CCL1, *tr. by* Anne Birrell

At Fifty.   Vivian Shipley.   ExTi

At fifty a white-headed old man.   Flying from Trouble.   Tu Fu [*or* Du Fu].   CCL1, *tr. by* Florence Ayscough *and* Amy Lowell

At fingertip control.   Kites at the Washington Monument.   Greg Williamson.   NAPBL

At first a childhood, limitless and free.   Imaginary Career.   Rainer Maria Rilke.   BBASP, *tr. by* Stephen Mitchell

At first, as you know, the sky is incidental.   Cloud Painter.   Jane Flanders.   PoA 2002

At first, come back, I'd nothing else to do.   Another Lazarus.   Sally Roberts Jones.   TCAWP

At first, for the man and woman.   Two Trees.   Ellen Bryant Voigt.   CAP-8; InGu

At first from your verse.   To Dennis Brutus.   Kofi Awoonor.   HBAPE

At first glance the coast of islands.   Painting the Islands.   Michael Crummey.   Coast

At first he had felt the scrape of a little murmur, his own throat struggling.   Motion Pictures: 4.   Barbara Guest.   BodElec

At first he refused to deliver junk mail because it was stupid, all.   Appointed Rounds.   Louis Jenkins.   RaBo

At first he thought only of home, and Penelope.   Odysseus's Secret.   Stephen Dunn.   PML

At first I don't recognize him.   In Line at Pancho's Tacos.   Bill Mohr.   SUP

At first, I had no time for their half-built temples.   Manora.   Pimone Triplett.   NAPBL

At first I laughed to hide my nervousness.   Learning to Laugh.   Allison Joseph.   PasH

At first I lost it in your beard.   Poem for the Man Who Said Shit.   David Clewell.   OPRER

At first, I played the game as I was given to play the game.   Where I Stand with Regard to the Game.   Joe Wenderoth.   LegDan

At first I spent hours gazing at the black and white horse.   Only Yak in Batesville, Virginia, The.   Oni Buchanan.   IIR; LegDan

At first I thought I would feel.   Nothing Could Take Away the Bear-King's Image.   Ray A. Young Bear.   HATNAP

At first I thought there was a superfine.   Fleming Helphenstine.   Edwin Arlington Robinson.   OxBSo

At first / I was land.   Mother Ireland.   Eavan Boland.   PoA 2002

At first I was overly cautious, procedure being all-important.   Voyage, The.   Charles Wright.   MotU

At first in that place, at all times, above the earth.   *Unknown*.   APN-2 *Fr.* Walam Olum; or, Red Score [of the Lenâpé], The [*or* The Wallam Olum; The Red Score or Painted History of the Lenni Lenape].

At first it seemed a swaying field of flowers.   Archive Film Material.   Ruth Fainlight.   HP

At first it was a small cold palmful.   Feeding the Bat.   Hilary Llewellyn-Williams.   TCAWP

At first it was an imperceptible tremor of the skin.   Divorce, The.   Hans Magnus Enzensberger.   WoPoe, *tr. by* Herbert Graf

At first, it was only a trickle.   Dixit Insipiens.   Carolyn Kizer.   Vesp

At first light, you ride.   Winter Night Farewell.   Chia Tao.   CSKM, *tr. by* Mike O'Connor

At first my mother balked I already had.   Sea Monkeys, The.   Barbara J. Orton.   NeAmPo

At first nobody could bear the heat, like.   In Andrea's Garden.   Susan Hampton.   BMAP

At first not frail because she was younger. At first comprised.   **Fall for.** *Informal.* 1. To become infatuated with; fall suddenly in love with. 2. To be tricked or deceived by; be taken in by.   Amy Newman.   IAoNAP

At first purling of light.   Letter from McCarty's Farm.   Ellen Kort.   IPoFL

At First She Came to Me Pure.   Juan Ramón Jiménez.   RaW; WED, *tr. by* Robert Bly

At first she led them out onto the floor.   Dance, The.   Irene McKinney.   PBCAP

At first she refused to sing.   Bessie Smith at Roy Thomson Hall.   Michael Ondaatje.   MotU

At first she thought the lump in the road.   Red String.   Minnie Bruce Pratt.   WiU

At first silence, a gas or two, a wind unchallenged.   Birth of God (from an Early Photograph), The.   James Ragan.   Vesp

At first the angel was pefectly wingless.   That Cold Summer.   Nin Andrews.   BAP-97

At first the dead.   Elegy.   Henriqueta Lisboa.   TCLAP, *tr. by* Hélcio Veiga Costa

At first the meaning won't come out from hiding.   Subway.   Miranda Field.   LegDan

At first the pains crawl cautious in me.   Pain, The.   Jeni Couzyn.   HAWP

At first the sound had no meaning.   April 13, 1865.   David Berman.   LegDan

At first the surprise.   Dancing with God.   Stephen Dunn.   NIP-4

At first there was nothing. Then a closed space.   Endymion.   Thomas Kinsella.   PBCIP

At first, there's a thin, bright Rider.   Apocalypse Dub.   Dennis Scott.   WaCA

At first they look like any other birds.   Cardinals in a Shower at Union Square.   Stanley Plumly.   BodElec

At first those closest to you shot holes in you.   Asylum.   Breyten Breytenbach.   VCWP, *tr. by* Stephen Gray

At first we heard the jingling of her ornaments.   Egyptian Dancer at Shubra.   Bernard Spencer.   NoAM

At first we look like nomads plodding.   Curlers at Dusk.   David Roderick.   MoASP

At first we see the tiny leaves.   Strawberry, The.   Maggie Pogue Johnson.   CBWP-4

At first your daybed was a piece of board.   Mike's.   Agnes Walsh.   Coast

At Five.   Oktavi.   BtF

At five each day I watch the sun ignite.   Three Poems for Violin.   Barbara Nickel.   ACAMVP

At five in the afternoon.   Lament for Ignacio Sánchez Mejías.   Federico García Lorca.   OBVE, *tr. by* Arthur Lloyd

At five in the afternoon.   Federico García Lorca.   WoPoe *Fr.* Lament for Ignacio Sanchez Mejias.

At five in the afternoon.   Lament for Ignacio Sánchez Mejías.   Federico García Lorca.   NAWM-7v2, *tr. by* J. L. Gili and Stephen Spender

At five in the morning.   Conversation Through the Door, A.   Anna Swirszczynska [*or* Swir].   AF, *tr. by* Czeslaw Milosz

At five this morn, when Phoebus raised his head.   Tunbridge Wells.   John Wilmot, 2d Earl of Rochester.   OBSV

At Flores in the Azores Sir Richard Grenville lay.   Alfred Tennyson.   OBWP *Fr. Revenge*, The.

At Flowering-Brightness Monastery in Yung-Ch'ung District.   Po Chü-i.   NDACCP, *tr. by* David Hinton

At Fort Clark.   Carol Coffee Reposa.   TiP2

At Fortress Monroe, Virginia.   Dave Jeddie Smith.   CAP-8

At Forty.   A. K. Ramanujan.   VCWP

At Forty.   Yevgeny Aleksandrovich Yevtushenko.   RusPo, *tr. by* Robert Arthur Douglas Ford

At forty-one, I am uncertain of more things.   Waiting for the Results of a Pregnancy Test.   Maria Gillan.   BRtP

At forty-six I am still the baby.   Late Arrivals.   Sybil Kollar.   FFC

At 4:00 a.m. the two.   Allen Ginsberg.   WhBo

At four in the morning he wakes.   More a Man Has the More a Man Wants, The.   Paul Muldoon.   ModIr

At four o'clock / in the gun-metal blue dark.   Roosters.   Elizabeth Bishop.   APT-2; ChIV-2; NALW; NAMCP V.2; OxBoAm

At Fourth and Main in Liberal, Kansas, 1932.   William Stafford.   CAP-8

At Francis Allen's on the Christmas Eve.   Alfred Tennyson.   NAEL-6v2; NAEL-7v2 *Fr.* Morte d'Arthur.

At Frank 'n' Helen's.   Constance Urdang.   PBCAP

At Funchal.   Tomas Tranströmer.   MotU; WED, *tr. by* Robert Bly

At Galway Races.   William Butler Yeats.   WoPoe

At General Electric, Where They Eat Their / Young.   Robert Farr.   SpirFl

At Gen's Embarkation for Yuan China.   Muso Soseki.   EaWin, *tr. by* W. S. Merwin

At Gettysburg.   Linda Pastan.   CFP

At girls who wear glasses. (LL)   News Item.   Dorothy Parker.   AmWit; APT-1; NALW; NAMCP V.2; OxBoAm

At Gold Hill Monastery.   Su Tung-p'o.   NDACCP, *tr. by* Kenneth Rexroth

At Golgotha I stood alone.   Edwin John Ellis.   OBMV *Fr.* Himself.

At Graceland with a Six Year Old, 1985.   David Wojahn.   AllShUp; PBCAP *Fr.* Mystery Train: A Sequence.

At Grass.   Philip Larkin.   HarvBoo; NPeEn; OxBEV; WeW-3

At Guaracara Park.   Eric Roach.   WoPoe

At Gull Lake; August, 1810.   Duncan Campbell Scott.   BrAP

At Guthrie, Texas, snow-rimed afterthought.   Winter at the Intersection.   Chris Willerton.   TiP2

At half my age.   Tempus Fugit.   Richard Harteis.   OtW

At Half past Three, a single Bird.   Emily Dickinson.   APN-2; MoAmPo; NAWM-7v2

At half-past eight o'clock, booms, hencoops, spars.   Lord Byron.   NPBRoP; NPeEn *Fr.* Don Juan.

At hame it's hard to feel. (LL) Parley of Beasts. Hugh MacDiarmid. ChIV-1; MoBrPo; NAMCP V.1; NoAM; OBMV

At Hans Christian Andersen's Birthplace, Odense, Denmark. Maurice Lindsay. EdScPo

At Harper's Ferry Just before the Attack. Edward W. Williams. CBCWP

At Heaven's Border, the autumn clouds are thin. After Rain. Tu Fu [or Du Fu]. CrYelRi, tr. by Sam Hamill

At Henry's bier let some thing fall out well. John Berryman. CAP-8; EMP; NoP-4; NoP-5 Fr. Dream Songs.

At her departure his disdain return'd. Homer. OBVE Fr. Iliad, The.

At Her Feet. Violet Fane. PoBW

At her from every stranger's hand. (LL) Palm Reader, The. Nicholas Christopher. NoP-4; NoP-5

At her last maquero's / Adulteries. (LL) Ezra Pound. MoAmPo; NAAPv.2 Fr. Hugh Selwyn Mauberley (Life and Contacts).

At his cramped desk. Star-Fix. Marilyn Nelson Waniek. ESEAA; LTA

At his desk, the boy. Cryptographiku No. 1. Bob Grumman. AnSo

At His Execution. Rudyard Kipling. ChIV-2

At His Father's Grave. John Ormond. OBWVE

At his request, after death, his brain was removed. Walt Whitman's Brain Dropped on Laboratory Floor. Thomas Lux. ViWalt

At Home. John Quarles. SacPr

At Home. Christina Georgina Rossetti. VWP

At Home. Wang An-shih. CrYelRi, tr. by Sam Hamill

At home, abroad, and everywhere. (LL) Another. Anne Bradstreet. EMWP; LW; NAAL-3

At home at Annika's place. At Annika's Place. Siv Widerberg. NTCP, tr. by Verne Moberg

At Home from Church. Sarah Orne Jewett. APN-2

At home I have a blue piano. My Blue Piano. Else Lasker-Schüler. PoCho, tr. by Eavan Boland

At home I have had to live as an alien. Wales Re-visited. Harry Guest. TCAWP

At home, in my flannel gown, like a bear to its floe. 90 North. Randall Jarrell. HarvBoo; NAMCP V.2; NoAM; NoP-5; PtR; StAl; VCAP

At Home in the Summer Mountains. Yu Xuanji. WPoS, tr. by Jane Hirshfield

At home my aged mother. Should I Earn My Daily Bread, or Should I Write a Poem? Bishwabimohan Shreshtha. PML, tr. by Michael James Hutt

At home the sea is in the town. Sea Eats the Land at Home, The. Kofi Awoonor. EmeKit

At home we pray every morning, we. Gwendolyn Brooks. OxWW Fr. Ulysses.

At Homecoming we cheered for game's-end. Regardless of the Final Score. Debra Nystrom. LiTh

At Honey Street in Ostrova. Jerome Rothenberg. AmWaPo; PFTM-2 Fr. Khurbn.

At Hongbub Temple. Daegak Euchon. BecRai, tr. by Kim Daljin, Kim Won-Chung and Christopher Merrill

At Hu-k'ou, Mourning for Kao Po-tsu. Ching An. CSKM, tr. by Jerome P. Seaton

At I-Chou, Climbing the Tower of Lung-Hsing Temple to View the High Northern Mountains. Chia Tao. CSKM, tr. by Mike O'Connor

At Iku's Embarkation for Yuan China. Muso Soseki. EaWin, tr. by W. S. Merwin

At instants I thought I merged with a deeper reality like a river the sea. At Instants I Thought. Jacques Dupin. YaTCFP, tr. by Stephen Romer

At intervals, the. Node. Imamu Amiri Baraka. EGAG

At Ithaca. "H. D." ColAP

At its bend the river thrashes. Riverbend. Marin Georgiev. CSCBP, tr. by Georgi Belev and Lisa Sapinkopf

At its own stable door. (LL) I like to see it lap the Miles. Emily Dickinson. APN-2; BrAP; GM; MoAmPo; NAAL-3; NAMCP V.1; NAWM-7v2; NoAM; NoP-4; NoP-5; OxBoAm; SoSe-8; TFi

At Jemez, at the crèche, we go to pray. Jemez Pueblo: December 26. Patricia Smith. ICANM

At Jhong-Jhou Train Station. G. Timothy Gordon. ArBi

At Kan's Embarkation for Yuan China. Muso Soseki. EaWin, tr. by W. S. Merwin

At Kenneth Rexroth's. Lawrence Ferlinghetti. WhBo

At Kino Viejo, Mexico. Alberto A. Ríos. NoAM

At Kisheneff two wicked men. Russia's Resentment. Lizelia Augusta Jenkins Moorer. CBWP-3

At Lac en Coeur. Louis Dudek. NLPA

At Lake Yi. Wang Wei. CrYelRi, tr. by Sam Hamill

At Lansdowne Bridge. Arthur Nortje. HBAPE; TSAP

At Last. John Montague. PBCIP Fr. Dead Kingdom, The.

At Last. Elizabeth Siddal. VWP

At last, at last the night. Soft Time of the Year, The. Hayden Carruth. PoCoUp

At last, by chance and guardian fancy led. Philip Freneau. NAAL-3; TCAPo Fr. House of Night, The.

At last, dearest Louisa, I take up my pen to address you. Arthur Hugh Clough. NoP-5 Fr. Amours de Voyage.

At last earnest sternness is transformed to sweet. Hatred Surely Does Not Kiss. Kaspar Stieler. GePo, tr. by George C. Schoolfield

At last free. Sumangalamata. WPoS

At last he is quiet; his harsh words. Smile for Daddy. Elizabeth Bartlett. Prnts

At last here is freedom for my poor, bedazzled head. In Which He Rejoices Over Having Discarded Love. Bálint Balassi. IQMS, tr. by Joseph Leftwich

At last I have a way to understand. Rāmprasād Sen. SinGod, tr. by Rachel Fell McDermott

At last I have found myself. (LL) I Return to the Place I Was Born. T'ao Ch'ien. NDACCP; WaAnP, tr. by Kenneth Rexroth

At last I'm taking off this coat. Honour Killing. Imtiaz Dharker. BeAl

At last it came into her mind, the answer. Precipice, The. Judith Wright. BMAP

At last I've broken Unmon's barrier! Daito. ZenPo, tr. by Takashi Ikemoto and Lucien Stryk

At last shee cals to mind where hangs a peece. William Shakespeare. PBRV

At last, snow, flocked. Epiphany. Martha Collins. Vesp

At last; so this is you, my dear! Christopher Found. Amy Levy. ViWPN

At last the secret is out, as it always must come in the end. At Last the Secret Is Out. W. H. Auden. GoPo

At last the silver birches look like Frost. Birches, Revisited: October. Ira Sadoff. PfSP

At Last the Women are Moving. Genevieve Taggard. BeAl

At last there came. Indian Summer. Hamlin Garland. APN-2

At last these two stout erles did meet. Unknown. FaBoWar Fr. Battle of Otterbourne, The.

At last they stand together, flushed. Curtain Call. William Trowbridge. SUP

At last Wayman gets the girl into bed. Wayman in Love. Tom Wayman. NIL-7; NIP-4

At last we killed the roaches. Lucille Clifton. CAP-8; PtR

At last you yielded up the album, which. Lines on a Young Lady's Photograph Album. Philip Larkin. BrAP

At last you'll know why you came. See Willow. James Bertolino. PoCoUp

At Least. Raymond Carver. GoPo

At least 100 seabirds attended my grandmother's funeral. My Grandmother's Funeral. Thomas Lux. WeW-3

At least I'll keep. (LL) Hiding Place. Richard Armour. NIL-7; NIP-4

At least quietly wrote something down. (LL) Passengers. Billy Collins. GoPo; OtW; PLBUT

At least that's. Vermont Has a High Suicide Rate. Richard Donze. BloBone

At least the mechanics are honest. Ode to My Car. Gig Ryan. BMAP

At least we can meet at the Indian Market. Promise! Mafika Pascal Gwala. NAfrP

At least we shall have descendants. (LL) To Pi Ssu Yao. Tu Fu [or Du Fu]. BLT; NDACCP, tr. by Kenneth Rexroth

At least we shall have roses, laughed my companion. Fortune. Mary Ursula Bethell. PoBW

At least you left me the green. Burden Lifters, The. Michael Waters. SwNoth

At least—to pray—is left—is left. Emily Dickinson. APN-2; NCAP; TCAPo

At length by so much importunity pressed [or press'd]. Lover, The; a Ballad. Lady Mary Wortley Montagu. NAEL-6v1; NAEL-7v1; NoP-4; NoP-5; OxBEV; PEW

At length I land upon the Strophades. Virgil. OWoS Fr. Aeneid (Dryden translation).

At length, my Lord, I have the bliss. Thomas Moore. OBSV Fr. Fudge Family in Paris, The.

At length the Muse her destin'd task resumes. Christopher Smart. Fr. Hop-Garden, The.

At length the Steam-Chiefs with replenish'd force. Thomas Baker. STuOW Fr. Steam Engine; or, The Power of the Flame, The.

At length their long kiss severed, with sweet smart. Dante Gabriel Rossetti. NAEL-6v2; NAEL-7v2 Fr. House of Life, The.

At length with jostling, elbowing, and the aid. Lord Byron. OBSV Fr. Vision of Judgment, The.

At Les Deux Magots. Maura Dooley. IrLP; LW

At Li's Mountain Hermitage. Wang Wei. CrYelRi, tr. by Sam Hamill

At London, Thames is a broad stream. Disaster to Steamer Victoria at London. James McIntyre. VerBaPo

At Long Last Love. Cole Porter. ReLy

At longsl last we came to the. Nathaniel Mackey. WoBe Fr. Song of the Andoumboulou.

At Lord's. Francis Thompson. OPOU

At low tide like this how sheer the water is. Bight, The. Elizabeth Bishop. APT-2; EmeKit; PoetW; VCAP

At Luca Signorelli's Resurrection of the Body. Jorie Graham. NAMCP V.2; NoP-5

At lunchtime I bought a huge orange. Orange, The. Wendy Cope. GoPo

At Lushan Temple. Ching An. CSKM, tr. by Jerome P. Seaton

At Maiden Castle in Dorset. Maiden Castle. Dorothy, Duchess of Wellington Wellesley. PoBW

At Maruža's. Imants Ziedonis. WoPoe, tr. by Barry Callaghan

At Mass. Unknown. IrLP, tr. by Robin Flower

At Melville's Tomb. Hart Crane. APT-2; HarvBoo; InoFa; MoAmPo; NAAL-5; NAMCP V.1; NoAM; NoP-4; NoP-5; OxBoAm; PoA 2002; WaAnP

At me—The Sea withdrew. (LL) By the Sea. Emily Dickinson. APN-2; NAAL-3; WeW-3

At midnight / An owl flies from my breast. Wailing. Abd al-Rahim Salih al-Rahim. IrPoTo, tr. by Saadi A. Simawe and Daniel Weissbort

At midnight, coming home, I passed a tiger. Coming Home Late at Night. Tu Fu [or Du Fu]. BLT

At midnight I walk over the bailey-bridge. Catching My Breath. Robert Minhinnick. TCAWP

At midnight I would hear my father rise. Lament at Night. H. Leivick. AWTN, tr. by Marie Syrkin

At midnight, in a cold bed, I cannot sleep. Cold Night. Po Chü-i. CrYelRi, tr. by Sam Hamill

At midnight, in his guarded tent. Fitz-Greene Halleck. APN-1 Fr. Marco Bozzaris.

At midnight, in the month of June. Sleeper, The. Edgar Allan Poe. BrAP; NAAL-3; NCAP

At midnight the memory of you is the only visitor. Unknown. SLW, tr. by Marjolijn De Jager, Sayd Bahodin Majrouh and André Velter

At midnight the teacher lectures on his throne. Reflections at Lake Louise. Allen Ginsberg. BBASP; WaAnP

At midnight they roused us. In the distance we heard. City of Anguish. Edwin Rolfe. AmWaPo

At midnight when the world's at rest. Unknown. SLW, tr. by Marjolijn De Jager, Sayd Bahodin Majrouh and André Velter

At midnight, your face in a dream brings a sigh. My Love's Dark Place Is Fragrant Like Narcissus. Ikkyu Sojun. ErotSp, tr. by Sam Hamill

At Midsummer. Norman Dubie. NoAM

At midsummer before dawn an orange light returns to the mountains. How We Are Spared. W. S. Merwin. CAP-8

At Moments Like This, I Always Blush. Ch'ôn Yanghûi. EcSo, tr. by Aimee N. Kwon

At morning the jackdaws creak and chatter. Vanitas. James Frank Dobie. TiP2

At morning's call. Welcoming the Dawn. Oliver Wendell Holmes. DiBP

At Mornington. Gwen Harwood. GPTC

At Moss Beach. Kim Addonizio. GeoHom

At Mother Teresa's. Naomi Shihab Nye. OPRER

At Mount Rushmore I look up into one. Loneliness of Lincoln, The. X. J. Kennedy. HHAm

At Mount Ssu-ming. Facing Snow and Writing What My Heart Embraces. Ching An. CSKM, tr. by Jerome P. Seaton

At Munsoo Temple. Daegam Tanyon. BecRai, tr. by Kim Daljin, Kim Won-Chung and Christopher Merrill

At my age to go ten thousand miles. Old and Traveling. Yuan Mei. GifTon, tr. by Jerome P. Seaton

At my dear Land of Story-Books. (LL) Land of Story-Books, The. Robert Louis Stevenson. ChAP; ITBLP; NePenScot

At My Doorstep. Ekaterina Iosifova. CSCBP, tr. by Georgi Belev and Lisa Sapinkopf

At My Father's Grave. Hugh MacDiarmid. HarvBoo; InoFa; NePenScot

At My Father's House. Nancy Travis. ISC

At My Mother's Funeral. Sabok. BecRai, tr. by Kim Daljin, Kim Won-Chung and Christopher Merrill

At My Study. Yun Söndo. CATKP, tr. by Chi-gyu Kim [or Kim Chonggil]

At my uncle's. Visitors. Unknown. SonAtl, tr. by Alan Brierly

At my wedding he came over the grass. Yew Berries. Ruth Padel. MFPA

At my windows no one has danced. At My Windows. Valentine Penrose. YaTCFP, tr. by Mary Ann Caws and Jean-Pierre Cauvin

At my words, "Christ was a man." Ishikawa Takuboku. PoCho, tr. by Sanford Goldstein and Seishi Shinoda

1. at nagasaki. Lucille Clifton. ESEAA

At Nature's Shrine. Henrietta Cordelia Ray. CBWP-3

At Navajo Monument Valley Tribal School (from the Photograph by Skeet Mcauley). Sherman Alexie. P180

At new moon on the crater / This summer. (LL) Burning Island. Gary Snyder. APSN; VCAP

At Night. Dennis Brutus. VCWP

At Night. Frances Darwin Cornford. MoBrPo

At Night. Jane Hirshfield. BodElec

At Night. Alice Thompson Meynell. OxAEP-2

At night. Defensive Driving. Giovanni Singleton. BtF

At Night. Sara Teasdale. APT-1

At night, a man is sitting at his desk in pain. Snapshot. Steve Kowit. PML

At night, a two year's widow. Open the Door. Miriam Sagan. ICANM

At night along this coast. At Moss Beach. Kim Addonizio. GeoHom

At night and in the wind and the rain. Refugees. Chaim Grade. HP, tr. by Marc Kaminsky

At night bare foot on flowers! Yvor Winters. NAAPv.2 Fr. Magpie's Shadow, The.

At night, beside you, awaken alone. (LL) Gin. David St. John. AmAlph; CAP-8

At night, by the fire. Domination of Black. Wallace Stevens. APT-1; MoAmPo; NAMCP V.1; OWoS; OxBoAm; TCAPo

At night Chinamen jump. Poem. Frank O'Hara. NAMCP V.2; NoAM; PmAP

At night, circling weightless, we dreamed of roses. Geoffrey Lehmann. BMAP Fr. Roses.

At night, coolness like water lapping. Ansel Talvikki. YaYoPo Fr. In Fragments, In Streams.

At night he lay awake and listened to. God Body. Beckian Fritz Goldberg. AmAlph

At night I dreamt I was back in Chang'an. Dreaming that I Went with Li and Yu to Visit Yuan Zhen. Po Chü-i. CCL1, tr. by Arthur Waley

At night, in my dream, I stoutly climbed a mountain. Dream of Mountaineering, A. Po Chü-i. BLT; CCL1, tr. by Arthur Waley

At night in rainless times small animals. Road Kill. Netta Gillespie. AmZen

At night, in the fish-light of the moon, the dead wear our white shirt. Homage to Paul Cézanne. Charles Wright. EMP; NAMCP V.2; VCAP

At night, in the winter, we'd drive. Getaway Car. Leanne O'Sullivan. NIrP

At night in Vinton County a Satanic cult. Offering. Debra Allbery. PBCAP

At Night Keep Still. Russell Atkins. EGAG

At night make me one with the darkness. Wendell Berry. UpMys Fr. Prayers and Sayings of the Mad Farmer.

At night / my mother opened a chest and took out. White Wedding Slippers. Anna Swirszczynska [or Swir]. AF, tr. by Czeslaw Milosz

At night on my bed I longed for. Bible, O.T. WPoS Fr. Song of Solomon.

At night on the radiant Rialto. Lilatu Laili. Amin Al-Rihani. NAAPv.2

At Night: "Our tree's shadow is green at night." Boris Hristov. CSCBP, tr. by Georgi Belev and Lisa Sapinkopf

At night packed in darkness and down. Winter Mirror II. Judith Mok. TuT, tr. by Michael O'Loughlin

At night she is. Machine, The. Kalman Hayzler. Prolet, tr. by Amelia Glaser

At night, sometimes, when I cannot sleep. John Montague. ModIr; NPeEn Fr. Chosen Light, A.

At night, sometimes, when I cannot sleep. Chosen Light, A. John Montague.

At night the child takes down. Smoke. Susan Mitchell. EmeKit

At night the day is constantly woken up. Work. Andrei Codrescu. PmAP

At night the dead come down to the river to drink. Dead, The. Susan Mitchell. P180

At night the fighter planes circle. Circling. Shelley Stenhouse. PA9/11

At night the honey-fungus takes over. Sodium Light. Fergus Allen. NIrP

At night the mountains look like huge. Moving Again. William Matthews. CAP-8

At night the suburban boulevards are full of snow; the bandits are. War. Max Jacob. AF, tr. by Michael Brownstein

At night the verandah is dark, the beds too numerous. Unknown. SLW, tr. by Marjolijn De Jager, Sayd Bahodin Majrouh and André Velter

At night they cross the border. Wreckers, The. Rafael Zepeda. SUP

At night what things will stalk abroad. Lux in Tenebris. Katharine Tynan Hinkson. SacPr

At night, when Beacon Hill. Green and Red, Verde y Rojo. Martín Espada. PueRic

At night, / with my wife. When the Leather Is a Whip. Martín Espada. LiTh

At Night: "Worries creep like insects." Stephanie Goldstein. PfS

At night / yes night. Loneliness. Amjad Nasir. BBASP, tr. by Charles Doria and May Jayyusi

At night you came and took my hand and we wandered together in my dream. Dreaming of Yuan Zhen. Po Chü-i. CCL1, tr. by Arthur Waley

At Nightfall, 1/27/91. Pinhas Sadeh. NRoS, tr. by Esther Raizen

At nightfall, in this place. Cilmeri. Gerallt Lloyd Owen. BBMWP, tr. by Joseph P. Clancy

At nightfall the sky was various. Two Lines from Paul Celan. Mark Halperin. GifTon

At nightfall, when the inquisitive elves in elf-pants. Lunatic of Lindley Meadow, The. August Kleinzahler. PmAP

At nine I knew what Jesus would do. Uncle. Julia Kasdorf. PBCAP

At nine year he is full bad. (LL) Properties of a Good Greyhound, The. Dame Juliana Berners. DiBP; WoPoe, *tr. by* Seamus Heaney

At ninety, the piano plays him. Sonata. Mark Cox. PoDa

At Ni-Yang Inn. Chia Tao. CSKM, *tr. by* Mike O'Connor

At noon I must have been conceived. Mikhail Alekseievich Kuzmin. CAGL, *tr. by* Michael Green

At noon, in the dead centre of a faith. Desertmartin. Tom Paulin. BeAl; ModIr; NPeEn; PBCIP; PNI

At noon in the desert a panting lizard. At the Bomb Testing Site. William Stafford. AtGh; NAMCP V.2; NIL-7; NIP-4; NoAM; OBWP; PoAgWa; WaAnP

At noon sneaky. Cold Lunch. William Corbett. PmAP

At noon they talk of evening and at evening. Cypresses. Robert Francis. APT-2

At Nootka Sound. Susan Musgrave. BrAP

At North Farm. John Ashbery. ColAP; HarvBoo; NAMCP V.2; OxBoAm; WaAnP

At old St. Ann's at Westcock, the church. John Thompson. Douglas Lochhead. Coast

At on of Apollonaire's Wednesdays I saw, sitting on the big divan. Greetings, Blaise Cendrars. Sonia Delaunay. CuPo

At once whatever happened starts receding. Whatever Happened? Philip Larkin. OxBSo

At one glance. Mihri Hatun. NaPG, *tr. by* Talat Sait Halman

At 102, Romance Comes Once a Year. Colleen J. McElroy. OxAAAP

At 100 Mile House the cowboys ride in rolling. Cariboo Horses, The. Alfred Wellington Purdy. BrAP; HeIP-4

At one point, you have to sift the sand to even glimpse. Minor Figure. Mary Ruefle. ExTi

At one time I lived. Visiting My Old Hut in Late Spring. Muso Soseki. EaWin, *tr. by* W. S. Merwin

At one time when life was real, your soul was one with my soul. Jelaluddin Rumi. NaPG, *tr. by* Talat Sait Halman

At one time your touches were clothing enough. Woods, The. Louise Erdrich. WaAnP

At Our Backs. Robert A. Fink. TiP2

At our gate he groaneth, groaneth. At Our Golden Gate. Joaquin Miller. APN-2

At Our Golden Gate. Joaquin Miller. APN-2

At our house there live. Surrender. William Larsen. WhBo

At our school sexes were colour-coded. Masculinity. Robert Crawford. PML

At Parting. Duo Duo. AF, *tr. by* Gregory Lee *and* John Cayley

At Parting. Edith Nesbit. OBGa

At Parting. Anne Ridler. FaBoWar; LW

At Parting. Wang Wei. CCL1, *tr. by* Witter Bynner

At Parting: "False love, since thou and I must sever." Robin Ernest William Flower. IrLP

At Pegasus. Terrance Hayes. AmPoNex

At Pemigewasset House. Tontine. Scott Hightower. PA9/11

At Pens-hurst. Edmund Waller. PBRV

At Piccadilly Circus. Vivian de Sola Pinto. OBMV

At Pleasure Bay. Robert Pinsky. NAAL-5

At Polwart on the Green. Polwart on the Green. Allan Ramsay. NPeEn; OxBEV

At prayer / Bead-swinging. Issa. ZenPo, *tr. by* Takashi Ikemoto and Lucien Stryk

At Present I Am Working as a Security Guard. Edison Dupree. OPRER

At Provincetown. Daniel Gerard Hoffman. YaYoPo

At Puri, the crows. Taste for Tomorrow. Jayanta Mahapatra. VCWP

At Queensferry. W. E. Henley. OxBSo

At Quincey's moat the squandering village ends. Almswomen. Edmund Charles Blunden. OBMV

At Rest in the Blast. Marianne Moore. MoAmPo

At Revolution's End. Lionel Abrahams. TSAP

At River's Head, birds swarm through willow flowers. Drinking with Elder Cheng the Eighth at Crooked River. Tu Fu [*or* Du Fu]. CrYelRi, *tr. by* Sam Hamill

At road's end I see power. Facades. Tomas Tranströmer. WoBe, *tr. by* Robin Fulton

At Rose's Range. R. S. Gwynn. TiP2

At St. Patrick's Day, and the Saint's death, plus 1,500 and 40 years, by the tradition. [Record]. Kenneth Irby. BAP-04

At Sainte-Marguerite. Trumbull Stickney. APN-2; TCAPo

At San Luis, on Good Friday. San Luis, New Mexico. Patricia Smith. ICANM

At Saxman, the totems slash down. Circle of Totems, The. Peggy Shumaker. PBCAP

At school I loved one picture's heavy greenness. Fosterling. Seamus Heaney. NoP-5

At school, I was a / squad-leader. I'd gotten enough votes. It meant. Each in a Place Apart. James McMichael.

At Sea. Richard Hovey. APN-2

At Seascale our shoes were full of sand. My Father's Shadow. Dorothy Nimmo. Prnts

At Seven a Son. Elaine Feinstein. HarvBoo

At seven I dreamed again and again. On Alabama Ave., Paterson, NJ, 1954. Rachel De Vries. UnSA

At seven you just nick it. Public Dinner, A. Thomas Hood. OBCoV

5. At Seventeen. Arthur Symons. OxBSo *Fr.* Violet.

At seventeen I should have asked boyfriends. Hunting. Janet Kauffman. ACAMVP

At seventeen I've come to read a poem. Twelve O'Clock. Carolyn Kizer. ExTi

At seventy miles an hour. Bull and Egret. Chinua Achebe. PFTM-2

At Seventy-Five: Rereading an Old Book. Hayden Carruth. TAPaP

At Shagger's funeral there wasn't much to say. At Shagger's Funeral. Bruce Dawe. NOBAu

At Shedd Aquarium. Robyn Schiff. LegDan

At sight of sparkling Bowls or beauteous Dames. Verses in Baretti's Commonplace Book. Samuel Johnson. OxAEP-1

At silo filling time the air was similarly wet. Silo Treading. Bruce Beaver. BMAP

At six a.m. and you will go to meet her. Your friend's arriving on the bus. Craig Arnold. BAP-04

At six A.M. the log cabins. Moose in the Morning, Northern Maine. Mona Van Duyn. ColAP

At six o'clock this morning. Four Poems in One. Anne Porter. GoPo

At six o'clock we were waiting for coffee. Miracle for Breakfast, A. Elizabeth Bishop. OxBoAm; PoA 2002

At Sixteen. Ann Darr. LW

At sixteen I was so vulnerable to every influence. At the Grave of My Guardian Angel: St. Louis Cemetery, New Orleans. Larry Levis. AmAlph

At sixteen, I worked after high school hours. Who Burns for the Perfection of Paper. Martín Espada. InvLad

At sixteen my mother had been a swimmer. Back to Back. Debra Kang Dean. NAPBL

At sixty Grandfather. Phone Booth at the Corner, The. Juan Delgado. TouFir

At slammed door and smoker's cough in the hall. (LL) Docker. Seamus Heaney. BrAP; HeIP-4

At South Fork Cemetery. Henry Taylor. LPSFW

At spring's end, I long for home. End to Spring, An. Li Ch'ing-chao. CrYelRi, *tr. by* Sam Hamill

At St. Sulpice. Erin Belieu. NAPBL

At start of spring I open a trench. Purification, A. Wendell Berry. TWF; UpMys

At stated .ic times. Composed in the Composing Room. Franklin Pierce Adams. NIL-7; NIP-4

At such a time, of year and day. Hill-Shade, The. William Barnes. OxBEV

At summer eve, when Heaven's ethereal bow. Thomas Campbell. *Fr.* Pleasures of Hope, The.

At Summer's End. Jean Janzen. GeoHom

At Summer's End. Charles Harper Webb. GeoHom

At summer's end, I come home to wilderness. Plenty. Naomi Feigelson Chase. PfS

At sun up I am up. Angel Butcher. Philip Levine. ColAP; WaAnP

At sunrise / on Kilimanjaro. Kilimanjaro Sunrise. Sŏ Chŏngju. CAMKP, *tr. by* David R. McCann

At Sunset. Henrietta Cordelia Ray. CBWP-3

At sunset from the top of the stair watching. Otranto. Barbara Guest. FTOS

At sunset I come out of the door. *Unknown.* ChinPo, *tr. by* Ye Weilian [*or* Yeh Wei-lien *or* Wai-lim Yip]

At Sunset I Strolled. *Unknown.* CCL1, *tr. by* John Frodsham

At sunset I strolled out of the front gate. At Sunset I Strolled. *Unknown.* CCL1, *tr. by* John Frodsham

At sun-up, inside. Snakeroot. J. L. Jacobs. AmPoNex

At Superstition mountain in the Sonoran desert. North America. Nanao Sakaki. WhBo

At Ta-an I Got Sick from Wine and Had to Lay Over for Half a Day. Governor Wang Invited Me to His Place Again. Lu Yu. ColAnChi, *tr. by* Burton Watson

At table I could not eat. Folded Wings. Pao Chao. CCL1, *tr. by* John Frodsham

At Tara today, in this awful hour. St. Patrick's Hymn Before Tara. James Clarence Mangan.

At ten A.M. the young housewife. Young Housewife, The. William Carlos Williams. APT-1; ColAP; HeIP-4; NAAL-5; NAAPv.2; NAMCP V.1; OxBoAm; WaAnP

At ten / before i knew. Objects of Desire. Monifa Atungaye Love. BtF

At ten I wanted fame. I had a comb. Behind Grandma's House. Gary Soto. UnSA

At Terezin. Teddy. INSAB

At that time Śāriputra danced for joy, then straightway rose and, joining his palms. Unknown. ColAnChi Fr. Lotus Sūtra.

At the age of empty spaces. How Do Your Eggs Want You (?). Pedro Juan Pietri. PueRic

At the Airport. Howard Nemerov. OtW

At the alder-darkened brink. Hamlen Brook. Richard Wilbur. HarvBoo; VCAP; WeW-3

At the Altar-Rail. Thomas Hardy. MoBrPo Fr. Satires of Circumstance in Fifteen Glimpses.

At the ancient pond. Basho. SoOfWa, tr. by Sam Hamill

At the ancient well. Buson. SoOfWa, tr. by Sam Hamill

At the antipodes of poetry, dark winter. Discovery of Thought, A. Wallace Stevens. APT-1

At the Ascension. Luís De León. SpanPo, tr. by James Edward Tobin

At the "Atlantic" Dinner, December 15, 1874. Oliver Wendell Holmes. OBCoV

At the Back of Progress . . . . Taslima Nasrin. VCWP

At the back of the bookshop a Karate expert. Enzensberger at 'Exiles'. John Tranter. BMAP

At the Back of the North Wind. George Macdonald.
"Where did you come from, baby dear?" ITBLP; WHSW

At the Ball Game. William Carlos Williams. BrAP; MoASP; NoAM

At the bank a week after the shooting. Ambivalent Nature of Healing, The. Ted Sexauer. WhBo

At the Barber Shop. Gentleman in the Barber Shop. S. Brandi Barnes. BtF

At the Beach. Elizabeth Alexander. FuFl

At the Beginning of Winter. Unknown. CCL1

At the beginning of winter a cold spirit comes. Unknown. CCL1

At the beginning / there was only. Traces. Beau Beausoleil. Eno

At the Black Edge. Ger Killeen. AmPoNex

At the blackboard I had missed. Zimmer's Head Thudding against the Blackboard. Paul Zimmer. PBCAP

At the Bomb Testing Site. William Stafford. AtGh; NAMCP V.2; NIL-7; NIP-4; NoAM; OBWP; PoAgWa; WaAnP

At the bottom of the ground a face emerging. Sickly Face at the Bottom of the Ground. Hagiwara Sakutaro. CAoMJL1, tr. by Hiroaki Sato

At the bottom of the sea. Me at the Bottom of the Sea. Alfonsina Storni. TCLAP, tr. by Andrew Rosing

At the bramble-end of the car lot, five wild turkeys. Turkeys in August. Gray Jacobik. UrbNat

At the break of dawn. Kakei. SoOfWa, tr. by Sam Hamill

At the brim, at the lip. Close. Robert Duncan. PmAP

At the British Museum. Richard Aldington. MoBrPo

At the British War Cemetery, Bayeux. Charles Causley. NAEL-6v2; NAEL-7v2; NoP-4; NoP-5; OBWP; PoWW

At the brookside I stroll. Tune: "The Dark Clouds of Ch'u" Visiting the Rainy Crag Alone. Hsin Ch'i-chi. ColAnChi, tr. by Jiaosheng Wang

At the burial of an epoch. Anna Andreyevna Akhmatova. FaBoWar; PoetW Fr. In 1940.

At the bus stop on the first frigid. Nobody's Hell. Douglas Goetsch. AmPoNex

At the Cafe Door. Constantine P. Cavafy. CAGL, tr. by Edmund Keeley and Philip Sherrard

At the Carnival. Anne Spencer. APT-1; NAAPv.2

At the Cascade. Henrietta Cordelia Ray. CBWP-3

At the Castle. Jerome Rothenberg. FTOS

At the Cave. Artur Miedzyrzecki. PoSu

At the Cavour. Arthur Symons. NPeEn

At the cemetery. Cemetery Gate. Georges Castera. OGAHCP, tr. by Boadiba and Jack Hirschman

At the cemetery, walnut grove plantation, south carolina, 1989. Lucille Clifton. CAP-8; LoL; NAMCP V.2

At the Center. Patricia Goedicke. PoDa

At the Center, Creator Hourglass. Eliza Kelley. RWB

At the Center of Injustice. Violeta Parra. TANSG, tr. by Karen Kerschen

At the center of the earth there is a mother. Our Mother. Susan Griffin. HW

At the city's heart stood the shrine to Dido's ghost. Catius As Conius Silius Italicus. RomPo Fr. Punica, The.

At the closing, he cut the final check. Conifer King, The. Michael Bugeja. UrbNat

At the Coast. Ray Ragosta. OnScMo

At the Commission. Ingrid de Kok. TSAP

At the Controls. Robert Vas Dias. OtW

At the Convent Gate. Charlotte Mew. VWP

At the Cookout. Charles Simic. PML

At the corner of Columbia Road & Bishop. To Be Held. Ron Schreiber. PrTe

At the corner of Rue des Fronforts and Main Street. Philosophy, A. Jean R. Désiré. OGAHCP, tr. by Boadiba and Jack Hirschman

At the corner of war and money. Bad Dream and the Friend. Gene Frumkin. ICANM

At the Crematorium, My Son Asks Why We're All Wearing Black. Mark Cox. NevBe

At the Crossroads. Thomas Kinsella. NoAM

At the Crossroads. Bill Knott. PBCAP

At the Crossroads. Mary Scott. ArBi

At the crosswalk. Office Depot Parking Lot. Del Ray Cross. FreRad

At the crucial moment she said yes. His hand in the back pocket. Widening, The. Carol Moldaw. NevBe

At the dark street corner. Guilt, Desire and Love. James Baldwin. CAGL

At the day camp years ago where we drove. Dawn. Betsy Sholl. LTA

At the dead of night by the side of the Sea. Sea-Side Cave, The. Alice Cary. APN-2; ColAP; NAAPv.1

At the Delicatessen Shop. Ernst Jandl. GTCP, tr. by Michael Hamburger

At the demolishing, this seat. Andrew Marvell. NOSC Fr. Upon Appleton House [To My Lord Fairfax].

At the Desk. Theodor Storm. WoPoe, tr. by Robert Bly

At the documentary level, a voice on tape. Topos. Jane Miller. GifTon

At the Door of Anticipation. Hala Mohammad. PoArWo, tr. by Cornelia Al-Khaled

At the Door of the Native Studies Director. Robert H. Davis. HATNAP

At the Draper's. Thomas Hardy. MoBrPo Fr. Satires of Circumstance in Fifteen Glimpses.

At the earliest ending of winter. Not Ideas about the Thing but the Thing Itself. Wallace Stevens. APT-1; OxBoAm; PFTM-2; SAmP; StAl

At the east where the black water lies stands the large corn. Corn Ceremony. Apache Oral Tradition. TCAPo

At the edge of all the ages. Song of Finis, The. Walter De la Mare. MoBrPo

At the edge of our woods. Building Walls. Todd Davis. ACAMVP; VisFro

At the edge of the forest. Ars Poetica. Primus St. John. TAPaP

At the Edge of the Great City. Oskar Loerke.
Down There. GTCP, tr. by Michael Hamburger
Envoi. GTCP, tr. by Michael Hamburger
Winter Evening, Berlin. GTCP, tr. by Michael Hamburger

At the edge of the Sahara. Call of the Fulani Maid. Kabura Zakama. NeNiPo

At the edge of town, daylilies the gold of old whiskey. Antichrist in Arkansas, The. T. R. Hummer. LPSFW

At the edge of your fingernail. Touch it. (LL) Touch It. Robert Mezey. CalPo; GeoHom

At the Egyptian Exhibit. Daniel Tobin. NAPBL

At the Electronic Frontier. Miguel Algarin. UnSA

At the End. Richard Ryan. PBCIP

At the end. (LL) Good Night, Willie Lee, I'll See You in the Morning. Alice Walker. InoFa; ISC; WeW-3

At the end a / "The Prisoner of Zenda." Prisoner of Zenda, The. Richard Wilbur. NBLV; OBCoV

At the end I remember it all. Only Death. Mary Doughtery Bartlett. ICANM

At the end of 1936 I reported to duty, a day-old baby in diapers. 1936–1986. Eitan Kalinski. NRoS, tr. by Esther Raizen

At the end of a crazy-moon night. Lal Ded. AWTN; WPoS, tr. by Coleman Barks

At the end of a freight train rolling away. Late Lights in Minnesota. Ted Kooser. BLT

At the end of a long-walled garden. Cottage Hospital, The. Sir John Betjeman. BrAP; InoFa; NAMCP V.1

At the end of a melancholy world. End of the World, The. João Cabral de Melo Neto. VCWP

At the end of a path, I built a thatch-roofed shack. Fire, Sixth Month, 408. T'ao Ch'ien. CrYelRi, tr. by Sam Hamill

At the end of delight, one. Limit. Diane Ward. FTOS

At the end of emotion and description there is a village. Which Religion Vouchsafes. Jane Miller. GifTon

At the end of every cigarette that burns there is of course. Eternity! Mary Ferrari. AHA

At the end of his act. Road Show. Geoff Page. BMAP

At the end of my suffering. Wild Iris, The. Louise Glück. ColAP; MoWP; NAMCP V.2; StAl

At the End of September. Sándor Petőfi. IQMS, tr. by Adam Makkai and Valerie Becker Makkai

At the End of Spring. Po Chü-i. CCL1, *tr.* by Arthur Waley

At the end of the battle. César Vallejo. TCLAP *Fr.* Spain, Take [Away] This Cup from Me [España, Aparta de Mí Este Cáliz].

At the end of the battle. César Vallejo. StAl *Fr.* Spain, Take Away This Cup from Me [España, Aparta de Mí Este Cáliz].

At the end of the first decade of the century, in first grade, Grandin, six years of age. First Grade. Jean Follain. MotU, *tr.* by Mary Feeney

At the end of the garden walk. Cold Green Element, The. Irving Layton. BrAP; NoP-4; NoP-5

At the end of the rainbow there's happiness. I'm Always Chasing Rainbows. Joseph McCarthy. ReLy

At the end of the road, in a drab chapel. Mother Tongue. Jon Stallworthy. NoAM

At the end of the row. Objection to Being Stepped On, The. Robert Frost. NBLV; OBCoV

At the End of the Weekend. Ted Kooser. PBCAP

At the end we prayed for death. Patient, The. Mary Karr. PoA 2002

At the Entrance. M. R. Peacocke. NLP

At the equinox when the earth was veiled in a late rain, wreathed with wet poppies, waiting spring. Continent's End. Robinson Jeffers. CalPo

At the Executed Murderer's Grave. James Wright. VCAP

At the Execution Ground. Sŏng [or Sung] Sammun. CATKP, *tr.* by Chi-gyu Kim [*or* Kim Chonggil]

At the exhausted lovers where they sleep. (LL) But That Is Another Story. Donald Justice. NoP-4; OxBoAm

At the Exhibition of Parables. Donald Revell. BodElec

At the Exiled King's River Pavilion. U'ng Bình. CaDao, *tr.* by John Balaban

At the factory I worked. Mexicans Begin Jogging. Gary Soto. CAP-8; LTA; PML; RWB

At the Faucet of June. William Carlos Williams. APT-1

At the [or de] feet o' Jesus. Feet o' Jesus. Langston Hughes. ISC

At the ferro-concrete bike sheds. Tattoo, The. Peter Finch. TCAWP

At the first peep of dawn she roused me. William Carlos Williams. TCAPo *Fr.* Wanderer, The: A Rococo Study.

At the first strokes of the fiddle bow. Wheel, The. Wendell Berry. RSR; UpMys

At the Fishhouses. Elizabeth Bishop. AmFaPo; APT-2; BeAl; CAP-8; Coast; ItP; NAAL-5; NALW; NAMCP V.2; OxBoAm; PoetW; PoPoPo; VCAP

At the Fishmonger's. Nikolai Alekseievich Zabolotsky. TCRusP, *tr.* by Alec Merivale

At the flea market across from the Commerce Speedway. Talismans. Maudelle Driskell. AllShUp

At the Florist's. Jacques Prévert. BeAl, *tr.* by Lawrence Ferlinghetti

At the Flyfisher's Shack. Sydney Lea. RA

At the font the black marble. Baroque. Marie-Claire Bancquart. MFP, *tr.* by Martin Sorrell

At the Foot of Mount Zion. Endre Ady. IQMS, *tr.* by Leslie A. Kery

At the foot of Old Hill. Van Horn. Steven Tye Culbert. TiP2

At the foot of the wall. Life Everlasting, The. Reginald Gibbons. Vesp

At the fort the flag flies all night long. Hill County Rest Home. Carol Coffee Reposa. TiP2

At the Frenchman's. Kendra Hamilton. BRtP

At the Freud Hilton. Campbell McGrath. AmPoNex

At the Frick. Anthony Hecht. GS

At the full face of the forest lies our little town. To the Red Lory. John Shaw Neilson. NOBAu

At the full length of all their chain. (LL) Unequal Fetters, The. Anne Finch, Countess of Winchilsea. BrAP; OxBEV

At the gate, I sit in a row of blue seats. Passengers. Billy Collins. GoPo; OtW; PLBUT

At the gate of an old temple, another spring ends. To a Friend. Im Ŏngnyŏng. CATKP, *tr.* by Chi-gyu Kim [*or* Kim Chonggil]

At the Gate of the Valley. Zbigniew Herbert. PoSu, *tr.* by Czeslaw Milosz

At the Gates. Kofi Awoonor. VCWP *Fr.* Night of My Blood (1971).

At the Gates of Aerea. René Char. BAP-04; MotU, *tr.* by Franz Wright

At the gathered ends of rooty paths. Island in the Evening, The. Fairfield Porter. PoA 2002

At the gathering of desire you made me a wine-cup. Nedim. OLP, *tr.* by Walter Andrews, Najaat Black and Mehmet Kalpakli

At the gathering of joy, the wine cup. Nabi. OLP, *tr.* by Walter Andrews, Najaat Black and Mehmet Kalpakli

At the Government Office Building. Taking Leave of Two Officials. Tu Fu [*or* Du Fu]. CrYelRi, *tr.* by Sam Hamill

At the Grave. Yi Kyŏngnim. EcSo, *tr.* by Peter H. Lee

At the Grave of My Brother: Bomber Pilot. William Stafford. PWW2

At the Grave of My Guardian Angel: St. Louis Cemetery, New Orleans. Larry Levis. AmAlph

At the great gate to the East. Chu-qi dong-men: At the Great Gate. *Unknown*. CCL1, *tr.* by Ezra Pound

At the greyhound bus stations, at airports, at silent wharfs. Exiles. Juan Felipe Herrera. CalPo

At the grocer's. (LL) Cariboo Horses, The. Alfred Wellington Purdy. BrAP; HeIP-4

At the Gwen John Exhibition. Charles McDonald. NLP

At the Hammersmith Palais. Alan Riddell. NOBAu

At the Havana Hilton. Sandra M. Castillo. TouFir

At the hayfield's edge, a few stalks. Quick and the Dead, The. Galway Kinnell. BAP-01

At the head of a march to the last new Jerusalem. (LL) James Russell Lowell. NAAPv.1; TCAPo *Fr.* Fable for Critics, A.

At the heart of the ridiculous, the sublime. (LL) Antarctica. Derek Mahon. NPeEn; PBCIP; StAl

At the height of the day, the fragile wing. Earth. Leanne O'Sullivan. NIrP

At the Hermitage of Master Fu. Wang Wei. CrYelRi, *tr.* by Sam Hamill

At the high school football game, the boys. Homecoming. Dorianne Laux. ExTi

At the hour when the heat of the day is overcome. Dante Alighieri. NAWM-5v1 *Fr.* Divina Commedia (Selections from Anthologies, in English).

At the House of Ghosts. Adrian C. Louis. MoASP

At the Immortal's Home. Rotten Axe-Handle Mountain. Huai Ku. CSKM, *tr.* by Paul Hansen

At the instant of drowning he invoked the three sisters. Three Fates, The. Rosemary Dobson. BMAP

At the Jackson Pollock Retrospective in L.A. Harold L. Johnson. BtF

At the Jewish Museum. Linda Pastan. TaR

At the Jewish New Year. Adrienne Rich. TaR

At the Justice Department November 15, 1969. Denise Levertov. AmWaPo *Fr.* Staying Alive.

At the Keyhole. Walter De la Mare. MoBrPo

At the large foot of a fair hollow tree. Country-Mouse, The. Abraham Cowley. NPeEn; OBVE

At the last moment, they said, my cousin held. Matter of Division, A. Frankie Paino. AmPoNex

At the last, tenderly. Last Invocation, The. Walt Whitman. MoAmPo

At the last turn in the path. Saying Farewell at the Monastery After Hearing the Old Master Lecture on "Return to the Source." Gary Snyder. WhBo

At the Lesbian and Gay Pride March we. Some of Us Wear Pink Triangles. Walta Borawski. CAGL

At the Lighthouse. Nikolai Nikolaevich Morshen. TCRusP, *tr.* by John Glad

At the lip of a big black vagina. Where I Live. Wanda Coleman. GeoHom

At the long tables of time. Jugs, The. Paul Celan. HP; OBVE, *tr.* by Christopher Middleton

At the Lord's Table waiting, robed and stoled. Incident, An. Frederick Tennyson. SacPr

At the Machine. Kalman Hayzler. Prolet, *tr.* by Amelia Glaser

At the Makeshift Aid Station. Tōge Sankichi. AtGh, *tr.* by Richard H. Minear

At the mental ward I chew. Recommitted. Juan Delgado. TouFir

At the mere sound of rushing wind. Open-Eyed Blind Man, An. Yi Yônju. EcSo, *tr.* by Yung-Hee Kim

At the mid hour of night, when stars are weeping, I fly. Echo. Thomas Moore. OBEV

At the midnight in the silence of the sleep-time. Epilogue. Robert Browning. NAEL-6v2

At the moment, I have thirty-three years on top of the table in my workroom. Cloister of the Shades, The. Blas de Otero. RaW, *tr.* by Hardie St. Martin

At the moment of death. About Death. Patricia K. Page. StAl

At the Moment of My Death. Chŏnggam, Great Master. CATKP, *tr.* by Peter H. Lee

At the moment the train passes throw. Josée Lapeyrère. SCFWP *Fr.* Apples.

At the Monument to Pierre Louÿs. Richard Howard. VCAP

At the Mosque. Chairil Anwar. PML; PoetW, *tr.* by Burton Raffel

At the Mountain-Lodge of the Buddhist Priest Ye Waiting in Vain for My Friend Ding. Meng Hao Jan. CCL1, *tr.* by Witter Bynner

At the mountain's top, I reach up. Nightrider. Tatamkulu Afrika. TSAP

At the Movie: Virginia, 1956. Ellen Bryant Voigt. LPSFW; LTA; NoAM

At the Movies. David Westheimer. TiP2

At the movies i always love the look. Sunday Matinee. Sybil Kollar. FFC

At the mythic coast, by the kitchen stove. Length of a Wave, The. Nick Laird. NIrP

At the Nachi Kannon Hall. Muso Soseki. EaWin, *tr.* by W. S. Merwin

At the New Mexico Viet Nam Veterans Memorial. Leroy V. Quintana. ICANM

At the New Moon: Rosh Hodesh. Marge Piercy. TaR

At the New Year. John Hollander. TaR

At the New Year. Kenneth Patchen. ItP *Fr.* Eight Early Poems.

At the news of your death. Lament for the Death of a Bullfighter. Joshua Beckman. AmPoNex

At the Nuclear Rally. Laura Boss. UnSA

At the Nu'uanu Reservoir Pool. Phyllis Thompson. ICANM

At the Office Early. Ted Kooser. PBCAP

At the offset it was calculated. Edoardo Sanguineti. ItPo *Fr.* Scartabello.

At the old pond. Buson. WoPoe, *tr. by* Tony Barnstone, Willis Barnstone *and* Haixin Xu

At the Olive Grove of the Resistance. Robert Hedin. GifTon

At the Opening of Oak Grove Cemetary Bridge. Thomas Lynch. PoDa

At the Other End of the Telescope. George Bradley. P180

At the outer edge again. Whooping Crane. James Cody. TiP2

At the outpost three years. Body Is Pain, The. *Vietnamese Oral Tradition.* CaDao, *tr. by* John Balaban

At the outset she still carried it quite well. Mary's Visitation. Rainer Maria Rilke. GI

At the park. Returned from California. Simon J. Ortiz. HATNAP

At the Party. Mikhail Alekseievich Kuzmin. CAGL, *tr. by* Simon Karlinsky

At the Party. Ursula K. Le Guin. FiBr

At the party she said. What's So Funny 'bout Peace, Love and Understanding. Robert Long. SwNoth

At the Pavelets radial-line station. Igor Moiseievich Irtenev. PML, *tr. by* Patrick Henry and Mark Nowak

At the Piano. Andrew Hudgins. UpMys
(Saints and Strangers.) RA

At the place of light. Prophetic Powers. *Unknown.* APN-2, *tr. by* Henry Rowe Schoolcraft

At the Playground. William Stafford. TLR

At the Poem. Clark Coolidge. AHA; NYP2

At the Poem Society a black-haired man stands up to say. Fresh Air. Kenneth Koch.

At the Poetry Conference: Berkeley After the New York Style. Robert Duncan. AHA

At the Poetry Reading. John Brehm. PoA 2002

At the Point. Robert Mezey. GeoHom

At the Poorhouse. Federico García Lorca. PFTM-1 *Fr.* Night (Suite for Piano and Poet's Voice).

At the Portals of the Future. Lines. Frances Ellen Watkins Harper. APN-2; NAAPv.1

At the post office he sees Joe McInnes. Quiet Desperation. Louis Simpson. CAP-8

At the Powwow. Cheryl Savageau. TWW

At the quarry's edge. King Lear. Peter Huchel. PoSu, *tr. by* Michael Hamburger

At the Railway Station, Upway. Thomas Hardy. PtR

At the Rainbow. Robert Vasquez. GeoHom

At the rapids father and boy pitch in a young birch. Woods Burial. John Peck. PoCoUp

At the rest stop on the way to Mississippi. Love of Travellers, The. Angela Jackson. BtF

At the retreat, Lee wasn't allowed. Nirvana. James Tate. BodElec

At the Rio Grande Near the End of the Century. Ray Gonzalez. TouFir

At the Ritz. Lynn Emanuel. OxBoAm

At the river's verge. Beautiful in Death. Martha E. (Martha Elizabeth Hotchkiss) Whitten. TiP2

At the Robert Frost Memorial. William Stafford. VisFro

At the roots of clouds a cutworm hollowing. Five Dawn Skies in November. David Wagoner. VCAP

At the round earth's imagined [*or* imagin'd] corners, blow. John Donne. BASC; BrAP; ChIV-2; ClHu; CtM; HeIP-4; MakPoe; NAEL-6v1; NAEL-7v1; NAWM-5v1; NoP-5; NOSC; NPeEn; OxAEP-1; OxBEV; OxBSo; RSR; SacPr; TFi; WaAnP; WoPoe *Fr.* Holy Sonnets.

At the Salvation Army. Simon J. Ortiz. NAAL-5 *Fr.* From Sand Creek.

At the same time. (LL) Prodigy. Charles Simic. AF; AmWaPo; EMP; NAMCP V.2; NoP-5; VCAP

At the San Francisco Airport. Yvor Winters. CalPo; HeIP-4; NIL-7; NIP-4; OxBoAm

At the School for the Gifted. Carol Muske-Dukes. ExTi

At the Scott Exhibition, Edinburgh Festival. Iain Crichton Smith. WaAnP

At the Sea. Rosmarie Waldrop. WoBe *Fr.* Hölderlin Hybrids.

At the seashore I came upon a golden shell. Seashell. Rubén Darío. SpanPo, *tr. by* Anita Volland

At the Seaside [*or* Sea-Side]. Robert Louis Stevenson. NTCP; TLR; WHSW

At the Shore. Mary Oliver. PoCoUp

At the side. Woman Washing. Patricia Bishop. Prnts

At the Siege of Corinth. Lord Byron. DiBP *Fr.* Siege of Corinth, The.

At the sight of the beauty that greets them, for the charm they have broken. (LL) London Snow. Robert Bridges. MoBrPo; NoAM; OxAEP-2; TFi

At the sight of water, my heart flows. At the Sight of Water. Kim Yŏngnang. CAMKP, *tr. by* Anthony, Brother of Taizé

At the silence of twilight's contemplative hour. Lines Written on Visiting a Scene in Argyleshire. Thomas Campbell. NPBRoP

At the *Six-Hiboux*, where the Acadian. Love Poem / Song Regarding Weymouth Falls. George Elliott Clarke. Coast

At the Sky's End, Thinking of Li Po. Tu Fu [*or* Du Fu]. ColAnChi, *tr. by* David Lattimore

At the slick edges of the mirror, without a trace. (LL) Shaving. Richard Blanco. AmPoNex; NAPBL

At the small end of an illness. World Contracted to a Recognizable Image, The. William Carlos Williams. APT-1

At the Smithville Methodist Church. Stephen Dunn. SUP

At the South Pole. Jean Earle. Prnts

At the south window, my back to a lamp. Village Snow, Sitting at Night. Po Chü-i. NDACCP, *tr. by* David Hinton

At the spring. To Light. Linda Hogan. HATNAP

At the St. Louis Institute of Music. Ronald Wallace. SUP

At the Stanley Spencer Exhibition. John Riley. Oth

At the start, something must be arbitrarily excluded. As We're Told. Rae Armantrout. AWPTFC

At the station exit, my bundle in hand. No More Hiroshimas. James Kirkup. RSaN

At the Stop. Zinaida Bykova. CRWP, *tr. by* Robert Reid

At the Stop Light, the Braided Blond Man. Anthony R. Vigil. AmPoNex

At the stormy moment of dawn. Swifts. Philippe Jaccottet. VCWP, *tr. by* Derek Mahon

At the Stream's Source in Spring: A Party. Wang Ch'ang-ling. CCL1, *tr. by* Stephen Owen

At the street bookstall in Karlsruhe, my father. Homage to Ferd. Holthausen. Gwen Harwood. NOBAu

At the Summit. Robert Phillips. Vesp

At the Swings. Henry Taylor. MPUn

At the Teahouse, 7 am. Holly Hughes. AmZen

At the Teahouse, 6 am. Holly Hughes. AmZen

At *The Tempest* with a Pregnant Wife. Charles Harper Webb. IaFF

At the Temple of Kuan Yin in the Rain. Su Tung-p'o. CrYelRi, *tr. by* Sam Hamill

At the Terminal. Patricia Hooper. OtW

At the Thatched Hall of the Ts'ui Family. Tu Fu [*or* Du Fu]. CrYelRi, *tr. by* Sam Hamill

At the Threshold of the Moon. Gigi Maria Ross. BtF

At the time I was born. Song of Longing. Chŏng Ch'ŏl. CATKP, *tr. by* David R. McCann

At the time I was four years old. House of the Hare, The. Naomi Mitchison. MoWP

At the time of night-prayer, as the sun slides down. Night and Sleep. Jelaluddin Rumi. WoPoe, *tr. by* Robert Bly

At the time of the White Dawn. Song of the Fallen Deer. *Unknown.* OBVE, *tr. by* Frank Russell

At the time the master disappeared. For Don Francisco Giner de Los Ríos. Antonio Machado Ruiz. RaW, *tr. by* Robert Bly

At the Top of My Voice. Vladimir Vladimirovich Mayakovsky.
"My most respected / comrades of posterity!" AF

At the top of the dune. Desolation. Dabney Stuart. PfSP

At the top of the hill you were Muriel. My Mother in Three Acts. Jane Cooper. ExTi

At the top of the house the apples are laid in rows. Moonlit Apples. John Drinkwater. OBMV

At the Tourist Center in Boston. Margaret Atwood. BrAP; NoP-4; NoP-5; WaAnP

At the Train Museum. Linda Pastan. GM

At the turn of the palace stair. (LL) "H. D." APT-1; HW; MoWP; NAAPv.2; NALW; NAMCP V.1; PFTM-1 *Fr.* Tribute to the Angels.

At the undulating head he aims. Emu Shot. Tjinapirrgarri. NOBAu, *tr. by* George von Brandenstein

At the Un-National Monument along the Canadian Border. William Stafford. BrAP; HeIP-4

At the Very Last Battle. Carmen Tafolla. TiP2

At the very mention of it there is one kind of person who laughs or looks. Weight of Sleep, The. W. S. Merwin. MotU

At the Vietnam Memorial. George Bilgere. PoA 2002

At the Wall. Vernice Wineera Pere. CFP

At the Washing of My Son. David Ray. RaBo

At the wedding of Prince Edward and Sophie Rhys-Jones. Official Versions. Mark Pawlak. PrTe

At the Well. Paul Blackburn. APSN; PFTM-2

At the Well. Leonard Nathan. PBCAP

At the wind that blew last night. *Unknown.* CATKP, *tr. by* Peter H. Lee

At the Window. "Rachel." FIT, *tr. by* Robert Friend

At the window frame concealing. Saint. Stéphane Mallarmé. NAWM-7v2, *tr. by* Henry Weinfield

At the Window in the Dark. Victor Hugo. SxFrPo, *tr. by* A. M. and E. H. Blackmore

At the window that veils her old. Saint. Stéphane Mallarmé. SxFrPo, *tr. by* A. M. and E. H. Blackmore

At the Zendo. Jinkag Haesim. BecRai, *tr. by* Kim Daljin, Kim Won-Chung and Christopher Merrill

At the Zoo. John Davies. AngWePo

At the Zoo. William Makepeace Thackeray. NTCP

At their backs. The ball turns in the darkening air. (LL) Old Men Playing Basketball. B. H. Fairchild. MoASP; P180; PoCho

At their urgent heels. (LL) Old Mythologies. John Montague. NoP-4; NoP-5

At them, too; but miss the reflection. (LL) Via Negativa. Ronald Stuart Thomas. InvLi; StAl

At thirteen already single-minded Abraham. John Hollander. OxBoAm *Fr.* Powers of Thirteen.

At Thirty. Kyoko Mori. SweBea

At Thirty-Three. Hans Magnus Enzensberger. VCWP, *tr. by* the author and Michael Hamburger

At this age of his when he wasn't here. Because We Need Good Maps. Forrest Hamer. ASA

At this height, Kansas. Reading *Moby-Dick* at 30,000 Feet. Tony Hoagland. OtW

At this hour exiles look for sleep in pills. An ambulance. Body Politic. Silvio Giussani. ItPo, *tr. by* Gayle Ridinger

At this hour the park offers only. HMS Glasshouse. Sean O'Brien. RSaN

At this hour the soul floats weightlessly. Poor Angels. Edward Hirsch. PoA 2002

At This Juncture. Blanca Wiethüchter. TANSG, *tr. by* Shaun Griffin and Emma Sepúlveda-Pulvirenti

At this lofty tower where the town ends, wilderness begins. From the City-Tower of Liuzhou To My Four Fellow-Officials at Zhang, Ding, Feng, and Lian Districts. Liu Tsung-yüan. CCL1, *tr. by* Witter Bynner

At this moment hundreds of women. Watch, The. Marge Piercy. BeAl

At this range, it's really monumental. Grass. Alfred Corn. WaAnP

At this resort. Ingrid de Kok. TSAP

At this speed, my friend, our origins are groundless. Transcanadian. Robert Hedin. GifTon

At this th' Impatient Hero sowrly smil'd. Homer. OBVE *Fr.* Iliad, The.

At this time there are few. Baby Is Born Out of a White Owl's Forehead—1972, A. Alice Notley. ExTi

At 3 A.M. Wendy Cope. LW

At three A.M., alone, not sleepy. Richard's Blues. Richard Cecil. SeSe

At 3 a.m. I run my tongue. Death's Head. Phyllis Gotlieb. IFF

At three in the afternoon. Meditation on Yellow. Olive Senior. WaCA

At three-thirty in the morning in America. Myra Sklarew. TaR *Fr.* Lithuania.

At thy approach, my cheek with blushes glows. Elizabeth Singer Rowe. PEW *Fr.* Paraphrase on the Canticles, A.

At Tikal. William Bronk. APSN

At times I fear. Portugal Laurel, The. John Wright. BloBone

At Times I Say: Let's Try to Be Joyous. Cristina Campo. CItWP, *tr. by* Cinzia Sartini Blum and Lara Trubowitz

At times, my longing for the beloved slays me. Mihri Hatun. OLP, *tr. by* Walter Andrews, Najaat Black and Mehmet Kalpakli

At times the heart looks toward open fields. Near Twelve Mile Point. Lance Henson. HATNAP

At Timon's Villa. Alexander Pope. *See* Timon's Villa.

At Timon's villa let us pass a day. Alexander Pope. NPeEn; OxBEV *Fr.* Epistle IV to Richard Boyle, Earl of Burlington.

At Toomebridge. Seamus Heaney. NAMCP V.2

At Toriwpn. Cho Chihun. CAMKP, *tr. by* David R. McCann

At Tsukiji Market Tokyo. Jerome Rothenberg. WoBe

At Twelve. Elizabeth McLagan. FiBr

At twelve, I quit reciting. Year I Was Diagnosed with a Sacrilegious Heart, The. Martín Espada. RWB; TouFir

At 12 o'clock in the afternoon. Epigram. Meleager. WoPoe, *tr. by* Peter Whigham

At twelve o'clock midnight, the lines are cut. Midnight Vigil. Fran Haraway. HHAm

At 28 I was still faithless. 28. Philip Levine. GeoHom

At 20 my daughter is still stealing. To Welcome a Changeling. Colleen J. McElroy. FiBr

At Twenty-Three Weeks She Can No Longer See Anything South of Her Belly. Thom Ward. GoPo

At Twilight. Hayyim Nahman Bialik. FIT, *tr. by* Robert Friend

At twilight I went into the street. Descending Figure. Louise Glück. NAMCP V.2

At twilight we come closest. Twilight Song. Kang Ŭn'gyo. EcSo, *tr. by* Ann Y. Choi

At various times, I have asked myself what reasons. Poem Written in a Copy of *Beowulf*. Jorge Luis Borges. PoetW, *tr. by* Alastair Reid

At Villequier. Victor Hugo. SxFrPo, *tr. by* A. M. and E. H. Blackmore

At Viscount Nelson's lavish funeral. 1805. Robert Graves. FaBoWar; OBCoV; OBSV

At Vshchizh. Fyodor Ivanovich Tyutchev. OBWP; OxBEV; WoPoe, *tr. by* Henry Gifford and Charles Tomlinson

At Waterfall Temple. Chang K'o-chiu. CrYelRi, *tr. by* Sam Hamill

At wells and dunghills. (LL) Anahorish. Seamus Heaney. HarvBoo; PBCIP

At westward window of a palace gray. My Lighthouses. Helen Hunt Jackson. APN-2; ColAP

At what time Jacob's race did leave of Egypt take. Mary Sidney Herbert, Countess of Pembroke. NoP-5 *Fr.* Psalms.

At whatever age he was, he was apt with that. Won't It Be Fine? Robert Creeley. BAP-97

At Whole-World-In-View-Hut. Muso Soseki. EaWin, *tr. by* W. S. Merwin

At Will Robers Beach. Timothy Steele. WeW-3

At Wilshire & Santa Monica I saw an opossum. Oldest Living Thing in L.A., The. Larry Levis. P180; UrbNat

At winter's end. Snowman Sniffles. N. M. Bodecker. TLR

At Woodlawn I heard the dead cry. Lost Son, The. Theodore Roethke. APT-2; NAMCP V.1; NoP-4; NoP-5; OxBoAm; TRP

At Woodward's Gardens. Robert Frost. PoA 2002

At words poetic, I'm so pathetic. You're the Top. Cole Porter. ReLy

At Work. Suzanne Gardinier. AmPoNex

At Work. Artur Miedzyrzecki. PoSu, *tr. by* John Batki and Artur Miedzyrzecki

At Worthing, an exile from Geraldine G———. My Life Is a———. Frederick Locker-Lampson. OBCoV

At year's end is there anything one can depend on? Harmonizing with a Poem by Left Assistant Yu Kao-chih Requesting Sick Leave. Shen Yüeh. ColAnChi, *tr. by* Richard Mather and Richard B. Mather

At Ynysddu. Graham Thomas. AngWePo

At Yorktown the church. At Yorktown. Charles Olson. FTtHH; HarvBoo

At your entreaty, I at last have writ. "Ephelia." PEW

At your funeral. Colors—Struck. Afaa Michael Weaver. BtF

Atalanta in Calydon. Algernon Charles Swinburne.
  Before the Beginning of Years. NAEL-6v2; NAEL-7v2
  (Chorus: "Before the beginning of years.") OBEV
  (Chorus from Atalanta in Calydon.) NoP-4; NoP-5
  When the Hounds of Spring. NAEL-6v2; NAEL-7v2; OBEV; OxBEV; TFi; WeW-3

Atavism. Elinor Wylie. NALW; PoA 2002

Atavistic: Traces after the Rain. Juan Felipe Herrera. TouFir

Ath I wath biking. Oh, Woe Ith Me! Bruce Lansky. ArBi

Atheism. Elizabeth Oakes-Smith.
  Annihilation. TCAPo

Atheling Grange; or, The Apotheosis of Lotte Nussbaum. William Plomer. OBNV

Athelstan King / Lord among Earls. Battle of Brunanburh. *Unknown*. CABP; FaBoWar; OBVE; OBWP, *tr. by* Alfred Tennyson

Athelstane. Priscilla Jane Thompson. CBWP-2

Athena. Amy Clampitt. PoA 2002

Athenian Garden, An. Trumbull Stickney. APN-2; NoP-4; NoP-5

Athenians' Answer, The. Elizabeth Singer Rowe. BASC

Athens. Vladimir Levchev. CSCBP, *tr. by* Georgi Belev and Lisa Sapinkov

Athens. John Milton. NOSC *Fr.* Paradise Regained [*or* Regain'd].

Athens and Jerusalem. Rose Drachler. TaR

Athletic tarantula, An. Thousand Marionettes, A. Sydney March. BtF

Atieno washes dishes. Freedom Song, A. Marjorie Oludhe Macgoye. HAWP; ItWoWo; WoPoe

Atieno yo. (LL) Freedom Song, A. Marjorie Oludhe Macgoye. HAWP; ItWoWo; WoPoe

Atlanta Exposition Ode. Mary Weston Fordham. CBWP-2; SWaP

Atlantic City Waiter. Countee Cullen. APT-2; NAMCP V.1

Atlantic closes, the sheet of time is rent. (LL) Pentecost. Gwyneth Lewis. MFPA; NeBrP

Atlantic is a sea of bones. Lucille Clifton. ESEAA

Atlantic is a stormy moat; and the Mediterranean, The. Eye, The. Robinson Jeffers. ItP; NoAM

Atlantis. W. H. Auden. OxAEP-2

Atlantis. Hart Crane. NAAL-5 *Fr.* Bridge, The.

Atlantis. Mark Doty.
  Michael's Dream. WiU
  New Dog. InoFa; WiU

Atlantis. Walter Helmut Fritz. GTCP, *tr. by* Reinhold Grimm

Atlantis. Joanna Fuhrman. AmPoNex

Atlantis. Slavko Mihalic. PoSu, *tr. by* Charles Simic

Atlas. U. A. Fanthorpe. BeAl

Atlas of the Difficult World, An. Adrienne Rich.
  "Catch if you can your country's moment, begin." NAAL-5
  "Dark woman, head bent, listening for something, A." GeoHom
  "Here is a map of our country." BeAl; NAAL-5; StAl; WaAnP
  "I know you are reading this poem." NAAL-5
  "Late summers, early autumns, you can see something that binds." NAAL-5; WaAnP
  "On this earth, in this life, as I read your story, you're lonely." NAAL-5
  "One night on Monterey Bay the death-freeze of the century." GeoHom; WaAnP
  "Soledad. = f. Solitude, loneliness, homesickness; lonely retreat." GeoHom
  "What homage will be paid to a beauty built to last." NAAL-5

ATM. Elizabeth Bachinsky. IFF

Atmosphere is incandescent, The. Atmosphere Is Incandescent, The. Rosalía de Castro. SpanPo, *tr. by* Edwin Morgan

Atmostphere for Poetry in Abilene, The. Robert A. Fink. TiP2

Atom bellies like a cauliflower, The. Jane Cooper. MakPoe *Fr.* After the Bomb Tests.

Atom bellies like a cauliflower, The. After the Bomb Tests. Jane Cooper.

Atom Bum, The. William Greenway. AtGh

Atomic Bride. Thomas Sayers Ellis. BAP-97; IIR; LegDan; NeAmPo

Atomic Factory, The. Gwilym R. Jones. *tr. by* Catherine Fisher

Quiet Valley, The. BBMWP, *tr. by* Catherine Fisher

Atomic Ghost. John Balaban. AtGh

Atomic Pantoum. Peter Meinke. WeW-3

Atomic Psalm. Maurya Simon. GifTon

Atoning Yesterday, The. Louise Imogen Guiney. SWaP

Atop the bamboo grove slants sunset's glow. After Snow, Longing for Elder Brother Hsi-ch'iao. Wang Shih-chieng. ColAnChi

Atop the fences where the four yards met. Fort. BeDoSh

Atossa. Matthew Arnold. TriCat

Atrides summon'd all to arms, to arms himself dispos'd. Homer. FaBoWar *Fr.* Iliad, The.

Atrium. Alessandro Ceni. ItPo, *tr. by* Gayle Ridinger

Atrocity / implies an audience of gods. Don McKay. NLPA *Fr.* Matériel.

Attack. Siegfried Sassoon. MoBrPo

Attack of the Squash People. Marge Piercy. NBLV

Attempt, An. Angela Ball. PoDa

Attempt at communication, An. Mafika Pascal Gwala. TSAP

Attempt at Jealousy, An. Craig Raine. NoAM

Attempt at Jealousy, An. Marina Ivanovna Tsvetayeva. TCRusP, *tr. by* Bob Perelman, Aleksandr Petrov and Shirley Rihner

Attempt at Jealousy, An. Marina Ivanovna Tsvetayeva. GPTC; OxBEV; WoPoe, *tr. by* Elaine Feinstein

Attempt to Locate. Sarah Cortez. TiP2

Attempt was made, The;—'tis needless to report. William Wordsworth. STuOW *Fr.* Excursion, The.

Attend my fable if your ears be clean. Roy Campbell. OBSV *Fr.* Wayzgoose, The.

Attend, ye mournful Parents, while. Another to Urania. Benjamin Colman. ChIV-1

Attending, The. Fred Chappell. RWB

Attention. Rae Armantrout. PmAP

Attention. Sa'di Yusuf. ItP, *tr. by* Khaled Mattawa

Attention, la perle au fond des siècles futurs aux roues de cuivre hurlantes. Je parle dans tous les âges. René Daumal. YaTCFP

Attention, shoppers. From within the inverted. Wolf Ridge. John Ashbery. BAP-04; VaPo

Attention was commanded through a simple, unadorned, unexplained, often decentered presence. Jealousy. Mei-Mei Berssenbrugge. OpBo; PmAP

Attention Young Bachelors. Violeta Parra. TANSG, *tr. by* Shaun Griffin and Emma Sepúlveda-Pulvirenti

Attention young bachelors. Attention Young Bachelors. Violeta Parra. TANSG, *tr. by* Shaun Griffin and Emma Sepúlveda-Pulvirenti

Attentive eyes, fantastic heed. Poet, A. Thomas Hardy. NAMCP V.1; NoAM

Attentive to the irredeemable. (LL) History. John Burnside. BeAl; PoAgWa

Attentively he heard us, while we spoke. Virgil. OBVE *Fr.* Aeneid [*or* Eneados *or* Aeneis], The.

Atthis, for you the thought of me has become hateful. Sappho. SaLy, *tr. by* Diane Rayor

Atthis, my darling, thou did'st stray. Michael Field. PoBW; ViWPN

Atthis, the immanence of death. (LL) Atthis, my darling, thou did'st stray. Michael Field. PoBW; ViWPN

Attic Landscape, The. Herman Melville. NCAP

Attic maid! with honey fed. To the Swallow. Euenus. OBVE, *tr. by* William Cowper

Attic room and window my ice skates on the wall. My Legs Señor. William S. Burroughs. BB

Attic, The. Marie Howe. ExTi

Atticus ("Peace to all such! but were there one whose fires"). Alexander Pope. OxBEV; TRP *Fr.* Epistle to Dr. Arbuthnot.

Attila József / I really love you. Attila József. Attila József. AF; MotU, *tr. by* John Batki

Attis. Catullus. OBVE; STV

Attitude. Magda Portal. TANSG, *tr. by* Shaun Griffin and Emma Sepúlveda-Pulvirenti

Attitude or, An. Alex Rawls. AnSo *Fr.* What's Your Sign?

Attitudes. Sotère Torregian. AHA

Attraction. Georgi Rupchev. CSCBP, *tr. by* Georgi Belev and Lisa Sapinkopf

Attraction. Ella Wheeler Wilcox. LW

Attraction comes from the mind. Clock. Douglas A. Martin. BeDoSh

Attractions. Alexander Shurbanov. PML, *tr. by* Ewald Osers

Attractive at that distance, hair fanning out. Double, The. Joan Aleshire. OPRER

Attribute all to the gods: often they raise. Archilochus. SaLy, *tr. by* Diane Rayor

Attributes of a Gentleman, The. Saint Ronald of Orkney. NePenScot, *tr. by* Paul Bibire

Au Aubade. Timothy Steele. CalPo

Au baptême / de la douleur. Tahar Bekri. YaTCFP *Fr.* Retour en Tunisie.

Au Café Noir. Mark McMorris. IAoNAP

Au pays des morts. Habib Tengour.
  Ombres 1. YaTCFP
  Ombres 2. YaTCFP
  Ombres 3. YaTCFP
  Ombres 10. YaTCFP

Au seuil / de l'ultime. Tahar Bekri. YaTCFP *Fr.* Retour en Tunisie.

Au Tombeau de Mon Père. Ronald McCuaig. NOBAu

Aubade. *Unknown.* NAWM-7v1, *tr. by* Peter Dronke

Aubade: "After the sadness of apples in August." Robin Behn. AmAlph

Aubade: "All day I've been searching for omens, flimsy as they are, and the cat." Mark Wunderlich. WiU

Aubade: "As I would free the white almond from the green husk." Amy Lowell. NAAPv.2; NIL-7

Aubade: "At break of dawn." W. H. Auden. CAGL *Fr.* Three Posthumous Poems.

Aubade: "Cold snap. Five o'clock." Richard Kenney. NoP-4; NoP-5

Aubade: "Dead woodchuck in the dog's mouth drooped, The." Catherine Imbriglio. IAoNAP

Aubade for Hope. Robert Penn Warren. MoAmPo

Aubade: "Geese flew by as you entered me, The." Kate C. Richardson. PasH

Aubade: "Hark! hark! the lark at heaven's gate sings." William Shakespeare. OBEV

Aubade: "Hours before dawn we were woken by the quake." William Empson. OxAEP-2; OxBEV

Aubade: "I work all day, and get half-drunk at night." Philip Larkin. AWTN; BodElec; BrAP; CABP; EMP; NAEL-6v2; NAEL-7v2; NAMCP V.2; NoP-4; NoP-5; PoetW; SoSe-8; StAl; TRP; WaAnP

Aubade: "It's all the same to morning what it dawns on." Nuala Ni Dhomhnaill. PBCIP, *tr. by* Michael Longley

Aubade: "Jane, Jane, / Tall as a crane." Dame Edith Sitwell. MoBrPo; NALW; NAMCP V.1; NoAM

Aubade: "Lark now leaves his watery [*or* wat'ry] nest, The." Sir William Davenant. *See* Lark Now Leaves His Watery [*or* Wat'ry] Nest.

Aubade: "Lights are out in the street, and a cool wind swings, The." Rosamund Marriott Watson. ViWPN

Aubade: Macedonia. Nicholas Samaras. YaYoPo

Aubade: "Man is squeezing oranges in my kitchen, A." Paula Cunningham. NIrP

Aubade: Opal and Silver. Mark Doty. HarvBoo

Aubade: "Over Govino Bay, looking up from the water's edge, the landscape resembles nothing so much as the hills above Genova." Charles Wright. MotU

Aubade: Some Peaches, After Storm. Carl Phillips. CAP-8

Aubade: "Waking is this easy." Marilyn Chin. NIP-4

Aubade: "World was very large, The. Then." Louise Glück. BodElec

Aubade, An. Irving Layton. WoPoe

Aubade, An: "As she is showering, I wake to see." Timothy Steele. PasH; RA

Aubade of the Singer and Saboteur, Marie Triste: 1941. Norman Dubie. AmWaPo

Aubade 1: "Five-thirty, little one, already light." Marilyn Hacker. FiBr

Aubade 2. Marilyn Hacker. FiBr

Aubade 2.   Geoffrey O'Brien.   PA9/11

A.U.C. 334: about this date.   Advice to Young Ladies.   Alec Derwent Hope.   NAMCP V.1; NoAM; NoP-4; NoP-5

Aucthour Maketh Her Wyll and Testament, The.   Isabella Whitney.   EMWP; NoP-4

 (Communication Which the Author Had to London, Before She Made Her Will, A.)   NoP-5

 (Will and Testament.)   NAEL-7v1

 (Wyll and Testament.)   PEW

Auction Sale, The.   Henry Reed.   MoBrPo

Auctioneer.   Carl Sandburg.   NOxBChV

Audacity of the Lower Gods.   Yusef Komunyakaa.   CAP-8

Auden, MacNeice, Day Lewis, I have read them all.   British Leftish Poetry, 1930–40.   Hugh MacDiarmid.   NAMCP V.1; NoAM

Auden's Face.   Fraser Sutherland.   Coast

Audible and Inaudible.   Yannis Ritsos.   AF, tr. by Minas Savas

Audible Still.   J. Adwaita Dèr Mouw.   TuT, tr. by Peter van de Kamp

Audible still, very very distant, is the night train.   Audible Still.   J. Adwaita Dèr Mouw.   TuT, tr. by Peter van de Kamp

Audible trout.   Girls on the Bridge.   Derek Mahon.   NoP-5

Audience, The.   Richard Silberg.   ASA

Auditor.   Gerardo Deniz.   RMCMP, tr. by Mónica de la Torre

Auditor Thinks about Female Nature, An.   Jamie Grant.   NOBAu

Auditory Hallucinations.   Joyce Mansour.   HAWP, tr. by Carol Cosman

Audre's Son.   John Alexander Frazier, Jr.   BtF

Audrey Causey.   Pavane on Mr Wray's Locations, A.   Tony Baker.   Oth

Audrey Hepburn moons big-eyed on the cover.   Guide to Holland, A.   Peter Sirr.   PBCIP

Audubon: A Vision.   Robert Penn Warren.   APT-2

 Dream He Never Knew the End of, The.   NAAPv.2

 Love and Knowledge.   NAAL-5; NAAPv.2

 Sign Whereby He Knew, The.   NAAPv.2

 Tell Me a Story.   FuPo; ItP; NAAL-5; NAAPv.2

 "Was not the lost dauphin, though handsome was only."   NAAL-5; NAMCP V.1

Audubon Drive, Memphis.   James Seay.   AllShUp; SwNoth

Audubon watched the flocks beat by for days.   Pigeons, The.   William Heyen.   CAP-8

Augher Clogher Fivemiletown.   Omagh Post Office Rhyme.   Unknown.   FaBoVe

Auguries of Innocence.   William Blake.   OxAEP-2; TFi

 "Bat that flits at close of eve, The."   UV

 Proverbial Philosophy.   DiBP

 Three Things to Remember.   OWoS

Augury.   Caitríona O'Reilly.   NIrP

Augury.   Sherod Santos.   PfSP

August.   Tade Ipadeola.   NeNiPo

August.   Henrietta Cordelia Ray.   CBWP-3

August.   Esta Spalding.   StAl

August.   Edmund Spenser.   Fr. Shepherd's Calender, The.

August.   William Stafford.   BodElec

August.   Pamela Stewart.   ExTi

August.   Elinor Wylie.   APT-1; MoAmPo

August 1, 1966.   Pat Stodghill.   TiP2

August 6, 1945.   Alison Fell.   PoAgWa; RSaN

August 6, 1950.   Tōge Sankichi.   AtGh, tr. by Richard H. Minear

August 22, 1939.   Kenneth Rexroth.   TAPaP

Aug. 29, 1967.   Joe Brainard.   AHA

August 29, 1999.   Alex Rawls.   AnSo Fr. What's Your Sign?

August 1914.   Isaac Rosenberg.   HarvBoo; NPeEn; OBWP; OxBEV; PoAgWa

August 1972.   Adrienne Rich.   BodElec

August 1990.   C. Mikal Oness.   GeoHom

August 2000.   Holley Blackwell.   AnSo

August 29: Charlie "Yardbird" Parker's birthday.   Bird Lives.   Faye Moskowitz.   MiVo

August a haze amniotic our dream aether and lens of distance. Tree sentinels in.   Christopher Dewdney.   FTOS Fr. Spring Trances in the Control Emerald Night.

August and the drive-in picture is packed.   Dear John Wayne.   Louise Erdrich.   UnSA

August: "August. / The opposing."   Federico García Lorca.   IPoFL; RaW, tr. by James Wright

August Bank Holiday.   Jacques Prévert.   MFP, tr. by Martin Sorrell

August, Beirut, 1982.   Mahmoud Darwish.   Eno, tr. by Ibrahim Muhawi

August day, An.   Times Square.   Alter Brody.   TaR

August dusk. We rest on the green porch.   Reynolds Price.   PoA 2002 Fr. Good Places.

August Fires.   Glover Davis.   GeoHom

August from My Desk.   Roland Flint.   OtW

August, goldenrod blowing. We walk.   Maple Syrup.   Donald Hall.   CAP-8

August Horizon.   Dennis Nurkse.   NevBe

August, in Brittany.   Poppies.   Nesta Wyn Jones.   BBMWP, tr. by Anthony Conran

August Insomnia.   Franz Wright.   AmAlph

August, Los Angeles, Lullaby.   Carol Muske-Dukes.   PBCAP; PtR

August Moon.   Cesare Pavese.   AF, tr. by William Arrowsmith

August Night.   Sara Teasdale.   MoAmPo

August Nights.   Jean Janzen.   GeoHom

August on Sourdough, a Visit from Dick Brewer.   Gary Snyder.   LoL; NAAL-5

August, on the Rented Farm.   Dave Jeddie Smith.   ColAP

August Rain.   Robert Bly.   MotU

August Rain, after Haying.   Jane Kenyon.   ExTi

August returns, but not with plenty crowned.   Drought.   Eric Duncan.   IFF

August Sleepwalker, The.   Bei Dao.   PFTM-2; VCWP tr. by Bonnie S. McDougall

August stretches into fall. Clouds spread.   Near the Mississippi.   Steve Gehrke.   AmPoNex

August the First; Court Martial. The Mother Speaks.   Marjorie Oludhe Macgoye.   HBAPE

August the First: The Shadow. Patel Speaks.   Marjorie Oludhe Macgoye.   HBAPE

August the First: The Watchman Speaks.   Marjorie Oludhe Macgoye.   HBAPE

August. The mums nod past, each a prickly heart on a sleeve. (LL)   Teach Us to Number Our Days.   Rita Dove.   ESEAA; NoAM

August. / The opposing.   August.   Federico García Lorca.   IPoFL; RaW, tr. by James Wright

August Third.   May Sarton.   GoPo

August Town.   Bob Stewart.   WaCA

August, 'twas the twenty-fifth.   Bars Fight [August 28, 1746].   Lucy Terry.   AmWaPo; NAAPv.1; WaAnP

August: "When the blackberries hang."   Mary Oliver.   NAMCP V.2

August Zero.   Jane Miller.   BodElec

Augusto Jandolo: On Excavating an Etruscan Tomb.   Tom Sleigh.   PtR

Augustus was a chubby lad;.   Story of Augustus Who Would Not Have Any Soup, The.   Heinrich Hoffmann.   NBLV

Aujourd'hui ce sont des mains que j'aime.   Chanson pour des fantômes et pour celles qui ont disparu.   Philippe Soupault.   YaTCFP

Auld freen and helper up the hill.   Poetical Epistle tae Cullybackey Auld Nummer.   Thomas Given.   FaBoVe

Auld Lang Syne.   Robert Burns.   NAEL-6v2; NAEL-7v2; NePenScot; NoP-5; NOSC; OBEV; OxAEP-2; OxBEV

Auld Nibor I'm three times, doubly, o'er your debtor.   Second Epistle to Davie.   Robert Burns.   NePenScot

Auld Noah was at hame wi' them a'.   Parley of Beasts.   Hugh MacDiarmid.   ChIV-1; MoBrPo; NAMCP V.1; NoAM; OBMV

Auld Reikie! wale o' ilka town.   Robert Fergusson.   NePenScot Fr. Auld Reikie, a Poem.

Auld Robin Gray.   Lady Anne Barnard (née Lindsay).   OBEV; OxBEV

Auld Sanct-Aundirans—Brand the Builder.   Tom Scott.   EdScPo

Auld wife sat at her ivied door, The.   Ballad.   Charles Stuart Calverley.   CABP; NBLV; OBCoV; OxAEP-2; UV

Aulus, my girlfriend's in a dreadful plight.   Martial.   RomPo, tr. by Anthony Reid

AUM MANI.   Mani-Mani Gatha.   Jackson Mac Low.   PFTM-1

Aún se queja su alma vagamente.   A Larra con Unas Violetas.   Luis Cernuda.   RaW

Aunt Annie said, "When I turned seventeen."   Legacies.   Emily Grosholz.   FFC

Aunt Chloe.   Frances Ellen Watkins Harper.

 Aunt Chloe's Politics.   NAAPv.1; NALW

 Church Building.   NAAPv.1

 Deliverance, The.   SWaP

 Learning to Read.   NAAPv.1; NALW

Aunt Chloe's Politics.   Frances Ellen Watkins Harper.   NAAPv.1; NALW Fr. Aunt Chloe.

Aunt Gilly.   Lexie Dean Robertson.   TiP2

Aunt Gilly was a Texas belle.   Aunt Gilly.   Lexie Dean Robertson.   TiP2

Aunt Hannah Jackson.   Fenton Johnson.   APT-1

Aunt Helen.   T. S. Eliot.   FTtHH; NPeEn

Aunt Jane.   Alden Nowlan.   IFF

Aunt Jane Allen.   Fenton Johnson.   OxAAAP

Aunt Jane, of whom I dreamed the nights it thundered.   Aunt Jane.   Alden Nowlan.   IFF

Aunt Jennifer's tigers prance across a screen. Aunt Jennifer's Tigers. Adrienne Rich. BrAP; ColAP; HeIP-4; NALW; NAMCP V.2; NIL-7; NIP-4; NoAM; NoP-4; NoP-5; OPOU; OxBoAm; TRP

Aunt Jessie. Wanda Coleman. GT

Aunt Laura Moves toward the Open Grave of Her Father. Joseph De Roche. HeIP-4

Aunt Lil. Paul Zweig. BodElec

Aunt Lily and Frederick the Great. Jean Nordhaus. PoDa

Aunt Lily stood / behind her candy counter / passing out Mary Janes, Hersheys, and advice. Candy Lady, The. Laura Boss. UnSA

Aunt Martha. Wil'um Lee. InTrad

Aunt Martha bustles. Old Houses. Melvin B. Tolson. GT

Aunt May. Robert A. Fink. TiP2

Aunt Rose—now—might I see you. To Aunt Rose. Allen Ginsberg. CLPP; ColAP; NAMCP V.2; NoAM; NoP-4; NoP-5; OxBoAm; PmAP; TaR; WaAnP

Aunt Sophie's Morning. James Tate. SUP

Aunt Sue has a head full of stories. Aunt Sue's Stories. Langston Hughes. APT-2; SAmP

Aunt Sue's Stories. Langston Hughes. APT-2; SAmP

Aunt Toni's Heart. Rafael Campo. RA

Auntie's Skirts. Robert Louis Stevenson. WHSW

Aura Lee. *Unknown.* NAAPv.1

Aurelia. Robert Malise Bowyer Nichols. OBMV

Aurelia, when your zeal makes known. Headache, The. Mary Leapor. PEW

Aurelius & Furius, true comrades. Catullus. NAWM-7v1 *Fr.* Carmina [Charles Martin Translation].

Aurelius! patron of starvelings. To Aurelius. Catullus. CAGL, *tr. by* Eugene O'Connor

Aureole, The / comes into my room. After Mayakovsky. Sotère Torregian. AHA

Aurora. Emily Dickinson. APN-2; NCAP; PCW

Aurora. Juan Ramón Jiménez. RaW

Aurora. Sir William Alexander, Earl of Stirling.
  "O happy Tithon! if thou know'st thy harp." OBEV
  Sonnet. NOSC

Aurora de Trasmuros. Juan Ramón Jiménez. RaW

Aurora Leigh. Elizabeth Barrett Browning. VWP
  "Critics say that epics have died out, The." BrAP; FaBoWar; NAEL-6v2; NAEL-7v2; NALW; NoP-4; NoP-5; WaAnP
  First Book: Young Aurora's Fostermother. NALW
  "My mother was a Florentine." NALW
  "So it was. / I broke the copious curls upon my head." BrAP
  Sweetness of England, The. OxAEP-2
  "Then, land!—then, England! oh, the frosty cliffs." NAEL-6v2; NAEL-7v2
  ""Then, must it be."" NALW
  "There he glowed on me." NAEL-6v2; NAEL-7v2
  "Times followed one another. Came a morn." NAEL-6v2; NAEL-7v2

Auroras of Autumn, The. Wallace Stevens. APT-1
  "Farewell to an idea . . . A cabin stands." NAMCP V.1
  "Farewell to an idea . . . The mother's face." NAMCP V.1

Aurore Bradaire, belle ti fille. Aurore Bradaire. *Unknown.* SSUS

Aurore se dissoudra, L'. Début de l'été, Le. Robert Melançon. YaTCFP

Aus Einem April. Frank O'Hara. HarvBoo

Auschwitz. János Pilinszky. IQMS, *tr. by* Peter Jay

Auschwitz. Salvatore Quasimodo. AF, *tr. by* Jack Bevan

Auschwitz, 1987. Adam Zych. HP, *tr. by* Hilda Schiff

Auspicious Arrival of Yung T'ao. Chia Tao. CSKM, *tr. by* Mike O'Connor

Auspicious flash of light—can you see, An. Auspicious Cloud. Master Naong. BecRai, *tr. by* Kim Daljin, Kim Won-Chung and Christopher Merrill

Austerities. Charles Simic. EmeKit

Austin. Karle Wilson Baker. TiP2 *Fr.* Some Towns of Texas.

Australia. Gary Catalano. NOBAu

Australia. Alec Derwent Hope. BMAP; BrAP; NAMCP V.1; NoAM; NoP-4; NoP-5

Australia 1970. Judith Wright. HarvBoo; MakPoe; NoAM

Australian Emigrant, The. Francis Fisher Browne. VWP *Fr.* Australian Emigrant, The.

Australian Garden, An. Peter Porter. BrAP; OBGa

Australorp. Edith Speers. NOBAu

Autant d'images-associations que je ne peux pas développer dans mes vers. Blaise Cendrars. YaTCFP *Fr.* Prose du Transsibérien et de la Petite Jeanne de France.

Authentic! Shadows of it, The. Matins. Denise Levertov. BrAP; NoAM

Author Loving These Homely Meats, The. John Davies of Hereford. NPeEn; OBCoV *Fr.* Scourge of Folly, The.

Author of American Ornithology Sketches a Bird, Now Extinct, The. David Wagoner. BLT

Author of light, revive my dying spright. Thomas Campion. InvLi

Author of the Jesus Papers Speaks, The. Anne Sexton. PFTM-2

Author of this is Ossian, The. *Unknown.* NePenScot, *tr. by* Derick Thomson

Author, The. Charles Churchill.
  "Gods! with what pride I see the titled slave." OBSV
  "When with much pains this boasted learning's got." OBSV

Author to Her Book, The. Anne Bradstreet. BASC; BrAP; ColAP; EMWP; MakPoe; NAAL-3; NAAL-5; NAAPv.1; NALW; NoP-4; NoP-5; OxBoAm; TCAPo; WaAnP

Author to His Body on Their Fifteenth Birthday, 29.ii.80, The. Howard Nemerov. NoAM

Author to His Book[e], The. Thomas Heywood. NOSC; WaAnP *Fr.* Apology for Actors, An.

Authoritarian School and How a Respectable Literary Genre Was Born, The. Gerardo Deniz. RMCMP, *tr. by* Mónica de la Torre

Authorities do not permit us, The. Joy. Susan Wicks. MFPA

Authors and actors and artists and such. Bohemia. Dorothy Parker. AmWit; APT-1; BrAP; NBLV

Authors and poets in prose and in rhyme. Night We Called It a Day, The. Tom Adair. ReLy

Author's Apology for His Book, The. John Bunyan.
  "When at the first I took my pen in hand." FaBoVe

Author's Club. Juan Ramón Jiménez. WED, *tr. by* Robert Bly

Author's Consent. Mahe Jabeen. HotL, *tr. by* V. Narayana Rao

Author's Dream to the Lady Mary, the Countess Dowager of Pembroke, The. Emilia Lanier and Aemilia Bassano Lanyer. BASC

Author's Early Life, The. Julia A. Moore.
  "And now, kind friends, what I have wrote." VerBaPo

Author's Epitaph, Made By Himself, The. Sir Walter Ralegh. *See* Even Such Is Time.

Authors of the Town, The. Richard Savage.
  "First, let me view what noxious nonsense reigns." OBSV

Authors [*or* Author's] Abstract of Melancholy, The. Robert Burton. NOSC *Fr.* Anatomy of Melancholy, The.

Author's Prayer. Ilya Kaminsky. LegDan

Author's Prologue. Dylan Thomas. ChIV-1
  (Prologue to The Collected Poems.) AngWePo

Author's Quietus, The. Henry Carey. FaBoVe

Author's Resolution, The. George Wither. *See* Shall I, Wasting in Despair.

Authorship. James Ball Naylor. GoPo; NBLV

Authours Epitaph, Made by Himself, The. Sir Walter Ralegh. NIL-7
  (Verses Found in His Bible in the Gatehouse at Westminster.) SacPr
  (Verses Made the Night before His Beheading.) CABP

Auto Mirror. Adam Zagajewski. BLT

Auto Wreck. Karl Shapiro. APT-2; NIL-7; NIP-4

Autobiographia. G. E. Patterson. P180

Autobiographia Literaria. Frank O'Hara. OxBoAm; PtR

Autobiographical. Abraham Moses Klein. BrAP; NoAM

Autobiographical Fragment. Kingsley Amis. OBCoV

Autobiographical Moment, An. Ya'ir Hurvits. PML, *tr. by* Lois Bar-yaacov

Autobiographical Poem. Elaine Equi. KGB

Autobiographical Response from a Provincial Wasteland (in Reply to a New Year's Greeting Sent with a Bouquet). Elizaveta Shakhova. ARWW, *tr. by* Catriona Kelly

Autobiography. Marilyn Bowering.
  4. IFF

Autobiography. John Burnside. NePenScot

Autobiography. Thom Gunn. NoAM

Autobiography. Joy Harjo. LTA

Autobiography. Louis MacNeice. ModIr; NPeEn; PNI

Autobiography. Paula Meehan. MoWP

Autobiography. Dan Pagis. PoSu

Autobiography. Dan Pagis. FIT, *tr. by* Robert Friend

Autobiography. Dan Pagis. AF; VCWP, *tr. by* Stephen Mitchell

Autobiography. Robert Viscusi. UnSA

Autobiography 2 (hellogoodbye). Michael Palmer. HarvBoo; WoBe

Autobiography: "All clocks are clouds." Michael Palmer. CalPo

Autobiography, An. Basil Bunting. HarvBoo; NAMCP V.1; NoAM; NoP-4; NoP-5; NPeEn *Fr.* Briggflatts [An Autobiography].

Autobiography, An. Ernest Rhys. OBEV; OBWVE

Autobiography, Chapter XLII: Three Days in Louisville. Jim Barnes. HATNAP

Autobiography, Chapter XVII: Floating the Big Piney. Jim Barnes. HATNAP

Autobiography: "First thing I can remember is a blue line, The. This was on the left." Margaret Atwood. MotU; OpeFie

Autobiography in Third Person. Betsy Sholl. ACAMVP

Autobiography of a Black Man. G. E. Patterson. AmPoNex

Autobiography of a Lungworm. Roy Fuller. NoAM

Autobiography of a Sloppy Sluggard. Kuan Kuan. PML, *tr. by* Zhang Cuo

Autobiography of John Doe, The. Jon Lavieri. OPRER

Autochthon. Sir Charles G. D. Roberts. IFF

Autocrat of the Breakfast Table, The. Oliver Wendell Holmes.

  Aestivation [an Unpublished Poem, by My Late Latin Tutor]. TCAPo

  Chambered Nautilus, The. APN-1; ColAP; CtM; ITBLP; NAAL-3; NAAPv.1; NCAP; NoP-4; NoP-5; OxBoAm; TCAPo; TFi; WaAnP

  Contentment. APN-1; OxBoAm

  Deacon's Masterpiece, The; or, The Wonderful "One-Hoss Shay." APN-1; BRP; ITBLP; NAAL-3; NAAPv.1; TCAPo; TFi

  Living Temple, The. APN-1

  Voiceless, The. APN-1

Autograph. Francisco Hernandez. PML, *tr. by* John Oliver Simon

Autograph on the Soul, The. Adah Isaacs Menken. CBWP-1

Autolycus as Peddler. William Shakespeare. NoSic; NPeEn *Fr.* Winter's Tale, The.

Autolycus's Song ("Jog on, jog on, the footpath way"). William Shakespeare. NoSic *Fr.* Winter's Tale, The.

Automat. David Ray. PoSol

Automatic Crystal, The. Aimé Césaire. SurPaPo, *tr. by* Clayton Eshleman and Annette Smith

Automatic Crystal, The. Aimé Césaire. YaTCFP, *tr. by* Mary Ann Caws and Jean-Pierre Cauvin and Patricia Terry

Automatic Text for Anne Ethuin. Elisabeth Lenk. SurWo, *tr. by* Gisela Baumhauer and Greta Wenziger

Automatically made Tony Anthony! (LL) Them & [uz]. Tony Harrison. NoP-4; NoP-5

Automne, L'. Jean Frémon. YaTCFP

Automne précéda l'été d'un jour, L'. Automne précéda l'été, L'. Venus Khoury-Gata. YaTCFP

Automobile, The. Russell Edson. RaBo; SUP

Automobile, The. Vladislav Felitsianovich Khodasevich. TCRusP, *tr. by* Daniel Weissbort

Automobiles. Iwan Llwyd. ATSWP, *tr. by* Robert Minhinnick

Automobiles of the Asylum. Philip Hammial. BMAP

Automotrici stutter along the branch lines. Off the Beaten Track. Peter Rafferty. NLP

Autonomy Is Jeopardy. Charles Bernstein. NAMCP V.2

Autonomy of the Mind. Tsering Wangno Dhompa. WANABP

Autopsy. James L. Foy. BloBone

Autopsy. Arthur Nortje. HBAPE

Autopsy, The. Odysseus Elytis. AF, *tr. by* Edmund Keeley and Philip Sherrard

Autopsychography. Fernando Pessoa. WoPoe, *tr. by* Keith Bosley

Autozobop. Boadiba. OGAHCP, *tr. by* the author and Jack Hirschman

Autre, L'. André Velter. YaTCFP

Autumn. Roy Campbell. MoBrPo; OBMV

Autumn. Alice Cary. APN-2

Autumn. Walter De la Mare. NPeEn

Autumn. Maurice Gilliams. TuT, *tr. by* Sean Dunne

Autumn. Autumn Moon Rising. Robert Grenier. Eno

Autumn. Friedrich Hölderlin. WoPoe *Fr.* Seasons, The.

Autumn. Thomas Ernest Hulme. NPeEn

Autumn. Alphonse Marie Louis de Lamartine. SxFrPo, *tr. by* A. M. and E. H. Blackmore

Autumn. Henry Wadsworth Longfellow. APN-1

Autumn. Archibald MacLeish. IllVoic

Autumn. Gabriela Mistral. SpanPo, *tr. by* Muriel Kittel

Autumn. Thomas Nashe. NoSic *Fr.* Summer's Last Will and Testament.

Autumn. Ngo Chi Lan. EaWin, *tr. by* W. S. Merwin and Nguyen Ngoc Bich

Autumn. Robert Peterson. GeoHom

Autumn. Alexander L. Posey. APN-2

Autumn: "On the first day of Autumn." Michael Schein. ArBi

Autumn ("I dwell alone—I dwell alone, alone.") Christina Georgina Rossetti. VWP

Autumn: "I saw old Autumn in the misty morn." Thomas Hood. OBEV; OxAEP-2

Autumn. Stevie Smith. *See* He Told His Life Story to Mrs. Courtly.

Autumn. James Thomson. *Fr.* Seasons, The.

Autumn. Mihály Tompa. IQMS, *tr. by* Watson Kirkconnell

Autumn. *Unknown.* OBMV

Autumn. *Unknown.* CCL1 *Fr.* Tzu Yeh Songs.

Autumn. Jean Starr Untermeyer. MoAmPo

Autumn. Yun Sŏndo. CATKP *Fr.* Angler's Calendar, The.

Autumn: "Autumn rains blow." *Vietnamese Oral Tradition.* CaDao, *tr. by* John Balaban

Autumn: "Autumn wind sweeps in through the windows, The." *Unknown.* CCL1, *tr. by* John Frodsham

Autumn: the ninth year of Yüan Ho. Temple, The. OBMV, *tr. by* Arthur Waley

Autumn: "November the 1st. Gold leaves." Charles Wright. GeoHom

Autumn 1710. *Unknown.* IQMS, *tr. by* Watson Kirkconnell

Autumn 1980. Marilyn Hacker. InoFa

Autumn: A Dirge. Percy Bysshe Shelley. TreFP

Autumn (A Fragment). Alexander Sergeyevich Pushkin. WoPoe, *tr. by* Edwin Morgan

Autumn Again. Sándor Petőfi. IQMS, *tr. by* Lydia Pasternak-Slater

Autumn already!—But why regret an eternal sun if we are embarked on. Arthur Rimbaud. PFTM-1

Autumn approaches. Basho. SoOfWa, *tr. by* Sam Hamill

Autumn Aspens: Cumbres Pass. Reg Saner. PoCoUp

Autumn Bees on Broccoli Blossoms Gone-by. Gary Margolis. PfSP

Autumn Begins in Martins Ferry, Ohio. James Wright. CAP-8; ColAP; EMP; HeIP-4; IJHIL; MoASP; NAAL-5; NAMCP V.2; NoAM; OxBoAm; StAl; VCAP; WaAnP; WeW-3

Autumn blast—wild boar. Urn. Takahashi Shinkichi. ZenPo, *tr. by* Takashi Ikemoto and Lucien Stryk

Autumn branches are bare, the sunlight weak, The. Waking from a Nap. Chungji. BecRai, *tr. by* Kim Daljin, Kim Won-Chung and Christopher Merrill

Autumn breezes. Buson. SoOfWa, *tr. by* Sam Hamill

Autumn Cancer. Kerry Hardie. BeAl; PoCu

Autumn, cloud blades on the horizon. Clear After Rain. Tu Fu [*or* Du Fu]. BLT; CCL1, *tr. by* Kenneth Rexroth

Autumn come / Cicada husk. Masaoka Shiki. ZenPo, *tr. by* Takashi Ikemoto and Lucien Stryk

Autumn comes to a river village. Yun Sŏndo. CATKP *Fr.* Angler's Calendar, The.

Autumn comes to rivers and lakes. Maeng Sasŏng. CATKP *Fr.* Four Seasons by the Rivers and Lakes.

Autumn constellations, The. Moon Festival. Tu Fu [*or* Du Fu]. NDACCP, *tr. by* Kenneth Rexroth

Autumn Cove. Li Po. ColAnChi, *tr. by* Burton Watson

Autumn, Crystal Eye. Margot Ruddock. OBMV

Autumn Day. Geng Wei. CCL1, *tr. by* Stephen Owen

Autumn Day. Rainer Maria Rilke. WoPoe, *tr. by* John Felsteiner

Autumn Day, An. Sun Ch'o. CCL1, *tr. by* John Frodsham

Autumn Day, An. Clara Ann Thompson. CBWP-2

Autumn days / are terrible and keen, The. Seeing Off a Guest at Captain Wang's Headquarters. T'ao Ch'ien. CCL1, *tr. by* William Acker

Autumn deepening. Basho. EMJL, *tr. by* Haruo Shirane

Autumn Distance. Jacques Réda. YaTCFP, *tr. by* Stephen Romer

Autumn Dusk at a Mountain Lodge. Wang Wei. ChinPo, *tr. by* Ye Weilian [*or* Yeh Wei-lien *or* Wai-lim Yip]

Autumn eats its leaf out of my hand: we are friends. Corona. Paul Celan. PoSu, *tr. by* Michael Hamburger

Autumn End. Luu Trong Lu. SonAtl, *tr. by* Duong Thu Huong, Mrs. S. Goldenhall, S. Goldenhall, Elisa Joy Holland and Sally Yang

Autumn / Even the birds. Basho. ZenPo, *tr. by* Takashi Ikemoto and Lucien Stryk

Autumn evening. (LL) This road. Basho. EH; NIL-7, *tr. by* Robert Hass

Autumn evening. Buson. EH, *tr. by* Yoel Hoffmann

Autumn evening. Issa. EH, *tr. by* Robert Hass

Autumn Evening. Robinson Jeffers. ChAP

Autumn evening / Knees in arms. Issa. ZenPo, *tr. by* Takashi Ikemoto and Lucien Stryk

Autumn Evening on the Great Lake. Wang Ch'ang-ling. CCL1, *tr. by* Stephen Owen

Autumn Evening: To Send to my Nieces and Nephews. Ch'i-chi. CSKM, *tr. by* Burton Watson

Autumn feels slowed down, The. Paula Becker to Clara Westhoff. Adrienne Rich. VCAP

Autumn Fires. Robert Louis Stevenson. NOxBChV

Autumn flowers. War Lament. *Unknown.* CrYelRi, *tr. by* Sam Hamill

Autumn Flowers. Jones Very. APN-1

Autumn frost, The. (LL) It would melt. Basho. ChAP; EH, *tr. by* Robert Hass

Autumn Garden. Dino Campana. STV, *tr. by* John Frederick Nims

Autumn going. Basho. EMJL, *tr. by* Haruo Shirane

Autumn has turned the dark trees toward the hill. Quail in Autumn. William Jay Smith. OWoS

Autumn hath all the summer's fruitful treasure. Thomas Nashe. NoSic *Fr.* Summer's Last Will and Testament.

Autumn in Korea. Black Hole. No Hyangnim. EcSo, *tr. by* Aimee N. Kwon

Autumn in New York. Vernon Duke. ReLy

Autumn is finished—yesterday a flash. First Morning. George Keithley. PoCoUp

Autumn is here and darkness comes earlier now; the rain is falling. Death of Sagittarius. Milán Füst. IQMS, *tr. by* Jess Perlman

Autumn is unquiet everywhere. Green Side, The. Jennifer Maiden. BMAP

Autumn is weary, halt, and old. October Redbreast, The. Alice Thompson Meynell. MoBrPo

Autumn Journal. Louis MacNeice.
  "And I remember Spain." OBWP; OxAEP-2
  "Close and slow, summer is ending in Hampshire." NPeEn
  "Nightmare leaves fatigue." ModIr; PNI
  "Now we are back to normal, now the mind is." OxAEP-2
  "September has come and I wake." NoP-4; NoP-5
  "Shelley and jazz and lieder and love and hymn-tunes." NPeEn
  "Sun shines easy, sun shines gay."
    Munich Agreement, The. RWPCtW
  "Which things being so, as we said when we studied."
  "I ought to be glad." OBCoV

Autumn Lament. Charles Baudelaire. MotU, *tr. by* Keith Bosley

Autumn Leaves. Marilyn Chin. ExTi; NAMCP V.2

Autumn Leaves. James Cushing. SeSe

Autumn Leaves. Clara Ann Thompson. CBWP-2

Autumn Leaves. Jones Very. APN-1

Autumn leaves that strew the brooks, The. Remembrance Sunday. Dennis Joseph Enright. NPeEn

Autumn Letter. No Hyangnim. EcSo, *tr. by* Aimee N. Kwon

Autumn Lines. Li Po. CCL1, *tr. by* David Young

Autumn Love. Li Ch'ing-chao. NDACCP

Autumn Meditation: 7. Tu Fu [*or* Du Fu]. CCL1, *tr. by* Stephen Owen

Autumn met me today as I walked over Castle Hill. Stand-To, The. Cecil Day Lewis. NoP-4; OBWP

Autumn moon. Issa. EH, *tr. by* Robert Hass

Autumn moon risen mid-sky, The. Border Guard, A. Hsiao Yen [*or* Emperor Wu of Liang]. CCL1, *tr. by* Anne Birrell

Autumn Moon Rising. Robert Grenier. Eno

Autumn moon / Tide foams. Basho. ZenPo, *tr. by* Takashi Ikemoto and Lucien Stryk

Autumn moonlight. Basho. EH, *tr. by* Robert Hass

Autumn Morning in Shokoku-ji, An. Gary Snyder. WeW-3 *Fr.* Four Poems for Robin.

Autumn Mountain Evening. Wang Wei. CCL1, *tr. by* Jerome P. Seaton

Autumn mountains: brocades of light. 166. Shih Shu. CSKM, *tr. by* James H. Sanford

Autumn Night. Tu Fu [*or* Du Fu]. EaWin, *tr. by* W. S. Merwin

Autumn Night: A Letter Sent to Ch'iu. Wei Ying-wu. ChinPo, *tr. by* Ye Weilian [*or* Yeh Wei-lien *or* Wai-lim Yip]

Autumn Night, An. Hsieh T'iao. CCL1, *tr. by* John Frodsham

Autumn Night Message: To Qiu. Wei Ying-wu. CCL1, *tr. by* Witter Bynner

Autumn nights, it seems. Ono no Komachi. WoPoe, *tr. by* Helen Craig McCullough

Autumn 1942. Roy Fuller. PoWW

Autumn, 1949: At the "Flower" Tea Room. Sŏ Chŏngju. CAMKP, *tr. by* David R. McCann

Autumn, 1939. Alun Lewis. PoWW

Autumn, On Retreat at a Mountain Temple. Lady Izumi. *See* In the Autumn, on Retreat at a Mountain Temple.

Autumn on the Riverbank. Chao Shan-ch'ing. CrYelRi, *tr. by* Sam Hamill

Autumn, once again enchanting. Autumn Again. Sándor Petőfi. IQMS, *tr. by* Lydia Pasternak-Slater

Autumn Path. Pao Hsien. CSKM, *tr. by* Paul Hansen

Autumn Ploughing. John Masefield. OxBEV

Autumn Pool. Po Chü-i. NDACCP, *tr. by* David Hinton

Autumn preceded summer by one day. Autumn Preceded Summer. Venus Khoury-Gata. YaTCFP, *tr. by* Marilyn Hacker

Autumn Prelude. Andrey Andreievich Voznesensky. RusPo, *tr. by* Robert Arthur Douglas Ford

Autumn Rain, The. Christopher Pearse Cranch. TCAPo

Autumn rains blow. Autumn. *Vietnamese Oral Tradition.* CaDao, *tr. by* John Balaban

Autumn Refrain. Wallace Stevens. APT-1; OxBoAm

Autumn resumes the land, ruffles the woods. Geoffrey Hill. NAEL-6v2; NAEL-7v2; NoAM; NoP-4; NoP-5; NPeEn *Fr.* Apology for the Revival of Christian Architecture in England, An.

Autumn Returns. Pablo Neruda. ConPit, *tr. by* Clayton Eshleman

Autumn River in Burning Tears. Pak Chaesam. CAMKP, *tr. by* David R. McCann and Jiwon Shin

Autumn Rose. Amal Moussa. PoArWo, *tr. by* Khaled Mattawa

Autumn Sequel. Louis MacNeice.
  Canto XX. ModIr

Autumn Sequence. Jan Freeman.
  Fifteen. OxWW

Autumn Shade. Edgar Bowers.
  "Awakened by some fear, I watch the sky." VCAP
  "I drive home with the books that I will read." VCAP
  "In nameless warmth, sun light in every corner." VCAP
  "Snow and then rain. The roads are wet. A car." VCAP

Autumn: "Shogun, always on the lookout for ways to increase his glory, The." Jean Frémon. YaTCFP, *tr. by* Cole Swensen

Autumn slipped into Paris yesterday. Autumn Slipped Into Paris. Endre Ady. IQMS, *tr. by* Anton N. Nyerges

Autumn smears the green hills. O my Dear Animals. Salvatore Quasimodo. SonAtl, *tr. by* Gregory Beaven and Favorita '68

Autumn Song. József Bajza. IQMS, *tr. by* Watson Kirkconnell

Autumn Song. Charles Baudelaire. SxFrPo, *tr. by* James McGowan

Autumn Song. Spencer Reece. LegDan

Autumn Song ("Long sobs of, The.") Paul Verlaine. SxFrPo, *tr. by* Martin Sorrell

Autumn Song ("Violins complain.") Paul Verlaine. WoPoe, *tr. by* Louis Simpson

Autumn Song ("With long sobs.") Paul Verlaine. NAWM-7v2, *tr. by* Carlyle Ferren MacIntyre

Autumn Sonnets, The. May Sarton.
  "If I can let you go as trees let go." PoBW

Autumn sunlight gilds the evening sky. Harmonizing with the Monk Heling's Poem "An Outing to the Kunming Pool." Yu Hsin. CCL1, *tr. by* John Frodsham

Autumn Sunrise. Antonio Machado Ruiz. RaW, *tr. by* Robert Bly

Autumn Sunset, An. Edith Wharton. APN-2

Autumn Supper. Dimitris Tsaloumas. BMAP

Autumn Testament. James Keir Baxter.
  "Bodies of the young are not the flower, The." BeAl

Autumn, the Nightwalk, the City, the River. David Wheatley. NIrP

Autumn this soon! But why hanker after an eternal sun. Farewell. Arthur Rimbaud. SxFrPo, *tr. by* Martin Sorrell

Autumn Thought. Choeui Eusoon. BecRai, *tr. by* Kim Daljin, Kim Won-Chung and Christopher Merrill

Autumn Thoughts. Han Yü. *tr. by* Burton Watson
  "Leaves fall turning turning to the ground." CCL1; WoPoe, *tr. by* Burton Watson
  "This morning I can't seem to get out of bed." CCL1, *tr. by* Burton Watson
  "When white dew descends on the hundred grasses." CCL1, *tr. by* Burton Watson

Autumn Thoughts. Mary E. Tucker. CBWP-1

Autumn Thoughts, Sent Far Away. Po Chü-i. NDACCP, *tr. by* David Hinton

Autumn Twilight in the Mountains. Wang Wei. NDACCP; WaAnP, *tr. by* Kenneth Rexroth

Autumn Valentine. Dorothy Parker. IJHIL

Autumn Verses. Rubén Darío. BLPSL, *tr. by* Rene de Costa, Rigas Kappatos and Eleni Paidoussi

Autumn Verses. Rubén Darío. SpanPo, *tr. by* Kate Flores

Autumn Violets. Christina Georgina Rossetti. ViWPN

Autumn Warrior. Barney Bush. HATNAP

Autumn was ripe. Beaches. Nesta Wyn Jones. BBMWP, *tr. by* Catherine Fisher

Autumn Wastes, The: 1 and 2. Tu Fu [*or* Du Fu]. CCL1, *tr. by* A. C. Graham

Autumn wastes are each day wilder, The. Autumn Wastes, The: 1 and 2. Tu Fu [*or* Du Fu]. CCL1, *tr. by* A. C. Graham

Autumn wind. Stanford M. Forrester. AmZen

Autumn Wind. Adriann Roland Holst. TuT, *tr. by* Desmond Egan

Autumn wind. Taneda Santoka. CAoMJL1, *tr. by* Burton Watson

Autumn Wind. Emperor Wu of Han. NDACCP, *tr. by* Kenneth Rexroth

Autumn wind / Across the fields. Onitsura. ZenPo, *tr. by* Takashi Ikemoto and Lucien Stryk

Autumn wind / Blasting the stones. Basho. ZenPo, *tr. by* Takashi Ikemoto and Lucien Stryk

Autumn wind blows drearily, The. Song of Yan, A. Ts'ao P'i. CCL1, *tr. by* John Frodsham

Autumn wind blows white clouds, The. Autumn Wind. Emperor Wu of Han. NDACCP, *tr. by* Kenneth Rexroth

Autumn wind / Gods, Buddha. Masaoka Shiki. ZenPo, *tr. by* Takashi Ikemoto and Lucien Stryk

Autumn wind / Mountain's shadow. Issa. ZenPo, *tr. by* Takashi Ikemoto and Lucien Stryk

Autumn wind rises; white clouds fly.   Autumn Wind, The.   Emperor Wu of Han.   CCL1, *tr. by* Arthur Waley

Autumn wind sweeps in through the windows, The.   Autumn.   *Unknown.*   CCL1, *tr. by* John Frodsham

Autumn wind: ten thousand trees wither.   Stone on the Hilltop, The.   Lu Yu.   ColAnChi, *tr. by* Burton Watson

Autumn Wind, The.   Emperor Wu of Han.   CCL1, *tr. by* Arthur Waley

Autumn wind / The beggar looks.   Issa.   ZenPo, *tr. by* Takashi Ikemoto and Lucien Stryk

Autumn winds blow along the river.   Grain-Barge Wife, The.   Wu Chia-chi.   ColAnChi, *tr. by* Jonathan Chaves

Autumn winds cry through mulberry branches.   Song by the Walls.   Wang Ch'ang-ling.   CCL1, *tr. by* Stephen Owen

Autumn winds descend and sweep.   Autumn 1710.   *Unknown.*   IQMS, *tr. by* Watson Kirkconnell

Autumn winds, swish-swish, sorrow killing men.   Old Song.   *Unknown.*   ChinPo, *tr. by* Ye Weilian [*or* Yeh Wei-lien *or* Wai-lim Yip]

Autumn Woods.   William Cullen Bryant.   APN-1

Autumn your bellringing, the apple of bright weeping.   Galina Ermoshina.   CRWP, *tr. by* Gerald Janecek

Autumnal.   Rubén Darío.   SpanPo, *tr. by* Anita Volland

Autumnal.   Mark Irwin.   PuP-23

Autumnal Equinox.   Svetlana Dengina.   CRWP, *tr. by* Daniel Weissbort

Autumnal full moon.   Basho.   SoOfWa, *tr. by* Sam Hamill

Autumnal Sketch, An.   August Kleinzahler.   PmAP

Autumnal[l], The.   John Donne.   BASC; FSCP; NOSC *Fr.* Elegies.

Autumn's born / Along a deep path.   Living on the Plain in Early Autumn.   Huai Ku.   CSKM, *tr. by* Paul Hansen

Autumn's colors spread their silk on the hill.   On Hearing the Song of the Geese.   Haewŏn.   BecRai, *tr. by* Kim Daljin, Kim Won-Chung and Christopher Merrill

Autumn's done; they have the golden corn in, The.   Trumbull Stickney.   APN-2

Autumn's End.   Christopher Buckley.   PfSP

Autumn's end: frost and dew become heavy.   Morning Walk in Autumn to South Valley Passing an Abandoned Village.   Liu Tsung-yüan.   ChinPo, *tr. by* Ye Weilian [*or* Yeh Wei-lien *or* Wai-lim Yip]

Autumn-time has come, The.   My Triumph.   John Greenleaf Whittier.   APN-1

Autumn-Time, Wind and the Planet Pluto.   Joseph Ceravolo.   NYP2

Aux buissons typographiques constitués par le poème sur une route.   Mûres, Les.   Francis Ponge.   YaTCFP

Aux défis de l'impossible.   Toast en réponse.   André Frénaud.   YaTCFP

Available Now: Archaic Torsos of Both Sexes.   Gregory Orr.   PoA 2002

Avalanche.   Quincy Troupe.   PFTM-2; SpirFl

Avalon.   Thomas Holley Chivers.   APN-1

Avant-garde snippet banal regarded both elements.   34th Merzgedicht in Memoriam Kurt Schwitters.   Jackson Mac Low.   PFTM-2

Avant-Garde, The.   Nance Van Winckel.   RoV

Avare.   Michel Leiris.   YaTCFP

Avatar, The.   Kerry Hardie.   NIrP; StAl

Ave Atque Vale.   Pennar Davies.   BBMWP, *tr. by* Joseph P. Clancy

Ave atque Vale.   Algernon Charles Swinburne.   NAEL-6v2; NAEL-7v2; OBEV

Ave atque Vale.   Rosamund Marriott Watson.   OBEV

Ave Atque Vale: "It gathers where the moody sky is bending."   Nora May French.   CalPo

Ave Caesar.   Robinson Jeffers.   NAMCP V.1; NoAM; OxBoAm

A've heard it said that bairns.   Crabbit Angels.   David Purves.   EdScPo

Ave Maria.   Hart Crane.   NoAM *Fr.* Bridge, The.

Ave Maria.   Frank O'Hara.   CLPP; HarvBoo; MakPoe; NoP-4; NoP-5; PmAP; PoPoPo; VCAP

Ave Maria Gratia Plena.   Oscar Wilde.   ChIV-2

Ave, Virgo! Gr-r-r—you swine! (LL)   Soliloquy of the Spanish Cloister.   Robert Browning.   BrAP; FaBoVe; NAEL-6v2; NAEL-7v2; NIL-7; NIP-4; NoP-4; NoP-5; OxBEV; UV

'Ave you 'eard o' the Widow at Windsor.   Widow at Windsor, The.   Rudyard Kipling.   NAEL-6v2; NAEL-7v2; NoAM

Avenge O Lord thy slaughtered [*or* slaughter'd] Saints, whose bones.   On the Late Massacre [*or* Massacher] in Piedmont [*or* Piemont].   John Milton.   BrAP; CABP; GSo; HeIP-4; NAEL-6v1; NIL-7; NoP-4; NoP-5; NPeEn; OBWP; OxBEV; OxBSo; PoPoPo; TFi; TRP; WaAnP; WeW-3

Avenger, The.   Samuel Carter.
  Incident in Italy.   STuOW

Avengers, The.   Edwin Markham.   MoAmPo

Avenir.   Henri Michaux.   YaTCFP

Avenue.   Robert Pinsky.   TaR

Avenue, The.   Frances Darwin Cornford.   LW

Avenue of tombs! I stand before, An.   In Père La Chaise.   Joaquin Miller.   APN-2

Avenue, The.   Paul Muldoon.   PBCIP

Avenue was green and long, and green, The.   Visit to Castletown House, A.   Michael Hartnett.   PBCIP

Avenues trot, The.   Tomas Tranströmer.   WoBe *Fr.* Haiku.

Average joe comes in, An.   Short-Order Cook.   Jim Daniels.   ReTh

Aves Tsu-kiou in aquaticis terris mas et foemina ambae vices agunt suas cantando.   *Unknown.*   CCL1 *Fr.* Guan-ju.

Aviary.   Mark DeFoe.   UrbNat

Aviary.   Medbh McGuckian.   MoWP

Aviary, The.   Saint-Pol Roux.   YaTCFP, *tr. by* Robin Magowan

Aviation.   Elaine Feinstein.   MoWP

Avid of life and love, insatiate vagabond.   Verlaine.   Richard Hovey.   APN-2

Avignon.   Remco Campert.   PoetW, *tr. by* Jeffery Paine

Avila.   John Yau.   BodElec

Avocado.   Gary Snyder.   PmAP; WhBo

Avocado Pit, The.   Carl Rakosi.   APT-2

Avoid.   Rachel Zucker.   IAoNAP

Avoid sharp swords and lovely women.   Risks.   Meng Chiao.   CCL1, *tr. by* Graeme Wilson

Avoid storms. And retirement parties.   Lines on Retirement, after Reading *Lear.*   David Wright.   IaFF

Avoid the reeking herd.   Eagle and the Mole, The.   Elinor Wylie.   CtM; MoAmPo; NAAPv.2; NALW

Avoiding fishnet.   Buson.   WoPoe, *tr. by* Tony Barnstone, Willis Barnstone *and* Haixin Xu

Avoiding News by the River.   W. S. Merwin.   GifTon

Aw wish my lover she was a cherry.   Pitman's Lovesong, A.   *Unknown.*   FaBoVe

Await us, weighing the unstripped bough. (LL)   Farewell to Van Gogh.   Charles Tomlinson.   NoP-4; NoP-5

Awaited—locally—a date. (LL)   Town, a town.   George Oppen.   APT-2; PFTM-1

Awake.   Mary Elizabeth Coleridge.   ViWPN

Awake, Aeolian lyre, awake.   Progress of Poesy, The.   Thomas Gray.   OBEV

Awake, and with attention hear.   34. Chapter of the Prophet Isaiah, The.   Abraham Cowley.   ChIV-1

Awake, arise, the hour is come.   Radical War Song, A.   Thomas Babington Macaulay, 1st Baron Macaulay.   OBSV

Awake at night.   Basho.   EH, *tr. by* Robert Hass

Awake at night.   Basho.   EH, *tr. by* Robert Hass

Awake, Awake! [Thou Heavy Sprite].   Thomas Campion.   ChIV-1

Awake but not yet up, too early morning.   Out of Sleep.   Allen Curnow.   BrAP

Awake! for morning in the bowl of night.   Rubáiyát of Omar Khayyám [of Naishápúr], The.   Omar Khayyám.   NPeEn; OxAEP-2; OxBEV; TAL; UV, *tr. by* Edward Fitzgerald

Awake! for Morning on the Pitch of Night.   Strugnell's Rubáiyát.   Wendy Cope.   UV

Awake I steal what they dream.   Sleepers.   Branko Miljkovic.   WoPoe, *tr. by* Charles Simic

Awake in a giant night.   Giant Night.   Anne Waldman.   AHA

Awake my Fanny! leave all meaner things.   John Wilkes.   EroLit *Fr.* Essay on Woman.

Awake, My Heart, to Be Loved.   Robert Bridges.   MoBrPo; OBEV

Awake, my heart's delight, awake.   Fair Melody, A: To Be Sung by Good Christians.   Hans Sachs.   GePo, *tr. by* Catherine Winkworth

Awake, my love, who sleep in the dawn!   Lady's Farewell, The.   Nuño Fernández Torneol.   WoPoe, *tr. by* Yvor Winters

Awake, my soul, and with the sun.   Morning Hymn.   Thomas Ken.   NOSC; SacPr

Awake, my soul! lift up thine eyes.   Call, The.   Anna Laetitia Barbauld.   SacPr

Awake, my St. John! leave all meaner things.   Alexander Pope.   NAEL-6v1; NAWM-7v2 *Fr.* Essay on Man, An.

Awake, O Lord, Awake Thy Saints.   Morgan Llwyd.   AngWePo

Awake, O Magyar nation, and open wide your eyes.   Verses of a True Hungarian Patriot, The.   *Unknown.*   IQMS, *tr. by* René Bonnerjea and Earl M. Herrick

Awake, [*or* Awake!] ye forms of verse divine!   Fitz-Greene Halleck and Joseph Rodman Drake.   APN-1 *Fr.* Croaker Papers, The.

Awake or sleeping (for I know not which).   Old-World Thicket, An.   Christina Georgina Rossetti.   VWP

Awake sad heart, whom sorrow ever drowns.   Dawning, The.   George Herbert.   NOSC

Awake! stir your bones! Rouse up!   Five O'Clock Whistle, The.   *Hawaiian Oral Tradition.*   NAAPv.1

Awake thy cloud-harp, angel of the rain!   Angel of the Rain.   Harriet McEwen Kimball.   TreFP

Awake, vain Man; 'tis time th' Abuse to see. Advice to His Grace. "Ephelia." EMWP

Awake, ye forms of verse divine! National Painting, The. Joseph Rodman Drake. GS

Awaked from the persistent dream. Wendell Berry. UpMys *Fr.* Sabbaths.

Awaken Hungarian youth! See how your national language. To Hungarian Youth. Dávid Baróti Szabó. IQMS, *tr. by* Matthew Mead and Ruth Mead

Awaken / Oh, boughs of passion. Awakening. Fawziyya Al-Sindi. PoArWo, *tr. by* Joseph T. Zeidan

Awaken them; they are knobs of sound. Sanskrit. Jayanta Mahapatra. VCWP

Awaken us to the long day of the spirit. Our Growing Day. Jean Toomer. NAAPv.2

Awakened at midnight. Basho. SoOfWa, *tr. by* Sam Hamill

Awakened at 3 A.M. Something Happened. Patricia Donegan. WhBo

Awakened by love, your body's animals want to get out. René Daumal. PFTM-1 *Fr.* Clavicles for a Great Poetic Game.

Awakened by some fear, I watch the sky. Edgar Bowers. VCAP *Fr.* Autumn Shade.

Awakened by the radiant beams of morn. Anxiety. Mary Julia Young. CenSon

Awakened in a Field. Juan Delgado. GeoHom

Awakened in the pitch of night. Rain Lover. Sakinah Carol Muhammad. OWABP

Awakened me from my slumber. (LL) Second Review of the Grand Army, A. Bret Harte. CBCWP; PCW

Awakened to this other bleakness. Falcon Drinking. Dimitris Tsaloumas. BMAP

Awakening. Elizabeth Abbot. ICANM

Awakening. Fawziyya Al-Sindi. PoArWo, *tr. by* Joseph T. Zeidan

Awakening. John G. de la Parra, Jr. BeDoSh

Awakening. Henrietta Cordelia Ray. CBWP-3

Awakening. Lucien Stryk. BodElec

Awakening, The. Alejandra Pizarnik. TCLAP, *tr. by* Frank Graziano and María Rosa Fort

Awakening from Drunkenness on a Spring Day. Li Po. TAL

Awakening of the Eremite, The. Luljeta Lleshanaku. WoBe, *tr. by* Henry Israeli

Awakening transports of an inner view of things. (LL) Roots and Branches. Robert Duncan. CalPo; FTOS

Awaking from a dream, you look for. Shadow, The. Luis Cernuda. CAGL, *tr. by* Rick Lipinski

Awaking on grass, sheep, goat. Sheep. Takahashi Shinkichi. ZenPo, *tr. by* Takashi Ikemoto and Lucien Stryk

Aware. D. H. Lawrence. MoBrPo; NAMCP V.1; NoAM

Aware. Denise Levertov. NAMCP V.2

Aware at first only of the dust of sound. Wild Geese Flying. Barbara Howes. OWoS

Aware that summer baked the water clear. Skykomish River Running. Richard Hugo. PoA 2002

Aware to the dry throat of the wide hell in the world. King David Dances. John Berryman. ChIV-1

Awash in chemicals: peptides and alkaloids, hormones and enzymes. Amra: The Neuropharmacology of Nirvana. Dale Pendell. WANABP

Away. Robert Creeley. ICANM

Away, away in the Northland. Legend of the Northland, A. Phoebe Cary. OBSP

Away! away! / Tempt me no more, insidious Love. Complaint, The. Mark Akenside. OBEV

Away, away! You are safer in the tomb. (LL) To a Shade. William Butler Yeats. NAEL-6v2; NAEL-7v2

Away, Delights. Francis Beaumont and John Fletcher. OBEV *Fr.* Captain, The.

Away despair! my gracious Lord doth heare. George Herbert. FSCP

Away down deep and away up high. At the Playground. William Stafford. TLR

Away down East, away down West. *Unknown.* TLR

Away Down in Sunbury. *Unknown.* SSUS

Away down into the shadowy depths of the Real I once lived. Myself. Adah Isaacs Menken. CBWP-1; NAAPv.1; ViWPN

Away, dull care, away! Toasting Song. S. Conant Foster. ArBi

Away, fear, with thy projects, no false fire. William Alabaster. NoSic (Away feare with thy projectes, noe false fyre.) NPeEn

Away from earth and its cares set free. Eternity. Josephine D. Henderson Heard. CBWP-4

Away from the city that hurts and mocks. I Cover the Waterfront. Edward Heyman. ReLy

Away from the literate river. San Antonio Nights. Bryce Milligan. TiP2

Away from the office and desk at last. Away from the Office. Willis Boyd Allen. ArBi

Away from the window. Away from Us. Ethan Gilsdorf. RWPCtW

Away from Us. Ethan Gilsdorf. RWPCtW

Away from you. Roger McGough. OBCoV *Fr.* Summer with Monika.

Away from you the seafloor's longitudinal. Peter Richards. IIR

Away, haunt thou not me. Arthur Hugh Clough. SacPr

Away in this chambered secret, I'll draw sound. In the Bathtub, to Mnemosyne. John Wheelwright. APT-2

Away into the rushing darkness. (LL) Rain Travel. W. S. Merwin. ColAP; GoPo

Away; let nought to Love displeasing. Winifreda. *Unknown.* OBEV

Away, melancholy, / Away with it, let it go. Away, Melancholy. Stevie Smith. BrAP, CABP

Away the horde rode, in a storm of hail. Uncertain Battle, The. David Gascoyne. PoWW

Away thou fondling motley humourist. John Donne. NoSic *Fr.* Satires.

Away to Canada. Joshua McCarter Simpson. "Grieve not, my wife—grieve not for me." TCAPo

Away to whoever it is will have you. (LL) Beast in the Space, The. William Sydney Graham. EmeKit; OxAEP-2; PoA 2002; StAl

Away we go on our wheels, boys. On the Road. Ninon Neckar. ArBi

Away with silks, away with lawn. Clothes Do But Cheat and Cozen [*or* Cousen] Us. Robert Herrick. ErotSp

Away with the curly, golden hair. To a Lady. Francisco de Terrazas. BLPSL, *tr. by* Rene de Costa, Rigas Kappatos and Eleni Paidoussi

Away with this pouting and sadness! Away with this Pouting. Thomas Moore. NPBRoP

Away, ye gay landscapes, ye gardens of roses! Lachin y Gair. Lord Byron. NePenScot

Awe. Bob Kaufman. OxAAAP

Awe at the first arrival. Guests. Cynthia Fuller. BeAl

Awe inspiring! Basho. EMJL, *tr. by* Haruo Shirane

Awe showing up before the curtain. A father's pedigree. Blue stripe. Gag. Robert Budde. PoPra

Awed I behold once more. Ralph Waldo Emerson. APN-1; ColAP

Awful. September 22nd. Vera Gheraducci. CItWP, *tr. by* Cinzia Sartini Blum and Lara Trubowitz

Awful but cheerful. (LL) Bight, The. Elizabeth Bishop. APT-2; EmeKit; PoetW; VCAP

Awful shadow of some unseen Power, The. Hymn to Intellectual Beauty. Percy Bysshe Shelley. HeIP-4; NAEL-6v2; NAEL-7v2; NOBRP; NoP-4; NoP-5; NPBRoP

Awhile meet Doubt and Faith. Burden of Easter Vigil, A. Lionel Pigot Johnson. SacPr

Awkward grammar appals a craftsman. A Dada bard. Christian Bök. OpeFie *Fr.* Chapter A.

Awkward on a hillock of grass. Forever the Snake. Jennifer Rankin. BMAP

Awoke in this. Perugia. Art Lange. PoMAP

Awoken: two eyes home. Proposal. Maggie Nelson. HeMarv

Ax heads and sledges, musket balls and elixir bottles. Treasure. Mark Cox. NevBe

Axe angles, An / from my neighbor's ashcan. Junk. Richard Wilbur. NoP-4; NoP-5; WaAnP; WeW-3

Axe Handles. Gary Snyder. CAP-8; ColAP; LoL; NAMCP V.2; NoAM; PmAP; PoPoPo; TWF; VCAP

Axe rang sharply 'mid those forest shades, An. Western Emigrant, The. Lydia Huntley Sigourney. SWaP

Axe rings in the wood, The. Remembered Morning. Janet Lewis. MakPoe; SoSe-8

Axe without a Handle. Great Master Wonhyo. BecRai, *tr. by* Kim Daljin, Kim Won-Chung and Christopher Merrill

Axe-fall, echo and silence. Noonday silence. Noonday Axeman. Les A. Murray. NAEL-7v2; NoP-4; NoP-5

Axeman. / Cut down my shade. Song of the Sterile Orange Tree. Federico García Lorca. SonAtl, *tr. by* Becca, Jenny Boarder, Thomas Boarder and Lisa Martin

Axes / After whose stroke the wood rings. Words. Sylvia Plath. NALW; OxBoAm; VCAP

Axiom. Walter Conrad Arensberg. APT-1

Axiom of Maria. Larissa Szporluk. NeAmPo

Axion Esti. Odysseus Elytis.

Axis around which the many-centered spiral unwinds is only the, The. Big L, The. Vera Hérold. SurWo, *tr. by* Guy Ducornet

Axle Song. Mark Van Doren. APT-2

Axolotl. Arthur Sze. AmAlph

Ay! / Ay!. Las calles lloran / Streets Are Crying. Francisco X. Alarcón. GeoHom

Ay, Ay, Ay, de la Grifa Negra. Julia de Burgos. *See* Ay, Ay, Ay of the Kinky-Haired Negress.

Ay, Ay, Ay of the Kinky-Haired Negress. Julia de Burgos. AmFaPo, *tr. by* Jack Agüeros

(Ay, Ay, Ay, de la Grifa Negra.) ItP

Ay, ay, ay, that am kinky-haired and pure black. Ay, Ay, Ay of the Kinky-Haired Negress. Julia de Burgos. AmFaPo, *tr. by* Jack Agüeros

Ay, Bashful Thou! Mor Nighean Uisdein. EMWP

Ay, beshrew you! by my fay. John Skelton. NoP-4; NoP-5

Ay, Democracy / Lops, lops; but where's her planted bed? Herman Melville. TCAPo *Fr.* Clarel: A Poem and Pilgrimage in the Holy Land.

Ay, gaze upon her rose-wreath'd hair. Revenge. Letitia Elizabeth Landon. NAEL-7v2; NOBRP; NPeEn

Ay, in the catalogue ye go for men. William Shakespeare. DiBP *Fr.* Macbeth.

Ay me, alas, heigh ho, heigh ho! Madrigal. Thomas Weelkes. NPeEn

Ay, screen thy favourite dove, fair child. Child Screening a Dove from a Hawk, A. Letitia Elizabeth Landon. NOBRP

Ay, so, God be wi' ye! Now I am alone. William Shakespeare. OxAEP-1 *Fr.* Hamlet.

Ay, tear her tattered ensign down! Old Ironsides. Oliver Wendell Holmes. AmWaPo; APN-1; BRP; NAAL-3; NAAPv.1; NCAP; OxBoAm; TCAPo; TFi

Ay, whaur's the snaws o langsyne? (LL) Ballat o the Leddies o Langsyne. François Villon. OBVE; OxBEV, *tr. by* Tom Scott

Aya! / Ayaya, it is beautiful, beautiful it is out-doors when the summer comes at last. Summer Song. *Unknown.* APN-2, *tr. by* Franz Boas

Ay[e], but to die, and go we know not where. William Shakespeare. WaAnP *Fr.* Measure for Measure.

Aye, 'e was buried the day before last. Curtain, The. Dyfnallt Morgan. BBMWP, *tr. by* Meic Stephens

Aye, there it is! It wakes to-night. Aye there it is! It wakes tonight. Emily Jane Brontë. NALW

(Aye there it is! It wakes tonight.) VWP

Aye, thou art welcome, heaven's delicious breath! October. William Cullen Bryant. APN-1

Aye, underneath yon shadowy side. Airey Force. Letitia Elizabeth Landon. RWP

Aye, well I know 'tis ghastly to descend that valley. On the Same Picture. Walt Whitman. GS

Aye! What a thing is the passing of Cronos, the angular-minded. John Cowper Powys. OBWVE *Fr.* Ridge, The.

Ayee! Ai! This is heavy earth on our shoulders. Burying Ground by the Ties. Archibald MacLeish. GM

Ayíasma. Gunnar Ekelof. WoPoe, *tr. by* W. H. Auden and Leif Sjöberg

Ayn el-Hilwe. Night. A child is crying. The quilt is pushed aside. Light flowing from two small feet. Hebron (Al-Khalil). Nasri Hajjaj. Eno, *tr. by* Ibrahim Muhawi

Azalea. Kang Ŭn'gyo. CAMKP, *tr. by* Tae Yang Kwak

Azalea Poem, The. Jack Coulehan. BloBone

Azaleas. Kim Sowŏl. CAMKP, *tr. by* David R. McCann

Azaleas and Dogwoods. Cyd Adams. TiP2

Aztec Father. Ray Gonzales. MAAN

Azure Because of You. Eduardo Carranza. BLPSL, *tr. by* Rene de Costa, Rigas Kappatos and Eleni Paidoussi

Azure, essence of change and horizons. Azuri. Askia Muhammad Touré. SpirFl

Azuri. Askia Muhammad Touré. SpirFl

B

b. Charles Bukowski. BodElec

B: Amazing! I did not think that they could speak this tongue. (LL) Black Boys Play the Classics. Toi Derricotte. ExTi; SpirFl

B.B. Blues. Mary Weems. SpirFl

B C D Goldfish, A. *Unknown.* NTCP

B' e d' aotromachd a rinn mo thàladh. Aotromachd. Meg Bateman. EdScPo

B Network, The. Haki R. Madhubuti. FuFl; IllVoic

B stands for Bear. When bears are seen. Joseph Hilaire Pierre Belloc. NoAM *Fr.* Moral Alphabet, A.

Baa, baa, black sheep, have you any wool? Mother Goose. OxBEV

Baalbeck. Nadia Tuéni. PoArWo

Bánk the Palatine. József Katona. *tr. by* Gavin Ewart and Paul Tabori

"Speak out, speak, well." IQMS, *tr. by* Gavin Ewart and Paul Tabori

Baap, nemesthe. Baap-Nemesthe Reggae Song. Dorothy Wong Loi Sing. WaCA

Baba Mostafa. Mimi Khalvati. Prnts

Babbitt and the Bromide, The. Ira Gershwin. OBCoV; ReLy

Babbitt met a Bromide on the avenue one day, A. Babbitt and the Bromide, The. Ira Gershwin. OBCoV; ReLy

Babble. César Vallejo. IJHIL, *tr. by* John Knoepfle

Babbling. Oswald de Andrade. TCLAP, *tr. by* Flavia Vidal

Babbling Ringwood. John Gay. DiBP *Fr.* Fables: First Series.

Babbling through your Benzedrine and beer! (LL) New York Seizures. Eugene B. Redmond. BRtP; FuFl

Babe Christabel. Gerald Massey.

"And thou hast stolen a jewel, Death." TreFP

Babe Jesus lay in Mary's lap. Christmas Carol, A. George Macdonald. SacPr

Babe Ruth Pointing. Timothy Kelly. MotU

Babe was born in the reign of George, A. Mervyn Laurence Peake. FaBoWar *Fr.* Rhyme of the Flying Bomb, The.

Babe was laid in the Manger, The. Nativity, A. Rudyard Kipling. ChrPo; GI

Babe, we are well met. Thou Swell. Lorenz Hart. ReLy

Babel. Giuseppe Ungaretti. PFTM-1

Babes on Broadway. Ralph Freed. ReLy

Babiaantje, The. Frank Templeton Prince. MoBrPo

Babies born blue. Formula for Blue Blues Babies. De Leon Harrison. EGAG

Babies Haven't Any Hair. Samuel Hoffenstein. NBLV

Babies, The. Sabrina Orah Mark. LegDan

Babies twist in their mothers' arms. The men. When a Beautiful Woman Gets on the Jutiapa Bus. Belle Waring. EmeKit; PBCAP

Babii Yar. Yevgeny Aleksandrovich Yevtushenko. HP; VCWP, *tr. by* George Reavey

Babits. Lőrinc Szabó. IQMS *Fr.* Cricket Music.

Baboon, The. Rhydwen Williams. OBWVE, *tr. by* R. Gerallt Jones

Baby. Carla Harryman.

Again. The. Time. BAP-04

Another Artifact. BAP-04

Baby. (For B and T). BAP-04

Baby. In Three Parts. BAP-04

Baby. N. Baseball. Song. BAP-04

Go. Down. Sun. BAP-04

Knowledge. BAP-04

Knowledge. BAP-04

Mutations. BAP-04

Mutations. BAP-04

Next. BAP-04

Note. BAP-04

The. Open. Box. BAP-04

The. Corner. Of. BAP-04

Tragedy. Reconsidered. BAP-04

Yelling. For. Fun. BAP-04

Baby. Ko Un. WhBo

Baby, The. Shin Kyŏngnim. CAMKP, *tr. by* Kevin O'Rourke

Baby, The. Rex Wilder. PoDa

Baby at her breast. Karai Senryū. EMJL, *tr. by* Makoto Ueda

Baby at the Bottom of the River. W. S. Rendra. WoPoe, *tr. by* Harry Aveling

Baby, Baby All the Time. Bobby Troup. ReLy

Baby bird has fallen from its tree and lies feebly peeping dead center of the bright circle under our streetlight, A. More Trouble with the Obvious. Michael Van Walleghen. IllVoic

Baby Boy is a veteran. Baby Boy. Afaa Michael Weaver. OxAAAP

Baby brackens make friendly bows to the clouds. Mountain Life. Hueng Guobin. BecRai, *tr. by* Kim Daljin, Kim Won-Chung and Christopher Merrill

Baby brother can't wait. Barbershop Ritual. Sharan Strange. InTrad; ISC

Baby carriage abandoned, A. Empress of Imagined Fertility, The. Leah Aini. DTA, *tr. by* Miriyam Glazer

Baby coughed and coughed, clearing its lungs, The. Christmas at Bristol. William Scammell. NLP

Baby Elephant, A. Nikolai Stepanovich Gumilyov. TCRusP, *tr. by* Carl R. Proffer

Baby, give me just. Errata. Kevin Young. LegDan

Baby has discovered a primal land of no name narcissism not because she knows the meaning of narcisssm. Carla Harryman. BAP-04 *Fr.* Baby.

Baby Hilary, Sir Edmund, The. Kathleen Leland Baker. NBLV

Baby, I ain't afraid to die. This World. Malvina Reynolds. ASA

Baby in another era was running from room to room with her arm thrust out. Carla Harryman. BAP-04 *Fr.* Baby.

Baby in the House, A. Patrick Williams. PNI

Baby Is Born Out of a White Owl's Forehead—1972, A. Alice Notley. ExTi

Baby, It's Cold Outside. Frank Loesser. ReLy

Baby looks at the snow piling up outside the window, The. Baby, The. Shin Kyŏngnim. CAMKP, *tr. by* Kevin O'Rourke

Baby. N. Baseball. Song. Carla Harryman. BAP-04 *Fr.* Baby.

Baby Poem Industry Poem, The. W. N. Herbert. NeBl

Baby Random. Belle Waring. PBCAP

Baby Song. Thom Gunn. AmFaPo; BeAl *Fr.* Three Songs.

Baby, the newborn, is the oldest, The. Name the Oldest Member of Your Family. Kalamu ya Salaam. OPRER

Baby Vallejo. David Rivard. SeSe

Baby Villon. Philip Levine. OxBoAm

Baby was going to sing and then sing twice. The song was later attenuated. Carla Harryman. BAP-04 *Fr.* Baby.

Babygirl. Mud Wit. Jeffrey Renard Allen. RD

Babylon. Alfred Tennyson. ChIV-1

Babylon: 539 B.C.E. Charles Reznikoff. ChIV-1

Babylon Revisited. Imamu Amiri Baraka. NoAM

Babylon that was beautiful is Nothing now. Babylon. Siegfried Sassoon. ChIV-1

Baby's Breath. Jabari Asim. FuFl

Baby's Debut, The. James Smith. NPBRoP

Baby's Dress, A. Hazel Hall. FiBr

Baby's Drinking Song. James Kirkup. NTCP

Baby's feet, like sea-shells pink, A. Algernon Charles Swinburne. WeW-3 *Fr.* Étude Réaliste.

Baby's Pantoum. Anne Waldman. FFC

Baby-Sermon, A. George Macdonald. NOxBChV; Spl

Babysitter's Devotion, The. Kevin Prufer. AmPoNex

Baby-Sitting. Gillian Clarke. TCAWP

Baccalaureate. David McCord. NBLV

Bacchae, The. Michael Donaghy. NeBrP

Bacchanal. Peter De Vries. NBLV

Bacchanal. Barbara J. Orton. NeAmPo

Bacchus. Ralph Waldo Emerson. APN-1; OBEV; OxBoAm; TCAPo

Bacchus. William Empson. NoAM

Bacchus in Tuscany. Francesco Redi. *tr.* by Leigh Hunt

 Bacchus's Opinion of Wine, and Other Beverages. OBVE, *tr.* by Leigh Hunt

Bacchus must now his power resign. Drinking-Song, A. Henry Carey. OBEV

Bach and the Sentry. Ivor Gurney. HarvBoo

Bach Fugue. Barker Fairley. IFF

Bachelor. William Meredith. NoAM; PoA 2002

Bachelor Song. Douglas Goetsch. PML; PoDa

Bachelors, The. Edward Cortez Garrett. ReBoTo

Back? T. Harri Jones. AngWePo; TCAWP

Back: "We try a new drug, a new combination." Jane Kenyon. IJHIL

Back. Alice Notley. Eno

Back. Sheila Wingfield. MoWP

Back again. Day one. Fingers blue with cold. I joined the lengthening queue. Slate Street School. Ciaran Carson. CABP

Back and forth, back and forth. Fall 1961. Robert Lowell. OBWP; OxBoAm; PoAgWa

Back and Side Go Bare, Go Bare. William Stevenson and John Still. HeIP-4; NAEL-6v1 *Fr.* Gammer Gurton's Needle.

Back at Cold Mountain. Han-shan (Cold Mountain). BB; CCL1; NDACCP, *tr.* by Gary Snyder

Back at the High Cloud Terrace. Yi Hwang. CATKP *Fr.* Twelve Songs of Tosan.

Back away from that, (she said). Fireworks on the Grass. Archilochus. WoPoe, *tr.* by Guy Davenport

Back before we all become "multicultural." Reading Room. Allison Joseph. NAPBL

Back down the steps I go out. Nathaniel Mackey. PFTM-2 *Fr.* Song of the Andoumboulou.

Back End. Peter Rafferty. NLP

Back End of the Horse, The. Paul Groves. TCAWP

Back Far Enough, Down Deep Enough. Constance Urdang. PBCAP

Back from being. You. *Unknown.* SonAtl, *tr.* by Rowena Astill, Alan Brierly and Abigail Herzen

Back from the line one night in June. Corporal Stare. Robert Graves. FaBoWar

Back from the palace of a famous king. Larkin Automatic Car Wash, The. Gavin Ewart. NoAM

Back from the sea now, back to their sources shall deep rivers. Ovid. RomPo *Fr.* Tristia.

Back from the spring in the green draw. Living in at Least Two Worlds. C. L. Rawlins. OPRER

Back from the Word-Processing Course, I Say to My Old Typewriter. Michael C. Blumenthal. NoAM

Back from the workbench and lamp, the tilt. Thinking of Red. Linda Bierds. AmAlph

Back home again on one of those bright mornings. Los Angeles after the Rain. Dana Gioia. UrbNat

Back home the black women are all beautiful. W. W. Imamu Amiri Baraka. HeIP-4

Back in 1935. Bud. William T. Crawley III. InTrad

Back in 1952. Sterling Brown. Ronald D. Palmer. BtF

Back in 1962 the world was. North and South. Linda France. NeBl

Back in Black Mountain / a child will smack your face. Black Mountain Blues. Bessie Smith. FTtHH; PFTM-1

Back in boyhood, game was all. Tennis Trophy. John Frederick Nims. PoA 2002

Back in My Day. Steve Fay. LiTh

Back in nineteen twenty-seven. Talking Dust Bowl. Woody Guthrie. APT-2

Back in *tachanka* days, when Red and Green. Makhno's Philosophers. John Streeter Manifold. NOBAu

Back in the Day. Lorenzo Thomas. AnSo; FuFl

Back in the Return. Huw Menai.
 Pieces of Coal. AngWePo
 "Where shall the eyes a darkness find." OBWVE

Back in the same room that an hour ago. Private Bottling, A. Don Paterson. EmeKit; NePenScot

Back in the second grade. Tap Dancing Lessons. Gerald Locklin. SUP

Back in the World. Ai. BAP-97

Back into the Jew-hating world. (LL) High Holy Days. Jane Shore. NoP-4; NoP-5

Back is the question. Back? T. Harri Jones. AngWePo; TCAWP

Back of Chicago the open fields—were you ever there? Evening Song. Sherwood Anderson. GM

Back on the Job. John G. Fisher. IFF

'Back on Times Square, Dreaming of Times Square'. Allen Ginsberg. CLPP

Back onto their pedestals. (LL) Autobiography 2 (hellogoodby). Michael Palmer. HarvBoo; WoBe

Back. Our dying keeps her alive. (LL) Singers Change, the Music Goes On, The. Linda Gregg. BAP-01; OxBoAm

Back out of all this now too much for us. Directive. Robert Frost. APT-1; ColAP; ItP; MakPoe; MoAmPo; NAAPv.2; NAMCP V.1; NoAM; NoP-4; NoP-5; OxBoAm; SAmP; StAl; TFi; WaAnP

Back path, steeped in musk and mint, A. Flower-Patterned Snake. Sŏ Chŏngju. VCWP, *tr.* by David R. McCann

Back Porch Fundamentalist. Maura Eichner. UpMys

Back road. Nzadi Z. Keita. BtF

Back Seat of My Mother's Car, The. Julia Copus. IFF; MFPA; NeBl; StAl

Back seat of the bus baby!, The. Metropolitan Metaphysics. James Flint. BRtP

Back Steps Lookout. Rhyll McMaster. BMAP

Back, the yoke, the yardage, The. Lapped seams. Shirt. Robert Pinsky. ColAP; FaoP; HarvBoo; NAAL-5; OxBoAm; StAl

Back Then. Yusef Komunyakaa. GT

Back then even the good girls got dizzy. Dizzy Girls in the Sixties. Gary Soto. ReTh

Back then I was still young. Blaise Cendrars. PFTM-1 *Fr.* Prose of the Trans-Siberian and of Little Jeanne of France, The.

Back then I was still young. Prose of the Trans-Siberian and of Little Jeanne of France, The. Blaise Cendrars. YaTCFP, *tr.* by Ron Padgett

Back then it seemed that wherever a girl took off her clothes the police would find her. Skin. Lucia Maria Perillo. IllVoic; P180

Back then when so much was clear. Tenderness. Stephen Dunn. NIP-4

Back through clouds. Train Tune. Louise Bogan. GM

Back through the Looking Glass to This Side. John Ciardi. NBLV

Back to Back. Debra Kang Dean. NAPBL

Back to Catfish. Belle Waring. SweBea

Back to it. Larry Eigner. FTOS

Back to the Blues. S. Brandi Barnes. BtF

Back to the cold transparent ham again! (LL) Sonnet to Vauxhall. Thomas Hood. NPeEn; OBCoV; OxBSo

Back to the First Bar. Emmy Bridgwater. SurWo

Back to the instruction manual which has made me dream of Guadalajara. (LL) Instruction Manual, The. John Ashbery. NAMCP V.2; NoAM; OxBoAm; YaYoPo

Back to the Land. On the Line. Emmy Bridgwater. SurWo

Back to the ordinary. (LL) Roe-Deer. Ted Hughes. NAMCP V.2; NoAM; NOxBChV; OxAEP-2

Back to the play of constant give and change. (LL) Missing, The. Thom Gunn. CAGL; EMP; NAMCP V.2; NoP-4; NoP-5; WaAnP

Back to Town. John Hollander. NAMCP V.2; NoAM

Back to work happy at the thought possibly so. (LL) Personal Poem. Frank O'Hara. CAP-8; CLPP; OxBoAm; PmAP

Back Trouble. Emily Grosholz. RA

Back water done rose around Sumner, now, The. High Water Everywhere. Charlie Patton. APT-1

Back When. Nance Van Winckel. RWB

Back when I used to be Indian. Battlefield. Mark Turcotte. PoA 2002

Back when I used to be Indian. Reflection. Mark Turcotte. PoDa

Back when it took all day to come up. Hearing. W. S. Merwin. NoAM

Back when the earth was new. Testimonial. Rita Dove. CAP-8

Back when we were children. Shin Tongyŏp. CAMKP *Fr.* Kŭm River.

Back when we were children. Kŭm River. Shin Tongyŏp. *tr. by* Anthony, Brother of Taizé

Back will go the head with the dark curls. Castanets. Bernard Spencer. WeW-3

Back wings, The. Between Walls. William Carlos Williams. APT-1; NAAPv.2

Back Yard, The. Peter Balakian. PfSP

Backdrop: The dining room at Stonington. James Merrill. NoAM *Fr.* Book of Ephraim, The.

Background, dark vine at the edge of the porch, The. (LL) Forties Flick. John Ashbery. FTOS; NoAM

Backgrounds. Moniza Alvi. NeBl

Backgrounds. Justin Quinn. NIrP

Backgrounds Observed. Jean Earle. TCAWP

Backing away bitten by a. Gu Cheng. WoBe *Fr.* Liquid Mercury.

Backing into the Future. Dick Gallup. BAP-97

Backing to breaking down. What Has Yet to Be Sung. Malkia Amala Cyril. AfrBLW

Backside to the Wind. Paul Durcan. PBCIP

Back-Up Singer, The. Dorothy Barresi. SwNoth

Backward & down into inbetween as Vicki says. Or as Robin teaches. Mean Drunk Poem. Sharon Thesen. BrAP

Backward Glance, A. David Wheatley. NIrP

Backward Sound. Nina Kossman. CRWP, *tr. by* the author

Backward, turn backward, O time, in your flight. Rock Me to Sleep[, Mother]. Elizabeth Akers Allen. APN-2; BRP; ITBLP; SWaP

Backward—as if retentive. Company, The. Robert Creeley. FTOS; OnScMo

Backwater Blues. Bessie Smith. NAAPv.2

Backwoodsman, The. James Kirke Paulding.
"Here lay dark Pittsburgh, from whose site there broke." APN-1
"In truth it was a landscape wildly gay." APN-1
"Neglected Muse! of this our western clime." APN-1
"'Tis true—yet 'tis no pity that 'tis true." APN-1
"'Twas sunset's hallow'd time—and such an eve." APN-1

Backyard. Diane Di Prima. PmAP; WaAnP

Backyard. John Tranter. BMAP

Backyard, dry flower half-border, unpeopled landscape. Disjecta Membra. Charles Wright. BAP-97

Backyard sun shower. Stanford M. Forrester. AmZen

Backyards and barnlots. Book of Galahad, The. Jack Spicer. FTOS

Backyards of America. Leonard Kress. RWB

Bacon's Epitaph, Made by His Man. John Cotton. TCAPo

Bacon-smell. Geranium-smell. Hangman's Room, The. János Pilinszky. PoSu, *tr. by* Peter Jay

Bad Alchemy. Dionisio D. Martinez. FaoP

Bad Aliens. Noelle Kocot. LegDan

Bad and Good. Alexander Resnikoff. NTCP

Bad Birds. William Trowbridge. UrbNat

Bad Blood. Arthur Rimbaud. MotU, *tr. by* Louise Varese

Bad Break!, A. W. T. Goodge. NOBAu

Bad day at the market for Canobie Dick, A. Story of Canobie Dick, The. Libby Houston. OBSP

Bad Days. Harvey Shapiro. PA9/11

Bad Days Will End, The. Penelope Rosemont. SurWo

Bad Dream. Louis MacNeice. NoAM

Bad Dream and the Friend. Gene Frumkin. ICANM

Bad Girl Blues. Wille ("Memphis Willie B.") Borum. FTtHH

Bad Government. Kuan Hsiu. WoPoe, *tr. by* Jerome P. Seaton

Bad habits. (LL) Cigarette Case. Stephen Kessler. CalPo; GeoHom

Bad Joke. Dorothy Barresi. SUP

Bad Karma. Mary Crockett Hill. AmPoNex

Bad Landlord, The. William Chamberlayne. NOSC *Fr.* Pharonnida.

Bad love last like a big. Poem About Heartbreak that Go on and on. June Jordan. StAl

Bad Luck Card. Langston Hughes. NoP-4; NoP-5; SAmP; TRP

Bad Luck to This Marching. Benjamin Hall Kennedy. OBCoV

Bad Luck with the Second Throw. Durs Grünbein. GTCP, *tr. by* Reinhold Grimm

Bad Man. Langston Hughes. NAMCP V.1

Bad men are seldom cheerful; but we see. Dealer and the Clerk, The. George Crabbe.

Bad Modernism. Michael Davidson. BAP-04

Bad money drives out good. What Do You Want: A Meaningful Dialogue, or a Satisfactory Talk? Ogden Nash. OBCoV

Bad monkeys to the windows. (LL) My Husband, Before Leaving. *Unknown.* EaWin; WoPoe, *tr. by* J. Moussaieff Masson and W. S. Merwin

Bad Moon Rising. Ibrahim Muhawi. Eno

Bad Muse, The. Lawrence Raab. SUP

Bad Old Days, The. Kenneth Rexroth. NoAM

Bad Pilgrim Room, The. Jeffrey McDaniel. SUP

Bad Report—Good Manners. Spike Milligan. NOxBChV

Bad Season Makes the Poet Sad, The. Robert Herrick. BASC; CavPo; NAEL-6v1; NAEL-7v1

Bad (she said) was. Hymn To a Woman Under Interrogation. Reiner Kunze. PoSu, *tr. by* Ewald Osers

Bad Sir Brian Botany. Alan Alexander Milne. NOxBChV

Bad Taste. Going Baroque. Jean V. Gier. ReBoTo

Bad Time for Poetry. Bertolt Brecht. PoSu, *tr. by* Ralph Manheim and John Willett

Bad Time for the Sublime, A. Kay Ryan. OxBoAm

Bad Times. Lenard D. Moore. BRtP

Bad Times Song. Jean Garrigue. OxBoAm

Bad times: / The cars pass. George Oppen. APT-2; PFTM-1

Bad Truth. Jane Rohrer. BodElec

Bad Verse I sing, and since 'twere best, I deem. Proem. Charles Lee. STuOW

Bad Weather at the Airport. Kurt J. Fickert. OtW

Badger, The. Gwynn Ap Gwilym. BBMWP, *tr. by* Grahame Davies

Badger, The. John Clare. FaBoVe

Badger grunting on his woodland track, The. Badger, The. John Clare. FaBoVe

Badger is the thirteenth astrological sign, The. Disasterology. Jeffrey McDaniel. LaCa; NeAmPo

Badgers, The. Seamus Heaney. ModIr

Badly-Chosen Lover. Rosemary Tonks. EmeKit; MoWP; StAl

Badman of the Guest Professor. Ishmael Reed. EGAG; SSLK

Baffled. William Wordsworth. STuOW *Fr.* Anecdote for Fathers [Showing how the Art of Lying may be Taught].

Baffled for just a day or two. Baffled for just a day or two. Emily Dickinson. PoBW

Bafflement. J. Eirian Davies. BBMWP, *tr. by* Sion Eirian

Baffling Picture. Lajos Kassák. IQMS, *tr. by* Edwin Morgan

Bag Lady's Body in the Financial District, A. Arthur Powers. RWB

Bag of Mice. Nick Flynn. AmPoNex; NAPBL

Bag which was left and not only taken but turned away was not found, A. Gertrude Stein. MotU; TCAPo *Fr.* Tender Buttons.

Bag Woman. Dudley Randall. NoAM

Bagatelle. HSü Ling. CCL1, *tr. by* Anne Birrell

Bagel, The. David Ignatow. P180

Baggot Street Deserta. Thomas Kinsella. NAMCP V.2; NoAM

Baghdad. Michael Gizzi. OnScMo

Baghdad, that captive, forgotten. City Ravaged by Silence, The. Buland Al-Haidari. IrPoTo, *tr. by* Hussein Kadhim and Christopher Merrill

Bagpipe Music. Ciaran Carson. ModIr

Bagpipe Music. Louis MacNeice. BeAl; BrAP; CABP; EMP; HarvBoo; MakPoe; NAEL-6v2; NAEL-7v2; NAMCP V.1; NBLV; NoAM; NoP-4; NoP-5; OBSV; OxBEV; TFi; UV

Bagpipes at the Biltmore. Robert Conquest. OBCoV

Bags on backs, wrapped in red mackinaws. City-Hotel. Alfred Des Rochers. SonAtl, *tr. by* Gregory Beaven, Kurt Ganzl and Tim Rauenbusch

Bagsche's Complaint. Sir David Lyndsay. DiBP

Bahnhofstrasse. James Joyce. NPeEn

Bailey Gatzert: The First Grade, 1945. Lonny Kaneko. LTA

Baileys, The. George Crabbe. STuOW *Fr.* Tales of the Hall.

Bailiff of a fertile garden plot, The. *Unknown.* PriapPo *Fr.* Priapus Poems, The.

Bailiff, The. T. Glynne Davies. BBMWP, *tr. by* Joseph P. Clancy

Bailiff, why your useless plaints about. *Unknown.* RompPo *Fr.* Priapean Corpus, The.

Bait for the stricken, stale, red-checked eyes. Outside You Cannot Breathe. Jasper Bernes. IAoNAP

Bait, The. Eric Chock. OpBo

Bait[e], The. John Donne. NAEL-6v1; NAEL-7v1; NOSC; WaAnP

Baize Queens. Jane Holland. NeBl

Bajada, La. Arthur Sze. NevBe

Bajji. Rashidah Ismaili. HAWP

Bajla Gelblung. Report. Johannes Bobrowski. GTCP, *tr.* by Reinhold Grimm

Bajo el árbol de la noche la escritura fragua la luz. Traslación de dominio. María Rivera. SPV

Bajo el higo es octubre. Bertha Beninu. Natalia Toledo. RMCMP

Bajo los puros muertos, a veces, brotan flores. Flores Bajo los Muertos. José Luis Hidalgo. RaW

Baked and cleaned. Grandmother. Siv Cedering Fox. PBCAP

Baked Oysters Rockefeller. Marjorie M. Evasco. ReBoTo

Baked the day she suddenly dropped dead. Tony Harrison. NAEL-6v2; NAEL-7v2; NAMCP V.2 *Fr.* School of Eloquence, The.

Baker hadn't yet unfastened the iron shutters of his shop when the, The. Leaves of Hypnos No. 128. René Char. AF, *tr.* by Cid Corman

Baker's Tale, The. Lewis Carroll. NAEL-6v2; NAEL-7v2; OxAEP-2 *Fr.* Hunting of the Snark, The.

Balaam's Blessing. Bible, *O.T.* OBVE *Fr.* Numbers.

Balade. Charles, Duc d' Orléans. NAWM-7v1, *tr.* by Sarah Spence

Balade: "Hide [*or* Hyd], Absalon, thy gilte tresses clere." Geoffrey Chaucer. OBEV *Fr.* Legend of Good Women, The.

Balade whych Anne Askewe made and sange whan she was in Newgate, The. Anne Askew. *See* Ballad Which Anne Askew[e] Made and Sang When She Was in Newgate, The.

Balalaĭka. Pierre Albert-Birot. CuPo

Balance. James Harris. PasH

Balance. Marilyn Nelson. RA; FFC

Balance and Beauty. Clarence Major. FTOS

Balance checkbook. / Rid lawn of onion grass. Things to Do. James Schuyler. OxBoAm

Balancing Act. Elsa Cross. RMCMP, *tr.* by Margaret Sayers Peden

Balancing as metal, its sound, the metal in its sound. Economics of Metonymy. Skip Fox. AnSo

Balancing. Austere. Life. Keith Waldrop. PmAP *Fr.* Shipwreck in Haven, A.

Balancing on Oriental spike heels. Three Gypsies. Shalin Hai-Jew. UnSA

Balancing Out. Margaret Avison. GPPA

Balancing Zero. V. B. Price. ICANM

Balanide 2. Paul Verlaine. CAGL, *tr.* by Alan Stone

Balboa, the Entertainer. Imamu Amiri Baraka. NoAM

Balcony. César Moro. AHA, *tr.* by Frances LeFevre

Balcony, The. Louise Glück. CAP-8

Balcony, violet shade on stucco fruit in a plastic bowl on the iron raggedy legged table, grapes and sliced melon, saucers a knife, wine, A. Eye, The. Adrienne Rich. PrTe

Bald. Bill Zavatsky. FaoP

Bald head with the fringe, The. Jane Beeson. NewEx

Bald heads forgetful of their sins. Scholars, The. William Butler Yeats. NoP-4; NoP-5

Bald Mountain. Wang An-shih. ColAnChi, *tr.* by Victor H. Mair

Bald Mountain Zaum-Poems. *Unknown.* PFTM-1

Bald tire. Garry Gay. CalPo

Bald Truth, The. Bob Hicok. MAAN

Baldanders. Christopher Reid. NPeEn

Bald-bare, bone-bare, and ivory yellow: skull. U.S. Sailor with the Japanese Skull, The. Winfield Townley Scott. APT-2; ICANM; OxBoAm

Balder. Sydney Thompson Dobell.
    Chanted Calendar, A. OBEV

Bald-Headed Man, A. Bhartrihari. WoPoe, *tr.* by Barbara Stoler Miller

Bald-headed man, his pate, A. Bald-Headed Man, A. Bhartrihari. WoPoe, *tr.* by Barbara Stoler Miller

Balding, already quite round. Saturday with Dad. Liz Houghton. Prnts

Baleful phantoms underground, The. (LL) Low Barometer. Robert Bridges. CABP; NoAM

Baleful Return. Ramón López Velarde. TCLAP, *tr.* by Victor Tulli

Bali Hai Calls Mama. Marilyn Nelson Waniek. ISC

Balitaw. Bataan Faigao. ReBoTo

Balkan. Gabriel Spera. PoA 2002

Balkans and Balconies. Ani Ilkov. CSCBP *Fr.* Orbis Tertius.

Balkis was in her marble town. Lascelles Abercrombie. MoBrPo *Fr.* Judith.

Ball, almost, The. Basketball. Ronald Wallace. PBCAP

Ball bearings fell out, The. April '68. Elouise Loftin. EGAG

Ball dribbles off the green and into the drink, The. Moonshine. David Wheatley. NIrP

Ball drops from a high place, its orbit spent, A. Last Cigar. Peter Gizzi. VaPo

Ball no question makes of Ayes and Noes, The. Omar Khayyám. CABP *Fr.* Rubáiyát of Omar Khayyám [of Naishápúr], The.

Ball Poem, The. John Berryman. ChAP; MoAmPo; NoAM

Ball, The. Wisława Szymborska. BeAl, *tr.* by Stanislaw Baranczak and Clare Cavanagh

Ball will bounce, but less and less, A. It's not. Juggler. Richard Wilbur. UpMys

Ballad. W. H. Auden. *See* O What Is That Sound [Which So Thrills the Ear].

Ballad: A Song in the Night. Pao Chao. CCL1, *tr.* by Joseph R. Allen

Ballad: Alice Brand. Sir Walter Scott. OxAEP-2

Ballad: "As I was walkin' the jungle round, a-killin' of tigers an' time." Guy Wetmore Carryl. NBLV

Ballad: "Auld wife sat at her ivied door, The." Charles Stuart Calverley. CABP; NBLV; OBCoV; OxAEP-2; UV

Ballad: Time of Roses. Thomas Hood. OBEV; OxAEP-2

Ballad: Between the Boxcars [1923]. Robert Penn Warren.
    "He was formidable, he was, the little booger." GM
    "I can't even remember the name of the one who fell." GM

Ballad: "Forgive me if i laugh." Sonia Sanchez. FuFl; PoDa

Ballad: "He passed by with another." Gabriela Mistral. PtR, *tr.* by Doris Dana

Ballad: "He was strolling with another woman." Gabriela Mistral. BLPSL, *tr.* by Rene de Costa, Rigas Kappatos and Eleni Paidoussi

Ballad: "He went by with another." Gabriela Mistral. SpanPo, *tr.* by Muriel Kittel

Ballad: "I put my hat upon my head." Samuel Johnson. OxAEP-1; UV

Ballad: "I want to know the unity in all things and the difference." A. R. Ammons. OxBoAm

Ballad: "If the man who turnips cries." Samuel Johnson. OxAEP-1

Ballad: "Tender infant, meek and mild, The." Samuel Johnson. OxAEP-1

Ballad: "Knight went down to the river's rim, A." Gerda Mayer. OBSP

Ballad: "Mary, fate lent me a moment of pleasure." John Clare. NPBRoP

Ballad by Hans Breitmann. Charles Godfrey Leland. APN-2; TCAPo

Ballad for Apothecaries, A. Anne Stevenson. RSaN

Ballad for Bill Pickett, A. William D. Barney. TiP2

Ballad for Dialectical Materialism. Ivan Radoev. CSCBP, *tr.* by Georgi Belev and Lisa Sapinkopf

Ballad for Gloom. Ezra Pound. MoAmPo

Ballad for the Future. Ivan Radoev. CSCBP, *tr.* by Georgi Belev and Lisa Sapinkopf

Ballad from Childhood. Audre Lorde. WaAnP

Ballad in Imitation of "The Prince of Huainan." Pao Chao. CCL1, *tr.* by Burton Watson

Ballad, The: "In those days, wasy of feinting and of tenderness." Michel Deguy. YaTCFP, *tr.* by Clayton Eshleman

Ballad of a Bombardier from Texas. Goldie Capers Smith. TiP2

Ballad of a Bun, A. Sir Owen Seaman. UV

Ballad of a Little Lamp. René Depestre. YaTCFP, *tr.* by Joan Dayan

Ballad of a Nun, A. John Davidson. MoBrPo; UV

Ballad of a Shadow. Alice Oswald. MFPA

Ballad of Agincourt, The. Michael Drayton. FaBoWar

Ballad of Alcohol Valley, The. Ronny Someck. IrPoTo, *tr.* by Vivian Eden

Ballad of an Old Woman [*with music*]. Frank A. Collymore. NOxBChV

Ballad of Aunt Geneva, The. Marilyn Nelson. RA

Ballad of Aunt Geneva, The. Marilyn Nelson Waniek. FFC; GT

Ballad of Barnaby, The. W. H. Auden. OBNV *Fr.* Six Commissioned Texts.

Ballad of 'Beau Brocade', The. Austin Dobson. OxAEP-2

Ballad of Biddy Early, The. Nancy Willard. FFC

Ballad of Billie Potts, The. Robert Penn Warren. FuPo

Ballad of Billy Rose, The. Leslie Norris. AngWePo

Ballad of Birmingham [*with music*]. Dudley Randall. HeIP-4; ISC; NIL-7; NIP-4; NoAM; NoP-4; NoP-5; SoSe-8; WaAnP

Ballad of Black/Essence. Eugene B. Redmond. OxAAAP

Ballad of Black Grief. Federico García Lorca. STV, *tr.* by John Frederick Nims

Ballad of Bouillabaisse, The. William Makepeace Thackeray. OBEV; OxAEP-2

Ballad of Christmas, A. Walter De la Mare. OBCP

Ballad[e] of Dead Ladies, The. François Villon. OBVE, *tr.* by Dante Gabriel Rossetti

Ballad of East and West, The. Rudyard Kipling. OBNV

Ballad of Echolocation, The. Ryan Knighton. IFF

Ballad of Father Gilligan, The. William Butler Yeats. IrV; MoBrPo

Ballad of George R. Sims, The. Sir John Betjeman. OBCoV; UV

Ballad of Going Down to the Store, A. Miron Bialoszewski. BLT, *tr.* by Czeslaw Milosz

Ballad of Hampstead Heath, The. James Elroy Flecker. MoBrPo

Ballad of Hector in Hades [*with music*]. Edwin Muir. HarvBoo; NAMCP V.1; NoAM

Ballad of Hell, A. John Davidson. MoBrPo

Ballad of Indolence. Herman De Coninck. TuT, *tr.* by Eamon Grennan

Ballad of Jan Palach, Student and Heretic. Ondra Lysohorsky. AF, *tr.* by Ewald Osers

Ballad of John Barleycorn, the Ploughman, and the Furrow, The.　George Mackay Brown.　BeAl

Ballad of John Cable and Three Gentlemen.　W. S. Merwin.　MakPoe; YaYoPo

Ballad of John Nameless, The.　Maurice Carpenter.
"One day I went to London."　RSaN

Ballad of Joking Jesus, The.　James Joyce.　ChIV-2

Ballad of Kansas, The [El corrido de Kiansis].　Unknown.
Kansas 1.　NAAPv.1

Ballad of Keith of Ravelston, The.　Sydney Thompson Dobell.　OBEV Fr. Nuptial Eve, A.

Ballad of Ladies Lost and Found.　Marilyn Hacker.　FFC; InoFa; VCAP

Ballad of Late Annie, The.　Gwendolyn Brooks.　ColAP

Ballad of Long Bank, The.　Li Po.　WoPoe, tr. by Elling O. Eide

Ballad of Love through the Ages.　Carlos Drummond de Andrade.　PML, tr. by Mark Strand

Ballad of Mrs. Noah, The.　Robert Duncan.　NoAM

Ballad: Of Motion.　Billy Mills.　Oth

Ballad of Mulan, The.　Unknown.　ColAnChi, tr. by Arthur Waley

Ballad of Mulan, The.　Unknown.　CCL1, tr. by John Frodsham

Ballad of Noah's Daughter.　Rossana Ombres.　NeIt

Ballad of O'Bruadir, The.　Frederick Robert Higgins.　OBMV

Ballad of Old Women & of How They Are Constrained To Simulate Youth In Order To Avoid Shocking the Young.　Norman Talbot.　NOBAu

Ballad of One Doomed to Die.　Federico García Lorca.　AWTN, tr. by Langston Hughes

Ballad of Orange and Grape.　Muriel Rukeyser.　ChAP; NoAM; NoP-4; NoP-5; WaAnP

Ballad of Passive Paederasty, A.　Aleister Crowley.　CAGL

Ballad of Reading Gaol, The.　Oscar Wilde.　OBNV; OxAEP-2; TFi
　1.　CABP; MoBrPo; NoAM; NPeEn; OBMV; OxBEV; UV; WaAnP
　3.　WaAnP
　"For oak and elm have pleasant leaves."　MakPoe; NoAM
　"He does not sit with silent men."　NPeEn; OxBEV
　"There is no chapel on the day."　NoAM
　"Yet each man kills the thing he loves."　OxBEV

Ballad of Religion and Marriage, A.　Amy Levy.　NPeEn; ViWPN; VWP

Ballad of Remembrance, A.　Robert Earl Hayden.　ESEAA

Ballad of Sally in Our Alley, The.　Henry Carey.　See Sally in Our Alley.

Ballad of Selling a Child [with music].　Wang Chiu-ssu.　ColAnChi, tr. by Jonathan Chaves

Ballad of Sue Ellen Westerfield, The.　Robert Earl Hayden.　ESEAA; NoAM

Ballad of the Army Carts, The.　Tu Fu [or Du Fu].　WoPoe, tr. by David Lattimore

Ballad of the Army Wagons, The.　Tu Fu [or Du Fu].　CCL1, tr. by Arthur Cooper

Ballad of the Bayonet, A.　Ernest Bryll.　FaBoWar, tr. by Czeslaw Milosz

Ballad of the Bird-Bride.　Rosamund Marriott Watson.　ViWPN; VWP

Ballad of the Bright Angel.　Bruce Berger.　GeoH

Ballad of the Cadger.　May Kendall.　ViWPN

Ballad of the D-Day Dodgers.　Hamish Henderson.　RSaN

Ballad of the Despairing Husband.　Robert Creeley.　RaBo

Ballad of the Dogs.　Lars Gustafsson.　WoPoe, tr. by Philip Martin

Ballad of the Emeu, The [with music].　Bret Harte.　NBLV

Ballad of the Gasfitter.　Gerrit Achterberg.　LWR, tr. by John M. Coetzee

Ballad of the General Strike.　Hugh MacDiarmid.　RSaN

Ballad of the Girl Whose Name Is Mud.　Langston Hughes.　SAmP

Ballad of the Goodly Fere.　Ezra Pound.　ChIV-2; MoAmPo

Ballad of the Government Granary Clerk.　Ho Ching-ming.　ColAnChi, tr. by Jonathan Chaves

Ballad of the Grapes.　George Sterling.　CalPo

Ballad of the Hidden Dragon.　Chinese Oral Tradition.
How Liu Chih-yüan Bade San-niang Good-bye and Joined the Army in T'ai-yüan.　ColAnChi, tr. by James I. Crump and M. Doleželová-Velingerová

Ballad of the Homing Man, The.　Ernest Rhys.　AngWePo

Ballad of the Ichthyosaurus.　May Kendall.　ViWPN

Ballad of the Landlord.　Langston Hughes.　WaAnP

Ballad of the Life and Times of Joe Louis, A.　Calvin C. Hernton.　FTtHH

Ballad of the Lonely Masturbator, The.　Anne Sexton.　WaAnP

Ballad of the Magic Glasses.　Maura Stanton.　FFC

Ballad of the Maiden of Lan-ling.　Chin Ho.　ColAnChi, tr. by Victor H. Mair

Ballad of the Man Who's Gone.　Langston Hughes.　SAmP

Ballad of the Mulberry Road.　Unknown.　ChinPo, tr. by Ye Weilian [or Yeh Wei-lien or Wai-lim Yip]

Ballad of the Mulberry Road, A.　Unknown.　NDACCP, tr. by Ezra Pound

Ballad of the Night.　Y. A. Rontsh.　Prolet, tr. by Amelia Glaser

Ballad of the Oedipus Complex.　Lawrence Durrell.　OBCoV

Ballad of the Orioles in the Fields.　Ts'ao Chih.　ColAnChi, tr. by Hans H. Frankel

Ballad of the Orphan Boy, The.　Unknown.　CCL1, tr. by Anne Birrell

Ballad of the Oysterman, The.　Oliver Wendell Holmes.　TCAPo

Ballad of the Pink-Brown Fence, The.　Milton Acorn.　IFF

Ballad of the Rainmaker.　Maik Nwosu.　NeNiPo

Ballad of the Sad Young Men, The.　Fran Landesman.　ReLy

Ballad of the Salvation Army.　Kenneth Fearing.　AmWit

Ballad of the Scarecrow Christ.　Elder Olson.　ChIV-2

Ballad of the Several Past.　Wyatt Prunty.　WaAnP

Ballad of the Shape of Things, The.　Sheldon Harnick.　ReLy

Ballad of the Shrieking Man, The.　James Fenton.　EmeKit

Ballad Of The Solitary Diner.　Todd Swift.　OpeFie

Ballad of the Taxi Driver's Cap.　Hamish Henderson.　RSaN

Ballad of the Tempest.　James Thomas Fields.　TreFP

Ballad of the Ten Casino Dancers.　Cecília Meireles.　TCLAP, tr. by James Merrill

Ballad of the Three Spectres.　Ivor Gurney.　OBWP

Ballad of the Two Left Hands.　Douglas Dunn.　RSaN

Ballad of the Underpass.　Patricia Beer.　HarvBoo

Ballad of the Were-Wolf, A.　Rosamund Marriott Watson.　ViWPN; VWP

Ballad of the Yorkshire Ripper, The.　Blake Morrison.
"Ower t'ills o Bingley."　FaBoVe

Ballad of Trees and the Master, A.　Sidney Lanier.　APN-2; ChIV-2; ColAP; ITBLP; TCAPo

Ballad of Villon and Fat Madge, The.　François Villon.　OBVE

Ballad of William Sycamore, The.　Stephen Vincent Benét.　MoAmPo

Ballad of Yukon Jake, The.　Edward E., Jr. Paramore.　TCAPo

Ballad on Seeing a Pupil of the Lady Gongsun Dance the Sword Mime.　Tu Fu [or Du Fu].　CCL1, tr. by Arthur Cooper

Ballad on the Investigation of a Disaster.　Yao Chen.　ColAnChi, tr. by Victor H. Mair

Ballad on the Marriage of Philip and Mary, A.　John Heywood.
"Egles byrde hath spred his wings, The."　PBRV

Ballad: The Boatman's Song.　Pao Chao.　CCL1, tr. by Joseph R. Allen

Ballad Values (2).　C. S. Giscombe.　RD

Ballad Which Anne Askew[e] Made and Sang When She Was in Newgate, The.　Anne Askew.　CABP; EMWP; NoP-4; NoP-5; NoSic; SacPr; WaAnP
(Balade whych Anne Askewe made and sange whan she was in Newgate, The.)　NPeEn; PBRV
(Lines In Prison.)　SacPr

Ballade 1.　Eustache Deschamps.　WoPoe, tr. by David Curzon and Jeffrey Fiskin

Ballade 2.　Eustache Deschamps.　WoPoe, tr. by David Curzon and Jeffrey Fiskin

Ballade at Thirty-Five.　Dorothy Parker.　AmWit; APT-1

Ballade for the Duke of Orléans.　Richard Wilbur.　WoPoe

Ballade: "Hide, Absalom, thy gilte tresses clear."　Geoffrey Chaucer.　WoPoe Fr. Legend of Good Women, The.

Ballade: "I was in blossom when I was a child."　Charles, Duc d' Orléans.　WoPoe, tr. by Tony Barnstone, Haixin Xu and Willis Barnstone

Ballade: "Tell me where, in what country, where."　François Villon.　STV, tr. by John Frederick Nims

Ballade, La: "En ce temps-là, façons de feinte et de tendresse, la peste ayant figure d'ennui dans les villes."　Michel Deguy.　YaTCFP

Ballade Made in the Hot Weather.　W. E. Henley.　MoBrPo

Ballade of an Omnibus.　Amy Levy.　ViWPN

Ballade of Broken Flutes.　Edwin Arlington Robinson.　APN-2

Ballade of Dead Actors.　W. E. Henley.　OBMV

Ballade of Dead Gentlemen.　Clive Staples Lewis.　OBCoV

Ballade of Hell and of Mrs. Roebeck.　Joseph Hilaire Pierre Belloc.　NPeEn

Ballade of Lost Objects [with music].　Phyllis McGinley.　NBLV

Ballade of Lovers.　May Probyn.　VWP

Ballade of Poetic Material.　Helen Smith Bevington.　AmWit

Ballade of Schopenhauer's Philosophy.　Franklin Pierce Adams.　AmWit

Ballade of Suicide, A.　G. K. Chesterton.　NBLV; OBCoV

Ballade of the Chinese Lover.　Stuart Merrill.　APN-2

Ballade of the Devout Husband, The.　Arthur Waugh.　ArBi

Ballade of the Ladies of Time Past.　François Villon.　WoPoe, tr. by Richard Wilbur

Ballade of the Men Who Were Hanged.　François Villon.　WoPoe, tr. by Fred Chappell

Ballade of the Moment After.　Paul Goodman.　BodElec

Ballade of the New God.　Thomas M. Disch.　RA

Ballade of the Outcasts.　Stuart Merrill.　APN-2

Ballade of the Poetic Life.　Sir John Collings Squire.　OBMV

Ballade of the Under Side.　Don Marquis.　AmWit Fr. Archys Life of Mehitabel.

Ballade to End With, A.　François Villon.　WoPoe, tr. by Richard Wilbur

Ballade to His Mistress. François Villon. WeW-3, *tr. by* Norman Cameron

Ballade Tragique à Double Refrain. Max Beerbohm. OBSV

Ballad[e] [upon a Wedding], A. Sir John Suckling. BASC; NAEL-7v1; NoP-4; NoP-5; WaAnP

Ballade van de gasfitter. Gerrit Achterberg. LWR

Ballads of the Wheel. Clinton Scollard. ArBi

Ballant o' the Laird's Bath, The. Douglas Young. EdScPo

Ballat o the Hingit. François Villon. OBVE, *tr. by* Tom Scott

Ballat o the Leddies o Langsyne. François Villon. OBVE; OxBEV, *tr. by* Tom Scott

Ballat [*or* Ballad] of Our Lady, [Ane]. William Dunbar. NePenScot

Ballata II: Last Song: from Exile [*with music*]. Guido Cavalcanti. WoPoe, *tr. by* George Sutherland Fraser

Ballerina. Rosario Ferré. TANSG, *tr. by* Nancy Diaz

Ballerina. Bob Russell. ReLy

Ballet of the Fifth Year, The. Delmore Schwartz. APT-2

Ball-games of the north-western tribes, The. Some Sporting Motifs. Maurice Riordan. NIrP

Ballin' the Jack. Jim Burris. ReLy

Balliol Rhymes. *Various authors.*
    On the Hon. George Nathaniel Curzon, Commoner of Balliol. OBCoV

Balloon, A / is going up. Twelve Poems. Larry Fagin. AHA

Balloon Heart. Beth Gylys. AmPoNex

Balloons. Dan Pagis. FIT, *tr. by* Robert Friend

Ballot, The. John Pierpont. APN-1 *Fr.* Word from a Petitioner.

Ballplayer. Evie Schockley. P180

Ballroom was filled with fashion's throng, The. Bird in a Gilded Cage, A. Arthur J. Lamb. NAAPv.2; TCAPo

Balls. Anne McNaughton. RaBo

Balls and Hoops. Martin Sorescu. PML, *tr. by* Adam J. Sorkin and Irina Grigorescu Pan and Lidia Vianu

Ball's Bluff. Herman Melville. AmWaPo; CBCWP; FaBoWar; OBWP; OxBoAm

Ballybunion. B. J. Atwood-Fukuda. FreRad

Ballygrand Widow. Deborah Randall. BeAl; NeBl

Ballymurphy painted white, inside and out. Jerusalem. David Morley. NLP

Balmy as summer. It won't last. Sunday Morning Through Binoculars. Eamon Grennan. PBCIP

Balmy comforts that are fled, The. Song. Tune, The Heavy Hours. Anne Batten Cristall. RWP

Baltazar Beats His Tutor at Scrabble. Belle Waring. ExTi

Balthasar's Song. William Shakespeare. NoSic; UV *Fr.* Much Ado about Nothing.

Balthazar's Poem. Chris Searle. RSaN

Baltic Sea froze in 1307, The. Birds flew north. Annual of the Dark Physics, An. Norman Dubie. BodElec

Baltimore. Afaa Michael Weaver. BtF

Baltimore Buzz. Noble Sissle. ReLy

Baltimore evening I saw, The. Soul Music. Baron Wormser. LTA; SwNoth

Baltimore Oriole. Baltimore Oriole. Paul Francis Webster. ReLy

Balulalow. John James *and* Robert Wedderburn. OBEV

Bam Chi Chi Lala. Lorna Goodison. NAMCP V.2

Bambalam. Shambhala. Ghost of Fusion, The. Andrew Duncan. VaPo

Bamboo. Hagiwara Sakutaro. CAoMJL1, *tr. by* Hiroaki Sato

Bamboo. Stephen Mitchell. WhBo

Bamboo. Eric Rolls. NOBAu

Bamboo by Li Ch'e Yun's Window, The. Po Chü-i. NDACCP, *tr. by* Kenneth Rexroth

Bamboo cold creeps into my room, The. Sleepless Nights. Tu Fu [*or* Du Fu]. CrYelRi, *tr. by* Sam Hamill

Bamboo Elegy: Two. Edmond Yi-teh Chang. OpBo

Bamboo Forest. Master Naong. BecRai, *tr. by* Kim Daljin, Kim Won-Chung and Christopher Merrill

Bamboo Garden. Muso Soseki. EaWin, *tr. by* W. S. Merwin

Bamboo Grove. Wang Wei. ChinPo, *tr. by* Ye Weilian [*or* Yeh Wei-lien *or* Wai-lim Yip]

Bamboo hat, straw coat—. Buson. SoOfWa, *tr. by* Sam Hamill

Bamboo Hermitage. Pou Kuksa. BecRai

Bamboo hut and a plum tree bower, A. Bamboo Hut, The. Nguyễn Trãi. WoPoe, *tr. by* Nguyen Ngoc Bich

Bamboo Lane House. Wang Wei. NDACCP, *tr. by* Gary Snyder

Bamboo Mat. Yüan Chěn. CrYelRi; ErotSp, *tr. by* Sam Hamill

Bamboo path leads through the First Stage, A. Climbing Pien-chueh Temple. Wang Wei. ColAnChi, *tr. by* Stephen Owen

Bamboo path leads up from the lowland, A. Climbing to the Monastery of Perception. Wang Wei. CCL1, *tr. by* Pauline Yu

Bamboo stick, the sight of you. Kim Kwanguk. CATKP, *tr. by* Peter H. Lee

Bamboo Tree. Jinkag Haesim. BecRai, *tr. by* Kim Daljin, Kim Won-Chung and Christopher Merrill

Bamboo tree near Sosang River, A. Reply to King Sunjo's Poem on Bamboo. Chunghur Hyujung. BecRai, *tr. by* Kim Daljin, Kim Won-Chung and Christopher Merrill

Bamboo-Midst Cottage. Wang Wei. NDACCP, *tr. by* David Hinton

Bamboos Grow Well Under Good Rule, The. *Unknown.* WoPoe, *tr. by* Ezra Pound

Bamboo's shadow sweeps the yard, The. For the Great Zen Master Sagum. Jinkag Haesim. BecRai, *tr. by* Kim Daljin, Kim Won-Chung and Christopher Merrill

Banana tree, The. Basho. SoOfWa, *tr. by* Sam Hamill

Banana Trees. Li Ch'ing-chao. NDACCP, *tr. by* Kenneth Rexroth

Bananas down at the Safeway, The. High-Class Bananas, The. Gary Gildner. PBCAP

Bananas ripe and green, and ginger-root. Tropics in New York, The. Claude McKay. APT-1; GT; MakPoe; NAAPv.2; NAMCP V.1; NoAM; OxBoAm

Banaras Is Another Name for the World. George Kalamaras. Vesp

Banat Museum. Elke Erb. OnScMo, *tr. by* Rosmarie Waldrop

Band plays an intro. Lady's Way. Reuben Jackson. GT

Bandaa sti bianni. Natalia Toledo. RMCMP

Bandaa stinu nga rucueza guriá yoo. Bandaa sti bianni. Natalia Toledo. RMCMP

Bandaged Shoulder, The. Constantine P. Cavafy. PtR, *tr. by* Edmund Keeley and Philip Sherrard

Banding near the South Texas Coast, Late April. Chip Dameron. TiP2

Bandstand. Michael S. Harper. SeSe

Bang Bang Bang. Amadou Diallo from Guinea to the Bronx Dead on Arrival. Carlos Raul Dufflar. BRtP

Bang Bang Bang. History of the Flood, The. John Heath-Stubbs. NOxBChV

Bang bang you're dead fifty bullets in you head. Children's Games. Malkia Amala Cyril. InTrad

Banging out a symphony. Soundtrack. Kevin Young. LegDan

Bangkok Gang, The. Maxine W. Kumin. NAMCP V.2

Baniano. Elsa Cross. RMCMP

Banished travelers—eighteen of us. First Reaching Huanzhou. Shen Quanqi. CCL1, *tr. by* Stephen Owen

Banishment of Poverty by His Royal Highness James Duke of Albany, The. Francis Sempill.
    "Pox fa that pultron Povertie." NePenScot

Banjo maker in the mountains, A. Grain of Sound, The. Robert Morgan. GoPo

Bank of the Magnolias, The. Pei Di and Wang Wei. CCL1 *Fr.* Wheel River.

Banking Potatoes. Yusef Komunyakaa. NoP-4; NoP-5

Banks are steep, the. Drought. Water too low. Wye Below Bredwardine, The. John Powell Ward. TCAWP

Banks o' Doon, The ("Ye banks and braes o' bonie [*or* bonnie] Doon.") Robert Burns. BrAP; OxBEV

Banks o' Doon, The ("Ye flowery banks o' bon[n]ie Doon.") Robert Burns. NAEL-6v2; NoP-5; NPBRoP

    (Bonie Doon.) NoP-4; WaAnP

Banks of the Condamine, The. *Unknown.* NOBAu

Banneker. Rita Dove. ESEAA; NAAL-5; NoAM; OxAAAP

Banner Bearer, The. William Carlos Williams. PoCho

Banners of the Heart. Fawziyya Al-Sindi. PoArWo, *tr. by* Joseph T. Zeidan

Banns. Don Domanski. Coast

Banquet. Ruth Bidgood. TCAWP

Banquet: *Dissertation 2, Canzone 1*, The. Dante Alighieri. WoPoe,

Banquet, The. Letitia Elizabeth Landon. TreFP

Banquet, The. John Milton. NOSC *Fr.* Paradise Regained [*or* Regain'd].

Banquet was a bonza, a rare recherché feed, The. Thank you, Mr Rason, for the Apples. E. G. Murphy. OBCoV

Bantams in Pine-Woods. Wallace Stevens. NAAPv.2; NAMCP V.1; NoAM; OxBoAm; SAmP

Banyan. Elsa Cross. TANSG, *tr. by* Patricia Dubrava

Banyan. Elsa Cross. RMCMP, *tr. by* Margaret Sayers Peden

Banyan roots almost reach. Singapore, July 4th. Sascha Feinstein. AmPoNex

Baobab. Alvin Aubert. FuFl

Baobab Tree 1996, The. Susan Hahn. PoA 2002

Baptism [*with music*]. Claude McKay. NAAPv.2

Bar. Langston Hughes. APSN

Bar Mitzvah, The. Philip Schultz. TaR

Bar of Michael Angelo, The. (LL) Alfred Tennyson. NAEL-6v2; NAEL-7v2 *Fr.* In Memoriam A. H. H.

Bar on the Piccola Marina, A. Noël Coward. NBLV

Barabbas, Judas Iscariot. Morning After, The. Dorothy, Duchess of Wellington Wellesley. OBMV

Baraja. David Huerta. RMCMP

Baraka says. Sea Shells. Lorna Lowe. BtF

Barbara [*with music*]. Jacques Prévert. AF; GPTC, *tr. by* Harriet Zinnes

Barbara. Jacques Prévert. MFP; YaTCFP, *tr. by* Martin Sorrell

Barbara. Jacques Prévert. YaTCFP

Barbara Allen's Cruelty. *Unknown. See* Bonny Barbara Allan.

Barbara Frietchie. John Greenleaf Whittier. AmWaPo; APN-1; CBCWP; ColAP; HHAm; ITBLP; NCAP; OxBoAm; PCW; TFi

Barbara remember. Barbara. Jacques Prévert. MFP; YaTCFP, *tr. by* Martin Sorrell

Barbarian. Mohammed Khaïr-Eddine. PFTM-2, *tr. by* Pierre Joris

Barbarian pass is filled with windblown sand, The. Li Po. ChinPo, *tr. by* Ye Weilian [*or* Yeh Wei-lien *or* Wai-lim Yip]

Barbarian Suite. Marilyn Chin. OpBo

Barbarians in a garden, softness does. In the Grounds. Douglas Dunn. NoP-4; NoP-5

Barbarians sweep down from the Carpathians. Lamb of Peace, the Ram of War, The. William Witherup. AtGh

Barbarians were a kind of solution, The. (LL) Waiting for the Barbarians. Constantine P. Cavafy. GPTC; WoPoe, *tr. by* Edmund Keeley and Philip Sherrard

Barb'd blossoms of the guarded gorse. Song of Winter, A. Emily Jane Pfeiffer. OBWVE

Barbecues smoke is rising at Legge's Camp; it is steaming into the midday air. Les A. Murray. NAMCP V.2 *Fr.* Buladelah-Taree Holiday Song Cycle, The.

Barbed wire looks incredibly evil still, The. Hartmanswillerkopf. Naomi Mitchison. RSaN

Barbed-wire / is the cloak of saints. Our Ashes. Horst Bienek. AF

Barbells of the Gods, The. Mark Cox. OPRER

Barber is cutting the hair, A. Self-Portrait at Thirty-Nine. Ted Kooser. PBCAP

Barbershop Ritual. Sharan Strange. InTrad; ISC

Barbie and Ken Maximize Their Options. Barbara Crooker. RWB

Barbie at the end of the mind, The. Of Mere Plastic. David Trinidad. KGB

Barbie Doll. Marge Piercy. BrAP; NIL-7; NIP-4; WaAnP

Barbie Says Math is Hard. Kyoko Mori. InvLad; ReTh

Barbie's Ferrari. Lynne McMahon. P180; RWB

Barbies, Las. Madeline Alviso. BeDoSh

Barbie's Molester. Denise Duhamel. ReTh

Barbizon Hotel for Women, The. Nicole Brossard. PFTM-2 *Fr.* Barbizon, The.

Barbizon, The. Nicole Brossard. *tr. by* Barbara Godard
    Barbizon Hotel for Women, The. PFTM-2, *tr. by* Barbara Godard
    Temptation, The. PFTM-2, *tr. by* Barbara Godard

Barcarolle. May Probyn. VWP

Barcelona. Alan Jenkins. NeBrP

Barcelona Days. Jaime Manrique. WiU, *tr. by* Edith Grossman

Barco Entra, Opaco y Negro, El. Juan Ramón Jiménez. RaW

Barco que nunca atraca, El. (LL) Refugee Ship. Lorna Dee Cervantes. NAMCP V.2; PoPoPo

Bard, The [A Pindaric Ode]. Thomas Gray. OxAEP-1

Bard and *vato*. Juan Martínez, Juan Nobody, Juan All. Heriberto Yépez. RMCMP, *tr. by* Mónica de la Torre

Bard whom pilf'red pastorals reknown, The. Alexander Pope. OBSV *Fr.* Epistle to Dr. Arbuthnot.

Bardo. Tsering Wangno Dhompa. WANABP

Bardo of Leaving. Janet Rodney. WANABP

Bardo of Perception. Janet Rodney. WANABP

Bardo of Sleep and Dream. Janet Rodney. ICANM

Bardo of the Threshold. Janet Rodney. ICANM

Bardo of War and Peace. Janet Rodney. ICANM

Bardo of Writing. Janet Rodney. WANABP

Bards of passion and of mirth. Ode. John Keats. OBEV; OxAEP-2

Bards of Wales, The. János Arany. IQMS, *tr. by* Peter Zollman

Bare Almond-Trees. D. H. Lawrence. FaBoVe

Bare Arms of Trees, The. John Tagliabue. GoPo

Bare birch mountainside. Ray McNiece. AmZen

Bare Bones. Kenward Elmslie. NYP2

Bare branches tremble, The. Tzu Yeh. WoPoe, *tr. by* Chung Ling and Kenneth Rexroth

Bare bulb, a scatter of nails, The. Ulster Twilight, An. Seamus Heaney. PBCIP

Bare earth. The defenseless. Closed. Vicente Aleixandre. RaW, *tr. by* W. S. Merwin

Bare Fig-trees. D. H. Lawrence. FaBoVe

Bare Floors. Melanie Hope. WiU

Bare oaks rock, and snowcrust tumbles down, The. Thoughts Before Dawn. John Balaban. AmWaPo

Bare Places. Douglas Burnet Smith. Coast

Bare Rocks and Stars. *Vietnamese Oral Tradition.* CaDao, *tr. by* John Balaban

Bare Wind, A. Pak Mogwŏl [*or* Mokwŏl]. CAMKP, *tr. by* Kevin O'Rourke

Bare Windows. Martha Rhodes. ExTi

Barefaced baby with the three minute dream. Song: Miss Penelope Burgess, Balling the Jack. Thomas McGrath. MiVo

Barefoot Boy, The. John Greenleaf Whittier. APN-1; BRP

Barefoot except for my skin. Will, The. Buland Al-Haidari. IrPoTo, *tr. by* Hussein Kadhim and Christopher Merrill

Barefoot/extinguish at will. Dana Lisa Lustig. AnSo

Barefoot Homiletics, after Wittgenstein and Boswell. Alan Dugan. BodElec

Barefoot in the City. Lisa Buscani. AmPoNex

Barefoot Necklace. Elouise Loftin. EGAG

Barefoot / they went through. They. Shin Kyŏngnim. CAMKP, *tr. by* Kevin O'Rourke

Bare-handed, I hand the combs. Stings. Sylvia Plath. NALW

Barely a twelvemonth after. Horses, The. Edwin Muir. BeAl; CABP; EmeKit; HeIP-4; MoBrPo; NAMCP V.1; NePenScot; NoAM; NPeEn; PoAgWa; TRP; WaAnP; WeW-3

Barely anything to say, everything said. Michael Palmer. APSN

Barely eight, already you are entering. Barely Eight. Rebecca Baggett. PfS

Barely fifty, but already my face is old, hair white. Running from Trouble. Tu Fu [*or* Du Fu]. CrYelRi, *tr. by* Sam Hamill

Barely light when I set off alone. First Time Going to School All by Myself. Browning Porter. NevBe

Barely through. For Thurman Thomas. Reuben Jackson. ISC

Barely tolerated, living on the margin. Soonest Mended. John Ashbery.) NAAL-5; NAMCP V.2; NoP-5; OxBoAm; PoetW; VCAP

Bargain, The. Cyrus Cassells. TAPaP *Fr.* Magician-Made Tree, The.

Bargain, The. Caradog Prichard. BBMWP, *tr. by* Joseph P. Clancy

Bargain, The. Sir Philip Sidney. BLPJKO; OBEV; OxAEP-1

Bargain at Half the Price, A. Henry Taylor. LPSFW

Bargain with the Watchman. Eva Salzman. MFPA

Bark of the rubgub [*or* rubagub] tree. (LL) Charles Edward Carryl. GoPo; NBLV *Fr.* Davy and the Goblin.

Bark went forth, with the morning's smile, A. Francis Fisher Browne. VWP *Fr.* Australian Emigrant, The.

Barking dogs, by lane and wood, The. John Clare. DiBP *Fr.* Shepherd's [*or* Shepheards] Calendar, The.

Barking sound the shepherd hears, A. Fidelity. William Wordsworth. DiBP

Barks the melancholy dog. Wakeful in the Township. Elizabeth Riddell. NOBAu

Bark-stripped and leafless. Disguised. Martha Rhodes. UrbNat

Barley-Break , A. Sir John Suckling. BASC; CavPo

Barley-reaping song / Smith's hammer. Takai Kito. ZenPo, *tr. by* Takashi Ikemoto and Lucien Stryk

Barley's season / Dust mutes. Tan Taigi. ZenPo, *tr. by* Takashi Ikemoto and Lucien Stryk

Barman vaulted the counter, The. True Story Ending in False Hope, A. Pearse Hutchinson. PBCIP

Barn, The. Edmund Charles Blunden. MoBrPo

Barn, The. Elizabeth Jane Coatsworth. OBCP

Barn, The. "Rachel." FIT, *tr. by* Robert Friend

Barn and the Down, The. Edward Thomas. OxBEV

Barn Owl. Leslie Norris. AngWePo

Barnes and Noble in Evansville, Indiana, mostly sells coffee, The. Poetry in America. Julia Kasdorf. ACAMVP

Barney Bigard. Suzanne Noguere. FFC

Barn's burnt down. Masahide. ZenPo, *tr. by* Takashi Ikemoto and Lucien Stryk

Barns huddle over the horns. November Harvest. Anita Endrezze. HATNAP

Barnsley and District. Donald Davie. NoAM

Barnyard, The. Yvor Winters. APT-2

Barometer of my moods today, mayfly. Mayfly. Louis MacNeice. ModIr

Baron has decided to mate the monster, The. Bride of Frankenstein, The. Edward Field. HeIP-4; ReTh; SUP

Barones an burgeises and bondemen als. William Langland. FaBoVe *Fr.* Vision of Piers Plowman, The.

Baron-Samedi. René Depestre. PFTM-2 *Fr.* Rainbow for the Christian West, A.

Baroque. Marie-Claire Bancquart. MFP, *tr. by* Martin Sorrell

Baroque Cell, A. David Huerta. RMCMP, *tr. by* Mark Schafer

Baroque Comment. Louise Bogan. APT-2

Baroque Excess of Pig Latin and. Jill Hartman. PoPra

Baroque Exterior. "Ern Malley." BMAP

Baroque Sunburst, A. Amy Clampitt. ColAP

Baroque Wall-Fountain in the Villa Sciarra, A. Richard Wilbur. ColAP; GS; NoP-4; NoP-5; OBGa; OxBoAm; VCAP

Barque of phosphor. Fabliau of Florida. Wallace Stevens. PoA 2002

Barrage. Ruth Garnett. BtF

Barred Owl, A. Richard Wilbur. NAMCP V.2

Barred owls scream in the black pines, The. Owls. Louise Erdrich. TRP

Barrel-Organ, The. Alfred Noyes. BRP; MoBrPo

Barrels of blue potato-spray, The. Spraying the Potatoes. Patrick Kavanagh. CABP

Barrels of chains. Sides of beef stacked in vans. Measuring the Tyger. Jack Gilbert. BeAl

Barren grassland, A. *Unknown*. NAAPv.2

Barren Moors, The. William Ellery Channing. APN-1

Barren patch to the right of the cemetery, A. Reading Hamlet. Anna Andreyevna Akhmatova. PoetW, *tr*. by Max Hayward and Stanley Kunitz

83: Barren Spring. Dante Gabriel Rossetti. NoP-4 *Fr*. House of Life, The.

Barren Tree, The. Llewelyn Wyn Griffith.

　"From his own solitude to the world unheeding." OBWVE

Barrenness. T. H. Parry-Williams. BBMWP, *tr*. by Richard Poole

Barrier, The. Louis Lavater. NOBAu

Barrio Beateo. Jesse F. García. UnSA

Barry, the St. Barnard. Samuel Rogers. DiBP *Fr*. Italy.

Bars. Nicolás Guillén. TCLAP, *tr*. by Eric Orozco

Bars burn again across your eyes. Doors. Dartmoor. David Gwenallt Jones. BBMWP, *tr*. by Emyr Humphreys

Bars Fight [August 28, 1746]. Lucy Terry. AmWaPo; NAAPv.1; WaAnP

Bars of Kangnam were dark, damp, and desolate, The. What Is History? 1. Ko Chônghûi. EcSo, *tr*. by Catherine J. Kim

Barter. Sara Teasdale. ITBLP; SoSe-8

Bartley Costello, eighty years old. Gaeltacht. Pearse Hutchinson. ModIr; PBCIP

Bartók. Gyula Illyés. IQMS, *tr*. by Robert C. Kenedy

Bartók. László Nagy. IQMS, *tr*. by Adam Makkai

Bartok and the Geranium. Dorothy Livesay. BrAP

Barton in the Beans. Joanne Limburg. NeBl

Baruch Spinoza. Jorge Luis Borges. WoPoe, *tr*. by Willis Barnstone

Baruch Spinoza of Amsterdam / was seized by a desire to reach God. Mr. Cogito Tells about the Temptation of Spinoza. Zbigniew Herbert. GI, *tr*. by John Carpenter and Bogdana Carpenter

Bas Bleu; Or, Conversation, The. Hannah More.

　"Long was Society o'er-run." PEW

Base Details [*with music*]. Siegfried Sassoon. BrAP; FaBoWar; MoBrPo; NPeEn; OxBEV; PLBUT

Base metal hanger by your master's thigh! One Writing against His Prick. *Unknown*. NOSC

Base of All Metaphysics, The. Walt Whitman. APN-1

Base Stealer, The [*with music*]. Robert Francis. NTCP; PML

3. The Base. Don McKay. NLPA *Fr*. Matériel.

Baseball. Paul Hoover. MoASP

Baseball. Linda Pastan. MoASP

Baseball. Christopher Stanard. SpirFl

Baseball and Classicism. Tom Clark. ASA; PmAP

Baseball and Writing. Marianne Moore. FaBoA; MoASP

Baseball Canto. Lawrence Ferlinghetti. MoASP

Based on a volume of / Japanese prints. (LL) From the Grove Press. Anthony Hecht. AmWit; OBCoV

Basel Square. Aharon Shabtai. WoBe, *tr*. by Peter Cole

Baseline pressure. Ulli Freer. Oth *Fr*. Dents.

Basement, The. Alan Shapiro. TaR

Basement Tale, A. Brian Bartlett. Coast

Bash on Basho: Six of the Best. Geoffrey Holloway. NLP

Bashed up? Seen to be Done. Oumar Ba. SonAtl, *tr*. by Olivier Barlet, Paul Boorde, P. Ellis, Kurt Ganzl and Saul Goode

Bashert. Irena Klepfisz.

　(Bashert.) AF

　"These words are dedicated to those who died." TaR

Basho 1. Cees Nooteboom. TuT, *tr*. by Michael O'Loughlin

Basho 2. Cees Nooteboom. TuT, *tr*. by Michael O'Loughlin

Basho 3. Cees Nooteboom. TuT, *tr*. by Michael O'Loughlin

Basho 4. Cees Nooteboom. TuT, *tr*. by Michael O'Loughlin

Bashō, A Departure. Robert Hass. LoL

Bashō, coming. Snow Party, The. Derek Mahon. HarvBoo; ModIr; NAMCP V.2; NPeEn; PBCIP; PNI; WaAnP

Basho ("Old man among the reeds mistrust of the poet.") Cees Nooteboom. LWR, *tr*. by John M. Coetzee

Basho ("Oude man tussen het riet achterdocht van de dichter.") Cees Nooteboom. LWR

Basho, please take me. Journey with Basho, A. David Ray. AmZen

Bashō says the body is composed of one hundred bones and nine openings. Midsummer. Nicholas Christopher. UrbNat

Basia. Johannes Secundus. *tr*. by Wayland Young

　Kisses, The. EroLit, *tr*. by Wayland Young

　"Not alwayes give a melting kiss." OBVE

Basic Con, The. Lew Welch. CalPo; OxBoAm

Basic Science. Fanny Howe. ExTi

[Basic system code]. Sandy Baldwin. AnSo

Basics. James Dickey. BodElec

Basin Pond. Tu Mu. CCL1, *tr*. by R. F. Burton

Basis then, of belief: base 10? base alphabet? base, The. St. Anzas IX. B. P. Nichol. FTOS

Basket Case. Basil T. Paquet. AmWaPo; FaBoWar

Basket Of Summer Fruit, A. Charles Harpur. NOBAu

Basket with Blue Ox. Nance Van Winckel. RoV

Basketball. Nikki Giovanni. NOxBChV

Basketball. Louis Jenkins. MoASP

Basketball. Ronald Wallace. PBCAP

Basketball is like this for young Indian boys, all arms and legs. Defending Walt Whitman. Sherman Alexie. AmPoNex; ViWalt

Baskets. Louise Glück. AFaM

Baskets of ripe fruit in air. Gardener Janus Catches a Naiad. Dame Edith Sitwell. MoBrPo; OBGa

Basking close to the sun as they are able. Goldfish in the Garden Pond. Valerie Worth. NOxBChV

Basking Shark. Norman Alexander MacCaig. NePenScot

Bas-Relief. Carl Sandburg. ColAP

Bass, The. John A. Stone. BloBone

Bass was. Low End, The. Tomás Riley. BRtP

Bastard from the Bush, The. *Unknown*. NOBAu

Bastard Son is born with a tooth in his mouth and hair on his. Paavo Haavikko. WoPoe *Fr*. Winter Palace, The.

Bastard, The. Richard Savage.

　"In gayer hours, when high my fancy ran." OBSV

Bastardly boy, sprung from some coward's loins. Christopher Marlowe. FaBoWar *Fr*. Tamburlaine the Great, Part 2.

Bastille, a Vision, The. Helen Maria Williams. RWP

Bastó sólo una mirada. En el Ritz de Meknés. Manuel Ulacia. RMCMP

Bat. Emily Dickinson. NAAL-3

Bat, The. Jane Kenyon. LoL

Bat, The. Ruth Pitter. MoWP

Bat, The. Theodore Roethke. APT-2; ChAP

Bat flits, A. Buson. EH, *tr*. by Robert Hass

Bat is born, A. Bats. Randall Jarrell. ChAP; GoPo; NTCP

Bat is dun with wrinkled Wings, The. Bat, The. Emily Dickinson. NAAL-3

Bat Messenger, The. Gurram Jashuva. HotL, *tr*. by V. Narayana Rao

Bat that blocks at close of play, The. Joyce Johnson. UV

Bat that flits at close of eve, The. William Blake. UV *Fr*. Auguries of Innocence.

Bateau de *shatang* avec des rames de *mulan*, Un. En Bateau. Li Po. CCL1, *tr*. by Marie-Jean-Léon, Marquis d'Hervey de Saint-Denys

Batellis [*or* Batalis] and the man I will descrive. Virgil. OBVE *Fr*. Aeneid [*or* Eneados *or* Aeneis], The.

Bath. John Godfrey. FTOS

Bath. John Knoepfle. IllVoic

Bath. Amy Lowell. NAAPv.2

Bath, A. Mookam Choinul. BecRai, *tr*. by Kim Daljin, Kim Won-Chung and Christopher Merrill

Bath: "Kindness, an Irish lilt in her voice." Myra Schneider. PoCu

Bath of Aphrodite. Brewster Ghiselin. APT-2

Bath, The. Robin Becker. PBCAP

Bath, The. Ron Butlin. EdScPo

Bath, The. Anne Portugal. *tr*. by Serge Gavronsky

　"Ah! it's chic to be the Dauphin." SCFWP, *tr*. by Serge Gavronsky

　"And don't you budge the skin hasn't settled." SCFWP, *tr*. by Serge Gavronsky

　"And who really cares about the temperature." SCFWP, *tr*. by Serge Gavronsky

　"As she was lighting up her cigarette." SCFWP, *tr*. by Serge Gavronsky

　"Because a ship." SCFWP, *tr*. by Serge Gavronsky

　"But in your place." SCFWP, *tr*. by Serge Gavronsky

　"Day at a country fair, A." SCFWP, *tr*. by Serge Gavronsky

　"In return can't you see that the only." SCFWP, *tr*. by Serge Gavronsky

　"It's better to know her name." SCFWP, *tr*. by Serge Gavronsky

"My Susanna." SCFWP, *tr.* by Serge Gavronsky

"No curtain." SCFWP, *tr.* by Serge Gavronsky

"She who would take a bath." SCFWP, *tr.* by Serge Gavronsky

"Susanna is drenched." SCFWP, *tr.* by Serge Gavronsky

Bath, The. Gary Snyder. CAP-8; FaoP; NAMCP V.2; PmAP; VCAP

Bath, The: August 6, 1945. Kimiko Hahn. AtGh

Bath Tub Thought. Jack Kerouac. WhBo

Bath when you're born. Issa. EH, *tr.* by Robert Hass

Bathed by tree filtered sun. Zoo. Shuntaro Tanikawa. PoetW, *tr.* by Harold Wright

Bather, The. Charles Simic. PoDa

Bathers, The. Lorenzo Thomas. EGAG

Bathhouse, The. Boris Abramovich Slutsky. TCRusP, *tr.* by Daniel Weissbort

Bathing Girls, The. Tracey Herd. NeBl

Bathing My Mother. Frances Wilson. Prnts

Bathing the summer night. Bath, The: August 6, 1945. Kimiko Hahn. AtGh

Bathroom. Elaine Feinstein. HarvBoo

Bathroom. Fanny Howe. ExTi

Bathroom, The. Group Therapy. Carolyn M. Rodgers. ISC

Baths of Caracalla, The. Famous Baths and Bathers. Carolyn Wells. AmWit

Bathsheba came out to the sun. Telling the Bees. Lizette Woodworth Reese. SWaP

Bathtub is white and full of strips, The. Kenneth Koch. NAMCP V.2; NoAM *Fr.* Days and Nights.

Bathtub [*or* Bath Tub], The. Ezra Pound. NIP-4; TRP; WeW-3

Bathtub Panopticon. Joshua Clover. CalPo

Batman, big shot, when you gave the order. Kid. Simon Armitage. BeAl

Baton Rouge. Terre Haute. Boise. (LL) In the Elementary School Choir. Gregory Djanikian. OPRER; UnSA

Batouque. Aimé Césaire. GPTC, *tr.* by Clayton Eshleman and Annette Smith

Batrachomyomachia; The Battle of the Frogs and Mice. *Unknown, formerly at. to* Homer.

"Ascend my shoulders, firmly keep thy seat." OBVE, *tr.* by Thomas Parnell

Bats. Randall Jarrell. ChAP; GoPo; NTCP

Bats. Mary Oliver. HeIP-4

Bats [*with music*]. Dave Jeddie Smith. NoAM; RoV; WaAnP

Bats flitting here and there. Buson. EH, *tr.* by Robert Hass

Bats flying. Issa. EH, *tr.* by Robert Hass

Bats have no bankers and they do not drink. John Berryman. EmeKit *Fr.* Dream Songs.

Bats have not heard a word of their literary reputation. Enquiry Concerning the Bat, An. José Emilio Pacheco. TCLAP, *tr.* by Alastair Reid

Batter a fences down. Blue 2. Wopko Jensma. TSAP

Batter my heart, three-personed [*or* three person'd] God; for you. John Donne. BASC; BrAP; CABP; ClHu; FSCP; GSo; HeIP-4; InvLi; NAEL-6v1; NAEL-7v1; NIL-7; NIP-4; NoP-4; NoP-5; NOSC; NPeEn; OxAEP-1; OxBSo; PBRV; PoPoPo; SacPr; SoSe-8; TFi; WaAnP *Fr.* Holy Sonnets.

Batter'd, wreck'd old man, A. Prayer of Columbus. Walt Whitman. NCAP

Battered and shiny like the moon. (LL) Shampoo, The. Elizabeth Bishop. APT-2; HarvBoo; OxBoAm; PtR; StAl; VCAP

Battered, black branches, gale-rattled; and. Night-time. Ricardo Jaimes Freyre. SonAtl, *tr.* by Lisa Martin and Eva Asensio Vicente

Battered packets pull out for faraway thought-places, The. Hot Ports. Léon Laleau. SonAtl, *tr.* by Hannah Bourgein, Carrol F. Coates, Kurt Ganzl and Pierre Laleau

Battered Toddler, Page B6. Ellen Doré Watson. OPRER

Batteries Out of Ammunition. Rudyard Kipling. InoFa; WoPoe *Fr.* Epitaphs of the War [1914–1918].

Battery. Diane Glancy. LiTh

Battery. Robin Morgan. GifTon

Battery woman. Pierre McOrlan. MFP, *tr.* by Martin Sorrell

Batting averages. Light Forms. Robert Trammell. TiP2

Batting of the salt-bag quilt commencing its long mope unto, The / death. (LL) What No One Could Have Told Them. C. D. Wright. GPPA; PoChi

Battle. John Davidson. CABP

Battle. Homer. OBVE *Fr.* Iliad, The.

Battle. Aleksandr Petrovich Tkachenko. ItGoST, *tr.* by Maia Tekses

Battle, The. Abraham Abulafia. WoPoe, *tr.* by Stanley Moss

Battle, The. Gwendolyn Brooks. FTtHH

Battle, The. Dan Pagis. FIT, *tr.* by Robert Friend

Battle, The. Louis Simpson. AmWaPo; NAMCP V.2; OBWP; PoWW

Battle About a Dog, The. Hector Boece [*or* Boethius]. DiBP *Fr.* Buik of the Cronicles of Scotland.

Battle at Horizon. Ben Marcus. HeMarv

Battle at the Edge of the Falls. César Moro. BLPSL, *tr.* by Rene de Costa, Rigas Kappatos and Eleni Paidoussi

Battle Autumn of 1862, The. John Greenleaf Whittier. AmWaPo; CBCWP; PCW

Battle boomed, and no reply came back, The. (LL) Christ and the Soldier. Siegfried Sassoon. NoP-4; NoP-5

Battle comes again, The. The charging host. John Neal. AmWaPo *Fr.* Battle of Niagara, The.

Battle Cry of Freedom, The. *Unknown.* NAAPv.1

Battle Hymn. Rita D. Costello. RWB

Battle Hymn of the Republic, The. Rafael Campo. NeAmPo

Battle Hymn [*or* Battle-Hymn] of the Republic, The. Julia Ward Howe. AmWaPo; APN-1; BRP; CBCWP; HHAm; NAAPv.1; NoP-5; OBWP; OxBoAm; SWaP; TCAPo; TFi

(Battle-Hymn of the Republic, The.) ColAP; FaBoA; NoP-4; PCW

Battle Hymn, The. Stephen Crane. AmWaPo

Battle is joined on the open plain. Sedulius Scottus. FaBoWar *Fr.* Defeat of the Norsemen, The.

Battle of Adobe Walls. Chris Willerton. TiP2

Battle of Argoed Llwyfain, The [*with music*]. Taliesin. OBWVE, *tr.* by Anthony Conran

Battle of Aughrim, The. Richard Murphy.

Casement's Funeral. ModIr; PBCIP

Luttrell. PBCIP

Rapparees. PBCIP

Slate. PBCIP

Battle of Blenheim, The. Robert Southey. BRP; CABP; FaBoWar; NPBRoP; OBWP; TFi; WaAnP

(After Blenheim.) OxAEP-2; UV

Battle of Brunanburh [*see trs.* Brunanburg *and* Battle of Brunanburh]. *Unknown.* CABP; FaBoWar; OBVE; OBWP, *tr.* by Alfred Tennyson

Battle of Brunanburh. *Unknown.*

"Hēr Æþoelstān cyning, eorla drihten." CABP

Battle of Flodden, The. *Unknown.* NoSic *Fr.* Scot[t]ish Field[e].

Battle of Gettysburg, The. Edgar Lee Masters. CBCWP

Battle of Inverlochy, The. *Unknown.* EMWP

Battle of Johnny Freedom, The. Damon McLaughlin. RWB

Battle of Maldon, The. *Unknown.* OBWP, *tr.* by Kevin Crossley-Holland

Battle of Maldon, The. *Unknown. tr.* by Michael Alexander

"Courage shall grow keener, clearer the will." WoPoe, *tr.* by Michael Alexander

Battle of Murfreesboro. Allen Tate. FaBoA

Battle of Naseby, The. Thomas Babington Macaulay, 1st Baron Macaulay. FaBoWar; OxAEP-2

Battle of Niagara, The. John Neal. AmWaPo

"Battle comes again, The. The charging host." AmWaPo

"Fresher and fresher comes the air. The blue." APN-1

"It is that hour when listening ones will weep." APN-1

"O save thy children blue Ontario!" APN-1

"There's a fierce gray Bird, with a bending beak." APN-1

Battle of Otterbourne, The. *Unknown.*

"At last these two stout erles did meet." FaBoWar

[Battle of Otterburn, The] [Version from Minstrelsy of the Scottish Border]. *Unknown.* IBB; NePenScot

Battle of the Baltic. Thomas Campbell. OBEV

Battle of the Stars. Adah Isaacs Menken. CBWP-1

Battle of Valcour Island, The. Richard Kenney. YaYoPo

Battle of Waun Gaseg, The. Llywelyn ab y Moel. OBWVE, *tr.* by H. Idris Bell

Battle of Wills Disguised, A. Marge Piercy. HeIP-4

Battle on the Blackbird's Field, The. Vasco [*or* Vasko] Popa. PoSu; WoPoe *Fr.* Blackbird's Field, The.

Battle, Over and Over Again, The. Safiya Henderson-Holmes. UnSA

Battle rent a cobweb diamond-strung, The. Range-finding. Robert Frost. NIL-7; NIP-4; NoAM; OBWP

Battle Report. Bob Kaufman. ISC

Battle Report. Harvey Shapiro. PWW2

Battle Song. Ebenezer Elliott. OxAEP-2

Battle Summers, The. Herman Melville. APN-2

Battle swayed, The. Christopher Logue. FaBoWar *Fr.* War Music.

Battle waged strong, The. Release, The. Adah Isaacs Menken. CBWP-1

Battle Won Is Lost [*with music*]. Phillip William George. HHAm

Battle-Cry of Freedom, The. George Frederick Root. CBCWP

Battlefield. Richard Aldington. OBWP

Battlefield. Mark Turcotte. PoA 2002

Battle-Hymn of the Republic, The. Julia Ward Howe. *See* Battle Hymn [*or* Battle-Hymn] of the Republic, The.

Battle-Retrospect. Amos Niven Wilder.

"Those sultry nights we used to pass outdoors." YaYoPo

Battles of Joshua. *Unknown.* VerBaPo

Battle's uncertain work begins; and move. Luis de Camões [or Camoëns or Camoëns]. FaBoWar *Fr.* Lusiads, The.

Battlesfield, The. Angel González. RaW, *tr. by* Herbert Baird and William Stafford

Battue of Berlin, The. Harry Graham.
    "It was a winter's morning." UV

Batyushkov. Osip Emilevich Mandelstam. OBVE

Baubles, bangles. Baubles, Bangles, and Beads. George Forrest and Robert Wright. ReLy

Baucis and Philemon. Ovid. NOSC *Fr.* Metamorphoses.

Baucis and Philemon. Ovid. OBVE *Fr.* Metamorphoses.

Baudelaire, dead broke, nonetheless allowed himself. Baudelaire's Ablutions. Roger Fanning. NAPBL

Baudelaire took the train. Radiant Silhouette III. John Yau. OpBo

Baudelaire's Ablutions. Roger Fanning. NAPBL

Baudelaire's Spleen. Jaime Manrique. WiU

Bavarian Gentians. D. H. Lawrence. BrAP; CABP; HarvBoo; NAEL-6v2; NAEL-7v2; NAMCP V.1; NoAM; NoP-4; NoP-5; NPeEn; OxBEV; PoPoPo; TFi; TRP; WaAnP

Baviad, The. William Gifford.
    "Lo, Della Crusca! In his closet pent." NOBRP

Bay, The [*with music*]. James Keir Baxter. BrAP; HarvBoo; StAl

Bay breeze, The. Salt. George Barlow. GT

Bay Fight, The. Henry Howard Brownell. PCW

Bay Psalm Book, The. Bible, *O.T.* tr. by Richard Mather
    Psalm 121. GoPo, *tr. by* Michael Wigglesworth
    Psalm 23. TCAPo

Bay the color of steel, of a warship, The. Rain. Roo Borson. NoP-4

Bay undz is es geven andersh. I knew nothing. My Mother's Sabbath Days. Irena Klepfisz. TaR

Bayer's children's aspirin is cheaper. Aspirin. Elizabeth Alexander. AmPoNex

Baying, The. James Bertolino. UrbNat

Bayonet, The. James Copeland. EdScPo

Bayonet Training. Vernon Scannell. FaBoWar

Bayou Arabic Argot. Jessica Freeman. AnSo

Bay's little waves licked the ankles, The. Grandmother. Eva Salzman. MFPA

Baz and the Freedom of the Press. Kevin Cadwallender. RSaN

BC:AD. U. A. Fanthorpe. OBCP; OxBEV

BE-. Sharon Bryan. PoDa

Be a beggar, be a thief. Be Anything (But Be Mine). Irving Gordon. ReLy

Be a child forever. Gail Wronsky. PoChi *Fr.* Sor Juana's Last Dream.

Be a facilitator, not a roadblock, says the lady who runs the news stand. Spring Forward, Fall Back. Alpay Ulku. AmPoNex

Be a Painter. Joe Lothamer. GeoH

Be a witness. On Non-Violence & Observation. Jim Cohn. WhBo

Be all serene, thou dull inclement Sky. On a Friend's Taking a Journey. Elizabeth Teft. PoBW

Be an unlikely treasure hoard. (LL) *Unknown.* APT-1; HeIP-4; NoP-4; NoP-5; OxBoAm; TCAPo; WaAnP; WoPoe *Fr.* Ripostes of Ezra Pound.

Be Anything (But Be Mine). Irving Gordon. ReLy

Be Attentive. Natan Zach. PoSu, *tr. by* Peter Everwine and Shulamit Yasny-Starkman

Be attentive to this trembling shade. Be Attentive. Natan Zach. PoSu, *tr. by* Peter Everwine and Shulamit Yasny-Starkman

Be bold! That's one way. Be Bold! That's One Way. Archilochus. WoPoe, *tr. by* Guy Davenport

Be born a saint; or keep. Be Born a Saint. Pearse Hutchinson. PBCIP

Be Brothers. Ifi Amadiume. HAWP

Be Careful. *Unknown.* NBLV

Be Careful. Natan Zach. PoSu

Be Careful of the Lilies! Jean Bleakney. NIrP

Be careful. Open your life. Be Careful. Natan Zach. PoSu

Be Careful When You Go Looking for a Madonna Cuz You Just Might Find a Woman. Pat Russell. BtF

Be composed—be at ease with me—I am Walt Whitman, liberal and lusty as Nature. To a Common Prostitute. Walt Whitman. MoAmPo

Be curst the time of Bullen's fatal birth. John Banks. STuOW *Fr.* Anna Bullen.

Be dark enough thy shades, and be thou there content. (LL) Introduction, The: "Did I, my lines intend for public[k] view." Anne Finch, Countess of Winchilsea. BrAP; EMWP; NAEL-6v1; NAEL-7v1; NALW; NoP-4; NoP-5; WaAnP

Be easy, October. No cackle hen, horse neigh, tree sough, duck quack. (LL) Patrick Kavanagh. EMP; ModIr; NAMCP V.1; NoAM; NoP-4; NoP-5; NPeEn *Fr.* Great Hunger, The.

Be extra careful by this door. Whisperer, The. Mark Van Doren. MoAmPo

Be faithful Go. (LL) Envoy of Mr. Cogito, The. Zbigniew Herbert. ItP; PoetW; WoPoe, *tr. by* Carpenter Bogdana, Bogdana Carpenter and John Carpenter *and* Bogdana Carpenter

Be from the Court of Love, and Reason torn. Mary Sidney Wroth, Countess of Montgomery. BASC

Be gentle when the wind and dark waves come. When the Wind and Dark Waves Come. David J. Rothman. GeoH

Be given to him who triumphs in his right. Mary Sidney Wroth, Countess of Montgomery. BASC

Be gone, have done! Down, wanton, down! (LL) Down, Wanton, Down! Robert Graves. BrAP; HarvBoo; HeIP-4; NAEL-6v2; NAEL-7v2; NAMCP V.1; NoAM

Be good! / Be good! (LL) Langston Hughes. NAAL-5; NAMCP V.1 *Fr.* Three Songs about Lynching.

Be good, my Lord, since you can not be pretty. (LL) Lord Barrenstock. Stevie Smith. NALW; NBLV; OBSV

Be good to those who come after us. (LL) Eavesdropper. Breyten Breytenbach. PML; PoetW, *tr. by* Ernst van Heerden

Be happy, my love, I shall take charge of our cares. *Unknown.* SLW, *tr. by* Marjolijn De Jager, Sayd Bahodin Majrouh and André Velter

Be He Ezra Pound, Kennedy, or King. Belle Randall. GifTon

Be in me as the eternal moods. Ezra Pound. MoAmPo *Fr.* Ripostes of Ezra Pound.

Be Indomitable, O My Heart. Nezahualcoyotl. WoPoe, *tr. by* Thelma D. Sullivan

Be indomitable, O my heart! Be Indomitable, O My Heart. Nezahualcoyotl. WoPoe, *tr. by* Thelma D. Sullivan

Be it right or wrong, these men among. Nut-brown Maid, The. *Unknown.* NoSic; OBEV

Be it so, for I submit; his doom is fair. John Milton. NAWM-5v1 *Fr.* Paradise Lost.

Be kind and tender to the Frog. Frog, The. Joseph Hilaire Pierre Belloc. ChAP; NOxBChV; NTCP

Be kind to her. To End Her Fear. John Freeman. OBMV

Be land ready. Be Ready. Carl Sandburg. NOxBChV

Be Like the Bird. Victor Hugo. Spl

Be literal a moment. Recollect. Seamus Heaney. PoetW *Fr.* Squarings.

Be loved, my beloved. Spell for Jealousy. Jeni Couzyn. BrAP; HAWP

Be many, and a blessing to mankind. (LL) William Wordsworth. NAEL-6v2; NAEL-7v2 *Fr.* Prelude, The; Growth of a Poet's Mind [1850 version; Selections from Anthologies].

Be merciful to me, a fool! (LL) Fool's Prayer, The. Edward Rowland Sill. APN-2; ITBLP

Be my stillborn son my son. Mulatto Lullaby. Ralph Dickey. ESEAA

Be near me when my light is low. Alfred Tennyson. BrAP; CABP; HeIP-4; NAEL-6v2; NAEL-7v2; NAWM-7v2; NoP-5; WaAnP *Fr.* In Memoriam A. H. H.

Be not afeard: the isle is full of noises. William Shakespeare. OxAEP-1 *Fr.* Tempest, The.

Be not afraid of my body. (LL) As Adam Early in the Morning. Walt Whitman. APN-1; ChIV-1; ColAP; NAAPv.1; SAmP; WaAnP

Be not deaf to the sound that warns. Alfred Tennyson. STuOW *Fr.* Printed in "The Times," May 1859.

Be of Good Cheer. Robert Creeley. BodElec

Be off, or I'll kick you downstairs! (LL) Lewis Carroll. ChAP; NPeEn; OBCoV; OxBEV; TFi *Fr.* Alice's Adventures in Wonderland.

Be perpendicular to the basket. Foul Shots: A Clinic. William Matthews. MoASP

Be plain in dress and sober in your diet. Summary of Lord Lyttleton's 'Advice to a Lady', A. Lady Mary Wortley Montagu. OxBEV

Be quiet awful woman. Calming Kali. Lucille Clifton. HW

Be quiet, heart! home! home! (LL) Lordly Hudson, The. Paul Goodman. APT-2; OxBoAm; PoCho

Be, rather than be called, a child of God. On an Infant Which Died before Baptism. Samuel Taylor Coleridge. SacPr

Be Ready. Carl Sandburg. NOxBChV

Be reckoned [or reckon'd] but with herbs and flowers [or flow'rs]. (LL) Garden, The. Andrew Marvell. BASC; BrAP; ClHu; FSCP; MakPoe; NAEL-6v1; NAEL-7v1; NIL-7; NiP-4; NoP-5; NOSC; NPeEn; OBGa; OxBEV; PBRV; PoPoPo; TFi; TRP; WaAnP

Be respectful / Sparrows. Issa. ZenPo, *tr. by* Takashi Ikemoto and Lucien Stryk

Be sad, be cool, be kind. Long Shadow of Lincoln: A Litany, The. Carl Sandburg. CBCWP

Be Sad, My Heart. Francis Quarles. NIP-4

Be Seeing You. Vasco [or Vasko] Popa. PoSu *Fr.* Raw Flesh.

Be silent, hide yourself. Silentium. Fyodor Ivanovich Tyutchev. WoPoe, *tr. by* Charles Tomlinson

Be silent, you still music of the spheres. On a Gentlewoman that Sung and Played upon a Lute. William Strode. NOSC

Be so—ashamed of thee. (LL)   What Soft—Cherubic Creatures.   Emily Dickinson.   APN-2; MoAmPo; NALW; TCAPo

Be still, my Blessed Babe, though cause thou hast to mourn.   Lulla Lullaby.   William Byrd.   ChIV-2

Be Still, My Soul.   Katharina von Schlegel.   SacPr, tr. by Jane L. Borthwick

Be still, my soul, be still; the arms you bear are brittle.   A. E. Housman.   MoBrPo Fr. Shropshire Lad, A.

Be still, my soul: the Lord is on thy side.   Be Still, My Soul.   Katharina von Schlegel.   SacPr Fr. tr. by Jane L. Borthwick

Be still. The Hanging Gardens were a dream.   Trumbull Stickney.   APN-2; WoPoe

Be still. / Wait. (LL)   Lost Son, The.   Theodore Roethke.   APT-2; CAP-8; NAMCP V.1; NoP-4; NoP-5; OxBoAm; TRP

Be still, while the music rises about us; the deep enchantment.   At a Concert of Music.   Conrad Potter Aiken.   MoAmPo

Be still with me, as all bells are still!   Ingeborg Bachmann.   VCWP

Be Strong.   Maltbie Davenport Babcock.   ITBLP; SoSe-8

Be strong, brother!   Imre Madách.   IQMS Fr. Tragedy of Man.

Be sure observe where brown Ostrea stands.   John Gay.   OxBEV Fr. Trivia; or, The Art of Walking the Streets of London.

Be sure to invite me.   Kim Yuk.   CATKP, tr. by Peter H. Lee

Be thanked, O plumage of paradise, be praised. (LL)   For the Sisters of the Hôtel Dieu.   Abraham Moses Klein.   BrAP; NoP-4

Be that as it may, it may be that it is as it will be.   Sounds of the Resurrected Dead Man's Footsteps (#1).   Marvin Bell.   IaFF

Be the medicine. (LL)   Ode to Meaning.   Robert Pinsky.   MakPoe; OxBoAm

Be the mistress of my choice.   Robert Herrick.   CavPo

Be the proud Thames of trade the busy mart!   To the River Arun.   Charlotte Smith.   RWP

Be the same day, the day of my life. (LL)   Man Meets a Woman in the Street, A.   Randall Jarrell.   NoP-4; NoP-5

Be this the fate.   Curse on a Closed Gate, A.   Unknown.   IrV, tr. by James H. Cousins

Be this was said a grondyn dart leit he glide.   Virgil.   NPeEn Fr. Aeneid [or Eneados or Aeneis], The.

Be thorough in your scholarship.   Tiruvalluvar.   WoPoe Fr. Kural, The.

Be thou to others kind and true.   Isaac Watts.   NOxBChV

Be thou, with snowy plumage soft.   Unknown.   RWP Fr. Aged Bard's Wish, The.

Be thy continuing line. (LL)   Heaven conserve thy course in quietness.   Unknown.   APSN; NDACCP, tr. by Ezra Pound

Be tied to the halberds, or grating, and whipped.   Lay of the Lash, The.   Unknown.   FaBoWar

Be tremblingly fearful.   Yao's Warning.   Unknown.   CCL1, tr. by James Legge

Be uncovered! / Hoe with look life! Sun rises.   Wild Provoke of the Endurance Sky.   Joseph Ceravolo.   BodElec; NYP2

Be unexpected Friends. (LL)   "Remember me" implored the Thief!   Emily Dickinson.   ChIV-2; SacPr

Be where I may when death brings in his bill.   Wish, A.   John Clare.   NPBRoP

Be wise as thou art cruel; do not press.   William Shakespeare.   NoSic Fr. Sonnets.

Be with baby under baby.   Carla Harryman.   BAP-04 Fr. Baby.

Be with me, Beauty, for the fire is dying.   On Growing Old.   John Masefield.   MoBrPo

Be with me, Luis de San Angel, now.   Hart Crane.   NoAM Fr. Bridge, The.

Be with me when I lie down; you promised me this in an earlier life. (LL)   It's True I Went to the Market.   Mirabai.   WED; WPoS, tr. by Robert Bly

Be your words made (good sir) of Indian ware.   Sir Philip Sidney.   NoSic Fr. Astrophil and Stella.

Be yourself: show your flyblown eyes.   You.   Dennis O'Driscoll.   StAl

Beach.   Sophia De Mello Breyner.   VCWP, tr. by Ruth Fainlight

Beach.   Tiziano Rossi.   ItPo, tr. by Gayle Ridinger

Beach.   Takahashi Shinkichi.   ZenPo, tr. by Takashi Ikemoto and Lucien Stryk

Beach, The.   Douglas Goetsch.   AmPoNex

Beach, The.   Suzanne Matson.   PfS

Beach, The.   Peter Scupham.   HarvBoo

Beach after a train, The. (LL)   Easter: Wahiawa, 1959.   Cathy Song.   FTtHH; OpBo

Beach at Noon, The.   Fred Cogswell.   Coast

Beach Burial.   Kenneth Slessor.   BrAP

Beach Glass [with music].   Amy Clampitt.   MoWP; NAMCP V.2; NoAM; NoP-4; NoP-5; VCAP

Beach grass tangled by wind—the sound rushes.   Eastern Long Island.   Marvin Bell.   PfSP

Beach House.   Stanley Noyes.   ICANM

Beach, Later.   Dennis Saleh.   GeoHom

Beach Red.   Peter Bowman.

    "Rejoice, O young man, in thy youth (Keep down, down)."   PWW2

2. Beach Roses.   Mark Doty.   AmAlph Fr. Fog Argument.

Beach was emptying like an hourglass, The.   Collaboration: A Day at the Beach.   Anthony Caleshu.   NIrP

Beachcomber stalks out of the froth, A.   Seascape.   Stanley Noyes.   ICANM

Beaches.   Nesta Wyn Jones.   BBMWP, tr. by Catherine Fisher

Beaches.   Zachary Scott Robbins.   BtF

Beaches of Chile were only a nickname, The.   Sparkling Beaches, The.   Raúl Zurita.   TCLAP, tr. by Jack Schmitt

Beachhead.   Samuel Menashe.   PWW2

Beachy Head.   Hilary Davies.   Prnts

Beachy Head.   Charlotte Smith.   RWP

    "Early worshipper at Nature's shrine, An."   MakPoe; NPBRoP

    "I once was happy, when while yet a child."   PEW

Beacon.   Vladimir Levchev.   CSCBP, tr. by Georgi Belev and Lisa Sapinkopf

Beacon.   Pedro Serrano.   RMCMP, tr. by Geoff Hargreaves

Beacon, The.   Richard Wilbur.   UpMys

Beacon Arms.   Jim Behrle.   FreRad

Beacons from the abode where the Eternal are. (LL)   Adonais; An Elegy on the Death of John Keats.   Percy Bysshe Shelley.   CABP; InoFa; NAEL-6v2; NAEL-7v2; NOBRP; NoP-4; NoP-5; OxAEP-2; TFi; WaAnP

Bead.   John Redmond.   NIrP

Bead of sweat.   Heat.   Onika Simon.   BeDoSh

Beads of ice hang from the coral tree.   Silence at the End of the World.   Amber Coverdale Sumrall.   AtGh

Beagles.   Paul Muldoon.   GPPA

Beak / by wing and weight.   Banding near the South Texas Coast, Late April.   Chip Dameron.   TiP2

Beaks evolved for gutter cracks, handouts.   Pigeons.   Daniel Tobin.   UrbNat

Beaks of Eagles, The.   Robinson Jeffers.   NAAPv.2

Beale Street Blues.   William Christopher Handy.   APT-1

Beall Mountain Seasonal.   Linda Pastan.   PfSP

Beam 30, The Garden.   Ronald Johnson.   FTOS Fr. Ark.

Beam 7.   Ronald Johnson.   APSN Fr. Ark.

Beam 4.   Ronald Johnson.   APSN Fr. Ark.

Beam of light in the mouth of azure, A.   Scene for the Mornings Preceding the Fire, A.   Ghada El-Shafa'i.   PoArWo, tr. by Atef Abu-Seif and Nathalie Handal

Beam 25, A Bicentennial Hymn.   Ronald Johnson.   APSN Fr. Ark.

Beaming flowers in the thicket.   Orchard Pavilion.   Wang Pin-chih.   ChinPo, tr. by Ye Weilian [or Yeh Wei-lien or Wai-lim Yip]

Beams.   Audre Lorde.   ESEAA; NoAM

Beams.   Paul Verlaine.   SxFrPo, tr. by Martin Sorrell

Bean Eaters, The.   Gwendolyn Brooks.   AFaM; AmFaPo; ESEAA; HeIP-4; HHAm; MoWP; NAAL-5; NALW; NAMCP V.2; NoP-4; NoP-5; PoPoPo; TRP; WaAnP; WeW-3

Bean Flower.   Unknown.   CCL1 Fr. Cai-ge [Translations].

Bean Spasms.   Ted Berrigan.   AHA; PmAP

Beans.   Sean Dunne.   ModIr Fr. Sydney Place.

Bean-Stalk, The.   Edna St. Vincent Millay.   NOxBChV

Beanstalk Country, The.   Tennessee Williams.   APT-2

Beanstalk, Meditated Later, The [with music].   Judith Wright.   NoAM

Beanstalks, in any breeze, are a slack church parade.   Broad Bean Sermon, The.   Les A. Murray.   BMAP; EmeKit; HarvBoo; MakPoe

Beanville. Tea.   Everywhere Is out of Town.   Kevin Young.   FuFl

Bear, The.   Robert Frost.   MoAmPo; NoAM

Bear, The.   Galway Kinnell.   CAP-8; MakPoe; StAl; TRP; VCAP; WaAnP

Bear, The [with music].   N. Scott Momaday.   HATNAP

Bear, The.   Yi Chinmyông.   EcSo, tr. by Carolyn U. So

Bear: A Totem Dance As Seen by Raven.   Peter Blue Cloud.   HATNAP

Bear at the Dump, The.   William Matthews.   PfSP

Bear barged into the boozer, The.   Other Side of the Mountain, The.   Kit Wright.   StAl

Bear: beware, from the last days.   Seasons.   Philip Booth.   PfSP

Bear down / My Mother Country.   Deliverance.   Amelia Blossom Pegram.   HAWP

Bear Fat.   Linda Hogan.   AFaM

Bear Fur.   Takamura Kotaro.   CAoMJL1, tr. by Leith Morton

Bear in mind / That death is a drum.   Drum.   Langston Hughes.   APT-2; MoAmPo; NAMCP V.1

Bear in the illustrated book of animals is fat and doesn't speak, The.   Bear, The.   Yi Chinmyông.   EcSo, tr. by Carolyn U. So

Bear mother / gives suck to the stars.   Federico García Lorca.   PFTM-1 Fr. Night (Suite for Piano and Poet's Voice).

Bear mother, supple.   Artemis.   V. B. Price.   ICANM

Bear my first thought, as waking, I hear.   Night Walking.   Robert Penn Warren.   BodElec

Bear of the Human Family, A.   Kazuko Shiraishi.   WoBe, tr. by Samuel Grolmes and Yumiko Tsumura

Bear on Main Street, The.   Dan Gerber.   PoDa

Bear on the Delhi Road, The.   Earle Birney.   BrAP; HeIP-4; NoAM; NoP-4; NoP-5

Bear [or Bare] that breath[e]s [or breaks] the northern blast the.   Upon a Wasp Chilled [or Child] with Cold.   Edward Taylor.   NAAL-3; NAAL-5; NAAPv.1; OxBEV

Bear puts both arms around the tree above her, The.   Bear, The.   Robert Frost.   MoAmPo; NoAM

Bear with me.   Elvis P. and Emma B.   Elizabeth Ash Vélez.   AllShUp

Bear-Baiting.   Samuel Butler.   DiBP Fr. Hudibras.

Bear-Baiting Cur, The.   William Shakespeare.   DiBP Fr. King Henry VI, Pt. II.

Beard and Bicycle.   Guy Boas.   ArBi

Bearded Callistratus wedded rugged Afer.   Martial.   CAGL Fr. Epigrams.

Bearded Oaks.   Robert Penn Warren.   APT-2; ColAP; EMP; FuPo; InGu; MoAmPo; NAAL-5; NAMCP V.1; NoAM; NoP-4; NoP-5; PoA 2002

Bearer of Evil Tidings, The.   Robert Frost.   NoAM; SAmP

Bearer, The.   Hayden Carruth.   PoA 2002

Bearers' Song.   T'ao Ch'ien.   ChinPo, tr. by Ye Weilian [or Yeh Wei-lien or Wai-lim Yip]

Bearhug.   Michael Ondaatje.   BeAl

Bearhug, The.   Nick Laird.   NIrP

Bearing no flowers.   Chiyojo.   NIL-7, tr. by Daniel C. Buchanan

Bearing so little ammunition. (LL)   School Children, The.   Louise Glück.   ColAP; ItP; NAMCP V.2; PoPoPo; WeW-3

Bearing the bandages, water and sponge.   Walt Whitman.   FaBoWar Fr. Wound-Dresser, The.

Bearing the golden bough of Argicida. So that. (LL)   Ezra Pound.   BrAP; NAAPv.2; NAMCP V.1; NoP-5; WaAnP Fr. Cantos.

Bearing the lustre of a full moon.   Bhartrihari.   EroLit, tr. by Barbara Stoler Miller

Bearing Witness.   Ellen Bass.   LiTh

Bears are kept by hundreds within fences, are fed cracked, The.   Elizabeth's War with the Christmas Bear.   Norman Dubie.   AmAlph; NAMCP V.2; NoAM

Beast in Man, The.   George Clutesi.   HATNAP

Beast in the Space, The.   William Sydney Graham.   EmeKit; OxAEP-2; PoA 2002; StAl

Beast with Two Backs, The.   Andrew Taylor.   NOBAu

Beasts.   Richard Wilbur.   BrAP

Beasts, cattle, have words, neither minor nor many.   Les A. Murray.   UpMys Fr. Walking to the Cattle Place.

Beasts in the schoolroom, whose transparent faces, The.   Blues for Warren.   Thomas McGrath.   AF

Beasts in their major freedom.   Beasts.   Richard Wilbur.   BrAP

Beasts of England, The.   Andy Croft.   RSaN

Beat at the air till the light blows out. (LL)   I Only Am Escaped Alone to Tell Thee.   Howard Nemerov.   HeIP-4; NoAM

Beat! Beat! Drums!   Walt Whitman.   CBCWP; FaBoWar; HeIP-4; NAAL-3; NAAL-5; NCAP; NoP-4; NoP-5; OBWP

Beat Drum, Beat Heart.   Sheila Wingfield.
Part Three: Women in Love.
"Where is the lumber-room of what was important?"   MoWP

Beat hell out of it.   William Carlos Williams.   APT-1 Fr. Paterson.

Beat out continuance in the choking veins.   Blood is Justified, The.   Muriel Rukeyser.   StAl; YaYoPo

Beat the knife on the plate and the fork on the can.   Going In to Dinner.   Edward Richard Burton Shanks.   OBMV

Beat upon it till it break. (LL)   Sub Contra.   Louise Bogan.   APT-2; WaAnP

Beaten Track, The.   Steve Benson.   FTOS

Beating and beating at an intractable metal. (LL)   Blackberrying.   Sylvia Plath.   BeAl; NAAL-5; NAMCP V.2; NoAM; PoPoPo

Beating, beating. (LL)   Lines to a Nasturtium.   Anne Spencer.   APT-1; InGu

Beating drum presses for my life, The.   At the Execution Ground.   Sŏng [or Sung] Samnun.   CATKP, tr. by Chi-gyu Kim [or Kim Chonggil]

Beating, The.   Ann Stanford.   SoSe-8

Beating the drum.   Tattoo, The.   Ania Walwicz.   BMAP

Beating the Drum in Reverse.   Miroslav Valek.   ArBi, tr. by David Short

Beating the Heat at Jade Lake.   Ching An.   CSKM, tr. by Jerome P. Seaton

Beating Time.   Barbara Kingsolver.   TWF

Beatings.   Joan Larkin.   WiU

Beatitudes.   Bruce Dawe.   GI

Beatitudes, The.   Bible, N.T.   OBVE Fr. St. Matthew.

Beatnik's Monologue, The.   Andrey Andreievich Voznesensky.   TCRusP, tr. by Daniel Weissbort

¡Beato sillón! La casa.   Beato Sillón.   Jorge Guillén.   RaW

Beatrice.   J. Bernlef.   TuT, tr. by Peter van de Kamp

Beatrice lay naked on the narrow bed.   Plot, The.   William Dickey.   YaYoPo

Beatrix Potter.   Lee Upton.   AmA!ph

Beats the golden bird no more. (LL)   Edna St. Vincent Millay.   APT-1; InoFa; MoAmPo Fr. Memorial to D. C..

Beattie is Three.   Adrian Mitchell.   StAl

Beau and the Bird.   William Cowper.   DiBP

Beau and the Water Lily.   William Cowper.   DiBP

Beau Ideal, The.   Jessie Pope.   FaBoWar

Beaufort, fair Beaufort, thou art a favored spot.   General Robert Smalls.   Josephine D. Henderson Heard.   CBWP-4

Beauharnois (1).   Margaret Atwood.   PoetW Fr. Four Small Elegies.

Beauharnois (3).   Margaret Atwood.   PoetW Fr. Four Small Elegies.

Beauharnois, Glengarry (2).   Margaret Atwood.   PoetW Fr. Four Small Elegies.

Beauing, belling, dancing, drinking.   Rakes of Mallow, The.   Unknown.   OBCoV

Beaulieu.   Clarence Major.   FTOS

Beaumaris Bay.   Richard Llwyd.
  Beaumaris Bay.   AngWePo

Beaumaris Bay.   Richard Llwyd.   AngWePo Fr. Beaumaris Bay.

Beaumont: Class Reunion.   Dave Oliphant.
  "Too talented to give a hot damn."   TiP2

Beaumont smells like the pursuit of.   Yankees in East Texas.   Joe Benevento.   RWB

Beaumont to Detroit: 1943.   Langston Hughes.   AmWaPo

Beau's Reply.   William Cowper.   DiBP

Beauteous Ethel's father has a, The.   Piazza Tragedy, A.   Eugene Field.   NBLV

Beauteous thou art, the spirit knows not how.   Elsewhere.   Michael Field.   VWP

Beauties of Nature, The.   Robert Burns.   TreFP

Beautiful. Diminutive.   Carlos Drummond de Andrade.   TCLAP, tr. by Virginia de Araújo

Beautiful, The.   E. H. Burrington.   TreFP

Beautiful, The.   Mary E. Tucker.   CBWP-1

Beautiful, accomplished, splendid—if he can be had—and brave.   Verses Written by Alis Daughter of Gryffydd Son of Iefan When Her Father Asked Her What Sort of Husband She Would Like.   Alis Ferch Gruffyd ab Ieuan ap Lleywelyn Fychan.   EMWP

Beautiful, also, are the souls of my people. (LL)   My People.   Langston Hughes.   APT-2; NOxBChV; OxAAAP; TWF

Beautiful American Poem, The.   Josh Bell.   RWB

Beautiful & dangerous. (LL)   Slam, Dunk, & Hook.   Yusef Komunyakaa.   ISC; MoASP

Beautiful As.   Lucie Thésée.   SurWo, tr. by Myrna Bell Rochester

Beautiful as a high foamy wave spurting in a crystal ball.   Beautiful As.   Lucie Thésée.   SurWo, tr. by Myrna Bell Rochester

Beautiful as a tiered cloud, skysails set and shrouds twanging.   Clipper-Ships.   John Gould Fletcher.   TCAPo

Beautiful as the flying legend of some leopard.   Judith of Bethulia.   John Crowe Ransom.   APT-1; NoAM

Beautiful Beeshareen Boy, The.   Mathilde Blind.   VWP

Beautiful bird we rinsed the soap from gently, A.   To the Horizon.   Michael Savitz.   FreRad

Beautiful Black Men.   Nikki Giovanni.   WaAnP

Beautiful, black-eyed boy.   Beautiful Beeshareen Boy, The.   Mathilde Blind.   VWP

Beautiful boy, flower fair.   To an English Boy.   Hilary.   EroLit, tr. by John Boswell

Beautiful Changes, The.   Richard Wilbur.   NAAL-5; NIL-7; OxBoAm

Beautiul, clear, July light.   Dante Park.   Miguel Algarin.   PueRic

Beautiful day, The. V.   Alfred B. Spellman.   EGAG

Beautiful Days.   Mary Kinzie.   ExTi

Beautiful, delicate bright gazelle, The.   Love-song.   Walter James Turner.   OBMV

Beautiful element of unreason under it? (LL)   Black Earth.   Marianne Moore.   APT-1; NAMCP V.1

Beautiful Evelyn Hope is dead!   Evelyn Hope.   Robert Browning.   TreFP

Beautiful excess of Jesus on the waters, The.   To Swim, to Believe.   Maxine W. Kumin.   CAP-8; MoASP; PoCho

Beautiful Eyes.   Louise Grassi Whitney.   PfS

Beautiful from his tail-tip.   Fox, The.   Mary Oliver.   PoCoUp

Beautiful girl, fifteen years old, A.   Woman's Sorrow, A.   Im Che.   CATKP, tr. by Peter H. Lee

Beautiful his peacock crown.   In Praise of Krishna.   Ruskhan.   WoPoe, tr. by Stephen Schaffer and Allen Shapiro

Beautiful House, The.   Laura Moriarty.   ASA

Beautiful Imogene is finally alone, The.   Harold and Imogene.   Paul Violi.   ReTh

Beautiful in death.   San Jacinto.   Mirabeau Buonaparte Lamar.   TiP2

Beautiful in Death.   Martha E. (Martha Elizabeth Hotchkiss) Whitten.   TiP2

Beautiful in the foregone drawing-room and the dance. Jane Austen. Patricia Beer. CABP

Beautiful IRELAND! Who will preach to thee? Who Will Show Us Any Good? Lady Jane Francesca Wilde. VWP

Beautiful landscape, The. Garden at the General's Residence, The. Muso Soseki. EaWin, *tr.* by W. S. Merwin

Beautiful light down there. Evening Change. John Haines. GifTon

Beautiful Lunacy! that shapest flight. Thomas Tod Stoddart. NOBRP *Fr.* Death-Wake, The; or, Lunacy.

Beautiful man and his wife, The. Window Dressing. William Peskett. PNI

Beautiful man is sleeping under a pine tree, A. Monk's Dream. Dave Etter. SeSe

Beautiful Melite, in the throes of middle age. Agathias. ErotSp, *tr.* by Sam Hamill

Beautiful miracle. Love Is Just Around the Corner. Leo Robin. ReLy

Beautiful Mistress, A. Thomas Carew. CavPo

Beautiful morning, A; we go down to the arena, A. Wednesday. Lisa Robertson. VaPo

Beautiful music! / Dangerous rhythm! Continental (You Kiss While You're Dancing), The. Herb Magidson. ReLy

Beautiful must be the mountains whence ye come. Nightingales. Robert Bridges. MoBrPo; OBEV; OBMV; TFi

Beautiful Nahid rose up and in her clear voice cried, The. *Unknown.* SLW, *tr.* by Marjolijn De Jager, Sayd Bahodin Majrouh and André Velter

Beautiful names, The. Quilt Complex. Ricardo Pau-Llosa. RWB

Beautiful new railway bridge of the Silvery Tay. William McGonagall. VerBaPo *Fr.* Address to the New Tay Bridge, An.

Beautiful Ones, The. Gonzalo Rojas. BLPSL, *tr.* by Rene de Costa, Rigas Kappatos and Eleni Paidoussi

Beautiful or ugly it doesn't matter. Beautiful or Ugly It Doesn't Matter. Valentine Penrose. SurWo, *tr.* by Roy Edwards

Beautiful Person, The. Ssu-ma Hsiang-ju. CCL1, *tr.* by John A. Scott

Beautiful Railway Bridge of the Silvery Tay! Railway Bridge of the Silvery Tay, The. William McGonagall. NePenScot

Beautiful Railway Bridge of the Silvery Tay! William McGonagall. VerBaPo *Fr.* Railway Bridge of the Silvery Tay, The.

Beautiful Railway Bridge of the Silv'ry Tay! William McGonagall. UV *Fr.* Tay Bridge Disaster, The.

Beautiful railway bridge of the silv'ry Tay!/ Alas! I am very sorry to say. Tay Bridge Disaster, The. William McGonagall. VerBaPo

Beautiful River. Robert Lowry. APN-2

Beautiful Sea, The. Mary E. Tucker. CBWP-1

Beautiful Signor. Cyrus Cassells. WiU

Beautiful solution, The. When Torrid Rhymes with Forehead. Ray DiPalma. FTOS

Beautiful Soup, so rich and green. Lewis Carroll. UV *Fr.* Alice's Adventures in Wonderland.

Beautiful star in heav'n so bright. Star of the Evening. James M. Sayles. UV

Beautiful summer night, A. Summer Night. BLT, *tr.* by Willis Barnstone

Beautiful Texas. Wilbert Lee O'Daniel. TiP2

Beautiful, The! what is not perfect here below. Beautiful, The. Mary E. Tucker. CBWP-1

Beautiful Toilet, The. Mei Sheng. NDACCP; OBVE, *tr.* by Ezra Pound

Beautiful Train, The. William Empson. OxAEP-2

Beautiful, visitors used to say. Dusting. Daniel Hall. YaYoPo

Beautiful? wasn't she beautiful? (LL) To my last period. Lucille Clifton. BeAl; NAMCP V.2; PoCu

Beautiful woman, A. Poetry. Ismail. HotL, *tr.* by V. Narayana Rao

Beautiful World, The. Albert Verwey. TuT, *tr.* by Tony Curtis and Tony Curtis

Beautiful Wreckage. William Daniel Ehrhart. AmWaPo

Beautiful yellow cassia, so tender. To the Tune: Partridge Sky. Li Ch'ing-chao. CrYelRi, *tr.* by Sam Hamill

Beautiful Young Nymph Going to Bed, A. Jonathan Swift. EroLit; NoP-5; NPeEn; OxBEV

Beautifully Janet slept. Janet Waking. John Crowe Ransom. APT-1; ColAP; FuPo; InGu; MoAmPo; NoAM; PtR; WaAnP

Beauty. Laurence Binyon. MoBrPo

Beauty. Madison Cawein. APN-2

Beauty. Thomas Stanley. OBVE

Beauty. Jones Very. SacPr

Beauty. Walt Whitman. WeW-3

Beauty [*with music*]. Elinor Wylie. APT-1

Beauty, A. Kim Suyŏng. CAMKP, *tr.* by Young-Jun Lee

Beauty Accurst. Richard Le Gallienne. RACG

Beauty and Her Visitors. Winthrop Mackworth Praed. NOBRP

Beauty and majesty are fallen at odds. Richard Barnfield. OxBSo *Fr.* Cynthia, with Certain[e] Sonnets.

Beauty and Mind. Fazil Hüsnü Daglarca. NaPG, *tr.* by Talat Sait Halman

Beauty and Sadness. Cathy Song. NAMCP V.2; NoAM

Beauty and the Beast. Olga Broumas. YaYoPo

Beauty and the Beast. Gillian Conoley. BodElec; RoV

Beauty and the Beast. Rita Dove. ESEAA; NoAM

Beauty and the Beast. George R. Sims.
 "He gazed on the face of the high-born maid." VerBaPo

Beauty and the Prince Formerly Known as Beast. Eleanor Brown. NeBl

Beauty Bathing. Anthony Munday. OBEV *Fr.* Primaleon of Greece.

Beauty clear and fair. John Fletcher. NOSC; OBEV *Fr.* Elder Brother, The.

Beauty does not come cheap. Cocksucker's Blues. Justin Chin. WiU

Beauty his transient eyes descried. (LL) Image-Maker, The. Oliver St. John Gogarty. OBEV; OBMV

Beauty I love, yet more than this I love. Faint Love. Arthur Symons. CABP

Beauty in Trouble. Robert Graves. OBCoV

Beauty is Elsewhere. Boyce House. TiP2

Beauty is not enough; who wishes to be fair. Petronius Arbiter. RomPo, *tr.* by J. P. Sullivan

Beauty Is the Straw. Amy Witting. NOBAu

Beauty is the straw I clutch at, but to say straw. Beauty Is the Straw. Amy Witting. NOBAu

Beauty is truth, truth beauty,—that is all / Ye know on earth, and all ye need to know. (LL) Ode on a Grecian Urn. John Keats. BLPJKO; BrAP; ClHu; HeIP-4; MakPoe; NAEL-6v2; NAEL-7v2; NAWM-7v2; NIP-4; NOBRP; NoP-5; NPBRoP; OBEV; OxBEV; TFi; WaAnP

Beauty itself lies here, in whom alone. Epitaph. Thomas Randolph. BASC

Beauty, I've seen you. Poetics. Yusef Komunyakaa. WaAnP

Beauty no more the subject be. Song, The. Thomas Nabbes. NOSC

Beauty of Ilona Zrínyi, The. István Gyöngyösi. IQMS, *tr.* by Watson Kirkconnell

Beauty of Israel is slain[e] upon thy high places, The. Bible, *O.T.* NPeEn; OBVE; OBWP *Fr.* Second Samuel.

Beauty of Job's Daughters, The. Jay Macpherson. ChIV-1; IFF

Beauty of manhole covers—what of that?, The. Manhole Covers. Karl Shapiro. NAMCP V.2; NoAM

Beauty of red bark, The. Ruispiri—A Comic Ballad. Bulat Shalvovich Okudzhava. RusPo, *tr.* by Robert Arthur Douglas Ford

Beauty of songs your absence I should not show. Sonnet. Bernadette Mayer. PmAP

Beauty of the Husband, The. Anne Carson.
 He She We They You You You I Her So Pronouns Begin the Dance Called Washing. NoP-5
 Homo Ludens. MoWP

Beauty of the rose, The. (LL) Poet's Lot, The. Letitia Elizabeth Landon. NPBRoP; RWP

Beauty of the South!, The. Tune: "Memories of the South." Po Chü-i. ColAnChi, *tr.* by Jiaosheng Wang

Beauty of the world hath made me sad, The. Wayfarer, The. Padraic Pearse. IrV

Beauty of Things, The. Robinson Jeffers. APT-1; PoA 2002

Beauty of women, their weakness, those pale hands. Paul Verlaine. SxFrPo, *tr.* by Martin Sorrell

Beauty of wood-boys and wood-men their clear untrimmed faces, The. Walt Whitman. CA *Fr.* Song of the Broad-Axe [*or* Broad-Ax].

Beauty renders Hermes pleasing. *Unknown.* PriapPo *Fr.* Priapus Poems, The.

Beauty Rituals 2000. Nwenna Kai. BRtP

Beauty Rohtraut. Eduard Friedrich Mörike. OBVE, *tr.* by George Meredith

Beauty runs a pawnshop. Pawnshop, The. Chu Hsiang. WoPoe, *tr.* by Kai-yu Hsu

Beauty sat bathing by a spring. Anthony Munday. OBEV *Fr.* Primaleon of Greece.

Beauty so sudden for that time of year. (LL) November Cotton Flower. Jean Toomer. ColAP; NAAPv.2; NAMCP V.1; NoAM; OxBoAm

Beauty [*or* Beautie], sweet love, is like the morning dew[e]. Samuel Daniel. NoSiC; OBEV *Fr.* Sonnets to Delia.

Beauty, That Lying Bitch. Paula McLain. AmPoNex

Beauty, whispered the leaves to the night. Penyberth. Gwynn Ap Gwilym. BBMWP, *tr.* by Joseph P. Clancy

Beauty's Transitoriness. Christian Hofmann von Hofmannswaldau. GePo, *tr.* by George C. Schoolfield

Be-Bop. Sterling Plumpp. FuFl

Be-Bop Boys. Langston Hughes. APSN; APT-2

Be-bop flows. Flow, The. Lynne d Johnson. BRtP

Be-Bop is precise clumsiness. Be-Bop. Sterling Plumpp. FuFl

Bebop Trumpet. Layding Lumumba Kaliba. BRtP

Be-bopping to Juarez. Attempt to Locate. Sarah Cortez. TiP2

Becalmed in the Tropics. Eliza Cook. STuOW; VerBaPo *Fr.* Song of the Seaweed.

Because. Kate Light. AmPoNex

Because.   James Philip McAuley.   BMAP; NOBAu; StAl

Because a bit of colour is a public service.   I Shall Paint My Nails Red.   Carole Satyamurti.   StAl

Because a ship.   Anne Portugal.   SCFWP *Fr.* Bath, The.

Because a thermal motif heard.   Dennis Phillips.   FTOS *Fr.* Etudes.

Because a wife can be expected to endure.   Suburban Crimes 3.   David Starkey.   LiTh

Because a witty writer of this time.   Sir John Harington.   DiBP *Fr.* Epigrams.

Because a woman had eaten something.   Floating Rib, The.   Lucia Maria Perillo.   PoDa

Because all this food is grown in the store.   Picketing Supermarkets.   Tom Wayman.   NIP-4

Because altruists are the least sexy.   From the Manifesto of the Selfish.   Stephen Dunn.   GoPo

Because Americans love seafood I can.   Shark Wrangler Goes to Church, The.   Jeni Olin.   FreRad

Because as they cut it was that special green, they decided.   Two Brothers in a Field of Absence.   Cynthia MacDonald.   NIP-4

Because Charles couldn't.   Jeanne Duval's Confession.   Yusef Komunyakaa.   BAP-97

Because Duke's voice.   Twilight Seduction.   Yusef Komunyakaa.   SeSe

Because each part of our face carries its own kind of information, takes its.   Plagiarism.   Ben Marcus.   HeMarv

Because / Each species is specialized.   Why There Are No Unicorns.   Judith Ortiz Cofer.   PfSP; PueRic

Because God couldn't figure how to be.   David Citino.   UpMys *Fr.* Sister Mary Appassionata Lectures the Pre-Med Class.

Because he can speak, because he can use his words, a whole headful.   Language Animal, The.   Thomas Lux.   AmAlph

Because he got me once and he let me go, O yes, Lord! (LL)   Nobody Knows the Trouble I've Had.   *Unknown.*   APN-2; NAAPv.1; SSUS

Because he had spoken harshly to his mother.   Revelation.   Robert Penn Warren.   NoAM

Because he has been reading *Autobiography of a Yogi.*   Elvis Decides to Become a Monk.   Fleda Brown.   MAAN

Because he has swept the creeks of consciousness.   Buddha Is Lord of Our Town.   John Gilgun.   AmZen

Because he is thinking so hard about his ode, because his mind is full.   Matthea Harvey.   IAoNAP *Fr.* Thermae.

Because he loved his rooster, and his wife.   Grandfather's Mint.   Edward Cortez Garrett.   ReBoTo

Because he loved men and sought their welfare.   *Various authors.*   CATKP *Fr.* Songs of Flying Dragons.

Because he played games seriously.   Competition.   Stephen Dunn.   MoASP

Because he seemed to walk with an intent.   James Thomson.   NePenScot *Fr.* City of Dreadful Night, The.

Because he took a stand for peace.   Martin Luther King.   Aileen Fisher and Olive Rabe.   HHAm

Because he was a butcher and thereby.   Reuben Bright.   Edwin Arlington Robinson.   APN-2; GSo; MoAmPo; NAMCP V.1; NCAP; NoP-4; NoP-5; OxBoAm

Because he was a soldier in Germany.   Highway.   Glenna Luschei.   ICANM

Because her brood is stolen away. (LL)   Alfred Tennyson.   NAEL-6v2; NAEL-7v2; NAWM-7v2 *Fr.* In Memoriam A. H. H.

Because he's lost the way.   Case in Point, A.   August Kleinzahler.   PmAP

Because his bright nature.   *Various authors.*   CATKP *Fr.* Songs of Flying Dragons.

Because his nose and face were one festering sore.   Orf.   Ted Hughes.   NAMCP V.2; NoAM

Because his soul was great. (LL)   Private of the Buffs; or, The British Soldier in China.   Sir Francis Hastings Doyle.   FaBoWar; OBEV

Because his soup was cold, he needs must sulk.   House-Mates.   Leon Gellert.   NOBAu

Because I am broke again.   Luck's Shining Child.   George Garrett.   InGu

Because I am done with this thing called work.   Robinson's Resignation.   Simon Armitage.   HarvBoo

Because I am it's a race thing trip.   Chong Xiong.   BRtP

"Because I am mad about women."   Wild Old Wicked Man, The.   William Butler Yeats.   RaBo

Because I am not a state, I have.   On Artistic Freedom in the Nationalist Era.   Salman Masalha.   PML, *tr. by* Vivian Eden

Because I am shattered. (LL)   Red Poppy, The.   Louise Glück.   MoWP; OxBoAm; PtR

Because I breathe not love to every one.   Sir Philip Sidney.   NoSic *Fr.* Astrophil and Stella.

Because I brought him here.   By Accident.   Jane O. Wayne.   InvLad

Because I cannot.   Like Leaving an Umbrella Somewhere.   Chŏng Hyŏnjong.   CAMKP, *tr. by* John M. Frankl

Because I can't see what's right before my.   Poem Without Beginning or End.   Patrick Warner.   Coast

Because I come from the West Indies.   Palm Tree King.   John Agard.   EmeKit; Oth

Because I could forever, my theatrical body.   Three Panels Depending on the Heart.   Timothy Donnelly.   LegDan

Because I could sing to High Heaven.   Caedmon.   Aidan Carl Mathews.   PBCIP

Because I did not love it enough.   On the Sixth Day the Word Is Taken from Me.   Lisa Beskin.   PoDa

Because I did not marry a bomb.   Vigil at a Missile Silo, A.   Mark Sanders.   AtGh

Because I do not give a damn. (LL)   Observation.   Dorothy Parker.   APT-1; NAMCP V.1; OxBoAm

Because I do not hope to turn again.   T. S. Eliot.   SacPr *Fr.* Ash Wednesday [*or* Ash-Wednesday].

Because I don't want you to shear my fleece. (LL)   Answer to the Parson, An.   William Blake.   NBLV; WoPoe

Because I feel that, in the Heavens above.   To My Mother.   Edgar Allan Poe.   NAAPv.1

Because I flew through the glass door when.   My Wrist Split Open.   Steve Healey.   LegDan

Because I grew up vaguely Methodist.   I Can't Become a Buddhist.   Adrienne Su.   NAPBL

Because I had loved so deeply.   Compensation.   Paul Laurence Dunbar.   APN-2; NAAPv.1

Because I have a luncheon date. (LL)   In Westminster Abbey.   Sir John Betjeman.   FaBoWar; HarvBoo; NAMCP V.1; NBLV; NIL-7; NIP-4; NoAM; OBSV; OxAEP-2

Because I have had occasion to remember, quote, paraphrase, I dedicate this poem to Anyone and Anything.   Louis Zukofsky.   APT-2; NAMCP V.1 *Fr.* Poem Beginning "The."

Because I knew I would be walking her.   Do you remember the scene in *The Godfather* where James Caan says, "Now make sure that the gun gets stashed in the rest room—I don't want my kid brother walking out of there with nothing but his dick in his hand"?   Gerald Locklin.   SUP

Because I know this is going to be painful.   So Far Off and Yet Here.   C. D. Wright.   CAP-8

Because I lay my.   Why Is God Love, Jack?   Allen Ginsberg.   FTOS (Because I lay my / head on pillows.)   CLPP

Because I left him there so you could see.   After the End.   Ann Townsend.   AmPoNex

Because I Let Go Your Hands.   Osip Emilevich Mandelstam.   TCRusP, *tr. by* John Glad

Because I liked you better.   Because I liked you better.   A. E. Housman.   CAGL; NPeEn; OxBEV

Because I love my father.   Portrait of My Father and His Grandson.   Richard Jones.   IllVoic

Because I oft, in dark abstracted guise.   Sir Philip Sidney.   CABP; NoSic *Fr.* Astrophil and Stella.

Because I once beat you up.   For a Far-out Friend.   Gary Snyder.   BB

Because I Paced My Thought.   John Hewitt.   PNI

Because I send Thee *all.* (LL)   To His Savior [*or* Saviour]. The New Years [*or* yeers] Gift.   Robert Herrick.   ChIV-2; NAEL-6v1

Because I, this poor one.   Natasha, the White Donkey, and I.   Paek Sŏk.   CAMKP, *tr. by* Kyunghwan Choi

Because I was afraid to lose you.   Omnivore.   Harryette Mullen.   OxAAAP

Because I was brought up in a working class family.   Art.   Denise Duhamel.   AmPoNex

Because I was content with these poor fields.   Musketaquid.   Ralph Waldo Emerson.   APN-1

Because I was 37 and he was 10.   Bass, The.   John A. Stone.   BloBone

Because I was to think otherwise. Because.   Species of Audibles.   Saskia Hamilton.   IIR

Because I was too much with myself.   Secret, The.   Peter Cooley.   PoCoUp

Because I'd seen a man.   Air, The.   Andrew Hudgins.   InvLad

Because if you existed.   You Are Not Poetry.   Rosario Castellanos.   TCLAP, *tr. by* Maureen Ahern

Because if you existed.   Poetry Is Not You.   Rosario Castellanos.   TANSG, *tr. by* Magda Bogin

Because i'm tall my legs are long my left leg's lame.   Paper Memorial Stone.   Yi Sang.   CAMKP; PFTM-1, *tr. by* Walter Lew

Because I'm writing about the snow not the sentence.   Fifth Prose.   Michael Palmer.   NoP-4; OxBoAm; PmAP

Because in Vietnam the vision of a Burning Babe.   Advent 1966.   Denise Levertov.   APSN

Because it hadn't seemed enough.   Home Movies: A Sort of Ode.   Mary Jo Salter.   WaAnP

Because it has a very important moral, which is, don't be a discoverer, be a promoter. (LL)   Columbus.   Ogden Nash.   EMP; FaBoA; NAAPv.2; NoP-4; NoP-5

Because it has no pure products. Learning to Love America. Shirley Lim. GeoHom

Because it is a gray day but not snowy, because traffic grinds by outside. Long, Disconsolate Lines. Jane Cooper. InoFa

Because it is the garden. What is left to us. You Must Believe in Spring. Jan Zwicky. OpeFie

Because it isn't harmonious. Reasons for Loving the Harmonica. Julie Kane. MiVo

Because it means looking into the sun, people can barely see. Festival of Giovedo Grasso, The. Matthea Harvey. IAoNAP

Because it might hurt, and because looseness. Red. Lance Larsen. AmPoNex

Because it seems the only way to save the roses. Only One of My Deaths. Dean Young. P180

Because it tells me most when it is most alone. Hide. Caitríona O'Reilly. NIrP

Because it was the first thing. Hospital Corners. Alison Townsend. SweBea

Because I've seen their musculature joined. Why I Believe in Angels. Rick Mulkey. AmPoNex

Because Jim insulted Harry eight years previous. On the Home Front—1942. Edwin Denby. OxBoAm

Because life's too short to blush. About Face. Alice Fulton. AllShUp

Because My Baby don't Mean Maybe Now. Walter Donaldson. ReLy

Because my faltering feet may fail to dare. Her Faith. Joseph Hilaire Pierre Belloc. SacPr

Because my husband would not read my poems. My Husband Discovers Poetry. Diane Lockward. PoDa

Because my Lord was born to suffer. Sor Juana Inés de la Cruz. WoPoe; WPoS Fr. Fifth Villancico, in Alternating Voices, Written for the Feast of the Nativity in Puebla, 1689, The.

Because my love has wave and foam for speech. Mourner, The. Nora May French. CalPo

Because my mother was too beautiful. Pall. Laura Kasischke. AmPoNex

Because my mouth. Minstrel Man. Langston Hughes. AmFaPo; ItP

Because my name is Lazarus and I live. (LL) Convert, The. G. K. Chesterton. ChIV-2; SacPr

Because my song was bold. Summary for Alastor. Laura Riding Jackson. FuPo; WoPoe

Because nobody visits this old man. Silly Song, A. Hwansung Jian. BecRai, tr. by Kim Daljin, Kim Won-Chung and Christopher Merrill

Because nothing else can be done. Midnight Supper. Ruth L. Schwartz. NeAmPo

Because of a promise I cannot break. Goodbye to the Old Friends. Henry Taylor. InGu; LPSFW

Because of body's hunger are we born. Sehnsucht. Anna Wickham. MoBrPo

Because of Certain Things. Hamhur Kiwha. BecRai, tr. by Kim Daljin, Kim Won-Chung and Christopher Merrill

Because of Clothes. Laura Riding Jackson. APT-2; OxBoAm

Because of Duties, Zimmer Had Forgotten the Forest. Paul Zimmer. AtGh

Because of how we are wed, enjoined, huddled. Concerning Violence. Ruth Garnett. BtF

Because of its erotic and cool underparts and the sunset emblazoned on its. Grid Erectile. Christopher Dewdney. FTOS

Because of its erotic and cool underparts and the sunset emblazoned on its membranous back. Its electric litheness. Cenozoic Asylum, The [1982 Version]. Christopher Dewdney. NLPA

Because of lake-water damage and otter dung. (LL) Margin Prayer from an Ancient Psalter. Ian Duhig. EmeKit; NeBl

Because of love and because of making love. My Son. Yehuda Amichai. WoPoe, tr. by Barbara Harshav and Benjamin Harshav

Because of My Father's Job. James Masao Mitsui. NIL-7; OpBo; UnSA

Because of spring there are babies everywhere. Delicious Babies. Penelope Shuttle. MoWP

Because of the menace. Weather. Linda Pastan. GoPo

Because of the Rain. Jinkag Haesim. BecRai, tr. by Kim Daljin, Kim Won-Chung and Christopher Merrill

Because of the steelworks. On the Buses with Dostoyevsky. Geoff Hattersley. NeBl

Because of the tailbone. Night, Work. Yi Sanghûi. EcSo, tr. by Jennifer M. Lee

Because of these men's courage, no smoke rose. Simonides. WoPoe, tr. by Peter Jay

Because of these reveries. (LL) Ezra Pound. MoAmPo; NAAPv.2 Fr. Hugh Selwyn Mauberley (Life and Contacts).

Because of thieves, a dog barked all night through. Master and the Dog, The. Ignacy Krasicki. WoPoe, tr. by Jerzy Peterkiewicz and Burns Singer

Because of this love. Unknown. ArkPo, tr. by Helen Craig McCullough

Because of your nose, like a leaf blade. Wheel, The. Molly Peacock. RA

Because one of us will die. (LL) Orchid Flower, The. Sam Hamill. AmZen; WANABP

Because one's husband is different from one's self. Causes. Mona Van Duyn. OxBoAm

Because our world has music, and we dance. World Well Lost 4, The. Marc André Raffalovich. CAGL

Because passion is the absence we speak. Linda Zisquit. DTA Fr. Unopened Letters.

Because passion is the silence we share. Linda Zisquit. DTA Fr. Unopened Letters.

Because robbers poisoned the people. Various authors. CATKP Fr. Songs of Flying Dragons.

Because, separated from us by a language. Landlady in Bangkok, The. Karen Swenson. GifTon

Because she desired him. Red Trousseau. Carol Muske-Dukes. BodElec

Because she had a face that wasn't fair. Ordinary Country Girl, An. Dean Phelps. RWB

Because she is the most popular doll. Bicentennial Barbie. Denise Duhamel. AmPoNex

Because she shares the bedroom with the baby. Single Parent. Connie Bensley. BeAl

Because she wants to touch him. Parable of the Four-Poster. Erica Jong. GoPo; LW

Because she was a white girl. Death of Janis Joplin, The. Robert Phillips. SwNoth; TiP2

Because she was wrong. Prawns de Jo. Selima Hill. MoWP

Because somebody's father bought a house. Sears Catalogue, The. Alan Michael Parker. RWB

Because spring brings its miserable green and painful red. Song to the Tune "Ting Feng Po." Liu Yung. WoPoe, tr. by Sam Hamill

Because spring brings miserable green and painful red. Song. Liu Yung. CrYelRi, tr. by Sam Hamill

Because still on the youthful wing. Nameless Love, The. John Henry Mackay. CAGL, tr. by Hubert Kennedy

Because struggling for riches and fame does not compare with leisure. After Getting Drunk in a Hermitage on Chiri Mountain. Suk Mumyong. BecRai, tr. by Kim Daljin, Kim Won-Chung and Christopher Merrill

Because that heckler was a joke. Testimony. Suzanne Wise. LegDan

Because the body is a map. Persephone in America. Alison Townsend. FiBr

Because the cockpit, like the snowy village in a paperweight. Black Box. William Matthews. OtW

Because the Eye Is a Flower Whose Root is the Hand. Dennis Schmitz. TAPaP

Because the film is running backwards. Woman in the Film, The. Lesley Dauer. NAPBL

Because the geeks and jocks were set in stone. Why I Skip My High School Reunions. Craig Arnold. AmPoNex

Because the girl Nastasia. God. Bella Akhatovna Akhmadulina. RusPo, tr. by Robert Arthur Douglas Ford

Because the govenment burdened the people. Various authors. CATKP Fr. Songs of Flying Dragons.

Because the greatest of these is love. Beloved's Face, The. Risto Ahti. PML, tr. by Herbert Lomas

Because the languages are enclosed and heated. Cliff Notes. Bob Perelman. PmAP

Because the male will be. Leviticus (Chapter 7, Verse 2-5). Manuela Fingueret. MirDau, tr. by Roberta Gordenstein

Because the mind is forever building its model airplane. At St. Sulpice. Erin Belieu. NAPBL

Because the mind's eye lit the sun. (LL) Blue Swallows, The. Howard Nemerov. MakPoe; NoP-4; NoP-5; OWoS

Because the moonlight deceives. Moon Haze. Amy Lowell. NAAPv.2

Because the past is in love the way. Third Body. Beckian Fritz Goldberg. AmAlph

Because the Poor Have Nothing. Violeta Parra. TANSG, tr. by Karen Kerschen

Because the question was, "Where am I?" Sailor, The. Safaa Fathy. PoArWo, tr. by S. V. Atalla

Because the rosy condition. I'm Gonna Slap Those Doctors. Jack Coulehan. BloBone

Because the shad. Shadblow. Linda Pastan. PoDa

Because the shells were screechinng overhead. (LL) Breakfast. Wilfrid Wilson Gibson. FaBoWar; OBMV

Because the smoke. For Paul Celan and Primo Levi. Harvey Shapiro. TaR

Because the stake was driven. Rocks. Takahashi Shinkichi. ZenPo, tr. by Takashi Ikemoto and Lucien Stryk

Because the straitjacket was short on me. Misery. Rumen Leonidov. CSCBP, tr. by Georgi Belev and Lisa Sapinkopf

Because the universe, it seems. In the Age of the Radio Telescope. James Scruton. PoA 2002

Because the wind has changed, because I guess.   Clearing the Title.   James Merrill.   HarvBoo

Because the Wind Remembers.   Frank Mkalawile Chipasula.   HBAPE

Because the winds are too strong, our Captain announces, his voice like an oracle.   We're Not Going to Malta.   Richard Blanco.   LegDan

Because the wolves wrought havoc.   *Various authors.*   CATKP *Fr.* Songs of Flying Dragons.

Because the wooden lawn statues.   On the Lawn at the Drug Rehab Center.   Jane Mead.   LaCa

Because the world had failed us / both. (LL)   Tragedy of the leaves, The.   Charles Bukowski.   CalPo; SUP

Because. then.   Textile 11.   Marjorie Welish.   VaPo

Because there are avenues.   After Tonight.   Gary Soto.   NAMCP V.2; NoAM

Because there are no children in his house, there is nothing.   Dream of the Jacklighter, The.   Dave Jeddie Smith.   RoV

Because there are too many pages in novels.   What Comes after Because.   Kelli Russell Agodon.   RWB

Because there is safety in derision.   Apparitions, The.   William Butler Yeats.   TRP

Because there was a man somewhere in a candystripe silk shirt.   Homage to the Empress of the Blues.   Robert Earl Hayden.   APT-2; ESEAA; NAAL-5; NAMCP V.2; OxAAAP; OxBoAm

Because there was disquiet in the wind.   This Poor Man.   W. J. Gruffydd.   OBWVE, *tr. by* Gwyn Jones

Because there was disquiet in the wind.   This Poor Man.   W. J. Gruffydd.   BBMWP, *tr. by* Anthony Conran

Because they are large, round and bluey.   Why the Elgin Marbles Must be Returned to Elgin.   W. N. Herbert.   EdScPo

Because they are secretly Jewish and eat matzoh on Saturday.   Why We Fear the Amish.   Robin Becker.   BodElec

Because they are shame, and cannot flee from it.   Wild Turkeys; The Dignity of the Damned.   Brigit Pegeen Kelly.   ExTi; IllVoic

Because they could feel the deforestation of the Amazon.   Why Young Men Wore Their Hair Long in the Sixties.   Jeff Poniewaz.   RWB

Because They Hesitated Between Roses and Darkness.   Venus Khoury-Gata.   PoArWo, *tr. by* Lucy McNair

Because they loaded their rifles with rain.   Because They Hesitated Between Roses and Darkness.   Venus Khoury-Gata.   PoArWo, *tr. by* Lucy McNair

Because they're both Italian, and I prefer sneakers to boots, sneakers to wing tips.   14 Reasons Why I Mention Mario Lanza to the Man I Love Every Chance I Get Tonight.   Jim Elledge.   IllVoic

Because this evening Miss Hoang Yen.   Her Life Runs Like a Red Silk Flag.   Bruce Weigl.   AF

Because this graveyard is a hill.   Visions and Interpetations.   Li-Young Lee.   NIP-4

Because this is the literature of ideas I cannot smoke a cigar.   Carla Harryman.   BAP-04 *Fr.* Baby.

Because this is the moment.   Inside, The.   David Wojahn.   YaYoPo

Because, this month, when napkins, pretty spoons.   Roman Presents.   Martial.   OBCP, *tr. by* James Michie

Because thou hast the power and own'st the grace.   Elizabeth Barrett Browning.   CenSon *Fr.* Sonnets from the Portuguese.

Because thou't not an oak.   Planting the Poplar.   Louise Imogen Guiney.   NAAPv.1

Because we are doing better.   Letters from the Front.   Michael Klein.   WiU

Because we are strangers. (LL)   Gaeltacht.   Pearse Hutchinson.   ModIr; PBCIP

Because we hooked up most days courtesy.   Long-Distance Call to Gregg, Who Lived with AIDS as Long as He Could.   Alfred Corn.   WiU

Because we live in the browning season.   Kopis'taya.   Paula Gunn Allen.   HATNAP

Because we lived our several lives.   House, The.   Mary Oliver.   WaAnP

Because we love, this day, this age, more times than once.   Because.   Kate Light.   AmPoNex

Because We Need Good Maps.   Forrest Hamer.   ASA

Because we suspected / the pillow would say "I know."   Lady Ise.   WoPoe, *tr. by* Irma Brandeis and Etsuko Teraski

Because we were 18 and still wonderful in our bodies.   Why I'm in Favor of a Nuclear Freeze.   Christopher Buckley.   AtGh

Because We're Here.   *Unknown.*   FaBoWar

Because we're running out of time.   By Heart.   Ruth Sharman.   Prnts

Because we've had more than our share.   Oldies But Goodies.   Grace Bauer.   MiVo

Because, without these, I would be a stranger here. (LL)   Studying the Language.   Eiléan Ní Chuilleanáin.   EmeKit; NPeEn

Because yesterday morning from the steamy window.   Happiness.   Robert Hass.   CAP-8

Because you are beautiful I will have to tell you a number / of my secrets.   Open Secrets.   Gwendolyn MacEwen.   LW

Because you are four years old.   Lola Ridge.   TCAPo *Fr.* Alley, The.

Because you are going.   Emily Dickinson.   MoAmPo

Because you are old and departing I have wetted my handkerchief.   Seeing Hsia Chan off by River.   Po Chü-i.   TAL

Because You Asked about the Line between Prose and Poetry.   Howard Nemerov.   OxBoAm; VCAP; WeW-3

Because you climbed your bed.   Childhood Wall.   Ahmed Taha.   AnVo, *tr. by* Mohamed Enani

Because you have thrown of[f] your Prelate Lord.   On the New Forcers of Conscience Under the Long Parliament.   John Milton.   BASC; NAEL-6v1; NOSC; PBRV

Because You love cremation grounds.   Rāmlāl Dāsdatta.   SinGod, *tr. by* Rachel Fell McDermott

Because You Mentioned the Spiritual Life.   Stephen Dunn.   BodElec; Vesp

Because you never know who you're talking to. (LL)   In Search of Aunt Jemima.   Crystal Williams.   AmPoNex; BtF

Because you turn.   Love Poem (2).   Walter Helmut Fritz.   GTCP, *tr. by* Reinhold Grimm

Because you will suffer soon and die, your choices.   Ghetto.   Michael Longley.   EmeKit; NoP-4; NoP-5; PNI

Because your blazing eyes my bale have bred. (LL)   For That He Looked Not upon Her.   George Gascoigne.   NoP-4; NoP-5

Because your eyes are slant and slow.   Prophetic Soul.   Dorothy Parker.   LW

Because your hearts are ice.   1914–1918 The Young to the Old.   W. J. Gruffydd.   BBMWP, *tr. by* Robert Minhinnick

Because You're American.   Kevin Stein.   ReTh

Because you're an infant in arms.   Pledge.   Gerwyn Williams.   BBMWP, *tr. by* the author and Richard Poole

Because Zen and Doctrine have the same origin and taste.   To the Old Reverend Monk, Hwasung.   Soyo Taeneung.   BecRai, *tr. by* Kim Daljin, Kim Won-Chung and Christopher Merrill

Beckon.   Gillian Conoley.   BodElec

Beckoner of hotheads, brag-tester, lord of the demi-suicides.   Immortal, An.   Les A. Murray.   UpMys

Become as little children.   Sylvia Townsend Warner.   FaBoWar

Become at last a bee.   Bee, A.   Peter Didsbury.   EmeKit

Become Becoming.   Li-Young Lee.   FaoP

Become essential, man, for if the world should flee.   "Angelus Silesius."   GePo *Fr.* Cherubical Wanderer, The.

Become the prey of the world. (LL)   Vultures Grow Impatient, The.   Amina Saïd.   HAWP; NAfrP, *tr. by* Eric Sellin

Become Your Face.   Marianne Vitale.   HeMarv

Becomes at last no meaning and no place. (LL)   Stoic, The: For Laura Von Courten.   Edgar Bowers.   CalPo; PWW2

Becoming a Buddha.   Seido Ray Ronci.   AmZen

Becoming a Farmer.   Tu Fu [*or* Du Fu].   CrYelRi, *tr. by* Sam Hamill

Becoming a hare terrified me.   Dialogue with Herz.   Antonio Porta.   ItPo, *tr. by* Gayle Ridinger

Becoming a Redwood.   Dana Gioia.   GeoHom; PfSP

Becoming Milton.   Coleman Barks.   RaBo; RaF

Becoming of Age.   Simon Armitage.   HarvBoo

Becoming Water.   Kang Ŭn'gyo.   EcSo, *tr. by* Ann Y. Choi

Becune Point.   Derek Walcott.   PoA 2002

Bed.   Kendra Borgmann.   PoDa

Bed, The.   Moniza Alvi.   MFPA

Bed, The.   Ray DiPalma.   FTOS

Bed, The.   Alec Derwent Hope.   NoAM

Bed! Bed! I couldn't go to bed!   I Could Have Danced All Night.   Alan Jay Lerner.   ReLy

Bed Book, The.   Sylvia Plath.   "Most Beds are Beds."   ChAP

Bed by the Window, The.   Robinson Jeffers.   APT-1

Bed Hangings.   Susan Howe.   "Revisionist work in."   VaPo

Bed in Summer.   Robert Louis Stevenson.   BLPJKO; BRP; NBLV

Bed in the Wilderness, The.   Geoffrey O'Brien.   PA9/11

Bed is left open to a mirror, A.   Floating Trees.   C. D. Wright.   AmAlph; InGu

Bed of Forget-Me-Nots, A.   Christina Georgina Rossetti.   VWP

Bed of the railway links me to these days of hell, The.   Blues.   Pierre Martory.   KGB, *tr. by* John Ashbery

Bed shared, The.   Life Sentence.   János Pilinszky.   IQMS, *tr. by* Peter Jay

Bed upstairs for seven years made for us in Hanover, Mass., The.   William Corbett.   AHA *Fr.* Columbus Square Journal.

Bed we loved in was a spinning world, The.   Anne Hathaway.   Carol Ann Duffy.   NoP-5

Bed with Mirrors.   Gonzalo Rojas.   TCLAP, *tr. by* Christopher Maurer

Bedbugs, The.   Issa.   EH, *tr. by* Robert Hass

Bedecked.   Victoria Redel.   MAAN

Bedouin Eyes. Dima Hilal. PoArWo

Bedouin Song. Bayard Taylor. APN-2; TCAPo

15: Bedouin Wind. Nathaniel Mackey. PFTM-2 *Fr.* Song of the Andoumboulou.

Bedraggled. Glamorous. Old as coyote breath. Michael McClure. WANABP *Fr.* Plum Stones.

Bedridden Peasant, The. Thomas Hardy. InvLi

Bedrooms. Sandra McPherson. ExTi

Beds. Charlie Smith. BAP-97

Beds, The. Elizabeth Spires. CAP-8

Beds are countries of delight. Beds of Purification. Jorge Debravo. BLPSL, H *tr. by* Rene de Costa, Rigas Kappatos and Eleni Paidoussi

Bedsheet is suspended on the clothesline, A. White, Mauve, Yellow. Anne Simpson. Coast

Bedside. Clive Matson. PasH

Bedside. Diana O'Hehir. InoFa

Bedside Reading. Seamus Heaney. IrLP; NoP-5 *Fr.* Glanmore Revisited.

Bedside Wreaths. Titiola Shoneyin. NeNiPo

Bed-Sitting Room, The. W. H. Davies. TCAWP

Bedtime. Ian Hamilton Finlay. EdScPo

Bedtime Stories. Silvia Curbelo. TouFir

Bedtime Story. Beckian Fritz Goldberg. AmAlph

Bedtime Story [*with music*]. George MacBeth. EmeKit; SoSe-8

Bedtime Story. Lilian Moore. NTCP

Bedtime Story. Lee Upton. AmAlph

Bedtime tears / and evening sorrow. Small Rains. N. M. Bodecker. Spl

Bee. Philip Booth. PoCoUp

Bee. X. J. Kennedy. Spl

Bee. Patricia Pogson. NLP

Bee. Ivan Tsanev. CSCBP, *tr. by* Georgi Belev and Lisa Sapinkopf

Bee, A. Basho. EH, *tr. by* Robert Hass

Bee, A. Peter Didsbury. EmeKit

Bee, The. James Dickey. AmFaPo

Bee, The. Emily Dickinson. MoAmPo

Bee Elk. Clark Coolidge. NYP2

Bee! I'm expecting you! Letter to Bee. Emily Dickinson. OxBoAm; SAmP; TLR

Bee is not afraid of me, The. Emily Dickinson. APN-2

Bee Meeting, The. Sylvia Plath. HarvBoo; NALW

Bee of my mind, The. Kamalākānta Bhattācārya. SinGod, *tr. by* Rachel Fell McDermott

Bee rolls in the yellow rose, A. Couple, A. May Swenson. NAMCP V.2

Be[e] ye my fictions; but her story. (LL) Wishes. To His (Supposed) Mistress[e]. Richard Crashaw. BASC; NOSC; OBEV; OxAEP-1

Be[e] you all pleased [*or* pleas'd]? your pleasures grieve not[t] me[e]. Mary Sidney Wroth, Countess of Montgomery. NOSC *Fr.* Pamphilia to Amphilanthus.

Bee-boy, *merops apiaster,* on sultry thundery days, The. Part of the Bee's Body Embedded in the Flesh, The. Carol Frost. CAP-8

Beech boles whiten in the swollen stream, The. Autumn, 1939. Alun Lewis. PoWW

Beech Tree, The. Michael Longley. NAMCP V.2

Beehive. Jean Toomer. GT; OxBoAm

Beehive Cell [*with music*]. Richard Murphy. OxBSo

Beehive source. Song, The. Anne Baring. HW

Beekeeper. Barbara J. Orton. NeAmPo

Beekeepers' boxes. Mount Bromley Hymn. John Peck. PoCoUp

Beelah Viaduct, The. John Close. STuOW

Beelzebub Chronicles, The. Artress Bethany White. BtF

Been so much so many. I Should Run for Cover But I'm Right Here. Harris Schiff. AHA

Been watching this jive. Gumba, gumba, gumba. Mafika Pascal Gwala. TSAP

Beeny Cliff. Thomas Hardy. CABP; OxAEP-2

Beer. Gerald Locklin. SUP

Beer Bottles. Lindley Williams Hubbell. APT-2

Beer, malt liquor talks. Aunt Martha. Wil'um Lee. InTrad

Beer. Milk. The Dog. My Old Man. Kim Addonizio. RoV

Bees. Emily Dickinson. NAAL-3

Bees and a honeycomb in the dried head of a horse in a pasture corner—a skull in the tall grass and a buzz and a buzz of the yellow honey-hunters. In Tall Grass. Carl Sandburg. PoA 2002

Bees are Black, with Gilt Surcingles—. Bees. Emily Dickinson. NAAL-3

Bees are flying, The. They taste the spring. (LL) Wintering. Sylvia Plath. MoW; NALW

Bees at my hive anticipate her hands. Robert Sheppard. Oth *Fr.* Empty Diaries/Twentieth Century Blues 24.

Bees build around red liver. Czeslaw Milosz. HP; PoSu; VCWP *Fr.* Voices of Poor People.

Bees Stumble. Molly McQuade. PoDa

Bees, The. Christopher Merrill. PfSP

Beethoven [*with music*]. Henrietta Cordelia Ray. CBWP-3

Beethoven. John Hall Wheelock. PoA 2002

Beethoven as an innovative genius. (LL) Another Reason Why I don't Keep a Gun in the House. Billy Collins. OxBoAm; SUP

Beethoven: Op. 95. Karen Solie. OpeFie

Beethoven, Opus 111. Amy Clampitt. NAMCP V.2; NIP-4; NoP-4; NoP-5

Beethoven's Ears. Bobi Jones. ATSWP, *tr. by* Robert Minhinnick

Beethoven's Old Age. István Vas. IQMS, *tr. by* Daniel Gerard Hoffman

Beethoven's Romance in G. David Wright. ACAMVP

Beethoven's Sixth Symphony. Steve Benson. FTOS

Beetle Light. Madeline DeFrees. GifTon

Beetle loves his unpretending track, The. William Wordsworth. STuOW *Fr.* Liberty [*sequel to* Gold and Silver Fishes in a Vase].

Beetle that lies on its back, A. Old Revolution. Hans Magnus Enzensberger. GTCP, *tr. by* Reinhold Grimm

Before. W. E. Henley. MoBrPo *Fr.* In Hospital.

Before. Khaled Mattawa. NeAmPo

Before. Sean O'Brien. EmeKit

Before. May Probyn. VWP

Before a Cornfield. Gottfried Benn. WoPoe, *tr. by* Harvey Shapiro

Before a Departure in Spring. W. S. Merwin. PoDa

Before a going and coming that goes on forever. (LL) Elegy for Alto. Christopher Okigbo. HBAPE; VCWP

Before a grotto of blue-tinted rock. At the Frick. Anthony Hecht. GS

Before a heaping, steaming breakfast was delivered. White Wedding. Gordon Rodgers. Coast

Before a January dawn, under a moondog sky. Emma Lee Warrior. *See* It's a good thing Dad deserted Mom.

Before a man goes to sleep a man takes off. Six Local Poems. David Avidan. FIT, *tr. by* Robert Friend

Before a Painting. James Weldon Johnson. GT

Before a Statue of Achilles. George Santayana. APN-2

Before anything could happen. Lyre. Donald Revell. RoV

Before Bed. Mary Ruefle. PoCho

Before Completion. Arthur Sze. ICANM

"Before Dawn." Tom Clark. BodElec

Before dawn all the first born. Smitten. Rod Mengham. VaPo

Before dawn in a back alley. In Burning Thirst. Kim Chiha. CAMKP, *tr. by* David R. McCann

Before Disaster. Yvor Winters. OxBoAm

Before Easter. Mihály Babits. IQMS, *tr. by* Peter Zollman

Before ever I knew men were hunting me. Black Huntsmen, The. Irving Layton. WoPoe

Before falling to the scythe. Peter Levitt. WhBo

Before first light, we would open the nets. Ansel Talvikki. YaYoPo *Fr.* In Fragments, In Streams.

Before Gereint, foe's affliction. Gereint ab Erbin. *Unknown.* OBWVE, *tr. by* Joseph P. Clancy

Before Gereint, the enemy's punisher. *Unknown.* WoPoe *Fr.* Black Book of Carmarthen, The.

Before God's last *Put out the Light* was spoken. (LL) Once by the Pacific. Robert Frost. APT-1; GSo; HeIP-4; MoAmPo; NIL-7; PtR; TRP; WeW-3

Before going to bed. December Moon. May Sarton. GoPo

Before hatred ate my heart. Caliban. J. P. Dancing Bear. IaFF

Before he collapsed. (LL) Passion of Ravensbrück. János Pilinszky. AF; GI; HP; PoSu, *tr. by* Ted Hughes

Before he died. Conversions. Neal Bowers. AllShUp

Before he went to feed with owls and bats. John Keats. ChIV-1

Before her wandering feet. (LL) Rose of the World, The. William Butler Yeats. MoBrPo; NAEL-6v2; NAEL-7v2

Before his butchered legions in the snow. (LL) Russia 1812. Victor Hugo. FaBoWar; OBWP, *tr. by* Robert Lowell

Before his immense window high as a cathedral window, the great unre-. Great Unrestrained Sadist, The. Hans Arp. PFTM-1

Before I arrived. Issa. SoOfWa, *tr. by* Sam Hamill

Before I began life this time. Last Poem. Ted Berrigan. NYP2

Before I could arrive at this moment when the earth. Sonata of Love's History. Richard Jackson. MAAN

Before I could call myself Ángel González. Before I Could Call Myself Ángel González. Angel González. VCWP, *tr. by* Steven Ford Brown and Revuelta Gutierrez

Before I ever saw this room. Sun-crossed. Cornelia Veenendaal. PfS

Before I fell in love with you. True Love. Jeremy Young. IrLP

Before I go / I'm supposed to get a last wish.   I Take Back Everything I've Said. Nicanor Parra. PoCho, *tr. by* Miller Williams

Before I got my eye put out. Emily Dickinson. APN-2

Before I have begun to live. (LL)   Lines Written in Kensington Gardens. Matthew Arnold. NAEL-6v2; NAEL-7v2

Before I knew there were men. My Life with Horses. Polly Clark. NeBl; StAl

Before I laughed with him. What She Said. Maturai Eruttalan Centamputan. WoPoe, *tr. by* A. K. Ramanujan

Before I met you no one attracted me. Let's Begin. Otto Harbach. ReLy

Before / I opened my mouth. On Reading Poems to a Senior Class at South High. David Chapman Berry. SoSe-8

Before i paint on the hard rotten zinc I think. Zinc. Yasser Musa. OWABP

Before I sigh my last gasp, let me breathe. Will, The. John Donne. NoSic

Before I Was Born. Lewis Warsh. PA9/11

Before I woke I knew her gone. Robert Malise Bowyer Nichols. OBMV *Fr.* Flower of Flame, The.

Before, it was a fascinating game. Day of the Dead. Rigoberto González. AmPoNex

Before it was quite unsheathed from reality. (LL) Hurt Hawks. Robinson Jeffers. APT-1; ChAP; ColAP; EMP; HarvBoo; MoAmPo; NAAPv.2; NAMCP V.1; NoAM; NoP-4; NoP-5; OWoS; OxBoAm; TFi; TRP; WaAnP

Before John and Maria's Wedding. Hilda Raz. ExTi

Before leaving there's always a get-together. The. Leslie Kaplan. SCFWP *Fr.* Règne.

Before light became time. *Unknown.* WoPoe *Fr.* Omoro Sōshi, The.

Before Lord God made the sea and the land. Lost in the Stars. Maxwell Anderson. ReLy

Before man came to blow it right. Aim Was Song, The. Robert Frost. SoSe-8

Before men walked. Taliesin and the Mockers. Vernon Watkins. AngWePo

Before money and California. Confessions. Anthony McCann. IIR

Before my back was bent I was eloquent. *Unknown.* OBWVE *Fr.* Hateful Old Age.

Before my bed the moonlight glitters. Quiet Night Thought. Li Po. CCL1, *tr. by* Elling O. Eide

Before my brother-in-law lost his telephone job. World Without End. Kevin Stein. SwNoth

Before my cheeks were fairly dry. Child's Party, A. Sarah Morgan Bryan Piatt. SWaP

Before my drift-wood fire I sit. Burning Drift-Wood. John Greenleaf Whittier. APN-1

Before my eyes would often pass. Parable of the Poet's Reward. Ivan Radoev. CSCBP, *tr. by* Georgi Belev and Lisa Sapinkopf

Before my face the picture hangs. Robert Southwell. NoSic *Fr.* Upon the Image of Death.

Before my feet the ploughshare rolls the earth. Winter Ploughing. William Everson. ASA

Before my fourth birthday my father. Hula Skirt, 1959, The. Kimiko Hahn. UnSA

Before my mother left she lost both rings. Joan Michelson. Prnts *Fr.* Departures.

Before *my* train comes round. (LL) Underground. May Kendall. ViWPN; VWP

Before Night Comes. Léopold Sédar Senghor. VCWP, *tr. by* Melvin Dixon

Before night comes I think of you and for you before I fall. Before Night Comes. Léopold Sédar Senghor. VCWP, *tr. by* Melvin Dixon

Before Olympus. John Gould Fletcher. MoAmPo

Before Our Encounter. Margherita Guidacci. CItWP, *tr. by* Cinzia Sartini Blum and Lara Trubowitz

Before our headlights the coyote. Arizona Nocturne. Carlos Reyes. UrbNat

Before our human dream (or terror) wove. Sea, The. Jorge Luis Borges. TCLAP, *tr. by* John Updike

Before prayer in the schools we had the Crusades. Just Yesterday. Mark Bibbins. LegDan

Before rhombus, before scalene. Contributors to Geometry: Cold Hands. Adam Dickinson. PoPra

Before September 11. 9/14/01. David Lehman. PA9/11

Before She Died. Karen Chase. P180

Before she has her floor swept. Portrait by a Neighbor. Edna St. Vincent Millay. BLPJKO; ItWoWo

Before she let me love her. Brief Encounter. Norman J. Loftis. SpirFl

Before she sleeps with Jim. (LL) Interpretation of a Poem by Frost. Thylias Moss. NAMCP V.2; VisFro

Before, she used to need a translator. Body Language. Linda France. NeBl

Before she walked into the river. Lorna Crozier. LW *Fr.* Last Testaments.

Before Sleep [*with music*]. Anne Ridler. SacPr

Before Summer Rain. Rainer Maria Rilke. WoPoe, *tr. by* Mark Rudman

Before Sunrise. Arthur Sze. WANABP

Before sunrise the stork was there. Lake Morning in Autumn. Douglas Livingstone. NoP-4

Before That. Michael Blackburn. BeAl

Before the 1820 rising in the West of Scotland a network of. Tom Leonard. Oth

Before the Anæsthetic; or, A Real Fright. Sir John Betjeman. HarvBoo

Before the ants. Eclogue and Elegy. Maura Eichner. UpMys

Before the Attack. Semyon Petrovich Gudzenko. TCRusP, *tr. by* Denis Johnson and Shirley Rihner

Before the basil blackened. Before plates. Elegy. Marianne Boruch. AmAlph

Before the Beginning. Christina Georgina Rossetti. InvLi; SacPr

Before the Beginning: Maybe God and a Silk Flower Concubine Perhaps. Pattiann Rogers. PuP-23

Before the Beginning of Years. Algernon Charles Swinburne. NAEL-6v2; NAEL-7v2 *Fr.* Atalanta in Calydon.

Before the beginning Thou hast foreknown the end. Before the Beginning. Christina Georgina Rossetti. InvLi; SacPr

Before the Birth of One of Her Children. Anne Bradstreet. AmFaPo; ColAP; EMWP; NAAL-3; NAAL-5; NAAPv.1; NoP-4; NoP-5; OxBoAm; PEW; SacPr

Before the Brain Surgery. Paula Tatarunis. BloBone

Before the day ends. Morning of the Last Farewell, The. Miyazawa Kenji. CAoMJL1, *tr. by* Hiroaki Sato

Before the day is everywhere. Martha Blake. Austin Clarke. ModIr; OxBEV

Before the days of self service. Fast Gas. Dorianne Laux. GeoHom; SUP

Before the dream is gone. For Emma. Luigi Fontanella. NeIt, *tr. by* Michael Palma

Before the dumb hoof. In the blood, Winnowing. Carl Phillips. WiU

Before the dusk grows deeper. Dusk. Joseph Ceravolo. NYP2; OxBoAm

Before the Eiffel was complete. Song of the Eiffel Tower. David Shapiro. BodElec

Before the Feast of Shushan. Anne Spencer. NAAPv.2

Before the firmament was ever formed. Singing of the Source of Holy Church. Wu Li. ColAnChi, *tr. by* Jonathan Chaves

Before the first war news or pain killers of the year. Introducing *New Year's SOLUTIONS*, from Saint Terri's Inc. Joe-Anne McLaughlin-Carruth. NevBe

Before the game. Last Shot. Jon Veinberg. PoDa

Before the glare o' dawn I rise. Shearer's Wife, The. Louis Esson. NOBAu

Before the hearse Death's chaplain seem'd to go. Philip Freneau. TCAPo *Fr.* House of Night, The.

Before the holidaymakers comes the spring. Derek Mahon. TRP

Before the indifferent beak could let her drop? (LL) Leda and the Swan. William Butler Yeats. BrAP; CABP; ClHu; EMP; EroLit; GSo; HarvBoo; HeIP-4; MoBrPo; NAEL-6v2; NAEL-7v2; NAMCP V.1; NAWM-7v2; NIL-7; NIP-4; NoAM; NoP-4; NoP-5; NPeEn; OWoS; OxAEP-2; OxBEV; OxBSo; PoPoPo; SoSe-8; TFi; TRP; WaAnP; WeW-3

Before the last curve of the day. Valerio Magrelli. ItPo, *tr. by* Gayle Ridinger

Before the Law. Franz Kafka. PFTM-1

Before the Law stands a doorkeeper. Before the Law. Franz Kafka. PFTM-1

Before the leaf could shake off the bird droppings. Leaf Struck by Bird Droppings. Yi Hyangji. EcSo, *tr. by* Catherine J. Kim

Before the library, Sister Suzy. Acanthus. Lawrence L. White. IAoNAP

Before the light went out. (LL) Reading by Mechanic Light. Thomas McGrath. BodElec; GifTon

Before the Mirror. Elizabeth Stoddard. SWaP

Before the Mirror. Algernon Charles Swinburne. OBEV *Fr.* Before the Mirror.

Before the mirror of a cement toilet in a trailer park at Doolin. Irish Woman Washing. Laima Sruoginis. PoDa

Before the mists descended on your body. Epitaph for a Poet. Homero Aridjis. PoetW; STV; TCLAP, *tr. by* John Frederick Nims

Before the Moone should cirlcewise close both hir hornes in one. Ovid. NPeEn *Fr.* Metamorphoses.

Before the parade passes by. Before the Parade Passes By. Jerry Herman. ReLy

Before the Peak of Returning Joy the sand was like snow. Song of War, A. Li Po. TAL

Before the plums fell asleep. On the Way to Mind. Milo De Angelis. NeIt, *tr. by* Lawrence Venuti

Before the plums slept. Towards the Mind. Milo De Angelis. ItPo, *tr. by* Gayle Ridinger

[Before the Rape]. William Shakespeare. NoSic *Fr.* Rape of Lucrece, The.

Before the revival of quartz pinks and icy blues. Silver Sands, The. Richard Blanco. AmPoNex; NAPBL

Before the Roman came to Rye or Caesar conquered Gaul. Rolling Chinese Wall, The. Roger Woddis. UV

Before the Roman came to Rye or out to Severn strode. Rolling English Road, The. G. K. Chesterton. OBEV; OBMV; OxAEP-2; UV

Before the Scales, Tomorrow. Otto René Castillo. AF, *tr. by* Barbara Paschke and David Volpendesta

Before the sirens started, he was late. Tube Ride to Martha's. Matthew Sweeney. ModIr

Before the six[t]h day of the next new year. On the Card[e]s, and Dice. Sir Walter Ralegh. ChIV-2

Before the Snake. Nathaniel Tarn. ICANM

Before the solemn bronze Saint Gaudens made. Ode in Time of Hesitation, An. William Vaughn Moody. APN-2; CBCWP; NAAPv.1

Before the spectacled professor snipped. Richard Murphy. BeAl; ModIr *Fr.* Price of Stone, The.

Before the stout harvesters falleth the grain. Summer Shower, The. Thomas Buchanan Read. TreFP

Before the Stuff Comes Down. Gary Snyder. HeIP-4

Before the tongue wags. Scold's Mask. Miranda Field. LegDan

Before the War. Margaret Atwood. MotU

Before the white chrysanthemum. Buson. EH, *tr. by* Robert Hass

Before the wig and the dress coat. Amor America (1400). Pablo Neruda. PoetW, *tr. by* Jack Schmitt

Before their light can reach us. (LL) Triage. Margot Schilpp. AmPoNex; PoDa

Before their time? They too will die. (LL) Alfred Tennyson. NAEL-6v2; NAEL-7v2 *Fr.* In Memoriam A. H. H.

Before there is a breeze again. Judith Ortiz Cofer. ExTi *Fr.* Three Poems in Memory of Mamá (Grandmother).

Before there was a trace of this world of men. Bibi Hayati. WPoS

Before these Wars. Carol Rumens. Prnts

Before they were married, Opa slept. Body Remembers, The. Julia Kasdorf. ACAMVP

Before this autumn wind. Issa. SoOfWa, *tr. by* Sam Hamill

Before this bridge we took the long way around. At the Opening of Oak Grove Cemetery Bridge. Thomas Lynch. PoDa

Before this grief, mountains must bend down. Dedication. Anna Andreyevna Akhmatova. PFTM-1

Before this world's great frame, in which all things. Hymn of Heavenly Love, An. Edmund Spenser. SacPr

Before tomorrow's timeless beauty of ripples. Tune-Up. Carl Dennis. PfSP

Before Twilight. Eyezion. Anne Batten Cristall. RWP

Before We Drown. Adrien Stoutenburg. CalPo

Before we go to Paradise by way of Kensal Green. (LL) Rolling English Road, The. G. K. Chesterton. OBEV; OBMV; OxAEP-2; UV

Before we got you off to school. Starting School. Annie Foster. NLP

Before we met and you what I had passed. (LL) Meeting and Passing. Robert Frost. OxBoAm; OxBSo

Before we pushed off for Moon in Mañana land. For Dear Life. Alane Rollings. OPRER

Before when you left you would always forget. Patrizia Cavalli. NeIt

Before, whenever I talked to myself, I used to say. Parable of the Unfaithful Wife. Rosario Castellanos. TANSG, *tr. by* Magda Bogin

Before words, mathematics nested in the Kananaskis. Parabola. Karen Solie. PoPra

Before you arrive, forget. Africa Says. Carl Phillips. PoPoPo

Before you ask for justice. Make sure. Paavo Haavikko. WoPoe *Fr.* Fifteen Epigrams in Praise of the Tyrant.

Before You Came. Faiz Ahmad Faiz. PoetW, *tr. by* Agha Shahid Ali

Before you came things were just what they were. Before You Came. Faiz Ahmad Faiz. PML; WoPoe, *tr. by* Naomi Lazard

Before you can learn the trees, you have to learn. Learning the Trees. Howard Nemerov. VCAP

Before you cry out, Stop—you'll fall on your back. Meteor. Ivan Davidkov. CSCBP, *tr. by* Georgi Belev and Lisa Sapinkopf

Before You Cut Loose. Simon Armitage. EmeKit

Before you know what kindness really is. Kindness. Naomi Shihab Nye. BeAl; IJHIL

Before You Leave. Ai. GT

Before you left for the Lucky Strike. Waitress's Kid, The. Peggy Shumaker. PBCAP

Before you, mother Idoto. Christopher Okigbo. NAMCP V.2 *Fr.* Heavensgate.

Before you praise Spring's advent note. Quatrain. Tu Fu [*or* Du Fu]. TAL

Before you start an argument. Good Time Charlie. Johnny Burke. ReLy

Before you thought of Spring. Emily Dickinson. SAmP

Before you up the mountain go. William Wordsworth. VerBaPo *Fr.* Thorn, The.

Before you were born. Baby. Ko Un. WhBo

Before your face in the moonlight my face. Soyŏng Problems. Yi Sang. PFTM-1

Before your waking I only knew. Before Your Waking. Anna Gréki. HAWP, *tr. by* Anita Barrows

Before-snow sky lasted like the perpetual twilight, The. Annotation in Her Last Court Diary. Kimiko Hahn. ExTi

Beg your pardon, Lord Priapus. *Unknown.* PriapPo *Fr.* Priapus Poems, The.

Began the year by seeing the rat uncheesed. Bio-Rodent-Oriole. Edwin Torres. HeMarv

Beggar, The. Francisco Brines. RaW, *tr. by* Rachel Benson

Beggar, The. Murad Mikha'il. IrPoTo, *tr. by* Christina Coyle and Sadok Masliyah

Beggar Love. Adriann Roland Holst. TuT, *tr. by* Desmond Egan

Beggar Maid, The. Sydney E. Jerrold. SacPr

Beggar on the corner is blind and bent over, A. On the Street Corner. L. Mattes. Prolet, *tr. by* Amelia Glaser

Beggar Outside Cape Town Station, A. Sarah Ruden. AmPoNex

Beggar to Beggar Cried. William Butler Yeats. NoAM; OxAEP-2

Beggar Woman. Charles Reznikoff. OxBoAm

Beggar Woman of Naples, The [*with music*]. Max Jacob. MotU; PoCho, *tr. by* John Ashbery

Beggar's Bush. John Fletcher.

Beggar's Holiday, The. NOSC

Beggar's Opera, The. John Gay.

Act 1, Scene viii, Air X—"Thomas, I Cannot," etc.. NoP-5

(Act 1, Scene ix, Air XI—'"A Soldier and a Sailor.") NoP-4; NoP-5

(Act 1, Scene xiii, Air XVI—"Over the Hills and Far Away.") NoP-5

Act II, Scene iv, Air IV—Cotillion. NoP-4; NoP-5

Act II, Scene xv, Air XXII—"The Lass of Patie's Mill." NoP-5

Act III, Scene xiii, Air XXVII—"Greensleeves." NAEL-6v1; NoP-5

Song. NAEL-6v1; NPeEn; OxBEV

"Virgins are like the fair flower in its lustre." NIL-7

Would You Have a Young Virgin? NAEL-6v1

Beggar's Song. A. Van Jordan. LegDan

Begging Another, on Colour of Mending the Former. Ben Jonson. NAEL-7v1 *Fr.* Celebration of Charis in Ten Lyric[k] Pieces [*or* Peeces], A.

Begging for Change in Winter. Rafael Campo. MoW

Begging silently with a paper cup under the viaduct. Old Indian Granny, The. Chrystos. ReEnLa

Begin. Brendan Kennelly. StAl

Begin afresh, afresh, afresh. (LL) Trees, The: "Trees are coming into leaf, The." Philip Larkin. BeAl; HarvBoo; NoAM; NoP-4; NoP-5; OPOU

Begin Again. Susan Coolidge. ITBLP

Begin again to the summoning birds. Begin. Brendan Kennelly. StAl

Begin and never cease! (LL) While Shepherds Watched [Their Flocks by Night]. Nahum Tate. ChrPo; NOSC; SacPr; UV

Begin christmas season with bonfires. Season, The. Anne MacNaughton. ICANM

Begin like tearing the sheet in whose folds you watched yourself sleeping. Begin Like Tearing. Jacques Dupin. YaTCFP, *tr. by* Stephen Romer

Begin the Beguine. Cole Porter. ReLy

Begin to gleam across the mournful plain? (LL) Raven Days, The. Sidney Lanier. APN-2; TCAPo

Begin to love the world. (LL) World Truffle. Sarah Lindsay. BeAl; PoDa

Begin with the Heron and the Bat. Mary Sue Koeppel. AmZen

Begin with Zeus, Aratus said; but, Muse. Strato. CAGL, *tr. by* Daryl Hine

Begin[ne] with Jove; then is the work[e] half[e] done. Evensong. Robert Herrick. BASC

Beginner, The. Lyn Hejinian. VaPo

Beginner in meditation, The. Chogyam Trungpa. WhBo

Beginner's Guide to the Ocean, A. Ogden Nash. AmWit

Beginner's Mind. Shunryu Suzuki. WhBo

Beginning. Harvena Richter. ICANM

Beginning. James Wright. ColAP; VCAP

Beginning, A. Richard Jones. IllVoic

Beginning, The. Viswanatha Satyanarayana. CFP *Fr.* Ramayana.

Beginning at my car's left headlight. Spider. Joan Swift. UrbNat

Beginning at the End: Capital/Capitol Punishment. Richard Bartee. BRtP

Beginning by Value. Christopher Gilbert. GT

Beginning from the Field. Gennady Aygi. WoBe, *tr. by* Peter France

Beginning from you, Phoebus, I shall tell the glory. Argonautica, The. Apollonius Rhodius. HePo, *tr. by* Barbara Hughes Fowler

Beginning / House repairs in. Yaba. EMJL *Fr.* Plum Blossom Scent.

Beginning is often splendid, The. Abel's Brothers. Ferial J. Ghazoul. IrPoTo

Beginning of a Beautiful Day (A Symphony), The. Daniil Kharms. AF; MotU, *tr. by* George Gibian

Beginning of art, The. Basho. EH, *tr. by* Robert Hass

Beginning of Summer. Robert Melançon. YaTCFP, *tr. by* Philip Stratford

Beginning of the Book, The. Edmond Jabès. AF, *tr. by* Rosmarie Waldrop

Beginning of the End, The. Roddy Lumsden. NeBl

Beginning of Things, The. Fatima Lim-Wilson. ReBoTo

Beginning of this year in spring is twisted, The. Spring Memorandum, A: Fort Knox. Robert Duncan. PWW2

Beginning Speech. Adonis. PoCho, tr. by John Heath-Stubbs and Lena Jayyusi and W. S. Merwin

Beginning to dangle beneath. In the Marble Quarry. James Dickey. LPSFW; NoP-4

Beginning to fear his own unworthiness. Soldier of Urbina, A. Jorge Luis Borges. PoetW, tr. by Alastair Reid

Beginning to Forget. Gwyneth Lewis. ATSWP, tr. by Robert Minhinnick

Beginning when I was six I became my father's accomplice. Robert Malise Bowyer Nichols. CLPP Fr. Get-Away.

Beginning with a Stain. Alice Notley. PmAP

Beginning with sonnets for Ted Berrigan. At the Poetry Conference: Berkeley After the New York Style. Robert Duncan. AHA

Beginnings. Robert Earl Hayden. NAAL-5

Beginnings. Peter Sirr. PBCIP

Beginnings. Afaa Michael Weaver. PBCAP

Beginnings are brutal, like this accident. Each Sound. Dorianne Laux. NevBe

Beginnings of poetry. Basho. EMJL, tr. by Haruo Shirane

Beg-Innish. John Millington Synge. IrV; MoBrPo

Begins again, not by our doing or desiring. (LL) Easter: "Even this suburb has overcome Death." Howard Nemerov. NoP-4; WaAnP

Begins another. (LL) Arrivants. Musaemura Bonus Zimunya. HBAPE; NAfrP

Begins here, the ciphered forest. Raul Bopp. TCLAP Fr. Black Snake.

Begins to live / That day. (LL) Word is dead, A. Emily Dickinson. PtR; SAmP; TCAPo

Begins with the saxophone's chromatic weather. Getting Even. Mark Fleckenstein. MiVo

Begone, calm. Spell of Weather, A. Eve Merriam. CA

Begotten by the meeting of rock with rock. Sea Holly. Conrad Potter Aiken. APT-1

Begrimed by trains. Native Soil. Marin Georgiev. CSCBP, tr. by Georgi Belev and Lisa Sapinkopf

Beguines who hear these words. Unknown. WPoS Fr. Soul Speaks, The.

Behaving Like a Jew. Gerald Stern. BodElec; InvLad; LoL; TaR

Behavior of Mirrors on Easter Island, The. Julio Cortázar. TCLAP, tr. by Paul Blackburn

Behavior of the pigeon, The. Buson. EH, tr. by Robert Hass

Behind a locked door. Political Prisoner. Fadil Azzawi. IrPoTo, tr. by Melissa Brown and Salaam Yousif

Behind a rail car warehouse, the bronze Lenins. Avant-Garde, The. Nance Van Winckel. RoV

Behind Bars, Sel. Fadwa Tuqan. AF, tr. by Hatem Hussaini

Behind every arras. Polonius. Miroslav Holub. WoPoe, tr. by Ian Milner

Behind Eyelids. Pierre Reverdy. MotU, tr. by Michael Benedikt

Behind Grandma's House. Gary Soto. UnSA

Behind grandmother's house is the verandah. Grandmother's Verandah. Sŏ Chŏngju. CAMKP, tr. by David R. McCann

Behind her big fan. Tête-à-Tête. May Probyn. NPeEn; VWP

Behind him lay the gray Azores. Columbus. Joaquin Miller. APN-2; BRP; CalPo

Behind him, on the news. Two Quarters, Two Nickels, and the Jacket of the One Album He Ever Recorded—America Welcomes Home the Desert Sax—Are in the Open Felt-Lined Case On the Platform of the Astor Place Subway Station: Gulf War 1. Chuck Wachtel. PrTe

Behind his wife stood, ever fixed alone. Abraham Cowley. NPeEn Fr. Davideis.

Behind Ise Shrine. Basho. SoOfWa, tr. by Sam Hamill

Behind its snout like a huge button. Photo of the Author with a Favorite Pig. William Matthews. WaAnP

Behind Me. Martha Rhodes. ExTi

Behind me, and will not go away. (LL) Follower. Seamus Heaney. CABP; IPoFL; PNI; PtR

Behind me are the fifteen years I've spent in prisons. Prison to Prison. Nazim Hikmet. NaPG, tr. by Talat Sait Halman

Behind me, Ovranopolis softens in the distance. Crossing the Strait. Nicholas Samaras. TWW

Behind me the sunken face of a woman. You Figure It Out. Betsy Sholl. PfS

Behind: me, wag. (LL) John Berryman. BrAP; CAP-8; ColAP; EMP; HarvBoo; HeIP-4; NAMCP V.2; NoAM; NoP-4; NoP-5; OxBoAm; PoetW; PtR; TRP; VCAP; WaAnP Fr. Dream Songs.

Behind Me—dips Eternity. Emily Dickinson. APN-2

Behind my side of the headboard. Lobengula: Having a son at 38. Nikky Finney. SpirFl

Behind our shield of health, each. Onlookers. Luci Shaw. SacPr

Behind shut doors, in shadowy quarantine. First Time, The. Karl Shapiro. APT-2; NAMCP V.2

Behind Sokolnik station, where there's a butcher's shop. Monastery. Yevgeny Borisovich Rein. TCRusP, tr. by Daniel Weissbort

Behind Stowe. Elizabeth Bishop. BLPJKO

Behind that stone before. Whole Story, The. Margaret Avison. GPPA

Behind the Church of St. Gerald. Tomorrow's Hope. Bob Lapierre. OGAHCP, tr. by Boadiba and Jack Hirschman

Behind the counter at the dry cleaner's. Journal. Amy Fusselman. HeMarv

Behind the gate of light. Season of Beginning and End. Zuhur Dixon. CFP, tr. by Patricia Alanah Byrne and Salma Khadra Jayyusi

Behind the gates of sunset. (LL) Eden. Emily Grosholz. FFC; RA

Behind the glass door. Long Afternoon, The. Louis Simpson. BodElec

Behind the Headlines. Raymond Garlick. TCAWP

Behind the heart. Parable of the Voices. Robert Bringhurst. TAPaP

Behind the House. Mahmoud Sharaf. AnVo, tr. by Mohamed Enani

Behind the house the upland falls. After the Pleasure Party [Lines Traced under an Image of Amor Threatening]. Herman Melville. APN-2; NAAL-3; OxBoAm

(Fear me, virgin whosoever.) NCAP

Behind the image. I.E. Claude Royet-Journoud. OnScMo, tr. by Keith Waldrop

Behind the left ear a scar. Men Who Killed My Brother, The. Edward Bartók-Baratta. LiTh

Behind the Line. Edmund Charles Blunden. OxBEV

Behind the Line. Ivor Gurney. HarvBoo

Behind the Mountain. Unknown. CCL1, tr. by Marsha Wagner

Behind the mountain I cultivated a garden and planted herbs and sunflowers. Behind the Mountain. Unknown. CCL1, tr. by Marsha Wagner

Behind the Nationalist's Flag. F. Richard Thomas. RWB

Behind the screen door. My Father Breaks the Neighbor's Nose. Hayan Charara. AmPoNex

Behind the silence is sound. Night. Frances Bellerby. MoWP

Behind the small, fixed windows of the album. Life of a Salesman. Emily Grosholz. RA

Behind the smooth texture. Like an Animal. Jimmy Santiago Baca. AF

Behind the Veil. Andrew Lansdown. NOBAu

Behind the veil, behind the veil. (LL) Alfred Tennyson. BrAP; NAEL-6v2; NAEL-7v2; NAWM-7v2; NoP-5; NPeEn; WaAnP Fr. In Memoriam A. H. H.

Behind the vivarium glass. Eagle Rock. Tomas Tranströmer. WoBe, tr. by Robin Fulton

Behind the window, in that room where rain. Waiting for the End of Time. Kelly Cherry. LPSFW

Behind their mortgaged houses. (LL) Men at Forty. Donald Justice. CAP-8; EMP; InGu; ItP; NAMCP V.2; NoAM; NoP-4; NoP-5; OxBoAm; VCAP

Behind us, Glencoe of the Slaughter. Rannoch Moor. Alison Fell. EdScPo

Behind us the poplars lingered, the horses' neighs. Returning from the Fair. Ivan Davidkov. CSCBP, tr. by Georgi Belev and Lisa Sapinkopf

Behind you the door sweeps breath after breath of summer air into the great cool hall. Astronomy. David Walker. MotU

Behind you: the owl, whose eyes. Robert Bringhurst. PoCoUp Fr. Conversations with a Toad.

Behold. Unknown. WoPoe, tr. by Alfons L. Korn and Mary Kawena Pukui

Behold a Shaking. Christina Georgina Rossetti. "Blessed that flock safe penned in Paradise." WPoS

Behold, behold, the day shall come when as. Lybica. Jane Seager. EMWP

Behold, God of Abraham, God of mercy. Elie Wiesel. HP Fr. Ani Maamin, A Song Lost and Found Again.

Behold her ancestors (a pious race). Mrs. Warner Arrives Above [or An Elegiac Thought on Mrs. Anne Warner]. Isaac Watts. STuOW

Behold her lip, how thin it is; her nose. Shrew, The. Rowland Watkyns. AngWePo

Behold her, single in the field. Solitary Reaper, The. William Wordsworth. CABP; ClHu; HeIP-4; NAEL-6v2; NAEL-7v2; NOBRP; NoP-4; NoP-5; NPBRoP; OBEV; OxAEP-2; OxBEV; PoPoPo; SoSe-8; TFi; WaAnP; WeW-3

Behold how every man, drawn with delight. Samuel Daniel. NoSic Fr. Musophilus; or, Defence of All Learning.

Behold, how Sodom swaggers in its Pride. George Lesley. CAGL Fr. Fire and Brimstone; or, The Destruction of Sodom.

Behold, I send thee to the heights of song. To W. S. M. Arthur W. Monroe. APN-2

Behold me, I pray thee, with all thine whole reason. John Skelton. ChIV-2

Behold me waiting—waiting for the knife. W. E. Henley. MoBrPo Fr. In Hospital.

Behold, my servant shall deal prudently. Bible, O.T. NAWM-5v1 Fr. Isaiah.

Behold My Treasures, Darling. Endre Ady. IQMS, tr. by Adam Makkai

Behold my treasures, my darling. Behold My Treasures, Darling. Endre Ady. IQMS, *tr.* by Adam Makkai

Behold, our bodies are laid out—a long, long row. Behold, Our Bodies are Laid Out. Haim Guri. NRoS, *tr.* by Esther Raizen

Behold Pelides with his yellow hair. Before a Statue of Achilles. George Santayana. APN-2

Behold, she said, a falling star! Ephemeron. Annie Fields. PoBW

Behold That Bay. *Unknown.* CCL1 *Fr.* Qi-yu [Translations].

Behold that bay, which is formed by the winding of the river KI. *Unknown.* CCL1 *Fr.* Qi-yu [Translations].

Behold that tree, in Autumn's dim decay. Anna Seward. WoRP *Fr.* Sonnets.

Behold the brave fellow who sits in his Yellow. All-night Taxi Stand, The. Kenneth Slessor. BMAP

Behold the critic, pitched like the *castrati.* Theodore Roethke. OBCoV *Fr.* Three Epigrams.

Behold the Deeds! Henry Cuyler Bunner. NBLV

Behold the dread Mt. Shasta, where it stands. Mount Shasta. John Rollin Ridge. APN-2; CalPo

Behold the feeble deer, what war they rage. Martial. DiBP *Fr.* Epigrams.

Behold the gloomy tyrant's awful form. Winter. Anne Hunter. CenSon

Behold, the grave of a wicked man. Stephen Crane. APN-2; NoP-4; NoP-5; OxBoAm

Behold the great Creator makes. Psalm for Christmas Day. Thomas Pestel. SacPr

Behold the horned goat of Bacchos, how lordly. Anyte. SaLy, *tr.* by Diane Rayor

Behold, the King of glory now is come. Laurence Clarkson. PBRV *Fr.* Single Eye All Light, no Darkness, A.

Behold the Lilies of the Field. Anthony Hecht. EmeKit

Behold, the old earth is young again! Sibyl, The. Agnes Mary Frances Robinson. VWP

Behold the rocky wall. Two Streams, The. Oliver Wendell Holmes. APN-1

Behold the Thin Green. Andrea Zanzotto. VCWP

Behold the tormented and the fallen angel. Beethoven. John Hall Wheelock. PoA 2002

Behold the way our fine-feathered friend. My Funny Valentine. Lorenz Hart. ReLy

Behold the woes of matrimonial life. Geoffrey Chaucer. *Fr.* Canterbury Tales, The.

Behold the wreckage. Make the Bed. Stephen Cushman. AWTN

Behold these woods, and mark, my sweet. Pastoral Courtship, A. Thomas Randolph. BASC

Behold This and Always Love It. Meridel Le Sueur. HW

Behold this Creature's Form and State. Irish Greyhound, The. Katherine Philips. DiBP

Behold this little volume here enrolled. On the Bible. *Unknown.* NOSC

Behold this needle; when the *Arctick* stone. Francis Quarles. PBRV

Behold this swarthy face, these gray eyes. Behold This Swarthy Face. Walt Whitman. APN-1; NAAPv.1

Behold what blessings Wealth to life can lend! Alexander Pope. OxBEV *Fr.* Epistle III, to Allen Lord Bathurst.

Behold what hap *Pigmalion* had to frame. Samuel Daniel. PBRV *Fr.* Sonnets to Delia.

Behold, whatever wind prevail. Mid-Day Moon, The. John Banister Tabb. APN-2

Behold where Beauty walks with Peace! California Christmas, A. Joaquin Miller. CalPo

Behold! wood into bird and bird to wood again. Boomerang. William Hart-Smith. NOBAu

Behold yon reach of the river KI. *Unknown.* CCL1 *Fr.* Qi-yu [Translations].

Behold young Raphael coming back. Raphael. Priscilla Jane Thompson. CBWP-2

Beholde, how good and joyfull a thinge it is, brethren to dwell to gether in unitye. Bible, *O.T.* OBVE

Beholde me, I pray thee, with all thi hole reson. John Skelton. SacPr

Beholde this fle. Barnabe Googe. NPeEn

Beho[u]ld, a silly [*or* sely *or* little] tender babe. New Prince, New Pomp[e]. Robert Southwell. ChrPo; NoSic; SacPr; WaAnP

Beho[u]ld the father is His daughter's son[ne]. Nativity of Christ[e], The. Robert Southwell. OxBEV

Béibuga luma inarúni. Beiguga Luma Inaruni. Marcela Lewis. OWABP

Bei-feng: Cold Is the North Wind. *Unknown.* CCL1, *tr.* by Burton Watson

Beiguga Luma Inaruni. Marcela Lewis. OWABP

Beija-Flor. Diane Ackerman. NIP-4

Beijing Spring. Marilyn Chin. ExTi

Being. Carol Frost. PfSP

Being. Adriann Roland Holst. TuT, *tr.* by Paula Meehan

Being a big favorite of the Muses, I'll appeal to. Let's Do This Poem (1.26). Horace. WED, *tr.* by Robert Bly

Being a boy from the hills, brought up. Welshman in Exile Speaks, The. T. Harri Jones. AngWePo; OBWVE

Being a colored poet. Jacket Notes. Ishmael Reed. UnSA

Being a deer means grazing, suddenly lifting the head. Being. Carol Frost. PfSP

Being a Monster. Lawrence Raab. OPRER

Being a person. Lady Izumi. WoPoe, *tr.* by Steven D. Carter

Being a Wife. Selima Hill. BeAl; EmeKit

Being alone is the next best thing. Evensong. Marc Cohen. KGB

Being an Immigrant. Matilde Salganicoff. MirDau, *tr.* by Celeste Kostopulos-Cooperman

Being Aware. Dennis Cooper. PmAP

Being Beauteous. Arthur Rimbaud. SxFrPo, *tr.* by Martin Sorrell

Being black in America. Lonely Eagles. Marilyn Nelson Waniek. ESEAA

Being Called For. Rosemary Dobson. BMAP

Being driven after the hearse thru suburbs. H. T. Louis Zukofsky. NAAPv.2

Being eaten. (LL) Elements of Composition. A. K. Ramanujan. NAMCP V.2; VCWP

Being Exit in the World. Calvin C. Hernton. EGAG

Being finer than my soul, I fear, A. (LL) Palace-Burner, The. Sarah Morgan Bryan Piatt. NAAPv.1; NCAP; SWaP

Being Free. Leanne O'Sullivan. PoCu

Being given a lover's key is an intimate gesture. Vicki and Daphne. Cheryl Clarke. WiU

Being helpless. *Unknown.* ArkPo, *tr.* by Edwin A. Cranston

Being (Human). John Fitzgerald. BBMWP, *tr.* by Joseph P. Clancy

Being human, don't ever say what happens tomorrow. Simonides. SaLy, *tr.* by Diane Rayor

Being idle in the wooden building, I opened a window. *Unknown.* ASA, *tr.* by Him Mark Lai

Being in earnest. Allen Fisher. Oth *Fr.* Stepping Out.

Being in Love. Marvin Bell. InvLad; StAl

Being invited to a clumsy tea ceremony. Disagreeable Things. *Unknown.* EMJL, *tr.* by Edward Putzar

Being Jewish in a Small Town. Lyn Lifshin. UnSA

Being just your sort of con. (LL) Sacrificial Wolf. Anne Rouse. MFPA; NeBl

Being made into words even as we speak. (LL) Poetry: "Invited onto the grounds of the god." Jane Miller. GifTon; TAPaP

Being my self captived here in care. Sonnet 73: 'Being my self captived here'. Edmund Spenser. AEP

Being neither white nor black? (LL) Cross. Langston Hughes. ColAP; GT; HarvBoo; NAMCP V.1; NoP-4; NoP-5; SAmP; SoSe-8

Being old is not so bad. You wake up. Nobody Here But Us. Richard Garcia. OPRER; TouFir

Being polite to your official guests. (LL) Easter Hymn. Alec Derwent Hope. ChIV-2; GI

Being set on the idea. Atlantis. W. H. Auden. OxAEP-2

Being Sick Together. Elaine Equi. IllVoic

Being sleepless at midnight. Sleepless at Midnight. Juan Chi. CCL1, *tr.* by Michael Bullock and C. J. Chen

Being so bad, how did he get to be king? King Claudius. Kirkpatrick Dobie. EdScPo

Being the child of a Mad Mother. Dīnrām. SinGod, *tr.* by Rachel Fell McDermott

Being the Third Song of Urias. Ken Smith. StAl

Being There. Thomas Sayers Ellis. AmPoNex

Being told that it is impossible. Peaceful Life. Dainin Katagiri. WhBo

Being tongue tied is what. Tongue Tied. ReBoTo

Being, whose flesh dissolves. To the Unseeable Animal. Wendell Berry. UpMys

Being with her now is a kind of boredom. Throes. Anthony Thwaite. PoCu

Being you, you cut your poetry from wood. Egg Boiler, The. Gwendolyn Brooks. CAP-8

Being your slave, what should I do[e] but tend. William Shakespeare. CAGL; NoSic; OBEV *Fr.* Sonnets.

Beings of the Mind, The. Felicia Dorothea Hemans. RWP

Beirut. Claire Gebeyli. PoArWo, *tr.* by Mona Takyeddine Amyuni

Beirut. Nadia Tuéni. PoArWo

Bejeweled makeup, cloud-coiffure, training golden garments. Palace Poem. Ts'ao Ching-chao. WoPoe, *tr.* by Nancy Hodes and Tung Yuan-fang

Bela. Gerald Stern. BodElec

Belated Lament. Attila József. IQMS, *tr.* by John P. Sadler

Belatedly, for kit's 11th birthday. Roy Kiyooka. NLPA *Fr.* Pear Tree Pomes.

Belex his flint adjusts and rights. By the Jordan. Herman Melville. NCAP

Belfast Confetti [*with music*]. Ciaran Carson. NPeEn; PNI

Belfast Tune. Joseph Brodsky. VCWP

Belgian, with cumbrous tread and iron boots.   Malines.   James Kenneth Stephen.   OBCoV

Belied at top and bottom, pinched at the waist.   Robert B. Shaw.   PoA 2002 *Fr.* Chronometrics.

Belief.   "Angelus Silesius."   GePo *Fr.* Cherubical Wanderer, The.

Belief.   Philip Levine.   ColAP

Belief [*with music*].   Josephine Miles.   NoAM

Belief, great mustard seed, sends mountains to the sea.   "Angelus Silesius." GePo *Fr.* Cherubical Wanderer, The.

Belief to regulate. (LL)   Last Night that She Lived, The.   Emily Dickinson. HeIP-4; NAAL-3

Believe Me.   Esther Ettinger.   DTA, *tr. by* Mariana Barr

Believe me, children!   Let's Eat Stars.   Nanao Sakaki.   WhBo

Believe me, I knew you, though faintly, and I loved, I loved you / All. (LL) Gwendolyn Brooks.   CAP-8; ESEAA; IllVoic; ISC; MoWP; NAAL-5; NALW; OxAAAP; OxBoAm; PoPoPo *Fr.* Street in Bronzeville, A.

Believe Me, If All Those Endearing Young Charms.   Thomas Moore.   NAEL-6v2; NAEL-7v2

Believe me, she grew more beautiful from moment to moment.   Believe Me. Esther Ettinger.   DTA, *tr. by* Mariana Barr

Believe me, sir, I'd like to spend whole days.   Martial.   OBVE; RomPo, *tr. by* James Vincent Cunningham

Believe that we bloom upon this stalk of time.   Muriel Rukeyser and Leif Sjoberg.   YaYoPo *Fr.* Night Flight : New York.

Believe the automatic righteousness.   Against the War in Vietnam.   Wendell Berry.   WaAnP

Believe those sounds and you're aiming a bomb. (LL)   On Hearing a New Escalation.   Richard Hugo.   AmWaPo; PoA 2002

Believer, O shall I die? / O my army, shall I die?   Shall I Die?   *Unknown.* SSUS

Believers' Best Buy.   Roger Woddis.   UV

Believer's Riddle, The.   Ralph Erskine.
  "I though from condemnation free."   SacPr
  "Mine arms embrace my God, yet I."   SacPr
  "My life's a maze of seeming traps."   SacPr
  "My life's a pleasure and a pain."   SacPr
  "To tell the world my proper name."   SacPr

Believing each simple thing passes from a perception that is less clear.   Pear. Susan Stewart.   AmAlph

Believing in the Absurd.   Harold Norse.   CLPP

Believing Mind, The.   Seng-ts'an.   CCL1, *tr. by* Graeme Wilson

Belinda frown'd, Thalestris call'd her Prude. (LL)   Alexander Pope.   NPeEn; OxBEV *Fr.* Rape of the Lock, The: An Heroi-Comical Poem in Five Cantos.

Belinda lived in a little white house.   Tale of Custard the Dragon, The.   Ogden Nash.   ITBLP; MakPoe

Belinda's Petition.   Rita Dove.   PtR

Belisarius.   Henry Wadsworth Longfellow.   APN-1

Belize Cemetery, The.   Mary Gomez Parham.   OWABP

Belizean Dawn, A.   Corinth Morter-Lewis.   OWABP

Belizeans: Unite to Build our Nation.   George Cadle Price.   OWABP

Bell, The.   Richard Jones.   P180

Bell, The.   Peter Levitt.   WhBo

Bell Barrow.   Duncan Glen.   EdScPo

Bell da Ring.   *Unknown.*   SSUS

Bell diphthonging in an atmosphere, A.   Dubious Night, A.   Richard Wilbur. UpMys

Bell in the mountain-temple sounds the coming of night, A.   Returning at Night to Lumen Mountain.   Meng Hao Jan.   CCL1, *tr. by* Witter Bynner

Bell is full of wind, The.   Roberto Juarroz.   VCWP *Fr.* Sixth Vertical Poetry.

Bell of Linh Mu Pagoda tolls, The.   Ship of Redemption.   *Vietnamese Oral Tradition.*   CaDao, *tr. by* John Balaban

Bell Speech.   Richard Wilbur.   MoAmPo

Bell struck one, and shook the silent tower, The.   Fair Elenor.   William Blake. NPBRoP

Bell / Too softly and too slowly tolled, The.   Kenneth Rexroth.   PFTM-1 *Fr.* Prolegomenon to a Theodicy, A.

Bell Tower.   Léonie Adams.   MoAmPo; OxBoAm

Bell wakes me at 6 in the pale spring dawn, The.   Letter from Pretoria Central Prison.   Arthur Nortje.   BrAP; HBAPE

Bell was not a jar, when, The.   Suicide Rates, The.   Lewis Warsh.   AHA; FTOS

Bella and the Golem.   Rossana Ombres.   CItWP, *tr. by* Cinzia Sartini Blum and Lara Trubowitz

Bella Donna Iu.   Li Yü.   NDACCP, *tr. by* William Carlos Williams

Bell-Birds.   Henry Clarence Kendall.   NOBAu

Belle Dame sans Merci, La [A Ballad].   John Keats.   BrAP; BRP; CABP; ClHu; CtM; HeIP-4; NAEL-6v2; NAEL-7v2; NAWM-7v2; NOBRP; NoP-4; NoP-5; NPBRoP; NPeEn; OBEV; OBSP; OxAEP-2; OxBEV; PoPoPo; SoSe-8; TFi; TRP; UV; WaAnP; WoPoe

Belle Isle Men, The.   Anthony Butts.   AmPoNex

Belle Isle, 1949.   Philip Levine.   ColAP; NAMCP V.2; VCAP; WaAnP

Belle Layotte [*tr. of Creole slave song*].   George Washington Cable.   APN-2

Belle Layotte.   *Unknown.*   SSUS

Belle of the Ball-Room, The.   Winthrop Mackworth Praed.   NOBRP *Fr.* Every Day Characters.

Bellman himself they all praised to the skies—, The.   Lewis Carroll.   OBCoV *Fr.* Hunting of the Snark, The.

Bellocq's Ophelia.   Natasha Trethewey.   FuFl; NeAmPo

Bellow- / ing skull heavy with brains.   Self-Portrait, Double Exposed.   Joanie Mackowski.   PoDa

Bellringing was another.   To My Father.   Tony Curtis.   AngWePo; TCAWP

Bellrope.   Robert Morgan.   BLT

Bell-rope that gathers God at dawn, The.   Broken Tower, The.   Hart Crane. APT-2; ColAP; MoAmPo; NAAPv.2; NAMCP V.1; NoAM; NoP-4; OxBoAm; PoPoPo; WaAnP

Bells.   Jimmy Santiago Baca.   FTtHH

Bells, The.   Rosalía de Castro.   SpanPo, *tr. by* Edwin Morgan

Bells, The.   Edgar Allan Poe.   APN-1; BRP; ChAP; IJHIL; ITBLP; NAAPv.1; TCAPo; TFi; TreFP

Bells and drums lie cold, The.   Hidden Tears.   Wei Chuang.   CCL1, *tr. by* Lois Fusek

Bells. Bells. Bells.   Earth Mother.   Sonia Sanchez.   ItWoWo

Bells for John Whiteside's Daughter.   John Crowe Ransom.   APT-1; BrAP; ColAP; FuPo; HarvBoo; HeIP-4; InGu; MakPoe; MoAmPo; NAAPv.2; NAMCP V.1; NIL-7; NIP-4; NoAM; NoP-4; NoP-5; OxBoAm; TFi; WaAnP; WeW-3

Bells gathered like bells What are.   Captive and Able.   Hoa Nguyen. WANABP

Bells of Heaven, The.   Ralph Hodgson.   MoBrPo; OBEV

Bells of hell go ting-a-ling-a-ling, The.   *Unknown.*   OBCoV *Fr.* Soldiers' Songs of the First World War.

Bells of San Blas, The.   Henry Wadsworth Longfellow.   APN-1

Bells of Shandon, The.   Francis Sylvester Mahony.   OBEV (Shandon Bells, The.)   OxAEP-2

Bells of St. Michael.   Mary Weston Fordham.   CBWP-2

Bells of Sunday rang us down, The.   Song.   John Ciardi.   PWW2

Bells of the Armistice wake his family, The.   Last Look in the Sambre Canal, A.   John Bensko.   YaYoPo

Bells of waiting Advent ring, The.   Christmas.   Sir John Betjeman.   ChrPo; OBCP

Bells. The word gongs my skull.   Bells.   Jimmy Santiago Baca.   FTtHH

Belly Button Song.   Menna Elfyn.   ATSWP, *tr. by* Robert Minhinnick

Belly Dancer.   Diane Wakoski.   NALW; NoAM

Belly to the bar, bare chest heaving under the open laces.   Walt Whitman at Pfaff's: A Fantasy.   Phil Tabakow.   ViWalt

Belong to the enormous bliss of American death. (LL)   Rhapsody.   Frank O'Hara.   NAMCP V.2; NoAM

Belong to the life of a railroad man. (LL)   Casey Jones.   T. Lawrence Seibert. GM; ITBLP

Belong to the life of a railroad man. (LL)   *Unknown.*   APT-1; TCAPo

Belonging.   Rafael Campo.   AmPoNex; WiU

Belonging.   Leslie Norris.   TCAWP

Belonging.   Jay Parini.   PfSP

Belonging to a New Family [*with music*].   Mohammad Bennis.   NAfrP, *tr. by* Charles Doria and Sharif Elmusa

Belongings.   A. V. Christie.   AmPoNex

Belongings.   Catherine Davis.   FFC

Beloved.   Iyamide Hazeley.   NAfrP

Beloved! amid the earnest woes.   To F——.   Edgar Allan Poe.   APN-1

Beloved has found.   Fewer Than Music.   Donald Revell.   RoV

Beloved husband, greatest part of our soul.   Elizabeth Hoby, Wife, to Thomas Hoby, Knight, Her Husband.   Elizabeth Cooke Hoby.   EMWP

Belovd, it is good.   Dream Song.   *Unknown.*   OBVE, *tr. by* Francis Densmore

Beloved, it is morn!   Song.   Emily Hickey.   SacPr

Beloved, may your sleep be sound.   Lullaby.   William Butler Yeats.   OBMV

Beloved, men in thick green coats came crunching.   Letter, The.   Mary Ruefle. AmAlph

Beloved, my Belovèd, when I think.   Elizabeth Barrett Browning.   CenSon *Fr.* Sonnets from the Portuguese.

Beloved, My Glory in Thee is Not Ceased.   Michael Field.   VWP

Beloved, Now I Love God First.   Michael Field.   PoBW

Beloved on the earth. (LL)   Late Fragment.   Raymond Carver.   IJHIL; StAl

Beloved Ones, The.   Eunice Juaquina Watkins-Cothran.   BtF

Beloved person must I think, The.   Akimine.   TAL *Fr.* Kokin Shu.

Beloved Spic.   Martín Espada.   OPRER

Beloved sweetheart bastard. Not a day since then.   Havisham.   Carol Ann Duffy.   MoWP

Beloved, The.   David Roberts.   OBWVE, *tr. by* H. Idris Bell

Belovèd, thou hast brought me many flowers.   Elizabeth Barrett Browning.   CenSon; LW; OxBSo *Fr.* Sonnets from the Portuguese.

Beloved, what do you want of me?   Marguerite Porete.   WPoS

Belovëd, when I saw thee sleeping there.   To———, Sleeping.   Adah Isaacs Menken.   PoBW

Beloved, You Must Not Die.   Yosano Akiko.   CAoMJL1, *tr. by* Janine Beichman

Beloved's Face, The.   Risto Ahti.   PML, *tr. by* Herbert Lomas

Beloveds, yours skins is a boundary separating yous from the rest of yous.   December 1, 2002.   Juliana Spahr.   LegDan

Below.   Federico García Lorca.   PFTM-1 *Fr.* Night (Suite for Piano and Poet's Voice).

Below deck.   Galley Oars.   Ali ibn Hariq.   WoPoe, *tr. by* Christopher Middleton

Below Fourth of July Mine.   Andrew Schelling.   AmZen

Below Freezing.   Tomas Tranströmer.   VCWP, *tr. by* Robert Bly

Below its floor, mint.   Fountain.   Elizabeth Robinson.   AmPoNex

Below Loughrigg.   Fleur Adcock.   BrAP

Below me, always below me is water.   Water.   Francis Ponge.   GPTC, *tr. by* Beth Archer

Below me treetops and a crow.   Cliff, The.   Gregory Orr.   PfSP

Below the Cellar of the Yellow House There Is Another Set of Stairs.   Robin Behn.   AmAlph

Below the gardens and the darkening pines.   At Carmel Highlands.   Janet Lewis.   PoA 2002

Below the mountain.   Self-portrait.   Yun Tongju.   CAMKP, *tr. by* David R. McCann

Below, the river spread to meet sea and sky. (LL)   On Brooklyn Bridge I saw a man drop dead.   Charles Reznikoff.   APT-2; NAAPv.2; NAMCP V.1

Below the Ruweisat Ridge. (LL)   Death Valley.   Sorley MacLean.   FaBoWar; NePenScot; PoAgWa

Below the Surface-Stream.   Matthew Arnold.   NPeEn

Below the thunders of the upper deep.   Kraken, The.   Alfred Tennyson.   CtM; NAEL-6v2; NAEL-7v2; NoP-4; NoP-5

Below us, as far on as eye could see. (LL)   If I were loved, as I desire to be.   Alfred Tennyson.   GSo; OxBSo

Below White Cliffs.   Abigail Albrecht.   GeoHom

Belphoebe and Timias.   Edmund Spenser.   NAEL-6v1; NAEL-7v1 *Fr.* Faerie Queene, The.

Belshazzar! from the banquet turn.   To Belshazzar.   Lord Byron.   ChIV-1

Belshazzar had a Letter.   Emily Dickinson.   ChIV-1

Belshazzar saw this blue.   Up There.   Ruth Stone.   ExTi

Belshazzer's Feast [*with music*].   Eloise Bibb.   CBWP-4

Belvedere Marittimo.   Greg Williamson.   AmPoNex; NeAmPo

Bemidji.   John Redmond.   NIrP

Ben Barley.   Gerard Benson.   UV

Ben Barley was a barman stout.   Ben Barley.   Gerard Benson.   UV

Ben Battle was a soldier bold.   Faithless Nelly Gray.   Thomas Hood.   NOBRP; UV

Ben Bolt.   Thomas Dunn English.   APN-1

Ben, do not leave the stage.   Answer to Master [*or* Mr.] Ben Jonson's Ode, to Persuade Him Not to Leave the Stage, An.   Thomas Randolph.   BASC

Ben Franklin again, down by the esplanade.   Ducks Are for Our Happiness.   Gerald Stern.   PfSP

Ben Hur.   Joe Weil.   BRtP

Ben Jonson Entertains a Man from Stratford.   Edwin Arlington Robinson.   MoAmPo

Ben Webster: "Did You Call Her Today?"   Ron Welburn.   SeSe

Ben Zen Poems.   Tom Montag.
   "Monk's bowl, The."   AmZen

Bench Marks.   Drew Milne.
   "Sweet shift go slow go."   VaPo

Bench of Boors, The.   Herman Melville.   APN-2; AWTN; NAAL-3; SoSe-8

Bench, the sewermouth, the hydrant placed, The.   Northern Boulevard.   Edwin Denby.   NYP2

Benches are hard and the professor is not all that bright either, The.   Authoritarian School and How a Respectable Literary Genre Was Born, The.   Gerardo Deniz.   RMCMP, *tr. by* Mónica de la Torre

Bend back thy bow, O Archer, till the string.   Archer, The.   Arthur James Marshall Smith.   BrAP

Bend down and touch lightly with my lips the white face in the coffin. (LL)   Reconciliation.   Walt Whitman.   AmWaPo; APN-1; FaBoWar; MoAmPo; NAAL-3; NAAL-5; NAAPv.1; NoP-4; NoP-5; OBWP; OxBoAm; PCW; WeW-3; WoPoe

Bend down my strange face to yours and forgive you. (LL)   All My Pretty Ones.   Anne Sexton.   NAMCP V.2; NoAM; OxBoAm

Bend in the River.   Simon J. Ortiz.   HATNAP; PoPoPo

Bend in the river followed us for days, The.   Twenty-four Logics in Memory of Lee Hickman.   Michael Palmer.   BodElec

Bend of the gulf.   Elena Clementelli.   CItWP *Fr.* Etruscan Notebook.

Bend thy bow, Dian! shoot thy silver shaft.   New Moon, The.   William Gilmore Simms.   APN-1

Bendin' knees a-achin', Body racked wid pain, I wishi I was a child of God.   O'er the Crossing.   *Unknown.*   SSUS

Bending above the spicy woods which blaze.   October.   Helen Hunt Jackson.   APN-2

Bending, I bow my head.   Combing.   Gladys Cardiff.   GifTon

Bending the Bow.   Robert Duncan.   HarvBoo

Bending the Light.   Tom Koontz.   VisFro

Bends all his powers, even unto Stella's grace. (LL)   Sir Philip Sidney.   CABP; NoSic *Fr.* Astrophil and Stella.

Beneath a gas-mantle that the moths bombard.   West, The.   Michael Longley.   PBCIP

Beneath a sable vaile, and Shadowes deepe.   Mans Knowledge, Ignorance in the Misteries of God.   William Drummond of Hawthornden.   SacPr

Beneath all the statistics.   New York.   Federico García Lorca.   RaBo; RaW; WED, *tr. by* Robert Bly

Beneath an old wall, that went round an old castle.   Poor Singing Dame, The.   Mary Robinson.   NAEL-7v2

Beneath any common belief.   Night Blindness.   Jocelyn Emerson.   IAoNAP

Beneath Aphrodite's golden portico you now lie.   Moiro.   SaLy, *tr. by* Diane Rayor

Beneath both the feet of Boötes you may see.   Aratus.   HePo *Fr.* Phaenomena.

Beneath Cold Mountain.   Michael Hannon.   GeoHom

Beneath Her Ribs.   Hwang Insuk.   EcSo, *tr. by* Peter H. Lee

Beneath its canopy of poisoned air. (LL)   On a Line from Valéry.   Carolyn Kizer.   FFC; GifTon

Beneath its wings.   Sappho.   SaLy, *tr. by* Diane Rayor

Beneath me this dark garden plunges, buoyant.   Villa d'Este.   Edwin Denby.   OBGa

Beneath my feet the pier shifts.   Redondo.   Ron Koertge.   CalPo

Beneath My Hand and Eye the Distant Hills, Your Body.   Gary Snyder.   NAAL-5

Beneath my weight, the duckboards bow.   Mermaid Tank, The.   Stephen Knight.   NeBl; StAl

Beneath our feet and o'er our head.   Holy Field, The.   Henry Hart Milman.   SacPr

Beneath our windows. (LL)   It Being Forbidden.   Martha Rhodes.   KGB; NAPBL

Beneath Searchlights.   Andrew Hudgins.   UpMys

Beneath the blossoms with a pot of wine.   Drinking Alone in the Moonlight.   Li Po.   ColAnChi; WoPoe, *tr. by* Elling O. Eide

Beneath the blossoms with a pot of wine.   Drinking Alone in the Moonlight.   Li Po.   CCL1, *tr. by* Elling O. Eide

Beneath the brushed wing of the mallard.   Lint.   Rita Dove.   AmAlph; TRP

Beneath the cross of Jesus.   Elizabeth Cecilia Clephane.   SacPr

Beneath the fabric of leaves.   Spring, The.   Ellen Bryant Voigt.   LPSFW

Beneath the flakes of Russian snow.   Tatiana Bek.   CRWP, *tr. by* Robert Reid

Beneath the fort where Osceola starved.   Old Slavemarket: St. Augustine, Fla.   George Garrett.   LPSFW

Beneath the lamp of my cheek's glow, in your hands I am.   Erin Mouré.   NLPA *Fr.* Wittgenstein Letters to Mel Gibson's Braveheart, The.

Beneath the machete we close our eyes.   Shall We Gather at the River?   Monifa Atungaye Love.   LiTh

Beneath the pines I asked his servant boy.   Looking for the Recluse and Not Finding Him.   Chia Tao.   CCL1, *tr. by* Stephen Owen

Beneath the Pole of Proud Raven.   Jana Harris.   SUP

Beneath the sagging roof.   Ezra Pound.   MoAmPo; NAAPv.2 *Fr.* Hugh Selwyn Mauberley (Life and Contacts).

Beneath the sculptured for which late you wore.   Maida.   Sir Walter Scott.   DiBP

Beneath the Shadow of the Freeway.   Lorna Dee Cervantes.   PBCAP

Beneath the Stars.   Vytautas Bloze.   PML, *tr. by* Jonas Zdanys

Beneath the tree of night writing forges.   Transfer of Title.   María Rivera.   SPV, *tr. by* Jen Hofer

Beneath the Tree of Vision's where we'll meet.   Young Girl Sleeping.   Jean Cocteau.   YaTCFP, *tr. by* Alfred Corn

Beneath the trees.   Memoriae Positum R. G. Shaw.   James Russell Lowell.   CBCWP

Besieged Serenity. Vasco [*or* Vasko] Popa.
  Echo. PoSu
  Journey. PoSu
Beso, El. Angelina Weld Grimké. NAAPv.2
Bess. Linda Pastan. GoPo
Bessie. Alvin Aubert. SeSe
Bessie Smith at Roy Thomson Hall. Michael Ondaatje. MotU
Bessie Smith's Funeral. Alvin Aubert. SeSe
Best. Gregory Orr. PoDa
Best? Siv Widerberg. NTCP, *tr. by* Verne Moberg
Best, The. Elizabeth Barrett Browning. OxBEV
Best and brightest, come away. To Jane: The Invitation. Percy Bysshe
  Shelley. NAEL-6v2; NPBRoP; NPeEn
Best be done before the last degree. Lao Tzu. WoPoe *Fr.* Tao Te Ching.
Best clock. Best carpet. Best three chairs. Study. Tony Harrison. CABP
Best Friend, The. W. H. Davies. OBMV
Best Is Yet to Come, The. Carolyn Leigh. ReLy
Best Medecines, The. Friedrich von Logau. SoSe-8, *tr. by* Henry Wadsworth
  Longfellow
Best of all is to be idle. Against Whatever It Is That's Encroaching. Charles
  Simic. ColAP
Best of all was listening to a hush, The. First Nights. Grace Schulman.
  NevBe
Best of Life Is But, The. Li Po. CCL1, *tr. by* H. A. Giles
Best of thy sex! if sacred friendship can. To Phylocles, Inviting Him to
  Friendship. "Ephelia." NOSC
Best slave, The. Alcestis on the Poetry Circuit. Erica Jong. NALW
Best Slow Dancer, The [*with music*]. David Wagoner. NoAM; VCAP
Best thing about dying is it frees you, The. On Death. Maurice Manning.
  LegDan
Best Thing in the World, The. Elizabeth Barrett Browning. VWP
Best thing in the world, The. Tune: "A Thousand Autumns." Huang T'ing-
  chien. ColAnChi, *tr. by* James Robert Hightower
Best Things in Life Are Free, The. Lew Brown, B. G. DeSylva and Ray
  Henderson. ReLy
Best time for a poet is when spring is new, The. Early Spring East of Town.
  Yang Chu-Yuan. TAPaP, *tr. by* Red Pine
Best way to insult God, The. Anne Carson. BodElec *Fr.* Truth About God,
  The.
Bestiary. Oliver Reynolds. TCAWP *Fr.* Tone Poem.
Bestiary for the Fingers of My Right Hand. Charles Simic. P180
Best-loved Night!, The. (LL) Hymn to the Night. Henry Wadsworth
  Longfellow. APN-1; NAAPv.1; TCAPo
Bestow a blessing on the young men; because the time has come. Prayer.
  Haim Guri. NRoS, *tr. by* Esther Raizen
Bestows profound benefits on her practitioner. Erin Mouré. NLPA *Fr.*
  Wittgenstein Letters to Mel Gibson's Braveheart, The.
Bestrew the benches: for my bride and me. *Unknown.* WoPoe *Fr.* Elder Edda,
  The.
Beth Gelert. Richard Henry Horne. DiBP
Beth Gelert. William Robert Spencer. DiBP
Beth Gèlert; or, The Grave of the Greyhound. William Robert Spencer.
  OBNV
Bethel, Horeb, Engedi, Soar. Exile: Welsh Service from Daventry. Llewelyn
  Wyn Griffith. AngWePo
Bethlehem. Marina Ivanovna Tsvetayeva. GI, *tr. by* Nina Kossman
Bethlehem in Germany. Advent Calendar. Gjertrud Schnackenberg. ChrPo
Bethsabe's Song. George Peele. ChIV-1; NoSic; NPeEn; OxBEV
Betjeman, 1984. Charles Causley. UV
Betrayal. Adam Zagajewski. VCWP, *tr. by* Renata Gorczynski
Betrayed. Luljeta Lleshanaku. WoBe, *tr. by* Henry Israeli
Betrayed by KC. Jenny Mueller. IAoNAP
Betrayed woman, like an outgrown shirt. Betrayed. Luljeta Lleshanaku.
  WoBe, *tr. by* Henry Israeli
Betrothal of Saint Catherine, The. *Unknown. tr. by* René Bonnerjea
  "And when thus the night availed." IQMS, *tr. by* René Bonnerjea
Better Answer, A. Matthew Prior. *See* Answer to Cloe [*or* Chloe] Jealous.
Better Answer to Cloe [*or* Chloe] Jealous, A. Matthew Prior. *See* Answer to
  Cloe [*or* Chloe] Jealous.
Better Days. Essex Hemphill. CAGL
Better hurry along. (LL) Alexander's Ragtime Band. Irving Berlin.
  NAAPv.2; ReLy; TCAPo
Better not to go back to the village. Malefic Return, The. Ramón López
  Velarde. OBVE, *tr. by* Samuel Beckett
Better Resurrection, A. Christina Georgina Rossetti. ViWPN; VWP
Better stuffed in a bag; drowned. W. D. Snodgrass. BodElec *Fr.* Führer
  Bunker, The.
Better than a closet martinet. What Happened? John Wieners. FTOS

Better than a dream, it left gargantuan. My Bomb. Beckian Fritz Goldberg.
  ExTi
Better than any of you, poems. Envoy. Eleanor Ross Taylor. InGu
Better Than Crying. Ishikawa Takuboku. CAoMJL1, *tr. by* Leith Morton
Better the crime, / the suicides of lovers, the incest committed. Octavio Paz.
  PoetW *Fr.* Sunstone.
Better this way: it's you with nothing to hold on to. Elena Fanailova. CRWP,
  tr. by Stephanie Sandler
Better to be the rock above the river. La Crosse at Ninety Miles an Hour.
  Richard Eberhart. APT-2
Better to dream away this profound June dusk. Returning a Lawn to the Field
  It Was. Brendan Galvin. PoCoUp
Better to see your cheek grown hollow. Madman's Song. Elinor Wylie.
  MoAmPo
Better to wonder if ten thousand angels. World History. Carl Dennis.
  OxBoAm
Better trust all and be deceived. Faith. Frances Anne Kemble. SWaP
Better yet write the exam. (LL) B Network, The. Haki R. Madhubuti. FuFl;
  IllVoic
Better—than Music! For I—who heard it. Emily Dickinson. APN-2
Betty. Paul Mariani. SwNoth
Betty Barnes, the Book-Burner. Rosamund Marriott Watson. ViWPN
Betty by the Sea. Ronald McCuaig. NOBAu
Betuix [*or* Betwix] twell houris and ellevin [*or* eleven]. Amendis [*or* Amends]
  to the Telyouris [*or* Tailors] and Sowtaris [*or* Soutaris *or* Soutars *or*
  Shoemakers]. William Dunbar. OBSV
Between. Vladimir Holan. PoSu, *tr. by* Ian Milner and Jarmila Milner
Between. Ágnes Nemes Nagy. IQMS, *tr. by* Alan Dixon
Between. Ágnes Nemes Nagy. VCWP, *tr. by* Hugh Maxton
Between. Micheal O'Siadhail. StAl
Between. Christian Karlson Stead. PoetW
Between a centipede and a flamingo. Difference. János Pilinszky. IQMS, *tr.
  by* Peter Jay
Between a sleep and a sleep. (LL) Algernon Charles Swinburne. NAEL-6v2;
  NAEL-7v2 *Fr.* Atalanta in Calydon.
Between a Tyrant and a King. Difference Between a King and a Tyrant, The.
  Timothy Kendall. NoSic
Between Acts. Janice Lowe. InTrad
Between Aphorisms. Dorothy E. Reid. YaYoPo
Between arid mountains. Lake. Octavio Paz. TCLAP, *tr. by* Rachel Benson
Between Bombardments: A Journal. Karen Alkalay-Gut.
  "Instead of his leash." DTA
  "So we begin to plan." DTA
  "Some people terrified for their lives cut." DTA
  "Think of the children in Baghdad." DTA
  "Tonight we wait for the alarm." DTA
  "Unable to move." DTA
Between chameleons. Nora. Nengi Ilagha. NeNiPo
Between Chimneys. Abraham Sutskever. MotU, *tr. by* Ruth R. Wisse
Between city and heaven dear bird a coin. Thoroughfares await them.
  Michele Leggott. VaPo
Between clackstones. Abdourahman A. Waberi. SonAtl, *tr. by* Harry B.
  Dunbar, Kurt Ganzl, Saul Goode, Christophe Mirambeau and Ronald
  Squires
Between contractions. Two Ice Storms. Charles Behlen. TiP2
Between Days. Yusef Komunyakaa. ESEAA
Between dreams and day an immense distance. First Light. Lisa Suhair
  Majaj. PoArWo
Between dusk and dawn the weather is constantly changing. Written on the
  Lake on My Way Back to the Retreat at Stone Cliff. Hsieh Ling-yün.
  CCL1, *tr. by* John Frodsham
Between each layer of tattered, broken flesh. Burial Detail. Andrew Hudgins.
  CBCWP
Between extremities. Vacillation. William Butler Yeats. NAMCP V.1;
  NoAM
Between flocculent elbows, the soft peony wings. (LL) One of the Strangest.
  May Swenson. APT-2; OWoS
Between going and staying the day wavers. Between Going and Staying.
  Octavio Paz. PoCho; TCLAP, *tr. by* Eliot Weinberger
Between great coloured vanes the butterflies. Wings. Judith Wright.
  NOBAu
Between here and sky aloof. Bill Lavender. AnSo *Fr.* Pentacl.
Between his hands. *Unknown.* EaWin, *tr. by* J. Moussaieff Masson and W. S.
  Merwin
Between hope and failure. Inna L'vovna Lisnyanskaya. CRWP, *tr. by* Ruth
  Fainlight
Between Hovers. Michael Longley. ModIr
Between hunger and love? (LL) Mundus et Infans. W. H. Auden. MoBrPo;
  NoAM

Between Language and Desire. Silvia Curbelo. TouFir

Between life and death, I lie. Third, A. Moishe Nadir. Prolet, *tr. by* Amelia Glaser

Between living and dreaming. Antonio Machado Ruiz. WED *Fr.* Moral Proverbs and Folk Songs.

Between May and June. Kim Chôngnan. EcSo, *tr. by* Peter H. Lee

Between me and the sunset, like a dome. Man against the Sky, The. Edwin Arlington Robinson. TCAPo

Between me and the sunset, the whole of life. Present Evening, The. Eugenio Florit. TCLAP, *tr. by* Hoffman Reynolds Hays

Between me and the world. Bouquet, A. Bei Dao. PtR, *tr. by* Bonnie S. McDougall

Between midnight and Reno. Secret Life of Musical Instruments, The. C. D. Wright. CAP-8

Between my finger and my thumb. Digging. Seamus Heaney. BeAl; NAEL-6v2; NAEL-7v2; NAMCP V.2; NoP-4; NoP-5; WaAnP

Between one moment and the next she stopped speaking. Jaime Sabines. MotU *Fr.* Adam and Eve.

Between Our Folding Lips. Thomas Edward Brown. VerBaPo

Between Ourselves. Audre Lorde. ISC

Between Ourselves and the Dead! (LL) Under the Light, yet under. Emily Dickinson. FaBoVe; NAAPv.1; NCAP

Between painting a roof yesterday and the hay. Independence Day. Wendell Berry. UpMys

Between pale office workers. Looking Out to Sea Again on the Uptown Express. Sanford Fraser. UrbNat

Between pillage and rape this relief. News. William Kloefkorn. LiTh

Between pond and sheepbarn, by maples and watery birches. Sister on the Tracks, A. Donald Hall. GM

Between present and future happiness the abyss gapes. Tuti's Ice Cream. Chairil Anwar. PoetW, *tr. by* Burton Raffel

Between pride and myself scars on the look-out. Fires Smouldering Under Winter. Pierre Reverdy. AHA, *tr. by* Georges Guy and Kenneth Koch

Between Saint and Witch. Kim Sŭnghŭi. EcSo, *tr. by* K. Kim Richards and Steffen Richards

Between sandbanks marsh reflecting twilight clouds. Birthday Party. Kusano Shimpei. PFTM-1

Between Scylla and Charybdis. Yunna Petrovna Moritz. ItGoST, *tr. by* Daniel Weissbort

Between Seasons. Li-Young Lee. TRP

Between Sickle and Sword. Yekhi'el Mar. NRoS, *tr. by* Esther Raizen

Between the Acts. Elise Paschen. IllVoic

Between the bars and netting wire of. Shame. Ku Sang. CAMKP, *tr. by* Kevin O'Rourke

Between the boughs of a tall tree the sun rises like a persimmon in the gray sky. One Wintry Day. Pyong-hwa Cho. PoetW, *tr. by* Peter H. Lee

Between the brown hands of a server-lad. Maundy Thursday. Wilfred Owen. NPeEn; OxBSo

Between the conscious and the unconscious, the mind has put up a swing. What Made Kabir a Servant. Kabir. WED, *tr. by* Robert Bly

Between the dark and the daylight. Children's Hour, The. Henry Wadsworth Longfellow. APN-1; BRP; ChAP; ITBLP; TCAPo; WHSW

Between the Devil and the Deep Blue Sea. Ted Koehler. ReLy

Between the fear. Age of Terror. Denise Levertov. PFTM-2

Between the foam and the tide. To a Boy. Nancy Morejón. TANSG, *tr. by* Joy Renjirian-Burgy

Between the form of Life and Life. Emily Dickinson. APN-2

Between the gulfs, where Laurence drains the world. Joel Barlow. AmWaPo *Fr.* Columbiad, The.

Between the houses of the day. To a Voyager. Mohammed Dib. YaTCFP, *tr. by* Ronnie Scharfman

Between the idea and the word. Between. Vladimir Holan. PoSu, *tr. by* Ian Milner and Jarmila Milner

Between the legs of the bitch of God. Amorous. Alfonso D'Aquino. RMCMP, *tr. by* Rebecca Seiferle

Between the Lines. Belinda Zubicueta Carmona. TANSG, *tr. by* Celeste Kostopulos-Cooperman

Between the lines. Between the Lines. Belinda Zubicueta Carmona. TANSG, *tr. by* Celeste Kostopulos-Cooperman

Between the Lines [*Yesterday, just before being transported back to prison, I committed a terrible gaffe. Two people came out of the interrogation room. One of them, tall, elegant, speaking a very cultivated French, looked so tormented, as though about to break down. I asked him with concern: 'Vous ont-ils malmené?' 'Quiça?' 'Mais eux.'* He looked at me, shrugged his shoulders and walked on. Then the Germany sentry said: 'But that's a Gestapo man.'*]. Michael Hamburger. HP

Between the Moon and the Sun. Dave Jeddie Smith. BodElec

Between the pale blue of the morning sky. Dawn on the Willamette. Ella Higginson. SWaP

Between the railway and the mine. Blackberry, The. Norman Nicholson. MoBrPo

Between the sheets, upon the chairs. Wedding, The. Alfonso D'Aquino. RMCMP, *tr. by* Rebecca Seiferle

Between the stone huts of the vineyard hill. Deaf Mute Girl, The. István Vas. IQMS, *tr. by* Charles Abraham Wagner

Between the supercilious litany of ultra. Fairytale Land of Um, The. Jean Bleakney. NIrP

Between the Traveller and the Setting Sun. Henry David Thoreau. NAAPv.1

Between the two, I get as much as I lose. (LL) Dream of Mountaineering, A. Po Chü-i. BLT; CCL1, *tr. by* Arthur Waley

Between the warm wind's. Meadow in Spring. Gregory Orr. PfSP

Between the Wars. Robert Hass. VCAP

Between the waves. Basho. EMJL, *tr. by* Haruo Shirane

Between the wet trees and the sorry steeple. W. H. Louise Imogen Guiney. APN-2

Between the World and Me. Richard Wright. FTtHH; ISC; SSLK

Between to live and to think. Cloister. Gabriel Zaid. TCLAP, *tr. by* Mónica Hernández-Cancio

Between TV and computer screens. Middle Age, The. Roger Fanning. NevBe

Between two fears, that is, between two loves. Poetic License. Leonard Nolens. TuT, *tr. by* Michael O'Loughlin

Between two fires. (LL) Conflict, The. Cecil Day Lewis. MoBrPo; NoP-4

Between Two Lovers. Sonia Edwards. BBMWP, *tr. by* Sally Roberts Jones

Between two rivers. Langston Hughes. APT-2 *Fr.* Lenox Avenue Mural.

Between us and the farthest star. Philippe Jaccottet. StAl *Fr.* Lessons.

Between verandah railings light is creeping. Winter Dawn. Xiao Zihui. CCL1, *tr. by* John Frodsham

Between Walls. William Carlos Williams. APT-1; NAAPv.2

Between water and sky. (LL) Reflections at Lake Louise. Allen Ginsberg. BBASP; WaAnP

Between What I See and What I Say. Octavio Paz. TCLAP, *tr. by* Eliot Weinberger

Between what was. What Might Have Been. Kate Y. A. Bone. EdScPo

Between Worlds. Jacqueline Berger. AmPoNex

Between Worlds. Adam Hill. Vesp

Between Worlds. Benjamin Alire Sáenz. TiP2

Between Your Sheets. Lady Mary Wortley Montagu. LW; PEW

Between your sheets you soundly sleep. Between Your Sheets. Lady Mary Wortley Montagu. LW; PEW

Betweene the Spyder and the gentle Bee. (LL) Edmund Spenser. NoP-4; NoP-5; PBRV; WaAnP *Fr.* Amoretti.

Betweenpie mountains—lights a lovely mile. (LL) My Own Heart Let Me More Have Pity On. Gerard Manley Hopkins. MoBrPo; NoP-4; NoP-5

Betwene Mershe and Averil. *Unknown.* WaAnP

Betwixt two ridges of plow[e]d [*or* ploughed] land sat [*or* lay] Wat. Hunting of the Hare, The. Margaret Lucas Cavendish, Duchess of Newcastle. BASC; FaBoVe; NAEL-7v1; NOSC

BE2c is my 'bus; therefore I shall want, The. Pilot's Psalm, The. *Unknown.* PoWW

Beulah Railway, The. *Unknown.* GM

Beverley's Saga. Grace Nichols. WaCA

Beverly Hills, Chicago. Gwendolyn Brooks. CAP-8; ESEAA; OxAAAP *Fr.* Womanhood, The.

Beware. Kenneth Fearing. APT-2; NAAPv.2

Beware. Marina Ivanovna Tsvetayeva. WoPoe, *tr. by* David McDuff

Beware: Do Not Read This Poem [*with music*]. Ishmael Reed. NIP-4

Beware of a black. Voudou Mama. Mawiyah Kai el-Jamah Bomani. BtF

Beware of gnawing the ideogram of nothingness. Karasumaru-Mitsuhiro. ZenPo, *tr. by* Takashi Ikemoto and Lucien Stryk

Beware of the machinery of longevity. Wendell Berry. UpMys *Fr.* Prayers and Sayings of the Mad Farmer.

Beware of the month Lenaion, bad days. Hesiod. WoPoe *Fr.* Works and Days.

Beware of thinking nothing's there. Virtual Particles. Frank Wilczek. NBLV

Beware the Cuckoo. Ernest G. Moll. NOBAu

Beware the cuckoo, though she bring. Beware the Cuckoo. Ernest G. Moll. NOBAu

Beware! The Israelite of old, who tore. Warning, The. Henry Wadsworth Longfellow. APN-1; ChIV-1; NCAP; PCW; TCAPo

Beware the Kleptomaniac. Kleptomaniac, The. Roger McGough. NOxBChV

Beware the shadowy booman in the evening garden. Booman. Carmelita McGrath. Coast

Beware. There are fawns. Kydios. WoPoe, *tr. by* Sam Hamill

Bewick Finzer. Edwin Arlington Robinson. MoAmPo

Bewilderment. Georgi Rupchev. CSCBP, *tr. by* Georgi Belev and Lisa Sapinkopf

Bewilderment is Love. Lesley Dauer. PoDa

Bewitched, Bothered and Bewildered. Lorenz Hart. APT-2

Beyond. Jamie McKendrick. PoCu

Beyond any. No Precedent. Muso Soseki. EaWin, *tr. by* W. S. Merwin

Beyond barred windows. Washing Stream, The. Li Ch'ing-chao. ErotSp, *tr. by* Sam Hamill

Beyond, beyond the mountain line. Dreams. Cecil Frances Alexander. NOxBChV

Beyond Compare. Marshall Barer. ReLy

Beyond Fear. Odia Ofeimun. HBAPE

Beyond fences. Mafika Pascal Gwala. TSAP

Beyond Freedom. Michael Hannon. GeoHom

Beyond Harm. Sharon Olds. BeAl

Beyond Having. Ray Gonzalez. TouFir

Beyond here there's no map. Heading Out. Philip Booth. PoA 2002

Beyond is where the passersby end. Elena Suntsova. CRWP, *tr. by* Nika Skandiaka

Beyond Kerguelen. Henry Clarence Kendall. NOBAu

Beyond Knowledge. Alice Thompson Meynell. ChIV-1

Beyond Light. Muso Soseki. EaWin, *tr. by* W. S. Merwin

Beyond living and dreaming. Antonio Machado Ruiz. WED *Fr.* Moral Proverbs and Folk Songs.

Beyond Phigalia. Alec Derwent Hope. BMAP

Beyond Poetry. Shakuntala Hawoldar. HAWP

Beyond Recall. Sharon Bryan. P180

Beyond serenity / Gray kites. Tan Taigi. ZenPo, *tr. by* Takashi Ikemoto and Lucien Stryk

Beyond Siberia again Siberia. Regina Derieva. CRWP, *tr. by* Kevin Carey

Beyond silence, icy silence. Blessing of Snow, The. Netta Gillespie. AmZen

Beyond that first domestic kiss. Epithalamion. Terese Svoboda. ExTi

Beyond that shadowy nest of red madrones. (LL) What Could Happen. Dorianne Laux. BodElec; GeoHom; RoV

Beyond the Blue Horizon. Leo Robin. ReLy

Beyond the breakers. Joyce Mansour. MFP, *tr. by* Martin Sorrell

Beyond the broad river. / Mai-ram-bo, mai-ram-bo. (LL) Song for a Fallen Warrior. *Unknown.* AmWaPo; APN-2, *tr. by* John Mason Browne

Beyond the Chiltern coast, this church. Edlesborough. Anne Ridler. SacPr

Beyond the East Gate. *Unknown.* TAL

Beyond the empty crossroads store. Green-Eyed Boy after Reading Whitman and Sandburg. Dave Etter. ViWalt

Beyond the far infrared, microwaves heat our coffee. St. Brigid's day opens. Imbolc. Jeanne Shannon. ICANM

Beyond the forbidding fence. Keiho Soga. NAAPv.2

Beyond the Hudson's. Undertaking in New Jersey, The. George Oppen. GPTC; OxBoAm

Beyond the Image. Henriqueta Lisboa. TCLAP, *tr. by* Hélcio Veiga Costa

Beyond the Image: plot of what is unutterable. Beyond the Image. Henriqueta Lisboa. TCLAP, *tr. by* Hélcio Veiga Costa

Beyond the iron gates set into the walls. Cemetery in the City. Luis Cernuda. RaW, *tr. by* Robert Bly

Beyond the last window. Blind. Vincente Huidobro. CuPo

Beyond the low marsh-meadows and the beach. Pines and the Sea, The. Christopher Pearse Cranch. ColAP

Beyond the night. Night. Marjorie Agosin. ExTi

Beyond the park, at River's Head. Drinking at Crooked River. Tu Fu [*or* Du Fu]. CrYelRi, *tr. by* Sam Hamill

Beyond the people. Escape Artist, The. Kevin Young. GT; AmPoNex

Beyond the point where the rivers. Old Man Advancing. Muso Soseki. EaWin, *tr. by* W. S. Merwin

Beyond the rapture and the dread? (LL) Abduction, The. Stanley Kunitz. CAP-8; WeW-3

Beyond the red traffic light, young chestnut leaves. Czeslaw Milosz. BodElec *Fr.* Lithuania, After Fifty-two Years.

Beyond the ridge there is a field of grass. Field Beyond the Ridge. George Scarbrough. LPSFW

Beyond the riverbank, dredgers. Windy Day. No Hyangnim. EcSo, *tr. by* Aimee N. Kwon

Beyond the silent aurochs-haunted forests. Cape of Wild Flies, A. Bernard Bador. ConPit, *tr. by* Clayton Eshleman

Beyond the snatch of time, my daily life. Juo. ZenPo, *tr. by* Takashi Ikemoto and Lucien Stryk

Beyond the steady rock the steady sea. Fable, The. Yvor Winters. APT-2

Beyond the view of crossroads ringed with breath. Rubaiyat. Mimi Khalvati. MFPA

Beyond the waste of commerce there are hills. Office Window. Llewelyn Wyn Griffith. AngWePo

Beyond the World. Muso Soseki. EaWin, *tr. by* W. S. Merwin

Beyond Vermont's green hills, against the skies. Richard Henry Wilde. APN-1 *Fr.* Hesperia.

Beyond: "Whenever I love a woman." Fazil Hüsnü Daglarca. NaPG, *tr. by* Talat Sait Halman

Beyond where the wild geese fly. Yun Sŏndo. CATKP *Fr.* Angler's Calendar, The.

Beyond Words. Robert Frost. Spl; WeW-3

Bgawk! / There goes that Polly again! Poem for El Lissitzky. Ron Padgett. NYP2

Bhagavad-Gita, The. *Unknown. tr. by* Barbara Stoler Miller

  "Arjuna, his war flag a rampant monkey." WoPoe, *tr. by* Barbara Stoler Miller

  "Arjuna sat dejected." WoPoe, *tr. by* Barbara Stoler Miller

  "Hear father yet thou Long-Armed Lord! these latest words I say." TAL

  "Learn now, dear Prince! how, if thy soul be set." TAL

  "Now will I open unto thee—whose heart." TAL

  "Tell me." WoPoe, *tr. by* Barbara Stoler Miller

  "Therefore, who doeth work rightful to do." TAL

  "This, for my soul's peace, have I heard from Thee." TAL

  "Who is that BRAHMA? What that Soul of Souls." TAL

Bhakti Yogi Buys a Bike, The. Gus Ferguson. ArBi

Bias of the will betray, The. (LL) Ralph Waldo Emerson. APN-1; TCAPo *Fr.* Quatrains.

Bibelforscher, Die. Waldo Williams. BBMWP, *tr. by* Rowan Williams

Bible Buckle, The. Rozell Caldwell. BtF

Bible Defence of Slavery. Frances Ellen Watkins Harper. APN-2; NAAPv.1

Bible is an antique Volume, The. Emily Dickinson. APN-2; ChIV-1; NAAL-3; NoP-4; NoP-5

Bible Lesson. Harvey Shapiro. TaR

Bible. Poland. Lodz Ghetto. Nineteen hundred forty one. Micrographic Manuscript, Miniature (2). Esther Ettinger. DTA, *tr. by* Mariana Barr

Bible. Spain. Saragossa. Fourteen hundred and something. Micrographic Manuscript, Miniature (1). Esther Ettinger. DTA, *tr. by* Mariana Barr

Bible Study. Gloria C. Oden. ESEAA; GT

Bible, The [*with music*]. Lizelia Augusta Jenkins Moorer. CBWP-3

Biblical Also-Rans. Charles Harper Webb. SUP

Biblical Meditations. Yehuda Amichai. WoPoe, *tr. by* Barbara Harshav and Benjamin Harshav

Biblical Winnipeg. Clive Holden. PoPra

Bibliographers, The. Geoffrey Hill. UpMys

Bibliolaters. James Russell Lowell.

  God Is Not Dumb. ChIV-1

Bibliothèque. Pierre Alféri. YaTCFP

"Biby's" Epitaph. *Unknown.* NOxBChV,

Bic lighter, A. Tee. Reuben Jackson. UnSA

Bicameral. Linda Gregerson. AmAlph

Bicameralization, The. Ralph Adamo.

  16. AnSo

  17. AnSo

Bicause I have the still kept fro lyes and blame. Petrarch. OBVE

Bicentennial Anti-Poem for Italian-American Women. Daniela Gioseffi. FTtHH; UnSA

Bicentennial Barbie. Denise Duhamel. AmPoNex

Bickering. Elke Erb. OnScMo, *tr. by* Rosmarie Waldrop

Bicycle [for Derek Peat]. David Malouf. ArBi; BMAP

Bicycle. Livingston Taylor. ArBi

Bicycle, The. James Brown. ArBi

Bicycle, The. Risa Lichtman. ArBi

Bicycle, The. James Reaney. ArBi

Bicycle, The. Stan Rice. ArBi

Bicycle and I, The. *Unknown.* ArBi

Bicycle Days. Robin Becker. ArBi

Bicycle Dream. Lauris Edmond. ArBi

Bicycle Glee Song, A. Glory Anna. ArBi

Bicycle Poem. Noelle Kocot. IIR

Bicycle Race in *Beowulf*, The. David Galef. ArBi

Bicycle Racers, The. Ann Townsend. AmPoNex; NeAmPo

Bicycle Ride, The. Henry Israeli. ArBi

Bicycle rolls on the road, A. Malcolm de Chazal. SurPaPo *Fr.* Sens Plastique.

Bicycle Slow Race, The. Claire Bateman. ArBi

Bicycle Song (For Women). Robert Williams Buchanan. ArBi

Bicycle Sprint. Pamela Alexander. ArBi

Bicycle Thief, The. Bill Berkson. AHA

Bicycler's Song, A. *Unknown.* ArBi

Bicyclers, The. Harriet Monroe. ArBi

Bicycles. Andrey Andreievich Voznesensky. ArBi, *tr. by* Anselm Hollo

Bicycles and the Apex, The. George Oppen. CalPo

Bicycles go by in twos and threes, The. Inniskeen Road: July Evening. Patrick Kavanagh. NAMCP V.1; NoAM; NPeEn; OxBSo; StAl

Bicycles lie, The. Bicycles. Andrey Andreievich Voznesensky. ArBi, *tr. by* Anselm Hollo

Bicycles! Tricycles! John Banister Tabb. ArBi

Bicycle's upturned. Father, The. Only Dream, The. Semezdin Mehmedinović. PML, *tr. by* Antonela Glavinic and Kathleen Jamie

Bicycling Away from the Library. William Hedrington. ArBi

Bid a strong ghost stand at the head. Prayer for My Son, A. William Butler Yeats. OxAEP-2; RaBo

Bid for a new majority, The. No Transport. Tony Lopez. Oth

Bid me Good Morning. (LL) Life. Anna Laetitia Barbauld. NAEL-6v2; NAEL-7v2; NoP-4; NoP-5; OBEV; OxAEP-1

Bid me remember, O my gracious Lord. Mary Elizabeth Coleridge. SacPr *Fr.* Death.

Bid me strike a match and blow. (LL) In Memory of Eva Gore-Booth and Con Markievicz. William Butler Yeats. GPTC; NAMCP V.1; NoAM; NPeEn; OBMV

Bid me to live, and I will live. To Anthea, Who May Command Him Anything. Robert Herrick. BASC; NOSC; OBEV; OxBEV

Bidding Farewell to Secretary Chou. Yu Hsin. CrYelRi, *tr. by* Sam Hamill

Bidding Spell. Penn Kemp. IFF

Bidin' My Time. Ira Gershwin. ReLy

Biding Farewell to My Cousin, Haeil, on His Return Home. Buhyu Sunsoo. BecRai, *tr. by* Kim Daljin, Kim Won-Chung and Christopher Merrill

Bids Farewell to Lesbos. Mary Robinson. CenSon; RWP

Bids spheres and atoms in just order move. (LL) Hand and Foot, The [*or* Hand and the Foot, The]. Jones Very. APN-1; SacPr

Bien m'en souvient. (LL) John Skelton. NoP-4; NoP-5 *Fr.* Phyllyp Sparowe [*or* Philip Sparrow *or* Phillip Sparow].

Bienvenido Poem for Sophie. Sandra Cisneros. TiP2

Big animals: despondent / at table: unsated, The. Poem. Paul Klee. PFTM-1

Big as a down duvet the night. Lullaby. Molly Peacock. PasH

Big Baboon, The. Joseph Hilaire Pierre Belloc. MoBrPo

Big Bad Art Thing, The. Carter Ratcliff. KGB

Big Bar. Kenward Elmslie. PmAP

Big Bend: Lion Warning. Jane Epton Seale. TiP2

Big Billie Potts was big and stout. Ballad of Billie Potts, The. Robert Penn Warren. FuPo

Big Bluejay Composition. Ron Padgett. PmAP

Big Boy came / Carrying a mermaid. Catch. Langston Hughes. NoAM

Big Boy Rich wants to mek a profit. De Rich Getting Rich. Benjamin Zephaniah. RSaN

Big Cars. Jane Flanders. PBCAP

Big Cars. Wesley McNair. PoA 2002

Big Chill Variations. Reuben Jackson. UnSA

Big core into the spreading nettles, The. (LL) My Grandfather and His Apple-Tree. John Ormond. AngWePo; TCAWP

Big Daddy Lipscomb, who used to help them up. Say Good-bye to Big Daddy. Randall Jarrell. MoASP

Big doors of the country barn stand open and ready, The. Walt Whitman. ColAP; ITBLP; WaAnP *Fr.* Song of Myself.

Big dumb animal states. Michael McClure. WANABP *Fr.* Plum Stones.

Big e, The. Ernst Jandl. OnScMo, *tr. by* Guy Bennet

Big Fire at the Architectural College, The. Andrey Andreievich Voznesensky. CLPP, *tr. by* Anselm Hollo

Big fish on the line. George Stanley. NLPA *Fr.* Mountains and Air.

Big Fort Island Buddha. Mac Lojowski. AmZen

Big Girls. Tracey Herd. MFPA

Big Glen, The. Colette Ni Ghallchóir. NIrP, *tr. by the author*

Big God. Big World Look Out. Jeneanne Collins. BRtP

Big guns go boom! (for Mark Prejsnar). Dana Lisa Lustig. AnSo

Big House Revisited, The. Tony Medina. SpirFl

Big Jigsaw. Chris Forhan. NAPBL

Big John. Norman J. Loftis. SpirFl

Big John's Tears Fall to the River. Siobhan Campbell. MFPA

Big L, The. Vera Hérold. SurWo, *tr. by* Guy Ducornet

Big living room is crowded, the. Fifties Rock Party, 1985. Judith Berke. SwNoth

Big man in batakari, The. Steps. Kojo Laing. NAfrP

Big Momma. Haki R. Madhubuti. AmFaPo

Big muddy daddy my daddys gris-gris to the world, A. Mud Water Shango. GT; SeSe

Big Mystical Circus, The. Jorge de Lima. GPTC, *tr. by* Dudley Poore

Big No-No, The. Chris Greenhalgh. NeBl

Big orange whale came up the Clyde, A. Big Orange Whale, The. Matt McGinn. EdScPo

Big Parade, The. Stephen Knight. NeBl; TCAWP

Big piece has been cut out of the fir hedge now (the garden fence), A. No, That Can't Be. Erica Pedretti. MotU, *tr. by* Stuart Friebert

Big rats! Big rats! *Unknown.* ColAnChi *Fr.* Classic of Odes.

Big Rig the Baroque Sky. Tessa Rumsey. LegDan

Big river goes east, The. Lyrics to the Tune "The Charms of Niennu": At the Red Cliff I Ponder Over Antiquity. Su Tung-p'o. WoPoe, *tr. by* David Lattimore

Big Rock Candy Mountains, The [*with music*]. *Unknown.* FaBoA

Big Rock-Candy Mountain, The. Louis Edward Sissman. GM

Big rocks into pebbles. Rocks. Florence Parry Heide. NTCP

Big Scales, The. Olav H. Hauge. WED, *tr. by* Robert Bly

Big ship sails on the alley alley oh, The. Big Ship Sails, The. *Unknown.* FaBoVe

Big Ship Sails, The. *Unknown.* FaBoVe

Big sleep, the high window, The. John Whitworth. NewEx

Big Spectacular Play. Louis Aragon. YaTCFP, *tr. by* Mary Ann Caws and Jean-Pierre Cauvin

Big steel tourist shield says maybe, The. On a Field Trip at Fredericksburg. Dave Jeddie Smith. LPSFW; PoPoPo

Big sweet muscles of an athlete's dream, The. Massacre of the Innocents. Alec Derwent Hope. GI

Big Swimming. Edwin Ford Piper. APT-1

Big Tease. Ania Walwicz. BMAP

Big Thicket Words. James Cody. TiP2

Big toe located on each of the two feet of man, The. Rule and Its Exception, The. Russell Edson. OxBoAm

Big tom was a black nigga man. River Town Packin House Blues. Quincy Troupe. LoL

Big White Dress, The. Lisa Rosenberg. PoDa

Big white sheet of paper. Seen from an Island in Godavari. Ismail. HotL, *tr. by* V. Narayana Rao

Big Wind. Theodore Roethke. ColAP; HarvBoo; TRP; WaAnP

Big with great purposes and proud, they sat. Homer. OBVE *Fr.* Iliad, The.

Big words. Del Ray Cross. FreRad

Big Words, The. Brendan Kennelly. EmeKit

Big World Look Out. Jeneanne Collins. BRtP

Big yellow woman. Laurel Street, 1950. Dorothy Perry Thompson. SpirFl

Big young bareheaded woman, A. Proletarian Portrait. William Carlos Williams. BLT; OxBoAm; SAmP

Big Zeb Johnson. Everett Hoagland. GT; OxAAAP

Bigamy. Roy McFadden. PNI *Fr.* Memories of Chinatown.

Big-ball elephant. Elephant. *Unknown.* SonAtl, *tr. by* Brenda Ginever, Malcolm Ginever and David Mahundiri

Big-Business. (LL) Thus / Hides the. George Oppen. APT-2; PFTM-1

Bigger fish have country cousins here, The. Frank Ormsby. PNI *Fr.* Northern Spring, A.

Bigger half, The? There's no such thing. Twice the Man. Aidan Rooney-Céspedes. NIrP

Bigger thomas. Big House Revisited, The. Tony Medina. SpirFl

Biggest snowstorm to hit Denver in twenty years, The. Poem for Salt. Leroy V. Quintana. P180

Bight, The. Elizabeth Bishop. APT-2; EmeKit; PoetW; VCAP

Biglow Papers, The. James Russell Lowell.
  ('Cruetin Sarjunt, The.) TCAPo
  Introduction.
    "Old Joe is gone, who saw hot Percy goad." TCAPo
  Letter, A ("Thrash away, you'll hev to rattle"). AmWaPo
  Letter Six—The Pious Editors' Creed. APN-1; NCAP

Bigness of cannon, The. E. E. Cummings. MoAmPo

Big-nose looks best in mountain-coarse clothes. My Man Pa Replies. Li Ho. ColAnChi, *tr. by* Burton Watson

Big-uddered piebald cattle low. Christmas Holiday. Alun Lewis. PoWW

Bike Ride on a Roman Road. Alice Oswald. NeBrP

Bike Ride with Older Boys. Laura Kasischke. ArBi

Bilbao Churchyard. Bobi Jones. ATSWP, *tr. by* Robert Minhinnick

Bilbea. Carl Sandburg. APT-1

Bilbea, I was in Babylon on Saturday night. Bilbea. Carl Sandburg. APT-1

Bilberries. Gerda Mayer. Spl

Bilingual Instructions. Harryette Mullen. PrTe

Bilingual Means Having Two Tongues. David Johnson. ICANM

Bilingual Sestina. Julia Alvarez. ExTi; FFC; WaAnP

Bill. P. G. Wodehouse. ReLy

Bill Bailey, Won't You Please Come Home. Hughie Cannon. NAAPv.2

Bill collectors gather. Ain't We Got Fun. Raymond B. Egan and Gustave Kahn. ReLy

Bill Gets Burned. Howard Phelps Putnam. APT-2; OxBoAm

Bill gripped the can in both hands and dashed it upward. Ashes. Andrew Hudgins. CAP-8

Bill hated the separation implied by the term. Nature Poetry. Meg Kearney. UrbNat

Bill (Original Version). P. G. Wodehouse. ReLy

Bill, Posted, A. BAP-97

Bill / Was ill. Careless Talk. Mark Hollis. NBLV

Bill Williams was in Hell without a guide. Bill Gets Burned. Howard Phelps Putnam. APT-2; OxBoAm

Billboard-poetry: ambiguous, harsh, journalistic. Commentary on an Old Review. Géza Szöcs. ConPit, tr. by Enikö Bollobás and Clayton Eshleman

Billie Holiday. Sterling Plumpp. IllVoic

Billie Holiday Chronicles, The. Patricia Jones.
    Birth of Rhythm and Blues, The. ReTh

Billie Holiday's burned voice. Canary. Rita Dove. ESEAA; LoL; OxAAAP; SeSe; VCAP

Billie in Silk. Angela Jackson. ReTh; SeSe

Billie's Blues. Alfred Corn. CAGL

Billions of maggots are being sucked into a whirlpool. Dance. Chông Hwajin. EcSo, tr. by Julie C. Park

Billowing cloth napkin still tucked into my collar, The. Going Wrong in the House of Neptune. David Clewell. MAAN

Billowing clouds surging across the heavens. Tune: "Fisherman's Pride." Li Ch'ing-chao. ColAnChi, tr. by Jiaosheng Wang

Billy. Oktavi Allison. BRtP

Billy. Linda McCarriston. LoL

Billy Batter. Dennis Lee. TLR

Billy Budd, Foretopman. Herman Melville.
    Billy in the Darbies. APN-2; NCAP; WoPoe

Billy in one of his nice new sashes. Harry Graham. NBLV; NOxBChV Fr. Some Ruthless Rhymes.

Billy rode on pinto horse. Outlaws. Whitney Montgomery. TiP2

Billy the Kid broke a man. Prison, San Elizario, Texas, The. Ray Gonzales. TiP2

Billygoat watches me work. Keith Abbott. WhBo

Billy's Famous Lounge. Joe Wenderoth. NAPBL

Biluuza ti ridxi. Huadxí que ziyaba. Víctor Terán. RMCMP

Biluxe / ne ngasi nga laani. Biluxe. Víctor Terán. RMCMP

Binary. Chris Wallace-Crabbe. OBCoV

Bind your straight hair. Thessalian. Winifred Bryher. PoA 2002

Binds all wounds. True Love. Kathleen Norris. UpMys

Bindweed. J. B. Bryan. ICANM

Bing Crosby was singing "White Christmas." When I First Saw Snow. Gregory Djanikian. UnSA

Bingen on the Rhine. Caroline Elizabeth Norton. TreFP

Binnorie; or, The Two Sisters. Unknown. OBEV

Binsey Poplars (Felled 1879). Gerard Manley Hopkins. NAEL-6v2; NAEL-7v2; NAMCP V.1; NoAM; PtR

¿Binti te wajwal mak ay yan a wajwal. Ak'a ta majtanal te lotil. Pedro Pérez Conde. RMCMP

Bio / autography (or, 18th-Century Multiculturalism). Evie Shockley. PoDa

Bio 7. David Moolten. BloBone

Biografía Incompleta. Gerardo Diego. RaW

Biografía, Poesía y Destino. León Felipe. RaW

Biographia Literaria. Joan Retallack. FTOS

Biographical News. Daria Menicanti. CItWP, tr. by Cinzia Sartini Blum and Lara Trubowitz

Biography. Imamu Amiri Baraka. EGAG

Biography. Mariella Bettarini. CItWP, tr. by Cinzia Sartini Blum and Lara Trubowitz

Biography: "Dog scatters her body in sleep, The." Michael Ondaatje. NAMCP V.2; NoAM

Biography of a Woman, The. Ferenc Juhász. ConPit, tr. by Clayton Eshleman and Gyula Kodolanyi

Biography, Poetry, Destiny. León Felipe. RaW, tr. by W. S. Merwin

Biological Imperative. Joan Houlihan. IAoNAP

Biological Light. Primus St. John. GifTon

Biology Teacher. Zbigniew Herbert. PoSu, tr. by John Carpenter and Bogdana Carpenter

Bio-Rodent-Oriole. Edwin Torres. HeMarv

Biplane shuttles through the telegraph wires, The. Sunday. Philippe Soupault. PFTM-1

Biral Biral. Lionel Fogarty. VaPo

Biral came down one day. Biral Biral. Lionel Fogarty. VaPo

Birch bark. Lorine Niedecker. FTOS Fr. Lake Superior.

Birch bark, soundings in the linden wood. Standing at Pasternak's Table, Peredelkino. James Ragan. TWW

Birch begins to crack its outer sheath, The. Young Birch, A. Robert Frost. SAmP

Birch Canoe. Carter Revard. NoP-4

Birches. Robert Frost. AmFaPo; APT-1; BrAP; FaBoVe; HarvBoo; HeIP-4; ITBLP; MoAmPo; NAAL-5; NAAPv.2; NAMCP V.1; NoAM; NoP-4; NoP-5; OxBoAm; PoPoPo; SAmP; SoSe-8; TCAPo; TFi; TRP; WaAnP

Birches falling down the hillside. (LL) For My Grandmother, Bridget Halpin. Michael Hartnett. ModIr; PBCIP

Birches, Revisited: October. Ira Sadoff. PfSP

Birches stand in their beggar's row, The. February: The Boy Breughel. Norman Dubie. AmAlph

Bird. Kim Addonizio. UrbNat

Bird. James E. Cherry. BtF

Bird. Joy Harjo. SeSe

Bird. Frieda Hughes. NeBl

Bird. Ágnes Nemes Nagy. PoSu, tr. by Bruce Berlind

Bird. Karen Press. TSAP

Bird. Yona Volach. DTA, tr. by Miriyam Glazer

Bird, A. Sheila Wingfield. MoWP; StAl

Bird, The. Robert Greacen. PNI

Bird, The. Moyshe-Leyb Halpern. OxBoAm, tr. by John Hollander

Bird, The. "St.-John Perse." OWoS, tr. by Robert Fitzgerald

Bird, The. Michael Savitz. FreRad

Bird, The. Henry Vaughan. OBEV

Bird, The. Susan M. Whitmore. AmPoNex

Bird and man. Unknown. SonAtl, tr. by Serone Bell, Andy Cox and Patricia Jabbeh Wesley

Bird / and shadow of bird. Bird. Karen Press. TSAP

Bird and the Bell, The. Christopher Pearse Cranch. APN-1

Bird and Waterfall Music. Wang Wei. NDACCP, tr. by Kenneth Rexroth

Bird at Dawn, The [with music]. Harold Monro. MoBrPo

Bird Bee. Bob Cobbing. Oth

Bird came down the Walk, A. Emily Dickinson. AmFaPo; APN-2; ColAP; HeIP-4; ITBLP; MoAmPo; NAAL-3; NAAL-5; NAAPv.1; NAMCP V.1; NAWM-7v2; NCAP; NoAM; NoP-4; NoP-5; NTCP; OxBoAm; SAmP; TFi

Bird carrying the wind in his wings, The. What Freedom Said. Georgi Borisov. CSCBP, tr. by Georgi Belev and Lisa Sapinkopf

Bird chase bird. Bush Telegram. Tom Pickard. Oth

Bird chirped at my window this morning, A. April. Amy Lowell. PoBW

Bird Close to Old Houses, A. Aliyah Abdul-Salaam. AnVo, tr. by Mohamed Enani

Bird does not live / charles christopher parker is dead. Assassination of Charlie Parker, The. Arthur Brown. SeSe

Bird dressed as solitude and tears. Bird dressed as solitude and tears. Jeannette Miller. TANSG, tr. by Paula Vega

Bird family. Joanne Kyger. WhBo

Bird flew tangent-wise to the open window, A. Bird, The. Robert Greacen. PNI

Bird had come to the very end of its song, The. End of the World, The. Miroslav Holub. BeAl, tr. by Ewald Osers

Bird half wakened in the lunar moon, A. On a Bird Singing in its Sleep. Robert Frost. APT-1

Bird in a Gilded Cage, A. Arthur J. Lamb. NAAPv.2; TCAPo

Bird in the hand, A. What My Teachers Taught Me I Try to Teach My Students. Maura Eichner. UpMys

Bird is meditation, The. Bird is Meditation, The. Amina Saïd. HAWP, tr. by Eric Sellin

Bird Language. Christopher Pearse Cranch. APN-1

Bird Lives. Faye Moskowitz. MiVo

Bird, most ardent for life of all our blood kin, The. Bird, The. "St.-John Perse." OWoS, tr. by Robert Fitzgerald

Bird Nests. Angela Shaw. NeAmPo

Bird of Death. Sharon Olinka. TWW

Bird of Endless Time, The. James Laughlin. WeW-3

Bird of Fire, The. Alda Merini. CItWP, tr. by Cinzia Sartini Blum and Lara Trubowitz

Bird of the tropic! thou, who lov'st to stray. To the White Bird of the Tropic. Helen Maria Williams. CenSon

Bird of the woodland, sing me a song. To the Mock-Bird. Mary Weston Fordham. CBWP-2

Bird on a Jaunt. T. Harri Jones. TCAWP

Bird, probably a grackle, got caught in, A. Turning Prose into Poetry. Bernadette Mayer. NYP2

Bird rests in the air, the stone rests on the land, The. "Angelus Silesius." GePo Fr. Cherubical Wanderer, The.

Bird saw the young Burara girls, twisting their strings, making string figures, The. Unknown. NOBAu Fr. Goulburn Island Song Cycle.

Bird sings from the tree, A. Heartsong. Khaled Mattawa. BAP-97; NAPBL; NeAmPo

Bird Sips Water. Keith Bosley. Spl

Bird Song. William Carlos Williams. SAmP

Bird Song, The. Mrs. Henry Linden. CBWP-4

Bird, start up your moan, your whine. Svetlana Ivanova. CRWP, *tr. by* Angela Livingstone

Bird Starver's Cry. *Unknown.* FaBoVe

Bird swerved dapple-white in the blue sky, The. Winged in Gold. Euros Bowen. OBWVE, *tr. by* the author

Bird that I don't know, A. Country Life, A. Randall Jarrell. MoAmPo

Bird, the long throat bent back, and the eyes in hiding. (LL) Winter Swan. Louise Bogan. APT-2; ColAP; OWoS; OxBoAm

Bird, to Its Young, The. Mihály Tompa. IQMS, *tr. by* Watson Kirkconnell

Bird with the Coppery, Keen Claws, The. Wallace Stevens. OxBoAm

Bird, you sing and sing. Kukutis in the Reich's Guard House. Marcelijus Martinaitis. TWW, *tr. by* Laima Sruoginis

Birdbones. David Brendon Hopes. UpMys

Birdcatcher, The. Ralph Hodgson. MoBrPo

Bird-cherry was my wife, The. Yury Timofeievich Galanskov. TCRusP, *tr. by* Olive Dehn

Bird-creole or the billowing froth of bride song. Iain Sinclair. Oth *Fr.* Ebbing of Kraft, The.

Bird-Cry Creek. Wang Wei. NDACCP, *tr. by* David Hinton

Birdfoot's Grampa. Joseph Bruchac. UnSA

Birdie McReynolds. Samuel Hoffenstein. NBLV

Birdland. Allen Fisher. Oth

Bird-Language. W. H. Auden. OWoS

Birdless heaven, seadusk, one lone star, A. Tutto è Sciolto. James Joyce. OBMV

Birds: "They don't plow, nor do they sow." Alexander Gerov. CSCBP, *tr. by* Georgi Belev and Lisa Sapinkopf

Birds. John Giorno.

"This is a field book." AHA

Birds. Frieda Hughes. NeBl; StAl

Birds. Robinson Jeffers. APT-1; NAAPv.2

Birds. Judith Wright. NoP-4

Birds. Subnarcosis. Andrea Zanzotto. ItPo, *tr. by* Gayle Ridinger

Birds, The. Linda Pastan. PfSP

Birds against the April wind, The. What the Birds Said. John Greenleaf Whittier. APN-1; OxBoAm

Birds and Fishes. Robinson Jeffers. NAAL-5; NoP-4; NoP-5; WaAnP

Birds and leaves disconnect in Fall. Zimmer in Fall. Paul Zimmer. CA

Birds and sunlight. Yellow. De Leon Harrison. EGAG

Birds are everywhere, and hardly sing, The. Native American Birds, The. Annie Finch. RWB

Birds are gone to bed the cows are still, The. Hares at Play. John Clare. WoPoe

Birds are in the air at ease. Birds Are in the Air at Ease. Francisco de Quevedo y Villegas. SpanPo, *tr. by* William M. Davis

Birds are in the bushes and the wolf is at the door, The. (LL) Everything in Its Place. Arthur Guiterman. AmWit; NBLV; OBCoV

Birds are speckled and tame tonight, The. Gareth Alban Davies. BBMWP *Fr.* Ruins.

Birds at Winter Nightfall. Thomas Hardy. MoBrPo

Birds cannot walk, beasts cannot fly. You're No Exception. Yüan Chěn. CCL1, *tr. by* John A. Scott

Birds even in the city. New York. Steven Blevins. PoCoUp

Birds fan, grubs snout. Treeback. *Unknown.* SonAtl, *tr. by* Ian Bevan, Nancy Gallas, Kurt Ganzl, Lorna MacIntosh, Bill Matthews and Tai Walker

Bird's fire-fangled feathers dangle down, The. (LL) Of Mere Being. Wallace Stevens. APT-1; BLPJKO; NAAPv.2; NAMCP V.1; NoP-4; NoP-5; OxBoAm; PtR; WoPoe

Birds fly away, The. Pei Di and Wang Wei. CCL1 *Fr.* Wheel River.

Birds / Fly into the depths of our existence. Seed, The. Tomasz Jastrun. AF, *tr. by* Michael March *and* Jaroslaw Anders

Birds go to sleep by the sweet, wild twist of her song, The. (LL) Outlaw of Loch Lene, The. Jeremiah Joseph Callanan. IrLP; OBEV, *tr. by* Jeremiah Joseph Callanan

Birds have long been silent, The. Cult of Love, The. Hadewijch. NAWM-7v1, *tr. by* Peter Dronke

Birds have vanished down the sky, The. Zazen on Ching-t'ing Mountain. Li Po. CrYelRi, *tr. by* Sam Hamill

Birds have vanished into the sky, The. Birds have Vanished, The. Li Po. BLT, *tr. by* Sam Hamill

Birds have vanished, The. Snowy River. Liu Tsung-yüan. CrYelRi, *tr. by* Sam Hamill

Birds: "I'm living in one place so long." Maxine Hong Kingston. FaoP

Birds in human shape. Tomas Tranströmer. WoBe *Fr.* Haiku.

Birds in Snow. "H. D." APT-1; PoA 2002; WaAnP

Birds in the Graveyard. Helon Habila. NeNiPo

Birds in the high Hall-garden. Alfred Tennyson. NAEL-6v2 *Fr.* Maud [A Monodrama].

Birds just passed over. Wounded Self-Portrait, A. Homero Aridjis. WoBe, *tr. by* George McWhirter

Birds Know. Myra Cohn Livingston. CalPo

Birds know how to lift their wings. Birds Know. Myra Cohn Livingston. CalPo

Birds Leaving. Johanna Kruit. TuT, *tr. by* Medbh McGuckian

Birds / living in the cage. Birds. Gensui. NAAPv.2

Birds Love the Net. Kondepudi Nirmala. HotL, *tr. by* V. Narayana Rao

Birds' Nest. John Clare. OWoS

Birds Nest. Gloria Fuertes. RaBo; RaW, *tr. by* Philip Levine

Birds nest in my arms. Birds Nest. Gloria Fuertes. RaBo; RaW, *tr. by* Philip Levine

Birds' Nests. Edward Thomas. OWoS

Birds of Detroit. Greg Pape. PBCAP

Birds of Passage. Valerie Thornton. EdScPo

Birds of Passage, The. Jones Very. NCAP

Birds of Prey. Claude McKay. APT-1

Birds of spring. Kitahara Hakushū. CAoMJL1, *tr. by* Donald Keene

Birds' Refuge, The. Sojourner Kincaid Rolle. GeoHom

Birds sang in the wet trees, The. Wet Evening in April. Patrick Kavanagh. BeAl; OPOU

Birds singing. Jack Kerouac. WhBo

Bird's Song, A. Dame Edith Sitwell. NALW

Birds suddenly dropped dead. Fata Morgana in Flanders. Willem M. Roggeman. TuT, *tr. by* Gabriel Rosenstock

Birds That Woke Us: An Urban Pastoral, The. Jeffrey Harrison. UrbNat

Birds, we're birds. Paddle-song. *Unknown.* SonAtl, *tr. by* Mo Alexander, Edward Astley and Karun Badel

Birds with bones of glass, The. Words, The. Michael Palmer. WoBe

Bird-Shooting. Eugenio Montale. ItPo, *tr. by* Gayle Ridinger

Bird-Singing Stream. Wang Wei. ChinPo, *tr. by* Ye Weilian [*or* Yeh Wei-lien *or* Wai-lim Yip]

Birdsong. *Unknown, fr. Terezin Concentration Camp.* INSAB

Birdsong 2. *Unknown, fr. Terezin Concentration Camp.* INSAB

Birdsong for September 11, 2001. Vivian Shipley. RWB

Birdsong from Inside the Egg. Timothy Donnelly. LegDan

Birdsong Torrent. Wang Wei. CCL1, *tr. by* Jerome P. Seaton

Birdsong Valley. Wang Wei. CrYelRi, *tr. by* Sam Hamill

Birdsongs that sound like the steady determined tapping. Zen Living. Dick Allen. PoA 2002

Birdwatchers of America [*with music*]. Anthony Hecht. NAMCP V.2; NoAM

Birdwatching at Fan Lake [*with music*]. Anita Endrezze. HATNAP

Bird-witted. Marianne Moore. APT-1

Birmingham. Louis MacNeice. MoBrPo; OxAEP-2

Birth. Elizabeth Bartlett. MoWP

Birth. Gioconda Belli. TANSG, *tr. by* Steven F. White

Birth. Louise Erdrich. NoP-4; NoP-5

Birth. Kelly Elaine Navies. BRtP

Birth, 1975. Cheryl Van Dyke. GifTon

Birth, A. N. Revathi Devi. HotL, *tr. by* V. Narayana Rao

Birth, The. Paul Muldoon. EmeKit

Birth and Death of Bette Davis, The. Jackie Kay. MoWP

Birth and the grave, that are not as they were. (LL) Alastor; or, The Spirit of Solitude. Percy Bysshe Shelley. NAEL-6v2; NAEL-7v2

Birth, by analogy, is a counterexample to. Reservation. Jean Day. ASA

Birth: "Camels pregnant." Bernard Bador. ConPit, *tr. by* Clayton Eshleman

Birth Day. Elise Paschen. P180

Birth Day. Andrew Waterman. PML

Birth days: as of the spirit. Birthday Triptych. Peter Scupham. HarvBoo

Birth in a narrow room, The. Gwendolyn Brooks. NoP-4; NoP-5

Birth is Death, Death is Birth [*epigram*]. Friedrich von Logau. GePo, *tr. by* George C. Schoolfield

Birth of a Coachman. Paul Durcan. PBCIP

Birth of a Nation. Milton Arana. OWABP

Birth of God (from an Early Photograph), The. James Ragan. Vesp

Birth of Jesus, The [*with music*]. Josephine D. Henderson Heard. CBWP-4

Birth of KNO₃, The. Erasmus Darwin. STuOW *Fr.* Economy of Vegetation, The.

Birth of Love. Robert Penn Warren. APT-2; VCAP

1. The Birth of Mary. Rainer Maria Rilke. WED *Fr.* Life of the Virgin Mary, The.

Birth of Rhythm and Blues, The. Patricia Jones. ReTh *Fr.* Billie Holiday Chronicles, The.

Birth of Sohráb, The. Firdowsi. TAL *Fr.* Shahnamah, The.

Birth of the Bike, The. *Unknown.* ArBi

Birth of the Blues, The. Lew Brown, B. G. DeSylva and Ray Henderson. ReLy

Birth of the Foal. Ferenc Juhász. WoPoe, *tr. by* David Wevill

Birth of the Smile, The. Rainer Maria Rilke. EroLit, *tr. by* J. B. Leishman

Birth of the Squire; an Eclogue, The. John Gay. NAEL-6v1

Birth of the Sun, The. Pablo Antonio Cuadra. TCLAP, *tr. by* Thomas Merton

Birth of Time, The. Josephine D. Henderson Heard. CBWP-4

Birth of Tragedy, The. Irving Layton. BrAP; NoAM; NoP-4; NoP-5

Birth of Venus. Constance Urdang. PoA 2002

Birth of Venus, The. Muriel Rukeyser. NALW

Birth, old age. Ly Ngoc Kieu. WPoS

Birth Postponed, A. Mailabattula Satish Chandar. HotL, *tr. by* V. Narayana Rao

Birth Room, The. Dennis Nurkse. NevBe

Birth Stone. Lorna Goodison. VCWP

4. Birth Story. Brent MacLaine. Coast *Fr.* Story of My Land, The.

Birth: "These mountains: blackness, silence, and snow." Georg Trakl. WED, *tr. by* Robert Bly

Birth Wail, The. Henrietta Tindal. VWP

Birthday. Christine Hume. AmPoNex

Birthday. Gerald Stern. PfSP

Birthday: "I have fallen to the ground." Dianne Edenfield Edwards. ICANM

Birthday, A. Christina Georgina Rossetti. CABP; LW; NAEL-6v2; NAEL-7v2; NALW; OBEV; PEW; TFi; UV; ViWPN; VWP

Birthday, A. Anne Rouse. MFPA

Birthday Cake. Paul Goodman. BodElec

Birthday Card to My Mother. Philip Appleman. GoPo

Birthday Crown, The. William, Archbishop of Armagh Alexander. SacPr

Birthday greetings / From a friend. Birthday Wishes to a Physician. Lizelia Augusta Jenkins Moorer. CBWP-3

Birthday Ode, 1732. Colley Cibber.
"Let there be light!" STuOW

Birthday Party. Kusano Shimpei. PFTM-1

Birthday Party on Old Orchard Road, A. Vivian Shipley. LiTh

Birthday Party, The. Josephine Jacobsen. OxBoAm

Birthday Poem. Steve Sanfield. WhBo

Birthday Poem, A. James Simmons. PNI

Birthday Sonnet. Elinor Wylie. MoAmPo

Birthday Sonnet for Grace. Bernadette Mayer. PmAP

Birth-Day, The. Mary Robinson. WoRP

Birthday, The: "I'm driving tonight into November." Elizabeth Morgan. P180

Birthday Triptych. Peter Scupham. HarvBoo

Birthday Wishes to a Husband [*with music*]. Lizelia Augusta Jenkins Moorer. CBWP-3

Birthday Wishes to a Minister of the Gospel [*with music*]. Lizelia Augusta Jenkins Moorer. CBWP-3

Birthday Wishes to a Physician. Lizelia Augusta Jenkins Moorer. CBWP-3

Birthdays. Mother Goose. NBLV

Birth-Dues. Robinson Jeffers. MoAmPo

Birth-Hour. Lindley Williams Hubbell. YaYoPo

Birthing. Cornelius Eady. FuFl

Birthmark. Khadar Mohiuddin. HotL, *tr. by* V. Narayana Rao

Birthnight: To F, The. Walter De la Mare. NPeEn

Birthplace. Nikolai Kanchev. CSCBP, *tr. by* Georgi Belev and Lisa Sapinkopf

Birthplace, The. Seamus Heaney. ModIr

Birthright, The. Peter Davison. YaYoPo *Fr.* Breaking of the Day, The.

Births. Pablo Neruda. BeAl, *tr. by* Stephen Mitchell

Births were nothing new in New Hope. At Our Backs. Robert A. Fink. TiP2

Biscuit, a basket. Hattie went to Market, A. Hattie Went to Market. Leslie Simon. FFC

Bishop Hatto. Robert Southey. OBNV; OBSP

Bishop Hatto and the Rats. Robert Southey. OxAEP-2

Bishop James A. Shorter. Josephine D. Henderson Heard. CBWP-4

Bishop Orders His Tomb at Saint Praxed's Church, The. Robert Browning. BrAP; CABP; HeIP-4; NAEL-6v2; NAEL-7v2; NAWM-7v2; NoP-4; NoP-5; NPeEn; TFi

Bishop Reading. J. D. McClatchy. KGB

Bishop tells us: "When the boys come back", The. "They." Siegfried Sassoon. NAEL-6v2; NAEL-7v2; NoP-4; NoP-5; OBSV; OBWP

Bismark. John Jay Chapman. APN-2

Bison Crossing Near Mt. Rushmore. May Swenson. GoPo

Bison, The. Joseph Hilaire Pierre Belloc. NoAM

Bistro Styx, The. Rita Dove. NoP-4; NoP-5

Bit by bit; thus. Bit by Bit. Hans Faverey. TuT, *tr. by* Peter van de Kamp

Bit of aluminum and glass in the middle of asphalt, A. Message from the Photo-Mat. Lawrence Goeckel. ICANM

Bit of Brass, A. Padraic Fallon. ModIr; NPeEn

Bit of jungle in the street, A. Alley Cat. Esther Valck Georges. Spl

Bit of Marble, A. Clinton Scollard. APN-2

Bit of rice in a string bag, A. Bit of Rice, A. Jean Valentine. AFaM

Bit of talcum, A. Reflection on Babies. Ogden Nash. NBLV

Bit of vanity, but mostly pride, A. (LL) In a few days now when two memories meet. James Vincent Cunningham. APT-2; OxBoAm

Bitch. Carolyn Kizer. GifTon; OxBoAm; PoA 2002; StAl

Bitch, A. Anna Swirszczynska [*or* Swir]. GifTon, *tr. by* Czeslaw Milosz and Leonard Nathan

Bitch opened the tent fly. Cough Drops. Sergio Kisielewsky. PML, *tr. by* John Oliver Simon

Bitcherel. Eleanor Brown. MFPA; NeBl; StAl

Bite. Tracy Ryan. StAl

Bite back passion. Spring now sets. Li Shang-yin. CCL1; WoPoe, *tr. by* A. C. Graham

Bite into the Onion. Marge Piercy. AFaM

Biting air. Winter Days. Gareth Owen. OBCP

Biting at her unfeathered heels. (LL) Anorexia. Alice Jones. AFaM; BloBone

Biting Back. Patricia Smith. GT

Biting winds, dark clouds, monkeys howling in the trees. Summit, A. Tu Fu [*or* Du Fu]. CrYelRi, *tr. by* Sam Hamill

Bits. Jean Dorcely Dede. OGAHCP, *tr. by* Boadiba and Jack Hirschman

Bits and Pieces, The. Chris Wallace-Crabbe.
Opener. BMAP

Bits of prosody fall near what remains of me. Broken Cup, The. Sharon Thesen. IFF

Bits of Reminiscence. "Shu Ting." VCWP, *tr. by* Carolyn Kizer and Y. H. Zhao

Bitsy cotton bathing-costume, A. Lake Balaton. Ágnes Nemes Nagy. IQMS, *tr. by* Hugh Maxton

Bitten to dust are the savage feathers of fire. To a Seaman Dead on Land. Kay Boyle. PoA 2002

Bitter. Ifi Amadiume. HAWP; NAfrP

Bitter Angel. Amy Gerstler. MotU; PmAP

Bitter Angel. Amy Gerstler. CalPo

Bitter batter boop! Last Cry of the Damp Fly, The. Dennis Lee. NTCP

Bitter, bitter jewel. "H. D." NALW *Fr.* Tribute to the Angels.

Bitter Cold. *Unknown.* NDACCP, *tr. by* Kenneth Rexroth

Bitter Cold: A Song. Ts'ao Ts'ao. ChinPo, *tr. by* Ye Weilian [*or* Yeh Wei-lien *or* Wai-lim Yip]

Bitter cold. No one is abroad. Bitter Cold. *Unknown.* NDACCP, *tr. by* Kenneth Rexroth

Bitter Cup, A. Mihály Vörösmarty. IQMS, *tr. by* Watson Kirkconnell

Bitter for remembrance of the healing which has passed. (LL) Lincoln. John Gould Fletcher. CBCWP; MoAmPo

Bitter Fruit of the Tree. Sterling Allen Brown. NoP-4; NoP-5; OxBoAm

Bitter Harvest. Tzu Yeh. CrYelRi, *tr. by* Sam Hamill

Bitter Mangoes, The. George Scurfield. FaBoWar

Bitter my life in times like these. War. Hedd Wyn. BBMWP, *tr. by* Gillian Clarke

Bitter night. The westwind. Winter Storm. Lucien Stryk. UrbNat

Bitter pinecone may be eaten, The. Empty Purse, The. Tu Fu [*or* Du Fu]. TAL

Bitter Poem, A. Sri Sri. HotL, *tr. by* V. Narayana Rao

Bitter River, The. Langston Hughes. NAMCP V.1

Bitter Sanctuary. Harold Monro. OBMV

Bitter Thoughts. Gerald Stern. PfSP

Bitter Withy, The. *Unknown.* NoP-4; NoP-5

Bitter Wood. Martin Carter. WoPoe

Bittermelon. Alan Chong Lau. WhBo

Bitterness of death is on me now, The. Cup, The. Jones Very. APN-1

Bitterness out of me, The. (LL) Bitter. Ifi Amadiume. HAWP; NAfrP

Bittersweet Growing Up the Red Wall. Robert Kelly. PmAP

Bitweene Merch and Averil. *Unknown.* NAEL-6v1

Bitwene March and Aperil. *Unknown.* OHMEL

Bivouac on a Mountain Side. Walt Whitman. NoAM

Bix to Buxtehude to Boulez. Victor Dog, The. James Merrill. NAMCP V.2; NoAM; NoP-4; NoP-5

Bizarre? / mysterioso? Thelonious. Reuben Jackson. ESEAA

Bizerta. George Campbell Hay. NePenScot

Björn Olinder's Pictures. Michael Longley. StAl

Bkln. Elouise Loftin. EGAG

Black. Maxine Chernoff. PmAP *Fr.* Japan.

Black. Grace Nichols. Oth

Black above the world. Imperial Airways. Louis Untermeyer. OtW

Black ambush, or Blowfish, resurrection and rage. (LL) Blowfish and Mudtoad. Dave Jeddie Smith. CAP-8; NAMCP V.2

Black and Blue (What Did I Do to Be So Black and Blue?). Andy Razaf. ReLy

Black and Divided or Chittlins and Caviar. Nicole Breedlove. InTrad

Black and serious, they are dropping down one by one to the top of the walnut tree. Committee, The. Ann Stanford. CalPo

Black and White. Jean Bleakney. NIrP

Black and White. Shirley Lim. UnSA

Black and White. Machiraju Savithri. HotL, tr. by V. Narayana Rao

Black and white castle makes all the difference, A. Angers. Bernard Noël. YaTCFP, tr. by Rosemary Lloyd

Black and white cat. Diane Di Prima. WhBo

Black and White Galaxie, The. Afaa Michael Weaver. UnSA

Black and white, The. Eugenio Montale. WoPoe Fr. Motets [Mottetti].

Black Angel / Doing what she's gotta do. Singer, The. Gerald William Barrax. ESEAA

Black Art. Imamu Amiri Baraka. ESEAA

Black Art, The. Anne Sexton. PoA 2002

Black Artist's role in America is to aid in the destruction / of America as he knows it, The. State/meant. Imamu Amiri Baraka. BB

Black as an iris, as an iris sucking up the. Marina Ivanovna Tsvetayeva. PoCho Fr. Insomnia.

Black as my night, anonymous here. American Memory of Africa, An. Kofi Awoonor. HBAPE

Black as snow and ice as cool / Miles stood horn-handed while. Boxcar. Terrance Hayes. AmPoNex

Black at that depth. Pacific Lament. Charles Olson. NAMCP V.2

Black Autumn. Aida Cartagena de Portalatin. TANSG, tr. by Daisy Cocco De Filippis

Black Back-Ups, The. Kate Rushin. ReTh

Black Banana House. Gavin Moses. InTrad

Black Bean Soup. Lucien Stryk. BodElec

Black bear does a strange and shuffling dance, The. Bear: A Totem Dance As Seen by Raven. Peter Blue Cloud. HATNAP

Black bear sits alone, A. Galway Kinnell. RaBo Fr. Lastness.

Black Beauty, A Praise. David Romtvedt. AtGh

Black beauty, which above that common light. Sonnet of Black Beauty. Edward Herbert, 1st Baron Herbert of Cherbury. NoP-5; NOSC

Black beds gain the most potent. Shadow Beds. Delmira Agustini. TANSG, tr. by Mark McCaffrey

Black bird, black voice. In the Orchard. Anne Stevenson. ColAP; WaAnP

Black bird on a black and snowy branch, A. Igor Vladimirovich Chinnov. TCRusP, tr. by John Glad

Black black black black black. Photoheliograph (For Lady A.). Harry Crosby. APT-2

Black Blot, The. Hedd Wyn. BBMWP, tr. by Gillian Clarke

Black Book of Carmarthen, The. Unknown. tr. by Ernest Rhys and Gwyn Williams
Gereint Son of Erbin. WoPoe, tr. by Gwyn Williams
Song of the Graves, The. OBMV

Black bottom stomp. Wopko Jensma. TSAP

Black Bourgeoisie. Imamu Amiri Baraka. ESEAA

Black Box. William Matthews. OtW

Black Box, The. Gavin Ewart. OBCoV

Black Boys Play the Classics. Toi Derricotte. ExTi; SpirFl

Black, brother, nigga. Haiku. C. Yaphet Brinson. BtF

Black Buoy. Robert H. Davis. HATNAP

Black, Byzantine eyes. Absent from Dances 1925. Stephanie Strickland. ExTi

Black car, A. May 28, 1945. S. L. Wisenberg. AtGh

Black cat yawns, The. Cat. Mary Britton Miller. TLR; WHSW

Black cats creep across my path. Everything Happens to Me. Tom Adair. ReLy

Black City, The. Breyten Breytenbach. PoetW, tr. by Leon de Kock and Sonia van Schalwyk

Black clad and mithered he harries his weight. Lamper, The. Maggie Hannan. NLP

Black clouds have risen in my sky. Rāmprasād Sen. SinGod, tr. by Rachel Fell McDermott

Black Clouds—Spilled Ink. Su Tung-p'o. ColAnChi, tr. by Burton Watson

Black Cloud, The. Langston Hughes. WaAnP

Black Cock, The. Ishmael Reed. ISC

Black Cockatoos. Judith Wright. OWoS

Black Coffee. Sonny Burke and Paul Francis Webster. ReLy

Black Cottage, The. Robert Frost. CBCWP

Black Cove. Ch'ôn Yanghûi. EcSo, tr. by Aimee N. Kwon

Black Crispus Attucks taught. Dark Symphony. Melvin B. Tolson. ColAP; SSLK

Black crows in the burnt mauve grass, as intimate as rotting rice. Oranges. Frank O'Hara. AHA

Black Cryptogram. Michael S. Harper. OxAAAP

Black Cup, The. César Vallejo. WoPoe, tr. by Tony Barnstone, Haixin Xu and Willis Barnstone

Black Dada Nihilismus. Imamu Amiri Baraka. PFTM-2

Black Dahlia. Michael McClure. Eno

Black Dog is Sleeping on Top of the Light, A. León Felipe.
"I am no one: a man." RaW, tr. by Hardie St. Martin

Black Drag Queen. A. Van Jordan. BtF

Black Dream, you come. Sappho. SaLy, tr. by Diane Rayor

Black Earth. Marianne Moore. APT-1; NAMCP V.1

Black English. Richard Katrovas. LTA

Black Experience, The. Mwatabu Okantah. BtF

Black Finger, The. Angelina Weld Grimké. NAAPv.2

Black fish under the bridge was so long I mistook it, The. Goldfish. Sinéad Morrissey. NIrP

Black flag, A. (LL) Transparent. Ronny Someck. Eno; IrPoTo, tr. by Vivian Eden

Black flies have not yet arrived, and our dog. Lion of God in Vermont in May. Pamela White Hadas. PfSP

Black flies kept nagging in the heat, The. Tao and Unfitness at Inistiogue on the River Nore. Thomas Kinsella. NPeEn; PBCIP

Black Flower. Walter Pavlich. TWW

Black fool, why winter here? These frozen skies. Advice to a Raven in Russia [December, 1812]. Joel Barlow. AmWaPo; NAAL-3; OBWP

Black fox loped out of the hills, The. Dream of a Black Fox. Brendan Kennelly. PBCIP

Black girl black girl. Blackberry Sweet. Dudley Randall. ISC; SoSe-8; WeW-3

Black Girl Tap Dancing. Lenard D. Moore. FuFl

Black grayed into white a nightmare of bicycling. Michael Dransfield. See Black greyed into white a nightmare of bicycling.

Black greyed into white a nightmare of bicycling. That Which We Call a Rose. Michael Dransfield. NOBAu
(Black grayed into white a nightmare of bicycling.) BMAP

Black grows the sudden sky, betokening rain. Sudden Shower. John Clare. OxAEP-2

Black Hair. Gary Soto. CAP-8; MoASP; UnSA

Black Hair. Unknown. EroLit

Black hair and red cheeks: for how long? Cui Shaoxuan. WPoS

Black hair of my Chinese doctor, The. Medicine. Tony Hoagland. PoCu

Black Hairs, The. Heinz Pasman. RaBo, tr. by Robert Bly

Black hands shucked. Gristmill. Yusef Komunyakaa. LPSFW

Black hat stingy brim, Th. Canto 10: Wooten. Tom Weatherly. EGAG

Black haw is in flower again, The. Song from the Traffic. Margaret Bell Houston. TiP2

Black Heart. Kwame Dawes. WaCA

Black Heart as Ever Green, The. Carolyn M. Rodgers. IllVoic

Black heart with wings of fire. Black Heart. Miguel de Unamuno. RaW, tr. by Hardie St. Martin

Black heralds, The. César Vallejo. BeAl, tr. by Gordon Brotherston and Edward Dorn

Black Heralds, The. César Vallejo. PoCho, tr. by Rebecca Seiferle

Black Hole. No Hyangnim. EcSo, tr. by Aimee N. Kwon

Black Hole, The. Robert Pack. OtW

Black Huntsmen, The. Irving Layton. WoPoe

Black ice on the motorway. M4. Emyr Lewis. ATSWP, tr. by Robert Minhinnick

Black in a tentlike cloak, at rest. Incident in Transylvania. Roger McDonald. BMAP

Black Irish Blues. Joe-Anne McLaughlin-Carruth. OPRER

Black iron fence closes the graves in, its ovals delicate as wine stems, A. Visiting Emily Dickinson's Grave with Robert Francis. Robert Bly. MotU

Black is not. Poem Looking for a Reader, A. Haki R. Madhubuti. ISC

Black is the night. What Is Black? Mary O'Neill. NTCP

Black Jackets. Thom Gunn. HeIP-4; NAEL-6v2; NAEL-7v2; NoP-4; NoP-5

Black Java Pepper. Arthur Sze. OpBo

Black key. White key. No. Unrelenting Flood. William Matthews. BodElec

Black king dance out front of the crowd. Four Poems. Velemir Khlebnikov. PFTM-1

Black knight. To Josh Gibson (Legendary Slugger of the Old Negro Baseball League). George, Jr. Mosby. ISC

Black Kőrös. József Erdélyi. IQMS, tr. by Alan Dixon

Black Lace Bra Kind of Woman. Sandra Cisneros. TiP2

Black Lace Fan My Mother Gave Me, The. Eavan Boland. HarvBoo; ModIr; MoWP; NPeEn

Black Lady, A. Elouise Loftin. EGAG

Black lake, black boat, two black, cut-paper people. Crossing the Water. Sylvia Plath. BrAP; CAP-8

Black Leather Because Bubmlebees Look Like It. Diane Wakoski. P180

Black Light. Peter Markus. AmPoNex

Black like me. (LL) Dream Variation[s]. Langston Hughes. APT-2; ISC; ITBLP; NoP-4; NoP-5; OxAAAP; OxBoAm; SAmP; SSLK

Black, long-tailed, The. Yellow Season, The. William Carlos Williams. MoAmPo

Black Love Black Hope. Doughtry Long. SeSe

Black Magicians / Come home: the pink meat image. Change, The: *Kyoto-Tokyo Express*. Allen Ginsberg. APSN

Black maid, complain not that I fly. Boy's Answer to the Blackmoor, The. Henry King, Bishop of Chichester. NoP-5

Black Maid to the Fair Boy, The. Henry Reynolds. NOSC

Black Male, 6'2", 28, wearing drooping baggy jeans. Usual Suspects, The. Reginald Harris. BRtP

Black man. Brother John. Michael S. Harper. OxAAAP

Black Man Go Back To The Old Country. High Modes: Vision as Ritual: Confirmation. Michael S. Harper. FuFl

Black Man Talks of Reaping, A. Arna Bontemps. APT-2; ColAP; NAAPv.2; SSLK; WaAnP

Black Man's Sonata, A. Afaa Michael Weaver. UnSA

Black Maps. Mark Strand. PoA 2002

Black March. Stevie Smith. EmeKit

Black Mary Janes, white-ruffled sox. Yesterday. Mary Weems. SpirFl

Black Meat. Jean Follain. BLT

Black men? (LL) Black Woman. Naomi Long Madgett. GT; ISC

Black men are the tall trees that remain. Portraiture. Anita Scott Coleman. OxAAAP

Black men only laughed, The. (LL) Father (Part 1). Harryette Mullen. OxAAAP; TiP2

Black mesh torn by the rock shelf's clinging. Mending. Joe Denham. OpeFie

Black Messengers, The. César Vallejo. PoetW; TCLAP, *tr. by* Rachel Benson

Black milk of daybreak we drink it at evening. Deathfugue. Paul Celan. AF; ItP; PoSu, *tr. by* John Felstiner

Black milk of daybreak we drink it at nightfall. Fugue of Death. Paul Celan. OBVE; PoetW, *tr. by* Christopher Middleton

Black milk of daybreak we drink it at sundown. Death Fugue. Paul Celan. GPTC; HP; VCWP; Wafne. Michael Hamburger

Black milk of morning we drink you at dusktime. Death Fugue, A. Paul Celan. CLPP; GifTon; PFTM-2, *tr. by* Jerome Rothenberg

Black Mood. Rosalía de Castro. STV, *tr. by* John Frederick Nims

Black Mood. Rosalía de Castro. WeW-3

Black moon geese fly high. Lu Lun. CCL1, *tr. by* Man Wong

Black Mother Praying. Owen Dodson. ISC

Black Mother Woman. Audre Lorde. OxAAAP

Black Mountain Blues. Bessie Smith. FTtHH; PFTM-1

Black mountains pricked with pointed pine. Watershed, The. Alice Thompson Meynell. VWP

Black mudbank pushes them out like hotel fire. Fiddlers. Dave Jeddie Smith. CAP-8; NAMCP V.2

Black Mulberries. Bedri Rahmi EyuboĞlu. NaPG, *tr. by* Talat Sait Halman

Black my beginning. Elizabeth Bewick. NewEx

Black- / ness. Combination II. Helmut Heissenbüttel. PFTM-2, *tr. by* Jerome Rothenberg

Black night spies upon my window, The. Gestures From My Window. Yolanda Bedregal. TANSG, *tr. by* Carolyne Wright

Black Night, The. Antar. WoPoe, *tr. by* Desmond O'Grady

Black November Turkey, A. Richard Wilbur. OWoS

Black, numb fingernails, The. (LL) On a Field Trip at Fredericksburg. Dave Jeddie Smith. LPSFW; PoPoPo

Black on Black. Bruce A. Jacobs. BtF

Black one, last as usual, swings her head, The. Fetching Cows. Norman Alexander MacCaig. NoP-4

Black Orchid. David Jauss. SeSe

Black Pacific. "Shahid, come here, quick." A ship. Purse-Seiner *Atlantis*, The. Agha Shahid Ali. AmAlph

Black peak at Xuan Loc, The. It Is Monsoon at Last. Basil T. Paquet. AmWaPo

Black Piano, The. Endre Ady. IQMS, *tr. by* Adam Makkai

Black Pine Tree in an Orange Light. Sylvia Plath. BodElec

Black Poet Leaps to His Death, A. Etheridge Knight. BodElec

Black Poets should live—not leap. For Black Poets Who Think of Suicide. Etheridge Knight. HeIP-4; LTA; OxAAAP; WaAnP

Black Poets, The. Charles Bukowski. LTA

Black poets / young, The. Black Poets, The. Charles Bukowski. LTA

Black Poppy (At the Temple). David St. John. BodElec

Black Postcards. Tomas Tranströmer. WoPoe, *tr. by* Joanna Bankier

Black Power. Raymond R. Patterson. OxAAAP

Black Queen Blues. Mari E. Evans. OxAAAP

Black Queen raised high, The. Evening Chess. Charles Simic. OxBoAm

Black Rape. Michelle T. Clinton. InTrad

Black reapers with the sound of steel on stones. Reapers. Jean Toomer. APT-2; ColAP; GT; InGu; NAAPv.2; NAMCP V.1; NIL-7; NoAM; NoP-4; NoP-5; OxBoAm; PtR; SoSe-8; TRP; WaAnP; WeW-3

Black Revolver. Jarret Keene. LiTh

Black riders came from the sea. Stephen Crane. APN-2; NAAPv.1; NoP-4; NoP-5

Black Riders, The. César Vallejo. RaBo; WED, *tr. by* Robert Bly

Black River, The. C. S. Giscombe. RD

Black Riviera, The. Mark Jarman. GeoHom

Black Road Over Which Green Trees Grow. Thomas Lux. AmAlph

Black rock, cross (how the north wind has rolled), The. Tomb. Stéphane Mallarmé. SxFrPo, *tr. by* A. M. and E. H. Blackmore

Black Rook in Rainy Weather. Sylvia Plath. BrAP; NIL-7; NoP-4

Black Runner, The. Angelina Weld Grimké. NAAPv.2

Black Sampson, The [*with music*]. Josephine D. Henderson Heard. CBWP-4; SWaP

Black Samson of Brandywine. Paul Laurence Dunbar. AmWaPo

Black sand. Dolores Dorantes. SPV, *tr. by* Jen Hofer

Black Series. Brenda Hillman. BodElec

Black Sheep, The. Gojko Djogo. AF, *tr. by* Michael March *and* Dušan Puvaić

Black Silhouettes of Shrimpers. Dave Jeddie Smith. NAMCP V.2

Black Silk. Tess Gallagher. EmeKit

Black Silk Pajamas. Danton R. Remoto. ReBoTo

Black Slip. Terry Wolverton. SUP; WiU

Black Snake. Raul Bopp. *tr. by* Renato Rezende

"Begins here, the ciphered forest." TCLAP, *tr. by* Renato Rezende

"I pass the swamp borders." TCLAP, *tr. by* Renato Rezende

"I wake up." TCLAP, *tr. by* Renato Rezende

"Sky very blue." TCLAP, *tr. by* Renato Rezende

"This is the rotten-breathed forest." TCLAP, *tr. by* Renato Rezende

Black Snake, The. Mary Oliver. NAMCP V.2

Black Soap. Sandra McPherson. VCAP

Black Soldier, A. Lenard D. Moore. BtF

Black Stone Lying on a White Stone. César Vallejo. PoCho; TCLAP; WED, *tr. by* Robert Bly and John Knoepfle

Black Stone on a White Stone. César Vallejo. WoPoe, *tr. by* Willis Barnstone

Black, such a soul in exile slowly makes its way towards. Secret in Broad Daylight. Habib Tengour. YaTCFP, *tr. by* Mary Ann Caws *and* Jean-Pierre Cauvin

Black Sunday, April 14, 1935. Naomi Stroud Simmons. TiP2

Black swallows swooping or gliding. Skaters, The. John Gould Fletcher. MoAmPo

Black swallows will return, The. Black Swallows Will Return, The. Gustavo Adolfo Bécquer. BLPSL, *tr. by* Rene de Costa, Rigas Kappatos and Eleni Paidoussi

Black swans with wings over their eyes. For Martin Luther King. Charles Fort. LTA

Black Tambourine. Hart Crane. NAMCP V.1; NoAM

Black Tax. Nzadi Z. Keita. BtF

Black Thorn, The. J. Eirian Davies. BBMWP, *tr. by* Sion Eirian

Black Thought, A. Juan Ramón Jiménez. RaW, *tr. by* Ralph Nelson and Rita García Nelson

Black thought came into my head, A. Black Thought, A. Juan Ramón Jiménez. RaW, *tr. by* Ralph Nelson and Rita García Nelson

Black Top River Fires / A Corona. Mary Rising-Higgins. ICANM

Black Train, The. Thomas McGrath. GM

Black Tulips. Martha Vertreace. IllVoice

Black unicorn is greedy, The. Black Unicorn, The. Audre Lorde. OxAAAP

Black Vahine. To Vahine (Painted by Gaugin). Enrique Molina. BLPSL, *tr. by* Rene de Costa, Rigas Kappatos and Eleni Paidoussi

Black village of gravestones. Heptonstall. Ted Hughes. OxAEP-2

Black Vulture, The. George Sterling. APT-1; ASA; CalPo

Black Walnut Tree, The. Mary Oliver. MakPoe

Black Water Creek. Walter Holland. BeDoSh

Black water. White waves. Furrows snowcapped. Seamus Heaney. NAMCP V.2; NoAM *Fr.* Station Island.

Black Wet, The. W. N. Herbert. NeBl

Black widows have crawled up under the skirts. Diana Hartog. NLPA *Fr.* Oasis.

Black windows, The. Her arms. Six/Nine/Forty-Four. David St. John. AmAlph

Black Winds, The. William Carlos Williams. APT-1

Black Winter. Frank Stewart. AmWaPo

Black Woman. Naomi Long Madgett. GT; ISC

Black woman comes up to me at break in the writing, A. For Black Women Who Are Afraid. Toi Derricotte. ExTi; FuFl

Black Women with Jewish Names. James Coleman. BtF

Blackamoors, The. Rowland Watkyns. AngWePo

Black-and-white magpie. Tomas Tranströmer. WoBe *Fr.* Haiku.

Blackberries. Yusef Komunyakaa. CAP-8

Blackberries. Francis Ponge. WED, *tr. by* Robert Bly

Blackberries. Francis Ponge. YaTCFP, *tr. by* Serge Gavronsky

Blackberries. Maurina Sherman. GeoHom

Blackberry Eating. Galway Kinnell. BeAl; CAP-8; InvLad; NIL-7; NIP-4; SoSe-8; WaAnP

Blackberry Sweet. Dudley Randall. ISC; SoSe-8; WeW-3

Blackberry, The. Norman Nicholson. MoBrPo

Blackberrying. Sylvia Plath. BeAl; NAAL-5; NAMCP V.2; NoAM; PoPoPo

Blackberry-Picking [*For Philip Hobsbaum*]. Seamus Heaney. ChAP; PtR

Blackbird, The. W. E. Henley. MoBrPo *Fr.* Echoes.

Blackbird, The. *Unknown.* IrV, *tr. by* Kuno Meyer

Blackbird, The. Humbert Wolfe. NOxBChV

Blackbird, blackbird. Bye Bye Blackbird. Mort Dixon. ReLy

Blackbird, blackbird, where's. Killer Blues. Calvin Forbes. IllVoic

Blackbird sang, the skies were clear and clean, The. At Queensferry. W. E. Henley. OxBSo

Blackbird Singing, A. Ronald Stuart Thomas. OBWVE

Blackbird Spring. William Heyen. CAP-8

Blackbird swooped, The. Snowy Sky. Takahashi Shinkichi. ZenPo, *tr. by* Takashi Ikemoto and Lucien Stryk

Blackbird that lives in the graveyard, The. On Derry's Walls. Kerry Hardie. NIrP

Blackbird's farewell song, The. (LL) Vasco [*or* Vasko] Popa. PoSu; WoPoe *Fr.* Blackbird's Field, The.

Blackbird's Field, The. Vasco [*or* Vasko] Popa. *tr. by* Anne Pennington

Battle on the Blackbird's Field, The. PoSu; WoPoe, *tr. by* Anne Pennington

Blackbirds to a swan. In Praise of a Sword Given Him by His Prince. Colman mac Lenini. WoPoe, *tr. by* Richard O'Connell

Blackbirds whistle over the young. American Century, The. Kenneth Rexroth. PoChi

Black-blue shadows on red-brown bricks. Shadows. Avrom Viktor. Prolet, *tr. by* Amelia Glaser

Blackboard in my mind holds words eye dream, A. And Syllables Grow Wings There. Quincy Troupe. SpirFl

Blackboard is erased in the attic, The. Rain Moving In. John Ashbery. NoP-4

Blackboard's white turned dark, The; I. Relief of Myopia, The. U. A. Fanthorpe. Spl

Blackbottom. Toi Derricotte. BtF; GT; LTA; OxAAAP; PBCAP

Blackcock, The [*or* The Black Cock]. Joanna Baillie. WoRP

Blackcurrant River. Arthur Rimbaud. SxFrPo, *tr. by* Martin Sorrell

Blacke is the beauty of the brightest day. Christopher Marlowe. OxBEV *Fr.* Tamburlaine the Great, Part 2.

Blackened and bleeding, helpless, panting, prone. Chicago. Bret Harte. APN-2

Blackened iron, The. Rain in May. Jane Hirshfield. GeoHom

Black-faced [*or* fac'd] house will love, A. (LL) On the Baptized Ethiopian. Richard Crashaw. ChIV-2; NoP-4; NoP-5, *tr. by* Richard Crashaw

Black-haired girl, The. Yawn, The. Paul Blackburn. P180

Blackie Thinks of His Brothers. Stanley Crouch. GT; OxAAAP

Blackjack. Steven Heighton. IFF

Black'm saut'm rough'm glower'm saw. Riddle. *Unknown.* FaBoVe

Blackman came walking I. Dreadwalk. Dennis Scott. WaCA

Blackman in the Desecrated Synagogue—Living in the Last Days. David Henderson. EGAG

Blackness. Primer for Blacks. Gwendolyn Brooks. ISC

Blackout. John Tranter.

"Burden of noise, of infections, A." VaPo

"Hang up a yellow shirt—you cause joy." VaPo

"Some sports are odious, but." VaPo

"Tell me we will drink water, and drink to me." VaPo

"Thunder heard—speak to ourselves." VaPo

"Wild stinking fire, love and death." VaPo

Blacks in frame houses. Song: I Want a Witness. Michael S. Harper. LTA

Blackshadow Chestnut. Conrad Ferdinand Meyer. SonAtl, *tr. by* Kurt Ganzl, Markus Jaigirder and Monique Tyler

Blacksmith's boy went out with a rifle, The. Legend. Judith Wright. NOBAu

Blacksmith's Shop, The. H. C. Artmann. MotU, *tr. by* Stuart Friebert

Blacksmiths, The. *Unknown.* WoPoe, *tr. by* Wesli Court

Blackstone Rangers, The. Gwendolyn Brooks. ESEAA; NAMCP V.2; NoAM

Blackstone Rangers, The. Gwendolyn Brooks.

Gang Girls. IllVoic

Blacktail Row. Liu Yu Hsi. CrYelRi, *tr. by* Sam Hamill

Blackthorn. Euros Bowen. OBWVE, *tr. by* the author

Blacktop yellow stripe down the middle. Requiem for James Byrd, Jr. H. Palmer Hall. TiP2

Blackwater Mountain [*with music*]. Charles Wright. NAMCP V.2

Bladder Song. Leonard Nathan. BLT

Blade days—, The. Invisible Autumn. Joseph Ceravolo. FTOS

Blade of Grass, A. Srirangam Narayana Babu. HotL, *tr. by* V. Narayana Rao

Blade of Grass, A. Otto Orban. MotU, *tr. by* George Szirtes

Blade touches the fish heart, over, The. Gutting the Salmon. Robert Adamson. BMAP

Blades. C. K. Williams. CAP-8

Blades and slime, the limits, The. Dario Villa. ItPo, *tr. by* Gayle Ridinger

Blaen Cwrt. Gillian Clarke. AngWePo

Blah, Blah, Blah. Ira Gershwin. ReLy

Blah-Blah. Harryette Mullen. OxAAAP

Blake. Lucille Clifton. ExTi

Blame It on My Youth. Edward Heyman. ReLy

Blame it on the weather, the news. Blues, The. Mark Vinz. MiVo

Blame not my lute, for he must sound [*or* sssnd *or* Sownde]. Blame Not My Lute. Sir Thomas Wyatt. NAEL-7v1; NoP-5

Blame not thyself too much, I said, nor blame. Alfred Tennyson. NAEL-6v2; NAEL-7v2 *Fr.* Princess, The.

Blame of the day comes knotted in the pad of night, The. One of Essence's Entrances. Clark Coolidge. NYP2

Blame the spring wind. (LL) I had not fastened my sash over my gown. Tzu Yeh. EroLit; WoPoe, *tr. by* Chung Ling and Kenneth Rexroth

Blame the Vicar. Sir John Betjeman. SacPr

Blames, for Rane and Diane. Glenn Sheldon. MiVo

Blaming Sons. Ch'ien T'ao. ColAnChi, *tr. by* Burton Watson

Blanca's Red Lips. Gloria Vando. TouFir

Blanco. Octavio Paz. *tr. by* Eliot Weinberger

"Stirring / a steering / a seedling, A." PFTM-2, *tr. by* Eliot Weinberger

Blanco. Gary Soto. GeoHom

Blanco está sobre lo verde, Lo. Nieve, La. Jorge Guillén. RaW

Blander than snow and slow to be cruel. (LL) Vermin. William Matthews. BAP-97; OxBoAm

Blandeur. Kay Ryan. CalPo; OxBoAm

Blank, A. Thom Gunn. NAMCP V.2

Blank Abandon of Beds, The. Star Black. KGB

Blank Misgivings. Andrew Crozier. VaPo

Blank Misgivings of a Creature Moving About in Worlds Not Realized. Arthur Hugh Clough.

"Here am I yet, another twelvemonth spent." CenSon

"Though to the vilest things beneath the moon." OxBSo

"Yes, I have lied, and so must walk my way." CenSon

Blank Sonnet. George Elliott Clarke. Coast; OpeFie

Blank to Fill in on the Visa of Pollen. Aimé Césaire. WoPoe, *tr. by* Gregson Davis

Blank wall is singing, A. In a Hand Not My Own. Bill Berkson. NYP2

Blanket Hog. Paul B. Janeczko. TLR

Blanket, its weight, while we were growing, The. In the Lungs. Milo De Angelis. NeIt, *tr. by* Lawrence Venuti

Blank-looking elephant in the Central Park Zoo, The. Elephant's Piggy Bank, The. Takamura Kotaro. CAoMJL1, *tr. by* Leith Morton

Blason, A. Alec Derwent Hope. NOBAu

Blasphemous wretch! How canst thou think or say. Sarah Fyge Egerton. PEW *Fr.* Female Advocate Or, An Answer to a Late Satyr*, The.

Blasphemy, A. Rodney Jones. IllVoic; WeW-3

Blast from Freedom's Northern hills, upon its Southern way, The. Massachusetts to Virginia. John Greenleaf Whittier. NAAPv.1

Blast of anniversary excitement, true. Edoardo Cacciatore. ItPo *Fr.* Full Powers: Five Warning Signs.

Blasted Fields of Clover Bring Harrowing and Regretful Sighs. Mark Bibbins.

"Now the sea moves up the lawn for him as those nearby view his life passing before their eyes." BAP-04

"Stacked circles (rain down) say green it releases nothing. Bundled wires." BAP-04

Blasted horn, do do di do, A. Courtyard Noises from the North, Twenty-fourth Precinct. Colette Inez. UrbNat

Blasted / I was a 15/yr old junkie. 1980–1990: A Poet's Personal Review. Asha Bandele. InTrad

Blasted with sighs, and surrounded with tears. Twickenham [*or* Twicknam] Garden. John Donne. BASC; OBGa

Blasts of Autumn as they scatter round, The. Written in October. Charlotte Smith. NoP-4; NoP-5

Blasts of wind amidst autumn rains. Rill of the House of the Luans. Wang Wei. ChinPo, *tr.* by Ye Weilian [*or* Yeh Wei-lien *or* Wai-lim Yip]

Blat. . .blat. . .water. In the Woods. *Unknown.* SonAtl, *tr.* by Lester Browne, J.P. Coyne and Meagan Pfelz

Blaupunkt (choruses Pepper Adams never took). Percy Johnston. EGAG

Blaze awake in the night and detest. Sleep's Underside. Melissa Kirsch. AWTN

Blaze of promise everywhere, The. (LL) Always. Mark Strand. EmeKit; NoP-4; NoP-5; TRP

Blazing in darkness, all they wish to see. (LL) Magi, The. Louise Glück. GI; HarvBoo; PoA 2002

16. Blazing Nirvana. David McFadden. NLPA

Blazing stanchions and the corporate lights—, The. Euclid Avenue. Harry Clifton. PBCIP

Blazon. Dinah Berland. SUP

Blazon Pronounced by the Huntsman, The. Jacques du Fouilloux. DiBP, *tr.* by George Turberville

Ble. Oskar Pastior. OnScMo, *tr.* by Rosmarie Waldrop

Bleach in the foot-bathtub. Sunday Morning, 1950. Irene McKinney. PBCAP

Bleached wood massed in bone piles, The. Kalaloch. Carolyn Forché. NoAM; YaYoPo

Bleak the February light. Kingdom of Heaven. Léonie Adams. MoAmPo

Bleaklow. Pauline Stainer. NeBl

Bleat. Barbara Guest. FTOS

Bleecker Street. Hugh Seidman. BodElec

Bleeding. May Swenson. NALW

Bleeding Nun, The. *Unknown.* NOBRP

Bleeding to death. The counter-attack had failed. (LL) Counter-Attack. Siegfried Sassoon. MoBrPo; OxAEP-2; PoWW

Blenheim Oranges. Edward Thomas. *See* Gone, Gone Again.

Bless me with forgiveness, Lord, for all my sins of youth. He Pleads for Forgiveness Before His Intended Marriage. Bálint Balassi. IQMS, *tr.* by Joseph Leftwich

Bless my life—its inks. Prayer. Carolyne Wright. SweBea

Bless the Lord, O my soul. O Lord my God. Bible, *O.T.* NAWM-5v1 *Fr.* Psalms.

Bless the red door open wide. Widow's Winter. Marilyn Bowering. IFF

Bless this my house under the pitch pines. On New Year's Day. Marge Piercy. MoW

Bless your writer's hand, Sir, and its paternal blues. To Afaa Michael S. Weaver. Major L. Jackson. FuFl

Blesse me! what damps are here? how stiffe an aire? Charnel-house, The. Henry Vaughan. FSCP

Blesse thee, Lord, because I GROW. Paradise. George Herbert. SacPr

Blessed angell not a word replies, The. Ludovico Ariosto. OBVE *Fr.* Orlando Furioso.

Blessed are the files marked action in the inward tray. Beatitudes. Bruce Dawe. GI

Blessed are the lovers. Most Ancient Names of Fire, The. Roberto Sosa. ErotSp, *tr.* by Jo Anne Engelbert

Blessed are the ones going forth, happy are they that they are armed Jews. Poem of Blessing. Uri Zvi Greenberg. NRoS, *tr.* by Esther Raizen

Blessed are the poor[e] in spirit for theirs is the kingdom[e] of heaven. Bible, *N.T.* OBVE *Fr.* St. Matthew.

Blessed Are They That Sow. Avraham Ben Yitzhak. WoPoe, *tr.* by Robert Mezey

Blessed are they that sow and shall not reap. Blessed Are They That Sow. Avraham Ben Yitzhak. WoPoe, *tr.* by Robert Mezey

Blessed Are They Who Sow and Do Not Reap. Avraham Ben Yitzhak. PoCho, *tr.* by Peter Cole

Blessed as the Gods! Sicilian Maid is he. Dreams of a Rival. Mary Robinson. CenSon; RWP

Blessed Assurance [*with music*]. Fanny Crosby. SWaP

Blessed be the name of the Lord. (LL) Few Days in the South in February, A. Eleanor Ross Taylor. CBCWP; InGu

Blessed be the Paps which Thou hast Sucked. Bible, *N.T.* ChIV-2; NOSC *Fr.* St. Luke.

Blessed be you beautiful. Quarter-Hour Between God and the Office. Lőrinc Szabó. IQMS, *tr.* by Egon F. Kunz

Blessed conversion, and a strange, A. Conversion of S. Paul, The. George Wither. ChIV-2

Blessed damozel leaned out, The. Blessed Damozel, The. Dante Gabriel Rossetti. BrAP; CABP; NAEL-6v2; NAEL-7v2; NoP-4; NoP-5; OBEV; OxAEP-2; TFi; WaAnP

Blessed Damozel was shocked, The. She fumed. Oh Keep the Poet Hence. Thomas Carper. PoA 2002

Blessed / in the light of the sun at the sight of the world. Epilogue. Charles Reznikoff. NAAPv.2

Blessed is the lord for bestowing on us these gifts which we are so unworthy of. Hymn to Hualien, A. Hung Hung. PML, *tr.* by Steve Bradbury

Blessed Is the Man. Marianne Moore. ChIV-1

Blessed is the man that walketh not in the assembly of the wicked. Psalm 1. Genrik Veniaminovich Sapgir. ItGoST, *tr.* by J. Kates

Blessed is yon shepherd on the turf reclined. Charlotte Smith. RWP

Blessed Lord, What It Is to Be Young. David McCord. NTCP

Blessed offender [*or* offendour], who thyself hast [*or* haist] tried [*or* try'd]. To Saint Mary Magdalen. Henry Constable. NoSic

Blessed Pentecost. *Hungarian Oral Tradition.* IQMS, *tr.* by Dermot Spence

Blessed Pentecost is here again that comes up new each year. Blessed Pentecost. *Hungarian Oral Tradition.* IQMS, *tr.* by Dermot Spence

Blessed sweet Pentecost's weather brightly glowing. For Wine Drinkers. Bálint Balassi. IQMS, *tr.* by René Bonnerjea

Blessed that flock safe penned in Paradise. Christina Georgina Rossetti. WPoS *Fr.* Behold a Shaking.

Blessed with a joy that only she. Gift of God, The. Edwin Arlington Robinson. MoAmPo

Blessednes of Brytaine, The. Morris Kyffin. AngWePo
  "Adore November's sacred seventeenth day." AngWePo

Blessednesse of Faithfull Soules by Death, The. William Drummond of Hawthornden. SacPr

Blessing. Reed Bye. AHA

Blessing. Imtiaz Dharker. BeAl; MoWP

Blessing, A: "Just off the highway to Rochester, Minnesota." James Wright. AmFaPo; CAP-8; ChAP; GoPo; MoAmPo; NAAL-5; NAMCP V.2; NoAM; NoP-4; NoP-5; OxBoAm; PoA 2002; PoPoPo; RaBo; StAl; TRP; VCAP

Blessing Attributed to Saint Clare, The. Clare of Assisi. BBASP, *tr.* by Regis J. Armstrong

Blessing in Disguise, A. John Ashbery. ColAP; ItP

Blessing of Snow, The. Netta Gillespie. AmZen

Blessing of your voice, your chaste touch, The. (LL) What I Learned from My Mother. Julia Kasdorf. ACAMVP; AmPoNex; GoPo; PBCAP; SweBea

Blessing on the house, A. Thomas A. Clark. Oth

Blessing on the printer's art!, A. Sarah Josepha Buell Hale. SWaP *Fr.* Three Hours; or, The Vigil of Love.

Blessing Over Bread, A. Dovid Seltzer. Prolet, *tr.* by Amelia Glaser

Blessing Poem. Demetria Martinez. ICANM

Blessing, The. Helen Dunmore. BeAl

Blessing the boats. Lucille Clifton. CFP

Blessing the House. Jim Daniels. SUP

Blessings. Mary Stewart Hammond.
  3. Paying Respects. InoFa

Blessings on all the kids who improve the signs in the subways. Graffiti. Edward Field. SUP

Blessings on the hunter and the hunted. Jubilee for the Bomb. Maureen Seaton. MAAN

Blessings on thee, little man. Barefoot Boy, The. John Greenleaf Whittier. APN-1; BRP

Blessings [*or* Blessing] on the hand of women! Hand That Rocks the Cradle Is the Hand That Rules the World, The. William Ross Wallace. ITBLP

Blessing's Precision. Christopher Howell. RWB

Blest age! when ev'ry Purling Stream. Torquato Tasso. BASC *Fr.* Aminta.

Blest are the moments, doubly blest. Hymn. William Wordsworth. SacPr

Blest be the day, and blest the month and year. Petrarch. NAWM-5v1; NAWM-7v1 *Fr.* Sonnets to Laura.

Blest is the tarn which towering cliffs o'ershade. Blest is the tarn which towering cliffs o'ershade. Sara Coleridge. VWP

Blest leaf! whose aromatic gales dispense. Isaac Hawkins Browne. UV *Fr.* Pipe of Tobacco, A.

Blest pair of *Sirens*, pledges of Heav'ns [*or* Heaven's] joy. At a Solemn Music[k]. John Milton. HeIP-4; OBEV; SacPr

Blest Poesy! Oh sent to calm. Helen Maria Williams. NOBRP *Fr.* Address to Poetry, An.

Blest privacy! Happy retreat, wherein. My Country Audit. Mildmay Fane, 2d Earl of Westmorland. NOSC

Blest solitude, be with me; even now, take me. To Solitude. Mihály Csokonai Vitéz. IQMS, *tr.* by Edmund Charles Blunden

Blew delicately down to death. (LL) April Mortality. Léonie Adams. APT-2; CtM; MoAmPo

Blew It. Michael Castro. SeSe

Blew out the golden light. (LL) Shall Then Another. Kenneth Mackenzie. BrAP; NOBAu

Blight. Arna Bontemps. ColAP

Blight. Ralph Waldo Emerson. APN-1; BrAP; NCAP; OxBoAm; TCAPo

Blight of Love, The [*with music*]. Mary E. Tucker. CBWP-1

Blighted laurel, and a moldering tomb!, A. (LL) To Phaon ("Can'st thou forget, O! Idol of my soul!") Mary Robinson. CenSon; RWP

Blighters. Siegfried Sassoon. NAMCP V.1; NoAM; OxBEV; PoWW

Blind. Vincente Huidobro. CuPo

Blind Bartimæus. Henry Wadsworth Longfellow. ChIV-2

Blind Beggar, The. Viswanatha Satyanarayana. HotL, tr. by V. Narayana Rao

Blind Boy's Pranks, The. William Thom. OBEV

Blind child clutches a 3" fish. Guard Duty. Dick Gallup. AHA

Blind City. Mona Saudi. PoArWo, tr. by Kamal Boullata

Blind Country. Katharine Tynan Hinkson. IrLP

Blind Date with the Muse. Stephen Dunn. NevBe

Blind fortune, if thou wants a guide. Fortune's Legacy. Unknown. NOSC

Blind from birth, they do not know, The. Some Lines Finished Just Before Dawn at the Bedside of a Dying Student It Has Snowed All Night. Miller Williams. InGu

Blind Goddess, The. Fadhila Chabbi. PoArWo, tr. by Yaseen Noorani

Blind horse trotting up an icy ledge, A. Kosen. ZenPo, tr. by Takashi Ikemoto and Lucien Stryk

Blind Irus' Wolf-Dog. Vincent Bourne. DiBP,

Blind loving wrestling touch! Sheathed hooded sharptoothed touch! Walt Whitman. CAGL Fr. Song of Myself.

Blind Man, The. Fazil Abdulovich Iskander. ItGoST, tr. by Avril Pyman

Blind Man, The. Judith Wright.
   Country Dance. BMAP

Blind Man at the Fair, The. Joseph Campbell. IrV

Blind man carried, A. Unknown. CATKP, tr. by Kevin O'Rourke

Blind Man's Dog, The. Samuel Jackson Pratt. DiBP Fr. Lower World, The.

Blind Men and the Elephant, The. John Godfrey Saxe. ITBLP

Blind Musicians, The. Unknown. TAL

Blind Musicians, the blind musicians, The. Blind Musicians, The. Unknown. TAL

Blind musicians, the blind musicians, The. Unknown. ColAnChi Fr. Classic of Odes.

Blind poet, fiddler, Raftery. For Raftery. Alan Alexander. NOBAu

Blind Solo [after A Love Supreme]. Afaa Michael Weaver. UnSA

Blind, The. Charles Baudelaire. SxFrPo, tr. by James McGowan

Blind woman was closer to the sea, The. Blaga Dimitrova. CSCBP Fr. Forbidden Sea.

Blind woman was more intimate with it, The. Blaga Dimitrova. BBASP, tr. by Heather McHugh

Blind woman—who by some miracle can, A. First Sight. Ellen Doré Watson. NevBe

Blind women, tireless, and the blind little boy. (LL) Robert Pinsky. NoAM; PoA 2002 Fr. Essay on Psychiatrists.

Blind Youth, The. Frank Wedekind. GTCP, tr. by Felix Pollak

Blindest buzzard that I know, The. Sketch, A. Christina Georgina Rossetti. VWP

Blindfold. Sunil Gangopadhyay. PML, tr. by Nandini Gupta

Blindfold I should to Myra run. Lady Sophia Burrell. LW Fr. Chloe and Myra.

Blindfold, The. Greta Stoddart. BeAl; MoWP

Blinding of Isaac Woodard, The. Woody Guthrie. PWW2

Blindman's Buff. Peter Viereck. MoAmPo

Blindman's Cries, The. Tristan Corbière. WoPoe, tr. by Martin James

Blindness we may forgive, but baseness we will smite. (LL) Ode in Time of Hesitation, An. William Vaughn Moody. APN-2; CBCWP; NAAPv.1

Blinds are up, the dusty screen breezing, The. In the Kitchen Dancing to Kitty Wells. Heather Sellers. SweBea

Blind-Sided. Rick Mulkey. AmPoNex

Blink. Cecilia Woloch. RaF

Blink Your Eyes. Sekou Sundiata. FaoP

Blinkered Mind, The. Amy Witting. NOBAu

Bliss. Jean Follain. YaTCFP, tr. by Stephen Romer

Bliss. Jay Parini. PfSP

Bliss of Heaven, Maria, shall be thine, The. Charles Tennyson Turner. CenSon

Blisses about my pilgrimage as pain. (LL) Hap. Thomas Hardy. BrAP; CABP; GSo; MoBrPo; NAEL-6v2; NAEL-7v2; NAMCP V.1; NoAM; NoP-4; NoP-5; OxBSo; WaAnP

Blissful dance. Scream. Allure of Forms, The. Coral Bracho. RMCMP; TAPaP, tr. by Mónica de la Torre

Blistered and dry was the desert I trod. Palm, The. Roy Campbell. MoBrPo

Blithe Fancy lightly builds with airy hands. After Reading Shakspere. Edwin Markham. APN-2

Blizzard. Bill Holm. MiVo

Blizzard, The. Roger McDonald. NOBAu

Blizzard, The: "Now that the worst is over, they predict." Phillis Levin. P180

Blkfern-jungal. Aileen Corpus. BMAP

Bloated and mesmerized by rasberries. Sentence. William Matthews. PfSP

Bloated face, A. with the fust. Anna Glazova. CRWP Fr. Cities.

Bloated with snow and bulging with prefab housing complexes, swollen at the edges. Driving Away. Chandra Mayor. PoPra

Bloating and Its Remedies. Jim Heynen. MotU

Block City. Robert Louis Stevenson. AmFaPo; NTCP

Block Island Ferry. Catherine Imbriglio. IAoNAP

Block of flats, somewhere in Turin. One Man. William Scammell. NLP

Block Party. Major L. Jackson. FuFl

Blockade Swallow, The. Olga Fiodorovna Berggolts. TCRusP, tr. by Daniel Weissbort

Blocks. Frank O'Hara. OxBoAm

Blocks rowdy with jays and strumpet sparrows. Aviary. Mark DeFoe. UrbNat

Blod. Aram Saroyan. AHA

Blōdmōnath. Jon Furberg. IFF

Blodwen, / Her name like the hours. Her Name like the Hours. Gloria Evans Davies. OBWVE

Bloke I know came rolling home as shickered as he could be, A. Shickered As He Could Be. Unknown. NOBAu

Blond. Joseph De Roche. HeIP-4

Blond Bombshell. Lynn Emanuel. OxBoAm

Blond boy in the red trunks is holding your head underwater, The. Primer for the Small Weird Loves, A. Richard Siken. LegDan

Blond guide was lecturing to the Germans, The. Kyoto 2—Ryoanji. William Kistler. WhBo

Blond guy, and I'll have / your nose. (LL) Upon Seeing an Ultrasound Photo of an Unborn Child. Thomas Lux. NevBe; SUP; WaAnP

Blond light blew away grayness, shadows, mists. Facing Bonnard. Aleksander Wat. BLT

Blond medallions of the aspen, The. Six. Caitríona O'Reilly. NIrP

Blond whose skin was translucent as a glass slipper, The. Blue Suede Shoes. Diane Wakoski. AllShUp

Blonde Ambition. Maureen Seaton. ReTh

Blonde neighbor lady tells my wife, The. Opposite of Green, The. Alvin Aubert. ISC

Blonde White Women. Patricia Smith. GT; UnSA

Blond-haired, green-eyed, Italian girl. Amazone. Mary Jo Bona. UnSA

Blondie. Jean Earle. TCAWP

Blood. Jeannette Armstrong. OpeFie

Blood. Judith Barrington. FiBr

Blood. Georges Castera. OGAHCP, tr. by Boadiba and Jack Hirschman

Blood. William Olsen. LiTh

Blood. Viki Radden. BtF

Blood. Lucien Stryk. BodElec

Blood. Franz Wright. AmAlph

Blood and Gold. Endre Ady. IQMS, tr. by Watson Kirkconnell

Blood and gold in leaves. Apocalyptic Yearnings. Michael Rothenberg. Eno

Blood and tears of the Ice Age. Puddle. Ryoko Shindo. CFP, tr. by Aoyami Miyuki and Leza Lowitz

Blood, blood! The lines of every printed sheet. George Henry Boker. APN-2; PCW

Blood Donor. Robert Morgan. AngWePo; TCAWP

Blood from our fingertips comes welling. Song of a Hungarian Jacobin. Endre Ady. IQMS, tr. by Sir Maurice Bowra

Blood from the shoulder drips from couch to floor. Judith. Félix Lope de Vega Carpio. WoPoe, tr. by Brian Soper

Blood Heifer. Dahlia Ravikovitch. DTA, tr. by Ariel Bloch and Chana Bloch

Blood is Justified, The. Muriel Rukeyser. StAl; YaYoPo

Blood Is the Argument. Gary Johnston. BRtP

Blood leaks from this woman, The. Mónica Nepote. SPV, tr. by Jen Hofer

Blood of Daybreak, The. Chŏng Hyŏnjong. CAMKP, tr. by John M. Frankl

Blood of Ishtar, The. Qadesha (Sacred Whore). Cosi Fabian. HW

Blood of my people courses through veins. Blood. Jeannette Armstrong. OpeFie

Blood of Others, The. Gioconda Belli. TANSG, tr. by Steven F. White

Blood only blood is able to beat to strike the right note. Whispered. Jiri Orten. AF, tr. by Lyn Coffin

Blood or Color. Marjorie Welish. FTOS; OnScMo

Blood puddles on the Spanish white floor. Almendares. Sandra M. Castillo. TouFir

Blood searching in his head without metaphor, The. (LL) Letters & Other Worlds. Michael Ondaatje. BrAP; NAMCP V.2; NoAM; NoP-4; NoP-5

Blood splatters itself on snow. Imprint of Microscopic Life Found in Arctic Stones. Patricia Goedicke. GifTon

Blood sprouts like early spring. Sunday Morning. Anne Rouse. NeBl

Blood stolen from my body before dawn. Sunrise. Yi Hyangji. EcSo, tr. by Catherine J. Kim

Blood surges in my temples. Wet Bodies. Franz Douskey. PasH

Blood Ties. Thelma Seto. TWW

Blood to Blood. Alvin Aubert. OxAAAP

Blood was her dress and her embassy. Self-portraits by Frida Kahlo. Joanna Rawson. BodElec

Bloodhounds on Arthur's Track. Edward Robert Bulwer-Lytton. DiBP *Fr.* Arthur.

Blood-inked political leaflets pelted Village streets. Demonstration: Women's House of Detention, 1965. Michael Waters. LiTh

Bloodletting. Anselm Berrigan. HeMarv

Bloodlines. Mary Loving Blanchard. TiP2

Bloods and bucks of this lewd town, The. Horace. *See* Ribald Romeos less and less berattle.

Blood-shotten through the bleak gigantic trees. Winter Twilight, A. John Banister Tabb. APN-2

Blood-splashed leaves cling to a porous moon-soaked walk. American Sonnet (46). Wanda Coleman. BtF

Blood-stained, continue cutting weeds and shade. (LL) Reapers. Jean Toomer. APT-2; ColAP; GT; InGu; NAAPv.2; NAMCP V.1; NIL-7; NoAM; NoP-4; NoP-5; OxBoAm; PtR; SoSe-8; TRP; WaAnP; WeW-3

Blood-stained fruit of labor, sweated out of Black slaves. On Sweet Coffee. Ábrahám Barcsay. IQMS, *tr. by* Thomas Kabdebo

Bloody Clock, A. Kim Hyesun. EcSo, *tr. by* Youngju Ryu

Bloody Hand. Ciaran Carson. PBCIP

Bloody knife blade, A. Richard Wright. APT-2

Bloody like night, splendid in terror, highstrung. Lament for the Stag. Pierre Jean Jouve. YaTCFP, *tr. by* Keith Waldrop

Bloody Masculinity. Ifi Amadiume. HAWP

Bloody men are like bloody buses. Bloody Men. Wendy Cope. BeAl; HarvBoo; NoP-4; NoP-5

Bloody men are like bloody cigarettes. And Another Bloody Thing. Clare Pollard. BeAl

Bloody Orkneys, The. Hamish Blair. EdScPo

Bloody Sire, The. Robinson Jeffers. PoA 2002; PWW2

Bloody trunk [*or* Bloudy trunck] of him who did possess[e], The. NOSC *Fr.* Il Pastor Fido.

Bloom of youth had faded from her face, The. Forsaken, The. Agnes Strickland. CenSon

Bloom on the fruit is perfect, The. At Les Deux Magots. Maura Dooley. IrLP; LW

Bloom-Girl. *Unknown.* SonAtl, *tr. by* Alan Brierly and B. Ouane

Blooming Death. . .Blossoms. Andre O. Hoilette. BRtP

Blooming in the Valley, A. Garrett McDowell. FuFl

Blooming in your childhood in the '30s. Snow. Maurya Simon. FiBr

Blooms and stiffens with desire. (LL) Good-Bye. Joan Larkin. LaCa; WiU

Bloomsbury Snapshot. Connie Bensley. OBCoV

Bloomsday Murders, 16 June 1997, The. Paul Durcan. StAl

Blossom. Stanley Plumly. LiTh

Blossom. May Probyn. VWP

Blossom, The. Eavan Boland. ItP

Blossom, The. William Shakespeare. OBEV *Fr.* Love's Labour's Lost.

Blossom[e], The. John Donne. NAEL-6v1; NAEL-7v1

Blossom at the End of the Body. Beckian Fritz Goldberg. AmAlph

Blossom that lov'st on shadowy banks to lie. Forget-Me-Not, The. Mary Russell Mitford. CenSon

Blossoming bulbs, pots swathed in pink and green. Easter Afternoon. Rachel Hadas. UrbNat

Blossoming myrtle tree. Woman's Ritornelle. Theodor Storm. WoPoe, *tr. by* James Wright

Blossoming plum! Issa. SoOfWa, *tr. by* Sam Hamill

Blossoming white in the rose garden. Blue Rose. Carol Muske-Dukes. ExTi

Blossoms at night. Issa. EH, *tr. by* Robert Hass

Blossoms in the Wind. Takajiro Ohnishi. FaBoWar

Blossoms lift the branches. Beautiful Days. Mary Kinzie. ExTi

Blossoms on the pear. Buson. TAL

Blot in the 'Scutcheon, A. Robert Browning.
  Earl Mertoun's Song. OBEV

Blouse of Felt. Amina Calil. BAP-01

Blow after blow is the farm's blight. Legacy. Ceri Wyn Jones. BBMWP, *tr. by* Dafydd Wyn Jones

Blow, Blow, Thou Winter Wind. Peter Meinke. IaFF

Blow, blow, thou winter wind. William Shakespeare. NoSiC; OBEV *Fr.* As You Like It.

Blow, blow, ye spicy breezes. Ambrose Bierce. APN-2 *Fr.* Devil's Dictionary, The.

Blow, Boys, Blow [*or* Blow, Bullies, Blow]. *Unknown.* FaBoVe

Blow, Bugle, Blow. Alfred Tennyson. *See* Splendour [*or*Splendor] Falls, The.

Blow / Ill wind. Ill Wind. Ted Koehler. ReLy

Blow of an ax. Buson. EH, *tr. by* Robert Hass

Blow Out the Lamp. Nanduri Subbarao. HotL, *tr. by* V. Narayana Rao

Blow out the lights, and come at last to bed. (LL) Sonnet: "All we need is fourteen lines, well, thirteen now." Billy Collins. CAP-8; PoA 2002

Blow them back on the branches. (LL) Our Little Sister is Worried. *Unknown.* NDACCP; WoPoe, *tr. by* Kenneth Rexroth

Blow, West Wind. Robert Penn Warren. ColAP; WaAnP

Blow, whistle / Blow away. Beyond the Blue Horizon. Leo Robin. ReLy

Blow, Winds. William Shakespeare. OxAEP-1 *Fr.* King Lear.

Blow, winds, and crack your cheek! rage! blow! William Shakespeare. OxAEP-1 *Fr.* King Lear.

Blow Your Trumpet, Gabriel. *Unknown.* APN-2; SSUS

Blowfish and Mudtoad. Dave Jeddie Smith. CAP-8; NAMCP V.2

Blowflies Buzz, The. *Unknown.* NOBAu, *tr. by* Catherine H. Berndt

Blowing Eggs. Anne Caston. NAPBL

Blowing out the candle. Ray McNiece. AmZen

Blowing softly over his eyelashes. Kettle Rooted to the Void. Anabel Torres. TANSG, *tr. by* Celeste Kostopulos-Cooperman

Blowing stones. Basho. EH, *tr. by* Robert Hass

Blowing ten thousand years ago. (LL) Languages. Carl Sandburg. APT-1; ColAP

"Blown Apart By Loss . . . ." Rita Dove. FFC

Blown apart by loss, she let herself go. "Blown Apart By Loss . . . ." Rita Dove. FFC

Blown away, flying and flying and flying. (LL) Venice Beach: Brief Song. Dorothy Barresi. SeSe; SwNoth

Blown by winds, the thistledown. Tu Fu [*or* Du Fu]. CrYelRi *Fr.* Random Pleasures.

Blown from Sleep's trumpet. (LL) Louse Hunting. Isaac Rosenberg. FaBoWar; NAEL-6v2; NAEL-7v2; NAMCP V.1; NoAM; NoP-4; NoP-5; OxAEP-2; OxBEV

Blown from the west. Buson. EH, *tr. by* Robert Hass

Blown[e] in the morning, thou shalt fade ere noon. Sir Richard Fanshawe. OBEV *Fr.* Il Pastor Fido.

Blows birthday candles for the world. (LL) Birth of Tragedy, The. Irving Layton. BrAP; NoAM; NoP-4; NoP-5

Blows the Wind Today. Robert Louis Stevenson. NPeEn
  (To S. R. Crockett.) NePenScot

Blows within his dream as lifting snow. Her Black Hair. Robert Pack. MoW

Blowzy dove, A. Beak wide open, on a khamsin day. Reflections on a Dove. Hamutal Bar Yosef. DTA, *tr. by* Shirley Kaufman

Blp. (LL) Loch Ness Monster's Song, The. Edwin Morgan. NePenScot; OPOU; StAl

BLS. G. E. Patterson. BRtP

Blue. Rafael Alberti. PoetW, *tr. by* Mark Strand

Blue. Elin ap Hywel. BBMWP, *tr. by* the author

Blue. Elin ap Hywel. ATSWP, *tr. by* Robert Minhinnick

Blue. Bryan Martin Davies. BBMWP, *tr. by* Elin ap Hywel

Blue. William Heyen. InoFa

Blue 2. Wopko Jensma. TSAP

Blue Again. Dorothy Fields. ReLy

Blue and sudden as beginning. Quilt, The. Chitra Divakaruni. FiBr

Blue and the Gray, The. Francis Miles Finch. APN-2; CBCWP; CtM; PCW

Blue and White. Mary Elizabeth Coleridge. OBEV

Blue and white. Poems at the Porthole. Lorine Niedecker. FTOS

Blue and white tie arrived at the man's neck through, The. Tell Us, Josephine. Ron Padgett. FTOS

Blue and yellow light, The. Training on the Peninsula. Brian Turner. ArBi

Blue Angel, The. Allen Ginsberg. BB

Blue Arm. Bernard Spencer. NoAM

Blue arm stuck out of the train's window, A. Watching Trains. Joanna Fuhrman. AmPoNex

Blue arrived. And its time was painted. Blue. Rafael Alberti. PoetW, *tr. by* Mark Strand

Blue as a new moon midnight. Fresh Mussels. Charles McDonald. NLP

Blue: "As through marble or the lining of." Carl Phillips. BtF; OxAAAP

Blue Bananas. Ron Padgett. NYP2

Blue Bayou. Langston Hughes. NAMCP V.1

Blue Bicycles. Charles Fishman. ArBi

Blue black and bow bent under, beautiful. Old Black Ladies Standing on Bus Stop Corners #2. Quincy Troupe. OxAAAP

Blue Black Pearl, A. Clairesa Clay. BRtP

Blue Blood. James Stephens. MoBrPo; OBCoV; OBMV

Blue, blue collar, my heart's delight. Zi-jin: The Student's Blue Collar or Lapel. *Unknown.* CCL1, *tr. by* Ezra Pound

Blue, blue is the grass about the river. Beautiful Toilet, The. Mei Sheng. NDACCP; OBVE, *tr. by* Ezra Pound

Blue blue the summit. Heaven Peak. Muso Soseki. EaWin, *tr. by* W. S. Merwin

Blue boat of morning and already. Tourism in the Late 20th Century. Silvia Curbelo. BodElec

Blue booby lives, The. Blue Booby, The. James Tate. NAMCP V.2; NoAM

Blue Book 18 Pages 1–4. Steve Benson. FTOS

Blue bus stopped too late, we were already on our way, The. Departure. Vincent Woods. NIrP

Blue Cage, A. Vincent Woods. NIrP

Blue City, The. Alfred Wellington Purdy. NoP-4

Blue Clay. Ellease Southerland. GT

Blue cloud sky. Tune: "Sumuche Dancers." Fan Chung-yen. ColAnChi, *tr. by* James Robert Hightower

Blue Collar Holiday. Jeni Olin. BAP-04; FreRad

Blue crane fishing in Cooloolah's twilight, The. At Cooloolah. Judith Wright. BMAP; HarvBoo

  (Blue crane fishing in Cooloola's twilight, The.) BrAP

Blue day / a blue jay, A. March. Elizabeth Jane Coatsworth. Spl

Blue Day Journey, The [*with music*]. Gwyn Jones. OBWVE

Blue Days. Rita Dove. ExTi

Blue Days. Sŏ Chŏngju. CAMKP, *tr. by* David R. McCann

Blue Deer. Pak Mogwŏl [*or Mokwŏl*]. CAMKP, *tr. by* Edward W. Poitras

Blue Diamond. Claudia Keelan. BodElec

Blue Dome, The. Deborah Randall. NeBl

Blue Elegies. George Elliott Clarke.

  1.5. Coast

Blue eraser dust. Organizing a Drawer. Yi Sanghûi. EcSo, *tr. by* Jennifer M. Lee

Blue eye-pupil in my park, A. Swan, The. Delmira Agustini. TANSG, *tr. by* Mark McCaffrey

Blue flax blossoming near the greenhouse. Apache Plume. Arthur Sze. AmAlph

Blue fluid in my limbs. Climbing Out. Diane Ackerman. OtW

Blue from Heaven, The. Stevie Smith. BrAP

Blue garbage truck goes by, A. Indiana. Reed Bye. AHA

Blue Girls. John Crowe Ransom. APT-1; BrAP; ColAP; MoAmPo; NoAM; NoP-4; NoP-5; WeW-3

  (Vanity of the Blue Girls, The.) FuPo

Blue go up & blue go down. American Lights, Seen from Off Abroad. John Berryman. OBCoV

Blue Grapes. Yi Yuksa. CAMKP, *tr. by* David R. McCann

Blue Grass. Howard Dietz. ReLy

Blue hairs suddenly grew in between the last sentences. Finger Paintings. Johnny Stanton. AHA

Blue Hat. Connie Voisine. FiBr

Blue Horses. Ed Roberson. GT

Blue Horses, The. James McAuley. BMAP

Blue in the west the mountain stands. Vickery's Mountain. Edwin Arlington Robinson. MoAmPo

18. Blue Irises. David McFadden. NLPA

Blue is for the troublemakers. Letters from School, The. Juan Delgado. TouFir

Blue is my sky peter. Unreturning, The. Alfred Goldsworthy Bailey. Coast

Blue is Our Lady's colour. Blue and White. Mary Elizabeth Coleridge. OBEV

Blue Is the Hero. Bill Berkson. AHA; NYP2

Blue Island Intersection. Carl Sandburg. MoAmPo

Blue Jacket, The. Marion Angus. NePenScot

Blue Jay. Paul Lake. RA

Blue jay scuffling in the bushes follows, The. On the Move. Thom Gunn. CalPo; NoP-4; NoP-5; OxAEP-2; TRP; WaAnP

Blue jay, The. In So Doing. Lawson Fusao Inada. WhBo

Blue Jay, The. D. H. Lawrence. NPeEn

Blue Juniata. Malcolm Cowley.

  Streets of Air, The. PoA 2002

Blue Kashmir, '74. Carol Muske-Dukes. AmAlph; PuP-23

Blue kingfisher dives on you in fire, The. (LL) Colloquy in Black Rock. Robert Lowell. MoAmPo; OxBoAm

Blue laguna rocks and quivers, The. Port of Holy Peter. John Masefield. OBMV

Blue landing lights make. Our Ground Time Here Will Be Brief. Maxine W. Kumin. NAMCP V.2; OtW

Blue leather harness slips off glistening shoulders. Radiant Silhouette I. John Yau. OpBo

Blue Light, The. Kathleen Norris. UpMys

Blue Meridian, The. Jean Toomer.

  Brown River, Smile. BLPJKO

Blue Mist. Sergey Aleksandrovich Yesenin. RusPo, *tr. by* Robert Arthur Douglas Ford

Blue mist. Snow plenitude. Blue Mist. Sergey Aleksandrovich Yesenin. RusPo, *tr. by* Robert Arthur Douglas Ford

Blue mists surround the mountains now. Lines Written on a Farewell View of the Franconia Mountains at Twilight. Henrietta Cordelia Ray. CBWP-3

Blue Monday. Calvin Forbes. ESEAA

Blue Monday. Langston Hughes. SAmP

Blue Monday. Diane Wakoski. NALW; PmAP

Blue Monday. Al Young. SpirFl

Blue Moon. Lorenz Hart. ReLy

Blue Moon. Mimi Khalvati. MFPA

Blue mountains speak of my desire. Hwang Chini. CATKP, *tr. by* Peter H. Lee

Blue mountains to the north of the walls. Taking Leave of a Friend. Li Po. NDACCP; PoCho; WaAnP, *tr. by* Ezra Pound

Blue mouth of the shark, The. Coming. Robert Kelly. PmAP

Blue Movies. Maurya Simon. GifTon

Blue of the heaps of beads poured into her breasts. Blue Monday. Diane Wakoski. NALW; PmAP

Blue Paisley Shirt, The. Thomas William Shapcott. BMAP

Blue parakeet named Julie, A. Things That Have Escaped Me. Jesse Lee Kercheval. SUP

Blue Pencil, The. John, Duke of Buckingham and Normandy Sheffield. STuOW *Fr.* Ode on the Death of Mr. Henry Purcell.

Blue, pink and yellow houses, and, afar. Tropical Town. Salomon De la Selva. NAAPv.2

Blue Plate Tea Room: Sestina, The. John Ridland. VisFro

Blue Poles. Jim Carroll. AHA

Blue Poles, a longtime painting, mute, manic, American. At the Jackson Pollock Retrospective in L.A. Harold L. Johnson. BtF

Blue Pond at Berkovitsa. Vladimir Levchev. CSCBP, *tr. by* Georgi Belev and Lisa Sapinkopf

Blue rain. Phantasmagoria. Sinan Anton. IrPoTo, *tr. by* the author

Blue Rapids. Lu Yu. ColAnChi, *tr. by* Burton Watson

Blue Ridge [*with music*]. Ellen Bryant Voigt. LPSFW; NoAM

Blue River. Muhammad ibn Ghalib al-Rusafi. WoPoe, *tr. by* Cola Franzen

Blue Rock, The. Sojourner Kincaid Rolle. GeoHom

Blue Room, The. Richard Edwards. Spl

Blue Room, The. Lorenz Hart. ReLy

Blue Rose. Carol Muske-Dukes. ExTi

Blue seagulls yell insults. Seagulls. Daria Menicanti. CItWP, *tr. by* Cinzia Sartini Blum and Lara Trubowitz

Blue Shade. Aaron Shurin. FTOS

Blue Skies. Irving Berlin. ReLy

Blue skies and drinking water. (LL) In the Next Galaxy. Ruth Stone. BeAl; StAl

Blue skies played house against. Nushu. Margaret Randall. ICANM

Blue Skies, White Breasts, Green Trees. Gerald Stern. BodElec

Blue sky blue water. Home. Calvin Forbes. GT

Blue sky in a human face. Mac Wellman. HeMarv *Fr.* Rat Minaret: Miniaturist-Divan, The.

Blue Sky in Morning. Rob MacKenzie. Oth

Blue snow is turning black, The. Poem. Aleksandr Trifonovich Tvardovsky. RusPo, *tr. by* Robert Arthur Douglas Ford

Blue Song. Mary Macleod. NePenScot, *tr. by* Robert Crawford

Blue Suburban. Howard Nemerov. ColAP

Blue Suede Shoes. Ai. ReTh

Blue Suede Shoes. Diane Wakoski. AllShUp

Blue Swallows, The. Howard Nemerov. MakPoe; NoP-4; NoP-5; OWoS

Blue Symphony. John Gould Fletcher. APT-1

Blue Tail Fly or Jimmy Cracked Corn, The. Daniel Decatur Emmett. TCAPo

Blue tail-feathers and markings of gold on a pair of mandarin ducks. News So Seldom Comes. Wen T'ing-yün. CCL1, *tr. by* Glen Baxter

Blue Terrance, The. Terrance Hayes. LegDan

Blue Texarkana. Glenn Stokes. EGAG

Blue That Isn't Even Blue or in Any Case, A. Amelia Rosselli. CItWP, *tr. by* Cinzia Sartini Blum and Lara Trubowitz

Blue. The green. The river-bed, The. Scene, The. Ágnes Nemes Nagy. PoSu, *tr. by* Bruce Berlind

Blue thigh of daybreak, sweetened, fall apart—. Michael Masse. Sam Witt. NeAmPo

Blue! 'Tis the Life of Heaven, the Domain. John Keats. OxBSo

Blue Tit on a String of Peanuts. Norman Alexander MacCaig. CABP

Blue vein, bright on her temple, pitifully beating, The. (LL) Boy with His Hair Cut Short. Muriel Rukeyser. NALW; NAMCP V.2; NoAM; NoP-5

Blue Water. Li Po. CrYelRi; ErotSp, *tr. by* Sam Hamill

Blue water ripples the well at the corner of the mossy rock. Evening on the Mountain: Song to the Moon in the Well. Yi Kyubo. WoPoe, *tr. by* Kevin O'Rourke

Blue whale swam through blue air in the basement, The.   Ghost Shirt, The. Lucia Maria Perillo.   BAP-01

Blue Willow.   Jody Gladding.   P180

Blue Wind, The.   Nadja.   SurWo, *tr.* by Richard Howard

Blue woman climbed out and kissed him, The.   Lake.   Georgi Belev.   CSCBP, *tr. by* the author and Lisa Sapinkopf

Blue world, A.   World of Lightning, A.   Mahmoud al-Braikan.   IrPoTo, *tr.* by Saadi A. Simawe and Ellen Doré Watson

Bluebeard.   Mark Bibbins.   WiU

Bluebeard.   Edna St. Vincent Millay.   APT-1; NAAPv.2

Bluebeard's Closet.   Rose Terry Cooke.   APN-2; NAAPv.1; TCAPo

Bluebells for Love [*with music*].   Patrick Kavanagh.   IrLP

Blueberry City.   Virginia Hamilton Adair.   AFaM

Bluebird in Cutleaf Beech.   Wendy Wilder Larsen.   KGB

Bluebird not a bluejay, A.   New Poem.   Holley Blackwell.   AnSo

Blue-black of a winter morning.   Waking Up Twice.   Jack Anderson.   PasH

Bluebonnets.   Gail Mazur.   CFP

Blue-Eyed Exterminator, The.   Josephine Jacobsen.   OxBoAm

Bluefish boil the water silver; they tangle in the chase.   Blues: Late August. Cleopatra Mathis.   ExTi

Blue-Fly, The.   Robert Graves.   NAEL-6v2; NAEL-7v2; NAMCP V.1; NoAM

Blue-geese, white-geese, you may say.   "H. D."   APT-1 *Fr.* Flowering of the Rod, The.

Bluegrass.   Jean Nordhaus.   PfSP

Blue-handed, with difficult string.   Winter Rose, The.   Gillian Ferguson. NeBl

Bluejay and the Mockingbird, The.   Howard Nemerov.   BodElec

Blueness of the Day, The.   David Mura.   OPRER

Blueness of the hour, The.   Sonnet.   Frank O'Hara.   AHA

Blueprint for Disaster.   Christian Morgenstern.   WoPoe, *tr.* by David R. Slavitt

Blueprints.   Madeline DeFrees.   ExTi

Blue-rinsed pool is full of rhythmic, lone strokers, The.   Going Swimmingly. Katherine Pierpoint.   MoWP

Blues.   Edward Kamau Brathwaite.   GT

Blues.   James A. Emanuel.   SeSe

Blues.   Suzanne Gardinier.   AmPoNex

Blues.   Pierre Martory.   KGB, *tr.* by John Ashbery

Blues.   B. P. Nichol.   IFF

Blues.   Sonia Sanchez.   GT

Blues.   Christine Wiesenthal.   IFF

Blues, The.   Langston Hughes.   TLR

Blues, The.   Mark Vinz.   MiVo

Blues 1.   Barry Wallenstein.   SeSe

Blues 2.   Barry Wallenstein.   SeSe

Blues and blues.   Remembered.   Sterling Plumpp.   GT

Blues at 1.   Dorothy Perry Thompson.   SpirFl

Blues at Dawn.   Langston Hughes.   SAmP

Blues begins to moan in her stomach never quite full, A.   Drummond's Lover Sings the Blues.   Norman Weinstein.   WaCA

Blues blow in their purity, The.   Blue Monday.   Al Young.   SpirFl

Blues del SIDA / AIDS Blues.   Francisco X. Alarcón.   GeoHom

Blues Don't Change, The [*"Now I'll tell you about the Blues. All Negroes like Blues. Why? Because they was born with the Blues. And now everybody have the Blues. Sometimes they don't know what it is."*].   Al Young. ESEAA; GT

Blues for a Melodeon.   Phyllis McGinley.   AmWit

Blues for Aunt Ruth.   Norita Dittberner-Jax.   MiVo

Blues for Bird.   Linda France.   NeBl

Blues for Elliot Sharp.   Ronny Someck.   IrPoTo, *tr.* by Vivian Eden

Blues for Franks Wooten / House of the Lifting of the Head.   Tom Weatherly. GT

Blues for the Lonely*.   Jeremy Robson.   SeSe

Blues for the Nightowl.   Elton Glaser.   PBCAP

Blues for Warren.   Thomas McGrath.   AF

Blues for Zoot.   Sascha Feinstein.   AmPoNex

Blues: "I meet you again in public. I."   Honor Moore.   PfS

Blues in "C."   Ron Overton.   SeSe

Blues in the Night.   Johnny Mercer.   APT-2; ReLy

Blues lady / with the beaded face.   Grinding Vibrato.   Jayne Cortez. OxAAAP

Blues: Late August.   Cleopatra Mathis.   ExTi

Blues meant Swiss-Up, The.   Riding Across John Lee's Finger.   Stanley Crouch.   GT

Blues: My Baby's Gone.   Alfred B. Spellman.   EGAG

Blues Spiritual for Mammy Prater.   Dionne Brand.   WaAnP

Blues: "Those five or six young guys."   Derek Walcott.   EMP

Blues: "Tops of the higher peaks, The."   Kenneth Rexroth.   NAMCP V.1

Blues Variations.   Lorenzo Thomas.   AnSo

Blues Villanelle for Sonny Criss.   Sascha Feinstein.   AmPoNex

Bluesky.   Pierre Albert-Birot.   CuPo

Bluesman.   Charlie R. Braxton.   BRtP

Bluesman in pungent mood, The.   Tobacco Warehouse Blues.   Houston A., Jr. Baker.   SeSe

Bluesman's Blues, A.   Lenard D. Moore.   ISC

Blue-Stocking Revels; or, The Feast of the Violets.   Leigh Hunt. Canto 2.
   Aphrodite Adiposa.   STuOW

Bluesy.   Gestures: A Game Anglican.   Ernst Jandl.   OnScMo

Bluetits.   Ruth Smith.   Prnts

Bluff Knoll Sublimity.   John Kinsella.   VaPo

Blunting, The.   Richard Eberhart.   BodElec

Blunts.   Major L. Jackson.   LegDan; SpirFl

Blurb for *Anna Livia Plurabelle*, A.   James Joyce.   OBCoV

Blurb for *Haveth Childers Everywhere*, A.   James Joyce.   OBCoV

Blurred Edge.   Barbara Guest.   NYP2

Blurred grey streak and he is gone, A.   Lizard.   Norman Kreitman.   EdScPo

Blurred in a whirlwind, a mighty cloud of dust.   Indignation.   José Santos Chocano.   TCLAP, *tr.* by Andrew Rosing

Blurring a definition. Quick! you are old. (LL)   Realization, The.   Yvor Winters.   APT-2; HarvBoo

Blush and blow, blush and blow.   Sad Spring-Song.   Sarah Morgan Bryan Piatt.   NCAP

Blusterer of a bull, A.   Summer Bull.   Valerie Gillies.   EdScPo

Bo Tree.   Patricia Pogson.   Prnts

Boädicea.   Alfred Tennyson.
   "Hear Icenian, Catieuchlanian, hear Coritanian, Trinobant!"   FaBoWar

Board-blinded windows knew what happened, The.   Another Nameless Prostitute Says the Man is Innocent.   Martín Espada.   ViWalt

Boarded the train there's no getting off. (LL)   Metaphors.   Sylvia Plath. HeIP-4; NAMCP V.2; SoSe-8

Boarded up churches.   Going Home.   Toneka Nathene Bonitto-Burwell.   BtF

Boarders look so good and new, The.   Legend of the Crossing-Sweeper.   May Kendall.   VWP

Boasting of My Son.   Li Shang-yin.   ColAnChi, *tr.* by James J. Y. Liu

Boat, a.   Jordan Davis.   HeMarv

Boat, The.   Ferenc Kazinczy.   IQMS, *tr.* by Watson Kirkconnell

Boat, The.   Francis Ponge.   MotU, *tr.* by Cid Corman

Boat, The.   Anne Sexton.   NAAL-5 *Fr.* Death of the Fathers, The.

Boat Builder.   Tammy Armstrong.   Coast

Boat docked in at Liverpool, The.   Arrival 1946.   Moniza Alvi.   BeAl

Boat Down the River of Yellow Silt, A.   Kimiko Hahn.   ExTi

Boat floats over shadow, two boys were aboard, A.   *Unknown.*   NDACCP, *tr. by* Ezra Pound

Boat has the smell of oil, and something whirrs all the time like an obsessive thought, The.   Start of a Late Autumn Novel.   Tomas Tranströmer. MotU, *tr.* by Robert Bly

Boat is chafing at our long delay, The.   Song.   John Davidson.   OBEV

Boat moored, lunch in a lonely village, The.   Dappled Horse, The.   Mei Yao Ch'en.   ColAnChi, *tr.* by Burton Watson

Boat of sandalwood and oars of magnolia, A.   Boating Song.   Li Po.   TAL

Boat of Stars.   Li Ch'ing-chao.   ErotSp, *tr.* by Sam Hamill
   (To the Tune: Boat of Stars.)   CrYelRi

Boat on the Pacific, A.   Najaat Al-Udwany.   PoArWo, *tr.* by Moulouk Berry and Ali Farghaly

Boat on the River of Heaven. (LL)   Kenneth Rexroth.   APSN; APT-2; NAAPv.2; NAMCP V.1 *Fr.* Love Poems of Marichiko, The.

Boat on the Shore.   Andrey Andreievich Voznesensky.   RusPo, *tr.* by Robert Arthur Douglas Ford

Boat People.   Yusef Komunyakaa.   AF; PoPoPo

Boat Poem.   Bernard Spencer.   EmeKit

Boat pulls upon its tether, shifts its body from one foot to the other, The.   Boat, The.   Francis Ponge.   MotU, *tr.* by Cid Corman

Boat rocks at anchor by the misty island, The.   Mooring on Chien-Te River. Meng Hao Jan.   NDACCP, *tr.* by Gary Snyder

Boat slows, moors by beach-run in smoke, A.   Stayover at Chien-Teh River. Meng Hao Jan.   ChinPo, *tr.* by Ye Weilian [*or* Yeh Wei-lien *or* Wai-lim Yip]

Boat Song [*with music*].   Henrietta Cordelia Ray.   CBWP-3

Boat Song.   Sir Walter Scott.   OxAEP-2

Boat that did not rock or wobble once, A.   Seamus Heaney.   ModIr *Fr.* Squarings.

Boat tilts on your image on the waves, The.   Romantic Movement, The.   Philip Lamantia.   CLPP

Boathouse, The.   Robert Minhinnick.   AngWePo

Boating at Dusk.   Song Ikp'il.   CATKP, *tr.* by Chi-gyu Kim [*or* Kim Chonggil]

Boating Song. Li Po. TAL

Boatman, The. Jay Macpherson. BrAP

Boatpond, broken off, looks back at the sky, The. X. Jean Valentine. ExTi

Boats. Bernadette Mayer. FTOS

Boats are careened in the harbour. Here is a bed. (LL)   Sailing to an Island. Richard Murphy. ModIr; PBCIP

Boat's Blueprint, The. Ian Hamilton Finlay. NePenScot

Boats in a Fog. Robinson Jeffers. NAAPv.2; NoP-4; NoP-5; WaAnP (Boats in Fog.) BLT

Boats' lights in the dawn going so swiftly the, The. Charles Olson. BodElec Fr. Maximus Poems, The.

Boat's tarred and shellacked to a water-repellant finish, The. Reed Boat, A. Yusef Komunyakaa. AmAlph

Boatswain! Tempest, The. William Shakespeare.

Boatswain, His One Friend. Lord Byron. DiBP

Boaz Asleep. Victor Hugo. SxFrPo

Bob marley new king of the music. Bob Marley New King of the Music. Anthony McNeill. WaCA

Bob Marley's Dead. Rachel Manley. WaCA

Bob Southey! You're a poet—poet-laureate. Lord Byron. OBSV Fr. Don Juan.

Bob Wills LP is on the turntable, A. At the Movies. David Westheimer. TiP2

Bob / You make me move in an ancient way. Stepping to da Muse/Sic. Afua Cooper. WaCA

Bobbin Stops, The. István Sinka. IQMS, tr. by Adam Makkai

Bobbing on the breeze blown waves. Way of the Water-Hyacinth, The. Zawgee. AmFaPo; ItP, tr. by Lyn Aye

Bobs on the water. Boat-like can cleave it. In Praise of the Body. Anna Hajnal. IQMS, tr. by Kenneth McRobbie

Bocas: A Daughter's Geography. Ntozake Shange. WaAnP

Boda, La. Alfonso D'Aquino. RMCMP

Bodas de las Flores se Dan Sobre el Estigma, Las. El polen se desprende al comenzar la aurora y en un solo momento la vida se redime y entonces se retira. María Baranda. RMCMP

Boddhisattva Doctrine: Enter / Nirvana only when all beings, sentient. John Cage. APSN Fr. Diary: How to Improve the World (You Will Only Make Matters Worse).

Bodega, Goodbye [with music]. Edwin Honig. NoAM

Bodhidharma Crossing the Graywolf River on a Ry-Krisp. Tim McNulty. GifTon

Bodhidharma Never Came to Hatboro. Tyler Doherty. WANABP

Bodhisattva Vow. Adam Yauch. WhBo

Bodhisattva Vows. Albert Saijo. WhBo

Bodhisattva vows to be the last one off the sinking ship. Bodhisattva Vows. Albert Saijo. WhBo

Bodies of men and women engirth me, and I engirth them, The. Walt Whitman. APN-1 Fr. Leaves of Grass [1855 Version, Complete Text].

Bodies of the young are not the flower, The. James Keir Baxter. BeAl Fr. Autumn Testament.

Bodies of Water. Greg Williamson. NAPBL; NeAmPo

Bodies, The. Elizabeth Spires. NIL-7

Bodies / tidal waves. Ana Istarú. TANSG, tr. by Mary Jane Treacy

Bodiless. Robert Budde. PoPra

Bodily music. (LL) Year's End. Marilyn Hacker. NAMCP V.2; WiU

Bodo. Thomas Lux. OPRER

Body. Robert Creeley. FTOS

Body and Mind. Conrad Hilberry. GM

Body and mind, we used to think, were two. Body and Mind. Conrad Hilberry. GM

Body, and soul. (LL) Jet Set Melodrama. Michael Brownstein. AHA; FTOS

Body and Soul. B. H. Fairchild. MAAN; MoASP; SUP

Body and Soul. Frank Eyton, Edward Heyman and Robert Sour. ReLy

Body and Soul. Luciana Notari. CItWP, tr. by Cinzia Sartini Blum and Lara Trubowitz

Body and Soul: Poem for Two Readers. John Taggart. FTOS

Body and the Soul, The. Vicente Aleixandre. RaW, tr. by Robert Bly

Body as Braille, The. Lorna Dee Cervantes. NAMCP V.2

Body as Dictionary, as Bible, The. Matt Robinson. Coast

Body as What Is Remembered. Tsering Wangno Dhompa. WANABP

Body Asking Shadow. Han-shan (Cold Mountain). BB; CCL1; NDACCP, tr. by Gary Snyder (Cold Mountain Poems.) ASA

Body asking shadow, how do you keep up? (LL) Body Asking Shadow. Han-shan (Cold Mountain). BB; CCL1; NDACCP, tr. by Gary Snyder

Body Bags. R. S. Gwynn. RA

Body Beside the Ties, The. Kenneth Patchen. CLPP

Body beside your body sleeps like death, The. Sleep of the Insomniac, The. William Virgil Davis. YaYoPo

Body Cavity. Martin Ross. IIR

Body Count. Leonard Nathan. PBCAP

Body Doubled. Lynne Cohen. PfS

Body escapes, The. Josée Lapeyrère. SCFWP Fr. Skirt, The.

Body full of blood. Tracie Morris. RD Fr. Myomectomy Cycle, The.

Body has its own story, The. She. Lynn Emanuel. BodElec

Body held in front of me. (LL) Elder Sister, The. Sharon Olds. CAP-8; NIL-7; NIP-4

Body I am is the purest instrumentation of desire I know, The. Roy Kiyooka. NLPA Fr. Pear Tree Pomes.

Body in Youth, The. Ellen Hinsey. YaYoPo

Body Inside the Soul, The. Bell Hooks. ISC

Body is Fragile, The. Tony Trigilio. AmZen

Body is immobile, left behind, The. Octet Before Winter. Claire Malroux. VCWP, tr. by Marilyn Hacker

Body Is Pain, The. Vietnamese Oral Tradition. CaDao, tr. by John Balaban

Body is something you need in order to stay. Living in the Body. Joyce Sutphen. GoPo

Body is the body of the Buddha, The. Ten Thousand Sutras. Sam Hamill. ErotSp

Body Language. Linda France. NeBl

Body Language. Sylvia Kantaris. LW

Body, long oppressed, The. This Corruptible. Elinor Wylie. MoAmPo

Body Mutinies, The. Lucia Maria Perillo. IllVoic

Body my house. Question. May Swenson. APT-2; GPTC; NAMCP V.2; OxBoAm; PtR

Body of a woman, white hills, white thighs. Body of a Woman. Pablo Neruda. ErotSp; PoCho; TCLAP, tr. by W. S. Merwin

Body of a woman, white hills, white thighs. Body of a Woman. Pablo Neruda. RaBo; WED, tr. by Robert Bly

Body / of / Benjamin Franklin, The. Epitaph. Benjamin Franklin. TCAPo

Body of God, The. D. H. Lawrence. ChIV-2

Body of Liberties, The. Peter Gurnis. OnScMo

Body of man is evolved to a brain, The. For Maulana Karenga & Pharoah Sanders. Imamu Amiri Baraka. APSN

Body of man is like a flicker of lightning, The. Body of Man, The. Van Hanh. EaWin; WoPoe, tr. by W. S. Merwin and Nguyen Ngoc Bich

Body of Man, The. Van Hanh. EaWin; WoPoe, tr. by W. S. Merwin and Nguyen Ngoc Bich

Body of morning glorious. Malva Flores. RMCMP Fr. Nomad House.

Body of my love. (LL) Cast Off, The. Marge Piercy. NAMCP V.2; NoAM

Body of the Beloved, The. Jorge Carrera Andrade. tr. by Rene de Costa, Rigas Kappatos and Eleni Paidoussi
   "Your body is a garden, a bush of flowers." BLPSL, tr. by Rene de Costa, Rigas Kappatos and Eleni Paidoussi
   "Your body is a golden temple." BLPSL, tr. by Rene de Costa, Rigas Kappatos and Eleni Paidoussi
   "Your body is bathed eternally." BLPSL, tr. by Rene de Costa, Rigas Kappatos and Eleni Paidoussi

Body of thirst will stand in morning rain, A. Harvest: A Line Drawing. Gregory Pardlo. BRtP

Body [or B o d y]. James Merrill. CAP-8; NAMCP V.2; OxBoAm

Body Politic. Silvio Giussani. ItPo, tr. by Gayle Ridinger

Body prone—almost flat, The. Inquest, By Hand. Jim Schley. NevBe

Body refuses to die, The. Memory, The. Jane Mead. LaCa

Body Remembers, The. Julia Kasdorf. ACAMVP

Body sinks and rises, A. Deer, The. Shara McCallum. NAPBL

Body, Soul, And Godhead. "Angelus Silesius." GePo Fr. Cherubical Wanderer, The.

Body swims half-hidden, The. Harmony in Blue. Mary O'Donoghue. NIrP

Body, The: A Fancy. Margaret Lucas Cavendish, Duchess of Newcastle. STuOW

Body: What bodies else but Man's did Nature make. Dialogue betwixt the Body and the Mind, A. Margaret Lucas Cavendish, Duchess of Newcastle. PEW

78: Body's Beauty. Dante Gabriel Rossetti. NAEL-7v2 Fr. House of Life, The.

Body's Speech, The. Unknown. IrLP, tr. by Frank O'Connor

Body-Snatcher. Ambrose Bierce. APN-2 Fr. Devil's Dictionary, The.

Boeing. Angela Agali. NeNiPo

Boerum Hill Tanka. Kimiko Hahn. PA9/11

Bofors A. A. Gun, The. Gavin Ewart. PoWW

Bog Queen. Seamus Heaney. NAMCP V.2; NoAM; RACG

Bogey-Wife, The. Kathleen Jamie. NeBrP

Bog-Face. Stevie Smith. NPeEn

Bogland. Seamus Heaney. HeIP-4; NAMCP V.2; NoAM; PBCIP; PNI; PoetW; PoPoPo

Bogomil in Languedoc. John Mathias. AmWaPo

Bogyman. Fleur Adcock. MoWP

Bohemia. Dorothy Parker. AmWit; APT-1; BrAP; NBLV

7. Bohemian Carp. Justin Quinn. NIrP Fr. Days of the New Republic.

Bohemians, The. Ivor Gurney. FaBoWar

Bohol's Tarsier Population. Clovis L. Nazareno. ReBoTo

Boi Vě os Homens, Um. Carlos Drummond de Andrade. IPoFL

Boiled Peanuts. Eleanor Ross Taylor. AFaM

Boiling over inwardly. Archpoet's Confession, The. Unknown. WoPoe, tr. by Phillip Holland

Boiling, The. Kevin Young. OxAAAP

Boiling Water, The. Kenneth Koch. ItP

Boise was my first city. Sunday Morning Walk. Vern Rutsala. NevBe

Bojangles of Harlem. Dorothy Fields. ReLy

Bold Benbow rubs his jovial eyes. Chancery Morals. Winthrop Mackworth Praed. NOBRP

Bold, cautious, true, and my loving comrade. (LL) As Toilsome I Wander'd Virginia's Woods. Walt Whitman. APN-1; BLT; NAAL-3; PoAgWa

Bold Hannibal himself force-marched beneath. Crossing the Alps. Ken Morrice. EdScPo

Bold red-head a quick. Cassin's Finch. Anne MacNaughton. ICANM

Bold Robin has robed him in ghostly attire. Thomas Love Peacock. OxAEP-2 Fr. Maid Marian.

Bolder Youth, grown of capable arms, A. Anne Finch, Countess of Winchilsea. FaBoWar Fr. All Is Vanity.

Boldest thing I ever did was to save a savior, The. Oration, The. Carolyn Kizer. PoDa

Bolding Vedas! Shanks New Nisa! Place-Names of China. Alan Bennett. UV

Boldness in Love. Thomas Carew. CavPo

Bolero at Armageddon. David Huerta. RMCMP, tr. by Mark Schafer

Bolero en Aramgedón. David Huerta. RMCMP

Boleros #21. Jay Wright. ICANM

Boleros #31. Jay Wright. ICANM

Boleros #36. Jay Wright. MoW

Bolivia: Another End of Ace. Tom Raworth. PFTM-2

Boll-weevil's coming, and the winter's cold. November Cotton Flower. Jean Toomer. ColAP; NAAPv.2; NAMCP V.1; NoAM; OxBoAm

Bolt and bar the shutter. Mad as the Mist and Snow. William Butler Yeats. RaBo

Bolt / In the frame. George Oppen. APT-2; PFTM-1

Bolt of lightning in its naked hand, A. (LL) Selves, The. Patricia K. Page. BrAP; GPPA

Bolt, The. Mary Kinzie. ExTi; PtR

Bolt-hole of brigandage, old keep. Old Roscoff. Tristan Corbière. WoPoe, tr. by Derek Mahon

Bomb. Gregory Corso. AtGh

Bomb bays open and they kick. Atom Bum, The. William Greenway. AtGh

Bomb is primed to go off at one twenty, The. One Twenty Pub, The. Wisława Szymborska. StAl, tr. by Dennis O'Driscoll

Bomb said to a city, A. Nina Kossman. CRWP, tr. by the author

Bomb Then, Bomb Now. Bruce Andrews. PmAP

Bomb will explode in the bar at twenty past one, The. Terrorist, He Watches, The. Wisława Szymborska. PoSu

(Bomb will go off in the bar at one twenty p.m, The.) AF

Bomb will go off in the bar at one-twenty, The. Terrorist Is Watching, A. Wisława Szymborska. WoPoe, tr. by Austin Flint

Bombardment. D. H. Lawrence. FaBoWar

Bombed in London. Rudyard Kipling. InoFa; WoPoe Fr. Epitaphs of the War [1914–1918].

Bomber climb out on the roof. Bomber, The. Robert Lowell. PWW2

Bomber, The. Brian Vrepont. NOBAu

Bombing. Paul Rodenko. TuT, tr. by Mary E. O'Donnell

Bombing at about ninety miles an hour with the exhaust skittering. Cocktails. Ciaran Carson. ModIr; PBCIP

Bombing of the Town of Kralupy, The. Jaroslav Seifert. tr. by Ewald Osers Candlestick, The. AF, tr. by Ewald Osers Never Again. AF, tr. by Ewald Osers

Bombs are falling darkly for our fate, The. (LL) Full Moon: New Guinea. Karl Shapiro. APT-2; PWW2

Bombs are not falling yet, The. Forecast. Kelly Cherry. RWB

Bombshell. Tracey Herd. NeBl

Bon, c'est la chaleur. Été, L'. Pascalle Monnier. YaTCFP

Bonanza Creek. John E. Smelcer. PoCoUp

Bond and Free. Robert Frost. APT-1

Bond of live things everywhere, The. (LL) Cutting greens. Lucille Clifton. AFaM; ESEAA; GT; IPoFL; NAMCP V.2

Bond, The. Bob Hicok. LiTh

Bond, The. Nuala Ni Dhomhnaill. PBCIP, tr. by Medbh McGuckian

Bondage. Gyula Illyés. IQMS, tr. by Dorren Bell

Bondmen, and helots, and serfs were we. Cry of the Oppressed, The. Henrietta Tindal. VWP

Bonds. Guillaume Apollinaire. CuPo

Bonds of Affection. Letitia Elizabeth Landon. TreFP

Bonds of Friendship, The. Simon Dach. GePo, tr. by Ingrid Waløe-Engel

Bone. C. K. Williams. CAP-8; UrbNat

Bone Die, The. Maggie Hannan. NLP

Bone driller of every abscess. Humbly, He Speaks to His Tools. Venus Khoury-Gata. PoArWo, tr. by Lucy McNair

Bone Prison, The. E. Howard Harries. AngWePo

Bone Scan. Gwen Harwood. HarvBoo

Bone that has no Marrow, The. Emily Dickinson. SacPr

Bone-build of the eyebrows has a mule's, The. Self-Portrait. Rainer Maria Rilke. PoCho

Bone-chilling snow on a thousand peaks. Han-shan Te-ch'ing. CSKM, tr. by Red Pine

Bone-Flower Elegy. Robert Earl Hayden. APT-2; NAMCP V.2; NoAM

Bone-idle, I lie listening to the rain. Dejection [Ode]. Derek Mahon. PBCIP; WoPoe

Bones. Ted Hughes. HarvBoo

Bones. Carl Sandburg. TCAPo

Bones. / Adobe. Museum Piece (ca. Now). Teresa Palma Acosta. TiP2

Bones and Drums. Ron Welburn. SeSe

Bones float in raised stone. Kalamu ya Salaam. SpirFl Fr. New Orleans Haiku.

Bones I can understand. One after another. South Shore (Aberystwyth), The. Bobi Jones. BBMWP, tr. by Anthony Conran

Bones in a sand cliff. So I could say frigidity prevails. Salisbury Plain. Elizabeth Robinson. AmPoNex

Bones in your foot that were shattered, The. Prayer. Richard Lambert. PoCu

Bones is a crazy pony. Bones. Ted Hughes. HarvBoo

Bones of birds are full of air, The. End of a Season. Thomas McGrath. BodElec

Bones of Lazarus. John Bensko. YaYoPo

Bones of My Father, The. Etheridge Knight. BodElec; OxAAAP

Bones of Zhuangzi, The. Chang Heng. CCL1, tr. by Arthur Waley

Bones show through images. Dark Senses. Tom Raworth. Oth

Bones that cannot bear the light, The. (LL) Genesis. Geoffrey Hill. ChIV-1; HarvBoo

Bones will represent time, The. (LL) Bush. Josephine Jacobsen. NoP-4; NoP-5

Boney. Unknown. FaBoVe

Bonfire in April. Norman Kreitman. EdScPo

Bonfires, The. Rudyard Kipling. NPeEn

Bong, Mr., bong Mr., bong, Mr., bong. (LL) Dirge: "1-2-3 was the number he played but today the number came 3-2-1." Kenneth Fearing. AmWit; APT-2; NAAPv.2; NIL-7; NIP-4; OxBoAm

Bonhoeffer in his skylit cell. Christmas Trees. Geoffrey Hill. ChrPo; UpMys

Bonie Doon. Robert Burns. See Banks o' Doon, The.

Bonk'abajahile. Mafika Pascal Gwala. TSAP

Bonn´n Buí, An. Derek Mahon. NAMCP V.2 Fr. Yellow Book, The.

Bonnard's Nudes. Raymond Carver. GoPo

Bonneville. Jenny Mueller. IAoNAP

Bonnie, bonnie bairn who sits poking in the ase, The. Castles in the Air. James Ballantine. TreFP

Bonnie Broukit Bairn, The. Hugh MacDiarmid. EdScPo; FaBoVe; HarvBoo; NePenScot

Bonnie Charlie's now awa. Will Ye No Come Back Again? Carolina Oliphant, Baroness Nairne. NePenScot

Bonnie House o' Airlie, The. Unknown. OBEV

Bonnie Lesley. Robert Burns. OBEV

Bonnie [or Bonny] Kilmeny gaed up the glen. James Hogg. OBEV; OxAEP-2 Fr. Queen's Wake, The.

Bonny Barbara Allan. Unknown. HeIP-4; NAEL-6v1; NAEL-7v1; NePenScot; NoP-5

(Barbara Allen's Cruelty.) OBEV

Bonny Barbara Allan [with music]. Unknown. HeIP-4

Bonny Earl of Murray, The [Version from Tea-Table Miscellany]. Unknown. NAEL-6v1; NAEL-7v1; NOSC; OBEV

Bonny Heck. William Hamilton. DiBP

Bonny Kilmeny gaed up the glen. James Hogg. NePenScot Fr. Queen's Wake, The.

Bonny [*or* Bonnie] Dundee. Sir Walter Scott. UV *Fr.* Doom of Devorgoil, The.

Bony cow of youth walked by, The. Queen candidates trod through the mud and straw. Third Farming Poem. Brenda Coultas. HeMarv

Bony, pubescent, boys body pulled. Black Banana House. Gavin Moses. InTrad

Boogie: 1 a.m. Langston Hughes. APSN; APT-2; NAMCP V.1

Boogie Woogie Bugle Boy. Hughie Prince and Don Raye. ReLy

Book, The. William Drummond of Hawthornden. ChIV-1

  (Booke of the World, The.) SacPr

Book, The. Edmond Jabès. AF, *tr. by* Rosmarie Waldrop

Book, The. Henry Vaughan. AngWePo; BASC; InvLi; PBRV

Book Concluding with As A Wife Has a Cow a Love Story, A. Gertrude Stein.

  Beside. MotU

  Cousin, A. MotU

  Emily. OxBoAm

  Fifty. OxBoAm

  Fish. OxBoAm

  Had a Horse. MotU; OxBoAm

  In English. OxBoAm

  In Question. OxBoAm

  Key to Closet. MotU; OxBoAm

  Longer. MotU

  Much Later. OxBoAm

  Not Surprising. OxBoAm

  Pink. MotU

  There. OxBoAm

  Wish, A. OxBoAm

Book does not begin, he replied, The. Beginning of the Book, The. Edmond Jabès. AF, *tr. by* Rosmarie Waldrop

Book Ends. Tony Harrison. NAEL-6v2; NAEL-7v2; NAMCP V.2 *Fr.* School of Eloquence, The.

Book, for Growing Old, The. Yves Bonnefoy. PoetW, *tr. by* Emily Grosholz

Book, for Growing Old, The. Yves Bonnefoy. YaTCFP, *tr. by* Richard Pevear

Book Full of Pictures, A. Charles Simic. NoP-4; NoP-5

Book: "Its leaves flutter, they thrive or wither, its outspread." Robert Pinsky. PoDa

Book of a Thousand Eyes, The. Lyn Hejinian.

  "There was once an angel who had a neighbor, and this neighbor was ambitious." FaoP

Book of Books, The. Sir Walter Scott. ChIV-1

Book of Company which, The. Autobiography 2 (hellogoodby). Michael Palmer. HarvBoo; WoBe

Book of Dreams, The. Richard Garcia. TouFir

Book of Ephraim, The. James Merrill.

  "Backdrop: The dining room at Stonington." NoAM

  "Correct but cautious, that first night, we asked." NoP-4; NoP-5

  Lost in Translation. NAMCP V.2; NoAM; NoP-4; NoP-5; OxBoAm; VCAP

  "Zero hour. Waiting yet again." NAMCP V.2

Book of Exits, miraculously copied, The. Real Thing, The. Eiléan Ní Chuilleanáin. ModIr; MoWP

Book of Galahad, The. Jack Spicer. FTOS

Book of Glass, A. David Shapiro. PmAP

Book of Hand Shadows, The. Marianne Boruch. P180

Book of How, The. Merrill Moore. MoAmPo

Book of Human Anomalies, The. Albert Goldbarth. OPRER

Book of Jonah, The. Mihály Babits. IQMS, *tr. by* István Tótfalusi

Book of Lies, The [*with music*]. James Tate. YaYoPo

Book of Matches. Simon Armitage.

  "Mother, any distance greater than a single span." BeAl

Book of Music, A. Jack Spicer. APSN; CalPo; OxBoAm

Book of My Enemy Has Been Remaindered, The. Clive James. OBCoV

Book of poems lay open, A. Book of Poems. Pak Tujin. CAMKP, *tr. by* Edward W. Poitras

Book of Questions, The. Edmond Jabès. *tr. by* Rosmarie Waldrop

  Book of the Living, The. PFTM-2, *tr. by* Rosmarie Waldrop

  Have you seen how a word is born and dies? PFTM-2, *tr. by* Rosmarie Waldrop

  Jew answers every question with another question, The. PFTM-2, *tr. by* Rosmarie Waldrop

  "To be in the book. To figure in the book of questions, to be part of it." PFTM-1, *tr. by* Rosmarie Waldrop

Book of Questions, The. Pablo Neruda. *tr. by* William O'Daly

  "And what did the rubies say." GifTon, *tr. by* William O'Daly

  "And when light was forged." TAPaP, *tr. by* William O'Daly

  "How did the grapes come to know." GifTon, *tr. by* William O'Daly

  "Tell me, is the rose naked." GifTon, *tr. by* William O'Daly

  "Who works harder on earth." GifTon, *tr. by* William O'Daly

Book of Routh. Carolyn Beard Whitlow. FFC

Book of Sharp Silhouettes, The. Molly Bendall. NAPBL

Book of Style, The. Molly Bendall. PoDa

Book of summer is the butterfly, A. Butterfly, The. John Fuller. Spl

Book of the Dead Man #1, The. Marvin Bell. GifTon

Book of the Dead Man #33, The. Marvin Bell. PoA 2002

Book of the Dead Man (#13), The. Marvin Bell. Vesp

Book of the Dead Man #43, The. Marvin Bell. GifTon

Book of the Dead Man #58, The. Marvin Bell. OPRER; TaR

Book of the Dead Man #87, The. Marvin Bell. PuP-23

Book of the Dead, The. Muriel Rukeyser. APT-2

Book of the Duchesse, The. Geoffrey Chaucer.

  Fawning Whelp, The. DiBP

  I Have of Sorwe So Grete Woon. PtR

Book of the Living, The. Edmond Jabès. PFTM-2 *Fr.* Book of Questions, The.

Book of the Sabbath is sealed like an unwritten dream, The. Excerpts from the Sabbath Dream Book. Esther Ettinger. DTA, *tr. by* Mariana Barr

Book of Thel, The. William Blake. NAEL-6v2; NAEL-7v2; NoP-5; WaAnP

  "Eternal gates' terrific porter lifted the northern bar, The." OxBEV

Book of Urizen [*or* First Book of Urizen], The. William Blake. NOBRP

Book of Verses underneath the Bough, A. Omar Khayyám. CABP; OBEV; TRP; WoPoe *Fr.* Rubáiyát of Omar Khayyám [*of* Naishápúr], The.

Book of Wisdom, The. Robert Lowell. ChIV-1

Book of Yolek, The. Anthony Hecht. HP; MakPoe; NAMCP V.2; NoP-4; NoP-5; OxBoAm; TaR; WaAnP; WeW-3

Book remained at the edge of his dead waist, A. César Vallejo. TCLAP *Fr.* Spain, Take [Away] This Cup from Me [España, Aparta de Mí Este Cáliz].

Book reviews. Waking Up. Yolanda Palis. ReBoTo

Book that can only be read in the dark, A. (LL) At Funchal. Tomas Tranströmer. MotU; WED, *tr. by* Robert Bly

Book was writ[t] of late called [*or* call'd] *Tetrachordon*, A. On the Detraction Which Followed upon My Writing Certain Treatises. John Milton. OxBSo

Bookbuying in the Tenderloin. Robert Hass. YaYoPo

Booke of *Common Pray'r* excels the rest, The. Francis Quarles. PBRV *Fr.* Divine Fancies.

Booke of the World, The. William Drummond of Hawthornden. *See* Book, The.

Booker T. and W. E. B. Dudley Randall. NoAM

Booker Washington Trilogy, The. Vachel Lindsay.

  John Brown. MoAmPo

  (Negro Sermon—Simon Legree, A.) MoAmPo

Bookful Blockhead, The. Alexander Pope. OBSV *Fr.* Essay on Criticism, An.

Bookmark, A. Thomas M. Disch. GoPo; RA

Books. Aneirin Talfan Davies. BBMWP, *tr. by* Catherine Fisher

Books, The. (LL) He Was Lucky. Anna Swirszczynska [*or* Swir]. CFP; HP; PoSu, *tr. by* Magnus J. Krynski and Robert A. Maguire

Books as Answer. Haki R. Madhubuti. FuFl

Books of Ovid's changed shapes, The. In the Praise of Music. Humphrey Gifford. NoSic

Books of the Dead, The. Marta Kornblith. MirDau, *tr. by* Roberta Gordenstein

Books of the Old Testament, The. Thomas Russell. ChIV-1

Bookshop in Winter. Margo Lockwood. PfS

Bookstore. Toi Derricotte. ExTi

Bookworm. *Unknown.* WoPoe *Fr.* Riddles (Exeter Book).

Boom! Howard Nemerov. NBLV; NIL-7; NIP-4

Boom above my knees lifts, and the boat, The. Sailing to an Island. Richard Murphy. ModIr; PBCIP

Booman. Carmelita McGrath. Coast

Boomerang. William Hart-Smith. NOBAu

Boomerang: A Blatantly Political Poem. Quincy Troupe. AF

Boon nature scattered, free and wild. Sir Walter Scott. OxAEP-2 *Fr.* Lady of the Lake, The.

Booster. Bill Berkson. NYP2

Boot Theory. Richard Siken. LegDan

Booth led boldly with his big bass drum. General William Booth Enters into Heaven. Vachel Lindsay. APT-1; ChIV-2; ColAP; MoAmPo; NAAPv.2; PoA 2002; TCAPo

Boots. Rudyard Kipling. BRP; MoBrPo

Boots and Saddles. Louis Simpson. BodElec

Boots are being polished. Where Will You Be? Patricia Parker. AfrBLW

Boots of Spanish Leather. Bob Dylan. NoP-5

Booty from the German War [*epigram*]. Friedrich von Logau. GePo, *tr. by* George C. Schoolfield

Booze Turns Men into Women [*with music*]. Bernadette Mayer. NYP2

Bop for Laotzu. Hester G. Storm. WhBo

Boppin' is Safer than Grindin'.   Thulani Davis.   GT

Bops bright. (LL)   Chord.   Langston Hughes.   APSN; OxBoAm

Bora Ring.   Judith Wright.   NAMCP V.2; NoAM

Borde es una boca finísima, una escisión aguda y deslumbrante, El.   Peces de piel fugaz.   Coral Bracho.   RMCMP

Border.   Francisco X. Alarcón.   CalPo

Border.   Gillian Clarke.   HarvBoo; MoWP

Border.   Taslima Nasrin.   VCWP

Border, The.   Martha Collins.   ExTi

Border, The ("Leaping from the eucalyptus branch, the wild desert pigs.")   Joanna Rawson.   AmPoNex

Border, The ("Sliding from half-up the eucalyptus trees, the wild desert pigs practice flight.")   Joanna Rawson.   BodElec

Border Affair, A.   Charles Badger, Jr. Clark.   APT-1

Border collie has been bred to keep, A.   Our Dog Chasing Swifts.   U. A. Fanthorpe.   Spl

Border Guard, A.   Hsiao Yen [or Emperor Wu of Liang].   CCL1, tr. by Anne Birrell

Bordered with rushes white on blue. (LL)   Kimono, The.   James Merrill.   CAP-8; ColAP; WaAnP

Borderland—that's where, if one knew how, The.   Life of Art, The.   Denise Levertov.   BodElec

Borderlands.   Louise Imogen Guiney.   TCAPo

Borders.   Margaret Randall.   ICANM

Borders.   Afaa Michael Weaver.   GT

Borders, Cages and Walls.   Homero Aridjis.   PoCoUp, tr. by George McWhirter

Borders / Stretch my slender vision.   Bloodlines.   Mary Loving Blanchard.   TiP2

Bore him the greetings of the deathless dead! (LL)   Cranes of Ibycus, The.   Emma Lazarus.   APN-2; NAAPv.1

Boreas.   Samuel Rowlands.   NoSic

Bored and impatient in the monster's mouth. (LL)   Dying.   Robert Pinsky.   PoA 2002; VCAP

Bored by Ascham and Zeno.   Glad Eye, The.   Paul Muldoon.   NoAM

Bored. confused actually. have started several letters.   Four Lines of a Black Love Letter between Teachers.   Ed Roberson.   EGAG

Bored with cards, chess or novel.   Love Rats.   Cheryl Follon.   BeAl

Boredom, and the horror, and the glory, The. (LL)   In Memory of the Unknown Poet, Robert Boardman Vaughn.   Donald Justice.   CAP-8; NAMCP V.2; NoAM; WaAnP

Boredom / the fog rolls over the bay.   Big words.   Del Ray Cross.   FreRad

Borges and I.   Jorge Luis Borges.   MotU, tr. by James E. Irby

Borges and Myself.   Jorge Luis Borges.   PoetW, tr. by Norman Thomas Di Giovanni

Borgia, thou once wert [or were] almost too august.   On Seeing a Hair of Lucretia Borgia.   Walter Savage Landor.   NPeEn; PtR; WeW-3

Boricua.   Jose Angel Figueroa.   PueRic

Boricua: you.   Boricua.   Jose Angel Figueroa.   PueRic

Boring executors approach their locks, The.   Poem against Catholics.   James Fenton and John Fuller.   OBSV

Borinkins in Hawaii.   Víctor Hernández Cruz.   PueRic

Born.   Brother Yao.   BtF

Born, born, we know how it goes. (LL)   Holy Family.   Muriel Rukeyser.   ChIV-2; MoAmPo

Born by the mediterranean.   Ghaflah—the sin of forgetfulness.   Dima Hilal.   PoArWo

Born for Poetry.   Chellapilla Venkata Sastri.   HotL, tr. by V. Narayana Rao and David Shulman

Born in another country, under a different flag.   Irish Requiem, An.   Michael O'Loughlin.   PBCIP

Born in Winter.   Francis Quarles.   NOSC

Born into a World Knowing.   Susan Griffin.   PoChi; WhBo

Born of the sorrowful of heart.   Countee Cullen.   SSLK Fr. Four Epitaphs.

Born of Woman.   Wisława Szymborska.   GI

Born on a sunday.   Mama Dot.   Frederick D'Aguiar.   Oth

Born on a tabletop in Joe's cafeé.   Davy Crockett.   Unknown.   FaBoVe

Born on the run, ambushed by sword and flame.   Epitaph for Mariana Gryphius, His Brother Paul's Little Daughter.   Andreas Gryphius.   PoAgWa; WoPoe, tr. by Christopher Benfey

Born salesman, A.   And One for My Dame.   Anne Sexton.   NoP-4; NoP-5

Born to the beauties of the flooding nocturnes.   Chiedu Ezeanah.   NeNiPo Fr. Song of Songs.

Born Too Soon.   James Fenton and John Fuller.   OBCoV

Born with a monocle he stares at life.   En Monocle.   Donald Evans.   APT-1

Born Yesterday.   Philip Larkin.   NoP-5

Borne by the darkness.   Tomas Tranströmer.   WoBe Fr. Haiku.

Borne over deep seas in swift ship.   Catullus.   WoPoe,

Borodino.   Mikhail Yuryevich Lermontov.   FaBoWar, tr. by Frances Darwin Cornford and Esther Polinowsky Salaman

Borough, The.   George Crabbe.
  Amusements.
    (Evening Sail, The.)   TreFP
    Winter Views Serene.   WoPoe
  General Description.
    Letter 1.   CABP
  Peter Grimes.   NPBRoP; OBNV
    "Alas! for Peter not an helping Hand."   NoP-4; NoP-5; NPeEn; OxBEV
  Prisons.
    Condemned Man, The.   NPeEn
  Vicar, The—The Curate, etc.
    Vicar, The.   OBSV

Borrow me borrow my life.   Procedure.   Ann Lauterbach.   BodElec

Borrowed this dust. (LL)   Passing Through.   Stanley Kunitz.   BodElec; LoL

Borrowing my house / From insects.   Issa.   ZenPo, tr. by Takashi Ikemoto and Lucien Stryk

Bosch.   Rafael Alberti.   WoPoe, tr. by Carolyn Tipton

Bosegran.   Kathleen Jamie.   GPPA

Bosom of his Father and his God, The. (LL)   Elegy Written in a Country Churchyard.   Thomas Gray.   BrAP; BRP; CABP; ClHu; HeIP-4; InoFa; MakPoe; NAEL-6v1; NAEL-7v1; NIL-7; NoP-4; NoP-5; NPeEn; OBEV; OxAEP-1; OxBEV; PoPoPo; TFi; TreFP; UV; WaAnP; WeW-3

Bosporus laps on Europe's shores, The.   Constantinople.   Mihály Csokonai Vitéz.   IQMS, tr. by Kenneth White

Bosque se adormeció, El.   Crisálida.   Francisco Segovia.   RMCMP

Boss Communication.   Mari E. Evans.   SeSe

Boss gets on my nerves, The.   Gentleman Is a Dope, The.   Oscar Hammerstein, II.   ReLy

Boss i went.   Don Marquis.   OBCoV Fr. Archy and Mehitabel.

Boss of all bosses of the universe.   To the One Upstairs.   Charles Simic.   StAl

Boss Rat.   Unknown.   WoPoe, tr. by John S. Major

Boss rat, boss rat.   Boss Rat.   Unknown.   WoPoe, tr. by John S. Major

Boss, The.   James Russell Lowell.   NCAP

Bossed around in the sack but honey don't you be tellin me what to do.   You Know I Like to Be.   Chrystos.   WiU

Bosses of Rome, The.   Giuseppe Gioacchino Belli.   PoCho, tr. by Miller Williams

Boston.   John Collins Bossidy.   NBLV; OBCoV

Boston.   Edwin Arlington Robinson.   APN-2

Boston.   George Starbuck.   AmWit

Boston Ballad, A.   Walt Whitman.   APN-1 Fr. Leaves of Grass [1855 Version, Complete Text].

Boston Beguine, The.   Sheldon Harnick.   ReLy

Boston Common.   John Berryman.   CBCWP

Boston Evening Transcript, The.   T. S. Eliot.   APT-1; TCAPo

Boston Hymn.   Ralph Waldo Emerson.   CBCWP; InvLi; PCW; TCAPo

Boston, sooty in memory, alive with a.   After Symond's Venice.   John Wieners.   AHA

Boston Year.   Elizabeth Alexander.   GT; OPRER

Bot now the haisty, egir, and wild Dido.   Virgil.   OBVE Fr. Aeneid [or Eneados or Aeneis], The.

Botanic Garden, The.   Erasmus Darwin.
  Loves of the Plants, The.
    "CARYO's sweet smile DIANTHUS proud admires."   NOBRP
    Eliza at the Battle.   STuOW
    "Fair Chunda smiles amid the burning waste."   NOBRP
    Fine Figure of a Nymph.   STuOW
    "On DOVE's green brink the fair TREMELLA stood."   NOBRP
    "Weak with nice sense, the chaste MIMOSA stands."   NOBRP
    "Where cool'd by rills and curtain'd round by woods."   NOBRP
  Kew.   OBGa

Botanical Fanaticism.   Thylias Moss.   TRP

Botany.   Dan Beachy-Quick.   IAoNAP

Both born in the same year of the Hsien-t'ung era.   Quietly Discussing My Thoughts with the Collator of Texts Ts'ui.   Ch'i-chi.   CSKM, tr. by Burton Watson

Both gloomy and dark was the shadowy night.   Song.   Anne Batten Cristall.   RWP

Both grandfather and father worked.   Tale of Red-Haired Motele, Mister Inspector, Rabbi Isaiah and Commissar Blokh, The.   Iosif Pavlovich Utkin.   TCRusP, tr. by Denis Johnson and Kathy Lewis

Both her mourner and her tomb. (LL)   On the Countess Dowager of Pembroke.   William Browne.   BASC; TFi

Both movies star actresses better known.   On Viewing Two Different Date Rape Movies.   Allison Joseph.   LiTh

Both my grandmas came from far away. Both My Grandmothers. Edward Field. CA

Both of the object seen, and eye that sees. (LL) NAEL-6v2; NAEL-7v2 *Fr.* Prelude, The; Growth of a Poet's Mind [1850 version; Selections from Anthologies].

Both of us are getting worse. Dance of the Cherry Blossom. Jackie Kay. EmeKit; PoCu

Both of us wordless against the dawn and death. (LL) My Grandmother Died in the Early Hours of the Morning. T. Harri Jones. AngWePo; TCAWP

Both robbed of air, we both lie in one ground. Hero and Leander. John Donne. NoSic; SoSe-8

Both sacred wisdom. Withered Zen. Muso Soseki. EaWin, *tr.* by W. S. Merwin

Both the year's, and the day's deep midnight is. (LL) Nocturnal[l] upon Saint Lucy's [*or* S. Lucy's *or* S. Lucies] Day, Being the Shortest Day, A. John Donne. BASC; CABP; NAEL-6v1; NAEL-7v1; NoP-4; NoP-5; NOSC; OxAEP-1; TFi

    (Both the yeares, and the dayes deep midnight is.) (LL) NPeEn; OxBEV; PBRV

Both were dwellers. Reluctant prophet. Luci Shaw. SacPr

Both whom one fire had burnt, one water drowned. (LL) Hero and Leander. John Donne. NoSic; SoSe-8

Both Yesterday and Today. Georges Castera. OGAHCP, *tr.* by Boadiba and Jack Hirschman

Both Your Mothers [*for Bieta*]. Jerzy Ficowski. HP; PoSu, *tr.* by Keith Bosley

Bothie of Tober-na-Vuolich, The [A Long-Vacation Pastoral]. Arthur Hugh Clough.

    Highland Glen near Loch Ericht, A. FaBoVe

    "I have been kissed before, she added, blushing slightly,." FaBoVe

    "Somewhat more splendid in dress, in a waistcoat work of a lady." FaBoVe

Botticellian Trees, The. William Carlos Williams. NAMCP V.1

Botticelli's St. Sebastian. Brigit Pegeen Kelly. ExTi

Bottle contained a little amber and a little, The. Some Glow on the Sill. Clark Coolidge. FTOS

Bottle in the Sea. George Seferis. WoPoe *Fr.* Mythistorima.

Bottle of Suze, A. Pablo Picasso. PFTM-1

Bottle, The. Ralph Knevet. ChIV-2

Bottled [New York]. Helene Johnson. APT-2

Bottle-neck. Kit Robinson. FTOS

Bottles are for sleeping in. Bottles in the Zoological Museum. William Peskett. PNI

Bottles in the Zoological Museum. William Peskett. PNI

Bottom. Arthur Rimbaud. MotU, *tr.* by Louise Varese

Bottom of the sea is cruel, The. (LL) Hart Crane. ColAP; NAAL-5; OxBoAm; WaAnP; WoPoe *Fr.* Voyages.

Bottom of things is neither life nor death, The. Roberto Juarroz. VCWP *Fr.* Vertical Poetry.

Bottomed by tugging combs of water. Swan, The. William Robert Rodgers. PNI

Bottomless pits. There's one in Castleton. Tony Harrison. HarvBoo; NAEL-6v2; NAEL-7v2; RSaN *Fr.* School of Eloquence, The.

Bottom's Dream. Leon Stokesbury. IaFF

Bottoms of my shoes, The. Jack Kerouac. WhBo

Boudica. Paol Keineg. OnScMo, *tr.* by Keith Waldrop

Bouge of Court, The. John Skelton.

    "Sail is up, Fortune ruleth our helm, The." NoSic

    "Ye remembre the gentylman ryghte nowe." OxBEV

Bough Well Bounds The Vowel Bounds Well, A. Ken Harris. AnSo

Boughs, the boughs are bare enough, The. Winter with the Gulf Stream. Gerard Manley Hopkins. NoAM

Bought a dozen years ago. Zuni Ring. David St. John. RoV

Bought at the drug store, very cheap; and later pawned. Green Light. Kenneth Fearing. OxBoAm

Bought myself a ticket, the ticket freed me. Yonder Tree, The. Joshua Weiner. PtR

Boulevard unfurls and yawns, The. Boulevard, The. Léon-Paul Fargue. MotU, *tr.* by Lydia Davis

Boult to Marina. "Ern Malley." BMAP

Bounce to Fop. Alexander Pope. DiBP

Bound. Odetta D. Norton. BtF

Bound each to each by natural piety. (LL) My Heart Leaps Up [When I Behold]. William Wordsworth. ChAP; ITBLP; NAEL-6v2; NAEL-7v2; NOBRP; NoP-4; NoP-5; PoPoPo; SacPr; TFi; WaAnP

Bound, hungry to pluck again from the thousand. For the Twentieth Century. Frank Bidart. KGB; OxBoAm

Bound I. Insubordinate / us. (LL) Nathaniel Mackey. FTOS; OxAAAP *Fr.* Song of the Andoumboulou.

Bound in the women who chain by. For Grizzel McNaught (1709–1792). Anne Finch. FFC

Bound in those icy chains by thee. (LL) Take, Oh, Take Those Lips Away. John Fletcher. NoP-4; NoP-5

Bound No'th Blues. Langston Hughes. NAAPv.2

Bound to Go. *Unknown.* SSUS

Bound to my heart as Ixion to the wheel. Dame Edith Sitwell. MoBrPo *Fr.* Three Poems of the Atomic Bomb.

Bound upon the accursed tree. Crucifixion, The. Henry Hart Milman. SacPr

Boundaries. José Emilio Pacheco. PoetW; STV; TCLAP, *tr.* by John Frederick Nims

Boundary. Pedro Serrano. RMCMP, *tr.* by Geoff Hargreaves

Bounden Duty. James Tate. BAP-04; OxBoAm

Bounding Line. Genevieve Taggard. APT-2

Boundless shaping Power, A. Lao Tzu. WoPoe *Fr.* Tao Te Ching.

Boundless will to ease us, A. (LL) To Cloe. George, Baron Lansdowne Granville. NBLV; OxBEV

Boundless—in the boundless, weed-ridden. T'ao Ch'ien. NDACCP *Fr.* Burial Songs.

Boundless—this vast heap earth. Elegy for Myself. T'ao Ch'ien. NDACCP, *tr.* by David Hinton

Bounty [*with music*]. Josephine Miles. NoAM

Bounty. Robert Pack. PfSP

Bounty of Our Age, The. Henry Farley. NOSC

Bouquet, A. Bei Dao. PtR, *tr.* by Bonnie S. McDougall

Bouquet of Belle Scavoir. Wallace Stevens. MoAmPo

Bouquet of Dead Flowers. David Eggleton. PML

Bouquet of Objects, A. Elaine Equi. PmAP

Bouquet of thyme in December, a tendril of sage on the snow, A. Dowry of Maubergeonne, The. René Char. MotU, *tr.* by Franz Wright

Bouquet of zephyr-flowers hitched to a hitching, A. You at the Pump. Frank O'Hara. FTOS

Bouquets. Robert Francis. ChAP

Bourbons. Walter Savage Landor. OBSV

Bourgeois Poet, The. Karl Shapiro.

    "Bourgeois poet closes the door of his study and lights his pipe, The." BodElec; IllVoic

    "Each in her well-lighted picture window, reading a book or magazine." BodElec

    "I drove three thousand miles to ask a question. No answer, naturally." BodElec

    "Look of shock on an old friend's face after years of not meeting, The." BodElec

    "Of love and death in the Garrison State I sing." BodElec

    "Oriental, you give and give. No Christian ever gave like you." BodElec

    "Prophets say to Know Thyself: I say it can't be done, The." BodElec

    "Quintana lay in the shallow grave of coral." BodElec

    "Rice around the lingam stone will be distributed in the dying sun, The." BodElec

    "Teachers of culture hate science but the teachers of science do not hate culture, The." BodElec

    "To make the child in your own image is a capital crime." BodElec

    "World is my dream, says the wise child, ever so wise, The." BodElec

'Bout th' husband oak [*or* oke], the vine. William Habington. NPeEn *Fr.* Castara.

Bout with Burning. Vassar Miller. MoAmPo

Bova. Mary O'Donoghue. NIrP

Bow and Arrow. Derec Llwyd Morgan. BBMWP, *tr.* by Joseph P. Clancy

Bow, daughter of Babylon, bow thee to dust! Babylon. Alfred Tennyson. ChIV-1

Bow to Allah. Brian G. Gilmore. ISC

Bow-bent luminous ice peak refraction. March Crescent Moon Song. Andrew Schelling. WANABP

Bowed by the weight of centuries he leans. Man with the Hoe, The. Edwin Markham. APN-2; BRP; CalPo; GS; MoAmPo; NAAPv.1; OxBoAm; TCAPo; TFi

Bowed down with age I seek my native place. Return, The. Ho Ch'e Ch'ang. CCL1, *tr.* by H. A. Giles

Bowells of the Earth my bowells hide, The. Lucy Hastings, Countess of Huntingdon. EMWP

Bower among the Beans, The. Emily Jane Pfeiffer. ViWPN

Bower of Bliss, The. Edmund Spenser. NAEL-6v1; NAEL-7v1; OBGa *Fr.* Faerie Queene, The.

Bower of Blisse Destroyed, The. Edmund Spenser. NPeEn

Bower of Pleasure, The. Mary Robinson. CenSon; RWP

3. The Bower of Pleasure. Mary Robinson. NPBRoP *Fr.* Sappho and Phaon.

Bower of Roses, A. Louis Simpson. PWW2

Bowing. Paul S. Piper. AmZen

Bowing "New Sabbath" or "Mount Ephraim." (LL) Church Romance, A. Thomas Hardy. OxAEP-2; OxBSo

Bowl for the bishop, a crushed and bitter bowl, A. Almería. Pablo Neruda. FaBoWar, *tr.* by Donald D. Walsh

Bowl he starts with, The. Man, The. His Bowl. His Raspberries. Claudia Rankine. GT

Bowl of Mul Kimch'i, A. Chŏng Hwajin. EcSo, *tr.* by Julie C. Park

Bowl Over, Wheel. Edmund Vale. ArBi

Bowl, The. John Wilmot, 2d Earl of Rochester. OxAEP-1

Bowl with Pine Cones. Kinereth Gensler. PfS

Bowlegged lady crawled across the river on cables. Brooklyn Bridge. Matthew Rohrer. NeAmPo

Bowlers Anonymous. Stephen Dobyns. CAP-8

Bowls. Marianne Moore. APT-1

Bowmen, The. Paavo Haavikko. WoPoe, *tr.* by Anselm Hollo

Box. Michele Glazer. IAoNAP

Box, A. Gertrude Stein. NAAPv.2 *Fr.* Tender Buttons.

Box, A ("Large box is handily made of what is necessary to replace any substance, A.") Gertrude Stein. MoWP *Fr.* Tender Buttons.

Box, The. Matthew Sweeney. BeAl

Box, The. Mark Turpin. ASA

Box Comes Home, A. John Ciardi. AmWaPo; PWW2

Box is only temporary, The. (LL) Arrival of the Bee Box, The. Sylvia Plath. NALW; NAMCP V.2; NPeEn; OxBoAm

Box of surinam toad glass hill. Soda Gong. Clark Coolidge. NYP2

Boxcar. Terrance Hayes. AmPoNex

Boxcars drift by / clanking, The. David Young. GM

Boxers, The. Andrew Feld. LegDan

Boxes, The. Solitude. 'Enayat Jaber. PoArWo, *tr.* by Wen Chin Ouyang

Boxing Day. Yusef Komunyakaa. ISC

Boxing Match, The. David Ignatow. MoASP

Boxwoods planted in the park spelled LIVE, The. Christ as a Gardener. Andrew Hudgins. UpMys

Boy. Mary Kinzie. FFC

Boy, The. Marilyn Hacker. ExTi; WiU

Boy, The. David Trinidad. BeDoSh

Boy, about eleven or twelve, The. Testimony: The United States (1901–1910) Recitative/The South. Charles Reznikoff. FTOS

Boy accepted them, The. Daedalus: The Dirge. George Oppen. FTOS

Boy, Allegorically Deployed. Reginald Shepherd. RD

Boy and horse, a similar brain: the horse doesn't cry when its rider lies in the dust. Theognis. CAGL *Fr.* Second Book of Theognis, The.

Boy and the girl loved each other very much, The. They saw the world. Boy and the Girl, The. Todd Colby. HeMarv

Boy and the Girl, The. Todd Colby. HeMarv

Boy and the girl toss the white ball, The. Beach, The. Suzanne Matson. PfS

Boy at the Paterson Falls. Toi Derricotte. BtF; PBCAP

Boy at the Window. Richard Wilbur. GoPo; MoW; NAMCP V.2; OxBoAm; RaBo

Boy bears a gray shield, The. Irina Shostakovskaya. CRWP, *tr.* by Daniel Weissbort

Boy Behind a Window. Luis Cernuda. RaW, *tr.* by Hardie St. Martin

Boy Breaking Glass [*with music*]. Gwendolyn Brooks. ESEAA; NAMCP V.2; NoAM; NoP-4; NoP-5; PtR

Boy, bring my morning porridge. Cho Chonsŏng. CATKP *Fr.* Four Songs Calling a Boy.

Boy, bring my sedge cape and bamboo hat. Cho Chonsŏng. CATKP *Fr.* Four Songs Calling a Boy.

Boy Changed into a Stag Clamours at the Gate of Secrets, The. Ferenc Juhász. IQMS, *tr.* by David Wevill

Boy Crazy. Maurya Simon. GeoHom

Boy Crying in the Night. Carlos Drummond de Andrade. PML, *tr.* by Mark Strand

Boy Died in My Alley, The [*with music*]. Gwendolyn Brooks. NAMCP V.2; NoAM

Boy Exploded on the Corner Today, A. Seth Tucker. LiTh

Boy Friend, The. Sandy Wilson. ReLy

Boy from Brooklyn used to cruise on summer nights, A. Perpetually Attempting to Soar. Mary Ruefle. AmAlph

Boy, gather your straw basket. Cho Chonsŏng. CATKP *Fr.* Four Songs Calling a Boy.

Boy, gather your straw basket. Four Songs Calling a Boy. Hanu. CATKP, *tr.* by Peter H. Lee

Boy Girl Game, The. Jody Helfand. BeDoSh

Boy hammers a piece of lead pipe, A. Streak, The. Julia Kasdorf. AmPoNex

Boy I can remember when February. New Constructions. John Ashbery. KGB

Boy I knew, A. Shot Down at Night. John Frederick Nims. PWW2

Boy I Never Met, The. Lesley-Anne Bourne. Coast

Boy in a Hospital. Diana Helen Melhem. PoArWo

Boy in the girl's ear says, Kiss me until, The. Twentieth Century Children (5): Blood-Kissing. Beckian Fritz Goldberg. AmAlph

Boy is amazed to see his father home from work in the afternoon with a bandaged finger, A. Transmutation. Gael Turnbull. BeAl

Boy is aware that the tree is alive, The. Poetics. Cesare Pavese. TAPaP, *tr.* by Geoffrey Brock

Boy Juggling a Soccer Ball, A. Christopher Merrill. MoASP; PML

Boy just like you took me out to see them, A. What the End Is For. Jorie Graham. AtGh; NoP-4; PoPoPo

Boy, lead a cow to the northern village. Cho Chonsŏng. CATKP *Fr.* Four Songs Calling a Boy.

Boy Leading a Horse. Geoffrey Nutter. IAoNAP

Boy of Egremond, The. Samuel Rogers. NOBRP

Boy of fifteen or sixteen carrying a bundle of peonies, A. In the Old Capital. Sŏ Chŏngju. CAMKP, *tr.* by David R. McCann

Boy of twelve, shaping a fuselage, The. Models. Howard Nemerov. AF

Boy on a Swing. Mbuyiseni Oswald Mtshali. NIL-7

Boy parks his red fire engine, The. Squad I. Tim Suermondt. PA9/11

Boy, presuming on his intellect, A. At Woodward's Gardens. Robert Frost. PoA 2002

Boy rehearsing the Continental Stroll, The. American Bandstand. Michael Waters. SwNoth

Boy Removes All Traces from His Room, The. Naomi Shihab Nye. MAAN

Boy Shepherds' Simile, The [*with music*]. David Bottoms. PoA 2002

Boy sits in the classroom, The. Learning Experience. Marge Piercy. NAMCP V.2; NoAM

Boy skips flat stones out to sea—each does fine, A. Notations of Ten Summer Minutes. Norman Alexander MacCaig. EmeKit; NPeEn

Boy Sleeping. Ann Lauterbach. PmAP

Boy stood on the burning deck, The. Casabianca. Felicia Dorothea Hemans. BRP; NAEL-6v2; NAEL-7v2; NOBRP; NoP-5; NPBRoP; NPeEn; RWP; ViWPN; VWP

Boy stops outside my window, A. Chu Ŭisik. CATKP, *tr.* by Peter H. Lee

Boy strides boldly from his June of youth, The. Gwilym R. Tilsley. BBMWP *Fr.* Ode in Praise of the Coalminer, An.

Boy, the way Glenn Miller played. Those Were the Days. Lee Adams. ReLy

Boy told me, A. Rider, The. Naomi Shihab Nye. ArBi

Boy Unable to Speak, The. Federico García Lorca. WED, *tr.* by Robert Bly

Boy was bright, like the retarded girl, The. Leonard. Jeffrey McDaniel. AmPoNex

Boy was going to take the bus out, The. Elvis Lives. Charles Bukowski. AllShUp

Boy who Dreamed the Country Night, The. Christopher Koch. NOBAu

Boy who fell into the Morning Glory Pool, The. Morning Glory Pool. Sandra McPherson. MotU

Boy who played and talked and read with me, A. Exile. Donald Hall. NoP-4; NoP-5

Boy with a fair-curled head, The. Henry Cuyler Bunner. VerBaPo *Fr.* In School House.

Boy With a Headset. Edward Hirsch. RoV

Boy with Book of Knowledge. Howard Nemerov. NoP-4; NoP-5

Boy with His Hair Cut Short. Muriel Rukeyser. NALW; NAMCP V.2; NoAM; NoP-5

Boy with the Empty Cage, The. José Hierro. RaW, *tr.* by Rachel Benson

Boy yell, bull elephant charge. Inmates. Maggie Hannan. NLP

Boy, yes, you with the teasing glances. Fragment 360. Anacreon. CAGL, *tr.* by Alfred Corn

Boycycle, The. S. Conant Foster. ArBi

Boyish sleep. Hamlin Garland. APN-2

Boy—okay, it's me—wears a fringed, A. Adoration of the Magi, The. Andrew Hudgins. UpMys

Boy's Afraid of the Live Tiger, The. Cesare Greppi. ItPo, *tr.* by Gayle Ridinger

Boy's Answer to the Blackmoor, The. Henry King, Bishop of Chichester. NoP-5

Boys are an inextricable maze. To Theodorus et al. Rhianos. CAGL, *tr.* by Daryl Hine

Boys came back, The. Bands played and flags were flying. Fight to a Finish. Siegfried Sassoon. RSaN

Boy's father dies, This. Shadow-Casting. James Galvin. MoASP

Boys Go to Ask a Neighbor for Some Apples, The. Jim Heynen. MotU

Boys have gone out to gather bracken. Chŏng Ch'ŏl. CATKP, *tr.* by Peter H. Lee

Boys have to slash their fingers to become brothers. Anointing, An. Thylias Moss. GT; MotU; ReTh

Boys / I don't promise you nothing. Admonitions. Lucille Clifton. NALW

Boys i mean are not refined, The. E. E. Cummings. OxBoAm

Boys in Dresses. Yusef Komunyakaa. CAP-8

Boys in sporadic but tenacious droves. Horse Chestnut Tree, The. Richard Eberhart. MoAmPo

Boys in the Backroom, The. Frank Loesser. ReLy

Boys kicking a ball on a vast square beneath an obelisk. Above Us. Julia Hartwig. BLT

Boys' members, Diodorus, come in three. Strato. CAGL, *tr. by* Daryl Hine

Boys of Ch'ien-t'ang practice riding the bore, The. Song of Surfing on the Bore. Cheng Hsieh. ColAnChi, *tr. by* Jonathan Chaves

Boys of Summer, The. E. Ethelbert Miller. SpirFl

Boys' Own. Brendan Cleary. NeBl

Boy's Room. George Oppen. OxBoAm

Boy's Song, A. James Hogg. NOxBChV; OBEV; OxAEP-2

Boy's Summer, A. Paul Laurence Dunbar. CA

Boys, the Broom Handle, the Retarded Girl, The. Alicia Ostriker. ExTi

Bo-zhou: Like a Lonely Bark. *Unknown.* CCL1, *tr. by* V. W. X.

Bo-zhou: That Boat of Cypress Wood. *Unknown.* CCL1, *tr. by* James Legge

Bozzy and Piozzi. "Peter Pindar."
    Town Eclogue, A. OBCoV

Brace a broomstick across the neck. How My Mother-in-Law Instructed Me in Slaughter. Sarah Kennedy. SweBea

Bracelet of Grass, The. William Vaughn Moody. APN-2; NAAPv.1; TCAPo

Bracelet, The. John Donne. NoSic

Bracelet to Julia, The. Robert Herrick. BASC; OBEV

Bracelets. William Strode. NOSC

Bracelets jingle every time. Love Poem, A. Vagura. WoPoe, *tr. by* Peter Dent and Edwin Gerow

Bracelets on my arms, jewelry around my neck. *Unknown.* SLW, *tr. by* Marjolijn De Jager, Sayd Bahodin Majrouh and André Velter

Bracketed by a diesel switcher and five. Note on the L and N. Richmond Lattimore. GM

Brackish reach of shoal off Madaket, A. Quaker Graveyard in Nantucket, The. Robert Lowell. ColAP; MakPoe; NAAL-5; NAMCP V.2; NoAM; NoP-5; VCAP; WaAnP

Bradshaw, Nebraska near York, forty-eight miles. Teaching, Hurt. Hilda Raz. PfSP

Brady Street, San Francisco. Michael Lassell. WiU

Brag, sweet tenor bull. Basil Bunting. HarvBoo; NAMCP V.1; NoAM; NoP-4; NoP-5; NPeEn *Fr.* Briggflatts [An Autobiography].

Braggart Duck. Takahashi Shinkichi. ZenPo, *tr. by* Takashi Ikemoto and Lucien Stryk

Brahma. Ralph Waldo Emerson. APN-1; ColAP; CtM; NAAPv.1; NoP-4; NoP-5; OBEV; OxBoAm; TCAPo; TFi; UV

Brahma. Andrew Lang. UV

Brahmin, The. James F. Montgomery.
    "Once on the mountain's balmy lap reclined." NOBRP

Braid Claith. Robert Fergusson. OxBEV

Braid of creation / trembles. (LL) Snakes of September, The. Stanley Kunitz. ColAP; WaAnP

Braided Creek. James Harrison and Ted Kooser.
    "Rabbit is born, The." TAPaP

Braids twist and tie. Broken Ends Broken Promises. Maria Fernandez. BRtP

Braille for Left Hand. Octavio Armand. TCLAP, *tr. by* Carol Maier

Brain forgets, but the blood will remember, The. Dark Chamber, The. Louis Untermeyer. MoAmPo

Brain of the Spider, The. Paul Zimmer. PfSP

Brain on Ice [The El Train Poem]. Michael Warr. UnSA

Brain throws [out] its voice, The. Ask-Vubba: A Decalogue. Tyrone Williams. RD

Brain, within its Groove, The. Emily Dickinson. NCAP; NoAM; SAmP

Brainsick race that wanton youth ensues, The. *Unknown.* NoSic

Brainstorm. Howard Nemerov. OxBoAm; TRP

Braly Street. Gary Soto. GeoHom; UnSA

Brambleberry, The. Sándor Weöres. IQMS, *tr. by* Adam Makkai and Valerie Becker Makkai

Brambu Drezi. Jake Berry.
    Book 3.
    "In the clutch of blind embryo." AnSo

Bran, a chaff, a very barley [y]awn, A. Edward Taylor. ChIV-2; NOSC; TCAPo; WaAnP *Fr.* Preparatory Meditations Before My Approach to the Lord's Supper.

Bran at the Island of Women. *Unknown.* WoPoe, *tr. by* Greg Delanty

Bran you're flabbergast. Bran at the Island of Women. *Unknown.* WoPoe, *tr. by* Greg Delanty

Branch which sways on a rounded sand dune, and from which my heart gathers [a harvest of] fire, A. At Taliq. HiArP, *tr. by* James T. Monroe

Branches of a Mabinogi. Meirion Pennar. BBMWP, *tr. by* Martin Davis

Branches of grape-vine thick as ankles. Elm Tree in Paddington, An. Robert Adamson. BMAP

Branches' snow is like the cotton fluff, The. Element Mother, The. Lorine Niedecker. FTOS

Brancusi's Golden Bird. Mina Loy. APT-1; HarvBoo; MoWP; NAAPv.2; NAMCP V.1

Brand Plucked from the Anti-tank Fire, A. Ramy Ditzanny. NRoS, *tr. by* Esther Raizen

Brandan's Last Voyage. Kenneth White. EdScPo

Brandy Station, Virginia. David Moolten. BloBone

Brandy, who got it from a blood transfusion. Twelfth Floor West. Marilyn Hacker. ExTi; NAMCP V.2

Branksome's Heir and the Hound. Sir Walter Scott. DiBP *Fr.* Lay of the Last Minstrel, The.

Branwen was buried here, so long ago. At Branwen's Grave. Dudley G. Davies. AngWePo

Branwen's Starling [*with music*]. R. Williams Parry. OBWVE, *tr. by* Gwyn Jones

Brass and parrots' feathers. Oshun, the River Goddess. *Unknown.* WoPoe, *tr. by* Ulli Beier

Brass Knuckles. Stuart Dybek. PBCAP

Brass Spittoons. Langston Hughes. MoAmPo; NoAM

Brass-green bird with grass, A. Smooth Gnarled Crape Myrtle. Marianne Moore. APT-1

Brats. X. J. Kennedy. NBLV

Brave. Jeanette Lynes. Coast

Brave as a postage stamp, he went his way. Philippe Soupault. PFTM-1, *tr. by*

Brave comrade, answer! When you joined the war. George Henry Boker. APN-2

Brave Coward, The. Menke Katz. Prolet, *tr. by* Amelia Glaser

Brave Dog's Challenge, The [Epode 6]. Horace. DiBP *Fr.* Epodes.

Brave flowers, that I could gallant it like you. Contemplation upon Flowers, A. Henry King, Bishop of Chichester. OBEV; PtR

Brave Grant, thou hero of the war. General Grant—the Hero of the War. George Moses Horton. CBCWP

Brave infant of Saguntum, clear. To the Immortal Memory and Friendship of That Noble Pair, Sir Lucius Cary and Sir H. [*or* Henry] Morison. Ben Jonson. BASC; CABP; NAEL-6v1; NAEL-7v1; NoP-4; NoP-5; NOSC; PBRV

Brave lads in olden musical centuries. Alcaics; to H. F. B. Robert Louis Stevenson. OBEV

Brave Man and Brave Woman. Mrs. Henry Linden. CBWP-4

Brave Man, The. Wallace Stevens. SAmP

Brave man with a sword!, The. (LL) Ballad of Reading Gaol, The. Oscar Wilde. OBNV; OxAEP-2; TFi

Brave Page Boys, The. Julia A. Moore.
    "Enos Page the youngest brother." VerBaPo

Brave Rover. Max Beerbohm. NBLV

Brave Sparrow. Michael Collier. UrbNat

Brave, wise, and Venus' son. (LL) In a Bye-Canal. Herman Melville. APN-2; NCAP

Braver Deeds. Gary Young.
    "It's Sunday, October ninth, and the earth here is barren after harvest." GeoHom

Braveries. Robert Pinsky. HarvBoo

Bravest Battle, The. Joaquin Miller.
    "Bravest battle that ever was fought, The." ITBLP

Bravura Lament. Daniel Halpern. PoDa

Braw, snortin', roarin', fearsome beastie. To a Bull Moose. Eugene O'Neill. UV

Brawling of a sparrow in the eaves, The. Sorrow of Love, The [1927 Version]. William Butler Yeats. BrAP; NAEL-6v2; NAEL-7v2; OxBEV

Brazen hypnotics glitter here;. Hart Crane. SeSe

Brazen Tongue. William Rose Benét. MoAmPo

Brazil. Bill Manhire. HarvBoo

Brazil, January 1, 1502. Elizabeth Bishop. BLT; NAMCP V.2; NoAM; PoetW; PoPoPo; VCAP

Brazos de Dios. Paul Foreman. TiP2

Breach in the Wall, The. *Unknown.* EMWP

Bread. Stanley Burnshaw. APT-2

Bread. Michael Hartnett. ModIr

Bread: "I'm standing in elm shadow." William Heyen. ViWalt

Bread. Brendan Kennelly. PBCIP

Bread. W. S. Merwin. VCAP

Bread and I, The. Yi Yŏnju. EcSo, *tr. by* Yung-Hee Kim

Bread and Water. Shirley Kaufman. CFP

Bread and Wine. Nina Cassian. AWTN, *tr. by* Andrea Deletant and Brenda Walker

Bread and Wine. Friedrich Hölderlin.
  "Oh friend, we arrived too late." RaBo

Bread goes up so bread goes up again. Inflation. Nicanor Parra. AF, *tr. by*
  Miller Williams

Bread Loaf, late August, the chemistry. Final Poem, The. Maxine W. Kumin.
  VisFro

Bread Man, The. Lucinda Roy. GT

Bread of this World; Praises III, The. Thomas McGrath. RaBo

Bread to Stone. Joy Kogawa. IFF

Bread: "When my daughter makes bread, a cloud of flour." Sharon Olds.
  SweBea

Breadcrumbs falling from the table. Inga Kuznetsova. CRWP, *tr. by* Max
  Nemtsov

Breaded Fish. A. K. Ramanujan. NoP-4; NoP-5

Breaded Meat, Breaded Hands. Michael S. Harper. ISC

Bread-oh, bread-oh, ten-cent bread . . . . Bread Man, The. Lucinda Roy. GT

Bread-Word Giver. John Wheelwright. ChIV-2

Break. Colette Bryce. NIrP

Break. Ben Howard. UrbNat

Break, The. Delmira Agustini. TANSG, *tr. by* Mark McCaffrey

Break, Break, Break. Alfred Tennyson. BrAP; BRP; ClHu; HeIP-4; NAEL-
  6v2; NAEL-7v2; NIL-7; NIP-4; NoP-4; NoP-5; SoSe-8; TFi; TreFP;
  WaAnP; WeW-3

Break It on Down. Brian Henry. WaAnP

Break of Dawn, The. Thomas Sayers Ellis. InTrad

Break of Day. John Donne. CtM; NAEL-6v1; NAEL-7v1; SoSe-8

Break of Day in the Trenches. Isaac Rosenberg. CABP; EMP; HarvBoo;
  MoBrPo; NAEL-6v2; NAEL-7v2; NAMCP V.1; NIL-7; NoAM; NoP-4;
  NoP-5; NPeEn; OBWP; OxAEP-2; OxBEV; PoA 2002; PoAgWa; PoWW;
  TFi; WaAnP

Break Open the Door. Rabindranath Tagore. ItP; PtR *Fr.* Gitanjali.

Break the law! Preparing the Nets at New Stuyahok. John Brandi. AtGh

Breakdancing. Jorie Graham. BodElec

Breaker breaking on the beach, The. (LL) Alfred Tennyson. NAEL-6v2;
  NAEL-7v2 *Fr.* In Memoriam A. H. H.

Breakers' jumbled yard: valley, The. Port Talbot. John Davies. AngWePo

Breakfast. Joe Denham. OpeFie

Breakfast. Wilfrid Wilson Gibson. FaBoWar; OBMV

Breakfast. Jacques Prévert. BeAl, *tr. by* Lawrence Ferlinghetti

Breakfast. William Carlos Williams. SAmP

Breakfast enjoyed. Basho. SoOfWa, *tr. by* Sam Hamill

Breakfast is drunk down...Damp earth. Our Daily Bread. César Vallejo.
  TCLAP, *tr. by* James Wright
  (Breakfast is drunk down . . . Damp earth.) GI

Breakfast on the Balcony. Yevgeny Borisovich Rein. TCRusP, *tr. by* Daniel
  Weissbort

Breakfast over, islanded by noise. Woman in Kitchen. Eavan Boland.
  WaAnP

Breakfast Poem. Clare Pollard. NeBl

Breakfast with Cats. Molly Peacock. KGB

Breaking. Phyllis Webb. BrAP

Breaking a Willow-Branch. Unknown. CCL1, *tr. by* John Frodsham

Breaking and Entering: A Very Short Novel in Verse. Bobby Byrd. ICANM

Breaking from under that thy cloudy veil. Edward Herbert, 1st Baron Herbert
  of Cherbury. OxAEP-1

Breaking Ground. Thom Gunn. OBGa

Breaking in song. (LL) Returning to Goleufryn. Vernon Watkins. AngWePo;
  OBWVE

Breaking of the Day, The. Peter Davison.
  Birthright, The. YaYoPo
  Dead Sea, The. YaYoPo
  Delphi. YaYoPo
  Gift of Tongues, The. YaYoPo

Breaking Points. Eamon Grennan. ModIr

Breaking the Chain. Tony Harrison. UV

Breaking the Rock Down. Ralph Angel. BodElec

Breaking up the clouds. (LL) Pushing. Christopher Gilbert. LTA; SoSe-8

Breaking waves dashed high, The. Landing of the Pilgrim Fathers [in New
  England], The. Felicia Dorothea Hemans. BRP; HHAm; ITBLP; NAEL-
  6v2; NAEL-7v2; NoP-4; NoP-5

Breaking with honey buds, shall ever equal. (LL) Express, The. Stephen
  Spender. BrAP; HeIP-4; MoBrPo; NAMCP V.1; NIL-7; NoAM

Breaks like the Atlantic Ocean on my head. (LL) Man And Wife. Robert
  Lowell. ColAP; VCAP

Bream swam by the tramcar window, A. Near Shinobazu Pond. Takahashi
  Shinkichi. ZenPo, *tr. by* Takashi Ikemoto and Lucien Stryk

Breast. Julia Copus. PoCu

Breast Examination. Wanda Coleman. GT

Breast / nursery. Truth. *Unknown.* SonAtl, *tr. by* Abdul Kalam Azad

Breast to my breast. Self-Love. Joan Larkin. FiBr

Breastès round, and long small armès twain, The. (LL) Smiling Mouth [and
  Laughing Eyen Grey], The. Charles, Duc d' Orléans. NoP-4; NoP-5

Breasting the thick brushwood that hid my track. Wet Day, A. Andrew
  Young. NePenScot

Breasts. Maxine Chernoff. PmAP; ReTh

Breasts. Charles Simic. RaBo; WaAnP

Breasts. Gary Snyder. WANABP

Breasts of all the women crumpled like gas bags when, The. State Will Be
  Served Even By Poets, The. Julian Beck. PFTM-2

Breath. Bill Berkson. NYP2

Breath. Reginald Gibbons. BodElec

Breath. Daniel Gray-Kontar. BRtP

Breath. (LL) Paul Laurence Dunbar in The Tenderloin. Ishmael Reed.
  EGAG; ESEAA

Breath. Pierre Reverdy. YaTCFP, *tr. by* Mary Ann Caws *and* Jean-Pierre
  Cauvin and Patricia Terry

Breath. Deema K. Shehabi. PoArWo

Breath clamber-short, face sun-peeled, stones. Red-Tail Hawk and Pyre of
  Youth. Robert Penn Warren. InGu

Breath He Holds, The. Rick Noguchi. NeAmPo

Breath is warm. Dirty Dreams and God Smiling. Alane Rollings. IllVoic

Breath leaves the sentences and does not come back, A. Losing a Language.
  W. S. Merwin. BeAl; EMP; NoP-4; NoP-5

Breath like a house fly batters the shut mouth. Mark Jarman. WaAnP *Fr.*
  Unholy Sonnets.

Breath of balm from foreign branches pressed, The. Martial. RomPo, *tr. by*
  Anthony Reid

Breath of balm—of orange bloom!, A. Retrospect. Ina Coolbrith. CalPo

Breath of Nature, The. Chuang Tzu. BBASP; WaAnP, *tr. by* Thomas Merton

Breath of Spring. Damp, dug up beds. Breath of Spring. Sarah Fel-Yelin.
  Prolet, *tr. by* Amelia Glaser

Breath opens operatic breaches in the walls, A. Common Nocturne. Arthur
  Rimbaud. MotU, *tr. by* Louise Varese

Breath the trees the bridge, The. Flame. C. D. Wright. AmAlph

Breathcrystal. Paul Celan. PFTM-2, *tr. by* Pierre Joris

Breathe by oneself or have something breathed. Organic Music. Takehisa
  Kosugi. WhBo

Breathe in and out, legs in stirrups, bottom up, eyes focused on a faded happy
  face tacked to the ceiling. Clog of Her Body, The. Diana García.
  TouFir

"Breathe light into the page," he said. Lesson in Anatomy, A. Liz Rosenberg.
  NIL-7

Breathe my breath also through these songs. (LL) Chanting the Square Deific.
  Walt Whitman. APN-1; NAAL-3

Breathers of wisdom won without a quest. Frogs, The. Archibald Lampman.
  BrAP

Breathes there the [*or* a] Man with soul so dead. Sir Walter Scott. ITBLP;
  NePenScot; OxBEV; SoSe-8; TFi *Fr.* Lay of the Last Minstrel, The.

Breathing. (LL) Orchids. Theodore Roethke. ColAP; HarvBoo; TRP;
  WaAnP

Breathing air with snow falling through it. Thoughts Breathing in a Blizzard.
  "Antler." PoCoUp

Breathing Exercises. Leonard Nathan. PBCAP

Breathing in. Balancing Zero. V. B. Price. ICANM

Breathing, the Endless News, The. Rita Dove. CAP-8; PoA 2002

Breathless she stood, her graceful head bent low. Listening Nydia. Henrietta
  Cordelia Ray. CBWP-3

Breathless Storm. Michael Burkard. BodElec

Breathless swimmer in that cold green element, A. (LL) Cold Green Element,
  The. Irving Layton. BrAP; NoP-4; NoP-5

Breathless, we flung us on the windy hill. Hill, The. Rupert Brooke.
  BLPJKO; MoBrPo; OxBSo

Breath's slow, The. Changing Room. John A. Scott. BMAP

Brébeuf and His Brethren. Francis Reginald Scott. IFF

Brechfa Chapel. Roland Mathias. AngWePo

Brecht. Heiner Müller. GTCP, *tr. by* Reinhold Grimm

Bredon Hill. A. E. Housman. MoBrPo; NAEL-6v2; OxAEP-2; SoSe-8; UV
  Fr. Shropshire Lad, A.

Breed's described, The: Now, Satire, if you can. Daniel Defoe. OBSV *Fr.*
  True-born Englishman, The.

Breeze, A. / At sea. Non Dimenticar. Bill Berkson. AHA

Breeze blew fair, the waving sea, The. Charnel Ship, The. Lucretia Davidson.
  TreFP

Breeze grew strong, the waves show'd crests of foam, The. Thomas Baker.
  STuOW *Fr.* Steam Engine; or, The Power of the Flame, The.

Breeze has passed, The. Spring at Wu Ling. Li Ch'ing-chao. ErotSp, *tr. by*
  Sam Hamill

Breeze in Translation.   Belle Waring.   PBCAP

Breeze is fresh, The.   Ryokan.   EMJL, tr. by Burton Watson

Breeze is springing up, A. Mark yon grey cloud.   Sea-View, A.   Ann Radcliffe.   RWP

Breeze sent a wrinkling darkness.   Waiting for the Storm.   Timothy Steele.   MakPoe

Breeze soft, sun frail, spring still early.   To the Tune "The Bodhisattva's Headdress."   Li Ch'ing-chao.   NDACCP, tr. by Kenneth Rexroth

Breeze stirs banana leaves behind the house, A.   Complaining about the Second Wife.   Vietnamese Oral Tradition.   CaDao, tr. by John Balaban

Breeze strokes the water of the spring, A.   Takushitsu.   EaWin, tr. by W. S. Merwin

Breeze tells me, loved one, The.   Breeze Tells Me, Loved One, The.   Antonio Machado Ruiz.   SpanPo, tr. by James Duffy

Breeze, you who blow from the mountainside where my lover fights.   Unknown.   SLW, tr. by Marjolijn De Jager, Sayd Bahodin Majrouh and André Velter

Breezes sigh, rising over bright tiled steps.   Evening near Serpent River.   Tu Fu [or Du Fu].   CrYelRi, tr. by Sam Hamill

Breezin' Along with the Breeze.   Haven Gillespie.   ReLy

Breezy Delicious Day.   Edwin Torres.   HeMarv

Breitmann in Paris.   Charles Godfrey Leland.   APN-2

Brenin Gwalia.   John Roderick Rees.   BBMWP, tr. by the author

Brennbaum.   Ezra Pound.   MoAmPo; NAAPv.2 Fr. Hugh Selwyn Mauberley (Life and Contacts).

Brent; a Poem to Thomas Palmer Esq.   William Diaper.
    "Had mournful Ovid been to Brent condemned."   OBSV
    "Happy are you, whom Quantock overlooks."   OBSV

Brer Rabbit, You's de Cutes' of 'Em All.   James Weldon Johnson.   APT-1

Bresson's Movies.   Robert Creeley.   NoP-4; NoP-5; PmAP

Brethren, behold, how suddenly he died.   Funeral Oration.   Dezső Kosztolányi.   IQMS, tr. by Geroge Gömöri and Clive Wilmer

Brethren, I know that many of you have come here today.   Fundamentals.   Ian Duhig.   NeBl; NeBrP

Brethren, The.   Seamus Deane.   PNI

Breughel's Winter.   Rutger Kopland.   VCWP, tr. by James Brockway

Brevity.   Friedrich Hölderlin.   NAWM-7v2, tr. by Christopher Middleton

Brevity.   Judith Wright.   HarvBoo Fr. Notes at Edge.

Brevity of Embraces.   Armanda Guiducci.   CItWP, tr. by Cinzia Sartini Blum and Lara Trubowitz

Brewed tacita of espresso, A.   Donatilia's Unrequited Love Remedy.   Virgil Suárez.   AmPoNex

Brewer's Man, The.   Leonard Alfred George Strong.   OBCoV

Brewing of Soma, The.   John Greenleaf Whittier.
    "Dear Lord and Father of mankind."   SacPr

Breyten Prays for Himself.   Breyten Breytenbach.   PoetW; VCWP, tr. by Denis Hirson

Brian O Linn had no breeches to wear.   Unknown. See Bryan O'Lynn was a Dutchman born.

Brian O'Linn.   Unknown.   NBLV
    (Brian O Linn.)   OBCoV
    (Bryan O'Lynn.)   FaBoVe

Brian's new shoes. She asked me of his whereabouts. They're putting a new door in.   They're Putting a New Door In.   Brian Kim Stefans.   BAP-04

Briar, a blunder, a, A.   Index.   Bernadette Mayer.   NYP2

Briar Rose (Sleeping Beauty).   Anne Sexton.   MoWP

Briar Rose Waltz.   Cynthia Cruz.   IAoNAP

Bric-à-Brac.   Dorothy Parker.   APT-1

Brick.   Kristin Kovacic.   SweBea

Brick distinguishes this country.   Amsterdam Letter.   Jean Garrigue.   VCAP

Brick or bracking that would.   Composition with Wire.   Mark Prejsnar.   AnSo

Brick-dust in sunlight.   Roy Fisher.   NPeEn Fr. City.

Bricklayer's Lunch Hour, The.   Allen Ginsberg.   MotU

Bricolage: Versicolor.   Anna Rabinowitz.   PA9/11

Bridal Ballad.   Edgar Allan Poe.   STuOW

Bridal Morn, The.   Unknown.   WoPoe

Bridal Rites.   Rebecca McClanahan.   MPUn

Bridal Song, A: "Roses, their sharp spines being gone."   John Fletcher and William Shakespeare.   NOSC; NoSic Fr. Two Noble Kinsmen, The.

Bridal Song: "Cynthia, to thy power."   Francis Beaumont and John Fletcher.   OBEV Fr. Maid's Tragedy, The.

Bridal Song: "O come, soft rest of cares, come Night."   George Chapman.   OBEV Fr. Hero and Leander.

Bridal Veil, The.   Alice Cary.   TCAPo

Bride, The.   Bella Akhatovna Akhmadulina.   MPUn

Bride, The.   Vladislav Felitsianovich Khodasevich.   TCRusP, tr. by Daniel Weissbort

Bride, The.   D. H. Lawrence.   InoFa; NAMCP V.1; NoAM

Bride, The.   Alicia Ostriker.   TaR

Bride and a groom sitting in an open buggy, A.   Rain Effect.   Mary Ruefle.   AmAlph

Bride and Groom Lie Hidden for Three Days.   Ted Hughes.   StAl

Bride disappears, The. After twenty minutes of searching.   Impossible Marriage, The.   Donald Hall.   OxBoAm

Bride of Abydos, The.   Lord Byron.
    "Zuleika mute and motionless."   NPBRoP

Bride of Frankenstein, The.   Edward Field.   HeIP-4; ReTh; SUP

Bride of Lammermoor, The.   Sir Walter Scott.
    Lucy Ashton's Song.   NAEL-6v2; NPeEn; OBEV; OxAEP-2; OxBEV; WoPoe

Bride of Long Division, The.   Christopher Howell.   RoV

Bride of Quietness, The.   Kelly Cherry.   FFC

Bride of the Greek Isle, The.   Felicia Dorothea Hemans.   RWP

Bride of the Iconoclasts, The.   Benjamin Paul Blood.
    "Stop!—Gaze thro' this hushed gallery! The air."   APN-2

Bride she is winsome and bonny, The.   Song: Woo'd and married and a'.   Joanna Baillie.   NAEL-6v2; NAEL-7v2; NoP-4; NoP-5

Bride Song.   Christina Georgina Rossetti.   OBEV Fr. Prince's Progress, The.

Bride: Virginity, virginity, where have you gone leaving me behind?   Sappho.   SaLy, tr. by Diane Rayor

Bride wore a gown, The.   Catherine Bowman.   ExTi Fr. El Paso Times "World of Women," The.

Bridegroom, beloved of my heart.   Unknown.   WPoS

Bridegroom, dear to my heart.   Ancient Sumerian Oral Tradition.   EroLit, tr. by Samuel Noah Kramer

Bridegroom of forty-one, / who tomorrow goes off to war, The.   Siberian Wooing.   Yevgeny Aleksandrovich Yevtushenko.   VCWP, tr. by Albert C. Todd and James Ragan

Bridegroom with his bride!, The. (LL)   St. Agnes' Eve.   Alfred Tennyson.   OBEV; SacPr

Bride-Night Fire, The.   Thomas Hardy.
    "O Tim, my own Tim I must call 'ee—I will!"   FaBoVe

Brides Come to Yuba City, The.   Chitra Divakaruni.   FTtHH; OpBo; UnSA

Bride's Day.   Susan Howe.   FTOS

Bride's Farewell, The.   Felicia Dorothea Hemans.   TreFP

Bride's Hours, A.   Jean Valentine.   MPUn

Brides of Elvis, The.   David Ray.   AllShUp

Bride's Tragedy, The.   Thomas Lovell Beddoes.
    "Who speaks? Who whispers there? A light! A light!"   NPBRoP

Bridge.   Bill Berkson.   Eno

Bridge.   Katri Vala.   SonAtl, tr. by Marja Heininen, Ursula Hobday and Phoebe Ravenhall

Bridge, The.   Victor Hugo.   SxFrPo, tr. by A. M. and E. H. Blackmore

Bridge, The.   Henry Wadsworth Longfellow.   APN-1; ITBLP; NAAPv.1; OxBoAm

Bridge, The.   O. V. de L. Milosz.   BLT

Bridge, The.   Alicia Ostriker.   ExTi Fr. Mastectomy Poems, The.

Bridge, The.   Charles Reznikoff.   OxBoAm

Bridge, The.   John Banister Tabb.   APN-2

Bridge, The.   Charlotte Zolotow.   CA

Bridge, The.   Hart Crane.   APT-2; NAMCP V.1
    Atlantis.   NAAL-5
    Ave Maria.   NoAM
    Cape Hatteras.   MoAmPo
        Power.   MoAmPo
        "Stars scribble on our eyes the frosty sagas."   OtW
    Powhatan's Daughter.
        Dance, The.   MoAmPo; NAAL-5
        Harbor Dawn, The.   MoAmPo; NoAM; OxBoAm
        River, The.   GM; MoAmPo; NAAL-5; OxBoAm
        Van Winkle.   MoAmPo; NAAPv.2
    (Proem: To Brooklyn Bridge.)   HeIP-4; NoAM; NoP-5; WaAnP; WeW-3
    To Brooklyn Bridge.   AmFaPo; ChIV-1; ClHu; ColAP; EMP; FaBoA; HarvBoo; MakPoe; MoAmPo; NAAL-5; NAAPv.2; NoP-4; OxBoAm; PoPoPo; TFi; TRP
    Tunnel, The.   MoAmPo; NAAL-5; OxBoAm

Bridge, and a hot concrete road, A.   Desert of Love, The.   János Pilinszky.   IQMS; OBVE, tr. by Ted Hughes

Bridge at noon.   Changing Borders.   Robert Bonazzi.   TiP2

Bridge, fallen, A. And so.   Through Clouds, Their Whispers.   Martha Rhodes.   NAPBL

Bridge in the South.   Jorge Teillier.   TCLAP, tr. by Carolyne Wright

Bridge is certainly the simplest answer, The.   Manly Ferry.   John Philip.   NOBAu

Bridge of my solitude.   Song.   Emilio Prados.   RaW, tr. by Robert Mezey

Bridge of Old Wonders.   Muzaffar Nawwab.   IrPoTo, tr. by Carol Bardenstein

Bridge of Sighs, The. Thomas Hood. BRP; OBEV; OxAEP-2; TreFP

Bridge of volumes, The. World in Yellow, A. Marcel Duchamp. PFTM-1

Bridge Poem, The. Kate Rushin. TWF

Bridge under our wheels moaned, some said, because it was built in a time, The. Cricket Mountain. Khaled Mattawa. NAPBL

Bridge View. Daniel Tobin. NevBe

Bridge Where the Moon Crosses, The. Muso Soseki. EaWin, *tr.* by W. S. Merwin

Bridge-Guard in the Karroo. Rudyard Kipling. OBWP

Bridges. Leslie Norris. TCAWP

Bridges: "My first bridge was a log—a slippery one across a muddy creek." Carlos Reyes. NevBe

Bridges that, a little because of absence. For the Princess Hello. David Shapiro. OxBoAm

Brief Autumnal. *Unknown.* WeW-3, *tr.* by Dudley Fitts

Brief Curriculum. Reiner Kunze. PoSu, *tr.* by Michael Hamburger

Brief Ectasy. Luciana Notari. CItWP, *tr.* by Cinzia Sartini Blum and Lara Trubowitz

Brief Encounter. Norman J. Loftis. SpirFl

Brief Entanglements. Richard Garcia. TouFir

Brief harp of the larches. To Friend-Tree of Counted Days. René Char. YaTCFP, *tr.* by William Carlos Williams

Brief History of Light, A. Caitríona O'Reilly. MoWP; NIrP

Brief History of the City. Robert Peterson. GeoHom

Brief in the light of streetlamp, then back again. Late Apollo. Carl Phillips. AmAlph

Brief Journey West, The. Howard Nemerov. NoAM

Brief Lessons in Eroticism 1. Gioconda Belli. ErotSp; TANSG, *tr.* by Steven F. White

Brief Letter to Donald Walsh (in memoriam). Angel Cuadra. AF, *tr.* by Katherine Rodriguez Nieto

Brief Lives. Olive Senior. EmeKit

Brief meeting today, A. For Ko Who Has Come Back from China. Muso Soseki. EaWin, *tr.* by W. S. Merwin

Brief Note from Jerusalem, A. Gabriel Preil. FIT, *tr.* by Robert Friend

Brief, on a flying night. Chimes. Alice Thompson Meynell. MoBrPo

Brief procession, The. Bessie Smith's Funeral. Alvin Aubert. SeSe

Brief Reflection on Accuracy. Miroslav Holub. StAl, *tr.* by Miroslav Holub

Brief Reflection on Brief Reflections. Miroslav Holub. MotU, *tr.* by Stuart Friebert and Dana Hábová

Brief reflection on the greatness of God. Yana Tokareva. CRWP, *tr.* by Daniel Weissbort

Brief reflections are indeed brief reflections. Accordingly, they are not poems. Brief Reflection on Brief Reflections. Miroslav Holub. MotU, *tr.* by Stuart Friebert and Dana Hábová

Brief Thoughts on cats Growing on Trees. Miroslav Holub. PoSu, *tr.* by Ian Milner and Jarmila Milner

Brief Thoughts on Cracks. Miroslav Holub. PoSu, *tr.* by Ian Milner and Jarmila Milner

Brief Thoughts on Floods. Miroslav Holub. PoSu, *tr.* by Ian Milner and Jarmila Milner

Brief To Butterick. Stephen Rodefer. VaPo

Brief Viper. Alfonso D'Aquino. RMCMP, *tr.* by Rebecca Seiferle

Brief was the meeting,—tear-stained, full of fears. To A.H.B. Margaret Witter Fuller. PoBW

Brief Wyoming Meditation. Diane Di Prima. BB

Briefcase, The. Paul Muldoon. CABP; NAMCP V.2

Briefly Eavesdropping on Walt Whitman, Virginia, 1863. Tim Suermondt. ViWalt

Briefly It Enters, and Briefly Speaks. Jane Kenyon. AFaM; HW

Brieves from the Book of Kells. R. T. Smith. PoA 2002

Briggflatts [An Autobiography]. Basil Bunting.
    Autobiography, An. HarvBoo; NAMCP V.1; NoAM; NoP-4; NoP-5; NPeEn
    "Poet appointed dare not decline."
      "Loaded with mail of linked lies." FaBoWar
    "Riding silk, adrift at noon." WoPoe

BRight. No Thanks, No. 70. E. E. Cummings. PFTM-1

Bright after Dark. Pearse Hutchinson. PBCIP

Bright, all white and blue. Andreyevsky Church, The. Nikolai Nikolaevich Morshen. TCRusP, *tr.* by John Glad

Bright and beautiful art thou. October. Mary Weston Fordham. CBWP-2

Bright and early we went down to the fishmarket. Words from Confinement. Cesare Pavese. AF, *tr.* by William Arrowsmith

Bright angels on the water, / Hovering by the light. Social Band, The. *Unknown.* SSUS

Bright as a single poppy in a field. Alfred Raymond Bellinger. YaYoPo

Bright as the day, and like the morning fair. Cloe. George, Baron Lansdowne Granville. NIP-4; OxBEV

Bright as the light that burns at night. Venetia. Adah Isaacs Menken. CBWP-1

Bright autumn moon. Six Ways, The. Issa. EH, *tr.* by Robert Hass

Bright BABE! Whose awfull beautyes make. Richard Crashaw. FSCP

Bright bird lighted in the sheltered yard, A. J S L. R. Williams Parry. BBMWP, *tr.* by Emyr Humphreys

Bright books! the perspectives to our weak sights. To His Books. Henry Vaughan. BASC

Bright burnished day, they are laying fresh roof down. Men Roofing. Eamon Grennan. PBCIP

Bright cards above the fire bring no friends near. Christmas 1944. Denise Levertov. AF

Bright cars hazarded, The. (LL) In California. Donald Davie. NAMCP V.2; NoAM

Bright Cigar-Shaped Object Hovers Over Mount Pleasant, A. John Kinsella. NeBl

Bright, consuming Spirit. No power on earth so great as Thee. Song of Hungarrda, The. Ngunaitponi. NOBAu

Bright Day, A. W. H. Davies. OBWVE

Bright enamoured youth above, The. Love's Mystery. Joseph Beaumont. NOSC

Bright eyes, sweet lips, with many fevers fill. Desire. Ada Cambridge. OxBSo

Bright Field, The. Ronald Stuart Thomas. AngWePo; TCAWP

Bright, glowing Sappho! child of love and song. Ode to Sappho. Elizabeth Oakes-Smith. ColAP

Bright hard day over habour where sea, A. Winter Lanscape—Halifax. Douglas Lochhead. NIP-4

Bright healthful waves flow forth to each glad wanderer free. (LL) To [*or the* Poet] Wordsworth. Felicia Dorothea Hemans. NPBRoP; RWP

Bright leaps a living brook! (LL) From the Flats. Sidney Lanier. APN-2; NoP-4; NoP-5

Bright Light of Responsibility, The. Jennifer L. Knox. BAP-97

Bright Lights of Sarajevo, The. Tony Harrison. EmeKit

Bright lure seized, the old hook bitten, The. (LL) Next Poem, The. Dana Gioia. NoP-4; NoP-5

Bright mirror I braved: the devil in it, The. Cleopatra to the Asp. Ted Hughes. RACG

Bright moon like frost, The. Tune: "Always Having Fun." Su Tung-p'o. ColAnChi, *tr.* by James Robert Hightower

Bright moon, oh how white it shines, The. *Unknown.* CCL1,

Bright moon slowly, slowly rises, The. Slowly, Slowly Poem, The. Yüan Hung-tao. ColAnChi, *tr.* by Jonathan Chaves

Bright moon soars over the Mountain of Heaven, The. Moon over the Mountain Pass, The. Li Po. TAL

Bright Moon, The. *Unknown.* CCL1,

Bright moonlight shines through the trees. Busy in the Spring. Tzu Yeh. CrYelRi; ErotSp, *tr.* by Sam Hamill

Bright Morning, A. George Crabbe. STuOW *Fr.* Tales of the Hall.

Bright over Europe fell her golden hair. (LL) Letty's Globe. Charles Tennyson Turner. NPeEn; OBEV; OxBEV; OxBSo

Bright pearl, kingfisher plume bed drapes. Parody of the Other Woman. Shen Manyuan. CCL1, *tr.* by Anne Birrell

Bright Queen of Heaven, God's Virgin Spouse. Knot, The. Henry Vaughan. BASC; RSR

Bright Receding. Heather Ramsdell. AmPoNex; IAoNAP

Bright sea, The. From the Seashore. Anna Petrovna Bunina. NAWM-7v2, *tr.* by Pamela Perkins

Bright shadows of true Rest! some shoots of bliss[e]. Son-Days [dayes]. Henry Vaughan. AngWePo; NOSC

Bright silver penny, A. (LL) Silver Penny, The. Walter De la Mare. NOxBChV; OBMV

Bright Star. Běkes. IrPoTo

Bright Star. John Keats. AWTN; CABP; CenSon; GSo; MakPoe; NAEL-6v2; NAEL-7v2; NAWM-7v2; NIL-7; NIP-4; NoP-4; NoP-5; NPBRoP; NPeEn; OxBSo; TFi; WaAnP

Bright sun rests on the mountain, is gone, The. Hooded Crane Tower. Wang Chih-huan. CCL1, *tr.* by Stephen Owen

Bright sun sinks / beyond the western ridge, The. T'ao Ch'ien. CCL1, *tr.* by William Acker

Bright Sunlight. Amy Lowell. APT-1

Bright town, tossed by waves of time to a hill. Ode to Swansea. Vernon Watkins. OBWVE

Bright Venus, who across the heavens stray. Bright Venus, Who Across the Heavens Stray. Louise Labé. AWTN, *tr.* by Graham Martin

Bright vocabularies are transient as rainbows. Precious Moments. Carl Sandburg. MoAmPo

Bright / with the armpit-dazzle of a lioness. Christopher Okigbo. NAMCP V.2 *Fr.* Heavensgate.

Brighter shall shine the stars which still remain. (LL)   Word for the Hour, A. John Greenleaf Whittier.   NCAP; PCW

"Brighter than a thousand suns"—that blinding glare.   Judith Wright.   HarvBoo Fr. Shadow of Fire: Ghazals, The.

Brightest and Best of the Sons of the Morning.   Reginald Heber.   SacPr

Brightest planet of the ETERNAL SPHERE!, The. (LL)   [Sonnet] Conclusive. Mary Robinson.   CenSon; RWP

Bright-footed Thetis did the sphere aspire.   Homer.   NoSic Fr. Iliad, The.

Bright-harnest [or Bright-harnessed] Angels sit in order serviceable. (LL)   On the Morning of Christ's Nativity.   John Milton.   BASC; ChrPo; NAEL-6v1; NAEL-7v1; NoP-4; NoP-5; PBRV; WaAnP

Brightlines.   Unknown.   SonAtl, tr. by H. Younde

Brightness.   Maggie Nelson.   HeMarv

Brightness of rain wavering.   Polderland.   Hendrik Marsman.   TuT, tr. by Seamus Deane

Brigitte Bardot in Grangetown.   Tony Curtis.   TCAWP

Brigomaglos, a Christian, Speaks.   Frances Horovitz.   MoWP

Brill.   Clark Coolidge.   PmAP

Brillan las luces hasta el horizonte.   Mar Egeo.   Manuel Ulacia.   RMCMP

Brilliance.   Mark Doty.   BeAl; PoCu

Brilliant— / A day that is less than zero.   Alicia Ostriker.   ExTi Fr. Mastectomy Poems, The.

Brilliant, bright—the flowers of the cold season!   Pavilion for Listening to Fragrance, The.   Chang Yü.   WoPoe, tr. by Jonathan Chaves

Brilliant day, deserted house. (LL)   Sentence, The.   Anna Andreyevna Akhmatova.   AmFaPo; ItP, tr. by Judith Hemschemeyer

Brilliant moon.   Issa.   SoOfWa, tr. by Sam Hamill

Brilliant Moon, A.   Wen T'ing-yün.   CCL1, tr. by Glen Baxter

Brilliant moon has just now reached the zenith of the night, A.   Brilliant Moon, A.   Wen T'ing-yün.   CCL1, tr. by Glen Baxter

Brilliant now, they seem to tremble and ring out. (LL)   Window at Key West, A.   Honor Moore.   KGB; WiU

Brilliant Sad Sun.   William Carlos Williams.   HarvBoo; NAAPv.2

Brilliant Sky.   Jean Joubert.   GifTon, tr. by Denise Levertov

Brilliant stills of food, the cozy, The.   Ladies' Home Journal, The.   Sandra M. Gilbert.   FuFl

Brilliant, this day—a young virtuoso of a day.   Celebration.   Denise Levertov.   NAMCP V.2

Brilliant tropical death yes, A. (LL)   Tropical Death.   Grace Nichols.   InoFa; NAMCP V.2

Brilliant Windows.   Larry Kramer.   GeoHom

Brilliantly philosophising.   Brilliantly Philosophising.   Hanny Michaelis.   TuT, tr. by Peter van de Kamp

Brimmed Whole.   Tu Fu [or Du Fu].   NDACCP, tr. by David Hinton

Brimming Water.   Tu Fu [or Du Fu].   CCL1; NDACCP, tr. by Kenneth Rexroth

Brindled, where what's left of the light finds him, he cowers.   Erasure.   Carl Phillips.   AmAlph

Bring all men to His bliss! Amen. (LL)   Unknown.   NAEL-6v1; NAEL-7v1; NAWM-7v1 Fr. Sir Gawain and the Green Knight [Marie Borroff Translation].

Bring back the life.   Give me the Red on the Black of the Bullet (for Claude Reece Jr.).   Jayne Cortez.   LTA

Bring, bring to deck my brow, ye Sylvan girls.   She Endeavors to Fascinate Him.   Mary Robinson.   CenSon; RWP

Bring, bring, to deck my brow, ye sylvan girls.   Mary Robinson.   NPBRoP Fr. Sappho and Phaon.

Bring dreams of Christ to dusky cane-lipped throngs. (LL)   Georgia Dusk. Jean Toomer.   APT-2; InGu; NAAL-5; NAAPv.2; NAMCP V.1; NoAM; NoP-4; NoP-5; OxBoAm

Bring flowers to crown the cup and lute.   Letitia Elizabeth Landon.   VWP Fr. New Monthly Magazine, 44 286–8.

Bring flowers, young flowers, for the festal board.   Bring Flowers.   Felicia Dorothea Hemans.   TreFP

"Bring forth the horse!" The horse was brought.   Lord Byron.   TreFP Fr. Mazeppa.

Bring forth the prisoner.   Dialogue, A.   Elizabeth Newell.   EMWP

Bring from the craggy haunts of birch and pine.   Song.   John Todhunter.   IrV

Bring her down.   Song to the Alpaca.   Denise Y. Arnold.   PoCoUp

Bring Kateen-beug and Maurya Jude.   Beg-Innish.   John Millington Synge. IrV; MoBrPo

Bring me all of your dreams.   Dream Keeper, The.   Langston Hughes.   ItP

Bring me my garland, bring me a wreath.   Maniac's Song, The.   Ann Taylor.   NOBRP

Bring me the sunflower for me to transplant.   Bring Me the Sunflower. Eugenio Montale.   PtR, tr. by George Kay

Bring me the sunflower, I'll plant it here.   Eugenio Montale.   PoetW, tr. by William Arrowsmith

Bring me the sunset in a cup.   Emily Dickinson.   APN-2; MoAmPo

Bring Me the Sweat of Gabriela Sabatini.   Clive James.   PML

Bring me the woes your days have bestowed.   Bring Me Your Woes.   Sarah Barkan.   Prolet, tr. by Amelia Glaser

Bring me wine, but wine which never grew.   Bacchus.   Ralph Waldo Emerson. APN-1; OBEV; OxBoAm; TCAPo

Bring Me Your Woes.   Sarah Barkan.   Prolet, tr. by Amelia Glaser

Bring On the Wine.   Li Po.   CCL1, tr. by Elling O. Eide

Bring out the tall tales now that we told.   Ghost Story.   Dylan Thomas. OBCP

Bring rain.   Santo Domingo Corn Dance.   Lynn Riggs.   APT-2

Bring Roses and Cardamom (2.3).   Horace.   WED, tr. by Robert Bly

Bring snow-white lilies, pallid heart-flushed roses.   Pantheist's Song of Immortality, The.   Constance Naden.   ViWPN; VWP

Bring Tara quickly, Mountain.   Andha Candī.   SinGod, tr. by Rachel Fell McDermott

Bring the camera closer in.   Focus.   Documentary.   Joseph Stroud.   InoFa

Bring the good old bugle, boys, we'll sing another song.   Marching through Georgia.   Henry Clay Work.   APN-2; CBCWP

Bring them to me. Bring them to me. Bring them to me.   Unknown.   APN-2 Fr. Minnetare Songs.

Bring us in no browne bred, fore that is mad of brane.   Bring Us In Good Ale. Unknown.   OBCoV; WaAnP

(Bryng us in no broun breed, for that is made of bren.)   OHMEL

Bringers of Beethoven, The.   Reiner Kunze.   PoSu, tr. by Gordon Brotherston and Gisela Brotherston

Bringing a Dead Man Back into Life.   Russell Edson.   TRP

Bringing Back the Draft.   E. Ethelbert Miller.   FuFl

Bringing My Son to the Police Station to Be Fingerprinted.   Shoshauna Shy. P180; PoDa

Bringing on tears shed only for myself. (LL)   Cruising with the Beach Boys. Dana Gioia.   GeoHom; PoA 2002; RWPCtW; SwNoth

Bringing Our Sheaves with Us.   Elizabeth Akers.   TreFP

Bringing the Geranium in for Winter.   Gillian Allnutt.   MoWP

Bringing the plants inside that flourished.   Wintering Over at the End of the Century.   Alvin Greenberg.   UrbNat

Bringing Zeus to His Knees.   Antler.   AtGh

Brinkwomanship.   Leontia Flynn.   NIrP; StAl

Brisk chaunticleer his mattins had begun.   Christopher Smart.   NPeEn

Bristol, thine heart hath throbbed to glory: slaves.   To the Right Hon. and Right Revd. Fredrick, Earl of Bristol, Bishop of Derry, Etc., Etc.   Ann Yearsley. RWP

Brit exclaims "O to build character in a playground riddled with hazards!", A. Golfers in the Family.   Mónica de la Torre.   LegDan

Britain.   Oliver Goldsmith.   NPeEn Fr. Traveller, The; or, A Prospect of Society.

Britain 1967.   Anna Mendelssohn.   VaPo

Britain Street: Saint John, New Brunswick.   Alden Nowlan.   Coast

Britain's Remembrancer Canto 4.   George Wither.
   "If by mischance the people in the street."   PBRV

Britannia, free from foes and foreign kings.   Seneca.   RomPo, tr. by Anthony James Boyle

Britannia Rejecta.   Henry Kirke White.   STuOW Fr. Time: A Poem.

Britannia's daughters, much more fair than nice.   Love of Fame, the Universal Passion.   Edward Young.   OBSV

Britannia's Pastorals.   William Browne.
   Golden Age: Flower-weaving, The.   NPeEn
   Golden Age, The.   NOSC
   (Hail, Thou my Native Soil.)   OxAEP-1
   Memory.   OBEV
   Morning.   NOSC
   "Shall I tell you whom I love?"   NOSC

Brither-men wha eftir us live on.   Ballat o the Hingit.   François Villon. OBVE, tr. by Tom Scott

British Church, The.   George Herbert.   AngWePo

British Columbia.   William Stafford.   GifTon

British Connection, The.   Padraic Fiacc.   PNI

British Garden, A.   Wes Magee.   OBGa

British Grenadiers, The.   Unknown.   FaBoWar

British Journalist, The.   Humbert Wolfe.   OBCoV; OxBEV

British Leftish Poetry, 1930–40.   Hugh MacDiarmid.   NAMCP V.1; NoAM

British Museum Reading Room, The.   Louis MacNeice.   BrAP; GoPo; MoBrPo

British Prison Ship, The.   Philip Freneau.
   "Two hulks on Hudson's stormy bosom lie."   TCAPo

Britomart in the House of the Enchanter Busyrane.   Edmund Spenser.   NPeEn Fr. Faerie Queene, The.

Brittania's Pastorals Book 2.   William Browne.
   "Happyer those times were, when the Flaxen clew."   PBRV

Brixton groans. Intercity Dub. Jane King. WaCA

brken promises. Sibby Anderson-Thompkins. InTrad

Bro Duncanson. C. S. Giscombe. GT *Fr.* (from the "In" Sequence).

Bro, they been callin[g] that sister by the wrong name. (LL) Gwendolyn Brooks. Haki R. Madhubuti. ESEAA; FTtHH; OPRER

Broad and far-reaching, the level plain. Desolate City, The: A Rhapsody. Pao Chao. CCL1, *tr.* by Burton Watson

Broad and flat. Flat Mountain. Muso Soseki. EaWin, *tr.* by W. S. Merwin

Broad beach / Sea wind and the sea's irregular rhythm, The. Afternoon: Amagansett Beach. John Hall Wheelock. APT-1

Broad Bean Sermon, The. Les A. Murray. BMAP; EmeKit; HarvBoo; MakPoe

Broad sun-stoned beaches. Midsummer, Tobago. Derek Walcott. MakPoe; OPOU; VCWP

Broad-Ax, The. Walt Whitman. MoAmPo *Fr.* Song of the Broad-Axe [*or* Broad-Ax].

Broad-backed hippopotamus, The. Hippopotamus, The. T. S. Eliot. NAEL-6v2; OBMV; SacPr; TCAPo

Broadcast. Philip Larkin. RWPCtW

Broadcasting to the G.B.P. D. H. Lawrence. RWPCtW

Broader leaves collect, The. Dew at the Edge of a Leaf. Marvin Bell. InvLad

Broadway. Walt Whitman. NAAL-3

Broadway. Evening. Signs in the sky that make one dizzy with color. Moon, The. Juan Ramón Jiménez. MotU, *tr.* by Hoffman Reynolds Hays

Broadway Idyl, A. Mary E. Tucker. CBWP-1

Broadway Melody. Arthur Freed. ReLy

Broadway Morning. Menna Elfyn. BBMWP, *tr.* by Gillian Clarke

Broadway Opening. Miguel Algarin. PueRic

Broagh. Seamus Heaney. FaBoVe; ModIr; NPeEn

Brocade City lies in dust and smoke. Becoming a Farmer. Tu Fu [*or* Du Fu]. CrYelRi, *tr.* by Sam Hamill

Brocade threads and summer reeds. Song for a Young General. Tu Fu [*or* Du Fu]. CrYelRi, *tr.* by Sam Hamill

Brocades and damasks and tabbies and gauzes. Jonathan Swift. IrV

Broceliande. Marilyn Hacker. ExTi

Brock. Paul Muldoon. NoAM; NoP-4

Broke the horizontal. Hank Lazer. AnSo *Fr.* Days.

Broken ALTAR, Lord, thy servant rear[e]s, A. Altar, The. George Herbert. AngWePo; BASC; CABP; ChIV-1; NAEL-6v1; NAEL-7v1; NoP-4; NoP-5; NOSC; WaAnP

Broken and Beirut. Suheir Hammad. PoArWo

Broken Appointment, A. Thomas Hardy. HarvBoo; NAEL-6v2; NAEL-7v2; NAMCP V.1; NoAM; NoP-4; NoP-5; PtR

Broken bay leaf. Olive pit. Unswept, The. Sharon Olds. ASA

Broken Boat, A. Tu Fu [*or* Du Fu]. CrYelRi, *tr.* by Sam Hamill

Broken Bowl, The. James Merrill. PoA 2002

Broken Chain, The. Dora Greenwell. VWP

Broken clocks and watches were my father's hobby. Clockwork. Donny O'Rourke. PML

Broken Cup, The. Sharon Thesen. IFF

Broken Dark, The. Robert Earl Hayden. AWTN; GT

Broken Doll, The. Nuala Ni Dhomhnaill. ModIr, *tr.* by John Montague

Broken down, somewhere near Bakersfield. To an Exeter City Cocktail Waitress. Jon Veinberg. GeoHom

Broken Ends Broken Promises. Maria Fernandez. BRtP

Broken Field, The. Sara Teasdale. APT-1

Broken Friendship. Mary Elizabeth Coleridge. VWP

Broken Glass. Victoria Edwards Tester. ICANM

Broken Glish. Pablo Neruda. RD

Broken Heart. Henrietta Cordelia Ray. CBWP-3

Broken Heart, The. John Donne. FSCP

Broken Heart, The. John Ford.
  Love's Martyrs. NOSC

Broken Helix. Dina Ben-Lev. AmPoNex

Broken Home, The. James Merrill. BrAP; ColAP; EMP; GPTC; NAAL-5; NAMCP V.2; NoAM; NoP-4; NoP-5; PoPoPo

Broken in pieces all asunder. Affliction (4). George Herbert. CABP; NOSC

Broken Lampstand, The. Wu Wei-yeh. ColAnChi, *tr.* by Jonathan Chaves

Broken Men, The. Rudyard Kipling. HarvBoo

Broken Mirror, The. Bob Perelman. FTOS

Broken Moon. Carole Satyamurti. BeAl; MoWP

Broken Necklace. Jill Bamber. Prnts

Broken Oar, The. Henry Wadsworth Longfellow. OxBSo

Broken pillar of the wing jags from the clotted shoulder, The. Hurt Hawks. Robinson Jeffers. APT-1; ChAP; ColAP; EMP; HarvBoo; MoAmPo; NAAPv.2; NAMCP V.1; NoAM; NoP-4; NoP-5; OWoS; OxBoAm; TFi; TRP; WaAnP

Broken sandstone slabs litter the shore, The. Stalingrad: 1942. Norman Nicholson. RSaN

Broken shadow gestured winter. Mother's Pearls. Bao-Long Chu. AmWaPo

Broken Silence. Louis M. Abbey. BloBone

Broken sods, a whipped flag, The. Burial, A. Seamus Deane. PNI

Broken Sonnets. Kim Addonizio. OPRER

Broken Tablets. Hsi Chou. CSKM, *tr.* by Paul Hansen

Broken, The. W. S. Merwin. MotU

Broken Tower, The. Hart Crane. APT-2; ColAP; MoAmPo; NAAPv.2; NAMCP V.1; NoAM; NoP-4; OxBoAm; PoPoPo; WaAnP

Broken Vase, The. Victor Hugo. SxFrPo, *tr.* by A. M. and E. H. Blackmore

Broken View, A. Robert Francis. APT-2

Broken-down hotel on an inhospitable sea, A. Far from Home. Nicholas Christopher. NoP-4; NoP-5

Broken-Face Gargoyles. Carl Sandburg. MoAmPo

Bronchitis. David Bottoms. PML

Bronco Busting, Event #1. May Swenson. APT-2

Brontë Sisters, The. Anna Semionovna Prismanova. ARWW, *tr.* by Catriona Kelly

Bronx. Joseph Rodman Drake. APN-1

Bronx Park. Richard Foerster. UrbNat

Bronze by gold heard the hoofirons, steelyringing. James Joyce. PFTM-1 *Fr.* Ulysses.

Bronze clock brought, The. Four Small Elegies. Margaret Atwood. PoetW

Bronze David of Donatello, The. Randall Jarrell. InGu

Bronze god running, The. At Guaracara Park. Eric Roach. WoPoe

Bronze Horseman, The. Alexander Sergeyevich Pushkin. *tr.* by D. M. Thomas Tale of St. Petersburg, A. WoPoe, *tr.* by D. M. Thomas

Bronze soldier hitches a bronze cape, The. In Memoriam Francis Ledwidge. Seamus Heaney. NAMCP V.2; NoAM

Bronze stones and cold scales. Tobacco Pickers. Kočo Racin. SonAtl, *tr.* by Broz Koneski

Bronzeville Mother Loiters in Mississippi, A. Meanwhile, a Mississippi Mother Burns Bacon. Gwendolyn Brooks. ESEAA; FuFl; IllVoic

Bronzeville Woman in a Red Hat. Gwendolyn Brooks. NALW
  (Bronzeville Woman in a Red Hat / Hires Out to Mrs. Miles.) GT

Brooding on the eightieth letter of *Fors Clavigera.* Geoffrey Hill. NAMCP V.2 *Fr.* Mercian Hymns.

Brook; An Idyl, The. Alfred Tennyson. OxAEP-2

Brook and road. Simplon Pass, The. William Wordsworth. NPeEn

——Brook and road, The. William Wordsworth. CABP *Fr.* Prelude, The; Growth of a Poet's Mind [1805 version; Selections from Anthologies].

Brook gives me, The. Strolls. A. R. Ammons. PoA 2002

Brook glides on to the river, The. Reverie. Henrietta Cordelia Ray. CBWP-3

Brooklyn. Afaa Michael Weaver. SpirFl

Brooklyn Anchorage. Lisa Jarnot. VaPo

Brooklyn Botanic Garden, The. Timothy Liu. UrbNat

Brooklyn Bridge. Matthew Rohrer. NeAmPo

Brooklyn Bridge. William Jay Smith. CA

Brooklyn Bridge, Brooklyn Bridge. Brooklyn Bridge. William Jay Smith. CA

Brooklyn Narcissus. Paul Blackburn. PmAP

Broom. Deborah Digges. SweBea

Broom, broom, man of a broom; Valentino-slick lurking overly-casual cornerly in the realm of the potted palm. Tango. Oliver Pitcher. EGAG

Broom, The; or, The Flower of the Desert. Giacomo Leopardi. *tr.* by John Heath-Stubbs and Arturo Vivante
  "Upon the arid shoulder." WoPoe, *tr.* by John Heath-Stubbs

Broon hens keckle and bouk, The. Hugh MacDiarmid. FaBoVe

Brotha saul. Seitlhamo Motsapi. TSAP

Brotha saul (furtha meditashuns). Seitlhamo Motsapi. TSAP

Brother. Gudmundur Bödvarsson. PML, *tr.* by Alan Boucher

Brother, The. Franz Wright. MotU

Brother and Sister. Lewis Carroll. NOxBChV

Brother and Sister. "George Eliot." NALW

Brother and Sisters. Judith Wright. BMAP

Brother Ass, Brother Ass, you are full of fancies. James Keir Baxter. HarvBoo *Fr.* Jerusalem Sonnets.

Brother Ben. John Rybicki. AmPoNex

Brother Body. Peter Cooley. OPRER

Brother / came back with the roses. Brother is a Star. Rachel E. Harding. BtF

Brother, Can You Spare a Dime? E. Y. Harburg. APT-2; NAAPv.2; ReLy

Brother Fire. Louis MacNeice. AF; NAMCP V.1; NoAM

Brother, Guide Me Home. *Unknown.* SSUS

Brother, I Am Here. "Shu Ting." GifTon, *tr.* by Carolyn Kizer and Y. H. Zhao

Brother, I will not howl challenges. We Are Equals. Gwendoline C. Konie. HAWP

Brother, if on the heels of war Western man. My Brother. Mikhail Naimy. NAAPv.2, tr. by Sharif Elmusa and Gregory Orfalea

Brother: / I'll look for you in the back of corners. Sent. Hérib Campos Cervera. SonAtl, tr. by Eleanor Davidson

Brother is a Star. Rachel E. Harding. BtF

Brother, it seems, you have been beaten. Struggle for Life. Frigyes Karinthy. IQMS, tr. by Peter Zollman

Brother John. Michael S. Harper. OxAAAP

Brother Man the Rasta. Edward Kamau Brathwaite. BrAP; NAMCP V.2 Fr. Arrivants: A New World Trilogy, The.

Brother men who come along now, we. Ballade of the Men Who Were Hanged. François Villon. WoPoe, tr. by Fred Chappell

Brother Moses Gone. Unknown. SSUS

Brother, my brother, whither do you pass? To a Face in a Crowd. Robert Penn Warren. FuPo

Brother nightwatchman I have shared your way. Nightwatchman. Deborah Randall. NeBl

Brother of the blowfly. Ode to the Maggot. Yusef Komunyakaa. CAP-8

Brother of the Streets. Sam Cornish. TRP

Brother Ovid, my classical leanings run thin. Intrusion of Ovid, The. Paul Guest. PoDa

Brother, there dwell, yon northern hill below. George Crabbe. STuOW Fr. Tales of the Hall.

Brother / This world. Rāmprasād Sen. SinGod, tr. by Rachel Fell McDermott

Brother, thou art gone before us: and thy saintly soul is flown. Where the Wicked Cease from Troubling, and the Weary Are at Rest. Henry Hart Milman. SacPr

Brother, today I sit on the brick bench outside the house. To My Brother Miguel. César Vallejo. PoetW; TCLAP, tr. by John Knoepfle and James Wright

Brother we are like weeds growing. David Craig. UpMys Fr. Prothalamion.

Brother where dost thou dwell? Henry David Thoreau. NCAP

Brother Wolverine. Mary Tallmountain. FiBr

Brother, / word has come, a grey decade after. Sunderland Nights. Peter Armstrong. PML

Brother, you who have the light, tell me where mine is. Melancholy. Rubén Darío. SpanPo, tr. by Anita Volland

Brotherhood. Thomas Kinsella. HarvBoo Fr. Notes.

Brotherhood. Octavio Paz. LoL, tr. by Eliot Weinberger

Brotherhood: "First boy to fall in, The." Yehoshua November. IJHIL

Brotherhood in Pain. Robert Penn Warren. OxBoAm

Brotherhood of Men. Richard Eberhart. PoWW

Brotherless Sisters. Unknown. WoPoe, tr. by Charles Simic

Brothers. Heinrich Lersch. FaBoWar, tr. by Christopher Middleton

Brothers, and a Sermon. Jean Ingelow.
Pups and the Fish, The. DiBP

Brothers and Sisters. Michael Foley. PNI

Brothers are kneeling. Haiku for My Brothers. Ira B. Jones. BtF; FTtHH

Brothers bop & pop and be-bop in cities locked up. B Network, The. Haki R. Madhubuti. FuFl; IllVoic

Brothers Grimm grew weaker and flickered, blue light, The. California Girlhood, A. Alice Notley. PmAP

Brothers in sacrifice, hail! To the idealistic killers. Lionel Abrahams. TSAP

Brothers, let us discover our hearts again. Open Letter. Owen Dodson. OxAAAP

Brothers Loving Brothers. Vega. ISC

Brothers met who many a year had past, The. Tales of the Hall. George Crabbe.

Brothers rebelled against one another, The. Various authors. CATKP Fr. Songs of Flying Dragons.

Brothers rolling around in the big back seat. Vacation, 1969. Dorothy Barresi. SwNoth

Brothers, The. Edwin Muir. HeIP-4

Brothers, / this big woman. Song at Midnight. Lucille Clifton. ErotSp; OxAAAP; UnSA

Brought by the breeze. "Shunzei's daughter." ArkPo, tr. by Robert H. Brower and Earl Miner

Brought crazy still. (LL) On Induction of the Hand. Clark Coolidge. NYP2; PmAP

Brought for us so low. (LL) Christmas Eve. Christina Georgina Rossetti. ChrPo; RSR

Brought gifts / home for me. My Daddy, Whenever He Went Some Place. David Huddle. PBCAP

Brought here in slave ships and pitched overboard. Love Your Enemy. Yusef Iman. GI

Brought in by pulling you under the arms. Incarnation. Joan Houlihan. IAoNAP

Brought low in Kyoto. How to Survive Nuclear War. Maxine W. Kumin. AtGh

Brought to bed by sickness, cut off from men. Replying to a Poem from My Cousin Huilian. Hsieh Ling-yün. CCL1, tr. by Burton Watson

Brought to burning eyelids sleep. (LL) Nuit Blanche, La. Rudyard Kipling. MoBrPo; UV

Brought Up. Sam Gardiner. NIrP

Brought up as I was to ask of the weather. Point Grey. Daryl Hine. BrAP

Brought up on underage drink drunk. Brought Up. Sam Gardiner. NIrP

Brow of a horse in that moment when, The. Anastasia and Sandman. Larry Levis. BAP-97

Brow / The brown beam. Trakl. Johannes Bobrowski. GTCP, tr. by Michael Hamburger

Brown, A. Gertrude Stein. NAAPv.2; NAMCP V.1 Fr. Tender Buttons.

Brown and black leather of all the dead comrades, The. (LL) Shoes of Dead Comrades, The. Jackie Kay. NeBrP; RSaN

Brown and furry / Caterpillar in a hurry. Caterpillar, The. Christina Georgina Rossetti. FaBoVe

Brown bare island stretched to July sailing winds. Mykonos. Edwin Denby. NYP2

Brown berry of a man, bald head, A. My Father's Dreams. Cynthia Fuller. Prnts

Brown Bess. Rudyard Kipling. FaBoWar

Brown Bomber. Sam Cornish. BtF

Brown bread and delicious moon. (LL) August: "August. / The opposing." Federico García Lorca. IPoFL; RaW, tr. by James Wright

Brown, brittle, wait-a-bit weeds. Indian Cave Jerry Ramsey Found, The. William Stafford. NoAM

Brown Circle. Louise Glück. CFP

Brown Curtain, The. Alberto Giacometti. SurPaPo, tr. by Mary Ann Caws and Jean-Pierre Cauvin

Brown enormous odor he lived by, The. Prodigal, The. Elizabeth Bishop. APT-2; ChIV-2; GI

Brown gas-fog, white. Denise Levertov. AmWaPo Fr. Staying Alive.

Brown gingham, pink, and skirts of Alice blue. (LL) In an Iridescent Time. Ruth Stone. MoAmPo; NALW; OxWW

Brown Girl, Blonde Okie. Gary Soto. NOxBChV

Brown Girl Dead, A. Countee Cullen. GT; InoFa

Brown harbour of our land. Far from the Beach. Alda do Espirito Santo. HAWP, tr. by Jacques-Noël Gouat

Brown is the flat gestation of a maze. Sonnet. Karen Volkman. IAoNAP

Brown lilac, roses filled with rain. World on Sunday. James McAuley. BMAP

Brown lived at such a lofty farm. Brown's Descent; or, The Willy-Nilly. Robert Frost. MoAmPo

Brown mare that ran until fatigued, The. Dirty Nylons. Na Hûidôk. EcSo, tr. by Peter H. Lee

Brown of her—her eyes, her hair, her hair[!], The. (LL) Farmer's Bride, The. Charlotte Mew. CABP; LW; MoBrPo; MoWP; NALW; NoP-4; NoP-5; RACG; VWP

Brown of Ossawatomie. John Greenleaf Whittier. NCAP

Brown owls come here in the blue evening. Frances Densmore and Tohono O'odham. NAAPv.1; SWaP Fr. Songs for Treating Sickness, Sung durring the Four Parts of the Night.

Brown Pot. Ray Gonzalez. TouFir

Brown rat has taken up residence with me, A. Little Citizen, Little Survivor. Hayden Carruth. GoPo; OPRER

Brown River, Smile. Jean Toomer. BLPJKO Fr. Blue Meridian, The.

Brown, sad-coloured hillside, where the soil, A. Sower, The. Sir Charles G. D. Roberts. BrAP

Brown scrub oak leaf, The. Jemez Mountains Meditation. Jim Cohn. WhBo

Brown Skin Girl. Tommy McClennan. FaBoVe

Brown spiders dwell in the kivas. New Mexico. Douglas Kent Hall. ICANM

Brown took 5 rounds from an AK-47. Dead Weight. Jim Nye. AmWaPo

Brown which is not liquid not more so is relaxed and yet there is change, a news is pressing, A. Gertrude Stein. NAAPv.2; NAMCP V.1 Fr. Tender Buttons.

Brown wrist and hand with its raw knuckles and blue nails, The. Machinist, Teaching His Daughter to Play the Piano, The. B. H. Fairchild. PoDa

Brown-dappled fawn, The. Fawn in the Snow, The. William Rose Benét. MoAmPo

Browning of leaves, The. La Querida. Bino A. Realuyo. ReBoTo

Brown's Descent; or, The Willy-Nilly. Robert Frost. MoAmPo

Br-r-r-am-m-m, rackety-am-m, OM, Am. What the Motorcycle Said. Mona Van Duyn. NIL-7; NIP-4

Bruce and Nina. Clarence Major. BodElec

Bruce and the Bloodhound. John Barbour. DiBP Fr. Bruce, The.

Bruce and the Bluegills. David Marlatt. AmPoNex

Bruce did-in 24 bluegills with a big spoon. Bruce and the Bluegills. David Marlatt. AmPoNex

Bruce Ismay's Soliloquy. Derek Mahon. PNI

Bruce, The. John Barbour.
  Book 16: Bruce in Ireland halts his army at Limerick so that a laundrywoman may give birth.
  "Syne went thai southwart in the land." NePenScot
  Bruce and the Bloodhound. DiBP
  Freedom [*or* Fredome]. NePenScot; OBEV; TreFP

Bruckner. Rayne Mackinnon. EdScPo

Brudder George is agwine to glory. Sin-Sick Soul, The. *Unknown.* SSUS

Brudder, guide me home an' I am glad. Brother, Guide Me Home. *Unknown.* SSUS

Brudder Moses gone to de promised land. Brother Moses Gone. *Unknown.* SSUS

Brueghel in Naples. Dannie Abse. NIP-4

Brueghel's Winter. Walter De la Mare. GS

Brugge. Franz Wright. MotU

Bruise. Robert Budde. PoPra

Bruise of This, The. Mark Wunderlich. NeAmPo; P180

Bruised Children. Janice W. Hodges. BtF

Bruised in the grapple with trade. Victor, The. Louis Untermeyer. STuOW

Bruised Reed Shall Ne Not Break, A. Christina Georgina Rossetti. OxAEP-2

Bruisingly cradled in a Harvard chair. Louis Edward Sissman. NoP-4; NoP-5 *Fr.* Dying: An Introduction.

Bruja: Witch. Pat Mora. FiBr

Brush of evening colours, A. To the Tune "Intoxicated with Shadows of Flowers." Yü Ch'ing-tsêng. EroLit, *tr. by* Chung Ling and Kenneth Rexroth

Brush of sunlight on the dry grass. Scarcity. Joanna Klink. IAoNAP

Brush the dark bangs on my forehead aside, kiss my beauty mark. *Unknown.* SLW, *tr. by* Marjolijn De Jager, Sayd Bahodin Majrouh and André Velter

Brush Up Your Shakespeare. Cole Porter. OBCoV; ReLy

Brushing back the curls from your famous brow. Copulating Gods, The. Carolyn Kizer. BrAP

Brushing flies. Buson. EH, *tr. by* Robert Hass

Brushwood door to the hermitage is closed even in daylight, The. Living at Eunjok Hermitage. Mookam Choinul. BecRai, *tr. by* Kim Daljin, Kim Won-Chung and Christopher Merrill

Brussels: Simple Frescos 1. Paul Verlaine. SxFrPo, *tr. by* Martin Sorrell

Brussels: Simple Frescos 2. Paul Verlaine. SxFrPo, *tr. by* Martin Sorrell

Brut, The. Layamon.
  "Arthur was mortally wounded, grievously badly." NAEL-7v1
  Arthur's Dream. NAEL-7v1

Brutal shuddering machines, yellow, bite into given earth. Landscape Gardeners, The. Geoffrey Grigson. OBGa

Brutal to Love. Queen of Carthage, The. Louise Glück. AmFaPo

Brute Image. John Ashbery. NoP-4; NoP-5

Brute Strength. Wanda Coleman. PmAP

Brutish recall. Echo. Robert Creeley. BodElec

Brutus. Abraham Cowley. BASC

Brutus' Last Song [*song*]. Christiania Whitehead. NeBl

Bryan and Pereene. James Grainger. STuOW

Bryan, Bryan, Bryan, Bryan. Vachel Lindsay. APT-1; FTtHH

Bryan Ferry. B.D. Love. SwNoth

Bryan O'Lynn. *Unknown. See* Brian O'Linn.

Bryan O'Lynn was a Dutchman born. Brian O'Linn. *Unknown.* NBLV
  (Brian O Linn had no breeches to wear.) OBCoV

Bryce & Tomlins. Kenneth Fearing. APT-2

Bryng us in no broun breed, for that is made of bren. *Unknown. See* Bring us in no browne bred, fore that is mad of brane.

Bubba Esther, 1888. Ruth Whitman. TaR

Bubble. Trebor Healey. BeDoSh

Bubble, The. Richard Crashaw. PBRV *Fr.* Bulla.

Bubble of Air. Muriel Rukeyser. TaR

Bubbled baby gave an abrupt burp, The. Edmund Wilson. OBCoV *Fr.* Easy Exercises in the Use of Difficult Words.

Bubbled with brimming kisses at my mouth. (LL) Dante Gabriel Rossetti. NAEL-6v2; OxBSo *Fr.* House of Life, The.

Bubbles. Celia de Fréine. NIrP, *tr. by the* author

Bubble-wrap the chimney like a vase. Moving House. Jacob Polley. BeAl

Bubbling brook doth leap when I come by, The. Nature. Jones Very. ColAP

Bubeleh, / if you will be. Old Lovers. Carl Rakosi. NAAPv.2

Buchenwald. Fedya Filkova. CSCBP, *tr. by* Georgi Belev and Lisa Sapinkopf

Buck in the Snow, The. Edna St. Vincent Millay. ColAP; MoWP; NALW; NoP-4; NoP-5; WaAnP

Buckdancer's Choice. James Dickey. HeIP-4; NAMCP V.2; NoAM; NoP-4; NoP-5

Bucket of azaleas, A. Basho. EH, *tr. by* Robert Hass

Bucket, The. Rose Romano. UnSA

Bucket, The. Samuel Woodworth. *See* Old Oaken Bucket, The.

Buckets in my head stand open, The. Buckets in My Head, The. Lucie Thésée. SurWo, *tr. by* Myrna Bell Rochester

Buckets in My Head, The. Lucie Thésée. SurWo, *tr. by* Myrna Bell Rochester

Buckles. Joy Lahey. AnSo

Buckroe, After the Season, 1942. Virginia Hamilton Adair. APT-2

Bucolic. Aimé Césaire. VCWP

Bud. William T. Crawley III. InTrad

Bud Powell, Paris, 1959. William Matthews. OxBoAm

Bud, The / stands for all things. Saint Francis and the Sow. Galway Kinnell. AmFaPo; BeAl; ChAP; NAAL-5; OxBoAm; P180; TWF

Budd, The. Edmund Waller. PBRV

Buddha. Jack Kerouac. BB

Buddha. Vachel Lindsay. NAAPv.2

Buddha and Brahma. Henry Adams. APN-2

Buddha and I, The. Atanu Dey. WhBo

Buddha and the Seven Tiger Cubs. Henri Cole. NAMCP V.2

Buddha, Birdbath, Hanging Plant. Peter Skrzynecki. PML

Buddha / Cherry flowers. Hoitsu. ZenPo, *tr. by* Takashi Ikemoto and Lucien Stryk

Buddha in the Woodpile, A. Lawrence Ferlinghetti. WANABP

Buddha Inside the Light. Rainer Maria Rilke. WED, *tr. by* Robert Bly

Buddha Is Lord of Our Town. John Gilgun. AmZen

Buddha is neither asian nor male. she could be an african woman. Amy Champ. WhBo

Buddha, known to men by many names, The. Buddha and Brahma. Henry Adams. APN-2

Buddha Law / Shining. Issa. ZenPo, *tr. by* Takashi Ikemoto and Lucien Stryk

Buddha of Sökkuram, The. Shirley Kaufman. GifTon

Buddha too. Masaoka Shiki. CAoMJL1, *tr. by* Burton Watson

Buddha took some Autumn leaves. Kenneth Rexroth. BLT *Fr.* City of the Moon, The.

Buddha's death-day / Old hands. Basho. ZenPo, *tr. by* Takashi Ikemoto and Lucien Stryk

Buddha's ears are droopy touch his shoulders. Hoa Nguyen. WANABP

Buddha's Nirvana / Beyond flowers. Issa. ZenPo, *tr. by* Takashi Ikemoto and Lucien Stryk

Buddha's Satori. Muso Soseki. EaWin, *tr. by* W. S. Merwin

Buddhist approach to packing up after the gig, The. Third Street Promenade; Full Moon, Sunday Night, Santa Monica. Al Young. WhBo

Buddhist Barbie. Denise Duhamel. SUP

Buddhist Monk Cut and Burned His Own Flesh to Make The Rains Stop—A Man From His Native Place Asked Me to Write a Poem to Send to Him, A. Hsü Wei. ColAnChi, *tr. by* Jonathan Chaves

Buddhist Retreat Behind Broken-Mountain Temple, A. Ch'ang Chien. CCL1, *tr. by* Witter Bynner

Buddhist Ruminations. *Unknown.* WhBo, *tr. by* Diane Di Prima

Budding floweret blushes at the light, The. Thomas Chatterton. OxAEP-1 *Fr.* Aella; a Tragycal Enterlude.

Buddy Bolden Cylinder, The. William Matthews. SeSe

Buddy, can you spare a dime? (LL) Brother, Can You Spare a Dime? E. Y. Harburg. APT-2; NAAPv.2; ReLy

Buddy, have you heard? (LL) Deferred. Langston Hughes. APSN; APT-2

Buddy Holly. David Wojahn. SwNoth

Buddy Holly Poem, The. Maurice Kilwein Guevara. TouFir

Buddy Holly Watching *Rebel Without a Cause*, Lubbock, Texas, 1956. David Wojahn. PBCAP *Fr.* Mystery Train: A Sequence.

Budger of history Breake of time You Bomb. Bomb. Gregory Corso. AtGh

Budgie Finds His Voice. Wendy Cope. UV

Budging the sluggard ripples of the Somme. Hospital Barge at Cérisy. Wilfred Owen. HarvBoo; TCAWP

Buds from winter's frost-work lift, The. Coming of Spring, The. Henrietta Cordelia Ray. CBWP-3

Buffalo. Eugenio Montale. ArBi, *tr. by* Jonathan Galassi

Buffalo. Molly Peacock. OxBoAm

Buffalo are coming. We will feed and feast. We wish to be fortunate and we expect it, The. *Unknown.* APN-2 *Fr.* Minnetare Songs.

Buffalo Bill opens a pawn shop on the reservation. Evolution. Sherman Alexie. NAMCP V.2; NeAmPo; PoPoPo

Buffalo Bill 's / defunct / who used to. Buffalo Bill's Lament. E. E. Cummings. HeIP-4; InoFa; NAMCP V.1; NIP-4; OxBoAm; StAl; WaAnP

Buffalo Bill's Lament. E. E. Cummings. HeIP-4; InoFa; NAMCP V.1; NIP-4; OxBoAm; StAl; WaAnP
  (Buffalo Bill's.) NAAL-5; NAAPv.2; NIL-7; TCAPo

Buffalo burned sage. Kin. Ruth Forman. AmPoNex

Buffalo Clouds over the Maestro Hoon. Norman Dubie. AmAlph

Buffalo Dreams. Bart Edelman. RWB

Buffalo Dusk. Carl Sandburg. ChAP

Buffalo Evening. Robert Creeley. BodElec

Buffalo Gals [see also Lubly Fan by Cool White]. Unknown. APN-2

Buffalo Poem #1. Geary Hobson. UrbNat

Buffaloes are gone, The. Buffalo Dusk. Carl Sandburg. ChAP

Buffeted by the waves. Archilochus. SaLy, tr. by Diane Rayor

Bufo. Alexander Pope. OBSV Fr. Epistle to Dr. Arbuthnot.

Bug, flower, bird on slipware fired and fluted. Syrinx. James Merrill. OxBoAm

Bugle blows, setting the marchers moving, The. Army Ballad. Wang Wei. ColAnChi, tr. by Stephen Owen

Bugler boy from barrack (it is over the hill), A. Bugler's First Communion, The. Gerard Manley Hopkins. NoAM

Bugs. Mary Ann Hoberman.
  Combinations. OBSP

Bugs. Unknown. HHAm

Bugs. Unknown. IFF

Bui Doi, Dust of Life. Yusef Komunyakaa. AmWaPo

Buick. Karl Shapiro. OxBoAm

Buie Annajohn was the king's black mare. Buie Annajohn. Bliss Carman. IFF

Buik of the Cronicles of Scotland. tr. by William Stewart
  Battle About a Dog, The. DiBP, tr. by William Stewart

Build a House in Paradise. Unknown. SSUS

Build cities. Turn. Andrée Chedid. PoArWo, tr. by Lucy McNair

Build it here. Sonnet with Lock and Key. Jasper Bernes. IAoNAP

"Build me straight, O worthy Master!" Building of the Ship, The. Henry Wadsworth Longfellow. CBCWP

Build over me no marble monument. Alcestis to Admetus. Mary Elizabeth Coleridge. ViWPN

Builder demolishes houses, The. Dialectics. Edvard Kocbek. PoSu

Builders, why do you stand looking out to sea? Belizeans: Unite to Build our Nation. George Cadle Price. OWABP

Building. Gwendolyn Brooks. BRtP

Building. Gary Snyder. BB

Building an Outhouse. Ronald Wallace. PBCAP

Building in Stone. Sylvia Townsend Warner. MoBrPo

Building Nicole's Mama. Patricia Smith. SpirFl

Building of a New Church, The. Unknown. HHAm

Building of Carthage, The. Virgil. OBVE Fr. Aeneid [or Eneados or Aeneis], The.

Building of the Ship, The. Henry Wadsworth Longfellow. CBCWP
  "And as he laboured, his mind ran o'er." FaBoWar
  "Then the Master." NAAL-3

Building of the Skyscraper, The. George Oppen. CalPo; OxBoAm

Building the Bridge. Will Allen Dromgoole. WeW-3

Building the cart again. (LL) Ox Cart Man. Donald Hall. GoPo; IPoFL; LoL

Building the Compost. Helena Minton. PfS

Building the Dam. Reuel Denney. YaYoPo

Building: The New London Hospital. Bill Griffiths.
  Fragment 1. Oth
  Fragment 4. Oth
  Fragment 9. Oth
  Fragment 11. Oth
  Fragment 12. Oth
  Fragment 13. Oth
  Fragment 18. Oth
  Shepherd's Calendar. Oth
  Shepherd's Calendar cont'd. Oth
  Ship, The. Oth
  South Song. Oth

Building upon the Sand. Eliza Cook. TreFP

Building Walls. Todd Davis. ACAMVP; VisFro

Buildings and Grounds. Henry Taylor. LPSFW

Buildings are at their stations, untimely, The. Elegy for New York, The. Douglas Crase. MakPoe

Buildings of the, The. Sherley Anne Williams. GeoHom Fr. Iconography of Childhood, The.

Built and placed it in my body. Infant Spouse, The. Joan Houlihan. IAoNAP

Built by Hank Wurlitzer, 7 ft. 8 inches, to house the first petrocommunications system. Big Bar. Kenward Elmslie. PmAP

Built for a cotton king, who loved the view. Richard Murphy. ModIr Fr. Price of Stone, The.

Buladelah-Taree Holiday Song Cycle, The. Les A. Murray.
  "Barbecues smoke is rising at Legge's Camp; it is steaming into the midday air." NAMCP V.2
  "Forests and State Forests, all down off the steeper country; mosquitoes are always living in there." NAMCP V.2
  "It is good to come out after driving and walk on the bare grass." NAMCP V.2
  "Now the sun is an applegreen blindness through the swells, a white blas on the sea face, flaking and shoaling." NAMCP V.2

Bulahdelah—Taree Holiday Song Cycle, The. Les A. Murray.
  "People are eating dinner in that country north of Legge's Lake, The." BMAP

Bulbs do not winter well, The. January Ovaries. Susan Hahn. ExTi

Bulging yellow clouds. Richard Wright. APT-2

Bulin File, The. Gu Cheng. tr. by Eva Hung
  Bulin is Dead, It Seems. PFTM-2, tr. by Eva Hung
  Bulin Met Bandit. PFTM-2, tr. by Eva Hung
  Discovery. PFTM-2; VCWP, tr. by Eva Hung

Bulk of it, The / In air. Chartres. George Oppen. OxBoAm

Bulk of these years is already gone out of mind, The. Orientius. WoPoe Fr. Poem on Divine Providence.

Bulk[e]ley, Hunt, Willard, Hosmer, Meriam, Flint. Hamatreya. Ralph Waldo Emerson. NAAPv.1; OxBoAm; TCAPo

Bulkhead sweating, and under naked bulbs, The. Mess Deck. Alan Ross. FaBoWar; PoWW

Bull, The. Ralph Hodgson. MoBrPo; OBMV

5 The Bull. Conor O'Callaghan. NIrP Fr. Loose Change.

Bull, The. Judith Wright. BrAP

Bull and Egret. Chinua Achebe. PFTM-2

Bull Calf, The. Irving Layton. BrAP

Bull does not know you, nor the fig tree, The. Federico García Lorca. WoPoe Fr. Lament for Ignacio Sanchez Mejias.

Bull Moose, The. Alden Nowlan. BeAl; BrAP

Bull moose waits, A. Across the River. Brian Henry. PoDa

Bull of Bryncelyn, The. Alan Llwyd. BBMWP, tr. by Joseph P. Clancy

Bulla. Richard Crashaw.

Bubble, The. PBRV

Bull-Baiting. Edward Lovibond. DiBP

Bulldozers come, they rip, The. Marge Piercy. NBLV Fr. Sand Roads.

Bullet, A / slams. Claude Anshin Thomas. WhBo

Bullet entered between the eyes, The. How It All Comes Back. William Daniel Ehrhart. AmWaPo

Bullet Hole Man. Nancy D. Tolson. BRtP

Bulletin. Binyo Ivanov. CSCBP, tr. by Georgi Belev and Lisa Sapinkopf

Bulletin board flutters with a flair, The. First Poem. Marvin Bell. NevBe

Bullets whip the air this last afternoon. Conjectural Poem. Jorge Luis Borges. TCLAP, tr. by Norman Thomas Di Giovanni

Bullfight. Pedro Serrano. RMCMP, tr. by Geoff Hargreaves

Bullfrog. Brendan Galvin. PoCoUp

Bullhead. John Engels. MoASP

Bullock / slowly, The. Federico García Lorca. PFTM-1 Fr. Night (Suite for Piano and Poet's Voice).

Bull-roarer, The. Gerald Stern. CAP-8

Bully [Boston, Massachusetts, 1987]. Martín Espada. LTA

Bulosan Listens to a Recording of Robert Johson. Alfred Encarnacion. OpBo (Bulosan Listens to a Recording of Robert Johnson.) LTA; UnSA

Bumper to Bumper. Harryette Mullen. RD

Bumblebee, You Saw Big Mama. Jayne Cortez. SurWo

Bumbler for sure, A. Bee. Philip Booth. PoCoUp

Bummer, A. Michael Casey. PoAgWa

Bumping on an Ass. Wang the Zealot. CCL1, tr. by C. H. Kwock and Vincent McHugh

Bun. Tom Clark and Ron Padgett. AHA

Buna. Primo Levi. AF, tr. by Ruth Feldman and Brian Swann

Bunch of drifter sons hollered, A. Bunch of Drifter Sons Hollered, A. Gottfried Benn. PFTM-1

Bunch of frightened rookies, A. This Is the Army, Mr. Jones. Irving Berlin. ReLy

Bunch of grapes leaves Bacchus satisfied, A. Unknown. PriapPo Fr. Priapus Poems, The.

Bunch of Grapes, The. George Herbert. ChIV-1; NAEL-6v1; NAEL-7v1; NOSC

Bunch of Pictures Back from the Drugstore, A: The Four Good Ones. Robert Masterson. ICANM

Bunch of the boys were whooping it up in the Malamute saloon, A. Shooting of Dan McGrew, The. Robert W. Service. BrAP; BRP; EdScPo; UV

Bunch of winecups stand on the dining table, A. In Memoriam: Dedicated to My Father. Wang Xiaolong. PML, tr. by Michelle Yeh

Bunches of carnations in a tin pitcher. Joke, A. Aleksander Wat. BLT

Bunchgrass or the months-dry wheat. Yard, The. David Baker. PfSP

Bundaberg Rum. W. N. Scott. NOBAu

Bundle in the gutter had its skull, The. Dust. Douglas Livingstone. TSAP

Bundle the piles of verbose missives. Kim Kwanguk. CATKP, *tr. by* Peter H. Lee

Bundled by Tuc's tight jagged. Notes on a Visit to Le Tuc d'Audoubert. Clayton Eshleman. PmAP

Bundles. Carl Sandburg. MoAmPo

Bundles for Them. Gertrude Stein. PFTM-1

Bungalow in Quogue. P. G. Wodehouse. ReLy

Bungalows, God said, Day 1, and up they sprang like buttercups. Retro Creation. Aidan Rooney-Céspedes. BeAl; NIrP

Bungle-man, The. *Unknown.* SonAtl, *tr. by* Ashley Barai and John Ellman

Bungler, The. Amy Lowell. LW

Bunk Johnson Blowing. Muriel Rukeyser. SeSe

Bunkers, The. Michael O'Loughlin. PBCIP *Fr.* Shards, The.

Bunthorne's Song. William Schwenck Gilbert. CABP *Fr.* Patience.

Buoy-Bell, The. Charles Tennyson Turner. GSo

Burden. Peter Kane Dufault. NoP-4; NoP-5

Burden, The. Anne Caston. NAPBL

Burden Lifters, The. Michael Waters. SwNoth

Burden of Easter Vigil, A. Lionel Pigot Johnson. SacPr

Burden of noise, of infections, A. John Tranter. VaPo *Fr.* Blackout.

Burdened. Ella Wheeler Wilcox. SWaP

Burdened with family feelings, I went. Burnt. Boris Abramovich Slutsky. HP, *tr. by* Daniel Weissbort

Burdens. Laura Riesco. TANSG, *tr. by* Shaun Griffin and Emma Sepúlveda-Pulvirenti

Burdock. Madness. Adelaide Crapsey. NAAPv.2

Bureau 2. Josephine Miles. NALW

Burgeoning trees are thick with leaves, The. East Wind. Ou-yang Hsiu. NDACCP, *tr. by* Kenneth Rexroth

Burger box and a burger too, a chipbox, A. David Wheatley. NIrP *Fr.* Sonnets to James Clarence Mangan.

Burial. Edna St. Vincent Millay. InoFa

Burial. Judith W. Steinberg. PfS

Burial, A. Seamus Deane. PNI

Burial, The. Ellen Bryant Voigt. InoFa

Burial, The. John Webster. NOSC *Fr.* Devil's Law Case, The.

Burial Clothes. Jessica Smucker Falcón. ACAMVP

Burial Code. Laurel Smith. VisFro

Burial Detail. Andrew Hudgins. CBCWP

Burial Flags. Ralph Nixon Currey. PoWW

Burial in the East. Pablo Neruda. TRP, *tr. by* Ben Belitt

Burial: "Like a sister who borrows." Rebecca McClanahan. PoDa

Burial Mound. Anne Marie Macari. MotU

Burial of a Fairy Queen. Mary E. Tucker. CBWP-1

Burial of Latané, The. John Reuben Thompson. CBCWP

Burial of Sir John Moore, The. Charles Wolfe. FaBoWar; GoPo; IrV; NOBRP; OBEV; OBWP; OxAEP-2; OxBEV; TFi; TreFP; UV

Burial of the Dog. Susan Musgrave. NoAM

Burial of the Spirit of a Young Poet. Richard Hughes. MoBrPo

Burial Path. Ruth Bidgood. AngWePo

Burial Practice. Srikanth Reddy. LegDan

Burial Songs. T'ao Ch'ien. *tr. by* David Hinton
  3. NDACCP, *tr. by* David Hinton

Burials. Amelia Blossom Pegram. HAWP

Buried. Michael Ondaatje.
  "To be buried in times of war." NAMCP V.2

Buried 2. Michael Ondaatje.
  "Heat of explosions, The." NAMCP V.2

Buried above ground. (LL) Lines Written During a Period of Insanity. William Cowper. IJHIL; NoP-4; NoP-5; NPeEn

Buried alive. Labyrinth. Jaime Torres Bodet. TCLAP, *tr. by* Sonja Karsen

Buried Birds, The. Ida G. M. Gerhardt. TuT, *tr. by* Medbh McGuckian

Buried Graves, The. Brad Leithauser. NoP-4; NoP-5; WaAnP

Buried in a morning Cloud. (LL) Katherine Philips. *See* Bury'd in a morning Cloud.

Buried inside, page three, below the fold. Woman Holding a Fox. David Yezzi. PoDa

Buried Life, The. Matthew Arnold. BrAP; NAEL-6v2; NAEL-7v2

Buried Light. Yusef Komunyakaa. AmAlph

Buried Poem, The. Ismail. HotL, *tr. by* V. Narayana Rao

Buried shrine disgorges through its foul, The. Tomb of Charles Baudelaire, The. Stéphane Mallarmé. SxFrPo, *tr. by* A. M. and E. H. Blackmore

Buried Stream, The. James Keir Baxter. HarvBoo

Burke. Samuel Taylor Coleridge. CenSon *Fr.* Effusions.

Burlesque dancer, The. Striptease. Andrey Andreievich Voznesensky. TCRusP, *tr. by* Daniel Weissbort

Burlesque upon the Great Frost. Charles Cotton.
  "But, to leave fooling, I assure ye." OBCoV

Burlington Bertie from Bow. William Hargreaves. OBCoV

Burly, dozing, humble-bee. Humble-Bee, The. Ralph Waldo Emerson. APN-1; NAAPv.1; NCAP

Burma-Shave Roadside Signs. *Unknown.* OBCoV *Fr.* Advertising Rhymes.

Burmese Figures. *Unknown.* EaWin, *tr. by* W. S. Merwin

Burn. Mary Dalton. Coast

Burn, alight, radiance tension flows, sheets. Kind of Ransom. Marla Jernigan. AnSo

Burn drowns steadily in its own downpour, The. Waterfall. Seamus Heaney. HeIP-4

Burn generations. People of Fire. Nidaa Khoury. DTA, *tr. by* Karen Alkalay-Gut

Burn Ovid with the rest. Lovers will find. Penal Law. Austin Clarke. ModIr; OxBEV

Burn Rubber on Me. Derrick X. BtF

Burn the generations. People of Fire. Nidaa Khoury. PoArWo, *tr. by* Linda Zisquit

Burn the soiled ones in the boiler. Women's Blood. Vicki Feaver. MoWP

Burned and dusty garden said, The. Athenian Garden, An. Trumbull Stickney. APN-2; NoP-4; NoP-5

Burned by cigarettes. The chair beside it. (LL) More Fun In The New World. Karen Solie. OpeFie; PoPra

Burned in the Test. Wilma Elizabeth McDaniel. CalPo

Burning, The. N. Scott Momaday. HATNAP

Burning Babe, The. Robert Southwell. ChrPo; HeIP-4; NAEL-6v1; NAEL-7v1; NoSic; OBCP; OBEV; OxAEP-1; OxBEV; SacPr; TFi; TRP; WaAnP; WoPoe

Burning / burning / burning / there was finally something. Crow's Last Stand. Ted Hughes. HarvBoo

Burning, burning, I drift and tread. Yunus Emre. NaPG, *tr. by* Talat Sait Halman

Burning Bush. Alison Apotheker. PoCoUp

Burning dinner is not incompetence but war. (LL) What's That Smell in the Kitchen? Marge Piercy. NBLV; NIL-7; NIP-4

Burning Drift-Wood. John Greenleaf Whittier. APN-1

Burning Field, The. Velemir Khlebnikov. TCRusP *Fr.* Laundress, The.

Burning Graves at Netherton, The. Roy Fisher. Oth

Burning Hills. Michael Ondaatje. NoAM

Burning in secret. Burning in Secret. "Shunzei's daughter." WoPoe, *tr. by* Steven D. Carter

Burning Interior, A. David Shapiro. BAP-04

Burning Island. Gary Snyder. APSN; VCAP

Burning Multitude, The. Menna Elfyn. ATSWP, *tr. by* Robert Minhinnick

Burning my h[e]art who had him kindly warm[e]d. (LL) Mary Sidney Wroth, Countess of Montgomery. NPeEn; OxBSo; PBRV *Fr.* Pamphilia to Amphilanthus.

Burning My Manuscripts. Yi Kyubo. CATKP, *tr. by* Kevin O'Rourke

Burning of Bustin's Island, The. Jim Carroll. AHA

Burning of Margaret Moone, The. Mary Doughtery Bartlett. ICANM

Burning of Paper instead of Children, The. Adrienne Rich. HarvBoo; VCAP

Burning of the Books, The. Bertolt Brecht. PoSu, *tr. by* John Willeh

Burning of the Leaves, The. Laurence Binyon.
  "Now is the time for the burning of the leaves." NPeEn

Burning Off. Geoffrey Dutton. NOBAu

Burning Oneself out. Adrienne Rich. BodElec

Burning Oneself to Death. Takahashi Shinkichi. ZenPo, *tr. by* Takashi Ikemoto and Lucien Stryk

Burning Shewolf. Vasco [*or* Vasko] Popa. PFTM-2; VCWP, *tr. by* Charles Simic

Burning Shit at An Khe. Bruce Weigl. AF; AmWaPo

Burning Spear wails with a hole, a hollow, in his voice. Music. Rohan B. Preston. WaCA

Burning the Cat. W. S. Merwin. NIP-4

Burning the Christmas Greens. William Carlos Williams. APT-1; ChrPo; NAAL-5; NAMCP V.1; NoAM

Burning the Dreams. Muriel Rukeyser. AF

Burning the Letters. Randall Jarrell. MoAmPo

Burning the Small Dead. Gary Snyder. NAMCP V.2

Burning the Water Hyacinth. Audre Lorde. AFaM

Burning under the bleached scalp; behind dry lips / a loaded gun. (LL) Face to Face. Adrienne Rich. NAMCP V.2; NoAM

Burning Want. Les A. Murray. HarvBoo

Burning Wheel, The. Aldous Leonard Huxley. ChIV-1

Burnished, burned-out, still burning as the year. Public Garden, The. Robert Lowell. BrAP; OBGa

Burnt. Boris Abramovich Slutsky. HP, *tr. by* Daniel Weissbort

Burnt Child, The. W. S. Merwin. NoAM

Burnt Lands. GSo

Burnt Norton. T. S. Eliot. APT-1; HarvBoo; MoAmPo; NAAL-5 *Fr.* Four Quartets.

Burnt out year, The. New Year Letter. Edward Kamau Brathwaite. GT

Burnt Ship, A. John Donne. FaBoWar; OBWP

Burnt Sienna. Norman Henry, II Pritchard. GT

Burnt sienna and sun they lie. Monarchs Steering. Shirley Lim. GeoHom

Burnt sugar skeletons. Memorial. Charmaine A. Gill. BtF

Burragorang. Nan McDonald. NOBAu

Burro once, sent by express, A. Advice to Travelers. Walker Gibson. NBLV

Burroughs. Robert Glück. WiU

Burrowing deep into earth until the grave is complete. Wolf. Peter Blue Cloud. HATNAP

Burrowing into the grass. Last Farewell to Kukutis. Marcelijus Martinaitis. TWW, *tr. by* Laima Sruoginis

Burrowing with his teeth. History of the Caesars, A. Isidor Schneider. APT-2

Burrowing Yankees. *Unknown.* AmWaPo; NAAPv.1

Burst agonized and clear! (LL) Success is counted sweetest. Emily Dickinson. APN-2; ColAP; GoPo; HeIP-4; MoAmPo; NAAL-3; NAAL-5; NAAPv.1; NoP-4; NoP-5; OxBoAm; PoAgWa; PoPoPo; SAmP; TCAPo; TFi

Burst of iris so that, A. Iris. William Carlos Williams. WeW-3

Burst of passion skims. History. Lucien Stryk. Vesp

Burst, to illumine our tempestuous day. (LL) England in 1819. Percy Bysshe Shelley. CenSon; NAEL-6v2; NAEL-7v2; NAWM-7v2; NoP-4; NoP-5; NPBRoP; OxAEP-2; OxBEV; OxBSo; PoPoPo; TFi

Bursting like an old wineskin. Inside Out. Jenna Johnson. MAAN

Bursting ripe plum, A. Richard Wright. APT-2

Burthen of my anger on my soul. Wheat-miners. Michael Field. ViWPN

Bury and Dig. Minnie Bruce Pratt. PoBW

Bury Her at Even. Michael Field. OBMV

Bury in order the snow-melt. Night at Tongbak Temple. Pak Chaesam. CAMKP, *tr. by* David R. McCann and Jiwon Shin

Bury Me in a Free Land. Frances Ellen Watkins Harper. ColAP; ISC; NAAPv.1; TCAPo; WaAnP

Bury me in my pink pantsuit, you said—and I did. Fare, The. Molly Peacock. ExTi; InoFa

Bury Me with a Band. Ofelia Zepeda. ReEnLa

Bury my heart at Wounded Knee. (LL) American Names. Stephen Vincent Benét. APT-2; FaBoA; OxBoAm

Bury the Great Horse. Douglas Garman. UV *Fr.* Ode on the Death of Haig's Horse.

Bury this old Illinois farmer with respect. Illinois Farmer. Carl Sandburg. HHAm

Bury'd in a morning Cloud. (LL) Epitaph on her Son H. P. at St. Syth's Church [where her body also lies Interred]. Katherine Philips. CABP; MakPoe; NoP-4; NoP-5; NOSC; PBRV; PEW

(Buried in a morning Cloud.) (LL) CABP; NoP-4; PBRV; PEW; WaAnP

Burying. Paul Ruffin. TiP2

Burying Ground by the Ties. Archibald MacLeish. GM

Bus, The. Leonard Cohen. HeIP-4

Bus comes and I'm ready, The. Muse Is Gone, The. Robert Long. MAAN

Bus driver from Delhi to Agra, A. Mud. George Kalamaras. BAP-97

Bus Driver Poem, The. Khaled Mattawa. AmPoNex

Bus Driver, The. Netta Gillespie. AmZen

Bus Driver, The. Hédi Kaddour. PML; YaTCFP, *tr. by* Marilyn Hacker

Bus driver tore my ticket, The. Fidel in Ohio. Martín Espada. TouFir

Bus I just got off of, The. Truth: I Have Five Fingers on Each Hand! Imad Fouad. AnVo, *tr. by* Mohamed Enani

Bus poems, The. Del Ray Cross. FreRad

Bus Ride. Kate Daniels. PBCAP

Bus Ride. Harvey Shapiro. PrTe

Bus Station, The. Sean Dunne. ModIr *Fr.* Sydney Place.

Bus was taking me, The. To S.V. György Petri. VCWP, *tr. by* Geroge Gömöri and Clive Wilmer

Bus Window. June Jordan. EGAG

Buses came late, each driver sullen. Christmas Bells, Saigon. Walter McDonald. AF

Bush. Josephine Jacobsen. NoP-4; NoP-5

Bush, a gathering smoke, The. Blackthorn. Euros Bowen. OBWVE, *tr. by* the author

Bush bangs, The. Match that Darkened the Sun, The. *Unknown.* SonAtl, *tr. by* Richard Blecker and Etienne Karekezi

Bush land scrub land. Country North of Belleville, The. Alfred Wellington Purdy. BrAP

Bush Navigator: The Last Morning of Hands. Peggy Shumaker. PBCAP

Bush of loo brush, A. Curly Kale. David Lindley. NLP

Bush Speaks, The. Ernest G. Moll. NOBAu

Bush Telegram. Tom Pickard. Oth

Bush, The. James Nicholas. BBMWP, *tr. by* Joseph P. Clancy

Bush warbler. Basho. EH, *tr. by* Robert Hass

Bush-bristling juniper and you the thorn. Génèvres Hérissez, et Vous, Houx Espineux. Pierre de Ronsard. WoPoe, *tr. by* Donald Davie

Bushed. Earle Birney. BrAP; NoAM; NoP-4; NoP-5

Bushranger, A. Kenneth Slessor. NOBAu

Bushwoman stands here. *Unknown.* SonAtl, *tr. by* B.A. Gathousi, Brenda Ginever, Malcolm Ginever and B. J. Sefhako

Busie old foole, unruly Sunne. John Donne. *See* Busy old fool, unruly sun.

Business Girls. Sir John Betjeman. UV

Business Man's Lair, A. George Crabbe. STuOW *Fr.* Tales of the Hall.

Business of Health, The. Jennifer Timoner. ICANM

Business of Love is Cruelty, The. Dean Young. SUP

Business of Poetry, The. Harold Norse. CLPP

Business Personals. John Ashbery. BodElec

Business Reverses. Edgar Lee Masters. ChIV-2

Busses, The. Frederick Morgan. PoDa

Bus-Stop on the Somme, The. David Rowbotham. NOBAu

Buster Keaton Looks in the Woods for His Love Who is a Real Cow. Rafael Alberti. GPTC, *tr. by* Mark Strand

Buster's Last Hand. Jennifer O'Grady. AmPoNex

Bustle in a House, The. Emily Dickinson. HeIP-4; NAAL-3; NAAL-5; NAAPv.1; NoP-4; NoP-5; SacPr; SAmP

Bustopher Jones: The Cat About Town. T. S. Eliot. OBCoV; TriCat

Busts of the great composers glimmered in niches. Mrs. Snow. Donald Justice. NoP-4

Busty never asked me why I came around. Pigeons. Conor O'Callaghan. NIrP

Busy, curious, thirsty fly. On a Fly Drinking out of [*or* from] His Cup. William Oldys. OBEV; OxAEP-1; OxBEV

Busy Days of My Nights, The. Bob Hicok. AmAlph

Busy Heart, The. Rupert Brooke. MoBrPo

Busy in my skin in my house, I receive. Flesh. Lionel Abrahams. TSAP

Busy in the Spring. Tzu Yeh. CrYelRi; ErotSp, *tr. by* Sam Hamill

Busy old fool, unruly sun. Sun Rising, The. John Donne. BASC; CABP; ClHu; FSCP; HeIP-4; NAEL-6v1; NAEL-7v1; NIL-7; NIP-4; NoP-4; NoP-5; NOSC; PoPoPo; TFi; WaAnP; WeW-3

(Busie old foole, unruly Sunne.) BrAP; PBRV

Busy old lady, charitable tray. Reason for Refusal. Martin Bell. FaBoWar

Busy with Many Jobs. Tadeusz Rózewicz. PoSu, *tr. by* Adam Czerniawski

Busy with very urgent jobs. Busy with Many Jobs. Tadeusz Rózewicz. PoSu, *tr. by* Adam Czerniawski

But. Vladimir Holan. PoSu, *tr. by* Ian Milner and Jarmila Milner

But a dream within a dream? (LL) Dream within a Dream, A. Edgar Allan Poe. NCAP; OxBoAm; TCAPo

But a solitary gull between earth and heaven? (LL) Thoughts on a Night Journey. Tu Fu [*or* Du Fu]. TAPaP; WaAnP, *tr. by* Arthur Sze

But accept it for friendship's sake. (LL) Cave of Making, The. W. H. Auden. FaBoVe; OxAEP-2

But ae braithless note. Sydney Goodsir Smith. OBVE *Fr.* Gangrel Rymour and the Pairdon of Sanct Anne, The.

But ah, Desire still cries, "give me some food." (LL) Sir Philip Sidney. NAEL-6v1; NAEL-7v1; NoP-4; NoP-5; NoSic *Fr.* Astrophil and Stella.

But ah! he left the thorn wi' me. (LL) Banks o' Doon, The ("Ye banks and braes o' bonie [*or* bonnie] Doon.") Robert Burns. BrAP; OxBEV

But ah! what glories yon blue vault emblaze? Hymn to Indra, A. Sir William Jones. NOBRP

But ah! when first to breathe man does begin. On Time, Death, and Eternity. Robert Peter. VerBaPo

But ain't it long, and ain't it good and thick. *Unknown.* PriapPo *Fr.* Priapus Poems, The.

But, alas, who less[e] could do[e] that found so good occasion? (LL) Think'st thou to seduce me then. Thomas Campion. NAEL-7v1; OxAEP-1

But Alive. Lee Adams. ReLy

But all he was is overworn. (LL) Alfred Tennyson. BrAP; CAGL; HeIP-4; NAEL-6v2; NAEL-7v2; NAWM-7v2; NoP-5 *Fr.* In Memoriam A. H. H.

But all is new unhallowed ground. (LL) Alfred Tennyson. ChrPo; NAEL-6v2; NAEL-7v2 *Fr.* In Memoriam A. H. H.

But all must be endured, since even a poor. (LL) In my eyes he matches the gods, that man who. Sappho. ASA; PoCho, *tr. by* Jim Powell

But all time roars outside this room. (LL) Thom Gunn. AmFaPo; BeAl *Fr.* Three Songs.

But all too late, grief's out of date. Michael Wigglesworth. NAAL-3 *Fr.* Day of Doom, The [First Section].

But always, without fail THE NECK. (LL) Travel[l]er's Curse after Misdirection[, The]. Robert Graves. MoBrPo; NBLV; OBCoV

But anxious cares the pensive nymph oppressed. Alexander Pope. OxAEP-1 *Fr.* Rape of the Lock, The: An Heroi-Comical Poem in Five Cantos.

But are not of? (LL) Midnight on the Great Western. Thomas Hardy. OxAEP-2; WoPoe

But art? / It is pure and intense play. Antonio Machado Ruiz. WED *Fr.* Moral Proverbs and Folk Songs.

But Artemis, my girls. Telesilla. SaLy, *tr. by* Diane Rayor

But as green / As anything: / As spring. (LL) Louis Edward Sissman. NoP-4; NoP-5 *Fr.* Dying: An Introduction.

But as long-liv'd as present love. (LL) Of English Verse. Edmund Waller. CABP; NOSC

But as my friend, take to a younger bed. Sappho. SaLy, *tr. by* Diane Rayor

But ask for it. (LL) Tiara. Mark Doty. MakPoe; WaAnP

But ask whatever else, and we will dare! (LL) Ode Recited at the Harvard Commemoration (July 21, 1865). James Russell Lowell. APN-1; CBCWP; OBWP; PCW

But at last there came the day, the hour of shovels and buckets. Angels of the Ruins, The. Rafael Alberti. AF, *tr. by* Geoffrey Connell

But at night, when there is most need. Atrium. Alessandro Ceni. ItPo, *tr. by* Gayle Ridinger

But at the common table. (LL) Te Deum. Charles Reznikoff. ChIV-1; NAAPv.2; NAMCP V.1; OxBoAm

But, baby, where are you? (LL) Ballad of Birmingham. Dudley Randall. HeIP-4; ISC; NIL-7; NIP-4; NoAM; NoP-4; NoP-5; SoSe-8; WaAnP

But be contented: when that fell arrest. William Shakespeare. NAEL-6v1; NAEL-7v1; OxAEP-1; PBRV; WaAnP *Fr.* Sonnets.

But Beautiful. Johnny Burke. ReLy

But Beautiful is the dog lost. But Beautiful. Michael Burkard. LaCa

But better get used to dreams too. (LL) China. Bob Perelman. FTOS; PFTM-2

But Bird. Paul Zimmer. AtGh; SeSe

Bow and die. (LL) Why did baby die. . .? Christina Georgina Rossetti. InoFa; VWP

But break, my heart, for I must hold my tongue! (LL) William Shakespeare. OxAEP-1; WaAnP *Fr.* Hamlet.

But bright—as if the soul had come for the night. Dream: Flight of a Dragonfly. Gennady Aygi. ItGoST, *tr. by* Peter France

But brims the poisoned well. (LL) Fragments of a Lost Gnostic Poem of the Twelfth [or 12th] Century. Herman Melville. APN-2; NoP-4; PoPoPo; TCAPo

But bring us in good ale! (LL) Bring Us In Good Ale. *Unknown.* OBCoV; WaAnP

But can see better there, and laughing there. Gwendolyn Brooks. ColAP *Fr.* Notes from the Childhood and the Girlhood.

But can you waft across the British tide. Faliscus Grattius. DiBP *Fr.* Cynegeticon Liber.

But can you waft across the British tide. Roman Tribute, A. John Whitaker. DiBP

But chief of all. John Milton. *See* Chief of all.

But clasp'd to his bosom, the infant was dead. (LL) Erl-King, The. Johann Wolfgang von Goethe. OBVE; STV

But could it come up into a limestone to correct, teeth. Clark Coolidge. FTOS

But could not hear it speak. (LL) Border. Gillian Clarke. HarvBoo; MoWP

But Custard keeps crying for a nice safe cage. (LL) Tale of Custard the Dragon, The. Ogden Nash. ITBLP; MakPoe

But day by day I spin my shroud. (LL) Arachne. Rose Terry Cooke. APN-2; NAAPv.1

But Death intenser—Death is Life's high mead. (LL) Why Did I Laugh Tonight? John Keats. CenSon; NAEL-6v2; NAEL-7v2

But Dionysos had no healing physic for his comrade fallen, of dancing he thought no more. Nonnus. CAGL *Fr.* Dionysiaca.

But discover it no more. (LL) Eden is that Old-Fashioned House. Emily Dickinson. ChIV-1; NALW

But dispossessed of breath. (LL) Syrinx. Amy Clampitt. NAMCP V.2; NoP-4; NoP-5

But do not let us quarrel any more. Andrea del Sarto. Robert Browning. NAEL-6v2; NAEL-7v2; NoP-4; NoP-5

But do not let your ignorance. Wendell Berry. UpMys *Fr.* Testament.

But do you really want to see Whitman's house instead of Roosevelt's? Walt Whitman. Juan Ramón Jiménez. ViWalt; WED, *tr. by* Robert Bly

But Don John of Austria rides home from the Crusade. (LL) Lepanto. G. K. Chesterton. FaBoWar; MoBrPo; OBMV; OBNV

But don't want to; I still don't want to know. (LL) X-Ray. Dannie Abse. AngWePo; BloBone; PoA 2002

But drives a blue car through the / stars. (LL) Two Years Later. John Wieners. PmAP; RaBo

But dropped like Adamant. (LL) 'Twas warm—at first—like Us. Emily Dickinson. APN-2; InoFa; NAWM-7v2; NCAP; SoSe-8

But dwell in darkness, for your god is blind. George Chapman. OxBSo *Fr.* Coronet for His Mistress Philosophy, A.

But each morning he starts out. Day Break. Joseph Somoza. ICANM

But—'e'll never be the man 'is Father woz. (LL) Chorus of a Song That Might Have Been Written by Albert Chevalier. Max Beerbohm. OBCoV; UV

But end at where we came. Floating Epitaphs, Their Possible Explanations in Poro Point. Alejandrino Hufana. ReBoTo

But ere I could fly thence, it pierced my heart. (LL) Sir Philip Sidney. NAEL-7v1; NoSic *Fr.* Astrophil and Stella.

But ere sterne conflict mixt both strengths, faire Paris stept before. Homer. OBVE *Fr.* Iliad, The.

But even leaving, longing to be back. Escaping from Autopia. Chryss Yost. GeoHom

But every section road is blacktopped now. Where I Grew Up. Jeff Gundy. ACAMVP

But everyone looks at the horse. (LL) Horse. Chase Twichell. ExTi; StAl

But, fair Iëmpsar (wife of Potiphar). Joshua Sylvester. ChIV-1 *Fr.* Maidens Blush, The.

But fate and gloomy night encompass thee around. (LL) To the Memory of Mr Oldham. John Dryden. BASC; BrAP; NAEL-6v1; NAEL-7v1; NIL-7; NIP-4; NoP-4; NoP-5; NOSC; NPeEn; OxAEP-1; OxBEV; PoPoPo; TFi; TRP; WaAnP

But fear, thirst, hunger, and this huddled chill. (LL) Montana Pastoral. James Vincent Cunningham. APT-2; MoAmPo; OxBoAm

But finding nothing, sullenly withdrew. (LL) Range-finding. Robert Frost. NIL-7; NIP-4; NoAM; OBWP

But first one must free oneself. Patrizia Cavalli. NeIt; VCWP, *tr. by* Patrizia Cavalli and Robert McCraken

But for a woodpecker. Basho. SoOfWa, *tr. by* Sam Hamill

But for her green. Hill-track, The. Kathleen Jamie. MoWP; NeBrP

But for His bride. (LL) World, The (1). Henry Vaughan. ChIV-2; FSCP; NAEL-6v1; NAEL-7v1; NoP-5; NOSC; NPeEn; OxAEP-1; OxBEV; PBRV; SacPr; TFi; WaAnP

But for Lust. Ruth Pitter. NPeEn

But for pictures. Robert Frost. Lex Runciman. VisFro

But, for such as our earth is now, it lasted long. (LL) Season of Phantasmal Peace, The. Derek Walcott. EmeKit; GPTC; NAMCP V.2; PoetW; PoPoPo; VCWP

But for their powers, accept my piety [or pietie]. (LL) To William Camden. Ben Jonson. BASC; NAEL-6v1; NAEL-7v1; NOSC; NPeEn

But for these apertures. Witter Bynner. APT-1

But to for make it spring again. (LL) Hock-Cart, or Harvest Home, The. Robert Herrick. BASC; NAEL-6v1; NAEL-7v1; NOSC; OxAEP-1

But for two, even mornings'. Beware. Marina Ivanovna Tsvetayeva. WoPoe, *tr. by* David McDuff

But for your terror. To Death. Oliver St. John Gogarty. OBMV

But frankly, gayly shall we get the gods. (LL) Meditation at Kew. Anna Wickham. MoBrPo; NALW

But from it fly. (LL) John Fletcher and William Shakespeare. NOSC; NoSic *Fr.* Two Noble Kinsmen, The.

But get some color and music out of life? (LL) Investment, The. Robert Frost. APT-1; GoPo

But go, now, and tell Death he must watch you, and not let you walk in your sleep. (LL) Giving Back the Flower. Sarah Morgan Bryan Piatt. APN-2; NAAPv.1

But God is Silent / Psalm 114. Bible, *O.T.* InvLi; UpMys

But God was seen no longer any more. (LL) He said: If in his image I was made. Trumbull Stickney. APN-2; OxBoAm; TCAPo

"But good Sir, look here"—said he. Mihály Fazekas. IQMS *Fr.* Matt the Gooseherd.

But gripped, gripped and is now a cenotaph. (LL) Relic. Ted Hughes. EMP; NAEL-6v2; NAEL-7v2; NoP-4

But hark! the cry is Astur. Thomas Babington Macaulay, 1st Baron Macaulay. OBWP *Fr.* Lays of Ancient Rome.

But he did for them both by his plan of attack. (LL) General, The. Siegfried Sassoon. FaBoWar; InoFa; NAEL-6v2; NAEL-7v2; NAMCP V.1; NoAM; NoP-4; NoP-5; NPeEn; OBWP; OxBEV; PoAgWa

But he didn't catch me. (LL) Little Turtle, The. Vachel Lindsay. BLPJKO; NOxBChV; NTCP; OBSP

But / He said. For Kinna 2. Christine Ama Ata Aidoo. HAWP

But hear. If you stay, and the child be born. Thomas Hardy. MoBrPo *Fr.* Satires of Circumstance in Fifteen Glimpses.

But helpless Pieces of the Game He plays. Omar Khayyám. CABP *Fr.* Rubáiyát of Omar Khayyám [of Naishápúr], The.

But her arm—damp, small. Mary Kinzie. FFC

But her favorite poems take place underwater. Sam Truitt. AmPoNex *Fr.* Anamorphosis Eisenhower.

But her sweet odour did them all excel[l]. (LL)   Edmund Spenser.   NAEL-6v1; OxBSo *Fr.* Amoretti.

But here no cannon thunders to the gale.   William Wordsworth.   CenSon *Fr.* River Duddon [A Series of Sonnets], The.

But here's the piece, made up to sell.   Landscape, The.   George Daniel. NOSC

But high up—my river of spirits.   Going to Sleep in Childhood.   Gennady Aygi.   ItGoST, *tr.* by Peter France

But his actual candle blazed with artifice. (LL)   Quiet Normal Life, A.   Wallace Stevens.   NAAL-5; NoAM

But his parents said look it is fall. (LL)   Fall, The: "There was a man who found two leaves and came indoors holding them out saying to his parents that he was a tree."   Russell Edson.   MotU; OxBoAm

But how alien, alas, at the streets of the city of grief.   Rainer Maria Rilke.   StAl *Fr.* Duino Elegies, The [Stephen Mitchell Translation].

But how am I to tell you.   How Am I To Tell You.   Carlos Bousoño.   RaW, *tr.* by Hardie St. Martin

But how can I tell their story / if I was not there?   Vocabulary.   Ariel Dorfman.   AF, *tr.* by Ariel Dorfman and Edith Grossman

But How It Came from Earth.   Conrad Potter Aiken.   MoAmPo

But how much more unfortunate are those.   Joseph Hilaire Pierre Belloc.   UV

But how thoroughly departmental. (LL)   Departmental.   Robert Frost.   HeIP-4; MoAmPo; NAAL-5; PtR; SoSe-8

But I accept a greeting at a place I've never seen, leaning.   Lyn Hejinian.   PfS *Fr.* Sight.

But I am an / Un-steam-soft-able, un-boil-through-able.   Yellow Bell Coda.   Kuan Han-ch'ing.   ColAnChi, *tr.* by Wayne Schlepp

But I am completely nourished. (LL)   Decade, [A].   Amy Lowell.   MoAmPo; NAAPv.2; NALW; NAMCP V.1; OxBoAm; PasH; PoBW

But I Am Growing Old and Indolent.   Robinson Jeffers.   APT-1; ColAP

But I / am not an isolated god.   Wall of Dreams (2).   Ahmed Taha.   NAfrP, *tr.* by Clarissa C. Burt

But I am not someone of spiteful.   Sappho.   SaLy, *tr.* by Diane Rayor

But I am—other than me—I am the gentle cricket.   Chameleon.   Daria Menicanti.   CItWP, *tr.* by Cinzia Sartini Blum and Lara Trubowitz

But I bruise easy. (LL)   Farm Woman, The: 1942.   Naomi Mitchison.   EdScPo; RSaN

But I can't squeeze more love into their stone. (LL)   Tony Harrison.   NAEL-6v2; NAEL-7v2; NAMCP V.2 *Fr.* School of Eloquence, The.

But I could not both live and utter it. (LL)   My life has been the poem I would have writ.   Henry David Thoreau.   APN-1; NAAPv.1; NCAP; TCAPo

But I don't care where the water goes if it doesn't get into the wine. (LL)   Wine and Water.   G. K. Chesterton.   ChIV-1; MoBrPo

But I forget.—My pilgrim's shrine is won.   Lord Byron.   NAEL-6v2; NAEL-7v2 *Fr.* Childe Harold's Pilgrimage.

But I haven't come to that—and I hope I never shall—and that's the Village Poor House! (LL)   Our Village—by a Villager.   Thomas Hood.   FaBoVe; OBSV

But I only looked at the screen.   Ultra Sound.   Penelope Shuttle.   PoCu

But I remember his hands. (LL)   Fifth Grade Autobiography.   Rita Dove.   ISC; NIL-7; NIP-4

But I shall be gone. (LL)   Sound of Trees, The.   Robert Frost.   APT-1; NoAM

But I shall stay at home. (LL)   Country Boy in Winter, A.   Sarah Orne Jewett.   APN-2; ColAP

But I sing the excellence of heroes.   Korinna [*or* Corinna].   SaLy, *tr.* by Diane Rayor

But I still don't know what the joke is, to tell them. (LL)   Toyland.   Roy Fisher.   HarvBoo; NPeEn

But I was *born* to other things. (LL)   Alfred Tennyson.   NAEL-6v2; NAEL-7v2 *Fr.* In Memoriam A. H. H.

But I was dead, an hour or more.   Escape.   Robert Graves.   MoBrPo

But I was glad I recorded for him / The melancholy. (LL)   Wet Evening in April.   Patrick Kavanagh.   BeAl; OPOU

But I was old if you add the things I suffered. (LL)   Epitaph for Mariana Gryphius, His Brother Paul's Little Daughter.   Andreas Gryphius.   PoAgWa; WoPoe, *tr.* by Christopher Benfey

But I was young and foolish, and now am full of tears. (LL)   Down by the Salley Gardens.   William Butler Yeats.   IrV; NAEL-6v2; NAEL-7v2; NoAM; NPeEn; OBEV; PoPoPo; SoSe-8

But if he came straight for me.   Pernette De Guillet.   EroLit *Fr.* Élegie.

But if I should ask the king?   Answering A Child.   Sarah Morgan Bryan Piatt.   NCAP

But if the cause be not good, the King himself hath a.   William Shakespeare.   RaF *Fr.* King Henry V.

But if they'd give us toys and twice the stuff.   Christmas at the Orphanage.   Bill Knott.   OPRER

But if thou wilt not pittie my complaint.   Richard Barnfield.   CAGL *Fr.* Affectionate Shepherd [*or* Shephearde], The.

But if through genuine tenderness of heart.   John Armstrong.   OBGa *Fr.* Art of Preserving Health, The.

But if we could see and hear, this Vision—were it not He? (LL)   Higher Pantheism, The.   Alfred Tennyson.   CABP; InvLi

But if you break the bloody glass you won't hold up the weather. (LL)   Bagpipe Music.   Louis MacNeice.   BeAl; BrAP; CABP; EMP; HarvBoo; MakPoe; NAEL-6v2; NAEL-7v2; NAMCP V.1; NBLV; NoAM; NoP-4; NoP-5; OBSV; OxBEV; TFi; UV

But I'm driving.   Your Character is Your Destiny.   Erin Belieu.   ExTi

But I'm minded on it againe.   Ye haue heard this yarn afore.   Peter Reading.   EmeKit

But in real life, I begin. But Doug.   Real Life.   Frances Driscoll.   PfS

But in That Sleep of Death What Dreams May Come?   Mary Elizabeth Coleridge.   VWP

But in the dome of mighty Mars the red.   Geoffrey Chaucer.   OBWP *Fr.* Canterbury Tales, The.

But in the end one tires of the high-flown.   About the Phoenix.   James Merrill.   NoAM

But in the last days it shall come to pass.   Bible, *O.T.*   FaBoWar *Fr.* Micah.

But in this country / there is war. (LL)   Lorna Dee Cervantes.   *See* There is war.

But in your place.   Anne Portugal.   SCFWP *Fr.* Bath, The.

But is for others undiminished somewhere. (LL)   Sad Steps.   Philip Larkin.   BrAP; NAEL-6v2; NAEL-7v2; NAMCP V.2; NoAM; NoP-4; NoP-5; WaAnP

But is there an edge.   Inside Long Treks.   Lewis Warsh.   AHA

But Islands of the Blessed, bless you, son.   Answer, An.   Robert Frost.   OBCoV

But it could be worse. (LL)   Sonnet for Minimalists.   Mona Van Duyn.   FFC; WeW-3

But it could not be brought to see what it.   Country Autumns, The.   Clark Coolidge.   AHA

But it is sadder than that, much, much sadder.   Body and the Soul, The.   Vicente Aleixandre.   RaW, *tr.* by Robert Bly

But it was just one of those things. (LL)   Just One of Those Things.   Cole Porter.   APT-1; ReLy

But it was the shadowed street-side she chose.   Child with Pillar Box and Bin Bags.   Kathleen Jamie.   GPPA

But it works every time. (LL)   Margaret Atwood.   NIL-7; NIP-4; PoA 2002; WeW-3 *Fr.* Songs of the Transformed.

But its radiocarbon ticks.   Hardy's "Shelley's Skylark."   Daniel Hall.   YaYoPo

But, John, have you seen the world, said he.   Angle of Vision.   Robert Rendall.   EdScPo

But Jove against the Greeks sent forth his son.   Homer.   FaBoWar *Fr.* Iliad, The.

But just to see a chapel like this room.   But Just to See.   Cyprian Norwid.   WoPoe, *tr.* by Jerzy Peterkiewicz, Burns Singer and Jon Stallworthy

But keep that earlier, wilder image bright. (LL)   To Cole, the Painter, Departing for Europe.   William Cullen Bryant.   ColAP; TCAPo

But kiss him & give him both drink and apparel. (LL)   William Blake.   NBLV; OBSV *Fr.* Songs of Experience.

But know not what's *resisted*. (LL)   Address to the Unco Guid, or the Rigidly Righteous.   Robert Burns.   ChIV-1; OxBEV

But, knowing now that they would have her speak.   Defense of Guenevere, The.   William Morris.   NAEL-6v2; NAEL-7v2

But known of what he died. (LL)   Workbox, The.   Thomas Hardy.   NAEL-6v2; NAEL-7v2

But leave, because I cannot as I should! (LL)   To John Donne ("Donne, the delight of Phoebus, and each Muse.")   Ben Jonson.   NAEL-6v1; NAEL-7v1

But leave the Wise to wrangle, and with me.   Omar Khayyám.   OxBEV *Fr.* Rubáiyát of Omar Khayyám [of Naishápúr], The.

But left the thorn wi' me. (LL)   Robert Burns.   *See* And sae was pu'd or [*or* ere] noon!

But let one of you hear this.   Korinna [*or* Corinna].   SaLy, *tr.* by Diane Rayor

But like crow I collect the shine of anything beautiful I can find. (LL)   Path to the Milky Way Leads Through Los Angeles, The.   Joy Harjo.   NAMCP V.2; StAl

But listen.   Go on, tell me the season is over.   Alan Wearne.   BMAP

But lo! at length the day is lingered out.   Francis Thompson.   OBMV *Fr.* Sister Songs.

But lo! the great Deliverer sails.   On the Landing of William III [*or* A Hymn of Praise for Three Great Salvations].   Isaac Watts.   STuOW

But look a trial down from some far height.   Full Vision.   Henrietta Cordelia Ray.   CBWP-3

But look / but look.   Nelly Sachs.   AF

But look how they blaze in the light. (LL)   Girls.   Lauris Edmond.   ArBi; BeAl

But look in your mirror for the other one.   Antonio Machado Ruiz.   RaBo; WED *Fr.* Moral Proverbs and Folk Songs.

But love survives the venom of the snake. (LL)   In Hospital: Poona (1).   Alun Lewis.   AngWePo; OBWVE; TCAWP

But love whilst that thou mayst [or maist] be loved [or lov'd] again[e]. (LL) Samuel Daniel. NoP-4; NoSic Fr. Sonnets to Delia.

But love whilst that thou mayst [or maist] be loved [or lov'd] again. Samuel Daniel. NoP-4; NoP-5; NoSic Fr. Sonnets to Delia.

But lovers are like umbrellas arnt they? Accoutrement. 'Marnia. LW

But may be ravenously unripped in hell? (LL) Algernon Charles Swinburne. OxBSo; UV Fr. Heptalogia, The.

But Men loved Darkness[e] Rather Than [or Then] Light. Richard Crashaw. ChIV-2

But minds me o' my Jean. (LL) Of A' the Airts [the Wind Can Blaw]. Robert Burns. NoP-4; NoP-5

But Money gives me pleasure all the time. (LL) Fatigue. Joseph Hilaire Pierre Belloc. NBLV; UV

But most avoid Italia's coast. Notice to Tourists. Della Cruscans. STuOW

But most by numbers judge a poet's song. Alexander Pope. NIL-7; NIP-4 Fr. Essay on Criticism, An.

But, Mother, I say, I am dying. (LL) Distance from Loved Ones. James Tate. MotU; OxBoAm

But Mozart did. Aleatory. Mary Zeppa. MiVo

But My Blood. Rose Romano. UnSA

But my brother is bitter, and he does not hear. (LL) Sterling Allen Brown. See All you need know is: you must not be bitter.

But my guests will long remember them. (LL) Autumn Twilight in the Mountains. Wang Wei. NDACCP; WaAnP, tr. by Kenneth Rexroth

But Nancy still with me. (LL) In a Letter to A.R.C. on Her Wishing to Be Called Anna. Matilda Barbara Betham-Edwards. PoBW; WoRP

But nearer than Guardian Angel. "H. D." NAAPv.2; NALW; NAMCP V.1 Fr. Tribute to the Angels.

But neither stops her song. (LL) I Ask My Mother to Sing. Li-Young Lee. IllVoic; InvLad; LoL; OpBo; PoCho; UnSA

But night, the reserved, the reticent, gives more than it takes. (LL) As One Put Drunk into the Packet-Boat. John Ashbery. NAMCP V.2; VCAP

But no diminishment, as in "fancy" and "open fifths" and "environmental sweepstakes." (LL) Sunrise with Sea Monster. Charles North. FTOS; NYP2

But no, it isn't over for them yet. What the Dark Proposes. Charles Martin. PfSP

But no point explaining to those who abstain. (LL) Drinking Alone in the Moonlight. Li Po. ColAnChi; WoPoe, tr. by Elling O. Eide

But nobody ever does. That's what cracks me up. (LL) Slowly I Open My Eyes. Amy Gerstler. MotU; SUP

But nodded off enough. All the Flutterlings Gone. Del Ray Cross. FreRad

But none of these, none of these. "H. D." NAAPv.2; NAMCP V.1 Fr. Tribute to the Angels.

But none shall thus lament for me! (LL) Lament of the Captive, The. Richard Henry Wilde. APN-1; ColAP; TCAPo

But not because we were girls. (LL) Barbie Says Math is Hard. Kyoko Mori. InvLad; ReTh

But Not for Me. Ira Gershwin. ReLy

But not in our alley! (LL) Sally in Our Alley. Henry Carey. OBEV; OxAEP-1

But not on a shell, she starts. Paltry Nude Starts on a Spring Voyage, The. Wallace Stevens. PoA 2002

But nothing happens. (LL) Exposure. Wilfred Owen. NAMCP V.1; NoAM; OBWP; PoWW; TCAWP

But nothing promised that is not performed. (LL) To Juan at the Winter Solstice. Robert Graves. HarvBoo; MoBrPo; NAEL-6v2; NAEL-7v2; NAMCP V.1; NoAM; NoP-4; NoP-5; NPeEn; RaBo; WaAnP

But now a sport more formidable. Samuel Butler. DiBP Fr. Hudibras.

But now had Hesper from the Hero's sight. Joel Barlow. APN-1 Fr. Columbiad, The.

But now hear what meat there needs eat thou must. Alexander Barclay. NoSic Fr. Eclogues.

But now I am home again there is nobody I know. (LL) Fairy Story. Stevie Smith. NOxBChV; OBSP

But now I feel hunger, which declares. John Milton. InvLi Fr. Paradise Regained [or Regain'd].

But now I have a will, yet want a wit. Intellectual Powers of the Soul, The. John Davies. SacPr

But now it's the Yiddish itself I'm forgetting. Shoyn Fergéssin: "I've Forgotten" in Yiddish. Albert Goldbarth. TaR

But now lead on. John Milton. NPeEn Fr. Paradise Lost.

But now Mr. Ferritt. And Mr. Ferritt. Judith Wright. MoBrPo

But now my boys, leave off, and list to me. Christopher Marlowe. FaBoWar Fr. Tamburlaine the Great, Part 2.

But now, no longer deaf to honour's call. Homer. OBVE Fr. Iliad, The.

But now Sarpedon watching his comrades drop and die. Homer. NAWM-7v1 Fr. Iliad, The.

But now that I am used to pain. Pibroch. J. D. McClatchy. OxBoAm

But now the stillness of this touching scene. Albery Allson Whitman. NAAPv.1 Fr. Octoroon, The.

But now they all end in the sky. (LL) Artemis in Echo Park. Eloise Klein Healy. CalPo; GeoHom

But now this man of hell toward me turned. Philip Freneau. NAAL-3 Fr. House of Night, The.

But O, my Muse, what numbers wilt thou find. Joseph Addison. OBWP Fr. Campaign, The.

But of all plagues, the greatest is untold. Juvenal. BASC Fr. Satires.

But of all the plagues, the greatest is untold. Juvenal. OBSV Fr. Satires.

But of course the poem is not an assertion. Do you see? When I wrote. Impossible Indispensability of the Ars Poetica, The. Hayden Carruth. TAPaP

But, of course, they didn't film that. (LL) Cameo Appearance. Charles Simic. NAMCP V.2; NoP-5; OxBoAm

But of the beautiful disrelation of the spiritual. (LL) Dam Neck, Virginia. Richard Eberhart. NAAPv.2; PoWW

But often on the mountain peaks when. Alcman. SaLy, tr. by Diane Rayor

But oh, that we could sleep up there. (LL) Sleeping on the Ceiling. Elizabeth Bishop. APT-2; OBGa

But on she went—on to the cabin sped. Albery Allson Whitman. NAAPv.1 Fr. Octoroon, The.

But on the third day Christ arose. Herman Melville. APN-2 Fr. Clarel: A Poem and Pilgrimage in the Holy Land.

But one apocalyptic lion's whelp (in flesh). There Is No Opera like "Lohengrin." John Wheelwright. OxBoAm

But only able. Josée Lapeyrère. SCFWP Fr. Skirt, The.

But only God can make a tree. (LL) Trees. Joyce Kilmer. APT-1; BRP; ChAP; ITBLP; PoA 2002; TCAPo; UV

But only God can make a tree. Very Short Poem. Raymond Souster. IFF

But Only Not to think. Irina Ratushinskaya. AF

But only not to think about the journey. But Only Not to think. Irina Ratushinskaya. AF

But only three in all God's universe. Elizabeth Barrett Browning. CenSon Fr. Sonnets from the Portuguese.

But oye, my heart will grow grey hairs. Brian Merriman. IrLP Fr. Midnight Court, The.

But peace, I must not quarrel with the will. John Milton. NoP-5 Fr. Samson Agonistes.

But perfectly random and coastal. Dennis Phillips. FTOS Fr. Exile.

But Perhaps God Needs the Longing. Nelly Sachs. WPoS,

But perhaps God needs the longing, wherever else should it dwell. Nelly Sachs. WPoS,

But pinned to the heart of darkness a tattered fire-flag flies. (LL) Stand-To, The. Cecil Day Lewis. NoP-4; OBWP

But proves at night a bed of down. (LL) Upon the Sudden Restraint of the Earl[e] of Somerset, Then Falling from Favor [or Favour]. Sir Henry Wotton. NOSC; NPeEn; OxBEV

But Roaring Bill (who killed him) thought it right. (LL) Pacifist, The. Joseph Hilaire Pierre Belloc. FaBoWar; OBCoV; PoAgWa

But shall not question much. (LL) Twice. Christina Georgina Rossetti. OBEV; VWP

But she got all the rainbow. (LL) Abraham Got All the Stars N the Sand. Ruth Forman. AmPoNex; OxAAAP

But she is not kind. (LL) In Mind. Denise Levertov. NAAL-5; NALW

But shines himself till they are seen no more. (LL) Impromptu: To Lady Winchelsea Occasioned by four Satirical Verses on Women Wits, In The Rape of the Lock. Alexander Pope. NAEL-7v1; NoP-4; NoP-5; WaAnP

But sickness is catching; lovers, permit me entrance. (LL) Urban Gallery. Rachel Wetzsteon. AmPoNex; NeAmPo

But silence, burnt dust on the valves, and whisky. (LL) Private Bottling, A. Don Paterson. EmeKit; NePenScot

But silence, nought can praise her. (LL) Dialogue between two shepherds, Thenot and Piers, in praise of ASTRÆA. Mary Sidney Herbert, Countess of Pembroke. EMWP; NAEL-6v1

But So as by Fire. George Oppen. APT-2 Fr. Some San Francisco Poems.

But some do say, We marvel much, that you can sit Silent. Something about Silence. Elizabeth Hincks. EMWP

But something about her was perfect. (LL) Sleeping with Artemis. Josh Bell. LegDan; PoDa

But something went wrong with the plan: I am still on the train. (LL) Observation Car. Alec Derwent Hope. NAMCP V.1; NoAM

But speech. Friedrich Hölderlin. WoPoe Fr. Hymns and Fragments.

But still be a Woman to you. (LL) Song: "When thy beauty appears." Thomas Parnell. IrLP; OBEV; OxAEP-1

But still regard the destitute. (LL) Lord, Hear My Prayer. John Clare. BBASP; ChIV-1

But stories somehow lengthen when begun. (LL) Beppo; a Venetian Story. Lord Byron. OBNV; OBSV

But suh, you've made a mistake. Oh, yes suh! I can't be.   Sidney, Looking for her Mother.   Dolores Kendrick.   ISC

But sun me in the Capitol. (LL)   Mithridates.   Ralph Waldo Emerson.   APN-1; NCAP

But sweet sister death has gone debauched today and stalks.   David Jones.   NPeEn; OBWP; OxAEP-2 Fr. In Parenthesis.

But tarries yet the Cause for which He died. (LL)   Christmas Ghost-Story, A.   Thomas Hardy.   ChrPo; OBWP

But tell me, child, your choice; what shall I buy You?   Handsome Heart, The.   Gerard Manley Hopkins.   FaBoVe

But tell me if the man whom I see here.   Dante Alighieri.   NAWM-7v1 Fr. Divine Comedy, The (Mandelbaum Translation).

But That Is Another Story.   Donald Justice.   NoP-4; OxBoAm

But that was nothing to what things came out.   Welsh Incident.   Robert Graves.   OBSP; OxBEV; WaAnP

But that which most I wonder at, which most.   Innocence.   Thomas Traherne.   BASC; CABP; ChIV-2; NOSC

But that's how it is in this world. One minute battling traffic. Next, head.   Such a Way to Go.   Martha Silano.   AmPoNex

But the choir-boy is happy and gay. (LL)   Low Church.   Stanley J. Sharpless.   NBLV; OBCoV

But the clover is honey and sun and the smell of sleep. (LL)   Nebuchadnezzar.   Elinor Wylie.   ChIV-1; MoAmPo

But the eagle will never fly. (LL)   America.   Henry Dumas.   ChAP; OxAAAP

But the fleet hours pass pitilessly fleeter.   Alfred Austin.   VerBaPo Fr. Human Tragedy, The.

But the future is different.   Future, The.   Angel González.   VCWP, tr. by Steven Ford Brown and Revuelta Gutierrez

But the glory of the Lord is all in all. (LL)   Dominus Illuminatio Mea.   Richard Doddridge Blackmore.   OBEV; SacPr

But the particulars, the cats. Because it is obvious that the streetcar banks into the turn.   Proportions of the Street, The.   Ágnes Nemes Nagy.   MotU, tr. by Bruce Berlind

But the sun point-blank (the very air massacred by the blink of an eye) all faces.   Dominique Grandmont.   OnScMo Fr. Down Here.

But the way you work.   Much of Your Poetry Is Beautiful.   Brenda Walcott.   BRtP

But the windy beating of the sea. (LL)   Shore Grass.   Amy Lowell.   APT-1; NAMCP V.1

But the Wine-press of Los is eastward of Golgonooza, before the Seat.   William Blake.   NOBRP Fr. Milton.

But the world shall end when I forget. (LL)   Itylus.   Algernon Charles Swinburne.   NPeEn; UV

But the years are gone. There are no more years. (LL)   Psalm and Lament.   Donald Justice.   CAP-8; GPTC

But their dreams are all inscrutable by eight or nine. (LL)   Some Dreams They Forgot.   Elizabeth Bishop.   ItP; NoAM

But then an even greater sense of the inexpressible.   Mario Luzi.   ItPo Fr. In the Dark Body of Metamorphosis.

But then, flaking off bit by bit, it dissolves--this.   Requiem in C.   Biagio Cepollaro.   ItPo, tr. by Gayle Ridinger

But then, in the imaginary trajectory of a white automobile.   Four.   Ofelia Perez Sepúlveda.   SPV, tr. by Jen Hofer

But there are.   John Keats.   NPeEn Fr. Endymion: A Poetic Romance.

But there is no joy in Mudville—Mighty Casey has struck out. (LL)   Casey at the Bat.   Ernest Lawrence Thayer.   ChAP; ITBLP

But there is no road through the woods. (LL)   Way Through The Woods, The.   Rudyard Kipling.   BrAP; ChAP; HarvBoo; NAMCP V.1; NoAM; NOxBChV; OBEV; OxAEP-2; WHSW; WoPoe

But there was the larger pattern.   Enough to Say.   Lisa Lubasch.   IIR

But there will be life.   Death to the Gold Mine!   Lindiwe Mabuza.   HAWP

But there—something rests on your hand and even.   Sapphics for Patience.   Anne Finch.   FFC

But they come by tens. (LL)   Old Lem.   Sterling Allen Brown.   APT-2; NAMCP V.1

But they have been dreamed too, in quiet rooms.   Other Places, The.   Charles E. Butler.   YaYoPo

But they knew they were on duty, replacing.   Pope's Carnations Knew Him.   Thom Gunn.   OBGa

But they're salesmen. (LL)   Moroccans with the carpets, The.   Patrizia Cavalli.   NeIt; VCWP, tr. by Kenneth Koch

But this is our desire, and of its worth.   Gyroscope, The.   Muriel Rukeyser.   YaYoPo

But this one's flesh. He isn't coming back. (LL)   Dead Christ.   Andrew Hudgins.   RA; UpMys

But this security in Jove the great sea-rector spied.   Homer.   NOSC Fr. Iliad, The.

But though full noble is my theme.   Edward Young.   STuOW Fr. Resignation.

But till that morning, ain't no one gonna harm you.   Susan Glickman.   BeAl

But times were stormy on the old plantation.   Albery Allson Whitman.   NAAPv.1 Fr. Octoroon, The.

But 'tis to love, as I love you. (LL)   Friendship Between Ephelia and Ardelia.   Anne Finch, Countess of Winchilsea.   NALW; NoP-4; NoP-5; PoBW

But to die their creature and be thankful. (LL)   Last of the Fire Kings, The.   Derek Mahon.   BeAl; NAMCP V.2; PNI

But to drink the entire sea. (LL)   Kenneth Rexroth.   NAMCP V.1; PoCho Fr. Love Poems of Marichiko, The.

But, to leave fooling, I assure ye.   Charles Cotton.   OBCoV Fr. Burlesque upon the Great Frost.

But to live in the tragic world forever. (LL)   Story About Chicken Soup, A.   Louis Simpson.   PoWW; UnSA

But to our story let us now return.   Albery Allson Whitman.   NAAPv.1 Fr. Octoroon, The.

But to our tale: the Donna Inez sent.   Lord Byron.   NAEL-6v2; NAEL-7v2 Fr. Don Juan.

But to the bad children, Christmas does not come. (LL)   Curse on Herod, A.   Amy Witting.   ChIV-2; NOBAu

But turning toward Ololon in terrible majesty Milton.   William Blake.   OxAEP-2 Fr. Milton.

But 'twas a famous victory. (LL)   Battle of Blenheim, The.   Robert Southey.   BRP; CABP; FaBoWar; NPBRoP; OBWP; TFi; WaAnP

But u are tired mes chers sweet dreams tomorrow night. (LL)   James Merrill.   NoP-4; NoP-5 Fr. Book of Ephraim, The.

But war his overturning trumpet blew.   Frederick Goddard Tuckerman.   APN-2 Fr. Sonnets.

But was I the first martyr, who.   Stephen to Lazarus.   Clive Staples Lewis.   ChIV-2; SacPr

But we have none! but we have none! (LL)   George Darley.   NAEL-6v2; NPeEn Fr. Syren Songs.

But we have to see behind all them, there is something.   They Receive Instructions Against Chile.   Pablo Neruda.   AF

But we left him alone with his glory. (LL)   Burial of Sir John Moore, The.   Charles Wolfe.   FaBoWar; GoPo; IrV; NOBRP; OBEV; OBWP; OxAEP-2; OxBEV; TFi; TreFP; UV

But we never give Pain or complain. (LL)   Breyten Prays for Himself.   Breyten Breytenbach.   PoetW; VCWP, tr. by Denis Hirson

But weep to have that which it fears to lose. (LL)   William Shakespeare.   AEP; HeIP-4; NoSic; OxAEP-1; TreFP Fr. Sonnets.

But were always a rose. (LL)   Rose Family, The.   Robert Frost.   BLPJKO; NIL-7

But westward, look, the land is bright. (LL)   Say Not the Struggle Nought Availeth.   Arthur Hugh Clough.   BrAP; ITBLP; NAEL-6v2; NAEL-7v2; NoP-4; NoP-5; OBEV; OxBEV; SacPr; TFi

But what an idea she'd gotten into her head.   Silvana Colonna.   ItPo, tr. by Gayle Ridinger

But what does it mean? What are we going to do? (LL)   It's No Use Raising a Shout.   W. H. Auden.   OBMV; OxBoAm

But what flowers is not his face.   My Love is Like a Lily.   Kim Ly Bui-Burton.   PasH

But what is more thought than a dark over the sun?   What is Thought but Won't Hold Still.   Clark Coolidge.   FTOS

But what is strength without a double share.   John Milton.   ChIV-1 Fr. Samson Agonistes.

But what lovers we were, what lovers.   Wreck, The.   Don Paterson.   PoDa

But, what of that? (LL)   I reason, Earth is short.   Emily Dickinson.   APN-2; BeAl; NCAP; TCAPo

But what sad use the world has made.   Sadakichi.   NAAPv.1 Fr. My Rubaiyat.

But what underneath him lies. (LL)   Fulke, 1st Baron Brooke Greville.   CABP; NOSC; NoSic Fr. Caelica.

But what we feel is the wind in our faces. (LL)   Walk, A.   Rainer Maria Rilke.   RaBo; WED, tr. by Robert Bly

But whaur's the Minister? (LL)   Last Lauch.   Douglas Young.   EdScPo; NBLV

But when at end.   M. S. 1544.   Jacqueline Risset.   YaTCFP, tr. by Jennifer Moxley

But when I have closed my eyes.   But When I Have.   Claude De Burine.   YaTCFP, tr. by Martin Sorrell

But when one stops to think back a moment.   Berysh Vaynshteyn.   Prolet Fr. America.

But when the Golden-thron'd Aurora made.   Unknown.   OBVE Fr. Homeric Hymns.

But when the misbegotten child had grown.   Ovid.   NAWM-7v1 Fr. Metamorphoses.

But when to mischief mortals bend their will.   Alexander Pope.   OxAEP-1 Fr. Rape of the Lock, The: An Heroi-Comical Poem in Five Cantos.

But when you are sad, think, Heaven could give no more. (LL)   At Parting.   Anne Ridler.   FaBoWar; LW

But where they may return with hono[u]r's grace.   Mary Sidney Wroth, Countess of Montgomery.   BASC; NoP-5

But wherefore did he take away the crown? William Shakespeare. OxAEP-1 *Fr.* King Henry IV, Pt. II.

But where's the bloody horse? (LL) On Some South African Novelists. Roy Campbell. MoBrPo; OBCoV; OxAEP-2; OxBEV

But where's the man who counsel can bestow. Alexander Pope. OxAEP-1 *Fr.* Essay on Criticism, An.

But which way is redemption? (LL) Downtown Boom. Lorenzo Thomas. RD; TiP2

But who advances next, with cheerful grace. Ambrose Philips. STuOW *Fr.* To the Right Honourable Charles Lord Halifax [one of the Lords Justices appointed by his Majesty].

But who killed the Jews? (LL) Riddle: "From Belsen a crate of gold teeth." William Heyen. HP; SoSe-8

But whose initial? Left here, illuminated. Annunciation in an Initial R. Angie Estes. ExTi

But why did he do it, Grandpa? I said. Robert Penn Warren. AmWaPo; CBCWP *Fr.* Day Dr. Knox Did It, The.

'But why do you go?' said the lady, while both sat under the yew. Elizabeth Barrett Browning. *See* "But why do you go?" said the lady, while both sat[e] under the yew.

"But why do you go?" said the lady, while both sat[e] under the yew. Lord Walter's Wife. Elizabeth Barrett Browning. NPeEn

('But why do you go?' said the lady, while both sat under the yew.) VWP

But winter and rough weather. (LL) William Shakespeare. NoSic; OBEV *Fr.* As You Like It.

But with herself she kindly did confer. Ovid. DiBP *Fr.* Metamorphoses.

But with long use her tears are dry. (LL) Alfred Tennyson. NAEL-6v2; NAEL-7v2; NAWM-7v2 *Fr.* In Memoriam A. H. H.

But with regard to me, I'll satisfy. Dante Alighieri. NAWM-7v1 *Fr.* Divine Comedy, The (Mandelbaum Translation).

But without need of them, being at home. (LL) Emigrants. Jane Griffiths. NeBl; StAl

But Woe is mee! who have so quick a Sent. Edward Taylor. TCAPo *Fr.* Preparatory Meditations Before My Approach to the Lord's Supper.

But words were lost, now aimed at Lena's ear. Albery Allson Whitman. NAAPv.1 *Fr.* Octoroon, The.

But you are not all the avenger. Gunnar Ekelof. PFTM-2 *Fr.* Mölna Elegy.

But you are so thin. Error of the Hydrographers, An. Ben Doyle. IIR

But you believe nothing, with the evidence lost. (LL) Blow, West Wind. Robert Penn Warren. ColAP; WaAnP

But you know what's. Epilogue(At the Proper Distance). Mariella Bettarini. CItWP, *tr.* by Cinzia Sartini Blum and Lara Trubowitz

But you like none, none you, for constant heart. (LL) William Shakespeare. NoSic; OBEV; OxAEP-1; OxBEV *Fr.* Sonnets.

But you were always ambitious. (LL) They Eat Out. Margaret Atwood. NAMCP V.2; NoAM

But you will die to-day. (LL) Her Strong Enchantments Failing. A. E. Housman. OxBEV; WoPoe

But you will last very long. (LL) Scented Herbage of My Breast. Walt Whitman. APN-1; NAAL-3; OxBoAm

But young men think it is, and we were young. (LL) Epitaph: "Here dead lie we because we did not choose." A. E. Housman. HarvBoo; OxBEV; Spl

But your distrust of the journey, of all that you hear, of arrival. (LL) Dissidence. Anthony Walton. NAPBL; RD

But your face I could never see. (LL) Knight and Shepherd's Daughter, The. *Unknown.* NoP-4; NoP-5

But your imagining was wrong. Silvana Colonna. ItPo, *tr.* by Gayle Ridinger

Butane, Kerosene, Gasoline. Ann Townsend. NAPBL

Butch once remarked to me how sinister it was. That Pull from the Left. Louise Erdrich. NoAM

"Butch" Weldy. Edgar Lee Masters. APT-1 *Fr.* Spoon River Anthology.

Butcher debones the violets, The. Curdled Skulls. Bernard Bador. ConPit, *tr.* by Clayton Eshleman

Butcher had prepared the leg of the lamb, The. Robert Duncan. APSN *Fr.* Passages.

Butcher of Abbeville, The. *Unknown.* NAWM-7v1, *tr.* by Ned Dubin

Butcher Shop. Carla Faesler Bremer. SPV, *tr.* by Jen Hofer

Butcher Shop. Charles Simic. AF

Butcher, the baker, the grocer, the clerk, The. There's No Business Like Show Business. Irving Berlin. ReLy

Butchering must be wholesale and the smell, The. Poem to Gentiles. Maxwell Bodenheim. TaR

Butcher's Meat by Loti. Jude Stéfan. YaTCFP, *tr.* by Marilyn Hacker

Butchers, The. Michael Longley. ModIr; NPeEn *Fr.* Odyssey.

Butcher's Wife, The. Louise Erdrich. HATNAP; NoP-4; NoP-5

Butchertown. William Loran Smith. LaCa

Butchery of the innocent, The. Sunday Papers. Charles Simic. WaAnP

Butler and the Gentleman, The. Anna Wickham. RSaN

Butt Cast in the Sea, A. Cemal Süreya. NaPG, *tr.* by Talat Sait Halman

Butt stay my thoughts, make end, geve fortune way. Sir Walter Ralegh. NPeEn *Fr.* Ocean's Love to Cynthia, The.

Butter Charm. *Unknown.* FaBoVe

Butter liver (as from Eve) fill our men. (LL) Hour Farther. Robert Desnos. MFP; YaTCFP, *tr.* by Martin Sorrell

Butter moon is white, The. To Selah. George Elliott Clarke. OpeFie

Butterflies. Patricia Grace. IPoFL

Butterflies. Angelina Weld Grimké. GT

Butterflies. Inagaki Chikai and Nomura Akitari. CAoMJL1, *tr.* by Leith Morton

Butterflies a-wing. Sadakichi. NAAPv.1 *Fr.* Haikai.

Butterflies butterflies. Stop on the rape-flower leaves! Butterflies. Inagaki Chikai and Nomura Akitari. CAoMJL1, *tr.* by Leith Morton

Butterflies Love Flowers. Li Ch'ing-chao. ErotSp, *tr.* by Sam Hamill (To the Tune: Butterflies Love Flowers.) CrYelRi

Butterflies of Anxiety. Najaat Al-Udwany. PoArWo, *tr.* by Moulouk Berry and Ali Farghaly

Butterflies under Persimmon. Mark Jarman. MAAN

Butterflies, white butterflies, in the sunshine. Butterflies. Angelina Weld Grimké. GT

Butterfly. Buson. EH, *tr.* by Robert Hass

Butterfly. Chang Pi. CCL1, *tr.* by John A. Scott

Butterfly. D. H. Lawrence. BLT; NAMCP V.1; NoAM

Butterfly. Nelly Sachs. PoCho, *tr.* by Matthew Mead and Ruth Mead

Butterfly, The. Margaret Avison. BrAP

Butterfly, The. Pavel Friedmann. HP, *tr.* by Dennis Silk

Butterfly, The. Pavel Friedmann. INSAB

Butterfly, The. John Fuller. Spl

Butterfly, The. Hô Sugyông. EcSo, *tr.* by Youngju Ryu

Butterfly attending the embroidered flowers, A. (LL) Linen Industry, The. Michael Longley. IrLP; ModIr; NoP-4; NoP-5; PBCIP; PNI; StAl

Butterfly Bones; or, Sonnet against Sonnets. Margaret Avison. BrAP

Butterfly, butterfly, butterfly, butterfly. Butterfly Song. *Unknown.* OBVE; TLR, *tr.* by Frances Densmore

Butterfly came to die, A. Etel Adnan. PoArWo *Fr.* Spring Flowers Own, The.

Butterfly Effect, The. Harry Humes. BAP-97

Butterfly frozen in stone, A. Shakir Li'aibi. IrPoTo, *tr.* by Ralph Saverese and Saadi A. Simawe

Butterfly Garden, The. Alfred Noyes. OBGa

Butterfly is the eye, The. Camouflage. Marianne Boruch. BAP-97

Butterfly Net, The. John Bensko. YaYoPo

Butterfly on Rock. Irving Layton. BrAP; NoAM

Butterfly Song. *Unknown.* OBVE; TLR, *tr.* by Frances Densmore

Butterfly, the wind blows sea-ward, strong beyond the garden wall! Butterfly. D. H. Lawrence. BLT; NAMCP V.1; NoAM

Butterfly / Time of late spring. Butterfly. Chang Pi. CCL1, *tr.* by John A. Scott

Butterfly to His Love, The. Ann Radcliffe. RWP *Fr.* Mysteries of Udolpho, The.

Butterfly upon the Sky, The. Emily Dickinson. NOxBChV

Butterflying. Tatiana De la Tierra. BeDoSh

Butterfly's Ball [and the Grasshopper's Feast], The. William Caldwell Roscoe. NOBRP; OxBEV

Butterfly's Dream, The. Hannah Flagg Gould. SWaP

Buttocks shivered against you. (LL) Kenneth Rexroth. APSN; NAMCP V.1 *Fr.* Love Poems of Marichiko, The.

Button, A. Sensation Type and His Friends, The. Michael Davidson. FTOS

Button Up Your Overcoat. Lew Brown, B. G. DeSylva and Ray Henderson. ReLy

Button-grass flats, pale through the drizzle: my eyes. High Country. Tim Thorne. BMAP

Buttoning my sweater over the huge splotch. First Date in Twenty-Five Years. Ellen Doré Watson. NevBe

Buttons. Tessa Rose Chester. MFPA

Buttons. Carl Sandburg. AmWaPo

Buttons and Bows. Ray Evans and Jay Livingston. ReLy

Buwayb. River and Death, The. Badr Shakir al-Sayyab. PFTM-2, *tr.* by Pierre Joris

Buxom young fellow from London came down, A. Nine Times a Night. *Unknown.* EroLit

Buy a book in brown paper. Blurb for *Anna Livia Plurabelle*, A. James Joyce. OBCoV

Buy it! But it! Kagawa Kageki. EMJL, *tr.* by Haruo Shirane

Buy, lads, or else your lasses cry: Come Buy. (LL) William Shakespeare. NoSic; NPeEn *Fr.* Winter's Tale, The.

Buy our little magazine. Do It Yourself. Joan Aiken. NOxBChV

Buying. Jean Follain. BLT, *tr.* by Heather McHugh

Buying a Cycle. Walter Parke. ArBi

Buying Fish. Susan Wicks. MFPA

Buying Flowers. Po Chü-i. TAL

Buying leeks. Buson. EH, *tr. by* Robert Hass

Buzz frantic. Buzz in the Window. Ted Hughes. NAMCP V.2; NoAM

Buzz in the Window. Ted Hughes. NAMCP V.2; NoAM

Buzz Plane, The. Robert Francis. OtW

Buzz subsides. I have come on stage, The. Boris Leonidovich Pasternak. AF

Buzz you into unisex twilight. Amazon Club. Kenward Elmslie. PmAP

Buzzard has nothing to fault himself with, The. In Praise of Self-Deprecation. Wisława Szymborska. BLT

Buzzards of my boyhood days are back again, The. Pembrokeshire Buzzards. Tony Curtis. TCAWP

Buzzards over Pondy Woods, The. Pondy Woods. Robert Penn Warren. MoAmPo

Buzz-saw snarled and rattled in the yard, The. Out, Out—. Robert Frost. AmFaPo; APT-1; ColAP; HarvBoo; HeIP-4; InoFa; ItP; NAAL-5; NAMCP V.1; OxBoAm; SoSe-8; TCAPo; TRP; WaAnP

By a bank as I lay. Dawn. *Unknown.* NoSic

By a bold people's stubborn arms oppressed. Virgil. BASC *Fr.* Aeneid [*or* Eneados *or* Aeneis], The.

By a breathless cay. Arere, Eiroworowin and Eomakan. *Unknown, tr. by* Ross Arthur, Solange Petit-Skinner and Steve Trussell

By a departing light. Emily Dickinson. APN-2

By a freak of the lustful that spreads like a disease. Old Home, The. Amanda Ros. VerBaPo

By a great, swift water. Aleksander Wat. AF; WoPoe *Fr.* Persian Parables.

By a I. Clark Coolidge. WhBo

By a lake below the mountain. Lady of Trees, The. Mary Elizabeth Coleridge. VWP

By a mad miracle I go intact. Street Song. Sylvia Plath. MiVo

By a peninsula the painter sat. Conduct. Samuel Greenberg. OxBoAm

By a peninsula the wanderer sat and sketched. Emblems of Conduct. Hart Crane. OxBoAm

By a route obscure and lonely. Dream-Land [*or* Dreamland]. Edgar Allan Poe. APN-1; BrAP; NAAL-3

By a Swimming Pool Outside Siracusa. Billy Collins. CAP-8

By a Waterfall. David Wagoner. NAMCP V.2

By a way wandering as I went. Thank God for All. John Lydgate. SacPr

By a Ways. Marc Matthews. WaCA

By a ways through mento prayers. By a Ways. Marc Matthews. WaCA

By absorption I mean engrossing, engulfing. Charles Bernstein. PFTM-2 *Fr.* Artifice of Absorption.

By Accident. Jane O. Wayne. InvLad

By Accident, Blinked. Lionel Fogarty. VaPo

By accident, I gaze at. View from the Roof, Waverly Place. Cornelius Eady. InvLad

By admonitions taught. (LL) Answer, The [*To Pope's* Impromptu]. Anne Finch, Countess of Winchilsea. NAEL-7v1; NALW; NoP-4; NoP-5; WaAnP

By All Lights: 1959. B. H. Boston. GeoHom

By all love's soft, yet mighty powers. Song. John Wilmot, 2d Earl of Rochester. BASC

By all means sing of love, but if you do. Truest Poetry Is the Most Feigning, The [*or,* Ars Poetica for Hard Times]. W. H. Auden. WaAnP

By an unfaded stupa. Kakei. EMJL *Fr.* Mad Verse.

By an Unknown Poet from Eastern Europe, 1955. György Petri. VCWP, *tr. by* Geroge Gömöri and Clive Wilmer

By and by. Epitaph on a Waiter. David McCord. APT-2; NBLV; NIP-4; OBCoV

By archy / the roach that scurries. Don Marquis. AmWit *Fr.* Archys Life of Mehitabel.

By art a poet is not made. For a Poet. George Wither. ChIV-2

By becoming a Cabinet Minister. (LL) On the Birth of His Son. Su Tung-p'o. OBVE; WoPoe, *tr. by* Arthur Waley

By Bicycle. Matthea Harvey. ArBi

By Blue Ontario's Shore. Walt Whitman. APN-1 Poet, The. MoAmPo

By Canada I have always been fascinated. Canada. Matthew Zapruder. LegDan

By candlelight, I read your poems. Reading Yuan Chen on a Boat. Po Chü-i. CrYelRi, *tr. by* Sam Hamill

By Chance. Sŏng Hon. CATKP, *tr. by* Chi-gyu Kim [*or* Kim Chonggil]

By chance I heard about the marriage contract. Finit. Máire Mhac an tSaoi. IrLP, *tr. by* the author

By chance I was alone in my bed the morning. Three Ways of Recovering a Body. Helen Dunmore. MoWP; StAl

By channels of coolness the echoes are calling. Bell-Birds. Henry Clarence Kendall. NOBAu

By chapel bare, with walls sea-beat. Haglets, The. Herman Melville. APN-2

By constantly greater beings. (LL) Man Watching, The. Rainer Maria Rilke. RaBo; WED, *tr. by* Robert Bly

By curvèd bank. *Unknown.* NDACCP, *tr. by* Ezra Pound

By custom doomed to folly, sloth and ease. Epistle to Mr. Pope Occasioned by His Characters of Women, An. Anne, Viscountess Irwin Ingram. NAEL-7v1

By dark severance the apparition head. Painted Head. John Crowe Ransom. APT-1; FuPo; NAMCP V.1; NoAM

By day his world extends, far, knotted, hot. Boy. Mary Kinzie. FFC

By day she spreads her broomstick. Street Flower in Big D. Frances E. Neidhardt. TiP2

By day she woo[e]s me, soft, exceeding fair. World, The. Christina Georgina Rossetti. NALW; PEW; ViWPN

By day the bat is cousin to the mouse. Bat, The. Theodore Roethke. APT-2; ChAP

By day the skyscraper looms in the smoke and sun and has a soul. Skyscraper. Carl Sandburg. HHAm

By Day, the Soul o'erborn by Life's Career. Edward Young. *Fr.* Night Thoughts.

By day these men ask nothing, and obey. Infantry. Alun Lewis. PoWW

By degree the lights go down. In the Theatre. Paulette Roeske. Vesp

By Derwent's rapid stream as oft I strayed. By Derwent's Rapid Stream. Anna Seward. CenSon; NPBRoP

By destiny compell'd, and in despair. Virgil. FaBoWar *Fr.* Aeneid (Dryden translation).

By divination came the Dorians. In Arcadia. Lawrence Durrell. MoBrPo

By dream[e]s, each one into a several [*or* sev'rall] world. (LL) Dream[e]s. Robert Herrick. NAEL-6v1; NAEL-7v1; OPOU; Spl

By duty bound, and not by custom led. To the Memory of My Dear and Ever Honored Father Thomas Dudley Esq. Who Deceased July 31, 1653, and of His Age 77. Anne Bradstreet. NAAL-3

By easy slope to west as if it had. Cheyenne Mountain. Helen Hunt Jackson. APN-2; NAAPv.1

By far the greater half have I seen through. Half-and-Half Song, The. Li Mi-an. ColAnChi, *tr. by* Lin Yutang

By fate, not option, frugal Nature gave. Xenophanes. Ralph Waldo Emerson. APN-1

By feathers green, across Casbeen. Phoenix, The. Arthur Christopher Benson. OBEV

By fifty, you know who you are and, more. Fifty-Fifty. Al Young. SpirFl

By Fire or Flood. David Lindley. NLP

By first light the pines struck down into the meadow. Landslide. John Engels. PfSP

By flowering pear. Buson. SoOfWa, *tr. by* Sam Hamill

By Forced Marches. Michael Hofmann. HarvBoo

By Forty-Sixth. Fernando D'Almeida. NAfrP, *tr. by* Faustine Boateng Gyima

By God. Anne Carson. BodElec; OxBoAm; WoBe *Fr.* Truth About God, The.

By God penis, you must be guarded. Penis, The. Dafydd ap Gwilym. EroLit; WoPoe, *tr. by* Dafydd Johnston

By good luck I was granted a meeting with you. Epithalamium. *Unknown.* CCL1, *tr. by* John Frodsham

By Halves. Bill Berkson. NYP2

By hand, all by her graceful brown hand. (LL) When a Beautiful Woman Gets on the Jutiapa Bus. Belle Waring. EmeKit; PBCAP

By Hatred out of Envy by Despair. (LL) Epigram: "I had gone broke, and got set to come back." James Vincent Cunningham. MoAmPo; VCAP

By Heart. John Hollander. NAMCP V.2

By Heart. Ruth Sharman. Prnts

By Her Aunt's Grave. Thomas Hardy. MoBrPo *Fr.* Satires of Circumstance in Fifteen Glimpses.

By his commandment hee maketh the snow to fall apace. Bible, Apocrypha. OBVE *Fr.* Ecclesiasticus.

By his left shoulder, as he sat up again. Lazarus. Ágnes Nemes Nagy. IQMS, *tr. by* Ila Egon

By holding my mirror out of the window I see. Motho Ke Motho Ka Batho Babang (A Person Is a Person Because of Other People). Jeremy Cronin. AF

By homely Anguish strung. (LL) I like a look of Agony. Emily Dickinson. APN-2; BrAP; HeIP-4; NAAL-3; NAAL-5; NoP-4; NoP-5; PoPoPo; TCAPo

By its nobship sailing upside down. Mollusc. Les A. Murray. NAMCP V.2; UpMys

By its own nature. Magnificent Peak. Muso Soseki. EaWin, *tr. by* W. S. Merwin

By its shape, like thrushes in clear evenings. (LL) Bride, The. D. H. Lawrence. InoFa; NAMCP V.1; NoAM

By June our brook's run out of song and speed. Hyla Brook. Robert Frost. APT-1; CtM; NAMCP V.1; TCAPo

By landscape reminded once of his mother's figure. Adolescence. W. H. Auden. OxBEV

By light of lit memoirs. Poem In Progress. Ken Harris. AnSo

By looking too long on your perfect face. Pierre de Ronsard. EroLit *Fr.* Sonnets to Helen.

By love. (LL) Various multitudes contained by the loves of my love, The. Anselm Berrigan. HeMarv; IIR

By Monday morning it seems certain. Missing. Tracey Herd. MFPA

By moonlight. Buson. EH, *tr. by* Robert Hass

By moonlight I sit all alone. Yi Sunsin. CATKP, *tr. by* Richard Rutt

By mourning beauty crowned[!]. (LL) Ode: "Sleep sweetly in your humble graves." Henry Timrod. CBCWP; ColAP; MakPoe; NAAPv.1

By my cold, clean, whispering spring. (LL) I, Hermes, have been set up. Anyte. OBVE; WoPoe, *tr. by* Kenneth Rexroth

By my faith, but I think ye're all makers of bulls. Irishman's Epistle to the Officers and Troops at Boston, The. *Unknown.* NAAPv.1

By my father. (LL) Self-Portrait. A. K. Ramanujan. NAMCP V.2; NoP-4; NoP-5; PML; PoetW

By my further dying. (LL) Wind Suffers [of Blowing], The. Laura Riding Jackson. NAAPv.2; NoP-4; NoP-5; NPeEn

By My Skin. Leontia Flynn. NIrP

By natural instinct they change their Lord. (LL) John Dryden. ChIV-1; OBSV *Fr.* Absalom and Achitophel.

By nature fierce, at length subdued and mild. Samuel Jackson Pratt. DiBP *Fr.* Lower World, The.

By naughty boys. (LL) Pigtail. Tadeusz Rózewicz. BeAl; HP; PoSu, *tr. by* Adam Czerniawski

By Night. Philip Jerome Cleveland. SacPr

By Night. Robert Francis. APT-2

By night, ghosts roam Aunt Ermyn's. Ooh My Soul. Charles Harper Webb. NevBe

By night I saw the *Hunter's moon.* Indian Gone!, The. Josiah D. Canning. APN-1

By night they haunted a thicket of April mist. Spectral Lovers. John Crowe Ransom. APT-1; HeIP-4

By night we lingered [*or* linger'd] on the lawn. Alfred Tennyson. NAEL-6v2; NAEL-7v2; NAWM-7v2; NoP-5; WaAnP *Fr.* In Memoriam A. H. H.

By night within my bed, I roamed here and there. Michael Drayton. ChIV-1 *Fr.* Most Excellent Song Which Was Solomon's, The.

By nightfall kids had come across them: every sidewalk on the block was scribbled with obscenities and hearts. (LL) Tar. C. K. Williams. AtGh; VCAP

By none but me can the tale be told. White Ship, The. Dante Gabriel Rossetti. OBNV

By noon, the bestial roar of surplus-driven labor. Silence, 2. Stefan Brecht. CLPP

By noon the heat became unbearable. Tea. Ch'u Ch'uang I. CCL1; NDACCP, *tr. by* Kenneth Rexroth

By noon we'll be deep into it. Conjugal Visits. Al Young. CalPo

By now I know most of the faces. Search Party. W. S. Merwin. PoA 2002

By now I'm dead. Make what you will of that. After the Last Words. Scott Cairns. UpMys

By now it's like returning to a foreign town, especially. In Port Talbot. John Davies. TCAWP

By now, the satchel's leather has reclaimed its living redolence. Steerage. Albert Goldbarth. TaR

By now when you say I *stop somewhere waiting for you.* Whoever You Are. W. S. Merwin. NoP-5

By numbers here from shame or censure free. Samuel Johnson. NPeEn; OBSV; OxAEP-1 *Fr.* London: A Poem in Imitation of the Third Satire of Juvenal.

By ones, by twos. (LL) Good world, A. Issa. EH; ZenPo, *tr. by* Takashi Ikemoto and Lucien Stryk

By our first strange and fatal[!] interview. John Donne. CABP; FSCP; NAEL-6v1; NAEL-7v1; NoSic; NPeEn; OxAEP-1 *Fr.* Elegies.

By Perfection fooled too long. Perfection. Oliver St. John Gogarty. IrLP

By Proxy. Amos Russel Wells. ArBi

By proxy his bomb exploded, his valour shone. (LL) From the Irish. James Simmons. ModIr; PBCIP; PNI

By reason good, good reason her to love. (LL) Sir Philip Sidney. NAEL-6v1; NAEL-7v1 *Fr.* Astrophil and Stella.

By reason of two and poore of one. God and Man Set as One. *Unknown.* SacPr

By rights one should experience holy dread. Eros. Timothy Steele. RA

By river and lakes at odds with life I journeyed, wine my freight. Easing My Heart. Tu Mu. CCL1, *tr. by* A. C. Graham

By Saint [*or* Saynt] Mary, my lady. John Skelton. NoSic; NPeEn; OBEV *Fr.* Garland [*or* Garlande *or* Garlands] of Laurel[l], The.

By Saturday cleanup. Bidding Spell. Penn Kemp. IFF

By scribbled names on walls, by telephone number. Village Spa. Phyllis McGinley. OBCoV

By six he's started. I wake to a wince and arrh. Demolisher. Alan Gould. BMAP

By some sad means, when reason holds no sway. Philip Freneau. TCAPo *Fr.* House of Night, The.

By St. Thomas Water. Charles Causley. OBSP

By Starlight on Narin Strand. Jean Bleakney. NIrP

By strangers' coasts and waters, many days at sea. Catullus. WoPoe, *tr. by* Robert Fitzgerald

By Stubborn Stars. Kenneth Leslie. Sonnet. IFF; OxBSo

By Su Creek Pavilion. Su Creek Pavilion. Tai Shu-lun. CCL1, *tr. by* Stephen Owen

By sundown we came to a hidden village. Conquerors. Henry Treece. OBWVE; TCAWP

By taking the impressions of watch-cases he discovered, one day. William McGonagall. VerBaPo *Fr.* Sprig of Moss, The.

By that long scan of waves, myself call'd back, resumed upon myself. Walt Whitman. NAAL-3 *Fr.* Fancies at Navesink.

By that precious pearl without a stain. (LL) *Unknown.* NoP-4; NoP-5 *Fr.* Pearl or Perle.

By that swamp's shore. Ze-bi: By That Swamp's Shore. *Unknown.* CCL1, *tr. by* Arthur Waley

By that the Ma[u]nciple hadde his tale al ended. Geoffrey Chaucer. NAEL-6v1; NAEL-7v1 *Fr.* Canterbury Tales, The.

By the ascension [*or* Assention] of thy Lawn, see All. (LL) To Dianeme ("Show [*or* Shew] me thy feet; show [*or* shew] me thy legs, thy thighs.") Robert Herrick. CavPo; NOSC

By the Bivouac's Fitful Flame. Walt Whitman. AmWaPo; BLT; NAMCP V.1; NoAM; NoP-4

By the blue taper's trembling light. Night Piece on Death. Thomas Parnell.

By the child dying at his mother's side. Five Sorrowful Mysteries, The. Francis Jammes. GI, *tr. by* Jeffrey Fiskin

By the Danube. Attila József. IQMS, *tr. by* Peter Zollman

By the dry road the fathers cough and spit. Brief Journey West, The. Howard Nemerov. NoAM

By the east window, laughing, she leans on a couch of white jade. (LL) For the Dancer of the King of Wu, When She Is Half Drunk. Li Po. CCL1; TAL, *tr. by* Robert Payne

By the end of the longest day of the year he could not stand it. Summer Solstice, New York City. Sharon Olds. FaoP

By the excellence of his work the workman is a neighbor. Wendell Berry. UpMys *Fr.* Prayers and Sayings of the Mad Farmer.

By the field of the crab-trees my love and I were walking. By the Field of the Crab-Trees. Frederick Robert Higgins. IrLP

By the first of August. I Remember. Anne Sexton. LW

By the flow of the inland river. Blue and the Gray, The. Francis Miles Finch. APN-2; CBCWP; CtM; PCW

By the gas-fire, kneeling. Olga Poems. Denise Levertov. NAMCP V.2; InoFa

By the gate with star and moon. Medallion. Sylvia Plath. HeIP-4

By the hearth a holier Lar! (LL) Celia's Home-Coming. Agnes Mary Frances Robinson. OBEV; VWP

By the images of things. Epoch. Vladimír Holan. PoSu, *tr. by* Ian Milner and Jarmila Milner

By the injustice of the skies for punishment? (LL) Cold Heaven, The. William Butler Yeats. InoFa; IrLP; NAMCP V.1; NoAM; NPeEn

By the Jordan. Herman Melville. NCAP

By the lake at Armenonville in the Bois de Boulogne. Armenonville. Edna St. Vincent Millay. NoP-4; NoP-5

By the lamplit stall I loitered, feasting my eyes. Sight. Wilfrid Wilson Gibson. MoBrPo

By the light of the moon. (LL) So We'll Go No More A-Roving. Lord Byron. BrAP; CABP; ChAP; ClHu; CtM; HeIP-4; IJHIL; MakPoe; NAEL-6v2; NAEL-7v2; NePenScot; NoP-4; NoP-5; OPOU; TFi; WoPoe

By the light of the night. Journey of the Shadow, The. Nada El-Hage. PoArWo, *tr. by* Nathalie El-Hani

By the Light of the Silvery Moon. Edward Madden. NAAPv.2; ReLy

By the Looking-Glass. Augusta Davies Webster. VWP

By the Margin of the Great Deep. George Russell. OBEV

By the Nape. Sandra Alcosser. ExTi

By the nature of this world. Wearing. Beau Beausoleil. Eno

By the new Boot's, a tool-chest with flagpoles. Kingsley Amis. NoAM *Fr.* Evans Country, The.

By the North Gate, the wind blows full of sand. Lament of the Frontier Guard. Li Po. APT-1; NAMCP V.1; NDACCP; NPeEn; OBVE; OBWP; PoAgWa, *tr. by* Ezra Pound

By the Ōi River. Ozawa Roan. EMJL, *tr. by* Peter Flueckiger

By the old Moulmein Pagoda, lookin' lazy at [*or* eastward to] the sea. Mandalay. Rudyard Kipling. BRP; HarvBoo; MoBrPo; NPeEn; OxAEP-2

By the old temple. Basho. EH, *tr. by* Robert Hass

By the Pacific Ocean. Joaquin Miller. CalPo

By the Pond. Roy Fisher. *Fr.* City.

By the Potomac. Thomas Bailey Aldrich. PCW
  (Accomplices.) AmWaPo

By the public hook for the private eye. River Song. Weldon Kees. OxBoAm

By the rain and oakleaves on the domino. (LL) Box Comes Home, A. John Ciardi. AmWaPo; PWW2

By the River. Martin Birnbaum. Prolet, *tr. by* Amelia Glaser

By the river a lone pine. Yun Sŏndo. CATKP *Fr.* Angler's Calendar, The.

By the river of stars, its brightness. *Unknown. See* She weaves and ends no pattern to day.

By the river of stars, its brightness. [Version 2]. *Unknown.* NDACCP, *tr. by* Ezra Pound

By the Rivers. Shirley Kaufman. GifTon; TAPaP

"By the Rivers of Babylon." Mary Weston Fordham. CBWP-2

By the rivers of Babylon there we sat down and wept. Psalm 137. Genrik Veniaminovich Sapgir. ItGoST, *tr. by* J. Kates

By the rivers of Babylon, there we sat down, yea, we wept, when [*or* then] we remembered Zion. Bible, *O.T.* NAWM-5v1 *Fr.* Psalms.

By the Rivers of Babylon We Sat Down and Wept. Lord Byron. ChIV-1

By the rivers of salt. (LL) By the Rivers. Shirley Kaufman. GifTon; TAPaP

By the Road to the Air-Base. Yvor Winters. NAAPv.2; NAMCP V.1
  (By The Road to the Sunnyvale Air-Base.) APT-2

By the road to the contagious hospital. Spring and All. William Carlos Williams. APT-1; ChAP; ColAP; EMP; MakPoe; NAAL-5; NAAPv.2; NAMCP V.1; NoAM; OxBoAm; PoPoPo; TCAPo; TFi; TRP

By The Road to the Sunnyvale Air-Base. Yvor Winters. *See* By the Road to the Air-Base.

By the roots of my hair some god got hold of me. Hanging Man, The. Sylvia Plath. OxBoAm; VCAP

By the rude bridge that arched the flood. Concord Hymn. Ralph Waldo Emerson. AmWaPo; BRP; ClHu; ColAP; CtM; FaBoA; HeIP-4; NAAPv.1; NoP-4; NoP-5; OBWP; OxBoAm; PoPoPo; TCAPo; TFi; WaAnP

By the rushy-fringèd bank. John Milton. OxBEV *Fr.* Comus; a Masque Presented at Ludlow Castle.

By the Same. Charlotte Smith. CenSon; RWP

By the Same. To Solitude. Charlotte Smith. CenSon; RWP

By the Sea. Emily Dickinson. APN-2; NAAL-3; WeW-3
  (I Started Early, Took My Dog.) ColAP; NAAPv.1

By the sea. Muso Soseki. EaWin, *tr. by* W. S. Merwin

By the Sea. Christina Georgina Rossetti. NPeEn

By the sea the autumn sun sinks. In the Chinhae Camp. Yi Sunsin. CATKP, *tr. by* Peter H. Lee

By the sea's side hear the dark-vowelled birds. (LL) Especially When the October Wind. Dylan Thomas. AngWePo; MoBrPo; OBWVE; OxAEP-2

By the Sea-Wall. Vincent O'Sullivan. IrLP

By the second / night of the storm, the ground had grown. Currents. Rose Solari. AmPoNex

By the sewage puddles of Sabra and Shatila. You Can't Kill a Baby Twice. Dahlia Ravikovitch. VCWP

By the shores of Gitche[e] Gumee. Henry Wadsworth Longfellow. NoP-5 *Fr.* Song of Hiawatha, The.

By the Skin of Our Luck. Mark Bibbins. IIR

By the Sound. John Hollander. MakPoe

By the Statue of King Charles [*or* I] at Charing Cross. Lionel Pigot Johnson. MoBrPo; OBEV; OBMV

By the Swanannoa. William Gilmore Simms. APN-1

By the time I get myself out of bed, my wife has left. Tuesday, June 4, 1991. Billy Collins. PoDa

By the time I got to them, the woman was stoned. Burden, The. Anne Caston. NAPBL

By the time the priest started into his sermon. Divorce Referendum, Ireland, 1986, The. Paul Durcan. PBCIP

By the time they are finished. Oya Now. Ifi Amadiume. NAfrP

By the time we missed you dusk was settling in. For Roland, Presumed Taken. Jim Barnes. LiTh

By the time you swear you're his. Unfortunate Coincidence. Dorothy Parker. AmWit; LW; NoP-4; NoP-5; OxBoAm

By the verge of the sea a man finds a gelatinous creature. Chimera. Carol Frost. CAP-3

By the Water. Jinkag Haesim. BecRai, *tr. by* Kim Daljin, Kim Won-Chung and Christopher Merrill

By the water. (LL) Edge of the ocean, The. George Oppen. APT-2; PFTM-1

By the waters of Babylon we sat down and wept. Psalm 137. *Unknown.* WoPoe, *tr. by* Miles Coverdale
  (By the waters of Babylon we sat downe and weapte.) NPeEn; OBVE

By the way cortez forcibly gold-filled. How Could All That Have Happened Here? Everett Hoagland. FuFl

By the way we met. William Shakespeare. OBCoV *Fr.* Comedy of Errors, The.

By the Well of Living and Seeing. Charles Reznikoff.
  "During the Second World War, I was going home one night." PWW2
  "Highway I was walking on, The." FTOS

By the West Pavilion, on a thousand feet of cliff. Midnight. Tu Fu [*or* Du Fu]. CCL1, *tr. by* A. C. Graham

By the whole heave and settle of the sea. (LL) Frederick Goddard Tuckerman. APN-2; TCAPo *Fr.* Sonnets.

By the Winding River. Tu Fu [*or* Du Fu]. CCL1, *tr. by* Kenneth Rexroth

By the women of Marblehead! (LL) Skipper Ireson's Ride. John Greenleaf Whittier. APN-1; NAAPv.1; NCAP

By their blight, from strand to strand? (LL) Lines: "At the Portals of the Future." Frances Ellen Watkins Harper. APN-2; NAAPv.1

By their nephews and their nieces. (LL) Good and Bad Children. Robert Louis Stevenson. ChAP; OBCoV

By their shadows. (LL) Sun-Dial, The. Adelaide Crapsey. APT-1; NAAPv.2

By then, by the time my brother. Not Knowing. Gary Soto. NoP-4; NoP-5

By thine own named town made famous in thy fall. Michael Drayton. NOSC *Fr.* Polyolbion [*or* Poly-Oobion].

By thinking American, I mean made. (LL) Thinking American. Hayan Charara. AmPoNex; PrTe

By this fire I still can feel the wind. Blues. Suzanne Gardinier. AmPoNex

By this Leander being near the land. Christopher Marlowe. NPeEn *Fr.* Hero and Leander.

By this mighty arm his rights shall be obtained! (LL) Black Sampson, The. Josephine D. Henderson Heard. CBWP-4; SWaP

By this, she hears the hounds are at a bay. William Shakespeare. DiBP *Fr.* Venus and Adonis [Complete Text *and* Selections from Anthologies].

By this the Northerne wagoner had set. Edmund Spenser. NoP-5; NoSic *Fr.* Faerie Queene, The.

By this the sun had sucked up the vast deep. Michael Drayton. NOSC *Fr.* Noah's Flood.

By this time. Mid-Year Report: For Haruko. June Jordan. ReTh

By this time had they reached the Stygian pool. Ben Jonson. NOSC *Fr.* On the Famous Voyage.

By this time long-gowned Lumen walked abroad. William Rankins. OBSV *Fr.* Satyrus Peregrinans.

By this title, the book declares itself, and the amount of riches that it conceals. A—B—on the Learned Bartholo Sylva. Anne Cooke Bacon. EMWP

By Those Eyes Where Sweet Expression. Lady Caroline Lamb. RWP

By Three Kinds of Flowers I'm Challenged. *Hungarian Oral Tradition.* IQMS, *tr. by* Adam Makkai

By thunders of white silence, overthrown. (LL) Hiram Powers' "Greek Slave." Elizabeth Barrett Browning. GS; NALW; ViWPN

By touching what we were. (LL) Gift, The: "I was wrong when I compared the mask of my own face." Rebecca Seiferle. ICANM; PoChi

By trivial breath, over the whole world's length. (LL) Self-portrait. Elinor Wylie. APT-1; NAAPv.2

By twisting shoreline and deep pool. Song of the Fisherman, The. Kao Shih. CCL1, *tr. by* Stephen Owen

By vew of her he ginneth to revive. Edmund Spenser. CAGL *Fr.* Faerie Queene, The.

By viewing nature, nature's handmaid, art. John Dryden. BASC *Fr.* Annus Mirabilis.

By vulgar Eros long misled. Song. Sarah Ponsonby. PoBW

By wagon, in the first temperate dry-out of summer. It. Linda Bierds. AmAlph

By warm blood of bird. Spell to Protect Our Love. Jeni Couzyn. HAWP

By Water Divined. Kathleene West. GifTon

By Wauchopeside. Hugh MacDiarmid. OxAEP-2

By way of a leak. Times Square Water Music. Amy Clampitt. UrbNat

By way of a vanished bridge we cross this river. Garden Shukkei-en, The. Carolyn Forché. AtGh; ExTi; WaAnP

By way of inventing a rivulet on the roof and continuing to struggle with the burning floor tiles. Deluge. Laura Solórzano. SPV, *tr. by* Jen Hofer

By Way of Preface. Edward Lear. *See* How Pleasant to Know Mr. Lear.

By what eternal streams. (LL) To One in Paradise. Edgar Allan Poe. NCAP; OBEV; OxBoAm

By what sends. Children's Rhymes. Langston Hughes. NOxBChV

By which our dreams and daily scenes stay separate. (LL) And Forgive Us Our Traspasses. Sinéad Morrissey. MoWP; NIrP

By Woundsday when a tongue-pierced Asian. Penance and the Work Week. Gaylord Brewer. Vesp

By Yangtze and Han. Tu Fu [*or* Du Fu]. CrYelRi, *tr. by* Sam Hamill

By your life, do you know whether it is the violence of the south winds dashing against my saddle, or the backs of excellent camels? Ibrāhīm ibn Abī al-Fath Ibn Khafāja. HiArP, *tr. by* James T. Monroe

By your side I am beautiful with my mouth extended and my open arms. *Unknown.* SLW, *tr. by* Marjolijn De Jager, Sayd Bahodin Majrouh and André Velter

Bye and bye. (LL) Chillen Get Shoes. Sterling Allen Brown. APT-2; NoP-4; NoP-5

Bye, baby bunting. Mother Goose. OxBEV

Bye Bye Barbara. Sally Bellerose. PfS

Bye Bye Blackbird. Mort Dixon. ReLy

Bye Bye Blackbird. John James. Oth

Bye! / I'm going to a place so thoroughly remote. Radical Departure, A. James Tate. WaAnP

Bypass, The. Conor O'Callaghan. NIrP

Bypassing Rue Descartes. Czeslaw Milosz. FaoP; VCWP, *tr. by* Renata Gorczynski and Robert Hass

By-Products. Baron Wormser. ReTh

Byre. Norman Alexander MacCaig. EdScPo

Byrnies, The. Thom Gunn. NoAM

Byron. J. Gordon Coogler. VerBaPo

Byron: a Critical Survey [*or* Lord Byron's Life]. Julia A. Moore. STuOW

Byron and Shelley and Keats. Pig's-Eye View of Literature, A. Dorothy Parker. APT-1; BrAP

By-street was bathed in sun, The. Andrey Bely. PFTM-1 *Fr.* Dramatic Symphony, The.

Bytuene Mersh and Averil. *Unknown.* NoP-4

Bytuene Mershe and Averil. *Unknown.* OBEV

Bytwene Mersh and Averil. *Unknown.* NoP-4; NoP-5

Byzantium. William Butler Yeats. HarvBoo; MoBrPo; NAEL-6v2; NAEL-7v2; NAMCP V.1; NAWM-7v2; NIL-7; NIP-4; NoAM; NoP-4; NoP-5; OxBEV; WaAnP

Byzantium / I come not from. Byzantium I Come Not From. Ray Bradbury. IllVoic

BZZZZZZZ. Amy Gerstler. PmAP

C

C. C. Rider. Lucille Clifton. GT

C. calls to tell me Mercury is in retrograde, so watch out. Just last night, walking. Chapel of the Miraculous Medal. Mark Wunderlich. NAPBL

"C" ing in Colors: Blue. Safiya Henderson-Holmes. SpirFl

"C" ing in Colors: Red. Safiya Henderson-Holmes. SpirFl

C. L. M. John Masefield. InoFa; MoBrPo

C Major of this life: so, now I will try to sleep, The. (LL) Abt Vogler. Robert Browning. NAEL-6v2; NAEL-7v2

C / olumbus from his after-. Colombe. Edward Kamau Brathwaite. VCWP

C. T. at the Five Spot. Thulani Davis. SeSe

C33. Hart Crane. CAGL

Ça. Pierre Reverdy. YaTCFP

Ca gunaa rusianda. Natalia Toledo. RMCMP

Cabal at Nickey Nackeys, The. Aphra Behn. NOSC

Cabalga la voz. Escucho los alientos, la salivación. Poema del habla. Laura Solórzano. SPV

Cabalistic Rabbis, The. Rosita Kalina. MirDau, *tr. by* Roberta Gordenstein

Cabalists, The. Angelina Muñiz Huberman. MirDau, *tr. by* Aurora Camacho

Caballo de acero, El. Dana Gelinas. SPV

Cabaret. Sterling Allen Brown. APT-2

Cabaret. Fred Ebb. ReLy

Cabaret McGonagall. W. N. Herbert. NeBrP

Cabato. Ray Gonzalez. TouFir

Cabbage, The. Ruth Stone. PoChi

Cabbage Butterfly, The. Henri Cole. UrbNat

Cabeza, where are your clothes? Roberto Meets Cabeza de Vaca in the Desert. Ray Gonzales. TiP2

Cabin gives off the odor, The. Life One Leads, The. Gabriel Celaya. RaW, *tr. by* Robert Mezey and Hardie St. Martin

Cabin in the Clearing, A. Robert Frost. APT-1

Cabin in the Sky. John Latouche. ReLy

Cabin morning, probes of wind after rain. Where. William Heyen. AmZen

Cabin-Boy, The. George, 2d Duke of Buckingham Villiers. NOSC

Cabinet of Seeds Displayed, A. Howard Nemerov. NoP-5

Cable Ship, The. Harry Edmund Martinson. WED, *tr. by* Robert Bly

Cables are made near the window. The cables have. Leslie Kaplan. SCFWP *Fr.* L'Excès-L'usine.

Cables to the Ace. Thomas Merton.
   "I am about to make my home." WhBo

Cabralism. The civilization of the donées. The willing and the exportation. Babbling. Oswald de Andrade. TCLAP, *tr. by* Flavia Vidal

Cachorros, Los. Pura López Colomé. RMCMP

Cacoëthes Scribendi. Oliver Wendell Holmes. NBLV; OBCoV

"Cacophony?!"—Let it be that! If in. Bartók. Gyula Illyés. IQMS, *tr. by* Robert C. Kenedy

Cactus. Sam Gardiner. NIrP

Cactus poachers work quickly. Diptych. Tony Towle. PA9/11

Cactuses. Jean-Joseph Rabéarivelo. SonAtl, *tr. by* Audrey Cooper, W. Ender and Celia Martin

Cada Puerco Tiene Su Sábado. Martín Espada. TouFir

Cada Vez Que Paso. Miguel Hernández. RaW

Cadáver Ínfimo. Angel González. RaW

Cadaver Politic. Tom Paulin. PNI

Caddo Mounds, The. Violette Newton. TiP2

Cadgwith. Lionel Pigot Johnson. SacPr

Cadidi Laaga Lua. Natalia Toledo. RMCMP

Cae Iago: May Day. Roland Mathias. TCAWP

Cae la tarde. Tenochtitlán Blues. Manuel Ulacia. RMCMP

Caedmon. Denise Levertov. BrAP; ItP; NAMCP V.2; NoAM; NoP-4; NoP-5; PoCho

Caedmon. Aidan Carl Mathews. PBCIP

Caedmon's Hymn. Caedmon. NoP-5, *tr. by* John Pope

Caedmon's Hymn. Caedmon. PoCho, *tr. by* Unknown

Cædmon's Hymn, West Saxon Version. Caedmon. NoP-5

Caelica. Fulke Greville, 1st Baron Brooke.
   Sonnet 7. NoSic
   Sonnet 23. WoPoe
   Sonnet 27. PBRV
   Sonnet 38. NAEL-6v1
   Sonnet 40. NoP-4; NoP-5
   Sonnet 45. NPeEn; PBRV
   Sonnet 56. CABP; NOSC; NoSic
   Sonnet 69. NoSic; PtR
   Sonnet 78. PBRV
   Sonnet 82. PtR
   Sonnet 84. NPeEn
   Sonnet 85. NoSic; NPeEn
   Sonnet 86. NoSic
   Sonnet 87. CABP; NOSC; NoSic
   Sonnet 88. NOSC; NoSic
   Sonnet 89. SacPr
   Sonnet 90. WaAnP
   Sonnet 97. NoSic; SacPr
   Sonnet 98. NoSic
   Sonnet 99. CABP; NOSC; NoSic; NPeEn; PBRV
   Sonnet 100. NAEL-7v1; NPeEn
   Sonnet 101. WaAnP
   Sonnet 103. SacPr
   Sonnet 105. NOSC; NoSic; SacPr
   Sonnet 109. ChIV-1; NoSic
   "I, with whose colors [*or* colours] Myra dressed [*or* dress'd *or* drest] her head." NoSic; OBEV; OxBEV; PBRV
   "You little stars that live in skies." NoP-4; NoP-5

Caelica, I overnight was finely used. Fulke Greville, 1st Baron Brooke. NAEL-6v1 *Fr.* Caelica.

Caernarfon Circus, 1969. T. E. Nicholas. BBMWP, *tr. by* Robert Minhinnick

Caernarfon, 2 July [*or* July 2] 1969. T. Glynne Davies. BBMWP; OBWVE, *tr. by* Joseph P. Clancy

Caesar and Brutus. Anne Finch, Countess of Winchilsea. EMWP

Caesar's back, and they've built him a throne to sit on. Brutus' Last Song. Christiania Whitehead. NeBl

Caesar's Palace. Moorer Denies Holyfield in Twelve. Olena Kalytiak Davis. AmPoNex; MoASP

Cæsura. John Ashbery. ChIV-1

Caesura. Kenneth Mackenzie. BeAl; BrAP; NOBAu; PoCu

Cafe. Czeslaw Milosz. PoSu, *tr. by* Jan Darowski

Café du Dôme. Else Von Freytag-Loringhoven. APT-1; SurPaPo

Café of Situations, The. Martin Johnston. BMAP *Fr.* In Transit: A Sonnet Square.

Café with the hotwire, The. Back to Catfish. Belle Waring. SweBea

Caffe Mediterraneum. John Oliver Simon. ASA

Cage. Salman Masalha. PML, *tr. by* Vivian Eden

Cage, The. John Berryman. PoA 2002

Cage, The. Geoffrey Chaucer. OWoS *Fr.* Canterbury Tales, The.

Cage, The. John Montague. PNI *Fr.* Rough Field, The.

Cage, The. James Stephens. OxBEV

Cage, The.   Rosamund Marriott Watson.   VWP

Cage of Voices, The.   Horace Gregory.   APT-2

Cage wrote 4'33."   Pedagogy.   Lin Max.   MiVo

Caged Bird.   Maya Angelou.   BrAP; WeW-3

Caged Bird, A.   Sarah Orne Jewett.   APN-2; ColAP; NAAPv.1

Caged Birds.   Ignacy Krasicki.   WoPoe, tr. by Jerzy Peterkiewicz and Burns Singer

Caged Goldfinch, The.   Thomas Hardy.   OWoS

Caged Skylark, The.   Gerard Manley Hopkins.   MoBrPo; OBMV; OWoS; SoSe-8

Caged Stone.   Martha Vertreace.   IllVoic

Cages, The.   Jerry McGuire.   AnSo

Cages, The.   James Tate.   YaYoPo

Cahoots.   Carl Sandburg.   APT-1

Cai-bin: I Pluck the Grass.   Unknown.   CCL1

Cai-fan: Pluck the Quince.   Unknown.   CCL1, tr. by Ezra Pound

Cai-ge [Translations].   Unknown.   CCL1
  Bean Flower.   CCL1, tr. by Man Wong
  Taedium.   CCL1, tr. by Ezra Pound

Cain.   Lucille Clifton.   NAMCP V.2

Cain.   Irving Layton.   BrAP

Cain: A Mystery.   Lord Byron.
  "And now I will convey thee to thy world."   NOBRP
  "Hear, Jehovah! / May the eternal serpent's curse be on him!"   NOBRP
  "Oh! thou dead / And everlasting witness! whose unsinking."   ChIV-1

Cain lifts Crow, that heavy black bird.   Crow Testament.   Sherman Alexie.   NAMCP V.2

Cain the Immortal [with music].   Yusuf Al-Khal.   PFTM-2, tr. by Sargon Boulus and Samuel Hazo

Cain't nobody tell me any different.   Song No. 3.   Sonia Sanchez.   FFC; NOxBChV

Cairo Jag.   Keith Douglas.   HarvBoo; PoWW

Cairo's taxi drivers speak to me in English.   Echo and Elixir 2.   Khaled Mattawa.   LegDan

Caisson.   Maurice Riordan.   NIrP

Cai-wei: We Pick Ferns, We Pick Ferns.   Unknown.   CCL1, tr. by Burton Watson

Cajun.   Sheryl St. Germain.   OPRER

Cake in the oven, clothes out on the line.   Rockin' A Man, Stone Blind.   Carolyn Beard Whitlow.   FFC

Cakes Continue to Rise.   Rick Agran.   AmPoNex

Calamity and conflagration! Strife!   Scythinus.   CAGL, tr. by Daryl Hine

Calamity in London; Family of Ten Burned to Death.   William McGonagall.   VerBaPo

Calamity of seals begins with jaws, The.   Seals at High Island.   Richard Murphy.   ModIr; PBCIP

Calbharaigh.   Sorley MacLean.   EdScPo

Calcined stones come back, The.   Homecoming of Love Amongst Illustrious Ruins.   Rafael Alberti.   CLPP, tr. by Kenneth Rexroth

Caleb Barnes.   David Wright.   NLP

Caledonian Antisyzygy, The.   Hugh MacDiarmid.   OxBEV

Calendar full, future unknown, The.   Black Postcards.   Tomas Tranströmer.   WoPoe, tr. by Joanna Bankier

Calendar is ironic, The. The stripper dances.   Dancing Sunshine Lounge, The.   Thomas Rabbitt.   ReTh

Calenture, The.   Randolph Stow.   BMAP

Calf.   Katrina Porteous.   BeAl; NeBl

Calf and the Ox, The.   Avianus.   WoPoe, tr. by David R. Slavitt

Calgary Bay.   Margaret Gillies Brown.   EdScPo

Caliban.   Edward Kamau Brathwaite.   HarvBoo

Caliban.   J. P. Dancing Bear.   IaFF

Caliban in the Coal Mines.   Louis Untermeyer.   MoAmPo

Caliban upon Setebos; or, Natural Theology in the Island.   Robert Browning.   NAEL-6v2; NAEL-7v2; OxAEP-2

Caliban's Books.   Michael Donaghy.   EmeKit; NeBrP

Caliban's Journal.   Suniti Namjoshi.   RACG

Calico cat lies, The.   Michael McClure.   WANABP Fr. Touching the Edge: Dharma Devotions.

Calico Pie.   Edward Lear.   NOxBChV

Calico summer, The.   Moon/light quarter/back sack.   Samuel F. Reynolds.   SpirFl

Calidarium (hot room).   Matthea Harvey.   IAoNAP Fr. Thermae.

California.   Paul Hoover.   BAP-97

California.   John Rollin Ridge.
  "And shall we view these miracles and more."   APN-2; CalPo

California.   David St. John.   SwNoth

California, 1852.   Sharyn Jeanne Skeeter.   ISC

California Christmas, A.   Joaquin Miller.   CalPo

California Coast.   Jean V. Gier.   ReBoTo

California Colors: A Song.   Charlotte Perkins Stetson Gilman.   CalPo

California Dreaming.   Carol Lem.   GeoHom

California Dreaming.   Rochelle Nameroff.   SwNoth

California Dreaming.   Charles Wright.   CAP-8

California Entertainment, 1936.   Wilma Elizabeth McDaniel.   GeoHom

California Girlhood, A.   Alice Notley.   PmAP

California, Here I Come.   B. G. DeSylva and Al Jolson.   ReLy

California Hills in August.   Dana Gioia.   CalPo

California Light.   Sherley Anne Williams.   CalPo; GeoHom

California Madrigal.   Bret Harte.   APN-2

California night. The Devil's wind.   In Chandler Country.   Dana Gioia.   GeoHom

California Peninsula: El Camino Real.   Al Young.   GeoHom; GT

California Poem.   Chryss Yost.   GeoHom

California rolls into.   Delia Rexroth.   Kenneth Rexroth.   CalPo; PoCho

California, She Replied.   Kathy Fagan.   GeoHom

California Spring.   Charles Wright.   ColAP

California: "To come again into the place of revolutionary."   Hayden Carruth.   TAPaP

California Twilight.   Charles Wright.   GeoHom

California: "What the hell am i doing anyway?"   Gerald Locklin.   CalPo

California Winter.   Edward Rowland Sill.   APN-2

Californians say No.   Bilingual Instructions.   Harryette Mullen.   PrTe

Calinda.   Unknown.   SSUS

Call.   Sarah Kirsch.   PFTM-2 Fr. Kite-Flying.

Call.   Noémia da Sousa.   HAWP, tr. by Jacques-Noël Gouat

Call, A.   Thomas Holley Chivers.   STuOW

Call, A (1876).   Julia A. Moore.   STuOW Fr. Hurrah for Cooper and Cary.

Call, The.   Anna Laetitia Barbauld.   SacPr

Call, The.   John Hall.   NOSC

Call, The.   Robert Harris.   BMAP

Call, The.   Dennis Haskell.   NOBAu

Call, The.   George Herbert.   SacPr

Call, The.   Aaron Kurtz.   Prolet, tr. by Amelia Glaser

Call, The.   Charlotte Mew.   PoCho

Call, The.   Thomas Osbert Mordaunt.   OBEV

Call, The.   Sir Walter Scott. See Sound, Sound the Clarion.

Call, The.   Unknown.   OBEV

Call a ruined shoe, the sandal.   Last Poem, Snow Tree.   Norman Dubie.   NAMCP V.2

Call and Response.   DJ Renegade.   BtF

Call and Response.   Ken Harris.   AnSo

Call Awe, then, what you will, long long ago.   Freight.   John Frederick Nims.   GM

Call back your odours, lonely flowers.   Night-Blooming Flowers.   Felicia Dorothea Hemans.   NOBRP

Call Boy.   Sterling Allen Brown.   GM

Call, by all means, but just once.   Voice.   Ann Sansom.   NeBl

Call for more pens, more paper, and more ink. (LL)   Cacoëthes Scribendi.   Oliver Wendell Holmes.   NBLV; OBCoV

Call for the Robin-Redbreast and the Wren.   John Webster.   NOSC; NPeEn; OxAEP-1; OxBEV; TFi Fr. White Devil, The.

Call for Vertical Integration in the Eye of the Storm, A.   Lee Ann Brown.   VaPo

Call her walking-mort; say where she goes.   Walking-Mort, The.   Djuna Barnes.   APT-1

Call in the Midst of the Crowd, A.   Alfred Corn.
  Fire: The People.   VCAP

Call in the midst of the crowd, A.   Walt Whitman.   ColAP Fr. Song of Myself.

Call in your reporters.   Guess Who's in Town? (Nobody but That Gal of Mine).   Andy Razaf.   ReLy

Call It Fear.   Joy Harjo.   ICANM; NAAL-5

Call it iron discipline. But for months.   NyQuil.   Raymond Carver.   LaCa

Call it the refrigerator's hum at night.   Villanelle for the Middle of the Night.   Jacqueline Osherow.   MakPoe

Call it the solstice, call it.   Summer Solstice.   Enos D. Watts.   Coast

Call it treason, but I'm eating my way.   Peach.   Lance Larsen.   AmPoNex

Call Me Irresponsible.   Sammy Cahn.   ReLy

Call me Ishmael.   Herman Melville.   GoPo Fr. Moby Dick.

Call Me Mister.   Harold Rome.   ReLy

Call me old-fashioned, but I'm never mean.   Eater of Wives, The.   Linda France.   MFPA

Call me Polyxena, the wife of Archelaus.   Dioscorides.   HePo Fr. Epigrams.

Call Me 'Shortchange'.   Joel Dailey.   AnSo

Call me What You Will.   Introduction to Eden.   Matthea Harvey.   IAoNAP

Call not thy wanderer home as yet. Germinal. George Russell. MoBrPo; OBEV; OBMV

Call of Nature, The [*with music*]. Tony Harrison. NoAM

Call of Poetry. Sri Sri. HotL, *tr. by* V. Narayana Rao

Call of the Desirous. José Lezama Lima. TCLAP, *tr. by* Willis Barnstone

Call of the Fulani Maid. Kabura Zakama. NeNiPo

Call of the Lake, The. Andrey Andreievich Voznesensky. VCWP

Call of the Soul, The. *Unknown.* WoPoe, *tr. by* Ronald Perry

Call of the Wild, The. Kalamu ya Salaam. FuFl

Call out. Call loud: 'I'm ready! Come and find me!'. Hide and Seek. Vernon Scannell. NOxBChV

Call out the colored girls. For the Record. Audre Lorde. ESEAA; InoFa

Call the roller of big cigars. Emperor of Ice-Cream, The. Wallace Stevens. APT-1; BeAl; BrAP; EMP; HeIP-4; InoFa; NAAL-5; NAAPv.2; NAMCP V.1; NAWM-7v2; NIL-7; NIP-4; NoAM; NoP-4; NoP-5; OxBoAm; PoPoPo; PtR; TCAPo; TFi; TRP; WaAnP; WeW-3

Call the strange spirit that abides unseen. William Lisle Bowles. NPBRoP *Fr.* Coombe Ellen.

Call, The: "When I heard the voice on the telephone." Carol Muske-Dukes. WaAnP

Call to Arms. "Lu Hsün." WoPoe, *tr. by* William R. Schultz

Call to Lieutenants. Sebestyén Tinódi. *tr. by* Joseph Leftwich
 "You, who are lieutenants in the army." IQMS, *tr. by* Joseph Leftwich

Call to the Muse. James Grainger. STuOW *Fr.* Sugar Cane, The.

Call yourself alive? Look, I promise you. Temptation. Nina Cassian. AF; StAl, *tr. by* Andrea Deletant and Brenda Walker

Callaloo. Chezia Thompson Cager. FTtHH

Callas. Edward Field. BodElec

Call—call—and bruise the air. Expression. Isaac Rosenberg. MoBrPo

Called Back. Emily Dickinson. MoAmPo

Called dog men. Royals. James Schuyler. FTOS

Called him "Big Joe" yes and Joe Turner it was his name. Hayden Carruth. GifTon *Fr.* Sleeping Beauty, The.

Called on Hermes. Still Waiting for My Winter Coat: A Sequence of Fragments. Hipponax. WoPoe, *tr. by* Anselm Hollo

Called out on Christmas Eve for a working-party. Devil on Ice. Donald Davie. NoAM

Called Up: Tinker to Evers to Chance. Dorothy Barresi. MoASP

Caller Herrin'. Carolina Oliphant, Baroness Nairne. WoRP

Caller Oysters. Robert Fergusson. NePenScot

Callers. Christine Evans. TCAWP

Calles, un jardín. Vida Urbana. Jorge Guillén. RaW

Calligram, 15 May 1915. Guillaume Apollinaire. OBWP, *tr. by* O. Bernard

Calligraphy of Birds. Larry Smith. AmZen

Calligraphy of geese. Buson. EH, *tr. by* Robert Hass

Callin buddy. Callin Buddy / Bolden. Callin Buddy. SeSe

Calling, A. Maxine W. Kumin. PoA 2002

Calling, A. W. S. Merwin. BodElec

Calling, The. Ai. MAAN

Calling, The. Luis Palés Matos. BLPSL, *tr. by* Rene de Costa, Rigas Kappatos and Eleni Paidoussi

Calling, The. Ronald Stuart Thomas. PoetW

Calling the Doctor (1000 A.D.). Nizami Arudi. WoPoe, *tr. by* Omar S. Pound

Calling Out the Names. Carol Gordon. FiBr

Calling the White Donkey. Ray Gonzalez. TouFir

Calling Up the Spirit of the Lost Child. Maggie Penn. TWW

Calliope. John Skelton. OxBEV

Calloused grass lies hard, The. By the Road to the Air-Base. Yvor Winters. NAAPv.2; NAMCP V.1

Callow eagle in its downy nest, The. Aspiration. Emily Jane Pfeiffer. ViWPN

Calls from the Outside World. Robert Hershon. PrTe

Calls through the valleys of Hall. (LL) Song of the Chattahoochee. Sidney Lanier. APN-2; ColAP; TCAPo

Calm, The. Dulce Maria Loynaz. TANSG, *tr. by* Alan West

Calm, The. John McAuliffe. NIrP

Calm, The/ Cool face of the river. Suicide's Note. Langston Hughes. APT-2; NAMCP V.1; OxAAAP; PoPoPo; SAmP

Calm, activity—each has its use. At times. Soen. ZenPo, *tr. by* Takashi Ikemoto and Lucien Stryk

Calm and lit up. Marcelina. Natalia Toledo. RMCMP, *tr. by* Alberto A. Ríos

Calm and lovely paradise, A. Nathaniel Parker Willis. APN-1 *Fr.* Melanie.

Calm as that second summer which precedes. Charleston. Henry Timrod. AmWaPo; APN-2; CBCWP; ColAP; OxBoAm; PCW; TCAPo

Calm comes from burning. Etymological Dirge. Heather McHugh. ExTi; FaoP

Calm down. No one's listening. Of course. Bad Muse, The. Lawrence Raab. SUP

Calm hair, meandering in pellucid gold. (LL) On Seeing a Hair of Lucretia Borgia. Walter Savage Landor. NPeEn; PtR; WeW-3

Calm in the half-light. Muted Tones. Paul Verlaine. SxFrPo, *tr. by* Martin Sorrell

Calm in the Vegetable Beard of Time. Hoa Nguyen. WANABP

Calm is the morn without a sound. Alfred Tennyson. BrAP; HeIP-4; NAEL-6v2; NAEL-7v2; NAWM-7v2; NoP-5; NPeEn; OxBEV; WaAnP *Fr.* In Memoriam A. H. H.

Calm moon, A. Basho. EH, *tr. by* Robert Hass

Calm Night Thought. Li Po. NDACCP, *tr. by* Ezra Pound

Calm on the bosom of thy God. Felicia Dorothea Hemans. OBEV *Fr.* Siege of Valencia, The.

Calm rocks to sleep in your usual place. Larisa Berezovchuk. CRWP, *tr. by* Richard McKane

Calm was the sea to which your course you kept. To W. P. George Santayana. TCAPo

Calm wind blows, A. Verb, The. Nedelcho Ganev. CSCBP, *tr. by* Georgi Belev and Lisa Sapinkopf

Calm[e], The. John Donne. NoSic; PBRV

Calm[e] was the day, and through the trembling air [*or* ayre]. Prothalamion. Edmund Spenser. BrAP; NoSic; NPeEn; OBEV; OxAEP-1; OxBEV; TFi; WoPoe

Calming Kali. Lucille Clifton. HW

Calmly grass becomes a wave. Hoa Nguyen. IIR

Calor irradiado—lo mismo por una fogata campestre, El. Teoría cuántica. Alberto Blanco. RMCMP

Calvary. Edwin Arlington Robinson. GI; MoAmPo

Calvary. *Unknown.* NAWM-7v1

"Calvary." William Butler Yeats.
 "I am Judas." GI

Calvary: "My eye is not on Calvary." Sorley MacLean. EdScPo; NePenScot

Calvary Path, A. Denise Levertov. UpMys

Calvary Way. May Miller. OxAAAP

Calverly's. Edwin Arlington Robinson. APT-1; NAAPv.1; NAMCP V.1; NoAM

Calvin Klein's Obsession. Ciaran Carson. EmeKit

Calvinist Sang. Alexander Scott. EdScPo

Calvinist, The. Kenneth Steven. EdScPo

Calv'ry's tragedy is ended. Empty Tomb, The. Clara Ann Thompson. CBWP-2

Calypso. Edward Kamau Brathwaite. BrAP; HarvBoo; NAMCP V.2

Calypso. Olga Broumas. CAP-8

Calypso. Ernst Jandl. PFTM-2

Calypso. Shara McCallum. AmPoNex

Calyx sweet X, crossroads, meetingplace. For CALYX. Ursula K. Le Guin. FiBr

Camarada arrived at his village. Homecoming. Joao Pedro. NAfrP, *tr. by* Don Burness

Cambodia. James Fenton. AF; PoAgWa; StAl

Cambodian kids speak English faster, The. Conspiracy, The. Robert Hill Long. OPRER

Cambria. John Davies of Hereford.
 "Great Grandame Wales, from whom those ancestors." AngWePo

Cambridge in the Long. Amy Levy. ViWPN

Cambridge ladies who live in furnished souls, The. E. E. Cummings. BrAP; HeIP-4; MakPoe; NAAPv.2; NAMCP V.1; NoAM; NoP-4; NoP-5; TCAPo; WaAnP

Cambridge Songs. *Unknown.* *tr. by* Fred Chappell and David Ferry
 Heriger and the False Prophet. WoPoe, *tr. by* Fred Chappell
 Levis Exsurgit Zephirus. WoPoe, *tr. by* David Ferry

Cambridge Street, summer. Days of 1981. Mark Doty. ReTh

Camden, 1892. Jorge Luis Borges. ViWalt, *tr. by* Willis Barnstone

Camden, most reverend head, to whom I owe. To William Camden. Ben Jonson. BASC; NAEL-6v1; NAEL-7v1; NOSC; NPeEn

Came a stranger late among us. In Memory of James M. Rathel. Josephine D. Henderson Heard. CBWP-4

Came along / a mountain path. Taneda Santoka. CAoMJL1, *tr. by* Burton Watson

Came buffalo heads. Dirty Money. Christine Hume. AmPoNex

Came by sporting a nowhere hat. At the Entrance. M. R. Peacocke. NLP

Came early with. Revival. Kevin Young. OxAAAP

Came fresh transfigurings of freshest blue. (LL) Sea Surface Full of Clouds. Wallace Stevens. APT-1; MoAmPo

Came in a pink. Slicker. David Trinidad. BeDoSh

Came in my full youth to the midnight cave. Ajanta. Muriel Rukeyser. APT-2; MoAmPo

Came kennelled in my head. (LL) How Came What Came Alas. HeidiLynn Nilsson. NeAmPo; PoDa

Came Neptunus / his mind leaping. Ezra Pound. APSN; APT-1; NAAPv.2; NAMCP V.1; PFTM-2 *Fr.* Cantos.

Came north. Mississippi on the Doorstep. Sam Cornish. BtF

Came out by the same door where in I went. (LL) Omar Khayyám. CABP; TRP *Fr.* Rubáiyát of Omar Khayyám [of Naishápúr], The.

Came the hammer, so to speak. How Came What Came Alas. HeidiLynn Nilsson. NeAmPo; PoDa

Came the relief. "What, sentry, ho!" Relieving Guard. Bret Harte. PCW

Came to an island farctate with feculence. Peter Reading. StAl *Fr.* Evagatory.

Came to dead water. Field of Light, A. Theodore Roethke. PtR; WaAnP

Came to me like a. Lovers Total Recall. Tracie Morris. BtF

Came to me— / Who? Rudaki. OBVE; OxBEV; WoPoe, *tr. by* Basil Bunting

Came to my side, and put down his head in love. (LL) Dream, The. Louise Bogan. MoAmPo; NALW; NoAM

Camel. Takahashi Shinkichi. ZenPo, *tr. by* Takashi Ikemoto and Lucien Stryk

Camel. *Unknown.* SonAtl, *tr. by* Una Awis, Michael Eastman and Ali Nazret

Camel. When your foothhuds flag. Camel. *Unknown.* SonAtl, *tr. by* Una Awis, Michael Eastman and Ali Nazret

Cameleon Lover, The. *Unknown.* TCAPo

Cameleon's Defence, The. *Unknown.* TCAPo

Camellia. Henriqueta Lisboa. TCLAP, *tr. by* Hélcio Veiga Costa

Camellia, The. Buson. EH, *tr. by* Robert Hass

Camellia, The. William Stanley Roscoe. CenSon

Camellia, it's that moist and sensitive. It runs, instead, so pure through my veins. Camellia, It's that Moist and Sensitive. Killarney Clary. MotU

Camellia Sabina. Marianne Moore. AFaM

Camellia tips, The. Buson. SoOfWa, *tr. by* Sam Hamill

Camelot. Alan Jay Lerner. ReLy

Camel's Complaint, The. Charles Edward Carryl. NOxBChV

Camel's hump is an ugly lump, The. Rudyard Kipling. NOxBChV *Fr.* Just-So Stories.

Camel's humps, The. Camel. Takahashi Shinkichi. ZenPo, *tr. by* Takashi Ikemoto and Lucien Stryk

Camels of the Kings. Leslie Norris. OBCP

Camels pregnant. Birth. Bernard Bador. ConPit, *tr. by* Clayton Eshleman

Camelus Saltat. George Meredith. OxBSo

Camelus Saltat: Continued. George Meredith. OxBSo

Cameo. Natasha Trethewey. NeAmPo

Cameo Appearance. Charles Simic. NAMCP V.2; NoP-5; OxBoAm

Cameo in Sudden Light. Lorenzo Thomas. FTOS

Cameo, The. Edna St. Vincent Millay. GPTC; MoAmPo

Camera is cousin of the gun, as, The. South Central: Notes toward a Shooting Script. Jasper Bernes. IAoNAP

Camera Obscura. Valerie Martínez. NAPBL

Camera Obscura. Robin Robertson. Flags of Autumn. EdScPo

Camera pans a gorgeous snow-filled landscape: rolling hills, large black trees, a frozen river, The. Cinema Vérité: The Death of Alfred, Lord Tennyson. Tom Andrews. MotU

Caminando. Víctor Hernández Cruz. PFTM-2

Camino Real. Adrienne Rich. BodElec

Camme and I listened to Nat King Cole and she sweetly lay her head. We Encounter Nat King Cole as We Invent the Future. Joy Harjo. ReTh

Camões, alone, of all the lyric race. Luís de Camões. Roy Campbell. OxAEP-2

Camouflage. Marianne Boruch. BAP-97

Camouflaged, they detach lengths of sea and sky. Destroyers in the Arctic. Alan Ross. PoWW

Camouflaging the Chimera. Yusef Komunyakaa. AmAlph

Camp. Janet Fisher. MFPA

Camp, The. Mary Robinson. NOBRP

Camp 1940. Léopold Sédar Senghor. PoetW, *tr. by* Melvin Dixon

Camp Fire. Alfonsina Storni. TANSG, *tr. by* Mark McCaffrey

Camp in the Prussian Forest, A. Randall Jarrell. FaBoWar; HP; MoAmPo; OBWP; PoWW; PWW2

Camp of Souls, The. Isabella Valancy Crawford. BrAP

Camp Story. Michael S. Harper. OxAAAP

Campagna. John Peck. HarvBoo

Campaign [*with music*]. Ciaran Carson. PNI

Campaign, The. Joseph Addison. Poem to His Grace the Duke of Marlborough, A. OBWP

Campaigning. John William DeForest. "I heard the bullet's hiss." PCW

Campbell's Black Bean Soup. Kevin Young. NeAmPo

Campèa. Andrea Zanzotto. VCWP

Campesino looked at the air, A. Problems With Hurricanes. Víctor Hernández Cruz. PmAP

Campesinos. Juan Delgado. GeoHom

Campesino's Lament, The. Judith Ortiz Cofer. PueRic; TouFir

Campfire. Anna Lindtová. INSAB

Camphor Laurel. Judith Wright. BMAP

Campidoglio. Robert Garioch. OBVE

Camping Clean. Reg Saner. PoCoUp

Campo. Antonio Machado Ruiz. RaW

Campo de Batalla, El. Angel González. RaW

Campo desnudo. Sola. Cerrada. Vicente Aleixandre. RaW

Camps, The. Hayden Carruth. GifTon

Camps hold [*or held*] their distance—[of] brown chestnuts and grey smoke, The. Derek Walcott. PoetW *Fr.* Midsummer.

Campsite. Chris Willerton. TiP2

Camptown Races. Stephen Collins Foster. TCAPo

Campus on the Hill, The. W. D. Snodgrass. NoAM

Can a mote of sunlight defeat its purpose. Anew 21. Louis Zukofsky. APT-2; NAAPv.2

Can a person atone for pure bewilderment? Yom Kippur Sonnet, with a Line from Lamentations. Jacqueline Osherow. PoCho

Can a sad song take the place of crying? Sad Song. *Unknown.* CCL1, *tr. by* Burton Watson

Can acupuncture cure the sadness of organs. Toxicity. Erin Mouré. BeAl

Can America be reckoned as the country of the free? Negro Ballot, The. Lizelia Augusta Jenkins Moorer. CBWP-3

Can blot the star that shines on Paris now. (LL) Verlaine. Edwin Arlington Robinson. APN-2; NCAP

Can centre both the worlds of Heaven and Hell. (LL) Stanzas: "Often rebuked, yet always back returning." Emily Jane Brontë. BrAP; CtM; NALW; OBEV; OxBEV; PEW; VWP

Can death be faithful or the grave be just. Resurrection, The. Nathaniel Wanley. NPeEn

Can even the soundest or loftiest notion. Love in the Abstract. Robert R. Calder. EdScPo

Can even winter's crystal gems be spared. (LL) December. Christopher Pearse Cranch. APN-1; TCAPo

Can fish be wives and wives and wives and have as many as that. Gertrude Stein. OxBoAm *Fr.* Book Concluding with As A Wife Has a Cow a Love Story, A.

Can five hundred paintings be created in one stroke? Kazuaki Tanahashi. WhBo

Can get across it if I try. (LL) I May, I Might, I Must. Marianne Moore. AmFaPo; ChAP

Can God delight in such a sight. Michael Wigglesworth. NAAL-3 *Fr.* Day of Doom, The [First Section].

Can I explain this to you? Your eyes. Knife, The. Keith Douglas. NoAM

Can I forget the sweet days that have been. Days That Have Been. W. H. Davies. AngWePo

Can I forget thee? No, while mem'ry lasts. On Parting with a Friend. Mary Weston Fordham. CBWP-2

Can I get the damned words to come into my mouth. (LL) Muse. Jo Shapcott. NeBrP; StAl

Can I go on loving anyone at fifty. Book of Wisdom, The. Robert Lowell. ChIV-1

Can I look back, and view with tranquil eye. Mary Tighe. CenSon

Can I not come to Thee, my God, for these. To His Ever-Loving God. Robert Herrick. OxBEV

Can I not sin, but thou wilt be. To His Conscience. Robert Herrick. ChIV-1; NAEL-6v1; NAEL-7v1; NoP-4; NoP-5; WaAnP

Can I see another's woe. William Blake. InvLi; OxAEP-2 *Fr.* Songs of Innocence.

Can I see him. (LL) My Love Has Departed. *Chippewa Oral Tradition.* NAAL-5; OBVE, *tr. by* Frances Densmore

Can I Tell You My Love with a Portrait. Nikolai Alekseievich Klyuyev. TCRusP, *tr. by* John Glad

Can I Tempt You to a Pond Walk? James Schuyler. PoA 2002

Can invent the equal. (LL) Marine Surface, Low Overcast. Amy Clampitt. GPTC; OxBoAm

Can it be. Living Alone with Jesus. Maxine W. Kumin. UnSA

Can it be right to give what I can give? Elizabeth Barrett Browning. CenSon *Fr.* Sonnets from the Portuguese.

Can It Be True That One Lives on Earth? Nezahualcoyotl. WoPoe, *tr. by* Thelma D. Sullivan

Can it be true that one lives on earth? Can It Be True That One Lives on Earth? Nezahualcoyotl. WoPoe, *tr. by* Thelma D. Sullivan

Can it be true, that we can meet. Slumbering Passion. Josephine D. Henderson Heard. CBWP-4

Can jamrock. Is Culcha Weapon? Brian Meeks. WaCA

Can life's best consciousness of joy. Questioning. Henrietta Cordelia Ray. CBWP-3

Can love exist without mortality? Love and the Years. Alfred Allen. IrLP

Can man forget this story? (LL) Hymn[e] on the Nativity [*or* Nativitie] of My Saviour, A. Ben Jonson. ChIV-2; SacPr

Can nothing serve thy turne but summum ius. Upon a Booke Written at the Beginning of the Parliament 1640. Anna Norman Ley. EMWP

Can nothing settle my uncertain breast. Galatians 6.14. Francis Quarles. ChIV-2

Can one make works which are not works of "art"? Speculations. Marcel Duchamp. PFTM-1

Can one recognize a dream as comic? I mean from inside the dream interpret an image and laugh? Gospel According to How We Throw Stones. Catherine Imbriglio. IAoNAP

Can one take captives by writing. Lyn Hejinian. FTOS *Fr.* Guard, The.

Can Pigeons Be Heroes? Ruth L. Schwartz. WiU

Can seriously affect your heart. (LL) This Poem. Elma Mitchell. BeAl; PoCu

Can someone / Called Daughter of a Stone. Rāmprasād Sen. SinGod, *tr. by* Rachel Fell McDermott

Can someone make my simple wish come true? Lonely Hearts. Wendy Cope. OBCoV; WaAnP

Can still propose the old labors. (LL) Heroes. Robert Creeley. NoP-4; NoP-5; OxBoAm

Can the bald lie? The nature of skin says not. Hairless. Jo Shapcott. PoCu

Can the German language crack and snore and rumble, thunder. German Language, The. Friedrich von Logau. GePo, *tr. by* George C. Schoolfield

Can the lover share his soul. Epithalamium. Walter James Turner. OBMV

Can the Mole Take. Cecil Day Lewis. OBMV

Can there be a collision between picture and application? Steve McCaffery. FTOS *Fr.* Evoba.

Can there be a moon in heaven to-night. Isabelle. James Hogg. NPBRoP

Can these movements which move themselves. Belly Dancer. Diane Wakoski. NALW; NoAM

Can this be justice. Bible, *O.T.* AHA *Fr.* Psalms [David Rosenberg Adaption].

Can This Be Love? Paul James. ReLy

Can this decay, but is beginning ever. (LL) Doing, a filthy pleasure is, and short. Petronius Arbiter. ErotSp; NPeEn; OBVE; OxBEV; WoPoe, *tr. by* Ben Jonson

Can this hard earth break wide. In Topaz. Toyo Suyemoto. ASA; NAAPv.2

Can this sin live. (LL) Slaveship[s]. Lucille Clifton. ESEAA; OPRER

Can Tie Shoes but Won't. Thomas Lux. AmAlph

Can turn a heart to dust. (LL) Longing for Someone. Li Po. CrYelRi; ErotSp, *tr. by* Sam Hamill

Can Vei La Lauzeta Mover. Bernard [*or* Bernart] de Ventadour *or* Ventadorn. APSN, *tr. by* Paul Blackburn

Can we imagine our rewards. (LL) Picture of Little J. A. in a Prospect of Flowers, The. John Ashbery. PmAP; WaAnP

Can we not force from wid[d]owed poetry. Elegy upon the Death of the Dean of [St.] Paul's, Dr. John Donne, An. Thomas Carew. BASC; CABP; CavPo; NAEL-6v1; NAEL-7v1; NoP-4; NoP-5; WaAnP

Can we slip away. Escape. Colette Ni Ghallchóir. NIrP, *tr. by* the author

Can We Talk? Laini Mataka. BtF

Can you break it? move. (LL) Twist, The. Alfred B. Spellman. EGAG; ISC

Can you claim to win. Nabíncandra Cakrabartī. SinGod, *tr. by* Rachel Fell McDermott

Can you feel the swell. Early Triangles. Ron Padgett. FTOS; NYP2

Can you hear it. Cricket at Central California Women's Facility. Dixie Salazar. GeoHom

Can you hear it/ a *faint echo/ vespers from the book of ancestry/ once bound.* What we have lost. Duriel Harris. SpirFl

Can you hear it? Somebody's reading a poem to me over the telephone. Somebody Consoles Me with a Poem. Sandor Csoori. GifTon; TAPaP, *tr. by* Len Roberts and László Vértes

Can you hear me? Under my name I am. Gloria Gervitz. MirDau *Fr.* Yiskor.

Can you hear the owl? Sitting Alone One Cold June Night Before an Empty Whiskey Bottle a Coffee Pot & an Oil Stove with a Window through which I Watched the Flames. James Koller. AHA

Can You Imagine. Artur Miedzyrzecki. PoSu

Can you imagine the air filled with smoke? Smoke. Philip Levine. MakPoe

Can you keep the unquiet physical-soul from straying, hold fast to the Unity, and never quit it? Lao Tzu. CCL1 *Fr.* Way and Its Power, The.

Can you recall the playful brushwood fire. Fires. József Kiss. IQMS, *tr. by* Peter Zollman

Can you tell me where my car is. How Fast. Martha Rhodes. NAPBL

Can you tell that I'm unhappy. Ain't It a Shame About Mame. Johnny Burke. ReLy

Can you type? Jake said. Working at the Wholesale Curtain Showroom. Ed Ochester. SUP

Cana. Thomas Merton. ChIV-2

Cana. Peter Steele. GI

Canada. Matthew Zapruder. LegDan

Canadian Authors Meet, The. Francis Reginald Scott. BrAP

Canadian Boat Song, A. Thomas Moore. TreFP

Canadian Boat Song ("Fair these broad meads—these hoary woods are grand.") *Unknown.* OBEV

Canadian Boat Song ("Listen to me, as when ye heard our father.") *Unknown.* OBEV

Canadian Love Song. Alden Nowlan. StAl

Canal Bank Walk. Patrick Kavanagh. MoBrPo; NAMCP V.1; NoAM; NoP-4; NoP-5

Canal flows quietly, The. Soliloquy. Eugenio Montale. ItPo, *tr. by* Gayle Ridinger

Canal Street. Bernard Heidsieck. *tr. by* Nicholas Zürbrugg

Canal Street 33/14. PFTM-2, *tr. by* Nicholas Zürbrugg

Canal Street 39/27. PFTM-2, *tr. by* Nicholas Zürbrugg

Canals, The. The liquor coming through. Joshua Beckman. LegDan

Canary. Rita Dove. ESEAA; LoL; OxAAAP; SeSe; VCAP

Canary. William Heyen. PfSP

Canary Man and You, The. Rick Alley. AmPoNex

Canberra in April. J. R. Rowland. NOBAu

Cancellation of a Construction Project. David Huerta. RMCMP, *tr. by* Mark Schafer

Cancer and Nova. Hyam Plutzik. AmFaPo

Cancer ate her like horse piss eats deep snow, The. (LL) Funeral, The. Norman Dubie. NAMCP V.2; NoAM

Cancer Diagnosis. Marjorie Maddox. IaFF

Cancer Hospital, The. Roy Fuller.

Your Absence. OxBSo

Cancer Winter. Marilyn Hacker. RA

Canción de Despedida. Emilio Prados. RaW

Canción del Naranjo Seco. Federico García Lorca. RaW *Fr.* Canciones para Terminar.

Canción: "Me colmó el sol del poniente." Juan Ramón Jiménez. RaW

Canción: "Puente de mi soledad." Emilio Prados. RaW

Canción: "Quisiera cantar: ser flor." Rafael Alberti. RaW

Cancion: "When I am the sky." Denise Levertov. NALW

Cancionero *Diario Poético* 1928–1936. Miguel de Unamuno.

199. RaW

206. RaW

312. RaW

313. RaW

Canciones. Kenneth Zamora Damacion. OPRER

Canciones para Terminar. Federico García Lorca.

Canción del Naranjo Seco. RaW

Candelaria and the Sea Turtle. Gladys Cardiff. HATNAP

Candescent Lies the Air. Rosalía de Castro. NAWM-7v2, *tr. by* S. Griswold Morley

Candescent lies the air. Candescent Lies the Air. Rosalía de Castro. NAWM-7v2, *tr. by* S. Griswold Morley

Candid Camera. Angelo Lumelli. ItPo, *tr. by* Gayle Ridinger

Candid Man, The. Stephen Crane. MoAmPo

Candid, Warhol. Campbell's Black Bean Soup. Kevin Young. NeAmPo

Candish deriv'd from Noble Parentage. Epitaph for Richard Cavendish, Engraved on his Monument in Hornsey Church. Margaret Russell Clifford, Countess of Cumberland. EMWP

Candle. Penelope Rosemont. SurWo

Candle, A. Sir John Suckling. BASC

Candle, The. Hsiao Yen [*or* Emperor Wu of Liang]. CCL1, *tr. by* Anne Birrell

Candle, The. Francis Ponge. MotU, *tr. by* Cid Corman

Candle, The. Francis Ponge. WED, *tr. by* Robert Bly

Candle at Canterbury, A. Tessa Rose Chester. MFPA

Candle burned out, my boat is windblown, The. Dreaming of My Wife. Yüan Chěn. CrYelRi, *tr. by* Sam Hamill

Candle burns in the room, The. Yi Kae. CATKP, *tr. by* Peter H. Lee

Candle, climb upward. Just for Today. Ervin Drake. ReLy

Candle Dies, A. Wei Chuang. CCL1, *tr. by* Lois Fusek

Candle dies, and incense fades by the closed curtains, A. Candle Dies, A. Wei Chuang. CCL1, *tr. by* Lois Fusek

Candle for the ship's breakfast, A. Candle Poem. Helen Dunmore. BeAl

Candle in a Glass, A. Marge Piercy. TaR

Candle in a long street, A. Hamra Night. Sa'di Yusuf. FaBoWar, *tr. by* Abdullah Al-Udhari

Candle in my hand, A. (LL) Night in Al-Hamra. Sa'di Yusuf. BeAl; PoAgWa, *tr. by* Khaled Mattawa

Candle in the bathroom burns all night, The. Courtly Love. T. R. Hummer. WaAnP

Candle Indoors, The. Gerard Manley Hopkins. ChIV-2; OxAEP-2

Candle light blue banners incense. Land O'Lakes, Wisconsin: Vajrayana Seminary. Allen Ginsberg. BBASP

Candle light shines low on the dark window, The. For My Brother Hagok. Hŏ Nansŏrhŏn. WoPoe, *tr. by* Kichung Kim

Candle lit in darkness of black waters, A. On the Lake. Victoria Mary Sackville-West. OBMV

Candle on the long road, A. Night in Al-Hamra. Sa'di Yusuf. BeAl; PoAgWa, *tr. by* Khaled Mattawa

Candle Poem. Helen Dunmore. BeAl

Candle that went berserk, The. Search Party. Mary Ruefle. AmAlph

Candle-flowers two-fold flames like fragrant trees. On the Third Day I Wait on the Emperor at a Banquet and Describe the Reflection of the Candles in the Serpentine. Yu Chien-wu. CCL1, *tr. by* John Frodsham

Candle-grease congealed, dark-streaked with wick-soot. Electric Light. Seamus Heaney. NAMCP V.2

Candlelight. Tony Hoagland. PoDa

Candlelight Dinner. Oscar Hahn. PML, *tr. by* James Hoggard

Candles. Constantine P. Cavafy. BeAl, *tr. by* Edmund Keeley and Philip Sherrard

Candles are burning, The. Poet's Resurrection, The. Jenő Dsida. IQMS, *tr. by* Peter Zollman

Candle's Fly, The. Moses Glyn Jones. BBMWP, *tr. by* Mike Jenkins

Candles. Red tulips, ninety cents the bunch. Evening Musicale. Phyllis McGinley. AmWit; OBCoV

Candles splutter; and the kettle hums, The. Still Small Voice, The. Abraham Moses Klein. IFF

Candlestick, The. Jaroslav Seifert. AF *Fr.* Bombing of the Town of Kralupy, The.

Candor. John Graham-Pole. BloBone

Candour of the gods is in thy gaze, The. George Santayana. APN-2 *Fr.* Sonnets.

Candour spurned, and art rewarded. (LL) January, 1795. Mary Robinson. NAEL-7v2; NPBRoP; OxBEV; WoRP

Candy. Mack David, Alex Kramer and Joan Whitney. ReLy

Candy / Is dandy. Reflections on Ice-breaking. Ogden Nash. APT-2; NAAPv.2; NBLV; NIL-7; NoP-4; NoP-5

Candy Lady, The. Laura Boss. UnSA

Candy Man, The. Leslie Bricusse. ReLy

Candy man was guid tae me, The. Candy Man, The. *Unknown.* FaBoVe

Candy Poem, The. Amy Lingafelter. FreRad

Candy-throated Carib, The. *Unknown.* SonAtl, *tr. by* Lester Browne and Myrna Teirrel

Canefield and the Sea, The. João Cabral de Melo Neto. TCLAP, *tr. by* Louis Simpson

Canicula. Mary Kinzie. FFC

Canine Immortality. Robert Southey. DiBP

Canis Major. Robert Frost. MoAmPo

Canker'd, cursed creature, crabbed, corbit kittle,. Sir Thomas Maitland's Satyr upon Sir Niel Laing. Sir Thomas Maitland. NePenScot

Canna. Takahashi Shinkichi. ZenPo, *tr. by* Takashi Ikemoto and Lucien Stryk

Cannery Town in August. Lorna Dee Cervantes. NAMCP V.2; NoAM

Cannibal. Thom Gunn. NOxBChV *Fr.* Three for Children.

Cannibal Hymn, The. *Unknown. tr. by* Tony Barnstone, Haixin Xu and Willis Barnstone

"Sky is a dark bowl, the stars die and fall, The." WoPoe, *tr. by* Tony Barnstone, Haixin Xu and Willis Barnstone

Cannibal Women in the Avocado Jungle of Death. Maureen Seaton. ExTi

Canning Cellar, Early Sixties. Judith Vollmer. SweBea

Cannon Hill. Sandra Hochman. YaYoPo

Cannot Be. Susan Howe. NAMCP V.2 *Fr.* Thorow.

Cannot for less be told. (LL) Elixir [*or* Elixer], The. George Herbert. BASC; NoP-4; NoP-5; NOSC; SacPr

Cannot quite expect that. You ain't ruined, said she. (LL) Ruined Maid, The. Thomas Hardy. FaBoVe; HeIP-4; NAEL-6v2; NAEL-7v2; NBLV; NIL-7; NoP-5; TFi; TRP

Cannot, the tempest tells me, disappoint. (LL) Rain: "Rain, midnight rain, nothing but the wild rain." Edward Thomas. FaBoWar; GPTC; HarvBoo; MakPoe; NAEL-6v2; NAEL-7v2; NAMCP V.1; NoP-4; NoP-5; NPeEn; OBWP; OxBEV; PoAgWa; PoWW; WaAnP

Canoe picks up speed, The. August Horizon. Dennis Nurkse. NevBe

Canoeing, The. Russell Edson. MotU

Canoeing Up Cabarga Creek. Philip Whalen.

"Silence in the middle of traffic." Eno

Canoer, The. Diane Wakoski. HeIP-4

Canon 4. Cristina Campo. CItWP *Fr.* Tiger's Absence.

Canonization, The. John Donne. BASC; BrAP; CABP; FaBoVe; FSCP; NAEL-6v1; NAEL-7v1; NAWM-5v1; NIL-7; NIP-4; NoP-4; NoP-5; NOSC; NPeEn; PBRV; PoPoPo; SoSe-8; TFi; TRP; WaAnP; WoPoe

Canon's Yeoman's Tale, The. Geoffrey Chaucer. *Fr.* Canterbury Tales, The.

Canopic old Egyptian jugs. Instructions for Your New Osiris. Lorenzo Thomas. PmAP

Canopy of nerve ends. Epiderm. Michael Dransfield. BMAP

Canst thou draw out Leviathan with an hook[e]? Bible, *O.T.* OBVE *Fr.* Job.

Can'st thou forget, O! Idol of my soul! To Phaon. Mary Robinson. CenSon; RWP

Canst thou forget, oh idol of my soul. Mary Robinson. NPBRoP *Fr.* Sappho and Phaon.

Canst thou, so keen of feeling! urge my fate. Rush to the Lakes, The [*or* Anna Matilda]. Robert Merry. STuOW

Can't be a model, there'd be times I. Alan Wearne. BMAP *Fr.* Nightmarkets, The.

Can't find what you can't see / can you? (LL) American History. Michael S. Harper. ESEAA; NAAL-5; NAMCP V.2; NoAM; PoPoPo

Cant. 5.6 & c. Elizabeth Singer. ChIV-1

Can't Help Lovin' Dat Man. Oscar Hammerstein, II. ReLy

Can't let go of it. to live is to drive. to have it function. I Live for My Car. Wanda Coleman. SUP

Can't mouse in. (LL) Popcorn-can cover. Lorine Niedecker. NAAPv.2; NAMCP V.1

Can't Oh. Del Ray Cross. FreRad

"Can't see out of my left eye." Spinning. Alfred Wellington Purdy. NoAM

Can't seem to wake you, kid, guess it. Body Beside the Ties, The. Kenneth Patchen. CLPP

Can't sleep. Taboo. Cherryl "Blue." Floyd-Miller. BtF

Can't swim; uses credit cards and pills to combat. Difference Between Pepsi and Coke, The. David Lehman. PmAP; ReTh

Can't Tell. Nellie Wong. ItWoWo; LTA; OpBo

Can't use no teenager, especially. Enactment, The. Rita Dove. FuFl

Can't We Be Friends? Paul James. ReLy

Can't we two go walkin' together. Heather on the Hill, The. Alan Jay Lerner. ReLy

Can't wring blood from. Lepidoptery. James Sherry. FTOS

Can't you just see them. Radio Cricket. Gavin Ewart. RWPCtW

Can't You See? Segun Akinlolu. NeNiPo

Cantares. Juan Gregorio Regino. RMCMP, *tr. by* Eliot Weinberger

Cantares. Juan Gregorio Regino. RMCMP

Cantares Mexicanos. *Unknown.*

   Chalcan Female Song. PFTM-1

Cantata. Jack Spicer. APSN

Cantata, 8: "Early March, trickle and rush of ice melt in mountains." Katrina Roberts. NevBe

Cante Jondo. Yusef Komunyakaa. BodElec

Canter has two stride patterns, one on the right lead and one on the left, each a mirror image of the other, The. Flying Change, The. Henry Taylor. InGu

Canterbury Tales, The. Geoffrey Chaucer.

   Canon's Yeoman's Tale, The.

     "Also ther was a disciple of Plato." SacPr

   Chaucer's Retraction. NAEL-6v1; NAEL-7v1

   (Cock and the Hen, The.) OBNV

     Chauntecleer. OWoS

     Rape of Chanticleer, The. DiBP

     "There liv'd, as Authors tell, in Days of Yore." OBVE

   Franklin's Introduction, The. NAEL-6v1

   Franklin's Prologue, The. NAEL-6v1

   Franklin's Tale, The. NAEL-6v1

   General Prologue, The. NAEL-6v1; NAEL-7v1; NoP-5; WaAnP

     "Knight [*or* Knyght] ther[e] was, and that a worthy man, A." UV

     Monk, A. OBCoV

     Parson and the Plowman Described, The. SacPr

     Pitiful Prioress, The. DiBP

     Prioresse, A. BrAP; NPeEn

     "Somonour was ther with us in that place, A." OBCoV

   Knight's Tale, The.

     "But in the dome of mighty Mars the red." OBWP

     Lycurgus' Alauns. DiBP

     "On t'other side there stood destruction bare." FaBoWar, *tr. by* John Dryden

     Saturn. NPeEn

     Temple of Mars, The. NPeEn

     "Ther saugh I first the derke ymaginyng." PoAgWa

   Man of Law's Epilogue, The. NAEL-7v1

   Manciple's Tale, The.

     Cage, The. OWoS

     "Lat take a cat, and fostre him [*or* hym] wel[l] with milk." TriCat

   Miller's Prologue, The. NAEL-6v1; NAEL-7v1

Miller's [*or* Milleres] Tale, The.   NAEL-6v1; NAEL-7v1
  Alysoun.   NPeEn
Nun's Priest's [*or* Nonne Preestes] Tale, The.   NAEL-6v1; NAEL-7v1
  Chauntecleer.   OWoS
  Rape of Chanticleer, The.   DiBP
  "There liv'd, as Authors tell, in Days of Yore."   OBVE
Pardoner's Introduction, The.   NAEL-6v1; NAEL-7v1; WaAnP
Pardoner's Prologue, The.   NAEL-6v1; NAEL-7v1; WaAnP
Pardoner's Tale, The.   NAEL-6v1; NAEL-7v1; WaAnP
  "These [*or* Thise] rioteres [*or* riotoures] thre[e] of which[e] I tell[e]."   NPeEn; OBNV
  "Whan they han goon nat fully half a mile."   OxBEV
Parson's Introduction, The.   NAEL-6v1; NAEL-7v1
Wife of Bath, The.
  "If poor (you say) she drains her husband's purse."   OBSV
Wife of Bath's Prologue, The.   NAEL-6v1; NAEL-7v1; NoP-5
  "Experience, though noon auctoritee."   OxBEV; RACG
  "My fourthe housbonde was a revelour."   NPeEn
Wife of Bath's Tale, The.   NAEL-6v1; NAEL-7v1; NoP-5
Cantica: Our Lord Christ: Of Order.   Saint Francis of Assisi.   OBVE, *tr. by* Dante Gabriel Rossetti
Canticle.   David Shapiro.   OxBoAm
Canticle for Abba Jacob, A.   Marilyn Nelson Waniek.   FFC
Canticle for Good Friday.   Geoffrey Hill.   ChIV-2; UpMys
Canticle: "Let others speak." [*with music*].   Joseph Bruchac.   ViWalt
Canticle of the Brother Sun, The.   Saint Francis of Assisi.   BBASP, *tr. by* Regis J. Armstrong and Ignatius C. Brady
Canticle of the Creatures.   Saint Francis of Assisi.   WoPoe, *tr. by* James Schuyler
Canticle of the Void, The.   Paul Murray.   InvLi
Canticle of the Way.   Xuanjue.
  Heart's Mirror Clear.   CCL1, *tr. by* Jerome P. Seaton
  Let Them Mock!   CCL1, *tr. by* Jerome P. Seaton
  One Moon Seen, The.   CCL1, *tr. by* Jerome P. Seaton
  Roar of the Lion.   CCL1, *tr. by* Jerome P. Seaton
Canticle: "Sharks tooth is perfect for biting, The. The Intent."   Michael McClure.   CalPo
Canticle to the Waterbirds, A.   William Everson.   APSN; APT-2; GeoHom
Cantiga de Amigo.   Pero Meogo.   WoPoe, *tr. by* Keith Bosley
Cantinas, The.   Malcolm Lowry.
  Delirium in Vera Cruz.   NoP-4; NoP-5
Cantonese Love-Songs.   *tr. by* Cecil Clementi
  Lament for Fortune's Frailty, A.   ColAnChi, *tr. by* Cecil Clementi
Cantor.   Guillaume Apollinaire.   CuPo
Cantos.   Ezra Pound.
  Canto 1.   BrAP; NAAPv.2; NAMCP V.1; NoP-5; WaAnP
  Canto 2.   APT-1; MoAmPo; NAAPv.2; NAMCP V.1; NoAM; NoP-5
  Canto 4.   APT-1
  Canto 7.   NAMCP V.1; NoAM
  Canto 13.   APT-1; NAAPv.2; OxBoAm; WaAnP
  Canto 14.
    "Slough of unamiable liars."   NAMCP V.1
  Canto 17.   APT-1; OBMV
  Canto 30.   HarvBoo
  Canto 32.   PFTM-1
  Canto 36.   APT-1; OBVE
  Canto 45.   APT-1; ColAP; HarvBoo; NAAL-5; NAAPv.2; NAMCP V.1; NoP-5; OxBoAm
  Canto 47.   APT-1
  Canto 49.   APT-1; PFTM-1
  Canto 51.   PFTM-1
  Canto 74.
    "Enormous tragedy of the dream in the peasant's bent, The."   AF
  Canto 80.
    "Tudor indeed is gone and every rose."   WoPoe
  Canto 81.   APT-1; HarvBoo; NAMCP V.1; NoAM; RaBo
    "What thou lovest well remains."   OxBoAm; RaBo; WaAnP; WoPoe
    "Yet / Ere the season died a-cold."   NAAPv.2
  Canto 83.
    "Nor can who has passed a month in the death cells."   PWW2
  Canto 90.   APSN; APT-1
  Canto 115.
    "Scientists are in terror, The."   APSN
  Canto 116.   APSN; APT-1; NAAPv.2; NAMCP V.1; PFTM-2
  Canto 117 et seq., Notes for.   APT-1
Cantus Amoris 2.   Richard Rolle of Hampole.   SacPr

Cantus Troili.   Geoffrey Chaucer. *See* Song of Troylus, The.
Canvas square, The.   At the Gwen John Exhibition.   Charles McDonald.   NLP
Canyon, Texas Sestina.   E. A. Mares.   ICANM
Canzone: "Consider the three functions of the tongue."   Marilyn Hacker.   NoAM
Canzone: "Ganz."   Ernst Jandl.   OnScMo
Canzone: "No better lost than any other woman."   Marilyn Hacker.   NoAM
Canzone: Of the Gentle Heart.   Guido Guinicelli.   OBVE, *tr. by* Dante Gabriel Rossetti
Canzonet.   Mary Robinson.   NOBRP
Canzonetta: A Bitter Song to His Lady.   Pier Moronelli da Fiorenza.   OBVE, *tr. by* Dante Gabriel Rossetti
Cao-chong: Hopper-Grass.   *Unknown*.   CCL1, *tr. by* Ezra Pound
Cap and Bells, The: ("Jester walked in the garden, The.")   William Butler Yeats.   MoBrPo; NAMCP V.1; NoAM
Cap and Bells, The: ("Queen was beloved by a jester, A.") .   William Butler Yeats.   MoBrPo; NoAM
Cape Ann.   T. S. Eliot.   NAEL-6v2; NoAM *Fr.* Landscapes.
Cape Breton.   Elizabeth Bishop.   Coast
Cape Breton in Autumn.   David Helwig.   Coast
Cape Cod.   George Santayana.   APN-2
Cape Enrage.   Lynn Davies.   Coast
Cape Hatteras.   Hart Crane.   MoAmPo *Fr.* Bridge, The.
Cape of Good Hope, The.   Jean Cocteau.   CuPo
Cape of Wild Flies, A.   Bernard Bador.   ConPit, *tr. by* Clayton Eshleman
Capel Calvin.   Idris Davies.   AngWePo
Capelin Scull.   Michael Crummey.   Coast
Capernaum.   Lewis Spence.   EdScPo
Capital.   John Tripp.   AngWePo
Capital, The.   W. H. Auden.   NAMCP V.1
Capital is a cave for wandering knights, The.   First Poem of Wandering Immortals.   Kuo P'o.   CCL1, *tr. by* John Frodsham
Capital ladies are gloomy this year, The.   Dames of Washington.   Grace Duffie Boylan.   ArBi
Capital Punishment.   Sherman Alexie.   PrTe
Capital Punishment.   Nina Cassian.   PoSu, *tr. by* Nina Cassian
Capital ship for an ocean trip, A.   Charles Edward Carryl.   GoPo; NBLV *Fr.* Davy and the Goblin.
Capitalist Poem #36.   Campbell McGrath.   NAPBL
Capitalist Projections.   Brenda Coultas.   HeMarv
Capitalization of "Clue", The.   Ray Ragosta.   OnScMo
Capitals.   Raymond Garlick.   AngWePo
Capitol, The.   Innokenty Fiodorovich Annensky.   WoPoe, *tr. by* Stephen Berg
Cap. 10 Lib. 2.   Blas de Otero.   RaW
Caporiestas dance in la Marqueta Modelo square.   Saudades.   Jacqueline Johnson.   BtF
Capper Kaplinski at the North Side Cue Club.   Hayden Carruth.   MoASP
Capriccio of Roman Ruins and Sculpture with Figures, A.   J. D. McClatchy.   GS
Capriccios.   Jaime Sabines.   TCLAP, *tr. by* Claudine-Marie D'Angelo
Caprichosa.   Angelina Weld Grimké.   PoBW
Capricorn pear tree, A.   Roy Kiyooka.   NLPA *Fr.* Pear Tree Pomes.
Capstone.   Ethan Paquin.   LegDan
Capsule.   John Giorno.   AHA
Capt. Smith and Pocahontas [*with music*].   Eloise Bibb.   CBWP-4
Captain Amasa Delano's Dilemma.   Yusef Komunyakaa.   BodElec
Captain America at Home.   Jarret Keene.   RWB
Captain calls his crew to the deck, The.   Landing of Rochambeau, The.   Michael Davidson.   FTOS; OnScMo
Captain Carpenter rose up in his prime.   Captain Carpenter.   John Crowe Ransom.   APT-1; FuPo; MoAmPo; NAAPv.2; NoAM; OxBoAm; TRP; WoPoe
Captain Cook.   *Aborigine Oral Tradition.*   NOBAu, *tr. by* Percy Mumbulla
Captain Fox.   Robert Greacen.   PNI
Captain Fox sits reading metaphysics.   Captain Fox.   Robert Greacen.   PNI
Captain Lavender.   Medbh McGuckian.   NAMCP V.2
Captain oaks moves.   Captain Oaks.   Reed Bye.   AHA
Captain or Colonel, or Knight in Arms.   When the Assault Was Intended to the City.   John Milton.   OxBSo
Captain Quiros and Mr William Lane.   Terra Australis.   Douglas Stewart.   NOBAu
Captain Reece.   William Schwenck Gilbert.   OBCoV
Captain scans the ruffled zone, The.   Edward Edwin Foot.   VerBaPo *Fr.* Homeward-Bound Passenger Ship, The.
Captain scans the ruffled zone, The.   Edward Edwin Foot.   STuOW *Fr.* Homeward-Bound Passenger Ship, The.
Captain Stratton's Fancy.   John Masefield.   MoBrPo; OBEV

Captain, The. Francis Beaumont and John Fletcher.
  Away, Delights. OBEV

Captain, what do you think, I asked. Military Creed, The. Ernest Crosby. FaBoWar

Captain Who Walks on His Deck, The. Jelaluddin Rumi. WED, *tr.* by Robert Bly

Cap'tain Zombi. René Depestre. PFTM-2 *Fr.* Rainbow for the Christian West, A.

Captains among the ghosts, heroes among the Dead! (LL) Hymn to the Fallen. *Unknown.* FaBoWar; OBWP, *tr.* by Arthur Waley

Captains Courageous. Frank O'Hara. FTOS

Captain's Log. Todd Colby. HeMarv

Caption for a Miniature. Joanne Kyger. BB

Caption for "The Child from Vallecas" by Velázquez. León Felipe. RaW, *tr.* by Julio de la Torre

Captive. Rose Terry Cooke. NAAPv.1

Captive. Theognis. WoPoe, *tr.* by Richmond Lattimore

Captive and Able. Hoa Nguyen. WANABP

Captive Dove, The. Anne Brontë. VWP

Captive Escaped in the Wilds of America, The. Addressed to the Hon. Mrs. O'Neill. Charlotte Smith. CenSon

Captive is flung onto the blazing coals, The. Festival of Xócotl Huetzi or Tenth Month. Carla Faesler Bremer. SPV, *tr.* by Jen Hofer

Captive mahogany of a private Roman, The. Roman Elegies. Joseph Brodsky. VCWP, *tr.* by the author

Captive of the White City, The. Ina Coolbrith. NAAPv.1

Captives, bound in iron bands. Broken Chain, The. Dora Greenwell. VWP

Captive's Song. *Unknown.* APN-2, *tr.* by Fannie Reed Giffen

Captivity. Louise Erdrich. AmWaPo; HATNAP; NAMCP V.2; NoAM

Captivity. Amy Levy. ViWPN

Captivity, The. Oliver Goldsmith.
  Cause and Effect. STuOW
  Entry of the Villagers. STuOW
  (Memory.) OBEV
  Sombre Moment, A. STuOW

Capture of Larache, The. Luis de Góngora y Argote. SpanPo, *tr.* by Frances Fletcher

Captured Goddess, The. Amy Lowell. NAAL-5; NAAPv.2

Car, a girl, a community of believers, A. (LL) Some Kind of Crazy. Major L. Jackson. FuFl; SpirFl

Car Has Fallen from a Bridge, A. Kevin Prufer. LegDan

Car / I give you over to. Car Wash. Myra Cohn Livingston. NTCP

Car je suis La Belle France. (LL) Deodand, The. Anthony Hecht. NAMCP V.2; NoAM

Car locked, I started home across the grass. Crossing Lincoln Park. Karl Shapiro. IllVoic

Car lurches on goat paths, The. Returning North. Gjertrud Schnackenberg. BeAl

Car Music. Reed Bye. AHA

Car stopped by my house, A. Tune, The. Yousif al-Sa'igh. IrPoTo, *tr.* by Saadi A. Simawe

Car, then he moves, opening door suddenly, The. Edward. Honor Moore. WiU

Car Wash. Myra Cohn Livingston. NTCP

Carafe, that is a blind glass, A. Gertrude Stein. MoWP; NAAPv.2; NAMCP V.1 *Fr.* Tender Buttons.

Caravaggio. Michelangelo Coviello. *tr.* by Gayle Ridinger
  Self-Portrait. ItPo, *tr.* by Gayle Ridinger

Caravaggio: Swirl and Vortex. Larry Levis. GeoHom

Caravan [*with music*]. Michael Longley. ModIr; PNI

Caravan heading east on Highway 6, A. Highway 6. Timothy Liu. AmPoNex

Carbon Dioxide. Ágnes Nemes Nagy. IQMS, *tr.* by Adam Makkai

Carcass, A. Charles Baudelaire. NAWM-7v2, *tr.* by James McGowan

Carcass, A. Charles Baudelaire. SxFrPo, *tr.* by James McGowan

Card table in the library stands ready, A. James Merrill. NAMCP V.2; NoAM; NoP-4; NoP-5; OxBoAm; VCAP *Fr.* Book of Ephraim, The.

Card-Dealer, The. Dante Gabriel Rossetti. BrAP

Cardiff Castle. Taliesin Williams.
  "Tourist, as he views the place, The." AngWePo

Cardinal Ideograms. May Swenson. NoP-4; NoP-5

Cardinal Newman. Christina Georgina Rossetti. NAEL-6v2; NAEL-7v2

Cardinals in a Shower at Union Square. Stanley Plumly. BodElec

Cardio Room, Young Women's Christian Association. Karen Solie. OpeFie

Card-Players, The. Philip Larkin. BLT

Cardplayers, The. Jack Spicer. APSN

Cards and Kisses. John Lyly. *See* Cupid and My Campaspe Played.

Cards are shuffled and the deck, The. Patrick Kavanagh. NPeEn *Fr.* Great Hunger, The.

Cards were sent, The. Registration of 1918. *Unknown.* NAAPv.2

Care about Wales? Well, I do and I don't. This One. T. H. Parry-Williams. BBMWP, *tr.* by Emyr Humphreys

Care awey, awey, awey / Care awey for evermore! *Unknown.* OHMEL

Care awey, awey, awey / Murnyng awey. *Unknown.* OHMEL

Care of Sheep, the labours of the Loom, The. Fleece, The. John Dyer.

Care-Charmer Sleep. Bartholomew Griffin. NoSic *Fr.* Fidessa, More Chaste than Kind[e].

Care-charmer Sleep[e], son[ne] of the sable Night. Samuel Daniel. GSo; NAEL-6v1; NAEL-7v1; NIP-4; NoP-4; NoP-5; NoSic; NPeEn; OxAEP-1; OxBEV; OxBSo; TFi *Fr.* Sonnets to Delia.

Care-charmer sleepe, sweet ease in restles miserie. Bartholomew Griffin. NoSic *Fr.* Fidessa, More Chaste than Kind[e].

Career in vestige management, A. Manufacturing. Rae Armantrout. AWPTFC

Careers. Imamu Amiri Baraka. TRP

Careful! *Unknown.* SonAtl, *tr.* by Haike Frank and Abioseh Michael Porter

Careful, hold on, do not be discouraged! *Unknown.* SLW, *tr.* by Marjolijn De Jager, Sayd Bahodin Majrouh and André Velter

Careful Husband, The. The Earl of Longford. IrLP

Careful suburban dead turn their backs, The. Sacrificial Wolf. Anne Rouse. MFPA; NeBl

Careful that these *Frisbees.* Giulia Niccolai. ItPo *Fr.* Frisbees.

Careful the things you say. Children Will Listen. Stephen Sondheim. TWF

Careful[l] observers may foretel[l] the hour. Description of a City Shower, A. Jonathan Swift. BrAP; HeIP-4; NAEL-6v1; NAEL-7v1; NIL-7; NoP-4; NoP-5; NPeEn; OBSV; WaAnP

Carefully dissected her knee. (LL) Miss Gee. W. H. Auden. UV; WaAnP

Carefully measuring out the pace. (LL) Girl on a Tractor. Joyce Sutphen. GoPo; IPoFL

Carefully section by section. Project. Piera Oppezzo. CItWP, *tr.* by Cinzia Sartini Blum and Lara Trubowitz

Careless Content. John Byrom. OBCoV

Careless Love. Stanley Kunitz. FaBoWar; PWW2

Careless man, my father. Tenth-Year Elegy. Neal Bowers. PoA 2002

Careless Talk. Mark Hollis. NBLV

Carentan O Carentan. Louis Simpson. AmWaPo; OBWP; PWW2; WoPoe

Caress in the dark, A. Handkerchief Kiss. Menna Elfyn. MoWP

Cargoes [*with music*]. John Masefield. BLPJKO; BRP; CABP; MoBrPo; OBEV; OBMV; TFi

Caria and Philistia considered. Cry Faugh! Robert Graves. MoBrPo

Caribbean Islands. Michel-Ange Hyppolite. OGAHCP, *tr.* by Boadiba and Jack Hirschman

Caribbean Sea. Gabriela Mistral. TANSG, *tr.* by Maria Giachetti [*or* Jacketti] and Maria Jacketti

Cariboo Horses, The. Alfred Wellington Purdy. BrAP; HeIP-4

Carillonneur. Ricardo M. de Ungria. ReBoTo

Caring for My Lover. Jelaluddin Rumi. WoPoe, *tr.* by Willis Barnstone

Caritas. Olga Broumas. CAP-8
  "With the clear." WiU

Carl Hamblin. Edgar Lee Masters. OBSV *Fr.* Spoon River Anthology.

Carlos bites the end of his pencil. Lost Parrot, The. Naomi Shihab Nye. TiP2

Carlos, calm down, love. don't Kill Yourself. Carlos Drummond de Andrade. WoPoe, *tr.* by Mark Strand

Carlos, keep calm, love. don't Kill Yourself. Carlos Drummond de Andrade. PoCho; TCLAP, *tr.* by Elizabeth Bishop

Carlsbad Caverns, then I moved to. Memorandum. Nanao Sakaki. AtGh

Carlton, Patrick and I. Boys of Summer, The. E. Ethelbert Miller. SpirFl

Carlyle combined the lit'ry life. Dorothy Parker. NALW *Fr.* Pig's-Eye View of Literature, A.

Carmarthen hills are green and low. Carmarthenshire. Dudley G. Davies. AngWePo

Carmarthenshire. Dudley G. Davies. AngWePo

Carmel. Dennis Schmitz. GeoHom

Carmel he seeks: the wandering maid he found. Anne Batten Cristall. RWP *Fr.* Thelmon and Carmel; An Irregular Poem.

Carmel Highlands. Janet Lewis. *See* At Carmel Highlands.

Carmel Point. Robinson Jeffers. APT-1; ASA; BLT; CalPo; NAAL-5; NAMCP V.1; NoAM; NoP-4; WaAnP; WhBo

Carmelita. D. A. Feinfeld. BloBone

Carmelita. Mirabeau Buonaparte Lamar. TiP2

Carmen. Théophile Gautier. WoPoe, *tr.* by John Theobald

Carmen. Newman Levy. AmWit

Carmen: 11. Catullus. WoPoe, *tr.* by Frederick Morgan

Carmen Ancillae. John Hollander. YaYoPo

Carmen is thin—a touch of bister. Carmen. Théophile Gautier. WoPoe, *tr.* by John Theobald
Carmen Possum. *Unknown.* NBLV
Carmen Saeculare. Charles Hubert Sisson. OBVE, *tr. by* Christopher Smart
Carmen Triumphale. Henry Timrod. PCW
Carmencita loves Patrick. Little Song. Langston Hughes. TLR
Carmencita said I had a small ibon. In Tagalog Ibon Means Bird. Nick Carbó. AmPoNex
Carmina. Catullus. *tr. by* Sir Walter Alexander Raleigh and Peter Whigham (Attis.) OBVE; STV
Carmen 31. AmFaPo
(*Carmina*, XXXIX.) OBVE, *tr. by* Peter Whigham
(*Carmina*, LV.) OBVE, *tr. by* Peter Whigham
(*Carmina*, LXIX.) OBVE
(*Carmina*, LXX.) OBVE
(*Carmina*, LXXII.) OBVE
(*Carmina*, LXXXV.) OBVE
(*Carmina*, XCII.) OBVE
(*Carmina*, VIII.) OBVE, *tr. by* Peter Whigham
(*Carmina*, LXXV.) OBVE
(*Carmina*, X.) OBVE, *tr. by* Peter Whigham
(*Carmina*, XIII.) OBVE, *tr. by* Peter Whigham
(Grief.) RaBo; RaF
"Lesbia / live with me." EroLit, *tr. by* Peter Whigham
  Sun May Set, The. NoSic; OBVE
(My Sweetest Lesbia [Let Us Live and Love].) HeIP-4; NoSic; OBVE; TFi; WeW-3, *tr. by* Peter Whigham
  Sun May Set, The. NoSic; OBVE
(Yacht, The.) OBVE, *tr. by* Peter Whigham
Carmina Burana. *Unknown.* *tr. by* Richmond Lattimore, David Parlett and Kenneth Rexroth
"Come, come, my companion." GePo
Dum Diana Vitrea. WoPoe, *tr. by* Richmond Lattimore
"I am constantly wounded." WoPoe, *tr. by* Kenneth Rexroth
Under the Linden Tree. EroLit, *tr. by* David Parlett
Carmina [Charles Martin Translation]. Catullus. *tr. by* Charles Martin
  2. NAWM-7v1, *tr. by* Charles Martin
  5. NAWM-7v1; WoPoe, *tr. by* Charles Martin
  8. NAWM-7v1, *tr. by* Charles Martin
  11. NAWM-7v1, *tr. by* Charles Martin
  51. NAWM-7v1, *tr. by* Charles Martin
  58. NAWM-7v1, *tr. by* Charles Martin
  70. NAWM-7v1, *tr. by* Charles Martin
  72. NAWM-7v1, *tr. by* Charles Martin
  75. NAWM-7v1, *tr. by* Charles Martin
  76. NAWM-7v1, *tr. by* Charles Martin
  83. NAWM-7v1, *tr. by* Charles Martin
  85. NAWM-7v1, *tr. by* Charles Martin
  86. NAWM-7v1, *tr. by* Charles Martin
  87. NAWM-7v1, *tr. by* Charles Martin
  109. NAWM-7v1, *tr. by* Charles Martin
Carmina V and VII [To the Same]. Ben Jonson. *See* To the Same [Celia].
Carnal Knowledge. Dannie Abse. BloBone
Carnal Knowledge I. Gwen Harwood. BMAP
Carnal Knowledge 2. Gwen Harwood. HarvBoo
Carnation. Lily, Lily, Rose. Susan Wood. TiP2
Carnations. Theodore Roethke. BLT
Carnicería. Carla Faesler Bremer. SPV
Carnies. Debra Allbery. PBCAP
Carnival. Primus St. John. GT
Carnival at the River. Robert Greacen. PNI
Caro mio, Pulcinello, kindly hear my wail of woe. Nocturne at Danieli's, A. Sir Owen Seaman. UV
Caro ragazzo, yes, sure, let's meet. Part of a Letter to the Codignola Boy. Pier Paolo Pasolini. VCWP, *tr. by* David Stivender *and* J. D. McClatchy
Caro those last few poems are dynamite. Telegram from the Muse, A. William Matthews. PoA 2002
Carol. Ben Jonson. ChrPo
Carol, A. Cecil Day Lewis. ChrPo
Carol, A. Donald Hall. ChrPo
Carol: "Deep in the fading leaves of night." William Robert Rodgers. OBCP
Carol, every violet has. Alfred Noyes. MoBrPo *Fr.* Flower of Old Japan, The.
Carol, for Candlemas Day. *Unknown.* NOSC
Carol for the Last Christmas Eve. Norman Nicholson. NOxBChV; OBCP
Carol: "Mary laid her Child among." Norman Nicholson. OBCP
Carol of Agincourt, A. *Unknown.* NoP-4; NoP-5; WaAnP

Carol of Patience. Robert Graves. OBCP
Carol of the Poor Children, The. Richard Middleton. OBCP
Carol of the Three Kings. W. S. Merwin. ChrPo
Carol: "On vague hills the prophet bird." W. S. Merwin. YaYoPo
Carol: "Villagers all, this frosty tide." Kenneth Grahame. RSR *Fr.* Wind in the Willows, The.
Carol: "While shepherds watched their flocks by night." "Saki." UV
Carolina. Henry Timrod. APN-2; CBCWP; PCW
Carolina, Carolina / At last they've got you on the map. Charleston. Cecil Mack. ReLy
Carolina gave me Dinah. Dinah. Sam M. Lewis and Joe Young. ReLy
Carolina in the Morning. Gustave Kahn. ReLy
Carolina mourns to-day. For he, the gifted. Tribute to Capt. F. W. Dawson. Mary Weston Fordham. CBWP-2
Caroline. *Unknown.* SSUS
Caroline Street, Cardiff. John Tripp. TCAWP
Caroline von Günderode. Alejandra Pizarnik. SurWo, *tr. by* Natalie Kenvin
Caroling softly souls of slavery. (LL) Song of the Son. Jean Toomer. InGu; ISC; MakPoe; NAAPv.2; NAMCP V.1; NIL-7; NIP-4; OxAAAP
Carousel jargon accounting for the iconoclasm, accounting for the jury pillage. Lesion. Robert Budde. PoPra
Carp. Dionisio D. Martinez. TouFir
Carp and sturgeon dazzle the silver. Along the Charles. Kenneth Rosen. UrbNat
Carp, The. *Vietnamese Oral Tradition.* CaDao, *tr. by* John Balaban
Carpe Diem: "Though pretty, it rarely worked, lining seduction." Rodney Jones. LPSFW
Carpe Diem: Time Flies. Marilyn Krysl. PuP-23
Carpenter bangs long nails, The. God Vacuums the Pool. Gail Martin. SweBea
Carpenter is intent on the pressure of his hand, The. El Greco: Espolio. Earle Birney. BrAP
Carpenter's Complaint, The. Edward Baugh. OBCoV
Carpenter's Son, The. John Berryman. ChIV-2
Carpenter's Son, The. A. E. Housman. ChIV-2; MoBrPo; OxAEP-2; UV *Fr.* Shropshire Lad, A.
Carpenter's Song, A. Im Yŏngjo. CAMKP, *tr. by* Edward W. Poitras
Carpet. Nancy Morejón. TANSG, *tr. by* Joy Renjilian-Burgy
Carpet, The. Olav H. Hauge. WED, *tr. by* Robert Bly
Carpos and Calamos. Nonnus. *Fr.* Dionysiaca.
Carrefour. Amy Lowell. LW
Carriage brushes through the bright, The. Solo for Ear-Trumpet. Dame Edith Sitwell. MoBrPo
Carrickfergus. Louis MacNeice. NAEL-6v2; NAMCP V.1; NoAM; PNI
Carrie Monro. Julia A. Moore.
  Hic Finis Rapto 4. STuOW
Carried her unprotesting out the door. Gwendolyn Brooks. InoFa; NAMCP V.2; NoP-4; NoP-5; OxAAAP; WeW-3 *Fr.* Womanhood, The.
Carried sky first. Earth, The. Amina Saïd. YaTCFP, *tr. by* Mary Ann Caws *and* Jean-Pierre Cauvin
Carriers of the Dream Wheel. N. Scott Momaday. ColAP; WaAnP
Carrie's age was twenty-three. Julia A. Moore. STuOW *Fr.* Carrie Monro.
Carrion Comfort. Gerard Manley Hopkins. BBASP; BrAP; CABP; GSo; HeIP-4; ItP; MakPoe; NAEL-6v2; NAEL-7v2; NAMCP V.1; NoAM; NoP-4; NoP-5; TFi; WaAnP
Carrion Crow, The. Eliza Cook.
  "I plunged my beak in the marbling cheek." VerBaPo
Carrots. Lorna Crozier. OpeFie
Carrots are fucking. Carrots. Lorna Crozier. OpeFie
Carrousel Tune [*with music*]. Tennessee Williams. NBLV
Carrowmore. Lucie Brock-Broido. AWPTFC; PoPoPo
Carry it on now. Tradition, The. Assata Shakur. BRtP
Carry me ackee go a Linstead market. Linstead Market. *Unknown.* FaBoVe
Carry Me Back to Old Virginny. James A. Bland. APN-2; TCAPo
Carry me back to old Virginny. Notes for a Southern Road Map. Phyllis McGinley. NBLV
Carry me down into that liquid again. Late Afternoon. Molly Fisk. PasH
Carry pride in your fist. When You Leave. Juan Delgado. TouFir
Carry quickly into daylight the excited birds. (LL) Undertaking in New Jersey, The. George Oppen. GPTC; OxBoAm
Carrying a bunch of marigolds. Negro Woman, A. William Carlos Williams. SAmP
Carrying her full cargo of roses. (LL) Big Wind. Theodore Roethke. ColAP; HarvBoo; TRP; WaAnP
Carrying my daughter to bed. Gravity. Kim Addonizio. RoV
Carrying My Mind Around. *Tlingit Oral Tradition.* TCAPo
Carrying My Wife. Moniza Alvi. NeBl

Carrying my world. Father. Myra Cohn Livingston. NTCP

Carrying the Kodak prints. Peace Corps Volunteer Comes Home, The. Carolyne Wright. RoV

Carrying their packages of groceries in particular. Old Men and Old Women Going Home on the Street Car. Merrill Moore. MoAmPo

Cars stuck in the snow. Ngodup Paljor. WhBo

Cart was circulating under the moon, The. Snowcone Vendor. Josaphat Robert Large. OGAHCP, *tr. by* Boadiba and Jack Hirschman

Cart With Four Oxen,The. Sándor Petőfi. IQMS, *tr. by* Ila Egon

Carta. Tedi López Mills. RMCMP

Cartagena. Gary Snyder. BB

Carthage. Najaat Al-Udwany. PoArWo, *tr. by* Moulouk Berry and Ali Farghaly

Carthusians. Ernest Dowson. NAEL-6v2; NAEL-7v2

Cartload of Shoes, A. Abraham Sutskever. HP, *tr.* David G. Roskies

Cartografía. Antonio Deltoro. RMCMP

Cartographies of Silence. Adrienne Rich. WaAnP

Cartography. Louise Bogan. TRP

Cartography. Antonio Deltoro. RMCMP, *tr. by* Christian Viveros-Fauné

Cartoon Physics, Part 1. Nick Flynn. BeAl; LegDan; NAPBL; P180; PoDa

Cartoon Physics, Part 2. Nick Flynn. NAPBL

Carts clang and clatter. Ballad of the Army Carts. Tu Fu [*or* Du Fu]. WoPoe, *tr. by* David Lattimore

Cary Grant was dying all that time. What It Was Like the Night Cary Grant Died. Eloise Klein Healy. WiU

Caryophyllaceae / like a scroungy, The. Spring Coming. A. R. Ammons. HeIP-4

CARYO's sweet smile DIANTHUS proud admires. Erasmus Darwin. NOBRP *Fr.* Botanic Garden, The.

Casa de Olga, La. Natalia Toledo. RMCMP

Casa Guidi Windows. Elizabeth Barrett Browning. "I heard last night a little child go singing." PEW; VWP

Casa, La. Rosemary Catacalos. TiP2

Casa nómada. Malva Flores. "Cuerpo de maravilla." RMCMP

Casabianca. Elizabeth Bishop. NIL-7; NoP-5; WoPoe

Casabianca. Felicia Dorothea Hemans. BRP; NAEL-6v2; NAEL-7v2; NOBRP; NoP-5; NPBRoP; NPeEn; RWP; ViWPN; VWP

Cascade of night aches pray we might. When you say no. Merilene M. Murphy. BtF

Cascades of Death. Angelina Muñiz Huberman. MirDau, *tr. by* Aurora Camacho

Cascadilla Falls. A. R. Ammons. OxBoAm

Cascando. Samuel Beckett. IrLP; ModIr

Case, The. Karen Volkman. LegDan

Case Against Mist, The. Mark Halliday. SUP

Case at Sessions, A. Walter Savage Landor. OBSV

Case for the Miners, The. Siegfried Sassoon. RSaN

Case History. Dannie Abse. TCAWP

Case in Point, A. August Kleinzahler. PmAP

Case of the Same Name, A. Giampiero Neri. ItPo, *tr. by* Gayle Ridinger

Case Study. Nissim Ezekiel. PML

Casement's Funeral. Richard Murphy. ModIr; PBCIP *Fr.* Battle of Aughrim, The.

Caserta Garden. Richard Wilbur. OBGa

Casey at the Bat. Ernest Lawrence Thayer. ChAP; ITBLP

Casey Jones. T. Lawrence Seibert. GM; ITBLP

"Cash flow" "liquid assets" "pooling our resources." Money As Water. Kurt Brown. SUP

Cash or Turtle or Heaven. Reginald Gibbons. Vesp

Cash Positive. Peter McDonald. PNI

Cashel of Munster. William English. IrLP; IrV; OBEV, *tr. by* Sir Samuel Ferguson

Casi todos / Almost all. Blues del SIDA / AIDS Blues. Francisco X. Alarcón. GeoHom

Casida of Sobbing. Federico García Lorca. AF, *tr. by* Robert Bly

Casida of the Dark Doves. Federico García Lorca. WoPoe, *tr. by* Edwin Honig

Casida of the Rose. Federico García Lorca. WED, *tr. by* Robert Bly

Casino. Richard Tipping. BMAP

Casino. S. L. Wisenberg. PfS

Casket Song, A. William Shakespeare. NoSic; TFi *Fr.* Merchant of Venice, The.

Cass Romanski, 23, and his fiancée made dinner at his family. 10 Dead Friends. Dennis Cooper. WiU

Cassandra. Louise Bogan. APT-2; MoAmPo; NALW; NAMCP V.1

Cassandra. Elena Chizhova. ARWW, *tr. by* Catriona Kelly

Cassandra. William Dickey. YaYoPo

Cassandra. Robinson Jeffers. APT-1; HeIP-4

Cassandra. Edwin Arlington Robinson. APT-1; NoAM; OxBoAm

Cassandra and Friend. Norman Henry, II Pritchard. GT

Cassandra to Agamemnon. Nina Kossman. CRWP, *tr. by the author*

Cassandra's kind. Three To's and an Oi. Heather McHugh. ExTi

Cassation on a Theme by Jacques Dupin. Harry Mathews. NYP2

Cassette tape, The. T.A.P.O.A.F.O.M. Thomas Sayers Ellis. BAP-01

Cassin's Finch. Anne MacNaughton. ICANM

—Cassiopeia at Noon. Michelle Boisseau. ExTi

Cassock, bands and hymn-book too. (LL) Impromptu. Samuel Wilberforce. NBLV; OWoS

Cast Away. Christopher Pilling. NLP

"Cast down your bucket where you are." Atlanta Exposition Ode. Mary Weston Fordham. CBWP-2; SWaP

Cast off all shame. Jana Bai. WPoS

Cast Off, The. Marge Piercy. NAMCP V.2; NoAM

Cast on the turbid current of the street. Julia Ward Howe. SWaP *Fr.* Lyrics of the Street.

Cast on this shore at end of year. Indian Summer. Lizette Woodworth Reese. SWaP

Cast our caps and cares away. John Fletcher. NOSC *Fr.* Beggar's Bush.

Cast Shadows. Marcel Duchamp. PFTM-1

Cast thy bread upon the waters. Bible, *O.T.* OBVE *Fr.* Ecclesiastes.

Castalian Scots, nou may ye cry, Allace! Fair Cop, A. Robert Garioch. OBCoV

Castanets. Bernard Spencer. WeW-3

Castara. William Habington. Cogitabo Pro Peccato Meo. ChIV-1 Cupio Dissolvi. ChIV-2 Nox Nocti Indicat Scientiam. BASC; NPeEn; OBEV; OxBEV Perdam Sapientiam Sapientum. ChIV-2 Solum Mihi Superest Sepulchrum. ChIV-1; NOSC To a Wanton. NOSC To Castara, *Being to Take a Journey.* NOSC To Castara, upon an Embrace. NPeEn To Roses in the Bosom[e] of Castara. NOSC; OBEV To the Moment Last Past. OxBSo *Upon* Castara's *Departure.* NOSC

Castaway, A. Augusta Davies Webster. "Poor little diary, with its simple thoughts." NPeEn; ViWPN

Castaway, The. William Cowper. BrAP; NAEL-6v1; NAEL-7v1; NOBRP; NoP-4; NoP-5; NPeEn; OxBEV; PoPoPo; TRP

Castaways, The. Claude McKay. APT-1

Casti Connubi. Marco Martos. PML, *tr. by* Margaret Greer

Castilian. Elinor Wylie. ColAP

Casting. Kevin Young. GT

Casting All Your Care upon God, for He Careth for You. Thomas Washbourne. SacPr

Casting and Gathering. Seamus Heaney. NoP-4; NoP-5

Casting Sequences. Marjorie Welish. FTOS

Casting, up a salt creek in the sea-rank air. San Pedro Road. Robert Hass. GeoHom

Castle Howard, the Seat of the Rt. Hon. Charles, Earl of Carlisle. Anne, Viscountess Irwin Ingram.

Castle Howard, the Seat of the Rt. Hon. Charles, Earl of Carlisle. OBGa

Castle in Lynn, A. Linda McCarriston. LoL

Castle in the Fire, The. Mary Jane Carr. ChAP

Castle of Chillon, The. Letitia Elizabeth Landon. CenSon

Castle of Indolence Stanzas, The. William Wordsworth. "With him there often walked in friendly wise." NPBRoP

Castle of Indolence, The. James Thomson. Leper-House and the Impenitents, The. NePenScot

Castle, The. Patricia K. Page. IFF

Castle to castle. Caernarfon, 2 July [*or* July 2] 1969. T. Glynne Davies. BBMWP; OBWVE, *tr. by* Joseph P. Clancy

Castle was nigh, with its towers so high, The. Pathetic Lament, A. Eliza Cook. VerBaPo

Castles in the Air. James Ballantine. TreFP

Castles of crystal. Trams. Dame Edith Sitwell. NOxBChV

Castor's loose on the buttoned chair, A. Blues for a Melodeon. Phyllis McGinley. AmWit

Castration. Nigel Jenkins. AngWePo; TCAWP

Castration of the Pen. Erica Jong. NALW

Castro Street. Art Beck. CalPo

Casts light for a shadow. (LL) Song: "You are as gold." "H. D." APT-1; MoAmPo; TCAPo

Casual Line, A. Chungji. BecRai, *tr.* by Kim Daljin, Kim Won-Chung and Christopher Merrill

Casual Wear. James Merrill. BeAl; NIP-4 *Fr.* Topics.

Casually. (LL) Don't worry, spiders. Issa. ChAP; EH, *tr.* by Robert Hass

Casually licking the bottom of the bag salt from their fingers. (LL) Saints. Arielle Greenberg. BAP-04; LegDan

Casualties. Robert Herrick. BASC

Casualties are not only those who are dead, The. Casualties, The. John Pepper Clark Bekedermo. HBAPE; PLBUT

Casualties, The. John Pepper Clark Bekedermo. HBAPE; PLBUT

Casualty. Seamus Heaney. ModIr; NAEL-6v2; NAEL-7v2; NAMCP V.2; PBCIP

Casualty. Langston Hughes. APT-2

Casualty. Michael Longley. NAMCP V.2

Casualty. Edwin Rolfe. APT-2

Casus Belli. Caroline Finkelstein. PfS

Cat. Emily Dickinson. SAmP

Cat. Mary Britton Miller. TLR; WHSW

Cat, The. Rose Fyleman. NOxBChV

Cat, The. Ogden Nash. WHSW

Cat, The. *Vietnamese Oral Tradition.* CaDao, *tr.* by John Balaban

Cat and Mirror. Chase Twichell. BeAl

Cat and the Moon, The. William Butler Yeats. CtM; HarvBoo; WHSW

Cat and the Pig, The. Gerard Benson. NOxBChV

Cat and the Weather. May Swenson. WeW-3

Cat came / sleepily from a thick shrub and stopped and shook its head, A. James McMichael. GeoHom *Fr.* Four Good Things.

Cat composed as an uncut pie, A. In the Barn. Roger Fanning. OPRER

Cat I live with is an animal, The. Domestic Cat, A. Edwin Denby. NYP2

Cat, if you go outdoors you must walk in the snow. On a Night of Snow. Elizabeth Jane Coatsworth. MoAmPo

Cat in the Snow. Aileen Fisher. NTCP

Cat is "in time", A. Lyn Hejinian. AWPTFC *Fr.* Writing Is an Aid to Memory.

Cat of Carlyshe Kynde, A. John Skelton. TriCat

Cat of Cats, The. William Brighty Rands. NOxBChV

Cat rubs his body, The. December Nap. Dennis Saleh. GeoHom

Cat runs the dripping fence. Drizzle. Takahashi Shinkichi. ZenPo, *tr.* by Takashi Ikemoto and Lucien Stryk

Cat shattered the casserole, The. Cat, The. *Vietnamese Oral Tradition.* CaDao, *tr.* by John Balaban

Cat sits on the back of the sofa looking, The. Sixth of January, The. David Budbill. GoPo

Cat stands at the fridge. Sister Cat. Frances Mayes. P180

Cat takes a look at the weather. Cat and the Weather. May Swenson. WeW-3

Cat vomits, The. Someone covers it with a paper towel and waits. Spots. Estella Lauter. SweBea

Cat Washing. Linda Molony. NOBAu

Cat went here and there, The. Cat and the Moon, The. William Butler Yeats. CtM; HarvBoo; WHSW

Cat! who hast passed [*or* pass'd] thy grand climacteric. To a Cat. John Keats. CenSon; OxBSo; TriCat; NPBRoP

Catacombs in San Callisto, The. Rolf Jacobsen. BLT, *tr.* by Roger Greenwald

Catalogue. Rosalie Moore.

Catalog [*or* Catalogue]. ITBLP; NTCP

Catalogue Army. Naomi Shihab Nye. ReTh

Catalogue of the Birds. Geoffrey Chaucer. NPeEn *Fr.* Parlement of Foules, The.

Catalpa leans toward lofty phoenix. Pure Wife, A. Yan Yanzhi. CCL1, *tr.* by Anne Birrell

Catalyst. Zoila Ellis. OWABP

Cataract Isle, The. Christopher Pearse Cranch. APN-1

Cataract of Death far thundering from the heights, The. (LL) Mezzo Cammin. Henry Wadsworth Longfellow. APN-1; ColAP; GSo; NAAL-3; NAAPv.1; NCAP; TCAPo

Cataract of Lodore, The. Robert Southey. NPBRoP

Catastrophe. Cornelius Whur. STuOW; VerBaPo *Fr.* Armless Artist, The.

Catch. George Bilgere. RaF

Catch [*with music*]. Robert Francis. RaBo

Catch. Langston Hughes. NoAM

Catch, A. Henry Aldrich. NOSC

Catch, The. Raymond Carver. MoASP

Catch, The. Sandy Feinstein. IaFF

Catch, The. Stanley Kunitz. APT-2; NAMCP V.1; PtR

Catch, The. Laura Mullen. IAoNAP

Catch, The. Rebecca Seiferle. ExTi

Catch, The. Richard Wilbur. WeW-3

Catch a moth in the Amazon; pin it under glass. Every Where and Every When. Arthur Sze. FTtHH; OpBo

Catch eels in the rocks below the Palace of the Legion of Honor. Things to Do Around San Francisco. Gary Snyder. OxBoAm

Catch if you can your country's moment, begin. Adrienne Rich. NAAL-5 *Fr.* Atlas of the Difficult World, An.

Catch me glassy vapid. Downtime. Lisa Buscani. AmPoNex

Catch, my Uncle Jack said. Elizabeth. Michael Ondaatje. NoAM

Catch not my breath, O clamorous heart. Alfred Tennyson. NAEL-6v2 *Fr.* Maud [A Monodrama].

Catches her into its way. (LL) Remembered Morning. Janet Lewis. MakPoe; SoSe-8

Catches tigers / In red weather. (LL) Disillusionment of Ten O'Clock. Wallace Stevens. APT-1; ItP; NAAPv.2; NAMCP V.1; NoAM; OxBoAm; SAmP; SoSe-8; TCAPo; TRP

  (In red weather.) (LL) ChAP; NAAL-5

Catching My Breath. Robert Minhinnick. TCAWP

Catching the Scent. Anne Haines. PfS

Catching Webs. Judith Beveridge. NOBAu

Catechism of the Sea. Christopher Buckley. MAAN

Categories, The. Russell Edson. SUP

Category Mistakes in Biochemistry. Rob MacKenzie. Oth

Category of crime known as false accusation sentenced me to death, The. Publications Law. Yi Sang. CAMKP, *tr.* by Edward Mack

Caterpillar. Annie Foster. NLP

Caterpillar, A. Basho. EH, *tr.* by Robert Hass

Caterpillar, The. Christina Georgina Rossetti. FaBoVe

Caterpillar, The. Miller Williams. InGu

Caterpillar ("How soft a Caterpillar steps—.") Emily Dickinson. SAmP

Caterpillar. "I'm learning / To crawl." (LL) Tickle Rhyme, The. Ian Serraillier. NTCP; Spl

Caterpillars. Aileen Fisher. TLR

Caterpillar's Lullaby. Jane Yolen. Spl

Catharine of Arragon [*with music*]. Eloise Bibb. CBWP-4

Catharine Plouffe. Susan Frances Harrison. IFF

Cathedral bells were tolling. I'll Be Seeing You. Irving Kahal. ReLy

Cathedral Builders. John Ormond. GoPo; NoP-4; NoP-5; TCAWP

Cathedral: "For hours I held one of my son's infant twins." Deena Linett. NevBe

Cathedral. Full of awe and reverence. To Liberty. Ágnes Nemes Nagy. IQMS, *tr.* by Ila Egon

Cathedral in the Thrashing Rain. Takamura Kotaro. CAoMJL1, *tr.* by Hiroaki Sato

Cathedrals sway in the blue face of the steel. Citizen. Julia Fields. GT

Catherine. Karla Kuskin. NTCP

Catherine said "I think I'll bake." Catherine. Karla Kuskin. NTCP

Catherine, though not from fortune's glittering stores. On Some Violets Planted in My Garden by a Friend. Elizabeth Cobbold. CenSon

Cathleen. Nuala Ni Dhomhnaill. ModIr, *tr.* by Paul Muldoon

Cathleen Sweeping. George Johnston. IFF

Catholic. Fanny Howe. BAP-04

Catholic Bells, The. William Carlos Williams. SAmP

Catholic Love. Charles Wesley. SacPr

Cathy. Beatrix Gates. WiU *Fr.* Triptych.

Catlike. Kate Y. A. Bone. EdScPo

Cat-naps take in pipe-bowl light. (LL) Bench of Boors, The. Herman Melville. APN-2; AWTN; NAAL-3; SoSe-8

Cato. Joseph Addison.

  Cato's Soliloquy.

  Soul, The. TreFP

Cats. Charles Baudelaire. TriCat, *tr.* by Dugald Sutherland MacColl

Cats. Eleanor Farjeon. WHSW

Cats and Dogs [*with music*]. N. M. Bodecker. TLR

Cats, contagious with sleep, bake. Summer Afternoon in Solon, Iowa. Stuart Dybek. PoDa

Cat's Cradle. Lynne Wycherley. Prnts

Cats hurry to cross our path. Explanation of a Sign. Pyotr Vegin. TCRusP, *tr.* by Daniel Weissbort

Cats making love. Basho. EH, *tr.* by Robert Hass

Cat's Meat. Harold Monro. OBMV

Cats of Kilkenny, The. *Unknown.* ChAP

Cats of morning awaken, sultry and feral, The. Walt Whitman Encounters the Cosmos with the Cats of New York. Gail White. ViWalt

Cat's Second Song, The. Nancy Willard. FFC

Cats sleep / Anywhere. Cats. Eleanor Farjeon. WHSW

Cats sleep fat and walk thin. Rosalie Moore. ITBLP; NTCP *Fr.* Catalogue.

Cat's song, The. Marge Piercy. BrAP

Cat's wife, A. Basho. EMJL, *tr.* by Haruo Shirane

Cats wind together in the barn, The. Angels. Louise Erdrich. UpMys

Cats—A Retrospective. Paula Cunningham. NIrP

Cattails Along Red River. Joy Lahey. AnSo

Cattle. Berta Hart Nance. TiP2

Cattle Brands. Vaida Stewart Montgomery. TiP2

Cattle Loading. Gordon Mackay-Warna. NOBAu, tr. by George von Brandenstein

Cattle out of their byres are dungy still, lambs. Gorse Fires. Michael Longley. NoP-4; NoP-5

Cattle Show. Hugh MacDiarmid. MoBrPo; OBMV; OxBEV

Cattle-count. Unknown. SonAtl, tr. by Kurt Ganzl and Saul Goode

Cattle-trains edge along the river, bringing morning on a white vibration. Ceiling Unlimited. Muriel Rukeyser. MoAmPo

Cattle-trains edge along the river, bringing morning on a white vibration, The. Muriel Rukeyser. OtW Fr. Tunnel, The.

Catullus, what keeps you from killing yourself? No good reason. What for? Catullus. WoPoe, tr. by Charles Martin

Cauchemars. Marie Étienne. YaTCFP

Caucus how fun to get it going and done. Meditatio Lectoris. Rodrigo Toscano. BAP-04

Caught. Carole Bernstein. AmPoNex

Caught and composed, motionless blue, behind. Desire of Water, The. Mark Jarman. PoA 2002

Caught, April 2002—A Prayer for Peace. Hettie Jones. PrTe

Caught between catastrophe and habit. Shoreline After Storm. Eamon Grennan. PoCoUp

Caught between two streams of traffic, in the gloom. T. S. Eliot. Robert Lowell. NoAM

Caught caterpillar. Landscapes. Pauline Kaldas. PoArWo

Caught in a cloud this morning, this barn. For the Barn at Bread Loaf. William Stafford. BodElec

Caught in an anger exact as a machine! (LL) Tired and Unhappy, You Think of Houses. Delmore Schwartz. APT-2; ItP; MoAmPo

Caught in coastal weather, came. Sound and Cerement. Nathaniel Mackey. BAP-04

Caught in my mittens' mohair barbs. Microscope in Winter, The. Sandra McPherson. VCAP

Caught in the centre of a soundless field. Myxomatosis. Philip Larkin. NoAM

Caught in the Swamp. Joseph Ceravolo. BodElec; NYP2

Caught me sittin. All is One for Monk. Imamu Amiri Baraka. ISC

Caught still as Absalom. Chagrin. Isaac Rosenberg. HarvBoo; MoBrPo

Caught—the bubble. Sonnet. Elizabeth Bishop. APT-2; WaAnP

Cauld blaws the wind frae east to west. Up in the Morning Early. Robert Burns. OPOU

Cauld, grey waater heaves on the neap tide. Itherness. Ellie McDonald. CABP

Cauldron, The. David Huerta. RMCMP, tr. by Mark Schafer

Cauliflowers. Paul Muldoon. ModIr; NAMCP V.2

Causality and Chance in Love. Karen Press. TSAP

Cause acquits you not, but I that wink, The. (LL) Ovid. NPeEn; OBVE Fr. Elegies.

Cause and Effect. Oliver Goldsmith. STuOW Fr. Captivity, The.

Cause and Effect. Matthew Prior. NBLV

Cause i'm from dixie too. Evie Shockley. RD

Cause of this stab in my side. Tryst, The. Unknown. OBWVE, tr. by Joseph P. Clancy

Cause you don't love me. Bad Luck Card. Langston Hughes. NoP-4; NoP-5; SAmP; TRP

Causes. Mona Van Duyn. OxBoAm

Causes are in Time; only their issue, The. Allegory of the Wolf Boy, The. Thom Gunn. HarvBoo

Caustic Soda. Liz Houghton. Prnts

Caution, The. Catherine Cockburn. LW

Cautionary Limerick. Unknown. NBLV

Cautious and Incantatory. Gwensways. Eugene B. Redmond. SpirFl

Cautious Gunslinger, The. Edward Dorn. PmAP Fr. Gunslinger.

Cautiously bubbles that spring water. Unknown. ColAnChi Fr. Classic of Odes.

Cavafy in Redondo. Mark Jarman. GeoHom

Cavalier Lyric. James Simmons. UV

Cavalier's Farewell, The. Guillaume Apollinaire. WoPoe, tr. by Anne Greet

Cavalry Crossing a Ford. Walt Whitman. AmWaPo; BLT; BrAP; CBCWP; FaBoA; HeIP-4; NAAL-3; NAAL-5; NAAPv.1; NAMCP V.1; NCAP; NoAM; NoP-4; NoP-5; PCW; SAmP; TCAPo; TFi; TRP; WaAnP

Cave. John Montague. ModIr Fr. Cave of Night, The.

2. The Cave. David Brendon Hopes. UpMys Fr. Five Neo-Platonic Commentaries.

Cave of AIDS, The. Mark Scott. PoA 2002

Cave of bronze amplifier of the storms. Alice Rahon. SurWo, tr. by Nancy Deffebach and Vanina Deler

Cave of Despair, The. Edmund Spenser. OBNV Fr. Faerie Queene, The.

Cave of Making, The. W. H. Auden. FaBoVe; OxAEP-2

Cave of Night, The. John Montague. Cave. ModIr

Cave of the Thousand Pines. Muso Soseki. EaWin, tr. by W. S. Merwin

Cave we found, but vacant all within, The. Homer. OBVE Fr. Odyssey.

Cavern, The. Charles Tomlinson. ICANM

Caverns. Madison Cawein. APN-2

Caviar of death between bread, The. Christmas Fare. Dilys Wood. Prnts

Cavour. Menella Bute Smedley. VWP

Caw Caw, Caw Caw Caw. Fauve. Arthur Sze. WhBo

Caw caw caw crows shriek in the white sun over grave stones. Allen Ginsberg. BB

Caxtons are mechanical birds with many wings. Martian Sends a Postcard Home, A. Craig Raine. NAEL-6v2; NAEL-7v2; NAMCP V.2; NoAM; NoP-4; NoP-5; NPeEn; WaAnP

Cayenne. Angela Jackson. SweBea

Cayenne in our blood. Kalamu ya Salaam. SpirFl Fr. New Orleans Haiku.

Ce glacier qui grince. Lumière de la lame, La. André Du Bouchet. YaTCFP

Ce sont les premiers beaux jours. Été, L'. Pascalle Monnier. YaTCFP

Ce toit tranquille, où marchent des colombes. Cimetière marin, Le. Paul Valéry. YaTCFP

Ce triangle d'eau qui a soif. Amour sans trêve, L'. Antonin Artaud. YaTCFP

Céanne. Jean Tardieu. YaTCFP, tr. by David Kelley

Cease then, my song, cease the unequal lay. (LL) On Imagination. Phillis Wheatley. NAAPv.1; NoP-5; OxWW; RWP

Cease then my tongue, and lend unto my mind. Edmund Spenser. InvLi Fr. Hymn[e] of Heavenly Beauty [or Beautie], An.

Ceasefire. Jane Bailey. FiBr

Ceasefire. Michael Longley. NAMCP V.2; StAl

Ceaseless weaving of the uneven water, The. Aphrodite Vrania. Charles Reznikoff. APT-2

Cebolla es escarcha, La. Nanas de la Cebolla. Miguel Hernández. RaW

Cebolla / luminosa redoma. Oda a la Cebolla. Pablo Neruda. IPoFL

Ceci n'est pas une pipe. Del Ray Cross. FreRad

Cecil B. De Mille. Nicolas Bentley. OBCoV

Cedar. David Tokuyu Reid-Marr. WhBo

Cedar, The. Han G. Hoekstra. TuT, tr. by Peter van de Kamp

Cedar and jagged fir. Lonely Land, The. Arthur James Marshall Smith. BrAP

Cedar Cove. John Steffler. Coast

Cedar umbrella / Off to Mount Yoshino. Basho. ZenPo, tr. by Takashi Ikemoto and Lucien Stryk

Cedar Waxwing, The. Carole Oles. PfSP

Cedars. Nadia Tuéni. PoArWo

Cedary Fragrance, A. Jane Hirshfield. WANABP

Céilí. Ciaran Carson. PBCIP

Ceiling of hell was fastened with thick gold nails, The. Wallpaper of Mr. R. K., The. Max Jacob. MotU, tr. by Andrei Codrescu

Ceiling Unlimited. Muriel Rukeyser. MoAmPo; OtW Fr. Tunnel, The.

Celan. James Brasfield. PoDa

Celandine. Edward Thomas. TCAWP

Celda barroca, Una. David Huerta. RMCMP

Celebrants chanted, The. Four Ways of Dying. Steve Chimombo. HBAPE; NAfrP

Celebrate this unlikely oracle. Groundhog Day. Lynn Ungar. IPoFL

Celebrated Missing Link, The. On the Antiquity of Warfare. George Starbuck. AmWit

Celebrated white-cap spelling bee was won by a spelling bee, The. Celebrated White-Cap Spelling Bee, The. Bob Kaufman. EGAG

Celebration. Joseph Ceravolo. FTOS

Celebration. Gzar Hantoosh. IrPoTo, tr. by Saadi A. Simawe and Ellen Doré Watson

Celebration. Denise Levertov. NAMCP V.2

Celebration. Nuala Ni Dhomhnaill. BeAl

Celebration. Gene Shuford. TiP2

Celebration: Birth of a Colt [with music]. Linda Hogan. HATNAP

Celebration: "How wonderful, Tomasito!" Thomas McGrath. GifTon; PoChi

Celebration of Charis in Ten Lyric[k] Pieces [or Peeces], A. Ben Jonson. NAEL-6v1; OxAEP-1
    Another Lady's Exception, Present at the Hearing. NAEL-7v1
    Begging Another, on Colour of Mending the Former. NAEL-7v1
    Her Man Described by Her Own[e] Dictamen. NAEL-7v1
    Her Triumph. BASC; NAEL-7v1; NoP-4; NoP-5; NOSC; NPeEn

His Excuse for Loving. NAEL-7v1; NOSC; PtR

How He Saw Her. NAEL-7v1

(Triumph of Charis, The.) TFi

(Triumph, The.) OBEV

Urging Her of a Promise. NAEL-7v1

What He[e] Suffered. NAEL-7v1

Celebration of Home Birth: November 15th, 1981, A. Sandra Maria Esteves. PueRic

Celebration of the Body. Daisy Zamora. LoL, *tr. by* Dinah Livingston

Celebrities. Alain Bosquet. PML, *tr. by* William Jay Smith

Celeste called work to leave a message. Calls from the Outside World. Robert Hershon. PrTe

Celestial Alphabet Event [Poem is an image.]. Jacques Gaffarel. PFTM-1

Celestial choir! enthroned [*or* enthron'd] in realms of light. To His Excellency General Washington. Phillis Wheatley. AmWaPo; NAAL-3; NAAL-5; NAAPv.1

Celestial City, The. Giles, the Younger Fletcher. ChIV-2; NOSC; SacPr *Fr.* Christ's Victory and Triumph.

Celestial Emperor, The. Howard Nemerov. BodElec

Celestial Evening, October 1967. Charles Olson. NAAL-5 *Fr.* Maximus Poems, The.

Celestial Music. Louise Glück. BBASP; CAP-8; OxBoAm

Celestial Surgeon, The. Robert Louis Stevenson. MoBrPo

Celestial, The. Elizabeth Spires. CAP-8

Celia Celia. Adrian Mitchell. OPOU

Celia Singing. Thomas Stanley. NOSC

Celia's Home-Coming. Agnes Mary Frances Robinson. OBEV; VWP

Celibacy. Austin Clarke. ModIr

Cell Angel. Menna Elfyn. BBMWP; MoWP, *tr. by* Gillian Clarke

Cell is but two metres long, A. Eighteen Dead, The. Jan Campert. TuT, *tr. by* Mary E. O'Donnell

Cell, The. Oskar Davico. SonAtl, *tr. by* Merica Delic, Kurt Ganzl, Ursula Hobday, Sladjana Josic, Ljubica Marasanov and Ziva Pecavar

Cell, The. Lucille Day. ASA *Fr.* Self-Portrait at the Health Museum.

Cell, The. Lyn Hejinian.

"In the dark sky there." FTOS

"It is the writer's object." NAMCP V.2

"Yesterday I saw the sun." NAMCP V.2

Cellist, / easy on that bow. Instructions to the Player. Carl Rakosi. APT-2; MiVo

Cello never made it, lost, The. Quartet. Leonard Nathan. Vesp

Cello on the bed, A. Still Life. Georgi Rupchev. CSCBP, *tr. by* Georgi Belev and Lisa Sapinkopf

Cells. Rudyard Kipling. FaBoWar

Celluloid of a photograph holds them well, The. Six Young Men. Ted Hughes. OBWP; PoAgWa; PoWW

Celtic History, A. William Neill. EdScPo

Celts, The. Stevie Smith. NoP-4; NoP-5

Celui qui est assis penché en avant sur le banc n'est pas toi. Pêche Lunaire. Greta Knutson. YaTCFP

Cement sky we were slow to get. Nathaniel Mackey. RD *Fr.* Song of the Andoumboulou.

Cementerio en la Ciudad. Luis Cernuda. RaW

Cementerio Está Cerca, El. Miguel Hernández. RaW

Cement-grey floors and walls. On the Island. Dennis Brutus. AF

Cemetery, A. Emily Dickinson. MoAmPo

Cemetery at Loch End, Catalone, Cape Breton, The. Douglas Lochhead. Coast

Cemetery at Petit Saconnex, The. Deema K. Shehabi. PoArWo

Cemetery Gate. Georges Castera. OGAHCP, *tr. by* Boadiba and Jack Hirschman

Cemetery in Punta Arenas. Enrique Lihn. TCLAP; VCWP, *tr. by* David Unger

Cemetery in the City. Luis Cernuda. RaW, *tr. by* Robert Bly

Cemetery in the Mind, The. Dambudzo Marechera. NAfrP

Cemetery Lies Near, The. Miguel Hernández. RaW, *tr. by* James Wright

Cemetery Nights [*with music*]. Stephen Dobyns. CAP-8; StAl

Cemetery of the Whales, The. Yevgeny Aleksandrovich Yevtushenko. RusPo, *tr. by* Robert Arthur Douglas Ford

Cemetery Reef. Elizabeth Spires. CAP-8

Cempasúchil, copal—en la parte alta de librero bajo—libamen, oblación. Angélica Tornero. SPV

Cempasúchil, copal—on the top part of the low bookcase—libation, offering. Angélica Tornero. SPV, *tr. by* Jen Hofer

Cena de un 10 de Abríl. Carla Faesler Bremer. SPV

Cenci, The. Percy Bysshe Shelley.

Final Moments. NPBRoP

Ceniza en Oxford. Francisco Brines. RaW

Cenotaph. John Yau. PmAP

Cenotaph stands in the Park, The. Greenwood's. Michael Sharkey. NOBAu

Cenotaph, The. Charlotte Mew. OxAEP-2

Cenozoic Asylum, The [1982 Version]. Christopher Dewdney. NLPA

Cenozoic Asylum, The [2002 Version]. Christopher Dewdney. OpeFie

Censored. Blas de Otero. RaW, *tr. by* Hardie St. Martin

Censoria. Blas de Otero. RaW

Censorship. John Ciardi. NBLV

Census man, The. Madam and the Census Man. Langston Hughes. SAmP

Census of Animal Bodies: Driving Home. Madeline DeFrees. UrbNat

Centaur, The. May Swenson. APT-2; ItP; NAMCP V.2

Centenary Ode, A: Inscribed to Little Crow, Leader of the Sioux Rebellion in Minnesota, 1862. James Wright. AmWaPo; NAMCP V.2

Centennial Celebration, The. Julia A. Moore.

Noble Structure, A. STuOW

Centennial For Whitman. Richard Eberhart. ViWalt

Centennial of Melville's birth this morning. Japanese City. Kenward Elmslie. NYP2; PmAP

Centennial Year for the Spirits. Sister Elizabeth Hope Goodwin. FTtHH

Center. Josephine Miles. OxBoAm

Centered. P. Inman. FTOS

Centipede. Rita Dove. InvLad

Centipede, The. *Unknown.* OBSP

Centipede adown the street, The. Don Marquis. AmWit; NBLV *Fr.* Archy and Mehitabel.

Central America. Jackson Mac Low. Eno

Central Standard Time. Kevin Young. AmPoNex

Centre in a table, A. Gertrude Stein. NAMCP V.1 *Fr.* Tender Buttons.

Centre of equal daughters, equal sons. America. Walt Whitman. FaBoA

Centrifuge, The. Billy Collins. BAP-04

Centuries. Ronald Stuart Thomas. CABP

Centuries of Meditations. Thomas Traherne.

"Corn was Orient and Immortal Wheat, which never should, The." NPeEn

Centuries of silence gone, now let me weave a celebration, The. After the Mute Centuries. Waldo Williams. BBMWP, *tr. by* Rowan Williams

Centuries to come. Future. Henri Michaux. YaTCFP, *tr. by* Mary Ann Caws *and* Jean-Pierre Cauvin and Patricia Terry

Centurion, A. Will M. Carleton. ArBi

Centurion of the Thirtieth, A. Rudyard Kipling. *Fr.* Puck of Pook's Hill.

Century of Hands. Michael Davidson. FTOS

Century Plant. David C. Yates. TiP2

Century, The. Francisco Aragon. RWB

Century's Decline, The. Wisława Szymborska. CFP, *tr. by* Stanislaw Barańczak and Clare Cavanagh

Century's no longer new, The. Toast to 2,000, A. Richard Percival Lister. OBCoV

Ceremonies for Christmas[se]. Robert Herrick. OBCP

Ceremoniously an egg. Egg Hatches Out a Flame, An. Drahomira Vandas. SurWo, *tr. by* Guy Ducornet

Ceremony. Georgi Rupchev. CSCBP, *tr. by* Georgi Belev and Lisa Sapinkopf

Ceremony. William Stafford. CAP-8

Ceremony. Richard Wilbur. NAAL-5; NAMCP V.2; NoAM

Ceremony after a Fire Raid. Dylan Thomas. AF

Ceremony by the Sea, A. Richard Eberhart. PWW2

Ceremony must be found, The. Speaking of Poetry. John Peale Bishop. APT-1; InGu

Ceremony upon Candlemas Eve. Robert Herrick. OBCP

Ceres and Proserpina. Ovid. NAWM-7v1 *Fr.* Metamorphoses.

Ceriserie. Joshua Clover. BAP-01

Cerrada. Vicente Aleixandre. RaW

Cerré Mi Puerta al Mundo. Emilio Prados. RaW

Certain branches cut. October. Denise Levertov. TRP

Certain Country, A. Yosano Akiko. CAoMJL1, *tr. by* Janine Beichman

Certain day became a presence to me, A. Variation on a Theme by Rilke. Denise Levertov. StAl

Certain Evening, A. G. K. Chesterton. OxAEP-2

Certain evenings a little before the golden. Excursion to the Planet Mercury. Alice Oswald. MoWP

Certain fiction bit me, A. Birthmark. Khadar Mohiuddin. HotL, *tr. by* V. Narayana Rao

Certain kind of man asks the same questions, A. Not Knowing Nijinsky or Diaghilev. Rachel Zucker. LegDan

Certain Lady, A [*with music*]. Dorothy Parker. NIL-7; NIP-4

Certain landscapes insist on fidelity. Leaving Sonora. Agha Shahid Ali. NAMCP V.2

Certain Light, A. Marie Howe. FaoP

Certain Maxims of Archy. Don Marquis.
  "I once heard the survivors." NBLV

Certain names have been ruined forever. Itinerary. Reginald Shepherd. RD

Certain of no definition, we few. Agnostic's funeral prayer. Lionel Abrahams. TSAP

Certain overcoat lived at home for many years, A. Overcoat, The. Alda Merini. CItWP, *tr.* by Cinzia Sartini Blum and Lara Trubowitz

Certain painter, leaving in the morning, A. Saddled Ass, The. Jean de La Fontaine. NBLV, *tr.* by Deems Taylor

Certain people would not clean their buttons. Bohemians, The. Ivor Gurney. FaBoWar

Certain precautions, obstacles. Religious Art. Charlie Smith. PA9/11

Certain Questions for Monsieur Renoir. John Ormond. AngWePo

Certain saurian species, notably the skink, are capable of shedding their tails in self-defense when threatened. Three Small Parables for My Poet Friends. Stanley Kunitz. OxBoAm

Certain Sickness, Deep Love. Yi Kyŏngnim. EcSo, *tr.* by Peter H. Lee

Certain sort of bravery, A. Thomas Hardy. FaBoWar *Fr.* Dynasts, The.

Certain things here are quietly American. Derek Walcott. NAEL-6v2; NAEL-7v2; NoP-4; NoP-5 *Fr.* Midsummer.

Certain words disappear from a language. Louisiana Perch. Ron Padgett. FTOS; NYP2

Certaine manière je. Jacques Roubaud. YaTCFP

Certaine Verses Written by the Said Ladie Jane with a Pinne. Lady Jane Grey Dudley. EMWP

Certainly they are the same weathered trees. From the Field. Lenard D. Moore. GT

Certainly you've missed this on your reading list. Rilke's Letter from Rome. Star Black. KGB

Certains disent: regardez ce qui se passe en coulisse. Dans l'air limpide. Michel Houellebecq. YaTCFP

Certainties in huge colors. Nadia Tueni. CFP, *tr.* by Elaine Gardiner

Certainty. Octavio Paz. TCLAP, *tr.* by Charles Tomlinson

Certainty that cheated me, The. There Is Music Going Down the Stairs. Ali Mansour. AnVo, *tr.* by Mohamed Enani

Certificate of Live Birth. Kimberly M. Blaeser. UnSA

Certified Public Accountant recalls the Early 1950s, The. Robert A. Fink. TiP2

'Cession's stahted on de gospel way, De. Spiritual, A. Paul Laurence Dunbar. SacPr

C'est en vain que je vois les arbres toujours verts. Octobre. Paul Claudel. YaTCFP

C'est l'aube. Et cette lampe a-t-elle donc fini. Tâche d'espérance, La. Yves Bonnefoy. YaTCFP

C'est l'hiver. Humide et froid. Blanc ou gris. Hiver, L'. Pascalle Monnier. YaTCFP

C'est vrai que je croyais en la ferveur immense de vivre. Cheval, Le. Tristan Tzara. YaTCFP

Cestello Annunciation, The. Andrew Hudgins. UpMys

Cet espace il te faut l'abandonner à sa propre fructification. Parle. Pierre Albert Jourdan. YaTCFP

Ceylon. Nishiwaki Junzaburo. CAoMJL1, *tr.* by Hosea Hirata

Ceyx and Alcyone. Ovid. NoSic *Fr.* Metamorphoses.

Cézanne. Gertrude Stein. OxBoAm

Cézanne. Jean Tardieu. YaTCFP

Cézanne at Aix. Charles Tomlinson. NAMCP V.2

Cha Till Maccruimein (Departure of the 4th Camerons). Ewart Alan Mackintosh. FaBoWar

Chacun à son goût. Dorothy Molloy. NIrP

Chaff, The. W. S. Merwin. CAP-8

Chagrin. Isaac Rosenberg. HarvBoo; MoBrPo

Ch'ai-kuan Mountain Pass. Wang Shih-chieng. ColAnChi, *tr.* by Richard John Lynn

Chain, The. Maxine W. Kumin. TaR

Chain Mail. Elliot Fried. SUP

Chain mail hand, a titanic dustpan, A. Dragging Bottom. Harry Thurston. Coast

Chain of green mountains appears through a white cloud, A. Cloudy Mountain. Pou Kuksa. BecRai, *tr.* by Kim Daljin, Kim Won-Chung and Christopher Merrill

Chain of memory is resurrection I am a vain man, The. Charles Olson. APSN

Chain of Pearl, A. Lady Diana Primrose.
  Eight Pearle, The: Science. EMWP

Chain Store Daisy. Harold Rome. ReLy

Chained. Rayaprolu Subbarao. HotL, *tr.* by V. Narayana Rao

Chained bodies. Middle Passage. Sonya Brooks. InTrad

Chained in the market-place he stood. African Chief, The. William Cullen Bryant. ColAP

Chains, chains. Slave Boat. Obu Udeozo. NeNiPo

Chains of hell that hold his friend, The. (LL) Horace. NAEL-6v1; NAEL-7v1 *Fr.* Odes.

Chair. Hagiwara Sakutaro. PFTM-1

Chair. Susan Howe.
  "Plain chair or two back." AWPTFC

Chair and bed red. Reds in the Bed. Peter Finch. Oth

Chair by the Window, The. Anne Winters. BeAl *Fr.* Elizabeth Near and Far.

Chair in the Meadow, The. William Stafford. BodElec

Chair she sat in, like a burnished throne, The. T. S. Eliot. HarvBoo *Fr.* Waste Land, The.

Chairmaker, The. Siobhan Campbell. IrLP; MFPA

Chairperson of the board. Global Inequalities. Jayne Cortez. PrTe

Chairs. Valerie Worth. NTCP

Chairs in Snow. Elwyn Brooks White. ChAP

Chairs move by themselves, and books. Alzheimer's. Bob Hicok. AmPoNex; BeAl; P180; PoCu

Chalazion. Allison Joseph. NAPBL

Chalcan Female Song. *Unknown.* PFTM-1 *Fr.* Cantares Mexicanos.

Chaldean Ruins, The. Dunya Mikhail. PoArWo, *tr.* by Samira Kawar

Chalk and Soot. Wassily Kandinsky. PFTM-1

Chalk Draw Ranch. Sherry Craven. TiP2

Chalk mark sex of the nation, on walls we drummers. Three Modes of History and Culture. Imamu Amiri Baraka. BrAP; ESEAA; OxAAAP; PmAP

Challenge, A. Charles MacKay. STuOW *Fr.* Volunteers, The.

Challenge to the Reader, A. Tad Richards. SwNoth

Chamber is there!, The. (LL) Bluebeard's Closet. Rose Terry Cooke. APN-2; NAAPv.1; TCAPo

Chamber maid. Christening Pot Boiler. Christopher Meredith. TCAWP

Chamber Music. Li Shang-yin. CCL1, *tr.* by James J. Y. Liu

Chamber Music. Carl Phillips. NAPBL

Chambered Nautilus. Linda Hogan. BodElec

Chambered Nautilus, The. Oliver Wendell Holmes. APN-1; ColAP; CtM; ITBLP; NAAL-3; NAAPv.1; NCAP; NoP-4; NoP-5; OxBoAm; TCAPo; TFi; WaAnP *Fr.* Autocrat of the Breakfast Table, The.

Chambre dans l'espace, La. René Char. YaTCFP

Chameleon. Daria Menicanti. CItWP, *tr.* by Cinzia Sartini Blum and Lara Trubowitz

Chameleon, The. Judith Ortiz Cofer. PfSP

Chameleon, The. Matthew Prior. OBSV

Chameleon was wrong, The. Death Song, A. Steve Chimombo. HBAPE

Chameleons are fine. Natalya Belchenko. CRWP, *tr.* by Robert Reid

Chamois Hunter's Love, The. Felicia Dorothea Hemans. RWP; VWP

Chamouni at Sunrise. Frederike Brün. SacPr, *tr.* by Timothy Dwight

Champagne goes straight to my head. Thinking of You, Hiroshima. Betsy Sholl. PBCAP

Champagne Rosée. John Kenyon. OBEV

Champion Chant. Rohan B. Preston. WaCA

Champs d'Honneur. Ernest Hemingway. AmWaPo; IllVoic; PoA 2002

"Champs Elysées of Broadway" says the awning. Elysian Fields. Marilyn Hacker. RA

Chan eil mo shùil air Calbharaigh. Calbharaigh. Sorley MacLean. EdScPo

Chance. Ai. ExTi

Chance and chance and thereby starlit. Animula. George Oppen. FTOS

Chance And Essence. "Angelus Silesius." GePo *Fr.* Cherubical Wanderer, The.

Chance befuddles prophets. Chance Child. Saunders Lewis. BBMWP, *tr.* by Joseph P. Clancy

Chance Child. Saunders Lewis. BBMWP, *tr.* by Joseph P. Clancy

Chance Encounter with a Wounded Man Playing a Theremin. Dara Wier. MAAN

Chance encounter—he'd, A. All Messages Have Been Played. John Ashbery. VaPo

Chance had an egg break in earthly Paradise. Egg, An. Max Jacob. YaTCFP, *tr.* by Mary Ann Caws and Jean-Pierre Cauvin

Chance led me once, when idling through the street. *Unknown.* CAGL *Fr.*

Chance Meeting of Two Men, A. Alberto A. Ríos. PML

Chance Meetings. Conrad Potter Aiken. TCAPo

Chance sight on a windowsill, the fly sits warming its back. Cold Fly, A. Yang Wan-li. NDACCP, *tr.* by David Hinton

Chance to meet is difficult, The. Chance to Meet Is Difficult, The. Li Shang-yin. WoPoe, *tr.* by Arthur Sze

Chancelor's Gravel-Drive, The. Po Chü-i. CCL1; WoPoe, *tr.* by Arthur Waley

Chance-passing nurse grumbling about some visitor—He ought to stop smoking!, A. Brand Plucked from the Anti-tank Fire, A. Ramy Ditzanny. NRoS, *tr.* by Esther Raizen

Chancery Morals. Winthrop Mackworth Praed. NOBRP

Chances. Taylor Graham. CalPo

Chances of Magic, The.   Keith Waldrop.   OnScMo

Chances "R."   Allen Ginsberg.   CAGL

Chandeliers.   Alexander Pomerantz.   Prolet, tr. by Amelia Glaser

Chandeliers: we make hanging lights.   Chandeliers.   Alexander Pomerantz. Prolet, tr. by Amelia Glaser

Chandlery.   Peter Didsbury.   NeBrP

Chanel № 5.   Robyn Schiff.   LegDan

Chang Chih-ho, in the 8th century, lost his post under the Emperor.   Changs. Eliot Weinberger.   WANABP

Chang'an.   Lu Chao-lin.   CCL1, tr. by Stephen Owen

Chang'an's broad avenues.   Chang'an.   Lu Chao-lin.   CCL1, tr. by Stephen Owen

Change / as.   Asalteris.   Norman Henry, II Pritchard.   EGAG

Change, The [with music].   Samuel Chimsoro.   NAfrP

Change, The.   A. A. Hedge Cole.   ReEnLa

Change, The.   Tony Hoagland.   BeAl

Change, The.   Henry King, Bishop of Chichester.   NOSC

Change, The.   Denise Levertov.   BAP-97

Change, The: Kyoto-Tokyo Express.   Allen Ginsberg.   APSN

Change blots out change,—their very memory dies.   Richard Henry Wilde. APN-1 Fr. Hesperia.

Change hands.   Currency.   Craig Watson.   OnScMo

Change is the law. The new must oust the old.   Last of His Tribe.   Oodgeroo of the tribe Noonuccal.   BMAP

Change Me, Some God, Into That Breathing Rose!   William Wordsworth. CenSon Fr. River Duddon [A Series of Sonnets], The.

Change, move, dead clock, that this fresh day.   Small Prayer.   Weldon Kees. PoA 2002

Change of Address.   Kathleen Fraser.   CalPo

Change of tone, the human hope gone gray, The. (LL)   Arrangements with Earth for Three Dead Friends.   James Wright.   NIL-7; NIP-4

Change onward from ours to that of beings who walk other spheres, The. (LL) World below the Brine, The.   Walt Whitman.   APN-1; NoP-4

Change Partners.   Irving Berlin.   ReLy

Change Should Breed Change.   William Drummond of Hawthornden.   OBEV

Change sun by sun and fling and laugh.   Ian Patterson.   VaPo Fr. Hardihood.

Change thy minde since she doth change.   Robert Devereux, 2d Earl of Essex. PBRV

Change: "Use to be eye would be laying there."   Quincy Troupe.   PML

Changed in a trice you find me.   Bicycle Song (For Women).   Robert Williams Buchanan.   ArBi

Changed Man, The.   Robert Phillips.   GoPo

Changed to Himself at last by eternity.   Tomb of Edgar Allan Poe, The. Stéphane Mallarmé.   SxFrPo, tr. by A. M. and E. H. Blackmore

Changeling, The.   Judith Ortiz Cofer.   NIL-7; TouFir

Changeling, The.   John Greenleaf Whittier.   MakPoe

Changes.   May Probyn.   VWP

Changes.   Kiki Wainwright.   OGAHCP, tr. by Boadiba and Jack Hirschman

Changes—Eight.   Norman J. Loftis.   EGAG

Changes—Five.   Norman J. Loftis.   EGAG

Changes—One.   Norman J. Loftis.   EGAG

Chang'gu: A Poem Written on the Twenty-Seventh Day of the Fifth Month.   Li Ho.   CCL1, tr. by John Frodsham

Changing.   Daphne Rock.   Prnts

Changing Address Books.   Michael S. Glaser.   UnSA

Changing Borders.   Robert Bonazzi.   TiP2

Changing clothes / But not.   Issa.   ZenPo, tr. by Takashi Ikemoto and Lucien Stryk

Changing Diapers.   Gary Snyder.   RaBo

Changing guests, each in a different mood, The.   Dante Gabriel Rossetti. NAEL-6v2 Fr. House of Life, The.

Changing Room.   John A. Scott.   BMAP

Changing the Oil.   Eloise Klein Healy.   WiU

Changing the Wheel.   Bertolt Brecht.   PoSu, tr. by Michael Hamburger

Changing What We Mean.   Eloise Klein Healy.   WiU

Changing: "Your unmistakable breasts, plain, finely wrinkled."   Jason Shinder. NevBe

Ch'ang-Kan Village Song.   Li Po.   NDACCP, tr. by David Hinton

Chango.   René Depestre.   PFTM-2 Fr. Rainbow for the Christian West, A.

Ch'ang-O.   Li Shang-yin.   ChinPo, tr. by Ye Weilian [or Yeh Wei-lien or Wai-lim Yip]

Changs.   Eliot Weinberger.   WANABP

Channel Boat, The.   Yosano Akiko.   WoPoe, tr. by Janine Beichman

"What shall I wear to sleep in alone?"   WoPoe, tr. by Janine Beichman

Channel caves in his hand like weak cushion, The.   Pure and Applied.   Gig Ryan.   VaPo

Channel Firing.   Thomas Hardy.   BrAP; CABP; HarvBoo; HeIP-4; NAEL-6v2; NAEL-7v2; NAMCP V.1; NIL-7; NIP-4; NoAM; NoP-4; NoP-5; OxAEP-2; OxBEV; PoAgWa; PoPoPo; PoWW; SoSe-8; TFi; WaAnP

Channel flaps like a tent, The.   Sea 6.   Chŏng Chiyong.   CAMKP, tr. by Kevin O'Rourke

Channing and Thoreau.   James Russell Lowell.   TCAPo Fr. Fable for Critics, A.

Chanson.   Ernst Jandl.   OnScMo; PFTM-2

Chanson Dada.   Tristan Tzara.   PFTM-1

Chanson Delice.   Beatrice E. Harmon.   YaYoPo

Chanson d'Outre Tombe.   Philip Whalen.   BB

Chanson: "Il naissait un poulain sous les feuilles de bronze."   "St.-John Perse."   YaTCFP

Chanson: "Mon cheval arrêté sous l'arbre plein de tourterelles."   "St.-John Perse."   YaTCFP

Chanson Philosophique.   Timothy Steele.   PoA 2002

Chanson pour des fantômes et pour celles qui ont disparu.   Philippe Soupault. YaTCFP

Chant.   Roundness.   Pierre Drieu la Rochelle.   CuPo

Chant.   Ron Schreiber.   PrTe

Chant for Dark Hours.   Dorothy Parker.   AmWit; ItWoWo

Chant for Reapers.   Wilfrid Thorley.   OBEV

Chant from the Iroquois Book of Rites.   Unknown.   APN-2, tr. by Horatio Hale

Chant of Lamentation.   Haunani-Kay Trask.   FiBr

Chant of praise for the idi amin dada.   Wopko Jensma.   TSAP

Chant of the Frontiersman.   Wang Ch'ang-ling.   NDACCP, tr. by William Carlos Williams

Chant to the Fire-fly.   William Ellery Channing.   TCAPo

Chant to the Fire-Fly.   Unknown.   APN-2, tr. by Henry Rowe Schoolcraft

Chantars No Pot Gaire Valer.   Bernard [or Bernart] de Ventadour or Ventadorn. APSN, tr. by Paul Blackburn

Chanted Calendar, A.   Sydney Thompson Dobell.   OBEV Fr. Balder.

Chanticleer.   Celia Laighton Thaxter.   NOxBChV

Chanting Buddha's name.   Unknown.   SoOfWa, tr. by Sam Hamill

Chanting Cherubs, The [A Group by Greenough].   Richard Henry Dana. APN-1

Chanting of banishment, / exhaling flame.   Elegy for the Time at Hand. Adonis.   AF, tr. by Samuel Hazo

Chanting the square deific, out of the One advancing, out of the sides. Chanting the Square Deific.   Walt Whitman.   APN-1; NAAL-3

Chants Democratic and Native Americans: 5.   Walt Whitman.   APN-1

Chants to the Deity.   Unknown.   APN-2, tr. by Henry Rowe Schoolcraft

Chao-Mong-Mu freely laid his hands over the sky.   Sermon.   Emanuel Carnevali.   APT-2

Chaos.   Still Life: The Table.   Theo Van Doesburg.   PFTM-1

Chaos of mountains upon mountains, A.   Tu Fu [or Du Fu].   ChinPo, tr. by Ye Weilian [or Yeh Wei-lien or Wai-lim Yip]

Chaos overshadows us.   Anne Carson.   WoBe Fr. Truth About God, The.

Chaos rumoured.   B. P. Nichol.   PFTM-2 Fr. Martyrology 7, The.

Chaos's Window.   Murilo Mendes.
   "Everything happens / In an Egypt of aerial corridors."   Eno, tr. by Chris Daniels

Chaotic sun on asphalt camouflages.   Argument.   Jonathan Galassi.   KGB

Chapala still remembers the foreigner.   Foreigner, A.   Witter Bynner.   APT-1

Chapel of the Miraculous Medal.   Mark Wunderlich.   NAPBL

Chapel's cowbell, The.   Crusoe's Island.   Derek Walcott.   VCWP

Chaplin and Others.   Alan Llwyd.   BBMWP, tr. by Joseph P. Clancy

Chaplinesque.   Hart Crane.   APT-2; HeIP-4; NAAL-5; NAAPv.2; NAMCP V.1; NoAM; OxBoAm

Chapmen.   Unknown.   FaBoVe

Chapped Lips.   Dean Young.   SUP

Chappell—you who love to jest.   How to Do It.   Martial.   WoPoe, tr. by Fred Chappell

Chapter 1.   Lao Tzu.   CCL1 Fr. Way and Its Power, The.

Chapter 2 (Fragment).   Bible, O.T.   NOSC Fr. Paraphrase Upon Job, A.

Chapter 4.   Lao Tzu.   CCL1 Fr. Way and Its Power, The.

Chapter 5.   Lao Tzu.   CCL1 Fr. Way and Its Power, The.

Chapter 6.   Lao Tzu.   CCL1 Fr. Way and Its Power, The.

Chapter 9.   Lao Tzu.   CCL1 Fr. Way and Its Power, The.

Chapter 10.   Lao Tzu.   CCL1 Fr. Way and Its Power, The.

Chap. 10 Book 2.   Blas de Otero.   RaW, tr. by Hardie St. Martin

Chapter 2: "Stopping before the steps, the young monk gushed."   Tung Chieh-yüan.   ColAnChi Fr. Master Tung's Western Chamber Romance.

Chapter 3: Parable.   Unknown.   ColAnChi Fr. Lotus Sūtra.

Chapter 42.   Bible, O.T.   ChIV-17 Fr. Paraphrase Upon Job, A.

Chapter 2, Book 35.   John Ashbery.   BodElec

Chapter 38, Part 3.   Derek Walcott.   NoP-5 Fr. Omeros.

Chapter 7: Black Bottom.   Jackie Kay.   MoWP Fr. Adoption Papers, The.

Chapter A. Christian Bök.
  "Awkward grammar appals a craftsman. A Dada bard." OpeFie
Chapter and Verse. Gonzalo Rojas. TCLAP, *tr.* by Christopher Maurer
Chapter E. Christian Bök.
  "Enfettered, these sentences repress free speech. The." OpeFie
  "Greek schemers seek egress *en ténèbres*, then enter the melee." IFF
Chapter Heading. Ernest Hemingway. PoA 2002
Chapter I. Christian Bök.
  "Writing is inhibiting. Sighing, I sit, scribbling in ink." OpeFie
Chapter II. Elizabeth Singer Rowe. PEW *Fr.* Paraphrase on the Canticles, A.
Chapter IV. Elizabeth Singer Rowe. PEW
Chapter O. Christian Bök.
  "Loops on bold fonts now form lots of words for books." OpeFie
Chapter One. Stephanie Brown. BodElec; SUP
Chapter U. Christian Bök.
  "*Kultur* spurns Ubu—thus Ubu pulls stunts. Ubu shuns." OpeFie
Chapter V. Elizabeth Singer Rowe. PEW
Chapter XXIII: Of Marriage. Rosmarie Waldrop. PFTM-2 *Fr.* Key into the Language of America, A.
Chapter XXIV: Concerning Their Coyne. Rosmarie Waldrop. PFTM-2 *Fr.* Key into the Language of America, A.
Chaque case a sa voisine. Chaque case. Anne Portugal. YaTCFP
character. Detonation. Francesco Cangiullo. PFTM-1
Character. Taslima Nasrin. VCWP
Character and beauty. (LL) Minks, The. Toi Derricotte. FuFl; UrbNat
Character of a Happy Life, The. Sir Henry Wotton. BASC; NOSC; OBEV; OxBEV; SacPr
Character of a Roundhead, The [*with music*]. *Unknown.* NOSC; WaAnP
Character of Holland, The. Andrew Marvell. BASC
Character of Love Seen as a Search for the Lost, The. Kenneth Patchen. CLPP
Character of Sir Robert Walpole, The. Jonathan Swift. WaAnP
Charcoal fire. Issa. IllVoic *Fr.* Issa: A Suite of Haiku.
Chard Whitlow. Henry Reed. MoBrPo; NBLV; NoP-4; NoP-5; OBCoV; UV
Chardin Exhibition, The. Edward Hirsch. RoV
Charge, A. Herbert Trench. OBEV
Charge at Waterloo. Sir Walter Scott. FaBoWar
Charge of the Goddess, The. Doreen Valiente. HW, *tr.* by Starhawk
Charge of the Light Brigade, The. Alfred Tennyson. BRP; CABP; ChAP; FaBoWar; NAEL-6v2; NAEL-7v2; NoP-4; NoP-5; OBWP; OxAEP-2; OxBEV; TFi; UV
Charge to students of the Tao, A. 149. Shih Shu. CSKM, *tr.* by James H. Sanford
Charge to the Poets, A. William Whitehead.
  "If nature prompts you, or if friends persuade." OBSV
Charges the Indians five bucks a head to enter. (LL) Evolution. Sherman Alexie. NAMCP V.2; NeAmPo; PoPoPo
Charioteer of Delphi, The. James Merrill. GS
Charioteer, The. Faye George. PoA 2002
Chariots horses draperies certitudes. (LL) Adrienne Rich. NoP-4; NoP-5 *Fr.* Eastern War Time.
Charis one day in discourse. Ben Jonson. NAEL-7v1 *Fr.* Celebration of Charis in Ten Lyric[k] Pieces [*or* Peeces], A.
Charisma. Ai. ExTi
C[h]aritas Nimia; or, The Dear[e] Bargain. Richard Crashaw. NOSC
Charity [*with music*]. Henrietta Cordelia Ray. CBWP-3
Charity and Humility. Henry More. SacPr
Charity Overcoming Envy. Marianne Moore. GS
Charity's Eye. Nizami Ganjavi. DiBP,
Charlatan, The. Unsi Al-Haj. PFTM-2, *tr.* by Pierre Joris
Charlene-N-Booker 4Ever. Forrest Hamer. GeoHom
Charles and Bruce, Geoff and Ron and Nancy. All Friends Together. Ronald Albert Simpson. NOBAu
Charles Augustus Chaytor. You Can't Make Love by Wireless. George Grossmith and P. G. Wodehouse. ReLy
Charles Augustus Fortescue [*with music*]. Joseph Hilaire Pierre Belloc. NoAM
Charles II. Andrew Marvell. OBSV *Fr.* Last Instructions to a Painter, The.
Charles! my slow heart was only sad, when first. Sonnet to a Friend Who Asked How I Felt When the Nurse First Presented My Infant to Me. Samuel Taylor Coleridge. CenSon
Charles on Fire. James Merrill. CAP-8; HeIP-4; OxBoAm
Charles on the Trevisan, night bridge. Self-Portrait. Charles Wright. OxBoAm
Charles river reaps here like a sickle, The. Professor Kelleher and the Charles River. Desmond O'Grady. PBCIP
Charles Sumner [*with music*]. Henrietta Cordelia Ray. CBWP-3

Charles the King, our Emperor, the great. *Unknown.* NAWM-5v1; NAWM-7v1 *Fr.* Song of Roland, The.
Charles, the last king of Britain. Morgan Llwyd.
  "Law was ever above kings, The." AngWePo
Charles used to watch Naomi, taking heart. Laboratory Poem. James Merrill. CAP-8
Charles—and I say it wond'ring—thou must know. To Charles Diodati. John Milton. OxBSo, *tr.* by William Cowper
Charleston. Cecil Mack. ReLy
Charleston. Henry Timrod. AmWaPo; APN-2; CBCWP; ColAP; OxBoAm; PCW; TCAPo
Charleston. Afaa Michael Weaver. RWB
Charleston Baskets. Carole Boston Weatherford. FiBr
Charleston, Charleston. Charleston. Cecil Mack. NAAPv.2
Charleston Gals. *Unknown.* SSUS
Charleston, South Carolina. Christopher Nickelson. BtF
Charley du Bignon [*with music*]. Mary E. Tucker. CBWP-1
Charley Parker Looked like Buddha. Jack Kerouac. BB
Charlie and Joe. John Redmond. NIrP
Charlie Chaplin. Charlie Chaplin Poem, The. Osip Emilevich Mandelstam. PFTM-1
Charlie Chaplin. Sadiq Sharshar. AnVo, *tr.* by Mohamed Enani
Charlie Chaplin Poem, The. Osip Emilevich Mandelstam. PFTM-1
Charlie Douglas. Katrina Porteous. NeBl
Charlie is my Darling. James Hogg. NePenScot
Charlie, our one hope, called the chucos from Braly Street. Effects of Abstract Art, The. Gary Soto. GeoHom
Charlie Parker's on the off ramp. Valentine's Day. Kenneth May. SeSe
Charlie said he wanted to die. Beatrix Gates. WiU *Fr.* Triptych.
Charlie Wolf used to whittle skinning knives. Halcyon Days. Jim Barnes. VCAP
Charlotte Brontë. Paul Hamilton Hayne. APN-2
Charlotte was dug out of my body. Caterpillar. Annie Foster. NLP
Charlottetown Harbour. Milton Acorn. Coast
Charm. *Unknown.* EMWP
Charm for What Looks Like. Kathy Fagan. RWB
Charm me asleep, and melt me so. To Music, to Becalm His Fever. Robert Herrick. OBEV
Charm of the Highway Strip, The. Jim Behrle. FreRad
Charm of the Nine Healing Herbs. *Unknown.* WoPoe, *tr.* by David Cloutier
Charm Rhyme, A. *Unknown.* FaBoVe
Charm, The. Rita Dove. OxAAAP
Charm to Destroy the Male Child of the Laird of Parkis. Isabel Gowdie. EMWP
Charm'd by thy suffrage, shall I yet aspire. To a Friend. Charlotte Smith. RWP
Charmed by a girl's soft ears. Downy Hair. Takahashi Shinkichi. ZenPo, *tr.* by Takashi Ikemoto and Lucien Stryk
Charming oysters I cry. Oysters. Jonathan Swift. ErotSp
Charming Woman, The. Helen Selina Blackwood, Countess of Dufferin and Clandeboye. VWP
Charmion's Lament [*with music*]. Eloise Bibb. CBWP-4
Charms of Small Women. Juan, Archpriest of Hita Ruiz. BLPSL, *tr.* by Rene de Costa, Rigas Kappatos and Eleni Paidoussi
Charnel Ground, The. Allen Ginsberg. BB; BodElec
Charnel Ship, The. Lucretia Davidson. TreFP
Charnel-house, The. Henry Vaughan. FSCP
Charon. Louis MacNeice. NAMCP V.1; OxBEV; PNI
Charon. Virgil. OBVE *Fr.* Aeneid [*or* Eneados *or* Aeneis], The.
Charon. Virgil. NPeEn *Fr.* Aeneid [*or* Eneados *or* Aeneis], The.
Charon. Zonas. PoDa, *tr.* by Brooks Haxton
Charon's Cosmology. Charles Simic. PoPoPo; WaAnP
Charon's Song. Charles Murray. EdScPo
Chart Indent. Richard Eberhart. BodElec
Chart Showing Rain, Winds, Isothermal Lines and Ocean Currents. Louise Owen. YaYoPo
Charter Flight into the Past, A. Hans Sahl. GTCP, *tr.* by Reinhold Grimm
Chartist Meeting. Mike Jenkins. AngWePo
Chartist's Complaint, The. Ralph Waldo Emerson. NCAP
Chartres. George Oppen. OxBoAm
Chartres. Edith Wharton. APN-2
Chartres of Gowrie, The. Don Paterson. NePenScot
Chase, The. Sir Walter Scott. NePenScot *Fr.* Lady of the Lake, The.
Chase, The. William Somerville.
  "First let the kennel be the huntsman's care." DiBP
Chase, The. Richard Tayson. AmPoNex

Chase of Jessy, The.   William Shenstone.   STuOW *Fr.* Describing the Sorrow of an Ingenuous Mind on the Melancholy Event of a Licentious Amour [*or* Elegy 26].

Chase of the Metaphor, The.   Bible, *O.T.*   STuOW *Fr.* Paraphrase on the Book of Job, A.

Chased round and round.   Akera Kanko.   EMJL, *tr. by* Haruo Shirane

Chasing Memory.   Tripuraneni Srinivas.   HotL., *tr. by* V. Narayana Rao

Chasing on the margins of pond-waters, the sun.   J. D. McClatchy.   WiU *Fr.* First Steps.

Chasm.   Mary Gomez Parham.   OWABP

Chasm, The.   Suji Kwock Kim.   AmWaPo

Chaste Crocale by two boys, Astacus and Idas.   Titus Calpurnius Siculus.   RomPo *Fr.* Eclogues.

Chaste Maiden, shining scarlet, The.   *Unknown.*   ColAnChi *Fr.* Classic of Odes.

Chaste Stranger, The.   James Tate.   NoAM

Chastity Belt.   Yusef Komunyakaa.   KGB

Chastity ("I Mean That Too, But Yet a Hidden Strength").   John Milton.   NOSC *Fr.* Comus; a Masque Presented at Ludlow Castle.

Chateau de Soupir, 1917.   Malcolm Cowley.   AmWaPo

Château Jackson.   Louis MacNeice.   OxBEV

Château noir et blanc fait la différence, Un.   Angers.   Bernard Noël.   YaTCFP

Château, The.   Henry Reed.   NoP-4

Chateaux en Espagne.   Henrietta Cordelia Ray.   CBWP-3

Chatsworth.   Charles Cotton.   OBGa *Fr.* Wonders of the Peak, The.

Chattanooga Choo-Choo.   Mack Gordon.   ReLy

Chattels.   Celia de Fréine.   NIrP, *tr. by* the author

Chatte-Show Host came with us, yclept Wogan, A.   Chaucer: The Wogan's Tale.   Stanley J. Sharpless.   UV

Chaucer.   Henry Wadsworth Longfellow.   APN-1; HeIP-4; OBEV; TCAPo; TFi; WoPoe

Chaucer, Langland, Douglas, Dunbar, with all your.   Ode to the Medieval Poets.   W. H. Auden.   GoPo

Chaucer: The Wogan's Tale.   Stanley J. Sharpless.   UV

Chaucer's Retraction.   Geoffrey Chaucer.   NAEL-6v1; NAEL-7v1 *Fr.* Canterbury Tales, The.

Chaucer's Wordes unto Adam, his Owne Scriveyn.   Geoffrey Chaucer.   NAEL-6v1; NAEL-7v1

   (To His Scribe Adam.)   NoP-4; NoP-5

   (Words unto Adam, His Own Scriveyn.)   CABP

Chauffeur, Le.   Hédi Kaddour.   YaTCFP

Chaunt of the Brazen Head, The.   Winthrop Mackworth Praed.
   "I think the thing you call Renown."   OBSV

Chauntecleer.   Geoffrey Chaucer.   OWoS *Fr.* Canterbury Tales, The.

Chaunts of Life.   Mathilde Blind.   VWP *Fr.* Ascent of Man, The.

Chaunts of the Brazen Head, The. II.   Winthrop Mackworth Praed.   NOBRP

Chauvinist.   Norman Alexander MacCaig.   NPeEn

Che Fece . . . Il Gran Rifiuto.   Constantine P. Cavafy.   BeAl, *tr. by* Edmund Keeley and Philip Sherrard

Che Sara Sara.   Rose Terry Cooke.   NAAPv.1; SWaP

Cheap Gas.   Brenda Hillman.   RoV

Cheap movie theaters, saloons, fly-by-night markets.   Shadow, The.   Tōge Sankichi.   AtGh, *tr. by* Richard H. Minear

Cheap Replicas of the Eiffel Tower.   Elton Glaser.   PBCAP

Cheap Repository: The Story of Sinful Sally. Told by Herself.   Hannah More.   RWP

Cheap Seats, the Cincinnati Gardens, Professional Basketball, 1959.   William Matthews.   MoASP; PML

Cheap, The / screwdriver reams the cheap.   Tools: An Ode.   Andrew Hudgins.   PML

Cheared with this hope, to Paris I returned.   William Wordsworth.   NAEL-6v2; NAEL-7v2

Cheat of Cupid; or, The Ungentle Guest, The.   Robert Herrick.   OBVE

Cheat, The.   Joseph Beaumont.   NOSC

Cheated Heart.   Arthur Rimbaud.   SxFrPo, *tr. by* Martin Sorrell

Check every outflash, every ruder sally.   Alfred Tennyson.   CenSon

Check One.   Regie Cabico.   ReBoTo; WiU

Check to Song.   Edward Robert Bulwer-Lytton.   *See* Going Back Again.

Check Up.   Patricia Donegan.   WhBo

Check Yourself.   Lowell Fulson.   ASA

Checkmark.   Stratis Haviaras.   MotU

Cheek by cheek on our pillow[s].   Lament.   *Unknown.*   ErotSp, *tr. by* Sam Hamill

Cheek of earth and say, There, there, child. (LL)   Snow: "Today the snow is drifting."   Philip Levine.   ColAP; UrbNat; WaAnP

Cheek to Cheek.   Irving Berlin.   ReLy

Cheekbone footprint husk if only they could write.   Centered.   P. Inman.   FTOS

Cheekbones goes business.   Poetry fro Dummies.   Joel Dailey.   AnSo

Cheer Up, My Mates.   Abraham Cowley.   OxAEP-1

Cheer up, my mates, the wind does fairly blow.   Cheer Up, My Mates.   Abraham Cowley.   OxAEP-1

Cheered as the woods (where new waked choirs they meet).   Sir William Davenant.   DiBP *Fr.* Gondibert.

Cheerful Girls at Smiller's Bar, 1971, The.   Jack A. Mapanje.   HBAPE; NAfrP

Cheerleaders.   Lisa Coffman.   AmPoNex

Cheerly firme Vesta, clad in verdant Green.   To Their Most Excellent Majesty of Great Brittaines Monarchy.   Mary Fage.   EMWP

Cheers.   Charles McDonald.   NLP

Cheese for the Archdeacon, A.   Thomas Hughes.   AngWePo

Chefs and saints may still appear to blithe it. (LL)   Moon Landing.   W. H. Auden.   EmeKit; OxAEP-2

Chekhov, my country is Ward 6.   Ward 6.   Tanure Ojaide.   HBAPE

Chelsea.   Eric Johnson.   NevBe

Chembank Card.   David S. Mills.   InTrad

Chemical names, bird names, names of fire.   Saying Your Names.   Richard Siken.   LegDan

Chemical tapestry of your brain, The.   In Ignorant Cadence.   Maura Stanton.   YaYoPo

Chemicals ripen the citrus.   In California.   Donald Davie.   NAMCP V.2; NoAM

Chemin de Fer.   Elizabeth Bishop.   StAl

Chemin de l'ermitage, Le.   Anne-Marie Albiach.
   "Contours d'une délinéation s'exercent sur le visage masqué et les membres, Les."   YaTCFP

Chemise.   Kay Ryan.   CalPo

Chemotherapy.   Julia Darling.   BeAl

Chen and Wei are brimming, The.   *Unknown.*   ChinPo, *tr. by* Ye Weilian [*or* Yeh Wei-lien *or* Wai-lim Yip]

Chen-gong: King's Serfs.   *Unknown.*   CCL1, *tr. by* Man Wong

Chengtu.   Tu Fu [*or* Du Fu].   TAL

Chepstow: A Poem.   Edward Davies.   OBWVE
   "Will no young British bard, on rhyme intent."   AngWePo

Cherished Daughter, The.   *Unknown.*   WoPoe, *tr. by* Nguyen Ngoc Bich

Chernobyl.   Mary Jo Salter.   AtGh; FFC

Chernobyl, / Eniwetok.   Radioactive.   Janine Canan.   HW

Chernobyl Icon.   Gwyneth Lewis.   NeBl *Fr.* Parables & Faxes.

Cherokee Love Song, A.   John Rollin Ridge.   APN-2

Cherokee, The [*with music*].   Mary Weston Fordham.   CBWP-2

Cherokee War-Song, Version 1.   *Unknown. See* From the South.

Cherokee War-Song, Version 2.   *Unknown. See* From the South: 2.

Cherries.   Michael C. Blumenthal.   PfSP

Cherries.   Joe Lamb.   RaBo

Cherries; a Parable, The.   Thomas Moore.   OBSV

Cherry.   Stuart Dybek.   PBCAP

Cherry blossom, The.   Wendy Cope.   PoCho

Cherry blossoms.   Issa.   IllVoic *Fr.* Issa: A Suite of Haiku.

Cherry blossoms.   Sobaku.   ZenPo, *tr. by* Takashi Ikemoto and Lucien Stryk

Cherry blossom's dance through the night, The. (LL)   Dance of the Cherry Blossom.   Jackie Kay.   EmeKit; PoCu

Cherry blossoms / dizzying.   Nishiyama Soin.   ZenPo, *tr. by* Takashi Ikemoto and Lucien Stryk

Cherry blossoms fall. (LL)   From all these trees.   Basho.   EH; SoOfWa, *tr. by* Sam Hamill

Cherry blossoms fallen.   Buson.   EH, *tr. by* Robert Hass

Cherry blossoms? / In these parts.   Issa.   ZenPo, *tr. by* Takashi Ikemoto and Lucien Stryk

Cherry blossoms, The.   Onitsura.   SoOfWa

Cherry bowl with a blue revolver, A.   Cherry Bowl with Blue Revolver: Neo-American Landscape.   Juan Felipe Herrera.   TouFir

Cherry Bowl with Blue Revolver: Neo-American Landscape.   Juan Felipe Herrera.   TouFir

Cherry Laurel, The.   Russell Thornton.   IFF

Cherry Robbers.   D. H. Lawrence.   MoBrPo

Cherry Trees, The.   Edward Thomas.   NAEL-6v2; NAEL-7v2; OBWP; Spl

Cherry-Blossom Wand, The.   Anna Wickham.   MoBrPo

Cherry-blossoms may be white, The.   Cherry-Tree.   József Erdélyi.   IQMS, *tr. by* Watson Kirkconnell

Cherrylog Road.   James Dickey.   ColAP; NIL-7; NIP-4; WaAnP; WeW-3

Cherry-ripe, ripe, ripe, I cry.   Cherry-ripe [*or* Cherrie-ripe].   Robert Herrick.   BASC; OBEV

Cherry-Tree.   József Erdélyi.   IQMS, *tr. by* Watson Kirkconnell

Cherry-Tree Carol, The.   *Unknown.*   ChrPo; HeIP-4; MakPoe; TFi
   (Joseph Was an Old Man.)   OBCP

Cherry-Tree Carol, The.   *Unknown.*   SacPr

Cherubical Wanderer, The.   "Angelus Silesius." *tr. by* George C. Schoolfield

Abomination Of Evil, The. GePo

Belief. GePo

Body, Soul, And Godhead. GePo

Chance And Essence. GePo

Each In His Own. GePo

God Is Nothing Physical. GePo

God Is To Me What I Desire. GePo

I Am As God And God As I. GePo

Light Exists In The Fire, The. GePo

Love. GePo

Man Is The Highest Thing. GePo

More Abandoned, The More Divine, The. GePo

One Knows Not What One Is. GePo

Only His Son Is With God. GePo

Rose, The. GePo

Secret Virginity, The. GePo

Sin. GePo

Spiritual Alchemy, The. GePo

Spiritual Ark And The Manna-Vessel, The. GePo

Spiritual Impregnation, The. GePo

Take Therefore That You May Have. GePo

To St. Augustine. GePo

Treasure Lies In the Cornerstone, The. GePo

Virtue's Goal Is God. GePo

Whoever Has Become All Divine. GePo

Cherwell, how pleased along thy willowed edge. To the River Cherwell. William Lisle Bowles. CenSon

Chess. Jorge Luis Borges. PoetW, *tr. by* Alastair Reid

Chess Game, A. Paul Goodman. OxBoAm

Chess I'm eager to play. Attributes of a Gentleman, The. Saint Ronald of Orkney. NePenScot, *tr. by* Paul Bibire

Chess Piece Cornered. John Kinsella. BMAP

Chess Play, The. Nicholas Breton. NoSic

Chessboard was reflected in her eyes, The. Chess Game, A. Paul Goodman. OxBoAm

Chest starts up again, The. (LL) David Wojahn. P180; PBCAP *Fr.* Mystery Train: A Sequence.

Chest X-Ray. Paula Tatarunis. BloBone

Chester. William Billings. *See* Let Tyrants Shake Their Iron Rod.

Chestnut by the eaves. Basho. EH, *tr. by* Robert Hass

Chestnut Casts His Flambeaux, The. A. E. Housman. BrAP; NAEL-6v2; NAEL-7v2

Chestnut they said had stood for seventy years, The. End of an Age, The. Robin Fulton. EdScPo

Chestnut Tree Deciding to Fly in May, The. Bobi Jones. BBMWP, *tr. by* Joseph P. Clancy

Chestnut tree's fearful, The. It stirs. Chestnut Tree Deciding to Fly in May, The. Bobi Jones. BBMWP, *tr. by* Joseph P. Clancy

Chestnuts roasting on an open fire. Christmas Song, The. Robert Wells. ReLy

Chestnuts shine through the cloven rind, The. Song. Thomas Bailey Aldrich. TreFP

Cheval, Le. Tristan Tzara. YaTCFP

Chevrolet fires past two blond children, The. American Tragedy. Joe Bolton. AmPoNex

Chewing [of] the Cud, The. Robert Herrick. ChIV-1

Chewing squash. Mixed. Tess Gallagher. AmZen

Cheyenne Mountain. Helen Hunt Jackson. APN-2; NAAPv.1

Chez Jane. Frank O'Hara. ColAP; NoAM; PoA 2002

Chez toi, Mahmout. Satire. Ibn Sharaf. WoPoe, *tr. by* Leticia Garza-Falcón and Christopher Middleton

Ch[i/o]mp. Ernst Jandl. OnScMo, *tr. by* Ben Friedlander

Chi River Gardens and Fields. Wang Wei. CrYelRi, *tr. by* Sam Hamill

Ch'iang Village. Tu Fu [*or* Du Fu]. CrYelRi, *tr. by* Sam Hamill

Chiapas [*with music*]. Gary Soto. NoAM

Chicago. Margaret Walker Alexander. GT

Chicago. Bret Harte. APN-2

Chicago. Susan Marshall. FTtHH

Chicago. Edgar Lee Masters.

"This is the city of great doges hidden." TCAPo

Chicago. Lola Ridge. PoA 2002

Chicago. Carl Sandburg. AmFaPo; APT-1; BRP; ColAP; EMP; FaBoA; FTtHH; IllVoic; MoAmPo; NAAL-5; NAAPv.2; NAMCP V.1; NoAM; NoP-4; NoP-5; OxBoAm; PoA 2002; TCAPo; TFi; TRP; WaAnP

Chicago Blues. Rohan B. Preston. AmPoNex

Chicago Charlie was a good time Romeo. Kansas City Kitty. Edgar Leslie. ReLy

Chicago Exposition Ode. Mary Weston Fordham. CBWP-2

Chicago "Manuel of Style" is really neat, The. John Tranter. NoAM *Fr.* Crying in Early Infancy.

Chicago, Oct. 8, 1969—I found myself carefully examining. Observations of Egyptian Artifacts. Britton Wilkie. AHA

Chicago on the Day Brother Increases His Chances of Reaching Age 21. Taiyon J. Coleman. BRtP

Chicago Poem. Lew Welch. BB

Chicago River. Jun Fujita. NAAPv.2

Chicago/3 Hours. PueRic

Chicago Zen. A. K. Ramanujan. NAMCP V.2

Chicago's avenues, as white as Poland. Derek Walcott. UrbNat *Fr.* Midsummer.

Chicana. Edward H. Garcia. TiP2

Chi-chi (Already across the stream). *Unknown.* ColAnChi *Fr.* I Ching [*or* The Book of Changes *or* The Classic of Changes].

Chick feed is what I eat. Muso Soseki. EaWin, *tr. by* W. S. Merwin

Chick Webb and Billy Strayhorn. Dancers. Afaa Michael Weaver. OxAAAP

Chickadee Encounter. Don McKay. OpeFie

Chickamauga. Charles Wright. PoA 2002

Chickcharnies. *Unknown.* SonAtl, *tr. by* Edward Kamau Brathwaite, Lester Browne, Eden Marshall and Myrna Teirrel

Chicken. Kim Addonizio. BAP-04

Chicken. Gertrude Stein. NAAPv.2; NAMCP V.1 *Fr.* Tender Buttons.

Chicken ("Alas a doubt in case of more go to say what it is cress. What is it. Mean. Potato. Loaves.") Gertrude Stein. NAMCP V.1 *Fr.* Tender Buttons.

Chicken Bucket. Jennifer L. Knox. FreRad

Chicken Guts. Jean Janzen. ACAMVP

Chicken. How shall I tell you what it is. Presentation of Two Birds to My Son, A. James Wright. YaYoPo

Chicken ("Pheasant and chicken, chicken is a peculiar bird.") Gertrude Stein. NAAPv.2; NAMCP V.1 *Fr.* Tender Buttons.

Chicken, The. Vladimir Holan. PoSu, *tr. by* Ian Milner and Jarmila Milner

Chicken & Sex. That's what I need constantly. I am quite insistent. Chicken & Sex. Brendan Cleary. NeBl

Chicken, she chided early, should not wait. Gwendolyn Brooks. ColAP *Fr.* Notes from the Childhood and the Girlhood.

Chicken ("Stick stick call then, stick stick sticking, sticking with a chicken. Sticking in a extra succession, sticking in.") Gertrude Stein. NAMCP V.1 *Fr.* Tender Buttons.

Chicken thaws, blood, A. Eden. Claudia Rankine. GT

Chickens. (LL) Red Wheelbarrow, The. William Carlos Williams. APT-1; BLPJKO; BLT; BrAP; ChAP; ColAP; EMP; HarvBoo; HeIP-4; MoAmPo; NAAL-5; NAAPv.2; NAMCP V.1; NIL-7; NIP-4; NoAM; NoP-4; NoP-5; OxBoAm; SAmP; SoSe-8; TFi; TRP; TWF; WaAnP; WeW-3

Chickens cannot, The. Killing the Animals. Wesley McNair. P180

Chickens Everywhere. Richard Garcia. SUP

Chickens, The. Home to Roost. Kay Ryan. OxBoAm

Chickens, The. *Unknown.* TLR

Chicory and Daisies. William Carlos Williams. APT-1

Chief Defect of Henry King, The. Henry King, Who Chewed Bits of String, and Was Early Cut Off in Dreadful Agonies. Joseph Hilaire Pierre Belloc. NBLV; OBCoV; OxAEP-2

Chief of all. John Milton. NOSC *Fr.* Samson Agonistes.

Chief of Medicine, The. Arthur Ginsberg. BloBone

Chief of the civil administration, The. Pilate. Donald Davie. GI

Chiefly to Mind Appears. Cecil Day Lewis. MoBrPo

Chieftain Iffucan of Azcan in caftan. Bantams in Pine-Woods. Wallace Stevens. NAAPv.2; NAMCP V.1; NoAM; OxBoAm; SAmP

Chieftain to the Highlands bound, A. Lord Ullin's Daughter. Thomas Campbell. NOBRP; NPBRoP

Ch'ien (Heaven). *Unknown.* ColAnChi *Fr.* I Ching [*or* The Book of Changes *or* The Classic of Changes].

Chiffchaff and celandine, The. Masque of May, The. John Millington Synge. IrLP

Child. Sylvia Plath. NAAL-5

Child, A. Mary Lamb. *See* Parental Recollections.

Child, The. Judith Wright. BMAP

Child between them on the street. W. D. Snodgrass. NAMCP V.2 *Fr.* Heart's Needle.

Child between them on the street, The. W. D. Snodgrass. NoP-5 *Fr.* Heart's Needle.

Child Bride. Garnett Kilberg Cohen. MPUn

Child brought blue clay from the creek, The. Image, The. Robert Hass. BLT; CAP-8

Child Burial. Paula Meehan. EmeKit; InoFa; MakPoe; ModIr

Child calling and calling, The. Evening. Karen Volkman. NIL-7

Child came to the dark library, The. Saturday in the '20s, A. Jean Earle. AngWePo

Child Christ at the Top of the Stairs. James Ragan. TWW

Child clings to the prettily patterned lattice, The. Suddenly, the Yard Where Rice and Yeast Brew. Chŏng Hwajin. EcSo, *tr. by* Julie C. Park

Child colors in his coloring book all day, A. Institutions. Kim Sŭnghŭi. EcSo, *tr. by* K. Kim Richards and Steffen Richards

Child Compassion, The. Margot Ruddock. OBMV

Child cried out in the darkness, A. Ballad of the Night. Y. A. Rontsh. Prolet, *tr. by* Amelia Glaser

Child / Curious and innocent, A. To Robert Louis Stevenson. W. E. Henley. MoBrPo

Child Dancing, The. Gwendolyn MacEwen. BrAP

Child, Do Not Throw This Book About. Joseph Hilaire Pierre Belloc. NoAM

Child, dream of a pomegranate tree. Winter Garden. Janet Lewis. APT-2

Child Dying, The. Edwin Muir. PoWW; WoPoe

Child gives her mother a drawing of Heaven, The. Making Babies. Hilary Llewellyn-Williams. TCAWP

Child had got two bullets in the head, The. Night of the Fourth: A Recollection, The. Victor Hugo. SxFrPo, *tr. by* A. M. and E. H. Blackmore

Child had longings all unspoken, The. In the Toy Shop. May Kendall. ViWPN

Child Hunting Tales, A. Magdy El-Gabry. AnVo, *tr. by* Mohamed Enani

Child, I'd curl up small at night, A. Ultrasound at 13 Weeks. Kona Macphee. BeAl

Child, in love with prints and maps, The. Voyage, The. Charles Baudelaire. NAWM-7v2, *tr. by* Charles Henri Ford

Child in the City, A. Lucien Stryk. UrbNat

Child in the New Delhi Sun. Garrett McDowell. BtF

Child Is Born, A. Mailabattula Satish Chandar. HotL, *tr. by* V. Narayana Rao

Child is Born, A. Elina Wechsler. MirDau, *tr. by* Darrell Lockhart

Child is born amonges man, A. Hand by Hand We Shall Us Take. *Unknown.* OHMEL

Child is born in blood, O child of blood, The. (LL) New Year's Day. Robert Lowell. ChrPo; TRP

Child is born, they cry, a child, A. Christmas. Stevie Smith. ChrPo

Child is Not a Knife, A. Göran Sonnevi. PFTM-2, *tr. by* Rika Lesser

Child is not dead, The. Child Who Was Shot Dead by Soldiers at Nyanga, The. Ingrid Jonker. HAWP; WoPoe, *tr. by* Jack Cope, Uys Krige and William Plomer

Child is pursuing a butterfly, A. Lilac Petals. Kim Ch'unsu [*or* Chun-soo]. CAMKP, *tr. by* Anthony, Brother of Taizé

Child is Revenant to the Man, The. Vincent Buckley. BMAP

Child is silent, The. Winter report. Lionel Abrahams. TSAP

Child, Is Thy Father Dead? Ebenezer Elliott. NOBRP

Child Life [*with music*]. Mary E. Tucker. CBWP-1

Child Maximilian in a White Frock, The. Shortened History in Pictures, A. Jamie McKendrick. OxBSo

Child 'midst ancient mountains I have stood, A. Felicia Dorothea Hemans. CenSon *Fr.* Sonnets, Devotional and Memorial.

Child my mother, A. Hair. Breda Sullivan. Prnts

Child need not be very clever, A. Grandpa Is Ashamed. Ogden Nash. OBCoV

Child not yet is lulled to rest, The. Cradle-Song at Twilight. Alice Thompson Meynell. NPeEn; VWP

Child of Adam. Viola C. White. YaYoPo

Child of distress, who meet'st the bitter scorn. To the Poor. Anna Laetitia Barbauld. NoP-4; NoP-5

Child of Europe. Czeslaw Milosz. AF, *tr. by* Jan Darowski

Child of my heart! My sweet, beloved first-born! To My Child. Barry Cornwall. CenSon

Child of my love! though thou be bright as day. Shadow. Mary Elizabeth Coleridge. VWP

Child of my parents, sister of my soul. William Wordsworth. NPBRoP *Fr.* Prelude, The; Growth of a Poet's Mind [1805 version; Selections from Anthologies].

Child of my winter, born. W. D. Snodgrass. MoAmPo *Fr.* Heart's Needle.

Child of that hour when rock and ocean meet. (LL) Hatteras Calling. Conrad Potter Aiken. ColAP; InGu

Child of the clouds! remote from every taint. William Wordsworth. CenSon *Fr.* River Duddon [A Series of Sonnets], The.

Child of the Earth. Don Domanski. Coast

Child of the Sun. Lillian M. Fisher. HHAm

Child of the sun, in whom his rays appear. La Gialletta Gallante, or the Sunburned Exotic Beauty. Edward Herbert, 1st Baron Herbert of Cherbury. NOSC

Child of Wonder. Bill Pearlman. ICANM

Child on the Shore, The. Ursula K. Le Guin. ASA

Child on Top of a Greenhouse. Theodore Roethke. NoP-4; NoP-5; NOxBChV; PtR

Child once wandered the earth, A. Moon Daughters. Artress Bethany White. BtF

Child said *What is the grass?* fetching it to me with full hands, A. Walt Whitman. ColAP; ITBLP; NoP-4; NoP-5; SAmP *Fr.* Song of Myself.

Child screams in his room, Rage, The. Unjustly Punished Child. Sharon Olds. PBCAP

Child Screening a Dove from a Hawk, A. Letitia Elizabeth Landon. NOBRP

Child should always say what's true, A. Whole Duty of Children. Robert Louis Stevenson. NBLV

Child sleeps in the daytime, The. Child Waking. Edith Jay Scovell. MoWP

Child stood in the shed, The. The child went mad. Carpenter's Son, The. John Berryman. ChIV-2

Child that his strength upbore. St Christopher. Austin Clarke. ModIr

Child, the current of your breath is six days long. Unknown Girl in the Maternity Ward. Anne Sexton. NoAM

Child this Day is Born, A. *Unknown.* ChrPo

Child to His Sick Grandfather, A. Joanna Baillie. CABP; RACG; WoRP

Child Waking. Edith Jay Scovell. MoWP

Child We Won't Have Is Crowding Us in the Front, The. Lyn Lifshin. PfS

Child went out one day, A. I Eat Kids Yum Yum! Dennis Lee. TLR

Child Who Was Shot Dead by Soldiers at Nyanga, The. Ingrid Jonker. HAWP; WoPoe, *tr. by* Jack Cope, Uys Krige and William Plomer

Child, with many a childish wile. To Cupid. Joanna Baillie. LW

Child with Pillar Box and Bin Bags. Kathleen Jamie. GPPA

Child, You New Man. Malka Lee. Prolet, *tr. by* Amelia Glaser

Childe Harold's Pilgrimage. Lord Byron.

   Canto 4.

     "And thou, who never yet of human wrong." NAEL-6v2; NAEL-7v2

     "But I forget.—My pilgrim's shrine is won." NAEL-6v2; NAEL-7v2

     "Egeria! sweet creation of some heart." NOBRP

     "I stood in Venice, on the Bridge of Sighs." CtM; NAEL-6v2; NAEL-7v2

     "Or view the Lord of the unerring bow." GS

     "Roll on, thou deep and dark blue ocean—roll!" NOBRP

     "What from this barren being do we reap?" NOBRP

   Canto 3.

     "In my youth's summer I did sing of One." NOBRP

     "Is thy face like thy mother's, my fair child!" NAEL-6v2; NAEL-7v2

     "Lake Leman woos me with its crystal face." NAEL-6v2; NAEL-7v2; NOBRP; NPBRoP; WaAnP

     Revelry by Night. NPBRoP

     "Sky is changed!—and such a change! Oh night, The." NOBRP

     "Stop!—for thy tread is on an Empire's dust!" NAEL-6v2; NAEL-7v2

     "There is a very life in our despair." NOBRP

     "There sunk the greatest, nor the worst of men." NAEL-6v2; NAEL-7v2

     ('Tis to Create.) NPBRoP

   "Come, blue-eyed maid of heaven!—but thou, alas!" NOBRP

   Lake Leman. BrAP

   Ocean, The.

     (Address to the Ocean.) ITBLP

     Apostrophe to the Ocean. OxAEP-2

     (Ocean, The.) TFi

     "Roll on, thou deep and dark blue ocean—roll!" UV

     (Solitude.) TreFP

   "Oh, thou! in Hellas deemed of heavenly birth." NAEL-6v2; NAEL-7v2

   There Was a Sound of Revelry by Night. FaBoWar; OBWP; OxAEP-2; TFi

Childe Maurice hunted the Silver Wood. *Unknown.* OBSP

Child[e] My Choice [*or* Choyse], A. Robert Southwell. OxBEV; SacPr

Childe Roland to the Dark Tower Came. Robert Browning. NAEL-6v2; NAEL-7v2; NAWM-7v2; NoP-4; NoP-5; OBNV; PoPoPo; WaAnP

Childhood. Edith Bruck. AF

Childhood. Syl Cheney-Coker. NAfrP

Childhood. Frances Darwin Cornford. OxBEV

Childhood. Chitra Divakaruni. OpBo

Childhood. Nikolai Stepanovich Gumilyov. TCRusP, *tr. by* Joseph Kiegel

Childhood. Hoda Hussein. PoArWo, *tr. by* Cornelia Al-Khaled

Childhood. Edwin Muir. HeIP-4; NePenScot; NoP-4; NoP-5; NPeEn

Childhood. Barbara Ras. GoPo

Childhood. Rainer Maria Rilke. GTCP, *tr. by* Felix Pollak

Childhood. Ann Stanford. PoChi

Childhood. Sharan Strange. GT

Childhood. Thomas Traherne. SacPr

Childhood. Henry Vaughan. NOSC

Childhood [*with music*]. Margaret Abigail Walker. NoP-4; NoP-5

Childhood Around 1950, A. Alan Williamson. ASA; FaoP

Childhood, boyhood, young manhood.   Robert Duncan.   FTOS *Fr.* Poems from the Margins of Thom Gunn's Moly.

Childhood Fled.   Charles Lamb.   CenSon

Childhood in Jacksonville, Florida.   Jane Cooper.   ExTi

Childhood in the Country, A.   Maisha Baton.   ICANM

Childhood Is the Kingdom Where Nobody Dies.   Edna St. Vincent Millay.   NALW

Childhood memory: those pears, A.   Sofiya Parnok.   ARWW, *tr. by* Catriona Kelly

Childhood of the Ancients.   Andrew Hudgins.   InvLad

Childhood Painting Lesson.   Henry Rago.   WHSW

Childhood remembrances [*or* memories] are always a drag.   Nikki-Rosa. Nikki Giovanni.   FaBoA; FuFl; GT; HeIP-4; InGu; ISC; OxAAAP; SSLK; UnSA

Childhood says, so free of guile.   Blind Youth, The.   Frank Wedekind.   GTCP, *tr. by* Felix Pollak

Childhood Stories.   Matthew Rohrer.   LegDan; NAPBL

Childhood Wall.   Ahmed Taha.   AnVo, *tr. by* Mohamed Enani

Childhood was full of storms.   Round Room, The.   Harvena Richter.   ICANM

Childhood's House.   Miranda Field.   LegDan

Childhood's Retreat [*with music*].   Robert Duncan.   NAMCP V.2; NoAM

Childish.   Gerardo Deniz.   PoChi; RMCMP, *tr. by* Mónica de la Torre

Childish Prank, A.   Ted Hughes.   CABP; NPeEn

Childless couple, The.   Restoration.   Jeffrey Skinner.   PBCAP

Childlessness.   Henri Cole.   NAMCP V.2

Childlessness.   James Merrill.   ColAP

Children.   Carolyn Kizer.   PoChi

Children.   Pinkie Gordon Lane.   FuFl

Children.   Charles Reznikoff.   FTOS

Children.   Teaching the Children.   Myra Sklarew.   CFP

Children, The.   Robert Minhinnick.   AngWePo

Children, The.   William Carlos Williams.   SAmP

Children are blooming like black flowers, The.   AIDS Education, Seventh Grade.   Ruth L. Schwartz.   NeAmPo

Children are dumb to say how hot the day is.   Cool Web, The.   Robert Graves.   BrAP; HarvBoo; NAEL-6v2; NAEL-7v2; NAMCP V.1; NoAM; OxBEV; WoPoe

Children Are Laughing, The.   Gwendolyn MacEwen.   IFF

Children aren't happy with nothing to ignore.   Parent, The.   Ogden Nash.   Spl

Children at Christmas in 1945.   Vladimir Holan.   AF, *tr. by* C. G. Hanzlicek *and* Dana Habova

Children Band, The.   Sir Aubrey De Vere.   OBEV

Children, billy goat, have put crimson reins, The.   Anyte.   HePo *Fr.* Epigrams.

Children born of fairy stock.   I'd Love to Be a Fairy's Child.   Robert Graves.   ChAP

Children, brown as earth, continue to laugh away.   Main Temple Street, Puri.   Jayanta Mahapatra.   VCWP

Children cried "Mummy!, The."   Tadeusz Rózewicz.   AF; GI

Children Disinterred.   Marion Albina Bigelow.

"Come, lowly ones, and take your places now."   VerBaPo

Children Do Linger.   *Unknown.*   SSUS

Children do not grow up.   Biting Back.   Patricia Smith.   GT

Children / don't harm the flea.   Issa.   ZenPo, *tr. by* Takashi Ikemoto and Lucien Stryk

Children go forward with their little satchels, The.   School Children, The. Louise Glück.   ColAP; ItP; NAMCP V.2; PoPoPo; WeW-3

Children Go, The.   Kenneth Mackenzie.   BMAP

Children Going Home.   Gwendolyn Brooks.

Jamal; Nineteen Cows In a Slow Line Walking.   ESEAA

Kojo: I Am A Black.   ESEAA

Merle; Uncle Seagram.   ESEAA

Novelle; My Grandmother Is Waiting For Me To Come Home.   ESEAA

Tinsel Marie; The Coora Flower.   ESEAA

(Uncle Seagram.)   FuFl; IllVoic

Children gone, grown into other arms, The.   Last Marriage, A.   Virginia Hamilton Adair.   BeAl; StAl

Children have brought their wood turtle, The.   No.   Mark Doty.   EmeKit

Children, if you dare to think.   Warning to Children.   Robert Graves.   NoP-4; NoP-5; NOxBChV; NPeEn; OxBEV; TWF

Children Imagining a Hospital.   U. A. Fanthorpe.   PoCu

Children imitating cormorants.   Issa.   EH, *tr. by* Robert Hass

Children in Armour.   Geoffrey Adkins.   FaBoWar

Children in Slavery.   Eliza Lee Cabot Follen.   SWaP

Children in the Arbor.   Glover Davis.   GeoHom

Children of Love.   Harold Monro.   MoBrPo

Children of my happier prime.   Immolated.   Herman Melville.   NCAP

Children of Nonti, The.   Mafika Pascal Gwala.   TSAP

Children of Saigon, The.   Walter McDonald.   AF

Children of the Atomic Age.   Dominador I. Ilio.   ReBoTo

Children of the Disappeared.   Valerie Martínez.   TouFir

Children of the early / Countryside.   Penobscot.   George Oppen.   HarvBoo

Children of the Future.   Jalauddin Mansur Nuriddin.   SpirFl

Children of the Mist.   Rosamund Marriott Watson.   VWP

Children of the Night, The.   Edwin Arlington Robinson.   APN-2; NAAPv.1

Children of the Owl and the Pussy-Cat, The.   Edward Lear.   OBCoV

Children of the Planet.   Blas de Otero.   RaW, *tr. by* Hardie St. Martin

Children of the Poor, The.   Gwendolyn Brooks.   PoA 2002 *Fr.* Womanhood, The.

Children of the Sun.   Fenton Johnson.   TCAPo

Children of the Working Class.   John Weiners.   BB

Children of the world.   César Vallejo.   TCLAP *Fr.* Spain, Take [Away] This Cup from Me [España, Aparta de Mí Este Cáliz].

Children of wealth in your warm nursery.   Children of Wealth.   Elizabeth Daryush.   MoWP; NPeEn; OxBEV; OxBSo; RSaN

Children of Zeus.   Hesiod.   WoPoe *Fr.* Theogony.

Children on Top of the Hill.   No Hyegyông.   EcSo, *tr. by* Ann Y. Choi

Children picking up our bones.   Postcard from the Volcano, A.   Wallace Stevens.   APT-1; GPTC; NAMCP V.1; NoAM; PoCho; SAmP; WeW-3

Children play with dolls and toys.   Observations.   Luvuyo Mkangelwa.   NAfrP

Children Playing Checkers at the Edge of the Forest.   Adrienne Rich.   WeW-3

Children run shouting, The.   Glimpses.   Philippe Jaccottet.   VCWP, *tr. by* Derek Mahon

Children run through streets of garbage.   Pantoum of the Working Classes. Sean Thomas Dougherty.   LiTh

Children saved their money, The.   Three-Liners.   Nina Gorlanova.   CRWP, *tr. by* Daniel Weissbort

Children / this is the blood.   Brother of the Streets.   Sam Cornish.   TRP

Children under, say, *ten*, shouldn't know.   Cartoon Physics, Part 1.   Nick Flynn.   BeAl; LegDan; NAPBL; P180; PoDa

Children Walking Home from School through Good Neighborhood [*with music*]. Donald Justice.   CAP-8; NIL-7; NIP-4

Children were around my feet like dogs, The.   Seventh Birthday of the First Child.   Sharon Olds.   PBCAP

Children were shouting together, The.   Frolic.   George Russell.   MoBrPo

Children, when was.   Napoleon.   Miroslav Holub.   ChAP; PoSu, *tr. by* Kaca Plakova

Children who were shot in Johannesburg, The.   Choice, The.   Ellen K. Kuzwayo.   CFP, *tr. by* Toi Derricotte

Children, why do you fear, why turn away?   For Miriam.   Marjorie Oludhe Macgoye.   HAWP

Children Will Listen.   Stephen Sondheim.   TWF

Children, you are very little.   Good and Bad Children.   Robert Louis Stevenson.   ChAP; OBCoV

Children—or.   Or a Play.   Leslie Scalapino.   FTOS

Children's Ball-Bouncing Song.   *Unknown.*   NOBAu

Children's Book of Knowledge, The.   Jesse Lee Kercheval.   SUP

Children's Children.   Sterling Allen Brown.   APT-2

Children's Games.   Malkia Amala Cyril.   InTrad

Children's Hour, The.   Henry Wadsworth Longfellow.   APN-1; BRP; ChAP; ITBLP; TCAPo; WHSW

Children's Letters, The.   Dorothy Livesay.   NALW

Children's poet's own child is dying, A.   Tale.   Georgi Belev.   CSCBP, *tr. by* the author and Lisa Sapinkopf

Children's Rhymes and Parodies.   *Unknown.*   NOBAu

Children's Rhymes ("By what sends.") [*see also* "Children's Rhymes ('When I was a chile we used to play')"].   Langston Hughes.   NOxBChV

Children's Train, The.   Dorianne Laux.   GM

Children's voices in the orchard.   T. S. Eliot.   NoAM; WeW-3 *Fr.* Landscapes.

Child's a plaything for an hour, A.   Parental Recollections.   Mary Lamb.   OxBEV

Child's Address to the Kentucky Mummy, The.   Hannah Flagg Gould.   SWaP

Child's Birthday, A.   Henry Rago.   IllVoic

Child's Christmas Day, A.   *Unknown.*   OBCP

Child's Christmas in Puerto Rico, A.   Aurora Levins Morales.   PueRic

Child's Dream, A.   Frances Darwin Cornford.   NOxBChV

Child's fingers breaking the wings at the joint, The.   This, too.   Karen Press.   TSAP

Child's Grace, A.   Robert Herrick.   See Grace for a Child.

Child's Grave, Hale County, Alabama [*with music*].   Jim Simmerman.   WeW-3

Child's hair rays, The.   Civilian Histories.   Lee Upton.   AmAlph

Child's Parliament.   Chenjerai Hove.   HBAPE

Child's Party, A.   Sarah Morgan Bryan Piatt.   SWaP

Child's Song.   Sir Thomas More.   ChAP

Child's Song in Spring.   Edith Nesbit.   NOxBChV

Child's Story, The. Elizabeth Jennings. HarvBoo

Child's teeth click against the marble, The. Tale of Me, The. Eiléan Ní Chuilleanáin. Prnts

Child's Thought, A. Bertha Moore. VerBaPo

Child's Thought of God, A. Elizabeth Barrett Browning. InvLi

Chile. Otto Orban. MotU, tr. by George Szirtes

Chile is bordered on the north by Peru. At the Center of Injustice. Violeta Parra. TANSG, tr. by Karen Kerschen

Chilean Cigarette Pack, The. Ai Ch'ing. WoPoe, tr. by Hualing Nieh

Chilean People, The. Gareth Alban Davies. BBMWP, tr. by the author

Chile's distant and it's a lie. 6. Raúl Zurita. TCLAP, tr. by Jack Schmitt

Chile's flag has three colors. Flag of Chile, The. Teresa de Jesús. AF, tr. by Maria Proser, Arlene Scully and James Scully

Chill, A. Bella Akhatovna Akhmadulina. TCRusP, tr. by Kathy Lewis and Bob Perelman

Chill autumn dusk, The. Richard Wright. APT-2

Chill Core. Dana Levin. LegDan

Chill summer day, the sky, A. John Morgan. ArBi Fr. Cyclist, The.

Chilled in this Irish pub I wish my loves. John Berryman. CAP-8 Fr. Dream Songs.

Chilled through, I wake up. Kenneth Rexroth. APT-2; NAAPv.2; NAMCP V.1 Fr. Love Poems of Marichiko, The.

Chillen Get Shoes. Sterling Allen Brown. APT-2; NoP-4; NoP-5

Chilling autumn rains. Basho. SoOfWa, tr. by Sam Hamill

Chill-rushing, / Hush-hushing, / Hush—hushing. (LL) Main-Deep, The. James Stephens. MoBrPo; OBMV

Chills. Bella Akhatovna Akhmadulina. ItGoST, tr. by F. D. Reeve

Chill-to-the-bone, A. Tomas Tranströmer. WoBe Fr. Haiku.

Chillun', listen here to me. All God's Chillun Got Rhythm. Gustave Kahn. ReLy

Chilly and overcast afternoon, A. Memory from Childhood. Antonio Machado Ruiz. RaW; WED, tr. by Robert Bly

Chilly early Saturday, my study. Passion. Michael Ryan. BodElec

Chilly Night, A. Christina Georgina Rossetti. VWP

Chilly nights. Masaoka Shiki. CAoMJL1, tr. by Burton Watson

Chilterns, The. Rupert Brooke. MoBrPo

Chimera. Silvia Eugenia Castillero. SPV, tr. by Jen Hofer

Chimera. Carol Frost. CAP-8

Chimes. Alice Thompson Meynell. MoBrPo

Chimes. Michael Smith. PBCIP

Chimes of Neverwhere, The. Les A. Murray. UpMys

Chimney is a hole in the roof, The. White and Black Bones, The. Konrad Bayer. PFTM-2, tr. by Malcolm Green

Chimney Ranch. Diana Hartog. NLPA Fr. Oasis.

Chimney Sweeper, The ("Little black thing among the snow, A.") William Blake. BrAP; NAEL-6v2; NAEL-7v2; NAWM-7v2; NPBRoP Fr. Songs of Experience.

Chimney Sweeper, The ("When my mother died I was very young.") William Blake. BrAP; HeIP-4; ItP; NAEL-6v2; NAEL-7v2; NAWM-7v2; NPBRoP; OxAEP-2; SoSe-8; TFi Fr. Songs of Innocence.

Chimney Swifts. Mark Jarman. PfSP

Chimneys. Ruth Bidgood. AngWePo

Chimneys: colder. Reindeer Report. U. A. Fanthorpe. OBCP

Chimneys, rank on rank, The. Evening. Richard Aldington. MoBrPo

Chimneys smoke despite each adverse breeze, The. Tŷ'r Ysgol. T. H. Parry-Williams. BBMWP, tr. by Joseph P. Clancy

Chin Music. Alan Soldofsky. MoASP

China. Dorianne Laux. LW

China. Bob Perelman. FTOS; PFTM-2

China Camp, California. Kim Addonizio. GeoHom

China island dream. Empire Smoke, Forgeries, Salient and The Ritz. Ray DiPalma. FTOS

China, I've Lost My Key. Liang Xiaobin. PML, tr. by Michelle Yeh

China Maniacs. May Probyn. VWP

China Observed Through Greek Rain in Turkish Coffee. Henrik Nordbrandt. VCWP, tr. by Henrik Norbrandt and Alexander Taylor and Alexander Taylor

Chinaberry, The. Andrew Hudgins. CAP-8

Chinaberry Trees, The. Andrew Hudgins. LPSFW

Chinatown. George Stanley. NLPA Fr. Mountains and Air.

Thank You Father. Yu Jian. PML, tr. by Ron Padgett and Wang Ping

Shao and the South. Unknown. tr. by Ezra Pound
  "Three stars, five stars rise over the hill." NDACCP, tr. by Ezra Pound

Chinese and a Japanese?, A. (LL) Notes for a Poem on Being Asian American. Dwight Okita. NIL-7; UnSA

Chinese Ballad [with music]. Mao Tse-tung. OxBEV, tr. by William Empson

Chinese Courtesy. Paul Engle. PoA 2002 Fr. Images of China.

Chinese Dragons. David Bottoms. GifTon

Chinese Drawings. Witter Bynner.
  "What though they conquer us?" NoP-4; NoP-5

Chinese Figures 1. Unknown. EaWin, tr. by W. S. Merwin

Chinese Figures 2. Unknown. EaWin, tr. by W. S. Merwin

Chinese Figures 3. Unknown. EaWin, tr. by W. S. Merwin

Chinese Garden, The. Horace Gregory. OBGa

Chinese Hot Pot. Wing Tek Lum. UnSA

Chinese Journal. Charles Wright. NoP-5

Chinese Landscape Above Caracas. John Yau. BodElec

Chinese magicians had conjured their chance. Tiles. Witter Bynner. APT-1; TCAPo

Chinese Man in Smyrna, A. Sharon Olinka. BRtP

Chinese Nightingale. William Carlos Williams. NAAPv.2

Chinese Nightingale, The. Vachel Lindsay. MoAmPo

Chinese Ode, A. Unknown. CCL1 Fr. Qi-yu [Translations].

Chinese Quatrains (The Woman in Tomb 44). Marilyn Chin. NAMCP V.2

Chinese stripper we've come to see comes on stage, The. Chinese Stripper. Robert Masterson. ICANM

Chinese tell time in a cat's eyes, The. Clock, The. Charles Baudelaire. MotU, tr. by Edward K. Kaplan

Chinese Villanelle. John Yau. PmAP; WaAnP

Ching Chong Chinaman. Chinks. Lawson Fusao Inada. FTtHH

Ch'ing Ming—Clear Bright. Oriole Song. Hsueh Chao-yun. CrYelRi, tr. by Sam Hamill

Chingis Khan left his camp on Mount Chasutu. Unknown. WoPoe Fr. Secret History of the Mongols, The.

Chingwe's Hole, you devoured the Chief's prisoners. Glory Be to Chingwe's Hole. Jack A. Mapanje. HBAPE

Chinks. Lawson Fusao Inada. FTtHH

Chinless and slouched, gray-faced, and slack of jaw. For an Early Retirement. Donald Hall. PoA 2002

Chin-ling Post Station. Wen T'ien-hsiang. ColAnChi, tr. by Michael A. Fuller

Chinoiserie. Kay Sage. SurWo

Chinook Songs. Unknown. APN-2, tr. by Franz Boas

Ch'in's First Emperor ravaged the sense. Peach-Blossom Spring. T'ao Ch'ien. NDACCP, tr. by David Hinton

Chip chip cherry. Riddle. Unknown. FaBoVe

Chip City. Linda France. MFPA

Chipmunk, The. Herman Melville. NCAP

Chipmunks jump, and / Greensnakes slither. Valentine. Donald Hall. NTCP

Chipped and splintered marble dust. Baltimore. Afaa Michael Weaver. BtF

Chipped flange on the dangling pipe bringing in our cooking gas, A. Lyn Hejinian. NAMCP V.2 Fr. Oxota: A Short Russian Novel.

Chippewa Music. tr. by Frances Densmore.
  I Am Walking. APT-1
  I Have Found My Lover. APT-1
  My Love Has Departed. APT-1
  Sky Will Resound, The. APT-1
  Song of Spring, A. APT-1,
  Song of the Butterfly, The. APT-1
  Sound Is Fading Away, The. APT-1

Chironomy. Takehisa Kosugi. WhBo

Chirping. Yi Kyôngnim. EcSo, tr. by Peter H. Lee

Chirping / Grasshopper. Kawai Chigetsu [or Chigetsu-Ni]. ZenPo, tr. by Takashi Ikemoto and Lucien Stryk

Chisel, chipping in, The. Tombstones. A. R. Ammons.

Chisel slid, I hit my little knuckle, The. Michael Haslam. Oth Fr. Continual Song.

Chiswick. Thomas Maurice. OBGa Fr. Richmond Hill.

Chitchat with the Junior League Women. Gary Soto. PoDa

Chitterling King, The. Melvin B. Tolson. EGAG

Chittlin's. Cornelius Eady. BtF

Chivalry. John Lundberg. LiTh

Chivo. Cecilio Garcia-Camarillo. ICANM

Chkk! chkk! hopper-grass. Cao-chong: Hopper-Grass. Unknown. CCL1, tr. by Ezra Pound

C[h]loe. Alexander Pope. OBSV Fr. Epistle [II,] to a Lady[: Of the Characters of Women].

Chloe and Myra. Lady Sophia Burrell. LW Fr. Chloe and Myra.

Chloe, by your command, in verse I write. Letter from Artemisa in the Town, to Chloe [or Cloe], in the Country, A. John Wilmot, 2d Earl of Rochester. NPeEn

Chloe Divine. Thomas D'Urfey. OBEV

Chloe or her modern sister, Lil. Chloe or. Laura Riding Jackson. APT-2

Chloe, we are finally Americans now. Chloe, we are here! (LL) Elegy for Chloe Nguyen. Marilyn Chin. FaoP; UnSA

Chloe, why wish you that your years. To Chloe, Who Wished Herself Young Enough for Me. William Cartwright. NOSC; OxAEP-1

Chloe's a nymph in flowery groves. Chloe Divine. Thomas D'Urfey. OBEV

Chloe's father is a professor of linguistics. Elegy for Chloe Nguyen. Marilyn Chin. FaoP; UnSA

Chloris, forbear a while. Song. Henry Bold. NOSC

Chloris in the Snow. William Strode. See On Chloris Walking in the Snow.

Cho-Fu-Sa. Tanya Larkin. FreRad; IIR

Chockablock Once a man was traveling through the woods, and. Charles Olson. FTOS

Chocolate Confessions. Magdalena Gomez. PueRic

Chocolate Soldier. Ian Duhig. NeBrP

Chocolates. Louis Simpson. OBCoV

Choice. David Bromige. FTOS

Choice. Emily Dickinson. NAAL-3

Choice. Liu K'o-hsiang. PML, tr. by Michelle Yeh

Choice, A. Paul Laurence Dunbar. OxBoAm

Choice, The. Ellen K. Kuzwayo. CFP, tr. by Toi Derricotte

Choice, The. John Masefield. MoBrPo Fr. Lollingdon Downs.

Choice, The. George Wither. OBEV

Choice, The: "I watched Odysseus go on board the flagship." Theo Dorgan. PML

Choice, The: "Intellect of man is forced to choose, The." William Butler Yeats. NoAM; WaAnP

73: The Choice ("Think thou and act; to-morrow thou shalt die"). Dante Gabriel Rossetti. ChIV-2; OBEV Fr. House of Life, The.

72: The Choice ("Watch thou and fear; to-morrow thou shalt die"). Dante Gabriel Rossetti. ChIV-2 Fr. House of Life, The.

71: The Choice ("Eat thou and drink; to-morrow thou shalt die"). Dante Gabriel Rossetti. ChIV-2 Fr. House of Life, The.

Choice, Inanna and the Galla. Pem Kremer. HW

Choices. Tess Gallagher. AmZen

Choir. Cecil Taylor. EGAG

Choir, The. Olga Broumas. CAP-8

Choir of angels glorified the hour, A. Anna Andreyevna Akhmatova. GI

Choirist. Pierre Alféri. YaTCFP, tr. by Cole Swensen

Choise of valentines, The. Thomas Nashe. PBRV

Choke-and-Rob it's a Choke-and-Rob nation. If you must. Ether. Laurence Lieberman. LiTh

Choked sunset. Roads. Peter Huchel. AF, tr. by Daniel S. Simko

Choked sunset glow. Roads. Peter Huchel. HP; PoSu, tr. by Michael Hamburger

Choker's Lane. Kenneth Slessor. BMAP

Chokes the garden. (LL) Idea of Trust, The. Thom Gunn. HarvBoo; ItP; NPeEn

Choking. Saniyya Salih. PoArWo, tr. by Kamal Boullata

Choking through the whole attack. (LL) Champs d'Honneur. Ernest Hemingway. AmWaPo; IllVoic; PoA 2002

Cholera. Nazik al-Mala'ika. PoArWo, tr. by Husain Haddawy and Nathalie Handal

Cholera Camp. Rudyard Kipling. FaBoWar

Chomei at Toyama. Basil Bunting.
"I have been noting events for forty years." NPeEn

Chŏngsŏn Arirang. Korean Oral Tradition. CATKP, tr. by David R. McCann

Choose. Carl Sandburg. Spl; StAl

Choose another where open to follow. Who Are You. Marla Jernigan. AnSo

Choose any angle you like, she said. Bicameral. Linda Gregerson. AmAlph

Choose one version. Turn it. Let it go. See how it spins. Way It Goes, The. Vona Groarke. NIrP

Choose, said God. (LL) Anne Carson. OxBoAm; WoBe Fr. Truth About God, The.

Choose Something like a Star. Robert Frost. APT-1; BLPJKO; MoAmPo
(Take Something Like a Star.) WaAnP

Choose the colour that hits the mark. Ad Miró. Pierre Alechinsky. PFTM-2, tr. by Michael Fineberg

Choose two from old Bibles, humbly beautiful quilts. How to Write the New Mennonite Poem. Jeff Gundy. ACAMVP

Choose Your Garden. Erin Belieu. ExTi

Choosing a Mast. Roy Campbell. NoP-4

Choosing plain words. Sikong Tu. CCL1 Fr. Twenty-Four Modes of Poetry.

Choosing Shoes [with music]. Ffrida Wolfe. ChAP

Choosing the Blues. Angela Jackson. ISC

Choosing the coffin. Arrangements. Alan Williamson. InoFa

Choosing the gelding, younger, more placid. Sending the Mare to Auction. Jana Harris. FiBr

Choosing Their Names. Thomas Hood. NOxBChV

Chopin. Marilyn Nelson. RA

Chopin Preludes, Opus 28. J. R. Solonche. MiVo

Choppers. Dale Ritterbusch. AmWaPo

Chopping Wood. Geoffrey Cook. Coast

Chops Are Flyin [Chops are flyin everywhere / and there's nothin says Louis / but old Duke left in there. / Get away, Duke, get away!]. Stanley Crouch. GT

Chopsticks. Alan Jenkins. PML

Chord. Langston Hughes. APSN; OxBoAm

Chord [or Cord] of Hope, The. Mikhail Naimy. tr. by Sharif Elmusa and Gregory Orfalea
"Hope is agony." NAAPv.2, tr. by Sharif Elmusa and Gregory Orfalea

Chords. Eamer O'Keefe. Prnts

Chords Passages 14. Robert Duncan. FTOS

Choreograph of the Robed Sheep. Maryhelen Snyder. ICANM

Choreographed escape a charged resolve to repel the hour. Bruise. Robert Budde. PoPra

Chores. Maxine W. Kumin. IPoFL

Choric Song. Alfred Tennyson. HeIP-4

Choricos. Richard Aldington. PoA 2002

Choriste. Pierre Alféri. YaTCFP

Chortle, laugh, in a laughter of storm. Acrobat of Pain. João da Cruz e Sousa. TCLAP, tr. by Flavia Vidal

Chorus. Euripides. OBEV Fr. Medea.

Chorus. Seneca. NPeEn Fr. Hercules Furens.

Chorus. Percy Bysshe Shelley. See World's Great Age, The.

Chorus: "Before the beginning of years." Algernon Charles Swinburne. See Before the Beginning of Years.

Chorus for Survival. Horace Gregory.
"Among the shades I heard my father's father." APT-2
Ask No Return. MoAmPo
"Meek Shall Disinherit the Earth,The." APT-2

Chorus from Atalanta in Calydon. Algernon Charles Swinburne. See When the Hounds of Spring.

Chorus: "If I drink water while this doth last." Thomas Love Peacock. NBLV Fr. Crotchet Castle.

Chorus of a Song That Might Have Been Written by Albert Chevalier. Max Beerbohm. OBCoV; UV

Chorus of dark angels, A. Savannah Brass. Verneda Sagay-Lights. BtF

Chorus of Nymphs, A. Andrey Andreievich Voznesensky. VCWP, tr. by Vera Dunham and H. W. Tjalsma

Chorus of Priests. Fulke, 1st Baron Brooke Greville. See Chorus Sacerdotum.

Chorus of the Archangels, The. Johann Wolfgang von Goethe. OBVE Fr. Faust.

Chorus of the Dead. Nelly Sachs. PFTM-1

Chorus of the Rescued. Nelly Sachs. PoSu

Chorus of the Stars. Nelly Sachs. BBASP; PFTM-1, tr. by Michael Roloff

Chorus of the weeds, unnameably, The. Weeds as Partial Survivors. Alan Dugan. YaYoPo

Chorus Primus of Bashaws or Cadis. Fulke, 1st Baron Brooke Greville. NOSC Fr. Mustapha.

Chorus Sacerdotum. Fulke Greville, 1st Baron Brooke. NAEL-6v1; NAEL-7v1; OxBEV Fr. Mustapha.

Chorus: "That rain-strewn night in the woods, the chorus, chorus." David Wagoner. MiVo

Chorus: "'Tis not enough for one that is a wife." Elizabeth Cary, Countess of Falkland. EMWP

Chorus: "To throw away the key and walk away." W. H. Auden. MoBrPo

Chorus: "Worlds on worlds are rolling ever." Percy Bysshe Shelley. HeIP-4; NAEL-6v2; NAEL-7v2 Fr. Hellas.

Choruses from "The Rock." T. S. Eliot.
"Eagle soars in the summit of heaven, The." OBMV
"I journeyed to the suburbs, and there I was told." UV

Chorus-leading, splashing out the wine. (LL) Postcard from North Antrim, A. Seamus Heaney. PBCIP; PNI

Chosen. Marilyn Nelson. ExTi

Chosen. Marilyn Nelson Waniek. FFC

Chosen Light, A. John Montague.
11 rue Daguerre. ModIr; NPeEn

Chosen People, The. W. N. Ewer. OBCoV

Chosen to Be Water. Christopher Gilbert. SwNoth

Chosen to walk in Heavenly places. Hope. Sydney E. Jerrold. SacPr

Chott. J. D. McClatchy. PfSP

Chough and crow to roost are gone, The. Outlaw's Song, The. Joanna Baillie. OBEV

Chrestus, your balls are depilated. Martial. CAGL Fr. Epigrams.

ChrisEaster. Molly Peacock. FFC

Christ and Our Selves. Francis Quarles. SacPr

Christ and the Soldier. Siegfried Sassoon. NoP-4; NoP-5

Christ as a Gardener. Andrew Hudgins. UpMys

Christ, as a light. James Clarence Mangan. SacPr Fr. St. Patrick's Hymn Before Tara.

Christ at the Apollo, 1962. Michael Waters. SwNoth

Christ Bearing the Cross by El Greco. David Craig. UpMys

Christ began his sermon in shabby clothing. Two People : 1. Yi Sang. CAMKP, *tr. by* Edward Mack

Christ bends, protects his groin. Thorns gouge. Ecce Homo. Andrew Hudgins. UpMys

Christ child lay on Mary's lap, The. Christmas Carol. G. K. Chesterton. OBCP

Christ Child, The [*with music*]. Mary Weston Fordham. CBWP-2

Christ, / come down from your cross and wash your hands. Irreverent Epistle to Jesus Christ. Romelia Alarcón de Folgar. TANSG, *tr. by* Alison Ridley

Christ Crucified. Richard Crashaw. OBEV

Christ has been done to death. Dutch Interiors. Jane Kenyon. ExTi

"Christ has risen." Whoever believes that. Czeslaw Milosz. GI *Fr.* Six Lectures in Verse.

Christ home, Christ and his mother and all his hallows. (LL) Starlight Night, The. Gerard Manley Hopkins. MoBrPo; NAEL-6v2; NAEL-7v2

Christ, I have read, did to His chaplains say. Salutation. Robert Herrick. CavPo; ChIV-2

Christ in Alabama. Langston Hughes. NAAPv.2

Christ in the Universe. Alice Thompson Meynell. MoBrPo; OxAEP-2; VWP

Christ is a Dixie Nigger. Frank Marshall Davis. APT-2

Christ is a nigger, / Beaten and black. Christ in Alabama. Langston Hughes. NAAPv.2

Christ is now risen again. Of the Resurrection. Miles Coverdale. ChIV-2

Christ is our Rock, who in a rock is lain. Holy Sepulchre, The. Rowland Watkyns. BASC

Christ / It's been more than a year now since I stopped thinking about You. Newspaper. Blaise Cendrars. YaTCFP, *tr. by* Ron Padgett

Christ, keep me from the self-survey. Christopher Smart. SacPr *Fr.* Hymns for the Amusement of Children.

Christ of His gentleness. In the Wilderness. Robert Graves. ChIV-2; MoBrPo

Christ Our All in All. Christina Georgina Rossetti. "Thy lovely saints do bring Thee love." SacPr

Christ pleads with His Sweet Leman. *Unknown.* SacPr

Christ Seen by Flemish Painters. Elizabeth Jennings. HarvBoo

Christ the Apple-Tree. *Unknown.* TCAPo

Christ, the End. Gaylord Brewer. Vesp

Christ! / the thing. Dad and Me. Geraint Jarman. BBMWP, *tr. by* Peter Finch

Christ to seek the lost was sent. Sympathy. Lizelia Augusta Jenkins Moorer. CBWP-3

Christ Triumphant. *Unknown.* NPeEn; SacPr; WeW-3

Christ / Voici plus d'un an que je n'ai plus pensé à Vous. Journal. Blaise Cendrars. YaTCFP

Christ was not sad, i' th' garden, for His own. Robert Herrick. CavPo

Christ was obedient unto his father. Catherine Parr, Lady Borough. EMWP *Fr.* In Contemplation of My Wretched Life.

Christ was the Word that spake it. *Unknown.* NoSic

Christ! What are patterns for? (LL) Patterns. Amy Lowell. AmFaPo; AmWaPo; APT-1; MoAmPo; NoP-4; NoP-5; WHSW

Christ, when he died. Christ's Victory. Richard Crashaw. SacPr

Christ who knows all His sheep. Good Shepherd, The. Richard Baxter. SacPr

Christ, whose glory fills the skies. Morning Hymn. Charles Wesley. NPeEn

Christ, you walked on the sea. In the Twentieth Century. James Philip McAuley. ChIV-2

Christabel. Samuel Taylor Coleridge. NAEL-6v2; NAEL-7v2; NOBRP

Christ-cut: the cedar. Passion Week. William Everson. SacPr

Christen Lyndesay to Ro. Hudsone. Christian Lindsay. EMWP

Christening Pot Boiler. Christopher Meredith. TCAWP

Christening the Prince. Edward Edwin Foot. State Occasion, A. STuOW

Christ[e]'s Childhood[e]. Robert Southwell. ChIV-2

Christian constellations run, The. Circle, The. Lizelia Augusta Jenkins Moorer. CBWP-3

Christian Epigram. *Unknown.* WoPoe, *tr. by* John Peck

Christian Ethics. Thomas Traherne. (Contentment Is a Sleepy Thing.) BBASP

Christian! going, gone!, A. Christian Slave, The. John Greenleaf Whittier. TCAPo

Christian Loses His Burden. John Bunyan. SacPr *Fr.* Pilgrim's Progress, The.

Christian Pilgrim's Hymn. William Williams. SacPr

Christian Science Minotaur, The. Christopher Howell. RoV

Christian Slave, The. John Greenleaf Whittier. TCAPo

Christian Virtues. Charlotte Perkins Stetson Gilman. SWaP

Christianite [*with music*]. William Stafford. NoAM

Christians, awake, salute the happy morn. John Byrom. SacPr *Fr.* Hymn.

Christina. Anna Ruth Ediger Baehr. ACAMVP

Christina. Dora Greenwell. VWP

Christina the Astonishing: Virgin. David Citino. UpMys

Christis Kirk on the Grene. *Unknown.* NePenScot

Christlike is my behaviour. Aldous Leonard Huxley. OBCoV *Fr.* Antic Hay.

Christmas. Sir John Betjeman. ChrPo; OBCP

Christmas. Gerardo Deniz. RMCMP, *tr. by* Mónica de la Torre

Christmas. George Herbert. ChrPo; NOSC

Christmas. George Herbert. RSR

Christmas. Leigh Hunt. OBCP

Christmas. Peter McDonald. PNI

Christmas. Dunya Mikhail. IrPoTo, *tr. by* Liz Winslow

Christmas. John Frederick Nims. ChrPo

Christmas. Stevie Smith. ChrPo

Christmas. Henry Timrod. APN-2

Christmas, The. Doll. Myra Cohn Livingston. TLR

Christmas 1956. György Petri. VCWP, *tr. by* Geroge Gömöri and Clive Wilmer

Christmas, 1957. The Dell-Vikings and the Diamonds. Sound Systems. Ronald Wallace. SwNoth

Christmas 1961. Murilo Mendes. Eno, *tr. by* Chris Daniels

Christmas after the summer, The. Nativity. Aidan Rooney-Céspedes. NIrP

Christmas, Again I desert my younger brothers. Multiple Floor, The. Jeffrey McDaniel. LaCa

Christmas alone, by choice, with a tin. Palindromic. Ken Babstock. OpeFie

Christmas at Bristol. William Scammell. NLP

Christmas at Sea. Robert Louis Stevenson. ChrPo; NePenScot

Christmas at the Orphanage. Bill Knott. OPRER

Christmas Ballad. San Juan de la Cruz. STV, *tr. by* John Frederick Nims

Christmas, Belfast. Robert Coles. BloBone

Christmas Bells. Henry Wadsworth Longfellow. ChrPo; OBCP

Christmas Bells, Saigon. Walter McDonald. AF

Christmas Bills. Joseph Hatton. OBCP

Christmas, bloody Christmas, we would say. Festive Tolls. Lesley Duncan. EdScPo

Christmas Card. Ted Hughes. OBCP

Christmas Card, After the Assassinations, A. Mona Van Duyn. ChrPo

Christmas Card to a Friend Who Might Be Dead. Gareth Alban Davies. BBMWP, *tr. by* the author and Mike Jenkins

Christmas Carol, A. George Macdonald. SacPr

Christmas Carol, A. Christina Georgina Rossetti. RSR

Christmas Carol, A: "God rest you merry gentlemen." G. K. Chesterton. UV

Christmas Carol, A: "In the bleak mid-winter." Christina Georgina Rossetti. OxBEV; RSR; SacPr; VWP

Christmas Carol, A: "It is close to a quarter of a century since then." T. H. Parry-Williams. BBMWP, *tr. by* Joseph P. Clancy

Christmas Carol, A: "Shepherds went their hasty way, The." Samuel Taylor Coleridge. ChrPo

Christmas Carol, A: "There's a song in the air!" Josiah Gilbert Holland. SacPr

Christmas Carol: "Christ child lay on Mary's lap, The." G. K. Chesterton. OBCP

Christmas Carol: "Close to a quarter of a century since then." T. H. Parry-Williams. OBWVE, *tr. by* Joseph P. Clancy

Christmas Childhood, A. Patrick Kavanagh. ModIr

Christmas comes like this: Wise men. Christmas Comes to Moccasin Flat. James Welch. NoAM

Christmas Comes to Moccasin Flat. James Welch. NoAM

Christmas Day. Roy Fuller. OBCP

Christmas Day. Christopher Smart. OBCP *Fr.* Hymns and Spiritual Songs for the Fasts and Festivals of the Church of England.

Christmas Day. Andrew Young. OBCP

Christmas Day [Is Come]. Luke Wadding. NOSC

Christmas day is come; let all prepare for mirth. Christmas Day [Is Come]. Luke Wadding. NOSC

Christmas Day. 1696. Nicholas Hasluck. NOBAu *Fr.* Rottnest Island.

Christmas Day; the Family Sitting. John Meade Falkner. ChIV-2

Christmas day was the least of it then, when I grew wild on the. Child's Christmas in Puerto Rico, A. Aurora Levins Morales. PueRic

Christmas Day: "What sudden blaze of song." John Keble. RSR

Christmas Dinner. Michael Rosen. OBCP

Christmas dinner was at two, The. Summer Christmas in Australia, A. Douglas Brook Wheelton Sladen. OBCP

Christmas East of the Blue Ridge. Charles Wright. LPSFW

Christmas Eve. Patricia Beer. OBCP

Christmas Eve. Marina Boroditskaya. CRWP, *tr. by* Ruth Fainlight

Christmas Eve. Walter De la Mare. ChrPo

Christmas Eve. Sascha Feinstein. SeSe

Christmas Eve [*with music*]. Lizelia Augusta Jenkins Moorer. CBWP-3

Christmas Eve. Christina Georgina Rossetti. ChrPo; RSR

Christmas Eve, 2003. Paul S. Piper. AmZen

Christmas Eve, and twelve of the clock. Oxen, The. Thomas Hardy. CABP; ChAP; ChrPo; CtM; HarvBoo; MoBrPo; NAMCP V.1; NoAM; OBCP; OxAEP-2; PoCho; SoSe-8; TFi; TRP; WeW-3

Christmas Eve: My Mother Dressing. Toi Derricotte. BtF

Christmas Eve: Nuyorican Café. Miguel Algarin. PueRic

Christmas Eve, South, 1865 [*with music*]. Mary E. Tucker. CBWP-1

Christmas Family Reunion [*with music*]. Peter De Vries. NBLV

Christmas Fare. Dilys Wood. Prnts

Christmas future is far away. Have Yourself a Merry Little Christmas. Ralph Blane and Hugh Martin. ReLy

Christmas Ghost, A. Priscilla Jane Thompson. CBWP-2

Christmas Ghost-Story, A. Thomas Hardy. ChrPo; OBWP

Christmas hath a darkness. Christmas Eve. Christina Georgina Rossetti. ChrPo; RSR

Christmas hath made an end. Carol, for Candlemas Day. *Unknown.* NOSC

Christmas Holiday. Alun Lewis. PoWW

Christmas Hymn, A. Richard Wilbur. ChIV-2; ChrPo; OBCP

Christmas in Africa. Jeni Couzyn.
  "One autumn afternoon when I was nine." CFP

Christmas in Biafra (1969) [*with music*]. Chinua Achebe. ChrPo

Christmas in Europe: 1945. J. M. Edwards. BBMWP, *tr. by* Robert Minhinnick

Christmas in India. Rudyard Kipling. ChrPo

Christmas Is Coming. Anthony Hecht. ChrPo

Christmas is coming [*or* a-coming], / And the geese are getting fat. *Unknown.* NTCP

Christmas is here. Mahogany Tree, The. William Makepeace Thackeray. ChrPo

Christmas is my name, far have I gone, have I gone, have I gone. Song Bewailing the Time of Christmas, So Much Decayed in England, A. *Unknown.* NoP-4; NoP-5
  (Christmas is my name, Farr have I gone, have I gone, have I gone.) PBRV

Christmas Is Really for the Children. Steve Turner. OBCP

Christmas Landscape. Laurie Lee. OBCP

Christmas Lullaby for a New-Born Child. Yvonne Gregory. NOxBChV

Christmas Morn. *Unknown.* OBCP

Christmas Morning. Elizabeth Madox Roberts. MoAmPo

Christmas Mourning. Vassar Miller. ChIV-2; MoAmPo

Christmas Night. Lawrence Sail. OBCP

Christmas night. The three of us. Foxes. Frieda Hughes. NeBl

Christmas 1944. Denise Levertov. AF

Christmas 1970. Spike Milligan. OBCP

Christmas: 1924. Thomas Hardy. OBCP

Christmas Poem, A. Dick Davis. ChrPo

Christmas Present for My Mother. Sue MacIntyre. Prnts

Christmas Rede. Jane Barlow. SacPr

Christmas Revel, A. Dafydd Bach ap Madog Wladaidd. OBWVE

Christmas Rhyme: North Tyrone. *Unknown.* FaBoVe

Christmas Robin, The. Robert Graves. ChrPo

Christmas Rush, The [*with music*]. Clara Ann Thompson. CBWP-2

Christmas Shopping. Louis MacNeice. OBCP

Christmas Shopping. Carter Revard. UrbNat

Christmas Song, The. Robert Wells. ReLy

Christmas Sonnet, A. Edwin Arlington Robinson. ChrPo

Christmas, South, 1866. Mary E. Tucker. CBWP-1

Christmas Spider, The. Michael Richards. Spl

Christmas Star, The. Boris Leonidovich Pasternak. WoPoe, *tr. by* Nina Kossman

Christmas Story, A. Alan Shapiro. TaR

Christmas Thank You's. Mick Gowar. OBCP

Christmas Times [*with music*]. Maggie Pogue Johnson. CBWP-4

Christmas Tree. Stanley Cook. OBCP

Christmas Tree. Laurence Smith. OBCP

Christmas Tree, A. William Burford. SoSe-8

Christmas Tree, The. Patricia Beer. OBCP

Christmas Tree, The. Cecil Day Lewis. ChrPo

Christmas Tree, The. Lizelia Augusta Jenkins Moorer. CBWP-3

Christmas Trees. Geoffrey Hill. ChrPo; UpMys

Christmas twigs crispen and needles rattle, The. New Year's Poem. Margaret Avison. BrAP

Christmas was in the air and all was well. Karma. Edwin Arlington Robinson. APT-1; HeIP-4; MoAmPo

Christophe. Russell Atkins. EGAG

Christopher. Sydney E. Jerrold. SacPr

Christopher Found. Amy Levy. ViWPN

Christopher Robin Changes Guard with Dylan Thomas. Bill Greenwell. UV

Christopher Robin goes / Hoppity, hoppity. Hoppity. Alan Alexander Milne. NTCP

Christopher Smart. Stanley Shaw. UV

Christopher Street 1979. Walter Holland. CAGL

Christ's blessing on the newly born! (LL) My Sister's Sleep. Dante Gabriel Rossetti. NAEL-6v2; NAEL-7v2

Christ's Cross. Mugrón, Abbot of Iona. NePenScot, *tr. by* Thomas Owen Clancy

Christ's cross across this face. Christ's Cross. Mugrón, Abbot of Iona. NePenScot, *tr. by* Thomas Owen Clancy

Christ's Flock of Lambs there also stands. Michael Wigglesworth. TCAPo *Fr.* Day of Doom, The [First Section].

Christ's Passion. Abraham Cowley. ChIV-2; SacPr

Christ's Prayer in Gethsemane. *Unknown.* SacPr

Christs Prophesie of the destruction of this Cittie. Thomas Deloney. ChIV-2 *Fr.* Destruction of Jerusalem, The.

Christ's Reply. Edward Taylor. NAAL-3 *Fr.* God's Determinations [touching his Elect].

Christ's Sadness. Robert Herrick. CavPo

Christ's teeth ascended with him into heaven. Michael Longley. ModIr; NPeEn *Fr.* Wreaths.

Christ's Twin. Louise Erdrich. CAP-8

Christ's Victory. Richard Crashaw. SacPr

Christ's Victory and Triumph. Giles Fletcher, the Younger.
  "As when the cheerfull Sunne, elamping wide." PBRV

Celestial City, The. ChIV-2; NOSC; SacPr

Christ's Victory on Earth.
  (Enchantress' Song, The.) NOSC
  Wooing Song. OBEV
  Mercy Replies to Justice. SacPr

Christus Natus Est. Countee Cullen. ChIV-2; ChrPo

Chromatin. J. H. Prynne. PFTM-2

Chronic Appendicitis. Luljeta Lleshanaku. WoBe, *tr. by* Henry Israeli

Chronic Meanings. Bob Perelman. OxBoAm; PmAP

Chronica. Else Lasker-Schüler. PFTM-1

Chronicle. Mei-Mei Berssenbrugge. OpBo

Chronicle. David Wheatley. NIrP

Chronicle of Sigismund, The. Sebestyén Tinódi. *tr. by* Michael Beevor
  "I've heard it sung—it may be true or no." IQMS, *tr. by* Michael Beevor

Chronicle, The; a Ballad. Abraham Cowley. OxAEP-1

Chronometrics. Robert B. Shaw.
  4. Hourglass. PoA 2002

Chronos, Chronos, mend thy pace. Secular Masque, The. John Dryden. BASC; NAEL-6v1; NPeEn; OxAEP-1; OxBEV

Chrysalides. Thomas Kinsella. ModIr

Chrysalis. Sherwin Bitsui. LegDan

Chrysalis. Francisco Segovia. RMCMP, *tr. by* Michael Wiegers

Chrysalis, A. Emily Jane Pfeiffer. ViWPN

Chrysanten, De / die in de vaas op de tafel. Chrysanten, roeiers. Hans Faverey. LWR

Chrysanten, roeiers. Hans Faverey. LWR

Chrysanthemum growers. Buson. EH, *tr. by* Robert Hass

Chrysanthemum scent. Basho. EMJL, *tr. by* Haruo Shirane

Chrysanthemums. Ko Ŭn. CAMKP, *tr. by* Kevin O'Rourke

Chrysanthemums. Irene McKinney. PBCAP

Chrysanthemums in the Eastern Garden, The. Po Chü-i. CCL1, *tr. by* Arthur Waley

Chrysanthemums, The / standing in the vase on the table. Hans Faverey. LWR

Ch'ü Yüan's "sorrow." Chang Yang-hao. ColAnChi, *tr. by* Jerome P. Seaton

Chuang Tzu and Hui Tzu*. Dick Barnes. GI

Chuang Tzu and Hui Tzu were hundreds of years old. Chuang Tzu and Hui Tzu*. Dick Barnes. GI

Chuang Tzu beats a bowl. After the Symbols. Gus Blaisdell. ICANM

Chuck Berry. Cornelius Eady. FaoP

Chuck it, Smith ! (LL) Antichrist, or the Reunion of Christendom; an Ode. G. K. Chesterton. OBSV; OxAEP-2

Chuck Man. Wanda Coleman. SUP

Quatrain: In Late Sun. Tu Fu [*or* Du Fu]. CCL1, *tr. by* Burton Watson

Chung Tzu. *Unknown.* WoPoe, *tr. by* Arthur Waley

Chungnan ranges near the imperial capital. Mount Chung-Nan. Wang Wei. ChinPo, *tr. by* Ye Weilian [*or* Yeh Wei-lien *or* Wai-lim Yip]

Chunks of night. Shadows. Patricia Hubbell. Spl

Chunks of wall are yellow. Paper 8. Dominique Batraville. OGAHCP, *tr. by* Boadiba and Jack Hirschman

Chupa neza za guibá. Na tacha. Natalia Toledo. RMCMP

Chuparosa. Juan Delgado. AmPoNex

Chu-qi dong-men: At the Great Gate. *Unknown*. CCL1, *tr. by* Ezra Pound

Church Bells. Clara Ann Thompson. CBWP-2

Church bells howitzers aloft to oust who suspect they've come as idea of beauty must. Impatient Heart, The. Bruce Andrews. FTOS

Church Bells, The [*with music*]. Mrs. Henry Linden. CBWP-4

Church Bells, The. Bishop Richard Mant. SacPr

Church Boiler, The. David Scott. NLP

Church Building. Frances Ellen Watkins Harper. NAAPv.1 *Fr.* Aunt Chloe.

Church Echoes. May Kendall. ViWPN

Church facing north, A. Stained Glass Window. Adelia Prado. TCLAP, *tr. by* Marcia Kirinus

Church Festivals. Christopher Harvey. NOSC

Church Full of Objections. Anthony Caleshu. NIrP

Church Going. Philip Larkin. BrAP; CABP; EMP; HarvBoo; HeIP-4; MoBrPo; NAEL-6v2; NAEL-7v2; NAMCP V.2; NIL-7; NIP-4; NoAM; NoP-4; NoP-5; SoSe-8; TFi; WaAnP

Church is a business, and the rich, The. After Lorca. Robert Creeley. CAP-8; OxBoAm; PmAP

Church is an iceberg, The. Winter Night. Charles Simic. MoW

Church: "I've come to kneel before you, while you're falling down." Nikolai Kanchev. CSCBP, *tr. by* Georgi Belev and Lisa Sapinkopf

Church Ladies. Nancy Travis. ISC

Church Militant, The. George Herbert.
     "Religion stands on tip-toe in our land." PBRV

Church Monuments. George Herbert. BASC; NAEL-6v1; NAEL-7v1; NOSC; NPeEn; TRP

Church no matter how big is the idea of space but not space—they, The. Cloister or "vietato toccare le rose." Rachel Zucker. IAoNAP

Church of a Dream, The. Lionel Pigot Johnson. CABP; OBMV

Church of Heaven's triumphal Car, The. Live, Evil Veil. John Wheelwright. ChIV-1

Church Romance, A. Thomas Hardy. OxAEP-2; OxBSo

Church steeple fingers the sky, The. Asleep in the City. Michael Smith. PBCIP

Churches of Rome and of England, The. John Dryden. UV *Fr.* Hind and the Panther, The.

Church-Floor[e], The. George Herbert. NOSC

Church-Music[k]. George Herbert. AmFaPo

Church's One Foundation, The. Samuel John Stone. SacPr; UV

Church's publication, The. Believers' Best Buy. Roger Woddis. UV

Churchyard. Robert Hass. MotU

Churchyard under Snow. David Scott. NLP

Churning Day. Seamus Heaney. ModIr

Ciampino: Envoi. Edwin Denby. NYP2

Cicada. Eclipse. HW

Cicada. Yi Illo. CATKP, *tr. by* Peter H. Lee

Cicada Blue. Charles Wright. KGB

Cicada chirp / Fan peddler. Kikaku. ZenPo, *tr. by* Takashi Ikemoto and Lucien Stryk

Cicada: "I lay with my heart under me." Adrien Stoutenburg. CalPo

Cicada shell, A. Basho. EH, *tr. by* R. H. Blyth and Robert Hass

Cicada Song. Liu Yung. CrYelRi, *tr. by* Sam Hamill

Cicadas. Hsüeh T'ao [*or* Xue Tao]. CCL1, *tr. by* Jeanne Larsen

Cicadas are singing in the mulberry forest, The. Chant of the Frontiersman. Wang Ch'ang-ling. NDACCP, *tr. by* William Carlos Williams

Cicada's autumn song is lonely, The. Cicada Song. Liu Yung. CrYelRi, *tr. by* Sam Hamill

Cicadas, the cicadas are singing, Rameses, The. About Limits. Tatiana Shcherbina. CRWP, *tr. by* Derek Walcott

Cid Calls His Vassals Together, The. They'll Go into Exile with Him. *Unknown*. WoPoe *Fr.* Excerpts from *The Poem of the Cid*.

Cid Enters Burgos, The. *Unknown*. WoPoe *Fr.* Excerpts from *The Poem of the Cid*.

Cid Ruy Díaz came into Burgos, The. *Unknown*. WoPoe *Fr.* Excerpts from *The Poem of the Cid*.

Ciel de fer s'est abattu, Le. Épitaphe, temps de guerre. Marguerite Yourcenar. YaTCFP

Cielo, El. Ernesto Lumbreras. RMCMP

Cielo, El / puede venirse abajo esta mañana. Ernesto Lumbreras. RMCMP

Cielo es un *sauce desbordado*, El. Entre sus ramas el sol es una oropéndola. Cielo, El. Ernesto Lumbreras. RMCMP

Cielo Min. Natalia Toledo. RMCMP, *tr. by* Alberto A. Ríos

Cielo Min. Natalia Toledo. RMCMP

Cigar bands and glinting, dimestore lockets. (LL) Who I Think You Are. Elizabeth Alexander. FFC; RA

Cigarette. Kim Sowŏl. CAMKP, *tr. by* David R. McCann

Cigarette Case. Stephen Kessler. CalPo; GeoHom

Cigarette holder. Satin Doll. Johnny Mercer. ReLy

Cigarettes. Lucille Clifton. PoChi

Cigarettes in my mouth. End of an Ethnic Dream, The. Jay Wright. SeSe

Cigarettes (marijuana), more. George Stanley. NLPA *Fr.* Mountains and Air.

Cigarettes snuffed down a sleeve, a candy bar slid to the hip, bags of. Long Coats with Deep Pockets. Sean Thomas Dougherty. AmPoNex

Cilmeri. Gerallt Lloyd Owen. BBMWP, *tr. by* Joseph P. Clancy

Cimetière marin, Le. Paul Valéry. YaTCFP

Cincinnati. Mitsuye Yamada. UnSA

Cinco. Eduardo Milán.
     "Ahora que no hay yo, vamos al yo general." RMCMP

Cinderella. Randall Jarrell. VCAP

Cinderella. Anne Sexton. BrAP; HeIP-4

Cinderella boiled up borscht. Stepmother, The. Tatiana Shcherbina. ItGoST, *tr. by* J. Kates

Cinders. Roger McGough. StAl

Cinders of the desert, The. (LL) But Bird. Paul Zimmer. AtGh; SeSe

Cinema Point. Philip Mead. BMAP

Cinema Verité. Dana Levin. LegDan

Cinema Vérité: Jacques Derrida and God's *Tsimtsum*. Tom Andrews. MotU

Cinema Vérité: The Death of Alfred, Lord Tennyson. Tom Andrews. MotU

Cinema Vérité: William Makepeace Thackeray Follows His Bliss. Tom Andrews. MotU

Cinema Yosemite. Del Ray Cross. FreRad

Cinema—an asian girl with an african name. Rifacimento. Paul Violi. PmAP

Cinéma-palace. Philippe Soupault. YaTCFP

Cineplex is showing a monster movie: our autobiography, The. Without Presumptions. Chris Forhan. NAPBL

Cinnabar cockerels sport resplendent hues. Cockfight. Liu Cheng. ColAnChi, *tr. by* Robert Joe Cutter

Cinnamon Peeler, The. Michael Ondaatje. StAl

Cinq Ans Après. Frank Gelett Burgess. OBCoV; TFi
     (Confession.) NBLV
     (Purple Cow, The: Suite.) APN-2

Cinquain: A Warning. Adelaide Crapsey. *See* Warning, The.

Cinquevalli. Edwin Morgan. HarvBoo; NePenScot

Circa. Tom Mitchelson. BRtP

Circadian. Joanna Klink. IAoNAP

Circe. Carol Ann Duffy. NeBrP

Circe. Louis MacNeice. OBMV

Circe. Augusta Davies Webster.
     Circe. VWP

Circe. Gabriel Zaid. TCLAP, *tr. by* Andrew Rosing

Circe / Mud Poems. Margaret Atwood.
     "I made no choice / I decided nothing." NALW
     "It's the story that counts." NALW
     "Men with the heads of eagles." NAMCP V.2; NoAM
     "People come from all over to consult me, bringing their limbs." NALW
     "This story was told to me by another traveller." NALW

Circe's Power. Louise Glück. OxBoAm

Circle. 'Enayat Jaber. PoArWo, *tr. by* Wen Chin Ouyang

Circle, The. Lizelia Augusta Jenkins Moorer. CBWP-3

Circle, The. Keith Wilson. AmWaPo

Circle and Obsession of Walls. Elena Clementelli. CItWP, *tr. by* Cinzia Sartini Blum and Lara Trubowitz

Circle Drawn in Water. Franz Wright. AmAlph

Circle Jerk. Andrei Codrescu. PmAP

Circle of dancing gopis. (LL) On Flower Wreath Hill. Kenneth Rexroth. APT-2; BodElec

Circle of the Golem, The. Angelina Muñiz Huberman. MirDau, *tr. by* Aurora Camacho

Circle of Totems, The. Peggy Shumaker. PBCAP

Circle, triangle, square. Shin Yu Pai. AmZen

Circle without end and without God, The. (LL) Diameter of the Bomb, The. Yehuda Amichai. BeAl; PoAgWa; PoSu, *tr. by the author and* Ted Hughes

Circled by a circle. Horizon. Mac Lojowski. AmZen

Circles. Harry Behn. CA

Circles. Ralph Waldo Emerson. APN-1; TCAPo

Circles. Carl Sandburg. HHAm

Circling. Shelley Stenhouse. PA9/11

Circling a patch / of grass. (LL) Plan, The. Rae Armantrout. AWPTFC; BAP-01

Circling by the fire. Stories. J. Patrick Lewis. NOxBChV

Circling the Daughter. Etheridge Knight. OxAAAP

Circlings. Leonard Nathan. PML

Circuit of Apollo, The. Anne Finch, Countess of Winchilsea. NALW

Circular and reforming in the glow and liquid fragment. (LL) Year of the Olive Oil, The. Charles North. FTOS; NYP2

Circular Fate. Askhari. InTrad

Circumambulating Arunachala. Gary Snyder. BB

Circumcising Pandora. Mirlande Jean-Gilles. BtF

Circumcision. Tawfiq Rafat. PML

Circumference between. (LL) At Half past Three, a single Bird. Emily Dickinson. APN-2; MoAmPo; NAWM-7v2

Circumstance. Butch Hancock. WhBo

Circumstance. John Townsend Trowbridge. APN-2

Circumstance, The. Hart Crane. PFTM-1

Circus Animals' Desertion, The. William Butler Yeats. BeAl; BrAP; HarvBoo; MakPoe; NAEL-6v2; NAEL-7v2; NAMCP V.1; NAWM-7v2; NIP-4; NoAM; NoP-4; NoP-5; TFi

Circus Circus swarms with us: floors strewn. Rumpelstiltskin Convention. Charles Webb. ReTh

Circus Nerves and Worries. Kenward Elmslie. NYP2

Circus of the City, The. Colleen J. McElroy. OxAAAP

Circus, The ("I remember when I wrote The Circus.") Kenneth Koch. OxBoAm; PmAP

Circus, The ("We will have to go away, said the girls in the circus.") Kenneth Koch. OxBoAm

Circus-Postered Barn, The. Elizabeth Jane Coatsworth. MoAmPo

Circus-Rider to Ringmaster. Thomas Hardy. RACG

Cirrostratus. CS. Geraldine Monk. Oth

Citadel. Edward Kamau Brathwaite. VCWP

Citation and Examination of William Shakespeare, The. Walter Savage Landor. Maid's Lament, The. OBEV; TreFP

Cities. Anna Glazova. tr. by Max Nemtsov
    Berlin. CRWP, tr. by Max Nemtsov
    Venice. CRWP, tr. by Max Nemtsov

Cities. Arthur Rimbaud. MotU, tr. by Louise Varese

Cities and Thrones and Powers. Rudyard Kipling. BrAP; NOxBChV Fr. Puck of Pook's Hill.

Cities are walled. It is a cruel land. Memory. Babette Deutsch. PoA 2002

Cities break up, The. Adonis. PoetW Fr. Desert, The.

Cities burn behind us; the lake glitters. Nostalgia of the Lakefronts. Donald Justice. InGu; NoP-5

Cities came from twelve girls, The. Sampler City. Christine Hume. LegDan

Cities Have Been Cut Off at the Feet, The. Hans Arp. MotU, tr. by Bethany Schneider

Cities of grass. Fort walls. The dumbstruck palace. His Dawn Vision. Seamus Heaney. PoetW

Cities of the Plain. Edgar Lee Masters. TCAPo

Cities of the Plain, The. John Greenleaf Whittier. ChIV-1; NCAP

Cities, The. George Russell. OBMV

Citizen. Julia Fields. GT

Citizen BOR Speaking. H. H. Tilley.
    "Democracy, my grannie's foot!" FaBoWar

Citizens and Sky. Phillis Levin. FFC

City. Sir John Betjeman. HarvBoo

City. Roy Fisher.
    By the Pond.
    "Brick-dust in sunlight." NPeEn
    Starting to Make a Tree.

City. Angel González. VCWP, tr. by Steven Ford Brown and Revuelta Gutierrez

City. Langston Hughes. SSCS

City. Arthur Rimbaud. SxFrPo, tr. by Martin Sorrell

City. Michael Smith. PBCIP

City a Wrecked Ship, The. Amal Dunqul. NAfrP, tr. by Sharif Elmusa and Thomas G. Ezzy

City Afternoon. John Ashbery. HeIP-4; NIP-4

City Animals. Chase Twichell. UrbNat

City as Hero, The. Weldon Kees. PWW2

City asleep / City asleep. Felice Holman. SSCS

City Baseball. Liz Rosenberg. CA

City Beneath the City, The. Eloise Klein Healy. GeoHom

City branching blindly through the clouds, The. Citizens and Sky. Phillis Levin. FFC

City by the Sea, The [with music]. Josephine D. Henderson Heard. CBWP-4

City cactus. Discovery. Zhao Zhenkai. VCWP, tr. by Chen Maiping and Bonnie S. McDougall

City Child, The. Alfred Tennyson. NOxBChV

City Christmas. Phyllis McGinley. ChrPo; OBCoV

City Dark, The. Robert Pinsky. PfSP

City Elegies. Robert Pinsky.
    Everywhere I Go, There I Am. PfSP

City, etched in the black metal of sunset, is called Resurrection, city of my birth, The. Winter Landscape. Alfonsas Nyka-Niliunas. MotU, tr. by Jonas Zdanys

City Evening. Frederick van Eeden. SonAtl, tr. by Gary and Francina VanderLinden

City, Evening, and an Old Man: Me, The. "Dhoomil." WoPoe, tr. by Vinay Dharwadker

City forsaken by its dwellers, A. Nostalgia, or a Painful Return to Memories. Stefan Tsanev. CSCBP, tr. by Georgi Belev and Lisa Sapinkopf

City Garden, A. William Stanley Braithwaite. GT

City Gent [with music]. Craig Raine. NoAM

City Goddess. Leah Korican. HW

City Guard, The. (LL) Daft Days, The. Robert Fergusson. CABP; NPeEn; OxAEP-1; OxBEV

City has tits in rows, The. Grotesque. William Carlos Williams. TCAPo

City in death with the streets caved in and the traffic lights / still, A. Catacombs in San Callisto, The. Rolf Jacobsen. BLT, tr. by Roger Greenwald

City in the Sea, The. Edgar Allan Poe. APN-1; BrAP; NAAL-3; NAAPv.1; NCAP; NoP-4; NoP-5; OxBoAm; TCAPo; TFi; TRP

City in Which I Love You, The. Li-Young Lee. ChIV-1

City in You. Michael Hill. BtF

City is covered with places you, The. City, The. Eddy Van Vliet. VCWP, tr. by John Van Tiel

City is crossed by the river, The. Landscape of the Capibaribe River. João Cabral de Melo Neto. VCWP, tr. by Richard Zenith

City is free of sin, The. Pierre Albert-Birot. CuPo

City is silent, The. Dawn Over the Mountains. Tu Fu [or Du Fu]. NDACCP, tr. by Kenneth Rexroth

City Johannesburg [with music]. Mongane Wally Serote. NAfrP; TSAP

City Life. Alvin Greenberg. UrbNat

City Life. Jorge Guillén. RaW, tr. by Charles Guenther

City Lights. Roo Borson. BeAl

City Limits. Ted Kooser. GM

City Limits, The. A. R. Ammons. EMP; GPTC; InGu; NAMCP V.2; NoAM; NoP-4; NoP-5; OxBoAm; PoPoPo; VCAP

City Limits, The. Attila József. IQMS, tr. by Anton N. Nyerges

City Lyrics. Nathaniel Parker Willis. APN-1

City Midnight Junk Strains. Allen Ginsberg. OxBoAm

City Morning, The. Sir William Davenant. NOSC Fr. Gondibert.

City Mouse and the Garden Mouse, The. Christina Georgina Rossetti. NTCP Fr. Sing-Song.

City mouse darts from the paws of night, A. Of Night. Molly Peacock. IFF

City mouse lives in a house, The. City Mouse and the Garden Mouse, The. Christina Georgina Rossetti. NTCP

City of Anguish. Edwin Rolfe. AmWaPo

City of Beggars, The. Alfred Hayes. FaBoWar; PWW2

City of Choan, The. Li Po. NDACCP, tr. by Ezra Pound

City of Dreadful Night, The. James Thomson.
    "Anear the centre of that northern crest." GS
    Part 2. NePenScot
    Part 17. NePenScot
    Part 21. NePenScot

City of Home is reached only in dreams, The. City of Home, The. Thomas William Shapcott. BMAP

City of Home, The. Thomas William Shapcott. BMAP

City of Men. Aaron Shurin. FTOS

City of No Reprieve. Willard Gellis. RWB

City of orgies, walks and joys. City of Orgies. Walt Whitman. APN-1; CAGL; ErotSp; NAAPv.1

City of Salt, The. Gregory Orr. BodElec

City of summer you inhabit a fluff-light city of little claws. Elena Suntsova. CRWP, tr. by Nika Skandiaka

City of swarming, city full of dreams. Seven Old Men, The. Charles Baudelaire. SxFrPo, tr. by James McGowan

City of tense and stricken faces. Jackson, Mississippi. Margaret Abigail Walker. InGu

City of the End of Things, The. Archibald Lampman. BrAP; IFF

City of the Grail, The. Henry E. G. Rope. SacPr

City of the Moon, The. Kenneth Rexroth.
    "Buddha took some Autumn leaves." BLT

City of the Silent, The. William Gilmore Simms.
"With ruder pomp, in more barbaric taste." APN-1
City opens its streets, The. Transparent Life, The. Luigi Fontanella. NeIt, tr. by W. S. Di Piero
City Out of the Boy, The. Jeffrey Skinner. UrbNat
City Park. Christine Crow. SSCS
City Park Merry-Go-Round. Eli W. Mandel. IFF
City Pigeons. Helen Chasin. WeW-3
City plum is not a plum, A. Christina Georgina Rossetti. NPeEn
City Ravaged by Silence, The. Buland Al-Haidari. IrPoTo, tr. by Hussein Kadhim and Christopher Merrill
City Seems, A. Laura Riding Jackson. HarvBoo
City seems between us, A. It is only love. City Seems, A. Laura Riding Jackson. HarvBoo
City squats on my back, The. Route Six. Stanley Kunitz. APT-2
City stir——wind on eardrum. Appalling Heart. Else Von Freytag-Loringhoven. NAAPv.2
City stirred about me softly and distant, The. Hours of the Day, The. George Dillon. IllVoic
City That Does Not Sleep. Federico García Lorca. RaW, tr. by Robert Bly
City, The. Constantine P. Cavafy. PLBUT; WoPoe, tr. by Rae Dalven
City, The. Constantine P. Cavafy. AmFaPo; BeAl, tr. by Edmund Keeley and Philip Sherrard
City, The. Meirion MacIntyre Huws. BBMWP, tr. by Geriant Løvgreen
City, The. Eddy Van Vliet. VCWP, tr. by John Van Tiel
City Tree, The. Isabella Valancy Crawford. BrAP
City Under Snow. Gwyn Williams. AngWePo
City used to grow, The. No Man's Land. José Ángel Valente. RaW, tr. by Hardie St. Martin
City Visions. Emma Lazarus. APN-2; NAAPv.1; SWaP
City where I knew you was swift, The. Elegy for a Soldier. Marilyn Hacker. WaAnP
City With Towers. Vitězslav Nezval. PFTM-1
City Without Smoke. Edwin Denby. NYP2
City-Hotel. Alfred Des Rochers. SonAtl, tr. by Gregory Beaven, Kurt Ganzl and Tim Rauenbusch
City's Coat of Arms, The. László Nagy. IQMS, tr. by Adam Makkai
Cityscape. Mary Crow. LiTh
City-Storm. Harold Monro. MoBrPo
Ciudad se ponía, La. Tierra de Nadie. José Ángel Valente. RaW
Ciudad sin Sueño. Nocturno del Brooklyn Bridge. Federico García Lorca. RaW
Civil Blood. Jill Breckenridge.
General John Cabell Breckinridge. CBCWP
Civil Elegies. Dennis Lee.
1. BrAP
Civil Rights. Ira Sadoff. LTA
Civil servant scrawls across, A. Justin Quinn. NIrP Fr. Days of the New Republic.
Civil Servant, The. Michael Longley. ModIr Fr. Wreaths.
Civil Song. Pier Paolo Pasolini. VCWP, tr. by Norman MacAfee and Luciano Martinengo
Civil Status. Antonin Artaud. ConPit, tr. by Albert James Arnold and Clayton Eshleman
Civil War [Bellum Civile] or Pharsalia. Lucan.
"All great things crush themselves; such end the gods." NoSic, tr. by Christopher Marlowe
Book 5. RomPo, tr. by Jane Wilson Joyce
"Just and fit actions, Ptolemy (he saith)." OBVE, tr. by Ben Jonson
"O wastfull riot, never well content." OBVE, tr. by Sir Walter Ralegh
"Thee Pompey thy past deeds by turns infest." OBVE, tr. by Nicholas Rowe
"When Caesar saw his army prone to war." NoSic, tr. by Christopher Marlowe
Civil War, The. Stephanie Farrow. FiBr
Civil War, The. Suzanne Rhodenbaugh. CBCWP
Civil war photo. George Oppen. APT-2; PFTM-1
Civil War Veteran from Indiana Recalls Visiting with Walt Whitman in a Washington Hospital, A. Norbert Krapf. ViWalt
Civil Wars, The. Samuel Daniel.
Book 2.
"Place there is, where proudly raised there stands, A." NoSic
Book 8.
"It was upon the twilight of that day." OBWP
Civilian and Soldier. Wole Soyinka. AF; PoetW
Civilian Histories. Lee Upton. AmAlph
Civilisation. János Arany. IQMS, tr. by Peter Zollman
Civilisation is hooped together, brought. Meru. William Butler Yeats. GSo; NAMCP V.1; NoAM; OxBSo; PoPoPo

Civilization. Bill Kushner. PA9/11
Civilization (Bongo, Bongo, Bongo). Bob Hilliard. ReLy
Civilization Day. Noelle Kocot. LegDan
Civilizations are viscous. History shipwrecks, Gold slips from God no. Disdained Apparitions. René Char. AF, tr. by Paul Mann
Civilization—spurns—the Leopard! Emily Dickinson. TCAPo
Civilizing the Filipino. Nick Carbó. AmPoNex
Clack your beaks you cormorants and kittiwakes. Canticle to the Waterbirds, A. William Everson. APSN; APT-2; GeoHom
Clacking and gouging when huddled. Snapshot of a Crab-Picker among Barrels Spilling Over, Apparently at the End of Her Shift. Dave Jeddie Smith. NoAM
Clacking my teeth only when you are here. Nothing in Art. J. Kates. IaFF
Claflin's Alumni [with music]. Lizelia Augusta Jenkins Moorer. CBWP-3
Claim to Fame. Beau Sia. HeMarv
Claiming Kin. Ellen Bryant Voigt. WaAnP
Claiming the Dust. Jean Janzen. ACAMVP; GeoHom
Claims no particular status in space, or being of its own. (LL) Jealousy. Mei-Mei Berssenbrugge. OpBo; PmAP
Clair de Lune. Gwen Harwood. BMAP
Clair de Lune. Jules Laforgue. WoPoe, tr. by William Jay Smith
Clairvoyant Journal. Hannah Weiner.
"How can I describe anything when all these interruptions keep arriving and then." PmAP
"I SEE words on my forehead IN THE AIR." AHA
Mar 7 SIGNAL. PFTM-2
Clambering up the Cold Mountain path. Cold Mountain Path, The. Han-shan (Cold Mountain). CCL1; NDACCP, tr. by Gary Snyder
Clammy midnight, moonless mist. Glasgow Green. Edwin Morgan. EdScPo
Clamor. Ann Lauterbach. PmAP
Clan is all together, eating Passover matzoh, joking, The. This Passover or the Next I Will Never Be in Jerusalem. Hilton Obenzinger. FTtHH
Clan Meeting: Births and Nations: A Blood Song [with music]. Michael S. Harper. NoAM
Clang! Clang! Clang! Firemen, The. James Keir Baxter. NOxBChV
Clang lace rug anhingas dream ragtime. Michelle Granguad Creating Anagrams. Paul Lloyd and Rosemary Lloyd. YaTCFP
Clanranald's Galley. Alexander MacDonald. tr. by Hugh MacDiarmid Incitement for Rowing to Sailing-place. NePenScot, tr. by Hugh MacDiarmid
Clap Your Hands for Herod. Josef Hanzlik. OBCP, tr. by Ian Milner
Clapping Chant, A. Unknown. FaBoVe
Clapping, The. Linda Gregg. BodElec
Clara conciencia de lo que ha perdido, Una. Príncipe de Aquitania, En Su Torre Abolida. Jaime Gil de Biedma. RaW
Clara, your house. Fischerhude, 2001. Sujata Bhatt. NeBrP
Clare he was to those who knew him well. Tribute to a Mohogany Cutter. J. Alexander Bennett. OWABP
Clarel: A Poem and Pilgrimage in the Holy Land. Herman Melville.
Afterward. APN-2
Concerning Hebrews. APN-2
Cypriote, The. TCAPo
Dirge. APN-2; NCAP
Easter. APN-2
Epilogue. APN-2; NCAP; TCAPo
Hostel, The. APN-2
"Ah! / These under-formings in the mind." TCAPo
Inscription, The. APN-2
Southern Cross. TCAPo
Medallion, The. APN-2
New-Comer, A.
Ungar's Harangue. TCAPo
Of Mortmain. APN-2
Pillow, The. APN-2
Prelusive.
"In Piranesi's rarer prints." TCAPo
Recluse, The. APN-2
(Shepherd's Dale, The.) TCAPo
Symphonies. APN-2
Ungar and Rolfe.
"They felt how far beyond the scope." TCAPo
Via Crucis. APN-2; NCAP
Clari, the Maid of Milan. John Howard Payne.
Home, Sweet Home! APN-1; BRP; TCAPo
Claridad del silencio. Francisco Segovia. RMCMP
Clarinet. Terrance Hayes. IIR
Claritas: / sun. Studies in Light. Diane Di Prima. PFTM-2

Claritas. The dry-eyed Latin word. Seamus Heaney. HarvBoo *Fr.* Seeing Things.

Clarity. 'Enayat Jaber. PoArWo, *tr. by* Wen Chin Ouyang

(Clarity! clarity!) a semblance of motion, omniscience. Ted Berrigan. PFTM-2 *Fr.* Sonnets, The.

Clarity of Silence. Francisco Segovia. RMCMP, *tr. by* Michael Wiegers

Clark Kent, Naked. Fred Moramarco. PML

Clark's nutcracker hid a seed. Below Fourth of July Mine. Andrew Schelling. AmZen

Clash o the kintra claik, The. Spik o' the Lan, The. Sheena Blackhall. EdScPo

Clash of salutation. As keels thrust into shingle. Geoffrey Hill. NAMCP V.2; NoAM; NoP-4 *Fr.* Mercian Hymns.

Clasp, The. Sharon Olds. BodElec

Clasp you the God within yourself. Last Round, The. Anna Wickham. MoBrPo

Claspe, The. Margaret Lucas Cavendish, Duchess of Newcastle. PBRV

Clasped around warm weeks in tents. Actually Swallowed. Douglas Messerli. FTOS

Class. Fred Ebb. ReLy

Class. Patricia Kirkpatrick. PfS

Class A, Salem, the Rookie League. Gary Fincke. MoASP

Class begins when I let go of the order of things. This is a class for anyone. Voucher. Michael Portnoy. HeMarv

Class Bully. Thomas Keiter. SwNoth

Class Dress. Dorothy Barresi. SUP

Class has dropped its books, The. The janitor's. War Poetry. Kate Clanchy. StAl

Class is irrelevant in here. Knowing Our Place. Carole Satyamurti. StAl

Class Song of '91 [*with music*]. Eloise Bibb. CBWP-4

Classic Ballroom Dances. Charles Simic. CAP-8; NAMCP V.2; WaAnP; WeW-3

Classic of Odes. *Unknown. tr. by* Jeffrey Riegel

"Big rats! Big rats!" ColAnChi

"Blind musicians, the blind musicians, The." ColAnChi, *tr. by* Jeffrey Riegel

"Cautiously bubbles that spring water." ColAnChi, *tr. by* Jeffrey Riegel

"Chaste Maiden, shining scarlet, The." ColAnChi, *tr. by* Jeffrey Riegel

"Common people are very weary, The." ColAnChi, *tr. by* Jeffrey Riegel

"Extensive the lands flanking that southern mountain." ColAnChi, *tr. by* Jeffrey Riegel

"Foxes move in pairs." ColAnChi, *tr. by* Jeffrey Riegel

"How do you cut an ax-handle?" ColAnChi, *tr. by* Jeffrey Riegel

"In the seventh month, declining is the Fire Star." ColAnChi, *tr. by* Jeffrey Riegel

"It takes a very stupid dolt." ColAnChi, *tr. by* Jeffrey Riegel

"Kuan-kuan call the ospreys." ColAnChi, *tr. by* Jeffrey Riegel

"Large-headed beauty, head so alluring, The." ColAnChi, *tr. by* Jeffrey Riegel

"Lofty trees of the south, The." ColAnChi, *tr. by* Jeffrey Riegel

"Make quiet, so quiet, your awesome bearing." ColAnChi, *tr. by* Jeffrey Riegel

"On the offering mound, a dead roe." ColAnChi, *tr. by* Jeffrey Riegel

"One who first gave birth to our people, The." ColAnChi, *tr. by* Jeffrey Riegel

"Please, Sir Second-born." ColAnChi, *tr. by* Jeffrey Riegel

"Restored Terrace is new and fresh, The." ColAnChi, *tr. by* Jeffrey Riegel

"So plentiful, the babes-in-a-pot." ColAnChi, *tr. by* Jeffrey Riegel

"Swallow flies away, The." ColAnChi, *tr. by* Jeffrey Riegel

"That peachtree so frail." ColAnChi, *tr. by* Jeffrey Riegel

"Throw me a quince." ColAnChi, *tr. by* Jeffrey Riegel

"Towering is that southern mountain." ColAnChi, *tr. by* Jeffrey Riegel

Classic Water. David Berman. IIR

Classical Head, The. John Forbes. BMAP

Classics Society. Tony Harrison. NoP-4; NoP-5 *Fr.* School of Eloquence, The.

Classified Ads. Gerardo Deniz. RMCMP, *tr. by* Mónica de la Torre

Classroom at the Mall, The. R. S. Gwynn. RA

Clattering hoofs of horses, glitter of metal. Near the Mill. Hayim Lenski. FIT, *tr. by* Robert Friend

Claud Cockburn. Thomas McCarthy. PBCIP

Claude Allen. *Unknown.* APT-1

Claude Monet's Water Landscapes. Liliane Welch. Coast

Claude to Eustace: "I am in love, meantime, you think; no doubt you would think so." Arthur Hugh Clough. FaBoVe; NPeEn *Fr.* Amours de Voyage.

Claude to Eustace: "These are the facts. The uncle, the elder brother, the squire." Arthur Hugh Clough. FaBoVe *Fr.* Amours de Voyage.

Claude to Eustace: "Yes, we are fighting at last, it appears. This morning, as usual." Arthur Hugh Clough. NPeEn; OxAEP-2 *Fr.* Amours de Voyage.

Claude to Eustace—*from Bellagio.* Arthur Hugh Clough. FaBoVe *Fr.* Amours de Voyage.

Claudette Colvin Goes to Work. Rita Dove. FuFl; NAMCP V.2

Claudia Petrovna. Claudia Petrovna. Yury Pavlovich Odarchenko. TCRusP, *tr. by* Theodore Weiss

Claudy [*with music*]. James Simmons. PBCIP

Claus von Stauffenberg. Thom Gunn. OBWP

Clause for a Covenant. Constance Carrier. APT-2

Claustro de las Sombras, El. Blas de Otero. RaW

Claustrophobia. Sean O Riordain. ModIr, *tr. by* Patrick Crotty

Claustrophobia of sand and stone: a walled heat, A. Three Ways of Looking at God. Robin Robertson. StAl

Clavicles for a Great Poetic Game. René Daumal.

    Clavicles for a Great Poetic Game. PFTM-1

Clay. Imamu Amiri Baraka. ESEAA

Clay. Charles Olson. APT-2 *Fr.* Maximus Poems, The.

Clay and Star. Ivan Davidkov.

    3. CSCBP, *tr. by* Georgi Belev and Lisa Sapinkopf

Clay Cup, The. Mirza Asadullah Khan Ghalib. WED, *tr. by* Robert Bly and Sunil Dutta

Clay Image. Takahashi Shinkichi. ZenPo, *tr. by* Takashi Ikemoto and Lucien Stryk

Clay Jug, The. Kabir. WED, *tr. by* Robert Bly

Clay kept the river we had to cross red. Dove Hunting Each Labor Day. James Hoggard. TiP2

Clay Pipes, The. Cathal Ó Searcaigh. ModIr, *tr. by* Seamus Heaney

Clay pot broken in 7 places, A. Clay Pot Broken, A. Lyonel Trouillot. OGAHCP, *tr. by* Boadiba and Jack Hirschman

Clay trinkets that I knead here on the threshold. Old Dedication. Luciana Frezza. CItWP, *tr. by* Cinzia Sartini Blum and Lara Trubowitz

Clean. Ann Turner. SSCS

Clean as a lady. Tulip. Humbert Wolfe. MoBrPo

Clean bones crying in the flesh, The. (LL) Full Moon. Elinor Wylie. NALW; NoP-4; NoP-5; StAl

Clean, deserted cave in the rock, A. Deciding to Live in an Empty Cave on Kumgang Mountain. Hueung Powoo. BecRai, *tr. by* Kim Daljin, Kim Won-Chung and Christopher Merrill

Clean fall wind. Autumn Lines. Li Po. CCL1, *tr. by* David Young

Clean is the autumn wind. Verses. Li Po. TAL

Clean otter, I have not seen other, The. Into the Ark. John Blight. BMAP

Clean People, The. Jim Heynen. GifTon

Clean people worry me, The. Clean People, The. Jim Heynen. GifTon

Clean rice, handstitch. What They Did by Lamplight. Kimberly M. Blaeser. SweBea

Clean Sheets. Lisa D. Chavez. AmPoNex

Clean that god damned room already. Deena November. IJHIL

Clean the spittoons, boy. Brass Spittoons. Langston Hughes. MoAmPo; NoAM

Clean up the mess, it is no mess of mine. (LL) Surgical Moves. Rachel Wetzsteon. AmPoNex; ExTi

Cleaned, lubed and wiped. Lesson, The. James Brown. ArBi

Cleaning. Rick Alley. AmPoNex

Cleaning. Karel Soudijn. TuT, *tr. by* Peter van de Kamp

Cleaning a Fish. Dave Jeddie Smith. NoAM

Cleaning Indian Dahl. Jane O. Wayne. InvLad

Cleaning out my refrigerator. Down on My Knees. Ginger Andrews. SweBea

Cleaning the Cistern. Anna Ruth Ediger Baehr. ACAMVP

Cleaning the Elephant. Henri Cole. BeAl

Cleaning the Well [*with music*]. Fred Chappell. InGu

Cleaning yellowtail. Yamaguchi Seishi. CAoMJL1, *tr. by* Alfred H. Marks and Takashi Kodaira

Cleanness of the path. Two Epilogues. Gennady Aygi. WoBe, *tr. by* Peter France

Clear After Rain ("Autumn, cloud blades on the horizon.") Tu Fu [*or* Du Fu]. BLT; CCL1, *tr. by* Kenneth Rexroth

Clear after Rain ("Long after rainfall, Sorceress Hills grow dark.") Tu Fu [*or* Du Fu]. CrYelRi, *tr. by* Sam Hamill

Clear air, the tree's shadow and your shadow, The. Order and the Days, The. Alicia Galaz Vivar. TANSG, *tr. by* Oliver Welden

Clear and Colder. Robert Frost. OBCoV

Clear Ankor, on whose silver-sanded shore. Michael Drayton. NOSC *Fr.* Idea.

Clear as air, the western waters. Grave of Rury, The. Thomas William Hazen Rolleston. IrV

Clear autumn. Beside the well, cold *wu* trees. I pass. Overnight at Headquarters. Tu Fu [*or* Du Fu]. NDACCP, *tr. by* David Hinton

Clear autumn opens endlessly away. Landscape. Tu Fu [*or* Du Fu]. NDACCP, *tr. by* David Hinton

Clear bright morning, with its scented air, The. Fair Morning, The. Jones Very. GSo

Clear brown eyes, kindly and alert, with 20-20 vision, The. Portrait. Kenneth Fearing. APT-2; MoAmPo

Clear Channel. Lorenzo Thomas. FTOS

Clear, clear—clearest! Moan. ZenPo, *tr. by* Takashi Ikemoto and Lucien Stryk

Clear Day and No Memories, A. Wallace Stevens. OxBoAm

Clear Form Clashes, The. Giulia Niccolai. CItWP, *tr. by* Cinzia Sartini Blum and Lara Trubowitz

Clear form of your face, The. Scream is a Kind of Coffin, The. Paz Molina. TANSG, *tr. by* Steven F. White

Clear, fresh, sweet waters, where she who alone seems lady. Petrarch. NAWM-7v1 *Fr.* Sonnets to Laura.

Clear in the blue, the moon! Ryuzan. ZenPo, *tr. by* Takashi Ikemoto and Lucien Stryk

Clear in the clearness of your eternal love. (LL) Prayer to Go to Paradise with the Donkeys, A. Francis Jammes. GPTC; WoPoe, *tr. by* Richard Wilbur

Clear Midnight, A. Walt Whitman. AWTN; SAmP; Spl

Clear mirage beyond the immaculate dune. Ablution. Angelina Muñiz Huberman. MirDau, *tr. by* Aurora Camacho

Clear mirror, The. Beyond Light. Muso Soseki. EaWin, *tr. by* W. S. Merwin

Clear moments are so short. Moment. Adam Zagajewski. StAl, *tr. by* Renata Gorczynski

Clear night in harvest time, A. I Pass the Night at General Headquarters. Tu Fu [*or* Du Fu]. NDACCP, *tr. by* Kenneth Rexroth

Clear night, thumb-top of a moon, a back-lit sky. Clear Night. Charles Wright. GeoHom; NAMCP V.2; StAl; VCAP

Clear out your. Alex Rawls. AnSo *Fr.* What's Your Sign?

Clear river curves around our village, The. In a Village by the River. Tu Fu [*or* Du Fu]. CrYelRi, *tr. by* Sam Hamill

Clear sac. Fish R Us. Mark Doty. FaoP

Clear Skies, Still Sea. *Vietnamese Oral Tradition.* CaDao, *tr. by* John Balaban

Clear stream, meanders by the village, flowing. Village by the River. Tu Fu [*or* Du Fu]. CCL1, *tr. by* Jerome P. Seaton

Clear the brown path, to meet his coulter's gleam! Ploughman, The. Oliver Wendell Holmes. CA

Clear the Way. Charles MacKay. TreFP

Clear the way there Jonathan! Walt Whitman. APN-1 *Fr.* Leaves of Grass [1855 Version, Complete Text].

Clear Valley. Muso Soseki. EaWin, *tr. by* W. S. Merwin

Clear View in Summer. Valentin Iremonger. ModIr

Clear vowels rise like balloons, The. (LL) Morning Song: "Love set you going like a fat gold watch." Sylvia Plath. BeAl; ColAP; HarvBoo; HeIP-4; ItWoWo; NAAL-5; NAMCP V.2; NIL-7; NIP-4; NoP-4; NoP-5; PoPoPo; VCAP; WaAnP

Clear water. Basho. EH, *tr. by* Robert Hass

Clear water in a brilliant bowl. Poems of Our Climate, The. Wallace Stevens. APT-1; NAMCP V.1; NoP-4; NoP-5; OxBoAm; SoSe-8

Clear weather of juniper, The. Sloe Gin. Seamus Heaney. PNI

Clearances. Seamus Heaney. EMP; NAMCP V.2; PBCIP; PNI
  "I thought of walking round and round a space." NoP-5
  "In the last minutes he said more to her." InoFa; NoP-5; PNI
  "Polished linoleum shone there. Brass taps shone." InoFa
  "She taught me what her uncle once taught her." NoP-5
  "When all the others were away at Mass." BeAl; BLT; InoFa; ItP; NoP-5; PML; PNI

Clearances, The. Iain Crichton Smith. NePenScot

Cleared by its flowing, dip the flood water up. *Unknown.* NDACCP, *tr. by* Ezra Pound

Clearer Now the Days Are Passing. Georg Heym. GTCP, *tr. by* Reinhold Grimm

Clearing. Lawson Fusao Inada. WhBo

Clearing, The. Carl Phillips. BAP-01

Clearing, The. Tomas Tranströmer. MotU, *tr. by* Robert Bly

Clearing, The: "Always in that clearing." Richard Foerster. PoDa

Clearing a Space. Brendan Kennelly. BeAl

Clearing Away. Andrew Taylor. BMAP

Clearing customs. Returning from Italy. Denise Calvetti Michaels. IPoFL

Clearing for the Plough. Ernest G. Moll. NOBAu

Clearing Out. Val Warner. EdScPo

Clearing Poems. Patrick Friesen.
  2. ACAMVP
  4. ACAMVP
  15. ACAMVP

Clearing the break in the trail, making it all the way from. Sombreo Beach, Vancouver Island, BC. Carrie Boden. BeDoSh

Clearing the Title. James Merrill. HarvBoo

Clearly through my tears I see. Clearly Through My Tears. Susan Love Fitts. IJHIL

Clearly, we are a part of the performance, slowing our. Air Show: F-16s above Cleveland. Mary Quade. OtW

Clears the morning of doves. Wind in the Trees, The. Cathy Song. OpBo

Clearsightedness. Andrew Salkey. RSaN

Clear—the senses bright—sitting in the black chair—Rocker. Michael McClure. BB *Fr.* Peyote Poem.

Cleaving, The. Li-Young Lee. OpBo; RoV

"He gossips like my grandmother, this man." IllVoic

Cleikit. David Purves. EdScPo

Clem Maverick. R. G. Vliet.
  Goodnight sweet prince. TiP2

Clemena, if you are indeed. To Clemena. Elizabeth Thomas. PoBW

Clementine. *Unknown.* NAAPv.1

Clenched ignorant against the sky! (LL) Armadillo, The. Elizabeth Bishop. APT-2; BrAP; ColAP; NAAL-5; NAMCP V.2; NIL-7; NoAM; NoP-4; NoP-5; VCAP; WaAnP

Cleomenes. John Dryden.
  (One Happy Moment.) OBEV

Cleopatra. Anna Andreyevna Akhmatova. FaBoWar; PoetW, *tr. by* Max Hayward and Stanley Kunitz

Cleopatra. Adrianne Marcus. IaFF

Cleopatra. William Wetmore Story. APN-1

Cleopatra to the Asp. Ted Hughes. RACG

Cleopatterer. P. G. Wodehouse. ReLy

Clepington Catastrophe, The. William McGonagall.
  "Accidents will happen by land and by sea." VerBaPo

Clerance. Ciaran Carson. BeAl

Cleric, The. Seamus Heaney. ModIr *Fr.* Sweeney Redivivus.

Clerihews. Edmund Clerihew Bentley.
  "After dinner Erasmus." OBCoV
  "Dinner-time? said Gilbert White." OBCoV
  George III. NPeEn
  "How vigilant was Spenser." OBCoV
  "Intrepid Ricardo, The." OBCoV
  "No, sir, said General Sherman." OBCoV
  Sir Christopher Wren. NBLV
  Sir Humphry Davy. OxBEV
  "Susaddah! exclaimed Ibsen." OBCoV
  "When their lordships asked Bacon." OBCoV
  "Wynkyn de Worde." OBCoV

Clerk Saunders [*diff. vers.*]. *Unknown.* NePenScot; OBEV

Clerks pretend to be shepherds, and under, The. Peire Cardenal. WoPoe, *tr. by* Paul Blackburn

Clerk's Tale, The. Spencer Reece. LegDan

Clerks, The. Edwin Arlington Robinson. APN-2; MoAmPo

Cleveland, Angels, Ogres, Trolls. David Citino. UpMys

Clever and Poor. V. Penelope Pelizzon. AmPoNex; PoDa

Clever Daughter, The. Susan Wicks. MFPA

Clever Woman, A. Mary Elizabeth Coleridge. ViWPN; VWP

Cliché can be true: You hate to open the paper. Insomnia: The Distances. Sydney Lea. RA

Click, click, forever click, click. Ballad of Mulan, The. *Unknown.* ColAnChi, *tr. by* Arthur Waley

Click Go the Shears. *Unknown.* NOBAu

Clickety-clack. Song of the Train. David McCord. NTCP

Cliff, The. On the Wall of Cloud-Friend Hut. Muso Soseki. EaWin, *tr. by* W. S. Merwin

Cliff, The. Gregory Orr. PfSP

Cliff, The. David Rowbotham. NOBAu

Cliff Dwelling, A. Robert Frost. APT-1

Cliff Klingenhagen. Edwin Arlington Robinson. APN-2; MoAmPo; NCAP

Cliff Notes. Bob Perelman. PmAP

Cliffs of scarlet cloud gleam in the west. Return, The. Tu Fu [*or* Du Fu]. TAL

Clifton Chapel. Sir Henry John Newbolt. OBEV

Clifton Grove. Henry Kirke White.
  Evening Sin, The. STuOW

Clikclakclikclak! Changes. Kiki Wainwright. OGAHCP, *tr. by* Boadiba and Jack Hirschman

Climacteric. Ralph Waldo Emerson. TCAPo *Fr.* Quatrains.

Climate succumbing continuously as water gathered. Nebraska. Barbara Guest. FTOS

Climate, The. Edwin Denby. NYP2

Climb aboard a butterfly and take off on the breeze. Dreamer's Holiday, A. Kim Gannon. ReLy

Climb at court for me that will. Seneca. OBVE *Fr.* Thyestes.

Climb Mount Fuji. Issa. EH, *tr. by* Robert Hass

Climb Mount Fuji. Avedik Issahakian. ChAP

Climb the tower so I can see in four directions. Climbing the Tower. Wang Ts'an. CCL1, *tr. by* Burton Watson

Climb / through my hair, climb in. Rapunzel. Olga Broumas. ReTh

Climbed high, to gaze upon the sea. Ancient Air. Li Po. BLT

Climbing. Lucille Clifton. GT; LoL

Climbing. Gloria Fuertes. RaW, *tr. by* Philip Levine

Climbing. Jennifer Maiden. BMAP

Climbing. C. Mikal Oness. GeoHom

Climbing a Tall Building on an Autumn Evening: I Gaze to Where the South River Touches the Shixing Road. Chang Chiu-ling. CCL1, *tr. by* Stephen Owen

Climbing Down the Snowy Mountain. Muso Soseki. EaWin, *tr. by* W. S. Merwin

Climbing Enlightenment Mountain. Hueung Powoo. BecRai, *tr. by* Kim Daljin, Kim Won-Chung and Christopher Merrill

Climbing from Merthyr through the dew of August mornings. Leslie Norris. ArBi *Fr.* Small War, A.

Climbing Gannett [*with music*]. Roberta Hill Whiteman. HATNAP

Climbing in Autumn for a View from the Temple on the Terrace of General Wu. Liu Ch'ang-ch'ing. CCL1, *tr. by* Witter Bynner

Climbing My Grandfather. Andrew Waterhouse. BeAl

Climbing of Snowdon. William Wordsworth. NPBRoP

Climbing on the Double Ninth Day. Tu Fu [*or* Du Fu]. ChinPo, *tr. by* Ye Weilian [*or* Yeh Wei-lien *or* Wai-lim Yip]

Climbing Out. Diane Ackerman. OtW

Climbing Pien-chueh Temple. Wang Wei. ColAnChi, *tr. by* Stephen Owen

Climbing Sears Tower. Dennis Schmitz. IllVoic

Climbing stone after stone. Yagul. John Brandi. ICANM

Climbing Stone Drum Mountain. Hsieh Ling-yün. CrYelRi, *tr. by* Sam Hamill

Climbing Suilven. Norman Alexander MacCaig. HarvBoo

Climbing the canyon even as. Daphne Marlatt. NLPA *Fr.* Touch to My Tongue.

Climbing the hill a coil of snakes. Michael Field. ViWPN

Climbing the Ling-ying Terrace and Looking North. Po Chü-i. BLT; CCL1, *tr. by* Arthur Waley

Climbing the mountain pass. Yuko Kawano. CFP, *tr. by* Aoyami Miyuki, Leza Lowitz and Akemi Tomioka

Climbing the peak of Tamalpais the loose. George Oppen. ASA *Fr.* Some San Francisco Poems.

Climbing the Ridge. Rosemerry Wahtola Trommer. GeoH

Climbing the southern slope of Cold Mountain? (LL) I can't stand these birdsongs. Han-shan (Cold Mountain). BB; NDACCP, *tr. by* Gary Snyder

Climbing the stairway gray with urban midnight. Effort at Speech. William Meredith. WaAnP

Climbing the Stork Pavilion. Wang Chih-huan. ColAnChi, *tr. by* Richard W. Bodman

Climbing the Tower. Wang Ts'an. CCL1, *tr. by* Burton Watson

Climbing the wax tree. Sky. Takahashi Shinkichi. ZenPo, *tr. by* Takashi Ikemoto and Lucien Stryk

Climbing through the January snow, into the Lobo canyon. Mountain Lion. D. H. Lawrence. FaBoVe

Climbing to the Monastery of Perception. Wang Wei. CCL1, *tr. by* Pauline Yu

Climbing Xie Tiao's North Tower at Xuan in Autumn. Li Po. CCL1, *tr. by* Elling O. Eide

Climbing You. Erica Jong. PoA 2002

Climbing Yun-lung Mountain. Su Tung-p'o. CrYelRi, *tr. by* Sam Hamill

Clin d'oeil. Benjamin Péret. YaTCFP

Clinchfield Station. Charles Wright. LPSFW

Cling to your knife. (LL) Valentine: "Not a red rose or a satin heart." Carol Ann Duffy. BeAl; EdScPo

Clinging to the bell. Buson. SoOfWa, *tr. by* Sam Hamill

Clinic Day. Diana Fitzgerald Bryden. OpeFie

Clinic in a Dangerous Season 1, A. Yi Yônju. EcSo, *tr. by* Yung-Hee Kim

Clinic in a Dangerous Season 7, A. Yi Yônju. EcSo, *tr. by* Yung-Hee Kim

Clinic in a Dangerous Season 8, A. Yi Yônju. EcSo, *tr. by* Yung-Hee Kim

Clinic, The. Grace Herman. BloBone

Clio. Martha Sansom.
    "Honour, that Guardian Angel, can alone." LW

Clip cuticle; drink orange juice. Philip Whalen. WANABP *Fr.* Epigrams & Imitations.

Clip cuticle; drink orange juice. Epigrams & Imitations. Philip Whalen.

Clipper-Ships. John Gould Fletcher. TCAPo

Clipping the same sad alnage of the years. (LL) Clerks, The. Edwin Arlington Robinson. APN-2; MoAmPo

Clippings. Kimiko Hahn. ExTi

Clips from the battlefield. Iraqi Evening, An. Yousif al-Sa'igh. IrPoTo, *tr. by* Chuck Miller and Saadi A. Simawe

Cloak, The. Robert Graves. HarvBoo

Cloak, The. James McAuley. BMAP

Cloak, The. Norman Henry, II Pritchard. GT

Cloak of Dawn. Amadou Lamine Sall. NAfrP

Clock. Clock, The. Jorge Carrera Andrade. TCLAP, *tr. by* Michael Surman

Clock. Douglas A. Martin. BeDoSh

Clock. Valerie Worth. TLR

Clock, The. Charles Baudelaire. WoPoe, *tr. by* Roy Campbell

Clock, The. Charles Baudelaire. MotU, *tr. by* Edward K. Kaplan

Clock, The. Jorge Carrera Andrade. TCLAP, *tr. by* Michael Surman

Clock, calm, evil god that makes us shiver, The. Clock, The. Charles Baudelaire. WoPoe, *tr. by* Roy Campbell

Clock in the Square, A. Adrienne Rich. HeIP-4

Clock Plods On, The. Valentine Ackland and Sylvia Townsend Warner. PoBW

Clock plods on, The. Clock Plods On, The. Valentine Ackland and Sylvia Townsend Warner. PoBW

Clock says "When will it be morning?", The. After Lorca. Ted Hughes. PoA 2002

Clock stopped, A. Emily Dickinson. APN-2; NAAL-3; NAAL-5; NoP-4; NoP-5; TCAPo

Clock strikes one that just struck two, The. Emily Dickinson. APN-2

Clock struck twelve; o'er half the globe, The. Duellist, The. Charles Churchill.

Clock struck twelve times. . .and it was a spade, The. Clock Struck Twelve Times, The. Antonio Machado Ruiz. WED, *tr. by* Robert Bly

Clock within us, speaking time, The. Making Love, Killing Time. Anne Ridler. SacPr

Clock-A-Clay. John Clare. NAEL-6v2; NAEL-7v2

Clockface. Rhyll McMaster. BMAP

Clockface. Judith Thurman. Spl

Clocks. Julio Cortázar. MotU, *tr. by* Paul Blackburn

Clocks. Sinéad Morrissey. MoWP; NIrP

Clocks are sorry, the clocks are very sad, The. Psalm and Lament. Donald Justice. CAP-8; GPTC

Clocks belled twelve. Main Street showed otherwise. Owl. Sylvia Plath. OWoS

Clocks blue seconds fold over me. Paregoric Babies. Jim Carroll. PmAP

Clocks out of order. Studies. Carlos Pellicer. TCLAP, *tr. by* Donald Justice

Clock's so huge you can watch the minute hand, The. Grand Central Station, 20 December 1987. Bruce Bawer. RA

Clocks strike in the distance. On My Child's Death. Joseph, Freiherr von Eichendorff. WoPoe, *tr. by* W. D. Snodgrass

Clocks strike, The. Death of the Wild Warrior. Daniil Kharms. TCRusP, *tr. by* Robin Milner-Gulland

Clock's untiring fingers wind the wool of darkness, The. Cradle Song. Louis MacNeice. MoBrPo

Clockwise and counter-clockwise turning. (LL) Poem Beginning with a Line by Pindar, A. Robert Duncan. PmAP; VCAP

Clockwork. Donny O'Rourke. PML

Clockwork beings, winding out their lives. Insects. Isidor Schneider. APT-2

Clockwork Doll. Dahlia Ravikovitch. FIT, *tr. by* Robert Friend

Clockwork skating Wordsworth on the ice, A. Xmas for the Boys. Gavin Ewart. OBSV

Clod & the Pebble, The. William Blake. NAEL-6v1; NAEL-7v2; NoP-4; NoP-5; NPBRoP; NPeEn; OxAEP-2; OxBEV; TFi *Fr.* Songs of Experience.

Clods' friability lulls iron to sleep. August Stramm. PFTM-1

Clods, return to your place. Prayer at the Winter Thanksgiving. *Unknown.* CCL1, *tr. by* James Legge

Cloe. George Granville, Baron Lansdowne. NIP-4; OxBEV

Cloe to Artimesa. *Unknown.* PoBW

Cloe's the wonder of her sex. To Cloe. George Granville, Baron Lansdowne. NBLV; OxBEV

Clog of Her Body, The. Diana García. TouFir

Clogged and soft and sloppy eyes. Gwendolyn Brooks. ColAP *Fr.* Notes from the Childhood and the Girlhood.

Cloister. Conrad Potter Aiken. MoAmPo

Cloister. Gabriel Zaid. TCLAP, *tr. by* Mónica Hernández-Cancio

Cloister of the Shades, The. Blas de Otero. RaW, *tr. by* Hardie St. Martin

Cloister or "vietato toccare le rose." Rachel Zucker. IAoNAP

Cloister, The. William Matthews. CAP-8

Cloodburst an' soarin' mune. Cloudburst and Soaring Moon. Hugh MacDiarmid. NAMCP V.1; NoAM

Cloosmit the herring, hosts in the night. Ko-Ishin-Mit Goes Fishing. George Clutesi. HATNAP

Clora come view my Soul, and tell. Gallery, The. Andrew Marvell. BASC; NoP-4; PBRV

Cloris' Charms Dissolved by Eudora. Anne Killigrew. BASC

Clorox bleaching my fingernails lady-white. Maid. Sarah Kennedy. SweBea

Close. Carol Ann Duffy. EdScPo

Close. Robert Duncan. PmAP

Close. Andrew Motion. HarvBoo; StAl

Close analysis revealed the existence of a key. Case of the Same Name, A. Giampiero Neri. ItPo, *tr.* by Gayle Ridinger

Close and slow, summer is ending in Hampshire. Louis MacNeice. NPeEn *Fr.* Autumn Journal.

Close by the shore, the shore. *Unknown.* WoPoe *Fr.* Mourning Songs of Greece.

Close by those meads, for ever crowned with flow'rs. Alexander Pope. OBSV *Fr.* Rape of the Lock, The: An Heroi-Comical Poem in Five Cantos.

Close Call. X. J. Kennedy. PoDa

Close cleaving unto Silence, into sound. Whisper. John Banister Tabb. APN-2

Close his eyes; his work is done! Dirge for a Soldier. George Henry Boker. PCW

Close of day. Zinaida Bykova. CRWP, *tr.* by Robert Reid

Close Shave. Jackie Kay. MoWP

Close the dim eyes, for expression hath left them. Lines on a Dead Girl. Priscilla Jane Thompson. CBWP-2

Close to a house on a piece of ground. Garden, The. Bernadette Mayer. FTOS

Close to a quarter of a century since then. Christmas Carol. T. H. Parry-Williams. OBVVE, *tr.* by Joseph P. Clancy

Close to Me. Gabriela Mistral. TANSG, *tr.* by Maria Giachetti [*or* Jacketti]

Close to Me. Gabriela Mistral. TCLAP, *tr.* by Doris Dana

Close to the gates a spacious garden lies. Homer. OBGa; OBVE *Fr.* Odyssey.

Close to the gates of Paradise I flee. Eve. Ella Higginson. SWaP

Close to the old houses. Bird Close to Old Houses, A. Aliyah Abdul-Salaam. AnVo, *tr.* by Mohamed Enani

Close to the road, we sit down one day. Close to the Road. Antonio Machado Ruiz. WED, *tr.* by Robert Bly

Close to the top. Problem, The. Thom Gunn. NAMCP V.2

Close to the west the great ocean is singing. Two Rain Songs (Papago). Winged Serpent. IPoFL

Close up the casement, draw the blind. Shut Out That Moon. Thomas Hardy. NAMCP V.1; NoAM

Close Woven. Sikong Tu. CCL1 *Fr.* Twenty-Four Modes of Poetry.

Close your eyes and you're stoned, child, here on River Road. Trick Noir. Brian Teare. LegDan

Close your eyes over my sins. Géza Páskándi. IQMS *Fr.* Language Memory.

Closed. Vicente Aleixandre. RaW, *tr.* by W. S. Merwin

Closed car—closed in glass. George Oppen. APT-2; PFTM-1

Closed Discussion about the Future. Tim Griffin. FreRad

Closed like confessionals, they thread. Ambulances. Philip Larkin. BrAP; NAEL-6v2; NAEL-7v2; NoP-4; NoP-5

Closed over wounds. (LL) Roads. Peter Huchel. HP; PoSu, *tr.* by Michael Hamburger

Closed Town, The. *Unknown, fr. Terezin Concentration Camp.* INSAB

Closed window looks down, A. Ka 'Ba. Imamu Amiri Baraka. ISC; PmAP

Closed World, The. Denise Levertov. NoP-4

Closer. Albert Goldbarth. PoA 2002

Closer, closer / to paradise—. Issa. ZenPo, *tr.* by Takashi Ikemoto and Lucien Stryk

Closer in. C. S. Giscombe. GT *Fr.* (from the "In" Sequence).

Closer, listen, I love you. (LL) This Is What I Wanted to Sign Off With. Alden Nowlan. PoCu; StAl

Closer to a bell than a bird. Rotary. Christina Pugh. P180

Closer to Home. Floyd Skloot. UrbNat

Closer together, as if you could make me whole. (LL) Mirror of Matsuyama, The. Sharon Hashimoto. CFP; OpBo

Closer we draw to the summit, the more the height of the cuckoo-flowers dwindles, The. Paengnokdam: White Deer Lake. Chŏng Chiyong. CAMKP, *tr.* by Anthony, Brother of Taizé

Closest our family ever came to red hair, The. One Red-haired Summer, The. Andrea Potos. FiBr

Close-up. A. R. Ammons. PoA 2002

Close-up on a Sharp-shinned Hawk. Don McKay. BeAl

Closing, A. May Miller. ISC

Closing cycle rich in good, The. (LL) Alfred Tennyson. ChrPo; NAEL-6v2; NAEL-7v2 *Fr.* In Memoriam A. H. H.

Closing Time. Eric Muirhead. TiP2

Closure. Douglas Messerli. FTOS

Closure Opening Its Trap. Suzanne Wise. AmPoNex

Clote, The. William Barnes. FaBoVe; NPeEn

Cloth, A. Gertrude Stein. TCAPo *Fr.* Tender Buttons.

Clothed in buckskin, clothed in homespun. Pioneers. Aileen Fisher and Olive Rabe. CA

Clothes. Wisława Szymborska. PoSu, *tr.* by Grazyna Drabik and Sharon Olds

Clothes. *Unknown.* SonAtl, *tr.* by P. Nbe Ondo

Clothes, The. Julia Copus. NeBl

Clothes Do But Cheat and Cozen [*or* Cousen] Us. Robert Herrick. ErotSp

Clothes make no sound when I tread ground. Cynewulf. WoPoe *Fr.* Riddles (Exeter Book).

Clothes Make the Man. Jack Conway. NBLV

Clothes Maketh the Man. Theodore Weiss. NoAM

Clothes must play a part. Lovely to Look At. Dorothy Fields and Jimmy McHugh. ReLy

Clothes Without the Monk, The. Silvio Giussani. ItPo, *tr.* by Gayle Ridinger

Clothesline. Laurie Kutchins. SweBea

Clothesline post is set, The. Lorine Niedecker. APT-2

Cloud. Takahashi Shinkichi. ZenPo, *tr.* by Takashi Ikemoto and Lucien Stryk

Cloud, The. Dulce Maria Loynaz. TANSG, *tr.* by Alan West

Cloud, The. Percy Bysshe Shelley. BrAP; CABP; NAEL-6v2; NAEL-7v2; NoP-4; NoP-5; NPBRoP

Cloud, The. Derek Walcott. ChIV-1

Cloud, The: "It's darker and cooler." Ekaterina Iosifova. CSCBP, *tr.* by Georgi Belev and Lisa Sapinkopf

Cloud above lotus / It too. Boryu. ZenPo, *tr.* by Takashi Ikemoto and Lucien Stryk

Cloud around tree outside window, in. Recollections of Being. Nathaniel Tarn. WANABP

Cloud creates the face of a man who, happening to look up, recognizes it as his own, A. Cloud Creates, A. David Ignatow. PoA 2002

Cloud Fantasy. Henrietta Cordelia Ray. CBWP-3

Cloud fields change into furniture. Emphasis Falls on Reality, An. Barbara Guest. AWPTFC; FTOS; PmAP

Cloud Game, The. William Reichard. AmPoNex

Cloud Hairdress. Chao Luan-luan. CCL1, *tr.* by Chung Ling and Kenneth Rexroth

Cloud hides the sun, A. A photograph. After Reading the Book of Splendor. Emily Warn. GifTon

Cloud in Trousers, A. Vladimir Vladimirovich Mayakovsky. TCRusP, *tr.* by Kathy Lewis and Bob Perelman

Cloud, journey of water through the sky. Cloud, The. Dulce Maria Loynaz. TANSG, *tr.* by Alan West

Cloud Messenger, The. Kalidasa. *tr.* by Eleanor Edgerton and Franklin Edgerton

"High on the Mount of Rama a yaksha dwelt, who for." WoPoe, *tr.* by Eleanor Edgerton and Franklin Edgerton

Cloud Mountain. Muso Soseki. EaWin, *tr.* by W. S. Merwin

Cloud moved close, A. The bulk of the wind shifted. Visitant, The. Theodore Roethke. TRP

Cloud no bigger than a button, A. Old Champagne Glass. Eddy Van Vliet. VCWP

Cloud of Dusk, A. Michael Burkard. BAP-04

Cloud of Unknowing, The. Christopher Edgar. BAP-01

Cloud Painter. Jane Flanders. PoA 2002

Cloud peaks. Basho. EMJL, *tr.* by Haruo Shirane

Cloud possessed the hollow field, A. High Tide at Gettysburg, The. Will Henry Thompson. CBCWP

Cloud-puffball, torn tufts, tossed pillows flaunt forth, then chevy on an air-. That Nature Is a Heraclitean Fire and of the Comfort of the Resurrection. Gerard Manley Hopkins. FaBoVe; NAEL-7v2; NoP-4; NoP-5; PFTM-1

Cloud Rains. Oumarou Watta. NAfrP

Cloud Song [*with music*]. Henrietta Cordelia Ray. CBWP-3

Cloud that drifted days ago, The. Cloud That Drifted, The. Feng Yen-ssu. CCL1, *tr.* by John Minford

Cloud That Drifted, The. Feng Yen-ssu. CCL1, *tr.* by John Minford

Cloud Unfolding, The. Ernesto Trejo. FTtHH; LTA

Cloud-backed heron will not move, The. Heron, The. Vernon Watkins. AngWePo; TCAWP

Cloudburst and Soaring Moon. Hugh MacDiarmid. NAMCP V.1; NoAM

Cloud-capped peaks fill the eyes. On a Visit to Ch'ung Chen Taoist Temple. Yü Hsüan-chi. ColAnChi, *tr.* by Chung Ling and Kenneth Rexroth

Clouded Evening, Late September. Sydney Lea. RA

Clouded Morning, The ("Morning comes, and thickening clouds prevail, The.") Jones Very. GSo

Clouded Skies. Philippe Jaccottet. YaTCFP, *tr.* by David Constantine and Mark Treharne

Clouded Sky. Miklós Radnóti. GifTon; HP, *tr. by* Stephen Berg, F. J. Marks, S. J. Marks and Steven Polgar

Clouded with snow / The cold winds blow. Winter. Walter De la Mare. OBMV

Cloudless summer day—. Haiku. Lenard D. Moore. SpirFl

Clouds. Complete Sound-Poems of Hugo Ball, The. Hugo Ball. PFTM-1

Clouds. Rupert Brooke. OBEV; OBMV

Clouds. Denise Levertov. VCAP

Clouds. Stanley Moss. BodElec

Clouds. Francis Webb. BMAP

Clouds. Sándor Weöres. IQMS, *tr. by* Edwin Morgan

Clouds above the Sea. Philip Levine. PML

Cloud's Anchor, The. Ian Hamilton Finlay. NePenScot

Clouds and the stars didn't wage this war, The. For the Record. Adrienne Rich. NIL-7; NIP-4; VCAP

Clouds are arriving now. Evening Clouds. Olav H. Hauge. WED, *tr. by* Robert Bly

Clouds are marshalling across the sky, The. Meditations. Margaret Fuller. NAAPv.1; SWaP

Clouds as I see them, rising, The. Clouds. Denise Levertov. VCAP

Clouds carry in another of June's remonstrances, The. Last week. Cloud Game, The. William Reichard. AmPoNex

Clouds chinked together vertebrae fashion. Summer Begins Outside Dalhart, Texas. Mary Vanek. TiP2

Clouds circle the moon. Love Song. Ma Chih-yüan. CrYelRi, *tr. by* Sam Hamill

Clouds come and go, The. Basho. SoOfWa, *tr. by* Sam Hamill

Clouds do not send their rain down endlessly. Grieving Too Long (2.9). Horace. WED, *tr. by* Robert Bly

Clouds dream and disappear. Wistaria. Witter Bynner. APT-1

Clouds Gathering. Charles Simic. ColAP

Clouds grow thickest when the summit's nigh, The. (LL) Slow Through the Dark. Paul Laurence Dunbar. GSo; SacPr

Clouds had made a crimson crown, The. Moment, A. Mary Elizabeth Coleridge. LW; PEW

Clouds have gathered, and gathered, The. To-Em-Mei's "The Unmoving Cloud." T'ao Ch'ien. NDACCP, *tr. by* Ezra Pound

Clouds have rolled away, The. Yun Sŏndo. CATKP *Fr.* Angler's Calendar, The.

Clouds now and then. Basho. OxBEV, *tr. by* Anthony Thwaite

Clouds of blossoms. Basho. EH, *tr. by* Robert Hass

Clouds of cherry blossoms! Basho. SoOfWa, *tr. by* Sam Hamill

Clouds of dust arise, rolling up from earth. *Unknown.* APN-2 *Fr.* Hako, The.

Clouds of Evening. Robinson Jeffers. MoAmPo

Clouds of incense, people close together. Sunlight streaming from the rotunda. Three Churches. Patricia Y. Ikeda. MotU

Clouds of mosquitoes / It would be bare. Issa. ZenPo, *tr. by* Takashi Ikemoto and Lucien Stryk

Clouds of the earth, The. Snowdonia after Chernobyl. BBMWP, *tr. by* Joseph P. Clancy

Clouds out of darkness. Second Coming, The. Suzanne Benton. HW

Clouds pass over, endless. Passover: the Injections. William Heyen. HP

Clouds, piled in rows like merchandise, The. Millinery District. Charles Reznikoff. APT-2

Clouds release the hillsides and wake the scenes of spring. Han-shan Te-ch'ing. CSKM, *tr. by* Red Pine

Clouds ripped open; a rainbow. Clouds Ripped Open. Antonio Machado Ruiz. RaW, *tr. by* Robert Bly

Clouds run, but the sky stands still. Reply to a Poem by Donglim. Pyungyang Ungee. BecRai, *tr. by* Kim Daljin, Kim Won-Chung and Christopher Merrill

Clouds seen and unseen. Tune: "Traveler Welcoming the Immortal." Chang K'o-chiu. ChinPo, *tr. by* Ye Weilian [*or* Yeh Wei-lien *or* Wai-lim Yip]

Clouds, shadows searching for what cast them. (LL) Tornados. Thylias Moss. GT; MakPoe

Clouds shouldered a path up the mountains, The. Drought, The. Gary Soto. NAMCP V.2; NoAM

Clouds spout upon her. Rain on a Grave. Thomas Hardy. OxAEP-2

Clouds stand in protest of morning. Public Radio Plays Eddie Harris. A. Van Jordan. LegDan

Clouds that drift so far and free. Wife's Thoughts, The. Hsü Kan. CCL1, *tr. by* Burton Watson

Clouds, The. Basho. EH, *tr. by* Robert Hass

Clouds, The. Thomas M. Disch. RA

Clouds, The. Mirabai. WED, *tr. by* Robert Bly

Clouds, The. Sándor Petőfi. *tr. by* W. H. Auden and Peter Zollman

"Farmer puts his field under the plow, The." IQMS, *tr. by* Peter Zollman

"Glorious night! / The giant moon, the tiny evening star." IQMS, *tr. by* Peter Zollman

"How many drops has the ocean sea?" IQMS, *tr. by* Peter Zollman

"How will the earth die? . . . will she freeze? will she burn?" IQMS, *tr. by* Peter Zollman

"Humankind has not declined!" IQMS, *tr. by* Peter Zollman

"I often wonder who will find." IQMS, *tr. by* Peter Zollman

"If all the hearts that shrivelled in their graves." IQMS, *tr. by* Peter Zollman

"Is the spirit the true lover of the flesh?" IQMS, *tr. by* Peter Zollman

"Sorrow? A Great Ocean." IQMS, *tr. by* W. H. Auden

"What happens to laughter." IQMS, *tr. by* Peter Zollman

"What's the merriest burial ground?" IQMS, *tr. by* Peter Zollman

Clouds, the source of rain, one stormy night, The. Lost in Heaven. Robert Frost. MoAmPo

Clouds were mountains, that day, behind the real mountains, The. View from Skates in Berkeley, The. Quincy Troupe. UnSA

Cloudy Day. Jimmy Santiago Baca. LoL

Cloudy Morning. Joseph McCarthy, Jr. ReLy

Cloudy morning dark as night. Cloudy Morning. Joseph McCarthy, Jr. ReLy

Cloudy Mountain. Pou Kuksa. BecRai, *tr. by* Kim Daljin, Kim Won-Chung and Christopher Merrill

Clover. Sidney Lanier. APN-2; ColAP

"Now comes the Course-of-things, shaped like an Ox." TCAPo

Clover fills the darkness quickly. Axiom of Maria. Larissa Szporluk. NeAmPo

Clover-rich, lugged close to the thorax and twirling heart. In the Beeyard. Linda Bierds. AmAlph

Clover's simple Flame, The. Emily Dickinson. APN-2

Clown, The. Renée Gregorio. ICANM

Clownfish. Lavinia Greenlaw. MoWP

Clown's Song, The. William Shakespeare. NoSic; TFi *Fr.* Twelfth Night.

Cloyed with the torments of a tedious night. Mary Sidney Wroth, Countess of Montgomery. BASC

Club, The. Mitsuye Yamada. FiBr

Club House. Janice Lowe. InTrad

Club Midnight. Charles Simic. BodElec

Clues / 1. Outside it snows. Ancestors. Karen Press. TSAP

Clues to what they remembered had been pasted into an album, The. Cenotaph. John Yau. PmAP

Clump of Gods, The. Tracy Philpot. IAoNAP

Clustering atop a leggy stem. Primula veris. Randolph Healy. Oth

Clutching the ward's wall rail. I'll See You Down the Lane. Alison Pryde. Prnts

Clyde Peeling's Reptiland in Allenwood, Pennsylvania. Kevin Young. NeAmPo

C'mon said the pilot and. Small Plane in Kansas. Thom Gunn. OtW

C'mon ye auld buggers, one by one. Den of the Old Men. Kathleen Jamie. GPPA

14. The CN Tower. David McFadden. NLPA

Coach Class Seats. Charles Harper Webb. PoDa

Coach in Effigy. Jack Ridl. LiTh

Coach waits, long, hot in the sun, The. Croeso i Gymru. Philip Owens. AngWePo

Coal. Audre Lorde. ESEAA; NAAL-5; NALW; NAMCP V.2; NoAM; NoP-4; NoP-5; VCAP

Coal Age. Emily Wilson. LegDan

Coal Fire in Winter, A. Thomas McGrath. ErotSp; GifTon; RaBo

Coal Miners, The. James Ballowe. IllVoic

Coal, shale, iron and steel. Even Solomon. Dennis O'Donnell. EdScPo

Coal Train. Jay Parini. GM

Co-alcoholic. Joan Larkin. LaCa

Coalmen, The. László Nagy. IQMS, *tr. by* Tony Connor

Coals go out, The. Galway Kinnell. RaBo *Fr.* Middle of the Way.

Coarse bread and water's most their fare. Roger Williams. *See* Course bread and water's most their fare.

Coarse/ jocosity/ catches the crowd. Don Marquis. APT-1 *Fr.* Archy and Mehitabel.

Coarse rigors. Stephanie Williams. AnSo

Coast, The. Gonzalo Rojas. PML, *tr. by* John Oliver Simon

Coast hills at Sovranes Creek, The. Place for No Story, The. Robinson Jeffers. APT-1

Coast of Texas, The. Isabel Nathaniel. TiP2

Coastal. Mark Doty. PtR

Coastal. Valerie Martínez. AmPoNex

Coastline never alters for the fisherman, The. Coastline, The. Eddy Van Vliet. VCWP, *tr. by* Matthew Blake

Coastline, The. Eddy Van Vliet. VCWP, *tr. by* Matthew Blake

Coat. Vicki Feaver. LW

Coat. Meirion MacIntyre Huws. BBMWP, *tr. by* Grahame Davies

Coat, A.   William Butler Yeats.   NAEL-6v2; NAEL-7v2; NAMCP V.1; NoAM; OxAEP-2; PtR

Coat, The.   Dewi Stephen Jones.   BBMWP, *tr. by* the author

Coat, The.   Dennis Lee.   TLR

Coated with blood, he canters home.   My Father's First Fight.   Deborah DeNicola.   NevBe

Cobalt.   Rolf Jacobsen.   BLT, *tr. by* Roger Greenwald

Cobble and Pebble in the teeth. Fang and Club upon.   Narrative Charm for Ibbotroyd.   Maggie O'Sullivan.   Oth; PFTM-2

Cobb's Barns.   Anne Babson Carter.   PoSol

Cobra Pilot.   Don Receveur.   OtW

Cobré la Rienda.   Juan Ramón Jiménez.   RaW

Cobweb.   Haniel Long.   APT-1

Cobweb, The.   Raymond Carver.   BLT

Cobwebs.   Melinda Goodman.   WiU

Cobwebs.   Christina Georgina Rossetti.   CABP; NAEL-6v2; NAEL-7v2; NALW; VWP

Coca-Cola and Coco Frío.   Martín Espada.   ReTh; UnSA

Cocaine Mad-Scream Article #33 LoveSong.   Gylan Kain.   BRtP

Cochineals and fig colours ripple.   Dining Out.   Judith Beveridge.   BMAP

Cock and the Fox, The.   Robert Henryson.   NAEL-7v1

Cock and the Hen, The.   Geoffrey Chaucer.   *See* Nun's Priest's [*or* Nonne Preestes] Tale, The.

Cock and the Pearl, The.   Max Jacob.
   "I thought he was bankrupt."   PFTM-1

Cock crows—cock-a-doodle-doo!—the east grows bright, The.   On the Hall of Precious Virtue.   Yang Shih-ch'i.   ColAnChi, *tr. by* Jonathan Chaves

Cock- / ed and forever loaded. Bonecrusher, meatgrinder, brain-.   Black Revolver.   Jarret Keene.   LiTh

Cock has crow'd an hour ago, The.   Morning Quatrains, The.   Charles Cotton.   NOSC

Cock I never see, The.   African Morning.   Mwatabu Okantah.   BtF

Cock is crowing, The.   Written in March [While Resting on the Bridge at the Foot of Brother's Water].   William Wordsworth.   ChAP; NAEL-6v2; NTCP

Cock that crowed this dawn up, heard, The.   Copernicus.   Robert David Fitzgerald.   NOBAu

Cock, warm roosting 'mid his feathers mates, The.   Winter's Day, A.   Joanna Baillie.   NAEL-7v2; WoRP

Cock, warm roosting midst his feathered dames, The.   Joanna Baillie.   *Fr.* Winter Day, A.

Cock-a-Doo.   Stevie Smith.   OWoS

Cockatoo.   Pam Bridgeman.   Prnts

Cock-Crow.   Edward Thomas.   MoBrPo; NPeEn

Cock-crowing.   Henry Vaughan.   BASC; NAEL-7v1; NPeEn; PBRV

Cocked Finger, The.   Stephen Dunn.   AtGh

Cocked up a squint eye and said, "I bloody did that." (LL)   Cathedral Builders.   John Ormond.   GoPo; NoP-4; NoP-5; TCAWP

Cockermouth.   David Wright.   NLP

Cockeyed Neruda dancing on a strobe.   In California with Neruda.   Shirley Lim.   GeoHom

Cockfight.   Liu Cheng.   ColAnChi, *tr. by* Robert Joe Cutter

Cockfight Marathon.   Frank Etienne. *tr. by* Boadiba and Jack Hirschman
   "They tear Alele's tongue out."   OGAHCP, *tr. by* Boadiba and Jack Hirschman

Cockfighter's Daughter, The.   Ai.   BeAl

Cockfights in the basements.   Side 26.   Víctor Hernández Cruz.   PueRic

Cockle-antarctica / has been cast up onto the shore.   Olga Zondberg.   CRWP, *tr. by* Daniel Weissbort

Cockles.   Einir Jones.   BBMWP, *tr. by* Joseph P. Clancy

Cocklorel would needs have the devil his guest.   Ben Jonson.   NOSC *Fr.* Gypsies Metamorphosed, The.

Cockney of the North, The.   Harry Graham.   UV

Cockney's Garden, The.   Edgar Bateman.   OBGa

Cock-phoenix, cock-phoenix goes back to his hometown.   Cock-Phoenix, Hen-Phoenix.   Ssu-ma Hsiang-ju.   ColAnChi, *tr. by* Anne Birrell

Cock-Phoenix, Hen-Phoenix.   Ssu-ma Hsiang-ju.   ColAnChi, *tr. by* Anne Birrell

Cockroaches of Liberation.   Martín Espada.   TouFir

Cocks and Mares.   Ruth Stone.   RaBo

Cocksucker's Blues.   Justin Chin.   WiU

Cocktail is a pleasant drink, The.   R-E-M-O-R-S-E.   George Ade.   NBLV; OBCoV

Cocktails.   Ciaran Carson.   ModIr; PBCiP

Cocktails / and signs of.   Louis Zukofsky.   APT-2 *Fr.* 29 Poems.

Cocktails for Two.   Sam Coslow.   ReLy

Coco-de-Mer.   W. N. Herbert.   NePenScot

Coconut / has the moon inside.   Philippine Figures.   *Unknown*.   EaWin, *tr. by* W. S. Merwin

Cocoons.   Sean Thomas Dougherty.   AmPoNex

Cod inert as an old boot.   Mid-Channel.   Gwen Harwood.   BMAP

Coda.   Marilyn Hacker.
   Conclusion.   NoAM
   ("Did You Love Well What Very Soon You Left?")   RA

[Coda & discography].   D. A. Powell.   LegDan

Coda: The Higher Keys.   James Merrill.
   "Empty perfection, as I take you in."   NoAM

Coda: Thelonius Monk, d. 17 February 1982.   Neil Powell.   WaAnP

Coda: "There's little in taking or giving."   Dorothy Parker.   AmWit; APT-1

Coda: "We have lived as ectoplasm."   "Ern Malley."   BMAP

Code key.   John Cayley.   PFTM-2 *Fr.* Reveal Code: Indra's Net 8.

Code, The.   Robert Frost.   OBNV
   (Code, The—Heroics.)   PoA 2002

Code, The.   Robert Morgan.   PoDa

Code, The—Heroics.   Robert Frost.   *See* Code, The.

Codex.   Stephen Rodefer.   PmAP

Codicil.   Derek Walcott.   NoAM

Codicil: Including the cost of a monument and inscription.   M. Travis Lane.   Coast

Cod-liver oil is rich in vitamin D.   Sound of Silence, The.   Srirangam Narayana Babu.   HotL, *tr. by* V. Narayana Rao

Coeur de Lion.   Richard I, Coeur de Lion.   *See* Ja Nul Homs Pris Ne Ira a Raison.

Coeval with man.   Oliver Goldsmith.   STuOW *Fr.* Captivity, The.

Coffee.   Wanda Coleman.   BrAP; ISC

Coffee.   James Vincent Cunningham.   MoAmPo

Coffee.   David St. John.   MotU

Coffee and cigarettes in a clean cafe.   Small Comfort.   Katha Pollitt.   P180

Coffee bowl called Part of Poland bursts, The.   Jack's Pigeon.   R. F. Langley.   HarvBoo

Coffee grinder.   Paul Dermée.   CuPo

Coffee Imp, The.   Bella Akhatovna Akhmadulina.   ItGoST, *tr. by* F. D. Reeve

Coffee in the Afternoon.   Alberto A. Ríos.   P180

Coffee, Markets, Blossoms.   Gary Snyder.   WANABP

Coffee Rancher, The.   *Unknown*.   SonAtl, *tr. by* Alan Brierly

Coffee Song (They've Got an Awful Lot of Coffee in Brazil), The.   Bob Hilliard.   ReLy

Coffee Table Blues.   Duncan Mercredi.   PoPra

Coffee turned cold in the pot.   Quiet Evening, Home Away.   Joann Balingit.   ReBoTo

Coffer with the Poisonous Snake, The.   Mirabai.   WED, *tr. by* Robert Bly

Coffin bearing the face of a boy, A.   Mirror for the Twentieth Century, A.   Adonis.   AF, *tr. by* Abdullah Al-Udhari

Coffin Worm, The.   Ruth Pitter.   MoBrPo; MoWP

Coffins.   Eli Alon.   NRoS, *tr. by* Esther Raizen

Coffins. / Coffins from Beirut.   Coffins.   Eli Alon.   NRoS, *tr. by* Esther Raizen

Cogitabo Pro Peccato Meo.   William Habington.   ChIV-1 *Fr.* Castara.

Cogito Ergo.   Jerzy Ficowski.   PoSu, *tr. by* Frank J. Corliss, Jr. and Grazyna Sandel

Cognac.   Michael Waters.   PoDa

Cohabiting.   Stephen Dunn.   CAP-8

Cohorts of charabancs fanfared Offa's province and his concern, negotiating the by-ways from Teme to Trent. Their windshields dripped butterflies. Stranded on hilltops they signalled with plumes of steam. Twilight menaced the land.   Geoffrey Hill.   OxBEV *Fr.* Mercian Hymns.

Coiled, scaly.   Farewell to Vinaya Master Ts'ung, Traveling in the West.   Heng Chao.   CSKM, *tr. by* Paul Hansen

Coiling a rope on the steel deck. (LL)   On the water, solid.   George Oppen.   APT-2; PFTM-1

Coimhthional Hiort.   Derick Thomson.   EdScPo

Coin, The.   Edwin Morgan.   NePenScot *Fr.* Sonnets from Scotland.

COIN / chip of the closed,—L O S T world, toward whose unseen grasses.   Coin for Joe, with the Image of a Horse, A; c. 350-325 BC.   Frank Bidart.   NAMCP V.2

Coin for Joe, with the Image of a Horse, A; c. 350-325 BC.   Frank Bidart.   NAMCP V.2

Coin is madaidhean-allaidh.   Sorley MacLean.   EdScPo

Coincidence.   Aida Gelbtrunk.   MirDau, *tr. by* Roberta Gordenstein

Coincidentally.   Frederic W. Platt.   BloBone

Coins handsome as Nero's; of good substance and.   Geoffrey Hill.   NAMCP V.2; NoAM *Fr.* Mercian Hymns.

Coins in the hand.   On Her Decision to Stop Wearing Clothes.   Mahadevi.   ErotSp; WPoS, *tr. by* Jane Hirshfield

Coins of Van-Lich.   *Vietnamese Oral Tradition*.   CaDao, *tr. by* John Balaban

Coition's brief, a nasty cheat.   Petronius Arbiter.   RomPo, *tr. by* J. P. Sullivan

Cokaigne Fantasy. Arthur Leslie Morton. RSaN

Cokboy. Jerome Rothenberg. PmAP

Coke. Philip Dacey. SUP

Cold: "Snow. No roofs this morning, alps, ominous message." Anne Stevenson. PfSP

Cold, The. Yvor Winters. APT-2

Cold, A / Dead face is. Morning Stroll, A. Yi Sanghûi. EcSo, tr. by Jennifer M. Lee

Cold Again, The. Paul De Roux. YaTCFP, tr. by Stephen Romer

Cold air drains down from the peaks. In the Mountains as Autumn Begins. Wen T'ing-yün. CCL1, tr. by Kenneth Rexroth

Cold airs from the river creep, The. Children of the Mist. Rosamund Marriott Watson. VWP

Cold and single over the map of language. (LL) Illuminations. Louise Glück. HarvBoo; NALW

Cold and the cranes. Joseph Ceravolo. FTOS

Cold April and the neighbor girl. Coastal. Mark Doty. PtR

Cold Are the Crabs. Edward Lear. NAEL-6v2; NAEL-7v2

Cold as Heaven. Judith Ortiz Cofer. ExTi Fr. Three Poems in Memory of Mamá (Grandmother).

Cold as No Plea. Death Sentence, The. Stevie Smith. NoP-4; NoP-5

Cold as the moon, he'd number. January. Baron Wormser. GoPo

Cold before dawn. Earth Sky Sea Trees Birds House Beasts Flowers. Kenneth Rexroth.

Cold begins in the ears by breaking sticks. Cryo. Adam Dickinson. PoPra

Cold bugle calls, and the city moves on, A. (LL) Armistice Day. Charles Causley. NAEL-6v2; NAEL-7v2; NoP-4; NoP-5; OBWP

Cold chain of life presseth heavily on me tonight, The. Fragment. Adah Isaacs Menken. CBWP-1

Cold chills invade my body. Happy New Year. Miguel Algarin. PueRic

Cold cliff. Laughing at Myself 1. Ching An. CSKM, tr. by Jerome P. Seaton

Cold, cold! / Cold tonight is broad Moylurg. Song of Winter, A. Unknown. IrV, tr. by Kuno Meyer

Cold, cold room with cold, cold girls, A. Morse Lesson. Joy Corfield. FaBoWar

Cold, cold the year draws to its end. Unknown. CCL1,

Cold! cold! 'tis a chilly clime. Robert Southey. NOBRP Fr. Thalaba the Destroyer.

Cold comes about, The. North Dakota, North Light. N. Scott Momaday. HATNAP

Cold coming we had of it, A. Journey of the Magi. T. S. Eliot. BrAP; ChrPo; GI; HeIP-4; ItP; MoAmPo; NAAL-5; NAEL-6v2; NAEL-7v2; NAMCP V.1; NIL-7; NIP-4; NoP-4; NoP-5; OBCP; OBMV; OxBoAm; StAl; TFi; TRP

Cold crests with deep-cut corridors. Shared Existence. Ivan Teofilov. CSCBP, tr. by Georgi Belev and Lisa Sapinkopf

Cold / December nights I'd go. Touched. Olga Broumas. GifTon

Cold evenings: red tongues and shadows. Mpondo's smithy, Transkei. Douglas Livingstone. TSAP

Cold felt cold until our blood, The. Phantasia for Elvira Shatayev. Adrienne Rich. ItP; NALW

Cold floors. Endurance. Dennis Brutus. VCWP

Cold Fly, A. Yang Wan-li. NDACCP, tr. by David Hinton

Cold food, homework, and hair. Rooms with a radiator and no books. Elements of Night. C. D. Wright. AmAlph

Cold fountain, cold fountain, refreshing with love. Cold Fountain, Cold Fountain. Unknown. BLPSL, tr. by Rene de Costa, Rigas Kappatos and Eleni Paidoussi

Cold, gray dawn of the morning after, The. (LL) R-E-M-O-R-S-E. George Ade. NBLV; OBCoV

Cold Green Element, The. Irving Layton. BrAP; NoP-4; NoP-5

Cold has put blue horses where lambs were, The. Blue Horses. Ed Roberson. GT

Cold Heaven, The. William Butler Yeats. InoFa; IrLP; NAMCP V.1; NoAM; NPeEn

Cold hungry Seamen, tho' they oft endure. Meditations on Persecution. Mary Mollineux. EMWP

Cold in the earth—and the deep snow piled above thee! Remembrance. Emily Jane Brontë. BrAP; CABP; MakPoe; NAEL-6v2; NAEL-7v2; NoP-4; NoP-5; NPeEn; OxAEP-2; OxBEV; PEW; PoPoPo; TFi; VWP; WeW-3

Cold in the house. To ABCs and from Rimbaud. Camille Martin. AnSo

Cold in the North (After Yueh-Fu). Li Ho. ChinPo, tr. by Ye Weilian [or Yeh Wei-lien or Wai-lim Yip]

Cold Landscape. Augusta Peaux. TuT, tr. by Tony Curtis

Cold Lost Marbles. William S. Burroughs. BB

Cold Lunch. William Corbett. PmAP

Cold marble, The. Memorium. Ed Robeson. Eno

Cold Meat. N. Revathi Devi. HotL, tr. by V. Narayana Rao

Cold Meteorite, The. William Reed Huntington. APN-2

Cold, moist, young phlegmy Winter now doth lie. Winter. Anne Bradstreet. MoW

Cold mornings, he would warm his hands. Coroner. Elton Glaser. PBCAP

Cold Mountain. Chiao-jan. CCL1, tr. by Stephen Owen

Cold Mountain. Han-shan (Cold Mountain). CCL1, tr. by Gary Snyder

Cold Mountain and Cold Mountain became the same thing in the mind. In Praise of Han Shan. Charles Wright. BAP-04; OxBoAm

Cold Mountain has many hidden wonders. Han-shan (Cold Mountain). NDACCP, tr. by Gary Snyder

Cold Mountain is a house [after Han-shan]. House Without Walls. Han-shan (Cold Mountain). BB; CCL1; NDACCP; WoPoe, tr. by Gary Snyder

Cold Mountain Path, The. Han-shan (Cold Mountain). CCL1; NDACCP, tr. by Gary Snyder

Cold Mountain Poem No. 158. Han-shan (Cold Mountain). WoPoe, tr. by E. Bruce Brooks

Cold Mountain Poems. Han-shan (Cold Mountain). See Body Asking Shadow.

Cold Mountain, The. Wang Wei. TAL

Cold mountain turns dark green. Cold Mountain, The. Wang Wei. TAL

Cold Night. Po Chü-i. CrYelRi, tr. by Sam Hamill

Cold night in a cell. Cell, The. Oskar Davico. SonAtl, tr. by Merica Delic, Kurt Ganzl, Ursula Hobday, Sladjana Josic, Ljubica Marasanov and Ziva Pecavar

Cold night: the wild duck. Basho. EH, tr. by Robert Hass

Cold Quilt. Michael McFee. PoA 2002

Cold Rain Comes, A. Na Hûidôk. EcSo, tr. by Peter H. Lee

Cold rain on the river. Parting with Hsin Chien at Hibiscus Tavern. Wang Ch'ang-ling. NDACCP, tr. by Gary Snyder

Cold rain starting, A. Basho. EH, tr. by Robert Hass

Cold rapid hands. Dawn. Octavio Paz. ItP, tr. by Charles Tomlinson

Cold remote islands, The. Night. Louise Bogan. APT-2; NAMCP V.1; NoP-4; NoP-5; WaAnP

Cold River. Joan Larkin. WiU

Cold rosy dawn in New York City. American Express. Ted Berrigan. NYP2

Cold, Sharp Lamentation. Douglas Hyde. OBMV, tr. by Augusta, Lady Gregory and Lady Gregory

Cold snap. Five o'clock. Aubade. Richard Kenney. NoP-4; NoP-5

Cold Sparrows. Yang Wan-li. NDACCP, tr. by David Hinton

Cold Spring, A. Elizabeth Bishop. ColAP; ItP

Cold stars and the whores. (LL) Street Corner College. Kenneth Patchen. APT-2; CLPP; MoAmPo

Cold / the clammy cement. Dennis Brutus. AF

Cold transparent ham is on my fork, The. Sonnet to Vauxhall. Thomas Hood. NPeEn; OBCoV; OxBSo

Cold War. Sara London. PoDa

Cold was the night wind, drifting fast the snow[s] fell. Widow, The. Robert Southey. NOBRP; UV

Cold, wet, Garand rifle in my hands, A. (LL) Still Life. Anthony Hecht. AmWaPo; NoP-4; NoP-5; PWW2

Cold wind, and the rain. Feng-yu: Cold Wind, and the Rain. Unknown. CCL1, tr. by Ezra Pound

Cold wind hastens the deep night, A. On Hearing a Pipe. Buhyu Sunsoo. BecRai, tr. by Kim Daljin, Kim Won-Chung and Christopher Merrill

Cold wind hurls itself at, A. Paul Verlaine. SxFrPo, tr. by Martin Sorrell

Cold wind out of the wilderness, A. Thinking of Li Po. Tu Fu [or Du Fu]. CrYelRi, tr. by Sam Hamill

Cold winds rise from the edge of heaven. At the Sky's End, Thinking of Li Po. Tu Fu [or Du Fu]. ColAnChi, tr. by David Lattimore

Cold winter sunlight stuns the window. To the Tune: Partridge Sky. Li Ch'ing-chao. CrYelRi, tr. by Sam Hamill

Cold Wood. Alan Shapiro. WaAnP

Cold world awakens. (LL) If the Owl Calls Again. John Haines. GifTon; HeIP-4

Cold, yes / But don't test. Sokan. ZenPo, tr. by Takashi Ikemoto and Lucien Stryk

Cold-day cicada's cutting creak. Tune: "Bells in the Rain." Liu Yung. ChinPo, tr. by Ye Weilian [or Yeh Wei-lien or Wai-lim Yip]

Colder. Erica Jong. LW

Coldest winter's day I remember, The. Leaving San Francisco. Marilyn Chin. CalPo; GeoHom

Cole Porter. Dionisio D. Martinez. TouFir

Colebrook Dale. Anna Seward.

"Scene of superfluous grace, and wasted bloom." PEW

Coleridge. Washington Allston. APN-1

Coleridge. Medbh McGuckian. MoWP

Coleridge. Theodore Watts-Dunton. GSo

Coleridge Crossing the Plain of Jars [1833]. Norman Dubie. AmAlph

Coleridge received the Person from Porlock. Thoughts about the Person from Porlock. Stevie Smith. NAEL-6v2; NAEL-7v2; NAMCP V.1; NoAM; NoP-4; NoP-5

Colic Passion, The. Jolanda Insana. *tr. by* Cinzia Sartini Blum and Lara Trubowitz

"No fear of losing my sanity." CItWP, *tr. by* Cinzia Sartini Blum and Lara Trubowitz

Colin Clout. John Skelton.

"Doctors that learned be." OBSV

"For though my rhyme be ragged." OBCoV

"Over this the foresayd lay." PBRV

Spirituality vs. the Temporality, The. NAEL-6v1

Colin, well fits thy sad cheer this sad stound. Pastoral Eclogue upon the Death of Sir Philip Sidney Knight, A. Lodowick Bryskett. NoSic

Colin, you can tell my words are crippled now. James Keir Baxter. HarvBoo *Fr.* Jerusalem Sonnets.

Colina verde, una colina verde, Una. Ernesto Lumbreras. RMCMP

Coliseum, The. Edgar Allan Poe. APN-1

Collaboration: A Day at the Beach. Anthony Caleshu. NIrP

Collaboration: Between Countries. Anthony Caleshu. NIrP

Collaboration: Letter to Charlie Chaplin. Peter Orlovsky. CLPP

Collaboration: Migration Patterns. Anthony Caleshu. NIrP

Collaboration: Storming the Beaches. Anthony Caleshu. NIrP

Collaboration, The. Tony Hoagland. SUP

Collaborators / naked Vichy women. Photo Taken in Winter, 1944. Barbara Unger. TWW

Collage. Shara McCallum. NAPBL

Collage for Richard Davis—Two Short Forms, A. De Leon Harrison. EGAG

Collapsed addict mother, passed out, The. Path Marked with Breadcrumbs, A. Tony Lopez. Oth

Collapses by the water cooler. (LL) Office Party. Phyllis McGinley. ChrPo; OBSV

Collapsing in the middle of the day. Become Your Face. Marianne Vitale. HeMarv

Collar Inscription, A. Alexander Pope. *See* Epigram Engraved on the Collar of a Dog Given [*or* Which I Gave] to His Royal Highness.

Collar, The. George Herbert. BASC; BrAP; CABP; ClHu; FaBoVe; FSCP; HeIP-4; InvLi; ItP; NAEL-6v1; NAEL-7v1; NIL-7; NIP-4; NoP-4; NoP-5; NOSC; NPeEn; OBWVE; PBRV; PoPoPo; SacPr; TFi; WeW-3

Collarbone [*or* Collar-Bone] of a Hare, The. William Butler Yeats. OxAEP-2

Colleagues are impressed. Alex Rawls. AnSo *Fr.* What's Your Sign?

Collecting is a basic human trait. The great collectors. Papilio. Carol Frost. PfSP

Collection Day. Natasha Trethewey. SpirFl

Collection of Emblemes, Ancient and Moderne, A. George Wither.

Husbandman, The. NOSC

Marigold, The. NOSC; SacPr

Planting. NOSC

Spade and the Wreath, The. NOSC

Spade, The. NOSC

Collection of White Poems. Kitasono Katsue. CAoMJL1, *tr. by* John Solt

Collection, The. Zhao Zhenkai. VCWP, *tr. by* Chen Maiping and Bonnie S. McDougall

Collective Invention, The. Chris Wallace-Crabbe. BMAP

Collective Search. Patrick Sylvain. InTrad

Collector's Marginalia, The. Peter Sirr. PBCIP

Collects her motions into shape. (LL) Nude Descending a Staircase. X. J. Kennedy. NIP-4; PoA 2002

College Colonel, The. Herman Melville. AmWaPo; CBCWP; FaBoWar; NAAPv.1; NaP; OBWP; PCW; WaAnP

College Formal: Renaissance Casino. Langston Hughes. APT-2

Collier, The. Vernon Watkins. OBWVE; TCAWP

Collier's Wife, The. D. H. Lawrence. FaBoVe

Collins. Lionel Pigot Johnson. OxAEP-2

Colloam [*with music*]. P. Inman. FTOS

Colloquial Reply, A: To Any Newsboy. Vachel Lindsay. AmWit

Colloquy in Black Rock. Robert Lowell. MoAmPo; OxBoAm

Colloquy with God, A. Sir Thomas Browne. SacPr *Fr.* Religio Medici.

Colloquy with John Keats ['And the Lord destroyeth the imagination of all them that had not the truth with them' Odes of Solomon 24.8]. "Ern Malley." BMAP

Cologne. Samuel Taylor Coleridge. NBLV

Colombe. Edward Kamau Brathwaite. VCWP

Colombine. Paul Verlaine. SxFrPo, *tr. by* Martin Sorrell

Colon Bay. *Unknown.* FaBoVe

Colonel. Andrew Hudgins. UpMys

Colonel. Kate Llewellyn. NOBAu

Colonel Chartres. John Arbuthnot. OBSV

Colonel Cold strode up the Line. Winter Warfare. Edgell Rickword. FaBoWar; OBWP; PoWW

Colonel Fantock. Dame Edith Sitwell. MoBrPo; OBMV

Colonel Fazackerley Butterworth-Toast. Charles Causley. NOxBChV

Colonel in a casual voice, The. Gallantry. Keith Douglas. NAEL-6v2; NAEL-7v2; NAMCP V.1; NoAM; NoP-4; NoP-5; OBWP; WaAnP

Colonel, The. Carolyn Forché. AmWaPo; MakPoe; MotU; NAMCP V.2; OBWP; OxBoAm; PoAgWa; SoSe-8; WaAnP

Colonels live there, commuters to the Pentagon. Springfield, Virginia. Anne Rouse. StAl

Colonel's Soliloquy, The. Thomas Hardy. FaBoWar; OBWP

Colonial Nomenclature. John Dunmore Lang. NOBAu

Colonial Troops Transport, The. *Vietnamese Oral Tradition.* CaDao, *tr. by* John Balaban

Colonists / unearth their wealth. Shaman Breaks. Gerald Vizenor. HATNAP

Colonization in Reverse. Louise Bennett. NAMCP V.2; OBCoV

Colonus' Praise. Sophocles. OBVE *Fr.* Oedipus at Colonus.

Colony, The. John Hewitt. ModIr

Colophon. Oliver St. John Gogarty. OBMV

Colophon. Dean Young. PoDa

Color, Caste, Denomination. Emily Dickinson. NAAPv.1

Color of coral and of your lips, The. From the French. Charles North. FTOS

Color of violence is black, The. Endangered Species. Ai. ESEAA

Color Sergeant, The [(On an Incident at the Battle of San Juan Hill)]. James Weldon Johnson. GT

Colorado Desert Night. Sam Gardiner. NIrP

Colored Blues Singer. Countee Cullen. OxBoAm

Colored cowboy named Nat Love. Deadwood Dick. Elizabeth Alexander. RA

Colored pictures. Charles Olson. NoAM *Fr.* Maximus Poems, The.

Colored pictures/ of all things to eat: dirty. Charles Olson. NoAM *Fr.* Maximus Poems, The.

Colored Soldiers, The. Paul Laurence Dunbar. APN-2; CBCWP

Colorful frames are erected beside the Yellow River, The. Li K'ai-hsien. ColAnChi *Fr.* Watching the Swinging.

Coloring. Mark DeCarteret. AmPoNex

Coloring. Ron Koertge. SUP

Colorizing: Turner Broadcasting Enterprises, Computer Graphics Division, Burbank, California, 1987. David Wojahn. PBCAP *Fr.* Mystery Train: A Sequence.

Colorless dawns. Dawn, The. Ricardo Jaimes Freyre. TCLAP, *tr. by* Victor Tulli

Colors. Fortunato Depero. PFTM-1

Colors are words' little sisters. They can't become soldiers. Cobalt. Rolf Jacobsen. BLT, *tr. by* Roger Greenwald

Colors calm you this afternoon: green. Going Back Through Color. Rafael Alberti. RaW, *tr. by* Mark Strand

Colors it, the rose / is predicated. (LL) William Carlos Williams. HarvBoo; PoA 2002 *Fr.* Paterson.

Colors of Desire, The. David Mura. LoL

Colors of Night, The. N. Scott Momaday. MotU

Colors of the Dark One have penetrated Mira's body; all the other colors washed out, The. Why Mira Can't Go Back to Her Old House. Mirabai. WED; WPoS, *tr. by* Robert Bly

"Colors" starring Patti, Grandma, & me at twenty-five. Jeni Olin. FreRad

Colors Without Objects. May Swenson. APT-2

Colors without objects—colors alone—. Colors Without Objects. May Swenson. APT-2

Colors—Struck. Afaa Michael Weaver. BtF

Colorstruck. Askhari. InTrad

Colosseum. Katie Ford. LegDan

Colossians 3:3. George Herbert. ChIV-2

Colossus, The. Sylvia Plath. BrAP; MoWP; NALW; NAMCP V.2; NoAM; NoP-4; NoP-5; VCAP; WoPoe

Colour. Tony Marinho. NeNiPo

Colour of silence, The. Shield of Perseus, The. Andrew Duncan. VaPo

Colour of the Old Man's Eyes, The. Judy Gahagan. Prnts

Colour of the olives who shall say?, The. Tuscan Olives. Agnes Mary Frances Robinson. VWP

Coltherdscleugh and Cauldcleuchheid. Half-Inch Tweeddale, The. Lillias Scott Forbes. EdScPo

Coltish horseplay of the locker room, The. Feast of Stephen, The. Anthony Hecht. NoAM; VCAP

Coltrane and My Father. Ralph Sneeden. SeSe

Colum Cille's Greeting to Ireland. *Unknown.* IrV, *tr. by* Kuno Meyer

Columbarium. Judi Benson. InoFa

Columba's Song. Edwin Morgan. HarvBoo

Columbia, all hail! Chicago Exposition Ode. Mary Weston Fordham. CBWP-2

Columbia, fairest nation of the world. Homes for All. Phoebe Cary. SWaP

Columbiad, The. Joel Barlow.
  "But now had Hesper from the Hero's sight." APN-1
Columbiad, The. APN-1
  "From Mohawk's mouth, far westing with the sun." APN-1
  "From slavery then your rising realms to save." TCAPo
  "From sultry Mobile's gulf-indented shore." APN-1
  "He spoke; and silent tow'rd the northern sky." APN-1
  Hostilities Between France and England Extended to America. Braddock's Defeat. AmWaPo
  "Now graceful truce suspends the burning war." APN-1
  Progress of the Colonies. Troubles with the Natives. AmWaPo
Columbian poet, whom we've all respected. Letter to an American Visitor. Alex Comfort. FaBoWar
Columbine High School / Littleton, CO. Albert Goldbarth. LiTh
Columbine, The. Jones Very. ColAP; GSo; WaAnP
Columbus. Walter Helmut Fritz. GTCP, tr. by Reinhold Grimm
Columbus. Ogden Nash. EMP; FaBoA; NAAPv.2; NoP-4; NoP-5
Columbus. Muriel Rukeyser. AF
Columbus. J. Slauerhoff. TuT, tr. by Desmond Egan
Columbus: "Behind him lay the gray Azores." Joaquin Miller. APN-2; BRP; CalPo
Columbus Circle Swing. William Jay Smith. PWW2
Columbus Day. Jimmie Durham. HATNAP; LTA
Columbus may have worked the wind. America Is Hard to See. Robert Frost. FaBoA
Columbus Square Journal. William Corbett.
  "Bed upstairs for seven years made for us in Hanover, Mass., The." AHA
Column Intended by Buonaparte for a Triumphal Edifice in Milan, Now Lying by the Way-Side in the Simplon Pass, The. William Wordsworth. OxBSo Fr. Memorials of a Tour of the Continent; 1820.
Column of lemon sky lit one hill, A. Civil War, The. Suzanne Rhodenbaugh. CBCWP
Columns constructed from delirious dust. Lovely Stuff. Diane Ward. PmAP
Com all ye Nymphs and evrey Swaine. Off the Dutchesse. Elizabeth Taylor. EMWP
Com Home Agayne. Unknown. SacPr
Com, shuppere holy gost, of-sech oure thouhtes. William Herebert. SacPr
Coma. Mimi Khalvati. PoCu; Prnts
Comatas. Harry Mathews. NYP2
Comb and the Mirror, The. Elizabeth Spires. FFC
Comba lánguida, La. Miguel de Unamuno. RaW Fr. Cancionero Diario Poético 1928–1936.
Combat, The [with music]. Edwin Muir. MoBrPo
Combat, The. Sir Walter Scott. Fr. Lady of the Lake, The.
Combat of Ferdia and Cúchulainn. Unknown. WoPoe Fr. Táin, The.
Combat raged not long, but ours the day, The. Burial of Latané, The. John Reuben Thompson. CBCWP
Combe, The. Edward Thomas. RSaN
Combed by the cold seas, Bering and Pacific. Love Letter from an Impossible Land. William Meredith. PWW2
Comber, The. Michael Longley. NAMCP V.2
Combination II. Helmut Heissenbüttel. PFTM-2, tr. by Jerome Rothenberg
Combinations. Mary Ann Hoberman. OBSP Fr. Bugs.
Combing. Gladys Cardiff. GifTon
Combing of my hair by grandma, The. Shower. Leah Aini. DTA, tr. by Linda Zisquit
Combing the papers for summer jobs. Hunger. Sharan Strange. FuFl
Combing. The poem of the act of the mind. (LL) Of Modern Poetry. Wallace Stevens. ColAP; NAAL-5; NAAPv.2; NAMCP V.1; NoAM; OxBoAm; WaAnP
Combustion Engine. Katherine Pierpoint. MFPA
Come a brimmer (my bullies) drink whole ones or nothing. Alexander Brome. PBRV Fr. Prisoners, The.
Come alive in her ears. (LL) Studs. Michael S. Harper. CAP-8; ESEAA
Come all ye jolly shepherds. When the Kye Comes Hame. James Hogg. NPBRoP
Come all ye rounders, for I want you to hear. Casey Jones. T. Lawrence Seibert. GM; ITBLP
Come all you gallant poachers, that ramble free from [or void of] care. Van Dieman's Land. Unknown. NOBAu
Come all you Lachlan men, and a sorrowful tale I'll tell. Streets of Forbes, The. Jack McGuire. NOBAu
Come all you sporty fellows. Stackalee. Unknown. APN-2
Come all you very merry London girls that are disposed to travel. Maidens of London's Brave Adventures, Or, a Boon Voyage Intended for the Sea, The. Laurence Price. NOSC
Come all young girls, both far and near, and listen unto me. Female Transport, The. Unknown. NOBAu

Come along in then, little girl! From a Very Little Sphinx. Edna St. Vincent Millay. NOxBChV
Come Along, Moses. Unknown. SSUS
Come along, Moses, don't get lost, don't get lost. Come Along, Moses. Unknown. SSUS
Come along, 'tis the time, ten or more minutes past. Arthur Hugh Clough. OBCoV; OBSV Fr. Spectator ab Extra.
Come and. Issa. EMJL, tr. by Haruo Shirane
Come and be a flower on my chest. Unknown. SLW, tr. by Marjolijn De Jager, Sayd Bahodin Majrouh and André Velter
Come, And Be My Baby. Maya Angelou. OPOU
Come and celebrate with me. (LL) Rondel: "Now that I am fifty-six." Muriel Rukeyser. NoP-4; NoP-5
Come and kiss me without thinking of the danger. What does it matter if they kill you? Unknown. SLW, tr. by Marjolijn De Jager, Sayd Bahodin Majrouh and André Velter
Come and let us live my Deare. Catullus. See Lesbia / live with me.
Come and listen to the chiming. Bells of St. Michael. Mary Weston Fordham. CBWP-2
Come and read to me tonight. Ka Hale / The Nurturing Place. Kalehua Parrilla Kim. FiBr
Come and See My Little Toys. BtF
Come and see my shining palace built upon the sand! (LL) Second Fig. Edna St. Vincent Millay. AmWit; APT-1; BLPJKO; NALW; NoP-4; NoP-5; PoA 2002
Come as ye dottilt, brain-deid lunks. Cabaret McGonagall. W. N. Herbert. NeBrP
Come Away, Come Away, Death. William Shakespeare. See Clown's Song, The.
Come Away, Come, Sweet Love. John Dowland. NoSic
Come away! come, sweet love! To His Love. Unknown. NoP-4; NoP-5
Come back / Before you get to the king-tree. Song for the Dying. Seminole Oral Tradition. NAAPv.1
Come Back Clean. Ella Wheeler Wilcox. VerBaPo
Come back, come back again. Dancer. Unknown. SonAtl, tr. by Alex Emmanar, Colin Foster and Sam Gordon
Come back early or never come. (LL) Autobiography. Louis MacNeice. Modlr; NPeEn; PNI
Come Back, Elvis, Come Back to Holyoke. Mary A. Koncel. ReTh
Come Back to Me. Alan Jay Lerner. ReLy
Come back to me! my life is young. Karazah to Karl. Adah Isaacs Menken. CBWP-1
Come back to me, O ye, my children. Mother's Recall. Mary Weston Fordham. CBWP-2
Come back to me, riddled with holes from a dark rifle's bullets. Unknown. SLW, tr. by Marjolijn De Jager, Sayd Bahodin Majrouh and André Velter
Come back to me, who wait and watch for you. Christina Georgina Rossetti. OxBSo Fr. Monna Innominata.
Come back to, this is your hand. (LL) You Begin. Margaret Atwood. NoP-4; NoP-5
Come, balm of night, oh nightingale. Hans Jakob Christoffel von Grimmelshausen. GePo
Come, balmy sleep! tired Nature's soft resort! To Sleep. Charlotte Smith. CenSon; NAEL-6v2; NAEL-7v2; RWP
Come, be my camera. Documentary. Claribel Alegría. LoL; VCWP
Come be with me like jewelry around my neck. Unknown. SLW, tr. by Marjolijn De Jager, Sayd Bahodin Majrouh and André Velter
Come, blessed ones, and sit on thrones. Michael Wigglesworth. NAAL-3 Fr. Day of Doom, The [First Section].
Come, blue-eyed maid of heaven!—but thou, alas! Lord Byron. NOBRP Fr. Childe Harold's Pilgrimage.
Come, boy, bring us. Anacreon. SaLy, tr. by Diane Rayor
Come, Break with Time. Louise Bogan. MoAmPo
Come, bring with a noise. Ceremonies for Christmas[se]. Robert Herrick. OBCP
Come, brother, come. Let's lift it. Cotton Song. Jean Toomer. APT-2; NAAPv.2
Come, brother, roll, roll! (LL) Cotton Song. Jean Toomer. APT-2; NAAPv.2
Come, brothers, everyone together. Mahendranāth Bhattācārya. SinGod, tr. by Rachel Fell McDermott
Come butter come! Butter Charm. Unknown. FaBoVe
Come carders an spinners an wayvers as weel. Factory Workers' Song. Unknown. FaBoVe
Come child, and with your sunbeam gaze assign. Green Eye, The. James Merrill. PoA 2002
Come close or run away. Charlatan, The. Unsi Al-Haj. PFTM-2, tr. by Pierre Joris
Come close to me, dear friends; still closer; thus! Paracelsus. Robert Browning.

Come close to me, my love. *Unknown.* SLW, *tr. by* Marjolijn De Jager, Sayd Bahodin Majrouh and André Velter

Come closer to me. Walt Whitman. APN-1 *Fr.* Leaves of Grass [1855 Version, Complete Text].

Come, come, dear Night, Love's mart of kisses. George Chapman. NoSic *Fr.* Hero and Leander.

Come, come, for the rosebower has blossomed; come, come, for the beloved has arrived. Jelaluddin Rumi. BBASP, *tr. by* A. J. Arberry

Come, come, my companion. *Unknown.* GePo *Fr.* Carmina Burana.

Come, come, this Parthenon of desire is set. Gabriel's News (37). Khwaja Shams-ad-din Muhammad Hafiz. WED, *tr. by* Robert Bly and Leonard Lewisohn

Come! Come! Though I call. Onitsura. NIL-7, *tr. by* Daniel C. Buchanan

Come, come, you will never find a friend like me. Jelaluddin Rumi. NaPG, *tr. by* Talat Sait Halman

Come, Connal, acushla, turn the clay. Potato-Digger's Song, The. Thomas Caulfield Irwin. IrV

Come Dance with Kitty Stobling [*with music*]. Patrick Kavanagh. HarvBoo; NAMCP V.1; NoAM; NPeEn

Come darkest night, be[e]coming sorrow best. Mary Sidney Wroth, Countess of Montgomery. BASC; EMWP; NOSC *Fr.* Pamphilia to Amphilanthus.

Come, dark-eyed Sleep, thou child of Night. And on My Eyes Dark Sleep by Night. Michael Field. LW; OBMV

Come, dear children, let us away. Forsaken Merman, The. Matthew Arnold. NAEL-6v2; NAEL-7v2; OBNV; OBSP

Come, Death, I'd have a word with thee. Motley. Walter De la Mare. PoWW

Come, dit l'Anglais à l'Anglais, et l'Anglais vient. Comme. Robert Desnos. YaTCFP

Come, divine lyre, speak to me. Sappho. SaLy, *tr. by* Diane Rayor

Come, don't let us be foolish. Sing, My Heart. Ted Koehler. ReLy

Come down and sleep in this tree, in this tree. In This Tree. Jacques Roubaud. YaTCFP, *tr. by* Rosmarie Waldrop

Come down, angel, and trouble the water. Let God's Saints Come In. *Unknown.* SSUS

Come down Canyon Creek trail on a summer afternoon. How to Regain Your Soul. William Stafford. EMP; PoA 2002

Come down from heaven to meet me when my breath. Invocation. Siegfried Sassoon. MoBrPo

Come down, O Christ, and help me! reach thy hand. E Tenebris. Oscar Wilde. ChIV-2; GSo; MoBrPo; NAEL-6v2; NAEL-7v2; OxAEP-2

Come down, O maid, from yonder mountain height. Alfred Tennyson. NAEL-6v2; NAEL-7v2; NPeEn; OBEV; OxBEV *Fr.* Princess, The.

Come down to Kew in lilac-time (it isn't far from London!). (LL) Barrel-Organ, The. Alfred Noyes. BRP; MoBrPo

Come dreadful child. Vampiro Nox. Marianne van Hirtum. SurWo, *tr. by* Guy Flandre and Peter Wood

Come, drunks and drug-takers; come, perverts unnerved! Several Voices Out of a Cloud. Louise Bogan. APT-2; NALW

Come each maiden lend an ear. Cheap Repository: The Story of Sinful Sally. Told by Herself. Hannah More. RWP

Come 'ere [*or* Com' mere], boy! (LL) Brass Spittoons. Langston Hughes. MoAmPo; NoAM

Come evening once again, season of peace. William Cowper. NAEL-6v1; NAEL-7v1 *Fr.* Task, The.

Come, fair one, be kind. George Farquhar. IrLP *Fr.* Recruiting Officer, The.

Come feed with me and be my love. Passionate Profiteer to His Love, The. "Sagittarius." OBCoV

Come, fill the Cup, and in the fire of Spring. Omar Khayyám. TRP; UV *Fr.* Rubáiyát of Omar Khayyám [of Naishápúr], The.

Come Fly with Me. Sammy Cahn. ReLy

Come, friendly bombs, and fall on Slough. Slough. Sir John Betjeman. HarvBoo; MoBrPo; NAMCP V.1; NoAM; OxAEP-2

Come from China in a barrel of water, sell. Goldfish in the Charles River. Lewis Hyde. UrbNat

Come from the woods with the citron flowers. Bride of the Greek Isle, The. Felicia Dorothea Hemans. RWP

Come, gaze with me upon this dome. E. E. Cummings. NoAM

Come, gentle sleep, death's image though thou art. Thomas Wharton, the Younger. OBVE

"Come girlies and fellas, as quick as you can." Mutton Bird Man. Rhyll McMaster. NOBAu

Come, give me kisses, Rhodope. Paulus Silentiarius. ErotSp, *tr. by* Sam Hamill

Come give me needle stitchcloth silke and haire. Gentlewoman yt Married a Yonge Gent Who After Forsooke Whereuppon She Tooke Hir Needle in Which She Was Excelent and Worked upon Hir Sampler Thus, A. *Unknown.* EMWP

Come Go With Me. *Unknown.* SSUS

Come God / Be man woman child old one. On a Weekend in September. Vassar Miller. TiP2

Come, Gorgo, put the rug in place. Michael Field. ViWPN; VWP

Come Green Again. Winfield Townley Scott. ICANM

Come, heavy souls, oppressed that are. Casting All Your Care upon God, for He Careth for You. Thomas Washbourne. SacPr

Come here, closer, and fold. Remembering. Stephen J. Lyons. PasH

Come here, I want to show you something. Sightseeing. Rita Dove. GT

Come here. Let me finger your hair. And Everywhere Offering Human Sound. Joan Houlihan. IAoNAP

Come here, my love, the crown of my home. Tribal Chieftain. NaPG, *tr. by* Talat Sait Halman

Come here, said Turnbull, till you see the sadness. Switch. Sean O Riordain. ModIr; StAI, *tr. by* Patrick Crotty

Come hither all sweet maidens soberly. On a Leander Gem which Miss Reynolds, My Kind Friend, Gave Me. John Keats. ItP

Come hither my boy tell me what thou seest here. Lacedemonian Instruction. William Blake. WoPoe

Come hither, womankind and all their worth. Kissing. Edward Herbert, 1st Baron Herbert of Cherbury. NOSC

Come, hoist the sail, the fast let go! Pleasure Boat, The [*or* Pleasure-Boat, The]. Richard Henry Dana. APN-1

Come, Holy Spirit. Veni Creator. Czeslaw Milosz. BeAl, *tr. by* the author and Robert Pinsky

Come Home, Father[!]. Henry Clay Work. APN-2; NAAPv.1

Come home with white gulls waving across gray. Winter Landscape. Stephen Spender. MoBrPo

Come Hymen come, for here to thee we bring. Luis de Góngora y Argote. SpanPo *Fr.* Solitudes, The.

Come, I will make the continent indissoluble. For You O Democracy. Walt Whitman. APN-1; CAGL; UV

Come if you dare, reivers and raiders! Charles MacKay. STuOW *Fr.* Volunteers, The.

Come In. Robert Frost. APT-1; MoAmPo; NoP-4; NoP-5; OxBoAM; RaBo; TRP

Come in at the low-silled window. Being Called For. Rosemary Dobson. BMAP

Come in, Aunt Jemima. Wintah Styles, De. Maggie Pogue Johnson. CBWP-4

Come in, friend, if I may be so bold. There Is But One True Friend. John Fitzgerald. BBMWP, *tr. by* Joseph P. Clancy

Come onto Animal Presence. Denise Levertov. AmFaPo; HeIP-4

Come into the Army, Maud. "Sagittarius." UV

Come into the garden, Fred. Alley Cat Love Song. Dana Gioia. P180

Come into the Garden, Maud. Alfred Tennyson. OxAEP-2; OxBEV; UV; WoPoe *Fr.* Maud [A Monodrama].

Come into the orchard, Anne. Algernon Charles Swinburne. UV

Come into the Whenceness Which. Whenceness of the Which. *Unknown.* UV

Come join hand in hand, brave Americans all. Liberty Song, The. John Dickinson. NAAPv.1

Come, let me sound thy depths, unquiet sea. To My Own Heart. Maria Jane Jewsbury. VWP

Come, let us build a temple to oblivion. Tabernacle. D. H. Lawrence. ChIV-1

Come, let us dance and sing. Song. Anne Batten Cristall. RWP

Come, let us down. Ode: Hastening His Friend into the Country. Eldred Revett. NOSC

Come, let us join this festal lay. Rally Song. Mary Weston Fordham. CBWP-2

Come, let us now resolve at last. Reconcilement, The. John, Duke of Buckingham and Normandy Sheffield. OBEV

Come, let us tell the weeds in ditches. Last Hill in a Vista. Louise Bogan. OxBoAm

Come, let's adore the King of Love. Love of Christ, The. John Austin. SacPr

Come, let's find the secret of the clear waters. Ransom, The. René[e] Vivien. YaTCFP, *tr. by* Mary Ann Caws and Jean-Pierre Cauvin

Come, let's go / snow-viewing. Basho. ZenPo, *tr. by* Takashi Ikemoto and Lucien Stryk

Come, let's grant joy to this heart of ours that founders in distress. Song. Nedim. NaPG, *tr. by* Talat Sait Halman

Come listen to me, you gallants so free. Robin Hood and Allen [*or* Allin] -a-Dale. *Unknown.* OxAEP-1

Come little babe, come silly soule. Nicholas Breton. RACG *Fr.* Arbor of Amorous Devises, The.

Come, little infant, love me now. Young Love. Andrew Marvell. OxAEP-1

Come Live with Me. Leontia Flynn. NIrP

Come, live with me and be my love. Cecil Day Lewis. NIP-4; OBMV; WaAnP *Fr.* Two Songs.

Come live with me and be my love. Bacchanal. Peter De Vries. NBLV

Come live with me and be my love. Further Proposal, A. Allen Ginsberg. NIL-7

Come, live with me and be my love. Samuel Hoffenstein. NBLV Fr. Invocation.

Come live with me[e] and be my Love. Passionate Shepherd to His Love, The. Christopher Marlowe. AEP; BLPJKO; CABP; ClHu; HeIP-4; ITBLP; MakPoe; NAEL-6v1; NAEL-7v1; NBLV; NIL-7; NIP-4; NoP-4; NoP-5; NoSic; OBEV; OxAEP-1; OxBEV; PoPoPo; TFi; TRP; WaAnP; WeW-3; WoPoe

    (Come live with me and be my Love.) AEP; CABP; NoP-4; PoPoPo

Come live with me and be my love. War Resisters' Song. Thomas McGrath. AtGh

Come live with me and be my mate. Come Live with Me. Leontia Flynn. NIrP

Come live with me[e], and be[e] my love. Bait[e], The. John Donne. NAEL-6v1; NAEL-7v1; NOSC; WaAnP

Come, lowly ones, and take your places now. Marion Albina Bigelow. VerBaPo Fr. Children Disinterred.

Come, Madam, come, all rest my powers defy [or defie]. John Donne. BASC; FSCP; NAEL-6v1; NAEL-7v1; NoP-4; NoP-5; NoSic; PBRV Fr. Elegies.

Come May, the empire of the earth assume. To May. Jane West. CenSon

Come, memory, let us seek them there in the shadows. (LL) On the Death of Friends in Childhood. Donald Justice. ColAP; NAMCP V.2; OxBoAm

Come, Muse, migrate from Greece and Ionia. Walt Whitman. MoAmPo Fr. Song of the Exposition.

Come, my Ardelia, to this bower. Retired Friendship, To Ardelia, A. Katherine Philips. BASC

Come, my auld towzy trusty friend. My Auld Hector. James Hoggard. DiBP

Come, my beloved. Bible, O.T. WPoS Fr. Song of Solomon, The.

Come, my beloved. From the Garden. Anne Sexton. LW

Come, my beloved, come quickly and be close to me! Unknown. SLW, tr. by Marjolijn De Jager, Sayd Bahodin Majrouh and André Velter

Come my Celia, let us prove. Ben Jonson. AEP; BrAP; NIL-7; NoP-4; NoP-5; NPeEn; OBVE; OxBEV; PoPoPo; TFi; WaAnP Fr. Volpone.

Come, my Corinna, come, let's go[e] a-Maying. (LL) Corinna's Going a-Maying. Robert Herrick. AEP; BASC; BrAP; CABP; NAEL-6v1; NAEL-7v1; NIP-4; NoP-4; NoP-5; NOSC; OBEV; OxBEV; PBRV; PoPoPo; TFi; WaAnP

Come (my dear) whilst youth conspires. Time Recover'd. Thomas Stanley. OBVE

Come / my love. Let's Go to Hell. Srirangam Narayana Babu. HotL, tr. by V. Narayana Rao

Come, my love, let me embrace you. Unknown. SLW, tr. by Marjolijn De Jager, Sayd Bahodin Majrouh and André Velter

Come, my love, let us go to bed together. Unknown. SLW, tr. by Marjolijn De Jager, Sayd Bahodin Majrouh and André Velter

Come, my Lucasia, since we see. Friendship's Mystery[s], to my dearest Lucasia. Katherine Philips. BASC; BrAP; NAEL-7v1; PBRV; PEW

Come, my songs, let me express our baser passions. Ezra Pound. PoA 2002 Fr. Lustra.

Come, my Way, my Truth, my Life. Call, The. George Herbert. SacPr

Come, nationals in exile. Jihad. Thelma Seto. TWW

Come night! come, Romeo! come, thou day in night! William Shakespeare. BLPJKO Fr. Romeo and Juliet.

Come not the earliest petal here, but only. Quiet. Marjorie Lowry Christie Pickthall. SacPr

Come Not the Seasons Here. Edwin John Pratt. NoP-4; NoP-5

Come now, bees, you want to, don't you? Foxgloves. Gerry Cambridge. EdScPo

Come now, come here. To the Man Holding a Sickle. Pak Sôwôn. EcSo, tr. by Julie C. Park

Come now ye rural deities and show. Sir John Clerk, of Penicuik. OBGa Fr. Country Seat, The.

Come, O thou traveller unknown. Wrestling Jacob. Charles Wesley. OBEV; OxAEP-1

Come, oh love's great sorrow! Unknown. SLW, tr. by Marjolijn De Jager, Sayd Bahodin Majrouh and André Velter

Come on all of you big strong men. I-Feel-Like-I'm Fixin'-To-Die Rag. Joe McDonald. ASA

Come on along and listen to. Lullaby of Broadway. Al Dubin. ReLy

Come on, babe. And All That Jazz. Fred Ebb. ReLy

Come on, don't be afraid you'll spoil me. Serenade. Emanuel Carnevali. APT-2

Come on down, Hemlin, guess what I have for you. Keep coming down. Hemlin. Ilse Aichinger. MotU, tr. by Stuart Friebert

Come on, good fellow, make an end. Dialogue between Death and Youth, A. Unknown. NoSic

Come on, my companions, the triumph display. Oliver Goldsmith. STuOW Fr. Captivity, The.

Come on, my partners in distress. Charles Wesley. NoP-4; NoP-5; WaAnP

Come on Percy, my pillion-proud, be. Cyril Connolly. OBCoV Fr. Where Engels Fears to Tread.

Come on, sir; he[e]re's the place: stand still. William Shakespeare. OxAEP-1; OxBEV Fr. King Lear.

Come on the wings of great desire. No Obligation. Victoria Mary Sackville-West. PoBW

Come on then my sweet. Over a Drink. Mererid Puw Davies. BBMWP, tr. by the author

Come on, ye critics! Find one fault who dare. On Mr. Edward Howard, upon His British Princes. Charles Sackville, 6th Earl of Dorset. OBSV

Come on, you...Do you want to live forever? (LL) Losers. Carl Sandburg. MoAmPo; NoAM

Come on, you too, whoo/do, we can do it. On the Removal of the Fascist American Right from Power. Etheridge Knight. BodElec

Come onto my pathway one more time. Unknown. SLW, tr. by Marjolijn De Jager, Sayd Bahodin Majrouh and André Velter

Come out come out come out. Moon Eclipse Exorcism. Unknown. WoPoe, tr. by Armand Schwerner

Come out from the bath. (LL) Bath, The. Gary Snyder. CAP-8; FaoP; NAMCP V.2; PmAP; VCAP

Come out, love—the night is enchanting! City Lyrics. Nathaniel Parker Willis. APN-1

Come out of Crete / and find me here. Horses in Flowers. Sappho. OBVE; WoPoe, tr. by Guy Davenport

Come out of the swamp! Tomas Tranströmer. WoBe Fr. Haiku.

Come out to view. Basho. SoOfWa, tr. by Sam Hamill

Come Over and Help Us; a Rhapsody. John Wheelwright. APT-2

Come pass me the cup quickly and hand it on. Khwaja Shams-ad-din Muhammad Hafiz. BBASP, tr. by R.M. Rehder

Come Peace, on snowy pinions. Ode to Peace. Mary Weston Fordham. CBWP-2

Come people; Aaron's drest [or dresst or dressed]. (LL) Aaron. George Herbert. BASC; ChIV-1; FSCP; NOSC; SacPr

Come pity [or pitie] us, all ye, who see. Widow's Tears [or Widdowes Teares]; or, Dirge of Dorcas, The. Robert Herrick. ChIV-2

Come play with me. To a Squirrel at Kyle-Na-No. William Butler Yeats. ChAP

Come play with me said the sun. Play. Frank Asch. NTCP

Come practice your whorish gestures in the graveyard, Ramona. Poem to Line My Casket with, Ramona. Josh Bell. IIR; LegDan

Come praise Colonus' horses and come praise. Sophocles. OBVE Fr. Oedipus at Colonus.

Come! Put by Pelops' Isle. Come! Put by Pelops' Isle. Alcaeus. WoPoe, tr. by Fred Beake

Come quick, come quick, come quick, come quick! (LL) Watch, The. Frances Darwin Cornford. MoBrPo; PtR

Come quick / down dim tracks. Soul Call. Unknown. SonAtl, tr. by Caroline O'Sullivan and Anne Swann

Come quickly, my love, so I can give you my mouth! Unknown. SLW, tr. by Marjolijn De Jager, Sayd Bahodin Majrouh and André Velter

Come, radishes, rosy against your greens. Three from the Market. Sandra McPherson. AFaM

Come Rain or Come Shine. Johnny Mercer. ReLy

Come, Reason, come! Each nerve rebellious bind. Mary Robinson. NPBRoP; CenSon; RWP Fr. Sappho and Phaon.

Come right in this house, Will Johnson! Mrs. Johnson Objects. Clara Ann Thompson. CBWP-2

Come, saints and sinners, hear me tell. Frederick Douglass. NAAL-3; NAWM-7v2 Fr. Narrative of the Life of Frederick Douglass, an American Slave.

Come, see / real flowers. Basho. ZenPo, tr. by Takashi Ikemoto and Lucien Stryk

Come See the Place Where the Lord Lay. Richard Crashaw. ChIV-2

Come show thy Durham Breast. Emily Dickinson. NCAP

Come! show your jolly tricks, and be possessed. Francis Saltus Saltus. VerBaPo Fr. Masters, The.

Come sing with me in chorus: it's nothing, all we know. Antonio Machado Ruiz. STV

Come, sisters, come! The shower's past. To Sisters on a Walk in the Garden, after a Shower. Jane Johnston Schoolcraft. NAAPv.1

Come Sleep! O sleep the certain knot of peace. Sir Philip Sidney. GSo; NAEL-6v1; NAEL-7v1; NoSic; OxAEP-1; OxBSo; TFi; WaAnP Fr. Astrophil and Stella.

Come sleep, thou ease of sickness, want, and care. Of Sleep. Martha, Lady Giffard. EMWP

Come slowly—Eden! Emily Dickinson. FaBoVe; NALW; NCAP; TCAPo

Come So Far as You Can Feel. Gültekin SamanoḠlu. NaPG, *tr.* by Talat Sait Halman

Come, soft Eolian harp, while zephyr plays. Mary Robinson. NPBRoP; CenSon; RWP *Fr.* Sappho and Phaon.

Come, sons of summer, by whose toil[e]. Hock-Cart, or Harvest Home, The. Robert Herrick. BASC; NAEL-6v1; NAEL-7v1; NOSC; OxAEP-1

Come soon, soon! (LL) To Night. Percy Bysshe Shelley. NAEL-6v2; NAEL-7v2; TFi

Come, sportive fancy, come with me and trace. Poet's Garret, The. Mary Robinson. RWP

Come, spring is young. Farmer's Song, The. Abburi Ramakrishna Rao. HotL, *tr.* by V. Narayana Rao

Come spur[re] away. Ode to Master [or Mr.] Anthony Stafford to Hasten Him into the Country, An. Thomas Randolph. BASC; NOSC; OBEV

Come, stack arms, men! Pile on the rails. Stonewall Jackson's Way. John Williamson Palmer. CBCWP

Come, stir the fire. Safe. James Walker. OBCP

Come suddenly, O Lord, or slowly come. Take ye heed, watch and pray: for ye know not when the time is. Mark 13:33. Jones Very. ChIV-2

Come, sweetheart mine. My Melancholy Baby. George Norton. ReLy

Come swiftly, soul. Call of the Soul, The. *Unknown.* WoPoe, *tr.* by Ronald Perry

Come take up your hats, and away let us haste. Butterfly's Ball [and the Grasshopper's Feast], The. William Caldwell Roscoe. NOBRP; OxBEV

Come tell me, was it all for nought. Borodino. Mikhail Yuryevich Lermontov. FaBoWar, *tr.* by Frances Darwin Cornford and Esther Polinowsky Salaman

Come the quick trumpet of the Judgement Day? (LL) Lament for a Leg. John Ormond. AngWePo; NoP-4; NoP-5; OBWVE

Come, then, and mounted on the wings of Love. Thomas Carew. EroLit *Fr.* Rapture, A.

Come then, as ever, like the wind at morning! Invocation to Youth. Laurence Binyon. OBEV

Come then, my dear—although I warn you now. Between Aphorisms. Dorothy E. Reid. YaYoPo

Come, Thou Almighty King. Charles Wesley. SacPr

Come, thou dost say to Angels. Advent. Christina Georgina Rossetti. RSR

Come, thou Fount of ev'ry blessing. Robert Robinson. SacPr

Come, thou monarch of the vine. William Shakespeare. NoSic *Fr.* Antony and Cleopatra.

Come thou, who art the wine and wit. His Winding-Sheet. Robert Herrick. BASC; OBEV

Come Thunder. Christopher Okigbo. HBAPE; NAMCP V.2; VCWP; WaAnP

Come tip a few with me. Alcaeus. WoPoe, *tr.* by Sam Hamill

Come to Agbarha. Where Everybody is King. Tanure Ojaide. NAfrP

Come to Calvary's holy mountain. James F. Montgomery. SacPr

Come to guard us, come to bless us. Triple Benison, The. Henrietta Cordelia Ray. CBWP-3

Come to me. Tefillin. Yona Volach. DTA, *tr.* by Aryeh Cohen and Miriyam Glazer

Come to me, as you come. Kenneth Rexroth. APSN *Fr.* Love Poems of Marichiko, The.

Come to me from Krete to this holy. Sappho. SaLy, *tr.* by Diane Rayor

Come to me God. Surrender. Amitiyah Elayne Hyman. BtF

Come to me God; but do not come. To God. Robert Herrick. CavPo; RSR

Come to me here. Wife of Chieftain. NaPG

Come to me in my dreams, and then. Longing. Matthew Arnold. SoSe-8

Come to me in the silence of the night. Echo. Christina Georgina Rossetti. LW; NoP-4; NoP-5; PEW; PoBW; VWP

Come to me. It's time you were here. Quickly. Come to Me. Han Yong'un [or Yongwun]. CAMKP, *tr.* by Sammy Solberg

Come to me, leaving the Peloponnesos. Alcaeus. SaLy, *tr.* by Diane Rayor

Come to me only with playthings now. Murmurings in a Field Hospital. Carl Sandburg. IllVoic

Come to me, Pan, with your wind-wild laughter. Song for a Forgotten Shrine to Pan. John Chipman Farrar. YaYoPo

Come to me so I can touch you and embrace you. *Unknown.* SLW, *tr.* by Marjolijn De Jager, Sayd Bahodin Majrouh and André Velter

Come to me There is something. Mina Loy. NAMCP V.1 *Fr.* Love Songs to Joannes.

Come to me with your triumphs and your woes. Beings of the Mind, The. Felicia Dorothea Hemans. RWP

Come to see the camellia. Camellia. Henriqueta Lisboa. TCLAP, *tr.* by Hélcio Veiga Costa

Come to Sunny Prestatyn. Sunny Prestatyn. Philip Larkin. NAMCP V.2; NoAM; OBCoV

Come to term the started child shocks. Multipara: Gravida 5. Marie Ponsot. CLPP

Come to the park they say is dead and see. Stefan George. GTCP, *tr.* by Kenneth Gee

Come to the Waldorf-Astoria. Langston Hughes. NAAPv.2

Come to the window. At Twilight. Hayyim Nahman Bialik. FIT, *tr.* by Robert Friend

Come to the window! You're the painter used. Requiescam. Trumbull Stickney. ColAP

Come to these lonely woods to die alone? Dying Raven, The. Richard Henry Dana. APN-1

Come to your heaven, you [or yowe] heavenly choirs [or quires]. New Heaven, New War[re]. Robert Southwell. ChIV-2
  (Come to your heaven, you heavenly choirs.) NoP-4; NoP-5
  (This little Babe so few dayes olde.) NPeEn

Come too late to see. In the Room I. Prnts

Come, try your skill, kind gentlemen. Gipsy Girl, The. Ralph Hodgson. MoBrPo

Come unto these yellow sands. William Shakespeare. NOSC; NoSic; NPeEn; OBEV; SoSe-8; TFi *Fr.* Tempest, The.

Come up and see me sometime. (LL) Invitation. Grace Nichols. MoWP; NAMCP V.2

Come up and see me sometime. Grace Nichols. EroLit *Fr.* Invitation.

Come up from the fields father, here's a letter from our Pete. Come Up from the Fields Father. Walt Whitman. AmWaPo; APN-1; CBCWP; FaBoWar; HHAm; MoAmPo; OBWP; SAmP

Come Up, Methuselah. Cecil Day Lewis. OBMV

Come up, thou red thing. Southern Night. D. H. Lawrence. NAMCP V.1

Come up with me, American love. Pablo Neruda. PFTM-2 *Fr.* Heights of Macchu Picchu, The.

Come, walk with me. Emily Jane Brontë. WaAnP

Come wander through the city, drink wine. Yahya Beg. OLP, *tr.* by Walter Andrews, Najaat Black and Mehmet Kalpakli

Come, warm your hands. Driftwood. Witter Bynner. APT-1

Come we shepheards whose blest Sight. In the Holy Nativity of Our Lord God. Richard Crashaw. NAEL-6v1; NAEL-7v1

Come, wed me, Lady Singleton. Lady "Rogue" Singleton. Stevie Smith. OPOU

Come what may. Issa. EMJL, *tr.* by Herschel Miller

Come, "Will," let's be good friends again. Sunshine after Cloud. Josephine D. Henderson Heard. CBWP-4

Come Wisdome Sweet. Morgan Llwyd. AngWePo

Come wisdome sweet, my spirit meet, for at thy feet I fall. Come Wisdome Sweet. Morgan Llwyd. AngWePo

Come with Me. Robert Bly. NoAM

Come with Me into those things that have felt this despair for so long. Come with Me. Robert Bly. NoAM

Come with me out into the road, my wheel. To the Wheel. Charles E. Pratt. ArBi

Come with me to the second story warehouse. Second Story Warehouse. Edward Hirsch. NevBe

Come worthy Greek, Ulysses, come. Ulysses and the Siren [or Syren]. Samuel Daniel. NAEL-6v1; NoP-4; NoP-5; OBEV; OxAEP-1
  (Come worthy Greeke, Ulisses come.) OxBEV

Come ye hither all, whose taste. Invitation, The. George Herbert. ChIV-1

Come, ye thankful people, come. Harvest Home. Henry Alford. SacPr

Come, ye thankful people, come. Come, Ye Thankful People, Come. George J. Elvey. HHAm

Come ye, whose hearts the tyrant sorrows wound. Stanzas Written Under Aeolus' Harp. Amelia Alderson Opie. NPBRoP

Come, yellow broom. Glimpse, A. Robert Duncan. FTOS

Come you, ascend the ladder; all come in; all sit down. Invocation to the Uʼ wannami. *Unknown.* APN-2, *tr.* by Matilda Coxe Stevenson

Come you, cartoonists. Halsted Street Car. Carl Sandburg. IllVoic

Comeahead then comeahead. Love Song of Tommo Frogley. Roger Crawford. UV

Comedian as the Letter C, The. Wallace Stevens. TCAPo

Comedian, holding a chunk of flaming shale, The. Why That's Bob Hope. William Hathaway. ReTh

Comedy, A. William Browne. DiBP *Fr.* Shepherd's Pipe, The.

Comedy of Errors, The. William Shakespeare.
  "By the way we met." OBCoV

Comedy Tonight. Stephen Sondheim. ReLy

Come—go— / here not too. *Unknown.* SonAtl, *tr.* by Abdul Kalam Azad

Comencemos por el principio. Mapas. Alberto Blanco. RMCMP

Comes after Yes. (LL) Yes. Muriel Rukeyser. MakPoe; StAl

Comes down, white as an avalanche. Stroke. Arthur Ginsberg. BloBone

Comes easy as turning to look. Camping Clean. Reg Saner. PoCoUp

Comes home dull with coal-dust deliberately. Her Husband. Ted Hughes. HarvBoo

Comes like an idiot, babbling and strewing flowers. (LL) Spring: "To what purpose, April, do you return again?" Edna St. Vincent Millay. APT-1; MoAmPo; NAMCP V.1; NoP-4; NoP-5

Comes not the springtime here.   Come Not the Seasons Here.   Edwin John Pratt.   NoP-4; NoP-5

Comes of his own accord to me.   He That None Can Capture.   May Swenson.   LW

Comes out like a ribbon lies flat on the brush. (LL)   Poem, or Beauty Hurts Mr. Vinal.   E. E. Cummings.   FaBoA; HarvBoo; MoAmPo; NAAL-5; NAAPv.2; PFTM-1; TRP

Comes the day, when he must die.   Muspilli.   *Unknown*.   GePo, *tr. by* Carroll Hightower

Comes the Gods to imitate! (LL)   Grasshopper, The.   Anacreon.   NOSC; OBVE, *tr. by* Thomas Stanley

Comes the time when it's later.   Wicker Basket, A.   Robert Creeley.   NAMCP V.2; NoAM

Comes to gather you from clocks and says *be moon*.   Sea by Dusk.   Joanna Klink.   IAoNAP

Comes to Rest.   Constantine P. Cavafy.   CAGL, *tr. by* Edmund Keeley and Philip Sherrard

Comes to us from a distance.   Music of the Altai Mountains.   Kelvin Corcoran.   Oth

Comet.   Federico García Lorca.   PFTM-1 *Fr.* Night (Suite for Piano and Poet's Voice).

Comet.   Matthew Rohrer.   NAPBL

Comet, The.   Gurajada Apparao.   HotL, *tr. by* V. Narayana Rao

Comet, The.   Maurice Riordan.   NIrP

Comet, The.   Maria Luisa Spaziani.   NeIt, *tr. by* Beverly Allen

Comet, The.   János Vajda.   IQMS, *tr. by* Watson Kirkconnell

Comet and Treefrog.   Jarold Ramsey.   PoCoUp

Comet Come.   Norman Nicholson.   NLP

Comet of stillness princess of what is over.   Vixen.   W. S. Merwin.   GPTC

Comet was travelling in the north-western sky, The.   Comet, The.   Maurice Riordan.   NIrP

Comets are like scythes, they do not hold.   Now and Again: An Autobiography of Basket.   Angie Estes.   ExTi

Comet's pulsing rose, The. (LL)   Seamus Heaney.   NPeEn; PBCIP; PNI; WaAnP *Fr.* Singing School.

Comfort.   Elizabeth Barrett Browning.   SacPr

Comfort.   Maura Stanton.   SoSe-8

Comfort in Puirtith.   Helen B. Cruickshank.   EdScPo

Comfort myself when that my hap is nought. (LL)   Petrarch.   NoSic; OxBSo *Fr.* Sonnets to Laura.

Comfort of the former, The.   He's running.   (We) Promenade.   Sharon Kraus.   PA9/11

Comfort that does not comprehend. (LL)   Return, The.   Edna St. Vincent Millay.   MoAmPo; NAMCP V.1; NoAM

Comfort to a Youth That Had Lost His Love.   Robert Herrick.   OBEV

Comfort ye, comfort ye my people.   Bible, *O.T.*   OBVE *Fr.* Isaiah.

Comforter, The.   Thomas Moore.   SacPr

Comfortless, so let evening come. (LL)   Let Evening Come.   Jane Kenyon.   BeAl; GoPo; MakPoe; OxBoAm; PoCu; PtR

Comfort-Maker.   Jerry W., Jr. Ward.   ISC

Comic.   Heather Fuller.   Eno

Comic Look at Damocles, A.   Bill Knott.   BodElec

Comice.   Joseph Stroud.   PoChi

Comin' thro' the Rye.   Robert Burns.   UV

Coming.   Robert Kelly.   PmAP

Coming.   Philip Larkin.   MoBrPo

Coming.   Heather McHugh.   EmeKit

Coming.   Kenneth Rexroth.   GoPo *Fr.* Air and Angels.

Coming and Going.   Robert Francis.   TLR

Coming and going like the dew. (LL)   Body of Man, The.   Van Hanh.   EaWin; WoPoe, *tr. by* W. S. Merwin and Nguyen Ngoc Bich

Coming and going these several seasons.   Abiku.   John Pepper Clark Bekederemo.   HBAPE

Coming around the corner of the dark trail . . . what was wrong with the.   Inquisitors, The.   Robinson Jeffers.   MoAmPo

Coming Ashore.   Lamont B. Steptoe.   FuFl

Coming at an end, the lovers.   Book of Music, A.   Jack Spicer.   APSN; CalPo; OxBoAm

Coming at Night to a Fisherman's Hut.   Chang Chi.   BLT

Coming back.   Buson.   EH, *tr. by* Robert Hass

Coming Back of an Assassinated Poet, The.   Rafael Alberti.   RaW, *tr. by* Mark Strand

Coming Back to the Cave.   Rachel Wetzsteon.   AmPoNex

Coming back to the cave is when the hard part.   Coming Back to the Cave.   Rachel Wetzsteon.   AmPoNex

Coming by evening through the wintry city.   At a Bach Concert.   Adrienne Rich.   NIL-7; NIP-4; YaYoPo

Coming Down.   Rick London.   Eno

Coming Down Cleveland Avenue.   James Tate.   YaYoPo

Coming Down from Derry Hill.   Maggie Hannan.   NLP

Coming down into an air brown as whiskey, the plane.   Autobiography, Chapter XLII: Three Days in Louisville.   Jim Barnes.   HATNAP

Coming Downtown.   Marilyn Hacker.   PoBW

Coming east we left the animals.   River at Wolf, The.   Jean Valentine and Anne Frydman.   LaCa

Coming Forth.   Scott Cairns.   UpMys

Coming Forth By Day.   Philip Whalen.   AHA

Coming from Kansas.   Myra Cohn Livingston.   CalPo; NOxBChV

Coming from Montreal.   Upstate.   Simon J. Ortiz.   LTA

Coming from the pool.   Prey.   Peter Makuck.   UrbNat

Coming from the south.   Six Ten Sixty-Nine.   Conyus.   GT

Coming, going, the waterfowl.   Dogen.   ZenPo, *tr. by* Takashi Ikemoto and Lucien Stryk

Coming Home.   Tess Gallagher.   LaCa

Coming Home.   Elizabeth Tibbetts.   SweBea

Coming Home, *Detroit*, 1968.   Philip Levine.   UrbNat

Coming home from work.   Chogyam Trungpa.   WhBo

Coming Home Late at Night.   Tu Fu [*or* Du Fu].   BLT

Coming Homeward out of Spain.   Barnabe Googe.   NoSic (Commynge Home-warde out of Spayne.)   NPeEn

Coming, I clench my hands.   Dankyo-Myorin.   ZenPo, *tr. by* Takashi Ikemoto and Lucien Stryk

Coming in off the dock after writing.   Station.   Sharon Olds.   PBCAP

Coming into History.   Jeanne Murray Walker.   PoA 2002

Coming into Their Own.   Sheenagh Pugh.   AngWePo

Coming late, as always.   Poem, The.   W. S. Merwin.   CAP-8

Coming of Age.   Ursula K. Le Guin.   Stanza 4.   GoPo

Coming of Age.   Michael Palma.   UnSA

Coming of Archy, The.   Don Marquis.   TCAPo "Expression is the need of my soul."   APT-1

Coming of Arthur, The.   Alfred Tennyson.   NAEL-7v2 *Fr.* Idylls of the King.

Coming of Enkidu, The.   *Unknown*.   CAGL *Fr.* Epic of Gilgamesh, The.

Coming of Good Luck, The.   Robert Herrick.   NPeEn; OxBEV; Spl

Coming of Grendel, The.   *Unknown*.   OPOU *Fr.* Beowulf.

Coming of John, The.   Amus Mor.   SeSe

Coming of Spring, The.   Henrietta Cordelia Ray.   CBWP-3

Coming of Teddy Bears, The.   Dennis Lee.   TLR

Coming of the Cold, The.   Theodore Roethke.   OBCP

Coming of the First Aeroplanes, The.   Dick Allen.   OtW

Coming of the Plague, The.   Weldon Kees.   ChIV-1; StAl

Coming of the Wee Malkies, The.   Stephen Mulrine.   EdScPo

Coming of War, The; Actaeon.   Ezra Pound.   PoA 2002

Coming of Wisdom with Time, The.   William Butler Yeats.   HarvBoo; SoSe-8

Coming Off a Depression, She Prepares for Venice.   A. V. Christie.   NAPBL

Coming [*or* Comming] to kiss[e] her lips [*or* lyps], such grace I found.   Edmund Spenser.   NAEL-6v1; OxBSo *Fr.* Amoretti.

Coming out. All right? Mama might worry. (LL)   To My Brother Miguel.   César Vallejo.   PoetW; TCLAP, *tr. by* John Knoepfle and James Wright

Coming out of the station he expected.   Return to Hiroshima.   Lucien Stryk.   AtGh

Coming Out on Solid Ground After the Ice Age.   Gary Paul Nabhan.   PoCoUp

Coming out with your clutch of postcards.   Leaving the Tate.   Fleur Adcock.   BrAP

Coming Over Coldwater.   Carol Muske-Dukes.   GeoHom

Coming Right Up.   A. R. Ammons.   OBCoV

Coming Storm, The.   Herman Melville.   APN-2

Comin[g] thro' [*or* through] the Rye.   Robert Burns.   FaBoVe; GoPo; OxAEP-2

Coming through the Craigs o' Kyle.   Jean Glover.   RACG

Coming through the rye.   Rose Farmer, The.   Herman Melville.   APN-2

Coming to a stream, I wash my feet.   Mountain Excursion.   Jinkag Haesim.   BecRai, *tr. by* Kim Daljin, Kim Won-Chung and Christopher Merrill

Coming to bed I come upon them lying.   XX.   Craig Arnold.   NAPBL

Coming to Spain on the first day of the fighting.   Muriel Rukeyser.   AmWaPo *Fr.* Letter to the Front.

Coming to the farm that winter afternoon.   Burragorang.   Nan McDonald.   NOBAu

Coming to the net (for arthur ashe_.   Brian G. Gilmore.   BtF; SpirFl

Coming to This [*with music*].   Mark Strand.   VCAP

Coming to You.   Daphne Marlatt.   PoBW

Coming to you.   Daphne Marlatt.   NLPA *Fr.* Touch to My Tongue.

Coming together.   Recreation.   Audre Lorde.   NIL-7

Coming up England by a different line.   I Remember, I Remember.   Philip Larkin.   HarvBoo

Coming Up for Air. David Waltner-Toews. Woods. IFF

Coming up from the subway. After Work. Richard Jones. GoPo

Coming up from underground. Daphne Marlatt. NLPA *Fr.* Touch to My Tongue.

Coming was an empty promise, you have gone, and left no footprint. Li Shang-yin. CCL1, *tr. by* A. C. Graham

Coming Woman, The. Mary Weston Fordham. CBWP-2; SWaP

Comings and Goings. Ann Townsend. NAPBL

Comma a Portrait, The. Pamela Alexander. AmAlph

Commander Lowell. Robert Lowell. NAMCP V.2

Commander of a camp, among his amusements, as in other camps, The. Charles Reznikoff. NAMCP V.1 *Fr.* Holocaust.

Commanding pow'r, whose hand with plastic art. Statue of the Dying Gladiator, The. Felicia Dorothea Hemans. RWP

Commandments. Judith Hemschemeyer. FiBr

Commandments, The. Lamea Abbas Amara. PoArWo, *tr. by* Mike Maggio

Comme. Robert Desnos. YaTCFP

Comme au-dessus du ciel il y a le ciel et après la vie la vie,—au-delà du regard il y a le regard. Cézanne. Jean Tardieu. YaTCFP

Comme si c'était nous que le jour halait. Labeur du jour. Paul De Roux. YaTCFP

Commencer. Jacques Dupin. YaTCFP

Commencer comme on déchir un drap. Commencer. Jacques Dupin. YaTCFP

Commendatory Sonnets. Edmund Spenser.
   To the Right Worshipfull, My Singular Good Frend, Master Gabriell Harvey, Doctor of the Lawes. NoSic

Commendatory Verses to Edmund Spenser's Fairy Queen. Sir Walter Ralegh.
   (Methought I Saw the Grave Where Laura Lay.) NAEL-6v1; NAEL-7v1
   (Vision upon the Fairy Queen, A.) NoP-4; NoP-5
   Vision upon This Concei[p]t of the Faerie [*or* Faery] Queen[e], A. NoSic

Comment. Dorothy Parker. AmWit; LW; NBLV; NIL-7; NIP-4; OBCoV

Comment on Curb. Langston Hughes. APSN; APT-2; OxBoAm *Fr.* Lenox Avenue Mural.

Comment on My Host, A. Mark Solomon. OPRER

Comment on this: in the real scheme of things, poetry is marginal. Richard Jones. TAPaP

Commentary. Hyam Plutzik. TaR

Commentary. Andrew Schelling. AmZen

Commentary on an Old Review. Géza Szöcs. ConPit, *tr. by* Enikö Bollobás and Clayton Eshleman

Commentary Text Commentary Text Commentary Text. David Shapiro. PmAP

Comments upon my last book of poesy. Charles Bukowski. OxBoAm

Commerce and the Man. Ricardo M. de Ungria. ReBoTo

Commercial Leech Farming Today. Thomas Lux. BodElec

Commercials exaggerate. James McManus. IllVoic *Fr.* Who Needs Two.

Commination, A. Alec Derwent Hope. ChIV-2

Comming to kisse her lyps, (such grace I found). Edmund Spenser. *See* Coming [*or* Comming] to kiss[e] her lips [*or* lyps], such grace I found.

Commingling sky, A. Freely Espousing. James Schuyler. FTOS; NoP-4; NoP-5

Commission. Ezra Pound. BrAP

Commissioner bet me a pony, The—I won, The. Robert, Viscount Sherbrooke Lowe. NOBAu *Fr.* Songs of the Squatters.

Commissioners believe that everything. Ordnance Survey in the Northern Counties. Mick North. NLP

Commit thou all thy griefs And ways into his hands. Commit thy way unto the Lord. Paul Gerhardt. SacPr

Commit thy way unto the Lord. Paul Gerhardt. SacPr

Committee, The. Ann Stanford. CalPo

Committee's fat, The. Un-American Investigators. Langston Hughes. HHAm

Common and Particular. David Constantine. PoCu

Common Cormorant [*or* Shag], The. Christopher Isherwood. NBLV; NoxBChV

Common Dust. Georgia Douglas Johnson. NAAPv.2

Common Fate of Books, The. Margaret Lucas Cavendish, Duchess of Newcastle. PBRV

Common feelings. Living. Jaime Torres Bodet. TCLAP, *tr. by* Sonja Karsen

Common Form. Rudyard Kipling. HarvBoo; InoFa; NPeEn; PoAgWa; WoPoe *Fr.* Epitaphs of the War [1914–1918].

Common Ground. Michael Murphy. NIrP

Common man I might have been, The. In Brief. Angel Cuadra. AF, *tr. by* Katherine Rodriguez Nieto

Common miracle. Miracle Mart. Wisława Szymborska. PoSu, *tr. by* Adam Czerniawski

Common Nocturne. Arthur Rimbaud. MotU, *tr. by* Louise Varese

Common Occurrence, A [*with music*]. Priscilla Jane Thompson. CBWP-2

Common Path, The. Glyn Jones. AngWePo

Common people are very weary, The. *Unknown.* ColAnChi *Fr.* Classic of Odes.

Common People, The. Rowland Watkyns. AngWePo; BASC

Common Prayer. Lynn Ungar. AFaM

Common Road, The. Silas H. Perkins. ITBLP

Common Sacrifice to Honour fall, A. (LL) Homer. NPeEn; OBVE *Fr.* Iliad, The.

Common Sense. Alan Brownjohn. NoP-5; NOxBChV *Fr.* Pitman's Common Sense Arithmetic, 1917.

Common speech is, spend and God will send, The. Magnum Vectigal Parsimonia. George Gascoigne. NoSic

Common, The. Gail Mazur. UrbNat

Common Things. Paul Laurence Dunbar. GT

Common Woman, The. Judy Grahn.
   Detroit Annie, Hitchhiking. ASA
   Ella, in a Square Apron, Along Highway 80. NALW
   Nadine, Resting on Her Neighbor's Stoop. NALW

Commonplace I sing, The. Commonplace, The. Walt Whitman. MoAmPo

Commonplace, The. Walt Whitman. MoAmPo

Commonwealth, Common Poverty. Gloria Vando. TouFir

Communal Living. Alice Jones. BloBone

Communication to the City Fathers of Boston. George Starbuck. YaYoPo

Communication Which the Author Had to London, Before She Made Her Will, A. Isabella Whitney. *See* Aucthour Maketh Her Wyll and Testament, The.

Communion. Sarah Maguire. MFPA

Communiqués from Yalta, The. R. P. Blackmur. APT-2

Communism [*with music*]. Ella Wheeler Wilcox. SWaP

Communist, half a world away, A. People's Republic, The. John A. Vanek. RWB

Communist Poem, 1935. Valentine Ackland. RSaN

Community. Sally Roberts Jones. AngWePo

Community College in the Rain. David Berman. LegDan

Community College Revises Its Curriculum in Response to Changing Demographics, The. Martín Espada. LiTh

Community School. Sheikh Selman. IrPoTo, *tr. by* Muhamad Tawfiq Ali

Commuted Sentence, The. Stevie Smith. OxAEP-2

Commuter. Lisel Mueller. GM

Commuter. Elwyn Brooks White. HHAm; NBLV

Commuters. Betsy Hearne. SSCS

Commynge Home-warde out of Spayne. Barnabe Googe. *See* Coming Homeward out of Spain.

Como la hormiga testaruda lleva su carga sosteniéndose en ella. Abrazada a una Lágrima. Luis Rosales. RaW

Como lo Siento. Lorna Dee Cervantes. NoAM

Como Moisés en lo alto del monte. Como Moisés Es el Viejo. Vicente Aleixandre. RaW

Como Moisés Es el Viejo. Vicente Aleixandre. RaW

Como se fue el maestro. A Don Francisco Giner de los Ríos. Antonio Machado Ruiz. RaW

Como un espejo la tarde llega. Corrida. Pedro Serrano. RMCMP

Como un fantasma que de pronto se asoma. Ante el Espejo. Vicente Aleixandre. RaW

Como una piedra sin mano, el azar. Arcano 10: La Fortuna. Veronica Volkow. RMCMP

Compact sat in parliament, The. 1838. Dennis Lee. IFF

Companies advertise their brands. Return to Normalcy. Joanna Fuhrman. PrTe

Companion, The. Mary Low. SurWo

Companion, The. Edwin Arlington Robinson. NoAM

Companion, The. *Unknown.* ArBi

Companions. Tade Ipadeola. NeNiPo

Companion's Progress, A. Paul Laurence Dunbar. GT

Company had advertised for men to unload a steamer across the river. It was six o'clock in the morning, snowing and still dark. Testimony. Charles Reznikoff. NAAPv.2; PFTM-1

Company I Keep, The. Nissim Ezekiel. BrAP

Company of mountains, an upthrust of mountains, A. Kinloch Ainort. Sorley MacLean. HarvBoo

Company, The. Robert Creeley. FTOS; OnScMo

Compare your body to a room. Five Weeks. Lee Ranaldo. HeMarv

Compared to the condos of the living. Fabio Morabito. RMCMP, *tr. by* Geoff Hargreaves

Compared with loss of thee will not seem so. (LL) William Shakespeare. NoSic; OBEV; OxAEP-1; RaF *Fr.* Sonnets.

Compared with this a grave or tomb. Pelleas and Melisande. Newman Levy. AmWit

Comparison, A. John Chipman Farrar. WHSW

Comparison, A [*with music*]. Ágnes Nemes Nagy. IQMS, *tr.* by Alan Dixon

Comparison betwixt a Whore and a Booke, A. John Taylor. "Me thinks I heare some Cavillers object." PBRV

Comparison of Hands One Day Late Summer El Sobrante. Wendy Rose. HATNAP

Comparison of His Thoughts to Pearls. William Drummond of Hawthornden. NePenScot

Comparison of the Life of Man, A [*with music*]. Richard Barnfield. NoSic

Comparison, The. John Donne. BASC *Fr.* Elegies.

Compass. Elizabeth Alexander. NAPBL

Compass. Jorge Luis Borges. PoetW, *tr.* by Richard Wilbur

Compass jokingly, The. Leaving Home. Bei Dao. WoBe, *tr.* by Iona Man-Cheong and Eliot Weinberger

Compass of the Dying. Laurence Lieberman. IllVoic

Compass Room, The: East. Thalia Field. IIR

Compassion's Bird. Jay Wright. ESEAA

Compendium Notes. Malinda Markham. IAoNAP

Compensation. Paul Laurence Dunbar. APN-2; NAAPv.1

Compensation. Robinson Jeffers. MoAmPo

Compensation. Henrietta Cordelia Ray. CBWP-3

Compensation ("Why should I keep holiday.") Ralph Waldo Emerson. APN-1

Compensation ("Wings of Time are black and white, The.") Ralph Waldo Emerson. APN-1

Competition. Stephen Dunn. MoASP

Competitive product you said you'd send, The. (LL) Consumer's Report, A. Peter Porter. EmeKit; NoP-4; NoP-5

Complacencies of the peignoir, and late. Sunday Morning. Wallace Stevens. APT-1; BBASP; ColAP; EMP; HarvBoo; HeIP-4; MoAmPo; NAAL-5; NAAPv.2; NAMCP V.1; NAWM-7v2; NIL-7; NIP-4; NoAM; NoP-4; NoP-5; OxBoAm; PoA 2002; PoPoPo; SAmP; SoSe-8; TCAPo; TFi; TRP; WaAnP

Complacent they tell us, hard hearts and derisive. Woman's Future. May Kendall. ViWPN; VWP

Complacent Tortoise, The. Brian Patten. OBSP

Complaining. George Herbert. ChIV-1

Complaining about the Second Wife. *Vietnamese Oral Tradition*. CaDao, *tr.* by John Balaban

Complaint. William Carlos Williams. SAmP

Complaint, A. William Wordsworth. NPBRoP

Complaint by Night of the Lover Not Beloved, A. Henry Howard, Earl of Surrey. OBVE

Complaint for a Sorcerer. Susy Hare. SurWo

Complaint for M and M, A. Kay Boyle. SurPaPo *Fr.* Complaint for Mary and Marcel, A.

Complaint for Mary and Marcel, A. Kay Boyle. Complaint for M and M, A. SurPaPo

Complaint from a Lady's Chamber. Wang Ch'ang-ling. ChinPo, *tr.* by Ye Weilian [*or* Yeh Wei-lien *or* Wai-lim Yip]

Complaint Near the Jade Stairs. Hsieh T'iao. CrYelRi, *tr.* by Sam Hamill

Complaint near the Jade Steps. Li Po. *See* Resentment Near the Jade Steps.

Complaint of a Lover Rebuked. Petrarch. HeIP-4; OBVE *Fr.* Sonnets to Laura.

Complaint of a Lover, The. Anne Killigrew. BASC

Complaint of Thames 1647 When the Best of Kings Was Imprisoned by the Worst of Rebels at Holmbie, The. Hester Lee Pulter. EMWP

Complaint of the Absence of Her Lover Being upon the Sea. Henry Howard, Earl of Surrey. *See* Seafarer, The.

Complaint of the Black Knight, The. John Lydgate. OBGa *Fr.* Complaint of the Black Knight, The.

Complaint of the Black Knight, The. John Lydgate. OBGa

Complaint of the Fair Armoress [*or* Armouress], The. François Villon. OBVE, *tr.* by Algernon Charles Swinburne

Complaint of the Jade Staircase. Hsieh T'iao. CCL1, *tr.* by John Frodsham

Complaint of Troilus, The. Geoffrey Chaucer. OBEV *Fr.* Troilus and Criseyde [*or* Criseide].

Complaint on the Oblivion of the Dead. Jules Laforgue. WoPoe, *tr.* by William Jay Smith

Complaint, The. Mark Akenside. OBEV

Complaint to His Purse. Geoffrey Chaucer. NoP-4; NoP-5

Complaint: To the Muse. Philip Whalen. BB

Complaynt [*or* Compleynt *or* Complaint] of the Comoun [*or* Common] Weill of Scotland, The. Sir David Lyndsay. PBRV *Fr.* Dreme, The.

Conplected. Teri Ellen Cross. BRtP

Complements. Like figures in statuary. Sun and Moon. Mary Kinzie. FFC

Complete Cynic, The. Keith Preston. NBLV

Complete Destruction. William Carlos Williams. SAmP

Complete earth, A. Avocado Pit, The. Carl Rakosi. APT-2

Complete Semen Study. Michael Ryan. BodElec

Complete Sound-Poems of Hugo Ball, The. Hugo Ball. PFTM-1

Complete the picture. (LL) William Carlos Williams. GS; OxBoAm *Fr.* Pictures from Brueghel.

Complete Thought I - XXV. Barrett Watten. PFTM-2

Complete with photomatic *stimmung*. Our Lady. John Godfrey. PmAP

Complete with Starry Night and Bourbon Shots. Albert Goldbarth. BAP-97

Completely. (LL) Apollo and Marsyas. Zbigniew Herbert. PoSu; WoPoe, *tr.* by Czeslaw Milosz and Peter Dale Scott

Completely blind. Kitahara Hakushū. CAoMJL1, *tr.* by Margaret Benton Fukasawa

Completely round is the perfect pearl. Ballad of the Shape of Things, The. Sheldon Harnick. ReLy

Completion of, The. Alex Rawls. AnSo *Fr.* What's Your Sign?

Completion of the Fiddle, The. Milton Acorn. Coast

Complex Mechanism of the Break, The. Jorie Graham. AWPTFC

Compleynt, compleynt I hearde upon a day. Ezra Pound. HarvBoo *Fr.* Cantos.

Compliance Engineering. Ron Silliman. BAP-04 *Fr.* VOG.

Complicated and Innovative Orthopedic Surgery. Ramy Ditzanny. NRoS, *tr.* by Esther Raizen

Complicated Shadows. Stephen Corey. PasH

Compose compose beds. Sacred Emily. Gertrude Stein. NAMCP V.1

Composed as I am, like others. Elements of Composition. A. K. Ramanujan. NAMCP V.2; VCWP

Composed at the Request of a Lady, and Descriptive of Her Feelings. Maria Gowen Brooks. APN-1

Composed at the West Wall of Tsou-p'ing Three Days After the Festival of Pure Brightness. Wang Shih-chieng. ColAnChi, *tr.* by Richard John Lynn

Composed at thirty, my funeral oration: Here lies. Funeral Oration, A. David Wright. InoFa

Composed by nature, time, human art. Reminder, The. Denise Levertov. PoCoUp

Composed by the Sea-Side, near Calais, August, 1802. William Wordsworth. CenSon

Composed During a Walk on the Downs, in November 1787. Charlotte Smith. OxBSo

Composed in One of the Valleys of Westmoreland, on Easter Sunday. William Wordsworth. ChIV-2

Composed in the Composing Room. Franklin Pierce Adams. NIL-7; NIP-4

Composed in the Tower before his execution. More Light! More Light! Anthony Hecht. AF; EmeKit; EMP; GPTC; HP; NoAM; NoP-4; OBWP; PWW2; TaR; VCAP

Composed Near the Bay Bridge (after a wild party). Marilyn Chin. ExTi

Composed on a Journey Homeward; the Author Having Received Intelligence of the Birth of a Son. Samuel Taylor Coleridge. *See* Sonnet Composed on a Journey Homeward; the Author Having Received Intelligence of the Birth of a Son, 20 September 1796.

Composed Playfully on New Year's Day. Yi Kyubo. CATKP, *tr.* by Kevin O'Rourke

Composed upon Westminster Bridge, September 3, 1802. William Wordsworth. BrAP; CABP; CenSon; ChAP; ClHu; CtM; GSo; HeIP-4; ITBLP; MakPoe; NAEL-6v2; NAEL-7v2; NAWM-7v2; NOBRP; NoP-4; NoP-5; NPeEn; OPOU; OxBEV; OxBSo; TFi; WaAnP (Westminster Bridge.) NPBRoP

Composing. "Anvari." WoPoe, *tr.* by Dick Davis

Composing scales beside the rails. Harmonious Heedlessness of Little Boy Blue, The. Guy Wetmore Carryl. AmWit

Composite. Cornelius Eady. FuFl

Composite. (LL) Bringing My Son to the Police Station to Be Fingerprinted. Shoshauna Shy. P180; PoDa

Composition. Hugh Seidman. BodElec

Composition in Drunkenness. Chang Yüeh. CCL1, *tr.* by Stephen Owen

Composition in Retrospect. John Cage. "You can't be serIous she said." APT-2

Composition of the Chalcans, A. *Unknown*. PFTM-1 *Fr.* Cantares Mexicanos.

Composition was shy, The. After. Gillian Conoley. RoV

Composition with Wire. Mark Prejsnar. AnSo

Compositions in harmony. Big Bluejay Composition. Ron Padgett. PmAP

Compositor, The. Greg Delanty. WaAnP

Comprehension Questions. Christine Hume. LegDan

Comprehensive [*with music*]. Carol Ann Duffy. RSaN

Compromise. Akhtar-ul-Iman. WoPoe, *tr.* by Vinay Dharwadker and C. M. Naim

Computation, The. John Donne. NoSic; SoSe-8

Computer Aided Design: Creation. Jackie Hardy. NeBl

Computer chip malfunctions, A. A micro. Spuyten Duyvil. Honor Moore. AtGh

Computers Are Poets Too.   Mererid Puw Davies.   BBMWP, tr. by the author
Computer's First Christmas Card, The.   Edwin Morgan.   NOxBChV; OxBEV
Comrade [with music].   Philippe Soupault.   PFTM-1
Comrade Jesus.   Sarah Norcliffe Cleghorn.   APT-1
Comrade Laugher.   Paul Potts.   RSaN
Comrades, leave me here a little, while as yet 't is early morn.   Granny's House.   Phoebe Cary.   APN-2
Comrades, leave me here a little, while as yet 'tis early morn.   Locksley Hall.   Alfred Tennyson.   NAEL-6v2; NAEL-7v2
Comus; a Masque Presented at Ludlow Castle.   John Milton.
    Chastity ("I Mean That Too, But Yet a Hidden Strength").   NOSC
    Echo.   OBEV
    Farewell of the Attendant Spirit.   OBEV; OxAEP-1
    (Comus' Summons.)   NOSC
    Mask, A.   OxAEP-1
      "Nay, lady, sit; if I but wave this wand."   OxAEP-1
    (Sabrina.)   OBEV
    Sabrina Fair.   OxBEV; WoPoe
    (Sabrina's Song.)   NOSC
    (Song.)   NoP-5; OxAEP-1
    (Song.)   NoP-5
    Song.   OxBEV
    (Spirit's Epilogue, The.)   NOSC
    Star That Bids the Shepherd Fold, The.   NPeEn; OBEV
Comus's Song.   Ben Jonson.   OBCoV
Con dos tijeretazos cayó su pantycelyn.   Edipo al cubo.   Gerardo Deniz.   RMCMP
Con la langua de Príapo y las manos obvias y corteses.   Inventario.   Pedro Serrano.   RMCMP
Con Los Pájaros.   Juan Delgado.   AmPoNex
Con Palabras Distintas.   José Ángel Valente.   RaW
Con sólo dos o tres estambres revientan las flores masculinas. Ascienden desde el fondo de sí mismas, candentes y jugosas. A mano suelta se revuelcan, se crían bajo este cielo a medias entre luz y sombra.   María Baranda.   RMCMP
Con su manto de nylon.   Virgen de Plástico.   Gloria Fuertes.   RaW
Con tanto ruido.   Acto.   Gerardo Deniz.   RMCMP
Con tus manos hiciste libres.   Niño de la Jaula Vacía, El.   José Hierro.   RaW
Con una quietud intolerante.   Seres patológicos.   David Huerta.   RMCMP
Conceit.   Mervyn Laurence Peake.   Spl
Conceit Begotten by the Eyes.   Sir Walter Ralegh.   NoSic
Conceived on a mattress of human hair.   Innocence.   Wisława Szymborska.   PoSu, tr. by Jan Darowski
Concentrate upon her attributes.   Close-up on a Sharp-shinned Hawk.   Don McKay.   BeAl
Concentrating.   Michael Hulse.   PML
Concentration.   Sikong Tu.   CCL1 Fr. Twenty-Four Modes of Poetry.
Concentration Camp Blues.   Henry Dumas.   SeSe
Concentration Constellation.   Lawson Fusao Inada.   GeoHom
Concept is interesting, The: to see, as though reflected.   Wet Casements.   John Ashbery.   NAMCP V.2; OxBoAm
Concept like "I," which I am told by many, A.   I Brood about Some Concepts, for Example.   Alicia Ostriker.   PBCAP
Conception.   Joseph Ceravolo.   FTOS
Conception.   Waring Cuney.   APT-2
Conception: "Death did not come to my mother."   Josephine Miles.   CalPo; ColAP; OxBoAm
Concern.   Steve Sanfield.   WhBo
Concerning a Girl.   Shuntaro Tanikawa.   VCWP, tr. by Harold Wright
Concerning a nun, composer and herbalist.   Short History of Illumination, A.   Matthew Rohrer.   AmPoNex
Concerning Dragons.   H. D. C. Pepler.   NOxBChV
Concerning Hebrews.   Herman Melville.   APN-2 Fr. Clarel: A Poem and Pilgrimage in the Holy Land.
Concerning Himself.   Paul Fleming.   GePo, tr. by George C. Schoolfield
Concerning My Neighbors, the Hittites.   Charles Simic.   VCAP
Concerning Paradise.   Christopher Buckley.   GeoHom
Concerning That Prayer I Cannot Make.   Jane Mead.   LaCa; PLBUT
Concerning the Afterlife, the Indians of Central California Had Only the Dimmest Notions.   Robert Hass.   LoL
Concerning the Atoms of the Soul.   John Glenday.   NeBrP
Concerning the Fruit-bringing Autumn Season.   Catharina Regina von Greiffenberg.   GePo, tr. by George C. Schoolfield
Concerning the Henbane Bird.   Will Alexander.
    "I cannot say that I am phenomena by model."   Eno
Concerning the Infanticide, Marie Farrar.   Bertolt Brecht.   WoPoe, tr. by Hoffman Reynolds Hays
Concerning the Islands Newly Discovered.   Joy Katz.   NeAmPo

Concerning the King of Sweden.   Georg Rudolph Weckherlin.   GePo, tr. by George C. Schoolfield
Concerning the Rehabilitation of the Disabled from the Wars of Israel.   Arye Sivan.   NRoS, tr. by Esther Raizen
Concerning the Wolffsbrunnen near Heidelberg.   Martin Opitz.   GePo, tr. by George C. Schoolfield
Concerning Violence.   Ruth Garnett.   BtF
Concerning your letter in which you ask.   With Mercy for the Greedy.   Anne Sexton.   CAP-8; MoWP; NIL-7; VCAP
Concert.   Josephine Miles.   NALW
Concert.   Helen G. Quigless.   EGAG
Concert Choir.   Beth McGrath.   MiVo
Concert in the Old School Garret.   Unknown, fr. Terezin Concentration Camp.   INSAB
Concert Party: Busseboom.   Edmund Charles Blunden.   FaBoWar
Concert, The.   Lisel Mueller.   MiVo
Concert-hall was crowded the night of the Crash, The.   Paper Anniversary.   Muriel Rukeyser.   NoAM
Concerts in those days were that much longer.   Looking for 78's in the 40's.   Hugh Macpherson.   EdScPo
Concession to Perpetuity No. 166.   Rod Mengham.   VaPo
Conch.   Zbigniew Herbert.   StAl, tr. by Bogdana Carpenter and John Carpenter and Bogdana Carpenter
Conch.   Eva Salzman.   MoWP
Conch from Sicily, A.   Alfred Corn.   NoP-5
Conchie, The.   R. F. Palmer.   FaBoWar
Conchita debemos to speak totalmente in English.   Doña Josefina Counsels Doña Concepción Before Entering Sears.   Maurice Kilwein Guevara.   AmPoNex
Conciencia Plena.   Juan Ramón Jiménez.   RaW
Conciousness.   Ágnes Nemes Nagy.   IQMS, tr. by Dorren Bell
Concise History of Music, A.   Thomas M. Disch.   OxBoAm
Concluding Aria.   Gertrude Stein.   PFTM-2 Fr. Mother of Us All, The.
Conclusion.   Geoffrey Chaucer.   WoPoe Fr. Troilus and Criseyde [or Criseide].
Conclusion.   Ovid.   OBVE Fr. Metamorphoses.
Conclusion.   Percy Bysshe Shelley.   NPeEn Fr. Sensitive Plant, The.
Conclusion: "But here no cannon thunders to the gale."   William Wordsworth.   CenSon Fr. River Duddon [A Series of Sonnets], The.
Conclusion: "Did you love well what very soon you left?"   Marilyn Hacker.   NoAM Fr. Coda.
Conclusion: "Image dance of change, An."   Siegfried Sassoon.   MoBrPo
Conclusion: "In one of those excursions (may they ne'er)."   William Wordsworth.   NAEL-6v2; NAEL-7v2 Fr. Prelude, The; Growth of a Poet's Mind [1850 version]; Selections from Anthologies].
Conclusion, The.   John Dryden.   BASC Fr. Religio Laici.
Conclusion, The.   Sir Walter Ralegh.   See Even Such Is Time.
Conclusion Is Not Drawn, The.   Nicole Espagnol.   SurWo, tr. by Myrna Bell Rochester
Conclusion of a Letter to the Rev. Mr. C———, The.   Mary Barber.   CABP
Conclusion of the Matter, The.   Christopher Smart.   ChIV-1 Fr. Hymns for the Amusement of Children.
Conclusion to Book 1.   Mary Robinson.   RWP Fr. Progress of Liberty, The.
Concord Hymn.   Ralph Waldo Emerson.   AmWaPo; BRP; ClHu; ColAP; CtM; FaBoA; HeIP-4; NAAPv.1; NoP-4; NoP-5; OBWP; OxBoAm; PoPoPo; TCAPo; TFi; WaAnP
    (Hymn[:] Sung at the Completion of the Concord Monument, April 19, 1836.)   APN-1; NAAL-3
Concordat Proviso Ascendant.   Christopher Dewdney.
    "She is liquid darkness occult with desire."   FTOS
Concordiam in Populo.   Bernard O'Donoghue.   BeAl
Concrete Delivery Delayed by Goose and Gosling Crossing, Late March, Mallett's Bay.   Richard Kenney.   PfSP
Concrete Seascape.   William Harmon.   PoDa
Concrete tendonitis bare floor hard muscle.   Watching a Dance Rehearsal in a Calgary Theatre with a Concrete Floor.   Suzette Mayr.   PoPra
Concubine, The.   Vietnamese Oral Tradition.   CaDao, tr. by John Balaban
Condemn me not for making such a coil.   Margaret Lucas Cavendish, Duchess of Newcastle.   PEW
Condemn me not, I make so much ado.   Margaret Lucas Cavendish, Duchess of Newcastle.   NoP-5
Condemn'd by Fate to way-ward Curse.   Sot-Weed Factor, The.   Ebenezer Cook.   TCAPo
Condemned.   Cecil Day Lewis.   See Tempt Me No More.
Condemned.   Philippe Soupault.   AF, tr. by Eden Paul
Condemned Man, The.   George Crabbe.   NPeEn Fr. Borough, The.
Condemned [or Condemn'd] to hope's delusive mine.   On the Death of Dr [or Mr] Robert Levet [a Practiser in Physic].   Samuel Johnson.   ChIV-2; NAEL-6v1; NAEL-7v1; NoP-4; NoP-5; NPeEn; OBEV; OxAEP-1; OxBEV; TFi; WaAnP

Condemned Site. Mona Van Duyn. MakPoe

5. Condemns its Power. Mary Robinson. NPBRoP *Fr.* Sappho and Phaon.

Condensed History of Beauty, A. Maurice Manning. LegDan

Condensery. (LL) Poet's Work. Lorine Niedecker. APT-2; HarvBoo; NAAPv.2; NAMCP V.1; OxBoAm; PoCho

Condicional. Gerardo Diego. RaW

Condition. Mahdi Muhammad Ali. IrPoTo, *tr.* by Salaam Yousif

Condition: hydroplane. Moon. Giovanni Raboni. ItPo, *tr.* by Gayle Ridinger

Condition of Women, The. Hồ Xuân Hương. PoChi, *tr.* by John Balaban

Condo. Louise Glück. BodElec

CONDOLENCES . . . from our swollen lips laden with condolences. Elegy for Slit-Drum. Christopher Okigbo. HBAPE

Condom Tree, The. Chase Twichell. EmeKit

Condominium, stiff bamboo. Urban Love Poem. Marilyn Chin. FaoP

Condor. David Tokuyu Reid-Marr. WhBo

Conduct. Samuel Greenberg. OxBoAm

Conductor, The. Dezső Kosztolányi. IQMS, *tr.* by Leslie A. Kery

Conductor, The. Adam Sol. IFF

Conductor's hands were black with money, The. Charon. Louis MacNeice. NAMCP V.1; OxBEV; PNI

Confabulation. John A. Stone. BloBone

Confederacy. Elise Paschen. FFC

Confederate Flags, The. Ambrose Bierce. AmWaPo; CBCWP

Confederate Memorial Day. *Unknown.* CBCWP

Confederate Veteran Tries to Explain the Event, A. Robert Penn Warren. AmWaPo; CBCWP *Fr.* Day Dr. Knox Did It, The

Conference, A. Renée Weiss and Theodore Weiss. BodElec

Conference among ourselves we called, A. George Gascoigne. OBWP *Fr.* Fruits of War, The.

Conference of the Birds, The. Farid-uddin Attar. *tr.* by Afkham Darb, Afkham Darbandi and Dick Davis

"World's birds gathered for their conference, The." WoPoe, *tr.* by Afkham Darbandi and Dick Davis

Confess: it's my profession. Loneliness of the Military Historian, The. Margaret Atwood. OpeFie

Confessio. Alan Jackson. EdScPo

Confessio Amantis. John Gower. *tr.* by John Gower
    Pygmaleon. NPeEn; OxBEV
    Rape of Lucrece, The. NPeEn, *tr.* by John Gower

Confession. Frank Gelett Burgess. *See* Cinq Ans Après.

Confession. Pearl Cleage. ISC

Confession. Stephen Dobyns. GoPo; SUP

Confession. Paul Gallico. TriCat

Confession. Susan Hahn. IllVoic

Confession. Alice Lee. ReEnLa

Confession. George Oppen. HarvBoo

Confession. Suzanne Wise. LegDan

Confession, A. Jenő Dsida. IQMS, *tr.* by Geroge Gömöri and Clive Wilmer

Confession, A. *Poets of the Tixall Circle.* EMWP

Confession, The. The Archpoet. *tr.* by Helen Waddell
    "Never yet could I endure." EroLit, *tr.* by Helen Waddell

Confession for Forgiveness, A. *Unknown.* IrV, *tr.* by Alfred Perceval Graves

Confession: "I held your sins against you for so long." Eli Goodwin. BtF

Confession #1. Ryan Van Cleave. NevBe

Confession of Cleopas, The. Eric Pankey. GI

Confession of Faith. Elinor Wylie. APT-1; MoAmPo

Confession of Gluttony. William Langland. NAEL-6v1; NAEL-7v1 *Fr.* Vision of Piers Plowman, The.

Confession of My Images. Barbara Guest. AWPTFC

Confession of the Highway / The Hermit Speaks. Garrett Kaoru Hongo. GeoHom *Fr.* Cruising 99.

Confessional. Tom Breidenbach. KGB

Confessional, The. Frederick William Faber. CenSon

Confessional, The. Nathaniel Parker Willis. APN-1

Confessional Poem. Louis Jenkins. RaBo

Confessions. Iman Mirsal. NAfrP, *tr.* by Clarissa C. Burt

Confessions: "Before money and California." Anthony McCann. IIR

Confessions from the Last Cloud. Jose Angel Figueroa. PueRic

Confessions of a Pisciphobe. Ruth Maassen. PfS

Confessions of an Old Believer. Jim Burns. RSaN

Confidentially Yours. Wopko Jensma. TSAP

Configurations. Aimé Césaire.
    "Nothing ever delivers but the opacity of words." ConPit, *tr.* by Clayton Eshleman and Annette Smith

Configurations. Grace Nichols. LW

Confined Love. John Donne. BASC

Confined / to a tent of soldiers. Self-Defense. Luljeta Lleshanaku. WoBe, *tr.* by Henry Israeli

Confinement. Ann Sansom. NeBl

Confirmation, The. Karl Shapiro. APT-2

Confiscating Salt. Wang An-shih. ColAnChi, *tr.* by Burton Watson

Conflation of rapture and regret, The. Asylum of Gestures. Carl Hancock Rux. HeMarv

Conflict, The. Cecil Day Lewis. MoBrPo; NoP-4

Conflict Between the Eyes and the Gaze, The. César Vallejo. ConPit, *tr.* by Clayton Eshleman

Conflict of Convictions, The. Herman Melville. APN-2; CBCWP

Confluence. John Knoepfle. IllVoic

Confluences at San Francisco. Elton Glaser. PBCAP

Confluent water mirror red clouds. Viewing the Three Lakes. Hsieh T'iao. ChinPo, *tr.* by Ye Weilian [*or* Yeh Wei-lien *or* Wai-lim Yip]

Confounding deities, not men. (LL) Nebuchadnezzar's Kingdom-Come. David Rowbotham. ChIV-1; NOBAu

Confrontation with a Bouquet. Maggie Bevan. Prnts

Confronting a longing. Poem to My Death. Julia de Burgos. TCLAP, *tr.* by Grace Schulman

Confronting each other the pictures stare. Royal Portraits, The. William Dean Howells. APN-2

Confronting the solitude. Song to Be Written on a Wave. José Emilio Pacheco. STV, *tr.* by John Frederick Nims

Confucianist is versed in the Six Arts, The. Juan Chi. ColAnChi *Fr.* Songs of My Soul.

Confused leaves fall, fluttering fragrant steps. Tune: "Walk on the Imperial Street." Fan Chung-yen. ChinPo, *tr.* by Ye Weilian [*or* Yeh Wei-lien *or* Wai-lim Yip]

Confused with my life, that is commonplace and solitary. (LL) Next Day. Randall Jarrell. AmFaPo; HarvBoo; NAMCP V.2; NoAM; NoP-4; NoP-5; VCAP; WeW-3

Confusion. Christopher Hervey. UV

Confusion of song. On the radio. Clouded Evening, Late September. Sydney Lea. RA

Confusion of times if not of place, though you understood when i said no, A. Touch to My Tongue. Daphne Marlatt. NLPA

Conga. Betty Comden and Adolph Green. ReLy

Conga. Allen Fisher. PFTM-2

Congo, The. Vachel Lindsay. APT-1; MoAmPo

Congratulations. Well done. Greetings. Gwyn Thomas. BBMWP, *tr.* by the author

Congratulatory Poem to Her Sacred Majesty Queen Mary, Upon Her Arrival in England, A. Aphra Behn. EMWP

Congregation was scandalised, The. Robert Sat. Tom Matthews. PNI

Congress of the Insomniacs, The. Charles Simic. EmeKit

Congressmen Came Out To See Bull Run. Stephen Vincent Benét. CBCWP *Fr.* John Brown's Body.

Congruence of the complement is vain, if it exists, The. (LL) To a Steam Roller. Marianne Moore. APT-1; MoAmPo; NAMCP V.1; NoP-5; OxBoAm; PoPoPo

Coniagui Women. Audre Lorde. NALW

Conifer King, The. Michael Bugeja. UrbNat

Conjectural Poem. Jorge Luis Borges. TCLAP, *tr.* by Norman Thomas Di Giovanni

Conjecture. (LL) Moon Is the Number 18, The. Charles Olson. APT-2; HarvBoo; PFTM-2

Conjugal. Russell Edson. PmAP

Conjugal Visits. Al Young. CalPo

Conjugation of the Paramecium, The. Muriel Rukeyser. NAMCP V.2

Conjugation of the verb: to blow. Fredrica Africa Payne. BRtP

Conjunction of Jupiter and Venus, The. William Cullen Bryant. APN-1

Conjunctions. Eamon Grennan. PBCIP

Conjure up demons from the main. Poet is Piqued, The [*or* Anna Matilda]. Robert Merry. STuOW

Conjure with me: three letters. Richard Skinner. NewEx

Conjured. Sterling Allen Brown. NoP-4; NoP-5

Conjured. Robert Nathaniel Dett. IFF

Conjurer. And of himself as God. (LL) Witch Doctor. Robert Earl Hayden. GPTC; NAMCP V.2; NoAM

Conjurer, The. Maura Stanton. YaYoPo

Conjurer's Honor. Joel Brouwer. RWB

Conjuring Against Alien Spirits. Quincy Troupe. ISC

Conkerbells. Mary Dalton. OpeFie

Connary, Blodgett, Day, Hapgood. Paul Goodman. BodElec

Connected with County, and landed estates. Western Brothers. RWPCtW *Fr.* We're Frightfully BBC.

Connecticut Road Song. Anna Hempstead Branch. TCAPo

Connecticut, with much at stake. New England Pilgrimage. Phyllis McGinley. AmWit

Connecting Light. Susan Michie. Prnts

Connection in Bridgend. John Tripp. TCAWP

Connoisseur of Chaos. Wallace Stevens. NAAPv.2; PFTM-1

Connoisseur of Jews, The. Jerome Rothenberg. TaR

Connoisseur of pearl, A. African China. Melvin B. Tolson. ColAP

Connoisseuse of Slugs, The. Sharon Olds. LW

Connor in the Wind and Rain with His Coat on. Paula McLain. AmPoNex

Connor is four and every day brings a clutch. Connor in the Wind and Rain with His Coat on. Paula McLain. AmPoNex

Connuche. Catron Grieves. ReEnLa

Conqueror Worm, The. Edgar Allan Poe. APN-1; NCAP; TCAPo

Conquerors. Henry Treece. OBWVE; TCAWP

Conquerors, The: The Black Troops in Cuba. Paul Laurence Dunbar. AmWaPo

Conquest. Sion Eirian. BBMWP Fr. Adolescent Experiences.

Conquest. Pauli Murray. GT

Conquest, The. Oliver St. John Gogarty. OBMV

Conquest of Granada, The. John Dryden.
   "'Tis war again, and I am glad 'tis so." FaBoWar

Conquest [or His Lady's Might]. Philippe Desportes. NoSic, tr. by Unknown

Conquistador. Archibald MacLeish.
   Prologue. NoAM

Conrad in Twilight. John Crowe Ransom. FuPo

Conrail Wax Museum. Manuel Ulacia. RMCMP, tr. by Indran Amirthanayagam

Conrail Wax Museum. Manuel Ulacia. RMCMP

Conscience. Victor Hugo. SxFrPo, tr. by A. M. and E. H. Blackmore

Conscience. Meirion MacIntyre Huws. BBMWP, tr. by Geriant Løvgreen

Conscientious Objector. Edna St. Vincent Millay. FaBoWar

Conscientious Objector, The. Karl Shapiro. PLBUT

Conscious. Wilfred Owen. PoWW

Conscious Lovers, The. Sir Richard Steele.
   Love-Sick Maid, The. IrLP

Consciousness requires the immaculate "separateness" of objects of its attention. Immaculate Perception, The. Christopher Dewdney. OpeFie

Conscript. Peter De Vries.
   3. PoA 2002

Conscript Goes, The. William Sydney Graham. FaBoWar

Conscription, The. Tu Fu [or Du Fu]. CCL1, tr. by E. H. Parker

Conscripts. Siegfried Sassoon. BrAP

Consecration. Murdoch O'Daly. IrV, tr. by Eleanor Hull

Consecration, A. John Masefield. MoBrPo

Consensus Series. Jennifer Scappettone.
   D. Eno

Consent. Carol Frost. OPRER

Consents to his inexorable will. (LL) Playboy. Richard Wilbur. CAP-8; NAMCP V.2; NoAM

Consequences. William Meredith. VCAP

Conservancies. Josephine Miles. AFaM

Conservation. Sikong Tu. CCL1 Fr. Twenty-Four Modes of Poetry.

Conservation of Energy, The. Chana Bloch. CFP

Conservatory Pond, Central Park, New York, New York. Joel Brouwer. AmPoNex

Conservatrix of Milesien. Ezra Pound. NAAPv.2 Fr. Hugh Selwyn Mauberley (Life and Contacts).

Conserving the Magnitude of Uselessness. A. R. Ammons. NoAM

Consider. W. H. Auden. OxAEP-2

Consider. Andrew Hudgins. UpMys

Consider a coral or guano atoll. Manichean Geography I. Tom Paulin. PNI

Consider / a girl who keeps slipping off. Briar Rose (Sleeping Beauty). Anne Sexton. MoWP

Consider abroad, how closely it brushes. Foreign. Kate Clanchy. MFPA

Consider Famous Men, Dai Bach. Idris Davies. OBWVE

Consider his song. Brian Coffey. ModIr Fr. For What For Whom Unwanted.

Consider honestly. Jeepney. Gemino H. Abad. ReBoTo

Consider Icarus, pasting those sticky wings on. To a Friend Whose Work Has Come to Triumph. Anne Sexton. CAP-8; OtW

Consider: if we measured the Four Oceans. Man. Chuang Tzu. SonAtl, tr. by Peter Aldman, Alek Stamnitz and P. L. Win

Consider Kyffin, now—as Welsh. Consider Kyffin. Raymond Garlick. TCAWP

Consider, my soul, this texture. Two Meditations. Rosario Castellanos. PFTM-2, tr. by Julian Pulley

Consider my state: what I am. Testament. Saleem Peeradina. Vesp

Consider, O my soul, what morn is this! Meditation for Christmas, A. Selwyn Image. OBEV

Consider Phlebas, who was once handsome and tall as you. (LL) T. S. Eliot. NPeEn; OBVE; OxBEV Fr. Waste Land, The.

Consider, please, this dish of ratatouille. Ratatouille. Douglas Dunn. BeAl

Consider, scholar, when you enter here. Thoughts in the Library. Mihály Vörösmarty. IQMS, tr. by Hymen H. Hart

Consider that the thing has died before we proved it ever lived. Death of the Loch Ness Monster, The. Gwendolyn MacEwen. StAl

Consider the egg. It's a miracle. Eggomania. Felicia Lamport. NBLV

Consider the Garden. Michael Collier. PfSP

Consider the Grass Growing. Patrick Kavanagh. StAl

Consider the infinite fragility of an infant's skull. Arguments. Lisa Suhair Majaj. PoArWo

Consider the Lillies of the Sea. Anne Porter. APT-2

Consider the sea's insatiate lust. Island, The. Brendan Kennelly. PBCIP

Consider the sea's listless chime. Sea-Limits, The. Dante Gabriel Rossetti. NAEL-6v2

Consider the significance. Wire. Rod Moran. NOBAu

Consider the three functions of the tongue. Canzone. Marilyn Hacker. NoAM

Consider them, my soul, they are a fright! Blind, The. Charles Baudelaire. SxFrPo, tr. by James McGowan

Consider These, for We Have Condemned Them. Cecil Day Lewis. RSaN

Consider this and in our time. Consider. W. H. Auden. OxAEP-2

Consider Well. Sir Thomas More. SacPr

Considerable Speck, A. Robert Frost. MoAmPo; SAmP

Consideration. Bryan Martin Davies. BBMWP, tr. by Elin ap Hywel

Considering How Exaggerated Music Is. Leslie Scalapino. FTOS

Considering Poverty and Homelessness. Robert Sund. GifTon

Considering the graveness. State of Seige. Teresa Calderón. TANSG, tr. by Celeste Kostopulos-Cooperman

Considering the Snail. Thom Gunn. NAEL-6v2; NAEL-7v2; OxBEV; PtR; StAl

Considering Tulips. Mieke Tillema. TuT, tr. by Medbh McGuckian

Consolation. Tanure Ojaide. EmeKit

Consolation. David Rivard. SwNoth

Consolation. Dimitris Tsaloumas. BMAP

Consolation Aria. Johann Christian Günther. GePo, tr. by George C. Schoolfield

Consolation: "I wend to the sea." Micheál Fanning. IrLP

Consolation of Philosophy, The ("De Consolacione Philosophie"). Boethius. tr. by Queen of England Elizabeth I, Henry Vaughan, Helen Waddell and John Walton
   "All human kind on earth." NoSic
   "Happy he whose eyes have view'd." OBVE
   Heu Quam Precipiti. OBMV
   Huc omnes pariter. OBMV
   Lib. 2. Metrum 5. NOSC; OBVE
   "O thou whose pow'r o'er moving worlds presides." OBVE
   "Though countless as the Grains of Sand." OBVE

Consolation: "Yes, let us speak, with lips confirming." William Larminie. IrLP Fr. Fand.

Consolations Before an Affair, Upper West Side. Noelle Kocot. BAP-01

Consolations of Philosophy. Derek Mahon. HarvBoo

Console her. with larkspur, delphinium, Galanthus (milk blooms, piercing snow, white). Sylva Legris. PoPra Fr. Negative Garden.

Consorting with Angels. Anne Sexton. MoWP; NALW

Conspiracy: "Violin which is following me, A." Jack Spicer. APSN; CalPo

Conspiracy, The. Robert Hill Long. OPRER

Constable Calls, A. Seamus Heaney. ArBi; EmeKit Fr. Singing School.

Constable's Clouds for Keats. Stanley Plumly. BodElec

Constance Hately. Edgar Lee Masters. APT-1 Fr. Spoon River Anthology.

Constancy. Michael Field. ViWPN; VWP

Constancy. Elsa Gidlow. PoBW

Constancy. John Wilmot, 2d Earl of Rochester. OBEV

Constancy to an Ideal Object. Samuel Taylor Coleridge. NAEL-6v2; NOBRP

Constancy[e]. Sidney Godolphin. NOSC

Constant Bride, The. Mary Jo Bang. NAPBL

Constant keeping-past of shaken trees. Dante Gabriel Rossetti. NPeEn Fr. Trip to Paris and Belgium, A.

Constant Lover, A [or The]. Sir John Suckling. BASC; CavPo; NAEL-6v1; NAEL-7v1; NBLV; NoP-4; NOSC; NPeEn; OxAEP-1; OxBEV; PBRV Fr. Poem with the Answer, A.

Constant Memories. Patrick Sylvain. InTrad

Constant North, The. J. F. Hendry. EdScPo; GoPo

Constant Penelope Sends to Thee. Unknown. NAEL-6v1,

Constant Penelope sends to thee, careless Ulysses. *Unknown.* NoSic; NPeEn, *tr. by* Ovid

Constant, The. A. R. Ammons. WeW-3

Constant welcome floors me, The. Constant Welcome, The. Siobhan Campbell. MFPA

Constant Welcome, The. Siobhan Campbell. MFPA

Constantinople. Mihály Csokonai Vitéz. IQMS, *tr. by* Kenneth White

Constantly I write this happily. Lyn Hejinian. NAMCP V.2 *Fr.* Happily.

Constantly Risking Absurdity. Lawrence Ferlinghetti. CalPo; PmAP

Constellation Frigidaire, The. Kim Roberts.
   Darkness Was Upon the Face of the Deep. AmPoNex
   Tilt, The. AmPoNex

Constellation of Dead Brothers. Victor Serge. AF, *tr. by* James Brook

Constellation: Prose Poem. Bruno Schulz. ArBi, *tr. by* Celina Wieniewska

Constellation Quilt, The. Mei-Mei Berssenbrugge. OpBo

Constellations, The. William Cullen Bryant. APN-1

Constellations in the corners. Having unwound their masters' togas. Matthea Harvey. IAoNAP *Fr.* Thermae.

Constellations of Self, The. Tracy Philpot. IAoNAP

Constellations rise, The. (LL) Well, The. Jay Macpherson. BrAP; NoP-4

Constipation. Breyten Breytenbach. PoetW, *tr. by* A. J. Coetzee

Constipation. Ronald Wallace. SUP

Constrained Response. Maxianne Berger. IFF

Construction of the Museum. Michael Palmer. BodElec; WoBe

Construction Papers. Greta Goetz.
   "Pianist looks like an airline pilot who's afraid to land, The." FreRad

Constructions weaken in the vortex of dust. Horizon. Laura Solórzano. SPV, *tr. by* Jen Hofer

Construed entity too, A. All's All. A. R. Ammons. NoP-5

Consult your tongue like a weather forecast. In the Waiting Room. Linda France. PoCu

Consultation. Jayne Cortez. SurWo

Consulting summer's clock. Emily Dickinson. SAmP

Consulting the omens. Kamalākānta Bhattācārya. SinGod, *tr. by* Rachel Fell McDermott

Consume their flesh before they die. (LL) Octopus. Caitríona O'Reilly. NIrP; StAl

Consumer's Report, A. Peter Porter. EmeKit; NoP-4; NoP-5

Consummate summer. Rome. Peter Huchel. GTCP, *tr. by* Reinhold Grimm

Consumptive man, The. Richard Wright. APT-2

Consumptive, The. Priscilla Jane Thompson. CBWP-2

Contact. Alison Chisholm. Prnts

Contact Sheet. Michael Murphy. NIrP

Container of Stars. Pat Reed. WANABP

Containing little or nothing. House Face. D. A. Powell. IAoNAP

Contains a complete eye of water. (LL) Glass Bubbles, The. Samuel Greenberg. APT-1; OxBoAm

Conte à mon chien. Caroline Anne Bowles Southey.
   Tale of the Reign of Terror, A. DiBP

Contemns its Power. Mary Robinson. CenSon

Contemns Philosophy. Mary Robinson. CenSon; RWP

Contémplalos. / Dormidos, con un aire de aldea. Soldados se Duermen, Los. Rafael Alberti. RaW

Contemplate all this work of Time. Alfred Tennyson. BrAP; NAEL-6v2; NAEL-7v2; NAWM-7v2 *Fr.* In Memoriam A. H. H.

Contemplating Hell. Bertolt Brecht. WoPoe, *tr. by* Robert Firmage

Contemplating hell, as I once heard it. Contemplating Hell. Bertolt Brecht. WoPoe, *tr. by* Robert Firmage

Contemplating the sky. Tranquil Night. Luís De León. SpanPo, *tr. by* Edwin Morgan

Contemplation Is Mourning. Tim Lilburn. OpeFie

Contemplation on Bassets Down-Hill by the Most Sacred Adorer of the Muses Mrs. A. K., A. Anne Kemp. EMWP

Contemplation upon Flowers, A. Henry King, Bishop of Chichester. OBEV; PtR

Contemplations. Anne Bradstreet. ColAP; NAAL-3; NAAL-5; NAAPv.1; TCAPo
   "Shall I then praise the heavens, the trees, the earth." NOSC
   "When I behold the heavens as in their prime." OxBoAm

Contemplations of Mary. Roy McFadden. PNI

Contemporáneos. Antonio Deltoro. RMCMP

Contemporania. Ezra Pound.
   Tenzone. PoA 2002

Contemporaries. Antonio Deltoro. RMCMP, *tr. by* Christian Viveros-Fauné

Contemporary. Hortense King Flexner. PoA 2002

Contemporary. Alejandrino Hufana. ReBoTo

Contemporary American Poetry. Alan Feldman. BAP-01

Contemporary Criticism, A. William Wetmore Story.
   "He thanked me for my kindness, disagreed." APN-1

Contemporary Culture and the Letter "K." Alfred Corn. NoP-4

Contemporary Folk Songs. Yi Chehyŏn. CATKP, *tr. by* Peter H. Lee
   "At a wash place by the stream under a drooping willow." CATKP, *tr. by* Peter H. Lee
   "I carve a small rooster from wood." CATKP, *tr. by* Peter H. Lee
   "Long ago in Silla, Venerable Ch'ŏyong." CATKP, *tr. by* Peter H. Lee
   "Magpie chatters in a flowering bough by the hedge, A." CATKP, *tr. by* Peter H. Lee

Contemporary Jezebel, The. Elin Llwyd Morgan. BBMWP, *tr. by* the author and Richard Poole

Contemporary Muse, The. Edgell Rickword. OBSV

Contemporary Poet, A. Steve Wilson. AmPoNex

Contend in a sea which the land partly encloses. Yachts, The. William Carlos Williams. APT-1; BrAP; HeIP-4; MoAmPo; NAAPv.2; NAMCP V.1; NoAM; NoP-4; NoP-5; SAmP; TFi

Contend to beare his bodie to his soule. (LL) Feltons Epitaph. *Unknown.* NPeEn; PBRV

Contending / Temple bell. Takai Kito. ZenPo, *tr. by* Takashi Ikemoto and Lucien Stryk

Content and Resolute. William Drummond of Hawthornden. NPeEn; PBRV

Content and Ri[t]ch[e]. Robert Southwell. ChIV-2; NoSic

Content of History Will be Poetry, The. Edward Sanders. PFTM-2 *Fr.* Investigative Poetry.

Content though blind, had I no better guide. (LL) To Mr. Cyriack Skinner upon His Blindness. John Milton. NOSC; NPeEn

Content with chipped bowl and tattered robe. Tosui Unkei. ZenPo *tr. with* Takashi Ikemoto and Lucien Stryk

Contented that such hap[p]inesses move. (LL) Mary Sidney Wroth, Countess of Montgomery. BASC; NAEL-7v1; PEW *Fr.* Pamphilia to Amphilanthus.

Contenteder—to die. (LL) My Portion is Defeat—today. Emily Dickinson. APN-2; FaBoWar; OBWP; PCW

Contention of Ajax and Ulysses, The. James Shirley.
   (Dirge.) NoP-4; NoP-5

Contentment. William Cowper. ChIV-2 *Fr.* Olney Hymns.

Contentment. Oliver Wendell Holmes. APN-1; OxBoAm *Fr.* Autocrat of the Breakfast Table, The.

Contentment Is a Sleepy Thing. Thomas Traherne. BBASP

Contentment: "Strung along back elm." J. B. Bryan. ICANM

Contentment, to a Friend. Charlotte MacCarthy. PoBW

Contentment: "Why am I." Brian MacGuigan. IrLP

Contentment: "Woke up to the finches crowing." Miriam Sagan. WANABP

Contents of an Ink-bottle, The. Mary Elizabeth Coleridge. VWP

Continent as the Letter M, The. Douglas Crase. OxBoAm

Continent o Venus. Alexander Scott. EdScPo

Continental Walk. Allen Fisher. PFTM-2

Continental (You Kiss While You're Dancing), The. Herb Magidson. ReLy

Continent's Edge. Mark Wunderlich. WiU

Continent's End. Robinson Jeffers. CalPo

Continual Song. Michael Haslem.
   84 01. Oth
   No Bloody Matter 43 42. Oth
   01 84. Oth
   30 55. Oth

Continually they cackle thus. Sir Osbert Sitwell. PoWW *Fr.* How Shall We Rise to Greet the Dawn?

Continue; I'll discover where you sweat (Kierkegaard). John Cage. PFTM-2 *Fr.* Diary: How to Improve the World (You Will Only Make Matters Worse).

Continued Song of Longing. Chŏng Ch'ŏl. CATKP, *tr. by* Peter H. Lee

Continues in the Same State of Feeling. Francisco de Quevedo y Villegas. BLPSL, *tr. by* Rene de Costa, Rigas Kappatos and Eleni Paidoussi

Continuity. George Russell. MoBrPo

Continuity of Life. William Bell Scott. OxBSo

Continuous. Tony Harrison. NPeEn

Continuous Time. Milo De Angelis. NeIt, *tr. by* Lawrence Venuti

Continuum. Allen Curnow. HarvBoo

Contortionist. Lee Upton. AmAlph

Contour of an outline constrains the masked face and the limbs, The. Hermitage Road, The. Anne-Marie Albiach. YaTCFP, *tr. by* Keith Waldrop

Contours. Noël Coward. UV

Contours d'une délinéation s'exercent sur le visage masqué et les membres, Les. Anne-Marie Albiach. YaTCFP *Fr.* Chemin de l'ermitage, Le.

Contra, The. Sandra M. Castillo. TouFir

Contraband. Denise Levertov. BLT

Contraband. Lamont B. Steptoe. FuFl

Contract. (For The Destruction and Rebuilding of Paterson), A. Imamu Amiri Baraka. FTOS

Contract is over and yet, The. *Hawaiian Oral Tradition.* NAAPv.2

Contract Mucker, The. Wilson H. Thomson. IFF

Contracting Universe, The. William J. Tait. EdScPo

Contradiction. Alice Cary. NAAPv.1

Contradictions: Tracking Poems. Adrienne Rich.
  "Dear Adrienne, / I feel signified by pain." PoCu
  "My mouth hovers across your breasts." LW; NIL-7

Contrail's white scimitar unsheathes, A. Jihad. J. D. McClatchy. AmWaPo

Contraption,—that's the bizarre, proper slang. John Davidson. NePenScot Fr. Crystal Palace, The.

Contrary Motion. Elizabeth Garrett. NeBl

Contrary Theses (I). Wallace Stevens. SAmP

Contrast, A. James Russell Lowell. NCAP

Contrast, A. Menella Bute Smedley. VWP

Contrast, The. Royall Tyler.
  "Father and I went to camp." NAAL-3
  "Marblehead's a rocky place." NAAL-3
  Prologue. NAAL-3
  Song. NAAL-3

Contrasts. Blaise Cendrars. CuPo

Contrasts. Iain Crichton Smith. NePenScot

Contrefable d'Orphée. Marie-Claire Bancquart. YaTCFP

Contretemps, A. Robert Pollok. STuOW Fr. Course of Time, The.

Contribution on Pornography, A. Wisława Szymborska. PoSu, tr. by Adam Czerniawski

Contribution to Statistics, A. Wisława Szymborska. PtR; TWF, tr. by Stanisław Barańczak and Clare Cavanagh

Contributors to Geometry: Cold Hands. Adam Dickinson. PoPra

Contrite Heart, The. William Cowper. NPeEn

Contrition. Ralph Knevet. ChIV-2

Contrition. Henry More. NOSC Fr. Psychozoia, or, the Life of the Soul.

Control. Janice W. Hodges. BtF

Control of the passes was, he saw, the key. Secret Agent, The. W. H. Auden. NAMCP V.1

Controlling Factors. Mary Ruefle. ExTi

Conundrum of the Workshops, The. Rudyard Kipling. MoBrPo

Convalescence. David McCord. AmWit

Convalescing in London. Thomas M. Disch. RA

Convenience. Richard Murphy. ModIr Fr. Price of Stone, The.

Convent in '45, The. Maria Luisa Spaziani. NeIt, tr. by Beverly Allen

Convent Threshold, The. Christina Georgina Rossetti. NALW; NoP-4; NoP-5; VWP

Conventions of the time. Earthly Love. Louise Glück. NAMCP V.2

Convergence of the Twain, The. Thomas Hardy. BrAP; CABP; GPTC; HarvBoo; HeIP-4; MakPoe; MoBrPo; NAEL-6v2; NAEL-7v2; NAMCP V.1; NIL-7; NIP-4; NoAM; NoP-4; NoP-5; NPeEn; OxBEV; PoPoPo; TFi; WaAnP

Convergences / of the spirit! What. Pavane. Ronald Stuart Thomas. HarvBoo

Conversation. Buson. NTCP

Conversation. Mihangel Morgan. BBMWP; BeAl, tr. by Martin Davis

Conversation. Ágnes Nemes Nagy. IQMS, tr. by Adam Makkai

Conversation. Dan Pagis. VCWP, tr. by Stephen Mitchell

Conversation, A. Gisèle Prassinos. PFTM-1

Conversation among the Mountains. Li Po. CCL1, tr. by David Young

Conversation begins, A / with a lie. And each. Cartographies of Silence. Adrienne Rich. WaAnP

Conversation between Me and the Women. Anna Petrovna Bunina. ARWW, tr. by Sibelan Forrester

Conversation between Two Sisters, One Choosing an Aged Man, and the Other Choosing Youth, A. Angharad Pritchard. EMWP

Conversation Class. Dorothy Molloy. NIrP

Conversation Galante. T. S. Eliot. TCAPo

Conversation in Front of a Helicopter. Rosario Murillo. CLPP, tr. by Alejandro Murguía

Conversation in Gibraltar 1943. Charles Causley. PoWW

Conversation in Woodside. Kim Addonizio. GeoHom

Conversation of prayers about to be said, The. Conversation of Prayer, The. Dylan Thomas. NoP-4; NoP-5; OxAEP-2

Conversation of the Deaf, The. Bobi Jones. BBMWP, tr. by Joseph P. Clancy

Conversation Piece. Eunice De Souza. NAMCP V.2

Conversation Through the Door, A. Anna Swirszczynska [or Swir]. AF, tr. by Czesław Miłosz

Conversation with a Cat. Yelena Shwarts. CRWP, tr. by Stephanie Sandler

Conversation with a Japanese Student. Eleanor Wilner. GifTon

Conversation with a New York Poet. Lev Vladimir Loseff. TCRusP, tr. by Henry Pickford

Conversation with a Survivor. Erich Fried. BeAl, tr. by Stuart Hood

Conversation with cancer, The. Death Who. Philip Hodgins. BMAP

Conversation with Death, A. Sileas Na Ceapaich. EMWP

Conversation with Duke Ellington and Louis (Pops) Armstrong. Carmen D. Lucca. BRtP

Conversation with Isadora Duncan. Molly Bendall. AmPoNex

Conversation with the Sun Bittern. Ansel Talvikki. PoDa

Conversational Melody, A Good Verse, A. Nikolai Alekseievich Klyuyev. TCRusP, tr. by John Glad

Conversations are simple: about food, The. Under the Window: Ouro Prêto. Elizabeth Bishop. VCAP

Conversations in Courtship. *Unknown.* tr. by Ezra Pound and Noel Stock
  Pleasant Songs of the Sweetheart Who Meets You in the Fields. WoPoe, tr. by Ezra Pound and Noel Stock

Conversations in the Mountains. Li Po. RaBo; TAL, tr. by Robert Payne

Conversations in the struggle. Pamela Plummer. BRtP

Conversations with a Toad. Robert Bringhurst.
  "Behind you: the owl, whose eyes." PoCoUp

Conversations with Louis. Jane Duran. MoWP

Conversations with Strangers. George Buchanan. PNI

Conversion. Jodi Braxton. EGAG

Conversion of S. Paul, The. George Wither. ChIV-2

Conversion of Saint Paul, The. Michael Waters. Vesp

Conversion of stones into bread would be a supernatural miracle, The. W. H. Auden. GI Fr. "Prolific and the Devourer," The.

Conversions. Neal Bowers. AllShUp

Convert, The. G. K. Chesterton. ChIV-2; SacPr

Conveying the effects of atmosphere. Appalachian Trees Encircled by Police Tape. Greg Williamson. NeAmPo

Convict held his breath in the shadow of the doorway as the, The. Downward Mobility. Lewis Warsh. BAP-97

Convict of Clonmel, The. *Irish Oral Tradition.* IrV, tr. by Jeremiah Joseph Callanan

Conviction. T. H. Parry-Williams. BBMWP, tr. by Richard Poole

Conviction fills the body. Radio. Barrett Watten. PmAP

Conviction (iv). Stevie Smith. LW

Convicts' Rum Song. *Unknown.* FaBoVe; NOBAu

Convict's Tour to Hell, A. Francis MacNamara. NOBAu

Convinced by Sorrow. Elizabeth Barrett Browning. SacPr Fr. Cry of the Human, The.

Convito. Dante Alighieri. tr. by Howard Nemerov (Banquet: *Dissertation 2, Canzone 1,* The.) WoPoe, tr. by Howard Nemerov

Convolvulus Tricolor. Leslie Adrienne Miller. SweBea

Convoy. Bruce Weigl. MotU

Convoy Escort. Rudyard Kipling. WoPoe Fr. Epitaphs of the War [1914–1918].

Convoy under a continent of storm, A. Amphibians. Robert Fitzgerald. PWW2

Convulsed, foaming immortal blood: farewell. (LL) Professor's Song, A. John Berryman. BrAP; HeIP-4; NoAM

Convulsions came; and, where the field. Apparition, The—A Retrospect. Herman Melville. APN-2; NAAPv.1; NCAP; TCAPo

Cook admired the native courage, made. Rex Ingamells. NOBAu Fr. Great South Land, The.

Cook County. Archibald MacLeish. IllVoic

(Weather.) MoAmPo

Cookie Poem, The. Jeff Gundy. ACAMVP

Cookies for Peace. Hal Sirowitz. PA9/11

Cooking. Ayin Adams. BRtP

Cooking Catalogue. Jill Breckenridge. SweBea

Cooking, it seems, is not your forte. Hungary. Sándor Petőfi. IQMS, tr. by Peter Zollman

Cooking Lesson. Zarina Mullan Plath. SweBea

Cooking to Music. Edward Kleinschmidt. MiVo

Cool as from underground springs and pure enough to drink. (LL) Man-Moth, The. Elizabeth Bishop. APT-2; MoAmPo; NALW; NAMCP V.2; NoAM

Cool black night thru the redwoods. First Party at Ken Kesey's with Hell's Angels. Allen Ginsberg. PmAP; TRP

Cool breeze. Issa. EMJL, tr. by Haruo Shirane

Cool breezes—I sleep by the open window. *Unknown.* CCL1 Fr. Tzu Yeh Songs.

Cool brisk fingers in my hair. April in Hollywood. Wanda Coleman. GeoHom

Cool Cat. Michael Myer. TriCat

Cool, clear autumn morning, so still. Skywriting. Jamie Grant. EmeKit

Cool, damp forest shakes, The. Snakes. Nikolai Alekseievich Zabolotsky. TCRusP, *tr. by* Denis Johnson and Kathy Lewis

Cool fall night, A. Basho. EH, *tr. by* Robert Hass

Cool inaccessible air. Lola Ridge. APT-1 *Fr.* Ghetto, The.

Cool it is, and still. Basho. TAL

Cool Nights. Yvor Winters. NAAPv.2 *Fr.* Magpie's Shadow, The.

Cool of bamboo invades my room, The. Restless Night. Tu Fu [*or* Du Fu]. CCL1, *tr. by* Burton Watson

Cool perfume of bamboo pervades my room. Summer Night. Tu Fu [*or* Du Fu]. TAL

Cool shades and dews are round my way. Scene on the Banks of the Hudson, A. William Cullen Bryant. NAAPv.1

Cool small evening shrunk to a dog bark and the clank of a bucket, A. Full Moon and Little Frieda. Ted Hughes. HarvBoo; NPeEn; OPOU; StAl

Cool surface, The. Jerry Kilbride. WhBo

Cool Tombs. Carl Sandburg. APT-1; HeIP-4; MoAmPo; NAMCP V.1; NoAM; TCAPo; TFi

Cool Web, The. Robert Graves. BrAP; HarvBoo; NAEL-6v2; NAEL-7v2; NAMCP V.1; NoAM; OxBEV; WoPoe

Coole Park and Ballylee, 1931. William Butler Yeats. NoAM; OBGa; OBMV

Coole Park, 1929. William Butler Yeats. CABP; OBMV

Coolie. Sándor Weöres. IQMS, *tr. by* Edwin Morgan

Coolie cane chop. Coolie. Sándor Weöres. IQMS, *tr. by* Edwin Morgan

Coolin, The. James Stephens. IrLP

Cool-matted silvery bed; but no dreams, A. She Sighs on Her Jade Lute. Wen T'ing-yün. CCL1, *tr. by* Witter Bynner

Coolness. Basho. EH, *tr. by* Robert Hass

Coolness. Basho. EMJL, *tr. by* Haruo Shirane

Coolness. Buson. EH; NIL-7, *tr. by* Robert Hass

Coolness, like the evening tide. Brother, I Am Here. "Shu Ting." GifTon, *tr. by* Carolyn Kizer and Y. H. Zhao

Coolness of melons. Basho. EH, *tr. by* Robert Hass

Coolun, The. Maurice Dugan. IrV, *tr. by* Sir Samuel Ferguson

Coombe Ellen. William Lisle Bowles.
   "Call the strange spirit that abides unseen." NPBRoP

Coons in the Corn. Alice Ewing Vail. TiP2

Cooper. James Russell Lowell. TCAPo *Fr.* Fable for Critics, A.

Cooper, whose name is with his country's woven. Red Jacket. Fitz-Greene Halleck. APN-1

Cooper's Hill. Sir John Denham. CABP; PBRV
   "Here should my wonder dwell, and here my praise." NAEL-6v1; NOSC; NPeEn
   "O could I flow like thee, and make thy stream." NPeEn
   Thames from Cooper's Hill, The. OxAEP-1; OxBEV

Coora Flower, The. Gwendolyn Brooks. IllVoic; NAAL-5; NIL-7; NoP-4

Coordinating cities gulls still gull, and, arms binged with wine, as wine. Ted Greenwald. FTOS *Fr.* Licorice Chronicles.

Coordinating Conjunction. John Hollander. PoA 2002

Coorie Doon. Matt McGinn. EdScPo

Coosaponakeesa (Mary Mathews Musgrove Bosomsworth), Leader of the Creeks, 1700–1783. Rayna Green. AmWaPo

Cop pulls a car over to tag investigation, something dull. While Watching *Cops* I Think of You. Virginia Chase Sutton. MAAN

Cop, The / with the gun full of faulkner. 7-30-96. Erren Geraud Kelly. BtF

Copa de Oro (The California Poppy). Ina Coolbrith. ASA

Copacetic Mingus. Yusef Komunyakaa. OxAAAP

Copano, 1834. Bryce Milligan. TiP2

Copernicus. Robert David Fitzgerald. NOBAu

Cope's Coney Island Café has a steak. Canyon, Texas Sestina. E. A. Mares. ICANM

Copier. *Unknown.* SonAtl, *tr. by* Colin Thewley

Coplas. AF, *tr. by* Robert Bly

Coplas about the Soul Which Suffers with Impatience to See God. San Juan de la Cruz.
   "I live without inhabiting/ Myself." OBVE

Coppers. Boris Abramovich Slutsky. TCRusP, *tr. by* Daniel Weissbort

Cop's face for an odd second, The. Pharoah's Army Got Drowned. Lynn Domina. OPRER

Coptic Socks. Roy Fuller. OBCoV

Copula. John Cope. GeoH

Copular y llover me recuerdan la noche blanca de un sauce. Reunión de violonchelos. Ernesto Lumbreras. RMCMP

Copulating Gods, The. Carolyn Kizer. BrAP

Copy of an Intercepted Despatch from His Excellency Don Strepitoso Diabolo. Thomas Moore. OBSV

Copy [*or* copie] out on[e]ly that, and save expense. (LL) Jordan (2). George Herbert. BASC; CABP; FSCP; NAEL-6v1; NAEL-7v1; NOSC; OBWVE; PBRV; SacPr

Copyright Renewal Under the Texaco Star. Jeffrey Dye. PoDa

Copy-writer's Dream, The. Bruce Dawe. BMAP

Coquetting through chiffon and rose bouquets. Tan Chanteuse, The. Carole Boston Weatherford. FuFl

Coral. Katie Donovan. NIrP

Coral and shells are heaped until it seems. Clouds, The. Thomas M. Disch. RA

Coral Grove, The. James Gates Percival. APN-1; ColAP

Coral Reef, The. John Blight. NOBAu

Coral toy, A. (LL) Emmett Till. James A. Emanuel. NIL-7; NIP-4

Coral-footed pigeons chortle in the rafters of the loading shed, The. Wake of Plenty, The. Roy Scheele. MotU

Coralie. Frederick Goddard Tuckerman. NCAP

Corals and Shells. William Bronk. APSN

Corazón mecánico. Josué Ramírez. RMCMP

Corazón negro con alas. Miguel de Unamuno. RaW *Fr.* Cancionero *Diario Poético* 1928–1936.

Cord. Gu Cheng. WoBe *Fr.* Liquid Mercury.

Cord, The. Leanne O'Sullivan. P180

Cordate head meanders through himself, The. Pit Viper. N. Scott Momaday. HATNAP

Cordeilla. Ann Lauinger. IaFF *Fr.* Three Songs for *King Leir*.

Cordelia, we needed more from you. Ordeal of Love, The. Joan Raymund. IaFF

Córdoba. / Distant and alone. Song of the Rider. Federico García Lorca. WED, *tr. by* Robert Bly

Cordon Negro. Essex Hemphill. CAGL

Cords. Kiren Shoman. OWABP

Cords made of cries. Bonds. Guillaume Apollinaire. CuPo

Core. Kim Chiha. CAMKP, *tr. by* Kevin O'Rourke

Core of every core, the kernel of every kernel, The. Buddha Inside the Light. Rainer Maria Rilke. WED, *tr. by* Robert Bly

Corfu appears, and then the distant blue. On the Ferry, Toward Patras. Emily Grosholz. RA

Coridon's Song. John Chalkhill. NOSC

Corinna at the Capitol. Felicia Dorothea Hemans. VWP

Corinna Bathes. George Chapman. OxAEP-1 *Fr.* Ovid's Banquet of Sense.

Corinna, from Athens, to Tanagra. Walter Savage Landor. OBEV *Fr.* Pericles and Aspasia.

Corinna In Vendome. Pierre de Ronsard. WoPoe, *tr. by* Robert Mezey

Corinna, pride of Drury Lane. Beautiful Young Nymph Going to Bed, A. Jonathan Swift. EroLit; NoP-5; NPeEn; OxBEV

Corinna's Going a-Maying. Robert Herrick. AEP; BASC; BrAP; CABP; NAEL-6v1; NAEL-7v1; NIP-4; NoP-4; NoP-5; NOSC; OBEV; OxBEV; PBRV; PoPoPo; TFi; WaAnP

Corinne's Last Love-Song. Lady Jane Francesca Wilde. IrLP; VWP

Coriolan. T. S. Eliot.
   Triumphal March. AmWaPo; OBWP

Coriolanus. William Shakespeare.
   "Madam, the Lady Valeria is come to visit you." OxAEP-1
   "Read it not, noble lords." OxAEP-1
   "Why dost not speak?" OxAEP-1

Coriolis Effect, The. Chuck Wachtel. PrTe

Cormorant. Peter Preece. AngWePo

Cormorant. Lucien Stryk. IllVoic

Cormorant, The. Rosanna Warren. PfSP

Cormorant carries the universe, The. Drowning Water. Don Domanski. Coast

Cormorant fishing / How stirring. Basho. ZenPo, *tr. by* Takashi Ikemoto and Lucien Stryk

Cormorant in Its Element, The [*with music*]. Amy Clampitt. NoP-4; NoP-5

Cormorant still screams, The. Late. Louise Bogan. APT-2

Cormorant-boat, The. Shunzei. WoPoe, *tr. by* Valerie Durham

Cormorants. John Kinsella. OWoS

Cormorants. Thomas O'Grady. Coast

Corn. Bernadette Mayer. NYP2

Corn, The [*with music*]. Daniel David Moses. HATNAP

Corn Ceremony. *Apache Oral Tradition.* TCAPo

Corn Children. Carol Lee Sanchez. HW

Corn, corn, sweet Indian corn. William W. Cook. VerBaPo *Fr.* Indian Corn.

Corn grows large, the rushes tall, The. Autumn on the Riverbank. Chao Shan-ch'ing. CrYelRi, *tr. by* Sam Hamill

Corn is a small hard seed. Corn. Bernadette Mayer. NYP2

Corn is universal. Seed. Ruth Stone. PoChi

Corn King beckoning to his Spring Queen, The. (LL) Girl in a Library, A. Randall Jarrell. InGu; NoAM

Corn Song. *Unknown.* APN-2, *tr. by* Henry Rowe Schoolcraft

Corn was Orient and Immortal Wheat, which never should, The. Thomas Traherne. NPeEn *Fr.* Centuries of Meditations.

Cornbread blues. Vincent Woodward. BtF

Corneal Graft. Anne Ridler. MoWP

Corneille's Pompey. Katherine Philips.
   Cornelia's Defiance. NOSC

Cornelian, The. Lord Byron. CAGL; TreFP

Cornelia's Defiance. Katherine Philips. NOSC *Fr.* Corneille's Pompey.

Cornelius sighs . . . the lines I write. Martial. RomPo, *tr. by* Peter Whigham

Corner. Amal Dunqul. PML, *tr. by* Sharif Elmusa and Thomas G. Ezzy

Corner *bodega* run by El Chino Chan, The. Rice Comes to El Volcán. Virgil Suárez. AmPoNex

Corner Boy's Farewell. Burns Singer. HarvBoo

Corner of the farmhouse, worn by wind, The. Uncle with Landscape—Kansas, 1954. Benjamin Vogt. RWB

Cornered and trapped, The. For Mack C. Parker. Pauli Murray. WaAnP

Cornering, holds it in spidery light. (LL) At Lansdowne Bridge. Arthur Nortje. HBAPE; TSAP

Corners. Kate Y. A. Bone. EdScPo

Corners. Stephen Dunn. PoA 2002

Cornerstone, A. Marble pilings. Curbstones and brick. It Was Raining in Delft. Peter Gizzi. IIR

Cornflowers. Ella Krylova. CRWP, *tr. by* Yury Drobyshev and Carol Rumens

Cornflowers, cornflowers, / little blue-eyed beacons. Cornflowers. Ella Krylova. CRWP, *tr. by* Yury Drobyshev and Carol Rumens

Corniche. Les A. Murray. NAMCP V.2

Cornkind. Frank O'Hara. CLPP

Cornucopia. Christopher Pearse Cranch. APN-1

Corona. Paul Celan. PoSu, *tr. by* Michael Hamburger

Coronach. Tracey Herd. NeBl

Coronado at Rio Grande Del Norte. Arthur M. Sampley. TiP2

Coronado Points. Alan Birkelbach. TiP2

Coronal, A. William Carlos Williams. OxBoAm; TCAPo

Coronation ceremony was in Belize this time, The. Mosquito Kingdom. Ernesto Cardenal. VCWP, *tr. by* Donald D. Walsh

Coronemus Nos Rosis Antequam Marcescant. Thomas Jordan. OBEV

Coroner. Elton Glaser. PBCAP

Coroner's Inquest. W. D. Snodgrass. OxBEV

Coronet, The. Andrew Marvell. BASC; BrAP; FSCP; NAEL-6v1; NAEL-7v1; NoP-4; NoP-5; NOSC; PBRV; SacPr

Coronet for His Mistress Philosophy, A. George Chapman.
   "But dwell in darkness, for your god is blind." OxBSo
   "For words want art and art wants words to praise her." OxBSo
   "Her look doth promise and her life assure." OxBSo
   "Love flows not from my liver but her living." OxBSo
   "Muses that fame's loose feathers beautify." OxBSo
   "Nor riches to the virtues of my love." OxBSo
   "Of her removed and soul-infused regard." OxBSo
   "So her close beauties further blaze her fame." OxBSo
   "To living virtues turns the deadly vices." OxBSo

Corporal. Ambrose Bierce. AmWit; APN-2 *Fr.* Devil's Dictionary, The.

Corporal Stare. Robert Graves. FaBoWar

Corporal Who Killed Archimedes, The. Miroslav Holub. PoSu, *tr. by* Ian Milner and Jarmila Milner

Corporeal. Robert Ayres. OPRER

Corporeal summer, no marvel is lost. True Western Summer. Hildegarde Flanner. APT-2

Corpse and Mirror III. John Yau. ReTh

Corpse of a Cat, The. Hagiwara Sakutaro. CAoMJL1, *tr. by* Hiroaki Sato

Corpse with streaming hair, A. (LL) Ballad of Hector in Hades. Edwin Muir. HarvBoo; NAMCP V.1; NoAM

Corpsebeach. Snorri Sturluson. SonAtl

Corpses, The. Lynn Emanuel. ExTi

Corpus Inscriptionum Latinarum 14.3565. *Unknown.* PriapPo, *tr. by* Richard W. Hooper

Corral de muertos, entre pobres tapias. En un Cementerio de Lugar Castellano. Miguel de Unamuno. RaW

Correct but cautious, that first night, we asked. James Merrill. NoP-4; NoP-5 *Fr.* Book of Ephraim, The.

Correct my fault[e]s, protect my life, direct me when I die [*or* dye]! (LL) Child[e] My Choice [*or* Choyse], A. Robert Southwell. OxBEV; SacPr

Correct temperatures, perfect sweetness. Evidence of Life. Afaa Michael Weaver. NevBe

Correction of proofs + desires in speed. Filippo Tommaso Marinetti. PFTM-1 *Fr.* Zang Tumb Tuuum.

Corrections. Thomas Heise. LegDan

Correlation which unites the human condition. Allen Fisher. Oth *Fr.* Emergent Manner.

Correspondence. Ilse Aichinger. GTCP, *tr. by* Michael Hamburger

Correspondence. Judith Ortiz Cofer. PueRic

Correspondence [*with music*]. Henri Coulette. PoA 2002

Correspondence between Mr. Harrison in Newcastle and Mr. Sholto Peach Harrison in Hull. Stevie Smith. NBLV

Correspondence School Instructor Says Goodbye to His Poetry Students, The. Galway Kinnell. NoAM; NoP-4; NoP-5; PoA 2002

Correspondences. Charles Baudelaire. NAWM-7v2, *tr. by* Richard Wilbur

Correspondences. Charles Baudelaire. SxFrPo, *tr. by* James McGowan

Correspondences. Christopher Pearse Cranch. APN-1

Correspondences. Anne Stevenson.
   Daughter's difficulties as a wife, A: Mrs Ruben Chandler to her mother in New Orleans. MoWP

Corrida. Pedro Serrano. RMCMP

Corrido Blanco. Alfred Arteaga. ASA

Corrido of "Gregorio Cortez." *Unknown.* NAAPv.2

Corrido of the Uprooted Ones. *Unknown.* NAAPv.2

Corrugated iron shack. One room, A. Cradle, The. Roland Robinson. NOBAu

Corruption. Freddy Macha. NAfrP

Corruption. Srikanth Reddy. LegDan

Corruption. Henry Vaughan. NAEL-6v1; NAEL-7v1; NOSC

Corsair, The. Lord Byron.
   "O'er the glad waters of the dark blue sea."
   "Unlike the heroes of each ancient race." NOBRP

Corset Mystère, Le. André Breton. YaTCFP

Corsons Inlet. A. R. Ammons. ColAP; InGu; NAAL-5; NAMCP V.2; NoAM; NoP-4; NoP-5; OxBoAm; VCAP; WaAnP

Cors-y-Gwaed: Fenland of Blood. A. G. Prys-Jones. AngWePo

Cortège. Paul Verlaine. OBVE, *tr. by* Arthur Symons

Cortège of Daughters, A. Elizabeth Smither. BeAl

Cortes Swamp, The. Clovis L. Nazareno. ReBoTo

Cortez's Horse. Pat Mora. UnSA

Cosas, Las. Gloria Fuertes. RaW

Cosas, nuestras cosas, Las. Cosas, Las. Gloria Fuertes. RaW

Cosas que se tocan sonidos materiales surcaron. Angélica Tornero. SPV

Cosmetics do no good. Cosmetics Do No Good. Steve Kowit. BLT

Cosmic Realities Vanilla Tobacco Wakings. Tristan Tzara. YaTCFP, *tr. by* Mary Ann Caws and Jean-Pierre Cauvin

Cosmogony. *Unknown.* WoPoe, *tr. by* Richard Taylor

Cosmology. *Unknown.* WoPoe, *tr. by* J. Moussaieff Masson and W. S. Merwin
   (Goddess Laksmi, The.) HW

Cosmopolitan Poetry. János Arany. IQMS, *tr. by* Madeline Mason

Cosmos in London. Arthur Nortje. HBAPE

Cosmos shows his power, The. Cosmos Shows His Power, The. Manuel González Prada. SpanPo, *tr. by* William M. Davis

Cosmus hath more discoursing in his head. Sir John Davies. NoSic *Fr.* Epigrams.

Cossacks snatched him from his mother, The. My Greatgreatuncle the Archbishop. Ruth Whitman. TaR

Cossante. Pero Meogo. WoPoe, *tr. by* Yvor Winters

Cost of Seriousness, The [*with music*]. Peter Porter. NoAM

Cost of Truth, The. Carlos Bousoño. RaW, *tr. by* Lewis Hyde

Cost you your railway lines, washing lines, sex on billboards. To Look Out Once from High Windows. Sinéad Morrissey. MFPA

Costanza. Felicia Dorothea Hemans. RWP

Costumes are a kind of late-colonial, The. Totalled. Peter McDonald. PNI

Côte de Liesse. Daryl Hine. NoP-4

Cotillion. Carl Phillips. WiU

Cottage for Sale, A. Larry Conley. ReLy

Cottage Hospital, The. Sir John Betjeman. BrAP; InoFa; NAMCP V.1

Cottage in Grasmere Vale, A. Dorothy Wordsworth. *See* Peaceful Our Valley, Fair and Green.

Cottage in the Wood, A. Russell Edson. MotU

Cottage Pictures. Samuel Jackson Pratt. OBGa

Cottage Song. John Drinkwater. UV

Cottage Street, 1953. Richard Wilbur. BodElec; CAP-8; NoP-5; PoPoPo

Cottage, The. Jones Very. APN-1

Cotter's Saturday Night [nscribed to Robert Aiken [*or* R. A****], Esq.], The. Robert Burns. NOBRP; TreFP

Cotton. Harry Edmund Martinson. WED, *tr. by* Robert Bly

Cotton and Gladiolas. Joy Lahey. AnSo

Cotton Boll, The. Henry Timrod. APN-2

Cotton eyes soaking up blood. Blue Monday. Calvin Forbes. ESEAA

Cotton Flannelette. Les A. Murray. PoetW

Cotton in a Pill Bottle. Dean Young. ASA

Cotton Mather. Rosemary Benét and Stephen Vincent Benét. APT-2

Cotton Song. Jean Toomer. APT-2; NAAPv.2

Cottonwood Country. Louise Glück. WaAnP

Cou'd our first father, at his toilsome plough. Anne Finch, Countess of Winchilsea. *See* Could our first father, at his toilsome plough.

Cou'd we stop the time that's flying. Unequal Fetters, The. Anne Finch, Countess of Winchilsea. BrAP; OxBEV

Cougar. Brendan Galvin. UrbNat

Cough, A. Philip Whalen. WANABP *Fr.* Epigrams & Imitations.

Cough Drops. Sergio Kisielewsky. PML, *tr. by* John Oliver Simon

Cough twilight sheepskin coat, A. Guard. Viktor Krivulin. TCRusP, *tr. by* Daniel Weissbort

Could a man in your position. Where is Talcott Parsons Now? Sophie Hannah. MFPA

Could anyone among us. On a Clear Day You Can See Forever. Alan Jay Lerner. ReLy

Could be the missing word. (LL) Emmanuel Hocquard. OnScMo; YaTCFP *Fr.* At Christmas.

Could but compose man's image and his cry. (LL) Sorrow of Love, The [1927 Version]. William Butler Yeats. BrAP; NAEL-6v2; NAEL-7v2; OxBEV

Could conquer hate. (LL) Dangerous Doubts. Lorenzo Thomas. AnSo; FuFl

Could hardly tell what name were thine. (LL) Alfred Tennyson. NAEL-6v2; NAEL-7v2 *Fr.* In Memoriam A. H. H.

Could I but live again. Pisgah-Sights. II. Robert Browning. ChIV-1

Could I but ride indefinite. Emily Dickinson. SAmP

Could I have come back to you to wince. Visiting Zomba Plateau. Jack A. Mapanje. NAfrP

Could I leave her! I stayed behind. (LL) Second Thoughts. Michael Field. LW; ViWPN

Could it be, Bud. For Bud. Michael S. Harper. ESEAA; FaoP

Could it be Madness—this? (LL) First Day's Night had come, The. Emily Dickinson. IJHIL; NCAP; TRP

Could man be drunk for ever. A. E. Housman. NAEL-6v2; OBMV

Could not once blinding me, cruel[l], suffice? Samson to His Delilah. Richard Crashaw. ChIV-1

Could not snap the spectrum up for food as you have done. (LL) To a Chameleon. Marianne Moore. APT-1; NoP-5

Could our first father, at his toilsome plough. Adam Posed. Anne Finch, Countess of Winchilsea. ChIV-1; NoP-4; NoP-5

  (Cou'd our first father, at his toilsome plough.) NPeEn

  (Could our first father, at his toilsome plow.) NoP-4

Could take that / from him. (LL) William Carlos Williams. NAMCP V.1; NoAM *Fr.* Pictures from Brueghel.

Could the West creep in to your idea of happiness—abundance. Glass Heart. Dana Levin. LegDan

Could to my sight that heavenly face restore. (LL) Surprised by Joy. William Wordsworth. CABP; CenSon; GSo; NAEL-6v2; NAEL-7v2; NoP-4; NoP-5; NPBRoP; OxBSo; TFi

Could ye come back to me, Douglas, Douglas. Douglas, Douglas, Tender and True. Dinah Maria Mulock Craik. TreFP

  (Could you come back to me, Douglas, Douglas.) LW

Could you bid an acorn. Lover's Reply to Good Advice. Richard Hughes. MoBrPo

Could you come back to me, Douglas, Douglas. Dinah Maria Mulock Craik. *See* Could ye come back to me, Douglas, Douglas.

Could you not drink her gaze like wine? Card-Dealer, The. Dante Gabriel Rossetti. BrAP

Couldn't sleep last night! Conjured. Robert Nathaniel Dett. IFF

Coumbite. Hilario Batista Felix. OGAHCP, *tr. by* Boadiba and Jack Hirschman

Council Pool's chockablock, The. Debbie and Co. John Tranter. BMAP

Counsel of Birds, The. Ed Robeson. Eno

Counsel of Moderation, A. Francis Thompson. MoBrPo

Count. Ernst Jandl. OnScMo, *tr. by* James Sherry

Count and the Lady, The. Edward Robert Bulwer-Lytton. STuOW *Fr.* Count Rinaldo Rinaldi.

Count Carrots. Gerda Mayer. OBSP

Count each affliction, whether light or grave. Sorrow. Aubrey Thomas De Vere. SacPr

Count, if you can, every leaf on every tree. Anacreon. WoPoe, *tr. by* Sam Hamill

Count me among those almonds your eyes. Unworn. Dan Beachy-Quick. LegDan

Count Ossie. Opal Palmer Adisa. WaCA

Count Rinaldo Rinaldi. Edward Robert Bulwer-Lytton.

  Count and the Lady, The. STuOW

Count the number of times boards crack. Insomnia. Wyatt Prunty. RA

Count Your Blessings. Mrs. Henry Linden. CBWP-4

Countdown. Ron Penoyer. OtW

Countdown takeoff. To the Moon and Back. William Plomer. OBCoV

Counter-Attack. Siegfried Sassoon. MoBrPo; OxAEP-2; PoWW

Counter-Attack. Siegfried Sassoon.

  "Good-morning, good-morning! the General said." EMP

Counterblast against Garlic, A. Horace. NBLV *Fr.* Epodes.

Counter-Example, The. David Shapiro. PmAP

Counterfable of Orpheus. Marie-Claire Bancquart. MFP, *tr. by* Martin Sorrell

Counterfeit Earth!, The. Albert Goldbarth. ReTh

Counterfeiter, The. Michael Davitt. PBCIP, *tr. by* Philip Casey

Counterfeiter, The. Greg Williamson. AmPoNex; RA

Counterlove, A. *Unknown.* NoSic

Counterparts. Stephen Dobyns. PoA 2002

Counterpoint. Ronald Stuart Thomas.

  "To be alive then." BeAl

Counter's crackle piles up the digits. Willowherb. Peter Rafferty. NLP

Countess of Anglesey lead Captive by the Rebels, at the Disforresting of Pewsam, The. Sir William Davenant. PBRV

Countess P———'s Advice for New Girls. Natasha Trethewey. LegDan

Countesse of Pembroke's Arcadia, The. Sir Philip Sidney.

  (Bargain, The.) BLPJKO; OBEV; OxAEP-1

  Delight of Solitariness, The. NoSic

  Epithalamium: "Let mother Earth." OxAEP-1

  Madrigal. NoSic

  "My Muse what ails this ardour."

  My Sheep Are Thoughts. NoSic

  "My true love hath my heart [*or* hart], and I have his." NoSic; NPeEn; OxBEV; PtR; TFi; UV

  Sestina: "Farewell, O Sun." WaAnP

  "Since wailing is a bud of causeful sorrow." MakPoe

  "What length of verse can serve brave *Mopsa*'s good to show?" NoP-4; NoP-5

  Ye Goat-herd Gods. NAEL-6v1; NoSic

  (Ye Goatherd Gods.) NoP-4; NoP-5

Counting. Fleur Adcock. BeAl

Counting. Mark Bibbins. WiU

Counting. Judith Ortiz Cofer. PueRic

Counting. Issa. EMJL, *tr. by* Haruo Shirane

Counting. Philip Larkin. PoetW

Counting Breaths. Denise Lassaw-Paljor. WhBo

Counting my numberless fingers. (LL) Mountain Talk. A. R. Ammons. LPSFW; OxBoAm

Counting Sheep. Hamish Brown. EdScPo

Counting Sheep. Russell Edson. SUP

Counting Small-Boned Bodies. Robert Bly. AmWaPo

Counting the Beats. Robert Graves. HarvBoo; OxAEP-2; WeW-3; WoPoe

Counting the Children. Dana Gioia. RA

Counting the eyes that see. (LL) Message on Cape Cod, The. Afaa Michael Weaver. GT; PBCAP

Counting the Mad [*with music*]. Donald Justice. InGu; NIP-4; NoP-4; NoP-5; TRP

Counting the singles carefully. (LL) After Midnight. Louis Simpson. BLT; NoAM

Counting the Years. Anne Marie Macari. MotU

Counting-out Rhyme. Edna St. Vincent Millay. NOxBChV; SoSe-8

Countless birds. Simonides. SaLy, *tr. by* Diane Rayor

Countries and Explanations. Robert Pinsky. StAl *Fr.* Explanation of America, An.

Countries still trapped within the snare of servitude. On the Changes in France. János Batsányi. IQMS, *tr. by* Matthew Mead and Ruth Mead

Country. Diana Helen Melhem.

  "Person place thing tree." PoArWo

  "To write the country." PoArWo

Country, A. Fawziyya Abu Khalid. PoArWo, *tr. by* Farouk Mustafa

Country at My Shoulder, The. Moniza Alvi. MoWP

Country Autumns, The. Clark Coolidge. AHA

Country Bedroom, The. Frances Darwin Cornford. MoBrPo

Country beneath / the earth has a green sun, The. Procedures for Underground. Margaret Atwood. NALW

Country boy, A. Love Song of a Red Cap. Sam Cornish. BtF

Country Boy, City Girl. Brenda Black White. TiP2

Country Boy in Winter, A. Sarah Orne Jewett. APN-2; ColAP

Country Bus at Night. Chŏng Hyŏnjong. CAMKP, *tr. by* Kevin O'Rourke

Country Bus Station. Shin Kyŏngnim. CAMKP, *tr. by* David R. McCann

Country Clergyman's Trip to Cambridge, The. Thomas Babington Macaulay, 1st Baron Macaulay. OBSV

Country climb is the best disgrace, a couple of practices any of them in order is so left, A. (LL)   Gertrude Stein.   NAAPv.2; NAMCP V.1 *Fr.* Tender Buttons.

Country Dance.   Dame Edith Sitwell.   NAMCP V.1; NoAM *Fr.* Façade.

Country Dance.   Judith Wright.   BMAP *Fr.* Blind Man, The.

Country Dance, A.   Charles Tennyson Turner.   OxBEV

Country Fair.   Charles Simic.   EmeKit; OxBoAm; P180

Country Fair.   Fay M. Yauger.   TiP2

Country Faith, The.   Norman Gale.   OBEV

Country Funeral.   Carlos Pezoa Velíz.   SonAtl, *tr. by* Lisa Martin and Eva Asensio Vicente

Country God, A.   Edmund Charles Blunden.   MoBrPo

Country? have lost our pride / as nationals no man can die for billboards / as have for freedom.   Spring 61.   Lenore Kandel.   BB

Country here-abouts, The.   Wire Song.   Mark Todd.   GeoH

Country I was born and lived in undergoes rapid and flagrant change, A. Usonian Journals 2000.   Adrienne Rich.   PrTe

Country Lassie, The.   *Unknown.*   TreFP

Country Life.   Chenjerai Hove.   HBAPE

Country Life, A.   Randall Jarrell.   MoAmPo

Country Life, A.   Katherine Philips.   BASC

Country Midwife, The: A Day.   Ai.   GT

Country North of Belleville, The.   Alfred Wellington Purdy.   BrAP

Country of a Thousand Years of Peace, The.   James Merrill.   NoP-4

Country of Dust, The.   Vahan Tekeyan.   AF, *tr. by* Diana Der Hovanessian and Marzbed Margossian

Country of early October had no fruit, The.   Words of Evening, The.   Yves Bonnefoy.   VCWP, *tr. by* Richard Pevear

Country of hunchbacks!—where the strong, straight spine.   Sonnet to Gath. Edna St. Vincent Millay.   MoAmPo

Country of Marriage, The.   Wendell Berry.   InGu

Country of my father, The.   Father Country.   Tyehimba Jess.   BtF

Country of No Lack.   Jean Starr Untermeyer.   MoAmPo

Country of Origin.   Maureen Hurley.   AtGh

Country or Western Music.   Gerald Early.   BodElec

Country Pastor, The.   Timothy Dwight.   SacPr

Country Pathway, A.   James Whitcomb Riley.
    "I come upon it suddenly, alone."   CA

Country Press [*with music*].   Rosemary Dobson.   NOBAu

Country rings around with loud alarms, The.   John Dryden.   OBSV *Fr.* Cymon and Iphigenia.

Country Road, A.   Li Ho.   CrYelRi, *tr. by* Sam Hamill

Country Roads.   Rolf Jacobsen.   WED, *tr. by* Robert Bly
    (Rubber.)   BLT

Country Scene.   Hồ Xuân Huong.   TAPaP, *tr. by* John Balaban

Country School.   Allen Curnow.   HarvBoo

Country School, The.   *Unknown.*   TCAPo

Country Seat, The.   Sir John, of Penicuik Clerk.   OBGa *Fr.* Country Seat, The.

Country Seat, The.   Sir John, of Penicuik Clerk.
    Country Seat, The.   OBGa

Country Song.   William Shakespeare.   NoSic; OBEV; TFi *Fr.* As You Like It.

Country Song, A.   Douglas Stewart.   NOBAu

Country Stars.   William Meredith.   VCAP

Country Summer.   Léonie Adams.   MoAmPo

Country that rejoices at formal outward propriety, A.   Certain Country, A. Yosano Akiko.   CAoMJL1, *tr. by* Janine Beichman

Country Thought.   Sylvia Townsend Warner.   MoBrPo

Country Town, A.   Philip James Bailey.
    (True Measure of Life, The.)   TreFP

Country Where Snow Has Not Yet Fallen, A.   No Hyangnim.   EcSo, *tr. by* Aimee N. Kwon

Country where the billboards have claws, A.   Sunland.   Edmond Jabès. YaTCFP, *tr. by* Keith Waldrop

Country Wife, The.   Dana Gioia.   RA

Country Wisdoms.   Maggie Anderson.   PBCAP

Country without a Mythology, A.   Douglas Le Pan.   BrAP

Country Without a Post Office, The.   Agha Shahid Ali.   AmAlph; NAMCP V.2
    "I read them, letters of lovers, the mad ones."   BeAl

Country-Mouse, The.   Abraham Cowley.   NPeEn; OBVE

Countryside sleeps, trembling, The.   Countryside Sleeps, Trembling, The. Juan Ramón Jiménez.   SpanPo, *tr. by* Eloise Roach

County.   Katayoon Zandvakili.   AmPoNex

County of Mayo, The.   Thomas Flavell.   OBEV, *tr. by* George Fox

Coup.   Leonard Nathan.   CalPo

Coupl'a jiggers of moonlight and add a star.   Moonlight Cocktail.   Kim Gannon.   ReLy

Couple, A.   May Swenson.   NAMCP V.2

Couple Having Breakfast in the Deli, The.   Jeanette I. Winthrop.   PfS

Couple in the Next Room, The.   John Ashbery.   BodElec

Couple of Swells, A.   Irving Berlin.   OBCoV; ReLy

Couple painted on the Bridal Shop, The.   Two Centuries in One Day.   Eloise Klein Healy.   GeoHom

Couple slumps on a veranda opening flat cokes, A.   Personal Ad.   Joanna Fuhrman.   AmPoNex

Couple that walked, The.   David Kherdian.   UrbNat *Fr.* Taking the Soundings on Third Avenue.

Couples.   Kate Jennings.   BMAP

Couplet: February 24, 1847.   Henry Wadsworth Longfellow.   APN-1

Couplets.   Yehuda Amichai.   FIT, *tr. by* Robert Friend

Couplets.   Robert Mezey.
    "She thinks if she puts out, her sainthood will be recognized."   CalPo

Couplets, Rare, Medium, and Well-Done.   Samuel Hoffenstein.
    Sexes, The.   AmWit

Couplings.   Menna Elfyn.   BBMWP, *tr. by* Joseph P. Clancy

Couplings buckled, cracked, collapsed.   Wreck of the Circus Train, The. Hayden Carruth.   GM

Courage!   John G. de la Parra, Jr.   BeDoSh

Courage.   Boris Leonidovich Pasternak.   FaBoWar, *tr. by Unknown*

Courage.   Anne Sexton.   GoPo; PLBUT; TWF

Courage: "Courage is the price that life exacts for granting peace."   Amelia Earhart.   OtW

Courage! I say. Thus exhorting myself.   Self-Exhortation on Military Themes. Alan Dugan.   PWW2

Courage is the price that life exacts for granting peace.   Courage.   Amelia Earhart.   OtW

Courage my Soul, now learn to wield.   Dialogue Between The Resolved Soul and Created Pleasure, A.   Andrew Marvell.   FSCP

Courage, or One of Gene Horner's Fiddles.   Lisa Coffman.   AmPoNex

Courage shall grow keener, clearer the will.   *Unknown.*   WoPoe *Fr.* Battle of Maldon, The.

Courage that my mother had, The.   Edna St. Vincent Millay.   NALW

Courage to let go of the door, the handle, The.   Maggid.   Marge Piercy.   TaR

Courage to wait, The.   Greater Courage.   Natan Zach.   PoSu, *tr. by* Peter Everwine and Shulamit Yasny-Starkman

Courageous know, The.   Not Courageous.   Marie Luise Kaschnitz.   GTCP, *tr. by* Reinhold Grimm

Courageousness.   Imamu Amiri Baraka.   EGAG

Coureurs de Bois.   Douglas Le Pan.   BrAP

Course bread and water's most their fare.   Observation Generall from Their Eating, Etc., The.   Roger Williams.   SacPr
    (Coarse bread and water's most their fare.)   TCAPo

Course of a Life, The.   Yehuda Amichai.   BBASP, *tr. by* Chana Bloch

Course of a Particular, The.   Wallace Stevens.   APT-1

Course of the sea over my entry, The.   Sea and You, The.   Julia de Burgos. TANSG, *tr. by* Heather Rosario Sievert

Course of Time, The.   Robert Pollok.
    Book 7.
       Contretemps, A.   STuOW
       Proximities.   STuOW
    Book 8.
       Once-Over, The.   STuOW

Course Prescribed, The.   William Wordsworth.   STuOW *Fr.* Excursion, The.

Coursier de Jeanne d'Arc, Le.   Linda McCarriston.   FaoP

Coursing in emptiness.   Lal Ded.   WPoS

Coursing, The.   Michael Drayton.   DiBP *Fr.* Polyolbion [*or Poly-Oobion*].

Court is deep, deep, deep, how deep, The.   Lyric to the Tune "Immortal by the River."   Li Ch'ing-chao.   WoPoe, *tr. by* Julie Landau

Court lady Addresses Her Lover, A.   Edward De Vere, 17th Earl of Oxford. NoSic

Court of Divine Justice, The.   Peter Klappert.   YaYoPo *Fr.* Pieces of the One and a Half Legged Man.

Court of Love, The.   *Unknown.*
    "On May-day, when the lark began to rise."   NoSic

Courteous Indian, The.   Roger Williams.   NOSC

Courteous pagan shall condemn[e], The.   Courteous Indian, The.   Roger Williams.   NOSC

Courteous people, A.   Executioners.   Paul Engle.   PoA 2002 *Fr.* Images of China.

Courtesan to a Young Customer, A.   Kshetrayya.   WoPoe, *tr. by* V. Narayana Rao, A. K. Ramanujan and David Shulman

Courtesan to Her Lover, A.   Kshetrayya.   WoPoe, *tr. by* V. Narayana Rao, A. K. Ramanujan and David Shulman

Courtesy.   Alexander Gerov.   CSCBP, *tr. by* Georgi Belev and Lisa Sapinkopf

Courtesy, A Trenchant Grace, A [*for Jim Giumentaro (1959–1992) and for Terry Pitzner*].   Cyrus Cassells.   GT; WiU

Courthouse Graffiti for Two Voices. Martín Espada. InvLad

Courtier's Life, The. Sir Thomas Wyatt. NoSic

Courting the Faerie Queen. Margaret Lucas Cavendish, Duchess of Newcastle. NOSC

Courtling, I rather thou shouldst utterly. To Censorious Courtling. Ben Jonson. NOSC

Courtly Love. T. R. Hummer. WaAnP

Courtney, Mentioned in Passing, Years After. Robyn Sarah. NoP-5

Courtship [with music]. Mark Strand. PoPoPo

Courtship of Inanna and Dumuzi, The. Ancient Sumerian Oral Tradition. tr. by Diane Wolkstein and Samuel Noah Kramer

"Word they had spoken, The." EroLit, tr. by Diane Wolkstein and Samuel Noah Kramer

Courtship Song. Unknown. CCL1 Fr. Guan-ju.

Courtship, The. Ann Beresford. LW

Courtyard is warmed by the coming of spring, The. Drumbeats. Yi Inbok. WoPoe, tr. by Kevin O'Rourke

Courtyard Noises from the North, Twenty-fourth Precinct. Colette Inez. UrbNat

Courtyard, The. Eddy Van Vliet. VCWP, tr. by John Van Tiel

Courtyard was hazy, The. Miraculous Marriage of Zarife Dominquez. Patricia Dubrava. MPUn

Courtyards in Delft. Derek Mahon. ModIr; NPeEn; PBCIP; PNI

Cousin, A. Gertrude Stein. MotU Fr. Book Concluding with As A Wife Has a Cow a Love Story, A.

Cousin Coat. Sean O'Brien. NeBrP; NoP-5

Cousin from Maine, knowing, The. Eating the Cookies. Jane Kenyon. AFaM

Cousin, I think the shape of a marriage. For a Wedding. Kate Clanchy. MFPA

Cousin Kate. Christina Georgina Rossetti. VWP

Cousin Mary. Wanda Coleman. GT; OxAAAP

Cousin Richard had escaped his clothes. Ethel Rosenberg and Me. Judith Werner. FiBr

Cousin Sidney. Dannie Abse. AngWePo

Cousin to Clare washing. Preciosilla. Gertrude Stein. NAAPv.2; NAMCP V.1

Cousin Vivian stayed single. Vivian, Take 57. BtF

Cove of the Wall of Meng, The. Pei Di and Wang Wei. CCL1 Fr. Wheel River.

Covenant. Douglas Crase. WaAnP

Covenant. Jorie Graham. AWPTFC

Covenanting Country. Sir Alec Cairncross. EdScPo

Coventry. Conor O'Callaghan. NIrP

Coventry Cathedral. István Vas. IQMS, tr. by Geroge Gömöri and Clive Wilmer

Cover me with your everlasting arms. Frances Anne Kemble. CenSon; SWaP

Cover my head. Buson. EH, tr. by Robert Hass

Cover Photograph. Marilyn Nelson. InvLi

Cover the windows with rods don't let it in it arrived with the delirium. Minute Amphibian. Silvia Eugenia Castillero. SPV, tr. by Jen Hofer

Cover up / Oh, quickly cover up. Mask, The. Laura Riding Jackson. HarvBoo

Cover us with your pools of fir. (LL) Oread. "H. D." APT-1; BrAP; ColAP; HeIP-4; MoAmPo; MoWP; NAAL-5; NAAPv.2; NALW; NAMCP V.1; NoAM; NPeEn; OxBoAm; PoPoPo; TCAPo

Cover your arms. Elbows. Minnie Bruce Pratt. WiU

Cover your teeth. (LL) Kalaloch. Carolyn Forché. NoAM; YaYoPo

Covered Dish. Kristin Kovacic. SweBea

Covered with Dew. Ana Blandiana. PoDa, tr. by Luciana Costea, Dona Rosu and Kathleen Snodgrass

Covered with rags and cardboard and nothing. Women's Room in Pennsylvania Station, The. Kate Daniels. GM

Covers it, like a stone covered [or cover'd] in grass. (LL) Sestina: Of the Lady Pietra degli Scrovigni. Dante Alighieri. MakPoe; NPeEn; OBVE, tr. by Dante Gabriel Rossetti

Cow. Selima Hill. StAl

Cow, The. Ogden Nash. NBLV; NoP-4; NoP-5

Cow, The. Robert Louis Stevenson. NTCP; TLR; WHSW

Cow Boy. Vincente Huidobro. PFTM-1

Cow eats green grass, The. Response to Rimbaud's Later Manner. Thomas Sturge Moore. CABP; OBMV

Cow in Apple Time, The. Robert Frost. MoAmPo

Cow of morning spurted, The. Last Vision of Eoghan Rua Ó Súilleabháin, The. Michael Hartnett. PBCIP

Cow Perseverance,The. Frederick D'Aguiar. NeBrP

Cow Worship. Gerald Stern. LoL

Coward. Maurya Simon. ExTi

Coward, The. Rudyard Kipling. HarvBoo; InoFa; NPeEn; WoPoe Fr. Epitaphs of the War [1914–1918].

Coward, The. Kate Rushin. BRtP

Cowardice. Amado Nervo. BLPSL, tr. by Rene de Costa, Rigas Kappatos and Eleni Paidoussi

Cowbell sounds, The. Rumination. Dabney Stuart. PfSP

Cowboy and the Farmer Should Be Friends, The. Robert Hershon. PoDa

Cowboy Film. Tom Matthews. PNI

Cowboy Sayings. Unknown. CA

Cow-boy still cuts short the day, The. John Clare. DiBP Fr. Shepherd's [or Shepheards] Calendar, The.

Cowboynomics. Jose Angel Figueroa. BRtP

Cowboys' Christmas Ball, The. William Lawrence Chittenden. TiP2

Cowboy's Lament, The [see also St. James Infirmary and The Bad Girl's Lament]. Unknown. APN-2; ChAP; FaBoA

Cowgirl. Pat LittleDog. TiP2

Cow-hoof imprint, A. Skyline. Jean Toomer. NAAPv.2

Cowhorn-crowned, shockheaded, cornshuck-bearded. Knight, Death, and the Devil, The. Randall Jarrell. GS; WeW-3

Cowlady cowlady. Ladybird. Unknown. FaBoVe

Cowpasture and the ragged line. Abbey Cwmhir. Harri Webb. AngWePo

Cowper's Grave. Elizabeth Barrett Browning. OxAEP-2

Cowries shells and kola nuts. Moonlight on the Lake. Kunle Adebajo. NeNiPo

Cows. Julia Alvarez. PfSP

Cows. Peter Kocan. NOBAu

Cows. James Reeves. NOxBChV; NTCP

Cows and Alabama Folklore. Kathryn Takara. FTtHH

Cows at Night, The. Hayden Carruth. GifTon; PoA 2002

Cows graze across the hill. Cows. Peter Kocan. NOBAu

Cows in Trouble. Steve Martin. MotU

Cow's moo and the goat's meheh carry down, The. Crimea. Olga Sulchinskaya. CRWP, tr. by Richard McKane

Cows on a narrow fringe of marshland browsing. Magyar Scene Through Magyar Eyes, A. Gyula Juhász. IQMS, tr. by Godfrey Turton

Cows they had, many, drifting like heavy clouds in the meadow. Russell Edson. MotU

Coxcomb, The. Joseph Hall. OxAEP-1

Coy like a lovebird, she flirts with hundreds, she with that lovely face. Ilhami, Sultan Selim III. NaPG, tr. by Talat Sait Halman

Coy Nature (which remain'd, though aged grown). Ode upon Doctor Harvey. Abraham Cowley. NPeEn

Coyne's. John Ennis. PBCIP

Coyote. Jim Linebarger. TiP2

Coyote eats chunks of the moon, A. I Can't Get Started. Ai. GT

Coyote Fragments. Lance Henson. HATNAP

Coyote Makes the First People. Peter Blue Cloud. FTtHH

Coyote, Skunk, and the Prairie Dogs. Navajo Oral Tradition. NAAL-5

Coyote stopped to drink at a big lake and saw his reflection. Coyote Makes the First People. Peter Blue Cloud. FTtHH

Coyotes are howling, The. Coyotes. George John Whyte-Melville. NOxBChV

Coyotes at Eyebrow Lake, Saskatchewan. David Waltner-Toews. ACAMVP

Coyote's song, A. New Realism. Joseph Ceravolo. PmAP

Coyotismo. Janice Gould. ReEnLa

Cozy comfortable homey homelike. Mantra for a Classless Society, or Mr. Roget's Neighborhood. Harryette Mullen. WANABP

Crab. Angela Dove. Prnts

Crab, The. Dennis O'Donnell. EdScPo

Crab Apple Jelly. Vicki Feaver. BeAl

Crab, the clot, the muzzle or the knife, The. Darwinian preface, A. Douglas Livingstone. TSAP

Crabapple Blossoms. Peter Sanger. Coast

Crabapple Brook. Hsüeh T'ao [or Xue Tao]. CCL1, tr. by Jeanne Larsen

Crab-Apple Crisis, The. George MacBeth. AtGh

Crabapple holding in arms. Spell to Be Said After Illness. Jane Hirshfield. AFaM

Crabapples. Michael Van Walleghen. IllVoic

Crabbed Age and Youth. William Shakespeare. NoSic; OBEV

Crabbit Angels. David Purves. EdScPo

Crab-Boil. Rita Dove. CAP-8

Crabs. Marge Piercy. NBLV

Crabs. Dennis Saleh. GeoHom

Crabs in their shells, because they cannot play. Armour. Aldous Leonard Huxley. OxBSo

Crabs lie to themselves, The. Crabs. Dennis Saleh. GeoHom

Crack, The. Carla Faesler Bremer. SPV, tr. by Jen Hofer

Crack, The. Clark Coolidge. PmAP

Crack, The. Denise Levertov. NALW

Crack! a man is crooning to the cement. Meridian Hill Terrace. Wendy S. Walters. BtF

Crack! crack! As the Flower of the Grass. May Probyn. VWP

Crack has overtaken your immune defenses. Sandra. Demetrice A. Worley. SpirFl

Crack inside my breast split through bone, A. Crack Inside My Breast, A. Juan Felipe Herrera. PfSP

Crack is moving down the wall, The. Weldon Kees. StAl *Fr.* Five Villanelles.

Crack of a starting pistol. Jean Jaurès. Geoffrey Hill. NAMCP V.2 *Fr.* Mystery of the Charity of Charles Péguy, The.

Crack ran through our hearthstone long ago, A. Refugees, The. Edwin Muir. NoAM

Crack the Whip. Carol Muske-Dukes. AmAlph

Cracked Bell, The. Charles Baudelaire. SxFrPo, *tr. by* James McGowan

Cracked Looking Glass. Jean Garrigue. VCAP

Cracked Portraits. Agha Shahid Ali. OpBo

Cracking Walnuts. Maria Jastrzebska. Prnts

Cracking whips, off to the wine shop. Streets of Ch'ang-an. Ch'u Kuang-hsi. ColAnChi, *tr. by* Burton Watson

Crackle of parched grass bent by wind, The. Peter Davison. YaYoPo *Fr.* Breaking of the Day, The.

Crackling embers on the hearth are dead, The. Night. Hartley Coleridge. OxBSo

Cracks in your palms are filled with wind and salt, The. Salt. Patricia Y. Ikeda. MotU

Crackup, last day of Carnival, first of Lint. Martin Johnston. BMAP *Fr.* In Transit: A Sonnet Square.

Cradle, The. Roland Robinson. NOBAu

Cradle Hymn, A. Isaac Watts. OBEV

Cradle Logic of Autumn, The [En mi país otoño nace de una flor seca, de algunos pájaros . . . o del vaho penetrante de ciertos ríos de la llanura]. Jay Wright. OxBoAm

Cradle Song. Nicholas Breton. *See* Sweet lullabie, A.

Cradle Song, A: "Angels are stooping, The." William Butler Yeats. NOxBChV

Cradle Song, A: "Sleep, sleep, beauty bright." William Blake. OBEV

Cradle Song, A: "Sweet dreams form a shade." William Blake. OBCP *Fr.* Songs of Innocence.

Cradle Song: "Clock's untiring fingers wind the wool of darkness, The." Louis MacNeice. MoBrPo

Cradle Song: "Reapers and sowers, gleaners and drovers." Jim Schley. GoPo

Cradle Song: "Sleep, my darling, sleep." Louis MacNeice. IrLP

Cradle-Song at Twilight. Alice Thompson Meynell. NPeEn; VWP

Craft of mine and delight. To My Craft. Ágnes Nemes Nagy. IQMS, *tr. by* Hugh Maxton

Crafty Butcher, The. Susan Hampton. BMAP; NOBAu

Crags stand in the mountains before us. Memorial Service. Ayin Tur-Malka. NRoS, *tr. by* Esther Raizen

Cramped, and the bright sun shining on its tusks. (LL) Gratitude. Louise Glück. OxBoAm; TRP

Cramped like sardines on the Queens, and sedated. Tourists. Howard Moss. NoP-4; NoP-5; OBCoV

Crane, The. Charles Tomlinson. MoBrPo

Crane Calls. *Unknown.* WoPoe, *tr. by* Constance A. Cook

Crane calls in Nine Marshes. Crane Calls. *Unknown.* WoPoe, *tr. by* Constance A. Cook

Crane in Reeds. William Heyen. PoCoUp

Crane is not indigenous, The. Water Birds. Cynthia Harper. TiP2

Cranes, The. Po Chü-i. CCL1; OBVE; OWoS, *tr. by* Arthur Waley

Crane's legs, The. Basho. EH, *tr. by* Robert Hass

Cranes of Ibycus, The. Emma Lazarus. APN-2; NAAPv.1

Cranes on the Seashore. Linda Gregerson. AmAlph

Cranmer and the Bread of Heaven. Anne Ridler. SacPr

Crash in the living room is not, The. Perfect Circle. Richard Lemm. Coast

Crash of rhinos, A. Paisley Rekdal. LegDan

Crashing down mossy walls. Middle Age. Arlene L. Mandell. PasH

Craswall [*with music*]. Roland Mathias. OBWVE

Crate, The. Francis Ponge. MotU, *tr. by* Cid Corman

Crater. Lisa Williams. AmPoNex

Crater Face. Denise Duhamel. BRtP; LiTh

Crawl into fridges and suffocate. Lost. children have been known to. Jill Hartman. PoPra

Crawled near my mind's poor birds. (LL) Trumbull Stickney. APN-2; NAAPv.2 *Fr.* Dramatic Fragments.

Crawlin' aboot like a snail in the mud. Image o' God, The. Joe Corrie. ChIV-1; RSaN

Crawling down headfirst into the hole. Tunnels. Yusef Komunyakaa. AmAlph

Craze Field, The. Les A. Murray. UpMys

Crazed [*with music*]. Mary E. Tucker. CBWP-1; RACG

Crazed Woman, The. Jeannette Miller. TANSG, *tr. by* Paula Vega

Crazy as white shines in summer. City Baseball. Liz Rosenberg. CA

Crazy Blues. Perry Bradford. NAAPv.2

Crazy Boys. Beverly McLoughland. HHAm

Crazy Dog Events. Jerome Rothenberg. RaBo

Crazy Girl, The. Sharan Strange. InTrad

Crazy Horse Monument. Peter Blue Cloud. HATNAP; UnSA

Crazy Horse Speaks. Sherman Alexie. UnSA

Crazy in the Heart. William Engvick. ReLy

Crazy Jane Goes to Painting Class. Jane Hilberry. FiBr

Crazy Jane on God [*fr.* Words for Music Perhaps]. William Butler Yeats. RACG

Crazy Jane Talks with the Bishop [*fr.* Words for Music Perhaps]. William Butler Yeats. CABP; NAEL-6v2; NAEL-7v2; NAMCP V.1; NoAM; NoP-4; NoP-5; OxAEP-2; PoPoPo; TRP

Crazy Kate. William Cowper. NAEL-6v1; NAEL-7v1; NPBRoP *Fr.* Task, The.

Crazy Mary dreams the city while she's awake. Circus of the City, The. Colleen J. McElroy. OxAAAP

Crazy Menu. Tess Gallagher. InoFa

Crazy Mind. Kamalākānta Bhattācārya. SinGod, *tr. by* Rachel Fell McDermott

Crazy Mother, The. Margherita Guidacci. CItWP, *tr. by* Cinzia Sartini Blum and Lara Trubowitz

Crazy Rhythm. Irving Caesar. ReLy

Crazy Satan. Murad Mikha'il. IrPoTo, *tr. by* Christina Coyle and Sadok Masliyah

Crazy She Calls Me. Bob Russell. ReLy

Crazy strings: they neigh, and boom and whine. Black Piano, The. Endre Ady. IQMS, *tr. by* Adam Makkai

Crazy Weather. John Ashbery. ColAP

Crazy with love, the birds fold. Crazy with Love. Paul Zimmer. PfSP

Crazy Woman, The. Gwendolyn Brooks. ItWoWo; NALW

Creaking of the universe must be, for those, The. Revealing Oneself to a Woman. Bin Ramke. YaYoPo

Creamy Breasts. Chao Luan-luan. CCL1; EroLit; NDACCP, *tr. by* Chung Ling and Kenneth Rexroth

Create Desire. Karen Volkman. KGB; NAPBL

Create me a world. Ekaterina Vlasova. CRWP, *tr. by* Peter France

Created, The. Jones Very. APN-1; InvLi

Creating history (their very words). Eighth Army at the Chongchon, The. Rolando Hinojosa. TiP2

Creation. Ifi Amadiume. HAWP

Creation. Sir Richard Blackmore.

   Possibilities. STuOW

   Possibilities. STuOW

Creation. Jeni Couzyn. HAWP

Creation. Donald Evans. BBMWP, *tr. by* Gillian Clarke

Creation. Mary Weston Fordham. CBWP-2

Creation. Robin Gurr. NOBAu

Creation. John Milton. NOSC *Fr.* Paradise Lost.

Creation. Eunice Odio. TCLAP, *tr. by* Martha Collins

Creation. Eunice Odio. *tr. by* Arthur Natella

   "I'm at the point of hurting myself and listening to myself." TANSG, *tr. by* Arthur Natella

Creation. Simon J. Ortiz. ColAP; HATNAP

Creation. Trinity Site, New Mexico. 5:30 A.M. July 16th, 1945. Benjamin Alire Sáenz. AtGh

Creation, The. Cecil Frances Alexander. *See* All Things Bright and Beautiful.

Creation, The. James Weldon Johnson. AmFaPo; APT-1; ChIV-1; InGu; ISC; MoAmPo; NAMCP V.1; OxAAAP; OxBoAm; SacPr; SSLK

Creation, 3:30 p.m., the Fifth Day. Diana Hartog. NLPA *Fr.* Oasis.

Creation Continues. Carol Fonesca Galvez. OWABP

Création de soi, La. André Frénaud. YaTCFP

Creation Hymn. *Unknown.* WoPoe *Fr.* Rig Veda.

Creation Hymn. *Unknown.* WoPoe *Fr.* Vedic Hymns.

Creation Is a Cycle. Empress. BRtP

Creation Myth on a Moebius Band. Howard Nemerov. OBCoV

Creation Night. Harry Edmund Martinson. WED, *tr. by* Robert Bly

Creation of the Earth, The. *Navajo Oral Tradition.* TCAPo

Creation Story, The. Joy Harjo. WaAnP

Creation's and Creator's crowning good. Coventry Patmore. CABP *Fr.* Unknown Eros, The.

Creation's issue congealing (and one woman's). (LL) Canticle for Good Friday. Geoffrey Hill. ChIV-2; UpMys

Creations mildest charms are there combined. Oliver Goldsmith. NPeEn *Fr.* Traveller, The; or, A Prospect of Society.

Creative Poverty. László Szabédi. IQMS, *tr. by* J. G. Nichols

Creator / If in eternal life. Springwater, Part 105. Bingxin. CFP, *tr. by* Michelle Yeh

Creator is to be remembred in due time, The. Bible, *O.T. See* Remember Now Thy Creator.

Creator Spirit, by whose aid. Veni Creator Spiritus. Charlemagne and Hrabanus Maurus. SacPr, *tr. by* John Dryden

Creator Spirit, who dost lightly hover. Little Prayers. Paul Goodman. PLBUT

Creatrix. Anna Wickham. MoBrPo

Creature, The. Harri Gwynn. *tr. by* Robert Minhinnick "Welcome / Black beetle." BBMWP, *tr. by* Robert Minhinnick

Creature Has a Purpose, The. Thomas Lux. BodElec

Creatures in the Zoo. Babette Deutsch. APT-2

Creatures preach to St Francis, The. Pauline Stainer. MoWP

Creatures that live in a wave, glass-housed. Garfish. John Blight. BMAP

Creatures that rustle in the shadows, all the crooked. Green Light. Rolf Jacobsen. AtGh, *tr. by* Roger Greenwald

Creatures that we met this morning, The. Discovery of the New World. Carter Revard. SoSe-8

Creciendo Hacia la Tierra. Luis Rosales. RaW

Credentials. Mark Halliday. SUP

Credo. Fiona Farrell. BeAl

Credo. Maxine W. Kumin. ExTi

Credo. Andrew Zawacki. IAoNAP; LegDan

Credo: "I believe there is something else." Matthew Rohrer. IIR

Credo: "I cannot find my way." Edwin Arlington Robinson. ITBLP; MoAmPo; OxBoAm

Credo: "My friend from Asia has powers and magic, he plucks a blue leaf from the young blue-gum." Robinson Jeffers. MoAmPo; OxBoAm

Creed. Belkis Cuza Malé. TANSG, *tr. by* Pamela Carmell

Creed for Free Women, A. Elsa Gidlow. HW

Creed of a Graffiti Writer, The. Steven Bonafide Rojas. BRtP

Creek, The. Roland Robinson. NOBAu

Creek's easy purr, The. Waterfall. Bruce Berger. NevBe

Creeping and healing. (LL) Minimal, The. Theodore Roethke. NAMCP V.1; NoAM; OxBoAm

Creeping serrate line of dusty red, A. Fighting Fire. Hamlin Garland. APN-2

Cremation. Agha Shahid Ali. InoFa

Cremation. Robinson Jeffers. BLT (It nearly cancels my fear of death.) NAAPv.2

Cremation of Sam McGee, The. Robert W. Service. BRP; IFF; OBCoV; OBNV; TCAPo; WaAnP

Crematorium. Sir John Betjeman. PoA 2002

Crêpe de Chine. Mark Doty. FaoP

Crepe paper Christmas. Teaching Poetry at Votech High, Santa Fe, the Week John Lennon Was Shot. Paula Gunn Allen. ReTh

Crept like a frightened girl. (LL) Harlot's House, The. Oscar Wilde. ItP; MoBrPo; NAEL-6v2; NAEL-7v2; NoAM

Crepuscule. Angela Shaw. NeAmPo

Crepuscule with Muriel. Marilyn Hacker. AFaM

Crepuscule with Nellie. Charles Simic. SeSe

Crescendo. James Grainger. STuOW *Fr.* Sugar Cane, The.

Crescendoes are indigo scarves. Gonsalves. Ron Welburn. SeSe

Crescent Moon. Ch'ôn Yanghûi. EcSo, *tr. by* Aimee N. Kwon

Crescent moon. Issa. EH, *tr. by* Robert Hass

Crescent moon, A. Ana Istarú. TANSG, *tr. by* Shaun Griffin and Emma Sepúlveda-Pulvirenti

Crescent moon shines, The. Crescent Moon, The. Mei Yao Ch'en. NDACCP, *tr. by* Kenneth Rexroth

Crest Jewel, The. James Stephens. MoBrPo

Crested iris by the front gate waves, The. Fog. Mark Doty. FaoP

Crests of foam where the milch-kine fed. Flood of Is in Brittany, The. Augusta Davies Webster. ViWPN

Creusa. Virgil. NoSic *Fr.* Aeneid [*or* Eneados *or* Aeneis], The.

Crevice, A! shouts the Emperor in his sleep. Emperor's Dream, The. Zbigniew Herbert. MotU, *tr. by* Czeslaw Milosz

Crew of *Apollo* 8, The. Elaine V. Emans. OtW

Crib Goch. T. Rowland Hughes. BBMWP, *tr. by* Catherine Fisher

Crib, The. Robert Finch. OBCP

Cricket. Issa. EH, *tr. by* Robert Hass

Cricket. Seido Ray Ronci. AmZen

Cricket. Dafydd Rowlands. BBMWP, *tr. by* Meic Stephens

Cricket. Ivan Tsanev. CSCBP, *tr. by* Georgi Belev and Lisa Sapinkopf

Cricket, The. Hwang Tonggyu. CAMKP, *tr. by* Kevin O'Rourke

Cricket, The. Tu Fu [*or* Du Fu]. CrYelRi, *tr. by* Sam Hamill

Cricket, The. Frederick Goddard Tuckerman. APN-2; NAAPv.1; NCAP; TCAPo

Cricket at Central California Women's Facility. Dixie Salazar. GeoHom

Cricket, be. Issa. WED, *tr. by* Robert Bly

Cricket calls while I am sitting, lost, A. Invitation to the Cricket. Holly Hughes. AmZen

Cricket did not actually seek the hearth, The. Mary Oliver. PoCoUp *Fr.* West Wind.

Cricket is so small a thing, The. Cricket, The. Tu Fu [*or* Du Fu]. CrYelRi, *tr. by* Sam Hamill

Cricket Mountain. Khaled Mattawa. NAPBL

Cricket Music. Lőrinc Szabó. *tr. by* Watson Kirkconnell, Edwin Morgan and John Gordon Nichols
Babits. IQMS, *tr. by* J. G. Nichols
English Poetry. IQMS, *tr. by* J. G. Nichols
Moment, The. IQMS, *tr. by* Watson Kirkconnell
On a Raft. IQMS, *tr. by* Watson Kirkconnell
Shame. IQMS, *tr. by* J. G. Nichols
To Forget? IQMS, *tr. by* Watson Kirkconnell
Tranquil Miracle, The. IQMS, *tr. by* Watson Kirkconnell
With Flute, with Violin. IQMS, *tr. by* Watson Kirkconnell

Cricket on a rubbish-tip, A. Winter Cricket. John Heath-Stubbs. OBCP

Cricket that sang these last few evenings, The. Cricket, The. Hwang Tonggyu. CAMKP, *tr. by* Kevin O'Rourke

Cricketer, The. Kashyap Bhattacharya. PML

Cricketer's Retirement Day, The. Julia Copus. NeBl

Crickets. David McCord. NTCP

Crickets chirping in the dark, The. Samuel Hoffenstein. AmWit *Fr.* Songs about Life and Brighter Things Yet.

Crickets, green-faced. Binyo Ivanov. CSCBP, *tr. by* Georgi Belev and Lisa Sapinkopf

Cricket-song. Lorine Niedecker. FTOS

Crickhowel. Richard Hall. AngWePo

Cried a scientist watching this creature dart by. Hummingbird. X. J. Kennedy. NOxBChV

Cried Innocence, "Mother, my thumbs, my thumbs!" Tortured, The. May Sarton. FFC

Crier, The. Michael Drayton. NOSC

Cries of London, The. *Unknown.* OPOU

Cries of the Newsboy. Edith Matilda Thomas. SWaP

Cries of wild geese. Issa. ZenPo, *tr. by* Takashi Ikemoto and Lucien Stryk

Cries We Make, The (64). Khwaja Shams-ad-din Muhammad Hafiz. WED, *tr. by* Robert Bly and Leonard Lewisohn

Crime. Robert Penn Warren. FuPo

Crime Against Nature. Minnie Bruce Pratt. WiU

Crime and Punishment. Paul Lake. RA

Crime and Punishment. János Pilinszky. IQMS, *tr. by* Adam Makkai

Crime at Its Best. Stoddard King. NBLV

Crime Club. Weldon Kees. OxBoAm

Crime of the Ages, The. Augusta Cooper Bristol. APN-2; PCW

Crime Was in Granada, The. Antonio Machado Ruiz. SpanPo, *tr. by* Kate Flores

Crimea. Vladimir Vladimirovich Mayakovsky. RusPo, *tr. by* Robert Arthur Douglas Ford

Crimea. Olga Sulchinskaya. CRWP, *tr. by* Richard McKane

Crimean Heroes, The. Walter Savage Landor. FaBoWar

Criminal. Stephen Dunn. MoASP

Criminal Justice System. Rebecca Wolff. RWB

Criminal, you took a great piece of my life. Badly-Chosen Lover. Rosemary Tonks. EmeKit; MoWP; StAl

Crimped clouds swim full low, The. Bowl Over, Wheel. Edmund Vale. ArBi

Crimson Tent. John Dos Passos. PoA 2002

Crimson / the crape-myrtle. Saitō Mokichi. CAoMJL1, *tr. by* Amy Vladek Heinrich

Criole Candjo [*tr. of Creole slave song*]. George Washington Cable. APN-2

Cripple Creek. *Unknown.* APN-2

Crippled beggar who lives, The. "Zelda." FIT, *tr. by* Robert Friend

Crisálida. Francisco Segovia. RMCMP

Crisis is on me, A. My soul is mute. Ironical Elegy, Composed in Those Terribly Sad Moments When I Cannot Write. Andrey Andreievich Voznesensky. RusPo, *tr. by* Robert Arthur Douglas Ford

Crispus Attucks. Robert Earl Hayden. ESEAA

Cristal Automatique. Aimé Césaire. YaTCFP

Cristo Yacente de Santa Clara (Iglesia de la Cruz) en Palencia, El. Miguel de Unamuno.
"Este Cristo español que no ha vivido." RaW

Critic. Elwyn Brooks White. NBLV *Fr.* Definitions.

Critic, The. Frank O'Hara. OxBoAm

Critic, The. C. K. Williams. OPRER

Critic leaves at curtain fall, The. Elwyn Brooks White. NBLV *Fr.* Definitions.

Critic objects to their "misterian" qualities, A. Heat Bird, The. Mei-Mei Berssenbrugge. OnScMo

Critical Condition. Yi Sang. *tr. by* Walter Lew
    Precipice. CAMKP; PFTM-1, *tr. by* Walter Lew

Critical mass came over me, A. Depression, The. Ira Sadoff. BodElec

Criticism. Ebenezer Elliott. CenSon

Critics and Connoisseurs. Marianne Moore. APT-1; BrAP; NAAPv.2; NAMCP V.1; NoAM; OxBoAm

Critics say that epics have died out, The. Elizabeth Barrett Browning. BrAP; FaBoWar; NAEL-6v2; NAEL-7v2; NALW; NoP-4; NoP-5; WaAnP *Fr.* Aurora Leigh.

Critique. Anthony Barnett. Oth

Crivens! This is jist typical. Maw Broon Visits a Therapist. Jackie Kay. MFPA

Croak of a raven hoar, The! Mammon Marriage. George Macdonald. SacPr

Croaked the Eagle: "Nevermore." "Sagittarius." UV

Croaker Papers, The. Fitz-Greene Halleck and Joseph Rodman Drake. National Painting [*or* Paintings], The. APN-1

Croatan. Tom Weatherly. EGAG

Crocodile, A. Thomas Lovell Beddoes. NPeEn; OxBEV *Fr.* Last Man, The.

Crocodile, The. Lewis Carroll. BLPJKO; ChAP; NBLV; OxBEV; TFi; UV *Fr.* Alice's Adventures in Wonderland.

Crocodile attacks with a glance, The. Crocodile 1–15. Yang Lian. PFTM-2, *tr. by* Mabel Lee

Crocus (after snow), The. Patrick Warner. Coast

Crocus Air. Winfield Townley Scott. APT-2

Crocus armies from the dead, The. Veni Coronaberis. Geoffrey Hill. NoP-4; NoP-5

Crocuses and Crown-of-Thorns. Enos D. Watts. Coast

Croeso i Gymru. Philip Owens. AngWePo

Cro-Kill. Anthony Lawrence. NOBAu

Cro-Magnons. Lawrence Ferlinghetti. BB

Cromwell. Brendan Kennelly.
    Three Tides. ModIr
    Vintage. ModIr

Cromwell, our chief [*or* cheif] of men, who through a cloud. To the Lord General Cromwell. John Milton. NAEL-6v1; NoP-5; NOSC; WaAnP; PBRV; GSo; NoP-4; PoPoPo

Cromwell: The Last Portrait. David Lindley. NLP

Crone I Will Become, The. Jean Hegland. FiBr

Crone, The. Karolina Pavlova. ARWW, *tr. by* Catriona Kelly

Cronies. Lyubomir Levchev. PML, *tr. by* Theodore Weiss

Cronopio receives his medical degree and opens a practice in the calle Santiago del Estero, A. Therapies. Julio Cortázar. MotU, *tr. by* Paul Blackburn

Crooked Afro. Frank X. Walker. SpirFl

Crooked ear, crooked ear, / Walker at night. Corn Song. *Unknown.* APN-2, *tr. by* Henry Rowe Schoolcraft

Crooked in the skyward angle of a pyramid. Prey. Michael Dorris. PoCoUp

Crooked, like bough the march wind bends wallward across the sleet. Lavender Woman, The. Lizette Woodworth Reese. APN-2

Crooked River Meditation. Tu Fu [*or* Du Fu]. CrYelRi, *tr. by* Sam Hamill

Croon. Langston Hughes. PFTM-1

Crootey Songo. Bob Kaufman. EGAG; FTtHH

Crop of sweat and blood, of African slave labour. On Sweet Coffee. Ábrahám Barcsay. IQMS, *tr. by* Peter Zollman

Crops like hedgehogs, high-crown'd hats. Modern Male Fashions. Mary Robinson. NOBRP

Crops were made, the leaves, The. History. Wendell Berry. LPSFW

Croquet by Moonlight. Julia A. Moore.
    "On a moonlight evening, in the month of May." VerBaPo

Cross. Langston Hughes. ColAP; GT; HarvBoo; NAMCP V.1; NoP-4; NoP-5; SAmP; SoSe-8

Cross. Patricia K. Page. StAl

Cross, The. Allen Tate. ChIV-2; MoAmPo

Cross, The. Yun Tongju. CAMKP, *tr. by* Kay Richards and Steffen Richards

Cross Burning Black. Willie Abraham Howard Jr. BtF

Cross Country. Rod Moran. NOBAu

Cross Country. Ann Sansom. MFPA

Cross Cut. Peter Davison. ColAP

Cross of oak twigs marks the place, A. Snake, The. Michael Collier. WaAnP

Cross of Snow, The. Henry Wadsworth Longfellow. APN-1; AWTN; ColAP; GSo; HeIP-4; NAAPv.1; NoP-4; NoP-5; TCAPo

Cross Questions. John Wheelwright. APT-2

Cross staggered him, The. At the cliff-top. Canticle for Good Friday. Geoffrey Hill. ChIV-2; UpMys

Cross the Aegean without me, then, Messalla. Cross the Aegean Without Me, Then, Messalla. Tibullus. WoPoe, *tr. by* Humphrey Clucas

Cross, the Cross, The. Tortoise-Shell. D. H. Lawrence. FaBoVe; NAEL-6v2; NAEL-7v2; OxAEP-2

Cross the fork the zigzag—a few straight lines, The. XYZ. Robert Pinsky. OxBoAm

Cross, The ("I must go on, till in my tearful line.") Jones Very. NCAP

Crossed, and the florid black found. (LL) Oregon. Bob Kaufman. EGAG; GT

Crossed Apple, The. Louise Bogan. HeIP-4; NALW

Crossed out *delete* and wrote his patient *stet.* (LL) Proof, The. Richard Wilbur. InvLi; UpMys

Crossed over on the other shore. Heartstopping. Nicole Espagnol. SurWo, *tr. by* Myrna Bell Rochester

Crossed over the river, and the river went dry. Crossroads. Forrest Hamer. PoDa

Crossed Threads. Helen Hunt Jackson. APN-2

Crossed-Over, Fiend-Snitched, X-ed Out. Mary Jo Bang. BAP-01

Crosses his blond eyes to think of you. Dracula. Lorenzo Thomas. AHA

Cross-framed square of kitchen light, A. Back Steps Lookout. Rhyll McMaster. BMAP

Crossing. Pamela Alexander. AmAlph

Crossing. Nin Andrews. AmZen

Crossing. Buson. EH, *tr. by* Robert Hass

Crossing: "Have we always been close to." Karen McKinnon. ICANM

Crossing. Diane Ward. FTOS

Crossing a bridge in our VW bus. Accident, An. Gjertrud Schnackenberg. ArBi

Crossing a summer. EMJL, *tr. by* Haruo Shirane

Crossing Alone the Nighted Ferry. A. E. Housman. HarvBoo; NoP-4; NoP-5; NPeEn; OxBEV

Crossing at rush hour the Walt Whitman Bridge. Modern Poet, A. Howard Nemerov. ViWalt

Crossing Brooklyn Ferry. Walt Whitman. APN-1; ColAP; FaBoA; NAAL-3; NAAL-5; NAMCP V.1; NCAP; NoAM; NoP-4; NoP-5; OxBoAm; WaAnP

Crossing Brooklyn Ferry from Staten Island. New Boy, The. Peter E. Murphy. OPRER

Crossing Ching-Men to See a Friend Off. Li Po. ChinPo, *tr. by* Ye Weilian [*or* Yeh Wei-lien *or* Wai-lim Yip]

Crossing Disappearing behind Them. Marjorie Welish. PmAP

Crossing half the sky. Basho. SoOfWa, *tr. by* Sam Hamill

Crossing Kansas by Train. Donald Justice. StAl *Fr.* American Sketches (for William Carlos Williams).

Crossing Lincoln Park. Karl Shapiro. IllVoic

Crossing Out. Fanny Howe. PfS

Crossing Over. Raylene Hinz-Penner. ACAMVP

Crossing Over. William Meredith. NoAM

Crossing quay crossing customs the end is here *that's it! no more!*. Omphalos. Michele Leggott. VaPo

Crossing Rice Fields at Nightfall. Ko Ŭn. CAMKP, *tr. by* Anthony, Brother of Taizé

Crossing the Alps. Ken Morrice. EdScPo

Crossing the Alps ("Upturning with a band.") William Wordsworth. NPBRoP *Fr.* Prelude, The; Growth of a Poet's Mind [1805 version; Selections from Anthologies].

Crossing the Atlantic. Anne Sexton. NoAM

Crossing the autumn moor. Buson. EH, *tr. by* Robert Hass

Crossing the Bar. Alfred Tennyson. BrAP; BRP; ChIV-2; ClHu; HeIP-4; InoFa; ITBLP; NAEL-6v2; NAEL-7v2; NoP-4; NoP-5; OBEV; SacPr; SoSe-8; TFi; TWF

Crossing the Border. Gu Cheng. WoBe, *tr. by* Joseph R. Allen

Crossing the Border. Norman Alexander MacCaig. HarvBoo

Crossing the Border, First Series. Tu Fu [*or* Du Fu]. *tr. by* David Lattimore
    "Drawing a bow you must draw a strong one." WoPoe, *tr. by* David Lattimore

Crossing the keyboards of the palace. Viktor Krivulin. ItGoST, *tr. by* Michael Molnar

Crossing the Loch. Kathleen Jamie. EdScPo; MoWP

Crossing the Mountain, I Follow the Chin-chu River. Hsieh Ling-yün. CrYelRi, *tr. by* Sam Hamill

Crossing the mountains. Soldiers. Ucha Sakhltkhutsishvili. PML, *tr. by* the author and Al Zolynas

Crossing the porch in the hazy dusk. Candlelight. Tony Hoagland. PoDa

Crossing the River. Monica Raymond. PfS

Crossing the River. Patrizia Vicinelli. ItPo *Fr.* Foundations of Being, The.

Crossing the River to Juárez. Pat LittleDog. TiP2

Crossing the Road. Walter McDonald. PML

Crossing the Square. Grace Schulman. ExTi

Crossing the Strait. Nicholas Samaras. TWW

Crossing the Straits. Richard Greene. Coast

Crossing the street. Broken Home, The. James Merrill. BrAP; ColAP; EMP; GPTC; NAAL-5; NAMCP V.2; NoAM; NoP-4; NoP-5; PoPoPo

Crossing the Valley. Fadil Azzawi. IrPoTo, tr. by Ralph Saverese and Saadi A. Simawe

Crossing the Water. Sylvia Plath. BrAP; CAP-8

Crossing the Yang-Chia Bridge Once More. Ching An. CSKM, tr. by Jerome P. Seaton

Crossing the Yellow River. Wang Wei. CrYelRi, tr. by Sam Hamill

Crossing there under the trees with leaden pace. False Enchantment. Jean Starr Untermeyer. MoAmPo

Crossing Walt Whitman Bridge. Daniel Gerard Hoffman. ViWalt

Crossings. Linda Hogan. BodElec

Cross-Road Epitaph, A. Amy Levy. VWP

Crossroads. Forrest Hamer. PoDa

Crossroads, The. Maria Luisa Spaziani. CItWP, tr. by Cinzia Sartini Blum and Lara Trubowitz

Crossroads in the Past. John Ashbery. BAP-01

Cross-tree, The. Robert Herrick. CavPo; ChIV-2

Crosswalk or neighbourhood watch, the shape and colour of habit. Tattoo. Robert Budde. PoPra

Crotchet Castle. Thomas Love Peacock.
    Chorus. NBLV
    Priest and the Mulberry-Tree, The. OxAEP-2

Crouch'd on the pavement close by Belgrave Square. West London. Matthew Arnold. GSo

Crouched in its giant green the Indian hid. Vacant Lot. Dudley Randall. NoAM

Crouched on one knee one. Autumn Warrior. Barney Bush. HATNAP

Crouched on their women woven saddle rugs. Great Horse Fair, The. Desmond O'Grady. PBCIP

Crouched over and across from the waiting girl, (dabbing nail polish where nylon hell broke loose). Washington Square: August Afternoon. Oliver Pitcher. EGAG

Crouching, I'm like some sneakthief, eye. Ritual. Gwyneth Lewis. ATSWP, tr. by Robert Minhinnick

Crow. Robert Grenier. PmAP

Crow. Ted Hughes.
    That Moment. UV

Crow. Yunna Petrovna Moritz. ItGoST, tr. by Daniel Weissbort

Crow. Viktor Aleksandrovich Sosnora. ItGoST, tr. by Dinara Georgeoliani and Mark Halperin

Crow, A. Basho. EH, tr. by Robert Hass

Crow, The. Issa. EH, tr. by Robert Hass

Crow and the Birds. Ted Hughes. HarvBoo

Crow and the Fox, The. Reed Whittemore. BodElec

Crow came to our house one time, A. Crow. Yunna Petrovna Moritz. ItGoST, tr. by Daniel Weissbort

Crow flew guiltily off. (LL) Crow's First Lesson. Ted Hughes. NAMCP V.2; NoAM

Crow is my name. (LL) Song of the Crows. Chippewa Oral Tradition. NAAL-5; NAAPv.2

Crow Is Walking. Grace Butcher. PoA 2002

Crow or crowd with its detached features of twig bark and plunder walks to, The. Allegory. Carla Harryman. FTOS

Crow pecks protein from the asphalt smear. Requiem on I-89. Maxine W. Kumin. CAP-8

Crow realized God loved him. Crow's Theology. Ted Hughes. GI

Crow sits on the prayerflagpole, A. Who Eats Who? Allen Ginsberg. BodElec

Crow Testament. Sherman Alexie. NAMCP V.2

Crow went on laughing. (LL) Childish Prank, A. Ted Hughes. CABP; NPeEn

Crowd. Cole Swensen. OnScMo

Crowd and Not Evening Or Light. Leslie Scalapino.
    Series—3, The. PmAP

Crowd at the ball game, The. At the Ball Game. William Carlos Williams. BrAP; MoASP; NoAM

Crowd at the ballpark sing, the cantor sings, The. Uncreation, The. Robert Pinsky. NAMCP V.2

Crowded Street, The. William Cullen Bryant. NCAP

Crowded Trolley Car, A. Elinor Wylie. SacPr

Crowded with beauties is thy lovely vale. Crickhowel. Richard Hall. AngWePo

Crowding out everything else. (LL) Immigrant Picnic. Gregory Djanikian. PoA 2002; PoDa

Crowding this beach. Stone Speech. Charles Tomlinson. NPeEn

Crowding time back in a corner. (LL) Remembrance of Strange Hospitality. Yelena Shwarts. ItGoST; StAl; VCWP, tr. by Michael Molnar

Crowdoll. L. S. Asekoff. BodElec

Crowds amassed with sudden bursts of, The. Victoria Station. Luigi Fontanella. NeIt, tr. by Michael Palma

Crowds cheer silently for hours. Watching Ants Play Soccer in Central Park. Anthony Piccione. UrbNat

Crowds Cheered as Gloom Galloped Away, The. Matthea Harvey. IAoNAP

Crowds, the cheers, the broken leg, the death, The. Morenz. Tim Bowling. IFF

Crowing of the Red Cock, The. Emma Lazarus. TaR

Crown and Country. Jackie Kay. MFPA

Crown me with roses whilest I live. Abraham Cowley. OBVE Fr. Epicure ("Underneath this myrtle shade, The").

Crown of glory unto woman's brow, The. (LL) Joan of Arc, in Rheims. Felicia Dorothea Hemans. RWP; ViWPN

Crown Prince of Dullness, The. John Dryden. NOSC; OBCoV; OxBEV Fr. Mac Flecknoe [or, A Satire upon the True-Blue Protestant Poet T. S.].

Crowned in hydrogen, it travels incognito. To the Sun. Tom Sleigh. UrbNat

Crowned with a feathered helmet. Pride. Yusef Komunyakaa. PoA 2002

Crowned with snows to catch the morning's fire. (LL) Snow: "Who affirms that crystals are alive?" John Davidson. EdScPo; NePenScot; NPeEn

Crowning a bluff where gleams the lake below. Pontoosuce. Herman Melville. APN-2; NCAP; TCAPo

Crows. Carole Glasser Langille. IFF

Crows. David McCord. MoAmPo

Crows. Mary Oliver. MoW

Crows. Lizette Woodworth Reese. APT-1; TCAPo

Crows. Mariana Romo-Carmona. WiU

Crows, The. Louise Bogan. ItP; NAAPv.2; NALW

Crows, The. David McCord. MoAmPo

Crows, a hoarse cone in the wind, The. Crows at Paestum. George Garrett. InGu

Crow's / Abandoned nest. Basho. ZenPo, tr. by Takashi Ikemoto and Lucien Stryk

Crows and Grackles Grackles. Hoa Nguyen. WANABP

Crows are cawing, The. Coming and Going. Robert Francis. TLR

Crows at Dusk. Li Po. CrYelRi, tr. by Sam Hamill

Crows at Paestum. George Garrett. InGu

Crows cawed, The. just before. dawn. Landscape Painting. Diane Glancy. TWW

Crow's First Lesson. Ted Hughes. NAMCP V.2; NoAM

Crows hastening to their nests, The. Yun Söndo. CATKP Fr. Angler's Calendar, The.

Crows have come back for April, The. In the Bog behind My House. Ira Sadoff. PfSP

Crows in a Strong Wind. Cornelius Eady. ESEAA; InvLad

Crow's Last Stand. Ted Hughes. HarvBoo

Crows on City Walls. Unknown. ColAnChi, tr. by Anne Birrell

Crows on city walls. Crows on City Walls. Unknown. ColAnChi, tr. by Anne Birrell

Crows resting. Basho. EMJL, tr. by Haruo Shirane

Crow's Theology. Ted Hughes. GI

Crow's-Eye View. Yi Sang. CAMKP, tr. by Walter Lew
    Poem No. 1. CAMKP, tr. by Walter Lew
    Poem No. 2. CAMKP; PFTM-1, tr. by Walter Lew
    Poem No. 3. CAMKP; PFTM-1, tr. by Walter Lew
    Poem No. 5. CAMKP; PFTM-1, tr. by Walter Lew
    Poem No. 7. CAMKP; PFTM-1, tr. by Walter Lew
    Poem No. 9. CAMKP, tr. by Walter Lew
    Poem No. 10: Butterfly. CAMKP; PFTM-1, tr. by Walter Lew
    Poem No. 13. CAMKP, tr. by Walter Lew
    Poem No. 15. CAMKP; PFTM-1, tr. by Walter Lew

Crucible and its contents vaporize, The. (LL) Dear World. Paula Gunn Allen. FiBr; HATNAP

Crucified. Francis Quarles. NOSC

Crucified Lord, you swim upon your cross. Geoffrey Hill. NAEL-6v2; NoAM; NoP-5 Fr. Lachrimae; or Seven Tears Figured in Seven Passionate Pavans.

Crucifix, The. Daniel Berrigan. UpMys

Crucifix in a Deathhand. Charles Bukowski. PmAP

Crucifixion. Hayden Carruth. BodElec; PLBUT

Crucifixion (Montgomery, Alabama). Andrew Hudgins. UpMys

Crucifixion of Our Blessed Lord. Christopher Smart. ChIV-2 Fr. Hymns and Spiritual Songs for the Fasts and Festivals of the Church of England.

Crucifixion, The. Mary Weston Fordham. CBWP-2

Crucifixion, The. Alice Thompson Meynell. SacPr

Crucifixion, The. Henry Hart Milman. SacPr

Crucifixion Will Not Take Place, The. Elma Mitchell. EdScPo

Crucify Him! Giles Fletcher, the Elder. SacPr

'Crucify Him, Crucify Him!' Hark. Will You Crucify Your King? Michael Field. ViWPN

Cruel, but composed and bland. Atossa. Matthew Arnold. TriCat

Cruel disease! Can there for beauty be. Verses Sent to Mr Bevil Higgons, on His Sickness and Recovery from the Small-pox, in the Year 1693. Catherine Cockburn. EMWP

Cruel girls we loved, The. Mothers and Daughters. David Campbell. BMAP

Cruel people, who see how an old man leads me to his bed. Unknown. SLW, tr. by Marjolijn De Jager, Sayd Bahodin Majrouh and André Velter

Cruel the roar of the city ways. Cries of the Newsboy. Edith Matilda Thomas. SWaP

CRUEL, you pull away too soon your lips whenas you kiss me. Unknown. NoSic

Cruelest thing I did to my younger sister, The. Our Other Sister. Jeffrey Harrison. PoDa

Cruellest thing they did, The. Finale. Judith Wright. EmeKit

Cruelties. Robert Herrick. CavPo

Cruelty. don't talk to me about cruelty. Lucille Clifton. BodElec

Cruelty has a Human heart. William Blake. ChIV-1; NAEL-6v2; NAEL-7v2; NoP-4; NoP-5 Fr. Songs of Experience.

Cruelty of ages past affects us now, The. MMDCCXIII½. Lorenzo Thomas. WhBo

Cruelty, the Vandals Say. Alan Michael Parker. NeAmPo

Cruelty Without Beauty. Denise Riley. MoWP

'Cruetin Sarjunt, The. James Russell Lowell. See Letter, A ("Thrash away, you'll hev to rattle").

Cruising. Gig Ryan. BMAP

Cruising a Hungry World. Scott Hightower. BeDoSh

Cruising for Prostitutes. Jennifer L. Knox. FreRad

Cruising 99. Garrett Kaoru Hongo.
    Confession of the Highway / The Hermit Speaks. GeoHom
    Porphyry of Elements, A. GeoHom

Cruising with the Beach Boys. Dana Gioia. GeoHom; PoA 2002; RWPCtW; SwNoth

Crum Appointment, The. Lizelia Augusta Jenkins Moorer. CBWP-3

Crumbled Paper for Future Poems. Fawzi Karim. IrPoTo, tr. by Chuck Miller and Saadi A. Simawe

Crumbled rock of London is dripping under, The. Sonnet. Roy Fuller. PoA 2002

Crumble-Knees, The. Russell Edson. SUP

Crumbling Infrastructure, The. Thomas M. Disch. OxBoAm

Crumbling is not an instant's Act. Emily Dickinson. TCAPo

Crumpled like an embroidered pillowcase. Kinged. Shalin Hai-Jew. UnSA

Crunch, The. Gerda Mayer. OBSP

Cruse of Tears, The. A Russian Legend. Emily Jane Pfeiffer. ViWPN

Crush. Rigoberto González. BeDoSh

Crush of age is turning my hair white, The. For the Beach Gulls. Po Chü-i. NDACCP, tr. by David Hinton

Crushed Flower, The. Mary E. Tucker. CBWP-1

Crushes them all. (LL) Ultima Ratio. Friedrich Georg Jünger. UpMys; WoPoe, tr. by Les A. Murray

Crushin. StacyLynn. BtF

Crusoe. Paul Valéry. PFTM-1

Crusoe had provided all the necessaries and was more or less at leisure in. Crusoe. Paul Valéry. PFTM-1

Crusoe in England. Elizabeth Bishop. APT-2; EmeKit; FaBoVe; NAMCP V.2; OxBoAm; PoPoPo; RACG

Crusoe's Island. Derek Walcott. VCWP

Crust on Fresh Snow. Rolf Jacobsen. WoPoe, tr. by Olav Grinde

Crustaceans. Roy Fuller. NoAM

Crutch slipping towel over. Changing. Daphne Rock. Prnts

Crutches. Nikki Giovanni. PfS

Crux. Bill Knott. PoCho

Cry, The. Ronald Stuart Thomas. StAl

Cry, The: "Then, everything slept." Larry Levis. NevBe

Cry Faugh! Robert Graves. MoBrPo

Cry from Childhood, A. Valeri Petrov. PML, tr. by Richard Wilbur

Cry "God for Harry, England, and Saint George!" (LL) William Shakespeare. OxAEP-1; WaAnP Fr. King Henry V.

Cry I bring down from the hills, The. You and I Are Disappearing. Yusef Komunyakaa. AmAlph; PoCho

Cry Me a River. Wopko Jensma. TSAP

Cry no more, wild geese. Riding a Mule. Kim Ch'unsu [or Chun-soo]. CAMKP, tr. by Anthony, Brother of Taizé

Cry of a People. Mary Evelyn Moore Davis. SWaP

Cry of a Stone, A [or The]. Anna Trapnell.
    "O he is a rest that requires." PBRV
    "Therefore John read how that thou wouldst." ChIV-2

Cry of Blood, and of a Broken Covenant, The. Sir William Mure.
    "O Heavens! O Earth! heer I must pause a space." PBRV

Cry of the Animals, The. Mary Howitt. VWP

Cry of the Children, The. Elizabeth Barrett Browning. NAEL-7v2; OxAEP-2; ViWPN; VWP

Cry of the deer / Where at its depths. Otsuyu. ZenPo, tr. by Takashi Ikemoto and Lucien Stryk

Cry of the guitar, The. Guitar, The. Federico García Lorca. SpanPo, tr. by Rachel Benson and Robert O'Brien

Cry of the Human, The. Elizabeth Barrett Browning.
    Convinced by Sorrow. SacPr

Cry of the Oppressed, The. Henrietta Tindal. VWP

Cryin' [or Crying] "Jean, Jean, Jean!" (LL) Tam i' the Kirk. Violet Jacob. EdScPo; NePenScot

Crying. Galway Kinnell. ChAP; NTCP

Crying and crying. Richard Wright. NoP-5

Crying as you sleep. (LL) Nightsweats. Richard Tayson. AmPoNex; WiU

Crying Asia! that famous place. Marriage of Hector and Andromache, The. Sappho. OBVE, tr. by Guy Davenport

Crying in Early Infancy. John Tranter.
    "Chicago "Manuel of Style" is really neat, The." NoAM
    "Giving up women is worse than animal laxatives." NoAM
    "Sweat is a style of the body." NoAM
    "They burn the radio and listen to the blues." NoAM

Crying only a little bit. Crying. Galway Kinnell. ChAP; NTCP

Crying Ospreys. Unknown. CCL1 Fr. Guan-ju.

Crying to the end "I have not finished." (LL) Geoffrey Hill. NAMCP V.2; NoAM Fr. Funeral Music.

Crying white candle, A. Haunted, The. Brad Leithauser. RA

Cryo. Adam Dickinson. PoPra

Cryptogram, The. David Lindley. NLP

Cryptographiku for Jim L5ftwich. Bob Grumman. AnSo

Cryptographiku for Wallace Stevens. Bob Grumman. AnSo

Cryptographiku No. 1. Bob Grumman. AnSo

Crypto-Jews, The. Robin Becker. ExTi; OPRER; TaR

Crystal, The. George Barker. OBMV

Crystal, The. Sidney Lanier. TCAPo

Crystal Cabinet, The. William Blake. NPBRoP; NPeEn

Crystal Chandeliers. David Ignatow. BodElec

Crystal, flawless beauty on the brows, A. Portrait, A. Michael Field. VWP

Crystal Gazer, The. Sara Teasdale. MoAmPo

Crystal Lithium, The. James Schuyler. PmAP; VCAP

Crystal Moment. Edward Weismiller. YaYoPo

Crystal Night. Denise Levertov. TaR

Crystal Palace, The. John Davidson.
    "Contraption,—that's the bizarre, proper slang." NePenScot

Crystal Palaces, The. Sir Richard Blackmore. STuOW Fr. Prince Arthur.

Crystal parting the meads. River in the Meadows, The. Léonie Adams. MoAmPo

Crystal Text, The. Clark Coolidge.
    "Where is the wonder to not know?" PFTM-2

Crystal willow, a poplar of water, A. Octavio Paz. WoPoe Fr. Sunstone.

Crystals. Thylias Moss. NAMCP V.2

Crystals like Blood. Hugh MacDiarmid. HarvBoo

CS. Geraldine Monk. Oth

Csongor and Tünde. Mihály Vörösmarty. tr. by Peter Zollman
    Soliloquy of the Night, The. IQMS, tr. by Peter Zollman

Csontváry. László Nagy. IQMS, tr. by Geroge Gömöri and Kenneth McRobbie

Cu Chuimne in his youth. Epitaph for Cu Chuimne. Unknown. WoPoe, tr. by Thomas Kinsella

¿Cuál coro? Eduardo Milán. RMCMP

Cuántas veces al entrar a la plaza y ver desde una de las calles que en ella desembocan. Contemporáneos. Antonio Deltoro. RMCMP

Cuando amanece alguien con gracia, de tan sencillas. Eugenio de Luelmo. Claudio Rodríguez. RaW

Cuando el tecolote canta, el indio muere. Consuelo de Aerenlund. OPRER

Cuando era primavera en España. Cuando Era Primavera. Emilio Prados. RaW

Cuando he llegado de noche. Incidentes Domésticos. Miguel de Unamuno. RaW

Cuando llegue la noche y sea la sombra un báculo. Creciendo Hacia la Tierra. Luis Rosales. RaW

Cuando llueve, y reviso mis papeles, y acabo. Momentos Felices. Gabriel Celaya. RaW

Cuando se quita del labio usted el epíteto escupiéndolo al rostro de la amada. Ignorancia. Gerardo Deniz. RMCMP

Cuando un niño nos mira serio. Fotografía de Niño. Carlos Sahagún. RaW

Cuando ya nada se espera personalmente exaltante. Poesía Es un Arma Cargada de Futuro, La. Gabriel Celaya. RaW

Cuatro. Ofelia Perez Sepúlveda. SPV

Cuatro ("Pero luego, en el trayecto imaginario de un automóvil blanco.") Ofelia Perez Sepúlveda. SPV

Cuatrocientos zontles de distancia. Cantares. Juan Gregorio Regino. RMCMP

Cuauhtemoc. Frank Lima. BodElec

Cuba. Sandra M. Castillo. TouFir

Cuba. Tapa Kearney.
    "Lifenet Intense feeling Burroughs; face." AHA

Cuba. Paul Muldoon. ModIr; PNI; StAl

Cuba, Crocodiles, Rain. Keith Armstrong. RSaN

Cuba Libre. Imamu Amiri Baraka. BB

Cuba, 1962. Ai. ESEAA

Cuban-American Gothic. Virgil Suárez. AmPoNex

Cubano / I was but a child when you marched. For Fidel Castro. Sandra Maria Esteves. PueRic

Cubes. Langston Hughes. APT-2

Cubic and rinsed. Paul Christensen. TiP2 Fr. Houston: An Ode.

Cubic inch of some stars, A. Blue Tit on a String of Peanuts. Norman Alexander MacCaig. CABP

Cubist Portrait. Marjorie Allen Seiffert. PoA 2002

Cubran las ventanas con alcándaras que no entre llegó con el delirio. Diminuto Anfibio. Silvia Eugenia Castillero. SPV

Cubs, The. Pura López Colomé. RMCMP, tr. by Forrest Gander

Cuchulain Comforted. William Butler Yeats. PoCho

Cuchulainn. Michael O'Loughlin. PBCIP

Cucina. Martine Bellen. TAPaP

Cuckoo. Robert Desnos. PFTM-1

Cuckoo. Woljo Toan. BecRai, tr. by Kim Daljin, Kim Won-Chung and Christopher Merrill

Cuckoo, A. Basho. EMJL, tr. by Haruo Shirane

Cuckoo, The. Basho. EMJL, tr. by Haruo Shirane

Cuckoo, The. Gerard Manley Hopkins. MoBrPo

Cuckoo, The. Kim Sowŏl. CAMKP, tr. by David R. McCann

Cuckoo, The. Unknown. FaBoVe

Cuckoo and Skylark. Sŏ Chŏngju. CAMKP, tr. by David R. McCann

Cuckoo and the gowk, the. Riddle. Unknown. FaBoVe

Cuckoo, cherry tree. Unknown. FaBoVe

Cuckoo cries, A. Basho. SoOfWa, tr. by Sam Hamill

Cuckoo, / Cuckoo. Cuckoo, The. Kim Sowŏl. CAMKP, tr. by David R. McCann

Cuckoo, glad cuckoo, Oh! where wilt thou rest to-night? Cuckoo Song. Henrietta Cordelia Ray. CBWP-3

Cuckoo on my breast will not be silent: her songs are green, The. Blue Cage, A. Vincent Woods. NIrP

Cuckoo singing. Issa. EH, tr. by Robert Hass

Cuckoo sings, The. Issa. EH, tr. by Robert Hass

Cuckoo sings / To me, to the mountain. Issa. ZenPo, tr. by Takashi Ikemoto and Lucien Stryk

Cuckoo snatches at the hairy worm, The. Food of Birds, The. Brewster Ghiselin. APT-2

Cuckoo Song. Henrietta Cordelia Ray. CBWP-3

Cuckoo Song, The. Unknown. See Sumer Is Icumen [or Ycomen] In.

Cuckoo-bird-castle-in-the-clouds. Twentieth Century Fresco. Sándor Weöres. IQMS, tr. by Adam Makkai

Cuckoo's crying / Nothing special to do. Issa. ZenPo, tr. by Takashi Ikemoto and Lucien Stryk

Cuckoo-spit. Katherine Pierpoint. MoWP

Cuckoo-spit on cowparsley. Cuckoo-spit. Katherine Pierpoint. MoWP

Cucumber, The. Nazim Hikmet. VCWP

Cucumbers. Lorna Crozier. OpeFie

Cucumbers hide. Cucumbers. Lorna Crozier. OpeFie

Cucumbers of Wolverhampton, The. Ifor Ap Glyn. BBMWP, tr. by Nigel Jenkins

Cuddie [or Cuddy], for shame hold up thy heavy[e] head. Edmund Spenser. NAEL-6v1; NAEL-7v1 Fr. Shepherd's Calender, The.

Cuddled in the dark. 4½ Months: Halfway Song. George Barlow. ISC

Cudgeled Husband, The. Jonathan Swift. NBLV

Cuerda sobre un abismo. Equilibrismo. Elsa Cross. RMCMP

Cuerpo de maravilla. Malva Flores. RMCMP Fr. Casa nómada.

Cuerpo dechado de dioscurismo sobre la mediocridad heliconia de este verso. Musa. Gerardo Deniz. RMCMP

3, Cuerpo Presente. Federico García Lorca. RaW Fr. Llanto por Ignacio Sánchez Mejías.

Cuerpo y el Alma, El. Vicente Aleixandre. RaW

Cui Bono? Horace Smith. NOBRP

Cuillin, The. Rayne Mackinnon. EdScPo

Culbin Sands. Andrew Young. EdScPo

Culebras. Habian cruzado las plantas amarillas del jardín para beber la luz ajadas con la cifra de la certeza. Éxtasis. María Baranda. RMCMP

Cult of Love, The. Hadewijch. NAWM-7v1, tr. by Peter Dronke

Cultivation. Ed Friedman. PrTe

Cultivation. Mrs. Henry Linden. CBWP-4

Cultivation of Orchids, The. Dionisio D. Martinez. TouFir

Cultivator. Judith Ortiz Cofer. PfSP

Cultural Trip, A. Opal Palmer Adisa. GT

Culture. Alfred Kreymborg. APT-1

Culture and Anarchy. Adrienne Rich. NALW

Culture as Exhibit. "Ern Malley." BMAP

Culture Drift. Anne Waldman. AHA

Culture Nervous. Ricardo M. de Ungria. ReBoTo

Culture whirls by us so fast, The. George Stanley. NLPA Fr. Mountains and Air.

Cultures. Gloria Anzaldúa. UnSA

Culture's beginnings. Basho. WoPoe, tr. by Sam Hamill

Culture's beginnings. Basho. SoOfWa

Cum here, Mandy, what's you chewin'. When Daddy Cums from Wuk. Maggie Pogue Johnson. CBWP-4

Cumae. Merrill Moore. FuPo

Cumberland, The. Henry Wadsworth Longfellow. CBCWP; PCW

Cumberland Gap. Unknown. APN-2

Cumberland Station. Dave Jeddie Smith. LPSFW

Cuncta Semper. Rodolfo Di Biasio. NeIt, tr. by Stephen Sartarelli

Cunning and art he did not lack. Allansford Pursuit, The. Unknown. WoPoe, tr. by Robert Graves

Cunning Painter, that with curious care, The. Joshua Sylvester. PBRV Fr. Saluste du Bartas' Devine Weekes.

Cunt is a spiderweb, The. Canto Twenty-Four. Tonino Guerra. PML, tr. by Adria Bernardi

Cup, The. Jones Very. APN-1

Cup of Clear Water, A. Thich Tue Sy. WhBo

Cup of cocoa steams in the mirror, A. Mirror, The. Boris Leonidovich Pasternak. TCRusP, tr. by Bogdan Boychuk and Mark Rudman

Cup of Coffee, a Sandwich, and You. Al Dubin and Billy Rose. ReLy

Cup of Coffee, The. Carole Bernstein. AmPoNex

Cup takes its sweet joy and tells how it touches, The. Meleager. HePo, tr. by Barbara Hughes Fowler

Cup, you come here! Tune: "Spring in the Ch'in Garden." Hsin Ch'i-chi. ColAnChi, tr. by James Robert Hightower

Cupboard, The. Walter De la Mare. NTCP

Cupid. Bernard O'Dowd. NOBAu

Cupid. Clare Rossini. MAAN

Cupid a Plowman. Moschus. OBVE,

Cupid abroad was lated in the night. Night Visitor, A. Robert Greene. NoSic

Cupid and My Campaspe Played. John Lyly. NoSic Fr. Alexander and Campaspe.

Cupid as he lay among. Wounded Cupid, The. Robert Herrick. OBVE

Cupid, in Myra's faire bewitching eyes. Fulke Greville, 1st Baron Brooke. PBRV Fr. Caelica.

Cupid Lost. Mary Sidney Wroth, Countess of Montgomery. See Sonnet 2: "Late in the Forest I did Cupid See."

Cupid's Call. James Shirley. NOSC

Cupid's Wrongs Vindicated. Martin Parker.
    "Thou knowst I lov'd thee well." PBRV

Cupio Dissolvi. William Habington. ChIV-2 Fr. Castara.

Cupolas flame, in Moscow where I live. Marina Ivanovna Tsvetayeva. TCRusP Fr. Poems to Blok.

Cupping her chin and lying there, the Bren. Defensive Position. John Streeter Manifold. MoBrPo

Cups. Gwen Harwood. EmeKit; HarvBoo

Cups #5. Robin Blaser. ASA

Cups we drink from are the skulls of arabs, The. Black Dahlia. Michael McClure. Eno

Cur foretells the knell of parting day, The. Ambrose Bierce. AmWit; APN-2 Fr. Devil's Dictionary, The.

Curandera, La. Diana García. TouFir

Curanderas. Natalia Toledo. RMCMP

Curdled Skulls. Bernard Bador. ConPit, tr. by Clayton Eshleman

Cure, The. Aidan Rooney-Céspedes. NIrP

Cure, The. Eugene Wildman. OPRER

Cure at Porlock, A. Amy Clampitt. NoAM

Cure at Troy, The. Seamus Heaney.
"Human beings suffer." PLBUT; TWF

Cure of my unquietness. Martial. RomPo, tr. by Peter Whigham

Cures. David Rivard. AllShUp; SwNoth

Curfew. Teresa de Jesús. AF, tr. by Maria Proser, Arlene Scully and James Scully

Curfew. Henry Wadsworth Longfellow. APN-1

Curfew Breakers, The. Samuel Chimsoro. NAfrP

Curfew Must Not Ring Tonight [or To-Night]. Rose Hartwick Thorpe. APN-2; BRP; SWaP

Curfew tolls the hour of locking up, The. Elegy in Newgate. William Cobbett. UV

Curfew tolls the knell of parting day, The. Elegy Written in a Country Churchyard. Thomas Gray. BrAP; BRP; CABP; ClHu; HeIP-4; InoFa; MakPoe; NAEL-6v1; NAEL-7v1; NIL-7; NoP-4; NoP-5; NPeEn; OBEV; OxAEP-1; OxBEV; PoPoPo; TFi; TreFP; UV; WaAnP; WeW-3

Curfew tolls the knell of parting day, The. Thomas Gray. UV Fr. Elegy Written in a Country Churchyard.

Curie / of the laboratory. Gertrude Stein. Mina Loy. APT-1; MoWP; NAAPv.2; NAMCP V.1; OxBoAm

Curing. Marlynn Rosario. PoCu

Curing Homosexuality. Jim Everhard. CAGL

Curiosity. Alastair Reid. SoSe-8; WaAnP

Curiosity, it means. Woman peeking. Explaining the Origin of My Name. Fatima Lim-Wilson. AmPoNex

Curious. Langston Hughes. APT-2

Curious concept—afterwards, A. Patricia K. Page. GPPA Fr. Alphabetical.

Curious Experiments. Pamela White Hadas. PfSP

Curious knot God made in paradise, A. Upon Wedlock and Death of Children. Edward Taylor. ColAP; NAAL-3; NAAL-5; NAAPv.1; NoP-4; NoP-5; SacPr; TCAPo

Curious tale that threaded through the town, A. Le Loupgarou. Derek Walcott. OxBSo

Curious, the assembly that forms before a door, a large door always. Jews in Hell. Tom Mandel. PmAP

Curl Up and Diet. Ogden Nash. OBCoV

Curled here, my cat is riding this couch. What Keeps Animals Sane? Douglas Goetsch. PA9/11

Curled like a foetus. On the Head of a Pin. Thomas McGrath. GifTon

Curlers at Dusk. David Roderick. MoASP

Curlews [Lift]. Ted Hughes.
"Out of the maternal watery blue lines." OWoS

Curl-grass, curl-grass. Juan-er: Curl-Grass. Unknown. APT-1; CCL1, tr. by Ezra Pound

Curling barbed wire. Huerfano Valley Seed Songs. Andrew Schelling. AmZen

Curling: Old Murrayfield Ice Rink. Angus Calder. EdScPo

Curling on the Bottom of My Mother's Bed. Lyn Lifshin. PfS

Curling them around. Cutting greens. Lucille Clifton. AFaM; ESEAA; GT; IPoFL; NAMCP V.2

Curling your antics 'round the springhouse. Tiff Belt Parley. David Thomas Roberts. AnSo

Curly had once seen arrows poisoned. Poison. William Heyen. RaF

Curly Kale. David Lindley. NLP

Curly-haired nomad boy, A. Song: Dragons at Midnight. Li Ho. CCL1, tr. by John Frodsham

6. The Current. Tom Sleigh. InoFa Fr. Work, The.

Currant bushes, the leaves of the currant, The. Indian Summer. Boris Leonidovich Pasternak. RusPo, tr. by Robert Arthur Douglas Ford

Currency. Craig Watson. OnScMo

Currency Lads may fill their glasses, The. Lass in the Female Factory, The. Unknown. NOBAu

Current Account. Haim Guri. NRoS, tr. by Esther Raizen

Current "Now, Voyager" Fantasy. Remy Holzer. OPRER

Currents. Rose Solari. AmPoNex

Curriculum Vitae. Ingeborg Bachmann. PFTM-2, tr. by Jerome Rothenberg

Curriculum vitae. Marie-Claire Bancquart. MFP, tr. by Martin Sorrell

Curriculum Vitae. Robert Gray. NOBAu

Curriculum Vitae. Lawrence Joseph. PBCAP

Curriculum Vitae. Lisel Mueller. IllVoic

Curry spice in the air. Caroline Street, Cardiff. John Tripp. TCAWP

Curse. Frank Bidart. OxBoAm

Curse, The. Robert Francis. APT-2

Curse, The. András Szkhárosi Horvát. tr. by Adam Makkai
"Dreadful are the happenings of our evil ages." IQMS, tr. by Adam Makkai

Curse, The. John Millington Synge. OBCoV

Curse for a Nation, A. Elizabeth Barrett Browning. NALW; ViWPN

Curse! Joy! Writing!, A. Natalya Gorbanevskaya. TCRusP, tr. by Daniel Weissbort

Curse of Kehama, The. Robert Southey.
Kehama's Curse. NOBRP

Curse of the Cat Woman. Edward Field. WeW-3

Curse on a Closed Gate, A. Unknown. IrV, tr. by James H. Cousins

Curse on a Thief, A. X. J. Kennedy. RaF

Curse on Herod, A. Amy Witting. ChIV-2; NOBAu

Curse on Mine-Owners, A. Unknown. RaF

Curse on the lover with shyness as plausible cover for his black lies, A. Spells. Eva Salzman. BeAl

Curse the thorns of fate, and damn as well its roses. Curse the Thorns of Fate. Rûhî. OLP; WoPoe, tr. by Walter Andrews, Najaat Black and Mehmet Kalpakli

Curse upon Edward, The. Thomas Gray. OBEV

Cursed is a Man. György Sárközi. IQMS, tr. by Roy Fuller

Cursed is a man in his forsaken years. Cursed is a Man. György Sárközi. IQMS, tr. by Roy Fuller

Cursing his eyes' erasing motion. Sickness & the Magnet, The. Christine Hume. IAoNAP

Cursive crawl, the squared-off characters, The. Writing. Howard Nemerov. VCAP

Curtain, The. Darl Macleod Boyle. YaYoPo

Curtain, The. Dyfnallt Morgan. BBMWP, tr. by Meic Stephens

Curtain Call. William Trowbridge. SUP

Curtain of cloud hangs, A. Muso Soseki. EaWin, tr. by W. S. Merwin

Curtain of daybreak is hanging, The. Unknown. APN-2 Fr. Mountain Chant, The.

Curtains. Ruth Stone. BeAl; InoFa; StAl

Curtains. David Wagoner. OxBoAm

Curtains in the House of the Metaphysician, The. Wallace Stevens. PoA 2002

Curtains part to reveal the equal parts. Exquisite Alchemy. Debra Taub. SurWo

Curtains were half drawn, the floor was swept, The. After Death. Christina Georgina Rossetti. NAEL-6v2; NAEL-7v2; NALW

Curtis Fuller. Rick Madigan. SeSe

Curve of the two steel spring-up prongs on. Wild Edge, The. Gary Snyder. NAMCP V.2

Curve of the Water. Hilda Morley. PmAP

Curve of your lips, The. Olga Popova. ItGoST, tr. by J. Kates

Curved pelvic bone dug up, The. Children of the Disappeared. Valerie Martínez. TouFir

Curves of beauty are not softly wrought, The. Palaestral Study, A. Edward Cracroft Lefroy. CAGL

Curzon! thou shouldst be living at this hour. Sonnet to the "Most Distinguished Chancellor" that Oxford Has Had. UV

Cushie Butterfield. George Ridley. FaBoVe

Cusp of Desire, The. Maysoun Saqr Al-Qasimi. PoArWo, tr. by Subhi Hadidi and Nathalie Handal

Custard is this. Gertrude Stein. NAAPv.2 Fr. Tender Buttons.

Custody. Thomas Lynch. BeAl

Custom. Carol Frost. MoASP

Custom. Carl Phillips. AmAlph

Custom Job: Hank Williams, Jr., and the Death Car, 1958. David Wojahn. PBCAP Fr. Mystery Train: A Sequence.

Customer #! Jessica Freeman. AnSo

Customs of the Country. Del Marie Rogers. TiP2

Cut. David J. Feela. ArBi

Cut. Sylvia Plath. CAP-8; EmeKit; MoWP; NAMCP V.2

Cut and drilled into, the blue cliff. Ridiculing the Monk Who Builds a Stupa. Jungkwan Haean. BecRai, tr. by Kim Daljin, Kim Won-Chung and Christopher Merrill

Cut brambles long enough. Sun Bu-er. WPoS

Cut Flower, A. Karl Shapiro. WeW-3

Cut Grass. Philip Larkin. NoAM

Cut mats are even. Laura Cashdollars. Bernadette Mayer. NYP2

Cut off these hands, cut off these feet. Wakayama Bokusui. CAoMJL1, tr. by Janine Beichman

Cut Pages, The. Roy Fisher.
"He paints words with the past." Oth
"To origin, which is another patch of sun." VaPo

Cut parents away, cut children away! Annihilation. Ko Un. WhBo

Cut the Grass. A. R. Ammons. WeW-3

Cut the lemon and let two drops fall into the glass. Naked Face. Yannis Ritsos. PFTM-2, tr. by Kimon Friar and Kostas Myrsiades

Cut the pear or I cut the pear. On Entries Emptiness. Dennis Phillips. FTOS

Cut the peony. Buson. EH, tr. by Robert Hass

Cut yer name across me backbone. Convicts' Rum Song. *Unknown.* FaBoVe; NOBAu

Cute Petite. Barry MacSweeney. VaPo

Cutting, A. Ou-yang Hsiu. CrYelRi, *tr. by* Sam Hamill

Cutting Back the Ifugao Past. Al Robles. ReBoTo

Cutting greens. Lucille Clifton. AFaM; ESEAA; GT; IPoFL; NAMCP V.2

Cutting off all to her thoughts. Her name Is 'Dooti'. Mongane Wally Serote. TSAP

Cutting Prow, The. Edward Sanders. PmAP

Cutting Sod-Land. George Scarbrough. LPSFW

Cutting the Cake. Virginia Hamilton Adair. AFaM

Cutting the Jewish Bride's Hair. Ruth Whitman. TaR

Cutting the throat of the sacrificial goat. What Her Girl-Friend Said. Peruñcattan. WoPoe, *tr. by* A. K. Ramanujan

Cutting, they called it. Castration. Nigel Jenkins. AngWePo; TCAWP

Cuttings. Nick Laird. NIrP

Cuttings (Sticks-in-a-drowse droop over sugary loam). Theodore Roethke. APT-2; IPoFL; NAAL-5; NAMCP V.1; NoAM; OBGa; WaAnP

Cuttings (later) ("This urge, wrestle, resurrection of dry sticks.") Theodore Roethke. APT-2; CAP-8; NAAL-5; NAMCP V.1; NoAM; OBGa; TRP; VCAP; WaAnP

(Cuttings (This urge, wrestle, resurrection of dry sticks).) ColAP

Cutty Wren, The. *Unknown.* UV

Cuz he's black and poor. About Atlanta. Ntozake Shange. ISC

Cuz' mama played jazz. Daniel Gray-Kontar. SpirFl

Cuzaani biaani ndani yudu. Yudu. Natalia Toledo. RMCMP

Cwa een like milk-wort and bog-cotton hair! Milk-Wort and Bog Cotton. Hugh MacDiarmid. EdScPo

Cwmchwefri. T. Harri Jones. AngWePo

Cwmrhydyceirw Elegiacs. Vernon Watkins. PoA 2002

Cyanide jar seals life, as sonnets move, The. Butterfly Bones; or, Sonnet against Sonnets. Margaret Avison. BrAP

Cyanogen Seas Are Surging. Sadakichi. NAAPv.1

Cyclamens. Michael Field. ViWPN; VWP

Cycle. Gottfried Benn. PFTM-1

Cycle. Bobbi Sykes. BMAP

Cycle Akhmatova, The. Marina Ivanovna Tsvetayeva. " . . . In my melodious city cupolas burn." AF

Cycle #22. B. P. Nichol. OpeFie

Cycle of Community. Margaret Avison. GPPA

Cycle of Inanna: The Courtship of Inanna and Dumazi, The. *Unknown. tr. by* Samuel Noah Kramer and Diane Wolkstein

"Inanna spoke." WoPoe, *tr. by* Samuel Noah Kramer and Diane Wolkstein

Cycle of life is a worrisome thing, The. On Covering the Bones of Chang Chin, the Hired Man. Liu Tsung-yüan. WoPoe, *tr. by* Jan W. Walls

Cycle of Months (Menstruation). Shuntaro Tanikawa. PFTM-2, *tr. by* Harold Wright

Cycle of Six Lyrics. Kenneth Koch.

O Pearl and Breasted World. PoA 2002

Cycles. Alison Brackenbury. ArBi

Cycles. Nzadi Z. Keita. BtF

Cycles in Flight: The Racing Bike. Allison A. deFreese. ArBi

Cycles of Donji Vakuf. Tony Harrison. FaBoWar

Cycling the Rosental. William Daniel Ehrhart. ArBi

Cyclist, The. John Morgan.

"Chill summer day, the sky, A." ArBi

Cyclist, The. Marge Piercy. NAMCP V.2; NoAM

Cycloid dimensions gripped. Wheels. Douglas Livingstone. TSAP

Cyclolotry. *Unknown.* ArBi

Cyclone. Remi Raji Oyelade. NeNiPo

Cyclone, howling because one of the lances, The. Derek Walcott. NAMCP V.2 *Fr.* Omeros.

Cyclones. Anna Hajnal. IQMS, *tr. by* Laurence James

Cyclop! if any ask thee who imposed. Homer. NOSC *Fr.* Odyssey.

Cyclops. Ovid. OBVE *Fr.* Metamorphoses.

Cyclus. Toeti Herarty. WoPoe, *tr. by* Harry Aveling

Cyder. John Philips.

Apple-Culture. OxAEP-1

Cymbals, the drummer, the tasteful buzzing brushes, The. Mom Used to Listen to Erroll Garner. Everett Goodwin. BtF

Cymbeline. William Shakespeare.

(Aubade: "Hark! hark! the lark at heaven's gate sings.") OBEV

(Fidele.) OBEV

Dirge for Fidele. ClHu; NoSic; OxAEP-1; SoSe-8; TFi

(Fear No More the Heat o' the Sun.) BrAP; ITBLP; NAEL-6v1; NoP-4; NoP-5; PoPoPo; PtR; WaAnP

"Hark, hark! the lark at heaven's gate sings." ITBLP; NIL-7; NIP-4; NoSic;

TFi; UV; NOSC

"How found you him?" OxAEP-1

"Pray you fetch him hither." NPeEn

(Song.) NOSC

Cymon and Iphigenia. John Dryden. OBNV

Militia, The. OBSV

Cymru. David Gwenallt Jones. OBWVE, *tr. by* Gwyn Jones

Cynara. Ernest Dowson. *See* Non Sum Qualis Eram Bonae sub Regno Cynarae.

Cynddylan on a Tractor. Ronald Stuart Thomas. AngWePo; TCAWP

Cynegetica. Oppian of Apamea [*or* Pella].

Greek Compliment, A. DiBP

Cynegeticon Liber. Faliscus Grattius.

Roman Tribute, A. DiBP, *tr. by* John Whitaker

Cynic, The. St. George Tucker.

"Once at a merry wedding feast." NBLV

Cynic Satire, A. John Marston. NoSic *Fr.* Satires.

Cynical Portraits. Louis Paul. NBLV

Cynotaph, The. Richard Harris Barham. DiBP

Cynthia in the Snow. Gwendolyn Brooks. TLR

Cynthia Matz, with my finger in your cunt. Each Day. David Ignatow. BodElec

Cynthia on Horseback. Philip Ayres. OxBSo

Cynthia, to thy power. Francis Beaumont and John Fletcher. OBEV *Fr.* Maid's Tragedy, The.

Cynthia, with Certain[e] Sonnets. Richard Barnfield.

"Beauty and majesty are fallen at odds." OxBSo

"Sighing, and sadly sitting by my Love." CAGL; PBRV

"Sometimes I wish that I his pillow were." PBRV

"Sporting at fancie, setting light by love." CAGL

"Sweet Corrall lips, where Nature's treasure lies." CAGL

"Thus was my love, thus was my Ganymed." CAGL

Cynthia's Revels. Ben Jonson.

(Echo's Lament for Narcissus.) OxAEP-1

Echo's [*or* Eccho's] Song. NOSC

Hymn[e] to Cynthia. NOSC

(Hymn to Diana.) OBEV; TFi

(Queen and Huntress.) NAEL-6v1; NAEL-7v1; NoP-4; NoP-5

(Slow, Slow, Fresh Fount [Keep Time with My Salt Tears].) NAEL-6v1; NAEL-7v1; NIP-4; NoP-4; NoP-5; TFi

Cypress. Aleksandr Semionovich Kushner. ItGoST, *tr. by* Paul Graves and Carol Ueland

Cypress Boat. *Unknown.* WoPoe, *tr. by* Constance A. Cook

Cypress on the Mound, The. *Unknown.* CCL1,

Cypresses. Robert Francis. APT-2

Cypresses. D. H. Lawrence. NAEL-6v2; NAEL-7v2

Cypriote, The. Herman Melville. TCAPo *Fr.* Clarel: A Poem and Pilgrimage in the Holy Land.

Cyriack, this three years['] day these eyes, though clear. To Mr. Cyriack Skinner upon His Blindness. John Milton. NOSC; NPeEn

Cyril Connolly. Enemies of Promise. Edmund Wilson. OBCoV

Cythera. David Ferry. GS

Cytherea. Carlos Montemayor. BLPSL, *tr. by* Rene de Costa, Rigas Kappatos and Eleni Paidoussi

Cywydd o Fawl. Harri Webb. AngWePo; TCAWP

Czar's Last Christmas Letter, The: A Barn in the Urals. Norman Dubie. NoAM; PoChi

Czech Dream. Lee Harwood. Oth

D

D. Jeffrey McDaniel. NeAmPo

D. G. Rossetti. Dorothy Parker. NALW *Fr.* Pig's-Eye View of Literature, A.

Da da buy buy. (LL) Lilies of the Field. Anne Rouse. MFPA; NeBl

Da / Phallic mystère. Cecil Taylor. EGAG

Dándole la mano a Mongo. Martín Espada. SeSe

Dab / Your death. State of the Union. Ben Friedlander. Eno

Dacca Gauzes, The. Agha Shahid Ali. BeAl; NAMCP V.2; NIL-7; NoP-4; NoP-5

Dachau Shoe, The. W. S. Merwin. AmWaPo; MotU

Dactyls. Vladislav Felitsianovich Khodasevich. TCRusP, *tr. by* Mary Jane White

Dad. Elaine Feinstein. InoFa; Prnts

Dad. Return, The. Joanne Limburg. NeBl

Dad a da da. Aborigine Sound Poem. *Unknown.* PFTM-1

Dad and Me. Geraint Jarman. BBMWP, *tr. by* Peter Finch

Dad gave me a desk, Mom a bed. Leaving Home. Yi Hyangji. EcSo, *tr.* by Catherine J. Kim

Dad, how good it would have been. Two Doors. Hwang Insuk. EcSo, *tr.* by Peter H. Lee

Dad is busy. *Unknown.* SonAtl, *tr.* by Tashi Delek, George van Driem and David Yang

Dad pushed my mother down the cellar stairs. Those Paperweights with Snow Inside. Molly Peacock. RA

Dad was a nurseryman. 30 Miles from J-Town. Amy Uyematsu. GeoHom

Dada, having only a few years or months or days to live, looks for a law-. Artichokes. Georges Ribemont-Dessaignes. PFTM-1

Dada Manifesto on Feeble and Bitter Love. Tristan Tzara. PFTM-1

Dad-Baby, The. Amanda Dalton. NeBl

Daddy. Sylvia Plath. BeAl; BrAP; CAP-8; ColAP; HeIP-4; HP; MakPoe; MoWP; NAAL-5; NALW; NAMCP V.2; NIL-7; NIP-4; NoAM; NoP-4; NoP-5; OxBoAm; PoPoPo; TFi; VCAP; WaAnP

Daddy. Bobby Troup. ReLy

Daddy, ain't you heard? (LL) Langston Hughes. APSN; APT-2; OxBoAm *Fr.* Lenox Avenue Mural.

Daddy and I are always here, you know. God Is Dead—Nietzche. Elizabeth Bartlett. Prnts

Daddy, daddy, you bastard, I'm through. (LL) Daddy. Sylvia Plath. BeAl; BrAP; CAP-8; ColAP; HeIP-4; HP; MakPoe; MoWP; NAAL-5; NALW; NAMCP V.2; NIL-7; NIP-4; NoAM; NoP-4; NoP-5; OxBoAm; PoPoPo; TFi; VCAP; WaAnP

Daddy, / don't let your dog. Warning. Langston Hughes. PFTM-1

Daddy don't smile. Crooked Afro. Frank X. Walker. SpirFl

Daddy drove with us kids in the back. October 27th. Vera Gheraducci. CItWP, *tr.* by Cinzia Sartini Blum and Lara Trubowitz

Daddy 43 but look 40. Abraham Got All the Stars N the Sand. Ruth Forman. AmPoNex; OxAAAP

Daddy / is hot butter corn bread in the winter. Waitin on Summer. Ruth Forman. SpirFl

Daddy Out Hitch-Hiking at 3:30 A.M. John Balaban. TAPaP

Daddy says the world. Drum, The. Nikki Giovanni. TWF

Daddy was a Belgian and so was Mammy too. Little Belgian Orphan, A. Amanda Ros. VerBaPo

Daddy would drop purple-veined vines. Banking Potatoes. Yusef Komunyakaa. NoP-4; NoP-5

Daddy's Friends. Esther Iverem. GT

Da-di-da, da-di-da, da-da-dee. Call Me Mister. Harold Rome. ReLy

Dae what ye wull ye canna parry. Hugh MacDiarmid. OxAEP-2 *Fr.* Drunk Man Looks at the Thistle, A.

Dae ye think there is nae saftness in ma breist? Feminist. Janet Paisley. EdScPo

Daedal of my death, A. Madrigal. William Drummond of Hawthornden. NOSC

Daedalus. Tom Dawe. Coast

Daedalus. Stephen Knight. TCAWP

Daedalus. Ovid. OBVE *Fr.* Metamorphoses.

Daedalus. Alastair Reid. WaAnP

Daedalus: The Dirge. George Oppen. FTOS

Dæmonic and the Celestial Love, The. Ralph Waldo Emerson. APN-1 *Fr.* Initial, Dæmonic, and Celestial Love.

Daffadowndilly. Mother Goose. NTCP

Daffodil. Waldo Williams. OBVWE, *tr.* by Gwyn Jones

Daffodil Song, The. Michael Drayton. AEP

Daffodils. Ted Hughes. NAEL-7v2; NoP-5

Daffodils. Karen Volkman. NeAmPo

Daffodils. William Wordsworth. *See* I Wandered Lonely as a Cloud.

Daffodils, The. William Wordsworth. *See* I Wandered Lonely as a Cloud.

Daffy-down-dilly is new come to town [*or* Daffadowndilly has come up to town]. Daffadowndilly. Mother Goose. NTCP

Daft Days, The. Robert Fergusson. CABP; NPeEn; OxAEP-1; OxBEV

Dafydd. Dylan Iorwerth. BBMWP *Fr.* Sand.

Dafydd ap Gwilym Resents the Winter. Rolfe Humphries. WoPoe

Dafydd's Seagull and the West Wind. Glyn Jones. TCAWP

Daguerreotype Taken in Old Age. Margaret Atwood. NoAM

Dahomey. Audre Lorde. PfS

Dai horse neighs against the bleak wind of Etsu, The. South-Folk in Cold Country. Li Po. NDACCP; OBVE, *tr.* by Ezra Pound

Dai K lives at the end of a valley. One is not quite sure. Synopsis of the Great Welsh Novel. Harri Webb. AngWePo; TCAWP

Dai, Live. Jon Dressel. AngWePo

Daily Daily, The. Nicolás Guillén.

National Police Headquarters. PFTM-1

Daily dawns another day. Inscription for the Ceiling of a Bedroom. Dorothy Parker. AmWit

Daily going out, The. Waterpot. Grace Nichols. RSaN

Daily Grind. BJ Ward. IaFF

Daily Habits. Heberto Padilla. VCWP

Daily Living. Rosemary Dobson.

Folding the Sheets. ItWoWo; NOBAu

Daily Papers. Marguerite Yourcenar. YaTCFP, *tr.* by Martin Sorrell

Daily Record for thirty-five years, The. (LL) Long Branch Song, A. Robert Pinsky. NoP-4; NoP-5

Daily Ritual. Shirley Kaufman. TAPaP

Daily Space. João Cabral de Melo Neto. VCWP

Daily Task. Belinda Zubicueta Carmona. TANSG, *tr.* by Celeste Kostopulos-Cooperman

Daily the indispensable is taught to elude us, while we are furnished according to our wishes. Good-Bye Shirts, The. W. S. Merwin. MotU

Daily to a profession—paid thinking. Two Women. Carol Rumens. MoWP

Daily to turn in Paul's, and help the trade. (LL) On English Monsieur. Ben Jonson. AEP; NBLV; NoP-4; NoP-5

Daily warmth we, The. John Cage. APSN *Fr.* Diary: How to Improve the World (You Will Only Make Matters Worse).

Daily we say to ourselves. Some Kind of Thanks. Menna Elfyn. ATSWP, *tr.* by Robert Minhinnick

Dainty Baby Austin! King of Oo-Rinktum-Jing, The. James Whitcomb Riley. NOxBChV

Dainty little maiden, whither would you wander? City Child, The. Alfred Tennyson. NOxBChV

Dainty Miss Apathy. Pooh! Walter De la Mare. OBCoV

Dainty Terms for Fratricide. Samuel Taylor Coleridge. NPBRoP *Fr.* Fears in Solitude [Written in April, 1798, during the Alarm of an Invasion].

Dairy Cows of Maria Cristina Cortes. Sherod Santos. PfSP

Daisies, daisies, in a field of daisies? (LL) Hogwash. Robert Francis. NIL-7; NIP-4; TRP

Daisy. Francis Thompson. MoBrPo; OBEV

Daisy. William Carlos Williams. MoAmPo

Daisy, The. Marya Alexandrovna Zaturenska. MoAmPo

Daisy and Lily. Dame Edith Sitwell. MoWP *Fr.* Façade.

Daisy follows soft the Sun, The. Emily Dickinson. NAAPv.1

Daisy: / garden aster of a shrubby habit. Michaelmas. Veronica Forrest-Thomson. HarvBoo

Daisy-cutter has wasted some, thinks Cloe O'Brien almost flinching. Flower, Pal Mal Comic Book. Leslie Scalapino. Eno

Dakota: October, 1822, Hunkpapa Warrior. Rod Taylor. WeW-3

Dalei Riverbank. Pao Chao. CCL1, *tr.* by Kang-i Sun Chang

Dali. Mahmoud Sharaf. AnVo, *tr.* by Mohamed Enani

Dallas. Dave Oliphant. TiP2

Dalliance of the Eagles, The. Walt Whitman. HeIP-4; NAAL-3; NAAPv.1; NoP-4; NoP-5; SAmP; TCAPo; TRP; WaAnP

Dalliance with Salt Sides, A. Clark Coolidge. NYP2

Dam Bellona, The. Der Blinde Junge. Mina Loy. APT-1; HarvBoo; NAMCP V.1

Dam Neck, Virginia. Richard Eberhart. NAAPv.2; PoWW

Damachi. Philip Whalen. AHA

Damages, Two Hundred Pounds. William Makepeace Thackeray. OBSV

Damascus. Gwendolyn MacEwen. StAl *Fr.* T. E. Lawrence Poems, The.

Damastes (Also Known As Procrustes) Speaks. Zbigniew Herbert. PoSu, *tr.* by John Carpenter and Bogdana Carpenter

Dame Edith Evans to. Said. George Starbuck. AmWit

Dame Lud dwelt deep in the haunted shade. Huntsman, The. Helen Adam. APT-2

Dame Nature, the goddess, one very bright day. On the Late Improvements at Nuneham, the Seat of the Earl of Harcourt. William Whitehead. OBGa

Dames. Al Dubin. ReLy

Dames of Washington. Grace Duffie Boylan. ArBi

Damien. George Young. BloBone

Damis erected this mound for his dead steadfast. Anyte. SaLy, *tr.* by Diane Rayor

Damn it all! all this our South stinks peace. Sestina: Altaforte. Ezra Pound. APT-1; ColAP; MakPoe; MoAmPo; OxBoAm; TCAPo; WaAnP

Damn it, honey, neither one of us. In the Twenty-Fifth Year of Marriage, It Goes On. Alicia Ostriker. PBCAP

Damn that celibate farm, that cracker-box house. Censorship. John Ciardi. NBLV

Damn the snow. Elegy for Thelonious. Yusef Komunyakaa. ESEAA

Damn Yankees. Richard Adler and Jerry Ross.

Heart. ReLy

Damn you dark poisons. Sleep (Second Version). Georg Trakl. GTCP, *tr.* by Robert Firmage

Damn you, lady, get out of my blood for good. Damn You, Lady. Robin Morgan. PfS

Damn'd for thy false Apostasy. (LL)   To My Inconstant Mistress [*or* Mistris]. Thomas Carew.   CavPo; NoP-4; OBEV; TFi

(Damned for thy false apostasy.) (LL)   NoP-4; WaAnP

DAMON and Phyllis squared.   *Unknown.*   NoSic

Damon the Mower.   Andrew Marvell.   BASC; NAEL-6v1; NAEL-7v1; NOSC

Damon's Lament for His Clorenda, Yorkshire, 1654.   Lupercio Leonardo de Argensola.   WoPoe, *tr. by* Geoffrey Hill

Damp gardenias pause.   Havana.   Laurel Ann Bogen.   SUP

Damp Hips of the Women, The.   Elisabeth Harvor.   Coast

Damp night overwhelmed Phoebus at the western gates.   Publius Papinius Statius.   RomPo *Fr.* Thebais [*or* Thebaid].

Damp wind, the innocent.   Gethsemane.   David Craig.   UpMys

Damp[e], The.   John Donne.   NOSC

Dampness, and things drift out of focus.   Viper Light.   Barbara Leslie Jordan. ExTi

Damsel came in midnight rain, A.   Thomas Love Peacock.   OxAEP-2 *Fr.* Maid Marian.

Damsel of Peru, The.   William Cullen Bryant.   APN-1

Danae and Perseus.   Simonides.   WoPoe, *tr. by* Richmond Lattimore

Danaïds, The.   Mihály Babits.   IQMS, *tr. by* Peter Zollman

Dança Mortal.   H. C. ten Berge.   TuT *Fr.* Lusitanian Variant, The.

Dance.   Sandy Shreve.   IFF

Dance.   Yamamura Bochō.   CAoMJL1, *tr. by* Leith Morton

Dance, The.   Marjorie Agosin.   TCLAP, *tr. by* Cola Franzen

Dance, The.   Hart Crane.   MoAmPo; NAAL-5 *Fr.* Bridge, The.

Dance, The.   Gareth Alban Davies.   OBWVE, *tr. by* Gwyn Jones

Dance, The.   Cornelius Eady.   GT

Dance, The.   Daniel Halpern.   ChAP

Dance, The.   HSü Ling.   CCL1, *tr. by* Anne Birrell

Dance, The.   Irene McKinney.   PBCAP

Dance, The.   Siamanto.   AF, *tr. by* Peter Balakian and Nevart Yaghlian

Dance, The.   C. K. Williams.   GoPo

Dance, The: "In Brueghel's great picture, The Kermess."   William Carlos Williams.   APT-1; BrAP; HarvBoo; HeIP-4; NAAL-5; NAAPv.2; NAMCP V.1; NIL-7; NIP-4; NoAM; NoP-4; PoPoPo; SAmP; SoSe-8; TFi; WaAnP

Dance, The ("When the snow falls the flakes.")   William Carlos Williams. NAAL-5

Dance and twitch for hours. (LL)   Angel Butcher.   Philip Levine.   ColAP; WaAnP

Dance, ballerina, dance.   Ballerina.   Bob Russell.   ReLy

Dance begins: to end about a form, The.   Desert Music, The.   William Carlos Williams.   APSN

Dance: "Billions of maggots are being sucked into a whirlpool."   Chông Hwajin.   EcSo, *tr. by* Julie C. Park

Dance Bodies #1.   Eugene B. Redmond.   ISC

Dance, dance in this museum case.   Love Song to Eohippus.   Peter Viereck. MoAmPo

Dance Figure.   Ezra Pound.   HeIP-4; MoAmPo

Dance Floor on the Mountain, The.   Pentti Saarikoski. "Winter solstice."   VCWP

Dance Hall.   Geoffrey Philp.   WaCA

Dance Hall: Version.   Geoffrey Philp.   WaCA

Dance in the township hall is nearly over, The.   Judith Wright.   BMAP *Fr.* Blind Man, The.

Dance Lesson, A.   A. Van Jordan.   SpirFl

Dance of Death.   Hwang Insuk.   EcSo, *tr. by* Peter H. Lee

Dance of Husbands in Bathrobes, The.   David Kirby.   SUP

Dance of Sister Rain.   Eugène Marais.   SonAtl, *tr. by* Joost Daalder, Peter Daskler and Alistair Turner

Dance of the Cherry Blossom.   Jackie Kay.   EmeKit; PoCu

Dance of the Greased Women, The.   Tristan Tzara.   PFTM-1 *Fr.* Poemes Negres.

Dance of the Infidels.   Al Young.   ESEAA; SeSe

Dance of the Letters.   Vince Gotera.   FTtHH; OpBo

Dance of the Macabre Mice.   Wallace Stevens.   PFTM-1

Dance of the Magyars, The.   Ádám Pálóczi Horváth.   IQMS, *tr. by* J. G. Nichols

Dance of the Sevin Deidly Synnis [*or* Seven Deadly Sins], The.   William Dunbar.   NePenScot

Dance of the starlings above the sleeping village, The.   Massacre of the Innocents, The (after Brueghel).   Holger Teschke.   GTCP, *tr. by* Reinhold Grimm

Dance Pianist, The.   Angela Ball.   ExTi

Dance, room, quiet.   My Flesh in its Sweat.   Giancarlo Majorino.   ItPo, *tr. by* Gayle Ridinger

Dance She Does, The.   Harryette Mullen.   ISC

Dance to your [*or* thee] daddy.   Mother Goose.   FaBoVe

Dance: "When I wait."   Yi Sanghûi.   EcSo, *tr. by* Jennifer M. Lee

Dance with me . . . dance with me . . . we are the song . . . we.   Three/Quarters Time.   Nikki Giovanni.   CA

Dance with Nothing On, with Nobody Around, A.   Mas-oud Shouman.   AnVo, *tr. by* Mohamed Enani

Dance with you, my sweet brown Harlem girl. (LL)   Juke Box Love Song. Langston Hughes.   OxBoAm; SAmP

Dance with your tongue, Poet, make an entrechat.   Medrano Academy.   Blaise Cendrars.   CuPo

Danced in the evenin'.   Jenny in Love.   Dolores Kendrick.   ESEAA

Danced round the dreadful thing in fiendish glee. (LL)   Lynching, The.   Claude McKay.   APT-1; ColAP; GT; InoFa; NAAL-5; NAMCP V.1

Dancer.   Martinus Nijhoff.   TuT, *tr. by* Desmond Egan

Dancer.   *Unknown.*   SonAtl, *tr. by* Alex Emmanar, Colin Foster and Sam Gordon

Dancer, The.   Joseph Campbell.   OBMV

Dancer, The.   Margaret Holley.   PoDa

Dancer—, The.   Maggie O'Sullivan.   PFTM-2 *Fr.* Doubtless.

Dancer, The.   Walter James Turner.   NOBAu; OBMV

Dancers.   Afaa Michael Weaver.   OxAAAP

Dancers Exercising.   Amy Clampitt.   NoAM

Dancers trace the ceiling couplets and feathers bands cat suit bird suit a woman.   Watching a Dance Rehearsal in a Calgary Theatre with a Concrete Floor 2. Suzette Mayr.   PoPra

Dancer's world, A.   Twist, The.   Alfred B. Spellman.   EGAG; ISC

Dances and Songs of the Winter Ceremonial.   *Unknown.*   APN-2, *tr. by* Franz Boas

Dances like Italy, imagining red. (LL)   Walt Whitman at Bear Mountain. Louis Simpson.   TRP; ViWalt

Dances of Death.   Aleksandr Aleksandrovich Blok. "Night: a street, a streetlight; drugstore."   TCRusP, *tr. by* Denis Johnson and Kathy Lewis "Night, street, a lamp, a chemist's window."   OBVE, *tr. by* Peter France and Jon Stallworthy

Dancin' Our Lives Away.   Lorena M. Craighead.   InTrad

Dancing, The.   Gerald Stern.   CAP-8; LoL; UnSA

Dancing a Spell.   Marjorie M. Evasco.   ReBoTo

Dancing after Sanchez.   Staci Lightburn.   BRtP

Dancing at Oakmead Road.   Maura Dooley.   NeBl

Dancing away from your cars by the frond of the sea I live.   Man, The. Kenneth Koch.   BAP-04

Dancing Bear, The.   Rachel Lyman Field.   NTCP

Dancing between the darkness of dawn and twilight.   Spring in Palo Duro Canyon.   Jerry Craven.   TiP2

Dancing bones on reason's day.   Dancing Bones.   George Bowering.   BrAP

Dancing Concerning a Form of Women, A.   Robert Duncan.   FTOS

Dancing Dog, The.   Michael Drayton.   DiBP

Dancing Girl.   Walther von der Vogelweide.   NAWM-7v1, *tr. by* Peter Dronke

Dancing Girl, The.   Letitia Elizabeth Landon.   CenSon

Dancing Girl, The.   Yosano Akiko.   CAoMJL1, *tr. by* Janine Beichman

Dancing in Menopause.   Dorothy Perry Thompson.   SpirFl

Dancing in my city.   Tatamkulu Afrika.   TSAP

Dancing in Odessa.   Ilya Kaminsky.   LegDan

Dancing in Paradise.   Achy Obejas.   WiU

Dancing in the dark.   Dancing in the Dark.   Howard Dietz.   ReLy

Dancing in the Dark.   Demetrice A. Worley.   SpirFl

Dancing in Vacationland.   Stephen Dobyns.   EmeKit

Dancing Justified.   Sir John Davies.   NAEL-6v1

Dancing may do this and that.   T'ain't No Sin to Dance Around in Your Bones. Edgar Leslie.   ReLy

Dancing on Beethoven's Birthday.   Edith Rylander.   MiVo

Dancing on the Ceiling.   Lorenz Hart.   ReLy

Dancing Pleiads and eternal men, The. (LL)   Bacchus.   Ralph Waldo Emerson. APN-1; OBEV; OxBoAm; TCAPo

Dancing Speech of O-No'-Sa, The.   *Iroquois Oral Tradition.*   NAAPv.1

Dancing Sunshine Lounge, The.   Thomas Rabbitt.   ReTh

Dancing the Tarantella at the County Farm.   Sandra Alcosser.   ExTi

Dancing There.   Thomas Meyer.   AnSo

Dancing to the Track Singers at the Nightclub.   Judith Berke.   SwNoth

Dancing with Demons.   Christine de Luca.   EdScPo

Dancing with God.   Stephen Dunn.   NIP-4

Dancing with Rex.   Beth Cuthand.   ReEnLa

Dandelion.   Neil Curry.   NLP

Dandelion.   Juan Delgado.   AmPoNex

Dandelion.   Alexander Gerov.   CSCBP, *tr. by* Georgi Belev and Lisa Sapinkopf

Dandelion.   Frigyes Karinthy.   IQMS, *tr. by* Peter Zollman

Dandelion Bone.   Boris Hristov.   CSCBP, *tr. by* Georgi Belev and Lisa Sapinkopf

Dandelion Greens.   Jane Flanders.   AFaM; IPofFL

Dandelion Puffs. *Wintu Oral Tradition.* NAAPv.1 *Fr.* Six Dream Songs.

Dandelions. Gerda Mayer. Spl

Dandelions. Craig Raine. NoAM

Dandelions. Will D. Stanton. SoSe-8

Dandelions blooming in fives and threes. Buson. EMJL *Fr.* Spring Breeze on the Kema Embankment.

Dane Tree, The. Alfred Noyes. RWPCtW

Danes all told my husband, "Your French wife", The. Question of Identity, The. Kristin Lattany. OxAAAP

Dang Me. Bruce Andrews.
  3. BAP-04
  4. BAP-04
  5. BAP-04

Danged down to hell her loathsome carriage [/ *Desunt nonnulla*]. (LL) Hero and Leander. Christopher Marlowe. NAEL-6v1; NAEL-7v1; NoP-5; NoSic

Danger. Helen Hunt Jackson. NAAPv.1

Danger, Men in Trees. Doris Safie. PoArWo

Danger of Writing Defiant Verse, The. Dorothy Parker. AmWit

Dangereux avril. Teresa Palma Acosta. TiP2

Dangerous Doubts. Lorenzo Thomas. AnSo; FuFl

Dangerous Games. Carolyn Kizer. ASA

Dangerous Hats. Richard Garcia. TouFir

Dangerous Life. Lucia Maria Perillo. IllVoic

Dangerous Things. *Unknown.* EMJL, *tr. by* Edward Putzar

Dangerous to hear, is that melodious tongue. Describes Phaon. Mary Robinson. CenSon; RWP

Dangerous to hear is that melodious tongue. Mary Robinson. NPBRoP *Fr.* Sappho and Phaon.

Dangerous World, The. Naomi Replansky. PoBW

Dangers of Looking Back, The. Cynthia MacDonald. AFaM

Dangers of the Journey to the Happy Land. Joseph Ceravolo. NYP2

Daniel at Breakfast. Phyllis McGinley. OBSV

Daniel Boone. Rosemary Benét and Stephen Vincent Benét. APT-2

Daniel in the lion's den. Nebuchadnezzar's Kingdom-Come. David Rowbotham. ChIV-1; NOBAu

Daniel Jazz, The. Vachel Lindsay. APT-1

Daniel Webster's Horses. Elizabeth Jane Coatsworth. MoAmPo

Daniel's Duck. Kerry Hardie. NIrP

Daniel's hands rub my back. Daniel's Hands. Niama Leslie JoAnn Williams. BtF

Danish Wit. John Hollander. NBLV

Dank, dark basement entered cautiously from the rear, A. Practice: For Derek Walcott. Thomas Sayers Ellis. NAPBL; NeAmPo

Dank fens of cedar, hemlock branches gray. Frederick Goddard Tuckerman. APN-2; OxBoAm *Fr.* Sonnets: First Series, 1854–1860.

Dannemora Contraband. Jackie Warren-Moore. SpirFl

Dannie Abse, Douglas Dunn. On Consulting "Contemporary Poets of the English Language." Anthony Thwaite. OxBEV

Danny. Malcolm Cowley. PoA 2002

Danny Deever. Rudyard Kipling. BRP; FaBoWar; InoFa; MoBrPo; NAEL-6v2; NAEL-7v2; NAMCP V.1; NoAM; NPeEn; OxBEV; TFi

Danny Drolet. Fowler Street. Tony Gloeggler. NevBe

Dans ce miroir. Miroir. Guillaume Apollinaire. YaTCFP

Dans cet arbre. Jacques Roubaud. YaTCFP

Dans la lumière du jour. Marcelin Pleynet. YaTCFP

Dans la maison refermée. Églogue. Jean Follain. YaTCFP

Dans l'abîme doré, rouge, glacé, doré, l'abîme où gîte la douleur. Tête Pleine de Beauté, La. Pierre Reverdy. YaTCFP

Dans l'air limpide. Michel Houellebecq. YaTCFP

Dans le brouillard qui entoure les arbres, les feuilles leur sont dérobées. Arbres se défont à l'intérieur d'une sphère de brouillard, Les. Francis Ponge. YaTCFP

Dans le ciel des hommes, le pain des étoiles. Lutteurs. René Char. YaTCFP

Dans les champs ou sur la colline. Pierre Reverdy. YaTCFP

Dans une quincaillerie de détail en province. Quincaillerie. Jean Follain. YaTCFP

Dans une ville noire entraînée par le temps. Jours, Les. Jean Tardieu. YaTCFP

Danse Africaine. Langston Hughes. NAAPv.2

Danse Russe. William Carlos Williams. AmFaPo; NAAPv.2; NAMCP V.1; NoP-5; OxBoAm; RaBo; SAmP

Danse solitaire sur les méandrews du tapis rouge. Réunion. Max Jacob. YaTCFP

Dante. Anna Andreyevna Akhmatova. PoetW, *tr. by* Max Hayward and Stanley Kunitz

Dante. William Cullen Bryant. APN-1

Dante. Robert Duncan.

Dante. Henry Wadsworth Longfellow. NCAP

Dante. Henrietta Cordelia Ray. CBWP-3

Dante Gabriel Rossetti. Dorothy Parker. NALW *Fr.* Pig's-Eye View of Literature, A.

Dante Park. Miguel Algarín. PueRic

Danube orchards, The. Denise Levertov. TaR

Danube to the Severn gave, The. Alfred Tennyson. NAEL-6v2; NAEL-7v2; NAWM-7v2; NoP-5 *Fr.* In Memoriam A. H. H.

Danza gozosa. Grito. Deleite de las formas, El. Coral Bracho. RMCMP

Daphnaïda. Edmund Spenser.
  Elegy, An. OBEV

Daphne. Elisabeth Langgässer. GTCP, *tr. by* Irmgard Hunt

Daphne. John Lyly. NoSic *Fr.* Midas.

Daphne and Apollo. Ovid. OBVE *Fr.* Metamorphoses.

Daphne and Laura and So Forth. Margaret Atwood. PoDa

Daphne with Her Thighs in Bark. Eavan Boland. AFaM

Daphne with her thighs in bark. Ezra Pound. NAAPv.2 *Fr.* Hugh Selwyn Mauberley (Life and Contacts).

Daphnis and Chloe. Haniel Long. APT-1

Daphnis dearest, wherefore weave me. Appeal. Edith Nesbit. LW

Daphnis to Ganymede. Richard Barnfield. CAGL *Fr.* Affectionate Shepherd [or Shephearde], The.

Dapper Street. J. C. Bloem. TuT, *tr. by* Desmond Egan

Dappled Horse, The. Mei Yao Ch'en. ColAnChi, *tr. by* Burton Watson

Dappled sky, a world of meadows, A. Jean Ingelow. PEW *Fr.* Divided.

Dapple-throned Aphrodite. Prayer to my lady of Paphos. Sappho. HW, *tr. by* Mary Barnard

Dar es-Salaam: Harbour of Peace. Breyten Breytenbach. AF, *tr. by* Denis Hirson

Dar es-Salaam: it's when night is darkest. Dar es-Salaam: Harbour of Peace. Breyten Breytenbach. AF, *tr. by* Denis Hirson

Dardanus...was son of Zeus the Lord of the clouds. Homer. CAGL *Fr.* Iliad, The.

Dare frame thy fearful symmetry? (LL) William Blake. BBASP; BrAP; BRP; ChAP; ClHu; CtM; HeIP-4; ITBLP; MakPoe; NAEL-6v2; NAEL-7v2; NAWM-7v2; NIL-7; NIP-4; NOBRP; NoP-4; NoP-5; NOxBChV; NPBRoP; NPeEn; OBEV; OPOU; OxBEV; PoPoPo; SoSe-8; TFi; WaAnP; WHSW *Fr.* Songs of Experience.

Dare to Be Different. Venus Harris. BRtP

Dare you see a Soul *at the White Heat?*. Emily Dickinson. APN-2; NALW; OxBoAm; TCAPo; WPoS

Daredevil. Stuart Dybek. MAAN

Daredevil. Ania Walwicz. BMAP

Daredevil riding on the concrete lip. Bicycle Racers, The. Ann Townsend. AmPoNex; NeAmPo

Darest thou my muse present thy Battlike winge. To the Kinges Most Excellent Majestye. Lady Anne Harris Southwell. EMWP

Daring to live for the impossible. (LL) Muriel Rukeyser. NALW; PoCho; TaR *Fr.* Letter to the Front.

Dark. Hoa Nguyen. WANABP

Dark, The. Myra Cohn Livingston. TLR

Dark, The. Richard Poole. AngWePo

Dark against the sky yonder distant line. *Unknown.* APN-2 *Fr.* Hako, The.

Dark and brooding beyond the Great Wall. Ji Gate. Kao Shih. CCL1, *tr. by* Stephen Owen

Dark and Deep. Norbert Krapf. VisFro

Dark and pillowy cloud, the sallow trees, The. Composed During a Walk on the Downs, in November 1787. Charlotte Smith. OxBSo

Dark and silent. House in Rome. Snorri Hjartarson. PML, *tr. by* Alan Boucher

Dark Angel. Kevin Hart. StAl

Dark Angel, The. Lionel Pigot Johnson. MoBrPo; OBMV; OxAEP-2

Dark angel who art clear and straight. Serenade: Any Man to Any Woman. Dame Edith Sitwell. NALW

Dark Angel, with thine aching lust. Dark Angel, The. Lionel Pigot Johnson. MoBrPo; OBMV; OxAEP-2

Dark Area. Russell Atkins. GT

Dark Between, The. Philip Schultz. PoA 2002

Dark birds flutter at my fingertips. Monsoon Song. James Cordeiro. PoDa

Dark Blood. Margaret Abigail Walker. NALW

Dark blood of the folk, The. (LL) Night of Battle. Yvor Winters. PoA 2002; PWW2

Dark breast feathers of a future storm. (LL) Crazy Horse Monument. Peter Blue Cloud. HATNAP; UnSA

Dark brown, distant. Towers, The. José María Eguren. TCLAP, *tr. by* Iver Lofving

Dark brown is the river. Where Go the Boats? Robert Louis Stevenson. NOxBChV; NTCP; TLR; WHSW

Dark cave, that ever dost cool shades retain. Ludovico Ariosto. NOBRP *Fr.* Orlando Furioso.

Dark Chamber, The. Louis Untermeyer. MoAmPo

Dark changes guard, The. Rounds, The. G. E. Murray. IllVoic

Dark chocolate fungus, A. Walking, when the Lake of the Air is Blue with Spring. J. S. Harry. BMAP

Dark Christmas on Wildwood Road, The. Morris Gilbert Bishop. ChrPo

Dark clouds are gathering. The trick knee aches. Neighboring Storms. Greg Williamson. AmPoNex

Dark clouds have rolled clean away. Tune: "Rouged Lips" Rain Just Over on the Night of the Lantern Preview. Wu Wen-ying. ColAnChi, *tr. by* Jiaosheng Wang

Dark comes early now on Saturdays, The. Footballers in the Snow. Martin Mooney. NIrP

Dark Comes On in Blocks, in Cubes, The. Thomas Lux. AmAlph

Dark Continent, The. Sean Manzano Labrador. BAP-04

Dark corsage I can't. Bite. Tracy Ryan. StAl

Dark dawn. I hear screams in my sleep but don't quite wake. September 11. Pat Reed. Eno

Dark / days are past. Mysteries, The. "H. D." APT-1

Dark Days, The. Greg Williamson. NeAmPo

Dark, deep, and cold the current flows. Plaint. Ebenezer Elliott. OBEV; SacPr

Dark, deeply. A red. Inside the River. James Dickey. PoA 2002

Dark dwelling place of meaning. Words. Elsa Cross. RMCMP, *tr. by* Margaret Sayers Peden

Dark eagles, sleep and death, The. Mourning. Georg Trakl. WED, *tr. by* Robert Bly

Dark Edge of Europe, The. Desmond O'Grady. "Twist of cloth on the flat stones, A." PBCIP

Dark Existence. Brenda Hillman. BodElec

Dark eyed, / O woman of my dreams. Dance Figure. Ezra Pound. HeIP-4; MoAmPo

Dark falls on this mid-western town. Love. Eavan Boland. HarvBoo

Dark Fates, The. Dezső Kosztolányi. IQMS, *tr. by* Lydia Pasternak-Slater

Dark Girl. Arna Bontemps. APT-2

Dark gods if all our days. Idris Davies. TCAWP *Fr.* Gwalia Deserta.

Dark grey, a very dark grey, a quite dark grey is monstrous ordinarily, A. Gertrude Stein. MoWP *Fr.* Tender Buttons.

Dark Harbor. Mark Strand.
"I am sure you would find it misty here." CAP-8
"Is it you standing among the olive trees." NAMCP V.2; NoP-4; NoP-5
"It is a dreadful cry that rises up." PoCho
"It is true, as someone has said, that in." NoP-4; NoP-5
"There is a road through the canyon." CAP-8; NAMCP V.2
"When after a long silence one picks up the pen." CAP-8

Dark head sits brooding its, A. Nathaniel Mackey. FTOS *Fr.* Song of the Andoumboulou.

Dark Horse. Phillis Levin. FFC

Dark Horses. Thomas O'Grady. Coast

Dark house, by which once more I stand. Alfred Tennyson. BrAP; HeIP-4; InoFa; NAEL-6v2; NAEL-7v2; NAWM-7v2; NoP-5; NPeEn; OxBEV; SoSe-8; WaAnP *Fr.* In Memoriam A. H. H.

Dark House, The. *Unknown.* NTCP

Dark in a corner of the room. Dark in a Corner of the Room. Gustavo Adolfo Bécquer. SpanPo, *tr. by* Kate Flores

Dark is soft, like fur. Rhyme for Night. Joan Aiken. TLR

Dark is the hour, long the night. Christmas Eve. Walter De la Mare. ChrPo

Dark ivy draws a wave across the yard. Daughter's Fever, A. David Bottoms. PoChi

Dark Laughter. Melvin B. Tolson. EGAG

Dark lintels, the blue and foreign stones, The. Adrienne Rich. NALW; NoAM *Fr.* Twenty-one Love Poems.

Dark meadow invites me, a. Dark Meadow Invites Me, A. José Lezama Lima. TCLAP, *tr. by* Willis Barnstone

Dark Mirror. Calvin Forbes. GT

Dark Morning, The. Thomas Merton. PoA 2002

Dark Night. San Juan de la Cruz. WoPoe, *tr. by* Frank Bidart

Dark Night, The. San Juan de la Cruz. BBASP; STV; WeW-3, *tr. by* Kieran Kavanaugh and Otilio Rodriquez
(Obscure Night of the Soul, The.) OBMV

Dark o'clock. Bed, The. Ray DiPalma. FTOS

Dark One, / all I request is a portion of love. Mirabai. ErotSp, *tr. by* Andrew Schelling

Dark one, / how can I sleep? Mirabai. AWTN

Dark paths are the way. Michael McClure. WANABP *Fr.* Touching the Edge: Dharma Devotions.

Dark Pines under Water. Gwendolyn MacEwen. BeAl; BrAP

Dark plume fetch me from yon blasted yew, A. William Wordsworth. CenSon *Fr.* River Duddon [A Series of Sonnets], The.

Dark Portrait, A. Lawrence Ferlinghetti. PmAP

Dark Prayer. Gregory Orr. PfSP

Dark precedes the sun, The. Sun Mass. Kim Sŭnghŭi. CAMKP, *tr. by* Anthony, Brother of Taizé

Dark Prophecy: I Sing of Shine. Etheridge Knight. ESEAA; LTA; PBCAP

Dark pure blue, deep in the light, the sea shakes white-flecked. Delos. Edwin Denby. NYP2

Dark rivers cry cities snivel. Flood Songs. Olga Khvostova. CRWP, *tr. by* Tatyana Retivova

Dark Room, The. Enrique Lihn. TCLAP; VCWP, *tr. by* David Unger

Dark Rosaleen. Owen Roe MacWard and Hugh O'Donnell. IrV; OBEV; OxAEP-2, *tr. by* James Clarence Mangan

Dark scissors of his legs, The. Jogger on Riverside Drive, 5:00 A.M., The. Agha Shahid Ali. MoASP

Dark sea spreads over the garden, A. (LL) Vespertilio. Linda Bierds. AmAlph; ExTi

Dark Senses. Tom Raworth. Oth

Dark shards, The. Dolores Dorantes. SPV, *tr. by* Jen Hofer

Dark shards from the grass, your voice in pieces, so far, belief. (LL) Los Angeles, The Angels. James Harms. NeAmPo; PuP-23

Dark Side, The. Adelaide Anne Procter. SacPr

Dark Side of Dazzle, The. Sean Brendan-Brown. LiTh

Dark Spaces: Thoughts on All Souls Day. John Knoepfle. IllVoic

Dark speckle, half with down, half feathered. Fledgling. Anthony Conran. AngWePo

Dark specks whirr like lint alive in the sunlight. Ephemeridae. Daniel Gerard Hoffman. YaYoPo

Dark Stag, The. Isabella Valancy Crawford. BrAP

Dark Star, Black Star. Rikki Ducornet. SurWo

Dark storms of the afternoon persist. Fossil Fuel. John Dickson. PoA 2002

Dark streets are deserted, The. After Midnight. Louis Simpson. BLT; NoAM

Dark Summer. Louise Bogan. APT-2; ItP

Dark Symphony. Melvin B. Tolson. ColAP; SSLK
"They tell us to forget." NAAPv.2

Dark the Star. Susan Stewart. AmAlph

Dark Thing Inside the Day, A. Linda Gregg. BLT; OxBoAm

Dark, thinned, beside the wall of stone. In Time of Grief. Lizette Woodworth Reese. APN-2

Dark thought is revealed in the twists and curves. Koja Râgıb Pasha. OLP, *tr. by* Walter Andrews, Najaat Black and Mehmet Kalpakli

Dark to me is the earth. Dark to me are the heavens. Desolate City, The. *Unknown.* OBEV, *tr. by* Wilfrid Scawen Blunt

Dark torch. Michele Leggott. VaPo

Dark Underfoot. Thom Ward. AmPoNex

Dark was before my eyes. There lay the abyss. Bridge, The. Victor Hugo. SxFrPo, *tr. by* A. M. and E. H. Blackmore

Dark was the dawn, and o'er the deep. Negro Girl, The. Mary Robinson. RWP

Dark was the sky, and not one friendly star. Philip Freneau. TCAPo *Fr.* House of Night, The.

Dark waters of the beginning. Christopher Okigbo. NAMCP V.2 *Fr.* Heavensgate.

Dark which canopies the dawning skies, The. Light Invested. Carlos A. Angeles. ReBoTo

Dark whispers. Night Gives Old Woman the Word. Gail Tremblay. HATNAP; ItWoWo

Dark with power, we remain. Dark with power. Wendell Berry. InGu

Dark woman, head bent, listening for something, A. Adrienne Rich. GeoHom *Fr.* Atlas of the Difficult World, An.

Dark wrath of people, The. Georg Trakl. AF

Dark, wrinkled as a purple pink. Obscur et froncé. Arthur Rimbaud. EroLit, *tr. by* Kenneth McLeish

Dark young pine, at the center of the earth originating. Shootingway Ceremony Prayer. *Unknown.* WoPoe; WPoS, *tr. by* Gladys A. Reichard

Dark-blue clouds of night, in dusky lines, The. Summer's Day, A. Joanna Baillie. WoRP

Dark-breasted flesh of a swan, The. Back. Sheila Wingfield. MoWP

Darkened copies of all trees, The. (LL) Emphasis Falls on Reality, An. Barbara Guest. AWPTFC; FTOS; PmAP

Darkened Mind, The. James Russell Lowell. NCAP

Darkening Hotel Room. Alfred Corn. VCAP

Darkening leaves, the. Tomas Tranströmer. WoBe *Fr.* Haiku.

Darkening room with light, The. (LL) Robert Penn Warren. APT-2; NAMCP V.1 *Fr.* Island of Summer.

Darker by far than any coalpit stone. (LL)　Edward Taylor.　NAAL-3; NAAPv.1; NOSC; OxBEV; OxBoAm; TCAPo; WaAnP *Fr.* God's Determinations [touching his Elect].

Darker then the colorless beards of old men.　Song of Myself by Walt Whitman.　Alex Rawls.　AnSo

Dark-Eyed Gentleman, The.　Thomas Hardy.　MoBrPo; NBLV

Darkfall of your voice is tired, The.　Opaque Copper.　Roberto Guillermo Monzón.　SonAtl, *tr.* by Eleanor Davidson

Dark-green upon distant heights.　Prologue at Sixty.　W. H. Auden.　NAMCP V.1

Dark-haired girl, who holds my thoughts entirely, The.　Peggy Browne. Turlough Carolan.　OxBEV, *tr.* by Austin Clarke

Darkling Summer, Ominous Dusk, Rumorous Rain.　Delmore Schwartz. APT-2

Darkling swallows will come again, The.　Darkling Swallows Will Come Again, The.　Gustavo Adolfo Bécquer.　SpanPo, *tr.* by Kate Flores

Darkling Thrums.　Clark Coolidge.　NYP2

Darkling Thrush, The.　Thomas Hardy.　AmFaPo; BrAP; CABP; ClHu; CtM; HarvBoo; MoBrPo; NAEL-6v2; NAEL-7v2; NAMCP V.1; NIL-7; NIP-4; NoAM; NoP-4; NoP-5; NPeEn; OBEV; OWoS; OxBEV; PoPoPo; SoSe-8; TFi; WaAnP; WoPoe

Darkmotherscream.　Andrey Andreievich Voznesensky.　RaBo, *tr.* by Robert Bly, Vera Dunham and H. W. Tjalsma

Darkness.　Lord Byron.　CABP; NAEL-6v2; NAEL-7v2; NPBRoP; TreFP Abdiel.　DiBP

Darkness.　Paavo Haavikko. "Days become years. Years."　VCWP

Darkness, The.　Charles E. Butler.　YaYoPo

Darkness and stars i' the mid-day! they invite.　Rhapsody, A.　Henry Vaughan. NAEL-6v1

Darkness and Void was all: myself alone.　Mihály Vörösmarty.　IQMS *Fr.* Csongor and Tünde.

Darkness begins a / retreat.　After Christmas.　Michael Richards.　OBCP

Darkness broke into my life, and I knew.　Delivery.　Armanda Guiducci. CItWP, *tr.* by Cinzia Sartini Blum and Lara Trubowitz

Darkness, but.　Recurrence.　Michael White.　GifTon

Darkness came early, though not yet cold.　Apple-raid, The.　Vernon Scannell. NOxBChV

Darkness comes out of the earth.　Twilight.　D. H. Lawrence.　OBMV

Darkness crumbles away, The.　Break of Day in the Trenches.　Isaac Rosenberg.　CABP; EMP; HarvBoo; MoBrPo; NAEL-6v2; NAEL-7v2; NAMCP V.1; NIL-7; NoAM; NoP-4; NoP-5; NPeEn; OBWP; OxAEP-2; OxBEV; PoA 2002; PoAgWa; PoWW; TFi; WaAnP

Darkness descends, do you see our hutment slowly dissolving?　Seventh Eclogue.　Miklós Radnóti.　IQMS, *tr.* by Peter Zollman

Darkness falls like a wet sponge.　Picture of Little J. A. in a Prospect of Flowers, The.　John Ashbery.　PmAP; WaAnP

Darkness has called to darkness, and disgrace.　As a Plane Tree by the Water. Robert Lowell.　BrAP; MoAmPo

Darkness in the room was like enormous riches, The.　Rainer Maria Rilke. RaBo

Darkness is for the poor, and thorough cold.　Christmas Is Coming.　Anthony Hecht.　ChrPo

Darkness is not dark, nor sunlight the light of the sun.　Foal.　Vernon Watkins. AngWePo

Darkness of trees, The.　George Oppen.　APT-2 *Fr.* Some San Francisco Poems.

Darkness or stillness. Essence, foundation. Soul, indescribable.　Leafy Plant of Wisdom, A.　Kim Chŏngnan.　EcSo, *tr.* by Peter H. Lee

Darkness rolls upward, the.　Blue Symphony.　John Gould Fletcher.　APT-1

Darkness stares from everywhere and no one's here.　Last Poem, The.　Jiri Orten.　AF, *tr.* by Lyn Coffin

Darkness Was Upon the Face of the Deep.　Kim Roberts.　AmPoNex *Fr.* Constellation Frigidaire, The.

Darkness wears off, and, dawning into light.　Figures on the Frieze, The. Alastair Reid.　WaAnP

Darkness with white spots.　Five-0.　Ras Baraka.　InTrad

Darktown Strutter's Ball, The.　Shelton Brooks.　ReLy

Darling can you kill me: with your mickeymouse pillows.　D. A. Powell. NeAmPo

Darling, dearest foal-hide flask.　Love Song to the Foal-Hide Flask.　Mihály Csokonai Vitéz.　IQMS, *tr.* by Thomas Kabdebo and Valerie Becker Makkai

Darling, each morning a blooded rose.　Corinna In Vendome.　Pierre de Ronsard.　WoPoe, *tr.* by Robert Mezey

"Darling," he said, "I never meant."　Forgetfulness!　Josephine D. Henderson Heard.　CBWP-4

Darling, he said, I never meant.　Two Truths.　Helen Hunt Jackson.　LW

Darling, how long before this breath will cease?　Evanishings.　Mary E. Tucker.　CBWP-1

Darling of Gods and Men, beneath the gliding stars.　Lucretius.　WoPoe *Fr.* De Rerum Natura (On the Nature of Things).

Darling, on the moving stairs.　And No Regrets.　Lex Banning.　NOBAu

Darling, pardon my confusion.　What Is There to Say?　E. Y. Harburg.　ReLy

Darling, the plates have been cleared away.　Beauty and the Beast.　Rita Dove. ESEAA; NoAM

Darling, there is nothing between us that cannot be.　Miss Havisham's Letter. Julia Copus.　MFPA

Darling, there's the tree you run to.　On the Street Where You Live.　Alan Jay Lerner.　ReLy

Darling / we are Forces of Production.　Forces of Production.　Nirasana Kavulu.　HotL, *tr.* by V. Narayana Rao

Darling, we'll both have equal shares in the sweet love you offer.　Catullus. NAWM-7v1 *Fr.* Carmina [Charles Martin Translation].

Darling—I am not what I appear.　Double.　Elizabeth Garrett.　MoWP

Darn That Dream.　Eddie DeLange.　ReLy

Dar's a skool in West Virginny.　To Professor Byrd Prillerman.　Maggie Pogue Johnson.　CBWP-4

Dar's plenty t'ings to write erbout.　Dat Mule ob Brudder Wright's.　Maggie Pogue Johnson.　CBWP-4

Dart of Izdabel prevails! 'twas dipt, The.　Dying Indian, The.　Joseph Warton. OxAEP-1

Dart—an idea.　Flit.　Mark Doty.　AmAlph

Darting here and there.　Buson.　SoOfWa, *tr.* by Sam Hamill

Dartmoor.　David Gwenallt Jones.　BBMWP, *tr.* by Emyr Humphreys

Darwin.　Lorine Niedecker.　APSN; APT-2

Darwin in 1881.　Gjertrud Schnackenberg.　NoAM; NoP-4; NoP-5

Darwinian preface, A.　Douglas Livingstone.　TSAP

Darwinism.　Agnes Mary Frances Robinson.　VWP

Darwinism in the Kitchen.　*Unknown.*　NBLV

Darwin's Unfinished Notes to Emma.　Amy Newman.　IAoNAP

Das Kapital.　Imamu Amiri Baraka.　PFTM-2

Dash down yon cup of Samian wine! (LL)　Lord Byron.　BLPJKO; OBEV; OxAEP-2 *Fr.* Don Juan.

Dash him to dust, and let the world repose. (LL)　Advice to a Raven in Russia [December, 1812].　Joel Barlow.　AmWaPo; APN-1; NAAL-3; OBWP

Dash It.　Annie Dillard.　UpMys

Dash of rain upon, A.　Chŏng Ch'ŏl.　CATKP, *tr.* by Peter H. Lee

Dash to the peak anaesthetizers, The.　Bluff Knoll Sublimity.　John Kinsella. VaPo

Dashing thro' the snow in a one-horse open sleigh.　Jingle Bells.　James S. Pierpont.　TCAPo

Dashing White Sergeant, The.　John Burgoyne.　FaBoWar

Dasius, chucker-out / at the Turkish Baths.　Martial.　OBVE

Dass Cap'm Cayetano.　Song of Cayetano's Circus, The.　George Washington Cable.　APN-2

Dat Mule ob Brudder Wright's.　Maggie Pogue Johnson.　CBWP-4

Data.　Joseph Ceravolo.　BodElec

Data in the glass jar: some ten scorpions, The.　In the Laboratory.　Dan Pagis. PoSu, *tr.* by Robert Friend

Date Nut Bread.　Ann Townsend.　SweBea

Date palm and the cypress, The.　Leaving Eden.　Nadya Aisenberg.　OPRER

Date With Robbe-Grillet, A.　Elaine Equi.　PmAP

Dateline Hyderabad.　Ajanta.　HotL, *tr.* by V. Narayana Rao

Dates.　Michael Ondaatje.　BrAP

Dat's Love (Habanera).　Oscar Hammerstein, II.　ReLy

Datta. Dayadhvam. Damyatta. / Shantih shantih shantih. (LL)　Waste Land, The.　T. S. Eliot.　APT-1; CABP; MoAmPo; NAAL-5; NAAPv.2; NAEL-6v2; NAEL-7v2; NAMCP V.1; NAWM-7v2; NoAM; NoP-4; NoP-5; OxAEP-2; OxBoAm; TCAPo; TFi; WaAnP

Datura the serpent, The.　Datura the Serpent, The.　Valentine Penrose. SurWo, *tr.* by Myrna Bell Rochester

Dauber.　John Masefield. Rounding the Horn.　MoBrPo

Daughter.　Susan Griffin.　PoChi

Daughter.　Olesya Nikolayeva.　ItGoST, *tr.* by Paul Graves and Carol Ueland

Daughter.　Ellen Bryant Voigt.　StAl

Daughter, lying on a snow-white bed.　To My Daughter.　N. Balamani Amma. CFP, *tr.* by N. Balamani Amma

Daughter of earth and child of the wave be appeased.　William Everson. NoAM *Fr.* Tendril in the Mesh.

Daughter of Genius! while thy tuneful lays.　Occasioned by Reading Mrs. M. Robinson's Poems.　Martha Hanson.　CenSon

Daughter of gods and men, great ruling will.　Klytemnestra.　Emily Jane Pfeiffer.　ViWPN

Daughter of Hyria, land of lovely dances.　Korinna [*or* Corinna].　SaLy, *tr.* by Diane Rayor

Daughter of Liberty! whose knife.　Hymn to the Guilotine.　"Peter Pindar." NOBRP

Daughter of music. Song for the Year's End, A. Louis Zukofsky. TaR

Daughter of th' Italian heaven! Corinna at the Capitol. Felicia Dorothea Hemans. VWP

Daughter of the Cavaliers, A. Old Belle, An. Lizette Woodworth Reese. SWaP

Daughter of Twilight. Quadroon, The. William Edward Burghardt DuBois. NAAPv.1

Daughter of Zeus who sets free, I beseech you, Fortune. Pindar. WaAnP *Fr.* Olympian Odes, The.

Daughter of Zion. Alden Nowlan. Coast

Daughter pail slipper sale underwail. Sand. Hannah Weiner. PFTM-2

Daughter, take this amulet. Mwana Kupona Msham. HAWP *Fr.* Poem to Her Daughter.

Daughter, That Picture of You. Keith Gilyard. SpirFl

Daughter to that good Earl[e], once President. To the Lady Margaret Ley. John Milton. OBEV

Daughter, while you rest. Baby's Breath. Jabari Asim. FuFl

Daughter-Mother-Maya-Seeta. Reetika Vazirani. NAPBL

Daughters, 1900. Marilyn Nelson Waniek. FFC; WaAnP

Daughter's difficulties as a wife, A: Mrs Ruben Chandler to her mother in New Orleans. Anne Stevenson. MoWP *Fr.* Correspondences.

Daughter's Fever, A. David Bottoms. PoChi

Daughters, in the wind's boisterous roughing. Vernal Equinox. Ruth Stone. MoAmPo

Daughters of Albion hear her woes, and ec[c]ho back her sighs, The. (LL) Visions of the Daughters of Albion. William Blake. CABP; NAEL-6v2; NAEL-7v2; NPBRoP

(Daughters of Jerusalem.) Chapter V. Elizabeth Singer Rowe. PEW

Daughters of Time, the hypocritic Days. Days. Ralph Waldo Emerson. APN-1; ColAP; HeIP-4; NAAL-3; NAAPv.1; NCAP; NoP-4; NoP-5; OxBoAm; TCAPo; TFi

Daughters—and live / with diabetes. (LL) Big Zeb Johnson. Everett Hoagland. GT; OxAAAP

Daughter-to-Father Talk. Kamilah Aisha Moon. BRtP

Daumenbreite. John Redmond. NIrP

Daunce of Death, The. John Lydgate.
"O thow Minstral that cannest so note and pipe." OxBEV

Dauntless the slug-horn to my lips I set. Tony Lopez. Oth *Fr.* Assembly Point D.

Dauphins, poulpes, poissons. Minoen récent 1 (Aiguières d'Hagia Triada). Lorand Gaspar. YaTCFP

Dave rode across a bridge. *Unknown.* WoPoe *Fr.* Three Swedish Spells.

Daventry calling. . .Dark and still. Dane Tree, The. Alfred Noyes. RWPCtW

David. Charles Reznikoff. ChIV-1

David and Bathsheba in the Public Garden. Robert Lowell. ChIV-1

David and Goliath. Priscilla Jane Thompson. CBWP-2

David and Goliath. P. Hately Waddell. ChIV-1

David and Goliath. Michael Drayton.
"Our sacred Muse, of Israel's Singer sings." ChIV-1

David and his three captains bold. David in the Cave of Adullam. Charles Lamb. ChIV-1

David Cassidy picks me on *The Dating Game.* David Cassidy Then. Dennis Cooper. ReTh; WiU

David Cassidy Then. Dennis Cooper. ReTh; WiU

David Garrick. Oliver Goldsmith. NPeEn; OxBEV *Fr.* Retaliation.

David Guest. Martin Bell. RSaN

David in the Cave of Adullam. Charles Lamb. ChIV-1

David Leaves the Saints for Paterson. Martín Espada. PueRic

David means beloved. Name, A. Linda Pastan. TaR

David ross called up from syracuse and wanted to know if. David Antin. PmAP

David sang to his hook-nosed harp. King David. Stephen Vincent Benét. ChIV-1

David Walker (1785–1830). Rita Dove. OxAAAP; WaAnP

David, we must have looked comic, sitting. Elegy for David Beynon. Leslie Norris. AngWePo; TCAWP

Davideis. Abraham Cowley.
  Gabriel's Appearance. NOSC
  Archangel's Toilet, An. STuOW
  Lot's Wife. NPeEn
  "Michal her modest flames sought to conceal." ChIV-1
  (Music.) OxAEP-1
  (Number, Weight, and Measure.) NOSC
  "So covetous Ballaam with fond intent." ChIV-1

David's arm hung near-paralyzed. David Leaves the Saints for Paterson. Martín Espada. PueRic

David's Epitaph on Jonathan. Francis Quarles. ChIV-1

David's Lament. Bible, *O.T.* NPeEn; OBVE; OBWP *Fr.* Second Samuel.

David's Lament for Jonathan. Peter Abelard. NAWM-5v1

David's Night in Veliès. James Merrill. HarvBoo

David's Peccavi. Robert Southwell. ChIV-1

David's Rumor. Liam Rector. OPRER

David's Sister. Peter Schjeldahl. AHA

Davy and the Goblin. Charles Edward Carryl.
  (Nautical Ballad, A.) APN-2
  Walloping Window-Blind, The. GoPo; NBLV

Davy Crockett. *Unknown.* FaBoVe

Daw, The / The rook, and magpie, to the grey-grown oaks. James Thomson. NPeEn *Fr.* Seasons, The.

Dawdling with yellow tummy: I act on a mechanism outside in contrast to. Instant Control. Michael Portnoy. HeMarv

Dawn. Nirmalprabha Bardoloi. CFP, *tr. by* D. N. Bezbarua

Dawn. Gordon Bottomley. MoBrPo

Dawn. Buson. EH, *tr. by* Robert Hass

Dawn. Hopper: In the Cafe. W.R. Elton. PoSol

Dawn. John Ford. OBEV *Fr.* Lover's Melancholy, The.

Dawn. Angelina Weld Grimké. APT-1; NAAPv.2

Dawn. Ella Higginson. SWaP

Dawn. Philippe Jaccottet. VCWP

Dawn. Emyr Lewis. *tr. by* the author
  Mad Magnet of a Wild Wind. BBMWP, *tr. by* the author
  Stale Spit is the Morning Train. BBMWP, *tr. by* the author
  "This is my book, in my hand." BBMWP, *tr. by* the author

Dawn. Gabriela Mistral. TANSG, *tr. by* Maria Giachetti [*or* Jacketti] and Maria Jacketti

Dawn. Octavio Paz. ItP, *tr. by* Charles Tomlinson

Dawn. Arthur Rimbaud. SxFrPo, *tr. by* Martin Sorrell

Dawn. Betsy Sholl. LTA

Dawn. Lucien Stryk. InvLad

Dawn. *Unknown.* NoSic

Dawn. Robert Penn Warren. BodElec

Dawn. William Carlos Williams. APT-1; MoAmPo

Dawn . . . and the city's lifeless dirt turns grey. Serenade at Dawn. Árpád Tóth. IQMS, *tr. by* Jess Perlman

Dawn, The. Ricardo Jaimes Freyre. TCLAP, *tr. by* Victor Tulli

Dawn, The. Alfred Tennyson. NAEL-6v2

Dawn, The. William Butler Yeats. BLPJKO

Dawn and dusk. Man Who Reads Homer, A. Nishiwaki Junzaburo. WoPoe, *tr. by* Masaya Saito

Dawn: and foot on the cold stair treading or. Aubade for Hope. Robert Penn Warren. MoAmPo; FuPo

Dawn and night of fighting, lovers like actual wars. Sonnet: Kamikaze. Bernadette Mayer. FTOS

Dawn; and the jew's-harp's sawing seesaw song. Pilots, Man Your Planes. Randall Jarrell. MoAmPo

Dawn: "Angel, robed in spotless white, An." Paul Laurence Dunbar. NAAPv.1; OxBoAm

Dawn at that hour. Virgil. WoPoe *Fr.* Aeneid [*or* Eneados *or* Aeneis], The.

Dawn Behind Night. Isaac Rosenberg. RSaN

Dawn birds on Somerset, The. For Daniel Beels, Third Generation Bricklayer. John Rybicki. AmPoNex

Dawn brings with it, The. Juan Ramón Jiménez. SpanPo; WoPoe *Fr.* Ten Short Poems.

Dawn broke. The pile of clouds kept growing softer. Stag of Irisoda, The. Lajos Áprily. IQMS, *tr. by* Adam Makkai

Dawn Chorus. Mary Holtby. UV

Dawn cicadas choke back sobs. Listening to a Monk Play the Reed Pipes. Hsüeh T'ao [*or* Xue Tao]. ColAnChi, *tr. by* Jeanne Larsen

Dawn comes and with it nostalgia. Along the Banks of the Charles. Adelina da Silva. NAftP, *tr. by* Don Burness

Dawn comes out of its vast silence. I Am Consecrated to the Coming One. Wafaa' Lamrani. PoArWo, *tr. by* Richard McKane and Tahia Abdel Nasser

Dawn coming on. Taneda Santoka. CAoMJL1, *tr. by* Burton Watson

Dawn crack of sounds known, The. This Earth, My Brother. Kofi Awoonor. VCWP

Dawn departs, the morning is begun, The. My Mother. Claude McKay. OxAAAP

Dawn Dissolves the Monsters. Paul Éluard. AF, *tr. by* Lloyd Alexander

Dawn drizzle [*or* Dawndrizzle] ended dampness steams from. Anglo Saxon Street. Earle Birney. HeIP-4; NIL-7

Dawn Fairy, The. Dunya Mikhail. PoArWo, *tr. by* Samira Kawar

Dawn fog separated into two parts, The. Ledge, The. Harry Mathews. NYP2

Dawn for you is night and darkness is light;[now] the girls of enjoyable company shy away, contrary to the days of youth. Hāzim al-Qarṭājannī. HiArP, tr. by James T. Monroe

Dawn had not streak'd the spacious veil of night. Before Twilight. Eyezion. Anne Batten Cristall. RWP

Dawn Has Arisen, Our Welfare Is Assured. Unknown. WoPoe Fr. Rig Veda.

Dawn Has Arisen, Our Welfare Is Assured. Unknown. WoPoe Fr. Vedic Hymns.

Dawn Has Yet to Ripple In. Melville Cane. MoAmPo

Dawn in El Paso. Carol Coffee Reposa. TiP2

Dawn in New York. Claude McKay. APT-1

Dawn is a fisherman, his harpoon of light. Dawn is a Fisherman. Raymond Barrow. OWABP

Dawn is grey here, she went on to tell him. It was not always like this, The. Henri Michaux. GPTC Fr. I Am Writing to You from a Far-Off Country.

Dawn Landscape. Tu Fu [or Du Fu]. NDACCP, tr. by David Hinton

Dawn leaves the bed of Dark and climbs the sky. Virgil. EroLit Fr. Aeneid [or Eneados or Aeneis], The.

Dawn lightly laid her rosy hand. (LL) Ballad of a Nun, A. John Davidson. MoBrPo; UV

Dawn moon struggles to shine its light, The. On Failing the Examination. Meng Chiao. ColAnChi, tr. by Burton Watson

Dawn of a pleasant morning in May. Lee to the Rear. John Randolph Thompson. CBCWP

Dawn of Freedom. Roland A. Parks. OWABP

Dawn of Love, The. Henrietta Cordelia Ray. CBWP-3

Dawn of the Navajo Woman, The. Terry Blackhawk. PoDa

Dawn: off from the south cliff. Scene from South Hill to North Hill Passing the Lake. Hsieh Ling-yün. ChinPo, tr. by Ye Weilian [or Yeh Wei-lien or Wai-lim Yip]

Dawn on the drab North Sea! North Sea. Jeffery Day. PoWW

Dawn on the East Coast. Alun Lewis. OBWP

Dawn on the Mountain. Wang Wei. NDACCP, tr. by Ezra Pound

Dawn on the Willamette. Ella Higginson. SWaP

Dawn Outside the City Walls. Juan Ramón Jiménez. RaW, tr. by Robert Bly

Dawn Over the Mountains. Tu Fu [or Du Fu]. NDACCP, tr. by Kenneth Rexroth

Dawn overtook Scheherazade and she fell silent. Telling, The. Andrew Hudgins. RA

Dawn Presented Itself Bare-Armed and Immodest. Amelia Rosselli. CItWP, tr. by Cinzia Sartini Blum and Lara Trubowitz

Dawn Rhythms. Margit Kaffka. IQMS, tr. by Paul Tabori

Dawn rolled up slowly what the night unwound. By the Sound. John Hollander. MakPoe

Dawn: "Rolling snow turned peach-color." Miyazawa Kenji. WhBo

"Dawn", said a stranger, "look, the cloud is tinted with blood." Dawn Rhythms. Margit Kaffka. IQMS, tr. by Paul Tabori

Dawn sifting through the trees, granulated sugar, everything hanging on that first step. Daylight. David Walker. MotU

Dawn! The Dawn! The crimson-tinted, comes, The. Dawn in New York. Claude McKay. APT-1

Dawn, the gulls weep for the Jews. I Decide Not to Have Children. Marilyn Nelson. InoFa

Dawn, The: "To Be / Immortal." Charles North. NYP2

Dawn to dusk, the weather constantly changed. Written on the Lake While Returning to Stone Cliff Hermitage. Hsieh Ling-yün. CrYelRi, tr. by Sam Hamill

Dawn Wail for the Dead. Oodgeroo of the tribe Noonuccal. BMAP

Dawn was apple-green, The. Green. D. H. Lawrence. HarvBoo; MoBrPo

Dawn where the, where the. Alba. Laura Mullen. IAoNAP

Dawn will dissolve. Beginning of Summer. Robert Melançon. YaTCFP, tr. by Philip Stratford

Dawn, with Cardinals. Jeffrey Levine. PoDa

Dawning of morn, the daylight's sinking, The. Thee, Thee, Only Thee. Thomas Moore. IrLP

Dawning of the Day, The. Edward Walsh. IrLP

Dawning sun shines upon the royal wheat fields, The. Pheasant on His Morning Flight, A. Hsiao Kang. ColAnChi, tr. by Victor H. Mair and Tsu-Lin Mei

Dawning, The. George Herbert. NOSC

Dawn's Carol. Henrietta Cordelia Ray. CBWP-3

Dawn's orb orange-raw shining over Palisades. We Rise on Sun Beams and Fall in the Night. Allen Ginsberg. CLPP

Dawn's promising skies. And This Is My Beloved. George Forrest and Robert Wright. ReLy

Dawnsong! Askia Muhammad Touré. FTtHH

Dawnward I wake. In darkness wait. Dawn. Robert Penn Warren. BodElec

Day! / Faster and more fast. Pippa Passes. Robert Browning.

Day: "That was the day that went too far." Colette Bryce. NIrP

Day 1: Portrait of the Artist, Small-kid Time. R. Zamora-Linmark. ReBoTo

Day 20. Bruce Beaver. BMAP Fr. Odes and Days.

Day, A. William Leroy Stidger. SoSe-8

Day, The / is ready to close. Saturday Night in the Village. Giacomo Leopardi. OBVE; WoPoe, tr. by Robert Lowell

Day absent of sun, troubles in over plush hilltops, The. Gray Day in January in La Jolla. Quincy Troupe. OxAAAP; PrTe

Day after Chasing Porcupines. James Welch. NoAM; WaAnP

Day after Conference, The. Josephine D. Henderson Heard. CBWP-4

Day after day. Sister, You Cannot Think a Baby Out! Irène Assiba d'Almeida. HAWP

Day after Day. Rabindranath Tagore. OBMV Fr. Gitanjali.

Day after day I have come and sat. Dead Boy's Portrait and His Dog, The. Gerald Massey. DiBP

Day after day, I learn to be grateful. Solitude Dinner. Renée Gregorio. ICANM

Day after day I live, deer for company. To a Friend. Pyŏn Wŏngyu. CATKP, tr. by Peter H. Lee

Day after day I sit and write. Advice to Young Ladies. Ann Plato. SWaP

Day after day it goes on. How Much Longer? Robert Mezey. OBWP

Day after day, O lord of my life, shall I stand before thee face to face? Rabindranath Tagore. OBMV Fr. Gitanjali.

Day after day we stood in helpless fields. 'Tis Sixty Years Since. Maurice Lindsay. EdScPo

Day After Sunday, The. Phyllis McGinley. AmWit; MoAmPo; OBSV

Day and Night. Aimé Césaire. NAWM-7v2, tr. by Gregson Davis

Day and night. Day and Night. Juan Chi. CCL1, tr. by Michael Bullock and C. J. Chen

Day and Night. Haniel Long. APT-1

Day and Night. Eugenio Montale. AF, tr. by William Arrowsmith

Day and night are never weary. Greek Epigram. Ezra Pound. MoAmPo

Day and Night Handball. Stephen Dunn. MoASP

Day and night she dances. Shulamit in Her Dreams. Marcia Falk. TaR

Day assimilating to night, The. Sunset Over Llŷn. Sion Aled. BBMWP, tr. by Grahame Davies

Day at a country fair, A. Anne Portugal. SCFWP Fr. Bath, The.

Day at a Time [For the artist of environment, time too must be flexible]. Michael Dransfield. BMAP

Day at Home, A. Zoya Ezrokhi. CRWP, tr. by Daniel Weissbort

Day at School, A. Andrea M. Wren. InTrad

Day at the Seaside, A. John Glenday. NeBrP

Day befo' Thanksgibin', De. Maggie Pogue Johnson. CBWP-4

Day before Christmas. Marchette Chute. NTCP

Day Before Spring, The. Lizette Woodworth Reese. SWaP

Day before those silver planes, The. Insistence of Beauty, The. Stephen Dunn. CAP-8

Day began early: we are embarking from the jetty of great white stones and palm trees, The. Tattoos in the Water. Efraín Bartolomé. RMCMP, tr. by Asa Zatz

Day begins to droop, The. Winter Nightfall. Robert Bridges. MoBrPo; OBEV

Day being humid and my head, The. Ovid. WoPoe Fr. Amores.

Day Break. Joseph Somoza. ICANM

Day breaks—the first rays of the riising Sun, stretching her arms, The. Unknown. NOBAu Fr. Dulngulg Song Cycle, The.

Day by Day. Sammy Cahn. ReLy

Day by Day. Sir Richard of Chichester. SacPr

Day by day I'm falling more in love with you. Day by Day. Sammy Cahn. ReLy

Day closes, / Time to feast and rest. Yun Sŏndo. CATKP Fr. Angler's Calendar, The.

Day creeps down. The moon is creeping up. Man on the Dump, The. Wallace Stevens. APT-1; NAMCP V.1; NAWM-7v2; NoAM; OxBoAm

Day dawns with scent of must and rain, The. Mirror in February. Thomas Kinsella. MakPoe; NAMCP V.2; NoAM

Day Death Comes, The. Faiz Ahmad Faiz. PoetW, tr. by Naomi Lazard

Day Dr. Knox Did It, The. Robert Penn Warren.
  Confederate Veteran Tries to Explain the Event, A. AmWaPo; CBCWP

Day Draws Near, The. Augusta, Lady Gregory. IrLP

Day Dream, A. Emily Jane Brontë. NALW

Day ends at the end of land, The. Pine Island. Reginald Gibbons. RWB

Day ends that way, with brilliant colors, so lovely, without, The. Not Even Mythology. Yannis Ritsos. AF, tr. by Edmund Keeley

Day ends with the blur, The. Pismo, 1959. Robert Vasquez. GeoHom

Day for Anne Frank, A. C. K. Williams. TaR

Day grows old, the low-pitched lamp hath made, The. Yet a Little While Is the Light With You. Francis Quarles. ChIV-2

Day had been a day of wind and storm, The. After a Tempest. William Cullen Bryant. APN-1

Day has blinked, the streets are awash with blue, The. Excitement. Polly Clark. NeBl

Day has her star, as well as Night. Two Stars, The. W. H. Davies. MoBrPo

Day has no blood to give you, The. Prayer to the Boys of San Antonio. Ray Gonzalez. LiTh

Day! hast thou two faces. Chartist's Complaint, The. Ralph Waldo Emerson. NCAP

Day He Died, The. Ted Hughes. OxAEP-2

Day I did not know, The. Meeting Bandits. Yŏngjae, Monk. CATKP, tr. by Peter H. Lee

Day I watched them carry her, The. Ballad of the Underpass. Patricia Beer. HarvBoo

Day in an' day oot on his auld farrant loom. Song for February, A. Thomas Given. FaBoVe

Day in August, A. Frank Ormsby. PBCIP; PNI

Day in October. Rainer Maria Rilke. WED, tr. by Robert Bly

Day in the Life of . . . , A. Conyus. GT

Day in—day out. Day In—Day Out. Johnny Mercer. ReLy

Day is a woman who loves you, The. Open. Driving Montana. Richard Hugo. AmFaPo

Day is dark and dreary, The. If. Franklin Pierce Adams. APT-1

Day is done, and the darkness, The. Day Is Done, The. Henry Wadsworth Longfellow. APN-1; BRP; ChAP; ITBLP; NAAPv.1; NCAP; TreFP

Day Is Done, The. Phoebe Cary. APN-2

Day is done; the twilight grows more dark, The. István Gyöngyösi. IQMS Fr. János Kemény.

Day is drawing to its fall, A. First Sight of Her and After. Thomas Hardy. FaBoVe

Day Is Dying in the West. Mary Artemisia Lathbury. SacPr

Day is ending. My Blue Heaven. George Whiting. ReLy

Day is ending, The. Afternoon in February. Henry Wadsworth Longfellow. APN-1; ColAP

Day Is Gone and All Its Sweets Are Gone, The. John Keats. CenSon (Day Is Gone, The.) NPBRoP

Day is mad, The. Mad is the house. Mad the bedsheets. Erotica 12. Yannis Ritsos. PFTM-2, tr. by Kimon Friar

Day is o'er and twilight's shade, The. Gerarda. Eloise Bibb. CBWP-4

Day is over and its cares and woes, The. Good Night, Sweetheart. Jimmy Campbell, Reginald Connelly and Ray Noble. ReLy

Day is past, the sun is set, The. Evening. Thomas Miller. NOxBChV

Day is through, The. Tomorrow Is Another Day. Gustave Kahn. ReLy

Day is warm. Yun Sŏndo. CATKP Fr. Angler's Calendar, The.

Day Labor. Heather Fuller. Eno

Day Lady Died, The. Frank O'Hara. CAP-8; EMP; InoFa; ItP; NAMCP V.2; NoAM; NoP-4; NoP-5; OxBoAm; PFTM-2; PmAP; RaBo; SwNoth; TRP; VCAP; WaAnP

Day, like our souls, is fiercely dark. Battle Song. Ebenezer Elliott. OxAEP-2

Day Lilies: Instructions and an Elegy. Christopher Merrill. PfSP

Day Lily and the Fox, The. Emily Hiestand. OPRER

Day Long After, A. Kim Sowŏl. CAMKP, tr. by David R. McCann

Day must bring an ending of the self, A. Raindrops. György Sárközi. IQMS, tr. by Roy Fuller

Day my daughter leaves for California, The. Living at the Frost Place. Sue Ellen Thompson. VisFro

Day my girl is lost for an hour, The. Quest, The. Sharon Olds. P180

Day of Atonement. Charles Reznikoff. ChIV-1

Day of Doom, The [First Section]. Michael Wigglesworth.
  "All filthy facts, and secret acts." NAAL-3
  "All silence keep, both goats and sheep." NAAL-3
  "But all too late, grief's out of date." NAAL-3
  "Can God delight in such a sight." NAAL-3
  "Christ's Flock of Lambs there also stands." TCAPo
  "Come, blessed ones, and sit on thrones." NAAL-3
  "For at midnight brake forth a Light." TCAPo
  "Glorious Judge will priviledge, The." TCAPo
  "Had your intent been to repent." NAAL-3
  "Others argue, and not a few." NAAL-3
  "Still was the night, serene and bright." ColAP; NAAL-3; TCAPo
  "These words appall and daunt them all." NAAL-3
  "They rush from Beds with giddy heads." TCAPo
  "They wring their hands, their caitiff-hands." NAAL-3
  "Thus all men's pleas the Judge with ease." NAAL-3
  "Thus everyone before the throne." NAAL-3; TCAPo
  "Thus he doth find of all mankind." NAAL-3
  "Thus shall they lie, and wail, and cry." NAAL-3
  "Unto the saints with sad complaints." NAAL-3

  "With cords of love God often strove." NAAL-3
  "Wond'rous crowd then 'gan aloud, A." NAAL-3

Day of Doom, The: Or, A Poetical Description of the Great and Last Judgment. Michael Wigglesworth.
  Day of Doom, The: Verses 208–224. NAAPv.1
  Day of Doom, Verses 1–10, The.
    "Still was the night, serene and bright." NAAPv.1
  Day of Doom, Verses 201–210, The.
    "Whom having brought, as they are taught." NAAPv.1

Day of Foreboding. Stanley Kunitz. NAMCP V.1

Day of Judgement. Henry Vaughan. ChIV-2

Day of Judgement, The. Jonathan Swift. ChIV-1; NPeEn; OBSV; OxBEV

Day of Judg[e]ment, The; an Ode [Attempted in English Sapphic]. Isaac Watts. ChIV-2; NoP-4; NoP-5; OBEV; OxBEV

Day of Judgment is here, The. So Bring the Order for My Execution. Faiz Ahmad Faiz. VCWP, tr. by Agha Shahid Ali

Day of Judgment, The. Thomas of Celano. OBVE,

Day of Judgment, The. Unknown. SSUS

Day of My Death, The. Pier Paolo Pasolini. VCWP, tr. by Max Hayward

Day of reckoning came, The. With bearing fine. Albery Allson Whitman. NAAPv.1 Fr. Octoroon, The.

Day of sea in the sky, made. Day of Sea. Sophia De Mello Breyner. VCWP, tr. by Ruth Fainlight

Day of the Dead. Rigoberto González. AmPoNex

Day of vast dreaming. Unknown. NAAPv.2

Day off in dark suit and hat. Zapruder. Thomas Sayers Ellis. LegDan

Day on the Planet, A. Brian Morse. NOxBChV

Day on which you, The. Enumeration. Ilse Aichinger. AF, tr. by Allen H. Chappel

Day One: Above the river I hear. Hay. Maxine W. Kumin. BodElec

Day perched at ground-level. More Rain. Ben Scammell. NLP

Day plain and un-cluttered. Geometry of the Figure. Mark McMorris. OnScMo

Day pounds hard against our temple doors, The. Cooking to Music. Edward Kleinschmidt. MiVo

Day seawater swilled my lungs, The. Does It Go Like this? Maura Dooley. NeBl

Day she went 5 for 5 against Vic Raschi, The. (LL) Baseball and Classicism. Tom Clark. ASA; PmAP

Day slow in going, A. Buson. EH, tr. by Robert Hass

Day so happy, A. Gift. Czeslaw Milosz. BeAl; PoCho; TWF; WhBo, tr. by the author

Day Song. Lance Henson. HATNAP

Day Surgery Pre-Op. Helena Minton. PfS

Day that Eliot died I stood, The. Thanks in Winter. Harri Webb. AngWePo

Day that I was crowned, The. Emily Dickinson. TCAPo

Day that they stole her tiger's-eye ring, The. On Becoming a Tiger. Lorna Goodison. GT

Day the Audience Walked Out on Me, and Why, The. Denise Levertov. BrAP

Day the gardeners planted, The. For Beauty. Susan Hahn. ExTi

Day the minister ran off with the choir director, The. Scandal, The. Robert Bly. GoPo

Day the Soviet Union collapsed I, I, The. Hwang Jiwoo. CAMKP Fr. Melancholy.

Day the two old women were dissecting two birds, The. Richard Brought His Flute. Nancy Morejón. TCLAP, tr. by Kathleen Weaver

Day the War Ended, The. Randall Swingler. RSaN

Day the wind was hardly, A. Letter VI. William Sydney Graham. EdScPo

Day they baptised, The. Gwyneth Lewis. BBMWP Fr. Wholeness.

Day They Cleaned Up the Border, The: El Salvador, February, 1981. Wendy Rose. AmWaPo; HATNAP

Day They Eulogized Mahalia, The. Audre Lorde. ReTh

Day they strung the cable from America to Europe, The. Cotton. Harry Edmund Martinson. WED, tr. by Robert Bly

Day to the reedy marsh had closed her eye. János Arany. IQMS Fr. Toldi.

Day took such a time to pass, The. Note. Dimitris Tsaloumas. BMAP

Day Trip. Carole Satyamurti. OPOU

Day turns to evening on the lake. Hayim Lenski. FIT, tr. by Robert Friend

Day very solid February 12th, 1944, A. Hayden Carruth. StAl Fr. Paragraphs.

Day wanes. Rotation 1. Kang Ŭn'gyo. EcSo, tr. by Ann Y. Choi

Day was clear as fire, The. Killer, The. Judith Wright. BMAP

Day was close, overcast like a grey belly, The. Winter. Philip Salom. NOBAu

Day was cloudy. No one could come to a decision, The. Last Day, The. George Seferis. PoetW, tr. by Edmund Keeley and Philip Sherrard

Day was cloudy, The. No one could come to a decision. George Seferis. AF Fr. Last Day, The.

Day was here when it was his to know, The. New Tenants, The. Edwin Arlington Robinson. NoAM

Day was nearly finished drawing clothes, The. Inscription. Stephen Rodefer. OnScMo

Day we die, The. Day We Die, The. *Southern Bushmen Oral Tradition.* BLT; WoPoe, *tr. by* Arthur Markowitz

Day We Visited New Orleans, The. Robert Bly. KGB

Day when Charmus ran with five, The. Nicarchus of Alexandria. AmWit *Fr.* Variations of Greek Themes.

Day Which Endures Not, A. A. G. Prys-Jones. OBWVE, *tr. by* Anthony Conran

Day will come when I will, The. Farewell to a Southern Melody, A. Huang O. WoPoe, *tr. by* Chung Ling and Kenneth Rexroth

Day will see your face. (LL) Rainbow at Night. Antonio Machado Ruiz. AF; BLT; WED, *tr. by* Robert Bly

Day Within a Day. Fazil Hüsnü Daglarca. NaPG, *tr. by* Talat Sait Halman

Day Without Night. Louise Glück. TaR

Day you fly to Tennessee, the snow, The. When You Can't Leave Me Anymore. Lynn Davies. Coast

Day you mean one more. (LL) Low Road, The. Marge Piercy. BeAl; TWF

Day you moved out of my life, The. 1/Vacant. Nadir Lasana Bomani. BtF

Day Zimmer Lost Religion, The. Paul Zimmer. PBCAP

Daybreak. Richard Henry Dana. APN-1

Daybreak. Philippe Jaccottet. MFP, *tr. by* Martin Sorrell

Daybreak. Juan Ramón Jiménez. RaW, *tr. by* Ralph Nelson and Rita García Nelson

Daybreak. Henry Wadsworth Longfellow. ITBLP

Daybreak. Sterling Plumpp. OxAAAP

Daybreak. *Unknown, at. to* John Donne. OBEV

Daybreak / has that sadness of arriving. Daybreak. Juan Ramón Jiménez. RaW, *tr. by* Ralph Nelson and Rita García Nelson

Daybreak / mingles blood. Daybreak. Philippe Jaccottet. MFP, *tr. by* Martin Sorrell

Daybreak: "On the tidal mud, just before sunset." Galway Kinnell. BLT; ChAP

Daybreak. Christiania Whitehead. NeBl

Daybreak, a van. Daybreak in Seoul. Kim Hyesun. EcSo, *tr. by* Youngju Ryu

Daybreak in Alabama. Langston Hughes. FaBoA

Daybreak in late spring, I embark at Ba Gorge. Arriving at Ba Gorge in the Morning. Wang Wei. WoPoe, *tr. by* Tony Barnstone, Willis Barnstone and Xu Haixin

Daybreak in Seoul. Kim Hyesun. EcSo, *tr. by* Youngju Ryu

Daybreak is still far away, The. Agonia Christiana. János Pilinszky. IQMS, *tr. by* Adam Makkai

Daybreak until nightfall. Her Long Illness. Donald Hall. GoPo

Daybreak wakes. Sterling Plumpp. FuFl *Fr.* Mary.

Daycare in a Doublewide. Janet Norman Knox. RWB

Day-dream, A. Mary Elizabeth Coleridge. VWP

Daydream of Ants, The. Tanure Ojaide. NAfrP

Daydreaming on the Trail. Miyazawa Kenji. PFTM-1

Daydreams Have Endlessly Turning Paths. Antonio Machado Ruiz. RaW, *tr. by* Robert Bly

Dayeinu—they said. Rosita Kalina. TANSG, *tr. by* Celeste Kostopulos-Cooperman

Daylight. Mariana Romo-Carmona. WiU

Daylight. David Walker. MotU

Daylight. . . / no one notices. Stanford M. Forrester. AmZen

Daylight announces. Sunrise Comes to Second Avenue. Thylias Moss. TRP

Daylight changed without you. Daylight. Mariana Romo-Carmona. WiU

Daylight fades, like the close of a long stemmed tiger lily. 9 PM Summer. Mary Sue Koeppel. AmZen

Daylight. For everyone but me. *Nap.* Dreams by No One's Daughter. Leslie Ullman. PBCAP

Daylight, full of small dancing particles. Jelaluddin Rumi. LoL, *tr. by* Coleman Barks

Daylights. Rosanna Warren. NoAM

Day-long bluster of the storm was o'er, The. Drowned Spaniel, The. Charles Tennyson Turner. DiBP

Day-long cold hard rain drove, The. Surviving. James Welch. HATNAP

Day-Long Day. Tino Villanueva. TiP2

Daylong this tomcat lies stretched flat. Esther's Tomcat. Ted Hughes. OxBEV

Days. Ralph Waldo Emerson. APN-1; ColAP; HeIP-4; NAAL-3; NAAPv.1; NCAP; NoP-5; OxBoAm; TCAPo; TFi

Days. Philip Larkin. NPeEn; OxAEP-2; OxBEV; PoetW; WaAnP; WoPoe

Days. Hank Lazer.

   28. AnSo

Days. Jean Tardieu. YaTCFP, *tr. by* David Kelley

Days. Gary Young.

   Four Poems. GeoHom

Days and months do not wish to tarry, The. T'ao Ch'ien. CCL1, *tr. by* William Acker

Days and Nights. Kenneth Koch.

   Days and Nights.

      "I certainly have lost something." NoAM

   Stones of Time, The. NAMCP V.2; NoAM

Days are beautiful, The. Hum. Ann Lauterbach. OxBoAm

Days are gone, when beauty bright, The. Thomas Moore. IrLP

Days are sad, it is the holy tide, The. Holy Tide, The. Frederick Tennyson. OBEV; SacPr

Days become years. Years. Paavo Haavikko. VCWP *Fr.* Darkness.

Days can be sunny. I Got Rhythm. Ira Gershwin. ReLy

Day's End. S. N. Masuri. SonAtl, *tr. by* Zaniah Marshallsay, Anne Swann and Kitty Yuen Ching

Day's End. Alden Nowlan. Coast

Day's End. Ann Townsend. SweBea

Day's end. Robins tweep. Day's End. S. N. Masuri. SonAtl, *tr. by* Zaniah Marshallsay, Anne Swann and Kitty Yuen Ching

Day's Ending. Sara Teasdale. NAAPv.2

Days Gone By. Gu Cheng. WoBe, *tr. by* Joseph R. Allen

Days Gone By, The. James Whitcomb Riley. APN-2

Days grow long, the mountains, The. South Wind. Tu Fu [*or* Du Fu]. BLT, *tr. by* Kenneth Rexroth

Days heap upon us. All plain. All clouds except a narrow opening at the top of the sky. Tuesday. Lisa Robertson. OpeFie

Day's in dread of losing her bright features, The. Ausiàs March. STV

Days in the wind. Gu Cheng. WoBe *Fr.* Liquid Mercury.

Days Inn. Linda Smukler. WiU

Days Into Flatspin is Ken Babstock's most formbidable masterpiece to date. Darren Wershler-Henry. PoPra *Fr.* Ten Out of Ten, or, Why Poetry Criticism Sucks in 2003.

Day's Labor, The. Paul De Roux. YaTCFP, *tr. by* Stephen Romer

Days like Prose. Alan Michael Parker. NeAmPo

Days must be hot to make the cotton white. Summer Nights in Texas. Grace Noll Crowell. TiP2

Day's noise was draining away in my mind, The. Man in the Middle of the Street. Petronius Arbiter. WoPoe, *tr. by* Tim Reynolds

Days of 1908. Constantine P. Cavafy. WoPoe, *tr. by* James Merrill

Days of 1908. Constantine P. Cavafy. PFTM-1, *tr. by* Edmund Keeley and Philip Sherrard

Days of 1968. Edward Hirsch. OxBoAm

Days of 1981. Mark Doty. ReTh

Days of 1994. James Merrill. OxBoAm

Days of Adam were 930 years, The. Dennis Joseph Enright. OBCoV *Fr.* Paradise Illustrated.

Days of April '43. George Seferis. PoetW, *tr. by* Edmund Keeley and Philip Sherrard

Days of calm. An invalid's mild diversions. Last Days in Camden. Robert B. Shaw. ViWalt

Days of My Mother, The. Laurel Mills. SweBea

Days of my youth left me long ago, The. Chrysanthemums in the Eastern Garden, The. Po Chü-i. CCL1, *tr. by* Arthur Waley

Days of 1964. James Merrill. NAMCP V.2; OxBoAm; VCAP

Days of 1935. James Merrill. OxBoAm

Days of our ghosthood were these, The. Ghosts, The. Edith Jay Scovell. HarvBoo

Days of Rain. Li Ho. CrYelRi, *tr. by* Sam Hamill

Days of the New Republic. Justin Quinn.

   7. Bohemian Carp. NIrP

   12. Graffiti. NIrP

Days of Yore, The. Douglas Thompson. TreFP

Day's pain seeps. Sleepless. Tatamkulu Afrika. TSAP

Days pass on that face, The. Gregorio Scalise. ItPo, *tr. by* Gayle Ridinger

Day's Ration, The. Ralph Waldo Emerson. APN-1

Days shorten, the south blows wide for showers now, The. Salmon Fishing. Robinson Jeffers. APT-1; NAAPv.2

Days That Have Been. W. H. Davies. AngWePo

Days to come stand in front of us. Candles. Constantine P. Cavafy. BeAl, *tr. by* Edmund Keeley and Philip Sherrard

Days Too Short. W. H. Davies. MoBrPo

Days when I laughed, The. Hakkaku. NAAPv.2

Days wrap themselves around me, The. Ode to Your Back. Gloria Vando. TouFir

Dayseye hugging the earth, The. Daisy. William Carlos Williams. MoAmPo

Daystar. Rita Dove. AmFaPo; BeAl; NIL-7; NIP-4; OxWW

Daytime Dream. Tu Fu [*or* Du Fu]. WoPoe, *tr. by* Eva Shan Chou

Day—Towards Evening. Gennady Aygi. WoBe, *tr. by* Peter France

Dazzle of ocean was their first infatuation, The. Brief History of Light, A. Caitríona O'Reilly. MoWP; NIrP

Dazzled [*or* Dazel'd] thus with height of place. Upon the Sudden Restraint of the Earl[e] of Somerset, Then Falling from Favor [*or* Favour]. Sir Henry Wotton. NOSC; NPeEn; OxBEV; PBRV

Dazzling and tremendous how quick the sun-rise would kill me. Walt Whitman. ColAP *Fr.* Song of Myself.

Dazzling blue days. Blue Days. Sŏ Chŏngju. CAMKP, *tr. by* David R. McCann

DC Nocturne. Kenneth Carroll. AmPoNex

D-Day, 1994. Jack Coulehan. BloBone

DDD. Bruce Andrews. FTOS

De. Robert Alan Jamieson. FaBoVe

De Aegypto. Ezra Pound. APT-1

De Amore Suo. Catullus. OBVE, *tr. by* Richard Lovelace

De aquí no se va nadie. Pie Para el Niño de Vallecas de Velázquez. León Felipe. RaW

De Carlo Lots, The. Anne Waldman. AHA

De ceux qui préférant à leurs regrets les fleuves. Seine de Paris, La. Jean Tardieu. YaTCFP

De Cœnatione Micae. Martial. RomPo, *tr. by* Robert Louis Stevenson

De cómo Robert Schumann fue vencido por los demonios. Francisco Hernandez. RMCMP

De Consolatione Philosophiae. Boethius. *tr. by* Henry Vaughan
Lilb. 2. Metrum 4. FSCP, *tr. by* Henry Vaughan

De la ventana. Ana Belén López Pulido. SPV

De la Vida en Provincias. Carlos Sahagún. RaW

De l'horizon il se. Vu de ce côté-ci. Anne Portugal. YaTCFP

De los Años Cuarenta. Jaime Gil de Biedma. RaW

De los cientos de muertes que me habitan. Muerte en la Tarde. Angel González. RaW

De maiden mit nodings on. (LL) Ballad by Hans Breitmann. Charles Godfrey Leland. APN-2; TCAPo

De mirada fija. En un baño de vapor. Manuel Ulacia. RMCMP

De Morte. Sir Henry Wotton. BASC; NOSC

De Natura Rerum. Yves Bonnefoy. VCWP, *tr. by* Lisa Sapinkopf

De Pisis--Piacenza Papers. Franco Buffoni. ItPo, *tr. by* Gayle Ridinger

De plus en plus femme. Pierre Jean Jouve. YaTCFP

De Ponto. Ovid. OBVE, *tr. by* Henry Vaughan

De Principe Bono et Malo. Sir Thomas More. PBRV

De Profundis. Thomas Campion. InvLi

De Profundis. George Gascoigne.
"From depth of dole, wherein my soul doth dwell." SacPr; ChIV-1
"Skies gan scowl, o'ercast with misty clouds, The." ChIV-1

De Profundis. David Gascoyne. PoWW

De Profundis. László Kálnoky. IQMS, *tr. by* Edwin Morgan

De Profundis. Georg Trakl. WoPoe, *tr. by* James Wright

De Puero Balbutiente. Thomas Bastard. NoSic; OxBEV

De Puerorum osculis. Giles de Gillies. CAGL

De qué país eres tú. De Qué País. Luis Cernuda. RaW

De railroad bridge's. Homesick Blues. Langston Hughes. GM; MoAmPo

De Ramis Cadunt Folia (Love in Winter). *Unknown.* WoPoe, *tr. by* Phillip Holland

De Regimine Principum. Thomas Hoccleve.
Lament for Chaucer. OBEV

De Rerum Natura (On the Nature of Things). Lucretius. *tr. by* Basil Bunting, John Dryden, John Wilmot, 2d Earl of Rochester and W. H. Mallock
Against the Fear of Death (The Latter Part of the Third Book). *tr. by* John Dryden
"What has this bugbear death to frighten man." NPeEn; OBVE, *tr. by* John Dryden
Beginning of the First Book, The [Address to Venus]. *tr. by* John Dryden
"Delight of Humane kind, and Gods above." OBVE, *tr. by* John Dryden
Concerning the Nature of Love (From The Fourth Book). *tr. by* John Dryden
"Thus, therefore, he who feels the fiery dart." EroLit, *tr. by* John Dryden
"When Love its utmost vigour does imploy." NPeEn; OxBEV, *tr. by* John Dryden
"Darling of Gods and Men, beneath the gliding stars." WoPoe, *tr. by* Basil Bunting
Elements Changeable, The. OBVE, *tr. by* Thomas Creech
"Gods, by right of Nature, must possess, The." NPeEn, *tr. by* John Wilmot, 2d Earl of Rochester

De Rich Getting Rich. Benjamin Zephaniah. RSaN

De Sade. John Fuller. NBLV

De sol a sol. Haroldo de Campos. PFTM-2 *Fr.* Transient Servitude.

De Souza Prabhu. Eunice De Souza. FaBoVe; NAMCP V.2

De sun give a light in de heaven all round. Give Up the World. *Unknown.* SSUS

De talles' tree in Paradise. Blow Your Trumpet, Gabriel. *Unknown.* APN-2; SSUS

De tu garganta. Tarde caía, La. Víctor Terán. RMCMP

De Two-Nineteen done took mah baby away. Mamie's Blues. "Jelly Roll." Morton. NAAPv.2

Dea ex Machina. John Updike. UV

Deacon's Masterpiece, The; or, The Wonderful "One-Hoss Shay." Oliver Wendell Holmes. APN-1; BRP; ITBLP; NAAL-3; NAAPv.1; TCAPo; TFi *Fr.* Autocrat of the Breakfast Table, The.

Dead, The. René Arcos. FaBoWar, *tr. by* Christopher Middleton

Dead, The. Mathilde Blind. GSo

Dead, The. Billy Collins. StAl

Dead, The. José María Eguren. TCLAP, *tr. by* Iver Lofving

Dead, The. Miroslav Holub. StAl, *tr. by* Ewald Osers

Dead, The. David Gwenallt Jones. BBMWP, *tr. by* Anthony Conran

Dead, The. Mark Strand. HeIP-4

Dead, The. Jones Very. APN-1; NoP-4; NoP-5; OxBoAm; SacPr; TCAPo

Dead, The: "At night the dead come down to the river to drink." Susan Mitchell. P180

Dead, The: "Dead come, looking for their shoes, The." Ellery Akers. InoFa

Dead! the gloroius Dead!—And shall they rise?, The. Magic Glass, The. Felicia Dorothea Hemans. NOBRP

Dead, The ("These hearts were woven of human joys and cares.") Rupert Brooke. SoSe-8

Dead abide with us, The! Though stark and cold. Dead, The. Mathilde Blind. GSo

Dead and divine and brother of all, and here again he lies. (LL) Sight in Camp [in the Daybreak Gray and Dim], A. Walt Whitman. BLT; CBCWP; InoFa; NAAL-3; NAAL-5; NoAM; SAmP

Dead are always looking down on us, they say, The. Dead, The. Billy Collins. StAl

Dead are always searched, The. Enemy Dead, The. Bernard Gutteridge. FaBoWar; PoWW

Dead are gone and with them we cannot converse, The. *Unknown.* CCL1,

Dead are horizontal and motionless, The. Ancestor Worship. Emyr Humphreys. AngWePo

Dead are selfish, The. Diatribe Against the Dead. Angel González. VCWP, *tr. by* Steven Ford Brown and Revuelta Gutierrez

Dead Armadillos. Gail White. UrbNat

Dead at Clonmacnois [*or* Clonmacnoise], The. Angus O'Gillan. OBEV; OBMV, *tr. by* Thomas William Hazen Rolleston

Dead at Villers-Bretonneux, The. Inscription at Villers-Bretonneux. Geoff Page. NOBAu

Dead beetle lies on a country road, A. Seen From Above. Wisława Szymborska. PoSu, *tr. by* Grazyna Drabik and Sharon Olds

Dead before Death. Christina Georgina Rossetti. NAEL-6v2; NAEL-7v2; NALW

Dead birds. Pet Shop. Philip Whalen. WhBo

Dead birds fell, but no one had seen them fly, The. Some Dreams They Forgot. Elizabeth Bishop. ItP; NoAM

Dead Boy. John Crowe Ransom. FuPo; HarvBoo; NAMCP V.1; NoAM; NoP-4

Dead Boy's Portrait and His Dog, The. Gerald Massey. DiBP

Dead Brother, The. *Hungarian Oral Tradition.* IQMS, *tr. by* Adam Makkai

Dead Butterfly, The. Denise Levertov. NoP-4

DEAD CAN SING, THE. For the Dead Lecturer. Diane Di Prima. BB

Dead can sleep, The. I Am Dead But I Know the Dead Are Not Like This. Charles Bukowski. PmAP

Dead Cartesian, The. Chris Wallace-Crabbe. PoA 2002

Dead cats, and turnip-tops, come tumbling down the flood. (LL) Description of a City Shower, A. Jonathan Swift. BrAP; HeIP-4; NAEL-6v1; NAEL-7v1; NIL-7; NoP-4; NoP-5; NPeEn; OBSV; WaAnP

Dead Center. Alfred A. Yuson. ReBoTo

Dead center of an open field there is a flowering tree. Flowering Tree. Yi Sang. CAMKP, *tr. by* Walter Lew

Dead Child Speaks, A. Nelly Sachs. HP; PoSu

Dead Christ. Andrew Hudgins. RA; UpMys

Dead Christ Lying in the Church of Santa Clara (Church of the Cross) in Palencia, The. Miguel de Unamuno. *tr. by* Philip Levine
"This Spanish Christ that hasn't lived." RaW, *tr. by* Philip Levine

Dead Chrysanthemums. Ber Grin. Prolet, *tr. by* Amelia Glaser

Dead Cities. Madison Cawein. APN-2

Dead Cleopatra lies in a crystal casket. Conrad Potter Aiken. PoA 2002 *Fr.* Discordants.

Dead cold spots in the air. Beckon. Gillian Conoley. BodElec

Dead come, looking for their shoes, The. Dead, The. Ellery Akers. InoFa

Dead cones upon the altar [*or* alder] shook. (LL)   In Memory of Jane Fraser [*or* Frazer].   Geoffrey Hill.   NAEL-6v2; NAEL-7v2; NAMCP V.2; NIL-7; NoAM; UpMys

Dead Cow Farm.   Robert Graves.   FaBoWar; PoWW

Dead dandelions, bald as drumsticks.   Dandelions.   Craig Raine.   NoAM

Dead darkness falls.   Sun.   *Unknown.*   SonAtl, *tr. by* Alan Brierly and F. Murphy

Dead Do Not Want Us Dead, The.   Jane Hirshfield.   AmZen; WANABP

Dead Erect, The.   Malika O'Lahsen.   HAWP

Dead Eyes.   Syl Cheney-Coker.   NAfrP

Dead for twelve minutes, the plumber in Akron.   Dead Man Interview.   Neal Bowers.   PoA 2002

Dead Friend, The.   Agnes Mary Frances Robinson.   VWP

Dead Gallop.   Pablo Neruda.   TCLAP, *tr. by* John Felstiner

Dead grow more intractable every day, The.   Soldier's Rest.   Roque Dalton. TCLAP, *tr. by* Richard Schaaf

Dead gull in the road, A.   Charles Reznikoff.   APT-2

Dead Hand.   W. S. Merwin.   CAP-8

Dead hangs the fruit on that tall tree.   Burial of the Spirit of a Young Poet. Richard Hughes.   MoBrPo

Dead have remembered, The.   Posthumous Rehabilitation.   Tadeusz Różewicz. HP, *tr. by* Adam Czerniawski

Dead Heroes, The.   Isaac Rosenberg.   MoBrPo

Dead Horse Bay.   Robert Adamson.   NOBAu

Dead Horse in Field.   Robert Penn Warren.   BodElec

Dead Horse, The.   Cecília Meireles.   TCLAP, *tr. by* James Merrill

Dead Host's Welcome, The.   John Fletcher.   OxAEP-1 *Fr.* Lover's Progress, The.

Dead House Sonnet.   Brian Teare.   LegDan

Dead Idyll.   César Vallejo.   BLPSL, *tr. by* Rene de Costa, Rigas Kappatos and Eleni Paidoussi

Dead in a Bereft Horah.   Yekhi'el Khazak.   NRoS, *tr. by* Esther Raizen

Dead in Europe, The.   Robert Lowell.   WoPoe

Dead in Frock Coats, The.   Carlos Drummond de Andrade.   PFTM-1

Dead in other lands are settled, The.   Order of the Dead, The.   John Pepper Clark Bekederemo.   HBAPE

Dead in the cold, a song-singing thrush.   Last Rites.   Christina Georgina Rossetti.   FaBoVe; NPeEn

Dead in the rice paddies, dead on the nameless hills. (LL)   Ode for the American Dead in Korea.   Thomas McGrath.   AmWaPo; StAl

Dead in the Sierras.   Joaquin Miller.   CalPo

Dead in There.   Langston Hughes.   APSN; NAMCP V.1

Dead in via, The.   La Préface.   Charles Olson.   APT-2; PFTM-2

Dead is he? Yes, our stranger guest said dead.   Augusta Davies Webster. ViWPN *Fr.* Medea in Athens.

Dead Kingdom, The.   John Montague.

Flowering Absence, A.

Family Conference.   ModIr

Flowering Absence, A.   PBCIP

Locket, The.   PBCIP

Silver Flask, The.

At Last.   PBCIP

Last Journey.   ModIr; PBCIP; PNI

Silver Flask, The.   PNI

Dead Landscape.   Attila József.   WoPoe, *tr. by* Edwin Morgan

Dead Language.   Johannes Bobrowski.   WoPoe, *tr. by* Matthew Mead and Ruth Mead

Dead Language Lesson.   A. E. Stallings.   PoA 2002

Dead leaves are falling in the dormant air.   Bridge, The.   O. V. de L. Milosz. BLT

Dead leaves scent the hall with nutmeg.   Hungry as the Sea.   Melanie Kenny. IaFF

Dead Letter From Out of Town.   David Wagoner.   OxBoAm

Dead Letter Office, The.   Maxine Chernoff.   SUP

Dead Liebknecht, The.   Hugh MacDiarmid.   OBVE

Dead living in their memories, The.   Source, The.   Jon Stallworthy.   PML

Dead Love.   Elizabeth Siddal.   LW

Dead loves that were born for me. (LL)   Stony Grey Soil.   Patrick Kavanagh. HarvBoo; ModIr

Dead Man Asks for a Song, The.   *Unknown.*   WoPoe, *tr. by* Willard Trask

Dead Man Interview.   Neal Bowers.   PoA 2002

Dead man is introduced back into life. They take him to a country fair, to a, The.   Bringing a Dead Man Back into Life.   Russell Edson.   TRP

Dead man likes it when the soup simmers and the kettle hisses, The.   Book of the Dead Man #87, The.   Marvin Bell.   PuP-23

Dead man steps over sweaty sleepers.   Let's Live Cheerfully.   Takahashi Shinkichi.   ZenPo, *tr. by* Takashi Ikemoto and Lucien Stryk

Dead man thinks he is alive when he sees blood in his stool, The.   Book of the Dead Man #1, The.   Marvin Bell.   GifTon

Dead Man's Corner.   Robert Silliman Hillyer.   APT-2

Dead Man's Dump.   Isaac Rosenberg.   NAEL-6v2; NAEL-7v2; NAMCP V.1; NoAM; NoP-5; OBWP; PoWW; WaAnP

Dead Mole, A.   Andrew Young.   NePenScot

Dead moths fell from the sky. Swirling swarms buried traffic lights.   Cocoons. Sean Thomas Dougherty.   AmPoNex

Dead Mouth, High Weather, Mixture.   Jon Gill Bentley.   ICANM

Dead Nation, The.   DeWitt Clinton Duncan [Too-qua-stee].   NAAPv.1

Dead Never Fight against Anything, The.   Pattiann Rogers.   SUP

Dead now the water-lily's scent, kingfisher gloss of leaf.   West Wind Ferries Grief, The.   Li Ching.   CCL1, *tr. by* Alan Ayling and Duncan Mackintosh

Dead of Winter.   Salvatore Quasimodo.   WoPoe, *tr. by* George Garrett

Dead on the War Path.   *Unknown.*   FaBoWar, *tr. by* Herbert J. Spinden

Dead! One of them shot by the sea in the east.   Mother and Poet.   Elizabeth Barrett Browning.   InoFa; NAEL-6v2; NALW; ViWPN; VWP

Dead person, I wander, A.   Exile.   Ingeborg Bachmann.   PoSu, *tr. by* Daniel Huws

Dead Pianist, The.   Sean Dunne.   ModIr *Fr.* Sydney Place.

Dead piled up, thick, fragrant, on the fire escape, The.   Autumn Leaves. Marilyn Chin.   ExTi; NAMCP V.2

(My dead piled up, thick, fragrant, on the fire escape.)   PoPoPo

Dead Poet, The.   Lord Alfred Bruce Douglas.   GSo

Dead Ponies.   Brenda Chamberlain.   OBWVE

Dead ringing of distant steps, The.   Dust.   Negar.   CRWP, *tr. by* Richard McKane

Dead rising from the boiling seas, The. (LL)   Fears of the Eighth Grade.   Toi Derricotte.   GT; LiTh

Dead Sea, The.   Peter Davison.   YaYoPo *Fr.* Breaking of the Day, The.

Dead Sea Poems, The.   Simon Armitage.   NeBrP

Dead Seal [near McClure's Beach], The.   Robert Bly.   CAP-8

Dead shall seem to live again!, The. (LL)   Song: "What voice is this, thou evening gale!"   Joanna Baillie.   RWP; WoRP

Dead shalt thou lie; and nought.   Sapphic Fragment.   Sappho.   OBVE, *tr. by* Thomas Hardy

Dead Soldiers.   James Fenton.   AF; FaBoWar; NAMCP V.2; NoAM; NoP-4; NoP-5; OBWP

Dead Soldiers, The.   Max Plowman.   PoWW

Dead Statesman, A.   Rudyard Kipling.   FaBoWar; NBLV; OPOU; PoWW; WoPoe *Fr.* Epitaphs of the War [1914–1918].

Dead Stepfather, The.   Terry Wolverton.   WiU

Dead Still.   Andrey Andreievich Voznesensky.   PasH, *tr. by* Richard Wilbur

Dead time. Hollow depression interred invalid to resurgence, reistant.   Theresa Hak Kyung Cha.   PFTM-2 *Fr.* Dictée.

Dead to the Living, The.   Edith Nesbit.   VWP

Dead Turk, A.   Li Kuang-t'ien.   WoPoe, *tr. by* Kai-yu Hsu

Dead, was all he answered. (LL)   Death of the Hired Man, The.   Robert Frost. APT-1; HeIP-4; MoAmPo; NAAL-5; NAAPv.2; NoP-4; OxBoAm; SAmP; TCAPo

Dead Water.   Wen Yi-tuo [*or* Wen I-to].   PFTM-1; WoPoe, *tr. by* Arthur Sze

Dead Weight.   Jim Nye.   AmWaPo

Dead Weight of the Land, The.   Tedi López Mills.   RMCMP, *tr. by* Esther Allen

Dead Wingman, The.   Randall Jarrell.   PoWW

Dead Woman.   Pablo Neruda.   StAl, *tr. by* Brian Cole

Dead woodchuck in the dog's mouth drooped, The.   Aubade.   Catherine Imbriglio.   IAoNAP

Deadman's Shoes.   Kate Clanchy.   MFPA

Dead's right grain, The.   Future and the Ancestor, The.   Andrée Chedid. HAWP, *tr. by* Mirène Ghossein and Samuel Hazo

Dead-Tryst, The.   Katharine Tynan Hinkson.   IrLP

Deadwood Dick.   Elizabeth Alexander.   RA

Deaf and Blind, The.   Paul Éluard.   WoPoe, *tr. by* Paul Auster

Deaf Dancing to Rock, The.   Lisel Mueller.   SwNoth

Deaf, he hears his own nature.   To an Old, Deaf, and Blind Monk.   Jungkwan Ilson.   BecRai, *tr. by* Kim Daljin, Kim Won-Chung and Christopher Merrill

Deaf Lantern.   Alejandra Pizarnik.   MirDau, *tr. by* Celeste Kostopulos-Cooperman

Deaf Mute Girl, The.   István Vas.   IQMS, *tr. by* Charles Abraham Wagner

Deaf to God, who calls and walks.   Doomsday Morning.   Genevieve Taggard. MoAmPo

Deafening peal, A.   Yakusai, Layman.   ZenPo, *tr. by* Takashi Ikemoto and Lucien Stryk

Deaf-Mute in the Pear Tree.   Patricia K. Page.   NAMCP V.2; NoAM; NoP-4; NoP-5

Deafness.   Richard Ryan.   PBCIP

Deal table where he wrote, so small and plain, The.   Birthplace, The.   Seamus Heaney.   ModIr

Dealer and the Clerk, The. George Crabbe.
   Miser's Only Friend, The. DiBP

Dealer in shirt-sleeves told his assistant Jenny, The. Newcombe at the Croydon Gallery. Arthur Nortje. HBAPE

Dealer is dailiness, and the asking, The. Blackjack. Steven Heighton. IFF

Dealing Scraps. Ruth Garnett. ISC

Dean, adult education may seem silly. Lucretius versus the Lake Poets. Robert Frost. OBCoV

Dean Bourn, a Rude River in Devon, by Which Sometimes He Lived. Robert Herrick. *See* To Dean-bourn, a Rude River in Devon, by Which Sometimes He Lived.

Dean of the University said, The. May 1968. Sharon Olds. NIP-4
   (When the Dean said we could not cross campus.) AmWaPo; CAP-8

Dean-Bourn, farewell; I never look to see. To Dean-bourn, a Rude River in Devon, by Which Sometimes He Lived. Robert Herrick. PBRV

Dear ———. Prageeta Sharma. IIR

Dear Adrienne, / I feel signified by pain. Adrienne Rich. PoCu *Fr.* Contradictions: Tracking Poems.

Dear Albert. This is a wholesome town. Really. Cherries grow. Letter to Goldbarth from Big Fork. Richard Hugo. BodElec

Dear Alice! you'll laugh when you know it. Talented Man, The. Winthrop Mackworth Praed. CABP

Dear America. Jeffrey McDaniel. LegDan; RWB

Dear, and so worthy both by your desert. William Alabaster. OxBSo

Dear Ann is gone unto her Rest. Short Testimony for Anne Whitehead, A. Jane Sowle. EMWP

Dear Antigone. Letter. Leonard Nathan. CalPo; PBCAP

Dear Arthur: In a country where a wealthy handful. Letter to Oberg from Pony. Richard Hugo. BodElec

Dear Auntie / Oh, what a nice jumper. Christmas Thank You's. Mick Gowar. OBCP

Dear Babe, whose meaning by fond looks expressed. Thomas Russell. CenSon

Dear Bill: I've made a. Reply (crumped on her desk). Florence H. Williams. WaAnP

Dear Bobbi: God, it's cold. Unpredicted, of course, by forecast. Letter to Hill from St. Ignatius. Richard Hugo. BodElec

Dear Boy George. Amy Gerstler. SUP

Dear Boy, What a superlative day for a funeral. Micheál Mac Liammóir. Paul Durcan. PBCIP

Dear boy, you will not hear me speak. Pangloss's Song: A Comic-Opera Lyric. Richard Wilbur. NBLV; NoAM

Dear Brother at home. Letter from Spain. Langston Hughes. NAAPv.2

Dear Brother, Would You Know the Life. Ralph Waldo Emerson. APN-1
   (Letter, A.) OxBoAm

Dear Bubble. Joel Dailey. AnSo

Dear child, first-born, what I could give outright. Hand-Shadows. Jarold Ramsey. NIP-4

Dear Child, My Darling Daughter. *Hungarian Oral Tradition.* IQMS, *tr. by* Anthony Edkins

"Dear children," they asked in every town. Wise Men Ask the Children the Way, The. Heinrich Heine. OBCP, *tr. by* Geoffrey Grigson

Dear Clem, / we got the word. R. G. Vliet. TiP2 *Fr.* Clem Maverick.

Dear Cloe [*or* Chloe], how blubber'd is that pretty face! Answer to Cloe [*or* Chloe] Jealous. Matthew Prior. OxBEV

Dear common flower, that grow'st beside the way. To the Dandelion. James Russell Lowell. NAAL-3

Dear Cousin Min, yuh miss sinting. Independence Dignity. Louise Bennett. NAMCP V.2

Dear D., I'm in a place where history. Out Here. Roger Mitchell. PoCoUp

Dear, damn'd, distracting Town, farewell! Farewell to London in the Year 1715, A. Alexander Pope. OBCoV

Dear Dark Head. *Irish Oral Tradition.* IrV,

Dear Daughter, / Can you be fifty-three this. From The Lost Letters of Frederick Douglass. Evie Shockley. RD

Dear dear dear beat. To Allen Ginsberg & Co. Luciana Frezza. CItWP, *tr. by* Cinzia Sartini Blum and Lara Trubowitz

Dear Derrida. David Kirby. BAP-01

Dear Dick: In order to xerox your book I had to break. Letter to Hugo from Later. Jane Hirshfield. GeoHom

Dear Dick: You know all that pissing and moaning around I've. Letter to Blessing from Missoula. Richard Hugo. BodElec

Dear DJD, at a rundown gas station in Circle, just off the rez a dead porcupine lay. Letter to David James Duncan, February 16, 2003. Mandy L. Smoker. PrTe

Dear Doctor. Too Heavy. Julia Darling. PoCu

Dear Doctor Baron, Aberdeen. To Robert Baron. Arthur Johnston. NePenScot, *tr. by* Robert Crawford

Dear Doctor, here comes a young virgin untainted. Humble Petition of a Beautiful Young Lady, The. *Unknown.* IrLP

Dear Dr. Hormone feed me for my dinner. Triolet for the Amphetamine Afflicted. Susan McCaslin. IFF

Dear Doctor of St Mary's. Song upon Miss Harriet Hanbury, Addressed to the Revd Mr Birt. Sir Charles Hanbury Williams. OBCoV

Dear Doll, while the tails of our horses are plaiting. Thomas Moore. NOBRP *Fr.* Fudge Family in Paris, The.

Dear driver, you made every journey a joy ride. Driver. Menna Elfyn. BBMWP, *tr. by* Anthony Conran

Dear Ellen, when you read these lines, O, throw them not aside! Lines to Ellen, the Factory Girl. Ellen Johnston. VWP

Dear Eustatio, I write that you may write me an answer. Arthur Hugh Clough. FaBoVe; NoP-5; OxAEP-2 *Fr.* Amours de Voyage.

Dear Ez. Christopher Pilling. NLP

Dear famish not what you yourself gave food. Mary Sidney Wroth, Countess of Montgomery. BASC

Dear fellow infidel, let's pray. Wing and Prayer. Jack Marshall. GeoHom

Dear Female Heart. Stevie Smith. ItWoWo; NALW

Dear Frank, Here is a poem. Josephine Miles. NALW

Dear Frère Jacques. Letter to a Benedictine Monk. Marilyn Nelson Waniek. GT

Dear friend, be silent and with patience see. To My Noble Friend Master William Browne: Of the Evil Time. Michael Drayton. CABP

Dear Friend, "Called away" from my country. Fabergé's Egg. Elizabeth Spires. PoA 2002

Dear friend, far off, my lost desire. Alfred Tennyson. CAGL; NAEL-6v2; NAEL-7v2 *Fr.* In Memoriam A. H. H.

Dear friend, I have a certain fear. Na Hyesôk's Complex. Kim Sŭnghŭi. EcSo, *tr. by* K. Kim Richards and Steffen Richards

Dear Friend, let me plunge into the sea of love. Yunus Emre. NaPG, *tr. by* Talat Sait Halman

Dear friend of my pain he told himself, "since I." Hearing about the Virtual Destruction of Pain. Nathaniel Tarn. WANABP

Dear Friend, since you have chosen to associate. Tennyson's Poems. Josephine D. Henderson Heard. CBWP-4; SWaP

Dear friend, sit down: the tale is long and sad. Love Unknown. George Herbert. WaAnP

Dear friend, / You bitterly reproach me for my performance at the Vieux-Colombier. Letter to André Breton. Antonin Artaud. ConPit, *tr. by* Clayton Eshleman

Dear friends. If we must lie, let's not lie around. (LL) Lies. Martha Collins. ExTi; PuP-23

Dear friends, if you'll be ruled by me. To My Friends Against Poetry. Jane Barker. BASC

Dear friends, left darkling in the long eclipse. Prelude to a Volume Printed in Raised Letters for the Blind. Oliver Wendell Holmes. APN-1

Dear friends: the snowflakes. Any Blue Movie. Dave Brinks. AnSo

Dear friends, we are gathered together. Tribute to the Bride and Groom, A. Priscilla Jane Thompson. CBWP-2

Dear gentle soul, who went so soon away. Do This Favour For Me. Luis de Camões [*or* Camõens *or* Camoëns]. WoPoe, *tr. by* Roy Campbell

Dear God, allow me to recall my works. Sergey Gandlevsky. ItGoST, *tr. by* Philip Metres

Dear God, for the rest of my life. Tourist Stricken at the Uffizi. Richard Outram. IFF

Dear God / i didn't kill the butterfly. Burials. Amelia Blossom Pegram. HAWP

Dear God, I didn't know that Cytherea was bathing. Rufinus. HePo, *tr. by* Barbara Hughes Fowler

Dear God, in shadows now and nothing but, come to think of it. Next to Last Prayer. Pimone Triplett. LegDan

Dear God, Our Heavenly Father, Gracious Lord. Mark Jarman. P180 *Fr.* Unholy Sonnets.

Dear God! there is no sadder fate in life. Burdened. Ella Wheeler Wilcox. SWaP

Dear gods, set me free from all the pain. Agamemnon. Aeschylus. NAWM-5v1, *tr. by* Robert Fagles

Dear guests, you now have seen Love's corpse-light shine. (LL) George Meredith. NAEL-6v2; NAEL-7v2; NoP-5; NPeEn; WaAnP *Fr.* Modern Love.

Dear head, four days ahead of love's day. For Tom. Richard Caddel. Oth

Dear head to one side, in summer dusk, Olga. Trastevere: A Dedication. Edwin Denby. NYP2

Dear, I Love. Todd Colby. HeMarv

Dear, in the terrible hour. More than They that Watch for the Morning. May Probyn. VWP

Dear. It's like camp, our ivy union. Letters from Camp. Arielle Greenberg. IIR

Dear Jack. William Makepeace Thackeray. OBCoV

Dear Jesse Helms. Lucille Clifton. GifTon

Dear John, Dear Coltrane. Michael S. Harper. CAP-8; FaoP; FuFl; ISC; LoL; NAAL-5; NAMCP V.2; NIL-7; NIP-4; VCAP

Dear John: Great to see your long-coming, well-crafted book. Letter to Haislip from Hot Springs. Richard Hugo. BodElec

Dear John Wayne. Louise Erdrich. UnSA

Dear Kenward, / What a pearl. James Schuyler. FTOS

Dear kindly Sergeant Krupke. Gee, Officer Krupke. Stephen Sondheim. ReLy

Dear Lela is my joy and crown. Lela's Charms. Lizelia Augusta Jenkins Moorer. CBWP-3

Dear lesbia / —i'm thankful i didn't have to choose. Roy Kiyooka. NLPA *Fr.* Pear Tree Pomes.

Dear letters, fond letters. Love Letters. Josephine D. Henderson Heard. CBWP-4; SWaP

Dear Literary Hero. Fan Letter, A. Amy Gerstler. BAP-97; BodElec

Dear little Bog-Face. Bog-Face. Stevie Smith. NPeEn

Dear little friend, who, day by day. To the Tormentors. Lewis Morris. DiBP

Dear Liz: Here's where I degraded myself for the last time. Letter to Libbey from St. Regis. Richard Hugo. BodElec

Dear Lizbie Browne. To Lizbie Browne. Thomas Hardy. FaBoVe; OxAEP-2

Dear Lord and Father of mankind. John Greenleaf Whittier. SacPr *Fr.* Brewing of Soma, The.

Dear Lord, / I offer this prayer for a good death. Prayer for a Good Death, A. Toni Kan. NeNiPo

Dear Lord, receive my son, whose winning love. Sir John Beaumont. OBEV *Fr.* Of My Dear Son, Gervase Beaumont.

Dear love, I am resolved with thee to live. Posy, A. Sir Robert Aytoun. NOSC

Dear Lyltsen, when I'm with thee. Lovelight. Gysbert Japicx. WoPoe, *tr. by* Rod Jellema

Dear Mama, / Good Day. Sonny's Lettah. Linton Kwesi Johnson. RSaN

Dear Mama, / Time I pay rent and get my food. Langston Hughes. APT-2 *Fr.* Lenox Avenue Mural.

Dear March, Come in. Emily Dickinson. CtM

Dear Margie, hello. It is 5:15 a.m. Ted Berrigan. PmAP *Fr.* Sonnets, The.

Dear master, was it really for this you died? Cranmer and the Bread of Heaven. Anne Ridler. SacPr

Dear matted squirrel tongue. Radiant Silhouette V. John Yau. OpBo

Dear Michele: Once, according to a native, this town. Letter to Birch from Deer Lodge. Richard Hugo. BodElec

Dear Michiko, / Do songs sound different in prison? Letters from Poston Relocation Camp (1942–45). David Mura. LTA

Dear Mike: We didn't have a chance. Our starter had no change. Letter to Mantsch from Havre. Richard Hugo. MoASP

Dear miles of love, the Solomon barefoot machine is quinting! Irresistible. Kenneth Koch. AHA

Dear Miss Roper, It seems, George Vernon, before we left Rome, said. Arthur Hugh Clough. FaBoVe *Fr.* Amours de Voyage.

Dear Moly, why so oft in tears? Horace. OBVE *Fr.* Odes.

Dear Mother. Henry Cuyler Bunner. VerBaPo *Fr.* Their Wedding Journey.

Dear Mother, dear Mother, the Church is cold. William Blake. NBLV; OBSV *Fr.* Songs of Experience.

Dear Mother, Thank you for the egg cosy. Sister Agnes Writes to Her Beloved Mother. Paul Durcan. OBCoV

Dear Mozart. Reed Bye. AHA

Dear Mr Pitt, I'm told. Church Boiler, The. David Scott. NLP

Dear Mr. Whitman. Mark Kraushaar. ViWalt

Dear mum's old picture. Dezső Kosztolányi. IQMS *Fr.* Laments of a Poor Little Child.

Dear my friend and fellow-student, I would lean my spirit o'er you! Lady Geraldine's Courtship. Elizabeth Barrett Browning.

Dear native brook! wild streamlet of the West! Sonnet to the River Otter. Samuel Taylor Coleridge. CenSon; OxBSo

Dear Nobody's Business. James Galvin. WaAnP

Dear Obour / Our crossing was without. Letter from Phillis Wheatley, A. Robert Earl Hayden. ESEAA; NoAM

Dear old equivocal and closest friend. Author to His Body on Their Fifteenth Birthday, 29.ii.80, The. Howard Nemerov. NoAM

Dear one, forgive my appearing before you like this. Victorian Hangman Tells His Love, A. Bruce Dawe. NoAM

Dear other self, so silent, swift and sure. To My Cycle. Adriel Vere. ArBi

Dear Parents. Letters in the Family. Adrienne Rich. NIL-7

Dear pear tree. Roy Kiyooka. NLPA *Fr.* Pear Tree Pomes.

Dear Pops. Conversation with Duke Ellington and Louis (Pops) Armstrong. Carmen D. Lucca. BRtP

Dear pursuing presence. Hindu to His Body, A. A. K. Ramanujan. PoetW

Dear Queenie, though it breaks my heart. Handmaid of Religion, The. Edgell Rickword. OBSV

Dear ras / i greet de lyaans. Brotha saul. Seitlhamo Motsapi. TSAP

Dear ras / is me pleasure. Brotha saul (furtha meditashuns). Seitlhamo Motsapi. TSAP

Dear reader, though my uncombed verse be queer. *Unknown.* PriapPo *Fr.* Priapus Poems, The.

Dear, red-faced father God who lit your mind. (LL) To His Dead Body. Siegfried Sassoon. NAMCP V.1; NoAM

Dear relatives and friends, when my last breath. Wendell Berry. UpMys *Fr.* Testament.

Dear San: Everybody doesn't write poetry. Feeling and Form. Marilyn Hacker. NoAM

Dear school of my childhood. Lines to an Old School-House. Priscilla Jane Thompson. CBWP-2

Dear Serious Novel. Exchange of Letters. Wendy Cope. OBCoV

Dear Shaka, / I have never written to you. I have never spoken to you. Epistle to the Revolutionary Bible, An. Andrea Roberts. BRtP

Dear Sir. Walter De la Mare. OBCoV

Dear Sir, I'm so anxious to hear of your health. New York Tory, to His Friend in Philadelphia, A. Philip Freneau. AmWaPo

Dear Sir, your astonishment's odd. Reply, A. *Unknown.* NBLV; OxBEV

Dear Sirs. Dwight Okita. UnSA

Dear Sirs: Is it not time we formed a Boston. Communication to the City Fathers of Boston. George Starbuck. YaYoPo

Dear Sister, my resentment had not been. Virgil. OBVE *Fr.* Aeneid [*or* Eneados *or* Aeneis], The.

Dear sisters in the Lord. Request from Tante Tina to the Mennonite Women's Missionary Society to Put Salman Rushdie on the Prayer List, A. David Waltner-Toews. ACAMVP

Dear smoke: It puzzles. Orphean Song. Sally Keith. LegDan

Dear Stars, Rock Me to Sleep. István Sinka. IQMS, *tr. by* Adam Makkai

Dear Stella, 'mid the pious sorrow. Anna Seward. PEW

Dear Steward. Sleeper. Patricia Pogson. NLP

Dear Superman. Ron Koertge. SUP

Dear thoughts are in my mind. Lark in the Clear Air, The. Sir Samuel Ferguson. IrLP

Dear Uncle Stranger. Conrad Potter Aiken. ColAP; NoAM

Dear uplands, Chester's favorable fields. Clover. Sidney Lanier. APN-2; ColAP

Dear Vi: You were great at the Roethke festival this summer. Letter to Gale from Ovando. Richard Hugo. BodElec

Dear Voyager: / This is to thank you for. Open Letter to Voyager II, An. John Updike. OtW

Dear wallace stevens. Roy Kiyooka. NLPA *Fr.* Pear Tree Pomes.

Dear Walt, / The Cheyennes didn't get their lands. February 12, 1865. Bruce Cutler. ViWalt

Dear waves, what will you do for me this year? Gerald Stern. InvLad *Fr.* Lucky Life.

Dear Webster. Connie Fife. ReEnLa

Dear, when we sit in that high, placid room. Touché. Jessie Redmond Fauset. NAAPv.2

Dear, why do you say you love. Song, A: On His Mistress. Sir Robert Aytoun. NOSC

"Dear, why should you command me to my rest." Michael Drayton. GSo

Dear, wild illusions of creative mind! To the Visions of Fancy. Ann Radcliffe. CenSon

Dear World. Paula Gunn Allen. FiBr; HATNAP

Dear you, / the letter I haven't written explains. She Sends Him a Postcard of the Sea. Lesley-Anne Bourne. Coast

Dear you: the lights here ask. Letters from the North Star. Kevin Young. NeAmPo

Dear You, whoever you are, if you show me your belly button, I'll love you. Love Song for the Belly Button 1. Kim Sŭnghŭi. EcSo, *tr. by* K. Kim Richards and Steffen Richards

Dear zeke, / i've just left your house where you and rebecca served a dinner of peace. Letter to Ezekiel Mphahlele. Sonia Sanchez. FuFl

Dearborn North Apartments Chicago, Illinois. Lola Haskins. P180; PoDa

Deare Cosen pardon me, if I mistowke. LD Ansure, The. Lady Dorothy Shirley. EMWP

Deare Infant, 'twas thy Mother's Fault. Mrs Thimelby, on the Death of Her Only Child. Gertrude Aston Thimelby. EMWP

Dear[e] love, for nothing less[e] than thee. Dream[e], The. John Donne. OBEV

Dearest brother, the charcoal brazier with the turtleshell pattern, the one you so cherished, cracked yesterday. My Brother and the Brazier. Im Hwa. CAMKP, *tr. by* Jiwon Shin

Dearest Evelyn, I often think of you. Jungle Husband, The. Stevie Smith. HarvBoo; NBLV; NIL-7; NIP-4

Dearest, it was a night. Birthnight: To F, The. Walter De la Mare. NPeEn

Dearest Louisa, Enquire if you please about Mr. Claude. Arthur Hugh Clough. FaBoVe *Fr.* Amours de Voyage.

Dearest love, listen. Dearest Love. Salma Khadra Jayyusi. CFP; PoArWo, *tr. by* Charles Doria

Dearest, note how these two are alike. Machines. Michael Donaghy. NeBrP; StAl

Dearest [*or* Dearest] if I by my deserving. Mary Sidney Wroth, Countess of Montgomery. EMWP *Fr.* Pamphilia to Amphilanthus.

Dearest Reader. Michael Palmer. CAP-8; FTOS

Dearest, the cloud hast left thy brow. To My Husband—December 1844. Margaret Moffette Lea Houston. TiP2

Dearest, the cockroaches are having babies. Love from a Foreign City. Lavinia Greenlaw. EmeKit; MFPA; MoWP

Dearest, when thou desirest to buy a ring. Ring Sonnet. Betty Scott Stam. SacPr

Dearest, you come suddenly, and suddenly, dearest, you depart. Dearest, You Come Suddenly and Suddenly You Depart. Walafrid Strabo. CAGL, *tr. by* John Boswell

Dearly beloved Cousin, these. Epistle of Deborah Dough, The. Mary Leapor. BrAP; NoP-4

Dearly beloved gentle girl. Walther von der Vogelweide. GePo

Dearly beloved, I mean today. Pastor Praises the Creator, The. UpMys

Death. Maxwell Bodenheim. APT-1

Death. Mary Elizabeth Coleridge. ViWPN

"Bid me remember, O my gracious Lord." SacPr

Death. Peter France. TCRusP, *tr. by* Gennady Aygi

Death. Roy Fuller. NoAM

Death. Thomas Hood. GSo

Death. Marilyn. Ōoka Mokoto. PFTM-2, *tr. by* Thomas Fitzimmons

Death. Rainer Maria Rilke. PFTM-1

Death. *Unknown.* OBWVE, *tr. by* Aneirin Talfan Davies

Death. *Unknown.* RaBo

Death. Henry Vaughan. ChIV-1

Death. Henry Vaughan. AngWePo

Death. Joe Wenderoth. AmPoNex

Death. William Butler Yeats. OxAEP-2

Death: "Death, thou wast once an uncouth hideous thing." George Herbert. FSCP; NAEL-6v1; NAEL-7v1; NoP-4; NoP-5; PtR

Death: "Going to sleep, I cross my hands on my chest." Bill Knott. PBCAP; PoCho

Death / is entering and leaving. Malaguena. Federico García Lorca. WED, *tr. by* Robert Bly

Death: "I have seen come on." John A. Stone. InoFa

Death, A: "In the end you want the clean dimensions of it mentioned." Thomas Lynch. PoA 2002

Death, an Ode. John Forbes. BMAP

Death and Burial of Cock Robbin, The. *Unknown.* OWoS

Death and Co. Sylvia Plath. EmeKit

Death and darkness, get you packing. Easter Hymn. Henry Vaughan. ChIV-2; SacPr

Death and Empedocles 444 B.C.. Horace Gregory. PoA 2002

Death, and it is broken. Instrument, The. Kathleen Jessie Raine. PoA 2002

Death and Morphine. Heinrich Heine. WoPoe *Fr.* Dying in Paris.

Death and Resurrection. Priscilla Jane Thompson. CBWP-2

Death and the Dancer. Muriel Rukeyser. AF

Death and the Good Citizen. A. K. Ramanujan. PoetW

Death and the Lady. Léonie Adams. MoAmPo

Death and the Turtle. May Sarton. GoPo

Death and Transfiguration of Fourteenth Street. Kenneth Fearing. AmWit

Death as Death. Laura Riding Jackson. NAMCP V.1

Death as History. Jay Wright. ESEAA

Death Asphodel. Jean Valentine. ExTi

Death at least gives separation repose. Dreaming of Li Po. Tu Fu [*or* Du Fu]. NDACCP; WoPoe, *tr. by* David Hinton

Death at Winson Green, A. Francis Webb. BMAP

Death Baby, The. Anne Sexton.

Dreams. NAMCP V.2

Death be not proud, though some have called thee. John Donne. BASC; BLPJKO; BrAP; HeIP-4; InoFa; ITBLP; NAEL-6v1; NAEL-7v1; NAWM-5v1; NIL-7; NIP-4; NoP-5; NOSC; NPeEn; OPOU; OxAEP-1; OxBEV; OxBSo; PtR; RSR; SacPr; SoSe-8; TRP; WaAnP; WeW-3 *Fr.* Holy Sonnets.

Death be not proud, thy hand gave not this blow. Elegy. Lucy Harington, Countess of Bedford. EMWP

Death Bed. Thomas Kinsella. PBCIP

Death Bed, The. Waring Cuney. APT-2

Death before forty's no bar. Lo! Obit on Parnassus. F. Scott Fitzgerald. AmWit; NBLV

Death Bells. Lightnin' Hopkins. APT-2

Death bursts. Belize Cemetery, The. Mary Gomez Parham. OWABP

Death by Fruit. Kay Ryan. PoDa

Death by Heroin of Sid Vicious, The. Paul Durcan. BeAl; NPeEn

4. Death by Water. T. S. Eliot. NPeEn; OBVE; OxBEV *Fr.* Waste Land, The.

Death Camp. Irena Klepfisz. TaR

Death can be so lazy at times. Death of a Lady. John Pepper Clark Bekedermo. HBAPE

Death, can you too be enamored? To Death. Johann Wilhelm Ludwig Gleim. GePo, *tr. by* George C. Schoolfield

Death comes in strange forms and contrasting images. Catius As Conius Silius Italicus. RomPo *Fr.* Punica, The.

Death covers up nakedness. Anna Gorenko. CRWP, *tr. by* Peter France

Death dancers perilously close to the living. Footnote. Douglas Kent Hall. ICANM

Death, Dark Agent. Jotie T'Hooft. TuT, *tr. by* Seán Lysaght

Death, dark doer and soft hand. Death, Dark Doer. Jotie T'Hooft. TuT, *tr. by* Peter van de Kamp

Death Described by His True Effects. George Chapman. NOSC *Fr.* Eugenia.

Death devours all lovely things. Passer Mortuus Est. Edna St. Vincent Millay. MoAmPo

Death did not come to my mother. Conception. Josephine Miles. CalPo; ColAP; OxBoAm

Death does not come from outside. Death is within. Death does not come from outside. Jaan Kaplinski. StAl, *tr. by* Hildi Hawkins

Death draws me to her. Matter. Alexander Gerov. CSCBP, *tr. by* Georgi Belev and Lisa Sapinkopf

Death for me is the transformation of the human spirit. October Death. Kiamsha Madelyn Leeke. BtF

Death fought; before giving in. (LL) Sacrifice, The. Frank Bidart. InoFa; VCAP

Death found strange beauty on the polished brow. Death of an Infant. Lydia Huntley Sigourney. SWaP; TCAPo

Death Fugue. Paul Celan. GPTC; HP; VCWP; WoPoe, *tr. by* Michael Hamburger

Death Fugue, A. Paul Celan. CLPP; GifTon; PFTM-2, *tr. by* Jerome Rothenberg

Death gapes to its hinges. (LL) Harbach 1944. János Pilinszky. AF; HP; PoSu; WoPoe, *tr. by* Janos Csokits and Ted Hughes

Death, get out of here! Rāmprasād Sen. SinGod, *tr. by* Rachel Fell McDermott

Death gives way sometimes. Friendship. Fedya Filkova. CSCBP, *tr. by* Georgi Belev and Lisa Sapinkopf

Death had come / And taken them all in times gone by. *Unknown.* NoP-5 *Fr.* Beowulf [Heaney Translation].

Death Has No Features of His Own. Gwen Harwood. NOBAu

Death ("He's dead / the dog won't have to.") William Carlos Williams. InoFa; NAMCP V.1

Death, I Speak of It. Claire Lejeune. YaTCFP, *tr. by* Judy Cockran and Renée Linkhorn

Death in a war. Leave-Taking. Eli Alon. NRoS, *tr. by* Esther Raizen

Death in an ancient country was a simple passport. Reuel Denney. YaYoPo *Fr.* Elegy on the Pilot.

Death in Four Voices. Buland Al-Haidari. IrPoTo, *tr. by* Hussein Kadhim and Christopher Merrill

Death in Larkspur Canyon, A. Richard Garcia. UrbNat

Death in Leamington. Sir John Betjeman. MakPoe; NoP-4; NoP-5; OxAEP-2

Death in Life. Thomas Vaux, 2d Baron Vaux of Harrowden. NoSic

Death in Mexico. Denise Levertov. NAAL-5

Death in so many. Without Shadow. Rudy Bee Graham. EGAG

Death in the Afternoon. Angel González. RaW, *tr. by* David Ignatow

Death in the Aquarium. Richard Hugo. CAP-8

Death in the Dawn. Wole Soyinka. NAMCP V.2 *Fr.* Idanre and Other Poems (1967).

Death in the Desert, A. Charles Tomlinson. ICANM

Death in the Evening. Miroslav Holub. PoSu, *tr. by* George Theiner

Death in the Flower. Letitia Elizabeth Landon. RWP

Death in the Kitchen. Thomas Hood. NPeEn

Death in Venice. Gareth Alban Davies. BBMWP, *tr. by* the author

Death in Venice. Jim Wilson. EdScPo

Death is a dead, at least that's what Freud said. Einstein & Freud & Jack. Howard Nemerov. PoCho

Death is a Dialogue between. Emily Dickinson. WPoS

Death Is a Matter of Mathematics. Barry Amiel. FaBoWar; PoWW

Death is all things we see awake. Anne Waldman. Eno *Fr.* Worry Yr Logos: Conversant You Speak to the Dead.

Death is always waiting, among the years. It's Always Waiting. José Luis Hidalgo. RaW, *tr. by* Hardie St. Martin

Death is another milestone on their way. Funeral, The. Stephen Spender. MoBrPo; NAMCP V.1; NoAM

Death is before me today. Death Is Before Me Today. *Unknown.* WoPoe, *tr. by* W. S. Merwin

Death is in the air—. Anniversary. Dorothy Hewett. BMAP

Death is in your house, but I'm out here. Heartless Art, The. Tony Harrison. NoP-4; NoP-5

Death is not death, for death is but the borning day. Birth is Death, Death is Birth. Friedrich von Logau. GePo, *tr. by* George C. Schoolfield

Death is not the worst of it. Worst of it, The. Craig Reynolds. CAGL

Death is patient as a chess set. Porcelain Childhood. Katherine Sánchez. LiTh

Death Is Sitting at the Foot of My Bed. Oscar Hahn. TCLAP, *tr. by* Sandy McKinney

Death is talking on the phone, long distance to somebody. Hear That Phone Ringing? Sounds Like a Long Distance Call. Joseph Stroud. CalPo

Death is the strongest of all living things. Warning to One. Merrill Moore. MoAmPo

Death is the supple Suitor. Emily Dickinson. NALW; NCAP

Death is the Tranquil Night. Heinrich Heine. WoPoe,

Death Is Your Salvation. Nidaa Khoury. DTA, *tr. by* Shirley Kaufman and Roger Tavor

Death knocks all night at my door. Journey to the Place of Ghosts. Jay Wright. GT; VCAP

Death leans forward and. Tomas Transtrømer. WoBe *Fr.* Haiku.

Death, let me praise you now. Laudare. Constance Carrier. APT-2

Death lies dead. (LL) Forsaken Garden, A. Algernon Charles Swinburne. NoP-4; NoP-5; NPeEn; OBGa; OxAEP-2

Death loved him the best. (LL) Envy. Adelaide Anne Procter. NPeEn; VWP

Death loves rich people. Funny Poem. Bill Knott. PBCAP

Death Month, August, wears a driver out, The. Origin of Fear, The. Robert McDowell. CalPo

Death, My Companion*. Alec Brock Stevenson. FuPo

Death News. Allen Ginsberg. BB

Death. Nothing is simplier. One is dead. Realization, The. Yvor Winters. APT-2; HarvBoo

Death of a Farmyard. Geoffrey Grigson. EmeKit

Death of a Fly. Johann Wolfgang von Goethe. STV, *tr. by* John Frederick Nims

Death of a Gardener. Phoebe Hesketh. OBGa

Death of a Grandmother. Harvey Shapiro. TaR

Death of a Grandparent. Mrs. Jennette Bonneau. Mary Weston Fordham. CBWP-2

Death of a Horse. Michael Longley. NAMCP V.2

Death of a Lady. John Pepper Clark Bekedermo. HBAPE

Death of a Naturalist. Seamus Heaney. NAMCP V.2; NoAM; OxBEV; WaAnP; WeW-3

Death of a Oaxaquenian. Malcolm Lowry. CLPP

Death of a Pair of Shoes. Jorge Guillén. RaW, *tr. by* Philip Levine

Death of a Poet. Charles Causley. EmeKit

Death of a Soldier, The [*also incl. in* "Lettres d'un Soldat"]. Wallace Stevens. AmWaPo; APT-1; NAAPv.2; NAMCP V.1; OBWP; OxBoAm; SAmP; SoSe-8

Death of a Species. Anthony Conran. AngWePo

Death of a Toad, The. Richard Wilbur. BrAP; NAAL-5; NAMCP V.2; NoAM; PoA 2002; PtR

Death of a Vermont Farm Woman. Barbara Howes. MoAmPo

Death of a Whale. John Blight. BMAP

Death of a Young Son by Drowning. Margaret Atwood. BrAP; NIL-7

Death of Abraham Lincoln, The. William Cullen Bryant. *See* Death of Lincoln, The.

Death of Adam, The. Elma Mitchell. EdScPo

Death of Adonis, The. Philip Ayres. OBVE

Death of Adonis, The. William Shakespeare. NoSic

Death of Adonis, The. Theocritus. NPeEn, *tr. by* Philip Ayres

Death of Allegory, The. Billy Collins. WeW-3

Death of an Infant. Lydia Huntley Sigourney. SWaP; TCAPo

Death of an Irishwoman. Michael Hartnett. EmeKit; PBCIP; StAl

Death of an Ox, The [*with music*]. Abraham Sutskever. MotU, *tr. by* Ruth R. Wisse

Death of Anselmo Luna, The. Alberto A. Ríos. NAMCP V.2

Death of Antinoüs. Mark Doty. PoA 2002

Death of Antoñito el Camborio. Federico García Lorca. SpanPo, *tr. by* Robert O'Brien

Death of Art O'Leary, The. Eibhlin Dubh O'Connell. *tr. by* Patrick Galvin Your Grave Disfigures Me. WoPoe, *tr. by* Patrick Galvin

Death of Chet Baker, The. Miller Williams. SeSe

Death of Cleopatra. William Shakespeare. OxAEP-1 *Fr.* Antony and Cleopatra.

Death of Crazy Horse, The. Lucille Clifton. ESEAA

Death of Dr. King. Sam Cornish. OxAAAP

Death of Enkidu, The. *Unknown*. CAGL *Fr.* Epic of Gilgamesh, The.

Death of Gladys Presley, The. Fleda Brown Jackson. AllShUp

Death of Grant, The. Ambrose Bierce. CBCWP

Death of Guillaume Apollinaire, The. Tristan Tzara. YaTCFP, *tr. by* Mary Ann Caws and Jean-Pierre Cauvin

Death of Hector, The. Homer. NAWM-7v1 *Fr.* Iliad, The.

Death of Hektor, The. Brian Coffey.

"Homer where born where buried of whom the son." ModIr

Death of Huskisson, The. Thomas Baker. STuOW *Fr.* Steam Engine; or, The Power of the Flame, The.

Death of Irish, The. Aidan Carl Mathews. PBCIP

Death of Isadora Duncan, The. Dionisio D. Martinez. TouFir

Death of Janis Joplin, The. Robert Phillips. SwNoth; TiP2

Death of John Berryman,The. William Dickey. BAP-97; InoFa

Death of Karen Klausner, The. Charlie Vermont. AHA

Death of King George V. Sir John Betjeman. OxBEV

Death of Kings, The. William Shakespeare. TRP *Fr.* King Richard II.

Death of Lincoln, The. William Cullen Bryant. NAAPv.1
(Abraham Lincoln.) NAAL-3
(Death of Abraham Lincoln, The.) CBCWP

Death of Lord and Lady Dalhousie, The. William McGonagall.
"Alas! Lord and Lady Dalhousie are dead, and buried at last." VerBaPo

Death of Luco. Ann Yearsley. NPBRoP *Fr.* On the Inhumanity of the Slave Trade.

Death of Man. "Arudra." HotL, *tr. by* V. Narayana Rao

Death of Marilyn Monroe, The. Sharon Olds. HeIP-4; InoFa; ReTh

Death of Moses, The. "George Eliot." ChIV-1

Death of My Father, The. Yehuda Amichai. FIT, *tr. by* Robert Friend

Death of My Father, The. Robert J. Gibbs. Coast

Death of my poor father, The. Lorine Niedecker. APT-2

Death of Myth-making, The. Sylvia Plath. PoA 2002

Death of Old Men, The. *Unknown*. SonAtl, *tr. by* Charles Dendi and S. Marne

Death of Orpheus, The. Ovid. WoPoe *Fr.* Metamorphoses.

Death of Othello. William Shakespeare. OxAEP-1 *Fr.* Othello.

Death of Pan, The. Gyula Reviczky. IQMS, *tr. by* Watson Kirkconnell

Death of Parcy Reed, The [Version from Richardsons' Borderers' Table Book]. *Unknown*. IBB

Death of Poetry, The. Bob Holman. BRtP

Death of Priam, The. Virgil. OBVE *Fr.* Aeneid [*or* Eneados *or* Aeneis], The.

Death of Priam, The. Virgil. NPeEn *Fr.* Aeneid [*or* Eneados *or* Aeneis], The.

Death of Sagittarius. Milán Füst. IQMS, *tr. by* Jess Perlman

Death of Saint Marinus, The. *Unknown*. SonAtl, *tr. by* Alessandro Della Balda and Robert Gasparoni

Death of Santa Claus, The. Charles Webb. P180

Death of Saul, The. Philip Levine. ChIV-1

Death of Shakespeare, The. Gyula Juhász. IQMS, *tr. by* J. G. Nichols

Death of Sir Nihil, book the *n*th. Tywater. Richard Wilbur. TRP; UpMys

Death of Slavery, The. William Cullen Bryant. CBCWP; PCW

Death of Sohráb, The. Firdowsi. TAL *Fr.* Shahnamah, The.

Death of Sophocles, The. Anna Andreyevna Akhmatova. PoetW, *tr. by* Max Hayward and Stanley Kunitz

Death of the Ball Turret Gunner, The. Randall Jarrell. AmWaPo; BrAP; ClHu; ColAP; EMP; HarvBoo; HeIP-4; InGu; InoFa; MoAmPo; NAAL-5; NAMCP V.2; NIL-7; NIP-4; NoAM; NoP-4; NoP-5; OBWP; OtW; OxBoAm; PoAgWa; PoPoPo; PoWW; PtR; PWW2; SoSe-8; TFi; VCAP; WaAnP

Death of the Bird, The. Alec Derwent Hope. BMAP

Death of the Day. Walter Savage Landor. NoP-4

Death of the Farm Workers' Cat. Rigoberto González. AmPoNex

Death of the Fathers, The. Anne Sexton.
Boat, The. NAAL-5
How We Danced. NAAL-5; NAMCP V.2

Death of the Flowers, The. William Cullen Bryant. TreFP

Death of the Hired Man, The. Robert Frost. APT-1; HeIP-4; MoAmPo; NAAL-5; NAAPv.2; NoP-4; OxBoAm; SAmP; TCAPo

Death of the King's Canary, The. William Empson.
"Not your winged lust but his must now change suit." UV

Death of the Kiss. Pura López Colomé. RMCMP, *tr. by* Forrest Gander

Death of the Loch Ness Monster, The. Gwendolyn MacEwen. StAl

Death of the Man in the Field, The. Haim Guri. NRoS, *tr. by* Esther Raizen

Death of the Pilot Whales, The. Peter Meinke. PBCAP

Death of the Polar Explorers. Gabriel Gbadamosi. HBAPE

Death of the Race Car Driver, The. Norman Dubie. MoASP

Death of the Sheriff, The. Robert Lowell. MoAmPo

Death of the Wild Warrior. Daniil Kharms. TCRusP, *tr. by* Robin Milner-Gulland

Death of thelma sayles, The. Lucille Clifton. OxAAAP

Death of Thomas Merton. Harry Clifton. PBCIP

Death of Time. Robert Penn Warren. BodElec

Death of Turnus, The. Virgil. NAWM-5v1; NAWM-7v1 *Fr.* Aeneid [*or* Eneados *or* Aeneis], The.

Death of water is the birth of air, The. (LL) Create Desire. Karen Volkman. KGB; NAPBL

Death of Yesugei, The. *Unknown.* WoPoe *Fr.* Secret History of the Mongols, The.

Death on Columbus Day. James Tate. YaYoPo

Death on Village Creek, A. H. Palmer Hall. TiP2

Death! / Plop. Tragedy, A. Théophile Julius Henry Marzials. VerBaPo

Death Plucks My Ear. Virgil. WoPoe, *tr. by* Oliver Wendell Holmes

Death plucks my ear and says. Death Plucks My Ear. Virgil. WoPoe, *tr. by* Oliver Wendell Holmes

Death Poems in September. Diane Di Prima. BB

Death rides a silencer. What is left. Nzadi Z. Keita. BtF

Death Rode a Pinto Pony. Whitney Montgomery. TiP2

Death says to the darkness, hey, buddy. Bad Joke. Dorothy Barresi. SUP

Death Scene, A. Emily Jane Brontë. OxAEP-2

Death Sentence, The. Stevie Smith. NoP-4; NoP-5

Death separation: sobs hard to swallow. Dreaming of Li Po. Tu Fu [*or* Du Fu]. ChinPo, *tr. by* Ye Weilian [*or* Yeh Wei-lien *or* Wai-lim Yip]

Death slap, A. Terrorist, The. Sergey Stratanovsky. ItGoST, *tr. by* J. Kates

Death Song. *Unknown.* APN-2, *tr. by* Henry Rowe Schoolcraft

Death Song, A. Steve Chimombo. HBAPE

Death Song, A. Paul Laurence Dunbar. InoFa; OxAAAP

Death Song, A [*with music*]. William Morris. NAEL-6v2

Death Song for Aijuk, Dreamed by Paulinaq. Paulinaoq. WoPoe,

Death Song for Owain ab Urien. Taliesin. OBWVE, *tr. by* Anthony Conran

Death Stands Above Me, Whispering Low. Walter Savage Landor. NoP-4

Death Stayed. Terese Svoboda. PoDa

Death stepped out of the television. Gods Ash Their Cigarettes, The. S. K. Kelen. BMAP

Death stoops over me. Tomas Tranströmer. WoBe *Fr.* Haiku.

Death Struck Him. Konstantin Mikhailovich Simonov. RusPo, *tr. by* Robert Arthur Douglas Ford

Death struck him like a bullet, silent. Death Struck Him. Konstantin Mikhailovich Simonov. RusPo, *tr. by* Robert Arthur Douglas Ford

Death Sunyata Chant: A Rite for Passing Over. Diane Di Prima. BB; WANABP

Death surrounds itself with the living. Mississippi. E. Ethelbert Miller. GT

Death, that is small respecter of distinction. Trainwrecked Soldiers. John Frederick Nims. GM

Death the Barber. William Carlos Williams. OxBoAm

Death the dancer poked his skull. We Show You That Death as a Dancer. Hamish Henderson. PoWW

Death the nimble, life the shy. Shortest Day. Arthur Leslie Morton. RSaN

Death the Painter. Anthony Hecht. NoP-4; NoP-5

Death, thou wast once an uncouth hideous thing. Death. George Herbert. FSCP; NAEL-6v1; NAEL-7v1; NoP-4; NoP-5; PtR

Death, though [*or* tho] I see him not, is near. Age. Walter Savage Landor. OxBEV

Death to the first-born sons, always. Miriam's Song. Eleanor Wilner. FiBr; TaR

Death to the Gold Mine! Lindiwe Mabuza. HAWP

Death to the killers, bringing light to life. (LL) Not Palaces. Stephen Spender. MoBrPo; NoAM

Death to the Lady said. Death and the Lady. Léonie Adams. MoAmPo

Death Valley. Sorley MacLean. FaBoWar; NePenScot; PoAgWa

Death was hours ago but already words. Murder. Lucy Grealy. KGB

Death was there, sitting by the roadside. Climbing. Gloria Fuertes. RaW, *tr. by* Philip Levine

Death wasn't the only thing aboveboard in New Orleans. Summer the Beatles Went Over Seven Minutes on a Single, The. Doyle Wesley Walls. SwNoth

Death Who. Philip Hodgins. BMAP

Death, who'ld not change prerogatives with thee. Elegy upon the Lady Venetia Digby, An. Thomas Randolph. BASC

Death, why so cruel [*or* soe crewill]? What! no other way. Bacon's Epitaph, Made by His Man. John Cotton. TCAPo

Death will come and have your eyes. Death Will Come. Theo Dorgan. IrLP

Death will not correct. Proofs. Tadeusz Rózewicz. PoSu; StAl, *tr. by* Adam Czerniawski

Death Without End. José Gorostiza. *tr. by* Rachel Benson
"Filled with myself, walled up in my skin." TCLAP, *tr. by* Rachel Benson

Death Words. Les A. Murray. UpMys *Fr.* Walking to the Cattle Place.

Death, you have made it your pleasure. Las! Mort Qui T'a Fait Si Hardie. Charles, Duc d' Orléans. WoPoe, *tr. by* Fred Chappell

Death, you're more successful than America. Death, an Ode. John Forbes. BMAP

Death-Bed, A. Rudyard Kipling. OxBEV; PoWW

Death-Bed, The. Thomas Hood. InoFa; OBEV; TreFP

Death-Bed, The. Siegfried Sassoon. AF

Deathbed Song. Buhyu Sunsoo. BecRai, *tr. by* Kim Daljin, Kim Won-Chung and Christopher Merrill

Deathbed Song. Chunghur Hyujung. BecRai, *tr. by* Kim Daljin, Kim Won-Chung and Christopher Merrill

Deathbed Song. Hueung Powoo. BecRai, *tr. by* Kim Daljin, Kim Won-Chung and Christopher Merrill

Deathbed Song. Jungkwan Haean. BecRai, *tr. by* Kim Daljin, Kim Won-Chung and Christopher Merrill

Deathbed Song. Pou Kuksa. BecRai, *tr. by* Christopher Merrill

Deathbed Song. Soyo Taeneung. BecRai, *tr. by* Kim Daljin, Kim Won-Chung and Christopher Merrill

Deathbed Song. Woljo Toan. BecRai, *tr. by* Kim Daljin, Kim Won-Chung and Christopher Merrill

Deathbeds. Annie Dillard.
"This is too tight; loosen it a little. I pray." UpMys

Deathfugue. Paul Celan. AF; ItP; PoSu, *tr. by* John Felstiner

Deathplace, A. Louis Edward Sissman. NoP-4; NoP-5; PoDa

Deaths and Engines. Eiléan Ní Chuilleanáin. ModIr

Death's Blue-Eyed Girl. Linda Pastan. InoFa

Death's Boots. Geoff Hattersley. NeBl

Death's carnival was at its height, Amman. Elegy of a Knight. Fadwa Tuqan. PoArWo, *tr. by* Samira Kawar

Death's Door. Thom Gunn. InoFa

Death's Echo. W. H. Auden. IJHIL

Deaths everywhere. George Oppen. APT-2; PFTM-1

Deaths ("First thing I forgot was your voice, The.") Pedro Salinas. RaW, *tr. by* W. S. Merwin

Death's Guerdon. Lizette Woodworth Reese. APN-2

Death's Head. Phyllis Gotlieb. IFF

Death's Jest Book. Thomas Lovell Beddoes.
"And what's your tune?" NPeEn
(Dirge.) OxBEV
(If Thou Wilt Ease Thine Heart.) WaAnP
Old Adam, the Carrion Crow. TFi
(Sailors' Song.) OxAEP-2
(Song.) NAEL-6v2
Song by Isbrand. OxBEV
Song on the Water. WoPoe
(Wolfram's Dirge.) OBEV; OxAEP-2

Deaths of Orphues and Hercules, The. Seneca. OBVE *Fr.* Medea.

Death's pale cold orb has turned to an eclipse. Avalon. Thomas Holley Chivers. APN-1

Death's Secret. Gösta Ågren. StAl, *tr. by* David McDuff

Death's stone rolled away from mouth and eyes. Christina the Astonishing: Virgin. David Citino. UpMys

Death's the classic look. It goes. Death's the Classic Look. John Ciardi. PoA 2002

Death's Valley. Walt Whitman. GS

Death-Wake, The; or, Lunacy. Thomas Tod Stoddart.
"Beautiful Lunacy! that shapest flight." NOBRP
"He sate like winter o'er the wasted year." NOBRP
Song. NOBRP

Deathwatch. Michael S. Harper. NAAL-5; NAMCP V.2

Deb at the Ham Slicer. Cynthia Gallaher. SUP

Debajo de las multiplicaciones. Nueva York. Oficina y Denuncia. Federico García Lorca. RaW

Debasement is the password of the base. Answer, The. Bei Dao. AF; PFTM-2, *tr. by* Bonnie S. McDougall

Debate between Jane Vaughan of Caergai and Cadwaladr the Poet. Jane Vaughan. EMWP

Debate with the Rabbi. Howard Nemerov. TaR

Debbie: An Epic. Lisa Robertson. NLPA

Debbie and Co. John Tranter. BMAP

Debe de vivir arriba un vecino al cual nunca conoceremos. Superior. Gerardo Deniz. RMCMP

Debits and Credits. Rudyard Kipling.
We and They. NAMCP V.1; NoAM

Debridement. Michael S. Harper. NoAM

Debridement is the word you want to check. One Page in *The American Heritage Dictionary.* Carole Oles. PoA 2002

Debris of Life and Mind. Wallace Stevens. SAmP

Debt, The. Paul Laurence Dunbar. ColAP; NAAPv.1

Debt is Paid, A. A. Van Jordan. BtF

Debt is paid, The. Past, The. Ralph Waldo Emerson. WoPoe

Debts. Jessie Belle Rittenhouse. TCAPo

Début de l'été, Le. Robert Melançon. YaTCFP

Decade, [A]. Amy Lowell. MoAmPo; NAAPv.2; NALW; NAMCP V.1; OxBoAm; PasH; PoBW

Decade and the small world in chrysalis, A. Nightbook. Dan Beachy-Quick. IAoNAP

Decadence; or, The Umbrella. William Wordsworth. STuOW

Decalogue of the Artist. Gabriela Mistral. TCLAP, tr. by Doris Dana

Decease, Release. Robert Southwell. NoSic; NPeEn

Deceav'd and undeceav'd to be. Self-Deceaver, The. Juan Perez de Montalvan. OBVE, tr. by Thomas Stanley

Deceit in the Park. Patrick Hare. OBGa

Deceiver Time. Luis de Góngora y Argote. SpanPo, tr. by James Edward Tobin

Deceiving Words. Leonor Scliar-Cabral. MirDau, tr. by Regina Igel

Deceiving World. Robert Greene. NoSic

December. John Clare. OBCP

December. John Clare. ChrPo

  "Glad Christmas comes, and every hearth." OBCP

December. Lucille Clifton. NOxBChV

December. Christopher Pearse Cranch. APN-1; TCAPo

December [with music]. Josephine D. Henderson Heard. CBWP-4

December [with music]. Maurice Kenny. HATNAP

December [with music]. Henrietta Cordelia Ray. CBWP-3

December. Miriam Van hee. TuT, tr. by Joan McBreen

December/ no signs of a Chicago winter/ no boulder-sized clumps of snow. For My Father. Duriel Harris. SpirFl

December 1, 1994. Gerald Stern. PoDa

December 1, 2002. Juliana Spahr. LegDan

December 4, 2002. Juliana Spahr. LegDan

Dec. 7, 1941. Josephine Miles. OxBoAm

Dec. 28, 1974. James Schuyler. OxBoAm

December 31, 1999. Alex Rawls. AnSo Fr. What's Your Sign?

December 14, 1979: A Poetry Reading. Stanislaw Baranczak. AF, tr. by Magnus J. Krynski

December 15th. Vera Gheraducci. CItWP, tr. by Cinzia Sartini Blum and Lara Trubowitz

December 1972: First Winter Ascension of the Sass Maor. Liliane Welch. Coast

December 25, 1991. Rose Solari. AmPoNex

December 31. Ahmed Taha. NAfrP, tr. by Clarissa C. Burt

December 7 Always Brings Christmas Early. Amy Uyematsu. LTA

December 7 always brings christmas early. December 7 Always Brings Christmas Early. Amy Uyematsu. LTA

December. An arctic wind, new. Wall Calendar. Dan Pagis. VCWP, tr. by Tsipi Keller

December, and all its dark rains. Annie Dillard. UpMys Fr. Feast Days.

December at the feet of December. Key and the Tree, The. Alessandro Ceni. ItPo, tr. by Gayle Ridinger

December Evening, '72. Tomas Tranströmer. WED, tr. by Robert Bly

Dec. 5th 1644 Upon Robin Austins Recovery of the Smal Pox and General Popams Son John Diing of Them. Katherine Austen. EMWP

December: "God gave a sign—and the." Jan Smrek. SonAtl, tr. by Ursula Hobday, Ziva Pecavar and Tamara Romanyk

December in Hanoi. Why Nothing Changes for Miss Ngo Thi Thanh. Bruce Weigl. AmAlph

December: "It snows." Charles Simic. OxBoAm

December Journal. Charles Wright. InGu

December Moon. May Sarton. GoPo

December Morning [sonnet]. Anna Seward. CenSon

December Nap. Dennis Saleh. GeoHom

December 9th. Eileen Myles. PmAP

December of My Springs, The. Nikki Giovanni. GT

December Offensive. Anna Enquist. TuT, tr. by Peter van de Kamp

December Pastures. Andrey Andreievich Voznesensky. RusPo, tr. by Robert Arthur Douglas Ford

December: Prayer to St. Nicholas. John Heath-Stubbs. OBCP

December 30th. Ivor Gurney. NAEL-6v2

December through the high. Geese, The. R. Williams Parry. BBMWP, tr. by Anthony Conran

December 12th. Zachary Scott Robbins. BtF

December 21st. Jean Valentine. CAP-8

December's Husbandry. Thomas Tusser. NoSic Fr. Five Hundred Points of Good Husbandry.

Decent docent doesn't doze, The. History of Education. David McCord. AmWit; APT-2

Deception [with music]. Josephine D. Henderson Heard. CBWP-4

Deception. Kim Sujang. WoPoe, tr. by Kevin O'Rourke

Deceptions. Philip Larkin. HarvBoo; OxAEP-2

Dechtire. Thomas MacGreevy. IrLP

Decidedly we are out of the world. No longer any sound. Arthur Rimbaud. AWTN Fr. Night of Hell.

Deciding Not to Go to India (147). Khwaja Shams-ad-din Muhammad Hafiz. WED, tr. by Robert Bly and Leonard Lewisohn

Deciding to Live in an Empty Cave on Kumgang Mountain. Hueung Powoo. BecRai, tr. by Kim Daljin, Kim Won-Chung and Christopher Merrill

Decisions, The. Rick Bursky. ReTh

Deck of Cards. David Huerta. RMCMP, tr. by Mark Schafer

Decked out in flannels and gripping my mitt. 4th Base. Gary Gildner. MoASP

Decks awash, / Mast-top dipping. Archilochus. OBVE

Declaration at Forty. Judson Crews. ICANM

Declaration of Hate. Efraín Huerta. TCLAP, tr. by Todd Dampier

Declaration of Love to Kurt Cobain. Hector Avellán. PML, tr. by Marco Morelli

Declaration of the Death of John Lewes, A. Thomas Gilbart. NoSic

Declaration of the Word as Such. Aleksei Eliseievich Kruchyonykh. PFTM-1

Declare, O mind, from fond desires excluded. Counterlove, A. Unknown. NoSic

Declare to man it was not sent in vain. (LL) Latter Rain, The ("Latter rain, it falls in anxious haste, The.") Jones Very. APN-1; TCAPo

Decline. Georg Trakl. WoPoe, tr. by Robert Firmage

Decline of Gaelic, The. Meg Bateman. MoWP

Decline of Love, The. William E. H. Lecky. IrLP

Declining Sun. Bahaa Awwad. AnVo, tr. by Mohamed Enani

Decommissioning. Katrina Porteous. NeBl

Decomposition with Laughter. Homero Aridjis. TCLAP, tr. by Jerome Rothenberg

Decoration. Louise Bogan. MoAmPo

Decoration Day [with music]. Josephine D. Henderson Heard. CBWP-4

Decorations climbing up the loft on a wobbly ladder. My Christmas; Mum's Christmas. Sarah Forsyth. OBCP

Decorator is mixing his plaster, The. Moon over Prague. Vitězslau Nezval. AF, tr. by Ewald Osers

Decoy. John Ashbery. OxBoAm

Decreed a light. September Morning. Colette Inez. PA9/11

Decrescendo. Larry Levis. SwNoth

Dedicace. Aleister Crowley. CAGL

Dedicated Spirit, A. William Wordsworth. NPBRoP

Dedicated to death. And this is you. (LL) Conrad Potter Aiken. APT-1; NAAPv.2; OxBoAm Fr. Preludes for Memnon; or, Preludes to Attitude.

Dedicated to Dr. W. H. Sheppard [with music]. Maggie Pogue Johnson. CBWP-4

Dedicated to the domestics. Nzadi Z. Keita. BtF

Dedicated to the Hermit Cui. Ch'ien Ch'i. CCL1, tr. by Jerome P. Seaton

Dedicated to the Right Rev'd D. A. Payne [with music]. Mary Weston Fordham. CBWP-2

Dedicated to You. Reetika Vazirani. TAPaP

Dedication. Anna Andreyevna Akhmatova. PFTM-1

Dedication. Henry Wadsworth Longfellow. TCAPo

Dedication. Rochelle Owens. PFTM-2

[Dedication]. Louis Zukofsky. NAMCP V.1 Fr. Poem Beginning "The."

Dedication: "Bob Southey! You're a poet—poet-laureate." Lord Byron. OBSV Fr. Don Juan.

Dedication Day [with music]. Maggie Pogue Johnson. CBWP-4

Dedication Day Poem [with music]. Lizelia Augusta Jenkins Moorer. CBWP-3

Dedication: "Hans, there are moments when the whole mind." James Merrill. OxBoAm

Dedication: "Health to great Gloucester—from a man unknown." Charles Churchill. OBSV

Dedication: "I would the gift I offer here." John Greenleaf Whittier. APN-1

Dedication: "If you would let me leave." Unknown. CATKP, tr. by Peter H. Lee

Dedication: "You whom I could not save." Czeslaw Milosz. AF; BeAl; PoAgWa; WoPoe, tr. by the author

Dedication: "Tall unpopular men." Oliver St. John Gogarty. OBMV

Dedication to G**** H******* Esq, A. Robert Burns.
  "Morality, thou deadly bane." OBSV

Dedication of the Cook. Anna Wickham. MoBrPo; NALW

Dedication to Hunger. Louise Glück.
  From the Suburbs. NALW

Dedication: to the Count of Niebla. Luis de Góngora y Argote. SpanPo Fr. Fable of Polyphemus and Galatea.

Dedicatory Sonnet to S. T. Coleridge. Hartley Coleridge. CenSon

Dedicatory (to My Wife). Antonio Cisneros. PML, *tr.* by Carol A. Klee

Dee dee da dee da. Gu Cheng. WoBe *Fr.* Liquid Mercury.

Deeds Done and Suffered by Light. Clayton Eshleman. APSN

Deep. Patricia Pogson. Prnts

Deep among ten thousand peaks I sit alone cross-legged. Han-shan Te-ch'ing. CSKM, *tr.* by Red Pine

Deep among the green valley grasses. Im Che. CATKP, *tr.* by Peter H. Lee

Deep and hidden, cicadas. Farewell to T'ien Cho on Retreat on Hua Mountain. Chia Tao. CSKM, *tr.* by Mike O'Connor

Deep and inscrutable singular Name. (LL) Naming of Cats, The. T. S. Eliot. AmWit; NBLV

Deep, and silent, and wide. Louisa Sarah Bevington. PEW *Fr.* Two songs.

Deep Are the Wells. Dezső Kosztolányi. IQMS, *tr.* by Egon F. Kunz

Deep as this hour, ready again to sleep. (LL) Night Feeding. Muriel Rukeyser. NAMCP V.2; NoP-4; NoP-5

Deep autumn. Basho. EH, *tr.* by Robert Hass

Deep autumnal green has soaked the earth. Jewish Cemetery, Frankfurt. Jenni Daiches. EdScPo

Deep blue sea baby. Gaia. Gary Snyder. GifTon

Deep calleth unto deep. Dial Call. Christopher Darlington Morley. NBLV

Deep, Deep in the Shade of the Court. Ou-yang Hsiu. ErotSp, *tr.* by Jerome P. Seaton

Deep, deep in the shade of the court. Deep, Deep in the Shade of the Court. Ou-yang Hsiu. ErotSp, *tr.* by Jerome P. Seaton

Deep Ecology. Michael C. Blumenthal. PfSP

Deep grief wringing the heart. At Gen's Embarkation for Yuan China. Muso Soseki. EaWin, *tr.* by W. S. Merwin

Deep in a vale, a stranger now to arms. American Soldier, The. Philip Freneau. AmWaPo

Deep in an orchard, under hawthorn leaves. Aubade. *Unknown.* NAWM-7v1, *tr.* by Peter Dronke

Deep in her seventh month, my sister dozes. Debra Bruce. FFC *Fr.* ("The Light They Make").

Deep in knowledge. (LL) Drapery Factory, Gulfport, Mississippi, 1956. Natasha Trethewey. FuFl; SpirFl

Deep in Mountain caves. Walking Around Watching the Miners Digging. Tachibana Akemi. EMJL, *tr.* by Burton Watson

Deep in the fading leaves of night. Carol. William Robert Rodgers. OBCP

Deep in the Forest. *Unknown.* WoPoe, *tr.* by James Harrison

Deep in the forest of Tangle. Forest of Tangle, The. Charles Causley. BeAl

Deep in the forest there is a pond. Deep in the Forest. *Unknown.* WoPoe, *tr.* by James Harrison

Deep in the grass the crickets sing. Written on the Seventh Day of the Seventh Month. Li Ch'ing-chao. NDACCP, *tr.* by Kenneth Rexroth

Deep / in the heart. Anatomy. Kevin Young. OxAAAP

Deep in the leafy fierceness of the wood. Apollo and Daphne. Yvor Winters. APT-2

Deep in the Mountain Wilderness. Wang Wei. NDACCP, *tr.* by Kenneth Rexroth

Deep in the night I woke: she, near me, held. Alfred Tennyson. EroLit *Fr.* Princess, The.

Deep in the peacefulness of life. Beth Gelert. Richard Henry Horne. DiBP

Deep in the Pit. Neeltje Maria Min. TuT, *tr.* by Peter van de Kamp

Deep in the put where her bones lie. Deep in the Pit. Neeltje Maria Min. TuT, *tr.* by Peter van de Kamp

Deep in the shadows of his room. Lesson of Night, A. Charles Ghigna. MiVo

Deep in the shady sadness of a vale. Hyperion. John Keats.

Deep in the wave is a coral grove. Coral Grove, The. James Gates Percival. APN-1; ColAP

Deep in the winter plain, two armies. Two Armies. Stephen Spender. OBWP

Deep in the woods, beyond the shuffle. Ruined House, The. Jay Parini. VisFro

Deep in weeds, on a smooth chunk of stone. Graffito. James Merrill. OxBoAm

Deep in Winter. Tu Fu [*or* Du Fu]. CCL1, *tr.* by A. C. Graham

Deep in your heart understand. Manly Love. Donald Malloch. CAGL

Deep inside me at my core is where my mother lives. Cassia Berman. HW

Deep inside wood sleeps primal fire. Wood and Fire. Kuong Viet. WoPoe, *tr.* by Huynh Sanh Thong

Deep intelligence living at peace would have, The. (LL) Life at War. Denise Levertov. CAP-8; WaAnP

Deep into the midst of a great, dark, wood. Snail's Lesson, The. Priscilla Jane Thompson. CBWP-2

Deep Mining. Irene McKinney. PBCAP

Deep night. On a small road through the woods. Happy Walk. No Hyegyông. EcSo, *tr.* by Ann Y. Choi

Deep on the convent-roof the snows. St. Agnes' Eve. Alfred Tennyson. OBEV; SacPr

Deep one night in October, '76. Loss of My Twins, The. U Sam Oeur. PML, *tr.* by Ken McCullough

Deep Peach Glades. Emperor Li Cunxu. CCL1, *tr.* by C. H. Kwock and Vincent McHugh

Deep Pool, the. James Laughlin. PoDa

Deep Purple. Mitchell Parish. ReLy

Deep river, Lord; I want to cross over into camp ground. (LL) Deep River. *Unknown.* APN-2; SacPr

Deep river, my home is over Jordan. Deep River. *Unknown.* APN-2; SacPr

Deep Rock. Jeffrey Renard Allen. RD

Deep seated enemies of spontaniety, The. Dear Bubble. Joel Dailey. AnSo

Deep Shit. Daniel Tobin. NAPBL

Deep Song. Antonio Machado Ruiz. SpanPo, *tr.* by John Crow

Deep Spring. *Unknown.* SacPr

Deep waters silent roul, so Grief like mine. Elegy on the Earl of Rochester. Anne Wharton. NOSC

Deep Well. Roland Robinson.
   "I am at Deep Well where the spirit-trees." NOBAu

Deep winter night; deep in the night you sit singing, The. Ballad: A Song in the Night. Pao Chao. CCL1, *tr.* by Joseph R. Allen

Deep within the shadows. Lament for a Courtesan. Li Ho. CrYelRi, *tr.* by Sam Hamill

Deep Youth, you've got the Victory. Ms. Cousins' Rap. Linda Cousins. BRtP

Deeper I go, The. Taneda Santoka. CAoMJL1, *tr.* by Burton Watson

Deeper Than a Dream. Peter Blue Cloud. AtGh

Deeper than sleep but not so deep as death. Night Feeding. Muriel Rukeyser. NAMCP V.2; NoP-4; NoP-5

Deeper the drifts now, rain and sun won't ease. After Ovid, Tristia. Peter Scupham. HarvBoo

Deepest Well in Madras, The. N. V. M. Gonzalez. ReBoTo

Deep-Freeze. Nuala Ni Dhomhnaill. MoWP

Deeply enclaved gnon spirited away from araldite. Photrum. Anna Mendelssohn. VaPo

Deeply Immoral Arrogant and Ignorant. Joanne Kyger. Eno

Deep-sea bathing (inna reggae dancehall). Deep-Sea Bathing (Inna Reggae Dancehall). Rohan B. Preston. AmPoNex; WaCA

Deep-Sea Pearl, The. Edith Matilda Thomas. PoBW

Deepstep Come Shining. C. D. Wright.
   "Meanwhile the cars continued in a persistent flow down." AmAlph; ExTi

Deep-Toned Jowler, The. James Hogg. DiBP *Fr.* Mador of the Moor.

Deer. Juan José Arreola. MotU, *tr.* by W. S. Merwin

Deer. No Ch'ŏnmyŏng. CAMKP, *tr.* by David R. McCann

Deer, The. David Baker. PfSP

Deer, The. Shara McCallum. NAPBL

Deer and the Snake, The. Kenneth Patchen. MoAmPo

Deer are just thankful it's over, The. Thanksgiving. Liz Rosenberg. PBCAP

Deer Camp. Wang Wei. NDACCP, *tr.* by Gary Snyder

Deer carcass hangs from a rafter, The. Gathering the Bones Together. Gregory Orr. InoFa

Deer Cloud. Susan Clements. UnSA

Deer Dancer. Joy Harjo. NAMCP V.2

Deer Enclosure. Wang Wei. ColAnChi, *tr.* by Richard W. Bodman and Victor H. Mair

Deer Enclosure, The. Pei Di and Wang Wei. CCL1 *Fr.* Wheel River.

Deer feed on. Upon Leaving the Parole Board Hearing. Conyus. GT

Deer in rain / Three cries. Buson. ZenPo, *tr.* by Takashi Ikemoto and Lucien Stryk

Deer is humble, lovely as God made her, The. Deer and the Snake, The. Kenneth Patchen. MoAmPo

Deer Lay Down Their Bones, The. Robinson Jeffers. APT-1; GPTC; NoAM

Deer licking. Issa. EH, *tr.* by Robert Hass

Deer looks through you to the other side, A. Iain Crichton Smith. HarvBoo *Fr.* Deer on the High Hills--a Meditation.

Deer on a Beach. Anne Simpson. Coast

Deer on the High Hills--a Meditation. Iain Crichton Smith.
   "Deer looks through you to the other side, A." HarvBoo

Deer Park. John Montague. PBCIP

Deer Park. Wang Wei. CrYelRi, *tr.* by Sam Hamill

Deer Park. Wang Wei. WhBo

Deer Sing. *Unknown. tr.* by Ezra Pound
   Fraternitas. OBVE, *tr.* by Ezra Pound

Deer walking quietly on the soft red earth. (LL) New Apartment. Linda Hogan. HATNAP; UnSA

Deer was on Linwood and I asked the forest, A. Once a Green Sky. Bob Hicok. AmAlph

Deer were bounding like blown leaves, The.   Fire on the Hills.   Robinson Jeffers.   CalPo; OxBoAm; RaBo

Deere to my soule, then leave me not forsaken.   Henry Constable.   NPeEn

Deer-tracks—I followed them: made.   Air Street.   David Morley.   NLP

Defeat.   Witter Bynner.   APT-1; PWW2

Defeat of the Norsemen, The.   Sedulius Scottus. *tr.* by James Carney
"Battle is joined on the open plain."   FaBoWar, *tr.* by James Carney

Defeat of Turnus, The.   Virgil.   OBVE *Fr.* Aeneid [*or* Eneados *or* Aeneis], The.

Defeated.   Robert Bly.   StAl

Defence of Fort McHenry.   Francis Scott Key. *See* Star-Spangled Banner, The.

Defend It.   Ágnes Nemes Nagy.   IQMS, *tr.* by Alan Dixon

Defend it, call it a thing of worth.   Defend It.   Ágnes Nemes Nagy.   IQMS, *tr.* by Alan Dixon

Defend the bad against the worse. (LL)   Where Are the War Poets?   Cecil Day Lewis.   NAMCP V.1; NoP-4; NoP-5; OBWP

Defending Walt Whitman.   Sherman Alexie.   AmPoNex; ViWalt

Defending you, my country, hurts.   Battle Hymn of the Republic, The.   Rafael Campo.   NeAmPo

Defense of Fort McHenry.   Francis Scott Key. *See* Star-Spangled Banner, The.

Defense of Guenevere, The.   William Morris.   NAEL-6v2; NAEL-7v2

Defense of the Alamo, The.   Joaquin Miller.   AmWaPo

Defense Rests.   Vassar Miller.   MoAmPo

Defensive Driving.   Giovanni Singleton.   BtF

Defensive Position.   John Streeter Manifold.   MoBrPo

Defensive Rapture.   Barbara Guest.   AWPTFC; FTOS

Deferment.   Marcel Duchamp.   PFTM-1

Deferred.   Langston Hughes.   APSN; APT-2

Deferred / overlong? (LL)   Tell Me.   Langston Hughes.   APSN; SAmP

Defiant flirtation.   In London.   Harris Khalique.   PML

Deficiency implies.   Argument for an Elemental Aesthetic.   Andrew Zawacki.   IAoNAP

Defining Moment.   Liz Ahl.   RWB

Defining Time.   Carl Dennis.   PoA 2002

Definition of a Waterfall.   John Ormond.   AngWePo

Definition of Love, The.   Andrew Marvell.   BASC; BrAP; FSCP; ITBLP; NAEL-6v1; NAEL-7v1; NoP-4; NoP-5; NOSC; NPeEn; OBEV; OxBEV; PBRV; PtR; TFi; WaAnP

Definition of Swan, The.   Geoffrey Nutter.   IAoNAP

Definition of Weather.   Matthea Harvey.   LegDan

Definition of Your Attraction.   János Pilinszky.   StAl, *tr.* by Peter Jay

Definitions.   Elwyn Brooks White.
Critic.   NBLV

Definitions for Mendy.   David Antin.   APSN

Definitivamente.   Noche Triste de Octubre, 1959.   Jaime Gil de Biedma.   RaW

Definitve Journey, The.   Juan Ramón Jiménez.   SpanPo, *tr.* by Angel Flores

Deflect.   Anne Carson. *See* Flexion of God.

Deflection Toward the Relative Minor.   Forrest Gander.   OPRER

Deformed Transformed, The.   Lord Byron.
Part 3.
"When the lion was young."   STuOW
Part 1.
"To horse! to horse! my coal-black steed."   STuOW

Deft, practised, eager.   Usquebaugh.   Wendy Cope.   UV

Defying Gravity.   Roger McGough.   EmeKit

Defying the power of speech, the Law Commission on Mount Vulture!   Myoyu.   ZenPo, *tr.* by Takashi Ikemoto and Lucien Stryk

Degree Four [*with music*].   Nathaniel Mackey.   ESEAA

Degrees.   Kevin Young.   AmPoNex

Degrees of Gray in Philipsburg.   Richard Hugo.   CAP-8; ItP; NAMCP V.2; NoAM; OxBoAm; TRP; VCAP; WaAnP

Dehorning the Yearlings.   LuAnn Keener.   FiBr

Deid is now that dyvour and dollin in erd.   William Dunbar.   RACG *Fr.* Tretis [*or* Book] of the Tua Mariit Wemen [*or* Two Married Women] and the Wedo[w] [*or* Widow], The.

Deid sall ye ligg, and ne'er a memorie.   Douglas Young.   OBVE

Deign, Laura—now again the rainy season's here.   Girl with Mind Wandering.   Paul Valéry.   STV, *tr.* by John Frederick Nims

Deil [*or* De'il] cam fiddling through the town, The.   De'il's [*or* Deil's] Awa wi' th' [*or* the] Exciseman, The.   Robert Burns.   OBCoV

Dein aschenes Haar Sulamith. (LL)   Deathfugue.   Paul Celan.   AF; ItP; PoSu, *tr.* by John Felstiner

Deirdre.   James Stephens.   OBMV

Deirdre's [*or* Deidre's] Lament for the Sons of Usnach.   *Unknown.*   IrLP, *tr.* by Sir Samuel Ferguson

Déjà Vu.   Shirley Kaufman.   DTA

Dejad las Puertas Abiertas.   Juan Ramón Jiménez.   RaW

Dejection: An Ode.   Samuel Taylor Coleridge.   BrAP; HeIP-4; NAEL-6v2; NAEL-7v2; NAWM-7v2; NOBRP; NoP-4; NoP-5; NPBRoP; NPeEn; OxAEP-2; PoPoPo; TFi; WaAnP

Dejection [Ode].   Derek Mahon.   PBCIP; WoPoe

Déjeuner, Le.   Carol Snow.   AFaM

Déjeuner Sur l'Herbe.   Bruce Beaver.   BMAP

Déjeuner sur l'herbe.   Tu Fu [*or* Du Fu].   BLT, *tr.* by Carolyn Kizer

Del Camino.   Antonio Machado Ruiz.
"En la desnuda tierra del camino."   RaW
"¿Mi Amor? . .¿Recuerdas, dime."   RaW
"Sobre la tierra amarga."   RaW

Del estilo de vida "poco común" de los indios cucapá citados por R. W. Haly Hardy, teniente Británico explorando el Golfo de California.   Heriberto Yépez.   RMCMP

Delacroix pentit Chopin's heid.   Ye Mongers Aye Need Masks for Cheatrie.   Sydney Goodsir Smith.   EdScPo

Delacroix's Version.   Kirsten Dierking.   IaFF

Delante de mi casa hay una viña.   Desconocido Atrae También a los Cobardes, Lo.   Gloria Fuertes.   RaW

Delaware.   David G. W. Scott.   RWB

Delay.   Elizabeth Jennings.   NIL-7; NIP-4; OPOU; StAl

Delay has Danger.   George Crabbe.   NOBRP *Fr.* Tales of the Hall.

Delayed Love Poem to Odem, Texas.   Richard Sale.   TiP2

Delaying Relevance.   Ben Marcus.   HeMarv

Deleite de las formas, El.   Coral Bracho.   RMCMP

Deletreo mi casa en árbol de nueva muerte. Deletreo domingo de claras.   Poema mudo.   Laura Solórzano.   SPV

Delia.   Samuel Daniel.
Sonnet 1.   NoP-4; NoP-5
Sonnet 2.   NoP-4; NoP-5; WaAnP
Sonnet 5.   AEP
Sonnet 6.   GSo; NoP-5; OBEV
Sonnet 9.   GSo
Sonnet 12.   OBEV
Sonnet 13.   PBRV
Sonnet 35.   OBEV
Sonnet 39.   NoP-4; NoSic
Sonnet 40.   NoP-4; NoP-5; NoSic
Sonnet 41.   AEP; NAEL-6v1; NAEL-7v1; NoP-4; NoSic; OBEV
Sonnet 42.   NoSic; PBRV
Sonnet 43.   NoSic
Sonnet 50.   NoSic; OBEV
Sonnet 51.   OBEV
Sonnet 54.   GSo; NAEL-6v1; NAEL-7v1; NIP-4; NoP-4; NoP-5; NoSic; NPeEn; OxAEP-1; OxBEV; OxBSo; TFi
Sonnet 55.   GSo; NAEL-6v1; NAEL-7v1; NoP-5; NoSic; OBEV; PBRV; WaAnP
Sonnet 59.   NoP-5

Delia.   Henry Wadsworth Longfellow.   TCAPo

Delia Rexroth ("California rolls into.")   Kenneth Rexroth.   CalPo; PoCho

Delia Rexroth ("Under your illkempt yellow roses.")   Kenneth Rexroth.   NAMCP V.1; OxBoAm

Deliberate.   Amy Uyematsu.   CalPo

Deliberate as scrimshaw.   Cat Washing.   Linda Molony.   NOBAu

Deliberately, long ago / the carcasses.   From an Old House in America.   Adrienne Rich.   TRP

Deliberation.   Jelaluddin Rumi.   LoL, *tr.* by Coleman Barks

Deliberation and flow bend.   Allen Fisher.   Oth *Fr.* Stepping Out.

Delicacy was drawn out like the finest wire.   Nedim.   OLP, *tr.* by Walter Andrews, Najaat Black and Mehmet Kalpakli

Delicate Adonis is dying, Kytheria—what should we do?   Sappho.   SaLy, *tr.* by Diane Rayor

Delicate, delicate, delicate, delicate—now! (LL)   Base Stealer, The.   Robert Francis.   NTCP; PML

Delicate eyes that blinked blue Rockies all ash.   On Neal's Ashes.   Allen Ginsberg.   BB; PmAP

Delicate hands fashioned this portrait: good Prometheus.   Erinna.   SaLy, *tr.* by Diane Rayor

Delicate old injuries, the spines of names and leaves.. (LL)   Indian Boarding School: The Runaways.   Louise Erdrich.   CAP-8; HATNAP; NoAM; UnSA

Delicate triangles in the afternoon. (LL)   Early Triangles.   Ron Padgett.   FTOS; NYP2

Delicate young Negro stands, A.   Anonymous Drawing.   Donald Justice.   HeIP-4

Delicately bordered by poplars. (LL)   In the Dordogne.   John Peale Bishop.   APT-1; OBWP; PoWW

Delicately Sloping Neck, The.   Miguel de Unamuno.   RaW, *tr.* by Hardie St. Martin

Delicious Babies.   Penelope Shuttle.   MoWP

Delicious, *fine* Sugar Hill. (LL)   Harlem Sweeties.   Langston Hughes.   NoP-4; NoP-5

Delicious Looking!   Issa.   EMJL, *tr.* by Haruo Shirane

Delight in books from evening.   Francis Daniel Pastorius.   NOSC

Delight in Disorder.   Robert Herrick.   BASC; BrAP; CABP; CavPo; ClHu; ErotSp; HeIP-4; NAEL-6v1; NAEL-7v1; NIL-7; NIP-4; NoP-4; NoP-5; NOSC; NPeEn; OBEV; OxAEP-1; OxBEV; PBRV; TFi; TRP; TWF; WaAnP; WeW-3

Delight of Humane kind, and Gods above.   Lucretius.   OBVE *Fr.* De Rerum Natura (On the Nature of Things).

Delight of Solitariness, The.   Sir Philip Sidney.   NoSic *Fr.* Countesse of Pembroke's Arcadia, The.

Delight, then sorrow.   Basho.   SoOfWa, *tr.* by Sam Hamill

Delighted That the Monk Ch'ien-chou Has Come a Long Way to Visit Me.   Ch'i-chi.   CSKM, *tr.* by Burton Watson

Delightful land—ah, now with general voice.   Helen Maria Williams.   NPBRoP *Fr.* To Dr Moore, in Answer to a Poetical Epistle Written by Him in Wales.

Delightful to be on the Hill of Howth.   Colum Cille's Greeting to Ireland.   *Unknown.*   IrV, *tr.* by Kuno Meyer

Delighting in the sobbed oriental note. (LL)   Autobiographical.   Abraham Moses Klein.   BrAP; NoAM

Delights of the Door, The.   Francis Ponge.   RaBo; WED, *tr.* by Robert Bly

Delilah.   Primo Levi.   PML, *tr.* by Ruth Feldman

Delineaments of the Giants, The.   William Carlos Williams.   NoAM *Fr.* Paterson.

Delirious the drought raved birds stretched on the fence.   Remember.   Ion Caraion.   AF, *tr.* by Marguerite Dorian *and* Elliott B. Urdang

Delirium.   Norman J. Loftis.   SpirFl

Delirium in Vera Cruz.   Malcolm Lowry.   NoP-4; NoP-5 *Fr.* Cantinas, The.

Delirium was: to fall from the furrow.   Peninsula.   Jenny Mueller.   IAoNAP

Deliverance.   Salomon De la Selva.   NAAPv.2

Deliverance.   Amelia Blossom Pegram.   HAWP

Deliverance, The.   Frances Ellen Watkins Harper.   SWaP *Fr.* Aunt Chloe.

Delivered at the Knighting of Lord Durgling by Great Bruce-Jean.   Jean Toomer.   GT

Delivered out of raw continual pain.   St. Peter and the Angel.   Denise Levertov.   SacPr

Deliverer, The.   John Milton.   OBEV; OxAEP-1 *Fr.* Samson Agonistes.

Delivering the Times, 1952-1944.   David Huddle.   PBCAP

Delivery.   Armanda Guiducci.   CItWP, *tr.* by Cinzia Sartini Blum and Lara Trubowitz

Delivery.   Alicia Galaz Vivar.   TANSG, *tr.* by Dave Oliphant

DeLiza drive the car to fetch, Alexis.   DeLiza Spend the Day in the City.   June Jordan.   NAMCP V.2; NoAM

Delos.   Edwin Denby.   NYP2

Delos.   Lawrence Durrell.   OxAEP-2

Delos [*with music*].   Bernard Spencer.   NoAM

Delphi.   Peter Davison.   YaYoPo *Fr.* Breaking of the Day, The.

Delphi, coming around the corner of the house.   Delphi, Coming Around the Corner.   Jane Mead.   BodElec

Delphos, Ohio.   Campbell McGrath.   NeAmPo

Delta.   Adrienne Rich.   HarvBoo; LoL; NIL-7; NIP-4

Delta.   Margaret Abigail Walker.   YaYoPo

Delta, The / Itch of cayenne.   Keith Cartwright.   AmPoNex

Deluge.   Laura Solórzano.   SPV, *tr.* by Jen Hofer

Deluge, The.   William Dixon Cocker.   EdScPo

Deluge, 1939, The.   Saunders Lewis.   BBMWP, *tr.* by Anthony Conran

Deluge 1939, The [*with music*].   Saunders Lewis.   OBWVE, *tr.* by Gwyn Morgan

Delusive Hope! more transient than the ray.   Sappho Rejects Hope.   Mary Robinson.   CenSon; RWP

Dem say him born.   For Don Drummond.   Lorna Goodison.   WaCA

Dem say too many words mad him.   Words Is Not Enough.   Bob Stewart.   WaCA

Demain sera le même jour.   Abdellatif Laâbi.   YaTCFP

Demand.   Piera Oppezzo.   CItWP, *tr.* by Cinzia Sartini Blum and Lara Trubowitz

Demanding that I explain / my treachery. (LL)   Blonde White Women.   Patricia Smith.   GT; UnSA

Demands my soul, my life, my all.. (LL)   Hymn: "When I survey the wondrous cross."   Isaac Watts.   OxAEP-1; SacPr

Demands of the Muse.   Vernon Watkins.   PoA 2002

DeMarco said the special bus.   Knot Hole Gang, The.   Brendan Galvin.   MoASP

Demas, in Love with This Present World.   Kristin Fogdall.   PoDa

Demented underneath the moon, I watch.   Asylum.   Rafael Campo.   NeAmPo

Dementia.   John Cope.   GeoH

Dementia.   Norman Dubie.   AmAlph

Démesure de la poésie.   Jacques Garelli.   YaTCFP

Demeter.   Genevieve Taggard.   HW

Demeter and Cora.   Dora Greenwell.   VWP

Demeter, Waiting.   Rita Dove.   BodElec

Demeter's Blessing.   Burleigh Muttén.   HW

Demeter's Song.   Starhawk.   HW

Demo and Thermion Both Slay Me.   Philodemus.   WoPoe, *tr.* by George Economou

Demo and Thermion both slay me.   Demo and Thermion Both Slay Me.   Philodemus.   WoPoe, *tr.* by George Economou

Demockery.   Ngoma.   BRtP

Democracy.   Lawrence Okezie Chibueze Anene.   NeNiPo

Democracy.   Derick Burleson.   PoA 2002

Democracy.   Suzanne Gardinier.   NeAmPo

Democracy.   Langston Hughes.   NAAL-5

Democracy / come! come!!   Democracy.   Lawrence Okezie Chibueze Anene.   NeNiPo

Democracy, my grannie's foot!   H. H. Tilley.   FaBoWar *Fr.* Citizen BOR Speaking.

Democracy will not come.   Langston Hughes.   NAAL-5

Democratic Vistas.   David Berman.   LegDan

Demographics.   Catherine Bowman.   ExTi; SUP

Demolisher.   Alan Gould.   BMAP

Demolition crew are petulant, The.   What's Going On.   Lavinia Greenlaw.   NoP-5

Demolition of the Cathedral at Chartres.   Steve Martin.   MotU

Demon Colors, Dark.   Göran Sonnevi.   PFTM-2, *tr.* by Rika Lesser

Demon colors, dark.   Demon Colors, Dark.   Göran Sonnevi.   PFTM-2, *tr.* by Rika Lesser

Demon in the morning, The.   Epigram.   Callimachus.   WoPoe, *tr.* by Stanley Lombardo and Diane Rayor

Demon Lover, The.   *Unknown.*   TFi; WeW-3

Demon [*or Daemon*] Lover.   *Unknown.*   WeW-3

Demons.   Diabolus in Musica.   Lawrence F. O'Brien.   MiVo

Demons.   Alexander Sergeyevich Pushkin.   WoPoe, *tr.* by D. M. Thomas

Demons of the Cities, The.   Georg Heym.   WoPoe, *tr.* by Peter Viereck

Demons were more beautiful than the angels, The.   How the Demons Were Assimilated and Became Productive Citizens.   A. E. Stallings.   PoDa

Demonstration.   Hanan Mikha'il.   CFP, *tr.* by Kamal Boullata

Demonstration.   Hugh Seidman.   PoA 2002

Demonstration, The.   Thomas Traherne.   BASC

Demonstration: Women's House of Detention, 1965.   Michael Waters.   LiTh

Den of the Old Men.   Kathleen Jamie.   GPPA

Den—for the beast, A.   Marina Ivanovna Tsvetayeva.   TCRusP *Fr.* Poems to Blok.

Denial[l].   George Herbert.   BASC; FSCP; NAEL-6v1; NAEL-7v1; NoP-4; NoP-5; NPeEn; PBRV

Denials.   Eric Gamalinda.   ReBoTo

Denied, / Like Bessie.   Of Walter White's Father in the Rain.   Houston A. Baker, Jr.   SeSe

Denied, The.   Lisa Sewell.   AmPoNex

Denigration.   Harryette Mullen.   PrTe

Denmark sleeps soundly.   Hamlet's Lost Monologue.   László Kálnoky.   IQMS, *tr.* by Kenneth McRobbie and Zita McRobbie

Dennis was hearty when Dennis was young.   Grand Match, The.   Moira O'Neill.   IrV

Dénouement.   Lyubomir Levchev.   CSCBP, *tr.* by Georgi Belev and Lisa Sapinkopf

Dense, dense dust on the bed.   Green, Green Riverside Grass.   Shen Yüeh.   CCL1, *tr.* by Anne Birrell

Dense flowers, a riot of stamens.   Walking Alone by the Riverbank Seeking Flowers.   Tu Fu [*or Du Fu*].   CCL1, *tr.* by Stephen Owen

Dented spider like a snowdrop white, A.   In White.   Robert Frost.   TRP

Dentists continue to water their lawns even in the rain.   Great Society, The.   Robert Bly.   NAMCP V.2; NoAM

Dentologia; a Poem on the Diseases of the Teeth and Their Proper Remedies.   Solyman Brown.

"Her lips disclosed to view."   VerBaPo

Denton.   Dave Oliphant.   TiP2

Dents.   Ulli Freer.

"Baseline pressure."   Oth

Denuded is the earth.   Denuded Is the Earth.   Antonio Machado Ruiz.   SpanPo, *tr.* by Edward F. Gahan

Denying they have been. (LL)   Snow, The.   Emily Dickinson.   MoW; SoSe-8; WHSW

Deo Optimo Maximo. Louise Imogen Guiney. SacPr

Deodand, The [*with music*]. Anthony Hecht. NAMCP V.2; NoAM

Deor. *Unknown*. WoPoe, *tr.* by Peter Russell

Departed Youth. Hannah Cowley. CABP

Departing from Ch'in-chou. Tu Fu [*or Du Fu*]. CrYelRi, *tr.* by Sam Hamill

Departing from Yiyang in the Early Morning. Wang Po. CCL1, *tr.* by Stephen Owen

Departing in Early Morning. Tu Mu. CrYelRi, *tr.* by Sam Hamill

Departmental. Robert Frost. HeIP-4; MoAmPo; NAAL-5; PtR; SoSe-8

Departure. Gerrit Achterberg. TuT, *tr.* by Peter van de Kamp

Departure. Louise Glück. GM

Departure. Edna St. Vincent Millay. MoAmPo

Departure. Bulat Shalvovich Okudzhava. ItGoST, *tr.* by Ronnie Apter and Mark Herman

Departure. Coventry Patmore. OBEV *Fr.* Unknown Eros, The.

Departure. Pierre Reverdy. CuPo

Departure. Arthur Rimbaud. SxFrPo, *tr.* by Martin Sorrell

Departure. Mai Sayigh. PoArWo, *tr.* by Lena Jayyusi and W. S. Merwin and Naomi Shihab Nye

Departure. Edgar Silex. NAPBL

Departure. Wang Wei. TAL

Departure. Mildred Weston. FFC

Departure. Vincent Woods. NIrP

Departure, The. William Vaughn Moody. APN-2

Departure, The. Trumbull Stickney. ColAP

Departure and Departure and. George Bruce. EdScPo

Departure Aria. Johann Christian Günther. GePo, *tr.* by George C. Schoolfield

Departure in Middle Age. Roland Mathias. OBWVE

Departure of the Good Daemon, The. Robert Herrick. BASC; NPeEn

Departure of the Prodigal Son, The. Rainer Maria Rilke. GI

Departures. David Helwig. Coast

Departures. Joan Michelson.
    Rings. Prnts

Departures. Linda Pastan. GoPo

Departure's Girl-Friend. W. S. Merwin. OxBoAm

Dependence! heavy, heavy are thy chains. To Dependence. Charlotte Smith. CenSon

Dependencies, The. Howard Nemerov. VCAP

Dependency on and. Novelist Speaks, The. Ann Lauterbach. KGB

Depending on the Angle. Jean Bleakney. NIrP

Depiction of Childhood. Franz Wright. BLT *Fr.* After Picasso.

Deported. *Unknown*. NAAPv.2

Deposed. John Alexander Frazier, Jr. BtF

Deposition, The. Colette Bryce. MoWP

Deposition from Love, A. Thomas Carew. BASC; CavPo

Depreciating Her Beauty. Wilfrid Scawen Blunt. OBMV *Fr.* Love Sonnets of Proteus, The.

Depressed by a Book of Bad Poetry, I Walk toward an Unused Pasture and Invite the Insects to Join Me. James Wright. EmeKit

Depressed like cabin air & passing out. Vanishing Point. Jeni Olin. FreRad

Depression. Isabel Joshlin Glaser. HHAm

Depression. János Pilinszky. IQMS, *tr.* by Peter Jay

Depression. Sonia Sanchez. ESEAA

Depression, The. David Gwenallt Jones. BBMWP, *tr.* by Anthony Conran

Depression, The. Ira Sadoff. BodElec

Depression Days. Pat Mora. UnSA

Depression in Winter. Jane Kenyon. LoL

Depressive Episode. Janet Holmes. ExTi

Depth of Field. Linda Bierds. ExTi

Depth or the duration of his woe, The. (LL) On Being Cautioned against Walking on an Headland Overlooking the Sea, Because It Was Frequented by a Lunatic. Charlotte Smith. CenSon; NAEL-7v2; NPeEn; WoRP

Depth Sounding, Lake Windermere. Christopher Dewdney. OpeFie

Depths of Fields. Luis Cabalquinto. ReBoTo

Depths of winter copy those of age, The. After the Solstice. Daryl Hine. PoA 2002

Der Blinde Junge. Mina Loy. APT-1; HarvBoo; NAMCP V.1

Der teufel's los in Bal Mabille. Breitmann in Paris. Charles Godfrey Leland. APN-2

Derailment. William Heyen. PoCoUp

Derailment: A Delirium. Steve Chimombo. HBAPE

Derbyshire Born, Monmouth Is My Home. Clifford Dyment. AngWePo

Derelict, The. Rudyard Kipling. NoAM

Dere's an ol' man called de Mississippi. Ol' Man River. Oscar Hammerstein, II. APT-2; ReLy

Dere's No Hidin' Place Down Dere. *Unknown*. APN-2

Dere's no rain to wet you. I Want to Go Home. *Unknown*. SSUS

Derrat slegelations, flo goof baber. Crootey Songo. Bob Kaufman. EGAG; FTtHH

Dervorgilla's supremely lovely daughter. Portrait with Background. Oliver St. John Gogarty. OBMV

Des fêtes. Annie Le Brun. YaTCFP

Dés, Les / éphémèrement unis. Maldonne. Michel Leiris. YaTCFP

Des mots sur un plan. Mural. Dominique Fourcade. OnScMo

Des rites. Annie Le Brun. YaTCFP

Des vols de perroquets traversent ma tête quand je te vois de profil. Clin d'oeil. Benjamin Péret. YaTCFP

Des yeux, puis une bouche. Récitation de l'oubli, La. Franck André Jamme. YaTCFP

Desahucio. Rafael Alberti. RaW

Désamère. Alice Notley.
   "Overhead at night, above the planet." PFTM-2

Descano, California. Chryss Yost. GeoHom

Descant. Jane Mayes. PasH

Descartes and the Splendor of *a Real Drama of* Everyday Life. In Six Parts. Joanne Kyger. AHA

Descend, embrace this daughter. Dialogue with the Dead. Amelia Rosselli. PFTM-2, *tr.* by Lawrence R. Smith

Descend et dors dans cete arbre, dans cet arbre. Dans cet arbre. Jacques Roubaud. YaTCFP

DESCEND from heaven O muse Melpomene. Epitaph of Our Late Queen Mary, An. George Cavendish. NoSic

Descend from Heaven [*or Heav'n*], Urania, by that name. John Milton. NAEL-6v1; NOSC *Fr.* Paradise Lost.

Descend, while three birds watch and the fourth flies. (LL) Winter Landscape. John Berryman. GS; HarvBoo; MoAmPo; OxBoAm

Descended of an ancient line. Horace. NPeEn; OBVE *Fr.* Odes.

Descender. David Huerta. RMCMP

Descending by the mountain-side. Guide and Guard. Herman Melville. NCAP

Descending Chestnut Ridge. Donald Davidson. FuPo *Fr.* Hermitage.

Descending Figure. Louise Glück. NAMCP V.2

Descending in the dark? (LL) Man Born to Farming, The. Wendell Berry. InGu; IPoFL

Descending just in time for the revival. Holy Ghost Flies into Second Baptist on Airline Highway in Baton Rouge, The. Kathleen Crown. FiBr

Descending Through Dragon Gate. Tu Fu [*or Du Fu*]. CrYelRi, *tr.* by Sam Hamill

Descending to the cave where the Archangel / made his announcement. Nazareth. Rosario Castellanos. GI, *tr.* by Magda Bogin

Descent. David Huerta. RMCMP, *tr.* by Mark Schafer

Descent. Esther Jansma. BeAl, *tr.* by the author and James Brockway

Descent. Robyn Selman. TaR

Descent and Defeat. Georg Trakl. WED, *tr.* by Robert Bly

Descent beckons, The. Descent, The. William Carlos Williams. APT-1; NAAPv.2; SAmP; WeW-3

Descent in Broad Daylight. Rutger Kopland. LWR, *tr.* by John M. Coetzee

Descent of Odin, The. Thomas Gray. OxAEP-1

Descent, The. James Tate. YaYoPo

Descent, The. William Carlos Williams. APT-1; NAAPv.2; SAmP; WeW-3

Desciendo a la blancura de esta mano, esta mesa. Descender. David Huerta. RMCMP

Desconocido Atrae También a los Cobardes, Lo. Gloria Fuertes. RaW

Describe the Borough—though out idle tribe. George Crabbe. CABP *Fr.* Borough, The.

Describe: The Rain on Dasaswamedh Ghat. Allen Ginsberg. BB; FTOS

Describes her Bark. Mary Robinson. CenSon; RWP

10. Describes Phaon. Mary Robinson. NPBRoP; CenSon; RWP *Fr.* Sappho and Phaon.

Describes Rationally the Irrational Effects of Love [*with music*]. Sor Juana Inés de la Cruz. SpanPo, *tr.* by Samuel Beckett

6. Describes the Characteristics of Love. Mary Robinson. NPBRoP; CenSon; RWP *Fr.* Sappho and Phaon.

Describes the Fascinations of Love. Mary Robinson. CenSon; RWP

Describing a Dream for Someone. Wang Seng-ju. ColAnChi, *tr.* by Anne Birrell

Describing the Sorrow of an Ingenuous Mind on the Melancholy Event of a Licentious Amour [*or Elegy 26*]. William Shenstone.
   Chase of Jessy, The. STuOW

Description of a City Shower, A. Jonathan Swift. BrAP; HeIP-4; NAEL-6v1; NAEL-7v1; NIL-7; NoP-4; NoP-5; NPeEn; OBSV; WaAnP

Description of an Irish Feast, The. Hugh MacGowran. OBCoV, *tr.* by Jonathan Swift

Description of an Irish Feast, The. Hugh MacGowran. OBVE,

Description of Cooke-ham [*or* Cookham], The. Emilia Lanier and Aemilia Bassano Lanyer. BASC; CABP; NAEL-6v1; NAEL-7v1; NoP-4; NoP-5; PBRV; WaAnP
"Now let me come unto that stately tree." MakPoe
"Yet you (great lady) mistress of that place." OBGa
Description of Elizium, The. Michael Drayton. PBRV *Fr.* Muses' Elysium [*or* Elizium].
Description of Elysium. James Agee. YaYoPo
Description of His Ugly Lady, A. Thomas Hoccleve. WaAnP
Description of London, A. John Bancks. OBCoV
Description of Love, A. Sir John Beaumont. NOSC
Description of Perfect Beauty. Christian Hofmann von Hofmannswaldau. GePo, *tr. by* George C. Schoolfield
Description of Sir Geoffrey Chaucer, The. Robert Greene. NoSic *Fr.* Greene's Vision.
Description of Some Confederate Soldiers, A. Randall Jarrell. CBCWP
Description of Spring, Wherein Each Thing Renews Save Only the Lover. Petrarch. *See* Soote Season, The.
Description of the Contrarious Passions in a Lover. Petrarch. OBVE *Fr.* Sonnets to Laura.
Description of the horrible Famine within *the Cittie of* Jerusalem. Thomas Deloney. FaBoWar *Fr.* Destruction of Jerusalem, The.
Description of the Morning, A. Jonathan Swift. BrAP; HeIP-4; NIL-7; NoP-4; NoP-5; OxAEP-1; OxBEV; PoPoPo; SoSe-8; TFi
Description of the Shepherd and His Wife, The. Robert Greene. NoSic
Description of Tyme, A. Alexander Montgomerie. OxBEV
Description of Virtue. Nicholas Grimald. NoSic
Descriptions (of Living Elsewhere). Tracy Philpot. IAoNAP
Descriptive Passages. William Matthews. BodElec
Descriptive Poetry. Friedrich Hölderlin. WoPoe, *tr. by* Vyt Bakaitis
Desde el umbral de un sueño me llamaron. Antonio Machado Ruiz. RaW
Desde esta luz en que incide, con delicada. Desde esta luz. Coral Bracho. RMCMP
Desde mi núcleo tenso trazo un itinerario circular, un mismo resonar de madeja apretada a mi abdomen. Madeja. Silvia Eugenia Castillero. SPV
Desdemona is sobbing in the bedroom, a hole. How Mother Courage Saves Desdemona. Jeanne Murray Walker. IaFF
Desdichada. Muriel Rukeyser. StAl
Dese all my fader's children. These Are All My Father's Children. *Unknown.* SSUS
Dese days, I doh even bada combing out mi locks. Calypso. Shara McCallum. AmPoNex
Desert, The. Adonis.
Diary of Beirut Under Siege, 1982, The. PoetW
Desert, The. Al-Munsif Al-Wahaybi. PML, *tr. by* Salma Khadra Jayyusi and Naomi Shihab Nye
Desert, The. Edmond Jabès. AF, *tr. by* Rosmarie Waldrop
Désert à l'essai. Jean Grosjean. YaTCFP
Desert Backyard. Rita Dove. AmAlph
Desert caller, The. Eyeful Glances. Niyi Osundare. HBAPE
Desert Center. Margaret Erwin Schevill. ASA
Desert Crossing. Dambudzo Marechera. NAfrP
Desert Cry, A. Magdalena Gomez. PueRic
Desert Flowers. Jeanne Bryner. SweBea
Desert Flowers. Keith Douglas. HarvBoo; NPeEn
Desert Has Many Teachings, The. Mechthild von Magdeburg. WPoS, *tr. by* Jane Hirshfield
Desert, II, The. Edmond Jabès. AF, *tr. by* Rosmarie Waldrop
Desert Music, The. William Carlos Williams. APSN
Desert, Not Wastleand. Robert Burlingame. TiP2
Desert of Love, The. János Pilinszky. IQMS; OBVE, *tr. by* Ted Hughes
Desert 1. Monica Mansour [*or* Mansur]. MirDau, *tr. by* Celeste Kostopulos-Cooperman
Desert or riverbank, a girl finds a stone. Shape of Things, The. Phyllis Thompson. ICANM
Desert Places. Robert Frost. APT-1; BrAP; HarvBoo; MoAmPo; NAAL-5; NAAPv.2; NAMCP V.1; NoAM; OxBoAm; SoSe-8; TRP
Desert Reservation. Barry Lopez. GifTon
Desert Run Scenario. Kathleen Norris. UpMys
Desert Song. John Ash. HarvBoo
Desert Storm. Kofi Anyidoho. PML
Desert Storm. Volker Braun. GTCP, *tr. by* Reinhold Grimm
Desert Symphony. Cherie Forman Spencer.
Night. TiP2
Desert was drifting its sands, The. For Everyone His Own Tree. Fadil Azzawi. IrPoTo, *tr. by* Ralph Saverese and Saadi A. Simawe
Desert Wisdom. Reg Saner. PoCoUp
Deserted. Madison Cawein. TCAPo

Deserted Angel, The. Anna Hajnal. IQMS, *tr. by* Jeannette Nichols
Deserted Died. Thomas Erskine, 1st Baron Erskine. DiBP
Deserted harbour stillness. Every stone. Seamus Heaney. PoetW *Fr.* Squarings.
Deserted here, the old house. Old House, The. Franta Bass. INSAB
Deserted Home, The. *Unknown.* IrV, *tr. by* Kuno Meyer
Deserted House. Dorothy, Duchess of Wellington Wellesley. Epilogue. OBMV
Deserted Orchard. Frances Mary Frost. YaYoPo
Deserted street, shadows of trees and houses, locked doors—. Vista. Faiz Ahmad Faiz. VCWP, *tr. by* Agha Shahid Ali
Deserted syntax gears up absolute, A. Bodiless. Robert Budde. PoPra
Deserted Village. Johannes Bobrowski. GTCP, *tr. by* Reinhold Grimm
Deserted Village, The. Oliver Goldsmith. NAEL-6v1; NAEL-7v1; NoP-4; NoP-5; OxAEP-1; TFi
"Ill fares the land, to hastening ills a prey." OBSV; UV
"Sweet was the sound, when oft at evening's close." NPeEn
Village Preacher, The.
"Near yonder copse, where once the garden smiled." TreFP
"Yes! let the rich deride, the proud disdain." OBSV
Deserter, A. Charles Reznikoff. TRP
Deserter, The. Ai. BodElec
Deserter, The. John Philpot Curran. OxAEP-1
Deserter, The. Gilbert Frankau. FaBoWar
Deserter, The. A. E. Housman. OBMV
Deserter, The. *Unknown.* FaBoWar
Desertmartin. Tom Paulin. BeAl; ModIr; NPeEn; PBCIP; PNI
Désespoir a trois paires de jambes, Le. Ma déraison d'être. Gherasim Luca. YaTCFP
Desfallecen las construccions en la vorágine del polvo. Horizonte. Laura Solórzano. SPV
Desgarrada la nube; el arco iris. Antonio Machado Ruiz. RaW
Desiderata on a Desert Island. Jasper Bernes. IAoNAP
Desiderato. William Johnson Cory. CAGL
Desideria. William Wordsworth. *See* Surprised by Joy.
Desiderium. John Byrom. *See* My Spirit Longeth for Thee.
Design. Robert Frost. APT-1; BrAP; ColAP; HeIP-4; NAAL-5; NAAPv.2; NAMCP V.1; NIL-7; NoAM; NoP-4; NoP-5; OxBoAm; OxBSo; PoPoPo; RaBo; SAmP; SoSe-8; TFi; TRP; WaAnP
Design. Mary Oliver. PoCoUp
Design for a Quilt. John Ormond. AngWePo; TCAWP
Design for a Tomb. John Ormond. TCAWP
Design, or chance, makes others wive. Of the Marriage of the Dwarfs. Edmund Waller. NPeEn
Designs on your blouse are flickering wildly, The. One Second. Innokenty Fiodorovich Annensky. WoPoe, *tr. by* Stephen Berg
Désillusion. Lady Jane Francesca Wilde. VWP
Desire. Claribel Alegría. LoL
Desire. Linda Bierds. AmAlph
Desire. Ada Cambridge. OxBSo
Desire. Kathy Fagan. GeoHom
Desire. Paul Hoover. PmAP
Desire. Langston Hughes. NAAPv.2; OxAAAP
Desire. Molly Peacock. RA
Desire. Kim Ports. PasH
Desire [*with music*]. George Russell. OBMV
Desire. Kurt Schwitters. PFTM-1
Desire: "There is a small wrought-iron balcony." David St. John. FaoP
Desire. Connemara Wadsworth. PasH
Desire 1. Thulani Davis. ISC
Desire, / with faith. Hope Chest. Stephanie Williams. AnSo
Desire as Light as a Shuttle. Joyce Mansour. HAWP, *tr. by* Mary Beach
Desire consumes hunger; hunger consumes blind jealousy. As My Will Concurred Not To My Being, It Were But Right and Equal to Reduce Me to My Dust. Yi Sanghûi. EcSo, *tr. by* Jennifer M. Lee
Desire has failed, desire has failed. Grasshopper Is a Burden. D. H. Lawrence. FaBoVe
Desire Loosening. Alcman. WoPoe, *tr. by* Rosanna Warren
Desire loosening. Desire Loosening. Alcman. WoPoe, *tr. by* Rosanna Warren
Desire Moving Through the Maps of the Material. Adonis. *tr. by* Allen Hibbard and Osama Isber
"Eiffel tower, The." PFTM-2, *tr. by* Allen Hibbard and Osama Isber
"It came to pass—." PFTM-2, *tr. by* Allen Hibbard and Osama Isber
"It is my desire moving." PFTM-2, *tr. by* Allen Hibbard and Osama Isber
"My passion is full of seeds issuing secretly from heraclitus and nietzsche." PFTM-2, *tr. by* Allen Hibbard and Osama Isber
"No, my body is neither a pelican nor a water lily." PFTM-2, *tr. by* Allen Hibbard and Osama Isber

Desire never leaves. How To Be Here? Tim Lilburn. OpeFie

Desire of Dominion. Timothy Kendall. NoSic

Desire of Water, The. Mark Jarman. PoA 2002

Desire, though thou my old companion art. Sir Philip Sidney. NAEL-6v1; NAEL-7v1; NoP-5 *Fr.* Astrophil and Stella.

Desire to us. Desire. Langston Hughes. NAAPv.2; OxAAAP

Desire was a quotation from someone. Michael Palmer. APSN

Desired, the snow falls upward. Michael Palmer. FTOS *Fr.* Letters to Zanzotto.

Desire's a Desire. Selima Hill. StAl

Desire's destroyed my life; what gifts have I. Khwaja Shams-ad-din Muhammad Hafiz. WoPoe *Fr.* Three Poems on Friendship.

Desires of Men and Women. John Berryman. BrAP

Desire's Persistence. Jay Wright. ESEAA

Desiring his imprisoned Muse to enlarge. On the Doctors' Telling Him that till He Left off Making Verses He Was Not Fit to be Discharged. James Carkesse. NOSC

Desiring nought but how to kill desire. (LL) Thou Blind Man's Mark. Sir Philip Sidney. HeIP-4; NAEL-6v1; NAEL-7v1

Desirous is one who gets away from his mother. Call of the Desirous. José Lezama Lima. TCLAP, *tr. by* Willis Barnstone

Desk, The [*with music*]. David Bottoms. WeW-3

Desnos Reading the Palms of Men on Their Way to the Gas Chambers. Stephen Berg. TaR

Desolate City, The. *Unknown.* OBEV, *tr. by* Wilfrid Scawen Blunt

Desolate City, The: A Rhapsody. Pao Chao. CCL1, *tr. by* Burton Watson

Desolate Field, The. William Carlos Williams. APT-1

Desolate inn is like that cottage in the old town, The. Watching the Rain at Hoeduk Inn. Chungji. BecRai, *tr. by* Kim Daljin, Kim Won-Chung and Christopher Merrill

Desolate wind from the city, A. Gunnar Ekelof. PFTM-2 *Fr.* Mölna Elegy.

Desolation. Jack Davis. BMAP

Desolation. John Henry, Cardinal Newman. SacPr

Desolation [*with music*]. *Unknown.* OBWVE, *tr. by* Aneirin Talfan Davies

Desolation: "At the top of the dune." Dabney Stuart. PfSP

Desolation Is a Delicate Thing. Elinor Wylie. MoAmPo

Desolation Row. Bob Dylan. OxBoAm

Despair: "It seems to be DARK all the time." John Berryman. ViWalt

Despair. Maxine W. Kumin. FFC

Despair. Meng Chiao. CrYelRi, *tr. by* Sam Hamill

Despair, anger, grief. Black Java Pepper. Arthur Sze. OpBo

Despair has prevented praise, but praise shall rise again. Venerating Senses Save Us. Jonathan Griffin. Oth

Despair has three pairs of legs. My Folly of Being. Gherasim Luca. YaTCFP, *tr. by* Michael Tweed

Despair is big with friends I love. Consequences. William Meredith. VCAP

Despairing Lover, The. William Walsh. NBLV

Desperate soldier's hands which kill all things. (LL) Place Pigalle. Richard Wilbur. HeIP-4; PWW2

Desperate Vitality, A. Pier Paolo Pasolini. *tr. by* Pasquale Verdicchio
  "As in a film by Godard: alone." PFTM-2, *tr. by* Pasquale Verdicchio

Despise poetry, and you'll be named to office. Despair. Meng Chiao. CrYelRi, *tr. by* Sam Hamill

Despise the World. *Unknown.* WaAnP

Despite her sixty years Aunt Hannah Jackson rubs on other people's clothes. Aunt Hannah Jackson. Fenton Johnson. APT-1

Despite his caricatures. Melvin B. Tolson. NAAPv.2 *Fr.* Harlem Gallery.

Despite that I overslept. That's Not in My Job Description. Paul Beatty. NeAmPo

Despite the grisly wounds portrayed in prints. Christ at the Apollo, 1962. Michael Waters. SwNoth

Despite the reigning darkness. Great Masturbator, The. Salvador Dali. PFTM-1

Despite the ruddy down upon your cheek. Strato. CAGL, *tr. by* Daryl Hine

Despondency, an Ode. Robert Burns. NPBRoP

Despondency and Aspiration. Felicia Dorothea Hemans. RWP

Despondent. Sikong Tu. CCL1 *Fr.* Twenty-Four Modes of Poetry.

Desponding Phyllis has endured. Phyllis [*or* Phillis] [*or* Progress of Love, The]. Jonathan Swift. OBCoV; OBSV

Despot treads thy sacred sands, The. Carolina. Henry Timrod. APN-2; CBCWP; PCW

Despot's heel is on thy shore, The. My Maryland. James Ryder Randall. CBCWP; PCW

Destierro terminó ya, El. Última Tierra en el Destierro. Jorge Guillén. RaW

Destination: Tule Lake Relocation Center, May 20, 1942. James Masao Mitsui. OpBo

Destinies. Hashim Shafiq. IrPoTo, *tr. by* Saadi A. Simawe and Ellen Doré Watson

Destiny. Eloise Bibb. CBWP-4

Destiny. Rosario Castellanos. CFP; TANSG, *tr. by* George Bogin

Destiny. Maria Luisa Spaziani. NeIt, *tr. by* Beverly Allen

Destiny, not guilt, was enough. Ovid. WaAnP *Fr.* Metamorphoses [Hughes Translation].

Destroy. Alice Notley. Eno

Destroy the heavy yoke beneath which you are bound! To Germany. Georg Rudolph Weckherlin. GePo, *tr. by* George C. Schoolfield

Destroyers in Collision. Rudyard Kipling. InoFa *Fr.* Epitaphs of the War [1914–1918].

Destroyers in the Arctic. Alan Ross. PoWW

Destroying life alone, not peace! (LL) Lines Written in the Bay of Lerici. Percy Bysshe Shelley. NAEL-6v2; NAEL-7v2

Destruction. Shakuntala Hawoldar. CFP; HAWP

Destruction. Joanne Kyger. BLT; GoPo

Destruction. Takahashi Shinkichi. AtGh; ZenPo, *tr. by* Takashi Ikemoto and Lucien Stryk

Destruction of Daughters. Lee Upton. AmAlph

Destruction of Jerusalem, The. Thomas Deloney.
  Christs Prophesie of the destruction of this Cittie. ChIV-2
  Description of the horrible Famine within *the Cittie of* Jerusalem. FaBoWar

Destruction of Psara, The. Dionysios Solomos. WoPoe, *tr. by* Edmund Keeley and Philip Sherrard

Destruction of Sennacherib, The. Lord Byron. BRP; CABP; ChAP; ChIV-1; FaBoWar; HeIP-4; NoP-4; NoP-5; OBWP; OxAEP-2; TFi; WeW-3; WoPoe

Destruction of Sodom, The. Daryl Hine. ChIV-1

Destruction of the beloved by the lover, The. With Passion without Compassion. Oscar Hahn. BLPSL, *tr. by* Rene de Costa, Rigas Kappatos and Eleni Paidoussi

Destruction of the Grecian Fort, The. Homer. OBVE *Fr.* Iliad, The.

Destruction of the Mir, The. Lucia Maria Perillo. RoV

Destruction that brings an eagle from heaven is better than mercy, The. (LL) Fire on the Hills. Robinson Jeffers. CalPo; OxBoAm; RaBo

Desultory Thoughts in London. Charles Lloyd.
  "Where have I wander'd, London, from thy haunts?" NOBRP

Desvanecida, ahogada. Recuerdo. Emilio Prados. RaW

Detach, Invading. Ron Padgett. FTOS

Detached by Saarinen or God. Dulles Airport. Eugene McCarthy. OtW

Detached, he said. Habitat Photo. Joy Lahey. AnSo

Detail. Eamon Grennan. StAl

Detail. Charles North. NYP2

Detail and distinguishing odor, The. Human Excrement. Stanley Plumly. PfSP

Detail from "Set for a Southern Gothic." Brian Teare. LegDan

Detail, of course, The. Interstate 80. Michael Anania. IllVoic

Detailed History of the Western World. Joe Wenderoth. AmPoNex

Details didn't concern me. Brief reflection on the greatness of God. Yana Tokareva. CRWP, *tr. by* Daniel Weissbort

Detain nature in facsimile across nonchalance, against the grain. What is an. Detained by Rest. Marjorie Welish. VaPo

Detained by Rest. Marjorie Welish. VaPo

Detected little things: a peach pit basket watch chain charm, an ivory cross wound. Father or Son. James Schuyler. FTOS

Detenido en la tensa turbulencia del aire. Neblina veraniega. David Huerta. RMCMP

Deteriora. William Johnson Cory. CAGL

Determinate Inflorescence: Ephemera. Liz Waldner. PoDa

Determination of Time. Alena Nádvorníková. SurWo

Determined, Dared, and Done. (LL) Song to David, A. Christopher Smart. NAEL-6v1; NAEL-7v1; OBWVE

Determines to Follow Phaon. Mary Robinson. CenSon; RWP

Determinism. Maurice Evan Hare. OBCoV

Detestable race, continue to expunge yourself, die out. Apostrophe to Man. Edna St. Vincent Millay. NAAL-5; NALW

Detonation. Francesco Cangiullo. PFTM-1

Detour. Michael Longley. BeAl; NAMCP V.2

Detouring through the rooms were men and fumes. Ivano Fermini. ItPo, *tr. by* Gayle Ridinger

Detroit Addendum. Murray Jackson. OxAAAP

Detroit Annie, Hitchhiking. Judy Grahn. ASA *Fr.* Common Woman, The.

Detroit just sits there. Idea of Detroit, The. Jim Gustafson. FTtHH

Detroit 1958. Al Young. ESEAA

Detroit popped in the window. Entering Detroit. Víctor Hernández Cruz. PueRic

Detroit River. Constance Fenimore Woolson. APN-2

Detroit, Tomorrow. Philip Levine. PoA 2002

Deucalion and Pyrrha, sole survivors of the Flood, renew Creation by casting stones behind them. Ovid. NPeEn *Fr.* Metamorphoses.

De—um majorettes. Ken Edwards. Oth *Fr.* Five Nocturnes, after Derek Jarman.

Deuteronomy. Bible, *O.T.*
"For the Lordes parte is his folke." OBVE

Deuteronomy 30.19. Francis Quarles. ChIV-1

Deutschland. Hugh Maxton. PBCIP

Deuxieme Sexe, La. Lucia Maria Perillo. RoV

Deva-like Barbarian. Wen T'ing-yün. ColAnChi, *tr. by* Lois Fusek

Development: "I learned to fuck one summer in a burgeoning subdivision." Joel Brouwer. NevBe

Development, The. Marge Piercy. NBLV *Fr.* Sand Roads.

Devil, A. Zbigniew Herbert. MotU, *tr. by* Czeslaw Milosz

Devil, The. Bosch. Rafael Alberti. WoPoe, *tr. by* Carolyn Tipton

Devil, The. Robert Southey. NOxBChV

Devil and the Princess. *Unknown.* NBLV

Devil beating his wife, The. Devil Beating His Wife. Ron Rash. LiTh

Devil below was ringing his knell, The. (LL) Inchcape Rock, The. Robert Southey. NPBRoP; OBNV; OBSP; OxAEP-2

Devil damn thee black, thou cream-faced loon—, The. Paul Dehn. OBCoV *Fr.* Potted Swan.

Devil, having nothing else to do, The. On Lady Poltagrue, A Public Peril. Joseph Hilaire Pierre Belloc. MoBrPo; OBCoV

Devil in Texas, The. *Unknown.* NBLV

Devil is a gentleman, and asks you down to stay, The. Aristocrat, The. G. K. Chesterton. OBCoV

Devil is dead, good people all!, The. Devil's Funeral, The. Mary Elizabeth Coleridge. NALW

Devil may endure but just being a man, A. Suicide of an Unemployed Person, The. Kodama Kagai. CAoMJL1, *tr. by* Leith Morton

Devil now knew his proper cue, The. Percy Bysshe Shelley. OBSV *Fr.* Peter Bell the Third.

Devil on Ice. Donald Davie. NoAM

Devil take her, The. (LL) Sir John Suckling. BASC; CavPo; ClHu; HeIP-4; ITBLP; NAEL-6v1; NAEL-7v1; NBLV; NIL-7; NIP-4; NoP-4; NoP-5; NPeEn; OBEV; OxAEP-1; OxBEV; TFi; WaAnP *Fr.* Aglaura.

Devil take the human race!, The. Ill Humor. Johann Wolfgang von Goethe. STV, *tr. by* John Frederick Nims

Devilish and the dark, the dying and diseas'd, The. Rounded Catalogue Divine Complete, The. Walt Whitman. NAAL-3

Devils, The. Charles Simic. OxBoAm

Devil's Advice to Story-Tellers, The. Robert Graves. NAEL-6v2; NoAM

Devil's Destroying Angel Exploded, The. Tom Pickard. Oth

Devil's Dictionary, The. Ambrose Bierce.
    Alone. APN-2
    Body-Snatcher. APN-2
    Corporal. AmWit; APN-2
    Egotist. APN-2
    Elegy. AmWit; APN-2
    Freedom. APN-2
    Gorgon. APN-2
    Hypochondriasis. APN-2
    Lead. APN-2
    Nose. APN-2
    Orthography. APN-2; CalPo
    Prospect. APN-2
    Rimer. APN-2
    Safety-Clutch. APN-2

Devil's Funeral, The. Mary Elizabeth Coleridge. NALW

Devil's Law Case, The. John Webster.
    Burial, The. NOSC
    (Vanitas Vanitatum.) OBEV

Devil's Symbol, The. Haytham El-Shawwaf. AnVo, *tr. by* Mohamed Enani

Devil's Thoughts, The. Samuel Taylor Coleridge and Robert Southey. NPBRoP; OBSV

Devil's Workshop, The. Yusef Komunyakaa. PoA 2002

Devisioun of the Eirth, The. Sir David Lyndsay. NePenScot *Fr.* Dreme, The.

Devolution. Molly Peacock. FFC

Devonshire Street W.1. Sir John Betjeman. NPeEn

Devotion. Thomas Campion. *See* Follow Thy Fair Sun[ne] [Unhappy Shadow].

Devotion. Thomas Campion. OBEV

Devotion. Paul Fleming. GePo, *tr. by* F. Warnke

Devotion. Dan Pagis. MotU, *tr. by* Stephen Mitchell

Devotions in Confidence. Margot Schilpp. AmPoNex

Devoured by a clock on his way to work. (LL) Cloud Unfolding, The. Ernesto Trejo. FTtHH; LTA

Devouring Time, blunt thou the lion's [*or* Lyons] paw[e]s. William Shakespeare. HeIP-4; NAEL-6v1; NAEL-7v1; NoSic; OxAEP-1; PBRV *Fr.* Sonnets.

Devout but highly imaginative Jesuit, A. Almost Spring, Driving Home, Reciting Hopkins. Maxine W. Kumin. ExTi

Devout like a Branch. Cristina Campo. CItWP, *tr. by* Cinzia Sartini Blum and Lara Trubowitz

Devout Lover, A. Thomas Randolph. OBEV

Dew and the clouds, The. (LL) I Found It. Fadwa Tuqan. BBASP; CFP, *tr. by* Patricia Alanah Byrne, Salma Khadra Jayyusi and Naomi Shihab Nye

Dew at the Edge of a Leaf. Marvin Bell. InvLad

Dew, clear as gilt jewels, hangs under the garden grass-blades. Wine. Li Po. NDACCP, *tr. by* Ezra Pound

Dew, clinging / To potato field. Masaoka Shiki. ZenPo, *tr. by* Takashi Ikemoto and Lucien Stryk

Dew falls, the sky is a long way up, the brimming waters are quiet, The. Autumn Night. Tu Fu [*or* Du Fu]. EaWin, *tr. by* W. S. Merwin

Dew in the morning, dust at noon. Barefoot Homiletics, after Wittgenstein and Boswell. Alan Dugan. BodElec

Dew is aflame on the flowers and trees, The. Having to Part From His Mistress at Dawn. Bálint Balassi. IQMS, *tr. by* Yakov Hornstein

Dew on a Dusty Heart. Jean Starr Untermeyer. MoAmPo

Dew on the bramble / Thorns. Buson. ZenPo, *tr. by* Takashi Ikemoto and Lucien Stryk

Dew on the secret orchid. Grave of Little Su, The. Li Ho. WoPoe, *tr. by* A. C. Graham

Dew on the Shallot. *Unknown.* CCL1, *tr. by* Anne Birrell

Dew sate on *Julia's* haire. Robert Herrick. PBRV

Dew spread / The seeds of hell. Issa. ZenPo, *tr. by* Takashi Ikemoto and Lucien Stryk

Dew Sweet Law, The. Joanne Kyger. WANABP

Dew whitens the jade steps. Resentment Near the Jade Steps. Li Po. ErotSp, *tr. by* Sam Hamill

Dewdrops are the gems of morning. Old Man's Sigh, The. A Sonnet. Samuel Taylor Coleridge. CenSon

Dewey Square, 1956. Percy Johnston. EGAG

Dewpoint and a level field. Or slick. Elegant. Linda Gregerson. AmAlph

Dew-rinsed. Cicadas. Hsüeh T'ao [*or* Xue Tao]. CCL1, *tr. by* Jeanne Larsen

Dewy morn / These saucepans. Buson. ZenPo, *tr. by* Takashi Ikemoto and Lucien Stryk

Dexter Gordon's tenor sax. February in Sydney. Yusef Komunyakaa. ESEAA; InGu; NAMCP V.2

Dey want me to help score d ambush. (LL) Badman of the Guest Professor. Ishmael Reed. EGAG; SSLK

Dey was talkin' in de cabin, dey was talkin' in de hall. When Dey 'Listed Colored Soldiers. Paul Laurence Dunbar. CBCWP

Dharma. Billy Collins. OxBoAm

Dharma is like an Avocado!, The. Avocado. Gary Snyder. PmAP; WhBo

Dharma spring of the Sixth Patriarch, The. Hui-neng's Pond. Muso Soseki. EaWin, *tr. by* W. S. Merwin

Dharmakaya. Philip Whalen. WANABP

D-Hour. Lawrence Okezie Chibueze Anene. NeNiPo

Di Brook Di Dry. Jag Chenkó. OWABP

Di sun si it all aready. History of Dub Poetry, The. "Mbala." WaCA

Día de Los Muerto. Cynthia Harper. TiP2

Día empezó temprano: en el embarcadero de grandes piedras blancas y palmeras nos embarcamos hoy, El. Tatuajes en el Agua. Efraín Bartolomé. RMCMP

Diabolus in Musica. Lawrence F. O'Brien. MiVo

Diagnosis. Carole Satyamurti. StAl

Diagnosis. Terence Winch. PoDa

Diagnosis, The. James Tate. BAP-01

Diagnosis: My Mother's Breast. Lisa Fishman. AmPoNex

Diagonal plane of low grey white cloud moving. Stephen Ratcliffe. ASA

Dial, The. Thomas Cole. APN-1

Dial Call. Christopher Darlington Morley. NBLV

Dialectic. Victor Serge. AF, *tr. by* James Brook

Dialectical Materialism. Bruce Weigl. AmAlph

Dialectics. Edvard Kocbek. PoSu

Dialectique. Hugh Maxton. IrLP

Dialog. Jean Garrigue. OxBoAm

Dialogue. Jared Angira. NAfrP

Dialogue. Richard Lovelace. CavPo

Dialogue. James McAuley. BMAP

Dialogue. Adrienne Rich. NIL-7; TWF

Dialogue, A. George Herbert. FSCP; NOSC; OBEV

Dialogue, A. Lizelia Augusta Jenkins Moorer. CBWP-3

Dialogue, A. Elizabeth Newell. EMWP

Dialogue, The. Funso Aiyejina. NAfrP

Dialogue between a Squeamish Cotting Mechanic and His Sluttish Wife, in the Kitchen. Edward Ward. WaAnP *Fr.* Nuptial Dialogues.

Dialogue between Death and Youth, A. *Unknown.* NoSic

Dialogue between Father and Daughter. Robert Browning. OBCoV

Dialogue between Old England and New, A. Anne Bradstreet. BASC; EMWP

Dialogue Between The Resolved Soul and Created Pleasure, A. Andrew Marvell. FSCP

Dialogue between the Soul and [the] Body, A. Andrew Marvell. BASC; BrAP; FSCP; NAEL-6v1; NAEL-7v1; NoP-4; NoP-5; OxAEP-1; OxBEV; SoSe-8; TFi

Dialogue between two shepherds, Thenot and Piers, in praise of ASTRÆA. Mary Sidney Herbert, Countess of Pembroke. EMWP; NAEL-6v1

Dialogue betwixt God and the Soul, A. Sir Henry Wotton. SacPr

Dialogue betwixt Man, and Nature, A. Margaret Lucas Cavendish, Duchess of Newcastle. PBRV

Dialogue betwixt the Body and the Mind, A. Margaret Lucas Cavendish, Duchess of Newcastle. PEW

Dialogue betwixt Time and a Pilgrim[e], A. Aurelian Townshend. NPeEn; OxBEV

Dialogue No. 5. Dmitry Aleksandrovich Prigov. ItGoST, *tr. by* Robert Reid

Dialogue of Self and Soul, A. William Butler Yeats. MoBrPo; NAEL-6v2; NAEL-7v2; NAMCP V.1; NoAM

  "Living man is blind and drinks his drop, A." RaBo

Dialogue of the Colours. Buland Al-Haidari. IrPoTo, *tr. by* Hussein Kadhim and Christopher Merrill

Dialogue of Thunder. Christine Hume. AmPoNex

Dialogue with Herz. Antonio Porta. ItPo, *tr. by* Gayle Ridinger

Dialogue with the Dead. Amelia Rosselli. PFTM-2, *tr. by* Lawrence R. Smith

Dialysis. Lucille Clifton. FuFl

Diamant qu'il ne t'a pas donné c'est parce qu'il l'a eu à la fin de sa vie, Le. Diamant qu'il ne t'a pas donné, Le. Paul Éluard. YaTCFP

Diameter of the bomb was thirty centimeters, The. Diameter of the Bomb, The. Yehuda Amichai. BeAl; PoAgWa; PoSu, *tr. by* the author and Ted Hughes

Diamond Cutter. Seido Ray Ronci. AmZen

Diamond Cutters, The. Adrienne Rich. ItP

Diamond he didn't give you, because he only had it as his life was ending, The. Diamond He Didn't Give You, The. Paul Eluard and Andre Breton. YaTCFP, *tr. by* Mary Ann Caws and Jean-Pierre Cauvin

Diamonds Are a Girl's Best Friend. Leo Robin. ReLy

Diamonds are forever so I gave you quartz. Hardness Scale, The. Joyce Peseroff. TRP

Diamonds are mined . . . oil is discovered. Poem (for Langston Hughes), A. Nikki Giovanni. SSLK

Diana. Henry Constable.

  Of his Mistress, upon Occasion of her Walking in a Garden. NIL-7; NIP-4; OBGa

  "Uncivil sickness, hast thou no regard." OxBSo

Dianae Sumus in Fide. Biancamaria Frabotta. CItWP, *tr. by* Cinzia Sartini Blum and Lara Trubowitz

Diane Arbus, New York. Nicole Cooley. AmPoNex

Diapers for My Father. Alice Friman. IaFF

Diaries. Ben Scammell. NLP

Diary. Gerald Stern. OPRER

Diary. Mary Wilson. Spl

Diary, The. Johann Wolfgang von Goethe. STV, *tr. by* John Frederick Nims

Diary Entry, January Seven. Elke Erb. OnScMo, *tr. by* Rosmarie Waldrop

Diary: How to Improve the World (You Will Only Make Matters Worse). John Cage.

  Abundance. APSN

  "Boddhisattva Doctrine: Enter / Nirvana only when all beings, sentient." APSN

  "Continue; I'll discover where you sweat (Kierkegaard)." PFTM-2

  "Daily warmth we, The." APSN

  "Get it, / she said, so it's unknown which parent." APSN

  "Hearing of past actions." APSN

  "Lazy dog (a bomb containing ten), The." APSN

  "LET'S CALL IT THE / COLLECTIVE CONSCIOUSNESS (WE'VE GOT." APSN

  "Mother wrote to say: "Stay / in Europe. Soak up as much beauty as you."" APSN

  "Since the / Spirit's omnipresent, there's a difference." APSN

  "The / children have a society of their own." APSN

  "They dance the world as." APSN

  "To / know whether or not art is contemporary." APSN

  "We've / poisoned our food, polluted our air." APSN

Diary Moon. Paul Farley. NeBrP

Diary of a Rough Trade Angel. Lisa Jarnot. OnScMo

Diary of Beirut Under Siege, 1982, The. Adonis. PoetW *Fr.* Desert, The.

Diary Theme, The. Allen Fisher. Oth *Fr.* Emergent Manner.

Diary (Underworld). Rachel Zucker. LegDan

Diary us a few hoops. Lyn Hejinian. AWPTFC *Fr.* Writing Is an Aid to Memory.

Diaspora. S. V. Atalla. PoArWo

Diatribe Against the Dead. Angel González. VCWP, *tr. by* Steven Ford Brown and Revuelta Gutierrez

Dibbukim (Dibbiks). Jerome Rothenberg. PFTM-2 *Fr.* Khurbn.

Dibuja una letra. Ana Belén López Pulido. SPV

Dic Siôn Dayfydd. Thomas Jacob Thomas. OBWVE, *tr. by* H. Idris Bell

Dice / momentarily together. Misdeal. Michel Leiris. YaTCFP, *tr. by* Keith Waldrop

Dice of Love are, The. Anacreon. SaLy, *tr. by* Diane Rayor

Dick, a Maggot. Jonathan Swift. NBLV

Dick and Colin at the Salmon Nets. Naomi Mitchison. MoWP

Dick Briggs a wealthy farmer's son. Dick Briggs from Australia. Charles Robert Thatcher. NOBAu

Dick Briggs from Australia. Charles Robert Thatcher. NOBAu

Dick Cheney's Heart. Ben Friedlander. Eno

Dick, I went back to those rocks today. Note from Capri to Richard Ryan on the Adriatic Floor. Richard Hugo. PWW2

Dick o' the Cow. *Unknown.* IBB

Dick Tracy's Yellow Hat. Peter Orlovsky. BB

Dick, you were right. I steered clear of that town. Dead Letter From Out of Town. David Wagoner. OxBoAm

Dickery Dean. Dennis Lee. TLR

Dickhead. Tony Hoagland. MAAN

Dickinson. Anne Finch. FFC

Dickinson's Blue Sleeve. Yi Sanghûi. EcSo, *tr. by* Jennifer M. Lee

Dictator, The. Lajos Kassák. IQMS, *tr. by* Paul Tabori

Dictator, hiding behind a nihilist's mask, A. Dragon, The. Abdul Wahab Al-Bayati. IrPoTo, *tr. by* Farouk Abdel Wahab

Dictators. Péter Zilahy. PML, *tr. by* Judith Sonnabend

Dictators, The. Pablo Neruda. AF, *tr. by* Robert Bly

Dictée. Theresa Hak Kyung Cha.

  Elitere Lyric Poetry. PFTM-2

Dictionaries have no entry for the sort of love we praise, The. Captain Who Walks on His Deck, The. Jelaluddin Rumi. WED, *tr. by* Robert Bly

Dictionary definition of change, The. Age of Plastic, The. John Forbes. BMAP

Dictionary for the New Century. Kimberly M. Blaeser. SweBea

Dictionary is oracle bone. No entry falls between devout. High Up the Thunder Gods, Downstairs the Hunger. Andrew Schelling. AmZen

Dictum: For a Masque of Deluge. W. S. Merwin. YaYoPo

Did a wind come just as you got up or were. Dysraphism. Charles Bernstein. FTOS

Did all the lets and bars appear. March into Virginia, The. Herman Melville. NCAP

Did Hamlet mean to kill Polonius? Diane and I sit at a table. After the Trial of Hamlet, Chicago. Sherman Alexie. PrTe

Did he have eyes and, if so, did he look. Martial. RomPo, *tr. by* Anthony Reid

Did he really have to go? Quiver of Questions, A. Titiola Shoneyin. NeNiPo

Did he strike soundings off Vecta Insula? David Jones. HarvBoo; NAMCP V.1; NoAM *Fr.* Anathemata, The.

Did her skin smell. Of Woman Torn. Suheir Hammad. PoArWo

Did I boast of liberty? Mary Sidney Wroth, Countess of Montgomery. LW; PEW *Fr.* Urania.

Did I create that sky? Yes, for, if it was. Jack Kerouac. CLPP *Fr.* Scripture of the Golden Eternity, The.

Did I evah tell you, Sonny. Uncle Jimmie's Yarn. Priscilla Jane Thompson. CBWP-2

Did I Fall in Love? Orhan Veli Kanik. NaPG, *tr. by* Talat Sait Halman

Did I go there enough? Was it enough when I tried. Clapping, The. Linda Gregg. BodElec

Did I? Is it? ID. Heather McHugh. OxBoAm

Did I love thee? I only did desire. Rondo. George Moore. IrLP

Did I Miss Anything? Tom Wayman. P180

Did I, my lines intend for public[k] view. Introduction, The. Anne Finch, Countess of Winchilsea. BrAP; EMWP; NAEL-6v1; NAEL-7v1; NALW; NoP-4; NoP-5; WaAnP

Did I not *once* have a pleasant childhood, heroic and fabulous. Morning. Arthur Rimbaud. SxFrPo, *tr. by* Martin Sorrell

Did I not tell you, my soul, "By Cypris, you will be caught." Meleager. HePo, *tr. by* Barbara Hughes Fowler

Did I step on your train? Before. May Probyn. VWP

Did I tell you I wanted one of those leashes you see at the mall. Leash. Lisa Glatt. SUP

Did I tell you of a strange dream I had? Inland sea, The. Jenny Joseph. MoWP

Did I write that I'll endure this. Women. Kim Hyesun. EcSo, *tr.* by Youngju Ryu

Did it better: pathetic in bathtub, post-. Self-Portrait as Somebody Else. Laura Mullen. ExTi

Did it matter? They were only for me. (LL) Kenneth Rexroth. APSN; APT-2 *Fr.* Love Poems of Marichiko, The.

Did it not tremble with the strings! Edgar Allan Poe. *See* Unless it trembled with the strings.

Did it once issue from the carver's hand. W. H. Auden. OxBSo *Fr.* Voyage, A.

Did John's Music Kill Him? Alfred B. Spellman. EGAG; SeSe

Did love him faithfully. (LL) Uncle Ananias. Edwin Arlington Robinson. MoAmPo; NIP-4

Did Not. Thomas Moore. IrLP

Did not produce a bumper crop. (LL) First Spring in California, 1936. Wilma Elizabeth McDaniel. CalPo; GeoHom

Did she drink tea? Yes, please. And after. Star's Whole Secret, The. Mary Jo Bang. NAPBL

Did / Somebody / Die? (LL) World War II. Langston Hughes. APT-2; PoPoPo

Did the earth stretch out. You, for My Meditation. Sara de Ibáñez. TCLAP, *tr.* by Andrew Rosing

Did the Harebell loose her girdle. Emily Dickinson. FaBoVe; NCAP

Did the people of Viet Nam. What Were They Like? Denise Levertov. HeIP-4; NIP-4; OBWP; PoAgWa

((1) Did the people of Viet Nam use lanterns of stone?) FTtHH; NAAL-5

Did the sun dip into the water this morning. How the Tortoise Knew It Was Her Time. Joan I. Siegel. PoCoUp

Did the water splash me or did I dive in? I am dying to know. The truth. Dive, The. Mimi Goese. HeMarv

Did their Catullus walk that way? (LL) Scholars, The. William Butler Yeats. NoP-4; NoP-5

Did then the bold slave rear at last the sword. Robert Southey. CenSon

Did these flyers. Media on War: or, the Square Root of Vietnam. Clarence Major. EGAG

Did we not underwrite them when we were born? (LL) Elegy for Minor Poets. Louis MacNeice. CABP; PNI

Did we suprise our teachers who had niggling doubts about the picayune brains of small black children. Denigration. Harryette Mullen. PrTe

Did Ye See Me? Robert Garioch. OBCoV

Did yet inspire a cheer, which he forbore to check. (LL) Lord Byron. NAEL-6v2; NAEL-7v2 *Fr.* Childe Harold's Pilgrimage.

Did you ask dulcet rhymes from me? To a Certain Civilian. Walt Whitman. CBCWP; FaBoWar

"Did You Call Me, Father?" Mary E. Tucker. CBWP-1

Did you eever iver ever. Hand-clapping Rhyme. *Unknown.* NTCP

Did You Ever Cross Over to Sneden's. Alec Wilder. ReLy

Did You Ever Hear an English Sparrow Sing? Bertha Johnston. ITBLP

Did you ever notice when a ride gets long. Never Eat Oranges! John Nelson. GeoH

Did you ever see someone coldcock a blind nun? Election Day, 1984. Carolyn Kizer. ExTi; GifTon

Did you ever see the day. On the Prince's Death, to the King. Sir Robert Aytoun. NOSC

Did you ever see two Yankees [part up on a foreign shore]. Give My Regards to Broadway. George M. Cohan. NAAPv.2; ReLy; TCAPo

Did you ever sit and ponder, sit and wonder, sit and think. Life's a Funny Proposition after All. George M. Cohan. ReLy

Did you ever stop to figure that this very life we lead. Nothing New Beneath the Sun. George M. Cohan. ReLy

Did you get the photo I sent? The horse? I would take her with me. Fourteen Things We're Allowed to Bring to the Underworld. Mark Wunderlich. LegDan

Did you go to the school by the river? Did You Ever Cross Over to Sneden's. Alec Wilder. ReLy

Did you hear. Arrival. Fedya Filkova. CSCBP, *tr.* by Georgi Belev and Lisa Sapinkopf

Did you hear about Lumumba? Lumumba Blues. Raymond R. Patterson. BRtP

Did you hear, *I heard.* Elsewhere. Larissa Szporluk. LegDan

Did you hear it? I have to look back: one eye, the gleam in black. Prime Time. Barry Silesky. LiTh

Did you hear of the curate who mounted his mare. Thomas Love Peacock. OxAEP-2 *Fr.* Crotchet Castle.

Did you know in China. Wedding, A. W. B. Keckler. IIR

Did you know it too all night long? Expectation. Ida G. M. Gerhardt. TuT, *tr.* by Peter van de Kamp

Did you light furtive aggregate late-flow samples. J. H. Prynne. VaPo *Fr.* Red D Gypsum.

Did you like the city the water wrought drop by drop in the center of the pines? Federico García Lorca. CAGL *Fr.* Sonetos del Amor Oscuro [Sonnets of Dark Love].

Did you love well what very soon you left? Marilyn Hacker. NoAM *Fr.* Coda.

"Did You Love Well What Very Soon You Left?" Marilyn Hacker. *See* Conclusion: "Did you love well what very soon you left?"

Did you pass that old man on the stair? Turning, The. Janet Paisley. EdScPo

Did you re-do? (LL) Music for Homemade Instruments. Harryette Mullen. AWPTFC; BAP-01

Did you run your fingers through your kids' hair? (LL) For My Torturer, Lieutenant D. Leila Djabali. CFP; HAWP, *tr.* by Anita Barrows

Did you say I've got a to learn? Teach Me Tonight. Sammy Cahn. ReLy

Did you see him go by here tonight? Stranger, The. Aldo Palazzeschi. PFTM-1

Did you take me because you loved me? Kenneth Rexroth. APSN; APT-2 *Fr.* Love Poems of Marichiko, The.

Did you then celebrate. Certain Questions for Monsieur Renoir. John Ormond. AngWePo

Did you wake me? Encounter. Rick Fournier. PasH

Didactic Piece. Louise Bogan. NoAM

Didactic Poem on the Nature of History, A.D. 1954. Helmut Heissenbüttel. PFTM-2, *tr.* by Jerome Rothenberg

Diddly Squat From Cyberspace. Kenward Elmslie. NYP2

Didn't Chet Baker know. Speed Ball. Yusef Komunyakaa. SeSe

Didn't He Ramble. James Simmons. PNI

Didn't like jazz, he once claimed. William Carlos Williams. Cornelius Eady. GT

Didn't My Lord Deliver Daniel? *Unknown.* APN-2

Didn't no / tracy chapman song echo in haunting a capella. Perspective. Lisa Pegram. BtF

Didn't think of the clasp. Memory. Robert Burns. MoASP

Didn't we have a lovely evening? Let's Put Out the Lights and Go to Sleep. Herman Hupfeld. ReLy

Didn't you like the way the ants help. Why Regret? Galway Kinnell. OxBoAm

Dido by Night. Virgil. OBVE *Fr.* Aeneid [*or* Eneados *or* Aeneis], The.

Dido, Queen of Carthage. Christopher Marlowe.
"Grecian soldiers, tired with ten years' war." FaBoWar

Dido: Swarming. Kathleen Spivack. PoA 2002

Dido to Her Sister Anna. Virgil. OBVE *Fr.* Aeneid [*or* Eneados *or* Aeneis], The.

Dido's Suicide. Virgil. OBVE *Fr.* Aeneid [*or* Eneados *or* Aeneis], The.

Didst fettle for the great grey [*or* gray] drayhorse his bright and battering sandal! (LL) Felix Randal. Gerard Manley Hopkins. FaBoVe; MoBrPo; NAEL-6v2; NAEL-7v2; NoAM; NoP-4; NoP-5; OBEV; OxAEP-2; OxBSo; PoPoPo; TFi; WeW-3; WoPoe

Didst thou not find the place inspired [*or* inspir'd]. Upon My Lady Carlisle's Walking in Hampton Court Garden. Sir John Suckling. NoP-5; CABP; CavPo; NoP-4

Didst Thou one end of air's wide curtain hold. Bible, *O.T.* STuOW *Fr.* New Version of the Psalms of David, Fitted to the Tunes Used in Churches, A.

Didyme waved an olive branch at me. Asclepiades. ErotSp, *tr.* by Sam Hamill

Did-You-Come-Yets of the Western World, The. Rita Ann Higgins. StAl

Die Ego Self! Drowning in the Last Days of Luxury. Edwin Torres. HeMarv

Die for it, too. (LL) Basic Con, The. Lew Welch. CalPo; OxBoAm

Die is cast, and we must part, The. Parting, The. Josephine D. Henderson Heard. CBWP-4

Die is cast, come weal, come woe, The. Marriage. Mary Weston Fordham. CBWP-2

DIE not before thy day, poor man condemned. *Unknown.* NoSic

Die single, and thine image dies with thee. (LL) William Shakespeare. NAEL-6v1; NAEL-7v1; NoP-4; NoP-5 *Fr.* Sonnets.

Die soon. (LL) We Real Cool. Gwendolyn Brooks. AmFaPo; CAP-8; EMP; ESEAA; FuFl; HeIP-4; HHAm; IllVoic; ItP; MakPoe; NAAL-5; NALW; NAMCP V.2; NIL-7; NoP-4; NoP-5; OxAAAP; OxBoAm; PoA 2002; PoPoPo; RaBo; SoSe-8; TFi; TRP; WaAnP; WeW-3

Die, wild country, like the eaglehawk. Australia 1970. Judith Wright. HarvBoo; MakPoe; NoAM

Die Zauberflöte. Rosamund Marriott Watson. ViWPN

Dieback. Elizabeth Dodd. UrbNat

Died once must all be died again? (LL) Stephen to Lazarus. Clive Staples Lewis. ChIV-2; SacPr

Diehards, The. Ruth Pitter. OBGa

Dieppe [*author's tr. of his* Dieppe ("Encore le dernier reflux")]. Samuel Beckett. YaTCFP, *tr.* by the author

Dies Iræ. Thomas Babington Macaulay, 1st Baron Macaulay. ChIV-2

Dies irae dreadful day. Irae. Edward Kamau Brathwaite. NAMCP V.2

Dies Ire-Dies Pacis. John Oxenham. SacPr

Dies Merini. Alda Merini. CItWP, *tr. by* Cinzia Sartini Blum and Lara Trubowitz

Diesel fumes rise. Dinner on the Miami River. Greg Pape. PBCAP

Diesel to Yesterday. John Tripp. AngWePo

Diet. John Armstrong. VerBaPo *Fr.* Art of Preserving Health, The.

Diet, The. Bruce Meyer. IFF

Dieter bit his sealskin mitts, and pulled. Bush Navigator: The Last Morning of Hands. Peggy Shumaker. PBCAP

Difference [*with music*]. T. Harri Jones. OBWVE

Difference. János Pilinszky. IQMS, *tr. by* Peter Jay

Difference, The. Elizabeth Delmore. NLP

Difference, The. Jackie Hardy. NeBl

Difference, The. Dorothy Livesay. BrAP

Difference Between a King and a Tyrant, The. Timothy Kendall. NoSic

Difference between Despair, The. Emily Dickinson. NAAL-3; TCAPo

Difference Between Night and Day, The. Bin Ramke. YaYoPo

Difference Between Pepsi and Coke, The. David Lehman. PmAP; ReTh

Difference between poetry and rhetoric, The. Power. Audre Lorde. NoAM; WaAnP

Difference between you and me, The. Half-Breed. Cherríe Moraga. UnSA

Difference Betwixt King and Subjects, The. Robert Herrick. BASC

Difference is spreading, The. (LL) Gertrude Stein. MoWP; NAAPv.2; NAMCP V.1 *Fr.* Tender Buttons.

Difference to me!, The. (LL) William Wordsworth. BrAP; HeIP-4; InoFa; NAEL-6v2; NAEL-7v2; NIL-7; NIP-4; NoP-5; NPBRoP; NPeEn; OxAEP-2; UV; WeW-3 *Fr.* Lucy.

Differences between rich and poor, king and queen. Rank. Lincoln Kirstein. FaBoA; OBWP; OxBoAm; PWW2

Differences in Dogs. William Shakespeare. DiBP *Fr.* Macbeth.

Different. Marga Kool. TuT, *tr. by* Joan McBreen

Different History, A. Sujata Bhatt. HarvBoo

Different Horizon. Aimé Césaire. VCWP

Different Love Poem / We Need a Change, A. Ntozake Shange. UnSA *Fr.* Okra to Greens /.

Different Morning Altogether, A. Dima Hilal. PoArWo

Different Ones #6—Future Possibilities (An Aids Soliloquy). Viki Akiwumi. InTrad

Different Ship, A. Pablo Neruda. WoPoe, *tr. by* Ben Belitt

Different sky, A. Sail Away. Noël Coward. ReLy

Different Strokes Bar, San Francisco, The. Forrest Hamer. GeoHom

Different Voice, The. Frieda Hughes. NeBl

Different yet the same as before. (LL) "H. D." NAAPv.2; NALW; NAMCP V.1 *Fr.* Tribute to the Angels.

Difficult and Weighty Question, A. Janus Pannonius. IQMS, *tr. by* Adam Makkai

Difficult Body. Mark Wunderlich. NAPBL; Vesp

Difficult, isn't it?, to love these high-topped. On a Stanza by Rilke. Thomas Swiss. PoDa

Difficult Music, The. Reginald Shepherd. NeAmPo

Difficult to believe, a knife ensures the voice. Last Living Castrato, The. Jennifer Grotz. LegDan

Difficult to know whether humans are inordinately anxious. Risk. C. K. Williams. PoA 2002

Difficult to manage. (LL) Broagh. Seamus Heaney. FaBoVe; ModIr; NPeEn

Difficult to say what all of this is all about. Poor Boy: Portrait of a Painting. John Ash. HarvBoo

Difficult verse I dislike that comes hard, and the easy writ easy. Hard and Easy. Ferenc Kazinczy. IQMS, *tr. by* Watson Kirkconnell

Difficult with You. Anna Cascella. CItWP, *tr. by* Cinzia Sartini Blum and Lara Trubowitz

Difficulties at Love. *Vietnamese Oral Tradition.* CaDao, *tr. by* John Balaban

Difficulty Along the Way. Lew Welch. WhBo

Difficulty That Is Marriage, The. Paul Durcan. IrLP

Difficulty to think at the end of day, The. Rabbit Is King of the Ghosts, A. Wallace Stevens. NAMCP V.1; NoAM

Difficulty was, it was, The. In the Beginning Was a Word. Robert Graves. PoA 2002

Diffugere Nives. Horace. *See* Ode 4.7: "Snow dissolv'd no more is seen, The."

Diffugere Nives. A. E. Housman. AmFaPo

Dig And Be Dug / In Return. (LL) Motto. Langston Hughes. ItP; NAMCP V.1

Digamos que dormido, a la intemperie. Cuatro. Ofelia Perez Sepúlveda. SPV

Digger's Song, The. Barcroft Henry Boake. NOBAu

Diggers' Song, The. *Unknown.* PBRV

Digger's Song, The [*with music*]. Gerrard Winstanley. BASC; NOSC

Digging. Donald Hall. CAP-8

Digging. Seamus Heaney. BeAl; NAEL-6v2; NAEL-7v2; NAMCP V.2; NoP-4; NoP-5; WaAnP

Digging. Edward Thomas. MoBrPo

Digging a new. Relics. Robyn Sarah. NoP-5

Digging deep in the garden. Planting Roses. Phillis Levin. FFC

Digging for China. Richard Wilbur. BrAP

Digging for Indians. Gary Gildner. PBCAP

Digging in the Streets of Gold. Barry Seiler. UnSA

Digging into the apple. Hunger. Jack Gilbert. BeAl

Digging of Deep Wells, The. Hugh MacDonald. Coast

Digging Out the Buddha Relic. Muso Soseki. EaWin, *tr. by* W. S. Merwin

Digging Sing, A. *Unknown.* FaBoVe

Digging Soil. Peter Gruffydd. AngWePo

Digging / toward a Lenten extreme. Year. Milo De Angelis. NeIt, *tr. by* Lawrence Venuti

Digging up weeds by the little hedge. Elaine Randell. Oth

Digging was always my worst work. Grandfather in the Garden. Robert Minhinnick. OBGa

Diggins-Oh, The. *Unknown.* NOBAu

Dignity of Labor, The. Robert Bersohn. NBLV

Digo *lagarto* y un bloque de la roca se desprende. Intermedio con cinco cocodrilos. Efraín Bartolomé. RMCMP

Digs in Escondido Canyon, The. Walter McDonald. PoA 2002

Dih dred ded. Ahdri Zhina Mandiela. WaCA

Dike, a flower bed, a bare linden tree, A. Igor Khomin. TCRusP, *tr. by* Daniel Weissbort

Dike of the Cormorants. Wang Wei. CCL1, *tr. by* Jerome P. Seaton

Dikes on Fundy Bay. Liliane Welch. Coast

Dile a Nemrod, me dijo, "que devuelva." Suspensión de una obra. David Huerta. RMCMP

Dilection [*with music*]. Ernst Jandl. OnScMo, *tr. by* Anselm Hollo

Dilemma. David Budbill. GoPo

Dilemma. Phoebe Hesketh. Prnts

Dilemma, The. Sir John Collings Squire. OBCoV

Dilemma of the Elm. Genevieve Taggard. MoAmPo

Dill. Keith Ratzlaff. ACAMVP

Dilly Dilly Piccalilli. Clyde Watson. NTCP

Diluvio. Laura Solórzano. SPV

Dim as the borrowed beams of moon and stars. Religio Laici. John Dryden

Dim boy claps because the others clap, The. Freaks at Spurgin Road Field, The. Richard Hugo. NoAM; PoCho; SoSe-8

Dim burnt the lamp, and now the phantom Death. Philip Freneau. TCAPo *Fr.* House of Night, The.

Dim dawn behind the tamarisks—the sky is saffron-yellow. Christmas in India. Rudyard Kipling. ChrPo

Dim Lady. Harryette Mullen. IaFF

Dim light of daybreak now. Dawn Wail for the Dead. Oodgeroo of the tribe Noonuccal. BMAP

Dim Light Splits the Woods in Two Distinct Lines, The. Biancamaria Frabotta. CItWP, *tr. by* Cinzia Sartini Blum and Lara Trubowitz

Dim the light in your faces: be passionless in the room. Image, The. Richard Hughes. OBMV

Dim vales—and shadowy floods. Fairyland [*or* Fairy-Land]. Edgar Allan Poe. APN-1; NAAL-3; OxBoAm

Dime after Dime. Mary Weems. SpirFl

Dime, Antonio, recuerdas que en el año 14. Evocación Para Grabarla en una Caja de Música. Luis Rosales. RaW

Dime for Jesus who had died for men, A. (LL) Karma. Edwin Arlington Robinson. APT-1; HeIP-4; MoAmPo

Dimensionless. Rain/Light. Christopher Buckley. PfSP

Dimensions. Laura Riding Jackson. FuPo

Dimensions are dizzying; peaks, The. Landscape. Marguerite Bouvard. PfS

Diminished and enlarged. Are they the same? (LL) Return to Scalpay. Norman Alexander MacCaig. NePenScot; NoP-5

Diminutive. Carlos Drummond de Andrade. TCLAP, *tr. by* Virginia de Araújo

Diminutive. Nancy Steele. GifTon

Diminuto Anfibio. Silvia Eugenia Castillero. SPV

Dimples. Sasabune. NAAPv.2

Dimples / so clearly seen. Dimples. Sasabune. NAAPv.2

Dimpling its tranquil surface. (LL) Charlotte Smith. NOBRP; NoP-4; NoP-5 *Fr.* Beachy Head.

Dimply damsel, sweetly smiling. Ode: To Miss Margaret Pulteney [Daughter of Daniel Pulteney, Esq., in the Nursery]. Ambrose Philips. OxAEP-1; STuOW; UV

Din / who am i floating. Dedication. Rochelle Owens. PFTM-2

Din of wagons, The! Whinnying horses! Ballad of the Army Wagons, The. Tu Fu [*or* Du Fu]. CCL1, *tr. by* Arthur Cooper

Din of work is subdued, The. Lullaby, A. W. H. Auden. NAMCP V.1; NoAM

Din quiets, The. I step onto the boards. Hamlet. Boris Leonidovich Pasternak. GI; WoPoe, tr. by Nina Kossman

Dinah. Sam M. Lewis and Joe Young. ReLy

Dinakdakan. Maria Luisa B. Aguilar-Cariño. ReBoTo

Dinas Emrys. Brian Morris. AngWePo

Diner. RoByn Baron. BRtP

Ding, dong, bell. Mother Goose. OxBEV

Ding, dong, bell. (LL) William Shakespeare. NoSic; TFi Fr. Merchant of Venice, The.

Ding Repair. Peter Gizzi. VaPo

Ding-Donging. Laura Riding Jackson. NAMCP V.1; NoP-4; NoP-5

Dingty diddlety. Mother Goose. FaBoVe

Dingy donkey, formal and unchanged, A. Fable, A. John Hookham Frere. UV

Dining. Douglas Dunn. InoFa

Dining Out. Judith Beveridge. BMAP

Dining Out with Doug and Frank. James Schuyler. OxBoAm

Dining-Room Tea. Rupert Brooke. MoBrPo

Dinky Di. *Unknown.* NOBAu

Dinna bathir wi thi braiggil o wir lends. Coco-de-Mer. W. N. Herbert. NePenScot

Dinner. Laura Kasischke. SweBea

Dinner, The. Rosario Morales. PueRic

Dinner at Le Caprice. Rachel Wetzsteon. RA

Dinner at the Hotel de la Tigresse Verte. Donald Evans. TCAPo

Dinner for the Devil. Ben Jonson. NOSC Fr. Gypsies Metamorphosed, The.

Dinner Guest, The. Ann Townsend. SweBea

Dinner Guest: Me. Langston Hughes. LTA; NoP-5; SSLK

Dinner in the Sun. Donald Berger. NAPBL

Dinner must be dished at one, The. John Gay. DiBP Fr. Fables: Second Series.

Dinner on an April 10th. Carla Faesler Bremer. SPV, tr. by Jen Hofer

Dinner on the Miami River. Greg Pape. PBCAP

Dinner Together. Diana Rivera. InvLad

Dinner was over, the tablecloth gone, The. Poem on the Supposition of the Book Having Been Published and Read, A. Elizabeth Hands. WoRP

"Dinner-time?" said Gilbert White. Edmund Clerihew Bentley. OBCoV Fr. Clerihews.

Dinogad's smock is pied, pied. Song to a Child. *Unknown.* WoPoe, tr. by Anthony Conran

Dinogad's speckled petticoat. Dinogad's Petticoat. *Unknown.* OBWVE, tr. by Gwyn Williams

Dinogon. Michael Portnoy. HeMarv

Dinosaurs. Valerie Worth. NTCP

Dinosaurs are not all dead, The. Steam Shovel. Charles Malam. NTCP

Dint. Tony Lopez. VaPo

Dio de sí nuestra barca, marineros. Thalassa. José Luis Rivas. RMCMP

Diogenes. Morris Gilbert Bishop. NBLV

Diogenes. Lamiah Abbas Imara. IrPoTo, tr. by Basima Qattan Bezirgan and Elizabeth Fernea

Diogenes, that wise old bird. Complete Cynic, The. Keith Preston. NBLV

Diogenes Tries to Forget. Mary Karr. PoA 2002

Diomede Mourns His Fate and That of His Friends to the Latian Ambassador Who Seeks His Alliance against Aeneas. Virgil. OBVE Fr. Aeneid [or Eneados or Aeneis], The.

Dionysiaca. Nonnus. tr. by W. H. D. Rouse

  Carpos and Calamos. tr. by W. H. D. Rouse

    "But Dionysos had no healing physic for his comrade fallen, of dancing he thought no more." CAGL, tr. by W. H. D. Rouse

    "Eros came near in the horned shape of a shaggy Silenos." CAGL, tr. by W. H. D. Rouse

    "Where Carpos wandered and died, I will fall headlong." CAGL, tr. by W. H. D. Rouse

  Dionysus and Ampelos. CAGL, tr. by W. H. D. Rouse

Dionysus. Genrik Veniaminovich Sapgir. ItGoST, tr. by J. Kates

Dionysus and Ampelos. Nonnus. CAGL Fr. Dionysiaca.

Diorama. Jenny Mueller. IAoNAP

Dip down upon the northern shore. Alfred Tennyson. NAEL-6v2; NAEL-7v2; WaAnP Fr. In Memoriam A. H. H.

Dip your head in the basin & go. Shakin All Over. John James. Oth

Diphthongs are honey, the dentals are resin, The. Learning the Language. Brewster Ghiselin. APT-2

Diplomacy: The Father. W. D. Snodgrass. BrAP

Dipped now in Ocean, the She-Bear's stellar guardian. Ovid. RomPo Fr. Tristia.

Dipper Territory. James Aitchison. EdScPo

Dipsychus [and the Spirit]. Arthur Hugh Clough.

  I Dreamt a Dream. NAEL-6v2

  "There is no God, the wicked saith." BrAP; CABP; NoP-4; NPeEn; OxBEV; SacPr; WaAnP

Diptych. Dewi Stephen Jones. BBMWP, tr. by Joseph P. Clancy

Diptych. Tony Towle. PA9/11

Diptych: Jesus and the Stone. Charles Baxter. BBASP

Diques invisibles para las palabras. Cartografía. Antonio Deltoro. RMCMP

Dirce. Walter Savage Landor. NAEL-6v2; NoP-4; NoP-5; NPeEn; OBEV; OxAEP-2; OxBEV; TFi; WeW-3; WoPoe Fr. Pericles and Aspasia.

Dire Cure. William Matthews. EMP

Dire one and desired one. Ode to Meaning. Robert Pinsky. MakPoe; OxBoAm

Diré un día: bienvenido. Encuentro, El. José Hierro. RaW

Direct address to the swans: you, whose feet. You, Failed Pronoun. Eleanor Wilner. ExTi

Direct stare will get you exactly nowhere, The. Horatio. Nan Cohen. IaFF

Directions. Joseph Stroud. GoPo

Directions, The. Christopher Gilbert. GT

Directions for Carrying Explosive Nuclear Wastes through Metropolitan New York. June Jordan. AtGh

Directions for Understanding Modern Jazz Criticism. Kalamu ya Salaam. FuFl

Directions in Our Blood [with music]. Barney Bush. HATNAP

Directions to the Maze. Ken Harris. AnSo

Directive. Robert Frost. APT-1; ColAP; ItP; MakPoe; MoAmPo; NAAPv.2; NAMCP V.1; NoAM; NoP-4; NoP-5; OxBoAm; SAmP; StAl; TFi; WaAnP

Director, The. Edmund George Valpy Knox. OBCoV

Diremos hoy del amor cosas verdades. Merlín. Gerardo Deniz. RMCMP

Dirge. Thomas Lovell Beddoes. OxBEV

Dirge: "Calm on the bosom of thy God." Felicia Dorothea Hemans. OBEV Fr. Siege of Valencia, The.

Dirge: "From a friend's friend I taste friendship." Stevie Smith. HarvBoo; NPeEn

Dirge: "I reached the middle of the mount." Ralph Waldo Emerson. TCAPo

Dirge: "It is harm to me and anguish." Mary Macleod. EMWP

Dirge: "1-2-3 was the number he played but today the number came 3-2-1." Kenneth Fearing. AmWit; APT-2; NAAPv.2; NIL-7; NIP-4; OxBoAm

Dirge: "Ring out your bells [or belles], let mourning shows [or shewes] be spread." Sir Philip Sidney. NoSic

  (Dirge.) OxAEP-1

  (Ring Out Your Bells.) NoP-4; NoP-5

Dirge: "Stay, Death. Not mine the Christus-wand." Herman Melville. APN-2; NCAP Fr. Clarel: A Poem and Pilgrimage in the Holy Land.

Dirge. William Shakespeare. See Clown's Song, The.

Dirge. James Shirley. NoP-4; NoP-5

Dirge. Sir Philip Sidney. See Dirge: "Ring out your bells [or belles], let mourning shows [or shewes] be spread."

Dirge, A. George Croly. SacPr

Dirge, A. John Webster. See Call for the Robin-Redbreast and the Wren.

Dirge, A ("Calm on the bosom of thy God"). Felicia Dorothea Hemans. See Dirge: "Calm on the bosom of thy God."

Dirge, A: "Rough wind, that moanest loud." Percy Bysshe Shelley. NAEL-7v2

Dirge, A: "Why were you born when the snow was falling?" Christina Georgina Rossetti. OxBEV

Dirge for a Soldier. George Henry Boker. PCW

Dirge for Fidele. William Shakespeare. ClHu; NoSic; OxAEP-1; SoSe-8; TFi Fr. Cymbeline.

Dirge for McPherson, A. Herman Melville. CBCWP

Dirge for the Living. Rosalie Moore. YaYoPo

Dirge for the New Sunrise. Dame Edith Sitwell. MoBrPo Fr. Three Poems of the Atomic Bomb.

Dirge for Two Generals. Yejong, King of Koryŏ. CATKP, tr. by Peter H. Lee

Dirge for Two Veterans. Walt Whitman. APN-1; BLT; CBCWP; ItP; MoAmPo

Dirge in Jazz Time. Vassar Miller. FFC

Dirge in Woods. George Meredith. NAEL-6v2; OBEV

Dirge of Jephthah's Daughter, The. Robert Herrick. ChIV-1

Dirge of O'Sullivan Bear. *Unknown.* IrV,

Dirge of St. Malo, The [tr. of Creole slave song]. George Washington Cable. APN-2

Dirge of the Three Queens. John Fletcher *and* William Shakespeare. OBEV

Dirge on the Death of Art O'Leary. Eileen O'Connell. IrV, tr. by Eleanor Hull

Dirge Without Music. Edna St. Vincent Millay. AmFaPo; BrAP; GoPo; InoFa

Dirt. StacyLynn. BtF

Dirt. Chase Twichell. PfSP

Dirt and / clean them clean them clean them. Streetcleaner's Lament, The. Patricia Hubbell. SSCS

Dirt grows up, The. Litany. Kevin Young. IIR

Dirt to Dirt. Hugh Seidman. BodElec

Dirtiest, downstream of Team, The. Grey Wagtail on the Tyne. Colin Simms. Oth

Dirty Dozens, The. Speckled Red (Rufus Perryman). FTtHH

Dirty Dreams and God Smiling. Alane Rollings. IllVoic

Dirty Floor, The. Edward Field. SUP

Dirty girl, / Thumb stump. (LL) Cut. Sylvia Plath. CAP-8; EmeKit; MoWP; NAMCP V.2

Dirty Money. Christine Hume. AmPoNex

Dirty Nylons. Na Hûidôk. EcSo, *tr. by* Peter H. Lee

Dirty sex violence of TV. Peter Reading. NeBrP *Fr.* Stet.

Dirty tears are falling. (LL) Walking Around. Pablo Neruda. RaBo; WED, *tr. by* Robert Bly

Dirty Thirties, The. Lorna Crozier. IFF

Dirty word hops in the cage of the mind like the Pondicherry vulture, The. Dirty Word, The. Karl Shapiro. PoA 2002

Dîs Aliter Visum; or, Le Byron de Nos Jours. Robert Browning. NAEL-6v2

Dis, Blaise, sommes-nous bien loin de Montmartre? Blaise Cendrars. YaTCFP *Fr.* Prose du Transsibérien et de la Petite Jeanne de France.

Dis Da Me. Philip Lewis. OWABP

Dis is gospel weathah sho'. Song of Summer. Paul Laurence Dunbar. APN-2

Dis is one recitation. Language. Marc Matthews. WaCA

Disabled. Wilfred Owen. FaBoWar; NAEL-6v2; NAEL-7v2; NAMCP V.1; NIL-7; NoAM; OBWVE; PoPoPo

Disabled Debauchee, The. John Wilmot, 2d Earl of Rochester. BASC; NAEL-6v1; NAEL-7v1; NoP-4; NoP-5; NPeEn; OBSV

Disabled garment worker, The. In the Age of Postcapitalism. Lawrence Joseph. PBCAP

Disagreeable Things. *Unknown.* EMJL, *tr. by* Edward Putzar

Disappearances, The. Vijay Seshadri. BeAl; StAl

Disappeared, The. Iwan Llwyd. BBMWP, *tr. by* Grahame Davies

Disappeared Woman V. Marjorie Agosin. TANSG, *tr. by* Cola Franzen

Disappearing Island, The. Seamus Heaney. BodElec

Disappearing Music for Face. Mieko Shiomi. WhBo

Disappointed, my will to serve the State. Planting Bamboos. Po Chü-i. CCL1, *tr. by* Arthur Waley

Disappointed Wife, The. Mehetabel Wright. LW

Disappointment [*with music*]. Mary E. Tucker. CBWP-1

Disappointment, A. Joanna Baillie. WoRP

Disappointment, The. Aphra Behn. BASC; BrAP; CABP; EMWP; EroLit; NAEL-7v1; NALW; NoP-4; NoP-5; NOSC; PEW; WaAnP

Disappointments of Childhood, The. Michael C. Blumenthal. PoA 2002

Disarmed. Elin ap Hywel. ATSWP, *tr. by* Robert Minhinnick

Disarmed with so genteel an air. Answer, The [*To Pope's* Impromptu]. Anne Finch, Countess of Winchilsea. NAEL-7v1; NALW; NoP-4; NoP-5; WaAnP

Disarticulated / arm torn out. Last Affair: Bessie's Blues Song. Michael S. Harper. ESEAA; FuFl

Disaster [*with music*]. Charles Stuart Calverley. NBLV (Disasters.) DiBP

Disaster at Sea. Edward Edwin Foot. STuOW *Fr.* Homeward-Bound Passenger Ship, The.

Disaster to Steamer Victoria at London. James McIntyre. VerBaPo

Disasterology. Jeffrey McDaniel. LaCa; NeAmPo

Disasters. Charles Stuart Calverley. *See* Disaster.

Disasters. Henry Wadsworth Longfellow. TreFP

Disasters. George Oppen. BodElec

Disasters come not singly. Disasters. Henry Wadsworth Longfellow. TreFP

Disasters numb within us, The. Life at War. Denise Levertov. CAP-8; WaAnP

Discharged Soldier, The. William Wordsworth. NPBRoP

Disciples Asleep at Gethsemane. Paul Kane. GI

Discipline. Mary Ursula Bethell. PoBW

Discipline. George Herbert. FSCP; NAEL-6v1; NAEL-7v1; NoP-4; NoP-5; OBEV; OxAEP-1

Discipline of Marriage, The. Chana Bloch. FaoP

Disciplined in the school of hard campaigning. Horace. OBWP

Disconcerting Object. J. Bernlef. TuT, *tr. by* Peter van de Kamp

Disconnections. Silvana Colonna. ItPo, *tr. by* Gayle Ridinger

Disconsolate Morning. Elizabeth Madox Roberts. APT-1

Discontent. Han Yü. CCL1, *tr. by* H. A. Giles

Discontent, The. Anne Killigrew. BASC

Discord in Childhood. D. H. Lawrence. HarvBoo; IJHIL

Discordants. Conrad Potter Aiken.
"Dead Cleopatra lies in a crystal casket." PoA 2002
"Music I heard with you was more than music." ItP; OxBoAm

Discords. Fabio Doplicher. NeIt, *tr. by* Dana Gioia

Discourse of Beasts, A. Margaret Lucas Cavendish, Duchess of Newcastle. BASC; PEW

Discourse of Melancholy, A. Margaret Lucas Cavendish, Duchess of Newcastle. NOSC

Discourse of the Good Thief, The. Nicanor Parra. GI, *tr. by* Miller Williams

Discourse on an Ornament. Hong Yunsuk. CAMKP, *tr. by* Genell Y. Poitras

Discourse on Colonialism. Aime Cesaire and Rene Depestre.
"How did you come to develop the concept of Negritude?" PFTM-1

Discourse on Method, The. Heberto Padilla. VCWP

Discourse on Peace, The. Jacques Prévert. CLPP, *tr. by* Lawrence Ferlinghetti

Discover Me [*for Pam, Rosa and Joan*]. Opal Palmer Adisa. GT

Discovered in Mid-Ocean. Stephen Spender. MoBrPo

Discoveries, Trade Names, Genitals, and Ancient Instruments. Carl Rakosi. APT-2

Discovering America Again. Lorenzo Thomas. RD

Discovering Lasseter. Conal Fitzpatrick. NOBAu

Discovery. Gu Cheng. PFTM-2; VCWP *Fr.* Bulin File, The.

Discovery. Brian Henry. AmPoNex

Discovery. Víctor Hernández Cruz. PueRic

Discovery. Hilda Schiff. HP

Discovery. Zhao Zhenkai. VCWP, *tr. by* Chen Maiping and Bonnie S. McDougall

Discovery, The. Gwendolyn MacEwen. BrAP

Discovery of America, The. James Logie Robertson. NePenScot

Discovery of the New World. Carter Revard. SoSe-8

Discovery of the Pacific, The. Thom Gunn. HeIP-4

Discovery of Thought, A. Wallace Stevens. APT-1

Discredit. Sianne Ngai. OnScMo

Discredited for some time to come. (LL) War Has Been Given a Bad Name. Bertolt Brecht. BeAl; HP; PoAgWa; PoSu, *tr. by* John Willett

Discreet Prayer, A. Dionisio D. Martinez. TouFir

Discrimination. *Unknown.* NAAPv.2

Discrimination angulaire, Une. Localité. Claude Royet-Journoud. YaTCFP

Disdain Punished. John Dryden. NOSC *Fr.* Theodore and Honoria, From [*Fables Ancient and Modern from*] Boccace.

Disdain Returned. Thomas Carew. BASC; CavPo

Disdained Apparitions. René Char. AF, *tr. by* Paul Mann

Disdirected, The. Louis Reyes Rivera. BRtP

Disease has attacked, A. Pecos Bill in Decline. Stephen Harrigan. TiP2

Disease That Arrives at Death. No Hyegyông. EcSo, *tr. by* Ann Y. Choi

Disease with floating moustaches, The. Lovely Monster. Joyce Mansour. SurWo, *tr. by* Guy Flandre and Peter Wood

Disembodied Voices of Women, The. Craig Arnold. NAPBL

Disentangling our lives. X-Ray, The. Andrew Elliott. PNI

Disfigure me, Lord. Take pity on me. Antipsalm. Novica Tadic. VCWP, *tr. by* Charles Simic

Disfortune. Joe Wenderoth. AmPoNex

Disgraced and mortal. (LL) Wellfleet Whale, The. Stanley Kunitz. CAP-8; NoAM

Disguised. Martha Rhodes. UrbNat

Disguised as a mutant. Stage and Screen, 1989. Carol Muske-Dukes. BodElec

Disguises. Thomas Edward Brown. SacPr

Disguises, The. Patricia K. Page. PoCho

Disgusted with crimes that are piffling and messy. Crime at Its Best. Stoddard King. NBLV

Dish for a Poet, A. *Unknown.* OBCP

Dishes all want to break, The. Note from a Loving Wife. Mariahadessa Ekere Tallie. RaF

Dishes, The. Josée Lapeyrère. SCFWP, *tr. by* Serge Gavronsky
"Faucet the benefactor, The." SCFWP, *tr. by* Serge Gavronsky
"Fleeing bracelets." SCFWP, *tr. by* Serge Gavronsky

Dish-eyed in the basement. Wood Stove Sunday. Tammy Armstrong. Coast

Dishonest Mailmen, The. Robert Creeley. OxBoAm

Dishwater. Ted Kooser. WaAnP

Disillusion for Rubén Darío. Nancy Morejón. TCLAP, *tr. by* Kathleen Weaver

Disillusionment [*with music*]. Virginia Graham. NBLV

Disillusionment, did you slip from my body and return with wine? One at Rest, The. Hô Sugyông. EcSo, *tr. by* Youngju Ryu

Disillusionment of Ten O'Clock. Wallace Stevens. APT-1; ItP; NAAPv.2; NAMCP V.1; NoAM; OxBoAm; SAmP; SoSe-8; TCAPo; TRP

Disintegrate Me. Denise Riley. Oth *Fr.* Seven Strangely Exciting Lies.

Disintegrated angel on these hills. (LL) Alloy. Muriel Rukeyser. NAMCP V.2; NoAM

Disinterred Warrior, The. William Cullen Bryant. AmWaPo

Disjecta Membra. Charles Wright. BAP-97

Dislocated by a bureaucratic operation—the census—the Virgin and the. Christmas 1961. Murilo Mendes. Eno, *tr.* by Chris Daniels

Disloyal Lines to an Alumnus. Edmund Wilson. OBCoV

Dismantled Ship, The. Walt Whitman. TCAPo

Dismantling the Silence. Charles Simic. WaAnP

Dismissal of the Koyemshi. *Zuni Oral Tradition.* NAWM-7v2 *Fr.* Shalako.

Dismissed as plink plonk. I can't repeat. Webern. Christopher Pilling. NLP

Dismount and drink this wine. To See a Friend Off. Wang Wei. CCL1; ChinPo, *tr.* by Ye Weilian [*or* Yeh Wei-lien *or* Wai-lim Yip]

Dismounted, o'er wine we had said our last say. Goodbye to Meng Haoran. Wang Wei. CCL1, *tr.* by H. A. Giles

Dismounting I give you wine to drink. Farewell. Wang Wei. CCL1, *tr.* by Pauline Yu

Disney didn't tell you. Pocahontas. Ed Ochester. SUP

Disney's Cinderella. Tennessee Reed. FTtHH

Disobedience. Alan Alexander Milne. NOxBChV; NTCP; TLR; UV

Disorder, The. Marilyn Chin. LoL

Disorder and Frailty. Henry Vaughan. ChIV-1

Disown. Rae Armantrout. FTOS

Dispensary, The. Sir Samuel Garth. OBSV

Dispersal of It. Anne Waldman. AHA

Dispersed and prepared to land in the city. (LL) Watching for Dolphins. David Constantine. HarvBoo; StAl

Displaced Person. Christopher Davis. RWB

Display of Mackerel, A. Mark Doty. AmAlph

Display thy breasts, my Julia, there let me. Upon Julia's Breasts. Robert Herrick. NoP-4; NoP-5; WaAnP

Dispossess me of belief. This Black Rich Country. A. R. Ammons. LPSFW

Dispossessed words. Karen Press. TSAP

Disproportionate. Timothy Geiger. AmPoNex

Dispute of the Heart and Body of François Villon, The. François Villon. OBVE, *tr.* by Algernon Charles Swinburne

Disquiet issues from the clouds—omens for us all—and at night. Miracle. Nikolai Kanchev. CSCBP, *tr.* by Georgi Belev and Lisa Sapinkopf

Disquieting muses again, The: what are "leftovers?". Business Personals. John Ashbery. BodElec

Disquieting Muses, The. Sylvia Plath. NALW; NAMCP V.2

Disregard [*with music*]. Ai. NoAM

Disregarding the curse. Arch of Titus. Barry Goldensohn. PoA 2002

Dissatisfaction invites me nowhere. Hangover. Arthur Nortje. TSAP

Dissecting Uncle Sorrow. Rick Alley. AmPoNex

Disseminating their / Circumference. (LL) Poets light but Lamps, The. Emily Dickinson. APN-2; HeIP-4; TCAPo

Dissert, A. Margaret Lucas Cavendish, Duchess of Newcastle. PEW From "Nature's Dessert." STuOW

Dissidence. Anthony Walton. NAPBL; RD

Dissidents, The. Catherine Obianuju Acholonu. HAWP

Dissimulation's inside. Vigil. Jocelyn Emerson. IAoNAP

Dissolve. Rita Dove. PfSP

Dissolving Presence, A. Sándor Weöres. IQMS, *tr.* by Adam Makkai and Donald E. Morse

Dissonance. Amy Lowell. APT-1; NAAPv.2

Dissonance Royal Traveller. Barbara Guest. NYP2

Dissonances. Giusi Busceti. ItPo, *tr.* by Gayle Ridinger

Disswasion hearing her assigne my helpe. Rachel Speght. PBRV *Fr.* Dream[e], The [*or* A].

Distánciamela, Espejo. Pedro Salinas. RaW

Distaff Side, The. Harry Clifton. PBCIP

Distance. Adisa Vera Beatty. FuFl

Distance. N. Revathi Devi. HotL, *tr.* by V. Narayana Rao

Distance. Peter Everwine. GeoHom; PoCho

Distance. Helen Hunt Jackson. SWaP

Distance. Luciana Notari. CItWP, *tr.* by Cinzia Sartini Blum and Lara Trubowitz

Distance. Eugene B. Redmond. SeSe

Distance. Mary Jo Salter. ExTi

Distance. David Wojahn. YaYoPo

Distance. Andrea Zanzotto. VCWP

Distance and a Certain Light. May Swenson. APT-2

Distance / and a certain light. Distance and a Certain Light. May Swenson. APT-2

Distance between Bodies, The [*with music*]. Bill Manhire. HarvBoo

Distance Between Zero and One, The. David Keplinger. AmPoNex

Distance de l'automne. Jacques Réda. YaTCFP

Distance from Loved Ones. James Tate. MotU; OxBoAm

Distance is at bay, and emptiness has gone. Peaceable Kingdom. Barbara Leslie Jordan. ExTi

Distance is money just out of reach. Homeric Interim. Reginald Shepherd. RD

Distance laid its static on us as mothers. On Nursing. Jenny Factor. PoChi

Distance Learning. Geoff Ward. VaPo

DISTANCE, OVERTURE. "Theatre." Anne-Marie Albiach. MFP, *tr.* by Martin Sorrell

Distance that lies from here, The. Space Song. Alfonso Cortes. TCLAP, *tr.* by Thomas Merton

Distances. Eavan Boland. HarvBoo

Distances. Otto René Castillo. AF, *tr.* by Margaret Randall

Distances. Katherine Gallagher. Prnts

Distances. Philippe Jaccottet. StAl; VCWP, *tr.* by Derek Mahon

Distances, The. Henry Rago. IllVoic

Distant, The. Yannis Ritsos. VCWP, *tr.* by Edmund Keeley

Distant clouds, trees deep into mist. Unsent. Tu Mu. NDACCP, *tr.* by David Hinton

Distant dove flutters, A. Distant Dove. Judah Ha-Levi. WoPoe, *tr.* by Gabriel Levin

Distant Drum, The. Calvin C. Hernton. GT

Distant Footsteps, The. César Vallejo. RaBo, *tr.* by James Wright and John Knoepfle

Distant Fury of Battle, The. Geoffrey Hill. FaBoWar; NoP-4; NoP-5; WaAnP

Distant Howling. Miroslav Holub. StAl, *tr.* by Ewald Osers

Distant mountains, The. Issa. SoOfWa, *tr.* by Sam Hamill

Distant Runners, The. Mark Van Doren. MoAmPo

Distant sea, memory. Thirst for the Sea. Magda Portal. TANSG, *tr.* by Shaun Griffin and Emma Sepúlveda-Pulvirenti

Distant View from a Grass Hill. Gensei. WoPoe, *tr.* by Burton Watson

Distinct Call of the Alligator, The. Betsy Sholl. PBCAP

Distinction. Paul Laurence Dunbar. SacPr

Distinction was never yours. Before That. Michael Blackburn. BeAl

Distinguish carefully between these two. Justice of the Peace, The. Joseph Hilaire Pierre Belloc. OBSV

Distinguished the belt feed lever from the belt holding pawl. (LL) Fury of Aerial Bombardment, The. Richard Eberhart. AmWaPo; APT-2; BrAP; HeIP-4; InoFa; NAAPv.2; NAMCP V.1; NIL-7; NIP-4; NoAM; NoP-4; NoP-5; OBWP; OtW; PoAgWa; PoWW; PWW2; WaAnP

Distinguishes the fair and the shameful. Simonides. SaLy, *tr.* by Diane Rayor

Distorted Sun. Akira Togawa. NAAPv.2

Distracted daughters, disoriented sons. Grandma. Thandiwe Shiphrah. BtF

Distracted Puritan, The. Richard Corbet. BASC; OBCoV

Distracted with care. Despairing Lover, The. William Walsh. NBLV

Distressed: single cane, I return. *Unknown.* ChinPo, *tr.* by Ye Weilian [*or* Yeh Wei-lien *or* Wai-lim Yip]

Distribution of Poetry. Jorge de Lima. PFTM-1

Disturbed by the chatter. Neighbour's Pear Tree. Tony Curtis. AngWePo

Disturbing the Sallies Forth [*with music*]. Clark Coolidge. FTOS

Disturbs me like a requiem. (LL) Old Tongue, The. Herbert Williams. AngWePo; TCAWP

Disused Shed in Co. Wexford, A. Derek Mahon. CABP; EmeKit; ModIr; NAMCP V.2; NoP-4; NoP-5; NPeEn; PBCIP; PNI; StAl

Ditch, The. Lee Upton. IaFF

Ditches. Karen Kipp. BodElec

Ditchley Portrait, The. Allen Fisher. Oth *Fr.* Emergent Manner.

Dittie to the Same Subject, A. Dame Gertrude More. EMWP

Ditties Lamentation for the cruelty of this age. *Unknown.* BASC

Ditty, A: In Praise of Eliza, Queen of the Shepherds. Edmund Spenser. OBEV *Fr.* Shepherd's Calender, The.

Ditty: "If you refuse me once, and think again." Edward Herbert, 1st Baron Herbert of Cherbury. NOSC

Ditty: "Why dost thou hate return instead of love." Edward Herbert, 1st Baron Herbert of Cherbury. NOSC

Dīvāni Shamsi Tabrīz. Jelaluddin Rumi. "Man of God is drunken without wine, The." TAL

Dive. Langston Hughes. APT-2

Dive, The. Mimi Goese. HeMarv

Dive could come who was its fledgling first, The. Nijinsky. Parker Tyler. PoA 2002

Dive from 45,000 Feet. Enid Shomer. OtW *Fr.* World Goes Black, The.

Divels, there many be, and Gods but one. (LL) Fulke Greville, 1st Baron Brooke. NOSC; NoSic; SacPr *Fr.* Caelica.

Diver does not abandon, A. Ono no Komachi. WoPoe, *tr.* by Mariko Aratani and Jane Hirshfield

Diver for the NYPD Talks to His Girlfriend, A. Richard Garcia. TouFir; UrbNat

Diver, The. Robert Earl Hayden. MoASP

Diver, The. Felicia Dorothea Hemans. TreFP

Diver, The. Christopher Merrill. MoASP

Diver-Bird. Mike Jenkins. TCAWP

Diverne stands in the kitchen as they dance. Diverne's Waltz. Marilyn Nelson Waniek. FFC

Diverne wanted to die, that August night. Chosen. Marilyn Nelson Waniek. FFC; ExTi

Diverne's Waltz. Marilyn Nelson Waniek. FFC

Divers, The. Peter Quennell. MoBrPo

Divers Doth Use. Sir Thomas Wyatt. NAEL-6v1; NAEL-7v1

Divers[e] [or Dyvers] doth[e] use, as I have heard and kno[w]. Sir Thomas Wyatt. OxBEV

Diverse strangers flower and diverge. Crossing Disappearing behind Them. Marjorie Welish. PmAP

Diverting History of John Gilpin, The. William Cowper. OBNV

Dives, when you and I go down to Hell. To Dives. Joseph Hilaire Pierre Belloc. ChIV-2; OBSV

Divested of his testicles and eyes? (LL) Death the Painter. Anthony Hecht. NoP-4; NoP-5

Divestment of Beauty. Laura Riding Jackson. APT-2; HarvBoo

Divide your bread in two. Heavenly Jerusalem, Jerusalem of the Earth. Leah Goldberg. FIT, tr. by Robert Friend

Divided. Jean Ingelow. VWP

"Dappled sky, a world of meadows, A." PEW

Divided by the Han River. Yu Xuanji. CCL1, tr. by Genevieve Wimsatt

Divided Child, The. Derek Walcott.

"Ajax, / lion-coloured stallion from Sealey's stable." PoetW

Divides forever. One. John Roberts. ASA

Dividing for a monarch entering his city. (LL) Derek Walcott. NAEL-7v2; NoP-4 Fr. Omeros.

Dividing time equally between earths, there in the coldness. Circadian. Joanna Klink. IAoNAP

Divina Commedia. Henry Wadsworth Longfellow. APN-1; BrAP; TCAPo

Divina Commedia. Dante Alighieri. tr. by Henry Cary, Alistair Elliot, Seamus Heaney, Susan Mitchell, Armand Schwerner and Arturo Vivante

Inferno: Canto 1. NAWM-5v1, tr. by John Ciardi

"And now we walked along the solid mire." OBVE

"And so from bridge to bridge we went, talking." WoPoe, tr. by Susan Mitchell

"Middle of life's journey; I, The." STV

"Through me come into the city full of pain." WoPoe, tr. by Armand Schwerner

Ugolino. OxBEV, tr. by Seamus Heaney

Paradiso.

"Glory of Him who moves all things rays forth, The." NAWM-5v1

"That sun that breathed love's fire into my youth." NAWM-5v1

"Then, in the form of a white rose, the host." NAWM-5v1

Purgatorio.

"As the day stands when the Sun begins to glow." NAWM-5v1

"At the hour when the heat of the day is overcome." NAWM-5v1

"Earnest to explore within and all around." OBVE

"For better waters now the little bark." NAWM-5v1

"When the Septentrion of the First Heaven." NAWM-5v1

Divine Comedy, The. Dante Alighieri. tr. by Allen Mandelbaum

Inferno. NAWM-7v1, tr. by Allen Mandelbaum

Paradiso. tr. by Allen Mandelbaum

"Virgin Mary, daughter of your Son." NAWM-7v1, tr. by Allen Mandelbaum

Purgatorio. tr. by Allen Mandelbaum

"And now, with the reflected lights that glow." NAWM-7v1, tr. by Allen Mandelbaum

"But tell me if the man whom I see here." NAWM-7v1, tr. by Allen Mandelbaum

"But with regard to me, I'll satisfy." NAWM-7v1, tr. by Allen Mandelbaum

"I have at times seen all the eastern sky." NAWM-7v1, tr. by Allen Mandelbaum

"Natural thirst that never can be quenched." NAWM-7v1, tr. by Allen Mandelbaum

"To course across more kindly waters now." NAWM-7v1, tr. by Allen Mandelbaum

Divine destroyer, pity me no more. Richard Lovelace. CavPo

Divine Fancies. Francis Quarles.

"Booke of Common Pray'r excels the rest, The." PBRV

"I saw him dead; I saw his Body fall." PBRV

"I wish a greater knowledge, then t'attaine." PBRV

Divine Image, The. William Blake. BBASP; ChAP; InvLi; NAEL-6v2; NAEL-7v2; NOBRP; NoP-4; NoP-5; NPBRoP; OxBEV; WaAnP Fr. Songs of Innocence.

Divine Meditations. William Alabaster.

(Ego Sum Vitis.) OxBEV

Divine Meditations. John Donne. Fr. Holy Sonnets.

Divine Mission, A. George Eveleigh. STuOW Fr. Science Revealed.

Divine Mistress, A. Thomas Carew. CavPo

Divine mystery. Sogetsuni. SoOfWa, tr. by Sam Hamill

Divine Oracles, tell me when. In Acknowledgment of the Praises of European Writers. Sor Juana Inés de la Cruz. SpanPo, tr. by Constance Urdang

Divine Presence, The. Adelaide Anne Procter. SacPr

Divine Rapture, A. Francis Quarles. OBEV

Divine Revenge [epigram]. Friedrich von Logau. GePo, tr. by George C. Schoolfield

Divine sea rocks its, The. Rocking. Gabriela Mistral. TANSG, tr. by Maria Giachetti [or Jacketti] and Maria Jacketti

Divine Sonnet, A. William Alabaster. NoSic

Divine Thalia strike th' Harmonious Lute. On the Soft and Gentle Motions of Eudora. Anne Killigrew. PoBW

Divine, to the Divinitiy. (LL) Dark Angel, The. Lionel Pigot Johnson. MoBrPo; OBMV; OxAEP-2

Divine Weeks and Works, The. Guillaume de Salluste Du Bartas. tr. by Joshua Sylvester

"Eden," The First Part of the First Day of the Second Week. tr. by Joshua Sylvester

"Adam, quoth He, the beauties manifold." InvLi, tr. by Joshua Sylvester

Fourth Day of the First Week, The. tr. by Joshua Sylvester

Zodiac, The. NOSC, tr. by Joshua Sylvester

Tower of Babel, The. NoSic, tr. by Joshua Sylvester

Divine Will. Michael Waters. Vesp

Divine Wooer, The. Phineas Fletcher. SacPr

Divinely Superfluous Beauty. Robinson Jeffers. HeIP-4; MoAmPo

Diving. Charlotte Brontë. PEW

Diving into the Wreck. Adrienne Rich. CAP-8; ColAP; EmeKit; HarvBoo; HeIP-4; MakPoe; MoWP; NAAL-5; NALW; NAMCP V.2; NIL-7; NIP-4; NoAM; NoP-4; NoP-5; OxBoAm; OxWW; PoPoPo; StAl; TWF; WaAnP

Diving over the vibrating floor. Closed Discussion about the Future. Tim Griffin. FreRad

Divinity. George Herbert. NOSC

Division. Michael Chitwood. PoDa

Division of Labor. Feyyaz Kayacan. WoPoe, tr. by Feyyaz Fergar

Division of O'Dowd, The. Alan Wearne. BMAP Fr. Nightmarkets, The.

Divorce. Joel Brouwer. LegDan

Divorce. Anna Wickham. MoBrPo; NALW

Divorce, The. Hans Magnus Enzensberger. WoPoe, tr. by Herbert Graf

Divorce and Mr. Circe. David Gewanter. NAPBL

Divorce 19th-century Style. Colette Ni Ghallchóir. NIrP, tr. by the author

Divorce Referendum, Ireland, 1986, The. Paul Durcan. PBCIP

Divorce Referendum, The. Sarah Maguire. MFPA

Divorced. Don Share. OPRER

Divorced, but friends again at last. Onion, Memory, The. Craig Raine. NAEL-6v2; NAEL-7v2; NAMCP V.2; NoAM; NoP-4; NoP-5

Divorced woman, The. EMJL, tr. by Haruo Shirane

Divorcee. C. Webster Wheelock. SoSe-8

Divorcing. Denise Levertov. NALW

Dixie [or Dixie's Land]. Daniel Decatur Emmett. APN-1; CBCWP; TCAPo; FaBoA

Dixit Insipiens. Carolyn Kizer. Vesp

DIY. Grahame Davies. BBMWP, tr. by the author

Dizains, Les. Maurice Scève. WoPoe, tr. by Phillip Lopate

Dizzy Girls in the Sixties. Gary Soto. ReTh

Djanbun's the platypus. He was a man one time. Platypus, The. Aborigine Oral Tradition. NOBAu

Djeni. Seitlhamo Motsapi. TSAP

Djinns, The. Victor Hugo. SxFrPo, tr. by A. M. and E. H. Blackmore

Do all condole my woe. (LL) Anne, Duchess of Arundel Howard. NOSC; WaAnP Fr. Good Shepherd's Sorrow for the Death of His Beloved Son, The.

Do all who lie down expect to awake? Resurrection of the Body, The. Eric Pankey. PoA 2002

Do but consider this small dust. Hour-Glass, The. Ben Jonson. NIP-4

Do chóireoinn leaba duit. Leaba Shíoda. Nuala Ni Dhomhnaill. CABP

Do, Do, Do. Ira Gershwin. ReLy

Do I begin at the here and now. From Rosary. Barbara Tran. PuP-23

Do I ever ask myself why I live here? I'm Rooted. René Philoctete. OGAHCP, *tr. by* Boadiba and Jack Hirschman

Do I hold the past in my hands. Olga Ivanova. CRWP, *tr. by* Jenefer Coates

Do I look angry? He screamed. I Have to Go Now. Maggie Estep. HeMarv

Do I need to (need to). Of Deaths, Days, Futures, Nations. Jen Hofer. Eno

Do I remember Punch?—Listen—I'll tell you. Punch, the Immortal Liar. Conrad Potter Aiken.

"Do I see a hat in the road?" I said. Old Sussex Road, The. Ian Serraillier. NTCP

Do I seem as cheerful. You Make Me Feel So Young. Mack Gordon. ReLy

Do I still desire virginity? Sappho. SaLy, *tr. by* Diane Rayor

Do I still like to think. November 19. David Lehman. PoDa

Do I think of you often, my husband wants to know. In the Spring of No Letters. Marlene Cookshaw. IFF

Do It Again. B. G. DeSylva. ReLy

Do It Yourself. Joan Aiken. NOxBChV

Do leän down low in Linden Lea. (LL) My Orcha'd in Lindèn Lea. William Barnes. FaBoVe; NPeEn; OxBEV

Do limits build. By Halves. Bill Berkson. NYP2

Do make thee blush at any time / Blame not my lute. (LL) Blame Not My Lute. Sir Thomas Wyatt. NAEL-7v1; NoP-5

Do men suppose, when God's free-giving hand. George Wither. NOSC *Fr.* Collection of Emblemes, Ancient and Moderne, A.

Do nettles mar the month of May. Nettles in May. Euros Bowen. BBMWP; OBWVE, *tr. by* the author and Joseph P. Clancy

Do nettles mutilate May. Nettles in May. Euros Bowen. BBMWP, *tr. by* Joseph P. Clancy

Do not. Hayyim Nahman Bialik. FIT, *tr. by* Robert Friend

Do not ask me, dear friend, how I spent my leisure. Unfinished Letter to My Lady. Dániel Berzsenyi. IQMS, *tr. by* Peter Zollman

Do not bathe her in blood. Abortion, An. Frank O'Hara. AHA

Do Not Be Afraid of No. Gwendolyn Brooks. ColAP; PtR *Fr.* Notes from the Childhood and the Girlhood.

Do not be always looking on the fire. Indian Counsel. Edwin Ford Piper. APT-1

Do not be angry if I tell you. Sofa, The. Medbh McGuckian. PBCIP; PNI

Do not be offended because. Excuse for Not Returning the Visit of a Friend, An. Mei Yao Ch'en. NDACCP, *tr. by* Kenneth Rexroth

Do not beguile my heart. Complaining. George Herbert. ChIV-1

Do not boast of your speed. Hwang Chini. CATKP, *tr. by* Peter H. Lee

Do not call me with many words. Do not call me with desperate vows. First Smile. Nathan Alterman. FIT, *tr. by* Robert Friend

Do not crouch to-day and worship. Present, The. Adelaide Anne Procter. TreFP

Do not crush me in your arms. *Unknown.* SLW, *tr. by* Marjolijn De Jager, Sayd Bahodin Majrouh and André Velter

Do not despair. For Johnny. John Pudney. OBWP

Do not enforce the tired wolf. John Crowe Ransom. MoAmPo *Fr.* Sixteen Poems in Eight Pairings.

Do not ensnarl me in a sphere of nouns. Love Is Not a Word. Eugene B. Redmond. FTtHH

Do Not Expect Again a Phoenix Hour. Cecil Day Lewis. MoBrPo; NoAM

Do not fear to put thy feet. John Fletcher. NOSC *Fr.* Faithful Shepherdess, The.

Do not fill postcards with memories. Face Lost in the Wilderness. Fadwa Tuqan. AF, *tr. by* Naomi Shihab Nye

Do not forget that you live in the midst of the animals. Only if Love Should Pierce You. Salvatore Quasimodo. StAl, *tr. by* Jack Bevan

Do Not Get Up. Ishikawa Takuboku. CAoMJL1, *tr. by* Leith Morton

Do Not Go Gentle into That Good Night. Dylan Thomas. AmFaPo; BrAP; CABP; ChAP; ClHu; CtM; EMP; HarvBoo; HeIP-4; InoFa; ITBLP; MakPoe; MoBrPo; NAEL-6v2; NAEL-7v2; NAMCP V.2; NIL-7; NIP-4; NoAM; NoP-4; NoP-5; NPeEn; OxAEP-2; PoPoPo; SoSe-8; StAl; TCAWP; TFi; TRP; UV; WaAnP; WeW-3

Do Not Go Sober. Roger Woddis. UV

Do not go sober into that dim light. Do Not Go Sober. Roger Woddis. UV

Do not grieve, little birds. Song Sun. CATKP, *tr. by* Peter H. Lee

Do Not Have Pity. Aimé Césaire. NAWM-7v2, *tr. by* Gregson Davis

Do not hold me too closely in your arms. *Unknown.* SLW, *tr. by* Marjolijn De Jager, Sayd Bahodin Majrouh and André Velter

Do not imagine that Jack and Rose apart. Jack's Letter. John Crowe Ransom. BrAP

Do not imagine that the exploration. Discovery, The. Gwendolyn MacEwen. BrAP

Do not jeer at the child, when with a whip and spur. To the German People. Friedrich Hölderlin. WoPoe, *tr. by* Robert Bly

Do not laugh at my tower. Warm Invitation, A. Yüan Chiu-ts'ai. WoPoe, *tr. by* Henry Hart

Do not let any woman read this verse! Deirdre. James Stephens. OBMV

Do not let your blood. Kim Namjo. CAMKP *Fr.* Love's Cursive.

Do not look at me. *Unknown.* ArkPo, *tr. by* Edwin A. Cranston

Do not look for him. Elegy. Leonard Cohen. BrAP; HeIP-4

Do not lose sight. You Who Occupy Our Land. Maria Manuela Margarido. HAWP, *tr. by* Allan Francovich

Do Not Make Things Too Easy. Martha Baird. LW

Do not pluck me. Do Not Pluck Me. *Unknown.* CCL1, *tr. by* Marsha Wagner

Do not ponder too much. Do Not Ponder Too Much. Stefan George. WoPoe, *tr. by* Stanley Burnshaw

Do not press my hands. Intimate. Gabriela Mistral. SpanPo, *tr. by* Kate Flores

Do Not Put Dead Monkeys in the Freezer. Martín Espada. TouFir

Do not say "Godspeed" to me, wicked heart. Callimachus. HePo, *tr. by* Barbara Hughes Fowler

Do not seek too much fame. Old Song. *Unknown.* RaBo

Do Not Speak Keresan to a Mescalero Apache. Arthur Sze. TAPaP

Do not speak to us of dreams, speak to us of autumn in. Gardens of Ravished Psyche, The. George Barker. OBGa

Do Not Stop Me! Angela Miri. NAfrP

Do not stop me! / I burn. Do Not Stop Me! Angela Miri. NAfrP

Do not think anything alien to mankind which may befall one. Certaine verses written by the said ladie Jane with a pinne. Lady Jane Grey Dudley. EMWP

Do not think I am not grateful for your small. Gratitude. Louise Glück. OxBoAm; TRP

Do Not Throw Away. Lin Huiyin. CFP, *tr. by* Michelle Yeh

Do not torment me, woman. Reconciliation. Brendan Kenneally. IrLP

Do not trust in these deceptive words. Sydney Lea. Vesp

Do not try so hard. Lesson. Barbara Winder. MiVo

Do not weep, maiden, for war is kind. War Is Kind. Stephen Crane. AmWaPo; APN-2; FaBoWar; NAAPv.1; NoP-4; NoP-5; OBWP; RaBo; TCAPo; WaAnP

Do People moulder equally. Emily Dickinson. ChIV-2

Do Sink. George Bowering. NLPA

Do sit down, Metro. Get up and set. Friends in Private. Herodas. HePo, *tr. by* Barbara Hughes Fowler

Do Skyscrapers ever grow tired. Skyscrapers. Rachel Lyman Field. ChAP; NOxBChV; SSCS

Do. Start. 527. Hwang Jiwoo. CAMKP, *tr. by* Young-Jun Lee and Scott Swaner

Do the Baby Cake-Walk. Clyde Watson. NTCP

Do the Dead Know What Time It Is? Kenneth Patchen. MoAmPo

Do the Others Speak of Me Mockingly, Maliciously? Delmore Schwartz. APT-2; ChIV-1

Do the people. Poem for Teacup Mantlepiece Poets Palpitating Poot Booty Plagiarists Imprisoned in Ivy League White Supremacist Mental Biological Warfare Labs. Tony Medina. InTrad

Do these gnarled and twisted trees. Hardwood. Linda Pastan. PfSP

Do they call Virtue [*or* Vertue] there ungratefulness[e]? (LL) Sir Philip Sidney. AEP; CABP; GSo; HeIP-4; NAEL-6v1; NAEL-7v1; NoP-4; NoP-5; NoSic; NPeEn; OxAEP-1; OxBEV; OxBSo; TFi; TRP; WaAnP *Fr.* Astrophil and Stella.

Do they let you still keep your crutches when. Crux. Bill Knott. PoCho

Do they whisper behind my back? Do they speak. Do the Others Speak of Me Mockingly, Maliciously? Delmore Schwartz. APT-2; ChIV-1

Do things then happen. Melting Milk. Bill Berkson. PmAP

Do This Favour For Me. Luis de Camões [*or* Camões *or* Camoëns]. WoPoe, *tr. by* Roy Campbell

Do this piece with a portrait of your dearest one. Portrait Piece. Mieko Shiomi. WhBo

Do this with. Five Senses. Denise Clegg. ICANM

Do We Not Hear Thy Footfall? Amy Carmichael. SacPr

Do we reach the sea with clocks. Deaf and Blind, The. Paul Éluard. WoPoe, *tr. by* Paul Auster

Do we see in what we see. In the Stealth of Stillness. Thurayya Al-Urayyid. PoArWo, *tr. by* Farouk Mustafa

Do what we can, summer will have its flies. True and Obscure Definitions of Fly, Domestic and Otherwise. Christine Hume. IAoNAP

Do what you are going to do, and I will tell about it. (LL) I Go Back to May 1937. Sharon Olds. BLT; EmeKit; FaoP; GoPo; LoL; MoWP; NIL-7; WaAnP

Do What You Can. Lawrence Joseph. PBCAP

Do what you can. (LL) On Angels. Czeslaw Milosz. AF; BBASP; WaAnP, *tr. by* the author

Do what you come for, captain, with your news. To Captain Hungry. Ben Jonson. FaBoWar

Do with me, God! as Thou didst deal with John. To God. Robert Herrick. ChIV-2

Do, writing books, she also said that he smiles a lot and kinda got good teeth. (LL) Poet: What Ever Happened to Luther? Haki R. Madhubuti. SpirFl; UnSA

Do ye hear the children weeping, O my brothers. Cry of the Children, The. Elizabeth Barrett Browning. NAEL-7v2; OxAEP-2; ViWPN; VWP

Do ye, o congregation. Psalm 58. Bible, *O.T.* NoP-4; NoP-5, *tr. by Unknown*

Do ye quail but to hear, Carolinians. Ode. William Gilmore Simms. PCW

Do you ask what the birds say? The sparrow, the dove. Answer to a Child's Question. Samuel Taylor Coleridge. ITBLP; NOxBChV; NPBRoP

Do you been or did you never? Ha! Red-Headed Intern, Taking Notes. Ramon Guthrie. APT-2

Do you believe in a God. Ordinary God. Donald Davie. InvLi

Do you believe in charms and spells. It Could Happen to You. Johnny Burke. ReLy

Do you believe that I am like the autumn wind. Alfred de Musset. WoPoe *Fr.* Night in May, A.

Do you blame me that I loved him? Double Standard, A. Frances Ellen Watkins Harper. NAAPv.1

Do you care to remedy the faces of the gods? Make white. Eduardo Milán. RMCMP, *tr. by* Roberto Tejada

Do you carrot all for me? Do you carrot all for me? *Unknown.* ChAP

Do you envy, my comrades-in-arms. Viktor Aleksandrovich Sosnora. TCRusP, *tr. by* Daniel Weissbort

Do You Fear the Wind? Hamlin Garland. ITBLP

Do you give yourself to me utterly. Sleep. Kenneth Slessor. BMAP

Do you have any scissors I could borrow? *No, I'm sorry I don't.* No Sorry. Catherine Bowman. BAP-97; RaF; SUP

Do you have hope for the future? Thanks, Robert Frost. David Ray. VisFro

Do you have the Poems of Han-shan in your house? Tahoe Nocturne. Sherod Santos. GeoHom

Do You Hear How They Beg for Realities? Pedro Salinas. RaW, *tr. by* W. S. Merwin

Do you know a dark man? My Exorcist Mother. Patricia Adelman. Prnts

Do you know a land. Such a Land. Sŏ Chŏngju. CAMKP, *tr. by* David R. McCann

Do you know, Daphne, of this old romance. To J—Y Colonna. Gérard de Nerval. WoPoe, *tr. by* Richard Sieburth

Do you know the old man who. Wild Flower Man, The. Lu Yu. NDACCP, *tr. by* Kenneth Rexroth

Do you know the story of Hamelin Town? Rat Trap. Mick Gowar. NOxBChV

Do you know what happened in August here? Anna Deavere Smith. OxWW *Fr.* Fires in the Mirror.

Do you know what is bad? Bad and Good. Alexander Resnikoff. NTCP

Do you know what was waiting beyond those steps of the harp calling you from another time, other days? Sonata. Alvaro Mutis. TCLAP, *tr. by* Sophie Cabot Black and Maria Negroni

Do you know why the old woman sings? Why the Old Woman Limps. Lupenga Mphande. HBAPE

Do you know you have asked for the costliest thing. Woman's Question, A. Lena Lathrop. ITBLP

Do you live in North London? Is it you? (LL) Lonely Hearts. Wendy Cope. OBCoV; WaAnP

Do you love her? Inquisition. Gloria Wade-Gayles. ISC

Do you love me? Do you love me? Question and Answer. Alasdair Maclean. EdScPo

Do you make me notice you! (LL) Reminder, The. Thomas Hardy. ChAP; OBCP

Do you more than we? (LL) "Is It Nothing to You?" May Probyn. OBEV; SacPr

Do you need an explanation. Russian God, The. Petr Andreevich Vyazemsky. WoPoe, *tr. by* Alan Myers

"Do you not find something very strange about him?" Assassination, The. Robert Silliman Hillyer. MoAmPo

Do you not hear the sighing of a willow in Japan. In Japan Beyond. Yonejiro (Yone) Noguchi. NAAPv.2

Do You Not Know that I Need to Touch You. Frances Horovitz. LW

Do You Not Love Me. Sergey Aleksandrovich Yesenin. RusPo, *tr. by* Robert Arthur Douglas Ford

Do you not love me, do you not pity me. Do You Not Love Me. Sergey Aleksandrovich Yesenin. RusPo, *tr. by* Robert Arthur Douglas Ford

Do you not see that we pitched our tent on the banks of night. Female. Muhammad Al-Ghuzzi. NAfrP, *tr. by* John Heath-Stubbs and May Jayyusi

Do you not see the riverside grass. Pao Chao. ChinPo *Fr.* Weary Road, The.

Do you not see the young men off to war. Pao Chao. ChinPo *Fr.* Weary Road, The.

Do you recall the fancies of many years ago. To My Brother. Letitia Elizabeth Landon. NPBRoP

Do you remember 1926? That summer of soups and speeches. Idris Davies. RSaN *Fr.* Gwalia Deserta.

Do you remember all the sunny places. Recollections. Caroline Elizabeth Norton. NPBRoP

Do you remember an Inn. Tarantella. Joseph Hilaire Pierre Belloc. BLPJKO; MoBrPo; OBMV; UV

Do you remember an Inn. New Tarantella. Paul Griffin. UV

Do you remember an inn, Miranda? It lost its licence of course. Footnote to Belloc's "Tarantella." John Heath-Stubbs. OBCoV

Do You Remember Ch'ŏongp'a Street? Ch'oe Sŭngja. EcSo, *tr. by* Mickey Hong

Do you remember Don Quixote. Imagination. Johnny Burke. ReLy

Do you remember / how I made you sit. Exchanges in Italy. Mary Twomey. IrLP

Do you remember how we went. To Another Housewife. Judith Wright. NALW

Do you remember, I wonder. Christmas Card to a Friend Who Might Be Dead. Gareth Alban Davies. BBMWP, *tr. by* the author and Mike Jenkins

Do you remember, mountains of grey. Roncesvalles. Iorwerth Cyfeilog Peate. BBMWP, *tr. by* Nigel Jenkins

Do you remember Mr. Goodbeare, the carpenter. Elegy for Mr. Goodbeare. Sir Osbert Sitwell. MoBrPo

Do You Remember 1926? Do You Remember 1926? Idris Davies. AngWePo; OBWVE

Do you remember, O Delphic Apollo. Edgar Lee Masters. APT-1 *Fr.* Spoon River Anthology.

Do you remember that night. Do You Remember That Night. *Unknown.* WoPoe, *tr. by* George Petrie

Do You Remember That Night? *Unknown.* IrLP, *tr. by* Eugene O'Curry

Do you remember that still summer evening. Golden Room, The. Wilfrid Wilson Gibson. VisFro

Do you remember that you wanted to be a Marguerite. Marguerite. Rubén Darío. SpanPo, *tr. by* Anita Volland

Do you remember the love? Arbor. Carrie St. George Comer. LegDan

Do you remember the night Abraham first saw. Night Abraham Called to the Stars, The. Robert Bly. OxBoAm; PoCho

Do you remember the ritual of candle-wax. Sliding. Sam Adams. AngWePo

Do you remember the scene in *The Godfather* where James Caan says, "Now make sure that the gun gets stashed in the rest room—I don't want my kid brother walking out of there with nothing but his dick in his hand"? Gerald Locklin. SUP

Do you remember the storming column. Storming Column, The. John William DeForest. PCW

Do you remember? We were in a room. Raiment We Put On, The. Kelly Cherry. FFC

Do you say the wind blew last night. Yu Ŭngbu. CATKP, *tr. by* Peter H. Lee

Do you see? Evening falls, fringed with barbed-wire. Seventh Eclogue. Miklós Radnóti. ConPit; PFTM-1, *tr. by* Clayton Eshleman and Gyula Kodolanyi

Do you see me! 'One with this world'. *Unknown.* FaBoA, *tr. by* A. L. Kroeber

Do you see that hummingbird. Grain of Sand. Fanny Carrión de Fierro. TANSG, *tr. by* Sally Cheney Bell

Do You See the Town? Hugo von Hofmannsthal. AmFaPo, *tr. by* Anne Adams

Do you see the town, how it rests over there. Do You See the Town? Hugo von Hofmannsthal. AmFaPo, *tr. by* Anne Adams

Do you see this square old yellow Book, I toss. Robert Browning. FaBoVe *Fr.* Ring and the Book, The.

Do you seriously want peace or a good meal. Hunger, A. Benjamin Saltman. P180

Do you think. Peter Coyote. WhBo

Do You Think? Josephine D. Henderson Heard. CBWP-4

Do you think I know what I'm doing? Jelaluddin Rumi. IJHIL; LoL, *tr. by* Coleman Barks

Do you think of me as I think of you. L.E.L.'s Last Question. Elizabeth Barrett Browning. VWP

Do you think that odes and sermons. Edgar Lee Masters. GeoHom *Fr.* Spoon River Anthology.

Do you think they wanted sex? asks the naïve girl in the film. Six, Sex, Say. Barbara Hamby. PoDa

Do you think we might go to hell too? Igor Vladimirovich Chinnov. TCRusP, *tr. by* John Glad

'Do you think we'll ever get to see Earth, sir?'. Sheenagh Pugh. TCAWP

"Do you think you will hug the shore, Captain, to-day?" Hugging the Shore. Mary E. Tucker. CBWP-1

Do you too soon forget the brown. Looking Up from Aeroplanes. W. N. Herbert. EdScPo

Do you understand the concept? The marvel? Tender at the neck.   Constant Bride, The.   Mary Jo Bang.   NAPBL

Do You Wonder Why I Am Sleepy.   James Purdy.   CAGL

Do Your Best [*with music*].   Mrs. Henry Linden.   CBWP-4

Do yuh hear that whistle down the line?   On the Atchison, Topeka and the Santa Fe.   Johnny Mercer.   ReLy

Doab of the Tatshenshini river and the Alsek lake, a long spit of.   Raven's Beak River at the End.   Gary Snyder.   PfSP

Doan raise no kite is good friday.   Mama Dot Warns Against an Easter Rising.   Frederick D'Aguiar.   Oth

Dobbs Ferry in autumn. I with my pen.   With Walter and Amati.   Gabriel Preil.   FIT, *tr. by* Robert Friend

Dobbs Ferry possesses a rat which slips out of his lair at night and.   Coming of Archy, The.   Don Marquis.   TCAPo

Doch doch I assure thee. (LL)   Enueg 2.   Samuel Beckett.   ItP; NoAM

Dockens afore his Peers.   Charles Murray.   NePenScot

Docker [*with music*].   Seamus Heaney.   BrAP; HeIP-4

Dockery and Son.   Philip Larkin.   PoetW

Dockery was junior to you.   Dockery and Son.   Philip Larkin.   PoetW

Docks at the foot of Christopher Street, The.   Gay Life.   Ron Schreiber.   PrTe

Doctor, The.   Dannie Abse.   BloBone

Doctor, The.   Mary Dalton.   OpeFie

Doctor, The.   Roger Woddis.   UV

Doctor asked her what she wanted done, The.   Edna St. Vincent Millay.   NALW *Fr.* Sonnets from an Ungrafted Tree.

Doctor came to take his pulse and said, The.   Diamond Cutter.   Seido Ray Ronci.   AmZen

Doctor disrobed, The.   Karai Senryū.   EMJL, *tr. by* Makoto Ueda

Doctor Faustus.   Christopher Marlowe.   NAEL-7v1
   End of Doctor Faustus, The.   FaBoVe; HeIP-4
   "Had I as many souls as there be stars."   SacPr
   Was This the Face.   BLPJKO

Doctor Fell.   Martial.   NBLV; OBCoV; OBVE; OxBEV, *tr. by* Thomas Brown (On the Occasion of One Dr. Fell's Challenge to Translate an Epigram of Matrial's.)   WoPoe

Doctor flicks on a light, The.   Murmur, The.   Arthur Sze.   PoChi

Doctor Foster went to Gloucester.   *Unknown.*   OxBEV

Doctor Frolic.   Robert Pinsky.   NoAM

Doctor gave them what they thought was enough, The.   Between Worlds.   Jacqueline Berger.   AmPoNex

Dr Hanagan.   Ann O'Neill.   PoCu

Doctor has prepared, The.   Karai Senryū.   EMJL, *tr. by* Haruo Shirane

Doctor in a clean, starched band, The.   Reasons That Induced Dr. Swift to Write a Poem Called "The Lady's Dressing-Room", The.   Lady Mary Wortley Montagu.   NAEL-7v1

Dr. Jack.   Thomas Stanley.   BtF

Doctor Johnson.   Soame Jenyns.   OBSV

Dr. King's photograph.   Report from the Skull's Diorama.   Yusef Komunyakaa.   LTA

Doctor, Lawyer, Indian Chief.   Paul Francis Webster.   ReLy

Doctor loves the patient, The.   Bed, The.   Alec Derwent Hope.   NoAM

Doctor Meyers.   Edgar Lee Masters.   APT-1; IllVoic *Fr.* Spoon River Anthology.

Dr. Nigel Bruce Watson Counting.   Russell Edson.   MotU

Dr. Nigel Bruce Watson sat before a long piece of sunlight on the floor.   Dr. Nigel Bruce Watson Counting.   Russell Edson.   MotU

Doctor, of great skill and fame, A.   Fair and Softly goes far or, The Wary Physician.   Laetitia Pilkington.   PEW

Doctor punched my vein, The.   Scyros.   Karl Shapiro.   PWW2

Doctor put her on a soft diet, then, The.   Death of Gladys Presley, The.   Fleda Brown Jackson.   AllShUp

Doctor to his retinue of interns and residents.   Scene: A Bedside in the Witches' Kitchen.   Ramon Guthrie.   APT-2

Doctor Who Sits at the Bedside of a Rat, The.   Josephine Miles.   OxBoAm

Doctor, you say there are no haloes.   Monet Refuses the Operation.   Lisel Mueller.   IllVoic

Doctor's face on a December day, The.   On Dutch's Death.   Robert Coles.   BloBone

Doctors failed to banish Viet Nam forever, The.   At the New Mexico Viet Nam Veterans Memorial.   Leroy V. Quintana.   ICANM

Doctor's fortunate indeed, A.   Physicians' Fortune, The.   Friedrich von Logau.   GePo, *tr. by* George C. Schoolfield

Doctors that learned be.   John Skelton.   OBSV *Fr.* Colin Clout.

Documentary.   Claribel Alegría.   LoL; VCWP

Documentary.   Joseph Stroud.   InoFa

Documentary Film.   "Ern Malley."   BMAP

Documentary Film.   Holger Teschke.   GTCP, *tr. by* Reinhold Grimm

Dodona: Asked of the Oracle.   Amy Clampitt.   PoA 2002

Doe, The.   Patrick Phillips.   NevBe

Does a man ever give up hope, I wonder.   Truth at Last.   Edward Rowland Sill.   APN-2

Does a word as a widow in the brain.   Elegy for Sir Ifor Williams.   Anthony Conran.   AngWePo

Does anybody mind if I don't live in a house that is quaint?   No Wonder Our Fathers Died.   Ogden Nash.   AmWit

Does Anyone Know This Feeling.   J. Adwaita Dèr Mouw.   TuT, *tr. by* Peter van de Kamp

Does anyone know this feeling: it's not the blues.   Does Anyone Know This Feeling.   J. Adwaita Dèr Mouw.   TuT, *tr. by* Peter van de Kamp

Does Anyone Know Where Roque Dalton Spent His Final Night?   Gaspar Aguilera Díaz.   PML, *tr. by* John Oliver Simon

Does he cock his weather-ear, enquiringly.   David Jones.   TCAWP *Fr.* Sleeping Lord, The.

Does he see himself reflected in me? In these hours, does he see the face of his hours reflected? (LL)   Hours Continuing Long.   Walt Whitman.   NAAPv.1; PoPoPo

Does he think of me in the merry throng.   Question, The.   Josephine D. Henderson Heard.   CBWP-4

Does It Go Like this?   Maura Dooley.   NeBl

Does It Matter?   Siegfried Sassoon.   MoBrPo; PoWW

Does it really matter, really, if it's true or not.   Singing to Tony Bennett's Cock.   Victoria Redel.   KGB

Does my old friend remember me? (LL)   Alfred Tennyson.   NAEL-6v2; NAEL-7v2 *Fr.* In Memoriam A. H. H.

Does my voice reach you? You are.   Light Years and the Love Lost in the Oleanders.   Alane Rollings.   WeW-3

Does my voice sound strange? I am sitting.   Talking to You Afterwards.   Peter Porter.   BMAP

Does not mean silence.   To Play Pianissimo.   Lola Haskins.   MiVo

Does now like one of them appear. (LL)   Upon Appleton House [To My Lord Fairfax].   Andrew Marvell.   BASC; NAEL-7v1

Does Poetry Matter?   Christopher Bursk.   PoA 2002

Does the brush paint, or does the ink? Or does the paper.   Kazuaki Tanahashi.   WhBo

Does the day break.   Dawn.   Nirmalprabha Bardoloi.   CFP, *tr. by* D. N. Bezbarua

Does the Eagle know what is in the pit?   Book of Thel, The.   William Blake.   NAEL-6v2; NAEL-7v2; NoP-5; WaAnP

Does the fawn of al-imā know that he has kindled the heart of a lover in which he dwelt.   Ibrāhīm Ibn Sahl al-Isrāīlī.   HiArP, *tr. by* James T. Monroe

Does the mouth refuse?   Russians Breathing.   Philip Hammial.   NOBAu

Does the Pope sit alone.   Pope at 7:00 P.M., The.   Eloise Klein Healy.   SUP

Does the road wind up-hill all the way?   Uphill [*or* Up-Hill].   Christina Georgina Rossetti.   BrAP; CABP; CtM; NAEL-6v2; NAEL-7v2; NALW; NoP-4; NoP-5; OBEV; PEW; PoPoPo; SacPr; TFi; WaAnP; WeW-3

Does the sound or the silence make.   Would You Think?   John Wheelwright.   APT-2; OxBoAm

Does the trick worth forty wenches. (LL)   Song: "Love a woman? You're [*or* Y'are] an ass."   John Wilmot, 2d Earl of Rochester.   NBLV; NOSC; WoPoe

Does this water.   At the Well.   Leonard Nathan.   PBCAP

Does thy life destroy. (LL)   William Blake.   BrAP; CABP; ClHu; HeIP-4; NAEL-6v2; NAEL-7v2; NAWM-7v2; NIL-7; NIP-4; NOBRP; NoP-4; NoP-5; NPBRoP; NPeEn; OPOU; OxAEP-2; OxBEV; PoPoPo; SoSe-8; TFi; TRP; WaAnP; WeW-3 *Fr.* Songs of Experience.

Does your mother realize.   You Must Have Been a Beautiful Baby.   Johnny Mercer.   ReLy

Doesn't he realize / that I am not / like the swaying kelp.   Ono no Komachi.   WoPoe, *tr. by* Ikuko Atsumi and Kenneth Rexroth

Doesn't it break your heart.   Baby, The.   Rex Wilder.   PoDa

Doesn't know why he's such a strong swimmer.   River God, The.   Vicki Feaver.   MoWP

Doesn't particularly like you, but gives up, and comes in. (LL)   Resemblance Between Your Life and a Dog, The.   Robert Bly.   CAP-8; OxBoAm

Dog.   Billy Collins.   WaAnP

Dog.   Lawrence Ferlinghetti.   NAMCP V.2

Dog.   Ingrid Jonker.   HAWP, *tr. by* Jack Cope and William Plomer

Dog.   Harold Monro.   MoBrPo

Dog, A.   Gertrude Stein.   NAMCP V.1 *Fr.* Tender Buttons.

Dog, The.   W. H. Davies.   MoBrPo

Dog, The.   Attila József.   MotU, *tr. by* John Bakti

Dog, The.   Stanley Moss.   BodElec

Dog, The.   Ogden Nash.   Spl

Dog, The.   Susan Fromberg Schaeffer.   PoCoUp

Dog, The [*with music*].   Gerald Stern.   BeAl; WeW-3

Dog, The.   C. K. Williams.   BodElec

Dog: "Why do you watch me so sadly and inquisitively." Stefan Tsanev. CSCBP, *tr. by* Georgi Belev and Lisa Sapinkopf

Dog and I are both grown old, The. Grown Old Together. William Lisle Bowles. DiBP

Dog and the Shadow, The. Aesop. DiBP, *tr. by* Aphra Behn

Dog Asleep. William Stafford. OtW

Dog Bark, The. Mary Jo Bang. NAPBL

Dog bark, the engine of a truck, an airplane hidden by the trees and rooftops, A. Lyn Hejinian. OxBoAm *Fr.* My Life.

Dog barked itself, The. Dog Which Barked Itself Out, The. Tymoteusz Karpowicz. PoSu, *tr. by* Bogdan Czaykowski and rzej Busza

Dog barked; then the woman stood in the doorway, and hearing iron strike stone down the steep road, The. Roan Stallion. Robinson Jeffers. NAAPv.2

Dog barking, A. Buson. EH, *tr. by* Robert Hass

Dog beneath the Skin, The. W. H. Auden.
  "We are girls of differnt ages." UV

Dog beside the threshold lies, The. John Clare. DiBP *Fr.* Shepherd's [*or* Shepheards] Calendar, The.

Dog Called Chance, A. Paula Cunningham.
  Hats. NIrP
  "I've jouked into a pub." NIrP
  Poem. NIrP
  Red Wine Stain from Malin to Mizen Head, A. NIrP

Dog Called Elderly, A. Adrian Mitchell. StAl

Dog Day Lesson. John Hughes. PNI

Dog Days. Derek Mahon. OPOU

Dog Days. Katherine Soniat. PoCoUp

Dog Days and Delta Nights. Franz Douskey. PasH

Dog Days, Jerusalem. Rita Dove. AmAlph

Dog disappears, A / across a small lake. Song of Autumn, A. Joseph Ceravolo. NYP2

Dog Fight. Eric Rolls. NOBAu

Dog Fox Field [The test for feeblemindedness was, they had to make up a sentence using the words dog, fox and field.]. Les A. Murray. BMAP

Dog in his day is born and, The. Names in the Bark. Rod Mengham. VaPo

Dog in the Manger, The. Aesop. DiBP, *tr. by* Aphra Behn

Dog Incog, The. William Hamilton. DiBP

Dog it was that died, The. (LL) Oliver Goldsmith. NBLV; OBNV; OxAEP-1; TFi *Fr.* Vicar of Wakefield, The.

Dog Latin. *Unknown.* DiBP

Dog of Art, The. Denise Levertov. NAMCP V.2; NoAM; WaAnP

Dog of St. Bernard's, The. Caroline Fry. DiBP

Dog Parted from Her Master. Hsüeh T'ao [*or* Xue Tao]. CCL1; WoPoe, *tr. by* Jeanne Larsen

Dog scatters her body in sleep, The. Biography. Michael Ondaatje. NAMCP V.2; NoAM

Dog searches until he finds me, The. Jane Kenyon. LoL *Fr.* Having It Out with Melancholy.

Dog shit. Stanford M. Forrester. AmZen

Dog Show. Laurie Anderson. OxWW

Dog Star. Gerry Gomez Pearlberg. WiU

Dog Star, The. William Drummond of Hawthornden. DiBP

Dog starved at his master's gate, A. William Blake. DiBP *Fr.* Auguries of Innocence.

Dog stops barking after Robinson has gone, The. Robinson. Weldon Kees. NoP-5; OxBoAm; StAl

Dog Suicide. Wanda Coleman. GeoHom

Dog That I Am. Gerald Stern. BAP-04

Dog trots freely in the street, The. Dog. Lawrence Ferlinghetti. NAMCP V.2

Dog Was Crying Tonight in Wicklow Also, A. Seamus Heaney. PoA 2002

Dog was in a hurry, The. It smelled the trees. Large raindrops were already falling. (LL) End of Dodona II, The. Yannis Ritsos. VCWP; WoPoe, *tr. by* Edmund Keeley

Dog was there, outside her door, The. Dog, The. W. H. Davies. MoBrPo

Dog Which Barked Itself Out, The. Tymoteusz Karpowicz. PoSu, *tr. by* Bogdan Czaykowski and rzej Busza

Dog who with his prey the River swam, The. Dog and the Shadow, The. Aesop. DiBP, *tr. by* Aphra Behn

Dogalypse. Andrey Andreievich Voznesensky. CLPP

Dogen. Robert Bringhurst.
  "Under the sunrise the mountains." PoCoUp

Dogged Persistence. Molly Peacock. PfS

Dogger, Rockall, Malin, Irish Sea. Seamus Heaney. RWPCtW *Fr.* Glanmore Sonnets.

Doggerel by a Senior Citizen. W. H. Auden. NBLV

Doggerel for the Great Czech Phallometer. Richard Katrovas. MAAN

Doggin the Rockman. Paul Beatty. InTrad

Dog-God. Robin Becker. ExTi

Dogs: "We humans talk." Hamish Brown. EdScPo

Dogs. Laurie Duggan.
  South Coast Haiku. BMAP

Dogs. Kate Meads. RaF

Dogs. Rhydwen Williams. BBMWP, *tr. by* Nigel Jenkins

Dogs, The. Afaa Michael Weaver. PBCAP

Dog's / body zipped, A. At the Crossroads. Thomas Kinsella. NoAM

Dogs and Weather. Winifred Welles. BLPJKO

Dogs and Wolves. Sorley MacLean. EdScPo

Dogs are barking, The. Sculpture. Joseph Ceravolo. NYP2

Dogs Are Shakespearean, Children Are Strangers. Delmore Schwartz. NoAM

Dogs are supposed to be walked on a leash, children by the hand. Dogs Are Supposed. Erica Pedretti. MotU, *tr. by* Stuart Friebert

Dogs bark ably: in Accra, The. Many Worlds Are Walked Once. Kojo Laing. HBAPE

Dogs bark and in the house, wine, laughter. (LL) Dusk in My Backyard. Keith Wilson. BLT; ICANM

Dogs bark in the midst of gurgling water. On Visiting Taoist Recluse of Tai-Tien-Shan and Not Finding Him. Li Po. ChinPo, *tr. by* Ye Weilian [*or* Yeh Wei-lien *or* Wai-lim Yip]

Dogs bark where the river sings. Going to Visit a Taoist Recluse on Heaven's Mountain Only to Find Him Gone. Li Po. CrYelRi, *tr. by* Sam Hamill

Dog's Death. John Updike. GoPo; P180

Dogs Gambol. Novica Tadic. VCWP, *tr. by* Charles Simic

Dog's Grave, A. Ted Kooser. PoDa

Dogs guard each approach. Childhood's House. Miranda Field. LegDan

Dogs have dreams of Laika, her free soul. Dog Asleep. William Stafford. OtW

Dogs, hogs, leaks in the bogs—we never went back. (LL) Itinerary. Edwin Morgan. HarvBoo; OBCoV

Dogs in Dutch Paintings, The. David Graham. PoDa

Dogs in the Morning Light. Bruce Dawe. NoAM

Dogs of Montone, The. William Matthews. PfSP

Dogs of New York, The. Lee Meitzen Grue. UrbNat

Dogs of Nile, The. Jonathan Swift. DiBP

Dogs of war are loose and the rugged russian bear, The. G. W. Hunt. FaBoWar *Fr.* McDermott's War Song.

Dogs on a leash. David Kherdian. UrbNat *Fr.* Taking the Soundings on Third Avenue.

Dogs on Strike, The. John Gay. DiBP *Fr.* Fables: First Series.

Dogs on the Cliffs, The. Michael Burkard. BodElec

Dog's Song. Robert Wallace. TLR

Dog's Tragedy, A. William Wordsworth. DiBP

Dogs' Welcome, The. Winthrop Mackworth Praed. DiBP

Dogs yap, sirens wail through the city. Lacrimae Rerum. Patricia Goedicke. ExTi

Dogtown. James Harms. GeoHom

Dogwood blossoms drift down at evening. Watching Dogwood Blossoms Fall in a Parking Lot Off Route 46. August Kleinzahler. PoA 2002

Dogwood flakes / what is green. Variations Done for Gerald Van De Wiele. Charles Olson. APT-2; NoAM; NoP-4; NoP-5

Doin'. Atiba Kwabena. BRtP

Doing. Giancarlo Majorino. ItPo, *tr. by* Gayle Ridinger

Doing, a filthy pleasure is, and short. Petronius Arbiter. ErotSp; NPeEn; OBVE; OxBEV; WoPoe, *tr. by* Ben Jonson

Doing Good. Nancy Esposito. PfS

Doing leg-lifts in the field, my gaze. Face Up. Jonathan Holden. PfSP

Doing the Evolution Shuffle. Alice Fulton. PoA 2002

Doing the Reactionary. Harold Rome. ReLy

Doing Without. David Ray. P180

Dokusan: Visit to Katagiri Roshi. Diane Di Prima. AmZen

Dol and Roger. Laetitia Pilkington. PEW

Dolce. Kennette Wilkes. PasH

Dolce Far Niente. Fidelito Cortes. ReBoTo

Doll. Myra Cohn Livingston. TLR

Doll. Josephine Miles. FTtHH; NALW

Doll. John Wieners. FTOS

Doll and god grow stronger. (LL) Breathing, the Endless News, The. Rita Dove. CAP-8; PoA 2002

Doll Believers, The. Clarence Major. PoChi

Doll in the doll-maker's house, A. Dolls, The. William Butler Yeats. NoAM

Doll Museum, The. Carlyle Reedy. Oth

Doll Not Included. David Trinidad. WiU

Dolls, The. William Butler Yeats. NoAM

Dolls. David St. John. AmAlph

Doll's House, A. Kit Wright. EmeKit

Dolls Museum in Dublin, The. Eavan Boland. NAEL-7v2; NoP-4; NoP-5

Dolor. Theodore Roethke. BrAP; GPTC; HeIP-4; NAMCP V.1; NoAM; OPOU; OxBoAm; PoA 2002; StAl; TRP

Dolor de corazón. Pura López Colomé. RMCMP

Dolor, El. Francisco Brines. RaW

Dolores. Algernon Charles Swinburne.
  "O lips full of lust and of laughter." UV

Dolorous, here he made his stand. He Who Loved Beauty. Alec Brock Stevenson. FuPo

Dolphin. Robert Lowell. NAMCP V.2; NoAM; OxBoAm; VCAP; WaAnP

Dolphin, The. Maurya Simon. GeoHom

Dolphins. Bryn Griffiths. TCAWP

Dolphins, octopi, fish. Late Minoan I: (Ewers of Hagia Triada). Lorand Gaspar. YaTCFP, tr. by Ronnie Scharfman

Dolphins play, The. Thom Gunn. NOxBChV Fr. Three for Children.

Dome of Sunday, The [or A]. Karl Shapiro. MoAmPo; NoAM

Domestic Bliss. John Yau. OxBoAm

Domestic Blues. Teresa Calderón. TANSG, tr. by Celeste Kostopulos-Cooperman

Domestic carnage now filled the whole year. William Wordsworth. NAEL-6v2; NAEL-7v2 Fr. Prelude, The; Growth of a Poet's Mind [1850 version; Selections from Anthologies].

Domestic Cat, A. Edwin Denby. NYP2

Domestic Chat. Leigh Hunt. STuOW Fr. Legend of Florence, A.

Domestic Economy. Anna Wickham. ItWoWo

Domestic Humiliation. Allison Joseph. SweBea

Domestic Interior. Eavan Boland.
  Night Feed. NAMCP V.2

Domestic Love. George Croly. TreFP

Domestic love! not in proud palace halls. Domestic Love. George Croly. TreFP

Domestic Mysticism. Lucie Brock-Broido. PoPoPo

Domestic Poem. Helen Dunmore. MoWP

Domestic Poems. Thomas Hood.
  Parental Ode to My Son, A. OBCoV
  Serenade, A (Fragment). NBLV

Domestic Storm, A. Priscilla Jane Thompson. CBWP-2

Domestic Tranquility. Gerald William Barrax. GT

Domestic Work, 1937. Natasha Trethewey. PoDa; SpirFl; SweBea

Domesticated Egg, A. Hans Arp. MotU, tr. by Bethany Schneider

Domesticity of Giraffes, The. Judith Beveridge. BMAP

Domicilium. Thomas Hardy. OBGa

Domination of Black. Wallace Stevens. APT-1; MoAmPo; NAMCP V.1; OWoS; OxBoAm; TCAPo

Domination of Wallace Stevens (1925). Carl Rakosi.
  (Paraguay.) FTOS

Domingo. Antonio Deltoro. RMCMP

Domingo Limón. Alberto A. Ríos. NAAL-5

Domino Theory (or Snoop Dogg rules the world), The. Kenneth Carroll. SpirFl

Dominus Illuminatio Mea. Richard Doddridge Blackmore. OBEV; SacPr

Dompteur de lions se souvient, Le. Tristan Tzara. YaTCFP

Don and Sancho, Tramp and Tray. Dogs' Welcome, The. Winthrop Mackworth Praed. DiBP

Don de resbalar. José Luis Rivas. RMCMP

Don de soi-même, Le. Valery Larbaud. YaTCFP

Don, Don, Don, the drum is calling. Shantung. Hsi-tseng Tsiang. NAAPv.2

Don José Gorostiza Encounters El Cordobés. Jay Wright. ESEAA

Don Juan (After He'd Consumed Tons of Lipstick). Martin Sorescu. PML; PoDa, tr. by Adam J. Sorkin and Irina Grigorescu Pan

Don Juan had got out on Shooter's Hill. Lord Byron. FaBoVe Fr. Don Juan.

Don Juan. Lord Byron.
  Canto the First. NAEL-6v2; NAEL-7v2; CABP
    "I want a hero: an uncommon want." NoP-5
    Juan and Julia. NPBRoP
    Juan's Puberty. NPeEn
    "Poor Julia's heart was in an awkward state." NOBRP
    "They tell me 'tis decided; you depart." NOBRP
    "What is the end of fame? 'Tis but to fill." OBCoV
    "Young Juan wandered by the glassy brooks." OBCoV
  Canto the Second.
    "Alas for Juan and Haidee! They were." NePenScot
    "Alas! they were so young, so beautiful." OxBEV
    "Alas, they were so young, so beautiful." EroLit
    "But to our tale: the Donna Inez sent." NAEL-6v2; NAEL-7v2
    Don Juan's Spaniel. DiBP
    "How long in his damp trance young Juan lay." NAEL-6v2; NAEL-7v2
    "Nine souls more went in her: the long-boat still." OxBEV

Shipwreck, The. NPBRoP; NPeEn
    "There, breathless, with his digging nails he clung." OxAEP-2
  Canto the Third.
    "Haidée and Juan carpeted their feet." NOBRP
    "I know that what our neighbours call longueurs." OBSV
    (Isles of Greece, The.) NPBRoP
    "Isles of Greece, the isles of Greece!, The." BLPJKO; OBEV; OxAEP-2
  Canto the Fourth.
    "As boy, I thought myself a clever fellow." NAEL-6v2; NAEL-7v2
    "I leave Don Juan for the present, safe." NOBRP
  Canto the Seventh.
    ""Let there be light!" said God, and there was light!" OBWP
    "Oh, thou eternal Homer! I have now." FaBoWar
  Canto the Ninth.
    On Wellington. FaBoWar; OBSV; OxAEP-2
    "To be or not to be! That is the question." OBCoV
  Canto the Tenth.
    "Lawyer and the critic but behold, The." NePenScot
  Canto the Eleventh. NOBRP
    Juan in England. FaBoVe
    "To our theme. The man who has stood on the Acropolis." OBSV
  Dedication. OBSV
    Watch-Dog's Honest Bark, The. DiBP
  Fragment [on the Back of the Ms. of Canto I]. NAEL-6v2; NAEL-7v2; NoP-5; OxBEV
  "How long in his damp trance young Juan lay." NPBRoP
  "My poem's epic, and is meant to be." BrAP

Don Juan's Address to the Sunset. Robert Malise Bowyer Nichols. OBMV

Don Juan's Spaniel. Lord Byron. DiBP Fr. Don Juan.

Don Leon. Unknown.
  "Among the yeomen's sons on my estate." CAGL
  "Chance led me once, when idling through the street." CAGL
  "Sometimes I sauntered from my lone abode." CAGL
  "Statesmen, in your exalted station know." CAGL
  "Thou ermined judge, pull off that sable cap!" CAGL
  "Thus feverish fancies floated in my brain." CAGL
  "Tree we plant will, when its boughs are grown, The." CAGL
  "Women as women, me had never charmed." CAGL

Don Pullen at the Zanzibar Blue Jazz Cafe, 1994 [1997]. Major L. Jackson. SpirFl

Don Pullen at the Zanzibar Blue Jazz Café [2006]. Major L. Jackson. LegDan

Don Quixote and the Flour Mills. Safaa Fathy. AnVo, tr. by Mohamed Enani

Don Sebastian. John Dryden.
  To Account Rendered. STuOW

Don Surly, to aspire the glorious name. On Don Surly. Ben Jonson. NAEL-6v1; NAEL-7v1

Doña Josefina Counsels Doña Concepción Before Entering Sears. Maurice Kilwein Guevara. AmPoNex

Donahue's Sister. Thom Gunn. NoAM

Donald Evans. Witter Bynner. APT-1

Donal[l] Oge [or Og]: Grief of a Girl's Heart. Augusta, Lady Gregory. IrLP, tr. by Augusta, Lady Gregory and Lady Gregory

Donatello's Saint George. Louise Imogen Guiney. Fr. Knight Errant, The.

Donatilia's Unrequited Love Remedy. Virgil Suárez. AmPoNex

Dónde cae la nota entre las ramas tendidas. Mi voz fiel como la sombra. Tedi López Mills. RMCMP

Done. Minnie Bruce Pratt. BeAl

Done a Good Job. Y. A. Rontsh. Prolet, tr. by Amelia Glaser

Done is a battell [or battle] on the dragon blak [or black]. William Dunbar. NePenScot; NPeEn; OxBEV; SacPr

Done Is a Battle. William Dunbar. NoP-5

Done / noose. Count. Ernst Jandl. OnScMo, tr. by James Sherry

Done With. Ann Stanford. CalPo

Done with a long day's begging. Ryokan. WoPoe, tr. by Burton Watson

Dong, sounds the brass in the east. Henry David Thoreau. APN-1

Dong with a luminous Nose. (LL) Dong with a Luminous Nose, The. Edward Lear. NOxBChV; OxAEP-2; OxBEV

Dong with a Luminous Nose, The [with music]. Edward Lear. NOxBChV; OxAEP-2; OxBEV

Donkey, The [with music]. G. K. Chesterton. ChIV-2; GI; MoBrPo; OBEV

Donkey, The. Stevie Smith. HarvBoo

Donkey, The [1920 version]. G. K. Chesterton. WaAnP

Donkey and the Lapdog, The. Jean de La Fontaine. OBVE, tr. by Marianne Moore

Donkey Speculates, The. Kazuko Shiraishi. WoBe, tr. by Samuel Grolmes and Yumiko Tsumura

Donkeys in Anantapur. Ismail. HotL, tr. by V. Narayana Rao

Donkey's tail is very nice, A. Monotony Song, The. Theodore Roethke. ChAP

Donne, the delight of Phoebus, and each Muse. To John Donne. Ben Jonson. NAEL-6v1; NAEL-7v1

Donor. Lucille Clifton. FuFl

Don's Holiday. George Rostrevor Hamilton. OBCoV

Don't ape what must be born in one. Donkey and the Lapdog, The. Jean de La Fontaine. OBVE, *tr. by* Marianne Moore

Don't Ask. Ch'i-chi. *tr. by* Burton Watson
  Don't Ask [1]. CSKM, *tr. by* Burton Watson
  Don't Ask [5]. CSKM, *tr. by* Burton Watson
  Don't Ask [9]. CSKM, *tr. by* Burton Watson
  Don't Ask [11]. CSKM, *tr. by* Burton Watson

Don't ask any questions! Drunk Among the Flowers. Mao Wen-hsi. ColAnChi, *tr. by* Lois Fusek

Don't ask if I'm out of touch with human affairs. Ch'i-chi. CSKM *Fr.* Don't Ask.

Don't ask if I've ceased my wanderings. Ch'i-chi. CSKM *Fr.* Don't Ask.

Don't ask if I've ceased wanting anything. Ch'i-chi. CSKM *Fr.* Don't Ask.

Don't Ask Me for That Love Again. Faiz Ahmad Faiz. PoetW; VCWP, *tr. by* Agha Shahid Ali

Don't ask me just how it happened. I Got Lost in His Arms. Irving Berlin. ReLy

Don't ask me, my love, for that love again. (LL) Don't Ask Me for That Love Again. Faiz Ahmad Faiz. PoetW; VCWP, *tr. by* Agha Shahid Ali

Don't ask suspiciously. Muso Soseki. EaWin, *tr. by* W. S. Merwin

Don't ask us for the word to frame. Eugenio Montale. PoetW, *tr. by* Jonathan Galassi

Don't ask whose face it is when you see me. Humiliation in Its Disguises. Andrew Crozier. VaPo

Don't ask why I shut my gate. Ch'i-chi. CSKM *Fr.* Don't Ask.

Don't ask—knowing's taboo—what's in the cards, darling, for you, for me. Horace. STV

Don't assume each threat is uttered. *Unknown.* PriapPo *Fr.* Priapus Poems, The.

Don't be afraid. Matter of Control, A. Diana García. TouFir

Don't be afraid of the future. Life Is a Song, Let's Sing It Together. Joe Young. ReLy

Don't be ashamed. Alex Rawls. AnSo *Fr.* What's Your Sign?

Don't be dismayed, woman, by my fierce form. Annunciation. Primo Levi. AF; GI, *tr. by* Ruth Feldman

Don't be fooled by costumes: I am still an orphan. I move through his house by stealth. I thieve. My Neck a Toothsome Feeding Ground. Vespered Swarms Had Drunk of Me Before this New Batman. D. A. Powell. FaoP

Don't be mad. Joshua Beckman. IIR

Don't be mad at me because I have. Yellow Is Me, But All the Same Are We. Joan Adams. BtF

Don't be polite. How to Eat a Poem. Eve Merriam. ChAP

Don't be saddish. Peter Bailey. WhBo

Don't be stupid. Invitation to Forget. Erich Fried. GTCP, *tr. by* Stuart Hood

Don't be surprised that modest hermits. Hermit Thoughts. Thich Tue Sy. WhBo

Don't be too eager to ask. Horace. WoPoe *Fr.* Odes.

Don't Be Weary, Traveller. *Unknown.* SSUS

Don't believe Nicole. Zebra, The. Marie Laurencin. CuPo

Don't Blame Me. Dorothy Fields. ReLy

Don't block my way, friend. Mirabai. ErotSp, *tr. by* Andrew Schelling

Don't bother about the news! Aleksandr Semionovich Kushner. TCRusP, *tr. by* Daniel Weissbort

Don't Bring Lulu. Lew Brown and Billy Rose. ReLy

Don't bring out the straw mat. Don't Bring Out the Straw Mat. Han Kwak. WoPoe, *tr. by* Virginia Olsen Baron and Chung Seuk Park

Don't Burn. Edict Against Christianity (Section 12). *Unknown.* EMJL

Don't call this world adorable, or useful, that's not it. Where Does the Dance Begin, Where Does it End? Mary Oliver. CAP-8

Don't care what that hoodoo. Roots 1: big momma speaks to jimmy's wife. Cherryl "Blue." Floyd-Miller. BtF

Don't Cheapen Yourself. Jana Harris. SUP

Don't chop that pear tree. *Unknown.* CCL1; NDACCP *Fr.* Gan-tang [Translations].

Don't Come to Me with the Entire Truth. Olav H. Hauge. WED, *tr. by* Robert Bly

Don't complain too much. Your father. Advice to a Coming Child. Benjamin Scott Grossberg. LiTh

Don't. Crow and butcher bird. Sick Woman. John Kinsella. BMAP

Don't Cry, Scream. Haki R. Madhubuti. SeSe

Don't cut it to make a flute. Bamboo by Li Ch'e Yun's Window, The. Po Chü-i. NDACCP, *tr. by* Kenneth Rexroth

Don't despair my dear daughter! Don't Despair. Murad Mikha'il. IrPoTo, *tr. by* Christina Coyle and Sadok Masliyah

Don't die, Dad. Last Hellos, The. Les A. Murray. HarvBoo; PoCu

Don't do the things I've done. (LL) Disasterology. Jeffrey McDaniel. LaCa; NeAmPo

Don't, don't [*with music*]. Huan Fu. PML, *tr. by* Zhang Cuo

Don't dye it, don't pull it out. White Hair. Ch'i-chi. CSKM, *tr. by* Burton Watson

Don't even go to a movie show. Keepin' Out of Mischief Now. Andy Razaf. ReLy

Don't ever fear sweet Mary, beware of sweet Marie. (LL) Mary's a Grand Old Name. George M. Cohan. NAAPv.2; ReLy

Don't Ever Leave Me. Oscar Hammerstein, II. ReLy

Don't Expect Anything. Maj Ragain. AmZen

Don't expect obedience, promise-keeping, or rectitude. As Rich as Solomon (21). Khwaja Shams-ad-din Muhammad Hafiz. WED, *tr. by* Robert Bly and Leonard Lewisohn

Don't Explain. Betsy Sholl. ACAMVP

Don't extend your thought. Dandelion. Alexander Gerov. CSCBP, *tr. by* Georgi Belev and Lisa Sapinkopf

Don't fear me! There's the grey [*or* gray] beginning. Zooks! (LL) Fra Lippo Lippi. Robert Browning. BrAP; NAEL-6v2; NAEL-7v2; NoP-4; NoP-5; OxAEP-2; WaAnP

Don't Feel No Way. Kevin Powell. InTrad

Don't fill up on bread. Sentimental Moment or Why Did the Baguette Cross the Road? Robert Hershon. P180

Don't fly off, nightingale. Issa. ZenPo, *tr. by* Takashi Ikemoto and Lucien Stryk

Don't Forget. Stephen Berg. PoChi

Don't Forget. Alice Sadongei. HATNAP

Don't forget to ask him to send me all of his . . . / I should have given. Bernard Heidsieck. PFTM-2 *Fr.* Canal Street.

Don't Forget to Say No, Baby. Hoagy Carmichael. ReLy

Don't forget to say no, baby, while I'm with your Uncle Sam. Don't Forget to Say No, Baby. Hoagy Carmichael. ReLy

Don't forget when the sticks are ready for picking. Don't Forget. Alice Sadongei. HATNAP

Don't founder, my ship, tomorrow's hero guides you. On New Waters. Endre Ady. IQMS, *tr. by* Anton N. Nyerges

Don't Frighten Me. Anna Andreyevna Akhmatova. RusPo, *tr. by* Robert Arthur Douglas Ford

Don't frighten me with a terrible fate. Don't Frighten Me. Anna Andreyevna Akhmatova. RusPo, *tr. by* Robert Arthur Douglas Ford

Don't Get Around Much Anymore. Bob Russell. ReLy

Don't give everything. David Foster. NOBAu *Fr.* Fleeing Atalanta, The.

Don't give me food. Ernst Mirville. OGAHCP, *tr. by* Boadiba and Jack Hirschman

Don't give yo / right name no / No NO. (LL) Blackie Thinks of His Brothers. Stanley Crouch. GT; OxAAAP

Don't give you a second. Men in the Hoboken Bar, the. Jonathan Holden. MAAN

Don't go back, Ma, don't go back, Mother. Najrul Islām. SinGod, *tr. by* Rachel Fell McDermott

Don't go, don't go. I touch your soles. I'm sold to you. Don't Go, don't Go. Mirabai. WED, *tr. by* Robert Bly

Don't go 'round mopin', hopin'. (Up on Top of a Rainbow) Sweepin' the Clouds Away. Sam Coslow. ReLy

Don't grieve too long. Missing Supper. Tim Suermondt. PA9/11

Don't Grow Old. Allen Ginsberg.
  Father Death Blues. CLPP

Don't hitch your dear little cunt against that wall. Strato. EroLit, *tr. by* Kenneth McLeish

Don't hunt too anxiously a wilful hound. Advice to a Man Who Lost a Dog. Howard Baker. APT-2

Don't imitate me. Basho. EH, *tr. by* Robert Hass

Don't invite me to your pity party. RSVP. Danielle Pafunda. BAP-04

Don't kill that fly! Issa. EH, *tr. by* Robert Hass

Don't kill that fly! Avedik Issahakian. ChAP

Don't kill that poor fly! Issa. SoOfWa, *tr. by* Sam Hamill

Don't Kill Yourself. Carlos Drummond de Andrade. WoPoe, *tr. by* Mark Strand

Don't Kill Yourself. Carlos Drummond de Andrade. PoCho; TCLAP, *tr. by* Elizabeth Bishop

Don't knock on my door, little child. Motherhood. Georgia Douglas Johnson. NAAPv.2; OxAAAP

Don't know a man or woman can do it, tell the truth about love. She Attempts to Tell The Truth About True Romance. Kathy Fagan. ExTi

Don't know about the people. Issa. EH, *tr. by* Robert Hass

Don't know. But that's where we're going. (LL) Scattered Congregation, The. Tomas Tranströmer. RaBo; VCWP; WED, *tr.* by Robert Bly

Don't know if Danish or Russian. Ugly Duckling, The. Luis Lloréns Torres. NAAPv.2

Don't know / Nice, though. (LL) Ode on a Grecian Urn Summarized. Desmond Skirrow. NIL-7; NIP-4

Don't Know No English. Nicolás Guillén. PFTM-1

Don't know whose house don't know. We Write. Siva Reddy. HotL, *tr.* by V. Narayana Rao and A. K. Ramanujan

Don't know why / There's no sun up in the sky. Stormy Weather (Keeps Rainin' All the Time). Ted Koehler. ReLy

Don't laugh if my roof beams. Sin Hǔm. CATKP, *tr.* by Peter H. Lee

Dont le soleil parfois musique sur grand ciel d'ouvert. Dont le soleil. Danielle Collobert. YaTCFP

Don't let freezing hands play with these pearls. Meng Chiao. CCL1 *Fr.* Apricots Die Young.

Don't Let Me Eat Dinner. Jeni Olin. FreRad

Don't let me fall. Prayers: I. Kadya Molodovsky. WPoS, *tr.* by Kathryn Hellerstein

Don't let me leave you, I may die. Kseniya Marennikova. CRWP, *tr.* by Daniel Weissbort

Don't let your dog curb you! Warning: Augmented. Langston Hughes. APT-2

Don't Let's Be Beastly to the Germans. Noël Coward. ReLy

Don't let's talk about being in love, OK? Don't Let's Talk About Being in Love. Selima Hill. StAl

Don't lock me in wedlock, I want. About Marriage. Denise Levertov. NALW

Dont look at me, look at your own self. Max Carries the One. Bernadette Mayer. NYP2

Don't lower your eyes. Lady Freedom Among Us. Rita Dove. LoL

Don't lower your languid eyes, don't aim. Râsih Bey. OLP, *tr.* by Walter Andrews, Najaat Black and Mehmet Kalpakli

Don't make it harder for us, the hangman whispered. (LL) Execution, The. Alden Nowlan. BrAP; StAl

Don't make me go out eat goose. Ebenezer Californicus. August Kleinzahler. PmAP

Don't mind if you die. It's just your body's shape. On Death. Sándor Weöres. IQMS, *tr.* by Alan Dixon

Don't misunderstand us. Stare, The. Mun Chônghui. EcSo, *tr.* by Catherine J. Kim

Don't mock a pine. Inp'yŏng, Prince. CATKP, *tr.* by Peter H. Lee

Don't need bansaw. Cross Burning Black. Willie Abraham Howard Jr. BtF

Don't nothing go over. Eatonton Tableaux. Honorée Fanonne Jeffers. AnSo

Don't obey me!—the Master ordered the perplexed Golem. Ana Maria Shúa. MirDau *Fr.* Golem and Rabbi.

Don't offend. Carroll Arnett. LTA

Don't own so much clutter. Wendell Berry. UpMys *Fr.* Prayers and Sayings of the Mad Farmer.

Don't pile cruel cares upon those griefs. Stesichoros. SaLy, *tr.* by Diane Rayor

Don't play too much, don't play. Accompanist, The. William Matthews. P180

Don't prepare for tomorrow, enter the narrow lane. Yehuda Amichai. FIT, *tr.* by Robert Friend

Don't pretend I didn't warn you. *Unknown.* PriapPo *Fr.* Priapus Poems, The.

Don't put your daughter on the stage. (LL) Noël Coward. ReLy; UV *Fr.* Mrs Worthingtion.

Don't Quit. Edgar Albert Guest. TWF

Don't Rain on My Parade. Bob Merrill. ReLy

Don't read books! Don't Read Books! Yang Wan-li. ColAnChi, *tr.* by Jonathan Chaves

Don't read odes, boy, timetables. For a Senior College Textbook. Hans Magnus Enzensberger. PoSu

Don't read odes, son, read timetables. For the Primer of Senior High. Hans Magnus Enzensberger. GTCP, *tr.* by Reinhold Grimm and Felix Pollak

Don't remember nothing interesting. Short History of Bill Berkson, A. Frank O'Hara. AHA

Don't remove the glasses and plates. Instructions for a Waitress. Yehuda Amichai. PoSu, *tr.* by Harold Schimmel

Don't run anymore. Quiet. How softly it rains. After Paradise. Czeslaw Milosz. PML, *tr.* by the author and Robert Hass

Don't say cover-up, this man's not masked. My last modernist poem, #2 (or, mugshot). Evie Shockley. RD

Don't Say Goodbye to the Pork-Pie Hat. Larry Neal. ISC; SeSe

Don't say goodbye to the Porkpie Hat that rolled. Larry Neal. GT

Don't Say Goodnight to Etheridge Knight. Tony Medina. InTrad

Don't say it. Lionel Abrahams. TSAP

Don't say that I will depart tomorrow. Please Call Me by My True Names. Thich Nhat Hanh. WhBo

Don't say that repeated defeats. Anwar Kamel Celebrates Le Quatorze Juillet. Ahmed Taha. AnVo, *tr.* by Mohamed Enani

Don't say the daily struggle will get you down. It's All Yours. Dorothy Fields. ReLy

Don't say this to an old idol that's lost its nose. Paavo Haavikko. WoPoe *Fr.* Fifteen Epigrams in Praise of the Tyrant.

Don't say to me. On Wishes. Mahmoud Darwish. VCWP, *tr.* by Denys Johnson-Davies

Don't say you know poems are scripture. Instructions for Academic Poets Who Talk to God. Honorée Fanonne Jeffers. RD

Don't Skimp with Me Today. Mirza Asadullah Khan Ghalib. WED, *tr.* by Robert Bly and Sunil Dutta

Don't sleep, baby, keep your eyes. War Lullaby. Dora Teitelboim. Prolet, *tr.* by Amelia Glaser

Don't slip. The bark's been skinned off. Scotchman Salvage. Joe Denham. OpeFie

Don't / Slobber on the paper. And then it was. For Shunko Enjo. Philip Whalen. WANABP

Don't smile. So you won't become a Buddha. Paavo Haavikko. WoPoe *Fr.* Fifteen Epigrams in Praise of the Tyrant.

Don't steal. Thou'lt never thus compete. Ambrose Bierce. NBLV

Don't stop after beating the swords. Appendix to the Vision of Peace, An. Yehuda Amichai. PoSu, *tr.* by Glenda Abramson and Tudor Parfitt

Don't talk to me about trees having branches and roots. On Trees. Alan Dugan. NoAM

Don't talk to me of love. I've had an earful. In Paris with You. James Fenton. NoP-4; NoP-5; StAl

Don't tell me. For Thieves Only. Lois Red Elk. ReEnLa

Don't tell me not to fly. Don't Rain on My Parade. Bob Merrill. ReLy

Don't tell me what he did in some other country. Wife to a Friend, A. Kshetrayya. WoPoe, *tr.* by V. Narayana Rao, A. K. Ramanujan and David Shulman

Don't they really have. What She Said. Mamalatan. WoPoe, *tr.* by A. K. Ramanujan

Don't think, I said, that because I deny. Monodrama. Bill Knott. BodElec

Don't think it was all hate. Cry, The. Ronald Stuart Thomas. StAl

Don't think / that I don't know. Sous-Entendu. Anne Stevenson. LW

Don't think the stars and moon are all. David Brendon Hopes. UpMys *Fr.* Winter Birds.

Don't think we came to ask for wealth. Yenishehirli 'Avnî. OLP, *tr.* by Walter Andrews, Najaat Black and Mehmet Kalpakli

Don't Touch. Boris Leonidovich Pasternak. TCRusP, *tr.* by Bogdan Boychuk and Mark Rudman

Don't touch a man. Lessons in lying. Nzadi Z. Keita. BtF

Don't touch my corpse. Standing Coffin. Tamura Ryuichi. AF, *tr.* by Christopher Drake

"Don't touch!" my host cried. Tan Taigi. SoOfWa, *tr.* by Sam Hamill

Don't touch that. And stop your whining too. What I Heard at the Discount Department Store. David Budbill. RaBo; TRP

Don't touch that fruit, Eve. *Paradise Lost* as a Haiku. Stanley J. Sharpless. OBCoV

"Don't touch. Wet paint." the sign said. Don't Touch. Boris Leonidovich Pasternak. TCRusP, *tr.* by Bogdan Boychuk and Mark Rudman

Don't trace out your profile. Antonio Machado Ruiz. RaBo *Fr.* Moral Proverbs and Folk Songs.

Don't travel beyond. Immigrant. Arthur Nortje. BrAP; TSAP

Don't turn around, don't look back. Olga Fiodorovna Berggolts. TCRusP, *tr.* by Daniel Weissbort

Don't turn away where are you gazing. In the Field. David Miller. OnScMo

Don't use the telephone. To Edward Dahlberg. Jack Kerouac. WhBo

Don't wake me up from this sleep. You in My Dream. Nanduri Subbarao. HotL, *tr.* by V. Narayana Rao

Don't Wanna Write About the South. Harold Rome. ReLy

Don't wanna write about the South. Don't Wanna Write About the South. Harold Rome. ReLy

Don't want any millions. I'm Sitting on Top of the World. Sam M. Lewis and Joe Young. ReLy

Don't we talk of then are unsealed they efflorescing. Giant Philosophical Otters. Jackson Mac Low. FTOS

Don't weep, insects / Lovers, stars, themselves. Issa. ZenPo, *tr.* by Takashi Ikemoto and Lucien Stryk

Don't. / When I point. Words of Love. Carl Phillips. AmAlph

Don't worry. Philippe Jaccottet. MFP, *tr.* by Martin Sorrell

Don't worry and fret about the crops. Wendell Berry. UpMys *Fr.* Prayers and Sayings of the Mad Farmer.

Don't Worry 'Bout Me. Ted Koehler. ReLy

Don't worry bout me. Generation Gap. Tammy Lynn Pertillar. BtF

Don't worry I know you're dead.   Yoke, The.   Frank Bidart.   OxBoAm

Don't worry, nobody has the.   Secret, The.   Charles Bukowski.   RaBo

Don't worry please please how many times do I have to say it.   Ikkyu Sojun.   WoPoe *Fr.* Four Poems.

Don't worry, spiders.   Issa.   ChAP; EH, *tr.* by Robert Hass

Don't worry, you'll get there! You're close.   Don't worry.   Philippe Jaccottet.   MFP, *tr.* by Martin Sorrell

Don't worry. You're in darkness.   Instructions to a Seed.   David Curzon.   GI

Don't write poems about what's happening.   Looking for Poetry.   Carlos Drummond de Andrade.   ChAP, *tr.* by Mark Strand

Don't you believe it's enough that I'm stuck in this spot.   *Unknown.*   PriapPo *Fr.* Priapus Poems, The.

Don't you care for my love? she said bitterly.   Intimates.   D. H. Lawrence.   NBLV; RaBo

Don't you cut the brush.   Lady Otomo no Sakanoé.   ArkPo, *tr.* by Edwin A. Cranston

Don't you feel it's like being in the midst of a long novel?   On Being in the Midwest.   Diana Chang.   FiBr

Don't You Hear that Whistle Blowin'.   Denise Levertov.   GM

Don't you love my baby, mam.   Infant Song.   Charles Causley.   NOxBChV

Don't you remember sweet Alice, Ben Bolt.   Ben Bolt.   Thomas Dunn English.   APN-1

Don't you see how the Running Horse River flows along the edge of the Sea of Snow.   Song of the Running Horse River, A: Presented on Saying Farewell to the Army Going on Campaign to the West.   Ts'en Shen.   ColAnChi, *tr.* by Daniel Bryant

Don't you see that ship asailin', asailin', asailin'.   Old Ship of Zion, The [North Carolina version].   *Unknown.*   SSUS

Don't you see, there were limits.   Message.   Lola Haskins.   PfS

Doodle durdle caw caw.   Doodle durdle.   *Unknown.*   SonAtl, *tr.* by Michael Estin and Rovetta McKinney

Doom.   Rubén Darío.   SpanPo, *tr.* by Kate Flores

Doom is dark and deeper than any sea-dingle.   Wanderer, The.   W. H. Auden.   HarvBoo; NAMCP V.1; NoAM; WaAnP; WeW-3; WoPoe

Doom of a City, The.   James Thomson.

"Thy Church has long been becoming the Fossil of a Faith."   SacPr

Doom of Devorgoil, The.   Sir Walter Scott.

Bonny [*or* Bonnie] Dundee.   UV

Doomsday.   Maurya Simon.   ExTi

Doomsday.   Elinor Wylie.   NoP-4; NoP-5; SacPr

Doomsday Morning.   Genevieve Taggard.   MoAmPo

Doomsday of wind.   Door of Roses.   Munia Samara.   PoArWo, *tr.* by Amal Amireh

Doomsday, the Mysteries.   *Unknown. tr.* by Tony Harrison

Harrowing, The.   WoPoe, *tr.* by Tony Harrison

Door.   Valerie Worth.   CA

Door, A.   U. A. Fanthorpe.   NewEx

Door, The.   Carlos Bousoño.   RaW, *tr.* by Charles Guenther

Door, The.   David Constantine.   StAl

Door, The.   Miroslav Holub.   StAl, *tr.* by Ian Milner

Door, The.   Mark Strand.   NoAM

Door, The.   Leonard Alfred George Strong.   MoBrPo

Door, The.   Charles Tomlinson.   OxBEV

Door, The: anticipation of wisdom.   Kapka Kassabova.   StAl

Door, The: "It is hard going to the door."   Robert Creeley.   BrAP; NAAL-5; NAMCP V.2; NoAM

Door and the Window, The.   Henry Reed.   HarvBoo

Door behind me was you, The.   Tom Clark.   PmAP *Fr.* You.

Door by door.   Jerusalem, Timeless.   Luisa Futuransky.   MirDau, *tr.* by Celeste Kostopulos-Cooperman

Door can be nothing, A.   Northeast Suite.   Pamela Alexander.   AmAlph

Door has a creaking latch, The. (LL)   Ezra Pound.   MoAmPo; NAAPv.2 *Fr.* Hugh Selwyn Mauberley (Life and Contacts).

Door in the rock closed, The.   Open Sesame.   Edward Field.   SUP

Door is before you again and the shrieking, The.   Door, The.   Mark Strand.   NoAM

Door is open, The.   Full Moon.   Juan Ramón Jiménez.   WED, *tr.* by Robert Bly

Door is open, The. I shall not be intruding.   Old Pump-house, Llanwrtyd Wells.   Ruth Bidgood.   TCAWP

Door is shut, The.   Sense of Distance, A.   Charles Tomlinson.   ICANM

Door isn't locked. You walk, The.   In the Gloaming.   Jennifer Maiden.   BMAP

Door jambs still frames, The.   Grandmother's Farm.   Mark Todd.   GeoH

Door of Hope, The [*with music*].   Lizelia Augusta Jenkins Moorer.   CBWP-3

Door of Roses.   Munia Samara.   PoArWo, *tr.* by Amal Amireh

Door of the Cities.   Munia Samara.   PoArWo, *tr.* by Amal Amireh

Door Shed, The.   Sam Gardiner.   NIrP

Door still swinging to, and girls revive, The.   Dream of Fair Women, A.   Kingsley Amis.   NoAM

Door sunk in a hillside, with a bolt, A.   Icehouse in Summer, The.   Howard Nemerov.   NAMCP V.2; NoAM

Door swung open . . . , The.   Kenneth Mackenzie.   BMAP

Door swung open, The.   Door swung open . . . , The.   Kenneth Mackenzie.   BMAP

Door that someone opened wide, The.   Message, The.   Jacques Prévert.   WeW-3, *tr.* by John Frederick Nims

Door Thrown Open to Daisies.   Rick Agran.   AmPoNex

Door was an absurd thing, The.   Effectual Marriage, The.   Mina Loy.   MoWP

Door was bolted and the windows of my porch, The.   Milkman, The.   Isabella Gardner.   AFaM

Door was shut. I looked between, The.   Shut Out.   Christina Georgina Rossetti.   NALW

Doorkeeper has feet seven fathoms long, The.   Sappho.   SaLy, *tr.* by Diane Rayor

Doorkeeper of mountains and oak groves.   Poem for Artemis (3.22).   Horace.   WED, *tr.* by Robert Bly

Doorknockers with tags of old brocade can be lightly pulled, The.   High Noon.   Li Shang-yin.   CCL1, *tr.* by James J. Y. Liu

Doors.   Rosalie Moore.   YaYoPo

Doors are open, The. We must pass through.   Preface to I Am Rain.   Hilary Booth.   SurWo

Doors of dead roses close stargazing lilies a garden we grew.   As I Leave You.   Chrystos.   ReEnLa

Doors of Sleep, The.   Marion Angus.   EdScPo; NePenScot

Doors of the mall swing open wide, The.   Mall, The.   William Jon Watkins.   IaFF

Doors open by themselves, The.   Chicken, The.   Vladimir Holan.   PoSu, *tr.* by Ian Milner and Jarmila Milner

Doors open on the sands, doors open on exile.   "St.-John Perse."   AF *Fr.* Exile.

Doors swing out, and spill you down the stair.   After Carnival.   Peter Rafferty.   NLP

Doors, where my heart was used to beat.   Alfred Tennyson.   NAEL-6v2; NAEL-7v2; NoP-5 *Fr.* In Memoriam A. H. H.

Dooshi Sorou Soshite Matsu No Me Futori Shoka No Sora.   Violet Kazue De Cristoforo.   CalPo

Dope.   Imamu Amiri Baraka.   APSN

Dora Markus.   Eugenio Montale.   PoetW, *tr.* by William Arrowsmith

Dora Markus and Her Actors.   Gregorio Scalise.   ItPo, *tr.* by Gayle Ridinger

Dorcas.   George Macdonald.   SacPr

Doré V.   José Manuel del Pino.   PML, *tr.* by G. F. Racz

Doreen had a round face.   Doreen.   Janice Mirikitani.   UnSA

Doretha wore the short blue lace last night.   Reception, The.   June Jordan.   NAMCP V.2

Δωρια.   Ezra Pound.   MoAmPo *Fr.* Ripostes of Ezra Pound.

Doric's No Dodo.   Sheena Blackhall.   EdScPo

Dorinda's sparkling wit, and eyes.   On the Countess of Dorchester.   Charles, 6th Earl of Dorset Sackville.   OBEV

Doris.   William Congreve.   WaAnP

Doris, that could repell.   Snow-Ball, The.   Thomas Stanley.   NPeEn

Dorkion, sweet little tomboy.   Asclepiades.   EroLit, *tr.* by Kenneth McLeish

Dormice are sleeping in the preserving jar, tightly packed, five or six dormice, The.   Huge Person, The.   Günter Eich.   MotU, *tr.* by David Walker

Dormitory is full of radios fighting to be loud, The.   Granite Jaw.   Mark Taksa.   LiTh

Dornier, The.   Gladys Mary Coles.   TCAWP

Dorothy Wordsworth, dying, did not want to read.   My Sisters, O My Sisters.   May Sarton.   NALW

Dorothy's Dower.   Phoebe Cary.   NAAPv.1

Dos Geshray (The Scream).   Jerome Rothenberg.   FTOS; PFTM-2 *Fr.* Khurbn.

Dos Oysleydikn (The Emptying).   Jerome Rothenberg.   AmWaPo; PFTM-2 *Fr.* Khurbn.

Dosn't thou 'ear my 'erse's legs, as they canters awaäy?   Northern Farmer: New Style.   Alfred Tennyson.   NAEL-6v2; OBCoV; OxAEP-2

Dossers at the Imperial War Museum.   Joyce Herbert.   TCAWP

Dost see how unregarded now.   Sonnet.   Sir John Suckling.   BASC; CavPo; NOSC

Dost therefore swell and pout with pride.   Tyrant in Sleep, Naught Differeth from a Common Man, A.   Timothy Kendall.   NoSic

Dost thou forget.   William Shakespeare.   OxAEP-1 *Fr.* Tempest, The.

Dost thou look back on what hath been.   Alfred Tennyson.   NAEL-6v2; NAEL-7v2 *Fr.* In Memoriam A. H. H.

Do'st thou thinke we shall know one an other.   John Webster.   OxBEV *Fr.* Duchess of Malfi, The.

Dostoevsky.   Charles Bukowski.   GoPo

Dostoevsky's Russia. The moon.   Northern Elegies.   Anna Andreyevna Akhmatova.   GPTC, *tr.* by Judith Hemschemeyer

Dot a dot dot dot a dot dot. Weather. Eve Merriam. TLR

Dotage. George Herbert. SacPr

Doth die unknown, dazed with dreadful face. (LL) Stand Whoso List. Sir Thomas Wyatt. NAEL-7v1; NoP-4; NoP-5

Doth dye unknow[e]n, dazed with dreadful[l] face. (LL) Seneca. NoSic; NPeEn; OBVE; OxBEV Fr. Thyestes.

Doth Fortune play the huswife with me now? William Shakespeare. FaBoWar Fr. King Henry V.

Doth make my heart give to my tongue the lie! (LL) Sir Philip Sidney. NAEL-6v1; NAEL-7v1; NoP-4; NoP-5 Fr. Astrophil and Stella.

Doth time [or tyme] outlive. (LL) Bible, O.T. ChIV-1; OxBEV Fr. Psalms.

Double. Elizabeth Garrett. MoWP

Double Acrostich on Mrs Svsanna Blvnt, A. Thomas Jordan. NPeEn

Double Bed. Carol Rumens. LW

Double Crossing. Eva Salzman. MFPA

Double Dactyl. Chris Wallace-Crabbe. OBCoV

Double Dactyls. Eric Salzman. OBCoV

Double Dactyls. E. William Seaman. OBCoV; WeW-3

Double Dialogue: Homage to Robert Frost. Muriel Rukeyser. VisFro

Double Elegy [with music]. Michael S. Harper. ESEAA; NAMCP V.2; NoAM; WaAnP

Double Feature. Robert Earl Hayden. NoAM

Double Features. Ed Rossman. HHAm

Double Fortress, The. Alfred Noyes. SacPr

Double Helix. Sean Thomas Dougherty. AmPoNex

Double Life. Norman Alexander MacCaig. EdScPo

Double love torments me; I strain because of two boys, A. Angelo Poliziano. CAGL Fr. Greek Epigrams.

Double Mirror. Ann Stanford. CalPo

Double Rock, The [sonnet]. Henry King, Bishop of Chichester. NOSC

Double Song. Frank Mkalawile Chipasula. NAfrP

Double sorwe of Troilus to tellen, The. Geoffrey Chaucer. MakPoe Fr. Troilus and Criseyde [or Criseide].

Double Standard, A. Frances Ellen Watkins Harper. NAAPv.1

Double, The. Joan Aleshire. OPRER

Double Transformation, The. Oliver Goldsmith. OBCoV; OBNV

Double Trouble. David Trinidad. PmAP; SUP

Double Writing. Stephen Knight. NeBl

Doubled, this hedge-like structure should be trimmed unevenly through. Anorexia. Robert Budde. PoPra

Double-decker. Gilbert Ruddock. BBMWP, tr. by the author

Double-lived in regions new! (LL) Ode: "Bards of passion and of mirth." John Keats. OBEV; OxAEP-2

Doubletalk. Francisco Aragon. BeDoSh

Doubt. Mary Elizabeth Coleridge. NALW; ViWPN

Doubt. Fanny Howe. BAP-01

Doubt. Clara Ann Thompson. CBWP-2

Doubt, A. Sarah Morgan Bryan Piatt. NCAP

Doubt as to Identity. Unknown. DiBP

Doubt compares with everything: in pure air the constant ringing. Barrett Watten. ASA Fr. Real Estate.

Doubt crept into a heart one day, A. Doubt. Clara Ann Thompson. CBWP-2

Doubt, cypress crowned, upon a ruined arch. Elizabeth Oakes-Smith. TCAPo Fr. Atheism.

Doubt of Martyrdom, A. Sir John Suckling. See Sonnet: "O[h]! for some honest lover's ghost."

Doubt which ye misdeem, fair love, is vain, The. Edmund Spenser. See Doubt which ye misdeeme, fayre love, is vaine, The.

Doubt which ye misdeeme, fayre love, is vaine, The. Edmund Spenser. NAEL-6v1; NAEL-7v1 Fr. Amoretti.

Doubt you to whom my Muse these notes intendeth [or entendeth]. Sir Philip Sidney. OxAEP-1 Fr. Astrophil and Stella.

Doubter's Prayer, The. Anne Brontë. SacPr

Doubtful divines, lawyers that wrangle most. Robert Hayman. NOSC Fr. Owen's Epigrams.

Doubtful, I chose a bronze chrysanthemum. Leavetaking. Veronica Rospigliosi. Prnts

Doubtless. Maggie O'Sullivan.
"Dancer—, The." PFTM-2

Doubtless there are other roads. (LL) Wayfarer / Perceiving the pathway to truth, The. Stephen Crane. APN-2; MoAmPo

Douglas, Douglas, Tender and True. Dinah Maria Mulock Craik. TreFP

Douglas Tragedy, The. Unknown. NoP-4; NoP-5

Douglass. Paul Laurence Dunbar. CBCWP; GSo; NAAPv.1; WaAnP

Douglass, a Last Letter. Tim Seibles. MAAN; RD

Douglass was someone who. Frederick Douglass: 1817–1895. Langston Hughes. CBCWP; HHAm

Dour smuts, or unplanned. Moral. Dominique Fourcade. OnScMo

Dour thing in olive trees, The. Olive Trees. Bernard Spencer. NoAM

Dousing clean a thousand old cares. Night with a Friend, A. Li Po. CCL1, tr. by Burton Watson

Dove. Stanley Plumly. PfSP

Dove, The. Victor James Daley. NOBAu

Dove, The. Walter De la Mare. OWoS

Dove at Sundown. Catherine Bowman. MoASP

Dove burned in its whiteness, The. Island in the Light. Sara de Ibáñez. TCLAP, tr. by Inés Probert

Dove descending breaks the air, The. T. S. Eliot. SacPr Fr. Four Quartets.

Dove has brought an olive branch to eat, The. (LL) Where the Rainbow Ends. Robert Lowell. MoAmPo; PoetW

Dove Hunting Each Labor Day. James Hoggard. TiP2

Dove in the Magpie's Nest, The. Unknown. CCL1 Fr. Que-chao [Translations].

Dove of New Snow, The. Vachel Lindsay. MoAmPo

Dove peered in, The. Hymn to St. Maximinus, A. Hildegard von Bingen. NAWM-7v1, tr. by Peter Dronke

Dove purrs—over and over the dove, The. Dove-Love. Judith Wright. NAMCP V.2; NIL-7; NIP-4; NoAM

Dove, that weak and timid bird, The. Unknown. CCL1 Fr. Que-chao [Translations].

Dove walks with sticky feet, The. Pastoral. Kenneth Patchen. CLPP

Dove-cries on the tower stones, The. Song of the Dove, The. Alexander Robertson. APT-1

Dove-Love. Judith Wright. NAMCP V.2; NIL-7; NIP-4; NoAM

Dover Beach. Matthew Arnold. AmFaPo; BrAP; BRP; CABP; ClHu; CtM; HeIP-4; ITBLP; MakPoe; NAEL-6v2; NAEL-7v2; NIL-7; NIP-4; NoP-4; NoP-5; NPeEn; OxBEV; PoPoPo; TFi; WaAnP; WoPoe

Dover Beach. Tom Clark. OxBoAm

Dover Beach—a Note to That Poem. Archibald MacLeish. BrAP

Dover Bitch, The. Anthony Hecht. AmWit; NBLV; NIL-7; NIP-4; NoP-5 (Dover Bitch, The: A Criticism of Life?) OxBoAm; TRP; WaAnP

Dover Cliffs. William Lisle Bowles. OxAEP-2

Doves. C. K. Williams. WaAnP

Doves in the rain. Sisters. Haunani-Kay Trask. ReEnLa

Doves love a dying palm. They nestle in the loud fronds. They hum. Los Angeles, The Angels. James Harms. NeAmPo; PuP-23

Dove-twirl in the tall grass. Chickamauga. Charles Wright. PoA 2002

Dowager. John Montague. ModIr

Dowie Dens of Yarrow, The [Version from Blackwood's Magazine]. Unknown. IBB

Dowie Houms o' Yarrow, The [Hogg Version from Scotch Ballads, Materials for Border Minstrelsy; Scott's Minstrelsy]. Unknown. OBEV

Down. Mark Abley. IFF

Down. Robert Graves. BrAP

Down a broad river of the western wilds. Indian Woman's Death-Song, The. Felicia Dorothea Hemans. NoP-4; NoP-5; NPBRoP; PEW; RWP

Down again. I Sit. Susan Griffin. PoChi

Down aisles, to his side of the stage. (LL) On the Death of a Colleague. Stephen Dunn. InoFa; P180

Down all the lanterned Bagdad of our youth. On Reading the Life of Haroun Er Reshid. Madison Cawein. APN-2

Down along the Iran River. Iranian Song. Velemir Khlebnikov. TCRusP, tr. by Kathy Lewis and Bob Perelman

Down among the roots like a half-. Nuchal, a Fragment. Thomas Kinsella. PBCIP

Down at the bottom. Madrigal. Giovanni Raboni. ItPo, tr. by Gayle Ridinger

Down at the Pine Knot Junior. Good Life, The. Bobby Byrd. TiP2

Down below, everywhere, all. Central Standard Time. Kevin Young. AmPoNex

Down by the Carib Sea. James Weldon Johnson.
Sunset in the Tropics. APT-1; NAMCP V.1

Down by the Erie Canal. George M. Cohan. ReLy

Down by the Riverside. Unknown. NAAPv.2

Down by the salley gardens my love and I did meet. Down by the Salley Gardens. William Butler Yeats. IrV; NAEL-6v2; NAEL-7v2; NoAM; NPeEn; OBEV; PoPoPo; SoSe-8

Down by the sea lived a lonesome oyster. Tale of the Oyster, The. Cole Porter. ReLy

Down! Down! Eleanor Farjeon. NTCP

Down, down, down, to the bottom of hte map. Amy Lowell. NAAPv.2 Fr. Guns as Keys: And the Great Gate Swings.

Down, down, in millions, blending. Snow-Flakes, The. Priscilla Jane Thompson. CBWP-2

Down from the Country. John Blight. BMAP

Down from the mountain pastures, Pascual, the shepherd. Pascual the Shepherd. Dorothy Molloy. NIrP

Down from the purple mist of trees on the mountain. Bull Moose, The. Alden Nowlan. BeAl; BrAP

Down from the rain-soaked law. Barry MacSweeney. Oth *Fr.* Pearl.

Down from the stairs. Home: After a Poem by Frost. Steve Wilson. VisFro

Down from the window take the withered holly. Twelfth Night. Phyllis McGinley. APT-2

Down Here.

    1. OnScMo, *tr.* by Rosmarie Waldrop

Down hill, I see a tangle of lights. On a Hill Above Your House. Julia Alvarez. PfSP

Down home / he sets on a stoop. Neighbor. Langston Hughes. APSN; OxBoAm; PFTM-1

Down in a green and shady bed. Violet, The. Jane Taylor. WoRP

Down in a valley, by a forest's side. William Browne. OxBSo *Fr.* Visions.

Down in all the plain, in the tinder-dry cities. Children of the Atomic Age. Dominador I. Ilio. ReBoTo

Down in Atlanta. Slim in Atlanta. Sterling Allen Brown. APT-2; NAMCP V.1; NoP-4; NoP-5

Down in Banyantown where young. At 102, Romance Comes Once a Year. Colleen J. McElroy. OxAAAP

Down in front of Casey's old brown wooden stoop. Sidewalks of New York, The. James W. Blake. TCAPo

Down in Georgia there are peaches. Everything Is Peaches Down in Georgia. Grant Clarke. ReLy

Down in history we find it and in grandest works of art. Negro Heroines. Lizelia Augusta Jenkins Moorer. CBWP-3

Down in Kentucky. Blue Grass. Howard Dietz. ReLy

Down in the bass. Easy Boogie. Langston Hughes. APSN

Down in the cabin all things were gay. Thwarted. Priscilla Jane Thompson. CBWP-2

Down in the deep, dumb worlds are waiting, silent;. Letter to My Wife. Miklós Radnóti. AF

Down in the Depths. Cole Porter. ReLy

Down in the depths of this fair church. Church Echoes. May Kendall. ViWPN

Down in the flood of remembrance, I weep like a child for the past. (LL) Piano. D. H. Lawrence. BrAP; CABP; GoPo; HarvBoo; HeIP-4; MoBrPo; NAEL-6v2; NAEL-7v2; NAMCP V.1; NIL-7; NoAM; NoP-4; NoP-5; OPOU; TFi; TRP; WeW-3

Down in the orchard. Félix Lope de Vega Carpio. WoPoe *Fr.* Pentecost Castle, The.

Down in the pool room. True Blue Lou. Sam Coslow and Leo Robin. ReLy

Down in the south, by the waste without sail on it. Beyond Kerguelen. Henry Clarence Kendall. NOBAu

Down in the Valley. *Unknown.* GoPo

Down in Washington, D.C. Money Song, The. Harold Rome. ReLy

Down into his eyes. "You understand? Your heart." (LL) Forty Something. Robert Hass. NAMCP V.2; OxBoAm

Down into the earth's womb. "Novalis." WoPoe *Fr.* Hymns to the Night.

Down near The river. Spring of Work Storm. Joseph Ceravolo. FTOS

Down 99, south from Portland, then. South. M. L. Williams. GeoHom

Down now into the dark earth's womb. Yearning for Death. "Novalis." NAWM-7v2, *tr.* by Charles E. Passage

Down on My Knees. Ginger Andrews. SweBea

Down on my knees again, on the linoleum outside room six. Outside Room Six. Lynn Emanuel. ReTh

Down on the beach, the Punch and Judy show. Are You There, Mr Punch? William Neill. EdScPo

Down poured the rain; the closed window streamed. Storm, The. Margaret Stanley-Wrench. LW

Down Stream. Louise Imogen Guiney. SWaP

Down stucco sidestreets. Dublinesque. Philip Larkin. NoAM

Down sunk the sun, nor shed one golden ray. Holbein. Anne Batten Cristall. RWP

Down the Bay. Mary Dalton. OpeFie

Down the blue night the unending columns press. Clouds. Rupert Brooke. OBEV; OBMV

Down the close, darkening lanes they sang their way. Send-Off, The. Wilfred Owen. HarvBoo; MoBrPo; NPeEn; OBWP; OBWVE; OxBEV; PoWW; TCAWP

Down the dead streets of sun-stoned Frederiksted. Virgins, The. Derek Walcott. SoSe-8

Down the dim aisle of standing pullman coaches. Departure. Mildred Weston. FFC

Down the graveyard track. Country Funeral. Carlos Pezoa Velíz. SonAtl, *tr.* by Lisa Martin and Eva Asensio Vicente

Down the hall past the half. Visiting Hours Are Over. Chana Bloch. PoA 2002

Down the irrationally humped. Origins. Vincent Buckley. BMAP

Down the long hall she glistens like a star. Venus of the Louvre. Emma Lazarus. APN-2; GS; NAAPv.1; OxBoAm

Down the narrow Calle where the moonlight cannot enter. Venetian Nocturne. Agnes Mary Frances Robinson. VWP

Down the old high roads of inexhaustible light. (LL) Coal Fire in Winter, A. Thomas McGrath. ErotSp; GifTon; RaBo

Down the red stock route. Song for the Cattle. David Campbell. NOBAu

Down the road someone is practising scales. Sunday Morning. Louis MacNeice. MoBrPo; NAEL-6v2; NAEL-7v2; NIP-4; OxAEP-2; WaAnP

Down the rock chute into the tombs of the kings they grope these battling sandalled. This Is the Life. Louis MacNeice. NoAM

Down the season's avenue. Daphne Marlatt. NLPA *Fr.* Touch to My Tongue.

Down the slimy rope into the impossible! Poem Films Itself, The. J. S. Harry. BMAP

Down the stone stairs. After the Opera. D. H. Lawrence. BrAP

Down the street the ground is feeling so. Directions, The. Christopher Gilbert. GT

DOWN the valley gan he track. Palmer, The. Robert Greene. NoSic

Down the waves of the Yang-tse-Kiang. Ballade of the Chinese Lover. Stuart Merrill. APN-2

Down the winding lanes of Moscow, down its hopeless. Elegies on the Cardinal Points. Yelena Shwarts. VCWP, *tr.* by Michael Molnar

Down their carved [*or* chiselled] names the rain-drop ploughs. (LL) During Wind and Rain. Thomas Hardy. HarvBoo; InoFa; NAEL-6v2; NAEL-7v2; NIL-7; NoP-4; NoP-5; NPeEn; OxBEV; TFi; TRP

Down there. GYN-astics. Kemal Kurt. PML, *tr.* by Marilya Veteto-Conrad

Down There. Oskar Loerke. GTCP *Fr.* At the Edge of the Great City.

Down There on a Visit. Anthony Hecht. AmWit

Down through the tomb's inward arch. Ikon: The Harrowing of Hell. Denise Levertov. BodElec

Down to me quickly, down! I am such dust. Mummy Invokes His Soul, The. Michael Field. NPeEn; OxBSo; VWP

Down to our footprints advancing in pairs. (LL) Somebody Consoles Me with a Poem. Sandor Csoori. GifTon; TAPaP, *tr.* by Len Roberts and László Vértes

Down to the Dregs. César Vallejo. TCLAP, *tr.* by James Wright

Down to the Mire. *Unknown.* WPoS

Down to the Puritan marrow of my bones. Elinor Wylie. MoAmPo *Fr.* Wild Peaches.

Down to the shore. And smell of brine. Away from moss, fern, mortar, brick. Rosmarie Waldrop. WoBe *Fr.* Hölderlin Hybrids.

Down to the vale this water steers; how merrily it goes! Old Man by the Brook, The. William Wordsworth. TreFP

Down under the bridge you. Shakti. Rae Desmond Jones. BMAP

Down under the surface. Ffynnon Grandis. Einir Jones. BBMWP, *tr.* by Joseph P. Clancy

Down valley a smoke haze. Mid-August at Sourdough Mountain Lookout. Gary Snyder. ColAP; FaoP; LoL; NoP-4; OxBoAm; VCAP; WaAnP

Down, wanton, down! Have you no shame. Down, Wanton, Down! Robert Graves. BrAP; HarvBoo; HeIP-4; NAEL-6v2; NAEL-7v2; NAMCP V.1; NoAM

Down with All Candidates. Felix Morisseau-Leroy. OGAHCP, *tr.* by Boadiba and Jack Hirschman

Down with Love. E. Y. Harburg. ReLy

Down with the Money-Exchange. Carlos German Belli. TCLAP, *tr.* by Maureen Ahern and David Tipton

Down with the rosemary, and so. Ceremony upon Candlemas Eve. Robert Herrick. OBCP

Down you go alone, so late, into the surge-black fissure. (LL) You Will Know When You Get There. Allen Curnow. EmeKit; NoP-4

Down, you mongrel, Death! Poet and His Book, The. Edna St. Vincent Millay. MoAmPo

Downe in the depth of mine iniquity. Fulke, 1st Baron Brooke Greville. CABP; NOSC; NoSic; NPeEn; PBRV *Fr.* Caelica.

Downfall. Georg Trakl. AF, *tr.* by Daniel Simko

Downfall of the Gael, The. Fearflatha O'Gnive. IrV, *tr.* by Sir Samuel Ferguson

Down-Hearted Blues. Albert Hunter and Louie Austin. NAAPv.2

Down-hill on a Bicycle. Louis Untermeyer. ArBi

Downhill [*or* Down hill] I came, hungry, and yet not starved. Owl, The. Edward Thomas. AF; ChAP; NAEL-6v2; NAEL-7v2; NAMCP V.1; NIP-4; NoAM; NoP-4; NoP-5; OBWVE; OWoS; OxAEP-2; PoCho; TCAWP; TFi; TRP

Down—I got it all. Almost. W. D. Snodgrass. BodElec *Fr.* Führer Bunker, The.

Downland Crisis, A. Dominic Bevan Wyndham Lewis. "Ale they drink in Giggleswick, The." UV

Downpour. Daisy Zamora. CLPP, *tr.* by Barbara Paschke

Downriver rocks were rapids. Believe me. Losing a Boat on the Brazos. Walter McDonald. TiP2

Downriver, someone plays. River Flute. Po Chü-i. CrYelRi, *tr.* by Sam Hamill

Downstairs a clock had chimed, two o'clock only. Down. Robert Graves. BrAP

Downstairs I laugh, I sport and jest with all. L. E. L. Christina Georgina Rossetti. VWP

Downstairs neighbors quicken. Jesus Never Sleeps. David Graham. SwNoth

Downstream, and its upturned reflection in the water. (LL) Going Out for Cigarettes. Billy Collins. MAAN; OPRER

Downstream ("Drifting to meet us on the darkening stage.") [*diff. vers. of* "Downstream ('We gave our craft to the slow-moving stream')"]. Thomas Kinsella. HarvBoo; PBCIP

Downstream the raft plunged. In the Torrent. Johannes Bobrowski. WoPoe, *tr.* by Mark Rudman

Downtime. Lisa Buscani. AmPoNex

Downtown anywhere and between the roil. Homo Will Not Inherit. Mark Doty. AmAlph; HarvBoo; NAMCP V.2; OPRER; WiU

Downtown Boom. Lorenzo Thomas. RD; TiP2

Downtown Bus, The. Wyatt Prunty. PoDa

Downtown Los Angeles: / In the huge baroque lobby. Bagpipes at the Biltmore. Robert Conquest. OBCoV

Downtown, on the precinct wall. Field Trip. Carol Muske-Dukes. GeoHom

Downtown Sunday. Robert Crawford. OPRER

Downtown-Boy Uptown. David Henderson. EGAG

Downward Look, A. James Merrill. CAP-8; StAl

Downward Mobility. Lewis Warsh. BAP-97

Downward to darkness, on extended wings. (LL) Sunday Morning. Wallace Stevens. APT-1; BBASP; ColAP; EMP; HarvBoo; HeIP-4; MoAmPo; NAAL-5; NAAPv.2; NAMCP V.1; NAWM-7v2; NIL-7; NIP-4; NoAM; NoP-4; NoP-5; OxBoAm; PoA 2002; PoPoPo; SAmP; SoSe-8; TCAPo; TFi; TRP; WaAnP

Downy Hair. Takahashi Shinkichi. ZenPo, *tr.* by Takashi Ikemoto and Lucien Stryk

Dowry of Maubergeonne, The. René Char. MotU, *tr.* by Franz Wright

Dowsed coals fume and hiss after your meal, The. Book of Yolek, The. Anthony Hecht. HP; MakPoe; NAMCP V.2; NoP-4; NoP-5; OxBoAm; TaR; WaAnP; WeW-3

Dowser, The. Edwin Morgan. NoP-4; NoP-5; NPeEn

Doxology. Josephine D. Henderson Heard. CBWP-4

Doxology. Jim Powell. CalPo

Doyen of walls. Apologia (Nkomati). Wole Soyinka. HBAPE

Dozen Cocktails—Please, A. Else Von Freytag-Loringhoven. APT-1

Dozen dozen in her place, A. (LL) Sir John Suckling. BASC; CavPo; NAEL-6v1; NAEL-7v1; NBLV; NoP-4; NOSC; NPeEn; OxAEP-1; OxBEV; PBRV *Fr.* Poem with the Answer, A.

Dozen sparrows scuttled on the frost, A. France. Douglas Dunn. EdScPo

Dozens of girls would storm up. Embraceable You. Ira Gershwin. ReLy

Dozing on horseback / smoke from tea-fires. Basho. ZenPo, *tr.* by Takashi Ikemoto and Lucien Stryk

DP's. Lincoln Kirstein. AmWaPo

Dr Szasz, professor, sir. Footnote Extended, A. Dannie Abse. HP

Dr. Wasserman. Brenda Coultas. HeMarv

Drab and dingy bird, A. (LL) Self-Protection. D. H. Lawrence. NoP-4; NoP-5

Dracula. Salwa Al-Neimi. PoArWo, *tr.* by Subhi Hadidi

Dracula. Lorenzo Thomas. AHA

Dracula. Yi Sanghŭi. EcSo, *tr.* by Jennifer M. Lee

Draft Board at Shih-hao, The. Tu Fu [*or* Du Fu]. CrYelRi, *tr.* by Sam Hamill

Draft 55: Quiptych. Rachel Blau DuPlessis. BAP-04

Draft Horse, The. Robert Frost. APT-1; EmeKit; HeIP-4; SAmP; TRP; WoPoe

Draft of a Modern Love Poem. Tadeusz Rózewicz. PoSu; VCWP

Draft of a Reparations Agreement. Dan Pagis. HP; PoSu; WoPoe, *tr.* by Stephen Mitchell

Drafted. Su Wu. WaAnP, *tr.* by Kenneth Rexroth

Drafts. A. K. Ramanujan. NAMCP V.2

Drafty winds and fine rain. Spring Joy. Chu Shu-chen. NDACCP, *tr.* by Kenneth Rexroth

Dragged, drenched, from sleep, by horror. Mimesis. Elizabeth Garrett. MFPA

Dragging Bottom. Harry Thurston. Coast

Dragging him up the stairs to one who lies dead. (LL) Conversation of Prayer, The. Dylan Thomas. NoP-4; NoP-5; OxAEP-2

Dragon. Ruth Bidgood. AngWePo

Dragon Carries the Inscription "Kunigundula" and Is Led on a Leash, The. Hans Arp. MotU, *tr.* by Bethany Schneider

Dragon Gate cuts a wide gorge. Dragon Gate Gorge. Tu Fu [*or* Du Fu]. CrYelRi, *tr.* by Sam Hamill

Dragon Gate Gorge. Tu Fu [*or* Du Fu]. CrYelRi, *tr.* by Sam Hamill

Dragon of our dreams roared in the hills, The. Y Ddraig Goch. Henry Treece. TCAWP

Dragon Slaying. Zoltán Jékely. IQMS, *tr.* by George Szirtes

Dragon sleeps three winter months, A. Tu Fu [*or* Du Fu]. CrYelRi *Fr.* Random Pleasures.

Dragon Speaks, The. *Unknown.* NPeEn

Dragon, The. Abdul Wahab Al-Bayati. IrPoTo, *tr.* by Farouk Abdel Wahab

Dragon, The. He Does Not Give the Reader One Line of Information. Alex Marlowe. WhBo

Dragonfly. Tania Pryputniewicz. ArBi

Dragonfly. Gary Snyder. BLT

Dragonfly / Dead on the snow. Dragonfly. Gary Snyder. BLT

Dragonfly, The. Basho. EH, *tr.* by Robert Hass

Dragonfly, The. Louise Bogan. APT-2; HeIP-4

Dragonfly, The. Issa. EH, *tr.* by Robert Hass

Dragonfly, The. Stanley Kunitz. APT-2

Dragon-Fly, The. Walter Savage Landor. OBEV

Dragonfly at My Windowpane. Wole Soyinka. NAMCP V.2

Dragon-Gate House. Muso Soseki. EaWin, *tr.* by W. S. Merwin

Dragon's Breath. Hervey Allen. YaYoPo

Dragon-Steed, The. Sándor Weöres. IQMS, *tr.* by Adam Makkai and Donald E. Morse

Dragon-Watching in St. Louis. Carter Revard. OtW; UrbNat

Drainage. Peter Didsbury. StAl

Drained Cup, The. D. H. Lawrence. FaBoVe

Drainlayer. Duncan Bush. AngWePo

Drake he's in his hammock an' a thousand mile away. Drake's Drum. Sir Henry John Newbolt. FaBoWar; OBMV; UV

Drake pays court to the duck, The. Mikhail Yeryomin. ItGoST, *tr.* by J. Kates

Drake's Drum. Sir Henry John Newbolt. FaBoWar; OBMV; UV

Drama, The. Suliaman El-Hadi. SpirFl

Drama of our time is the coming of all men into one fate, The. Robert Duncan. PFTM-1 *Fr.* Rites of Participation.

Dramatic Fragments. Trumbull Stickney.
"Sir, say no more." APN-2; NAAPv.2

Dramatic Symphony, The. Andrey Bely.
"By-street was bathed in sun, The." PFTM-1

Dramatis personae. Pura López Colomé. RMCMP

Dramatis Personae. Pura López Colomé. RMCMP, *tr.* by Forrest Gander

Drank lonesome water. Lonesome Water. Roy Helton. APT-1; MoAmPo

Dransfield, who wrote. Eight xx. Laurie Duggan. BMAP

Drapery Factory, Gulfport, Mississippi, 1956. Natasha Trethewey. FuFl; SpirFl

Draw a bucket of water. *Unknown.* FaBoVe

Draw a line. Write a line. There. Lines. Martha Collins. P180

Draw a little closer, comrades! Fisherman's Story, The. Henrietta Cordelia Ray. CBWP-3

Draw a pail of water. *Unknown.* FaBoVe

Draw closer to me, God, than were I one. Prayer of an Unbeliever. Lizette Woodworth Reese. SacPr

Draw in your head and sleep the long way home. (LL) Hart Crane. ColAP; NAAL-5 *Fr.* Voyages.

Draw in your stools, good folk, for heating. Song of a Turf-sod. William A. Byrne. IrV

"Draw me," the cypress said. Childhood Painting Lesson. Henry Rago. WHSW

Draw near, / And list what with our council we have done. William Shakespeare. OxAEP-1 *Fr.* King Richard II.

Draw up his venetians and welcome the moon. (LL) Moonlight and Gas. Constance Naden. ViWPN; VWP

Drawer. Zbigniew Herbert. VCWP, *tr.* by Czeslaw Miosz and Peter Dale Scott

Drawerful of obscure tools, A. Casino. Richard Tipping. BMAP

Drawing. George Oppen. APT-2; PFTM-1

Drawing a bow you must draw a strong one. Tu Fu [*or* Du Fu]. WoPoe *Fr.* Crossing the Border, First Series.

Drawing each breath like a fine crystal of snow. (LL) Last Marriage, A. Virginia Hamilton Adair. BeAl; StAl

Drawing Hands. Greg Williamson. AmPoNex

Drawing the moon from a well. Well. Kim Chiha. CAMKP, *tr.* by David R. McCann

Drawing you, heavy with sleep to lie closer. Drawing You, Heavy With Sleep. Sylvia Townsend Warner. RSaN

Drawings of the Song Animals [*with music*]. Duane Niatum. HATNAP

Drawn by old Homer's hand, the rose. Evan Lloyd. AngWePo; OBWVE *Fr.* Powers of the Pen, The.

Drawn by Stones, by Earth, by Things That Have Been in the Fire. Marvin Bell. CAP-8; VCAP

Drawn on the blackboard. School and Nature. Jean Follain. BLT, *tr. by* W. S. Merwin

Drawn on the burden of light. Bleat. Barbara Guest. FTOS

Draws back his blade. (LL) White lotus. Buson. WoPoe; ZenPo, *tr. by* Takashi Ikemoto and Lucien Stryk

Dread. Sadiq al-Saygh. IrPoTo, *tr. by* Ralph Saverese and Saadi A. Simawe

Dread. Frederick D'Aguiar. WaCA

Dread. John Millington Synge. MoBrPo

Dread are the death-pale Kings. Still-Heart. Frank Pearce Sturm. OBMV

Dread of future foes exyle my present Joy, The. Queen of England Elizabeth I. EMWP

Dread song. "Not one of my seed" the words said. So Jah Sey. Kendel Hippolyte. WaCA

Dread Soveraign Charles! O King of Most Renown! Exultationis Carmen To the Kings Most Excellent Majesty upon His Most Desired Return. Rachel Jevon. EMWP

Dreadful are the happenings of our evil ages. András Szkhárosi Horvát. IQMS *Fr.* Curse, The.

"Dreadful Has Already Happened, The." Mark Strand. NoAM; VCAP

Dreadful schism in the British nation, A. (LL) Tony Harrison. NoP-4; NoP-5 *Fr.* School of Eloquence, The.

Dreadlocks. Tara Betts. BRtP

Dreadlocks gone. For Bob Marley. John Agard. WaCA

Dreadtalk. Frederick D'Aguiar. WaCA

Dreadwalk. Dennis Scott. WaCA

Dream. Maria Arrillaga. TANSG

Dream [*with music*]. Richard Watson Dixon. OxBEV

Dream. Mikhail Yuryevich Lermontov. WoPoe, *tr. by* W. K. Matthews

Dream: "I see you displaced, condensed, within my dream." Josephine Miles. PoA 2002

Dream: "I'm doing this poetry reading with Simone." Joanne Kyger. WhBo

Dream: "Sea was in front of me, The." No Hyangnim. EcSo, *tr. by* Aimee N. Kwon

Dream: "When the trees began to calcify, and the birds to coalesce with the branches." Georgi Belev. CSCBP, *tr. by* the author and Lisa Sapinkopf

Dream. Vahan Tekeyan. AF, *tr. by* Diana Der Hovanessian and Marzbed Margossian

Dream 8. Cecilio Garcia-Camarillo. ICANM

Dream, A [*or* The]. William Allingham. IrV

Dream, A. Anna Andreyevna Akhmatova. TCRusP, *tr. by* Daniel Weissbort

Dream, A. William Blake. NOBRP *Fr.* Songs of Innocence.

Dream, A. Maggie Pogue Johnson. CBWP-4

Dream, A. Evan Jones. NOBAu

Dream, A. Sir John Suckling. ChIV-2

Dream, A. Charles Tennyson Turner. OxBSo

Dream, A. Charles Williams. OBEV

Dream, The. Aphra Behn. RACG *Fr.* Voyage to the Isle of Love, A.

Dream, The. Louise Bogan. MoAmPo; NALW; NoAM

Dream, The. Irving Feldman. TaR; VCAP

Dream, The. Robert Earl Hayden. ESEAA

Dream, The. Marie Howe. LaCa

Dream, The. Ben Jonson. NOSC

Dream, The. Felix Pollak. RaBo

Dream, The. Theodore Roethke. NIL-7

Dream[e], The [*or* A]. Rachel Speght. BASC; EMWP
  "*Disswasion* hearing her assigne my helpe." PBRV
  "My grief, quoth I, is called Ignorance." NAEL-7v1

Dream, The; An Epistle to Mr. Dryden. Elizabeth Thomas. EMWP

Dream, The: "And once again I was within that house." John Peale Bishop. InGu

Dream, The: "Let us slip into." Olav H. Hauge. WED, *tr. by* Robert Bly

Dream, a glittering saw blade, A. Four stumps. Recurring Nightmare, A: My Amputation. Pak Sôwôn. EcSo, *tr. by* Julie C. Park

Dream, A / we dreamed. Perpetuum Mobile: The City. William Carlos Williams. APT-1

Dream, after Reading Dante's Episode of Paolo and Francesca, A. John Keats. NOBRP

Dream and Poetry. Hu Shih. WoPoe, *tr. by* Kai-yu Hsu

Dream at Night, A. Mei Yao Ch'en. BLT, *tr. by* Kenneth Rexroth

Dream Avenue. Charles Simic. StAl

Dream Boogie. Langston Hughes. APSN; NAMCP V.1; OxAAAP; OxBoAm; PFTM-1; SSLK

Dream Boogie: Variation. Langston Hughes. APSN; NAMCP V.1; OxBoAm; SSLK

Dream Broke, A. William Cartwright. NOSC

Dream Cloud. Lindiwe Mabuza. HAWP

Dream Come True. Molly Peacock. RA

Dream Deferred. Langston Hughes. *See* Harlem.

Dream Dream, The. Michael Davidson. FTOS

Dream Dust. Langston Hughes. IPoFL

Dream/Eaters. Shirley Bradley LeFlore. SpirFl

Dream/eaters on the edge. Dream/Eaters. Shirley Bradley LeFlore. SpirFl

Dream Fears. Bessie Rayner Parkes. PoBW

Dream: Flight of a Dragonfly. Gennady Aygi. ItGoST, *tr. by* Peter France

Dream He Never Knew the End of, The. Robert Penn Warren. NAAPv.2 *Fr.* Audubon: A Vision.

Dream in a dream the heavy soul somewhere. Canto Amor. John Berryman. MoAmPo

Dream in Barcelona. Meret Oppenheim. YaTCFP, *tr. by* Mary Ann Caws and Jean-Pierre Cauvin

Dream Keeper, The. Langston Hughes. ItP

Dream: "Last night in sleep." Jean R. Désiré. OGAHCP, *tr. by* Boadiba and Jack Hirschman

Dream Lover. Mark DeFoe. SwNoth

Dream Maiden, A. Harriet Hamilton King. VWP

Dream May 18, 1958. Peter Orlovsky. BB

Dream of a Baseball Star. Gregory Corso. BB; PmAP

Dream of a Black Fox. Brendan Kennelly. PBCIP

Dream of a Butterfly, The. Hurbak Myungjo. BecRai, *tr. by* Kim Daljin, Kim Won-Chung and Christopher Merrill

Dream of a Language that Speaks. Michael Palmer. WoBe

Dream of a Slave. Gavin Ewart. EmeKit

Dream of a Snow Flower, The. Shakir Samawi. IrPoTo, *tr. by* Chuck Miller and Saadi A. Simawe

Dream of a summer day: a hearse. Summer Day, A. Robert Greacen. PNI

Dream of a trophy. Ingrid de Kok. TSAP

Dream of battle on a windy night, A. Old Soldier. Louis Simpson. PWW2

Dream of Birth, The. Judith Ortiz Cofer. PueRic

Dream of Blue Eyes, A. Frederick William Faber. CenSon

Dream of Burial, A. James Wright. InoFa

Dream of Christopher Columbus, The. Juan Felipe Herrera. TouFir

Dream of Comparison, A. Stevie Smith. MoWP

Dream of Dying, A. Leslie Monsour. FFC

Dream of Elfland, A [*with music*]. Henrietta Cordelia Ray. CBWP-3

Dream of Eugene Aram [the Murderer], The. Thomas Hood. NPBRoP

Dream of Evil (First Version). Georg Trakl. GTCP, *tr. by* Robert Firmage

Dream of Fair Women, A. Kingsley Amis. NoAM

Dream of Fair Women, A. Alfred Tennyson.
  Iphigenia in Extremis. STuOW

Dream of Frida, A. Judyth Hill. ICANM

Dream of Glass Bangles, A. Agha Shahid Ali. OpBo

Dream of Hanging, A. Patricia Beer. EmeKit

Dream of Husbands, A [*with music*]. Alberto A. Ríos. NoAM

Dream of Instant Total Representation, The. Anselm Hollo. PmAP

Dream of Jealousy, A. Seamus Heaney. NoP-4; NoP-5

Dream of Mango, A. Rohan B. Preston. BtF

Dream of Mimesis, A. Katherine Lederer. BodElec

Dream of Mountaineering, A. Po Chü-i. BLT; CCL1, *tr. by* Arthur Waley

Dream of Pairing. Ntozake Shange. GT

Dream of people altogether singing. Altogether Singing. John Beecher. InGu

Dream of Retarded Children, A. Robert Bly. LoL

Dream of Rimbaud. Patti Smith. OxBoAm

Dream of Sappho, A. Ella Higginson. SWaP

Dream of the Caiman, The. José Santos Chocano. TCLAP, *tr. by* Andrew Rosing

Dream of the Closeness of Venus, A. James ("Jim.") Grabill. AtGh

Dream of the Condor, The. José Santos Chocano. TCLAP, *tr. by* Andrew Rosing

Dream of the Evil Servant. Reetika Vazirani. NAPBL

Dream of the Hair Burning Smell. Jana Harris. AtGh

Dream of the Jacklighter, The. Dave Jeddie Smith. RoV

Dream of the Just, The. Dana Gelinas. SPV, *tr. by* Jen Hofer

Dream of the Quartz Pebble, The. Vasco [*or* Vasko] Popa. PoSu *Fr.* Quartz Pebble, The.

Dream of the Ring: The Great Jack Johnson, A. George Barlow. ESEAA; MoASP

Dream of the river, The. Wakening. Robert Melançon. YaTCFP, *tr. by* Philip Stratford

Dream of the Rood, The. *Unknown*. NePenScot, *tr. by* Robert Crawford

Dream of the Unified Field, The. Jorie Graham. NAMCP V.2

Dream of the White-headed Boy, A. Colette Ni Ghallchóir. NIrP, *tr. by* the author

Dream of Trains, A. Mark Van Doren. GM

Dream of Tsuang Tsi, The. Lőrinc Szabó. IQMS, *tr. by* Adam Makkai

Dream of Wearing Shorts Forever, The. Les A. Murray. EmeKit
Dream of William Carlos Williams, A. Robert Bly. BodElec
Dream On. James Tate. BodElec; OxBoAm; PtR
Dream 1: the Bush Garden. Margaret Atwood. BrAP
Dream Painter, The. Stanley Noyes. ICANM
Dream Poem. Mary Jo Bona. UnSA
Dream Prison. Barbara Myers. IFF
Dream Question, A. Thomas Hardy. ChIV-1
Dream: Queue for Paraffin. Gennady Aygi. ItGoST, *tr. by* Peter France
Dream Recalling a Temptation, A. Maysoun Saqr Al-Qasimi. PoArWo, *tr. by* Subhi Hadidi and Nathalie Handal
Dream Song. Lewis Alexander. WHSW
Dream Song. *Unknown.* OBVE, *tr. by* Francis Densmore
Dream Songs. John Berryman.
    129.   CAP-8
    145.   NAMCP V.2; NoP-4; NoP-5
    149.   NAMCP V.2; NoAM
    153.   NAMCP V.2
    (155).   BeAl; NoP-4
    (157).   StAl
    172.   CAP-8
    312.   InoFa; NAMCP V.2; NoAM; TRP
    366.   CAP-8
    382.   CAP-8; EMP; NoP-4; NoP-5
    47. April Fool's Day, or St. Mary Egypt.   CAP-8; ChIV-2
    "Bats have no bankers and they do not drink."   EmeKit
    (Dream Song 4.)   PoPoPo
Dream Song 14.   BrAP; CAP-8; ColAP; EMP; HarvBoo; HeIP-4; NAMCP V.2; NoAM; NoP-4; NoP-5; OxBoAm; PoetW; PtR; TRP; VCAP; WaAnP
Dream Song 22: "Of 1826."   IJHIL
Dream Song 26.   CAP-8; HarvBoo
Dream Song 29.   BrAP; CAP-8; HarvBoo; NAAL-5; NAMCP V.2; NoP-4; NoP-5; OxBoAm; VCAP
Dream Song 45.   PoPoPo
Dream Song 61.   HarvBoo; OxBoAm
Dream Song 255.   HarvBoo
Dream Song 384.   BrAP; CAP-8; InoFa; NAMCP V.2; PoPoPo; VCAP
Dream Song 8.   HarvBoo
Dream Song 55.   ChIV-2
    324. Elegy for W. C. W., the Lovely Man, An.   EMP; MakPoe; NoP-4; NoP-5; WaAnP
    4th Song.   CAP-8; ColAP; EmeKit; NAMCP V.2; NoP-4; NoP-5; VCAP
    "God bless Henry. He lived like a rat."   OxBoAm
    (He stared at ruin.)   NAAL-5
    Henry sats in de bar and was odd.   PoPoPo; VCAP
    76: Henry's Confession.   EMP; NAMCP V.2; NoAM; VCAP
    "Henry's mind grew blacker the more he thought."   OxBoAm
    "Henry's pelt was put on sundry walls."   NoAM; TRP
    "Huffy Henry hid the day."   ColAP; EMP; NAMCP V.2; NoP-4; NoP-5; VCAP
    "I am, outside. Incredible panic rules."   VCAP
    "I'm scared a lonely. Never see my son."   NoP-4; NoP-5
    Lay of Ike, The.   OxBoAm
    89. Op. Posth. No. 12.   CAP-8
    91. Op. Posth. No. 14.   CAP-8
    "Seedy Henry rose up shy in de world."   VCAP
    219: So Long? Stevens.   NAMCP V.2
    Tears Henry Shed for Poor Old Hemingway (235).   OxBoAm
    "That's enough of that, Mr Bones. *Some* lady you make."   EMP; VCAP
    37: Three around the Old Gentleman.   NAMCP V.2
    "Thunder & the flaw of their great quarrel, The."   VCAP
    "Turning it over, considering, like a madman."   NoAM
Dream Songs Concluded. Maura Eichner. UpMys
Dream that stole o'er us in the time. Charlotte Brontë. PEW *Fr.* Retrospection.
Dream Thief. Nathaniel Mackey. GT
Dream tree, Polly's tree, A. Polly's Tree. Sylvia Plath. AmFaPo
Dream Variation[s]. Langston Hughes. APT-2; ISC; ITBLP; NoP-4; NoP-5; OxAAAP; OxBoAm; SAmP; SSLK
Dream Vision. James Vincent Cunningham. APT-2
Dream Vision, A. Yvor Winters. NAAPv.2
Dream was dead in me before we reached Damascus, The. Gwendolyn MacEwen. StAl *Fr.* T. E. Lawrence Poems, The.
Dream within a Dream, A. Edgar Allan Poe. NCAP; OxBoAm; TCAPo
Dream within a Song, A [*with music*]. Henrietta Cordelia Ray. CBWP-3
Dreamboat coalman filmed in silk-white ashes. (LL) Two Lorries. Seamus Heaney. EMP; NoP-5

Dreame, Ane. Alexander Montgomerie. NePenScot
Dream[e], The. John Donne. OBEV
Dreamer Meets Conscience and Reason. William Langland. NAEL-6v1; NAEL-7v1 *Fr.* Vision of Piers Plowman, The.
Dreamers? Louisa Sarah Bevington. VWP
Dreamers. Siegfried Sassoon. GSo; MoBrPo; NAMCP V.1; NoAM
Dreamer's Holiday, A. Kim Gannon. ReLy
Dream[e]s. Robert Herrick. NAEL-6v1; NAEL-7v1; OPOU; Spl
Dreaming. Fleur Adcock. OxBSo
Dreaming at the Rexall Drug. Robin Becker. ReTh
Dreaming Bean, The. Katherine Pierpoint. MoWP
Dreaming Child, The. Felicia Dorothea Hemans. NOBRP; NPBRoP
Dreaming, dreaming the night, the street, the stairway. Nocturne of the Statue. Xavier Villaurrutia. TCLAP, *tr. by* Dana Stangel
Dreaming Frankenstein. Liz Lochhead. MoWP
Dreaming Horse. Silvia Curbelo. TouFir
Dreaming I sat by the fire last night. Saturday Tub, The. Mary Gilmore. NOBAu
Dreaming I see you infinitely superposed upon yourself. Dreaming I See You. André Breton. SurPaPo, *tr. by* Jean-Pierre Cauvin and Mary Ann Caws
Dreaming in the Shanghai Restaurant [*with music*]. Dennis Joseph Enright. EmeKit
Dreaming My Dad. John Hegley. PoCu
Dreaming of Hair. Li-Young Lee. BodElec
Dreaming of Li Po ("Death at least gives separation repose.") Tu Fu [*or Du Fu*]. NDACCP, *tr. by* David Hinton
Dreaming of Li Po ("Death separation: sobs hard to swallow.") Tu Fu [*or Du Fu*]. ChinPo, *tr. by* Ye Weilian [*or Yeh Wei-lien or Wai-lim Yip*]
Dreaming of Li Po ("Parted by death, we'd strangle on our tears.") Tu Fu [*or Du Fu*]. CrYelRi, *tr. by* Sam Hamill
Dreaming of Long Ago. Po Chü-i. NDACCP, *tr. by* David Hinton
Dreaming of My Wife. Yüan Chĕn. CrYelRi, *tr. by* Sam Hamill
Dreaming of Yuan Zhen. Po Chü-i. CCL1, *tr. by* Arthur Waley
Dreaming Over a Page. Lewis Warsh. AHA
Dreaming that I Went with Li and Yu to Visit Yuan Zhen. Po Chü-i. CCL1, *tr. by* Arthur Waley
Dreaming the flower I have never seen. (LL) Moly. Thom Gunn. CABP; NAMCP V.2; NoAM; NPeEn
Dreaming Up Mother. Robert Adamson. BMAP
Dreaming, waking, the beggar maid. Beggar Maid, The. Sydney E. Jerrold. SacPr
Dream-Land [*or Dreamland*]. Edgar Allan Poe. APN-1; BrAP; NAAL-3; NCAP
Dream-Language of Fergus, The [*with music*]. Medbh McGuckian. MoWP; NAMCP V.2
Dream-Pedlary. Thomas Lovell Beddoes. OBEV; OxAEP-2
Dreams. Cecil Frances Alexander. NOxBChV
Dreams. Langston Hughes. PtR
Dreams. Helen Hunt Jackson. APN-2
Dreams. Myŏngok. WoPoe, *tr. by* Okhee Yoo and Michael Stephens
Dreams: "Oh! That my young life were a lasting dream!" Edgar Allan Poe. NCAP; OxBoAm
Dreams: "Surely I heard a voice—surely my name." Caroline Elizabeth Norton. NPBRoP
Dreams. Anne Sexton. NAMCP V.2 *Fr.* Death Baby, The.
Dreams. Henry Timrod. APN-2
Dreams Are Also Wounds. Breyten Breytenbach. VCWP, *tr. by* André Brink
Dreams Are the Royal Road to the Unconscious. Paul Goodman. PoA 2002
Dreams aren't coming, The. Selected Poses. Anselm Berrigan. Eno
Dreams by No One's Daughter. Leslie Ullman. PBCAP
Dreams fled away, this country bedroom, raw. Another September. Thomas Kinsella. CABP; HarvBoo; NoP-4; NoP-5
Dreams in German. David Martin. NOBAu
Dreams in Harrison Railroad Park. Nellie Wong. CFP; OpBo
Dreams of a Rival. Mary Robinson. CenSon; RWP
Dreams of Beauty [*with music*]. Adah Isaacs Menken. CBWP-1
Dreams of Delight, Farewell. Mary Tighe. NOBRP *Fr.* Psyche.
Dreams of the One, The. Lőrinc Szabó. IQMS, *tr. by* Edwin Morgan
Dreams, said the dog. Dialog. Jean Garrigue. OxBoAm
Dreamsters. Ani Ilkov. CSCBP, *tr. by* Georgi Belev and Lisa Sapinkopf
Dreamt blood. (LL) Biography: "Dog scatters her body in sleep, The." Michael Ondaatje. NAMCP V.2; NoAM
Dreamt I today [*or to-day*] the dream of yesternight. George Santayana. APN-2 *Fr.* Sonnets.
Dreamt I was a poet. La Bodega Sold Dreams. Miguel Piñero. PueRic
Dreamt Up. Dennis Cooper. WiU
Dreamtigers. Jorge Luis Borges. PtR, *tr. by* Alastair Reid

Dreamtime, / The first ones lived, those of long ago. Lalai (Dreamtime). Sam Woolagoodjah. NOBAu

Dreamwood. Adrienne Rich. PoA 2002

Dream-Work, The. Harry Mathews. NYP2

Dreamy and docile you sit. Grooming. Katie Donovan. NeBl

Drear cell, along whose lonely bounds. Bastille, a Vision, The. Helen Maria Williams. RWP

Drearie trumpet blew a dreadfull blast, The. Torquato Tasso. PBRV *Fr.* Godfrey of Bulloigne; or, The Recoverie of Jerusalem [Gerusalemme Liberata].

Dreary Change, The. Sir Walter Scott. NAEL-6v2

Dreary days are over. Long Ago (And Far Away). Ira Gershwin. ReLy

Dregs. Ernest Dowson. OBMV

Dreme, The. Sir David Lyndsay.
Complaynt [*or* Compleynt *or* Complaint] of the Comoun [*or* Common] Weill of Scotland, The. PBRV
Devisioun of the Eirth, The. NePenScot

Drenched with the silver salvage of the mornfrost. (LL) History. Robert Lowell. ColAP; PoetW; VCAP

Dresden. Ciaran Carson. ModIr; NPeEn; PBCIP; PNI

Dresdener:. Remembering Dresden. Van K. Brock. HP

Dress, The. Mark Strand. CAP-8

Dress, The. C. K. Williams. BeAl; StAl

Dress of Fire, A. Dahlia Ravikovitch. VCWP

Dress to know her socks off, spent all day looking for just the right. I Bought a New Red. Chrystos. WiU

Dressed and left for work. (LL) Reject Jell-O. Lucille Day. CalPo; MPUn

Dressed in the colours of a country day. From the Painting "Back from Market" by Chardin. Eavan Boland. PBCIP

Dressed mainly in black and with hair. Hopkins Enters the Roman Catholic Church. David Scott. NLP

Dressing Up. Jackie Kay. MoWP

Drew trips over his shadow by the pool. Gwyneth Lewis. NeBl; StAl

Dried Flowers. Carmen Celia Beltrán. NAAPv.2

Dried leaves as I bow and pass smiling. (LL) Young Housewife, The. William Carlos Williams. APT-1; ColAP; HeIP-4; NAAL-5; NAAPv.2; NAMCP V.1; OxBoAm; WaAnP

Dried salmon. Basho. EMJL, *tr. by* Haruo Shirane

Dried salmon. Basho. WED, *tr. by* Robert Bly

Dried vines, an old tree, evening crows. Tune: "Sky-Pure Sand." Ma Chih-yüan. ChinPo, *tr. by* Ye Weilian [*or* Yeh Wei-lien *or* Wai-lim Yip]

Drier than the sun-dried raisins. *Unknown.* PriapPo *Fr.* Priapus Poems, The.

Drifter. Marilyn Nelson. BtF

Drifter off Tarentum, A. Rudyard Kipling. PoWW; WoPoe *Fr.* Epitaphs of the War [1914–1918].

Drifters. Bruce Dawe. BMAP; NoAM

Drifter's Brand, A. Art Coelho. RWB

Drifting from above, the palms seem to sink. Last Night in Havana. Richard Blanco. NAPBL

Drifting off the wheel of a past. First Spring. Duane Niatum. HATNAP

Drifting officials alone. Harmonizing a Spring Poem by Premier Lu of Chin-Ling. Tu Shen-yen. ChinPo, *tr. by* Ye Weilian [*or* Yeh Wei-lien *or* Wai-lim Yip]

Drifting scent of the Georgia pines. Robert Earl Hayden. OxAAAP

Drifting to meet us on the darkening stage. Downstream. Thomas Kinsella. HarvBoo; PBCIP

Drifting to the hostel for the night. (LL) Seamus Heaney. NAMCP V.2; NoAM *Fr.* Station Island.

Drifts That Bar My Door [*with music*]. Adah Isaacs Menken. CBWP-1

Driftwood. Witter Bynner. APT-1

Drift-Wood. Clara Ann Thompson. CBWP-2

Driftwood and Seacoal. Andrew Crozier. Oth

Drill sergeants break up the only road we've got, The. Good Science. Ken Edwards. Oth

Drilling in Russell Square. Edward Richard Burton Shanks. OBMV

Drill's the Thing. *Unknown.* FaBoWar

Drimeh Kundan. *Unknown. tr. by* Armand Schwerner
"Queen wept but thought: It is not appropriate to show such grief, The." WoPoe, *tr. by* Armand Schwerner

Drimin Donn Dílis. John Walsh. IrV

Drink all you want in the rose-garden. Who cares what they say! Leylâ Hanim. NaPG, *tr. by* Talat Sait Halman

Drink and Agriculture. Dave Etter. IllVoic

Drink and be merry, merry, merry boys. Song, The. Thomas Morton. NAAL-3

Drink and be whole again beyond confusion. (LL) Directive. Robert Frost. APT-1; ColAP; ItP; MakPoe; MoAmPo; NAAPv.2; NAMCP V.1; NoAM; NoP-4; NoP-5; OxBoAm; SAmP; StAl; TFi; WaAnP

Drink and dance and laugh and lie. Flaw in Paganism, The. Dorothy Parker. NBLV

Drink, my horse, while we cross the autumn water! Under a Border-Fortress. Wang Ch'ang-ling. CCL1, *tr. by* Witter Bynner

Drink of Milk, A. John Montague. ModIr; PNI

Drink of Spring, A. John Ennis. PBCIP

Drink of Water, A. Seamus Heaney. TRP

Drink On [*with music*]. Mary E. Tucker. CBWP-1

Drink only to excess. Baghdad. Michael Gizzi. OnScMo

Drink to me only with thine eyes [*adapted from the Greek of Philostratus*]. Song. To Celia. Ben Jonson. AmFaPo; ClHu; NAEL-6v1; NAEL-7v1; NoP-4; NoP-5; NOSC; OxAEP-1; OxBEV; SoSe-8; TFi; UV; WaAnP

Drink when thirsty, eat when hungry. Zen Sermon. Xuanjian. CCL1, *tr. by* Graeme Wilson

Drink...with me, Melanippos. Why (think that). Alcaeus. SaLy, *tr. by* Diane Rayor

Drinker's Wife Writes Back, The. Jean Valentine. LaCa

Drinking. *Unknown.* NPeEn; OBEV; OBVE; OxAEP-1; OxBEV, *tr. by* Abraham Cowley

Drinking All Night, Sleeping All Day. Li Ho. CrYelRi, *tr. by* Sam Hamill

Drinking Alone. Wang Fan-chih. CrYelRi, *tr. by* Sam Hamill

Drinking Alone. Wang Ji. CCL1, *tr. by* Stephen Owen

Drinking Alone in Moonlight. Li Po. TAL

Drinking Alone in the Moonlight. Li Po. CCL1; ColAnChi; WoPoe, *tr. by* Elling O. Eide

Drinking Alone in the Rainy Season. T'ao Ch'ien. CrYelRi, *tr. by* Sam Hamill

Drinking Alone on a Spring Night. An Jung-Söp. TAPaP, *tr. by* Sung-Il Lee

Drinking Alone under Moonlight. Li Po. TAL

Drinking Alone with the Moon. Li Po. APT-1; ASA, *tr. by* Witter Bynner and Kang-hu Kiang

Drinking Alone with the Moon. Li Po. CrYelRi, *tr. by* Sam Hamill

Drinking Art, The. Robert Minhinnick. AngWePo; TCAWP

Drinking at Crooked River. Tu Fu [*or* Du Fu]. CrYelRi, *tr. by* Sam Hamill

Drinking Beer with Sir. Cindy Goff. LaCa

Drinking Fountain, The. Robert Duncan. CLPP

Drinking, I sing of peace and of equality. Drinking Song. Ts'ao Ts'ao. CrYelRi, *tr. by* Sam Hamill

Drinking in the Mountains with a Recluse. Li Po. NDACCP, *tr. by* David Hinton

Drinking into deep night at East Slope, sober then drunk. Tune: "Immortal by the River." Su Tung-p'o. ChinPo, *tr. by* Ye Weilian [*or* Yeh Wei-lien *or* Wai-lim Yip]

Drinking Mojitos in Cuba Libre. Harryette Mullen. RD

Drinking of wine is not pleasing to me, The. Abū Bakr ibn Muhammad ibn Ahmad al-Anṣārī al-Ishbīlī Al-Abyad. HiArP, *tr. by* James T. Monroe

Drinking on East Slope at night. Listening to the River. Su Tung-p'o. TAL

Drinking party in spring's shade, The. Sober, Remaining. Hô Sugyông. EcSo, *tr. by* Youngju Ryu

Drinking Sappho Brand Ouzo. Martin Johnston. BMAP *Fr.* In Transit: A Sonnet Square.

Drinking Song. Robert Burns. NePenScot; NPeEn

Drinking Song. Silvia Curbelo. TouFir

Drinking Song. Robert Fergusson. OxAEP-1

Drinking Song. Richard Brinsley Sheridan. NPeEn; OxBEV *Fr.* School for Scandal, The.

Drinking Song. Randall Swingler. RSaN

Drinking Song. Ts'ao Ts'ao. CrYelRi, *tr. by* Sam Hamill

Drinking Song, A. The Peniarth Poet.
"Loke that none of you departe." AngWePo

Drinking Song, A. William Shakespeare. NoSic *Fr.* Antony and Cleopatra.

Drinking Spree Beneath the Open Sky. Slavko Mihalic. PoSu, *tr. by* Peter Kastmiler

Drinking Together. Li Po. NDACCP, *tr. by* William Carlos Williams

Drinking together among mountain blossoms, we. Drinking in the Mountains with a Recluse. Li Po. NDACCP, *tr. by* David Hinton

Drinking While Driving. Raymond Carver. LaCa

Drinking Wine. T'ao Ch'ien. *tr. by* David Hinton
3. NDACCP, *tr. by* David Hinton

Drinking Wine. *Unknown.* ChinPo, *tr. by* Ye Weilian [*or* Yeh Wei-lien *or* Wai-lim Yip]

Drinking Wine ("He looked, and gave me beauty.") Wisława Szymborska. FiBr, *tr. by* Grazyna Drabik and Sharon Olds

Drinking Wine with a Mountain Hermit. Li Po. CrYelRi, *tr. by* Sam Hamill

Drinking with a Friend, Among the Mountains. Li Po. CCL1, *tr. by* Jerome P. Seaton

Drinking with Elder Cheng the Eighth at Crooked River. Tu Fu [*or* Du Fu]. CrYelRi, *tr. by* Sam Hamill

Drinking-Song, A.   Henry Carey.   OBEV

Drinks are okay.   Friendliest Thing (Two People Can Do), The.   Ervin Drake.   ReLy

Drinks in the Town Square.   Rachel Wetzsteon.   AmPoNex; NeAmPo

Drip in darkness like a leaking pipe in the cellar. (LL)   Evening Hawk.   Robert Penn Warren.   APT-2; ColAP; InGu; NAMCP V.1; NoP-4; NoP-5; OWoS; VCAP; WaAnP

Dripping with sweat he bends down.   One-Armed Man in the Undergrowth, The.   Bertolt Brecht.   PoSu, *tr. by* Derek Bowman

Dripping / words / off.   (Ryokan's scroll).   Louis Zukofsky.   APT-2

Drive.   Maggie Hannan.   NeBl

Drive a Tractor [*with music*].   *Unknown.*   NBLV

Drive Friendly.   Robert Phillips.   TiP2

Drive from Elgin to the hospital, The.   Harvest in March, The.   W. N. Herbert.   BeAl

Drive on, sharp wings, and cry above.   Redshanks, The.   Julian Bell.   OBMV

Drive stakes, shoot gradese.   Job No. 75-14.   Clemens Starck.   PoDa

Drive to Lone Ranger, A.   Ray A. Young Bear.   AF

Drive-In, The.   R. S. Gwynn.   RA

Drivel.   Emyr Lewis.   BBMWP, *tr. by* the author

Driven are the only ones to read, The.   Reading *Pericles* in New London.   Alfred Corn.   IaFF

Driven by a godawful wind. (LL)   You and I Are Disappearing.   Yusef Komunyakaa.   AmAlph; PoCho

Driven by a Strange Desire.   Mónica de la Torre.   IIR; LegDan

Driver.   Menna Elfyn.   BBMWP, *tr. by* Anthony Conran

Driver rubbed at his nettly chin, The.   To the Four Courts, Please.   James Stephens.   MoBrPo

Driver, what stream is it? I asked, well knowing.   Lordly Hudson, The.   Paul Goodman.   APT-2; OxBoAm; PoCho

Driving a cardboard automobile without a license.   #2.   Lawrence Ferlinghetti.   PoDa

Driving across the Bay Bridge at 50 m.p.h.   Picnic on the Bay Bridge.   Morton Marcus.   GeoHom

Driving along the motorway.   Glad of These Times.   Helen Dunmore.   BeAl

Driving an orange bug, passes.   At the Stop Light, the Braided Blond Man.   Anthony R. Vigil.   AmPoNex

Driving and Drinking.   David Lee.

"This all happened before."   GifTon

Driving around, I will waste more time. (LL)   Driving to Town Late to Mail a Letter.   Robert Bly.   CAP-8; HeIP-4

Driving Away.   Chandra Mayor.   PoPra

Driving down 54th St at 3 am, we were.   Misdemeanor.   Sharon Zetter.   BeDoSh

Driving During a Shower.   Kim Hyesun.   EcSo, *tr. by* Youngju Ryu

Driving from Stephenville in the late October.   That Night We Were Ravenous.   John Steffler.   Coast

Driving goats into a valley.   Driving Goats Into a Valley.   *Unknown.*   CCL1, *tr. by* John Frodsham

Driving home I see the white heron on one leg.   Out Whistling.   Dave Jeddie Smith.   PfSP

Driving Home the Cows.   Kate Putnam Osgood.   CBCWP

Driving home to River Heights after a hard day's work on a new mystery.   Unexpected Adventure, An.   Amy Gerstler.   SUP

Driving Home to See the Folks.   Anthony Sobin.   MAAN

Driving in a Snowstorm, King Salmon to Naknek.   Richard Dauenhauer.   GifTon

Driving in Oklahoma [*with music*].   Carter Revard.   HATNAP

Driving Montana.   Richard Hugo.   AmFaPo

Driving my bad news the back way home.   Night Owl.   M. Wyrebek.   PoCho

Driving My Chariot Through the Northern Suburbs Gate.   Ruan Yu.   CCL1, *tr. by* John Frodsham

Driving north before Cochiti exit, he visualizes.   Bajada, La.   Arthur Sze.   NevBe

Driving north out of town today.   Wanting You.   Terra Hunter.   PasH

Driving on the road to Stinson Beach.   Promising Author.   Carolyn Kizer.   GeoHom

Driving over the limit.   Stone Pond.   Ellen Bryant Voigt.   LPSFW

Driving Past My Exit.   Alan Michael Parker.   LegDan

Driving the freeway while.   Last song, The.   Charles Bukowski.   GoPo

Driving the last stretch before the home stretch, past the lake.   Childhood.   Barbara Ras.   GoPo

Driving the Midwest.   Ray McNiece.   AmZen

Driving the perfect fuel, its thermonuclear wings.   Hummingbirds.   Ruth Stone.   ExTi

Driving the perfect length of Ireland.   To a Cuckoo at Coolanlough.   Medbh McGuckian.   PBCIP

Driving through Minnesota during the Hanoi Bombings.   Robert Bly.   InoFa

Driving through new england.   Lucille Clifton.   ESEAA

Driving to Katoomba.   Merlinda Bobis.   ReBoTo

Driving to the Hospital.   Kate Clanchy.   BeAl

Driving to the Winnebago pow-wow, across Iowa in the August evening.   Indian Car.   Catron Grieves.   ReTh

Driving to Town Late to Mail a Letter.   Robert Bly.   CAP-8; HeIP-4

Driving to work.   Fringe-Area Reception.   Halvard Johnson.   MiVo

Driving Towards Houston.   Paul Christensen.   TiP2

Driving up highway 99.   Children in the Arbor.   Glover Davis.   GeoHom

Driving West in 1970.   Robert Bly.   PoA 2002

Driving with Dominic in the Southern Province We See Hints of the Circus.   Michael Ondaatje.   NAMCP V.2; NoP-5

Drizzle.   Cornelius Eady.   PfSP

Drizzle.   Takahashi Shinkichi.   ZenPo, *tr. by* Takashi Ikemoto and Lucien Stryk

Drizzle, The.   China Observed Through Greek Rain in Turkish Coffee.   Henrik Nordbrandt.   VCWP, *tr. by* Henrik Norbrandt and Alexander Taylor

Dromedary has one hump, The.   How to Tell a Camel.   J. Patrick Lewis.   TLR

Drone of airplane neared, and dimmed away, The.   Immanent.   Walter De la Mare.   PoA 2002

Drone v. Worker.   Ebenezer Elliott.   OBSV

Droning a drowsy syncopated tune.   Weary Blues, The.   Langston Hughes.   BrAP; ColAP; EMP; FaBoA; HarvBoo; ISC; NAAPv.2; NAMCP V.1; NoAM; NoP-4; NoP-5; OxBoAm; PoPoPo; SAmP

Droning autumn rain.   Richard Wright.   NoP-5

Drooling Madness at St. Liz.   Charles Bukowski.   BodElec

Drop by bright red drop. (LL)   Child Burial.   Paula Meehan.   EmeKit; InoFa; MakPoe; ModIr

Drop by Drop.   *Unknown.*   CCL1, *tr. by* Marsha Wagner

Drop by drop and drip by drip, rain on the winding banks.   Drop by Drop.   *Unknown.*   CCL1, *tr. by* Marsha Wagner

Drop dies in the river, The.   Ghazal 5.   Mirza Asadullah Khan Ghalib.   EaWin, *tr. by* Aijaz Ahmad and W. S. Merwin

Drop, drop, slow tears, and bathe those beauteous feet.   Hymn.   Phineas Fletcher.   SacPr

Drop my new pen.   Keith Abbott.   WhBo

Drop of dew, A.   On Reading Jules Renard's Diary.   Miguel de Unamuno.   RaW, *tr. by* Robert Bly and Hardie St. Martin

Drop your lids, little architect. Admit the bats of wisdom into your head. (LL)   Lullaby: "Sleep, little architect. It is your mother's wish."   Joan Murray.   OxBoAm; YaYoPo

Dropped a hook, east of Plankbridge.   Written on the Painting "Cold River Snow."   Ching An.   CSKM, *tr. by* Jerome P. Seaton

Dropped into the Ether Acre.   Emily Dickinson.   NCAP

Dropped off the tip of the tongue.   Dialogue of Thunder.   Christine Hume.   AmPoNex

Dropping down through tired skies.   Leaf from a Log Book, A.   H. Babcock.   OtW

Dropping Leaflets.   Jena Osman.   Eno

Dropping over the snow like tongueless bells. (LL)   For My Mother.   Ellen Bryant Voigt.   NIP-4; StAl

Dropping the Euphemism.   Bob Hicok.   AmAlph

Drops of blood drip on the earth.   Where are the Men Chased Away by that Mad Wind?   Alda do Espirito Santo.   HAWP, *tr. by* Jacques-Noël Gouat

Drops of Water.   Ella Wheeler Wilcox.

"And he held me fast, and he said, At last."   VerBaPo

Dropt in her Lap from some once lovely Head. (LL)   Omar Khayyám.   CABP; CtM; TRP *Fr.* Rubáiyát of Omar Khayyám [of Naishápúr], The.

Drought.   Eric Duncan.   IFF

Drought.   J.G. Mocoancoeng.   WoPoe, *tr. by* Philip Bryant and Mongane Wally Serote

Drought.   Joan I. Siegel.   PoCoUp

Drought, malevolent stepmother.   Natalya Gorbanevskaya.   TCRusP, *tr. by* Daniel Weissbort

Drought seems to go on forever, The.   Subterranean.   Michael Hannon.   GeoHom

Drought: Sure Signs in Merkle, Texas.   Robert A. Fink.   TiP2

Drought, The.   Gary Soto.   NAMCP V.2; NoAM

Drought Year [*with music*].   Judith Wright.   NAMCP V.2; NoAM

Drouth, The.   Jon Dressel.   AngWePo

Drouth, The.   Charles Augustus Keeler.   ASA

Drove all day from San Diego.   August Fires.   Glover Davis.   GeoHom

Drover, A [*with music*].   Padraic Colum.   MoBrPo; OBMV

Drover's Boy, The.   Ted Egan.   NOBAu

Drowned.   Gordon Rodgers.   Coast

Drowned Children, The.   Louise Glück.   NAMCP V.2; OxBoAm; VCAP

Drowned Radio, The.   Charles Bennett.   RWPCtW

Drowned River, The.   Dolores Kendrick.   FuFl

Drowned Sailor, The.   Judith Ortiz Cofer.   PueRic

Drowned Spaniel, The.   Charles Tennyson Turner.   DiBP

Drowned truck-driver was propped on the slab, A.   Little Aster.   Gottfried
Benn.   PFTM-1

Drowned Woman.   Elinor Wylie.   NAAPv.2

Drowning / I felt for a moment reaching towards me.   Epitaphs.   Charles
Reznikoff.   APT-2; NAMCP V.1

Drowning done right is simply a question which doesn't hold its answer at bay.
I Loved Ophelia.   Catherine Imbriglio.   IAoNAP

Drowning Horses.   Joy Harjo.   NAAL-5 *Fr.* She Had Some Horses.

Drowning in the Last Days of Luxury.   Edwin Torres.   HeMarv

Drowning in Wheat.   John Kinsella.   PoA 2002

Drowning is not so pitiful.   Emily Dickinson.   NCAP

Drowning / no end to it.   Old Women and Love.   Kay Smith.   Coast

Drowning of the Facts of a Life, The.   Michael S. Harper.   ESEAA

Drowning, The.   David Lehman.   MAAN

Drowning Water.   Don Domanski.   Coast

Drownproofing Lesson.   Robin Behn.   AmAlph

Drowsy sun went slowly to his rest, The.   Evening.   James Stephens.
MoBrPo

Drugged and Hooded into a Prose Poem.   Anselm Berrigan.   Eno

Drugs.   Dennis Cooper.   PmAP

Drugs.   Jacquie Jones.   ISC

Drugs of War, The.   Les A. Murray.   BMAP

Drugstore.   Peter Schjeldahl.   AHA

Drugstore Trolls.   Maura Stanton.   SUP

Druids and Shakespeare, The.   Midsummer's Eve.   Deborah Leiter.   IaFF

Druidstone.   Dylan Iorwerth.   BBMWP *Fr.* Sand.

Drum.   Langston Hughes.   APT-2; MoAmPo; NAMCP V.1

Drum anda wheel.   Cycle #22.   B. P. Nichol.   OpeFie

Drum heartbeat is present / An external behavior.   Unconsciously.   Ken
Edwards.   Oth

Drum: *Leo's Tool & Die, 1950.*   Philip Levine.   NAMCP V.2

Drum on your drums, batter on your banjos.   Jazz Fantasia.   Carl Sandburg.
MoAmPo; NAAPv.2

Drum skin whip.   Prelude.   Edward Kamau Brathwaite.   WaAnP

Drum, The.   Nikki Giovanni.   TWF

Drum, The.   John Scott of Amwell. *See* Ode: "I hate that drum's discordant
sound."

Drumbeat is constant as surf, The.   At Bon Odori.   James Masao Mitsui.
OpBo

Drumbeats.   Yi Inbok.   WoPoe, *tr. by* Kevin O'Rourke

Drumlin Woodchuck, A.   Robert Frost.   APT-1; NoAM

Drummed their boots on the camion floor.   Riparto d'Assalto.   Ernest
Hemingway.   AmWaPo

Drummer Hodge.   Thomas Hardy.   BrAP; FaBoWar; HarvBoo; NAEL-6v2;
NAEL-7v2; NAMCP V.1; NoAM; NoP-4; NoP-5; OBWP; OxAEP-2;
WeW-3

Drummer lad who marched away, The.   Old Story.   Kenneth Fearing.   AmWit

Drummer, The.   Bruce Beaver.   BMAP

Drummer, The.   Philip Dacey.   MiVo

Drummond's Lover Sings the Blues.   Norman Weinstein.   WaCA

Drums mutter for war, and soon we must begin, The.   Advice for a Journey.
Sidney Keyes.   PoWW

Drums of My Fathers.   E. Roy Cayetano.   OWABP

Drunk Among the Flowers.   Mao Wen-hsi.   ColAnChi, *tr. by* Lois Fusek

Drunk and weeping. It's another.   Nights.   Harvey Shapiro.   PA9/11

Drunk as drunk on turpentine.   Pablo Neruda.   PasH; WoPoe *Fr.* Red Bird.

Drunk, I let my skiff.   Tune: "Rouged Lips."   Ch'in Kuan.   ColAnChi, *tr. by*
Jiaosheng Wang

Drunk I lie asleep.   Yun Sŏndo.   CATKP *Fr.* Angler's Calendar, The.

Drunk, I scurry up a hillside.   Climbing Yun-lung Mountain.   Su Tung-p'o.
CrYelRi, *tr. by* Sam Hamill

Drunk in the Furnace, The.   W. S. Merwin.   NAMCP V.2; NoAM; NoP-4;
NoP-5; WaAnP

Drunk in the kitchen, I ring God.   Telephoning God.   Gary Soto.   PBCAP

Drunk Man Looks at the Thistle, A.   Hugh MacDiarmid.
"Dae what ye wull ye canna parry."   OxAEP-2
Farewell to Dostoevski.   NAEL-6v2; NAEL-7v2
"Language that but sparely floo'ers, The."   NePenScot
"O wha' the bride that cairries the bunch."   NPeEn
Yet Ha'e I Silence Left.   NAEL-6v2; NAEL-7v2

Drunk Man, The.   *Unknown.*   NOBAu

Drunk on Dragon Hill tonight.   On Dragon Hill.   Li Po.   CrYelRi, *tr. by* Sam
Hamill

Drunk on the blossoming plum.   To an Ancient Tune.   Chu Tun-ju.   CrYelRi,
tr. by Sam Hamill

Drunk who lives across the street from us, The.   Neighbor.   Richard Hugo.
GifTon

Drunkard, A [*with music*].   Fei Ma.   PML, *tr. by* Zhang Cuo

Drunkard Promise, A.   Stephanie Williams.   AnSo

Drunkard's Address to a Bottle of Whiskey, A.   Joseph Sheridan Le Fanu.   IrV

Drunkards are rolling in slowly, those who hold to wine are approaching, The.
Drunkards, The.   Jelaluddin Rumi.   WED, *tr. by* Robert Bly

Drunkard's Wife, The.   Mary E. Tucker.   CBWP-1

Drunken Boat.   Arthur Rimbaud.   SxFrPo, *tr. by* Martin Sorrell

Drunken Boat, The.   Arthur Rimbaud.   NAWM-7v2, *tr. by* Stephen Stepanchev

Drunken Boat, The.   Arthur Rimbaud.   ConPit, *tr. by* Clayton Eshleman

Drunken Boat [*or* Barge], The.   Arthur Rimbaud.
"Hearing the thunder of the intransitive weirs."   WoPoe, *tr. by* Derek Mahon

Drunken Fisherman, The.   Robert Lowell.   ChIV-2

Drunken guest clings to my sleeve, The.   To a Drunken Guest.   CATKP, *tr. by*
Peter H. Lee

Drunken Lyricist, The.   Gerry Cambridge.   EdScPo

Drunken Memories of Anne Sexton.   Alan Dugan.   BodElec

Drunken Merchant, The.   Milán Füst.   IQMS, *tr. by* Jess Perlman

Drunken Winter.   Joseph Ceravolo.   NYP2; OxBoAm

Drunkenness.   "Anvari."   WoPoe, *tr. by* Geoffrey Squires

Drunkenness [*epigram*].   Friedrich von Logau.   GePo, *tr. by* George C.
Schoolfield

Dry as the first of August.   Partitions.   Franco Buffoni.   ItPo, *tr. by* Gayle
Ridinger

Dry birch tree stood, The.   Maya Borisova.   TCRusP, *tr. by* Daniel Weissbort

Dry brown coughing beneath their feet, The.   Gwendolyn Brooks.   CAP-8;
ESEAA; OxAAAP *Fr.* Womanhood, The.

Dry creekbeds littered with buckeyes, fallen.   Like Memory, Caverns.
Elizabeth Dodd.   AmPoNex

Dry Eleven Months.   John Berryman.   BodElec

Dry heat of the Tassajara canyon.   Letter to Jeanne (at Tassajara).   Diane Di
Prima.   BB

Dry in the sun by corner of K'i.   Bamboos Grow Well Under Good Rule, The.
Unknown.   WoPoe, *tr. by* Ezra Pound

Dry Loaf.   Wallace Stevens.   RaBo

Dry River.   *Unknown.*   FaBoVe

Dry River Bed.   Andrew Salkey.   WoPoe

Dry riverbed, A.   Issa.   EH, *tr. by* Robert Hass

Dry Rivers—Arizona.   Ramona Wilson.   ReEnLa

Dry Root in a Wash [*with music*].   Simon J. Ortiz.   HATNAP

Dry Salvages, The.   T. S. Eliot.   NoP-4 *Fr.* Four Quartets.

Dry self-portrait.   Lionel Abrahams.   TSAP

Dry Spell of Faith, A.   Timothy Geiger.   AmPoNex

Dry summers flaw the leaf to a rose flame.   Nature Note: The California Poison
Oak.   Helen Pinkerton.   CalPo

Dry Tree.   Muso Soseki.   EaWin, *tr. by* W. S. Merwin

Dry tree with an empty honeycomb, A.   James McAuley.   BMAP *Fr.* Hero and
the Hydra, The.

Dry wafer.   This Day.   Denise Levertov.   UpMys

Dry wind flies from the desert, A.   Spring in Placitas.   Mary Doughtery
Bartlett.   ICANM

Dry World.   Dieter Weslowski.   InvLad

Dry-Foot Bwoy.   Louise Bennett.   NAMCP V.2

Drying pollack at the end of the eaves.   Sound of the Mountain Bird.   Paek
Sŏk.   CAMKP, *tr. by* Kyunghwan Choi

Drying Spit Blues.   Jayne Cortez.   EGAG

Dryness is upon the house, A.   In Honor of David Anderson Brooks, My
Father.   Gwendolyn Brooks.   OxAAAP

D's giving a talk called 'Poets on Poets'. I nearly didn't go.   Poet on 'Poets to
Poets', A: And Other Poems.   Mererid Puw Davies.   BBMWP, *tr. by* the
author

Du Bartas: His Divine Weeks and Works.   Joshua Sylvester.
Acrostiteliostichon.   OxBSo
"If patience true could termine passions warr."   OxBSo
"Rare type of gentrie, and true Vertues Starr."   OxBSo

Du rouge au vert tout le jaune se meurt.   Fenêtres, Les.   Guillaume
Apollinaire.   YaTCFP

Du triangle des trottoirs de la place partent tous les fils et la faux de l'arc-enciel.
S'entre-bâille.   Pierre Reverdy.   YaTCFP

Dual Call, The.   Abubakar Othman.   NeNiPo

Dualism in Ralph Ellison's Invisible Man.   Ishmael Reed.   EGAG; ESEAA

Dubbed Out.   Jean Binta Breeze.   WaCA

Dubious Night, A.   Richard Wilbur.   UpMys

Dubious "Old Kriss," A.   James Whitcomb Riley.

Dublinesque.   Philip Larkin.   NoAM

Duc Thanh brought me three fish.   Three Fish.   Bruce Weigl.   AmAlph

Duchess of Dogs.   Stephanie Williams.   AnSo

Duchess of Malfi, The. John Webster. NAEL-7v1

"Do'st thou thinke we shall know one an other." OxBEV

(Shrouding of the Duchess of Malfi, The.) OBEV

"Thou wretched thing of blood." OxBEV

"What death?" OxBEV

Duchesses. David Campbell. NOBAu

Duchess's Lullaby, The. Lewis Carroll. NBLV; UV *Fr.* Alice's Adventures in Wonderland.

Duck. Valerie Worth. NTCP

Duck fats rot in the roasting pan, The. Gwendolyn Brooks. ColAP *Fr.* Notes from the Childhood and the Girlhood.

Duck lives forever. Braggart Duck. Takahashi Shinkichi. ZenPo, *tr. by* Takashi Ikemoto and Lucien Stryk

Duck patrol is waddling down the odd-number side of Raglan, The. Army. Ciaran Carson. PBCIP

Duck's Ditty. Kenneth Grahame. NOxBChV; NTCP; WHSW *Fr.* Wind in the Willows, The.

Duckling, Swan. Jim Elledge. SwNoth

Ducks Are for Our Happiness. Gerald Stern. PfSP

Ducks bobbing on the water. Issa. EH, *tr. by* Robert Hass

Duckweed. Leopold Staff. PoSu, *tr. by* Adam Czerniawski

Duda. Víctor Terán. RMCMP

Dudley Randall. Ahmos, II Zu-Bolton. BRtP

Due East, far West. Guns as Keys: And the Great Gate Swings. Amy Lowell.

Due of the Dead, The. William Makepeace Thackeray. FaBoWar; OBWP

Due the hilot, faithful to my father. From the Raw. Alejandrino Hufana. ReBoTo

Due to an urgent trip and a lack of foresight on my part, it became necessary one night. Unpublished Man, The. Rafael Pérez Estrada. PML, *tr. by* Steven J. Stewart

Due to the tragic lowness of my brow. Red, Hot and Blue. Cole Porter. ReLy

Duel. H. C. ten Berge. TuT *Fr.* Lusitanian Variant, The.

Duel, The. Eugene Field. APN-2; ITBLP; NOxBChV; TFi

Duellist, The. Charles Churchill.

"First (entitled to the place), The." OBSV

Duende. Tracy K. Smith. LegDan

Duende. Virgil Suarez. PML

Duenna, The. Richard Brinsley Sheridan.

"Oh, the days when I was young." OxAEP-1

Song. IrLP

Thou Canst Not Boast of Fortune's Store. IrLP

Duesenberg, 1929. Herbert Morris. PoA 2002

Duet. Betsy Colquitt. TiP2

Duet. Lady Caroline Lamb. RWP

Duet. Theodore Roethke. OBCoV

Duet, A. Thomas Sturge Moore. OBEV

Duet for a Chair and a Table. Jack Spicer. APSN

Duets. Caitríona O'Reilly. NIrP

Dufferin, Simcoe, Grey (4). Margaret Atwood. PoetW *Fr.* Four Small Elegies.

Dug out just before sunrise. Great Piece of Turf, The. Rita Dove. PfSP

Dug-Out, The. Siegfried Sassoon. MoBrPo

Duh, duh, duh, DUM! (LL) Double Dactyls. E. William Seaman. OBCoV; WeW-3

Duino Elegies, The. Rainer Maria Rilke. *tr. by* David Young

Ninth Elegy. *tr. by* David Young

"Earth, isn't this / what you want: / rising up." IPoFL, *tr. by* David Young

Duino Elegies, The. Rainer Maria Rilke. *tr. by* Robert Kelly

Eight Elegy, The. BeAl, *tr. by* Robert Kelly

Duino Elegies, The. Rainer Maria Rilke. *tr. by* Stephen Mitchell

Tenth Elegy, The. *tr. by* Stephen Mitchell

"But how alien, alas, at the streets of the city of grief." StAl, *tr. by* Stephen Mitchell

Duke and I 2, The. Charles Ducal. TuT, *tr. by* Desmond Egan

Duke Ellington Dream, The. Paul Zimmer. PBCAP

Duke Is the Lad [to Frighten a Lass], The. Thomas Moore. OBCoV

Duke Of Buccleuch, The. J. A. Phelp. NOBAu

Duke: royall letcher; goe, gray hayrde adultery. Cyril Tourneur. OxBEV *Fr.* Revenger's Tragedy, The.

Duke was in his hammock and a thousand miles away, The. Great Poll-Tax Victory of '88, The. Noel Petty. UV

Duke's Song, The. Mary Sidney Wroth, Countess of Montgomery. RACG

Duke's World. Imamu Amiri Baraka. SpirFl

Duke's World / is the explanation. Duke's World. Imamu Amiri Baraka. SpirFl

Dulce et Decorum Est. Wilfred Owen. AmFaPo; BrAP; CABP; EMP; FaBoWar; HarvBoo; HeIP-4; InoFa; ItP; MoBrPo; NAEL-7v2; NAMCP V.1; NIL-7; NIP-4; NoAM; NoP-4; NoP-5; OBWP; OxBEV; PoAgWa; PoPoPo; PoWW; RaBo; TCAWP; TFi; TRP; WaAnP

Dulce it is, and *decorum,* no doubt, for the country to fall, to. Arthur Hugh Clough. FaBoWar; OxAEP-2; PoAgWa; WaAnP *Fr.* Amours de Voyage.

Dulce Lignum, Dulces Clavos. Carol Muske-Dukes. MotU

Dull and unthinking! had'st thou none but me. Upon a Bookseller. John Oldham. BASC

Dull as a bat, said my mother. Cousin Sidney. Dannie Abse. AngWePo

Dull, dull hungry cloth-head dullard! Each day. Pre-Breakfast Rant, A. Andrew Greig. BeAl

Dull. Dull indeed! What shall it e'er be thus? Edward Taylor. ChIV-1 *Fr.* Preparatory Meditations Before My Approach to the Lord's Supper.

Dull evening in a run-down village, A. Earth Poem. Mahmoud Darwish. AF, *tr. by* Abdullah Al-Udhari

Dull people, A. From Colony to Nation. Irving Layton. BrAP; NIL-7

Dull rattle of shutters being lowered, The. Anatoly Steiger. TCRusP, *tr. by* Paul Schmidt

Dull Sonnet. Henry Reed. OxBEV

Dull to myself [*or* my self] and almost dead to these. Bad Season Makes the Poet Sad, The. Robert Herrick. BASC; CavPo; NAEL-6v1; NAEL-7v1

Dull unwashed windows of eyes. Poem Some People Will Have to Understand, A. Imamu Amiri Baraka. GT; RaBo

Dull water spirit—and Protean god. Fog. Henry David Thoreau. APN-1

Dulled by the slow glare of the yellow bulb. Wartime Dawn, A. David Gascoyne. NPeEn

Dulles Airport. Eugene McCarthy. OtW

Dulngulg Song Cycle, The. *Unknown. tr. by* Ronald M. Berndt

Sunrise Sequence. NOBAu

Duluth, Minnesota. Connie Wanek. UrbNat

Dum Diana Vitrea. *Unknown.* WoPoe *Fr.* Carmina Burana.

Dumas. Jabari Asim. InTrad

Dumb. Hildegarde Flanner. APT-2

Dumb Advocate, A. *Unknown.* DiBP

Dumb Animal. Sonnet L'Abbé.

"Shyness, the delay to say, The." OpeFie

Dumb, / bloodied, the severed. John Montague. PBCIP *Fr.* Rough Field, The.

Dumb: for they flamed, and it was me they burned. (LL) Some Eyes Condemn. Edward Thomas. NoAM; OxBSo

Dumb Insolence. Adrian Mitchell. NOxBChV

Dumb World, The. W. H. Davies. OBWVE

Dumbfounding, The. Margaret Avison. BrAP

Dumka, The. B. H. Fairchild. GoPo

Dummer the Shepherd Sacrific'd. Cotton Mather. SacPr *Fr.* Epitaph.

Dump, The. Yelena Shwarts. ItGoST, *tr. by* Catriona Kelly and Michael Molnar

Dumping (left over from the autumn). Enemy Encounter. Padraic Fiacc. PNI

Dumpy little man, The. Nostalgia. Aharon Shabtai. WoBe, *tr. by* Peter Cole

D'un et de deux, de tous. Paul Éluard. YaTCFP

Dun shades quiver down the lone long fallow. Poem for Max Nordau, A. Edwin Arlington Robinson. APN-2

Dunbar, 1650. Sidney Keyes. FaBoWar

Dunbar Attacks His Rival. William Dunbar. NePenScot *Fr.* Flyting of Dumbar [*or* Dunbar] and Kennedie [*or* Kennedy], The.

Duncan's class met last night and more talk. Joanne Kyger. WhBo

Dunce. Jacques Prévert. MFP, *tr. by* Martin Sorrell

Dunciad, The. Alexander Pope.

Book the Fourth.

"O Muse! relate (for you can tell alone)." OxBEV

To Dr. Jonathan Swift. OxAEP-1

"Yet, yet a moment, one dim ray of light." NAEL-6v1; NAEL-7v1

Idle Pursuits. OBSV

"Now crowds on crowds around the goddess press." NAEL-6v1; NAEL-7v1

Reign of Chaos, The. NoP-4; NoP-5

"Then thick as locusts black'ning the ground." NPeEn

Triumph of Dullness, The. NAEL-6v1; NAEL-7v1; NPeEn

Dundee. John Burnside. NePenScot

D'une certaine manière je voudrais. Certaine manière je. Jacques Roubaud. YaTCFP

Dune Road, Southampton. Frederick Seidel. BeAl

Dung Beetle, The. Pennar Davies. BBMWP, *tr. by* Joseph P. Clancy

Dung-beetle. Breyten Breytenbach. PoetW, *tr. by* André Brink

Dungle sublime. Ronaldo V. Wilson. BtF

Dunna thee tell me it's his'n, mother. Whether or Not. D. H. Lawrence. MoBrPo

Duns Scotus's Oxford. Gerard Manley Hopkins. CABP; NAEL-6v2; NAEL-7v2; NoAM; OBMV; OxAEP-2

Dunt Dunt Dunt Pittie Pattie. *Unknown.* FaBoVe

Duomo, The. Maria Luisa Spaziani. NeIt, *tr. by* Beverly Allen

Duo-Tang. Kenward Elmslie. AHA; FTOS

Duplicity of Women, The. John Lydgate. WaAnP

Duras son las bancas, y el profesor tampoco tan lúcido. Escuela autoritaria y cómo nació un respetable género de literatura, La. Gerardo Deniz. RMCMP

Dürer: Innsbruck, 1495. "Ern Malley." BMAP

Dürer rides into the mountains. Dissolve. Rita Dove. PfSP

Dürer would have seen a reason for living. Marianne Moore. APT-1; ColAP; FTtHH; HarvBoo; NAAPv.2; NAMCP V.1; NoAM; NoP-4; NoP-5; OxBoAm; PoA 2002; PoPoPo *Fr.* Part of a Novel, Part of a Poem, Part of a Play.

Durer's *Apollo.* Darrell Bourque. Vesp

Dürer's 'Young Hare'. Norah Hill. Prnts

Duressor. Larissa Szporluk. AmPoNex

Durham. Tony Harrison. NoAM

"Durham," "Devonia," "Allendale,"—their houses, those. Summer Cloud, A. Waldo Williams. OBWVE, *tr. by* Joseph P. Clancy

Durham, "Devonia," "Allendale"—those are their houses. Summer Cloud, A. Waldo Williams. BBMWP, *tr. by* Anthony Conran

During a Friend's Illness. Gennady Aygi. WoBe, *tr. by* Peter France

During a war the poets turn to war. Ordonnance. Thomas McGrath. GifTon

During an Illness. Vladimir Holan. WoPoe, *tr. by* Ian Milner and Jarmila Milner

During dark. Having Lost My Son, I Confront the Wreckage. Wanda Coleman. BRtP

During his great speech the prosecutor. Trial, The. Zbigniew Herbert. AF; PoetW, *tr. by* Bogdana Carpenter and John Carpenter

During lecture garbage truck drums. Norman Fischer. WANABP *Fr.* Success.

During March while hoeing long rows. Hoeing. Gary Soto. PBCAP

During my Joe McCarthy childhood. Pink Diapers. Donna Brook. PrTe

During my sister's birth. Coming Down from Derry Hill. Maggie Hannan. NLP

During our consecration here, let's be careful not to make this thing that we use every day too pearly. Assiette, The (The Plate). Francis Ponge. WED, *tr. by* Robert Bly

During Recess. Giovanna Pollarolo. TANSG, *tr. by* Marjorie Agosin

During recess in the fifth grade. Foreplay. Tony Gloeggler. NevBe

During Saturn's reign I believe that Chastity still. Juvenal. RomPo *Fr.* Satires.

During the day, even if I shuddered from awkwardness, I repressed it. In the Subway—Getting Used to Ugliness 3. Kim Chŏngnan. EcSo, *tr. by* Peter H. Lee

During the Eclipse. Pascale Petit. PoCu

During the final minutes of the raid. Mushroom Clouds. John Engman. AtGh

During the First International Elvis Conference in Oxford. Elvis Reads The Wild Swans at Coole. Fleda Brown Jackson. AllShUp

During the last nights of my father's life. My Father's Clothes. Pascale Petit. Prnts

During the month that I was living at Honfleur I had not yet seen the sea. Jetty, The. Henri Michaux. MotU, *tr. by* Richard Ellmann

During the reign of King Yao, Heaven sent down countless good omens. Transformation Text on the Boy Shun's Extreme Filial Piety. *Chinese Oral Tradition.* ColAnChi, *tr. by* Richard W. Bodman

During the Second World War, I was going home one night. Charles Reznikoff. PWW2 *Fr.* By the Well of Living and Seeing.

During the winter of course. Elephant in Winter, The. Michael Van Walleghen. UrbNat

During War, the Timeless Air. John Seed. Oth

During Wind and Rain. Thomas Hardy. HarvBoo; InoFa; NAEL-6v2; NAEL-7v2; NIL-7; NoP-4; NoP-5; NPeEn; OxBEV; TFi; TRP

During your absence, when I swept the floor. Roy Fuller. OxBSo *Fr.* Cancer Hospital, The.

Durring the act, when our minds tend to wander. (LL) Reading Pornography in Old Age. Howard Nemerov. NAMCP V.2; NoAM

Dusk. Basho. EH, *tr. by* Robert Hass

Dusk. Frank Mkalawile Chipasula. HBAPE *Fr.* Nightsong.

Dusk. Angelina Weld Grimké. APT-1; NAAPv.2

Dusk. Gabriela Mistral. TANSG, *tr. by* Maria Giachetti [*or* Jacketti]

Dusk: "Before the dusk grows deeper." Joseph Ceravolo. NYP2; OxBoAm

Dusk. Summer Recital. Cynthia S. Pederson. MiVo

Dusk. Shuntaro Tanikawa. PoetW, *tr. by* Harold Wright

Dusk. *Unknown, fr. Terezin Concentration Camp.* INSAB

Dusk / Above the / water hang the. Swan and Shadow. John Hollander. NoP-4; NoP-5; OxBoAm; PoA 2002; VCAP

Dusk, The. Robert Gray. BMAP

Dusk and the Wife. A. V. Christie. PoDa

Dusk arrives. The monastery garden. Twilight in the Garden. Wang Wei. WaAnP, *tr. by* Jay Parini

Dusk Coming on outside ———, New York. Stanley Plumly. PfSP

Dusk dark / On Railroad Avenue. Railroad Avenue. Langston Hughes. APT-2

Dusk, deserted road, and suddenly. Goat. Jo Shapcott. StAl

Dusk. Enormous clouds press down on the town. Moguer. Juan Ramón Jiménez. RaW, *tr. by* Hardie St. Martin

Dusk flew in on the wings of evening, The. Dusk. *Unknown, fr. Terezin Concentration Camp.* INSAB

Dusk— / He's spearing from a boat. Lorine Niedecker. FTOS

Dusk in Creason's Park comes on slow. Late Afternoon, Late in the Twentieth Century. Jeffrey Skinner. PBCAP

Dusk in My Backyard. Keith Wilson. BLT; ICANM

Dusk in the Country [*with music*]. Harry Edmund Martinson. WED, *tr. by* Robert Bly

Dusk in Winter. W. S. Merwin. BLT; OxBoAm

Dusk, iridescent gasoline floats on the. Going Back to the River. Marilyn Hacker. WiU

Dusk: July. Marilyn Hacker. FFC

Dusk must become your light. Sitting with Lester Young. Paul Zimmer. SeSe

Dusk of Autumn: Writing What My Heart Embraces. Ching An. CSKM, *tr. by* Jerome P. Seaton

Dusk of Horses, The. James Dickey. ColAP

Dusk sifted into my breathless room, The. Deep Song. Antonio Machado Ruiz. SpanPo, *tr. by* John Crow

Dusk, the ivy thick with sparrows. Temple Near Quang Tri, Not on the Map. Bruce Weigl. AmAlph

Dusk-haired and gold-robed o'er the golden wine. For 'The Wine of Circe' by Edward Burne Jones. Dante Gabriel Rossetti. UV

Dusking year, in cosmic measure, ushers in shorter days. Night Up in the Tower. Tu Fu [*or* Du Fu]. ChinPo, *tr. by* Ye Weilian [*or* Yeh Wei-lien *or* Wai-lim Yip]

Dusky sky fades into blue, The. Paean to the Dawn, A. Bayard Taylor. CAGL

Dust. Wendell Berry. PoA 2002

Dust. Rupert Brooke. MoBrPo

Dust. Dorianne Laux. SUP

Dust: "Bundle in the gutter had its skull, The." Douglas Livingstone. TSAP

Dust: "Dead ringing of distant steps, The." Negar. CRWP, *tr. by* Richard McKane

Dust. Judith Wright. HarvBoo *Fr.* Shadow of Fire: Ghazals, The.

Dust and clay. Ascension Hymn. Henry Vaughan. NOSC

Dust and old plaster on our heads descend. In the Church of Marosszentimre. Zoltán Jékely. IQMS, *tr. by* J. G. Nichols

Dust Bowl. P. Inman.

"Field dodd." FTOS

Dust for you, but never my mouth again. *Unknown.* SLW, *tr. by* Marjolijn De Jager, Sayd Bahodin Majrouh and André Velter

Dust Hath Closed Helen's Eye. Anthony Raftery. IrV,

Dust is the only Secret. Emily Dickinson. TCAPo

Dust may never settle, The. (LL) When I Think About America Sometimes (I Think of Ralph Kramden). Dorothy Barresi. ExTi; ReTh

Dust motes float, The. Dust. Wendell Berry. PoA 2002

Dust of all the saints of the ages, The. Cymru. David Gwenallt Jones. OBWVE, *tr. by* Gwyn Jones

Dust of Mexico, The. David Johnson. ICANM

Dust of Poems, The. Nathan Yonathan. NRoS, *tr. by* Esther Raizen

Dust of Silence. Oliver Pitcher. EGAG

Dust of Snow. Robert Frost. APT-1; ChAP; NAAPv.2; NAMCP V.1; OxBoAm; PtR; SAmP; SoSe-8; WaAnP; WeW-3

Dust on the Mantel: Sonnet. Jacqueline Osherow. InoFa

Dust Storm. Gray Jacobik. BAP-97

Dust Storm, The. Yusuf Rakha. AnVo, *tr. by* Mohamed Enani

Dust Storm Disaster. Woody Guthrie. APT-2

Dust takes you from the stranger's company. Gaius Valerius Flaccus. RomPo *Fr.* Argonautica, The.

Dust to Dust. Thomas Hood. NBLV

Dust Truck Blues. Iwan Llwyd. BBMWP, *tr. by* Geraint Løvgreen

Dust World. Adrian C. Louis. UnSA

Dusting. Rita Dove. AmAlph; ESEAA; HeIP-4; NAAL-5; NAMCP V.2; NoP-5; PoA; WaAnP *Fr.* Thomas and Beulah.

Dusting. Daniel Hall. YaYoPo

Dusting. Marilyn Nelson Waniek. PfSP

Dusty, with some skeleton of. Yahrtzeit Light, The. Lyn Lifshin. UnSA

Dutch Interiors. Jane Kenyon. ExTi

Dutch Lover, The. Aphra Behn.
  (Song: The Willing Mistriss.) PEW
  (Willing Mistress, The.) NALW
  (Willing Mistress, The.) LW
Dutch Lullaby, A. Eugene Field. *See* Wynken, Blynken, and Nod.
Dutch Proverb, A. Matthew Prior. OBCoV
Duties and Vocations. Jane Satterfield. SweBea
Duties of the Student. Kuan Chung. ColAnChi *Fr.* Kuan Tzu.
Duty, or Truth at Work [*with music*]. Lizelia Augusta Jenkins Moorer. CBWP-3
Duty Surviving Self-Love. Samuel Taylor Coleridge. NPeEn
Duty to Tyrants. Robert Herrick. BASC
Duw gwyddiad mai da y gweddai. Dafydd ap Gwilym. CABP *Fr.* Mis Mai.
Dux Bellorum. Max Winter. NeAmPo
Dwarf barefooted, chanting, The. Peasants, The. Alun Lewis. OxBEV; PoWW; TCAWP
Dwarf Birches. Yevgeny Aleksandrovich Yevtushenko. TCRusP, *tr.* by Peter Levi and Robin Milner-Gulland
Dwarfs are born constantly. (LL) Henri Michaux. GPTC; MotU *Fr.* I Am Writing to You from a Far-Off Country.
Dwell in this stone who once was tenant of flesh. Design for a Tomb. John Ormond. TCAWP
Dwell of a sound for a while, The. Textures. William Stafford. BodElec
Dwell thou, a warning to the coming times. (LL) Death of Slavery, The. William Cullen Bryant. CBCWP; PCW
Dweller in hollow places, hills and rocks. Echo. Madison Cawein. APN-2
Dwelling. Emily Warn. GifTon
Dwelling by a Stream. Liu Tsung-yüan. CCL1, *tr.* by Witter Bynner
Dwelling in poverty / I have few human contacts. In Reply to a Poem by Liu Chaisang. T'ao Ch'ien. CCL1, *tr.* by William Acker
Dwelling in the Mountains. Hsieh Ling-yün. *tr.* by David Hinton
  "Here where I live." NDACCP, *tr.* by David Hinton
Dwelling-Place, The. Henry Vaughan. NOSC
Dwells within the soul of every Artist. Unexpressed. Adelaide Anne Procter. SacPr
Dwindle in loss. (LL) Her Garden. Donald Hall. BAP-01; OxBoAm
Dxi ne gueela. Na Victórica litru. Natalia Toledo. RMCMP
Dxiibi Guidxa. Natalia Toledo. RMCMP
Dyeing. Mabel Tobrise. NAfrP
Dyfed Devastated? Thomas James Jones. BBMWP, *tr.* by Jon Dressel
Dying [*with music*]. Adah Isaacs Menken. CBWP-1
Dying. Robert Pinsky. PoA 2002; VCAP
Dying. Tōge Sankichi. PFTM-2 *Fr.* Poems of the Atomic Bomb.
Dying: An Introduction. Louis Edward Sissman.
  "Bruisingly cradled in a Harvard chair." NoP-4; NoP-5
Dying Art, A. Derek Mahon. ModIr
Dying Away. William Meredith. NAMCP V.2; NoAM
Dying Child, The. Mary Howitt. VWP
Dying Child, The. Letitia Elizabeth Landon. VWP
Dying Christian to His Soul, The. Alexander Pope. *See* Ode: The Dying Christian to His Soul.
Dying, darling, is the easy bit. Fifty paracetamol. New Bride, The. Catherine Smith. BeAl
Dying firelight slides along the quirt, A. End of the Weekend, The. Anthony Hecht. WeW-3
Dying Gaul, The. Desmond O'Grady. PBCIP
Dying Girl, The [*with music*]. Mary Weston Fordham. CBWP-2
Dying Husband's Farewell, The. Phineas Fletcher. SacPr
Dying In. Peter Dale Scott. ASA
Dying in Paris. Heinrich Heine. *tr.* by Robert Lowell
  Death and Morphine. WoPoe, *tr.* by Robert Lowell
  "Every idle desire has died in my breast." WoPoe, *tr.* by Robert Lowell
  "My zenith was luckily happier than my night." WoPoe, *tr.* by Robert Lowell
Dying Indian, The. Joseph Warton. OxAEP-1
Dying on the grass. Dying In. Peter Dale Scott. ASA
Dying Oscar. David Macbeth Moir. DiBP
Dying Raven, The. Richard Henry Dana. APN-1
Dying Song. Anton Ulrich. GePo, *tr.* by George C. Schoolfield
Dying Speech of an Old Philosopher. Walter Savage Landor. *See* I Strove With None.
Dying Swan, The. Thomas Sturge Moore. OBMV
Dying Swan, The. Alfred Tennyson. OWoS
Dying Viper, A. Michael Field. CABP
Dying wasps stagger wide of the mark. Flames and Leaves. Caitríona O'Reilly. NIrP
Dying with Amish Uncles. Julia Kasdorf. PBCAP

Dying with the Wrong Name [Three parts of an unfinished poem]. Sam Hamod. UnSA
Dying Words of Stonewall Jackson, The. Sidney Lanier. APN-2; CBCWP; PCW
Dying Year, The [*with music*]. Clara Ann Thompson. CBWP-2
Dyke View Berry Farm. Leonard Neufeldt. ACAMVP
Dykes, The. Rudyard Kipling. HarvBoo; OBWP
Dylan. Thomas James Jones. BBMWP, *tr.* by Jon Dressel
Dylan is about the Individual against the whole of creation. Is About. Allen Ginsberg. BAP-97
Dylan Thomas at Tenby. Raymond Garlick. TCAWP
Dylan, Two Days [*for Dylan Corbett*]. Patricia Smith. GT
Dynamic marking cuts through the fill-up. Allen Fisher. Oth *Fr.* Stepping Out.
Dynamite. Peter Schjeldahl. MotU
Dynamizer and the Oscilloclast, The. Jack Coulehan. BloBone
Dynamo Stadium, 1980. Aleksandr Petrovich Tkachenko. ItGoST, *tr.* by Maia Tekses
Dynasts, Part 2, The. Thomas Hardy.
  "Something stands here to peril our advance." FaBoWar
Dynasts, The. Thomas Hardy.
  Albuera. FaBoWar
  "Certain sort of bravery, A." FaBoWar
  Eve of Waterloo, The. FaBoWar; OBWP
  Night of Trafalgar, The. MoBrPo; OBMV
  "What are you thinking, that you speak no word?" FaBoWar
Dyne. René Char. MotU, *tr.* by Franz Wright
Dysraphism. Charles Bernstein. FTOS
Dzogbese Lisa has treated me thus. Songs of Sorrow. Kofi Awoonor. HBAPE
D-Zug. Julian Croft. NOBAu

E

E- / gypt. Journeys, The. Edward Kamau Brathwaite. HarvBoo
E. D. in Commendation of the Author and His Choise. "E. D." EMWP
E. D. in Prayse of Mr. W. Fouler Her Friend. "E. D." EMWP
E get one dream. I Wan Bi President. Ezenwa-Ohaeto. NAfrP
E is in Heaven. Dixie Salazar. GeoHom
E. P. Ode Pour l'Election de Son Sepulchre. Ezra Pound. *See* Hugh Selwyn Mauberley.
E Pur Si Muove. George Bradley. YaYoPo
E Questa Vita Un Lampo. Peter Riley. Oth
E. S. L. Charles Martin. RA
E stands for egg. Joseph Hilaire Pierre Belloc. NoAM *Fr.* Moral Alphabet, A.
E Tenebris. Oscar Wilde. ChIV-2; GSo; MoBrPo; NAEL-6v2; NAEL-7v2; OxAEP-2
'E was warned agin 'er. Sergeant's Weddin', The. Rudyard Kipling. OBCoV
Each Afternoon. Idea Vilariño. TANSG, *tr.* by Louise B. Popkin
Each afternoon draws to a close. Each Afternoon. Idea Vilariño. TANSG, *tr.* by Louise B. Popkin
Each and All. Ralph Waldo Emerson. APN-1; ColAP; NAAL-3; NAAL-5; NAAPv.1; NCAP; OxBoAm; TCAPo; TreFP
Each blessed lady that in virtue spends. To All Virtuous Ladies in General. Emilia Lanier and Aemilia Bassano Lanyer. BASC
Each body has its art, its precious prescribed. Still Do I Keep My Look, My Identity. Gwendolyn Brooks. OxBoAm
Each body has its art, its precious prescribed. Gwendolyn Brooks. IllVoic *Fr.* Gay Chaps at the Bar.
Each Bone of the Body. Frankie Paino. FaoP
Each book has a title and all chapters have numbers and each page has a number. Compass Room, The: East. Thalia Field. IIR
Each burning deed and thought! (LL) Village Blacksmith, The. Henry Wadsworth Longfellow. APN-1; BRP; UV
Each care decays, and yet my sorrow springs. (LL) Soote Season, The. Petrarch. BrAP; NAEL-6v1; NAEL-7v1; NoP-4; NoP-5; NoSic; WaAnP
Each care-worn face is but a book. Strangers, The. Jones Very. APN-1
Each certain kind of weather or of light. Black Cockatoos. Judith Wright. OWoS
Each cough is an underground nuclear explosion. Remedios. Demetria Martinez. ICANM
Each Day. David Ignatow. BodElec
Each day I long so much to see. One Who Is at Home, The. Franciso Albanez. RaBo, *tr.* by Robert Bly
Each day I see them carefully grow old and feed. Sunny Prestatyn. John Davies. TCAWP

Each day, I take the lift from the sublet down to the ground floor.   Beds, The.   Elizabeth Spires.   CAP-8

Each day into the upper air.   Election Reflection.   M. Keel Jones.   NBLV

Each day it seems fiery winds blew but now at last the great hand has come to my waist.   Yi Sang.   CAMKP *Fr.* Crow's-Eye View.

Each day mowed.   Man into Whose Yard You Should Not Hit Your Ball, The.   Thomas Lux.   P180

Each day, the autumn, eating a little further.   Autumn Cancer.   Kerry Hardie.   BeAl; PoCu

Each day the gold sun comes over the hill.   Sun, The.   Georg Trakl.   WED, *tr. by* Robert Bly

Each day the road splits into dozens of branches. Before me.   Anam Street 2—Outside the Cinema.   Yi Kyôngnim.   EcSo, *tr. by* Peter H. Lee

Each day the tide withdraws; chills us; pastes.   Wreaths.   Geoffrey Hill.   PoA 2002

Each day the time grows less, the hours.   Winter 9.   Patrick Lane.   BrAP

Each dream is an afterimage of a woman leaving. (LL)   Dionisio D. Martinez.   NoP-4; NoP-5 *Fr.* What the Men Talk About When the Women Leave the Room.

Each drifting snowflake.   Snow Valley.   Muso Soseki.   EaWin, *tr. by* W. S. Merwin

Each droplet contains a message.   It Is Raining Today.   Sandra Maria Esteves.   PueRic

Each evening.   Dirt.   StacyLynn.   BtF

Each evening, ducks paddle, egrets fly.   Venturing Out.   *Vietnamese Oral Tradition.*   CaDao, *tr. by* John Balaban

Each evening, I watch the clouds flying.   Evening.   *Vietnamese Oral Tradition.*   CaDao, *tr. by* John Balaban

Each evening Master Lu sets his fish traps.   Mandarin Who Couldn't Do Anything, The.   *Vietnamese Oral Tradition.*   CaDao, *tr. by* John Balaban

Each face in the street is a slice of bread.   Bread.   W. S. Merwin.   VCAP

Each fall this town empties, leaving me.   Emptying Town.   Nick Flynn.   AmPoNex; LegDan; NAPBL

Each falling petal diminishes spring.   Crooked River Meditation.   Tu Fu [*or* Du Fu].   CrYelRi, *tr. by* Sam Hamill

Each form of beauty's but the new disguise.   Unimaginative, The.   Madison Cawein.   APN-2

Each friend turned out to be an enemy.   Khwaja Shams-ad-din Muhammad Hafiz.   WoPoe *Fr.* Three Poems on Friendship.

Each from Different Heights.   Stephen Dunn.   StAl

Each Happiness Ringed by Lions.   Jane Hirshfield.   ExTi

Each has a foot-square paper napkin stuck.   Coach Class Seats.   Charles Harper Webb.   PoDa

Each hour has some glory all its own.   Hour's Glory, The.   Henrietta Cordelia Ray.   CBWP-3

Each house had its ghost. Graves opened to his voice.   Sigmund Freud.   Howard Nemerov.   PoA 2002

Each in a Place Apart.   James McMichael.   "My parents had teased that if I ever."   GeoHom

Each in her well-lighted picture window, reading a book or magazine.   Karl Shapiro.   BodElec *Fr.* Bourgeois Poet, The.

Each In His Own.   "Angelus Silesius."   GePo *Fr.* Cherubical Wanderer, The.

Each in his Proper gloom.   My Own Fate.   Lionel Pigot Johnson.   SacPr

Each inmost peece in me is thine.   Bible, *O.T.*   NPeEn *Fr.* Psalms.

Each instant comes with a price, the blue-edged bill.   Cradle Logic of Autumn, The.   Jay Wright.   OxBoAm

Each island marks the limits of the sight.   Desiderata on a Desert Island.   Jasper Bernes.   IAoNAP

Each Life Converges to some Centre.   Emily Dickinson.   TCAPo

Each man me telleth I change most my device.   Sir Thomas Wyatt.   AEP

Each man on this slow train.   Farewell to You.   Elizabeth Alexander.   GT

Each minute the last minute. (LL)   Living.   Denise Levertov.   BLT; GoPo; OPOU; StAl

Each Moment a White Bull Steps Shining into the World.   Jane Hirshfield.   PoDa

Each moment is infinite and complete.   Moment.   Angela Jackson.   BtF

Each Moment is Surrounded.   Ray DiPalma.   PmAP

Each Moment of the long-liv'd Day.   Catullus.   OBVE

Each morn / From the straw raincoat.   Ransetsu.   ZenPo, *tr. by* Takashi Ikemoto and Lucien Stryk

Each Morning.   Imamu Amiri Baraka.   ESEAA *Fr.* Hymn for Lanie Poo.

Each morning a missionary advertise with neon sign.   Civilization (Bongo, Bongo, Bongo).   Bob Hilliard.   ReLy

Each morning, as soon as the arbors drink in the dew, the hospital doors swing open.   Lepers.   Aloysius Bertrand.   MotU, *tr. by* James Weeks

Each morning, his baby fingers clack.   What We Need Words For.   Rebecca Seiferle.   PoChi; TAPaP

Each morning I finish my coffee.   Lullaby.   Jon Mukand.   BloBone

Each morning / I go down.   Imamu Amiri Baraka.   ESEAA *Fr.* Hymn for Lanie Poo.

Each morning she is wheeled into the picture.   Living in the La Brea Tar Pits.   Nancy Vieira Couto.   PBCAP

Each morning they pass over.   Starling Migration, The.   Jeffrey Skinner.   PBCAP

Each naked branch, the yellow leaf or brown.   Robe, The.   Jones Very.   NCAP

Each night, as I step beyond the four.   Amadou.   James E. Cherry.   BRtP

Each night, I braid my daughter's hair.   They Were Alone in the Winter.   Luci Tapahonso.   ItWoWo

Each night plows instead of no head.   Female Torso.   Frank O'Hara.   AHA

Each night she fills, from the fabled.   Mrs McKellar, Her Martyrdom.   Kathleen Jamie.   EdScPo

Each night with moist leaves.   Bamboo Elegy: Two.   Edmond Yi-teh Chang.   OpBo

Each now dropped / Lay your hands upon me, you in the black bent grass, the body in motion.   Psalm.   Catherine Imbriglio.   IAoNAP

Each of them must have terrified.   In Memory of the Utah Stars.   William Matthews.   CAP-8; MoASP

Each of these microscopic points and lines is in itself a complete world;.   Universe of the Rose.   Chimako Tada.   VCWP, *tr. by* Kirsten Vidaeus

Each of us has some bodily trait that's well known.   *Unknown.*   PriapPo *Fr.* Priapus Poems, The.

Each of us holds a locked razor. (LL)   Waking in the Blue.   Robert Lowell.   AmFaPo; MoAmPo; NAMCP V.2

Each of us pursues his trade.   Scholar and the Cat, The.   *Unknown.*   WoPoe, *tr. by* Frank O'Connor

Each one making possible the next. (LL)   From a Survivor.   Adrienne Rich.   LoL; NALW

Each one showed me his gold medal.   Viet Kong.   William Trowbridge.   ReTh

Each one the shape of its soul.   Mesquite.   Robert A. Fink.   TiP2

Each perfect rose that unfolded yesterday.   Ecstasy.   Amado Nervo.   TCLAP, *tr. by* Sue Standing

Each person is a world, peopled.   Gunnar Ekelof.   WED *Fr.* Études.

Each photographed face.   Valerio Magrelli.   NeIt

Each picture was a painted memory.   Hour in a Studio, An.   Richard Watson Gilder.   APN-2

Each ray of sunshine is seven minutes old.   Snow on the Desert.   Agha Shahid Ali.   AmAlph

Each Saturday, our father downtown to work.   Arrowhead Christian Center and No-Smoking Luncheonette.   Janet Sylvester.   ReTh

Each Sentence Is Into the Fast.   Joe Wenderoth.   BodElec

Each small gleam was a voice.   Stephen Crane.   APN-2

Each sockeye of adulterous claim.   Little Hans.   Steve McCaffery.   FTOS

Each Sound.   Dorianne Laux.   NevBe

Each star a rung.   Prison Evening, A.   Faiz Ahmad Faiz.   BeAl; VCWP, *tr. by* Agha Shahid Ali

Each steamy night.   Sea-palms.   *Unknown.*   SonAtl, *tr. by* P. Alleyne, Tim Hillier, Terence Madeleine, Jean-Claude Mahoune, Christopher Morau and Alan Starr

Each Step.   Jane Hirshfield.   WhBo

Each storm-soaked flower has a beautiful eye.   Rain.   Vachel Lindsay.   RaBo

Each summer I would coddle a bottle of cognac.   Cognac.   Michael Waters.   PoDa

Each Sunday I climb the mountain to picnic.   Picnic.   Nellie Wong.   OpBo

Each tear that fell.   If I Were Earth.   Henry Dumas.   OxAAAP

Each that I loved is now my enemy.   Epigrams: A Journal.   James Vincent Cunningham.

Each Time.   Edgar Anawrok.   GifTon

Each time.   Each Time.   Edgar Anawrok.   GifTon

Each time breath draws through me.   This Body.   Michael Cuddihy.   GifTon

Each time footsteps.   Karai Senryū.   EMJL, *tr. by* Makoto Ueda

Each time I come back.   This Familiarity.   Eli Clare.   PfS

Each time I come over a rise.   Sierra Noon.   C. G. Hanzlicek.   GeoHom

Each Time I Pass.   Miguel Hernández.   RaW, *tr. by* Hardie St. Martin

Each time I passed his place I looked.   I Stand at the Window and Wave My Arms About.   Angela Cooke.   ArBi

Each time I study the works of great writers, I flatter myself I know how their minds worked.   Rhymeprose on Literature.   Lu Chi.   ColAnChi, *tr. by* Achilles Fang

Each Time That Almost.   Vittorio Sereni.   PML, *tr. by* Marcus Perryman and Peter Robinson

Each tree stands alone in stillness.   Ted Berrigan.   NYP2 *Fr.* Sonnets, The.

Each volcano lifts its profile.   Volcanoes, The.   José Santos Chocano.   TCLAP, *tr. by* Andrew Rosing

Each way the turn.   Turn, The.   Robert Creeley.   FTOS

Each week, our great Aunt Doris came to teach me piano. Largo. Deryn Rees-Jones. TCAWP

Each wishing for the sword that severs all. (LL) George Meredith. CABP; GSo; NAEL-6v2; NAEL-7v2; NoP-4; NoP-5; NPeEn; WaAnP *Fr.* Modern Love.

Each woman is moved. Love Story in Subtitles. Nancy Mitchell. LaCa

Each word carefully. Sam Hamill. TAPaP *Fr.* Tao of Poetry, A.

Each year, come the late autumn evenings. Autumn Evening: To Send to my Nieces and Nephews. Ch'i-chi. CSKM, *tr. by* Burton Watson

Each year I hoped they'd keep, knew they would not. (LL) Blackberry-Picking. Seamus Heaney. ChAP; PtR

Each year it is but a peck of rice. Basho, Boncho and Mukai Kyorai. WoPoe *Fr.* Linked-Verse Sequence Throughout the Town, The.

Each year the monuments grew larger. Monuments, The. John Ash. EmeKit

Each year when the trees turn white. Santa Claus. Harry Edmund Martinson. PML, *tr. by* Leif Sjöberg and William Jay Smith

Each year when the vile bugs come round. Bugs. *Unknown.* IFF

Eager baby voice outside my door, The. (LL) Augusta Davies Webster. ViWPN; VWP *Fr.* Mother and Daughter.

Eager breath, An. First Portrait of My Son. Alaide Foppa. TANSG, *tr. by* Celeste Kostopulos-Cooperman

Eager I'd traverse Lybia's plain. Some Terrify Lions [*or* Anna Matilda]. Robert Merry. STuOW

Eager note on my door said "Call me", The. Poem. Frank O'Hara. NAMCP V.2; NoAM; OxBoAm; PmAP

Eager Spring. Gordon Bottomley. MoBrPo

Eager to become. *Unknown.* NAAPv.2

Eagle Above Us, The. *Unknown.* WoPoe, *tr. by* Willard Trask

Eagle and a squirrel, An. A bull and a sage. Book of Hand Shadows, The. Marianne Boruch. P180

Eagle and Me, The. E. / Harburg. ReLy

Eagle and the Beetle, The. Jean de La Fontaine. OBVE, *tr. by* Elizur Wright

Eagle and the Mole, The. Elinor Wylie. CtM; MoAmPo; NAAPv.2; NALW

Eagle is my power, The. Eagle-Feather Fan, The. N. Scott Momaday. NoP-4; NoP-5

Eagle of Pengwern. *Unknown.* WoPoe, *tr. by* Gwyn Williams

Eagle Poem. Joy Harjo. HATNAP; NAAL-5; WeW-3

Eagle Rock. Tomas Transtromer. WoBe, *tr. by* Robin Fulton

Eagle shall die, The. Dumas. Jabari Asim. InTrad

Eagle soars in the summit of heaven, The. T. S. Eliot. OBMV *Fr.* Choruses from "The Rock."

Eagle Song. Gordon Bottomley. MoBrPo *Fr.* Suilven and the Eagle.

Eagle That Is Forgotten, The. Vachel Lindsay. APT-1; MoAmPo

Eagle, The. Alfred Tennyson. ChAP; ClHu; HeIP-4; ITBLP; NAEL-6v2; NAEL-7v2; NoP-4; NoP-5; NTCP; OWoS; TFi; TRP; WaAnP

Eagle! why soarest thou above that tomb? Spirit of Plato. *Unknown.* OBVE

Eagle Youth. Karle Wilson Baker. OtW

Eagle-Feather Fan, The. N. Scott Momaday. NoP-4; NoP-5

Eagles. James Dickey. BodElec

Eagles at Dollywood. Stephen Powers. RWB

Eagles gather on the place of death, The. Eagles, The. Jones Very. TCAPo

Eagle's nest on the head of an old redwood on one of the precipice-footed ridges, An. Beaks of Eagles, The. Robinson Jeffers. NAAPv.2

Eagles, The. Jones Very. TCAPo

Ear Injured by Hearing Things, An. Steve Jonas. EGAG

Ear of a Goat, The. Tony Marinho. NeNiPo

Ear struck from within, roaring. (LL) Paterson: The Falls. William Carlos Williams. APT-1; ColAP

Ear Training. Sekou Sundiata. SpirFl

Eardrums of the deaf are already broken; they like it loud, The. They. Deaf Dancing to Rock, The. Lisel Mueller. SwNoth

Earl and the Girl, The. Charles MacKay. STuOW *Fr.* Man's Heart, A.

Earl Mertoun's Song. Robert Browning. OBEV *Fr.* Blot in the 'Scutcheon, A.

Earle of Somerset. Sir Henry Wotton. *See* Upon the Sudden Restraint of the Earl[e] of Somerset, Then Falling from Favor [*or* Favour].

Earlier, to be ready, I hoovered the carpet. On Reading Rumi. Mimi Khalvati. MFPA

Earliest Crows in Mineral. Jennifer Timoner. ICANM

Earliest Known Representation of a Storm in Western Art, The. Lavinia Greenlaw. MFPA

Earliest Spring. William Dean Howells. OBEV
(In Earliest Spring.) APN-2

Early. Jean-Baptiste Tati-Loutard. WoPoe, *tr. by* Eric Sellin

Early Affection. George Moses Horton. TCAPo

Early Afterlife, An. Linda Pastan. ExTi

Early April on Broadway, south of Union Square. Seeing Off a Friend. Stephen Dobyns. EmeKit

Early Arrival: Sydney. Vivian Smith. NOBAu

Early Aspirations. William Bell Scott. CenSon

Early Autumn. Johnny Mercer. ReLy

Early bird may catch the worm, The. Samuel Hoffenstein. NBLV *Fr.* As the Crow Flies, Let Him Fly.

Early blossoms—could a single. Permanence in Change. Johann Wolfgang von Goethe. STV, *tr. by* John Frederick Nims

Early Copper. Carl Sandburg. HeIP-4

Early cricket sings clear, then stops, An. Evening Rain. Po Chü-i. NDACCP, *tr. by* David Hinton

Early dawn. Basho. EMJL, *tr. by* Haruo Shirane

Early dawn shows the maroon and tan shell. Bedside. Clive Matson. PasH

Early Days. John Stuart Williams. TCAWP

Early Death. Hartley Coleridge. OBEV

Early Departure from White Emperor Fortress. Li Po. CCL1, *tr. by* Elling O. Eide

Early, each morning, Martha Blake. Martha Blake at Fifty-one. Austin Clarke. ModIr; NPeEn

Early electric people had domesticated the wild ass, The. Electric Orchard, The. Paul Muldoon. HarvBoo

Early Electric! With what radiant hope. Metropolitan Railway, The. Sir John Betjeman. OxAEP-2

Early English everlasting. Mina Loy. NAMCP V.1 *Fr.* Anglo-Mongrels and the Rose.

Early Evening. Edward Byrne. ViWalt

Early evening, five minutes before. Modern Love. Jan Beatty. SweBea

Early evening hill is a lantern's lamp, The. Loop-the-Loop in Prospect Park (1905). Gerry Gomez Pearlberg. WiU

Early Evening Quarrel. Langston Hughes. SAmP

Early fall. Basho. EH, *tr. by* Robert Hass

Early, / four o' clock. Bedside Wreaths. Titiola Shoneyin. NeNiPo

Early Frost. Leslie Norris. AngWePo

Early germ. Plague Victims Catapulted Over Walls Into Besieged City. Thomas Lux. AmAlph; KGB

Early Graves, The. Friedrich Gottlieb Klopstock. GePo, *tr. by* J. W. Thomas

Early History of a Writer. Charles Reznikoff.
"I had been bothered by a secret weariness." APT-2
"When my grandfather was about fifty, he fell sick." NAMCP V.1

Early Images of Heaven. Sharon Olds. CAP-8

Early in the day reports said our planes. Kind of Shadow That Calls Out Fate, The. Tony Hoagland. AmWaPo

Early in the evening they come hooting about. Tohono O'odham. NAAPv.1 *Fr.* Songs for Treating Sickness, Sung durring the Four Parts of the Night.

Early in the morning. Lungi Crossing. Iyamide Hazeley. NAfrP

Early in the Morning. Li-Young Lee. LoL

Early in the Morning. Louis Simpson. TRP; WaAnP

Early in the morning. Jules Supervielle. MFP, *tr. by* Martin Sorrell

Early in the morning. *Unknown.* SSUS

Early in the spring-time a huntsman full of sorrow. Miklós Zrínyi. IQMS *Fr.* Idyll.

Early in the war they began to show up on Sundays. Names of Summer, The: A War Memory. Harold L. Johnson. BtF

Early Instruments. Don McKay. OpeFie

Early Irish Triads. *Unknown.* IrV, *tr. by* Alfred Perceval Graves

Early, Late. Philip Fried. PA9/11

Early light on the meadow. Prey. Ken Gerner. GifTon

Early Lynching. Carl Sandburg. ChIV-2; MoAmPo

Early March, trickle and rush of ice melt in mountains. Cantata, 8. Katrina Roberts. NevBe

Early may fly the Babylonian wo[e]. (LL) On the Late Massacre [*or* Massacher] in Piedmont [*or* Piemont]. John Milton. BrAP; CABP; GSo; HeIP-4; NAEL-6v1; NIL-7; NoP-4; NoP-5; NPeEn; OBWP; OxBEV; OxBSo; PoPoPo; TFi; TRP; WaAnP; WeW-3

Early mist. Conversion. Jodi Braxton. EGAG

Early morning glows. *Unknown.* ErotSp, *tr. by* Sam Hamill

Early Morning Landing. Charles Bruce. Coast

Early morning over Rouen, hopeful. Rouen. May Wedderburn Cannan. NAEL-6v2; NAEL-7v2; OBWP

Early Morning Test Light over Nevada, 1955. Robert Vasquez. AtGh; GeoHom

Early Morning, The. Joseph Hilaire Pierre Belloc. Spl; TLR

Early morning was Japanese. You could feel the faintly. Early Morning Was. John Smith. Coast

Early mornings the baby nudges. Shotgun. Patti See. MPUn

Early Morning—Ucross, Wyoming. Christopher Buckley. PfSP

Early Noon. Ingeborg Bachmann. AF, *tr. by* Mark Anderson

Early November. Ursula Krechel. GTCP, *tr. by* Reinhold Grimm

Early on a pleasant day. Mocking-Bird, The. Joseph Rodman Drake. APN-1

Early on a Saturday afternoon, in autumn, a grown man takes off his shirt. What Surprises Him. Dinty Moore. MAAN

Early on I wished to seek out famous mountains. Returning to My Garden Home: In Respectful Response to the Master of Hua-yang. Shen Yüeh. ColAnChi, *tr.* by Richard Mather and Richard B. Mather

Early on Lammas Morning. Nighean Dhonnchadh. EMWP

Early on the morning of Monday. Omens. *Unknown.* WoPoe, *tr.* by Alexander Carmichael

Early on you introduced me to young women in bars. To World War Two. Kenneth Koch. BAP-01; OxBoAm; PWW2

Early Plum Blossoms. Ch'i-chi. CSKM, *tr.* by Burton Watson

Early Poem. Laura Solórzano. SPV, *tr.* by Jen Hofer

Early Poems. Donald Justice. *See* About My Poems.

Early Rising. Tu Fu [*or* Du Fu]. CrYelRi, *tr.* by Sam Hamill

Early Romance, Japanese Garden (*In the Heart of the City*). Michele Glazer. IAoNAP

Early September, the weather temperate again. White Settlement. William Wenthe. TiP2

Early Spring. Sidney Keyes. MoBrPo

Early Spring at the Capital, Sent to the Honorable Kuan. Hsi Chou. CSKM, *tr.* by Paul Hansen

Early Spring East of Town. Yang Chu-Yuan. TAPaP, *tr.* by Red Pine

Early spring's sweet blush, The. Early Spring. Eloise Bibb. CBWP-4

Early summer rain. Buson. EH, *tr.* by Robert Hass

Early sun grazes. Whale in the Web, The. Bill O'Daly. GifTon

Early sun on fields. Fast Car On Nebraska I-80: Visting Teacher. Hilda Raz. ExTi

Early Sunday Morning [*with music*]. John A. Stone. PoSol

Early this morning when you knocked upon my door. Me and the Devil Blues. Robert Johnson. APT-2; OxBoAm

Early Thoughts of Winter. Maxine W. Kumin. ExTi

Early to bed and early to rise. Early to Bed. Mary Mapes Dodge. SWaP

Early to Bed, Early to Rise. Mark Ford. NeBrP

Early Triangles. Ron Padgett. FTOS; NYP2

Early Unfinished Sketch. Austin Clarke. ModIr

Early Warning. Frederick Turner. TiP2

Early worshipper at Nature's shrine, An. Charlotte Smith. MakPoe; NPBRoP *Fr.* Beachy Head.

Early-morning breath, The. Zen Mountain Center. David Tokuyu Reid-Marr. WhBo

Earnest, earthless, equal, attuneable, vaulty, voluminous, . . . stupendous. Spelt from Sibyl's Leaves. Gerard Manley Hopkins. NAMCP V.1; NPeEn; OxBEV; OxBSo

Earnest elements of nature. (LL) Boats in a Fog. Robinson Jeffers. NAAPv.2; NoP-4; NoP-5; WaAnP

Earnest Liberal's Lament, The. Ernest Hemingway. OBSV

Earnest to explore within and all around. Dante Alighieri. OBVE *Fr.* Divina Commedia (Selections from Anthologies, in English).

Earnestly talking to themselves. All Those People. Marianne Boruch. AmAlph

Earning a Dinner. Matthew Prior. NBLV

Earning high wages? Yus. Munition Wages. Madeline Ida Bedford. FaBoWar

Earphones. Richard Church. RWPCtW

Earplugs. Francisco Aragon. BeDoSh

Earrings Dangling and Miles of Desert. Gary Snyder. APSN *Fr.* Mountains and Rivers without End: The Market.

Ear's Delight, The. George Chapman. NoSic *Fr.* Ovid's Banquet of Sense.

Ears like a walnut's broken shell. Babysitter's Devotion, The. Kevin Prufer. AmPoNex

Ear-string, An. William Strode. NOSC

Earth. Leanne O'Sullivan. NIrP

Earth. Jules Supervielle. MFP, *tr.* by Martin Sorrell

Earth. Ann Taylor. NOxBChV

Earth. Derek Walcott. StAl

Earth, The. David Gwenallt Jones. OBWVE, *tr.* by Dyfnallt Morgan

Earth, The. Christopher Pilling. NLP

Earth, The. Amina Saïd. YaTCFP, *tr.* by Mary Ann Caws *and* Jean-Pierre Cauvin

Earth, The. Jones Very. APN-1

Earth and heaven endure forever. Substance, Shadow, and Spirit. T'ao Ch'ien. ColAnChi, *tr.* by James Robert Hightower

Earth and I Gave You Turquoise. N. Scott Momaday. HATNAP

Earth and Rain, the Plants & Sun. Simon J. Ortiz. NAAL-5

Earth Angel. Jeffrey Skinner. PBCAP

Earth at Its Origin. Anne Hébert. YaTCFP, *tr.* by Mary Ann Caws *and* Jean-Pierre Cauvin

Earth becomes home, their natural element. (LL) Young Girls. Patricia K. Page. BrAP; StAl

Earth between two lights. Twilight Under Pine Ridge. Robert Mezey. GeoHom

Earth Chorus. Juan Felipe Herrera. FTtHH

Earth; consisting of earthenware, The. Hans Faverey. LWR, *tr.* by John M. Coetzee

Earth continues to be round, The. Relationships. Mahe Jabeen. HotL, *tr.* by V. Narayana Rao

Earth, critical earth. Syliva Legris. PoPra *Fr.* Negative Garden.

Earth, crowded, cries: "Too many men!" Ralph Waldo Emerson. STuOW *Fr.* Alphonso of Castile.

Earth does not understand her child. Return, The. Edna St. Vincent Millay. MoAmPo; NAMCP V.1; NoAM

Earth Dream. Esther Shumyatsher. Prolet, *tr.* by Amelia Glaser

Earth Dweller. William Stafford. BeAl; IPoFL

Earth, Ephemera. That Which Is Fugitive, That Which Is Medicinally Sweet or Alterable to Gold, That Which Is Substantiated by Unscientific Means. Valerie Wohlfeld. YaYoPo

Earth exhales, The. (LL) Slough. Sir John Betjeman. HarvBoo; MoBrPo; NAMCP V.1; NoAM; OxAEP-2

Earth expanding right hand and left hand, The. Walt Whitman. AmFaPo *Fr.* Song of the Open Road.

Earth grown old, yet still so green. Advent. Christina Georgina Rossetti. ChrPo

Earth has a taste for us, in its unknowing, The. What Begins Bitterly Becomes Another Love Poem. G. C. Waldrep. LegDan

Earth has done this to itself, The. It heaved its rock. Purgatory Chasm. Timothy Donnelly. PoDa

Earth has many keys, The. Emily Dickinson. APN-2

Earth has not anything to show [*or* shew] more fair. Composed upon Westminster Bridge, September 3, 1802. William Wordsworth. BrAP; CABP; CenSon; ChAP; ClHu; CtM; GSo; HeIP-4; ITBLP; MakPoe; NAEL-6v2; NAEL-7v2; NAWM-7v2; NOBRP; NoP-4; NoP-5; NPeEn; OPOU; OxBEV; OxBSo; TFi; WaAnP

(Earth hath not anything to show more fair.) PoPoPo

Earth hath one spot on which none may intrude. Albery Allson Whitman. NAAPv.1 *Fr.* Octoroon, The.

Earth his bones, the heavens possess his ghost, The. (LL) Wyatt Resteth Here. Henry Howard, Earl of Surrey. NoP-4; NoP-5

Earth, I Get Everything From You. Edvard Kocbek. PoCho, *tr.* by Michael Scammell

Earth in beauty dressed. Her Anxiety. William Butler Yeats. OPOU

Earth in her mercy permits us to repeat. Wedding Song. Patricia Storace. FFC

Earth is a beautiful place, The. Third Sermon on the Warpland, The. Gwendolyn Brooks. SeSe

Earth is a cipher. I read. Scanning an Afternoon in Winter. Carole Glasser Langille. Coast

Earth is a hard text to read; but the king. Bibelforscher, Die. Waldo Williams. BBMWP, *tr.* by Rowan Williams

Earth Is a Living Thing, The. Lucille Clifton. HW

Earth is a place on which England is found, The. G. K. Chesterton. OBSV *Fr.* Songs of Education.

Earth is a prison to man all his life, The. Prison, The. Shmuel HaNagid. WoPoe, *tr.* by T. Carmi

Earth is a stadium. Especially after rain, the gulls. Sue MacLeod. Coast

Earth is at the same time mother, The. Hildegard von Bingen. HW

Earth is at the same time, The. Earth is at the same time mother, The. Hildegard von Bingen. HW

Earth is beautiful, The. Song of the Earth. *Navajo Oral Tradition.* NAAPv.1

Earth Is Blue like an Orange, The. Paul Eluard and Andre Breton. YaTCFP, *tr.* by Mary Ann Caws and Jean-Pierre Cauvin

Earth is bright through the boughs of the moon like a dead planet, The. Archibald MacLeish. APT-1

Earth is burning, The. Rea Nikonova. CRWP, *tr.* by Gerald Janecek

Earth is dry and they live wanting, The. Duende. Tracy K. Smith. LegDan

Earth is full of anger, The. Hymn before Action. Rudyard Kipling. FaBoWar

Earth is hard enough, The. Moon's Cadaver, The. Clara Silva. TANSG, *tr.* by Celeste Kostopulos-Cooperman

Earth is immemorial in death, The. (LL) Philadelphia: Spring, 1985. Sonia Sanchez. ESEAA; FuFl

Earth is raw with this one note. Crows. Lizette Woodworth Reese. APT-1; TCAPo

Earth, isn't this / what you want: / rising up. Rainer Maria Rilke. IPoFL *Fr.* Duino Elegies, The [David Young Translation].

Earth keeps some vibration going, The. Edgar Lee Masters. IllVoic; NAMCP V.1; NoAM *Fr.* Spoon River Anthology.

Earth, like a girl, sipped the rains, The.　Summer.　Judah Ha-Levi.　NAWM-7v1, *tr.* by William M. Davis

Earth Magician shapes this world.　Creation of the Earth, The.　*Navajo Oral Tradition.*　TCAPo

Earth Man.　Lynne Wycherley.　Prnts

Earth may change from summer green to winter white, The.　Nothing Ever Changes My Love for You.　Jack Segal.　ReLy

Earth Mother.　Sonia Sanchez.　ItWoWo

Earth, mountains, rivers—hidden in this nothingness.　On Joshu's Nothingness.　Saisho.　ZenPo, *tr.* by Takashi Ikemoto and Lucien Stryk

Earth Movers, The.　Christopher Cokinos.　UrbNat

Earth moves, The.　Good Nights.　Saundra Sharp.　SpirFl

Earth, My Likeness.　Walt Whitman.　APN-1

Earth, ocean, air, belovèd brotherhood!　Alastor; or, The Spirit of Solitude.　Percy Bysshe Shelley.　NAEL-6v2; NAEL-7v2

Earth offers its greeting, with a paternal kiss.　Return, The.　Julio Herrera y Reissig.　TCLAP, *tr.* by Andrew Rosing

Earth owls in ancient burrows clumpt.　Sentinels, The.　Robert Duncan.　HarvBoo

Earth place / Water place.　Lure.　Susan Musgrave.　BrAP

Earth Poem.　Mahmoud Darwish.　AF, *tr.* by Abdullah Al-Udhari

Earth Quake.　Ruth Stone.　ExTi

Earth quivers wherever I go, The.　Thou Gaia Art I.　Heide Göttner-Abendroth.　HW

Earth rais'd up her head.　William Blake.　ChIV-1; NAEL-6v2; NAEL-7v2; NAWM-7v2; NOBRP; NPBRoP *Fr.* Songs of Experience.

Earth Remembers, The.　Ágnes Nemes Nagy.　MotU, *tr.* by Hugh Maxton

Earth revives, The.　Earthquake.　Kuo Mo-jo.　WoPoe, *tr.* by Harold Acton and Ch'en Shih-hsiang

Earth, river, mountain.　Dangai.　ZenPo, *tr.* by Takashi Ikemoto and Lucien Stryk

Earth Screaming.　Esther Iverem.　GT

Earth shows her face to the moon, The.　Eclipse II.　Linda Hogan.　HATNAP

Earth Sky Sea Trees Birds House Beasts Flowers.　Kenneth Rexroth.
　"Long lifetime, A."　BLT

Earth smells dank, the weeds grow rank, The.　Witch's Last Ride, The.　Emily Jane Pfeiffer.　ViWPN

Earth spins to my fingertips and, The.　Globe in [North] Carolina, The.　Derek Mahon.　PBCIP

Earth Spirit, The.　William Ellery Channing.
　"Then spoke the Spirit of the Earth."　TCAPo

Earth stopped. The Holy City hit a mountin.　Joshua.　X. J. Kennedy.　ChIV-1

Earth, Take Me Back.　John Hall Wheelock.　APT-1

Earth that creates all that lives, The.　Eternity.　Sándor Weöres.　IQMS, *tr.* by Adam Makkai and Donald E. Morse

Earth, that drinks rain, refreshes the trees.　In Defence of Drunkards.　Jan Kochanowski.　WoPoe, *tr.* by Jerzy Peterkiewicz and Burns Singer

Earth that lightly covers her, The. (LL)　Upon a Child That Died [or Dyed].　Robert Herrick.　NoP-4; NoP-5; WaAnP

Earth Verse.　Gary Snyder.　WhBo

Earth was my home, but even there I was a stranger.　Flight of Apollo, The.　Stanley Kunitz.　OPRER; OtW; TaR

Earth was young, the world was fair, The.　Saxon Legend of Language, The.　Mary Weston Fordham.　CBWP-2

Earth which I breathe in the heavy night.　Mole, The.　Christine D'Haen.　TuT, *tr.* by Dennis O'Driscoll

Earth will flame and glow, The.　Afterwards.　Moishe Nadir.　Prolet, *tr.* by Amelia Glaser

Earth with thunder torne, with fire blasted, The.　Fulke Greville, 1st Baron Brooke.　NoSic *Fr.* Caelica.

Earth won't entirely have given us up, The. (LL)　Saint's Logic.　Linda Gregerson.　ExTi; PoDa

Earthen Jugs.　Gabriela Mistral.　SpanPo, *tr.* by Kate Flores

Earthen Lot, The.　Tony Harrison.　NPeEn

Earthen shadow lay on men's endeavor, An.　Flight, The.　Babette Deutsch.　OtW

Earthly Beauty, An.　Jane Hirshfield.　PLBUT

Earthly Joy.　Sydney E. Jerrold.　SacPr

Earthly Light.　Marcia Southwick.　PuP-23

Earthly Love.　Louise Glück.　NAMCP V.2

Earthly Paradise, The.　William Morris. *See* Apology, An.

Earthly Paradise, The.　William Morris.
　Apology, An.　NAEL-6v2
　(Earthly Paradise, The.)　NoP-4; NoP-5

Earthly Turmoil.　Caradog Prichard. *tr.* by Martin Davis
　"This is my testament, the voice of one."　BBMWP, *tr.* by Martin Davis

Earthquake.　Kuo Mo-jo.　WoPoe, *tr.* by Harold Acton and Ch'en Shih-hsiang

Earthquake.　Li K'ai-hsien.　*tr.* by Jonathan Chaves
　"Earthquake covered Shansi and Shensi, The."　ColAnChi, *tr.* by Jonathan Chaves

Earthquake.　*Unknown.*　PoCho, *tr.* by Burton Raffel

Earthquake Blues.　Ishmael Reed.　FTtHH

Earthquake covered Shansi and Shensi, The.　Li K'ai-hsien.　ColAnChi *Fr.* Earthquake.

Earthquake of 1886, The [*with music*].　Josephine D. Henderson Heard.　CBWP-4

Earthquake Weather.　Janice Gould.　GeoHom

Earthquakes could be caused.　Tabloid News.　Blythe Nobleman.　ReTh

Earth's Answer.　William Blake.　ChIV-1; NAEL-6v2; NAEL-7v2; NAWM-7v2; NOBRP; NPBRoP *Fr.* Songs of Experience.

Earth's axle creaks; the year jolts on; the trees.　Mythology.　Andrew Motion.　NeBrP

Earth's Bondman.　Betty Page Dabney.　OtW

Earth's Lyric.　APN-2

Earthstar.　Arthur Sze.　AmAlph

Earthworker's God is Healed, The.　Bernadette Mayer.　FTOS

Earthworm.　Robert Francis.　APT-2

Earthworm, The [*with music*].　Harry Edmund Martinson.　RaBo, *tr.* by Robert Bly

Earthy Anecdote.　Wallace Stevens.　SAmP

Earwigs.　Edward Newman.　VerBaPo

Ease.　Po Chü-i.　Spl, *tr.* by Arthur Waley

Ease; the hand on the sword-hilt. (LL)　Evening, water in a glass, The.　George Oppen.　APT-2; PFTM-1

Easing a savior's birth. (LL)　Cecil Day Lewis.　MoBrPo; OBMV *Fr.* Magnetic Mountain, The.

Easing My Heart.　Tu Mu.　CCL1, *tr.* by A. C. Graham

East.　Johannes Bobrowski.　GTCP, *tr.* by Michael Hamburger

East.　Conor O'Callaghan.　NIrP

East and West.　Ernest Francisco Fenollosa.
　Separated East, The.　APN-2
　Separated West, The.
　　"Soul of my inner face, face of my race."　APN-2
　　"West provokes the East, The. The iron arm."　APN-2

East Anglian Bathe.　Sir John Betjeman.　NoP-4; NoP-5

East Coast Journey.　James Keir Baxter.　NoP-4; NoP-5

East Fifth Street (N.Y.).　Bob Kaufman.　EGAG

East Gate, The.　*Unknown.*　ChinPo, *tr.* by Ye Weilian [*or* Yeh Wei-lien *or* Wai-lim Yip]

East Jesus.　Kevin Young.　FuFl

East of Easter.　Neil Astley.　RSaN

East of me, west of me, full summer.　After Reading Tu Fu, I Go Outside to the Dwarf Orchard.　Charles Wright.　ItP

East of the Passes there were loyal knights.　Graveyard Song.　Ts'ao Ts'ao.　CCL1, *tr.* by John Frodsham

East of the strait.　Muso Soseki.　EaWin, *tr.* by W. S. Merwin

East of the sun's slant, in the vineyard that never failed.　Harvest.　Gary Soto.　PBCAP

East of the Town.　Wei Ying-wu.　CCL1, *tr.* by Witter Bynner

East of town, the countryside unwrinkles and smooths out.　Stray Paragraphs in February, Year of the Rat.　Charles Wright.　NAMCP V.2

East or West?　Charles Tennyson Turner.　OxBSo

East Peak.　Muso Soseki.　EaWin, *tr.* by W. S. Merwin

East River's Charm.　Samuel Greenberg.　OxBoAm

East saint africa.　11-Haiku-Poem for a Magnificent Million.　Eugene B. Redmond.　FuFl

East Seventh Street.　Mark Wunderlich.　WiU

East Song.　Alvaro Mutis.　TCLAP, *tr.* by Sophie Cabot Black and Maria Negroni

East Texas Blues.　Mary Loving Blanchard.　TiP2

East Wind.　Ou-yang Hsiu.　NDACCP, *tr.* by Kenneth Rexroth

East wind blows in the street to-day, The.　March Day in London, A.　Amy Levy.　VWP

East wind fans a gentle breeze, The.　Solitary Carouse on a Day in Spring, A.　Li Po.　CCL1, *tr.* by Robert Kennaway Douglas

East wind finds the gap bringing rain, The.　Return, The: An Elegy.　Robert Penn Warren.　APT-2

East wind, moving with a chillness, The.　Dyfed Devastated?　Thomas James Jones.　BBMWP, *tr.* by Jon Dressel

East wind sighs, the fine rains come, The.　Li Shang-yin.　CCL1, *tr.* by A. C. Graham

East winds have blown the grass green in Ying-chou.　Poem Composed at the Command of the Emperor.　Li Po.　ChinPo, *tr.* by Ye Weilian [*or* Yeh Wei-lien *or* Wai-lim Yip]

East winds to greet my mother when she came. Escorting My Mother Home: A Short Song for the Road. Rai San'yo. EMJL, *tr. by* Burton Watson

Easter ("I got me flowers to straw [*or* strew *or* strow] Thy [*or* the] way.") George Herbert. OBEV; OxBEV

(Song, The.) NAEL-7v1

Easter. Herman Melville. APN-2 *Fr.* Clarel: A Poem and Pilgrimage in the Holy Land.

Easter. Adelia Prado. TANSG, *tr. by* Ellen Doré Watson

Easter: "Even this suburb has overcome Death." Howard Nemerov. NoP-4; WaAnP

Easter. Edmund Spenser. *See* Sonnet 68: "Most glorious Lord of Life that on this day."

Easter 1916. William Butler Yeats. BrAP; HarvBoo; HeIP-4; IrV; NAEL-6v2; NAEL-7v2; NAMCP V.1; NAWM-7v2; NIL-7; NIP-4; NoAM; NoP-4; NoP-5; NPeEn; OBWP; OxAEP-2; PoPoPo; TFi; WaAnP

Easter Afternoon. Rachel Hadas. UrbNat

Easter again, and a small rain falls. Other Side of the River, The. Charles Wright. InGu; OxBoAm; VCAP

Easter at Christmas. Alun Lewis. PoWW

Easter baskets. Anatomy. Harryette Mullen. OxAAAP

Easter Bonnet, The [*with music*]. Clara Ann Thompson. CBWP-2

Easter Carol [*with music*]. Henrietta Cordelia Ray. CBWP-3

Easter Day. Oscar Wilde. OxAEP-2

Easter Feast. Stratis Haviaras. MotU

Easter for Joe. Kenward Elmslie. AHA

Easter has come around. W. D. Snodgrass. VCAP *Fr.* Heart's Needle.

Easter Hymn. Alec Derwent Hope. ChIV-2; GI

Easter Hymn. A. E. Housman. GI

Easter Hymn. Henry Vaughan. ChIV-2; SacPr

Easter Lesson, The. Jennifer Moxley. VaPo

Easter Light, The. Clara Ann Thompson. CBWP-2

Easter light in the convent garden. Latin Lesson, The. Eavan Boland. ModIr

Easter Morn [*with music*]. Josephine D. Henderson Heard. CBWP-4

Easter Morning. A. R. Ammons. NAAL-5; NAMCP V.2; NoAM; OxBoAm; PoA 2002; PoetW

Easter Morning. Amy Clampitt. ChIV-2

Easter Night. Alice Thompson Meynell. ChIV-2; SacPr

Easter 1984. Les A. Murray. ChIV-2; UpMys

Easter; or, Spring-Time [*with music*]. Lizelia Augusta Jenkins Moorer. CBWP-3

Easter Outing. Sally Carr. Prnts

Easter Parade. Irving Berlin. ReLy

Easter Pome. B. P. Nichol. OpeFie

Easter Revolt Painted on a Tablespoon, The. Maurice Kilwein Guevara. TouFir

Easter ("Rise heart; thy Lord is risen. Sing his praise.") George Herbert. NAEL-6v1; NOSC

Easter Roses. Robert Grenier. FTOS *Fr.* Phantom Anthems.

Easter stars are shining, The. Flight to the City. William Carlos Williams. APT-1

Easter Sunday. Allen Ginsberg. FTOS

Easter Sunday. Janice Gould. GeoHom

Easter Sunday, 1985. Charles Martin. RA

Easter Sunday and my father plans a visit to one of the old missions along the Camino Real. Easter Sunday. Janice Gould. GeoHom

Easter: Wahiawa, 1959. Cathy Song. FTtHH; OpBo

Easter Wings. George Herbert. AngWePo; BASC; BrAP; CABP; ChIV-1; FSCP; HeIP-4; MakPoe; NAEL-6v1; NAEL-7v1; NIL-7; NIP-4; NoP-4; NoP-5; NOSC; PBRV; PoPoPo; SacPr; TFi; TRP; WaAnP; WeW-3; WoPoe

Eastern European Cooking. Charles Simic. NAMCP V.2

Eastern guard tower. Etheridge Knight. ESEAA; InGu; NIL-7 *Fr.* Haiku.

Eastern Long Island. Marvin Bell. PfSP

Eastern Sea, 100 fathoms. Lobster, The. Carl Rakosi. APT-2

Eastern Shore. Charles Bruce. IFF

Eastern Slope. Su Tung-p'o. *tr.* Burton Watson
"I planted rice before Spring Festival." ColAnChi, *tr. by* Burton Watson
"Little stream used to cross my land, A." ColAnChi, *tr. by* Burton Watson

Eastern Tempest. Edmund Charles Blunden. MoBrPo

Eastern War Time. Adrienne Rich.
"Memory lifts her smoky mirror: 1943." NoP-4; NoP-5
"Memory says: Want to do right? Don't count on me." TaR
"Woman wired in memories, A." NoP-5

Eastward goes the Yangtze! Tune: "Charming Nien-Nu." Su Tung-p'o. ChinPo, *tr. by* Ye Weilian [*or* Yeh Wei-lien *or* Wai-lim Yip]

Eastward Ho! A Succession. David Bromige. FTOS

Eastward in Eastanalle. George Scarbrough. LPSFW

Eastward, overlooking the Monolith. View of the Blue Sea. Ts'ao Ts'ao. ChinPo, *tr. by* Ye Weilian [*or* Yeh Wei-lien *or* Wai-lim Yip]

Eastward spurs tip backward from the sun, The. Nigger's Leap, New England. Judith Wright. NOBAu

East-West border is always wandering, The. East-West border, The. Jaan Kaplinski. StAl, *tr. by* Sam Hamill and Riina Tamm

East-West border, The. Jaan Kaplinski. StAl, *tr. by* Sam Hamill and Riina Tamm

East-West Dialog 2002. Mark Pawlak. PrTe

Easy as breath, without a trace of toil. For Robert Frost. Rhina P. Espaillat. VisFro

Easy Boogie. Langston Hughes. APSN

Easy Come, Easy Go. Edward Heyman. ReLy

Easy Exercises in the Use of Difficult Words. Edmund Wilson.
Lakeside. OBCoV
Nursery Vignette. OBCoV
Scène de Boudoir. OBCoV

Easy for almost anything to occur. Grudges. Stephen Dunn. PA9/11

Easy live and quiet die. (LL) Sir Walter Scott. NAEL-6v2; NPeEn; OBEV; OxAEP-2; OxBEV; WoPoe *Fr.* Bride of Lammermoor, The.

Easy Living. Leo Robin. ReLy

Easy Living. Afaa Michael Weaver. SpirFl

Easy Morning's Ride, An. (LL) Hummingbird, A. Emily Dickinson. APN-2; HeIP-4; NAAL-3; NAAL-5; NoP-4; NoP-5; SoSe-8; TCAPo

Easy on your drums. Dark Girl. Arna Bontemps. APT-2

Easy Puddings. Bernadette Mayer. AHA

Easy Rider Blues. Blind Lemon Jefferson. GM

Easy task it is to tread, An. Path of Independence, The. *Unknown.* TreFP

Eat bread. Drink wine. Try to sing the song. Maura Eichner. UpMys *Fr.* Out of Cana.

Eat the fire of the Lord. Pentecost. Gerrit Achterberg. TuT, *tr. by* Dennis O'Driscoll

Eat thou and drink; to-morrow thou shalt die. Dante Gabriel Rossetti. ChIV-2 *Fr.* House of Life, The.

Eat what you wish; I'll teach ye all to die. George Chapman. NOSC *Fr.* Eugenia.

Eat ye this bread, eat ye this bread. Song of the Eucharist, A. James Ryman. SacPr

Eat your banana, Annie dear. Sales Talk for Annie. Morris Gilbert Bishop. NBLV

Eat Your Heart Out, Edward Lear! Roger Woddis. UV

Eat[e], Eat[e] me, Soul, and thou shalt never die [*or* dy]. (LL) Edward Taylor. ChIV-2; ColAP; NAAL-3; NAAL-5; NAAPv.1; NoP-4; NoP-5; TCAPo *Fr.* Preparatory Meditations Before My Approach to the Lord's Supper.

Eaten by the Wolf. Alexei Remizov. MotU, *tr. by* Nancy Condee

Eater of Wives, The. Linda France. MFPA

Eating. Daphne Marlatt. NLPA *Fr.* Touch to My Tongue.

Eating almonds and drinking. Next and Last. Chase Twichell. AmZen

Eating Alone. Li-Young Lee. CAP-8; NAAL-5; NAMCP V.2; TRP; WeW-3

Eating an apple, I think of Emerson. Windfall. William Heyen. PoCoUp

Eating Bamboo-Shoots. Po Chü-i. CCL1; OBVE, *tr. by* Arthur Waley

Eating breakfast you notice. Have You Seen This Child. Franz Wright. AmAlph

Eating Chocolate Ice Cream: Reading Mayakovsky. Barbara Guest. AHA

Eating Clay. Minnie Bruce Pratt. ExTi

Eating Dinner at My Sister's. David Romtvedt. AtGh

Eating habits of the old man. Alan Chong Lau. WhBo

Eating in Hall. Alexander Barclay. NoSic *Fr.* Eclogues.

Eating Poetry. Mark Strand. NAMCP V.2; NoAM; PtR; StAl; WaAnP

Eating Roasted *Matsutake* Mushrooms. Ishikawa Jōzan. WoPoe, *tr. by* Jonathan Chaves

Eating spinach makes my teeth squeak. Vote, The. Del Ray Cross. FreRad

Eating the Cookies. Jane Kenyon. AFaM

Eating the living germs of grasses. Song of the Taste. Gary Snyder. WhBo

Eating the Pig. Donald Hall. BodElec

Eating through bread. Dick Cheney's Heart. Ben Friedlander. Eno

Eating Together. Li-Young Lee. CAP-8; IllVoic; InvLad; NAAL-5; NAMCP V.2

Eating Wild Mushrooms. Gary Young. GeoHom

Eatonton Tableaux. Honorée Fanonne Jeffers. AnSo

Eats me alive / Everytime. (LL) Eight Ways of Looking at Pussy. Letta Neely. BRtP; WiU

Eau-de-vie de Dantzick. Gold Leaf Brandy. Kinoshita Mokutarō. CAoMJL1, *tr. by* Leith Morton

Eaves. Ellis Jones. OBWVE, *tr. by* Anthony Conran

Eavesdropper. Breyten Breytenbach. PML; PoetW, *tr. by* Ernst van Heerden

Eavesdropper, The. Bliss Carman. BrAP

Eavesdropper, The. Jane O. Wayne. InvLad

Ebb. Sorley MacLean. NePenScot

Ebb and Flow, The. Edward Taylor. InvLi

Ebb slips from the rock, the sunken, The. Night. Robinson Jeffers. ColAP; MoAmPo

Ebb Tide. Marjorie Lowry Christie Pickthall. IFF

Ebbing of Kraft, The. Iain Sinclair.
  Serious of Photographs, A. Oth
  Snow Lip. Oth
  World's Oldest Comedian Is Dead. Oth

Ebbtide at Sundown. Michael Field. OxBSo; VWP

Ebbtide to me! *Unknown.* IrV

Ebb-tide to me as to the sea; old age brings me reproach. Hag of Beare, The. *Unknown.* OBVE, *tr. by* Augusta, Lady Gregory

Ebenezer Californicus. August Kleinzahler. PmAP

Ebon, fruitfilled Ebon. First Coconut Tree, The. *Unknown.* SonAtl, *tr. by* Jane Downing and Dirk Spennemann

Ecce Homo. David Gascoyne. ChIV-2; NoP-4; NoP-5; OBWP *Fr.* Miserere.

Ecce Homo. Andrew Hudgins. UpMys

Ecce Homo: "On the threshold of the black cave." Meirion Pennar. BBMWP, *tr. by* Martin Davis

Ecce homunculus c'est moi 'tis I. Branches of a Mabinogi. Meirion Pennar. BBMWP, *tr. by* Martin Davis

Ecce Puer. James Joyce. AmFaPo; ChIV-2; NoAM

Eccho, An. *Unknown.* AngWePo

Eccho, tell me: on what's religion grounded? . . . Roundhead. Eccho, An. *Unknown.* AngWePo

Eccho, what shall I do to my Nymphe, when I goe to behold her? Barnabe Barnes. MakPoe *Fr.* Parthenophil and Parthenophe.

Eccles Street, Bloomsday, 1982. Harry Clifton. PBCIP

Ecclesiastes. Bible, *O.T.*
  "Cast thy bread upon the waters." OBVE
  (Creator is to be remembrd in due time, The.) NPeEn
  (Ecclesiastes 3, 1–8.) CtM
  Remember Now Thy Creator. OBVE
  To Everything There Is a Season. BLPJKO; NAWM-5v1; OBVE
  "Vanity of vanities, saith the Preacher, vanity of vanities; all is vanity." NAWM-5v1

Ecclesiastes. G. K. Chesterton. ChIV-1; MoBrPo

Ecclesiastes. Derek Mahon. BeAl; ChIV-1; ModIr; PNI

Ecclesiastes 3, 1–8. Bible, *O.T. See* To Everything There Is a Season.

Ecclesiastical Sonnets. William Wordsworth.
  Mutability. CenSon; HeIP-4; NAEL-6v2; NAEL-7v2; NoP-4; NoP-5; OBEV
  Obligations of Civil to Religious Liberty. SacPr
  Persuasion. OWoS
  Point at Issue, The. SacPr

Ecclesiasticus. Bible, Apocrypha.
  "All flesh waxeth old as a garment." OBVE
  "By his commandment hee maketh the snow to fall apace." OBVE
  Our Fathers. OBVE

Echo. Ausonius. NPeEn, *tr. by* George Sandys

Echo. Madison Cawein. APN-2

Echo. Walter De la Mare. OBMV

Echo. Henriqueta Lisboa. TCLAP, *tr. by* Hélcio Veiga Costa

Echo. Audre Lorde. OxAAAP

Echo. John Milton. OBEV *Fr.* Comus; a Masque Presented at Ludlow Castle.

Echo ("At the mid hour of night, when stars are weeping, I fly.") Thomas Moore. OBEV
  (At the Mid Hour of Night.) IrLP

Echo ("Brutish recall.") Robert Creeley. BodElec

Echo ("How sweet the answer Echo makes.") Thomas Moore. NOBRP
  (Echoes.) OxAEP-2

Echo. Vasco [*or* Vasko] Popa. PoSu *Fr.* Besieged Serenity.

Echo. Christina Georgina Rossetti. LW; NoP-4; NoP-5; PEW; PoBW; VWP

Echo. George Santayana. APN-2

Echo. John Banister Tabb. APN-2

Echo always mocks the sound, The. Rabindranath Tagore. PoA 2002 *Fr.* Epigrams.

Echo, An. Sir William Alexander, Earl of Stirling. NOSC

Echo and A. Dan Beachy-Quick. IAoNAP

Echo and Elixir 1. Khaled Mattawa. LegDan

Echo and Elixir 2. Khaled Mattawa. LegDan

Echo Club, The. Bayard Taylor.
  Night the Eighth: Camerados. APN-2
  Night the Second: All or Nothing. APN-2
  Night the Sixth: Hadramaut. APN-2

Echo from Willow-Wood, An. Christina Georgina Rossetti. CABP

Echo, I ween, will in the wood reply. Gentle Echo on Woman, A. Jonathan Swift. NBLV

Echo of fireplace, An. Louise Herlin. MFP, *tr. by* Martin Sorrell

Echo of fireplace on the dividing wall, An. Echo of fireplace, An. Louise Herlin. MFP, *tr. by* Martin Sorrell

Echo of insects where the lamplight thins. At Ch'ang-ku, Reading: To Show to My Man Pa. Li Ho. ColAnChi, *tr. by* Burton Watson

Echo of mine, I am amenable. (LL) Mirror. James Merrill. BeAl; PoA 2002

Echo of the Ax, The. Al Pittman. PML

Echo of the clocktower, footstep. Prayer. Dana Gioia. NoP-4; NoP-5

Echo Reverie. Henrietta Cordelia Ray. CBWP-3

Echo to Narcissus. Michele Glazer. IAoNAP

Echo your thought in ours? "Destroy! Destroy!" (LL) Brother Fire. Louis MacNeice. AF; NAMCP V.1; NoAM

Echoes. W. E. Henley.
  Blackbird, The. MoBrPo
  (I. M. Margaritae Sorori.) CABP
  Invictus. AmFaPo; BRP; CABP; CtM; MoBrPo; NAEL-6v2; NAEL-7v2; OBEV; OBMV
  Margaritae Sororis. MoBrPo; OBEV
  "On the Way to Kew." MoBrPo
  "We'll go no more a-roving by the light of the moon." MoBrPo

Echoes. Emma Lazarus. APN-2; GSo; NAAPv.1

Echoes. Timothy Liu. ReTh

Echoes. Michael Longley. BeAl

Echoes. Audre Lorde. NoP-4; NoP-5

Echoes. Naomi Long Madgett. SeSe

Echoes. Thomas Moore. *See* Echo.

Echoes. John Banister Tabb. APN-2

Echoes. Ronald Stuart Thomas. OxAEP-2

Echoes of the Murder of Emmett Till. Ira B. Jones. InTrad

Echoes of Wheels. Furnley Maurice. NOBAu

Echoes of wheels and singing lashes. Echoes of Wheels. Furnley Maurice. NOBAu

Echoing [*or* Ecchoing] Green, The. William Blake. AmFaPo; NAEL-6v2; NAEL-7v2; NPBRoP; OxAEP-2 *Fr.* Songs of Innocence.

Echo's Bones. Samuel Beckett. NoAM

Echo's Complaint. Henrietta Cordelia Ray. CBWP-3

Echo's Lament for Narcissus. Ben Jonson. *See* Echo's [*or* Eccho's] Song.

Echo's [*or* Eccho's] Song. Ben Jonson. NOSC *Fr.* Cynthia's Revels.

Eclipse. John Haines. PoCoUp

Eclipse. Jonathan Johnson. AmPoNex

Eclipse. Ed Roberson. GT

Eclipse, The: "Having never been to a drive-in movie." Alan Michael Parker. NevBe

Eclipse and glory of her kind?, The. (LL) On His Mistress [*or* Mistris], the Queen of Bohemia. Sir Henry Wotton. BASC; NOSC; NPeEn; OxBEV; TFi

Eclipse, Kenwick, 1974. Tracy Ryan. NeBl

Eclipse of the Moon. Mary Susannah Robbins. PfS

Eclipse II. Linda Hogan. HATNAP

Eclipsed. Richard Meier. IIR

Eclogue 2: The Lament of Corydon for His Faithless Alexis. Virgil. CAGL *Fr.* Eclogues.

Eclogue 4: "Sicilian Muses, sing we greater things." Virgil. OBVE *Fr.* Eclogues.

Eclogue 1. Titus Calpurnius Siculus. RomPo *Fr.* Eclogues.

Eclogue 1. Baldomero Garcilaso de la Vega. *tr. by* Edwin Morgan
  "O waters running pure and crystal clear." SpanPo, *tr. by* Edwin Morgan

Eclogue 4: "Shell-bursting births, comas, and the mute." Andrea Zanzotto. Ifo ItPo, *tr. by* Gayle Ridinger

Eclogue 8. Francis Quarles. BASC

Eclogue and Elegy. Maura Eichner. UpMys

Eclogue: Clerk of the Weather. William Scammell. NLP

Églogue: "Dans la maison refermée." Jean Follain. YaTCFP

Eclogue for Christmas, An. Louis MacNeice. NAMCP V.1; NoAM; OBMV

Eclogue: "In the closed house." Jean Follain. YaTCFP, *tr. by* Stephen Romer

Eclogue: "Industry undressing in front of Agriculture." Michael Hofmann. HarvBoo

Eclogue: "Men talking, The." George Oppen. APT-2; FTOS

Eclogues. Alexander Barclay.
  "Miseries of Courtiers" by Æneas Sylvius Ricolomini, The.
    Eating in Hall. NoSic
  Winter. PBRV

Eclogues. Titus Calpurnius Siculus. RomPo, *tr. by* Guy Lee
  Eclogue 1. RomPo, *tr. by* Guy Lee
  Eclogue 2. RomPo, *tr. by* Guy Lee
  Eclogue 3. RomPo, *tr. by* Guy Lee
  Eclogue 4. RomPo, *tr. by* Guy Lee
  Eclogue 5. RomPo, *tr. by* Guy Lee

Eclogue 6.　RomPo, *tr. by* Guy Lee

Eclogue 7.　RomPo, *tr. by* Guy Lee

Eclogues.　Virgil. *tr. by* Charles Stuart Calverley, John Dryden and Byrne Fone

Eclogue 2: The Lament of Corydon for His Faithless Alexis.　CAGL, *tr. by* Byrne Fone

Eclogue 4.　OBVE, *tr. by* Sir John Beaumont

Ecolog.　Lawrence Ferlinghetti.　WhBo

Ecologue.　Eugenio Montale.　WoPoe, *tr. by* William Arrowsmith

Ecology.　Tony Hoagland.　FaoP

Economics of Gererosity, The.　Judyth Hill.　ICANM

Economics of Metonymy ("Balancing as metal, its sound, the metal in its sound.")　Skip Fox.　AnSo

Economics of Metonymy: sic transit.　Skip Fox.　AnSo

Economy is a puppeteer, The.　Toward a Portrait of the Undocumented.　Javier Omar Huerta.　RWB

Economy of Vegetation, The.　Erasmus Darwin.

　Birth of KNO₃, The.　STuOW

Ecosystem.　Anna Rabinowitz.　PoDa

Ecotone.　Ingrid de Kok.　TSAP

Écoute je ferai un poème mais ne ris pas.　Réalités cosmiques vanille tabac éveils.　Tristan Tzara.　YaTCFP

Ecstacy, An.　Richard Crashaw. *See* Song: "Lord, when the sense of Thy sweet grace."

Ecstasy.　María Baranda.　RMCMP, *tr. by* Mónica de la Torre

Ecstasy.　Amado Nervo.　TCLAP, *tr. by* Sue Standing

Ecstasy.　Sharon Olds.　EmeKit; MoWP; StAl

Ecstasy.　Yamamura Bochō.　CAoMJL1, *tr. by* Leith Morton

Ecstasy, The.　John Donne.　BASC; CABP; FSCP; NAEL-6v1; NAEL-7v1; NoP-4; NoP-5; OBEV; OxBEV; TFi; WaAnP

　(Exstasie, The.)　NPeEn

　(Extasie, The.)　BrAP

Ecstasy and its fellows.　Extasis.　Lawrence Ferlinghetti.　Eno

Ecstasy Notebook.　Thomas Lux.　MotU

Ecstasy of St Saviour's Avenue, The.　Neil Rollinson.　EmeKit

Ecstatic and in anguish over lost days.　Elegy.　Frank O'Hara.　AHA

Ecstatic bird songs pound.　Dawn.　William Carlos Williams.　APT-1; MoAmPo

Ecstatic conditioning—indexing anatomy.　Stitch.　Robert Budde.　PoPra

Ecstatic Longing.　Johann Wolfgang von Goethe.　STV, *tr. by* John Frederick Nims

Ecstatic love is an ocean, and the Milky Way is a flake of foam floating on that ocean.　Ecstatic Love Is an Ocean.　Jelaluddin Rumi.　WED, *tr. by* Robert Bly

Ecstatic thought's the thing.　Poetry.　Mary Elizabeth Fullerton.　GI; NOBAu

Ed.　James Copeland.　EdScPo

Ed.　Louis Simpson.　GoPo

Ed, / Like the dead.　Ed.　James Copeland.　EdScPo

Ed was in love with a cocktail waitress.　Ed.　Louis Simpson.　GoPo

Eddi, priest of St. Wilfrid.　Eddi's Service.　Rudyard Kipling.　OBCP

Eddie and the Birthday.　Michael Rosen.　NOxBChV

Eddie Priest's Barbershop and Notary.　Kevin Young.　AmPoNex; ISC; SpirFl

Eddie the spaghetti nut.　Jack Prelutsky.　ChAP

Eddie was a cute boy.　Realist of 1939–40, A.　Wilma Elizabeth McDaniel.　GeoHom

Eddi's Service.　Rudyard Kipling.　OBCP

Eden.　Jean Daive. *See* Woman measures, A.

Eden.　Emily Grosholz.　FFC; RA

Eden.　Leslie Norris.　ArBi *Fr.* Small War, A.

Eden.　Claudia Rankine.　GT

Eden.　James Simmons.　PNI

Eden.　Thomas Traherne.　ChIV-1

Eden.　David Woo.　OpBo

Eden a myth? But feel that leaping.　Beginning.　Harvena Richter.　ICANM

Eden, Eden.　Gwendolyn MacEwen.　BrAP

Eden is that old-fashioned House.　Eden is that Old-Fashioned House.　Emily Dickinson.　ChIV-1; NALW

Eden Rock.　Charles Causley.　NoP-4; NoP-5; NPeEn; StAl

Eden Says No.　Robert Johnstone.　PNI

"Eden," The First Part of the First Day of the Second Week.　Guillaume de Salluste Du Bartas. *Fr.* Divine Weeks and Works, The.

Edenic glory sequestered just outside.　Brooklyn Botanic Garden, The.　Timothy Liu.　UrbNat

Edgar.　Ann Lauinger.　IaFF *Fr.* Three Songs for *King Leir.*

Edgar A. Guest Syndicates the Old Woman Who Lived in a Shoe.　Louis Untermeyer.　MoAmPo

Edge.　Sylvia Plath.　BrAP; InoFa; NALW; NAMCP V.2; NPeEn; OxBoAm; PoPoPo; VCAP

Edge.　Kenneth Steven.　EdScPo

Edge, The.　Fred Cogswell.　IFF

Edge, The.　Rosemary Dobson.　NOBAu

Edge, The.　Louise Glück.　HarvBoo

Edge, The.　Paul Jamal.　BtF

Edge, The.　Andrey Andreievich Voznesensky.　RusPo, *tr. by* Robert Arthur Douglas Ford

Edge, The ("Long over whatever edge.")　Robert Creeley.　FTOS

Edge Guide for Impression.　Clarence Major.　EGAG

Edge of Autumn, The.　Michael Anania.　NoAM

Edge of Something, The.　Linda Gregg.　BodElec

Edge of the dome is slipping, The.　Fanny Howe.　FTOS *Fr.* O'Clock.

Edge of the light. (LL)　How Poetry Comes to Me.　Gary Snyder.　LoL; PoPoPo; WhBo

Edge of the ocean, The.　George Oppen.　APT-2; PFTM-1

Edge of the Roof, The.　Jelaluddin Rumi.　WED, *tr. by* Robert Bly

Edge of the sky, The.　Songs and Chants. *Unknown.*　APN-2, *tr. by* John Wesley Powell

Edge of town.　Taneda Santoka.　CAoMJL1, *tr. by* Burton Watson

Edge the word. Crow trembles in the knot. (LL)　Narrative Charm for Ibbotroyd.　Maggie O'Sullivan.　Oth; PFTM-2

Edge-Hill.　Richard Jago.

　Instructions on landscaping.　OBGa

Edges.　Robert Creeley.　WoBe

Edges of slave ships are narrow and difficult for footing, The.　Storm.　Brandon D. Johnson.　BtF

Edges of the gorges hack up sun and moon, The.　Meng Chiao.　CCL1 *Fr.* Laments of the Gorges.

Edgewater Hospital.　Albert Goldbarth.　PoA 2002

Edgewater Park.　Ruth L. Schwartz.　WiU

Edging back, I gaze to the west, long and deep my sighs. (LL)　Road to Shu Is Hard, The.　Li Po.　CCL1; WoPoe, *tr. by* Elling O. Eide

Edging each other towards consummation.　In the Borghese Gardens.　Charles Tomlinson.　OBGa

Edible World, The.　David Bromige.　FTOS

Edict Against Christianity (Section 12). *Unknown.*　EMJL

Edinburgh.　Robert Adamson.　EdScPo

Edinburgh after Flodden.　William Edmonstoune Aytoun.

　"Then the Provost he uprose."　OBWP

Edinburgh Castle.　Alan Bold.

　"As if a few odd bombs were bouncing around."　EdScPo

Edipo al cubo.　Gerardo Deniz.　RMCMP

Édit Funéraire.　Victor Segalen.　YaTCFP

Edith; a Tale of the Woods.　Felicia Dorothea Hemans.　RWP

Edith B——and her mother on a Sunday afternoon.　Liz Rosenberg.　UnSA *Fr.* Prose Poems.

'Edith is fair,' the painter said.　Two Artists, The.　Constance Naden.　ViWPN; VWP

Editing *Poetry.*　Karl Shapiro.　IllVoic

Editing *The Gazette of the Infinite.*　Michael Benedikt.　MotU

Editor, / Here are the lines my mind fathomed.　Prologue.　Dan Beachy-Quick.　LegDan

Editor, / *Mappemundi.* That word: I meant.　Afterword.　Dan Beachy-Quick.　LegDan

Editor said, The.　Dr. Jack.　Thomas Stanley.　BtF

Editor Whedon.　Edgar Lee Masters.　APT-1; OBSV; OxBoAm *Fr.* Spoon River Anthology.

Edlesborough.　Anne Ridler.　SacPr

Edmund Burke.　Oliver Goldsmith.　NPeEn; OxBEV *Fr.* Retaliation.

Edna St. Vincent Millay Exhorts Little Boy Blue.　Louis Untermeyer.　MoAmPo *Fr.* Mother Goose Up-to-Date.

Edna's Alphabet.　Barry Humphries.　OBCoV

Edna's Hymn.　Barry Humphries.　NOBAu

Edom o' Gordon [Foulis Version]. *Unknown.*　NePenScot

Education by Degrees.　Clarence Major.　EGAG

Education by Stone.　João Cabral de Melo Neto.　TCLAP, *tr. by* James Wright

Education in Wales.　Goronva Camlan.　AngWePo

Education regarding chills is not well handled in this country, The.　Henri Michaux.　GPTC; MotU *Fr.* I Am Writing to You from a Far-Off Country.

Educational ladder. (LL)　Alan Brownjohn.　NoP-5; NOxBChV *Fr.* Pitman's Common Sense Arithmetic, 1917.

Education's Martyr.　May Kendall.　VWP

Educators, The.　D. M. Black.　EdScPo

Edward.　Honor Moore.　WiU

Edward [*or* Edward, Edward]. *Unknown.*　ClHu; NoP-4; OBEV; OxBEV; SoSe-8; TFi; TRP

"Edward back from the Indian Sea."　Neglectful Edward.　Robert Graves.　MoBrPo

Edward Hopper. Anthony Rudolf. PoSol

Edward Hopper and the House by the Railroad. Edward Hirsch. PoSol

Edward Hopper, "Hotel Room," 1931. Larry Levis. PoSol

Edward Hopper Retrospective, The. Tony Quagliano. PoSol

Edward Hopper's "Lighthouse at Two Lights." Tony Quagliano. PoSol

Edward Hopper's Nighthawks, 1942. Joyce Carol Oates. PoSol

Edward Hopper's Seven A.M. John Hollander. PoSol

Edward Lear. W. H. Auden. OxAEP-2; OxBSo

Edward MacDermott. Mail King. Paul B. Janeczko. HHAm

Edward/ Paterson has grown older. William Carlos Williams. NoAM *Fr.* Paterson.

Edward the Dyke and Other Poems. Judy Grahn.
"In the place where." NALW

Edward the Second. Christopher Marlowe.
"Ah, wicked King! Accursed Gaveston!" CAGL
"Here is the form of Gaveston's exile." CAGL
"He's gone, and for his absence thus I mourn." CAGL
"My father is deceas'd. Come, Gaveston." CAGL
"Nephew, I must to Scotland. Thou stay'st here." CAGL

Edwin, The Minstrel. James Beattie. OxAEP-1

Edwin, your father has never ceased to be. Veterans of the Wars. Edgar Lee Masters. CBCWP

Ee calazi. Hammer-Song. *Unknown.* FaBoVe

Eeeveryyee time. Trips. Nikki Giovanni. CA

Eel, The. Eugenio Montale. PoetW, *tr. by* William Arrowsmith

Eel, The. Eugenio Montale. PoCho, *tr. by* Jonathan Galassi

Eel, The. Eugenio Montale. STV; WeW-3

Eel, The. Eugenio Montale. GPTC, *tr. by* Charles Wright

Eel, The. Ogden Nash. NTCP

Eel, coldwater, The. Eel, The. Eugenio Montale. PoetW, *tr. by* William Arrowsmith

Eel in the Cave, The. Robert Bly. GoPo

Eel, siren, The. Eel, The. Eugenio Montale. PoCho, *tr. by* Jonathan Galassi (Eel, the siren, The.) WoPoe

Eel, siren, The. Eel, The. Eugenio Montale. GPTC, *tr. by* Charles Wright

Eel, the siren, The. Eugenio Montale. *See* Eel, siren, The.

Eel, the siren, The. Eugenio Montale. *See* Eel, The.

Eel-Grass. Edna St. Vincent Millay. APT-1

Eemis-Stane, The. Hugh MacDiarmid. EdScPo; NAEL-6v2; NePenScot; NPeEn

E'en as a mastiff fell, whom grewnd more fell. Ludovico Ariosto. DiBP *Fr.* Orlando Furioso.

E'en as the sculptor chisels patiently. Tireless Sculptor, The. Henrietta Cordelia Ray. CBWP-3; SWaP

E'en from my heart the strings do break. (LL) When to Her Lute Corinna [*or* Corrina] Sings. Thomas Campion. NAEL-7v1; NoP-4; NoP-5; NoSic; WaAnP

(Ev'n from my heart the strings do break.) (LL) NAEL-6v1; NoP-4; WaAnP

Eena Mi Corner. Jean Binta Breeze. WaCA

Eeny meeny figgety fig. Tig. *Unknown.* FaBoVe

Ef ah could, ah sholy would. Railroad Section Leader's Song. *Unknown.* GM

Ef you / don't / Watch / Out! (LL) Little Orphant Annie. James Whitcomb Riley. APN-2; BRP; ChAP; ITBLP; NBLV; TCAPo

Effects. John McAuliffe. NIrP

Effects of Abstract Art, The. Gary Soto. GeoHom

Effectual Marriage, The. Mina Loy. MoWP

Effendi. Reed Bye. AHA

Effet de Neige. John Hollander. GS

Efficiency. Ralph Waldo Emerson. STuOW *Fr.* Alphonso of Castile.

Effigies, The. Felicia Dorothea Hemans. NOBRP

Effigy of a Nun. Sara Teasdale. NAAPv.2

Efflux of the soul is happiness, here is happiness, The. Walt Whitman. AmFaPo *Fr.* Song of the Open Road.

Effort at Speech. William Meredith. WaAnP

Effort at Speech. Ellen Bryant Voigt. WaAnP

Effort at Speech between Two People. Muriel Rukeyser. ItP; MoAmPo; NAAL-5; WaAnP

Effortless and uninscribed, the sky. Flight. Vona Groarke. NIrP

Effortlessly. Mechthild von Magdeburg. WPoS

Effusions. Samuel Taylor Coleridge.
Aeolian [*or* Eolian] Harp, The. NAEL-6v2; NAEL-7v2; NOBRP; NoP-4; NoP-5; NPBRoP; NPeEn
Burke. CenSon
Koskiusko. OxBSo
La Fayette. CenSon
Mrs. Siddons. CenSon

On a Discovery Made Too Late. CenSon; GSo

Pitt. CenSon

To a Young Ass. OxAEP-2

To the Autumnal Moon. CenSon

To the Honourable Mr. Erskine. CenSon

To the Rev. [*or* Reverend] W. L. Bowles. CenSon

Eficaz la pata de conejo, el no estar. Eduardo Milán. RMCMP

EFT. Roberta Swann. PoCoUp

Eftsoones they heard a most melodious sound. Edmund Spenser. OxBEV; PBRV *Fr.* Faerie Queene, The.

Egan O Rahilly. *Unknown.* OBMV, *tr. by* James Stephens

Egeria! sweet creation of some heart. Lord Byron. NOBRP *Fr.* Childe Harold's Pilgrimage.

Egg. C. G. Hanzlicek. GoPo

Egg. Linda Pastan. InvLad

Egg, An. Max Jacob. YaTCFP, *tr. by* Mary Ann Caws *and* Jean-Pierre Cauvin

Egg, The. Clarence Day. NBLV

Egg and the Machine, The. Robert Frost. MoAmPo

Egg Boiler, The. Gwendolyn Brooks. CAP-8

Egg Hatches Out a Flame, An. Drahomira Vandas. SurWo, *tr. by* Guy Ducornet

Egg is always being made, The. Grand Grand Mother is Returning. Judy Grahn. HW

Egg of fire. the egg of water. the egg of wind in the silk bag. the egg of air, The. Man, The. The Woman. Hans Arp. PFTM-1

Egg Thoughts. Russell Hoban. NTCP

Egg-and-Dart. Robert Finch. IFF

Eggleston was a taxi-driver. Cynical Portraits. Louis Paul. NBLV

Eggomania. Felicia Lamport. NBLV

Eggplant. Ibn Sara. WoPoe, *tr. by* Leticia Garza-Falcón and Christopher Middleton

Eggplants Have Pins and Needles, The. Novella Nikolaevna Matveyeva. TCRusP, *tr. by* Daniel Weissbort

Eggs. Sharon Olds. AFaM

Eggs. Gertrude Stein. NAMCP V.1 *Fr.* Tender Buttons.

Eggs. Susan Wood. SoSe-8

Eggs Laid by a Tiger. Antonio Deltoro. RMCMP, *tr. by* Christian Viveros-Fauné

Egg-yoke. Chivo. Cecilio Garcia-Camarillo. ICANM

Egil's Saga. *Unknown. tr. by* John Lucas
"I crossed the deep sea." WoPoe, *tr. by* John Lucas

Egles byrde hath spred his wings, The. John Heywood. PBRV *Fr.* Ballad on the Marriage of Philip and Mary, A.

Eglwys Newydd. John Tripp. AngWePo

Egnatius has fine teeth, and those. Catullus. OBVE,

Ego. Denise Duhamel. NeAmPo; SUP

Ego Flos. Guido Gezelle. TuT, *tr. by* Peter van de Kamp

Ego Sum Vitis. William Alabaster. OxBEV

Ego Tripping (There May Be a Reason Why). Nikki Giovanni. GT; InGu; ISC; RaBo; TWF

'Egoisme à Deux'. Louisa Sarah Bevington. VWP

Egoist, The. Anna Wickham. MoWP

Ego's reach is so strong, The. Shoplifter Hands. Diane Averill. FiBr

Egotist. Ambrose Bierce. APN-2 *Fr.* Devil's Dictionary, The.

Egret died the other night. Egret's Death and Funeral Preparations. *Vietnamese Oral Tradition.* CaDao, *tr. by* John Balaban

Egret Tree, The. Dave Jeddie Smith. PfSP

Egrets bear egret sons. Mother Egret. *Vietnamese Oral Tradition.* CaDao, *tr. by* John Balaban

Egret's Death and Funeral Preparations. *Vietnamese Oral Tradition.* CaDao, *tr. by* John Balaban

Egrets ("Snowy coats and snowy crests and beaks of blue jade.") Tu Mu. WoPoe, *tr. by* A. C. Graham

Egrets ("With snowy coats, snowy crests, and sapphire bills.") Tu Mu. CCL1, *tr. by* R. F. Burton

Egypt. "H. D." APT-1

Egypt. Keith Douglas. HarvBoo

Egyptian Dancer at Shubra. Bernard Spencer. NoAM

Egyptian Kites. Rex Warner. OWoS

Egyptian Pulled Glass Bottle in the Shape of a Fish, An. Marianne Moore. APT-1; NALW

Egyptian Register. "Ern Malley." BMAP

Egyptian woman. Christian Epigram. *Unknown.* WoPoe, *tr. by* John Peck

Egypt's Favorite. Sir Francis Hubert.
Joseph in Carcere. ChIV-1

Eh, jankh-bi, kaay fii, a woman calls. Tattoo, or Henna. Odetta D. Norton. BtF

Eh! Oranges, sweet little oranges / my lady! Marketwoman of Luanda. Maria Eugénia Lima. HAWP, *tr. by* Julia Kirst

Eheu! Rubén Darío. SpanPo, *tr. by* Anita Volland

Eheu! hic jacet Crony. Dog Latin. *Unknown*. DiBP

Eh-Ros-ka, the Warrior's Dance. *Unknown*. APN-2 *Fr.* War Dance.

Eia ergo. For this is Sion's twin city. Geoffrey Hill. *Fr.* Hymns to Our Lady of Chartres.

Eid Al-Fitr. Kerry Krause. AFaM

Eider are back, The. Men's Harbour, The. John Burnside. PML

Eidólons. Walt Whitman. APN-1

Eiffel Tower. Eiffel Tower. Vincente Huidobro. CuPo

Eiffel Tower, on the topmost platform, The. Going Down, Please. László Mécs. IQMS, *tr. by* Watson Kirkconnell

Eiffel tower, The. Adonis. PFTM-2 *Fr.* Desire Moving Through the Maps of the Material.

Eiga Monogatari, The. *Unknown. tr. by* Helen Craig McCullough and William H. McCullough
"Which is worse." WoPoe, *tr. by* Helen Craig McCullough and William H. McCullough

Eight Aspects of Melissa. Lawrence Durrell.
Visitations. MoBrPo

Eight Ball. Richard Jackson. SwNoth

8-Ball at the Twilite. David Baker. ReTh

Eight Days in April. Marilyn Hacker. FFC

Eight dollars for a dozen roses sold. Against Nature. Timothy Liu. LiTh

Eight Early Poems. Kenneth Patchen.
At the New Year. ItP

Eight Elegies. Rick Barot. LegDan

8:50 AM Ft. Lyons VAH. Simon J. Ortiz. NAAL-5 *Fr.* Poems from the Veterans Hospital.

8 / (in transit). Hank Lazer. AnSo *Fr.* New Spirit, The.

8 Little Theatres of the Cornices. Erin Mouré. BAP-04

Eight O'Clock. A. E. Housman. MoBrPo; NAMCP V.1; NoAM; SoSe-8

8 O'Clock Defeat, Approximately. Chris O. Cook. FreRad

Eight Pearle, The: Science. Lady Diana Primrose. EMWP *Fr.* Chain of Pearl, A.

Eight Phases of Contemplation. Giusi Busceti. ItPo, *tr. by* Gayle Ridinger

8:10 Ferry, The. Cemal Süreya. NaPG, *tr. by* Talat Sait Halman

8-track clicked through tunes as we two, The. Playland. Richard Foerster. SwNoth

Eight Ways of Looking at Pussy. Letta Neely. BRtP; WiU

Eight xx. Laurie Duggan. BMAP

Eight years difference in age seems now, The. Terminal. Thom Gunn. CAGL; OxBEV

Eighteen below: the black-capped chickadee. Rage. Peter Meinke. LiTh

Eighteen Dead, The. Jan Campert. TuT, *tr. by* Mary E. O'Donnell

1887. A. E. Housman. NIP-4 *Fr.* Shropshire Lad, A.

1815. Jeffrey Wainwright. NPeEn

1805. Robert Graves. FaBoWar; OBCoV; OBSV

1845. Jackson Mac Low. APSN *Fr.* Presidents of the United States of America, The.

1841 (I). Jackson Mac Low. APSN *Fr.* Presidents of the United States of America, The.

1841 (II). Jackson Mac Low. APSN *Fr.* Presidents of the United States of America, The.

Eighteen Hundred and Eleven, a Poem. Anna Laetitia Barbauld. NOBRP; RWP

1802. Mary Tighe. CenSon

1801. William Wordsworth. CenSon
(I Grieved for Bonaparté.) NPBRoP

1809. Jackson Mac Low. APSN *Fr.* Presidents of the United States of America, The.

1808 Wordsworth dies from fall while hiking in Scotland. Other Lives of the Romantics. Jane Flanders. PBCAP

1801. Jackson Mac Low. APSN *Fr.* Presidents of the United States of America, The.

Eighteen Poems. Hans Faverey. WoBe, *tr. by* Francis R. Jones
"Although is is forever." WoBe, *tr. by* Francis R. Jones
"As a woman might." WoBe, *tr. by* Francis R. Jones
"As simple as a drop of water." WoBe, *tr. by* Francis R. Jones
"As soon as I raise my eyes." WoBe, *tr. by* Francis R. Jones
"Extremely slowly the snail." WoBe, *tr. by* Francis R. Jones
"If the opening were forever." WoBe, *tr. by* Francis R. Jones
"Its only riddle: how." WoBe, *tr. by* Francis R. Jones
"More fleeting than my shadow is." WoBe, *tr. by* Francis R. Jones
"Muffled thud with which the strange cat, The." WoBe, *tr. by* Francis R. Jones
"Seldom has a panther's leap." WoBe, *tr. by* Francis R. Jones
"She has let herself fall on her bed." WoBe, *tr. by* Francis R. Jones
"Shortly before it is too late." WoBe, *tr. by* Francis R. Jones
"Then they went away too." WoBe, *tr. by* Francis R. Jones
"Time and again I have to love you." WoBe, *tr. by* Francis R. Jones
"Train scarcely slackens speed, The." WoBe, *tr. by* Francis R. Jones
"Vase, The." WoBe, *tr. by* Francis R. Jones
"What it is all about." WoBe, *tr. by* Francis R. Jones
"Why did she not stay where she is." WoBe, *tr. by* Francis R. Jones

1817. Jackson Mac Low. APSN *Fr.* Presidents of the United States of America, The.

1871. J. D. McClatchy. WiU *Fr.* First Steps.

1838. Dennis Lee. IFF

1837. Jackson Mac Low. APSN *Fr.* Presidents of the United States of America, The.

Eighteen to Twenty-One. David Trinidad.
"As one young guy screwed another young guy." WiU
"He said his name was Nick; later I learned." WiU
"More than anything, I wanted Charlie." WiU
"Tom used spit for lubricant and fucked me." WiU

1825. Jackson Mac Low. APSN *Fr.* Presidents of the United States of America, The.

1829. Jackson Mac Low. APSN *Fr.* Presidents of the United States of America, The.

Eighteen-Seventy. Arthur Rimbaud. *tr. by* Robert Lowell
Evil. OBWP
Napoleon after Sedan. OBWP
Poster of Our Dazzling Victory at Saarbrucken, A. OBWP
Sleeper in the Valley, The. OBWP
To the French of the Second Empire. OBWP

Eighteenth-Century Medical Illustration: The Infant in its Little Room. Ann Townsend. AmPoNex

Eighth Air Force. Randall Jarrell. NAMCP V.2; NoAM; NoP-4; NoP-5; OBWP; PoWW; PWW2; TRP; VCAP; WaAnP

Eighth and the Thirteenth, The. Alicia Ostriker. TaR

Eighth Army at the Chongchon, The. Rolando Hinojosa. TiP2

Eighth Dream, The. Tony Curtis. PML

Eighth Eclogue. Miklós Radnóti. IQMS, *tr. by* Peter Zollman

Eight Elegy, The. Rainer Maria Rilke. BeAl *Fr.* Duino Elegies, The [Robert Kelly Translation].

Eighth Inning, The. Donald Hall. MoASP

Eighth of Shostakovich, The. Eighth and the Thirteenth, The. Alicia Ostriker. TaR

Eighth Sky. Michael Palmer. FTOS

Eighth Symphony Interruptus. Brian Levison. RWPCtW

Eighties Meditation. Kay Murphy. SwNoth

Eight-Legged Colt, Chernobyl. Jerah Chadwick. AtGh

Eight-Mile Bike Ride, The. Philip Schultz. ArBi

84 01. Michael Haslam. Oth *Fr.* Continual Song.

80 papers / was all there was. Delivering the Times, 1952-1944. David Huddle. PBCAP

86 Pasteur Corner. Manuela Fingueret. MirDau, *tr. by* Celeste Kostopulos-Cooperman

'Eighty-nine was bad. Graves at Elkhorn. Richard Hugo. VCAP

Eighty-three years—at last. Kyurin-Eki. ZenPo, *tr. by* Takashi Ikemoto and Lucien Stryk

Eild. Robert Tannahill. NePenScot

Eileann Chanaidh. Kathleen Jessie Raine.
Highland Graveyard. EdScPo

Eileen Aroon. Gerald Griffin.
"When like the rising day." OBEV

Eileen's Vision. Eileen Myles. BodElec

Ein Complaint. Virginia Graham. OBCoV

Ein Leben. Dan Pagis. FIT, *tr. by* Robert Friend

Ein Leben. Dan Pagis. GPTC, *tr. by* Stephen Mitchell

Eine Kleine Snailmusik. May Sarton. NBLV

Einstein & Freud & Jack. Howard Nemerov. PoCho

Einstein's Bathrobe. Howard Moss. VCAP

Eire. William Drennan. IrV

Eisenhower Years, The. Paul Zimmer. PBCAP

Eisenhower's Visit to Franco, 1959. James Wright. PoAgWa

Either archival youths or Aegean men. Subterranean River Poem. Svetlana Ivanova. CRWP, *tr. by* Angela Livingstone

Either cockleshells from the Erythraian reef as gifts. Hedyla. SaLy, *tr. by* Diane Rayor

Either heard or taught. Song for a Thin Sister. Audre Lorde. OxWW

Either I want you on my bosom always. *Unknown*. SLW, *tr. by* Marjolijn De Jager, Sayd Bahodin Majrouh and André Velter

Either I'm swimming toward a floating discotheque its dancers. Treason's Choice. Philip Hammial. BMAP

Either in the hotel D'Lido in Managua. Temptation. Bruce Weigl. AmAlph

Either incognito and desperate. Lonely Tower, The. Tom Paulin. ModIr

Either my sight is getting worse. Recognition. Kate Clanchy. MFPA

Either/Or, the ground slants, and divides. Peter Riley. VaPo *Fr.* Excavations.

Either, over the shoulder enjoy leaning. don't. Against the Grain. Michael Brownstein. AHA

Either she was foul, or her attire was bad. Ovid. CABP; OBVE *Fr.* Elegies.

Either the lunches or the dead soldiers. (LL) Dead Soldiers. James Fenton. AF; FaBoWar; NAMCP V.2; NoAM; NoP-4; NoP-5; OBWP

Either Way. Tricia Corob. Prnts

Either you will / go through this door. Prospective Immigrants Please Note. Adrienne Rich. AmFaPo

(Either you will.) PoPoPo

Ejaculating into their vaginas—young girls of the western tribes. *Unknown.* NOBAu *Fr.* Goulburn Island Song Cycle.

Ejaculation. Elinor Wylie. APT-1

Ejected Wife, The. Yüan-ti. OBVE; OxBEV, *tr. by* Arthur Waley

El Alamein. Steve Crow. HATNAP

El Alamein. John Jarmain. FaBoWar

El Buen Samaritano keeps reappearing. Iwan Llwyd. ATSWP *Fr.* Woodstock.

El Camino Verde. Paul Blackburn. PmAP

El Curandero. Rafael Campo. BloBone

El Desdichado. Gérard de Nerval. WoPoe, *tr. by* Robert Duncan

El Día de los Muertos. Rafael Campo. RA

El Elvis. Wasabi Kanastoga. ReTh

El Elvis / puro pedo. El Elvis. Wasabi Kanastoga. ReTh

El Greco: Espolio. Earle Birney. BrAP

El Hombre. William Carlos Williams. NAAPv.2; SAmP; StAl

El Jibarito Moderno. Miguel Algarin. PueRic

El Malibú. Richard Blanco. AmPoNex

El Paso Monologue. Ishmael Reed. SpirFl

El Paso Times "World of Women," The. Catherine Bowman. "Bride wore a gown, The." ExTi

El periférico, or Sleep. Joshua Clover. NeAmPo

El Serape's floorshow finished at one. The lights. Elephant Hunt in Guadalajara. Jack Gilbert. BodElec

Elaine, pretending it was salt. E. Aitken. UV

Elaine sleeps most of the day. She's the prettiest invalid I've ever seen. True Bride, The. Amy Gerstler. PmAP

Elastics once snapped and hard buttons gone soggy lose their skill. lazily refuse to. Repeat the capitalism of narrative. Nicole Markotić. PoPra

Elba. Gerrit Kouwenaar. PFTM-2, *tr. by* Peter Nijmeijer

Elbow in Dumberland, An. Edwin Torres. HeMarv

Elbow Tree, The. Wyatt Prunty. PfSP

Elbows. Minnie Bruce Pratt. WiU

Elder, An. Our fathers were saved from the deaths. Babylon: 539 B.C.E. Charles Reznikoff. ChIV-1

Elder Brother, The. George Crabbe. *Fr.* Tales of the Hall.

Elder Brother, The. John Fletcher. "Beauty clear and fair." NOSC; OBEV

Elder Dubb. Edwin Torres. HeMarv

Elder Edda, The. *Unknown. tr. by* W. H. Auden, Eirikr Magnusson, Henry Adams Bellows, William Morris and Paul B. Taylor

First Lay of Gudrun, The. Gudrun Laments over Sigurd. OBVE

Lay [*or* Short Lay] of Sigurd, The. "And now one prayer." OBVE

(Part of the Lay of Sigrdrifa.) OBVE

Words of the All-Wise, The. WoPoe, *tr. by* W. H. Auden and Paul B. Taylor "Say, Dwarf, for it seems to me." OBVE, *tr. by* W. H. Auden and Paul B. Taylor

Elder Father, though thine eyes. Holy of Holies, The. G. K. Chesterton. SacPr

Elder lives by the side of the river, An. Juan Chi. ColAnChi *Fr.* Songs of My Soul.

Elder Sister, The. Sharon Olds. CAP-8; NIL-7; NIP-4

Elderblossom. Johannes Bobrowski. AF

Elderly Lady Crossing on Green. Wyatt Prunty. RA

Elderly white male, unresponsive, An. Rafael Campo. InoFa *Fr.* Ten Patients, and Another.

Elderly Woman, An. Mun Chônghui. EcSo, *tr. by* Catherine J. Kim

Elders, The. Charles Simic. FTtHH

Elders Are Gods, The. Tijan M. Sallah. BRtP; NAfrP

Eldorado. Edgar Allan Poe. APN-1; ChAP; ColAP; NAAPv.1; NCAP; NoP-4; NoP-5; NOxBChV; TCAPo

Eleanor (she spoiled in a British climate). Ezra Pound. NAMCP V.1; NoAM *Fr.* Cantos.

Eleanor's Letters. Donald Hall. GoPo

Elected Silence. Siegfried Sassoon. MoBrPo

Elected Silence, sing to me. Habit of Perfection, The. Gerard Manley Hopkins. ChIV-2; MoBrPo; NAMCP V.1; NoAM; OBEV; OBMV; OxAEP-2; SacPr; TFi

Elected virgins, The. Wedding in Hanover. Lorna Goodison. GT

Election. Oswald de Andrade. TCLAP, *tr. by* Flavia Vidal

Election, The. Leonard Nathan. ASA; PBCAP

Election Day. R. Zamora-Linmark. ReBoTo

Election Day, 1984. Carolyn Kizer. ExTi; GifTon

Election Eve, with Cat. Alex Skovron. BMAP

Election pincers. Mafika Pascal Gwala. TSAP

Election Reflection. M. Keel Jones. NBLV

Election Time. Lamont B. Steptoe. UnSA

Election Time. *Unknown.* UV

Elective Affinities. Jonathan Cott. AHA

Electra. György Petri. VCWP, *tr. by* Geroge Gömöri and Clive Wilmer

Electric Elegy. Adam Zagajewski. VCWP, *tr. by* Renata Gorczynski, Benjamin Ivry and C. K. Williams

Electric Light. Seamus Heaney. NAMCP V.2

Electric Orchard, The. Paul Muldoon. HarvBoo

Electrical Hierarchy, The. Konrad Bayer. PFTM-2 *Fr.* Philosopher's Stone, The.

Electrical, naked in the hot marble that filters from skin to clothes. Beautiful Ones, The. Gonzalo Rojas. BLPSL, *tr. by* Rene de Costa, Rigas Kappatos and Eleni Paidoussi

Electricity. Lavinia Greenlaw. MoWP; NeBrP

Electricity Breadthwise. Marcel Duchamp. PFTM-1

Electricity of Blossoms [*for Janet*]. Lorenzo Thomas. FTOS

Electroconvulsive Therapy. Elspeth Cameron Ritchie. BloBone

Electrocuting an Elephant. George Bradley. RaF

Electrolytes. Luljeta Lleshanaku. WoBe, *tr. by* Henry Israeli

Electronic Sound. May Swenson. APT-2

Elefantes nacen viejos, Los. Fabio Morabito. RMCMP

Elegance in the extreme. Elegance in the Extreme. Ntozake Shange. SeSe

Elegant. Linda Gregerson. AmAlph

Elegant Endings. Richard Blanco. LegDan

Elegant Things. *Unknown.* EMJL, *tr. by* Edward Putzar

Elegant Tongue, The. Terrance Hayes. LegDan

Elegant use of foliage and grace, An. Gertrude Stein. TCAPo *Fr.* Tender Buttons.

Elegía Incompleta, Una. José Ángel Valente. RaW

Elegía y Recuerdo de la Canción Francesa. Jaime Gil de Biedma. RaW

Elegiac Sonnet to a Mopstick. William Beckford. CenSon

Elegiac Stanzas: Suggested by a Picture of Peele Castle, in a Storm, Painted by Sir George Beaumont. William Wordsworth. NAEL-6v2; NAEL-7v2; NOBRP; NoP-4; NPBRoP; NPeEn; WaAnP

(Suggested by a Picture of Peele Castle, in a Storm, Painted by Sir George Beaumont.) GS

Elegiac Verse. Henry Wadsworth Longfellow. "Peradventure of old, some bard in Ionian Islands." APN-1

Elegiac Verse 12. Henry Wadsworth Longfellow. TCAPo

Elegiac western Imagination. Susan Howe. NAMCP V.2 *Fr.* Thorow.

Élégie. Pernette De Guillet. *tr. by* T. Anthony Perry "But if he came straight for me." EroLit, *tr. by* T. Anthony Perry

Elegie upon the Death of the Deane of Pauls, Dr. John Donne, An. Thomas Carew. *See* Elegy upon the Death of the Dean of [St.] Paul's, Dr. John Donne, An.

Elegie Written by the Lady A. S. to the Countesse of London Derrye Supposyenge Hir to be Dead by Hir Long Silence, An. Lady Anne Harris Southwell. EMWP

Elegies. André Marie de Chénier. *tr. by* David Curzon, Jeffrey Fiskin and Arthur Symons "Happy is he given to sage disciplines." WoPoe, *tr. by* David Curzon and Jeffrey Fiskin

Elegies. John Donne.

Autumnal[l], The. BASC; FSCP; NOSC

Comparison, The. BASC

His Picture. FSCP; OxAEP-1; PBRV

Love's Progress. BASC

"Nature's lay idiot [*or* ideot], I taught thee to love." BASC; NoP-4; NoP-5; OxAEP-1

"Oh, let me not serve so, as those men serve." BASC

On His Mistress [*or* Mistris]. CABP; FSCP; NAEL-6v1; NAEL-7v1; NoSic; NPeEn; OxAEP-1

Perfume, The. FSCP; NoSic

Sappho to Philaenis. RACG

To His Mistress Going to Bed. BASC; FSCP; NAEL-6v1; NAEL-7v1; NoP-4; NoP-5; NoSic; PBRV

(To His Mistris Going to Bed.) EroLit; OxAEP-1; OxBEV; WoPoe

Elegies. Douglas Dunn.

Thirteen Steps and the Thirteenth of March. InoFa; NoP-4; NoP-5

Elegies. Hugh Maxton. PBCIP

Elegies. Ovid. *tr. by* Christopher Marlowe

Elegy 1.4. CABP; NoSic, *tr. by* Christopher Marlowe

Elegy 1.5. CABP; ErotSp; NoSic; NPeEn; OBVE; OxAEP-1; OxBEV, *tr. by* Christopher Marlowe

Elegy 1.15. CABP; NoSic, *tr. by* Christopher Marlowe

Elegy 2.1. OBVE, *tr. by* Christopher Marlowe

Elegy 3.1. CABP, *tr. by* Christopher Marlowe

Elegy 3.6. CABP; OBVE, *tr. by* Christopher Marlowe

Elegy 3.13. NPeEn; OBVE, *tr. by* Christopher Marlowe

Elegies. Propertius. *tr. by* Kirby Flower Smith, Kenneth McLeish and Frederick Adam Wright

"Night's best of all. Night brings delight." EroLit, *tr. by* Kenneth McLeish

Elegies for Paradise Valley. Robert Earl Hayden. NAMCP V.2

Elegies for the Dead in Cyrenaica. Hamish Henderson.

First Elegy: End of a Campaign. EdScPo; PoWW; RSaN

Ninth Elegy: Fort Capuzzo. FaBoWar

Prologue. EdScPo

Elegies on the Cardinal Points. Yelena Shwarts. VCWP, *tr. by* Michael Molnar

Elegist, The. Geoff Page. BMAP

Elegy: "My Prime of Youth Is But a Frost of Cares." Chidiock Tichborne. *See* Tichborne's Elegy.

Elegy: "Alone, with harsh marine aloneness." José Gorostiza. TCLAP, *tr. by* Rachel Benson

Elegy: "April again, and it is a year again." Sidney Keyes. NoP-4; NoP-5

Elegy: "At first the dead." Henriqueta Lisboa. TCLAP, *tr. by* Hélcio Veiga Costa

Elegy: "Before the basil blackened. Before plates." Marianne Boruch. AmAlph

Elegy: "Cur foretells the knell of parting day, The." Ambrose Bierce. AmWit; APN-2 *Fr.* Devil's Dictionary, The.

Elegy: "Death be not proud, thy hand gave not this blow." Lucy Harington, Countess of Bedford. EMWP

Elegy: "Do not look for him." Leonard Cohen. BrAP; HeIP-4

Elegy: "Ecstatic and in anguish over lost days." Frank O'Hara. AHA

Elegy: "From the old settlements only the writings." Slavko Mihalic. PoSu, *tr. by* Charles Simic

Elegy: "I expected him to look dead in the casket." Richard Hugo. GM

Elegy: "I know but will not tell." Alan Dugan. NIL-7; NIP-4

Elegy: "It's a pity we have to suffer." Tom Clark. OxBoAm

Elegy: "It's true such reckless grace should never die." David St. John. RoV

Elegy: "I've won (lost) my day." Carlos Drummond de Andrade. TCLAP, *tr. by* Virginia de Araújo

Elegy: "Jackals prowl, the serpents hiss, The." Arthur Guiterman. AmWit

Elegy: "Lamp lost its master at home, The." Great Master Hyecho. BecRai, *tr. by* Kim Daljin, Kim Won-Chung and Christopher Merrill

Elegy: "Leaves have a sense of, The." Lewis Warsh. BodElec

Elegy: "Let them bury your big eyes." Edna St. Vincent Millay. APT-1; InoFa; MoAmPo *Fr.* Memorial to D. C..

Elegy: "No more, no more Jewish townships in Poland." [*in honour of the Warsaw Ghetto uprising, April 19, 1943*]. Antoni Slonimski. HP, *tr. by* Isaac Komen

Elegy: "O loveliest daughter of Hsieh." Yüan Chên. CrYelRi; ErotSp, *tr. by* Sam Hamill

Elegy: "Outworn year has altered his apparel, The." Miklós Zrínyi. IQMS, *tr. by* Watson Kirkconnell

Elegy: "Pages of history open, The. The dead enter." Sandra M. Gilbert. PoA 2002; WaAnP

Elegy: "Salt water. and faces dying." Frank O'Hara. AHA

Elegy: "There is a question." Max Winter. NeAmPo

Elegy: "They are lang deid, folk that I used to ken." Robert Garioch. EdScPo; NePenScot; NPeEn

Elegy: "Wander, my troubled soul, sigh mid the night thy pain." Anne Batten Cristall. RWP

Elegy: "We carved our names." Chang Chi. CrYelRi, *tr. by* Sam Hamill

Elegy: "We first lay down among flowers." Ikkyu Sojun. ErotSp, *tr. by* Sam Hamill

Elegy: "What remains of the suicide's voice is the last conversation." Edgar Silex. NAPBL

Elegy: "Who keeps the owl's breath? Whose eyes desire?" David St. John. AmAlph

Elegy: "Wind won't come to draw smiles in the sand of dreams, The." Yehuda Amichai. PFTM-2, *tr. by* Stephen Mitchell

Elegy. Constance Carrier. APT-2

Elegy. Arthur L. Clements. UnSA

Elegy. Black Autumn. Aida Cartagena de Portalatin. TANSG, *tr. by* Daisy Cocco De Filippis

Elegy. Carolyn Forché. ExTi; LoL

Elegy. Tomas Tranströmer. WoPoe, *tr. by* Robert Bly

Elegy. *Unknown. See* Lament: "Cheek by cheek on our pillow[s]."

Elegy 1.4: "Thy husband to a banquet goes with me." Ovid. CABP; NoSic *Fr.* Elegies.

Elegy 1.5: "In summer's heat[e] and mid-time of the day." Ovid. CABP; ErotSp; NoSic; NPeEn; OBVE; OxAEP-1; OxBEV *Fr.* Elegies.

Elegy 1.15: "Envy, why carp'st [*or* carpest] thou my time is spent so ill." Ovid. CABP; NoSic *Fr.* Elegies.

Elegy 2.1: "I, Ovid, poet of my wantonness." Ovid. OBVE *Fr.* Elegies.

Elegy 3.1: "Old wood stands uncut, of long years' space, An." Ovid. CABP *Fr.* Elegies.

Elegy 3.6: "Either she was foul, or her attire was bad." Ovid. CABP; OBVE *Fr.* Elegies.

Elegy 3.13: "Seeing thou art fair[e], I bar[re] not thy false playing." Ovid. NPeEn; OBVE *Fr.* Elegies.

Elegy 11: Ford. Eric Mottram. Oth

Elegy 2. Anacreon. CAGL, *tr. by* Peter Bing and Rip Cohen

Elegy 5. Sydney Goodsir Smith. EdScPo

Elegy: "About a year has passed. I've returned to the place of battle." Joseph Brodsky. AF, *tr. by* the author

Elegy, An: "Love, give me leave to serve thee, and be wise." Thomas Randolph. NOSC

Elegy, An: "She fell away in her first ages spring." Edmund Spenser. OBEV *Fr.* Daphnaïda.

Elegy, An: "Though beauty be the mark of praise." Ben Jonson. NoP-4; NoP-5; OBEV

Elegy as Evening, as Exodus. James Harms. GeoHom

Elegy at Mustang Island. Isabel Nathaniel. TiP2

Elegy before Death. Edna St. Vincent Millay. BrAP

Elegy, An: December, 1970. Edgar Bowers. InGu

Elegy for 6 So Far. Gig Ryan. BMAP

Elegy for a Bad Example. Rodney Jones. InGu

Elegy for a Cave Full of Bones. John Ciardi. PWW2

Elegy for a Child. Gregory Orr. BodElec

Elegy for a Dead Soldier. Karl Shapiro. OBWP

Elegy for a Forest Clear-Cut by the Weyerhaeuser Company. David Wagoner. NAMCP V.2; NoAM

Elegy for a Professor. Nicholas Samaras. TWW

Elegy for a Soldier. Marilyn Hacker. WaAnP

Elegy for a Woman of No Importance. Nazik al-Mala'ika. ItWoWo, *tr. by* Chris Knipp and Mohammed Sadiq

Elegy for Alto. Christopher Okigbo. HBAPE; VCWP

Elegy for an Unknown Soldier. James Keir Baxter. BrAP

Elegy for Bob Marley, An. William Matthews. SwNoth; WaAnP

Elegy for *Challenger*. Diane Ackerman. OtW

Elegy for Chloe Nguyen [(1955–1988)]. Marilyn Chin. FaoP; UnSA

Elegy for D.H. Lawrence, An. William Carlos Williams. WaAnP

Elegy for David Beynon. Leslie Norris. AngWePo; TCAWP

Elegy for Drowned Children. Bruce Dawe. BMAP; NOBAu

Elegy for Elvis. Richard Blessing. AllShUp; InoFa; SwNoth

Elegy for Faustina. Fergus Allen. ModIr

Elegy for His Daughter Ellen. Goronwy Owen. OBWVE, *tr. by* George Burrow

Elegy for Jane. Theodore Roethke. APT-2; BrAP; ColAP; InoFa; MoAmPo; NAMCP V.1; NoP-4; NoP-5; PoPoPo; PtR; TFi; TRP; WaAnP; WeW-3

Elegy for Jane Kenyon (2). Jean Valentine. PoDa

Elegy for Jim Larkin. Patrick Kavanagh. ModIr

Elegy for Joan. Anthony Walton. RD

Elegy for Joan the Mad One. Federico García Lorca. BLPSL, *tr. by* Rene de Costa, Rigas Kappatos and Eleni Paidoussi

Elegy for John, My Student Dead of AIDS. Robert Cording. PoA 2002

Elegy for Llywelyn Humphries. Meic Stephens. TCAWP

Elegy for Lyn James. Leslie Norris. OBWVE; TCAWP

Elegy for Mélusine from the Intensive Care Ward. Ramon Guthrie. APT-2

Elegy for Minor Poets. Louis MacNeice. CABP; PNI

Elegy (for MOVE and Philadelphia). Sonia Sanchez. ESEAA

Elegy for Mr. Goodbeare. Sir Osbert Sitwell. MoBrPo

Elegy for My Father. Mark Strand.

New Year, The. NAMCP V.2

Elegy for My Father, Who Is Not Dead. Andrew Hudgins. RA

Elegy for My Friend E. Galo. Raymond Mazisi Kunene. PoetW

Elegy for My Sister. Howard Moss. VCAP

Elegy for Myself. Ki Joon. GifTon, *tr. by* Sung-Il Lee

Elegy for Myself. T'ao Ch'ien. NDACCP, *tr. by* David Hinton

Elegy for N. N. Czeslaw Milosz. BodElec; GPTC, *tr. by* the author and Lawrence Davis

Elegy for Neal Cassady. Allen Ginsberg. CLPP

Elegy for New York, The. Douglas Crase. MakPoe

Elegy for Sir Ifor Williams. Anthony Conran. AngWePo

Elegy for Slit-Drum. Christopher Okigbo. HBAPE

Elegy for the Bee-god. Selima Hill. MoWP

Elegy for the Duke. Robert Patrick Dana. SeSe

Elegy for the Duke of Marmalade. Luis Palés Matos. TCLAP, *tr. by* Ellen G. Matilla and Diego de la Texera

Elegy for the Great Inca Atawallpa, The. *Unknown. tr. by* W. S. Merwin

"You all by yourself fulfilled." WoPoe, *tr. by* W. S. Merwin

Elegy for the Hurdler. Randall Mann. BeDoSh

Elegy for the Nightbound. Anthony Cronin. PBCIP

Elegy for the Revolution. Kofi Anyidoho. NAfrP

Elegy for the Time at Hand. Adonis. AF, *tr. by* Samuel Hazo

Elegy for the Unknown Soldier. Michael O'Loughlin. PBCIP

Elegy for the Unsaid. Simone Muench. RWB

Elegy for the Welsh Dead, in the Falkland Islands, 1982. Anthony Conran. TCAWP

Elegy for Thelonious. Yusef Komunyakaa. ESEAA

324. Elegy for W. C. W., the Lovely Man, An. John Berryman. EMP; MakPoe; NoP-4; NoP-5; WaAnP *Fr.* Dream Songs.

Elegy for Wright & Hugo. Norman Dubie. NoAM

Elegy for Yards, Pounds, and Gallons. David Wagoner. PoA 2002

Elegy for Your Absence. Eugenio Florit. TCLAP, *tr. by* Hoffman Reynolds m6 Hays

Elegy in a Country Churchyard. G. K. Chesterton. FaBoWar; MoBrPo; OBWP

Elegy in a Spider's Web. Laura Riding Jackson. PFTM-1

Elegy in an Abandoned Boatyard. Dave Jeddie Smith. VCAP

Elegy in August. Robert McDowell. PoDa

Elegy in Newgate. William Cobbett. UV

Elegy in the Manner of a Requiem in Memory of D.H. Lawrence. Walter Lowenfels.

    Among the Luminals. APT-2

Elegy Just in Case. John Ciardi. AmWaPo; PWW2

Elegy of a Knight. Fadwa Tuqan. PoArWo, *tr. by* Samira Kawar

Elegy of Fortinbras. Zbigniew Herbert. PoSu; VCWP; WoPoe, *tr. by* Czeslaw Milosz

Elegy of Our Times. Eugenio Montale. ItPo, *tr. by* Gayle Ridinger

Elegy of the Wind. Christopher Okigbo. VCWP

Elegy on a Broom Bush. Árpád Tóth. IQMS, *tr. by* Neville Masterman

Elegy on a Lady, Whom Grief for the Death of Her Betrothed Killed. Robert Bridges. OBEV

Elegy on a Maiden Name, An. Jane Cave. CABP

Elegy on a Young Airedale Bitch Lost Two Years Since in the Salt-Marsh. Yvor Winters. APT-2

Elegy on a Young Lady. Anne Batten Cristall. RWP

Elegy on a Young Warrior. Ponmutiyar. WoPoe,

Elegy on an X-ray Photo of My Skull. Yelena Shwarts. ItGoST; VCWP, *tr. by* Catriona Kelly and Michael Molnar

Elegy on Cynddylan, The. *Unknown.*

    "Stand out, maids, and look on the land of Cynddylan." OBWVE

Elegy on Mael Mhedha, his Wife. Muireadhach Albanach Ó Dálaigh. NePenScot, *tr. by* Thomas Owen Clancy

Elegy on Mr. William Smith. Thomas Chatterton.

    Mr. Smith is Dead. STuOW

Elegy on Reichenau. Walafrid Strabo. NAWM-7v1, *tr. by* Peter Godman

Elegy on the Death of a Mad Dog, An. Oliver Goldsmith. NBLV; OBNV; OxAEP-1; TFi *Fr.* Vicar of Wakefield, The.

Elegy on the Death of Her Husband. Anne, Duchess of Arundel Howard. NOSC; WaAnP *Fr.* Good Shepherd's Sorrow for the Death of His Beloved Son, The.

Elegy on the Death of Mr Sterne. Miles Peter Andrews. NOBRP

Elegy on the Dust. Thom Gunn. NoAM *Fr.* Misanthropos.

Elegy on the Earl of Rochester. Anne Wharton. NOSC

Elegy on the Pilot. Reuel Denney.

    "Death in an ancient country was a simple passport." YaYoPo

Elegy on Thomas Hood. Martin Fagg. UV

Elegy over a Tomb. Edward Herbert, 1st Baron Herbert of Cherbury. OBEV; OBWVE

Elegy Residence on Earth. Robert Hass. BodElec

Elegy That Was Never Finished, An. José Ángel Valente. RaW, *tr. by* Hardie St. Martin

Elegy to a Dissected Puppy, An. Georgia Bailey Parrington.

    "Sweet Dog! now cold and stiff in death." VerBaPo

Elegy to Aisha, An. Abdul Wahab Al-Bayati. IrPoTo, *tr. by* Farouk Abdel Wahab

Elegy to Atlantis. Tatyana Retivova. CRWP, *tr. by* Tatyana Retivova

Elegy to Myself. Ch'oe Kinam. CATKP, *tr. by* Chi-gyu Kim [*or* Kim Chonggil]

Elegy to the Memory of an Unfortunate Lady. Alexander Pope. OBEV

Elegy upon His Tomb in Herndon-Hill Church, Erected by His Wife, Who Speaks, an. James Howell. OBWVE

Elegy upon Old Freeman, An. Matthew Stevenson.

    "Here in this homely cabinet." NOSC

Elegy upon S[ir] W[alter] R[aleigh], An. Henry King, Bishop of Chichester. NOSC

Elegy upon the Death of His Own Father, An. Richard Corbet. NOSC

Elegy upon the Death of Mrs. A. Behn, the Incomparable Astrea, An. *Unknown.* EMWP

Elegy upon the Death of the Dean of [St.] Paul's, Dr. John Donne, An. Thomas Carew. BASC; CABP; CavPo; NAEL-6v1; NAEL-7v1; NoP-4; NoP-5; WaAnP

Elegy upon the Lady Venetia Digby, An. Thomas Randolph. BASC

Elegy with a Bridle in Its Hand. Larry Levis. AmAlph

Elegy with a Chimneysweep Falling Inside It. Larry Levis. AmAlph

Elegy with a Thimbleful of Water in the Cage. Larry Levis. AmAlph

Elegy Written after Reading the "Sorrows of Werter." Robert Merry. STuOW

Elegy Written in a Country Churchyard. Thomas Gray. BrAP; BRP; CABP; ClHu; HeIP-4; InoFa; MakPoe; NAEL-6v1; NAEL-7v1; NIL-7; NoP-4; NoP-5; NPeEn; OBEV; OxAEP-1; OxBEV; PoPoPo; TFi; TreFP; UV; WaAnP; WeW-3

    "Curfew tolls the knell of parting day, The." UV

Elegy Written in a Country Coal-Bin. Christopher Darlington Morley. AmWit

Element Mother, The. Lorine Niedecker. FTOS

Element that utters doves, angels and cleft flames. Air. Kathleen Jessie Raine. MoBrPo

Elemental. Marjorie M. Evasco. ReBoTo

Elemental. D. H. Lawrence. NoP-4; NoP-5

Elemental Journey: Anniversary Gift. Alicia Gaspar de Alba.

    4: The Niagara River Speaks Three Languages. FTtHH

    5: Rainstorm: The Gorge. FTtHH

Elementary. Muriel Spark. MoWP

Elementary School Classroom in a Slum, An. Stephen Spender. MoBrPo

Elementary school for six years. Autobiography of a Sloppy Sluggard. Kuan Kuan. PML, *tr. by* Zhang Cuo

Elements, The. W. H. Davies. MoBrPo

Elements, The. Tom Lehrer. UV

Elements, The. John Henry, Cardinal Newman. SacPr

Elements Changeable, The. Lucretius. OBVE *Fr.* De Rerum Natura (On the Nature of Things).

Elements have merged into solicitude, The. Racer's Widow, The. Louise Glück. MoASP

Elements of Composition. A. K. Ramanujan. NAMCP V.2; VCWP

Elements of Night. C. D. Wright. AmAlph

Elements of San Joaquin, The. Gary Soto. GeoHom; PBCAP

    Rain. NoAM

    Wind. NoAM

Elena. Pat Mora. NIL-7; UnSA

Elena's Song. Sir Henry Taylor. OBEV; RACG *Fr.* Philip van Artevelde.

Elephant. *Unknown.* SonAtl, *tr. by* Brenda Ginever, Malcolm Ginever and David Mahundiri

Elephant, The. Joseph Hilaire Pierre Belloc. BLPJKO

Elephant, The. Dan Chiasson. LegDan

Elephant, The. Carlos Drummond de Andrade. ItP, *tr. by* Mark Strand

Elephant asked another elephant if its tusks were mustaches, An. Elephant Tears. Russell Edson. SUP

Elephant Hunt in Guadalajara. Jack Gilbert. BodElec

Elephant in his tub, An. Twilight. Philippe Soupault. SurPaPo, *tr. by* Mary Ann Caws and Jean-Pierre Cauvin and Patricia Terry

Elephant in Winter, The. Michael Van Walleghen. UrbNat

Elephant of long service to a circus retired to a small cottage, An. Retirement of the Elephant, The. Russell Edson. SUP

Elephant on a ball presents a Shakespearean spectacle, An. Modern circus, The. Pierre McOrlan. MFP, *tr. by* Martin Sorrell

Elephant Rocks. Kay Ryan. ExTi

Elephant Tears. Russell Edson. SUP

Elephanté, mongo!, L'. Chant of praise for the idi amin dada. Wopko Jensma. TSAP

7. Elephants. David McFadden. NLPA

Elephants and birds of beauty and a gold-fish. Gertrude Stein. OxBoAm *Fr.* Book Concluding with As A Wife Has a Cow a Love Story, A.

Elephants are born old. Fabio Morabito. RMCMP, *tr.* by Geoff Hargreaves

Elephants Are Different to Different People. Carl Sandburg. MoAmPo

Elephants Are in the Yard, The. Indran Amirthanayagam. OpBo

Elephants Dying, The. Michael C. Blumenthal. NoAM

Elephants of Thailand perform their bows extremely well, The. Elephants of Thailand. Sŏ Chŏngju. WoPoe, *tr.* by David R. McCann

Elephant's Piggy Bank, The. Takamura Kotaro. CAoMJL1, *tr.* by Leith Morton

Elephants walking. Holding Hands. Lenore M. Link. NTCP

Eletelephony. Laura Elizabeth Richards. NBLV; NOxBChV; NTCP

Eleusis. Jim Leftwich. AnSo

Elevated above Queens mist gathers. Heading for Manhattan by Train. Ed Friedman. PrTe

Elevator: "Passing my floor." Sanford Fraser. NevBe

Elevator Music. Henry Taylor. GoPo; P180

Elevator operator. Mr. 'Gator. N. M. Bodecker. NTCP

Eleven. Archibald MacLeish. WeW-3

Eleven A.M. on My Day Off, My Sister Phones Desperate for a Babysitter. Sharon Hashimoto. OpBo

Eleven Addresses to the Lord. John Berryman.
(Address to the Lord.) GoPo
"If I say Thy name, art Thou there ? It may be so." ItP
"Master of beauty, craftsman of the snowflake." InvLi; PLBUT
"Sole watchman of the flying stars, guard me." ItP

11-Haiku-Poem for a Magnificent Million. Eugene B. Redmond. FuFl

Eleven o'clock and the bar is empty. Hat Factory, The. Paul Durcan. ModIr

Eleven o'clock, and the curtain falls. End of the Comedy. Louis Untermeyer. PoA 2002

Eleven Parts of Feeling. Nguyen Quang Thieu. PML
"My heart beats in the first spring." PML, *tr.* by Martha Collins

Eleven Poems on the Ten Vows of the Universally Worthy Bodhisattva. Kyunyŏ, Great Master. CATKP, *tr.* by Peter H. Lee
"Homage to the buddhas." CATKP, *tr.* by Peter H. Lee
"I bow before the buddhas." CATKP, *tr.* by Peter H. Lee
"I have committed errors." CATKP, *tr.* by Peter H. Lee
"I will at once follow the vows." CATKP, *tr.* by Peter H. Lee
"King of the bodhi tree, The." CATKP, *tr.* by Peter H. Lee
"Though all the buddhas." CATKP, *tr.* by Peter H. Lee
"To the majestic assembly of buddhas." CATKP, *tr.* by Peter H. Lee
"Truth of dependent origination tells me, The." CATKP, *tr.* by Peter H. Lee
"When the realm of living runs out." CATKP, *tr.* by Peter H. Lee
"With tongs I trim the lamp." CATKP, *tr.* by Peter H. Lee
"Would that all my good deeds." CATKP, *tr.* by Peter H. Lee

Eleven Rock Poems. Gustaf Sobin. PmAP

11 rue Daguerre. John Montague. ModIr; NPeEn *Fr.* Chosen Light, A.

Eleven Stars over Andalusia. Mahmoud Darwish. *tr.* by Agha Shahid Ali, Mona Anis, Ahmad Dallal and Nigel Ryan
On Our Last Evening on This Land. PoetW, *tr.* by Agha Shahid Ali, Mona Anis, Ahmad Dallal and Nigel Ryan

11/10 Again. Lucille Clifton. GT

Eleventh Vertical Poetry. Roberto Juarroz.
"Every word is a doubt." VCWP

Eleven-thirty and hot. Cyclist, The. Marge Piercy. NAMCP V.2; NoAM

Elf Shots. Peter Riley. Oth

Elfrida. László Arany. IQMS, *tr.* by Watson Kirkconnell

Elgar started it. Wireless, The. Desmond Graham. RWPCtW

El-Hajj Malik El-Shabazz. Robert Earl Hayden. ESEAA

Eli, Eli. Jack Foley. FTtHH

Eli, Eli. Judith Wright. BMAP; GI

Eliahu. Tamara Kamenszain. MirDau, *tr.* by Roberta Gordenstein

Elijah's Wagon knew no thill. Emily Dickinson. ChIV-1

Elinda's [*or* Ellinda's] Glove. Richard Lovelace. NOSC; CavPo

Elinor Frost's Marble-Topped Kneading Table. Pattiann Rogers. VisFro

Elinor Glyn. *Unknown.* OBCoV

Elinor White Frost Speaks. N. M. Brewka. VisFro

Elis. Georg Trakl. WoPoe, *tr.* by Robert Firmage

Elis, when the blackbird calls in the black forest. To the Child Elis. Georg Trakl. WoPoe, *tr.* by Robert Firmage

Elise. Alan Wearne. BMAP *Fr.* Nightmarkets, The.

Elise, I have your valentine with the red shoes. I have. Grandfather's Last Letter, A. Norman Dubie. PoChi

Elite Syncopations. Richard Garcia. TouFir

Elitere Lyric Poetry. Theresa Hak Kyung Cha. PFTM-2 *Fr.* Dictée.

Elites, levels, proletariat. Satis Passio. Les A. Murray. HarvBoo

Elixir [*or* Elixer], The. George Herbert. BASC; NoP-4; NoP-5; NOSC; SacPr

Eliza at the Battle. Erasmus Darwin. STuOW *Fr.* Botanic Garden, The.

Eliza Harris. Frances Ellen Watkins Harper. WaAnP

Eliza in Uncle Tom's Cabin. Eloise Bibb. CBWP-4

Elizabeth. Michael Ondaatje. NoAM

Elizabeth. Sylvia Townsend Warner. MoBrPo

Elizabeth Bishop, *Croton.* Mark Doty. AmAlph

Elizabeth, frigidly stretched. This Houre Her Vigill. Valentin Iremonger. ModIr

Elizabeth Gone. Anne Sexton. WaAnP

Elizabeth Hoby, Wife, to Thomas Hoby, Knight, Her Husband. Elizabeth Cooke Hoby. EMWP

Elizabeth lies here (alas for my heart), thus fated. Epicedium by Elizabeth Hoby, Their Mother, on the Death of Her Two Daughters Elizabeth and Anne, An. Elizabeth Cooke Hoby. EMWP

Elizabeth Looks at Robert. Jo Shapcott. MoWP

Elizabeth Near and Far. Anne Winters.
Chair by the Window, The. BeAl
Night Light. BeAl

Elizabeth of Bohemia. Sir Henry Wotton. *See* On His Mistress [*or* Mistris], the Queen of Bohemia.

Elizabeth / Szilágyi. Mother of King Matthias, The. János Arany. IQMS, *tr.* by Neville Masterman

"Elizabeth the Beloved." Elizabeth. Sylvia Townsend Warner. MoBrPo

Elizabeth Walters is my name. Elizabeth Walters. FaBoVe

Elizabethan and Nova Scotian Music. Charles North. NYP2; PmAP

Elizabethan Phrase, The. Philip Whalen. WANABP

Elizabeth's War with the Christmas Bear. Norman Dubie. AmAlph; NAMCP V.2; NoAM

Elk in Winter. Robert Pack. WaAnP

Elk, The Whelk, The. Robert Williams Wood. NBLV

Elkhart, Indiana. Todd Davis. ACAMVP

Elkhorn Slough. Abigail Albrecht. GeoHom

Ella, fell a. Hugh Lofting. NOxBChV

Ella, in a Square Apron, Along Highway 80. Judy Grahn. NALW *Fr.* Common Woman, The.

Ella Mi Fu Rapita! Gavin Ewart. NoAM

Elle est debout sur mes paupières. Amoureuse, L'. Paul Éluard. YaTCFP

Elle est venue de plus loin que les routes. Neige, La. Yves Bonnefoy. YaTCFP

Elle est—mais elle n'est qu'à minuit quand tous les oiseaux blancs. Elle est. Paul Éluard. YaTCFP

Elle lançait sa vieille vaisselle à la lune. Elle lançait sa vieille vaisselle. Venus Khoury-Gata. YaTCFP

Elle lui dit: Il fait très beau. Passé, Le. Jacques Roubaud. YaTCFP

Elle sait aussi qu'il avait dit: Les autre. Variations. Hédi Kaddour. YaTCFP

Ellen Craft. Honorée Fanonne Jeffers. AnSo

Ellen Learning to Walk. Frances Sargent Osgood. ColAP

Ellen West. Frank Bidart. NAMCP V.2; RACG

Ellenore. Gottfried August Bürger. *See* Lenora.

Ellin Thorne Songe. Ellin Thorne. EMWP

Ellington is dead. Elegy for the Duke. Robert Patrick Dana. SeSe

Ellis Britton was standing outside the churchhouse. Benediction. David Lee. GifTon

Ellis Island, September 1907. Andrea Hollander Budy. OPRER

Elm. Robert Hass. BodElec

Elm. Sylvia Plath. NAMCP V.2; NoAM; NoP-4; NoP-5; OxBoAm

Elm, laburnum, hawthorn, oak. Trees. Fleur Adcock. OBGa

Elm lies prone, its branches cut away, The. Waking. Anne Simpson. IFF

Elm Tree in Paddington, An. Robert Adamson. BMAP

Elm Tree on Lafayette Street, The. Rod Kessler. OPRER

Elms. Louise Glück. NoAM

Elms here are easy to talk about, The. Park Elms. Charles Ghigna. UrbNat

Éloge de Robert Desnos. Franck Venaille. YaTCFP

Éloge du Jade. Victor Segalen. YaTCFP

Eloi, Eloi, Lama Sabachthani? D. H. Lawrence. GI

Eloisa to Abelard. Alexander Pope. NAEL-6v1; NAEL-7v1; RACG

Elopement and civil wedding . . . the sham squire. Distaff Side, The. Harry Clifton. PBCIP

Elsa Wertman. Edgar Lee Masters. NAAPv.1; NAMCP V.1; NoAM *Fr.* Spoon River Anthology.

Else tears heap all within one clay-cold hill. (LL) To Emily Dickinson. Hart Crane. ColAP; NIL-7; NIP-4; NoAM; NoP-4; NoP-5; OxBoAm

Elsewhere. Lynn Emanuel. BodElec

Elsewhere. Michael Field. VWP

Elsewhere. Larissa Szporluk. LegDan

Elsewhere / a babe's first words might be. Going East. Ishmael Reed. ASA

Elsewhere, Things Tend. Claudia Rankine. AmPoNex

Elude me still, keep ever just before. Mystery. Lizette Woodworth Reese. SWaP

Elusive shadow of my substance, stay. Elusive Shadow of My Substance, Stay. Sor Juana Inés de la Cruz. SpanPo, *tr. by* Kate Flores

Elvin Jones Gretsch Freak. David Henderson. SeSe

Elvin's Blues. Michael S. Harper. LoL

Elvious Ricks grew up in sunlight. Penny Ballad of Elvious Ricks. R. G. Vliet. TiP2

Elvis. Sam Cornish. AllShUp

Elvis. Brian G. Gilmore. AllShUp

Elvis Acts as His Own Pallbearer. Fleda Brown Jackson. AllShUp

Elvis at the End of History. Fleda Brown Jackson. AllShUp

Elvis couldn't twitch a hip. All Shook Up. Don Bogen. AllShUp

Elvis Decides to Become a Monk. Fleda Brown. MAAN

Elvis Elevator, The. Terry Stokes. AllShUp

Elvis for the Ages, An. Lynne McMahon. AllShUp

Elvis from the Waist Up. Alice Fulton. AllShUp *Fr.* Wonder Stings Me More than the Bee.

Elvis Goes to the Army. Fleda Brown Jackson. AllShUp

Elvis, King of PTL TV. I Wannabe Your Queen. Susan Swartwout. SwNoth

Elvis kissed me once, she swears. Elvis Kissed Me. T. S. Kerrigan. GoPo

Elvis lay cool in his thick shadow. Elegy for Elvis. Richard Blessing. AllShUp; InoFa; SwNoth

Elvis Lives. Charles Bukowski. AllShUp

Elvis Moving a Small Cloud: The Desert Near Las Vegas, 1976. David Wojahn. AllShUp

Elvis P. and Emma B. Elizabeth Ash Vélez. AllShUp

Elvis Presley. Thom Gunn. AllShUp

Elvis Presley. Rochelle Nameroff. SwNoth

Elvis Presley is alive and well. Elvis. Brian G. Gilmore. AllShUp

Elvis Reads The Wild Swans at Coole. Fleda Brown Jackson. AllShUp

Elvis Sings Gospel. Fleda Brown Jackson. AllShUp

Elvis the Performing Octopus. Polly Clark. BeAl

Elwha River, The. Gary Snyder. NoAM

Elwood Collins: Summer of 1932. Dave Etter. IllVoic

Elysian Fields. Marilyn Hacker. RA

Elysian Garden. Carmen Boullosa. RMCMP, *tr. by* Geoff Hargreaves

Elysium is as far as to. Suspense. Emily Dickinson. MoAmPo; TCAPo

Em pom pee para me. Clapping Chant, A. *Unknown.* FaBoVe

Emaciated Teeth. Fatma Kandil. PoArWo, *tr. by* Khaled Mattawa

E-Mail. Reetika Vazirani. NAPBL

Emancipation. Priscilla Jane Thompson. CBWP-2

Emancipation Day. Lizelia Augusta Jenkins Moorer. CBWP-3

Emancipation Proclamation. William Heyen. PoCoUp

Emancipators, The. Randall Jarrell. PoA 2002

Embalmer. Rossana Ombres. NeIt

Embalmment. Michael Field. VWP

Embankment, The (The fantasia of a fallen gentleman on a cold, bitter night). Thomas Ernest Hulme. OPOU

Embarcation. Thomas Hardy. OBWP

Embarkation for Cythera. Lorenzo Thomas. EGAG

Embarkation for Cythera, The. David Ferry. GS

Embarkation, 1942. John Jarmain. PoWW

Embarrassed cold. Half-Season. Simone Yoyotte. SurWo, *tr. by* Myrna Bell Rochester

Embarrassed presently. Solitary. Samar Sen. WoPoe, *tr. by* Pritish Nandy

Embarrassed the moon with his curses & songs. (LL) Because of My Father's Job. James Masao Mitsui. NIL-7; OpBo; UnSA

Embarrassing Episode of Little Miss Muffet, The. Guy Wetmore Carryl. AmWit

Embarrassing with exclamations strange. Albery Allson Whitman. NAAPv.1 *Fr.* Octoroon, The.

Embassy to Achilles, The. Homer. NAWM-7v1 *Fr.* Iliad, The.

Embedded deep in our cells is ourselves and everyone else. December 4, 2002. Juliana Spahr. LegDan

Embers. Claudia Keelan. RoV

Embers of incense. Embers of Incense. Wen T'ing-yün. CCL1, *tr. by* John Minford

Embers of night flare up afresh. Twin Flames. James Broughton. PasH

Embers of the day are red, The. Evensong. Robert Louis Stevenson. ITBLP

Embers of wood in fire I'd be. Four Elements, The. Sándor Weöres. IQMS, *tr. by* Adam Makkai and Donald E. Morse

Embertide in Advent. David Middleton. PoDa

Emblazoned bleak in austral skies. Herman Melville. TCAPo *Fr.* Clarel: A Poem and Pilgrimage in the Holy Land.

Emblem. David Chaloner. VaPo

Emblem 51. Zbigniew Morsztyn. WoPoe, *tr. by* Jerzy Peterkiewicz and Burns Singer

Emblems (Fragments). Francis Quarles.

  (Divine Rapture, A.) OBEV

  (I Am My Beloved's, and His Desire Is towards Me.) NPeEn; OxAEP-1; SacPr

  "Whene'er the old exchange of profit rings." BASC; NOSC

  "Why dost thou shade thy lovely face? O[h] why." BASC; NOSC; OxAEP-1; SacPr

Emblems of Conduct. Hart Crane. OxBoAm

Emblems of Love. Lascelles Abercrombie.

  Epilogue. MoBrPo

  Hymn to Love. OBEV

  Woman's Beauty. MoBrPo

Embodied close, the lab'ring Grecian train. Homer. OBVE *Fr.* Iliad, The.

Embrace. Billy Collins. SUP

Embrace. Dulce Maria Loynaz. TANSG, *tr. by* Alan West

Embrace, The. Louis Aragon. YaTCFP, *tr. by* Edward Lucie-Smith

Embrace, The. Mark Doty. AmAlph; AmFaPo; BeAl; NAMCP V.2

Embrace of the Electric Eel. Pascale Petit. Prnts

Embrace the Blade. Joyce Mansour. HAWP, *tr. by* Carol Cosman

Embraceable You. Ira Gershwin. ReLy

Embracing in the road. Hawk's Shadow. Louise Glück. HarvBoo; StAl

Embracing the Multipede. Denise Levertov.

  "On the dream sidewalk." UpMys

Embroidered Memory. Lorene Zarou-Zouzounis. PoArWo

Embroideries. Sikong Tu. CCL1 *Fr.* Twenty-Four Modes of Poetry.

Embroidery must remain flat, The. Liliane Giraudon. SCFWP *Fr.* Poem with Incense Paper.

Embroidery's Secret, The. Han Yong'un [*or* Yongwun]. CAMKP, *tr. by* Sammy Solberg

Emerald in big clusters. High the Mount of Wu. Li Ho. ChinPo, *tr. by* Ye Weilian [*or* Yeh Wei-lien *or* Wai-lim Yip]

Emerald is as green as grass, An. Flint. Christina Georgina Rossetti. SacPr

Emergency. Julio Marzán. PueRic

Emergency Kit. Tanure Ojaide. EmeKit

Emergency Response. Karen Solie. OpeFie

Emergency Services. Jonathan Wonham. RWPCtW

Emergent Manner. Allen Fisher.

  Diary Theme, The. Oth

  Ditchley Portrait, The. Oth

  Machynlleth. Oth

  Murder One. Oth

Emerging from the Old Palace One Day. Kim Suyŏng. CAMKP, *tr. by* Ellie Choi

Emerging through the automatic doors. Library, The. Timothy Steele. RA

Emerson. James Russell Lowell. APN-1; NAAPv.1; OxBoAm; TCAPo *Fr.* Fable for Critics, A.

Emerson. Henrietta Cordelia Ray. CBWP-3

Emerson thought the bride had one eye. New England, Springtime. Norman Dubie. AmAlph

Emetic. Lawrence L. White. IAoNAP

Emigrant Irish, The. Eavan Boland. AmFaPo; EmeKit; MoWP

Emigrants. Janet Caird. EdScPo

Emigrants. Jane Griffiths. NeBl; StAl

Emigrants, The. Charlotte Smith. RWP

Emigrant's Son, The. Luis Andrade Silva. NAfrP, *tr. by* Don Burness

Emigration Trains, The. Thomas McCarthy. PBCIP

Emigravit. Helen Hunt Jackson. SWaP

Emigrée, The. Carol Rumens. BeAl

Emily. Catherine Imbriglio. IAoNAP

Emily. Gertrude Stein. OxBoAm *Fr.* Book Concluding with As A Wife Has a Cow a Love Story, A.

Emily, as I entered a real greenhouse. To Two of My Characters. John Updike. PoDa

Emily Dickinson. Wendy Cope. NIL-7

Emily Dickinson. Yury Ivask. TCRusP, *tr. by* William Tjalsma

Emily Dickinson, Bismarck and the Roadrunner's Inquiry. Ray A. Young Bear. HATNAP

Emily Dickinson in Southern California. X. J. Kennedy. NBLV; OBCoV

Emily Dickinson's Defunct. Marilyn Nelson Waniek. ESEAA

Emily is admitted admittedly, Emily is admittedly Emily is admittedly. Gertrude Stein. OxBoAm *Fr.* Book Concluding with As A Wife Has a Cow a Love Story, A.

Emily Sparks. Edgar Lee Masters. APT-1 *Fr.* Spoon River Anthology.

Emily Writes Such a Good Letter. Stevie Smith. OBCoV

Emily's Words. Leslie Monsour. FFC

Emine and Hamide. Hettie Jones. PrTe

Eminent Public Figure. Dezső Kosztolányi. IQMS, *tr. by* Peter Zollman

Emma and the Radio. James Priory. RWPCtW

Emma Zola à Wimbledon supposons. Jude Stéfan. YaTCFP

Emma Zola at Wimbledon Let's Say. Jude Stéfan. YaTCFP, *tr. by* Marilyn Hacker

Emmeline Grangerford's Ode to Stephen Dowling Bots, Dec'd. Mark Twain. NBLV *Fr.* Adventures of Huckleberry Finn, The.

Emmet is an ant (archaic), The. Emmet, The. Ogden Nash. OBCoV

Emmet, The. Ogden Nash. OBCoV

Emmett Till. James A. Emanuel. NIL-7; NIP-4

Emmett Till's ghost hangs between us. Midnight in Mississippi. M. Eliza Hamilton. BtF

Emotion. Ts'ao Chih. CCL1, *tr. by* John Frodsham

Emotion. Zhang Hua. CCL1, *tr. by* John Frodsham

Emotional the / fox at an am. Brill. Clark Coolidge. PmAP

Emotions are engaged, The. George Oppen. NAMCP V.1 *Fr.* Of Being Numerous.

Empedocles came coughing through the smoke. To the Thoughtful Reader. William Meredith. NoAM

Empedocles on Etna. Matthew Arnold.

   Hymn of Empedocles. OBEV

   "Through the black, rushing smoke-bursts." OBEV

Empedocles' Sandal. Habib Tengour. *tr. by* Pierre Joris

   "Traces/Renown/Shades/Urns/Life(s)/Epoch/Zenith." PFTM-2, *tr. by* Pierre Joris

Emperor, The. Jonathan Griffin. Oth

Emperor Hadrian on his Soul. Emperor Hadrian. WoPoe, *tr. by* Frederick Morgan

Emperor Hadrian to his Soul, The. Emperor Hadrian. RomPo,

Emperor Has No Clothes!, The. Kathleen Norris. UpMys

Emperor of China, The. Shirley Kaufman. BAP-01

Emperor of Ice-Cream, The. Wallace Stevens. APT-1; BeAl; BrAP; EMP; HeIP-4; InoFa; NAAL-5; NAAPv.2; NAMCP V.1; NAWM-7v2; NIL-7; NIP-4; NoAM; NoP-4; NoP-5; OxBoAm; PoPoPo; PtR; TCAPo; TFi; TRP; WaAnP; WeW-3

Emperor of the East, The. Philip Massinger.

   (Song.) OxAEP-1

Emperor prized beauty, and longed for a woman to topple a kingdom, The. Song of Everlasting Sorrow. Po Chü-i. WoPoe, *tr. by* Dore J. Levy

Emperor's Dream, The. Zbigniew Herbert. MotU, *tr. by* Czeslaw Milosz

Emperor's New Costume, Or the Case of the Missing Mask, The. Jalal Toufic. Eno

Emphasis Falls on Reality, An. Barbara Guest. AWPTFC; FTOS; PmAP

Emphasis on the dull and the glossy, The. Portrait. Mary Leader. NAPBL

Emphasize the "h," you ignorant ass. On Being Told I don't Speak Like a Black Person. Allison Joseph. OPRER

Emphatic we can be. How long they've been at it. (LL) *Ancestored-Back* Is the Overpresiding Spirit of This Poem. Albert Goldbarth. CAP-8; PoDa

Empieza a hervir. Las fauces del humo y del automóvil, encuentran su presa. Poema incesante. Laura Solórzano. SPV

Empire is no more! and now the lion & wolf shall cease. (LL) William Blake. NAEL-6v2; NAEL-7v2 *Fr.* Marriage of Heaven and Hell, The.

Empire of Dreams. Charles Simic. BLT; VCAP

Empire of Lights, The. John Glenday. NeBrP

Empire Smoke, Forgeries, Salient and The Ritz. Ray DiPalma. FTOS

Employment. George Herbert. FaBoVe

Emplumada. Lorna Dee Cervantes. NoAM; PBCAP

Empowered image Baudrillard. Robert Sheppard. Oth *Fr.* Empty Diaries/ Twentieth Century Blues 24.

Empress Herself Served Tea to Su Tung-Po, The. Lew Welch. BB

Empress Messalina, The. Juvenal. BASC *Fr.* Satires.

Empress of Imagined Fertility, The. Leah Aini. DTA, *tr. by* Miriyam Glazer

Empress of Sighs ("Mom and Dad have abandoned the family home and retired to Palm.") Beth Lisick. AmPoNex

Empress of Sighs ("Mom says getting to the new home is a snap.") Beth Lisick. BAP-97

Empress Receives the Head of a Taiping Rebel, The. Sarah Gorham. FFC

Empress Shōtoku Invents Printing in 1770. Teresa D. Cader. ExTi

Emptiness is a long story. 155. Shih Shu. CSKM, *tr. by* James H. Sanford

Emptiness of being a man is not like, The. Emptiness of Being a Man, The. João Cabral de Melo Neto. PoetW, *tr. by* Galway Kinnell

Emptiness of Man, The. João Cabral de Melo Neto. TCLAP, *tr. by* Galway Kinnell

Emptiness of the day, The. Roberto Juarroz. VCWP *Fr.* Fifth Vertical Poetry.

Empty. Vegunta Mohana Prasad. HotL, *tr. by* V. Narayana Rao

Empty almost weightless, onioned brain, The. Wasps' Nest. Mary Ruefle.

AmAlph

Empty bag of skin filling with desire. Taoist Song. Teng Yu-pin. CrYelRi, *tr. by* Sam Hamill

Empty Bed Blues. Bessie Smith. APT-2; OxBoAm

Empty bell, The. Secret. Pierre Reverdy. PFTM-1

Empty black haunted house. Empty Black Haunted House. Joyce Mansour. NAWM-7v2, *tr. by* Serge Gavronsky

Empty boat / drifts on and on at will, The. Written on the First Day of the Fifth Month. T'ao Ch'ien. CCL1, *tr. by* William Acker

Empty Cage, The. Lise Deharme. SurWo, *tr. by* Franklin Rosemont

Empty carousel in a deserted park, An. Gloria C. Oden. GT

Empty Chairs. Maxianne Berger. IFF

Empty Church, The. Ronald Stuart Thomas. AngWePo; EmeKit

Empty City, An. Mahmoud al-Braikan. IrPoTo, *tr. by* Ralph Saverese and Saadi A. Simawe

Empty coathangers. Leavetaking. Rita Wong. IFF

Empty Diaries/Twentieth Century Blues 24. Robert Sheppard.

   Empty Diary 1905. Oth

   Empty Diary 1936. Oth

   Empty Diary 1944. Oth

   Empty Diary 1954. Oth

   Empty Diary 1968. Oth

   Empty Diary 1987. Oth

   Empty Diary 1990. Oth

Empty Dwelling Places. Kenneth Patchen. PoA 2002

Empty foolscap, The. Lines. Barbara Nickel. ACAMVP

Empty Glen, The. R. Crombie Saunders. EdScPo

Empty holes in the fish-dying-becoming directions. Armand Schwerner. PFTM-2 *Fr.* Tablets, The.

Empty House. James Kimbrell. LegDan

Empty House. Yüan Chĕn. CrYelRi; ErotSp, *tr. by* Sam Hamill

Empty house, An. ToKoku. EMJL *Fr.* Mad Verse.

Empty House, The. Aida Gelbtrunk. MirDau, *tr. by* Roberta Gordenstein

Empty House, The. William Dean Howells. APN-2

Empty inside, it's always clean. Bamboo Hermitage. Pou Kuksa. BecRai

Empty Kettle. Louis Oliver. HATNAP; NAAPv.2

Empty Laird was called that 'cause. Layered, The. Nick Laird. NIrP

Empty lighthouse stood where the man who built it died, The. Isosceles Lighthouse, The. Alfred Goldsworthy Bailey. Coast

Empty Mirror. Kenneth Rexroth. OxBoAm

Empty mountain after fresh rains. Autumn Dusk at a Mountain Lodge. Wang Wei. ChinPo, *tr. by* Ye Weilian [*or* Yeh Wei-lien *or* Wai-lim Yip]

Empty mountain, after new rain. Autumn Mountain Evening. Wang Wei. CCL1, *tr. by* Jerome P. Seaton

Empty mountain: no man. Four Examples from the Poems of River Wang Deer Enclosure. Wang Wei. ChinPo, *tr. by* Ye Weilian [*or* Yeh Wei-lien *or* Wai-lim Yip]

Empty mountains. Deer Camp. Wang Wei. NDACCP, *tr. by* Gary Snyder

Empty or "empty" under title: part. Frames. Laura Mullen. IAoNAP

Empty out your pockets nighttime, Daddy. Who I Think You Are. Elizabeth Alexander. FFC; RA

Empty Page, The. Sara de Ibáñez. TCLAP, *tr. by* Andrew Rosing

Empty perfection, as I take you in. James Merrill. NoAM *Fr.* Coda: The Higher Keys.

Empty Place, An. Robert Bly. CAP-8

Empty Place, An. Sonia Edwards. BBMWP, *tr. by* Sally Roberts Jones

Empty Place at the Celebration, An. José Ángel Valente. RaW, *tr. by* Ralph Nelson and Hardie St. Martin

Empty Purse. Tu Fu [*or* Du Fu]. CrYelRi, *tr. by* Sam Hamill

Empty Purse, The. George Meredith.

   "He cancelled the ravaging Plague." VerBaPo

Empty Purse, The. Tu Fu [*or* Du Fu]. TAL

Empty room begins to growl, The. Vasco [*or* Vasko] Popa. PoSu *Fr.* Besieged Serenity.

Empty room is still the empty room, The. Empty Room, The. Hans Andreus. TuT, *tr. by* Desmond Egan

Empty room is still the empty room, The. Empty Room, The. Hans Andreus. TuT, *tr. by* Joan McBreen

Empty Shrine Buddha, The. Joanne Kyger. WhBo

Empty skies. And beyond, one hawk. Standing Alone. Tu Fu [*or* Du Fu]. NDACCP, *tr. by* David Hinton

Empty sky, a world of heather, An. Divided. Jean Ingelow. VWP

Empty Song, The. Liz Lochhead. EdScPo

Empty Streets. Hilmi Yavuz. NaPG, *tr. by* Talat Sait Halman

Empty the pain. Barefoot Necklace. Elouise Loftin. EGAG

Empty Tomb, The. Clara Ann Thompson. CBWP-2

Empty Vessel. Hugh MacDiarmid. EdScPo; NePenScot; NPeEn; OxBEV

Empty Walnut, The. Gabriela Mistral. TANSG, *tr. by* Maria Giachetti [*or* Jacketti]

Empty Warriors. Haki R. Madhubuti. RaBo

Emptying Town. Nick Flynn. AmPoNex; LegDan; NAPBL

Emu Shot. Tjinapirrgarri. NOBAu, *tr. by* George von Brandenstein

Emulation, The. Sarah Fyge Egerton. CABP; PEW

Emulation, The: A Pindarick Ode. *Unknown.* EMWP

En ausencia de progreso. ¿Hacia Donde? Ernesto Lumbreras. RMCMP

En avant / du centre. Pierre ou eau. André Du Bouchet. YaTCFP

En Bateau. Li Po. CCL1, *tr. by* Marie-Jean-Léon, Marquis d'Hervey de Saint-Denys

En Casa Ya. Miguel de Unamuno.
  Junto a la Laguna del Cristo, en la Aldehuela de Yeltes, una Noche de Luna Llena. RaW
  ¡Siémbrate! RaW

En ce monde. Épreuves du poète. Andrée Chédid. YaTCFP

En ce temps-là, façons de feinte et de tendresse, la peste ayant figure d'ennui dans les villes. Ballade, La. Michel Deguy. YaTCFP

En ce temps-là j'étais en mon adolescence. Blaise Cendrars. YaTCFP *Fr.* Prose du Transsibérien et de la Petite Jeanne de France.

En Cest Sonet Coind' a Leri. Arnaut Daniel. WoPoe,

En coma. Dolores Dorantes. SPV

En el callejón marino. Na Aurea. Natalia Toledo. RMCMP

En el desván antiguo de raída memoria. Precio de la Verdad. Carlos Bousoño. RaW

En el espejo del tiempo. Sobre él discurren con suavidad. Coral Bracho. RMCMP

En el piso de abajo el sufrimiento se extiende como el polvo. Vecinos. Antonio Deltoro. RMCMP

En el Principio, el Agua. Carlos Sahagún. RaW

En el Ritz de Meknés. Manuel Ulacia. RMCMP

En el silencio entreverado. Misterios del tacto, Los. Coral Bracho. RMCMP

En el Sol de Mi Barrio. Sandra M. Castillo. TouFir

En el umbral de madera. Agrícola. Natalia Toledo. RMCMP

En el Valle de Zapata. Veronica Volkow. RMCMP

En esta oscura mezquita tibia. Coral Bracho. RMCMP

En esta tarde llueve, y llueve pura tu imagen. En mi recuerdo el día se abre. Entraste. Llueve. Vicente Aleixandre. RaW

En este momento, tengo treinta y tres años encima de la mesa del despacho. Claustro de las Sombras, El. Blas de Otero. RaW

En Famille. Robert Creeley. BAP-01

En Famille. Dame Edith Sitwell. NALW *Fr.* Façade.

En la Calle Coahuila. Heriberto Yépez. RMCMP

En la Ceniza Hay un Milagro. Carlos Bousoño. RaW

En la desnuda tierra del camino. Antonio Machado Ruiz. RaW *Fr.* Del Camino.

En la humedad de mi lengua la espiral de la serpiente. Rosario. Pedro Serrano. RMCMP

En la mitad del barranco. Reyerta. Federico García Lorca. RaW

En la naturaleza sólo existen dos tipos de seres. Teorí de Fractales. Alberto Blanco. RMCMP

En la palma de mi mano. Víctor Terán. RMCMP

En la playa. Manuel Ulacia. RMCMP

En la profunda cueva. Dolores Dorantes. SPV

En la Tierra Seca. Pedro Salinas. RaW

En la ventana. Carla Faesler Bremer. SPV

En las rancias cantinas y fachadas de mala cara. En la Calle Coahuila. Heriberto Yépez. RMCMP

En Monocle. Donald Evans. APT-1

En Roma o en Paris. Millares 1965. Rafael Alberti. RaW

En Route. Alan Ross. FaBoWar

En Route to America. Soyen Shaku. WhBo

En su vitrina pende el pez. Lejano, es una lección de anatomía, un discurso de vida ajena. Imagen del Pez. Mónica Nepote. SPV, *tr. by* Jen Hofer

En turbante. Mandap. Elsa Cross. RMCMP

En un baño de vapor. Manuel Ulacia. RMCMP

En un Cementerio de Lugar Castellano. Miguel de Unamuno. RaW

En un cuarto a oscuras se enciende una vela. Teoría de conjuntos. Alberto Blanco. RMCMP

En un Vergier Soiz Folha D'Albespi. *Unknown.* WoPoe, *tr. by* Stanley Burnshaw

En una esquina blanca se oyen estas voces. Vagos en una esquina blanca. Ernesto Lumbreras. RMCMP

Enactment, The. Rita Dove. FuFl

Enamel Girl, The. Genevieve Taggard. MoAmPo

Encampment at Morning, An. W. S. Merwin. GifTon

Enchanted by the name of the mountain. Climbing Enlightenment Mountain. Hueung Powoo. BecRai, *tr. by* Kim Daljin, Kim Won-Chung and Christopher Merrill

Enchanted frame assures the image of a loved one, An. Veil. Marjorie Welish. OnScMo; PmAP

Enchanted is what they were. Animals Are Entering Our Lives. Lisel Mueller. ExTi

Enchanted Island, The. Letitia Elizabeth Landon. CABP; NOBRP

Enchanted Mistress, The. Egan O'Rahilly. IrLP, *tr. by* Augusta, Lady Gregory

Enchanted Princess, An. Rosamund Marriott Watson. ViWPN

Enchanted Shell, The. Henrietta Cordelia Ray. CBWP-3

Enchantment, The. Thomas Otway. OBEV

Enchantment, The. Theocritus. OBVE *Fr.* Idylls.

Enchantress' Song, The. Giles Fletcher, the Younger. *See* Wooing Song.

Encircled by freeway loops. Dallas. Dave Oliphant. TiP2

Enclosure. Christopher Gilbert. SwNoth

Encompass me, my lover. Constant North, The. J. F. Hendry. EdScPo; GoPo

Encore le dernier reflux. Dieppe. Samuel Beckett. YaTCFP

Encore le froid. Paul De Roux. YaTCFP

Encounter. Rick Fournier. PasH

Encounter. Mary Low. SurWo

Encounter. Czeslaw Milosz. ASA; BodElec; ChAP; GPTC; PoetW; StAl; WoPoe, *tr. by* the author and Lillian Vallee

Encounter. Marianne Poloskey. RWB

Encounter. Alfonsina Storni. TANSG, *tr. by* Mark McCaffrey

Encounter. August Stramm. PFTM-1

Encounter. Marion Strobel. LW

Encounter, An. Guido Cavalcanti. NAWM-7v1, *tr. by* James J. Wilhelm

Encounter at St. Martin's. Ken Smith. OPOU

Encounter at the Post Office Counter. Christopher Pilling. NLP

Encouragement. János Batsányi. IQMS, *tr. by* Matthew Mead *and* Ruth Mead

Encouragement. Mrs. Henry Linden. CBWP-4

Encouraging. Attila József. WoPoe, *tr. by* John Batki

Encroaching on the emptiness, riot of color. Cold Mountain. Chiao-jan. CCL1, *tr. by* Stephen Owen

Encroaching shadows. Tomas Tranströmer. WoBe *Fr.* Haiku.

Encuentro, El. José Hierro. RaW

Encyclopedia Botanica. Lee Ann Brown. VaPo

Encyclopedia of Rhythm and Blues, The. Anthony Walton. RD

End. Hugh Seidman. BodElec

End / conscience. Stéphane Mallarmé. PFTM-1 *Fr.* Le Livre.

End, An. Or a beginning. Late Snow. M. R. Peacocke. BeAl

End, The. Wilfred Owen. ChIV-1

End, The. Mark Strand. TRP

End and Beginning. Wisława Szymborska. PLBUT, *tr. by* Joseph Brodsky

End and the Beginning, The. Wisława Szymborska. CFP; StAl; VCWP, *tr. by* Stanislaw Barańczak and Clare Cavanagh

End and the Beginning, The. Wisława Szymborska. GPTC, *tr. by* Joanna Trzeciak

End came easy for most of us, The. Man from Washington, The. James Welch. HATNAP; NoAM; PoPoPo; RaBo; WaAnP

End is an Animal, The. Claudia Keelan. RoV

End of a line, The. Wishon Line, The. Sherley Anne Williams. GeoHom

End of a Love Affair, The. Edward C. Redding. ReLy

End of a Season. Thomas McGrath. BodElec

End of a Summer, The. Günter Eich. GTCP, *tr. by* Reinhold Grimm

End of a thing. December. Lucille Clifton. NOxBChV

End of a War, The. Sir Herbert Read. OBMV

End of an Age, The. Robin Fulton. EdScPo

End of an Ethnic Dream, The. Jay Wright. SeSe

End of Another Home Holiday. D. H. Lawrence. OxAEP-2

End of Art, The. Reiner Kunze. PoSu, *tr. by* Michael Hamburger

End of Civilization as We Know It, The. Colleen J. McElroy. UrbNat

End of Clonmacnois, The. *Unknown.* WoPoe, *tr. by* Frank O'Connor

End of Communism, The. Rodney Jones. IllVoic

End of Doctor Faustus, The. Christopher Marlowe. FaBoVe; HeIP-4 *Fr.* Doctor Faustus.

End of Dodona II, The. Yannis Ritsos. VCWP; WoPoe, *tr. by* Edmund Keeley

End of Ends . . . in God's Beginning's lost, The. (LL) Clover. Sidney Lanier. APN-2; ColAP

End of everything approaches, The. Doomsday. Elinor Wylie. NoP-4; NoP-5; SacPr

End of Fall, The. Francis Ponge. WED, *tr. by* Robert Bly

End of Human Reign on Bashan Hill, The. Bernadette Mayer. FTOS

End of January, The. Cathal McCabe. NIrP

End of July. John Peck. HarvBoo

End of love should be a big event, The. End of Love, The. Sophie Hannah. MFPA

End of March, The. Elizabeth Bishop. NAMCP V.2

End of my life, The. Palm Reader. Dabney Stuart. PfSP

End of Mythology, The.   Konstantin Pavlov.   CSCBP, *tr.* by Georgi Belev and Lisa Sapinkopf

End of "Pain", The.   Amanda Ros.   VerBaPo

End of spring, The.   Buson.   EH, *tr.* by Robert Hass

End of summer.   Stanford M. Forrester.   AmZen

End of Summer.   Stanley Kunitz.   LoL; MoAmPo

End of summer suggested the way, The.   Autumn Leaves.   James Cushing.   SeSe

End of the affair is always death, The.   Ballad of the Lonely Masturbator, The.   Anne Sexton.   WaAnP

End of the Affair, The.   E. San Juan, Jr.   ReBoTo

End of the Affair, The.   James Simmons.   PBCIP

End of the City, The.   Kevin Prufer.   LegDan

End of the Comedy.   Louis Untermeyer.   PoA 2002

End of the factory-window song. (LL)   Factory Windows Are Always Broken.   Vachel Lindsay.   AmWit; APT-1

End of the Flower World (A.D. 2300).   Stanley Burnshaw.   APT-2

End of the Game.   Artur Miedzyrzecki.   PoSu, *tr.* by John Batki and Artur Miedzyrzecki

End of the Journey, The.   May Probyn.   VWP

End of the Line, The.   Thomas McGrath.   GM

End of the line, The.   Philip Whalen.   WhBo

End of the Owls, The.   Hans Magnus Enzensberger.   BeAl, *tr.* by Jerome Rothenberg

End of the Picnic.   Francis Webb.   BMAP; NOBAu

End of the Questionnaire.   Dan Pagis.   PoSu, *tr.* by Robert Friend

End of the Reagan Era, The.   Peter Balakian.   ReTh

End of the Row.   Anne Born.   Prnts

End of the Suitors, The.   Homer.   OBVE *Fr.* Odyssey.

End of the War, The.   Ioan Alexandru.   FaBoWar, *tr.* by Brenda Walker and Andrea Deletant

End of the Weekend, The.   Anthony Hecht.   WeW-3

End of the World.   Jakov Van Hoddis.   GTCP, *tr.* by Irmgard Hunt

End of the World, The.   Gordon Bottomley.   MoBrPo

End of the World, The.   João Cabral de Melo Neto.   VCWP

End of the World, The.   Miroslav Holub.   BeAl, *tr.* by Ewald Osers

End of the World, The.   Archibald MacLeish.   BrAP; GSo; MoAmPo; NAMCP V.1; NoAM; OxBSo; TFi

End of the World, The.   Thomas McGrath.   AF

End of the World, The: To Embody.   Gherasim Luca.   YaTCFP, *tr.* by Mary Ann Caws and Jean-Pierre Cauvin

End of their journey, I descended too, The. (LL)   Traveller [*or* Traveler], The.   John Berryman.   GM; OxBoAm; PoA 2002

End of Winter.   Liz Rosenberg.   IJHIL

End or a Beginning, An.   Bei Dao.   AF, *tr.* by Bonnie S. McDougall

End to Myth, An.   Charles Buckmaster.   BMAP

End to Spring, An.   Li Ch'ing-chao.   CrYelRi, *tr.* by Sam Hamill

End to Spring, An ("Spring has vanished.")   Tzu Yeh.   CrYelRi, *tr.* by Sam Hamill

End to Spring, An ("Your leaving brought an end to spring.")   Tzu Yeh.   CrYelRi, *tr.* by Sam Hamill

End was dreadful, The. Inside a dam burst.   Her End.   Gwyneth Lewis.   MoWP, *tr.* by Richard Poole

End was dreadful, The. Inside, a dam burst.   Gwyneth Lewis.   BBMWP *Fr.* Language Murderer, The.

End was horrible, The. A vessel burst.   Last Minutes, The.   Gwyneth Lewis.   ATSWP, *tr.* by Robert Minhinnick

End was quick and bitter, The.   Quick And Bitter.   Yehuda Amichai.   VCWP

Endangered Nouns.   David Antin.   PFTM-2

Endangered Roots of a Person.   Wendy Rose.   ReEnLa

Endangered Species.   Ai.   ESEAA

Endangered Species.   William Cook.   FTtHH

Ended, ere it begun.   Emily Dickinson.   APN-2

Enderecé la fruta veraz.   Poema temprano.   Laura Solórzano.   SPV

Endimion.   John Lyly.
   "Pinch him, pinch him black and blue."   NoSic
   "Stand! Who goes there?"   NoSic; OBCoV

Ending.   Gavin Ewart.   NBLV; SoSe-8

Ending.   Eugene McCarthy.   HHAm *Fr.* Page of Short Poems, A.

Ending by Pound, An.   Tedi López Mills.   RMCMP, *tr.* by C. M. Mayo

Ending Poem.   Aurora Levins Morales and Rosario Morales.   PueRic

Ending up tending shop up in Fiesole. (LL)   Tourists.   Howard Moss.   NoP-4; NoP-5; OBCoV

Ending With a Line From *Lear*.   Marvin Bell.   PoChi

Endings.   Bill Pearlman.   ICANM

Endings always erase the traces of their plot.   Letter.   Tedi López Mills.   RMCMP, *tr.* by C. M. Mayo

Endless and indestructible. (LL)   Descent, The.   William Carlos Williams.   APT-1; NAAPv.2; SAmP; WeW-3

Endless blue mountains disperse, The.   On the Tower of Gathering Remoteness.   Su Tung-p'o.   TAL

Endless curve of sky, The.   Song to Come, The.   Doreen Baingana.   BtF

Endless détour. (LL)   On Inhabiting an Orange.   Josephine Miles.   NoAM; PoA 2002; WaAnP

Endless fields sit under snowy blankets, The.   Farewell to Várad.   Janus Pannonius.   IQMS, *tr.* by Adam Makkai

Endless horizons of wheat and corn.   End of the Reagan Era, The.   Peter Balakian.   ReTh

Endless infusions, silver strainers.   Sean Dunne.   ModIr *Fr.* Sydney Place.

Endless Journeys.   Pierre Reverdy.   WoPoe, *tr.* by John Ashbery

Endless lanes sunken in the clay.   Trenches, The.   Frederic Manning.   NOBAu; PoWW

Endless River Flows, An.   Kim Yŏngnang.   CAMKP, *tr.* by Anthony, Brother of Taizé

Endless sameness.   Paul Verlaine.   SxFrPo, *tr.* by Martin Sorrell

Endless, the white clouds. (LL)   To See a Friend Off.   Wang Wei.   CCL1; ChinPo, *tr.* by Ye Weilian [*or* Yeh Wei-lien *or* Wai-lim Yip]

Endless, waterway toward the southwest.   To Hsuan-Ch'eng, Past Hsin-Lin-P'u, Toward Pan-Ch'iao.   Hsieh T'iao.   ChinPo, *tr.* by Ye Weilian [*or* Yeh Wei-lien *or* Wai-lim Yip]

Endless worlds, The.   One Hut.   Muso Soseki.   EaWin, *tr.* by W. S. Merwin

Endlessly, endlessly the blue waves break.   Sea Spray.   Marion Margaret Boyd.   YaYoPo

Endow the fool with sun and moon.   Fool and Wise.   Coventry Patmore.   SacPr

Endowed fiction of a mouse ear.   Mac Wellman.   HeMarv *Fr.* Rat Minaret: Miniaturist-Divan, The.

Endowed with Ch———l's strength and Low———r's face. (LL)   Epistle from Mrs. Yonge to Her Husband.   Lady Mary Wortley Montagu.   NAEL-6v1; NAEL-7v1; NALW; NoP-4; NoP-5; NPeEn

Endowment Becoming Less An Institution, The.   Brian Blanchfield.   IIR

Endowment for Long Mornings in Bed, The.   Endowment Becoming Less An Institution, The.   Brian Blanchfield.   IIR

Ends.   Robert Frost.   TRP

Ends of all, who for the scene do write, The.   Ben Jonson.   ASA *Fr.* Epicoene; or, The Silent Woman.

Endsight [*for Union Carbide, A.D. Hope and Sir P. Hasluck, Askin, Clutha etc.*].   Michael Dransfield.   BMAP

Endsong.   Sion Eirian.   BBMWP *Fr.* Adolescent Experiences.

Endurance.   Dennis Brutus.   VCWP

Endurance of Poth, Texas, The.   Naomi Shihab Nye.   TiP2

Endure the wintry and the darkened days. (LL)   To Honora Sneyd.   Anna Seward.   CenSon; PoBW

Endure what life God gives and ask no longer span.   Sophocles.   OBMV *Fr.* Oedipus at Colonus.

Enduring like a tree under the curious stars. (LL)   Peasant, A.   Ronald Stuart Thomas.   AngWePo; OBWVE; OxBEV

Enduring Witness, the Mosques of Kattankudi.   Peter Michelson.   OPRER

Endymion.   Thomas Kinsella.   PBCIP

Endymion: A Poetic Romance.   John Keats.
   "But there are."   NPeEn
   "Peona! ever have I long'd to slake."   NAEL-6v2; NAEL-7v2
   Song of the Indian Maid.   OBEV
   "Wherein lies happiness? In that which becks."   NPBRoP

Eneas wonderit the greitnes of Cartaige.   Virgil.   OBVE *Fr.* Aeneid [*or* Eneados *or* Aeneis], The.

Enemies.   Tish Benson.   BRtP

Enemies.   Wendell Berry.   RaF

Enemies.   Sa'di Yusuf.   IrPoTo, *tr.* by Khaled Mattawa

Enemies.   Charlotte Zolotow.   HHAm

Enemies of Promise.   Edmund Wilson.   OBCoV

Enemy.   Beau Sia.   HeMarv

Enemy, The.   Randolph Stow.   NOBAu

Enemy Dead, The.   Bernard Gutteridge.   FaBoWar; PoWW

Enemy Encounter.   Padraic Fiacc.   PNI

Enemy was always identified in art by a lion, The.   Gentleman Compares His Virtue to a Piece of Jade, A.   Michael Ondaatje.   PoDa

Enemy's Eyes, The.   Emma Lee Warrior.   HATNAP

Energy.   Víctor Hernández Cruz.   PueRic

Energy in Sweden.   Kenneth Koch.   NoP-4; NoP-5

Energy—Absolute.   Sikong Tu.   CCL1 *Fr.* Twenty-Four Modes of Poetry.

Enfettered, these sentences repress free speech, The.   Christian Bök.   OpeFie *Fr.* Chapter E.

Enfidaville.   Keith Douglas.   PoWW

Enfield Falls.   A. R. Ammons.   LPSFW

Enfin: The secular order rises in time from its roots in the earth. Modern Western History. Britton Wilkie. AHA

Engima, The. Alan Bold. ArBi

Engine, The. Ella Wheeler Wilcox. APN-2

Engine Driver. Bobi Jones. ATSWP, *tr. by* Robert Minhinnick

Engine stops, The. Dust in a weary threat. Hunger. Attila József. IQMS, *tr. by* Watson Kirkconnell

Engineers' Corner. Wendy Cope. OBCoV

Engines of Gloom and Affection. John Yau. PmAP

England. Marianne Moore. MoAmPo

England and America. James Kenneth Stephen.
    On a Rhine Steamer. FaBoA; OBCoV

England! Awake! Awake! Awake! William Blake. NoP-4; NoP-5

England be your sepulchre. (LL) Song to the Men of England. Percy Bysshe Shelley. CABP; NAEL-6v2; NAEL-7v2; RSaN

England, 1802, I. William Wordsworth. *See* Written in London, September, 1802.

England, 1802, II. William Wordsworth. *See* London 1802.

England, His Love. Maurice Riordan. NIrP

England in 1819. Percy Bysshe Shelley. CenSon; NAEL-6v2; NAEL-7v2; NAWM-7v2; NoP-4; NoP-5; NPBRoP; OxAEP-2; OxBEV; OxBSo; PoPoPo; TFi
    (Sonnet: England in 1819.) BrAP; GSo

England, my England. W. E. Henley. MoBrPo; OBEV

England, my England--you have been my tutrix. W. H. Auden. OBSV *Fr.* Letter to Lord Byron.

England Nil. Anne Rouse. MFPA; NeBl

England's Alfred Abroad. Sir Owen Seaman. UV

England's Dead. Felicia Dorothea Hemans. NAEL-6v2; NAEL-7v2; NoP-4; NoP-5; WaAnP

England's Heroical Epistles. Michael Drayton.
    Owen Tudor to Queen Katherine. NoSic
    Queen Katherine to Owen Tudor. NoSic

England's sun was slowly setting o'er the hill-tops far away. Curfew Must Not Ring Tonight [*or* To-Night]. Rose Hartwick Thorpe. APN-2; BRP; SWaP

English, The. Sándor Sík. IQMS, *tr. by* James Turner

English Are So Nice!, The. D. H. Lawrence. NAMCP V.1; NoP-4; NoP-5; PoPoPo; RaBo

English Bards and Scotch Reviewers [1810 version]. Lord Byron.
    "Time was, ere yet in these degenerate days." NPBRoP

English Bards and Scotch Reviewers [1812 version]. Lord Byron.
    "As Sisyphus against the infernal steep." OBSV
    "Illustrious Holland! hard would be his lot." OBSV
    "Oh! Southey! Southey! cease thy varied song!" WaAnP

English Bull Dog, Dutch Mastiff, and Quail, The. Christopher Smart.
    Insular Prejudice. DiBP

English con Salsa. Gina Valdés. CalPo

English Cousin Comes to Scotland. Jackie Kay. NOxBChV

English Earthquake, The. Eva Salzman. MFPA

English Flavors. Laure-Anne Bosselaar. SUP

English Fleet Goes Out, The. John Dryden. STuOW *Fr.* Annus Mirabilis.

English, French, Italian. Chinoiserie. Kay Sage. SurWo

English Garden, The. William Mason.
    Alcander's Flower Garden. OBGa
    Some Early gardenists. OBGa

English Girl. *Unknown.* OBMV, *tr. by* E. Powys Mathers

English Girl Eats Her First Mango. John Agard. BeAl

English Graves, The. G. K. Chesterton. FaBoWar

English has all the sexual options. Hebrew. Yona Volach. DTA, *tr. by* Miriyam Glazer

English hymn writer. Anne Steele. Jean Balderston. MPUn

English Music. Geoff Ward.
    7. VaPo
    9. VaPo

English muskets went bim! bim!, The [*tr. of Creole slave song*]. George Washington Cable. APN-2

English Poetry. Lőrinc Szabó. IQMS *Fr.* Cricket Music.

English Poets. James McIntyre.
    "We have scarcely time to tell thee." VerBaPo

English Queen, The. Henry Lawson. NOBAu

English Rose. Mina Loy. NAMCP V.1 *Fr.* Anglo-Mongrels and the Rose.

English Sampler, An. Frederick D'Aguiar. Oth

English Teeth, English Teeth! Teeth. Spike Milligan. OPOU

English think it never happens here, The. Rebecca Baggett. FiBr *Fr.* Art of the Amish: A Quilt Exhibition.

English-Speaking Persons Will Find Translations. Michael S. Glaser. UnSA

Englishwoman, An. Sion Eirian. BBMWP *Fr.* Adolescent Experiences.

Englyns are akin to scampi. Englyns. Ifor Ap Glyn. BBMWP, *tr. by* Nigel Jenkins

Engpop, engpop, bop, plolo, plolo, bop, bop. (LL) Crootey Songo. Bob Kaufman. EGAG; FTtHH

Engraved on the Collar of a Dog, Which I Gave to His Royal Highness. Alexander Pope. *See* Epigram Engraved on the Collar of a Dog Given [*or* Which I Gave] to His Royal Highness.

Engraving, An. Aleksandr Petrovich Tkachenko. ItGoST, *tr. by* Maia Tekses

Engraving of Blake, An. Mary Kinzie. MakPoe

Engraving Twenty-Nine. Fadhila Chabbi. PoArWo, *tr. by* Yaseen Noorani

Enhances Nature now. (LL) Further in Summer than the Birds. Emily Dickinson. APN-2; NoP-4; NoP-5; OxBoAm

Enheduanna and Goethe. Amal Al-Juburi. PoArWo, *tr. by* Salih J. Altoma

Enia. Seitlhamo Motsapi. TSAP

Enigma. Catherine Maria Fanshawe. OBCoV

Enigma No. 6. Augusta Davies Webster. VWP

Enigma of the Stigma, or Vice Versa. Peter Johnson. Vesp

Enigmas, The. Jorge Luis Borges. PoCho, *tr. by* John Updike

Enigmas: "You've asked me what the lobster is weaving there with his golden feet?" Pablo Neruda. WED, *tr. by* Robert Bly

Enjoy his lust, eat well and play the flute? (LL) Soliloquy at Potsdam. Peter Porter. BrAP; NOBAu

Enjoy [*or* Injoy] such liberty. (LL) To Althea, from Prison. Richard Lovelace. BASC; CavPo; CtM; ITBLP; ItP; NAEL-6v1; NAEL-7v1; NIL-7; NoP-4; NoP-5; NOSC; NPeEn; OBEV; OxBEV; PBRV; TFi; WaAnP

Enjoying [*or* Injoying] of myself I lie [*or* lye]. (LL) Love Made in the First Age[: To Chloris]. Richard Lovelace. NAEL-6v1; NAEL-7v1

Enjoying Spring. Hwansung Jian. BecRai, *tr. by* Kim Daljin, Kim Won-Chung and Christopher Merrill

Enjoyment Body. Jonathan Cott. AHA

Enjoys with them "the Liberty it loved." (LL) To the Shade of Burns. Charlotte Smith. NoP-4; NoP-5; WaAnP

Enkindled Spring, The. D. H. Lawrence. NAMCP V.1; NoAM

Enlarge my Life with Multitude of Days. Juvenal. OxBEV *Fr.* Vanity of Human Wishes, The; The Tenth Satire of Juvenal [Imitated].

Enlightenment. Shih Shu. WoPoe, *tr. by* James H. Sanford

Enlightenment Song. Great Master Wonhyo. BecRai, *tr. by* Kim Daljin, Kim Won-Chung and Christopher Merrill

Enlisted Today. *Unknown.* CBCWP

Enlli. Christine Evans. TCAWP

Enmeshment. Lewis Warsh. FTOS

Enmeshment is an enter. Closure. Douglas Messerli. FTOS

Enniskillen. David Morley. NLP

Ennui. Larry Chittendon. TiP2

Enobarbus, Antony. William Shakespeare. OxAEP-1 *Fr.* Antony and Cleopatra.

Enoch. Jones Very. ChIV-1; TCAPo

Enoch Arden. Alfred Tennyson.
    Ocean-Spoil Alive, O! STuOW

Enoch, I walk about the earth the *angels* have defiled. Boleros #31. Jay Wright. ICANM

Enormous and solid. Grove, The. Octavio Paz. TCLAP, *tr. by* Elizabeth Bishop

ENORMOUS BLISS of American death, The. Reading Frank O'Hara in a Mexican Rainstorm. Michael McClure. BB

Enormous clock at the sandy mansion, An. Anna Glazova. CRWP *Fr.* Cities.

Enormous cloud-mountains that form over Point Lobos and into the sunset. Clouds of Evening. Robinson Jeffers. MoAmPo

Enormous engineering problems, The. Popular Mechanics. Charles Simic. EmeKit

Enormous Hand, The [*with music*]. Jorge de Lima. PFTM-1

Enormous mentality, The. Part of the Bridge. Peter Didsbury. NeBrP

Enormous rope of silence, An. (LL) Distance. Peter Everwine. GeoHom; PoCho

Enormous tragedy of the dream in the peasant's bent, The. Ezra Pound. AF *Fr.* Cantos.

Enormous tree-trunk crawling on the waves. Dream of the Caiman, The. José Santos Chocano. TCLAP, *tr. by* Andrew Rosing

Enos Page the youngest brother. Julia A. Moore. VerBaPo *Fr.* Brave Page Boys, The.

Enosis. Christopher Pearse Cranch. TCAPo

Enough. Thomas Kinsella. ModIr *Fr.* One Fond Embrace.

Enough: "Moon the color of an empty movie screen, A." Cindy Day Roberts. LaCa

Enough. Tracy Ryan. NeBl

Enough. Lucien Stryk. Vesp

Enough. Sara Teasdale. APT-1

Enough cloth is plenty and more, more is almost enough for that. Gertrude Stein. TCAPo *Fr.* Tender Buttons.

Enough for you. (LL)   For Bud. Michael S. Harper. ESEAA; FaoP

Enough Horses. Alvaro Cardona-Hine. ICANM

Enough kind Heaven! to purpose I have liv'd. To Mrs. W. on Her Excellent Verses. Aphra Behn. EMWP

Enough, my Muse, of earthly things. Christ's Passion. Abraham Cowley. ChIV-2; SacPr

Enough new ghosts now to mourn any war. Facing Snow. Tu Fu [or Du Fu]. NDACCP, tr. by David Hinton

Enough of air. A desert subject now. John Armstrong. VerBaPo Fr. Art of Preserving Health, The.

Enough of Grongar and the shady dales. Ruins of Rome, The. John Dyer. AngWePo

Enough of those who study the oblique. Good Resolution, A. Roy Campbell. OBSV

Enough praise, enough rope. (LL) Gift, The: "Older, more generous." N. Scott Momaday. NoP-4; NoP-5

Enough Rain for Agnes Walquist. Allen Grossman. BAP-01

Enough seen. The vision has been met in every air. Departure. Arthur Rimbaud. SxFrPo, tr. by Martin Sorrell

Enough the ordeal now, the snow- and hail-storms. Horace. WaAnP Fr. Odes.

Enough to fortify our care against the winter. (LL) Meadow, The. Peter Fallon. IPoFL; PBCIP

Enough to Say. Lisa Lubasch. IIR

Enough typing. Woman Writer Does Laundry, A. Anna Swirszczynska [or Swir]. TAPaP, tr. by Czeslaw Milosz and Leonard Nathan

Enough! we're tired, my heart and I. My Heart and I. Elizabeth Barrett Browning. VWP

Enough! Why should a man bemoan. Per Iter Tenebricosum. Oliver St. John Gogarty. OBMV

Enough women over thirty are at Redbones. Raising a Humid Flag. Thylias Moss. GT

Enquiry, The. Katherine Philips. OxBEV

Enquiry Concerning the Bat, An. José Emilio Pacheco. TCLAP, tr. by Alastair Reid

Enrica, 1865. Christina Georgina Rossetti. NALW

Enrich my resignation as I usurp those far. Enrich My Resignation. Hart Crane. PoA 2002

Enriching the Earth. Wendell Berry. InGu; WaAnP

Ensconced now in your heart, our mother. Nigeria of the Seventies. Molara Ogundipe-Leslie. HAWP

Ensembles. Dominique Fourcade. YaTCFP

Ensembles here, spacious: thus. Ensembles. Dominique Fourcade. YaTCFP, tr. by Cole Swensen

Ensembles ici, spacieux: ainsi. Ensembles. Dominique Fourcade. YaTCFP

Ensenada Wedding. Robert Thomas. FaoP

Ensnaring Flower of Psalms. Rossana Ombres. NeIt

Ensuing Copy the Late Printer Hath Been Pleased to Honour, by Mistaking It Among Those of the Most Ingenious and Too Early Lost Sir John Suckling, The. See Song: "When, dearest, I but think on [or of] thee."

Entallaron la piedra. Arcano 4: El Emperador. Veronica Volkow. RMCMP

Entangled. Mathilde Blind. VWP

Entangled. Jules Supervielle. BBASP, tr. by James Kirkup

Entanglement. Caitlin Maude. IrLP, tr. by Gabriel Fitzmaurice

Entelechy. Croatan. Tom Weatherly. EGAG

Entelechy on the Libidinal Fringe. E. San Juan, Jr. ReBoTo

Entendez ci de saint Brandent. Brandan's Last Voyage. Kenneth White. EdScPo

Enter and see this tomb, sirs, do not fear. Epitaph on Some Bottles of Sack and Claret Laid in Sand. Robert Wild. NOSC

Enter / at South Gate. Capsule. John Giorno. AHA

Enter Celia, with a Writing. Bin Ramke. RoV

Enter(f*#@ckin)tained. Nzinga Regtuinah Chavis. BRtP

Enter here and find your home. Eight Ways of Looking at Pussy. Letta Neely. BRtP; WiU

Enter mine host. To Whom. Peter Klappert. YaYoPo

Enter the dream-house, brothers and sisters, leaving. Newsreel. Cecil Day Lewis. MoBrPo

Enter the forest. Double Song. Frank Mkalawile Chipasula. NAfrP

Enter the Long Island Expressway at Brookhaven. Directions for Carrying Explosive Nuclear Wastes through Metropolitan New York. June Jordan. AtGh

Enter the story here: their battle lost. Story, The. Kevin Hart. BMAP

Enter with him. Legend. W. H. Auden. CAGL

Entered that brilliant intimate. Only Alice. Josephine Jacobsen. FFC

Entered to race, Barabbas was scratched. Passion of Jesus Considered as an Uphill Race, The. Alfred Jarry. PFTM-1

Entering a darkened room. Gathering at the Orchid Pavilion, The. Shin Yu Pai. WANABP

Entering a Wilderness Area. William Stafford. PfSP

Entering Chikso Falls. Ch'ôn Yanghûi. EcSo, tr. by Aimee N. Kwon

Entering Detroit. Víctor Hernández Cruz. PueRic

Entering Poetic Blindspots. Brian Schorn. OnScMo

Entering Quiao Gorge and Anju Creek. Chen Zi'ang. CCL1, tr. by Stephen Owen

Entering the churchyard. Steeplejack. Katherine Pierpoint. MFPA

Entering the hall, she meets the new wife. Ejected Wife, The. Yüan-ti. OBVE; OxBEV, tr. by Arthur Waley

Entering the Mare. Katie Donovan. NeBl

Entering your silence, my Lord. Troubled Awakening. Magdalena Gomez. PueRic

Entering—takes away, The. (LL) I had been hungry, all the Years. Emily Dickinson. AFaM; MoAmPo; NAAPv.1; NALW; SAmP; TCAPo; WPoS

Enters—and is lost in Balms. (LL) Come slowly—Eden! Emily Dickinson. FaBoVe; NALW; NCAP; TCAPo

Entertainer, The. Bruce Beaver. NOBAu

Entertaining the Canary. Charles Simic. CAP-8

Entertainment. Charles Reznikoff. NAMCP V.1 Fr. Holocaust.

Entertainment of War, The. Roy Fisher. BeAl

Enthrone thy Rosy-selfe within mine Eyes. (LL) Edward Taylor. ChIV-1; TCAPo Fr. Preparatory Meditations Before My Approach to the Lord's Supper.

Enthusiast, The. Herman Melville. ChIV-1; NAAL-3

Enthusiast, The. Arla. Anne Batten Cristall. RWP

Enthusiast, The. Songs of Arla. Anne Batten Cristall. RWP
  Song 1. RWP
  Song 3. RWP

Entire country is overrun with private property, The. Gypsy. Josephine Miles. NoAM

Entire day spent scrutinizing, An. Jigsaw Puzzle. Deborah Boe. PfS

Entire, more than entire have we been devastated! Tears of the Fatherland, Anno Domini 1636. Andreas Gryphius. GePo, tr. by George C. Schoolfield

Entirely. Louis MacNeice. StAl

Entirely an industry. Harley Davidson. Iwan Llwyd. ATSWP, tr. by Robert Minhinnick

Entirely You. Anton Korteweg. ArBi, tr. by the author

Entity of Its Word, An. Sam Pereira. BodElec

Entrain airport: New York, Chicago, west. Valediction to My Contemporaries. Horace Gregory. MoAmPo

Entraña. Silvia Eugenia Castillero. SPV

Entrance. Rainer Maria Rilke. AmFaPo, tr. by Edward Snow

Entrance. Rainer Maria Rilke. PoDa, tr. by Dana Gioia

Entrance and exit wounds are silvered clean. Recalling War. Robert Graves. AF; BrAP; HarvBoo; NAMCP V.1; NoAM; OBWP; PoWW

Entrancielo. Edwin Torres. BRtP

Entre la bruma iluminada. Visita al Turk's Head Pub. Manuel Ulacia. RMCMP

Entre las piernas de la perra de Dios. Amoroso. Alfonso D'Aquino. RMCMP

Entre las sábanas, sobre las sillas. Boda, La. Alfonso D'Aquino. RMCMP

Entre les maisons du jour. A un voyageur. Mohammed Dib. YaTCFP

Entre nosotros. Del estilo de vida "poco común" de los indios cucapá citados por R. W. Haly Hardy, teniente Británico explorando el Golfo de California. Heriberto Yépez. RMCMP

Entrepreneur chicken shed his tail feathers, surplus, The. Josephine Miles. NoAM

Entresol. Jaime Sabines. TCLAP, tr. by Claudine-Marie D'Angelo

Entries for a Possible Poem. Sargon Boulus. Eno

Entries on Light. Mimi Khalvati.
  "Knocking on the door." Prnts

Entropic Villanelle. Thomas M. Disch. RA

Entropy. Faith Shearin. SweBea

Entry. Diana Hartog. NLPA Fr. Oasis.

Entry into Jerusalem. Dmitry Aleksandrovich Prigov. ItGoST, tr. by Robert Reid

Entry of the Marines [or The Red Cross of England]. Eliza Cook. STuOW

Entry of the Villagers. Oliver Goldsmith. STuOW Fr. Captivity, The.

Enueg 1. Samuel Beckett. ItP

Enueg 2. Samuel Beckett. ItP; NoAM

Enumeration. Ilse Aichinger. AF, tr. by Allen H. Chappel

Envelope, The. Maxine W. Kumin. CFP; NALW

Envelope of Skin. Dorothy Molloy. NIrP

Enveloping Echo, The. Ion Caraion. AF, tr. by Marguerite Dorian and Elliott B. Urdang

Envenomed are my songs. Heinrich Heine. RaF, tr. by Walter Arndt

Enviable Isles, The. Herman Melville. NCAP

Envidia el corazón. Zenaida. Natalia Toledo. RMCMP

Envious and foul disease, could there not be. Epigram, An. To the Small-Pox. Ben Jonson. NOSC

Envious Dog that Brooding lay, An. Dog in the Manger, The. Aesop. DiBP, *tr. by* Aphra Behn

En-vi-RON-ment. Lee Bennett Hopkins. HHAm

Environs. Larry Eigner. FTOS

Envoi. James McAuley. BMAP

Envoi: "And although it will be." Caitríona O'Reilly. MoWP

Envoi: "Go, dumb-born book." Ezra Pound. *See* Envoi (1919).

Envoi: "God, thou great symmetry." Anna Wickham. MoBrPo

Envoi: "Must it be so? Should foreignness begin." Oskar Loerke. GTCP *Fr.* At the Edge of the Great City.

Envoi (1919). Ezra Pound. NAAPv.2; TCAPo *Fr.* Hugh Selwyn Mauberley (Life and Contacts).

Envoi: "Sun in the mouth of the day." Robley, Jr. Wilson. InvLad; PBCAP

Envoi: "There's a whisper down the field where the year has shot her yield." Rudyard Kipling. OBEV

Envoi: Waking After Snow. David Baker. PasH

Envoi: Washington Square Park. Myra Cohn Livingston. SSCS

Envoi: "Why did I bring you to this Hull." Douglas Dunn. EdScPo

Envoy. May Kendall. ViWPN

Envoy: "Better than any of you, poems." Eleanor Ross Taylor. InGu

Envoy: "Go, songs, for ended is our brief, sweet play." Francis Thompson. MoBrPo

Envoy: "If homely virtues draw from me a tune." James Weldon Johnson. SacPr

Envoy: "Little poem, the two of us know too much." George Garrett. InGu

Envoy: "They are not long, the weeping and the laughter." Ernest Dowson. *See* Vitae Summa Brevis Spem Nos Vetat Incohare Longam.

Envoy of Mr. Cogito, The. Zbigniew Herbert. ItP; PoetW; WoPoe, *tr. by* John Carpenter and Bogdana Carpenter

Envoy to Scogan. Geoffrey Chaucer. NPeEn

Envy. Charles Lamb and Mary Lamb. WoRP

Envy. Adelaide Anne Procter. NPeEn; VWP

Envy. Edmund Spenser. RaF *Fr.* Faerie Queene, The.

Envy of Other People's Poems. Robert Hass. RoV

Envy of Poor Lovers, The. Austin Clarke. IrLP

Envy the barrel's ability to contain nothing. Post-War Procession. Anita Lahey. IFF

Envy the mad killer who lies in the ditch and grieves. Crime. Robert Penn Warren. FuPo

Envy, why carp'st [*or* carpest] thou my time is spent so ill. Ovid. CABP; NoSic *Fr.* Elegies.

Envy with heavy heart asked for shrift. William Langland. NAEL-6v1; NAEL-7v1 *Fr.* Vision of Piers Plowman, The.

Envying the Art of the Cartographer. Edward Byrne. RWB

Envying the Children of San Francisco. Gary Soto. CAP-8

Enzensberger at 'Exiles'. John Tranter. BMAP

Eohippus. Larissa Szporluk. LegDan

Eous. Oliver Reynolds. TCAWP *Fr.* Tone Poem.

Ephemera Today on "All My Children." Connie Deanovich.
   "Natalie gets discovered in her pit by an old, drunken transient." ReTh

Ephemeridae. Daniel Gerard Hoffman. YaYoPo

Ephemeron. Annie Fields. PoBW

Ephraim Repenting. William Cowper. ChIV-1 *Fr.* Olney Hymns.

Epic. Patrick Kavanagh. CABP; HarvBoo; MakPoe; ModIr; NAMCP V.1; NoP-4; NoP-5; NPeEn; OxBSo

Epic of Gilgamesh, The. *Unknown. tr. by* David Ferry and N. K. Sandars
  Coming of Enkidu, The. CAGL, *tr. by* N. K. Sandars
  Death of Enkidu, The. CAGL, *tr. by* N. K. Sandars
  "In the early hours of the next morning dawning." WoPoe, *tr. by* David Ferry
  "In the early hours of the next morning dawning." WoPoe, *tr. by* David Ferry
  Lament of Gilgamesh for Enkidu, The. CAGL, *tr. by* N. K. Sandars
  "With the first light of the early morning dawning." WoPoe, *tr. by* David Ferry

Epic, The [Morte d'Arthur]. Alfred Tennyson. NAEL-6v2; NAEL-7v2 *Fr.* Morte d'Arthur.

Epicedium by Elizabeth Hoby, Their Mother, on the Death of Her Two Daughters Elizabeth and Anne, An. Elizabeth Cooke Hoby. EMWP

Epicoene; or, The Silent Woman. Ben Jonson.
  Prologue. ASA
  (Simplex Munditiis.) OBEV
  (Simplicity and Sweet Neglect.) OxAEP-1
  (Clerimont's Song.) BASC; NOSC
  (Still to Be Neat.) NoP-5
  Sweet Neglect, The. NAEL-6v1; NAEL-7v1; NIL-7; NoP-4; NPeEn; PoPoPo; TFi; WeW-3

Epicure, Dining at Crewe, An. Limerick. *Unknown.* NTCP

Epicure, The. Anacreon. OxAEP-1, *tr. by* Abraham Cowley

Epicure ("Underneath this myrtle shade, The"). Abraham Cowley. OBEV
  "Crown me with roses whilest I live." OBVE

Epicurean Ode, An. John Hall. NOSC; NPeEn

Epidemic. Charles Reznikoff. APT-2

Epiderm. Michael Dransfield. BMAP

Epifanía. Elsa Cross. RMCMP

Epigram. Callimachus. WoPoe, *tr. by* Stanley Lombardo and Diane Rayor

Epigram: "At 12 o'clock in the afternoon." Meleager. WoPoe, *tr. by* Peter Whigham

Epigram: "Fair Beatrice tucks her coat up somewhat high." John Taylor. NOSC

Epigram: "Golden one is gone from the banquets, The." "H. D." PoA 2002

Epigram: "Good Fortune, when I hailed her recently." James Vincent Cunningham. APT-2; VCAP

Epigram: "Here lies my wife. Eternal peace." James Vincent Cunningham. NIP-4

Epigram: "Here lies New Critic who would fox us." James Vincent Cunningham. APT-2; MoAmPo

Epigram: "I fish for minnows in the lake." Su Tung-p'o. NDACCP, *tr. by* Kenneth Rexroth

Epigram: "I had gone broke, and got set to come back." James Vincent Cunningham. MoAmPo; VCAP

Epigram: "King to Oxford sent a troop of horse, The." Sir William Browne. OxBEV

Epigram: "Look how yon lecher's legs are worn away." John Taylor. NOSC

Epigram: "Lusty wench as nimble as an eel, A." John Taylor. NOSC

Epigram: "Midas, they say, possessed the art of old." "Peter Pindar." NIL-7; NIP-4

Epigram: "Milo's from home; and, Milo being gone." Martial. OBVE, *tr. by* Elijah Fenton

Epigram: "On parent knees, a naked new-born child." Sir William Jones. OBEV

Epigram: "Says a Reverend Priest to a less Rev'rend friend." *Unknown.* NOBRP

Epigram: "There chanced to meet together in an inn." John Taylor. NOSC

Epigram: "Women, as some men say, unconstant be." George Wither. NOSC

Epigram: "World laid low, and the wind blew like a dust, The." *Unknown.* FaBoWar, *tr. by* Thomas Kinsella

Epigram: "You ask me how Contempt who claims to sleep." James Vincent Cunningham. VCAP

Epigram: "You wonder why Drab sells her love for gold?" James Vincent Cunningham. APT-2

Epigram 29: "Gentlewoman of the dealing trade, A." Samuel Rowlands. NOSC

Epigram, A Supposed Construction. John Taylor. NOSC

Epigram, An: "To John I ow'd great obligation." Matthew Prior. OBVE; OxBEV

Epigram, An. To the Small-Pox. Ben Jonson. NOSC

Epigram Engraved on the Collar of a Dog Given [*or* Which I Gave] to His Royal Highness. Alexander Pope. NTCP; OxBEV
  (Collar Inscription, A.) DiBP
  (Engraved on the Collar of a Dog, Which I Gave to His Royal Highness.) SoSe-8

Epigram for a Worm. Daria Menicanti. CItWP, *tr. by* Cinzia Sartini Blum and Lara Trubowitz

Epigram IV.v: Of Treason. Sir John Harington. *See* Of Treason.

Epigram: The Likeness. Martial. RomPo, *tr. by* Brian Hill

Epigram on Fasting. Jonathan Swift. OBVE

Epigram on Milton. John Dryden. *See* Lines Printed under the Engraved Portrait of Milton [In Tonson's Folio of the "Paradise Lost"].

Epigram on Scolding, An. Jonathan Swift. FaBoVe; NPeEn

Epigram: On Sir Roger Phillimore [*with music*]. *Unknown.* NBLV

Epigram: Political Reflexion. Howard Nemerov. NIP-4

Epigram: Respice Finem. Francis Quarles. OBEV

Epigram VII: Winifred. Hugh Crompton. NOSC

Epigram LXVII: Time, the Interpreter. Hugh Crompton. NOSC

Epigrams. Anyte.
  "Children, billy goat, have put crimson reins, The." HePo
  "For her locust, nightingale of the fields, and her cricket that slept." HePo
  "No longer, as before, will you wake at dawn and flap." HePo
  "No longer shall I exult in the floating seas and arch." HePo
  "Often on this her daughter's tomb did Cleina grieve." HePo
  "This tomb Damis built for his courageous horse." HePo

Epigrams. Bassus.
  "I'm not planning to turn into gold. Somebody else." HePo

Epigrams. Crinagoras.
"You toss now to the left; you toss now to the right." HePo
Epigrams: "Old dissembler who lived out his lie, An." James Vincent Cunningham.
Epitaph for Anyone, An. APT-2; OxBoAm
"Homer was poor. His scholars live at ease." WoPoe
"Time heals not: it extends a sorrow's scope." WoPoe
Epigrams. Sir John Davies.
"Amongst the poets Dacus numbered is." NoSic
"Cosmus hath more discoursing in his head." NoSic
"Fine youth Ciprius is more terse and neat, The." NoSic
In Cineam. DiBP
(In Cosmum.) NPeEn
"Philo the gentleman, the fortune teller." NoSic
"Titus the brave and valorous gallant." NoSic
Epigrams. Dioscorides.
"Call me Polyxena, the wife of Archelaus." HePo
"Eros, that bane of men, molded soft as marrow." HePo
"Lamisca, who breathed her last in lamentable pangs of labor." HePo
"They drive me mad, those rosy lips, forever prattling." HePo
Epigrams. Diotimus.
"Polyaenus' daughter, Scyllis, came to the wide gates." HePo
"What use to suffer in labor, give birth to children, if she." HePo
Epigrams. Erinna.
"I am the grave of Baucis the bride. Passing by." HePo
"Stele and my Sirens and mournful pitcher that hold." HePo
Epigrams. Sir John Harington.
Ambiguity. DiBP
In Praise of Bungey. DiBP
Epigrams. Martial. tr. by Brian Hill, William Matthews, Richard O'Connell, J. A. Pott, Richard E. Prior and Joseph S. Salemi
"Artemidorus sold his land to buy a boy." CAGL, tr. by Richard O'Connell
"Bearded Callistratus wedded rugged Afer." CAGL, tr. by Richard E. Prior
"Chrestus, your balls are depilated." CAGL, tr. by Joseph S. Salemi
Gallic Lap-Dog, The. DiBP, tr. by James Elphinston
"Here he is whom you read and clamor for." WoPoe, tr. by William Matthews
"If by chance, Flaccus, someone could offer me for the asking." CAGL, tr. by Richard E. Prior
Issa's Portrait. DiBP, tr. by James Elphinston
"Nasica raped the doctor's pretty lad." CAGL, tr. by Brian Hill
New Point of View, A. DiBP, tr. by James Elphinston
"Surrounded by eunuchs and limp as a tissue." WoPoe, tr. by William Matthews
"Ted's studio burnt down, with all his poems." WoPoe, tr. by William Matthews
Trusty Lydia, The. DiBP, tr. by James Elphinston
"Why is it modern poets are ignored." PoDa, tr. by William Matthews
"You lie and I concur. You "give."" WoPoe, tr. by William Matthews
"You often say my work is coarse. It's true." CAGL, tr. by J. A. Pott
"You sold a slave just yesterday." WoPoe, tr. by William Matthews
"Your slave boy's cock is aching, Naevolus." CAGL, tr. by Joseph S. Salemi
Epigrams. Mnasalces.
"Say, stranger, that this is the tomb of the mare Aethyia." HePo
Epigrams. Howard Nemerov.
(Epigram: Political Reflexion.) NIP-4
Epigrams. Philodemus.
"I fell in love with Demo of Paphos. No big surprise." HePo
"In the middle of the night I slipped away from my husband." HePo
"I've been in love. Who hasn't? I went out and got drunk." HePo
"O foot, O leg, O thighs for which I rightly died." HePo
"O two-horned moon, you love the parties that last all night." HePo
"Philaenion is small and swart, but her hair curls more." HePo
"Xanthippe's strumming, her chatter, her speaking eye, her song." HePo
Epigrams. Rabindranath Tagore.
"Echo always mocks the sound, The." PoA 2002
Epigrams: A Journal. James Vincent Cunningham.
History of Ideas. NIP-4; VCAP
Motto for a Sun Dial. APT-2
"Soft found a way to damn me undefended." APT-2
"This Humanist whom no beliefs constrained." APT-2
"Within this mindless vault." WoPoe

Epigrams & Imitations. Philip Whalen.
Actions of Buddha. WANABP
False Senryū. WANABP
From the Japanese of Kakinomoto Hitomaro. WANABP
Perpetuum Mobile. WANABP
Upon the Poet's Photograph. WANABP
Epigrams for My Father. Eugene B. Redmond. OxAAAP
Epigrams of Martial, The. Laurie Duggan.
One xxxvii. BMAP
Epigraph. William Blake. Spl Fr. Jerusalem.
Epil y Filiast. Harri Webb. AngWePo; TCAWP
Epilogue. Anna Andreyevna Akhmatova. PFTM-2 Fr. Poem without a Hero.
Epilogue. Alfred Tennyson. Fr. In Memoriam A. H. H.
Epilogue: "'O where are you going?' said reader to rider." W. H. Auden. NoAM; OxBEV; UV Fr. Five Songs.
Epilogue: "At the midnight in the silence of the sleep-time." Robert Browning. NAEL-6v2
Epilogue (At the Proper Distance). Mariella Bettarini. CItWP, tr. by Cinzia Sartini Blum and Lara Trubowitz
Epilogue: "Blessed / in the light of the sun at the sight of the world." Charles Reznikoff. NAAPv.2
Epilogue: "Carol, every violet has." Alfred Noyes. MoBrPo Fr. Flower of Old Japan, The.
Epilogue: "He is not dead nor liveth." Dorothy, Duchess of Wellington Wellesley. OBMV Fr. Deserted House.
Epilogue: "His money-making properties come back like a beach." Gig Ryan. VaPo
Epilogue: "I have crossed an ocean." Grace Nichols. NAMCP V.2
Epilogue: "I have seen flowers come in stony places." John Masefield. OxBEV
Epilogue: "If Luther's day expand to Darwin's year." Herman Melville. APN-2; NCAP; TCAPo Fr. Clarel: A Poem and Pilgrimage in the Holy Land.
Epilogue: "Journey back was a nightmare, The." Colette Bryce. NIrP
Epilogue: "My joys are those of the spare autumn birds." Dimitris Tsaloumas. PML
Epilogue: "My monument is done, my task is ended." Miklós Zrínyi. IQMS, tr. by Michael Hatwell
Epilogue: "On the first of the Feast of Feasts." Robert Browning. ChIV-2
Epilogue: "Our revels now are ended. These our actors." William Shakespeare. ASA; UV Fr. Tempest, The.
Epilogue: "Terence, this is stupid stuff." A. E. Housman. MoBrPo
Epilogue: "This advanced frontier." Charles Tomlinson. WoBe Fr. Zipangu.
Epilogue: "Those blessèd structures, plot and rhyme." Robert Lowell. HarvBoo; NAAL-5; NAMCP V.2; NoAM; NoP-4; NoP-5; OxBoAm; PoetW; PoPoPo; StAl; VCAP; WaAnP
Epilogue: "Time is a thing." Stephen Spender. MoBrPo
Epilogue: "Truly my Satan thou art but a dunce." William Blake. WeW-3 Fr. Gates of Paradise, The.
Epilogue: "Virtue may unlock hell, or even." Francis Thompson. MoBrPo Fr. Judgment in Heaven, A.
Epilogue: "Well, when all is said and done." George Russell. MoBrPo
Epilogue: "What shall we do for Love these days?" Lascelles Abercrombie. MoBrPo Fr. Emblems of Love.
Epilogue for Emilia. Rachel Beck. IaFF
Epilogue—the Last Journey. John Davidson. EdScPo
Epilogue to a Human Drama. Stephen Spender. AF
Epilogue to Alun Mabon [with music]. John Ceiriog Hughes. OBWVE, tr. by H. Idris Bell
Epilogue to Casualties. John Pepper Clark Bekedermo. HBAPE
Epilogue to "The Parson's Wedding." Thomas Killigrew. NOSC
Epilogue to the Satires, in Two Dialogues. Alexander Pope.
Art of Satire, The. OBSV
"Spare then the person, and expose the vice." OBSV
Triumph of Vice, The. NPeEn; OBSV
Epilogue to "The Sister." Oliver Goldsmith.
"Lud! what a group the motley scene discloses!" OBSV
Epilogue to Tyrannic[k] Love. John Dryden. OBCoV Fr. Tyrannic Love.
Epilogue was hers, The. Good Duke Speaks, The. Gilbert Allen. IaFF
Epiphanies, / and commas, commas. Natalya Gorbanevskaya. CRWP, tr. by Daniel Weissbort
Epiphanies of Light! (LL) Lemon Trees, The. Eugenio Montale. PoetW; WoPoe, tr. by William Arrowsmith
Epiphany. Martha Collins. Vesp
Epiphany. Christine D'Haen. TuT, tr. by Dennis O'Driscoll
Epiphany: "Unearthly lightning of presage." Robert Fitzgerald. ChrPo; PoCho
Epiphany. Pem Kremer. HW
Epiphany: "Sometimes you show yourself." Elsa Cross. RMCMP; TAPaP, tr. by Margaret Sayers Peden

Epiphany. Andrea Zanzotto. VCWP

Epiphany, 1937. George Seferis. GPTC, *tr. by* Edmund Keeley and Philip Sherrard

Epipsychidion. Percy Bysshe Shelley. NPBRoP

Episode of Hands. Hart Crane. CAGL; NIL-7

Episode 17. William Carlos Williams. APT-1 *Fr.* Paterson.

Episode two with Peter Jennings. Century, The. Francisco Aragon. RWB

Episodes with unusables. Arthur Nortje. TSAP

Epistemology. Richard Wilbur. NoAM

Epistemology, and all the afternoon. Days like Prose. Alan Michael Parker. NeAmPo

Epistle, An. Elizabeth Hands. PoBW

Epistle IV to Richard Boyle, Earl of Burlington. Alexander Pope.
    (At Timon's Villa.) OBSV
    Timon's Villa. NPeEn; OxBEV

Epistle Answering to One That Asked to Be Sealed of the Tribe of Ben, An. Ben Jonson. BASC

Epistle Containing the Strange Medical Experience of Karshish, the Arab Physician, An. Robert Browning. ChIV-2; NAEL-6v2; NAEL-7v2

Epistle from Alexander to Hephaestion in His Sickness, An. Anne Finch, Countess of Winchilsea. EMWP

Epistle from Mr Murray to Dr Polidori. Lord Byron. OBCoV

Epistle from Mrs. Yonge to Her Husband [*with music*]. Lady Mary Wortley Montagu. NAEL-6v1; NAEL-7v1; NALW; NoP-4; NoP-5; NPeEn

Epistle of Deborah Dough, The. Mary Leapor. BrAP; NoP-4

Epistle of Love and of Consolation unto Israel, An. Dorothy White. EMWP

Epistle on the Shipwreck. María Baranda. RMCMP, *tr. by* Mónica de la Torre

Epistle on Suicide. Bertolt Brecht. StAl, *tr. by* John Willett

Epistle III, to Allen Lord Bathurst. Alexander Pope.
    "Behold what blessings Wealth to life can lend!" OxBEV
    Sir Balaam. NPeEn

Epistle to a Friend, to Persuade Him to the Wars, An. Ben Jonson. FaBoWar
    "Wake, friend, from forth thy lethargy; the drum." FaBoWar

Epistle to a Lady, An. Mary Leapor. CABP

Epistle to a Patron, An. Frank Templeton Prince. HarvBoo; OxBEV

Epistle to Augusta. Lord Byron. NPBRoP

Epistle to Be Left in the Earth. Archibald MacLeish. APT-1; MoAmPo

Epistle to Dr. Arbuthnot. Alexander Pope. NAEL-6v1; NAEL-7v1; NoP-4; NoP-5; OxAEP-1; TFi
    Atticus ("Peace to all such! but were there one whose fires"). OxBEV; TRP
    "Bard whom pilf'red pastorals reknown, The." OBSV
    Bufo. OBSV
    "Lash like mine no honest man shall dread, A." NPeEn
    "Peace to all such! but were there one whose fires." NPeEn
    Sporus. OBSV; OxBEV
    "You think this cruel? take it for a rule." NPeEn

Epistle. To Enrique Caracciolo Trejo. Donald Davie. HarvBoo

Epistle to J.H. Reynolds. John Keats. NPBRoP *Fr.* To J. H. Reynolds, Esq.

Epistle to J. Lapraik, an Old Scotch Bard. Robert Burns.
    "While briers an' woodbines budding green." NPBRoP

Epistle to Lord Burlington. Alexander Pope. OBGa *Fr.* Epistle to Lord Burlington.

Epistle to Master John Selden, An. Ben Jonson. BASC

Epistle to Miss [*or* Miss Teresa] Blount, on Her Leaving the Town after the Coronation. Alexander Pope. NAEL-6v1; NAEL-7v1; NoP-4; NoP-5

Epistle to Mr. Cuthbert Jackson, An. Matthew Green. NoP-4; NoP-5 *Fr.* Spleen, The.

Epistle to Mr. Pope Occasioned by His Characters of Women, An. Anne, Viscountess Irwin Ingram. NAEL-7v1

Epistle to My Gardener. Nicolas Boileau-Despéaux. OBGa *Fr.* Epistle to My Gardener.

Epistle. To Prince Henrie]. Samuel Daniel.
    "Theare be great Prince, such as will tell you howe." PBRV

Epistle to the Rapalloan. Archibald MacLeish. PoA 2002

Epistle to the Revolutionary Bible, An. Andrea Roberts. BRtP

Epistle [II,] to a Lady[: Of the Characters of Women]. Alexander Pope. CABP; NAEL-6v1; NAEL-7v1; WaAnP
    C[h]loe. OBSV
    "Men, some to bus'ness, some to pleasure take." NPeEn; OBSV; oxBEV

Epistle Written in the Country to the Right Honourable the Lord Lovelace, An. Soame Jenyns.
    "In days, my Lord, when mother Time." OBSV

Epistles to Mr. Pope. Edward Young.
    "These labouring wits, like paviours, mend our ways." OBSV

Epistola del náufrago. María Baranda. RMCMP

Epi-strauss-ium. Arthur Hugh Clough. NAEL-6v2; NAEL-7v2

Epitafio. Ece Ayhan. WoPoe, *tr. by* Murat Nemet-Nejat

Epitaph. Marie-Claire Bancquart. MFP, *tr. by* Martin Sorrell

Epitaph: "For this she starred her eyes with salt." Elinor Wylie. MoAmPo

Epitaph: "Fortune's darling, king's content." *Unknown.* BASC

Epitaph: "Her grieving parents cradled here." Sylvia Townsend Warner. MoBrPo

Epitaph: "Here dead lie we because we did not choose." A. E. Housman. HarvBoo; OxBEV; Spl
    (Here Dead Lie We [Because We Did Not Choose].) NoP-4; NoP-5; WaAnP

Epitaph: "Here lies a man who was so bright." Robert Finch. IFF

Epitaph: "Here lies John Hughes and Sarah Drew." Lady Mary Wortley Montagu. CABP

Epitaph: "Here lies Sir Tact, a diplomatic fellow." Timothy Steele. NBLV

Epitaph: "I, an unwedded wandering dame." Sylvia Townsend Warner. MoBrPo

Epitaph: "I lived in those times. For a thousand years." Robert Desnos. PFTM-1

Epitaph: "I, Richard Kent, beneath these stones." Sylvia Townsend Warner. MoBrPo

Epitaph: "Like silver dew are the tears of love." Alfred Edgar Coppard. OBMV

Epitaph: "Malcolm Lowry." Malcolm Lowry. OBCoV

Epitaph: "My brother is skull and skeleton now." William Montgomerie. EdScPo

Epitaph: "My friend, judge not me." *Unknown.* NOSC

Epitaph: "Not the five feet of water to your chin." Charles Reznikoff. APT-2; OxBoAm

Epitaph: "One whom I knew, a student and a poet." Alex Comfort. MoBrPo

Epitaph: "Sir, you should notice me: I am the Man." Lascelles Abercrombie. MoBrPo

Epitaph: "So I may say." "H. D." APT-1; NAAPv.2; NAMCP V.1; OxBoAm

Epitaph: "Stop, Christian passer-by!—Stop, child of God." Samuel Taylor Coleridge. NAEL-6v2; NAEL-7v2; SacPr

Epitaph: "This is the end of him, here he lies." Amy Levy. NPeEn; PEW
    (Epitaph (On a Commonplace Person who Died in Bed).) CABP; VWP

Epitaph: "This stone, with not unpardonable pride." John Sparrow. OBCoV

Epitaph: "Time that brings [*or* bringes] all things to light." Thomas Morton. NOSC

Epitaph: "When Oxford gave thee two degrees in art." Mrs. Boughton. EMWP

Epitaph: "Young then, / we were bored already." Eleanor Wilner. ChIV-1

Epitaph. *Unknown.* WoPoe

Epitaph: "Again, traveller, you have come a long way led by that star." Thomas McGrath. RaBo

Epitaph: "Angler rose, he took his rod, The." Robert Louis Stevenson. OBCoV

Epitaph: "Beauty itself lies here, in whom alone." Thomas Randolph. BASC

Epitaph: "Beneath this stone lies William Burke." R. P. Weston. OBCoV

Epitaph: "Body / of / Benjamin Franklin, The." Benjamin Franklin. TCAPo

Epitaph: "Dummer the Shepherd Sacrific'd." Cotton Mather.
    "Dummer the Shepherd Sacrific'd." SacPr

Epitaph: "John Bird, a laborer, lies here." Sylvia Townsend Warner. MoBrPo

Epitaph, An. Thomas Carew. OBEV

Epitaph, An: "Erected by her sorrowing brothers." Clive Staples Lewis. OBCoV

Epitaph, An: "Here lies a most beautiful lady." Walter De la Mare. MoBrPo; OBEV

Epitaph, An: "I am a drowned man's tomb. There is a farmer's." Plato. PoCho, *tr. by* Burton Raffel

Epitaph, An: "I was buried near this dyke [*or* Dike]." William Blake. OBCoV

Epitaph, An: "Interr'd [*or* Interred] beneath this marble stone." Matthew Prior. NAEL-6v1; NAEL-7v1; OBCoV; OBSV

Epitaph, An: "Like thee I once have stemm'd the sea of life." James Beattie. OBEV

Epitaph, An: "My name—my country—what are they to thee." Paulus Silentiarius. OBVE,

Epitaph, An: On a Man for Doing Nothing. John Hoskyns. NOSC

Epitaph, An: "This is a drowned man's tomb. Sail on, stranger." Theodoridas. PoCho, *tr. by* Burton Raffel

Epitaph, An: "When I am gone." Josephine D. Henderson Heard. CBWP-4

Epitaph: André Breton. Philippe Soupault. SurPaPo, *tr. by* Mary Ann Caws and Patricia Terry

Epitaph for a Concord Boy. Stanley Young. ChAP

Epitaph for a Good Mouser. Anne Stevenson. Spl

Epitaph for a Poet. Homero Aridjis. PoetW; STV; TCLAP, *tr. by* John Frederick Nims

Epitaph for a Postal Clerk. X. J. Kennedy. NIL-7; NIP-4

Epitaph for a Scientist. Lex Banning. NOBAu

Epitaph for Anyone, An.   James Vincent Cunningham.   APT-2; OxBoAm *Fr.* Epigrams.

Epitaph for Cu Chuimne.   *Unknown.*   WoPoe, *tr. by* Thomas Kinsella

Epitaph for Etheridge Knight.   Melba Joyce Boyd.   BRtP

Epitaph for Jonathan Robbins.   Philip Freneau.   TCAPo

Epitaph for Mariana Gryphius, His Brother Paul's Little Daughter.   Andreas Gryphius.   PoAgWa; WoPoe, *tr. by* Christopher Benfey

Epitaph for [*or on*] Thomas Clere.   Henry Howard, Earl of Surrey.   NoSic; OxBSo

  (Epitaph on Thomas Clere.)   OBWP

  (Norfolk sprang thee, Lambeth holds thee dead.)   PBRV

  (Norfolk Sprung Thee, Lambeth Holds Thee Dead.)   NoP-4

Epitaph for Richard Cavendish, Engraved on his Monument in Hornsey Church.   Margaret Russell Clifford, Countess of Cumberland.   EMWP

Epitaph for Sir Lawrence Tanfield.   Lady Elizabeth Tanfield.   NOSC

  (Tomb of Sir Lawrence Tanfield obiit 30 Ap. 1625 erected by Lady Tanfield 1628.)   EMWP

Epitaph for Someone or Other.   James Vincent Cunningham.   APT-2; TRP; WoPoe *Fr.* Five Epigrams.

Epitaph for the Old Howard.   Byron Vazakas.   APT-2

Epitaph for the Race of Man.   Edna St. Vincent Millay.

  "Here lies, and none to mourn him but the sea."   HeIP-4

  "O Earth, unhappy planet born to die."   HeIP-4

  "See where Capella with her golden kids."   MoAmPo

Epitaph for the Western Intelligentsia.   Richard Allen.   NOBAu

Epitaph for Thomas Johnson, Huntsman. Charlton, Sussex.   *Unknown.*   NPeEn

Epitaph for Willie or Little Black Poet with No Future.   Sibby Anderson-Thompkins.   InTrad

[Epitaph] In Obitum M.S., X° Maij [*or* Maii], 1614.   William Browne.   OBEV

Epitaph in Time of War.   Marguerite Yourcenar.   YaTCFP, *tr. by* Martin Sorrell

Epitaph Intended for Sir Isaac Newton, in Westminster Abbey.   Alexander Pope.   *See* Intended for Sir Isaac Newton.

Epitaph: Justice.   Theocritus.   WoPoe, *tr. by* Fred Chappell

Epitaph of Dionysia.   *Unknown.*   OBEV

Epitaph of Graunde [*or* La Graunde] Amoure, The.   Stephen Hawes.   NoSic; OBEV *Fr.* Pastime of Pleasure, The.

Epitaph of John Jack.   Daniel Bliss.   TCAPo

Epitaph of Nearchos.   Ammianus.   WeW-3, *tr. by* Dudley Fitts

Epitaph of Our Late Queen Mary, An.   George Cavendish.   NoSic

Epitaph of Sir Griffith ap Rhys, The.   *Unknown.*   AngWePo

Epitaph (On a Commonplace Person who Died in Bed).   Amy Levy.   *See* Epitaph: "This is the end of him, here he lies."

Epitaph on a Hare.   William Cowper.   NoP-4; NoP-5; PoPoPo

Epitaph on a Jacobite.   Thomas Babington Macaulay, 1st Baron Macaulay.   *See* Jacobite's Epitaph, A.

Epitaph on a Living Woman.   Angelina Weld Grimké.   APT-1

Epitaph on a Party Girl.   Richard Usborne.   OBCoV

Epitaph on a Pessimist.   Thomas Hardy.   TRP

Epitaph on a Pet Cat.   Joachim Du Bellay.   TriCat, *tr. by* Ralph Nixon Currey

Epitaph on a Spaniel.   "Peter Pindar."   DiBP

Epitaph on a Tyrant.   W. H. Auden.   AF; HeIP-4; NoAM; OxBEV; WaAnP

Epitaph on a Waiter.   David McCord.   APT-2; NBLV; NIP-4; OBCoV

Epitaph on an Army of Mercenaries.   A. E. Housman.   FaBoWar; NAEL-6v2; NAEL-7v2; NAMCP V.1; NoP-4; NoP-5; NPeEn; OxBEV; PoAgWa; SoSe-8; WaAnP

Epitaph on an Unfortunate Artist.   Robert Graves.   OBCoV

Epitaph on Charles II.   John Wilmot, 2d Earl of Rochester.   WoPoe

Epitaph on Claudy Phillips, a Musician, An.   Samuel Johnson.   NPeEn; OxAEP-1

Epitaph on Elizabeth, L. H.   Ben Jonson.   NAEL-6v1; NIL-7; NIP-4; NoP-4; NoP-5; NOSC; OBEV

Epitaph on Erotion.   Martial.   RomPo, *tr. by* Leigh Hunt

Epitaph on her Son H. P. at St. Syth's Church [where her body also lies Interred].   Katherine Philips.   CABP; MakPoe; NoP-4; NoP-5; NOSC; PBRV; PEW

  (Epitaph on Her Son Hector Philips.)   CABP; WaAnP

Epitaph on Himself.   Matthew Prior.   OBCoV

Epitaph on Hogarth.   Samuel Johnson.   OxAEP-1

Epitaph on M. H., An.   Charles Cotton.   NPeEn

Epitaph on Mr W—.   Felicia Dorothea Hemans.   ViWPN

Epitaph on my Dear and Ever Honored Mother Mrs. Dorothy Dudley.   Anne Bradstreet.   NAAPv.1

Epitaph on S. P. [*or* Salomon Pavy], a Child of Queen Elizabeth's Chapel.   Ben Jonson.   NAEL-6v1; NAEL-7v1; NOSC; OBEV; OxBEV

  (Epitaph on S. P.)   TFi

Epitaph on Sir Philip Sidney Lying in St Paul's without a Monument, to be Fastned upon the Church Door.   Edward Herbert, 1st Baron Herbert of Cherbury.   NPeEn

Epitaph on Sir Thomas Wyatt.   Henry Howard, Earl of Surrey.   *See* Wyatt Resteth Here.

Epitaph on Sir William Dyer.   Lady Catherine Dyer.   *See* My Dearest Dust: Epitaph on the Monument of Sir William Dyer at Colmworth, 1641.

Epitaph on Some Bottles of Sack and Claret Laid in Sand.   Robert Wild.   NOSC

Epitaph on the Countess[e] Dowager of Pembroke.   William Browne.   *See* On the Countess Dowager of Pembroke.

Epitaph on the Duke of Buckingham.   James Shirley.   NPeEn

Epitaph on the Duke of Buckingham.   *Unknown.*   BASC; NPeEn; PBRV

Epitaph on the Earl of Strafford.   John Cleveland.   BASC; NOSC; NPeEn; OxBEV

Epitaph on the Favourite Dog of a Politician.   Joseph Hilaire Pierre Belloc.   OBSV

Epitaph on the Lady Mary Villiers ("Lady Mary Villiers lies, The.")   Thomas Carew.   OBEV

Epitaph on the Monument of Sir William Strode.   William Strode.   NOSC

Epitaph: On the Near-Death Experience.   Ellis Owen.   WoPoe, *tr. by* Anthony Conran

Epitaph on the Politician Himself.   Joseph Hilaire Pierre Belloc.   MoBrPo; NBLV; OBSV

Epitaph on the Tombstone of a Child, the Last of Seven that Died Before.   Aphra Behn.   CABP; NOSC; OxBSo

Epitaph on Thomas Clere.   Henry Howard, Earl of Surrey.   *See* Epitaph for [*or on*] Thomas Clere.

Epitaph: Tristran Tzara.   Philippe Soupault.   SurPaPo, *tr. by* Mary Ann Caws and Patricia Terry

Epitaph Upon a Child that Died.   Robert Herrick.   *See* Upon a Child That Died [*or* Dyed].

Epitaph upon a Young Married Couple, An.   Richard Crashaw.   *See* Epitaph Upon Husband and Wife Who Died and Were Buried Together, An.

Epitaph Upon Husband and Wife Who Died and Were Buried Together, An.   Richard Crashaw.   OBEV; OxAEP-1

  (Epitaph upon a Young Married Couple, An.)   NIL-7

Epitaph upon That Profound and Learned Casuist, the Late Ordinary of Newgate, An.   Thomas Brown.   OBSV

Epitaph upon Thomas, Lord Fairfax, An.   George, 2d Duke of Buckingham Villiers.   NOSC

Epitaph, uppon Cassandra Mac Willms Wife to Sr Thomas Ridgway Earle of London Derry by ye Lady A. S., An.   Lady Anne Harris Southwell.   EMWP

Epitaph: Zion.   Anne Carson.   NAMCP V.2

Épitaphe, temps de guerre.   Marguerite Yourcenar.   YaTCFP

Epitaphium Citharistriae.   Victor Gustave Plarr.   NBLV

Epitaphs.   Edmund Wilson.   APT-2

Epitaphs: "Drowning / I felt for a moment reaching towards me."   Charles Reznikoff.   APT-2; NAMCP V.1

Epitaphs of the War [1914–1918].   Rudyard Kipling.   NAMCP V.1; NoP-5; OBWP

  Batteries Out of Ammunition.   InoFa; WoPoe

  Bombed in London.   InoFa; WoPoe

  Common Form.   HarvBoo; InoFa; NPeEn; PoAgWa; WoPoe

  Convoy Escort.   WoPoe

  Coward, The.   HarvBoo; InoFa; NPeEn; WoPoe

  Dead Statesman, A.   FaBoWar; NBLV; OPOU; PoWW; WoPoe

  Destroyers in Collision.   InoFa

  Drifter off Tarentum, A.   PoWW; WoPoe

  Ex-Clerk.   HarvBoo

  Journalists.   HarvBoo

  R.A.F. (Aged Eighteen).   PoWW

  Refined Man, The.   NPeEn

  Servant, A.   HarvBoo; NPeEn

  Shock.   InoFa

  Sleepy Sentinel, The.   PoAgWa

  Son, A.   NPeEn; PoAgWa

  Unknown Female Corpse.   PoWW

Epith.   Carol Muske-Dukes.   MakPoe; PoDa

Epithalament.   Brenda Shaughnessy.   LegDan

Epithalamion: "Hark, hearer, hear what I do; lend a thought now, make believe."   Gerard Manley Hopkins.   CAGL

Epithalamion: "Singing, today I married my white girl."   Dannie Abse.   OBWVE

Epithalamium: "Aves Tsu-kiou in aquaticis terris mas et foemina ambae vices agunt suas cantando."   *Unknown.*   CCL1 *Fr.* Guan-ju.

Epithalamium: "By good luck I was granted a meeting with you."   *Unknown.*   CCL1, *tr. by* John Frodsham

Epithalamium: "Can the lover share his soul."   Walter James Turner.   OBMV

Epithalamium: "Hymen, god of marriage bed."   Joseph Rutter.   NOSC

Epithalamium: "Hymen hath together tied."   R. Hatton.   NOSC

Epithalamium: "Let mother Earth." Sir Philip Sidney. OxAEP-1 *Fr.* Countesse of Pembroke's Arcadia, The.

Epithalamium: "So you are married, girl. It makes me sad." Roy McFadden. IrLP; PNI

Epithalamion. Nancy Schoenberger. SwNoth

Epithalamion: "Ye learned sisters which have oftentimes." Edmund Spenser. NAEL-6v1; NAEL-7v1; NoP-5; NoSic; OBEV; OxAEP-1; WaAnP

Epithalamion. Terese Svoboda. ExTi

Epithalamium: "Waterbirds on / River islands!" *Unknown.* CCL1 *Fr.* Guan-ju.

Epithalamium, An. Joan Murray. YaYoPo

Epithalamion for Sarah and Tony. Jeff Mock. PoDa

Epithalamion, or Marriage Song on the Lady Elizabeth and Count Palatine Being Married on St. Valentine's Day, An. John Donne. ItP

Epithalamon Teratos. George Chapman. NoSic *Fr.* Hero and Leander.

Epithalamium: To Mistress M. A. Martin Lluellyn [*or* Lluelyn]. NOSC

Epithalamium for a Niece. Norman Nicholson. NLP

Epithalamium in Olive Drab. William Jay Smith. PWW2

Epithalamy. Alexander Brome. NOSC

Epithet. Judith McCombs. FiBr

Epoch. Vladimir Holan. PoSu, *tr. by* Ian Milner and Jarmila Milner

Epochs. Juan Gelman. TCLAP, *tr. by* Robert Marquez and Elinore Randall

Epode. "H. D." MotU

Epodes. Horace. *tr. by* John Dryden, Roswell Martin Field, Ben Jonson and *Unknown*

  Brave Dog's Challenge, The [Epode 6]. DiBP, *tr. by* Sir Theodore Martin

  Counterblast against Garlic, A. NBLV

  (Praises of a Countrie Life, The.) OBVE, *tr. by* Ben Jonson

  Praises of a Country Life, The. BASC, *tr. by* Ben Jonson

  To a Randy Old Woman. EroLit, *tr. by Unknown*

Épreuves du poète. Andrée Chédid. YaTCFP

Epygrams. John Heywood.

  "Wilt thou use turners craft still? ye by my trouth." PBRV

Epytaphe of the Death of Nicolas Grimoald, An. Barnabe Googe. NPeEn

Equal by the wind. (LL) Vox Angelica. Timothy Liu. NeAmPo; WiU

Equal Temperament. Lin Max. MiVo

Equal thrust and pattern, An. (LL) Louis MacNeice. NoP-4; NoP-5 *Fr.* Autumn Journal.

Equal to the Gods. Sappho. AmFaPo, *tr. by* Edward Sanders

Equality. Edwin Emanuel Bradford. VerBaPo *Fr.* Tree of Knowledge, The.

Equality. Hal Sirowitz. KGB

Equality, Father. Edith Bruck. AF

Equality, father! Your dream has come true. Edith Bruck. AF

Equanimity. Les A. Murray. NOBAu

Equator's hot, The. Cold Meat. N. Revathi Devi. HotL, *tr. by* V. Narayana Rao

Equilibrismo. Elsa Cross. RMCMP

Equilibrists, The. John Crowe Ransom. APT-1; FuPo; InGu; NoAM

Equinox. Elizabeth Alexander. ExTi

Equinox. Susan Musgrave. BrAP

Equinox 1980. Peter Davison. NoP-4; NoP-5

Equipoise: becalmed / Trees, a dome of kindness. Evening in Connecticut. Louis MacNeice. HarvBoo

Era claro en extremo. Río 1. José Luis Rivas. RMCMP

Era deforme como un ángel caído en un patio entre algodones. Cap. 10 Lib. 2. Blas de Otero. RaW

Era of Easy Meat at Locarno, An. George McWhirter. IFF

Era un aire suave: the calm and gentle air. Visit to the House of the Poet—Nicaragua, 1987—Homage to Rubén Darío on His Birthday, A. Thomas McGrath. BodElec

Era's End. Mairtin O Direain. ModIr, *tr. by* Patrick Crotty

Erased all paths to Saturday. Moon on Friday Night, The. Susan Goyette. Coast; OpeFie

Eraser. Juan Carlos Galeano. PML, *tr. by* Delia Poey

Erasing Stars. Stephen Kuusisto. TAPaP

Erasure. Carl Phillips. AmAlph

Erasure creates the light pouring down from the. Painting, The. Maryhelen Snyder. ICANM

Erat Hora. Ezra Pound. ItP

Erat Quaedam Mulier. Lady Mary Cheke. EMWP

Erato. Phyllis Thompson. ICANM

Erdywurble. Carole Satyamurti. Prnts

Ere all the world had grown so drear. Philosophy. Amy Levy. ViWPN

Ere God had built the mountains. William Cowper. ChIV-1 *Fr.* Olney Hymns.

Ere I freeze, to sing bravely. Poem of the Frost and Snow. Lewis Morris. OBWVE, *tr. by* Anthony Conran

Ere I know it—next moment I dance at the King's! (LL) Laboratory, The (Ancien Régime). Robert Browning. NAEL-6v2; NAEL-7v2; OBEV

Ere, in the northern gale. Autumn Woods. William Cullen Bryant. APN-1

Ere it passes, barefoot boy! (LL) Barefoot Boy, The. John Greenleaf Whittier. APN-1; BRP

Ere my heart beats too coldly and faintly. Truants, The. Walter De la Mare. MoBrPo

Ere on my bed my limbs I lay. Pains of Sleep, The. Samuel Taylor Coleridge. AWTN; NAEL-6v2; NAEL-7v2; NPBRoP

Ere Sleep Comes Down to Soothe the Weary Eyes. Paul Laurence Dunbar. APN-2; ColAP

Ere the cock has crowed. Forsaken Girl, The. Eduard Friedrich Mörike. WoPoe, *tr. by* Randall Jarrell

Ere the Golden Bowl Is Broken. Anna Hempstead Branch. TCAPo

Ere their story die. (LL) In Time of "The Breaking of Nations." Thomas Hardy. BrAP; ChIV-1; HarvBoo; MoBrPo; NAEL-6v2; NAEL-7v2; NAMCP V.1; NoAM; NoP-4; NoP-5; OBEV; OBWP; OPOU; OxAEP-2; PoWW; TFi; WeW-3

Ere we had reached the wished-for place, night fell. William Wordsworth. CenSon; NPBRoP

Ere yet our course was graced with social trees. William Wordsworth. CenSon *Fr.* River Duddon [A Series of Sonnets], The.

Ere yet they win that verge and line. Herman Melville. APN-2 *Fr.* Clarel: A Poem and Pilgrimage in the Holy Land.

Ere you proudly question ours! (LL) Negro's Complaint, The. William Cowper. CABP; ItP

Ere you were born, was beauty's summer dead. (LL) William Shakespeare. HeIP-4; NoSic; OBEV; OxAEP-1 *Fr.* Sonnets.

Erebuni. Nina Gabrielian. *tr. by* Peter France

  1. CRWP, *tr. by* Peter France

  2. CRWP, *tr. by* Peter France

  3. CRWP, *tr. by* Peter France

  4. CRWP, *tr. by* Peter France

Erect like a cherry tree without bark or blossoms. Nuptial Material. Pablo Neruda. ConPit, *tr. by* Clayton Eshleman

Erected by her sorrowing brothers. Epitaph, An. Clive Staples Lewis. OBCoV

Erections. Erin Belieu. ExTi

Eres hermosa como la piedra. Vals, El. Vicente Aleixandre. RaW

Eride ("Dull words that swim upon the page.") Trumbull Stickney.

  "Now in the palace gardens warm with age." APN-2

Erie Canal, The. William S. Allen. HHAm

  (Low Bridge, Everybody Down.) APN-2

E-ri-e, The. *Unknown.* TCAPo

Erik Satie, accused. Caritas. Olga Broumas. CAP-8

Erinna's Spinning. Margaret Junkin Preston. SWaP

Erin's Daughter. Lydia Huntley Sigourney. SWaP

Erl-King. Johann Wolfgang von Goethe. WoPoe, *tr. by* John Frederick Nims

Erl-King, The. Johann Wolfgang von Goethe. OBVE; STV

Erminia's steed this while his mistress bore. Torquato Tasso. NoSic *Fr.* Godfrey of Bulloigne; or, The Recoverie of Jerusalem [Gerusalemme Liberata].

Ernest. Malcolm Cowley. APT-2

Ernie Morgan found him, a small. Barn Owl. Leslie Norris. AngWePo

Eroding face of a knife spatters, The. Unknown Love. ADNAN Özer. NaPG, *tr. by* Talat Sait Halman

Erol Güney's Cat. Orban Veli Kanik. WoPoe, *tr. by* Talat Sait Halman

Erolog. Michael Palmer. FTOS

Eros. Robert Bridges. CABP

Eros. Ralph Waldo Emerson. APN-1

Eros. Michael Field. NAEL-7v2; VWP

Eros. Denise Levertov. AHA

Eros. Timothy Steele. RA

Eros at Temple Stream. Denise Levertov. NALW

[Eros] came from heaven wearing a purple cloak. Sappho. SaLy, *tr. by* Diane Rayor

Eros came near in the horned shape of a shaggy Silenos. Nonnus. CAGL *Fr.* Dionysiaca.

Eros, Ethos, Economuos. Aaron McCollough. IIR

Eros: have you never perchance felt. Public Prayer. Delmira Agustini. TANSG, *tr. by* Mark McCaffrey

Eros in His Striped Blue Shirt. Reginald Shepherd. WiU

Eros in His Striped Shirt. Beckian Fritz Goldberg. PfS

Eros, let me lead you, blind father. Another Race. Delmira Agustini. TCLAP, *tr. by* Karl Kirchwey

Eros Poesis. Tatiana Shcherbina. ItGoST, *tr. by* J. Kates

Eros seizes and shakes my very soul. Sappho. ErotSp, *tr. by* Sam Hamill

Eros, that bane of men, molded soft as marrow. Dioscorides. HePo *Fr.* Epigrams.

Eros, thou yet behold'st me? William Shakespeare. OxAEP-1 *Fr.* Antony and Cleopatra.

Eros Turannos. Edwin Arlington Robinson. AmFaPo; APT-1; HeIP-4; MoAmPo; NAAPv.1; NAMCP V.1; NoAM; NoP-4; OxBoAm; PoA 2002; PoPoPo; TCAPo; TFi; TRP; WoPoe

Eros: "Valley of the Usk, exactly mid-distant." John Powell Ward. RWPCtW

Eros, why should one or two small notes. Goad, The. Michael Field. VWP

Erosion. Claribel Alegría. TANSG, *tr.* by Darwin Flakoll

Erosion. Jorie Graham. FaoP

Erosion. Christopher Merrill. OPRER

Erosion. Linda Pastan. NIP-4

Erosion of rocks blooms, The. The world. Lyn Hejinian. ASA

Erosion of Utopia or Rigor of Patience? Biancamaria Frabotta. CItWP, *tr.* by Cinzia Sartini Blum and Lara Trubowitz

Erotic Collectibles. Wayne Koestenbaum.
    1980. WiU
    1992. WiU
    1977. WiU

Erotic Fruit. Stella Morotskaya. *tr.* by Vitaly Chernetsky
    Tomato. CRWP, *tr.* by Robert Reid

Erotic Philosophers, The. Carolyn Kizer. NoP-5; OxBoAm *Fr.* Pro Femina.

Erotic Suite. Olga Nolla. TANSG, *tr.* by Paula Vega

Erotic tension is almost palpable, The. Big No-No, The. Chris Greenhalgh. NeBl

Erotica 12. Yannis Ritsos. PFTM-2, *tr.* by Kimon Friar

Errand. David Morley. NLP

Errata. Jane Griffiths. NeBl

Errata. Charles Simic. CAP-8

Errata. Kevin Young. LegDan

Erratic, complicated shape, like a tool for some obsolete task, An. Bone. C. K. Williams. CAP-8; UrbNat

Error. / And its emotions. Essay on What I Think about Most. Anne Carson. WaAnP

Error of the Hydrographers, An. Ben Doyle. IIR

Erskineville. The sun came round a corner. Pioneer Lane. Michael Dransfield. NOBAu

Erst when I wandered far from those I loved. Charles Lloyd. CenSon

Erthe took of erthe, erthe wyth wogh. *Unknown.* OHMEL

Erudite demon, a fiend in topology, An. Möbius Strip-Tease. Alec Derwent Hope. OBCoV

Eruption: Pu'u Ō'ō. Garrett Kaoru Hongo. LoL

Es de noche, en mi studio. Miguel de Unamuno. RaW *Fr.* Incidentes Domésticos.

Es del continente, alrededor de ella todo es luz y yo la observo sobre la plancha en la imagen de su cuerpo. Tres. Ofelia Perez Sepúlveda. SPV

Es éste el olor. Este volar de partículas metálicas entre los dientes. País de la calle. Laura Solórzano. SPV

Es la lluvia, ya suelta, lo que miras desmelenarse por la enrejada ventana de madera. Don de resbalar. José Luis Rivas. RMCMP

Es lanzado el cautivo a las brasas ardientes. Fiesta de xócotl huetzi o décimo mes. Carla Faesler Bremer. SPV

Es un batimiento. Dolores Dorantes. SPV

Esau brought 13 halal chickens to her house last night. Last Days of a Slow Cooker. Mursalata Muhammad. FTtHH

Escalade (Paul-Émile Borduas, 1905-1960). Peter Sanger. Coast

Escalando. Gloria Fuertes. RaW

Escalator, The. Escalator. Gene Frumkin. ICANM

Escape. Kenneth Fearing. APT-2

Escape. Robert Graves. MoBrPo

Escape. Georgia Douglas Johnson. NAAPv.2

Escape. Colette Ni Ghallchóir. NIrP, *tr.* by the author

Escape. Elinor Wylie. MoAmPo

Escape Artist, The. Kevin Young. AmPoNex *Fr.* Escape Artist, The.

Escape from the weekday time. Which deadens and endures. (LL) Sunday Morning: "Down the road someone is practising scales." Louis MacNeice. MoBrPo; NAEL-6v2; NAEL-7v2; NIP-4; OxAEP-2; WaAnP

Escape is such a thankful Word. Emily Dickinson. OxBoAm

Escape Journey, 1988. Choman Hardi. BeAl

Escape, The. Mark Van Doren. MoAmPo

Escaped from Germany—. History and Reality. Stephen Spender. HP

Escaped the nets. Buson. EH, *tr.* by Robert Hass

Escapes unhurt beneath so warm a veil. (LL) William Cowper. NAEL-6v1; NAEL-7v1 *Fr.* Task, The.

Escapes unhurt beneath so warm a veil. (LL) William Cowper. NoP-4; NoP-5; NPBRoP; NPeEn *Fr.* Task, The.

Escaping from Autopia. Chryss Yost. GeoHom

Escapology. Ian Samuels. PoPra

Eschatology. Morris Gilbert Bishop. AmWit

Escort fish, Pompilos, sending sailors a fair sailing. Erinna. SaLy, *tr.* by Diane Rayor

Escorting My Mother Home: A Short Song for the Road. Rai San'yo. EMJL, *tr.* by Burton Watson

Escrito con Lluvia. Blas de Otero. RaW

Escritura en un diapasón gradual. Colina verde, una colina verde, Una. Ernesto Lumbreras. RMCMP

Escucha, San Pedro, esta pequeña historia. Llaves de santo. Ernesto Lumbreras. RMCMP

Escuela autoritaria y cómo nació un respetable género de literatura, La. Gerardo Deniz. RMCMP

Esenin's Suicide Note. Sergey Aleksandrovich Yesenin. CAGL, *tr.* by Simon Karlinsky

Eshu. Adesanya Alakoye. ISC

Eskimo Girl, The. David Ray. LTA

Eskimo occasion. Judith Rodriguez. BrAP; ItWoWo; NOBAu

Eskimo's Woman, The. Anabel Torres. TANSG, *tr.* by Celeste Kostopulos-Cooperman

Eso fue todo entonces. Peso muerto de la tierra, El. Tedi López Mills. RMCMP

Esope, myne Authour, makis mentioun. Robert Henryson. NePenScot *Fr.* Morall Fabillis of Esope the Phrygian, The.

España, Aparta de me Este Caliz. César Vallejo. *tr.* by Robert Bly
    Masses. PoCho; WED, *tr.* by Robert Bly

España Joven, Una. Antonio Machado Ruiz. RaW

Española Pantoum. Joan Logghe. ICANM

Espanto tonto. Natalia Toledo. RMCMP

Especially after rain, the gulls. Sue MacLeod. Coast

Especially in weeping. Valerio Magrelli. NeIt

Especially When the October Wind. Dylan Thomas. AngWePo; MoBrPo; OBWVE; OxAEP-2

Especie de, Una. Blas de Otero. RaW

Espectros. Jorge Fernández Granados. RMCMP

Espera Siempre. José Luis Hidalgo. RaW

Esperance! The twinge of moonlight in outer space. Blank Abandon of Beds, The. Star Black. KGB

Espío en el edificio. Piazza Gimma. Fabio Morabito. RMCMP

Esponja, La. Fabio Morabito. RMCMP

Esposito, Fiorani, Fogagnolo. To the Fifteen of Piazzale Loreto. Salvatore Quasimodo. AF, *tr.* by Jack Bevan

Espresso. Carol Lee Saffoti. UnSA

Esprit d'Escalier. John Wheelwright. APT-2

Espuma. Claudio Rodríguez. RaW

Esqueleto enterrado. Espanto tonto. Natalia Toledo. RMCMP

Essay, An. Semezdin Mehmedinović. PML, *tr.* by Antonela Glavinic and Kathleen Jamie

Essay on Concrete, An. Douglas Messerli. FTOS

Essay on Criticism, An. Alexander Pope. NAEL-6v1; NAEL-7v1; TFi
    Bookful Blockhead, The. OBSV
    "But most by numbers judge a poet's song." NIL-7; NIP-4
    "But where's the man who counsel can bestow." OxAEP-1

Essay on Criticism. OBCoV
    "Little learning is a dangerous [*or* dang'rous] thing, A." OxBEV
    "Of all the causes which conspire to blind." MakPoe; NoP-4; NoP-5; OxAEP-1; WaAnP
    Plain Fools. OBSV
    Servile Herd, The. OBSV
    "Some to Conceit alone their taste confine." OxAEP-1
    "Thus critics, of less judgment than caprice." BrAP

Essay on Death. Hayden Carruth. BodElec

Essay on Friendship. Mary Leapor.
    "To Artemisia.—'Tis to her we sing." PEW

Essay on Friendship, An. J. D. McClatchy.
    7. PoA 2002

Essay on Language. Wanda Coleman. PmAP

Essay on Liberation, An. David St. John. AmAlph

Essay on Man, An. Alexander Pope.
    "Awake, my St. John! leave all meaner things." NAEL-6v1; NAWM-7v2
    "Lo, the poor Indian! whose untutor'd mind." DiBP
    Paragon of Animals, The. NAEL-6v1; NAEL-7v1; SacPr; TFi
    "Placed on this isthmus of a middle state." WeW-3
    (Scale of Being, The.) WoPoe
    "See, through this air, this ocean, and this earth." InvLi
    "What would this Man? Now upward will he soar." HeIP-4

Essay on Psychiatrists. Robert Pinsky.
    Invocation. NoAM
    Lakeside Identification, A. NoP-4; NoP-5

Mad, The. NoAM

Peroration, Concerning Genius. NoAM

Physical Comparison With Professors and Others. NoP-4; NoP-5

Proposition. NoAM

Their Patients. NoAM

Their Philistinism Considered. NoAM

Their Seriousness, with Further Comparisons. NoAM

Their Speech, Compared with Wisdom and Poetry. NoAM; PoA 2002

Essay on What I Think about Most. Anne Carson. WaAnP

Essay on William Carlos Williams, An. Víctor Hernández Cruz. PmAP

Essay on Woman. John Wilkes.

"Awake my Fanny! leave all meaner things." EroLit

"He who the hoop's immensity can pierce." EroLit

"Pleased to the last, she likes the luscious food." EroLit

"Then, in the scale of Pricks, 'tis plain." EroLit

"Then, say not Man's imperfect, Heaven in fault." EroLit

Essay on Woman, An. Mary Leapor. BrAP; NAEL-7v1

Essay upon Good-Friday, An. Anne King. EMWP

Essays on Excess and Escape. Gaylord Brewer. LiTh

Esse. Czeslaw Milosz. MotU, tr. by the author and Robert Pinsky

Essence. Bernard Bador. ConPit, tr. by Clayton Eshleman

Essence. Judson Crews. ICANM

Essences. Antonio Porta. tr. by Gayle Ridinger

"Nearby creatures of the air." ItPo, tr. by Gayle Ridinger

"To become a tree." ItPo, tr. by Gayle Ridinger

"White bars from the window." ItPo, tr. by Gayle Ridinger

Essential oils—are wrung. Emily Dickinson. APN-2; SWaP; TCAPo

Essential Serbo-Coat. Ken Smith. PoAgWa

Essential Story, The. Charlie Smith. PoA 2002

Essential, The. Aleksandar Ristovic. BeAl, tr. by Charles Simic

Essentially description, night. 1978, Remembering 1962. C. S. Giscombe. GT

Esta Es Mi Tierra. Edison Coleman. OWABP

Esta tarde te alivian los colores: el verde. Retornos a Través de los Colores. Rafael Alberti. RaW

Estaba en una orilla de la orilla. Tercer Mundo. Christina Rivera-Garza. SPV

"Established" is a good word, much used in garden books. Time. Mary Ursula Bethell. OBGa

Establishment has taken to the hills. First Letter to an Irish Novelist. Roy McFadden. PNI

Estadio Chile. Víctor Jara. TCLAP, tr. by Joan Jara

Estate. Agi Mishol. DTA, tr. by Tsipi Keller

Estate bird, The. Loon, The. Michael S. Harper. ESEAA

Este Cristo español que no ha vivido. Miguel de Unamuno. RaW Fr. Cristo Yacente de Santa Clara (Iglesia de la Cruz) en Palencia, El.

Este otoño. Anuncio. Tedi López Mills. RMCMP

Estel. Julia Alvarez. ExTi

Estelí / this mountain town means something. Resurrection. Joy Harjo. HATNAP

Estes' Backyard, The. Pamela Stewart. UrbNat

Esther. Eve Merriam. TaR

Esther [a Young Man's Tragedy]. Wilfrid Scawen Blunt.

"When I hear laughter from a tavern door." OBMV

With Esther. OBEV; OBMV

Esther's Tomcat. Ted Hughes. OxBEV

Estío en Bidonville. Angel González. RaW

Esto no puede seguir así: sé sincero, uno. Eduardo Milán. RMCMP

Estranged in site. Parthenon, The. Herman Melville. NCAP

Estrangement. Jane Cooper. ExTi

Estray, The. Forceythe Willson. APN-2

Estrella's Prophecies #47. David Baratier. AmPoNex

Estrella's Prophecies #18. David Baratier. RWB

Estrellitas. Carlos Cumpian. IllVoic

Estrich, thou feather'd fool and easy prey. Richard Lovelace. CavPo

Estuary. Julie Fay. PoDa

Esyllt. Glyn Jones. AngWePo; OBMVE

Et cetera. (LL) Cheerful Girls at Smiller's Bar, 1971, The. Jack A. Mapanje. HBAPE; NAfrP

Et Homo Factus Est. Crucifixus. Saunders Lewis. BBMWP, tr. by Joseph P. Clancy

Et in Arcadia ergo points to everywhere. Some Versions of Pastoral. Steve McCaffery. BAP-04

Et in Leucadia Ego. Michael Davidson. PmAP

Et Incarnatus Est. William Langland. SacPr Fr. Vision of Piers Plowman, The.

Et le paon repartait se pavaner seul dans le parc. Franck André Jamme. YaTCFP Fr. Vie du scarabée, Le.

Et les soldats faisaient la haie? ILS LA FAISAIENT. (LL) T. S. Eliot. AmWaPo; OBWP Fr. Coriolan.

Et nous / tressons. Tahar Bekri. YaTCFP Fr. Retour en Tunisie.

Et Nox Facta Est. Victor Hugo. NAWM-7v2, tr. by Mary Ann Caws

Et Quidquid Aspiciebam Mors Erat. Robert Fitzgerald. APT-2

Etched Away From. Paul Celan. OBVE, tr. by Michael Hamburger

Etching. Samuel Greenberg. APT-1

Été, L' ("Bon, c'est la chaleur.") Pascalle Monnier. YaTCFP

Été, L' ("Ce sont les premiers beaux jours.") Pascalle Monnier. YaTCFP

Eternal, The. Blas de Otero. RaW, tr. by Hardie St. Martin

Eternal Aphrodite, Zeus's daugther, throne. Prayer to Aphrodite. Sappho. WoPoe, tr. by Alfred Corn

Eternal autumn rain—evening sounds. To the Tune: The Wine Spring. Li Hsun. CrYelRi; ErotSp, tr. by Sam Hamill

Eternal Controversy, The. Dean B. Lyman, Jr. YaYoPo

Eternal Dialogue. Tasos Leivaditis. PML, tr. by Minas Savvas

Eternal Dice, The. César Vallejo. PoetW, tr. by James Wright

Eternal Farewell. Ricardo Jaimes Freyre. TCLAP, tr. by Victor Tulli

Eternal Female ground! [or groan'd!] it was heard all over the Earth, The. William Blake. NAEL-6v2; NAEL-7v2 Fr. Marriage of Heaven and Hell, The.

Eternal gates lift up their heads, The. Hymn. Cecil Frances Alexander. SacPr

Eternal gates' terrific porter lifted the northern bar, The. William Blake. OxBEV Fr. Book of Thel, The.

Eternal God! maker of all. Book, The. Henry Vaughan. AngWePo; BASC; InvLi; PBRV

Eternal God—for whom who ever dare. John Donne. SacPr

Eternal Health. Sequence for the First Sunday in Advent. Unknown. RSR, tr. by L. William Countryman

Eternal Image, The. Ruth Pitter. MoBrPo

Eternal Justice: Morecambe Sands, Aug. 1794. William Wordsworth. NPBRoP Fr. Prelude, The; Growth of a Poet's Mind [1805 version; Selections from Anthologies].

Eternal Landscape, The. Lenard D. Moore. GT

Eternal lightning of Lenin's bones, The. (LL) Skeleton of the Future, The. Hugh MacDiarmid. MoBrPo; OBMV

Eternal Lord! eased of a cumbrous load. William Wordsworth. SacPr

Eternal Love, maintain thy life in me. (LL) Leave Me O Love. Sir Philip Sidney. AEP; GSo; HeIP-4; NIP-4; NPeEn; OxAEP-1; SacPr; TFi

Eternal Masculine. William Rose Benét. MoAmPo

Eternal Moment. Sándor Weöres. IQMS, tr. by Edwin Morgan

Eternal pain! (LL) Philomela. Matthew Arnold. OBEV; OWoS

Eternal power from whose allseeing eye. Baptina Palavicino Cromwell. EMWP

Eternal Power, of earth and air! Doubter's Prayer, The. Anne Brontë. SacPr

Eternal Present, The. Gabriel Preil. FIT, tr. by Robert Friend

Eternal reciprocity of tears, The. (LL) Insensibility. Wilfred Owen. BrAP; FaBoWar; NoP-4; NoP-5; OBWP; OxAEP-2; PoWW

Eternal Son, The. Li-Young Lee. RoV

Eternal Spirit of the chainless Mind! Sonnet on Chillon. Lord Byron. CenSon; GSo; NPBRoP

ETERNAL sprite, which art in heaven the love. To God the Holy Ghost. Henry Constable. NoSic

Eternal Three, The. Tove Ditlevsen. WoPoe, tr. by Inga Allwood, Martin Allwood and John Hollander

Eternall Mover, whose diffused glory. Sir Henry Wotton. SacPr

Eternall Truth, almighty, infinite. Fulke Greville, 1st Baron Brooke. NoSic; SacPr Fr. Caelica.

Eternally to be waiting for bloody news. Yunna Petrovna Moritz. CFP, tr. by Gerald S. Smith

Eternity. Hart Crane. NAAPv.2

Eternity: "She's neither ugly nor fearful." Alexander Gerov. CSCBP, tr. by Georgi Belev and Lisa Sapinkopf

Eternity! Mary Ferrari. AHA

Eternity. Josephine D. Henderson Heard. CBWP-4

Eternity. Robert Herrick. CavPo

Eternity. Kabir. WoPoe, tr. by Arvind Krishna Mehrotra

Eternity. James Whitcomb Riley. GSo

Eternity. Takahashi Shinkichi. ZenPo, tr. by Takashi Ikemoto and Lucien Stryk

Eternity. Sándor Weöres. IQMS, tr. by Adam Makkai and Donald E. Morse

Eternity Affirms the Hour. Robert Browning. SacPr

Eternity of God, The. Frederick William Faber. SacPr

Eternity of Pure Color. Pak Mogwŏl [or Mokwŏl]. CAMKP Fr. Nature of Gravel, The.

Eternity, thou thunderous word. Johann Rist. GePo *Fr.* Eternity, Thou Thunderous Word.

Eternity's Woods. Paul Zweig. BodElec

Eterno, Lo. Blas de Otero. RaW

Ethel in her crimson row boat. Chateaux en Espagne. Henrietta Cordelia Ray. CBWP-3

Ethel Rosenberg and Me. Judith Werner. FiBr

Ether. Laurence Lieberman. LiTh

Ether broke into the house. Red Dye. Barbara Guest. BodElec

Ether Insatiable. May Kendall. CABP

Ethics. Linda Pastan. WaAnP

Ethiopia. Kate Daniels. PBCAP

Ethiopia. Audre Lorde. AFaM

Ethiopia Unda a Jamaican Mango Tree. Opal Palmer Adisa. WaCA

Ethiopian Apocalypse of Don, The. Norman Weinstein. WaCA

Ethnogenesis. Henry Timrod. APN-2; PCW; TCAPo

Étoiles transhumantes; et le berger. Livre, pour vieillir, Le. Yves Bonnefoy. YaTCFP

Etosion achthos aroures. Robert Bridges. OxBEV

Étreinte, L'. Louis Aragon. YaTCFP

Etruscan Notebook. Elena Clementelli. *tr. by* Cinzia Sartini Blum and Lara Trubowitz

   "Bend of the gulf." CItWP, *tr. by* Cinzia Sartini Blum and Lara Trubowitz

   "Subterranean geography." CItWP, *tr. by* Cinzia Sartini Blum and Lara Trubowitz

Ettrick. Lady John Scott. LW; SoSe-8

Ettricke Foreste is a feir forestle. Sang of the Outlaw Murray, The. *Unknown.* IBB

Étude Réaliste. Algernon Charles Swinburne.

   "Baby's feet, like sea-shells pink, A." WeW-3

Études. Gunnar Ekelof.

   3. WED, *tr. by* Robert Bly

Etudes. Dennis Phillips.

   If It's Only Rhythm. FTOS

Etymological Dirge. Heather McHugh. ExTi; FaoP

Etymology. Olga Broumas. WiU

Eucalyptus and the pure scent / of rage. (LL) Poema para los Californios Muertos. Lorna Dee Cervantes. NAMCP V.2; PoPoPo

Eucalyptus, his mouth. Into the Next One. Valerie Martínez. AmPoNex

Euclid Alone Has Looked on Beauty Bare. Edna St. Vincent Millay. APT-1; BRP; GSo; HeIP-4; MoAmPo; NoP-4; NoP-5

Euclid Avenue. Harry Clifton. PBCIP

Eudiades. John Addington Symonds.

   "In years of old." CAGL

Eudoxia. Italo Calvino. MotU *Fr.* Invisible Cities.

Eugene Onegin Stanza, The. Vladimir Vladimirovich Nabokov. *See* On Translating "Eugene Onegin."

Eugene Wukasch, Texas Architect. Dave Oliphant. TiP2

Eugenia. George Chapman.

   Death Described by His True Effects. NOSC

Eugenio de Luelmo. Claudio Rodríguez. RaW, *tr. by* Philip Levine

Eugenio de Luelmo. Claudio Rodríguez. RaW

Eugenio Montale: The Eel. Paul Muldoon. GPPA

Eulalie—A Song. Edgar Allan Poe. STuOW

Eulogy: "This should be a eulogy without words." Amichai Israeli. NRoS, *tr. by* Esther Raizen

Eulogy: "Bereavement revolves in our garden like a sword." Moshe Tabenkin. NRoS, *tr. by* Esther Raizen

Eulogy, The. Carol Muske-Dukes. InoFa; PBCAP

Eulogy for Sister. Opal Moore. FuFl

Eulogy to a hell of a dame. Charles Bukowski. CalPo

Eulogy to W.H. Auden. Derek Walcott. ESEAA

Eumenides, The. Aeschylus. NAWM-5v1, *tr. by* Robert Fagles

Eunica scorned [*or* skorned *or* skornde] me, when her I would have sweetly kissed [*or* kist]. Theocritus. NoSic; OBVE *Fr.* Idylls.

Eunuch Unique. Francis Picabia. PFTM-1 *Fr.* Eunuch Unique.

Eupheme. Ben Jonson.

   Picture of the Body, The. NOSC

Euphony. Yusef Komunyakaa. ESEAA

Euphoria. Major L. Jackson. LegDan

Eureka. Maureen Duffy. PoBW

Euripides' Cave. Elizabeth Morgan. PoDa

Euripides the Athenian. George Seferis. PoetW, *tr. by* Edmund Keeley and Philip Sherrard

Europa. Rolfe Humphries. APT-2

Europa. Moschus. HePo, *tr. by* Barbara Hughes Fowler

Europa. Anatol Stern. PFTM-1

Europa and Jove. Ovid. NAWM-7v1 *Fr.* Metamorphoses.

Europe; A Prophecy. William Blake.

   "Five windows light the caverned man: through one he breathes the air." NPBRoP

Europe, Late. Dan Pagis. HP, *tr. by* Stephen Mitchell

Europe 1953. For Ethel Rosenberg. Adrienne Rich. AtGh

Europe, the 72d and 73d Year of These States. Walt Whitman. TCAPo

Europe the 72nd and 73rd Years of These States. Walt Whitman. APN-1 *Fr.* Leaves of Grass [1855 Version].

Europe was a mess: it will come back to you. In Mournful Praise and Memory of the French Song. Jaime Gil de Biedma. RaW, *tr. by* Timothy Baland

Europe's Prisoners. Sidney Keyes. PoWW

Euryalus and Nisus Meet Their Deaths. Virgil. NoSic *Fr.* Aeneid [*or* Eneados *or* Aeneis], The.

Eurydice. Rosita Copioli. CItWP, *tr. by* Cinzia Sartini Blum and Lara Trubowitz

Eurydice. Luciana Frezza. CItWP, *tr. by* Cinzia Sartini Blum and Lara Trubowitz

Eurydice. Louise Glück. BodElec

Eurydice. "H. D."

   "So you have swept me back." NALW

Eurydice went back to hell. Eurydice. Louise Glück. BodElec

Eutawville Lynching, The. Lizelia Augusta Jenkins Moorer. CBWP-3

Eutopia. Francis Turner Palgrave. OBGa

Eutychus. Rosemary Dobson. ChIV-2

"Eva!" again. (LL) Eve. Ralph Hodgson. ChIV-1; MoBrPo

Eva Braun. W. D. Snodgrass. BodElec *Fr.* Führer Bunker, The.

Eva, forma futuri. Andrea Zanzotto. ItPo *Fr.* Prophecies or Memories or Display-Board Newspapers.

Evacuee, The. R. Hewett Thomas. ItP

Evading believers, he hurries off down Pitt Street. (LL) Absolutely Ordinary Rainbow, An. Les A. Murray. HarvBoo; StAl

Evadne. "H. D." LW

Evagatory. Peter Reading.

   "Came to an island farctate with feculence." StAl

Evanescence. Hugo von Hofmannsthal. GTCP, *tr. by* Herman Salinger

Evanescent hue whose pearly gleam, An. Ideal, An. Henrietta Cordelia Ray. CBWP-3

Evangelical. Mary Ruefle. AmAlph

Evangeline: A Tale of Acadie. Henry Wadsworth Longfellow.

   Preamble to a Tale of Acadie. APN-1; NAAPv.1; NoP-4; TCAPo; UV

   "This is the forest primeval. The murmuring pines and the hemlocks." NoP-5

Evangeline made her. Straight Talk from Plain Women. Sherley Anne Williams. GT

Evanishings. Mary E. Tucker. CBWP-1

Evans. Ronald Stuart Thomas. OxBEV

Evans Country, The. Kingsley Amis.

   Aberdarcy: The Main Square. NoAM

Evans? Yes, many a time. Evans. Ronald Stuart Thomas. OxBEV

Evaporations. Ani Ilkov. CSCBP, *tr. by* Georgi Belev and Lisa Sapinkopf

Evarra and His Gods. Rudyard Kipling. MoBrPo

Evasive souls, of whom the wise lose track. Imaginative Life, The. Geoffrey Hill. NoAM

Eve. Jacob Fichman. FIT, *tr. by* Robert Friend

Eve. Ella Higginson. SWaP

Eve. Ralph Hodgson. ChIV-1; MoBrPo

Eve. Dorothy Livesay. ItWoWo; NALW

Eve. Julio Marzán. PueRic

Eve. Christina Georgina Rossetti. ChIV-1; NALW; NIL-7; NIP-4

Eve descends with radiant streaks, The. Song. Anne Batten Cristall. RWP

Eve Falling. Jane McVeigh. HW

Eve in Eden. Manuela Fingueret. MirDau, *tr. by* Roberta Gordenstein

Eve Names the Animals. Susan Donnelly. NIL-7

13: Eve No Longer Exists. Jaime Sabines. MotU *Fr.* Adam and Eve.

Eve of Christmas had arrived, The. Christmas Ghost, A. Priscilla Jane Thompson. CBWP-2

Eve of St. Agnes, The. John Keats. CABP; NAEL-6v2; NAEL-7v2; NOBRP; NoP-4; NoP-5; NPBRoP; NPeEn; OBNV; OxAEP-2; TFi; TRP; WaAnP

   "Her faltering hand upon the balustrade." OxBEV

   "Sudden a thought came like a full-blown rose." EroLit

Eve of St Mark, The. Geoffrey Hill. NPeEn; OxBEV *Fr.* Apology for the Revival of Christian Architecture in England, An.

Eve of Waterloo, The. Thomas Hardy. FaBoWar; OBWP *Fr.* Dynasts, The.

Eve Oh Eve. Taslima Nasrin. VCWP

Eve (Rachel). Michael S. Harper. ESEAA

Even Now You Are Leaving. Tess Gallagher. LaCa

Even on a spring morning. Shepherd in Capri. Nishiwaki Junzaburo. CAoMJL1, *tr. by* Hosea Hirata

Even on clear nights, lead the most supple children. Great Bear, The. John Hollander. ColAP; NoAM

Even on Sunday. Robin Blaser. FTOS

Even on the quietest days the distant. Ford Manor. Derek Mahon. PBCIP

Even on the smallest islands. Issa. EH, *tr. by* Robert Hass

Even opening my eyes. July Thirteenth. Jeanne Wells. PfS

Even Ornaments of Speech Are Forms of Deceit. Ron Koertge. PoDa

Even praying for the light of his jade-like hair. (LL) In Praise of a Gold and Silver Painted Scene of the Buddha Manifestation in the Pure Land of the West, with a Preface. Li Po. CCL1; WoPoe, *tr. by* Elling O. Eide

Even Samuel Johnson found that ending. Revised Versions, The. Lawrence Raab. PoDa

Even sex-hexed men mend nets. Big e, The. Ernst Jandl. OnScMo, *tr. by* Guy Bennet

Even so. (LL) Dirge in Woods. George Meredith. NAEL-6v2; OBEV

Even so distant, I can taste the grief. Deceptions. Philip Larkin. HarvBoo; OxAEP-2

Even so, one hand gropes out for another, again. (LL) After the Dinner Party. Robert Penn Warren. NAAL-5; PoCho

Even Solomon. Dennis O'Donnell. EdScPo

Even Such Is Time. Sir Walter Ralegh. TFi

(Author's Epitaph, Made By Himself, The.) NAEL-6v1; NAEL-7v1; NIL-7

(Conclusion, The.) OBEV

(Verses Made the Night before He Died [*or* Dyed].) NoSic

(Verses Written the Night before His Execution.) TRP

Even than all lovely lights and roses are? (LL) Frederick Goddard Tuckerman. APN-2; OxBoAm *Fr.* Sonnets: First Series, 1854–1860.

Even than we are. (LL) Apollo. Elizabeth Alexander. ExTi; PoA 2002

Even the abandoned husk of a person can sometimes. Figure in the Carpet, The. James Tate. BodElec

Even the barnacle has certain rights. This Octopus Exploits Women. James Fenton. NoAM

Even the croaking of frogs. Hakuro Wada. NAAPv.2

Even the dark end of Belmont Avenue. Walking by the Cliffside Dyeworks. Robert Carnevale. UnSA

Even the dirt kept breathing a small breath. (LL) Root Cellar. Theodore Roethke. CAP-8; ColAP; HarvBoo; HeIP-4; NoP-4; NoP-5; OxBoAm; VCAP

Even the dumplings / Are smaller. Morikawa Kyoroku. ZenPo, *tr. by* Takashi Ikemoto and Lucien Stryk

Even the Eagles Must Gather. Alma Villanueva. FFC

Even the fat slug. Everything in the Garden is Lovely. Alasdair Aston. OBGa

Even the flags seemed frozen. Remembering Frost at Kennedy's Inauguration. Linda Pastan. VisFro

Even the Gulls of the Cool Atlantic. Joan Murray. OxBoAm

Even the iris bends. Nuance. Amy Lowell. NAAPv.2

Even the last few, weeks off yet, misshapen as toes. (LL) Broad Bean Sermon, The. Les A. Murray. BMAP; EmeKit; HarvBoo; MakPoe

Even the long-dead are willing to move. Gentle Communion. Pat Mora. NIL-7; NIP-4

Even the longest day. Marina Dolia. CRWP *Fr.* Silence.

Even the man who is happy. Kalidasa. EaWin, *tr. by* J. Moussaieff Masson and W. S. Merwin

Even the most delicate. Forgiveness. Julia Copus. MoWP

Even the most die-hard liberals. Lonely Affair, A. Reuben Jackson. GT

Even the pole bean tendrils sought out and gripped their. Stories Are Made of Mistakes. James Galvin. TAPaP

Even the smell pulls her in. (LL) White Asparagus. Sujata Bhatt. HarvBoo; StAl

Even the stars wear out. Little Elegy. Keith Althaus. PoDa

Even the sugar is murmuring: "and do you remember how they came for you." Supper: House Outside Town. Gennady Aygi. WoBe, *tr. by* Peter France

Even the sun-clouds this morning cannot manage such skirts. Poppies in October. Sylvia Plath. NAMCP V.2; NoAM; OxBoAm; StAl

Even the tallest didn't remember. Gentleness of the Very Tall, The. Linda France. MFPA

Even the thin tube of Spanish saffron. Saffron. David St. John. RoV

Even the trees outside feel it, their fine branches. Even the Trees. Jackie Kay. MFPA; NeBrP

Even the walls are flowing, even the ceiling. Variation on Heraclitus. Louis MacNeice. NAMCP V.1; NoAM

Even the whales now. Even the Whales. Tom Matthews. PNI

Even the wind that should listen hums something lovely. Letter. Margit Szécsi. IQMS, *tr. by* Kenneth McRobbie

Even the worst intelligence must needs ride. Sir Gelli to R.S. Roland Mathias. AngWePo

Even the wrist's fast jack. Bone Die, The. Maggie Hannan. NLP

Even these long days. Basho. SoOfWa, *tr. by* Sam Hamill

Even this far from that burning place. History. Alpay Ulku. AmPoNex

Even this far, with two paper cups and miles of taut string, I could describe a ghost of myself. From San Diego. Chryss Yost. GeoHom

Even this suburb has overcome Death. Easter. Howard Nemerov. NoP-4; WaAnP

Even though I'm angry. Tenderness. Belinda Zubicueta Carmona. TANSG, *tr. by* Celeste Kostopulos-Cooperman

Even though my memory grew dim. So That We Do Not Forget. Buland Al-Haidari. IrPoTo, *tr. by* Hussein Kadhim and Christopher Merrill

Even though she don't have a job, Mami still words. Unemployed Mami. Willie Perdomo. InTrad

Even though they were rebellious. *Various authors.* CATKP *Fr.* Songs of Flying Dragons.

Even though you have a brushwood door. Written at the Dwelling of a Recluse. Chia Tao. CSKM, *tr. by* Mike O'Connor

Even to the end of the earth. Kim Namjo. CAMKP *Fr.* Love's Cursive.

Even to the icy winter, and the siege. (LL) Leningrad Cemetery, Winter of 1941. Sharon Olds. NIL-7; NIP-4

Even to thy pure and most most loving breast. (LL) Sonnet 110. William Shakespeare. AEP; NAEL-6v1; NAEL-7v1; NoSic; OxAEP-1 *Fr.* Sonnets.

Even today, the streets. Again at the Crossroads. Im Hwa. CAMKP, *tr. by* Jiwon Shin

Even tonight and I need to take a walk and clear. Poem About My Rights. June Jordan. ISC; NoAM; WaAnP

Even two weeks after her fall. Death in Mexico. Denise Levertov. NAAL-5

Even watching that Tina Turner movie. Burn Rubber on Me. Derrick X. BtF

Even what the hungry Wolf in Field would do. Mary Mollineux. EMWP, *tr. by* Henry Mollineux

Even when cross planks are nailed down. Leaving the Village. *Vietnamese Oral Tradition.* CaDao, *tr. by* John Balaban

Even when first her face. Someone Talking to Himself. Richard Wilbur. HarvBoo

Even when I fall asleep early. Insomnia. Lu Yu. NDACCP, *tr. by* Kenneth Rexroth

Even when they destroy you it will still be beautiful. Odysseus Elytis. GifTon *Fr.* With Light and With Death.

Even when you see through the lies, the lies they. Once a Shoot of Heaven. Beckian Fritz Goldberg. PuP-23

Even while chopping. Mukai Kyorai. EMJL, *tr. by* Haruo Shirane

Even whilst I watch him I am remembering. To T.A.R.H. Stephen Spender. CAGL

Even with insects. Issa. ASA; ChAP; EH, *tr. by* Robert Hass

Even your computer is haunted ruin, as your. Haunted Ruin, The. Robert Pinsky. NAMCP V.2

Even Your Escape Is a Bit Special. Anna Cascella. CItWP, *tr. by* Cinzia Sartini Blum and Lara Trubowitz

Even your friend, the radio, is still; even when her. X Minus X. Kenneth Fearing. OxBoAm

Evenfall, so slow on hills, hath shot, The. Lights of London, The. Louise Imogen Guiney. APN-2

Evening. Richard Aldington. MoBrPo

Evening. "H. D." APT-1; HarvBoo

Evening. Andreas Gryphius. GePo, *tr. by* George C. Schoolfield

Evening. Willem Kloos. TuT, *tr. by* Desmond Egan

Evening. Emma Lazarus. APN-2 *Fr.* Phantasies (After Robert Schumann).

Evening. Mark McMorris. AmPoNex

Evening. Thomas Miller. NOxBChV

Evening. John Milton. TreFP

Evening. James Stephens. MoBrPo

Evening. Ronald Stuart Thomas. HarvBoo

Evening. *Vietnamese Oral Tradition.* CaDao, *tr. by* John Balaban

Evening. Mihály Csokonai Vitéz. IQMS, *tr. by* Madeline Mason

Evening. Karen Volkman. NIL-7

Evening, An. Robert Mezey. GeoHom

Evening, The. Georg Trakl. PFTM-1, *tr. by* Robert Firmage

Evening, The: "With the ghostly shapes of dead heroes." Georg Trakl. WED, *tr. by* Robert Bly

Evening after evening. Meditation of 8/5/85. Jacques Roubaud. YaTCFP, *tr. by* Rosmarie Waldrop

Evening after Rain. Tu Fu [*or* Du Fu]. CrYelRi, *tr. by* Sam Hamill

Evening and Night. James Thomson. NAEL-6v1; NAEL-7v1 *Fr.* Seasons, The.

Evening and the flat land. Prairie Spring. Willa Sibert Cather. NAAPv.2

Evening, as slow thy placid shades descend. Sonnet 5. William Lisle Bowles. NOBRP

Evening at Tsarskoe Selo. Polina Barskova. CRWP, *tr.* by Peter France

Evening Before, The. José Ángel Valente. RaW, *tr.* by Hardie St. Martin

Evening before, The. (LL) Michael Wigglesworth. ColAP; TCAPo *Fr.* Day of Doom, The [First Section].

Evening, before the King's pavilion. At the Exiled King's River Pavilion. U'ng Bình. CaDao, *tr.* by John Balaban

Evening bell / Persimmons pelt. Masaoka Shiki. ZenPo, *tr.* by Takashi Ikemoto and Lucien Stryk

Evening Bells near a Temple. Ma Chih-yüan. CrYelRi, *tr.* by Sam Hamill

Evening breeze, The. Tenderly. Jack Lawrence. ReLy

Evening bridge / A thousand hands. Kikaku. ZenPo, *tr.* by Takashi Ikemoto and Lucien Stryk

Evening brings all home. For that we wait, The. Horatius Bonar. SacPr *Fr.* My Old Letters.

Evening came, a child was missing. Little Bell. Mary E. Tucker. CBWP-1

Evening Change. John Haines. GifTon

Evening Chess. Charles Simic. OxBoAm

Evening clears, The. Issa. EH, *tr.* by Robert Hass

Evening cloudburst, An. Buson. SoOfWa, *tr.* by Sam Hamill

Evening Clouds. Olav H. Hauge. WED, *tr.* by Robert Bly

Evening comes and everything is hushed, The. Family Circle. János Arany. IQMS, *tr.* by Neville Masterman

Evening Darkens Over, The. Robert Bridges. WaAnP

Evening dropped toward owl-call, The. Robert Penn Warren. LPSFW *Fr.* Some Quiet, Plain Poems.

Evening Ebb. Robinson Jeffers. NoAM

Evening falls / and you finish your trip. Tenochtitlán Blues. Manuel Ulacia. RMCMP, *tr.* by Indran Amirthanayagam

Evening forecast for the region, The. Nick Laird. NIrP

Evening. Gertrude. Anne Batten Cristall. RWP

Evening Halo of Light, An. Árpád Tóth. IQMS, *tr.* by Thomas Kabdebo

Evening Hawk. Robert Penn Warren. APT-2; ColAP; InGu; NAMCP V.1; NoP-4; NoP-5; OWoS; VCAP; WaAnP

Evening, I found lodging at Shihao. Pressgang at Shihao Village, The. Tu Fu [*or* Du Fu]. CCL1, *tr.* by Jerome P. Seaton

Evening in Connecticut. Louis MacNeice. HarvBoo

Evening in Terezin, An. Eva Schulzová. INSAB

Evening in the Country. John Ashbery. PoDa

Evening in the Garden, Clear after Rain. Ch'u Ch'uang I. CCL1; WaAnP, *tr.* by Kenneth Rexroth

Evening in the Sanitarium. Louise Bogan. GPTC; NALW; NIL-7; OxBoAm

Evening is clogged with gnats as the light fails. Alceste in the Wilderness. Anthony Hecht. PoA 2002

Evening is coming, the day wears on. *Unknown.* WoPoe *Fr.* Song of Roland, The.

Evening is dying, The. In the Fields. Antonio Machado Ruiz. RaW, *tr.* by Robert Bly

Evening Land, The. D. H. Lawrence. FaBoA

Evening lies down in my window, heavy and tired, The. Toye-Voye. Esther Shumyatsher. Prolet, *tr.* by Amelia Glaser

Evening Lull, An. Walt Whitman. NAAL-3

Evening moon. Issa. EH, *tr.* by Robert Hass

Evening Musicale. Phyllis McGinley. AmWit; OBCoV

Evening near Serpent River. Tu Fu [*or* Du Fu]. CrYelRi, *tr.* by Sam Hamill

Evening Nixon called his last troops off, The. April 30, 1975. John Balaban. AmWaPo

Evening oer the meadow seems to stoop, The. Mist in the Meadows. John Clare. NPeEn

Evening of the Mind, The. Donald Justice. VCAP

Evening of the Sixth Day, The. Rose Drachler. APT-2

Evening on Calais Beach. William Wordsworth. *See* It Is a Beauteous Evening.

Evening on Lesbos. Edna St. Vincent Millay. PoBW

Evening on the Mountain: Song to the Moon in the Well. Yi Kyubo. WoPoe, *tr.* by Kevin O'Rourke

Evening on the Potomac. Richard Hovey. APN-2

Evening Out, The. Ogden Nash. MoAmPo

Evening Prayer [*ad. fr.* Psalm 140, 141]. Thomas Merton. ChIV-1

Evening Prayer. Henrietta Cordelia Ray. CBWP-3

Evening Prayer, at a Girls' School. Felicia Dorothea Hemans. VWP

Evening prayer for the indelible one. Words of. Prayer for August 21. David Huerta. RMCMP, *tr.* by Mark Schafer

Evening primrose. Buson. EH, *tr.* by Robert Hass

Evening primrose. Kim Namjo. CAMKP, *tr.* by David R. McCann and Hyunjae Yee Sallee

Evening Primrose, The. Christopher Pearse Cranch. APN-1

Evening primrose dressed. Pollen. Wyn Cooper. UrbNat

Evening Quatrains. Charles Cotton. NOSC; NPeEn; OxBEV

Evening Rain. Po Chü-i. NDACCP, *tr.* by David Hinton

Evening rain drips on the steps. Tune: "Joy of Returning to the Fields." Huang T'ing-chien. ColAnChi, *tr.* by James Robert Hightower

Evening red and morning gray. *Unknown.* FaBoVe

Evening rises toward the mountain trails. Night in a Room by the River. Tu Fu [*or* Du Fu]. AWTN; CrYelRi, *tr.* by Sam Hamill

Evening Sail, The. George Crabbe. TreFP

Evening Scene, An. Bei Dao. VCWP, *tr.* by Chen Maiping and Bonnie S. McDougall

Evening Shower in Spring, An. Tu Fu [*or* Du Fu]. CCL1, *tr.* by John Francis Davis

Evening Sin, The. Henry Kirke White. STuOW *Fr.* Clifton Grove.

Evening slips you into it, has kept a place for you, The. Tonight of Yesterday. Vona Groarke. NIrP; StAl

Evening Song. Sherwood Anderson. GM

Evening Song. Sherwood Anderson. PoA 2002

Evening Song. Ralph J., Jr. Mills. IllVoic

Evening Song. Elizabeth Madox Roberts. APT-1

Evening Song. Jean Toomer. APT-2; GT

Evening Song. Philipp von Zesen. GePo, *tr.* by George C. Schoolfield

Evening Star. Edward Hirsch. TiP2

Evening Star. Francisco Segovia. RMCMP, *tr.* by Michael Wiegers

Evening Star, The. Pablo Antonio Cuadra. TCLAP, *tr.* by Ann McCarthy de Zavala and Grace Schulman

Evening Star, The. Henry Wadsworth Longfellow. APN-1

Evening Star who gathers everything. Sappho. SaLy; WPoS, *tr.* by Diane Rayor

Evening Stroll. Ema Saikō. WoPoe, *tr.* by Conrad Totman

Evening Stroll, The; or, The Poet. Henry Kirke White. STuOW

Evening sunlight aswim with the river mist. Harmonizing with Great Officer Yan's Poem "The Start of the Fine Weather." Yu Hsin. CCL1, *tr.* by John Frodsham

Evening traffic homeward burns. Before Disaster. Yvor Winters. OxBoAm

Evening Trumpet. Boris Hristov. CSCBP, *tr.* by Georgi Belev and Lisa Sapinkopf

Evening View as the Snow Clears. Chia Tao. CCL1, *tr.* by Stephen Owen

Evening View from Grass Hill. Gensei. WoPoe, *tr.* by Burton Watson

Evening Walk. Yannis Ritsos. MotU, *tr.* by Martin McKinsey

Evening Walk. Charles Simic. PoA 2002

Evening Walk, An. J. H. Prynne. PFTM-2

Evening Walk, The. Nazim Hikmet. AF

Evening, water in a glass, The. George Oppen. APT-2; PFTM-1

Evening will come. Evening—Sail. Ian Hamilton Finlay. NePenScot

Evening wind. Buson. EH, *tr.* by Robert Hass

Evening Wind. William Carpenter. PoSol

Evening Wind. Robert Mezey. PoSol

Evening with Stars. Srikanth Reddy. LegDan

Evening's End. Leon Stokesbury. BAP-97

Evenings ever more willing lapse into my world's evening. Denis Devlin. ModIr *Fr.* Memoirs of a Turcoman Diplomat.

Evening's getting cold and old, The. Valse Triste. Sándor Weöres. IQMS, *tr.* by W. Arthur Boggs

Evenings I hear. Plague of Starlings, A. Robert Earl Hayden. ESEAA; NoAM; WaAnP

Evening's late November, clouds hump and streak, The. Wild Night at Treweithan. Gwyn Williams. AngWePo; TCAWP

Evenings, listening hard. Backgrounds. Moniza Alvi. NeBl

Evening—Sail. Ian Hamilton Finlay. NePenScot

Evening-Star. Louise Bogan. APT-2

Evenlode, The. Joseph Hilaire Pierre Belloc. OxAEP-2

Evensong. Marc Cohen. KGB

Evensong. Paul Gerhardt. GePo, *tr.* by Ingrid Waløe-Engel

Evensong. Robert Herrick. BASC

Evensong. Robert Louis Stevenson. ITBLP

Event. Kim Addonizio. MoASP

Event, The. Rita Dove. ESEAA; NoAM

Event, The. Rita Dove. NAAL-5; NAMCP V.2 *Fr.* Thomas and Beulah.

Event, The. Thomas Sturge Moore. OBMV

Event for Late Afternoon. Mieko Shiomi. WhBo

Event he foresees for each of us—a reckoning, our own. (LL) Last Things. William Meredith. NAMCP V.2; NoAM

Event on the Street, An. Daniil Kharms. AF

Even-Tempered Girl Holds Her Breath, An. Lorenzo Thomas. AnSo

Events Like Palaces. Paz Molina. TANSG, *tr.* by Steven F. White

Events strangely irrelevant as. Party Crash. René Ricard. AHA

Ever a toiling *child* doth make us sad.   Caroline Elizabeth Norton.   VWP *Fr.* Voice from the Factories, A.

Ever a voice is pleading at my heart.   Voice of Memory in Exile, from a Home in Ashes, The.   William Gilmore Simms.   AmWaPo

Ever at night have I looked up for thee.   Planet Jupiter, The.   Epes Sargent.   APN-1

Ever expanding in the bosom of God, the human imagination! (LL)   William Blake.   NPBRoP; WaAnP *Fr.* Jerusalem.

Ever let the Fancy roam.   Fancy.   John Keats.   OBEV

Ever mine [*or* myn] hap[pe] is slack and slo[w] in coming [*or* commyng].   Petrarch.   OBVE

Ever perfect, ever in them- / selves eternal [*or*; eternall]. (LL)   Thomas Campion.   NAEL-6v1; NAEL-7v1; NoP-4; NoP-5; NOSC; TFi; TRP; WaAnP *Fr.* Observations in the Art of English Poesie.

Ever since childhood this constant traveler.   Ballad: The Boatman's Song.   Pao Chao.   CCL1, *tr. by* Joseph R. Allen

Ever since I left home.   Han-shan (Cold Mountain).   ColAnChi, *tr. by* Red Pine

Ever since i was knee high to a grasshopper they said i had cute cheeks.   Marble surfaces.   Joanne Burns.   BMAP

Ever since I was small.   Zombies.   Felix Morisseau-Leroy.   OGAHCP, *tr. by* Boadiba and Jack Hirschman

Ever since Miss Susan Johnson lost her jockey, Lee.   Yellow Dog Blues.   William Christopher Handy.   NAAPv.2

Ever since my heart took such a tumble.   Will You Still Be Mine?   Tom Adair.   ReLy

Ever since school.   My Last Name.   Nicolás Guillén.   TCLAP, *tr. by* Robert Marquez and David Arthur McMurray

Ever since the lucky night I found you.   Don't Blame Me.   Dorothy Fields.   ReLy

Ever since the painter depicted.   Finishing Touch.   Martha Serpas.   Vesp

Ever since the time when I was a lusty boy.   Realizing the Futility of Life.   Po Chü-i.   CCL1, *tr. by* Arthur Waley

Ever since they'd left the Tennessee ridge.   Rita Dove.   ESEAA; NAAL-5; NAMCP V.2; NoAM *Fr.* Thomas and Beulah.

Ever since you went away.   Poem Sent to a Traveler.   Pao Ling-hui.   CCL1, *tr. by* Anne Birrell

Ever singing "Die, oh die." (LL)   Phantom-Wooer, The.   Thomas Lovell Beddoes.   NAEL-6v2; WaAnP

Ever So, Between.   Valerie Martínez.   NAPBL

Ever the poet *from* the land.   Ralph Waldo Emerson.   TCAPo *Fr.* Quatrains.

Ever will the coward.   Brave Coward, The.   Menke Katz.   Prolet, *tr. by* Amelia Glaser

Ever-blissful Kali.   Kamalākānta Bhattācārya.   SinGod, *tr. by* Rachel Fell McDermott

Everest.   Kimiko Hahn.   PrTe

Ever-Fixed Mark, An.   Kingsley Amis.   NAMCP V.2; NoAM

Evergreen, atremble and unsaid. (LL)   Seamus Heaney.   IrLP; NoP-5 *Fr.* Glanmore Revisited.

Evergreen shadow and the pale magnolia, The.   Souls Lake.   Robert Fitzgerald.   APT-2

Evergreen, The.   John Frederick Nims.   APT-2

Everlasting Astronauts, The.   Tom Buchan.   EdScPo

Everlasting Gospel, The.   William Blake.
   "Vision of Christ that thou dost see, The."   ChIV-2
   "Was Jesus Chaste? or did he."   ChIV-2
   "Was Jesus Humble? or did he."   ChIV-2

Everlasting Mercy, The.   John Masefield.
   "From '41 to '51."   SacPr

Everlasting night, An. (LL)   Hymn[e] to Christ, at the Author's Last Going into Germany, A.   John Donne.   BASC; NAEL-6v1; NAEL-7v1; NOSC; NPeEn; OxAEP-1; SacPr

Everlasting omen of what is. (LL)   Often I Am Permitted to Return to a Meadow.   Robert Duncan.   ColAP; HarvBoo; NAMCP V.2; OxBoAm; PFTM-2; PmAP; WaAnP

Everlasting Quail.   Sam Witt.   NeAmPo

Everlasting universe of things, The.   Mont Blanc.   Percy Bysshe Shelley.   BrAP; NAEL-6v2; NAEL-7v2; NIP-4; NOBRP; NoP-4; NoP-5; NPBRoP

Everlasting Wrong, The.   Po Chü-i.   CCL1, *tr. by* H. A. Giles

Everly Brothers, The.   Floyd Skloot.   SwNoth

Evermore, wher-so-evere I be.   *Unknown.*   OHMEL

Everness.   Jorge Luis Borges.   TCLAP, *tr. by* Richard Wilbur

Every being is immortal, says the first Goddess.   Goddesses, The.   Janine Canan.   HW

Every Blessed Day.   Philip Levine.   BeAl

Every branch big with it.   Snow in the Suburbs.   Thomas Hardy.   MoBrPo; OBMV

Every Breath (I lied to myself).   Every Breath.   Claire Malroux.   YaTCFP, *tr. by* Marilyn Hacker

Every Bullet Has Its Billet.   *Unknown.*   FaBoWar

Every Cache.   Robert Johnstone.
   "He's a high clear forehead."   PNI
   "Various instants I'm not with you."   PNI

Every car drones a radio.   Mondrian's Forest.   Wendy Battin.   AmWaPo

Every Chapter of the World.   Dionne Brand.
   "Today then, her head is thudding."   OpeFie

Every child may joy to hear. (LL)   William Blake.   ChAP; ClHu; HeIP-4; NoP-4; NOxBChV; SoSe-8; TFi *Fr.* Songs of Innocence.

Every connection is a revelation.   In the Parlour.   Martin Mooney.   NIrP

Every corner or alley, every moment's good.   First Year.   Vittorio Sereni.   PML, *tr. by* Marcus Perryman and Peter Robinson

Every dawn, while the refugee camp is still asleep, I rise from my bed and before I go to the toilet.   Honey Fig.   Nasri Hajjaj.   Eno, *tr. by* Ibrahim Muhawi

Every Day.   Ingeborg Bachmann.   CFP; PoSu, *tr. by* Daniel Huws

Every Day.   Ingeborg Bachmann.   StAl, *tr. by* Peter Filkins

Every Day.   Ingeborg Bachmann.   GTCP, *tr. by* Reinhold Grimm and Irmgard Hunt

Every day.   Sun-Dial, The.   Adelaide Crapsey.   APT-1; NAAPv.2

Every day.   Heart and Soul.   Assotto Saint.   CAGL

Every day a wilderness—no.   Dusting.   Rita Dove.   AmAlph; ESEAA; HeIP-4; NAMCP V.2; PoA 2002

Every day a wilderness—no.   Rita Dove.   NAAL-5; NoP-5; WaAnP *Fr.* Thomas and Beulah.

Every day another broken heart.   Fat Chance.   Beth Gylys.   AmPoNex

Every day at work I see suited.   Stormy Lear.   Ken Pobo.   IaFF

Every Day Characters.   Winthrop Mackworth Praed.
   Belle of the Ball-Room, The.   NOBRP
   Vicar, The.   OBEV; OxAEP-2

Every day God pats my head and calls me.   Ophelia's Confession.   Tracey Herd.   BeAl; StAl

Every day I burn a stick of incense.   Joanne Kyger.   BB

Every day I create for you.   Last Flower, The.   Nova Ray.   WhBo

Every day I did not spend in solitude was wasted. (LL)   After Long Busyness.   Robert Bly.   CAP-8; OxBoAm

Every day I dig you up.   Habit.   Ruth Stone.   InoFa

Every day / i find a new life.   Daybreak.   Sterling Plumpp.   OxAAAP

Every day I peruse the box scores for hours.   Baseball and Classicism.   Tom Clark.   ASA; PmAP

Every day I see from my window.   Wild Oats.   Norman Alexander MacCaig.   NePenScot; NPeEn

Every day I try to do something that would make my mother proud of me.   David McFadden.   NLPA

Every Day, Matilde.   Pablo Neruda.   GifTon, *tr. by* William O'Daly

Every day on the way home from.   By the Winding River.   Tu Fu [*or* Du Fu].   CCL1, *tr. by* Kenneth Rexroth

Every day Ophelia.   Theatrum Mundi.   Günter Kunert.   GTCP, *tr. by* Reinhold Grimm

Every day our bodies separate.   Villanelle.   Marilyn Hacker.   MakPoe

Every day our name is changed.   Lake Song.   Colette Inez.   PLBUT

Every day, / She does this duty several times.   Aïda.   Alaa Khalid.   AnVo, *tr. by* Mohamed Enani

Every day / she tiptoes through a minefield of emotions.   N.   Kiini Ibura Salaam.   BRtP

Every day when I returned home.   Habitude.   Yousif al-Sa'igh.   IrPoTo, *tr. by* Chuck Miller and Saadi A. Simawe

Every evening a mother makes up another episode of the same story for her son.   Transmutation.   Gael Turnbull.   BeAl

Every evening, at the same time, Tea Boy comes into the shop.   Myth of Tea Boy, The.   Leontia Flynn.   NIrP

Every evening, bent over the bright.   Valerio Magrelli.   NeIt

Every evening now throughout the summer. (LL)   Cold Spring, A.   Elizabeth Bishop.   ColAP; ItP

Every evening when I come home.   Supper.   Yousif al-Sa'igh.   IrPoTo, *tr. by* Saadi A. Simawe

Every family has a genius.   Invaders from Mars.   Robert Glück.   WiU

Every fear is a desire. Every desire is fear.   Staffordshire Murderer, A.   James Fenton.   NeBrP

Every few nights I walk over here, screen door opened.   Empty House.   James Kimbrell.   LegDan

Every few weeks I see there is an empty chair in our local nursery.   Linor Goralik.   CRWP, *tr. by the* author and Robert Reid

Every few weeks or so, I make.   Queen of Swords, The.   Joanne Limburg.   NeBl

Every few years, down at the Florida Keys.   Death of the Pilot Whales, The.   Peter Meinke.   PBCAP

Every fool.   For Lester.   Reggie Timpson.   BtF

Every foolish drunken poet. Female Genitals, The. Gwerfyl Mechain. EroLit, *tr.* by Dafydd Johnston

Every Friday morning my grandfather. Ancestors. Edward Kamau Brathwaite. NoP-4; NoP-5

Every Friday night we watched the fights. Friday Night Fights, The. Ronald Wallace. PoA 2002

Every game that Harvey plays. Harvey Always Wins. Jack Prelutsky. NTCP

Every girl, without delay, listen intently. Debate between Jane Vaughan of Caergai and Cadwaladr the Poet. Jane Vaughan. EMWP

Every god is lonely, an exile. Breathing, the Endless News, The. Rita Dove. CAP-8; PoA 2002

Every green mountain is the cave of Amitābha Buddha. Enlightenment Song. Great Master Wonhyo. BecRai, *tr.* by Kim Daljin, Kim Won-Chung and Christopher Merrill

Every hour, every moment. "H. D." NALW; NAMCP V.1; NoAM *Fr.* Tribute to the Angels.

Every hour I am disappearing. Prayer. Carole Glasser Langille. Coast

Every Hour in the Day. *Unknown.* SSUS

Every idle desire has died in my breast. Heinrich Heine. WoPoe *Fr.* Dying in Paris.

Every inch of you, a terrible vision, not bear, but virgin! (LL) Elizabeth's War with the Christmas Bear. Norman Dubie. AmAlph; NAMCP V.2; NoAM

Every letter you've read in this whole book was written. Ovid. RomPo *Fr.* Tristia.

Every Life. Brenda Hillman. BodElec

Every life, as it dawns. Every Life. René Char. YaTCFP, *tr.* by James Wright

Every live and dead tree. (LL) Not Knowing. Gary Soto. NoP-4; NoP-5

Every long and wide expanse of sea. Every Wide and Long Expanse of Sea. Maurice Scève. WoPoe, *tr.* by Richard Sieburth

Every man can be like that. Old Man Is Like Moses, The. Vicente Aleixandre. GifTon, *tr.* by Lewis Hyde

(Like Moses on top of the mountain.) RaW

Every Man His Own Cross. Dick Barnes. CalPo

Every man wants to be a stud. Cocks and Mares. Ruth Stone. RaBo

Every map is out of date. Reclaiming our land. Karen Press. TSAP

Every mess I made is mine. Clean that god damned room already. Deena November. IJHIL

Every Metaphor. Milo De Angelis. ItPo, *tr.* by Gayle Ridinger

Every misconception, foolish. Lucille Day. ASA *Fr.* Self-Portrait at the Health Museum.

Every moment came with this fill in the blank quality. Drugged and Hooded into a Prose Poem. Anselm Berrigan. Eno

Every Month. Teresa Porzecanski. MirDau, *tr.* by Roberta Gordenstein

Every morn I lift my head. Ralph Waldo Emerson. APN-1 *Fr.* Monadnoc.

Every morning. Work We Hate and Dreams We Love. Jimmy Santiago Baca. LoL

Every Morning. Claire Malroux. VCWP, *tr.* by Marilyn Hacker

Every morning. Daily Habits. Heberto Padilla. VCWP

Every Morning After Killing Thousands of Angels. VCWP, *tr.* by Christopher Drake

Every morning after sleep. Beautiful World, The. Albert Verwey. TuT, *tr.* by Tony Curtis and Tony Curtis

Every morning, emerald trees. Tune: "Sheep on the Mountain Slope." Liu Chih. ChinPo, *tr.* by Ye Weilian [*or* Yeh Wei-lien *or* Wai-lim Yip]

Every morning he is astounded again. Terminally Ill. Anna Swirszczynska [*or* Swir]. PoSu

Every morning, I. Kenneth Rexroth. APSN; APT-2; NAAPv.2; NAMCP V.1 *Fr.* Love Poems of Marichiko, The.

Every morning I do this. I stop work, and through. Ghosts. William Carpenter. ReTh

Every morning I forget how it is. Poem. Charles Simic. CAP-8

Every morning I get up. To the Tune "A Floating Cloud Crosses Enchanted Mountain." Huang O. WoPoe, *tr.* by Chung Ling and Kenneth Rexroth

Every morning, I look in the mirror. Every Morning in the Mirror. Ch'ôn Yanghûi. EcSo, *tr.* by Aimee N. Kwon

Every morning I see him pedaling past. Engima, The. Alan Bold. ArBi

Every Morning in the Mirror. Ch'ôn Yanghûi. EcSo, *tr.* by Aimee N. Kwon

Every morning, man and wife, seated and washed. Casti Connubi. Marco Martos. PML, *tr.* by Margaret Greer

Every morning the curtain rises. Every Morning. Claire Malroux. VCWP, *tr.* by Marilyn Hacker

Every morning the sun comes, the sun. (LL) Arc Inside and Out, The. A. R. Ammons. NoAM; NoP-4; NoP-5

Every Morning The War Gets Up From Sleep. Fadil Azzawi. IrPoTo, *tr.* by Melissa Brown and Salaam Yousif

Every morning / the world / is created. Morning Poem. Mary Oliver. EMP

Every morning they hold hands. Suburban Lovers. Bruce Dawe. NOBAu

Every morning you return from a long. Morning Roar of the City, The. Slavko Mihalic. PoSu, *tr.* by Charles Simic

Every morning you used to play hooky. Once Upon a Time. Cahit Külebi. NaPG, *tr.* by Talat Sait Halman

Every need analyzed, each personal problem weighed, carefully, and solved according to the circumstance of. Bryce & Tomlins. Kenneth Fearing. APT-2

Every night, as my grandfather sat. Guild, The. Sharon Olds. PoA 2002; RaBo

Every night at this place. Ted's Bar and Grill. Jim Daniels. ReTh

Every night death counts on her fingers. Nocturnal. Romelia Alarcón de Folgar. TANSG, *tr.* by Alison Ridley

Every night I dream we're fighting, armies raise. General John Cabell Breckinridge. Jill Breckinridge. CBCWP

Every night I dream we're fighting, armies raised. Jill Breckinridge. CBCWP *Fr.* Civil Blood.

Every night I place this creature on my table. Last Iraq, The. Fadil Azzawi. IrPoTo, *tr.* by Salaam Yousif

Every night in the moonlight the foxes come down the hill. Foxes in Winter. Mary Oliver. MoW

Every night space junk falls from the sky. Destruction of the Mir, The. Lucia Maria Perillo. RoV

Every night when I went to bed. Brian Merriman. OBVE *Fr.* Midnight Court, The.

Every October it becomes important, no, *necessary*. Leaves. Lloyd Schwartz. UrbNat

Every October millions of little fish come along the shore. Birds and Fishes. Robinson Jeffers. NAAL-5; NoP-4; NoP-5; WaAnP

Every one loved King Matthias, when his charger he rode. King Matthias in Gömör. János Garay. IQMS, *tr.* by James Turner

Every one of these bodies, those in drag, those. Cotillion. Carl Phillips. WiU

Every [*or* Ev'ry] Time I Feel the [*or* de] Spirit. *Unknown.* APN-2

Every other day I am an invalid. Selves, The. Patricia K. Page. BrAP; GPPA

Every other weekend they go to their mother's. Custody. Thomas Lynch. BeAl

Every passage exists simply as a fragment. In the Sulphur Garden. David St. John. AmAlph

Every peak is a crater. This is the law of volcanoes. Adrienne Rich. NALW; NoAM *Fr.* Twenty-one Love Poems.

Every plant is burnt yellow. War Lament. *Unknown.* CrYelRi, *tr.* by Sam Hamill

Every poem. Regeneration. Leo Vroman. TuT, *tr.* by James Liddy

Every poem is a hesitation of history. Tenth.9. Roberto Juarroz. PoetW, *tr.* by Mary Crow

Every poem is made of air. Noise. Ferreira Gullar. TCLAP, *tr.* by Renato Rezende

Every season has its dead. Maurizio Cucchi. ItPo, *tr.* by Gayle Ridinger

Every shack has its girl-next-door. Every Shack. Anne Portugal. YaTCFP, *tr.* by Norma Cole

Every silver. 9.1.59: VI. Pablo Picasso. CLPP, *tr.* by Paul Blackburn

Every single instant begins another new year. At the New Year. John Hollander. TaR

Every so often he jumps, just to make it clear that he is essentially immobile. Toad, The. Juan José Arreola. MotU, *tr.* by W. S. Merwin

Every stance seemed crooked. He had. Saint Ras. Anthony McNeill. WaCA

Every step the sidewalks span. Men. Dora Teitelboim. Prolet, *tr.* by Amelia Glaser

Every stinking son of a bitch. Peace, So That. Greg Kuzma. AmWaPo

Every street kid in Bombay knows. My Required Tool. Justin Cain. MAAN

Every summer. Lemonade Stand. Myra Cohn Livingston. TLR

Every summer. Braly Street. Gary Soto. GeoHom; UnSA

Every Thing. Harold Monro. MoBrPo

Every thing that gains a shape. Plasnewydd Square. Christopher Meredith. TCAWP

Every Thursday, every Thursday. Plaza de Mayo. Dacia Maraini. CFP, *tr.* by Gail Wronsky

Every time I am bound towards you. Choking. Saniyya Salih. PoArWo, *tr.* by Kamal Boullata

Every time I approach this borrowed hearth I see the face. Flame On. Rebecca Wolff. IIR

Every Time I Climb A Tree. David McCord. NTCP

Every time I climb a tree. Five Chants. David McCord. NOxBChV

Every time I go by the train. Blind Beggar, The. Viswanatha Satyanarayana. HotL, *tr.* by V. Narayana Rao

Every time I hear that march from Lohengrin. Makin' Whoopee. Gustave Kahn. OBCoV

(Ev'rytime I hear that march from Lohengrin.) ReLy

Every time I see you. If You Want. Lenous Surprice. OGAHCP, *tr. by* Boadiba and Jack Hirschman

Every time I think about us women. Sacred Trees. Jayne Cortez. SurWo

Every time I tried to put the eight ball. Eight Ball. Richard Jackson. SwNoth

Every time the bucks went clattering. Earthy Anecdote. Wallace Stevens. SAmP

Every Time We Say Goodbye. James Cushing. SeSe

Every time you hear me sing this song. Railroad Blues, The. *Unknown.* GM

Every town with black Catholics has a St. Peter Claver's. St. Peter Claver. Toi Derricotte. LTA; PBCAP

Every village has its village idiot. It Took a Village. Stephanie Brown. AmPoNex

Every weekday morning heading east. Silver-Paced. Bruce Berger. UrbNat

Every Where and Every When. Arthur Sze. FTuHH; OpBo

Every Wide and Long Expanse of Sea. Maurice Scève. WoPoe, *tr. by* Richard Sieburth

Every wild she-bird has nest and mate in the warm April weather. Virgin Martyr, The. Ada Cambridge. NOBAu

Every Winged Fowl of the Air. Colette Bryce. NIrP

Every wise child is sad. Tearing the Page. Li-Young Lee. FaoP

Every woman has a tomb in her body. About Women. Ch'oe Sûngja. EcSo, *tr. by* Mickey Hong

Every word is a doubt. Roberto Juarroz. VCWP *Fr.* Eleventh Vertical Poetry.

Every year the harvest of its flowers will be reaped by others. (LL) Fēng Mèng-lung. ColAnChi; WoPoe *Fr.* Mountain Songs.

Every year without knowing it I have passed the day. For the Anniversary of My Death. W. S. Merwin. BeAl; CAP-8; ColAP; GoPo; NAMCP V.2; OxBoAm; PoPoPo; VCAP; WaAnP

Every year you said it wasn't worth the trouble. Crab Apple Jelly. Vicki Feaver. BeAl

Every young woman in the world. Young Woman's Complaint about Her Sweetheart, A. Elen Gwdman. EMWP

Everybody. Mark Levine. AmPoNex

Everybody can tell you the date of George Washington's birth. Watchman, What of the First First Lady? Ogden Nash. AmWit

Everybody else, then, going. Exeunt Omnes. Thomas Hardy. FaBoVe; UV

Everybody has a car. Philip Whalen. WANABP *Fr.* Epigrams & Imitations.

Everybody knows her, for they see her every day. Pay Your Debts. Mrs. Henry Linden. CBWP-4

Everybody loved Yona. Real Love Isn't What It Seems. Dahlia Ravikovitch. DTA, *tr. by* Chana Bloch

Everybody says. Edge, The. Paul Jamal. BtF

Everybody Says don't. Stephen Sondheim. ReLy

Everybody was going on talking the same talk. Mariya Kildibekova. CRWP, *tr. by* Roy Fisher

Everybody who's anybody longs to be a tree. Horse and Tree. Rita Dove. TRP

Everybody's singing, they call it that. Singing. Geoff Hattersley. NeBl

Everyday. Abd al-Rahim Salih al-Rahim. IrPoTo, *tr. by* Ralph Saverese and Saadi A. Simawe

Everyday. Indian Girl. Lenard D. Moore. GT

Everyday Alchemy. Genevieve Taggard. APT-2; NAAPv.2

Everyday / I think about dying. Survivor. Roger McGough. OBCoV

Everyday is a reenactment of the creation story. Post-colonial Tale, A. Joy Harjo. BodElec; PrTe

Everyday / it is hard. Those i love are sometimes white. Imani Tolliver. BtF

Everyday, we step off the bus. MacArthur High School. Lacey A. Dalby. BeDoSh

Everydays homecoming at sidewalk university / harlem campus. Independent Study. Paul Beatty. AmPoNex

Everyman. Siegfried Sassoon. MoBrPo

Everyman. *Unknown.* NAWM-5v1

Everyone agrees, / when you visit New Zealand. My Father in New Zealand. George Bowering. BrAP

Everyone at Lake Kearney had a nickname. Sway. Louis Simpson. NoAM

Everyone at the same time if everyone at the same time. Team Effort. Bob Hicok. AmAlph

Everyone cheered her on. Grandmother, Dead at 99 Years and 10 Months. William Matthews. PuP-23

Everyone / combines skins. On the Rails. Reed Bye. AHA

Everyone complains about the nose. Nose, The. Ruth Stone. InvLad

Everyone cries for love. Student's Tale, The. George Elliott Clarke. OpeFie

Everyone else may leave you, I will never leave you, fugitive. (LL) Under Voice, The. Jean Valentine. BodElec; CAP-8; ExTi

Everyone else says otherwise. They take me. I Was Born in Lucerne. Philip Levine. CAP-8

Everyone grumbled. The sky was gray. Daddy Fell into the Pond. Alfred Noyes. ChAP; NOxBChV

Everyone had to know something, and what they said. In Memory of Robert Frost. William Meredith. VisFro

Everyone has only one leg. Great Infirmities. Charles Simic. ChAP

Everyone hates the gaudy slave trader, with good reason. Gaudy Slave Trader. Wayne Koestenbaum. KGB

Everyone here wears a full head of dark hair. Mornings. Midlife. Robin Becker. BodElec

Everyone in Genthe's famous photographs of the San Francisco earthquake and fire is well dressed. Images of the San Francisco Disaster. Larry Kramer. GeoHom

Everyone in here hates. That is why this place is called a clinic. Cure, The. Eugene Wildman. OPRER

Everyone in me is a bird. In Celebration of My Uterus. Anne Sexton. CAP-8; NALW

Everyone in this room. Conference, A. Renée Weiss and Theodore Weiss. BodElec

Everyone knew about it before long. Nightjar. John McAuliffe. NIrP

Everyone knows. Dylan Iorwerth. BBMWP *Fr.* Sand.

Everyone knows it was swampland. Mickey Mouse. Christopher Murray. BeDoSh

Everyone knows that time unfolds. Wind Domes, The. Joyelle McSweeney. LegDan

Everyone knows that under her robes. Why a Woman Can't Be Pope. Sandra Kohler. FiBr

Everyone knows this world will not be ruined. İzzet Molla. OLP, *tr. by* Walter Andrews, Najaat Black and Mehmet Kalpakli

Everyone looked away. Father on My Shoulders. Harry Thurston. Coast

Everyone Sang. Siegfried Sassoon. MoBrPo; NAEL-6v2; NAEL-7v2; NAMCP V.1; NoAM; NoP-4; NoP-5; NPeEn; OBEV; OBWP; OPOU; StAl; WaAnP

Everyone says he's depressed. Friends. Bill Kushner. PA9/11

Everyone says / what they do. Life Is a Killer. John Giorno. PmAP

Everyone seems to be waiting for it. It. Roger Mitchell. PoCoUp

Everyone sees. Mugoku Osho's Snow Poem. Muso Soseki. EaWin, *tr. by* W. S. Merwin

Everyone silent, moving. . .Take my hand. / Speak to me. (LL) Effort at Speech between Two People. Muriel Rukeyser. ItP; MoAmPo; NAAL-5; WaAnP

Everyone stands alone at the heart of this earth. And Suddenly It Is Evening. Salvatore Quasimodo. WoPoe, *tr. by* J. Ruth Gendler

Everyone suddenly burst out singing. Everyone Sang. Siegfried Sassoon. MoBrPo; NAEL-6v2; NAEL-7v2; NAMCP V.1; NoAM; NoP-4; NoP-5; NPeEn; OBEV; OBWP; OPOU; StAl; WaAnP

Everyone waiting reading the coverless magazines. Angels of Mercy. Bob Hicok. AmAlph

Everyone Was Drunk. Jean Valentine. LaCa

Everyone was happier. But where did the sadness go? People wanted to know. Crowds Cheered as Gloom Galloped Away, The. Matthea Harvey. IAoNAP

Everyone who made love the night before. Saturday Morning. Hugo Williams. GoPo

Everyone Who Wants to Work Can. Brooke Wiese. OPRER

Everyone's born with an empty body. Drinking Alone. Wang Fan-chih. CrYelRi, *tr. by* Sam Hamill

Everyone's dancing where I live. Zali Gurevitch. FIT, *tr. by* Robert Friend

Everyone's flocking to Gajan. Mahendranāth Bhattācārya. SinGod, *tr. by* Rachel Fell McDermott

Everyone's here, and because I love old things, I've rented a grand. Old House Blues. William Kulik. BodElec

Everyone's on about Walter's willy. Underneath the Archers *or* What's All This about Walter's Willy? Kit Wright. OBCoV

Everyone's sick! The soldiers poison the air. (LL) From Trollope's Journal. Elizabeth Bishop. AmWaPo; CBCWP; PoAgWa

Everything about the young foreign taxidermist was overdone. Mustache, The. Sabrina Orah Mark. LegDan

Everything and Nothing. Jorge Luis Borges. PoetW, *tr. by* Anthony Kerrigan

Everything but everything. Snapshot. Lajos Kassák. IQMS, *tr. by* Edwin Morgan

Everything but His Face perishes. Rosa Mystica. John Gwyn Griffiths. BBMWP, *tr. by* Richard Poole

Everything can be grown from seed—only stipulation. Summer Seeming. John Riley. Oth

Everything / can be retouched. Need for Censorship, The. Reiner Kunze. PoSu, *tr. by* Michael Hamburger

Everything Changes. Cicely Herbert. OPOU

Everything closes in. The wind from sea. Thursday. Thomas James Jones. BBMWP, *tr. by* Jon Dressel

Everything! Counter and scales. Business Reverses. Edgar Lee Masters. ChIV-2

Everything crumbles like a spoon of salt in the meal's entropy. Ticklish Moments. Pedro Serrano. RMCMP, *tr.* by Geoff Hargreaves

Everything declines after reaching perfection, therefore let no man be beguiled by the sweetness of a pleasant life. Abū al-Baqā Sālih ibn Alī Rundī. HiArP, *tr.* by James T. Monroe

Everything: Eloy, Arizona, 1956. Ai. BodElec

Everything else remained the same. This is why, you said, there was no fiction. (LL) Rosmarie Waldrop. FTOS; PFTM-2 *Fr.* Reproduction of Profiles, The.

Everything ended with the Honeymoon. Loyal Housewife. Daisy Zamora. LoL, *tr.* by Margaret Randall

Everything fades, turning into grey. What Will Come of This? Jenő Dsida. IQMS, *tr.* by Adam Makkai

Everything falls asleep with sleep. Passenger Opposite, The. Elma Mitchell. NePenScot

Everything gets forgotten. Vyacheslav Kupriyanov. TCRusP, *tr.* by Pamela Davidson

Everything Good Between Men and Women. C. D. Wright. GPPA

Everything happens / In an Egypt of aerial corridors. Murilo Mendes. Eno *Fr.* Chaos's Window.

Everything Happens to Me. Tom Adair. ReLy

Everything Happens to (Monk and) Me. Brenda Marie Osbey. BodElec

Everything has a place. Landscape. Johanna Kruit. TuT, *tr.* by Micheal O'Siadhail

Everything has changed, though nothing has. After the Terror. Jay Parini. WaAnP

Everything has come true. The punishment fits the crime. Svetlana Kekova. ItGoST, *tr.* by Judith Hemschemeyer

Everything has its limit, including sorrow. To Urania. Joseph Brodsky. AF, *tr.* by the author and Joseph Brodsky

Everything has lasted till today. Unknown Soldier, The. Alun Lewis. MoBrPo

Everything has ripened. Listening to Dvorak's Serenade in E. Colette Inez. MiVo

Everything I can think of right now. Three Hymns for Aphrodite. V. B. Price. ICANM

Everything I do is against meaning. Against Meaning. Andrei Codrescu. PmAP

Everything I do is stitched with its color. (LL) Separation. W. S. Merwin. NoP-4; NoP-5

Everything I Have Is Yours. Harold Adamson. ReLy

Everything I Need to Know I Learned in Kindergarten. Martin Jude Farawell. OPRER

Everything I steal, I give away. Gift of Tongues, The. Sam Hamill. GifTon

Everything I want to say. Stinking Rose, The. Sujata Bhatt. HarvBoo

Everything I will learn in this life. Memory Span of a Goldfish Is Three Seconds, The. Traci Paris. ICANM

Everything in Its Place. Arthur Guiterman. AmWit; NBLV; OBCoV

Everything in matter changes its state. Three States and Three Kingdoms. Alberto Blanco. RMCMP, *tr.* by Joan Lindgren

Everything in motion! Wind of Our Going: Adagio Ma Non Troppo. Patricia Goedicke. MiVo

Everything in the Garden is Lovely. Alasdair Aston. OBGa

Everything is capable of being broken. Relative Heat Index. Alan Gilbert. FreRad

Everything is forgiven. After the First Snow. David Keller. NevBe

Everything Is Going to Be All Right. Derek Mahon. BeAl; PBCIP; PoCu

Everything is light. Archipelago (Interra Diocesan). A. Di Michele. AnSo

Everything is loud: the rasp of bed-sheets. My Life Asleep. Jo Shapcott. BeAl; NeBrP

Everything is natural, from the cotton summer. Bosegran. Kathleen Jamie. GPPA

Everything is out today. Larry Fagin. AHA *Fr.* Parade of the Caterpillars, The.

Everything Is Peaches Down in Georgia. Grant Clarke. ReLy

Everything is plundered, betrayed, sold. Anna Andreyevna Akhmatova. WPoS

Everything is quiet, and the night is clear. Reply to Sir Kukwon's "Sleeping in the Temple in Autumn." Daegak Euchon. BecRai, *tr.* by Kim Daljin, Kim Won-Chung and Christopher Merrill

Everything is real. Doin'. Atiba Kwabena. BRtP

Everything Is Swept Away by the Brief Year. Francisco de Quevedo y Villegas. SpanPo, *tr.* by Kate Flores

Everything is Your wish, Tara. Naracandra Rāy. SinGod, *tr.* by Rachel Fell McDermott

Everything leans, like tottering, hunched old women. Closed Town, The. *Unknown, fr. Terezin Concentration Camp.* INSAB

Everything opaque about us, perhaps. Anthony Wilson. NewEx

Everything passes and vanishes. William Allingham. NPeEn; OxBEV; WaAnP

Everything rubs me the wrong way. I can't stand dancing any more. Ghost Street. Milán Füst. IQMS, *tr.* by Jess Perlman

Everything she finds she drags home. Twentieth Century Children (2). Beckian Fritz Goldberg. AmAlph

Everything she wants she sees. Traveler. Valerie Martínez. TouFir

Everything shifts: orange hills. Tuscarora. Jan Heller Levi. PfS

Everything sounds funny in a funny magazine. Paper on Humor. Andrei Codrescu. PmAP

Everything stands wondrously multicolored. Woolworth's. Mark Irwin. GoPo

Everything started again in a harbor. Sea, the Memory, and the Woman, The. Seyfettin Başçillar. NaPG, *tr.* by Talat Sait Halman

Everything takes a longer time. The rains. I Want to Write like a Postcard. Rebecca Radner. WhBo

Everything That Acts Is Actual. Denise Levertov. NoAM

Everything that happens to me these days. Julia Alvarez. FFC *Fr.* ("33").

Everything That Man Esteems. William Butler Yeats. TWF *Fr.* Resurrection, The.

Everything that's happened once could happen again. (LL) Even the Trees. Jackie Kay. MFPA; NeBrP

Everything the Power of the World Does is Done in a Circle. Black Elk. AmFaPo

Everything this generation has told me. (LL) Isaiah by Kerosene Lantern Light. Robert Harris. ChIV-1; NOBAu

Everything to Declare. Frank Mkalawile Chipasula. NAfrP

Everything vanishes. The line of rain. Architecture of the Wings, The. Amy Newman. IAoNAP

Everything wants to be water. Ill-fated Water, The. Efraín Bartolomé. RMCMP, *tr.* by Asa Zatz

Everything was happening for the first time. As we travelled through. There. Philip Mead. BMAP

Everything was put to use. Seven Words, The. Jerzy Ficowski. PoSu, *tr.* by Keith Bosley and Krystyna Wandycz

Everything we don't understand. X. Amina Baraka. BRtP

Everything we know about death. Altruism. Dionisio D. Martinez. TouFir

Everything we look upon is blest. (LL) Dialogue of Self and Soul, A. William Butler Yeats. MoBrPo; NAEL-6v2; NAEL-7v2; NAMCP V.1; NoAM

Everything we stand up in. Spectrum. Aidan Carl Mathews. PBCIP

Everything white, the lake's cheek, turns. Trompe L'Oeil in Winter. Mary Ann Samyn. AmPoNex

Everything will be forsaken then. Apocrypha. János Pilinszky. PoSu, *tr.* by Ted Hughes

Everything You Own. Gerald Costanzo. GifTon

Everything you see, Reader, in the little book before you. To the Reader. Elizabeth Jane Leon. EMWP

Everything's a metaphor, some wise. History. Rita Dove. ExTi; FFC; WaAnP

Everything's Coming Up Roses. Stephen Sondheim. ReLy

Everything's equal now. Blue leash blue bike. School of Fish. Eileen Myles. WiU

Everything's just as it was: fine hard snow. Guest, The. Anna Andreyevna Akhmatova. RaBo; WoPoe, *tr.* by Vera Dunham and Jane Kenyon

Everything's / so far away. Sadness of Leaving, The. Eileen Myles. PmAP

Everytime a thunderstorm comes. My Mother is a God Fearing Woman. Cornelius Eady. ISC

Everytime you weep, I feel the surface. Letters from Home. Elmaz Abinader. PoArWo

Everywhere, a reason for caution. Wedding Gifts. Adrienne Su. NAPBL

Everywhere / At once. (LL) As for Poets. Gary Snyder. BB; PmAP; WhBo

Everywhere barricades. Bardo of War and Peace. Janet Rodney. ICANM

Everywhere else in the country, if someone asks. New Yorkers. Edward Field. GoPo

Everywhere, everywhere, following me. Bayard Taylor. APN-2 *Fr.* Echo Club, The.

Everywhere, *everywhere*, snow sifting down. Manna. Joseph Stroud. CalPo; GeoHom

Everywhere I go it's the same old thing. Kitchen. Twain Dooley. IJHIL

Everywhere I Go, There I Am. Robert Pinsky. PfSP *Fr.* City Elegies.

Everywhere I look in the garden. Déjeuner Sur l'Herbe. Bruce Beaver. BMAP

Everywhere Is out of Town. Kevin Young. FuFl

Everywhere of Silver, An. Emily Dickinson. TCAPo

Everywhere / soft breeze warm sunshine. Spring Cliff. Muso Soseki. EaWin, *tr.* by W. S. Merwin

Everywhere the. Jacques Roubaud. YaTCFP, *tr.* by the author

Everywhere the Earth Is Opening. Jennifer Richter. FiBr

Everywhere the material world is speaking to me. One Explanation of Beauty. Mark Wunderlich. AmPoNex

Everywhere there was a bush and a bird in it. Map. Michele Glazer. IAoNAP

Everywhere / they go. Plantings. Catalina Cariaga. AFaM

Everywhere / under objects. Everywhere the. Jacques Roubaud. YaTCFP, *tr. by the author*

Everywhere we are either moving away from. For the Woman with the Radio. Malena Mörling. AmPoNex

Everywhere You Eat. Kalamu ya Salaam. SpirFl *Fr.* New Orleans Haiku.

Eve's Apology in Defense of Women. Emilia Lanier. NAEL-7v1

Eve's Monologue. Bella Abramovna Dizhur. ItGoST, *tr. by* Sarah Bliumis

Eves of autumn. Brambleberry, The. Sándor Weöres. IQMS, *tr. by* Adam Makkai and Valerie Becker Makkai

Eve's Striptease. Julia Kasdorf. ACAMVP; NeAmPo

Eve-Song. Mary Gilmore. LW

Eveything I know about you, Grandma Susie. Everything I Know. Carmen Horst. ACAMVP

Eviction. Rafael Alberti. RaW, *tr. by* Rachel Benson

Eviction. Lucille Clifton. NTCP

Eviction. Michelle T. Clinton. ISC

Eviction Fight. N. D. Korman. Prolet, *tr. by* Amelia Glaser

Evidence. Joanna Fuhrman. AmPoNex

Evidence: "He brought her presents." Helen Lamb. EdScPo

Evidence. Dan Pagis. FIT, *tr. by* Robert Friend

Evidence. Toki Zenmaro. CAoMJL1, *tr. by* Makoto Ueda

Evidence everywhere: accumulation. On That Mountain. Rachel Hadas. ExTi

Evidence of *a woman's hard life*. Old Women. Judith Ortiz Cofer. PueRic

Evidence of Death's Voodoo—Inside and Outside the "Gun As Art Exhibit." Wendy Bishop. LiTh

Evidence of Life. Afaa Michael Weaver. NevBe

Evidence on Film, The. Ron Charach. BloBone

Evidence Read at the Trial of the Knave of Hearts. Lewis Carroll. NPeEn *Fr.* Alice's Adventures in Wonderland.

Evidence, The. Tom Leonard. Oth

Evidently she can't hear me. April 27, 1994. Donna Brook. PrTe

Evidently, She Says. Ginger Andrews. SUP

Evil. Langston Hughes. APT-2

Evil. Arthur Rimbaud. OBWP *Fr.* Eighteen-Seventy.

Evil. Arthur Rimbaud. FaBoWar, *tr. by* Norman Cameron

Evil Days, The. Dennis Joseph Enright. OBCoV

Evil Days, The. Boris Leonidovich Pasternak. GI, *tr. by* Nina Kossman

Evil, if rightly understood. On the Origin of Evil. John Byrom. NPeEn

Evil [*or* Evill] spirit, your beauty, haunts me still, An. Michael Drayton. NoSic *Fr.* Idea.

Evil Port. Bernard Bador. ConPit, *tr. by* Clayton Eshleman

Evil Raven, have paper pity upon those. Mac Wellman. HeMarv *Fr.* Rat Minaret: Miniaturist-Divan, The.

Evil Time. Hermann Hesse. IJHIL, *tr. by* James Wright

Evil was active in the land. "H. D." HarvBoo; NAAL-5 *Fr.* Walls Do Not Fall, The.

Evil word it is, An / This love. (LL) In Memory of Radio. Imamu Amiri Baraka. BB; NoP-4; NoP-5; RWPCtW

Ev'n from my heart the strings do break. (LL) Thomas Campion. *See* E'en from my heart the strings do break.

Ev'n God himself, being pressed for my sake. (LL) Bunch of Grapes, The. George Herbert. ChIV-1; NAEL-6v1; NAEL-7v1; NOSC

Evoba. Steve McCaffery.

"Can there be a collision between picture and application?" FTOS

Evocación Para Grabarla en una Caja de Música. Luis Rosales. RaW

Evocation of Recife. Manuel Bandeira. TCLAP, *tr. by* Candace Slater

Evocation to Record a Music Box. Luis Rosales. RaW, *tr. by* Ralph Nelson and Rita García Nelson

Evohé. Cristina Peri Rossi. *tr. by* Diana P. Decker

"Tired of women." TANSG, *tr. by* Diana P. Decker

Evolution. Sherman Alexie. NAMCP V.2; NeAmPo; PoPoPo

Evolution. Langdon Smith. BRP

Evolution. John Banister Tabb. APN-2

Evolution fall foul of. Mina Loy. NAMCP V.1 *Fr.* Love Songs to Joannes.

Evolution from the Fish. Robert Bly. NoAM

Evolution of Appetite. Kelleen Zubick. OPRER

Evolution of Lather, The. Michael Portnoy. HeMarv

Evolution on 38th Street. Jack Brannon. UrbNat

Evolutional Erotics. Constance Naden. ViWPN

Natural Selection. VWP

Scientific Wooing. VWP

Solomon Redivivus, 1886. VWP

Evolutionary Randomizer [unsuccessful]. Artificial Terra-cotta Skin Mutagen Mask of Humbaba/Humwawa. Sandy Baldwin. AnSo

Evolving Similarities. Ralph Angel. BodElec

Ev'ry day is a brand new day. If There Is Someone Lovelier Than You. Howard Dietz. ReLy

Ev'ry day seems like a year. Sometimes I'm Happy. Irving Caesar. ReLy

Ev'ry night the same encore. (LL) By the Light of the Silvery Moon. Edward Madden. NAAPv.2; ReLy

Ev'ry rolling stone gets to feel alone. Sentimental Journey. Bud Green. ReLy

Ev'ry state has something. Rhode Island Is Famous for You. Howard Dietz. ReLy

Ev'ry Time. Ralph Blane and Hugh Martin. ReLy

Ev'ry Time We Say Good-bye. Cole Porter. ReLy

Ev'rybody's building the big ships and the boats. Quinn the Eskimo. Bob Dylan. RaBo

Ev'ryone is on the make for something. Make with the Feet. Harold Adamson. ReLy

Ev'rything seems lovely. Because My Baby don't Mean Maybe Now. Walter Donaldson. ReLy

Ev'rything that happens in life. That's Entertainment. Howard Dietz. ReLy

Ev'rything went wrong. Always. Irving Berlin. ReLy

Ev'rytime I hear that march from Lohengrin. Gustave Kahn. *See* Every time I hear that march from Lohengrin.

Evyn as mery as I make myght. *Unknown.* EMWP

Ewan McLachlan, the rickety footbridge. For Ewan McLachlan. R. Gerallt Jones. BBMWP, *tr. by the author*

Ewe's Candy Canes Red Sea Outerbank. Jessica Freeman. AnSo

Ewigkeit. Jorge Luis Borges. WoPoe, *tr. by* Richard Wilbur

Ex- / track. Aram Saroyan. AHA

Ex Vermibus. Hugh MacDiarmid. CABP

Exact beat from, The. Hayden Carruth. StAl *Fr.* Paragraphs.

Exact Fares. David Morley. NLP

Exact Moment of His Death, The. Sharon Olds. NAMCP V.2

Exactly as the setting sun. Glass of Wine, A. Andrew Motion. NeBrP

Exactly at six every evening I go. Dog Days, Jerusalem. Rita Dove. AmAlph

Exactly half the phenomenal world is gone. Half Life. Paul Monette. InoFa

Exactly how to do it. (LL) Prayer to the Muse of Ordinary Life. Kate Daniels. ExTi; PoDa

Exactly like the upper life sleep has. As Endymion. Odysseus Elytis. GifTon, *tr. by* Olga Broumas

Exactly what I am. Amen. (LL) Prayer to Be with Mercurial Women. Roddy Lumsden. BeAl; EdScPo; NeBl

Exaggeration of Despair, The. Sherman Alexie. BAP-97; NeAmPo; PrTe

Exaltatio Humanae Naturae. William Alabaster. NoSic

Examination. StacyLynn. BtF

Examination at the Womb-Door. Ted Hughes. NAEL-6v2; NAEL-7v2; NoP-4; NoP-5

Examination Question. *Unknown.* OBCoV

Examination, The. Priscilla Jane Thompson. CBWP-2

Examining the I. Jean V. Gier. ReBoTo

Example, An. M. Wyrebek. AmPoNex

Example, The. W. H. Davies. MoBrPo

Example, The. Paul Zimmer. OPRER

Example often used to show ?? is x falling feet first into a singularity with a watch on, An. Shared Custody. Brenda Hillman. RoV

Exasperated, worn, you conjure a mansion. Desires of Men and Women. John Berryman. BrAP

Ex-Basketball Player. John Updike. TRP

Ex-Boyfriends Named Michael. Justin Chin. WiU

Excavation, The. Carl Hancock Rux. HeMarv

Excavations. Peter Riley.

169. VaPo

147. 67. VaPo

119. 3. VaPo

175. 123. VaPo

171. 115. VaPo

1134. 39. VaPo

149. Thesis. VaPo

Exceeding brightness of this early sun, The. Sun This March, The. Wallace Stevens. APT-1; HarvBoo

Exceeding sorrow / Consumeth my sad heart! O Mors! Quam Amara Est Memoria Tua Homini Pacem Habenti In Substantiis Suis. Ernest Dowson. OBMV

Excelente Balade of Charitie, An. Thomas Chatterton. OxAEP-1

Excellence in the Small. Tears Frozen on Your Face. Lorna Crozier. IFF

Excellent Brutus, of all human race. Brutus. Abraham Cowley. BASC

Excellent Epitaffe of Syr Thomas Wyat, An. Henry Howard, Earl of Surrey. NPeEn

Excellent Epitaph of Sir Thomas Wyatt, An. Henry Howard, Earl of Surrey. *See* Wyatt Resteth Here.

Excellent Wigglesworth, Remembered by some Good Tokens, The. Cotton Mather. SacPr

Excelsior [*see* Shades of Night, The *by* Housman *for par.*]. Henry Wadsworth Longfellow. BRP; GoPo; NAAL-3; OBSP; STuOW; TCAPo; UV

Excelsior. Walt Whitman. SAmP

Except for love everything. Tatiana Shcherbina. CRWP, *tr. by* J. Kates

Except for my body, who accompanies me. Psalm before Sleep. Peter Cooley. Vesp

Except for shoes. Impediment. Stephen Dunn. PoSol

Except for the dog, that she wouldn't have him put away, wouldn't let him die, I'd have liked her. Dog, The. C. K. Williams. BodElec

Except for what is very old (the failing). In the General Area of North Texas. Scott Cairns. TiP2

Except my hart which you beestow'd before. Mary Sidney Wroth, Countess of Montgomery. EMWP *Fr.* Pamphilia to Amphilanthus.

Except my h[e]art which you bestowed [*or* beestow'd] be[e]fore. (LL) Mary Sidney Wroth, Countess of Montgomery. BASC; EMWP *Fr.* Pamphilia to Amphilanthus.

Except on bodies. (LL) Ants on the Melon. Virginia Hamilton Adair. AFaM; StAl

Except ourselves, we have no other prayer. Without Ceremony. Vassar Miller. MoAmPo

Except the Heaven had come so near. Emily Dickinson. SAmP

Except to prove the sweetness of a shower. (LL) Tall Nettles. Edward Thomas. FaBoVe; MoBrPo; NPeEn; OxBEV

Excepting the diner. Donald Justice. GoPo; StAl *Fr.* American Sketches (for William Carlos Williams).

Exceptions. Felice Belle. BRtP

[Excerpts]. Yusef Komunyakaa. InoFa *Fr.* Songs for My Father.

Excerpts from *The Poem of the Cid. Unknown. tr. by* Paul Blackburn and John Hookham Frere

  Cid Calls His Vassals Together, The. They'll Go into Exile with Him. WoPoe, *tr. by* Paul Blackburn

  Cid Enters Burgos, The. WoPoe, *tr. by* Paul Blackburn

  "Franks come down the hill with a random course, The." FaBoWar, *tr. by* John Hookham Frere

  "Gentlemen, for this day's work our chance has not been ill." FaBoWar, *tr. by* John Hookham Frere

  No One Will Put the Cid up. Only a Small Girl Addresses Him and That to Tell Him to Go Away. The Cid Finds He Has to Make Camp Outside of Town, on the Sand of the Riverbank. WoPoe, *tr. by* Paul Blackburn

  Omens on the Road to Burgos. WoPoe, *tr. by* Paul Blackburn

Excerpts from the Sabbath Dream Book. Esther Ettinger. DTA, *tr. by* Mariana Barr

Excess of lemon, whether on the phone. Lair, The. Rachel Hadas. FFC

Excess of Poetry. Jacques Garelli. YaTCFP, *tr. by* Mary Ann Caws and Jean-Pierre Cauvin

Exchange of Feelings. Paul Verlaine. SxFrPo, *tr. by* Martin Sorrell

Exchange of Gifts, An. Alden Nowlan. StAl

Exchange of Hats, An. Stanley Moss. BodElec

Exchange of Letters. Wendy Cope. OBCoV

Exchanges. Ernest Dowson. OBMV

Exchanges in Italy. Mary Twomey. IrLP

Exchanging Hats. Elizabeth Bishop. NIL-7; OxBoAm

Excitation. Lorenzo Thomas. FTOS

Excite my breasts. Feathers. Jayne Cortez. SurWo

Excited as a sophisticated boy at his first. Matins and Lauds. Marie Ponsot. CLPP

Excitement. Polly Clark. NeBl

Exciting at first. Basho. EH, *tr. by* Robert Hass

Exclamation. Octavio Paz. ChAP, *tr. by* Eliot Weinberger

Ex-Clerk. Rudyard Kipling. HarvBoo *Fr.* Epitaphs of the War [1914–1918].

Excrement Poem, The. Maxine W. Kumin. GoPo

Excursion. Niyi Osundare. HBAPE

Excursion, The. William Wordsworth.

  Course Prescribed, The. STuOW

  Despondency Corrected.

    "I have seen / A curious child, who dwelt upon a tract." ITBLP

    "From the abstraction I was roused,—and how?" NAEL-7v2

    "Her cottage, then a cheerful object, wore." OBGa

  Wanderer, The.

    "Supine the Wanderer lay." NOBRP

Excursion of the Speech and Hearing Class, The. David Wagoner. VCAP

Excursion to Ravenna of A Young Girl with Her Parents. Rossana Ombres. Morning Hours. NeIt

Excursion to the Planet Mercury. Alice Oswald. MoWP

Excursions. Ray Ragosta. OnScMo

Excuse, The. Morgan Llwyd. AngWePo *Fr.* 1648.

Excuse and Explanation. Yevgeny Bunimovich. PML, *tr. by* Patrick Henry

Excuse for Not Returning the Visit of a Friend, An. Mei Yao Ch'en. NDACCP, *tr. by* Kenneth Rexroth

Excuse me. Half-caste. John Agard. Oth

Excuse me. I thought for a moment you were someone I know. I Thought It Was Harry. William Bronk. APSN; OxBoAm

Excuse me, pilgrim. Art of Getting Lost, The. Art Goodtimes. GeoH

Excuse, my lord, the liberty I take. Letter to Lord Byron. W. H. Auden.

Ex-Deputy Sheriff Remembers the Eastern Oklahoma Murderers, An. Jim Barnes.

  Summerfield. HATNAP

Exeat. Stevie Smith. NAEL-6v2; NAMCP V.1; NoAM

Execution, The. Walter Lowenfels. FTtHH

Execution, The. Alden Nowlan. BrAP; StAl

Execution of Madame du Barry, The. J. J. Bray. NOBAu

Execution of Memory, The. Jerzy Ficowski. HP, *tr. by* Keith Bosley

Execution of Montrose, The. William Edmonstoune Aytoun.

  "Morning dawned full darkly, The." NePenScot

Execution of the faithless maids. Homer. OBVE *Fr.* Odyssey.

Execution Poster, The. Mary Ruefle. AmAlph

Executioner of Flowers. Muhammad Al-Maghut. PFTM-2, *tr. by* May Jayyusi and Naomi Shihab Nye

Executioner yawned, The. From his axe the blood was still dripping. Imagerie d'Epinal. Aleksander Wat. AF

Executive Geochrone. Daniel Anderson. AmPoNex

Executive Privilege. Danny Shot. BRtP

Exegi Monumentum. Horace. WaAnP *Fr.* Odes.

Exemplary Nick. Sydney Smith. DiBP

Exeo in a spasm. Enueg 1. Samuel Beckett. ItP

Exequy, An. Peter Porter. NoAM; NoP-4; NoP-5

Exequy on [*or* upon] His Wife. Henry King, Bishop of Chichester. *See* Exequy, The.

Exequy, The. Henry King, Bishop of Chichester. NAEL-6v1

Exequy to His Matchless[e] Never to be Forgotten Friend [*or* Freind], An. Henry King, Bishop of Chichester. *See* Exequy, The.

Exercise No. 2. William Carlos Williams. SAmP

Exercises in Scriptural Writing (1925–1939). Carl Rakosi.

  Sandalwood Comes to My Mind. ChIV-1

Exert thy voice, sweet harbinger of Spring! To the Nightingale. Anne Finch, Countess of Winchilsea. NALW

Exeunt. Richard Wilbur. HeIP-4

Exeunt Omnes. Thomas Hardy. FaBoVe; UV

Exhaled, The. Katherine Swiggart. IaFF

Exhausted Bug, The. Robert Bly. BodElec

Exhausted by jogging. Ngodup Paljor. WhBo

Exhausted, he sees nothing now but the bars. Panther, The. Rainer Maria Rilke. PoCho, *tr. by* Robin Robertson

Exhausted, I sought. Basho. SoOfWa, *tr. by* Sam Hamill

Exhausted Inconsistency Floats Here, An. Giusi Busceti. ItPo, *tr. by* Gayle Ridinger

Exhausted, / time to find a lodging. Basho. EMJL, *tr. by* Haruo Shirane

Exhibits, The. Tracey Herd. MFPA

Exhilaration—is within. Emily Dickinson. TCAPo

Exhilarating, something I can't explain. Anthuriums, Pahoa. Joan Swift. PoCoUp

Exile. Ingeborg Bachmann. PoSu, *tr. by* Daniel Huws

3. Exile. İlhan Berk. NaPG *tr. by* Talat Sait Halman *Fr.* History of a Face, The.

Exile: "Here *exactly*—a little elbow room. Here, in this margin of poor housing." Scott Cairns. UpMys

Exile. Teresa Calderón. TANSG, *tr. by* Celeste Kostopulos-Cooperman

Exile. Hart Crane. NIL-7

Exile. Stephen Dobyns. OPRER

Exile. Hilde Domin. PoCho, *tr. by* Eavan Boland

Exile. Erich Fried. AF, *tr. by* Georg Rapp

Exile. Donald Hall. NoP-4; NoP-5

Exile. Anthony Hecht. TaR

Exile. John Milton. NOSC

Exile: "What happier fortune can one find." Frank O'Connor. IrLP

Exile. "St.-John Perse."

  "Doors open on the sands, doors open on exile." AF

Exile. Dennis Phillips.
    From Arena. FTOS.
Exile. Alejandra Pizarnik. TCLAP, *tr. by* Frank Graziano and María Rosa Fort
Exile. Danton R. Remoto. ReBoTo
Exile. Saniyya Salih. PoArWo, *tr. by* Kamal Boullata
Exile. Ellen Bryant Voigt. AWTN
Exile, The. Pablo Medina. OPRER
Exile, The: "He was not made for politics." Edwin Thumboo. PML
Exile in Japan. Su Man-shu. BLT, *tr. by* Kenneth Rexroth
Exile is ended now, The. Last Land of Exile. Jorge Guillén. RaW, *tr. by* Charles Guenther
Exile Is Stale Bread. Paul Laraque. OGAHCP, *tr. by* Boadiba and Jack Hirschman
Exile lingering here, An. (LL) Infelix. Adah Isaacs Menken. CBWP-1; NAAPv.1; TCAPo
Exile of Erin, The. *Unknown.* NOBAu
Exile of Rákóczi, The. *Unknown.* IQMS, *tr. by* Watson Kirkconnell
Exile, Representative. Breyten Breytenbach. AF, *tr. by* Denis Hirson
Exile: Welsh Service from Daventry. Llewelyn Wyn Griffith. AngWePo
Exiles. Abena Busia. NAfrP
Exiles: "At the greyhound bus stations, at airports, at silent wharfs." Juan Felipe Herrera. CalPo
Exiles. Diana Der Hovanessian. OPRER
Exiles. George Russell. MoBrPo
Exiles. *Unknown.* SonAtl, *tr. by* Rita Kelly and Michael Portas
Exiles, The. Iain Crichton Smith. HarvBoo; NePenScot
Exile's Letter. Li Po. APT-1; CCL1; NDACCP, *tr. by* Ezra Pound
Exile's Letter (Or: An Essay on Assimilation). Marilyn Chin. OpBo
Exile's Return, The. Slavko Mihalic. PoSu, *tr. by* Peter Kastmiler and Charles Simic
Exile's Reverie, The [*with music*]. Mary Weston Fordham. CBWP-2
Exiles see exiles everywhere. Elizabeth Bishop, *Croton.* Mark Doty. AmAlph
Exile's Song, The. Robert Gilfillan. TreFP
Exilics: Leaving Lochboisdale, 1919. Walter Perrie. EdScPo
Exist, without a man cook. (LL) Coming Woman, The. Mary Weston Fordham. CBWP-2; SWaP
Existence. Thich Nhat Hanh. WhBo
Existentially Speaking. Joe-Anne McLaughlin-Carruth. AFaM
Existing. Alejandra Pizarnik. MirDau, *tr. by* Roberta Gordenstein
Existing is not always appropriate. Fifth Floor. Miryana Basheva. CSCBP, *tr. by* Georgi Belev and Lisa Sapinkopf
Existing Psychically. Andrea Zanzotto. ItPo, *tr. by* Gayle Ridinger
Exists, like blinder or mistake. Doors. Rosalie Moore. YaYoPo
Exists there one, who carelessly can view. Second Evening. Mary F. Johnson. CenSon
Exit. Rita Dove. AmAlph; ExTi
Exit. Edwin Arlington Robinson. MoAmPo
Exit Amor. Virginia Hamilton Adair. APT-2
Exit, Pursued by a Bear. Kathleen Kirk. IaFF
Exit Wound. Jorie Graham. AWPTFC
Exits. Jean Earle. TCAWP
Exits. Patricia Pogson. NLP
Exits from Elmina Castle: Cape Coast, Ghana. Toi Derricotte. BtF
Exodus. Bible, *O.T.*
    "Let us synge unto the Lorde, for he is become glorious." OBVE
    Then Sang Moses. OBWP
Exodus. Horst Bienek. AF
Exodus. Jarret Keene. Vesp
Exodus. George Oppen. ChIV-1
Exodus. Charles Reznikoff. ChIV-1
Exodus. Robyn Selman. WiU
Exodus. Jaime Torres Bodet. TCLAP, *tr. by* Sonja Karsen
Exorcism. Dorothy Nimmo. Prnts
Exotic thumbalina, crayola flame. Stray Moth, Asleep. Joyce Peseroff. VisFro
Expansive puppets percolate self-unction. Canadian Authors Meet, The. Francis Reginald Scott. BrAP
Expatriates. Ronald Stuart Thomas. AngWePo
Expatriates. David Woo. OpBo
Expatriation. Mahdi Muhammad Ali. IrPoTo, *tr. by* Salaam Yousif
Expect Nothing Else from Me. Rita Joe. ReEnLa
Expectably slowed yet unthinking. Edges. Robert Creeley. WoBe
Expectation. Ida G. M. Gerhardt. TuT, *tr. by* Peter van de Kamp
Expected Guest, The. Sidney Keyes. PoWW
Expected. Pure gravy. And don't forget it. (LL) Gravy. Raymond Carver. BeAl; LaCa
Expected, the handsome, the one who needs us, The. (LL) Beauty and the Beast. Rita Dove. ESEAA; NoAM
Expecting no miracle, we found none. Return to DeKalb. Lucien Stryk. IllVoic
Expecting to see him anytime. Between Days. Yusef Komunyakaa. ESEAA
Expenditure of force leads to outward decay. Sikong Tu. CCL1 *Fr.* Twenty-Four Modes of Poetry.
Expense of spirit in a waste of shame, Th'. Garden of Proserpine, The. Veronica Forrest-Thomson. MoWP
Expense [*or* Expence] of spirit in a waste of shame, The [*or* Th']. William Shakespeare. BrAP; CABP; ErotSp; HeIP-4; NAEL-6v1; NAEL-7v1; NIL-7; NIP-4; NoP-5; NoSic; NPeEn; OBEV; OxAEP-1; OxBEV; PBRV; PoPoPo; TFi; WoPoe *Fr.* Sonnets.
Experience. Ralph Waldo Emerson. APN-1; TCAPo
Experience [*with music*]. Dorothy Parker. AmWit
Experience. Edith Wharton. APN-2
Experience had been set up, at an angle. (LL) Formation of Soils, The. Brenda Hillman. BAP-01; FaoP
Experience, though noon auctoritee. Geoffrey Chaucer. NAEL-6v1; NAEL-7v1; NoP-5; OxBEV; RACG *Fr.* Canterbury Tales, The.
Experience Too Late. Letitia Elizabeth Landon. RWP
Experiences as a taxi-driver in Venezuela. *Unknown.*
    "When I start my fast driving." EroLit
Experiment. Wisława Szymborska. PoSu, *tr. by* Magnus F. Krynski
Experiment Degustatory. Ogden Nash. ChAP
Experiment escorts us last. Emily Dickinson. APN-2
Experiment that Failed, An. William Wordsworth. STuOW *Fr.* Vaudracour and Julia.
Experimental Animals. Dennis O'Driscoll. StAl
Experiments in the Impersonal. Steve Wilson. AmPoNex
Experiments Lasted through the Winter, The. Sabrina Orah Mark. LegDan
Experiments with God. Karen Gershon. HP
Experts, The. Jack Myers. BodElec; TiP2
Experts at Veneers. Kenward Elmslie. NYP2
Experts say for me to do it well. Running. Brendan Galvin. MoASP
Expiation. Victor Hugo. *tr. by* Phillip Holland and Louis Simpson
    "It was snowing. For the first time, conquered." WoPoe, *tr. by* Louis Simpson
    "Waterloo! Waterloo! Waterloo! dismal plain!" WoPoe, *tr. by* Phillip Holland
Explain given to. Underneath (3). Jorie Graham. BodElec
Explain this to me as i conjure images of. Georgia avenue, washington d.c. Brian G. Gilmore. BRtP
Explaining. Evan X. Hyde. OWABP
Explaining Current Events to a One-Year-Old. Martha Silano. RWB
Explaining everything. (LL) Last Gods. Galway Kinnell. PasH; RaBo
Explaining Magnetism. Maura Dooley. MoWP
Explaining the Big One. William Stafford. PWW2
Explaining the Declaration. Hans Magnus Enzensberger. BeAl, *tr. by* David Constantine
Explaining the Origin of My Name. Fatima Lim-Wilson. AmPoNex
Explanation. William Barber. CAGL
Explanation. Explanation / tangent things. Larry Eigner. PFTM-2
Explanation. Christine Hume. LegDan
Explanation of a Sign. Pyotr Vegin. TCRusP, *tr. by* Daniel Weissbort
Explanation of America, An. Robert Pinsky.
    Part One: Its Many Fragments.
        Countries and Explanations. StAl
    Part Three: Its Everlasting Possibility.
        Serpent Knowledge. ColAP
Explanation / tangent things. Larry Eigner. PFTM-2
Explicating the Twilight. Jack Gilbert. WaAnP
Expliqué la razón. Abrí la boca de las palabras y el resoplido expresó su cuchillo. Poema de casa. Laura Solórzano. SPV
Exploded. To the ground. On his back. Arms apart. He. Eyes. Yevgeny Mikhailovich Vinokurov. TCRusP, *tr. by* Anthony Rudolf
Explore the beauty of our land. Odyssey, The. Sipho Sepamla. AF
Explorer of Aromas. Toyin Adewale. NeNiPo
Exploring the Dark Content. Harryette Mullen. OxAAAP
Explosion. Takahashi Shinkichi. AtGh; ZenPo, *tr. by* Takashi Ikemoto and Lucien Stryk
Explosion, The. Philip Larkin. BrAP; EmeKit; InoFa; ItP; MakPoe; NAEL-6v2; NAEL-7v2; NAMCP V.2; NoAM; NoP-4; NoP-5; NPeEn; OxAEP-2; WeW-3
Explosion names, An. 86 Pasteur Corner. Manuela Fingueret. MirDau, *tr. by* Celeste Kostopulos-Cooperman
Explosion your death, An. Silence. Claribel Alegría. TANSG, *tr. by* Darwin Flakoll

Explosive posters lit at night. Break of Dawn, The. Thomas Sayers Ellis. InTrad

Exposed meat bleeds among the flies inside the cases, The. Butcher Shop. Carla Faesler Bremer. SPV, *tr. by* Jen Hofer

Exposed to light. On Veronica. Rita Dove. AmAlph

Expository Tale on King Wu's Expedition against Chow. *Chinese Oral Tradition.*
    Scroll 1. ColAnChi, *tr. by* Liu Ts'un-yan

Expostulation, An. Isaac Bickerstaffe. OBCoV

Expostulation and Reply. William Wordsworth. NAEL-6v2; NAEL-7v2; NOBRP; NoP-5

Expostulation, The. Elizabeth Singer Rowe. PEW

Expostulatory Epistle to Lord Byron, An. Joseph Cottle.
    Virtue Protests [*or* Epistle to Lord Byron]. STuOW

Exposure. Seamus Heaney. NPeEn; PBCIP; PNI; WaAnP *Fr.* Singing School.

Exposure. Wilfred Owen. NAMCP V.1; NoAM; OBWP; PoWW; TCAWP

Express. Vicente Huidobro. PFTM-1

Express, The. Stephen Spender. BrAP; HeIP-4; MoBrPo; NAMCP V.1; NIL-7; NoAM

Express Train. Rolf Jacobsen. BLT, *tr. by* Roger Greenwald

Express Train. Ivan Tsanev. CSCBP, *tr. by* Georgi Belev and Lisa Sapinkopf

Express train 1256 races alongside hidden, remote villages. House. Express Train. Rolf Jacobsen. BLT, *tr. by* Roger Greenwald

Express train gropes and thrusts its way through darkness. Not a star is out. On Crossing the Rhine Bridge at Cologne by Night. Ernst Stadler. GTCP, *tr. by* Michael Hamburger

Expression. Isaac Rosenberg. MoBrPo

Expression is the need of my soul. Don Marquis. APT-1 *Fr.* Coming of Archy, The.

Expulsion. Lisa Sewell. AmPoNex

Expulsion from Eden, The. John Milton. OPOU *Fr.* Paradise Lost.

Expulsion of Hagar, The [*with music*]. Eloise Bibb. CBWP-4

Ex-Queen Among the Astronomers, The. Fleur Adcock. MoWP; NAEL-6v2; NAEL-7v2; NALW; NoP-4; NoP-5

Exquisite Alchemy. Debra Taub. SurWo

Exquisite stillness! What serenities! Don Juan's Address to the Sunset. Robert Malise Bowyer Nichols. OBMV

Exquisite world, powerful, joyous, splendid. To the Natural World: at 37. Genevieve Taggard. APT-2

Exstasie, The. John Donne. *See* Ecstasy, The.

Extasie, The. John Donne. *See* Ecstasy, The.

Éxtasis. María Baranda. RMCMP

Extasis. Lawrence Ferlinghetti. Eno

Extempore Effusion upon the Death of James Hogg. William Wordsworth. NAEL-6v2; NAEL-7v2; NPBRoP

Extempore—On Being Shown a Beautiful Country Seat Belonging to Maxwell of Cardoness. Robert Burns. OBGa

Extend, there where you venture and come back. Walk on the Moon. N. Scott Momaday. OtW

Extended Family. A. K. Ramanujan. NAMCP V.2

Extended malady of your metaphor has finally reached me, The. I Danced with You Once Only Onliest One. Ivan Arguelles. ASA

Extended Relations (1). Uduma Kalu. NeNiPo

Extending from her left ear down her jaw. S. W. Rafael Campo. BloBone

Extensive the lands flanking that southern mountain. *Unknown.* ColAnChi *Fr.* Classic of Odes.

Exterior formed in measure to match his mind, An. (LL) Marbod of Rennes. CAGL; EroLit *Fr.* Unyielding Youth, The.

Exterior—to Time. (LL) This was a Poet—It is That. Emily Dickinson. APN-2; NAAL-3; NAAL-5; NAAPv.1; NCAP; OxBoAm; TCAPo

Extermination of the Jews, The. Marvin Bell. TaR

Exterminator has arrived, The. He has not intruded. He was summoned. Blue-Eyed Exterminator, The. Josephine Jacobsen. OxBoAm

External promise is also internal, The. Love as Fear of Love in Laughter. Chris Stroffolino. IIR

External rituals mean nothing. Kamalākānta Bhattācārya. SinGod, *tr. by* Rachel Fell McDermott

Extinguish, One by One. Vicki Raymond. NOBAu

Extract. Paul Bowles. PoA 2002

Extract 9. Venice. Thomas Moore. OBSV *Fr.* Rhymes on the Road.

Extract from a Diary. János Pilinszky. PoSu, *tr. by* Peter Jay

Extracted. Aleida Rodríguez. FaoP, *tr. by* the author

Extraction. Anthony Barnett. OnScMo

Extracts. Hsi K'ang. CCL1 *Fr.* Lute, The: A Rhapsody.

Extracts. Zhou Xingsi. CCL1 *Fr.* Thousand Character Classic, The.

Extraño, en esta noche, he recordado. Mendigo, El. Francisco Brines. RaW

Extraordinary events befell my family. Bardo of the Threshold. Janet Rodney. ICANM

Extraordinary patience of things!, The. Carmel Point. Robinson Jeffers. APT-1; ASA; BLT; CalPo; NAAL-5; NAMCP V.1; NoAM; NoP-4; WaAnP; WhBo

Extravagance of Zoos, The. Craig Arnold. AmPoNex

EVA Psalm. Raymond Roseliep. OtW

Extreme scab take thee and thine, for me, The. (LL) To the Sour[e] Reader. Robert Herrick. NBLV; NoP-4; NoP-5

Extreme Unction. Ernest Dowson. MoBrPo; OBMV

Extremely slowly the snail. Hans Faverey. WoBe *Fr.* Eighteen Poems.

Extremes Ain't My Thing As Salaam Alaikum. Tufara Waller Muhammad. BRtP

Exudes from the dried fish and the brown jug and the bowl. (LL) Nature Morte. Louis MacNeice. NAMCP V.1; NoAM

Exult each patriot heart!—this night is shewn. Royall Tyler. NAAL-3 *Fr.* Contrast, The.

Exultation. Hywel ab Owain Gwynedd. OBWVE, *tr. by* Gwyn Williams

Exultation is the going. Emily Dickinson. APN-2; TCAPo

Exultationis Carmen To the Kings Most Excellent Majesty upon His Most Desired Return. Rachel Jevon. EMWP

Exulting in his Strength, he seems to dare. Virgil. OBVE *Fr.* Aeneid [*or* Eneados *or* Aeneis], The.

Ex-Voto for a Shipwreck. Aimé Césaire. PFTM-1

Eyam. Anna Seward. RWP

Eye. Nishiwaki Junzaburo. CAoMJL1, *tr. by* Hosea Hirata

Eye, The. Robinson Jeffers. ItP; NoAM

Eye, The. Adrienne Rich. PrTe

Eye, The. Richard Wilbur.
    2. UpMys

Eye after countless eye of the bomb. Vision of Hiroshima. Oscar Hahn. TCLAP, *tr. by* Sandy McKinney

Eye and Ear, The. Jones Very. APN-1

Eye and mouth. Robert Lowell. CAP-8

Eye Behind the I, The. Adam David Miller. ASA

Eye Blade. George Evans. AF

Eye can hardly pick them out, The. At Grass. Philip Larkin. HarvBoo; NPeEn; OxBEV; WeW-3

Eye change dreams at 42nd street, times square. Eye Change Dreams. Quincy Troupe. FaoP

Eye closes, An. Pierre Reverdy. PFTM-1

Eye / drinks the dry orange ground. Arizona Desert. Charles Tomlinson. ICANM

Eye in the center of the triangle. Temple. Natalia Toledo. RMCMP, *tr. by* Alberto A. Ríos

Eye is meant to see things, An. Someone Digging in the Ground. Jelaluddin Rumi. RaBo, *tr. by* Coleman Barks

Eye is static, the guns bebopping too. Heavy, The. Imamu Amiri Baraka. EGAG

Eye Like a Strange Balloon Mounts Toward Infinity, The. Mary Jo Bang. BAP-04

Eye Mask. Denise Levertov. BLT

Eye, murdered, is not yet dead, The. Blindman's Cries, The. Tristan Corbière. WoPoe, *tr. by* Martin James

Eye Occupation, The. Jennifer Timoner. ICANM

Eye of Creation, The. Angelina Muñiz Huberman. MirDau, *tr. by* Aurora Camacho

Eye of the earth; and what it watches is not our wars. (LL) Eye, The. Robinson Jeffers. ItP; NoAM

Eye of the future, gazing back, The. (LL) Answer. Bei Dao. PoetW; VCWP, *tr. by* Donald Finkel

Eye of the Tornado. James Hoggard. TiP2

Eye Poem. Harris Schiff. AHA

Eye Reflecting the Gold of Fall. Charles North. NYP2

Eye sees, but not itself, The. 4th Witness—The Petty Thieves. Ifi Amadiume. NAfrP

Eye sit here, now, inside my fast thickening breath. Reflections on Growing Older. Quincy Troupe. GT; OxAAAP

Eye that sees, The. Another Poetics. Octavio Armand. TCLAP, *tr. by* Carol Maier

Eye, the cauldron of morning. (LL) Ariel. Sylvia Plath. BrAP; ColAP; HeIP-4; NALW; NAMCP V.2; NoAM; NoP-4; NoP-5; VCAP

Eye to Eye. Alexander Gerov. CSCBP, *tr. by* Georgi Belev and Lisa Sapinkopf

Eye unacquitted by whatever it holds in allegiance, The. Didactic Piece. Louise Bogan. AmAlph

Eye use to write poems about burning. Boomerang: A Blatantly Political Poem. Quincy Troupe. AF

Eye, you see is contradictory in both parts, The. Placable Caps, The. Hannibal Vito Acconci. AHA

Eye you see is not, The. Antonio Machado Ruiz. SpanPo; WED, *Fr.* Moral Proverbs and Folk Songs.
Eyeball Works, The. Stephen Knight. NeBl
Eyebrow mounds dark, facing the spluttering lamp. Mating. Yang Wei-chen. ColAnChi, *tr. by* John Timothy Wixted
Eye-catching as a dog on a chain. Quality of Striving, The. Chase Twichell. AmZen
Eye-flattering fortune, look thou never so fair. Fortune. Sir Thomas More. SacPr
Eye-food whose flights having. *A in I* as was Blackening Read (Mandala). Ken Harris. AnSo
Eyeful Glances. Niyi Osundare. HBAPE
Eyeless labourer in the night, The. Woman to Man. Judith Wright. BMAP; BrAP; NoP-4; NoP-5; StAl
Eyelids meet, The. He'll catch a little nap. In the Smoking-Car. Richard Wilbur. GM; MoAmPo
Eyelids of eve fall together at last, The. Thomas Hardy. FaBoWar; OBWP *Fr.* Dynasts, The.
Eye-Opener. Malcolm Lowry. NoP-4; NoP-5
Eyes. Juan Gelman. TCLAP, *tr. by* Robert Marquez and Elinore Randall
Eyes. Yevgeny Mikhailovich Vinokurov. TCRusP, *tr. by* Anthony Rudolf
Eyes: "It seems nothing can provoke." Edip Cansever. NaPG, *tr. by* Talat Sait Halman
Eyes, The. Antonio Machado Ruiz. BeAl, *tr. by* Willis Barnstone
Eyes, The. Don Paterson. EdScPo
Eyes and Tears. Andrew Marvell. FSCP
Eyes are drawn to the dusty ground in fall, The. Empty Place, An. Robert Bly. CAP-8
Eyes caught by beauty, fancy by eyes caught. Husband of To-Day, The. Edith Nesbit. VWP
Eyes Fastened with Pins. Charles Simic. VCAP
Eyes in the Back of Her Head. Harryette Mullen. OxAAAP
Eyes in this place droop, The. Pastime Café. W. M. Ransom. GifTon
Eyes knees and of your Etcetera. (LL) My sweet old etcetera. E. E. Cummings. HeIP-4; NAMCP V.1; OBWP; PoAgWa
Eyes look front in humans, The. Teleology. May Swenson. VCAP
Eyes of clear serenity. Madrigal: Eyes of Clear Serenity. Gutierre de Cetina. SpanPo, *tr. by* Kate Flores
Eyes of gods! ye must have seen. Ralph Waldo Emerson. STuOW *Fr.* Alphonso of Castile.
Eyes of men running, falling, screaming. *Unknown.* OBWP
Eyes of mother-of-pearl, smell of quince. To Die. Sándor Weöres. IQMS, *tr. by* Edwin Morgan
Eyes of My Regret, The. Angelina Weld Grimké. IJHIL
Eyes of [*or* the] body, being blindfold by night, The. Valentine Ackland and Sylvia Townsend Warner. PoBW
Eyes of Soon Children. Honorée Fanonne Jeffers. AnSo
Eyes of the crow and the eye of the camera open, The. Memorial for the City. W. H. Auden.
Eyes of twenty centuries, The. Judas Iscariot. Stephen Spender. MoBrPo; NIP-4
Eyes open in the womb. The struggle arrives to turn darkness into. Grace. Umar Bin Hassan. BRtP
Eyes open on the beach. Christopher Okigbo. WaAnP *Fr.* Heavensgate.
Eyes open to a cry of pulleys, The. Love Calls Us to the Things of This World. Richard Wilbur. AmFaPo; BrAP; CAP-8; ColAP; EMP; HeIP-4; MoAmPo; NAAL-5; NAMCP V.2; NIL-7; NIP-4; NoAM; NoP-4; NoP-5; OxBoAm; TFi; UpMys; VCAP; WaAnP
Eye's roundness between the bars. Language Mesh. Paul Celan. VCWP, *tr. by* Michael Hamburger
Eyes shining in that half-sane stare. What It Comes Down To. Tim Seibles. TiP2
Eyes shining without mystery. Pantoum. John Ashbery. MakPoe
Eyes shut. Lapsed time. The 2 A.M. aquarium light. Talking Cure, The. Sherod Santos. LiTh
Eyes tall dark and skinny men. *Sexy Things*. Anne Waldman. AHA
Eyes that drew from me such fervent praise, The. Petrarch. NAWM-5v1 *Fr.* Sonnets to Laura.
Eyes that mock me sign the way, The. Bahnhofstrasse. James Joyce. NPeEn
Eyes, then a mouth. Recitation of Forgetting, The. Franck André Jamme. YaTCFP, *tr. by* John Ashbery
Eyes thieve with prickled stir. While Waiting for a Friend to Come to Visit a Friend in a Mental Hospital. Russell Atkins. EGAG
Eyes turn topaz, The. (LL) Hugh Selwyn Mauberley (Life and Contacts). Ezra Pound. APT-1; NAMCP V.1; NoAM; NoP-5
Eyes Watch the Stars. Christopher Okigbo. WaAnP *Fr.* Heavensgate.
Eyes whistling in the dark. Entrancielo. Edwin Torres. BRtP
Eyeshop, The. Okot P'Bitek. SonAtl, *tr. by* E. M. Dipuo

Eyesight of Wasps. Osip Emilevich Mandelstam. StAl, *tr. by* Elizabeth McKane and Richard McKane
Ez Malindy sings. (LL) When Malindy Sings. Paul Laurence Dunbar. APN-2; CtM; ISC; NAAPv.1
Ezek'el saw the wheel. *Unknown. See* Ezekiel saw de [*or* the] wheel.
Ezekiel. Bible, *O.T. tr. by* David Curzon
  Valley of Dry Bones, The. WoPoe, *tr. by* David Curzon
Ezekiel. John Greenleaf Whittier. ChIV-1
Ezekiel Saw de [*or* the] Wheel. *Unknown.* APN-2; NoP-4; NoP-5
Ezekiel Saw de Wheel. Honorée Fanonne Jeffers. AnSo
Ezequiel. Martín Espada. PrTe
Ezequiel, boy with the name of a prophet. Ezequiel. Martín Espada. PrTe
Ezili Impending. Rachel E. Harding. BtF
Ezra Pound. Robert Lowell. NoAM
Ezra, whom not with eye nor with ear have I ever. Epistle to the Rapalloan. Archibald MacLeish. PoA 2002

F

F.B.I. swooped in early, The. Lawson Fusao Inada. GeoHom *Fr.* Legends from Camp.
F.D.R. Jones. Harold Rome. ReLy
F. de Samara to A. G. A. Emily Jane Brontë. NALW
F is for Forecast. Eleanor Farjeon. RWPCtW
Fab Four Tour Deutschland: Hamburg, 1961. David Wojahn. PBCAP *Fr.* Mystery Train: A Sequence.
Fabergé's Egg. Elizabeth Spires. PoA 2002
Fable. Eugenio de Andrade. VCWP, *tr. by* Alexis Levitin
Fable: "Mountain and the squirrel, The." Ralph Waldo Emerson. APN-1; NBLV; OxBoAm; TFi
Fable. James Facos. NBLV
Fable: "Animal understands itself, The." Luiza Neto Jorge. SurWo, *tr. by* Jean R. Longland
Fable: "Once upon a time / there was a lonely wolf." János Pilinszky. OBVE; PoSu
Fable, A. John Hookham Frere. UV
Fable, A: "In Æsop's tales an honest wretch we find." Matthew Prior. NoP-4; NoP-5
Fable, The. Yvor Winters. APT-2
Fable 4. The Eagle and the Assembly of Animals. John Gay. *Fr.* Fables: First Series.
Fable 15. The Cook-Maid, the Turnspit, and the Ox. To a Poor Man. John Gay. *Fr.* Fables: Second Series.
Fable 21: The Rat-catcher and Cats. John Gay. OxAEP-1
Fable 30. The Setting-Dog and the Partridge. John Gay. *Fr.* Fables: First Series.
Fable 34. The Mastiff. John Gay. *Fr.* Fables: First Series.
Fable 44. The Hound and the Huntsman. John Gay. *Fr.* Fables: First Series.
Fable 46. The Cur, the Horse, and the Shepherd's Dog. John Gay. *Fr.* Fables: First Series.
Fable at the beginning of the monsoon, The. Monsoon Day Fable, A. Jayanta Mahapatra. VCWP
Fable for Critics, A. James Russell Lowell. NAAL-3
  Alcott. TCAPo
  Channing and Thoreau. TCAPo
  Cooper. TCAPo
  Emerson. APN-1; NAAPv.1; OxBoAm; TCAPo
  (Fable for Critics, A.) NCAP
  Hawthorne. TCAPo
  Holmes. TCAPo
  [James Russell] Lowell. NAAPv.1; TCAPo
  Philothea (Lydia Child). TCAPo
  Phoebus. TCAPo
  Poe and Longfellow. APN-1; OxBoAm; TCAPo
  "There are truths you Americans need to be told." OBSV
Fable of Polyphemus and Galatea. Luis de Góngora y Argote. *tr. by* Frances Fletcher
  Dedication: to the Count of Niebla. SpanPo, *tr. by* Frances Fletcher
  Polyphemus' Love Song. SpanPo, *tr. by* Frances Fletcher
Fable of the Ant and the Word. Mary Barnard. PoA 2002
Fable of the Hunter. Jorge Esquinca. PML, *tr. by* Robert Jones
Fable of the Mermaid and the Drunks. Pablo Neruda. StAl, *tr. by* Alastair Reid
Fable of the War, A. Howard Nemerov. AmWaPo; OBWP; PWW2
Fables. John Gay.
  Wild Boar and the Ram, The. NPeEn
Fables: First Series. John Gay.
  Fable 4. The Eagle and the Assembly of Animals.

Dogs on Strike, The.   DiBP

Fable 21. The Rat-Catcher and the Cats.   OxAEP-1

Fable 30. The Setting-Dog and the Partridge.
   Plain Words to the Spaniel.   DiBP

Fable 34. The Mastiff.
   Meddling Mastiff, The.   DiBP

Fable 44. The Hound and the Huntsman.
   Babbling Ringwood.   DiBP

Fable 46. The Cur, the Horse, and the Shepherd's Dog.
   Yelping Nuisance of the Way, The.   DiBP

Introduction to the Fables. The Shepherd and the Philosopher.
   Tray, the Exemplar.   DiBP

Fables of Critique.   Peter Gizzi.   VaPo

Fables of the Beginning and Remains of the Origin.   Cecilia Vicuña.
   WANABP

Fables: Second Series.   John Gay.
   Fable 15. The Cook-Maid, the Turnspit, and the Ox. To a Poor Man.
   Turnspit Taught, The.   DiBP

Fabliau of Florida.   Wallace Stevens.   PoA 2002

Fabrication of Ancestors.   Alan Dugan.   AmWaPo; CBCWP; NAMCP V.2;
   NoAM

Fabulación.   Elsa Cross.   RMCMP

Fabulation.   Elsa Cross.   RMCMP, tr. by Margaret Sayers Peden

Fabulists, The.   Rudyard Kipling.   OxBEV

Fabullus I will treat you handsomely.   Catullus.   OBVE

Façade.   Dame Edith Sitwell.
   Ass-Face.   OBMV
   Country Dance.   NAMCP V.1; NoAM
   En Famille.   NALW
   I Do Like to Be Beside the Seaside.   PFTM-1
   Sir Beelzebub.   MoBrPo; MoWP; NALW; OBCoV
   Trio for Two Cats and a Trombone.   NAEL-6v2
   Waltz.   MoWP

Facades.   Tomas Tranströmer.   WoBe, tr. by Robin Fulton

Face.   Sounds.   Wassily Kandinsky.   PFTM-1

Face.   Jean Toomer.   NoP-4; NoP-5

Face.   Yi Sang.   CAMKP, tr. by Edward Mack

Face, The.   Mahmoud al-Braikan.   IrPoTo, tr. by Ralph Saverese and Saadi A.
   Simawe

Face, The.   Randall Jarrell.   InGu

Face damp on a lover's thigh and scratchy.   Eating Clay.   Minnie Bruce Pratt.
   ExTi

Face down on the beach, head askew, the view.   Depending on the Angle.
   Jean Bleakney.   NIrP

Face from the Past, A.   Menella Bute Smedley.   VWP

Face haggard turning yellow and puffy.   Unknown.   NAAPv.2

Face, huge face on the screen.   Scene-Script.   Giancarlo Majorino.   ItPo, tr. by
   Gayle Ridinger

Face I can see to see my face, A.   Octavio Paz.   WoPoe Fr. Sunstone.

Face in the Depths of the Desert, The.   Rebecca Seiferle.   ICANM

Face in the Mirror, The.   Robert Graves.   CABP

Face is turned to Mecca, The.   Prayer.   Rudaki.   WoPoe, tr. by Geoffrey
   Squires

Face it. The stars have their own lives and care.   Twelve Gates.   Lorenzo
   Thomas.   EGAG

Face Lift.   Sylvia Plath.   BrAP

Face like a chocolate bar.   125th Street.   Langston Hughes.   APT-2; NAMCP
   V.1

Face Lost in the Wilderness.   Fadwa Tuqan.   AF, tr. by Naomi Shihab Nye

Face Mask.   Patricia Pogson.   NLP

Face of a Horse, The.   Nikolai Alekseievich Zabolotsky.   TCRusP, tr. by Kathy
   Lewis and Bob Perelman

Face of all the world is changed, I think, The.   Elizabeth Barrett Browning.
   CenSon Fr. Sonnets from the Portuguese.

Face of azure beams on the face, The.   As with Them.   Boris Leonidovich
   Pasternak.   TCRusP, tr. by Bogdan Boychuk and Mark Rudman

Face of Love, The.   Ingrid Jonker.   HAWP, tr. by Jack Cope

Face of the landscape is a mask, The.   Mask.   Stephen Spender.   MoBrPo

Face of the spring moon.   Issa.   EH, tr. by Robert Hass

Face reflected in the stream's, The.   Crossing the Yang-Chia Bridge Once More.
   Ching An.   CSKM, tr. by Jerome P. Seaton

Face shines, anchored in fog, A.   Things of the Blind.   Paz Molina.   TANSG,
   tr. by Steven F. White

Face sings, alone, The.   Poem for Willie Best, A.   Imamu Amiri Baraka.
   NAAL-5

Face: "Suddenly below my ankles."   No Hyegyông.   EcSo, tr. by Ann Y. Choi

Face the Animal.   Jean Follain.   BLT, tr. by Heather McHugh

Face to Face.   Thomas James Jones.   BBMWP, tr. by Jon Dressel

Face to Face.   Adrienne Rich.   NAMCP V.2; NoAM

Face to Face with My Lover on Daito's Anniversary.   Ikkyu Sojun.   ErotSp, tr.
   by Sam Hamill

Face Up.   Jonathan Holden.   PfSP

Face with red cavernous gashes and things possibly living in them, A.   Carla
   Harryman.   BAP-04 Fr. Baby.

Faced with his jaw, his cocked head, the stubble.   Fifteen.   Mendi Lewis
   Obadike.   RD

Face-down; odor.   Terror.   Denise Levertov.   MoWP

Faces.   John Ciardi.   WeW-3

Faces.   Walt Whitman.   APN-1 Fr. Leaves of Grass [1855 Version].

Faces greying faster than loam-crumbs on a harrow.   Judge Not.   Theodore
   Roethke.   ChIV-2; GI

Faces I Love, The.   Gerald Stern.   LoL

Faces of dolls, The.   Seifū.   NIL-7, tr. by Daniel C. Buchanan

Faces of the counted years.   Naked Face, The.   Andrée Chedid.   HAWP, tr. by
   Mirène Ghossein and Samuel Hazo

Faces on the porches, The.   Adirondack Return.   Jean Nordhaus.   PfSP

Faces with anticipated youth, The.   Faces, The.   Robert Creeley.   NoAM

Faceted grains of wisdom.   Mikhail Yeryomin.   TCRusP, tr. by John Glad

Facing Bonnard.   Aleksander Wat.   BLT

Facing His Own Death.   Narihira.   WoPoe Fr. Ise Monogatari, The.

Facing It.   Daniel Berrigan.   UpMys

Facing It.   Yusef Komunyakaa.   AmAlph; AmFaPo; AmWaPo; EMP; ESEAA;
   FTtHH; InoFa; ItP; NAMCP V.2; NoP-5; OxBoAm; PLBUT; PoAgWa;
   PoPoPo; StAl; TRP

Facing me, the blustering evening rain besprinkles the sky over the river.   Tune:
   "Eight Beats of a Kan-chou Song."   Liu Yung.   ColAnChi, tr. by James J.
   Y. Liu

Facing Snow and Writing What My Heart Embraces.   Ching An.   CSKM, tr.
   by Jerome P. Seaton

Facing Snow ("Enough new ghosts now to mourn any war.")   Tu Fu [or Du
   Fu].   NDACCP, tr. by David Hinton

Facing the palm of fire.   Meditation for this Day.   Antonio Machado Ruiz.
   CLPP, tr. by Kenneth Rexroth

Facing the Shadow.   Jinkag Haesim.   BecRai, tr. by Kim Daljin, Kim Won-
   Chung and Christopher Merrill

Facing the Snow ("New ghosts weep over lost battles.")   Tu Fu [or Du Fu].
   CrYelRi, tr. by Sam Hamill

Facing the Snow ("Northern snows invade the city.")   Tu Fu [or Du Fu].
   CrYelRi, tr. by Sam Hamill

Facing the Snow ("Weeping over battle, many new ghosts.")   Tu Fu [or Du Fu].
   CCL1, tr. by Stephen Owen

Facing the sun, untalkative, out of reach. (LL)   Here.   Philip Larkin.   NAMCP
   V.2; NPeEn

Facing up the truth of shooting stars.   Black and White.   Jean Bleakney.
   NIrP

Facing West from California's Shores.   Walt Whitman.   MoAmPo; NAAL-3;
   NAAL-5; NAAPv.1; NIL-7

Fact.   Langston Hughes.   APSN; OxBoAm; PFTM-1

Fact of life is it's no life-or-death matter, The.   There Is No Real Peace in the
   World.   Douglas Crase.   BodElec; OxBoAm

Fact that we survive it compels us, The.   Beyond Fear.   Odia Ofeimun.
   HBAPE

Fact: the cordially hated present.   Here 2.   Bob Perelman.   BAP-04

Faction Du Muet.   René Char.   MotU, tr. by Thomas Merton

Factory.   "Antler."
   "Machines waited for me, The."   CLPP

Factory.   "Antler."
   "Ungag our souls!! Unstrangle our souls!! Unsmother our souls!!"   CLPP

"Factory."   André Breton.   PFTM-1 Fr. Magnetic Fields, The.

Factory, The.   Lajos Kassák.   IQMS, tr. by Michael Kitka

Factory, The.   Letitia Elizabeth Landon.   NPBRoP

Factory, one goes there, The. Everything is there.   Leslie Kaplan.   SCFWP Fr.
   L'Excès-L'usine.

Factory, the factory universe, the one, The.   Leslie Kaplan.   SCFWP Fr.
   L'Excès-L'usine.

Factory Town on the 4th of July.   Susan Jelus.   RWB

Factory Windows Are Always Broken.   Vachel Lindsay.   AmWit; APT-1

Factory Workers' Song.   Unknown.   FaBoVe

Facts of Life, The.   Ronald Wallace.   PBCAP

Facts of Life, Ballymoney.   Eamon Grennan.   PBCIP

Faculty at Work, The.   John Dryden.   STuOW Fr. Threnodia Augustalis.

Faded.   Augusta Davies Webster.   VWP

Faded, and the hill slept. (LL)   He Fell among Thieves.   Sir Henry John
   Newbolt.   OBEV; OBWP

Faded hibiscus and its leaves.   Tune: "Sand of Silk-Washing Brook."   Wang
   Kuo-wei.   ColAnChi, tr. by Jiaosheng Wang

Faded Pictures [*with music*]. William Vaughn Moody. TCAPo

Faded the last red blossoms. Tune: "Butterflies Lingering over Flowers." Su Tung-p'o. ColAnChi, *tr.* by Jiaosheng Wang

Fading into tiny gray dots on UHF. (LL) Crater Face. Denise Duhamel. BRtP; LiTh

Fading Plum Blossoms. Li Ch'ing-chao. NDACCP, *tr.* by Kenneth Rexroth

Fading Skiff, The [*with music*]. Henrietta Cordelia Ray. CBWP-3

Fado Singer. Wole Soyinka. HBAPE

Fae. Timothy Steele. VisFro

Faenza. Dino Campana. MotU, *tr.* by Charles Wright

Faerie Queene, The. Edmund Spenser.

  Book 1, Canto 2. NoP-5; NoSic

  Book 2.

    "And in the midst of all, a fountaine stood." EroLit

  Book 2, Canto 12.

    Bower of Bliss, The. NAEL-6v1; NAEL-7v1; OBGa

    (Bower of Blisse Destroyed, The.) NPeEn

    "Eftsoones they heard a most melodious sound." OxBEV; PBRV

  Book 2, Canto 8. NoSic

  Book 3. NAEL-6v1; NAEL-7v1

    Britomart in the House of the Enchanter Busyrane. NPeEn

  Book 3.

    Belphoebe and Timias. NAEL-6v1; NAEL-7v1

    Book 3, Canto 11. NAEL-6v1; NAEL-7v1

    Book 3, Canto 12. NAEL-6v1; NAEL-7v1

    "First was Fancy, like a lovely boy, The." CAGL

    "Great enimy to it, and to all the rest." OxBEV

    "There now he lives in everlasting joy." CAGL

    Visit to Merlin, The. NAEL-6v1; NAEL-7v1

  Canto 1, Book 1. NoP-5

  Canto 5, Book 1. NoSic

  Cave of Despair, The. OBNV

  Envy. RaF

  [From Book 3]. PBRV

  Guyon's Voyage to the Bower of Bliss. NoSic

  "He making speedy way through spersed ayre." NoSic

  "He was to weet a man of full ripe years." UV

  House of Busyrane, The. NoSic

  Legend of the Knight of the Red Crosse, or of Holinesse, The. NAEL-7v1; NoP-5

  "Lo I the man, whose muse whilome did maske." NAEL-6v1; NAEL-7v1; WaAnP

    "By vew of her he ginneth to revive." CAGL

    "That darkesome cave they enter, where they find." OxBEV

  Mutability Claims to Rule the World. NoSic

  (Nature.) AEP

  Nature's Reply to Mutability. MakPoe

    "Then since within this wide great Universe." NPeEn

    "Nought vnder heauen so strongly doth allure." NoSic

  (Pageant of the Seasons and the Months, The.) OxAEP-1

  (Phaedria's Island: The Faerie Queene II.vi. 12–17.) AEP

  "Right well I w[r]ote most mighty Soueraine [*or* soueraine]." NoSic

  Song of Bliss. OBVE

  Vision of the Graces, The. NoSic

  "When I bethinke me on that speech whyleare." NoSic; NPeEn

  "Who travels [*or* trauels] by the wearie wandring way." OxAEP-1

Faery Chasm, The. William Wordsworth. CenSon; OxBSo *Fr.* River Duddon, The.

Fafnir. Alec Derwent Hope. BMAP

Fag Art. John Iozia. CAGL

Fag art sucks. Fag Art. John Iozia. CAGL

Fagots blazed, the caldron's smoke, The. Brewing of Soma, The. John Greenleaf Whittier.

Fail to meet by a moment, and a word. (LL) World and I, The. Laura Riding Jackson. APT-2; ColAP; HarvBoo; NAAPv.2; OxBoAm

Failed Memory Exercise. Rodney Jones. LPSFW

Failed Tribute to the Stonemason of Tor House, Robinson Jeffers. James Tate. OxBoAm

Failing in the Presence of Ants. Gary Soto. CAP-8; PoA 2002

Fails but still tries to rhyme with love. (LL) Second time the comet swung by, The. Gwyneth Lewis. NeBl; StAl

Failure. Dana Gioia. KGB

Failure. Katha Pollitt. OxBoAm

Failure [*with music*]. Henrietta Cordelia Ray. CBWP-3

Failure. Kay Ryan. OxBoAm

Failure. Lina Tibi. PoArWo, *tr.* by Subhi Hadidi and Nathalie Handal

Failure. Natan Zach. FIT, *tr.* by Robert Friend

Failure of an Invention. Safiya Henderson-Holmes. BRtP; UnSA

Failure of Language, The. Elon G. Eidenier. IaFF

Failure of Similes, The. Richard Foerster. PoA 2002

Failure, the longed-for valley, takes him in. (LL) In the Smoking-Car. Richard Wilbur. GM; MoAmPo

Failures. May Kendall. ViWPN; VWP

Failures in Infinitives. Bernadette Mayer. NYP2

Fain would I have a pretty thing. Proper Song, Entitled: Fain Would I Have a Pretty Thing to Give unto My Lady, A. *Unknown.* NoSic

Fain would I kiss my Julia's dainty leg. Her Legs. Robert Herrick. NOSC

  (I fain would kiss my Julia's dainty leg.) CavPo

Fain would I rival thee. To the Eagle. Mary Weston Fordham. CBWP-2

Fain Would I Wed. Thomas Campion. NAEL-6v1; NAEL-7v1

Fain would my Muse the flow'ry Treasures sing. Garden, The. Alexander Pope. OBGa

Faint, and final. (LL) Butcher's Wife, The. Louise Erdrich. HATNAP; NoP-4; NoP-5

Faint clouds caress the mountains. Farewell Song. Ch'in Kuan. CrYelRi, *tr.* by Sam Hamill

Faint Honey. James Purdy. CAGL

Faint Love. Arthur Symons. CABP

Faint moon in a heavy frost, The. *Unknown.* CATKP, *tr.* by Peter H. Lee

Faint Music. Robert Hass. CAP-8

Faint not—fight on! To-morrow comes the song. (LL) Be Strong. Maltbie Davenport Babcock. ITBLP; SoSe-8

Faint now in the evening pallor. Silver Jubilee. Llewelyn Wyn Griffith. OBWVE

Faint Thunder Drifts beneath the Willow. Ou-yang Hsiu. ErotSp, *tr.* by Jerome P. Seaton

Faint trickle of. Ryokan. EMJL, *tr.* by Burton Watson

Faint yellow rose, A. Issa. SoOfWa, *tr.* by Sam Hamill

Faint yet pursuing, faint yet still pursuing / Ever. (LL) Life's Parallels, A. Christina Georgina Rossetti. NAEL-6v2; NAEL-7v2

Faint-flushed buds awake within the cup, The. Awakening. Henrietta Cordelia Ray. CBWP-3

Fainting. Margaret Atwood. MotU

Faintly as tolls the evening chime. Canadian Boat Song, A. Thomas Moore. TreFP

Fair Amazon of Heaven who tookst in hand. To Saint Margaret. Henry Constable. NoSic

Fair Amoret is gone astray. Hue and Cry after Fair Amoret, A. William Congreve. NPeEn; OBEV; OxBEV

Fair and Fair. George Peele. OBEV *Fr.* Arraignment of Paris, The.

Fair and fair, and twice so fair. George Peele. OBEV *Fr.* Arraignment of Paris, The.

Fair and Scornful. *Unknown.* OBCoV

Fair and Softly goes far or, The Wary Physician. Laetitia Pilkington. PEW

Fair are the bells of this bright-flowering weed. Poet and Botanist. Constance Naden. ViWPN; VWP

Fair Beatrice tucks her coat up somewhat high. Epigram. John Taylor. NOSC

Fair bosom! fraught with virtue's richest treasure. Edmund Spenser. NIP-4 *Fr.* Amoretti.

Fair boy, alas, why fliest thou me. Black Maid to the Fair Boy, The. Henry Reynolds. NOSC

Fair cheek under a merry blue eye, two brows, A. Beloved, The. David Roberts. OBWVE, *tr.* by H. Idris Bell

Fair Chunda smiles amid the burning waste. Erasmus Darwin. NOBRP *Fr.* Botanic Garden, The.

Fair Cop, A. Robert Garioch. OBCoV

Fair Cynthia mounted on her sprightly pad. Cynthia on Horseback. Philip Ayres. OxBSo

Fair daffodils, we weep to see. To Daffodils. Robert Herrick. PtR

Fair daughter of that fleeting race. Nymph of the Fountain to Charlotte, The. Anne Grant. PoBW

Fair eastern star, that art ordained to run. Of the Epiphany. John Beaumont. SacPr

Fair Elenor. William Blake. NPBRoP

Fair Exchange. Aileen Fisher. NOxBChV

Fair fa' your honest, sonsie face. To a Haggis. Robert Burns. FaBoVe; NePenScot

Fair, Fair, Cry the Ospreys. *Unknown.* CCL1 *Fr.* Guan-ju.

Fair famous flood, which sometimes did divide. Sonnet: On the River Tweed. Sir Robert Aytoun. NOSC

  (Faire famous flood, which sometyme did devyde.) NePenScot

Fair Flower! Tune: "Partridge Sky." Li Ch'ing-chao. ColAnChi, *tr.* by Jiaosheng Wang

Fair flower, that dost so comely grow. Wild Honey Suckle, The. Philip Freneau. ColAP; ITBLP; NAAL-3; NAAPv.1; OxBoAm; TCAPo

Fair, fragile Una, golden-haired. Enchanted Shell, The. Henrietta Cordelia Ray. CBWP-3

Fair friend, 'tis true, your beauties move. Ben Jonson. NOSC

Fair Golden Age! When milk was th' on[e]ly food. Sir Richard Fanshawe. NOSC; OBVE *Fr.* Il Pastor Fido.

Fair gull on the water's bank. Seagull, The. Siôn Phylip. OBWVE, *tr. by* Joseph P. Clancy
  (Fair seagull on the water's edge, bright-feathered breast, rich your state.) PBRV

Fair Hills of Ireland, The. *Unknown.* OBEV, *tr. by* Sir Samuel Ferguson

Fair Hope with lucent light in her glad eyes. Quest of the Ideal, The. Henrietta Cordelia Ray. CBWP-3; SWaP

Fair Ilonka. Mihály Vörösmarty. IQMS, *tr. by* Watson Kirkconnell

Fair Ines. Thomas Hood. OBEV

Fair [*or* Fayre] is my love, and cruel[l] as she's [*or* sh'is] fair [*or* fayre]. Samuel Daniel. GSo; NoP-5; OBEV *Fr.* Sonnets to Delia.

"Fair is my love, when her fair golden hairs." Edmund Spenser. *See* Sonnet 81: "Fair [*or* Fayre] is my love, when her fair [*or* fayre] golden heares."

Fair lady, on that snowy neck and half-clad bosom. More Care for the Neck Than for the Intellect. J. Gordon Coogler. VerBaPo

Fair lake, thy lovely and thy haunted shore. Castle of Chillon, The. Letitia Elizabeth Landon. CenSon

Fair lovely maid, or if that title be. To the Fair Clarinda [*or* Clorinda], Who Made Love to Me, Imagin'd [*or* Imagined] More than Woman. Aphra Behn. BASC; CABP; EMWP; NALW; NIL-7; NoP-4; NoP-5; PEW; PoBW; WaAnP

Fair maid, had I not heard thy baby cries. To a Lofty Beauty, from Her Poor Kinsman. Hartley Coleridge. OxAEP-2

Fair maiden, fair maiden. Invocation to the Muse. Richard Hughes. MoBrPo

Fair Melody, A: To Be Sung by Good Christians. Hans Sachs. GePo, *tr. by* Catherine Winkworth

Fair Mildred wide her lattice threw. Mildred's Doves. Henrietta Cordelia Ray. CBWP-3

Fair Moon! You shining lady of the sombre night. To The Moon. Dávid Baróti Szabó. IQMS, *tr. by* Adam Makkai

Fair morn unbars her gates of gold. Dawn's Carol. Henrietta Cordelia Ray. CBWP-3

Fair Morning, The. Jones Very. GSo

Fair mouth's broken tooth, A. (LL) August 1914. Isaac Rosenberg. HarvBoo; NPeEn; OBWP; OxBEV; PoAgWa

Fair Musidora starry-eyed. Musidora's Vision. Henrietta Cordelia Ray. CBWP-3

Fair nights beneath the mellow moon. Maid of Ehrenthal, The. Henrietta Cordelia Ray. CBWP-3

Fair [*or* Fayre] is my love, when her fair [*or* fayre] golden heares. Edmund Spenser. NoP-5 *Fr.* Amoretti.

Fair[e] pledges of a fruitful tree. To Blossoms. Robert Herrick. BrAP; NAEL-6v1; NOSC; OBEV; TreFP

Fair Raiment. John Oxenham. SacPr

Fair, Rich, and Young. Sir John Harington. NIP-4

Fair rosa. *Unknown.* FaBoVe

Fair Rosa was a lovely child. Fair rosa. *Unknown.* FaBoVe

Fair seagull on the water's edge, bright-feathered breast, rich your state. Siôn Phylip. *See* Fair gull on the water's bank.

Fair seed time had my soul, and I grew up. William Wordsworth. NoP-5 *Fr.* Prelude, The; Growth of a Poet's Mind [1850 version].

Fair seed-time had my soul, and I grew up. William Wordsworth. OxAEP-2 *Fr.* Prelude, The; Growth of a Poet's Mind [1805 version].

Fair ship, that from the Italian shore. Alfred Tennyson. CAGL; NAEL-6v2; NAEL-7v2 *Fr.* In Memoriam A. H. H.

Fair Singer, The. Andrew Marvell. FSCP; NoP-4; NoP-5

Fair slim boy not made for this world's pain, A. Wasted Days. Oscar Wilde. CAGL

Fair Star of evening, Splendo[u]r of the west. Composed by the Sea-Side, near Calais, August, 1802. William Wordsworth. CenSon

Fair Summer Droops. Thomas Nashe. NoSic *Fr.* Summer's Last Will and Testament.

Fair summer droops, droop men and beasts therefore. Thomas Nashe. NoSic *Fr.* Summer's Last Will and Testament.

Fair these broad meads—these hoary woods are grand. Canadian Boat Song. *Unknown.* OBEV

Fair Virtue, the Mistress of Philarete [Selections from anthologies]. George Wither.
  (Author's Resolution, The.) OBEV
  Shall I, Wasting in Despair. OxAEP-1
  Sonnet. NOSC

Fair young face o'er which is only cast, A. Princess Victoria, The. Letitia Elizabeth Landon. RWP

Fair young fine-browed lass, A. When Her Father a Widower Asked What She Would Say to His Intention of Marrying a Young Girl. Alis Ferch Gruffyd ab Ieuan ap Lleywelyn Fychan. EMWP

Fair[e] as unshaded light; or as the day. To the Queen[e], Entertain[e]d at Night by the Countess[e] of Anglesey. Sir William Davenant. NOSC

Fair[e] daffodils [*or* daffadills], we weep to see. To Daffodils [*or* Daffadills]. Robert Herrick. BASC; NoP-4; NOSC; OBEV; OxAEP-1; TFi; TreFP

Faire famous flood, which sometyme did devyde. Sir Robert Aytoun. *See* Fair famous flood, which sometimes did divide.

Faire, fresshest erthly creature. *Unknown.* OHMEL

Faire Friend, 'tis true, your beauties move. Sidney Godolphin. NPeEn

Fairest day that ever yet has shone, The. Lost, The. Jones Very. APN-1; NoP-4; NoP-5

Fairest o' fair, O, hear my cry. Fine Fechtin Mouse, The. Sir Alexander Gray. EdScPo

Fairest summer hath its sudden showers, The. Shadows. John Clare. CenSon

Fairest thing I leave behind is sunlight, The. Praxilla. SaLy, *tr. by* Diane Rayor

Fairest things are those which live, The. Song. Mary Russell Mitford. NOBRP

Fairfax, whose name in arm[e]s through Europe rings. On the Lord Gen[eral] Fairfax at the Siege of Colchester. John Milton. NOSC

Fairfield County Fair in Lancaster, Ohio, The. Shots of Thackeray. Cinema Vérité: William Makepeace Thackeray Follows His Bliss. Tom Andrews. MotU

Fair-haired strapping fellow, six foot tall. Jack. Máire Mhac an tSaoi. IrLP

Fairies Are Dancing All Over the World, The. Michael Rumaker. CAGL

Fairies' Lullaby, The. William Shakespeare. NoSic *Fr.* Midsummer Night's Dream, A.

Fairies' Song, The. Jane Taylor. NOBRP

Fairies, The. William Allingham. NOxBChV; OBEV; TFi

Fairs, with fireworks. A mix of people. Leslie Kaplan. SCFWP *Fr.* Règne.

Fairy Land, 1. William Shakespeare. OBEV

Fairy Land, 2. William Shakespeare. *See* Fairies' Lullaby, The.

Fairy Maimounè, The. John Moultrie. NOBRP

Fairy Ring, The. Andrew Young. Spl

Fairy Scene. Jean Cocteau. CuPo

Fairy Song. William Butler Yeats. MoBrPo

Fairy squalls on the water. Flirrup. Mary Dalton. OpeFie

Fairy Story. Stevie Smith. NOxBChV; OBSP

Fairy Tale: "Little elf is dressed in a floppy cap, The." Ron Padgett. NYP2

Fairy Tale, A. Bogdan Boychuk. WoPoe, *tr. by* David Ignatow

Fairy Tales. "Shu Ting." VCWP

Fairy tales can come true. Young at Heart. Carolyn Leigh. ReLy

Fairyland [*or* Fairy-Land]. Edgar Allan Poe. APN-1; NAAL-3; OxBoAm

Fairytale Land of Um, The. Jean Bleakney. NIrP

Fait Accompli. Anne Waldman. BodElec

Faith. Frances Anne Kemble. SWaP

Faith [*epigram*]. Friedrich von Logau. GePo, *tr. by* George C. Schoolfield

Faith. Czeslaw Milosz. RaBo, *tr. by* Robert Hass, Robert Pinsky and Renata Gorcynski

Faith. Charles Harper Webb. Vesp

Faith ("There is no faith; the mountain stands within.") Jones Very. SacPr

Faith #1. Esther Iverem. InTrad

Faith Above Reason. William Drummond of Hawthornden. SacPr

"Faith" bleats—to understand! (LL) I should have been too glad, I see. Emily Dickinson. APN-2; SacPr

Faith Healers. Anne Rouse. NeBrP

Faith Healing. Philip Larkin. ChIV-2; GI; NAMCP V.2; NoAM; OxBEV

Faith, Hope, and Charity Are the Prospects of Manhood. Leigh Hunt. ChIV-2

Faith in Florida. Martha Serpas. Vesp

Faith is a fine invention. Emily Dickinson. APN-2; NAAL-3; NAAL-5; NAAPv.1; NCAP; NoP-4; NoP-5; OxBoAm; TCAPo

Faith Upon the Waters. Laura Riding Jackson. APT-2

Faith (wench) I cannot court thy sprightly eyes. Sir John Davies. PBRV

Faithful as enemy, or friend. (LL) Roosters. Elizabeth Bishop. APT-2; ChIV-2; NALW; NAMCP V.2; OxBoAm

Faithful Betrayal. Victor Segalen. YaTCFP, *tr. by* Timothy Billings and Christopher Bush

Faithful Daughter Dreams of Spring Break While Installing a Bird Feeder for Her Mother by a Window in the Courtyard of Safe Harbour, The. Vivian Shipley. ExTi

Faithful Mirror. Gyula Illyés. IQMS, *tr. by* Adam Makkai and Donald E. Morse

Faithful mother tongue, / I have been serving you. My Faithful Mother Tongue. Czeslaw Milosz. VCWP, *tr. by* the author, Robert Hass and Robert Pinsky

Faithful Shepherdess, The. John Fletcher.
  Hymn to Pan. OBEV
  River[-]God's Song, The. NOSC
  Satyr's Song, The ("Softly Gliding as I Go"). NOSC
Faithful, The. Jane Cooper. AmWaPo
Faithful watcher sits alone, A. Watcher, The. Clara Ann Thompson.
  CBWP-2
Faithful Wife, The. Patricia Beer. LW
Faithfullest Beast, The. Philipp Camerarius and Vera Moller. DiBP, tr. by
  John Molle
Faithfulness. Mirabai. WED, tr. by Robert Bly
Faith—is the Pierless Bridge. Emily Dickinson. NCAP
Faithless Knight, The. Caroline Elizabeth Norton. NPBRoP
Faithless Nelly Gray. Thomas Hood. NOBRP; UV
Faithless, perverse, and blind. Unbelief. Phoebe Cary. SacPr
Faithless Sally Brown. Thomas Hood. OBNV
Faithless Shepherdess, The. *Unknown.* OBEV
Faithless the watch that I kept: now I have none to keep. Rudyard Kipling.
  PoAgWa Fr. Epitaphs of the War [1914–1918].
Faithless Wife, The. Federico García Lorca. SpanPo, tr. by Robert O'Brien
  and Robert O'Brien
Faking out graciously. Fake would have numerics stop. Fog short. Fog. Short
  hop. Sentencing. Natalie Simpson. PoPra
Falcon. Rachel Hadas. ExTi
Falcon Drinking. Dimitris Tsaloumas. BMAP
Falcon gone to the gloom. Long Wind, the Dawn Wind. Ezra Pound. APT-1
Falcon hovers at the edge of the sky, A. I Stand Alone. Tu Fu [or Du Fu].
  CrYelRi, tr. by Sam Hamill
Falcon, The! His symmetrical confession. Ivan Teofilov. CSCBP, tr. by
  Georgi Belev and Lisa Sapinkopf
Falero, lero, loo. (LL) I Loved a Lass. George Wither. OBEV; VerBaPo
Fall: "It was a wing, it was a kiss." Silvia Curbelo. NevBe
Fall: "He always did that." Mahe Jabeen. HotL, tr. by V. Narayana Rao
Fall. George Cabot Lodge. APN-2
Fall. Conor O'Callaghan. NIrP
Fall: "This morning I found." Jane Mead. LaCa
Fall: "Leaves are falling, falling from trees, The." Robin Robertson. NeBrP
Fall, The. NOSC Fr. Il Pastor Fido.
Fall, The. Malak' Abd al-Aziz. HAWP, tr. by Pamela Vittorio
Fall, The. Fergus Allen. ModIr
Fall, The. Michael Anania. IllVoic
Fall, The: "There was a man who found two leaves and came indoors holding
  them out saying to his parents that he was a tree." Russell Edson. MotU;
  OxBoAm
Fall, The. John Kinsella. NeBl
Fall, The. Sarah Maguire. LW
Fall, The. Daniel David Moses. IFF
Fall, The. John Wilmot, 2d Earl of Rochester. ChIV-1
Fall, The. Edmund Waller. NOSC
Fall 1961. Robert Lowell. OBWP; OxBoAm; PoAgWa
Fall aster with firefly. Shin Yu Pai. AmZen
Fall back. To give ground; recede; retreat. Amy Newman. IAoNAP
Fall fizzles, wet, eel-ike, in thorny thickets. Tarry Awhile, Restless Bird.
  Walter Höllerer. GTCP, tr. by Irmgard Hunt
Fall for. *Informal.* 1. To become infatuated with; fall suddenly in love with. 2.
  To be tricked or deceived by; be taken in by. Amy Newman. IAoNAP
Fall from these beclouded skies. (LL) One Foot in Eden. Edwin Muir.
  EdScPo; NoAM
Fall, gáll themsélves, and gásh góld-vermílion. (LL) Windhover, The. Gerard
  Manley Hopkins. AmFaPo; BrAP; CABP; ClHu; MoBrPo; NAEL-6v2;
  NAEL-7v2; NAMCP V.1; NIL-7; NoAM; NoP-4; NoP-5; NPeEn; OWoS;
  OxAEP-2; OxBEV; OxBSo; PoPoPo; SacPr; TFi; TRP; WaAnP
Fall going. Basho. EH, tr. by Robert Hass
Fall in, that awkward squad, and strike no more. Conscripts. Siegfried
  Sassoon. BrAP
Fall is falling from electric burst, The. (LL) Who comes is occupied. George
  Oppen. APT-2; PFTM-1
Fall Is Here, The. Mrs. Henry Linden. CBWP-4
Fall, leaves, fall; die, flowers, away;. Song. Emily Jane Brontë. NPeEn
Fall of Because, The. David Baratier. AmPoNex
Fall of Hyperion, The; A Dream. John Keats. NAEL-6v2; NAEL-7v2
  "Then the tall shade, in drooping linens veiled." OxBEV
Fall of Leaves, The. Yvor Winters. APT-2
Fall of night. Basho. TAL
Fall of Rome, The. W. H. Auden. NPeEn; OxBEV
Fall of Zolnok, The. Sebestyén Tinódi. IQMS, tr. by George Burrow
Fall on Me. Kate Schmitt. IJHIL
Fall Returns, The. Clark Coolidge. AHA

Fall River. David Rivard. PBCAP
Fall River Song. Li Po. CrYelRi, tr. by Sam Hamill
Fall River Song. Li Po. CrYelRi, tr. by Sam Hamill
Fall silent! Cease to sing your tale. On Mankind. Mihály Vörösmarty.
  IQMS, tr. by Valerie Becker Makkai and Neville Masterman
Fall the deep curtains. Archer. "H. D." OxBoAm
Fall under. To succumb to; come under an influence or power. Amy Newman.
  IAoNAP
Fallen. Kate Schmitt. IJHIL
Fallen. Samira Vijghen. FTtHH
Fallen / angels. Homework Assignment on the Subject of Angels. Tadeusz
  Rózewicz. VCWP
Fallen Bodies. Gideon Ferebee. BtF
Fallen cold and dead. (LL) Walt Whitman. AmWaPo; APN-1; BRP; CBCWP;
  ChAP; HHAm; MakPoe; MoAmPo; PCW; SAmP; TCAPo; TFi Fr.
  Memories of President Lincoln.
Fallen cross beneath my belly, The. Hardest Part About Love, The. Imani
  Tolliver. BRtP
Fallen Elm, The [*with music*]. John Clare. RSaN
Fallen flowers rise. Haiku. Arakida Moritaké. SoSe-8, tr. by Harold G.
  Henderson
Fallen from heaven, lies across. River. Ted Hughes. NAEL-6v2; NoP-4
Fallen leaves hide the mountain path. On My Way Back to Kojokdae.
  Jungkwan Ilson. BecRai, tr. by Kim Daljin, Kim Won-Chung and
  Christopher Merrill
Fallen leaves / Raking. Tan Taigi. ZenPo, tr. by Takashi Ikemoto and Lucien
  Stryk
Fallen Maple Leaves. Gerry Cambridge. EdScPo
Fallen on a turf grown green. (LL) Somewhere Or Other. Christina Georgina
  Rossetti. FaBoVe; OxBEV
Fallen petals carpet the garden walk. Tune: "Spring in the Painted Hall."
  Ch'in Kuan. ColAnChi, tr. by Jiaosheng Wang
Fallen petals of red plum. Buson. EH, tr. by Robert Hass
Fallen red blossoms. Buson. SoOfWa, tr. by Sam Hamill
Fallen, so freshly fallen. Dragonfly, The. Stanley Kunitz. APT-2
Fallen Star, The. George Darley. OBEV
Fallen Tower of Siloam, The. Robert Graves. ChIV-2
Fallen Women. Audrey Poetker-Thiessen. ACAMVP
Fallen Yew, A. Francis Thompson. MoBrPo
Falling. Lesley Dauer. AmPoNex; NAPBL
Falling. James Dickey. InGu; NoAM
Falling. Joy Katz. NeAmPo
Falling Asleep. Siegfried Sassoon. MoBrPo
Falling Asleep over the Aeneid. Robert Lowell. MoAmPo
Falling Bricks. Jim Daniels. PML
Falling flower, The. Haiku. Arakida Moritaké. SoSe-8, tr. by Babette
  Deutsch
Falling flower, The. Arakida Moritaké. NIL-7, tr. by Babette Deutsch
Falling for Jesus. Enid Shomer. OPRER
Falling forever. Ochre Iron. Peter Blue Cloud. HATNAP
Falling from a sleeve. Wild Sleeve. Marjorie Welish. FTOS
Falling, I caught the curtain. On the Other Side. Czeslaw Milosz. PoSu, tr.
  by Jan Darowski
Falling in Love after Forty. Ruth L. Schwartz. NeAmPo
Falling in Love at Sixty-Five. Mona Van Duyn. NoP-4; NoP-5
Falling in Love with Love. Lorenz Hart. ReLy
Falling into Meditation. Gene Frumkin. ICANM
Falling of the Grain, The. William Everson.
  8. Advent. CalPo
Falling on my knees. Hymn to the Thousand-Eyed Sound Observer.
  Hüimyŏng. CATKP, tr. by Peter H. Lee
Falling Petals. Cho Chihun. CAMKP, tr. by Kyung-Ja Chun
Falling petals in the far temple are red rain, The. Pulil Hermitage. Chunghur
  Hyujung. BecRai, tr. by Kim Daljin, Kim Won-Chung and Christopher
  Merrill
Falling Snow. Amy Lowell. ColAP
Falling Star, The. Sara Teasdale. ChAP
Falling tears in my heart. Paul Verlaine. SxFrPo, tr. by Martin Sorrell
Fallow fields, dark pewter sky. Winter Drive. James Philip McAuley.
  BMAP; PoA 2002
Falls from mine eyes, which she dissolves in showers. (LL) Henry Constable.
  NIL-7; NIP-4; OBGa Fr. Diana.
Falls of Falloch, The. Sydney Tremayne. EdScPo
Falls of Glomach, The. Andrew Young. EdScPo
Falmouth. W. E. Henley. MoBrPo
False Arrest. Cornelius Eady. LTA
False Bay. Frank Templeton Prince. HarvBoo

False beauty who, although in semblance fair. Ballade to His Mistress. François Villon. WeW-3, *tr.* by Norman Cameron

False dreams, all false. Iliad. Humbert Wolfe. MoBrPo

False Enchantment. Jean Starr Untermeyer. MoAmPo

False, ere I come, to two or three. (LL) Song: "Go and catch a falling star." John Donne. BLPJKO; ClHu; FSCP; HeIP-4; NAEL-6v1; NAEL-7v1; NAWM-5v1; NIL-7; NIP-4; NoP-4; NoP-5; NOSC; NoSic; OBEV; OxAEP-1; PtR; SoSe-8; TFi; WaAnP; WoPoe

False...False. Malhas Thurayya. PoArWo, *tr.* by Nasser Farghaly

False Friends-like [*with music*]. William Barnes. NPeEn; OxBSo

False Gallia's sons, that hoe the ocean isles. James Grainger. STuOW *Fr.* Sugar Cane, The.

False glozing pleasures, casks of happiness. Dotage. George Herbert. SacPr

False life! a foil and no more, when. Quickness. Henry Vaughan. BBASP; NOSC

False love, since thou and I must sever. At Parting. Robin Ernest William Flower. IrLP

False Move. Grace Schulman. ExTi

False [*or* Faulce] hope which feeds but[t] to destroy, and spill. Mary Sidney Wroth, Countess of Montgomery. BASC; NAEL-6v1; NAEL-7v1; PEW *Fr.* Pamphilia to Amphilanthus.

False or true? Ev'ry Time. Ralph Blane and Hugh Martin. ReLy

False Poets and True. Thomas Hood. CenSon; NPBRoP

False Report, A. Robert Graves. OxBEV

False Security. Sir John Betjeman. NoAM; NoP-4; NoP-5

False Senryū. Philip Whalen. WANABP *Fr.* Epigrams & Imitations.

False Though She Be. William Congreve. OBEV

 (Song) OxBEV

Falsehood. William Cartwright. OBEV

Falstaff's Dream. Jackson Wheeler. IaFF

Fama had a wall clock, and each week he wound it VERY VERY CAREFULLY, A. Clocks. Julio Cortázar. MotU, *tr.* by Paul Blackburn

Fame [*with music*]. Josephine D. Henderson Heard. CBWP-4

Fame [*with music*]. Charlotte Mew. HarvBoo; NPeEn; VWP

Fame. Virgil. NPeEn; OBVE *Fr.* Aeneid [*or* Eneados *or* Aeneis], The.

Fame and Friendship. Austin Dobson. OBEV

Fame is a bee. Emily Dickinson. NoP-4; NoP-5; OxBoAm

Fame is a fickle food. Emily Dickinson. SAmP

Fame is a food that dead men eat. Fame and Friendship. Austin Dobson. OBEV

Fame, like a wayward girl, will still be coy. John Keats. CenSon *Fr.* Two Sonnets on Fame.

Fame, wisdom, love, and power were mine. 'All Is Vanity, Saith the Preacher'. Lord Byron. ChIV-1

Famed Telethusa, of the downtown mob. *Unknown*. PriapPo *Fr.* Priapus Poems, The.

Fames Away. Steve Carey. AHA

Fame's pillar here at last we set. Pillar of Fame, The. Robert Herrick. NIP-4

Familial [*with music*]. Jacques Prévert. CLPP; FaBoWar; PoAgWa, *tr.* by Lawrence Ferlinghetti

Familiar. Maria Luisa B. Aguilar-Cariño. ReBoTo

Familiar Epistle to J. B. Esq, A. Robert Lloyd.

 "Mark yon round parson, fat and sleek." OBSV

Familiar Story. Alan Shapiro. NIP-4

Familiar with, the tune. Something I'm Not. Liz Lochhead. NePenScot

Families, when a child is born. On the Birth of His Son. Su Tung-p'o. OBVE; WoPoe, *tr.* by Arthur Waley

Family. Ai. TiP2

Family. Nissim Ezekiel. OBCoV *Fr.* Songs for Nandu Bhende.

Family. Eirwyn George. BBMWP, *tr.* by Peter Finch

Family. Vona Groarke. BeAl

Family. Pak Mogwŏl [*or* Mokwŏl]. CAMKP, *tr.* by Edward W. Poitras

Family Affairs. Maya Angelou. OxAAAP

Family Album, A. Alter Brody. TaR

Family Circle. János Arany. IQMS, *tr.* by Neville Masterman

Family Conference. John Montague. ModIr *Fr.* Dead Kingdom, The.

Family Fool, The. William Schwenck Gilbert. NBLV *Fr.* Yeoman of the Guard.

Family Group, The. Madeline DeFrees. PoChi

Family History. Irving Feldman. VCAP

Family History, The. Nicole Cooley. AmPoNex

Family in Spring, The. Gary Soto. WaAnP

Family Is All There Is, The. Pattiann Rogers. NIP-4

Family Jewels [*for Washington, D.C.*]. Essex Hemphill. GT

Family man. Lionel Abrahams. TSAP

Family Man, The. Bruce Dawe. BMAP

Family Man, The. William Loran Smith. LaCa

Family Name, The [*with music*]. Charles Lamb. CenSon

Family of Love, The. James Philip McAuley.

 Song of Shem. ChIV-1

Family Photograph, The. Vona Groarke. MFPA

Family Photographs. Cecilio Garcia-Camarillo. ICANM

Family Portrait. Shuntaro Tanikawa. VCWP, *tr.* by Harold Wright

Family Portraits. Mary E. Tucker. CBWP-1

Family Procession, A. John Pepper Clark Bekedermo. HBAPE

Family Reunion [*with music*]. Louise Erdrich. HATNAP; NAMCP V.2; NoAM; WaAnP

Family reunion. Garry Gay. CalPo

Family Reunion [*with music*]. Maxine W. Kumin. AFaM; GoPo

Family reunion. Haiku. Lenard D. Moore. SpirFl

Family Reunion—Aunt Vern's Two Cents. Beth Gylys. AmPoNex

Family Romance. Joshua Clover. AmPoNex

Family Romance. Paul Hoover. IllVoic

Family Romance [*with music*]. Larry Levis. BodElec

Family Secrets. Toi Derricotte. OxAAAP; SpirFl

Family Stories. Dacia Maraini. CItWP, *tr.* by Cinzia Sartini Blum and Lara Trubowitz

Family story tells, and it was told true, The. Funnel. Anne Sexton. MoAmPo

Family treasures. *Unknown*. NAAPv.2

Family Tree. Yusef Komunyakaa. FaoP

Family Tree, The. Catalina Cariaga. ReBoTo

Family were gathered, The. Kisimiso. Musaemura Bonus Zimunya. HBAPE; NAfrP

Family won't go away. I keep pulling up to them. Family in Spring, The. Gary Soto. WaAnP

Famine Road, The [*with music*]. Eavan Boland. MoWP

Famine, The. Henry Wadsworth Longfellow. TreFP *Fr.* Song of Hiawatha, The.

Fam'ly cares call next upon the wife, The. Joanna Baillie. NePenScot *Fr.* Winter Day, A.

Famous. Naomi Shihab Nye. LoL

Famous and the dead have learned to fall between our eyes, The. Feral Floats the Form in Heaven and of Light. Joshua Clover. ASA

Famous Baths and Bathers. Carolyn Wells. AmWit

Famous battle happened in this valley, A. How We Made a New Art on Old Ground. Eavan Boland. PoA 2002

Famous don't have ages like you and me, The. John Birks Gillespie: An Appreciation and Reflection. Everett Goodwin. BtF

Famous Flames. Ron Padgett. NYP2

Famous might have been this scholar. Scholar's Cat, The. János Arany. IQMS, *tr.* by Neville Masterman

Famous monk dropped to this knees before a giant image and cried, A. Robert Glück. WiU *Fr.* Visit, The.

Famous Poems of the Past Explained. Bin Ramke. PoDa; RoV

Famous Polish poet calls Simone de Beauvoir a Nazi hag, The. Deuxieme Sexe, La. Lucia Maria Perillo. RoV

Famous Tay Whale, The. William McGonagall.

 "And my opinion is that God sent the whale in time of need." VerBaPo

Famous Women—Claudette Colbert. Kathleen de Azevedo. ReTh

Famously she descended, her red hair. Recollection, A. John Peale Bishop. InGu

Fan. Jinkag Haesim. BecRai, *tr.* by Kim Daljin, Kim Won-Chung and Christopher Merrill

Fan from Korea, A [*with music*]. Chu Yün-ming. ColAnChi, *tr.* by Jonathan Chaves

Fan Letter, A. Amy Gerstler. BAP-97; BodElec

Fan of smoke in the long, green-white revery of the sky, A. Death. Maxwell Bodenheim. APT-1

Fan of white silk, A. Fan-Piece, for Her Imperial Lord. Pan Chieh-yü. APT-1, *tr.* by Ezra Pound

 (O fan of white silk.) NDACCP

Fan, The. Eugenio Montale. AF, *tr.* by William Arrowsmith

Fanaticism? No. Writing is exciting. Baseball and Writing. Marianne Moore. FaBoA; MoASP

Fanatics have their dreams, wherewith they weave. Fall of Hyperion, The; A Dream. John Keats. NAEL-6v2; NAEL-7v2

Fancies at Navesink. Walt Whitman.

 "By that long scan of waves, myself call'd back, resumed upon myself." NAAL-3

 "Had I the choice to tally greatest bards." SoSe-8

Fancy. John Keats. OBEV

Fancy. Thomas Moore. CenSon

Fancy, A. Thomas Carew. NOSC

Fancy and Imagination. Henrietta Cordelia Ray. CBWP-3

Fancy Another Day Gone. Lorine Niedecker. FTOS

Fancy baby New Year, fancy baby mine, fancy. (LL) Gertrude Stein. MotU; OxBoAm *Fr.* Book Concluding with As A Wife Has a Cow a Love Story, A.

Fancy Cortex. Harryette Mullen. AWPTFC

Fancy Dress. Dorothea MacKellar. NOBAu

Fancy in Nubibus. Samuel Taylor Coleridge. CenSon

Fancy (quoth he) farewell, whose badge I long did bear. Green Knight's Farewell to Fancy, The. George Gascoigne. NoSic

Fancy, that Sleeping makes us reenjoy. On My Visitt to WS Which I Dreamt of That Night. Lucy Hutchinson. EMWP

Fancy the Copt. Coptic Socks. Roy Fuller. OBCoV

Fancy the Sunrise—left the door ajar! (LL) I know some lonely Houses off the Road. Emily Dickinson. APN-2; MoAmPo

Fancy! to thee, I pour a votive strain. To Fancy. Martha Hanson. CenSon

Fand. William Larminie.
  Consolation. IrLP

Fanfare. U. A. Fanthorpe. MoWP; Prnts *Fr.* Stations Underground.

Fanfare of drums, wooden bells: iron chapter. Thunder Can Break. Christopher Okigbo. HBAPE

Fanfare of glory. . . . And which of us dares to deny him?, A. (LL) Tetélestai. Conrad Potter Aiken. APT-1; MoAmPo

Fannie / lou / hamer / never / heard / of. Sam Cornish. LTA

Fanny was younger once than she is now. Fanny. Fitz-Greene Halleck.

Fan-Piece, for Her Imperial Lord. Pan Chieh-yû. APT-1, *tr. by* Ezra Pound

Fans. Baron Wormser. SwNoth

Fantasia. G. K. Chesterton. SacPr

Fantasie Metropolitan. Janet Holmes. ExTi

Fantasies of a Love-Thief. Bilhana. EroLit, *tr. by* Barbara Stoler Miller
  "Even now." EroLit, *tr. by* Barbara Stoler Miller

Fantastic! Eduard Veniaminovich Limonov. TCRusP *Fr.* Secret Notebook.

Fantastic Names of Jazz, The. Hayden Carruth. GoPo

Fantasy. Gérard de Nerval. WoPoe, *tr. by* Geoffrey Wagner

Fantasy, A. Mathilde Blind. PoBW; ViWPN; VWP

Fantasy, A. Louise Glück. NAMCP V.2

Fantasy of an African Boy. James Berry. RSaN

Fantoches. Paul Verlaine. OBMV, *tr. by* Arthur Symons

Far above the dome. It Pleases. Gary Snyder. FaoP

Far above us where a jay. Morning on the Lièvre. Archibald Lampman. BrAP

Far / and / wee. (LL) In Just. E. E. Cummings. BLPJKO; FaBoVe; HarvBoo; HeIP-4; MoAmPo; NAAL-5; NAMPv.2; NAMCP V.1; NIL-7; NIP-4; NoP-4; NOxBChV; PoPoPo; SoSe-8; WaAnP; WeW-3

Far Away. Blas de Otero. RaW, *tr. by* Hardie St. Martin

Far Away. *Unknown.* FaBoWar

Far Away and Long Ago. Rubén Darío. PFTM-1; SpanPo, *tr. by* Denise Levertov

Far away from those. Only the Sun. István Sinka. IQMS, *tr. by* William Price Turner

Far away stands Ch'ong ŭn Temple. Blue Deer. Pak Mogwŏl [*or* Mokwŏl]. CAMKP, *tr. by* Edward W. Poitras

Far away, still I was with you. Eugenio Montale. WoPoe *Fr.* Motets [Mottetti].

Far away, we saw three chimneys in the trees. Chimneys. Ruth Bidgood. AngWePo

Far back, related on my mother's side. Old Salt Kossabone. Walt Whitman. WaAnP

Far back when I went zig-zagging. Orion. Adrienne Rich. BrAP; NAMCP V.2; NIP-4; NoAM; NoP-4; NoP-5

Far be remov'd each painted scene! Invocation. To Horror. Hannah Cowley. NOBRP

Far behind the trees one could hear. Liliane Giraudon. SCFWP *Fr.* Poem with Incense Paper.

Far beyond the chalky pain. Cyclones. Anna Hajnal. IQMS, *tr. by* Laurence James

Far brighter than this gaudy melon-flower! (LL) Home-Thoughts, from Abroad. Robert Browning. CABP; ClHu; HeIP-4; NAEL-6v2; NAEL-7v2; NoP-4; NoP-5; OBEV; TFi; UV

Far but near. End. Hugh Seidman. BodElec

Far cliff Babylon, your natty dread future is a dole card. Far Cliff Babylon. Barry MacSweeney. Oth

Far Cry from Africa, A. Derek Walcott. AmFaPo; BrAP; ESEAA; HeIP-4; NAEL-6v2; NAEL-7v2; NAMCP V.2; NIL-7; NoAM; NoP-4; NoP-5

Far down, down through the city's great gaunt gut. Subway Wind. Claude McKay. APT-1

Far down, in the pool below me. Seal Cave. Brenda Chamberlain. TCAWP

Far enough down is China, somebody said. Digging for China. Richard Wilbur. BrAP

Far, far. Abba Kovner. HP *Fr.* 'My Little Sister'.

Far, Far a City Lies. Abba Kovner. HP *Fr.* 'My Little Sister'.

Far, far, far are my silver waters drawn. Song of the Oktahutchee. Alexander L. Posey. APN-2

Far far from gusty waves these children's faces. Elementary School Classroom in a Slum, An. Stephen Spender. MoBrPo

Far, far out lie the white sails all at rest. Ocean Musing, An. Henrietta Cordelia Ray. CBWP-3; SWaP

Far far the least of all, in want. Prisoners, The. Stephen Spender. MoBrPo

Far Field, The. Theodore Roethke. ColAP; NAMCP V.1; NoAM *Fr.* North American Sequence.

Far footfalls died away till none were left. (LL) Ball's Bluff. Herman Melville. AmWaPo; CBCWP; FaBoWar; OBWP; OxBoAm

Far from a cultural centre he was used. W. H. Auden. NoAM

Far from Home. Nicholas Christopher. NoP-4; NoP-5

Far from kingdoms. Patrizia Cavalli. NeIt; VCWP, *tr. by* Judith Baumel

Far from Love the Heavenly Father. Emily Dickinson. APN-2

Far from me and like the stars, the sea, and all the props of poetic legend. If You Knew. Robert Desnos. SurPaPo; YaTCFP, *tr. by* Mary Ann Caws *and* Jean-Pierre Cauvin

Far from the Beach. Alda do Espírito Santo. HAWP, *tr. by* Jacques-Noël Gouat

Far from the brine. Cockles. Einir Jones. BBMWP, *tr. by* Joseph P. Clancy

Far from the happy homeland I adore. (LL) On a Shipmate, Pero Moniz, Dying at Sea. Luis de Camões [*or* Camõens *or* Camoëns]. OxBEV; WoPoe, *tr. by* Roy Campbell

Far from the heart of culture he was used. W. H. Auden. *See* Far from a cultural centre he was used.

Far from the Kingdoms. Patrizia Cavalli. CItWP, *tr. by* Cinzia Sartini Blum and Lara Trubowitz

Far from the Rappahannock, the silent. Into the Dusk-Charged Air. John Ashbery. APSN

Far from the Vistula, along the northern plain. Auschwitz. Salvatore Quasimodo. AF, *tr. by* Jack Bevan

Far from the vulgar haunts of men. On the Same. Roy Campbell. OBCoV

Far from this world, O Lord, I flee. William Cowper. SacPr *Fr.* Olney Hymns.

Far from this atmosphere that music sounds. Music. Henry David Thoreau. APN-1

Far have I clamored in my mind. Charity and Humility. Henry More. SacPr

Far In. Rachel Loden. PasH

Far in a western brookland. A. E. Housman. NPeEn *Fr.* Shropshire Lad, A.

Far in the forest deep. Mauberes, The. *Unknown.* SonAtl, *tr. by* Dino Haddia, Malcolm Watkins and Phillip Waynes

Far in the Heavens my God retires. Incomprehensible, The. Isaac Watts. SacPr

Far in the land of sunny South. Southern Scene, A. Priscilla Jane Thompson. CBWP-2

Far in the past, dimly it comes back to me. White Night. Boris Leonidovich Pasternak. RusPo, *tr. by* Robert Arthur Douglas Ford

Far in the purple valleys of illusion. Purple Valleys, The. Madison Cawein. APN-2

Far inland from the sea the onion fields. Onion Fields. Robert Francis. APT-2

Far inland, he. Navigation. Philip Booth. PfSP

Far into the amber night of future these first. Stealth-pirates of Cyberia. Blair Ewing. BRtP

Far o'er the waves my lofty bark shall glide. Describes her Bark. Mary Robinson. CenSon; RWP

Far off a lonely hound. Hounds, The. John Freeman. OBMV

Far off, above the plain the summer dries. Second Air Force. Randall Jarrell. NAAL-5

Far off and deep in woodlands ways. In the Forest of Vaal. János Vajda. IQMS, *tr. by* Watson Kirkconnell

Far off brough, A. *Unknown.* FaBoVe

Far off I see the River at Meng Ford. Song of the Breaking of the Willow. *Unknown.* ColAnChi, *tr. by* Burton Watson

Far off is less distant than the ground, the biting bed. Fraction. André Du Bouchet. YaTCFP, *tr. by* Mary Ann Caws

Far off it is a rainy smudge against the sky. Oil Well Fire. Grace Ross. TiP2

Far off the sea is grey and still as the sky. Week-End by the Sea. Edgar Lee Masters. MoAmPo

Far off, the yellow suburbs fade. All the Radios. Conrad Potter Aiken. InGu

Far out of sight forever stands the sea. Slow Pacific Swell, The. Yvor Winters. APT-2; CalPo; ColAP; HarvBoo; NAMCP V.1

Far reach. Lorine Niedecker. APT-2

Far Rockaway. Iwan Llwyd. ATSWP, *tr. by* Robert Minhinnick

Far Rockaway. Delmore Schwartz. APT-2; OxBoAm

Far space. Listening to Master Yu Chao Play the Lute. Heng Chao. CSKM, *tr. by* Paul Hansen

Far spreads the land. It seems not to dim her. (LL) *Unknown.* APN-2; NAAPv.1 *Fr.* Mountain Chant, The.

Far swifter than e'er Atalanta flew. To Flight. S. Conant Foster. ArBi

Far up Cold Mountain slants a rocky path. Mountain Walk, A. Tu Mu. CCL1, *tr. by* R. F. Burton

Far up the dim twilight fluttered. Unknown God, The. George Russell. MoBrPo

Far up the River—hark! 'tis the loud shock. Flight of Wild Ducks, A. Charles Harpur. NOBAu

Far Within Us. Vasco [*or* Vasko] Popa.
  "Look that is that uninvited." PoSu
  "Streets of your glances, The." PoSu
  "These are your lips." PoSu

Fara Diddle Dyno [*madrigal*]. Thomas Weelkes. OBCoV

Farasa. Nicholas Samaras. TWW

Farce was ended, The. Get Out of Town. Cole Porter. ReLy

Fare, the. Molly Peacock. ExTi; InoFa

Fare Thee Well. Lord Byron. NOBRP; NPBRoP

Fare thee well! bright land of beauty. Farewell to Texas. Anna Word Spragins. TiP2

Fare Well. Walter De la Mare. NoP-4; NoP-5; OBEV; OxBEV

Fare Ye Well. *Unknown.* SSUS

Fareweel to a' our Scotish fame. Such a Parcel of Rogues in a Nation. Robert Burns. NePenScot

Farewel, this world! I take my leve for evere. *Unknown. See* Farewell, this world! I take my leve for ever.

Farewel to the World, A. Michael Wigglesworth. SacPr

Farewell. Robert Fitzgerald. APT-2

Farewell. Enrique Lihn. BLPSL, *tr. by* Rene de Costa, Rigas Kappatos and Eleni Paidoussi

Farewell. Adriaan Morriën. TuT, *tr. by* Peter van de Kamp

Farewell. Arthur Rimbaud. SxFrPo, *tr. by* Martin Sorrell

Farewell. Wang Wei. CCL1, *tr. by* Pauline Yu

Farewell, A [*or* The]. Robert Burns. OBEV

Farewell, A: "Good-bye!—no [*or* nay] do not grieve that it is over." Harriet Monroe. PoA 2002

Farewell, A. Coventry Patmore. OBEV *Fr.* Unknown Eros, The.

Farewell, A: "I have not won." Eithne Strong. IrLP

Farewell, A: "Farewell thou little Nook of mountain-ground." William Wordsworth. OBGa

Farewell, The. Guillaume Apollinaire. YaTCFP, *tr. by* Roger Shattuck

Farewell, The. Rosario Castellanos. TANSG, *tr. by* Magda Bogin

Farewell, The: "They say the ice will hold." Edward Field. P180

Farewell, The. Letitia Elizabeth Landon. RWP; VWP

Farewell, The: "Gone, gone,—sold and gone." John Greenleaf Whittier. NCAP

Farewell! a long farewell to thee. Fleet Marmion. Mary Russell Mitford. DiBP

Farewell, a Welcome, A. Lisel Mueller. OtW

Farewell! Adieu! Good-bye! So long! (LL) To a Thesaurus. Franklin Pierce Adams. AmWit; NBLV

Farewell, adieu, that courtly life. John Pickering. NoSic *Fr.* Horestes.

Farewell and adieu to you noble hearties. Tom Deadlight. Herman Melville. APN-2; NCAP

Farewell!—and never think of me. Song. Letitia Elizabeth Landon. VWP

Farewell: "At a certain point I lost track of you." Agha Shahid Ali. PoDa

Farewell awhile, beautiful Italy! Farewell to Italy. Frances Anne Kemble. VWP

Farewell dear babe, my heart's too much content. In Memory of My Dear Grandchild Elizabeth Bradstreet Who Deceased August, 1665, Being a Year and Half Old. Anne Bradstreet. BASC; ColAP; NAAL-3; NAAL-5; NAAPv.1

Farewell, dear love! Since thou wilt needs be gone. *Unknown.* NoSic

Farewell Dinner for My Uncle Li Yun, the Collator, at Xie Tiao's Tower in Xuan Prefecture. Li Po. CCL1, *tr. by* Elling O. Eide

Farewell, false Friend!—our scenes of kindness close! Anna Seward. CenSon

Farewell, False Love. Sir Walter Ralegh. *See* Farewell to False Love, A.

Farewell, false love, the oracle of lies. Farewell to False Love, A. Sir Walter Ralegh. NoSic

Farewell: "Farewell to the bushy clump close to the river." John Clare. NoP-4; NoP-5

Farewell. farewells. (LL) Farewell Stairway, The. Barbara Guest. AWPTFC; NYP2

Farewell for ever to last night. Niall Mor MacMuireadach. NePenScot, *tr. by* Derick Thomson

Farewell, for Two Years, to England, A. A Poem. Helen Maria Williams. RWP

Farewell! gay Summer! now the changing wind. On the Approach of Autumn. Amelia Alderson Opie. CenSon

Farewell, German radio with your green eye. Electric Elegy. Adam Zagajewski. VCWP, *tr. by* Renata Gorczynski, Benjamin Ivry and C. K. Williams

Farewell in a Dream. Stephen Spender. MoBrPo

Farewell, incomparable element. Hymn to Earth. Elinor Wylie. MoAmPo

Farewell! Like a bee. Basho. BLPJKO, *tr. by* Harry Behn

Farewell, love, and all thy law[e]s forever [*or* for ever]. Sir Thomas Wyatt. GSo; NAEL-6v1; NAEL-7v1; NoSic; OxBSo
  (Ffarewell, love, and all thy lawes for ever.) BrAP

Farewell my dearer half, joy of my heart. First Farewell to J.G. "Ephelia." NOSC

Farewell, my lute!—and would that I. Letitia Elizabeth Landon. NPBRoP; RWP; VWP *Fr.* Improvisatrice, The.

Farewell, my younger brother! *Unknown.* APN-2 *Fr.* Mountain Chant, The.

Farewell, My Youth. Yi Sanghûi. EcSo, *tr. by* Jennifer M. Lee

Farewell, my Youth! for now we needs must part. Ave atque Vale. Rosamund Marriott Watson. OBEV

Farewell now, poesy's secret cell, thy ordered grace. Farewell to Hendre Fechan. William Phylip. OBWVE, *tr. by* H. Idris Bell

Farewell, O Sun, Arcadia's clearest light. Sir Philip Sidney. WaAnP *Fr.* Countesse of Pembroke's Arcadia, The.

Farewell of the Attendant Spirit. John Milton. OBEV; OxAEP-1 *Fr.* Comus; a Masque Presented at Ludlow Castle.

Farewell once more,—and yet again farewell! George Henry Boker. APN-2 *Fr.* Sonnets: A Sequence on Profane Love.

Farewell Poem. *Unknown.* CrYelRi, *tr. by* Sam Hamill

Farewell Queen Mother Moore. John Watusi Branch. BRtP

Farewell, Rewards and Fairies. Richard Corbet. *See* Proper New Ballad Entitled [*or* Intituled] The Fairies' [*or* Faeryes] Farewell, or God-a-Mercy Will, A.

Farewell, rewards and fairies [*or* faeries]. Proper New Ballad Entitled [*or* Intituled] The Fairies' [*or* Faeryes] Farewell, or God-a-Mercy Will, A. Richard Corbet. BASC; NOSC; OxBEV; PBRV

Farewell Rhyme. Tu Fu [*or* Du Fu]. CrYelRi, *tr. by* Sam Hamill

"Farewell, Romance!" the Cave-men said. King, The. Rudyard Kipling. CABP

Farewell San Miguel, splendid with your harvested fields. Angela de Trejo. ASA, *tr. by* Antonio Mantilla Sanchez

Farewell! / Shadows and scenes that have, for many hours. Farewell, The. Letitia Elizabeth Landon. RWP; VWP

Farewell Song. Ch'in Kuan. CrYelRi, *tr. by* Sam Hamill

Farewell Song of Magic Strings. Li Ho. CCL1, *tr. by* John Frodsham

Farewell Stairway, The. Barbara Guest. AWPTFC; NYP2

Farewell sweet Boy, complaine not of my truth. Fulke, 1st Baron Brooke Greville. NPeEn *Fr.* Caelica.

Farewell (sweet Cooke-ham [*or* Cookham]) where I first obtained [*or* obtain'd]. Description of Cooke-ham [*or* Cookham], The. Emilia Lanier. BASC; CABP; NAEL-6v1; NAEL-7v1; NoP-4; NoP-5; PBRV; WaAnP

Farewell, that was my lef so dere. *Unknown.* EMWP

Farewell, then. It is finished. I forego. Wilfrid Scawen Blunt. OxBSo

Farewell, this world! I take my leve for ever. *Unknown.* NPeEn

Farewell! thou art too dear[e] for my possessing. William Shakespeare. CAGL; NAEL-6v1; NAEL-7v1; NoP-5; NoSic; OBEV; OxAEP-1; TFi *Fr.* Sonnets.

Farewell, thou child of my right hand and joy. On My First Son. Ben Jonson. AmFaPo; BASC; BrAP; CABP; ClHu; InoFa; MakPoe; NAEL-6v1; NAEL-7v1; NIL-7; NIP-4; NoP-4; NoP-5; NOSC; NPeEn; OxBEV; PBRV; PoPoPo; RaBo; SUP; TFi; TRP; WaAnP; WeW-3; WoPoe

Farewell, thou dimpled cherub, Joy. Joseph Warton. STuOW *Fr.* Ode against Despair.

Farewell thou fertyll soyle. Barnabe Googe. PBRV

Farewell thou little Nook of mountain-ground. Farewell, A. William Wordsworth. OBGa

Farewell, thou Thing, time-past so knowne, so dear. His Farewell [*or* Farewell] to Sack. Robert Herrick. NAEL-6v1; NAEL-7v1

Farewell to a Southern Melody, A. Huang O. WoPoe, *tr. by* Chung Ling and Kenneth Rexroth

Farewell to Allen University [*with music*]. Josephine D. Henderson Heard. CBWP-4

Farewell[l] to America, A. To Mrs. S. W. Phillis Wheatley. NoP-4; NoP-5

Farewell to an idea. . .A cabin stands. Wallace Stevens. NAMCP V.1 *Fr.* Auroras of Autumn, The.

Farewell to an idea. . .The mother's face. Wallace Stevens. NAMCP V.1 *Fr.* Auroras of Autumn, The.

Farewell to Arms, A. George Peele. *See* His Golden Lock[e]s [Time Hath to Silver Turned].

Farewell to barn and stack and tree. A. E. Housman. HarvBoo; MoBrPo *Fr.* Shropshire Lad, A.

Farewell to Dostoevski. Hugh MacDiarmid. NAEL-6v2; NAEL-7v2 *Fr.* Drunk Man Looks at the Thistle, A.

Farewell to English, A.   Michael Hartnett.
   "Her eyes were coins of porter and her West."   ModIr
Farewell to False Love, A.   Sir Walter Ralegh.   NoSic
   (Farewell, False Love.)   NAEL-6v1; NAEL-7v1
Farewell to Florida.   Wallace Stevens.   NoAM
Farewell to France.   Sarah Hamilton.   CenSon
Farewell to Hendre Fechan.   William Phylip.   OBWVE, tr. by H. Idris Bell
Farewell to Italy.   Frances Anne Kemble.   VWP
Farewell to Last Night.   Niall Mor MacMuireadach.   IrLP, tr. by Myles Dillon
Farewell to London in the Year 1715, A.   Alexander Pope.   OBCoV
Farewell to Love.   John Donne.   BASC
Farewell to Love.   Michael Drayton.   MakPoe; NOSC
Farewell to Maria.   Tadeusz Borowski.   HP, tr. by Tadeuszt Pióro
Farewell to Master Tan Returning to Min.   Chia Tao.   CSKM, tr. by Mike O'Connor
Farewell to Master Yu Chao.   Wen Chao.   CSKM, tr. by Paul Hansen
Farewell to Monk Chih-Hsing.   Chia Tao.   CSKM, tr. by Mike O'Connor
Farewell to Russia.   Lev Mak.   TCRusP, tr. by Daniel Weissbort
Farewell to Spring.   Wang Wei.   CCL1, tr. by John Francis Davis
Farewell to Texas.   Anna Word Spragins.   TiP2
Farewell to the bushy clump close to the river.   Farewell.   John Clare.   NoP-4; NoP-5
Farewell to the Court.   George Peele.   See His Golden Lock[e]s [Time Hath to Silver Turned].
Farewell to the Court.   Sir Walter Ralegh.   NoSic
Farewell to the Highlands.   Robert Burns.   See My Heart's in the Highlands.
Farewell to the Highlands, farewell to the North.   Robert Burns.   See My heart's in the Highlands, my heart is not here.
Farewell to the Land where the gloom of my Glory.   Napoleon's Farewell.   Lord Byron.   NPBRoP
Farewell to the Muse, A.   Maria Jane Jewsbury.   VWP
Farewell to the world, and to the night farewell.   Chikamatsu Monzaemon.   WoPoe Fr. Love Suicides at Sonezaki, The.
Farewell to Thee.   Queen Lili'u-o-ka-lani.   See Aloha'oe.
Farewell to T'ien Cho on Retreat on Hua Mountain.   Chia Tao.   CSKM, tr. by Mike O'Connor
Farewell to Várad.   Janus Pannonius.   IQMS, tr. by Adam Makkai
Farewell to Van Gogh.   Charles Tomlinson.   NoP-4; NoP-5
Farewell to Vinaya Master Ts'ung, Traveling in the West.   Heng Chao.   CSKM, tr. by Paul Hansen
Farewell to Wei Feng, Going to Far-South Mountain.   Hsi Chou.   CSKM, tr. by Paul Hansen
Farewell to Whitefoot.   Michael Drayton.   DiBP Fr. Shepherd's Garland, The.
Farewell to Worldly Joys, A.   Anne Killigrew.   BASC; CABP
Farewell to Yin Shu.   Li Po.   CrYelRi, tr. by Sam Hamill
Farewell to You.   Elizabeth Alexander.   GT
Farewell, too little and too lately known.   To the Memory of Mr Oldham.   John Dryden.   BASC; BrAP; NAEL-6v1; NAEL-7v1; NIL-7; NIP-4; NoP-4; NoP-5; NOSC; NPeEn; OxAEP-1; OxBEV; PoPoPo; TFi; TRP; WaAnP
Farewell, ungrateful traitor!   John Dryden.   RACG
Farewell, unkist! (LL)   Sir Thomas Wyatt.   NoP-4; NoP-5
Farewell! We lose ourselves in light. (LL)   Alfred Tennyson.   NAEL-6v2; NAEL-7v2 Fr. In Memoriam A. H. H.
Farewell, ye coral caves, ye pearly sands.   Suspects his Constancy.   Mary Robinson.   CenSon; RWP
Farewell, ye towering cedars, in whose shade.   Determines to Follow Phaon.   Mary Robinson.   CenSon; RWP
Farewell ye unsubstantial joys.   Farewell to Worldly Joys, A.   Anne Killigrew.   BASC; CABP
Farewells from Paradise.   Elizabeth Barrett Browning.   OBEV
Farm, A. A cannon on a hill.   Cannon Hill.   Sandra Hochman.   YaYoPo
Farm and black wood-stack stand, The.   Tristitia Ante.   Maurice Gilliams.   TuT, tr. by Sean Dunne
Farm Boy after Summer.   Robert Francis.   APT-2
Farm boys wild to couple.   Sheep Child, The.   James Dickey.   CAP-8; EmeKit; NAMCP V.2; NoAM; VCAP
Farm Implements and Rutabagas in a Landscape.   John Ashbery.   HarvBoo; NAMCP V.2; PmAP; WaAnP
Farm in the Green Mountains, A.   Dave Etter.   VisFro
Farm Is Yours, The.   León Felipe.   RaW, tr. by Hardie St. Martin
Farm never seemed the same after gramps died, The.   Memories.   Charles Bernstein.   BodElec
Farm Picture, A.   Walt Whitman.   BLT; TRP
Farm-to-Market #4.   Richard Sale.   TiP2
Farm Wife.   Ronald Stuart Thomas.   GoPo
Farm within farm, and in the centre, me. (LL)   Summer Farm.   Norman Alexander MacCaig.   NePenScot; NoP-5; NPeEn; StAl; WaAnP
Farm Woman, The: 1942 [with music].   Naomi Mitchison.   EdScPo; RSaN

Farm woman opens, A.   Female Ancestor.   Ann Elizabeth Hostetler.   ACAMVP
Farmer.   Prince Redcloud.   HHAm
Farmer, The.   Kees Ouwens.   TuT, tr. by Peter van de Kamp
Farmer, The.   Fredegond Maitland Shove.   SacPr
Farmer, The.   Ellen Bryant Voigt.   WeW-3
Farmer, The.   William Carlos Williams.   NAMCP V.1
Farmer and the Farmer's Wife, The.   Paul Gerhardt Hiebert.   NBLV
Farmer in deep thought, The.   Farmer, The.   William Carlos Williams.   NAMCP V.1
Farmer / Pointing the way.   Issa.   ZenPo, tr. by Takashi Ikemoto and Lucien Stryk
Farmer puts his field under the plow, The.   Sándor Petőfi.   IQMS Fr. Clouds, The.
Farmer Remembers the Somme, The.   Vance Palmer.   NOBAu
Farmer said, The.   Salting of Snow, A.   Hamish Brown.   EdScPo
Farmer Seth Atwood was past eighty when.   Well, The.   Howard Phillips Lovecraft.   APT-1
Farmer sings about the Fourth Moon, A.   Buried Light.   Yusef Komunyakaa.   AmAlph
Farmer sleeps under a printed stone, The.   Apple-Tree Man, The.   Charles Causley.   OBSP
Farmer, what's the point complaining.   Unknown.   PriapPo Fr. Priapus Poems, The.
Farmer with his weather-powers, The.   F is for Forecast.   Eleanor Farjeon.   RWPCtW
Farmer, worn from, The.   Farmer.   Prince Redcloud.   HHAm
Farmers.   Kathleen Peirce.   PBCAP
Farmers.   Wang Ji.   CCL1, tr. by Stephen Owen
Farmers are practical people, all right.   Music for the Cows.   Jim Johnson.   MiVo
Farmer's Boy, The.   Robert Bloomfield.
   "Now, ere sweet Summer bids its long adieu."   NPBRoP
   To Err Is Human.   DiBP
   Trouncer, the Foxes Foe.   DiBP
Farmer's Bride, The.   Charlotte Mew.   CABP; LW; MoBrPo; MoWP; NALW; NoP-4; NoP-5; RACG; VWP
Farmers come, come, The.   People from the Valley, The.   Keith Wilson.   ICANM
Farmer's Dance.   Shin Kyŏngnim.   CAMKP, tr. by David R. McCann
Farmer's Evidence, The.   Gwyneth Lewis.   ATSWP, tr. by Robert Minhinnick
Farmers' Life insurance agent, The.   Drought: Sure Signs in Merkle, Texas.   Robert A. Fink.   TiP2
Farmer's Pride, The.   Unknown.   WoPoe, tr. by Nguyen Ngoc Bich
Farmer's roadside, The.   Basho.   SoOfWa, tr. by Sam Hamill
Farmer's son is good and mad, The.   Recitative: "Farmer's son is good and mad," The.   Ronald McCuaig.   NOBAu
Farmer's Song, The.   Abburi Ramakrishna Rao.   HotL, tr. by V. Narayana Rao
Farmer's wife looked out of the dairy, The.   Rival, The.   Sylvia Townsend Warner.   MoBrPo
Farmhand lay all hidden, A.   Steinmar.   GePo
Farmhouse, The.   Reed Whittemore.   GoPo
Farmhouse: Three Poems.   Yi Kyubo.   CATKP, tr. by Kevin O'Rourke
   "Leaves of the mountain pear are red, The."   CATKP, tr. by Kevin O'Rourke
   "Loom importunes, The."   CATKP, tr. by Kevin O'Rourke
   "Village mill echoes, The."   CATKP, tr. by Kevin O'Rourke
Far-off a young State rises, full of might.   Farther.   John James Piatt.   APN-2
Far-Off Journey.   Ts'ao Chih.   CCL1, tr. by John Frodsham
Far-off, most secret, and inviolate Rose.   Secret Rose, The.   William Butler Yeats.   NAEL-6v2; NAEL-7v2
Far-Off Rose, A.   Josephine Preston Peabody.   TCAPo
Farragut, Farragut.   William Tuckey Meredith.   CBCWP
Farrar! to thee these early lays I owe.   Studley Park.   John Langhorne.   OBGa
Farther.   John James Piatt.   APN-2
Farther and farther down the green mountain. (LL)   On Parting with the Buddhist Pilgrim Ling-Ch'ĕ.   Liu Ch'ang-ch'ing.   CCL1; WoPoe, tr. by Witter Bynner
Farther east it wouldn't be on the map.   Midwest Town.   Ruth Delong Peterson.   CA
Farther he went the farther home grew, The.   For the Grave of Daniel Boone.   William Stafford.   NAMCP V.2
Farthest Thunder that I heard, The.   Emily Dickinson.   NAAL-3
Fascicle 34 Poem 9.   Emily Dickinson.   PFTM-1
Fascinación por lo que se ve y se oye desde la estatura, por las calles desde la banqueta.   Huevos puestos un por un tigre.   Antonio Deltoro.   RMCMP
Fascinating Rhythm.   Ira Gershwin.   ReLy
Fascinating the way our dreams.   In the Chariot Drawn by Dragons.   Michael Van Walleghen.   IllVoic

Fascination. Sikong Tu. CCL1 *Fr.* Twenty-Four Modes of Poetry.

Fascination for what is seen and heard from the heights, in the streets from the sidewalk. Eggs Laid by a Tiger. Antonio Deltoro. RMCMP, *tr. by* Christian Viveros-Fauné

Fascination in love of self, A. (LL) At the Poem. Clark Coolidge. AHA; NYP2

Fascination of What's Difficult, The. William Butler Yeats. NAEL-6v2; NAEL-7v2; NAMCP V.1; OxAEP-2

Fashion. Ada Cambridge. NOBAu

Fashionable women in luxurious homes. Anti-Suffragists, The. Charlotte Perkins Stetson Gilman. SWaP

Fashioned After the Manner of Master Geoffrey Chaucer in His Assembly of Fowls. Thomas Warton, the Elder. ChIV-1

Fast asleep on the wooden bench. Warru. Jack Davis. BMAP

Fast Break. Edward Hirsch. MoASP; P180; VCAP

Fast breaks. Lay ups. With Mercury's. Slam, Dunk, & Hook. Yusef Komunyakaa. ISC; MoASP

Fast Car On Nebraska I-80: Visting Teacher. Hilda Raz. ExTi

Fast Gas. Dorianne Laux. GeoHom; SUP

Fast train, The? The express? Miryana Basheva. CSCBP, *tr. by* Georgi Belev and Lisa Sapinkopf

Fast-anchor'd eternal O love! O woman I love! Fast-Anchor'd Eternal O Love! Walt Whitman. APN-1

Fasten the chamber! Bluebeard's Closet. Rose Terry Cooke. APN-2; NAAPv.1; TCAPo

Faster, Earth, Faster. Juan Ramón Jiménez. SpanPo, *tr. by* Eloise Roach

Faster, Faster/ O Circe, Godess. Strayed Reveller, The. Matthew Arnold.

Faster I find to the war[re] they arme them. (LL) Bible, *O.T.* BASC; OxBEV *Fr.* Psalms.

Faster than fairies, faster than witches. From a Railway Carriage. Robert Louis Stevenson. NePenScot

Fastidiously, with gloved and careful fingers. Lady Selecting Her Christmas Cards. Phyllis McGinley. ChrPo

Fat black bucks in a wine-barrel room. Congo, The. Vachel Lindsay. APT-1; MoAmPo

Fat black woman, The / could see through politicians. Fat Black Woman Versus Politics, The. Grace Nichols. MoWP

Fat Black Woman Versus Politics, The. Grace Nichols. MoWP

Fat black woman want, The. Tropical Death. Grace Nichols. InoFa; NAMCP V.2

Fat Budgie, The. John Lennon. NBLV

Fat Chance. Beth Gylys. AmPoNex

Fat in America. Heid E. Erdrich. AmPoNex

Fat Is Not a Fairy Tale. Jane Yolen. P180

Fat men go about the streets, The. Ballade of the Poetic Life. Sir John Collings Squire. OBMV

Fat of the Land, The. Ronald Wallace. FTtHH

Fat priest, The. Issa. EH, *tr. by* Robert Hass

Fat White Woman Speaks, The. G. K. Chesterton. OBCoV; UV

Fata Morgana in Flanders. Willem M. Roggeman. TuT, *tr. by* Gabriel Rosenstock

Fatal Birth, The. Ebenezer Elliott. OxBSo

Fatal Love [*with music*]. Matthew Prior. NBLV

Fatal sisters—death and cards and women, The. Dark Fates, The. Dezső Kosztolányi. IQMS, *tr. by* Lydia Pasternak-Slater

Fatal Volume, The. Marina Ivanovna Tsvetayeva. GI, *tr. by* Nina Kossman

Fatalist, The. Lyn Hejinian.
  "I arrived with biographical context." OxBoAm
  "Presences that constitute life do so by entering life, The." Eno
  "Time is filled with beginners. You are right. Now." FaoP

Fatality. Rubén Darío. TCLAP, *tr. by* Lysander Kemp

Fate. Carolyn Wells. SWaP

Fate brought me as husband a child I must raise. *Unknown.* SLW, *tr. by* Marjolijn De Jager, Sayd Bahodin Majrouh and André Velter

Fate fell upon a man. Fate. Helen B. Cruickshank. EdScPo

Fate, give me space to breathe, let me do. Fate Give Me Space. Sándor Petőfi. IQMS, *tr. by* Edwin Morgan

Fate is a cruel. Fate Is a Cruel and Proficient Potter. Vidya. WoPoe, *tr. by* Andrew Schelling

Fate of Vultures, The. Tanure Ojaide. NAfrP

Fate / Sent her to me. She's a Latin from Manhattan. Al Dubin. ReLy

Fates of Men. Peter Reading. PML

Fate's sister, fortune, favours those. Christopher Logue. FaBoWar *Fr.* War Music.

2. Fates Worse Than Death. Don McKay. NLPA *Fr.* Matériel.

Father. Ralph Dickey. ESEAA

Father. Myra Cohn Livingston. NTCP

Father. John Tripp. TCAWP

Father. Paul Zweig. BodElec

Father, The. Maura Eichner. UpMys

Father, The. Joshua Sylvester. InvLi; SacPr

Father, adonoi, author of all things. Anthony Hecht. PWW2 *Fr.* Rites and Ceremonies.

Father, and bard revered! to whom I owe. Dedicatory Sonnet to S. T. Coleridge. Hartley Coleridge. CenSon

Father and Daughter. Sonia Sanchez. FFC; GT

Father and Daughter. Cathy Song. OpBo

Father and Farther. Sherman Alexie. AmPoNex

Father and I drove to the sand-quarry across the ruined marshlands. Sand-Quarry with Moving Figures. Muriel Rukeyser. NoP-4

Father and I went down to camp. Yankee Doodle. *Unknown.* TCAPo

Father and I went to camp. Royall Tyler. NAAL-3 *Fr.* Contrast, The.

Father and mother watch an automobile with a just married sign on it growing smaller in a road. (LL) Automobile, The. Russell Edson. RaBo; SUP

Father and Son. DJ Renegade. BtF

Father and Son. Robert Greacen. PNI

Father and Son. Frederick Robert Higgins. OBMV

Father and Son. Stanley Kunitz. AF; TaR, *tr. by* Jack Bevan

Father Burns has given us Basil, his greyhound pup. Holy Land, The. Maurice Riordan. NIrP

Father calls me William, sister calls me Will. Jest 'fore Christmas. Eugene Field. ChrPo

Father Country. Tyehimba Jess. BtF

Father dead, loved one dead. Motionless Faces. Carlos Drummond de Andrade. PFTM-1

Father, dear father, come home with me now! Come Home, Father[!]. Henry Clay Work. APN-2; NAAPv.1

Father Death Blues. Allen Ginsberg. CLPP *Fr.* don't Grow Old.

Father dozes with a book of heroes. Circlings. Leonard Nathan. PML

Father, father, where are you going? William Blake. NoP-4; NoP-5; WaAnP *Fr.* Songs of Innocence.

Father from Asia. Shirley Lim. UnSA

Father, grant me yourself from Elysian springs. Publius Papinius Statius. RomPo *Fr.* Sylvae [*or Silvae*].

Father grew up here. Red Hills of Home. Chenjerai Hove. HBAPE; NAfrP

Father has a bus'ness. Second Hand Rose. Grant Clarke. ReLy

Father, have pity on me. *Arapaho Oral Tradition.* NAAL-5; NAAPv.2 *Fr.* Ghost-Dance Songs.

Father / (he calls himself). Anne Sexton. NAAL-5 *Fr.* Death of the Fathers, The.

Father, he cried, after the critics' chewing. Howard Nemerov. GI *Fr.* Gnomes.

Father, hello and goodbye. (LL) Elegy: "I know but will not tell." Alan Dugan. NIL-7; NIP-4

Father! I bless thy name that I do live. In Him We Live [and Move and Have Our Being]. Jones Very. APN-1

Father, I have sinned and I confess. In the Box. John Powell Ward. PML

Father, I know that all my life. My Times Are in Thy Hand. Anna L. Waring. SacPr

Father! I wait thy word—the sun doth stand. Son, The. Jones Very. NCAP

Father in heaven, after each lost day. Petrarch. NAWM-5v1; NAWM-7v1 *Fr.* Sonnets to Laura.

Father, it was an honor to be there, in the dugout. Poem for My Father; for Quincy Trouppe, Sr. Quincy Troupe. MoASP
  (Father, it was honor to be there, in the dugout.) AF

Father John's bread was made of rye. Rye Bread. William Stanley Braithwaite. GT

Father Knows Best. David Shapiro. OxBoAm

Father led me behind some mail-bags. My Father's Trapdoors. Peter Redgrove. PML

Father Mat. Patrick Kavanagh. ModIr

Father, Mother. Carlos German Belli. TCLAP, *tr. by* Maureen Ahern and David Tipton

Father, Mother. Father, Mother. Carlos German Belli. TCLAP, *tr. by* Maureen Ahern and David Tipton

Father, Mother, and me. Rudyard Kipling. NAMCP V.1; NoAM *Fr.* Debits and Credits.

Father / Mother Haibun #1. Fred Wah. NLPA *Fr.* This Dendrite Map: Father / Mother Haibun.

Father / Mother Haibun #2. Fred Wah. NLPA *Fr.* This Dendrite Map: Father / Mother Haibun.

Father / Mother Haibun #3. Fred Wah. NLPA *Fr.* This Dendrite Map: Father / Mother Haibun.

Father / Mother Haibun #4. Fred Wah. NLPA; OpeFie *Fr.* This Dendrite Map: Father / Mother Haibun.

Father / Mother Haibun #5. Fred Wah. IFF; NLPA *Fr.* This Dendrite Map: Father / Mother Haibun.

Father / Mother Haibun #6. Fred Wah. NLPA *Fr.* This Dendrite Map: Father / Mother Haibun.

Father / Mother Haibun #7. Fred Wah. NLPA *Fr.* This Dendrite Map: Father / Mother Haibun.

Father / Mother Haibun #8. Fred Wah. NLPA *Fr.* This Dendrite Map: Father / Mother Haibun.

Father / Mother Haibun #9. Fred Wah. NLPA *Fr.* This Dendrite Map: Father / Mother Haibun.

Father / Mother Haibun #10. Fred Wah. NLPA *Fr.* This Dendrite Map: Father / Mother Haibun.

Father / Mother Haibun #11. Fred Wah. NLPA; OpeFie *Fr.* This Dendrite Map: Father / Mother Haibun.

Father / Mother Haibun #12. Fred Wah. NLPA *Fr.* This Dendrite Map: Father / Mother Haibun.

Father / Mother Haibun #13. Fred Wah. NLPA *Fr.* This Dendrite Map: Father / Mother Haibun.

Father / Mother Haibun #14. Fred Wah. NLPA *Fr.* This Dendrite Map: Father / Mother Haibun.

Father / Mother Haibun #15. Fred Wah. NLPA *Fr.* This Dendrite Map: Father / Mother Haibun.

Father / Mother Haibun #16. Fred Wah. NLPA *Fr.* This Dendrite Map: Father / Mother Haibun.

Father / Mother Haibun #17. Fred Wah. NLPA *Fr.* This Dendrite Map: Father / Mother Haibun.

Father / Mother Haibun #18. Fred Wah. NLPA

Father / Mother Haibun #19. Fred Wah. NLPA *Fr.* This Dendrite Map: Father / Mother Haibun.

Father / Mother Haibun #20. Fred Wah. NLPA *Fr.* This Dendrite Map: Father / Mother Haibun.

Father / Mother Haibun #21. Fred Wah. NLPA *Fr.* This Dendrite Map: Father / Mother Haibun.

Father, Mother, Robert Henley, who hanged himself in the ninth grade, et al. Stephen Dunn. StAl

Father, 1952. Christopher Buckley. GeoHom

Father! no amaranths e'er shall wreathe my brow. Sara Coleridge. VWP

Father / —nothing now to be talked to. With Me. Yvonne Cullen. NIrP

Father of all! in every [*or* ev'ry] age. Universal Prayer, The [Deo Opt. Max.]. Alexander Pope. InvLi; NoP-4; NoP-5

Father of Famine. Richard Ryan. PBCIP

Father of Light! great God of Heaven! Prayer of Nature, The. Lord Byron. TreFP

Father of lights! what sunny [*or* sunnie] seed. Cock-crowing. Henry Vaughan. BASC; NAEL-7v1; NPeEn; PBRV

Father of love! Evening Prayer. Henrietta Cordelia Ray. CBWP-3

Father of My Country, The. Diane Wakoski. NoAM

Father of My Father. Lawson Fusao Inada. UnSA

Father of Rivers! standing by thy side. Richard Henry Wilde. APN-1 *Fr.* Hesperia.

Father of the Bride. Robin Metz. MAAN

Father of the Faithful said, The. Christopher Smart. ChIV-1 *Fr.* Hymns for the Amusement of Children.

Father of the Man. David Graham. SwNoth

Father of the Stethoscope, The. Back-Up Singer, The. Dorothy Barresi. SwNoth

Father of Women, A [Ad Sororem E. B.]. Alice Thompson Meynell. NALW; VWP

Father O'Fondle comes to town. Eli, Eli. Jack Foley. FTtHH

Father on My Shoulders. Harry Thurston. Coast

Father or Son. James Schuyler. FTOS

Father (Part 1). Harryette Mullen. OxAAAP; TiP2

Father rides the subway. Great Indian Father in the Subway. Diane Glancy. FiBr

Father Riley's Horse. Andrew Barton Paterson. NOBAu

Father said if I gave the boy who was teasing me. Cookies for Peace. Hal Sirowitz. PA9/11

Father sat by the chimney-post, A. Good and Better. *Unknown.* TreFP

Father Says So, The. *Sioux Oral Tradition. See* Songs of the Sioux.

Father says so, the father says so, The. (LL) *Sioux Oral Tradition.* NAAL-5; TCAPo *Fr.* Ghost-Dance Songs.

Father says so—*E'yayo!,* The. *Sioux Oral Tradition.* NAAL-5 *Fr.* Ghost-Dance Songs.

Father Son and Holy Ghost. Audre Lorde. ESEAA; NoAM

Father stands on a walkway talking, A. Folktale, A. Tonya Foster. FreRad

Father studied theology through the mail. Book Full of Pictures, A. Charles Simic. NoP-4; NoP-5

Father, this year's jinx rides us apart. All My Pretty Ones. Anne Sexton. NAMCP V.2; NoAM; OxBoAm

Father! Thy wonders do not singly stand. God Not Afar Off. Jones Very. InvLi

Father was a serf. Self-portrait. Sŏ Chŏngju. CAMKP, *tr. by* David R. McCann

Father was a serf, seldom came home at night. Self-Portrait. Sŏ Chŏngju. WoPoe, *tr. by* Peter H. Lee

Father was to her, and to me. Fever. Judith Ortiz Cofer. PueRic

Father, when I am in my grave, kind Father. Christina. Dora Greenwell. VWP

Father, who designs his babe a priest, The. William Cowper. OBSV *Fr.* Tirocinium; or, A Review of Schools.

Father who found this vibrant light. Whitman, Come Again to the Cities. Toi Derricotte. ViWalt

Father! whose hard and cruel law. Death of Grant, The. Ambrose Bierce. CBCWP

Father will descend, The. *Unknown.* APN-2 *Fr.* Ghost-Dance Songs.

Father William. Lewis Carroll. ChAP; NPeEn; OBCoV; OxBEV; TFi *Fr.* Alice's Adventures in Wonderland.

Father, you must have been. Offering. Thomas McGrath. RaBo

Father, you turn your hands toward me. Father from Asia. Shirley Lim. UnSA

Fatherhood. Joan Waddleton. Prnts

Fathering the Map. Robert Pack. PfSP

Fatherland in the Heights. Gyula Illyés. IQMS, *tr. by* Vernon Watkins

Fatherless and childless: not a who will know us. Dazzled afternoon won't we widow ourselves away. (LL) Who won't praise green. Each minute to caress each minute blade of spring. Green slice us open. D. A. Powell. NAPBL; NeAmPo

Fatherless Townships. Abiyah. BRtP

Fathers. Robert Creeley. FTOS

Fathers and brothers still excavate and sift for the remains of the dead. Boerum Hill Tanka. Kimiko Hahn. PA9/11

Fathers and Sons. Peter Cooley. MAAN

Fathers and Sons. Tom Leonard. CABP; NePenScot

Father's Day. E. Ethelbert Miller. OxAAAP

Father's Day. Aarian Pope. BRtP

Father's Day. Gloria Vando. TouFir

Father's Death, A. John Hewitt. PNI

Father's Hymn for the Mother to Sing. George Macdonald. SacPr

Fathers in the Snow. Jill Bialosky.
  "After father died." InoFa

Father's Love, The. Mary E. Tucker. CBWP-1

Fathers: naked, you stand for their big faces. This Is a Poem for the Dead. Michael Ryan. YaYoPo

Father's Old Blue Cardigan. Anne Carson. StAl

Father's Poem, A. Sarah Arsone. WhBo

Father's Shoes. Tyehimba Jess. BtF

Father's sickle is hanging. *Unknown.* WoPoe *Fr.* Two Swedish Riddles.

Father's Song. Gregory Orr. PoChi

Fathers, The: "Something's familiar about that villain." Elizabeth Holmes. P180

Father's Things. R. V. Bailey. Prnts

Father-Sequence. Luigi Fontanella. NeIt, *tr. by* Michael Palma

Fathoms they abide, The. (LL) She Rose to His Requirement—Dropt. Emily Dickinson. NAAPv.1; NALW

Fatigue. Joseph Hilaire Pierre Belloc. NBLV; UV

Fatima. Laura Kasischke. AmPoNex

Fat-kneed god! Feeder of mangy leopards! You Also, Gaius Valerius Catullus. Archibald MacLeish. NoAM

Fatness. Alan Ansen. GPTC

Fatted / on herbs, swollen on crabapples. Porcupine, The. Galway Kinnell. NAAL-5

Faucet she is dripping, The. Mañana (Is Soon Enough for Me). Dave Barbour and Peggy Lee. ReLy

Faucet the benefactor, The. Josée Lapeyrère. SCFWP *Fr.* Dishes, The.

Faulce hope which feeds butt to destroy, and spill. Mary Sidney Wroth, Countess of Montgomery. *See* Sonnet 35: "False [*or* Faulce] hope which feeds but[t] to destroy, and spill."

Fault, The. John Montague. *Fr.* Rough Field, The.

Fault, The. Carol Muske-Dukes. GeoHom

Faun Sees Snow for the First Time, The. Richard Aldington. MoBrPo

Faust. Johann Wolfgang von Goethe. *tr. by* David Luke, Louis MacNeice and Bayard Taylor
  Mystical Chorus. WoPoe, *tr. by* Louis MacNeice
  Prologue in Heaven.
    Chorus of the Archangels, The. OBVE, *tr. by* Bayard Taylor
  "Sight is my birthright." PtR, *tr. by* Stuart Atkins

Faustina, if that was your name, you are dead. Elegy for Faustina. Fergus Allen. ModIr

Faustus. Alec Derwent Hope. NOBAu

Fauve. Arthur Sze. WhBo

Fauviste. Donald Revell. BodElec

Favn in the Afternoon, A. Stéphane Mallarmé. SxFrPo, *tr. by* A. M. and E. H. Blackmore

Favola di Orfeo. Angelo Poliziano. *tr. by* Elizabeth Basset Welles
  "What song will ever be so sorrowful." CAGL, *tr. by* Elizabeth Basset Welles

Favorable Prospects. Norman Fischer. WANABP

Favored by Heaven are those, ordained to taste. Sonnet Introductory. Mary Robinson. CenSon; RWP

Favorite Little Shrine, A. Enrique Lihn. VCWP

Favorite Slave's Story, The [*with music*]. Priscilla Jane Thompson. CBWP-2; RACG

Favoured by Heaven are those, ordained to taste. Mary Robinson. NPBRoP *Fr.* Sappho and Phaon.

Favourite Stretch of Disused Railway, A. Tom Pow. EdScPo

Favourite Swain, The. Elizabeth Hands. WoRP

Fawn in the Snow, The. William Rose Benét. MoAmPo

Fawnia. Robert Greene. OBEV

Fawning Whelp, The. Geoffrey Chaucer. DiBP *Fr.* Book of the Duchesse, The.

Fawn's Foster-Mother. Robinson Jeffers. NAMCP V.1; NoAM

Fayre is my love, when her fayre golden heares. Edmund Spenser. *See* Fair [*or* Fayre] is my love, when her fair [*or* fayre] golden heares.

Fayre Summer droops, droope men and beasts therefore. Thomas Nashe. *See* Fair summer droops, droop men and beasts therefore.

Fay's reading Virginia Woolf: how a. Acrophobia. Nancy Means Wright. PfS

Fazal / all eyes on the clock. Fazal. Chiqui Vicioso. TANSG, *tr. by* Emma Jane Robinett

FB Eye Blues, The. Richard Wright. APT-2

Fe de vida. José Hierro. ConPit, *tr. by* Clayton Eshleman

Fear. Marjorie Agosin. ExTi

Fear. James Vincent Cunningham. APT-2

Fear: "Fear of the icy moon." Herbert Gassner. PML, *tr. by* Herbert Kuhner and Peter Tyran

Fear. George Oppen. BodElec

Fear. Eva Picková. INSAB; ItWoWo

Fear: "Fear passes from man to man." Charles Simic. CAP-8; WaAnP; WeW-3

Fear, A. Elizabeth Jennings. MoWP

Fear, The. Lascelles Abercrombie. OBMV

Fear, The. Andrew Young. EdScPo

Fear 2. Marjorie Agosin. ExTi

Fear and dreams. Rest Is Grace, The. János Pilinszky. IQMS, *tr. by* Adam Makkai

Fear and dwindle waste the ear. Ian Patterson. VaPo *Fr.* Hardihood.

Fear and Fame. Philip Levine. PoDa

Fear and the Monkey. William S. Burroughs. PFTM-2

Fear and Trembling. Robert Penn Warren. NAMCP V.1

Fear as old as Cain, The. (LL) Bora Ring. Judith Wright. NAMCP V.2; NoAM

Fear death?—to feel the fog in my throat. Prospice. Robert Browning. InoFa; ITBLP; NAEL-6v2; NAEL-7v2

Fear enters, exits, And your better self. Fear. Karl Krolow. GTCP, *tr. by* Reinhold Grimm

Fear (Extracts). Yevgeny Aleksandrovich Yevtushenko. RusPo, *tr. by* Robert Arthur Douglas Ford

Fear freedom. Wopko Jensma. TSAP

Fear God—obey his just decrees. Christopher Smart. ChIV-1 *Fr.* Hymns for the Amusement of Children.

Fear it has faded and the night. Schoolgirls Hastening. John Shaw Neilson. NOBAu

Fear me, virgin whosoever. Herman Melville. *See* Behind the house the upland falls.

Fear / nested. Fear. Marjorie Agosin. ExTi

Fear no longer for the lone grey birds. End of the Flower World (A.D. 2300). Stanley Burnshaw. APT-2

Fear No More. David Case. IaFF

Fear no more the heat o' the Sun. William Shakespeare. ClHu; NoSic; OxAEP-1; SoSe-8; TFi *Fr.* Cymbeline.

Fear No More the Heat o' the Sun. William Shakespeare. *See* Dirge for Fidele.

Fear not: for they that are with us are more than they that are with them. 2 Kings 6:16. Jones Very. ChIV-1

Fear not, shepherds, for I bring. Angel's Song. Charles Causley. OBCP

Fear of Madness, The. Lucretia Davidson. TCAPo

Fear of pain in this chained and welcoming port. (LL) Edward Kamau Brathwaite. NoP-4; NoP-5 *Fr.* Arrivants: A New World Trilogy, The.

Fear of poetry is the, The. Reading Time : 1 Minute 26 Seconds. Muriel Rukeyser. NIL-7

Fear of Shoplifting. Maureen Seaton. FFC

Fear Of Snakes. Lorna Crozier. OpeFie

Fear of Subways. Maureen Seaton. FFC

Fear of the Earth. Alex Comfort. MoBrPo

Fear of the Future. Gillian Ferguson. NeBl

Fear of the icy moon. Fear. Herbert Gassner. PML, *tr. by* Herbert Kuhner and Peter Tyran

Fear so pervasive it blocks even the hypnotically dissociated part from performing automatic writing, A. Emperor's New Costume, Or the Case of the Missing Mask, The. Jalal Toufic. Eno

Fear turns objects over in the darkness. Anna Andreyevna Akhmatova. ARWW, *tr. by* Catriona Kelly

Fear ws no longer that continuous presence that took pleasure in appropriating our surroundngs. Fear 2. Marjorie Agosin. ExTi

Feare no more the heate o'th'Sun. William Shakespeare. *See* Fear no more the heat o' the Sun.

Feare not, litle flocke, for it is your fathers good pleasure to give you the kingdome. Bible, *N.T.* OBVE *Fr.* St. Luke.

Fearful of beauty, I always went. Enamel Girl, The. Genevieve Taggard. MoAmPo

Fearful Symmetry. Basil Bunting. PoA 2002

Fearful Women. Carolyn Kizer. ExTi

Fearless Rider. Jim Clawson. ArBi

Fears and sorrows of this day, The. (LL) Lucasia, Rosania and Orinda Parting at a Fountain, July 1663. Katherine Philips. EMWP; PEW

Fears in Solitude [Written in April, 1798, during the Alarm of an Invasion]. Samuel Taylor Coleridge. OBWP
  Dainty Terms for Fratricide. NPBRoP
  "Thankless too for peace." FaBoWar; PoAgWa

Fears of the Eighth Grade [*with music*]. Toi Derricotte. GT; LiTh

Feast Day. W. S. Merwin. BodElec

Feast Day Dog. Anne MacNaughton. ICANM

Feast Days. Annie Dillard.
  Thanksgiving—Christmas 2. UpMys
  Thanksgiving—Christmas 3. UpMys

Feast o' Saint [*or* St.] Stephen, The. Ruth Sawyer. OBCP

Feast of San Silvestro, The. V. Penelope Pelizzon. AmPoNex

Feast of Stephen, The. Anthony Hecht. NoAM; VCAP

Feast of Stephen, The. Kevin Nichols. OBCP

Feast of the Poets, The. Leigh Hunt.
  "All on a sudden, there rose on the stairs." NPBRoP

Feast, The. Robert Duncan. APSN *Fr.* Passages.

Feast, The. Robert Hass. GoPo

Feast, The. Mary Ruefle. AmAlph

Feasted once. Deep Peach Glades. Emperor Li Cunxu. CCL1, *tr. by* C. H. Kwock and Vincent McHugh

Feastful sight, A. Rain at Noon-time. Molara Ogundipe-Leslie. CFP; HAWP

Feasting with Etang a Hundred Times Around. Al Robles. ReBoTo

Feat of Gardening, The. John Gardner. OBGa *Fr.* Feat of Gardening, The.

Feather, The. Lilian Bowes-Lyon. LW

Feathered Dancers. Kenward Elmslie. AHA; NYP2; PmAP

Feathered discs of asters trace, The. Maritime Pastoral. Ted Benttinen. PoCoUp

Feathered Robe, The. Gary Snyder. BodElec

Feathers. Jayne Cortez. SurWo

Feathers fan the spade. Nearness. David Lindley. NLP

Feathers in a fan, The. Man. Humbert Wolfe. MoBrPo

Feathers up fast, and steeples; then in clods. Fountain, The. Donald Davie. NoP-4; NoP-5

Feathery in the corner strikes three times the fox. Night Sentence. Christine Hume. IAoNAP

Feats of Arms, and famed heroick Host, The. Luis de Camões [*or* Camõens *or* Camoëns]. FaBoWar *Fr.* Lusiads, The.

Features unseen embers and tongs once worried. Arabian Night. James Merrill. NoP-5

Febrile is my fendish fent my practice spent in. Erin Mouré. NLPA *Fr.* Wittgenstein Letters to Mel Gibson's Braveheart, The.

February. John Heath-Stubbs. OBCP

February. Lisa Lewis. BodElec

February: "There is no kindness in me here. I ache to be kind, but the weather." Sinéad Morrissey. NIrP

February [*with music*]. Henrietta Cordelia Ray. CBWP-3

February: "One who lights the wood stove, The." Charles Simic. CAP-8

February 12, 1865. Bruce Cutler. ViWalt

2-26-91. Roland Flint. PoCho

February 8, 1980: And No One Has Warned Me.   Stanislaw Baranczak.   AF, *tr.* by Magnus J. Krynski

February Afternoon [*with music*].   Edward Thomas.   NAMCP V.1; NoAM; PoWW

February Days.   May Sarton.   APT-2

February Evening in Boston, 1971.   Denise Levertov.   TaR

February Evening in New York.   Denise Levertov.   NoAM

February, from a nook in the wall.   Seasons.   Giampiero Neri.   ItPo, *tr.* by Gayle Ridinger

February Ground.   Edward Dahlberg.   APT-2

February Ice Years.   Melinda Goodman.   WiU

February in Sydney.   Yusef Komunyakaa.   ESEAA; InGu; NAMCP V.2

February: Pemaquid Point.   Ira Sadoff.   PoSol

February 17th.   Ted Hughes.   NPeEn

February Sun.   Paul Rodenko.   TuT, *tr.* by Mary E. O'Donnell

February: The Boy Breughel.   Norman Dubie.   AmAlph

February: Thinking of Flowers.   Jane Kenyon.   LoL

February 18, 1999.   Alex Rawls.   AnSo *Fr.* What's Your Sign?

Fed back to the dot.   Loopy Dupes.   Andrew Crozier.   Oth

Federal Case.   Julie O'Callaghan.   StAl

Federation.   W. T. Goodge.   NOBAu

Federico García Lorca.   Working Habits.   George Starbuck.   AmWit

Fedora.   Italo Calvino.   MotU *Fr.* Invisible Cities.

Feeble Little Voice: All It Takes Is Barely Opening the Shutter, A.   Amelia Rosselli.   CItWP, *tr.* by Cinzia Sartini Blum and Lara Trubowitz

Feed Ma Lamz.   Tom Leonard.   EdScPo

Feed still thy self, thou fondling, with belief.   *Unknown.*   NoSic

Feed the sparrows, and they will feed you.   Petition.   Malinda Markham.   IAoNAP

Feed them with red flamboyán.   Take the Hearts of Children.   Sandra Maria Esteves.   PueRic

Feeder is red with sugared water, The.   Chuparosa.   Juan Delgado.   AmPoNex

Feeder, then was gone, The. (LL)   August, Los Angeles, Lullaby.   Carol Muske-Dukes.   PBCAP; PtR

Feeding Ducks.   Norman Alexander MacCaig.   HarvBoo

Feeding Frenzies.   C. G. Hanzlicek.   GeoHom

Feeding Frenzy.   Holly Iglesias.   SweBea

Feeding the Bat.   Hilary Llewellyn-Williams.   TCAWP

Feeding the Dog.   Russell Edson.   RaBo

Feeding the Sun.   Bill Knott.   PBCAP

Feeding the Worms.   Tania Rochelle.   NevBe

Feel and hear.   Billie Holiday.   Sterling Plumpp.   IllVoic

Feel for your bad fall how could I fail.   Sympathy, A Welcome, A.   John Berryman.   NoP-4

Feel Free.   Natasha Tarpley.   ISC

Feel me to do right, our father said on his deathbed.   Feel Me.   May Swenson.   InoFa

Feel my eye breaking. (LL)   Window, The.   Robert Creeley.   FTOS; NoAM; PmAP

Feel of Hands, The.   Thom Gunn.   OxBEV

Feel of it was hairy and coarse, The.   Pulling a Pig's Tail.   Dave Jeddie Smith.   PfSP

Feel of the Wind, The.   Gu Cheng.   WoBe *Fr.* Liquid Mercury.

Feel so low-down an' sad Lawd.   Friendless Blues.   Mercedes Gilbert.   NAAPv.2

Feel their age, and sigh for liberation. (LL)   Seed-Picture, The.   Medbh McGuckian.   ModIr; PNI

Feel, you said. How does this feel?   On the Line.   Ruth Padel.   MFPA; NeBrP

Feelin' fine, feelin' great.   Haven't Got a Worry.   Ray Evans and Jay Livingston.   ReLy

Feeling.   Nikolai Kanchev.   CSCBP, *tr.* by Georgi Belev and Lisa Sapinkopf

Feeling.   Bolivia: Another End of Ace.   Tom Raworth.   PFTM-2

Feeling, A.   Robert Creeley.   PoDa

Feeling and Form.   Marilyn Hacker.   NoAM

Feeling Fucked/Up Up.   Etheridge Knight.   GT; PBCAP; RaBo
   (Feeling Fucked Up.)   LaCa

Feeling Her End Would Come with Summer's End.   Rosalía de Castro.   SpanPo, *tr.* by Kate Flores

Feeling / if you ever sleep in a grave.   Reading Croce.   Meirion Pennar.   BBMWP, *tr.* by Martin Davis

Feeling it with me.   Walking on Water.   James Dickey.   ChIV-2

Feeling Jon is far more anxious for her, A.   Group.   John Berryman.   BodElec

Feeling like the onset of an evening, A: pregnant with growling thunder.   Logic of Queerness, The: (Releasing Your Ivy Evening Within).   Ron Palmer.   BeDoSh

Feeling over the window ledge.   No Part of the Hand Was Hungry.   Julie Kalendek.   PfS

Feeling Rosemary.   Jerry McGuire.   AnSo

Feeling that it is vaguely undignified.   Science and Human Behavior.   John Hollander.   YaYoPo

Feeling the Itch.   Fĕng Mĕng-lung.   ColAnChi; WoPoe *Fr.* Mountain Songs.

Feeling the vibrations coming out of the machines.   Termination.   Fred Voss.   SUP

Feeling Type and His Friends, The.   Michael Davidson.   FTOS

Feelings I don't have I don't have, The.   To Women, as Far as I'm Concerned.   D. H. Lawrence.   NPeEn; RaBo

Feelings of a Republican on the Fall of Bonaparte.   Percy Bysshe Shelley.   CenSon

Feelings of helplessness drove me to fantastic and ridiculous extremes.   Mei-Mei Berssenbrugge.   AWPTFC *Fr.* Four Year Old Girl.

Feels about his new poem.   I Know How Every Poet.   James Laughlin.   TAPaP

Feet o' Jesus.   Langston Hughes.   ISC

Feet of Spring Are on the Stair, The.   Rosalía de Castro.   NAWM-7v2, *tr.* by S. Griswold Morley

Feet of spring are on the stair, the.   Feet of Spring Are on the Stair, The.   Rosalía de Castro.   NAWM-7v2, *tr.* by S. Griswold Morley

Feet on the fender by firelight.   Roundel to My Pipe.   Emile Nelligan.   IFF, *tr.* by P. F. Widdows

Feet pulled in, sparrow dead.   Sparrow in Withered Field.   Takahashi Shinkichi.   ZenPo, *tr.* by Takashi Ikemoto and Lucien Stryk

Feet tied together.   [She Unties the Straps of Her Corselette Fire].   Jill Hartman.   PoPra

Feilire of Adamnan, The.   *Unknown.*   IrV, *tr.* by Patrick Joseph McCall

Feld, groes or goers, hus, doeg, dung.   Returning to Roots of First Feeling.   Robert Duncan.   PoA 2002

Felicia Hemans.   Letitia Elizabeth Landon.   NPBRoP

Félicité.   Jean Follain.   YaTCFP

Felicitous Life, A.   Czeslaw Milosz.   PoSu, *tr.* by the author and Lillian Vallee

Felicitous phenomenon! (LL)   O to Be a Dragon.   Marianne Moore.   APT-1; ChIV-1; NAAL-5; NALW

Felicity.   Isaac Watts.   SacPr

Felicity the healer isn't young.   Doctor Frolic.   Robert Pinsky.   NoAM

Felines.   Daria Menicanti.   CItWP, *tr.* by Cinzia Sartini Blum and Lara Trubowitz

Felipa, La Filosofa de Rincon que Nació a los 98 Años.   Jose Angel Figueroa.   PueRic

Félix Rándal the fárrier, O is he déad then? my dúty all énded.   Felix Randal.   Gerard Manley Hopkins.   FaBoVe; MoBrPo; NAEL-6v2; NAEL-7v2; NoAM; NoP-4; NoP-5; OBEV; OxAEP-2; OxBSo; PoPoPo; TFi; WeW-3; WoPoe
   (Felix Randal the farrier, O he is dead then? my duty all ended.)   CABP; InoFa; NAMCP V.1

Felix White Sr.'s Introduction to Wakjankaga.   *Winnebago Oral Tradition.*   NAAL-5

Fell fast I loitered still. (LL)   Apple Gathering, An.   Christina Georgina Rossetti.   CtM; NAEL-6v2; NAEL-7v2

Fell, in sense old, I mean, torn from the feathered womb.   Palm at the Entrance to the Arm, A.   Marla Jernigan.   AnSo

Felled Shadows.   Terri L. Jewell.   FiBr

Felling a tree.   Basho.   EH, *tr.* by Robert Hass

Felling a Tree.   Ivor Gurney.   FaBoVe

Felling of a Tree, The.   Jennifer Rahim.   CFP

Fellow compositors.   Printer's Error, The.   Aaron Fogel.   OxBoAm; P180

Fellow has a screw loose, The.   Conversation with a New York Poet.   Lev Vladimir Loseff.   TCRusP, *tr.* by Henry Pickford

Fellow Mortal, A.   John Masefield.   OxAEP-2

Fellow reading poetry at us wouldn't stop, The.   I Attend a Poetry Reading.   Steve Kowit.   SUP

Fellow who sits in the air-conditioned office, The.   At the Back of Progress.   Taslima Nasrin.   VCWP

Fellows, if you're on.   Nagasaki.   Mort Dixon.   ReLy

Fellowship.   Michael Field.   VWP

Fellowship in Grief.   Thomas Aird.   DiBP

Fellow-trees, bell so frail and brown.   Forest Divers.   Frank O'Hara.   BodElec

Felo de Se.   Richard Hughes.   OBMV

Felo de Se.   Amy Levy.   VWP

Felo de Se.   Elinor Wylie.   NAAPv.2

Felt here as joy. (LL)   In the Marble Quarry.   James Dickey.   LPSFW; NoP-4

Feltons Epitaph.   *Unknown.*   NPeEn; PBRV

Female.   Muhammad Al-Ghuzzi.   NAfrP, *tr.* by John Heath-Stubbs and May Jayyusi

Female Advocate Or, An Answer to a Late Satyr, The.   Sarah Fyge Egerton.   "Blasphemous wretch! How canst thou think or say."   PEW

Female Ancestor.   Ann Elizabeth Hostetler.   ACAMVP

Female body, its creases and declivities, The.   Dodona: Asked of the Oracle.   Amy Clampitt.   PoA 2002

Female Buddha. Kim Sŭnghŭi. EcSo, *tr.* by K. Kim Richards and Steffen Richards

Female Cousins at Thanksgiving. Paul Ruffin. TiP2

Female descent, The. Picnic. Jane Hirshfield. FiBr

Female Exile, The. Charlotte Smith. NPBRoP

Female Figure. Olga Sedakova. ItGoST, *tr.* by Catriona Kelly

Female Friend, The. Cornelius Whur. STuOW

Female Genitals, The. Gwerfyl Mechain. EroLit, *tr.* by Dafydd Johnston

Female Philosopher, The. Charlotte Dacre. NOBRP; RWP

Female prisoner in blue clothes, The. Spring of the Steel Bar Window. No Ch'ŏnmyŏng. CAMKP, *tr.* by Mickey Hong

Female Scriptural Characters. Rebekah Gumpert Hyneman. No. 5, Judith. SWaP

Female Seer Will Burn upon This Pyre, The. Elizabeth Alexander. SweBea

Female Socket. Nicole Espagnol. SurWo, *tr.* by Myrna Bell Rochester

Female spider / swept her legends into her palms. Roots of Blue Bells. Nia Francisco. HATNAP

Female Torso. Frank O'Hara. AHA

Female Transport, The. *Unknown.* NOBAu

Female Wits, The: A Song by a Lady of Quality. *Unknown.* NOSC

Females, Sacred and Profane. John Duncombe. STuOW *Fr.* Feminead, or Female Genius, The.

Femina Contra Mundum. G. K. Chesterton. OxAEP-2

Feminead, or Female Genius, The. John Duncombe. Females, Sacred and Profane. STuOW

Feminine Intuition. Stephanie Brown. AmPoNex; BAP-97

Feminine marvelous and tough. (LL) Ted Berrigan. NYP2; OxBoAm; PmAP *Fr.* Sonnets, The.

Femininity. Ray Evans and Jay Livingston. ReLy

Feminism. Carolyn M. Rodgers. OxAAAP

Feminism, baby, feminism. Male Rage Poem. Pier Giorgio Di Cicco. PML

Feminist. Janet Paisley. EdScPo

Feminist Poem Number One. Elizabeth Alexander. FaoP; NAPBL

Femme et Chatte. Paul Verlaine. OBVE, *tr.* by Arthur Symons

Femme Fatale. Suzanne Lummis. PoDa

Femmemasochism. Alicia Galaz Vivar. TANSG, *tr.* by Dave Oliphant

Fence can be seen from afar, The. Edmond Jabès. PFTM-2 *Fr.* Book of Questions, The.

Fence posts I set today, The. Re-stringing 100 Year Old Wire. John Collin Murphey. TiP2

Fence, The. Louise Erdrich. NAMCP V.2

Fence, The. Heather McHugh. FaoP

Fencewalled / circundressed. Dolores Dorantes. SPV, *tr.* by Jen Hofer

Fencing. Anthony Lawrence. NOBAu

Fenêtres, Les. Guillaume Apollinaire. YaTCFP

Feng-nian: Good Year. *Unknown.* CCL1, *tr.* by Man Wong

Feng-yu: Cold Wind, and the Rain. *Unknown.* CCL1, *tr.* by Ezra Pound

Fennel. Opal Palmer Adisa. ASA

Fennel. David Lindley. NLP

Feral Floats the Form in Heaven and of Light. Joshua Clover. ASA

Ferdia of the hosts. *Unknown.* WoPoe *Fr.* Táin, The.

Ferdinand De Soto lies. Distant Runners, The. Mark Van Doren. MoAmPo

Ferdinando and Elvira; or, The Gentle Pieman. William Schwenck Gilbert. OBCoV

Fergus of Galloway: Knight of King Arthur. William Malveisin. tr. by Mick Imlah

Fergus attempts to make off with the Sheild of Dunottar. NePenScot, *tr.* by Mick Imlah

Fermi Lab: Sisyphus of Quarks. Pearl Andelson Sherry. PoA 2002

Fern Hill. Dylan Thomas. AmFaPo; AngWePo; BrAP; CABP; ChAP; ClHu; EMP; GPTC; HarvBoo; HeIP-4; IPoFL; MoBrPo; NAEL-6v2; NAEL-7v2; NAMCP V.2; NIL-7; NIP-4; NoAM; NoP-4; NoP-5; OBWVE; PoPoPo; SoSe-8; TCAWP; TFi; TRP; WaAnP

Fern Kidnappings, The. Jeanette Lynes. Coast

Fern Song. Hildegarde Flanner. APT-2

Fernando has a basketball. Fernando. Marci Ridlon. NTCP

Ferniehirst Castle. Richard Hugo. NoAM

Ferns and the Night. John Ash. HarvBoo

Ferns in a Hollow of Absence. Alice Rahon. SurWo, *tr.* by Myrna Bell Rochester

Ferris Wheel, The. Wyatt Prunty. RA

Ferry. Louis Zukofsky. APT-2 *Fr.* 29 Poems.

Ferry departs, The. Buson. SoOfWa, *tr.* by Sam Hamill

Ferry drags, The. For the Lover. Maria Luisa B. Aguilar-Cariño. ReBoTo

Ferry Me Across. B. P. Nichol. FTOS

Ferry Me across the Water. Christina Georgina Rossetti. TLR *Fr.* Sing-Song.

Ferry of Lead, The. Iwan Goll. WoPoe, *tr.* by Galway Kinnell

Ferry to South Baymouth, The. Bruce Meyer. IFF

Ferry wades across the kyle, The. I drive. Return to Scalpay. Norman Alexander MacCaig. NePenScot; NoP-5

Ferryboat and the Traveler. Han Yong'un [*or* Yongwun]. CAMKP, *tr.* by Sammy Solberg

Fertile and rank and rich the coastal rains. William Everson. CalPo *Fr.* Falling of the Grain, The.

Fertile Muck, The. Irving Layton. NoAM

Fertility Test. Diana Fitzgerald Bryden. OpeFie

Fervent lover and the sage austere, The. Cats. Charles Baudelaire. TriCat, *tr.* by Dugald Sutherland MacColl

Fervid breath of our flushed Southern May, The. Evening on the Potomac. Richard Hovey. APN-2

Festal Song. *Unknown.* CrYelRi, *tr.* by Sam Hamill

Feste and the Fence Post. Daniel Williams. IaFF

Feste's Song. William Shakespeare. *See* Song: "When that I was and a little tiny boy."

Festival of Giovedo Grasso, The. Matthea Harvey. IAoNAP

Festival of Izcalli or Eighteenth Month. Carla Faesler Bremer. SPV, *tr.* by Jen Hofer

Festival of Xócotl Huetzi or Tenth Month. Carla Faesler Bremer. SPV, *tr.* by Jen Hofer

Festivals. Annie Le Brun. YaTCFP, *tr.* by Mary Ann Caws *and* Jean-Pierre Cauvin

Festive draperies override the claims of. Naming Day, A. Odia Ofeimun. HBAPE

Festive Tolls. Lesley Duncan. EdScPo

Festus Conrad. Melvin B. Tolson. GT

Fetch. Jeffrey Skinner. PoDa

Fetching Cows. Norman Alexander MacCaig. NoP-4

Fete. Guillaume Apollinaire. CuPo

Fete on the Lake. Molly Bendall. NAPBL

Fetish. Beckian Fritz Goldberg. AmAlph

Fetish. Christopher Reid. NeBrP

F[o]etus in an acrobat's womb, A. Alien. A. K. Ramanujan. NAMCP V.2

Feud, The. Sydney Lea. RA

Fever. Eavan Boland. NAMCP V.2

Fever. Judith Ortiz Cofer. PueRic

Fever. Jana Harris. FiBr

Fever. Sean O Riordain. ModIr, *tr.* by Patrick Crotty

Fever 103°. Sylvia Plath. NAMCP V.2; NoAM; OxBoAm; PoA 2002; VCAP

Fever Tune. Karel Van de Woestijne. TuT, *tr.* by Tony Curtis and Tony Curtis

Feverish Propositions. Rosmarie Waldrop. FTOS; PFTM-2 *Fr.* Reproduction of Profiles, The.

Feverish psyche gropes for an, A. Elegy for the Revolution. Kofi Anyidoho. NAfrP

Feverish room and that white bed, The. White Heliotrope. Arthur Symons. NPeEn

Few, The. J. M. Edwards. BBMWP, *tr.* by Robert Minhinnick

Few and Far Between. Dick Barnes. CalPo

Few are the moonlit nights that I've cared for. Last Stop. George Seferis. AF

Few Autobiographical Facts, A. Anna Barkova. ARWW, *tr.* by Catriona Kelly

Few broken things linger in my palm, A. Letter, The. Feriha Aktan. NaPG, *tr.* by Talat Sait Halman

Few dark notes from a jade flute, A. Listening to a Flute on a Spring Night in Lo-yang. Li Po. CrYelRi, *tr.* by Sam Hamill

Few days ago, A. Happy Day in My Life, A. Mircea Cărtărescu. PML, *tr.* by Sanda Agalida and Julian Semilian

Few days ago I bought three, A. Life in the Egg 3. Kim Sŭnghŭi. CAMKP, *tr.* by Anthony, Brother of Taizé

Few Days in the South in February, A. Eleanor Ross Taylor. CBCWP; InGu

Few days to turn the pages, A. Dirt to Dirt. Hugh Seidman. BodElec

Few Facts about Me, A. Charles North. NYP2; PmAP

Few Helpful Hints, A. Peter Sirr. ModIr

Few Last Lines of Laundry, A. Eamon Grennan. PoA 2002

Few miles from here, they've unearthed, A. Brandy Station, Virginia. David Moolten. BloBone

Few minutes ago, I stepped onto the deck, A. Cobweb, The. Raymond Carver. BLT

Few months obliterate, A. (LL) Basil Bunting. HarvBoo; NAMCP V.1; NoAM; NoP-4; NoP-5; NPeEn *Fr.* Briggflatts [An Autobiography].

Few of the Bird-Family, A. James Whitcomb Riley. NOxBChV

Few people had gone out to see if the trees, A. Antichromatic. Pamela Alexander. PfSP

Few Picnics in Illinois, A. Maura Stanton. IllVoic

Few puffs of white cloud, A. Suzan Oshos's Visit to My West Mountain Hut. Muso Soseki. EaWin, *tr.* by W. S. Merwin

Few sashay, a few finagle, A. I Knew I'd Sing. Heather McHugh. OxBoAm
Few, save the poor, feel for the poor. Poor, The. Letitia Elizabeth Landon. VWP
Few soft words of Russian, A. Peaceful Sentiment. Judy Kronenfeld. RWB
Few stripes that foreshorten the wall are indications for the police, The. That. Pierre Reverdy. YaTCFP, tr. by John Ashbery
Few strokes of ink and there it is, A. Reading the Japanese Poet Issa (1762–1826). Czeslaw Milosz. WoPoe, tr. by the author and Robert K. Haas
Few Things, A. Gerhard Rühm. PFTM-2, tr. by Rosmarie Waldrop
Few Things Can More Inflame. Cecil Day Lewis. OBMV
Few things for themselves, A. O Florida, Venereal Soil. Wallace Stevens. NAAPv.2; TCAPo
Few thought he was even a starter. Clement Attlee. OBCoV
Few times I've been knocked out cold, The. Lightweight. Jack Myers. SUP
Few vague clouds in the insane blue sky, A. 110 Degrees in Dallas. Frederick Turner. TiP2
Few verses, A. Pleasures. Radmila Lazić. PoCho, tr. by Charles Simic
Few women, sad and rouged, A. Far Away. Blas de Otero. RaW, tr. by Hardie St. Martin
Few words, A. Amazing Grace. Edward Smallfield. ASA
Few Words on the Soul, A. Wisława Szymborska. PoDa, tr. by Stanislaw Baranczak and Clare Cavanagh
Few yards out the drop, A. Learning to Swim at Poverty Beach. Peter E. Murphy. NevBe
Few years ago, I was moved by a story, A. One Day. Ch'ôn Yanghûi. EcSo, tr. by Aimee N. Kwon
Few years back and they told me Black, A. June Jordan. LTA; UnSA
Fewer. George Stanley. NLPA Fr. Mountains and Air.
Fewer Than Music. Donald Revell. RoV
Ffarewell, love, and all thy lawes for ever. Sir Thomas Wyatt. See Farewell, love, and all thy law[e]s forever [or for ever].
Ffarwell sweet infant; blissfull babe adieu. Greifes Farwell, to an Inherritor of Joy. Ann Williams. EMWP
F[f]rom depth of[f] sin[n] and from a deep [or diepe] despair [or dispaire]. Bible, O.T. NoSic; OBVE
Ffynnon Grandis. Einir Jones. BBMWP, tr. by Joseph P. Clancy
Fhir luraich's fhir àlainn. Meg Bateman. EdScPo
Fiascherino. Charles Tomlinson. NoAM
Fiasco, The. Walter Helmut Fritz. GTCP, tr. by Reinhold Grimm
Fiat Lux. Robert Crawford. NeBrP
Fiber Optics. Joseph Millar. PoDa
Ficción y las Cosas, La. Josué Ramírez. RMCMP
Fickle Fortune. Ferenc Faludi. IQMS, tr. by Watson Kirkconnell and J. G. Nichols
Fiction and the Reading Public. Philip Larkin. OBSV
Fictions. William Kulik. BodElec
Fiddleheads. Maureen Seaton. BAP-97; SUP
Fiddler Jones. Edgar Lee Masters. IllVoic; NAMCP V.1; NoAM Fr. Spoon River Anthology.
Fiddler of Dooney, The. William Butler Yeats. NBLV; OxAEP-2
Fiddler, The. Marion Angus. EdScPo
Fiddlers. Dave Jeddie Smith. CAP-8; NAMCP V.2
Fiddle's incomplete without the dance, The. Completion of the Fiddle, The. Milton Acorn. Coast
Fidel in Ohio. Martín Espada. TouFir
Fidele. William Collins. OBEV
Fidelity. William Wordsworth. DiBP
Fidelity Rewarded. Dora Greenwell. VWP
Fidessa, More Chaste than Kind[e]. Bartholomew Griffin. Care-Charmer Sleep. NoSic
Fiduciary. Randall Mann. PoDa
Fie on all courtesy, and unruly winds. Coxcomb, The. Joseph Hall. OxAEP-1
Fie [or Fy] tedious Hope, why do[e] you still rebel[l]? Mary Sidney Wroth, Countess of Montgomery. NOSC Fr. Pamphilia to Amphilanthus.
Fie, school of Patience, fie; your lesson is. Sir Philip Sidney. NAEL-6v1; NAEL-7v1 Fr. Astrophil and Stella.
Fiel de la balanza, El. Alberto Blanco. RMCMP
Field. Annie Foster. NLP
Field. Dana Levin. AmPoNex
Field, The. Mary Barnard. APT-2
Field, The. Christopher Pilling. NLP
Field, The: "Once I left the room." Tom Sleigh. PoDa
Field Beyond the Ridge. George Scarbrough. LPSFW
Field Day. William Robert Rodgers. PNI
Field dodd. P. Inman. FTOS Fr. Dust Bowl.
Field Guide to Western Intimacy. Tenaya Darlington. IIR
Field Hospital, A. Randall Jarrell. NoP-4; NoP-5

Field Hospital, The. Paul Muldoon. PNI
Field is large, the barn at hand, The. Morgan Llwyd. AngWePo Fr. 1648.
Field mouse follows its own shadow, The. Snowfall; a Poem about Spring. James Wright. NoAM
Field Mushrooms. W. S. Merwin. CAP-8
Field of bright mustard. Buson. EH, tr. by Robert Hass
Field of bright mustard. Buson. EH, tr. by Yoel Hoffmann
Field of cotton, A. Basho. EH, tr. by Robert Hass
Field of Folk, The. William Langland. NAEL-6v1; NAEL-7v1; NoP-5
Field of Glory, The. Edwin Arlington Robinson. MoAmPo
Field of Light, A. Theodore Roethke. PtR; WaAnP
Field of mustard, A. Buson. EH, tr. by Yoel Hoffmann
Field of oilseed rape, The. Field. Annie Foster. NLP
Field of Poppies, A. Barbara Baldwin. FiBr
Field of Red Tulips. Margot Scharpenberg. GTCP, tr. by the author
Field of the Cloth of Gold, The. Patrick Joseph Hartigan. NOBAu
Field of wind gave license for defeat, A. Spinazzola: Quella Cantina Là. Richard Hugo. PWW2
Field Poem. Gary Soto. PBCAP; WaAnP
Field Trip. Carol Muske-Dukes. GeoHom
Field Trip. Kevin Young. GT
Field upon field, field upon field, of snow. (LL) Wintry Mind, The. Witter Bynner. NoP-4; NoP-5
Field Upon Field Upon Field. Sergey Aleksandrovich Yesenin. TCRusP, tr. by Nigel Stott
Field-Glasses. Andrew Young. EdScPo
Field-Mouse, The. Gillian Clarke. MoWP
Fields Belong to Woman, The. Betty De Shong Meador. HW
Fields belong to woman, The. In her body, woman carries. Fields Belong to Woman, The. Betty De Shong Meador. HW
Fields flame with it, endless, blue, The. Indigo. Chitra Divakaruni. OpBo
Fields from Islington to Marybone, The. William Blake. OBNV Fr. Jerusalem.
Fields of flax and sweetcorn flash under a half-moon. Under the Big Top. Ted Genoways. PoDa
Fields of Learning [with music]. Josephine Miles. NoAM
Fields of Sorrow, The. Ausonius. WoPoe, tr. by Helen Waddell
Fields of this Summer. Gennady Aygi. WoBe, tr. by Peter France
Fields, Teruko-san, are threshed, The. A good. Hibakusha's Letter (1955), The. David Mura. AtGh; OpBo
Fields were bleached white, The. Patrick Kavanagh. NPeEn Fr. Great Hunger, The.
Fieldswirl, October. Dave Jeddie Smith. PfSP
Fier, my Savior, Fier. Satan's Camp a-Fire. Unknown. SSUS
Fierce calmness, A. Heat rises a bubble to the surface. Reaction To What You Said. Sonnet L'Abbé. OpeFie
Fierce Girl Playing Hopscotch. Alice Fulton. PoA 2002
Fierce musical cries of a couple of sparrowhawks hunting on the headland, The. Birds. Robinson Jeffers. APT-1; NAAPv.2
Fierce passions discompose the mind. William Cowper. ChIV-2 Fr. Olney Hymns.
Fierce they drove on, impatient to destroy. Homer. OBVE Fr. Iliad, The.
Fierce was the wild billow, Dark was the night. Anatolius. SacPr, tr. by John Mason Neale
Fiercely the battle raged and, sad to tell. Ambrose Bierce. AmWit; APN-2 Fr. Devil's Dictionary, The.
Fiery ball takes on oxygen, burning off, The. Reconciled Flame. Alessandro Ceni. ItPo, tr. by Gayle Ridinger
Fiery Darts of Satan stob my heart, The. Edward Taylor. TCAPo Fr. Preparatory Meditations Before My Approach to the Lord's Supper.
Fiery palm tree in front of me, The. Today's Meditation. Antonio Machado Ruiz. AF; WED, tr. by Robert Bly
Fiery songs, their five long toes trembling in the soaked earth, The. (LL) Johnson's Cabinet Watched by Ants. Robert Bly. NAMCP V.2; NoP-5; OxBoAm
Fiery unicorn snapped, The. Daichu. ZenPo, tr. by Takashi Ikemoto and Lucien Stryk
Fiesta de izcalli o décimo octavo mes. Carla Faesler Bremer. SPV
Fiesta de xócotl huetzi o décimo mes. Carla Faesler Bremer. SPV
Fife Tune. John Streeter Manifold. FaBoWar; NBLV; NOBAu
Fifteen. Jan Freeman. OxWW Fr. Autumn Sequence.
Fifteen. Michael McClure. WANABP Fr. Plum Stones.
Fifteen. Mendi Lewis Obadike. RD
Fifteen. Patricia Pogson. NLP
Fifteen. William Stafford. CAP-8
Fifteen: "Late that summer my girlfriend's boyfriend." Richard Frost. NevBe
Fifteen beds. Fifteen chairs with names. Pain Strikes Sparks on Me, the Pain of Terezin. Unknown, fr. Terezin Concentration Camp. INSAB

Fifteen Epigrams in Praise of the Tyrant. Paavo Haavikko. *tr.* by Anselm Hollo
"Before you ask for justice. Make sure." WoPoe, *tr.* by Anselm Hollo
"Don't say this to an old idol that's lost its nose." WoPoe, *tr.* by Anselm Hollo
"Don't smile. So you won't become a Buddha." WoPoe, *tr.* by Anselm Hollo
"Hades is an even worse place." WoPoe, *tr.* by Anselm Hollo
"How decisively." WoPoe, *tr.* by Anselm Hollo
"I always bow down deep before a small tree and a great tyrant." WoPoe, *tr.* by Anselm Hollo
"It has been proposed that the stars should be removed from sight." WoPoe, *tr.* by Anselm Hollo
"Look, life has been constructed this way to make sure." WoPoe, *tr.* by Anselm Hollo
"Plant trees. Exactly against this tree." WoPoe, *tr.* by Anselm Hollo
"Precisely the way you divide your small change between two." WoPoe, *tr.* by Anselm Hollo
"Take heart, Ovid. No sentence." WoPoe, *tr.* by Anselm Hollo
"Twice, three times." WoPoe, *tr.* by Anselm Hollo
"Tyrant inspires small poems, The." WoPoe, *tr.* by Anselm Hollo
"When the tyrant is young. Everyone waits." WoPoe, *tr.* by Anselm Hollo
"When you go to the tyrant. Keep your head on a platter." WoPoe, *tr.* by Anselm Hollo
Fifteen Haiku. Masaoka Shiki.
"Sprays of wisteria." CAoMJL1, *tr.* by Burton Watson
"Sprays of wisteria, The / arranged in a vase." CAoMJL1, *tr.* by Burton Watson
Fifteen men on the Dead Man's Chest. Robert Louis Stevenson. NPeEn *Fr.* Treasure Island.
Fifteen Million Plastic Bags. Adrian Mitchell. EmeKit; OBSV
Fifteen minutes or thereabouts. Thomas Kinsella. ModIr *Fr.* Anniversaries.
Fifteen times the better jock. Delayed Love Poem to Odem, Texas. Richard Sale. TiP2
Fifteen years ago beneath moonlight and flowers. Written by Chance. Li Ch'ing-chao. NDACCP, *tr.* by Kenneth Rexroth
15 years of loving. High Noon. John Wieners. AHA
Fifteen years old and naked, quivering. Tower. David Biespiel. NAPBL
15th Kühl-Psalm, The. Quirinus Kuhlmann. GePo, *tr.* by George C. Schoolfield
Fifteenth of May. Cherry blossom. The swifts. Swifts. Ted Hughes. OWoS
Fifteenth passes with drums and in armour, The. Centuries. Ronald Stuart Thomas. CABP
Fifth Amendment, The. Susan Hahn. ExTi
Fifth Book. Elizabeth Barrett Browning. PEW
Fifth Book: On Limitation. Nanni Cagnone. ItPo *Fr.* Vaticinio.
Fifth day of the New Year / was here before we knew it, The. Picnic by the Xie River, A. T'ao Ch'ien. CCL1, *tr.* by William Acker
Fifth Floor. Miryana Basheva. CSCBP, *tr.* by Georgi Belev and Lisa Sapinkopf
Fifth Grade Autobiography. Rita Dove. ISC; NIL-7; NIP-4
Fifth Inning, The. Donald Hall. MoASP
Fifth Letter. Nazim Hikmet. NaPG *Fr.* Letters to Taranta Babu.
Fifth month, golden plums are ripe. Evening in the Garden, Clear after Rain. Ch'u Ch'uang I. CCL1; WaAnP, *tr.* by Kenneth Rexroth
Fifth Movement: Autobiography. Louis Zukofsky. NAMCP V.1; PFTM-1; TaR *Fr.* Poem Beginning "The."
Fifth Ode of Horace. Lib. I, The. Horace. NPeEn; OxBEV; PBRV,
5.8.1942 / In Memory of Janusz Korczak. Jerzy Ficowski. HP, *tr.* by Keith Bosley
Fifth Philosopher's Song. Aldous Leonard Huxley. OBCoV
Fifth Prose. Michael Palmer. NoP-4; OxBoAm; PmAP
Fifth Stanzas. De Arte Poetica. Olga Sedakova. ARWW; ItGoST, *tr.* by Catriona Kelly
5th Tuesday. John Berryman. BodElec
Fifth Vertical Poetry. Roberto Juarroz.
"Emptiness of the day, The." VCWP
Fifth Villancico, in Alternating Voices, Written for the Feast of the Nativity in Puebla, 1689, The. Sor Juana Inés de la Cruz. *tr.* by Alan S. Trueblood
"Because my Lord was born to suffer." WoPoe; WPoS, *tr.* by Alan S. Trueblood
Fifth-Floor Window, The. Lola Ridge. APT-1; NAAPv.2
Fifties Rock Party, 1985. Judith Berke. SwNoth
Fifty. Gertrude Stein. OxBoAm *Fr.* Book Concluding with As A Wife Has a Cow a Love Story, A.
Fifty American cheerleaders booking uphill on Rue LePic. Bloodletting. Anselm Berrigan. HeMarv
50. *Because fields grew parking lots.* (LL) 50 Years in the Career of an Aspiring Thug. Suzanne Wise. AmPoNex; LegDan
Fifty cents apiece. Good Hot Dogs. Sandra Cisneros. NOxBChV

Fifty Faggots. Edward Thomas. MoBrPo; PoWW
50–50. Langston Hughes. NoAM
Fifty-Fifty. Al Young. SpirFl
Fifty fifty and fifty-one, she said she thought so. Gertrude Stein. OxBoAm *Fr.* Book Concluding with As A Wife Has a Cow a Love Story, A.
51st Highland Division's Farewell to Sicily, The. Hamish Henderson. EdScPo
Fifty foot trombone blows, A. Whale Breathing: Bartlett Cove, Alaska. Bill Holm. MiVo
59 / And the / Cancer creeped. Don't Say Goodnight to Etheridge Knight. Tony Medina. InTrad
59th Light Poem: for La Monte Young and Marian Zazeela—6 November 1982. Jackson Mac Low. PmAP
Fifty Quatrains. Michael Field. VWP
56 Westervelt. Maggie Nelson. AmPoNex
Fifty three years ago my father. Steak and Eggs. Bobby Byrd. ICANM
Fifty-three years / This clumsy ox has managed. Sekishitsu-Soei. ZenPo, *tr.* by Takashi Ikemoto and Lucien Stryk
Fifty Years. James Weldon Johnson. InGu
Fifty years have passed. Problem of Anxiety, The. John Ashbery. BAP-97
50 Years in the Career of an Aspiring Thug. Suzanne Wise. AmPoNex; 3m LegDan
Fig Curtain of Atherton, The. Michael Spence. PoCoUp
Fig for the Lower House, A. Patrick Carey. NOSC
Fig for Thee, Oh! Death, A. Edward Taylor. NAAL-3
Figaro here, Figaro there. Figaro. *Unknown.* Prolet, *tr.* by Amelia Glaser
Figgie Hobbin. Charles Causley. NOxBChV
Fight and Play. Sarah Kindman. Prolet, *tr.* by Amelia Glaser
Fight at Rorke's Drift, The. Emily Jane Pfeiffer. ViWPN
Fight in the Cave, The. Adam Lindsay Gordon. STuOW *Fr.* Wolf and Hound.
Fight! O My Young Men. D. H. Lawrence. RSaN
Fight of the Year, The. Robert McGough. OBCP
Fight on brave soldiers for the cause. Saints' Encouragement, The. Alexander Brome. BASC
Fight Song. Deborah Garrison. BeAl
Fight to a Finish. Siegfried Sassoon. RSaN
Fight was at its hottest, The. Rev. Andrew Brown, over the Hill to Rest. Josephine D. Henderson Heard. CBWP-4
Fight with a Water-Spirit. Norman Cameron. OxBSo
Fight with an Angel. Tadeusz Rózewicz. PoSu, *tr.* by Victor Contoski
Fight with Grendel. *Unknown.* NoP-5 *Fr.* Beowulf [Heaney Translation].
Fighters. René Char. YaTCFP, *tr.* by Thomas Merton
Fighters come, The. Libyan Airliner/Egyptian Acrobats/Israeli Air Circus [2004 version]. Sam Hamod. OtW
Fighters for Life. Michael Rosen. RSaN
Fighting Fire. Hamlin Garland. APN-2
Fighting on the South Frontier. Li Po. TAL
Fighting, south of the ramparts. *Unknown.* ChinPo, *tr.* by Ye Weilian [*or* Yeh Wei-lien *or* Wai-lim Yip]
Fighting South of the Wall. Li Po. WoPoe, *tr.* by Elling O. Eide
Fighting Words. Dorothy Parker. AmWit
Fights after School. Norman J. Loftis. SpirFl
Fights God for cursed Amalek? That hand. Meditatio Septima. Francis Quarles. ChIV-1
Figlio Maggiore. Robert Fitzgerald. NoP-4; NoP-5
Figs. D. H. Lawrence. EroLit
FigTree. Stephanie Strickland. ExTi
Fig-trees, weird fig-trees. Bare Fig-trees. D. H. Lawrence. FaBoVe
Figure and Ground. Christine Garren. PoDa
Figure in the Carpet, The. James Tate. BodElec
Figure Motioned with Its Mangled Hand toward the Wall behind It, The. Kenneth Patchen. APT-2
Figure on the Edge. Dabney Stuart. PfSP
Figure stood a crucifix against the door, The. Message from a Cross. Max Harris. NOBAu
Figured wheel rolls through shopping malls and prisons, The. Figured Wheel, The. Robert Pinsky. NAMCP V.2; NoAM
Figurehead. Dilys Rose. EdScPo
Figurehead, The. Léonie Adams. APT-2; OxBoAm
Figurehead, The. Maria Luisa Spaziani. NeIt, *tr.* by Beverly Allen
Figures, The. Robert Creeley. CAP-8
Figures, The. Robert Patrick Dana. PoDa
Figures for a Carrousel. Madeline DeFrees.
3. The Music. FiBr
Figures in an Ancient Ink. Carl Rakosi. APT-2
Figures in the Carpets. David Schloss.
[Kazak]. PoA 2002

Figures in the fields against the sky! Poem. Antonio Machado Ruiz. WoPoe, *tr.* by John Dos Passos

Figures of light and dark, these two are walking. Effet de Neige. John Hollander. GS

Figures on the Frieze, The. Alastair Reid. WaAnP

Filene's department store. Ladders. Elizabeth Alexander. FFC

Fileuse, La. Paul Valéry. YaTCFP

Filipino Boogie. Jessica Tarahata Hagedorn. UnSA

Filipino Woman, The. *Unknown*. NAAPv.2

Fill and Illumined. Joseph Ceravolo. ChIV-1; OxBoAm

Fill their bodies with their ghosts. Practicing Their Diffidence, the Vandals. Alan Michael Parker. LegDan

Fill thou my life, O Lord my God. Horatius Bonar. SacPr

Fill up my glass again! The anodyne. Tibullus. WoPoe *Fr.* Adde Merum Vinoque.

Fill up the silences of night and morn. (LL) False Poets and True. Thomas Hood. CenSon; NPBRoP

Fill with the angels of bread. (LL) Imagine the Angels of Bread. Martín Espada. PrTe; TouFir

Filled his great lungs with cool air. (LL) In My Father's House. George Barlow. ESEAA; OxAAAP

Filled out gourd rots, the, the. Motion's Holdings. A. R. Ammons. NAMCP V.2; NoAM

Filled with myself, walled up in my skin. José Gorostiza. TCLAP *Fr.* Death Without End.

Filled with old lovers, in the clutch of the chair. Girlfriends, The. Elizabeth Woody. ReEnLa

Filled with water. Family Portrait. Shuntaro Tanikawa. VCWP, *tr.* by Harold Wright

Filling her compact and delicious body. John Berryman. CAP-8; ColAP; EmeKit; NAMCP V.2; NoP-4; NoP-5; VCAP *Fr.* Dream Songs.

Filling Station. Elizabeth Bishop. NoP-4; NoP-5; PoetW; PtR; VCAP; WeW-3

Filling the Gap. Lawson Fusao Inada. FTtHH; OpBo

Filling the hollow of my throat. (LL) To My Father. Tony Curtis. AngWePo; TCAWP

Fills the white enamel bucket, overflows. Summer. Maura Eichner. UpMys

Film in a railway station, A. Fadil Azzawi. IrPoTo, *tr.* by Ralph Saverese and Saadi A. Simawe

Film Noir. Six One-Line Film Scripts. Tom Andrews. P180

Film Noir. Aram Saroyan. LiTh

Film Version, The. Barry Spacks. IaFF

Filming a motion picture. Cut. David J. Feela. ArBi

Filo walked out my door. Rainfall Piano. Luis J. Rodriguez. LiTh

Filter here, not innocence but guilt, The. (LL) Photos of a Salt Mine. Patricia K. Page. NAMCP V.2; NIP-4; NoAM

Fin and Oshin went out to hunt. Finn and Ossian Hunting. *Unknown*. DiBP

Fin de Siècle. Joe Bolton. AmPoNex

Fin-de-Siècle Cat. Oscar Wilde. TriCat *Fr.* Sphinx, The.

Fin du monde, La: Prendre corps. Gherasim Luca. YaTCFP

Final. Pablo Neruda. WoPoe, *tr.* by Ben Belitt

Final Battle for the Ryūkyū Islands, The. Takamura Kotaro. CAoMJL1, *tr.* by Leith Morton

Final Curtain. Gerwyn Williams. BBMWP, *tr.* by the author and Richard Poole

Final Curtain. Roger Woddis. UV

Final de Pound, Un. Tedi López Mills. RMCMP

Final Disposition. Jane Glazer. FiBr

Final Inch, The. Emily Dickinson. APN-2; NCAP

Final issues of heart and mind, The. (LL) Unbosoming. Michael Field. NAEL-7v2; VWP

Final Manuscript. Giannina Braschi. TANSG, *tr.* by Alan West

Final Minutes, The. Gwyneth Lewis. BBMWP *Fr.* Language Murderer, The.

Final Moments. Percy Bysshe Shelley. NPBRoP *Fr.* Cenci, The.

Final Notations. Adrienne Rich. BeAL; BrAP; PoA 2002; PoCu

Final Paean. Edward Young. STuOW *Fr.* Imperium Pelagi, or, The Merchant.

Final Poem, The. Maxine W. Kumin. VisFro

Final poem for the gently sifting public begins on the streets. Joshua Beckman. LegDan

Final Poems. Rabindranath Tagore. *tr.* by Wendy Barker
    Last Poems 10. PoCho, *tr.* by Wendy Barker
    Last Poems 13. PoCho, *tr.* by Wendy Barker

Final Question, The. Yousif al-Sa'igh. IrPoTo, *tr.* by Chuck Miller and Saadi A. Simawe

Final reductions. M. R. Peacocke. NLP

Final shadow that will close my eyes, The. Love Constant Beyond Death. Francisco de Quevedo y Villegas. AmFaPo, *tr.* by Willis Barnstone

Final Signs, The. Lenze L. Bouwers. TuT, *tr.* by Pat Boran

Final signs are weariness and might, The. Final Signs, The. Lenze L. Bouwers. TuT, *tr.* by Pat Boran

Final Soliloquy of the Interior Paramour. Wallace Stevens. APT-1; BBASP; ColAP; HarvBoo; NAAPv.2; WaAnP

Final Solution: Jobs, Leaving. Simon J. Ortiz. PFTM-2

Final Sonnet. Miguel Hernández. BLPSL, *tr.* by Rene de Costa, Rigas Kappatos and Eleni Paidoussi

Final Sonnet, A. Ted Berrigan. FTOS; PFTM-2; PmAP; WaAnP *Fr.* Sonnets, The.

Final Tree. Gabriela Mistral. TCLAP, *tr.* by Doris Dana

Final Vigil. Georg Heym. WoPoe, *tr.* by Peter Viereck

Finale. Sue Lenier. LW

Finale. Judith Wright. EmeKit

Finally, all the migrants are dead. Alba. Durs Grünbein. GTCP, *tr.* by Reinhold Grimm and Irmgard Hunt

Finally changed the calendar today to August. Sitting here this morning. Fred Wah. NLPA *Fr.* This Dendrite Map: Father / Mother Haibun.

Finally found a fellow. Murder, He Says. Frank Loesser. ReLy

Finally, from your house there is no view. Water Island. Howard Moss. NoP-4

Finally it was just me, and the katydids. Daddy Out Hitch-Hiking at 3:30 A.M. John Balaban. TAPaP

Finally, one arrives at the place. Golgotha. Andrew Lansdown. ChIV-2

Finally out of reach. Tessho. ZenPo, *tr.* by Takashi Ikemoto and Lucien Stryk

Finally retired pensionless. Big Momma. Haki R. Madhubuti. AmFaPo

Finally stays no more away. Consolation Aria. Johann Christian Günther. GePo, *tr.* by George C. Schoolfield

Finally / The butcher dog snaps at the golden ring. The. Finally. Meret Oppenheim. SurPaPo, *tr.* by Catherine Schelbert

Finally / the only one I want. Privacy. Olga Broumas. PasH

Finally the Rain. Carrington McDuffie. PoCoUp

Finally there are enough people to hug! At Mother Teresa's. Naomi Shihab Nye. OPRER

Finally, to forgo love is to kiss a leaf. Rescue the Dead. David Ignatow. WoPoe

Finally to make his mind up to go home. (LL) Prodigal, The. Elizabeth Bishop. APT-2; ChIV-2

Financial Note. Edward Robert Bulwer-Lytton. STuOW

Find easy voice to utter each aright. (LL) Once Alien Here. John Hewitt. CABP; PNI

Find Heaven and thee. (LL) Silence and Stealth of Day[e]s! Henry Vaughan. NAEL-6v1; NAEL-7v1; NPEeN

Find it in the letter the mailman refused. If You Cannot Find the Truth Right Where You Are, Where Do You Expect to Find It? Maj Ragain. AmZen

Find keys for that. (LL) Arioso Dolente. Anne Stevenson. NoP-5; Prnts

Find me, and turn thy back on heaven. (LL) Brahma. Ralph Waldo Emerson. APN-1; ColAP; CtM; NAAPv.1; NoP-4; NoP-5; OBEV; OxBoAm; TCAPo; TFi; UV

Find me in the grass. Spirit of the Place, The. Tony Curtis. AngWePo

"Find rest in Him!" One knows the parsons' tags. Charlotte Mew. ChIV-2 *Fr.* Madeleine in Church.

Find the fair Pierides! (LL) Garden Song, A. Austin Dobson. OBEV; OBGa

Find their sole voice [or speech] in that victorious brow. (LL) Shakespeare: "Others abide our question. Thou art free." Matthew Arnold. BrAP; GSo; HeIP-4; NoP-4; NoP-5; OBEV; OxAEP-2; OxBSo; PoPoPo

Find Uncle Fred's photograph. Well You Needn't. Dave Etter. SeSe

Find Work. Rhina P. Espaillat. PoA 2002

Finder, The. Robin Blaser. FTOS

Finders and reflections. What is not immediately present. Message No. 69. Holley Blackwell. AnSo

Fin-de-Siècle Identikit. Pierre Joris. PFTM-2

Finding. Celia Barry. Prnts

Finding a Horseshoe. Osip Emilevich Mandelstam. RusPo, *tr.* by Robert Arthur Douglas Ford

Finding a Long Gray Hair. Jane Kenyon. ItP; LoL

Finding a teacher to learn the truth is nothing special. To a Monk. Buhyu Sunsoo. BecRai, *tr.* by Kim Daljin, Kim Won-Chung and Christopher Merrill

Finding a whole woman there, in her one face. (LL) Who's Joking with the Photographer? Anne Stevenson. BeAL; MoWP

Finding all of the stops. (LL) San Sepolcro. Jorie Graham. MoWP; VCAP

Finding His Fist. Patricia Smith. SpirFl

Finding is the first Act. Emily Dickinson. TCAPo

Finding My Old Battalion Command Post. William Daniel Ehrhart. AmWaPo

Finding myself in the desert, I planted a luminous seed. I let go. Broken Glish. Pablo Neruda. RD

Finding the stars over and over again. County. Katayoon Zandvakili. AmPoNex

Finding What's Lost. Dorianne Laux. GeoHom

Finds a tree of unrecorded species. Literary Excellence. Robert Harris. BMAP

Finds ways enough to ease thine heaviness. (LL) Of Money. Barnabe Googe. NBLV; NoSic; SoSe-8

Fine and Dandy. Paul James. ReLy

Fine brick houses are crumbling, The. Butchertown. William Loran Smith. LaCa

Fine buildings in the fragrant forest face the tall pavilions. Jade Tree Blossoms in the Back Garden, A. Emperor Chen Shubao. CCL1, *tr. by* John Frodsham

Fine Day. Ivan Tsanev. CSCBP, *tr. by* Georgi Belev and Lisa Sapinkopf

Fine delight that fathers thought; the strong, The. To R. B. Gerard Manley Hopkins. OxAEP-2

Fine Fechtin Mouse, The. Sir Alexander Gray. EdScPo

Fine feelings under blockade! Cargoes just in from Kamschatka! Winter Coming On. Martin Bell. OBVE

Fine Figure of a Nymph. Erasmus Darwin. STuOW *Fr.* Botanic Garden, The.

Fine fish to net. Yu-li: Fine Fish to Net. *Unknown.* CCL1; OBVE, *tr. by* Ezra Pound

Fine flickering hungers of the brain, The. (LL) Moon Is Always Female, The. Marge Piercy. NoAM; WaAnP

Fine grass; slight breeze from bank. Traveler at Night Writes His Thoughts, A. Tu Fu [*or* Du Fu]. CCL1, *tr. by* Florence Ayscough and Amy Lowell

Fine Knacks for Ladies. John Dowland. NoP-4; NoP-5; NoSic; NPeEn; PBRV

Fine knacks for ladies, cheap, choice, brave and new! Fine Knacks for Ladies. John Dowland. NoP-4; NoP-5; NoSic; NPeEn; PBRV

Fine living. . .à la carte?? Advertisement for the Waldorf-Astoria. Langston Hughes. FTtHH

Fine Madam Would-Be, wherefore should you fear. To Fine Lady Would-Be. Ben Jonson. NoP-4; NOSC

Fine Occupation, A. Ryan Fitzpatrick. PoPra

Fine Old English Gentleman, The; New Version. Charles Dickens. OBSV; RSaN

Fine player was he, A. Fiddler, The. Marion Angus. EdScPo

Fine Romance, A. Dorothy Fields. OBCoV; ReLy

Fine suicide fled victoriously, The. Stéphane Mallarmé. SxFrPo, *tr. by* A. M. and E. H. Blackmore

Fine, white cowl. Nun's Dance, The. Cho Chihun. CAMKP, *tr. by* Kevin O'Rourke

Fine Work with Pitch and Copper. William Carlos Williams. OxBoAm

Fine youth Ciprius is more terse and neat, The. Sir John Davies. NoSic *Fr.* Epigrams.

Finger. Jackie Kay. NeBrP

Finger lifted to the eye, A. Music of the Spheres. Anthony Barnett. Oth

Finger of death touched me, The. He Is Gone. Anna Swirszczynska [*or* Swir]. CFP; PoSu, *tr. by* Czeslaw Milosz and Leonard Nathan

Finger Paintings. Johnny Stanton. AHA

Finger-nails. Paolo Buzzi. PFTM-1

Fingerprints. Iwan Llwyd. BBMWP, *tr. by* Geriant Løvgreen

Fingers— / gets away. (LL) Avocado. Gary Snyder. PmAP; WhBo

Fingers in the Bread. Joan Aleshire. NevBe

Fingers lie in the lap, The. Year's End. Ellen Bryant Voigt. NoAM

Fingers over the hedge, you move around. Near Speech, The. Mark McMorris. AmPoNex

Fingers Probe. Claire Malroux. VCWP, *tr. by* Marilyn Hacker

Fings Ain't Wot They Used t'Be. Lionel Bart. ReLy

Finis. Walter Savage Landor. *See* I Strove With None.

Finished. Ai. CAP-8

Finished. Kate Llewellyn. NOBAu

Finished Gentleman, A. Geoffrey Dutton. NOBAu

Finished Man, A. Richard Wilbur. NAMCP V.2

Finished Poem. Michelle Calhoun Green. BtF

Finished the stranger, with whom, late. César Vallejo. WoPoe, *tr. by* Rebecca Seiferle

Finishing Touch. Martha Serpas. Vesp

Finistère. Thomas Kinsella. PBCIP *Fr.* One.

Finit. Máire Mhac an tSaoi. IrLP, *tr. by* the author

Finite Intuition. Milo De Angelis. NeIt, *tr. by* Lawrence Venuti

Finite—to fail, but infinite to Venture. Emily Dickinson. TCAPo

Finlay's House (in Rousay). Ian Hamilton Finlay. EdScPo

Finn and Ossian Hunting. *Unknown.* DiBP

Finnegans Wake. James Joyce.
  "Hear, O hear, Iseult la belle! Tristan, sad hero, hear! The Lambeg drum." PFTM-2

Finnegan's Wake. *Unknown.* NBLV

Finnesburh Fragment, The. *Unknown.* OBWP, *tr. by* Kevin Crossley-Holland

Finney's Bar. Deborah Randall. StAl

Finnish Tango. Hans Magnus Enzensberger. GTCP, *tr. by* Reinhold Grimm

Fir. T.E. Jay. GifTon

Fir, bamboo. Autumn Path. Pao Hsien. CSKM, *tr. by* Paul Hansen

Fire! Willy Bal. WoPoe, *tr. by* Yann Lovelock

Fire. Mark O'Connor. NOBAu

Fire. Luis J. Rodriguez. UnSA

Fire. Ann Taylor. NOxBChV

Fire. *Unknown.* WoPoe *Fr.* Kalevala, The.

Fire: "What makes a fire burn." Judy Brown. TWF

Fire. Dorothy, Duchess of Wellington Wellesley. OBMV

Fire: "Probably I am an ordinary middle-class." Adam Zagajewski. PoCho, *tr. by* Renata Gorczynski

Fire, The. Robert Duncan. APSN *Fr.* Passages.

Fire, The. Sir Walter Scott. OBCP

Fire after Fire, The. Ken Harris. AnSo

Fire alight / in the other window as it. Open Air Where. Larry Eigner. PmAP

Fire and Brimstone; or, The Destruction of Sodom. George Lesley.
  "Behold, how Sodom swaggers in its Pride." CAGL

Fire and Embers. Leonor Scliar-Cabral. MirDau, *tr. by* Regina Igel

Fire and Ice. Robert Frost. APT-1; BrAP; BRP; ColAP; HeIP-4; MoAmPo; NAAL-5; NAAPv.2; NAMCP V.1; NoAM; OxBoAm; RaBo; SoSe-8; TFi; WaAnP

Fire and Ice by Robert Frost: an early draft. Ron Overton. VisFro

Fire and Rope, Bullet and Axe. Nikolai Semionovich Tikhonov. TCRusP, *tr. by* John Glad

Fire and St. Francis. Andrew Hudgins. UpMys

Fire Ants. Joseph Somoza. ICANM

Fire at Alexandria, The. Theodore Weiss. NoAM; PoA 2002; SAmP

Fire Barns. Jordan Davis. HeMarv

Fire: because it is quick, and can destroy. If You Could Write One Great Poem, What Would You Want It to Be About? Robert Pinsky. PoCho

Fire blows left of the outstretched. Of Children on Wood. Malinda Markham. IAoNAP

Fire darkens, the wood turns black, The. Song for the Sun That Disappeared behind the Rainclouds. *Unknown.* ChAP

Fire falls, the night, The. Summer Is a Poem by Ovid. Douglas G. Jones. NIP-4

Fire, Famine, and Slaughter. Samuel Taylor Coleridge. FaBoWar

Fire, fire, fire, fire! Thomas Campion. WoPoe

Fire high up in air, The. Bird's Song, A. Dame Edith Sitwell. NALW

Fire in Early Morning. Christiane Jacox Kyle. YaYoPo

Fire in leaf and grass, The. Living. Denise Levertov. BLT; GoPo; OPOU; StAl

Fire in My Meditation Burned [*with music*]. Henry Ainsworth. ChIV-1

Fire in the Heavens. Christopher John Brennan. NOBAu *Fr.* Quest of Silence, The.

Fire in the heavens, and fire along the hills. Christopher John Brennan. NOBAu *Fr.* Quest of Silence, The.

Fire in the window! flashes in the pane! Fire in the Window. Mary Mapes Dodge. SWaP

Fire is burning clear and blithely, The. Darkened Mind, The. James Russell Lowell. NCAP

Fire Is Laid, The. *Hungarian Oral Tradition.* IQMS, *tr. by* Dermot Spence

Fire is my companion, but I do not talk to it, it talks to me. Suburb of Long Suffering. Mary Ruefle. FaoP

Fire is out, and spent the warmth thereof, The. Dregs. Ernest Dowson. OBMV

Fire Island. May Swenson. PoA 2002

Fire Keeper. Bahiyyih Maroon. SpirFl

Fire more priceless than diamonds rare. Father's Love, The. Mary E. Tucker. CBWP-1

Fire of Drift-Wood, The. Henry Wadsworth Longfellow. APN-1; ITBLP; MakPoe; NAAL-3; NCAP; OxBoAm

Fire on the Hills. Robinson Jeffers. CalPo; OxBoAm; RaBo

Fire pit is cold the stone bed like ice, The. Han-shan Te-ch'ing. CSKM, *tr. by* Red Pine

Fire / poking / through the. Container of Stars. Pat Reed. WANABP

3. The Fire Sermon. T. S. Eliot. HarvBoo *Fr.* Waste Land, The.

Fire, Sixth Month, 408. T'ao Ch'ien. CrYelRI, *tr. by* Sam Hamill

Fire Station's Delight, The. Susan Hampton. NOBAu

Fire, the, lamp, and I, were alone together, The. Mary Elizabeth Coleridge. ViWPN; VWP

Fire: The People. Alfred Corn. VCAP *Fr.* Call in the Midst of the Crowd, A.

Fire, the suddenly discovered knowledge of love, The. (LL) Satan Says. Sharon Olds. OxBoAm; PBCAP

Fire Us with Ice, Burn Us with Snow. Mary Monk. LW

Fire/Water Blues. Darrell Stover. BtF

Fire, water, woman, are man's ruin! Dutch Proverb, A. Matthew Prior. OBCoV

Fire will not ask me to make its bed, The. Asseverations. Arthur Nortje. HBAPE

Fire, with well-dried logs supplied, The. Fire, The. Sir Walter Scott. OBCP

Firebell for Peace. Joyce Lee. NOBAu

Fire-blade split the known roof and the white ceiling, The. Vision of St. Michael and St. John, The. Jeremy Ingalls. YaYoPo

Firebombing, The. James Dickey. AmWaPo; OBWP; PWW2

Fire-charms of summer's flaming legion, The. Hungarian Summer [1918]. Gyula Juhász. IQMS, *tr. by* Adam Makkai

Firecrackers. Jerry Kilbride. WhBo

Firecrackers thundering day and night, and lightning silences. Any Two Wheels. Jane Miller. BodElec

1. Fired cook was deranged. Headlines. Harryette Mullen. RD

Fired Pot, The. Anna Wickham. LW; NPeEn

Fired Up!! Everett Hoagland. OxAAAP

Fired up over the chess, cards, poems. Having Led a Charmed Life, He Had to be Hanged Twice. Mac Wellman. FTOS

Fired with the music, Aikin, of thy lays. On Anna Laetitia Aikin. Mary Scott. RWP

Firefighters of Chernobyl, The. Xochiquetzal. Pauline Stainer. NeBl

Fire-flakes, flints: the same old stars. Stars Falling. Jay Parini. PfSP

Fireflies. Paul Fleischman. NOxBChV

Fireflies. José Gorostiza. TCLAP, *tr. by* Rachel Benson

Fireflies / Entering my house. Issa. ZenPo, *tr. by* Takashi Ikemoto and Lucien Stryk

Fireflies float noiseless. Canicula. Mary Kinzie. FFC

Fireflies floated up from the grass, The. On a Summer Night. Elmaz Abinader. CFP

Fireflies in a Jar. DJ Renegade. FuFl

Fireflies in the Garden. Robert Frost. BLPJKO; SAmP

Fireflies [*or* Fire-flies] come stagg'ring down the dark, The. (LL) Summer's Night, A. Paul Laurence Dunbar. APN-2; NAAPv.1; NoP-4; NoP-5

Firefly. Elizabeth Madox Roberts. NTCP

Firefly. Tu Fu [*or* Du Fu]. CrYelRi, *tr. by* Sam Hamill

Fire-fly, fire-fly! bright little thing. Chant to the Fire-fly. William Ellery Channing. TCAPo

Fire-fly, fire-fly, light me to bed. Chant to the Fire-Fly. *Unknown*. APN-2, *tr. by* Henry Rowe Schoolcraft

Firelight. Edwin Arlington Robinson. NoAM

Firelight. John Greenleaf Whittier. OBCP *Fr.* Snow-Bound [*or* Snow-Bound] [A Winter Idyl].

Firemen, The. James Keir Baxter. NOxBChV

Firemen, firemen! Help! X. J. Kennedy. CA

Firemen wax their mustaches at an alarm; walls with mirrors are habitually saved. Vanity, Wisconsin. Maxine Chernoff. SUP

Fireplace, The. Michael S. Harper. GT

Fires. József Kiss. IQMS, *tr. by* Peter Zollman

Fires, always fires after midnight. Summer at North Farm. Stephen Kuusisto. PoA 2002

Fire's army overruns Topanga's hills. Arson. Charles Harper Webb. GeoHom

Fires / Burn in my heart. Kenneth Rexroth. APSN; NAAPv.2 *Fr.* Love Poems of Marichiko, The.

Fire's here, that won't be forgotten. Log. David Bromige. FTOS

Fires in Illinois. John James Piatt. APN-2

Fires in the Mirror. Anna Deavere Smith. Roslyn Malamud the Coup. OxWW

Fires run through my body—the pain of loving you. *Kwakiutl Oral Tradition*. ErotSp, *tr. by* Sam Hamill

Fires Smouldering Under Winter. Pierre Reverdy. AHA, *tr. by* Georges Guy and Kenneth Koch

Firestarter. Dorianne Laux. RoV

Firestone. David Rivard. PBCAP

Fire-whip cracks, A. Animalistic balls spring over meadows. Domesticated Egg, A. Hans Arp. MotU, *tr. by* Bethany Schneider

Firewing. Breyten Breytenbach. VCWP, *tr. by* Ernst van Heerden

Firewood, iron-ware, and cheap tin trays. (LL) Cargoes. John Masefield. BLPJKO; BRP; CABP; MoBrPo; OBEV; OBMV; TFi

Fireworks. Chu Yohan. CAMKP, *tr. by* Kyung-Ja Chun

Fireworks. Valerie Worth. NTCP

Fireworks in steel. Fete. Guillaume Apollinaire. CuPo

Fireworks on the Grass. Archilochus. WoPoe, *tr. by* Guy Davenport

Fire-Worshippers, The. Thomas Moore. NPBRoP *Fr.* Lalla Rookh.

Firm and well-fixed foundation. (LL) Robert Herrick. *See* Jocund his Muse was; but his Life was chast.

Firm branches dip the blue, blue lips from the cold. (LL) Suicide Rates, The. Lewis Warsh. AHA; FTOS

Firm desire which enters, The. Arnaut Daniel. EroLit, *tr. by* Anthony Bonner

Firmament breaks up, The. In black eclipse. Word for the Hour, A. John Greenleaf Whittier. NCAP; PCW

Firmament on High. Laurence Goldstein. OtW

Firmness. Anthony Hecht. AmWit

Firs / born Xmas day. Christopher Reid. FaBoVe *Fr.* Memres of Alfred Stoker.

First. Douglas Florian. NOxBChV

First. Maurice Manning. LegDan

First: "For me it was Robin Hentz." Mark Halliday. NevBe

First. Sharon Olds. ExTi

First / A far thud. Fireworks. Valerie Worth. NTCP

First a razor then a fact. (LL) Fifth Prose. Michael Palmer. NoP-4; OxBoAm; PmAP

First a sea: soft sands, muds, and marls. What Happened Here Before. Gary Snyder. APSN

First Act was called the Daily Life, The. Thornton Wilder. ASA *Fr.* Our Town.

First Adventurer for her fame I stand, The. Delariviere Manley. EMWP *Fr.* Lost Lover, The.

First agency we went to, The. Waiting Lists, The. Jackie Kay. NeBl

First Amendment. Aliki Barnstone. RWB

First and last time I met, The. Drunken Memories of Anne Sexton. Alan Dugan. BodElec

First Anniversary of the Government under His Highness the Lord Protector, 1655, The. Andrew Marvell. BASC

First Anniversary of the Government under O.C, The. Andrew Marvell. "'Is this, saith one, the Nation that we read'." PBRV

First answer was incorrect, The. Art of Response, The. Audre Lorde. BrAP

First, are you our sort of a person? Applicant, The. Sylvia Plath. BeAl; EmeKit; NAMCP V.2; OxBoAm; PoPoPo

First, at a window of the vacant house. Windows, The. Chris Wallace-Crabbe. BMAP

First Atlantic Telegraph, The. Jones Very. NCAP

First Attempt in Rhyme, A. Thomas Hood. OBCoV

First battles brought forth, The. Two Poems about the First Battles. Yehuda Amichai. NRoS, *tr. by* Esther Raizen

First Beating. Lorna Dee Cervantes. TouFir

First Bird. Jon Gill Bentley. ICANM

First Birth. Sharon Olds. StAl

First Birthday After Death, The. John Collin Murphey. TiP2

First Birthday, The. Hartley Coleridge. CenSon

First Blood. Dorothy Molloy. NIrP

First Blood. Vegunta Mohana Prasad. HotL, *tr. by* V. Narayana Rao

First blow caught me sideways, my jaw, The. Beating, The. Ann Stanford. SoSe-8

First Blow-Job. Meg Kearney. NevBe

First Book, The. Rita Dove. LoL

First Book: Young Aurora's Fostermother. Elizabeth Barrett Browning. NALW *Fr.* Aurora Leigh.

First Books. Andrea Hollander Budy. NevBe

First Bookshelf. Patty Seyburn. LegDan

First born of *Chaos*, who so fair didst come. Abraham Cowley. OxAEP-1 *Fr.* Pindarique Odes.

First bout of Shanghai flu, sweat the bed without you. So Get Over It, Honey. Belle Waring. ExTi

First box held tiny yellow apples, The. Boat Down the River of Yellow Silt, A. Kimiko Hahn. ExTi

First boy to fall in, The. Brotherhood. Yehoshua November. IJHIL

First came Patchen. Blue Bananas. Ron Padgett. NYP2

First came the legions, then the colonists. Colony, The. John Hewitt. ModIr

First came the primrose. Sydney Thompson Dobell. OBEV *Fr.* Balder.

First Canzone. Nikolai Stepanovich Gumilyov. TCRusP, *tr. by* Mary Jane White

First Canzone of the Convito, The. Dante Alighieri. OBVE, *tr. by* Percy Bysshe Shelley

First cat that was ever killed by Care, The. (LL) New England. Edwin Arlington Robinson. HeIP-4; MoAmPo; PoPoPo

First chairs, east, west: meadowlarks. Morning Chamber Orchestra Near Piney Crick, Wyoming, 7 A.M., The. William Borden. MiVo

First Chance Twice. Fanny Howe. FTOS

First cherry blossoms. Sanpu. SoOfWa, *tr. by* Sam Hamill

First—Chill—then Stupor—then the letting go. (LL) After great pain a formal feeling comes. Emily Dickinson. APN-2; BrAP; HeIP-4; MoAmPo; NAAL-3; NAAL-5; NAAPv.1; NALW; NAMCP V.1; NAWM-7v2; NIL-7; NIP-4; NoAM; NoP-4; NoP-5; OxBoAm; OxWW; PoPoPo; PtR; SAmP; TCAPo; TFi; TRP

First cicada / Life is. Issa. ZenPo, *tr.* by Takashi Ikemoto and Lucien Stryk

First Circle, The. Kofi Awoonor. BrAP; HBAPE; VCWP

First Circle, The. S. K. Kelen. BMAP

First clear afternoon of Spring bursts, The. Games with My Daughter. Tony Curtis. TCAWP

First Coconut Tree, The. *Unknown.* SonAtl, *tr.* by Jane Downing and Dirk Spennemann

First Cold. A. R. Ammons. PfSP

First colour? Just like a captive, The. Three-Coloured Banner. János Pilinszky. PoSu, *tr.* by Peter Jay

First comes the logic of substitution. Secret Life of Gilbert Bond, The. Joan Retallack. FTOS

First Corinthians. Bible, *N.T.*
  Though I Speak with the Tongues of Men and Angels. BLPJKO

First Corinthians at the Crossroads [*with music*]. Bruce Dawe. NoAM

First country to die was normal in the evening, The. Last War, The. Kingsley Amis. OBSV

First Cycle of Love Poems. George Barker.
  My Joy, My Jockey, My Gabriel. MoBrPo

First dance. Patrick Friesen. NLPA *Fr.* Anna.

1st Dance—Making Things New—6 February 1964. Jackson Mac Low. FTOS; PFTM-2; PmAP *Fr.* Pronouns, The—A Collection of 40 Dances—For the Dancers.

First Date in Twenty-Five Years. Ellen Doré Watson. NevBe

First Day, The. Geriant Løvgreen. BBMWP, *tr.* by the author

First Day, The. Elizabeth Spires. CAP-8

First day from the weaving of the ling net, The. Net, The. George Mackay Brown. WaAnP

First day he was travelling in Asia, The. Shape-Changer, The. Chris Wallace-Crabbe. NOBAu

First day I shot dope, The. Summer Words of [*or* for] a Sistuh [*or* Sister] Addict. Sonia Sanchez. WaAnP

First day of false spring, I hit the street, The. Green Market, New York. Julia Kasdorf. NeAmPo

First day of kindergarten I slice my four-years' thumb. Susans. Susan Clements. UnSA

First day of spring. Basho. EH, *tr.* by Robert Hass

First Day of Spring, The. Pedro Juan Pietri. PueRic

First day of summer, The. Don't Expect Anything. Maj Ragain. AmZen

First day of the week he spoke to them, The. Eutychus. Rosemary Dobson. ChIV-2

First day of this month I saw. Snowdrops. George MacBeth. OBCP

First day she passed up and down through the Heavens, The. Petrarch. OBMV *Fr.* Sonnets to Laura.

First day the Germans came into the city, The. Massacres. Charles Reznikoff. APSN

First day we stood in gradations of high and low, The. Concert Choir. Beth McGrath. MiVo

First day when water, The. Winter Mirror. Judith Mok. TuT, *tr.* by Michael O'Loughlin

First daylight on the bittersweet-hung. Meridian. Amy Clampitt. NAMCP V.2; NIL-7

First Daylight Song. *Unknown.* APN-2 *Fr.* Mountain Chant, The.

First Days, The. James Wright. TRP

First Day's Night had come, The. Emily Dickinson. IJHIL; NCAP; TRP

First Days of Spring. Ryokan. WoPoe, *tr.* by Stephen Mitchell

First days of spring—the sky. First Days of Spring. Ryokan. WoPoe, *tr.* by Stephen Mitchell

First day's sun, The. Rabindranath Tagore. PoCho *Fr.* Final Poems.

First Death [*with music*]. Donald Justice. CAP-8

First Death. Ann Townsend. NeAmPo

First Death in Nova Scotia. Elizabeth Bishop. HarvBoo; InoFa

First death was coming like a horse. Like a Horse. Robin Behn. AmAlph

First, delicate apple-greens, The. Easter Outing. Sally Carr. Prnts

First Dimension of Skunk, The. Ray A. Young Bear. HATNAP

First, do no harm, the Hippocratic. Dire Cure. William Matthews. EMP

First: don't use the word *souls*. don't use the word *fire*. How to Write a Poem after September 11th. Nikki Moustaki. PA9/11

First Drift. Ron Padgett. FTOS

First Drink. Susan Browne. NevBe

First Early Mornings Together. Robert Pinsky. ColAP; WaAnP

First Eclogue. Baldomero Garcilaso de la Vega. *tr.* by Rene de Costa, Rigas Kappatos and Eleni Paidoussi
  "Oh, to my sobs, Galatea, you are harder than a stone." BLPSL, *tr.* by Rene de Costa, Rigas Kappatos and Eleni Paidoussi

First Elegy: End of a Campaign. Hamish Henderson. EdScPo; PoWW; RSaN *Fr.* Elegies for the Dead in Cyrenaica.

First Empathy. J. Allyn Rosser. NevBe

First English Wildcat, The. Colin Simms. Oth

First (entitled to the place), The. Charles Churchill. OBSV *Fr.* Duellist, The.

First Epistle of the First Book of Horace Imitated, The. Alexander Pope. Profiteers. OBSV

First / erase your name. Who Remains Standing? Andrée Chedid. CFP; HAWP; WoPoe, *tr.* by Mirène Ghossein and Samuel Haze

First Exercise. Michael Ryan. NevBe

First Extra, The. Amy Levy. ViWPN

First Farewell to J.G. "Ephelia." NOSC

First, feel, then feel, then. Young Soul. Imamu Amiri Baraka. OxAAAP

First few wounds are nearly invisible, The. Shooting a Farmhouse. Ted Kooser. PBCAP

First Fig. Edna St. Vincent Millay. AmWit; APT-1; BLPJKO; BRP; ChAP; NAAPv.2; NALW; NAMCP V.1; NIL-7; NoAM; NoP-4; NoP-5; OxBoAm; PoA 2002

First Fight. Then Fiddle. Gwendolyn Brooks. NIL-7; NIP-4; PtR *Fr.* Womanhood, The.

First firefly / Why turn away. Issa. ZenPo, *tr.* by Takashi Ikemoto and Lucien Stryk

First Flight. Daniel Gerard Hoffman. OtW

First, for kindness, we must assume the dark. Love among Lepers. Richard Ronan. BodElec

First form your artful looks with studious care. Charlotte Lennox. LW *Fr.* Art of Coquetry, The.

First Glasses. Jennifer Grotz. NevBe

First goal is to see the thing itself, The. Three Goals, The. David Budbill. GoPo

First Grade. Jean Follain. MotU, *tr.* by Mary Feeney

First Grade. Liam Rector. LiTh

First Green of Spring, The. David Budbill. BeAL; GoPo; IPoFL

First Grey Hair, The [*with music*]. Mary E. Tucker. CBWP-1

First Haircut. Richard Frost. NevBe

First Harvest. Monica Raymond. PfS

First having read the book of myths. Diving into the Wreck. Adrienne Rich. CAP-8; ColAP; EmeKit; HarvBoo; HeIP-4; MakPoe; MoWP; NAAL-5; NALW; NAMCP V.2; NIL-7; NIP-4; NoAM; NoP-4; NoP-5; OxBoAm; OxWW; PoPoPo; StAl; TWF; WaAnP

First he believes this meadow in all its abundance is his, entirely, with thousands of green surprises. Art of Reduction, The. Dan Pagis. MotU, *tr.* by Shirley Kaufman

First he fingers wet sand into the names. Eighth Dream, The. Tony Curtis. PML

First he was shivering on the shore in skins. Sophoclean. Seamus Heaney. PoAgWa

First hear, then repeat what I say: it's rhymed. Mene Tekel. Frigyes Karinthy. IQMS, *tr.* by Aaron Kramer

First, her tippet made of tulle. Taking Off Emily Dickinson's Clothes. Billy Collins. StAl

First horn lifts its arm over the dew-lit grass, The. House Slave, The. Rita Dove. AmAlph; NAMCP V.2; NoAM; OxAAAP

First horse I ever saw, The. Horse. Michael Waters. NevBe; UrbNat

First Horses, 1519. Victoria Edwards Tester. ICANM

First Hour. Sarah Josepha Buell Hale. *Fr.* Three Hours; or, The Vigil of Love.

First hunters who crossed Siberia, The. Country of Origin. Maureen Hurley. AtGh

First I am one. Mystery, The. Jeni Couzyn. HAWP

First I heard the voice throbbing across the river. Saint Clare. Louise Erdrich. UpMys

First I saw the white bear, then I saw the black. At the Zoo. William Makepeace Thackeray. NTCP

First, I think, like a pear, velvet-furred; a liquid bite. Quince, The. Michael Donhauser. SonAtl, *tr.* by Colin Brown, Kurt Ganzl, Ursula Hobday and Barbara Vogt

First I was born and it was tough on Mom. Story Often Told in Bars, A: The *Reader's Digest* Version. William Matthews. ReTh

First I went down to the street. Ballad of Going Down to the Store, A. Miron Bialoszewski. BLT, *tr.* by Czeslaw Milosz

First I would have a face exactly fair. How to Choose a Mistress. Edmond Prestwich. NOSC

First, I would have her be beautiful. Selecting a Reader. Ted Kooser. P180; PBCAP

First Ice, The. Andrey Andreievich Voznesensky. RusPo, *tr.* by Robert Arthur Douglas Ford

First idea was not our own, The. Adam. Wallace Stevens. ColAP *Fr.* Notes toward a Supreme Fiction.

First I'll find two pears. What I Want to Make for You. Natasha Sajé. SweBea

First Impression. Joe Wenderoth. NAPBL

First in the North. The black sea-tangle beaches. Mythical Journey, The. Edwin Muir. NoAM

First indication was this repeated tic, The, the latch jigging and clicking. Asylum. Ciaran Carson. PNI

First inroads were made in our 19-aughts. Contemporary Culture and the Letter "K." Alfred Corn. NoP-4

First is a park, The. Four-Light Window, A. Ágnes Nemes Nagy. VCWP, tr. by Hugh Maxton

First, it was more about mystery than about trying to get us to. Religion. Stephen Dunn. Vesp

First, it was the common magic. Marriage. Richard Frost. PoDa

First it was the secret place where I went to dream, end. Tire Hangs in the Woods, The. Dave Jeddie Smith. CAP-8

First Job Viper. Peter Wood. NevBe

First Kill. M. L. Williams. NevBe

First Kingdom, The. Seamus Heaney. PoetW Fr. Sweeney Redivivus.

First Kiss: "Afterwards you had that drunk, drugged look." Kim Addonizio. NevBe

First Kiss. April Lindner. GoPo

First Kiss: "Her mouth." Tim Seibles. NevBe

First Lady Challenges a Loa-as-Poem. James Richardson. RD

First Lay of Gudrun, The. Unknown. Fr. Elder Edda, The.

First Lesson [with music]. Philip Booth. GoPo

First Lesson in Unpopular Mechanics. Ken Babstock. OpeFie

First lesson is electricity, The. Art of Kissing, The. Mary Ann Samyn. AmPoNex

First Lesson: Winter Trees. Michael Waters. NevBe

First, let me say it is sickening, this syrupy public. Iago, the Poet. J. P. Dancing Bear. IaFF

First let me show you with the pointer. Map. Martin Sorescu. VCWP, tr. by Russell-Gebbett

First, let me view what noxious nonsense reigns. Richard Savage. OBSV Fr. Authors of the Town, The.

First let the kennel be the huntsman's care. William Somervile. DiBP Fr. Chase, The.

First let there be a tree, roots taking ground. Design for a Quilt. John Ormond. AngWePo; TCAWP

First Letter from Tamara A. Reiner Kunze. PoSu, tr. by Ewald Osers

First Letter to an Irish Novelist. Roy McFadden. PNI

1st Lt. John R. Fox: Rain of Fire. Jabari Asim. BtF

1st Lt. Vernon J. Baker: Hero on the Hill. Jabari Asim. BtF; FuFl

First, light. Grammar of Waking, A. Tonya Foster. FreRad

First Light. Lisa Suhair Majaj. PoArWo

First Light. Jim Powell. ASA

First Light: "Near Nunnerie, where Daer and Potrail meet." Stewart Conn. EdScPo

First light of morning, it gives you no warning. Those Which Were Pomp and Delight. Pedro Calderón de la Barca. WoPoe, tr. by Katherine Washburn

First light shook with ax blows to the frozen pond. Winter. Judy Jordan. AmPoNex

First line of this poem, The. Love Poem. Sabahattin Kudret Aksal. NaPG, tr. by Talat Sait Halman

First looked in November, trusted hearsay. Narrative of the Men and Women Who Became Stars. Nathaniel Tarn. ICANM

First Love. John Clare. GoPo; NoP-4; NoP-5; PoPoPo

First Love. Robert Creeley. ICANM

First Love. Elizabeth Jennings. LW

First Love. Caroline Elizabeth Norton. NPBRoP

First Love. Edwin Rolfe. AmWaPo; APT-2

First Love. Shimazaki Toson. CAoMJL1, tr. by Leith Morton

First Love. Vidyapati. ErotSp, tr. by Sam Hamill

First Love, Sixteen Years Old. Baron Wormser. NevBe

First man I called Sir, The. Epithet. Judith McCombs. FiBr

First Mango. Vince Gotera. ReBoTo

First March. Ivor Gurney. OxBEV

First Memory. Louise Glück. RaF

First Men on Mercury, The. Edwin Morgan. EdScPo; NePenScot

First Merseburg Spell. Unknown. GePo, tr. by Carroll Hightower

First Monday Scottsboro Alabama. Tom Weatherly. EGAG

First month, early auspicious, Dinghai day, The. Yun'er's Bell. Yun'er. WoPoe, tr. by Constance A. Cook

First month in Florida I couldn't get used. Faith in Florida. Martha Serpas. Vesp

First month of his absence, The. Song (On Seeing Dead Bodies Floating Off the Cape). Alun Lewis. NAEL-6v2; NoP-4; NoP-5; OBWP

First month of winter the blood of ours sons, The. Lament for Ch'en T'ao. Tu Fu [or Du Fu]. CrYelRi, tr. by Sam Hamill

First Morning. George Keithley. PoCoUp

First morning after anyone's death, is it important, The. Thomas Hardy. Norman Dubie. AmAlph

First morning of Three Mile Island: those first disquieting, uncertain, mystifying hours, The. Tar. C. K. Williams. AtGh; VCAP

First Movement. Padraic Fiacc. PNI

First Movement: "And out of olde bokes, in good feith." Louis Zukofsky. NAMCP V.1 Fr. Poem Beginning "The."

First music we don't hear but, The. Music of the Spheres. Robert Morgan. PoA 2002

First Night. Julia H. Ackerman. PasH

First Night, A [with music]. Peter Kane Dufault. NoP-4; NoP-5

First night at the monastery, The. Pine. Chase Twichell. WaAnP

First night back and rain falls, The. Yu No Send. Me No Come. Shara McCallum. BtF

First Night in the New House. Andrea Hollander Budy. NevBe

First night, the first night, The. Carol for the Last Christmas Eve. Norman Nicholson. NOxBChV; OBCP

First night you were gone. Place, Places. Melvin Dixon. ISC

First Nightmare Waking. Nicholas Samaras. NevBe

First Nights. Grace Schulman. NevBe

First nobody liked us; they said we smelled. American Dream: First Report. Joseph Papaleo. UnSA

First Nowell the angel did say, The. First Nowell, The. Unknown. ChrPo

First of all do you remember the way a bear goes through. Destruction. Joanne Kyger. BLT; GoPo

First of all, I could never get a straight answer. I'd ask, what day is it. Why He Had to Go. Justin Chin. AmPoNex

"First of all, it's all true." Creation. Simon J. Ortiz. ColAP; HATNAP

First of all, it's being nine years old and. What It's Like to Be a Black Girl (For Those of You Who Aren't). Patricia Smith. UnSA

First of all. The House has remained in its old spot. Nightmares. Marie Étienne. YaTCFP, tr. by Marilyn Hacker

First of December, The. Publius Papinius Statius. RomPo Fr. Sylvae [or Silvae].

First of that train which cursed the wave. To the First Slave Ship. Lydia Huntley Sigourney. ColAP

First of the gods I honor in my prayer is Mother Earth. Eumenides, The. Aeschylus. NAWM-5v1, tr. by Robert Fagles

First of the undecoded messages read: "Popeye sits in thunder", The. Farm Implements and Rutabagas in a Landscape. John Ashbery. HarvBoo; NAMCP V.2; PmAP; WaAnP

First of walkers come the Earwigs. Earwigs. Edward Newman. VerBaPo

First Offense. David Lehman. PmAP

First on TV, A. David Ignatow. RaBo

First One, The. Jeffrey McDaniel. NevBe

First pains came slow, The. First Death. Ann Townsend. NeAmPo

First Part: "Was it for this." William Wordsworth. NPBRoP Fr. Two-Part Prelude, The.

First Party at Ken Kesey's with Hell's Angels. Allen Ginsberg. PmAP; TRP

First Payment. Jon Mukand. BloBone

First Performance of the Rock 'n Roll Band Puce Exit. Kevin Stein. SwNoth

First person is an existentialist, The. 9-11-01. Fanny Howe. OxBoAm

First Person Omniscient. Jeffrey McDaniel. LaCa

First person plural is a house. Brian Teare. LegDan

First person to set foot on land was Noah's daughter, The. Ballad of Noah's Daughter. Rossana Ombres. NeIt

First, Plaintiff contracted with Defendant. Anonymous Wedding Photo. Jennifer O'Grady. AmPoNex

First Player's Monologue, The. Richard Hedderman. IaFF

First Poem: "Bulletin board flutters with a flair, The." Marvin Bell. NevBe

First Poem, The. Paavo Haavikko. PFTM-2 Fr. Winter Palace, The.

First Poem, The. Mark Van Doren. APT-2

1st Poem for Cuba. Sandra Maria Esteves. PueRic

First Poem for You. Kim Addonizio. CalPo

First Poem of Wandering Immortals. Kuo P'o. CCL1, tr. by John Frodsham

First Portrait of My Son. Alaide Foppa. TANSG, tr. by Celeste Kostopulos-Cooperman

First Prayer for the Hottentotsgod. Breyten Breytenbach. AF, tr. by Denis Hirson

First Proof. Traci Paris. ICANM

First Psalm (Posthumous). Bertolt Brecht. PFTM-1

First Quilt. Ann Townsend. AmPoNex

First Radio. Michael McFee. SwNoth

First Rain. Ward Abbott. ICANM

First Reaching Huanzhou. Shen Quanqi. CCL1, tr. by Stephen Owen

First Reader. Billy Collins. PoA 2002; TWF

First Reader Santee Training School, 1873, The. Diane Glancy. LTA

First real grip I ever got on things, The. Wheels within Wheels. Seamus Heaney. ArBi; ModIr

First rehearse the easy things. How to Disappear. Amanda Dalton. NeBl

First Relations. Pamela Alexander. PfSP

First resurrection, move forward. First Resurrection. Géza Páskándi. IQMS, *tr. by* Neville Masterman

First retainer / he gave to her, The. Marriage, A. Robert Creeley. RaBo (First retainer, The.) PoPoPo

First revelation: that everything is bent, double. Cages, The. Jerry McGuire. AnSo

First Robin. Jane Yolen. NOxBChV

First Rock and Roll Song of 1970, The. Pedro Juan Pietri. ReTh

First Rondeau: After a French Poet of the Fourteenth Century. Johann Nikolaus Götz. GePo, *tr. by* George C. Schoolfield

First Rule [*with music*]. Maurice Kenny. HATNAP

First rule is to pacify the wives, The. Gwyneth Lewis. MFPA; NeBrP *Fr.* Welsh Espionage.

First rule: it must stand all evening, The. House of Cards, The. Vern Rutsala. MotU

First Satire of the Second Book of Horace [Imitated], The. Alexander Pope. "With all a woman's virtues but the pox." OBSV

First second she reminds, The. Choirist. Pierre Alféri. YaTCFP, *tr. by* Cole Swensen

First Second, The. Ian Duhig. NeBl

First see those ample melons—brindled o'er. Basket Of Summer Fruit, A. Charles Harpur. NOBAu

First sentence: Her cheap perfume. Seduced by Analogy. Bob Perelman. FTOS

First Sex. Richard Tayson. WiU

First Shaman Song. Gary Snyder. PFTM-2 *Fr.* Myths and Texts.

First she sent him treasure. Ruth Fainlight. MoWP *Fr.* Sheba and Solomon.

First shivers of palm fronds lift over the French Quarter. New Orleans Engagement. Dave Jeddie Smith. LPSFW

First Sight. Philip Larkin. NTCP; PtR

First Sight: "Blind woman—who by some miracle can, A." Ellen Doré Watson. NevBe

First Sight of Her and After. Thomas Hardy. FaBoVe

First sign of fall: yellow chalk. School of Denial. Mary Ruefle. ExTi

First sign of spring, first blush. Cactus. Sam Gardiner. NIrP

First silver work of kindness, The. First Station, The. Jean Valentine. ExTi

First Six Verses of the Ninetieth Psalm, The. Robert Burns. ChIV-1

First Smile. Nathan Alterman. FIT, *tr. by* Robert Friend

First snow. Basho. EH; NIL-7, *tr. by* Robert Hass

First snow comes in on lorries from the north. Weather Report. Charles Tomlinson. HarvBoo

First snow / Head clear. Etsujin. ZenPo, *tr. by* Takashi Ikemoto and Lucien Stryk

First Snow in Alsace. Richard Wilbur. AmWaPo; NoP-4; NoP-5; OBWP; PWW2

First Snow on an Airfield. John Ciardi. PoA 2002

First snow, unrolling scrim, my dogs running. Aubade: Opal and Silver. Mark Doty. HarvBoo

First snow was sleet, The. It swished heavily. Sleet. Norman Alexander MacCaig. OBCP

First snow wet against the windshield. In the Third Month. David Ray. RaBo

First Snowfall: Intimations. Edward Hirsch. PfSP

First Snowfall [*or* Snow-Fall], The. James Russell Lowell. AmFaPo; ITBLP; MoW

First Snowflake. N. M. Bodecker. TLR

First Sober Morning, The. Cindy Goff. LaCa

First Solitude, The. Luis de Góngora y Argote. OBVE, *tr. by* Edward Meryon Wilson

First, some flakes. Old Poetess Makes a Child, The. Ken Harris. AnSo

First Song. Galway Kinnell. NAMCP V.2; NoP-4; NoP-5

First Song of Moses, The. George Wither. ChIV-1

First Song of the Exploding Stick. *Unknown.* APN-2 *Fr.* Mountain Chant, The.

First Song of the Thunder. *Unknown.* APN-2; TCAPo *Fr.* Mountain Chant, The.

First sorrow of autumn, The. Seven Sorrows, The. Ted Hughes. NAEL-6v2; NAEL-7v2

First Spring. Duane Niatum. HATNAP

First Spring Day, The. Christina Georgina Rossetti. FaBoVe

First Spring in California, 1936. Wilma Elizabeth McDaniel. CalPo; GeoHom

First Station, The. Jean Valentine. ExTi

First Steps. J. D. McClatchy. WiU

   1871. WiU

   1946, 1957. WiU

   1971. WiU

   "Spirit sets about its task, but slowly, The." WiU

First Stone, The. Vievee Francis. NevBe

First Sunday I missed Mass on purpose, The. Day Zimmer Lost Religion, The. Paul Zimmer. PBCAP

First Sunset at Outler's Ranch. Enid Shomer. NevBe

First surprise: I like it, The. Getting Older. Elaine Feinstein. HarvBoo

First take me in your arms and hold me tight. *Unknown.* SLW, *tr. by* Marjolijn De Jager, Sayd Bahodin Majrouh and André Velter

First take me into your arms and hold me close. *Unknown.* SLW, *tr. by* Marjolijn De Jager, Sayd Bahodin Majrouh and André Velter

First Thanksgiving. Myra Cohn Livingston. HHAm

First Thanksgiving, The. Jack Prelutsky. NTCP

First Thanksgiving of All. Nancy Byrd Turner. ChAP

First Thaw. Tessa Ransford. EdScPo

First, The. Grace Cavalieri. UnSA

First, the beginning, presupposed as a past, goes to ground like a foundation and doubles itself. Mei-Mei Berssenbrugge. AWPTFC *Fr.* Kali.

First the chemistry made their atoms wobble. Sadness of Couples, The. Barbara Ras. NAPBL

First the goat. Making of the Drum, The. Edward Kamau Brathwaite. EmeKit

First: / the little death. Duchess of Dogs. Stephanie Williams. AnSo

First the melody, clean and hard. How High the Moon. Lance Jeffers. SeSe

First the outer gate. Truth Hall. Muso Soseki. EaWin, *tr. by* W. S. Merwin

First the path stones, then the shadow. Memento of the Hours. Linda Bierds. RoV

First the pleasures fire the heart. From Belfast to Suffolk. William Peskett. PNI

First, the river unclothes them, washes. For the Drowned. Nick Norwood. TiP2

First the snare crack. Some Tentative Definitions 1. Kwame Dawes. WaCA

First their car broke down, then Darlene and Kaylee drank up all the butterscotch schnapps. Throne of Grace, The. Kathleen Norris. UpMys

First there came the general's wife. Army Dance, The. *Unknown.* FaBoWar

First there was putting hot-water bottles to it. Inevitable. Sir John Betjeman. MoBrPo

First there was the island. Sea and Other Stories, The. Jennifer Rankin. NOBAu

First, there was the waking. Migration. Jane Griffiths. BeAl; NeBl

First there were two of us, then there were three of us. Storm, The. Walter De la Mare. NOxBChV

First They Came for the Jews. Pastor Niemoller. BeAl; HP; PoAgWa, *tr. by Unknown*

First they got the panther. How the Big Thicket Got Smaller. Jerry Bradley. TiP2

First They Slaughtered the Angels. Lenore Kandel. BB

First they taught us earth. The Napoleonic death. Ballad of the Bayonet, A. Ernest Bryll. FaBoWar, *tr. by* Czeslaw Milosz

First Thing. Kit Robinson. FTOS

First Thing, The. Mohja Kahf. PoArWo

First thing I can remember is a blue line, The. This was on the left. Autobiography. Margaret Atwood. MotU; OpeFie

First thing i do is take a long drink of wine. (LL) Knees of a Natural Man. Henry Dumas. GT; OxAAAP

First thing I felt, The. Wings. Ku Sang. CAMKP, *tr. by* Kevin O'Rourke

First thing I forgot was your voice, The. Deaths. Pedro Salinas. RaW, *tr. by* W. S. Merwin

First things first. First. Douglas Florian. NOxBChV

First things first: dig in at the lake's edge. How to Wait. Kelly Cherry. LPSFW

First Things, Last Things. Peter Scupham. WaAnP

First think, my soul, if I have foes. George Wither. SacPr *Fr.* Prisoner's Lay, A.

First thirty-seven years, The. Karen Press. TSAP

First, this one: "Peetah, Peetah, Peetah!" Kong Breaks a Leg at the William Morris Agency. William Trowbridge. ReTh

First thought in my head waking up was, oh no. Untitled. Robin Pickering. BeDoSh

First thought, the roof's edge and a bird there, singing. Omens. Marianne Boruch. AmAlph

First through. Glass Box Puzzle No. 1. Andrew J. Baldwin. BtF

First time, The. Bare Floors. Melanie Hope. WiU

First Time, The. Karl Shapiro. APT-2; NAMCP V.2

First Time: 1950. Honor Moore. FFC

First Time at the Wheel. Kurt Brown. NevBe

First Time Going to School All by Myself. Browning Porter. NevBe

First time he kissed me, he but only kissed. Elizabeth Barrett Browning. CenSon; ITBLP; LW Fr. Sonnets from the Portuguese.

First time I flew over Florida I was amazed, The. Distinct Call of the Alligator, The. Betsy Sholl. PBCAP

First time I got high I stood in a circle, The. Blunts. Major L. Jackson. LegDan; SpirFl

First Time I Heard Elvis, The. Steven Huff. NevBe

First time I heard, The. Big Words, The. Brendan Kennelly. EmeKit

First time I held a gun, The. Gun, The. Jacqueline Berger. AmPoNex

First time I lied to my baby, I told him that it was his face on the baby food jar, The. How Lies Grow. Maxine Chernoff. IllVoic; PmAP; SUP

First time I remember waking up. Wendell Berry. GoPo

First time I robbed Tiffany's it was raining, The. First Time I Robbed Tiffany's, The. Norman Stock. NevBe

First time I saw hundreds of fiddlehead ferns boiling in an enormous pot I realized. Fiddleheads. Maureen Seaton. BAP-97; SUP

First time I saw my father defeated, The. Resisting Geometry. Ann Elizabeth Hostetler. ACAMVP

First time I see, The. Carmelita. D. A. Feinfeld. BloBone

First Time I Set Eyes on You, The. Unknown. CCL1, tr. by John Frodsham

First time I walked, The. Oranges. Gary Soto. CAP-8; NAMCP V.2; NoAM; WeW-3

First time I was born, it, The. Verse for First. Tseverin Furey. NevBe

First Time In. Ivor Gurney. FaBoVe; NAMCP V.1; NoP-4; NoP-5

First time in a sales booth. Trade Show. Miles A. Coon. NevBe

First time it occurred to me there are no orgasms in this world, The. Zen 101. Nin Andrews. AmZen

First time out. Lives. Derek Mahon. BeAl; EmeKit; ModIr; PBCIP

First Time Reading Freud. Douglas Goetsch. NevBe

First time that the sun rose on thine oath, The. Elizabeth Barrett Browning. CenSon; NAEL-6v2; NAEL-7v2 Fr. Sonnets from the Portuguese.

First time we went to bed, The. (LL) Close. Andrew Motion. HarvBoo; StAl

First to come, The. Song of the Crows. Chippewa Oral Tradition. NAAL-5; NAAPv.2

First to feast is love, The. On the scraps of love the fever feasts. Margherita Guidacci. CItWP Fr. Meditations and Maxims.

First Tooth, The. Charles Lamb and Mary Lamb. WoRP

First touch of hand in hand—Did one but know! (LL) Christina Georgina Rossetti. LW; OxBSo Fr. Monna Innominata.

First Trimester, The. Campbell McGrath. NeAmPo; UrbNat

First Turn to Me. Bernadette Mayer. PmAP

First Turtle. David Lee. NevBe

First TV in a Mennonite Family. Julia Kasdorf. AmPoNex

First unexpected pain is beautiful, The. Ivano Fermini. ItPo, tr. by Gayle Ridinger

1st Untitled Poem. Pedro Juan Pietri. PueRic

First View of the Islands, A. Jean V. Gier. ReBoTo

First Villancico, Written for the Nativity of Our Lord, Puebla, 1689, The. Sor Juana Inés de la Cruz. "Since Love is shivering." WPoS

First Walk on the Moon. May Swenson. RACG

First war resembles. First War. Shmuel HaNagid. WoPoe, tr. by Peter Cole

First Warning Sign: Epiphany. Edoardo Cacciatore. ItPo Fr. Full Powers: Five Warning Signs.

First was Fancy, like a lovely boy, The. Edmund Spenser. CAGL Fr. Faerie Queene, The.

First we carried out the faggot of steel stakes. Roy Fisher. Fr. City.

First we locked our fingers, wove them. My Blood Brother. Frank Mkalawile Chipasula. HBAPE; PML

1st Weather: / beside the sun, actually, and skinny enough to set on fire. Schubert, or: Notes on the Weather, Vienna. Friederike Mayröcker. OnScMo, tr. by Rosmarie Waldrop

First week the soil was clean, The. Digging for Indians. Gary Gildner. PBCAP

First Winter: Joy. Peggy Shumaker. PBCAP

First winter rain. Basho. EH, tr. by Robert Hass

First with a glass of water. Every Blessed Day. Philip Levine. BeAl

First word was, The. Nommo: how we come to speak. Devorah Major. BRtP

First World War Poets. Edward Bond. FaBoWar

First, worms begin with a man's mind. In the Background of Silence. Yusef Komunyakaa. CAP-8

First Year. Vittorio Sereni. PML, tr. by Marcus Perryman and Peter Robinson

First you bite your fingernails. And then you comb your hair again. And then you wait. And wait. American Rhapsody. Kenneth Fearing. APT-2; MoAmPo

First you must have. Instructions for Building Straw Huts. Yusef Komunyakaa. GT

First: "You stepped off the wrong train they made you flit through the city's mirror." Sezai Karakoç. NaPG, tr. by Talat Sait Halman

First, you think they are dead. Lobsters in the Window. W. D. Snodgrass. TRP

First, you took the parakeet out of its cage. Harm. Vickie Karp. KGB

First Zen Abbess of America, The. Nathaniel Tarn. WANABP

First-born. Fergus Allen. NIrP

Firstborn. Louise Glück. HarvBoo

First-Born, A. Kong Rong. CCL1, tr. by H. A. Giles

First-born, The. Jack Davis. BMAP

Firstborn Land, The. Ingeborg Bachmann. GTCP, tr. by Irmgard Hunt and Daniel Huws

First-Day Thoughts. John Greenleaf Whittier. APN-1

Firste fader and findere of gentilesse, The. Geoffrey Chaucer. NAEL-6v1

Firstforce or earth-driven godman; globe-song. Ballad of Black/Essence. Eugene B. Redmond. OxAAAP

First-Rate Wife, The. Cornelius Whur. STuOW

Firsts in No Particular Order. Kimiko Hahn. NevBe

Fisbo. Robert Malise Bowyer Nichols. "Talking of Ezra Pound and long-dead pantos." OBSV

Fischerhude, 2001. Sujata Bhatt. NeBrP

Fish. Moniza Alvi. NeBl

Fish. José Luis Hidalgo. RaW, tr. by Ralph Nelson

Fish. Mariana Romo-Carmona. WiU

Fish. Takahashi Shinkichi. ZenPo, tr. by Takashi Ikemoto and Lucien Stryk

Fish. Gertrude Stein. OxBoAm Fr. Book Concluding with As A Wife Has a Cow a Love Story, A.

Fish, The. Elizabeth Bishop. APT-2; BeAl; BrAP; CAP-8; ChAP; HarvBoo; HeIP-4; MoAmPo; MoASP; NAAL-5; NALW; NAMCP V.2; NoAM; NoP-4; NoP-5; PoetW; PoPoPo; TFi; TRP; WaAnP

Fish, The: "Wade / through black jade." Marianne Moore. APT-1; BrAP; ColAP; EMP; GPTC; MoAmPo; NAAPv.2; NAMCP V.1; NoAM; NoP-4; NoP-5; OxBoAm; WaAnP

Fish 2. Fidelito Cortes. ReBoTo

Fish / always accurately know where to move and when. Brief Reflection on Accuracy. Miroslav Holub. StAl, tr. by Miroslav Holub

Fish and Sauce. No Hyegyông. EcSo, tr. by Ann Y. Choi

Fish & styrofoam. At Tsukiji Market Tokyo. Jerome Rothenberg. WoBe

Fish Answers, A. Leigh Hunt. NBLV; NPeEn Fr. Fish, the Man, and the Spirit, The.

Fish are staying here, The. Heart Feels the Water. Joseph Ceravolo. NYP2

Fish are the first to return, The. Asylum. Quan Barry. PoDa

Fish bones walked the waves off Hatteras. Cottonmouth Country. Louise Glück. WaAnP

Fish can have mad cow disease and I have a problem. Whither Thou Goest. Bob Hicok. AmAlph

Fish cannot drown in water, A. Mechthild von Magdeburg. WPoS

Fish Cove. Blaise Cendrars. BLT, tr. by Monique Chefdor

Fish dangles in its glass case, The. Far-off, it's an anatomy lesson, the discourse of an alien life. Image of the Fish. Mónica Nepote. SPV, tr. by Jen Hofer

Fish Daughter, The. Pascale Petit. MoWP

Fish Dream, The. John Engels. AtGh

Fish (fly-replete, in depth of June). Heaven. Rupert Brooke. MoBrPo; NPeEn; OxBEV

Fish Food. John Wheelwright. APT-2

Fish / fowl. Paean to Place. Lorine Niedecker. APSN; APT-2; FTOS

Fish hit water nymphs, breaking surface, The. Late Spring in the Nuclear Age. Andrew Hudgins. AtGh

Fish I Remember. Suzanne Lummis. SUP

Fish in Deep Water, The (144). Khwaja Shams-ad-din Muhammad Hafiz. WED, tr. by Robert Bly and Leonard Lewisohn

Fish in the Net. János Pilinszky. IQMS, tr. by Adam Makkai

Fish in the Stone, The. Rita Dove. EmeKit

Fish in the Unruffled Lakes. W. H. Auden. MoBrPo Fr. Twelve Songs.

Fish in the unruffled lakes. W. H. Auden. MoBrPo Fr. Twelve Songs.

Fish of Fleeting Skin. Coral Bracho. RMCMP, tr. by Suzanne Jill Levine

Fish Pond, The [1993] ("Not full of fish—that's imprecise—but full.") Sydney Lea. PfSP

Fish R Us. Mark Doty. FaoP

Fish shop. Basho. WoPoe; ZenPo, tr. by Takashi Ikemoto and Lucien Stryk

Fish Shop Windows. Geoffrey Dutton. NOBAu

Fish Tea Rice. Linda Gregg. BeAl; ExTi

Fish, the Man, and the Spirit, The. Leigh Hunt. OBEV; OxBSo

Fish Answers, A. NBLV; NPeEn

"Man's life is warm, glad, sad, 'twixt loves and graves." NPeEn

To a Fish. NBLV; NPeEn

Fish took a notion, A. Tip-Toe Tail. Dixie Willson. NTCP

Fish weeps in the, The. Fish Weeps, The. *Unknown.* NDACCP, *tr. by* Kenneth Rexroth

Fishamble Street, the Civic Offices. David Wheatley. NIrP *Fr.* Sonnets to James Clarence Mangan.

Fishbone ground for cleaning, flagstone. Norway. Linda Gregerson. AmAlph

Fisher Jamie. John, 1st Baron Tweedsmuir Buchan. EdScPo

Fisher King. Imani Tolliver. BtF

Fisher Street. Thylias Moss. GT

Fisher Towers. Jenny Mueller. IAoNAP

Fisheris ar gon to the sea, The. For Cadging Fish. Isabel Gowdie. EMWP

Fisherman. Ou-yang Hsiu. BLT, *tr. by* Kenneth Rexroth

Fisherman, A. Sŏng Kan. CATKP, *tr. by* Chi-gyu Kim [*or* Kim Chonggil]

Fisherman, The. Johann Wolfgang von Goethe. STV, *tr. by* John Frederick Nims

Fisherman, The: "World was first a private park, The." [*with music*]. Jay Macpherson. BrAP

Fisherman, The. Janice Mirikitani. OpBo

Fisherman, The. Yunna Petrovna Moritz. TCRusP, *tr. by* Daniel Weissbort

Fisherman, The. William Butler Yeats. NAMCP V.1; NoAM

Fisherman at Byolam. Muyong Sooyon. BecRai, *tr. by* Kim Daljin, Kim Won-Chung and Christopher Merrill

Fisherman, Hey! *Hungarian Oral Tradition.* IQMS, *tr. by* Dermot Spence

Fisherman in wellingtons, A. Gaelic Stories. Iain Crichton Smith. NePenScot

"Fisherman's Honor," The. Li Ch'ing-chao. WPoS, *tr. by* Jane Hirshfield (Written to the Tune "The Fisherman's Honor.") WoPoe

Fisherman's hut, by the mouth of the river. Coming at Night to a Fisherman's Hut. Chang Chi. BLT

Fisherman's Pants, The. Thomas Lux. MotU

Fisherman's Rhyme. *Unknown.* FaBoVe

Fisherman's Song, A. Jinkag Haesim. BecRai, *tr. by* Kim Daljin, Kim Won-Chung and Christopher Merrill

Fisherman's Song, The. Thomas D'Urfey. NOSC

Fisherman's Story, The. Henrietta Cordelia Ray. CBWP-3

Fisherman's swapping a yarn for a yarn, The. Flower-Boat, The. Robert Frost. PoA 2002

Fisherman's Wife, The. Jody Gladding. YaYoPo

Fishermen. Song. Primus St. John. GT

Fishermen at Ballyshannon. Limbo. Seamus Heaney. NoAM

Fishermen from Ma Yuan. "Lucebert." TuT, *tr. by* Peter van de Kamp

Fishermen, hey! Fishermen, hey! Fisherman, Hey! *Hungarian Oral Tradition.* IQMS, *tr. by* Dermot Spence

Fishes are born in water. Man Is Born in Tao. Chuang Tzu. BLT, *tr. by* Thomas Merton

Fishes are climbing against the stream. (LL) Yun Sŏndo. CATKP; WoPoe *Fr.* Angler's Calendar, The.

Fishes in the shallows. Yun Sŏndo. CATKP *Fr.* Angler's Calendar, The.

Fishes / theirs fit. Tom Weatherly. EGAG

Fish-Hawk, The. John Hall Wheelock. APT-1

Fishing. Paula McLain. AmPoNex

Fishing. Dorothy, Duchess of Wellington Wellesley. OBMV

Fishing among the Learned. Nikky Finney. SpirFl

Fishing boat driving water. After Source of the Peach Blossom Stream. Wang Wei. ChinPo, *tr. by* Ye Weilian [*or* Yeh Wei-lien *or* Wai-lim Yip]

Fishing in the Keep of Silence. Linda Gregg. BodElec; GoPo

Fishing in Winter. Ralph Burns. MoASP

Fishing Lass of Hakin, The. Lewis Morris. AngWePo

Fishing the Dream. Mike Delp. MoASP

Fishing the White Water. Audre Lorde. GT

Fishing with Elvis. Dabney Stuart. AllShUp

Fishing-Tackle, The. Bertolt Brecht. PoSu, *tr. by* Lee Baxendall

Fishmonger. Marsden Hartley. APT-1

Fishnet. Robert Lowell. PoetW; VCAP

Fish's Nightsong. Christian Morgenstern. WeW-3

Fishy smell, A. Basho. EH, *tr. by* Robert Hass

Fission. Jorie Graham. NAMCP V.2; OxBoAm

Fission, I'm running very fast. (LL) Explosion. Takahashi Shinkichi. AtGh; ZenPo, *tr. by* Takashi Ikemoto and Lucien Stryk

Fist, The. Tatamkulu Afrika. TSAP

Fist, The. Derek Walcott. BeAl; ESEAA

Fist clenched round my heart, The. Fist, The. Derek Walcott. BeAl; ESEAA

Fist: Joe Louis The Brown. Brown Bomber. Sam Cornish. BtF

Fist meets the face as the stone meets water, The. Battery. Robin Morgan. GifTon

Fist of red fire, a flower, A. First Love. Elizabeth Jennings. LW

Fists. Peter Finch. TCAWP

Fists in their pockets, daggers in their eyes. (LL) Drinks in the Town Square. Rachel Wetzsteon. AmPoNex; NeAmPo

Fit As a Fiddle. Arthur Freed. ReLy

Fit Für Gaing Farth. Barbara Guest. AHA

Fit Music. Lorenzo Thomas. AHA

Fit of Rhyme against Rhyme, A. Ben Jonson. NoP-4; NoP-5; PBRV

Fit the First: The Landing. Lewis Carroll. WaAnP *Fr.* Hunting of the Snark, The.

Fit the Second: The Bellman's Speech. Lewis Carroll. OBCoV *Fr.* Hunting of the Snark, The.

Fitness expert. Big gym-man. Strato. EroLit, *tr. by* Kenneth McLeish

Fitting. Pauline Prior-Pitt. Prnts

Fitting, The. Edna St. Vincent Millay. NALW

Fitting Room, The. Angela Jackson. BtF

Fitting stone upon stone. (LL) Building Walls. Todd Davis. ACAMVP; VisFro

Fitzroy. Andrew Taylor. BMAP

Five. Eduardo Milán. *tr. by* Roberto Tejada

"Now that there's no self, let's proceed to the general self." RMCMP, *tr. by* Roberto Tejada

Five. Dennis Phillips. FTOS *Fr.* Twenty Questions.

5:46 train roars, waking me, The. Peace Be Still. Esther Iverem. BtF

Five A.M. Na Hŭidŏk. EcSo, *tr. by* Peter H. Lee

Five a.m., and I've been. Dawn. Lucien Stryk. InvLad

Five a.m. on East Fourteenth I'm out to eat. Sonnet. Tom Clark. AHA

Five A.M., the Fourth of July. Independence Day Letter. Donald Hall. NoP-5

Five Bells. Kenneth Slessor. BrAP; NOBAu

Five buds were on the parent tree. Family Portraits. Mary E. Tucker. CBWP-1

Five by seven, aged brown. Honor Card. Betsy Colquitt. TiP2

Five can't ketch me and ten can't hold me. 'Round the Corn, Sally. *Unknown.* SSUS

Five Chants. David McCord. NOxBChV

Five daughters, in the slant light on the porch. Daughters, 1900. Marilyn Nelson Waniek. FFC; WaAnP

Five Dawn Skies in November. David Wagoner. VCAP

Five Days Remaining, The (75). Khwaja Shams-ad-din Muhammad Hafiz. WED, *tr. by* Robert Bly and Leonard Lewisohn

Five Dogs. Mark Strand. PtR

Five Epigrams. James Vincent Cunningham. *tr. by* James Vincent Cunningham

Epitaph for Someone or Other. APT-2; TRP; WoPoe

Lip. OxBoAm

(Too Late.) WoPoe, *tr. by* James Vincent Cunningham

Five fathoms deep my father lies. Sea Bells. Miriam Waddington. BrAP

515 Madison Avenue. Rhapsody. Frank O'Hara. NAMCP V.2; NoAM

Five Fingers of the Hand, The. Aloysius Bertrand. MotU, *tr. by* James Weeks

Five Flights Up. Elizabeth Bishop. OxBoAm

Five Foot Two, Eyes of Blue (Has Anybody Seen My girl?). Sam M. Lewis and Joe Young. ReLy

Five from Three. Alice Jones. Vesp

Five geese deploy mysteriously. Bas-Relief. Carl Sandburg. ColAP

Five goddesses, permanent residents of the land of pure bliss. Philosophical Inquiry into the Nature of the Human Cock, A. Nin Andrews. AmZen

Five Holy Mountains are great works raised by spirits, The. Song of My Mountain Dwelling. Zhidun. CCL1, *tr. by* John Frodsham

Five hours, (and who can do it less in?). Lady's Dressing Room, The. Jonathan Swift. NAEL-7v1; NoP-4; NoP-5; WaAnP

527. Hwang Jiwoo. CAMKP, *tr. by* Young-Jun Lee and Scott Swaner

Five Hundred Points of Good Husbandry. Thomas Tusser.

Advice of Housewives. NoSic

December's Husbandry. NoSic

500,000 years ago sleepy chipmunks. American History in Context. Antler. WhBo

Five Hymns to Pain. Nazik al-Mala'ika. PoArWo, *tr. by* Husain Haddawy

Five inches from. Desire. Paul Hoover. PmAP

Five is the sum of this world figured by the senses. Interval of Five Tones Being the Dominant, An. Brooks Haxton. PoDa

Five Men. Cole Heinowitz. FreRad

Five Men. Zbigniew Herbert. PoSu, *tr. by* Peter Dale Scott

Five men pull straws. Fragging. Yusef Komunyakaa. AmAlph; ESEAA

Five miles beneath the fuselage I see. First View of the Islands, A. Jean V. Gier. ReBoTo

Five miles from Tatum down State 43. Pete's Poem. Cyd Adams. TiP2

Five miles to my mother's house.   That Saturday without a Car.   Stephen Dunn.   WaAnP

Five Minutes.   Norman Nicholson.   NLP

Five Minutes after the Air Raid.   Miroslav Holub.   PoAgWa, *tr.* by George Theiner

5 Minutes, Mr. Salaam.   Kalamu ya Salaam.   SpirFl

Five minutes with his paintings and I remember.   Fauviste.   Donald Revell.   BodElec

Five months after your death, I come like the others.   Elegy for a Forest Clear-Cut by the Weyerhaeuser Company.   David Wagoner.   NAMCP V.2; NoAM

Five Neo-Platonic Commentaries.   David Brendon Hopes.
   2. The Cave.   UpMys

Five Nights of Bleeding.   Linton Kwesi Johnson.   WaCA

Five Nocturnes, after Derek Jarman.   Ken Edwards.
   "About this time streetlamps flicker up like."   Oth
   "Art of definition—is this, An."   Oth
   "De—um majorettes."   Oth
   "Night falls on single vision zombies everywhere."   Oth
   "This juxtaposition of events without."   Oth

Five Note Range of Sorrow.   Honorée Fanonne Jeffers.   AnSo

Five Notebooks for Exit Art.   Cecilia Vicuña.   PFTM-2

Five O'Clock Opera.   Lavinia Greenlaw.   MFPA

Five O'Clock Whistle, The.   *Hawaiian Oral Tradition.*   NAAPv.1

Five Old Favorites.   James Merrill.
   Midnight Snack, The.   OxBSo

Five. One.   Laurie Duggan.   BMAP *Fr.* Ash Range, The.

Five Panels.   Mark Irwin.   PoDa

Five Poems about Poetry.   George Oppen.
   Gesture, The.   OxBoAm

Five Poems on Returning to Dwell in the Country.   T'ao Ch'ien.   CCL1, *tr.* by William Acker

Five rice dumplings.   Ransetsu.   ZenPo, *tr.* by Takashi Ikemoto and Lucien Stryk

Five rivers, like the fingers of a hand.   Ebenezer Elliott.   NOBRP *Fr.* Village Patriarch, The.

Five seasons without traveling to a festival, without walking.   Homage to Lester Flatt.   David Bottoms.   SwNoth

Five Senses.   Denise Clegg.   ICANM

Five Smooth Stones.   Deborah Digges.   ExTi

Five soldiers fixed by Mathew Brady's eye.   Looking into History.   Richard Wilbur.   VCAP

Five Sorrowful Mysteries, The.   Francis Jammes.   GI, *tr.* by Jeffrey Fiskin

Five Stages of Grief, The.   Linda Pastan.   WaAnP

Five summer days, five summer nights.   Blue-Fly, The.   Robert Graves.   NAEL-6v2; NAEL-7v2; NAMCP V.1; NoAM

Five things glimpsed unexpectedly.   Memorabilia.   Lexie Dean Robertson.   TiP2

5:30 a.m. / downtown ghetto Richmond.   Ghetto Dokusan.   Gary Rosenthal.   WhBo

5:32, The.   Phyllis McGinley.   APT-2 *Fr.* I Know a Village.

529 1983.   Gerda Mayer.   Spl

Five Urban Love Songs.   Kate Light.
   Safe-T-Man.   AmPoNex
   2. San Francisco.   PoDa

Five Verses for Shariputra Mugged Outside His Building.   Tony Trigilio.   AmZen

Five Villanelles.   Weldon Kees.
   Villanelle.   StAl

Five (was I?) when Edward Sanderlin, Ford Plant employee and nearby neighbor.   Dogs.   Kate Meads.   RaF

Five Ways to Kill a Man.   Edwin Brock.   BeAl

Five Weeks.   Lee Ranaldo.   HeMarv

Five windows light the cavern'd Man; thro' one he breathes the air.   Europe; A Prophecy.   William Blake.

Five windows light the caverned man: through one he breathes the air.   William Blake.   NPBRoP *Fr.* Europe; A Prophecy.

Five Wishes.   Anne Porter.   KGB

5-Year-Old Girls Encountered.   Katie Degentesh.   FreRad

Five years are vanished since I first poured out.   William Wordsworth.   *Fr.* Prelude, The; Growth of a Poet's Mind [1805 version].

Five years have passed [*or* past]; five summers, with the length.   Lines Composed a Few Miles above Tintern Abbey on Revisiting the Banks of the Wye During a Tour, July 13, 1798.   William Wordsworth.   AmFaPo; BrAP; CABP; HeIP-4; NAEL-6v2; NAEL-7v2; NAWM-7v2; NIL-7; NoP-4; NoP-5; NPeEn; OxAEP-2; OxBEV; PoPoPo; TFi

Five years out of school and preachy.   Naming It.   Leontia Flynn.   NIrP

Five years since you died and I am.   Letter to a Dead Father.   Richard Shelton.   PBCAP

Five yen each / A cup of tea.   Issa.   ZenPo, *tr.* by Takashi Ikemoto and Lucien Stryk

Five-0.   Ras Baraka.   InTrad

Five-Color.   Yang Chi.   WoPoe, *tr.* by Jonathan Chaves

Five-Finger Exercises.   T. S. Eliot.
   Lines for Cuscuscaraway and Mirza Murad Ali Beg.   NBLV; OBCoV; UV
   Lines to Ralph Hodgson Esqre.   NBLV

Five-thirty light fell onto the dining room table, The.   Leaving Home.   Sarah Rosenblatt.   AmPoNex

Five-thirty, little one, already light.   Aubade 1.   Marilyn Hacker.   FiBr

Five-thirty on a summer afternoon.   Topiary Rooster.   Chase Twichell.   WANABP

Five-Year Plan.   Victoria Chang.   SweBea

Fix.   Michael Dransfield.   NOBAu

Fix.   Alice Fulton.   PoDa

Fix bayonets, and die, as English soldiers do.   Isandula.   Hume Nisbet.   FaBoWar

Fix your eyes on any chance object. For instance.   Brotherhood in Pain.   Robert Penn Warren.   OxBoAm

Fixed Ideas.   Kenneth Slessor.   BMAP

Fixed in the fireplace.   Fireplace, The.   Michael S. Harper.   GT

Fixin' to Die.   Bukka White.   APT-2

Fixture, A.   Bill Berkson.   NYP2

Fizzle to / Donky Kong may.   Poem with Referees.   James Sanders.   AnSo

Flacas mujeres de los metalúrgicos, Las.   Flacas Mujeres, Las.   Gloria Fuertes.   RaW

Flag, The.   Pablo Neruda.   PoetW, *tr.* by Nathaniel Tarn

Flag, A! A flag! (LL)   Edgar Lee Masters.   AmWaPo; APT-1 *Fr.* Spoon River Anthology.

Flag let loose for a day of festivity, The.   John Gould Fletcher.   PoA 2002 *Fr.* Irradiations.

Flag Memoir.   Reg Saner.   AmWaPo

Flag of Chile, The.   Teresa de Jesús.   AF, *tr.* by Maria Proser, Arlene Scully and James Scully

Flag of Honeysuckle, A.   Andrew Hudgins.   LPSFW

Flaggy Shore, The.   Gwyneth Lewis.   NeBrP

Flags of all sorts.   Things We Dreamt We Died For.   Marvin Bell.   PoA 2002

Flags of Autumn.   Robin Robertson.   EdScPo *Fr.* Camera Obscura.

Flags of war like storm-birds fly, The.   Battle Autumn of 1862, The.   John Greenleaf Whittier.   AmWaPo; CBCWP; PCW

Flags Vex a Dying Face.   Emily Dickinson.   MoAmPo

Flag-Tree.   Dan Beachy-Quick.   IAoNAP

Flailed from the heart of water in a bow.   Ballade for the Duke of Orléans.   Richard Wilbur.   WoPoe

Flailing like a foal giraffe to keep his balance.   Sailing.   Richard Kenney.   YaYoPo

Flakes not of fabric but of words of fabric of words—scraps—remnants.   Bernard Heidsieck.   PFTM-2 *Fr.* Canal Street.

Flakes of lacquer, dust of bones.   Song of an Arrowhead from Changping.   Li Ho.   CCL1, *tr.* by John Frodsham

Flakes over grave and cairn.   Brother.   Gudmundur Bödvarsson.   PML, *tr.* by Alan Boucher

Flakes pour to the black dead.   In the Camp There Was One Alive.   Randall Jarrell.   HP

Flame.   Jayne Cortez.   OxAAAP

Flame.   Cauvin L. Paul.   OGAHCP, *tr.* by Boadiba and Jack Hirschman

Flame.   C. D. Wright.   AmAlph

Flame, A.   Adam Zagajewski.   PoCho, *tr.* by Clare Cavanagh

Flame, The.   I. D. Hooson.   BBMWP, *tr.* by Anthony Conran

Flame is full, The.   Soul, The.   Nedelcho Ganev.   CSCBP, *tr.* by Georgi Belev and Lisa Sapinkopf

Flame Ode.   Barry MacSweeney.   Oth

Flame On.   Rebecca Wolff.   IIR

Flame on the Spanish Stairs, A: John Keats in Rome.   Douglas Barbour.
   "I know now I always wanted to write, to."   IFF

Flame out, you glorious skies.   Dead Heroes, The.   Isaac Rosenberg.   MoBrPo

Flame-flower, day-torch, Mauna Loa.   Lines to a Nasturtium.   Anne Spencer.   APT-1; InGu

Flamenco Guitar.   Ruth L. Schwartz.   WiU

Flames.   Pearse Hutchinson.   BeAl

Flames.   Tōge Sankichi.   FaBoWar, *tr.* by Richard H. Minear

Flames and Dangling Wire.   Robert Gray.   BMAP; NOBAu

Flames and Leaves.   Caitríona O'Reilly.   NIrP

Flames from sun.   Magnificent Tomorrows.   Haki R. Madhubuti.   SpirFl

Flame's speech is confused, The. The muttering of the water is hollow.   A. Velichansky.   TCRusP, *tr.* by Daniel Weissbort

Flaming Heart, The. Richard Crashaw. NAEL-6v1; NAEL-7v1
  "Live in these conquering leaves; live all the same." OxAEP-1
  "O sweet incendiary! shew here thy art." NPeEn
  Upon the Book and Picture of the Seraphical Saint Teresa. OBEV; WoPoe
Flaming Heart vpon the Book and Picture of the Seraphicall Saint Teresa, (As She Vsvally Expressed with a Seraphim biside her), The. Richard Crashaw. See Flaming Heart, The.
Flaming Terrapin, The. Roy Campbell.
  "Maternal Earth stirs redly from beneath." MoBrPo
Flaming with anger and despair, Perseus is hunting Medusa. Apotheosis of Medusa. Pat Parnell. HW
Flamingo delouses its belly with the easy speed. Seriema Song. Albert Goldbarth. UrbNat
Flamingos Have Arrived in Ashtabula. Andrew Hudgins. LPSFW
Flamingos, The. Rainer Maria Rilke. OWoS, tr. by Stephen Mitchell
Flammonde. Edwin Arlington Robinson. NoAM
Flaneur [or Flâneur], The. Oliver Wendell Holmes. APN-1; NAAPv.1
Flanking Sheep in Mosedale. David Scott. NLP
Flap we our lips, praise Big Man. Cywydd o Fawl. Harri Webb. AngWePo; TCAWP
Flap your wings on my bare trees. Little Tales. Zakiyya Malallah. PoArWo, tr. by Wen Chin Ouyang
Flarebombs bloom on the dark sky. Witness Remains, The. Thich Nhat Hanh and Jane Hirshfield. WhBo
Flash. Lee Bennett Hopkins. SSCS
Flash, A. May Muzaffar. PoArWo, tr. by Tahia Abdel Nasser
Flash Cards. Rita Dove. ESEAA; LoL; PoPoPo
Flash Colonial Barman, The. William W. Coxon. NOBAu
Flash Crimson. Carl Sandburg. MoAmPo
Flash! flash! bang! bang! and we blazed away. Adam Lindsay Gordon. STuOW Fr. Wolf and Hound.
Flash lights from the wild gardens. (LL) Wild Gardens Overlooked by Night Lights. Barbara Guest. FTOS; PmAP
Flash me. Lee Ranaldo. HeMarv
Flash of lightning. Buson. EMJL, tr. by Haruo Shirane
Flash Point. Lorenzo Thomas. AnSo
Flashing and glimmering at the edge of the horizon. (LL) East Coast Journey. James Keir Baxter. NoP-4; NoP-5
Flashing their angry tears, here in Live Oak. (LL) Walking Down the Road. Adrienne Rich. NIL-7; NIP-4
Flashing wild horses of Europe. Ten to One to No. Joyce Mansour. SurWo, tr. by Mary Beach
Flashy and feisty, furious fun, this ostensibly. Constrained Response. Maxianne Berger. IFF
Flask of Brandy, A. Padraic Fallon. ModIr
Flat chord; and cordate. perennial sounding, earth and eyes. Syliva Legris. PoPra Fr. Negative Garden.
Flat end of sorrow here, The. First Circle, The. Kofi Awoonor. BrAP; HBAPE; VCWP
Flat, / Flat. St. Louis. Amy Lowell. NAAL-5
Flat Lake cold penetrates water-lily clothes. Han-shan Te-ch'ing. CSKM, tr. by Red Pine
Flat Lake's autumn water merges with the winter sky. Han-shan Te-ch'ing. CSKM, tr. by Red Pine
Flat Mountain. Muso Soseki. EaWin, tr. by W. S. Merwin
Flat on the bank I parted. John Montague. ModIr; NoP-4; NoP-5; PBCIP; PNI; StAl Fr. All Legendary Obstacles.
Flat One, A. W. D. Snodgrass. NAMCP V.2
Flat, white, and dangerous. Mango's Core, The. Patricia Blanco. AFaM
Flatlanders. Monica Youn. LegDan
Flattened your words against your speaking mouth. (LL) Hearing Your Words, and Not a Word among Them. Edna St. Vincent Millay. ColAP; NoAM
Flaubert in Egypt. Robert Penn Warren. NoAM
Flaubert wanted to write a novel. Style. Howard Nemerov. NoAM; OxBoAm
Flautist boasts but God's enraged—, The. Elegy on an X-ray Photo of My Skull. Yelena Shwarts. ItGoST; VCWP, tr. by Catriona Kelly and Michael Molnar
Flavio Gonzales, seventy-two, made jackhammer. Moon Is a Diamond, The. Arthur Sze. TAPaP
Flavor, The. I'm Sayin Though. Marco Villalobos. BRtP
Flaw, A. Michael Field. ViWPN; VWP
Flaw, The. Robert Lowell. HarvBoo
Flaw in Paganism, The. Dorothy Parker. NBLV
Flawless is the word, no doubt, for this third of May. Hourglass. Josephine Jacobsen. NoP-4; NoP-5
Flaxman. Margaret Fuller. APN-1
Flay the square with crowds. Girl with the Bad Rep, The. Kay Murphy. SwNoth

Flea flew by a bee, A. The bee. Mary Ann Hoberman. OBSP Fr. Bugs.
Flea, The. John Donne. AmFaPo; BASC; BrAP; FSCP; NAEL-6v1; NAEL-7v1; NBLV; NIL-7; NIP-4; NoP-4; NoP-5; NoSic; OxAEP-1; TFi; WaAnP
Fleadh Cheoil. Pearse Hutchinson. PBCIP
Fleance. Michael Longley. PNI
Fleas in my hut. Issa. EH, tr. by Robert Hass
Fleas, lice. Basho. EH, tr. by Robert Hass
Fleas, lice. Basho. EMJL, tr. by Haruo Shirane
Fleas, stink, pigs, mold. Rondeau. Eustache Deschamps. WoPoe, tr. by David Curzon and Jeffrey Fiskin
Flecha, tanto sol, Una. Tanta munición de rayos cruza. Cada punta pica, picotea. Astilla. Silvia Eugenia Castillero. SPV
Flecknoe, an English Priest at Rome. Andrew Marvell. BASC
Fled back unhinderd till she came into the vales of Har. (LL) Book of Thel, The. William Blake. NAEL-6v2; NAEL-7v2; NoP-5; WaAnP
Fled is that music—Do I wake or sleep? (LL) Ode to a Nightingale. John Keats. AmFaPo; BrAP; BRP; CABP; CIHu; HeIP-4; NAEL-6v2; NAEL-7v2; NAWM-7v2; NIL-7; NOBRP; NoP-4; NoP-5; NPBRoP; NPeEn; OBEV; OWoS; OxBEV; PoPoPo; SoSe-8; TFi; WaAnP
Fledgling. Anthony Conran. AngWePo
Fle[e] alway[i]s from[e] the snare [or snair]. (LL) Rondel of Luve [or Love], A. Alexander Scott. OBEV; OxBEV
Flee every friendship and live: a greater truth. Seneca. RomPo, tr. by Anthony James Boyle
Flee fro the prees and dwelle with soothfastnesse. Geoffrey Chaucer. NAEL-6v1; NAEL-7v1; NoP-4; NoP-5; SacPr
Flee, lovers, from Love, flee from his fire. Michelangelo Buonarroti. CAGL, tr. by James M. Saslow
Flee, stately Juno, Samos fro. Ludovic Lloyd. AngWePo Fr. Sidanen.
Flee trouble, as you desire: it will catch you and hold you in bondage. Soul of a Man, The. Ferenc Kazinczy. IQMS, tr. by Adam Makkai
Fleece, The. John Dyer.
  House Beautiful, The. STuOW
  Insensible Hottentot, The. STuOW
  Leeds for Pleasure. STuOW
  Pastoral. STuOW
  Treating Sheep Ailments.
  Pastoral. STuOW
Fleeing Atalanta, The. David Foster.
  "Alchemists say the Stone turns lead to gold." NOBAu
  "Don't give everything." NOBAu
  "Seeking heat men become cold, and look for meaning." NOBAu
Fleeing bracelets. Josée Lapeyrère. SCFWP Fr. Dishes, The.
Fleeing from my fellow-countrymen. 1940. Bertolt Brecht. HP, tr. by John Willet
Flee—into yourself, into the Churches, to the lavatories, to the Egypts, to Haiti. Beatnik's Monologue, The. Andrey Andreievich Voznesensky. TCRusP, tr. by Daniel Weissbort
Fleering snow, The. Winter (January / February 1978). Larry Eigner. PFTM-2
Flees the outhouse and a baby inherits the pain. (LL) Southern Birth. Kevin Powell. AmPoNex; InTrad
Fleet Astronomer can bore, The. Vanity [or Vanitie] (1). George Herbert. BASC; FSCP; NoP-4; NoP-5; NOSC
Fleet Marmion. Mary Russell Mitford. DiBP
Fleet ships encountering on the high seas. Good Ships. John Crowe Ransom. OxBSo; WeW-3
Fleeting Return. Juan Ramón Jiménez. BLPSL, tr. by Rene de Costa, Rigas Kappatos and Eleni Paidoussi
Fleetly hath passed the year; the seasons came. New Year, The. Nathaniel Parker Willis. TreFP
Fleming Helphenstine. Edwin Arlington Robinson. OxBSo
Flemington Racecourse. Kevin Hart. NOBAu
Flemish Beauty. Ansel Talvikki. AmPoNex
Flesh. Lionel Abrahams. TSAP
Flesh. Katie Ford. LegDan
Flesh, and cars, tar, dug holes beneath stone. Contract. (For The Destruction and Rebuilding of Paterson), A. Imamu Amiri Baraka. FTOS
Flesh and Fluids. Rupert M. Loydell. PoCu
Flesh and the Spirit, The. Anne Bradstreet. BASC; ChIV-2; NAAL-3; NAAPv.1; OxWW
Flesh, considered as cognitive region, as opposed to undifferentiated. Rosmarie Waldrop. PFTM-2 Fr. Key into the Language of America, A.
Flesh is heretic. Anorexic. Eavan Boland. NAMCP V.2
Flesh is sad, alas, The! And I have read. Sea Breeze. Stéphane Mallarmé. WoPoe, tr. by Louis Simpson
Flesh is sad—and I've read every book, The. Sea Breeze. Stéphane Mallarmé. SxFrPo, tr. by A. M. and E. H. Blackmore
Flesh of dark, The. Caliban. Edward Kamau Brathwaite. HarvBoo

Flesh of Miss Le'a's daughter. (LL)　California Light.　Sherley Anne Williams. CalPo; GeoHom

Flesh Tones.　Richmond Lattimore.　PoA 2002

Fleshes his dirty hunka tin I am right.　Burroughs.　Robert Glück.　WiU

Fleshing his dream of the beautiful, needful thing. (LL)　Frederick Douglass. Robert Earl Hayden.　CBCWP; ESEAA; ISC; NIL-7; NIP-4; OxAAAP; PoPoPo; PtR; VCAP

Fleshpot.　Martha Zweig.　PfS

Flexible.　William Kulik.　BodElec

Flexion of God.　Anne Carson.　BodElec *Fr.* Truth About God, The.

Flicker flies by.　Bend in the River.　Simon J. Ortiz.　HATNAP; PoPoPo

Flickering curtain, scintillations, junebugs.　Wavering.　Denise Levertov. PmAP

Flickering Mind.　Denise Levertov.　UpMys

Flickering shades.　Hunt by Night, The.　Derek Mahon.　HarvBoo

Flies.　Jack Kerouac.　CLPP

Flies and butterflies, children, bees.　At a Grave.　Martinus Nijhoff.　TuT, *tr. by* Desmond Egan

Flies, flies are on the plane tree, on the streets. (LL)　As a Plane Tree by the Water.　Robert Lowell.　BrAP; MoAmPo

Flies in the temple, The.　Issa.　EH, *tr. by* Robert Hass

Flies screaming like a jay. (LL)　Deaf-Mute in the Pear Tree.　Patricia K. Page. NAMCP V.2; NoAM; NoP-4; NoP-5

Flies, spilled tea.　Summer Retreat: Pema Osel Ling.　Diane Di Prima. AmZen

Flies swarming / What do they want of.　Issa.　ZenPo, *tr. by* Takashi Ikemoto and Lucien Stryk

Flight: "Series of white squares, each, A."　Pamela Alexander.　AmAlph; OtW

Flight.　Mahdi Muhammad Ali.　IrPoTo, *tr. by* Salaam Yousif

Flight.　Miranda Beeson.　PA9/11

Flight: "River slops under the bridge, The."　Neal Bowers.　PoDa

Flight.　Charles Stuart Calverley.　OBCoV

Flight.　B. H. Fairchild.　PoA 2002

Flight.　Sam Gardiner.　NIrP

Flight.　Vona Groarke.　NIrP

Flight.　Jorge Guillén.　BLT, *tr. by* Reginald Gibbons

Flight.　Louis Jenkins.　GoPo

Flight.　Suji Kwock Kim.　PoCho

Flight: "Outside the porthole life, or what is."　George Oppen.　OtW

Flight: "Summer night is flying, The."　Floyd Skloot.　PoDa

Flight: "Mother blackbird I've been feeding, The."　Sarah Wardle.　BeAl; PoCu

Flight.　Franz Wright.　AmAlph

Flight, The: "Earthen shadow lay on men's endeavor, An."　Babette Deutsch. OtW

Flight, The [*with music*].　Sara Teasdale.　LW

Flight as a Way of Life.　Ann Darr.　PWW2

Flight 828, now boarding at Gate 17. (LL)　Vacation.　Rita Dove.　OtW; SpirFl

Flight from Manhattan, The.　Les A. Murray.　BMAP *Fr.* Sydney Highrise Variations, The.

Flight from the Marriage Bed.　Lisa M. Carbone.　PasH

Flight impossible, a sick cicada.　Sick Cicada, A.　Chia Tao.　NDACCP, *tr. by* David Hinton

Flight in the Desert, The.　William Everson.　ChIV-2

Flight Instructor.　James Applewhite.　OtW

Flight is past: and man forgot, The. (LL)　Sic Vita.　Henry King, Bishop of Chichester.　BASC; NOSC

Flt #4372.　Jeanne Murray Walker.　OtW

Flight of Apollo, The.　Stanley Kunitz.　OPRER; OtW; TaR

Flight of fancy and breath of fresh air, A.　I Applied for the Board.　Jimmy Santiago Baca.　LoL

Flight of migrating birds froze in full sky, The.　It Was a Season Tattooed on the Forehead of the Earth.　Venus Khoury-Gata.　PoArWo, *tr. by* Lucy McNair

Flight of the Daughter, The.　Maisha Baton.　ICANM

Flight of the Duchess, The.　Robert Browning.

"And were I not, as a man may say, cautious."　OBCoV

Flight of the Itzás.　Chilam Balam.　WoPoe, *tr. by* Christopher Sawyer-Lauçanno

Flight of the Sparrow.　Takahashi Shinkichi.　ZenPo, *tr. by* Takashi Ikemoto and Lucien Stryk

Flight of Wild Ducks, A.　Charles Harpur.　NOBAu

Flight of Zalán, The.　Mihály Vörösmarty.　IQMS, *tr. by* Watson Kirkconnell

Flight out of Time.　Hugo Ball.

Flight out of Time.　PFTM-1

Flight to the City.　William Carlos Williams.　APT-1

Flint.　Christina Georgina Rossetti.　SacPr

Flip, Flop.　Denise Riley.　Oth *Fr.* Seven Strangely Exciting Lies.

Flippancies.　Richard Wilbur.

Star System, The.　NBLV

What's Good for the Soul is Good for Sales.　NBLV

Flipping eck, cor blimey, strewth.　Taking the Plunge.　John Mole. NOxBChV

Flip-top with brain.　Bird.　Frieda Hughes.　NeBl

Flirrup.　Mary Dalton.　OpeFie

Flirtation.　Rita Dove.　PoA 2002

Flirtation.　Li Ch'ing-chao.　WoPoe,

Flit.　Mark Doty.　AmAlph

Flitting, The.　John Clare.　OxAEP-2

Flitting, The [*with music*].　Medbh McGuckian.　PBCIP; PNI

Float aloft, thou stainless banner!　Hymn to the National Flag.　Margaret Junkin Preston.　PCW

Floating.　Kenneth Rexroth.　BodElec

Floating along the tops of the Sangre de Christos.　Give.　Mark Irwin. PoCoUp

Floating cloud follows the sun, The.　To Li Po.　Tu Fu [*or* Du Fu].　NDACCP, *tr. by* William Carlos Williams

Floating cloud is original nothingness, A.　Deathbed Song.　Woljo Toan. BecRai, *tr. by* Kim Daljin, Kim Won-Chung and Christopher Merrill

Floating Epitaphs, Their Possible Explanations in Poro Point.　Alejandrino Hufana.　ReBoTo

Floating, floating, the river waters.　Wang Chiu-ssu.　WoPoe *Fr.* After Reading the Poems of Master Han Shan.

Floating, floating weightless.　Swimming Pool.　Myra Cohn Livingston. NOxBChV

Floating Houses [*with music*].　David Wojahn.　WaAnP

Floating in clear solution in a dish.　In Glass.　Catherine Tufariello.　PoA 2002

Floating in God's brain.　Repairing the Hubble Telescope.　Robert Thomas. FaoP

Floating in the sac.　Learning to Smile.　Art Goodtimes.　GeoH

Floating Island at Hawkshead.　Dorothy Wordsworth.　NPeEn; PEW

Floating lights of the emergency vehicles circle wind, The.　All Saints Day, 2001.　Patricia Spears Jones.　PA9/11

Floating Metonymy 2.　Kim Sŭnghŭi.　EcSo, *tr. by* K. Kim Richards and Steffen Richards

Floating Metonymy 5.　Kim Sŭnghŭi.　EcSo, *tr. by* K. Kim Richards and Steffen Richards

Floating on the River Han.　Wang Wei.　ChinPo, *tr. by* Ye Weilian [*or* Yeh Wei-lien *or* Wai-lim Yip]

Floating perfectly through the net. (LL)　Fast Break.　Edward Hirsch. MoASP; P180; VCAP

Floating Poem, Unnumbered, The.　Adrienne Rich.　EroLit; NALW; NoAM; WaAnP *Fr.* Twenty-one Love Poems.

Floating Rib, The.　Lucia Maria Perillo.　PoDa

Floating that cypress boat.　Cypress Boat.　Unknown.　WoPoe, *tr. by* Constance A. Cook

Floating Trees.　C. D. Wright.　AmAlph; InGu

Floats an edge. (LL)　Defensive Rapture.　Barbara Guest.　AWPTFC; FTOS

Flock of, A / gulls flew.　A. R. Ammons.　NAMCP V.2 *Fr.* Tombstones.

Flock of birds leaving the side of the mountain, A.　Parable of Flight.　Louise Glück.　CAP-8

Flock of bright red lanterns, A / Has settled. (LL)　About an excavation. Charles Reznikoff.　NAMCP V.1; NTCP

Flock of pigeons rises over the roof, The.　Sky Harbor.　Norman Dubie. AmAlph

Flock of Sheep near the Airport, A.　Yehuda Amichai.　PML, *tr. by* Chana Bloch

Flocking together.　Vultures—in the Midst of War.　Shaku Chōkū.　CAoMJL1, *tr. by* Makoto Ueda

Flocks of Doves.　Carlos Pellicer.　TCLAP, *tr. by* Alexandra Migoya

Flocks of the wandering waves I hold, The.　Alfred Austin.　VerBaPo *Fr.* Wind Speaks, The.

Flocks went bleating; the roads, The.　Sorrowful Shadow, The.　Julio Herrera y Reissig.　TCLAP, *tr. by* Andrew Rosing

Flodden.　William Montgomerie.　EdScPo

Flood: "This had happened before: rain that began."　Claudia Emerson.　PoDa

Flood.　Tony Harrison.　InoFa

Flood.　James Joyce.　MoBrPo

Flood.　John McAuliffe.　NIrP

Flood, The.　Patricia Beer.　HarvBoo

Flood, The.　John Milton.　NOSC *Fr.* Paradise Lost.

Flood of Is in Brittany, The.　Augusta Davies Webster.　ViWPN

Flood Songs.　Olga Khvostova.　CRWP, *tr. by* Tatyana Retivova

Flood Water.　Unknown.　NOBAu, *tr. by* Mungayana Nundhirribala

Flood Year [*with music*]. Judith Wright. NAMCP V.2; NoAM

Flooded Valley, The. Roland Mathias. AngWePo

Flooding with a brilliant mist. To the Moon. Johann Wolfgang von Goethe. STV, *tr. by* John Frederick Nims

Floodlights come on: look, The. Not Responsible. Caroline Finkelstein. PoA 2002

Floods all the soul with its melodious seas. (LL) Milton. Henry Wadsworth Longfellow. GSo; NAAPv.1

Floods, by nature enemies to land, The. Ovid. OBVE *Fr.* Metamorphoses.

Flood-Tide below me! I see you face to face! Crossing Brooklyn Ferry. Walt Whitman. APN-1; ColAP; FaBoA; NAAL-3; NAAL-5; NAMCP V.1; NCAP; NoAM; NoP-4; NoP-5; OxBoAm; WaAnP

Floor, The. Yolanda Palis. ReBoTo

Floor in Goethe's House, The. Sŏ Chŏngju. CAMKP, *tr. by* David R. McCann

Floor / of the temple, The. Trance. "H. D." APT-1

Floor Plans. Maxine Scates. PBCAP

Floor Scrapers. Daniel Tobin. NAPBL

Floor shone from nightmare, The. Unable to Sleep in Frost's Bed in Franconia. Marvin Bell. VisFro

Floor the wall the wall meet, The. In Spite of How. Heather Ramsdell. IAoNAP

Floorboards creak, The. New Apartment. Linda Hogan. HATNAP; UnSA

Floor-show ends, lights dim, I tilt the bottle, The. Way Back Then. Fergus Allen. IrLP

Flopped on the fan. Issa. EH, *tr. by* Robert Hass

Flor de oro. Pedro Pérez Conde. RMCMP

Floral Apron, The. Marilyn Chin. LoL; SweBea

Flora's Plea to Mary. Juan Delgado. TouFir

Florence, powerful lily, sprint shoot. Spring mornings along the Arno. Florence. Dino Campana. MotU, *tr. by* Charles Wright

Florence: Sleeping in Fog. Adam Drinan. EdScPo

Florence Vane. Philip Pendleton Cooke. APN-1

Flores Bajo los Muertos. José Luis Hidalgo. RaW

Flores moradas. Revelación. Natalia Toledo. RMCMP

Florida. Campbell McGrath. NAPBL

Florida, La. Virgil Suárez. BAP-04

Florida Anasazi, The. Campbell McGrath. NAPBL

Florida Beach, The. Constance Fenimore Woolson. APN-2

Florida Road Workers. Langston Hughes. MoAmPo

Florilegium. Eric Tretheway. PfSP

Florio: A Tale, and The Bas-bleu; or, Conversation. Hannah More. RWP

Florist's Vade-Mecum, The. Samuel Gilbert.
  Florist's Vade-Mecum, The. OBGa

Flos Lunae. Ernest Dowson. OBMV

Flossie Cabanis. Edgar Lee Masters. APT-1 *Fr.* Spoon River Anthology.

Flounder. Natasha Trethewey. OxAAAP; TWW

Flourish of silver, A. Deer Park. John Montague. PBCIP

Flourish of sunlight in the room where, A. Claud Cockburn. Thomas McCarthy. PBCIP

Flow. Marcel Gerard. SonAtl, *tr. by* Gregory Beaven, Kurt Ganzl, Germaine Goetzinger, Christophe Mirambeau and Pascal Nicolay

Flow, The. Lynne D. Johnson. BRtP

Flow Chart. John Ashbery.
  "Still in the published city but not yet." PmAP
  "Suddenly they all stopped talking about it. Yet I." PFTM-2

Flow, flow the waves hated. Illusions. Ralph Waldo Emerson. APN-1

Flow of champagne, A. Wedding Party. William R. Lafleur. WhBo

Flow swiftly into thee, and in thee ever end. (LL) Upon Nothing. John Wilmot, 2d Earl of Rochester. NOSC; OBSV; OxAEP-1; OxBEV

Flower. Huan Fu. PML, *tr. by* Zhang Cuo

Flower. Kim Ch'unsu [*or* Chun-soo]. CAMKP, *tr. by* Kevin O'Rourke

Flower, A. Po Chü-i. TAL

Flower, The. George Herbert. AngWePo; BASC; BrAP; FSCP; NAEL-6v1; NAEL-7v1; NoP-4; NoP-5; NPeEn; OBGa; OxBEV; PBRV

Flower, The: "I think I grow tensions." Robert Creeley. CAP-8; PmAP

Flower an elaboration of the spiny leaves that will rasp your hand, The. Thistle. Roy Scheele. MotU

Flower and the Leaf, The. The Lady of the Arbour.
  Flower and the Leaf, The. OBGa

Flower blooms, A. Tanka. Kanoko Okamoto. CAoMJL1, *tr. by* Makoto Ueda

Flower bursts from stone. Stone Wall. Takahashi Shinkichi. ZenPo, *tr. by* Takashi Ikemoto and Lucien Stryk

Flower child. Statue, The. Luz Maria Umpierre. PueRic

Flower from a soldier's grave, A. (LL) To E. S. Salomon. Ambrose Bierce. CBCWP; PCW

Flower from Robert Kennedy's Grave, A. Edward Sanders. FTtHH

Flower Given to My Daughter, A. James Joyce. OBMV; PtR; RaBo

Flower handkerchief from the West that I left in my sleeve, The. Nagasaki Style. Kinoshita Mokutarō. CAoMJL1, *tr. by* Leith Morton

Flower Herding on Mount Monadnock. Galway Kinnell. HeIP-4; NoAM

Flower in the Crannied Wall. Alfred Tennyson. BBASP; BRP; ITBLP; NAEL-6v2; NAEL-7v2; TFi

Flower in the glass peanut bottle formerly in the kitchen crooked to take a place in the light, The. Transcription of Organ Music. Allen Ginsberg. ItP

Flower in the leaves, only as heaven pleases. Deep in Winter. Tu Fu [*or* Du Fu]. CCL1, *tr. by* A. C. Graham

Flower Is Looking, A. Harold Monro. MoBrPo *Fr.* Strange Meetings.

Flower is not visible, The. Yi Sang. CAMKP; PFTM-1 *Fr.* Critical Condition.

Flower Market, The. Po Chü-i. CCL1, *tr. by* Arthur Waley

Flower Master, The [*with music*]. Medbh McGuckian. ModIr; PNI

Flower No Flower. Po Chü-i. NDACCP, *tr. by* David Hinton

Flower No More Than Itself, A. Linda Gregg. BBASP; WaAnP

Flower of Air, The. Gabriela Mistral. TCLAP, *tr. by* Doris Dana

Flower of capital is small and white large and grey-green in a storm its petals sing, The. Flower of Capital, The. Michael Palmer. MotU

Flower of coincidence, The. Death of Karen Klausner, The. Charlie Vermont. AHA

Flower of drowsiness. Menace of the Flower, The. Alfonso Reyes. TCLAP, *tr. by* Samuel Beckett

Flower of Five Blossoms. Galway Kinnell. CAP-8

Flower of Flame, The. Robert Malise Bowyer Nichols.
  "Before I woke I knew her gone." OBMV

Flower of Gold. Pedro Pérez Conde. PoCho; RMCMP, *tr. by* Michael Wiegers

Flower of Mullein, A. Lizette Woodworth Reese. MoAmPo

Flower of Nut-Brown Maids, The. Eleanor Hull. IrLP

Flower of Old Japan, The. Alfred Noyes.
  Epilogue. MoBrPo

FLOWER of roses, angels' joy. Hymn to the Virgin. *Unknown.* NoSic

Flower of the flock. On Sweet Killen Hill. Tom MacIntyre. IrLP

Flower of the foam of the waves. Captive of the White City, The. Ina Coolbrith. NAAPv.1

Flower of the pear tree gathers and turns to fruit, The. At the End of Spring. Po Chü-i. CCL1, *tr. by* Arthur Waley

Flower of the vine! Stornelli and Strambotti. Agnes Mary Frances Robinson. VWP

Flower of waves, A. Lady Ise. WoPoe, *tr. by* Irma Brandeis and Etsuko Teraski

Flower, Pal Mal Comic Book. Leslie Scalapino. Eno

Flower Piece. Gerhard Rühm. PFTM-2, *tr. by* Rosmarie Waldrop

Flower planted on the sands, A. Wind to the Stones, The. Pak Nohae. CAMKP, *tr. by* Scott Swaner

Flower Poem. Alec Derwent Hope. BMAP

Flower Summit precipitous, overlooking the sea. Thinking of a Monk of Flower Summit on Mount T'ien-t'ai. Ch'i-chi. CSKM, *tr. by* Burton Watson

Flower that smiles today, The. Mutability. Percy Bysshe Shelley. NAEL-6v2; NoP-4; NoP-5

Flower vase on the general's table, A. General's Property, The. Samih Al-Qasim. PoAgWa, *tr. by* Abdullah Al-Udhari

Flower was offered [*or* offerd] to me, A. William Blake. NAEL-6v2; NAEL-7v2; NOBRP; NPBRoP *Fr.* Songs of Experience.

Flower-Boat, The. Robert Frost. PoA 2002

Flowered woods have dropped their springtime rose festoon, The. Flowered Woods, The. Li Yu [*or* Li Hou-Chu]. CCL1, *tr. by* Sam Houston Brock

Flowered Woods, The. Li Yu [*or* Li Hou-Chu]. CCL1, *tr. by* Sam Houston Brock

Flower-feasting bee, why do you touch upon. Meleager. HePo, *tr. by* Barbara Hughes Fowler

Flower-fed Buffaloes, The. Vachel Lindsay. GM; ItP; MoAmPo; TRP
  (Flower-Fed Buffalos, The.) CA

Flowering, A. Michael Longley. PML

Flowering Absence, A ("How can one make an absence flower.") John Montague. PBCIP *Fr.* Dead Kingdom, The.

Flowering of the Rod, The. "H. D."
  "Blue-geese, white-geese, you may say." APT-1
  "I go where I love and where I am loved." APT-1; HarvBoo
  "In resurrection, there is confusion." APT-1
  "O the beautiful garment." HarvBoo
  "Satisfied, unsatisfied." APT-1
  "So I would rather drown, remembering." APT-1
  "Yet resurrection is a sense of direction." APT-1

Flowering plum, A. Issa. SoOfWa, *tr. by* Sam Hamill

Flowering Quince. Winfield Townley Scott. APT-2

Flowering sea and the mountains in the moon's waning, The. Epiphany, 1937. George Seferis. GPTC, *tr.* by Edmund Keeley and Philip Sherrard

Flowering Tree. Yi Sang. CAMKP, *tr.* by Walter Lew

Flowerlike, The / animal perfume. Eros. Denise Levertov. AHA

Flower-Patterned Snake. Sŏ Chŏngju. VCWP, *tr.* by David R. McCann

Flowerpot. (LL) Poem: "As the cat." William Carlos Williams. ChAP; HarvBoo; NoP-4; NoP-5; OxBoAm; PoPoPo; SoSe-8

Flower-Quiet in the Rush-Strewn Sheiling. Austin Clarke. IrLP *Fr.* Vengeance of Fionn, The.

Flowers: "Right now I am the flower girl." Margaret Atwood. NoP-4; NoP-5

Flowers: "Some men never think of it." Wendy Cope. NoP-4; NoP-5

Flowers. Dennis Joseph Enright. OBGa

Flowers. Julie Fay. NAPBL

Flowers: "I have not missed the irony of this magnetism, my being." Raylene Hinz-Penner. ACAMVP

Flowers. Eileen Myles. PA9/11

Flowers. Leo Vroman. TuT, *tr.* by James Liddy

Flowers. William Wordsworth. CenSon *Fr.* River Duddon, The [A Series of Sonnets].

Flowers', The. Allan Graham. ICANM

Flowers, The. Robert Louis Stevenson. BLPJKO

Flowers, and tall-stalked grasses, and a bee. Ivan Alekseievich Bunin. GI; WoPoe, *tr.* by David Curzon and Vladislav L. Gucrassev

Flowers and Trees. Sir Walter Scott. OxAEP-2 *Fr.* Lady of the Lake, The.

Flowers and Water. Nancy Vieira Couto. PoDa

Flowers / are out. Flowers. Eileen Myles. PA9/11

Flowers beside the palace fade. Passing the Night. Tu Fu [*or* Du Fu]. CrYelRi, *tr.* by Sam Hamill

Flowers bloom. Gazing at Spring. Hsüeh T'ao [*or* Xue Tao]. WoPoe, *tr.* by Jeanne Larsen

Flowers bloom when it is warm. Yun Sŏndo. CATKP *Fr.* Songs of Five Friends.

Flowers by the Sea ("When over the flowery, sharp pasture's.") William Carlos Williams. APT-1; MoAmPo; NAMCP V.1; NoAM

Flowers droop. *Wintu Oral Tradition.* NAAPv.1 *Fr.* Six Dream Songs.

Flowers drown when the ground gets sodden. Forecast: Nadja. Susan Elmslie. IFF

Flower's Escape. Ron Padgett. NYP2

Flowers fall, unreasonable, out of space and counter point of time. Antistrophe. "H. D." MotU

Flower's fragrance is a woman's virtue, A. Orchid House, The. Medbh McGuckian. CABP

Flowers hang their heavy heads, The. (LL) Spring Rain. Tu Fu [*or* Du Fu]. CCL1; WaAnP, *tr.* by Kenneth Rexroth

Flowers have lost their withered red, The. Spring Scene. Su Tung-p'o. TAL

Flowers I called Christ's when I was four, The. (LL) Supernatural Love. Gjertrud Schnackenberg. MakPoe; NoAM; NoP-4; NoP-5; StAl; VCAP

Flowers in bud on the trees, The. On the Death of a New Born Child. Mei Yao Ch'en. WoPoe, *tr.* by Kenneth Rexroth

Flowers in legions bloomed around in forest, scrub, and marsh. Tasmanian Scenes. Louisa Meredith. NOBAu

Flowers in the Garden. Pyungyang Ungee. BecRai, *tr.* by Kim Daljin, Kim Won-Chung and Christopher Merrill

Flowers left thick at nightfall in the wood, The. In Memoriam (Easter, 1915). Edward Thomas. NoP-4; NoP-5; OBWP; OBWVE; PoAgWa; Spl

Flowers like a gangster's funeral. Viewing the Body. W. D. Snodgrass. CAP-8; InoFa

Flowers live faster than rotting of cherries. Anna Gorenko. CRWP, *tr.* by Peter France

Flowers lurk in the dusk by the palace walls. Spring Vigil in the Imperial Chancellery. Tu Fu [*or* Du Fu]. ChinPo, *tr.* by Ye Weilian [*or* Yeh Wei-lien *or* Wai-lim Yip]

Flowers. Masquerading as words. Confrontation with a Bouquet. Maggie Bevan. Prnts

Flowers need the sunshine. You're Gonna Lose Your Gal. Joe Young. ReLy

Flowers no longer fly in our city in March. Flowers No Longer Fly in Our City. Rong Zi. CFP, *tr.* by Michelle Yeh

Flowers nodding gaily, scent in air. Duet, A. Thomas Sturge Moore. OBEV

Flowers of autumn still bloom in the garden, The. At the End of September. Sándor Petőfi. IQMS, *tr.* by Adam Makkai and Valerie Becker Makkai

Flowers of ice. Snow. Muso Soseki. EaWin, *tr.* by W. S. Merwin

Flowers of Mildew. Tudor Arghezi. WoPoe, *tr.* by Michael Impey and Brian Swann

Flowers of Politics, I, The. Michael McClure. CalPo

Flowers of Red and Blue. Nezahualcoyotl. WoPoe, *tr.* by Stephen Berg

Flowers of Rhetoric. Morris Gilbert Bishop. AmWit

Flowers of the Field. John Keble. SacPr

Flowers of the Forest are a' wede away, The. (LL) Flowers of the Forest, The. Jane Elliot. NePenScot; NoP-4; NoP-5; OxBEV

Flowers of the Forest, The. Jane Elliot. NePenScot; NoP-4; NoP-5; OxBEV (Lament for Flodden, The.) OBEV

Flowers of Unceasing Coincidence, The. Robert Kelly.
 164. WhBo
 222. WhBo
 550. WhBo
 563. WhBo
 630. WhBo
 664. WhBo
 666. WhBo

Flowers offered to the Buddha. Buson. EH, *tr.* by Robert Hass

Flowers on one tree have opened, The. Plum Window. Muso Soseki. EaWin, *tr.* by W. S. Merwin

Flowers on the mountain bloom. Mountain Flowers. Kim Sowŏl. CAMKP, *tr.* by David R. McCann

Flowers through the window. Nantucket. William Carlos Williams. HarvBoo; OxBoAm; TRP; WeW-3

Flowers under the Dead. José Luis Hidalgo. RaW, *tr.* by Hardie St. Martin

Flowers upon your lips and hands. Love Poem. Maurice James Craig. IrLP

Flowers with six petals. Snow Garden. Muso Soseki. EaWin, *tr.* by W. S. Merwin

Flowers—at ease and tall. The king is dead. (LL) No Swan So Fine. Marianne Moore. BrAP; NALW; NoP-4; NoP-5; OxBoAm

Flower-sellers, Budapest. Kathleen Jamie. NePenScot

Flower-tinted cheek, the flowery close, A. Khwaja Shams-ad-din Muhammad Hafiz. TAL *Fr.* Odes.

Flowing winds brush Meandering Islet. Orchid Pavilion. Sun Ch'o. ChinPo, *tr.* by Ye Weilian [*or* Yeh Wei-lien *or* Wai-lim Yip]

Fluency. Adelia Prado. TCLAP, *tr.* by Marcia Kirinus

Fluid as water that all tones reflects. *Unknown.* NDACCP, *tr.* by Ezra Pound

Flukum couldn't stand the strain. Flukum. Etheridge Knight. ESEAA *Fr.* Two Poems for Black Relocation Centers.

Flung outward and up—disappearing suddenly! (LL) Spring Strains. William Carlos Williams. APT-1; TCAPo

Flunked out and laid-off. Eisenhower Years, The. Paul Zimmer. PBCAP

Flush / a Play. Leslie Scalapino. PmAP

Flush of fever in spring. The heart's. Rose Quartz. Leslie Ullman. ExTi

Flush or Faunus. Elizabeth Barrett Browning. DiBP; VWP

Flushed by the spirit of the genial year. James Thomson. OxAEP-1 *Fr.* Seasons, The.

Flushed, from my restless pillow I arose. Song of Arla, Written During Her Enthusiasm, A. Anne Batten Cristall. RWP

Flute, The. Sophia De Mello Breyner. VCWP, *tr.* by Ruth Fainlight

Flute, The. Hsiao Yen [*or* Emperor Wu of Liang]. CCL1, *tr.* by Anne Birrell

Flute, The. Oktay Rifat. WoPoe, *tr.* by Talat Sait Halman

Flûte Mystérieuse, La. Li Po. CCL1, *tr.* by Judith Gautier

Flute player, I've roamed so far in shadowed lands. Flute Player. Lorand Gaspar. YaTCFP, *tr.* by Ronnie Scharfman

Fluteplayers from Finmarken. Carl Rakosi. FTOS

Flutes echo from the far shore. At Lake Yi. Wang Wei. CrYelRi, *tr.* by Sam Hamill

Flux dehydrates my flesh, The. Common. 1668. Dom Moraes. EmeKit

Flux, efflorescence—whatever you care to call it! (LL) One. Carolyn Kizer. CAP-8; VCAP *Fr.* Pro Femina.

Fly. W. S. Merwin. ChAP; OWoS

Fly, The. Philip Ayres. OBVE

Fly, The. William Blake. *See* Little Fly.

Fly, The [*with music*]. Miroslav Holub. NPeEn; PoAgWa; PoetW; PoSu; StAl, *tr.* by Ian Milner and George Theiner

Fly, The. Y. Nokhem. Prolet, *tr.* by Amelia Glaser

Fly, The. Karl Shapiro. NAMCP V.2; NoAM; SoSe-8

Fly and the Ocean, The. Jean Tardieu. YaTCFP, *tr.* by David Kelley

Fly Away, Fly Away. Christina Georgina Rossetti. Spl

Fly by night / black galaxy / friendly galaxy. Lee Morgan. David Henderson. SeSe

Fly, dare take / The rice grain. Ransetsu. ZenPo, *tr.* by Takashi Ikemoto and Lucien Stryk

Fly down, Death: call me. Madboy's Song. Muriel Rukeyser. MoAmPo

Fly envious Time, till thou run out thy race. On Time. John Milton. OBEV; SacPr

Fly, fly, my friends. Sir Philip Sidney. NAEL-7v1; NoSic *Fr.* Astrophil and Stella.

Fly fro the presse, and dwell with sothfastnesse. Geoffrey Chaucer. TreFP

Fly from the soil whose desolating creed. To Persecuted Foreigners. Penina Moise and Edward N. Calisch. SWaP

Fly hence, shadows, that do keep. John Ford. OBEV *Fr.* Lover's Melancholy, The.

Fly is giving another sermon, The. Benediction. Stuart Dybek. UrbNat

Fly Me to the Moon (In Other Words). Bart Howard. ReLy

Fly stops on the window glass, The. In the Window. Carla Faesler Bremer. SPV, *tr. by* Jen Hofer

Fly swayed, A. Fly and the Ocean, The. Jean Tardieu. YaTCFP, *tr. by* David Kelley

Fly up in a sudden breeze. (LL) Youngest Daughter, The. Cathy Song. NoAM; WaAnP

Fly, with a deafening buzz, A. Fly, The. Y. Nokhem. Prolet, *tr. by* Amelia Glaser

Flyer's Fall. Wallace Stevens. SAmP

Flying. Michael Dransfield. BMAP

Flying. Florence Ripley Mastin. OtW

Flying. Pedro Serrano. RMCMP, *tr. by* Geoff Hargreaves

Flying above California. Thom Gunn. CalPo

Flying arrow hardly was aware, The. Deceiver Time. Luis de Góngora y Argote. SpanPo, *tr. by* James Edward Tobin

Flying at Night. Ted Kooser. OtW; PBCAP

Flying Change, The. Henry Taylor. InGu

Flying curved to the wind shear-waters turn their bodies in the wave. Summer. Kay Boyle. MotU

Flying Down to Rio. Edward Eliscu and Gustave Kahn. ReLy

Flying Dutchman, The. Walter McDonald. TiP2

Flying Fowl, and Creeping Things, Praise Ye the Lord. Isaac Watts. ChIV-1

Flying from Greece to see Moscow's dancing girl. Ciampino: Envoi. Edwin Denby. NYP2

Flying from the dry pall of the city. Gray Woods Exploding, The. Earle Birney. NoAM

Flying from Trouble. Tu Fu [*or* Du Fu]. CCL1, *tr. by* Florence Ayscough and Amy Lowell

Flying Home from Utah. May Swenson. OtW

Flying in / Before snow closed the airport. New Year's Eve in Bismarck, North Dakota. Kathleen Norris. UpMys

Flying Kangaroos. Coral Hull. PoCoUp

Flying light, flying light. Flying Light. Li Ho. WoPoe, *tr. by* Arthur Sze

Flying over America. Kalamu ya Salaam. BRtP

Flying, Reflying, Farming. Richard Hugo. OtW

Flying skeleton. Pāhkahkos. Louise Bernice Halfe. ReEnLa

Flying south, south, into the deepest south, there was the feeling of. South. Aurora Levins Morales. PueRic

Flying squirrel, A. Buson. EH, *tr. by* Robert Hass

Flying squirrel, A. Buson. SoOfWa, *tr. by* Sam Hamill

Flying up a valley in the Alps where the rock. Lufthansa. John Tranter. BMAP; NOBAu

Flying Wheel, The. Ernest De Lancey Pierson. ArBi

Flying word from here and there, A. Master, The. Edwin Arlington Robinson. CBCWP; MoAmPo

Flying-Man. Mother Goose. HHAm

Flying-man, Flying-man. Flying-Man. Mother Goose. HHAm

Flyover Elegies. Gwyneth Lewis. MFPA

Flypaper. Theodore Weiss. BodElec

Flyting o' Life and Daith, The. Hamish Henderson. EdScPo

Flyting of Dumbar [*or* Dunbar] and Kennedie [*or* Kennedy], The. William Dunbar.
Dunbar Attacks His Rival. NePenScot

Foal. Vernon Watkins. AngWePo

Foam. Roland Jones. WoPoe, *tr. by* Anthony Conran

Foam. Claudio Rodríguez. RaW, *tr. by* Robert Mezey

Foam. T. Arfon Williams. BBMWP, *tr. by* Emyr Lewis

Foaming white wave washes over a grave, A. Exultation. Hywel ab Owain Gwynedd. OBWVE, *tr. by* Gwyn Williams

Fo'c'sle Dreams. Joe Denham. OpeFie

Fog. Michelle Boisseau. ExTi

Fog. Amy Clampitt. MakPoe

Fog. Mark Doty. FaoP

Fog. Louise Imogen Guiney. APN-2

Fog. Lizette Woodworth Reese. APT-1

Fog: "Fog comes, The." Carl Sandburg. APT-1; BLPJKO; BRP; ChAP; HeIP-4; ITBLP; MoAmPo; NAAL-5; NAAPv.2; Spl; TCAPo; TFi; WaAnP

Fog. György Sárközi. IQMS, *tr. by* Roy Fuller

Fog. Henry David Thoreau. APN-1

Fog and thaw make the garden smell like Christmas. It's February But. Janet Fisher. MFPA

Fog Argument. Mark Doty. AmAlph
2. Beach Roses. AmAlph
1. Jade. AmAlph

Fog: big doped cats lazily. Fog. György Sárközi. IQMS, *tr. by* Roy Fuller

Fog comes, The. Fog. Carl Sandburg. APT-1; BLPJKO; BRP; ChAP; HeIP-4; ITBLP; MoAmPo; NAAL-5; NAAPv.2; Spl; TCAPo; TFi; WaAnP

Fog descends over the tidal surge and the shallow lagoons. Gary Young. GeoHom *Fr.* If He Had.

Fog drifts slowly down the hill, The. Night Piece, The. Thom Gunn. ASA

Fog hanged over the park, the night cold, and, clean. And, Hinges. Ted Greenwald. FTOS

Fog. He can see only this deep still fog. Winslow Homer. Winfield Townley Scott. APT-2

Fog heaved in like a headache only more ambitious. Romanticism. Spencer Short. IIR

Fog: "Hundreds of millions of years ago, days were many hours shorter." Mei-Mei Berssenbrugge. ICANM

Fog Land. Ingeborg Bachmann. WoPoe, *tr. by* Michael Hamburger

Fog lifting above the fields. Mussel Rock/Lowtide—Santa Cruz, California 1959. Jeff Tagami. OpBo

Fog lifts in the stream before me. Angler's Calendar, The. Yun Sŏndo. CATKP, *tr. by* Peter H. Lee

Fog lifts in the stream before me. Yun Sŏndo. CATKP *Fr.* Angler's Calendar, The.

Fog like cold sweat coated every inch of the ferry. Brian Bartlett. Coast *Fr.* Talking to the Birds.

Fog over the base: the beams ranging. Front, A. Randall Jarrell. NoP-4; NoP-5; OBWP; PoWW

Fog so thick the cows beyond the fence slide. Fieldswirl, October. Dave Jeddie Smith. PfSP

Fog thickens, The. Figurehead. Dilys Rose. EdScPo

Fog walks down the hill and finds our yard, The. Lost. John Burnside. EdScPo

Fogbound / in a hotel room. Leafsmoke. Marianne Bluger. IFF

Foggy Day (in London Town), A. Ira Gershwin. ReLy

Foggy night, a long silver train, someone's hand, A. Elegant Endings. Richard Blanco. LegDan

Fog-Horn. W. S. Merwin. CAP-8

Foghorn, A. Brenda Hillman. FaoP

Foghorns. Gillian Clarke. TCAWP

Fog-Talk. Philip Booth. BodElec

Fog-wreaths of doubt in blinding eddies drifted. One Reality, The. Frances Ridley Havergal. SacPr

Fold away all your bright-tinted dresses. Hospital Duties. *Unknown.* CBCWP

Fold it up carefully, lay it aside. Jacket of Gray, The. Caroline Augusta Ball. CBCWP

Folded close under deepening snow. (LL) First Snowfall [*or* Snow-Fall], The. James Russell Lowell. AmFaPo; MoW

Folded hands and darkened eyes. Stone, The. Walter De la Mare. WeW-3

Folded Skyscraper, A. William Carlos Williams.
Hemmed-in Males. APT-1

Folded Wings. Pao Chao. CCL1, *tr. by* John Frodsham

Folderol. Vona Groarke. StAl

Folding clothes / I think of folding you. Sorting Laundry. Elisavietta Ritchie. SoSe-8

Folding the paper money, tearing the bills. (LL) Struggle, The. Toi Derricotte. LTA; PBCAP

Folding the Sheets. Rosemary Dobson. ItWoWo; NOBAu *Fr.* Daily Living.

Fold-out map of Europe in my Filofax, The. Liminal. Sarah Maguire. MoWP

Foley Artist, The. Nick Drake. NeBl

Foliage of years, autumn of life. Missing Out. Eli Alon. NRoS, *tr. by* Esther Raizen

Folk Form. Rick London. Eno

Folk Song: "O I'm off to Hullaboola where the climate's never cooler." Bruce Beaver. OBCoV

Folk Tune. Esther Raab. FIT, *tr. by* Robert Friend and Shimon Sandbank

Folklore. Les A. Murray. PML

Folks ain't got no right to censuah othah [*or* uthah] folks about dey habits. Accountability. Paul Laurence Dunbar. APN-2; NAAPv.1

Folks are blessed who make the best of ev'ry day. Give Me the Simple Life. Harry Ruby. ReLy

Folks downstairs brought him home, The. Dylan, Two Days. Patricia Smith. GT

Folks, I'm telling you. Advice. Langston Hughes. NBLV; SAmP

Folks in Georgia's 'bout to go insane. Ballin' the Jack. Jim Burris. ReLy

Folks Who Live on the Hill, The. Oscar Hammerstein, II. ReLy

Folks, you've heard of scandalous vamps. Louisville Lou (The Vampin' Lady). Milton Ager and Jack Yellen. ReLy

Folktale, A: "Father stands on a walkway talking, A." Tonya Foster. FreRad

Follies of Adam, The. Theodore Roethke. ChIV-1

Follow Me. Nada El-Hage. PoArWo, *tr. by* Nathalie El-Hani

Follow me, the voice, the long, longed-for voice stops. In Our Only Time. C. D. Wright. AmAlph

Follow the clews. Song for Annie. Harry Gilonis. Oth

Follow the yellow brick road. We're Off to See the Wizard (The Wonderful Wizard of Oz). E. Y. Harburg. ReLy

Follow Thy Fair Sun[ne] [Unhappy Shadow]. Thomas Campion. NoP-4; NoP-5; NOSC; NoSic; NPeEn; OxBEV (Devotion.) OBEV

Follow your nose. Segue O Teu Destino. Fernando Pessoa. WoPoe, *tr. by* David Wright

Followed and cursed, the groaning man was led. (LL) George Crabbe. NoP-4; NoP-5; NPeEn; OxBEV *Fr.* Borough, The.

Followed mountains over a thousand miles. Night: Setting out from Shih-Kuan Pavilion. Hsieh Ling-yün. ChinPo, *tr. by* Ye Weilian [*or* Yeh Wei-lien *or* Wai-lim Yip]

Follower. Seamus Heaney. CABP; IPoFL; PNI; PtR

Following a Man. John Ash. HarvBoo

Following day, about th' eleventh hour, The. Edward Edwin Foot. STuOW *Fr.* Jane Hollybrand; or, Virtue Rewarded.

Following forbidden streets. Wraith-Friend, The. George Barker. OBMV

Following Her to Sleep. Jeffrey McDaniel. NeAmPo

Following, like a fist of purple kelp. (LL) St Bride's. Kathleen Jamie. MoWP; NePenScot

Following our own bent. Sikong Tu. CCL1 *Fr.* Twenty-Four Modes of Poetry.

Following the North Star Boogaloo. Quincy Troupe. FaoP

Following the Rhymes of Shao-pao Huang's Poem on Being Moved while Visiting the Farmers [*with music*]. Yang Shih-ch'i. WoPoe, *tr. by* Jonathan Chaves

Following the Road. Larry Smith. AmZen

Following their road of exit, they stooped over and came out. *Zuni Oral Tradition.* APN-2 *Fr.* History Myth of the Coming of the A'shiwi as Narrated by 'Kiáklo.

Follows the naked work, profoundly moved by it. (LL) Story of a Hotel Room. Rosemary Tonks. BeAl; LW; MoWP

Folly—. What Is the Word. Samuel Beckett. OxBEV

Folly. Henri Cole. NAMCP V.2

Folly and error, stinginess and sin. To the Reader. Charles Baudelaire. SxFrPo, *tr. by* James McGowan

Folly of Being Comforted, The. William Butler Yeats. HeIP-4; IJHIL; IrLP; NAEL-6v2; NAEL-7v2

Folly's Song. Thomas Dekker *and others.* NOSC

Fond man *Musophilus*, that thus dost spend. Samuel Daniel. NoSic; PBRV *Fr.* Musophilus; or, Defence of All Learning.

Fond man, that canst believe her blood. Thomas Carew. CavPo

Fond Memory. Eavan Boland. ModIr; NAMCP V.2

Fond nymphs, from us true pleasure learn. In Derision of a Country Life. Edward Ravenscroft. NOSC

Fond Painter, why woulds't thou my picture draw? Echo. Ausonius. NPeEn, *tr. by* George Sandys

Fondling and snuggling. Love Song. Kuan Yün-shih. CrYelRi, *tr. by* Sam Hamill

Fondly familiar is the look she gives. Caroline Elizabeth Norton. NPBRoP *Fr.* Voice from the Factories, A.

Food and Drink. Louis Untermeyer. MoAmPo

Food of Birds, The. Brewster Ghiselin. APT-2

Food of Love. Carolyn Kizer. RaBo

Food Packages: 1947. Adrienne Rich. TaR

Foods leave us cavities. (LL) W. D. Snodgrass. NAMCP V.2; NoAM *Fr.* Heart's Needle.

Fool, The. Kenneth Mackenzie. BMAP

Fool, a fool! I met a fool i' the forest, A. William Shakespeare. OBCoV *Fr.* As You Like It.

Fool and the Poet, The. Alexander Pope. NBLV

Fool and Wise. Coventry Patmore. SacPr

Fool[e], said my Muse to me, "look[e] in thy heart and write." (LL) Sir Philip Sidney. BrAP; CABP; GSo; NAEL-6v1; NAEL-7v1; NoP-4; NoP-5; NoSic; NPeEn; OxAEP-1; OxBEV; OxBSo; PBRV; TFi *Fr.* Astrophil and Stella.

Fool there was and he made his prayer, A. Vampire, The. Rudyard Kipling. OxBEV

Foolin' Myself. Jack Lawrence. ReLy

Fooling God. Louise Erdrich. ReEnLa; UpMys; WaAnP

Fooling Mom. Fěng Měng-lung. ColAnChi *Fr.* Mountain Songs.

Foolish Earthlings. Ron Koertge. SUP

Foolish gods are doing poppers while they sing along, The. Gods at Three A.M., The. Reginald Shepherd. NeAmPo; WiU

Foolish prater, what dost thou. Swallow, The. Abraham Cowley. OBEV; OxAEP-1

Foolish Thing. Michael Burkard. BodElec

Foolish Treasures. Lorenzo Thomas. AnSo

Foolishly I'd imagined for you your mother's. Raptor, The. Molly Peacock. PfS

Foolishly—simply existing. Orokahisasa Tada Ni Natsu No Hi O Kurashi Mukou Castle Rock. Violet Kazue De Cristoforo. CalPo

Fools and Wise Men [*epigram*]. Friedrich von Logau. GePo, *tr. by* George C. Schoolfield

Fool's Errand. Zachariah Wells. IFF

Fools Fall in Love. Irving Berlin. ReLy

Fools have power over wise men: each transactions, each affair. Fools and Wise Men. Friedrich von Logau. GePo, *tr. by* George C. Schoolfield

Fool's Prayer, The. Edward Rowland Sill. APN-2; ITBLP

Fools! Sit down and wait for them to crumble! (LL) On the Fly-Leaf of Pound's Cantos. Basil Bunting. HarvBoo; NAMCP V.1; NoAM

Foot, and gazing into the future. (LL) Why Brownlee Left. Paul Muldoon. EmeKit; NAMCP V.2; NoP-4; NoP-5; NPeEn; OxBSo; PBCIP; StAl; WaAnP

Foot cannot know, The. Marching Song. George Dillon. PoA 2002

Foot of the tower. An angle where the darkness, The. Thomas Kinsella. PBCIP *Fr.* Nightwalker.

Foot Race Song. *Unknown.* OBVE, *tr. by* Frank Russell

Football field rises, The. At Navajo Monument Valley Tribal School (from the Photograph by Skeet Mcauley). Sherman Alexie. P180

Football: "I take the snap from center, fake to the right, fade back." Louis Jenkins. MoASP; P180; RaBo

Football thuds upon the green field, The. Footballers. Zoltán Jékely. IQMS, *tr. by* J. G. Nichols

Footballers. Zoltán Jékely. IQMS, *tr. by* J. G. Nichols

Footballers in the Snow. Martin Mooney. NIrP

Footbinding. Patricia Beer. NoP-4

Footfalling. Laura Riding Jackson. NAMCP V.1

Footfalls of a Great Criminal, The. César Vallejo. ConPit, *tr. by* Clayton Eshleman

Footnote. Douglas Kent Hall. ICANM

Footnote at "Figure of Speech." Tina Darragh. FTOS

Footnote Extended, A [for Thomas Szasz's *Karl Kraus and the Soul Doctors*]. Dannie Abse. HP

Footnote on Monasticism, A: Dingle Peninsula. John Montague. BBASP

Footnote to Belloc's "Tarantella." John Heath-Stubbs. OBCoV

Footnote to Howl. Allen Ginsberg. CLPP

Footnote to Tennyson. Gerald Bullett. UV

Footnote to the Amnesty Report on Torture [*with music*]. Margaret Atwood. NAMCP V.2; NoAM

Footnotes. Arkadii Dragomoschenko. ItGoST, *tr. by* Elena Balashova and Lyn Hejinian

Footpaths Cross in the Rice Field. "Lin Ling." CFP, *tr. by* Chung Ling and Kenneth Rexroth

Footprint on the Air, A. Naomi Lewis. NOxBChV

Footprints. Esther Louise. BRtP

Footprints. Caitlin O'Donnell. WhBo

Footprints. Dan Pagis. VCWP, *tr. by* Stephen Mitchell

Footprints on the Glacier. W. S. Merwin. NoAM

Footprints tread. Distance. Luciana Notari. CItWP, *tr. by* Cinzia Sartini Blum and Lara Trubowitz

Footsole to scalp alive facing the window's black mirror. Late Ghazal. Adrienne Rich. HarvBoo

Footsteps climb whereas they decend. Anna Mendelssohn. VaPo

Footsteps of an Owl and His Lament, The. Viktor Aleksandrovich Sosnora. TCRusP, *tr. by* Kathy Lewis

Foot-Washing, The. A. R. Ammons. ChIV-2

Foot-Washing, The. George Ella Lyon. OxWW

Fop. William Cowper. DiBP

For. Gwyn Thomas. BBMWP, *tr. by the author*

For 5p at a village fête I bought. On First Looking into Chapman's Hesiod. Peter Porter. NOBAu

For a beggar's bowl. (LL) In the Garden of Time and Destiny. Nâbî. OLP; WoPoe, *tr. by* Walter Andrews, Najaat Black and Mehmet Kalpakli

For a Birthday. Sophie Jewett. PoBW

For a Bitter Season. George Garrett. LPSFW

For a centenary. Inga Kuznetsova. CRWP, *tr. by* Max Nemtsov

For a Child Expected. Anne Ridler. SacPr

For a Coming Extinction. W. S. Merwin. EMP; GifTon; NAMCP V.2; PoPoPo; VCAP

For a couple of hours, but I am not that person. (LL) How to Get There. Frank O'Hara. NoP-4; NoP-5

For a Cowper Paperweight. Charles North. NYP2

For a Daughter Gone Away. Brendan Galvin. GM

For a day and a night. Rock, The. Elizabeth Spires. ExTi

For a Dead Lady. Edwin Arlington Robinson. APT-1; HeIP-4; InoFa; MoAmPo; NAMCP V.1; NoAM; OxBoAm; TCAPo; TFi

For a face, and dark lines for arms. (LL) Sonnet: "Now I see them sitting me before a mirror." Michael Palmer. HarvBoo; MakPoe

For a Far-out Friend. Gary Snyder. BB

For a few thousand battered books. (LL) Ezra Pound. AmWaPo; HarvBoo; InoFa; MoAmPo; NPeEn; OxBoAm; PoAgWa; TRP; WaAnP Fr. Hugh Selwyn Mauberley (Life and Contacts).

For, a few years now. Greed. Bernice Reagon. FuFl

For a Five-Year-Old [with music]. Fleur Adcock. StAl

For a Fountain. Barry Cornwall. OBEV

For a Friend in Travail. Adrienne Rich. NAAL-5

For a good decade. Drunk in the Furnace, The. W. S. Merwin. NAMCP V.2; NoAM; NoP-4; NoP-5; WaAnP

For a Grotto. Mark Akenside. OBGa Fr. Inscriptions.

For a group shot, and the rock remains shattered in a star. (LL) Album—A Runthru. Clark Coolidge. AHA; FTOS; NYP2

For a housemaid. Karai Senryū. EMJL, tr. by Makoto Ueda

For a kid that's black? (LL) Merry-Go-Round. Langston Hughes. AmFaPo; BLPJKO; SAmP

For a Lady I Know. Countee Cullen. APT-2; HeIP-4; NAAPv.2; NAMCP V.1; NIL-7; NIP-4; SSLK; TRP Fr. Four Epitaphs.

For a Lady's Summons of Non-Entry. William Drummond of Hawthornden. NOSC

For a Lamb. Richard Eberhart. ColAP; SoSe-8

For a long, long time, she confided to him, we have been in combat with the sea. Henri Michaux. GPTC Fr. I Am Writing to You from a Far-Off Country.

For a long time. For Tetsu the New Head Priest of Erin-ji. Muso Soseki. EaWin, tr. by W. S. Merwin

For a long time he tried to survive. Vyacheslav Kupriyanov. TCRusP, tr. by Pamela Davidson

For a Long Time I Have Wanted to Write a Happy Poem. Richard Jackson. PfSP

For a long time now. Electrolytes. Luljeta Lleshanaku. WoBe, tr. by Henry Israeli

For a long time now I have not been able to listen. Gift, A. Jack Marshall. ASA

For a long time you have not existed. Who What. Michel Deguy. YaTCFP, tr. by Clayton Eshleman

For a long while I have lived with the hope. Wish, A. Olga Fiodorovna Berggolts. TCRusP, tr. by Daniel Weissbort

For a Lost Child. William Stafford. InoFa

For a man that's dedicated. Vote for Lunn. Unknown. FaBoVe

For a minute? (LL) You. D. H. Lawrence. NAMCP V.1; NoAM

For a moment all that it touches back to wonder. (LL) Beautiful Changes, The. Richard Wilbur. NAAL-5; NIL-7; OxBoAm

For a moment concentrate on a spider's brain. Brain of the Spider, The. Paul Zimmer. PfSP

For a moment, the idiot inside me who shouts death constantly blacks out. Talking About Things. Michael Ryan. YaYoPo

For a moment there is no periphery. Camera Obscura. Valerie Martínez. NAPBL

For a Monk Going West. Muso Soseki. EaWin, tr. by W. S. Merwin

For a Moose. Denise Lassaw-Paljor. WhBo

For a Mouthy Woman. Countee Cullen. ChIV-1

For a night—any night—that bends. Poem of the Dawn and the Night. Rodolfo Di Biasio. NeIt, tr. by Stephen Sartarelli

For a particular size of stone about the size of your fist. There Are Words. Gael Turnbull. Oth

For a piece of democracy. Bits. Jean Dorcely Dede. OGAHCP, tr. by Boadiba and Jack Hirschman

For a Poet. Countee Cullen. BLPJKO; ItP

For a Poet. George Wither. ChIV-2

For a Portrait of Annette Vallon. Andrey Andreievich Voznesensky. RusPo, tr. by Robert Arthur Douglas Ford

For a ráinbow fóoting it nor hé for his bónes rísen. (LL) Caged Skylark, The. Gerard Manley Hopkins. MoBrPo; OBMV; OWoS; SoSe-8

For a rolling head. (LL) Birds. Frieda Hughes. NeBl; StAl

For a saving grace, we didn't see our dead. War in the Air, The. Howard Nemerov. ColAP; EMP; OtW; PWW2; VCAP

For a Senior College Textbook. Hans Magnus Enzensberger. PoSu

For a single beautiful word. (LL) Parsley. Rita Dove. AmAlph; CAP-8; EMP; ESEAA; LoL; NAAL-5; NAMCP V.2; NIL-7; NoAM; NoP-4; NoP-5; PoPoPo; VCAP; WaAnP

For a single move a thousand. Immortals' Paduk Game. Pak Chaesam. CAMKP, tr. by David R. McCann and Jiwon Shin

For a Six Year Old. Ben Scammell. NLP

For a solemn opening. We Survived Them. Anna Swirszczynska [or Swir]. AF, tr. by Czeslaw Milosz

For a Stone Girl at Sanchi. Gary Snyder. BB

For a Texas Beauty. Jerry Bradley. TiP2

For A' That and A' That. Shirley Brooks. UV

For A' That and A' That ["Is there, for honest poverty"]. Robert Burns. BRP; NAEL-6v2; NePenScot; NPBRoP; OxAEP-2; OxBEV; TFi; TreFP; UV

(Is There for Honest Poverty.) ItP

(Song: For A' That and A' That.) CABP; NAEL-7v2

For a time. Jade. Phyllis Thompson. ICANM

For a Virgin Lady. Countee Cullen. MoAmPo

For a War Memorial. G. K. Chesterton. PoWW

For a Wedding. Kate Clanchy. MFPA

For a while a year is a long time. Wholes. Larry Eigner. PmAP

For a whole week. Roma Higgins. Dave Etter. IllVoic

For a Wife in Jizzen. Douglas Young. EdScPo

For a Woman with Child. James Vincent Cunningham. APT-2

For a Woman's Rights. Joette Harland-Watts. InTrad

For a Working Woman. Frances Moore. RSaN

For a Young Artist. Robert Earl Hayden. NoAM

For a Zen Seeker. Mookam Choinul. BecRai, tr. by Kim Daljin, Kim Won-Chung and Christopher Merrill

For Adelaide. Bessie Rayner Parkes. VWP

For Adolf Eichmann. Primo Levi. AF, tr. by Ruth Feldman and Brian Swann

For ages and ages. When Your Lover Has Gone. E. A. Swan. ReLy

For ages and ages, they couldn't have seemed less simpatico. Nature of Things, The. Kathleen Ossip. BAP-01

For Albert, the Terrible. Carlota Caulfield. TANSG, tr. by Chris Allen

For all of the horses butchered on the battlefield. Horses, The. Michael Longley. StAl

For all one flag, one flag for all. (LL) Atlanta Exposition Ode. Mary Weston Fordham. CBWP-2; SWaP

For all the saints who from their labors rest. Funeral Hymn. William Walsham Howe. SacPr

For all these years, my certain Zen. Ryushu Shutaku. ZenPo, tr. by Takashi Ikemoto and Lucien Stryk

For all true poetry is cruel. Constipation. Breyten Breytenbach. PoetW, tr. by A. J. Coetzee

For All Unwed Mothers. Robert Fleming. ISC

For All We Know. Sam M. Lewis. ReLy

For all we know / We may never meet again. For All We Know. Sam M. Lewis. ReLy

For all your days prepare. Preparedness. Edwin Markham. MoAmPo; NAAPv.1

For Allen Ginsberg. X. J. Kennedy. PoA 2002

For Alva Benson, and for Those Who Have Learned to Speak. Joy Harjo. HATNAP; UnSA

For an Album. Adrienne Rich. VCAP

For "An Allegorical Dance of Women" by Andrea Mantegna. Dante Gabriel Rossetti. CenSon

For An Amorous Lady. Theodore Roethke. NBLV

For an Approving God. (LL) Apparently with no surprise. Emily Dickinson. NAAL-3; NAAL-5; SAmP; SoSe-8; TCAPo

For an Early Retirement. Donald Hall. PoA 2002

For an End. Helen Pinkerton. CalPo

For an Island. Ko Ŭn. CAMKP, tr. by Anthony, Brother of Taizé

For an officer / in the old Capital, fox fur. Ezra Pound. OBVE

For and Against the Environment. D. M. Black. EmeKit

For Andrew [with music]. Fleur Adcock. BeAl

For Andrew Wood. James Fenton. NAMCP V.2

For Anne Gregory. William Butler Yeats. NAEL-6v2; NAEL-7v2; OxAEP-2

For Annie. Edgar Allan Poe. APN-1; ColAP; OBEV; TCAPo

Prone. STuOW

For anyone who is tired and still has to walk. (LL) Kinaxixi. Agostinho Neto. PoetW; WoPoe, tr. by W. S. Merwin

For Ares, gold-exchanger for the dead. Aeschylus. FaBoWar Fr. Agamemnon.

For Art Blakey and the Jazz Messengers. Keorapetse Kgositsile. SeSe

For as the harmony which sense admires. Fulke, 1st Baron Brooke Greville. NOSC Fr. Treatise of Monarchy, A.

For as the Soul's essential powers are three. Three Kinds of Life Answerable to the Three Powers of the Soul. John Davies. SacPr

For at midnight brake forth a Light. Michael Wigglesworth. TCAPo Fr. Day of Doom, The [First Section].

For aught that a lie saith, fear. (LL) Lake of Gaube, The. Algernon Charles Swinburne. CABP; NAEL-6v2

For auld lang syne. (LL) Auld Lang Syne. Robert Burns. NAEL-6v2; NAEL-7v2; NePenScot; NoP-5; NOSC; OBEV; OxAEP-5; OxBEV

For auld Robin Gray he is kind unto me. (LL) Auld Robin Gray. Lady Anne Barnard (née Lindsay). OBEV; OxBEV

For Aunt Cathy. Kevin Powell. InTrad

For authorities whose hopes. Paper Nautilus, The. Marianne Moore. HarvBoo; MakPoe; NAAL-5; NAAPv.2; NALW; NAMCP V.1

For aye the more he sought his way. Sir Walter Scott. DiBP *Fr.* Lay of the Last Minstrel, The.

For aye unsought-for slept among his ashes cold. (LL) Eve of St. Agnes, The. John Keats. CABP; NAEL-6v2; NAEL-7v2; NOBRP; NoP-4; NoP-5; NPBRoP; NPeEn; OBNV; OxAEP-2; TFi; TRP; WaAnP

For Babies Unborn. Tracy Clarke. InTrad

For Baby. Kim Namjo. CAMKP, *tr. by* David R. McCann and Hyunjae Yee Sallee

For Barbara, Who Brings a Green Stone in the Shape of a Triangle. Hilda Raz. PfSP

For Beautiful Mary Brown: Chicago Rent Strike Leader. June Jordan. OxAAAP

For Beauty. Susan Hahn. ExTi

For being unfaithful though ever true. Christopher Cook. NewEx

For Beirut I write. Beirut. Claire Gebeyli. PoArWo, *tr. by* Mona Takyeddine Amyuni

For beste of boon and blood. (LL) *Unknown.* NAEL-6v1

For better waters now the little bark. Dante Alighieri. NAWM-5v1 *Fr.* Divina Commedia (Selections from Anthologies, in English).

For Black Poets Who Think of Suicide. Etheridge Knight. HeIP-4; LTA; OxAAAP; WaAnP

For Black Women Who Are Afraid. Toi Derricotte. ExTi; FuFl

For Boats Only. Janine Pommy-Vega. PrTe

For Bob Marley. John Agard. WaCA

For Both of You, the Divorce Being Final. John Hollander. YaYoPo

For brave comportment, wit without offence. To His Honoured and Most Ingenious Friend Mr. Charles Cotton. Robert Herrick. NOSC

For Brigid. M. Travis Lane. Coast

For Brothas That Like to Holla. Kenneth Carroll. BtF

For, Brother, What Are We? Thomas Clayton Wolfe. RaBo

For Bud. Michael S. Harper. ESEAA; FaoP

For by tomorrow [*or* to morrow], I may think[e] so too. (LL) Woman's Constancy. John Donne. NBLV; NOSC

   (For by tomorrow, I may think so too.) (LL) FSCP; NoP-4

For C. K. at His Christening. Daniel Lawrence Kelleher. BLPJKO

For C.W.B. Elizabeth Bishop. GoPo

For C., Who Died of Childbirth at the Age of One Year and Eleven Months. Giovanni Raboni. ItPo, *tr. by* Gayle Ridinger

For Cadging Fish. Isabel Gowdie. EMWP

For CALYX. Ursula K. Le Guin. FiBr

For Carlos Charles Bucillio [*with music*]. Alice Sadongei. HATNAP

For Carole. Gary Snyder. WANABP

For centuries sadhus live and die. Circumambulating Arunachala. Gary Snyder. BB

For certain things must need be changed. Sadakichi. NAAPv.1 *Fr.* My Rubaiyat.

For change of solitude. (LL) Happiness Makes Up in Height for What It Lacks in Length. Robert Frost. MoAmPo; SoSe-8

For Christine at the Frost Farm. Daniel Tobin. VisFro

For Christmas Day. Joseph Hall. SacPr

For Christopher Isherwood and Chester Kallman. W. H. Auden. SacPr

For City Spring. Stephen Vincent Benét. NBLV

For Colored Girls Who Have Considered Suicide When the Rainbow Is Enuf. Ntozake Shange.

   One. FaoP

   "She waz sullen." ASA

For comfort on bad nights. Barton in the Beans. Joanne Limburg. NeBl

For Communism and for liberty. (LL) Full Moon at Tierz: Before the Storming of Huesca. John Cornford. OBWP; RSaN

For Consciousness [*with music*]. Mervyn Morris. WaCA

For conversation when we meet again. (LL) I, Being Born A Woman [and Distressed]. Edna St. Vincent Millay. APT-1; HarvBoo; LW; NAAPv.2; NALW; NAMCP V.1; NIL-7; NIP-4; NoP-4; NoP-5

For Cool Papa Bell. Tom Dent. ISC

For Craig Who Leapt Off a Cliff in to Hummingbird Light. Diane Wakoski. PmAP

For Daniel Beels, Third Generation Bricklayer. John Rybicki. AmPoNex

For Danton. Charles Tomlinson. HarvBoo

For Daughters of Magdalen. Countee Cullen. ChIV-2

For dawn, wind / off the river. Imamu Amiri Baraka. BB

For days after the wedding. Balloon Heart. Beth Gylys. AmPoNex

For days he has dumped a trail of tuna blood. Great White Shark, The. Arthur Sze. GifTon

For days I have wakened and felt immediately. Messenger, The. Thomas Kinsella.

For days you find it one long zero hour. Marking Time. Peter Steele. NOBAu

For Dear Life. Alane Rollings. OPRER

For Death, he taketh all away, but them he cannot take. (LL) Heraclitus. William Johnson Cory. OBEV; OxAEP-2; UV

For Death thou art a Mower too. (LL) Damon the Mower. Andrew Marvell. BASC; NAEL-6v1; NAEL-7v1; NOSC

For deep deer-copse beneath Mount Han. Ezra Pound. OBVE

For Deliverance from a Fever. Anne Bradstreet. NAAL-3; NAAPv.1; NALW

For Desire. Kim Addonizio. BeAl; SUP

For Diane di Prima. Michael McClure. WANABP *Fr.* Haiku Rows.

For Don Drummond. Lorna Goodison. WaCA

For Don Francisco Giner de Los Ríos. Antonio Machado Ruiz. RaW, *tr. by* Robert Bly

For Dorothy Wordsworth. Charles North. NYP2

For Douglas whom the cloud and eddy rejected. Funeral Oration, A. Drummond Allison. PoWW

For Du Fu. Li Po. CCL1, *tr. by* David Young

For Duke Ellington. Reuben Jackson. ESEAA

For each a golden age. The trees brimming. Childhood. Ann Stanford. PoChi

For each breath of the south-wind makes a new bamboo! (LL) Eating Bamboo-Shoots. Po Chü-i. CCL1; OBVE, *tr. by* Arthur Waley

For each ecstatic instant. Emily Dickinson. NAAL-3

For each morning a tune. Interior Music, The. Patricia Goedicke. MiVo

For each year of service. Zizwe. Tanya Tyler. BRtP

For Easter Island or Another Island. William Dickey. YaYoPo

For Edward Hopper, from the Floor. Lucia Maria Perillo. ExTi

For Edward Thomas Killed at Arras. Geoffrey Matthews. RSaN

For Elaine de Kooning. Hilda Morley. PmAP

For Eli Jacobson. Kenneth Rexroth. RaBo

For Emily (Dickinson). Maureen Owen. PmAP; ReTh

For Emma. Luigi Fontanella. NeIt, *tr. by* Michael Palma

For England's Sake. W. E. Henley.

   (England, my England.) MoBrPo; OBEV

For Eric Blair. Siùsaidh NicNèill. EdScPo

For Erwin Smith, Cowboy Photographer. Larry McMurtry. TiP2

For Esther. Stanley Plumly. GM

For Ethel Rosenberg. Adrienne Rich. AtGh

For Etheridge Knight. Lamont B. Steptoe. OxAAAP

For Etheridge Knight. Jackie Warren-Moore. SpirFl

For Euthanasia and Pain-Killing Drugs. Alan Dugan. NAMCP V.2

For ever hard to meet, and as hard to part. Li Shang-yin. CCL1, *tr. by* A. C. Graham

For every bird there is this last migration. Death of the Bird, The. Alec Derwent Hope. BMAP

For every chekeh of the guitar. Some Tentative Definitions 11. Kwame Dawes. WaCA

For Every Heart. Olga Broumas. ErotSp

For Every Man There's a Woman. Leo Robin. ReLy

For every ten bushels of paddy she harvests. Primary Lessons in Political Economy. Amitava Kumar. IPoFL

For every year, he grew a new tooth. Man Who Became Old, The. Alberto A. Ríos. NoAM

For every year of life we light. Birthday Poem, A. James Simmons. PNI

For Everyone His Own Tree. Fadil Azzawi. IrPoTo, *tr. by* Ralph Saverese and Saadi A. Simawe

For everyone / The swimmer's moment at the whirlpool comes. Swimmer's Moment, The. Margaret Avison. BrAP

For ev'ry man there's a woman. For Every Man There's a Woman. Leo Robin. ReLy

For Ewan McLachlan. R. Gerallt Jones. BBMWP, *tr. by* the author

For example, one could be a slinger of burgers at McDonald's. Worse. J. R. Solonche. VisFro

For example, taking the cement onto palettes, for the hoist. Bill Griffiths. Oth *Fr.* Building: The New London Hospital.

For Exmoor. Jean Ingelow. OBEV

For eyes he waves greentipped. Slug in Woods. Earle Birney. NoP-4

For F. M. Who Did Not Get Killed Yesterday on 57th Street. Malena Mörling. AmPoNex

For False Heart. Joseph Hilaire Pierre Belloc. MoBrPo

For Fatma and Her Co-Wives. Janeya K. Hisle. BtF

For Fausto Coppi (1916–60) et Tous les Copains de la Bicyclette. Jeff Cloves. ArBi

For fear of disturbing the men in heaven. (LL) Inscribed at Summit Temple. Li Po. CCL1; WoPoe, *tr. by* Elling O. Eide

For fear of finding something worse. (LL) Jim Who Ran Away from His Nurse, and Was Eaten by a Lion. Joseph Hilaire Pierre Belloc. NOxBChV; OBSP; OxAEP-2

For fellowship—at night. (LL) Mountains grow—unnoticed, The. Emily Dickinson. MoAmPo; SWaP

FOR few nights' solace in delicious bed. To St Mary Magdalen. Henry Constable. ChIV-2; NoSic

For "Fiddle-De-De." John Hollander. P180
  (For "Fiddle-De-Dee.") BAP-04

For Fidel Castro. Sandra Maria Esteves. PueRic

For five loathsome weeks. Kali Kolsson. SonAtl

For Five Minutes. Na Hûidôk. EcSo, tr. by Peter H. Lee

For five or six years I haven't been really emotional. Beriberi. Barbara Hamby. SUP

For Fog and Fate no charm is found. Rudyard Kipling. InoFa Fr. Epitaphs of the War [1914–1918].

For forty million years a warm, warm rain. Formation of Soils, The. Brenda Hillman. BAP-01; FaoP

For forty years I shunned the lust. For a Virgin Lady. Countee Cullen. MoAmPo

For forty years now, ever since. Live at the Village Vanguard. Bill Zavatsky. FaoP

For Frankenstein, of course, Hamlet's central. Hamlet Meets Frankenstein. Kevin Griffith. IaFF

For Freckle-Faced Gerald. Etheridge Knight. ESEAA

For Friendship. Robert Creeley. VCAP

For Fugitives. Frank Templeton Prince. HarvBoo

For Gary Snyder and Carole Koda. Michael McClure. WANABP Fr. Haiku Rows.

For gay bard, barren summer. Lament for Lleucu Llwyd. Llywelyn Goch ap Meurig Hen. OBWVE, tr. by Joseph P. Clancy

For Gen the New Head Priest of Erin-ji. Muso Soseki. EaWin, tr. by W. S. Merwin

For Gil and Other Incurables. Renée Weiss and Theodore Weiss. BodElec

For giving me my madness back, or nearly. (LL) Come Dance with Kitty Stobling. Patrick Kavanagh. HarvBoo; NAMCP V.1; NoAM; NPeEn

For Gloucester on Being Newly Blind. Michelle LaBarre. IaFF

For God, our God, is a gallant foe. Ballad for Gloom. Ezra Pound. MoAmPo

For God's sake. Revelations. Harry Thurston. Coast

For God's sake be careful or someone will hear you! (LL) Sacred and Profane Love, or, There's Nothing New under the Moon Either. Peter De Vries. NBLV; OBCoV

For God's sake marcke that Fly. Nulla Fides. Patrick Carey. OxBEV

For God's sake [or Godsake] hold your tongue, and let me love. Canonization, The. John Donne. BASC; BrAP; CABP; FaBoVe; FSCP; NAEL-6v1; NAEL-7v1; NAWM-5v1; NIL-7; NIP-4; NoP-4; NoP-5; NOSC; NPeEn; PBRV; PoPoPo; SoSe-8; TFi; TRP; WaAnP; WoPoe

For God's sake, reader! take them not for mine! (LL) Lord Byron. NAEL-6v2; NAEL-7v2 Fr. Don Juan.

For good is the life ending faithfully. (LL) Long love that in my thought doth harbo[u]r, The. Sir Thomas Wyatt. GSo; NAEL-6v1; NAEL-7v1; NoP-5
  (For goode is the liff, ending faithfully.) (LL) BrAP; NPeEn; OxBEV

For Grace, after a Party. Frank O'Hara. CAP-8

For grief. Exile. Saniyya Salih. PoArWo, tr. by Kamal Boullata

For Grizzel McNaught (1709–1792). Anne Finch. FFC

For Gwendolyn Brooks. Quraysh Ali Lansana. BRtP

For Gwendolyn Brooks: As I Civilize a Space. Dolores Kendrick. FuFl

For H. V. (1901–1927). Weldon Kees. NoP-5

For half a century. Roller Coaster. Nicanor Parra. PoCho; TCLAP, tr. by Miller Williams

For Hamlet. Peter Cooley. IaFF

For Hans Keller. Craig Raine. NoP-5

For Harry S Truman in Hell. David Ray. AtGh

For Hazel Hall, American Poet. Countee Cullen. APT-2

For H.D. Diane Di Prima. PmAP

For he was drowned, and I've the ague. (LL) Written After Swimming from Sestos to Abydos. Lord Byron. NAEL-6v2; NAEL-7v2; NBLV; NoP-4; NoP-5

For he was sick, and very bad. Julia A. Moore. STuOW Fr. John Robinson.

For he would never thus have flown. Lord Byron. STuOW Fr. Prisoner of Chillon, The.

For healthy cells please remember. Sappho's Gymnasium. T. Begley and Olga Broumas. PfS

For Heather, Entering Kindergarten [with music]. Roberta Hill Whiteman. HATNAP; NoAM

For Heaven and the future's sakes. (LL) Two Tramps in Mud Time. Robert Frost. APT-1; MoAmPo; NAMCP V.1; NoAM; OxBoAm; SAmP

For Heiner Muller: Poem 1. Safaa Fathy. AnVo, tr. by Mohamed Enani

For Heiner Muller: Poem 2. Safaa Fathy. AnVo, tr. by Mohamed Enani

For Heiner Muller: Poem 3. Safaa Fathy. AnVo, tr. by Mohamed Enani

For Helen, the journey is not complete without bridges. On the Train. Lynn Davies. Coast

For Her Children. Martha Rhodes. LaCa

For her gait, if she be walking. Song. William Browne. OBEV

For her, he says to me. On Class and Desire. Chuck Wachtel. PrTe

For her locust, nightingale of the fields, and her cricket that slept. Anyte. HePo Fr. Epigrams.

For Her Lover. Lady Ishikawa. AHA

For her sake once again I disinter. In Mayo. Michael Longley. IrLP

For her sake that died for me. (LL) Helen of Kirconnell. Unknown. OBEV; OxBEV

For her this rhyme is penned, whose luminous eyes. Edgar Allan Poe. NCAP

For Hettie. Imamu Amiri Baraka. GT

For him also I powrit out mony teiris. Mary Stuart, Queen of Scots. NePenScot Fr. Sonnets to Bothwell.

For him the Shannon opens. Swimmer, The. Brendan Kennelly. PBCIP; PML

For him who yearning longs for his beloved. (LL) Wife's Lament, The. Unknown. NoP-4; NoP-5, tr. by Richard Hamer

For His Father. William Meredith. PoA 2002

For his mind, I do[e] not care. Ben Jonson. NAEL-7v1 Fr. Celebration of Charis in Ten Lyric[k] Pieces [or Peeces], A.

For his religion it was fit. Samuel Butler. OBCoV; OBSV; OxBEV Fr. Hudibras.

For His Ring and Watch on the Night Stand [with music]. Gladys Cardiff. HATNAP

For Hokey and Henrietta. Norman Nicholson. NoP-4

For hoot of cold, for cold of hoot I die. (LL) Geoffrey Chaucer. See For hete of cold, for cold of hete I dye.

For hours at the end I kissed your temple stroked. No Goodbyes. Paul Monette. InoFa

For hours I held one of my son's infant twins. Cathedral. Deena Linett. NevBe

For hours I sat on our driveway beneath the dogwood tree. St. Francis Speaks to Me at a Young Age. Vic Coccimiglio. InvLad

For hours I've persistently watched my long legs. Ritual of My Legs. Pablo Neruda. ConPit, tr. by Clayton Eshleman

For how long have you wanted a magician. Caernarfon Circus, 1969. T. E. Nicholas. BBMWP, tr. by Robert Minhinnick

For how many hundreds of years. Floor in Goethe's House, The. Sŏ Chŏngju. CAMKP, tr. by David R. McCann

For I am rightful fellow of their band. Mentors. Gwendolyn Brooks. ESEAA

For I can say truthfully. "H. D." NAAPv.2 Fr. Tribute to the Angels.

For I can snore like a bullhorn. After Making Love We Hear Footsteps. Galway Kinnell. BeAl; CAP-8; ColAP; EMP; NAAL-5; NAMCP V.2; NIL-7; NIP-4; NoAM; NoP-4; NoP-5; PasH; RaBo; VCAP; WaAnP

For I cannot die nor live without you anymore. (LL) Seventh Eclogue ("Do you see? Evening falls, fringed with barbed-wire.") Miklós Radnóti. ConPit; PFTM-1, tr. by Clayton Eshleman and Gyula Kodolanyi

For I have read. Of Earthly Love. Susanna Valentine Mitchell. LW

For I Have Taught the Japanese. Lucia Maria Perillo. ExTi

For I lull nobody, and you will never understand me. (LL) To a Certain Civilian. Walt Whitman. CBCWP; FaBoWar

For I pray God to bless Polly in the blessing of Naomi. Christopher Smart. WaAnP Fr. Jubilate Agno.

For I prophesy that we shall have our horns again. Christopher Smart. ChIV-1 Fr. Jubilate Agno.

For I rejoice in my cat Matty. Jubilate Matteo. Gavin Ewart. UV

For I will consider my Cat Jeoffry. My Cat Jeoffry. Christopher Smart. BrAP; CABP; HeIP-4; NAEL-6v1; NAEL-7v1; NoP-4; NoP-5; NPeEn; OBWVE; OxAEP-1; PoPoPo; TriCat; TRP; WaAnP; WeW-3 Fr. Jubilate Agno.

For I will consider my dog Poochkin. Jubilate Canis. Erica Jong. WaAnP

For I will consider my lover, who shall remain nameless. My Lover. Wendy Cope. MoWP

For I will dare none. Good lord, walk dead still. (LL) On Something, that Walks Somewhere. Ben Jonson. BASC; NAEL-6v1; NAEL-7v1

For if it prosper, none dare call it Treason. (LL) Of Treason. Sir John Harington. NoSic; NPeEn; OBCoV; OxBEV; SoSe-8

For I'm sick at the heart, and I fain wa[l]d lie down. (LL) Lord Randal[l]. Unknown. CtM; HeIP-4; InoFa; NAEL-6v1; NAEL-7v1; NIL-7; NoP-4; NoP-5; NPeEn; OxBEV; PoPoPo; TFi; TRP; WaAnP; WeW-3

For I'me a parting now from you. (LL) To My Husband. "Eliza." EMWP; LW; PBRV

For Imelda. James Simmons. PNI

For Instance. Robert McAlmon. PoA 2002

For instance, for instance. In Waking Words. Dorothy Barresi. SweBea

For instance, the child skipping. No Boundaries. Liz Rosenberg. InvLad

For instance, the last time I saw my friend. Music We Dance To, The. Rebecca Seiferle. PoDa

For it seems to us worthy of record. (LL) Les Millwin. Ezra Pound. APT-1; OBCoV

For it was writ in heaven doubly Wright. (LL) Robert Frost. AmWit; WeW-3 Fr. Ten Mills.

For it will be as when a man going on a journey called his servants and entrusted to them his property. Jorge Luis Borges. GI Fr. St. Matthew.

For J. W. Rafael Campo. RA

For Jack Kerouac. Michael McClure. WANABP Fr. Haiku Rows.

For Jack Spicer. David Meltzer. ASA

For Jan as the End Draws Near. Carolyn Kizer. GeoHom

For Jan, with Love. David Lee. GifTon

For Joe Brainard. David Trinidad. WiU

For John Chappell. Gary Snyder. InoFa

For John Clare. John Ashbery. HarvBoo; MotU

For John Donne: Master Metaphysical. Alexander Trocchi. EroLit

For John F. Kennedy; His Inauguration. Robert Frost. BLPJKO

For Johnny. John Pudney. OBWP

For Jose Mercado Vasquez and Frances Roman Vasquez. Robert Vasquez. GeoHom

For Jude the Obscure. Peter Cooley. Vesp

For Jurij Koch. Robat Powell. BBMWP, tr. by the author

For Karen. Elizabeth Robinson. AmPoNex

For Kinna 2. Christine Ama Ata Aidoo. HAWP

For knighthood is not in the feats of war. Stephen Hawes. OBEV Fr. Pastime of Pleasure, The.

For Ko Who Has Come Back from China. Muso Soseki. EaWin, tr. by W. S. Merwin

For lack of Knowledge do my people die! My People are destroyed for lack of Knowledge.—Hosea 4:6. Jones Very. ChIV-1

For Lady and Prez. Theodore A. Harris. BRtP

For largest Woman's Heart I knew. Emily Dickinson. NAAPv.1

For Larry Levis in Memory. Luis Omar Salinas. GeoHom

For Laura. Mihály Vörösmarty. IQMS, tr. by Adam Makkai

For learned books, I read the grasses. Walking a Field into Evening. Larry Smith. AmZen

For LeRoi Jones. Steve Jonas. EGAG

For Lester. Reggie Timpson. BtF

For Letters. Yvonne Cullen. NIrP

For Lew Welch in a Snowfall. Gary Snyder. InoFa

For Life I Had Never Cared Greatly. Thomas Hardy. NAMCP V.1; NoAM

For listening and instructional purposes. Drive to Lone Ranger, A. Ray A. Young Bear. AF

For little dreams to go. (LL) Hold Fast Your Dreams. Louise Driscoll. ChAP; ITBLP

For Little Giffen, of Tennessee. (LL) Little Giffen. Francis Orrery Ticknor. CBCWP; PCW

For lo! the board with cups and spoons is crown'd. Alexander Pope. UV Fr. Rape of the Lock, The: An Heroi-Comical Poem in Five Cantos.

For Lolita Lebron. Sandra Maria Esteves. PueRic

For long. (LL) Mermaid Tank, The. Stephen Knight. NeBl; StAl

For long and in loneliness. (LL) I explain the silvered passing of a ship at night. Stephen Crane. APN-2; TCAPo

For long between the trenches a dead man lay in view. Brothers. Heinrich Lersch. FaBoWar, tr. by Christopher Middleton

For long years we have been haunting the quarter. Fuzuli. OLP, tr. by Walter Andrews, Najaat Black and Mehmet Kalpakli

For Lorine Niedecker in Heaven. Ralph J., Jr. Mills. IllVoic

For Louis Armstrong, A Ju-Ju. Sarah Webster Fabio. SeSe

For Love [(For Bobbie)]. Robert Creeley. NAMCP V.2; PmAP; VCAP

For love no time has she, or inclination. Soame Jenyns. OBSV Fr. Modern Fine Lady, The.

For love of Megan I danced all night. My Autobiography. Ted Berrigan. OxBoAm

For love there is no other drug, Nicias. Theocritus. HePo Fr. Idylls.

For love—I would. Warning, The. Robert Creeley. CAP-8

For Love's sake, kiss[e] me once again[e]. Ben Jonson. NAEL-7v1 Fr. Celebration of Charis in Ten Lyric[k] Pieces [or Peeces], A.

For Mack C. Parker. Pauli Murray. WaAnP

For Malcolm: After Mecca. Gerald William Barrax. OxAAAP

For Malcolm X. Margaret Abigail Walker. FTutHH; OxAAAP

For Malcolm's eyes, when they broke. Poem for Black Hearts, A. Imamu Amiri Baraka. NAMCP V.2; SSLK; WaAnP

For man is between the pinchers while his soul is shaping and purifying. Christopher Smart. ChIV-1 Fr. Jubilate Agno.

For man to tell how human life began. John Milton. ChIV-1 Fr. Paradise Lost.

For Man will hearken to his glozing lies. John Milton. InvLi Fr. Paradise Lost.

For many distant travelers. Acoma. William Oandasan. HATNAP

For many years. For a Monk Going West. Muso Soseki. EaWin, tr. by W. S. Merwin

For Many Years. Kemal Ozer. NaPG, tr. by Talat Sait Halman

For many years. (LL) Kisimiso. Musaemura Bonus Zimunya. HBAPE; NAfrP

For many years I did not make migration. Tougaloo Blues. Kelly Norman Ellis. SpirFl

For many years I wanted a child. Childlessness. Henri Cole. NAMCP V.2

For maple and for pine. Maple and the Pine, The. Robert Garioch. NPeEn

For Marilyn and Stan Brakhage. Michael McClure. WANABP Fr. Haiku Rows.

For Martin Luther King. Charles Fort. LTA

For Marxist dialectic: spouting, spouting. For. Gwyn Thomas. BBMWP, tr. by the author

For Mary McLeod Bethune. Margaret Abigail Walker. OxAAAP

For Mats and Laila. Tomas Tranströmer. MotU, tr. by Robert Bly

For Maulana Karenga & Pharoah Sanders. Imamu Amiri Baraka. APSN

For Maximino Palomo. Teresa Palma Acosta. TiP2

For me a perfectly ordinary. Routine Day Sonnet. A. K. Ramanujan. EmeKit

For me a tragedy's most important act is the sixth. Theater Impressions. Wisława Szymborska. VCWP

For Me and My Gal. E. Ray Goetz and Edgar Leslie. ReLy

For me it was an adventure. Loss of Control. Pat Mora. FiBr

For me it was Robin Hentz. First. Mark Halliday. NevBe

For me, it's a bit of cool hide. Madeleine, A. George Bilgere. PoDa

For me neither honey nor bee. Sappho. SaLy, tr. by Diane Rayor

For me the Muse a simple band design'd. To Mr. Hayley, on Receiving Some Elegant Lines from Him. Charlotte Smith. RWP

For me, the naked and the nude. Naked and the Nude, The. Robert Graves. SoSe-8

For me to lose you and for you to lose me, we both lose. Ernesto Cardenal. BLPSL, tr. by Rene de Costa, Rigas Kappatos and Eleni Paidoussi

For Medgar Evers. David Ignatow. LTA

For men and women soon the day draws near. Abu Sa'id Abul Khayr. WoPoe Fr. Four Poems on Death.

For Men to Tell How Human Life Began Is Hard, for Who Himself Beginning Knew? Desire with Thee Still Longer to Converse Induced Me as New-Waked from Soundest Sleep Soft on the Flow'ry Herb I Found Me Laid in Balmy Sweat. Yi Sanghûi. EcSo, tr. by Jennifer M. Lee

For Meng Hao-Jan. Li Po. WoPoe, tr. by Greg Whincup

For Mercy, Courage, Kindness, Mirth. Laurence Binyon. MoBrPo

For Michael Griffith, Murdered Dec. 21, 1986, Howard Beach, NY. Jeffrey Renard Allen. BRtP

For Michaela. David Rivard. MAAN

For Micha's Mother, Who Signs. Robert A. Fink. PoA 2002

For Midas, the Man from Akragas First in the Flute Match. Pindar. WoPoe Fr. Pythian Odes.

For Miriam. Marjorie Oludhe Macgoye. HAWP

For Mohammed Zeid, Age 15. Naomi Shihab Nye. P180

For Monk. Michael McClure. SeSe

For Mordecai Richler's Shalinsky Who Said "A Jew Is An Idea." Joseph Sherman. Coast

For more than five thousand years. At the Jewish New Year. Adrienne Rich. TaR

For more than sixty years he has been blind. War Blinded. Douglas Dunn. NePenScot; OBWP

For more than thirty years we hadn't met. Reunion. Carolyn Kizer. ExTi

For mortal love, that might not die of it. (LL) Oh, sleep forever in the Latmian cave. Edna St. Vincent Millay. GSo; MoAmPo; NALW; NoAM

For My Birthday. Attila József. IQMS, tr. by Earl M. Herrick

For My Birthday. Attila József. IQMS, tr. by Adam Makkai

For My Birthday. Attila József. IQMS, tr. by Istvan Fekete

For My Birthday. Attila József. IQMS, tr. by Anton N. Nyerges

For My Brother Hagok. Hŏ Nansŏrhŏn. WoPoe, tr. by Kichung Kim

For My Contemporaries. James Vincent Cunningham. APT-2; OxBoAm; VCAP; WaAnP

For My Daughter. Reginald Gibbons. LiTh

For My Daughter [with music]. Weldon Kees. OxBoAm; OxBSo; WaAnP

For My Dead Red-Haired Mother. Ruth Stone. OxBoAm

For My D.C. Girlfriends. Michelle Calhoun Green. BtF

For My Father. Duriel Harris. SpirFl

For My Father. Philip Schultz. TaR

For My Father's Grave. Yvor Winters. IllVoic

For my first poem there are specific images. Mr. Nabokov's Memory. Thomas McCarthy. ModIr

For My Grandmother. Countee Cullen. APT-2; MoAmPo; SSLK *Fr.* Four Epitaphs.

For My Grandmother, Bridget Halpin. Michael Hartnett. ModIr; PBCIP

For My Great-Grandfather: A Message Long Overdue. Maxine W. Kumin. UnSA

For my high school graduation. Class. Patricia Kirkpatrick. PfS

For My Mother. Doris Brett. NOBAu

For My Mother. Duriel Harris. BtF

For My Mother [*with music*]. Ellen Bryant Voigt. NIP-4; StAl

For My Mother: Genevieve Jules Creeley. Robert Creeley. TRP

For My Mother Magnetic Poetry Series. Gideon Ferebee. BtF

For My Own Monument. Matthew Prior. OBEV

For my people everywhere singing their slave songs repeatedly: their dirges and their ditties and their blues and jubilees. For My People. Margaret Abigail Walker. InGu; ISC; ItP; OxAAAP; SSLK; TWF; WaAnP

For my sins I live in the city of New York. Whitman in Black. Ted Berrigan. NYP2; ViWalt

For My Sister. Jannifer Traig. FTtHH

For My Sister Shura. Sergey Aleksandrovich Yesenin. TCRusP, *tr. by* Nigel Stott

For My Son. Muriel Rukeyser. TaR

For My Son Johnny. Anne Porter. OxBoAm

For My Son Noah, Ten Years Old. Robert Bly. GoPo; LoL; RaBo

For My Torturer, Lieutenant D. Leila Djabali. CFP; HAWP, *tr. by* Anita Barrows

For my 27th birthday: a poem longer than 10 lines in which pronouns appear. Giovanni Singleton. BtF

For my weak heart this living in the sorrow house is more than enough. Leftovers in the Cup. Mirza Asadullah Khan Ghalib. WED, *tr. by* Robert Bly and Sunil Dutta

For Mycea. Édouard Glissant. YaTCFP, *tr. by* Brent Hayes Edwards

For Myo's Departure for Anzen-ji. Muso Soseki. EaWin, *tr. by* W. S. Merwin

For Myo's Departure for Shofuku-ji. Muso Soseki. EaWin, *tr. by* W. S. Merwin

For Napoleon. (LL) Napoleon. Miroslav Holub. ChAP; PoSu, *tr. by* Kaca Plakova

For nearly a week that open-aired autumn. Ground Elder. Leonard Clark. OBGa

For never a begger need now despair, And every rogue has a chance. (LL) Speculators, The. William Makepeace Thackeray. OBCoV; OBSV

For never more to me the Spring of Hope returns! (LL) Written in October. Charlotte Smith. NoP-4; NoP-5

For New Year, Postumus, ten years ago. Roman Thank-You Letter, A. Martial. OBCP, *tr. by* James Michie

For nine months I had borne him in my womb. Labour. Kristina Rungano. HAWP

For no reason. Short Circuit. Daniel Hall. OWoS

For no specific reason I have become one of the city's unicorns. Wino Rhino. Harryette Mullen. AWPTFC

For none can call again[e] the passed [*or* passèd] time. (LL) Edmund Spenser. NoP-5; OBEV *Fr.* Amoretti.

For none can call againe the passèd time. (LL) Edmund Spenser. *See* For none can call again[e] the passed [*or* passèd] time.

For None see God and live. (LL) To pile like Thunder to its close. Emily Dickinson. APN-2; NCAP

For Norman Nicholson. David Scott. NLP

For nothing now can ever come to any good. (LL) W. H. Auden. CAGL; EMP; MoBrPo; OPOU *Fr.* Twelve Songs.

For now, and since first break of dawne the Fiend. John Milton. NPeEn *Fr.* Paradise Lost.

For oak and elm have pleasant leaves. Oscar Wilde. MakPoe; NoAM *Fr.* Ballad of Reading Gaol, The.

For once. Portrait of Jonah with woman. Marie-Claire Bancquart. MFP, *tr. by* Martin Sorrell

For once, I hardly noticed what I ate. Runaways Café II. Marilyn Hacker. NoAM

For Once, Then, Something. Robert Frost. APT-1; NAMCP V.1; NoAM; OxBoAm

For one brief day, did Queenie stay. Queenie. Mary Weston Fordham. CBWP-2

For one month I was imprisoned; my slippers never moved forward. *Unknown.* NAAPv.2

For One Must Want / To Shut the Other's Gaze. Jorie Graham. BodElec

For one short week I leave, with anxious heart. Eyam. Anna Seward. RWP

For One Who Gayly Sowed His Oats. Countee Cullen. APT-2; NAAPv.2

For other fruits my father was indifferent. My Father and the Fig Tree. Naomi Shihab Nye. IPoFL

For Our Lady of the Rocks By Leonardo da Vinci. Dante Gabriel Rossetti. GS

For our own private reasons. Reasons. Thomas James. PoCho

For over a week now, again and again. Mother. Attila József. IQMS, *tr. by* Vernon Watkins

For over ten years now. Maple Syrup Sonnet. Bernadette Mayer. NYP2

For over twenty years you prime. Century Plant. David C. Yates. TiP2

For papers are still papers. Tale, A. Ahmed Taha. AnVo, *tr. by* Mohamed Enani

For parents, the only way. Way of Pain, The. Wendell Berry. UpMys

For Paul. Eve Triem. APT-2

For Paul Celan and Primo Levi. Harvey Shapiro. TaR

For Paul Laurence Dunbar. Countee Cullen. SSLK *Fr.* Four Epitaphs.

For Paula Cooper. Jackie Warren-Moore. SpirFl

For P—Celtic: found text from Machen. Bill Griffiths. Oth

For people, islands give birth. For an Island. Ko Ŭn. CAMKP, *tr. by* Anthony, Brother of Taizé

For Peter, My Cousin. Barbara Nickel. IFF

For physic and farces his equal there scarce is. On Sir John Hill, M. D., Playwright. David Garrick. NBLV

For plucking out the feathers of rigid archangels. Final Sonnet. Miguel Hernández. BLPSL, *tr. by* Rene de Costa, Rigas Kappatos and Eleni Paidoussi

For poems the pay was a dollar. Autumn, 1949: At the "Flower" Tea Room. Sŏ Chŏngju. CAMKP, *tr. by* David R. McCann

For Pulling the Feathers from Icy Archangels. Miguel Hernández. WED, *tr. by* Robert Bly

For purposes of illusion. Theorem. Walter Conrad Arensberg. APT-1

For quite obviously they might yawn just as well elsewhere. (LL) Henri Michaux. GPTC; MotU *Fr.* I Am Writing to You from a Far-Off Country.

For R. J. C. (Summer, 1936). Margot Heinemann. RSaN

For Raftery. Alan Alexander. NOBAu

For rank, descent and title famed. Martial. RompO, *tr. by* J. P. Sullivan

For reasons any. Irapuato. Earle Birney. NIL-7

For repose I have sighed and have struggled; have sigh'd and have struggled in vain. Felo de Se. Amy Levy. VWP

For Rhoda. Delmore Schwartz. MoAmPo

For rice-planting women. Konishi Raizan. SoOfWa, *tr. by* Sam Hamill

For Richer, For Poorer. Emily Hickey. PoBW

For Righteousness' Sake. John Greenleaf Whittier. OxBoAm

For Rita's Daughter, Just Born. Eunice De Souza. NAMCP V.2

For Robert Desnos. Tristan Tzara. AF

For Robert Frost. Rhina P. Espaillat. VisFro

For Robert Frost. Galway Kinnell. VisFro

For Robert Frost, in the Autumn, in Vermont. Howard Nemerov. VisFro

For Roland, Presumed Taken. Jim Barnes. LiTh

For round about, the wals yclothed were. Edmund Spenser. PBRV *Fr.* Faerie Queene, The.

For Russell and Rowena Jelliffe. Langston Hughes. OxAAAP

For sale what the Jews have not sold, what neither nobility nor crime has tasted. Sales. Arthur Rimbaud. SxFrPo, *tr. by* Martin Sorrell

For Sanje, a Hermit. Daegak Euchon. BecRai, *tr. by* Kim Daljin, Kim Won-Chung and Christopher Merrill

For Santacruze the glad fleet takes her way. Andrew Marvell. FaBoWar *Fr.* Victory Obtained by Blake over the Spaniards, in the Bay of Santa Cruz in the Island of Teneriffe, 1657.

For Sappho/After Sappho. Carolyn Kizer. GifTon

For, see! where Winter comes, himself, confest. James Thomson. NePenScot *Fr.* Seasons, The.

For self-destruction. (LL) Psalm: "That from the seed of men." Peter Huchel. AF; AtGh, *tr. by* Daniel S. Simko

For sentimental reasons. Last Apple, The. Carol Coiffait. Prnts

For Services Rendered. F. G. Butterfield. FaBoWar

For seven years at school I named. Song of the Dead Soldier, The. Christopher Logue. FaBoWar

For seven years now Uludağ and I have been staring each other in the eye. About Mount Uludağ. Nazim Hikmet. WoPoe, *tr. by* Randy Blasing and Mutlu Konuk

For seventy-two years / I've kept the ox well under. Bokuo. ZenPo, *tr. by* Takashi Ikemoto and Lucien Stryk

For several *li*. Passing by a Mountain Village at Dusk. Chia Tao. CSKM, *tr. by* Mike O'Connor

For several months. P.C. Plod versus the Dale St. Dog Strangler. Roger McGough. OBSP

For shame, thou everlasting wooer. Antiplatonic[k], The. John Cleveland. NOSC

(For shame, thou everlasting Woer.) NPeEn; PBRV

For Sheridan [*with music*]. Robert Lowell. PoetW

For Sho the New Head Priest of Erin-ji. Muso Soseki. EaWin, *tr. by* W. S. Merwin

For Shunko Enjo. Philip Whalen. WANABP

For Sidney Bechet. Philip Larkin. NoP-4; NoP-5

For Simon Rodia: The sudden appearance, at once, of. Time Traveler's Potlatch. Philip Lamantia. CLPP

For Singing In Good Mood. Lebert Bethune. GT

For Sister Gwen Brooks. Sonia Sanchez. FuFl

For Sister Sue Ellen and Her Special Messenger. Toi Derricotte. ExTi

For six hundred years I have travelled. Clever Daughter, The. Susan Wicks. MFPA

For six months now I've washed her clothes. Service Wash. Deryn Rees-Jones. MFPA

For six years sitting alone. Buddha's Satori. Muso Soseki. EaWin, *tr. by* W. S. Merwin

For sixty days and upwards. Vicksburg. Paul Hamilton Hayne. PCW

For Sleep. Larry Eigner. FTOS

For Soldiers. Humphrey Gifford. FaBoWar; NoSic

For Some Future Day. Hans Andreus. TuT, *tr. by* Peter van de Kamp

For *some have entertained angels unawares.* (LL) "H. D." NALW; NAMCP V.1 *Fr.* Tribute to the Angels.

For some life is a fight. Fight and Play. Sarah Kindman. Prolet, *tr. by* Amelia Glaser

For some people the day comes. Che Fece. . .Il Gran Rifiuto. Constantine P. Cavafy. BeAl, *tr. by* Edmund Keeley and Philip Sherrard

For some semitropical reason. Tarantulas on the Lifebuoy. Thomas Lux. AmAlph

For some time I have been starving myself. Form. Colette Bryce. NIrP

For some time now, in the heart of Seoul. Story of a Sound, The. Kim Chiha. CAMKP, *tr. by* David R. McCann

For some twisted reason I. Juniper. Abbie Huston Evans. APT-1

For some we loved, the loveliest and the best. Omar Khayyám. TRP *Fr.* Rubáiyát of Omar Khayyám [of Naishápúr], The.

For some years he still would harden as he. Fall, The. Sarah Maguire. LW

For Song. Gerald Stern. BBASP

For South Bronx. Sandra Maria Esteves. PueRic

For sport my *Julia* threw a Lace. Silken Snake, The. Robert Herrick. PBRV

For Spring, by Sandro Botticelli, in the Accademia of Florence. Dante Gabriel Rossetti. GS

For Stuart Porter, Who Asked for a Poem That Would Not Depress Him Further. Jeffrey Skinner. PBCAP

For sunlight on the garden. (LL) Sunlight on the Garden, The. Louis MacNeice. HarvBoo; NAEL-6v2; NAEL-7v2; NAMCP V.1; NoP-4; NoP-5; NPeEn; OxAEP-2; PNI; TRP; WaAnP; WoPoe

For sure, *circa Regna tonat.* (LL) Who list his wealth and ease retain. Sir Thomas Wyatt. NAEL-7v1; NoSic

For Survival. Andrée Chedid. HAWP, *tr. by* Marie Ponsot

For Suzuki Roshi. Diane Di Prima. WANABP

For Sweet Honey in the Rock. Sonia Sanchez. FuFl

For T. S. E. Only. Hyam Plutzik. APT-2; TaR

For Taihei Osho. Muso Soseki. EaWin, *tr. by* W. S. Merwin

For Talking [Saint Didacus, 1968]. Denise Nico Leto. UnSA

For Teen-Age Boys Murdered in Texas: The Refusal to Dramatize Bloodlust. Kelly Cherry. LPSFW

For Tetsu the New Head Priest of Erin-ji. Muso Soseki. EaWin, *tr. by* W. S. Merwin

For That He Looked Not upon Her. George Gascoigne. NoP-4; NoP-5 (You must not wonder, though you think it strange.) GSo

For that I never knew you, I only learned to dread you. St. Roach. Muriel Rukeyser. PLBUT

For that is his knock at the door! (LL) Love Versus Learning. Constance Naden. ViWPN; VWP

For that rare, random descent. (LL) Black Rook in Rainy Weather. Sylvia Plath. BrAP; NIL-7; NoP-4

For that reason / I am a true Russian! (LL) Babii Yar. Yevgeny Aleksandrovich Yevtushenko. HP; VCWP, *tr. by* George Reavey

For That Reason We Are Also Not Obliged to Polish the Claws, Horns, and Weather Vanes. Hans Arp. MotU, *tr. by* Walter Howell III

For that you never acknowledged me, I acknowledge. Desdichada. Muriel Rukeyser. StAl

For the Angry White Student Who Wanted to Know. Wendy Rose. FTtHH

For the Anniversary Day of One's Conversion. Charles Wesley. SacPr

For the Anniversary of My Death. W. S. Merwin. BeAl; CAP-8; ColAP; GoPo; NAMCP V.2; OxBoAm; PoPoPo; VCAP; WaAnP

For the Assignment of the Spirit. Robert Duncan. WhBo

For the Baptist. William Drummond of Hawthornden. *See* Saint John Baptist.

For the Baptiste. William Drummond of Hawthornden. NPeEn; OxBEV; PBRV

For the Barn at Bread Loaf. William Stafford. BodElec

For the Barren Woman. Desanka Maksimovic. GI, *tr. by* Ivo Soljan

For the Beach Gulls. Po Chü-i. NDACCP, *tr. by* David Hinton

For the beauty of the earth. F. S. Pierpoint. SacPr

For the bees keep buzzing around the meat. City's Coat of Arms, The. László Nagy. IQMS, *tr. by* Adam Makkai

For the beginning and the end. Meditations 1. Duriel Harris. BtF

For the black plunge-line nightdress. (LL) Skunk, The. Seamus Heaney. NAEL-6v2; NAEL-7v2; NoP-4; NoP-5; StAl; WaAnP

For the blue flash and the moments. Ezra Pound. APT-1 *Fr.* Cantos.

For the Bones of Josef Mengele, Disinterred June 1985. Robert Bringhurst. NIP-4

For the breast. (LL) Miriam's Song. Eleanor Wilner. FiBr; TaR

For the Brothers Who Aint Here. Ras Baraka. InTrad

For the Bullies of West Morris High. Steven Cramer. PoA 2002

For the bursting forth of joys. (LL) Rain at Noon-time. Molara Ogundipe-Leslie. CFP; HAWP

For the caged bird / sings of freedom. (LL) Caged Bird. Maya Angelou. BrAP; WeW-3

For the Calvinists. Ben Howard. PoA 2002

For the Children. Gary Snyder. BeAl

For the Children or the Grown-ups? *Unknown.* OBCP

For the clouds above the garden in Papenburg. Homesick. Helmut Heissenbüttel. CLPP, *tr. by* Jerome Rothenberg

For the Color of My Mother. Cherríe Moraga. UnSA

For the Common Market. Michael Burn. OBCoV

For the Company Underground. Francis MacNamara. NOBAu

For the correct / yes. (LL) In Celebration of My Uterus. Anne Sexton. CAP-8; NALW

For the country will bring us no peace. (LL) Raleigh Was Right. William Carlos Williams. NIL-7; NIP-4; NoAM; PoA 2002; WaAnP; WoPoe

For the Courtesan Ch'ing Lin. Wu Tsao. WoPoe, *tr. by* Chung Ling and Kenneth Rexroth

For the cracked dish. Still Life with Endings. Ray Gonzalez. TouFir

For the cricket (nightingale of the field) and oak. Anyte. SaLy, *tr. by* Diane Rayor

For the cry from the well of "mama!" Irina Ratushinskaya. ItGoST, *tr. by* David McDuff

For the D. Anthony McNeill. WaCA

For the Dancer of the King of Wu, When She Is Half Drunk. Li Po. CCL1; TAL, *tr. by* Robert Payne

For the Dead. Kevin Prufer. AmPoNex

For the Dead Lecturer. Diane Di Prima. BB

For the Death of a Monk. Muso Soseki. EaWin, *tr. by* W. S. Merwin

For the Death of Vince Lombardi. James Dickey. MoASP

For the delights hereafter. (LL) Curse the Thorns of Fate. Rûhî. OLP; WoPoe, *tr. by* Walter Andrews, Najaat Black and Mehmet Kalpakli

For the dim regions whence my father[s] came. Outcast. Claude McKay. APT-1; NAAPv.2; NAMCP V.1; OxAAAP

For the disciple nothing had changed. The mood was still. John Ashbery. FTOS

For the doubling of flowers is the improvement of the gard'ner's talent. Christopher Smart. ChIV-2; NPeEn *Fr.* Jubilate Agno.

For the Drowned. Nick Norwood. TiP2

For the Drunk. Carole Oles. OPRER

For the end of the story sucks. Not air. Ground beneath Us, The. Patricia Goedicke. ExTi

For the eyes of the children. Sorrow Song. Lucille Clifton. BodElec; CFP

For the fairest maid in Hampton. Changeling, The. John Greenleaf Whittier. MakPoe

For the Fallen. Laurence Binyon. NPeEn; OBEV; OBWP "They went with songs to the battle, they were young." FaBoWar

For the Far-Out Experimental Writer. Víctor Hernández Cruz. PueRic

For the Father of Sandro Gulotta. Janet Lewis. APT-2

For the Field. Robyn Selman. TaR

For the Fighters—A Lament. Ayin Tur-Malka. NRoS, *tr. by* Esther Raizen

For the first time, I listen to a lost. Then. Roddy Lumsden. NeBl

For the first time in months. Grief Comes in Smallest Ways. Gailmarie Pahmeier. SweBea

For the first time in seven years. We Meet Again. Valerie Gillies. EdScPo

For the first time in what must be. Evening's End. Leon Stokesbury. BAP-97

For the first time, now for the first time seen. (LL) Green. D. H. Lawrence. HarvBoo; MoBrPo

For the first time she loved him from her heart. (LL) Return of Persephone, The. Alec Derwent Hope. BMAP; BrAP

For the first time since anyone remembers. Rhapsody on Main Street. Patrick Williams. PNI

For the first time the only. Rescue. James Tate. YaYoPo

For the first twenty years [or yeares], since yesterday. Computation, The. John Donne. NoSic; SoSe-8

For the first two years of her life I tried to kill her. For My Sister. Jannifer Traig. FTtHH

For the foul magenta of its gorgeous heart. (LL) Skunk Cabbage. Eric Ormsby. NoP-4; NoP-5

For the Fourth of July. Eliza Lee Cabot Follen. SWaP

For the Freedom Train. (LL) Dream Boogie: Variation. Langston Hughes. APSN; NAMCP V.1; OxBoAm; SSLK

For the Good of the Pythian Order. Mrs. Henry Linden. CBWP-4

For the Grave of a Peace-Loving Man. Hans Magnus Enzensberger. VCWP, tr. by the author, Hans Magnus Enzensberger and Michael Hamburger

For the Grave of Daniel Boone. William Stafford. NAMCP V.2

For the great flint to come singing into his heart. (LL) Bushed. Earle Birney. BrAP; NoAM; NoP-4; NoP-5

For the Great Zen Master Sagum. Jinkag Haesim. BecRai, tr. by Kim Daljin, Kim Won-Chung and Christopher Merrill

For the great-eyed sunflower you gave us. Song of the Tower of Skulls. Vasco [or Vasko] Popa. WoPoe, tr. by Anne Pennington

For the green turtle with her pulsing burden. Lament. Gillian Clarke. HarvBoo; TCAWP

For the guy too poor to be able to have a woman. I'm Writing a Poem. Emile Célestin-Mégie. OGAHCP, tr. by Boadiba and Jack Hirschman

For the historical ache, the ache passed down. To a Terrorist. Stephen Dunn. RaF

For The Holy Family, by Michelangelo, in the National Gallery. Dante Gabriel Rossetti. SacPr

For the huge. Whirl Wind Must, The. George Oppen. BodElec

For the Intellectuals. Jeremy Ingalls. YaYoPo

For the Jim Crow Mexican Restaurant in Cambridge, Massachusetts, Where My Cousin Esteban was Forbidden to Wait Tables Because He Wears Dreadlocks. Martín Espada. PrTe

For the Lady Olivia Porter; a Present upon a New Year's Day. Sir William Davenant. NOSC

For the Last Summer. Robert Wrigley. SwNoth

For the last time I wash the shirt. I Wash the Shirt. Anna Swirszczynska [or Swir]. BLT

For the Late R. F. Thom Gunn. VisFro

For the life. My Least Skirtable Deficiency. HeidiLynn Nilsson. NeAmPo

For the life of her she couldn't decide what to wear to the. For the Life of Him and Her. Reed Whittemore. GoPo

For the long wait till our meeting. (LL) Wings and Seeds: For My Birth Mother. Sandra McPherson. LoL; PoA 2002

For the Lord of Caves. Allama Prabhu. PFTM-1

For the Lordes parte is his folke. Bible, O.T. OBVE Fr. Deuteronomy.

For the love of his girlfriend. Van Gogh's Ear. Ismail. HotL, tr. by V. Narayana Rao

For the love of Mike! Café du Dôme. Else Von Freytag-Loringhoven. APT-1; SurPaPo

For the Lover. Maria Luisa B. Aguilar-Cariño. ReBoTo

For the Magdalene. William Drummond of Hawthornden. ChIV-2

For the Man I Met on Georgia Ave. Matthew Watley. BtF

For the man was she made by the Eden tree. Ballade of Lovers. May Probyn. VWP

For the man who. Robert Sheppard. Oth Fr. Empty Diaries/Twentieth Century Blues 24.

For the Marriage of Faustus and Helen. Hart Crane. APT-2; NoAM; OxBoAm

For the mighty wind arises, roaring seaward, and I go. (LL) Locksley Hall. Alfred Tennyson. NAEL-6v2; NAEL-7v2

For the Missing in Action. John Balaban. AF

For the Moment. Belkis Cuza Malé. TANSG, tr. by Pamela Carmell

For the moment, we've run out of starry nights. For the Moment. Belkis Cuza Malé. TANSG, tr. by Pamela Carmell

For the Nativity. John Heath-Stubbs. ChrPo

For the New York City Poet Who Informed Me That Few People Live This Way. Jeff Gundy. IllVoic

For the next legation I bite. Melanin. J. H. Prynne. PFTM-2

For the Old Highlands. Douglas Young. EdScPo

For the one. 'No' Madonnas, The. Gwyneth Lewis. TCAWP

For the One Who Would Take Man's Life in His Hands. Delmore Schwartz. MoAmPo

For the Other World. Ray Gonzalez. PoDa

For the Passing of Groucho's Pursuer. John Hollander. PoA 2002

For the people of that flow. George Oppen. NAMCP V.1 Fr. Of Being Numerous.

For the Pileated Woodpecker and Its Cousin, the Ivory-Billed, Who May or May Not Be Extinct. Lucia Maria Perillo. RoV

For the Poet Who Said Poets Are Struck by Lightning Only Two or Three Times [with music]. Peter Klappert. NBLV

For the Poets. Jayne Cortez. InoFa; PmAP

For the poet's biography. Poet's Biography. Belkis Cuza Malé. TANSG, tr. by Pamela Carmell

For the Poorman's nosegay is an introduction to a Prince. (LL) Christopher Smart. ChIV-2; NPeEn Fr. Jubilate Agno.

For the present there is just one moon. Present, The. Michael Donaghy. BeAl

For the Primer of Senior High. Hans Magnus Enzensberger. GTCP, tr. by Reinhold Grimm and Felix Pollak

For the Princess Hello. David Shapiro. OxBoAm

For the Reader (Blank Book). Laura Mullen. ExTi

For the Recluse Wei Pa. Tu Fu [or Du Fu]. NDACCP, tr. by David Hinton

For the Record. Audre Lorde. ESEAA; InoFa

For the Record. Roy McFadden. PNI

For the Record. Adrienne Rich. NIL-7; NIP-4; VCAP

For the sake of a Turkish woman from Shiraz, consumed in the deadly fumes. Ghazal. Mariya Galina. CRWP, tr. by Daniel Weissbort

For the Sake of Man. Mun Chônghui. EcSo, tr. by Catherine J. Kim

For the Sake of Man Again. Mun Chônghui. EcSo, tr. by Catherine J. Kim

For the sake of others, / disappear. (LL) Traveling Onion, The. Naomi Shihab Nye. AFaM; CAP-8; IPoFL; LoL

For the sake of the fleabane growing rose a little. Hats. Paul Muldoon and Gerald Stern. GPPA

For the Sake of Two Screws. Yi Yônju. EcSo, tr. by Yung-Hee Kim

For the sea. By which I mean the "open" sea. (LL) Briefcase, The. Paul Muldoon. CABP; NAMCP V.2

For the Second Time in Thirty-Three Years. Ch'oe Sûngja. EcSo, tr. by Mickey Hong

For the seven lakes, and by no man these verses. Ezra Pound. APT-1; PFTM-1 Fr. Cantos.

For the Seventh Day. Sandor Csoori. TAPaP, tr. by Len Roberts

For the shore, my heart beating in my mouth. (LL) Breaded Fish. A. K. Ramanujan. NoP-4; NoP-5

For the silence. (LL) High Noon at Los Alamos. Eleanor Wilner. AtGh; NoP-4; NoP-5

For the Sisters of the Hôtel Dieu. Abraham Moses Klein. BrAP; NoP-4

For the site of the Kingdom of Heaven. (LL) Loss of something ever felt I, A. Emily Dickinson. ChIV-2; NALW; NCAP

For the Sleepwalkers. Edward Hirsch. IllVoic; SUP

For the sound we revere. For Art Blakey and the Jazz Messengers. Keorapetse Kgositsile. SeSe

For the Spartan Dead at Thermopylai (480 B.C.). Simonides. PoAgWa, tr. by Peter Jay

For the Stepford Girl Groups. MiVo

For the Taking. Linda Gregerson. AmAlph

For the Thing we call Moon contains. Chords Passages 14. Robert Duncan. FTOS

For the three dead children. (LL) Lament for Tadhg Cronin's Children. Egan O'Rahilly. ModIr; PBCIP; WoPoe, tr. by Michael Hartnett

For the Time Being; a Christmas Oratorio. W. H. Auden.
Flight into Egypt, The.
After Christmas. ChrPo; MoBrPo; OBCP

For the train-wrecked, the puck-struck. One Petition Lofted into the Ginkgos. Gabriel Gudding. PoDa

For the Tree to Sing. Vladimir Alekseievich Soloukhin. TCRusP, tr. by Daniel Weissbort

For the Twentieth Century. Frank Bidart. KGB; OxBoAm

For the unbidden swish of morning curtains. Thankyou Note. Dannie Abse. TCAWP

For the Unfortunates. Kevin Prufer. LegDan

For the Union Dead. Robert Lowell. AmWaPo; BrAP; CAP-8; CBCWP; ColAP; EMP; FaBoA; HarvBoo; HeIP-4; NAAL-5; NAMCP V.2; NoAM; NoP-4; NoP-5; OBWP; OxBoAm; PoetW; PoPoPo; PtR; TFi; TRP; VCAP; WaAnP; WeW-3

For the voyage of oblivion awaits you. (LL) Ship of Death, The ("Now it is autumn and the falling fruit.") D. H. Lawrence. BrAP; GPTC; MoBrPo; NAEL-6v2; NAEL-7v2; NAMCP V.1; NoAM; NoP-4; NoP-5; OxAEP-2; OxBEV

For the Wandering Jews. Philip Schultz. TaR

For the way that plantains move in the rain. Plantains. Tu Mu. CCL1, tr. by R. F. Burton

For the White Lady Holding Me. Crystal Williams. AmPoNex

For the White Poets Who Would Be Indian. Wendy Rose. CalPo

For the white wine and red. (LL) Wine Bowl. "H. D." NoP-4; NoP-5

For the white-limbed heroes of Hellas ride by upon their horses. Ford Madox Ford. FaBoWar Fr. Antwerp.

For 'The Wine of Circe' by Edward Burne Jones. Dante Gabriel Rossetti. UV

For the Woman Who Dressed Up to Listen to Gigli on the Radio. Jane Duran. MFPA

For the Woman with the Radio. Malena Mörling. AmPoNex

For the word of God is a sword on my side—no matter what other weapon a stick or a straw. Christopher Smart. BBASP *Fr.* Jubilate Agno.

For the word which burns like Joan at the stake. Humble Litany. Aida Cartagena de Portalatin. TANSG, *tr. by* Emma Jane Robinett

For thee, and for myself, no quiet find. (LL) William Shakespeare. AWTN; CAGL; HeIP-4; NoSic *Fr.* Sonnets.

For thee I shall not die. I Shall Not Die for Thee. *Irish Oral Tradition.* IrV, *tr. by* Douglas Hyde

For thee was a house built. *Unknown.* TCAPo *Fr.* From the Anglo-Saxon.

For them to move. I want to see them again. (LL) Joy Addict, The. James Harms. NAPBL; NeAmPo

For there is no God found stronger than death; and death is a sleep. (LL) Hymn to Proserpine. Algernon Charles Swinburne. NAEL-6v2; NAEL-7v2

For there is one thing braver than all flowers. William Carlos Williams. PoA 2002

For these dead Birds sigh a prayer. (LL) Phoenix and the Turtle, The. William Shakespeare. NoP-5; NoSic; OBEV; OxAEP-1; OxBEV

For these I feel,—and feel that they are Love. (LL) Describes the Characteristics of Love. Mary Robinson. CenSon; RWP

For these vines. (LL) Vespers: "In your extended absence, you permit me." Louise Glück. CAP-8; OxBoAm

For they appeal from tyranny to God. (LL) Sonnet on Chillon. Lord Byron. CenSon; GSo; NPBRoP

For they know when their Shepherd is nigh. (LL) William Blake. ChAP; NPBRoP *Fr.* Songs of Innocence.

For they were deep in the earth and what is possible swiftly took hold. (LL) Orpheus and Eurydice. Jorie Graham. OxBoAm; VCAP

For Thieves Only. Lois Red Elk. ReEnLa

For thine is the kingdom / the power. D. H. Lawrence. GI

For thine own Duplicity. (LL) "Heavenly Father"—take to thee. Emily Dickinson. APN-2; InvLi

For things we never mention. Broken Men, The. Rudyard Kipling. HarvBoo

For thirteen days / she had threatened / and forced me dark. Friendly Town #3. Safiya Henderson-Holmes. UnSA

For thirty years. Teacher of Defeated Hebrew Language. Eitan Kalinski. NRoS, *tr. by* Esther Raizen

For thirty-five years, Father, you were a numb-fish. Embrace of the Electric Eel. Pascale Petit. Prnts

For this agility chance found. Ezra Pound. TCAPo *Fr.* Hugh Selwyn Mauberley (Life and Contacts).

For this and for all enclosures like it the archetype. Cave of Making, The. W. H. Auden. FaBoVe; OxAEP-2

For this, as well, I love black cypress; and I love. Cypress. Aleksandr Semionovich Kushner. ItGoST, *tr. by* Paul Graves and Carol Ueland

For this hell. Garden. Marina Ivanovna Tsvetaeva. RusPo, *tr. by* Robert Arthur Douglas Ford

For this I will be thine, my love! for this I will be thine! (LL) Chamois Hunter's Love, The. Felicia Dorothea Hemans. RWP; VWP

For this is the day of joy. Gaudeamus Igitur: A Valediction. John A. Stone. BloBone

For this particular silence. (LL) Memory of Elena, The. Carolyn Forché. LoL; NAMCP V.2; NoAM

For this poor wreath, give Thee a crown of praise. (LL) Wreath, A. George Herbert. NOSC; NPeEn

For this she starred her eyes with salt. Epitaph. Elinor Wylie. MoAmPo

For this you get a degree in the government. Deeply Immoral Arrogant and Ignorant. Joanne Kyger. Eno

For this your mother sweated in the cold. To Jesus on His Birthday. Edna St. Vincent Millay. ChIV-2; HeIP-4

For Thomas Moore. James Simmons. PBCIP

For Those Dead, Our Dead. Ernesto Cardenal. PoetW, *tr. by* Jonathan Cohen

For Those my unbaptized Rhymes [*or* Rhimes]. His Prayer for Absolution. Robert Herrick. SacPr

(For those my unbaptized rhymes.) CavPo

For those parallel destinies. Alice Rahon. SurWo, *tr. by* Nancy Deffebach and Vanina Deler

For those that never know the light. Children of the Night, The. Edwin Arlington Robinson. APN-2; NAAPv.1

For those this mausoleum is erected. Ambrose Bierce. CalPo

For those vicissitudes by which men die. (LL) La Gioconda; Leonardo Da Vinci, The Louvre. Michael Field. ViWPN

For Those Who Always Fear the Worst [*with music*]. *Unknown.* NBLV

For those who have lived. Lilacs. Sue Sinclair. Coast

For those who ran in the streets. For the Other World. Ray Gonzalez. PoDa

For Those Whom the Gods Love Less. Denise Levertov. BodElec

For those whose voices cry from ruins. City as Hero, The. Weldon Kees. PWW2

For Thoth. Martin Mooney. NIrP

For thou art not beloved. (LL) Revenge. Letitia Elizabeth Landon. NAEL-7v2; NOBRP; NPeEn

For thou didst die for me, O Son of God! Henry Hart Milman. SacPr *Fr.* Martyr of Antioch, The.

For though my rhyme be ragged. John Skelton. OBCoV *Fr.* Colin Clout.

For Though the Eaves Were Rabbeted. Henry David Thoreau. NCAP

For thoughts that curve like winging birds. I Yield Thee Praise. Philip Jerome Cleveland. SacPr

For three days. Zombie. Jean-Marie Willer Denis. OGAHCP, *tr. by* Boadiba and Jack Hirschman

For three hours I have been doing accounts. To Know Me? Jolanda Insana. CItWP, *tr. by* Cinzia Sartini Blum and Lara Trubowitz

For three years, diabolus in the scale. Ezra Pound. TCAPo *Fr.* Hugh Selwyn Mauberley (Life and Contacts).

For three years, out of key with his time. Hugh Selwyn Mauberley (Life and Contacts). Ezra Pound. APT-1; NAMCP V.1; NoAM; NoP-5

For Thurman Thomas. Reuben Jackson. ISC

For thus I leave the world, the flesh, and devil. (LL) John Donne. BASC; FaBoVe *Fr.* Holy Sonnets.

For Thus saith The Lord to the men of Judah and Jerusalem. Bible, *O.T.* OBVE *Fr.* Jeremiah.

For thy names sake, be my refuge. Voyce of Anne Askewe out of the 54. Psalme of David, Called, Deus in Nomine Tuo, The. Anne Askew. EMWP

For Thy Sake Let the World Call Me Fool. *Unknown.* SacPr

For thy soul's health to shed his dearest blood. (LL) Emilia Lanier. EMWP; NAEL-6v1; NALW; NOSC *Fr.* Salve Deus Rex Judaeorum.

For to a torche or to a taper the Trinite is likened. William Langland. SacPr *Fr.* Vision of Piers Plowman, The.

For to Admire. Rudyard Kipling. MoBrPo

For to please ourselves, truly, is more than we can. (LL) On an Unsociable Family. Elizabeth Hands. NPeEn; WoRP

For today we have naming of parts. (LL) Henry Reed. AmFaPo; BrAP; FaBoWar; MoBrPo; NAEL-6v2; NAEL-7v2; NoP-4; NoP-5; OxBEV; PoPoPo; RaBo; SoSe-8; TFi; UV; WaAnP *Fr.* Lessons of the War.

For Tom. Richard Caddel. Oth

For tomorrow's sake, don't skimp with me on wine today. Don't Skimp with Me Today. Mirza Asadullah Khan Ghalib. WED, *tr. by* Robert Bly and Sunil Dutta

For Tony, Embarking in Spring. Haniel Long. APT-1

For treuthe [*or* trewthe] telleth that love [*or* loue] is triacle to abate sinne [*or* of hevene]. William Langland. OBEV *Fr.* Vision of Piers Plowman, The.

For true report rung in his royall eares. Thomas Deloney. FaBoWar *Fr.* Destruction of Jerusalem, The.

For truth, and like the Preacher found it not. (LL) Sonnet: Lift Not the Painted Veil. Percy Bysshe Shelley. CenSon; GSo; NOBRP

For twelve days. German Army, Russia, 1943, The. Ai. MakPoe

For twenty years and more surviving after. Widows. Edgar Lee Masters. MoAmPo

For Two Children. David Malouf. BMAP

For two days I have not said a word. Seamstress, The. Zinaida Nikolayevna Gippius. ARWW, *tr. by* Catriona Kelly

For two days I've been crying. Novel, The. Richard Jones. GifTon

For Two Voices. Luis Cernuda. CAGL, *tr. by* Rick Lipinski

For Una. Robinson Jeffers. APT-1

For Uncle Jim's deep-fried, all-fat, real gone / whale steaks. (LL) Naughty Boy. Robert Creeley. HeIP-4; NAMCP V.2; NoAM

For us, all that's left. Attempt, An. Angela Ball. PoDa

For us, five writers, it's partly. Women Watching Basketball. Marisa De Los Santos. NAPBL

For us, too, there was a wish to possess. Idea, The. Mark Strand. CAP-8; NAMCP V.2; OxBoAm

For us who sometimes fly in dreams. Swinging Doors of Knocking-Wood Cowards: 8 for Us. Esther Louise. BtF

For vanished Hellas and Hebraic pain. (LL) Venus of the Louvre. Emma Lazarus. APN-2; GS; NAAPv.1; OxBoAm

For vein honour or for the worldes good. John Gower. SacPr *Fr.* Address to the King, An.

For vengeance, and the ashes of language. (LL) Lament: "For the green turtle with her pulsing burden." Gillian Clarke. HarvBoo; TCAWP

For Venus' ceston every line you make. (LL) Sonnet to the Noble Lady, the Lady Mary Wroth, A. Ben Jonson. NAEL-7v1; NoP-4; NoP-5

For vulgar praise, doth it too dearly [*or* dearely] buy. (LL) To My Book. Ben Jonson. NAEL-6v1; NAEL-7v1

For W. C. W ("Rhyme is after, The.") Robert Creeley. FTOS

For Walt Whitman. Patricia Goedicke. ViWalt

For Want. Ansel Talvikki. NeAmPo

For want of a flashlight. For Want. Ansel Talvikki. NeAmPo

For water. Samaki. Seitlhamo Motsapi. TSAP

For water-ices, cheap but good. Grace for Ice-Cream, A. Allan M. Laing. OBCoV

For we have thought the longer thoughts. Chapter Heading. Ernest Hemingway. PoA 2002

For we meet by one or the other. (LL) Choose. Carl Sandburg. Spl; StAl

For weariness my hand writes ill. Scribe, The: "For Weariness My Hand Writes Ill." *Unknown.* IrV, *tr. by* Alfred Perceval Graves

For weariness of life, not love of thee. (LL) To Heaven. Ben Jonson. BASC; ChIV-2; InvLi; NAEL-6v1; NAEL-7v1; NOSC; NPeEn; SacPr; TRP

For weeks before it comes I feel excited, yet when it. Afterthought. Elizabeth Jennings. NOxBChV; OBCP

For weeks I felt smaller and tame, as if Spanish had finally cut me down to size. Bilingual Means Having Two Tongues. David Johnson. ICANM

For weeks now. Haciendo Apenas la Recolección. Tino Villanueva. UnSA

For weeks on end it has rained in Texas. Red Raging Waters, The. Larry D. Thomas. TiP2

For weeks the poem of your body. Poem Unwritten, The. Denise Levertov. CAP-8

For weeks we've been promising. Miscarriage, Midwinter. Kate Clanchy. MoWP

For wele or wo I wyl not flee. *Unknown.* OHMEL

For what contend the wise?—for nothing less. William Wordsworth. SacPr *Fr.* Ecclesiastical Sonnets.

For What For Whom Unwanted. Brian Coffey.
  "And where now snow had." ModIr
  "Consider his song." ModIr

For what I gave. (LL) Tale of Sunlight, The. Gary Soto. CAP-8; NoAM

For What It's Worth. Benjamin Theolonius Sanders. BRtP

For what it's worth: Jacob Louslinger, white haired, stinking, dirty bearded. William Carlos Williams. MotU *Fr.* Kora in Hell.

For what service I was to the people! (LL) Edgar Lee Masters. NAAPv.1; NAMCP V.1; NoAM *Fr.* Spoon River Anthology.

For what the world admires I'll wish no more. Resolve, The. Mary Lee, Lady Chudleigh. BrAP

For what we owe to other days. Exit. Edwin Arlington Robinson. MoAmPo

For what we still had to lose. (LL) Take Good Care of Yourself. Mark Wunderlich. NeAmPo; ReTh; WiU

For Whatever Animals Dwell on Earth. Petrarch. AWTN, *tr. by* Robert M. Durling

For whatever did it—the cider. Cure at Porlock, A. Amy Clampitt. NoAM

For which the intricate Alps are a single nest. (LL) Connoisseur of Chaos. Wallace Stevens. NAAPv.2; PFTM-1

For which the sun sometimes music on vast sky of open. For Which the Sun. Danielle Collobert. YaTCFP, *tr. by* Michael Tweed

For whisper and orchestra. Eduard Veniaminovich Limonov. TCRusP *Fr.* Secret Notebook.

For Whitman. Diane Wakoski. ViWalt

For Who? [*with music*]. Mary Weston Fordham. CBWP-2

For Whom. Jonathan Denwood. RSaN

For whom and what is this foul slaughter done? For Whom. Jonathan Denwood. RSaN

For Whom the Bells Toll and Toll and Toll. John Nelson. GeoH

For whom the possessed sea littered, on both shores. Requiem for the Plantagenet Kings. Geoffrey Hill. CABP; NAEL-6v2; NAEL-7v2; NoAM

For whom there is no ornament. (LL) Nativity Poem. Louise Glück. GI; HarvBoo

For whore and rogue; and dog and bitch. (LL) Epigram on Scolding, An. Jonathan Swift. FaBoVe; NPeEn

For Whose Delight. Gael Turnbull. EdScPo

For Wilfred Owen. Freda Downie. StAl

For William Stafford. Henry Taylor. PoA 2002

For Willyce. Patricia Parker. PoBW

For Wine Drinkers. Bálint Balassi. IQMS, *tr. by* René Bonnerjea

For wishing to be King. (LL) Silvio's Complaint: A Song, to a Fine Scotch Tune. Aphra Behn. EMWP; RACG

For with his nail[e]s he'll dig them up again [*or* agen]. (LL) John Webster. NOSC; NPeEn; OxAEP-1; OxBEV; TFi *Fr.* White Devil, The.

For women grieve to think[e] they must be old[e]. (LL) Samuel Daniel. NoSic; OBEV *Fr.* Sonnets to Delia.

For words want art and art wants words to praise her. George Chapman. OxBSo *Fr.* Coronet for His Mistress Philosophy, A.

For years after we left Puerto Rico for the last time, I would wake. Immigrants. Aurora Levins Morales. PueRic

For years and years. Rivière du Loup. Alfred Goldsworthy Bailey. Coast

For years, copying other people, I tried to know myself. Jelaluddin Rumi. IJHIL, *tr. by* Coleman Barks and John Moyne

For years he had heard his father talk about work, about carbon. Black Light. Peter Markus. AmPoNex

For years he's gone over her parting words. No, Go On. Maura Dooley. LW

For years I dug in the earth. Muso Soseki. EaWin, *tr. by* W. S. Merwin

For years I fantasized pain. Beauty and the Beast. Olga Broumas. YaYoPo

For years I lived with the thought. Missing. Gardner McFall. OtW

For years I thought I knew, at the bottom of the dream. Meeting, The. Louise Bogan. NoAM

For years I wanted to trade. Falling for Jesus. Enid Shomer. OPRER

For years I was doomed to worship a contemptible woman. Viper, The. Nicanor Parra. TCLAP, *tr. by* W. S. Merwin

For years it was land working me, oil fields. 3 A.M. Kitchen: My Father Talking. Tess Gallagher. LaCa

For years my father practiced the violin. For Years My Father. Robert Alexander. MAAN

For years my heart asked me for Jamshid's cup. Ghazal 24: For Years My Heart Asked Me for Jamshid's Cup. Khwaja Shams-ad-din Muhammad Hafiz. WoPoe, *tr. by* Elizabeth Gray

For years now I have heard the cracking of. Studying Physics with My Daughter. Jeanne Murray Walker. WeW-3

For years, so long, I had imagined. West Pitch at the Falls. Marsden Hartley. APT-1

For years the dead. Change, The. Denise Levertov. BAP-97

For years the drops of belladonna in our eyes. Possible Man, The. A. V. Christie. NAPBL

For years the old Italians have been dying. Old Italians Dying, The. Lawrence Ferlinghetti.

For years they came in wonder, filing past. East of Easter. Neil Astley. RSaN

For years we scavenged among the dark sands. Hollow, The. Ricardo Pau-Llosa. Vesp

For You. Ted Berrigan. AHA

For You. Prince Otsu. AHA

For You. Carl Sandburg. MoAmPo

For you, Aitana child. Going Up the Rivers. Rafael Alberti. RaW, *tr. by* Rachel Benson

For you, be there. (LL) My Spirit Will Not Haunt the Mound. Thomas Hardy. FaBoVe; MoBrPo

For you beautiful ones my mind. Sappho. SaLy, *tr. by* Diane Rayor

For you fleas too. Avedik Issahakian. ChAP

For you, for you I am trilling these songs. (LL) For You O Democracy. Walt Whitman. APN-1; CAGL; UV

For you, I cry this paper down into words on Black feminism. For a Woman's Rights. Joette Harland-Watts. InTrad

For you I have emptied the meaning. Louis Zukofsky. NoAM

For you I have slept. Michael Ondaatje. NoP-4 *Fr.* Rock Bottom.

For you I have stored up an ocean of thought. Thinking of Someone. "Hsiung Hung." CFP, *tr. by* Chung Ling and Kenneth Rexroth

For you, little trumpet. Ode to the Computer. Inna L'vovna Lisnyanskaya. CRWP, *tr. by* Ruth Fainlight

For You, My Son. Horace Gregory. MoAmPo

For You O Democracy. Walt Whitman. APN-1; CAGL; UV

For you, O gulls. Richard Wright. APT-2

For you, *Robert*. It means *bright fame*. (LL) Early Morning Test Light over Nevada, 1955. Robert Vasquez. AtGh; GeoHom

For you to live, who need our merest touch. (LL) Richard Murphy. BeAl; ModIr *Fr.* Price of Stone, The.

For you too, my fleas. Issa. SoOfWa, *tr. by* Sam Hamill

For You, Walt Whitman. William Stafford. ViWalt

For you who loved me too. For Fugitives. Frank Templeton Prince. HarvBoo

For Your Birthday, Philip: And upon the Occasion of Becoming Abbot of the Hartford Street Zen Center. Joanne Kyger. WANABP

For your fleas too. Issa. EH, *tr. by* Robert Hass

For your offence. (LL) Thomas Lodge. NoSic; OBEV *Fr.* Rosalynde; or Euphues' Golden Legacy.

For Zenshin Ryufu Philip Whalen. Michael McClure. WANABP *Fr.* Haiku Rows.

Forbear bold Youth. Answer to Another Persuading a Lady to Marriage, An. Katherine Philips. WeW-3

Forbear, thou great good husband, little ant. Ant, The. Richard Lovelace. BASC

Forbearance. Samuel Taylor Coleridge. ChIV-2

Forbecause a prisoner lies. Ja Nul Homs Pris Ne Ira a Raison. Richard I, Coeur de Lion. WoPoe, *tr. by* Frank Templeton Prince

Forbid! Marcelijus Martinaitis. TWW, *tr. by* Laima Sruoginis

Forbid / Kukutis to drive. Forbid! Marcelijus Martinaitis. TWW, *tr. by* Laima Sruoginis

Forbidden. Unoma Nguemo Azuah. NeNiPo

Forbidden Love. Elizabeth Daryush. PoBW

Forbidden Sea. Blaga Dimitrova.
    8. CSCBP, *tr.* by Georgi Belev and Lisa Sapinkopf
    18. CSCBP, *tr.* by Georgi Belev and Lisa Sapinkopf

Forbidden to speak. Basho. EMJL, *tr.* by Haruo Shirane

Forc'd from home, and all its pleasures. Negro's Complaint, The. William Cowper. CABP; ItP

Force. *Unknown.* OBCoV *Fr.* Advertising Rhymes.

Force in the firmament, the strength in the green shoots, The. (LL) In Berlin, August 1945: Lehrte Bahnhof. Alun Llywelyn-Williams. BBMWP; OBWVE, *tr.* by Joseph P. Clancy

Force of Gravity, The. Luiza Neto Jorge. SurWo, *tr.* by Jean R. Longland

Force of Love, The. Samuel Jones. NPeEn

Force of reason, who shut up the shrill. Athena. Amy Clampitt. PoA 2002

Force That through the Green Fuse Drives the Flower, The. Dylan Thomas. BrAP; CABP; HarvBoo; MoBrPo; NAEL-6v2; NAEL-7v2; NAMCP V.2; NoAM; NoP-4; NoP-5; NPeEn; OBWVE; OxAEP-2; OxBEV; PtR; TFi; WaAnP

Forced Labour. Manuel González Prada. SonAtl, *tr.* by Dave French, Lisa Martin and Lisandro Pena

Forced March. Miklós Radnóti. AF

Forced March. Miklós Radnóti. IQMS, *tr.* by Peter Zollman

Forced March ("He is a fool who, collapsed on the ground, gets up and walks on.") Miklós Radnóti. ConPit, *tr.* by Clayton Eshleman and Gyula Kodolanyi

Forced March in Summer. Yehoshua Zafrir. NRoS, *tr.* by Esther Raizen

Forced Music, A. Robert Graves. MoBrPo

Forced Recruit, The. Elizabeth Barrett Browning. FaBoWar

Forced Retirement. Nikki Giovanni. PfS

Forced to cuddle but some heirloom of power and peril it must be. Token Enabler. Anselm Berrigan. BAP-04

Forces. Jean Valentine. LaCa

Forces, The. Michael C. Blumenthal. PML

Forces of Production. Nirasana Kavulu. HotL, *tr.* by V. Narayana Rao

Ford Castle: The Borders. Geoffrey Holloway. NLP

Ford Manor. Derek Mahon. PBCIP

Ford of Ch'u, knot for three Hsiang waters. Floating on the River Han. Wang Wei. ChinPo, *tr.* by Ye Weilian [*or* Yeh Wei-lien *or* Wai-lim Yip]

Ford pickup, painted red but rusted, straddled, The. I-35, South of Waco. William Virgil Davis. TiP2

Fording the River. Seamus Deane. PBCIP; PNI

Fore and Aft. Robert Montgomery. STuOW *Fr.* Omnipresence of the Deity, The.

Foreboding, The. Robert Graves. PoA 2002

Forecast. Kelly Cherry. RWB

Forecast. Duncan Forbes. RWPCtW

Forecast. Josephine Miles. NoAM

Forecast for a Quiet Night. Robin Fulton. EdScPo

Forecast: Nadja. Susan Elmslie. IFF

Forefathers. Edmund Charles Blunden. NoP-4; NoP-5; OBEV; OBMV

Forehead, Eyes, Cheeks, Nose, Mouth, and Chin. Mother Goose. FaBoVe

Forehead of No. (LL) Mind's Disguise, The. Rosalie Moore. APT-2; YaYoPo

Foreheads linked like antlers of furious elk. Your mouth and mine meshed. Fusion of Shadows, A. Marco Antonio Montes de Oca. MotU, *tr.* by Brian Swann

Foreign. Kate Clanchy. MFPA

Foreign. Carol Ann Duffy. HarvBoo

Foreign Address, The. Edward Young.
    With a Yo, Ho, Ho. STuOW
    Ye Nations, Tremble! Parliament has Met. STuOW

Foreign Game, A. Joseph Somoza. ICANM

Foreign Gate, The. Sidney Keyes.
    "Moon is a poor woman, The." NoP-4; NoP-5; OBWP

Foreign Land. Greta Knutson. SurWo, *tr.* by Penelope Rosemont

Foreign Relations. Fergus Allen. NIrP

Foreign Ruler, A. Walter Savage Landor. OBSV; OxBEV

Foreign Ways. Diana Chang. UnSA

Foreigner, A. Witter Bynner. APT-1

Foreigner Who Died in Juchitán, The. Pancho Na'car. WoPoe, *tr.* by Brian Swann

Foreigners, The. John Tutchin. BASC

Foreman drives by the fields counting his pickers, A. Campesinos. Juan Delgado. GeoHom

Foremost of false philosophies. Sea, False Philosophy. Laura Riding Jackson. APT-2

Forenoon. Summer Insects Described. James Thomson. NPeEn *Fr.* Seasons, The.

Forensics. Ben Doyle. LegDan

Foreplay. Tony Gloeggler. NevBe

Foreplay. Natasha Josefowitz. PasH

Forerunner. Raymond R. Patterson. FuFl

Forerunners. Ralph Waldo Emerson. APN-1; OBEV

Forerunners, The. George Herbert. AngWePo; FSCP; NAEL-6v1; NAEL-7v1; NoP-4; NoP-5; PBRV

Foreseen for so many years: these evils, this monstrous violence. May-June, 1940. Robinson Jeffers. MoAmPo

37. Foresees Her Death. Mary Robinson. CenSon; NPBRoP; RWP *Fr.* Sappho and Phaon.

Foresight. Lincoln Kirstein. OBWP; PoWW

Forest. Priscilla Borthwick. Prnts

Forest, The. Miroslav Holub. PoSu, *tr.* by George Theiner

Forest, The. Susan Stewart. AmAlph

Forest Divers. Frank O'Hara. BodElec

Forest drips and glows with green, The. Rainforest. Judith Wright. OPOU

Forest Family. Lawson Fusao Inada. WhBo

Forest grew drowsy, The. Chrysalis. Francisco Segovia. RMCMP, *tr.* by Michael Wiegers

Forest Hymn. William Cullen Bryant. TreFP *Fr.* Forest Hymn, A.

Forest Hymn, A. William Cullen Bryant. APN-1
    Forest Hymn. TreFP

Forest in winter, The! From edge to edge. Konstantin Iakovlevich Vanshenkin. TCRusP, *tr.* by Daniel Weissbort

Forest is crowded and a wounded, The. Chicago Blues. Rohan B. Preston. AmPoNex

Forest keeps its whole self to itself, The. Vegetal Animus. Francisco Segovia. RMCMP, *tr.* by Michael Wiegers

Forest Lake. Edith Södergran. WPoS, *tr.* by Stina Katchadourian

Forest Leaves in Autumn. John Keble.
    November. OBEV

Forest Murmurs [*after* Eduard Mörike]. Eduard Friedrich Mörike. WoPoe, *tr.* by Randall Jarrell

Forest of Tangle, The. Charles Causley. BeAl

Forest of the Dead, The. James Griffyth Fairfax. PoWW

Forest Road, The. Charlotte Mew. VWP

Forest Trees of the Sea. *Unknown.* WoPoe, *tr.* by Alfons L. Korn and Mary Kawena Pukui

Forest Utilization. Anthony Barnett. OnScMo

Forest would start when you held my hand, The. Melih Cevdet Anday. NaPG *Fr.* Horses Before Troy.

Forests and Caverns. Eleanor Percy Lee and Catherine Anne Warfield. SWaP

Forests and State Forests, all down off the steeper country; mosquitoes are always living in there. Les A. Murray. NAMCP V.2 *Fr.* Buladelah-Taree Holiday Song Cycle, The.

Forests are branches of a tree lying down. Flying Home from Utah. May Swenson. OtW

Forests break off. Mountains stretch on still. River Song, The. Wang Yung. ChinPo, *tr.* by Ye Weilian [*or* Yeh Wei-lien *or* Wai-lim Yip]

Forests I believed in, The. Illinois: At Night, Black Hawk's Statue Broods. James W. Rivers. PoA 2002

Foretold Futures. Giovanna Pollarolo. TANSG, *tr.* by Marjorie Agosin

Forever after with no tears. (LL) There is no hope. Idea Vilariño. CFP; TANSG, *tr.* by Louise B. Popkin

Forever Afternoon. Adam David Miller. FuFl

Forever Arima. Cheryl Boyce Taylor. WiU

Forever brigands and pirates, the Cretans are never just. Leonidas of Tarentum. HePo, *tr.* by Barbara Hughes Fowler

Forever / it dwells in the windows and doors. Time for Dejection. Hamda Khamees. PoArWo, *tr.* by Joseph T. Zeidan

Forever Martial. *Unknown.* WoPoe, *tr.* by John S. Major

Forever over now, forever, forever gone. Cameo, The. Edna St. Vincent Millay. GPTC; MoAmPo

Forever Parted: Graveyard. Gu Cheng. VCWP, *tr.* by Jerome P. Seaton

Forever the little thud of names, falling. Empty Dwelling Places. Kenneth Patchen. PoA 2002

Forever the Snake. Jennifer Rankin. BMAP

Forever we abandon. Unknown man, The. Fadil Azzawi. IrPoTo, *tr.* by Saadi A. Simawe

Forever witnessing. Going On. Daryl E. Jones. TiP2

Forevermore. Jones Very. NCAP

Foreward. Yun Tongju. CAMKP, *tr.* by Kay Richards and Steffen Richards

Forfeit their Paradise by their pride. (LL) Flower, The. George Herbert. AngWePo; BASC; BrAP; FSCP; NAEL-6v1; NAEL-7v1; NoP-4; NoP-5; NPeEn; OBGa; OxBEV; PBRV

Forfeiture, The. Henry King, Bishop of Chichester. NOSC

Forge, The. Seamus Heaney. NAEL-6v2; NAEL-7v2; NoP-4; NoP-5; OxAEP-2; WaAnP

Forge the contrary of this world. Movement. Andrée Chedid. HAWP, *tr. by* Mirène Ghossein and Samuel Hazo

Forget about you forget about you forget about you. (LL) Pygmy Headhunters and Killer Apes, My Lover and Me. Laurel Ann Bogen. CalPo; SUP

Forget he was alone in winter in some town. (LL) When My Dead Father Called. Robert Bly. GoPo; MAAN

Forget How to Remember How to Forget. John Hollander. PoDa

Forget it. (LL) Derek Walcott. *See* About love. If it's so tough, / forget it.

Forget maps at 10F each. Those before. Strangers: An Essay. Jim Elledge. SwNoth

Forget not this. (LL) Steadfastness. Sir Thomas Wyatt. FaBoVe; NoSic; OBEV

Forget Not Yet. Sir Thomas Wyatt. *See* Steadfastness.

Forget not yet the tried intent. Steadfastness. Sir Thomas Wyatt. FaBoVe; NoSic; OBEV

(Forget not yet the tryde entent.) NPeEn

Forget our pride, our faces, our common love. (LL) Do the Others Speak of Me Mockingly, Maliciously? Delmore Schwartz. APT-2; ChIV-1

Forget roadside crossings. How to See Deer. Philip Booth. GoPo

Forget that version, gist's. Stones (Istanbul, Robert Smithson). Ann Lauterbach. AWPTFC

"Forget thee?" If to dream by night and muse on thee by day. Forget Thee? John Moultrie. ITBLP

Forget What Did. Philip Larkin. NAMCP V.2; NoAM

Forget your life. Say *God is Great.* Get up. Say Yes Quickly. Jelaluddin Rumi. RaBo, *tr. by* Coleman Barks

Forgetfulness. Billy Collins. EMP; FaoP; PoA 2002; StAl

Forgetfulness. Hart Crane. HarvBoo; NIL-7; StAl

Forgetfulness! Josephine D. Henderson Heard. CBWP-4

Forgetfulness. The Earl of Longford. IrLP

Forgetfulness Is Not. Anna Cascella. CItWP, *tr. by* Cinzia Sartini Blum and Lara Trubowitz

Forget-Me-Not, The. Mary Russell Mitford. CenSon

Forgetting. Air. Pierre Reverdy. CuPo

Forgetting. Vahan Tekeyan. AF, *tr. by* Diana Der Hovanessian and Marzbed Margossian

Forgetting Begins, The. Gwyneth Lewis. BBMWP *Fr.* Language Murderer, The.

Forgetting God. Sir Thomas Seymour. NoSic

FORGETTING God. Forgetting God. Sir Thomas Seymour. NoSic

Forgetting, Love. Nathalie Handal. PoArWo

Forgetting the Sixties. Mark DeFoe. SwNoth

Forgetting. Yes, I will forget it all. Forgetting. Vahan Tekeyan. AF, *tr. by* Diana Der Hovanessian and Marzbed Margossian

Forgive a hick unable to compete. *Unknown.* PriapPo *Fr.* Priapus Poems, The.

Forgive and Live. Yusef Komunyakaa. BodElec

Forgive Me! Andrey Andreievich Voznesensky. RusPo, *tr. by* Robert Arthur Douglas Ford

Forgive me if I laugh. Ballad. Sonia Sanchez. FuFl; PoDa

Forgive me, if I wound your ear. In a Letter to A.R.C. on Her Wishing to Be Called Anna. Matilda Barbara Betham-Edwards. PoBW; WoRP

Forgive me if my eyes see. Pablo Neruda. GifTon, *tr. by* William O'Daly

Forgive me, insomniacs. I dozed off. I fell into a dream. For the Unfortunates. Kevin Prufer. LegDan

Forgive me, my child. Letters to Childhood. Mohammed Shehadeh. PoCho, *tr. by* Aziz Shihab

Forgive me, my delight. To Tanya at Christmas. Wendell Berry. UpMys

Forgive me not! Hate me and I shall know. Quatrain: Forgive Me Not. Lilla Cabot Perry. RaF

Forgive Me, Sire. Norman Cameron. OxBEV

Forgive me, soldier. Please. Yusef Komunyakaa. OxAAAP

Forgive me that I opened your door silently. Negar. CRWP, *tr. by* Richard McKane

Forgive, O Lord, my little jokes on Thee. Robert Frost. SAmP

Forgive these nigguhs that know not what they do. (LL) Riot. Gwendolyn Brooks. NALW; SSLK

Forgive your son! (LL) Ecce Puer. James Joyce. AmFaPo; ChIV-2; NoAM

Forgiveness. Julia Copus. MoWP

Forgiveness. Morton Marcus. RaF

Forgiveness. George Russell. IrLP; IrV

Forgiveness. John Greenleaf Whittier. GSo

Forgiveness Dream, The: Man from the Warsaw Ghetto. Jean Valentine. CFP

Forgiving. Alfred Tennyson. SacPr

Forgo the charming Muses! No, in spite. Elizabeth Singer Rowe. PEW *Fr.* To one that persuades me to leave the Muses.

Forgotten. *Unknown, fr. Terezin Concentration Camp.* INSAB

Forgotten Song. John Ashbery. HarvBoo

Forgotten? / What it was about? / What the matter was? Hollanditis. Simon Vinkenoog. CLPP, *tr. by* Charles McGeehan

Fork. Charles Simic. CAP-8; ChAP; ColAP; NAMCP V.2; PoPoPo; TRP; WaAnP; WeW-3

Forlorn. William Dean Howells. APN-2

Forlorn Queen, The. Bryan Guinness. IrLP

Form. Colette Bryce. NIrP

Form. Elsa Cross. RMCMP, *tr. by* Margaret Sayers Peden

Form. Heather McHugh. OxBoAm

Form a Band, Goddammit. Horehound Stillpoint. BeDoSh

Form and Feature. Sikong Tu. CCL1 *Fr.* Twenty-Four Modes of Poetry.

Form, as any taper, fine, A. Modern Female Fashions. Mary Robinson. NOBRP

Form in Void. Ikkyu Sojun. ZenPo, *tr. by* Takashi Ikemoto and Lucien Stryk

Form of Chiasmus, The; The Chiasmus of Forms. Michael Davidson. PmAP

Form of Women, A. Robert Creeley. ErotSp

Form of youth without blemish, is not such the form divine?, The. Song of My Soul. Ralph Chubb. CAGL

Form Rejection Letter. Philip Dacey. SUP

Form your letters slowly and well. Antonio Machado Ruiz. WED *Fr.* Moral Proverbs and Folk Songs.

Forma. Elsa Cross. RMCMP

Formal as a minuet or sonnet. Mystery Story. Howard Nemerov. NBLV

Formal Poem, A. Amal Moussa. PoArWo, *tr. by* Khaled Mattawa

Formalized / by middle age. Song of Bullets, The. Jessica Tarahata Hagedorn. FiBr

Formation of Soils, The. Brenda Hillman. BAP-01; FaoP

Formed to research why it had left but it never became clear. (LL) One Filament against the Firmament. Matthea Harvey. IAoNAP; PoDa

Former, A. Cowboy and the Farmer Should Be Friends, The. Robert Hershon. PoDa

Former Barn Lot. Mark Van Doren. MoAmPo

Former Beauties. Thomas Hardy. NoAM; OBMV *Fr.* At Casterbridge Fair.

Former Love, a Lover of Form, A. Carol Muske-Dukes. BodElec

Former National Republican Party Chairman. Portrait in Rhythm and Blues. Dick Lourie. PrTe

Former WWII Paratrooper Dreams of Suicide, 1977, A. Marianne Burke. RWB

Formerly a Slave. Herman Melville. APN-2

Formerly he had been a well-loved god. Naked among the Trees. Norman Cameron. OxBEV

Formerly I thought of you twice. Four Notions of Love and Marriage. N. Scott Momaday. HATNAP

Formerly: nim how matter. Numb to Number. Tina Darragh and P. Inman. Eno

Formerly, when we still parted the big rivers with our arms. Formerly, When We Still Parted the Big Rivers. Peter Rühmkorf. GTCP, *tr. by* Reinhold Grimm and Irmgard Hunt

Forming in globular. Red Pepper. Sue Sinclair. Coast

Forms, flames, and the flakes of flames. (LL) Nomad Exquisite. Wallace Stevens. APT-1; ColAP; WaAnP

Forms of Forts. Susan Stewart. AmAlph

Forms of Love, The. George Oppen. ItP

Formula for Blue Blues Babies. De Leon Harrison. EGAG

Formula for tragedy. Oliver Pitcher. EGAG

Formula to Cause Death. *Cherokee Oral Tradition.* NAAPv.1

Formula to Secure Love. *Cherokee Oral Tradition.* NAAPv.1

Formulaires. Mohammed Dib. *tr. by* Carol Lettieri and Paul Vangelisti

"Language sovereign secret incompatible submerged in the universal wound." PFTM-2, *tr. by* Carol Lettieri and Paul Vangelisti

Fornicator. A New Song, The. Robert Burns. NPeEn

Forsaken. Kim Sowŏl. CAMKP, *tr. by* David R. McCann

Forsaken, The. Duncan Campbell Scott. BrAP

Forsaken, The. Agnes Strickland. CenSon

Forsaken Brother, a Chippewa Tale, The. Jane Johnston Schoolcraft. My Brother, my brother. NAAPv.1

Forsaken Garden, A. Algernon Charles Swinburne. NoP-4; NoP-5; NPeEn; OBGa; OxAEP-2

Forsaken Girl, The [*after* Eduard Mörike]. Eduard Friedrich Mörike. WoPoe, *tr. by* Randall Jarrell

Forsaken Merman, The. Matthew Arnold. NAEL-6v2; NAEL-7v2; OBNV; OBSP

Forsaken of all comforts but these two. Upone Tabacco. Sir Robert Aytoun. WaAnP

Forsaken they would not see the prairies but only a cry. Even Forsaken They'd Flower. Raúl Zurita. TCLAP, *tr. by* Jack Schmitt

Forsaken Wife, The. Elizabeth Thomas. GoPo; LW

Forsaken woods, trees with sharp storms opressed. Robert Sidney. NoSic (Forsaken woods, trees with sharpe storms opprest.) NPeEn

Forsee or more control than robin or wren. (LL) Fifty Faggots. Edward Thomas. MoBrPo; PoWW

Forster says in Aspects of the Novel. In the Grove. Rachel Hadas. KGB

Fort. BeDoSh

Fort of Rathangan, The. *Unknown*. WoPoe, *tr.* by Kuno Meyer

Fort or Castle of Hope, The. Margaret Lucas Cavendish, Duchess of Newcastle.
"Some with sharp swords, to tell O most accursed!" PEW

Fort over against the oak-wood, The. Fort of Rathangan, The. *Unknown*. WoPoe, *tr.* by Kuno Meyer

Fort that never fell to guns has fallen, The. Historical Site. Arthur Powers. RWB

Forth Feasting. William Drummond of Hawthornden.
"What blust'ring noise now interrupts my sleep." NOSC

Forth from its scabbard, pure and bright. Sword of Robert Lee, The. Abram Joseph Ryan. CBCWP; PCW

Forth from my literal door I'm greeted. Report to the Stockholders. Reg Saner. PoCoUp

Forthrightness is good. Core. Kim Chiha. CAMKP, *tr.* by Kevin O'Rourke

Forthwith the sounds and seas, each creek and bay. John Milton. ChIV-1 *Fr.* Paradise Lost.

Forties Flick. John Ashbery. FTOS; NoAM

Fortnight. Pak Inhwan. CAMKP, *tr.* by Scott Swaner

Fortnight ago a report about town, A. Edward Robert Bulwer-Lytton. STuOW

Fortnight before Christmas Gypsies were everywhere, A. Gypsy, The. Edward Thomas. NAMCP V.1; NoAM; NoP-4

Fortress is immobile, The. Nina Gabrielian. CRWP *Fr.* Erebuni.

Fortress of stone, as unmoved as the arm and the beast of our builder! Vajdahunyad. Ferenc Kazinczy. IQMS, *tr.* by Watson Kirkconnell

Fortunate Traveller, The. Derek Walcott. NAMCP V.2; NoAM

Fortunately Australia has been given back to Aboriginals now. Memo to Us (Story). Lionel Fogarty. VaPo

Fortunately the skins. Judy Grahn. PasH

Fortunately, there are mitigating circumstances. Translation of Raimundo Luz, The: My Good Luck. Scott Cairns. UpMys

Fortune. Mary Ursula Bethell. PoBW

Fortune. Sir Thomas More. SacPr

Fortune. *Unknown*. HeIP-4

Fortune and misfortune have no fixed abode. Four Poems Written While Drunk. T'ao Ch'ien. CCL1, *tr.* by William Acker

Fortune and Virtue. Thomas Dekker *and others*. NoSic *Fr.* Old Fortunatus.

Fortune Cookie Blues. Amy Uyematsu. LTA

Fortune Cookies. Fred Moramarco. SUP

Fortune determines rise and fall. Wŏn Ch'ŏnsŏk. CATKP, *tr.* by Peter H. Lee

Fortune doth frown. Sir Thomas Wyatt. NoSic

Fortune hath taken away my love. Fortune Hath Taken Away. Sir Walter Ralegh. NoSic
(Fortune hath taken thee away, my love.) NoP-4; NoP-5; WaAnP

Fortune hath taken the away my love. Sir Walter Ralegh.
"Thus now I leave my love in fortunes {handes / bandes}." PBRV

Fortune is Bardolph's foe, and frowns on him. William Shakespeare. FaBoWar *Fr.* King Henry V.

Fortune smiles, cry holy day! [*or* holiday]. Thomas Dekker *and others*. NoSic *Fr.* Old Fortunatus.

Fortune Teller, The. Nizar Qabbani. PML, *tr.* by Issam A. Lakkis, Fred Moramarco and Al Zolynas

Fortune Teller, The [*with music*]. Fu'ad Rifqa. BBASP, *tr.* by Sargon Boulus and Samuel Hazo

Fortune that is wont to stumble often brought you honor, and a time in which you succored us has done you wrong, A. Abd al-Jabbār ibn Abī Bakr Ibn Hamdīs. HiArP, *tr.* by James T. Monroe

Fortune's darling, king's content. Epitaph. *Unknown*. BASC

Fortunes in knee breeches. H. C. ten Berge. TuT *Fr.* Lusitanian Variant, The.

Fortune's Legacy. *Unknown*. NOSC

40. Ronny Someck. IrPoTo, *tr.* by Vivian Eden

Forty Augusts—aye, and several more—ago. Voice of Things, The. Thomas Hardy. HarvBoo

40 Days and 40 Nights. Henri Cole. PoPoPo

Forty degrees from yesterday's argument for sun. Historia. Brian Clements. TiP2

Forty degrees. Not a soul on the beach. Island of Miracles. Catherine Phil MacCarthy. ArBi

Forty Fungi.
Orange Birch Bolete (Leccinum versipelle). Oth

40— Love. Roger McGough. OBCoV

'49 dawn set me high on a roaring yellow tractor, The. In Kansas. Carter Revard. HATNAP

'49 Merc, A. Kurt Brown. PoDa

49th Birthday Trip (What Are You On?). Samuel Menashe. P180

47° 28' N, 19° 1' E. Michael Murphy. NIrP

47.57. Carson Cistulli. FreRad *Fr.* Twenty-Six Friends, That's the Same as Your Age.

Forty Something. Robert Hass. NAMCP V.2; OxBoAm

42.24. Carson Cistulli. FreRad *Fr.* Twenty-Six Friends, That's the Same as Your Age.

Forty years, / forty years of hurt. Blue Black Pearl, A. Clairesa Clay. BRtP

Forty years / How sharp. Kaya Shirao. ZenPo, *tr.* by Takashi Ikemoto and Lucien Stryk

Forty years I've lived in the green hills. By Chance. Sŏng Hon. CATKP, *tr.* by Chi-gyu Kim [*or* Kim Chonggil]

Forty years separate me from her. 40. Ronny Someck. IrPoTo, *tr.* by Vivian Eden

Forty-eight years ago. Gas-poker, The. Thom Gunn. StAl

Forty-Five. Hayden Carruth. GoPo

Forty-five Minutes from Broadway. George M. Cohan. ReLy

Forty-love. Robert Frost at the Net. Daneen Wardrop. VisFro

Forty-nine years / —What a din! Uncho. ZenPo, *tr.* by Takashi Ikemoto and Lucien Stryk

Forty-one, Alone, No Gerbil. Sharon Olds. BeAl

Forty-one Seconds on a Sunday in June, in Salt Lake City, Utah. Quincy Troupe. MoASP

Forty-one years ago I did not see. When I Woke, Everything Was the Same but Different. Olive M. Ritch. PoCu

Forty-second Street. Al Dubin. ReLy

Forty-two years ago (to me if to no one else). Star-Gazer. Louis MacNeice. ModIr; NAEL-6v2; NAEL-7v2; NoP-4; NoP-5

Forward abrupt. Night and a Distant Church. Russell Atkins. EGAG

Forward March. Gerwyn Williams. BBMWP, *tr.* by the author and Richard Poole

Forward or Back. Aaron Shurin. FTOS

Forward to Nationhood. Reginal Faber. OWABP

Forward violet thus did I chide, The. William Shakespeare. OxAEP-1 *Fr.* Sonnets.

Forward Youth that would appear, The. Horatian Ode upon Cromwell's Return from Ireland, An. Andrew Marvell. BASC; CABP; FSCP; NAEL-6v1; NAEL-7v1; NoP-4; NoP-5; NOSC; NPeEn; OBEV; OBWP; OxAEP-1; OxBEV; PBRV; PoPoPo; TFi; WaAnP

Forwards in reverse, always holding their caps. (LL) Glasgow Schoolboys, Running Backwards. Douglas Dunn. BeAl; RSaN

Fosfórico / el sitio que hiela. Dolores Dorantes. SPV

Fossil, A. May Kendall. VWP

Fossil bones, splintered bits of pelvis. Sister Mary Appassionata Lectures the Science Class: Fossils, Physics, Apple, Heart. David Citino. UpMys

Fossil Fuel. John Dickson. PoA 2002

Fossil Garden, The. Emily Wilson. LegDan

Fosterling. Seamus Heaney. NoP-5

Fotografía de Niño. Carlos Sahagún. RaW

Foul canker of fair virtuous action. John Marston. NoSic *Fr.* Scourge of Villainy [*or* Villanie], The.

Foul fa' the breast first treason bred in. Hobie [*or* Hobbie] Noble. *Unknown*. IBB

Foul Line—1987. Colleen J. McElroy. LTA

Foul parent of fair child, swoll'n Breadtax! thou. Fatal Birth, The. Ebenezer Elliott. OxBSo

Foul Shots: A Clinic. William Matthews. MoASP

Found. Johann Wolfgang von Goethe. STV, *tr.* by John Frederick Nims

Found a family, build a state. Fragments of a Lost Gnostic Poem of the Twelfth [*or* 12th] Century. Herman Melville. APN-2; NoP-4; PoPoPo; TCAPo

Found Frozen. Helen Hunt Jackson. NAAPv.1

Found he had worsted God! (LL) Little East of Jordan, A. Emily Dickinson. ChIV-1; NoP-4; NoP-5

Found him, and set to barking. (LL) Bicycle Racers, The. Ann Townsend. AmPoNex; NeAmPo

Found in africa / dawned in freedom. Bio / autography (or, 18th-Century Multiculturalism). Evie Shockley. PoDa

Beating like drumbeats through the heart. (LL) Reflections on Growing Older. Quincy Troupe. GT; OxAAAP

Found in the Free Library. Eleanor Wilner. AmWaPo

Found Missing. Jasper Bernes. IAoNAP

Found Poem, North of Boston. Paul Marion. VisFro

Foundation. Henry Van Dyke. SacPr

Foundation Stone. Alejandra Pizarnik. TANSG, *tr.* by Susan Bassnett

Foundations. Leopold Staff. BLT, *tr.* by Czeslaw Milosz

Foundations. Leopold Staff. PoSu, *tr.* by Adam Czerniawski

Foundations, The. Jennifer Maiden. BMAP

Foundations of Being, The. Patrizia Vicinelli. *tr. by* Gayle Ridinger
　　Crossing the River. ItPo, *tr. by* Gayle Ridinger

Founded on rock and facing the night-fouled sea. Beacon, The. Richard
　　Wilbur. UpMys

Founder thou; these are thy race!, The. (LL) Experience. Ralph Waldo
　　Emerson. APN-1; TCAPo

Foundered Star. Jane Miller. ExTi

Founding of New Hampshire, The. Carl Rakosi. FTOS

Founding of Yuba City, The. Chitra Divakaruni. GeoHom

Foundling, The. Rebecca Seiferle. ICANM

Foundlings in the Yukon. A. K. Ramanujan. NAMCP V.2; PoetW

Found—my little angel. Sandro Penna. CAGL, *tr. by* John McRae

Found—Who Lost? Mary E. Tucker. CBWP-1

Fount, The. Rubén Darío. SpanPo, *tr. by* William M. Davis

Fountain. Benjamin Péret. YaTCFP, *tr. by* Mary Ann Caws *and* Jean-Pierre
　　Cauvin

Fountain. Elizabeth Robinson. AmPoNex

Fountain, The. William Cullen Bryant. APN-1

Fountain, The. William Cowper. ChIV-1

Fountain, The. Donald Davie. NoP-4; NoP-5

Fountain, The. James Russell Lowell. TreFP

Fountain, The. William Wordsworth. NPBRoP; OxAEP-2

Fountain, a House of Stone, A. Heberto Padilla. VCWP

Fountain in the orchard of my beloved. Flower of Gold. Pedro Pérez Conde.
　　PoCho; RMCMP, *tr. by* Michael Wiegers

Fountain in the plaza cascaded dirty water, The. San Jacinto Plaza. Ray
　　Gonzalez. UrbNat

Fountain of Cyanë, The. Donald Davie. HarvBoo

Fountain of living light. Hymn to Su'rya, A. Sir William Jones. NOBRP

Fountain of my spirit thirsts for your ruby, The. Baqi. OLP, *tr. by* Walter
　　Andrews, Najaat Black and Mehmet Kalpakli

Fountain plays, The. Memorial Fountain, The. Roy Fisher. NPeEn

Fountain, that springest on this grassy slope. Fountain, The. William Cullen
　　Bryant. APN-1

Fountain to which we, The. Bath. John Godfrey. FTOS

Fountain's Abbey. Letitia Elizabeth Landon. NPBRoP
　　(Fountains Abbey.) NPBRoP

Fountains are dry and the roses over, The. Manor Garden, The. Sylvia Plath.
　　HarvBoo

Fountains in the Sea. Martin Sorescu. VCWP, *tr. by* Seamus Heaney and
　　Joana Russell-Gebbett

Fountains mingle with the river, The. Love's Philosophy. Percy Bysshe
　　Shelley. ItP; OxAEP-2

Fountains of the boiling stars, the flowers on the foreland, the ever-returning
　　roses of dawn, The. (LL) Apology for Bad Dreams. Robinson Jeffers.
　　APT-1; MoAmPo

Fountains that frisk and sprinkle. Ballade Made in the Hot Weather. W. E.
　　Henley. MoBrPo

Four. Ofelia Perez Sepúlveda. SPV, *tr. by* Jen Hofer

4:30 a.m. with the woe adding up. Reality Organization. Albert Goldbarth.
　　CAP-8

Four a.m. call to the faithful wakes us, The. Noises in the Dark. Liz
　　Lochhead. EdScPo

Four a.m. in summertime. Lovely Morning Thought. Arthur Rimbaud.
　　SxFrPo, *tr. by* Martin Sorrell

Four about Apples. David Young. MotU

Four about Heavy Machinery. David Young. MotU

Four about Metaphysics. David Young. MotU

Four adobe walls. Bougainvillaeas. Stanzas for an Imaginary Garden. Octavio
　　Paz. OBGa

Four Ages of Man, The. Anne Bradstreet.
　　Old Age. TCAPo

4 A.M. Kenneth Fearing. APT-2

4AM. Tim Seibles. RD

Four a.m. At the reactor an alarm begins. Glow-boys. John Tranter. BMAP

4 a.m. freight comes pounding and shaking through the fall night, The. Don't
　　You Hear that Whistle Blowin'. Denise Levertov. GM

Four and a Half. John Holmes. APT-2

4½ Months: Halfway Song. George Barlow. ISC

Four and Twenty Soldiers. S. P. Shephard. BtF

Four be the things I am wiser to know. Inventory. Dorothy Parker. NBLV

Four Beats of the Heart. Sajidah al-Musawi. IrPoTo, *tr. by* Basima Qattan
　　Bezirgan and Elizabeth Fernea

Four Best Things, The. Robert Herrick. *See* Four[e] Things Make Us Happy
　　Here.

Four big Zimmerman farm boys rounded. 4-H. Adam Halbur. NevBe

Four Bird Songs. Simon J. Ortiz. HATNAP

Four Black Bogmen, The. Elder Olson. APT-2

Four blue stones in this thrush's nest. Nest, The. Andrew Young. Spl

Four boys have been arrested for killing geese. This is how it happened.
　　Predictions about a Black Car. Mark Wunderlich. LegDan

Four ("But then, in the imaginary trajectory of a white automobile.") Ofelia
　　Perez Sepúlveda. SPV, *tr. by* Jen Hofer

Four centuries of sleep they say. African Sleeping Sickness. Wanda Coleman.
　　PmAP; WaAnP

Four children. Picture. Bekes Jr. IrPoTo, *tr. by* Muhamad Tawfiq Ali

Four Crows at Dusk. Betsy Sholl. SUP

Four days the mother. Snow Monkey Argues with God, The. David Huddle.
　　PfSP

Four days to go until the twelfth, and the bonfire is fourteen feet high.
　　Thoughts in a Black Taxi. Sinéad Morrissey. MFPA

Four days with you, my father three months dead. Stream, The. Mona Van
　　Duyn. VCAP; WaAnP

Four Dead Sons. James Wright. BodElec

Four Deer. Eamon Grennan. ModIr

Four deer lift up their lovely heads to me. Four Deer. Eamon Grennan.
　　ModIr

Four Divine Animals. Takahashi Shinkichi. ZenPo, *tr. by* Takashi Ikemoto
　　and Lucien Stryk

Four Dream Songs. John Berryman.
　　3. To William Meredith. PoA 2002

Four Ducks on a Pond. William Allingham. IrV; OxAEP-2

Four Elements in Newfound-land, The. Robert Hayman. IFF

Four Elements, The. Sándor Weöres. IQMS, *tr. by* Adam Makkai and Donald
　　E. Morse

Four Epitaphs. Countee Cullen.
　　For a Lady I Know. APT-2; HeIP-4; NAAPv.2; NAMCP V.1; NIL-7; NIP-4;
　　　SSLK; TRP
　　For My Grandmother. APT-2; MoAmPo; SSLK
　　For Paul Laurence Dunbar. SSLK
　　(Lady I Know, A.) MoAmPo

Four Examples from the Poems of River Wang Deer Enclosure. Wang Wei.
　　ChinPo, *tr. by* Ye Weilian [*or* Yeh Wei-lien *or* Wai-lim Yip]

Four foot box, a foot for every year, A. (LL) Mid-Term Break. Seamus
　　Heaney. AmFaPo; BeAl; NIL-7; PoPoPo; WaAnP

Four for Sir John Davies. Theodore Roethke. APT-2; MoAmPo; NoAM

Four Good Things. James McMichael.
　　"Cat came / sleepily from a thick shrub and stopped and shook its head, A."
　　　GeoHom

4-H. Adam Halbur. NevBe

Four Horses, The. James Reeves. TLR

Four Hours. Denise Duhamel. LiTh

4 hours into the climb. Climbing Sears Tower. Dennis Schmitz. IllVoic

450 Years of Selective Memory (Smile). Ken McManus. BRtP

Four hundred hairs of a brush. Peter Levitt. WhBo

400-Meter Freestyle. Maxine W. Kumin. MoASP

Four hundred years ago. Good Luck. Oswald de Andrade. TCLAP, *tr. by*
　　Flavia Vidal

Four hundred zontles away. Cantares. Juan Gregorio Regino. RMCMP, *tr.
　　by* Eliot Weinberger

Four in the Morning. Wisława Szymborska. BLT

Four Japanese Paintings. Arthur Davison Ficke.
　　Wave Symphony, The. PoA 2002

Four Lines of a Black Love Letter between Teachers. Ed Roberson. EGAG

Four little words I send, indeed, mark them well. To your own son. One for a
　　Keepsake Album. Ferenc Kölcsey. IQMS, *tr. by* Adam Makkai

Four Men in a Car. Philip Dacey. PML

Four Minute History of Getting It Together in Order to Be Fabulous, Briefly, A.
　　Anselm Berrigan. HeMarv

Four Notions of Love and Marriage. N. Scott Momaday. HATNAP

Four November 9ths. Anne-Marie Levine. PA9/11

Four o'clock. Letters from Chankiri Prison. Nazim Hikmet. PFTM-1

Four O'Clock, New Year's Morning, New River Beach. Elisabeth Harvor.
　　Coast

Four of July. Robert Newton Peck. CA

Four of the Belt. Tom Leonard. BeAl

Four on a Sidewalk. *Unknown*. CA

IV, 1. To Venus. Horace. OBVE.

4 Or 5 Tadpoles. Kusano Shimpei. PFTM-1

Four or five years have passed since he left. Longing for a Man Faraway.
　　Jaewol Kyunghun. BecRai, *tr. by* Kim Daljin, Kim Won-Chung and
　　Christopher Merrill

Four pelicans went over the house. Pelicans. Robinson Jeffers. MoAmPo

Four Poems. Elizabeth Bishop.
　　Rain Towards Morning. OxBoAm

Four Poems. Ikkyu Sojun. *tr. by* Stephen Berg

"Don't worry please please how many times do I have to say it." WoPoe, *tr. by* Stephen Berg

"Nobody told the flowers to come up nobody." WoPoe, *tr. by* Stephen Berg

"Oh green green willow wonderfully red flower." WoPoe, *tr. by* Stephen Berg

"Ten years of whorehouse joy I'm alone now in the mountains." WoPoe, *tr. by* Stephen Berg

Four Poems. Velemir Khlebnikov. PFTM-1

Four Poems. Gary Young. GeoHom *Fr.* Days.

Four Poems. Gary Young. PfSP

Four Poems for Robin. Gary Snyder. NoAM; NoP-5

Autumn Morning in Shokoku-ji, An. WeW-3

(Four Poems for Robin.) BB

Four Poems in One. Anne Porter. GoPo

Four Poems on Death. Abu Sa'id Abul Khayr. *tr. by* Dick Davis

"For men and women soon the day draws near." WoPoe, *tr. by* Dick Davis

"His absence is the knife that cuts your throat?" WoPoe, *tr. by* Dick Davis

"If I've been dead for twenty years or so." WoPoe, *tr. by* Dick Davis

"I'm going to tell You something that is true." WoPoe, *tr. by* Dick Davis

Four Poems Written While Drunk. T'ao Ch'ien. CCL1, *tr. by* William Acker

Four Preludes on Playthings of the Wind. Carl Sandburg. MoAmPo

Four Quartets. T. S. Eliot.

Burnt Norton. APT-1; HarvBoo; MoAmPo; NAAL-5

4. WaAnP

Dry Salvages, The. NoP-4

"Where is there an end of it, the soundless wailing." AmFaPo

East Coker.

"Home is where one starts from. As we grow older." BeAl

"So here I am, in the middle way, having had twenty years." TWF

Little Gidding. CABP; NAAPv.2; NAEL-6v2; NAEL-7v2; NAMCP V.1; NAWM-7v2; NoAM; NoP-5; OxAEP-2; OxBoAm; TFi

"Ash on an old man's sleeve." NPeEn; OxBEV

"Dove descending breaks the air, The." SacPr

"What we call the beginning is often the end." BeAl

Four Quatrains. Jelaluddin Rumi.

"In the shambles of love, they kill only the best,." RaBo

"Tonight with wine being poured." RaBo

"Two strong impulses: One." RaBo

"Where is a foot worthy to walk a garden,." RaBo

Four Resurrections in the Valley of the Ghosts. Yehuda Amichai. VCWP, *tr. by* Benjamin Harshav *and* Barbara Harshav

Four Roses. Susan Wood. TiP2

Four sailors on the bus, dressed in blue denim shirts. Charles Reznikoff. NAAPv.2

Four Saints in Three Acts. Gertrude Stein.

"Pigeons on the grass alas." NAAPv.2; OWoS

Four Screen Shots. John Cayley. PFTM-2 *Fr.* Reveal Code: Indra's Net 8.

Four Seasons by the Rivers and Lakes. Maeng Sasŏng. CATKP, *tr. by* Peter H. Lee

Four Seekers of the Great Metaphor. Vladimir Levchev. CSCBP, *tr. by* Georgi Belev and Lisa Sapinkopf

Four skinheads stand. Allen Ginsberg. WhBo

Four Small Elegies. Margaret Atwood. PoetW

Four Songs Calling a Boy. Hanu. CATKP, *tr. by* Peter H. Lee

Four Sonnets about Food. Adrienne Su. NAPBL

Four southern regions. Summer Triangle. Derek Beaulieu. PoPra

Four talked about the pine tree. One defined it by genus, species, and variety. Conversation. Dan Pagis. VCWP, *tr. by* Stephen Mitchell

Four Tao philosophers as cedar waxwings. Waxwings. Robert Francis. APT-2; BLT; RaBo

Four teenaged girls walk don the middle. Somerville Saturday Night. Ron Schreiber. PrTe

Four Things Choctaw. Jim Barnes. HATNAP

4/30/92 for Rodney King. Lucille Clifton. ESEAA

(4) THOUGHT AND SPEECH CANNOT KEEP UP WITH THE EMO-. Declaration of the Word as Such. Aleksei Eliseievich Kruchyonykh. PFTM-1

Four times during the night your eyes like white butterflies. Four times during the night. Jeannette Miller. TANSG, *tr. by* Paula Vega

Four times the pitch is outside the strike zone. Aesthetics of the Bases Loaded Walk. Joe Wenderoth. AmPoNex

Four Trees—upon a solitary Acre. Emily Dickinson. APN-2

Four *Tz'u* from Tun-huang. *Unknown. tr. by* Elling O. Eide and Burton Watson

Tune: Eternal Longing. ColAnChi, *tr. by* Burton Watson

Tune: Eternal Longing. ColAnChi, *tr. by* Burton Watson

Tune: Eternal Longing. ColAnChi, *tr. by* Elling O. Eide

Tune: Magpie on the Branch. ColAnChi, *tr. by* Burton Watson

4 Variations On. Gerrit Kouwenaar. PFTM-2, *tr. by* Peter Nijmeijer

Four Ways of Dying. Steve Chimombo. HBAPE; NAfrP

Four weeks have passed since I left, and still. Letter Home. Natasha Trethewey. RD

Four wet winters and now the dry. Runoff. William Everson. NoAM

Four white heifers with sprawling hooves. Orotava Road, The. Basil Bunting. NoAM

Four Winds. Hal Porter. NOBAu

Four winds and seven seas have called me friend. From Life to Love. Countee Cullen. ChIV-1

Four winds contend on the sea's face. Vision of Beasts, A. John Heath-Stubbs. ChIV-1

Four Winds, The. Henry Wadsworth Longfellow. *Fr.* Song of Hiawatha, The.

Four words have the coins of Van-Lich. Coins of Van-Lich. *Vietnamese Oral Tradition.* CaDao, *tr. by* John Balaban

Four Year Old Girl. Mei-Mei Berssenbrugge.

1. AWPTFC

2. AWPTFC

4. AWPTFC

Four Years. Pamela Gillilan. StAl

Four years. Immortality. Samuel Marshak. RusPo, *tr. by* Robert Arthur Douglas Ford

Four years ago I met your death here. Letter from Chicago. May Sarton. NALW

Four years ago I started reading Proust. Bookmark, A. Thomas M. Disch. GoPo; RA

Four years each day with daily bread was blest. William Wordsworth. NPBRoP *Fr.* Salisbury Plain.

Four[e] Things Make Us Happy Here. Robert Herrick. Spl

(Four Best Things, The.) Spl

Fourfold cycle shifts to the Yin pitchpipes, The. Mooring by Jiangzhen in the Evening. Lo Pin-wang. CCL1, *tr. by* Stephen Owen

Fourfold Exercise for the Believer in His Lodging on Earth, A. Ralph Erskine. SacPr

Fourier what have they done with your keyboard. André Breton. PFTM-2 *Fr.* Ode to Charles Fourier.

Four-Leaf Clover. Ella Higginson. SWaP

Four-Light Window, A. Ágnes Nemes Nagy. VCWP, *tr. by* Hugh Maxton

Four-score and seven, so the papers say. Old Boatman of Death's River, The. R. Williams Parry. OBWVE, *tr. by* Joseph P. Clancy

Fourscore and seven years ago. Gettysburg Address, The. Abraham Lincoln. HHAm

Foursomes. Marvin K. White. BRtP

Fourteen. James A. Emanuel. OxAAAP

Fourteen. Michael McClure. WANABP *Fr.* Plum Stones.

Fourteen. David Wheatley. NIrP

Fourteen, a sonneteer thy praises sings. Sonnet upon Sonnets, A. Robert Burns. GSo

Fourteen and I knew from nothing. Sleep Walk. Christopher Buckley. SUP

Fourteen and still a boy. Hundred Worries, A. Tu Fu [*or* Du Fu]. CrYelRi, *tr. by* Sam Hamill

1492. Emma Lazarus. APN-2; NAAPv.1; OxBoAm; SWaP

Fourteen Irises for J. L. Gustaf Sobin. WoBe

14 Reasons Why I Mention Mario Lanza to the Man I Love Every Chance I Get Tonight. Jim Elledge. IllVoic

Fourteen small broidered berries on the hem. What the Sonnet Is. Eugene Lee-Hamilton. GSo

14 Songs and 1 Riddle. Robert Filliou.

"Homage in dance, An." PFTM-2

Fourteen Things We're Allowed to Bring to the Underworld. Mark Wunderlich. LegDan

1422 amsterdam avenue. Old Buildings, The. Pedro Juan Pietri. UnSA

14-Year-Old Convalescent Cat in the Winter, A. Gavin Ewart. OPOU

Fourteen years after you snuck. En el Sol de Mi Barrio. Sandra M. Castillo. TouFir

Fourteen years old, learning the alphabet. Reading Lesson, The. Richard Murphy. PBCIP

14 de julio. Sandra Cisneros. WaAnP

Fourteenth Ode. Sekeena Shaben. PoArWo

14th Street Was Gutted in 1968. Cheryl Clarke. UnSA

Fourteenth street, with a bad cold in its head. Death and Transfiguration of Fourteenth Street. Kenneth Fearing. AmWit

Fourteen-year-old boy is out rambling alone, A. Backside to the Wind. Paul Durcan. PBCIP

4th Base. Gary Gildner. MoASP

Fourth Day of the First Week, The. Guillaume de Salluste Du Bartas. Fr. Divine Weeks and Works, The.

Fourth Eclogue, The. Miklós Radnóti. IQMS, tr. by John Wain

Fourth Ecologue, The: Pollio. Virgil. WoPoe, tr. by David R. Slavitt

Fourth Floor, Dawn, Up All Night Writing Letters. Allen Ginsberg. HarvBoo; InvLad

4th of July. William Carlos Williams. PoA 2002

Fourth Rome, The. Nikolai Alekseievich Klyuyev. CAGL, tr. by Simon Karlinsky

Fourth Song, The. Francis Beaumont. NOSC Fr. Masque of the Inner Temple and Gray's Inne, The.

Fourth Street, San Rafael [with music]. Bill Berkson. NYP2

Fourth sunday, A. I am your courtier. Honorée Fanonne Jeffers. AnSo

Fourth Supreme, The. Allison Joseph. BtF

4th Weekend. John Berryman. BodElec

4th Witness—The Petty Thieves. Ifi Amadiume. NAfrP

Fourth World, The. Vincent Woods. NIrP

Four-Word Lines. May Swenson. OxBoAm

Fowk spik aboot Scots. Doric's No Dodo. Sheena Blackhall. EdScPo

Fowler Street. Tony Gloeggler. NevBe

Fowls [or Foweles or Fowles] in the Frith. Unknown. FaBoVe; NAEL-6v1; NoP-4; NoP-5

Fowre muckle angels wi their trumpets, stalkin. Judgment Day. Robert Garioch. OBVE

Fox. Adrienne Rich. NAMCP V.2

Fox, The. Dafydd ap Gwilym. NAWM-7v1, tr. by Richard Morgan Loomis

Fox, The. Kahlil Gibran. NAAPv.2

Fox, The. Philip Levine. SoSe-8

Fox, The. Mary Oliver. PoCoUp

Fox, The [with music]. R. Williams Parry. OBWVE, tr. by Gwyn Williams

Fox and the Ape Go to Court, The. Edmund Spenser. NoSic Fr. Mother Hubbard's Tale.

Fox and the Crow, The. Jean de La Fontaine. OBVE, tr. by Marianne Moore

Fox chewed his thoughtful paw, gnawed, The. Different Voice, The. Frieda Hughes. NeBl

Fox disguised, The. Buson. EMJL, tr. by Haruo Shirane

Fox Hunt, The. Henry Brooke. DiBP

Fox knew well, that before they tore him, The. John Masefield. OBNV Fr. Reynard the Fox.

Fox knows many. Strategy. Archilochus. WoPoe, tr. by Guy Davenport

Fox knows many things, The. Archilochus. SaLy, tr. by Diane Rayor

Fox looked at his shadow at sunrise and said, "I will have a", A. Fox, The. Kahlil Gibran. NAAPv.2

Fox pushes softly, blindly through me at night, The. Searching for Pittsburgh. Jack Gilbert. BeAl

Fox set out in hungry plight, The. Unknown. ChAP

Fox you didn't know you had, The. Scotch. Ruth Padel. MFPA

Foxes. Frieda Hughes. NeBl

Foxes in Winter. Mary Oliver. MoW

Foxes move in pairs. Unknown. ColAnChi Fr. Classic of Odes.

Foxfire. Dominique Parker. SpirFl

Foxfire. Andy Young. AnSo

Foxgloves. Gerry Cambridge. EdScPo

Foxlight. Pamela Alexander. AmAlph

1. Ipswich. AmAlph
2. Plum Island. AmAlph
3. Punta Blanca. AmAlph

Fox's Counsel, The. Huw Llwyd. OBWVE, tr. by Joseph P. Clancy

Fox's Trick, The. Shimazaki Toson. CAoMJL1, tr. by Leith Morton

Fra Bank to Bank, Fra Wood to Wood I Rin. Mark Alexander Boyd. OxBEV

(Fra bank to bank, fra wood to wood I rin.) WoPoe

(Sonet.) NPeEn; PBRV

(Sonet: "Fra bank [or banc] to bank [or banc], fra wood [or wod] to wood [or wod] I rin.") OBEV

(Venus and Cupid.) NePenScot

Fra Lippo Lippi. Robert Browning. BrAP; NAEL-6v2; NAEL-7v2; NoP-4; NoP-5; OxAEP-2; WaAnP

Fracas of light falling on apples. Josée Lapeyrère. SCFWP Fr. Apples.

Fractal Audition. Pimone Triplett. NAPBL

Fraction. André Du Bouchet. YaTCFP, tr. by Mary Ann Caws

Fradel Schtok. Irena Klepfisz. TaR

Frae great Apollo, poet say. Poet's Wish, The; an Ode. Allan Ramsay. OBVE

Fragging. Yusef Komunyakaa. AmAlph; ESEAA

Fragile. / A seven letter word. Fragile soy. Teresa Palma Acosta. TiP2

Fragile as a spider's web. Love. May Sarton. PoBW

Fragile Mimosa, through the flood of months. R. Bryn Williams. BBMWP,

Fragile Soy. Teresa Palma Acosta. TiP2

Fragment. Alessandro Ceni. ItPo, tr. by Gayle Ridinger

Fragment. Adelaide Crapsey. APT-1

Fragment. Ray DiPalma. FTOS

Fragment. Angelina Weld Grimké. NAAPv.2; OxBoAm

Fragment: "Cold chain of life presseth heavily on me tonight, The." Adah Isaacs Menken. CBWP-1

Fragment: "I lived on this earth in an age." Miklós Radnóti. IQMS, tr. by Geroge Gömöri and Clive Wilmer

Fragment: "This time the hold up man didn't know a video-sound camera hidden up in a corner." C. K. Williams. InoFa

Fragment: "As for him who." William Carlos Williams. Spl

Fragment: "I cannot find my way to Nazareth." Yvor Winters. OBSV

Fragment 1: "Adventure." Bill Griffiths. Oth Fr. Building: The New London Hospital.

Fragment 3: "All horizons are round." Helmut Heissenbüttel. GTCP, tr. by Christopher Middleton

Fragment 3. Sydney, Lady Morgan Owenson. PoBW

Fragment 4: "Little Jo wakes me up." Bill Griffiths. Oth Fr. Building: The New London Hospital.

Fragment 9: "I go to Zoo." Bill Griffiths. Oth Fr. Building: The New London Hospital.

Fragment 11: "My latest thought brick for an abundant supply for home and clothes." Bill Griffiths. Oth Fr. Building: The New London Hospital.

Fragment 12: "For example, taking the cement onto palettes, for the hoist." Bill Griffiths. Oth Fr. Building: The New London Hospital.

Fragment 13: "Maple." Bill Griffiths. Oth Fr. Building: The New London Hospital.

Fragment 18: "Met Noel at Cheshire Street." Bill Griffiths. Oth Fr. Building: The New London Hospital.

Fragment 36 [or Thirty-Six]: "I know not what to do." "H. D." BrAP; NALW; PoBW

Fragment 40: "Keep love and he wings." "H. D." BrAP

Fragment 10. The Boudoir. Sydney, Lady Morgan Owenson. RWP Fr. Lay of an Irish Harp, or Metrical Fragments, The.

Fragment 113: "Not honey, / not the plunder of the bee." "H. D." APT-1; NAAPv.2

Fragment 17. Anacreon. CAGL, tr. by Eugene O'Connor

Fragment 19. L'Amant Mutin. Sydney, Lady Morgan Owenson. RWP Fr. Lay of an Irish Harp, or Metrical Fragments, The.

Fragment 35. The Irish Jig. Sydney, Lady Morgan Owenson. RWP Fr. Lay of an Irish Harp, or Metrical Fragments, The.

Fragment 360. Anacreon. CAGL, tr. by Alfred Corn

Fragment 58: Night and Sleep. Alcman. WoPoe, tr. by Rosanna Warren

Fragment 652. Euripides. CAGL, tr. by John Addington Symonds

Fragment 68: "I envy you your chance of death." "H. D." NAAPv.2; NAMCP V.1

Fragment A. Christopher Smart. Fr. Jubilate Agno.

Fragment, A. William Wordsworth. NOBRP

Fragment, A: "Maiden, thou wert thoughtless once." Anne Brontë. VWP

Fragment, A: "Our fancies are but joys all unexprest." Henrietta Cordelia Ray. CBWP-3

Fragment, A: The Blind Man. Anne Batten Cristall. RWP

Fragment: August 4, 1856. Henry Wadsworth Longfellow. TCAPo

Fragment B. Christopher Smart. Fr. Jubilate Agno.

Fragment C. Christopher Smart. Fr. Jubilate Agno.

Fragment: December 18, 1847. Henry Wadsworth Longfellow. APN-1; TCAPo

Fragment for the Mother. Mariella Bettarini. CItWP, tr. by Cinzia Sartini Blum and Lara Trubowitz

Fragment (Found Inside My Mother). Nick Flynn. AmPoNex

Fragment from "The Maladjusted: A Tragedy" [with music]. Morris Gilbert Bishop. NBLV

Fragment of a Greek Tragedy. A. E. Housman. WoPoe

Fragment of a Poem on Hunting, A. Thomas Tickell.
  Fragment on Hunting-Dogs, A. DiBP

Fragment of a rainbow bright, A. Rainbow, The. John Keble. TreFP

Fragment of a Sonnet. Pierre de Ronsard. OBVE, tr. by Keats

Fragment of an English Opera. A. E. Housman. OBCoV

Fragment of an Ode to Maia Written on May Day, 1818. John Keats. OBEV

Fragment on Hunting-Dogs, A. Thomas Tickell. DiBP Fr. Fragment of a Poem on Hunting, A.

Fragment [on the Back of the Ms. of Canto I]. Lord Byron. NAEL-6v2; NAEL-7v2; NoP-5; OxBEV Fr. Don Juan.

Fragment: Where Is Tangwen Now? Glyn Jones. TCAWP

Fragmentary Stars. Léonie Adams. APT-2

Fragmented Address to the FBI. Diane Di Prima. BB

Fragmenti. Ezra Pound. PoA 2002

Fragmento. Ulli Freer. VaPo

Fragments. Gottfried Benn. AF, *tr. by* Vernon Watkins

Fragments: "Now there is a slit in the blue fabric of air." Stephen Dobyns. CAP-8

Fragments. Letitia Elizabeth Landon.
Secrets. VWP

Fragments: "Locke sank into a swoon." William Butler Yeats. NoAM

Fragments 1920–1921. Nikolai Stepanovich Gumilyov. TCRusP, *tr. by* Mary Jane White

Fragments from Dove Cottage Manuscript. William Wordsworth.
I Have Thoughts that Are Fed by the Sun. NPBRoP

Fragments join in me with their own music, The. (LL) Poem as Mask, The. Muriel Rukeyser. APT-2; NAAL-5; NALW; NAMCP V.2

Fragments of a Lost Gnostic Poem of the Twelfth [*or* 12th] Century. Herman Melville. APN-2; NoP-4; PoPoPo; TCAPo

Fragments of Ancient Poetry, Collected in the Highlands of Scotland. James Macpherson.
(2). NePenScot

Fragments of the Forgotten War. Suji Kwock Kim. AmWaPo

Fragments of the Night, The. José Lezama Lima. TCLAP, *tr. by* Willis Barnstone

Fragments, / Refuse of the soul. Fragments. Gottfried Benn. AF, *tr. by* Vernon Watkins

Fragments to Overcome Silence. Alejandra Pizarnik. TANSG, *tr. by* Susan Bassnett

Fragonard, / Your spiral women. George Oppen. APT-2; PFTM-1

Fragrance. Kay Sage. SurWo

Fragrance Comes from the Scent I Wear, The. *Unknown.* CCL1 *Fr.* Tzu Yeh Songs.

Fragrance is due to perfumes. *Unknown.* ChinPo, *tr. by* Ye Weilian [*or* Yeh Wei-lien *or* Wai-lim Yip]

Fragrance of Life, Odor of Death. Denise Levertov. AF

Fragrance of men. (LL) Kirkyard. George Mackay Brown. NePenScot; NPeEn

Fragrance of night, not to be defined, A. Fragrance of Night, A. Léon-Paul Fargue. YaTCFP, *tr. by* Wallace Stevens

Fragrance of red lotuses has faded, The. Plum Blossoms. Li Ch'ing-chao. ErotSp, *tr. by* Sam Hamill

Fragrance of the lotus, The. *Unknown.* WhBo

Fragrance of the Udumbara, The. Muso Soseki. EaWin, *tr. by* W. S. Merwin

Fragrance would call me out of the house, A. Catching Webs. Judith Beveridge. NOBAu

Fragrant fireweed grows in the rain. Country Road, A. Li Ho. CrYelRi, *tr. by* Sam Hamill

Fragrant Hands. Faiz Ahmad Faiz. VCWP, *tr. by* Agha Shahid Ali

Fragrant or "fragment," I still can't decide which. Multiple Choice. Douglas Burnet Smith. Coast

Fragrant with powder, moist with perspiration. Creamy Breasts. Chao Luanluan. CCL1; EroLit; NDACCP, *tr. by* Chung Ling and Kenneth Rexroth

Frail and tenuous mist lingers on baffled and intricate branches, A. Leaves. Frederic Manning. NOBAu

Frail as the leaves that quiver on the sprays. Homer. OBVE *Fr.* Iliad, The.

Frail duration of a flower, The. (LL) Wild Honey Suckle, The. Philip Freneau. ColAP; ITBLP; NAAL-3; NAAPv.1; OxBoAm; TCAPo

Frail, frail, lone-growing bamboo. *Unknown.* ColAnChi, *tr. by* Burton Watson

Frail multitude, whose giddy law is list. Crucify Him! Giles Fletcher, the Elder. SacPr

Frail sound of a tunic trailing, A. Poem. Antonio Machado Ruiz. WoPoe, *tr. by* John Dos Passos

Frail the white rose and frail are. Flower Given to My Daughter, A. James Joyce. OBMV; PtR; RaBo

Frailty, Thy Name is Woman. William Shakespeare. OxAEP-1; WaAnP *Fr.* Hamlet.

Frälein, can you. Christian Hawkey. IIR

Frame of Fear. Unoma Nguemo Azuah. NeNiPo

Frame of the world is suddenly rotated, The. Pin's Fee, or Painting with Star, A. David Shapiro. BodElec

Frame within frame, the evolving conversation. Dancers Exercising. Amy Clampitt. NoAM

Framed by the open window, a lone Stearman. Randolph Field, 1938. R. S. Gwynn. TiP2

Framed in her phoenix fire-screen, Edna Ward. Cottage Street, 1953. Richard Wilbur. BodElec; CAP-8; NoP-5; PoPoPo

Frames. Laura Mullen. IAoNAP

Framing. Michael Davidson. FTOS

Framing and line of your neck, The. Body as dictionary, as bible, The. Matt Robinson. Coast

Fran. Christopher Pilling. NLP

France: "Dozen sparrows scuttled on the frost, A." Douglas Dunn. EdScPo

France 1792. Helen Maria Williams. NPBRoP *Fr.* To Dr Moore, in Answer to a Poetical Epistle Written by Him in Wales.

France aids them now, a desperate game I play. Philip Freneau. TCAPo *Fr.* George the Third's Soliloquy.

France (Concluded). William Wordsworth. *Fr.* Prelude, The; Growth of a Poet's Mind [1850 version].

France underfoot like a worn-out carpet spread. Night at Dunkirk. Louis Aragon. FaBoWar, *tr. by* Malcolm Cowley and Rolfe Humphries

France's I am; my lookout's glum. Quatrain. François Villon. WoPoe, *tr. by* Richard Wilbur

Franchises in Flux. John Ashbery. VaPo

Francine's Room [*with music*]. Louise Erdrich. NoAM

Francis Ford Coppola and Anthropologist Interpreter Teaching Gartewienna Tribesmen to Sing "Light My Fire," Philippine Jungle, 1978. David Wojahn. ReTh

Francis Helps a Brother Who Is in Sin. David Craig. UpMys

Francis Meets a Leper. David Citino. UpMys

Francis walked in silence. Francis Helps a Brother Who Is in Sin. David Craig. UpMys

Francisco Velarde was here. Lolo Panchito was here. (LL) Madarika. Vince Gotera. OpBo; ReBoTo

François Villon. Bulat Shalvovich Okudzhava. TCRusP, *tr. by* Denis Johnson, Aleksandar Petrov and Shirley Rihner

Francus. Sir John Davies. OBCoV

Frank. Romance, A. Ernst Jandl. OnScMo, *tr. by* Brian Schorn

Frank Baker's my name, and a bachelor I am. *Unknown.* APN-2

Frank Costello eating spaghetti in a cell at San Quentin. Mafioso. Sandra M. Gilbert. UnSA

Frank O'Hara Five, Geoffrey Chaucer Nil. Geoff Hattersley. NeBl

Franked. Anna Mendelssohn. VaPo

Frankenstein naps on a golden bed. Frankenstein. Connie Deanovich. ReTh

Frankfurt. János Pilinszky. PoSu
(Frankfurt 1945.) AF

Frankie and Johnny [*or* Johnnie *or* Albert]. *Unknown.* APN-2; FaBoA; NAAPv.2; NIP-4; TCAPo

Frankie was a good waoman. Frankie and Albert. *Unknown.* APN-2

Franklin Hyde. Joseph Hilaire Pierre Belloc. NBLV

Franklin sailed a key-hung kite. Fable. James Facos. NBLV

Franklin's Introduction, The. Geoffrey Chaucer. NAEL-6v1 *Fr.* Canterbury Tales, The.

Franklin's Prologue, The. Geoffrey Chaucer. NAEL-6v1 *Fr.* Canterbury Tales, The.

Franklin's Tale, The. Geoffrey Chaucer. NAEL-6v1 *Fr.* Canterbury Tales, The.

Franks come down the hill with a random course, The. *Unknown.* FaBoWar *Fr.* Excerpts from *The Poem of the Cid.*

Frank's Song. Reed Bye. AHA

Frantic as a prentice poet. Niyi Osundare. HBAPE *Fr.* Moonsongs.

Frantic elk climb from the valleys to escape the flies, The. On the Elk, Unwitnessed. Alan Dugan. YaYoPo

Fraser rushes out to sea and you, where you are i am, The. Daphne Marlatt. NLPA *Fr.* Touch to My Tongue.

Frater Ave Atque Vale. Alfred Tennyson. NAEL-6v2; NoP-4; NoP-5

Fraternitas. *Unknown.* OBVE *Fr.* Deer Sing.

Fratricide. Abdula Peshew. IrPoTo, *tr. by* Muhamad Tawfiq Ali

Frau Bauman, Frau Schmidt, and Frau Schwartze. Theodore Roethke. APT-2; NAMCP V.1; NoAM

Fraudulent perhaps in that they gave. Swans. Lawrence Durrell. MoBrPo

Fray of Suport, The. *Unknown.* IBB

Freaks at Spurgin Road Field, The. Richard Hugo. NoAM; PoCho; SoSe-8

Freaky time. Charles Bukowski. OxBoAm

Fred. Ian Duhig. NeBl

Fred Pickering never asked why. Playground, The. Gregory Harrison. NOxBChV

Fred Sanford's on at 12. What I Am. Terrance Hayes. BtF

Fred, where is north? West-Running Brook. Robert Frost. APT-1; MoAmPo; NoP-4; NoP-5

Freddie Hubbard's music / is an hour late. Left Bank Jazz Society, The. Afaa Michael Weaver. UnSA

Freddie Hubbard's playing the cassette deck. Indian Song. Major L. Jackson. FuFl; WaAnP

Freddy. Stevie Smith. LW

Fredensborg. Friedrich Gottlieb Klopstock. GePo, *tr. by* George C. Schoolfield

Frederick Douglass. Paul Laurence Dunbar. CBCWP

Frederick Douglass. Robert Earl Hayden. CBCWP; ESEAA; ISC; NIL-7; NIP-4; OxAAAP; PoPoPo; PtR; VCAP

Frederick Douglass: 1817–1895. Langston Hughes. CBCWP; HHAm

Frederick Knieps, Physician of the Bed-Chamber to the Empress Theresa. Big Mystical Circus, The. Jorge de Lima. GPTC, *tr. by* Dudley Poore

Fredericksburg. Thomas Bailey Aldrich. AmWaPo; PCW; TCAPo

Frederiksted, Dusk [*with music*]. Derek Walcott. NoAM

Fredman's Epistlar, 1790. Carl Michael Bellman. *tr. by* Rika Lesser
  Fredman's Epistle No. 23. WoPoe, *tr. by* Rika Lesser

Fredman's Epistle No. 23. Carl Michael Bellman. WoPoe *Fr.* Fredman's Epistlar, 1790.

Free Abandonment Blues, The. Jean Valentine. BodElec

Free bird leaps, A / on the back of the wind. Caged Bird. Maya Angelou. BrAP; WeW-3

Free, black, & forty-one. (LL) John Berryman. NoP-4; NoP-5 *Fr.* Dream Songs.

Free evening fades, outside the windows fastened with decorative iron grilles, The. Evening in the Sanitarium. Louise Bogan. GPTC; NALW; NIL-7; OxBoAm

Free Fall. Karl Krolow. GTCP, *tr. by* Reinhold Grimm

Free Fantasia on Japanese Themes. Amy Lowell. MoAmPo

Free Fantasia: Tiger Flowers. Robert Earl Hayden. ESEAA

Free from all fogs but[t] shining fair[e], and clear [*or* cleere]. Mary Sidney Wroth, Countess of Montgomery. BASC; EMWP *Fr.* Pamphilia to Amphilanthus.

Free Grace. Charles Wesley. SacPr

Free I have my own self-reliance. I Drift in the Wind. Ingrid Jonker. HAWP, *tr. by* Jack Cope

Free Mercy. Philip Schultz. PA9/11

Free Old Man. Muso Soseki. EaWin, *tr. by* W. S. Merwin

Free One, A. W. H. Auden. OxAEP-2

Free Puerto Rico. Puerta Rica. Víctor Hernández Cruz. LoL

Free Radicals. James Sherry. FTOS

Free Rein. Laura Chester.
  "Search to get lost in a great big coat, The." OnScMo

Free Speech. Tom Clark and Lewis Warsh. AHA

Free Thought. Algernon Charles Swinburne. NPeEn

Free Throw. Mark Kraushaar. MoASP

Free to travel, he still couldn't be shown how lucky. David Walker (1785–1830). Rita Dove. OxAAAP; WaAnP

Free Union. André Breton. PFTM-1

Free Union. André Breton. NAWM-7v2, *tr. by* Mary Ann Caws and Jean-Pierre Cauvin

Free Union. André Breton. YaTCFP, *tr. by* Mary Ann Caws and Patricia Terry

Free Verse. Charles Reznikoff. APT-2; NAAPv.2

Free will-star is a hendiadys for dream. To the Readers. Maria Luisa Spaziani. CItWP, *tr. by* Cinzia Sartini Blum and Lara Trubowitz

Free-booter, The. George Darley. OxBSo

Freeborn Pindaric never does refuse. Samuel Wesley. VerBaPo *Fr.* Pindaricque on the Grunting of a Hog, A.

Free-coursing wind from the sky. Wind, The. Dafydd ap Gwilym. WoPoe, *tr. by* Daniel Huws

Freed like a miracle from bondage. In the Wilderness. Colville N. Young. OWABP

Freediving thirty to forty feet, only a few seconds to spare. Lobsters in the Brain Coral. Laurence Lieberman. IllVoic

Freedom. Ambrose Bierce. APN-2 *Fr.* Devil's Dictionary, The.

Freedom. Wimal Dissanayake. ChAP

Freedom. Ralph Waldo Emerson. APN-1

Freedom. Ethel Carnie Holdsworth. RSaN

Freedom. Emyr Lewis. *tr. by* Grahame Davies
  "In the imperfect time when we have the right." BBMWP, *tr. by* Grahame Davies
  "This is the city of lost things, thrown away." BBMWP, *tr. by* Grahame Davies

Freedom [*epigram*]. Friedrich von Logau. GePo, *tr. by* George C. Schoolfield

Freedom. Jan Struther. LW

Freedom. Anthony Thwaite. OxBSo

Freedom a Come Oh! [*with music*]. Unknown. FaBoVe

Freedom, as every schoolboy knows. Ambrose Bierce. APN-2 *Fr.* Devil's Dictionary, The.

Freedom at last. Cincinnati. Mitsuye Yamada. UnSA

Freedom at McNealy's. Priscilla Jane Thompson. CBWP-2; SWaP

Freedom Child—Tilla's Lullaby. Eintou Pearl Springer. CFP

Freedom comes slowly, but remember she. Freedom. Ethel Carnie Holdsworth. RSaN

Freedom Fighter. Antigone Kefala. BMAP; ItWoWo

Freedom in Peril. "Sagittarius." UV

Freedom is more than a word, more than the base coinage. *Nabara*, The. Cecil Day Lewis. OBNV

Freedom is seldom what you now believe. City Park Merry-Go-Round. Eli W. Mandel. IFF

Freedom is the ability to admit you were wrong. Techniques of Mass Persuasion. Geoffrey O'Brien. PA9/11

Freedom of the Moon, The. Robert Frost. APT-1

Freedom of the wholly mad, The. Phenomenology of Anger, The. Adrienne Rich. PFTM-2; WaAnP

Freedom [*or* Fredome]. John Barbour. NePenScot; OBEV; TreFP *Fr.* Bruce, The.

Freedom Ride. Rita Dove. FuFl

Freedom Song, A. Marjorie Oludhe Macgoye. HAWP; ItWoWo; WoPoe

Freedom to worship God! (LL) Landing of the Pilgrim Fathers [in New England], The. Felicia Dorothea Hemans. BRP; HHAm; ITBLP; NAEL-6v2; NAEL-7v2; NoP-4; NoP-5

Freedom Train. Langston Hughes. GM

Freehold. John Hewitt.
  Lonely Heart, The.
  "Once in a seaside town with time to kill." ModIr

Freely Espousing. James Schuyler. FTOS; NoP-4; NoP-5

Freely in Hidden Fire. Mirza Asadullah Khan Ghalib. WoPoe, *tr. by* Frances W. Pritchett

Freely tumultuous. (LL) Party on Shipboard. George Oppen. APT-2; PFTM-1

Freeman Field. Marilyn Nelson Waniek. ESEAA

Freestyle, on the First of Tishri. Enid Shomer. TaR

Freestyle (Why They don't Like Rap). Sonnet L'Abbé. OpeFie

Freeway 280. Lorna Dee Cervantes. NoAM; WeW-3

Freeze-Up. Michael Longley. CABP

Freeze-up annexes the sea even, The. Freeze-Up. Michael Longley. CABP

Freezing Pan, The. Helga Novak. MotU, *tr. by* Ann Maria Celona

Freight. Maura Dooley. StAl

Freight. John Frederick Nims. GM

Freight, The. Richard Jones. PoChi

Freight Cars. Stephen Dobyns. GM

Freight Train, Freight Train. Alvin Greenberg. GM

Freight Trains. Attila József. AF, *tr. by* John Batki

Freight trains are pulling in. Freight Trains. Attila József. AF, *tr. by* John Batki

Freighter, gay with rust, The. Jews at Haifa. Randall Jarrell. MoAmPo

Frelimo Oya. Let It Be. Musaemura Bonus Zimunya. NAfrP

French are glad to die for love, The. Diamonds Are a Girl's Best Friend. Leo Robin. ReLy

French Dress [*epigram*]. Friedrich von Logau. GePo, *tr. by* George C. Schoolfield

French Generals, The. Robert Bly. BAP-01

French Historie, The. Anne Dowriche.
  "So him at first *De Nance* commanded was to kill;." PBRV; WaAnP

French Lisette: A Ballad of Maida Vale. William Plomer. OBCoV

French Noel. William Morris. ChrPo

French Prisoner, The. János Pilinszky. IQMS, *tr. by* Peter Zollman

French Prisoner, The. János Pilinszky. PoSu, *tr. by* Janos Csokits and Ted Hughes

French Quarter Intimacies. Kalamu ya Salaam. SpirFl *Fr.* New Orleans Haiku.

French ships run in the new canal, The. Difficulties at Love. *Vietnamese Oral Tradition*. CaDao, *tr. by* John Balaban

Frenchie. Stephen Dobyns. BodElec

Frenzy softens the air. Radiant Silhouette IV. John Yau. OpBo

Frenzy, Sweet Little Child, You Sleep. Marcelle Ferry. SurWo, *tr. by* Myrna Bell Rochester

Frequently during my mornings of pain & reflection. So Many Books, So Little Time. Haki R. Madhubuti. BRtP

Frequently unasked questions. Charles Bernstein. NoP-5

Fresco. Martin Sorescu. VCWP, *tr. by* D. J Enright and Joana Russell-Gebbett

Fresco Come to Life. Boris Leonidovich Pasternak. AF

Fresco: Departure for an Imperialist War. Thomas McGrath. AF

Fresco of my life. (LL) Another Life. Frank Bidart. OxBoAm; VCAP

Fresh Air. Kenneth Koch.
  "Supposing that one walks out into the air." OBCoV

Fresh and fair the morn awaketh. Morn. Josephine D. Henderson Heard. CBWP-4

Fresh Cheese and Cream. Robert Herrick. BASC

Fresh clad from heaven in robes of white. In My Own Album. Charles Lamb. NPBRoP

Fresh fields and woods! the Earth's fair face. Retirement. Henry Vaughan. ChIV-1

Fresh figs blacken and sweeten.   All That in the Voice I Have Adopted for This Lie.   Michele Glazer.   IAoNAP

Fresh from the earth's insides.   Photo of a Rotary Crew, Sour Lake Oilfield, 1904.   Roger Jones.   TiP2

Fresh in their new wraps, earth and heaven.   On New Year's Day.   Nantembo.   ZenPo, *tr. by* Takashi Ikemoto and Lucien Stryk

Fresh Mussels.   Charles McDonald.   NLP

Fresh night, The. (LL)   God is Good. It Is a Beautiful Night.   Wallace Stevens.   APT-1; SAmP

Fresh peaks of salt and pepper hair.   Vallejo.   Maggie Nelson.   HeMarv

Fresh savannas of the Sangamon, The.   Painted Cup, The.   William Cullen Bryant.   APN-1

Fresh Spring the herald of love's [*or* loves] mighty king.   Edmund Spenser.   NoP-5; OBEV *Fr.* Amoretti.

Fresh Stain.   Tess Gallagher.   ExTi

Fresher and fresher comes the air. The blue.   John Neal.   APN-1 *Fr.* Battle of Niagara, The.

Freshly lit cigarette in his mouth.   Improvisation for Piano.   Afaa Michael Weaver.   UnSA

Fresno Truth, The.   Lawson Fusao Inada.   GeoHom

Fressh lusty beautee joyned wyth gentilesse.   *Unknown.*   OHMEL

Freud's Butcher.   Charles Bernstein.   BodElec

Friar had said his paternosters duly, The.   Necrological.   John Crowe Ransom.   FuPo; NAAPv.2

Frida Kahlo paints.   Tattooed Girl.   Monica A. Hand.   BtF

Frida sits coiffed (in whiteface), sits next to the canvas.   Frida's Album (*Frida Kahlo's Album*).   Elena Fanailova.   CRWP, *tr. by* Stephanie Sandler

Frida's Album (*Frida Kahlo's Album*).   Elena Fanailova.   CRWP, *tr. by* Stephanie Sandler

Friday before Labor Day, The.   In the Way Back.   Debra Kang Dean.   UnSA

Friday Night at the End of a Millennium, A.   Clare Pollard.
   "I enjoy dancing."   NeBl
   "On the first of January."   NeBl

Friday night. Beautiful jazz piano at Picante's. Two people in.   Piano Man.   Joyce Jenkins.   ASA

Friday Night Fights, The.   Ronald Wallace.   PoA 2002

Fridge clicks, hums; light flows across, The.   Joseph.   Timothy Steele.   RA

Friend, A.   Paul Klee.   PFTM-1

Friend, The.   Marge Piercy.   NALW

Friend, a poet, wrote me near the end, A.   Drouth, The.   Jon Dressel.   AngWePo

Friend after friend departs.   On the Loss of Friends.   James F. Montgomery.   SacPr

Friend, Ah You Have Changed!   Frank Mkalawile Chipasula.   HBAPE

Friend and Beloved.   Tim Seibles.   RD

Friend calls, says, A.   Suzy Wong's Been Dead a Long Time.   Kitty Tsui.   ReTh

Friend Cato.   Anna Wickham.   MoBrPo

Friend dies one night, A.   Drugs.   Dennis Cooper.   PmAP

Friend, henceforth to be reckoned the foremost among my comrades.   Ovid.   RomPo *Fr.* Tristia.

Friend, hope for the Guest while you are alive.   To Be a Slave of Intensity.   Kabir.   RaBo, *tr. by* Robert Bly

Friend, how I have missed you.   Scroll, The.   Kathleen Spivack.   PfS

Friend I can trust is the one who will let me have my death, The.   Ghazal.   Adrienne Rich.   WoPoe

Friend, I'm reading your old poems on the north terrace.   Antonio Cisneros.   TCLAP *Fr.* Loneliness.

Friend in my mountain-side demesne.   To a Gardener.   Robert Louis Stevenson.   OBGa

Friend is sometimes desert, A.   Eugenio de Andrade.   VCWP *Fr.* White on White.

Friend! My friend! You make me cry like a flower blooming at my love's grave.   Upon Reading Tagore's "The Gardener."   Han Yong'un [*or* Yongwun].   CAMKP, *tr. by* Sammy Solberg

Friend, now for ever gone.   To One Who Died in a Garret in Cardiff.   Huw Menai.   AngWePo

Friend of Humanity and the Knife Grinder, The.   George Canning *and* John Hookham Frere.   OBCoV; UV
   (Sapphics.)   NOBRP; NPeEn

Friend of Man, The.   *Unknown.*   DiBP

Friend of mine, A.   See, I hold her face in trembling, passionate hands. (LL)   Small Female Skull.   Carol Ann Duffy.   EmeKit; HarvBoo; MoWP

Friend of mine met the son of a man, A.   Six Characters in Search of Something.   Jamie McKendrick.   NeBrP

Friend once used to be, and still is, but only, A.   Story Having to Do with Walt Whitman, A.   Daisy Fried.   ViWalt

Friend of my father came to stay, A.   Stranger to a Small Child.   Ben Scammell.   NLP

Friend of Ronsard, Nashe and Beaumont.   On a Birthday.   John Millington Synge.   OBMV

Friend of the arts and artists, scholar, generous patron.   Ovid.   WoPoe *Fr.* Tristia.

Friend of the wise! and teacher of the good!   To William Wordsworth [1817 version].   Samuel Taylor Coleridge.   NAEL-6v2; NAEL-7v2

Friend of the wretched! wherefore should the eye.   Ode to Death.   Charlotte Smith.   NoP-4; NoP-5

Friend remarks to the Prophet, "Why is it."   Deliberation.   Jelaluddin Rumi.   LoL, *tr. by* Coleman Barks

Friend saw the rooms, A.   Boy's Room.   George Oppen.   OxBoAm

Friend told me, A.   Alone.   Michael S. Harper.   ISC

Friend who is concerned, The.   Destruction of Daughters.   Lee Upton.   AmAlph

Friend with no heart or theater, The.   Big Spectacular Play.   Louis Aragon.   YaTCFP, *tr. by* Mary Ann Caws

Friend, with regard to this same hare.   To the Rev. Mr. Powell.   Christopher Smart.   OBWVE

Friendless and faint, with martyred steps and slow.   Calvary.   Edwin Arlington Robinson.   GI; MoAmPo

Friendless Blues.   Mercedes Gilbert.   NAAPv.2

Friendliest Thing (Two People Can Do), The.   Ervin Drake.   ReLy

Friendly cow all red and white, The.   Cow, The.   Robert Louis Stevenson.   NTCP; TLR; WHSW

Friendly Skies.   Bruce A. Jacobs.   BtF

Friendly Town #1.   Safiya Henderson-Holmes.   UnSA

Friendly Town #3.   Safiya Henderson-Holmes.   UnSA

Friends.   Helen Hunt Jackson.   PoBW

Friends.   Bill Kushner.   PA9/11

Friends.   May Muzaffar.   PoArWo, *tr. by* Tahia Abdel Nasser

Friends.   William Butler Yeats.   NoAM

Friends: "Joseph is without doubt rent in pieces an evil beast hath devoured him."   Nathan Yonathan.   NRoS, *tr. by* Esther Raizen

Friends, The.   Bertolt Brecht.   PoSu, *tr. by* Michael Hamburger

Friends and High Places.   Jeffrey McDaniel.   LaCa

Friends are unhappy; their long night.   Winter Work.   Peter Fallon.   PBCIP

Friends Beyond.   Stella Davis.   RWPCtW

Friends Beyond.   Thomas Hardy.   FaBoVe; OBEV

Friends Departed.   Henry Vaughan. *See* They Are All Gone into the World of Light!

Friends in Private.   Herodas.   HePo, *tr. by* Barbara Hughes Fowler

Friends, last night I carefully watched my love.   Caring for My Lover.   Jelaluddin Rumi.   WoPoe, *tr. by* Willis Barnstone

Friends my own age all have kids they can't wait.   Without.   Bruce Berger.   OPRER

Friends of faces unknown and a land.   Only a Curl.   Elizabeth Barrett Browning.   TreFP

Friends / our dear sister.   Goodbye Party for Miss Pushpa T. S.   Nissim Ezekiel.   OBCoV

Friends, Romans, countrymen, lend me your ears.   William Shakespeare.   MakPoe; OxAEP-1; OxBEV; WaAnP *Fr.* Julius Caesar.

Friends, there has to be a limit.   *Unknown.*   PriapPo *Fr.* Priapus Poems, The.

Friends, wake up! Why do you go on sleeping?   Only Woman Awake, The.   Kabir.   WED, *tr. by* Robert Bly

Friends, when my latest bed of rest is made.   Thomas Doubleday.   CenSon

Friends whose names smell powdery.   Healthy Remedies.   Georges Henein.   SurPaPo, *tr. by* Mary Ann Caws *and* Jean-Pierre Cauvin

Friends—With a Difference.   Mary Elizabeth Coleridge.   VWP

Friendship.   Hartley Coleridge. *See* To a Friend.

Friendship.   Florence Converse.   PoBW

Friendship.   Dinah Maria Mulock Craik.   ITBLP

Friendship.   Margaretta Faugeres.   PoBW

Friendship: "Death gives way sometimes."   Fedya Filkova.   CSCBP, *tr. by* Georgi Belev and Lisa Sapinkopf

Friendship.   Katherine Mansfield.   PoBW

Friendship.   Cole Porter.   ReLy

Friendship.   Shel Silverstein.   NTCP

Friendship.   Anatoly Steiger.   TCRusP, *tr. by* Paul Schmidt

Friendship.   Mary Julia Young.   CenSon

Friendship, The.   Toi Derricotte.   PBCAP

Friendship After Love.   Ella Wheeler Wilcox.   APN-2; LW

Friendship, as some sage poet sings.   On the Aphorism "L'Amitié est l'Amour sans Ailes."   Charlotte Smith.   CABP; PEW

Friendship Between Ephelia and Ardelia.   Anne Finch, Countess of Winchilsea.   NALW; NoP-4; NoP-5; PoBW

Friendship for a Woman of Grace.   J. Greshoff.   TuT, *tr. by* Dennis O'Driscoll

Friendship! I hate thy name—my rankled heart.   Friendship.   Margaretta Faugeres.   PoBW

Friendship in Emblem[e], or the Seal[e], to my dearest Lucasia. Katherine Philips. CABP; EMWP; PBRV

Friendship's folly, to utter. Miscarriage. Joseph P. Clancy. AngWePo

Friendship's Mystery[s], to my dearest Lucasia. Katherine Philips. BASC; BrAP; NAEL-7v1; PBRV; PEW

Friend—the face I wallow toward. What I Like. Alice Fulton. WeW-3

Frightful Release, A. Gertrude Stein. MotU; TCAPo *Fr.* Tender Buttons.

Frigidarium (cold room). Matthea Harvey. IAoNAP *Fr.* Thermae.

Frigidity the hesitant. Cold, The. Yvor Winters. APT-2

Fringe-Area Reception. Halvard Johnson. MiVo

Fringed Gentians. Abbie Huston Evans. APT-1

Frisbees. Giulia Niccolai. *tr. by* Gayle Ridinger
   "Careful that these *Frisbees*." ItPo, *tr. by* Gayle Ridinger

Frisbees '88. Giulia Niccolai. *tr. by* Gayle Ridinger
   ""What's that?" the boy asks his mother, pointing to the flag." ItPo, *tr. by* Gayle Ridinger

Frisbees on Light. Giulia Niccolai. CItWP, *tr. by* Cinzia Sartini Blum and Lara Trubowitz

Frisco-City. Blaise Cendrars. BLT, *tr. by* Monique Chefdor

Frisky Lamb, A. Christina Georgina Rossetti. WHSW

Fritz. Gerald Stern. MiVo

Fr[o/i]sch. Ernst Jandl. OnScMo

Frog. Issa. WoPoe, *tr. by* Conrad Totman

Frog, A [*epigram*]. Friedrich von Logau. GePo, *tr. by* George C. Schoolfield

Frog, The. Joseph Hilaire Pierre Belloc. ChAP; NOxBChV; NTCP

Frog, The. Francis Ponge. BLT, *tr. by* Beth Archer

Frog, The. Francis Ponge. WED, *tr. by* Robert Bly

Frog, The [*with music*]. Unknown. NBLV; NOxBChV; NTCP

Frog and I. Issa. IllVoic *Fr.* Issa: A Suite of Haiku.

Frog I Saved from a Snake, The. Robert Sund. WhBo

Frog in the Swimming Pool, The. Debora Greger. NoP-4

Frog noise / suddenly stops. Lorine Niedecker. NAAPv.2

Frog Song. Hildegarde Flanner. APT-2

Frogs. Norman Alexander MacCaig. WaAnP

Frogs, The. Archibald Lampman. BrAP

Frogs and crickets. Revelation. Aaron Pope and Jodi A. Shaw. IFF

Frogs and snakes and a dead cat or two. Our Spring Needs Shoveling. Haniel Long. APT-1

Frogs sit more solid. Frogs. Norman Alexander MacCaig. WaAnP

Frogs time out of mind, The. Aesop's Fable of the Frogs. Jean de La Fontaine. OBVE, *tr. by* John Hookham Frere

Frolic. George Russell. MoBrPo

Frolic architecture of the snow, The. (LL) Snow-Storm [*or* Snowstorm], The. Ralph Waldo Emerson. APN-1; BrAP; ITBLP; MoW; NAAL-3; NAAPv.1; NCAP; NoP-4; NoP-5; OxBoAm; PoPoPo; TCAPo; TFi; TreFP; WaAnP

Frolic in the Snow, A. William Cowper. DiBP

Frolicsome Old Dog, The. John Clare. DiBP *Fr.* Shepherd's [*or* Shepheards] Calendar, The.

From '41 to '51. John Masefield. SacPr *Fr.* Everlasting Mercy, The.

From 66 to 70 A.D. Rome and Palestine tore. Wars of Imperialism. John Foulcher. NOBAu

From a Boat at Coniston. Norman Nicholson. NLP

From a Clinic Waiting Room. Amy Clampitt. WaAnP

From a Conversation During Divorce. Carol Rumens. EmeKit

From a determinable horizon. Axiom. Walter Conrad Arensberg. APT-1

From a Distance I Can See. Jennifer Moxley. IIR

From a distance, I watch. Practical Concerns. William J. Harris. EGAG

From a distance—twilight's distance, which is measureless. Night Fishing. Caroline Price. Prnts

From a documentary on marsupials I learn. Nurture. Maxine W. Kumin. CAP-8; PoA 2002

From a donkey, excuse me, one lesson is given. Fanny Howe. FTOS

From a Dream. Ch'in Kuan. CrYelRi, *tr. by* Sam Hamill

From a friend's friend I taste friendship. Dirge. Stevie Smith. HarvBoo; NPeEn

From A Funeral Song, Upon the Decease of Annes His Mother. Nicholas Grimald. NoP-4 *Fr.* Funeral Song, Upon the Decease of Annes His Mother, A.

From a German War Primer. Bertolt Brecht. AF

From a hand neither one of us could see. (LL) Kiss, The. Marie Howe. ExTi; FaoP

From a hummock in the Malookas. Hummock in the Malookas, A. Matthew Rohrer. AmPoNex

From a junto that longs for absolute power. Libera nos, Domine—Deliver Us, O Lord. Philip Freneau. OxBEV

From a Late Diary. Gabriel Preil. FIT, *tr. by* Robert Friend

From a Letter: About Snow. Toi Derricotte. SpirFl

From a letter thrown on the table a line comes which runs across the pine plank. Lines of the Hand, The. Julio Cortázar. MotU; TCLAP, *tr. by* Paul Blackburn

From a libation cup. Shang Cup. Louis Zukofsky. APT-2

From a little basket on the kitchen shelf I was about to. Concerning a Girl. Shuntaro Tanikawa. VCWP, *tr. by* Harold Wright

From a little town quickly passed over. (LL) Twirling. Jane Flanders. ItWoWo; PBCAP

From a London Bookshop. Unknown. NBLV

From a long way off I can see the cross-. Blueprints. Madeline DeFrees. ExTi

From a long-abandoned Mission. (LL) Lass of Aughrim, The. Paul Muldoon. NoAM; PBCIP

From a martin's / back. (LL) At Yorktown. Charles Olson. FTtHH; HarvBoo

From a Mooring on the Tonglu to a Friend in Yangzhou. Meng Hao Jan. CCL1, *tr. by* Witter Bynner

From a New Height. Andrea Zanzotto. PML, *tr. by* Ruth Feldman and Brian Swann

From a new peony. Sonnet for Minimalists. Mona Van Duyn. FFC; WeW-3

From a Notebook. James Merrill. MoW

From a Paris Hotel Room. Jennifer Bartlett. ICANM

From a passing train at twilight. Renewal Notice. Bruce Dawe. BMAP

From a Photograph. George Oppen. FTOS

From a pot of wine among the flowers. Drinking Alone with the Moon. Li Po. APT-1; ASA, *tr. by* Witter Bynner and Kang-hu Kiang

From a Railway Carriage. Robert Louis Stevenson. NePenScot

From a red tile roof. Richard Wright. APT-2

From a Republican Grave: Daniel Henry Deniehy, 1828–1865. Philip Mead. NOBAu

From a Revolutionary to J. L. Borges. Roque Dalton. TCLAP, *tr. by* Julie Schumacher

From a ruler that's a curse. Litany. Charles Cotton. OBSV

From a Sick Poetesse to Mrs St George on Her Feeding the Swans. *Poets of the Tixall Circle.* EMWP

From a small boat on a large river. Trying to Sleep After Studying Color Photos of Goma. Monifa Atungaye Love. BtF

From a Spanish Cloister. G. K. Chesterton. UV

From a Survivor. Adrienne Rich. LoL; NALW

From a Talk. Yevgeny Aleksandrovich Yevtushenko. CLPP, *tr. by* Anselm Hollo

From a thousand Chinese dinners, one cookie. Robert Mezey. RaBo *Fr.* Thousand Chinese Dinners, A.

From a thread in space, endless and unbroken. Without unravelling. Jacques Dupin. VCWP *Fr.* Songs of Rescue.

From a Train Window. Edna St. Vincent Millay. GM

From a Travel Diary. T. H. Parry-Williams. BBMWP, *tr. by* Anthony Conran

From a Vacant House. Mark Wunderlich. NeAmPo

From a Very Little Sphinx. Edna St. Vincent Millay. NOxBChV

From a well you mount up, dear child. Your head a pyre. Whisper in the Dark. Sándor Weöres. IQMS, *tr. by* Edwin Morgan

From a Woman's Life. Maura Eichner. UpMys

From a world more full of weeping than he can understand. (LL) Stolen Child, The. William Butler Yeats. NAEL-6v2; NAEL-7v2; NoP-4; NoP-5; WaAnP

From Abertillery and Aberdare. Angry Summer, The. Idris Davies. AngWePo

From above it's a dickie or a verdant tie skewed sideways, banana or schlong. Florida Anasazi, The. Campbell McGrath. NAPBL

From afar I beheld him. What Am I Chasing! Hala Mohammad. PoArWo, *tr. by* Cornelia Al-Khaled

From age seven I began to crave. Raspa. Orlando Ricardo Menes. RWB

From all my lame defeats and oh! much more. Apologist's Evening Prayer, The. Clive Staples Lewis. SacPr

From all the rooms, my father suddenly. Death of My Father, The. Yehuda Amichai. FIT, *tr. by* Robert Friend

From all these trees. Basho. EH; SoOfWa, *tr. by* Sam Hamill

From Altitude, the Diamonds. Richard Hugo. MoASP

From America comes the little huming-bird. Vermont Apollinaire. William Corbett. PmAP

From an airtight office window. Downpour. Daisy Zamora. CLPP, *tr. by* Barbara Paschke

From an Album. Genrik Veniaminovich Sapgir. ItGoST, *tr. by* J. Kates

From an Apocryphal Gospel. Jorge Luis Borges. GI *Fr.* Apocryphal Gospel, An.

From an ass to an analyst and back. Joyce Mansour. MFP, *tr. by* Martin Sorrell

From an Old House in America. Adrienne Rich. TRP

From anger into the pit of sleep. Wife to Husband. Fleur Adcock. BrAP

From Arena. Dennis Phillips. FTOS *Fr.* Exile.

From Ariadne's Crown. Shooting Star, A. Edith Matilda Thomas. ChAP

From as far away as china. Maria 2. Asaf Halet Çelebi. NaPG, *tr. by* Talat Sait Halman

From Asia, the stony Rife. Roadside Weeds. John Haines. PoCoUp

From Athens to Cairo. Sunil Gangopadhyay. PML, *tr. by* Nandini Gupta

From behind he looks like a man. China. Dorianne Laux. LW

From Behind the Closed Door. Buland Al-Haidari. IrPoTo, *tr. by* Hussein Kadhim and Christopher Merrill

From behind the gas mask. Siren of Love, A. Asher Reich. NRoS, *tr. by* Esther Raizen

From Belfast to Suffolk. William Peskett. PNI

From below, the waist-thick pine. Yggdrasill. Paul Muldoon. PBCIP

From Belsen a crate of gold teeth. Riddle. William Heyen. HP; SoSe-8

From between my own teeth I come out smoking. Hungry Man's Wheel, The. César Vallejo. PFTM-1

From beyond the grave. (LL) Proofs. Tadeusz Rózewicz. PoSu; StAl, *tr. by* Adam Czerniawski

From Bindle's opera house in the village. Edgar Lee Masters. APT-1 *Fr.* Spoon River Anthology.

From Birmingham to Bristol in a Boxcar. Carole Boston Weatherford. FuFl

From black branches. (LL) Love Song: "Sweep the house clean." William Carlos Williams. MoAmPo; SAmP

From blacked-out streets. Denise Levertov. TaR

From blossoms. Ode to the Lemon. Pablo Neruda. PoetW, *tr. by* Margaret Sayers Peden

From blossoms comes. From Blossoms. Li-Young Lee. BeAl; GoPo; IPoFL; RoV; StAl; TRP

From blue Loch Carron rise white and sheer. Among the Hebrides. Emily Jane Pfeiffer. ViWPN

From blue sky to green forest, bathing. Susannah Bathing. Ödön Palasovszky. IQMS, *tr. by* Kenneth McRobbie

From Bowling Green. Al Young. ESEAA

From brightening fields of ether fair-disclosed. James Thomson. *Fr.* Seasons, The.

From broken dreams. Relations: Old Light / New Sun / Postmistress / Earth / 04421. Philip Booth. GoPo

From Brooklyn, over the Brooklyn Bridge, on this fine morning. Invitation to Miss Marianne Moore. Elizabeth Bishop. NALW

From Bulgaria, the roll of thick, wild cannon blasts. Serbian Postcard 1. Miklós Radnóti. ConPit, *tr. by* Clayton Eshleman and Gyula Kodolanyi

From Bulgaria thick, wild cannon pounding rolls. Picture Postcards. Miklós Radnóti. AF

From burweed / Such a butterfly. Issa. ZenPo, *tr. by* Takashi Ikemoto and Lucien Stryk

From buttered gold to. Kalamu ya Salaam. SpirFl *Fr.* New Orleans Haiku.

From Canaan Joseph shall return, whose face. Khwaja Shams-ad-din Muhammad Hafiz. TAL *Fr.* Odes.

From Catullus Poem LI. B. P. Nichol. OpeFie

From child to youth; from youth to arduous man. Dante Gabriel Rossetti. SacPr *Fr.* House of Life, The.

From childhood's hour I have not been. Alone. Edgar Allan Poe. APN-1; ItP; NAAL-3; NAAPv.1

From Chin-Chu Creek, Past the Ridge, Along the Stream. Hsieh Ling-yün. ChinPo, *tr. by* Ye Weilian [*or* Yeh Wei-lien *or* Wai-lim Yip]

From Clee to heaven the beacon burns. A. E. Housman. NIP-4 *Fr.* Shropshire Lad, A.

From Colony to Nation. Irving Layton. BrAP; NIL-7

From coming apart at the ends. (LL) · Saturday Afternoon, When Chores Are Done. Harryette Mullen. ISC; OxAAAP

From counties far and wide the people come. State Fair. David Riley Russell. TiP2

From Cumberland's funerals, eldest son, I. Night Traffic Near Winchester, Virginia. Dave Jeddie Smith. LPSFW

From darkness where no stars shine. Observed Observer, The. Alan Gould. BMAP

From Death and dark Oblivion, ne'er the same. Ben Jonson. GS

From death to life thou mightst him yet recover. (LL) Michael Drayton. AEP; BASC; ClHu; GSo; HeIP-4; NAEL-6v1; NAEL-7v1; NoP-5; OPOU; OxBSo; SoSe-8; TFi; WaAnP *Fr.* Idea.

From deep below a world of eerie silence. Letter to My Spouse. Miklós Radnóti. IQMS, *tr. by* Peter Zollman

From deep within. Basho. EMJL, *tr. by* Haruo Shirane

From deepest need cry out, oh hungered heart! From Deepest Need. Quirinus Kuhlmann. GePo, *tr. by* George C. Schoolfield

From depth of dole wherein my soul doth dwell. George Gascoigne. ChIV-1; SacPr *Fr.* De Profundis.

From depth of grief. Mary Sidney Herbert, Countess of Pembroke. EMWP *Fr.* Psalms.

From depth of sinn and from a diepe despaire. Bible, *O.T.* OxBEV *Fr.* Psalms.

From Depths of Woe I Cry to You. Martin Luther. GePo, *tr. by* F. Samuel Janow

From Disaster. George Oppen. APT-2; NAMCP V.1

From early on I was nothing. From Early On I Was. Ch'oe Sûngja. EcSo, *tr. by* Mickey Hong

From Eastertide to Eastertide. Ballad of a Nun, A. John Davidson. MoBrPo; UV

From epigram to epic is the course. Strange Metamorphosis of Poets. Howard Nemerov. NoP-5

From Escomb, County Durham: July 1990. John Seed. Oth

From every corner fears resolves are yelling. Assault. Reinhold Grimm. GTCP, *tr. by* the author

From every direction. Basho. SoOfWa, *tr. by* Sam Hamill

From every limb the leaves are cast. De Ramis Cadunt Folia (Love in Winter). *Unknown.* WoPoe, *tr. by* Phillip Holland

From every place you cast your wandering eyes. Anne, Viscountess Irwin Ingram. OBGa *Fr.* Castle Howard, the Seat of the Rt. Hon. Charles, Earl of Carlisle.

From everything a little remained. Residue. Carlos Drummond de Andrade. GPTC; PoetW; VCWP, *tr. by* Mark Strand

From Exile [*with music*]. Dafydd Benfras. OBWVE, *tr. by* Anthony Conran

From fairest creatures we desire increase. William Shakespeare. HeIP-4; NAEL-6v1; NAEL-7v1; NoP-5; WaAnP *Fr.* Sonnets.

From fake astrologies, from customs a bit lugubrious. Taste. Pablo Neruda. ConPit, *tr. by* Clayton Eshleman

From Fanon. Sandra Maria Esteves. PueRic

From Far. Alain Veinstein. OnScMo, *tr. by* Robert Kocik

From far away, a mile or so. Bayonet Training. Vernon Scannell. FaBoWar

From Far Dakota's Cañons (June 25, 1876). Walt Whitman. AmWaPo

From far, from eve and morning. A. E. Housman. HeIP-4; MoBrPo; NoP-4; NoP-5 *Fr.* Shropshire Lad, A.

From far off I have brought medicines, she watches me because I am her son. Saitō Mokichi. WoPoe *Fr.* Mother Dies.

From far she's come, and very old. Age in Youth. Trumbull Stickney. ColAP

From far, with the child. From Far. Alain Veinstein. OnScMo, *tr. by* Robert Kocik

From Father to Son [*with music*]. Emyr Humphreys. AngWePo; OBWVE; TCAWP

From fealty to light. (LL) Enthusiast, The. Herman Melville. ChIV-1; NAAL-3

From Feathers to Iron. Cecil Day Lewis.
    Now She Is like the White Tree-Rose. MoBrPo

From Florrie Abraham Witness, December 1972. Jack A. Mapanje. HBAPE

For a Pastoral Family. Judith Wright.
    I To my Brothers. BMAP

From '41 to '51. Everlasting Mercy, The. John Masefield.

From frozen climes, and endless tracks [*or* tracts] of snow. Winter-Piece, A. Ambrose Philips. NPeEn

From furthest Spirit—God. (LL) On a Columnar Self. Emily Dickinson. APN-2; NoP-4; NoP-5

From garden-beds I tend, it is not far. Texas Cowboy. Karle Wilson Baker. TiP2

From gazelles' eyes the pupils dropped. War Diaries. Sami Mahdi. IrPoTo, *tr. by* Ferial J. Ghazoul

From ghoulies and ghosties. Things That Go Bump in the Night. *Unknown.* NTCP

From giving and giving and giving / food and birth. (LL) Bicentennial Anti-Poem for Italian-American Women. Daniela Gioseffi. FTtHH; UnSA

From gloomie shaddowes of eternall Night. Piers Gaveston [1619]. Michael Drayton.

From Gloucester Out. Edward Dorn. PmAP

From God's side even of such a simple thing? (LL) To a Daisy. Alice Thompson Meynell. MoBrPo; SacPr; VWP

From green and blue things and arguments that cannot be proven. (LL) Canal Bank Walk. Patrick Kavanagh. MoBrPo; NAMCP V.1; NoAM; NoP-4; NoP-5

From Green Mountain. William Reed Huntington. APN-2

From Greenland's Icy Mountains. Reginald Heber. SacPr

From Ground Zero. Everett Hoagland. FuFl

From Guinea to Haiti to Brooklyn. And the Saga Continues. Ted Wilson. BRtP

From harmony, from heavenly [*or* heav'nly] harmony. Song for St Cecilia's Day, 1687, A. John Dryden. BASC; NAEL-6v1; NAEL-7v1; NoP-5; NOSC; OBEV; OxAEP-1; TFi; TreFP; WoPoe

From haunt of man, from day's obtrusive glare. To the Bat. Ann Radcliffe. CenSon

From heaped-up mound of earth and from the heart. Poem of Jacobus Sadoletus on the Statue of Laocoon, The. Jacopo Sadoleto. GS, *tr. by* H. S. Wilkinson

From Hear to Air. Douglas Messerli. FTOS

From heart through mind into image. William Oandasan. HATNAP *Fr.* Past, The.

From Heaven Above to Earth I Come. Martin Luther. GePo

From Heaven's Gate to Hampstead Heath. Ballad of Hampstead Heath, The. James Elroy Flecker. MoBrPo

From her autumn-lotus mouth. Kamalākānta Bhattācārya. SinGod, *tr. by* Rachel Fell McDermott

From / her thoughts. (LL) Rain: "As the rain falls." William Carlos Williams. ItP; OxBoAm; WaAnP

From Heraclitus. Alan Dugan. PoA 2002

From here / all the way there. No One. Kim Chiha. CAMKP, *tr. by* David R. McCann

From here an empty echo penetrates to Hades. Erinna. SaLy, *tr. by* Diane Rayor

From here do I send. Medicine Songs. *Unknown.* APN-2, *tr. by* Francis La Flesche

From here, I can go anywhere. Eye Behind the I, The. Adam David Miller. ASA

From here it is necessary to ship all bodies east. Thomas McGrath. GifTon *Fr.* Letter to an Imaginary Friend.

From here it's five miles to the black top. Thirty-Five Miles to a Traffic Light. David Budbill. AmZen

From here, ten to fourteen rows of folding and branching. Complex Mechanism of the Break, The. Jorie Graham. AWPTFC

From here, the quay, one looks above to mark. Harbour Bridge, The. Thomas Hardy. NoAM

From here, this poem a neon pall over the tarry asphalt. Set for a Southern Gothic. Brian Teare. LegDan

From Here to Eternity. Mary Ruefle. AmAlph

From high above the birds look down and sing because they see. Street Ballad. George Barker. GoPo

From His Bed in the Capital City. David Berman. LegDan

From his brimstone bed at break of day. Devil's Thoughts, The. Samuel Taylor Coleridge and Robert Southey. NPBRoP; OBSV

From his brimstone bed at the break of day. Devil, The. Robert Southey. NOxBChV

From his own solitude to the world unheeding. Llewelyn Wyn Griffith. OBWVE *Fr.* Barren Tree, The.

From his wanderings far to eastward. Henry Wadsworth Longfellow. NCAP *Fr.* Song of Hiawatha, The.

From Homegrown: An Asian-American Anthology of Writers. Colleen J. McElroy. LTA

From Hot Springs Mountain. Basho. EMJL, *tr. by* Haruo Shirane

From inmost depths of clear dark blue. (LL) Upward Look, An. James Merrill. CAP-8; NAMCP V.2; PoPoPo

From inside the room. Climbing Down the Snowy Mountain. Muso Soseki. EaWin, *tr. by* W. S. Merwin

From its unknown source, a resurrection, a new spirit? (LL) Agony . . . A Resurrection, An. Assumpta Acam-Oturu. HAWP; NAfrP

From it[t] self[e] never turning [*or* turnynge]. (LL) As You Came from the Holy Land [of Walsingham]. *Unknown, sometimes at. to* Sir Walter Ralegh. NoSic; NPeEn; OBEV; OxAEP-2; OxBEV; PBRV; TFi

From just on puberty, I lived in funeral. Burning Want. Les A. Murray. HarvBoo

From lake Tung-t'ing we travel west. On the Way to Pa-ling. Yüan Mei. ColAnChi, *tr. by* Jonathan Chaves

From life. (LL) Release. Adelaide Crapsey. APT-1; NAAPv.2; OxBoAm

From life itself contentedly may part. (LL) To Death. Mary Tighe. CenSon; NPBRoP

From Life to Love. Countee Cullen. ChIV-1

From Lines in a Dream. Gennady Aygi. WoBe, *tr. by* Peter France

From Lines of Swinburne. Charles Bernstein. FTOS

From lips notched in the pinebranch bled. His Long Home. Rosanna Warren. ExTi

From Los Angeles Looking South. Eloise Klein Healy. WiU

From loud sound and still chance. Baroque Comment. Louise Bogan. APT-2

From low to high doth dissolution climb. William Wordsworth. CenSon; HeIP-4; NAEL-6v2; NAEL-7v2; NoP-4; NoP-5; OBEV *Fr.* Ecclesiastical Sonnets.

From Lo-yang's autumn willows. Farewell to Master Tan Returning to Min. Chia Tao. CSKM, *tr. by* Mike O'Connor

From many a lip came sounds of praise. Letitia Elizabeth Landon. RWP *Fr.* Improvisatrice, The.

From March 1979. Tomas Tranströmer. StAl, *tr. by* Robin Fulton

From me far off, with others all too near. (LL) William Shakespeare. AWTN; CAGL *Fr.* Sonnets.

From Merthyr to Dowlais the tramway climbs. Deluge, 1939, The. Saunders Lewis. BBMWP, *tr. by* Anthony Conran

From mighty Caesar, and his boundless grace. John, Duke of Buckingham and Normandy Sheffield. STuOW *Fr.* On Brutus, an Ode.

From mind to mind. Heavens, The. Denis Johnson. LaCa

From Mr Fowler sharpening farmers' saws. (LL) Kumquat for John Keats, A. Tony Harrison. BeAl; NoP-4; NoP-5; WaAnP

From Mohawk's mouth, far westing with the sun. Joel Barlow. APN-1 *Fr.* Columbiad, The.

From Molepolole and Morogoro. Reflexions on the Seizure of the Suez, and on a Proposal to Line the Banks of That Canal with Billboard Advertisements. Howard Nemerov. NBLV

From Momentary Work, A Wrench. Jean Day. FTOS

From momentary work, a wrench, to just fall forward. From Momentary Work, A Wrench. Jean Day. FTOS

From morning slumber a stir a shift a spinning motion of tossing. Maya Bejerano. DTA *Fr.* Hymns of Job.

From Mustapha. Fulke, 1st Baron Brooke Greville. *See* Chorus Sacerdotum.

From My Diary, 3. Vera Bulich. ARWW, *tr. by* Catriona Kelly

From My Diary, July 1914. Wilfred Owen. MoBrPo

From my face. And will obtain a blush. (LL) But first one must free oneself. Patrizia Cavalli. NeIt; VCWP, *tr. by* Patrizia Cavalli and Robert McCraken

From my father my strong heart. Gifts. Ronald Stuart Thomas. NPeEn

From my favorite place in the Chung-nan Mountains. Oxhead Temple. Ssu-k'ung Shu. ColAnChi, *tr. by* Hellmut Wilhelm

From my feet. (LL) Charles Olson. APT-2; NAAL-5; NAMCP V.2; PmAP *Fr.* Maximus Poems, The.

From My High Love. Kenneth Patchen. MoAmPo

From my high love I look at that poor world there. From My High Love. Kenneth Patchen. MoAmPo

From my high window I can watch. Winter in Minneapolis. Richard Ryan. PBCIP

From My Hut in Miura. Muso Soseki. EaWin, *tr. by* W. S. Merwin

From my lyre within the sky. (LL) Israfel. Edgar Allan Poe. APN-1; NAAL-3; NAAPv.1; TCAPo

From my mother, the antique mirror. Heritage. Linda Hogan. UnSA

From my mother—like others—I received the still-unopened letter. Topography. Josué Ramírez. RMCMP, *tr. by* Joan Lindgren

From My Mother's Home. Leah Goldberg. FIT, *tr. by* Robert Friend

From my mother's sleep I fell into the State. Death of the Ball Turret Gunner, The. Randall Jarrell. AmWaPo; BrAP; ClHu; ColAP; EMP; HarvBoo; HeIP-4; InGu; InoFa; MoAmPo; NAAL-5; NAMCP V.2; NIL-7; NIP-4; NoAM; NoP-4; NoP-5; OBWP; OtW; OxBoAm; PoAgWa; PoPoPo; PoWW; PtR; PWW2; SoSe-8; TFi; VCAP; WaAnP

From My Notebook. Pablo Neruda. TAPaP, *tr. by* Willis Barnstone

From My Study at the Mouth of the Valley: A Message to Censor Yang. Ch'ien Ch'i. CCL1, *tr. by* Witter Bynner

From my tensed nucleus I trace a circular itinerary, a single resonance of a skein passed to my abdomen. Skein. Silvia Eugenia Castillero. SPV, *tr. by* Jen Hofer

From my wife and household and fields. Air and Fire. Wendell Berry. LPSFW

From My Window. C. K. Williams. CAP-8

From my window I can see the moonlight stroking the smooth surface of the river. Dissonance. Amy Lowell. APT-1; NAAPv.2

From my youth up I never liked the city. I Return to the Place I Was Born. T'ao Ch'ien. NDACCP; WaAnP, *tr. by* Kenneth Rexroth

From narrow provinces. Moose, The. Elizabeth Bishop. NAAL-5; NALW; NoP-4; NoP-5; StAl; WaAnP

From Nature doth emotion come, and moods. William Wordsworth. *Fr.* Prelude, The; Growth of a Poet's Mind [1850 version; Selections from Anthologies].

From "Nature's Dessert." Margaret Lucas Cavendish, Duchess of Newcastle. STuOW *Fr.* Dissert, A.

From near the sea, like Whitman my great predecessor, I call. Ode: Salute to the French Negro Poets. Frank O'Hara. PFTM-2

From north, from south, from east, from west. Oliver Goldsmith. STuOW *Fr.* Captivity, The.

From Nothingness into a massive Being. Letter to a Zen Master. Han Wo. CCL1, *tr. by* Graeme Wilson

From now on. Kamalākānta Bhattācārya. SinGod, *tr. by* Rachel Fell McDermott

From Now On. James Harms. AmPoNex

From now on. Issa. EH, *tr. by* Robert Hass

From now on I'll call you England. Again. Deanna Ortiz. ICANM

From now on let birds tell you of our life. Letter of the 26th June. Philippe Jaccottet. MFP, *tr. by* Martin Sorrell

From now on, like a departure seen from a distance. Absence of Joaquín. Pablo Neruda. ItP, *tr. by* W. S. Merwin

From now till never, goodbye. Goodbye. Mihai Eminescu. SonAtl, *tr. by* Chris Constantinescu and Phoebe Ravenhall

From Now Until Chile. Emma Sepúlveda-Pulvirenti. TANSG, *tr. by* Shaun Griffin

From Number Nine, Penwiper Mews. Limerick. Edward Gorey. OBCoV

From ocean. For Barbara, Who Brings a Green Stone in the Shape of a Triangle. Hilda Raz. PfSP

From office confinement all year long. East of the Town. Wei Ying-wu. CCL1, *tr. by* Witter Bynner

From one darkness. Lady Izumi. WoPoe, *tr. by* Steven D. Carter

From one of the white throats which it hid among? (LL) Vision by Sweetwater. John Crowe Ransom. HarvBoo; OxBoAm

From one to another? (LL) Acting: "I most remember the class where we lie." Suzanne Cleary. BeAl; P180

From one unus'd in pomp of words to raise. To My Venerable Friend, the President of the Royal Academy. Washington Allston. APN-1

From Orford Ness to Shingle Street. Dawn on the East Coast. Alun Lewis. OBWP

From our corner window. Busses, The. Frederick Morgan. PoDa

From our high window we saw the towers. When the Towers Fell. Galway Kinnell. AmWaPo

From our low seat beside the fire. Call, The. Charlotte Mew. PoCho

From ourselves, for ourselves? (LL) As Difference Blends into Identity. Josephine Miles. NoAM; OxBoAm

From out of the waters it came with a moan. Beast in Man, The. George Clutesi. HATNAP

From out the font of being, undefiled. Mathilde Blind. ViWPN *Fr.* Ascent of Man, The.

From out the heart of Summer's joy. (LL) Pomona. William Morris. NPeEn; OxBEV; WoPoe

From out the heated city Cyclist takes. From Out the Heated City. S. Conant Foster. ArBi

From outside a hedge, a hen calls her chicks. Buson. EMJL *Fr.* Spring Breeze on the Kema Embankment.

From Pa-Ling, the sight of Ch'ang-an. Ascend the Three Mountains Toward the Evening: Looking Back at the Capital. Hsieh T'iao. ChinPo, *tr. by* Ye Weilian [*or* Yeh Wei-lien *or* Wai-lim Yip]

From Paris on a Postcard. Yosano Akiko. CAoMJL1, *tr. by* Janine Beichman

From Pent-up Aching Rivers. Walt Whitman. APN-1; EroLit; NAAL-3

From Persian looms the silk *he* wove. To Mr. Blanchard, the Celebrated Aeronaut in America. Philip Freneau. APN-1

From Place to Place forlorn I go. Sir Richard Steele. IrLP *Fr.* Conscious Lovers, The.

From plains that reel to southward, dim. Heat. Archibald Lampman. BrAP

From plane of light to plane, wings dipping through. Evening Hawk. Robert Penn Warren. APT-2; ColAP; InGu; NAMCP V.1; NoP-4; NoP-5; OWoS; VCAP; WaAnP

From Plane to Plane. Robert Frost. MoAmPo

From pointed pates hats fly into the blue. End of the World. Jakov Van Hoddis. GTCP, *tr. by* Irmgard Hunt

From red to green all the yellow dies away. Windows. Guillaume Apollinaire. CuPo

From relief to relief, the white lines, the white paper. Amelia Rosselli. ItPo, *tr. by* Gayle Ridinger

From Revelation and Defeat. Georg Trakl. MotU, *tr. by* Stuart Friebert

From *Rice*. Joan Logghe. ICANM

From Rich Uneasy America to My Friend Christopher Logue. Adrian Mitchell. SeSe

From Rivers, and from the Earth Itself. James Purdy. CAGL

From Rooftops, Kenji Takezo Throws Himself. Rick Noguchi. NeAmPo

From Room to Room. Jane Kenyon. LoL

From Rosary. Barbara Tran. PuP-23

From Ruin. Julie Suk. PoA 2002

From San Diego. Chryss Yost. GeoHom

From Sand Creek. Simon J. Ortiz.
"At the Salvation Army." NAAL-5

From Sappho to myself, consider the fate of women. Carolyn Kizer. CAP-8; VCAP *Fr.* Pro Femina.

From sea to shining sea! (LL) America the Beautiful. Katharine Lee Bates. APN-2; BLPJKO; FaBoA; HHAm; OxBoAm

From Shasta south to El Cajon. Drouth, The. Charles Augustus Keeler. ASA

From side to side the sufferer tossed. Message, The. Mathilde Blind. ViWPN

From slavery then your rising realms to save. Joel Barlow. TCAPo *Fr.* Columbiad, The.

From snow that melted only yesterday. (LL) Spring Pools. Robert Frost. APT-1; ColAP; CtM; NoAM; OxBoAm

From *So* Mountain. *Vietnamese Oral Tradition.* CaDao, *tr. by* John Balaban

From Some Time to This Place. José Emilio Pacheco. MotU, *tr. by* Philip Levine

From some unsought somewhere. Pain, The. John Graham-Pole. BloBone

From some void. Saturday Morning, A. Manuel A. Viray. ReBoTo

From somewhere over the houses, through the silence. Lovers. Witter Bynner. APT-1; ASA

From "Songs of a Wanderer." Aleksander Wat. BLT

From Soul to Soul. Árpád Tóth. IQMS, *tr. by* Watson Kirkconnell

From *Spoke / Aug 19.* Hannah Weiner. FTOS

From stone to bronze, from bronze to steel. From Stone to Steel. Edwin John Pratt. BrAP; NoP-4; NoP-5

From such a scene depart. (LL) Scale Force, Cumberland. Letitia Elizabeth Landon. NPBRoP; RWP

From sultry Mobile's gulf-indented shore. Joel Barlow. APN-1 *Fr.* Columbiad, The.

From Sunset to Star Rise. Christina Georgina Rossetti. VWP

From sweet weeping to a painful smile. Michelangelo Buonarroti. CAGL, *tr. by* James M. Saslow

From tape 2 "Kitch's Last Meal." Interior Scroll. Carolee Schneemann. PFTM-2

From 10. (LL) All Shook Up. Dan Sicoli. AllShUp; SwNoth

From Texas by electron. Searching for Mooncakes. Kathe Davis. AmZen

From that blest bed the hero came. Andrew Marvell. OBGa *Fr.* Upon Appleton House [To My Lord Fairfax].

From that far land to him? (LL) Indian Names. Lydia Huntley Sigourney. APN-1; ColAP; SWaP

From that last acre on oblivion's heap. Louis Untermeyer. MoAmPo *Fr.* Mother Goose Up-to-Date.

From that prominent bar in Secaucus, N.J. (LL) In a Prominent Bar in Secaucus [One Day]. X. J. Kennedy. GoPo; NBLV; NIL-7; NIP-4; TRP

From that time forth, Authority in France. William Wordsworth. *Fr.* Prelude, The; Growth of a Poet's Mind [1850 version].

From that which made us that which will make us again. (LL) Wheel, The. Edwin Muir. NAMCP V.1; NoAM

From that woman. Issa. SoOfWa, *tr. by* Sam Hamill

From the abstraction I was roused,—and how? William Wordsworth. NAEL-7v2 *Fr.* Excursion, The.

From the Admonitions of St. Theresa of Avila. István Vas. IQMS, *tr. by* George Szirtes

From the Anglo-Saxon. Henry Wadsworth Longfellow and *Unknown. tr. by* Henry Wadsworth Longfellow
  Grave, The. TCAPo, *tr. by* Henry Wadsworth Longfellow

From the Antique. Christina Georgina Rossetti. OxBEV; PEW

From the Arabic: An Imitation. Percy Bysshe Shelley. OBEV

From the archaic ships the green and red. Mathilde in Normandy. Adrienne Rich. YaYoPo

From the ash-colored steel of images. Spring and the Ashura. Miyazawa Kenji. PFTM-1

From the back it looks like a porch. For Esther. Stanley Plumly. GM

From the back of the old cow we went west. Road West, The. Vincent Woods. NIrP

From the Baptismal hour, thro' weal and woe. William Wordsworth. SacPr

From the barbed body, wires. Yearbook. Milo De Angelis. NeIt, *tr. by* Lawrence Venuti

From the bathing machine came a din. Limerick. Edward Gorey. AmWit; OBCoV

From the beginning. East Peak. Muso Soseki. EaWin, *tr. by* W. S. Merwin

From the beginning. Muso Soseki. EaWin, *tr. by* W. S. Merwin

From the beginning of time. Ballad of Love through the Ages. Carlos Drummond de Andrade. PML, *tr. by* Mark Strand

From the beginning of time. Mount Fuji [Selections, 1943]. Kusano Shimpei. CAoMJL1, *tr. by* Leith Morton

From the beginning, / We have been with you. Ancient Ones, The. Patricia Reis. HW

From the being of me, this. In/Vocation. Lawson Fusao Inada. WhBo

From the besieged Ardea all in post. Rape of Lucrece, The. William Shakespeare.

From the besieged hills. Vasco [*or* Vasko] Popa. PoSu *Fr.* St Sava's Spring.

From the black beach and broad expanse of sea. Thomas Parnell. ChIV-1 *Fr.* Hezekiah.

From the black forests inside my mother long ago. (LL) Of Poor B.B. Bertolt Brecht. GTCP; WoPoe, *tr. by* Michael Hamburger

From the black trunk I shake out. Yuba City School. Chitra Divakaruni. GeoHom; LTA; OpBo

From the Boat. Patricia Goedicke. ExTi

From the Book of Divine Consolation. Andrew Zawacki. IAoNAP

From the bough. Issa. BLT; ZenPo, *tr. by* Takashi Ikemoto and Lucien Stryk

From the boy's identification. Myself, Rousseau, a Few Others. William Meredith. YaYoPo

From the breath of these marble fish. From Their Eyes Adorned with Vitreous Sands. Coral Bracho. TANSG, *tr. by* Celeste Kostopulos-Cooperman

From the Bridge. Claribel Alegría. AF

From the bright realms, and happy fields above. To Cleone. Elizabeth Singer Rowe. PoBW

From the bright stars, or from the viewless air. To a Departed Spirit. Felicia Dorothea Hemans. RWP

From the brush pile I wrestled brittle limbs. Flag of Honeysuckle, A. Andrew Hudgins. LPSFW

From the bus I see graffiti. Kevin of the N.E. Crew. Elizabeth Alexander. FFC

From the Canton of Expectation. Seamus Heaney. ModIr

From the ceiling near the roof. Engraving of Blake, An. Mary Kinzie. MakPoe

From the Childhood of Jesus. Robert Pinsky. EmeKit; HarvBoo; OxBoAm; WaAnP

From the Chinese [*with music*]. Michael Smith. PBCIP

From the city: news. Basho. EMJL *Fr.* Plum Blossom Scent.

From the City-Tower of Liuzhou to My Four Fellow-Officials at Zhang, Ding, Feng, and Lian Districts. Liu Tsung-yüan. CCL1, *tr. by* Witter Bynner

From the colour the nature. Ezra Pound. APSN; APT-1 *Fr.* Cantos.

From the conception the increase. Cosmogony. *Unknown.* WoPoe, *tr. by* Richard Taylor

From the cool electric gaze of a Hollywood enigma. California. Paul Hoover. BAP-97

From the Country to the City. Elizabeth Bishop. PoA 2002

From the Cradle to the Graave, or, Through Working and Sweating, Suffering and Hardship, Even Through Prayyer into Damnation. Adolf Wolfli.
　"And now: And now: here begins Our Voyage, hunters and naturalists of indefatigable enthusiasm." PFTM-1

From the dark mood's control. Recovery, The. Edmund Charles Blunden. MoBrPo

From the Dark Tower. Countee Cullen. APT-2; BrAP; ColAP; MakPoe; NAAPv.2; WaAnP

From the dark woods that breathe of fallen showers. Zebras, The. Roy Campbell. MoBrPo; OxBSo

From the day he could talk, the son asked. Initiation, The. Shuja Nawaz. PML

From the days of my youth I loved music, and I have practiced it ever since. Hsi K'ang. CCL1 *Fr.* Lute, The: A Rhapsody.

From the deep shadow of the still fir-groves. Chamouni at Sunrise. Frederike Brün. SacPr, *tr. by* Timothy Dwight

From the desert I come to thee. Bedouin Song. Bayard Taylor. APN-2; TCAPo

From the desert west we jet back east. Jet Lag. Peter Makuck. OtW

From the distant fog. Prisoner's Song, A. Sinan Anton. IrPoTo, *tr. by* the author

From the Domain of Arnheim. Edwin Morgan. EmeKit

From the doorsill of a dream they called my name. From the Doorsill of a Dream. Antonio Machado Ruiz. WED, *tr. by* Robert Bly

From the dress-box's plashing tis. Catch, The. Richard Wilbur. WeW-3

From the Dressing-room. Medbh McGuckian. MoWP

From the dry, rattle-like dahlias. Forgive Me! Andrey Andreievich Voznesensky. RusPo, *tr. by* Robert Arthur Douglas Ford

From the dull confines of the drooping West. His Return to London. Robert Herrick. BASC; NAEL-6v1; NAEL-7v1

From the dust of my bosom! (LL) Edgar Lee Masters. CBCWP; MoAmPo; NAMCP V.1; NoAM; OxBoAm; TFi *Fr.* Spoon River Anthology.

From the earliest poets, the fashion stands. Persius. RomPo *Fr.* Satires.

From the end of the nose. Issa. EH, *tr. by* Robert Hass

From the explosion to the iron split. Pablo Neruda. GifTon, *tr. by* James Nolan

From the Field. Lenard D. Moore. GT

From the fires of Estrées. (LL) Fly, The. Miroslav Holub. NPeEn; PoAgWa; PoetW; PoSu; StAl, *tr. by* Ian Milner and George Theiner

From the first cave, the first farm, the first sage. Violence. Robert Lowell. NoAM

From the first dollar-a-night rooming house on Tremont. Hotels 1970. John Wieners. AHA

From the first it had been like a. Bronzeville Mother Loiters in Mississippi, A. Meanwhile, a Mississippi Mother Burns Bacon. Gwendolyn Brooks. ESEAA; FuFI; IllVoic

From the first shock of leaves their alliance. Park Poem. Paul Blackburn. PmAP

From the Flats. Sidney Lanier. APN-2; NoP-4; NoP-5

From the flower vendor I bought. Tune: "Magnolia Flowers." Li Ch'ing-chao and Jiaosheng Wang. ColAnChi

From the flurry of the uniformed garrison. Scene in a Café. Saunders Lewis. BBMWP, *tr. by* Joseph P. Clancy

From the Foel Eryr ridge the Wicklow Hills are pale. Family. Eirwyn George. BBMWP, *tr. by* Peter Finch

From the forests and highlands. Hymn of Pan. Percy Bysshe Shelley. OBEV

From the French. Charles North. FTOS

From the Frontier of Writing. Seamus Heaney. BrAP; CABP; ModIr; PoetW; PoPoPo

From the Garden. Anne Sexton. LW

From the Garden of the Women Once Fallen. Lorna Goodison. VCWP

From the garden you can see them going past below, the waitresses, the sales girls, arm in arm. Here. Erica Pedretti. MotU, *tr. by* Stuart Friebert

From the geyser ventilators. Business Girls. Sir John Betjeman. UV

From the Great Buddha's. Issa. SoOfWa, *tr. by* Sam Hamill

From the great trees the locusts cry. In August. Hamlin Garland. APN-2

From the Green Book of Yfan. Rolfe Humphries. APT-2

From the grey fires of South-east Asia. (LL) Newscast, The. Ian Hamilton. FaBoWar; NPeEn; PoAgWa

From the Grove Press. Anthony Hecht. AmWit; OBCoV

From the hag[g] and hungry [*or* hungrie] goblin. Tom o' Bedlam's Song. *Unknown.* BASC; NoP-4; NoP-5; NPeEn; TFi

From the half / of the sky. Approach of the Storm, The. *Chippewa Oral Tradition.* NAAL-5; NAAPv.2; OBVE, *tr. by* Frances Densmore

From the Hazel Bough. Earle Birney. BrAP; IFF; NIP-4

From the Healing Dark. Alma Villanueva. HW

From the heart of the earth. Wind of Liberty. Amélia Veiga. HAWP, *tr. by* Julia Kirst

From the heel / Of a half loaf. Austerities. Charles Simic. EmeKit

From the Heights. Li Shang-yin. CrYelRi, *tr. by* Sam Hamill

From the High Ground. Thomas Lux. AmAlph

From the high line spun over us, we hang on to. Confluences at San Francisco. Elton Glaser. PBCAP

From the high terrace porch I watch the dawn. On a View of Pasadena from the Hills. Yvor Winters. HarvBoo

From the hitchhiker whose head. This Thing We Learn from Others. Ingrid de Kok. TSAP

From the horizon there. Seen from Over Here. Anne Portugal. YaTCFP, *tr. by* Norma Cole

From the hospital solarium we watch row houses. Visiting Hour. Lynda Hull. LaCa

From the House of Yemanjá [*with music*]. Audre Lorde. NALW; NAMCP V.2; NoAM; NoP-4; NoP-5

From the Hymn to Inanna. Enheduanna. WPoS

From the "In" Sequence. C. S. Giscombe.
　Bro Duncanson. GT

From the Indians who welcomed the pilgrims. Winter in America. Gil Scott-Heron. ISC

From the Irish. Ian Duhig. NeBl

From the Irish. James Simmons. ModIr; PBCIP; PNI

From the Island of Manhattan to the Coast of Gold. Of Thee I Sing. Ira Gershwin. ReLy

From the Island to Europe. Island and Europe, The. Luis Andrade Silva. NAfrP, *tr. by* Don Burness

From the Japanese of Kakinomoto Hitomaro. Philip Whalen. WANABP *Fr.* Epigrams & Imitations.

From the Journals of the Frog Prince. Susan Mitchell. PtR

From the Lake. David St. John. MAAN

From the little copper tap marked 'cold'. (LL) Johnson Brothers Ltd. Rutger Kopland. BeAl; VCWP, *tr. by* James Brockway

From the local office, orders flying thicker than comb's teeth. Confiscating Salt. Wang An-shih. ColAnChi, *tr. by* Burton Watson

From the Lost Letters of Frederick Douglass. Evie Shockley. RD

From the Manifesto of the Selfish. Stephen Dunn. GoPo

From the Mark Prejsnar Playbook. James Sanders. AnSo

From the Market. Sandra McPherson. IPoFL *Fr.* Three from the Market.

From the McMichaels'. Four Good Things. James McMichael.

From the Meadow. Peter Everwine. GeoHom

From the meadows of bliss even the angel goes. Fredensborg. Friedrich Gottlieb Klopstock. GePo, *tr. by* George C. Schoolfield

From the middle of the pool. [Winter Sketches III]. Charles Reznikoff. PoA 2002

From the mind. Chiyojo. WPoS

From the mist came sounds of moving in Pant Glas. Ties. Eluned Phillips. BBMWP, *tr. by* Gillian Clarke

From the Moment I Picked Up Your Book. Ann Sansom. MFPA

From the moment I realized. Worry All the Time. Alison Morris. BtF

From the mountain's end, sight of coming smoke. Wu Yun. ChinPo, *tr. by* Ye Weilian [*or* Yeh Wei-lien *or* Wai-lim Yip]

From the Mouth of the Gxara.   Carole Boston Weatherford.   BtF

From the mouth of the Harlem Gallery.   Melvin B. Tolson.   NAAPv.2; NAMCP V.1; OxAAAP *Fr.* Harlem Gallery.

From the Nativity.   Adoration of the Kings, The.   William Carlos Williams.   ChrPo

From the Night-Window.   Douglas Dunn.   EdScPo

From the North Tower my westward gaze.   North Tower of Golden Fort, The.   Kao Shih.   CCL1, *tr. by* Stephen Owen

From the Novissimi.   Giulia Niccolai.   PFTM-2, *tr. by* Paul Vangelisti

From the Nursery.   Jane Kenyon.   LoL *Fr.* Having It Out with Melancholy.

From the old memories, the web that swims under the waves.   Resounding echo of the buddha's words, The.   Jessemyn Meyerhoff.   WhBo

From the old settlements only the writings.   Elegy.   Slavko Mihalic.   PoSu, *tr. by* Charles Simic

From the ominous petulance of the sea. (LL)   Severn Bore.   Catherine Fisher.   AngWePo; TCAWP

From the other world. (LL)   Milkweed.   James Wright.   ColAP; RaBo

From the Outland.   Peter Davison.   UrbNat

From the Outside [*with music*].   Mafika Pascal Gwala.   NAfrP

From the Painting "Back from Market" by Chardin.   Eavan Boland.   PBCIP

From the parrot's perch.   Our Square of Lawn.   Matthea Harvey.   LegDan

From the pier, at dusk, the dim.   Buried Graves, The.   Brad Leithauser.   NoP-4; NoP-5; WaAnP

From the piling's kelp I drew.   After You Left.   Heather McHugh.   BodElec

From the Porch.   John Koethe.   MakPoe

From the porch; from the hayrick where her prickled.   Mood Indigo.   William Matthews.   WeW-3

From the Porch of the Frost Place.   Gray Jacobik.   VisFro

From the porch, the world beyond.   Arson.   Nicole Cooley.   LiTh

From the Precious Tears of the Donkey.   Kazuko Shiraishi.   WoBe, *tr. by* Samuel Grolmes and Yumiko Tsumura

From the private ease of Mother's womb.   Thom Gunn.   AmFaPo; BeAl *Fr.* Three Songs.

From "The Prolific and the Devourer."   W. H. Auden.   GI *Fr.* "Prolific and the Devourer," The.

From the Provinces.   Ben Scammell.   NLP

From the quiet / Stone floor. (LL)   White. From the / Under arm of T.   George Oppen.   APT-2; PFTM-1

From the Raw.   Alejandrino Hufana.   ReBoTo

From the Republic of Conscience.   Seamus Heaney.   BodElec

From the river bank she saw the fields.   Heifer, The.   Andrew Crozier.   Oth

From the rocky-bound Atlantic to the south Pacific shore.   Wabash Cannonball, The.   Delmore Brothers.   GM

From the round window, everything is blue.   Ernesto Cardenal.   VCWP

From the ruins of that place. (LL)   Voice and Address.   Michael Palmer.   FTOS; PmAP

From the scaffold.   Last Platform, The.   Yury Timofeievich Galanskov.   TCRusP, *tr. by* Olive Dehn

From the Scythian cave came the heavenly horse.   Song of the Heavenly Horse.   Li Po.   CCL1, *tr. by* Elling O. Eide

From the Seashore.   Anna Petrovna Bunina.   NAWM-7v2, *tr. by* Pamela Perkins

From the seven small windows of my room.   For the Field.   Robyn Selman.   TaR

From the shadow of domes in the city of domes.   Piece of the Storm, A.   Mark Strand.   BeAl; CAP-8; WaAnP

From the shiny iron stove.   Easy Living.   Afaa Michael Weaver.   SpirFl

From the soft skin of the toy bride there arises now and then a milky fragrance.   I Wed a Toy Bride.   Yi Sang.   CAMKP, *tr. by* Walter Lew

From the sombre clouds fell slow.   Snow Song.   Henrietta Cordelia Ray.   CBWP-3

From the Songs of the Land of Zion and Jerusalem.   Yehuda Amichai.   NRoS, *tr. by* Esther Raizen

From the South.   *Unknown.*   TCAPo, *tr. by* William Ellery Channing (Cherokee War-Song, Version 1.)   AmWaPo

From the South: 2.   *Unknown.*   TCAPo, *tr. by* William Ellery Channing (Cherokee War-Song, Version 2.)   AmWaPo

From the south they came, Birds of War.   From the South: 2.   *Unknown.*   TCAPo, *tr. by* William Ellery Channing

From the south they come.   War Songs.   *Unknown.*   APN-2, *tr. by* Henry Rowe Schoolcraft

From the south they come.   From the South.   *Unknown.*   TCAPo, *tr. by* William Ellery Channing

From the sphere of our sorrow? (LL)   To—: "One word is too often profaned."   Percy Bysshe Shelley.   OBEV; OxAEP-2; TFi

From the Spirit of Phillis Wheatley to the Spirit of Thomas Jefferson (A Note 212 Years Later).   Karen Williams.   BtF

From the Spotted Night.   Ray A. Young Bear.   HATNAP

From the spreading sepsis that was once my balls. (LL)   Basket Case.   Basil T. Paquet.   AmWaPo; FaBoWar

From the start, the forces were unequal: Satan a grand seigneur in Heaven.   Homily.   Dan Pagis.   MotU, *tr. by* Stephen Mitchell

From the stately violence of the State.   Broken Mirror, The.   Bob Perelman.   FTOS

From the Suburbs.   Louise Glück.   NALW *Fr.* Dedication to Hunger.

From the sun. (LL)   Easter Morning.   A. R. Ammons.   NAAL-5; NAMCP V.2; NoAM; OxBoAm; PoA 2002; PoetW

From the Sun Itself [*with music*].   Roberta Hill Whiteman.   HATNAP

From the tawny light.   Everything That Acts Is Actual.   Denise Levertov.   NoAM

From the Technology of Tears.   Zbigniew Herbert.   BeAl, *tr. by* Peter Dale Scott

From the Telephone.   Florence Ripley Mastin.   LW

From the temple, deep in its tender bamboos.   On Parting with the Buddhist Pilgrim Ling-Ch'ě.   Liu Ch'ang-ch'ing.   CCL1; WoPoe, *tr. by* Witter Bynner

From the temples' incense of bygone Babylon.   To Poetry.   Nazik al-Mala'ika.   IrPoTo, *tr. by* Ferial J. Ghazoul

From the Theater of Wine.   Cyrus Cassells.   GifTon

From the Thirteenth Cantata of Metastasio.   Pietro Metastasio.   NPBRoP,

From the Three Emperors and Five Kings down to Hsia, Shang, and Chou.   *Chinese Oral Tradition.*   ColAnChi *Fr.* Expository Tale on King Wu's Expedition Against Chow.

From the Tibetan.   John Hewitt.   PNI

From the time of the womb.   Dīnrām.   SinGod, *tr. by* Rachel Fell McDermott

From the time you came into my house.   Sad Remembrance.   Mei Yao Ch'en.   ColAnChi, *tr. by* Burton Watson

From the top here.   X L E B.   Jack Hirschman.   CLPP

From the top of MountSinai.   Settlement.   David Avidan.   NRoS, *tr. by* Esther Raizen

From the top of this bank I am able.   Daybreak.   Christiania Whitehead.   NeBl

From "The Torah of the Void."   Rabbi Nahman of Bratzlav.   BLT, *tr. by* Zalman Schachter

From the train window at daybreak.   At Daybreak.   Adam Zagajewski.   VCWP, *tr. by* Renata Gorczynski, Benjamin Ivry and C. K. Williams

From the triangle of the sidewalks of the square all the wires start.   Is Ajar.   Pierre Reverdy.   YaTCFP, *tr. by* John Ashbery

From the unfathoming of his sickbed.   My Father Plaits His Granddaughter's Hair.   Joseph Sherman.   Coast

From the union of power and money.   Mad Farmer, Flying the Flag of Rough Branch, Secedes from the Union, The.   Wendell Berry.   PoCoUp

From the usual unreliable sources / real dead. (LL)   Sometime During Eternity.   Lawrence Ferlinghetti.   NoAM; NoP-4; NoP-5

From the vase.   Hans Faverey.   LWR, *tr. by* John M. Coetzee

From the very first coming down.   Letter, The.   W. H. Auden.   NoAM

From the Viking Museum.   John Peck.   HarvBoo

From the Wailing Wall.   Enid Shomer.   TaR

From the wan dream that was her waking day.   Edna St. Vincent Millay.   NALW *Fr.* Sonnets from an Ungrafted Tree.

From the Wave.   Thom Gunn.   NAEL-6v2; NAEL-7v2; NoP-4; NoP-5

From the west comes Harold, with a bitter smile.   Harold.   David Ignatow.   LTA

From the White Day to Take Me.   Francisco de Quevedo y Villegas.   SpanPo, *tr. by* Kate Flores

From the white day to take me, the ultimate.   From the White Day to Take Me.   Francisco de Quevedo y Villegas.   SpanPo, *tr. by* Kate Flores

From the white, inviolate solitude. (LL)   Skater, The.   Sir Charles G. D. Roberts.   BrAP; IFF

From the wilderness remote he breaks.   Red-Man, The.   Frank Prewett.   HATNAP

From the Willow Branches.   Salvatore Quasimodo.   WoPoe, *tr. by* Michael Egan

From the window.   Dog Days.   Katherine Soniat.   PoCoUp

From the window I saw the horses.   Horses.   Pablo Neruda.   BeAl, *tr. by* Stephen Mitchell

From the Window of a Plane.   Andrey Andreievich Voznesensky.   TCRusP, *tr. by* Daniel Weissbort

From the window of a train.   Night Coach.   Phillis Levin.   RA

From the window of the midnight-bound Vegas plane.   Jo Gravis in His Metal Garden.   Sinéad Morrissey.   NIrP

From the windows of a standing train.   Standing Trains, The.   Thomas McCarthy.   ModIr

From the windows of the house.   Dance of Husbands in Bathrobes, The.   David Kirby.   SUP

From the windowsill, the stillest.   Telling the Time.   Christine de Luca.   EdScPo

From the winter wind.   Michael Rosen.   Spl

From the woods at night. Richard Wright. APT-2

From the Year Of Our Lord 19**. Walt, I Salute You! Lynn Emanuel. MAAN; ViWalt

From Their Eyes Adorned with Vitreous Sands. Coral Bracho. TANSG, tr. by Celeste Kostopulos-Cooperman

From Then to Now. Kim Addonizio. LiTh

From these high walls I look at the town below. After Collecting the Autumn Taxes. Po Chü-i. BLT, tr. by Arthur Waley

From these parts. (LL) Blandeur. Kay Ryan. CalPo; OxBoAm

From thine eyrie, the crag. Fred Emerson Brooks. VerBaPo Fr. Old Eagle.

From this contriving flesh-land. Existing Psychically. Andrea Zanzotto. ItPo, tr. by Gayle Ridinger

From this deep chasm, where quivering sunbeams play. William Wordsworth. CenSon Fr. River Duddon [A Series of Sonnets], The.

From this distance thinking toward you. George Oppen. APT-2; PFTM-1

From this high place all things flow. Robert Penn Warren. OxBoAm; PoA 2002 Fr. Kentucky Mountain Farm.

From this high quarried ledge I see. Mountain over Aberdare, The. Alun Lewis. AngWePo; TCAWP

From this high window best, you see the briar rose. Space Between, The. Edith Jay Scovell. MoWP

From this I will not swerve nor fall nor falter. Ready for Flight. Eavan Boland. IrLP; OxBSo

From this light into which, with delicate. From This Light. Coral Bracho. RMCMP, tr. by Suzanne Jill Levine

From This Moment On. Cole Porter. ReLy

From this moment on, what is. Beacon Arms. Jim Behrle. FreRad

From this night on God let me eat. Night. Jean Valentine. AFaM

From this sheer wall the Indians watched the plain. South Rim: Big Bend National Park. Arthur M. Sampley. TiP2

From this tree-finned hill. Hill Fort, Caerleon. Sam Adams. AngWePo

From this ultimate dim Thule. (LL) Dream-Land [or Dreamland]. Edgar Allan Poe. APN-1; BrAP; NAAL-3

From this, unto the last of daies. (LL) Easter Hymn. Henry Vaughan. ChIV-2; SacPr

From those theaters, Claudia, from those feasts. Ernesto Cardenal. BLPSL, tr. by Rene de Costa, Rigas Kappatos and Eleni Paidoussi

From three dark places Christ came forth this day. Upon Christ's Nativity or Christmas. Rowland Watkyns. OBWVE

From thy compeers in genius wisely learn. Joseph Cottle. STuOW Fr. Expostulatory Epistle to Lord Byron, An.

From thy patient, who while here. Accompanying a Gift. Lizelia Augusta Jenkins Moorer. CBWP-3

From time one I've been reading slaughter. On Hearing a New Escalation. Richard Hugo. AmWaPo; PoA 2002

From time to time our love is like a sail. Wedding. Alice Oswald. BeAl; MFPA; MoWP; NeBrP

From tomorrow's mist-fall till Time be sped! (LL) Thomas Hardy. FaBoWar; OBWP Fr. Dynasts, The.

From Transylvanian peaks to far Tibet. Song about Kőrösi Csoma. Gyula Juhász. IQMS, tr. by Watson Kirkconnell

From Travancore to Tripoli. Ballad of the Oedipus Complex. Lawrence Durrell. OBCoV

From / tree after tree. In Praise of Ch'an Master Wang You Who Cares for the Bonnet Monkeys around His Mountain Studio. Shi Zhiyuan. CSKM, tr. by Paul Hansen

From Trollope's Journal. Elizabeth Bishop. AmWaPo; CBCWP; PoAgWa

From under the ground. Digging Out the Buddha Relic. Muso Soseki. EaWin, tr. by W. S. Merwin

From under the house. Richard Wright. APT-2

From up here in the crow's nest. Jesus Dies. Anne Sexton. PFTM-2; RACG

From up here, the insomniac. Distance. Mary Jo Salter. ExTi

From us, like appendicitis. Poem. Andrey Andreievich Voznesensky. RusPo, tr. by Robert Arthur Douglas Ford

From walk to walk, from shade to shade. Joseph Addison. STuOW Fr. Rosamond.

From Water-Tower Hill to the brick prison. Point Shirley. Sylvia Plath. NIL-7; NIP-4

From what country are you. From What Country. Luis Cernuda. RaW, tr. by John Haines

From what dripping cell, through what fairy glen. Drunkard's Address to a Bottle of Whiskey, A. Joseph Sheridan Le Fanu. IrV

From what i've been hearing. Letter. Keith Gilyard. SpirFl

From whence no paths return. Other World, The. Dmitry Vasil'evich Bobyshev. ItGoST, tr. by Michael Van Walleghen

From whence we come? Space. A Prose Poem Monologue. Sekou Sundiata. FaoP

From where, from whom? Why ask, in torment. Gift, The. John Ormond. TCAWP

From Where I Stand. Elena Georgiou. WiU

From where I stand now. 12 October. Myra Cohn Livingston. NTCP

From where I stand, Professor Pagels. Proton Decay. Robert Pack. ColAP

From where on earth do they keep reemerging. Rich, The. Hans Magnus Enzensberger. GTCP, tr. by Reinhold Grimm

From Where the Blues? Norman Henry Pritchard II. EGAG

From where you have come. Ana Istarú. TANSG, tr. by Shaun Griffin and Emma Sepúlveda-Pulvirenti

From which heaven did you return. Rain. Kim Chôngnan. EcSo, tr. by Peter H. Lee

From which the meteorite had removed his body. (LL) Orf. Ted Hughes. NAMCP V.2; NoAM

From white silk a whiff of wind and frost. Hawk in a Painting, A. Tu Fu [or Du Fu]. WoPoe, tr. by David Lattimore

From Whitsuntide to Whitsuntide. Ballad of a Bun, A. Sir Owen Seaman. UV

From whom, in happier hours, we wept to part. (LL) To the River Itchin, near Winton, William Lisle Bowles. CenSon; NAEL-6v2; OxBSo

From William Tyndale to John Frith. Edgar Bowers. InGu

From Winchester, twenty miles away! (LL) Sheridan's Ride. Thomas Buchanan Read. APN-2; CBCWP; PCW

From wing to outstretched. Units of Measurement. Blaga Dimitrova. CSCBP, tr. by Georgi Belev and Lisa Sapinkopf

From wonder to wonder. Jolanda Insana. CItWP Fr. Scream of Abû Nuwàs, The.

From Wynyard's Gap the livelong day. Trampwoman's Tragedy, A. Thomas Hardy. NAEL-6v2; NAEL-7v2; OBNV

From Year to Year the Contest Grew. James M. Whitfield. CBCWP Fr. Poem Written for the Celebration of the Fourth Anniversary of President Lincoln's Emancipation Proclamation, A.

From Yellow-Crane Tower, my old friend leaves the west. On Yellow-Crane Tower, Farewell to Meng Hao-Jan Who's Leaving for Yang-Chou. Li Po. NDACCP, tr. by David Hinton

From yon fair hill, whose woody crest. Verses Written in the Spring. Anne Batten Cristall. RWP

From you have I been absent in the spring. William Shakespeare. NAEL-6v1; NAEL-7v1; NoSic; OBEV; OxAEP-1 Fr. Sonnets.

From you I want more than I've ever asked. Adrienne Rich. AmFaPo; BeAl; LoL Fr. Not Somewhere Else, But Here.

From you I would love a child who could be a sword. Genesis. Alda Merini. CItWP, tr. by Cinzia Sartini Blum and Lara Trubowitz

"From Your Depths and Kneeling . . ." Teresa Calderón. TANSG, tr. by Celeste Kostopulos-Cooperman

From your mouth, from the well of your eyes I drink, from your belly, at your flanks. On Contact Opens Its Indigo Pit. Coral Bracho. PFTM-2, tr. by Forrest Gander

From your throat. It Was Early Evening. Víctor Terán. RMCMP, tr. by Donald Frischmann

From your work you will be able one day to gather yourself. (LL) Throw Yourself Like Seed. Miguel de Unamuno. PLBUT; RaBo; RaW, tr. by Robert Bly

From Zeus let us begin, him we mortals never. Aratus. HePo Fr. Phaenomena.

Front, A. Randall Jarrell. NoP-4; NoP-5; OBWP; PoWW

Front a mirror, The. Looking at an Old Mirror. Olav H. Hauge. WED, tr. by Robert Bly

Front door slipped from its latch and he, The. Scotch and Soda. Jenny Factor. CalPo

Front Line. Lyubomir Levchev. PML, tr. by Theodore Weiss

Front moved through last night, A. Oregon Inlet. Mary Beath. ICANM

Front wheel's off the mountainside, The. Either Way. Tricia Corob. Prnts

Front Window, The. Rae Desmond Jones. BMAP

Frontera. Francisco X. Alarcón. CalPo

Frontera / Border. Francisco X. Alarcón. GeoHom

Frontier. Oswald de Andrade. TCLAP, tr. by Flavia Vidal

Frontier Mystery. Berta Hart Nance. TiP2

Frontier of rage that exists, The. Frontier of Rage, The. Askia Muhammad Touré. ISC

Fronto, Father, Flaccilla, Mother, extend. Martial. RomPo, tr. by Peter Whigham

Frost: "Hospital garden on Sunday, A." Fedya Filkova. CSCBP, tr. by Georgi Belev and Lisa Sapinkopf

Frost. Found Poem, North of Boston. Paul Marion. VisFro

Frost. Floyd Skloot. VisFro

Frost. Laurence Snydal. VisFro

Frost, a star edges with its fire. (LL) Sea Violet. "H. D." APT-1; MoWP; NAMCP V.1; NoP-4; NoP-5

Frost and His Enemies. Robert Bly. VisFro

Frost and sun, as needed. Tatyana Rizdvenko. CRWP, tr. by Daniel Weissbort

Frost at Midnight. Mary Jo Salter. RA; VisFro

Frost at Midnight [1798 version]. Samuel Taylor Coleridge. NOBRP; NPBRoP; WaAnP

Frost at Midnight [1829 version]. Samuel Taylor Coleridge. BrAP; CABP; NAEL-6v2; NAEL-7v2; NOBRP; NoP-4; NoP-5; NPeEn; PtR; TFi

"Frost performs its secret ministry, The." OPOU

Frost bit deep, The. When heavy guns were dragged. Winter, Before the War. Waclaw Potocki. WoPoe, tr. by Jerzy Peterkiewicz and Burns Singer

Frost covers the reeds of the marsh. Kenneth Rexroth. APSN Fr. Love Poems of Marichiko, The.

Frost falls on my clothes. Yun Sŏndo. CATKP Fr. Angler's Calendar, The.

Frost has sealed. Tree in December. Melville Cane. MoAmPo

Frost in Miami. Peter Schmitt. VisFro

Frost Is All Over, The. Pearse Hutchinson. PBCIP

Frost meant fruit trees and their need. Good-by and Keep Cold. Robert Cooperman. VisFro

Frost of separation / Father, child. Ome Shushiki. ZenPo, tr. by Takashi Ikemoto and Lucien Stryk

Frost on the windowpanes; the sick. Eugenio Montale. WoPoe Fr. Motets [Mottetti].

Frost performs its secret ministry, The. Frost at Midnight [1829 version]. Samuel Taylor Coleridge. BrAP; CABP; NAEL-6v2; NAEL-7v2; NOBRP; NoP-4; NoP-5; NPeEn; PtR; TFi

Frost performs its secret ministry, The. Samuel Taylor Coleridge. OPOU Fr. Frost at Midnight [1829 version].

Frost performs its secret ministry, The. Frost at Midnight [1798 version]. Samuel Taylor Coleridge. NOBRP; NPBRoP; WaAnP

Frost, 1654, The: To Mr. W.L. Thomas Shipman.

"Streams are fettered, and with us as rare, The." NOSC

Frost Song. William Heyen. VisFro

Frost to Skellings. Edmund Skellings. VisFro

Frost To-night. Edith Matilda Thomas. TCAPo

Frost white across the river. Moored at Maple Bridge. Ching An. CSKM, tr. by Jerome P. Seaton

Frosts are Coming. László Nagy. IQMS, tr. by Alan Dixon

Frost's Last Lecture: A Tape: His Audience—1963. William Olsen. VisFro

Frosty Christmas Eve, A. Noel; Christmas Eve, 1913. Robert Bridges. ChrPo; OBCP; SacPr

Frosty Night, A. Robert Graves. MoBrPo

Frottage. Dean Young. BAP-97

Frown you? Frown on; your hour is past! Edward Young. STuOW Fr. Foreign Address, The.

Frozen, A / indian acorn. Zen Acorn. Harryette Mullen. WANABP

Frozen Drought. Peter Davison. MoW

Frozen Field, The. Sheenagh Pugh. TCAWP

Frozen, finished in suspension. (LL) Bolt, The. Mary Kinzie. ExTi; PtR

Frozen Greenhouse, The. Thomas Hardy. OBGa

Frozen lost dead with hunger. August Bank Holiday. Jacques Prévert. MFP, tr. by Martin Sorrell

Frozen Rain. Michael Longley. PBCIP

Frozen rain drop, The. Houston Haiku. Robert Phillips. TiP2

Frozen Stiff. Seán O Riordáin. ModIr, tr. by Patrick Crotty

Frozen Tarn. Catherine Fisher. TCAWP

Frozen Witness, The. Nick Piombino. FTOS

Fructus. Genevieve Taggard. APT-2

Fruit. Kenward Elmslie. FTOS

Fruit. Philippe Jaccottet. MFP, tr. by Martin Sorrell

Fruit and Flower Painter. Herman Melville. NCAP

Fruit is ruined, but the bread is baked, The. Oven. Laura Kasischke. NAPBL

Fruit of Knowledge, The. Robert Johnstone. PNI

Fruit of Loneliness. May Sarton. PoA 2002

Fruit of Sin, or a Lamentation for England, The. Julea Palmer. EMWP

Fruit Plummets from the Plum Tree. Unknown. WoPoe, tr. by Tony Barnstone, Willis Barnstone and Haixin Xu and Chou Ping

Fruit They Had in Common. Shin Yu Pai. WANABP

Fruitbowl 1. Imani E. Wilson. BtF

Fruitcake / material of stars run across flesh. Stone Free. Jim Brodey. AHA

Fruit-Gift, The. John Greenleaf Whittier. TCAPo

Fruits of War, The. George Gascoigne.

"Conference among ourselves we called, A." OBWP

"I set aside to tell the restless toil." FaBoWar

"Soldiers, behold, and captains, mark it well." FaBoWar

Fruit-vender church. Sunday. Jorge Carrera Andrade. TCLAP, tr. by Muna Lee

Frustrated. May Probyn. VWP

Frustration. Dorothy Parker. AmWit

Frutas: "Growing up in Miami any tropical fruit I ate." Ricardo Pau-Llosa. NevBe

Frutta di Mare. Geoffrey Scott. OBMV

Fry says a word. Brown Rosellen. FFC

Fúar liom an adhaighsi dh'Aodh. Winter Campaign, A. Eochaidh Ó Heóghusa. CABP

Fuchsias, twined around long stems, all the same height, about 1 m. Heimgarten. Erica Pedretti. MotU, tr. by Franz Wright

Fuck All Departments. Lionel Fogarty. VaPo

Fuck European girls. Things to Do in Holland. Beau Sia. HeMarv

Fuck I want to be bound by devotion! Tortured. African Sunday. Maureen Owen. PmAP

Fuck me, oh God, with ordinary things. Oh God, Fuck Me. Ruth L. Schwartz. BeAl

Fuck / Portraying. Doubletalk. Francisco Aragon. BeDoSh

Fuck thém. I wish you God. (LL) Last Hellos, The. Les A. Murray. HarvBoo; PoCu

Fuck you and your platitudes. She Replies to the Fat Crimson Bishop. Vincent Woods. NIrP

Fucking. Frederick Seidel. BodElec

Fudge Family in Paris, The. Thomas Moore.

"At length, my Lord, I have the bliss." OBSV

Letter 1. From Miss Biddy Fudge to Miss Dorothy————. NOBRP

"Oh Dick! You may talk of your writing and reading." OBCoV

Fue la pasada primavera. Impresión de Destierro. Luis Cernuda. RaW

Fue un tiempo de mentira, de infamia. A España toda. España Joven, Una. Antonio Machado Ruiz. RaW

Fuel. Naomi Shihab Nye. ExTi

Fuel filler cap. Instructions. Gary Snyder. NoP-5

Fueled. Marcie Hans. TWF

Fueled / by a million. Fueled. Marcie Hans. TWF

Fuente de huertos de mi amado. Flor de oro. Pedro Pérez Conde. RMCMP

Fugitive, The [with music]. Priscilla Jane Thompson. CBWP-2

Fugitive Pieces and Reminiscences of Lord Byron with Some Original Poetry, Letters and Recollections of Lady Caroline Lamb, ed. I. Nathan. Lady Caroline Lamb.

"Let the harp be mute for ever." RWP

William Lamb's Return from Paris, Asking Me My Wish. RWP

Fugitive returned on New Year's Eve, The. Festus Conrad. Melvin B. Tolson. GT

Fugitive Slaves. Gale Jackson. SpirFl

Fugitive Slave's Apostrophe to the North Star, The. John Pierpont. APN-1

Fugue. Carol Dine.

4. PfS

5. PfS

Fugue. Shara McCallum. NAPBL

Fugue. Stephen Perry. MiVo

Fugue: "Women are on their way." Robyn Sarah. IFF

Fugue for Phantoms. Robin Robertson. NeBrP

Fugue for Tinhorns. Frank Loesser. ReLy

Fugue of Death. Paul Celan. OBVE; PoetW, tr. by Christopher Middleton

Führer Bunker, The. W. D. Snodgrass.

Adolf Hitler—1 April, 1945. BodElec

Adolf Hitler—20 April, 1934; 1900 hours. BodElec

Eva Braun. BodElec

Hermann Fegelein. BodElec

Fuji at Sunrise. Ernest Francisco Fenollosa. NAAPv.1

Full and True Account of a Dreaded Fire, That Lately Broke Out in the Pope's Breeches, A. Unknown. EroLit

Full autumn moon / On the straw mat. Kikaku. ZenPo, tr. by Takashi Ikemoto and Lucien Stryk

Full be the year, abundant be the grain. Ezra Pound. OBVE

Full clear and bright the Christmas night range. Christmas Rede. Jane Barlow. SacPr

Full cloves, The. Shallot, A. Richard Wilbur. OxBoAm

Full Consciousness. Juan Ramón Jiménez. RaW, tr. by Robert Bly

Full day—. Today Tutu Is Beating the Same Burru As Me. Lebert Bethune. GT

Full deck gusts outside the playground, The. Mutability Checkers. Randolph Healy. Oth

Full doelful Tales have oft been told. Samuel Wesley. VerBaPo Fr. On Two Souldiers Killing One Another for a Groat.

Full eighteen years in sorrow I did lye. Revelation 8, March 31. Anne Wentworth. EMWP

Full face. Andrée Chedid. PoArWo, tr. by Lucy McNair

Full fathom [or fadom] five thy father lies. William Shakespeare. ClHu; NAEL-6v1; NoP-4; NoP-5; NoSic; OBEV; OxBEV; PoPoPo; TFi Fr. Tempest, The.

Full house tonight at the Kit-Kat Cinema. Charlie Chaplin. Sadiq Sharshar. AnVo, tr. by Mohamed Enani

Full in the hand, heavy. September Afternoon at Four O'Clock. Marge Piercy. NIP-4

Full Indian Rope Trick, The. Colette Bryce. MoWP; NIrP

Full little he thinks who has life's joy. Seafarer, The. *Unknown*. SacPr, *tr. by* Margaret Williams

Full many a glorious morning have I seen[e]. William Shakespeare. NAEL-7v1; NIL-7; NIP-4; NoP-4; NoP-5; NoSic; OxAEP-1; TFi; WeW-3 *Fr.* Sonnets.

Full Moon. Big Thicket Words. James Cody. TiP2

Full Moon. Robert Earl Hayden. GT

Full moon. Issa. EH, *tr. by* Robert Hass

Full Moon. Juan Ramón Jiménez. WED, *tr. by* Robert Bly

Full Moon ("Above the tower—a lone, twice-sized moon."). Tu Fu [*or* Du Fu]. NDACCP, *tr. by* David Hinton

Full Moon. Elinor Wylie. NALW; NoP-4; NoP-5; StAl

Full moon and a grey piece of the moon. Horsehoe Crab in Flagrante Delicto. Richard Price. EdScPo

Full Moon and Little Frieda. Ted Hughes. HarvBoo; NPeEn; OPOU; StAl

Full Moon at Tierz: Before the Storming of Huesca. John Cornford. OBWP; RSaN

Full moon creates a crystalpath, The. Landscape. Paul Van Ostaijen. TuT, *tr. by* Tony Curtis and Tony Curtis

Full moon easterly rising, furious, The. Love Story, A. Robert Graves. NAEL-6v2

Full moon illuminated large initial for letter M. Appalachian Book of the Dead 3, The. Charles Wright. AWTN

Full moon is partly hidden by cloud, The. Fable of the War, A. Howard Nemerov. AmWaPo; OBWP; PWW2

Full Moon: New Guinea. Karl Shapiro. APT-2; PWW2

Full moon. Our Narragansett gales subside. John Berryman. HarvBoo; OxBoAm *Fr.* Dream Songs.

Full moon ringed, The. Prince Shiki. SoOfWa, *tr. by* Sam Hamill

Full moon rising on the waters of my heart. Evening Song. Jean Toomer. APT-2; GT

Full moon slip swim. Moon and Farmstead. Sándor Weöres. IQMS, *tr. by* Edwin Morgan

Full moon was rising, The. Sappho. SaLy, *tr. by* Diane Rayor

Full of beauty, full of tension, to effort a stranger, a stripling. On the Statue of a Player at Svaika. Alexander Sergeyevich Pushkin. CAGL, *tr. by* Michael Green

Full of fear in my doubt, never at rest my pain. One For Balassi. Ferenc Kölcsey. IQMS, *tr. by* George Sutherland Fraser

Full of Hell. Baz and the Freedom of the Press. Kevin Cadwallender. RSaN

Full of her long white arms and milky skin. Equilibrists, The. John Crowe Ransom. APT-1; FuPo; InGu; NoAM

Full of life now, compact, visible. Full of Life Now. Walt Whitman. APN-1

Full of mercy, full of love. Prayer for Charity, A. Jeremy Taylor. SacPr

Full of sentiment, clever at mechanics, and we love our luxuries. (LL) Ave Caesar. Robinson Jeffers. NAMCP V.1; NoAM; OxBoAm

Full of simple sweetness and repetition. (LL) Supremes, The. Mark Jarman. GeoHom; SwNoth

Full of years and seasoned like a salt timber. Islandman. Brenda Chamberlain. AngWePo; OBWVE

Full oft doth Mat. with Topaz dine. Earning a Dinner. Matthew Prior. NBLV

Full oft, unknowning what they did. William Whitehead. DiBP

Full Orchestra. Kenneth Slessor. OxBSo

Full Powers: Five Warning Signs. Edoardo Cacciatore. *tr. by* Gayle Ridinger
  First Warning Sign: Epiphany. ItPo, *tr. by* Gayle Ridinger
  "Let's try another hand, let's redo the count." ItPo, *tr. by* Gayle Ridinger
  Second Warning Sign: the Game Heats Up. ItPo, *tr. by* Gayle Ridinger
  Third Warning Sign: An Endless Surprise. ItPo, *tr. by* Gayle Ridinger
  "Where do I stand and where do you? Seems like." ItPo, *tr. by* Gayle Ridinger

Full September moon sheds floods of light, The. September Night, A. George Marion McClellan. TCAPo

Full stop. Let's not. Far In. Rachel Loden. PasH

Full Supporting Programme. William Price Turner. EdScPo

Full twenty years have roll'd, ye rhiming band. Charge to the Poets, A. William Whitehead.

Full Vision. Henrietta Cordelia Ray. CBWP-3

Full well I know that she is there. Gertrude Stein. PoA 2002 *Fr.* Stanzas in Meditation.

Full well, Tibaldi, did thy kindred mind. On Seeing the Picture of Æolus by Pelegrino Tibalbi, in the Institute at Bologna. Washington Allston. APN-1

Full white the Bourbon lily blows. Thistle's Grown aboon the Rose, The. Allan Cunningham. NePenScot

Full wish of a moon. Cryptographiku for Jim L5ftwich. Bob Grumman. AnSo

Full year since, I took this eager city, A. Irishman in Coventry, An. John Hewitt. ModIr; PNI

Full-faced to the brisk sea gale, I breathe air. Beach at Noon, The. Fred Cogswell. Coast

Fullness. Latasha Natasha Diggs. BRtP

Fully occupied with growing—that's. Métier of Blossoming, The. Denise Levertov. MoWP

Fulmars. Robert W. Service. EdScPo

Fulmars are on Stac an Armainn, The. St Kildan Congregation. Derick Thomson. EdScPo

Fum and Hum, the Two Birds of Royalty. Thomas Moore. OBSV

Fumbling for the live nerve. Winter. Rae Armantrout. FTOS

Fumes from all kinds, The. Coming Down Cleveland Avenue. James Tate. YaYoPo

Fun to be Fooled. Ira Gershwin and E. Y. Harburg. ReLy

Function of Winter, The. Jay Parini. WaAnP

Fundamental Project of Technology, The. Galway Kinnell. AtGh; CAP-8

Fundamentals. Ian Duhig. NeBl; NeBrP

Fundoscopy. Maura Dooley. MoWP

Funeral. Carol Ann Duffy. InoFa

Funeral: "Naked in eastern mournin sun." Gary Lilley. BtF

Funeral. Clarence Major. BodElec

Funeral. Vaida Stewart Montgomery. TiP2

Funeral, The: "I see, under the canopy of death." Ward Abbott. ICANM

Funeral, The: "Her smile drains." Tatamkulu Afrika. TSAP

Funeral[1], The. John Donne. FSCP; HeIP-4; NAEL-6v1; NAEL-7v1; NAWM-5v1; NoP-4; NoP-5; OBEV; TFi

Funeral, The. Norman Dubie. NAMCP V.2; NoAM

Funeral, The. Miroslav Holub. MotU, *tr. by* Dana Hábová and David Young

Funeral, The. Stephen Spender. MoBrPo; NAMCP V.1; NoAM

Funeral Blues. W. H. Auden. *See* Song: "Stop all the clocks, cut off the telephone."

Funeral Eva. Koroneu. RaBo

Funeral grief song, The. Say Something: A Change Is Gonna Come. Mbali Umoja. BtF

Funeral Hymn. William Walsham Howe. SacPr

Funeral in Soweto. Wole Soyinka.
  "We wish only to bury our dead. Shorn." PoetW

Funeral in the East. Pablo Neruda. TRP, *tr. by* Robert Bly

Funeral is a wedding with God, A. Wedding. Ruth Forman. OxAAAP

Funeral March in B Flat. Female Socket. Nicole Espagnol. SurWo, *tr. by* Myrna Bell Rochester

Funeral Mass. Patricia K. Page. GPPA

Funeral Music. Geoffrey Hill.
  "Let mind be more precious than soul; it will not." UpMys
  "My little son, when you could command marvels." NAMCP V.2; NoAM; UpMys
  "Not as we are but as we must appear." NAMCP V.2; NoAM
  "They bespoke doomsday and they meant it by." UpMys

Funeral of Anton Fransch, The. Tatamkulu Afrika. TSAP

Funeral of Poetry, The. Karl Shapiro. APT-2; OxBoAm

Funeral of the German Emperor, The. William McGonagall.
  "As the procession passes the palace the blinds are drawn." VerBaPo

Funeral Oration. Dezső Kosztolányi. IQMS, *tr. by* Geroge Gömöri and Clive Wilmer

Funeral Oration. *Unknown*. IQMS, *tr. by* Alan Jenkins

Funeral Oration, A. Drummond Allison. PoWW

Funeral Oration, A. David Wright. InoFa

Funeral Oration as Pronounced by the Compassionate Buddha, The. Daniel Berrigan.
  "Assembled sirs. The courtesies afforded us by the Dali Lama." UpMys

Funeral Rites. Seamus Heaney. ModIr; PBCIP; PoetW

Funeral Sermon, Soweto. Wole Soyinka. VCWP

Funeral Song, Upon the Decease of Annes His Mother, A. Nicholas Grimald.
  From A Funeral Song, Upon the Decease of Annes His Mother. NoP-4
  "I, in your frutefull woomb conceyved, born was." PBRV

Funeraled Fare Well. Kalamu ya Salaam. SpirFl *Fr.* New Orleans Haiku.

Funeral[l] Rites of the Rose, The. Robert Herrick. NOSC; OBEV

Funerals are important. Exiles. Abena Busia. NAfrP

Funerals keep coming, The. Snow is Falling. Tomas Tranströmer. WoBe, *tr. by* Robin Fulton

Funerary Edict. Victor Segalen. YaTCFP, *tr. by* Mary Ann Caws *and* Jean-Pierre Cauvin and Patricia Terry

Funerary Portraits. Rosanna Warren. NoAM

Fungus Considered. Monica Berlin. MAAN

Funicello at 50. Klipschutz. ReTh

Funk. Mary Weems. SpirFl

Funk Lore. Imamu Amiri Baraka. UnSA

Funk Qualms. John Wilkinson. VaPo

Funnel. Anne Sexton. MoAmPo

Funnel-web spider, snake and octopus. Pelicans. Judith Wright. BMAP; OWoS

Funniest of all was birth. Vera Pavlova. CRWP Fr. Signs of Life.

Funny how the kid you always punched. Dogtown. James Harms. GeoHom

Funny Poem. Bill Knott. PBCAP

Funny to think you can still buy it now. Treacle. Paul Farley. NeBrP

Fur. William Heyen. PfSP

Fur Coats. James King Annand. EdScPo

Fürchte dich nicht, ich bin bei dir. (LL) Exequy, An. Peter Porter. NoAM; NoP-4; NoP-5

Furies, The. Anne Sexton. BodElec
  Fury of Cocks, The. OxBoAm
  Fury of Overshoes, The. NIL-7

Furious Boy, The. Toi Derricotte. OxAAAP

Furious Clarity, A. Gabriel Zaid. TCLAP, tr. by George McWhirter

Furious Cooking. Maureen Seaton. SUP; SweBea

Furious machines, difficult objects, dilapidate. Fames Away. Steve Carey. AHA

Furious sun of blind gold. Opened Orange of Light, The. Alfonso D'Aquino. RMCMP, tr. by Rebecca Seiferle

Furious'd Garb. Russell Atkins. EGAG

Furiously a crane. Shock. C. K. Williams. UrbNat

Furiously along the banks stormed Hannibal. Catius As Conius Silius Italicus. RomPo Fr. Punica, The.

Furius and Aurelius, aides to Catullus. Farewell. Robert Fitzgerald. APT-2

Furius and Aurelius, loyal friends. Carmen: 11. Catullus. WoPoe, tr. by Frederick Morgan

Furl sails into fishermen's cove. Tune: "Full Court of Fragrance." Yao Sui. ChinPo, tr. by Ye Weilian [or Yeh Wei-lien or Wai-lim Yip]

Furling my sail near the town of Huai. Mooring at Twilight in Yuyi District. Wei Ying-wu. CCL1, tr. by Witter Bynner

Furnace Blast, The. John Greenleaf Whittier. CBCWP

Furnace tolls the knell of falling steam, The. Elegy Written in a Country Coal-Bin. Christopher Darlington Morley. AmWit

Further. Nedelcho Ganev. CSCBP, tr. by Georgi Belev and Lisa Sapinkopf

Further Arrivals. Margaret Atwood. BrAP

Further in Summer than the Birds. Emily Dickinson. APN-2; NoP-4; NoP-5; OxBoAm

Further Instructions. Ezra Pound. PoA 2002 Fr. Lustra.

Further Proposal, A. Allen Ginsberg. NIL-7

Further Pulsations. Marvin Bell. PfSP

Furtherness. Mary Ruefle. BAP-01

Furthest Distances I've Travelled, The. Leontia Flynn. NIrP

Furtive blow, more like, A. There was I. Leda's Version. James Harrison. NIP-4

Fury. Lucille Clifton. LoL

Fury. Carol Frost. CAP-8

Fury of Cocks, The. Anne Sexton. OxBoAm Fr. Furies, The.

Fury of Overshoes, The. Anne Sexton. NIL-7; NIP-4 Fr. Furies, The.

Fury said to a mouse, That. Long Tale, A. Lewis Carroll. OBCoV

Fury said to a / mouse, That he. Lewis Carroll. NoxBChV; NoAM; OBCoV Fr. Alice's Adventures in Wonderland.

Fus time dem kar me go a Bellevue was fi di dactar an de lanlord operate, De. Riddym Ravings (The Mad Woman's Poem). Jean Binta Breeze. WaCA

Fuselage Installation. Juan Felipe Herrera. BodElec

Fuses I and II. Charles Baudelaire. PFTM-1

Fusion of Shadows, A. Marco Antonio Montes de Oca. MotU, tr. by Brian Swann

Futile Flight, Futile Fugue. Dulce Maria Loynaz. TANSG, tr. by Alan West

Futile Poem, A. Remco Campert. TuT, tr. by Theo Dorgan

Futility. Wilfred Owen. HarvBoo; MoBrPo; NAEL-6v2; NAEL-7v2; NAMCP V.1; NoAM; NoP-4; NoP-5; NPeEn; OBWP; PoAgWa; TCAWP; WaAnP

Future. Henri Michaux. YaTCFP, tr. by Mary Ann Caws and Patricia Terry

Future. Vicki Viidikas. BMAP

Future ain't what it used to be, The. Pharaoh. Jane Kenyon. LoL

Future and the Ancestor, The. Andrée Chedid. HAWP, tr. by Mirène Ghossein and Samuel Hazo

Future Debris. Heid E. Erdrich. AmPoNex

Future is for Tomorrow, The. Anna Gréki. HAWP, tr. by Mildred P. Mortimer

Future Martyr of Supersonic Waves. Juan Felipe Herrera. TouFir

Future Models May Have Infra-Red Sensors. Tom Raworth. Oth

Future of which we dream, The. S.L.A.M. Giovanna Pollarolo. TANSG, tr. by Marjorie Agosin

Future, past, the sea. Sea of Oblivion. Takahashi Shinkichi. ZenPo, tr. by Takashi Ikemoto and Lucien Stryk

Future Peace and Glory of the Church, The. William Cowper. InvLi Fr. Olney Hymns.

Future, The. Angel González. VCWP, tr. by Steven Ford Brown and Revuelta Gutierrez

Future Verdict, The. Ada Cambridge. NOBAu

Future will make you tall, The. (LL) Madre Sofía. Alberto A. Ríos. NAAL-5; NAMCP V.2; NoAM

Futures in Lilacs. Robert Hass. RoV

Future—turned his back, and walked away, The. (LL) Great Artist Reconsiders the Homeric Simile, The. John Tranter. BMAP; NoAM; NOBAu

Future—with what hands shall we pass you on? Ballad for the Future. Ivan Radoev. CSCBP, tr. by Georgi Belev and Lisa Sapinkopf

Futurism Wants to Transform the Variety Theater into a Theater of Amazement, Record-setting, and Body-madness. Filippo Tommaso Marinetti. PFTM-1 Fr. Variety Theater Manifesto, The.

Fuzzy Wuzzy was a bear. Unknown. NTCP

Fuzzy-Wuzzy. Rudyard Kipling. MoBrPo

Fy Satyre fie, shall each mechanick slave. John Marston. PBRV Fr. Scourge of Villanie, The.

G

G. K. Chesterton on His Birth [with music]. A. E. Housman. NBLV

Gabachos in the Photograph, The. Bobby Byrd. ICANM

Gabey's comin'. Lonely Town. Betty Comden and Adolph Green. ReLy

Gabi. Maria Luisa B. Aguilar-Cariño. ReBoTo

Gabion / Parapet. Susan Howe. NAMCP V.2 Fr. Thorow.

"Gables are not burning, The." Finnesburh Fragment, The. Unknown. OBWP, tr. by Kevin Crossley-Holland

Gabriel the rain-lover. Rain Poem. Gabriel Preil. FIT, tr. by Robert Friend

Gabriel turned at last into old Mr Preil. From a Late Diary. Gabriel Preil. FIT, tr. by Robert Friend

Gabriel's Appearance. Abraham Cowley. NOSC Fr. Davideis.

Gabriel's News (37). Khwaja Shams-ad-din Muhammad Hafiz. WED, tr. by Robert Bly and Leonard Lewisohn

Gacela del Amor Imprevisto. Federico García Lorca. RaW

Gacela of Unforeseen Love. Federico García Lorca. RaW, tr. by W. S. Merwin

Gacelas. Federico García Lorca.
  (Gacela del Amor Imprevisto.) RaW

Gadafi's Little Daughter. Einion Evans. BBMWP, tr. by Mike Jenkins

Gaea. William Stafford. PfSP

Gaelic is alive. Aonghas MacNeacail. NePenScot

Gaelic Long Tunes, The. Les A. Murray. UpMys

Gaelic Stories. Iain Crichton Smith. NePenScot

Gaeltacht. Pearse Hutchinson. ModIr; PBCIP

Gaffer Gray. Thomas Holcroft. OxAEP-1

Gaffer Speaks. Ghulam-Reza Ruhani. WoPoe, tr. by Omar S. Pound

Gag. Robert Budde. PoPra

Gagarin says, in ecstasy. Heel and Toe to the End. William Carlos Williams. OtW

Gaia. Gary Snyder. GifTon

Gaia, first-born daughter of Chaos. Lithuania, After Fifty-two Years. Czeslaw Milosz. tr. by the author and Robert Hass

Gaiety of Form, The. Robert Bly. BodElec

Gail. Hugh Seidman. KGB

Gaily bedight. Eldorado. Edgar Allan Poe. APN-1; ChAP; ColAP; NAAPv.1; NCAP; NoP-4; NoP-5; NOxBChV; TCAPo

Gaily they grow, the quiet throng. Heather Flowers. Eliseus Williams. OBWVE, tr. by Kenneth Hurlstone Jackson

Gal, I'm tellin you, I'm tired to frue. Lament of the Banana Man, The. Evan Jones. PML

Galactic anachronisms enslave assessments. Jackson Mac Low. WhBo

Galapagos. Neil Curry. NLP

Galataea. Callimachus.
  "Or rather the sacred fish with the golden faces." HePo, tr. by Barbara Hughes Fowler

Galatians 6.14. Francis Quarles. ChIV-2

Galaxea / be kind to Galileo Galilei. Listen Galaxea. Alvaro Cardona-Hine. ICANM

Galaxies. Alan Gould. NOBAu

Galaxy, The. Henry Wadsworth Longfellow. OxBSo

Gale at Dawn. William Everson. APT-2

Gale in April. Robinson Jeffers. MoAmPo

Gale ruffles the stream. Sikong Tu. CCL1 Fr. Twenty-Four Modes of Poetry.

Gale Sayers.　Ta-Nehisi Coates.　BtF
Gale: tiles, roofs whirling.　Beach.　Takahashi Shinkichi.　ZenPo, *tr. by* Takashi Ikemoto and Lucien Stryk
Gales.　Anne Stevenson.　Spl
Galilee Shore.　Allen Ginsberg.　ChIV-2; FTOS
Galileo.　János Székely.　IQMS, *tr. by* Geroge Gömöri and Adam Makkai
Galileo and the Bicycle.　*Unknown.*　ArBi
Galileo from his retreat.　Galileo and the Bicycle.　*Unknown.*　ArBi
Galileo is laughing at you.　For What It's Worth.　Benjamin Theolonius Sanders.　BRtP
Galileo's Wife.　Lavinia Greenlaw.　MoWP
Gallant Chateau.　Wallace Stevens.　MoAmPo
Gallant foeman in the fight, A.　Robert E. Lee.　Julia Ward Howe.　CBCWP
Gallantry.　Keith Douglas.　NAEL-6v2; NAEL-7v2; NAMCP V.1; NoAM; NoP-4; NoP-5; OBWP; WaAnP
(Galleons in sea-pomp) sails.　Armada of Thirty Whales, An.　Daniel Gerard Hoffman.　YaYoPo
Gallery.　Albert Goldbarth.　RWB; TaR
Gallery, The.　Sally Keith.　LegDan
Gallery, The.　Andrew Marvell.　BASC; NoP-4; PBRV
Gallery, The.　Tomas Tranströmer.　PFTM-2, *tr. by* Robin Fulton
Galley Oars.　Ali ibn Hariq.　WoPoe, *tr. by* Christopher Middleton
Galley of Count Arnaldos, The.　Henry Wadsworth Longfellow.　OBEV
Galley, The.　Petrarch.　OBVE; OxBEV; WeW-3 *Fr.* Sonnets to Laura.
Gallic Lap-Dog, The.　Martial.　DiBP *Fr.* Epigrams.
Gallio's Song.　Rudyard Kipling.　ChIV-2
Galloping collection of boards, The.　Somewhere.　Robert Creeley.　NoAM
Gallows, The [*with music*].　Edward Thomas.　MoBrPo; NAMCP V.1; NoAM
Gallows in my garden, people say, The.　Ballade of Suicide, A.　G. K. Chesterton.　NBLV; OBCoV
Gallowstree drops, The.　Jesus Unborn.　Anne Sexton.　PFTM-2
Galo sózinho não tece uma manhã, Um.　Tecendo a manhã.　João Cabral de Melo Neto.　IPoFL
Galoots.　Carl Sandburg.　APT-1
Galoots, you hairy, hankering.　Galoots.　Carl Sandburg.　APT-1
Galoshes.　Rhoda Warner Bacmeister.　NTCP
Gal's Cry for a Dying Lover.　Langston Hughes.　NAMCP V.1
Galveston.　Stanley E. Babb.　TiP2
Galveston.　Isabel Nathaniel.　TiP2
Gambier.　Joe Osterhaus.　AmPoNex; NAPBL
Gambit.　Tony Curtis.　AngWePo
Gamble.　Linda Hogan.　HATNAP
Gambling.　Vince Gotera.　OpBo
Gambling.　Dora Teitelboim.　Prolet, *tr. by* Amelia Glaser
Game, The.　Eavan Boland.　PtR
Game, The.　Edvard Kocbek.　PoSu, *tr. by* Michael Scammell and Veno Taufer
Game, The.　Stanley Kunitz.　PoA 2002
Game at Salzburg, A.　Randall Jarrell.　NoAM
2. A Game of Chess.　T. S. Eliot.　HarvBoo *Fr.* Waste Land, The.
Game of Chess, A.　Gwen Harwood.　MakPoe
Game of "just supposing", The.　Make Believe.　Oscar Hammerstein, II.　ReLy
Game Trail, The.　Mark Todd.　GeoH
Gamebagkeeper dealt detachable breath.　TM.　Ulli Freer.　Oth
Gameboy.　Regie Cabico.　WiU
Gamelia.　Susan M. Whitmore.　AmPoNex
Games.　Admiel Kosman.　PML, *tr. by* Lisa Katz
Games.　Vasco [*or Vasko*] Popa. *tr. by* Anne Pennington
　He.　PoSu; StAl, *tr. by* Anne Pennington
　Nail, The.　PoSu
　Seed, The.　PoSu
Games at the Hour of the Desert.　Manuela Fingueret.　MirDau, *tr. by* Roberta Gordenstein
Games were over now. The gathered armies scattered, The.　Homer.　NAWM-7v1 *Fr.* Iliad, The.
Games with My Daughter.　Tony Curtis.　TCAWP
Gammer Gurton's Needle.　William Stevenson *and* John Still. *tr. by* John Still
　Back and Side Go Bare, Go Bare.　HeIP-4; NAEL-6v1
　Jolly Good Ale and Old.　OBEV
Gandhabba #5.　Tom Weatherly.　EGAG
Gang Girls.　Gwendolyn Brooks.　IllVoic *Fr.* Blackstone Rangers, The.
Gang Girls are sweet exotics.　Gwendolyn Brooks.　IllVoic *Fr.* Blackstone Rangers, The.
Gang of labourers on the piled wet timber, A.　Morning Work.　D. H. Lawrence.　MoBrPo
Gang wanted to give Oedipus Rex a going away present, The.　Oedipus.　Josephine Miles.　SoSe-8

Gang was there when midnight came, The.　Joseph Moncure March.　APT-2 *Fr.* Wild Party, The.
Gangrel Rymour and the Pairdon of Sanct Anne, The.　Sydney Goodsir Smith.　"But ae braithless note."　OBVE
Gangrene.　Vanessa Haley.　PfS
Gangway / platform wharf.　Slate Roof Blues.　Jessica Freeman.　AnSo
Gan-tang [Translations].　*Unknown.*　CCL1
　Don't Chop That Pear Tree.　CCL1; NDACCP, *tr. by* Ezra Pound
　That Shady Crab.　CCL1, *tr. by* V. W. X.
Ganz.　Canzone.　Ernst Jandl.　OnScMo
Gao Tang Rhapsody, The.　Sung Yu.　CCL1, *tr. by* Arthur Waley
Gao-yang: In His Lambskin Coat.　*Unknown.*　CCL1, *tr. by* V. W. X.
Gap, The.　Annie Foster.　NLP
Gape, gape, gorlin'.　Ex Vermibus.　Hugh MacDiarmid.　CABP
Garage in Co. Cork, A.　Derek Mahon.　PBCIP
Garage Sale.　Brian Henry.　AmPoNex
Garage Sale as a Spiritual Exercise, The.　Thomas M. Disch.　GI
Garbage.　A. R. Ammons.
　"Garbage has to be the poem of our time because."　NAAL-5; NAMCP V.2
Garbage at the shore below the levee.　New Southern Exposure.　Hettie Jones.　PrTe
Garbage has to be the poem of our time because.　A. R. Ammons.　NAAL-5; NAMCP V.2 *Fr.* Garbage.
Garbage is bagged, deposited in the dump, and several, The.　Little Cape Cod Landscape.　Charles North.　FTOS
García Lorca tasted.　Drinking Fountain, The.　Robert Duncan.　CLPP
Garden.　Michael Bullock.　OBGa
Garden.　"H. D."　APT-1; NAMCP V.1; NoAM
Garden.　John Engels.　PfSP
Garden.　Dylan Iorwerth.　BBMWP *Fr.* Sand.
Garden: "Space, The."　Ok-Ku Kang.　WhBo
Garden.　Marina Ivanovna Tsvetayeva.　RusPo, *tr. by* Robert Arthur Douglas Ford
Garden.　John Greenleaf Whittier.　OBGa
Garden, A.　Andrew Marvell.　OBEV *Fr.* Upon Appleton House [To My Lord Fairfax].
Garden, The.　Rae Armantrout.　FTOS
Garden, The.　Franta Bass.　INSAB
Garden, The.　Joseph Beaumont.　NOSC
Garden, The.　Abraham Cowley.　OBGa
Garden, The.　Abraham Cowley.
　(Garden, The.)　OBGa
Garden, The.　William Cowper. *Fr.* Task, The.
Garden, The.　"H. D."　NoAM
　Heat.　HeIP-4; MoAmPo; TCAPo; TRP
Garden, The.　Dorianne Laux.　AtGh
Garden, The [*see also* Hortus].　Andrew Marvell.　BASC; BrAP; ClHu; FSCP; MakPoe; NAEL-6v1; NAEL-7v1; NIL-7; NIP-4; NoP-5; NOSC; NPeEn; OBGa; OxBEV; PBRV; PoPoPo; TFi; TRP; WaAnP
　(Thoughts in a Garden.)　OBEV
Garden, The.　Bernadette Mayer.　FTOS
Garden, The.　Harriet Monroe.　IllVoic
Garden, The [*in imitation of* Cowley].　Alexander Pope.　OBGa
Garden, The.　Victoria Mary Sackville-West.　OBGa
Garden, The.　James Shirley.　NOSC
Garden, The [*with music*].　Mark Strand.　ColAP; NoAM
Garden, The.　Joshua Sylvester.　OBGa
Garden, The.　Jones Very.　APN-1; OxBoAm
Garden, The ("How vainly men themselves amaze").　Andrew Marvell.　NIP-4
Garden, The: "I couldn't do it again."　Louise Glück.　NoP-4; NoP-5
Garden, The: "Just for a quarter of a day, I'd have you."　John Glenday.　NeBrP
Garden, The: "Like a skein of loose silk blown against a wall."　Ezra Pound.　APT-1; BrAP; HeIP-4; MoAmPo; NIL-7; NIP-4; NoP-4; NoP-5; OxBoAm; PoPoPo
Garden, The. Nothing catches fire. (LL)　Public Garden, The.　Robert Lowell.　BrAP; OBGa
Garden, The: "One sound. Then the hiss and whir."　Louise Glück.　VCAP
Garden Abstract.　Hart Crane.　OBGa
Garden at the General's Residence, The.　Muso Soseki.　EaWin, *tr. by* W. S. Merwin
Garden butterfly.　Issa.　EH, *tr. by* Robert Hass
Garden Calendar.　N. M. Bodecker.　TLR
Garden called Gethsemane / In Picardy it was, The.　Rudyard Kipling.　*See* Garden called Gethsemane.
Garden called Gethsemane, The.　Gethsemane.　Rudyard Kipling.　NPeEn
　(Garden called Gethsemane / In Picardy it was, The.)　GI

Garden Chidings. Louise Imogen Guiney. SWaP

Garden City Diner: Loving Back. Sherry Craven. TiP2

Garden did not bloom, The. Gethsemane A. D. Dolores Kendrick. FFC

Garden District Soubrette. Jessica Freeman. AnSo

Garden Fancies. Robert Browning. OBGa

Garden Fancies. Robert Browning.
(Garden Fancies.) OBGa

Garden flew round with the angel, The. Pleasures of Merely Circulating, The. Wallace Stevens. PtR

Garden Fragrance. Lam Thi My Da. PoCho, tr. by Martha Collins and Thuy Dinh

Garden God, The. Richard Eberhart. OBGa

Garden Hose, The. Beatrice Janosco. NTCP

Garden in September, The. Robert Bridges. OBGa

Garden inclosed is my sister, my spouse; a spring shut up, a fountain / sealed, A. Bible, O.T. OBGa Fr. Song of Solomon, The.

Garden is a loathsome thing, God wot, A. My Garden. P. R. Hines. UV

Garden is a lovesome thing, God wot!, A. My Garden. Thomas Edward Brown. OBEV; OBGa; UV

Garden is breathing out the air of Paradise today, The. On the Way to the Garden (77). Khwaja Shams-ad-din Muhammad Hafiz. WED, tr. by Robert Bly and Leonard Lewisohn

Garden Note I, Los Altos. Janet Lewis. APT-2

Garden Note II, March. Janet Lewis. APT-2

Garden of Eden (described in the Bible), The. Fall, The. Fergus Allen. ModIr

Garden of Eden, The. Ágnes Nemes Nagy. IQMS, tr. by Hugh Maxton

Garden of Friendship, The. Frances Sargent Osgood. PoBW

Garden of Gethsemane, The. Boris Leonidovich Pasternak. GI, tr. by Nina Kossman

Garden of Love, The. William Blake. ItP; NAEL-6v2; NAEL-7v2; NoP-4; NoP-5; NPBRoP; NPeEn; OBGa; OxAEP-2; OxBEV; PoPoPo; TFi; TRP Fr. Songs of Experience.

Garden of Proserpine, The. Veronica Forrest-Thomson. MoWP

Garden of Proserpine, The. Algernon Charles Swinburne. CABP; InoFa; NAEL-6v2; NAEL-7v2; NoP-4; NoP-5; OxBEV; TFi

Garden of Questions. Ivan Metodiev. CSCBP Fr. Songs for Orphans Big and Small.

Garden of Shanah. Sara Riwka Erlich. MirDau, tr. by Auristela Xavier

Garden of Shushan! Before the Feast of Shushan. Anne Spencer. NAAPv.2

Garden of the Muses: Iopas' Song, The. John Skelton. NPeEn Fr. Garland [or Garlande or Garlands] of Laurel[l], the.

Garden of the One, The. Salah Stétié. YaTCFP, tr. by Marilyn Hacker

Garden of Theophrastus, The. Peter Huchel. AF, tr. by Daniel Simko

Garden or gardin was, by measuring, The. Guillaume de Lorris. OBGa

Garden Party. Sir Herbert Read. OBGa

Garden Party, The. Donald Davie. OxBEV

Garden Poem. Ian Hamilton Finlay. OBGa

Garden Shukkei-en, The. Carolyn Forché. AtGh; ExTi; WaAnP

Garden Song, A. Austin Dobson. OBEV; OBGa

Garden Song, A. George R. Sims. OBCoV; OBGa

Garden Temple, The. Patrick Lane. IFF

Garden we walked in, The. Green Grass and Yellow Balloons. Etheridge Knight. GT

Garden where he broods is like a riddle, The. Wartburg, 1521–22, The. Timothy Steele. RA

Garden, Wilderness. Michael Hamburger. OBGa

Garden Window, The. Aaron Hill. OBGa

Garden Year, The. Sara Coleridge. ChAP

Garden-boy is leading the cranes home, The. (LL) Cranes, The. Po Chü-i. CCL1; OBVE; OWoS, tr. by Arthur Waley

Gardener. Robert Graves. OBGa

Gardener. Dom Moraes. OBGa

Gardener. A. H. Snow. OBGa

Gardener, The. Sidney Keyes. MoBrPo

Gardener, The. Ellen Kort. IPoFL

Gardener, The. Craig Raine. UV

Gardener, The. Robert Louis Stevenson. OBGa

Gardener, The. Rabindranath Tagore. OBMV

Gardener, The. Rowland Watkyns. NOSC

Gardener does not love to talk, The. Gardener, The. Robert Louis Stevenson. OBGa

Gardener Janus Catches a Naiad. Dame Edith Sitwell. MoBrPo; OBGa

Gardener to His God, The. Mona Van Duyn. RACG

Gardener wi' His Paidle; or, The Gardener's March, The. Robert Burns. OBGa

Gardeners. Douglas Dunn. OBGa

Gardener's Daughter, The. Alfred Tennyson. OBGa Fr. Gardener's Daughter, The.

Gardener's rule applies to youth and age, The. Adage. Henry James Byron. NBLV

Gardening. Tudur Dylan Jones. BBMWP, tr. by Elin ap Hywel

Gardening Chrysanthemums, I Think of [T'ao] Yüan-Ming. Ishikawa Jōzan. WoPoe, tr. by Jonathan Chaves

Gardening in the Tropics, you never know. Brief Lives. Olive Senior. EmeKit

Gardenng in the Tropics you hear poetry. Tropic Love. Olive Senior. WaAnP

Gardens [with music]. Neil Curry. OBGa

Gardens, The. Abbé Jacques de Lille. OBGa Fr. Gardens, The.

Gardens, gardens, and we are gardeners. Gardeners. Douglas Dunn. OBGa

Gardens No Emblems. Donald Davie. OBGa

Gardens of Alcinous, The. Homer. OBGa; OBVE Fr. Odyssey.

Gardens of Alcinous, The. Homer. OBVE Fr. Odyssey.

Gardens of Ravished Psyche, The. George Barker. OBGa

Gardens of the Villa D'Este, The. Anthony Hecht. ColAP; OBGa

Gardens of Zuñi, The. W. S. Merwin. GifTon

Garden's quit with me: as yesterday, The. Joseph Beaumont. See Garden's quit with me, The. As yesterday.

Garden's quit with me, The. As yesterday. Garden, The. Joseph Beaumont. NOSC

(Garden's quit with me: as yesterday, The.) OBGa

Gardens We Have Left. David Mura. OpBo

Gardin of Adonis, The. Edmund Spenser. NPeEn Fr. Faerie Queene, The.

Gare du Midi. W. H. Auden. StAl

Garfish. John Blight. BMAP

Garglers, The. Mark Cox. SUP

Gargoyle. Carl Sandburg. NAMCP V.1; NoAM

Garibaldian cape shot full of bullet holes, The. (LL) City of Beggars, The. Alfred Hayes. FaBoWar; PWW2

Garland briefer than a girl's, The. (LL) A. E. Housman. BrAP; ChAP; CtM; HeIP-4; InoFa; MoBrPo; NAEL-6v2; NAEL-7v2; NAMCP V.1; NIP-4; NoAM; NoP-4; NoP-5; PtR; SoSe-8; TFi; TRP; WaAnP; WeW-3 Fr. Shropshire Lad, A.

Garland for Advancing Years, A. William Bell Scott. GSo

Garland of Precepts, A [with music]. Phyllis McGinley. NBLV

Garland [or Garlande or Garlands] of Laurel[l], the. John Skelton.
Garden of the Muses: Iopas' Song, The. NPeEn
(Lullay, Lullay, Like a Child.) NAEL-6v1; NAEL-7v1
(To Mastres Margery Wentworthe.) OxBEV
To Mistress Margery Wentworth. OBEV
To Mistress [or Maystres] Isabell Pennell. NoSic; NPeEn; OBEV
To Mistress [or Maystres] Margaret Hussey. NAEL-6v1; NBLV; NoP-4; NoP-5; NoSic; OBEV; OxBEV; TFi; WaAnP
With Lullay, Lullay, Like a Child. NoSic

Garlands fade that Spring so lately wove, The. Sonnet Written at the Close of Spring [or Elegiac Sonnet]. Charlotte Smith. CenSon; RWP

Garlands of fatted words are strung through the city. Silence. Miroslav Holub. PoSu, tr. by Ian Milner and Jarmila Milner

Garlic, The. Bert Meyers. CalPo

Garments of God, The. Jessica Agnes Powers. InvLi

Garments worn in flying dreams, The. Windy City. Stuart Dybek. IllVoic; PoCho

Garnyvillo. Edward Lysaght. IrLP

Garrulous to the very last. (LL) After the Supper and Talk. Walt Whitman. MoAmPo; NAAL-3

Garvey's Head as Value. Norman Weinstein. WaCA

Gas. Gerry Gordon. MiVo

Gas. Sidney Wade. PoSol

Gas Drill. Tom Rawling. FaBoWar

Gas is good, The. Petit Guignol. Philip Hammial. BMAP

Gas Station Attendant. Brian G. Gilmore. SpirFl

Gas Station, The. C. K. Williams. CAP-8; VCAP

Gas was on in the Institute, The. Shropshire Lad, A. Sir John Betjeman. HarvBoo

Gasco. Günter Grass. CLPP, tr. by Jerome Rothenberg

Gascoigne's Good-Morrow. George Gascoigne. NoSic

Gascoigne's Lullaby [or Lullabie]. George Gascoigne. See Lullaby [or Lullabie] of a Lover, The.

Gascoigne's Memories. George Gascoigne.
No Hast But Good. NoSic

Gascoigne's [or Gascoygnes] Good-Night. George Gascoigne. NoSic

Gascoigne's Woodmanship. George Gascoigne. NoSic
(Gascoignes wodmanship.) PBRV
(Woodmanship.) NAEL-7v1

Gashed, from her long immobility on the sea-bed. Arrival of the Titanic, The. William Dickey. PoA 2002

Gasholders, russet among fields. Milldams, marpools. Geoffrey Hill. NAEL-7v2; NAMCP V.2; NoAM; NoP-4; NoP-5; NPeEn Fr. Mercian Hymns.

Gaslight. Rolf Jacobsen. WoPoe, tr. by Roger Greenwald

Gasmask, The. David Wheatley. NIrP

Gas-poker, The. Thom Gunn. StAl

Gassed underground the quiet Nazi way. (LL) Woodchucks. Maxine W. Kumin. CAP-8; NIL-7; NIP-4

Gassing the woodchucks didn't turn out right. Woodchucks. Maxine W. Kumin. CAP-8; NIL-7; NIP-4

Gastric Muse, The. John Armstrong. STuOW Fr. Art of Preserving Health, The.

Gate City Breakdown. Charles Wright. LPSFW

Gate closed, The. Key to Dreams. Georg Nikolic. IllVoic

Gate Gate Paragate Parasmgate Bodhi Svaha. C. Robert Lloyd. ICANM

Gate in a lane. Passing by Where Hsu, "The Wine-Flushed Immortal," Used to Live. Ching An. CSKM, tr. by Jerome P. Seaton

Gate Lodge. Richard Murphy. PBCIP

Gate of Universal Light, The. Muso Soseki. EaWin, tr. by W. S. Merwin

Gate, red lights revolving in the leaves. (LL) First Party at Ken Kesey's with Hell's Angels. Allen Ginsberg. PmAP; TRP

Gatehouse Salutation, The. Eleanor Touchet Davies. EMWP

Gateposts [with music]. Medbh McGuckian. MakPoe; ModIr; PBCIP

Gates. Georgi Borisov. CSCBP, tr. by Georgi Belev and Lisa Sapinkopf

Gates, The. Muriel Rukeyser. BodElec

Gates clanged and they walked you into jail, The. Conscientious Objector, The. Karl Shapiro. PLBUT

Gates fly open with a pretty sound, The. Under the Hill. Daryl Hine. MakPoe

Gates of Paradise, The. William Blake.
    Epilogue. WeW-3
    (To the Accuser Who Is the God of This World.) NPeEn; OxBEV

Gates of the town are closed. The princes, The. Prayer to the Gods of the Night. Unknown. WoPoe, tr. by David Ferry

Gateway buried deep in flowers. Tune: "Sand of Silk-Washing Brook" A Reminiscence. Wu Wen-ying. ColAnChi, tr. by Jiaosheng Wang

Gateway to the Sea—St. Andrews. George Bruce. EdScPo

Gathas. Robert Aitken. WhBo

Gathas. Unknown. WhBo

Gathasaptasati, The. Unknown. tr. by David Ray, Andrew Schelling and Martha Ann Selby
    Even He Was Abashed. WoPoe, tr. by Martha Ann Selby
    Lone Buck. WoPoe, tr. by Andrew Schelling
    Newly Wed Girl, The. WoPoe, tr. by David Ray
    These Women Plunder My Husband. WoPoe, tr. by David Ray
    Those Women. WoPoe, tr. by Martha Ann Selby
    You Love Her. WoPoe, tr. by David Ray

Gather a body to me. Charles Olson. BodElec Fr. Maximus Poems, The.

Gather for festival. "H. D." MoAmPo Fr. Songs from Cyprus.

Gather him to his grave again. Disinterred Warrior, The. William Cullen Bryant. AmWaPo

Gather noble death. Cumae. Merrill Moore. FuPo

Gather out of star-dust. Dream Dust. Langston Hughes. IPoFL

Gather 'round me. Accentuate the Positive. Johnny Mercer. ReLy

Gather round while I sing you of Wernher von Braun. Wernher von Braun. Tom Lehrer. OBCoV

Gather some wood and make a great fire! Unknown. SLW, tr. by Marjolijn De Jager, Sayd Bahodin Majrouh and André Velter

Gather the dead as the first dead scrape home. (LL) Guardians, The. Geoffrey Hill. NoP-4; NoP-5

Gather the pears of St. Peter before the first vespa begins to suck. Giorni. Edward Kleinschmidt. PoDa

Gather the sacred dust. Lines. Abram Joseph Ryan. APN-2

Gather ye bank-notes while ye may. Election Time. Unknown. UV

Gather ye rosebuds while ye may. On Lady A———. Nicolas Bentley. OBCoV

Gather ye Rosebuds while ye may. William Cole. AmWit Fr. Uncoupled Couplets.

Gather ye rose-buds while ye may. To the Virgins, to Make Much of Time. Robert Herrick. BASC; BrAP; CavPo; ClHu; CtM; HeIP-4; ITBLP; NAEL-6v1; NAEL-7v1; NBLV; NIL-7; NIP-4; NoP-4; NoP-5; NOSC; NPeEn; OBEV; OxAEP-1; OxBEV; PoPoPo; PtR; SoSe-8; TFi; UV; WaAnP

Gathered Ants. Tachibana Akemi. EMJL, tr. by Haruo Shirane

Gathered at the nation's sickbed. Conga. Allen Fisher. PFTM-2

Gathered at the River. Denise Levertov. AtGh

Gathered in the heavy heat of Indiana. Fat of the Land, The. Ronald Wallace. FTtHH

Gathered, warped, then straightened, marking new wands. (LL) Words: "Simple contact with a wooden spoon and the word, The." Barbara Guest. AWPTFC; FTOS; OxBoAm

Gathering. Basho. EH, tr. by Robert Hass

Gathering at the Orchid Pavilion, The. Shin Yu Pai. WANABP

Gathering at the River. Anne Caston. NAPBL

Gathering fuel in vacant lots. (LL) Preludes: "Winter evening settles down, The." T. S. Eliot. APT-1; BrAP; HeIP-4; NAAPv.2; NAMCP V.1; OBMV; OxBoAm; PtR; TCAPo; WeW-3

Gathering in the Days. Gareth Owen. NOxBChV

Gathering lotuses by Yeh River. Li Po. CrYelRi; ErotSp Fr. Women of Yueh.

Gathering Mushrooms. Paul Muldoon. HarvBoo; ModIr; NAEL-7v2; NoP-4; PBCIP; PNI

Gathering of the Grand Army, The. Charlotte L. Forten Grimke. AmWaPo

Gathering Place, The. Alan Alexander. NOBAu

Gathering the Bones Together. Gregory Orr. InoFa

Gathering the rains. Basho. EMJL, tr. by Haruo Shirane

Gathering the water-plants. Sikong Tu. CCL1 Fr. Twenty-Four Modes of Poetry.

Gathering the Wild Figs—Vizcaina, Gomera. Emilia Paredes. AFaM; IPoFL

Gaudeamus Igitur: A Valediction. John A. Stone. BloBone

Gaudy boat with wine on board: West Lake is at its best, A. Tune: "Gathering Mulberry Leaves." Ou-yang Hsiu. ColAnChi, tr. by James Robert Hightower

Gaudy Camp Follower, The. Jack Beeching. RSaN

Gaudy Gossip, The. Juvenal. BASC Fr. Satires.

Gaudy gossip, when she's set agog, The. Juvenal. BASC Fr. Satires.

Gaudy Slave Trader. Wayne Koestenbaum. KGB

Gauge. Langston Hughes. APSN

Gaugin ("His journalist.") Manuel Vázquez Montalbán. RaW, tr. by Robert Mezey

Gauguin. Derek Walcott. NoAM Fr. Midsummer.

Gauguin ("Periodista / su padre.") Manuel Vázquez Montalbán. RaW

Gauguin's White Horse. Vicki Hearne. GS

Gauley Bridge is a good town for Negroes, they let us stand. George Robinson: Blues. Muriel Rukeyser. RACG

Gaunt brown walls, The. W. E. Henley. NPeEn Fr. In Hospital.

Gaunt thing, The. Babylon Revisited. Imamu Amiri Baraka. NoAM

Gaunt tousled pine-trees. Tomas Tranströmer. WoBe Fr. Haiku.

Gaurus, you have a fault for which. Martial. RomPo, tr. by Dorothea Wender

Gave me things I. Swallow the Lake. Clarence Major. ESEAA; FTOS; GT; OxAAAP; PmAP

Gave to the dim harmonics voice and tongue? (LL) Harmonics. William Vaughn Moody. AmFaPo; APN-2

Gawaine and the Hound. Edward Robert Bulwer-Lytton. DiBP Fr. Arthur.

Ga-wash-truht in Mesita, in early fall. Hunter's Dance in Early Fall. Debra Haaland Toya. ReEnLa

Gawd save the Queen! (LL) Shillin' a Day. Rudyard Kipling. NAMCP V.1; NoAM

Gawking at clouds. (LL) End and the Beginning, The. Wisława Szymborska. CFP; StAl; VCWP, tr. by Stanislaw Barańczak and Clare Cavanagh

Gay, The. George Russell. OBMV

Gay and audacious crime glints in his eyes. In the Vices. Donald Evans. APT-1

Gay blade on the gentle hedgerow. Daffodil. Waldo Williams. OBWVE, tr. by Gwyn Jones

Gay Chaps at the Bar. Gwendolyn Brooks.
    Gay Chaps at the Bar. IllVoic
    My Dreams, My Works, Must Wait Till After Hell. IllVoic
    Still Do I Keep My Look, My Identity. IllVoic

Gay Full Story. Bernadette Mayer. PmAP

Gay Life. Ron Schreiber. PrTe

Gay little Girl-of-the-Diving-Tank. At the Carnival. Anne Spencer. APT-1; NAAPv.2

Gay Love and the Movies. Ralph Pomeroy. CAGL

Gay Poet, The. William Barber. CAGL

Gay Summer's Bliss, Good-bye. Dietmar von Aist [or Eist]. GePo, tr. by J. W. Thomas

Gay wrap, A. Luwani Dangriga. Zoila Ellis. OWABP

Gaylen got them to sit. Meeting Gaylen's 5th Grade Class. Miguel Algarin. PueRic

Gaza, creeps. Moment of Mourning, A. Donia El-Amal Ismail. PoArWo

Gaza, Undated. Rachel Tzvia Back. DTA

Gaze, The. Gu Cheng. WoBe, tr. by Joseph R. Allen

Gaze is no longer leveled, The. —Cassiopeia at Noon. Michelle Boisseau. ExTi

Gaze not on thy beauty's pride. Thomas Carew. CavPo

Gaze not upon my outside, friend. Apple Dumplings. Mary E. Tucker. CBWP-1

Gaze penetrates through the glass. Reflection on El Train Glass. Luis J. Rodriguez. IllVoic

Gazelle, The. Shmuel HaNagid. WoPoe, *tr. by* Peter Cole

Gazelle, The. Rainer Maria Rilke. PoCho, *tr. by* Robin Robertson

Gazelles have bound their hearts, The. Enderunlu Vâsıf. OLP, *tr. by* Walter Andrews, Najaat Black and Mehmet Kalpakli

Gazelles, The. Thomas Sturge Moore. OBMV

Gazing at Spring. Hsüeh T'ao [*or* Xue Tao]. WoPoe, *tr. by* Jeanne Larsen

Gazing on Lake Dongting. Liu Yu Hsi. CCL1, *tr. by* Stephen Owen

Gazing on the unmoving calm of an ancient Egyptian face. Mummification and Space Travel. Britton Wilkie. AHA

Gazing thro' her chamber window. Reflection. Christina Georgina Rossetti. VWP

Gazing upon him now, severe and dead. Edna St. Vincent Millay. APT-1; InoFa; NALW; NAMCP V.1 *Fr.* Sonnets from an Ungrafted Tree.

GDR. Frederick D'Aguiar.
   Now the Two Are One. WaCA

Géant Blanc Lépreux du paysage, Le. Tristan Tzara. YaTCFP

Gearshift Poem, The. Jane Rohrer. ACAMVP

Gebir. Walter Savage Landor.
   "Now to Aurora, borne by dappled steeds." NOBRP
   "Sleepless, with pleasure and expiring fears." NOBRP

Geburt des Monicakinds. Monica Ferrell. LegDan

Ged a bhiodh cuairt nan reul. Anoch is tu bhuam. Aonghas MacNeacail. EdScPo

Gee, but it's hard to love someone, when that someone don't love you. Down-Hearted Blues. Albert Hunter *and* Louie Austin. NAAPv.2

Gee, but it's tough to be broke, kid. I Can't Give You Anything but Love. Dorothy Fields. APT-2; ReLy

Gee! It's great, after bein' our late. Walkin' My Baby Back Home. Roy Turk. ReLy

Gee, Officer Krupke. Stephen Sondheim. ReLy

Geese, The [*with music*]. Jorie Graham. MoWP; NoP-5; WaAnP

Geese, The. R. Williams Parry. BBMWP, *tr. by* Anthony Conran

Geese are displeased, The. Wisdom of Geese, The. Nancy Willard. PfSP

Geese at Gregynog. R. Gerallt Jones. BBMWP, *tr. by* the author

Geese Blood. Barbara Guest. FTOS

Geese flew by as you entered me, The. Aubade. Kate C. Richardson. PasH

Geese flew over, The. Hokku. Toyo Suyemoto. NAAPv.2

Geese, fresh greens / Wait for you. Issa. ZenPo, *tr. by* Takashi Ikemoto and Lucien Stryk

Geese Gone Beyond. Gary Snyder. NoAM

Geese goosestepping in terror, their hissing peevish from the sedges, The. Bull of Bryncelyn, The. Alan Llwyd. BBMWP, *tr. by* Joseph P. Clancy

Geese have gone, The. No lack. Geese at Gregynog. R. Gerallt Jones. BBMWP, *tr. by* the author

Gegard. Fazil Abdulovich Iskander. ItGoST, *tr. by* Avril Pyman

Gem Creek. Muso Soseki. EaWin, *tr. by* W. S. Merwin

Gem Forest. Muso Soseki. EaWin, *tr. by* W. S. Merwin

Gem Mountain. Muso Soseki. EaWin, *tr. by* W. S. Merwin

Genaro was standing. Appointment, The. Louis Simpson. BodElec

Genau'r Glyn, every day from these to Rhys's halls. Ode to Rhys ap Maredudd of Tywyn. Dafydd Nanmor. OBWVE, *tr. by* H. Idris Bell

Genazzano at nightfall. Genazzano. Marie Luise Kaschnitz. GTCP, *tr. by* Reinhold Grimm

Gene sat on a rock, dangling our map. Route of the Táin, The. Thomas Kinsella. PBCIP

Genealogy. Joan Larkin. LaCa

Genealogy of Crosses, The. Andrey Andreievich Voznesensky. PFTM-2, *tr. by* Richard McKane

Genealogy of Women, The. Semonides. *tr. by* Peter Whigham
   "God in His Wisdom from the start." WoPoe, *tr. by* Peter Whigham

General, The. Siegfried Sassoon. FaBoWar; InoFa; NAEL-6v2; NAEL-7v2; NAMCP V.1; NoAM; NoP-4; NoP-5; NPeEn; OBWP; OxBEV; PoAgWa

General B. F. Butler. Ambrose Bierce. CBCWP

General becomes a sword, The. Having Died. Kim Kwangsŏp. WoPoe, *tr. by* David R. McCann

General Description. George Crabbe. *Fr.* Borough, The.

General Eclipse, The. John Cleveland. BASC

General Grant—the Hero of the War. George Moses Horton. CBCWP

General inspecting the trenches, The. Sir Alan Patrick Herbert. PoWW

General John Cabell Breckinridge. Jill Breckinridge. CBCWP *Fr.* Civil Blood.

General names, no other. Nanni Cagnone. ItPo, *tr. by* Gayle Ridinger

General Prologue, The. Geoffrey Chaucer. NAEL-6v1; NAEL-7v1; NoP-5; WaAnP *Fr.* Canterbury Tales, The.

General Review of the Sex Situation. Dorothy Parker. NAAPv.2

General Robert Smalls. Josephine D. Henderson Heard. CBWP-4

General Store. Rachel Lyman Field. ChAP

General Strike. Nancy Joyce Peters. SurWo

General, there's a battle. Song of the Juggler. Heberto Padilla. AF; BeAl, *tr. by* Andrew Hurley and Alastair Reid

General Walker is dead; killed in a road accident. Rest Due and Taken. Rolando Hinojosa. TiP2

General will be shot in the face, The. Respect for Law and Order, A. John Hughes. PNI

General William Booth Enters into Heaven. Vachel Lindsay. APT-1; ChIV-2; ColAP; MoAmPo; NAAPv.2; PoA 2002; TCAPo

General, your tank is a powerful machine. Bertolt Brecht. BeAl *Fr.* German War Primer, A.

General's Plaque, The. Hồ Xuân Hương. FaBoWar, *tr. by* Graeme Wilson

General's Property, The. Samih Al-Qasim. PoAgWa, *tr. by* Abdullah Al-Udhari

Generals Ride in Cars. *Unknown.* FaBoWar

Generation. Rae Armantrout. FTOS

Generation, A. Gu Cheng. PFTM-2; VCWP, *tr. by* Sam Hamill

Generation Gap. Tammy Lynn Pertillar. BtF

Generation of the Seeds, or the Origin of Corn, The. *Unknown.*
   "Lo! ye children of men and the Mother." APN-2

Generation will not know, The. Multiple-Theater. Heather Fuller. Eno

Generations. Siva Reddy. HotL, *tr. by* V. Narayana Rao

Generations 1. Sam Cornish. GT

Generations 2. Sam Cornish. GT

Generations of the virgin are tattooed on her unblemished belly, The. Poem of Any Virgin. Jorge de Lima. PFTM-1

Generations unfold from our faces. Bones and Drums. Ron Welburn. SeSe

Generic Elbows. Bernadette Mayer. FTOS

Genes confessing. (LL) Weakness, The. Toi Derricotte. GT; LTA

Genesis. Bible, *O.T.*
   "And God saw that the wickedness of man was great." NAWM-5v1
   "And Joseph was brought down to Egypt." NAWM-5v1
   "And Noah was six hundred years old when the flood of waters." NAWM-5v1
   "And the Lord God planted a garden eastward in Eden." OBGa
   "And the whole earth was of one language, and of one speech." NAWM-5v1
   "In the beginning God created the heaven and the earth." NAWM-5v1
   "Joseph, being seventeen years old, was feeding the flock with his brethren." NAWM-5v1
   "See, the smelle of my sone is as the smell of a feld." OBVE

Genesis. Geoffrey Hill. ChIV-1; HarvBoo
   "On the sixth day, as I rode." UpMys

Genesis [*with music*]. Evan Jones. PML

Genesis. Alda Merini. CItWP, *tr. by* Cinzia Sartini Blum and Lara Trubowitz

Genesis. Ali Smith. PoBW

Genesis XXIV. Arthur Hugh Clough. ChIV-1

Genesis 2. Etheridge Knight. BodElec

Genesis: A Retrospective. Peter Johnson. Vesp

Genesis (Chapter 7, Verse 5). Manuela Fingueret. MirDau, *tr. by* Roberta Gordenstein

Genesis Text for Larry Levis, Who Died Alone, A. Norman Dubie. MAAN

Genetics. Sinéad Morrissey. BeAl; MoWP; NIrP

Geneva was the wild one. Ballad of Aunt Geneva, The. Marilyn Nelson Waniek. FFC; GT; RA

Génèvres Hérissez, et Vous, Houx Espineux. Pierre de Ronsard. WoPoe, *tr. by* Donald Davie

Genial poets, pink-faced. Goodbye to Tolerance. Denise Levertov. NoAM

Genie in the Jar, The. Nikki Giovanni. SeSe

Genie serves a continental breakfast, angel brings the desired, A. Zealous. Joshua Clover. PuP-23

Genie's Prayer Under the Kitchen Sink. Rita Dove. RACG

Genius. Adah Isaacs Menken. CBWP-1; ViWPN

Genius. Margit Szécsi. IQMS, *tr. by* Agnes Arany-Makkai

Genius Child. Langston Hughes. PoPoPo

Genius Child. Kevin Powell. AmPoNex

Genius is power. Genius. Adah Isaacs Menken. CBWP-1; ViWPN

Genius Loci. Margaret Louisa Woods. OBEV

Genius of Africk! whether thou bestrid'st. James Grainger. PoSl *Fr.* Sugar Cane, The.

Genius of Fog at Ecola Creek Mouth. Sandra McPherson. ExTi

Genius of musings, who, the midnight hour. Time: A Poem. Henry Kirke White.

Genius, or Muse, whate'er thou art! whose thrill.   Robert Merry.   NOBRP *Fr.* Laurel of Liberty. A Poem, The.

Genius, technique—you'd swear the pair unsuited.   Nature and Art.   Johann Wolfgang von Goethe.   STV, *tr. by* John Frederick Nims

Genius: "Two old dancing shoes my grandfather."   Philip Levine.   CalPo; NoAM

Genius was 81, The.   Cutting Prow, The.   Edward Sanders.   PmAP

Genoa.   Dino Campana.   PFTM-1

Genoa salami on a bagel? Why not.   Seasonal Ramble.   Tony Towle.   PoDa

Genotype is her genetic constitution, The.   Mei-Mei Berssenbrugge.   AWPTFC *Fr.* Four Year Old Girl.

Gent, Nugget, Swank, and *Dude.*   Thirteen.   Ronald Wallace.   PBCAP

Gentile or Hebrew or simply a man.   Jorge Luis Borges.   GI

Gentle Anarchist, The.   Brunton Stephens.   NOBAu

Gentle Annie, willow wind, the West, A.   Four Winds.   Hal Porter.   NOBAu

Gentle as a maiden's dream.   Snow Storm, The.   Mary Weston Fordham.   CBWP-2

Gentle Breeze with a Whispered Cry, The.   Gustavo Adolfo Bécquer.   SpanPo, *tr. by* Alice Jane McVan

Gentle Check, The.   Joseph Beaumont.   NOSC

Gentle Communion.   Pat Mora.   NIL-7; NIP-4

Gentle day's flower.   Chogyam Trungpa.   WhBo

Gentle Echo on Woman, A.   Jonathan Swift.   NBLV

Gentle ghost.   Marina Ivanovna Tsvetayeva.   TCRusP *Fr.* Poems to Blok.

Gentle handed holy father, or whomever.   Zombie Sunday (Had We but World Enough and Time).   Josh Bell.   LegDan

Gentle Ithuriel led him round the skies.   Mr. Gunston is Shown round Heaven [*or* To the Dear Memory of Thomas Gunston, Esq.].   Isaac Watts.   STuOW

Gentle knight was pricking on the plaine, A.   Edmund Spenser.   NoP-5 *Fr.* Faerie Queene, The.

Gentle Locke sits down to write his famous treatise.   At Work.   Artur Miedzyrzecki.   PoSu, *tr. by* John Batki and Artur Miedzyrzecki

Gentle Owen was a man well set, The.   Owen Tudor.   Hugh Holland.   AngWePo

Gentle priestess of the Wise, A. (LL)   Forgiveness.   George Russell.   IrLP; IrV

Gentle purple-throated dove.   Wood Dove, The.   Ernest Francisco Fenollosa.   NAAPv.1

Gentle Shepherd, The.   Allan Ramsay.

   Act 1.

      Lover's Logic.   DiBP

      (Peggy.)   OBEV

      (Sang.)   OxBEV

Gentle slopes are green to remind you, The.   NAEL-6v2; NAEL-7v2 *Fr.* In Parenthesis.

Gentle squire would gladly entertain, A.   Joseph Hall.   NoSic *Fr.* Virgidemiarum.

Gentle sunlight of evening.   Heysel.   Robat Powell.   BBMWP, *tr. by* the author

Gentleman and the Lady, The.   Vivian Lamarque.   CItWP, *tr. by* Cinzia Sartini Blum and Lara Trubowitz

Gentleman Compares His Virtue to a Piece of Jade, A.   Michael Ondaatje.   PoDa

Gentleman in Front, The.   Vivian Lamarque.   CItWP, *tr. by* Cinzia Sartini Blum and Lara Trubowitz

Gentleman in the Barber Shop.   S. Brandi Barnes.   BtF

Gentleman in the Heart, The.   Vivian Lamarque.   CItWP, *tr. by* Cinzia Sartini Blum and Lara Trubowitz

Gentleman Is a Dope, The.   Oscar Hammerstein, II.   ReLy

Gentleman makes his way among clouds and moons, The.   Brief Note from Jerusalem, A.   Gabriel Preil.   FIT, *tr. by* Robert Friend

Gentleman who had been at Winchester said, The.   Butler and the Gentleman, The.   Anna Wickham.   RSaN

Gentlemen.   W. N. Ewer.   RSaN

Gentlemen, for this day's work our chance has not been ill.   *Unknown.* FaBoWar *Fr.* Excerpts from *The Poem of the Cid.*

Gentlemen: / It pleases me to inform you, by means of these lines, that death, more than a punishment.   Need to Die, The.   César Vallejo.   ConPit, *tr. by* Clayton Eshleman and Jorge Guzman

Gentlemen of the Press.   Crucifixion Will Not Take Place, The.   Elma Mitchell.   EdScPo

Gentlemen who have got to be classics and are now old with beards, The.   Letter to the Academy.   Langston Hughes.   AF

Gentlemen-Rankers.   Rudyard Kipling.   FaBoWar

Gentleness of the slant October light, The.   Where It Ends.   William Bronk.   APSN

Gentleness of the Very Tall, The.   Linda France.   MFPA

Gentlest air, thou breath of lovers.   Sigh, A.   Anne Finch, Countess of Winchilsea.   OxBEV

Gentlest fair, mourn, mourn no moe. (LL)   John Fletcher.   OBEV; OxAEP-1 *Fr.* Queen of Corinth, The.

Gentlewoman of the dealing trade, A.   Epigram 29.   Samuel Rowlands.   NOSC

Gentlewoman yt Married a Yonge Gent Who After Forsooke Whereuppon She Tooke Hir Needle in Which She Was Excelent and Worked upon Hir Sampler Thus, A.   *Unknown.*   EMWP

Gentlewomans Answer to One, that Sayd He Should Dye, if Shee Refuse His Desires, A.   *Unknown.*   EMWP

Gently, gently prithee, time.   *Unknown.*   NOSC

Gently I took that which ungently came.   Forbearance.   Samuel Taylor Coleridge.   ChIV-2

Gently shirred. (LL)   Rita Dove.   NAAL-5; NAMCP V.2 *Fr.* Thomas and Beulah.

Gently slide your hand inside my sleeves.   *Unknown.*   SLW, *tr. by* Marjolijn De Jager, Sayd Bahodin Majrouh and André Velter

Gently Stroke a Wound.   Joyce Mansour.   MFP, *tr. by* Martin Sorrell

Gently, the side wind blowing.   Yun Söndo.   CATKP *Fr.* Angler's Calendar, The.

Gentrification.   Erika Meitner.   RWB

Gents bounce thoroughly around in turn-of-the-century.   Dalliance with Salt Sides, A.   Clark Coolidge.   NYP2

Genuflection to Petty Officer First Class Leonette Masters.   Hettie Jones.   PrTe

Genuine, you are interested in poetry. (LL)   Poetry [1921 version]: "I, too, dislike it: there are things that are important beyond all this fiddle."   Marianne Moore.   AmFaPo; APT-1; ColAP; HeIP-4; MoAmPo; NAAL-5; NAAPv.2; NALW; NAMCP V.1; NIP-4; NoAM; NoP-4; NoP-5; OxBoAm; PoPoPo; TCAPo; TFi; WaAnP

Genus Infoelix Vitae.   Queen of England Elizabeth I.   EMWP

Genus Narcissus.   Natasha Trethewey.   LegDan

Geo-Bestiary #X.   James Harrison.   TAPaP

Geocentric.   Pattiann Rogers.   SUP

Geographical History, The.   Giulia Niccolai.   CItWP, *tr. by* Cinzia Sartini Blum and Lara Trubowitz

Geography.   Adisa Vera Beatty.   FuFl

Geography.   G. K. Chesterton.   OBSV *Fr.* Songs of Education.

Geography.   Kenneth Koch.   NAMCP V.2; NoAM

Geography.   Brenda Marie Osbey.   BodElec

Geography: a Song.   Howard Moss.   OBCoV

Geography I am learning, The.   Geography.   Brenda Marie Osbey.   BodElec

Geography Lesson.   Robin Morgan.   FiBr

Geography Lesson.   Carol Rumens.   BeAl; MoWP

Geography of dream is complex, The.   Difference Between Night and Day, The.   Bin Ramke.   YaYoPo

Geography of Lograire, The.   Thomas Merton.

   East.

      Place Names.   ChIV-1

Geological Hymn.   Joseph Ceravolo.   PmAP

Geologist, The.   Michael C. Blumenthal.   PfSP

Geology, A.   Brenda Hillman.   AWPTFC; GeoHom

Geometric, deformed, unnatural. (LL)   Venus Hottentot, The.   Elizabeth Alexander.   ESEAA; InTrad

Geometrical Place.   Günter Eich.   AF, *tr. by* David Young

Geometry.   Jenni Daiches.   EdScPo

Geometry.   Rita Dove.   HeIP-4; NAMCP V.2; PtR

Geometry Class.   Mark Bibbins.   AmPoNex; WiU

Geometry of the Figure.   Mark McMorris.   OnScMo

Geometry of the Soul.   Fawziyya Abu Khalid.   PoArWo, *tr. by* Farouk Mustafa

Geopolitical, The.   David Buuck.   Eno *Fr.* Stanzas in Mediation.

Georg Heym—The Almost Metaphysical Adventure.   Zbigniew Herbert.   PoetW, *tr. by* Bogdana Carpenter and John Carpenter *and* Bogdana Carpenter

Georg Trakl.   Else Lasker-Schüler.   PFTM-1

George [*with music*].   Dudley Randall.   NoAM

George III Enters Paradise.   Robert Southey.   STuOW *Fr.* Vision of Judgement,-A.

George and Genevieve Geronimo with a with whether they thought they were with whether.   George Hugnet.   Gertrude Stein.   NAAPv.2; NAMCP V.1; NoAM

George and me.   Letter to a Boy at School.   Anna Wickham.   NOxBChV

George Buchanan in Old Age.   James Logie Robertson.   EdScPo

George Burns likes to insist that he always.   Of Time and the Line.   Charles Bernstein.   FTOS; NIL-7; NoP-5; PFTM-2; PmAP; ReTh; WaAnP

George Burroughs.   Fred Cogswell.   Coast

George Copway's Dream Song.   *Unknown.*   APN-2, *tr. by* George Copway

George Crabbe.   Edwin Arlington Robinson.   APN-2; MoAmPo; NoP-4; NoP-5

George Genevieve in are ring. (LL)   George Hugnet.   Gertrude Stein. NAAPv.2; NAMCP V.1; NoAM

George Grosz.   Else Lasker-Schüler.   PFTM-1

George Hugnet.   Gertrude Stein.   NAAPv.2; NAMCP V.1; NoAM

George Robinson: Blues.   Muriel Rukeyser.   RACG

George Sand.   Dorothy Parker.   NALW; NAMCP V.1 *Fr.* Pig's-Eye View of Literature, A.

George the First was always reckoned.   Georges, The.   Walter Savage Landor. NIP-4; OBCoV; OBSV

George III.   Edmund Clerihew Bentley.   NPeEn *Fr.* Clerihews.

George the Third's Soliloquy.   Philip Freneau.
"France aids them now, a desperate game I play."   TCAPo

George Washington and the Loss of His Teeth.   Diane Wakoski.   PFTM-2

George Washington never owned a camel.   Jackson Mac Low.   APSN *Fr.* Presidents of the United States of America, The.

Georges, The.   Walter Savage Landor.   NIP-4; OBCoV; OBSV

Georgi Borisov in Paris.   John Balaban.   TAPaP

Georgia.   Philippe Soupault.   SurPaPo, *tr.* by Mary Ann Caws and Patricia Terry

Georgia.   Philippe Soupault.   YaTCFP

Georgia avenue, washington d.c.   Brian G. Gilmore.   BRtP

Georgia Dusk [*with music*].   Jean Toomer.   APT-2; InGu; NAAL-5; NAAPv.2; NAMCP V.1; NoAM; NoP-4; NoP-5; OxBoAm

Georgia on My Mind.   Stuart Gorrell.   ReLy

Georgiad, The.   Roy Campbell.
"Hail, mediocrity, beneath whose spell."   MoBrPo

Georgian Spring.   Roy Campbell.   OBSV

Georgics.   Virgil. *tr.* by John Dryden, Richmond Lattimore, Percy Bysshe Shelley, David R. Slavitt and William Wordsworth
Third Book of the Georgics, The. *tr.* by John Dryden
Uses of the Dog, The.   DiBP, *tr.* by John Dryden
Georgic 1.
"Therefore Philippi saw once more the Roman battalions."   APT-2, *tr.* by Richmond Lattimore
"Who dares deny the burning truth of the sun?"   WoPoe, *tr.* by David R. Slavitt
What crops the region will bear.   IPoFL, *tr.* by L. P. Wilkinson

Georgics of Heisod, The.   Hesiod. *tr.* by George Chapman
Winter.   NOSC, *tr.* by George Chapman

Georgina / don't cry.   Georgina.   Cauvin L. Paul.   OGAHCP, *tr.* by Boadiba and Jack Hirschman

Georgina Trevellyn to Luisa: "At last, dearest Louisa, I take up my pen to address you."   Arthur Hugh Clough.   NoP-5 *Fr.* Amours de Voyage.

Georgina Trevellyn to Luisa: "Dearest Louisa, Enquire if you please about Mr. Claude."   Arthur Hugh Clough.   FaBoVe *Fr.* Amours de Voyage.

Geranium.   Edward Dorn.   PmAP

Geranium, The.   Theodore Roethke.   EmeKit; WeW-3

Geranium and the Child.   Ece Ayhan.   PFTM-2, *tr.* by Murat Nemet-Nejat

Geranium Flame.   Lucile Adler.   ICANM

Geranium needs, The.   Holm Oak, The.   Mariella Bettarini.   CItWP, *tr.* by Cinzia Sartini Blum and Lara Trubowitz

Gerarda.   Eloise Bibb.   CBWP-4

Gereint ab Erbin.   *Unknown.*   OBWVE, *tr.* by Joseph P. Clancy

Gereint Son of Erbin.   *Unknown.*   WoPoe *Fr.* Black Book of Carmarthen, The.

Geriatric.   Ronald Stuart Thomas.   TCAWP

Geriatric, wizened, ancient man.   Trickster 1 (for Winston Rodney).   Kwame Dawes.   WaCA

Germ of new life, whose powers expanding slow.   To a Little Invisible Being Who Is Expected Soon to Become Visible.   Anna Laetitia Barbauld. NAEL-6v2; NAEL-7v2; WoRP

Germ, The.   Ogden Nash.   APT-2

German Army, Russia, 1943, The.   Ai.   MakPoe

German Frontier at Basel: 1942 and 1992, The.   Hilda Schiff.   HP

German Language, The [*epigram*].   Friedrich von Logau.   GePo, *tr.* by George C. Schoolfield

German Prisoners.   Joseph Lee.   FaBoWar

German Requiem, A.   James Fenton.   HarvBoo; NAEL-6v2; NAEL-7v2; NAMCP V.2; NoAM; NoP-5; NPeEn
"His wife nods, and a secret smile."   HP

German War Primer, A.   Bertolt Brecht.
"General, your tank is a powerful machine."   BeAl, *tr.* by David Constantine

Germans stood together under guard, The.   1945.   Ed Leeflang.   TuT, *tr.* by Peter van de Kamp

Germany of three confessions now shall keep a single one.   One Faith and No Faith.   Friedrich von Logau.   GePo, *tr.* by George C. Schoolfield

Germinal.   George Russell.   MoBrPo; OBEV; OBMV

Germinating sopranos in conservative head squares.   Middle-aged Irish Mothers.   Rita Ann Higgins.   MoWP

Gerontion.   T. S. Eliot.   APT-1; ColAP; NAAL-5; NAAPv.2; NAMCP V.1; NoAM; NPeEn; OxAEP-2; TCAPo; TFi; WaAnP
"Vacant shuttles / Weave the wind. I have no ghosts."   UV

Gertrude of Wyoming.   Thomas Campbell.
Part Two.   NPBRoP

Gertrude; or, Fidelity till Death.   Felicia Dorothea Hemans.   RWP

Gertrude Stein.   Mina Loy.   APT-1; MoWP; NAAPv.2; NAMCP V.1; OxBoAM

Gertrude Stein Rides the Town Down El.   Tom Postell.   EGAG

Gertrude to Hamlet.   Lee Upton.   IaFF

Ge-sheng: The Kudzu Spreads till It Darkens the Brier.   *Unknown.*   CCL1, *tr.* by Burton Watson

Gest of Robyn Hode.   *Unknown.*
"Lythe and listin, gentilmen."   NAEL-6v1

Gestalt Me Out!   Bruce Andrews.   FTOS

Gestalt me out! Slang to the point of meat-eating, imperative ornament, dislike. Gestalt Me Out!   Bruce Andrews.   FTOS

Gesture and Flight.   Ann Lauterbach.   BodElec

Gesture of an Ionic column returning your face.   Noli Me Tangere.   Jan Polkowski.   AF, *tr.* by Michael March and Jaroslaw Anders

Gesture, The.   George Oppen.   OxBoAm *Fr.* Five Poems about Poetry.

GESTURE THE GESTURE THE GESTURE THE GES-, THE.   Hymn to Saint Geryon.   Michael McClure.   PmAP

Gestures: A Game Anglican.   Ernst Jandl.   OnScMo

Gestures from My Window.   Yolanda Bedregal.   TANSG, *tr.* by Carolyne Wright

Get A Blank.   Directions for Understanding Modern Jazz Criticism.   Kalamu ya Salaam.   FuFl

Get a load.   Lorine Niedecker.   APT-2

Get away, they're all gone.   Chops Are Flyin.   Stanley Crouch.   GT

Get Blind Drunk.   Wang the Zealot.   CCL1, *tr.* by C. H. Kwock and Vincent McHugh and Vincent McHugh

Get drunk, get drunk.   Get Drunk.   Ho Ch'i-fang.   WoPoe, *tr.* by Kai-yu Hsu

Get drunk / Walk on water.   Things to Do in the Bible.   Elaine Equi.   IllVoic

Get High.   Charles Baudelaire.   MotU, *tr.* by Edward K. Kaplan

Get him up and be gone as one shaped awry; he disturbs the order here. (LL) Thomas Hardy.   ChIV-1; NAMCP V.1; NoAM *Fr.* In Tenebris.

Get It Again.   Mark Halliday.   PtR

Get it, / she said, so it's unknown which parent.   John Cage.   APSN *Fr.* Diary: How to Improve the World (You Will Only Make Matters Worse).

Get on top.   On Top of It All.   Keith Gilyard.   SpirFl

Get on with the festivities—let them say what they will.   Leylâ Hanim.   NaPG, *tr.* by Talat Sait Halman

Get out of me a little.   Death Is Your Salvation.   Nidaa Khoury.   DTA, *tr.* by Shirley Kaufman and Roger Tavor

Get out of my hut, you stealthy vermin! Leonidas'.   Leonidas of Tarentum. HePo, *tr.* by Barbara Hughes Fowler

Get Out of Town.   Cole Porter.   ReLy

Get out the lunch-box of your dreams.   Jim Crow Car.   Langston Hughes. GM

Get put gat eisnin monocotyledon.   Like Pornography.   Rob MacKenzie.   Oth

Get ready. (LL)   La Migra.   Pat Mora.   NIL-7; UnSA

Get so near. I started there. (LL)   Love.   Kate Clanchy.   BeAl; MoWP

Get the word and go.   Journey.   Eamon Grennan.   PoDa

Get thee a ship well-rigged and tight.   In Praise of Fidelia.   Mildmay Fane, 2d Earl of Westmorland.   NOSC

Get thee behind me. Even as, heavy-curled.   Dante Gabriel Rossetti.   ChIV-2 *Fr.* House of Life, The.

Get this.   Descriptive Poetry.   Friedrich Hölderlin.   WoPoe, *tr.* by Vyt Bakaitis

Get this straight, Joe, and don't get me wrong.   How Do I Feel?   Kenneth Fearing.   APT-2

Get Up!   Joseph Skipsey.   NPeEn

Get Up and Bar the Door.   *Unknown.*   HeIP-4; NePenScot; NoP-4; NoP-5

Get Up, Get Up.   *Unknown.*   NTCP

Get up, get up for shame! the blooming morn[e].   Corinna's Going a-Maying. Robert Herrick.   AEP; BASC; BrAP; CABP; NAEL-6v1; NAEL-7v1; NIP-4; NoP-4; NoP-5; NOSC; OBEV; OxBEV; PBRV; PoPoPo; TFi; WaAnP

Get up, get up, Mountain: no more sleep for you!   Āśutos Bhattācārya. SinGod, *tr.* by Rachel Fell McDermott

Get up, get up, you lazy-head.   Get Up, Get Up.   *Unknown.*   NTCP

"Get up!" "Marlene?" I smell the April rain.   Mark Stern Wakes Up. Frederick Feirstein.   RA

Get up, Mountain, get up!   *Unknown.*   SinGod, *tr.* by Rachel Fell McDermott

"Get up!" the caller calls, "Get up!"   Get Up!   Joseph Skipsey.   NPeEn

Get up, you old dog.   To the Man Inside.   Carl Rakosi.   BodElec

Get wild rapture instead? (LL)   Late Psalm.   Betsy Sholl.   ACAMVP; MAAN

Get ye hence, rebellious spirits.   Incantation.   Zinaida Nikolayevna Gippius. ARWW, *tr.* by Catriona Kelly

Get ye up from the wrath of God's terrible day! Cities of the Plain, The. John Greenleaf Whittier. ChIV-1; NCAP

Get your flag out of my face, it tickles! Last Will and Testament. Hans Magnus Enzensberger. PoSu

(Get Your Kicks On) Route 66! Bobby Troup. ReLy

Get your purse, have you got your keys? (LL) Secondhand Coat. Ruth Stone. NALW; NIL-7; NIP-4

Get yourself elected. Comrade Laugher. Paul Potts. RSaN

Ge-tan: Shade o' the Vine. *Unknown.* CCL1, *tr.* by Ezra Pound

Get-Away. Robert Malise Bowyer Nichols.
   "Beginning when I was six I became my father's accomplice." CLPP

Getaway Car. Leanne O'Sullivan. NIrP

Gethsemane: "Damp wind, the innocent." David Craig. UpMys

Gethsemane: "Moon swims to the fore in the pale heavens, The." Irina Ermakova. CRWP, *tr.* by Daniel Weissbort

Gethsemane. Rudyard Kipling. NPeEn

Gethsemane A. D. Dolores Kendrick. FFC

Gethsemani, KY. Ernesto Cardenal. *tr.* by Thomas Merton
   Like Empty Beer Cans. TCLAP, *tr.* by Thomas Merton

Gets in / the damp. Ana Belén López Pulido. SPV, *tr.* by Jen Hofer

Getting Away: Verses and Choruses for Various Voices. Wendell Berry. PoCoUp

Gettin[g] de Spirit [*with music*]. Una Marson. MoWP

Getting Dirty. Dorthi Charles. TLR

Getting Even. Mark Fleckenstein. MiVo

Getting in the Wood. Gary Snyder. NoAM

Getting It Wrong, Again. Steve Griffiths. AngWePo

Getting Lost in Nazi Germany. Marvin Bell. TaR

Getting Off the Ride. Mafika Pascal Gwala. TSAP

Getting Older. Elaine Feinstein. HarvBoo

Getting Out. Cleopatra Mathis. SoSe-8

Getting Out Alive. Rosario Morales. PueRic

Getting out of bed one day, you broke. Elegy for My Sister. Howard Moss. VCAP

Getting Over Robert Frost. Peter Davison. VisFro

Getting Ready. Jack Gilbert. BodElec

Getting the Message. Maxine W. Kumin. TaR

Getting the News. Helen Chasin. YaYoPo

Getting the right words in the right order. Trying to Make Music. David Wagoner. BAP-04

Getting There. Sylvia Plath. GM

Getting Through. Deborah Pope. PoA 2002

Getting to Know Her. Jacqueline Berger. AmPoNex

Getting to Sleep in New Jersey. John A. Stone. BloBone

Getting Up Ahead of Someone (Sun). Frank O'Hara. CAP-8

Getting Up in Winter. Emperor Ch'ien-wen of Liang. BLT, *tr.* by Kenneth Rexroth

Getting Warm. Rae Armantrout. FTOS

Getting your kids to climb. Robert Frost As Father. Sarah Katherine Mccann. VisFro

Getting Your Rocks Off. Melvin Dixon. CAGL

Get-Together Song. Ralph Waldo Emerson. STuOW *Fr.* Alphonso of Castile.

Gettysburg. Edgar Lee Masters. CBCWP

Gettysburg Address, The. Abraham Lincoln. HHAm

Gettysburg, July 1, 1863. Jane Kenyon. CBCWP

Gettysburg Ode. Bayard Taylor. CBCWP

Geyser, The. Ágnes Nemes Nagy. PoSu, *tr.* by Bruce Berlind

Ghaflah—the sin of forgetfulness. Dima Hilal. PoArWo

Ghastly ordeal it was, A. In. No Title. David Schubert. APT-2

Ghazal: "Only language of loss left in the world is Arabic, The." Agha Shahid Ali. AmAlph; PML
   (Arabic.) PoCho

Ghazal: "What will suffice for a true-love knot? Even the rain?" Agha Shahid Ali. AmAlph

Ghazal: "Where are you now? Who lies beneath your spell tonight." Agha Shahid Ali. NAMCP V.2

Ghazal: "For the sake of a Turkish woman from Shiraz, consumed in the deadly fumes." Mariya Galina. CRWP, *tr.* by Daniel Weissbort

Ghazal. Mirza Asadullah Khan Ghalib. WoPoe, *tr.* by Frances W. Pritchett

Ghazal. Adrienne Rich. WoPoe

Ghazal 1. John Thompson. Coast

Ghazal 5: "My white mare on the Punjabi plains, the stamp of her hooves." Kuldip Gill. IFF

Ghazal 5. Mirza Asadullah Khan Ghalib. EaWin, *tr.* by Aijaz Ahmad and W. S. Merwin

Ghazal 12. Mirza Asadullah Khan Ghalib. EaWin, *tr.* by Aijaz Ahmad and W. S. Merwin

Ghazal 13: "Where are your woo-trysts and your heart-wreches now, Ghalib?" Mirza Asadullah Khan Ghalib. SonAtl, *tr.* by Esfandiar Kiani and Sunil Sidpara

Ghazal 15. Mirza Asadullah Khan Ghalib. EaWin, *tr.* by Aijaz Ahmad and W. S. Merwin

Ghazal 21. Mirza Asadullah Khan Ghalib. EaWin, *tr.* by Aijaz Ahmad and W. S. Merwin

Ghazal 24: For Years My Heart Asked Me for Jamshid's Cup. Khwaja Shams-ad-din Muhammad Hafiz. WoPoe, *tr.* by Elizabeth Gray

Ghazal 25. Mirza Asadullah Khan Ghalib. EaWin, *tr.* by Aijaz Ahmad and W. S. Merwin

Ghazal 34. Mirza Asadullah Khan Ghalib. EaWin, *tr.* by Aijaz Ahmad and W. S. Merwin

Ghazal 37: "Now you have burned your books, you'll go with nothing." John Thompson. Coast

Ghazal 39: "If you laid out all the limbs from the Civil War hospital." James Harrison. ViWalt

Ghazal: Comet. Jacqueline Osherow. ExTi

Ghazal for Open Hands. Martín Espada. PrTe

Ghazal: Half-Way Through the Night. Khwaja Shams-ad-din Muhammad Hafiz. WoPoe, *tr.* by Geoffrey Squires

Ghazal of the Better-Unbegun. Heather McHugh. ExTi; FaoP

Ghazal of the Dark Death. Federico García Lorca. WED, *tr.* by Robert Bly

Ghazal of the Terrifying Presence. Federico García Lorca. WED, *tr.* by Robert Bly

Ghazal on signs of Love and Occupation. Philip Salom. BMAP

Ghede Poem. Nathaniel Mackey. PmAP

Ghetto. Michael Longley. EmeKit; NoP-4; NoP-5; PNI

Ghetto, The. Lola Ridge.
   1. APT-1
   6. APT-1

Ghetto Dokusan. Gary Rosenthal. WhBo

Ghetto Twilight. Alter Brody. TaR

Ghost. Nina Cassian. PoSu, *tr.* by Christopher Hewitt

Ghost. Daphne Marlatt. BrAP *Fr.* Steveston.

Ghost. Cathy Song. NAMCP V.2

Ghost, The. Rafael Alberti. RaW, *tr.* by Charles Guenther

Ghost, The. Charles Churchill.
   "Pomposo (insolent and loud)." OBSV

Ghost, The. Ágnes Nemes Nagy. PoSu, *tr.* by Bruce Berlind

Ghost, The. Fitz-James O'Brien. FaBoVe

Ghost, The [*after* Sextus Propertius]. Propertius. PoA 2002; WoPoe, *tr.* by Robert Lowell

Ghost, The. Iain Crichton Smith. NOxBChV

Ghost, The ("Peace in thy hands / Peace in thine eyes.") Walter De la Mare. MoBrPo

Ghost, The ("Who knocks? I, who was beautiful.") Walter De la Mare. InoFa; MoBrPo

Ghost at Anlaby, The. Randolph Stow. NOBAu

Ghost Birches. Chase Twichell. PfSP

Ghost Frost. Roger Weingarten. VisFro

Ghost in the dark hunts the author of "The Little Man", A. Nightmare, The. Abdul Wahab Al-Bayati. IrPoTo, *tr.* by Farouk Abdel Wahab

Ghost in the Martini, The [*with music*]. Anthony Hecht. NoP-4; NoP-5

Ghost is someone: death has left a hole, A. Ghost, The. Propertius. PoA 2002; WoPoe, *tr.* by Robert Lowell

Ghost Lights. H. Palmer Hall. TiP2

Ghost of a Chance. Adrienne Rich. OxBoAm

Ghost of a Ghost, The. Brad Leithauser. RA

Ghost of Abel, The. William Blake. ChIV-1

Ghost of Fadon, The. Joanna Baillie. NOBRP

Ghost of Fusion, The. Andrew Duncan. VaPo

Ghost of His Hand, The. Nancy Bennett. IFF

Ghost of Me. Andy Young. AnSo

Ghost of Santo Domingo, The. Suzanne Gardinier. NeAmPo

Ghost rose when the waves rose, A. Faith Upon the Waters. Laura Riding Jackson. APT-2

Ghost Ship. Tom French. NIrP

Ghost Shirt, The. Lucia Maria Perillo. BAP-01

Ghost Song. Jack Spicer. APSN

Ghost Stations. Carole Satyamurti. RSaN

Ghost Story. Dylan Thomas. OBCP

Ghost Street. Milán Füst. IQMS, *tr.* by Jess Perlman

Ghost Tantras. Michael McClure.
   "PLEASURE FEARS ME, FOOT ROSE, FOOT BREATH." BB
   "SILENCE THE EYES! BECALM THE SENSES!" PFTM-2
   "TREES ARE ELEPHANTS' HEADS, THE." PFTM-2

Ghost that loved a lady fair, A. Phantom-Wooer, The. Thomas Lovell Beddoes. NAEL-6v2; WaAnP

Ghost Town. Michael Longley. ModIr

Ghost with PCP eyes, A. On Display. Thomas Sayers Ellis. InTrad

Ghost-Dance Songs. *Unknown. tr. by* James Mooney

(Father Says So, The.) NAAPv.1

"Father says so—*E'yayo!*, The." NAAL-5

Give Me Back My Bow. NAAPv.1

"Give me my knife." NAAL-5

"Whole world is coming, The." NAAL-5; TCAPo

Whole World Is Coming, The. NAAPv.1

"I'yehe! my children—Uhi'yeye'heye!" NAAPv.2

Songs of the Arapaho. APN-2

Father, have pity on me. NAAL-5; NAAPv.2

"*He!* When I met him approaching." NAAL-5

Songs of the Kiowa. APN-2

Songs of the Paiute. APN-2

Songs of the Sioux. APN-2

"Father says so—*E'yayo!*, The." NAAL-5

Give Me Back My Bow. NAAPv.1

"Give me my knife." NAAL-5

"Whole world is coming, The." NAAL-5; TCAPo

Whole World Is Coming, The. NAAPv.1

Ghostly milkweed and the last laugh, The. (LL) Later Still. Philip Levine. ColAP; WaAnP

Ghostly Tree. Léonie Adams. APT-2; MoAmPo

Ghosts. Robert Bridges. OxBEV

Ghosts. William Carpenter. ReTh

Ghosts, The. Thomas Love Peacock. OBCoV

Ghosts, The. Edith Jay Scovell. HarvBoo

Ghosts are attacking me, crowding up from. Poet Haunted, The. Wendy Rose. ReEnLa

Ghosts Clap Hands. Wang the Zealot. CCL1, *tr. by* C. H. Kwock *and* Vincent McHugh and Vincent McHugh

Ghosts in the Stacks. Richard H. W. Dillard. PoDa

Ghosts not having. Underneath (2). Jorie Graham. BodElec

Ghosts of dryness are, The. (LL) Two Views of Two Ghost Towns. Charles Tomlinson. NAMCP V.2; NoAM

Ghosts of hedgers and ditchers. Ash Keys. Michael Longley. PBCIP

Ghosts of Luxury, The. Bruce Cohen. VisFro

Ghosts of our fathers flocking down at dusk. Egret Tree, The. Dave Jeddie Smith. PfSP

Ghosts of summer learn, The. Pastoral. George Garrett. InGu

Ghosts / of sweetwater. Verbal gun shots. Reggie Timpson. BtF

Ghosts of the Buffaloes, The. Vachel Lindsay. MoAmPo

Ghosts, Places, Stories, Questions. Vincent Buckley. NOBAu

Ghost-Who-Walks, The. Colleen J. McElroy. GT

Ghoul Care. Ralph Hodgson. MoBrPo

Ghurba. Rawia Morra. *tr. by* Magdi Abdelhadi

"Powerless." PoArWo, *tr. by* Magdi Abdelhadi

Gia. Tracey Herd. MFPA

Giant distant whales go by. (LL) Childish. Gerardo Deniz. PoChi; RMCMP, *tr. by* Mónica de la Torre

Giant Night. Anne Waldman. AHA

Giant Otters. Jackson Mac Low. FTOS

Giant Philosophical Otters. Jackson Mac Low. FTOS

Giant Red Woman. Clarence Major. GT

Giant Rocket. Wes Magee. NOxBChV

Giant Snail. Elizabeth Bishop. MotU *Fr.* Rainy Season; Sub-Tropics.

Giant Thunder, striding home. James Reeves. NOxBChV

Giant whispering and coughing from. Broadcast. Philip Larkin. RWPCtW

Giant Yellow. Maggie O'Sullivan. Oth

Giantess, The [*see also tr. by* Karl Shapiro, "When Nature once in lustful hot undress"]. Charles Baudelaire. OBVE, *tr. by* Roy Campbell

Giantess, The. Charles Baudelaire. OBVE, *tr. by* Roy Campbell

Giantesses, female fauna. Women of Rubens, The. Wisława Szymborska. PoSu; VCWP

Giants. Jane Miller. ExTi

Giants. David Shapiro. OxBoAm

Giants are much too beautiful. Giants. David Shapiro. OxBoAm

Giaour, The. Lord Byron. NOBRP

Gia's Song. Nora Naranjo-Morse. ReEnLa

Gibraltar. Wilfrid Scawen Blunt. OBEV

Gie her a *Haggis*! (LL) To a Haggis. Robert Burns. FaBoVe; NePenScot

Gi'e me a lass with a lump of land. Lass with a Lump of Land. Allan Ramsay. OxBEV

Gif ye kip the schule. I Winna Let On. James King Annand. NOxBChV

Gift: "How silly and how dear, how very dear." Ian Hamilton Finlay. EdScPo

Gift: "Day so happy, A." Czeslaw Milosz. BeAl; PoCho; TWF; WhBo, *tr. by* the author

Gift. Rabindranath Tagore. AmFaPo, *tr. by* William Radice

Gift, A. Jack Marshall. ASA

Gift, The. Lucille Clifton. CAP-8

Gift, The. Louise Glück. CFP; TaR

Gift, The. Kevin Hart. RSR

Gift, The. Jack Myers. TiP2

Gift, The. Amado Nervo. TCLAP, *tr. by* Sue Standing

Gift, The. John Ormond. TCAWP

Gift, The. Edgar Silex. NAPBL

Gift, The. William Stafford. ItP

Gift, The. Sara Teasdale. LW

Gift, The. William Carlos Williams. ChIV-2

Gift, The: "I was wrong when I compared the mask of my own face." Rebecca Seiferle. ICANM; PoChi

Gift, The: "Older, more generous." N. Scott Momaday. NoP-4; NoP-5

Gift, The: "They hung the lambs and cut their white throats. Blood." Andrew Hudgins. UpMys

Gift, The. To Iris, in Bow Street, Covent Garden. Oliver Goldsmith. IrLP

Gift, The: "To pull the metal splinter from my palm." Li-Young Lee. BodElec; CAP-8; LoL; NAMCP V.2; OpBo; RaBo; RoV; TWF; UnSA

Gift from Him who made me, A. (LL) Self-Mastery. Henrietta Cordelia Ray. CBWP-3; SWaP

Gift from Kenya. May Miller. OxAAAP

Gift Horse. Yusef Komunyakaa. GT

Gift of Children, The. Tiruvalluvar. WoPoe *Fr.* Kural, The.

Gift of God, The. Edwin Arlington Robinson. MoAmPo

Gift of Oneself, The. Valery Larbaud. YaTCFP, *tr. by* Mary Ann Caws *and* Jean-Pierre Cauvin and Patricia Terry

Gift of the Poem. Stéphane Mallarmé. AWTN, *tr. by* Kate Flores

Gift of Tongues, The. Peter Davison. YaYoPo *Fr.* Breaking of the Day, The.

Gift of Tongues, The. Sam Hamill. GifTon

Gift Outright, The. Robert Frost. BLPJKO; ColAP; FaBoA; HarvBoo; HHAm; MoAmPo; NAAL-5; NAMCP V.1; NoAM; NoP-4; NoP-5; OxBoAm; PoPoPo; TFi; TRP; WaAnP

Gifted with vision the snowman would see. Frank Fell. NewEx

Gifts. Mary Elizabeth Coleridge. VWP

Gifts. Juliana Horatia Ewing. LW

Gifts. Murray Jackson. OxAAAP

Gifts. Lenard D. Moore. SpirFl

Gifts. "Shu Ting." VCWP

Gifts. Ronald Stuart Thomas. NPeEn

Gifts. James Thomson. OBEV *Fr.* Sunday up the River.

Gifts. Thelma Tyfield. PoBW

Gifts Misused. Letitia Elizabeth Landon. VWP

Gifts of God, The. George Herbert. *See* Pulley, The.

Gigabyte Me—How Much RAM in Your Summer of Love? Edwin Torres. HeMarv

Gigantic Nymph! the fair Kleinhovia reigns. Erasmus Darwin. STuOW *Fr.* Botanic Garden, The.

Gij hebt de huizen achterom bereikt. Ballade van de gasfitter. Gerrit Achterberg. LWR

Gilbertian Cats. William Schwenck Gilbert. TriCat

Gilded Lapse of Time, A. Gjertrud Schnackenberg.

"Then Gabriel sent down a dream that I stood." StAl

Giles Johnson, Ph.D. Frank Marshall Davis. FTuHH

Giles likes it flat. Farm-to-Market #4. Richard Sale. TiP2

Gilgamesh went abroad in the world, but he met with none who could withstand his arms till he came to Uruk. *Unknown.* CAGL *Fr.* Epic of Gilgamesh, The.

Gille Machree. Gerald Griffin. IrV

Gilligan's Island. Tim Dlugos. ReTh

Gimme a Little Kiss (Will Ya, Huh?). Jack Smith and Roy Turk. ReLy

Gimme $25.00 / and the change. Request. Langston Hughes. APT-2; PFTM-1

Gin. David St. John. AmAlph; CAP-8

Gin a body meet a body. Comin' thro' the Rye. Robert Burns. UV

Gin a body meet a body. Rigid Body Sings. James Clerk Maxwell. UV

Gin I was God, Sittin' up there abeen. Gin I Was God. Charles Murray. EdScPo

Gineral B. is a sensible man. James Russell Lowell. OBCoV *Fr.* Biglow Papers.

Ginevra. Samuel Rogers. OxAEP-2 *Fr.* Italy.

Gingerbread man gave a gingery shout, The. Gingerbread Man, The. Rowena Bastin Bennett. ChAP

Ginger-flowers. Kenneth Mackenzie. BMAP

Ginger-haired girl in a blue sailor's jacket, A. Ginger-Haired Girl, The. Novella Nikolaevna Matveyeva. TCRusP, tr. by Daniel Weissbort

Gingham dog and the calico cat, The. Duel, The. Eugene Field. APN-2; ITBLP; NOxBChV; TFi

Ginny at a table of young men belly dancing. Soup Kitchen. Betsy Sholl. ACAMVP; PBCAP

Ginsberg, Ginsberg, burning bright. For Allen Ginsberg. X. J. Kennedy. PoA 2002

Ginsburg. Thomas C. Howell IV. BRtP

Gin-weary, temple on the pane. Up in the Air. Greg Williamson. AmPoNex

Giorni. Edward Kleinschmidt. PoDa

Giotto. Rafael Alberti. WoPoe, tr. by Carolyn Tipton

Giovanni da Fiesole on the Sublime. Richard Howard. GS

Giovanni Jacopo meditates. Douglas Livingstone. TSAP

Gipsies [or The Gipsy Camp]: "Snow falls deep; the forest lies alone, The." John Clare. NoP-5

(Gypsies.) NoP-4

Gipsy Girl, The. Ralph Hodgson. MoBrPo

Gipsy of the sea. Stormpetrel. Richard Murphy. ModIr

Gipsy Queen. John Alexander Chapman. OBEV

Gipsy-Night. Richard Hughes. OBWVE

Gipsy's Malison, The. Charles Lamb. OxBSo

Giraffe. Stanley Plumly. ChAP

Girandole. Gustaf Sobin. APSN

Girdle, A. William Strode. NOSC

Girdle is a grass leaf dried and curled, The. Birdbones. David Brendon Hopes. UpMys

Girl. Kelly Norman Ellis. SpirFl

Girl. Octavio Paz. STV, tr. by John Frederick Nims

Girl, A. Michael Field. NAEL-7v2; ViWPN; VWP

Girl, A. Ezra Pound. MoAmPo; NOxBChV Fr. Ripostes of Ezra Pound.

Girl, A / leans on the railing. Ana Belén López Pulido. SPV, tr. by Jen Hofer

Girl, The / walks carefully over the tracks. Adolescent Suicide, The. Jill Bialosky. LiTh

Girl and Baby Florist Sidewalk Pram Nineteen Seventy Something. Kenneth Koch. NoP-4

Girl and Her Companion, The. Unknown. CCL1, tr. by Marsha Wagner

Girl and her companion together search for the misty water, The. Girl and Her Companion, The. Unknown. CCL1, tr. by Marsha Wagner

Girl and I face each other, The. When We Were Good. Leanne O'Sullivan. NIrP

Girl asked you: What is poetry?, A. She Asked You. Vladimir Holan. PML, tr. by Ian Milner and Jarmila Milner

Girl at Her Devotions, A. Letitia Elizabeth Landon. VWP

Girl at the harbor! Girl from that foreign land! Pier of Yokohama under the Umbrella, The. Im Hwa. CAMKP, tr. by Jiwon Shin

Girl at the Window. Pinkie Gordon Lane. FuFl; GT

Girl attacked me once with a number 2 Eagle pencil, A. Blasphemy, A. Rodney Jones. IllVoic; WeW-3

Girl by the River, The. Alton Delmore. APT-2

Girl cat / So thin. Basho. ZenPo, tr. by Takashi Ikemoto and Lucien Stryk

Girl child / they took you so far away. Brother Wolverine. Mary Tallmountain. FiBr

Girl comes out, A. Morning. Franz Wright. AmAlph

Girl, don't be so haughty. Unknown. CATKP, tr. by Kevin O'Rourke

Girl dreams of her lover at night, The. Konstantin Iakovlevich Vanshenkin. TCRusP, tr. by Daniel Weissbort

Girl fishes up the sea, The. Greek Girl at Riis Beach, A. Frank O'Hara. BodElec

Girl fits her body, The. Night Vision. Lucille Clifton. BodElec; GifTon; UnSA

Girl, fourteen years old but bigger than me, The. Swing, The. Hwang O. CATKP, tr. by Chi-gyu Kim [or Kim Chonggil]

Girl Friend Poem # 3. C. D. Wright. CAP-8

Girl from the realm of birds florid and fleet. Something Like a Sonnet for Phillis Miracle Wheatley. June Jordan. NIL-7

Girl grew up to become a woman, The. Twenty Years. Đỗ Tấn Xuân. WoPoe, tr. by Nguyen Ngoc Bich

Girl Help. Janet Lewis. APT-2; CalPo; HeIP-4

Girl, / Her soul a deep-wave pearl, A. Girl, A. Michael Field. NAEL-7v2; ViWPN; VWP

Girl in a Fur-Trimmed Dress. Honor Moore. WiU

Girl in a Library, A. Randall Jarrell. InGu; NoAM

Girl in a Nightgown. Wallace Stevens. AmFaPo

Girl in the Boy's Dressing Room, The. Jody Helfand. BeDoSh

Girl in the Kitchen. "Vaidehi." CFP, tr. by A. K. Ramanujan

Girl in the tea shop, The. Tea Shop, The. Ezra Pound. HeIP-4

Girl is freezing in the telephone, A. First Ice, The. Andrey Andreievich Voznesensky. RusPo, tr. by Robert Arthur Douglas Ford

Girl, it is slow, the forgetting of a face. On Forgetting Your Father's Face. Crystal Williams. RD

Girl Machine. Kenward Elmslie. AHA; NYP2

Girl: Mommy do you remember yesterday when Daddy was talking about someone died. 5-Year-Old Girls Encountered. Katie Degentesh. FreRad

Girl Named Spring, A. Betsy Sholl. PBCAP

Girl no whiter than the Moors are. Unknown. PriapPo Fr. Priapus Poems, The.

Girl of Fifteen. James Weldon Johnson. GT

Girl of Mount Hua, The. Han Yü. ColAnChi, tr. by Burton Watson

Girl of Six from the Ghetto Begging in Smolna Street in 1942, A. Jerzy Ficowski. HP, tr. by Keith Bosley

Girl of the Red Mouth. Martin MacDermott. IrV

Girl of Yueh, The. Li Po. TAL

Girl on a Tractor. Joyce Sutphen. GoPo; IPoFL

Girl on the Land, The. Alice Thompson Meynell. VWP

Girl on the Quay at Rio, The. T. H. Parry-Williams. BBMWP, tr. by Richard Poole

Girl on the stairs listens to her father, A. Tours. Charles David Wright. AmAlph

Girl plays the piano, The. Capriccios. Jaime Sabines. TCLAP, tr. by Claudine-Marie D'Angelo

Girl Powdering Her Neck. Cathy Song. NoP-4

Girl Profligacy, A. Erin Mouré. NLPA Fr. Wittgenstein Letters to Mel Gibson's Braveheart, The.

Girl Refugee, The. Matilde Salganicoff. MirDau, tr. by Celeste Kostopulos-Cooperman

Girl sits on the hard ground, The. Photograph of the Girl. Sharon Olds. NAMCP V.2

Girl/Spit. Lisa Coffman. AmPoNex

Girl, stop pretending tragedy. Wicked Women. Vietnamese Oral Tradition. CaDao, tr. by John Balaban

Girl strapped in the bare mechanical crib, The. Song and Story. Ellen Bryant Voigt. InGu

Girl them a shock out, The. Some Tentative Definitions 4. Kwame Dawes. WaCA

Girl thinks if I can only manage, The. Marie Luise Kaschnitz. ItWoWo Fr. Return to Frankfurt.

Girl threw an apple to a cloud, A. Unknown. WoPoe, tr. by Charles Simic

Girl was swimming nude, The. On the Beach One Day. Fraser Sutherland. Coast

Girl, watch your cunt; boy, keep your ass from grief. Unknown. PriapPo Fr. Priapus Poems, The.

Girl, when his tongue is all sugar, suddenly. Sugar. Crystal Williams. RD

Girl Who Couldn't Be Loved, The. Lisa Jarnot. LegDan

Girl Who Loved the Sky, The. Anita Endrezze. HATNAP

Girl who sells melons beside the stream, The. Melon Girl. Mei Yao Ch'en. NDACCP, tr. by Kenneth Rexroth

Girl with all that raising, A. Ballad of the Girl Whose Name Is Mud. Langston Hughes. SAmP

Girl with Mind Wandering. Paul Valéry. STV, tr. by John Frederick Nims

Girl with the Bad Rep, The. Kay Murphy. SwNoth

Girl with the Binh Tien Hairdo, The. Vietnamese Oral Tradition. CaDao, tr. by John Balaban

Girl with the Dark Hair. Unknown. WoPoe, tr. by W. S. Merwin

Girl working the xerox in the stationery store, The. For Emily (Dickinson). Maureen Owen. PmAP; ReTh

Girl, you cut me up inside. To a Beauty, White, Pure, and Constant. Abu Bakr ibn Abd al-Malik Ibn Quzman. WoPoe, tr. by Leticia Garza-Falcón and Christopher Middleton

Girlfriend. Lori Tsang. BtF

Girlfriends. Carol Ann Duffy. HarvBoo

Girlfriends, The. Elizabeth Woody. ReEnLa

Girls. Lauris Edmond. ArBi; BeAl

Girls, The. Oni Buchanan. LegDan

Girls are drifting in their ponytails, The. He or She That's Got the Limb, That Holds Me Out on It. Susan Wheeler. ExTi

Girls / Brides / Tortoise. Erinna. SaLy, tr. by Diane Rayor

Girls Can We Educate We Dads? James Berry. NOxBChV

Girls, don't ever marry students! Good Scholars Make Bad Husbands. Unknown. WoPoe, tr. by Nguyen Ngoc Bich

Girls go by in their sailor suits, The. Sailor. Gerry Gomez Pearlberg. WiU

Girl's Hair, A. Dafydd ab Edmwnd. OBWVE, tr. by Gwyn Williams

Girl's Head, A. Katherine Gallagher. NOBAu

Girls of Llanbadarn, The. Dafydd ap Gwilym. OBWVE, tr. by Rolfe Humphries

Girls of the Light, The. José María Eguren. TCLAP, tr. by Iver Lofving

Girls of the Rodeo. Margie B. Boswell. TiP2

Girls of Yueh, The. Li Po. TAL

Girls on the Bridge. Derek Mahon. NoP-5

Girls outshout the machines, The. Charles Reznikoff. NAAPv.2

Girls planting paddy. Konishi Raizan. OxBEV, *tr. by* Anthony Thwaite

Girls scream. School's Out. W. H. Davies. OBMV

Girls Sitting Together Like Dolls. Christiania Whitehead. NeBl

Girl's Song. *Unknown.* WoPoe, *tr. by* Edwin Gladding Burrows

Girl's Song, A. *Unknown.* APN-2 *Fr.* Songs of the Kwakiutl Indians.

Girls still ride bicycles into Jhong-Jhou Train Station. At Jhong-Jhou Train Station. G. Timothy Gordon. ArBi

Girls today in society, The. Brush Up Your Shakespeare. Cole Porter. OBCoV; ReLy

Girls whose feet moved so fast, where did they go?, The. Old Women, The. Rolf Jacobsen. WED, *tr. by* Robert Bly

Girls Working in Banks. Karl Shapiro. WeW-3

Git out o' bed, you rascals. Call Boy. Sterling Allen Brown. GM

Gita Govinda, The. Jayadeva. *tr. by* Sir Edwin Arnold and Barbara Stoler Miller

   "Sandal and garment of yellow and lotus garlands upon his body of blue." TAL

   Song of Krishna: The Fourth Song, Sung with Raga "Ramakari." WoPoe, *tr. by* Barbara Stoler Miller

Gita says three *gunas*, The. To Phil Dow, in Oregon. Robert Hass. BodElec

Gitanjali. Rabindranath Tagore.

   Break Open the Door. ItP; PtR, *tr. by* the author

   Day after Day. OBMV

   I Have Got My Leave. OBMV

   If It Is Not My Portion. OBMV

   Let My Country Awake. ItP; PtR; TWF, *tr. by* the author

   On the Slope of the Desolate River. OBMV

   Thou Art the Sky. OBMV

Giuseppe, da barber, ees greata for "mash." Mia Carlotta. Thomas Augustin Daly. NBLV

Give. Mark Irwin. PoCoUp

Give a man a horse he can ride. James Thomson. OBEV *Fr.* Sunday up the River.

Give: A Sequence Reimagining Daphne & Apollo. Alice Fulton. AllShUp *Fr.* Give: A Sequence Reimagining Daphne & Apollo.

Give All to Love. Ralph Waldo Emerson. APN-1; ColAP; OBEV; OxBoAm; TCAPo

Give all you have been, or could be. (LL) Barter. Sara Teasdale. ITBLP; SoSe-8

Give Away the Lie. Pedro Pérez Conde. RMCMP, *tr. by* Michael Wiegers

Give birth to me again. Give birth to me again that I may know. Give Birth to Me Again That I May Know. Mahmoud Darwish. PML, *tr. by* Abdullah Al-Udhari

Give changing moods to even halcyon days. (LL) Ocean Musing, An. Henrietta Cordelia Ray. CBWP-3; SWaP

Give Ear, O Heavens, to That Which I Declare [*with music*]. Henry Ainsworth. ChIV-1

Give ear to my words, O Lord. Psalm 5. Ernesto Cardenal. PLBUT; TCLAP, *tr. by* Robert Marquez

Give, give me back that Trifle you despise. Request of Alexis, The. Sarah Dixon. LW

Give him coffee, said the general. Ainadamar. Nigel Jenkins. TCAWP

Give him the darkest inch your shelf allows. George Crabbe. Edwin Arlington Robinson. APN-2; MoAmPo; NoP-4; NoP-5

Give honour unto Luke Evangelist. Dante Gabriel Rossetti. SacPr *Fr.* House of Life, The.

Give Isaac the nymph who no beauty can boast. Richard Brinsley Sheridan. IrLP *Fr.* Duenna, The.

Give it all back, even what you were just handed. Lover Man. James Cushing. SeSe

Give it away? (LL) Living Memory. Adrienne Rich. OxBoAm; TRP

Give it up! / Give it up! There Must Be Somethin' Better Than Love. Dorothy Fields. ReLy

Give known or pin ware. Guillaume Apollinaire. Gertrude Stein. NAAPv.2; NAMCP V.1; OxBoAm

Give Me . . . I'll Give You. Maisun bint Bahdal. SonAtl, *tr. by* 'Ali Mahmud Taha

Give me a cottage on some Cambrian wild. Sonnet. Henry Kirke White. CenSon

Give me a doctor, partridge-plump. Give Me a Doctor. W. H. Auden. OBCoV *Fr.* Shorts [1948–1957].

Give me a golden pen, and let me lean. On Leaving Some Friends at an Early Hour. John Keats. CenSon

Give me a happy heart and suasive tongue. Happy Heart, A. Josephine D. Henderson Heard. CBWP-4

Give me a harsh land to wring music from. This Land. Ian Mudie. NOBAu

Give Me a Heart to Sing To. Ned Washington. ReLy

Give me a homeland. Issa. SoOfWa, *tr. by* Sam Hamill

Give me a hurly house: I'll give you this echo-high Hall. Give Me . . . I'll Give You. Maisun bint Bahdal. SonAtl, *tr. by* 'Ali Mahmud Taha

Give me a landscape made of obstacles. Rough Country. Dana Gioia. PfSP

Give me a thrill, says the reader. Fiction and the Reading Public. Philip Larkin. OBSV

Give me all the kisses of your mouth. Bible, *O.T.* ErotSp *Fr.* Song of Solomon, The [*or* The Song of Songs].

Give Me Back My Bow. *Sioux Oral Tradition.* NAAPv.1 *Fr.* Ghost-Dance Songs.

Give Me Confidence. Bairagi. HotL, *tr. by* V. Narayana Rao

Give me, fair sweet, the map, well-colourèd. John Davies of Hereford. OxBSo *Fr.* Wit's Pilgrimage.

Give me food. Mahārāja Rāmkrsna Rāy. SinGod, *tr. by* Rachel Fell McDermott

Give me, give me Buriano. Francesco Redi. OBVE *Fr.* Bacchus in Tuscany.

Give me hackneyed words because. Residence at C———. Lisa Robertson. OpeFie

Give Me Jesus. *Unknown.* SacPr

Give me leave to rail at you. Song. John Wilmot, 2d Earl of Rochester. NOSC

Give me Maeonian Homer's resonant tongue. Catius As Conius Silius Italicus. RomPo *Fr.* Punica, The.

Give me more love or more disdain. Mediocrity in Love Rejected. Thomas Carew. NoP-4; NoP-5; WaAnP

Give me my hand on his neck and his back to my breast. Veneer. Vona Groarke. NIrP

Give me my knife. *Sioux Oral Tradition.* NAAL-5 *Fr.* Ghost-Dance Songs.

Give me my robe, put on my crown; I have. William Shakespeare. OxAEP-1 *Fr.* Antony and Cleopatra.

Give me my Scallop[-]shell of quiet. Passionate Man[']s Pilgrimage, The. Sir Walter Ralegh. ChIV-2; NoP-5; NoSic; NPeEn; OxBEV; TFi

   (Give me my scallop-shell of quiet.) NoP-4

   (Give mee my Escallope shell of Quiett.) OxAEP-1

Give me new Phœnix [*or* Phoenix] wings to fly at my desire. (LL) On Sitting Down to Read *King Lear* Once Again. John Keats. CABP; GSo; NAEL-6v2; NAEL-7v2; NoP-4; NoP-5; NPBRoP; PoPoPo

Give me no gift! Less than thyself were nought. Broken Friendship. Mary Elizabeth Coleridge. VWP

Give me, O friend, the secret of thy heart. Rosa Rosarum. Agnes Mary Frances Robinson. PoBW

Give me, O indulgent fate! Anne Finch, Countess of Winchilsea. NOSC *Fr.* Petition for an Absolute Retreat, The.

Give me something to eat. Poor Crow! Mary Mapes Dodge. SWaP

Give me that old-time religion. Old-Time Religion. APN-2

Give me / the creeps. Ishikawa Takuboku. CAoMJL1, *tr. by* Carl Sesar

Give me the gloomy walk in summer-time. Give Me the Gloomy Walk. John Clare. NPBRoP

Give me the priest these graces shall possess. Priest of Christ, The. Thomas Ken. SacPr

Give me the Red on the Black of the Bullet (for Claude Reece Jr.). Jayne Cortez. LTA

Give me the right of way. Irish. Paul Celan. OBVE, *tr. by* Michael Hamburger

Give Me the Simple Life. Harry Ruby. ReLy

Give me the splendid silent sun with all his beams full-dazzling. Give Me the Splendid Silent Sun. Walt Whitman. CBCWP; MoAmPo

Give me the strongest cheese, the one that stinks best. For Desire. Kim Addonizio. BeAL; SUP

Give me the woman here. (LL) Sonnet: "O[h]! for some honest lover's ghost." Sir John Suckling. BASC; CavPo; OxBEV

Give me those flowers there, Dorcas. Reverend sirs. William Shakespeare. OxAEP-1 *Fr.* Winter's Tale, The.

Give Me Thy Heart. Adelaide Anne Procter. SacPr

Give me truths / For I am weary of the surfaces. Blight. Ralph Waldo Emerson. APN-1; BrAP; NCAP; OxBoAm; TCAPo

Give me wings, I'll reach a high heaven. Upon Reading Chuang Tzu. Chunggwan, Great Master. CATKP, *tr. by* Peter H. Lee

Give me your hand, my love, and let us go into the fields. *Unknown.* SLW, *tr. by* Marjolijn De Jager, Sayd Bahodin Majrouh and André Velter

Give me your hand. Place it on my bare breast. She Teaches Him to Reach Out. Martha Elizabeth. PasH

Give mee my Escallope shell of Quiett. Sir Walter Ralegh. *See* Give me my Scallop[-]shell of quiet.

Give *Mee* the *Free* and *Noble Stile.* Claspe, The. Margaret Lucas Cavendish, Duchess of Newcastle. PBRV

Give money me, take friendship whoso list. Of Money. Barnabe Googe. NBLV; NoSic; SoSe-8

Give my heart. (LL) Christmas Carol, A: "In the bleak mid-winter." Christina Georgina Rossetti. OxBEV; RSR; SacPr; VWP

Give My Regards to Broadway. George M. Cohan. NAAPv.2; ReLy; TCAPo

Give pardon, blessèd soul, to my bold cries. On the Death of Sir Philip Sidney. Henry Constable. OBEV

Give Peace a Chance. Judith W. Steinbergh. PfS

Give place, you ladies, and be gone! Praise of His Lady, A. John Heywood. OBEV

Give store of days, good Jove, give length of years. Juvenal. OBSV Fr. Satires.

Give the hungry. Fennel. Opal Palmer Adisa. ASA

Give the mourning doves any sun. Ruined Motel, The. Reginald Gibbons. BodElec

Give them my regards when you go to the school reunion. More of a Corpse Than a Woman. Muriel Rukeyser. NALW

Give them thy fingers, me thy lips to kiss. (LL) William Shakespeare. NAEL-6v1; NAEL-7v1; OxAEP-1 Fr. Sonnets.

Give thou my sacred relics burial [or Reliques Buriall]. (LL) His Return to London. Robert Herrick. BASC; NAEL-6v1; NAEL-7v1

Give three flowers to a maiden: one on her hair, one on her breast, one on her shame. Flower. Huan Fu. PML, tr. by Zhang Cuo

Give to barrows, trays, and pans. Art. Ralph Waldo Emerson. APN-1

Give to me the life I love. Vagabond, The. Robert Louis Stevenson. OxAEP-2

Give up. (LL) My Rival's House. Liz Lochhead. CFP; EdScPo; EmeKit

Give up erotic games, Kabir. Kabir. ErotSp, tr. by Sam Hamill

Give up on friends. No Pardon. Friedrich Hölderlin. WoPoe, tr. by Vyt Bakaitis

Give Up the World. Unknown. SSUS

Give up the world; give up self; finally, give up God. Instructions. Sheri Hostetler. ACAMVP

Give us grace. (LL) Welcome Eumenides. Eleanor Ross Taylor. InGu; NALW

Give us that grand word "woman" once again. Woman. Ella Wheeler Wilcox. SWaP

Give us this day. Give us this day and night. Lord's Prayer, The. Elizabeth Jennings. MoWP

Give us wholeness, for we are broken. Breaking. Phyllis Webb. BrAP

Give us your very best table, I swaggered, taking. Jet Set Melodrama. Michael Brownstein. AHA; FTOS

Give way, an ye be ravished by the sun. To Marygolds. Robert Herrick. CavPo; NAEL-6v1; NAEL-7v1

Give way, give way ye Gates, and win. Wassaile, The. Robert Herrick. PBRV

Give your longing to wound. Basho. WED, tr. by Robert Bly

Given all my worries over each day's trivia. Joachim Du Bellay. WoPoe Fr. Regrets.

Given away in poems, only their solitude kept. (LL) Correspondence School Instructor Says Goodbye to His Poetry Students, The. Galway Kinnell. NoAM; NoP-4; NoP-5; PoA 2002

Given Day, A. W. S. Merwin. NAMCP V.2

Given Flesh Returns Nothing but Bread, The. Aileen Kelly. ChIV-2

Given in Person Only. Mark Wunderlich. WiU

Given, not lent. Unto Us a Son Is Given. Alice Thompson Meynell. SacPr

Given the gift of ground the pear tree shaded every summer. Roy Kiyooka. NLPA Fr. Pear Tree Pomes.

Given the gift of its white blossoms the small yellow pears. Roy Kiyooka. NLPA Fr. Pear Tree Pomes.

Given the limitation of trees, what if each. New Language, The. Elizabeth Robinson. OnScMo

Given to Master Ch'ing-lun of Hsia Mountain. Chien Chang. CSKM, tr. by Paul Hansen

Given to the people, and my love was theirs. (LL) William Wordsworth. NAEL-6v2; NAEL-7v2 Fr. Prelude, The; Growth of a Poet's Mind [1850 version].

Given to Wen Chao. Hui Ch'ung. CSKM, tr. by Paul Hansen

Given What Manages. Cleopatra Mathis. ExTi Fr. Lessons.

Giving. Nora B. Cunningham. LW

Giving Back the Flower. Sarah Morgan Bryan Piatt. APN-2; NAAPv.1

Giving Birth, The. Jean-Michel Maulpoix. YaTCFP, tr. by Mark Polizzoti

Giving birth is like jazz, something from silence. Elizabeth Alexander. FaoP Fr. Neonatology.

Giving brilliant gourd-shell rattles / to everyone who comes. (LL) Grandfather at the Indian Health Clinic. Elizabeth Cook-Lynn. HATNAP; UnSA

Giving Buddha to all beings is giving to oneself. Taigen Dan Leighton. WhBo

Giving Potatoes. Adrian Mitchell. NBLV

Giving Thanks. Anne K. Smith. PasH

Giving the House Away. Julie King. SweBea

Giving up women is worse than animal laxatives. John Tranter. NoAM Fr. Crying in Early Infancy.

Giving Way. Johanna Kruit. TuT, tr. by Medbh McGuckian

Giving, while the rain lasts, soft noises. Eaves. Ellis Jones. OBWVE, tr. by Anthony Conran

Glace De, Une. Jacques Roubaud. YaTCFP

Glacier's Daughters, The. David Brendon Hopes. UpMys

Glaciers in the arms of trees. George Stanley. NLPA Fr. Mountains and Air.

Glad. W. H. Auden. CAGL Fr. Three Posthumous Poems.

Glad All Over. Patricia Spears Jones. BRtP

Glad at the Cold (1955). Alan Dugan. NoAM

Glad, but not flush'd with gladness. Algernon Charles Swinburne. OBEV Fr. Before the Mirror.

Glad Christmas comes, and every hearth. December. John Clare. ChrPo

Glad Eye, The. Paul Muldoon. NoAM

Glad of These Times. Helen Dunmore. BeAl

Glad Preamble, The. William Wordsworth. NPBRoP; WaAnP Fr. Prelude, The; Growth of a Poet's Mind [1805 version; Selections from Anthologies].

Glad Rag Doll. Jack Yellen. ReLy

Glad to Be Unhappy. Lorenz Hart. ReLy

Gladiator in his net, passing judgement on the crowd, A. (LL) Sonogram, The. Paul Muldoon. BeAl; NAMCP V.2; P180

Gladioli by the Sea. Oscar Hahn. TCLAP, tr. by Isabel Bize

Glads. Carl Phillips. CAP-8

Gladstone was still respected. Ezra Pound. MoAmPo; NAAPv.2 Fr. Hugh Selwyn Mauberley (Life and Contacts).

Glamis thou art, andd Cawdor; and shalt be. William Shakespeare. OxAEP-1 Fr. Macbeth.

Glamour of the end attic, the smell of old, The. Perdita. Louis MacNeice. PoA 2002

Glance. Dhabya Khamees. PoArWo, tr. by Clarissa C. Burt

Glance. Belkis Cuza Malé. TANSG, tr. by Pamela Carmell

Glance in White Space. Clark Coolidge. FTOS

Glances changed their source. Alice Rahon. SurWo, tr. by Nancy Deffebach and Vanina Deler

Glancing at the train from hills touched with autumn. Anguish. Andrey Andreievich Voznesensky. RusPo, tr. by Robert Arthur Douglas Ford

Glancing at the wicker. Elite Syncopations. Richard Garcia. TouFir

Glanmore Revisited. Seamus Heaney.
  Bedside Reading. IrLP; NoP-5
  Skylight, The. NoP-5; OxBSo

Glanmore Sonnets. Seamus Heaney.
  "Dogger, Rockall, Malin, Irish Sea." RWPCtW

Glans, high point of the soul. Balanide 2. Paul Verlaine. CAGL, tr. by Alan Stone

Glare from the brass horn makes sun-brown satin fit smoothly the girl by the window, The. Fancy Another Day Gone. Lorine Niedecker. FTOS

Glasgow. Alexander Smith.
  "Sing, Poet, 'tis a merry world." NePenScot

Glasgow Green. Edwin Morgan. EdScPo

Glasgow 1956. Gerald Mangan. EdScPo

Glasgow Schoolboys, Running Backwards. Douglas Dunn. BeAl; RSaN

Glasgow Sonnets. Edwin Morgan. RSaN

Glasnevin Cemetery. Michael O'Loughlin. PBCIP

Glass. Gillian Clarke.
  Migraine. Prnts

Glass. Diana Hartog. NLPA Fr. Oasis.

Glass. Anne Rouse. NeBl

Glass. Anne Finch, Countess of Winchilsea. OxBEV

Glass, The. Esther Ettinger. DTA, tr. by Mariana Barr

Glass, The. Carolyn Kizer. ErotSp

Glass, The. Edwin Morgan. HarvBoo

Glass, The. Sharon Olds. NIL-7; NIP-4

Glass Box Puzzle No. 1. Andrew J. Baldwin. BtF

Glass Bracelets, The. Kimiko Hahn. PrTe

Glass Bubbles, The. Samuel Greenberg. APT-1; OxBoAm

Glass Canyons. David Romtvedt. UrbNat

Glass door. Masaoka Shiki. CAoMJL1, tr. by Burton Watson

Glass Enclosure, The. Michael Brownstein. FTOS

Glass Essay, The. Anne Carson. NLPA
  Hero. NLPA
  Hot. NLPA
  I. NLPA
  Kitchen. NLPA
  Liberty. NLPA
  She. NLPA

Thou. NLPA

Three. NLPA

Whacher. NLPA

"Well there are many ways of being held prisoner." NAMCP V.2

Glass falls lower, The. Sad Green. Sylvia Townsend Warner. MoBrPo

Glass has been falling all the afternoon, The. Storm Warnings. Adrienne Rich. NAAL-5; NIL-7; NIP-4; PtR; YaYoPo

Glass Heart. Dana Levin. LegDan

Glass House. Diane Ward. PmAP

Glass in her hand is the only thing moving—, The. Photograph of a Bawd Drinking Raleigh Rye. Natasha Trethewey. NeAmPo

Glass Man, The. Scott Cairns. UpMys

Glass of Ancient Wine, A. Gzar Hantoosh. IrPoTo, *tr. by* Saadi A. Simawe and Ellen Doré Watson

Glass of Beer, A. James Stephens. NBLV; OBCoV; OBMV; OxBEV (Righteous Anger.) MoBrPo

Glass of Pure Water, The. Hugh MacDiarmid. PFTM-2

Glass of Water, A: "Here is a glass of water from my well." May Sarton. IJHIL; StAl

Glass of Water, The. Wallace Stevens. MoAmPo

Glass of Wine, A. Andrew Motion. NeBrP

Glass of wine, as it should be, the glass of wine, The. (LL) Before You Came. Faiz Ahmad Faiz. PML; WoPoe, *tr. by* Naomi Lazard

Glass on the picture from the Bible, The. Darkening Hotel Room. Alfred Corn. VCAP

Glass-Bottom Boat. Elizabeth Spires. CAP-8

Glassed with cold sleep and dazzled by the moon. Train Journey. Judith Wright. NoP-4; NoP-5

Glasshouse, The. Vona Groarke. NIrP

Glassine envelopes trampoline the pigmeat into a final awakening. Glass Enclosure, The. Michael Brownstein. FTOS

Glassworks. Margit Mikes. IQMS, *tr. by* Susanne K. Walther

Glassy Sea. W. S. Merwin. BodElec

Glaucopis. Richard Hughes. OBMV

Glaucus, pilot of the Nessus strait, born. On the Death of the Ferryman, Glaucus. Antiphilus. WoPoe, *tr. by* W. S. Merwin

Glaukos, look: already the deep sea is troubled. Archilochus. SaLy, *tr. by* Diane Rayor

Glazed glitter. Gertrude Stein. NAAPv.2 *Fr.* Tender Buttons.

Glazier, The. Stéphane Mallarmé. OBVE, *tr. by* Keith Bosley

Glazing the pale hair, the duplicate gray [*or* grey] standard faces. (LL) Dolor. Theodore Roethke. BrAP; GPTC; HeIP-4; NAMCP V.1; NoAM; OPOU; OxBoAm; PoA 2002; StAl; TRP

Glazunoviana. John Ashbery. VCAP

Gleamed a resplendent star. At Christmas-Tide. Henrietta Cordelia Ray. CBWP-3

Gleams a green lamp. Louis Zukofsky. APT-2 *Fr.* 29 Poems.

Gleaners of grain they did not sow. Rooks: December. Huw Menai. AngWePo

Gleaning the rice field. Buson. EH, *tr. by* Robert Hass

Glee-fulfiller, fruit-producer, cook who glad the year can feed. Concerning the Fruit-bringing Autumn Season. Catharina Regina von Greiffenberg. GePo, *tr. by* George C. Schoolfield

Glee—The great storm is over. Emily Dickinson. APN-2

Glenaradale. Walter Chalmers Smith. OBEV

Glenasmole. Fergus Allen. NIrP

Glenasmole translates as 'valley of the thrushes'. Glenasmole. Fergus Allen. NIrP

6. Glenn Gould's Hands: A Sonnet. Kate Braid. IFF *Fr.* Glenn Gould Poems.

Glenn on Monk's Mountain. Nathaniel Mackey. OxAAAP

Gliding, gleaming, speeding along. Swiftly We Fly. James Clarence Harvey. ArBi

Gliding through the still air, he made no sound;. Return of Persephone, The. Alec Derwent Hope. BMAP; BrAP

Gliding Toward the Lamps. Matthew Rohrer. NeAmPo

Glimmer farther away than the head, The. Adieu. Pierre Reverdy. CuPo

Glimmer of light high over Mount Diablo (silhouette flat across). Ron Silliman. ASA

Glimmerings of castrated history emerge from. Metaphysically Niggerish. Wanda Coleman. RD

Glimpse, A. Frances Darwin Cornford. OBMV

Glimpse, A. Robert Duncan. FTOS

Glimpse, A. Walt Whitman. APN-1; RaBo

Glimpse, A. John Wieners. FTOS

Glimpse from the Past. Ilse Aichinger. AF, *tr. by* Allen H. Chappel

Glimpse of God. Tatamkulu Afrika. TSAP

Glimpse of Love, A. Mary Tighe. NOBRP *Fr.* Psyche.

Glimpse of Starlings, A. Brendan Kennelly. PoCu; StAl

Glimpse of Terrain. Thomas Bolt. YaYoPo

Glimpse of your body, A. Mirabai. ErotSp, *tr. by* Andrew Schelling

Glimpse through an interstice caught, A. Glimpse, A. Walt Whitman. APN-1; RaBo

Glimpsed from the train, which takes shadow for truth. Glimpsed. Vladimir Holan. PoSu, *tr. by* Ian Milner and Jarmila Milner

Glimpsed world, halfway through the film, A. Malice of Innocence, The. Denise Levertov. BodElec

Glimpses. Christopher Gilbert. GT

Glimpses. Philippe Jaccottet. VCWP, *tr. by* Derek Mahon

Glimpses. William Stafford. BodElec

Glimpses of Infancy. Priscilla Jane Thompson. CBWP-2

Glinting like water. Mary Kinzie. FFC

Glisten in your pristine splendor. A*boriginal* Elegy: The Once and Future Queen. Askia Muhammad Touré. FuFl

Glistening like slices of winter melon. (LL) Lost Sister ("In China.") Cathy Song. NAMCP V.2; NoAM

Glistening, The. Deema K. Shehabi. PoArWo

Glitter of a northern kingdom. Mao Tse-tung. WoPoe, *tr. by* David Lattimore

Glitter of mica at the windy corners. Home Town Elegy. George Sutherland Fraser. EdScPo

Glitter of Nausicaä's. Homer in Basic. Kenneth Rexroth. NAMCP V.1

Glittering, adroit, the Sicilian wonder. Death and Empedocles 444 B.C. Horace Gregory. PoA 2002

Glittering and still shall come the awful night. (LL) Winter Evening. Archibald Lampman. BrAP; NIL-7

Glittering bridge. Bridge, The. Charlotte Zolotow. CA

Glittering cities. Tomas Tranströmer. WoBe *Fr.* Haiku.

Glittering colors of the day are fled, The. To the Moon. Helen Maria Williams. NoP-4

(Glitt'ring colors of the day are fled, The.) CenSon

Glittering leaves of the rhododendrons, The. Green Symphony. John Gould Fletcher. MoAmPo

Glittering of air, it glitters. Mystery. Octavio Paz. TCLAP, *tr. by* Muriel Rukeyser

Glitt'ring colors of the day are fled, The. Helen Maria Williams. *See* Glittering colors of the day are fled, The.

Global Inequalities. Jayne Cortez. PrTe

Global Rewards Redemption Centre, The. Gig Ryan. VaPo

Globe in [North] Carolina, The. Derek Mahon. PBCIP

Gloire de Dijon. D. H. Lawrence. NAMCP V.1; NoAM; WaAnP

Gloom of night had overspread the land, The. Nativity, The. Mary Weston Fordham. CBWP-2

Glooms of the live-oaks, beautiful-braided and woven. Sidney Lanier. NAAPv.1; NoP-5 *Fr.* Hymns of the Marshes.

Gloomy am I, oppressed and sad. Poet's Arbour in the Birchwood, The. Edward Williams. OBWVE, *tr. by* Kenneth Hurlstone Jackson

Gloomy grammarians in golden gowns. On [*or* Of] the Manner of Addressing Clouds. Wallace Stevens. PoA 2002

Gloomy hulls, in armour [*or* armor] grim, The. *Temeraire*, The. Herman Melville. APN-2; FaBoWar

(Gloomy hulls, in armor grim, The.) GS; NCAP

Gloomy minister of Hades who sail this stream. Leonidas of Tarentum. HePo, *tr. by* Barbara Hughes Fowler

Gloria. Bill Berkson. Eno

Gloria. Lincoln Kirstein. APT-2

Gloria mundi est. Unknown. NPeEn

Glories of the world struck me, made me aria, once, The. John Berryman. CAP-8; HarvBoo *Fr.* Dream Songs.

Glorified in full release upward— / songs cease. (LL) Dawn. William Carlos Williams. APT-1; MoAmPo

Glorious. Marla Jernigan. AnSo

Glorious days he had, and a chivalrous spirit. Old White Russian, An. Ch'en Meng-chia. WoPoe, *tr. by* Harold Acton and Ch'en Shih-hsiang

Glorious greks dois prayse their Homers quill, The. E. D. in Prayse of Mr. W. Fouler Her Friend. "E. D." EMWP

Glorious illuminations, made on high. Sir Richard Blackmore. STuOW *Fr.* Prince Arthur.

Glorious image of the Maker's beauty, The. Edmund Spenser. SacPr *Fr.* Amoretti.

Glorious Judge will priviledge, The. Michael Wigglesworth. TCAPo *Fr.* Day of Doom, The [First Section].

Glorious morning when spring blossoms into flower, A. Spring Blossoms into Flower. Unknown. CAoMJL1, *tr. by* Leith Morton

Glorious night! / The giant moon, the tiny evening star. Sándor Petőfi. IQMS *Fr.* Clouds, The.

Glorious Ruins. Tomislav Longinovic. PML

Glorious Strike of the Builders, The. *Unknown.* FaBoVe

Glorious Vision you adore, The. (LL) Love's Mirror. Constance Naden. ViWPN; VWP

Glory: "Sky with reddened eyelids foretells windy weather, The." Nikolai Kanchev. CSCBP, *tr. by* Georgi Belev and Lisa Sapinkopf

Glory, A. Hymn to the Sun. Akhenaton. WoPoe, *tr. by* John Perlman

Glory, The. Edward Thomas. HarvBoo

Glory Be to Chingwe's Hole. Jack A. Mapanje. HBAPE

Glory be to God for dappled things. Pied Beauty. Gerard Manley Hopkins. AmFaPo; BrAP; CABP; ChAP; ClHu; CtM; HeIP-4; InvLi; ITBLP; MoBrPo; NAEL-6v2; NAEL-7v2; NAMCP V.1; NIL-7; NoAM; NoP-4; NoP-5; NPeEn; OBEV; OBMV; OxAEP-2; OxBEV; PoCho; PoPoPo; RaBo; SacPr; SoSe-8; TFi; UV; WaAnP; WeW-3

Glory be to God for Hopkins' verse. Pied Beauty. Stanley J. Sharpless. UV

Glory Glory / Psalm 19. Bible, *O.T.* UpMys

Glory here Diggers all. (LL) Digger's Song, The. Gerrard Winstanley. BASC; NOSC

Glory Monster. Sandra Alcosser. PfSP

Glory of Him who moves all things rays forth, The. Dante Alighieri. NAWM-5v1 *Fr.* Divina Commedia.

Glory of Love, The. Billy Hill. ReLy

Glory of the beauty of the morning, The. Glory, The. Edward Thomas. HarvBoo

Glory of the Garden, The. Rudyard Kipling. OBGa

Glory of Women. Siegfried Sassoon. FaBoWar; NAEL-6v2; NAEL-7v2; NoP-4; NoP-5; OBWP; OxAEP-2; OxBSo

Glory to caesar! and glory to God in the highest! Viktor Krivulin. ItGoST, *tr. by* Michael Molnar

Glory to God, and praise, and love Be ever, ever given. For the Anniversary Day of One's Conversion. Charles Wesley. SacPr

Glory to the Father. Our Father. David Craig. UpMys

Glory to you, red star hero. Last Page of the Civil War. Vladimir Vladimirovich Mayakovsky. RusPo, *tr. by* Robert Arthur Douglas Ford

Glory Trumpeter, The. Derek Walcott. GT; NAEL-6v2; NAEL-7v2; NoP-4; NoP-5; SeSe

Gloss. Padraic Fiacc. PNI

Gloss. Brooks Haxton. PoCho

Gloss to Matthew V 27–28. Alec Derwent Hope. GI

Glossolalia. Angela Sorby. PoDa

Glossy Mail. Norman Kreitman. EdScPo

Gloucester Moors. William Vaughn Moody. APN-2; TCAPo

Glow, little glow-worm, fly of fire. Glow-Worm, The. Johnny Mercer. ReLy

Glow of it in early winter, the barn that Eric Bartlett and, The. What In Fire Did I, Firelover, Starter of Fires, Love? Lisa Jarnot. VaPo

Glow of my campfire is dark red and flameless, The. Kenneth Rexroth. APT-2 *Fr.* Toward an Organic Philosophy.

Glow of my campfire is dark red and flameless, The. Toward an Organic Philosophy. Kenneth Rexroth.

Glow Worm. Vicki Feaver. MoWP; StAl

Glow-boys. John Tranter. BMAP

Glowing blossoms we tended together, The. Cold Rain Comes, A. Na Hûidôk. EcSo, *tr. by* Peter H. Lee

Glowworm. David McCord. NTCP

Glow-Worm, The. Johnny Mercer. ReLy

Glowworm, The. Thomas Stanley. NOSC

Glowworm scatters flashes through the moss, A. Glowworm Scatters Flashes, A. Rosalía de Castro. NAWM-7v1, *tr. by* S. Griswold Morley

Gloze Upon This Text, *Dominus iis opus habet,* A. George Gascoigne. ChIV-2

Glue and a small amount of alum. Pictures of the Floating World. Miyazawa Kenji. PFTM-1

Glued to the window. Self-Portrait at Eleven on a Train. Homero Aridjis. WoBe, *tr. by* George McWhirter

Glutted, half asleep, browsing in. Grace of Geldings in Ripe Pastures, The. Maxine W. Kumin. CAP-8

Gluttony in the Ale-house. William Langland. NPeEn

Glyn Cynon Wood. *Unknown.* OBWVE, *tr. by* Gwyn Williams

Glyndwr, see thy comet flaming. Glyndwr's War Song. John Jones. AngWePo

Glyndwr's War Song. John Jones. AngWePo

Gnarly and bent and deaf's a pos'. Zeke. Leonard Alfred George Strong. MoBrPo

Gnat, The. Joseph Beaumont. NOSC

Gnat on My Paper. Richard Eberhart. APT-2

Gnawing through a shinbone, a high howl. Unlike, for Example, the Sound of a Riptooth Saw. Thomas Lux. AmAlph

Gnomes. Howard Nemerov.
Sacrificed Author, A. GI

Gnomic Verses. William Blake.
Abstinence Sows Sand All Over. OxBEV

Gnosis. Christopher Pearse Cranch. APN-1; ColAP

Gnostic Prelude. James McAuley. BMAP

Gnosticism. Anne Carson. BAP-04

Go ahead. Blade of Grass, A. Srirangam Narayana Babu. HotL, *tr. by* V. Narayana Rao

Go ahead, baby. Song for a Baby on Padre Island. Mayme Evans. TiP2

Go ahead / tear my books up in the library. Text XXX. Josaphat Robert Large. OGAHCP, *tr. by* Boadiba and Jack Hirschman

Go and ask Robin to bring the girls over. Vision by Sweetwater. John Crowe Ransom. HarvBoo; OxBoAm

Go and catch a falling star. Song. John Donne. BLPJKO; ClHu; FSCP; HeIP-4; NAEL-6v1; NAEL-7v1; NAWM-5v1; NIL-7; NIP-4; NoP-4; NoP-5; NOSC; NoSic; OBEV; OxAEP-1; PtR; SoSe-8; TFi; WaAnP; WoPoe
(Goe and catche a falling starre.) NBLV; OxBEV

Go and fight in Kabul, my love. *Unknown.* SLW, *tr. by* Marjolijn De Jager, Sayd Bahodin Majrouh and André Velter

Go and find *work.* (LL) What the Chairman Told Tom. Basil Bunting. BrAP; EmeKit; NAMCP V.1; NoP-4

Go and let it be known to all lovers. Yunus Emre. NaPG, *tr. by* Talat Sait Halman

Go and open the door. Door, The. Miroslav Holub. StAl, *tr. by* Ian Milner

Go Ask the Dead. Thomas McGrath. AF

Go away! Van Gogh. Fadhil Assultani. IrPoTo, *tr. by* Raghid Nahhas

Go away a bit my sadness. Time to Shine. Hamda Khamees. PoArWo, *tr. by* Joseph T. Zeidan

Go away, Death! Alfred Austin. VerBaPo *Fr.* Go Away, Death!

Go away then, my friend, and travel well! *Unknown.* SLW, *tr. by* Marjolijn De Jager, Sayd Bahodin Majrouh and André Velter

Go bind thou up young dangling apricots. William Shakespeare. OBGa *Fr.* King Richard II.

Go bow thy head in gentle spite. To a Lily. James Matthew Legaré. APN-2

Go, bring back the worthless stick. Fetch. Jeffrey Skinner. PoDa

Go by, its clear depths never change. (LL) Mountain Spring, A. Ch'u Ch'uang I. CCL1; NDACCP; WaAnP, *tr. by* Kenneth Rexroth

Go by! linked fin by fin! most odiously. (LL) Leigh Hunt. NBLV; NPeEn *Fr.* Fish, the Man, and the Spirit, The.

Go, cruel tyrant of the human breast! Supposed To Be Written by Werter. Charlotte Smith. CenSon; RWP

Go Down Death (A Funeral Sermon). James Weldon Johnson. ISC; OxAAAP; SacPr

Go Down, Moses [*see also* Let My People Go]. *Unknown.* NAAPv.1; NoP-4; NoP-5

Go down obscurely. Be of Good Cheer. Robert Creeley. BodElec

Go. Down. Sun. Carla Harryman. BAP-04 *Fr.* Baby.

Go down to Kew in lilac-time, in lilac-time, in lilac-time. Barrel-Organ, The. Alfred Noyes. MoBrPo

Go, draw aside the curtain, and discover. William Shakespeare. OxAEP-1 *Fr.* Merchant of Venice, The.

Go, dumb-born book. Ezra Pound. NAAPv.2; TCAPo *Fr.* Hugh Selwyn Mauberley (Life and Contacts).

Go farther! I let it serve to trample on. (LL) Elizabeth Barrett Browning. CenSon; OxAEP-2 *Fr.* Sonnets from the Portuguese.

Go fetch to me a pint o' [*or of*] wine. Silver Tassie, The. Robert Burns. OBEV; WoPoe

Go figure—it's a knitting performance every day. Little Heart to Heart with the Horizon, A. Alice Fulton. PfSP

Go find Avicenna. Calling the Doctor (1000 A.D.). Nizami Arudi. WoPoe, *tr. by* Omar S. Pound

Go first, my love, to avenge the martyrs' blood. *Unknown.* SLW, *tr. by* Marjolijn De Jager, Sayd Bahodin Majrouh and André Velter

Go fly a kite he writes. Ted Berrigan. BodElec

Go For Broke. André Breton. PFTM-1

Go, for they call you, Shepherd, from the hill. Scholar Gypsy, The. Matthew Arnold. NAEL-6v2; NAEL-7v2; NoP-4; NoP-5; OBEV; OxAEP-1; TFi

Go, for they call you, shepherd, from the hill. Matthew Arnold. WaAnP *Fr.* Scholar Gypsy, The.

Go;—for 'tis Memorial morning. Memorial Day. Clara Ann Thompson. CBWP-2

Go forth and bid the land rejoice. Carmen Triumphale. Henry Timrod. PCW

Go forth myn hert wyth my lady. Charles, Duc d' Orléans. NPeEn
(Go forth, myn herte, wyth my lady.) OHMEL

Go from me: I am one of those who fall. Mystic and Cavalier. Lionel Pigot Johnson. MoBrPo

Go from me, summer friends, and tarry not. From Sunset to Star Rise. Christina Georgina Rossetti. VWP

Go from me. Yet I feel that I shall stand. Elizabeth Barrett Browning. CenSon; LW; OBEV; OxAEP-2; PtR *Fr.* Sonnets from the Portuguese.

Go from the must-laden room. Advance of the Grizzly, The. Barbara Guest. BodElec

Go! go! go! seek some other where, importune me no more. (LL)   Queen of England Elizabeth I. *See* Importune me no more!

Go, grieving rimes of mine, to that hard stone.   Petrarch.   NAWM-5v1; NAWM-7v1 *Fr.* Sonnets to Laura.

Go her way, her quiet, quiet way.   Relinquishment.   Elsa Gidlow.   PoBW

Go herte, hurt wyth adversitee.   *Unknown.*   OHMEL

Go home, America.   Cowboynomics.   Jose Angel Figueroa.   BRtP

Go / home, drop, go, back.   Lefty.   Imamu Amiri Baraka.   EGAG

Go home, stupid.   Ultimatum: Kid to Kid.   Langston Hughes.   NOxBChV

Go! hunt the whiter ermine, and present.   For the Lady Olivia Porter; a Present upon a New Year's Day.   Sir William Davenant.   NOSC

Go, idle Boy! I quit thy pow'r.   Adieu and Recall to Love, The.   Robert Merry.   NOBRP

Go in the Wilderness.   *Unknown.*   SSUS

Go inside a stone.   Stone.   Charles Simic.   CAP-8; ChAP

Go into the Highways and Hedges, And Compel Them to Come In.   Aleister Crowley.   CAGL

Go into this mediating passage.   We Startle Things.   Beth Baruch Joselow.   Eno

Go, keep holiday far away.   Publius Papinius Statius.   RomPo *Fr.* Sylvae [*or* Silvae].

Go lack go lack use to her.   Gertrude Stein.   NAAPv.2 *Fr.* Tender Buttons.

Go Left Out of Shantiville.   Nathaniel Mackey.   OxAAAP

Go, litel bille, and do me recomaunde.   *Unknown.*   OHMEL

Go, litel boke, go, litel myn tragedye.   Geoffrey Chaucer.   NPeEn

Go, litel ryng, to that ilke swete.   *Unknown.*   OHMEL

Go Little Book.   Robert Louis Stevenson. *See* Wishes.

Go, little book, my little tragedy.   Geoffrey Chaucer.   WoPoe *Fr.* Troilus and Criseyde [*or* Criseide].

Go[e], lovely rose.   Song.   Edmund Waller.   BASC; CABP; ClHu; CtM; HeIP-4; NAEL-6v1; NAEL-7v1; NIL-7; NoP-4; NoP-5; NOSC; NPeEn; OBEV; OxAEP-1; OxBEV; PBRV; PoPoPo; SoSe-8; TFi; WaAnP; WeW-3; WoPoe

Go measure the distance from Cape Town to Pretoria.   Measure for Measure.   Sipho Sepamla.   AF

Go, my flock, go get you hence.   Sir Philip Sidney.   NoSic *Fr.* Astrophil and Stella.

Go, my Lord of the Mountains.   Kamalākānta Bhattācārya.   SinGod, *tr. by* Rachel Fell McDermott

Go, my songs, seek your praise from the young and from the intolerant.   Ité.   Ezra Pound.   MoAmPo

Go, my songs, to the lonely and the unsatisfied.   Commission.   Ezra Pound.   BrAP

Go, My Thought.   Ingeborg Bachmann.   PoSu, *tr. by* Mark Anderson

Go, my thought, as long as a word clear enough for flight.   Go, My Thought.   Ingeborg Bachmann.   PoSu, *tr. by* Mark Anderson

Go north up the T'ai-heng Mountains.   Bitter Cold: A Song.   Ts'ao Ts'ao.   ChinPo, *tr. by* Ye Weilian [*or* Yeh Wei-lien *or* Wai-lim Yip]

Go not too near a House of Rose.   Emily Dickinson.   MoAmPo; NIL-7; NIP-4

Go on, high ship, since now, upon the shore.   Farewell to Florida.   Wallace Stevens.   NoAM

Go on, / Muses, / and sing the Moon with her big wings.   *Unknown.*   HW *Fr.* Homeric Hymns.

Go on, tell me the season is over.   Alan Wearne.   BMAP

Go on the Scout they say.   Thorow.   Susan Howe.   APSN

Go on transforming a square canvas.   Painting to be Constructed in Your Head.   Yoko Ono.   WhBo

Go on working around my hairline with a blade.   Cruelty Without Beauty.   Denise Riley.   MoWP

Go, one of you, find out the forester.   William Shakespeare.   DiBP *Fr.* Midsummer Night's Dream, A.

Go out and camp somewhere. You're lying down.   Mapooram.   *Aborigine Oral Tradition.*   NOBAu, *tr. by* Fred Biggs

Go out in the midday sun.   (LL)   Mad Dogs and Englishmen.   Noël Coward.   NBLV; ReLy

Go out in this dear summertide.   Paul Gerhardt.   GePo, *tr. by* George C. Schoolfield

Go out with awe.   Writing on a Door, A.   *Unknown.*   CCL1, *tr. by* James Legge

Go pretty [*or* prettie] child and bear[e] this flower.   To His Saviour, a Child; a Present, by a Child.   Robert Herrick.   ChIV-2

Go, quiet as a shower.   Tomas Tranströmer.   WoBe *Fr.* Haiku.

Go, rose, my Chloe's bosom grace.   Love's Emblem.   John Clare.   NIL-7; NIP-4

Go, rural Naiad! wind thy stream along.   To the Naiad of the Arun.   Charlotte Smith.   CenSon; RWP

Go sad or sweet or riotous with beer.   Old Women, The.   George Mackay Brown.   EdScPo; NoP-4; NoP-5; WaAnP

Go, she pleaded, 'I'll be fine,' head flung.   Flight.   Sam Gardiner.   NIrP

Go sit yo ass down.   We Are the Young Magicians.   Ruth Forman.   AmPoNex

Go slow, my soul, to feed thyself.   Emily Dickinson.   APN-2

Go, solitary wood, and henceforth be.   On the Death of a Nightingale.   Thomas Randolph.   BASC

Go, songs, for ended is our brief, sweet play.   Envoy.   Francis Thompson.   MoBrPo

Go, Soul [*or* Goe soule], the body's [*or* bodies] guest.   Lie, The.   Sir Walter Ralegh.   NAEL-6v1; NAEL-7v1; NoP-4; NoP-5; NoSic; NPeEn; OxBEV; PBRV; PoPoPo; TFi; WaAnP

Go soule, go sweetest soule for ever blest.   Ludovico Ariosto.   OBVE *Fr.* Orlando Furioso.

Go, swallow, and tell, now that the summer is dying.   Cwmrhydyceirw Elegiacs.   Vernon Watkins.   PoA 2002

Go sway on a suspension bridge over a gorge.   Inflorescence.   Arthur Sze.   WANABP

Go t' School.   Day at School, A.   Andrea M. Wren.   InTrad

Go tell at Sparta, traveler passing by.   On the Spartan Dead at Thermopylae.   Simonides.   WeW-3, *tr. by* Peter Jay

Go tell it—What a Message.   Emily Dickinson.   OxBoAm

Go tell the king: the daedal.   Last Utterance of the Delphic Oracle, The.   *Unknown.*   OBVE, *tr. by* Kenneth Rexroth

Go tell the Spartans, thou that passest by.   Thermopylae.   Simonides.   OBVE; OBWP; WoPoe, *tr. by* William Lisle Bowles

Go, the rich *Chariot* instantly prepare.   Abraham Cowley.   CABP; PBRV *Fr.* Pindarique Odes.

Go there where you see your heart.   Go There.   Tontongi.   OGAHCP, *tr. by* Boadiba and Jack Hirschman

Go thou gentle whispering wind.   Prayer to the Wind, A.   Thomas Carew.   CavPo

Go thou to Rome,—at once the paradise.   Percy Bysshe Shelley.   CtM *Fr.* Adonais; An Elegy on the Death of John Keats.

Go through and down the steps.   Justin Quinn.   NIrP

Go through the pockets of the enemy wounded.   Love Letters of the Dead.   Douglas Street.   FaBoWar

Go to sleep inside my eyes.   *Unknown.*   SLW, *tr. by* Marjolijn De Jager, Sayd Bahodin Majrouh and André Velter

Go to sleep McKade.   Kenneth Fearing.   APT-2

Go to sleep, my baby goblin.   Mother Goblin's Lullaby.   Jack Prelutsky.   NOxBChV

Go to sleep—though of course you will not.   Goodnight, A.   William Carlos Williams.   MoAmPo

Go to the ant, you sluggard.   Proverbs 6:6.   David Curzon.   ChIV-1

Go to the patch some afternoon.   How to Make Rhubarb Wine.   Ted Kooser.   PBCAP

Go to the sea.   How to Get a Baby.   Judith Ortiz Cofer.   NIL-7; PueRic

Go to the western gate, Luke Havergal.   Luke Havergal.   Edwin Arlington Robinson.   APN-2; MoAmPo; NAAL-5; NAAPv.1; NAMCP V.1; NoAM; OxBoAm; TCAPo; TFi

Go to Venice; bring me back a mason jar of glass eyes. They shall multiply like shadflies. (LL)   C. D. Wright.   AmAlph; ExTi *Fr.* Deepstep Come Shining.

Go underneath the ancient rooms.   Search, The.   Inge Hoogerhuis.   HW

Go, wash thyself in Jordan—go, wash thee and be clean!   Naaman's Song.   Rudyard Kipling.   ChIV-1

Go when the friendly moon permits the tides.   Advice to a Clam-Digger.   Wilbert Snow.   APT-1

Go where the waters fall.   John Keble.   SacPr *Fr.* Waterfall, The.

Go where there is music.   Preparing to Live Among the Old.   Stephen Corey.   PoA 2002

Go where those others went to the dark boundary.   Envoy of Mr. Cogito, The.   Zbigniew Herbert.   ItP; PoetW; WoPoe, *tr. by* Carpenter Bogdana, Bogdana Carpenter and John Carpenter *and* Bogdana Carpenter

Goad, The.   Michael Field.   VWP

Goanna.   Anthony Lawrence.   PML

Goanna.   *Unknown.*   NOBAu, *tr. by* Mungayana Nundhirribala

Goanna chases grasshopper.   Goanna.   *Unknown.*   NOBAu, *tr. by* Mungayana Nundhirribala

Goat.   Jo Shapcott.   StAl

Goat, The.   Greg Delanty.   MAAN

Goat, The.   Umberto Saba.   WoPoe, *tr. by* Stephen Sartarelli

Goat and a sheep, with a fat pig, are, A.   Pig, Goat, Sheep.   Jean de La Fontaine.   WoPoe, *tr. by* Bruce Boone and Robert Glück

Goat God, The.   Cesare Pavese.   WoPoe, *tr. by* William Arrowsmith

Goat-bearded, crazy-hatted old wrong-noter.   Coda: Thelonius Monk, d. 17 February 1982.   Neil Powell.   WaAnP

Goat-foot choros the.   Japanese Presentation I and II.   Joan Retallack.   FTOS

Goats and Botanists.   William Shenstone.   STuOW *Fr.* Taking a View of the Country from His Retirement [*or* Elegy 21].

Goback goback farewell Loch Thom. (LL)   Loch Thom.   William Sydney Graham.   EdScPo; NePenScot

Gobble the news with seven grains. Landing on the Moon. Odia Ofeimun. EmeKit

Gobelins. Ellen Bryant Voigt. InGu

Goblet, The. Bayard Taylor. TreFP

Goblet of Wine, A. Pao Chao. CCL1, *tr. by* John Frodsham

Goblet of wine, A. Tune: "Sand of Silk-Washing Brook." Yen Shu. ColAnChi, *tr. by* Jiaosheng Wang

Goblin, The. Rose Fyleman. NTCP

Goblin, The. Jack Prelutsky. TLR

Goblin lives in our house, in our house, in our house, A. Goblin, The. Rose Fyleman. NTCP

Goblin Market. Christina Georgina Rossetti. BrAP; NAEL-6v2; NAEL-7v2; NALW; NOxBChV; OBNV; OxAEP-2; OxBEV; ViWPN; VWP; WaAnP
""Good folk," said Lizzie." FaBoVe

God. Bella Akhatovna Akhmadulina. RusPo, *tr. by* Robert Arthur Douglas Ford

God: "God is in the high notes." Maxine Chernoff. Vesp

God: "Numbers from one to ten, however, are called." Annie Dillard. UpMys

God. Samuel Greenberg. APT-1

God. Isaac Rosenberg. OxBEV

God: "I feel that God is traveling." César Vallejo. WED, *tr. by* Robert Bly

God. Boris Abramovich Slutsky. TCRusP, *tr. by* Daniel Weissbort

God (3). Marina Ivanovna Tsvetayeva. WPoS, *tr. by* Paul Graves

God, A. Ted Hughes. GI

God a great railway to heaven has planned. Beulah Railway, The. *Unknown.* GM

God, A Poem. James Fenton. NAMCP V.2; NoAM; NoP-4; NoP-5; OBCoV

God Almighty the First Garden Made. Kathleen Jamie. GPPA

God and His angels stroll in the garden. That Old-Time Religion. Peter Didsbury. NeBrP

God and Man Set as One. *Unknown.* SacPr

God and Saint [*or* Sanct] Peter was gangand be the way. How the First Hielandman of God Was Made. *Unknown.* OBSV

God and the devil in these letters. Postman's Bell Is Answered Everywhere, The. Horace Gregory. MoAmPo

God and the devil still are wrangling. For a Mouthy Woman. Countee Cullen. ChIV-1

God and the G-Spot. Ellen Bass. NevBe

God and the Holy Stones. Annie Foster. NLP

God be in my head. Knight's Prayer, The. *Unknown.* InvLi

(God be praised!) the Georges ended. (LL) Georges, The. Walter Savage Landor. NIP-4; OBCoV; OBSV

God be wyth Trouthe wher he be. *Unknown.* OHMEL

God being with thee when we know it not. (LL) It Is a Beauteous Evening. William Wordsworth. BrAP; BRP; CenSon; GSo; HeIP-4; NAEL-6v2; NAEL-7v2; NIP-4; NOBRP; NoP-4; NoP-5; NPBRoP; OxAEP-2; TFi

God, best at making in the morning, tossed. Morning Person. Vassar Miller. GoPo

God Bless America. John Fuller. OBSV

God bless Henry. He lived like a rat. John Berryman. OxBoAm *Fr.* Dream Songs.

God bless our good and gracious King. Impromptu on Charles II. John Wilmot, 2d Earl of Rochester. BASC; NBLV; OBSV; OxAEP-1

God bless the chick in Alaska. Prayer. Ginger Andrews. SUP

God Bless the Child. Arthur Herzog, Jr. and Billie Holiday. ReLy

God bless the king, God bless our faith's defender. John Byrom. SacPr

God bless the little feet that never go astray. My Darlings' Shoes. *Unknown.* TreFP

God bless this house and keep us all from hurt. War Memory, A. Lizette Woodworth Reese. AmWaPo

God Body. Beckian Fritz Goldberg. AmAlph

God breathed. Creation. Robin Gurr. NOBAu

God, burn the houses down. *Unknown.* SLW, *tr. by* Marjolijn De Jager, Sayd Bahodin Majrouh and André Velter

God, but I do. Paganly. Trinidad Tarrosa Subido. InvLi

God! but the interest! (LL) Debt, The. Paul Laurence Dunbar. ColAP; NAAPv.1

God by his Wisdome, and all seeing Pow'r. Alice Sutcliffe. EMWP *Fr.* Meditations of Man's Mortalitie; or, A Way to True Blessedness.

God caught his eye. (LL) Epitaph on a Waiter. David McCord. APT-2; NBLV; NIP-4; OBCoV

God, consider the soul's need. Death Song for Owain ab Urien. Taliesin. OBWVE, *tr. by* Anthony Conran

God Correctly Understood. J. Gordon Coogler. VerBaPo

God counts the rings. God Scrubs the Tub. Gail Martin. SweBea

God Coup, The. Anne Carson. BodElec; WoBe *Fr.* Truth About God, The.

God created his image. Fill and Illumined. Joseph Ceravolo. ChIV-1; OxBoAm

God decided he was tired. Budgie Finds His Voice. Wendy Cope. UV

God did forbid the Israelites, to bring. Ass[e], The. Robert Herrick. ChIV-1

God, do not let any woman die in exile! *Unknown.* SLW, *tr. by* Marjolijn De Jager, Sayd Bahodin Majrouh and André Velter

God do not seem entirely to be dead. (LL) DeLiza Spend the Day in the City. June Jordan. NAMCP V.2; NoAM

God does for virtue goal and urge and crown afford. "Angelus Silesius." GePo *Fr.* Cherubical Wanderer, The.

God does what she wants. She has very large. Yellow Dot, The. Robert Bly. CAP-8

God doesn't fit in. More Than Anything. Doreen Baingana. BtF

God doubtless makes her, and doth make her good. John Davies. SacPr *Fr.* Nosce Teipsum.

God, ever gracious God! Here I myself debase. Night Thoughts Concerning a Dream. Daniel Casper von Lohenstein. GePo, *tr. by* George C. Schoolfield

God exists. Instead. Fatima. Laura Kasischke. AmPoNex

God Fit, The. Anne Carson. BodElec; WoBe *Fr.* Truth About God, The.

God follows after the days. Clump of Gods, The. Tracy Philpot. IAoNAP

God, for a man that solicits insurance! (LL) Bohemia. Dorothy Parker. AmWit; APT-1; BrAP; NBLV

God, / for Mercy's sake. From "The Torah of the Void." Rabbi Nahman of Bratzlav. BLT, *tr. by* Zalman Schachter

God Forgotten. Nick Flynn. AmPoNex

God gave a sign—and the. December. Jan Smrek. SonAtl, *tr. by* Ursula Hobday, Ziva Pecavar and Tamara Romanyk

God gave an onomatopoeic quality to women's language. Anne Carson. WoBe *Fr.* Truth About God, The.

God Gave Safe Passage to the Animals through His Forest of Bright Spectrums. Jennifer L. Knox. FreRad

God give me strength to lead a double life. Prayer. Hugo Williams. EmeKit; NPeEn

God give the yellow man. God Give to Men. Arna Bontemps. ColAP

God Give to Men. Arna Bontemps. ColAP

God, give us a long winter. Flame, A. Adam Zagajewski. PoCho, *tr. by* Clare Cavanagh

God give us men! A time like this demands. Wanted. Josiah Gilbert Holland. SacPr

God got plenty o' room, got plenty o' room. God Got Plenty o' Room. *Unknown.* SSUS

God grant thee thine own wish, and grant thee mine. John Donne. OBVE

God guard me from those thoughts men think. Prayer for Old Age, A. William Butler Yeats. ItP

God had no emotions but wished temporarily. Anne Carson. OxBoAm; WoBe *Fr.* Truth About God, The.

God had no name. Anne Carson. BodElec; WoBe *Fr.* Truth About God, The.

God had released her. (LL) Widow, The. Robert Southey. NOBRP; UV

God has a Right Hand, but is quite bereft. Right Hand, The. Robert Herrick. CavPo

God has foure keyes, which He reserves alone. Gods Keyes. Robert Herrick. SacPr

God Has Mercy on Kindergarten Children. Yehuda Amichai. NRoS, *tr. by* Esther Raizen

God has mercy on kindergarteners. God Has Mercy on Kindergarten Children. Yehuda Amichai. NRoS, *tr. by* Esther Raizen

God has, of old, been speaking to you through his Seers. To the Hungarian People. János Edrosi Sylvester. IQMS, *tr. by* Adam Makkai

God Has Pity on Kindergarten Children. Yehuda Amichai. TWF, *tr. by* Stephen Mitchell

God has took their little treasure. Julia A. Moore. STuOW *Fr.* Little Henry.

God hath the whole world perfect made, and free. Pleasd with thy Place. Epictetus. NPeEn, *tr. by* George Chapman

God hath yeuen, of myghtis most. Seven Gifts of the Holy Ghost, The. John Audelay [*or* Awdelay]. SacPr

God have her soul, I can no better say. (LL) Oft in My Thought. Charles D'Orleans. NoP-4; NoP-5

God help me, liberal mothers. Russ Joy Little League. Douglas Carlson. MoASP

God help thee, Traveler, on thy journey far. Winter Traveler, The. Henry Kirke White. CenSon

God, how my mouth swam. Sparrow Hills. Robley, Jr. Wilson. PBCAP

God Hunger. Michael Ryan. BodElec

God, I have sought you as a fox seeks chickens. Sacrament. Alden Nowlan. StAl

God, I know nothing, my sense is all nonsense. Grace, A. Donald Hall. LoL

God, I need a job because I need money. Prayer. Alan Dugan. NoAM

God if he exists. Man Root, The. Kazuko Shiraishi. PFTM-2, *tr. by* Ikuko Atsumi and Kenneth Rexroth

God in Hiding, God of Faith. John Fitzgerald. BBMWP, *tr.* by Joseph P. Clancy

God in His Wisdom from the start. Semonides. WoPoe *Fr.* Genealogy of Women, The.

God in His wisdom made the fly. Ogden Nash. OBCoV

God in his wondrous grace a garden did sow. Airstrip St Athan. Iorwerth Cyfeilog Peate. BBMWP, *tr.* by Nigel Jenkins

God in the darkness, God beyond our knowing. Elizabeth J. Smith. RSR

God in wrath, A. Stephen Crane. NAAPv.1

God is a distant—stately Lover. Emily Dickinson. APN-2; NCAP

God is a grand heart cut. Anne Carson. BodElec; WoBe *Fr.* Truth About God, The.

God is a zealous pruner. Pruner, The. John Oxenham. SacPr

God is above the sphere of our esteem. What God Is. Robert Herrick. NOSC

God Is Dead—Nietzche. Elizabeth Bartlett. Prnts

God is good but. Notes. Thomas Kinsella.

God Is Good. It Is a Beautiful Night. Wallace Stevens. APT-1; SAmP

God is in the high notes. God. Maxine Chernoff. Vesp

God is love love in a dark park. K-Doe Codas. Brett Evans. AnSo

God is love. Then by inversion. James Vincent Cunningham. NIP-4; VCAP *Fr.* Epigrams: A Journal.

God is my staff, my path, my goal, my game, my fire. "Angelus Silesius." GePo *Fr.* Cherubical Wanderer, The.

God is near, and, The / difficult to grasp. Patmos. Friedrich Hölderlin. OBVE; WoPoe, *tr.* by David Gascoyne

God Is Not Dumb. James Russell Lowell. ChIV-1 *Fr.* Bibliolaters.

God is not dumb, that he should speak no more. James Russell Lowell. ChIV-1 *Fr.* Bibliolaters.

God is not offered to the senses. December Journal. Charles Wright. InGu

God Is Nothing Physical. "Angelus Silesius." GePo *Fr.* Cherubical Wanderer, The.

God is older than the sun and moon. Maximus. D. H. Lawrence. BLT

God is our strength and our refuge: therefore will we not tremble. Hexameters[; Paraphrase of Psalm XLVI]. Samuel Taylor Coleridge. ChIV-1

God is still glorified. Building in Stone. Sylvia Townsend Warner. MoBrPo

God is the first snow. He is a leaf, a mosquito. Tatyana Voltskaya. CRWP, *tr.* by Richard McKane

God is the great urge that has not yet found a body. Body of God, The. D. H. Lawrence. ChIV-2

God, is this then a sin? *Unknown.* SLW, *tr.* by Marjolijn De Jager, Sayd Bahodin Majrouh and André Velter

God Is To Me What I Desire. "Angelus Silesius." GePo *Fr.* Cherubical Wanderer, The.

God knows, I've looked in you enough. Organist Confesses to His Mirror, The. John Purser. EdScPo

God knows, teaching the Renaissance I could use it. Why I Don't Speak Italian. Arthur L. Clements. UnSA

God knows / We have our troubles, too. High to Low. Langston Hughes. APT-2; PoPoPo

God knows what happened to the candlestick. Jaroslav Seifert. AF *Fr.* Bombing of the Town of Kralupy, The.

God knows which God is the God God recognizes. (LL) Day After Sunday, The. Phyllis McGinley. AmWit; MoAmPo; OBSV

God Knows Why. *Unknown.* SonAtl, *tr.* by Alan Brierly, M. Ellison and Saul Goode

God lay dead in Heaven. Stephen Crane. APN-2

God leaned out of himself one day. Whole New Scene, A. John Fuller. NOxBChV

God, let me be with him if only for a moment. *Unknown.* SLW, *tr.* by Marjolijn De Jager, Sayd Bahodin Majrouh and André Velter

God like a kiss, God like a welcoming. Mark Jarman. InVLi *Fr.* Unholy Sonnets.

God Looks on Nature With a Glorious Eye. John Clare. BBASP

God love you now, if no one else will ever. Ode for the American Dead in Korea. Thomas McGrath. AmWaPo; StAl

God loves us all, I'm pleased to say. God's Love. Vikram Seth. TRP

God Lovingly Counterattacks. Jarret Keene. Vesp

God Lyaeus, Ever Young. John Fletcher. OBEV *Fr.* Tragedy of Valentinian, The.

God made man in His image, true. Why God Chose Robert Frost Over Elvis. Lynn Veach Sadler. VisFro

God made the bees. Mother Goose. Spl

God made the sex-shop keeper. Fiona Pitt-Kethley. UV

God made the sugar cane grow where it's hot. Bundaberg Rum. W. N. Scott. NOBAu

God made the wicked grocer. Song against Grocers, The. G. K. Chesterton. OBCoV

God makes a path, provides a guide. Roger Williams. SacPr

God mercifully forgets us for a few hours. God Forgotten. Nick Flynn. AmPoNex

God moves in a mysterious way. William Cowper. CABP; NoP-4; NoP-5; NPeEn; OxBEV; SacPr; TFi *Fr.* Olney Hymns.

God must have a big eye to see everything. Jack Spicer. PmAP *Fr.* Imaginary Elegies.

God my father spoke in the calm of evening. Peter Davison. YaYoPo *Fr.* Breaking of the Day, The.

God No / Date: 21 Aug 93. Call and Response. DJ Renegade. BtF

God Not Afar Off. Jones Very. InVLi

God of Abraham praise, The. Thomas Olivers. SacPr

God of day rolls his car up the slopes, The. Guido's Aurora. Henry David Thoreau. APN-1

God of Love, The. George MacBeth. EmeKit

God of mine, I am weeping for the life that I live. Eternal Dice, The. César Vallejo. PoetW, *tr.* by James Wright

God of our fathers, known of old. Recessional. Rudyard Kipling. BrAP; BRP; CABP; InvLi; MoBrPo; NAEL-6v2; NAEL-7v2; NAMCP V.1; NoAM; NoP-4; NoP-5; NPeEn; OBEV; OxAEP-2; OxBEV; TFi; UV; WaAnP

God of peace! before thee. Hymn of Freedom. Michael J. Barry. IrV

God of Pepper, The. Alan Michael Parker. NeAmPo

God of Roads. Yvor Winters. NAAPv.2 *Fr.* Magpie's Shadow, The.

God of Smoke listens idly in the heat, The. Backyard. John Tranter. BMAP

God of song and laughter long ago, The. But. Vladimir Holan. PoSu, *tr.* by Ian Milner and Jarmila Milner

God of the Flies. John Rimington. FaBoWar

God of War, The. Bertolt Brecht. AF, *tr.* by Michael Hamburger

God of your fathers, known of old. Post-Recessional. G. K. Chesterton. UV

God on a bike going twenty miles an hour. God on a Bike. Pat Winslow. ArBi

God Once Commanded Us, A. Leah Goldberg. FIT, *tr.* by Robert Friend

God only knows what he'd been doing. Painting or sewing? Parish. Norman Dubie. AmAlph

God our fathers formerly knew. Headlined in Heaven. Paul Grano. NOBAu

God Our Refuge. Richard Chenevix Trench. SacPr

God Packs Lunches. Gail Martin. SweBea

God pity me whom (god distinctly has). E. E. Cummings. SeSe

God placed the Russian peasant. Gentlemen. W. N. Ewer. RSaN

God, please let my youth go up in smoke! *Unknown.* SLW, *tr.* by Marjolijn De Jager, Sayd Bahodin Majrouh and André Velter

God, please rescue just that one! *Unknown.* SLW, *tr.* by Marjolijn De Jager, Sayd Bahodin Majrouh and André Velter

God, provide the "little horror" with an eternal sleep! *Unknown.* SLW, *tr.* by Marjolijn De Jager, Sayd Bahodin Majrouh and André Velter

God rest that Jewy woman. Song for the Clatter-Bones. Frederick Robert Higgins. ChIV-1; OBMV

God rest ye merry, gentlemen. God Rest Ye Merry, Gentlemen. *Unknown.* SacPr

(God rest you merry gentlemen.) ChrPo

God Rest You Merry. Dinah Maria Mulock Craik. UV

God rest you merry gentlemen. Christmas Carol, A. G. K. Chesterton. UV

God rest you merry gentlemen. *Unknown. See* God rest ye merry, gentlemen.

God said, "Let there be light, and there was light." Mysteries of Life. Mary E. Tucker. CBWP-1

God said to Abraham. Aida Gelbtrunk. MirDau, *tr.* by Roberta Gordenstein

God / save this country. Prayer, A. Devarakonda Balagangadhara Tilak. HotL, *tr.* by V. Narayana Rao

God Says Yes to Me. Kaylin Haught. BeAl; P180

God Scatters Beauty. Walter Savage Landor. InVLi

God Scrubs the Tub. Gail Martin. SweBea

God send eueric Preist ane wyfe. *Unknown.* NePenScot *Fr.* Gude and Godlie Ballatis, The.

God send the Devil is a gentleman. Knight Fallen on Evil Days, The. Elinor Wylie. MoAmPo

God send the land deliverance. Death of Parcy Reed, The [Version from Richardsons' Borderers' Table Book]. *Unknown.* IBB

God sende hem so[o]ne [a] verray pestilence! (LL) Geoffrey Chaucer. NAEL-6v1; NAEL-7v1; NoP-5 *Fr.* Canterbury Tales, The.

God sends his tasks. Visitation, The. Brigit Pegeen Kelly. YaYoPo

God Shed His Grace. Philip Stephens. AmPoNex

God sits on a chair of darkness in my soul. Garments of God, The. Jessica Agnes Powers. InVLi

God snaps your picture—don't look away. Archival Print, An. William Stafford. OxBoAm

God Speaks to the Soul. Mechthild von Magdeburg. WPoS, *tr.* by Oliver Davies

God spins the peanut butter thin. God Packs Lunches. Gail Martin. SweBea

God Stiff. Anne Carson. WoBe *Fr.* Truth About God, The.

God stopped and the car. Not Singing. Kate Daniels. PBCAP

God strengthen me to bear myself. Who Shall Deliver Me? Christina Georgina Rossetti. SacPr

God strikes His Church, But 'tis to this intent. Persecutions Purifie. Robert Herrick. SacPr

God, take this old husband away. *Unknown.* SLW, *tr. by* Marjolijn De Jager, Sayd Bahodin Majrouh and André Velter

God tempteth no one (as S. Aug'stine saith). Temptation. Robert Herrick. SacPr

God the Eater. Stevie Smith. NAMCP V.1

God, the Eternal! Infinite! All-wise! Cain: A Mystery. Lord Byron.

God, the mother. Spell for Birth. Jeni Couzyn. HAWP

God, the Port of Peace. John Walton. SacPr

God, the rabbis tell us, never assigns. Getting the Message. Maxine W. Kumin. TaR

God, this mud. Fear's habit. Water Buffalo. Yusef Komunyakaa. AmAlph

God, thou great symmetry. Envoi. Anna Wickham. MoBrPo

God, though [*or* although] this life is but a wraith. Prayer. Louis Untermeyer. MoAmPo

God thought of you, and so I am here. (LL) George Macdonald. ITBLP; WHSW *Fr.* At the Back of the North Wind.

God through the wrong end of a telescope. (LL) Of John Davidson. Hugh MacDiarmid. HarvBoo; NePenScot; OxBEV

God tole Hezykiah. Little Black Train Is A-Comin'. *Unknown.* GM

God tried to teach Crow how to talk. Crow's First Lesson. Ted Hughes. NAMCP V.2; NoAM

God Vacuums the Pool. Gail Martin. SweBea

God, we don't like to complain. Caliban in the Coal Mines. Louis Untermeyer. MoAmPo

God, what are you doing to me? *Unknown.* SLW, *tr. by* Marjolijn De Jager, Sayd Bahodin Majrouh and André Velter

God when He's angry here with any one. Gods Anger without Affection. Robert Herrick. InvLi

God who created me. Prayers. Henry Charles Beeching. OBEV; SacPr

God Who Loves You, The. Carl Dennis. BeAl; PoDa

God who mounts the winged winds, The. Homer. OBVE *Fr.* Odyssey.

God, whose law it is that he who learns must suffer. Aeschylus. BLPJKO *Fr.* Agamemnon.

God will cheat no one, not even the world of its triumph. (LL) W. H. Auden. ChrPo; MoBrPo; OBCP *Fr.* For the Time Being; a Christmas Oratorio.

God will have all or none; serve Him, or fall. Neutrality Loathsome. Robert Herrick. ChIV-1; NoP-4; NoP-5

God wills us free; man wills us slaves. Epitaph of John Jack. Daniel Bliss. TCAPo

God, you could grow to love it, God-fearing, God. Ecclesiastes. Derek Mahon. BeAl; ChIV-1; ModIr; PNI

God, you may render me blind from here on in. *Unknown.* SLW, *tr. by* Marjolijn De Jager, Sayd Bahodin Majrouh and André Velter

God, you may render me blind today! *Unknown.* SLW, *tr. by* Marjolijn De Jager, Sayd Bahodin Majrouh and André Velter

God-born before the Sons of God, she hurled. Music. Madison Cawein. APN-2

Godchild and Her Daughter, The. Last Happy Day, The. Naomi Long Madgett. FuFl

Goddam Street, The. Robert Coles. BloBone

Goddamn you, sliding around under. Untitled. Mandy Kahn. FTtHH

Goddès mother be. (LL) I Sing of a Maiden. *Unknown.* ChIV-2; TFi

    (Godes moder be.) (LL) CABP; NAEL-6v1; NoP-4; NoP-5; NPeEn; WaAnP

Goddesses of Wales. Goddesses. Elin ap Hywel. BBMWP, *tr. by* the author

Goddess Laksmi, The. Cosmology. *Unknown.* WoPoe, *tr. by* J. Moussaieff Masson and W. S. Merwin

    (Goddess Lakshmi, The.) EaWin

Goddess of chain link fences. City Goddess. Leah Korican. HW

Goddess of poetry. To the Moon. Yvor Winters. APT-2

Goddess of the Luo, The. Ts'ao Chih. CCL1, *tr. by* Burton Watson

Goddess of the Waters. Skin of Clouds. Thulani Davis. FTtHH

Goddesse bade the nymphs remove, The. *Unknown.* OBVE *Fr.* Vigil of Venus, The.

Goddesses. Elin ap Hywel. BBMWP, *tr. by* the author

Goddesses, The. Janine Canan. HW

Goddesses of the past. Goddesses. Elin ap Hywel. ATSWP, *tr. by* Robert Minhinnick

Gode sire, pray ich thee. *Unknown. See* Goode sire, praye ich thee.

Gode sire, preye I thee. *Unknown. See* Goode sire, praye ich thee.

Godes moder be. (LL) *Unknown. See* Goddès mother be.

God-Forgotten. Thomas Hardy. InvLi

Godfrey of Bulloigne; or, The Recoverie of Jerusalem [Gerusalemme Liberata]. Torquato Tasso. *tr. by* Edward Fairfax

    "All wilie sleights, that subtile women know." OxBEV, *tr. by* Edward Fairfax

    "Drearie trumpet blew a dreadfull blast, The." PBRV, *tr. by* Edward Fairfax

    "Erminia's steed this while his mistress bore." NoSic

    "Joyous birds, hid under greenewood shade, The." OBVE

    "Palace great is builded rich and round." NoSic

    "Sweet Armida tooke this charge on hand, The." OBVE

Godhorse. Kojo Laing. HBAPE

GOD-IN-HIMSELF / I feel the evil of absence in my eternal heart. Preface or The Drama of Absence in an Eternal Heart. Roger Gilbert-Lecomte. PFTM-1

Godlie Instructione for Old and Young, Ane. *Unknown.* EMWP

Godlike. Anselm Hollo. PmAP

Godlings are born racily. Nativities. U. A. Fanthorpe. NoP-4

Gododdin, The. Aneirin. *tr. by* Joseph P. Clancy and Desmond O'Grady

    "Lord of Gododdin will be praised in song, A." NePenScot, *tr. by* Joseph P. Clancy

    "Men went to Catraeth, keen their war-band." OBWVE

    "Men went to Gododdin, laughter-loving." OBWP

    "To Cattraeth's vale in glitt'ring row." OBVE

    "When a crowd of cares." NePenScot, *tr. by* Joseph P. Clancy

    "Youth." WoPoe, *tr. by* Desmond O'Grady

God-rendering voice of a storm. (LL) Of Politics, & Art. Norman Dubie. AmAlph; P180

Gods. Takahashi Shinkichi. ZenPo, *tr. by* Takashi Ikemoto and Lucien Stryk

Gods, The. Les A. Murray. WoPoe

God's Absence. Mechthild von Magdeburg. WPoS, *tr. by* Oliver Davies

God's all-unfathomed plan is quite fulfilled. (LL) Tireless Sculptor, The. Henrietta Cordelia Ray. CBWP-3; SWaP

God's anger mutter in the darkened heaven. (LL) Frederick Goddard Tuckerman. APN-2; NoP-5 *Fr.* Sonnets.

Gods Anger without Affection. Robert Herrick. InvLi

Gods are dead: no longer do we bring, The. Santa Decca. Oscar Wilde. OxBSo

Gods are everywhere. Gods. Takahashi Shinkichi. ZenPo, *tr. by* Takashi Ikemoto and Lucien Stryk

Gods are happy, The. Matthew Arnold. OBEV *Fr.* Strayed Reveller, The.

Gods Are Here, The. Jean Toomer. APT-2; OxBoAm

God's armies of Heaven, with pinions extended. Pro Patria. Adah Isaacs Menken. CBWP-1

Gods arrive, The. (LL) Give All to Love. Ralph Waldo Emerson. APN-1; ColAP; OBEV; OxBoAm; TCAPo

Gods Ash Their Cigarettes, The. S. K. Kelen. BMAP

Gods at Three A.M., The. Reginald Shepherd. NeAmPo; WiU

God's Beloveds Remain True. Anne Carson. WoBe *Fr.* Truth About God, The.

God's Blessing. Len Roberts. BodElec

God's blessing on poor ship-folk! Peace and prayer. Wanderers, The. Robert Williams Buchanan. OxBSo

God's blessings all are uniform. They Are the Same. Priscilla Jane Thompson. CBWP-2

God's Body. Sara Klugman. HW

Gods boundles bownties gods promise ever abyding. Bible, *O.T.* PBRV *Fr.* Psalms.

God's Bouquet of Undying Love. Anne Carson. WoBe *Fr.* Truth About God, The.

Gods, by right of Nature, must possess, The. Lucretius. NPeEn *Fr.* De Rerum Natura (On the Nature of Things).

Gods chase / Round vase. Ode on a Grecian Urn Summarized. Desmond Skirrow. NIL-7; NIP-4

God's child in Christ adopted—Christ my all. My Baptismal Birthday [*or* Birth-Day]. Samuel Taylor Coleridge. ChIV-2

God's Christ Theory. Anne Carson. OxBoAm; WoBe *Fr.* Truth About God, The.

God's City. Francis Turner Palgrave. SacPr

God's cows are in the fields. Monastery Orchard in Early Spring, The. Kathleen Norris. UpMys

God's Cutt-Off TV Screen's Vanishing Mirror Seems an Unshared Point. Christopher Davis. Vesp

God's Determinations [touching his Elect]. Edward Taylor.
    Christ's Reply. NAAL-3
    Joy of Church Fellowship Rightly Attended, The. NAAL-3
    Preface [to God's Determinations], The. NAAL-3; NAAPv.1; NOSC; OxBEV; OxBoAm; TCAPo; WaAnP
    Soul's Groan to Christ for Succo[u]r, The. NAAL-3

God's Electric Power. Mrs. Henry Linden. CBWP-4

God's evident, and may be said to be. Gods Presence. Robert Herrick. SacPr

God's Freedom Lovers. Ahmed Herdi. IrPoTo, *tr. by* Muhammad Ali

God's Gifts. Albrecht von Johannsdorf. GePo, *tr. by* F. C. Nicholson

God's Grandeur. Gerard Manley Hopkins. AmFaPo; BBASP; BrAP; CABP; ChAP; ClHu; GSo; ITBLP; ItP; MoBrPo; NAEL-6v2; NAEL-7v2; NAMCP V.1; NIL-7; NIP-4; NoAM; NoP-4; NoP-5; OxBEV; OxBSo; PoCho; PoPoPo; RaBo; SacPr; SoSe-8; TFi; WaAnP; WeW-3

God's Handiwork. Anne Carson. BodElec *Fr.* Truth About God, The.

Gods have taken alien shapes upon them, The. Exiles. George Russell. MoBrPo

Gods *Houses,* almost like *Troyes Ilion,.* John Taylor. PBRV *Fr.* Here followeth the unfashionable fashion, or the too too homely Worshipping of God.

Gods it is I ask to release me from this watch, The. Agamemnon. Aeschylus. *tr. by* Louis MacNeice

God's Justice. Anne Carson. OxBoAm; WoBe *Fr.* Truth About God, The.

Gods Keyes. Robert Herrick. SacPr

God's List of Liquids. Anne Carson. OxBoAm; WoBe *Fr.* Truth About God, The.

God's Love. Vikram Seth. TRP

God's Measurements. Laurence Lieberman. IllVoic

God's Mother. Anne Carson. OxBoAm; WoBe *Fr.* Truth About God, The.

God's Name. Anne Carson. BodElec; WoBe *Fr.* Truth About God, The.

God's nobleman, hearken. Vineyard Place in My Care, A. Saunders Lewis. BBMWP, *tr. by* D. Myrddin Lloyd

Gods of old are silent on their shore, The. Aristomenes. Lord Byron. NPeEn

Gods of the Copybook Headings, The. Rudyard Kipling. NoAM; OBSV

God's old angels made us peaceful. My New Angels. Sinéad Morrissey. MFPA

God's other eye is good and gold. So bright. Jack Spicer. PmAP *Fr.* Imaginary Elegies.

God's Penis. Jeffrey Harrison. MAAN

Gods Presence ("God's evident, and may be said to be.") Robert Herrick. SacPr

Gods Providence. Robert Herrick. SacPr

God's querulous calling. (LL) Theology. Ted Hughes. NAEL-6v2; NAEL-7v2; NoAM; NoP-4; NoP-5

God's refuted but the devil's not. Scarecrow, The. Charles Simic. OxBoAm

God's Residence. Emily Dickinson. SAmP; WPoS

Gods their god-like fun, The. (LL) Letter to My Sister. Anne Spencer. InGu; TCAPo

Gods themselves with us do dwell, The. (LL) Mower Against Gardens, The. Andrew Marvell. BASC; CABP; NAEL-6v1; NAEL-7v1; NIL-7; NoP-4; NoP-5; NOSC; NPeEn; OBGa; OxAEP-1; PBRV

God's twins (the testaments) speak loud. Morgan Llwyd. AngWePo *Fr.* 1648.

God's Two Dwellings. Thomas Washbourne. SacPr

God's undivided, One in Persons Three. To God. Robert Herrick. SacPr

God's unfinished work. (LL) Campesino's Lament, The. Judith Ortiz Cofer. PueRic; TouFir

God's Voice. Sunday Ayewanu. NeNiPo

God's Ways, Not Our Ways. Henrietta Cordelia Ray. CBWP-3

Gods who rule the ghosts; all silent shades. Virgil. NAWM-5v1; NAWM-7v1 *Fr.* Aeneid [*or* Eneados *or* Aeneis], The.

God's Will for You and Me. *Unknown.* SoSe-8

God's will is—the bud of the rose for your hair. We Two. Sarah Morgan Bryan Piatt. NAAPv.1

God's wind in the back. Tomas Tranströmer. WoBe *Fr.* Haiku.

Gods with Stainless Ears. Lynnette Roberts.
    Part 4: Cri Madonna. MoWP

Gods! with what pride I see the titled slave. Charles Churchill. OBSV *Fr.* Author, The.

God's Woman. Anne Carson. OxBoAm; WoBe *Fr.* Truth About God, The.

God's Work. Anne Carson. BodElec; OxBoAm; WoBe *Fr.* Truth About God, The.

God's World. Edna St. Vincent Millay. APT-1; ITBLP; MoAmPo

God's wounded hand. Denise Levertov. UpMys *Fr.* Showings, The: Lady Julian of Norwich, 1342-1416.

Gods Wrote, The. Keorapetse Kgositsile. GT; OxAAAP

Godspeed. John Greenleaf Whittier. GSo

Goe and catche a falling starre. John Donne. *See* Go and catch a falling star.

Goe hurtles soules, whom mischiefe hath opprest. Seneca. NPeEn *Fr.* Hercules Furens.

Goe little booke: thy selfe present. Edmund Spenser. NAEL-6v1; NAEL-7v1 *Fr.* Shepherd's Calender, The.

Go[e], smiling soul[e]s, your new-built cages break[e]. To the Infant Martyrs. Richard Crashaw. ChIV-2; NAEL-6v1; NAEL-7v1; NoP-4; NoP-5

Goe turne away those Cruell Eyes. Song. Captain Henry Cooke and Barbara Syms. EMWP

Go[e] wailing verse, the Infants of my love. Samuel Daniel. NoP-4; NoP-5; WaAnP *Fr.* Sonnets to Delia.

Goes all right. Korean Figures. *Unknown.* EaWin, *tr. by* W. S. Merwin

Goes flaring down to Baggot Street. (LL) Baggot Street Deserta. Thomas Kinsella. NAMCP V.2; NoAM

Goes on, and the moon in the breast of man is cold. (LL) Moon and the Night and the Men, The. John Berryman. GPTC; PWW2; VCAP

Goes out. Issa. EH, *tr. by* Robert Hass

Goes way back to the days / my father a young man. Cousin Mary. Wanda Coleman. GT; OxAAAP

Goethe and Brentano. Andrew Taylor. BMAP *Fr.* Travelling to Gleis-Binario.

Goethe in Weimar sleeps, and Greece. Memorial Verses. Matthew Arnold. CABP; NAEL-6v2; NAEL-7v2

Goethe, Racine, Neruda, Pushkin—next! Verse Translator. John Frederick Nims. PoA 2002

Gog. Ted Hughes. NAMCP V.2

Goggles and Helmet. Donald Hall. PoA 2002

Gogol explains his country as a troika. Robert Pinsky. StAl *Fr.* Explanation of America, An.

Gogol (his namesake). Personal Histories, The. Michael Burkard. BodElec

Goin' down the [*or* de] road, Lawd. Bound No'th Blues. Langston Hughes. NAAPv.2

Going [for my mother-in-law, Gladys]. Bruce Dawe. BMAP

Going. Philip Larkin. WoPoe

Going, The. Thomas Hardy. HarvBoo; InoFa; NAMCP V.1; OxAEP-2

Going abroad, he saw one day a hound was. Pythagorean, The. Xenophanes. DiBP, *tr. by* Sir Edwin Arnold

Going and Coming of Sequins. Joyce Mansour. PFTM-2, *tr. by* Molly Bendall

Going and Staying. Thomas Hardy. NAMCP V.1; NoAM

Going Back Again. Edward Robert Bulwer-Lytton. VerBaPo
    (Check to Song.) STuOW

Going Back Patiently. Frank Mkalawile Chipasula. HBAPE

Going Back Through Color. Rafael Alberti. RaW, *tr. by* Mark Strand

Going Back to Ireland. Violette Newton. TiP2

Going Back to the Convent. Madeline DeFrees. TAPaP

Going Back to the River. Marilyn Hacker. WiU

Going Baroque. Jean V. Gier. ReBoTo

Going Blind. Rainer Maria Rilke. BLT, *tr. by* Walter Arndt

Going Down Hill on a Bicycle. Henry Charles Beeching. ArBi; NOxBChV; OBEV

Going Down, Please. László Mécs. IQMS, *tr. by* Watson Kirkconnell

Going East. Ishmael Reed. ASA

Going Forth. Andrée Chedid. PoArWo, *tr. by* Lucy McNair

Going from us at last. Escape, The. Mark Van Doren. MoAmPo

Going, Going. Philip Larkin. NAMCP V.2; NoAM; OxAEP-2

Going Home. Catherine Obianuju Acholonu. HAWP

Going Home. Toneka Nathene Bonitto-Burwell. BtF

Going home. Buson. EH, *tr. by* Robert Hass

Going Home. Janice Gould. FiBr

Going Home. Wing Tek Lum. UnSA

Going Home. Derek Mahon. HarvBoo

Going Home. Patricia Pogson. NLP

Going Home Madly. Brooke Wiese. UrbNat

Going Home to Mayo, Winter, 1949. Paul Durcan. PBCIP

Going In to Dinner. Edward Richard Burton Shanks. OBMV

Going north meant Opal Fruits and Aztec bars. Legacy. Siobhan Campbell. MFPA

Going On. Daryl E. Jones. TiP2

Going On. Peter Reading.
    "These are the days of the horrible headlines." StAl
    "This is unclean: to eat turbots on Tuesdays." BeAl

Going on always on and on. *Unknown.* WoPoe, *tr. by* Charles O. Hartman

Going on boats but. Leslie Scalapino. PmAP *Fr.* Crowd and Not Evening Or Light.

Going Out and Coming In. Mary Evelyn Moore Davis. SWaP

Going Out for Cigarettes. Billy Collins. MAAN; OPRER

Going out of Town. N. Revathi Devi. HotL, *tr. by* V. Narayana Rao

Going out that evening with the garbage. Death in Larkspur Canyon, A. Richard Garcia. UrbNat

Going Out Through the North Gate of Chi. Pao Chao. ColAnChi, *tr. by* Daniel Bryant

Going out to fame and triumph. Going Out and Coming In. Mary Evelyn Moore Davis. SWaP

Going Postal. Paul Christensen. LiTh

Going Swimmingly. Katherine Pierpoint. MoWP

Going to Europe. Michael Lassell. WiU

Going to God with the Shepherds. L. William Countryman. RSR

Going to his room one night. Householder Departs from the City, The. Nathan Alterman. FIT, *tr. by* Robert Friend

Going to Jail. Tom Clark and Lewis Warsh. AHA

Going to Mass after Fifteen Years. Maxine Scates. PBCAP

Going to Norway. Jack Anderson. SUP

Going to Sea. Douglas Messerli. FTOS

Going to Sleep. Dorothy Livesay. IFF

Going to sleep, I cross my hands on my chest. Death. Bill Knott. PBCAP; PoCho

Going to Sleep in Childhood. Gennady Aygi. ItGoST, *tr. by* Peter France

Going to tend our family graves today. Going to Tend Our Family Graves. Issa. WoPoe, *tr. by* Harold Stewart

Going to the Palace with a Friend at Dawn. Tu Fu [*or* Du Fu]. CrYelRi, *tr. by* Sam Hamill

Going to Visit a Taoist Recluse on Heaven's Mountain Only to Find Him Gone. Li Po. CrYelRi, *tr. by* Sam Hamill

Going to Walden. Mary Oliver. WhBo

Going to Work. Nancy Mercado. PA9/11

Going Under. Carl Phillips. OxAAAP

Going Up. Sam Liptsin. Prolet, *tr. by* Amelia Glaser

Going up for the assault that morning. Walt. Ted Hughes. NoP-4

Going up for the jump shot. I Try to Turn in My Jock. David Hilton. MoASP

Going Up the Rivers. Rafael Alberti. RaW, *tr. by* Rachel Benson

Going Uptown to Visit Miriam. Víctor Hernández Cruz. PueRic

Going Without Saying. Bernard O'Donoghue. PoCu

Going Wrong in the House of Neptune. David Clewell. MAAN

Going-elsewhere of ripples incessantly shaping, The. (LL) Swimming Chenango Lake. Charles Tomlinson. NAMCP V.2; NoAM

Gold. Gurajada Apparao. HotL, *tr. by* V. Narayana Rao

Gold and al this worldës wyn. *Unknown.* NPeEn

Gold and whores a thousand years announced that. Kingdom, The. Barry Silesky. IllVoic

Gold armchair is witness to his calm, The. Boy's Afraid of the Live Tiger, The. Cesare Greppi. ItPo, *tr. by* Gayle Ridinger

Gold Band, The. *Unknown.* SSUS

Gold Coast Customs. Dame Edith Sitwell.

"One fantee wave." OBMV

Gold Digger's Song (We're in the Money), The. Harry Warren. ReLy

Gold Glade. Robert Penn Warren. TRP *Fr.* Promises.

Gold Glimmers and Fades. Wen T'ing-yün. CCL1, *tr. by* Glen Baxter

Gold in *Jesus and the Stone* fell, The. Diptych: Jesus and the Stone. Charles Baxter. BBASP

Gold Is the Son of Zeus: Neither Moth nor Worm May Gnaw It. Michael Field. OBMV

Gold Leaf Brandy. Kinoshita Mokutarō. CAoMJL1, *tr. by* Leith Morton

Gold on Oak Leaves. George Oppen. FTOS

Gold on Oak Leaves Said Young. George Oppen. BodElec

Gold or iv'ry's not intended. Horace. OBVE *Fr.* Odes.

Gold said her golden. Gold on Oak Leaves. George Oppen. FTOS

Gold survives the fire that's hot enough. Tony Harrison. EmeKit; HarvBoo; NAMCP V.2 *Fr.* School of Eloquence, The.

Gold tape gently billowing with her breathing. Mars and Venus. Rachel Hadas. GS

Gold that was my hair has turned, The. Marina Ivanovna Tsvetayeva. WPoS

Gold triangle is my enemy, The. Resurrection of the Flesh, The. Juan Felipe Herrera. TouFir

Gold vessels of fine wines. Hard Is the Journey. Li Po. CCL1, *tr. by* Arthur Cooper

Gol-darned Wheel, The. *Unknown.* ArBi

Goldbrown upon the sated flood. Flood. James Joyce. MoBrPo

Golden Age, The. William Browne. NOSC *Fr.* Britannia's Pastorals.

Golden Age, The. Sir Richard Fanshawe. NOSC; OBVE *Fr.* Il Pastor Fido.

Golden Age, The. Artur Miedzyrzecki. PoSu

Golden Age, The. Ovid. NAEL-6v1; NAEL-7v1 *Fr.* Metamorphoses.

Golden Age, The. Torquato Tasso. OBVE *Fr.* Aminta.

Golden Age: Flower-weaving, The. William Browne. NPeEn *Fr.* Britannia's Pastorals.

Golden Age, The. A Paraphrase on a Translation out of French. Torquato Tasso. BASC *Fr.* Aminta.

Golden Altar, The. *Unknown.* SSUS

Golden apples of the sun, The. (LL) Song of Wandering Aengus, The. William Butler Yeats. BLPJKO; ChAP; CtM; IrLP; IrV; MoBrPo; NAMCP V.1; PtR; RaBo; TFi; WaAnP

Golden Bells. Po Chü-i. BLT; CCL1, *tr. by* Arthur Waley

Golden Birch Grove's, The. Sergey Aleksandrovich Yesenin. TCRusP, *tr. by* Nigel Stott

Golden Book of Bovinities, The. Robert John Moore.

"We are nowhere near as calm as we probably appear." Coast

Golden Bough. Elinor Wylie. MoAmPo

Golden Bough: The Feather Palm. Susan Mitchell. ExTi

Golden Calf. Norman Alexander MacCaig. ChIV-1

Golden chrysanthemums just in bloom. Tune: "On the Trail of Sweet Incense." Li Ch'ing-chao. ColAnChi, *tr. by* Jiaosheng Wang

Golden cradle under you, and you young, A. He Meditates on the Life of a Rich Man. Douglas Hyde. OBMV, *tr. by* Augusta, Lady Gregory and Lady Gregory

Golden crocuses. Our Red Wheelbarrow. Larry Goodell. ICANM

Golden crow has risen—where will it go?, The. Western Peak. Master Naong. BecRai, *tr. by* Kim Daljin, Kim Won-Chung and Christopher Merrill

Golden dawn and trembling dusk find our brig lying off the coast opposite that villa and its outbuildings. Promontory. Arthur Rimbaud. SxFrPo, *tr. by* Martin Sorrell

Golden fingers stretching, spreading upwards. Belizean Dawn, A. Corinth Morter-Lewis. OWABP

Golden Fleece, The. Oscar Williams. PoA 2002

Golden Gate, The. Vikram Seth.

"How ugly babies are! How heedless." OBCoV

"Week ago, when I had finished, A." NoP-5

Golden girl / in a golden gown. College Formal: Renaissance Casino. Langston Hughes. APT-2

Golden Grove, The. Sergey Aleksandrovich Yesenin. RusPo, *tr. by* Robert Arthur Douglas Ford and R.A.D. Ford

Golden Grove, Carmarthen. Rowland Watkyns. AngWePo

Golden hinges of the year have turned, The. Parting. Frances Anne Kemble. PoBW

Golden Hours: Calais and the Rhone, July 1790. William Wordsworth. NPBRoP

Golden in July sun, her black hair floating. Midsummer Farewell. Jerry Craven. TiP2

Golden Island, The; or, the Darian Song. *Unknown.* EMWP

Golden Journey to Samarkand, The. James Elroy Flecker.

Prologue: "We Who with Songs Beguile Your Pilgrimage." OBMV; UV

Golden Jubilee of Wilberforce. Mrs. Henry Linden. CBWP-4

Golden light has presently, The. Evening Song. Philipp von Zesen. GePo, *tr. by* George C. Schoolfield

Golden Lotus, The. Diana Brebner.

"We are always surprised that pears survive." IFF

Golden Meadow, The. Kim Sowŏl. CAMKP, *tr. by* David R. McCann

Golden Mean, The. Henry Howard, Earl of Surrey. OBVE

Golden Mile-Stone, The. Henry Wadsworth Longfellow. NCAP

Golden mists o'er Cloudland wreathing. Fancy and Imagination. Henrietta Cordelia Ray. CBWP-3

Golden, New Mexico. Mark Ivey. ICANM

Golden one is gone from the banquets, The. Epigram. "H. D." PoA 2002

Golden Palomino Bites the Clock, The. Sotère Torregian.

"I could smell the river in." AHA

Golden Pheasant. Mating Pair. Golden Pheasant. William Hart-Smith. NOBAu

Golden Road to Barcelona: 1992, The. Martin Fagg. UV

Golden Room, The. Wilfrid Wilson Gibson. VisFro

Golden Sayings. Gérard de Nerval. WoPoe, *tr. by* Richard Sieburth

Golden slumbers kiss[e] your eyes. Golden Slumbers. Thomas Dekker *and others.* NoSic; OxAEP-1; OxBEV *Fr.* Pleasant Comedy of Patient Grissell [*or* Grissel *or* Grissill], The.

Golden spider of the sky, The. Solar Myth. Genevieve Taggard. MoAmPo

Golden State. Frank Bidart. NoAM

Golden sun upon his fiery wheels, The. Michael Drayton. NoSic *Fr.* Idea's Mirrour.

Golden Violet, The. Letitia Elizabeth Landon.

Song. NOBRP; NPBRoP

Song. NOBRP

Golden-Mantled Ground Squirrel. Sandra Alcosser. PfSP

Goldenrod. Mary Oliver. NIL-7

Goldenrod [*or* Golden-rod] is yellow, The. September [Days Are Here]. Helen Hunt Jackson. APN-2

Goldfinger. Leslie Bricusse. ReLy

Goldfish. Sinéad Morrissey. NIrP

Goldfish in the Charles River. Lewis Hyde. UrbNat

Goldfish in the Garden Pond. Valerie Worth. NOxBChV

Goldie Sapiens. P. J. Kavanagh. OBCoV

Goldilocks. Magi Gibson. EdScPo

Goldminers' Waltz, The. Aleksandr Arkadevich Galich. TCRusP, tr. by Gerry Smith

Golem, The. Jorge Luis Borges. PoetW, tr. by John Hollander

Golem and Rabbi. Ana Maria Shúa. tr. by Rhonda Buchanan

  Golem and Rabbi 5. MirDau, tr. by Rhonda Buchanan

  Golem and Rabbi 4. MirDau, tr. by Rhonda Buchanan

  Golem and Rabbi 3. MirDau, tr. by Rhonda Buchanan

Golf Links Lie So Near the Mill, The. Sarah Norcliffe Cleghorn. APT-1; NIP-4

Golfers in the Family. Mónica de la Torre. LegDan

Golgotha. Andrew Lansdown. ChIV-2

Goliardic Song. Anthony Hecht. OBCoV

Goliath and David. Robert Graves. FaBoWar

Goliath Poem. Terrance Hayes. AmPoNex

Golly, How Truth Will Out. Ogden Nash. MoAmPo

Gondibert. Sir William Davenant.

  City Morning, The. NOSC

  Lombard Stag-Hunt, The. DiBP

  Praise and Prayer. OBEV

Gondibert Book 2. Sir William Davenant.

  "There, when they thought they saw in well sought Books." PBRV

Gondoliers, The. William Schwenck Gilbert.

  There Lived a King. OBCoV

Gone. Mary Elizabeth Coleridge. OBEV; PoBW; VWP

Gone. Calvin Forbes. BtF

Gone. Mary E. Tucker. CBWP-1

Gone are my blues. Gold Digger's Song (We're in the Money), The. Harry Warren. ReLy

Gone are the coloured princes, gone echo, gone laughter. Ruin, The. Richard Hughes. OBMV

Gone Are the Days. Norman Alexander MacCaig. CABP

Gone are the drab monosyllabic days. Tilth. Robert Graves. OBSV

Gone are those three, those sisters rare. Three Sisters, The. Arthur Davison Ficke. TCAPo

Gone Are Those We Love. Fadwa Tuqan. CFP, tr. by Kamal Boullata

Gone Before. Christina Georgina Rossetti. PoBW

Gone for some time. Martin Mooney. NIrP

Gone from this bruk-spirit, kiss-me-arse place. (LL) Nigger Sweat. Edward Baugh. EmeKit; WaCA

Gone, Gone Again. Edward Thomas. OxAEP-2; PoWW

  (Blenheim Oranges.) NPeEn

Gone, gone,—sold and gone. Farewell, The. John Greenleaf Whittier. NCAP

Gone, I say and walk from church. Truth the Dead Know, The. Anne Sexton. ColAP; FTtHH; ItP; MoAmPo; NAMCP V.2; NoAM; NoP-4; NoP-5; VCAP

Gone is *Elizabeth*. Short and Sweet Sonnet Made by One of the Maids of Honour, upon the Death of Queen Elizabeth, which She Sewed upon a Sampler, in Red Silke, A. *Unknown*. EMWP

Gone is the romance that was so divine. What'll I Do? Irving Berlin. ReLy

Gone is the sound of my favorite misfortune, which even yesterday. Bakhyt Kenjeev. ItGoST, tr. by Nina Kossman

Gone Ladies. François Villon. WoPoe, tr. by Christopher Logue

Gone now the baby's nurse. Home After Three Months Away. Robert Lowell. PoetW

Gone the three ancient ladies. Frau Bauman, Frau Schmidt, and Frau Schwartze. Theodore Roethke. APT-2; NAMCP V.1; NoAM

Gone to seed, ailanthus, the poverty. Ornithology. Lynda Hull. SeSe

Gone, with all her sparkling beauty. Gone. Mary E. Tucker. CBWP-1

Gone with the Wind. Herb Magidson. ReLy

Goneys an' gullies an' all o' the birds o' the sea. Sea Change. John Masefield. OBMV

Gong Sheng had no life left to him. Last Poem. Hsieh Ling-yün. CCL1, tr. by John Frodsham

Gong sounds, curtain lowers. Farmer's Dance. Shin Kyŏngnim. CAMKP, tr. by David R. McCann

Gong's brown-golden tones no longer loud, A. Dream of Evil (First Version). Georg Trakl. GTCP, tr. by Robert Firmage

Gongula. Jerry McGuire. AnSo

Gongula. (LL) Papyrus. Ezra Pound. APT-1; PFTM-1

Gongyla. Sappho. SaLy, tr. by Diane Rayor

Gonna be so slammin. This Poem. Ruth Forman. SpirFl

Gonna change my life. Anne Waldman. AHA

Gonna find her. Searchin'. Jerry Leiber *and* Michael E. Stoller and Michael E. Stoller. FTtHH

Gonsalves. Ron Welburn. SeSe

Gonzales will always be. Poem for Gonzales, California, The. Morton Marcus. GeoHom

Good advice speaks from unlikely places, so you follow it. Radio Nebraska. Erin Belieu. NAPBL

Good aged Bale, that with thy hoary hairs. To Doctor Bale. Barnabe Googe. NoSic

Good and Bad. James Stephens. MoBrPo

Good and bad and right and wrong. Good and Bad. James Stephens. MoBrPo

Good and Bad are eminent teachers. Seung Sahn. WhBo

Good and bad are in my heart. Twins, The. James Stephens. RaBo

Good and Bad Children. Robert Louis Stevenson. ChAP; OBCoV

Good and Better. *Unknown*. TreFP

Good, and great God, can I not think[e] of thee. To Heaven. Ben Jonson. BASC; ChIV-2; InvLi; NAEL-6v1; NAEL-7v1; NOSC; NPeEn; SacPr; TRP

Good and great God! How should [*or* sho'd] I fear[e]. No Coming to God without Christ. Robert Herrick. SacPr

Good Angel, The. Rafael Alberti. RaW, tr. by John Haines

Good angels snatch'd him eagerly on high. John, Duke of Buckingham and Normandy Sheffield. STuOW *Fr.* Ode on the Death of Mr. Henry Purcell.

Good Appetite [*with music*]. Mark Van Doren. Spl

Good Attitude to Horses, A. Vladimir Vladimirovich Mayakovsky. TCRusP, tr. by P. Lemke

Good bailiff of my farm, that snug domain. Horace. OBVE

Good Catholic girl, she didn't mind the cleaning. Snow White and the Seven Deadly Sins. R. S. Gwynn. SoSe-8

Good Chinese American housewife has a five-year plan, A. Five-Year Plan. Victoria Chang. SweBea

Good Christian men, rejoice. *Unknown*. SacPr, tr. by John Mason Neale

Good Company. William Matthews. BodElec

Good Counsail. Geoffrey Chaucer. TreFP

Good Counsel. *Unknown*. OBWVE, tr. by Glyn Jones

Good Counsel to a Young Maid. Thomas Carew. CavPo

Good creatures, do you love your lives. I Counsel You Beware. A. E. Housman. StAl

Good "D." James McKean. MoASP

Good dame looked from her cottage, The. Leak in the Dike, The. Phoebe Cary. ITBLP

Good Devil, The. Kurt Brown. OPRER

Good Duke Speaks, The. Gilbert Allen. IaFF

Good evening, daddy! Boogie: 1 a.m. Langston Hughes. APSN; APT-2; NAMCP V.1

Good evening, little visitor. To Halley's Comet. Lionel Abrahams. TSAP

Good folk, go gain. God's Gifts. Albrecht von Johannsdorf. GePo, tr. by F. C. Nicholson

Good folk [*or* folke], for gold or hire [*or* hyre]. Crier, The. Michael Drayton. NOSC

"Good folk," said Lizzie. Christina Georgina Rossetti. FaBoVe *Fr.* Goblin Market.

Good for good is only fair. Good Counsel. *Unknown*. OBWVE, tr. by Glyn Jones

Good for Nothin' Joe. Ted Koehler. ReLy

Good for the wind, good for the night, good for the cold. Waltz of the Twenty-Year-Olds, The. Louis Aragon. FaBoWar, tr. by Malcolm Cowley and Rolfe Humphries

Good Fortune, when I hailed her recently. Epigram. James Vincent Cunningham. APT-2; VCAP

Good Friday. Rofel G. Brion. ReBoTo

Good Friday. Lucille Clifton. OxAAAP

Good Friday. João da Cruz e Sousa. TCLAP, tr. by Flavia Vidal

Good Friday. Kathleen Jessie Raine. BBASP

Good Friday ("Am I a stone and not a sheep.") Christina Georgina Rossetti. ChIV-2

Good Friday, Alice Liddell. Nicole Cooley. AFaM

Good Friday: For Lack of an Orchestra. Jack Spicer. APSN

Good Friday: Rex Tragicus, or, Christ Going to His Cross[e]. Robert Herrick. NOSC

Good Friday [*or* Goodfriday], 1613. Riding Westward. John Donne. BASC; BBASP; BrAP; ChIV-2; FSCP; NAEL-6v1; NAEL-7v1; NoP-4; NoP-5; NOSC; PBRV; SacPr; TFi; WaAnP

Good Friday was the day. Martyr, The. Herman Melville. CBCWP; ColAP; NCAP; TCAPo

Good Gifts. Dorothy Nimmo. BeAl

Good Girl. Molly Peacock. FFC

Good glory, give a look at Sporting Beasley. Sporting Beasley. Sterling Allen Brown. APT-2; NAMCP V.1

Good god, make me for thi love and thi desyre. Make Me Loathe Earthly Likings. *Unknown.* SacPr

Good God, What a Night That Was. Petronius Arbiter. PasH, *tr. by* Kenneth Rexroth

Good gray [*or* grey] guardians of art, The. Museum Piece. Richard Wilbur. NIL-7; NIP-4; TRP

Good Grease. Mary Tallmountain. UnSA

Good Grey Poet, The. Theodore Weiss. ViWalt

Good heaven [*or* Heav'n], I thank thee since it was designed. On Myself. Anne Finch, Countess of Winchilsea. NoP-4; NoP-5

Good Hot Dogs. Sandra Cisneros. NOxBChV

Good Hours. Robert Frost. MoW

Good house. Basho. EH, *tr. by* Robert Hass

Good house, and ground whereon, A. Salt Garden, The. Howard Nemerov. OBGa

Good Humor. Allison Joseph. SUP

Good is an orchard, the saint saith. Of an Orchard. Katharine Tynan Hinkson. SacPr

Good, it's hot. Summer. Pascalle Monnier. YaTCFP, *tr. by* Cole Swensen

Good King Matthias, whom we mourn. On The Death of King Matthias. *Unknown.* IQMS, *tr. by* Joseph Leftwich

Good King Wenceslas. *Unknown.* ChrPo; SacPr, *tr. by* John Mason Neale

Good King Wenceslas went out. Children's Rhymes and Parodies. *Unknown.* NOBAu

Good Kosciusko, thy great name alone. To Kosciusko. John Keats. CenSon

Good Langston sat too long to lift me. (LL) Reading Walt Whitman. Calvin Forbes. ESEAA; ViWalt

Good Life, The. Bobby Byrd. TiP2

Good Lord. Good Lord in That Heaven. *Unknown.* WPoS

Good Lord, behold this dreadful[l] enemy. Edward Taylor. NAAL-3 *Fr.* God's Determinations [touching his Elect].

Good Lord, in de manshans above. In the Mansions Above. *Unknown.* SSUS

Good Lord in That Heaven. *Unknown.* WPoS

Good Lord Saved Her, The. Anna Swirszczynska [*or* Swir]. PoSu

Good Loser, The. Sophie Hannah. HarvBoo

Good Luck. Oswald de Andrade. TCLAP, *tr. by* Flavia Vidal

Good Luck. Oliver St. John Gogarty. IrLP

Good Luck and Bad. Heinrich Heine. NBLV, *tr. by* John Hay

Good Luck Gold. Janet S. Wong. NOxBChV

Good luck is the gayest of all gay girls. Good Luck and Bad. Heinrich Heine. NBLV, *tr. by* John Hay

Good madam, when ladies are willing. To a Lady Making Love. Lady Mary Wortley Montagu. LW

Good Man in Hell, The. Edwin Muir. MoBrPo

Good Man Talking to Himself, A. Guiguis Shoukry. AnVo, *tr. by* Mohamed Enani

Good manners may in Seven Words be found. Of Courtesy. Arthur Guiterman. Spl

Good Man's Fate, A. William Loran Smith. LaCa

Good Marriage, A. Giovanna Pollarolo. TANSG, *tr. by* Marjorie Agosin

Good Men. Roberta Spear. GeoHom

Good men and women gone too soon to bed. (LL) Dear Uncle Stranger. Conrad Potter Aiken. ColAP; NoAM

Good Morning. Arthur Freed. ReLy

Good Morning. Carl Rakosi. FTOS

Good morning. . .morning of losses. Morning. Fadhil Assultani. IrPoTo, *tr. by* Raghid Nahhas

Good morning, Algernon: Good morning, Percy. On Mundane Acquaintances. Joseph Hilaire Pierre Belloc. OBCoV

Good Morning America. Frank Lima. PA9/11

Good morning, and How do you do? Ninety-Nine. Elizabeth Godley. NOxBChV

Good Morning Coffee Makes Vivid of the Vague; Suddenly You Have Hands and Eyes and Legs! Peter Sears. NevBe

Good morning, daddy! Dream Boogie. Langston Hughes. APSN; NAMCP V.1; OxAAAP; OxBoAm; PFTM-1; SSLK

Good morning, daddy! Langston Hughes. APSN; APT-2; OxBoAm *Fr.* Lenox Avenue Mural.

Good Morning, Fakhani. Sa'di Yusuf. IrPoTo, *tr. by* Khaled Mattawa

Good morning, fox of the cave. Fox's Counsel, The. Huw Llwyd. OBWVE, *tr. by* Joseph P. Clancy

Good morning, Fräulein! Armgart. "George Eliot."

Good Morning! / Good Morning streets and rifles. Good Morning, Fakhani. Sa'di Yusuf. IrPoTo, *tr. by* Khaled Mattawa

Good morning, Life—and all. Greeting, A. W. H. Davies. MoBrPo

Good morning Pearl; good morning John. Barry MacSweeney. Oth *Fr.* Pearl.

Good morning to the day; and, next, my gold. Ben Jonson. NAEL-7v1; OxBEV *Fr.* Volpone.

Good Morning—Midnight. Emily Dickinson. NALW

Good morrow bids the cock, th' owl bids good night. Of a Husbandman. Joshua Sylvester. NOSC

Good morrow to the day so fair. Mad Maid's Song, The. Robert Herrick. OBEV; RACG

Good morrow to thy sable beak. Blackcock, The [*or* The Black Cock]. Joanna Baillie. WoRP

Good Mr. Peeps or Peps or Pips. Gospel of Mr. Pepys, The. Christopher Darlington Morley. NBLV

Good News/Bad News. Betsy Sholl. PfS

Good news for the town of our birth! Letter to a Brother in Exile. Rosemary Catacalos. TiP2

Good news from the windy city: Thomas Edison's. Muddy Waters and the Chicago Blues. Cornelius Eady. ESEAA

Good news, member, good news, member, / don't you mind what Satan say. Good News, Member. *Unknown.* SSUS

Good Nigger. Leroy V. Quintana. ICANM

Good Night. Eleanor Farjeon. NOxBChV

Good Night. Thomas Hood. Spl

Good Night! Gilbert Sorrentino. FTOS

Good Night. William Carlos Williams. SAmP

Good Night, All You Ships at Sea, You. Jim Behrle. FreRad

Good Night Dear. Oscar Hahn. PML, *tr. by* James Hoggard

Good night Iris / It's time. (LL) Tinfoil. Joyce Mansour. MFP; YaTCFP, *tr. by* Martin Sorrell

Good night Marcus put out the light. To Marcus Aurelius. Zbigniew Herbert. VCWP, *tr. by* Czeslaw Miosz and Peter Dale Scott

Good Night, Star. Michael Earl Craig. IIR

Good Night, Sweetheart. Jimmy Campbell, Reginald Connelly and Ray Noble. ReLy

Good night to the Season—good night! (LL) Good Night to the Season. Winthrop Mackworth Praed. NPeEn; OBCoV; OxBEV

Good night to the Season! 'Tis over! Good Night to the Season. Winthrop Mackworth Praed. NPeEn; OBCoV; OxBEV

Good Night, Willie Lee, I'll See You in the Morning. Alice Walker. InoFa; ISC; WeW-3

Good Nights. Saundra Sharp. SpirFl

Good of the Chaplain to enter Lone Bay. Herman Melville. APN-2; NCAP; WoPoe *Fr.* Billy Budd, Foretopman.

Good Old Days, The. Barbara Fried. NBLV

Good Old Way, The. *Unknown.* SSUS

Good Ole Days, The. Harriet Wilkes Washington. BtF

Good Omen. Lewis Warsh. BodElec

Good people all attend now. Leigh Hunt. NPBRoP *Fr.* St James's Phenomenon, The.

Good people all, of every sort. Oliver Goldsmith. NBLV; OBNV; OxAEP-1; TFi *Fr.* Vicar of Wakefield, The.

Good Places. Reynolds Price.
  Hawk Hill. PoA 2002

Good prince? (Guardian of Flocks.) His bark. Good Princes and Bad. Sir Thomas More. WoPoe, *tr. by* Katherine Washburn

Good prince, what? The dog that keeps, A. Of a Good Prince and an Evil. Timothy Kendall. NoSic

Good Princes and Bad. Sir Thomas More. WoPoe, *tr. by* Katherine Washburn

Good Princes must be pray'd for: for the bad. Duty to Tyrants. Robert Herrick. BASC

Good Rain: A Night in Spring. Tu Fu [*or* Du Fu]. CCL1, *tr. by* Jerome P. Seaton

Good rain knows its season, A. Spring Rain. Tu Fu [*or* Du Fu]. CCL1; WaAnP, *tr. by* Kenneth Rexroth

Good rain knows its season, The. Good Rain: A Night in Spring. Tu Fu [*or* Du Fu]. CCL1, *tr. by* Jerome P. Seaton

Good Resolution, A. Roy Campbell. OBSV

Good Samaritan et Al, The. Stephen Mitchell. GI

Good Scholars Make Bad Husbands. *Unknown.* WoPoe, *tr. by* Nguyen Ngoc Bich

Good Science. Ken Edwards. Oth

Good Sense. César Vallejo. PoetW, *tr. by* Clayton Eshleman

Good Sheep. Heather Ramsdell. IAoNAP

Good Shepherd, The: Atlanta, 1981. Ai. RACG

Good Shepherd, have You skipped away, to leave. At the Ascension. Luís De León. SpanPo, *tr. by* James Edward Tobin

Good Shepherd, The. Richard Baxter. SacPr

Good Shepherd's Sorrow for the Death of His Beloved Son, The. Anne, Duchess of Arundel Howard.
  Elegy on the Death of Her Husband. NOSC; WaAnP

Good Ships. John Crowe Ransom. OxBSo; WeW-3

Good show, A. Atomic Bride. Thomas Sayers Ellis. BAP-97; IIR; LegDan; NeAmPo

Good sign, The. (LL) Jay Wright. ESEAA; TRP *Fr.* Logbook of Judgments.

Good snowman. Winter's End. Dan Pagis. FIT, *tr. by* Robert Friend

Good Son Jim. Russell Edson. SUP

Good speech is rarer than jade. It is rarer. Song of Ptahhotep, The. Robert Bringhurst. GifTon

Good sportsmanship we hail, we sing. Richard Armour. ChAP

Good Sunday. John Lucas. RSaN

Good Taste. Christopher Logue. OBSP

Good Teacher, The. Ray Amorosi. MotU

Good Teachers, The. Carol Ann Duffy. ItWoWo; NAMCP V.2

Good Thief, The. Tom Leonard. EdScPo

Good Thing Is, We Know, The. Antonio Machado Ruiz. SpanPo, *tr. by* William M. Davis

Good things go by so softly, The. Back to it. Larry Eigner. FTOS

Good things, that come of course, far less[e] do[e] please. Casualties. Robert Herrick. BASC

Good Tidings of Great Joy to All People. James F. Montgomery. SacPr

Good Time Charlie. Johnny Burke. ReLy

Good time of the year, The. Bernard [*or* Bernart] de Ventadour *or* Ventadorn. STV

Good Times. Lucille Clifton. FTtHH; HHAm; SoSe-8; TRP

Good times and bum times. I'm Still Here. Stephen Sondheim. ReLy

Good times were drunk times, The. Mardi Gras Premortem. Ann Townsend. NeAmPo

Good Vibrations Sound Studio. Miguel Algarin. PueRic *Fr.* Angelitos Negros: A Salsa Ballet.

Good Water. Patty Seyburn. AmPoNex

Good Will. Sharon Olds. CAP-8

Good Will to Men—Christmas Greetings in Six Languages. Dorothy Brown Thompson. OBCP

Good Woman. Heid E. Erdrich. SweBea

Good Woman of Szechwan, The. Bertolt Brecht.
    Epilogue. ASA, *tr. by* Eric Bentley

Good Woman's home makes up into beds, The. Good Woman. Heid E. Erdrich. SweBea

Good world, A. Issa. EH; ZenPo, *tr. by* Takashi Ikemoto and Lucien Stryk

Good year, / Much wheat much rice. Feng-nian: Good Year. *Unknown.* CCL1, *tr. by* Man Wong

Good Young Squire, The. Edward Edwin Foot. STuOW *Fr.* Jane Hollybrand; or, Virtue Rewarded.

Good, your worship, cast your eyes. Maunding Soldier; or, The Fruits of Warre Is Beggery, The. Martin Parker. FaBoWar

Good-by and Keep Cold. Robert Cooperman. VisFro

Goodby Betty,don't remember me. E. E. Cummings. BrAP

Good-by, my son, good-by. Wayward Son, The. Mrs. Henry Linden. CBWP-4

Good-by now to the streets and the clash of wheels and locking hubs. Teamster's Farewell, A. Carl Sandburg. IllVoic

Good-by, sweetheart, our days of bliss. Parting Lovers, The. Mrs. Henry Linden. CBWP-4

Goodby, you long black sonofabitch, he says. Elvis Goes to the Army. Fleda Brown Jackson. AllShUp

Goodbye: "From now till never, goodbye." Mihai Eminescu. SonAtl, *tr. by* Chris Constantinescu and Phoebe Ravenhall

Good-Bye. Joan Larkin. LaCa; WiU

Goodbye. Alun Lewis. AngWePo; NAEL-6v2; NoP-4; NoP-5; OBWP; PoWW; TCAWP

Goodbye. Adrian Mitchell. OPOU

Good-Bye. *Unknown.* SSUS

Good-bye, brother, good-bye brother, / If I don't see you more. Good-bye, Brother. *Unknown.* SSUS

Goodbye Christ. Langston Hughes. NAAPv.2

Goodbye, Goldeneye. May Swenson. NoP-4; NoP-5

Goodbye. I willgo. Buson. SoOfWa, *tr. by* Sam Hamill

Goodbye in the Shape of a Knot. Bob Hicok. AmAlph

"Goodbye" is not quite true; we'll meet tonight. Letter to My Mother. Suzanne Gardinier. NeAmPo

Goodbye, lady in Bangor, who sent me. Correspondence School Instructor Says Goodbye to His Poetry Students, The. Galway Kinnell. NoAM; NoP-4; NoP-5; PoA 2002

Good-bye, my brudder, goodbye, Hallelujah! Good-Bye. *Unknown.* SSUS

Good-bye, my Fancy! / Farewell dear mate, dear love! Good-Bye, My Fancy! Walt Whitman. NAAL-3; NAAPv.1; SAmP

Good-bye my fancy—(I had a word to say,). Good-Bye My Fancy. Walt Whitman. TCAPo

Goodbye, my friend, goodbye. Esenin's Suicide Note. Sergey Aleksandrovich Yesenin. CAGL, *tr. by* Simon Karlinsky

Good-bye!—no [*or* nay] do not grieve that it is over. Farewell, A. Harriet Monroe. PoA 2002

Good-bye / No use leading with our chins. I Wish You Love (Que Reste-t-il de Nos Amours?). Charles Trenet. ReLy, *tr. by* Albert A. Beach

Good-bye now sergeant sir. Reinforcements [1]. Raymond Queneau. YaTCFP, *tr. by* Keith Waldrop

"Goodbye, O sun," said Cleombrotus of Ambracia. Callimachus. HePo, *tr. by* Barbara Hughes Fowler

Goodbye, old friend, goodbye, goodbye. After Esenin. David St. John. RoV

Goodbye pale cold inconstant. Farewell, a Welcome, A. Lisel Mueller. OtW

Goodbye Party for Miss Pushpa T. S. Nissim Ezekiel. OBCoV

Goodbye, Post Office Square. Fanny Howe. OxBoAm

Goodbye said after a party, after the drive home, A. In Memory of Stevie Smith. Patricia Beer. MoWP

"Good-bye," said the river, "I'm going downstream." Howard Nemerov. WeW-3

Good-Bye Shirts, The. W. S. Merwin. MotU

Good-bye Summer. Jas. Mardis. TiP2

Goodbye to a Spaceman. Ojars Vacietis. SonAtl, *tr. by* Tamara Romanyk and Sharon Strauch

Goodbye to Meng Haoran. Wang Wei. CCL1, *tr. by* H. A. Giles

Goodbye to the Old Friends. Henry Taylor. InGu; LPSFW

Goodbye to the Old Life. Wesley McNair. P180

Goodbye to Tolerance. Denise Levertov. NoAM

Good-bye to Winter, I'll see you next year. Ho Hum. Edward Heyman. ReLy

Good-Bye, Valentine. Leslie Anne McIlroy. AmPoNex

Good-bye—and hail! my Fancy. (LL) Good-Bye, My Fancy! Walt Whitman. NAAL-3; NAAPv.1; SAmP

Goode sire, praye ich thee. I Am of Ireland. *Unknown.* NAEL-6v1; NAEL-7v1; NoP-5

(Gode sire, pray ich thee.) NPeEn; WaAnP

(Gode sire, preye I thee.) OHMEL

Good-for-nothings on a White Corner. Ernesto Lumbreras. RMCMP, *tr. by* Rebecca Seiferle

Goodhousekeeping #17. Safiya Henderson-Holmes. ISC

Goodland. *Unknown.* SonAtl, *tr. by* Vince Akland and Tracey Yuan

Good-morning, fellow-wheelman; here's a warm fraternal hand. Wheelmen's Song. Will M. Carleton. ArBi

Good-morning; good-morning! the General said. General, The. Siegfried Sassoon. FaBoWar; InoFa; NAEL-6v2; NAEL-7v2; NAMCP V.1; NoAM; NoP-4; NoP-5; NPeEn; OBWP; OxBEV; PoAgWa

Good-morning, good-morning! the General said. Siegfried Sassoon. EMP *Fr.* Counter-Attack.

Good-Morrow, The. John Donne. BASC; BrAP; CABP; ClHu; FaBoVe; FSCP; ItP; NAEL-6v1; NAEL-7v1; NAWM-5v1; NIL-7; NoP-4; NoP-5; NOSC; OxAEP-1; OxBEV; SoSe-8; TFi; WaAnP

Goodness and the Salt of the Earth. Thylias Moss. MotU

Goodness is hard on the body. Tout les Matins du Monde. Peter Gizzi. VaPo

Goodnight. James Shirley. NOSC

Goodnight, A. William Carlos Williams. MoAmPo

Goodnight, Achilles. Enrique Lihn. VCWP, *tr. by* Alastair Reid

Goodnight, Goodbye. Meg Kearney. NevBe

Goodnight Irene. *Unknown.* NAAPv.2

Goodnight, Mary. (LL) Tullynoe: Tête-à-Tête in the Parish Priest's Parlour. Paul Durcan. BeAl; ModIr; NPeEn; OBCoV

Goodnight sweet prince. R. G. Vliet. TiP2 *Fr.* Clem Maverick.

Goods produced in the factories of space and time, The. Five Days Remaining, The (75). Khwaja Shams-ad-din Muhammad Hafiz. WED, *tr. by* Robert Bly and Leonard Lewisohn

Goodsonnet. J. D. Smith. IaFF

Goody Blake and Harry Gill. William Wordsworth.
    Odd Case of Mr. Gill. STuOW

Goodyere, I am glad and grateful to report. To Sir Henry Goodyere. Ben Jonson. NOSC

Gooing babies, helpless pygmies. J. W. Scholl. VerBaPo *Fr.* Light-Bearer of Liberty, The.

Goops they lick their fingers, The. Table Manners. Frank Gelett Burgess. CalPo

Goose. Richard Emil Braun. NoAM

Goose Fish, The. Howard Nemerov. HeIP-4; NAMCP V.2; NIL-7; NIP-4; NoAM; NoP-4; NoP-5

Gooseberry's no doubt an oddity, The. Gooseberry Fool. Amy Clampitt. NoAM

Gooseflesh. Janet Fisher. MFPA

Goose-Girl, The. Edith Nesbit. VWP

Goran's Whispers. Nathalie Handal. PoArWo

Gorcheanu: The Three Laments. Aneirin. WoPoe, *tr. by* Desmond O'Grady

Gordian Knot. Constance Quarterman Bridges. OxAAAP

Gorée. Everett Hoagland. GT

Goree. Harriet Jacobs. SpirFl

Goree. Niyi Osundare. HBAPE

Gorée ten miles offshore beckons. Gorée. Everett Hoagland. GT

Gorey at the Biennale. Martin Johnston. BMAP

Gorgeous, and on fire. I have my kingdom. (LL) Homo Will Not Inherit. Mark Doty. AmAlph; HarvBoo; NAMCP V.2; OPRER; WiU

Gorgeous blossoms of that magic tree, The. To a Persian Boy in the Bazaar at Smyrna. Bayard Taylor. CAGL

Gorgeous grew the common walls about me. Impromptu. Mary Elizabeth Coleridge. VWP

Gorgeous Surfaces. Thomas Lux. AmAlph

Gorge's river all empty clarity, rain sweeps in, The. Night Rain at Luster Gap. Yang Wan-li. NDACCP, tr. by David Hinton

Gorgon. Ambrose Bierce. APN-2 Fr. Devil's Dictionary, The.

Gorilla Gorilla. Bruce Dawe. NoAM

Goring and the Death, The. Federico García Lorca. WoPoe Fr. Lament for Ignacio Sanchez Mejias.

Gorrión. Claudio Rodríguez. RaW

Gorse Fires. Michael Longley. NoP-4; NoP-5

Gorselight, yellow, the slopes. Matière de Bretagne. Paul Celan. WoPoe, tr. by Margaret Guillemin and Katherine Washburn

Gorselight, yellow, the slopes. Matière de Bretagne. Paul Celan. VCWP, tr. by Michael Hamburger

Gospel. Andrew Hudgins. UpMys

Gospel. Keith Ratzlaff. ACAMVP

Gospel According to Clairol, The. Rachel Loden. CalPo

Gospel According to How We Throw Stones. Catherine Imbriglio. IAoNAP

Gospel According to One Who Always Needs an Audience. Catherine Imbriglio. IAoNAP

Gospel According to the Middle. Catherine Imbriglio. IAoNAP

Gospel of Labor, The. Henry Van Dyke. SacPr

Gospel of Mr. Pepys, The. Christopher Darlington Morley. NBLV

Gospel Poem #1. David Craig. UpMys

Gospel Poem #2. David Craig. UpMys

Gospel Poem #3. David Craig. UpMys

Gospel train is moving, The. Gospel Train, The. Unknown. GM

Gospel Train, The. Unknown. GM

Gossip. Mrs. Henry Linden. CBWP-4

Gossip. Angela Sorby. AmPoNex

Go-Summer. Mary O'Donoghue. NIrP

Got a Home in That Rock [see also Home in That Rock and I Got a Home in Dat Rock]. Unknown. APN-2

Got a little rhythm, a rhythm, a rhythm. Fascinating Rhythm. Ira Gershwin. ReLy

Got a treasure map and a silver pick. Jump Rope Rhyme of the 49er Daughters. Wayde Compton. IFF

Got married. As March rain stopped. Joy of Love, The. Yi Hyangji. EcSo, tr. by Catherine J. Kim

Got to get / over you, out of here. Add-Water Instant Blues. Robin Morgan. PoA 2002

Got up. Passage, The. Rita Dove. ESEAA

Got up and dressed up. Jack Kerouac. PmAP Fr. Mexico City Blues.

Got up, went to school. Diary. Mary Wilson. Spl

Got your letter. And the crate of dead crows. Are you trying to tell me something? Divorce. Joel Brouwer. LegDan

Gota de rocío, Una. Miguel de Unamuno. RaW Fr. Cancionero Diario Poético 1928–1936.

Gothic flowers bedded themselves. Book of Sharp Silhouettes, The. Molly Bendall. NAPBL

Götterdämmerung. Rita Dove. ExTi

Götterdämmerung on the radio. October Opera for Kate. Angus Calder. EdScPo

Gouge, Adze, Rasp, Hammer. Chris Forhan. P180

Goulburn Island Song Cycle. Unknown.
  "Bird saw the young Burara girls, twisting their strings, making string figures, The." NOBAu
  "Ejaculating into their vaginas—young girls of the western tribes." NOBAu
  "They saw the young girls twisting their strings, Goulburn Island." NOBAu
  "They seize the young girls of the western tribes, with their swaying." NOBAu

Gourd now sprouts its bitter blade, The. Pao-you ku-ye: Bitter Blade. Unknown. CCL1, tr. by Arthur Cooper

Gourmand, The. Harry Graham. UV

Gourmet challenged me to eat, A. Experiment Degustatory. Ogden Nash. ChAP

Gourmet Kitchen means two ovens. Some Terms in Real Estate Defined. Richard Cecil. SUP

Gout. Lewis Warsh. FTOS

Govern a life. (LL) Words. Sylvia Plath. NALW; OxBoAm; VCAP

Government and Binding. Mark Prejsnar. AnSo

Government asks me to "check one", The. Check One. Regie Cabico. ReBoTo; WiU

Government Injunction [Restraining Harlem Cosmetic Co.]. Josephine Miles. OxBoAm

Government-bull yoked to a government-cart!, A. Chancelor's Gravel-Drive, The. Po Chü-i. CCL1; WoPoe, tr. by Arthur Waley

Governor interdicted: poetry is evicted, The. Beating Time. Barbara Kingsolver. TWF

Governor loves to go mapping—round and round, The. Sydney Cove, 1788. Peter Porter. BrAP; NoAM

Governor of Huaiyang, arm and leg to the ruler, The. In a Provincial Capital Sick in Bed. Hsieh T'iao. CCL1, tr. by Burton Watson

Gowk, The. William Soutar. EdScPo

Gowned and veiled for tribal ritual. Cutting the Cake. Virginia Hamilton Adair. AFaM

Goyng towards Spayne. Barnabe Googe. PBRV

Gráfico de la Petenera. Federico García Lorca.
  Seis Cuerdas, Las. RaW

Grab each other. (LL) Love Poem. Linda Pastan. NIL-7; NIP-4

Grab the beast by the horns. Stuart Henson. NewEx

Grab whatever cash he has. Madam to a Young Courtesan, The. Sarangapani. WoPoe, tr. by V. Narayana Rao, A. K. Ramanujan and David Shulman

Grace. Umar Bin Hassan. BRtP

Grace. Imtiaz Dharker. MoWP

Grace. Ralph Waldo Emerson. APN-1; InvLi; NCAP

Grace. Rafael Jesús González. IPoFL

Grace. George Herbert. ChIV-1

Grace. William Heyen. PfSP

Grace. Laura Kasischke. NAPBL

Grace. Adelia Prado. TCLAP, tr. by Marcia Kirinus

Grace. John Wilkinson. VaPo

Grace: "Its hair is a fine weed." C. D. Wright. CAP-8

Grace, A. Donald Hall. LoL

Grace at Kirkudbright [see also A Child's Grace]. Robert Burns. OxBEV

Grace before Meat. Robert David Fitzgerald. NOBAu

Grace for a Child. Robert Herrick. NAEL-6v1; TFi
  (Another Grace for a Child.) NAEL-7v1; NOSC
  (Child's Grace, A.) OBEV; OxAEP-1

Grace for Ice-Cream, A. Allan M. Laing. OBCoV

Grace length, a fresh uncertain sea we branch in. Black Top River Fires / A Corona. Mary Rising-Higgins. ICANM

Grace, Majesty, and the calm bliss of life. Two Worlds. Richard Watson Gilder. GS

Grace of Geldings in Ripe Pastures, The. Maxine W. Kumin. CAP-8

Grace of God and the Meth-Drinker, The. Sydney Goodsir Smith. NePenScot

Grace of old Greece the divine and the greatness of Rome the majestic. Our Tongue. Ferenc Kazinczy. IQMS, tr. by Watson Kirkconnell

Grace of the Way. Francis Thompson.
  "Now of that vision I, bereaven." MoBrPo

Grace of Tullies eloquence doth excell, The. Tony Harrison. NoP-4; NoP-5 Fr. School of Eloquence, The.

Grace That Comes by Violence, The. Anne Carson. WoBe Fr. Truth About God, The.

Grace to be born and live as variously as possible. Ted Berrigan. FTOS; NYP2; PFTM-2 Fr. Sonnets, The.

Grace to Be Said at the Supermarket. Howard Nemerov. SoSe-8

Graceful Divine, A. Edward Edwin Foot. STuOW Fr. Jane Hollybrand; or, Virtue Rewarded.

Graceful error may correct the cave, A. (LL) Mind. Richard Wilbur. OxBoAm; SoSe-8; VCAP

Graceful handsome youth, A. Han-shan (Cold Mountain). ColAnChi, tr. by Red Pine

Gracey Nugent. Turlough Carolan. IrLP; OxBEV, tr. by Austin Clarke

Graciela [with music]. Gary Soto. NAMCP V.2; NoAM

Gracing the tide-warmth, this seagull. Seagull, The. Dafydd ap Gwilym. OBWVE; TCAWP, tr. by Glyn Jones

Gracious Lady / Simple as when I asked your aid before. Prayer to the Virgin of Chartres. Henry Adams. APT-1

Gracious Saviour let me make. Thou Lovest Me. Josephine D. Henderson Heard. CBWP-4

Grackle, The. Ogden Nash. NBLV

Gradation. Charles Bernstein. FTOS

Gradual bud and bloom and seedfall speeded up. July 4th. May Swenson. PoA 2002

Gradual self-effacement of the dead, The. (LL) Song (On Seeing Dead Bodies Floating off the Cape). Alun Lewis. NAEL-6v2; NoP-4; NoP-5; OBWP

Gradually. Stuart Dybek. LiTh

Gradually. Elvira Levy. MirDau, *tr. by* Roberta Gordenstein

Gradually I got to aching so bad. Narrative Poem. Joe Wenderoth. LegDan

Gradually, the water that was dripping stopped. Homecoming. Anthony Caleshu. NIrP

Graduate student visits Einstein in his Princeton study, A. Antlia the Air Pump. Alan Robert Wilson. Coast

Graffiti. Julian Croft. NOBAu

Graffiti. Edward Field. SUP

Graffiti [*with music*]. Alice Archer Sewall James. NBLV

12. Graffiti. Justin Quinn. NIrP *Fr.* Days of the New Republic.

Graffiti. Jane Yolen. SSCS

Graffiti from the Gare Saint-Manqué. Marilyn Hacker. FaoP

Graffito. James Merrill. OxBoAm

Graffito in Meknès. Murilo Mendes. Eno, *tr. by* Chris Daniels

Grafted Bud, The. Mary Weston Fordham. CBWP-2

Grafted Tongue, A. John Montague. PBCIP *Fr.* Rough Field, The.

Grafts easily onto the animal air. (LL) Orpheus. Eurydice. Hermes. Joanna Klink. IAoNAP; LegDan

Grain Burning Far Away. Thomas Lux. AmAlph

Grain by grain, and gaining momentum with a shudder of sand down its flank. Diana Hartog. NLPA *Fr.* Oasis.

Grain elevators have stood empty for years, The. Quaker Oats. Rita Dove. MotU

Grain of Sand. Fanny Carrión de Fierro. TANSG, *tr. by* Sally Cheney Bell

Grain of sand, the beginning of the desert, The. Grain of Sand, The. Maria Luisa Spaziani. NeIt, *tr. by* Beverly Allen

Grain of Sound, The. Robert Morgan. GoPo

Grain of wheat, The. Sign of Your Father, The. Annie Dillard. UpMys

Grain-Barge Wife, The. Wu Chia-chi. ColAnChi, *tr. by* Jonathan Chaves

Grainfield. Ibn 'Iyad. WoPoe, *tr. by* Cola Franzen

Grammar. Tony Hoagland. P180

Grammar and fiction are one. (LL) Emmanuel Hocquard. OnScMo; YaTCFP *Fr.* At Christmas.

Grammar commences with a 5-line curse. Palladas. OBVE, *tr. by* Tony Harrison

Grammar Lesson, The. Steve Kowit. P180

Grammar of cause, The. Kenneth Rexroth. PFTM-1 *Fr.* Prolegomenon to a Theodicy, A.

Grammar of Light, The. Carol Ann Duffy. HarvBoo

Grammar of Waking, A. Tonya Foster. FreRad

Grammarian's Funeral, A. Robert Browning. NAEL-6v2; NAEL-7v2

Grammatic structure first, then phonetic values. On the Decipherment of "Linear B." Alfred Wellington Purdy. BrAP

Grand ancient, Gothic, mark this ample dome. Lake, The; Or, Modern Improvement in Landscape. Anna Seward. OBGa

Grand Army Plaza. June Jordan. ISC

Grand attempt some Amazonian dames, A. On a Fortification at Boston Begun by Women [American edition]. Benjamin Tompson. NOSC

Grand Canyon. Estelle E. Farley. BtF

Grand Canyon. Ken Pobo. RWB

Grand Canyon, The. Jean Garrigue. APT-2

Grand Central by Night. Yosl Grinshpan. Prolet, *tr. by* Amelia Glaser

Grand Central Hotel, The. Roy McFadden. PNI

Grand Central Station, 20 December 1987. Bruce Bawer. RA

Grand Central, with Soldiers, in Early Morning. Howard Nemerov. AmWaPo

Grand conglomerate hills of Araby, The. Bayard Taylor. APN-2 *Fr.* Echo Club, The.

Grand Conversation, The. Paul Muldoon. NAMCP V.2

Grand Diva. Thandiwe Shiphrah. BtF

Grand Entry, The [*with music*]. Gary Snyder. NoAM

Grand Get Together, The. Grace Birabwa Isharaza. CFP

Grand Grand Mother is returning. Judy Grahn. HW

Grand Jason and Steeple Jason, parts. Rockhopper, The. Kimiko Hahn. PrTe

Grand Match, The. Moira O'Neill. IrV

Grand Rapids Cricket Club, The. Julia A. Moore.
"When Mr. Dennis does well play." VerBaPo

Grand rough old Martin Luther. Twins, The. Robert Browning. FaBoVe

Grand Testament. François Villon. *tr. by* Peter Dale
"I love and serve my lady with a will." EroLit, *tr. by* Peter Dale

Grand treat. / A determination favorable for a mare. *Unknown*. ColAnChi *Fr.* I Ching [*or* The Book of Changes *or* The Classic of Changes].

Grand treat. / A favorable determination. *Unknown*. ColAnChi *Fr.* I Ching [*or* The Book of Changes *or* The Classic of Changes].

Grand-Dad, they say you're old and frail. Child to His Sick Grandfather, A. Joanna Baillie. CABP; RACG; WoRP

Granddaddy waited while men with spades. In Fields of Buffalo. Walter McDonald. TiP2

Granddaughter was a guerilla, The. Dream. Maria Arrillaga. TANSG

Granddaughters' bright smiles, chili dogs, and lemonade in the shade start. Baseball. Christopher Stanard. SpirFl

Grandes constructions, face au soleil, le ciel égal, sont visibles de la chambre tout au sommet du paysage, Les. Grandes Constructions, Les. Dora Maar. YaTCFP

Grandest ship-of-war which e'er to sea was known, The. She Is the Greatest Wealth. Georg Rudolph Weckherlin. GePo, *tr. by* George C. Schoolfield

Grandeur of Ghosts. Siegfried Sassoon. MoBrPo; OBMV

Grandeur of the tower was nothing at first, The. Bridge View. Daniel Tobin. NevBe

Grandeurs of his Babylonian heart, The. (LL) Francis Thompson. MoBrPo; OBMV *Fr.* Heart, The.

Grandfather. George Bowering. BrAP

Grandfather. Michael S. Harper. ESEAA; VCAP; WaAnP

Grandfather [*with music*]. Lance Henson. HATNAP, *tr. by* Lance Henson

Grandfather. Derek Mahon. OxBSo

Grandfather. Joseph Stroud. GeoHom

Grandfather / advised me. Poet's Work. Lorine Niedecker. APT-2; HarvBoo; NAAPv.2; NAMCP V.1; OxBoAm; PoCho

Grandfather and Grandmother in Love. David Mura. TRP

Grandfather at the Indian Health Clinic [*with music*]. Elizabeth Cook-Lynn. HATNAP; UnSA

Grandfather dear, young and simple. Morris Winchevsky. Ber Grin. Prolet, *tr. by* Amelia Glaser

Grandfather disappears into a field. The yard is empty. Silent threads of sunlight stream down. I'm a Dragonfly Caught in a Net. Chông Hwajin. EcSo, *tr. by* Julie C. Park

Grandfather, dying in November. Wild Grapes. Jean Janzen. ACAMVP

Grandfather Grandfather. Marlon D. Satchell. InTrad

Grandfather in the Garden. Robert Minhinnick. OBGa

Grandfather / Jabez Harry Bowering. Grandfather. George Bowering. BrAP

Grandfather Poem, A. William J. Harris. EGAG

Grandfather, we come to you now. Yahrzeit. Susan Fromberg Schaeffer. TaR

Grandfather-in-law. David Mura. LoL

Grandfathers, The [*or* After a Line by John Peale Bishop]. Donald Justice. NAMCP V.2

Grandfather's Cap, My. David St. John. MoASP

Grandfather's Clock. Henry Clay Work. ITBLP

Grandfather's Last Letter, A. Norman Dubie. PoChi

Grandfather's Mint. Edward Cortez Garrett. ReBoTo

Grandfather's Rockery. David Woo. OpBo

Grandfather's ten-gallon demijohn, The. Water from the Lamp Bottle. James Applewhite. LPSFW

Grandma. Thandiwe Shiphrah. BtF

Grandma and I used to go. Double Features. Ed Rossman. HHAm

Grandma, come back, I forgot. Morning Baking, The. Carolyn Forché. LoL

Grandma in the Shower. Dale M. Kushner. UnSA

Grandma Jenny never learned. Observance. Barbara Unger. TWW

Grandma lit the stove. History. Gary Soto. PBCAP

Grandma Mariana, washerwoman. Grandma Mariana. Alda do Espirito Santo. HAWP, *tr. by* Julia Kirst

Grandma Talk. Sonya Brooks. InTrad

Grandma's Bureau [*with music*]. Robert Morgan. WeW-3

Grandma's Man [*with music*]. James Welch. NoAM

Grandma's Zoo. Dorothy Molloy. NIrP

Grandmaster cuts faster. Adventures of Grandmaster Flash, The. DJ Renegade. BRtP

Grandmither, Think Not I Forget. Willa Sibert Cather. AmFaPo

Grandmother. Grace Cavalieri. UnSA

Grandmother. Regina DeCormier-Shekejian. TWW

Grandmother. Siv Cedering Fox. PBCAP

Grandmother. Eva Salzman. MFPA

Grandmother, The. Claribel Alegría. TANSG, *tr. by* Darwin Flakoll

Grandmother, The. Victor Hugo. TreFP

Grandmother, a Caribbean Indian, Described by My Father. Yvonne Sapia. NIL-7; UnSA

Grandmother: Crossing Jordan. Melvin Dixon. ESEAA

Grandmother, Dead at 99 Years and 10 Months. William Matthews. PuP-23

Grandmother Eliza. Nora Dauenhauer. FTtHH

Grandmother Emily Dickinson. Dickinson's Blue Sleeve. Yi Sanghûi. EcSo, *tr. by* Jennifer M. Lee

Grandmother had a cure for everything. Curing. Marlynn Rosario. PoCu

Grandmother hoed her garden black and blue. Dirty Thirties, The. Lorna Crozier. IFF

Grandmother Jackson. David Jackson. OBCP

Grandmother Living in Fear of Free Verse. Nina Corwin. VisFro

Grandmother of Russian Poetry: A Self-Portrait, The. Vera Merkureva. ARWW, *tr. by* Catriona Kelly

Grandmother plaited her granddaughter's hair and then she said, The. Butterflies. Patricia Grace. IPoFL

Grandmother Remembers, A. Janet Lewis. IllVoic

Grandmother, the same hot night you died. May Levine. Susan Fromberg Schaeffer. TaR

Grandmother walked over. Grandmother's Sea. Yi Yônju. EcSo, *tr. by* Yung-Hee Kim

Grandmother would sit me. Wrong Kitchen, The. Nikki Giovanni. FuFl

Grandmothers. Adrienne Rich. NAMCP V.2; NoAM

Grandmothers, The. Amy Lingafelter. FreRad

Grandmother's Farm. Mark Todd. GeoH

Grandmothers in Green and Orange. Frank R. Maloney. GifTon

Grandmothers Land. William Oandasan. HATNAP

Grandmother's love. Love Necessitates. Eugene B. Redmond. ISC

Grandmother's Sea. Yi Yônju. EcSo, *tr. by* Yung-Hee Kim

Grandmothers sing their song. Grandmothers' Song. Nellie Wong. FFC; MakPoe

Grandmother's Song. Nellie Wong. FFC; MakPoe

Grandmother's Spit. Andrew Hudgins. CAP-8

Grandmother's Verandah. Sŏ Chŏngju. CAMKP, *tr. by* David R. McCann

Grandmothers who wring the necks. Classic Ballroom Dances. Charles Simic. CAP-8; NAMCP V.2; WaAnP; WeW-3

Grandpa Is Ashamed. Ogden Nash. OBCoV

Grandpa took me along to the hospital. Curtains. David Wagoner. OxBoAm

Grandpapa. Harry Graham. OBCoV

Grandparents. Robert Lowell. ColAP; NAMCP V.2; WaAnP

Grands Seigneurs, Les. Dorothy Molloy. BeAl

Grandson of György Dózsa, The. Endre Ady. IQMS, *tr. by* Sir Maurice Bowra

Grange, The. Stevie Smith. OBCoV

Grania's Song to Diarmuid. *Unknown.* WoPoe, *tr. by* Frank O'Connor

Granite and Cypress. Robinson Jeffers. APT-1

Granite Jaw. Mark Taksa. LiTh

Grannie's Birthday. Eliza Ogilvy. VWP

Granny's here. Her mother's voice was bright. Big Girls. Tracey Herd. MFPA

Granny's House. Phoebe Cary. APN-2

Grant, I thee pray, such heat into mine heart. Prayer, A. Sir Thomas More. InvLi

Grant me a single summer, you lords of all. To the Fates. Friedrich Hölderlin. NAWM-7v2, *tr. by* Christopher Middleton

Grant me good rest tonight, O Lord. Prayer for Sleep, A. Michael Hartnett. BeAl

Grant of death, The. Anna Glazova. CRWP, *tr. by* Max Nemtsov

Grant that no Hobgoblins fright me. Prayer. John Day. Spl

Grant us, O God! great Ruler of the Skies! Translation of "Pax Bello Potior." *Unknown.* NOBRP, *tr. by* Unknown

Granted that what we summon is absurd. T. R. Donald Hall. OxBoAm

Granted, the choir. Salvation. Scott Cairns. UpMys

Granted, we die for good. Table Talk. Wallace Stevens. NoP-4; NoP-5

Grape Wine. Golden Bowls. Take Wine. Li Po. CCL1, *tr. by* Elling O. Eide

Grape wine is beautiful, The. Song of Liang-chou. Wang Han. WaAnP, *tr. by* Arthur Sze

Grapes Making. Léonie Adams. APT-2

Graph. Leroy McLucas. EGAG

Grappa in September. Cesare Pavese. RaBo, *tr. by* William Arrowsmith

Grashopper, The. Abraham Cowley. *See* Grasshopper, The.

Grasmere—a Fragment. Dorothy Wordsworth. *See* Peaceful Our Valley, Fair and Green.

Grasping clouds and standing on the edge of a rock. Pine Bark Bread. Hamhur Kiwha. BecRai, *tr. by* Kim Daljin, Kim Won-Chung and Christopher Merrill

Grass. Byok Namkung. WoPoe, *tr. by* Kevin O'Rourke

Grass. Alfred Corn. WaAnP

Grass. Blaga Dimitrova. CSCBP, *tr. by* Georgi Belev and Lisa Sapinkopf

Grass: "Oh praise the lowly stalk." Vera Pavlova. CRWP, *tr. by* Maura Dooley and Terence Dooley

Grass. Kim Suyŏng. CAMKP, *tr. by* Kevin O'Rourke

Grass. James Merrill. OxBoAm

Grass. Carl Sandburg. AmWaPo; ColAP; FaBoWar; InoFa; MoAmPo; NAAL-5; NAAPv.2; NAMCP V.1; NoAM; NoP-4; NoP-5; OBWP; OxBoAm; PoAgWa; PoPoPo; StAl; TCAPo; TFi; WaAnP

Grass, The. Emily Dickinson. ItP

Grass and the Sin, The. Larissa Szporluk. AmPoNex

Grass below—above the vaulted sky, The. (LL) I Am. John Clare. BBASP; CABP; NAEL-6v2; NAEL-7v2; NoP-4; NoP-5; NPeEn; OxBEV; PoPoPo; TFi; TRP; WoPoe

Grass by the River, The. Pao Chao. CCL1, *tr. by* John Frodsham

Grass by the River-Bank, The. *Unknown.* CCL1,

Grass Crust, The. Christiania Whitehead. NeBl

Grass cut trees need pruning. Maya to Herself and Then to Her Gardener. Reetika Vazirani. NAPBL

Grass Fingers. Angelina Weld Grimké. APT-1; NAAPv.2

Grass grew in vain, The. Bride, The. Vladislav Felitsianovich Khodasevich. TCRusP, *tr. by* Daniel Weissbort

Grass grows wild by Red Bird Bridge. Blacktail Row. Liu Yu Hsi. CrYelRi, *tr. by* Sam Hamill

Grass is rising, The. Tomas Tranströmer. WoBe *Fr.* Haiku.

Grass lies down, The. It fluttered. Grass. Kim Suyŏng. CAMKP, *tr. by* Kevin O'Rourke

Grass manoeuvres under passing swans. Picnic. Kenward Elmslie. FTOS

Grass on the Mountain, The. *Unknown.* APT-1, *tr. by* Mary Austin

Grass people bow, The. To Turn Back. John Haines. TRP

Grass purpled by fallen Judas flowers. In the Spring Garden. Geoffrey Grigson. OBGa

Grass resurrects to mask, to strangle. Distant Fury of Battle, The. Geoffrey Hill. FaBoWar; NoP-4; NoP-5; WaAnP

Grass rustle through dim woods. Lu Lun. CCL1, *tr. by* Man Wong

Grass skirt on the willow is yellow this morning, The. Running Loose around the Castle. Lee McCarthy. IaFF

Grass so little has to do, The. Grass, The. Emily Dickinson. ItP

Grass, summer grass. Grass. Byok Namkung. WoPoe, *tr. by* Kevin O'Rourke

Grass-covered path, The. Abode of the Unplanned Effect. Chia Tao. CSKM, *tr. by* Mike O'Connor

Grasse: The Olive Trees. Richard Wilbur. NoAM

Grassehopper, The. Anacreon. *See* Grasshopper, The.

Grasse-Hopper, The. Richard Lovelace. *See* Grasshopper, The [To My Noble Friend Mr Charles Cotton: Ode].

Grasses and trees. Joy Mountain. Muso Soseki. EaWin, *tr. by* W. S. Merwin

Grasses enclose the old palaces as waning sunlight shifts. Chin-ling Post Station. Wen T'ien-hsiang. ColAnChi, *tr. by* Michael A. Fuller

Grasshopper. Danielle Legros Georges. BRtP

Grasshopper, A. Tropicalia. Margaret Haley. YaYoPo

Grasshopper, The. Anacreon. NOSC; OBVE, *tr. by* Thomas Stanley (Grassehopper, The.) NPeEn

Grasshopper, The. Abraham Cowley. BASC; NOSC; OBVE; OxAEP-1 (Grashopper, The.) NPeEn

Grasshopper, The [To My Noble Friend Mr Charles Cotton: Ode]. Richard Lovelace. BASC; CavPo; NAEL-6v1; NAEL-7v1; NoP-4; NoP-5; NOSC; OBEV; TFi; WaAnP
(Grasse-Hopper, The.) NPeEn; PBRV
(To the Grasshopper.) OxAEP-1

Grasshopper and the Cricket, The. Leigh Hunt. *See* To the Grasshopper and the Cricket.

Grasshopper and the Cricket, The. Olga Sedakova. ItGoST, *tr. by* Catriona Kelly

Grasshopper Is a Burden. D. H. Lawrence. FaBoVe

Grasshopper thrice-happy! who. Grasshopper, The. Anacreon. NOSC; OBVE, *tr. by* Thomas Stanley

Grasshopper, your fairy [*or* tiny] song. Earth. John Hall Wheelock. MoAmPo

Grasshoppers. Roland Mathias. TCAWP

Grasshopper's among some grassy hills, The. (LL) On the Grasshopper and [the] Cricket. John Keats. CenSon; NIL-7; NIP-4; OxAEP-2

Grasshoppers click and whirr. Carnal Knowledge 2. Gwen Harwood. HarvBoo

Grasshoppers on the Bell. László Nagy. IQMS, *tr. by* Júlia Kada and Kenneth McRobbie

Grassy path, The. Written on the Wall at Master Wei Feng's. Pao Hsien. CSKM, *tr. by* Paul Hansen

Grassy Sound. A. R. Ammons. WaAnP

Gratiana Dancing [*or* Dauncing] and [*or* &] Singing. Richard Lovelace. OBEV
(Gratiana Dancing and Singing.) CavPo
(Gratiana dauncing and singing.) PBRV

Grating Parmesan. Barbara Crooker. SweBea

Gratitude. Louise Glück. OxBoAm; TRP

Gratitude. György Petri. VCWP, *tr. by* Geroge Gömöri and Clive Wilmer

Gratitude for gifts. Issa. SoOfWa, *tr. by* Sam Hamill

Gratitude to Mother Earth, sailing through night and day. Prayer for the Great Family. Gary Snyder. WeW-3

Gratitude to Old Teachers. Robert Bly. P180

Gratulatory to Mr. Ben Johnson for His Adopting of Him to Be His Son, A. Thomas Randolph. NPeEn

Grauballe Man, The. Seamus Heaney. BrAP; NAMCP V.2; OxBEV; PoetW

Grave, A. Marianne Moore. APT-1; HeIP-4; NAAPv.2; NAMCP V.1; NoAM; NoP-4; NoP-5; TFi; TRP; WeW-3

Grave, The. Robert Blair.
  All Impelled Onward Alike. OxAEP-1
  Grave-yard on a Stormy Night, The. OxAEP-1
  "Oft in the lone church-yard at night I've seen." OxAEP-1
  Peace the End of the Good Man. OxAEP-1

Grave, The. Unknown. TCAPo Fr. From the Anglo-Saxon.

Grave Bird, that sheltered in thy lonely bower. To the Owl. Thomas Russell. CenSon

Grave charge in Mayfair bathroom case. Headline History. William Plomer. OBCoV

Grave Doubts. Patricia Beer. NoP-4

Grave in Hollywood Cemetery, Richmond, A. Margaret Junkin Preston. CBCWP; PCW

Grave of a Poetess, The. Felicia Dorothea Hemans. NPBRoP; RWP; VWP

Grave of Little Su, The. Li Ho. WoPoe, tr. by A. C. Graham

Grave of Love, The. Thomas Love Peacock. OxAEP-2

Grave of my firstlove murdered by my brother, The. (LL) Ireland 1972. Paul Durcan. PBCIP; PoAgWa

Grave of Rury, The. Thomas William Hazen Rolleston. IrV

Grave the bard underground overseas, hand. Hedd Wyn. R. Williams Parry. BBMWP, tr. by Joseph P. Clancy

Grave Wedding of Lu Chong. Gan Bao. CCL1, tr. by Kenneth DeWoskin

Gravel rattles against the fenders of the van. Once on a Night in the Delta: A Report From Hell. Etheridge Knight. BodElec

Gravelly Run. A. R. Ammons. EMP; LPSFW; NAMCP V.2; NoAM; PoA 2002; PoDa; VCAP

Gravely. (LL) Have You Anything to Say in Your Defense? César Vallejo. PoetW; RaBo, tr. by James Wright

Graves, The. Lorine Niedecker. APT-2

Graves at Elkhorn. Richard Hugo. VCAP

Graves by the Sea, The. Paul Valéry. WoPoe, tr. by John Finlay

Graves grow deeper, The. Dead, The. Mark Strand. HeIP-4

Graves of a Household, The. Felicia Dorothea Hemans. NOBRP; NPBRoP; RWP; TreFP

Graves the rain makes wet and sleek, The. Unknown. OBWVE Fr. Stanzas of the Graves, The.

Graveside Memorial. Shin Kyŏngnim. CAMKP, tr. by Anthony, Brother of Taizé

Gravestone, August 8, 1968, A. Paul Goodman. BodElec

Gravestone upon the Floor in the Cloisters of Worcester Cathedral, A. William Wordsworth. SacPr

Graveyard, The. Unknown. SSUS

Graveyard by the Sea, The. Paul Valéry. STV, tr. by John Frederick Nims

Graveyard crows. Tune: "Unbroken." Chang K'o-chiu. ChinPo, tr. by Ye Weilian [or Yeh Wei-lien or Wai-lim Yip]

Grave-yard on a Stormy Night, The. Robert Blair. OxAEP-1 Fr. Grave, The.

Graveyard Song. Ts'ao Ts'ao. CCL1, tr. by John Frodsham

Gravity. Kim Addonizio. RoV

Gravity and Grace. Claudia Keelan. BodElec

Gravity, Death. Agi Mishol. DTA, tr. by Tsipi Keller

Gravity is one of the oldest tricks in the book. Defying Gravity. Roger McGough. EmeKit

Gravy. Raymond Carver. BeAl; LaCa

Gravy Train, The. R. R. Davidson. NOBAu

Gray are the pages of record. Black Samson of Brandywine. Paul Laurence Dunbar. AmWaPo

Gray autumn sky. Stanford M. Forrester. AmZen

Gray bark of the street. (LL) Street, The. Robert Pinsky. NAAL-5; NoP-4; NoP-5

Gray brick, ash, hand-bent railings, steps so big. Cumberland Station. Dave Jeddie Smith. LPSFW

Gray Day in January in La Jolla. Quincy Troupe. OxAAAP; PrTe

Gray despair. Old Mare, The. Elizabeth Jane Coatsworth. MoAmPo

Gray Folk, The. Edith Nesbit. PEW

Gray fox, female, nine pounds three ounces, A. One Should Not Talk to a Skilled Hunter about What Is Forbidden by the Buddha. Gary Snyder. CAP-8

Gray Fox, The. Gregory Orr. PfSP

Gray hairs being plucked. Basho. SoOfWa, tr. by Sam Hamill

Gray hairs, unwelcome monitors, begin. Dial, The. Thomas Cole. APN-1

Gray heron flies past, A. Splitting Wood Near Morris, Oklahoma on Robbie and Lesa McMurtry's Farm. Lance Henson. HATNAP

Gray Heron, The. Galway Kinnell. OWoS

Gray man comes down the foggy street, A. Remorse Dressed Up as Night. Luis Cernuda. RaW, tr. by Timothy Baland

Gray Poem. Peter Everwine. GeoHom

Gray rainwater lay on the grass in the late afternoon. Wednesday. Marvin Bell. VCAP

Gray She-Wolf, The. Unknown. WoPoe, tr. by W. S. Merwin

Gray skies are gonna clear up. Put on a Happy Face. Lee Adams. ReLy

Gray sky, mist, the trees black and wet. November Woods. S. J. Marks. BodElec

Gray smoke rose from the morning ground. Actual Vision of Morning's Extrusion. Alan Dugan. YaYoPo

Gray Squirrel, The. Humbert Wolfe. MoBrPo

Gray Stones and Gray Pigeons. Wallace Stevens. SAmP

Gray suit. Wrong Color. Christopher Stanard. SpirFl

Gray swept the angry waves. How the Cumberland Went Down. Silas Weir Mitchell. PCW

Gray thunder. First Rain. Ward Abbott. ICANM

Gray tide flows and flounders in the rocks, The. At Sainte-Marguerite. Trumbull Stickney. APN-2; TCAPo

Gray Waves. Leopoldo Lugones. TCLAP, tr. by Julie Schumacher

Gray whale / Now that we are sending you to The End. For a Coming Extinction. W. S. Merwin. EMP; GifTon; NAMCP V.2; PoPoPo; VCAP

Gray Woods Exploding, The. Earle Birney. NoAM

Gray-blue shadows lift. Starlight Scope Myopia. Yusef Komunyakaa. AF; AmAlph; AmWaPo; MakPoe; NAMCP V.2; RoV

Gray-haired man, The. Allen Ginsberg. WhBo

Graying chest hair emerging from his apron-top in tufts. First Light. Jim Powell. ASA

Graying poet of Camden, The. Whitman in a Corner. Paul Hoover. ViWalt

Graze on, my sheep; and let your souls defy. Eclogue 8. Francis Quarles. BASC

Grazing. Chiyojo. WPoS

Grazing. Ira Sadoff. BodElec

Greasy and grimy at day's end, the plumbers sat. Sodomy. Orlando Ricardo Menes. PML

Great all-seeing burning eye of day, The. Libra, September. John Taylor. NOSC

Great Amazon of God behold your bread. For Mary McLeod Bethune. Margaret Abigail Walker. OxAAAP

Great and bounteous Benefactor. Christopher Smart. ChIV-2 Fr. Hymns and Spiritual Songs for the Fasts and Festivals of the Church of England.

Great and glorious thing it is, A. Arithmetic on the Frontier. Rudyard Kipling. OBWP

Great are the fallen of Thermopylae. Greek Dead at Thermopylae, The. Simonides. FaBoWar, tr. by T. F. Higham

Great are the Hittites. Concerning My Neighbors, the Hittites. Charles Simic. VCAP

Great are the myths. . . .I too delight in them. Walt Whitman. APN-1 Fr. Leaves of Grass [1855 Version].

Great Artist Reconsiders the Homeric Simile, The. John Tranter. BMAP; NoAM; NOBAu

Great Bassist, The. Lawson Fusao Inada. OpBo

Great Bear, The. John Hollander. ColAP; NoAM

Great Bear, come down, shaggy night. Invocation of the Great Bear. Ingeborg Bachmann. VCWP, tr. by Mark Anderson

Great Big Bunch of You, A. Mort Dixon. ReLy

Great big houses with great big rooms. Little Things in Life, The. Irving Berlin. ReLy

Great Bird, The. Li Po. CrYelRi, tr. by Sam Hamill

Great blue ceremony of the air, The. Mary and the Bramble. Lascelles Abercrombie. OBMV

Great Blue Heron. Del Marie Rogers. TiP2

Great Blue Heron, The. Carolyn Kizer. InoFa; InvLad; WaAnP

Great blue mountain! Ghost. Mount Kearsarge. Donald Hall. LoL

Great Breath, The. George Russell. MoBrPo; OBEV; OBMV

Great Britain Through the Ice: Or, Premature Patriotism. Charles Tennyson Turner. OxBSo

Great Canzon, The. Dante Alighieri. ItP, tr. by Kenneth Rexroth

Great captain if you will! great Duke! great Slave! Wellington. Charles Harpur. NOBAu

Great citadels whereon the gold sun falls. John Berryman. WaAnP Fr. Sonnets to Chris.

Great city fell asleep, The. What Her Friend Said. Kollan Alici. WoPoe, tr. by A. K. Ramanujan

Great city has a hundred million rooms so any combination, The. Day at a Time. Michael Dransfield. BMAP

Great Cloak, The. John Montague.

Anchor.

Point, The. PNI

Same Gesture, The. ModIr; PNI

Separation.

Herbert Street Revisited. ModIr; PBCIP; PNI

Refrain. IrLP

Great Dancer there was, A. Ballad on Seeing a Pupil of the Lady Gongsun Dance the Sword Mime. Tu Fu [*or* Du Fu]. CCL1, *tr. by* Arthur Cooper

Great dark rush of mothering, The. Diana Brandt. ACAMVP

Great, dark skirts moving across Bering bridge. Muskoxen. Jeanette Lynes. Coast

Great Day. Edward Eliscu and Billy Rose. ReLy

Great death has made all his for evermore. (LL) Sonnet, A: "When you see millions of the mouthless dead." Charles Hamilton Sorley. EdScPo; FaBoWar; NPeEn; OBWP; OxBSo; PoAgWa; PoWW

Great desert, let your sweetness wake. (LL) Dowser, The. Edwin Morgan. NoP-4; NoP-5; NPeEn

Great Digest of Confucius, The. Ezra Pound. GifTon

Great Digest, The. Confucius. PFTM-1 *Fr.* Great Digest, The.

Great Doubters of History, The. Stephen Dobyns.

"Woman who kicked out the back window, The." BodElec

Great enimy to it, and to all the rest. Edmund Spenser. OxBEV *Fr.* Faerie Queene, The.

Great events are about to happen. Day of Foreboding. Stanley Kunitz. NAMCP V.1

Great Expectations. Charles Dickens.

Joe Gargery's Epitaph on His Father. FaBoVe

Great Father Eating His Children, The. Hesiod. RaBo *Fr.* Theogony.

Great Favorit Beheaded, A. *See* Fall, The.

Great Fetishes, The. Blaise Cendrars. PFTM-1

Great Figure, The. William Carlos Williams. HeIP-4; NAAPv.2; NAMCP V.1; NoAM; SAmP

Great Fires, The. Jack Gilbert. BeAl

Great folks are of a finer mould. Epigram on Scolding, An. Jonathan Swift. FaBoVe; NPeEn

Great Foreign Writer Visits Age-Old Temple, Greeted by Venerable Abbess, 1955. Anthony Thwaite. OBCoV

Great geometrical winter constellations, The. Requiem for the Spanish Dead. Kenneth Rexroth. CalPo

Great Giver has ended His disposing, The. Day of Atonement. Charles Reznikoff. ChIV-1

Great Glasshouse at the National Botanic Garden of Wales. Tudur Dylan Jones. BBMWP, *tr. by* Elin ap Hywel

Great God accept our gratitude. Doxology. Josephine D. Henderson Heard. CBWP-4

Great God of the exiled! *Unknown.* SLW, *tr. by* Marjolijn De Jager, Sayd Bahodin Majrouh and André Velter

Great Grandame Wales, from whom those ancestors. John Davies of Hereford. AngWePo *Fr.* Cambria.

Great Grandame Wales from whom those Ancestors. Cambria. John Davies of Hereford.

Great Grandfathers. Jane Duran. MoWP

Great grandmother / was a guinea woman. Guinea Woman. Lorna Goodison. NAMCP V.2

Great grandson of the old chief, The. He Told Me His Name Was Sitting Bull. Joy Harjo. WaAnP

Great hand King Wu. *Unknown.* NDACCP, *tr. by* Ezra Pound

Great Helmsman, The. David Woo. OpBo

Great Horse Fair, The. Desmond O'Grady. PBCIP

Great horse running in the fields. Horse. Gloria Anzaldúa. UnSA

Great horses of Yilderin, The. Horses of Yilderin, The. Kenneth Patchen. APT-2

Great humility fills me. Thank You, My Fate. Anna Swirszczynska [*or* Swir]. BLT

Great Hunger, The. Patrick Kavanagh.

1. EMP; ModIr; NAMCP V.1; NoAM; NoP-4; NoP-5; NPeEn

"Cards are shuffled and the deck, The." NPeEn

"Fields were bleached white, The." NPeEn

"Poor Paddy Maguire, a fourteen-hour day." ModIr; NPeEn

"We may come out into the October reality, Imagination." ModIr

Great Indian Father in the Subway. Diane Glancy. FiBr

Great Industrial Centre, A. Edith Nesbit. VWP

Great Infirmities. Charles Simic. ChAP

Great is my envy of you, earth, in your greed. Petrarch. NAWM-5v1 *Fr.* Sonnets to Laura.

Great is the sun, and wide [*or* wise] he goes. Summer Sun. Robert Louis Stevenson. MoBrPo

Great Is Thy Faithfulness. Thomas O. Chisholm. SacPr

"Great is thy faithfulness," O God my Father. Great Is Thy Faithfulness. Thomas O. Chisholm. SacPr

Great It May Be. Ceraman Kottampalattut. WoPoe, *tr. by* George L. Hart III

Great joy be to the sailor if he chart. Heureux Qui, Comme Ulysse, A Fait un Beau Voyage. Joachim Du Bellay. WoPoe, *tr. by* Anthony Hecht

Great labor was always to efface oneself, The. Lives of Alchemists, The. Charles Simic. KGB

Great Lament of My Obscurity Three, The. Tristan Tzara. PFTM-1

Great land and a wide land was the east land, A. *Unknown.* OBVE; TCAPo *Fr.* Walam Olum; or, Red Score [of the Lenâpé], The [*or* The Wallam Olum; The Red Score or Painted History of the Lenni Lenape].

Great learned lady, whom I long have known. To the Lady Arabella. Emilia Lanier. NOSC

Great learning (adult study, grinding corn in the head's mortar to fit), The. Great Digest of Confucius, The. Ezra Pound. GifTon

Great legend of the railways and reservoirs, the weariness of carriage, The. André Breton. PFTM-1 *Fr.* Magnetic Fields, The.

Great light cage has broken up in the air, The. Elizabeth Bishop. OxBoAm *Fr.* Four Poems.

Great light of compassion, The. Gate of Universal Light, The. Muso Soseki. EaWin, *tr. by* W. S. Merwin

Great Little One. John Fitzgerald. BBMWP, *tr. by* Joseph P. Clancy

Great lords, wise men ne'er sit and wail their loss. William Shakespeare. FaBoWar *Fr.* King Henry VI, Pt. III.

Great Love Duets. Lorenzo Thomas. AHA

Great Lover, The. Rupert Brooke. MoBrPo

Great machete blow of red pleasure right in the face there was blood, The. Miraculous Weapons, The. Aimé Césaire. PFTM-1

Great Masturbator, The. Salvador Dali. PFTM-1

Great men have been among us; hands that penned. William Wordsworth. OBEV

Great men want the four seas. I've only. T'ao Ch'ien. WoPoe, *tr. by* David Hinton

Great Moments. Gabriel Celaya. RaW, *tr. by* Robert Mezey

Great Monarch, whose feared hands the thunder fling. Paraphrase Upon Part of the CXXXIX Psalm, A. Thomas Stanley. ChIV-1

Great moon, white-westering past our battlement. Robert Penn Warren. *Fr.* Promises.

Great Mullen. William Carlos Williams. OxBoAm

Great Mutando, The. Deryn Rees-Jones. TCAWP

Great New York bridges reflect its faces, The. New York Face, A. Edwin Denby. APT-2

Great Northern. Dave Etter. GM

Great Odor of Summer, The. Nathaniel Tarn. ICANM

Great or small, you furnish your parts toward the soul. (LL) Crossing Brooklyn Ferry. Walt Whitman. APN-1; ColAP; FaBoA; NAAL-3; NAAL-5; NAMCP V.1; NCAP; NoAM; NoP-4; NoP-5; OxBoAm; WaAnP

Great Overdog, The. Canis Major. Robert Frost. MoAmPo

Great Pacific railway, The. Railroad Cars Are Coming, The. *Unknown.* HHAm

Great Painter! to thy soul aglow with thought. Raphael. Henrietta Cordelia Ray. CBWP-3

Great Palaces of Versailles, The. Rita Dove. ESEAA; NAMCP V.2; NoAM

Great Pan is not dead. Different History, A. Sujata Bhatt. HarvBoo

Great Pat Smith American Dreampoem, The. Patricia Smith. ICANM

Great Piece of Turf, The. Rita Dove. PfSP

Great pleasure of laziness . . . as it slides. Hibernation. Maurizio Cucchi. ItPo, *tr. by* Gayle Ridinger

Great Poll-Tax Victory of '88, The. Noel Petty. UV

Great Prayer. Alfonso Cortes. TCLAP, *tr. by* Thomas Merton

Great princes have great playthings. Some have played. William Cowper. FaBoWar *Fr.* Task, The.

Great pulsation passed. Glass lay around me, The. Rejoice in the Abyss. Stephen Spender. AF

Great Sadness, The. Federico García Lorca. PFTM-1 *Fr.* Night (Suite for Piano and Poet's Voice).

Great sage came to the vile West, The. Satori in Fauldhouse. Colin Will. EdScPo

Great sea, The. Shaman Song. Uvavnuk. WoPoe, *tr. by* Jane Hirshfield

Great sea, The. Uvavnuk. WPoS

Great Sir, having just had the good luck to catch. Copy of an Intercepted Despatch from His Excellency Don Strepitoso Diabolo. Thomas Moore. OBSV

Great sleeves of air, The. Between. Ágnes Nemes Nagy. VCWP, *tr. by* Hugh Maxton

Great Society, The. Robert Bly. NAMCP V.2; NoAM

Great South Land, The. Rex Ingamells.

"Cook admired the native courage, made." NOBAu

Great Spirit's lodge—you have heard of it. I will enter it, The.   Meda Songs.   *Unknown.*   APN-2, *tr. by* Henry Rowe Schoolcraft

Great spirits now on earth are sojourning.   Great Spirits Now on Earth.   John Keats.   CenSon

Great Spotted Woodpecker, The.   Gordon Meade.   EdScPo

Great Springtime.   Ko Ŭn.   CAMKP, *tr. by* Anthony, Brother of Taizé

Great stasis.   Norman Fischer.   WANABP *Fr.* Success.

Great stone hearth has gone, The.   Fire.   Dorothy, Duchess of Wellington Wellesley.   OBMV

Great stone, The / Above the river.   George Oppen.   NAMCP V.1 *Fr.* Of Being Numerous.

Great Stories of the Chair.   Ted Berrigan.   AHA

Great Storm, The.   Larry D. Thomas.   TiP2

Great Streets of silence led away.   Emily Dickinson.   APN-2

Great, the charming Strephon is no more, The. (LL)   On the Death of the Late Earl of Rochester.   Aphra Behn.   BASC; EMWP; NoP-4; NoP-5; WaAnP

Great thing is a refuge for itself, A.   Fifth Stanzas. De Arte Poetica.   Olga Sedakova.   ARWW; ItGoST, *tr. by* Catriona Kelly

Great thing, The / is not having.   Red Poppy, The.   Louise Glück.   MoWP; OxBoAm; PtR

Great Things Have Happened [*with music*].   Alden Nowlan.   BeAl

Great tiger, The.   Folk Tune.   Esther Raab.   FIT, *tr. by* Robert Friend and Shimon Sandbank

Great Time, A.   W. H. Davies.   MoBrPo

Great trouble and vexation.   Necessitie and Benefit of Affliction, The.   Anne Lok.   EMWP

Great Unaffected Vampires and the Moon.   Stevie Smith.   NoAM

Great Uncle Joe.   Apology.   Duane Niatum.   HATNAP

Great Unrestrained Sadist, The.   Hans Arp.   PFTM-1

Great uttering of the city is hushed, The.   City Evening.   Frederick van Eeden.   SonAtl, *tr. by* Gary and Francina VanderLinden

Great Void, vast and wide, that knows no boundary, The.   Wandering on Mount Tiantai.   Sun Ch'o.   CCL1, *tr. by* Burton Watson

Great Wagon, A.   Jelaluddin Rumi.   ErotSp, *tr. by* Coleman Barks

Great War, The.   Vernon Scannell.   OBWP

Great War Dance, The.   *Unknown.*   WoPoe, *tr. by* Constance A. Cook

Great Wave, The.   Sŏ Chŏngju.   CAMKP, *tr. by* David R. McCann

Great Waves Breaking with a Roar.   Gustavo Adolfo Bécquer.   SpanPo, *tr. by* John Haines

Great Way—simple as it is, The.   Speaking My Mind.   Chung-ch'ang T'ung.   CCL1, *tr. by* Burton Watson

Great Western Days.   Thomas Baker.   STuOW *Fr.* Steam Engine; or, The Power of the Flame, The.

Great white lilies in the grass, The.   Pallor.   Agnes Mary Frances Robinson.   VWP

Great White Shark, The.   Arthur Sze.   GifTon

Great whorl-centered sun, The.   Helianthus.   Constance Carrier.   APT-2

Great wind arises—billowing clouds fly, A.   Song of the Great Wind.   Liu Pang.   ColAnChi, *tr. by* Victor H. Mair

Great wind came forth, A.   Song of the Great Wind.   Liu Pang.   CCL1, *tr. by* Burton Watson

Great with Child.   Judith Arcana.   FiBr

Great Women Composers, The.   Gavin Ewart.   OBCoV

Great Zeus was reared in Krete and no one.   Moiro.   SaLy, *tr. by* Diane Rayor

Great-aunts have a corner, and wrinkled skin, The.   Language of Great-Aunts, The.   Alberto A. Ríos.   UnSA

Greater cats with golden eyes, The.   Greater Cats, The.   Victoria Mary Sackville-West.   OBMV; Spl

Greater cities are, The.   Poem.   Víctor Hernández Cruz.   PueRic

Greater Courage.   Natan Zach.   PoSu, *tr. by* Peter Everwine and Shulamit Yasny-Starkman

Greater Love.   Wilfred Owen.   MoBrPo; NAMCP V.1; NoAM; TFi

Greater than the readiness for sacrifice.   On the Readiness for Sacrifice.   Reuven ben Yoseph.   NRoS, *tr. by* Esther Raizen

Greater was our gain, our losse the more, The. (LL)   Anne Bradstreet.   OxBEV; TCAPo *Fr.* In Honour of that High and Mighty Princess Queen Elizabeth of Happy Memory.

Greatest bliss, The.   Kiss, The.   Charlotte Dacre.   CABP; NOBRP; WaAnP

Greatest delight, I sense, The.   Betrayal.   Adam Zagajewski.   VCWP, *tr. by* Renata Gorczynski

Greatest living poet, The.   Traffic Misdirector.   Pedro Juan Pietri.   PueRic

Greatest love?, The.   Like This (2).   Stevie Smith.   PtR

Greatest Love, The.   Anna Swirszczynska [*or* Swir].   PoSu

Greatest of all forms of wealth.   Tiruvalluvar.   WoPoe *Fr.* Kural, The.

Greatest self-made man in the world today, The.   Our Noble Booker T. Washington.   Mrs. Henry Linden.   CBWP-4

Great-grandfather Fray was a white man.   Gordian Knot.   Constance Quarterman Bridges.   OxAAAP

Greatgrandma's bending to pluck some vegetable.   Recipe.   Albert Goldbarth.   RWB

Great-grandmother who bears down on us, as if beholding the mote.   Ancestor, The.   Paul Muldoon.   GPPA

Greatly shining / The autumn moon floats in the thin sky.   Wind and Silver.   Amy Lowell.   HeIP-4; MoAmPo; Spl; TCAPo

Greatness in Little.   Richard Leigh.   NOSC

Great-Sledmakers, The.   Kenneth Patchen.   MotU

Grecian soldiers, tired with ten years' war.   Christopher Marlowe.   FaBoWar *Fr.* Dido, Queen of Carthage.

Greece.   Gunnar Ekelof.   BLT

Greed.   Giuseppe Gioacchino Belli.   WoPoe, *tr. by* Anthony Burgess

Greed.   Bernice Reagon.   FuFl

Greed and Aggression.   Sharon Olds.   RaBo

Greedy the people, The.   E. E. Cummings.   SoSe-8

Greek Architecture.   Herman Melville.   NoP-4

Greek Compliment, A.   Oppian of Apamea [*or* Pella].   DiBP *Fr.* Cynegetica.

Greek Dead at Thermopylae, The.   Simonides.   FaBoWar, *tr. by* T. F. Higham

Greek Epigram.   Ezra Pound.   MoAmPo

Greek Epigrams.   Angelo Poliziano.   *tr. by* James J. Wilhelm
   Love Song for Chrysokomos (Goldenlocks).   CAGL, *tr. by* James J. Wilhelm
   On the Love of Two Boys.   CAGL, *tr. by* James J. Wilhelm
   To Giovan Battista Buoninsegni.   CAGL, *tr. by* James J. Wilhelm

Greek Girl at Riis Beach, A.   Frank O'Hara.   BodElec

Greek History.   Olga Nolla.   TANSG, *tr. by* Paula Vega

Greek Metamorphosis.   Belkis Cuza Malé.   TANSG, *tr. by* Pamela Carmell

Greek schemers seek egress *en ténèbres*, then enter the melee.   Christian Bök.   IFF *Fr.* Chapter E.

"Greek Tragedy" of course is the sort of thing.   Robert Pinsky.   NoAM *Fr.* Essay on Psychiatrists.

Greeks Like Clouds, The.   Homer.   OBVE *Fr.* Iliad, The.

Greeks said: Never to be born is best, The.   Best.   Gregory Orr.   PoDa

Green: "Green silence softly."   Jeannette Armstrong.   OpeFie

Green ("Take this fruit, these flowers, these branches and leaves.")   Paul Verlaine.   SxFrPo, *tr. by* Martin Sorrell

Green.   Amy Clampitt.   PfSP

Green.   D. H. Lawrence.   HarvBoo; MoBrPo

Green.   Paul Verlaine.   WoPoe, *tr. by* Yvor Winters

Green and Gold.   Ani Ilkov.   CSCBP, *tr. by* Georgi Belev and Lisa Sapinkopf

Green and Red, Verde y Rojo.   Martín Espada.   PueRic

Green and silent spot, amid the hills, A.   Fears in Solitude [Written in April, 1798, during the Alarm of an Invasion].   Samuel Taylor Coleridge.   OBWP

Green arbor that I once knew, A.   Green Arbor, A.   Linda Beatrice Brown.   GT

Green arch of the bridge says sleep, The.   Sleep.   Jane Holland.   NeBl

Green arsenic smeared on an egg-white cloth.   L'Art, 1910.   Ezra Pound.   HeIP-4; TCAPo

Green as an afterthought. (LL)   Weathering Out.   Rita Dove.   AmAlph; CFP; ESEAA; NAMCP V.2; NoAM

Green as that summer fly.   Silk Robe.   Jeffrey Skinner.   PBCAP

Green Automobile, The.   Allen Ginsberg.   BB

Green Baize Couplets.   Conor O'Callaghan.   NIrP

Green be the turf above thee.   On the Death of Joseph Rodman Drake.   Fitz-Greene Halleck.   APN-1

Green Beret.   Ho Thien.   FaBoWar; PoAgWa, *tr. by Unknown*

Green beyond green, the grass along the river.   *Unknown.*   ChinPo, *tr. by* Ye Weilian [*or* Yeh Wei-lien *or* Wai-lim Yip]

Green bird came down being once only, A.   New Orleans.   Ralph Adamo.   AnSo

Green, blue, yellow, and red.   One, The.   Patrick Kavanagh.   MoBrPo

Green Boots n Lil Honeys.   Ruth Forman.   SpirFl

Green branch with a sadness of yellow fruit.   Tin Ujević.   SonAtl, *tr. by* Merica Delic, Ursula Hobday and Ziva Pecavar

Green Buddhas.   Watermelons.   Charles Simic.   OxBoAm; VCAP

Green bushes are bursting with giant flowers.   Asphyxiated Man, The.   Victor Serge.   AF, *tr. by* James Brook

Green Cadillac.   Eric Tretheway.   Coast

Green Candles.   Humbert Wolfe.   MoBrPo

Green catalpa tree has turned, The.   April Inventory.   W. D. Snodgrass.   BrAP; ColAP; EMP; GPTC; NAMCP V.2; NoAM; NoP-4; OxBoAm; TRP; VCAP; WaAnP

Green Chile.   Jimmy Santiago Baca.   NIL-7

Green Corn Season.   Diana García.   TouFir

Green Crab's Shell, A.   Mark Doty.   NAMCP V.2

Green elm with the one great bough of gold, The.   October.   Edward Thomas.   CABP; HarvBoo; NoAM

Green embellishment of human life.   Hope.   Sor Juana Inés de la Cruz. SpanPo, *tr.* by Kate Flores

Green Eye, The.   James Merrill.   PoA 2002

Green Eyed Monsters of the Valley Dusk, The.   Sherley Anne Williams. GeoHom

Green Field, The.   Robin Behn.   AmAlph

Green fields are like constructions of the mind which have, The.   At Parting. Duo Duo.   AF, *tr.* by Gregory Lee *and* John Cayley

Green figures move forward and the objects grow larger, The.   North.   Tony Towle.   PmAP

Green fingers, green hand, by now green man.   Garden, Wilderness.   Michael Hamburger.   OBGa

Green first thing each day sees waves.   Green Sees Things in Waves.   August Kleinzahler.   EmeKit

Green fold of a skirt green where.   Josée Lapeyrère.   SCFWP *Fr.* Skirt, The.

Green girl from the back country—employment was my quest, A.   Housemaid's Ballad, The.   Dōyaku Sensei, Master Artery.   EMJL, *tr.* by Haruo Shirane

Green gossip of the maidenhair, The.   Bruce Beaver.   BMAP *Fr.* Odes and Days.

Green grape, and you refused me.   Brief Autumnal.   *Unknown.*   WeW-3, *tr.* by Dudley Fitts

Green Grass.   *Unknown.*   FaBoVe

Green Grass and Yellow Balloons [*(for Alexandria Keller, a poet at four)*]. Etheridge Knight.   GT

Green grass spreads about like silk, The.   Prince Went Wandering, A.   Hsieh T'iao.   CCL1, *tr.* by John Frodsham

Green gravel green gravel.   Green Gravel.   *Unknown.*   FaBoVe

Green, green, green / Herbs splash.   Konishi Raizan.   ZenPo, *tr.* by Takashi Ikemoto and Lucien Stryk

Green, Green Is El Aghir.   Norman Cameron.   NePenScot; NPeEn; OBWP

Green, Green Riverside Grass.   Shen Yüeh.   CCL1, *tr.* by Anne Birrell

Green, green riverside grass.   Watering Horses at a Long Wall Hole. *Unknown.*   ColAnChi, *tr.* by Anne Birrell

Green, green riverside grass.   *Unknown.*   ColAnChi *Fr.* Nineteen Old Poems, The.

Green, green, / The cypress on the mound.   *Unknown.*   CCL1,

Green, green, / The grass by the river-bank.   *Unknown.*   CCL1,

Green, green willows hang, The.   Farewell Poem.   *Unknown.*   CrYelRi, *tr.* by Sam Hamill

Green grow the rashes, O; / Green grow the rashes, O; / The sweetest hours that e'er I spend.   Green Grow the Rashes [A Fragment].   Robert Burns. NAEL-6v2; NAEL-7v2; NoP-4; NoP-5; OxAEP-2

Green grow'th the holly.   *Unknown.*   ChrPo

Green Hair.   Elinor Wylie.   APT-1

Green has suddenly, The.   Fall of Leaves, The.   Yvor Winters.   APT-2

Green Hill, a Green Hill, A.   Ernesto Lumbreras.   RMCMP, *tr.* by Rebecca Seiferle

Green hills. (LL)   Turning Thirty, I Contemplate Students Bicycling Home. Rita Dove.   AmAlph; ArBi; ESEAA

Green hills—how can it be, The.   Yi Hwang.   CATKP *Fr.* Twelve Songs of Tosan.

Green, how I love you, green.   Sleepwalking Ballad, The.   Federico García Lorca.   WoPoe, *tr.* by Michael Hartnett

Green I love you green.   Sleepwalkers' Ballad.   Federico García Lorca. WeW-3, *tr.* by John Frederick Nims

Green. I want you green.   Somnambulist Ballad.   Federico García Lorca. SpanPo, *tr.* by Robert O'Brien

Green is the color of everything.   One West Coast.   Al Young.   GeoHom

Green is the grass on riverbanks.   *Unknown.*   WoPoe, *tr.* by Dell R. Hales

Green is the plane-tree in the square.   London Plane-Tree, A.   Amy Levy. PEW; ViWPN

Green is the valley, and fair the slopes around it.   Ruined Altar, A.   Rosamund Marriott Watson.   ViWPN

Green it's your green I love.   Sleepwalkers' Ballad.   Federico García Lorca. STV, *tr.* by John Frederick Nims

Green Jade Plum Trees in Spring.   Ou-yang Hsiu.   NDACCP, *tr.* by Kenneth Rexroth

Green Knight's Farewell to Fancy, The.   George Gascoigne.   NoSic

Green lamp flares on the table, The.   This Life.   Rita Dove.   GT

Green leaves.   Buson.   EH, *tr.* by Robert Hass

Green level of lily leaves, A.   To Paint a Water Lily.   Ted Hughes.   CABP

Green life brightens, The.   Phnom Penh Morning.   Yin Luoth.   SonAtl, *tr.* by Carole Gibson, Zaniah Marshallsay and Anne Swann

Green Light.   Kenneth Fearing.   OxBoAm

Green Light.   Rolf Jacobsen.   AtGh, *tr.* by Roger Greenwald

Green light came down from the heaven of the jackals.   Even Love.   Anne Marie Macari.   PoDa

Green lights strung in an apple tree.   Christmas Eve, 2003.   Paul S. Piper. AmZen

Green Little Shamrock of Ireland, The.   Andrew Cherry.   IrV

Green little vaulter in the sunny grass.   To the Grasshopper and the Cricket. Leigh Hunt.   CenSon; GSo; OxBSo

Green lotus on waves of transparent blue, A.   Lotus Lover, The.   Tzu Yeh. CrYelRi, *tr.* by Sam Hamill

Green mansion is a place of filth and shame, A.   *Unknown.*   NAAPv.2

Green Market, New York.   Julia Kasdorf.   NeAmPo

Green Mistletoe! / Oh, I remember now.   Winter.   Walter De la Mare.   OBMV

Green mountain lies beyond the north wall of the city, The.   Saying Farewell to a Friend.   Li Po.   TAL

Green mountains.   Muso Soseki.   EaWin, *tr.* by W. S. Merwin

Green mountains lie across the north wall.   Taking Leave of a Friend.   Li Po. ChinPo, *tr.* by Ye Weilian [*or* Yeh Wei-lien *or* Wai-lim Yip]

Green mountains rise to the north.   Taking Leave of a Friend.   Li Po. CrYelRi, *tr.* by Sam Hamill

Green Noise of Ohio Hardwoods, The.   Kathe Davis.   AmZen

Green Nostalgia.   Thế Lữ'.   WoPoe, *tr.* by Nguyen Ngoc Bich

Green of Jesus, The.   Spring Song.   Lucille Clifton.   IPoFL

Green of the distant meadows, lightly.   Tadeusz Borowski.   HP

Green One over There, The.   Katia Kapovich.   P180

Green parrot.   Echo.   Henriqueta Lisboa.   TCLAP, *tr.* by Hélcio Veiga Costa

Green pines and a rustic hut.   Sikong Tu.   CCL1 *Fr.* Twenty-Four Modes of Poetry.

Green Place, A.   Honor Moore.   FFC

Green plum.   Buson.   EH, *tr.* by Robert Hass

Green points on the shrub.   Elegy for D.H. Lawrence, An.   William Carlos Williams.   WaAnP

Green Pond, A.   Wei Chuang.   CCL1, *tr.* by Lois Fusek

Green pond and red flowers lie in the soft misty rain, A.   Green Pond, A.   Wei Chuang.   CCL1, *tr.* by Lois Fusek

Green pores of April grass.   Lilac.   Jeanne Shannon.   ICANM

Green Rain.   Dorothy Livesay.   NALW; NIP-4; NoP-4

Green River.   William Cullen Bryant.   APN-1; TCAPo "When breezes are soft and skies are fair."   ITBLP

Green River, The.   Lord Alfred Bruce Douglas.   OBEV

Green road lies this way, The.   El Camino Verde.   Paul Blackburn.   PmAP

Green roads that end in the forest, The.   Green Roads, The.   Edward Thomas. NAMCP V.1; NoAM

Green robe, green robe, lined with yellow.   Lü-yi: Green Robe.   *Unknown.* APSN; CCL1; NDACCP, *tr.* by Ezra Pound

Green Room, The.   Sydney Lea.   MAAN

Green rushes with red shoots.   Plucking The Rushes.   *Unknown.*   OBVE, *tr. by* Arthur Waley

Green rustlings, more-than-regal charities.   Royal Palm.   Hart Crane. MoAmPo; NAMCP V.1; NoAM

Green scapulars to wear over your shroud. (LL)   Strand at Lough Beg, The. Seamus Heaney.   NAMCP V.2; NoAM; NPeEn; OBWP

Green screams enfold my night. (LL)   African Dream.   Bob Kaufman.   GT; OxAAAP

Green sea clothes on.   Hints.   Giancarlo Majorino.   ItPo, *tr.* by Gayle Ridinger

Green Sees Things in Waves.   August Kleinzahler.   EmeKit

Green Side, The.   Jennifer Maiden.   BMAP

Green silence softly.   Green.   Jeannette Armstrong.   OpeFie

Green Sleeves [and Tartan Ties].   Robert Burns.   FaBoVe

Green Snake, when I hung you round my neck.   To the Snake.   Denise Levertov.   NAAL-5; PoA 2002

Green soaks into the dark trees.   Twilight in West Virginia: Six O'Clock Mine Report.   Irene McKinney.   PBCAP

Green spires stab the horizon.   First Bird.   Jon Gill Bentley.   ICANM

Green Street Mortuary Marching Band, The.   Lawrence Ferlinghetti.   GoPo

Green Symphony.   John Gould Fletcher.   MoAmPo

Green things are flowers too.   Poem.   Frank O'Hara.   PoA 2002

Green Trees that in the Forest grew. (LL)   Dialogue between the Soul and [the] Body, A.   Andrew Marvell.   BASC; BrAP; FSCP; NAEL-6v1; NAEL-7v1; NoP-4; NoP-5; OxAEP-1; OxBEV; SoSe-8; TFi

Green truck, The.   Wreckage along the River, The.   Jeff Knorr.   LiTh

Green Tuxedo, The.   Janet Holmes.   LiTh

Green upon green, grass along the river.   Water the Horses at a Breach in the Great Wall.   *Unknown.*   ChinPo, *tr.* by Ye Weilian [*or* Yeh Wei-lien *or* Wai-lim Yip]

Green Valley, The.   Sylvia Townsend Warner.   MoBrPo

Green willows and fragrant grass by the posthouse road.   Tune: "Spring in the Jade House."   Yen Shu.   ColAnChi, *tr.* by James Robert Hightower

Green woodpecker flying up and down, The.   Green Woodpecker's Nest, The. John Clare.   FaBoVe

Green Woodpecker's Nest, The.   John Clare.   FaBoVe

Green yellow dog up. i have not. i am. green red cat down. i is not. i is. Scraptures: 7th Sequence.   B. P. Nichol.   FTOS

Green-blue ground, The. On Gay Wallpaper. William Carlos Williams. APT-1; MoAmPo

Green-bodied, with small eyes of crimson fire. Moon-talk. Edgell Rickword. OxBSo

Green-coated elms stand placidly around. Scotland. Rayne Mackinnon. EdScPo

Greene's Groatsworth of Wit. Robert Greene. (Deceiving World.) NoSic

Greene's Mourning Garment. Robert Greene. Shepherd's Wife's Song, The. NoSic; RACG

Greene's Vision. Robert Greene. Description of Sir Geoffrey Chaucer, The. NoSic

Green-eyed and could not give them to her children. About this Woman. Judith Rodriguez. BMAP

Green-Eyed Boy after Reading Whitman and Sandburg. Dave Etter. ViWalt

Green-eyed Care. Old Cat Care. Richard Hughes. OBMV

Greengrocer, The. Michael Longley. ModIr Fr. Wreaths.

Greenhalgh's Pub. Julian Croft. NOBAu

Greenhouse Vanity, The. Les A. Murray. FaBoVe

Greenhouses and Gardens. David Lehman. PfSP

Greening Yang. Unknown. CCL1, tr. by Anne Birrell

Greening Yang starts to stir. Greening Yang. Unknown. CCL1, tr. by Anne Birrell

Greenly, blades of spring grass. Greenly the Earth. Chŏng Hyŏnjong. CAMKP, tr. by Kevin O'Rourke

Greenly the Earth. Chŏng Hyŏnjong. CAMKP, tr. by Kevin O'Rourke

Greenock at Night I Find You. William Sydney Graham. EdScPo

Green-shadowed people sit, or walk in rings. Spring. Philip Larkin. MoBrPo

Green-tinged pink tones fade. Brussels: Simple Frescos 1. Paul Verlaine. SxFrPo, tr. by Martin Sorrell

Greenwich Observatory. Sidney Keyes. MoBrPo

Greenwood's. Michael Sharkey. NOBAu

Greet the bights that gave me shelter. Old Fisherman, The. George Campbell Hay. EdScPo

Greet You. Claude De Burine. YaTCFP, tr. by Martin Sorrell

Greeting [with music]. Henrietta Cordelia Ray. CBWP-3

Greeting, A. W. H. Davies. MoBrPo

Greeting, Not Greeting. Angus Calder. EdScPo

Greeting Shekinah. Lynn Gottlieb. HW

Greeting to Lu Yu, A. Li Yeh. CCL1, tr. by Chung Ling and Kenneth Rexroth

Greeting to thee, O most trusty friend!, A. To My Own Face. Caroline Lindsay. VWP

Greetings. Gwyn Thomas. BBMWP, tr. by the author

Greetings, 260 thousand ccm. Murder Machine 43. Kurt Schwitters. PFTM-1

Greetings, Blaise Cendrars. Sonia Delaunay. CuPo

Greetings from My Shtetl (A Letter from Poland). Chaim Plotkin. Prolet, tr. by Amelia Glaser

Greetings from the Chateau. James Schuyler. FTOS

Greetings ladies, kith and kin. Judah Ha-Levi. WoPoe Fr. On the Sea.

Gregory's House. David Huddle. PBCAP

Greifes Farwell, to an Inherritor of Joy. Ann Williams. EMWP

Grenade. Francis Scarfe. FaBoWar

Grenadier. A. E. Housman. OBMV; OBWP

Grenadiers, The. Heinrich Heine. FaBoWar, tr. by Unknown

Grenoble Café. Jean Garrigue. APT-2; OxBoAm

Gretel in Darkness. Louise Glück. NoAM; NoP-4; NoP-5

Gretsch love / gretsch hate. Elvin Jones Gretsch Freak. David Henderson. SeSe

Grew more human & flawed. (LL) Smokehouse, The. Yusef Komunyakaa. NoP-4; NoP-5

Grew wilder. (LL) Bag of Mice. Nick Flynn. AmPoNex; NAPBL

Grey. Einir Jones. BBMWP, tr. by Joseph P. Clancy

Grey afternoon clouds, The. Sea-Sickness. Heinrich Heine. WoPoe, tr. by Vernon Watkins

Grey as a mouse. John Ronald Reuel Tolkien. NOxBChV

Grey cells either side of him. Cell Angel. Menna Elfyn. BBMWP; MoWP, tr. by Gillian Clarke

Grey courtyards where the imprisoned. Via Margutta. Maria Luisa Spaziani. NeIt, tr. by Beverly Allen

Grey Dawn. Julio Herrera y Reissig. TCLAP, tr. by Andrew Rosing

Grey Eye Weeping, A. Egan O'Rahilly. OBMV, tr. by Frank O'Connor

Grey gaunt days dividing us in twain, The. Minute before Meeting, The. Thomas Hardy. OxBSo

Grey haunted eyes, absent-mindedly glaring. Face in the Mirror, The. Robert Graves. CABP

Grey hills of that country fall away, The. Cadaver Politic. Tom Paulin. PNI

Grey horse, Death, in profile bears the young Titus, The. Polish Rider, The. Derek Walcott. WoPoe

Grey. Intangible drops. Sea. Marie-Claire Bancquart. MFP, tr. by Martin Sorrell

Grey is her sleep to-night. (LL) Highland Woman, A. Sorley MacLean. HarvBoo; NePenScot

Grey Islands, The. John Steffler. They All Save One Last Squirt. Coast

Grey Kirk in the Mearns. Gillian Ferguson. EdScPo

Grey Monk, The. William Blake. PtR

Grey monkeys gibber, ignorant and wise. Alun Lewis. FaBoWar Fr. Jungle, The.

Grey mountains, sea and sky. Even the misty. Sea Anemones, The. Gwen Harwood. BMAP

Grey over Riddrie the clouds piled up. King Billy. Edwin Morgan. EdScPo; NePenScot; NoP-4; NoP-5

Grey pier from where the snow bait falls. Grey Pier. Michel Deguy. YaTCFP, tr. by Clayton Eshleman

Grey Rider, The. Norah M. Holland. IFF

Grey [or gray] sea and the long black land, The. Meeting at Night. Robert Browning. BRP; CABP; FaBoVe; HeIP-4; ITBLP; NAEL-6v2; NAEL-7v2; OBEV; OPOU; OxBEV; SoSe-8; TFi

Grey sea turns in its sleep, The. Aberdeen. Robin Robertson. NePenScot

Grey the sky, and growing dimmer. Twilight. Louisa Sarah Bevington. PEW

Grey trees, grey skies, and not a star. Dawn. Angelina Weld Grimké. APT-1; NAAPv.2

Grey Wagtail on the Tyne. Colin Simms. Oth

Grey Woman. Gladys Cardiff. GifTon

Greyer than the tide below, the tower. Homage to Jack Yeats. Thomas MacGreevy. OBMV

Greyhound. Christopher Stahl. BeDoSh

Greyhound in Slip. Ludovico Ariosto. DiBP Fr. Orlando Furioso.

Greyhound should be headed like a snake, A. Properties of a Good Greyhound, The. Dame Juliana Berners. DiBP; WoPoe, tr. by Seamus Heaney

Greyhound Snowball, The. Unknown. DiBP

Greyhound which the hunters hold in slip, A. Ludovico Ariosto. DiBP Fr. Orlando Furioso.

Grid Erectile. Christopher Dewdney. FTOS

Grief. Robin Becker. TaR

Grief: "With eyes happy." Francisco Brines. RaW, tr. by David Ignatow

Grief. Elizabeth Barrett Browning. HeIP-4; NALW; NPeEn; OBEV; VWP

Grief. Catullus. RaBo; RaF

Grief. William Matthews. BeAl; CAP-8; PoCho

Grief. Ruth L. Schwartz. AmPoNex

Grief. Siamanto. AF, tr. by Peter Balakian and Nevart Yaghlian

Grief [with music]. Unknown. OBWVE, tr. by Aneirin Talfan Davies

Grief Comes in Smallest Ways. Gailmarie Pahmeier. SweBea

Grief counselor, The. Keith Abbott. WhBo

Grief is not apparel. Homocide. Essex Hemphill. GT

Grief isn't empty it's black and material I've seen it. I—Towards a Definition. Alice Notley. ExTi

Grief of little boys will make, The. Song for a Play. Dan Chiasson. LegDan

Grief of the coyote seems to make, The. Arizona Midnight. Robert Penn Warren. AmFaPo

Grief reached across the world to get me. Catullus. RaBo; RaF

Grief that troubled your life, The. Elegy: "O loveliest daughter of Hsieh." Yüan Chĕn. CrYelRi; ErotSp, tr. by Sam Hamill

Griefe was common, common were the Cryes, The. Miserable Estate of the World Before the Incarnation of God. William Drummond of Hawthornden. SacPr

Griefs of a little boy are forever, The. Four and a Half. John Holmes. APT-2

Grief's prodigals, where are you? Unthrifts, where? Upon Mr. Hopton's Death. Henry Halswell. NOSC

Griesly Wife, The. John Streeter Manifold. MoBrPo

Grieta, La. Carla Faesler Bremer. SPV

Grievances. Philip Whalen. WANABP

Grieve, ladies, so may God keep you. Lament for the Death of Guillén Peraza. Unknown. WoPoe, tr. by W. S. Merwin

Grieve not, dear love, although we often part. Grieve Not, Dear Love. John Digby. NOSC

Grieve not, my wife—grieve not for me. Joshua McCarter Simpson. TCAPo Fr. Away to Canada.

Grieved, I idle and doze. Tu Fu [or Du Fu]. CrYelRi Fr. Random Pleasures.

Grieved lands of Africa, The. Grieved Lands, The. Agostinho Neto. PoetW, tr. by Michael Wolfers

Grieved Lands, The. Agostinho Neto. PoetW, tr. by Michael Wolfers

Grieving for My Little Girl. Yi Kyubo. CATKP, tr. by Kevin O'Rourke

Grieving the sapless limbs, the shorn and shaken. (LL) Dead Boy. John Crowe Ransom. FuPo; HarvBoo; NAMCP V.1; NoAM; NoP-4

Grieving Too Long (2.9). Horace. WED, tr. by Robert Bly

Griffin calls to come and kiss him goodnight. Bearhug. Michael Ondaatje. BeAl

"Grill me some bones," said the Cobbler. At the Keyhole. Walter De la Mare. MoBrPo

Grim and gaunt the sergeant-major. Bayonet, The. James Copeland. EdScPo

Grim bulwarked hatred between heart and heart! (LL) 1492. Emma Lazarus. APN-2; NAAPv.1; OxBoAm; SWaP

Grim Cotton Mather. Cotton Mather. Rosemary Benét and Stephen Vincent Benét. APT-2

Grim in my tight black coat as the sleazy beetle. John Crowe Ransom. FuPo

Grim Sisters, The. Liz Lochhead. CABP; MoWP

Grim Skeleton. Allen Ginsberg. BodElec

Grim Skeleton come back and put me out of Action. Grim Skeleton. Allen Ginsberg. BodElec

Grim Town in a Steep Valley. Thomas Lux. AmAlph

Grimalkin. Thomas Lynch. EmeKit

Grin, A. Ted Hughes. EmeKit

Grin that wide. (LL) 125th Street. Langston Hughes. APT-2; NAMCP V.1

Grinding Vibrato. Jayne Cortez. OxAAAP

Griots Who Know Brer Fox, The. Colleen J. McElroy. OxAAAP

Grip down and begin to awaken. (LL) Spring and All. William Carlos Williams. APT-1; ChAP; ColAP; EMP; MakPoe; NAAL-5; NAAPv.2; NAMCP V.1; NoAM; OxBoAm; PoPoPo; TCAPo; TFi; TRP

Gripe. Lincoln Kirstein. PoWW

Gripped on the shoulder of the man in front. (LL) War Blinded. Douglas Dunn. NePenScot; OBWP

Gription. Paul Beatty. InTrad

Griselda. Evangeline Paterson. Prnts

Griselda stands at the window. Griselda. Evangeline Paterson. Prnts

Grist for Grace. Judyth Hill. ICANM

Gristmill. Yusef Komunyakaa. LPSFW

Grit. Geoff Page. NOBAu

Grizzly Bear. Mary Austin. BLPJKO

Grizzly Bear is huge and wild, The. Infant Innocence. A. E. Housman. Spl

Grizzly squab comrade, A. Worker, The. Nikolai Stepanovich Gumilyov. SonAtl, tr. by Tamara Romanyk

Gro-ink. Kopita, kopita, ko-pi-ta . . . konk. Nub. Chris Wallace-Crabbe. BMAP

Groans of nature in this nether world, The. William Cowper. NoP-5 Fr. Task, The.

Grocer's Dream, The. Giovanna Pollarolo. TANSG, tr. by Marjorie Agosin

Grodek ("All evening the autumn thickets.") Georg Trakl. SonAtl, tr. by Kurt Ganzl and Markus Jaigirder

Grodek ("At evening the woods of autumn are full of the sound.") Georg Trakl. WED, tr. by Robert Bly

Grodek ("In the evening the autumn woods ring.") Georg Trakl. AF, tr. by Daniel S. Simko

Grodek (Second Version). Georg Trakl. GTCP, tr. by Robert Firmage

Groin, come of age, his state sold out of hand. On Groin. Ben Jonson. NOSC

Grongar Hill. John Dyer. CABP; NoP-4; OxAEP-1

"Now, I gain the Mountain's Brow." NPeEn

Groom of the Animal-Bride. Paulann Petersen. FiBr

Groom of the Chamber's Religion in King Henry the Eighth's Time, A. Sir John Harington. NoSic; PBRV

Groom retails the favours of his lord, The. (LL) Sir Samuel Johnson. NPeEn; OBSV; OxAEP-1 Fr. London: A Poem in Imitation of the Third Satire of Juvenal.

Grooming. Katie Donovan. NeBl

Groove in black plastic got deeper, The. Rock 'n Roll. Peter Balakian. SwNoth

Grooves fill with moss, The. A. R. Ammons. NAMCP V.2 Fr. Tombstones.

Groping along the tunnel, step by step. Rear-Guard, The. Siegfried Sassoon. MoBrPo; NAEL-6v2; NAEL-7v2; NAMCP V.1; NoAM; OBWP; PoWW; WaAnP

Groping back to bed after a piss. Sad Steps. Philip Larkin. BrAP; NAEL-6v2; NAEL-7v2; NAMCP V.2; NoAM; NoP-4; NoP-5; WaAnP

Grossdaadi's Funeral. Julia Kasdorf. NeAmPo

Grotesque. William Carlos Williams. TCAPo

Grotesque and queerly huddled. Troop ship, The. Isaac Rosenberg. OxBEV; PoWW

Grotesques. Robert Graves. OBCoV

Ground Beneath Us, The. Patricia Goedicke. ExTi

Ground drops back, The. Aeroplane. Pudjipangu. NOBAu, tr. by George von Brandenstein

Ground Elder. Leonard Clark. OBGa

Ground is shadowy moist, The. Bending the Light. Tom Koontz. VisFro

Ground / itself would / hint, The. Kiche Manitou. Nathaniel Mackey. FTOS

Ground lapis for the sky, and scrolls of gold. Illumination. Anthony Hecht. ChrPo

Ground squirrels dart among. Oil Field Road off Clyte Escarpment. James Hoggard. TiP2

Ground Swell. Mark Jarman. GeoHom; MoASP

Ground / under a maple-tree. Sigil. "H. D."

Ground was frozen so hard, The. Dying with Amish Uncles. Julia Kasdorf. PBCAP

Ground wave. Ingrid de Kok. TSAP

Ground Zero. Sharon Doubiago. AtGh

Groundhog, The. Richard Eberhart. APT-2; BrAP; InoFa; MoAmPo; NAAPv.2; NAMCP V.1; NoAM; RaBo; TFi; TRP; WaAnP

Groundhog Day. Lynn Ungar. IPoFL

Groundhog on the mountain did not run, The. Incommunicado. Sylvia Plath. BodElec

Ground-Thumping Song. Unknown. ColAnChi, tr. by Burton Watson

Group. John Berryman. BodElec

Group of Musings, A. Henrietta Cordelia Ray. CBWP-3

Group of professional, A. Physics of Ochun, The. Víctor Hernández Cruz. PueRic

Group of six monks began their journey that same day, The. Story of How the Monk Tripiṭaka of the Great Country of T'ang Brought back the Sūtras, The. Unknown. ColAnChi, tr. by Charles J. Wivell

Group of them, A. Basho. EH, tr. by Robert Hass

Group Photo with Winter Trees. Greg Williamson. NoP-5

Group Portrait with Ukuleles. Keith Ratzlaff. ACAMVP

Group Therapy. Carolyn M. Rodgers. ISC

Groupie. Mark Bibbins. LegDan

Groups of God, The. Rainmakers, The. Robert Kelly. PmAP

Grove at Nemi, The. Susan Mitchell. ExTi

Grove is hush'd, the saffron-tinged clouds, The. Anne Batten Cristall. RWP Fr. Thelmon and Carmel; An Irregular Poem.

Grove of small trees, branches thick with berries, A. Charles Reznikoff. APT-2

Grove, The. Octavio Paz. TCLAP, tr. by Elizabeth Bishop

Groves of Blarney, The. Richard Alfred Millikin. OBGa

Groves of legendary holly; silverdark the ridged gleam. (LL) Geoffrey Hill. NAEL-7v2; NoP-4 Fr. Mercian Hymns.

Groves were God's first temples. Ere man learned, The. Forest Hymn, A. William Cullen Bryant. APN-1

Groves were God's first temples, The. Ere man learned. William Cullen Bryant. TreFP Fr. Forest Hymn, A.

Grow. Joseph Ceravolo. BodElec; NYP2

Grow not too high, grow not too far from home. Edna St. Vincent Millay. OxBSo

Grow old along with me! Rabbi Ben Ezra. Robert Browning. NAEL-6v2; NAEL-7v2

Grow to my lip, thou sacred kiss. Kiss, The. Thomas Moore. NOBRP

Grower of trees, the gardener, the man born to farming, The. Man Born to Farming, The. Wendell Berry. InGu; IPoFL

Growing Days, The. Rick Alley. AmPoNex

Growing into my name. Harriet Jacobs. SpirFl

Growing Old. Matthew Arnold. NAEL-6v2; NPeEn

Growing Old (1). Yüan Mei. WoPoe, tr. by Arthur Waley

Growing Old (2). Yüan Mei. WoPoe, tr. by Arthur Waley

Growing old through all these turbulent years. On Killing Myself. Hwang Hyŏn. CATKP, tr. by Chi-gyu Kim [or Kim Chonggil]

Growing older, I grow into the Tao. Hermitage at Chung-nan Mountain. Wang Wei. CrYelRi, tr. by Sam Hamill

Growing Pearl 1. Kim Sŭnghŭi. EcSo, tr. by K. Kim Richards and Steffen Richards

Growing tired of her hysterical gestures. On the Glittering Beaches. Tracey Herd. MFPA

Growing Toward the Earth. Luis Rosales. RaW, tr. by Ralph Nelson and Rita García Nelson

Growing Up. Jason Shinder. MAAN

Growing Up. William Stafford. CAP-8

Growing Up Haunted. Marge Piercy. TaR

Growing Up in a Jewish Neighborhood. Richard Chess. TaR

Growing up in Miami any tropical fruit I ate. Frutas. Ricardo Pau-Llosa. NevBe

Growing Up Italian. Maria Gillan. UnSA

Growing Up with a Sears Catalog in Benghazi, Libya. Khaled Mattawa. LegDan

Grown old are these strong elements of tragedy. One Hundred Lines for the Coast. Kojo Laing. HBAPE

Grown Old Together.   William Lisle Bowles.   DiBP

Grown quiet, I looked at his pink back, and thought. (LL)   Robert Pinsky.   NoP-4; NoP-5 *Fr.* Essay on Psychiatrists.

Grown-over slagheaps rise like burial mounds.   Shotts.   George MacBeth.   EdScPo

Grown-up.   Edna St. Vincent Millay.   AmWit; NAAPv.2; NAMCP V.1; NoAM

Grows deathless by the sacrifice [*or* sacrifise]. (LL)   Friendship's Mystery[s], to my dearest Lucasia.   Katherine Philips.   BASC; BrAP; NAEL-7v1; PBRV; PEW

Grows fainter and fades away. (LL)   Kenneth Rexroth.   APSN; APT-2; NAMCP V.1 *Fr.* Love Poems of Marichiko, The.

Growth.   Shuntaro Tanikawa.   PoetW, *tr. by* Harold Wright

Growth of Love, The.   Robert Bridges.

1.   NoAM

23.   MoBrPo

39.   NoAM

Gr-r-r—there go, my heart's abhorrence!   Soliloquy of the Spanish Cloister.   Robert Browning.   BrAP; FaBoVe; NAEL-6v2; NAEL-7v2; NIL-7; NIP-4; NoP-4; NoP-5; OxBEV; UV

Grr—what's that? A dog? A poet?   From a Spanish Cloister.   G. K. Chesterton.   UV

Grudge, The.   Dimitris Tsaloumas.   BMAP

Grudges.   Stephen Dunn.   PA9/11

Gruel heaped / In a perfect bowl.   Naito Joso.   ZenPo, *tr. by* Takashi Ikemoto and Lucien Stryk

Grunts, and drains it clean. (LL)   Drink of Milk, A.   John Montague.   ModIr; PNI

Gruoch.   Marion Lomax.   NeBl

Grussy's body lay for three days.   Burial Clothes.   Jessica Smucker Falcón.   ACAMVP

Gruyere—is being cleared of its forest—the mountains.   End to Myth, An.   Charles Buckmaster.   BMAP

Gryll Grange.   Thomas Love Peacock.

Love and Age.   OBEV

"Guan! Guan!" The fish-hawk.   *Unknown.*   CCL1 *Fr.* Guan-ju.

Guan-ju.   *Unknown.*   CCL1

Courtship Song.   CCL1, *tr. by* John Turner

Crying Ospreys.   CCL1, *tr. by* Gladys Yang and Yang Xianyi, Gladys Yang *and* Hu Shiguang

Epithalamium.   CCL1, *tr. by* Alexandre de Lacharme

Epithalamium.   CCL1, *tr. by* Arthur Cooper

Fair, Fair, Cry the Ospreys.   CCL1, *tr. by* Arthur Waley

"Guan!" Cries the Hawk.   CCL1, *tr. by* William McNaughton

Gwan! Gwan! Cry the Fish Hawks.   CCL1, *tr. by* Burton Watson

Hid! Hid!   CCL1, *tr. by* Ezra Pound

King Wen's Epithalamium.   CCL1, *tr. by* Clement Allen

Kuan Chü, The.   CCL1, *tr. by* James Legge

Kuan Kuan.   CCL1, *tr. by* Man Wong

Kuan ts'ü.   CCL1, *tr. by* Bernhard Karlgren

Kuan-kuan, the Ospreys.   CCL1, *tr. by* Ye Weilian [*or* Yeh Wei-lien *or* Wai-lim Yip]

Kwan Ts'eu.   CCL1, *tr. by* James Legge

Mallards, The.   CCL1, *tr. by* Robert Payne

Mouettes, Les.   CCL1, *tr. by* Marcel Granet

Ospreys, The.   CCL1, *tr. by* Evangeline Dora Edwards and Marcel Granet

Ospreys Woo, The.   CCL1, *tr. by* V. W. X.

Song of the Ospreys, The.   CCL1, *tr. by* "An Accomplished Friend of Ernst Faber"

Song of Welcome to the Bride of King Wen.   CCL1, *tr. by* William Jennings

Guaranteed hole in the forehead vast plain stretched before, of industry, or waste, sheltering nothing.   Peter Riley.   VaPo *Fr.* Excavations.

Guaranteed the canopy of the firmament above us. (LL)   Picnic, an Homage to Civil Rights, The.   Afaa Michael Weaver.   ISC; LTA; PoPoPo

Guard.   Viktor Krivulin.   TCRusP, *tr. by* Daniel Weissbort

Guard, A.   John Alexander Frazier, Jr.   BtF

Guard, The.   Lyn Hejinian.

"Can one take captives by writing."   FTOS

Guard at the Binh Thuy Bridge, The.   John Balaban.   AF

Guard Duty.   Dick Gallup.   AHA

Guard picks dead leaves from plants, The.   In an Urban School.   Toi Derricotte.   PBCAP

Guarded Wound, The.   Adelaide Crapsey.   APT-1; NAAPv.2

Guardian Angel.   Rolf Jacobsen.   RaBo; WED, *tr. by* Robert Bly

Guardian Angel, The.   Stephen Dunn.   OPRER

Guardian Angel of Not Feeling, The.   Jorie Graham.   ExTi

Guardian Angel of Self-Knowledge, The.   Jorie Graham.   MoWP

Guardian at the Gate, A.   John Clare.   DiBP *Fr.* Shepherd's [*or* Shepheards] Calendar, The.

Guardian Life.   Michael Klein.   WiU

Guardian of the gates.   Seva.   Elsa Cross.   RMCMP, *tr. by* Margaret Sayers Peden

Guardiana de las puertas.   Seva.   Elsa Cross.   RMCMP

Guardians, The.   Geoffrey Hill.   NoP-4; NoP-5

Guard-Room.   Peter Scupham.   WaAnP

Guatemala, Nicaragua, Salvador.   Yannis Ritsos.   PFTM-2 *Fr.* Second Series.

Gubbinal.   Wallace Stevens.   NAAPv.2

Gud Ber.   *Unknown.*   FaBoVe

Gude and Godlie Ballatis, The.   *Unknown.*

"God send euerie Preist ane wyfe."   NePenScot

"With huntis vp, with huntis vp."   NePenScot

Gude guide me, are ye hame again, and hae ye got nae wark?   Last Sark, The.   Ellen Johnston.   NePenScot

Gude Lord Scroop[e]'s to the huntin[g] gane.   Hughie [the] Gra[e]me [Version from Scott's Minstrelsy].   *Unknown.*   IBB

Gudeman's awa, for to fecht wi' the stranger, The.   *Unknown.*   CCL1 *Fr.* Jun-zi yu-yi.

Gudeman's come hame, an' his face weers a bloom, The.   Jun-zi yang-yang: The Gudeman's Come Hame (scoticè).   *Unknown.*   CCL1, *tr. by* James Legge

Gudewife sits i' the chimney-neuk, The.   Ballad of the Were-Wolf, A.   Rosamund Marriott Watson.   ViWPN; VWP

Gudrun Laments over Sigurd.   *Unknown.*   OBVE *Fr.* Elder Edda, The.

Gudrun of old days.   *Unknown. Fr.* Elder Edda, The.

Guélowâr! / We have listened to you, we have heard you.   Camp 1940.   Léopold Sédar Senghor.   PoetW, *tr. by* Melvin Dixon

Guendaranaxhii.   Xhoopa' diidxa' rui' xiinga guendaranaxhii.   Víctor Terán.   RMCMP

Guerilla Fighter.   Jofre Rocha.   NAfrP, *tr. by* Don Burness

Guess I'll Hang My Tears Out to Dry.   Sammy Cahn.   ReLy

Guess well, and that is well. Our age can find.   Alfred Tennyson.   OxBSo

Guess! / Where do you think I'm goin' when the winds start blowin' strong?   Way Down Yonder in New Orleans.   Henry Creamer.   ReLy

Guess Who.   Fred Chappell.   NBLV

'Guess who I saw last night?' was all she said.   Your Street Again.   Sophie Hannah.   MFPA

Guess Who I Saw Today.   Elisse Boyd.   ReLy

Guess who we have here!   Not-a.   Yosl Cutler.   Prolet, *tr. by* Amelia Glaser

Guess Who's in Town? (Nobody but That Gal of Mine).   Andy Razaf.   ReLy

Guest, A.   Tu Fu [*or* Du Fu].   ChinPo, *tr. by* Ye Weilian [*or* Yeh Wei-lien *or* Wai-lim Yip]

Guest, The.   Anna Andreyevna Akhmatova.   ErotSp, *tr. by* Max Hayward and Stanley Kunitz

Guest, The.   Anna Andreyevna Akhmatova.   RaBo; WoPoe, *tr. by* Vera Dunham and Jane Kenyon

Guest, The.   Wendell Berry.   UpMys

Guest, The.   Sheenagh Pugh.   TCAWP

Guest, The.   *Unknown.*   SacPr

(Preparations.)   OBEV

(Yet if his Majestie our Sovareigne lord.)   PBRV

(Yet If His Majesty, Our Sovereign Lord.)   NoP-4

Guest Arrives, A ("North and south of my cottage, spring waters everywhere.")   Tu Fu [*or* Du Fu].   ColAnChi, *tr. by* Victor H. Mair

Guest Arrives, A ("North of my lodge, south of my lodge, spring rivers all.")   Tu Fu [*or* Du Fu].   CCL1, *tr. by* Burton Watson

Guest Ellen at the Supper for Street People, The.   David Ferry.   NIP-4

Guest gone / I stroke the brazier.   Shozan.   ZenPo, *tr. by* Takashi Ikemoto and Lucien Stryk

Guest is inside you, and also inside me, The.   Guest Is Inside, The.   Kabir.   RaBo, *tr. by* Robert Bly

Guests.   Cynthia Fuller.   BeAl

Guests have arrived at last, The. The old.   Winter 6.   Patrick Lane.   BrAP

Guests in their summer colors have fled, The.   Last Picnic, The.   Stanley Kunitz.   AF

Guests moved restless, The.   Party, The.   Antigone Kefala.   BMAP

Guests of Space.   Anselm Hollo.

"Strong tendency towards silence, A."   PrTe

Guests on the sea: Our visit is short.   Guests on the Sea.   Mahmoud Darwish.   VCWP, *tr. by* Lena Jayyusi and W. S. Merwin

Gu-feng: The Valley Wind.   *Unknown.*   CCL1, *tr. by* Arthur Waley

Gu-feng.   *Unknown.*   CCL1

Valley Wind, The.   CCL1, *tr. by* Arthur Waley

Zephyr's Sigh, The.   CCL1, *tr. by* John Francis Davis

Guibá sit min.   Natalia Toledo.   RMCMP

Guide and Guard.   Herman Melville.   NCAP

Guide, and support, and cheer me to the end! (LL)   William Wordsworth.   NAEL-6v2; NAEL-7v2 *Fr.* Recluse, The.

Guide from St. Stephen the Sabaite, The. John Mason Neale. SacPr

Guide me, O thou great Jehovah. William Williams. OBWVE

Guide me, O thou great Redeemer. William Williams. SacPr

Guide me on my way. Princess Shokushi. ArkPo, *tr. by* Robert H. Brower and Earl Miner

Guide to Holland, A. Peter Sirr. PBCIP

Guide to the Other Gallery. Dana Gioia. RA; WaAnP

Guide to the Perplexed. David Malouf. NOBAu

Guide to the Underworld. Gunnar Ekelof. *tr. by* Rika Lesser
"Alone in the quiet night." WoPoe, *tr. by* Rika Lesser

Guide to Urban Birds, A. David B. Axelrod. UrbNat

Guiding hand raised, A. When Asked to Lie Down on the Altar. Eleanor Wilner. TaR

Guido, I wish that you and Lapo and I. Love and Poetry. Dante Alighieri. NAWM-7v1, *tr. by* James J. Wilhelm

Guidon flags flutter gaily [*or* gayly] in the wind, The. (LL) Cavalry Crossing a Ford. Walt Whitman. AmWaPo; BLT; BrAP; CBCWP; FaBoA; HeIP-4; NAAL-3; NAAL-5; NAAPv.1; NAMCP V.1; NCAP; NoAM; NoP-4; NoP-5; PCW; SAmP; TCAPo; TFi; TRP; WaAnP

Guido's Aurora. Henry David Thoreau. APN-1

Guie naxiñá yaase. Cadidi Laaga Lua. Natalia Toledo. RMCMP

Guie xiña yase / Xhidi badu dxaapa huiini. Ca gunaa rusianda. Natalia Toledo. RMCMP

Guiffre's Nightmusic. Thomas McGrath. SeSe

Guild, The. Sharon Olds. PoA 2002; RaBo

Guile and softness of the Saxon race, The. On the Welch. *Unknown.* AngWePo

Guillaume Apollinaire. Gertrude Stein. NAAPv.2; NAMCP V.1; OxBoAm

Guillotine is the masterpiece of the plastic arts, The. Head, The. Blaise Cendrars. CuPo

Guilt, Desire and Love. James Baldwin. CAGL

Guilty. Gustave Kahn. ReLy

Guilty, he does not always like his patients. Doctor, The. Dannie Abse. BloBone

Guilty, my Lord, what can I more declare? Edward Taylor. ChIV-1; TCAPo *Fr.* Preparatory Meditations Before My Approach to the Lord's Supper.

Guinea Woman. Lorna Goodison. NAMCP V.2

Guitar. David St. John. InvLad

Guitar, The. Federico García Lorca. SpanPo, *tr. by* Rachel Benson and Robert O'Brien

Guitar, The. Six Strings, The. Federico García Lorca. RaW, *tr. by* Donald Hall

Guitarist Tunes Up, The. Frances Darwin Cornford. SoSe-8

Guitarra, La. Federico García Lorca. RaW *Fr.* Gráfico de la Petenera.

Guitars I Used to Know, The. Jayne Cortez. FuFl

Guitars / with excavated rhythms. Guitars I Used to Know, The. Jayne Cortez. FuFl

Güler's Hours of Love. Necati Cumalı. NaPG, *tr. by* Talat Sait Halman

Gulf. Dhabya Khamees. PoArWo, *tr. by* Clarissa C. Burt

Gulf. Marion Lomax. NeBl

Gulf, The. Derek Walcott. NoP-4; NoP-5; PoetW; PoPoPo

Gull flicks down on a wave, A. Body is Fragile, The. Tony Trigilio. AmZen

Gull flies low across the darkening bay, A. Nocturne. James McAuley. BMAP

Gull Goes Up, A. Léonie Adams. OWoS

Gull inch-perfect over water, the busy crane, The. Gull inch-perfect over water, The. Louise Herlin. MFP, *tr. by* Martin Sorrell

Gull Lake set in the rolling prairie. At Gull Lake; August, 1810. Duncan Campbell Scott. BrAP

Gull on a Post. Jeremy Hooker. AngWePo

Gull on a post firm. Gull on a Post. Jeremy Hooker. AngWePo

Gull rides on the ripples of a dream, A. Walk in Late Summer, A. Theodore Roethke. APT-2

Gull shanty red rot. Vase of the Universe, The. Edwin Torres. HeMarv

Gull shrieks guided us, The. Seagulls. Judith Herzberg. TuT, *tr. by* Greg Delanty

Gull, up close, A. Seagulls. John Updike. OWoS

Gulling[e] Sonnets, The. Sir John Davies.
"As when the bright[e] Crulean firmament." NoSic
"My case is this." NoSic
"Sacred muse that first[e] made love divine [*or* devine], The." NoSic; OxBSo; PBRV
"What eagle can beho[u]ld her sunbright[e] eye." NoSic

Gulls. Jorie Graham. AWPTFC; BAP-01

Gulls at Cannon Beach. William Stafford. PoCoUp

Gull's Flight, The. Nigel Roberts. NOBAu

Gulls of the cool Atlantic tip the foam, The. Even the Gulls of the Cool Atlantic. Joan Murray. OxBoAm

Gulls when they fly move in a liquid arc. Gull Goes Up, A. Léonie Adams. OWoS

Gully of green, a laughing river, A. Asleep in the Valley. Paul Verlaine. SxFrPo, *tr. by* Martin Sorrell

Gum. Jean Toomer. APT-2; NAMCP V.1

Gum has no shade, The. Robert, Viscount Sherbrooke Lowe. NOBAu *Fr.* Songs of the Squatters.

Gum up the works, girls. Crossing Out. Fanny Howe. PfS

Gumba, gumba, gumba. Mafika Pascal Gwala. TSAP

Gumbo-limbo swoons in the arms of an oak, A. Prayer for the Everglades. Lola Haskins. RWB

Gum-trees Stripping. Judith Wright. BMAP

Gun, The. Jacqueline Berger. AmPoNex

Gun Emplacement: Sundown. Jeremy Ingalls. YaYoPo

Gun full swing the swimmer catapults and cracks, The. 400-Meter Freestyle. Maxine W. Kumin. MoASP

Gunga Din. Rudyard Kipling. BRP; MoBrPo

Gunner, The. Francis Webb. BMAP

Guns as Keys: And the Great Gate Swings. Amy Lowell.
"Down, down, down, to the bottom of hte map." NAAPv.2

Guns know what is what, but underneath, The. Memories of a Lost War. Louis Simpson. AmWaPo; OBWP; PWW2

Guns spell money's ultimate reason, The. Ultima Ratio Regum. Stephen Spender. AF; FaBoWar; NoP-4; NoP-5; OBWP; PoWW

Gunslinger. Edward Dorn.
"I met in Mesilla." PFTM-2
Idle Visitation, An. PmAP

Guraj Push. Essential Serbo-Coat. Ken Smith. PoAgWa

Gurgles, genderless. Women Laughing. U. A. Fanthorpe. ItWoWo; MoWP

Gurgling waters foam and play, The. On the rapids of the St. Lawrence. Henrietta Cordelia Ray. CBWP-3

Gurlie an gray the snell Fife shore. Sydney Goodsir Smith. NePenScot *Fr.* Armageddon in Albyn.

Gurney Tears. Audrey Shafer. BloBone

Gurteen. Padraic Fallon. ModIr *Fr.* Three Houses.

Gust of memory stirs faded letters, A. Igor Vladimirovich Chinnov. TCRusP, *tr. by* John Glad

Gust of wind, A. Buson. EH, *tr. by* Robert Hass

Gustave Thibon, How Simone Weil Appeared to Me/2. Stephanie Strickland. ExTi

Gustave Thibon, How Simone Weil Appeared to Me/3. Stephanie Strickland. ExTi

Gustave Thibon, How Simone Weil Appeared to Me/4. Stephanie Strickland. ExTi

Gustave Thibon, How Simone Weil Appeared to Me/5. Stephanie Strickland. ExTi

Gusts of wind. Pei Di and Wang Wei. CCL1 *Fr.* Wheel River.

Gusts of wind cruise like fish. Opening Day. David McKain. AtGh

Gut Catcher. Stan Platke. FaBoWar

Gut eats all day and lechers all the night. On Gut. Ben Jonson. NoP-4; NoP-5; NPeEn; PoPoPo

Gutenberg Inscription. Mihály Vörösmarty. IQMS, *tr. by* Peter Zollman

Gutting. Joe Denham. OpeFie

Gutting the Salmon. Robert Adamson. BMAP

Guttural Muse, The. Seamus Heaney. HarvBoo

Guttural sorrow of the refugees, The. (LL) British Museum Reading Room, The. Louis MacNeice. BrAP; GoPo; MoBrPo

Guttural stammer of the chopper blades, The. It's Only Rock and Roll but I Like It: The Fall of Saigon, 1975. David Wojahn. IllVoic; ReTh

Guy, The. Karai Senryū. EMJL, *tr. by* Haruo Shirane

Guy at the next table reminded her of her first serious boyfriend, The. Wreck of the *Platonic*, The. B. J. Atwood-Fukuda. FreRad

Guy who's sitting in is not an ass, The. Mark Stern. Frederick Feirstein. RA

Guyon's Voyage to the Bower of Bliss. Edmund Spenser. NoSic *Fr.* Faerie Queene, The.

Guys. Sheenagh Pugh. TCAWP

Gwalia Deserta. Idris Davies.
"Dark gods if all our days." TCAWP
"Do you remember 1926? That summer of soups and speeches." RSaN

Gwalia Deserta XV. AngWePo

Gwalia Deserta XXII. AngWePo

Gwalia Deserta XXVI. AngWePo

"There are countless tons of rock above his head." TCAWP

Gwan! Gwan! Cry the Fish Hawks. *Unknown.* CCL1 *Fr.* Guan-ju.

GWB in the Rain, The. Mary Stewart Hammond. KGB

Gwbert: Mackerel Fishing. Sam Adams. TCAWP

Gwen John's women only just. Retrospective. William Scammell. NLP

Gwendolyn Brooks. Haki R. Madhubuti. ESEAA; FtHH; OPRER

Gwendolyn Brooks. Anthony Walton. RD

Gwenllian. Myrddin ap Dafydd. BBMWP, *tr.* by Anthony Conran

Gwensways. Eugene B. Redmond. SpirFl

Gwine find a beauty shop. Kinky Hair Blues. Una Marson. MoWP

Gwine Follow. *Unknown.* SSUS

Gwine to march away in de gold band. Gold Band, The. *Unknown.* SSUS

Gwine to walk about Zion, I really do believe. Sabbath Has No End. *Unknown.* SSUS

Gwladys Rhys. W. J. Gruffydd. OBWVE, *tr.* by Myrddin Lloyd

Gwladys Rhys. W. J. Gruffydd. BBMWP, *tr.* by Robert Minhinnick

Gynae One. Christine Ama Ata Aidoo. HAWP

GYN-astics. Kemal Kurt. PML, *tr.* by Marilya Veteto-Conrad

Gyno-Text. Lola Lemire Tostevin. NLPA

György Bessenyei to Himself. György Bessenyei. IQMS, *tr.* by Watson Kirkconnell

Gypsies. John Clare. *See* Gipsies [*or* The Gipsy Camp]: "Snow falls deep; the forest lies alone, The."

Gypsies carry sacks of walnuts out of the groves, The. Coleridge Crossing the Plain of Jars [1833]. Norman Dubie. AmAlph

Gypsies Metamorphosed, The. Ben Jonson.
  Dinner for the Devil. NOSC

Gypsies on the Move. Charles Baudelaire. GS, *tr.* by Unknown

Gypsy. Josephine Miles. NoAM

Gypsy, The. Ezra Pound. NPeEn

Gypsy, The. Susan Stewart. CFP

Gypsy, The. Edward Thomas. NAMCP V.1; NoAM; NoP-4

Gypsy Hand. Miriam Sagan. ICANM

Gypsy in the Condemned Cell, A. Mihály Babits. IQMS, *tr.* by Peter Zollman

Gypsy Summer. Noelle Kocot. LegDan

Gypsy Teaches Her Grandchild Wolfen Ways, The. Susan Swartwout. ReTh

Gypsy's Evening Blaze, The. John Clare. CenSon

Gypsy's Window, The. Denise Levertov. CLPP

Gyre's Galax. Norman Henry, II Pritchard. EGAG

Gyres, The. William Butler Yeats. NAMCP V.1; NoAM

Gyroscope. Howard Nemerov. NAMCP V.2; NoAM

Gyroscope, The. Muriel Rukeyser. YaYoPo

H

H. Michael Palmer. BodElec

H. Antecessor. Joan Houlihan. IAoNAP

H. Chic. Virgil Suárez. NevBe

H is for High water. H E L P. Rosamond S. King. BtF

H. S. Mauberley (Life and Contacts) Part 1 by Ezra Pound. Alex Rawls. AnSo

H. Scriptures. Henry Vaughan. ChIV-2

H. Scriptures (1), The. George Herbert. BASC; ChIV-1

H. Scriptures (2), The. George Herbert. BASC; ChIV-2

H. T. Louis Zukofsky. NAAPv.2

Ha . . . No Shadows. Kim Suyŏng. CAMKP, *tr.* by Anthony, Brother of Taizé

Ha ha! ha ha! This world doth pass. Fara Diddle Dyno. Thomas Weelkes. OBCoV

Ha ha. You searching. Clear Channel. Lorenzo Thomas. FTOS

Ha! Original Sin! Ogden Nash. NBLV

Ha' we lost the goodliest fere o' all. Ballad of the Goodly Fere. Ezra Pound. ChIV-2; MoAmPo

Ha! whare ye gaun, ye crowlin' [*or* crowlan] ferlie! To a Louse [On Seeing One on a Lady's Bonnet at Church]. Robert Burns. FaBoVe; NAEL-6v2; NAEL-7v2; NePenScot; NOBRP

Hácese añicos el mundo en estado de sitio, uña sobrecogida que la mugre cubre, camino de silencio y destello final. Bolero en Aramgedón. David Huerta. RMCMP

Había la miseria. Elegía Incompleta, Una. José Ángel Valente. RaW

Había vivido mucho. Viejo y el Sol, El. Vicente Aleixandre. RaW

Habit. Natalie Clifford Barney. PoBW

Habit. Ruth Stone. InoFa

Habit. David Woo. OpBo

Habit of Perfection, The. Gerard Manley Hopkins. ChIV-2; MoBrPo; NAMCP V.1; NoAM; OBEV; OBMV; OxAEP-2; SacPr; TFi

Habit of staring, The. Habit. David Woo. OpBo

Habitable planets are unknown or too. Native's letter. Arthur Nortje. BrAP; HBAPE; TSAP

Habitat Photo. Joy Lahey. AnSo

Habitation. Margaret Atwood. WeW-3

Habitation, The. Ralph Knevet. NOSC

Habits: / false. shoals. Monstrous Pictures of Whales. Dennis Schmitz. GeoHom

Habits of the soul. (LL) Plague of Starlings, A. Robert Earl Hayden. ESEAA; NoAM; WaAnP

Habitude. Yousif al-Sa'igh. IrPoTo, *tr.* by Chuck Miller and Saadi A. Simawe

Ha-Borei, / You who create. Rosh Chodesh Tisheri. Vicki Hollander. HW

Habría cerrojos y círculos violetas. Celda barroca, Una. David Huerta. RMCMP

Habría una vez la perra más azul de la manada. Tres. Ofelia Perez Sepúlveda. SPV

Hacedor. Joseph Stroud. TAPaP

Hacho. Pedro Serrano. RMCMP

¿Hacia Donde? Ernesto Lumbreras. RMCMP

Haciendo Apenas la Recolección. Tino Villanueva. UnSA

Hacked, naked, roped to a pole. Photos. Hugh Seidman. BodElec

Hackney Coach, The. Endre Ady. IQMS, *tr.* by Anton N. Nyerges

Hackney Coachman, The; Or, The Way to Get a Good Fare. Hannah More. WoRP

Hacks with traps. Salon, Salon. Louis Cabri. PoPra

Had a definite flavour of gin. (LL) Limerick: "From the bathing machine came a din." Edward Gorey. AmWit; OBCoV

Had a Horse. Gertrude Stein. MotU; OxBoAm *Fr.* Book Concluding with As A Wife Has a Cow a Love Story, A

Had a / weed in it. (LL) Reflective. A. R. Ammons. OxBoAm; VCAP

Had anything been wrong, we should certainly have heard. (LL) Unknown Citizen, The. W. H. Auden. BrAP; HeIP-4; NAMCP V.1; NBLV; NIP-4; OBSV; SoSe-8; TRP

Had been cut in two. (LL) Kenneth Rexroth. APSN; APT-2; NAAPv.2 *Fr.* Love Poems of Marichiko, The.

Had broken and thrown away! (LL) Slave's Dream, The. Henry Wadsworth Longfellow. NAAL-3; NAAL-5

Had built this stack of thigh-bones, jaws and shins. (LL) In Kerry. John Millington Synge. IrLP; MoBrPo

Had crashed the right part of town. Esther. Eve Merriam. TaR

Had cut grooves too deeply across our backs. (LL) Hard Rock Returns to Prison from the Hospital for the Criminal Insane. Etheridge Knight. ESEAA; NIL-7; NIP-4; PBCAP; TRP

  (Had cut deep bloody grooves / Across our backs.) (LL) AF; GT; InGu

Had Damn'd him to the Hell of Impotence. (LL) Disappointment, The. Aphra Behn. BASC; BrAP; CABP; EMWP; EroLit; NAEL-7v1; NALW; NoP-4; NoP-5; NOSC; PEW; WaAnP

Had *Dorothea* liv'd when mortals made. Edmund Waller. PBRV

Had gone up to. Memory Gardens. Robert Creeley. FTOS

Had had the measure of nothing, or nothing if not smoke, and then wildfire. (LL) Imperial Measure. Vona Groarke. BeAl; MoWP; NIrP

Had he and I but met. Man He Killed, The. Thomas Hardy. ChAP; FaBoWar; HarvBoo; HeIP-4; ItP; MoBrPo; NIP-4; OBWP; TFi; WeW-3

Had he not drank them up for you. (LL) His Saviour[']s Words, Going to the Cross[e]. Robert Herrick. ChIV-2; SacPr

Had he sat there, a witness? Metal Denser Than, and Liquid, A. John Peck. BAP-01

Had I a man's fair form, then might my sighs. To ———: "Had I a man's fair form, then might my sighs." John Keats. CenSon; OxAEP-2

Had I as many souls as there be stars. Christopher Marlowe. SacPr *Fr.* Doctor Faustus.

Had I been an ox or horse. Wang An-shih. WoPoe *Fr.* In the Style of Han Shan and Shih Te.

Had I died? or was I. Hymn, The. Denise Levertov. BodElec

Had I died—but I did not. Afterthought. Caroline Finkelstein. PfS

Had I known, only known. Mentor. Timothy Murphy. PoDa

Had I known the time of separation was to come. *Unknown.* SLW, *tr.* by Marjolijn De Jager, Sayd Bahodin Majrouh and André Velter

Had I more carefully cultivated the Horatian pentameter, then. To Whom Else. George Barker. HarvBoo

Had I not loved. For an End. Helen Pinkerton. CalPo

Had I not perceived so much of worth in her. Legacy, The. Heinrich von Morungen. GePo, *tr.* by F. C. Nicholson

Had I remained in innocent security. Angellica's Lament. Aphra Behn. LW

Had I the choice to tally greatest bards. Walt Whitman. SoSe-8 *Fr.* Fancies at Navesink.

Had I the heavens' embroidered cloths. He Wishes for the Cloths of Heaven. William Butler Yeats. BLPJKO; ChAP; GoPo; MoBrPo; NAMCP V.1; NoAM; OBEV; PtR

Had I the use of thought equivalent. Fern Song. Hildegarde Flanner. APT-2

Had I the wings of a bird. Thoughts. Maggie Pogue Johnson. CBWP-4

Had Life remained one whole. Unit. Mary Elizabeth Fullerton. NOBAu

Had me a corn patch, back o' my place. Coons in the Corn. Alice Ewing Vail. TiP2

Had mournful Ovid been to Brent condemned. William Diaper. OBSV *Fr.* Brent; a Poem to Thomas Palmer Esq.

Had not the milder hand of Mercy broke. Mercy Tempering Justice. Francis Quarles. SacPr

Had not these me against myself defended. (LL) Grace. Ralph Waldo Emerson. APN-1; InvLi; NCAP

Had Robinson Crusoe never left the highest, or more correctly the most visible point of his island. Robinson Crusoe. Franz Kafka. MotU, *tr. by* Edwin Muir and Willa Muir

Had she come all the way for this. Haystack in the Floods, The. William Morris. CABP; NAEL-6v2; NAEL-7v2; NoP-4; NoP-5; OBNV; OxAEP-2

Had something to smile about. (LL) Sometimes When It Rains. Gcina Mhlophe. HAWP; NAfrP

Had somewhere to get to and sailed calmly on. (LL) Musée des Beaux Arts. W. H. Auden. BeAl; BrAP; CABP; ClHu; EMP; GS; HeIP-4; NAEL-6v2; NAEL-7v2; NAMCP V.1; NIL-7; NoAM; NoP-4; NoP-5; NPeEn; OxAEP-2; OxBEV; OxBoAm; PoPoPo; RaBo; RSaN; SoSe-8; TFi; TRP; WaAnP

Had sowed these fruits, and got the harvest in. (LL) To the Immortal Memory and Friendship of That Noble Pair, Sir Lucius Cary and Sir H. [*or* Henry] Morison. Ben Jonson. BASC; CABP; NAEL-6v1; NAEL-7v1; NoP-4; NoP-5; NOSC; PBRV

Had stayed at home behind me and was fast asleep in bed. (LL) My Shadow. Robert Louis Stevenson. ChAP; ITBLP; ItP; UV

Had the light. Clearing, The. Carl Phillips. BAP-01

Had the light on. (LL) Donald Justice. GoPo; StAl *Fr.* American Sketches (for William Carlos Williams).

Had to be was angry full of. Angry. Suki Wessling. ArBi

Had we but parted at the start. Samuel Hoffenstein. AmWit *Fr.* Love-songs, at Once Tender and Informative.

Had we but world enough, and time. To His Importunate Mistress. Peter De Vries. NBLV; NIL-7; NIP-4

Had we but World enough and Time. To His Coy Mistress. Andrew Marvell. AmFaPo; BASC; BrAP; CABP; ClHu; EroLit; ErotSp; FSCP; HeIP-4; NAEL-6v1; NAEL-7v1; NIL-7; NIP-4; NoP-4; NoP-5; NOSC; NPeEn; OBEV; OxAEP-1; OxBEV; PBRV; PoPoPo; TFi; TRP; UV; WaAnP; WoPoe

Had your intent been to repent. Michael Wigglesworth. NAAL-3 *Fr.* Day of Doom, The [First Section].

Haddock Fishermen. George Mackay Brown. NoP-4; NoP-5

Hades. Vegunta Mohana Prasad. HotL, *tr. by* V. Narayana Rao

Hades and Euclid (first version). Harry Edmund Martinson. WED, *tr. by* Robert Bly

Hades in Manganese. Clayton Eshleman. APSN

Hades is an even worse place. Paavo Haavikko. WoPoe *Fr.* Fifteen Epigrams in Praise of the Tyrant.

Hades withoot an Elysium. Scottish Mythology. Raymond Vettese. EdScPo

Hadn't heard of the atom bomb. Seals in Penobscot Bay, The. Daniel Gerard Hoffman. YaYoPo

Hadrian's Address to His Soul When Dying. Emperor Hadrian. OBVE, *tr. by* Byron

Hadrian's Lane. Ray DiPalma. FTOS

Hae ye cam here fae Passchendaele? Passchendaele. Angus Martin. EdScPo

Haesunja Asks for an Enlightenment Song. Master Naong. BecRai, *tr. by* Kim Daljin, Kim Won-Chung and Christopher Merrill

Hag and the Slavies, The. Jean de La Fontaine. OBVE, *tr. by* Edward Marsh

Hag of Beare, The. *Unknown.* OBVE, *tr. by* Augusta, Lady Gregory

Hag Riding. Lucille Clifton. ExTi

Hagar. Rosanna Warren. ExTi

Haggai. John Chagy. ChIV-1

Haggard daylight steer, The. (LL) Death of a Toad, The. Richard Wilbur. BrAP; NAAL-5; NAMCP V.2; NoAM; PoA 2002; PtR

Haglets, The. Herman Melville. APN-2

Hagomel. Uriel Ofek. NRoS, *tr. by* Esther Raizen

Haibun. Andrew Schelling. WANABP

Haibun Flycatcher. Andrew Schelling. AmZen; WANABP

Haibun is the Japanese literary form that mixes terse prose with compressed verse. Haibun the Migration of Haibun. Andrew Schelling. AmZen

Haida Cradle-Song. *Unknown.* TCAPo

Haidée and Juan carpeted their feet. Lord Byron. NOBRP *Fr.* Don Juan.

Haif hairt in hairt ye hairt of hairtis haill. *Unknown.* EMWP

Haiim, / Behold you have returned to your Mother. To the Memory of a Comrade. Hillel Omer. NRoS, *tr. by* Esther Raizen

Haikai. Sadakichi.
    1. NAAPv.1
    2. NAAPv.1

Haiku: "Lightning flashes, The!" Basho. SoSe-8, *tr. by* Earl Miner

Haiku: "Lightning gleam, A." Basho. SoSe-8, *tr. by* Harold G. Henderson

Haiku: "Black, brother, nigga." C. Yaphet Brinson. BtF

Haiku: "I think I'll die." Masaoka Shiki. CAoMJL1 *Fr.* Thirty-nine Haiku.

Haiku. Lenard D. Moore. SpirFl

Haiku. Lenard D. Moore. SpirFl

Haiku. Lenard D. Moore. SpirFl

Haiku: "Fallen flowers rise." Arakida Moritaké. SoSe-8, *tr. by* Harold G. Henderson

Haiku: "Falling flower, The." Arakida Moritaké. SoSe-8, *tr. by* Babette Deutsch

Haiku. Sonia Sanchez. ISC

Haiku: "Was it yesterday." Sonia Sanchez. FFC

Haiku: "Your voice unwrapping." Sonia Sanchez. FFC

Haiku: "Upon Kissing You after You Vomited." James Shea. IIR

Haiku. Tomas Transtrӧmer. WoBe, *tr. by* Robin Fulton
    "And blueweed, blueweed." WoBe, *tr. by* Robin Fulton
    "Ash-colored silence." WoBe, *tr. by* Robin Fulton
    "Avenues trot, The." WoBe, *tr. by* Robin Fulton
    "Birds in human shape." WoBe, *tr. by* Robin Fulton
    "Black-and-white magpie." WoBe, *tr. by* Robin Fulton
    "Borne by the darkness." WoBe, *tr. by* Robin Fulton
    "Chill-to-the-bone, A." WoBe, *tr. by* Robin Fulton
    "Come out of the swamp!" WoBe, *tr. by* Robin Fulton
    "Darkening leaves, The." WoBe, *tr. by* Robin Fulton
    "Death leans forward and." WoBe, *tr. by* Robin Fulton
    "Death stoops over me." WoBe, *tr. by* Robin Fulton
    "Encroaching shadows." WoBe, *tr. by* Robin Fulton
    "Gaunt tousled pine-trees." WoBe, *tr. by* Robin Fulton
    "Glittering cities." WoBe, *tr. by* Robin Fulton
    "Go, quiet as a shower." WoBe, *tr. by* Robin Fulton
    "God's wind in the back." WoBe, *tr. by* Robin Fulton
    "Grass is rising, The." WoBe, *tr. by* Robin Fulton
    "He writes, writes and writes." WoBe, *tr. by* Robin Fulton
    "Hear the swish of rain." WoBe, *tr. by* Robin Fulton
    "Here where the sun burned." WoBe, *tr. by* Robin Fulton
    "Here's a dark picture." WoBe, *tr. by* Robin Fulton
    "Hold on, nightingale!" WoBe, *tr. by* Robin Fulton
    "Humming in the mist." WoBe, *tr. by* Robin Fulton
    "I've been in that place." WoBe, *tr. by* Robin Fulton
    "My happiness swelled." WoBe, *tr. by* Robin Fulton
    "November sun, The." WoBe, *tr. by* Robin Fulton
    "On a rocky ledge." WoBe, *tr. by* Robin Fulton
    "On the balcony." WoBe, *tr. by* Robin Fulton
    "Perplexing forest." WoBe, *tr. by* Robin Fulton
    "Revelation, A." WoBe, *tr. by* Robin Fulton
    "Roof broke apart, The." WoBe, *tr. by* Robin Fulton
    "Sea is a wall, The." WoBe, *tr. by* Robin Fulton
    "See how I'm sitting." WoBe, *tr. by* Robin Fulton
    "Sitting on a shelf." WoBe, *tr. by* Robin Fulton
    "Something has happened." WoBe, *tr. by* Robin Fulton
    "Stag in blazing sun." WoBe, *tr. by* Robin Fulton
    "Station platform scene." WoBe, *tr. by* Robin Fulton
    "Sun disappears, The." WoBe, *tr. by* Robin Fulton
    "Those milestones, always." WoBe, *tr. by* Robin Fulton
    "Thoughts standing still, like." WoBe, *tr. by* Robin Fulton
    "Wall of hopelessness." WoBe, *tr. by* Robin Fulton
    "When the hour is here." WoBe, *tr. by* Robin Fulton
    "Wind slow and slow, A." WoBe, *tr. by* Robin Fulton
    "With hanging gardens." WoBe, *tr. by* Robin Fulton
    "Working up the slopes." WoBe, *tr. by* Robin Fulton

Haiku: "Just enough of rain." Richard Wright. APT-2

Haiku #3. Kim C. Lee. InTrad

Haiku # 135: "My butterfly breaths." Kalamu ya Salaam. BtF

Haiku: "Eastern guard tower." Etheridge Knight. ESEAA; InGu

Haiku for My Brothers. Ira B. Jones. BtF; FTtHH

Haiku Monument for Washington, D.C. Michael Redhill. IFF

Haiku Rows. Michael McClure.
    For Diane di Prima. WANABP
    For Gary Snyder and Carole Koda. WANABP
    For Jack Kerouac. WANABP
    For Marilyn and Stan Brakhage. WANABP
    For Zenshin Ryufu Philip Whalen. WANABP

Hail. Debra Kang Dean. NevBe

Hail. Seymour Mayne. IFF *Fr.* Word Sonnets.

Hail and beware the dead who will talk life until you are blue. Newly Discovered "Homeric" Hymn, A. Charles Olson. NoAM

Hail beauteous Chiswick! hail, sequestered seat! Thomas Maurice. OBGa *Fr.* Richmond Hill.

Hail, beauteous stranger of the grove [*or* wood]! To the Cuckoo. Michael Bruce. OBEV

Hail Bishop Valentine, whose day this is. Epithalamion, or Marriage Song on the Lady Elizabeth and Count Palatine Being Married on St. Valentine's Day, An. John Donne. ItP

Hail, Blushing Goddess, Beauteous Spring! Esther Vanhomrigh. LW

Hail! Dawn is shining glory doing. Kilaben Bay Song. *Unknown.* NOBAu, *tr. by* Perce Haslam

Hail, Derwent's beauteous pride! Ode to Borrowdale in Cumberland. Amelia Alderson Opie. RWP

Hail, Devon! In thy bosom let me rest. Written in Devonshire, Near the Dart. Anne Batten Cristall. RWP

Hail, fair youth, who seeks no bribe. To an English Boy. Hilary. CAGL, *tr. by* John Boswell

Hail Flag of the Union! Hail Flag of the free! Stars and Stripes. Mary Weston Fordham. CBWP-2

Hail, gentle spirits, who with magic wing. To Dreams. Mary Julia Young. CenSon

Hail! gentle youth, and do not deem me rude. Lines: To a Young Gentleman of Surpassing Beauty. Ellen Johnston. VWP

Hail, glorious day; mayst thou be writ in gold. Simon Ford. NOSC *Fr.* London's Resurrection.

HAIL graceful morning of eternal day. To the Blessed Virgin. William Alabaster. NoSic

Hail, happy bride, for thou art truly blest! On the Death of Mrs. Bowes. Lady Mary Wortley Montagu. LW

Hail, happy day, when smiling like the morn. To the Right Honourable William, Earl of Dartmouth. Phillis Wheatley. NAAL-5; NAAPv.1; NALW; OxBoAm

Hail, happy saint, on thine [*or* thy] immortal throne. On the Death of the Rev. Mr. George Whitefield [1770]. Phillis Wheatley. ColAP; NAAL-3; NAAL-5; NAAPv.1; SacPr; WaAnP

Hail, happy virgin! of celestial race. To Almystrea, on her Divine Works. Elizabeth Thomas. EMWP

Hail, holy Lead!—of human feuds the great. Ambrose Bierce. APN-2 *Fr.* Devil's Dictionary, The.

Hail holy Light, ofspring of Heav'n first-born. John Milton. OxBEV *Fr.* Paradise Lost.

Hail Ihesu, my creator, of the sorrowing, medicine! Cantus Amoris 2. Richard Rolle of Hampole. SacPr

Hail! land of the palmetto and the pine. Albery Allson Whitman. NAAPv.1 *Fr.* Octoroon, The.

Hail, Mary. *Unknown.* SSUS

Hail Matrimony, made of Love! William Blake. OxBEV *Fr.* Island in the Moon, An.

Hail, May Day, dedicated to holy delights, to joy as full as unadulterated. May Morning. George Buchanan. PBRV

Hail, mediocrity, beneath whose spell. Roy Campbell. MoBrPo *Fr.* Georgiad, The.

Hail, meek-eyed maiden, clad in sober grey. Ode to Evening. Joseph Warton. OxAEP-1

Hail mer- / ry, tricky, and clandestine. Ode to Pornography. Jack Anderson. PoA 2002

Hail Mother Full of Grace Power Is with Thee. Jennifer Berezan. HW

Hail, Muse! et caetera.—We left Juan sleeping. Lord Byron. *Fr.* Don Juan.

Hail, old patrician trees, so great and good! Of Solitude. Abraham Cowley. BASC

Hail peaceful Shade, whose sacred verdant side. Alicia D'Anvers. NOSC *Fr.* Academia; or The Humours of the University of Oxford.

Hail / peppered. Seymour Mayne. IFF *Fr.* Word Sonnets.

Hail, Priapus, primal father. Corpus Inscriptionum Latinarum 14.3565. *Unknown.* PriapPo, *tr. by* Richard W. Hooper

Hail! Richmond, hail! thy matchless beauties. *Unknown.* OBGa *Fr.* Richmond Gardens: A Poem.

Hail, Roma, daughter of Ares. Melinno. SaLy, *tr. by* Diane Rayor

Hail, sister springs! Weeper, The. Richard Crashaw. FSCP

Hail South Australia! blessed clime. Hail South Australia! *Unknown.* NOBAu

Hail, Thou my Native Soil. William Browne. OxAEP-1

Hail, thou once despised Jesus. *Unknown.* SacPr

Hail, thou sole Empress of the Land of wit. Pindarick To Mrs. Behn on her Poem on the Coronation, A. *Unknown.* EMWP

Hail to *Clarinda*, dear Euterpe Hail. To Mrs S. F. on Her Poems. Mary Pix. EMWP

Hail to the black! (LL) Song of the Smoke, The. William Edward Burghardt DuBois. ISC; SSLK

 (I am black.) (LL) APT-1; FTtHH

Hail to the coming time! (LL) Fine Old English Gentleman, The; New Version. Charles Dickens. OBSV; RSaN

Hail to the fields—with Dwellings sprinkled o'er. William Wordsworth. CenSon *Fr.* River Duddon [A Series of Sonnets], The.

Hail to the hero! Ernest Crosby. FaBoWar *Fr.* War and Hell.

Hail to thee, blithe Spirit! To a Skylark. Percy Bysshe Shelley. BrAP; BRP; NAEL-6v2; NAEL-7v2; NOBRP; NoP-4; NoP-5; NPBRoP; OBEV; OWoS; OxAEP-2; TFi; WaAnP

Hail to thee, merciful King, Saint Ladislas! Lay of King Saint Ladislas, The. *Unknown.* IQMS, *tr. by* Anthony Edkins

Hail to thy pencil! Well its glowing art. To Mr. Opie, On His Having Painted for Me the Picture of Mrs Twis. Amelia Alderson Opie. RWP

Hail to thy puggy nose, my Darling. Natal Address to My Child, March 19th 1844, A. Eliza Ogilvy. VWP

Hail, universal mother! lightly rest. Ovid. NOBRP *Fr.* Metamorphoses.

Hail, ye indomitable heroes, hail! Crimean Heroes, The. Walter Savage Landor. FaBoWar

Hail you, King's serfs! Chen-gong: King's Serfs. *Unknown.* CCL1, *tr. by* Man Wong

Hail[e], sister springs! Saint Mary Magdalene or The Weeper. Richard Crashaw. BASC; ChIV-2

Haill clanjamfrie!, The. (LL) Bonnie Broukit Bairn, The. Hugh MacDiarmid. EdScPo; FaBoVe; HarvBoo; NePenScot

Hailstone, The. Peter Didsbury. NPeEn

Hailstones. Basho. EH, *tr. by* Robert Hass

Hailstones drop loud, with a rattlesnake's song. (LL) Would You Think? John Wheelwright. APT-2; OxBoAm

Hailstones falling like sharp blue sky chips. Crazy Horse Monument. Peter Blue Cloud. HATNAP; UnSA

Hailstorm in May. Gerard Manley Hopkins. Spl

Hair. Nina Iskrenko. ItGoST, *tr. by* Patrick Henry, John High and Katya Olmsted

Hair. Breda Sullivan. Prnts

Hair and bacon grease, pearl button. Genie's Prayer Under the Kitchen Sink. Rita Dove. RACG

Hair beneath, The. Stand farther off then! Go. (LL) Elizabeth Barrett Browning. CenSon; LW; NALW; PEW; VWP *Fr.* Sonnets from the Portuguese.

Hair fanning out, he'll float upside down. Necromancy: The Last Days of Brian Jones, 1968. David Wojahn. SwNoth

Hair half gone grey, half blinded. Grandmother of Russian Poetry: A Self-Portrait, The. Vera Merkureva. ARWW, *tr. by* Catriona Kelly

Hair of the Field. Tony Barnstone. ViWalt

Hair oil, boiled sweets, chalk dust, squid's ink. Caliban's Books. Michael Donaghy. EmeKit; NeBrP

Hair on your body, The. David Hart. NewEx

Hair— / silver-gray. Face. Jean Toomer. NoP-4; NoP-5

Hair that I gloss down. Just Like the Legend. Léon Damas. PFTM-1

Hair the color of. Powwow. Carroll Arnett. LTA

Hair Tonic. Gisèle Prassinos. PFTM-1

Hair which boldly speaks in Bernice's despite, A. Description of Perfect Beauty. Christian Hofmann von Hofmannswaldau. GePo, *tr. by* George C. Schoolfield

Hairband, homespun, opera-hat, afghan. Motley. Peter Davison. NBLV

Hair-bowed Rose, deep in lush grass of the river. Profile of Rose. Glyn Jones. OBWVE

Hair—braided chestnut. Portrait in Georgia. Jean Toomer. APT-2; InGu; NAAPv.2; NAMCP V.1; NoP-4; NoP-5

Hairbrush. Selima Hill. BeAl

Hairbrush, The. Sandra Hochman. YaYoPo

Haircut. David Huddle. AmWaPo

Hairdresser's, The. Pierre McOrlan. MFP, *tr. by* Martin Sorrell

Hairdressing. Patricia Pogson. NLP

Hairless. Jo Shapcott. PoCu

Hairline Fracture, A. Amy Clampitt. NoAM

Hairnet! Scissors! Fine-teet comb! South Parade Peddler. Louise Bennett. NAMCP V.2

Hairs rush out of his nose and ears. Old Man. Geoffrey Holloway. NLP

Hairy Toe, The. *Unknown.* OBSP

Haiseau has yet another thing. Ring That Controlled Erections, The. *Unknown.* NAWM-7v1, *tr. by* Ned Dubin

Haiti. Chiqui Vicioso. TANSG, *tr. by* Daisy Cocco De Filippis

Haiti Tomorrow. Jean-Claude Martineau. OGAHCP, *tr. by* Boadiba and Jack Hirschman

Hakeldama. Zbigniew Herbert. GI, *tr. by* John Carpenter and Bogdana Carpenter

Hako, The. *Unknown. tr. by* Alice C. Fletcher

Mother Corn Assumes Leadership.

 "Mother with the life-giving power now comes." APN-2

Song of the Promise of the Buffalo. APN-2

Song to the Trees and Streams. APN-2

Ha-Kon-E-Crase, the Eagle Dance. *Unknown.* APN-2 *Fr.* War Dance.

Halcion. R. T. Smith. AWTN

Halcyon. "H. D."
    "I'm not here." MoAmPo

Halcyon Days. Jim Barnes. VCAP

Hale [*or* Hail], sterne superne, hale [*or* hail], in eterne. Ballat [*or* Ballad] of Our Lady, [Ane]. William Dunbar. NePenScot

Half. Gwyneth Lewis. BBMWP *Fr.* Wholeness.

Half. Julia Park Rodrigues. TWW

Half a bar, half a bar. Village Choir, The. *Unknown.* UV

Half a basin. Two Prison Poems. Ho Chi Minh. PoetW, *tr. by* Burton Raffel

Half a Double Sonnet. Mary Jo Salter. MakPoe

Half a league, half a league. Charge of the Light Brigade, The. Alfred Tennyson. BRP; CABP; ChAP; FaBoWar; NAEL-6v2; NAEL-7v2; NoP-4; NoP-5; OBWP; OxAEP-2; OxBEV; TFi; UV

Half a Lemon, Half a Cigarette, and Half a Desire to Have It Off. Haytham El-Shawwaf. AnVo, *tr. by* Mohamed Enani

Half an hour north of Grand Central. In Cheever Country. Dana Gioia. GM

Half an hour to dress, wide rubber hip boots. Fear and Fame. Philip Levine. PoDa

Half asleep. Fishing the Dream. Mike Delp. MoASP

Half asleep on the cold grass. For a Stone Girl at Sanchi. Gary Snyder. BB

Half Century. Maeve Kelly. IrLP

Half Choakt ith' Dust of our lewd Town. Alicia D'Anvers. EMWP *Fr.* Oxford-Act, The.

Half close your eyelids, loosen your hair. He Thinks of Those Who Have Spoken Evil of His Beloved. William Butler Yeats. NoAM

Half cracked open, my hands are stained with it. (LL) West Willow. Reginald Shepherd. AmPoNex; IllVoic

Half doun the hill, whaur fa's the linn. Gowk, The. William Soutar. EdScPo

Half hour for coffee, and at night, A. James Vincent Cunningham. APT-2

Half in a dream. Kenneth Rexroth. APSN; APT-2; NAMCP V.1 *Fr.* Love Poems of Marichiko, The.

Half Life. Paul Monette. InoFa

Half Measures. Thomas McGrath. BodElec

Half moon. Mendocino Memory. June Jordan. ASA

Half my childhood my father carried in his dusty pocket. Horseshoes. David Bottoms. PoA 2002

Half my friends are dead. Sea Canes. Derek Walcott. HeIP-4; InoFa

Half of America doubtless has the whole. Line Drive Caught by the Grace of God. Linda Gregerson. ExTi; MoASP

Half of his / body hung in. Spirits. Víctor Hernández Cruz. PueRic

Half of Life. Friedrich Hölderlin. OBVE

Half of Life, The. Friedrich Hölderlin. NAWM-7v2, *tr. by* Christopher Middleton

Half of my life is gone, and I have let. Mezzo Cammin. Henry Wadsworth Longfellow. APN-1; ColAP; GSo; NAAL-3; NAAPv.1; NCAP; TCAPo

Half of Spain occupied the whole of Spain. In the Forties. Jaime Gil de Biedma. RaW, *tr. by* Timothy Baland

Half of the people in the world. Yehuda Amichai. FIT, *tr. by* Robert Friend

Half past nine—high time for supper. In Praise of Cocoa, Cupid's Nightcap. Stanley J. Sharpless. NBLV

Half past three. The hour when all matter. Half Past Three. Luljeta Lleshanaku. WoBe, *tr. by* Henry Israeli

Half sleeping, for she has been traveling. Army of Lovers, An. Alicia Ostriker. AtGh

Half the day lost, staring. Meadow, The. Kate Knapp Johnson. P180

Half the time they munched the grass, and all the time they lay. Cows. James Reeves. NOxBChV; NTCP

Half-and-half affair, I grew from the union, A. Peter Davison. YaYoPo *Fr.* Breaking of the Day, The.

Half-and-Half Song, The. Li Mi-an. ColAnChi, *tr. by* Lin Yutang

Half-Ballad of Waterval. Rudyard Kipling. FaBoWar

Half-blind, hands shaking. Blues for Aunt Ruth. Norita Dittberner-Jax. MiVo

Half-Breed. Cherríe Moraga. UnSA

Half-caste. John Agard. Oth

Half-Caste Girl. Judith Wright. NALW

"Half-cracked" to Higginson, living. I Am in Danger—Sir. Adrienne Rich. HarvBoo; NAAL-5; NALW

Half-Dead. David Kirby. LiTh

Half-Done, Half-Turn. Jon Gill Bentley. ICANM

Half-ended melodies are purer. Variation. Bill Berkson. NYP2

Half-high, or tapering off at Summer's end. (LL) Frederick Goddard Tuckerman. APN-2; NoP-4; OxBoAm *Fr.* Sonnets.

Half-horse / half-woman. Yosano Akiko. CAoMJL1, *tr. by* Janine Beichman

Half-Inch Tweeddale, The. Lillias Scott Forbes. EdScPo

Halflife. Friedrich Hölderlin. WoPoe, *tr. by* Vyt Bakaitis

Half-Life of Sorrow, The. Roger Greenwald. AtGh

Half-numb, guzzling bourbon and Coke from coffee mugs. Body and Soul. B. H. Fairchild. MAAN; MoASP; SUP

Half-Open. Patricia Donegan. WhBo

Half-past eight Don Pullen just arrived. Don Pullen at the Zanzibar Blue Jazz Cafe, 1994 [1997]. Major L. Jackson. SpirFl

Half-past eight Don Pullen just arrived. Don Pullen at the Zanzibar Blue Jazz Café [2006]. Major L. Jackson. LegDan

Half-Season. Simone Yoyotte. SurWo, *tr. by* Myrna Bell Rochester

Half-sleeping, / my body pulls toward yours. Jane Hirshfield. PasH

Halftime. Adam Lefevre. MoASP

Halfway between childhood and manhood. Bicycle, The. James Reaney. ArBi

Half-way down you lose the sense of falling. Peacetime. Peter McDonald. ModIr

Half-Way Pause, A. Dante Gabriel Rossetti. OxBEV

Halfway Street, Sidcup. Fleur Adcock. Spl

Halfway through an afternoon. Hot Comb. Natasha Trethewey. SpirFl

Halfway Through the Book I'm Writing. Lynn Emanuel. ExTi

Half-way through the night. Ghazal: Half-Way Through the Night. Khwaja Shams-ad-din Muhammad Hafiz. WoPoe, *tr. by* Geoffrey Squires

Halfway up. Walking Past the Dugout of Felix McKittrick. Robert Burlingame. TiP2

Halieutica. Oppian [of Corycus]. *tr. by* William Diaper
    "Lamprey, glowing with uncommon fires, The." OBVE
    Loves of the Eel [*or* Fishes], The. NPeEn, *tr. by* William Diaper
    Loves of the Tortoise, The. NPeEn
    "Then from the teeming Filth, and putrid Heap." NPeEn,
    Sex-life of Fish, The. OBVE
    "When they in throngs a safe retirement seek." OBVE

Haligonian Market Cry. George Elliott Clarke. Coast

Hall of Ifor Hael, The. Evan Evans. OBWVE, *tr. by* Gwyn Williams

Hall of the Guardian God. Muso Soseki. EaWin, *tr. by* W. S. Merwin

Hallaig. Sorley MacLean. EdScPo; HarvBoo; NePenScot; NPeEn; WoPoe

Hallaig. Sorley MacLean. EdScPo

Hallelu, Hallelu. *Unknown.* SSUS

Hallelujah! Clifford Grey and Leo Robin. ReLy

Hallelujah, Bum Again. *Unknown.* GM

Hallelujah! / It works. American Football (A Reflection upon the Gulf War). Harold Pinter. PoAgWa

Hallelujah! kneel and sing / Praises to the heav'nly king. Bible, *O.T.* OBVE

Hallelujah; or, Britain's Second Remembrancer. George Wither.
    (To a Musician.) SacPr

Hallelujah Terrible. Matthew Lippman. BAP-97

Halley's Comet. Norman Nicholson. NoP-4; NoP-5

Halley's Comet crossed the jungle sky. Ansel Talvikki. YaYoPo *Fr.* In Fragments, In Streams.

Halloa! King Cheng. Yi-xi: Halloa! *Unknown.* CCL1, *tr. by* Man Wong

Hallow the threshold, crown the posts anew! On the Queen's Return from the Low Countries. William Cartwright. OBEV

Hallowed be Thy name—Halleluiah! Human Cry, The. Alfred Tennyson. InvLi

Halloween. Robert Burns. NOBRP; TreFP

Hallowe'en. Lizelia Augusta Jenkins Moorer. CBWP-3

Halloween 1967. Lewis Warsh. AHA

Halls are thronged, the grand staircase murmurous, The. Blessing, The. Helen Dunmore. BeAl

Hallucinatory Sunset, with Sons. Vicente Gerbasi. SonAtl, *tr. by* Eleanor Davidson

Hallucinogenic Bullfighter. Juan Felipe Herrera. BodElec

Halo Factory, The. Dave Brinks. AnSo

Halo of two eagles chortle, A. On the Eve of Aphrodite. Tracy Philpot. IAoNAP

Haloes, Not Hats [*or* A Vision of the Gods]. John Close. STuOW

Halsted Street Car. Carl Sandburg. IllVoic

Halt (Naïve). Dan Beachy-Quick. IAoNAP

Halt! Shoulder arms! Recover! As you were! Sonnet to Britain. William Edmonstoune Aytoun. OxBSo

Haltersick's Song. John Pickering. NoSic *Fr.* Horestes.

Ham and the Moon. Jesse Lee Kercheval. SweBea

Hamartia Symbolized by the Stray. Joel Brouwer. LegDan

Hamatreya. Ralph Waldo Emerson. APN-1; NAAL-3; NCAP

Hamatreya. Ralph Waldo Emerson. NAAPv.1; OxBoAm; TCAPo

Hambone and the Heart, The. Dame Edith Sitwell. OBMV

Hambone Gospel, A. Lamont B. Steptoe. OxAAAP

Hambone Two Tongue. David Chapman Berry. IaFF

Hamburg: the clock hands move upon their star. Galaxies. Alan Gould. NOBAu

Hamburger. August Kleinzahler. PmAP

Hamburger wizard. Chuck Berry. Cornelius Eady. FaoP

Hame, Hame, Hame, hame fain wad I be. Hame, Hame, Hame. Allan Cunningham. OBEV

Hamelin Town's in Brunswick. Pied Piper of Hamelin, The. Robert Browning. NOxBChV; OBNV; OBSP

Hamilton Greene. Edgar Lee Masters. NAAPv.1; NAMCP V.1; NoAM Fr. Spoon River Anthology.

Hamlen Brook. Richard Wilbur. HarvBoo; VCAP; WeW-3

Hamlet. Ciaran Carson. FaBoVe; ModIr; PNI

Hamlet. Boris Leonidovich Pasternak. GI; WoPoe, tr. by Nina Kossman

Hamlet [limerick]. Stanley J. Sharpless. NBLV

Hamlet at the Paris Aerobleu. Ryan Van Cleave. IaFF

Hamlet Meets Frankenstein. Kevin Griffith. IaFF

Hamlet Off-stage: Laertes Cool. David Chapman Berry. P180

Hamlet says, this is a place. George Stanley. NLPA Fr. Mountains and Air.

Hamlet. William Shakespeare. NAWM-5v1

  "Angels and ministers of grace defend us!" OxAEP-1

  "Ay, so, God be wi' ye! Now I am alone." OxAEP-1

  Frailty, Thy Name is Woman. OxAEP-1; WaAnP

  Hamlet's Soliloquy. OxAEP-1; OxBEV; TreFP; UV; WaAnP

  "Look here, upon this picture, and on this." OxAEP-1

  "Mote it is to trouble the mind's eye, A." OxAEP-1

  "My lord, as I was sewing in my closet." OxAEP-1

  "O! my offense is rank, it smells to heaven." OxAEP-1

  Ophelia's Death. OxAEP-1

  Ophelia's Song. NoSic

  Ophelia's Songs, 2 ("And will he not come again"). NoSic

  Song. NoSic

  (Song: "Tomorrow is Saint Valentine's Day.") NTCP

  "Why, let the strucken deer go weep." NoSic

Hamlet to Ophelia. Peter Cummings. IaFF

Hamlet's Lost Monologue. László Kálnoky. IQMS, tr. by Kenneth McRobbie and Zita McRobbie

Hamlet's Soliloquy. William Shakespeare. OxAEP-1; OxBEV; TreFP; UV; WaAnP Fr. Hamlet.

Hammer a nail into a mirror, a piece of. Painting To Hammer a Nail. Yoko Ono. WhBo

Hammer and Anvil. John Oxenham. SacPr

Hammer Falls, Is Falling, The. Marianne Boruch. AmAlph

Hammer, hammer. Hammer and Anvil. John Oxenham. SacPr

Hammer struck my nail, instead of nail, The. Almanac. May Swenson. APT-2

Hammers pound there above. Along Galeana Street. Octavio Paz. VCWP, tr. by Elizabeth Bishop

Hammers, The. Ralph Hodgson. MoBrPo

Hammer-Song. Unknown. FaBoVe

Hammock. Blaise Cendrars. CuPo

Hammock was a blue cocoon, The. Dream of Dying, A. Leslie Monsour. FFC

Hamnavoe. George Mackay Brown. EdScPo

Hamnavoe Market. George Mackay Brown. EmeKit; NePenScot

Hampstead Heath. Manuel Ulacia. RMCMP

Hampstead Heath. Manuel Ulacia. RMCMP, tr. by Indran Amirthanayagam

Hampstead Highgate Finchley Hendon Muswell hill: rage loud. William Blake. NOBRP Fr. Jerusalem.

Hampton Court. Antonio Cisneros. TCLAP Fr. Loneliness.

Hampton Court. Alexander Pope. OBSV Fr. Rape of the Lock, The: An Heroi-Comical Poem in Five Cantos.

Hampton Lock. Dave McClure. ArBi

Hamra Night. Sa'di Yusuf. FaBoWar, tr. by Abdullah Al-Udhari

Hamza Aweiwi, a Shoemaker in Hebron. Hayan Charara. PrTe

Han Shan in Santa Rosa. John Tarrant. WhBo

Ha'nacker Mill. Joseph Hilaire Pierre Belloc. MoBrPo

Hana-hana. Hana-Hana: Working. Hawaiian Oral Tradition. NAAPv.1

Hanbok. Pak Mogwŏl [or Mokwŏl]. CAMKP, tr. by Kevin O'Rourke

Hand. Nishiwaki Junzaburo. CAoMJL1, tr. by Hosea Hirata

Hand. Robert E. Penn. WiU

Hand. Takahashi Shinkichi. ZenPo, tr. by Takashi Ikemoto and Lucien Stryk

Hand, The. Bernard Bador. ConPit, tr. by Clayton Eshleman

Hand, The. Frank Lima. BodElec

Hand, The: "Brightness Falls from the Air." Gregory Orr. PoChi

Hand, The: "Teacher asks a question, The." Mary Ruefle. P180

Hand a shade of moonlight on the pillow, The. Non Ti Fidar. Louis Zukofsky. WaAnP

Hand and Foot, The [or Hand and the Foot, The]. Jones Very. APN-1; SacPr

Hand appeared out of the earth, A. Vasco [or Vasko] Popa. PoSu Fr. Quartz Pebble, The.

Hand burns resinous in the evening sky, The. Egyptian Register. "Ern Malley." BMAP

Hand by Hand We Shall Us Take. Unknown. SacPr

Hand by Hand We Shall Us Take. Unknown. OHMEL

Hand for Some Others, A. Geoffrey Holloway. NLP

Hand Further, The. Clark Coolidge. PmAP

Hand Game. Frances Boyle. IFF

Hand has her hair, A. Libido. Larissa Szporluk. AmPoNex

Hand in a crevice, the tongue at rest in the mouth, A. Shelburne Falls. Carrie St. George Comer. LegDan

Hand in the breast-pocket, The. (LL) Marriage. Marianne Moore. APT-1; ColAP; MoWP; NAAPv.2; NALW; OxBoAm

Hand is all heart, The. It hops around like a toad to prove its. Hand, The. Frank Lima. BodElec

Hand is writing these lines, A. Peter and Mother. David Schubert. OxBoAm

Hand Me Down Blues [for my brother George 1933–1971]. Calvin Forbes. GT

Hand Mirror. Daisy Zamora. LoL, tr. by Barbara Paschke

Hand of Snapshots, A. Louis MacNeice.

  Once-in-Passing, The. ModIr

Hand of the Lord held me transported, The. Unknown. WoPoe Fr. Ezekiel.

Hand of the wind's own lover, The. Caroline von Günderode. Alejandra Pizarnik. SurWo, tr. by Natalie Kenvin

Hand over hungry hand. (LL) Climbing. Lucille Clifton. GT; LoL

Hand reaches for the cocktail, it's in darkness, The. Glass House. Diane Ward. PmAP

Hand swinging the loops of paint—splashes—drips. Ode to Jackson Pollock. Michael McClure. PmAP

Hand that made us is Divine, The. (LL) Ode: "Spacious firmament on high, The." Joseph Addison. ChIV-1; NPeEn; OxBEV

Hand That Rocks the Cradle Is the Hand That Rules the World, The. William Ross Wallace. ITBLP

Hand that signed the paper felled a city, The. Hand That Signed the Paper, The. Dylan Thomas. FaBoWar; MoBrPo; NAMCP V.2; NoAM; NoP-4; NoP-5; OBWP; TCAWP

Hand That Swept the Sounding Lyre, The. Frances Sargent Osgood. NAAPv.1

Hand that tries to shake a hand, A. Nature. Marvin Bell. PfSP

Hand to Hand. Bruce Weigl. MotU

Hand trembling towards hand; the amazing lights. Sonnet Reversed. Rupert Brooke. OxBSo

Hand, with rhythmic and thoughtless motion, A. Web, The. Pierre Reverdy. YaTCFP, tr. by Mary Ann Caws and Jean-Pierre Cauvin and Patricia Terry

Handbag. Ruth Fainlight. OPOU; StAl

Handball Players at Brighton Beach, The. Irving Feldman. TaR

Handbell Choir, The. Jane Flanders. PBCAP

Handbook of Versification. Gilbert Sorrentino. PoA 2002

Hand-clapping Rhyme. Unknown. NTCP

Handful of red sand, from the hot clime, A. Sand of the Desert in an Hour-Glass. Henry Wadsworth Longfellow. NCAP

Handful of thatch, A. Old Hut. Muso Soseki. EaWin, tr. by W. S. Merwin

Handfuls of Wind. Laila Halaby. PoArWo

Handicap. Anthony Hecht. AmWit

Handicraft—After Marina Tsvetaeva. Duo Duo. PoetW, tr. by Michelle Yeh

Handing Down, The. Wendell Berry.

  Heaviness of His Wisdom, The. UpMys

Handing me the bread / dipped in the dish. Judas' Reproach. Nina Kossman. GI

Handkerchief Kiss. Menna Elfyn. MoWP

Handkerchief waving / goodbye. (LL) To a Daughter Leaving Home. Linda Pastan. ArBi; ItWoWo; NIL-7; NIP-4

Handle for the Flutist, A. Odia Ofeimun. HBAPE

Handless Clock. Raymond Radiguet. CuPo

Handmaid of Religion, The. Edgell Rickword. OBSV

Hand-Mirror, A. Walt Whitman. NAAL-3; NAAPv.1; NAMCP V.1; PoPoPo

Handnotes. Lyn Moir. Prnts

Handprint, small and negative, The. 12,000 Years Is Not Too Long. Carol Cullar. TiP2

Hand-Rolled Cigarettes. Yevgeny Aleksandrovich Yevtushenko. VCWP

Hands. Rin Ishigaki. WoPoe, tr. by Naoshi Koriyama and Edward Lueders and Edward Lueders

Hands. Robinson Jeffers. CalPo

Hands. Edvard Kocbek. PoSu, tr. by Michael Scammell and Veno Taufer and Michael Scammell

Hands. Victor Serge. AF, tr. by James Brook

Hands. Angela Shannon. BtF

Hands: "Hands were purified in fire." Chaim Schwartz. Prolet, *tr. by* Amelia Glaser

Hands, The. Marco Antonio Montes de Oca. MotU, *tr. by* Brian Swann

Hands, The. Daniel David Moses. IFF

Hands and feet. Allan Graham. ICANM

Hands and feet. Stigmata. Mitch Rayes. ICANM

Hands are touching. Nostalgia of the Infinite. Barbara Guest. BAP-04

Hands explore tentatively, The. Feel of Hands, The. Thom Gunn. OxBEV

Hands gripped hard on the desert, The. (LL) At the Bomb Testing Site. William Stafford. AtGh; NAMCP V.2; NIL-7; NIP-4; NoAM; OBWP; PoAgWa; WaAnP

Hands have no tears to flow. (LL) Hand That Signed the Paper, The. Dylan Thomas. FaBoWar; MoBrPo; NAMCP V.2; NoAM; NoP-4; NoP-5; OBWP; TCAWP

Hands in a thorn bush. Sion Eirian. BBMWP *Fr.* Adolescent Experiences.

Hands in the Motion of Prayer. Sojourner Kincaid Rolle. GeoHom

Hands in the Wind. Ted Kooser. UrbNat

Hands make love to thigh, breast, clavicle. Euphony. Yusef Komunyakaa. ESEAA

Hands must touch and handle many things, The. New Man, The. Jones Very. APN-1; TCAPo

Hands of God, The. D. H. Lawrence. ChIV-2; InvLi

Hands of Mary Joe, The. Mary Tallmountain. LoL

Hands of the Body without the Body, and Nothing to Hold, The. Katie Ford. LegDan

Hands of the Old Métis, The. Maurice Kilwein Guevara. NAPBL

Hands on the steering wheel. Revenge. Sadhu Binning. PML, *tr. by* the author

Hands so cold. Masaoka Shiki. CAoMJL1, *tr. by* Burton Watson

Hands were purified in fire. Hands. Chaim Schwartz. Prolet, *tr. by* Amelia Glaser

Hand's / writing the, A. Out of the Identical. Gustaf Sobin. PmAP

Hand-Shadows. Jarold Ramsey. NIP-4

Handshake, a lowered light, the chance to clear her table, A. Green Baize Couplets. Conor O'Callaghan. NIrP

Handshakes, The. Robert Crawford. NeBrP

Handsome Heart, The. Gerard Manley Hopkins. FaBoVe

Handsome horses O shiver and admire. Anaktoria. Sappho. WoPoe, *tr. by* Guy Davenport

Handsome Is as Handsome Does. James Wright. BodElec

Handsome man is good to look at, A. Sappho. SaLy, *tr. by* Diane Rayor

Hand-tinted, creamy olive skin. Taking It Back. Dixie Salazar. UnSA

Handy Mole who plied no shovel, A. Christina Georgina Rossetti. VWP

Hang and swinging hang and swinging. Eugen Gomringer. PFTM-2, *tr. by* Jerome Rothenberg

Hang at my hand as I write now. Verses for a First Birthday. George Barker. MoBrPo

HANG him, base gull; I'll stab him, by the Lord. Boreas. Samuel Rowlands. NoSic

Hang it all, Robert Browning. Ezra Pound. APT-1; MoAmPo; NAAPv.2; NAMCP V.1; NoAM; NoP-5 *Fr.* Cantos.

Hang out our banners on the outward walls. William Shakespeare. *See* To-morrow, and to-morrow, and to-morrow.

Hang Out the Flag. James Sterling Tippett. CA

Hang sorrow, cast away care. Song. *Unknown.* NOSC

Hang up a yellow shirt—you cause joy. John Tranter. VaPo *Fr.* Blackout.

Hang Up the Baby's Stocking! *Unknown.* OBCP

Hanging Fire. Audre Lorde. BrAP; NAMCP V.2; NIL-7; NIP-4; NoAM; NoP-4; PoPoPo; TRP

Hanging from the beam. Portent, The. Herman Melville. APN-2; CBCWP; ColAP; InoFa; NAAL-3; NAAPv.1; NCAP; NoP-4; NoP-5; OBWP; OxBoAm; PCW; TCAPo; WaAnP

Hanging in the balance. Fallen Bodies. Gideon Ferebee. BtF

Hanging luggage disturbs shadows in the water. Ascend Lu-Shan. Pao Chao. ChinPo, *tr. by* Ye Weilian [*or* Yeh Wei-lien *or* Wai-lim Yip]

Hanging Man, The. Sylvia Plath. OxBoAm; VCAP

Hanging man wandered out of a moonshine dream, The. Hume's Suicide of the External World. Christine Hume. LegDan

Hangman. Gunnar Ekelof. PFTM-1

Hangman. Philip Stephens. AmPoNex

Hangman / what will you do with my arms? Hangman. Gunnar Ekelof. PFTM-1

Hangman's Room, The. János Pilinszky. PoSu, *tr. by* Peter Jay

Hangover. Jeffery Conway. WiU

Hangover. Arthur Nortje. TSAP

Hangs and cannot wake itself. (LL) Laser. A. R. Ammons. NAMCP V.2; NoAM

Hangs heavy / down into trees: dawn. Haze. James Schuyler. OxBoAm

Hangs in the tank like a ruined balloon. Elvis the Performing Octopus. Polly Clark. BeAl

Hangs on and howls, biting at air. (LL) Vacuum, The. Howard Nemerov. NIL-7; NIP-4; StAl

Hangs. / whipped / blood. Biography. Imamu Amiri Baraka. EGAG

Hangzhou. Po Chü-i. CCL1, *tr. by* Marsha Wagner

Hank hasn't spoken since the trial began. Pieces of Henry. Taylor Graham. CalPo

Hank Mobley's. Cornelius Eady. SeSe

Hannibal ("Produce the urn that Hannibal contains"). Juvenal. OBVE *Fr.* Satires.

Hannibal ("Put Hannibal i' th' scale"). Juvenal. OBVE *Fr.* Satires.

Hannibal ("Throw Hannibal on the scales, how many pounds"). Juvenal. OBVE *Fr.* Satires.

Hanoch, Pallu, Hezron, Carmi. Biblical Also-Rans. Charles Harper Webb. SUP

Hanoi Market, The. Yusef Komunyakaa. AmAlph

Hans Breitmann as a Politician. Charles Godfrey Leland.
   "There's a liddle fact of hishdory vitch few hafe oondershtand." APN-2

Hans Breitmann gife a barty. Hans Breitmann's Party [*or* Barty]. Charles Godfrey Leland. OBCoV

Hans Breitmann's Party [*or* Barty]. Charles Godfrey Leland. OBCoV

Hans, there are moments when the whole mind. Dedication. James Merrill. OxBoAm

Hansel and Gretel. Barbara Noel-Scott. Prnts

Hansel, Gretel and Ruby Redlips. Anita Endrezze. HATNAP

Han-Shan Fashions a Myth. George Scarbrough. PoA 2002

Ha-nui / limped. Shin Tongyŏp. CAMKP *Fr.* Kŭm River.

Hap. Thomas Hardy. BrAP; CABP; GSo; MoBrPo; NAEL-6v2; NAEL-7v2; NAMCP V.1; NoAM; NoP-4; NoP-5; OxBSo; WaAnP

Happen. How Everything Happens (Based on a Study of the Wave). May Swenson. APT-2

Happen you come on your own. Seven Sides and Seven Syllables. Edouard J. Maunick. VCWP, *tr. by* Carolyn Kizer

Happening at Sordid Creek. Peter Porter. NoAM

Happening, The. Eight Phases of Contemplation. Giusi Busceti. ItPo, *tr. by* Gayle Ridinger

Happenings / (the telephone). (LL) Written structure. George Oppen. APT-2; PFTM-1

Happens upon the plug. (LL) Downward Look, A. James Merrill. CAP-8; StAl

Happie is he, that from all Businesse cleere. Horace. *See* Happy is he, that from all business clear.

Happie newyear god grant may ever stande. Sisters Newyearsgift from Elizabeth to Mary a Happie Mother of Good Children, The. Elizabeth Cromwell. EMWP

Happiest Man in the World, The. Gzar Hantoosh. IrPoTo, *tr. by* Saadi A. Simawe and Ellen Doré Watson

Happiest of the spaniel race. Advice to a Dog Painter. Jonathan Swift. DiBP

Happily. Lyn Hejinian.
   "Constantly I write this happily." NAMCP V.2
   "Manner in which we are present at this time to and fro appears, we come to point of view before us, The." AWPTFC

Happily I turn the earth. Tony Kushner. ASA *Fr.* Hydriotaphia.

Happiness. Raymond Carver. GoPo; PoA 2002; StAl

Happiness. Stephen Dunn. StAl

Happiness. Louise Glück. HarvBoo; WaAnP

Happiness: "Because yesterday morning from the steamy window." Robert Hass. CAP-8

Happiness. John Keble. TreFP

Happiness. Jane Kenyon. BeAl; PoA 2002; PoDa

Happiness. Alan Alexander Milne. AmFaPo; NOxBChV

Happiness. Robert Pollok. TreFP

Happiness. Carl Sandburg. IllVoic

Happiness. Michael Van Walleghen. VisFro

Happiness. Mihály Csokonai Vitéz. IQMS, *tr. by* Paul Tabori

Happiness. Crystal Williams. RD

Happiness comes with success. I've Got a Pocketful of Dreams. Johnny Burke. ReLy

Happiness: "In the hot white dome of air." Lee Upton. AmAlph

Happiness in the Trees. Joseph Ceravolo. OxBoAm

Happiness Is Just a Thing Called Joe. E. Y. Harburg. ReLy

Happiness Is the Art of Being Broken. Bruce Dawe. NoAM

Happiness is when. Tachibana Akemi. WoPoe *Fr.* Thirty Tanka.

Happiness Makes Up in Height for What It Lacks in Length. Robert Frost. MoAmPo; SoSe-8

Happy Among These Cliffs. Han-shan (Cold Mountain). CCL1; NDACCP, *tr. by* Gary Snyder

Happy and Contented in Your Hut. Francisco de Quevedo y Villegas. SpanPo, *tr. by* William M. Davis

Happy and mournful were the memories. Present, The. Maria Luisa Spaziani. CItWP, *tr. by* Cinzia Sartini Blum and Lara Trubowitz

Happy and Unhappy Families 1. Lisel Mueller. ExTi

Happy and Unhappy Families 2. Lisel Mueller. ExTi

Happy Arabia. Tom Matthews. PNI

Happy are men who yet before they are killed. Insensibility. Wilfred Owen. BrAP; FaBoWar; NoP-4; NoP-5; OBWP; OxAEP-2; PoWW

Happy are they and charmed in life. Memorial on the Slain at Chickamauga. Herman Melville. CBCWP

Happy are you, whom Quantock overlooks. William Diaper. OBSV *Fr.* Brent; a Poem to Thomas Palmer Esq.

Happy armchair! The house. Happy Armchair. Jorge Guillén. RaW, *tr. by* Charles Guenther

Happy art thou, whom God does bless. Abraham Cowley. OBGa

Happy As I Am. Steve Orlen. LiTh

Happy As the Day Is Long. Ted Koehler. ReLy

Happy band on the hill slope, A. Battle of Waun Gaseg, The. Llywelyn ab y Moel. OBWVE, *tr. by* H. Idris Bell

Happy be they which will believe, and never seek the rest. (LL) Sir Philip Sidney. NoP-4; NoP-5 *Fr.* Countess of Pembroke's Arcadia, The.

Happy Birthday. Frank Bidart. VCAP

Happy Birthday, A. Ted Kooser. PoCho

Happy bridegroom, the marriage that you prayed for. Sappho. SaLy, *tr. by* Diane Rayor

Happy Christmas to all, and to all a good night! (LL) Visit from St Nicholas, A. Clement Clarke Moore. APN-1; BLPJKO; BRP; ChAP; ChrPo; NTCP; OBCP; OxBoAm; TCAPo; TFi

Happy Day in My Life, A. Mircea Cărtărescu. PML, *tr. by* Sanda Agalida and Julian Semilian

Happy Days Are Here Again. Jack Yellen. ReLy

Happy Ending. Fleur Adcock. LW

Happy Farmer, The. Edward Williams.
"I live on my farm in a beautiful vale." AngWePo

Happy genius of my household?, The. (LL) Danse Russe. William Carlos Williams. AmFaPo; NAAPv.2; NAMCP V.1; NoP-4; NoP-5; OxBoAm; RaBo; SAmP

Happy, happy year is born, The. Ode upon the New Year. Nahum Tate. STuOW

Happy have no notion how time passes, The. Brontë Sisters, The. Anna Semionovna Prismanova. ARWW, *tr. by* Catriona Kelly

Happy he who has found wisdom. Bible, *O.T.* HW *Fr.* Proverbs.

Happy he whose eyes have view'd. Boethius. OBVE *Fr.* Consolation of Philosophy, The ("De Consolacione Philosophie").

Happy Heart, A. Josephine D. Henderson Heard. CBWP-4

Happy Heart, The. Thomas Dekker *and others.* NoSic *Fr.* Pleasant Comedy of Patient Grissell [*or* Grissel *or* Grissill], The.

Happy Hour. Walid Bitar. KGB

Happy Hours that Hurry Away. Gutierre de Cetina. SpanPo, *tr. by* Kate Flores

Happy hunters are coming back, The. Lion Lion. Tom Raworth. PFTM-2

Happy insect, what can be. Grasshopper, The. Abraham Cowley. BASC; NOSC; OBVE; OxAEP-1

Happy Is England! I Could Be Content. John Keats. CenSon; OxAEP-2

Happy is he given to sage disciplines. André Marie de Chénier. WoPoe *Fr.* Elegies.

Happy is he, that from all business clear. Horace. BASC *Fr.* Epodes.

Happy is the day which saw me when I was joined to my boyfriend. Pacifico Massimi. CAGL *Fr.* Hecateleguim.

Happy Letter, A. Hwang Tonggyu. CAMKP, *tr. by* Anthony, Brother of Taizé

Happy Life, A [Book 10, Epigram 47; *see also* "Things that make the happier life, are these, The," by Ben Jonson]. Martial. OBVE, *tr. by* Sir Richard Fanshawe

Happy Life (Martial X. xlvii), A. Martial. NOSC,

Happy Life of a Country Parson, The [*in imitation of* Swift]. Alexander Pope. UV

Happy Life, The. Martial. NoSic; OBVE, *tr. by* Henry Howard, Earl of Surrey
(Martial, the things that do attain.) NAEL-7v1
(Means to Attain the Happy Life, The.) OBEV
(My Friend, the Things That Do Attain.) NAEL-6v1

Happy Little Cripple, The. James Whitcomb Riley.
"I'm thist a little crippled boy, an' never goin' to grow." VerBaPo

Happy lover who has come, A. Alfred Tennyson. InoFa; NAEL-6v2; NAEL-7v2 *Fr.* In Memoriam A. H. H.

Happy Marriage. Taslima Nasrin. P180

Happy me! o happy sheepe! King James Version. *See* Lord is my shepherd; I shall not want, The.

Happy men that lose their heads, The. Fantasia. G. K. Chesterton. SacPr

Happy moments tell me, pray. Birth of Time, The. Josephine D. Henderson Heard. CBWP-4

Happy Morning. *Unknown.* SSUS

Happy New Year. Miguel Algarin. PueRic

Happy New Year, A. W. H. Auden. OBSV

Happy New Year, Anyway. Joanna Cole. NTCP

Happy One, The. Paul Klee. PFTM-1

Happy one, who is almost / an idiot, The. Happy One, The. Paul Klee. PFTM-1

Happy Pair, A. Priscilla Jane Thompson. CBWP-2

Happy Pair, The. Sir Charles Sedley.
Marriage and Money. OBSV

Happy people die whole, they are all dissolved in a moment, they have had what they wanted. Post Mortem. Robinson Jeffers. MoAmPo

Happy rain knows time and season. Spring Night, Happy Rain. Tu Fu [*or* Du Fu]. CCL1, *tr. by* Florence Ayscough *and* Amy Lowell

Happy Returns! the children say. Grannie's Birthday. Eliza Ogilvy. VWP

Happy Talk. Oscar Hammerstein, II. ReLy

Happy talk / Keep talkin' happy talk. Happy Talk. Oscar Hammerstein, II. ReLy

Happy that first white age! when wee. Boethius. NOSC; OBVE *Fr.* Consolation of Philosophy, The ("De Consolacione Philosophie").

Happy the man which, far from city care. Second Epode of Horace Translated, The. Thomas Randolph. BASC

Happy the Man, who his whole time doth bound. Old Man of Verona, The. Claudian. OBVE, *tr. by* Abraham Cowley

Happy the man who, safe on shore. Hurricane, The. Philip Freneau. TCAPo

Happy the man whose wish and care. Ode on Solitude. Alexander Pope. HeIP-4; NAEL-6v1; NIL-7; NOSC; SacPr; WaAnP

Happy the one who sighs for you by your side. Imitating an Ode by Sapho. Gertrudis Gomez de Avellaneda. BLPSL, *tr. by* Rene de Costa, Rigas Kappatos and Eleni Paidoussi

Happy the tree, that scarcely feels. Doom. Rubén Darío. SpanPo, *tr. by* Kate Flores

Happy the wild birds that can soar. Unfair to Men. *Unknown.* OBWVE, *tr. by* Gwyn Jones

Happy those early days [*or* dayes]! when I. Retreat[e], The. Henry Vaughan. BASC; CABP; ClHu; FSCP; NAEL-6v1; NAEL-7v1; NIP-4; NoP-4; NoP-5; NOSC; NPeEn; OBEV; OBWVE; OxBEV; PBRV; RSR; TFi

Happy Thought. Robert Louis Stevenson. BRP; Spl

Happy Time, The. Fred Ebb. ReLy

Happy to have saved us all. (LL) Hymnus Ad Patrem Sinensis. Philip Whalen. BB; WANABP

Happy to have these fish! Catch, The. Raymond Carver. MoASP

Happy traveler / Mosquito wick. Buson. ZenPo, *tr. by* Takashi Ikemoto and Lucien Stryk

Happy Walk. No Hyegyông. EcSo, *tr. by* Ann Y. Choi

Happy Warrior, The. Sir Herbert Read. FaBoWar

Happy Were He. Robert Devereux, 2d Earl of Essex. NoSic

Happy were he could finish forth his fare. Happy Were He. Robert Devereux, 2d Earl of Essex. NoSic

Happy who near you sigh, for you alone. Verses Made by Sappho, Done from the Greek by Boyleau, and from the French by a Lady of Quality. Sappho. EMWP

Happy ye leaves when as those lilly hands. Edmund Spenser. Sonnet 1. GSo; NAEL-6v1; NAEL-7v1; NoP-4; NoP-5

Happyer those times were, when the Flaxen clew. William Browne. PBRV *Fr.* Brittania's Pastorals Book 2.

Happy-go-lucky and lazy. We took things. God Lovingly Counterattacks. Jarret Keene. Vesp

Hara came and made off with my Gauri. Kamalākānta Bhattācārya. SinGod, *tr. by* Rachel Fell McDermott

Harbach 1944. János Pilinszky. AF; HP; PoSu; WoPoe, *tr. by* Janos Csokits *and* Ted Hughes and Ted Hughes

Harbingers are come, The. See, see their mark. Forerunners, The. George Herbert. AngWePo; FSCP; NAEL-6v1; NAEL-7v1; NoP-4; NoP-5; PBRV

Harbor, The. William Ellery Channing. APN-1

Harbor, The. Carl Sandburg. APT-1; ColAP; NAMCP V.1

Harbor Dawn, The. Hart Crane. MoAmPo; NoAM; OxBoAm *Fr.* Bridge, The.

Harbour. Frank Lima. AHA

Harbour Bridge, The. Thomas Hardy. NoAM

Harbour of Fowey, The. Sir Arthur Thomas Quiller-Couch. OBCoV

Hard Against the Soul. Dionne Brand.
"Then it is this simple. I felt the unordinary romance of." PoBW

Hard and Easy. Ferenc Kazinczy. IQMS, *tr. by* Watson Kirkconnell

Hard as hurdle arms, with a broth of goldish flue. Harry Ploughman. Gerard Manley Hopkins. EroLit

Hard as mine with another man? (LL) Attempt at Jealousy, An. Marina Ivanovna Tsvetaeva. GPTC; OxBEV; WoPoe, *tr.* by Elaine Feinstein

Hard by the lilied Nile I saw. Thomas Lovell Beddoes. NPeEn; OxBEV *Fr.* Last Man, The.

Hard calloused dreams. Wild Glee from Elsewhere. Joyce Mansour. SurWo

Hard cold rain a forest of wind, A. Han-shan Te-ch'ing. CSKM, *tr.* by Red Pine

Hard core nights are so. Kalamu ya Salaam. SpirFl *Fr.* New Orleans Haiku.

Hard Daddy. Langston Hughes. NAMCP V.1

Hard Drive. Paul Muldoon. KGB

Hard energy, like the stars. (LL) My Sad Captains. Thom Gunn. NAEL-6v2; NAEL-7v2; NAMCP V.2; NoAM; NoP-4; NoP-5; NPeEn; PoPoPo; WaAnP

Hard frosts march together. Frosts Are Coming. László Nagy. IQMS, *tr.* by Alan Dixon

Hard head, A. My Grandfather's Hammer. Charles Behlen. TiP2

Hard, heavy, slow, dark. Ikons, The. James Keir Baxter. BeAl

Hard hook-finger clutching down to the bottom, The. Creature Has a Purpose, The. Thomas Lux. BodElec

Hard, I say. Mostly I can't think how. My Mother's Hard Row to Hoe. Fred Chappell. InGu

Hard Is the Journey. Li Po. CCL1, *tr.* by Arthur Cooper

Hard is the stone, but harder still. Image-Maker, The. Oliver St. John Gogarty. OBEV; OBMV

Hard life of the young, The. (LL) Album: "This is a hard life you are living." Josephine Miles. APT-2; CalPo; ColAP

Hard luck means being born in Viet Nam. Good Nigger. Leroy V. Quintana. ICANM

Hard Put. Catie Rosemurgy. AmPoNex

Hard Road Blues. *Unknown.* FaBoVe

Hard Rock Returns to Prison from the Hospital for the Criminal Insane. Etheridge Knight. ESEAA; NIL-7; NIP-4; PBCAP; TRP

Hard rock was I, and she was water flowing. Water and the Rock, The. Fred Cogswell. Coast

Hard Rock / was / "known not to take no shit." Hard Rock Returns to Prison from the Hospital for the Criminal Insane. Etheridge Knight. ESEAA; NIL-7; NIP-4; PBCAP; TRP

Hard sand breaks, the. Hermes of the Ways. "H. D." NAAPv.2

Hard Song. J. Eirian Davies. BBMWP, *tr.* by Sion Eirian

Hard Structure of the World, The. Richard Eberhart. NoAM

Hard Surface Road. Michael Chitwood. MotU

Hard Times. John Ashbery. NoAM

Hard to image. Anacapa. Abigail Albrecht. GeoHom

Hard to picture, but these Goliath trees. Robeson at Rutgers. Elizabeth Alexander. OxAAAP

Hard to Place. Elaine Randell. Oth

Hard to pronounce and play, the OBOE. Oboe. Laurence McKinney. NBLV

Hard Traveling. Ku K'uang. CCL1, *tr.* by Stephen Owen

Hard water and square wheels. Written While Riding the Long Island Rail Road. May Swenson. GM

Hard work along can't drive blue northers off. Hawks in a Bitter Blizzard. Walter McDonald. TiP2

Hard? You don't know what hard is, boy. Childhood of the Ancients. Andrew Hudgins. InvLad

Hard-Boiled Egg. Jim Daniels. LiTh

Harden now thy tyred hart, with more than flinty rage. Catullus. OBVE,

Hardened Arm, The. Michael Chitwood. MotU

Hardened in a leaf? (LL) Sea Rose. "H. D." APT-1; HeIP-4; MoWP; NAAPv.2; NAMCP V.1; NIL-7; NoAM; NoP-4; NoP-5; OxWW; TRP; WaAnP

Hardening of the World, and the First Settlement of Men, The. *Unknown.* "That the earth be made safer for men, and more stable." APN-2

Hardest Part About Love, The. Imani Tolliver. BRtP

Hard-Hearted Hannah (The Vamp of Savannah). Charles Bates, Bob Bigelow and Jack Yellen. ReLy

Hardihood. Ian Patterson. VaPo

Hardin County. Charles Wright. LPSFW

Hardly a day goes by I don't think of him. Damien. George Young. BloBone

Hardly a ghost left to talk with. The slavs moved on. River Now, The. Richard Hugo. VCAP

Hardly the food revolt in "Potemkin." Fingers in the Bread. Joan Aleshire. NevBe

Hardly visible they rock, on a sigh of light. Evening. Willem Kloos. TuT, *tr. by* Desmond Egan

Hardness Scale, The. Joyce Peseroff. TRP

Hardships of tomorrow are put off, The. Procession, The. Sarah Rosenblatt. AmPoNex

Hardware Store. Jean Follain. YaTCFP, *tr.* by Marilyn Hacker

Hardware store, The. All day. Where We All Went. G. Travis Regier. RWB

Hardwood. Linda Pastan. PfSP

Hardwood sheathing, A. Great Fetishes, The. Blaise Cendrars. PFTM-1

Hardy's "Shelley's Skylark." Daniel Hall. YaYoPo

Hare, The. Silvia Eugenia Castillero. SPV, *tr.* by Jen Hofer

Hare, The. Gillian Clarke. TCAWP

Harebell and Pansy. Laurence Binyon. CABP

Harem, The. Maher Sabry. AnVo, *tr.* by Mohamed Enani

Harengs et bouleaux. Jude Stéfan. YaTCFP

Hares, The. Susan Miles. LW

Hares at Play. John Clare. WoPoe

Hare's Complaint, The. George Turberville. DiBP

Hark! Sacrifice, A. Robert Davenport. NOSC

Hark! ah, the nightingale. Philomela. Matthew Arnold. OBEV; OWoS

Hark, All Ye Lovely Saints. *Unknown.* NPeEn

Hark! for the beetle winds his horn. Fairies' Song, The. Jane Taylor. NOBRP

Hark! from the islet in the the stream the voice. *Unknown.* CCL1 *Fr.* Guan-ju.

Hark, hark, the bark as Fido springs. Dawn Chorus. Mary Holtby. UV

Hark, hark! the lark at heaven's gate sings. William Shakespeare. ITBLP; NIL-7; NIP-4; NoSic; TFi; UV *Fr.* Cymbeline.

Hark, hearer, hear what I do; lend a thought now, make believe. Epithalamion. Gerard Manley Hopkins. CAGL

Hark, how all the welkin rings! Glory to the King of Kings. Charles Wesley. SacPr

Hark how she laughs aloud. Richard Lovelace. CavPo

Hark how the Mower Damon sung. Damon the Mower. Andrew Marvell. BASC; NAEL-6v1; NAEL-7v1; NOSC

Hark, my Flora! Love doth call us. Song of Dalliance, A. William Cartwright. NOSC

Hark, my soul! it is the Lord. William Cowper. ChIV-2 *Fr.* Olney Hymns.

Hark[e]! now I hear[e] them—ding-dong, bell. (LL) William Shakespeare. ClHu; NAEL-6v1; NoP-4; NoP-5; NoSic; OBEV; OxBEV; PoPoPo; TFi *Fr.* Tempest, The.

Hark, now the drums beat up again. Over the Hills and Far Away, or, The Recruiting Officer. *Unknown.* FaBoWar

Hark! that's the nightingale. Pain or Joy. Christina Georgina Rossetti. OWoS

Hark! the Alleluias of the great salvation. Christina Georgina Rossetti. RSR

Hark!—the black squadrons wheeling down to death! (LL) Fredericksburg. Thomas Bailey Aldrich. AmWaPo; PCW; TCAPo

Hark! the flow of the four rivers. Farewells from Paradise. Elizabeth Barrett Browning. OBEV

Hark! the glad sound! the Savior comes. Philip Doddridge. RSR; SacPr

Hark! the herald angels sing, Glory to the newborn King. Charles Wesley. SacPr

Hark! the Mavis. Robert Burns. OBEV

Hark the sound of holy voices, chanting at the crystal sea. All Saints' Day, Nov. 1. Christopher Wordsworth. SacPr

Hark! the wood doves' moan. Lai. May Probyn. VWP

Hark, to the snow-fiend's voice afar. Snow-Fiend, The. Anne Batten Cristall. RWP

Hark to the whimper of the sea-gull. Sea-Gull, The. Ogden Nash. OWoS

Hark what a sound, and too divine for hearing. Hymn. Frederic William Henry Myers. SacPr

Harke, al[l] you ladies that do sleep [*or* doo sleepe]. Thomas Campion. NoSic; NPeEn; OxBEV

Harke how my Celia, with the choyce. Thomas Carew. NPeEn

Harlech Castle. John Corben. Spl

Harlem Dancer, The. Claude McKay. APT-1; ISC; NAAL-5; NAAPv.2; NAMCP V.1; NIL-7; NIP-4; NoAM; OxBoAm; TCAPo; WaAnP

Harlem Freeze Frame. Lebert Bethune. GT

Harlem Gallery. Melvin B. Tolson.

   Alpha. APT-2

   Chi.

     "Despite his caricatures." NAAPv.2

   Lambda. NAAPv.2; NAMCP V.1

   Mu. APT-2; NAMCP V.1; OxBoAm; PFTM-1

   Nu. NAMCP V.1

   Xi.

     "Hideho Heights, / a black Gigas." NAMCP V.1

Harlem Gallery, an Afric pepper bird, The. Melvin B. Tolson. APT-2 *Fr.* Harlem Gallery.

Harlem Haiku: A Scrapbook. Jabari Asim. InTrad

Harlem Happiness. Sterling Allen Brown. OxBoAm

Harlem is vicious / modernism. BangClash. Return of the Native. Imamu Amiri Baraka. APSN; ColAP; OxAAAP

Harlem, Montana. James Welch. HATNAP

(Harlem, Montana: Just Off the Reservation.) PoPoPo

Harlem: Neo-Image. Kevin Powell. AmPoNex

Harlem Shadows. Claude McKay. APT-1; ColAP; NAAL-5; NAAPv.2; TCAPo

Harlem: Sidewalk Icons. Oliver Pitcher.
"Man, in some lan." EGAG

Harlem Suite. Raymond R. Patterson. FuFl

Harlem Sweeties. Langston Hughes. NoP-4; NoP-5

Harlem to you! (LL) Langston Hughes. APSN; APT-2; OxBoAm Fr. Lenox Avenue Mural.

Harlem ("What happens to a dream deferred?") Langston Hughes. APSN; APT-2; BrAP; GT; HeIP-4; NAMCP V.1; NIL-7; NIP-4; NoP-4; NoP-5; OxBoAm; RaBo; SAmP; SSLK; WaAnP Fr. Lenox Avenue Mural.

Harley Davidson. Iwan Llwyd. ATSWP, tr. by Robert Minhinnick

Harlot's House, The. Oscar Wilde. ItP; MoBrPo; NAEL-6v2; NAEL-7v2; NoAM

Harm. Vickie Karp. KGB

Harmonics. William Vaughn Moody. AmFaPo; APN-2

Harmonie du Soir. Stephen Yenser. PoDa

Harmonies. Thomas Kinsella. ModIr

Harmonious Heedlessness of Little Boy Blue, The. Guy Wetmore Carryl. AmWit

Harmonious powers with Nature work. Floating Island at Hawkshead. Dorothy Wordsworth. NPeEn; PEW

Harmonizing a Spring Poem by Premier Lu of Chin-Ling. Tu Shen-yen. ChinPo, tr. by Ye Weilian [or Yeh Wei-lim or Wai-lim Yip]

Harmonizing with a Poem by Left Assistant Yu Kao-chih Requesting Sick Leave. Shen Yüeh. ColAnChi, tr. by Richard Mather and Richard B. Mather

Harmonizing with a Poem by the Registrar Guo. T'ao Ch'ien. CCL1, tr. by William Acker

Harmonizing with Great Officer Yan's Poem "The Start of the Fine Weather." Yu Hsin. CCL1, tr. by John Frodsham

Harmonizing with the Monk Heling's Poem "An Outing to the Kunming Pool." Yu Hsin. CCL1, tr. by John Frodsham

Harmony. Tom Postell. EGAG

Harmony. Andrea M. Wren. InTrad

Harmony in Blue. Mary O'Donoghue. NIrP

Harmony in the Kingdom. Vietnamese Oral Tradition. CaDao, tr. by John Balaban

Harmony of Evening, The. Charles Baudelaire. SxFrPo, tr. by James McGowan

Harold. David Ignatow. LTA

Harold and Imogene. Paul Violi. ReTh

Harold, are you asleep? Harold's Leap. Stevie Smith. StAl

Harold Wilson's Selected Poems. Mary Wilson.
"I went out of the conf'rence to get a pint of beer." UV

Harold's Leap. Stevie Smith. StAl

Harold's Walk. Geoffrey Lehmann. EmeKit

Harp, The. Ralph Waldo Emerson. APN-1

Harp, The. Ralph Knevet. ChIV-2

Harp, The. Po Chü-i. TAL

Harp/Desire. Katherine Soniat. MiVo

Harp music blows off the stand, The. Music in the Meadow. Alice Wirth Gray. MiVo

Harp of the North, Farewell! Sir Walter Scott. OxAEP-2

Harp of the North! that mouldering long hast hung. Sir Walter Scott. NePenScot Fr. Lady of the Lake, The.

Harp Song of the Dane Women. Rudyard Kipling. HarvBoo; NAMCP V.1; RACG Fr. Puck of Pook's Hill.

Harp That Once through Tara's Halls, The. Thomas Moore. CABP; NAEL-6v2; NAEL-7v2

Harp the Monarch Minstrel Swept, The. Lord Byron. ChIV-1

Harpe brève des mélèzes. Vers l'arbre-frère aux jours comptés. René Char. YaTCFP

Harpers Ferry. Adrienne Rich. BodElec

Harper's Song for Inherkhawy, The. Unknown. WoPoe, tr. by John L. Foster

Harpe's dead. Harpe's Head. John Knoepfle. IllVoic

Harpies, The. Virgil. OWoS Fr. Aeneid (Dryden translation).

Harpist, The. Jerry Kilbride. WhBo

Harpist believes there is music, The. Concert, The. Lisel Mueller. MiVo

Harpkin. Unknown. FaBoVe

Harpkin gaed up t'the hill. Harpkin. Unknown. FaBoVe

Harriet. Lucille Clifton. OxAAAP

Harriet. Audre Lorde. NAAL-5

Harriet ("Repeating fly, blueback, thumbthick—so gross, A.") Robert Lowell. NoP-4; NoP-5

Harriet Beecher Stowe. Paul Laurence Dunbar. PoPoPo

Harriet Beecher Stowe. Dorothy Parker. NALW Fr. Pig's-Eye View of Literature, A.

Harriet/ if i be you. Harriet. Lucille Clifton. OxAAAP

Harriet there was always somebody calling us crazy. Harriet. Audre Lorde. NAAL-5

Harriet Tubman. Sam Cornish. OxAAAP

Harriet Tubman. Unknown. HHAm

Harriet Tubman aka Moses. Samuel Allen. ISC

Harrigan. George M. Cohan. NAAPv.2

Harrison Street Court. Carl Sandburg. APT-1

Harrowing. Douglas Messerli. FTOS

Harrowing, The. Unknown. WoPoe Fr. Doomsday, the Mysteries.

Harry loves Myrtle—He has strong arms from the warehouse. Aphrodite Metropolis (3). Kenneth Fearing. AmWit

Harry Ploughman. Gerard Manley Hopkins. EroLit

Harry Pollit Was a Bolshie. Unknown. OBCoV

Harry S Truman Library, Independence, Missouri. Diane Glancy. AtGh

Harry Vaughan. John L. Thomas.
"His father did intend that Harry should." AngWePo

Harry, whose tuneful[1] and well-measured [or well-measur'd] song. To Mr. H. Lawes On His Airs. John Milton. NoP-4; NoP-5

Harry Williams. Edgar Lee Masters. AmWaPo; APT-1 Fr. Spoon River Anthology.

Harryette Mullen Lecture on the American Dream. Terrance Hayes. RWB

Harry's Bar Ballad. Giulia Niccolai. CItWP, tr. by Cinzia Sartini Blum and Lara Trubowitz

Harsh Metropolitan Season. Luciana Notari. CItWP, tr. by Cinzia Sartini Blum and Lara Trubowitz

Harsh with salt of the sea. (LL) Drover, A. Padraic Colum. MoBrPo; OBMV

Harshness. (LL) Microscope. Gwyn Thomas. BBMWP; OBWVE, tr. by Joseph P. Clancy

Hart Crane. Paul Engle. YaYoPo

Hartmanswillerkopf. Naomi Mitchison. RSaN

Hartwell Gardens. A. of Aylesbury Merrick. OBGa

Harvard Classics. Henri Cole. NAMCP V.2

Harvest. Blaise Cendrars. BLT, tr. by Monique Chefdor

Harvest. Gary Soto. PBCAP

Harvest. Stephen Caldwell Wright. BtF

Harvest, The. Morgan Llwyd. AngWePo Fr. 1648.

Harvest, The ("They love me not, who at my table eat.") Jones Very. SacPr

Harvest: A Line Drawing. Gregory Pardlo. BRtP

Harvest and Spring. Dic Jones. BBMWP, tr. by the author

Harvest Bow, The. Seamus Heaney. HarvBoo; ModIr; NoAM; PBCIP; PNI

Harvest Gathering. Phoebe Cary. SWaP

Harvest Home. Henry Alford. SacPr

Harvest Home. Bettye T. Spinner. TWF

Harvest in March, The. W. N. Herbert. BeAl

Harvest moon. Basho. EH, tr. by Robert Hass

Harvest moon. Buson. EH, tr. by Robert Hass

Harvest Moon, The. Henry Wadsworth Longfellow. APN-1

Harvest of Hate. Wole Soyinka. AF

Harvest of War. Catherine Obianuju Acholonu. HAWP; NAfrP

Harvest shall flourish in wintry weather, The. Merlins Prophecy. William Blake. WoPoe

Harvest Song. Jean Toomer. NoP-4; NoP-5; WaAnP

Harvest Time. Olav H. Hauge. WED, tr. by Robert Bly

Harvest won't save our barn from twisters. After the Random Tornado. Walter McDonald. TiP2

Harvesters, The. Mary Gilmore. NOBAu

Harvesting the Cows. Ellen Bryant Voigt. CAP-8

Harvest-mouse with caution walks, The. Rustler. William Stroud. Spl

Harvey Always Wins. Jack Prelutsky. NTCP

Harvey, the happy above happiest men. To the Right Worshipfull, My Singular Good Friend, Master Gabriel Harvey, Doctor of the Lawes. Edmund Spenser. NoSic

Harvey, the happy above happiest men. Edmund Spenser. NoSic Fr. Commendatory Sonnets.

Has a giant hand. My Psychic. James Kimbrell. LegDan

Has a gold tooth, sits long hours. Black Bourgeoisie. Imamu Amiri Baraka. ESEAA

Has a packet of chocolate and a souvenir of Tripoli. (LL) Cairo Jag. Keith Douglas. HarvBoo; PoWW

Has any one supposed it lucky to be born? Walt Whitman. ColAP; NAWM-7v2; WaAnP Fr. Song of Myself.

Has anyone seen the boy who used to come here? Has Anyone Seen the Boy? Jelaluddin Rumi. RaBo; WoPoe, *tr. by* Coleman Barks and John Moyne

Has bajado a la tierra, cuando nadie te oía. Has Bajado. José Luis Hidalgo. RaW

Has been written in mud and butter. Everything Good Between Men and Women. C. D. Wright. GPPA

Has death indeed cut off his breath. Wake. Yekhi'el Khazak. NRoS, *tr. by* Esther Raizen

Has done the lover mortal hurt. (LL) Vergissmeinnicht. Keith Douglas. EdScPo; FaBoWar; GoPo; HarvBoo; NAEL-6v2; NAEL-7v2; NAMCP V.1; NoAM; NoP-4; NoP-5; NPeEn; OBWP; OxBEV; PoAgWa; PoWW; SoSe-8; StAl; WoPoe

Has Faded in Part But Magnificent Also Late for RC / Mirrors. Robert Grenier. PmAP

Has fixed my mother and father in a garden. Photograph, The. Myra Schneider. Prnts

Has he walked away from the temple? Has he taken. You Keep Coming upon Your Breath at the Altar. George Kalamaras. Vesp

Has it ever happened. Interlaced Lines for the Same Moment. Ghada El-Shafa'i. PoArWo, *tr. by* Atef Abu-Seif and Nathalie Handal

Has it really been thirty years? To Abbot Min the Compassionate. Tu Fu [*or* Du Fu]. CrYelRi, *tr. by* Sam Hamill

Has left a note saying GONE AWAY. (LL) Ending. Gavin Ewart. NBLV; SoSe-8

Has never been what we are. (LL) As Hour and Year Collapsed. Joe Wenderoth. LegDan; NAPBL

Has not altered. Spenser's Ireland. Marianne Moore. NoAM

Has only just / begun. (LL) Charles Olson. APSN; ColAP *Fr.* Maximus Poems, The.

Has painted his hands blue. Logical Positivist, The. David Bromige. FTOS

Has Sabine winter brought you to your fireside. Persius. RomPo *Fr.* Satires.

Has set me softly down beside you. The poem is you. (LL) Paradoxes and Oxymorons. John Ashbery. FTOS; HeIP-4; NAMCP V.2; NoAM; NoP-5; PmAP; PoPoPo

Has the age of psychology really passed? Whatever Became Of: Freud? Edward Field. BodElec

Has the time come to draw up the accounts? Yevgeny Mikhailovich Vinokurov. TCRusP, *tr. by* Daniel Weissbort

Has vuelto a mí más viejo y triste en la dormida. Retornos de un Poeta Asesinado. Rafael Alberti. RaW

Hasard fit casser un oeuf dans le Paradis terrestre, Le. Oeuf, Un. Max Jacob. YaTCFP

Hasbrouck and the Rose. Howard Phelps Putnam. APT-2

Haschish, The. John Greenleaf Whittier. APN-1; NCAP

Haskell. Witter Bynner. NoP-4; NoP-5

Hassan. James Elroy Flecker.

   Hassan's Serenade. OBEV

   War Song of the Saracens. MoBrPo

Hassan's Serenade. James Elroy Flecker. OBEV *Fr.* Hassan.

Hast Never Come to Thee an Hour. Walt Whitman. SAmP

Hast power to say the Time in terms of tone. (LL) Sidney Lanier. APN-2; NCAP *Fr.* Street Cries.

Hast seen. Sir Edwin Arnold. DiBP

Hast thou a charm to stay the morning-star. Hymn before Sunrise, in the Vale of Chamouni. Samuel Taylor Coleridge. SacPr

Hast thou a cunning instrument of play. Preparation. Thomas Edward Brown. OBEV

'Hast thou come with the heart of thy childhood back? Return, The. Felicia Dorothea Hemans. RWP

Hast thou no Arm for Me? (LL) At least—to pray—is left—is left. Emily Dickinson. APN-2; NCAP; TCAPo

Hast thou no mercy, wind, that thou should'st tear from me. Mother's Lament, The. Mary E. Tucker. CBWP-1

Hast Thou seen her, great Jew. Highland Woman, A. Sorley MacLean. HarvBoo; NePenScot

Hast thou, spirit. William Shakespeare. OxAEP-1 *Fr.* Tempest, The.

Hasta luego and over you go and it's not. Border, The. Martha Collins. ExTi

Haste, hoist the sails! Fair blows the wind. Negro Boy's Tale, The. Amelia Alderson Opie. RWP

Haste Not! Rest Not! Johann Wolfgang von Goethe. TreFP, *tr. by* Unknown

Haste then, sweet love, our wishèd flight! (LL) To His Love. Unknown. NoP-4; NoP-5

Haste to the mighty ocean. August. Henrietta Cordelia Ray. CBWP-3

Hasten toward immense and earthly joy, the eyelids blinking as they. Waking. Tristan Tzara. AF

Hasty Pudding, The [complete text]. Joel Barlow.

   Canto 1. NAAL-3; NAAPv.1; OxBoAm; TCAPo

Hat. Tomasz Jastrun. AF, *tr. by* Daniel Bourne

Hat Factory, The. Paul Durcan. ModIr

Hat Lady, The. Linda Pastan. SoSe-8

Hatched from sleep, as we slipped out of orbit. Postcard from Greece, A. A. E. Stallings. PoA 2002

Hatchet was buried, the table made ready, The. Two Kinds of Welsh Bards. Endre Ady. IQMS, *tr. by* Neville Masterman

Hatching Thunder. Jacqueline Scott. OGAHCP, *tr. by* Boadiba and Jack Hirschman

Hate. James Stephens. MoBrPo

Hate Crime. Barry Ballard. LiTh

Hate Crimes. Joanne Lowery. LiTh

Hate Hitler? No, I spared him hardly a thought. IFF. Howard Nemerov. AmWaPo; BodElec; PWW2

Hate me or love, I care not, as I pass. Unicorn, The. Ruth Pitter. MoBrPo

Hate the people of this village. People of the Other Village, The. Thomas Lux. PoCho; StAl; SUP

Hated Rats, The. Nguyen Binh Khiem. WoPoe, *tr. by* Nguyen Ngoc Bich

Hateful Old Age. *Unknown.*

   "Before my back was bent I was eloquent." OBWVE

Hath melted like snow in the glance of the Lord! (LL) Destruction of Sennacherib, The. Lord Byron. BRP; CABP; ChAP; ChIV-1; FaBoWar; HeIP-4; NoP-4; NoP-5; OBWP; OxAEP-2; TFi; WeW-3; WoPoe

Hath no misfortune, but that Rich she is. (LL) Sir Philip Sidney. NAEL-6v1; NAEL-7v1 *Fr.* Astrophil and Stella.

Hath not the morning dawned with added light? Ethnogenesis. Henry Timrod. APN-2; PCW; TCAPo

Hath oftener [*or* oft'ner] left me mourning. (LL) Simon Lee, the Old Huntsman; with an incident in which he was concerned. William Wordsworth. NAEL-6v2; NAEL-7v2

Hath onely Anger an Omnipotence. Upon the Asse That Bore Our Saviour. Richard Crashaw. ChIV-2

Hath the Rain a Father? Jones Very. ChIV-1

Hath this world aught so fair as Stella is? (LL) Sir Philip Sidney. NAEL-7v1; NoP-5; NoSic *Fr.* Astrophil and Stella.

Hating. Kate Fetherston. MAAN

Hating Jews. Tom Wayman. LTA

Hatred. Gwendolyn B. Bennett. RaBo

Hatred and vengeance, my eternal portion. Lines Written During a Period of Insanity. William Cowper. IJHIL; NoP-4; NoP-5; NPeEn

Hatred I reserve for thee, The. Invective Against Denise, a Witch. Pierre de Ronsard. WoPoe, *tr. by* Anthony Hecht

Hatred Surely Does Not Kiss. Kaspar Stieler. GePo, *tr. by* George C. Schoolfield

Hats. Paula Cunningham. NIrP *Fr.* Dog Called Chance, A.

Hats. Paul Muldoon and Gerald Stern. GPPA

Hatteras Calling. Conrad Potter Aiken. ColAP; InGu

Hatters, The. Nan McDonald. NOBAu

Hattie House. Julia A. Moore.

   "She had blue eyes and light flaxen hair." VerBaPo

Hattie Went to Market. Leslie Simon. FFC

Haul the mainsail down. I have reached the harbour. My Portion. Dániel Berzsenyi. IQMS, *tr. by* Peter Zollman

Haul Your Paper Boats. Eugenio Montale. WoPoe, *tr. by* William Arrowsmith

Hauled hay bales all afternoon. Appaloosa Hail Storm. Gerald Hausman. GifTon

Haulier's Wife Meets Jesus on the Road Near Moone, The. Paul Durcan. ModIr

Hauling Over Wolf Creek Pass in Winter. Walter McDonald. AmWaPo

Haunch under the whip of douches in the slime. Spermal Chimney. Francis Picabia. PFTM-1

Haunted. Edith Nesbit. VWP

Haunted, The. Brad Leithauser. RA

Haunted Beach, The. Mary Robinson. NPBRoP; RWP

Haunted by poems beginning with I. Prologue. Audre Lorde. ESEAA

Haunted Country. Robinson Jeffers. APT-1

Haunted Heart. Howard Dietz. ReLy

Haunted Houses. Henry Wadsworth Longfellow. TCAPo

Haunted Importantly. Jack Gilbert. WaAnP

Haunted Oak, The. Paul Laurence Dunbar. ColAP; NAAPv.1

Haunted Palace, The [*fr.* The Fall of the House of Usher]. Edgar Allan Poe. APN-1; BrAP; NAAL-3; NAAPv.1; OxBoAm; TCAPo; TFi

Haunted Ruin, The. Robert Pinsky. NAMCP V.2

Haunted Streets. Mathilde Blind. ViWPN

Haunting. Andrew Steeves. Coast

Haunting the page of my passport. Paris Is Not the Same. Eric Maschwitz. ReLy

Haunting the Western Moor. (LL) Trampwoman's Tragedy, A. Thomas Hardy. NAEL-6v2; NAEL-7v2; OBNV

Haunting velvet blanket, A. Velvet Blanket. Marlon D. Satchell. InTrad

Haunts me night and day. (LL) Look, The. Sara Teasdale. APT-1; LW

Haunts of the Mirage. Bruce Berger. GeoH

Havana. Laurel Ann Bogen. SUP

Havana Birth. Susan Mitchell. OxBoAm

Havana Harbor. Nancy Morejón. TANSG, tr. by Joy Renjilian-Burgy

Have a being less durable even than he. (LL) Poplar Field, The. William Cowper. BrAP; OxBEV

Have a Jacuzzi and a Jenn-Aire in their condo. Barbie and Ken Maximize Their Options. Barbara Crooker. RWB

Have all built their nests in my beard! (LL) There Was an Old Man with a Beard. Edward Lear. NoP-5; NOxBChV; NPeEn; OPOU; TLR

Have begun opening their doors. (LL) I Wish in the City of Your Heart. Robley, Jr. Wilson. InvLad; P180

Have certain periods set, and hidden fates. (LL) Sonnet: "Dost see how unregarded now." Sir John Suckling. BASC; CavPo; NOSC

Have crawled too far! (LL) I know that He exists. Emily Dickinson. APN-2; NCAP

Have died, the Present teaches, but in vain! (LL) Robert Gould Shaw. Paul Laurence Dunbar. CBCWP; PoPoPo

Have ending. (LL) White Island, The: or Place of the Blest. Robert Herrick. NoP-4; NoP-5; NOSC; NPeEn

Have eyes to wonder, but lack tongues to praise. (LL) William Shakespeare. NAEL-6v1; NAEL-7v1; NoP-5; NoSic; OBEV; OxAEP-1; WoPoe Fr. Sonnets.

Have Feet, Will Dance. Dorothy Fields. ReLy

Have gathered them and will do never again. (LL) In Memoriam (Easter, 1915). Edward Thomas. NoP-4; NoP-5; OBWP; OBWVE; PoAgWa; Spl

Have hamburgers! Have hamburgers! (LL) Louisiana Perch. Ron Padgett. FTOS; NYP2

Have, have ye no regard, all ye. His Saviour['s] Words, Going to the Cross[e]. Robert Herrick. ChIV-2; SacPr

Have heard a kitten in the wilderness. (LL) Chaplinesque. Hart Crane. APT-2; HeIP-4; NAAL-5; NAAPv.2; NAMCP V.1; NoAM; OxBoAm

Have heard her massive sandal set on stone. (LL) Euclid Alone Has Looked on Beauty Bare. Edna St. Vincent Millay. APT-1; BRP; GSo; HeIP-4; MoAmPo; NoP-4; NoP-5

Have I a wife? Bedam I have! Brewer's Man, The. Leonard Alfred George Strong. OBCoV

Have I caught my heav'nly jewel. Sir Philip Sidney. NoSic Fr. Astrophil and Stella.

Have I except it comes from the sun? (LL) Waving Adieu, Adieu, Adieu. Wallace Stevens. NoP-4; NoP-5

Have I got a hut! Kukutis Describes His Hut. Marcelijus Martinaitis. TWW, tr. by Laima Sruoginis

Have I let my love. Lady Kasa. ArkPo, tr. by Edwin A. Cranston

Have I not blessed [or blest] thee? Then go forth; nor fear. To His Book[e]. Robert Herrick. BASC

Have I not seen the hills of Candahar. Albery Allson Whitman. APN-2 Fr. Twasinta's Seminoles; Or Rape of Florida.

Have I renounc't my faith, or basely sold. Upon an Unhandsome Gentlewoman, Who Made Love unto Him. Richard Corbet. BASC

Have lain there long before. (LL) Love's Last Lesson. Letitia Elizabeth Landon. NAEL-7v2; RWP

Have lasted all this while. (LL) Flowers: "Some men never think of it." Wendy Cope. NoP-4; NoP-5

Have minde upon my supplicacioun. (LL) Complaint to His Purse. Geoffrey Chaucer. NoP-4; NoP-5

Have mynde how I mankynde have take. James Ryman. OHMEL

Have neither part nor lot in me. (LL) Magdalen. Amy Levy. ViWPN; VWP

Have no use for any sweets of any kind. Honeysuckle Rose. Andy Razaf. ReLy

Have oon god in worshipe. Unknown. OHMEL

Have Pen, Will Travel. Charles Bernstein. NAMCP V.2

Have Pity. Claribel Alegría. TANSG, tr. by Darwin Flakoll

Have pity on our brother. Have Pity. Claribel Alegría. TANSG, tr. by Darwin Flakoll

Have saved them from the gas. (LL) It Out-Herods Herod. Pray You, Avoid It. Anthony Hecht. AF; NAMCP V.2; NIP-4; NoAM

Have Some Madeira, M'dear? Michael Flanders. OBCoV

Have the gods then loved me here on earth? Retreat. Árpád Tóth. IQMS, tr. by Watson Kirkconnell

Have the poets left a place. Black Night, The. Antar. WoPoe, tr. by Desmond O'Grady

Have the summer rains. Basho. EMJL, tr. by Haruo Shirane

Have the waves lost their way? Midnight Caller, The. Pak Sôwôn. EcSo, tr. by Julie C. Park

Have thine own way, Lord! Have thine own way! Adelaide A. Pollard. SacPr

Have to leave the city. Intermission from Monday. Pedro Juan Pietri. PueRic

Have to work after all. (LL) Necessity. Langston Hughes. APSN; RaBo

Have we always been close to. Crossing. Karen McKinnon. ICANM

Have we come this far. For Brothas That Like to Holla. Kenneth Carroll. BtF

Have We Had Easter Yet? Alison Pryde. BeAl

Have ye beheld (with much delight). Upon the Nipples of Julia's Breast. Robert Herrick. ErotSp; NAEL-6v1; NAEL-7v1; NOSC

Have ye e'er heard of gallant like young Lochinvar? (LL) Sir Walter Scott. ChAP; NAEL-6v2; NAEL-7v2; NePenScot; NPBRoP; OxAEP-2; TFi Fr. Marmion.

Have You Anything to Say in Your Defense? César Vallejo. PoetW; RaBo, tr. by James Wright

Have you been at Garnyvillo? Garnyvillo. Edward Lysaght. IrLP

Have you been in our wild west country? then. West Country, The. Alice Cary. APN-2; SWaP

Have you dug the spill. Harlem Sweeties. Langston Hughes. NoP-4; NoP-5

Have you ever. Massimo del Panino, Il. Del Ray Cross. FreRad

Have you ever awakened to find that you're glad to be awake? You're in Love. Bobby Troup. ReLy

Have you ever been ordered to strip. Solitary Confinement. Robert Walker. NOBAu

Have You Ever Faked an Orgasm? Molly Peacock. RA

Have you ever heard of lynching in the great United States? Lynching. Lizelia Augusta Jenkins Moorer. CBWP-3

Have you ever heard of the Sugar-Plum Tree? Sugar-Plum Tree, The. Eugene Field. ITBLP; NBLV

Have you ever noticed how her toes tickle. Her Eyes a Thousand Times Over. Chani DiPrima. HW

Have you ever seen. Gut Catcher. Stan Platke. FaBoWar

Have you ever seen the dawn of love? Lady's in Love with You, The. Frank Loesser. ReLy

Have you ever smelled summer? That Was Summer. Marci Ridlon. NTCP

Have you ever watched your old mother. Mother. Vladimir Holan. PoSu, tr. by Ian Milner and Jarmila Milner

Have you forgotten what we were like then. Animals. Frank O'Hara. GoPo; HarvBoo; StAl

Have you forgotten yet? Aftermath. Siegfried Sassoon. BLPJKO; MoBrPo; PoWW

Have you heard, my dear Anne, how my spirits are sunk? Lines by a Lady on the Loss of her Trunk. Richard Brinsley Sheridan. OBCoV

Have you heard, my friend, the slander that the Negro has to face? Immortality. Lizelia Augusta Jenkins Moorer. CBWP-3

Have you heard of a collier of honest renown. Patient Joe; or, The Newcastle Collier. Hannah More. WoRP

Have you heard of the Coffin Close, boys. Song of the Coffin Close. Kenneth White. EdScPo

Have you heard of the dreadful fate. Ashtabula Disaster, The. Julia A. Moore. VerBaPo

Have you heard of the wonderful one-hoss shay. Oliver Wendell Holmes. APN-1; BRP; ITBLP; NAAL-3; NAAPv.1; TCAPo; TFi Fr. Autocrat of the Breakfast Table, The.

Have you heard the music that no fingers enter into? Music without Strings, The. Kabir. WED, tr. by Robert Bly

Have you heard the story that gossips tell. John Burns of Gettysburg. Bret Harte. CBCWP; PCW

Have you his lovely image still in mind. Stefan George. EroLit, tr. by Ernst Morwitz and Carol North Valhope

Have you learn'd lessons only of those who admired you, and were tender with you, and stood aside for you? Stronger Lessons. Walt Whitman. RaF

Have you made your life worth? (LL) After Experience Taught Me. W. D. Snodgrass. CAP-8; OBWP

Have You Met Miss Jones? Lorenz Hart. ReLy

Have you never felt the fever of the. Whirling Wheel, The. Unknown. ArBi

Have you not heard the gossip and the rumour going around. Raphael de Leon. EroLit

Have you not seen the grass by the river? Grass by the River, The. Pao Chao. CCL1, tr. by John Frodsham

Have you not seen the young men. Rough Road, A. Pao Chao. CCL1, tr. by John Frodsham

Have you not seen them. Hard Traveling. Ku K'uang. CCL1, tr. by Stephen Owen

Have you not seen (you must remember). Henry Luttrell. NOBRP Fr. Letter to Julia, in Rhyme.

Have you noticed this desire. To Adam. Thandiwe Shiphrah. BtF

Have you read in the Talmud of old. Sandalphon. Henry Wadsworth Longfellow. TCAPo

Have you seen a person. Kim Kwanguk. CATKP, tr. by Peter H. Lee

Have you seen / hear or known surfeited under the unheard of tree the acquired. Balcony. César Moro. AHA, tr. by Frances LeFevre

Have You Seen How a Word Is Born and Dies? Edmond Jabès. PFTM-2 *Fr.* Book of Questions, The.

Have you seen my cousin? William Shakespeare. OxAEP-1 *Fr.* Troilus and Cressida.

Have you seen that Vigilante Man? Vigilante Man. Woody Guthrie. APT-2

Have you seen the well-to-do. Puttin' on the Ritz (Original Version). Irving Berlin. ReLy

Have you seen the well-to-do. Puttin' on the Ritz (Revised Version). Irving Berlin. ReLy

Have You Seen This Child. Franz Wright. AmAlph

Have you time for a story. Charity Overcoming Envy. Marianne Moore. GS

Have you with your white beard no shame? *Unknown.* SLW, *tr. by* Marjolijn De Jager, Sayd Bahodin Majrouh and André Velter

Have Yourself a Merry Little Christmas. Ralph Blane and Hugh Martin. ReLy

Haven of Rest. Mihály Tompa. IQMS, *tr. by* Dorren Bell

Haven't Got a Worry. Ray Evans and Jay Livingston. ReLy

Haven't I told you enough? (LL) When I Was Growing Up. Nellie Wong. OxWW; UnSA

Haven't you already filled. On Poetry. Franco Buffoni. ItPo, *tr. by* Gayle Ridinger

Haven't you heard the latest news about AIDS? Island of Lost Tears, The. Sky Gilbert. PML

Having a Coke with You. Frank O'Hara. VCAP

Having a crush was how I existed. Suburban Childhood, A. Liz Rosenberg. PBCAP

Having allowed my willow to dry out. Halcion. R. T. Smith. AWTN

Having been a farmer's daughter. Amaryllis. Ellen Bryant Voigt. AFaM

Having been born and brought up in Palestine and educated in the United States. Bad Moon Rising. Ibrahim Muhawi. Eno

Having been taught by fools, how else could I have ended up. On Fire. Andrew Feld. LegDan

Having been tenant long to a rich Lord. Redemption. George Herbert. BASC; CABP; FSCP; GSo; NAEL-6v1; NAEL-7v1; NoP-4; NoP-5; NOSC; NPeEn; OxBEV; OxBSo; PBRV; PoPoPo; SoSe-8; TFi; WeW-3

Having begun in thought there. Other. Robert Creeley. OxBoAm

Having built my city and named my god. Lenaia. Susan M. Whitmore. AmPoNex

Having caroused far into the night. Song of Ch'ŏyong. Ch'ŏyong. CATKP, *tr. by* Peter H. Lee

Having commanded Adam to bestow. Naming the Animals. Anthony Hecht. ChIV-1

Having Completed My Fortieth Year. John Tranter. BMAP

Having Cut the Sparrow's Heart. Malinda Markham. IAoNAP

Having Died. Kim Kwangsŏp. WoPoe, *tr. by* David R. McCann

Having done most shameful, unjust things. Alcaeus. SaLy, *tr. by* Diane Rayor

Having enjoyed his shower, the cake of soap. On His Birthday. Greg Williamson. NAPBL

Having fallen not knowing. Conscript Goes, The. William Sydney Graham. FaBoWar

Having fathomed Tao, you went to dwell among simple villages. Visiting the Recluse Cheng. Po Chü-i. NDACCP, *tr. by* David Hinton

Having given my clothes to a boy. Kim Ch'ŏnt'aek. CATKP, *tr. by* Peter H. Lee

Having given up hope for a high-wire act. Learning to Swim at Forty-Five. Colleen J. McElroy. FiBr; GT

Having gone upstairs. Mirror, A. Jean Follain. BLT

Having hauled down my pyjamas. Circumcision. Tawfiq Rafat. PML

Having heard that an official was coming to investigate the disaster. Ballad on the Investigation of a Disaster. Yao Chen. ColAnChi, *tr. by* Victor H. Mair

Having indulged in a spring dream, I sober up at dawn. Drinking Alone on a Spring Night. An Jung-Sŏp. TAPaP, *tr. by* Sung-Il Lee

Having interred [*or* interr'd] her infant-birth. Ode, upon a Question Moved, Whether Love Should Continue Forever?, An. Edward Herbert, 1st Baron Herbert of Cherbury. BASC; OxAEP-1; OxBEV

Having invented a new Holocaust. U. S. 1946 King's X. Robert Frost. NIP-4

Having It Out with Melancholy. Jane Kenyon. EMP; ExTi; IJHIL; PoA 2002
From the Nursery. LoL
In and Out. LoL
Often. LoL
Once There Was Light. LoL
Pardon. LoL
Suggestion from a Friend. LoL

Having Led a Charmed Life, He Had to Be Hanged Twice. Mac Wellman. FTOS

Having left behind its cutting. *Unknown.* RomPo *Fr.* Priapean Corpus, The.

Having let flow. Tanka. Kanoko Okamoto. CAoMJL1, *tr. by* Makoto Ueda

Having little to do with Eros. This Is Not Love's Offering. Shaun Griffin. PoDa

Having lived a wretched life, he died. Graveside Memorial. Shin Kyŏngnim. CAMKP, *tr. by* Anthony, Brother of Taizé

Having Lost My Son, I Confront the Wreckage. Wanda Coleman. BRtP

Having myself been scared silly when I was young. Thief, The. Alden Nowlan. RaBo

Having never been. On Trying to Imagine the Kiwi Pregnant. Clarence Major. GT

Having never been to a drive-in movie. Eclipse, The. Alan Michael Parker. NevBe

Having no force to fly. (LL) Pine boat a-shift. *Unknown.* APSN; APT-1; NDACCP; OBVE, *tr. by* Ezra Pound

Having not yet crossed the Yellow River, my heart is not at peace. *Unknown.* NAAPv.2

Having Our Tea. Bobi Jones. BBMWP, *tr. by* Joseph P. Clancy

Having oversold the spirit, having. Don McKay. NLPA *Fr.* Matériel.

Having planted a banana tree. Basho. EH, *tr. by* Robert Hass

Having Prayed for, and Made Much Mention of the Merchants, She Sings the Following Hymn to Them. Anna Trapnell. EMWP

Having Read Up on the Subject. Jane Holland. NeBl

Having reddened the plum blossoms. Buson. EH, *tr. by* Robert Hass

Having sat all morning at the bay window. Late Mr Charles Lynch Digresses, The. Paul Durcan. ModIr

Having slept, the cat gets up. Issa. EH, *tr. by* Robert Hass

Having Slept with a Man. Palladas. WoPoe, *tr. by* Peter Jay

Having so rich a treasury, so fine a hoard. Daisy, The. Marya Alexandrovna Zaturenska. MoAmPo

Having submitted your petition for dismissal. Svetlana Kekova. ItGoST, *tr. by* Judith Hemschemeyer

Having Sunk His Chin in His Hand. Francisco Brines. RaW, *tr. by* David Ignatow

Having the Wrong Name for Mr. Wright. Helen Barolini. UnSA

Having this day my horse, my hand, my lance. Sir Philip Sidney. NAEL-6v1; NAEL-7v1 *Fr.* Astrophil and Stella.

Having to Hide. Basho. EMJL *Fr.* Mad Verse.

Having to Part from His Mistress at Dawn. Bálint Balassi. IQMS, *tr. by* Yakov Hornstein

Having tried to use the. It Is Deep. Carolyn M. Rodgers. SSLK

Having used every subterfuge. Renewal, A. James Merrill. CAP-8; VCAP

Having wet me with love. Mirabai. ErotSp, *tr. by* Andrew Schelling

Having written every kind of poem. Tired Hunter, The. Gabriel Preil. FIT, *tr. by* Robert Friend

Havisham. Carol Ann Duffy. MoWP

Haw, Jimmy, dinnae mess wi me. Shore Crab. Gerry Cambridge. EdScPo

Haw Lantern, The. Seamus Heaney. HarvBoo; MakPoe; NoAM; PNI

Hawk. Mary Oliver. NAAL-5; NAMCP V.2; OWoS

Hawk, The. George Mackay Brown. BeAl; NoP-4; WaAnP

Hawk, The. Jelaluddin Rumi. WED, *tr. by* Robert Bly

Hawk above Felindre, The. Alan Llwyd. BBMWP, *tr. by* Joseph P. Clancy

Hawk above the House, The. Andrew Hudgins. LPSFW

Hawk Chant of the Saginaws. *Unknown.* APN-2, *tr. by* Henry Rowe Schoolcraft

Hawk drops to the treetop, A. On Exploration. James Galvin. TAPaP

Hawk Hill. Reynolds Price. PoA 2002 *Fr.* Good Places.

Hawk hovering over oak trees, A. Flodden. William Montgomerie. EdScPo

Hawk hovers in air, A. Loneliness. Tu Fu [*or* Du Fu]. CCL1, *tr. by* Kenneth Rexroth

Hawk hung low above the house, The. Hawk above the House, The. Andrew Hudgins. LPSFW

Hawk in a Painting, A. Tu Fu [*or* Du Fu]. WoPoe, *tr. by* David Lattimore

Hawk in golden space. Illegibility. Franz Wright. AmAlph

Hawk in the Rain, The. Ted Hughes. WaAnP

Hawk is present in its absence, The. Tom Montag. AmZen *Fr.* Plain Poems: A Fairwater Daybook.

Hawk over Inwood Road, A. A. C. Greene. TiP2

Hawk Roosting. Ted Hughes. BrAP; EMP; HeIP-4; OWoS; OxBEV; WaAnP

Hawk turns into the sun. Net of Place, The. Paul Blackburn. PFTM-2; PmAP

Hawk's Cry in Autumn, The. Joseph Brodsky. WaAnP, *tr. by* Alan Myers, the author and Joseph Brodsky

Hawks in a Bitter Blizzard. Walter McDonald. TiP2

Hawk's Shadow. Louise Glück. HarvBoo; StAl

Hawks turn their heads nimbly round, The. Hawk Chant of the Saginaws. *Unknown.* APN-2, *tr. by* Henry Rowe Schoolcraft

Hawthorn and Lavender. W. E. Henley.
13. OBMV
27. MoBrPo
38. OBMV

Hawthorn at Digiff. Ruth Bidgood. TCAWP

Hawthorn bares its fangs. Puncture Wounds: A Baiku. Rowena M. Love. ArBi

Hawthorn morning moving, The. Renewal by Her Element. Denis Devlin. ModIr

Hawthorne. James Russell Lowell. TCAPo *Fr.* Fable for Critics, A.

Hawthorne berries, The. David Kherdian. UrbNat *Fr.* Taking the Soundings on Third Avenue.

Hawthorne Metal, Detroit, 1939. Marcus Cafagña. MAAN

Hay. Maxine W. Kumin. BodElec

Hay días en que amanezco hermosa. Natalia. Natalia Toledo. RMCMP

Hay Fever. Alec Derwent Hope. NoAM

Hay for the Horses. Gary Snyder. BB; CAP-8; GoPo; LoL; TRP

Hay making. Joanna Baillie. OxAEP-2

Hay que bajar sin miedo. Hay que Bajar. José Luis Hidalgo. RaW

Hay scented, The. The cinnamon, the horsetail. Understory. Pamela Alexander. ExTi

Hay spread for. Hokko. NAAPv.2

Hay un silencio antiguo convertido en estatua. Teoría de Silencios. Gabriel Celaya. RaW

Hay una Luz que Cubre Todo el Campo. Francisco Brines. RaW

Hay veces que los hombres tristemente. Tres Poemas Sobre la Muerte. Carlos Bousoño. RaW

Hay Wagon. Lőrinc Szabó. IQMS, *tr. by* Godfrey Turton

Hay wagon passed through the town at night, The. Hay Wagon. Lőrinc Szabó. IQMS, *tr. by* Godfrey Turton

Haydon! forgive me that I cannot speak. To B.R. Haydon, with a Sonnet Written on Seeing the Elgin Marbles. John Keats. CenSon

Hayes, The. Emyr Lewis. ATSWP, *tr. by* Robert Minhinnick

Hayfork, The. Henry Taylor. PoDa

Haying. Wyatt Prunty. PfSP

Haylle, Comly and Clene. *Unknown.* OBEV

Haymakers. Deborah Randall. NeBl

Hay-Making. Gillian Clarke. AngWePo

Haymaking. Edward Thomas. MoBrPo

Haymaking. William Carlos Williams. NAMCP V.1; NoAM *Fr.* Pictures from Brueghel.

Haymarket, The. John Keene. FuFl

Haystack in the Floods, The. William Morris. CABP; NAEL-6v2; NAEL-7v2; NoP-4; NoP-5; OBNV; OxAEP-2

Hayyal al salat, hayyal al salat. Dual Call, The. Abubakar Othman. NeNiPo

Hazardous Waste. James Sherry. FTOS

Hazards of Imagery, The. Paul Violi. KGB

Haze. Carl Sandburg. TCAPo

Haze. James Schuyler. OxBoAm

Haze of gold, the Occident lights up, A. Baruch Spinoza. Jorge Luis Borges. WoPoe, *tr. by* Willis Barnstone

Hazed with harvest dust and heat. For the Missing in Action. John Balaban. AF

Hazel. Oliver Reynolds. FaBoWar

Hazel Goodwin Morrissey Brown. Sinéad Morrissey. MFPA; NIrP

Hazel Stick for Catherine Ann, A. Seamus Heaney. NoAM

Hazel Tells LaVerne. Katharyn Howd Machan. ReTh; SUP

Hazing (for tony new and albee). Brian G. Gilmore. BtF

Hazlitt calls Iago an artist. And. Iago. Arthur Powers. IaFF

Hazy mountain temple hides away behind the setting sun, A. Tune: "Sand of Silk-Washing Brook." Wang Kuo-wei. ColAnChi, *tr. by* Jiaosheng Wang

He. Stanley Kunitz. NoP-4; NoP-5

He. Vasco [*or* Vasko] Popa. PoSu; StAl *Fr.* Games.

He. *Unknown.* WoPoe *Fr.* Excerpts from *The Poem of the Cid.*

He admits he has been collecting old greeting cards. Almost Bashfully. Walter Helmut Fritz. GTCP, *tr. by* Reinhold Grimm

He adored the desk, its brown-oak inlaid with ebony. Geoffrey Hill. NAMCP V.2; NoAM; NoP-4 *Fr.* Mercian Hymns.

He ahold of my hand has completely satisfied me. (LL) Of the Terrible Doubt of Appearances. Walt Whitman. APN-1; CAGL

He all that time among the sewers of Troy. Troy. Edwin Muir. HarvBoo

He also told them a parable. William Carlos Williams. GI *Fr.* St. Matthew; He also told them a parable.

He always blinked too much. Remembering Dennis's Eyes. Geoff Hattersley. NeBl

He always did that. Fall. Mahe Jabeen. HotL, *tr. by* V. Narayana Rao

98: He and I. Dante Gabriel Rossetti. OxBSo *Fr.* House of Life, The.

He and I both nearing seventy. Delighted That the Monk Ch'ien-chou Has Come a Long Way to Visit Me. Ch'i-chi. CSKM, *tr. by* Burton Watson

He andado muchos caminos. Antonio Machado Ruiz. RaW

He andado perdido por el mundo pidiendo pan y luz. Me Voy Porque la Espiga y la Aurora No Son Mías. León Felipe. RaW

He appeared as I was standing at the lighted coals in my fireplace. Nijinski. George Seferis. MotU, *tr. by* Edmund Keeley and Philip Sherrard

He appeared, white as any angel. I Wouldn't Even Bleed. Benjamin Alire Sáenz. TiP2

He applies for a job. Variations on a Poem by Reznikoff. Louis Simpson. BodElec

He approaches her, trailing his whole fortune. Peacock Display. David Wagoner. OWoS

He arises. Oriane / the lurcher wants. Red Brick and Brown Stone. James Schuyler. BodElec

He arrived, confused, in groups at the harbours. Word, The. Colette Bryce. MoWP

He arrived, towing a crowd, and slept. David Constantine. HarvBoo

He ask'd, and hoped, through Christ. Do thou the same! (LL) Epitaph: "Stop, Christian passer-by!—Stop, child of God." Samuel Taylor Coleridge. NAEL-6v2; NAEL-7v2; SacPr

He asked her how she knew it was the same man. Parts of a Mystery. Charlotte Osgood Carter. AHA

He ate and drank the precious Words. Emily Dickinson. APN-2

He attempted *texas red light.* Random (Re-arrangeable) Study for *Views.* Tony Towle. PmAP

He avoids the momentous rhythm. Last Man, The. Thom Gunn. OxAEP-2 *Fr.* Misanthropos.

He bade me "Be Happy," he whisper'd "Forget me." He Bade Me Be Happy. Frances Sargent Osgood. TCAPo

He bar him up, he bar him down. *Unknown.* OHMEL

He bare hym up, he bare hym down. *Unknown.* NPeEn; OBEV; TFi

He bathes his soul in women's wrath. Irish Patriarch, The. Ruth Pitter. NALW

He battled against the king's enemy. *Various authors.* CATKP *Fr.* Songs of Flying Dragons.

He be a home mender and floor fixer. Wet Oak. Angela Shannon. BtF

He beat me with the hem of a kimono. Club, The. Mitsuye Yamada. FiBr

He believed that touch. St. Jacob's Church of the Hanging Hand. James Ragan. Vesp

He believes she is looking at him. (LL) Modern Love. Ann Townsend. LegDan; LiTh

He best can paint 'em, who shall feel 'em most. (LL) Eloisa to Abelard. Alexander Pope. NAEL-6v1; NAEL-7v1; RACG

He Bids His Beloved Be at Peace. William Butler Yeats. *See* Michael Robartes Bids His Beloved Be at Peace.

He blinks upon the hearth-rug. On a Cat Aging. Sir Alexander Gray. TriCat

He bore him up, he bore him down. *Unknown.* NAEL-6v1; NAEL-7v1; NoP-4; NoP-5

He bought me the fur thing five Winters ago. Take Back Your Mink. Frank Loesser. ReLy

He bows because he is nobody. Tennessee Waltz, The. James Haug. OPRER

He breathed deeply. Circle. 'Enayat Jaber. PoArWo, *tr. by* Wen Chin Ouyang

He breathed in air, he breathed out light. Goodbye. Adrian Mitchell. OPOU

He breathes before writing. . .then he writes without breathing. He Breathes before Writing. Jacques Dupin. YaTCFP, *tr. by* Stephen Romer

He brought her presents. Evidence. Helen Lamb. EdScPo

He brought our saviour to the western side. John Milton. NOSC *Fr.* Paradise Regained [*or* Regain'd].

He brushed against me, Father. Very gently. (LL) Cuba. Paul Muldoon. ModIr; PNI; StAl

He burnt up his desire. (LL) Adonis. Theocritus. NoSic; NPeEn, *tr. by* Theocritus and *Unknown*

He buys me a glass. Gameboy. Regie Cabico. WiU

He called her his willow. Every time he wanted to. He Called Her His Willow. Arnljot Eggen. PML, *tr. by* Nancy Coleman

He called his dog (that sometime had the praise). Michael Drayton. DiBP *Fr.* Shepherd's Garland, The.

He calls it their stage which echoes our first misrecognition of unity. Instances. Swan, The. Mei-Mei Berssenbrugge. OpBo

He came, a dark youth, singing in the dawn. James David Corrothers. WaAnP

He came after the reading, when all. Belonging. Leslie Norris. TCAWP

He came and took me by the hand. Mystery, The. Ralph Hodgson. InvLi; MoBrPo

He came apart in the open. Martin's Blues. Michael S. Harper. NAAL-5

He came back. Dry River Bed. Andrew Salkey. WoPoe

He came back and shot. He shot him. When he came. Incident. Imamu Amiri Baraka. AF; NoAM

He came from Malta. Maltese Dog, A. Tymnes. Spl; WoPoe, *tr. by* Edmund Charles Blunden

He came in. Triolet. Jack London. ASA

He came lilting down the brae with a blackthorn stick the thick of a shotgun. Bagpipe Music. Ciaran Carson. ModIr

He came over to London and straight away strode. Dinky Di. *Unknown.* NOBAu

He came to the depot a figure of shame. Conchie, The. R. F. Palmer. FaBoWar

He came to the desert of London town. William Blake. CABP

He Came unto His Own, and His Own Received Him Not. Mary Elizabeth Coleridge. ViWPN

He can bring down stars. Galileo's Wife. Lavinia Greenlaw. MoWP

He can only drink tea now, screwed and filed. Pink Slip at Tool & Dye. Dave Jeddie Smith. NoAM

He cancelled the ravaging Plague. George Meredith. VerBaPo *Fr.* Empty Purse, The.

He cannot imagine a doorknob. Feeling Type and His Friends, The. Michael Davidson. FTOS

He captured many thousand guns. Napoleon. William Makepeace Thackeray. FaBoWar

He catched at love, and filled his arms with bays. (LL) Story of Phoebus and Daphne, The. Edmund Waller. NAEL-6 v1; NAEL-7 v2; PBRV

He catches salamanders two centimeters long. Sarah Kirsch. PFTM-2 *Fr.* Kite-Flying.

He challenged her, went straight for her heart. Mortal Partner, The. René Char. YaTCFP, *tr. by* Nancy Kline

He changes into a bird, and that's. Gout. Lewis Warsh. FTOS

He circles slowly and the walls of the room. Baba Mostafa. Mimi Khalvati. Prnts

He clasps the crag with crookèd hands. Eagle, The. Alfred Tennyson. ChAP; ClHu; HeIP-4; ITBLP; NAEL-6v2; NAEL-7v2; NoP-4; NoP-5; NTCP; OWoS; TFi; TRP; WaAnP

He clicks off the reading lamp, and it is almost morning. Night Person, The. Richard Frost. AWTN

He climbed and, under the gray leaves. Olive Garden, The. Rainer Maria Rilke. GI

He climbed down the hill and went off somewhere. My Mother's Wedding. Boris Hristov. CSCBP, *tr. by* Georgi Belev and Lisa Sapinkopf

He closed the deal on the night. A real. Nocturnes. Dionisio D. Martinez. TouFir

He closes his eyes. Wink. Roger Gilbert-Lecomte. PFTM-1

He Comes Among. George Barker. OBMV

He comes from the mountains, he stands in the grove! Antichrist, The. Stefan George. WoPoe, *tr. by* Peter Viereck

He comes from the north. Three for Bear. Aimé Césaire. PFTM-1

He Comes Not To-night. Josephine D. Henderson Heard. CBWP-4

He comes to lie down in my bed and pretends I'm not here. He Comes to Lie Down. Naomi Feigelson Chase. PfS

He comes with autumn, when the leaves flake. Shoni Onions. Sheenagh Pugh. AngWePo

He Considers the Birds of the Air. Karl Kirchwey. GI

He could barely tell one from the other. (LL) Milkweed and Monarch. Paul Muldoon. NAEL-7v2; NoP-4; NoP-5; PoetW; WaAnP

He could be so far outside himself, generating body heat, far. Valley of the Shadow of the Dogs. Lisa Jarnot. VaPo

He could have come to tell us. Never Give a Bum an Even Break. James Welch. NoAM

He could help us out. Tennis in the City. Frank Higgins. MoASP

He could not be just particles of mist. Case against Mist, The. Mark Halliday. SUP

He could not imagine himself a hero at all. Country or Western Music. Gerald Early. BodElec

He could not imagine himself as Lear. Role of a Lifetime, The. Floyd Skloot. IaFF

He could see the little lake. Lake, The. James Stephens. MoBrPo

He could sing sweetly on a string. Orpheus. Elizabeth Madox Roberts. MoAmPo

He couldn't remember what propelled him. Man on a Fire Escape. Edward Hirsch. OxBoAm; UrbNat

He couldn't say it or write it or sign it or give it a name. Sounds of the Resurrected Dead Man's Footsteps (#3). Marvin Bell. Vesp

He courts her up there on the roof. Muse Is Always the Other Woman, The. Constance Urdang. PBCAP

He cracked them in half. Cracking Walnuts. Maria Jastrzebska. Prnts

He crawls to the edge of the foaming creek. Meeting the Mountains. Gary Snyder. NoAM

He cut a sappy sucker from the muckle rodden-tree. Whistle, The. Charles Murray. EdScPo

He cut the officer's head off. José's Japanese Sword. Ray Gonzalez. LiTh

He danced with tall grass. We Never Know. Yusef Komunyakaa. AmAlph; OxBoAm; WhBo

He dances on a toe. L'indifférent. Michael Field. ViWPN

He delights to play. Musical Saw. David Kresh. MiVo

He did enjoy the evening, gracious daughters. Face to Face. Thomas James Jones. BBMWP, *tr. by* Jon Dressel

He did his duty both by peers and peasants. King George V. Charles W. Hayward. NOBAu

He did not boast of his natural gifts. *Various authors.* CATKP *Fr.* Songs of Flying Dragons.

He did not hear her words. Child in the New Delhi Sun. Garrett McDowell. BtF

He did not want to be buried, you say. Burial Code. Laurel Smith. VisFro

He did not wear his scarlet coat. Ballad of Reading Gaol, The. Oscar Wilde. CABP; MoBrPo; NoAM; NPeEn; OBMV; OBNV; OxAEP-2; OxBEV; UV; TFi; WaAnP *Fr.* Ballad of Reading Gaol, The.

He did not wear his swallow tail. Gourmand, The. Harry Graham. UV

He Didn't Come Back. Nanduri Subbarao. HotL, *tr. by* V. Narayana Rao

He didn't, no he didn't think continually. Hand for Some Others, A. Geoffrey Holloway. NLP

He didn't say. Malcolm Spoke / Who Listened? Haki R. Madhubuti. ESEAA

He died before my children were born and I tell them about him sometimes. Angels of Wine, The. Jonas Zdanys. PML

He died, in our land where he came to stay. Foreigner Who Died in Juchitán, The. Pancho Na'car. WoPoe, *tr. by* Brian Swann

He died privately. Ram. Gillian Clarke. AngWePo

He dies vicariously on "Carol Burnett." Assassination of Robert Goulet as Performed by Elvis Presley: Memphis, 1968, The. David Wojahn. AllShUp; IllVoic

He "Digesteth Harde Yron." Marianne Moore. APT-1; NAAPv.2; NAMCP V.1; NoAM; OWoS

He dines alone surrounded by reflections. Witch Doctor. Robert Earl Hayden. GPTC; NAMCP V.2; NoAM

He disappeared in the dead of winter. In Memory of W. B. Yeats. W. H. Auden. AmFaPo; BrAP; GPTC; HeIP-4; MakPoe; MoBrPo; NAEL-6v2; NAEL-7v2; NAMCP V.1; NIL-7; NoAM; NoP-4; NoP-5; NPeEn; OxAEP-2; OxBoAm; TFi; TRP; WaAnP; WeW-3

He discovered the age of the sun and he knows. To a Mathematician. Jan Kochanowski. WoPoe, *tr. by* Jerzy Peterkiewicz and Burns Singer

He discovers himself on an old airfield. Old Pilot, The. Donald Hall. OtW

He Does Not Give the Reader One Line of Information. Alex Marlowe. WhBo

He does not sit with silent men. Oscar Wilde. NPeEn; OxBEV *Fr.* Ballad of Reading Gaol, The.

He doesn't act as though he cares. As Long As He Needs Me. Lionel Bart. ReLy

He doesn't forget. Shrewd waif. Sparrow. Claudio Rodríguez. RaW, *tr. by* Robert Mezey

He doesn't know the world at all. Birdsong. *Unknown, fr. Terezin Concentration Camp.* INSAB

He doesn't like it, of course. His Body. Sandra McPherson. LoL

He doesn't mind breathing dust. Mowing. Stuart Dybek. UrbNat

He Doeth All Things Well. Anne Brontë. SacPr

He doth not crave less time, but more. (LL) Time. George Herbert. NAEL-6v1; NAEL-7v1

He doth sit by us and moan. (LL) William Blake. InvLi; OxAEP-2 *Fr.* Songs of Innocence.

He draws a man. Picture of a Man. Calvin Forbes. ISC

He draws memory out of me with hands of fire. Penelope Shuttle. LW *Fr.* Passion.

He dreamed of / an open window. Dream, The. Felix Pollak. RaBo

He dreams of saxophones and hounds. Lugs Benedict on the Coast, 1934. Tom Rea. GifTon

He Dreams What Is Going On Inside His Head. Jonathan Cott. AHA

He dreams whole continents of tires aflame, the velvet *yes yes.* Sponge Boy. Stefi Weisburd. MAAN

He dreamt his ear was a small Africa. Vision of Salt & Water: Elijah's Horn. J. J. Blickstein. Vesp

He drew a circle that shut me out. Outwitted. Edwin Markham. CalPo; MoAmPo; NAAPv.1

He drew hundreds of women. Beauty and Sadness. Cathy Song. NAMCP V.2; NoAM

He drifts into a room of strangers. Leaving the Country. Wyn Cooper. OPRER

He drifts on blue water. Blue Water. Li Po. CrYelRi; ErotSp, *tr. by* Sam Hamill

He drinks because she scolds, he thinks.   Which the Chicken, Which the Egg?   Ogden Nash.   APT-2

He drowsed and was aware of silence heaped.   Death-Bed, The.   Siegfried Sassoon.   AF

He dwelt among 'apartments let'.   Jacob.   Phoebe Cary.   APN-2

He eats of the fruits of the great Speckle.   Ted Berrigan.   FTOS *Fr.* Sonnets, The.

He eats rain.   Fir.   T.E. Jay.   GifTon

He embraces his murderer to win him over.   He Embraces His Murderer.   Mahmoud Darwish.   BeAl, *tr. by* Sabri Hafiz and Sarah Maguire

He ended, and they both descend the hill.   John Milton.   NAWM-5v1; NAWM-7v1 *Fr.* Paradise Lost.

He ended; and thus *Adam* last reply'd.   John Milton.   HeIP-4 *Fr.* Paradise Lost.

He ended, nor the Argicide refus'd.   Homer.   OBVE *Fr.* Odyssey.

He enjoyed making masks.   Mask.   Sapardi Djoko Damono.   WoPoe, *tr. by* John H. McGlynn

He erects magic squares on yellow cards.   Provisional Measures.   Charles Stein.   AHA

He escape the lynch days. He survives.   Wole Soyinka.   HBAPE

He explained, and the band played on. (LL)   Mingus at The Showplace.   William Matthews.   OxBoAm; PoA 2002; SeSe

He falls.   To Etan: An Israeli Child from the Kibbutz Ma'oz Hayim.   Fadwa Tuqan.   CFP, *tr. by* Kamal Boullata

He feared money so much he was known.   Usual Immigrant Uncle Poem, The.   Askold Melnyczuk.   OPRER

He Fell among Thieves.   Sir Henry John Newbolt.   OBEV; OBWP

He fell for a beautiful.   Vasco [*or Vasko*] Popa.   PoSu *Fr.* Quartz Pebble, The.

He fell in love with the butcher's daughter.   Street.   Eiléan Ní Chuilleanáin.   EmeKit

He fell off a barn on his head.   Captains Courageous.   Frank O'Hara.   FTOS

He fell off his crane.   Report to the Stockholders.   John Beecher.   InGu

He felt at first.   Roman Study.   Louise Glück.   BodElec

He filled a fresh glass and sank down among us. (LL)   Charles on Fire.   James Merrill.   CAP-8; HeIP-4; OxBoAm

He filled a glass, held it before his eyes.   Albery Allson Whitman.   NAAPv.1 *Fr.* Octoroon, The.

He finds it in the yard.   Bird.   Kim Addonizio.   UrbNat

He finds the dusty gin.   His.   Martha Rhodes.   LaCa

He finds the God there far unlike his books. (LL)   Fulke, 1st Baron Brooke Greville.   NAEL-6v1; NAEL-7v1; OxBEV *Fr.* Mustapha.

He first deceased [*or* deceas'd]; she for a little tried [*or* tri'd].   Upon the Death of Sir Albert Morton's Wife.   Sir Henry Wotton.   BASC; NPeEn; OBEV; OxBEV; PBRV; WeW-3

He flattens his haunches deep.   Mountain Lion.   Barry Goldensohn.   MAAN

He flies as poets might. (LL)   Magpies in Picardy.   T. P. Cameron Wilson.   BLPJKO; FaBoWar

He flies not—but he coolly walks away. (LL)   On the Aphorism "L'Amitié est l'Amour sans Ailes."   Charlotte Smith.   CABP; PEW

He followed their lilting stanzas.   Local Poet, A.   John Hewitt.   ModIr; PNI

He forced his way into it, a near shave.   Life, A.   Janet Fisher.   MFPA

He fought like those Who've nought to lose.   Emily Dickinson.   PCW

He found a formula for drawing comic rabbits.   Epitaph on an Unfortunate Artist.   Robert Graves.   OBCoV

He found her by the ocean's moaning verge.   George Meredith.   NAEL-6v2; NAEL-7v2; NoP-4; NoP-5 *Fr.* Modern Love.

He frightens all the witches and the dragons in their lair.   Black Cock, The.   Ishmael Reed.   ISC

He from the wind-bitten North with ship and companions descended.   Rudyard Kipling.   PoWW; WoPoe *Fr.* Epitaphs of the War [1914–1918].

He fumbles at your Soul.   Emily Dickinson.   APN-2; LW; NAAL-3; NCAP; TCAPo; TRP

(He fumbles at your spirit.)   ColAP

He gathered for His own delight.   Ere the Golden Bowl Is Broken.   Anna Hempstead Branch.   TCAPo

He gave his strength and his loveliness for his country.   On a Soldier Killed in the Great War.   R. Williams Parry.   OBWVE, *tr. by* H. Idris Bell

He gave the solid rail a hateful kick.   Egg and the Machine, The.   Robert Frost.   MoAmPo

He gave us eyes to see them, And lips that we might tell, How great is God Almighty, Who has made all things well. (LL)   All Things Bright and Beautiful.   Cecil Frances Alexander.   SacPr; UV

(Who has made all things well!) (LL)   ChAP; VWP

He gazed and gazed and gazed and gazed.   Rhyme for a Child Viewing a Naked Venus in a Painting [of "The Judgement of Paris"].   Robert Browning.   NPeEn; OBCoV

He gazed on the face of the high-born maid.   George R. Sims.   VerBaPo *Fr.* Beauty and the Beast.

He gets / robbed, a knife in his chest and two.   Bond, The.   Bob Hicok.   LiTh

He gives her a black lace bra.   Good Gifts.   Dorothy Nimmo.   BeAl

He gives her all the configurations.   Configurations.   Grace Nichols.   LW

He gives me a handshake.   Big Chill Variations.   Reuben Jackson.   UnSA

He giveth his beloved-sleep. (LL)   Sleep, The.   Elizabeth Barrett Browning.   ChIV-1; OxAEP-2

He glanced at me one day—but then his mean.   Sadi.   WoPoe, *tr. by* Dick Davis

He gloried in the feats.   My Father's Heroes.   Allison Joseph.   SeSe

He goes. As I fall past, remember me. (LL)   Praying Drunk.   Andrew Hudgins.   RA; UpMys

He goes free of the earth.   Wendell Berry.   UpMys *Fr.* Three Elegiac Poems.

He gossips like my grandmother, this man.   Cleaving, The.   Li-Young Lee.   OpBo; RoV

He gossips like my grandmother, this man.   Li-Young Lee.   IllVoic *Fr.* Cleaving, The.

He got hauled in.   Autobiography of John Doe, The.   Jon Lavieri.   OPRER

He got up to play in the partable.   Real Toads.   Heidi Peppermint.   BAP-04

He grew old between the fires of Troy.   Euripides the Athenian.   George Seferis.   PoetW, *tr. by* Edmund Keeley and Philip Sherrard

He had a name.   Generations 1.   Sam Cornish.   GT

He had a tall cedar he wanted to cut for posts.   Old Man Climbs a Tree, The.   Wendell Berry.   PoCoUp

He had a very large number of friends. (LL)   Whenever I Make a New Poem.   Lew Welch.   BB; OxBoAm

He had always supposed he would die first.   Soon.   James Harms.   NeAmPo

He had been called many things by many men.   Traitor.   Pat Stodghill.   TiP2

He had been falling in the abyss some four thousand years.   Et Nox Facta Est.   Victor Hugo.   NAWM-7v2, *tr. by* Mary Ann Caws

He had been in paradise.   Mission Impossible.   Elizabeth Smither.   BeAl

He had begun to take.   Thong.   Joel Dailey.   AnSo

He had contempt that was divine.   Mess Boy, The.   Sydney Wilmer.   CAGL

He had determined to dance the presence of the dance. He had been in fact determined.   Presence of the Dance / The Resolution of the Music, The.   Robert Duncan.   FTOS

He had died only a few inches.   Least Corpse, The.   Angel González.   RaW, *tr. by* Robert Mezey

He had driven half the night.   Hay for the Horses.   Gary Snyder.   BB; CAP-8; GoPo; LoL; TRP

He had entered her heart.   Gentleman in the Heart, The.   Vivian Lamarque.   CItWP, *tr. by* Cinzia Sartini Blum and Lara Trubowitz

He had got, finally.   Poem for Speculative Hipsters, A.   Imamu Amiri Baraka.   NAMCP V.2; NoAM

He had his Thirty-nine Articles.   Fossil, A.   May Kendall.   VWP

He had left the villages far behind.   Trial Desert.   Jean Grosjean.   YaTCFP, *tr. by* Mary Ann Caws and Patricia Terry

He had lived a long time.   Old Man and the Sun, The.   Vicente Aleixandre.   RaW, *tr. by* W. S. Merwin

He had made a life of stone.   Geologist, The.   Michael C. Blumenthal.   PfSP

He had many to help him.   *Various authors*.   CATKP *Fr.* Songs of Flying Dragons.

He had no rights, they beat him up, you've got.   Rights.   Martha Collins.   LiTh

He had passed it.   Disconcerting Object.   J. Bernlef.   TuT, *tr. by* Peter van de Kamp

He had taken the right pills the night before.   Certain Light, A.   Marie Howe.   FaoP

He had the nerve to say *Let's be grown-up about this*.   New York Spring.   Linda France.   MFPA

He had to be four times cuckold. (LL)   Temperaments, The.   Ezra Pound.   NAMCP V.1; NoAM; OBCoV

He had to die they say.   Heaven's Ring.   Vasco [*or Vasko*] Popa.   VCWP, *tr. by* Charles Simic

He had worked out at Gold's Gym.   Stud, The.   Fred Voss.   SUP

He has a rather plain wife.   My Neighbor.   Roque Dalton.   AF, *tr. by* Richard Schaaf

He has a scar on his forehead and always sits apart.   Solitary Man.   Boris Hristov.   CSCBP, *tr. by* Georgi Belev and Lisa Sapinkopf

He has a ticking in his soul, and prays.   Peter Klappert.   YaYoPo *Fr.* Pieces of the One and a Half Legged Man.

He has an eye for cities. Among his rows.   Lewis Mumford.   George Buchanan.   PNI

He has become as / talkative as Bottom a weaver and says for.   Louis Zukofsky.   APSN *Fr.* A.

He has been awake.   My Father, Counting Sheep.   Kate Foley.   Prnts

He has built himself a cottage in a wood, near where the insect rubs its wings in song.   Cottage in the Wood, A.   Russell Edson.   MotU

He has chopped wood (very badly too) and carried logs for one.   Caliban's Journal.   Suniti Namjoshi.   RACG

He has finished a day's work.   Pornographer, The.   Robert Hass.   YaYoPo

He has five children, I'm papa. Dropping the Euphemism. Bob Hicok. AmAlph

He has gone. Last Journey. Enrique Gonzáles Martínez. TCLAP, tr. by Samuel Beckett

He has lain here for a terrible, motionless. David Wojahn. PBCAP; SwNoth Fr. Mystery Train: A Sequence.

He has leaned for hours against the veranda railing. Cross. Patricia K. Page. StAl

He has married again. His wife. Pot Burial. Tom Paulin. ModIr

He has never lost a child. He has never even. Credentials. Mark Halliday. SUP

He has not woo'd, but he has lost his heart. Country Dance, A. Charles Tennyson Turner. OxBEV

He has taken flight through the tropic day and the night. Perchance to Dream. Mary Low. SurWo

He has taught the Universe to realize itself. Alcoholic in the 3rd Week of the 3rd Treatment, The. John Berryman. BodElec

He has the lower part. Man with a Hole in His Face, The. Jack Coulehan. BloBone

He has three singles on the charts and in. David Wojahn. PBCAP Fr. Mystery Train: A Sequence.

He has two antennae. Gnat on My Paper. Richard Eberhart. APT-2

He has woven rose-vines. C33. Hart Crane. CAGL

He hath abolished the old drouth. Gerard Manley Hopkins. SacPr

He Hath Need of Rest. Josephine D. Henderson Heard. CBWP-4

He heard the bell toll, erratic. Francis Meets a Leper. David Citino. UpMys

He hears it not now, but used to notice such things? (LL) Afterwards. Thomas Hardy. HarvBoo; ItP; MoBrPo; NAMCP V.1; NoP-4; NoP-5; OxAEP-2; OxBEV; PoPoPo; TFi; WoPoe

He hears with gladdened heart the thunder. Robert Louis Stevenson. ITBLP

He held me bone-tight. He held me backward. My Pietà. Thomas Heise. LegDan

He Held Radical Light. A. R. Ammons. VCAP

He hit the backs of forty tailed deer. *Various authors.* CATKP Fr. Songs of Flying Dragons.

He hoes the grain under a midday sun. Pitying the Farmer. Li Shen. ColAnChi, tr. by Burton Watson

He holds a volume open in his hands. Boy with Book of Knowledge. Howard Nemerov. NoP-4; NoP-5

He hugs each policeman in turn. Walt Whitman at the Irish Festival, Syracuse, New York: Four Snapshots. Shane Seely. ViWalt

He hunched a broomstick. Canary Man and You, The. Rick Alley. AmPoNex

He in Christ's doctrine deals by way of trade. Portrait of a Bishop. Evan Lloyd. AngWePo

He invented a rainbow but lightning struck it. Bushed. Earle Birney. BrAP; NoAM; NoP-4; NoP-5

He is a fool who, collapsed on the ground, gets up and walks on. Forced March. Miklós Radnóti. ConPit, tr. by Clayton Eshleman and Gyula Kodolanyi

He is a parricide to his mother's name. In Praise of Women in General. Thomas Randolph. NOSC

He is a very inoffensive man. Sonnet 43. Eleanor Brown. MFPA

He is all bark and strung gut. Photo of Ron Carter, Playing His Bass. Cornelius Eady. BtF

He is almost a god, a man beside you. Sappho. ErotSp, tr. by Sam Hamill

He is an utter failure as a devil. Devil, A. Zbigniew Herbert. MotU, tr. by Czeslaw Milosz

He is blood, himself. Water of the Flowery Mill (II), The. Jerome Rothenberg. FTOS

He is breathing his last, my rebellion is dying. Surrender. "Rachel." FIT, tr. by Robert Friend

He is dead, the beautiful youth. Killed at the Ford. Henry Wadsworth Longfellow. CBCWP; PCW

He is eating some ice with colour. Ice In. Jacques Roubaud. YaTCFP, tr. by the author

He is 41, his mother 28. Blonder than Denmark, there isn't enough dye. Laurence Olivier's Hamlet. David Oliveira. IaFF

He is going to stop thinking. Dandelion. Juan Delgado. AmPoNex

He is gone. Tune: "Dreaming of Southland" Thinking of Someone. Liu Shih. ColAnChi, tr. by Kang-i Sun Chang

He Is Gone. Anna Swirszczynska [or Swir]. CFP; PoSu, tr. by Czeslaw Milosz and Leonard Nathan

He is gone on the mountain. Sir Walter Scott. Fr. Lady of the Lake, The.

He is gone to comfort others. (LL) He Is Gone. Anna Swirszczynska [or Swir]. CFP; PoSu, tr. by Czeslaw Milosz and Leonard Nathan

He is half bull. Christian Science Minotaur, The. Christopher Howell. RoV

He is handsome. *Unknown.* SonAtl, tr. by William Delaney, Nick Downes and David Edgens

He is, in truth, lacking in civility. Mary Stuart, Queen of Scots. EMWP

He is innocent, so he is happy. Bat Messenger, The. Gurram Jashuva. HotL, tr. by V. Narayana Rao

He is Jealous of the Heavens and the Earth. Petrarch. MoBrPo Fr. Sonnets to Laura.

He is knit with his doom. (LL) Germinal. George Russell. MoBrPo; OBEV; OBMV

He is languid as a fed lion. Scheherazade. Gillian Allnutt. NeBrP

He is learning at a rate of knots. For a Six Year Old. Ben Scammell. NLP

He Is Lightning. Jordan Davis. HeMarv

He is like a god. Catullus. ErotSp, tr. by Sam Hamill

He is lonely then within the pale of the palace. Commentary. Hyam Plutzik. TaR

He is lost to the small farms, lane by lane. (LL) Day in August, A. Frank Ormsby. PBCIP; PNI

He is my shadow. Veronique Tadjo. NAfrP, tr. by Faustine Boateng Gyima

He is no common man. Sketch of a Fetish. Kim Kwang-kyu. PML, tr. by Anthony, Brother of Taizé

He is not dead. (LL) Frederick Douglass: 1817–1895. Langston Hughes. CBCWP; HHAm

He is not dead nor liveth. Dorothy, Duchess of Wellington Wellesley. OBMV Fr. Deserted House.

He is not de[a]d that sometime [or somtyme] hath a fall. Sir Thomas Wyatt. OBVE

He is not quite dead. Armand Schwerner. PFTM-2; WoPoe Fr. Tablets, The.

He is not the man who goes over the wall. Man on the Edge. Heberto Padilla. VCWP

He is patient, he is not angry. *Yoruba Oral Tradition.* BLT

He is, perhaps, none of my business. Writer in sand, The. Lionel Abrahams. TSAP

He is quick, thinking in clear images. In Broken Images. Robert Graves. HarvBoo; NoP-4; NoP-5; TRP

He is repulsed [or repuls'd] indeed—but you are [or you're or you'r] undone. (LL) To the Noblest and Best of Ladies, the Countess of Denbigh. Richard Crashaw. NAEL-6v1; NAEL-7v1

He is Rosa without Rosa. Fountain. Benjamin Péret. YaTCFP, tr. by Mary Ann Caws

He is rust / in moonlight. Coyote Fragments. Lance Henson. HATNAP

He is simply chopping wood in my front yard. Walt Whitman. Wang Yin. ViWalt, tr. by Cheng Baolin and Richard Terrill

He is stark mad, who ever says. Broken Heart, The. John Donne. FSCP

He is sun-bright myth and Cosmic Light. O Lord of Light! A Mystic Sage Returns to Realms of Eternity! Askia Muhammad Touré. FuFl; SeSe; SpirFl

He is the love-wolf. *Unknown, fr. Egyptian hieroglyphics.* ErotSp, tr. by Barbara Hughes Fowler

He is the oldest grandfather. Memory Sire, The. Barney Bush. HATNAP

He is the source of hot forests. Cusp of Desire, The. Maysoun Saqr Al-Qasimi. PoArWo, tr. by Subhi Hadidi and Nathalie Handal

He is there, like Clouseau. Luke 14: A Commentary. Kathleen Norris. UpMys

He is wearing baggy shorts and a loud T-shirt. Boy With a Headset. Edward Hirsch. RoV

He is your friend. (LL) Turtle, The. William Carlos Williams. EmeKit; PtR; RaBo; SAmP

He journeys over the dark land. Vasco [or Vasko] Popa. PoSu; WoPoe Fr. St Sava's Spring.

He jumped off the box-car. All Purpose Country and Western Self Pity Song, The. Kit Wright. StAl

He jumps from behind, flying like a shard. Sarah Gorham. FFC Fr. Notes From a Chinese Love Manual.

He kicked the world, and lunging long ago. Horse, The. James Wright. YaYoPo

"He killed his parents." Majeski Plays the Saxophone. Martín Espada. SeSe

He killed in a cow mask. Murderer is a Cow, The. Gerard Woodward. BeAl

He kneels on the rumpled bed. Gail Morse. PasH

He knew it was waiting for him somewhere. My Father's Death. Constance Urdang. PBCAP

He knew nothing about death. Nani Worries about Her Father's Happiness in the Afterlife. Ana Castillo. FTtHH

He knew the stories he could tell. Survivor, Walking. Stephen Sandy. PoA 2002

He knew the wife, who quickly did admit. Albery Allson Whitman. NAAPv.1 Fr. Octoroon, The.

He laughed at death. Airman, The. *Unknown.* OtW

He lay down his hoe, left his cornfield on the side. Lonesome Texas. Bettye Hammer Givens. TiP2

He lay like someone fallen from a high. Request, The. Sharon Olds. BodElec

He lay on the bed, thinking. Man on the Bed, The. Debora Greger. PoSol

He lay on the couch night after night. Saturn. Sharon Olds. RaBo

He Leadeth Me. Joseph Henry Gilmore. SacPr

He leans over—well. Let's Say. Yusef Komunyakaa. RoV

He learns the grammar of this world each time. Portrait of the Marginalized. Ch'oe Sŭngja. EcSo, *tr. by* Mickey Hong

He left behind coins, for his lodging, and traces of / red mud. (LL) Geoffrey Hill. NAEL-7v2; NAMCP V.2; NoAM; NoP-4 *Fr.* Mercian Hymns.

He / left her. January 8, 1996. Kimmika L. H. Williams. BRtP

He left his application forms. Non-Emigrant, The. Lotte Kramer. Prnts

He left his pants upon a chair. Theodore Roethke. OBCoV *Fr.* Three Epigrams.

He left us a library. Dudley Randall. Ahmos, II Zu-Bolton. BRtP

He let go. Take-Off. Peter Thorpe. OtW

He lets me bury fingers in the lion's mane. Dreadlocks. Tara Betts. BRtP

He lies groaning on his bed. Radio Gibberish. Genrikh Sabgir. TCRusP, *tr. by* Daniel Weissbort

He lies in the soft earth under the grass. Tory, a Puppy. Mortimer Collins. DiBP

He lies on the sofa, listening to the baroness. Last Solo: Charlie Parker, Hotel Stanhope, March 12, 1955. David Jauss. MiVo

He lifted the wicker lid. Man Who Invented Pain, The. Craig Raine. EmeKit

He lifted up, among the actuaries. John Berryman. NAMCP V.2 *Fr.* Dream Songs.

He lights a cigarette. What Man Might Kill. Cortney Davis. PfS

He likes to do the kind of thing that shows. Beauty and the Prince Formerly Known as Beast. Eleanor Brown. NeBl

He listened at the porch that day. Year's Spinning, A. Elizabeth Barrett Browning. NAEL-6v2

He Lived amidst th' Untrodden Ways. Hartley Coleridge. UV

He lived—childhood summers. Lorine Niedecker. APT-2; ItP; NAAPv.2

He lived in a small farm-house. Refusal to Mourn, A. Derek Mahon. ModIr; PNI

He Lives Long Who Lives Well. Thomas Randolph. TreFP

He lives—he then unties the string. (LL) Warning to Children. Robert Graves. NoP-4; NoP-5; NOxBChV; NPeEn; OxBEV; TWF

He Llegado al Final de la Casa Donde Están la Cocina y el Baño. Luis Rosales. RaW

He loads his weapons, but the Lord God sees him. Mark Jarman. LiTh *Fr.* Unholy Sonnets.

He lolls in the supermarket. Portrait of a House Detective. Hans Magnus Enzensberger. HP; PoSu, *tr. by* Michael Hamburger

He looked about six or seven, only much too thin. Forgiveness Dream, The: Man from the Warsaw Ghetto. Jean Valentine. CFP

He looked, and gave me beauty. Drinking Wine. Wisława Szymborska. FiBr, *tr. by* Grazyna Drabik and Sharon Olds

He looked at me and I at him; We did not see the same. Past Perm and Glitz. Charlotte Renk. TiP2

He looked for mischief. Even-Tempered Girl Holds Her Breath, An. Lorenzo Thomas. AnSo

He looks as if he's a silhouette. Figure on the Edge. Dabney Stuart. PfSP

He looks back over the last metaphor. Great Artist Reconsiders the Homeric Simile, The. John Tranter. BMAP; NoAM; NOBAu

He looks into a glass. Lord, What is Man? Carl Rakosi. FTOS

He loved her so he wrote. Body Language. Sylvia Kantaris. LW

He loved his cabin: there. Salt Water Story. Richard Hugo. NoAM

He loved peculiar plants and rare. Education's Martyr. May Kendall. VWP

He loved statues with broken noses. Ancient Signs. Edward Hirsch. TaR

He loved the brook's soft sound. Peasant Poet, The. John Clare. WaAnP

He loved three things. Anna Andreyevna Akhmatova. RaBo

He loved to pull out his clasp-knife. Gardener. A. H. Snow. OBGa

He Loves. David Schirmer. GePo, *tr. by* George C. Schoolfield

He loves, but hates equally. (LL) Self-Portrait. Robert Creeley. NoAM; PmAP

He Loves in Vain. Christian Hofmann von Hofmannswaldau. GePo, *tr. by* George C. Schoolfield

He made a glass violin, because he wanted to see the music. Prologue to a Comedy. Wisława Szymborska. MotU, *tr. by* Krystyna Piorkowski

He made her do the same scene. Marilyn Climbs Out of the Pool. Tracey Herd. LW

He made peace with eternity. Second-Class Citizen. Slavko Mihalic. PoSu, *tr. by* Charles Simic

He made the whole Fleet love him, damn his eyes! (LL) 1805. Robert Graves. FaBoWar; OBCoV; OBSV

He Makes a House Call. John A. Stone. BloBone

He makes himself comfortable. Jackson Mac Low. FTOS; PFTM-2; PmAP *Fr.* Pronouns, The—A Collection of 40 Dances—For the Dancers.

He making speedy way through spersed ayre. Edmund Spenser. NoSic *Fr.* Faerie Queene, The.

Hé mandu / It was me. Ay, Bashful Thou! Mor Nighean Uisdein. EMWP

He marries the lilac from the Taurus Mountains. Mixed Marriage. Diana Der Hovanessian. TWW

He marvels at the regularity. Aerial Photograph, An. Thomas Carper. OtW

He may as well deny a world to me. (LL) Thomas Heywood. NOSC; WaAnP *Fr.* Apology for Actors, An.

He may go. (LL) Exeat. Stevie Smith. NAEL-6v2; NAMCP V.1; NoAM

He may our prophet, and our tutor prove. Mary Sidney Wroth, Countess of Montgomery. BASC; NoP-4; NoP-5

He means to cut down senseless craving. (LL) There's a naked bug at Cold Mountain. Han-shan (Cold Mountain). BB; WoPoe, *tr. by* Gary Snyder

He measures all the drops with wondrous skill. Bible, *O.T.* STuOW *Fr.* New Version of the Psalms of David, Fitted to the Tunes Used in Churches, A.

He Meditates on the Life of a Rich Man. Douglas Hyde. OBMV, *tr. by* Lady Augusta Gregory

He meets, by heavenly chance express. Coventry Patmore. OxAEP-2 *Fr.* Angel in the House, The.

He met a lady. Earle Birney. *See* I met a lady / on a lazy street.

He might be tethered. Self-Examination. Elaine Terranova. GifTon

He might be weak enough to suffer woe. (LL) John Donne. BASC; WaAnP *Fr.* Holy Sonnets.

He mishears 'Yorkshire'. Backward Glance, A. David Wheatley. NIrP

He motions me over with a question. Kidnap[p]er. Tess Gallagher. LaCa

He mounted her, growing between her thighs. Love-Cry. Brendan Kennelly. IrLP

He mounts his favorite steed of war. Mandan Chief, The. Fanny Crosby. SWaP

He moves his hips. One Night With a Stranger at 30. Lisa Glatt. AmPoNex

He must attend two dozen funerals. Eminent Public Figure. Dezső Kosztolányi. IQMS, *tr. by* Peter Zollman

He must be 30 or 31. Father, 1952. Christopher Buckley. GeoHom

He must have been one or two, I was five. Night Lake. Jean Valentine. LaCa

He Na Tye Woman. Paula Gunn Allen. HW

He neither knows, remembers—but instead / Sleeps, comforted. (LL) Field Hospital, A. Randall Jarrell. NoP-4; NoP-5

He Never Did That to Me. Noël Coward. NBLV

He Never Expected Much. Thomas Hardy. NAEL-6v2; NAEL-7v2; NAMCP V.1; NoAM

He never made the dive—not while I watched. Springboard, The. Louis MacNeice. PoA 2002

He Never Said a Mumblin' Word [*see also* Crucifixion: "They crucified my Lord, an' He never said a mumbalin' word"]. *Unknown.* APN-2

He never smiled, his friends said. Scott Joplin. Bill Holm. MiVo

He never spoke a word to me. Simon the Cyrenian Speaks. Countee Cullen. ChIV-2; MoAmPo; OxAAAP

He nice frum far, but far frum nice. Vicious Circle. Marsha Prescod. LW

He of the nautical whiskers and breezy black aria is back in strapping emotion-bent form. Darren Wershler-Henry. PoPra *Fr.* Ten Out of Ten, or, Why Poetry Criticism Sucks in 2003.

He only happy is, and wise. How to Ride Out a Storm. Mildmay Fane, 2d Earl of Westmorland. NOSC

He only wanted me for happiness. Wiederkehr. Rita Dove. BodElec

He only wanted to sleep, that wakeful. Anti-dithyrambics. John Peck. HarvBoo

He opened the four borders. *Various authors.* CATKP *Fr.* Songs of Flying Dragons.

He opens her. She can't have him. Riddles. Kathleen Peirce. PoDa

He opens his eyes with a cry of delight. Child's Christmas Day, A. *Unknown.* OBCP

He Opens Wide a Third Eye. Bei Dao. PFTM-2, *tr. by* Chen Maiping and Bonnie S. McDougall

He or She That's Got the Limb, That Holds Me Out on It. Susan Wheeler. ExTi

He [*or When he*] killed the noble Mudjokivis. George A. Strong. OBCoV; UV *Fr.* Song of Milkanwatha, The.

He owns a smoke shop, the bastard. My Other Life. Peter Serchuk. PoDa

He painted the mountain over and over again. Dearest Reader. Michael Palmer. CAP-8; FTOS

He paints sheep of the Sierras, the Pyrenees. Dream Painter, The. Stanley Noyes. ICANM

He paints words with the past. Roy Fisher. Oth *Fr.* Cut Pages, The.

He pales at pleasure. Prometheus. Robert Horan. YaYoPo

He passed by with another. Ballad. Gabriela Mistral. PtR, *tr. by* Doris Dana

He passed so peacefully in sleep, it seemed. Ophelia Writes Home. William Greenway. IaFF

He pays the whole, and yet am I not free. (LL) William Shakespeare. HeIP-4; OxAEP-1 *Fr.* Sonnets.

He pities me. (LL) Song of the Captive Sioux Woman. *Chippewa Oral Tradition.* NAAL-5; NAAPv.2

He placed all rest, and had no resting place.   Mary Sidney Herbert, Countess of Pembroke.   SacPr *Fr.* Our Saviour's Passion.

He played the juice harp and me. don't judge too harshly.   Beelzebub Chronicles, The.   Artress Bethany White.   BtF

He plays.   Advice.   Lee Cataldi.   BMAP

He plays *congas*.   Mi Negrito.   Anasuya Isaacs.   BRtP

He Pleads for Forgiveness Before His Intended Marriage.   Bálint Balassi.   IQMS, *tr. by* Joseph Leftwich

He plodded away through drifts of i / ce.   Pythagorean Silence.   Susan Howe.   FTOS

He Points Out the Brevity of Life, Unthinking and Suffering, Surprised by Death.   Francisco de Quevedo y Villegas.   WoPoe, *tr. by* Willis Barnstone

He praised my breasts so round and white.   Sighle of the Lovespot.   Joseph Campbell.   IrLP

He Praises His Wife.   *Unknown*.   IrLP,

He prayed for patience; Care and Sorrow came.   His Answer.   Clara Ann Thompson.   CBWP-2

He preached upon "Breadth" till it argued him narrow.   Emily Dickinson.   NAWM-7v2; SacPr

He preferred his glass eye to be of itself.   Millefiori.   Lavinia Greenlaw.   MFPA

He proposes things to the self as a way of proposing to himself.   Another.   Skip Fox.   AnSo

He protested all his life long.   Edgar Lee Masters.   APT-1; IllVoic *Fr.* Spoon River Anthology.

He provides his artists with calm, good board, and absolute isolation from hellish life. (LL)   What Mr. Cogito Thinks About Hell.   Zbigniew Herbert.   GPTC; VCWP; WoPoe, *tr. by* Bogdana Carpenter and John Carpenter

He pulls off into the picnic area.   Poet Gets Drowsy on the Road, The.   Frederick Turner.   TiP2

He Put the Belt Around My Life.   Emily Dickinson.   TRP

He put the coffee.   Breakfast.   Jacques Prévert.   BeAl, *tr. by* Lawrence Ferlinghetti

He puts four dimes into the slot.   Vending Machine.   Hans Magnus Enzensberger.   PoSu, *tr. by* the author

He ran a good shop, and he died.   Michael Longley.   ModIr *Fr.* Wreaths.

He ran the course and as he ran he grew.   Innocence.   Thom Gunn.   HP

He rang me up.   Dream of Hanging, A.   Patricia Beer.   EmeKit

He raped.   In the Tradition of Bobbitt.   Saundra Sharp.   SpirFl

He remembered this sunburnt river with its spindly.   Derek Walcott.   NAMCP V.2 *Fr.* Omeros.

He remembers the village after sunset as in.   Village After Sunset, The.   James Applewhite.   LPSFW

He reminds me of a man who once sold me a green tuxedo.   Green Tuxedo, The.   Janet Holmes.   LiTh

He Repeats the Song of Colin, a Discerning Shepherd [*or* Elegy 18].   William Shenstone.

    Home Industries First: The Song of Colin, a Discerning Shepherd, Lamenting the State of the Woollen Manufactory.   STuOW

He Resigns.   John Berryman.   HarvBoo; WeW-3

He rested through the winter, watched the rain.   Death of a Gardener.   Phoebe Hesketh.   OBGa

He retains a slight "Martian" accent, from the years of single phrases.   It Allows a Portrait in Line Scan at Fifteen.   Les A. Murray.   HarvBoo

He returned to grass two feet tall.   Exile, The.   Pablo Medina.   OPRER

He rides at their head.   College Colonel, The.   Herman Melville.   AmWaPo; CBCWP; FaBoWar; NAAPv.1; NCAP; OBWP; PCW; WaAnP

He rode a white horse.   Colonel.   Kate Llewellyn.   NOBAu

He rode into town upon a wild-eyed mountain horse.   Yellowjacket.   Peter Blue Cloud.   HATNAP

He rose again behind the stone. (LL)   Easter Night.   Alice Thompson Meynell.   ChIV-2; SacPr

He rose the morrow morn. (LL)   Rime of the Ancient Mariner, The (1798 version).   Samuel Taylor Coleridge.   CABP; HeIP-4; NAEL-6v2; NAEL-7v2; NoP-4; OBEV; OBNV; OxAEP-2; OxBEV; PoPoPo; TFi

He rose the morrow morn. (LL)   Rime of the Ancient Mariner (1817 version).   Samuel Taylor Coleridge.   NoP-5; WaAnP

He rose up on his dying bed.   Hope.   Langston Hughes.   APSN; OxBoAm; PFTM-1

He runs before the wise men: he.   He.   Stanley Kunitz.   NoP-4; NoP-5

He runs free in the furrow, flutters his wings in the air.   I Love, Love.   Gabriela Mistral.   BLPSL, *tr. by* Rene de Costa, Rigas Kappatos and Eleni Paidoussi

He runs like the rough satyr Sun. / Come away! (LL)   Dame Edith Sitwell.   NAMCP V.1; NoAM *Fr.* Façade.

He Said Discipline Is the Highest Form of Love.   Beckian Fritz Goldberg.   AmAlph

He said he would be back and we'd drink wine together.   Waiting for Icarus.   Muriel Rukeyser.   OtW; OxBoAm

He said he would come at moonrise.   Waiting for My Love.   Nŭngun.   CATKP, *tr. by* Peter H. Lee

He said he'd hurt himself against a wall or had fallen down.   Bandaged Shoulder, The.   Constantine P. Cavafy.   PtR, *tr. by* Edmund Keeley and Philip Sherrard

He said his name was Nick; later I learned.   David Trinidad.   WiU *Fr.* Eighteen to Twenty-One.

He said, "I love you."   Interpretations.   Baba Lukata.   BtF

He said I should try something harder.   Mask of Anger, A.   Lyn Hejinian.   FTOS

He said: If in his image I was made.   Trumbull Stickney.   APN-2; OxBoAm; TCAPo

He said, I'm just out of hospital.   R.A.F.   "H. D."   PWW2; WaAnP

He said in his mother's house, growing up.   Wallpaper.   Julia Alvarez.   BodElec

He said it doesn't look good.   What the Doctor Said.   Raymond Carver.   EmeKit

He said it two days ago.   Emmett Williams.   PFTM-2 *Fr.* Red Chair (for three voices), The.

He said my eyes were misty grey.   Steel Yourself.   Siùsaidh NicNèill.   EdScPo

He said "soul."   When He Said "Soul."   Hwang Insuk.   EcSo, *tr. by* Peter H. Lee

He sang of life, serenely sweet.   Poet, The.   Paul Laurence Dunbar.   NAAPv.1; TCAPo

He sat; and in the assembly next upstood.   John Milton.   FaBoWar *Fr.* Paradise Lost.

He sat by the boot shop window.   Playing for England.   David Scott.   NLP

He sat in a wheeled chair, waiting for dark.   Disabled.   Wilfred Owen.   FaBoWar; NAEL-6v2; NAEL-7v2; NAMCP V.1; NIL-7; NoAM; OBWVE; PoPoPo

He sat in his cell staring.   Baboon, The.   Rhydwen Williams.   OBWVE, *tr. by* R. Gerallt Jones

He sat up slowly, and around his left side.   Lazarus.   Ágnes Nemes Nagy.   PoSu, *tr. by* Frederic Will

He sat upon the rolling deck.   Sailor.   Langston Hughes.   PoA 2002

He sate like winter o'er the wasted year.   Thomas Tod Stoddart.   NOBRP *Fr.* Death-Wake, The; or, Lunacy.

He saw her from the bottom of the stairs.   Home Burial.   Robert Frost.   APT-1; ColAP; NAAPv.2; NAMCP V.1; NoP-5; OxBoAm; SoSe-8; TRP; WaAnP

He saw the bloated mess.   Drowned.   Gordon Rodgers.   Coast

He saw the iron wings of daybreak struggling.   In the Midwest.   Edward Hirsch.   PfSP

He saw the lean dogs beneath the wall.   Lord Byron.   DiBP *Fr.* Siege of Corinth, The.

He saw the skull within the looping.   Epitaph for a Scientist.   Lex Banning.   NOBAu

He saw the sun, the Light-giver, step down behind the oak.   Ballad of the Homing Man, The.   Ernest Rhys.   AngWePo

He saw thee Lord of all his creatures stand. (LL)   Created, The.   Jones Very.   APN-1; InvLi

He says again, "Good fences make good neighbo[u]rs." (LL)   Mending Wall.   Robert Frost.   APT-1; BrAP; BRP; ChAP; ClHu; CtM; EMP; HarvBoo; HeIP-4; ITBLP; MoAmPo; NAAL-5; NAAPv.2; NAMCP V.1; NoAM; NoP-4; NoP-5; OxBoAm; PoPoPo; RaF; SAmP; SoSe-8; TCAPo; TFi; WeW-3

He says he doesn't feel like working today.   My Erotic Double.   John Ashbery.   EMP; VCAP

He says. He smiles. He's sweet.   I Got Beat Up A Lot in High School.   Christopher Murray.   BeDoSh

He says, *My reign is in peace*, so slays.   Foreign Ruler, A.   Walter Savage Landor.   OBSV; OxBEV

He says that home is here.   At the Olive Grove of the Resistance.   Robert Hedin.   GifTon

He says / When they made this place.   Outside the Hospital.   Joe Wenderoth.   BodElec

He says you're a blackberry, dropped into his mouth.   Willing.   Paula McLain.   AmPoNex

He scanned me closely, Rufus, just as.   Martial.   RomPo, *tr. by* Peter Whigham

He scattered tarantulas over the roads.   Devil in Texas, The.   *Unknown*.   NBLV

He scorcheth down the Ripley Road.   Scorcher, The.   Edward F. Strange.   ArBi

He scorned his land, his tongue denied.   Dic Siôn Dafydd.   Thomas Jacob Thomas.   OBWVE, *tr. by* H. Idris Bell

He seemed to have been walking forever.   Distance Learning.   Geoff Ward.   VaPo

He seemed to know the harbour.   Shark, The.   Edwin John Pratt.   BrAP

He seems to be a god, that man.   Arbor, The.   Sappho.   WoPoe, *tr. by* Guy Davenport

He seems to me almost a god, or even.   He Seems to Me Almost a God. Catullus.   WoPoe, *tr. by* Robert Mezey

He seems white to me in the morning.   Ghost, The.   Rafael Alberti.   RaW, *tr. by* Charles Guenther

He sees me.   Ishikawa Takuboku.   CAoMJL1, *tr. by* Carl Sesar

He sees the gentle stir of birth.   Matthew Arnold.   NPeEn *Fr.* Resignation.

He Sees Through Stone.   Etheridge Knight.   GT; PBCAP

He sends word for them not to be in His place.   Eduardo Milán.   RMCMP, *tr. by* Roberto Tejada

He sent; and as he fled, he slew. (LL)   To a Lady: She Refusing to Continue a Dispute with Me.   Matthew Prior.   NoP-4; NoP-5

He set her on her steede, and forward forth did beare. (LL)   Edmund Spenser.   NoP-5; NoSic *Fr.* Faerie Queene, The.

He shakes the dust from off his feet.   Battle of Murfreesboro.   Allen Tate.   FaBoA

He shall be my jailer.   Drowned Woman.   Elinor Wylie.   NAAPv.2

HE SHE WE THEY YOU YOU YOU I HER SO PRONOUNS BEGIN THE DANCE CALLED WASHING.   Anne Carson.   NoP-5 *Fr.* Beauty of the Husband, The.

He shifted his trumpet, and only took snuff. (LL)   Oliver Goldsmith.   OBCoV; OxBEV *Fr.* Retaliation.

He shifts on the bed carefully, so as.   Man on the Hotel Room Bed, The.   Galway Kinnell.   VCAP

He Shook off the Beast.   Charles Wesley.   ChIV-2

He shot six roebucks.   *Various authors.*   CATKP *Fr.* Songs of Flying Dragons.

He should not have sent his son.   Meditations of Mr. Cogito on Redemption. Zbigniew Herbert.   GI, *tr. by* John Carpenter and Bogdana Carpenter

He showed me the painting he made of me.   What a Poet Does.   Chana Bloch.   FaoP

He shows me tonight.   Nobody.   Novica Tadic.   VCWP, *tr. by* Charles Simic

He shuddered briefly and stared down the long valley.   Return of Robinson Jeffers, The.   Robert Hass.   GeoHom

He shuffled my file.   Lilith and the Doctor.   Kathleen Norris.   HW

He sings in his father's arms, sings his father.   You Must Sing.   Li-Young Lee.   CAP-8; PLBUT

He sipped at a weak hock and seltzer.   Arrest of Oscar Wilde at the Cadogan Hotel, The.   Sir John Betjeman.   MoBrPo; NAMCP V.1; NoAM; NoP-4; NoP-5; NPeEn

He sits at the bar in the Alhambra.   Simple.   Naomi Long Madgett.   GT

He Sits Down on the Floor of a School for the Retarded.   Alden Nowlan.   StAl

He sits in front of the bright, blazing grate.   Old Freedman, The.   Priscilla Jane Thompson.   CBWP-2

He sits in the corner.   Corner.   Amal Dunqul.   PML, *tr. by* Sharif Elmusa and Thomas G. Ezzy

He sits on a bench.   Taxidermist at the Zoo, The.   Ruth Anderson Barnett.   UrbNat

He slammed the door shut. From under trees.   Outside in the Open.   Adriann Roland Holst.   TuT, *tr. by* Desmond Egan

He sleeps in the room next to mine, a wall between us.   Solitude Exercises.   Iman Mersal.   PoArWo, *tr. by* Khaled Mattawa

He sleeps on the top of a mast.   Unbeliever, The.   Elizabeth Bishop.   NAAL-5; NoAM

He slept in my bed.   Drugs.   Jacquie Jones.   ISC

He slept like a rock or a man that's dead. (LL)   Weary Blues, The.   Langston Hughes.   BrAP; ColAP; EMP; FaBoA; HarvBoo; ISC; NAAPv.2; NAMCP V.1; NoAM; NoP-4; NoP-5; OxBoAm; PoPoPo; SAmP

He slew the noble Mudjekeewis.   What Hiawatha Probably Did.   *Unknown.*   NBLV

He slowly replaced the receiver.   August Insomnia.   Franz Wright.   AmAlph

He smashed all the glass in the room (Bill: $50). (LL)   Malcolm Lowry.   NoP-4; NoP-5 *Fr.* Cantinas, The.

He smelled bad and was red-eyed with the miseries.   Portrait from the Infantry.   Alan Dugan.   AF; AmWaPo; PWW2

He smells of—what?   Balancing Out.   Margaret Avison.   GPPA

He smiles from his statue.   Sri Nityananda Mandir (The Temple of Nityananda).   Elsa Cross.   TANSG, *tr. by* Patricia Dubrava

He smokes his first Tiger.   Self-Portrait at Age Sixteen.   Homero Aridjis.   WoBe, *tr. by* George McWhirter

He snuggles his fingers.   After Winter.   Sterling Allen Brown.   GT

He sought the mountain and the loneliest height.   Jesus Praying.   Hartley Coleridge.   ChIV-2

He spake no dream, for as his words had end.   John Milton.   NOSC *Fr.* Paradise Regained [*or* Regain'd].

He speaks: My poor Penelope, my little lass.   Lullaby for Odysseus.   Irina Ermakova.   CRWP, *tr. by* Daniel Weissbort

He speaks of voyages.   Tour Guide: La Maison des Esclaves.   Melvin Dixon.   ESEAA; OxAAAP

He spins about (laughing) then shows.   Silvana Colonna.   ItPo, *tr. by* Gayle Ridinger

He spoke. And drank rapidly a glass of water. (LL)   Next to of course god america i.   E. E. Cummings.   FaBoA; NAAL-5; NAMCP V.1; NBLV; NoP-4; NoP-5; OBWP; OxBoAm; PoAgWa; PoWW; RaBo; StAl; TFi; WaAnP

He spoke; and silent tow'rd the northern sky.   Joel Barlow.   APN-1 *Fr.* Columbiad, The.

He spoke, and what he spoke was soon obeyed.   London Subverted by the Furies.   Abraham Cowley.   NOSC

He spoke in a thimble.   Presence of God, The.   David Craig.   UpMys

He spoke while sitting on what seemed to be.   Memory 2.   George Seferis.   PoetW, *tr. by* Edmund Keeley and Philip Sherrard

He stalls above me like an elephant. (LL)   To Speak of Woe That Is in Marriage.   Robert Lowell.   CAP-8; NAMCP V.2; NoAM; WaAnP

He stands against what looks like the other side.   David Ferry.   FaBoA

He stands and walks as if his knees were tensed.   Eastern Shore.   Charles Bruce.   IFF

He stands beside his ancient, lovely mistress.   Old Fisherman, The.   Emily Grosholz.   RA

He stands, cold in the morning wind.   Roll-Call in the Concentration Camp.   Dan Pagis.   FIT; PoSu, *tr. by* Robert Friend

He stands, stamps a little in his boots.   Roll Call, The.   Dan Pagis.   HP, *tr. by* Stephen Mitchell

He stands / Up and all.   He Is Lightning.   Jordan Davis.   HeMarv

He stared at ruin.   John Berryman.   *See* Dream Song 45.

He Stared at Ruin. Ruin stared straight back.   John Berryman.   PoPoPo *Fr.* Dream Songs.

He started coming on to me.   Unfaithful Wife, The.   Nuala Ni Dhomhnaill.   ModIr, *tr. by* Paul Muldoon

He starts a landslide shooting a.   Rabbit Shoeshine.   S. K. Kelen.   BMAP

He stepped ino the night aware.   Tired Man, The.   Suliaman El-Hadi.   SpirFl

He stepped off the plane shaking.   Uncle Good Intentions.   Susie Silook.   FTtHH

He steps down from the dark train, blinking; stares.   Ten Days Leave.   W. D. Snodgrass.   MoAmPo; PWW2

He steps out from the others.   Passion of Ravensbrück.   János Pilinszky.   AF; GI; HP; PoSu, *tr. by* Ted Hughes

He steps out from the others.   Passion of Ravensbrück, The.   János Pilinszky.   IQMS, *tr. by* Ted Hughes

He still believes by middle-age.   Traveler, The.   Duane Niatum.   HATNAP

He still may leave thy garland green. (LL)   Love and Friendship.   Emily Jane Brontë.   LW; PoBW

He stirs, beginning to awake.   Field Hospital, A.   Randall Jarrell.   NoP-4; NoP-5

He stood, a point / on a sheet of green paper.   Progressive Insanities of a Pioneer.   Margaret Atwood.   BrAP

He stood among a crowd at Drumahair [*or* Dromahair].   Man Who Dreamed of Faeryland, The.   William Butler Yeats.   NAEL-6v2; NAEL-7v2; NoAM
(He stood among a crowd at Drumahair.)   NoP-4

He stood, and heard the steeple.   Eight O'Clock.   A. E. Housman.   MoBrPo; NAMCP V.1; NoAM; SoSe-8

He stood by the piano for an hour, every Wednesday.   Mr Teller the Piano Teacher.   Jane Duran.   MFPA

He stood in the sulphur baths, his calves.   First.   Sharon Olds.   ExTi

He stood naked as one of the two windows.   Essay on Liberation, An.   David St. John.   AmAlph

He stood, the last—the last of all.   William Bingham Tappan.   VerBaPo *Fr.* Last Drunkard, The.

He stood wrapped in air.   Annunciation.   Anna Kamienska.   GI, *tr. by* David Curzon and Grażyna Drabik

He straight perceav'd himselfe to be my Lover. (LL)   Richard Barnfield.   CAGL; PBRV *Fr.* Cynthia, with Certain[e] Sonnets.

He strode young into the landscape of old age.   Dylan.   Thomas James Jones.   BBMWP, *tr. by* Jon Dressel

He sucks with greed the treacherous attraction.   Death of a Fly.   Johann Wolfgang von Goethe.   STV, *tr. by* John Frederick Nims

He summons Twinkling Indicator and Grand Yin.   Sweet Springs Palace, The.   Yang Hsiung.   CCL1, *tr. by* David Knechtges

He takes Earl Grey tea.   Taking Tea with My Father and Mother.   Pam Zinnemann-Hope.   Prnts

He takes me to see his mother. She lives in the.   Leslie Kaplan.   SCFWP *Fr.* Livre des ciels, Le.

He takes night as a kind of medicine.   Sinking.   Mark Bibbins.   PoDa

He tells me in Bangkok he's robbed.   Baby Villon.   Philip Levine.   OxBoAm

He tells me, "Your back."   Body As Braille, The.   Lorna Dee Cervantes.   NAMCP V.2

He thanked me for my kindness, disagreed.   William Wetmore Story.   APN-1 *Fr.* Contemporary Criticism, A.

He Thanks His Woodpile.   Lew Welch.   BB

He that but once too nearly hears. Coventry Patmore. NPeEn *Fr.* Victories of Love, The.

He that can trace a ship making her way. Heart Is Deep, The. Roger Wolcott. ChIV-1

He that for fear his Master did deny. To St. Peter and St. Paul. Henry Constable. NoSic

He that had come that morning. Ballad of John Cable and Three Gentlemen. W. S. Merwin. MakPoe; YaYoPo

He that is by Mooni now. Mooni. Henry Clarence Kendall. OBEV

He that is down, needs fear no fall. John Bunyan. OBEV; SacPr *Fr.* Pilgrim's Progress, The.

He that is weary, let him sit. Employment. George Herbert. FaBoVe

He that loves a rosy cheek. Disdain Returned. Thomas Carew. BASC; CavPo

He That None Can Capture. May Swenson. LW

He that of such a height hath built his mind. To the Lady Margaret, Countess [*or* Countesse] of Cumberland. Samuel Daniel. NOSC

He that saw hell in his melancholy dream. John Cleveland. NOSC *Fr.* Rebel Scot, The.

He that shuns love doth love himself the less. Mary Sidney Wroth, Countess of Montgomery. BASC

He that to number all the stars would seek. Guillaume de Salluste Du Bartas. NOSC *Fr.* Divine Weeks and Works, The.

He the ultimate shady dark Right. Skip The Byuppie. Ted Joans. FTtHH

He Thinks of Those Who Have Spoken Evil of His Beloved. William Butler Yeats. NoAM

He thinks she cannot see him through the window. Sunday Baking. Gailmarie Pahmeier. SweBea

He thinks that bearded iris. Stranger. Kerry Hardie. MoWP

He thinks when we die we'll go to China. Heaven. Cathy Song. NAAL-5; NIL-7; NoAM

He thought, but did not say. (LL) What He Thought. Heather McHugh. OxBoAm; P180; PtR; WaAnP

He thought he kept the universe alone. Most of It, The. Robert Frost. APT-1; BLT; NAMCP V.1; NoP-4; NoP-5; OxBoAm; TRP; WaAnP; WeW-3

He thought he saw an elephant [*or* a banker's clerk *or* a buffalo]. Lewis Carroll. WoPoe *Fr.* Sylvie and Bruno.

He thought it humanity's lot for ever to be persuading a huge rock up a mountainside. David Bromige. FTOS *Fr.* Tight Corners.

He thrashed the royal *erse* so that the *heid*. George Buchanan in Old Age. James Logie Robertson. EdScPo

He threw his cigarette in silence, then he said. L.R.D.G. J. G. Meddemmen. FaBoWar

He threw them out and slammed the gate shut. Eden. James Simmons. PNI

He tips hot water into a cup, stirs the powdered. Thermodynamics. Arthur Sze. WANABP

He tiptoes into the room almost as if he were an intruder. Annunciation, The. Stephen Mitchell. GI

He Told His Life Story to Mrs. Courtly. Stevie Smith. NBLV (Autumn.) LW

He told me he had spent. Shortening the Road. Michael Davitt. PBCIP, *tr. by* Philip Casey

He Told Me His Name Was Sitting Bull. Joy Harjo. WaAnP

He told me what I could see twenty feet away. First Glasses. Jennifer Grotz. NevBe

He told us, this may be the secret of heroism. (LL) Dying Away. William Meredith. NAMCP V.2; NoAM

He too has an eternal part to play. Historical Judas, The. Howard Nemerov. NoP-4

He too will soon go away. "Rachel." FIT, *tr. by* Robert Friend

He took / flight. Exile. Erich Fried. AF, *tr. by* Georg Rapp

He took her through a fire hydrant. Sex—A Five-Minute Briefing. Nina Iskrenko. ItGoST, *tr. by* Patrick Henry, John High and Katya Olmsted

He took her, trembling. Anniversaries. Thomas Kinsella.

He took her with a sigh. (LL) Love's Secret. William Blake. ITBLP; NPeEn; OxBEV

He took his sled and went back into the house. (LL) It had long been dark, though still an hour before supper-time. Charles Reznikoff. NAAPv.2; NAMCP V.1

He took one step. Blood Heifer. Dahlia Ravikovitch. DTA, *tr. by* Ariel Bloch and Chana Bloch

He touched me, so I live to know. Emily Dickinson. NCAP

He tramped in the fading light. Monk, The. Thomas Kinsella. BBASP

He trekked his body. Fleshpot. Martha Zweig. PfS

He tried so hard and is defeated. In the safehouse he lifts just the edge. Visit to the Cities of Cheese, A. Margaret Johnson. OnScMo

He tried to / climb a / ladder of light. Written for Love of an Ascension—Coltrane. Carolyn M. Rodgers. SeSe

He trudges the street of Blantyre. Tramp. Frank Mkalawile Chipasula. HBAPE

He tumbled from his weary wheel. Centurion, A. Will M. Carleton. ArBi

He turned and waved. Harold's Walk. Geoffrey Lehmann. EmeKit

He turns his back to dress; i've lost him. Memoirs of a Velvet Urinal. Michael Dransfield. BMAP

He Understands the Great Cruelty of Death. Petrarch. OBMV; OxBEV; WoPoe *Fr.* Sonnets to Laura.

He understood that words are living beings. Four Seekers of the Great Metaphor. Vladimir Levchev. CSCBP, *tr. by* Georgi Belev and Lisa Sapinkopf

He unto whom thou art so partial. Post-Obits and the Poets. Martial. OBVE; RomPo, *tr. by* Lord Byron

He visited, the man who takes your life. Visiting. Alan Jenkins. NeBrP

He wades in neoprene boots the tank's. Wild Salmon: Stillaguamish Tribal Hatchery. Joan Swift. PoCoUp

He waits at dusk, bamboo walking stick in hand. Visiting the Mountain Hermitage of a Monk at Gan-hua Monastery. Wang Wei. CrYelRi, *tr. by* Sam Hamill

He walked around and couldn't think of anything. Clark Coolidge. NYP2

He walked beside me smiling. Who Are You? Abd al-Rahim Salih al-Rahim. IrPoTo, *tr. by* Saadi A. Simawe and Daniel Weissbort

He walked out and left me flat. T'Ain't No Use. Herb Magidson. ReLy

He walks among us. He's a gentle soul. Revolutionary,The. Dezső Kosztolányi. IQMS, *tr. by* Peter Zollman

He walks around here. Berlioz in the Madhouse. Halvard Johnson. MiVo

He waltzes into the lane. Makin' Jump Shots. Michael S. Harper. ISC; MoASP

He wanders through the crooked streets. Aquí. Carmen Tafolla. TiP2

He wanted to rise up to the moment. Poet Lied, The. Odia Ofeimun. HBAPE

He wanted to tell her the weekend idea was "neat." Sestina. James Cummins. OxBoAm

He wants to be. Self-Portrait. Robert Creeley. NoAM; PmAP

He wants to be brought back to himself. To lose himself. As Is His Wont. Nance Van Winckel. RoV

He wants to go. Growing Up in a Jewish Neighborhood. Richard Chess. TaR

He wants to wonder not look so. Jerome in His Study. Clark Coolidge. FTOS

He warranted no better, I don't know. (LL) Mr Bleaney. Philip Larkin. NPeEn; OxBEV; PoPoPo; TRP; UV

He was a big man, says the size of his shoes. Abandoned Farmhouse. Ted Kooser. WeW-3

He was a blessing one never prays for—. Obituary. Steve Chimombo. HBAPE

He was a boy when first we met. Love Returned. Bayard Taylor. CAGL

He was a famous trumpet man from out Chicago way. Boogie Woogie Bugle Boy. Hughie Prince and Don Raye. ReLy

He was a gentleman sitting in front of a lady seated in. Gentleman in Front, The. Vivian Lamarque. CItWP, *tr. by* Cinzia Sartini Blum and Lara Trubowitz

He was a good boy. Uncle's First Rabbit. Lorna Dee Cervantes. NoAM

He was a huge. Time Heals All Wounds—But One. Vernon Rowe. BloBone

He was a large-eyed, Hunnish youth. Poet of the Hortobágy, The. Endre Ady. IQMS, *tr. by* Anton N. Nyerges

He Was a Man. Sterling Allen Brown. InGu

He was a poor man flying. Beethoven's Ears. Bobi Jones. ATSWP, *tr. by* Robert Minhinnick

He was a selfish shellfish. Idyll: "He was a selfish shellfish." Stoddard King. NBLV

He was a soldier in the army. Casualty. Langston Hughes. APT-2

He was a soldier or a Shaker. At least he was doing *something*. Chapter 2, Book 35. John Ashbery. BodElec

He was a South-of-Watford man. Looking North. Pamela Gillilan. Prnts

He was a trafficker in hearts. Wheels. Sarah Rabkin. RaF

He was a traveler west of the river,/ only he knew how lonely he was. *Unknown.* ColAnChi *Fr.* Four *Tz'u* from Tun-huang.

He was a traveler west of the river,/ then he took sick, lay an inch away from death. *Unknown.* ColAnChi *Fr.* Four *Tz'u* from Tun-huang.

He was a traveler west of the river,/ with wealth and eminence rare in this world. *Unknown.* ColAnChi *Fr.* Four *Tz'u* from Tun-huang.

He was a young god. Genesis. Evan Jones. PML

He Was Acquainted with Grief. Jones Very. SacPr

He was always the same. Portrait. Leopold Staff. PoSu, *tr. by* Adam Czerniawski

He was an Indiana corporal. At Chancellorsville. Andrew Hudgins. CBCWP

He was an upright man, a too-tight man. Woman Who Mistook Her Father for an Irishman, The. Nicki Jackowska. Prnts

He was arrested and detained. Soft Targets. Essex Hemphill. GT; OxAAAP

He was back. Said nothing. Homecoming. Wisława Szymborska. PoSu, *tr.* by Adam Czerniawski

He was bad at torture. Flubbed his first flaying. Good Devil, The. Kurt Brown. OPRER

He was born gray as a trough of concrete. Son of The House of a Thousand Chandeliers. Jennifer L. Knox. FreRad

He was born in Alabama. Gwendolyn Brooks. ESEAA; InoFa; NAMCP V.2; NoAM *Fr.* Street in Bronzeville, A.

He was born with the fingerpads of the blind. Prodigy, The. Lola Haskins. MiVo

He was but dust: how could he stand before him? Giles Fletcher, the Younger. SacPr *Fr.* Christ's Victory and Triumph.

He was captured in the Valley of Women. Man in the Valley of Women, A. Chris Greenhalgh. NeBl

He was carrying only. Flight. Mahdi Muhammad Ali. IrPoTo, *tr.* by Salaam Yousif

He was consistent from beginning to end. *Various authors.* CATKP *Fr.* Songs of Flying Dragons.

He was convinced that you had to eat the entire thing. Fruit They Had in Common. Shin Yu Pai. WANABP

He was dreaming of the factories across the water's fog. What Cannot Be Kept. Reginald Shepherd. GT

He was dying on the cross. On the Cross. Anna Kamienska. GI, *tr.* by David Curzon and Grażyna Drabik

He was formed of chicken blood and lightning. Christ's Twin. Louise Erdrich. CAP-8

He was formidable, he was, the little booger. Robert Penn Warren. GM *Fr.* Ballad: Between the Boxcars [1923].

He was found by the Bureau of Statistics to be. Unknown Citizen, The. W. H. Auden. BrAP; HeIP-4; NAMCP V.1; NBLV; NIP-4; OBSV; SoSe-8; TRP

He was good at telling. Diagnosis. Carole Satyamurti. StAl

He was heroic, fugitive, in love with the machinery. Marco Polo. Marvin Bell. BodElec

He was holding clean globes in his hands. (LL) Medgar Evers. Gwendolyn Brooks. ESEAA; NoP-4; NoP-5

He was just back. Vietnam. Clarence Major. HHAm; PoAgWa

He was lodging above in Coom. 'Mergency Man, The. John Millington Synge. NPeEn

He was lost!—not a shade of doubt of that. Little Lost Pup. Arthur Guiterman. ITBLP

He Was Lucky. Anna Swirszczynska [*or* Swir]. CFP; HP; PoSu, *tr.* by Magnus J. Krynski and Robert A. Maguire

He was my servant—and the better man. (LL) Rudyard Kipling. HarvBoo; NPeEn *Fr.* Epitaphs of the War [1914–1918].

He was no longer my father. Mirror, The. Michael Davitt. BeAl; PBCIP, *tr.* by Paul Muldoon

He was not a kind man. Agapé. Stephanie Brown. SUP

He was not a wise man. My Father. Manuela Fingueret. MirDau, *tr.* by Roberta Gordenstein

He was not ever completely working. (LL) Picasso. Gertrude Stein. NAAPv.2; NAMCP V.1

He was not made for politics. Exile, The. Edwin Thumboo. PML

He was out of work that year. Days of 1908. Constantine P. Cavafy. PFTM-1, *tr.* by Edmund Keeley and Philip Sherrard

He was preparing an Ulster fry for breakfast. Michael Longley. ModIr *Fr.* Wreaths.

He was quite a guy how he laughed like oh what's the name of the guy. Famous Women—Claudette Colbert. Kathleen de Azevedo. ReTh

He was reading late, at Richard's, down in Maine. Henry's Understanding. John Berryman. NAMCP V.2; NoAM; OxBoAm; PoCho; WoPoe

He was *really* / nowhere. (LL) Poem for Speculative Hipsters, A. Imamu Amiri Baraka. NAMCP V.2; NoAM

He was running with his friend from town to town. Minefield, The. Diane Thiel. AmWaPo; RaF

He was shaggy, sloppy, wet, his coat a yellow flame. Dog, The. Attila József. MotU, *tr.* by John Bakti

He was short and sturdy, one of dim Picton's Silurians. In Memory of Idris Davies. John Tripp. AngWePo

He was speaking other than with words. Speaking Other Than with Words. Luis Cernuda. RaW, *tr.* by Timothy Baland

He was straight and strong, and his eyes were blue. Lynmouth Widow, A. Amelia Josephine Burr. LW

He was strange weather, this luther. he read books, mainly poetry and sometimes. Poet: What Ever Happened to Luther? Haki R. Madhubuti. SpirFl; UnSA

He was strolling with another woman. Ballad. Gabriela Mistral. BLPSL, *tr.* by Rene de Costa, Rigas Kappatos and Eleni Paidoussi

He was the first always: Fortune. Envy. Adelaide Anne Procter. NPeEn; VWP

He was the first to see the snow. (LL) First Snow in Alsace. Richard Wilbur. AmWaPo; NoP-4; NoP-5; OBWP; PWW2

He was the last. Truly the last. Butterfly, The. Pavel Friedmann. HP, *tr.* by Dennis Silk

He was the one who saw me. Daphne and Laura and So Forth. Margaret Atwood. PoDa

He was the one who would not use his face. Thou Hast Blessed the Work of His Hands. Bin Ramke. RoV

He was the sort who *entertained*. Man Who Couldn't Believe, The. David Citino. UpMys

He Was the Word That Spake It. *Unknown.* OxBEV

He was the youngest son of a strange brood. Otto. Theodore Roethke. HarvBoo

He was tired of the old ladies. Shakespeare as a Waiter. BJ Ward. IaFF

He was to weet a man of full ripe years. Edmund Spenser. UV *Fr.* Faerie Queene, The.

He was too excited to fall asleep. Film Noir. Aram Saroyan. LiTh

He Was Too Good to Me. Lorenz Hart. ReLy

He was twelve years old. Green Beret. Ho Thien. FaBoWar; PoAgWa, *tr.* by *Unknown*

He was walking a frozen road. Music of Spheres. Jean Follain. BLT

He was walking from Bethany to Jerusalem. Miracle, The. Boris Leonidovich Pasternak. GI, *tr.* by Nina Kossman

He was washing the day's ink off his hands when he noticed a tiny mouth in the valley of his left palm. Good Teacher, The. Ray Amorosi. MotU

He watch her like a coonhound watch a tree. Balance. Marilyn Nelson Waniek. FFC; RA

He watched everything from his cross. Dulce Lignum, Dulces Clavos. Carol Muske-Dukes. MotU

He watched them as they walked towards the tree. Tree, The. Dorothy Auchterlonie. NOBAu

He waves his breakfast knife and screams he'll kill me. Paternity. Sydney Lea. PfSP

He wears Clarks Movers, his new shoes. News of the Changes. Bryan Aspden. AngWePo

He went by with another. Ballad. Gabriela Mistral. SpanPo, *tr.* by Muriel Kittel

He went down to the woodshed. No One Heard Him Call. Dorothy Aldis. TLR

He went to Arthur's Court, and play'd his part. Leigh Hunt. STuOW *Fr.* Story of Rimini, The.

He went / to the window. Beautiful day, The. V. Alfred B. Spellman. EGAG

He! When I met him approaching. When I Met Him Approaching. *Arapaho Oral Tradition.* NAAL-5; NAAPv.2 *Fr.* Ghost-Dance Songs.

He who at first a womans mind. Inconstancy. James Harrington. PBRV

He who bakes bread. Zen Baker. Jordan Jones. WhBo

He who believes that absence. Sonnet 41. Francisco de Medrano. BLPSL, *tr.* by Rene de Costa, Rigas Kappatos and Eleni Paidoussi

He who binds to himself a joy. William Blake. AmFaPo; NoP-4; NoP-5; SoSe-8; Spl *Fr.* Several Questions Answered.

He who could win the girl I love. Girl's Hair, A. Dafydd ab Edmwnd. OBWVE, *tr.* by Gwyn Williams

He who discovered. My Father Recounts a Story from His Youth. Kevin Prufer. AmPoNex

He who first stretched his nerves of subtile wire. Science and Poetry. James Russell Lowell. NCAP

He who has a yod in his name. Bella and the Golem. Rossana Ombres. CItWP, *tr.* by Cinzia Sartini Blum and Lara Trubowitz

He who has lost soul's liberty. Soul's Liberty. Anna Wickham. MoBrPo

He who has once been happy is for aye. Wilfrid Scawen Blunt. OBEV; OBMV *Fr.* Esther [a Young Man's Tragedy].

He who has seen my Mother. Najrul Islām. SinGod, *tr.* by Rachel Fell McDermott

He who holds that nothingness. Inscription over His Door. Gido. ZenPo, *tr.* by Takashi Ikemoto and Lucien Stryk

He who knew to serve as one of the oridnary soldiers. Memorial. Uri Zvi Greenberg. NRoS, *tr.* by Esther Raizen

He who knows how to shave the razor, will know how to erase the. Henri Michaux. PFTM-1 *Fr.* Slices of Knowledge.

He who knows not the Oba. Praise Song for the Oba of Benin. *Unknown.* WoPoe, *tr.* by John Bradbury

He Who Loved Beauty. Alec Brock Stevenson. FuPo

He, who navigated with success. Death of a Young Son by Drowning. Margaret Atwood. BrAP; NIL-7

He, who outbounded time and space. Greyhound Snowball, The. *Unknown.* DiBP

He who shuts off the rain. July. Margit Szécsi. IQMS, *tr.* by Agnes Arany-Makkai

He who sleeps on his palm / But even here, noiselessly. Seventh Heaven Can Be Seen at First Glance. Nikolai Kanchev. CSCBP, tr. by Georgi Belev and Lisa Sapinkopf

He Who splashed a thousand worlds with color. Quatrain. Ayn Al-Qozat Hamadani. BBASP, tr. by Nasrollah Pourjavady and Peter Lamborn Wilson

He who the hoop's immensity can pierce. John Wilkes. EroLit Fr. Essay on Woman.

He who thinks perchance to drown. Drunkenness. Friedrich von Logau. GePo, tr. by George C. Schoolfield

He who wants to leave. Love's Way. Kang Ŭn'gyo. CAMKP, tr. by Tae Yang Kwak

He Who Weeps Goes Not Alone. Rosalía de Castro. SpanPo, tr. by Kate Flores

He Whose Hand and Eye Are Gentle. Unknown. OBWVE, tr. by Kenneth Hurlstone Jackson

He whose not too honest fingers. Unknown. PriapPo Fr. Priapus Poems, The.

He, whose warm hand had often pressed. Unfortunate Gentleman, The. Cornelius Whur. STuOW

He will be sacrificed, the captive. Festival of Izcalli or Eighteenth Month. Carla Faesler Bremer. SPV, tr. by Jen Hofer

He will focus on a woman. Always a good idea. Where shall she sit? Matthea Harvey. IAoNAP Fr. Thermae.

He will outlast us, churning out his books. At the Scott Exhibition, Edinburgh Festival. Iain Crichton Smith. WaAnP

He will walk in as you're sitting down to a meal. (LL) Book of Yolek, The. Anthony Hecht. HP; MakPoe; NAMCP V.2; NoP-4; NoP-5; OxBoAm; TaR; WaAnP; WeW-3

He Wishes for the Cloths of Heaven. William Butler Yeats. BLPJKO; ChAP; GoPo; MoBrPo; NAMCP V.1; NoAM; OBEV; PtR

He wishes he could hug them like big friends from home. (LL) Stalin Epigram, The. Osip Emilevich Mandelstam. AF; WoPoe, tr. by Clarence Brown and W. S. Merwin

He with the beating wings. Dead Language. Johannes Bobrowski. WoPoe, tr. by Matthew Mead and Ruth Mead

He with whom I ran hand in hand. Woman Meets an Old Lover, A. Denise Levertov. BLT

He without hair, and thou without a crown. (LL) Fable, A: "In Æsop's tales an honest wretch we find." Matthew Prior. NoP-4; NoP-5

He woke, and wondered more: for there she lay. (LL) Dante Gabriel Rossetti. NAEL-6v2; NAEL-7v2 Fr. House of Life, The.

He woke at five and, unable. Physical Universe. Louis Simpson. CAP-8

He won't walk as a man ever again. (LL) On the Murder of Lieutenant José del Castillo by the Falangist Bravo Martinez, July 12, 1936. Philip Levine. AmWaPo; WaAnP

He would declare and could himself believe. Never Again Would Birds' Song Be the Same. Robert Frost. APT-1; NAMCP V.1; NIP-4; NoAM; NoP-4; NoP-5; OWoS; OxBoAm; SoSe-8

He would drink by himself. Casualty. Seamus Heaney. ModIr; NAEL-6v2; NAEL-7v2; NAMCP V.2; PBCIP

He would get the gold. Stroke. Hugh Seidman. BodElec

He would have to put out his smoke. Why Ralph Refuses to Dance. C. D. Wright. CAP-8

He would not lie uncovered. Burial of the Dog. Susan Musgrave. NoAM

He would not stay for me; and who can wonder? A. E. Housman. CAGL

He would rest his elbows. Robert Frost's Chair. Gary Metras. VisFro

He would tell you the grass this spring was a pale. Bravura Lament. Daniel Halpern. PoDa

He would travel. Sleeper. Ken Worpole. RSaN

He wouldn't sign the death warrant. Vitalina Tkhorzhevskaya. CRWP, tr. by Daniel Weissbort

He writes down something that he crosses out. (LL) Boy, The. Marilyn Hacker. ExTi; WiU

He Writes to the Soul. Christopher Howell. RoV

He writes, writes and writes. Tomas Tranströmer. WoBe Fr. Haiku.

He wrote that the light struck the window blind and she should have stopped there. Reading for Pleasure. Barbara Einzig and Jerome Rothenberg. OnScMo

He Wrote the History Book. Marianne Moore. APT-1

He wrote The I and the It. On the Death of a German Philosopher. Stevie Smith. OBCoV

He yawned and watched the lilac horns of his island. Derek Walcott. NAEL-7v2; NoP-4 Fr. Omeros.

Head and Torso of the Minotaur. John Reibetanz. IFF

Head at the Covers, A. Bill Berkson. NYP2

Head bent, walking through snow. 125th Street and Abomey. Audre Lorde. OxAAAP

Head Filled with Beauty, The. Pierre Reverdy. YaTCFP, tr. by Mary Ann Caws

Head full of fragrant vines. Medusa. Mariahadessa Ekere Tallie. BRtP

Head Itself. Laura Riding Jackson. PoA 2002

Head of a Doll. Charles Simic. NAMCP V.2

Head of a White Woman Winking. James Tate. BodElec

Head of Hair. Charles Baudelaire. SxFrPo, tr. by James McGowan

Head of Medusa. Marya Alexandrovna Zaturenska. MoAmPo

Head of Medusa on a Rotella of Michelangelo da Caravaggio, in the Gallery of the Grand Duke of Tuscany, The. GS, tr. by Unknown

Head of Pancho Villa, The. Ray Gonzales. TiP2

Head Over Heels in Love. Mack Gordon. ReLy

Head pillowed on arm. Buson. SoOfWa, tr. by Sam Hamill

Head pressed against the shoulder, thirty times, The. Tape Mark. Nanni Balestrini. PFTM-2, tr. by Lawrence R. Smith

Head. Red-handed, I leave the field. (LL) Strawberrying. May Swenson. NAMCP V.2; VCAP

Head That Once Was Crowned with Thorns, The. Thomas Kelly. SacPr

Head, The. Blaise Cendrars. CuPo

Head thrusts in as for the view, A. All Revelation. Robert Frost. APT-1

Headache, The. Mary Leapor. PEW

Heading for Manhattan by Train. Ed Friedman. PrTe

Heading for the Heights. Merryn Williams. Prnts

Heading Out. Philip Booth. PoA 2002

Heading Out West. John Balaban. OPRER

Heading over to Bulaan Alaaga's. Cutting Back the Ifugao Past. Al Robles. ReBoTo

Heading South. Tu Fu [or Du Fu]. CrYelRi, tr. by Sam Hamill

Heading south down the freeway making the switch. Really the Real. Gary Snyder. WANABP

Headlands. Jack Hirschman. CLPP

Headless, lacking foot and hand. Rudyard Kipling. PoWW Fr. Epitaphs of the War [1914–1918].

Headless limbless / it appears. Vasco [or Vasko] Popa. PoSu Fr. Quartz Pebble, The.

Headless man walks, lives, A. Sun. Michael Palmer.

Headless torsos, faceless lovers, friends of mine. (LL) Onion, Memory, The. Craig Raine. NAEL-6v2; NAEL-7v2; NAMCP V.2; NoAM; NoP-4; NoP-5

Headlights, large, round. Two pieces of shattered glass. (LL) Wreck in the Woods. Dave Jeddie Smith. NAMCP V.2; RoV

Headline History. William Plomer. OBCoV

Headlined in Heaven. Paul Grano. NOBAu

Headlines. Harryette Mullen. RD

Headlines chanting. Morning Ride. Lola Ridge. NAAPv.2

Headlong down the red dawn galloped. Battle of Adobe Walls. Chris Willerton. TiP2

Headmaster. John Tripp. AngWePo

Headmaster Abe. Ko Un. PML, tr. by Anthony, Brother of Taizé, Gary Gach and Yŏng-mu Kim

Headmaster Abe Sudomu, from Japan. Headmaster Abe. Ko Un. PML, tr. by Anthony, Brother of Taizé, Gary Gach and Yŏng-mu Kim

Heads beside roots, pressed against them, you sleep. Marin Georgiev. CSCBP Fr. Memory.

Heads each on each, the numb flowers drowse. You Never Ask. Unknown. SonAtl, tr. by Gris Klamas and Tina Ritson

Heads of strong old age are beautiful, The. Promise of Peace. Robinson Jeffers. MoAmPo

Headwaters. N. Scott Momaday. ICANM; NoP-4; NoP-5; WaAnP

Heald þu nu, hruse, nu hæleð ne mostan. Unknown. NoP-5 Fr. Beowulf [Anglo-Saxon].

Healed. Dorothy Parker. AmWit

Healers. Natalia Toledo. RMCMP, tr. by Alberto A. Ríos

Healing. D. H. Lawrence. RaBo

Healing. Daphne Marlatt. NLPA Fr. Touch to My Tongue.

Healing. Alicia Ostriker. ExTi Fr. Mastectomy Poems, The.

Healing Animal. Joy Harjo. SeSe

Healing Earthquakes. Jimmy Santiago Baca.
  Book 1: As Life Was; Poem Two. ICANM
  Book 3: La Guerra; Poem Thirteen. ICANM
  Book 5: Rebirth; Poem Twenty-Eight. ICANM
  Book 5: Rebirth; Twenty-Nine. ICANM

Healing Logic, A. M. Wyrebek. AmPoNex

Healing Notebooks, The. Kenny Fries.
  "I bed next to you, I feel your heartbeat." AmPoNex
  "Who knows the precise moment when the stream." AmPoNex

Healing Song. Unknown. OBVE, tr. by Frances Densmore

Healing the Mare. Linda McCarriston. LoL

Health, A. Edward Coote Pinkney. APN-1

Health Check. Penny Feinstein. PoCu

Health Forecast, The. Roger McGough. PoCu

Health in his rags, Content upon his face. On Seeing a Bird-Catcher. Eliza Cook. VWP

Health is the first good lent to men. Four[e] Things Make Us Happy Here. Robert Herrick. Spl

Health to great Gloucester—from a man unknown. Dedication. Charles Churchill. OBSV

Healthy Remedies. Georges Henein. SurPaPo, tr. by Mary Ann Caws

Healthy Spot, A. W. H. Auden. OxBoAm

Heap cassia, sandal-buds and stripes. Robert Browning. OBEV Fr. Paracelsus.

Heap earth upon it. (LL) Requiescat. Oscar Wilde. GoPo; IrV; MoBrPo

Heap on more grass was his request. Joseph Gwyer. VerBaPo Fr. On the Funeral of Dr. Livingston.

Heap on more wood!—the wind is chill. Sir Walter Scott. ChrPo; OBCP Fr. Marmion.

Heapt with leaves the midden hides my mirth. Roy Kiyooka. NLPA Fr. Pear Tree Pomes.

Hear. (LL) At the cemetery, walnut grove plantation, south carolina, 1989. Lucille Clifton. CAP-8; LoL; NAMCP V.2

Hear father yet thou Long-Armed Lord! these latest words I say. Unknown. TAL Fr. Bhagavad-Gita, The.

Hear from Heaven Today. Unknown. SSUS

Hear hear hear hear. Ronald Johnson. APSN Fr. Ark.

Hear! hear! hear! / Listen! the word. Mocking-Bird, The. Richard Hovey. APN-2

Hear Icenian, Catieuchlanian, hear Coritanian, Trinobant! Alfred Tennyson. FaBoWar Fr. Boädicea.

Hear it! Eventless inmesh. A stick collapses. Truth Put It. Marianne Vitale. HeMarv

Hear, Jehovah! / May the eternal serpent's curse be on him! Lord Byron. NOBRP Fr. Cain: A Mystery.

Hear me, great ones of Uruk. Unknown. CAGL Fr. Epic of Gilgamesh, The.

Hear me, / helper of mankind. Unknown. RaBo Fr. Homeric Hymns.

Hear me, my God, and hear me soon. Petition, The. Thomas Beedome. NOSC

Hear me [or Heare mee], O God! Hymn[e] to God the Father, A. Ben Jonson. BrAP; InvLi; NoP-4; NoP-5; NOSC; OxAEP-1; SacPr

Hear me out, my dear friends. Yunus Emre. NaPG, tr. by Talat Sait Halman

Hear me propitious, and defend my lays. (LL) To Maecenas. Phillis Wheatley. NAAL-5; WaAnP

Hear my voice where you are. Come Back to Me. Alan Jay Lerner. ReLy

Hear now a curious dream I dreamed last night. My Dream. Christina Georgina Rossetti. ViWPN; VWP

Hear, O hear, Iseult la belle! Tristan, sad hero, hear! The Lambeg drum. James Joyce. PFTM-2 Fr. Finnegans Wake.

Hear, O Israel! Adah Isaacs Menken. CBWP-1

Hear, O Israel! and plead my cause against the ungodly nation. Hear, O Israel! Adah Isaacs Menken. CBWP-1

Hear, O my people, and I will speak. Bible, O.T. InvLi Fr. Psalms.

Hear that echo, children. Swan Sequence, The. Unknown. WoPoe, tr. by Denis Goacher

Hear That Phone Ringing? Sounds Like a Long Distance Call. Joseph Stroud. CalPo

Hear that tree-lizard singin' out. Jarrangulli. Roland Robinson. NOxBChV

Hear the Bird of Day. David Campbell. NOBAu

Hear the dreary, dreary rain. Voices of the Rain. Henrietta Cordelia Ray. CBWP-3

Hear the music, the thunder of the wings. Love the wild swan. (LL) Love the Wild Swan. Robinson Jeffers. APT-1; MoAmPo; NoAM

Hear the sledges with the bells. Bells, The. Edgar Allan Poe. APN-1; BRP; ChAP; IJHIL; ITBLP; NAAPv.1; TCAPo; TFi; TreFP

Hear the swish of rain. Tomas Tranströmer. WoBe Fr. Haiku.

Hear the voice of the Bard! William Blake. ChIV-1; NAEL-6v2; NAEL-7v2; NAWM-7v2; NOBRP; NoP-4; NoP-5; NPBRoP; NPeEn; OxBEV; TFi Fr. Songs of Experience.

Hear them, hear them—all. Cage of Voices, The. Horace Gregory. APT-2

Hear! this is what I. For John Donne: Master Metaphysical. Alexander Trocchi. EroLit

Hear this my clarion call. Nommo. Zizwe Ngafua. BRtP

Hear what God the Lord hath spoken. William Cowper. InvLi Fr. Olney Hymns.

Hear, Ye Ladies [That Despise]. John Fletcher. OBEV Fr. Tragedy of Valentinian, The.

Heard by a Girl. Louise Bogan. APT-2

Heard de owl a hootin'. Gal's Cry for a Dying Lover. Langston Hughes. NAMCP V.1

Heard in air those words I later made me read. Flag-Tree. Dan Beachy-Quick. IAoNAP

Heard, not seen. Basho. SoOfWa, tr. by Sam Hamill

Heard over the radio. News Story. Clarence Major. EGAG

Heard riot in the emptied head. (LL) To Kill a Deer. Carol Frost. CAP-8; MoASP

Heard the pulse of you when all was still ringing little bells last night under my ear. (LL) I Heard You Solemn-Sweet Pipes of the Organ. Walt Whitman. APN-1; SAmP

Heard you that shriek? It rose. Slave Mother, The. Frances Ellen Watkins Harper. NAAPv.1; WaAnP

Heäre, The. William Barnes. DiBP

Hearing. W. S. Merwin. NoAM

Hearing a Mozart Duo at 36,000 Feet. Ruth Whitman. PfS

Hearing a Startled Bird During Stayover at Chin-Ch'ang Pavilion. Li Shang-yin. ChinPo, tr. by Ye Weilian [or Yeh Wei-lien or Wai-lim Yip]

Hearing a thud, as though a ball had struck. False Move. Grace Schulman. ExTi

Hearing about the Virtual Destruction of Pain. Nathaniel Tarn. WANABP

Hearing Bells at Night in the Mountains. Chang Yüeh. CCL1, tr. by Stephen Owen

Hearing Impairment. Les A. Murray. OBCoV

Hearing Loss. Christian Wiman. AmPoNex; PoDa

Hearing loss? Yes, loss is what we hear. Hearing Impairment. Les A. Murray. OBCoV

Hearing Music Through Dark Trees. Ethan Paquin. LegDan

Hearing of harvests rotting in the valleys. Paysage Moralisé. W. H. Auden. HarvBoo; MoBrPo

Hearing of Imperial Forces Retaking Ho-Nan and Ho-Pei. Tu Fu [or Du Fu]. ChinPo, tr. by Ye Weilian [or Yeh Wei-lien or Wai-lim Yip]

Hearing of past actions. John Cage. APSN Fr. Diary: How to Improve the World (You Will Only Make Matters Worse).

Hearing one saga, we enact the next. Remembering the 'Thirties. Donald Davie. HarvBoo; NAMCP V.2; NoP-4; NoP-5

Hearing the cuckoo's song in the spring field outside the window. On a Cuckoo's Song. Pyungyang Ungee. BecRai, tr. by Kim Daljin, Kim Won-Chung and Christopher Merrill

Hearing the Flute in the City of Loyang in a Spring Night. Li Po. ChinPo, tr. by Ye Weilian [or Yeh Wei-lien or Wai-lim Yip]

Hearing the Gibbons Call in Pa Gorge. Wen Chao. CSKM, tr. by Paul Hansen

Hearing the horizons endure. (LL) Horses, The. Ted Hughes. BeAl; NAMCP V.2; NoAM; WaAnP

Hearing the judges' well-considered sentence. After the Trial. Weldon Kees. MakPoe

Hearing the organ stray. Service. Peter Scupham. HarvBoo

Hearing the rain at last, I stepped out and saw the dark day. Finally the Rain. Carrington McDuffie. PoCoUp

Hearing the stones cry out under the horizons. (LL) Wind. Ted Hughes. HarvBoo; NAEL-6v2; NAEL-7v2; NoP-4; NoP-5

Hearing the thunder of the intransitive weirs. Arthur Rimbaud. WoPoe Fr. Drunken Boat [or Barge], The.

Hearing, this June day, the thin thunder. Home Thoughts from Abroad. William Robert Rodgers. OBCoV

Hearing Your Words, and Not a Word among Them. Edna St. Vincent Millay. ColAP; NoAM

Hearken all ye, 'tis the feast o' Saint Stephen. Feast o' Saint [or St.] Stephen, The. Ruth Sawyer. OBCP

Hearken, thou craggy ocean pyramid! To Ailsa Rock. John Keats. CenSon

Hearken to me, gentlemen. Unknown. OBNV

Hears thy voice right, now he is gone. (LL) Memorial Verses. Matthew Arnold. CABP; NAEL-6v2; NAEL-7v2

Hearsay / You've hid out. Sent to Huai Ku. Hsi Chou. CSKM, tr. by Paul Hansen

Hearse comes up the road, The. Twelve Minutes. J. C. Hall. InoFa

Hearse-dark grackles pockmark. Omens. Cyd Adams. TiP2

Heart. Richard Adler and Jerry Ross. ReLy Fr. Damn Yankees.

Heart. Catherine Bowman. ExTi

Heart. Maura Dooley. NeBl

Heart. Cheryl Savageau. PfS

Heart. David Scott. BeAl; PoCu

Heart. Dieter Weslowski. InvLad

Heart, The. Michael Drayton. NOSC

Heart, The. Francis Thompson.
All's Vast. MoBrPo; OBMV
"Heart you hold too small and local thing, The." OBMV

Heart, The: "Wild heart grew white in the forest, The." Georg Trakl. WED, tr. by Robert Bly

Heart, The. Patrick Warner. Coast

Heart, The. C. K. Williams. PoCu

Heart and Clock. Charles Reznikoff. NAMCP V.1

Heart and flesh. (LL) John Montague. ModIr; PNI Fr. Great Cloak, The.

Heart and Mind. Dame Edith Sitwell. LW

Heart and Soul. Assotto Saint. CAGL

Heart and the Severed Head, The. Rosita Copioli. CItWP, *tr.* by Cinzia Sartini Blum and Lara Trubowitz

Heart asks Pleasure—first, The. Emily Dickinson. APN-2; MoAmPo; NAAL-3; NoP-4; NoP-5; OxBoAm; PoPoPo; PtR; TCAPo

Heart Attack. Adam Ziemianin. PML, *tr.* by Amelia Gregorek and Jerzy Gregorek

Heart be content, though she be gone. Ostella forth of Town: To My Heart. John Tatham. NOSC

Heart beating, beating inside what I say *en inglés*. (LL) Bilingual Sestina. Julia Alvarez. ExTi; FFC; WaAnP

Heart broken from leaving you and the road of departure! Selections from "Quatrains." Kim Yŏngnang. CAMKP, *tr.* by Walter Lew

Heart cold in the breast with terror, grieving. Lament for Llywelyn ap Gruffudd. Gruffudd ab yr Ynad Coch. OBWVE, *tr.* by Joseph P. Clancy

Heart, Crown, and Mirror. Guillaume Apollinaire. *tr.* by Roger Shattuck Mirror. YaTCFP, *tr.* by Roger Shattuck

Heart dies of this sweetness, The. (LL) Brigit Pegeen Kelly. ExTi; IllVoic *Fr.* Southern Review, The.

Heart envies, The. Zenaida. Natalia Toledo. RMCMP, *tr.* by Alberto A. Ríos

Heart Escaping. László Kálnoky. IQMS, *tr.* by Kenneth McRobbie and Zita McRobbie

Heart Feels the Water. Joseph Ceravolo. NYP2

Heart holds its own heat, The. Hearthouse. John MacKenzie. Coast

Heart is both the cup and the wine, The. Nef'i. OLP, *tr.* by Walter Andrews, Najaat Black and Mehmet Kalpakli

Heart Is Deep, The. Roger Wolcott. ChIV-1

Heart is pleased when black down covers, The. Nejati. OLP, *tr.* by Walter Andrews, Najaat Black and Mehmet Kalpakli

Heart is sensual, though five eyes break, The. (LL) When All My Five and Country Senses See. Dylan Thomas. MoBrPo; NAMCP V.2; NoAM; PoA 2002

Heart is there, A. Reflection on the Paintings of Mark Rothko's Chapel, A. Eric Muirhead. TiP2

Heart Mountain, 1943. Lee Ann Roripaugh.
1. Kimiko Ozawa. AmWaPo

Heart, my heart churning with fathomless cares. Archilochus. SaLy, *tr.* by Diane Rayor

Heart, my lovely hobo, you. Heart, My Lovely Hobo. Sandra Cisneros. IllVoic

Heart of a Thirtyish Woman, The. Yosano Akiko. CAoMJL1, *tr.* by Janine Beichman

Heart of a woman goes forth with the dawn, The. Heart of a Woman, The. Georgia Douglas Johnson. ISC; NAAPv.2

Heart of autumn! Chipmunk, The. Herman Melville. NCAP

Heart of Autumn. Robert Penn Warren. APT-2; ColAP; FuPo; InGu; WaAnP

Heart of Herakles, The. Kenneth Rexroth. BLT *Fr.* Lights in the Sky are Stars, The.

Heart of Midlothian, The. Sir Walter Scott.
(Madge Wildfire Sings.) NPeEn
"Proud Maisie is in the wood." CABP; NAEL-6v2; NAEL-7v2; NePenScot; NOBRP; OBEV; OxBEV; RACG; TFi

Heart of Oak. David Garrick. FaBoWar

Heart of Rice Straw, A. Nellie Wong.
"Ma, my heart must be made of rice straw." UnSA

Heart of standing is we cannot fly, The. (LL) Aubade: "Hours before dawn we were woken by the quake." William Empson. OxAEP-2; OxBEV

Heart of Texas, The. James Cody. TiP2

Heart of the Matter. Susan Prospere. MakPoe

66: The Heart of the Night. Dante Gabriel Rossetti. SacPr *Fr.* House of Life, The.

Heart of the Quartz Pebble, The. Vasco [*or* Vasko] Popa. PoSu *Fr.* Quartz Pebble, The.

Heart of Time. Fanny Carrión de Fierro. TANSG, *tr.* by Sally Cheney Bell

Heart stood at the helm that night, The. Departure. Gerrit Achterberg. TuT, *tr.* by Peter van de Kamp

Heart Stumbles in Darkness, The. Nathaniel Tarn. WANABP

Heart that answers heart. Kim Namjo. CAMKP *Fr.* Love's Cursive.

Heart, The / a canned tulip. Surplus. Rebecca Reynolds. AmPoNex

Heart to hear, the balls bells tear a theater. Not A Ton Notation. Jerry McGuire. AnSo

Heart! We [*or* Heart, we] will forget him! Emily Dickinson. SAmP

Heart whose love is innocent!, A. (LL) She Walks In Beauty. Lord Byron. AmFaPo; BLPJKO; BrAP; BRP; CABP; HeIP-4; ITBLP; NAEL-6v2; NAEL-7v2; NePenScot; NOBRP; NoP-4; NoP-5; NPBRoP; OBEV; OxAEP-2; OxBEV; PoPoPo; PtR; TFi; WaAnP

Heart with Little or No Bedrock for Anchor, A. Vivian Shipley. ExTi

Heart, you bully, you punk, I'm wrecked, I'm shocked. One is One. Marie Ponsot. ExTi

Heart you hold too small and local thing, The. Francis Thompson. OBMV *Fr.* Heart, The.

Heartache. Pura López Colomé. RMCMP, *tr.* by Forrest Gander

Heart-affluence in discursive talk. Alfred Tennyson. NAEL-6v2; NAEL-7v2 *Fr.* In Memoriam A. H. H.

Heartbeats. Melvin Dixon. ESEAA

Heartbreak Hotel Piano-Bar. Richard Speakes. SwNoth

Heartbreaking white flowers come up sometimes. Flowers Under the Dead. José Luis Hidalgo. RaW, *tr.* by Hardie St. Martin

Heartease 3. Lorna Goodison. WaCA

Hearth, The. C. K. Williams. BeAl; WaAnP

Hearth Song. John Montague. PNI

Hearthouse. John MacKenzie. Coast

Hearthstone. Harold Monro. OBMV

Heart-Hungry. Josephine D. Henderson Heard. CBWP-4

Heartland. Jim Barnes. HATNAP

Heartland. Trent Busch. BAP-01

Heartland. Linda Hogan. UrbNat

Heartless Art, The. Tony Harrison. NoP-4; NoP-5

Heart-Mirror. Tess Gallagher. AmZen

Hearts. Melvin E. Lewis. BtF

Hearts, The. Robert Pinsky. VCAP

Hearts (1983). Laurie Duggan. BMAP *Fr.* Three Found Poems.

Heart's Abysses, The. Walter Savage Landor. OBSV

Heart's Counting Knows Only One, The. Jane Hirshfield. WhBo

Heart's Desire. Adelia Prado. TANSG, *tr.* by Ellen Doré Watson

Heart's Ease. Paul Hoover. PmAP

Heart's Ease. Mary E. Tucker. CBWP-1

Heart's Fine Gold, The. W. O. Bourne. TreFP

Heart's Garden, the Garden's Heart, The. Kenneth Rexroth.
"Water is always the same." WhBo

Heart's Graveyard Shift, The. Yusef Komunyakaa. InGu

Heart's Hunger. Karen Press. TSAP

Heart's mirror clear Reflects beyond fetter. Heart's Mirror Clear. Xuanjue. CCL1 *Fr.* Canticle of the Way.

Heart's Music. Thomas Campion. OBEV

Heart's Needle. W. D. Snodgrass.
"Child between them on the street." NAMCP V.2
"Child between them on the street, The." NoP-5
"Child of my winter, born." MoAmPo
"Easter has come around." VCAP
"Here in the scuffled dust." NoP-5
"I get numb and go in." CAP-8
"I thumped on you the best I could." NAMCP V.2; NoAM
"Late April and you are three; today." NoP-5; VCAP
"Vicious winter finally yields, The." NoP-5

Hearts thus intermixed speak, The. Friendship in Emblem[e], or the Seal[e], to my dearest Lucasia. Katherine Philips. CABP; EMWP; PBRV

Hearts-Ease. Walter Savage Landor. OxBEV

Heart-Shaped Island, A. J. P. Dancing Bear. IaFF

Heartsong. Jeni Couzyn. BeAl; HAWP

Heartsong. Khaled Mattawa. BAP-97; NAPBL; NeAmPo

Heartstopping. Nicole Espagnol. SurWo, *tr.* by Myrna Bell Rochester

Heartstring. Blessed wood. Copacetic Mingus. Yusef Komunyakaa. OxAAAP

Heat. Carol Cullar. TiP2

Heat. Maura Dooley. NeBl

Heat. "H. D." HeIP-4; MoAmPo; TCAPo; TRP *Fr.* Garden, The.

Heat. Denis Johnson. MakPoe; SwNoth

Heat. Archibald Lampman. BrAP

Heat. Kenneth Mackenzie. BMAP

Heat. Onika Simon. BeDoSh

Heat Bird, The. Mei-Mei Berssenbrugge. OnScMo

Heat Lightning in a Time of Drought. Andrew Hudgins. CAP-8
(Heat Lightning in Time of Drought.) UpMys

Heat of explosions, The. Michael Ondaatje. NAMCP V.2 *Fr.* Buried 2.

Heat of Midnight Tears, The. Mirabai. WED; WPoS, *tr.* by Robert Bly

Heat of the oven, The. Breaded Meat, Breaded Hands. Michael S. Harper. ISC

Heat oven to 375° lie. Mourning dove ragpicks bargemen. Jessica Freeman. AnSo

Heat / Rots your breath. Family Photographs. Cecilio Garcia-Camarillo. ICANM

Heat Sours, The. David Biespiel. AmPoNex

Heat standing tall as a door, you go outside, The. Antigua. Gary Soto. PoA 2002

Heat that feb ice. Spell melt. La Tormenta. Geraldine Monk. Oth

Heat waiting inside their mouths, The. (LL)   Perch, The.   Galway Kinnell. PML; PoDa

Heat Wave.   Irving Berlin.   ReLy

Heat wave, A / Blew right into town last week.   Heat Wave.   Irving Berlin. ReLy

Heat waves shimmering.   Basho.   EH, *tr. by* Robert Hass

Heat-blaze, white dazzle: and white is the dust.   Day Dr. Knox Did It, The. Robert Penn Warren.

Heath grass / Sandals.   Masaoka Shiki.   ZenPo, *tr. by* Takashi Ikemoto and Lucien Stryk

Heat-heavy creatures.   Mary Kinzie.   FFC

Heathen in free verse, A.   Shame of the Writers' Conference.   Allison Joseph. BtF

Heathen Pass-ee, The.   Arthur Clement Hilton.   UV

Heather, The.   Neil Munro.   EdScPo

Heather Flowers.   Eliseus Williams.   OBWVE, *tr. by* Kenneth Hurlstone Jackson

Heather on the Hill, The.   Alan Jay Lerner.   ReLy

Heave away, heave away! I'd rather court a yellow gal than work for Henry Clay.   Heave Away.   *Unknown.*   SSUS

Heave Me a Mountain, Lord! (Prayer from the Plainview Rest Home).   Jack E. Murphy.   TiP2

Heaven.   Chairil Anwar.   PML; PoetW, *tr. by* Burton Raffel

Heaven.   Rupert Brooke.   MoBrPo; NPeEn; OxBEV

Heaven.   George Herbert.   WoPoe

Heaven: "What was it I saw at the top."   Eleni Sikelianos.   IIR

Heaven.   Cathy Song.   NAAL-5; NIL-7; NoAM

Heaven.   Gary Soto.   SwNoth

Heaven and Earth.   Vera Pavlova.   CRWP, *tr. by* Maura Dooley and Terence Dooley

Heaven and Earth are ruthless.   Lao Tzu.   CCL1 *Fr.* Way and Its Power, The.

Heaven and Earth endure and do not perish.   Substance, Shadow, and Spirit. T'ao Ch'ien.   CCL1, *tr. by* William Acker

Heaven and Hell [*with music*].   Francis Thompson.   SacPr

Heaven and hell are men's unhappy inventions.   Taoist Song.   Teng Yu-pin. CrYelRi, *tr. by* Sam Hamill

Heaven and Hell, like the great auction galleries, have heaps of objects accumulated in their passageways.   Report on Heaven and Hell.   Silvina Ocampo.   MotU, *tr. by* Edith Grossman

Heaven as Anus.   Maxine W. Kumin.   CAP-8

Heaven Bell A-Ring.   *Unknown.*   SSUS

Heaven Bells, The.   *Unknown.*   SSUS

Heaven conserve thy course in quietness [fr. *the Chinese of the* Confucian Odes].   *Unknown.*   APSN; NDACCP, *tr. by* Ezra Pound

Heaven / doesn't kill me.   Taneda Santoka.   CAoMJL1, *tr. by* Burton Watson

Heaven gave him courage and wisdom.   *Various authors.*   CATKP *Fr.* Songs of Flying Dragons

Heaven had not won, nor earth so timely lost. (LL)   Epitaph for [*or on*] Thomas Clere.   Henry Howard, Earl of Surrey.   NoSic; OxBSo

Heaven has different Signs—to me.   Emily Dickinson.   RSR

Heaven has once again become valuable to me.   If I Leave You.   Alberto A. Ríos.   PoChi

Heaven / I'm in heaven.   Cheek to Cheek.   Irving Berlin.   ReLy

Heaven is Hers! / Earth is Hers!   Inanna's Chant.   Janine Canan.   HW

Heaven Is Just Another Country.   Jaime Jacinto.   ReBoTo

"Heaven"—is what I cannot reach!   Emily Dickinson.   PoBW

Heaven of Animals, The.   James Dickey.   CAP-8; ColAP; EmeKit; HeIP-4; InGu; InoFa; NAMCP V.2; NoAM; StAl; TRP; VCAP; WaAnP; WoPoe

Heaven opened wide / Her ever during gates, harmonious sound.   John Milton. ChIV-1; TreFP *Fr.* Paradise Lost.

Heaven Peak.   Muso Soseki.   EaWin, *tr. by* W. S. Merwin

Heaven Questions, The.   Ch'u Yüan.   *tr. by* Stephen Field

"In the beginning of old."   WoPoe, *tr. by* Stephen Field

Heaven sent a genius.   *Various authors.*   CATKP *Fr.* Songs of Flying Dragons

Heaven, the earth, and all the liquid main [*or* mayne], The.   Virgil.   OBVE *Fr.* Aeneid [*or* Eneados *or* Aeneis], The.

Heaven took my wife. Now it.   Sorrow.   Mei Yao Ch'en.   WoPoe, *tr. by* Kenneth Rexroth

Heaven, unmoved, weeps on forever.   Sunday Piece.   Jules Laforgue.   WoPoe, *tr. by* William Jay Smith

Heaven vows to keep him. (LL)   Epitaph on S. P. [*or* Salomon Pavy], a Child of Queen Elizabeth's Chapel.   Ben Jonson.   NAEL-6v1; NAEL-7v1; NOSC; OBEV; OxBEV

Heaven was impatient of our crimes.   Mr. Mead, Mr. Bates, and Mr. Gouge [*or* An Elegy on Mr. Thomas Gouge].   Isaac Watts.   STuOW

Heaven / was only half as far that night.   Lawrence Ferlinghetti.   CLPP

Heaven Will Protect the Working-Girl.   Edgar Smith.   ReLy

Heaven-Haven.   Gerard Manley Hopkins.   HeIP-4; MoBrPo; NoAM; OBEV; OxAEP-2; SoSe-8; TFi

Heavenly.   David Baker.   Vesp

Heavenly blue sky to look up to.   Late Light.   Joseph Somoza.   ICANM

"Heavenly Father"—take to thee.   Emily Dickinson.   APN-2; InvLi

Heavenly Feast, The.   Gjertrud Schnackenberg.   AFaM

Heavenly Jerusalem, Jerusalem of the Earth.   Leah Goldberg.   FIT, *tr. by* Robert Friend

Heavenly music, furred with praise, An. (LL)   Upon a Wasp Chilled [*or* Child] with Cold.   Edward Taylor.   NAAL-3; NAAL-5; NAAPv.1; OxBEV

Heavenly Questions.   Ch'u Yüan.   ColAnChi, *tr. by* Victor H. Mair

Heavenly River.   Tu Fu [*or* Du Fu].   CrYelRi, *tr. by* Sam Hamill

Heavenly River is muddy year-round.   Heavenly River.   Tu Fu [*or* Du Fu]. CrYelRi, *tr. by* Sam Hamill

Heavens, The.   Denis Johnson.   LaCa

Heavens! all China's on the ground, in pieces!   Broken Vase, The.   Victor Hugo.   SxFrPo, *tr. by* A. M. and E. H. Blackmore

Heavens allowed me, The.   At Whole-World-In-View-Hut.   Muso Soseki. EaWin, *tr. by* W. S. Merwin

Heavens are playing with the earth, The.   Larisa Miller.   CRWP, *tr. by* Richard McKane

Heavens are somber; the earth is yellow, The.   Zhou Xingsi.   CCL1 *Fr.* Thousand Character Classic, The.

Heavens bespeak the glory of God, The.   Glory Glory / Psalm 19.   Bible, *O.T.* UpMys

Heavens Cherubim High Horsed or The Meeting of the Two Sevens (May 1977).   Velma Pollard.   WaCA

Heavens declare the glory of God, The.   Bible, *O.T.*   NAWM-5v1 *Fr.* Psalms.

Heavens glorious Eie, which all the world surveyes.   Another on the Sun Shine. Lucy Hutchinson.   EMWP

Heaven's lips! I dreamed.   Gnosticism.   Anne Carson.   BAP-04

Heaven's mills are grinding slowly, but they grind exceeding small.   Divine Revenge.   Friedrich von Logau.   GePo, *tr. by* George C. Schoolfield

Heaven's Ring.   Vasco [*or* Vasko] Popa.   VCWP, *tr. by* Charles Simic

Heavens sense our burden, The.   Storm, The.   Jirka Polak.   INSAB

Heavens weep with their morning and evening rain clouds over those excellent lords, the Banū 'Abbād, The.   Muhammad ibn Īsá Ibn al-Labbānah. HiArP, *tr. by* James T. Monroe

Heavensgate.   Christopher Okigbo.

"Bright / with the armpit-dazzle of a lioness."   NAMCP V.2

"Dark waters of the beginning."   NAMCP V.2

Eyes Watch the Stars.   WaAnP

"I am standing above the noontide."   NAMCP V.2

Overture.   NAMCP V.2

Heavier.   Pierre Reverdy.   YaTCFP, *tr. by* John Ashbery

Heavier than a feather. (LL)   Marriage, A.   Ronald Stuart Thomas.   BeAl; TCAWP

Heaviest wheel rolls across our foreheads, The.   Terezin.   Mif.   INSAB

Heaviness May Endure for a Night, But Joy Cometh in the Morning.   Christina Georgina Rossetti.   SacPr

Heaviness of His Wisdom, The.   Wendell Berry.   UpMys *Fr.* Handing Down, The.

Heaving a sigh and then another sigh.   Ballad of Mulan, The.   *Unknown.* CCL1, *tr. by* John Frodsham

Heav'n it self would stoop to her. (LL)   John Milton.   OBEV; OxAEP-1 *Fr.* Comus; a Masque Presented at Ludlow Castle.

Heavnly Frame sets forth the Fame, The.   Bible, *O.T. See* Heavens declare the glory of God, The.

Heavy as the heart's clumsy logbook. (LL)   When Loneliness Is a Man.   Yusef Komunyakaa.   AWTN; OxAAAP

Heavy Bear Who Goes with Me, The.   Delmore Schwartz.   APT-2; ColAP; FTtHH; NAMCP V.2; NoAM; StAl *Fr.* Repetitive Heart, The.

Heavy blue veins streaked across my mother's legs, some of them bunched up into dark lumps at her ankles.   Heavy Blue Veins.   Luis J. Rodriguez. UnSA

Heavy bodies lunge, the broken language, The.   Old Men Playing Basketball. B. H. Fairchild.   MoASP; P180; PoCho

Heavy cart rumbles by, A.   Buson.   EH, *tr. by* Robert Hass

Heavy curtains in the waiting rooms.   Waiting-rooms.   David Vogel.   FIT, *tr. by* Robert Friend

Heavy dew. Thick mist. Dense grass.   Passing a Ruined Palace.   Wen T'ing-yün.   CCL1, *tr. by* Kenneth Rexroth

Heavy / footsteps of.   Museum.   Josep-Enric Dallerès.   SonAtl, *tr. by* Eleanor Davidson, Richard Hacken, Alberto José Miyara and Anna Platt

Heavy gate—violent, serene, consenting, suffering it all, The. (LL)   Lives of the Heart, The.   Jane Hirshfield.   ExTi; GoPo

Heavy Going.   John, Duke of Buckingham and Normandy Sheffield.   STuOW *Fr.* On Brutus, an Ode.

Heavy gold bracelets.   Like a Dog.   Cheryl Boyce Taylor.   BRtP

Heavy gray and white clouds surrounding the dark green mountaintops, The. Chinese Landscape above Caracas.   John Yau.   BodElec

Heavy Headed Dance, The. Jayne Cortez. BAP-97; FuFl

Heavy heart, Belovèd, have I borne. Elizabeth Barrett Browning. CenSon *Fr.* Sonnets from the Portuguese.

Heavy, heavy, heavy, hand and heart. Tenebrae. Denise Levertov. EMP; NoP-4; NoP-5

Heavy hippity hoppity hipster. Arts Are Black, The. Charlie R. Braxton. InTrad

Heavy mahogany door with its wrought-iron screen, The. Devonshire Street W.1. Sir John Betjeman. NPeEn

Heavy mirror carried. Miracle Glass Co. Charles Simic. MakPoe

Heavy mist, A. A muffled sea. Atheling Grange; or, The Apotheosis of Lotte Nussbaum. William Plomer. OBNV

Heavy rain crumbles a wall of my house, A. Night Rain: A Wall Collapses—Sent To My Neighbors. Yang Shih-ch'i. ColAnChi, *tr. by* Jonathan Chaves

Heavy reggae beat thumps. Reggae Prophecy. Marion Bethel. WaCA

Heavy sounds are over-sweet, The. City-Storm. Harold Monro. MoBrPo

Heavy, The. Imamu Amiri Baraka. EGAG

Heavy, to hurt those sacred seeds of thee. (LL) To His Dying Brother, Master William Herrick. Robert Herrick. CavPo; NOSC

Heavy Violets. Barbara Guest. FTOS

Heavy with leaves the garden bushes again. Clear View in Summer. Valentin Iremonger. ModIr

Heavy with the heat and silence. Henry Wadsworth Longfellow. APN-1 *Fr.* Song of Hiawatha, The.

Heavy-Petting Zoo, The. Clare Pollard. NeBl

Heavyweight champion of the world Mike Tyson. Today's News. Elizabeth Alexander. InTrad; ISC; OxAAAP

Hebe and Ganymede. *Unknown.* CAGL, *tr. by* John Boswell

Hebrew. Yona Volach. DTA, *tr. by* Miriyam Glazer

Hebrew culture resembles. Hebrew Culture. Aharon Shabtai. WoBe, *tr. by* Peter Cole

Hebrew, Greek or Latin, I have not. To Cotton Mather, from a Quaker. Thomas Maule. TCAPo

Hebrides, The. Michael Longley. PBCIP

Hebron. Diane Di Prima. Eno

Hebron (Al-Khalil). Nasri Hajjaj. Eno, *tr. by* Ibrahim Muhawi

Hecale. Callimachus.
    "As long as it was still noon and the earth." HePo, *tr. by* Barbara Hughes Fowler
    "South wind does not shed so great a cast, The." HePo, *tr. by* Barbara Hughes Fowler
    "They fell asleep but not for long, for soon." HePo, *tr. by* Barbara Hughes Fowler

Hecateleguim. Pacifico Massimi. *tr. by* James J. Wilhelm
    Book 1. *tr. by* James J. Wilhelm
        Advice to Paulinus. CAGL, *tr. by* James J. Wilhelm
    Book 2. *tr. by* James J. Wilhelm
        Love Song for Marcus, A. CAGL, *tr. by* James J. Wilhelm
    Book 5. *tr. by* James J. Wilhelm
        On Happiness. CAGL, *tr. by* James J. Wilhelm

Hecatodistichon. Anne Seymour Dudley, Jane Seymour and Margaret Seymour.
    "This sacred urn holds the ashes of the Queen of Navarre." EMWP

Hector. Valentin Iremonger. IrLP

Hector Arms. Homer. NOSC *Fr.* Iliad, The.

Hector Flees before Achilles. Homer. OBVE *Fr.* Iliad, The.

Hector Returns to Troy. Homer. NAWM-7v1 *Fr.* Iliad, The.

Hector, the captain bronzed, from simple fight. Geoffrey Scott. OBMV *Fr.* Skaian Gate, The.

Hector was there. Theophile also. In this light. Derek Walcott. WaAnP *Fr.* Omeros.

Hector's Child and the Plume. Homer. OBVE *Fr.* Iliad, The.

Hector's Defiance. Homer. NOSC *Fr.* Iliad, The.

Hecuba's Testament. Rosario Castellanos. STV, *tr. by* John Frederick Nims

He'd come to me from worlds deep down and settled in the dust. Stele for Lenz. Isabelle Hovald. OnScMo, *tr. by* Keith Waldrop

He'd play, after the bawdy songs and blues. When de Saints Go Ma'chin' Home. Sterling Allen Brown. NAAPv.2

Hedd Wyn. R. Williams Parry. BBMWP, *tr. by* Joseph P. Clancy

Hedda Gabler is lighting the lamps in a fury. Act One. Chana Bloch. ExTi

Hedge, A. Pine Shade. Muso Soseki. EaWin, *tr. by* W. S. Merwin

Hedge, The. Gwyneth Lewis. MFPA

Hedge breaks out in bud, The. Elaine Randell. Oth *Fr.* Snoad Hill Poems, The.

Hedge of trees surrounds me, A. Scribe, The. *Unknown.* IrV, *tr. by* Kuno Meyer

Hedgehog. Paul Muldoon. NAMCP V.2; NoAM; PBCIP; WaAnP

Hedgehog, The. David Gwenallt Jones. BBMWP, *tr. by* Joseph P. Clancy

Hedges are dazed as cock-crow, heaps of leaves, The. Departure in Middle Age. Roland Mathias. OBWVE

Heed us when we turn our eyes to heaven. Song to Heaven. Uri Zvi Greenberg. FIT, *tr. by* Robert Friend

Heedless and wilful, took their knights to bed. (LL) Sonnet: "Women have loved before as I love now." Edna St. Vincent Millay. HeIP-4; NALW; NIL-7; PoA 2002

Heedless of where the next bright bolt may fall. (LL) White Goddess, The. Robert Graves. HarvBoo; MoBrPo; NAEL-6v2; NAEL-7v2; NoP-4; NoP-5

Heel and Toe to the End. William Carlos Williams. OtW

Heel of Bernadette, The. Colette Bryce. NIrP

Heenie Majeski, Johnny Gee. Van Lingle Mungo. Dave Frishberg. ReLy

Heere uninterr'd suspendes though not to save. Feltons Epitaph. *Unknown.* NPeEn; PBRV

Heere we doe not lynger; thee vowd sollemnitye finnisht. Virgil. NoSic *Fr.* Aeneid [*or* Eneados *or* Aeneis], The.

Hegemon's Lament, The. Hsiang Chi. CCL1, *tr. by* Burton Watson

Heh Jimmy. Good Thief, The. Tom Leonard. EdScPo

Heidi men call me when their homes I visit. Song of the Seeress. *Unknown.* NAWM-5v1

Heifer, The. Andrew Crozier. Oth

Heigh in the hevynnis figure circulere. James I, King of Scotland. NePenScot *Fr.* Kingis Quair, The.

Heigh-ho / Summer comes along. Summer Is a-Comin' In. John Latouche. ReLy

Height. Nedelcho Ganev. CSCBP, *tr. by* Georgi Belev and Lisa Sapinkopf

Height. Rosalie Moore. APT-2

Height, Breadth, Depth. Kalamu ya Salaam. SpirFl *Fr.* New Orleans Haiku.

Height of the Season, The. Maxine W. Kumin. FFC

Height of trees. Geese Blood. Barbara Guest. FTOS

Height—Antiquity. Sikong Tu. CCL1 *Fr.* Twenty-Four Modes of Poetry.

Heights of Macchu Picchu, The. Pablo Neruda. *tr. by* John Felstiner, Nathaniel Tarn and David Young
    "Come up with me, American love." PFTM-2, *tr. by* Nathaniel Tarn
    "I come to speak through your dead mouth." PoCho, *tr. by* John Felstiner
    "Rise up, brother, be born with me." TCLAP, *tr. by* David Young
    "Stone upon stone, and man, where was he?" TCLAP, *tr. by* John Felstiner
    "Stone within stone, and man, where was he?" VCWP
    "Then up the ladder of the earth I climbed." TCLAP, *tr. by* Nathaniel Tarn

Heimgarten. Erica Pedretti. MotU, *tr. by* Franz Wright

Heiress, The. Raymond Garlick. TCAWP

Heiress, The. Carolina Oliphant, Baroness Nairne. NePenScot

Heirloom [*with music*]. Abraham Moses Klein. NIL-7

Heirloom. Kathleen Jessie Raine. NALW

Heirlooms. Walter McDonald. RWB

Heirlooms. Geoffrey Philp. WaCA

Heirs to these marshy lowlands. Cors-y-Gwaed: Fenland of Blood. A. G. Prys-Jones. AngWePo

Helas! Hung Hung. PML, *tr. by* Steve Bradbury

Hélas! Oscar Wilde. CAGL; GSo; MoBrPo; NAEL-6v2; NAEL-7v2

Held Back, Like a Bow Drawn Tight. Walter Höllerer. CLPP, *tr. by* Jerome Rothenberg

Held between wars / my lifetime. Käthe Kollwitz. Muriel Rukeyser. NALW

Held in the arms of rhythm and of sleep. (LL) Sonnet: "I am in need of music that would flow." Elizabeth Bishop. CtM; PoCu

Held in the tense turbulence of the air. Summer Mist. David Huerta. RMCMP, *tr. by* Mark Schafer

Held prisoner in the house. (LL) Sunday Afternoons. Yusef Komunyakaa. InGu; NoP-4; NoP-5

Held the wrong way either will take the finger. Blowfish and Mudtoad. Dave Jeddie Smith. CAP-8; NAMCP V.2

Held To. Gillian Allnutt. NeBrP

Heledd and Inge, when the torches are red. In Berlin, August 1945: Lehrte Bahnhof. Alun Llywelyn-Williams. BBMWP; OBWVE, *tr. by* Joseph P. Clancy

Helen. "H. D." APT-1; BrAP; ColAP; EMP; FTtHH; MoAmPo; NAAL-5; NAAPv.2; NALW; NAMCP V.1; NIL-7; NoAM; NoP-4; NoP-5; OxBoAm; PoPoPo

Helen [*with music*]. James Harrison. NBLV

Helen. Mary Lamb. NOBRP

Helen. Peter Meinke. PBCAP

Helen ("I am the blue! I come from the lower world.") Paul Valéry. OBVE, *tr. by* Robert Lowell

Helen ("It is I, O Azure, come from the caves below.") Paul Valéry. WoPoe, *tr. by* Richard Wilbur

Helen ("O Light, 'tis I, who from death's other shores.") Paul Valéry. OBVE

Helen and the Elders. Homer. NPeEn *Fr.* Iliad, The.

Helen Grown Old. Janet Lewis. APT-2

Helen in Egypt. "H. D."
   "I am not nor mean to be." WaAnP
   "This is the spread of wings." WoPoe

Helen like the Rose. Evan Lloyd. AngWePo; OBWVE *Fr.* Powers of the Pen, The.

Helen of Kirconnell [*see also* Where Helen Lies *by* Robert Burns]. *Unknown.* OBEV; OxBEV

Helen of Troy had a wandering glance. Words of Comfort to Be Scratched on a Mirror. Dorothy Parker. AmWit

Helen Paints a Room (1984). John A. Scott. BMAP

Helen suddenly saw a divine omen. Stesichoros. SaLy, *tr. by* Diane Rayor

Helen, thy beauty is to me. To Helen. Helen Smith Bevington. AmWit

Helen, thy beauty is to me. To Helen. Edgar Allan Poe. APN-1; BrAP; BRP; ClHu; ColAP; CtM; HeIP-4; NAAL-3; NAAL-5; NAAPv.1; NIP-4; NoP-4; NoP-5; OBEV; OxBoAm; PoPoPo; PtR; TCAPo; TFi; WaAnP; WeW-3

Helen Todd: My Birthname. Sandra McPherson. LoL

Helena's Humble Petition. William Shakespeare. DiBP *Fr.* Midsummer Night's Dream, A.

Helene and Heloise. Glyn Maxwell. NeBrP

Helen's Burning. Laura Riding Jackson. ColAP; NAAPv.2

Helen's Lamentation. Homer. OBVE *Fr.* Iliad, The.

Helianthus. Constance Carrier. APT-2

Helicopter cameras, The. Looters, The. Robert Minhinnick. TCAWP

Helicopter of the hill. Lark. Tom Earley. AngWePo

Helicopter Wrecked on a Hill. Christine Hume. BAP-97

Heliogabalus. John Hollander. NBLV

Helioptér of a skyscraper hotel. Mikhail Yeryomin. ItGoST, *tr. by* J. Kates

Heliotrope sprouts from your shoes, brother. Blue Suede Shoes. Ai. ReTh

Hell. W. H. Auden. WaAnP

Hell. Andreas Gryphius. WoPoe, *tr. by* Michael Hamburger

Hell is no other, but a soundlesse pit. Hell. Robert Herrick. SacPr

Hell. Peter Johnson. Vesp

Hell: "I died & went to Hell & it was nothing like L.A." Steve Kowit. CalPo; SUP

Hell. Edith Södergran. PFTM-1

Hell. Mátyás Nyéki Vörös. *tr. by* Watson Kirkconnell
   "Of what avail are palaces in hell." IQMS, *tr. by* Watson Kirkconnell

Hell blot black for alway the thought "Peace"! (LL) Sestina: Altaforte. Ezra Pound. APT-1; ColAP; MakPoe; MoAmPo; OxBoAm; TCAPo; WaAnP

Hell Gate. A. E. Housman. NoAM

He'll grow into his sleep so sound again. (LL) Ten Days Leave. W. D. Snodgrass. MoAmPo; PWW2

Hell ("Hell is no other, but a soundlesse pit.") Robert Herrick. SacPr

Hell Hound Blues. D. L. Crockett-Smith. OxAAAP

Hell is a city much like London. Percy Bysshe Shelley. OBSV *Fr.* Peter Bell the Third.

Hell is a red barn on a hill. Curse, The. Robert Francis. APT-2

Hell is neither here nor there. Hell. W. H. Auden. WaAnP

Hell Mural, The: Panel I. Ronald Wallace. AtGh

Hell to Pay. Susanne Doyle. CalPo; FFC

Hell, well, heaven. Mongane Wally Serote. TSAP

Hell where youth and laughter go, The. (LL) Suicide in the Trenches. Siegfried Sassoon. FaBoWar; PoAgWa; PoWW

Hellas. Desmond O'Grady.
   "Here, because of the shock, the sudden." PBCIP

Hellas. Percy Bysshe Shelley.
   (Chorus.) OxBEV
   Chorus. HeIP-4; NAEL-6v2; NAEL-7v2
   (Hellas.) OBEV
   (Last Chorus, The.) NPBRoP
   "World's great age begins anew, The." HeIP-4; NoP-4; NoP-5

Hellhound on My Trail. Robert Johnson. APT-2; PFTM-2

Hello. Kateb Yacine. SonAtl, *tr. by* Heather Goode, Saul Goode and Blanca Madani

Hello. Benjamin Péret. YaTCFP, *tr. by* Mary Ann Caws

Hello Again. Larry Fagin. AHA *Fr.* Parade of the Caterpillars, The.

Hello, Dolly! Jerry Herman. ReLy

Hello Goodbye. Sharon Thesen. BrAP

Hello Gozo, here we are. Dream of a Language that Speaks. Michael Palmer. WoBe

"Hello, hello, hello, sir." Jump-Rope Rhyme. *Unknown.* NTCP

Hello hello night again don't worry about it this is your caveman speaking. Automatic Crystal, The. Aimé Césaire. YaTCFP, *tr. by* Mary Ann Caws and Patricia Terry

Hello: "I am one anatomy and take turns. Sometimes after dinner I wrap them in a newspaper." Sabrina Orah Mark. LegDan

Hello. May I be alive in your dream of unconsciousness? Bun. Tom Clark and Ron Padgett. AHA

Hello! My Baby. Joseph E. Howard. NAAPv.2

Hello my life. Hello. Kateb Yacine. SonAtl, *tr. by* Heather Goode, Saul Goode and Blanca Madani

Hello sir i'm glad you're here we. Kentucky. M. Loncar. NAPBL

Hello Up There. Marge Piercy. NBLV

Hello, up there. Thank God you happened by. Italics, Mine. Greg Williamson. LegDan

Hello, Young Lovers. Oscar Hammerstein, II. ReLy

Hello. You've reached 385-2053. I'm very sorry I can't take your call now. Floating Metonymy 2. Kim Sŭnghŭi. EcSo, *tr. by* K. Kim Richards and Steffen Richards

Hellvellyn. Sir Walter Scott. ItP

Helmet and rifle, pack and overcoat. Battle, The. Louis Simpson. AmWaPo; NAMCP V.2; OBWP; PoWW

Helmet now an hive for bees becomes, The. Vote, The. Ralph Knevet. FaBoWar; NOSC
   (Helmett now an hive for Bees becomes, The.) NPeEn; PoAgWa

Helmsman, The. "H. D." GPTC; OxBoAm

Heloise. Biancamaria Frabotta. *tr. by* Cinzia Sartini Blum and Lara Trubowitz
   "Here dwells the whole and scattered." CItWP, *tr. by* Cinzia Sartini Blum and Lara Trubowitz

Help! X. J. Kennedy. CA

H E L P. Rosamond S. King. BtF

Help, a love, a you, a wife, A. (LL) Love Song: I and Thou. Alan Dugan. AmFaPo; NAMCP V.2; NoAM

Help, help all tongues to celebrate this wonder. Ben Jonson. NOSC *Fr.* Masque of Queens, The.

Help! How Minne has deserted me. Friedrich von Hausen. GePo

Help is a Discotheque. Eddie Bell. BtF

Help me, oh sapling of the tulip cheek. Nev'î. OLP, *tr. by* Walter Andrews, Najaat Black and Mehmet Kalpakli

Help, she is wailing. Lost. Bruce A. Jacobs. BtF

Help[e] me! help[e] me! now I call. To His Mistress[es]. Robert Herrick. ErotSp

Helping Hand, A. Miroslav Holub. PoSu, *tr. by* George Theiner

Helpless like this. Edward Kamau Brathwaite. NoP-4; NoP-5 *Fr.* Arrivants: A New World Trilogy, The.

Helpless on the meathook. Choice, Inanna and the Galla. Pem Kremer. HW

Helpstone. John Clare.
   "Thou far-fled pasture, long evanished scene." NPBRoP

Helsinore, Denmark. Maurya Simon. IaFF

Hemicránea. Claudia Hernández de Valle-Arizpe. *tr. by* Jen Hofer
   "It's not necessary for someone to die." RMCMP, *tr. by* Jen Hofer

Hemicránea. Claudia Hernández de Valle-Arizpe.
   "No es necesario que muera alguien." RMCMP

Hemingway. Cyril Dabydeen. PML

Hemingway's Hat. Vicki Feaver. MoWP

Hemispheres. Jessica Smucker Falcón. ACAMVP

Hemlin. Ilse Aichinger. MotU, *tr. by* Stuart Friebert

Hemlock at Sunset, A. Alec Brock Stevenson. FuPo

Hemlock in the Furrows [*with music*]. Adah Isaacs Menken. CBWP-1

Hemlock shakes in the rafter, the oak in the driving keel, The. (LL) Misgivings. Herman Melville. APN-2; NAAL-3; NCAP; OxBoAm; TCAPo

Hemlocks in Autumn. Edward Weismiller. YaYoPo

Hemmed-in Males. William Carlos Williams. APT-1 *Fr.* Folded Skyscraper, A.

Hemp . . . / A stick. Gauge. Langston Hughes. APSN

Hempstead, 1923. Carol Coffee Reposa. TiP2

Hen. Zbigniew Herbert. VCWP, *tr. by* Czeslaw Miosz and Peter Dale Scott

Hen, The. Ellen Bryant Voigt. CAP-8

Hen is the best example of what living constantly with humans, The. Hen. Zbigniew Herbert. VCWP, *tr. by* Czeslaw Miosz and Peter Dale Scott

Hen It Is a Noble Beast, The. William McGonagall. NBLV

Hen remarked to the mooley cow, The. Art. *Unknown.* NBLV

Hen Woman. Thomas Kinsella. ModIr; NPeEn; PBCIP

Hence, all you vain delights. John Fletcher. OBEV *Fr.* Nice Valor, The.

Hence, heart, with her that must depart. Alexander Scott. NePenScot; OBEV

Hence, hence, all you vain delights. Melancholy. Thomas Middleton. NOSC

Hence loathed Melancholy. L'Allegro. John Milton. BASC; NAEL-6v1; NAEL-7v1; NoP-4; NoP-5; NOSC; OBEV; PBRV; PoPoPo; TFi

Hence orient Nitre owes its sparkling birth. Erasmus Darwin. STuOW *Fr.* Economy of Vegetation, The.

Hence, stupid Peace! thy pride and song. Age of War, The. *Unknown.* NOBRP

Hence thro' the windings of the mazy wood. Gilbert West. OBGa *Fr.* Stowe, the Gardens of the Rt. Hon. Richard Lord Viscount Cobham.

Hence to deep Acheron they take their way. Virgil. NPeEn *Fr.* Aeneid [*or* Eneados *or* Aeneis], The.

Hence vain deluding joys. Il Penseroso. John Milton. BASC; NAEL-6v1; NAEL-7v1; NoP-4; NoP-5; NOSC; OBEV; TFi

Hence, vain intruder, haste away. To My Rival. Thomas Carew. OxBSo

Hence with your jeerings, petulant and low. Charles Tennyson Turner. CenSon

Hence ye profane: mell not with holy things. Satire VIII. Joseph Hall. ChIV-2

Hence ye prophane; I hate ye all. Horace. OBVE

Henceforth, from the Mind. Louise Bogan. NAAPv.2

Henchman, The. John Greenleaf Whittier. OBEV

Hendy hap ichabbe yhent, An. (LL) *Unknown.* NoP-4; NoP-5

Henhouse. Harry Edmund Martinson. WED, *tr. by* Robert Bly

Henri Rousseau and Friends. Michael Ondaatje. BrAP

Henri Toussaints. Cheryl Savageau. TWW

Henry V at the Siege of Harfleur. William Shakespeare. OxAEP-1; WaAnP *Fr.* King Henry V.

Henry V before Agincourt. William Shakespeare. BLPJKO *Fr.* King Henry V.

Henry and Mary. Robert Graves. NOxBChV

Henry by Night. John Berryman. EmeKit

Henry C. Calhoun. Edgar Lee Masters. *Fr.* Spoon River Anthology.

Henry got me with child. Edgar Lee Masters. APT-1; NAMCP V.1; NoAM; OxBoAm *Fr.* Spoon River Anthology.

Henry in Ireland to Bill underground. John Berryman. EMP; MakPoe; NoP-4; NoP-5; WaAnP *Fr.* Dream Songs.

Henry James at Newport. Weldon Kees. PoA 2002

Henry King, Who Chewed Bits of String, and Was Early Cut Off in Dreadful Agonies. Joseph Hilaire Pierre Belloc. NBLV; OBCoV; OxAEP-2

Henry Morgan's March on Panama. A. G. Prys-Jones. AngWePo

Henry Porter wore good clothes for his journey. Passage. Elizabeth Alexander. FuFl; ISC

Henry Sats in de Bar and Was Odd. John Berryman. PoPoPo; VCAP *Fr.* Dream Songs.

HENRY THE GRANDFATHER. Hannah Weiner. FTOS *Fr.* Little Books / Indians.

Henry was a young king. Henry and Mary. Robert Graves. NOxBChV

Henry was sick of winter, John dying of. Dream Songs Concluded. Maura Eichner. UpMys

Henry went over the edge of the bridge first; he always did. Death of John Berryman,The. William Dickey. BAP-97; InoFa

76: Henry's Confession. John Berryman. EMP; NAMCP V.2; NoAM; VCAP *Fr.* Dream Songs.

Henry's Fate. John Berryman. ColAP

Henry's mind grew blacker the more he thought. John Berryman. OxBoAm *Fr.* Dream Songs.

Henry's nocturnal habits were the terror of his women. Henry by Night. John Berryman. EmeKit

Henry's pelt was put on sundry walls. John Berryman. NoAM; TRP *Fr.* Dream Songs.

Henry's Understanding. John Berryman. NAMCP V.2; NoAM; OxBoAm; PoCho; WoPoe

Hens drift in early from the day's pecking, The. Henhouse. Harry Edmund Martinson. WED, *tr. by* Robert Bly

Hep! / Hé* bonjour* mes enfants**. Hep! Oliver Cadiot. YaTCFP

Hep-Cat Chung, 'ware my town. Jiang Zhong-zi: Hep-Cat Chung. *Unknown.* CCL1, *tr. by* Ezra Pound

Heptalogia, The. Algernon Charles Swinburne.

    Higher Pantheism in a Nutshell, The. CABP

    Sonnet for a Picture. OxBSo; UV

Heptonstall. Ted Hughes. OxAEP-2

Her. Stephen Chambers. EGAG

Her Address to the Moon. Mary Robinson. CenSon; RWP

24. Her Address to the Moon. Mary Robinson. NPBRoP *Fr.* Sappho and Phaon.

Hēr Æþoelstān cyning, eorla drihten. *Unknown.* CABP *Fr.* Battle of Brunanburh.

Her alien eyes. (LL) Cradle-Song at Twilight. Alice Thompson Meynell. NPeEn; VWP

Her angel looked upon God's face. Eternal Image, The. Ruth Pitter. MoBrPo

Her ankles are watches. George Oppen. APT-2; PFTM-1

Her Answer. John Bennett. ITBLP

Her Anxiety. William Butler Yeats. OPOU

Her apartment is a lesson in schematics. Reetika Arranges My Closet. Dorianne Laux. SweBea

Her arms around me—child. From a Photograph. George Oppen. FTOS

Her arms have the beauty. What He Said. Orerulavanar. WoPoe, *tr. by* A. K. Ramanujan

Her back in a line straight. Foul Line—1987. Colleen J. McElroy. LTA

Her Back to Me. Ed Stever. PasH

Her bare feet tell the neurasthenic: fake moustaches on that ostrich. Metal Coughdrops. Tristan Tzara. PFTM-1

Her beautiful hair for Yom Kippur festively tied. Torah Braids. Tamara Kamenszain. MirDau, *tr. by* Roberta Gordenstein

Her beauty bugs him. Rockstar Poet. Elizabeth Rees. PfS

Her beauty conquers all. (LL) Love's Emblem. John Clare. NIL-7; NIP-4

Her beauty, passive in despair. Philanthropist and the Jelly-fish, The. May Kendall. ViWPN; VWP

Her beauty, which we talk of. Helen's Burning. Laura Riding Jackson. ColAP; NAAPv.2

Her Bed. Robert Herrick. PBRV

Her Black Hair. Robert Pack. MoW

Her blacks crackle and drag. (LL) Edge. Sylvia Plath. BrAP; InoFa; NALW; NAMCP V.2; NPeEn; OxBoAm; PoPoPo; VCAP

Her Blindness in Grief. Sarah Morgan Bryan Piatt. NAAPv.1

Her Body. Daniel Halpern. BAP-97

Her body is not so white as. Queen Anne's Lace. William Carlos Williams. APT-1; BrAP; MoAmPo; NAAL-5; NAAPv.2; NAMCP V.1; NoAM; NoP-4; NoP-5; OxBoAm

Her Body Is Private. Eleanor Wilner. ExTi

Her body was braille, was scent bottles uncorked. Bouquet of Dead Flowers. David Eggleton. PML

Her boredom took her away. So simple. Ella Mi Fu Rapita! Gavin Ewart. NoAM

Her boyfriend stood guard—cat eyes on the lookout. Stringbeans. Kay Lindsey. BtF

Her breast is fit for pearls. Emily Dickinson. HeIP-4; PoBW

Her brothers take turns reading to her. Christina. Anna Ruth Ediger Baehr. ACAMVP

Her chair drawn to the door. Laundress, The. Thomas Kinsella. HarvBoo

Her charming steel-horse could not miss. J. Gordon Coogler. VerBaPo *Fr.* Lover's Return on a Bicycle, The.

Her chaunging lookes no colour longe can holde. Seneca. OBVE *Fr.* Medea.

Her cheek is flush'd with fever red. Dying Child, The. Letitia Elizabeth Landon. VWP

Her children fill toy ships, await dawn's majestic. Dark Side of Dazzle, The. Sean Brendan-Brown. LiTh

Her Confirmed Despair. Mary Robinson. CenSon; RWP

36. Her Confirmed Despair. Mary Robinson. NPBRoP *Fr.* Sappho and Phaon.

Her cottage, then a cheerful object, wore. William Wordsworth. OBGa *Fr.* Excursion, The.

Her Descending Down. Margaret Lucas Cavendish, Duchess of Newcastle. BASC; NOSC

Her Door. Mary Leader. GoPo

Her dress is soft green and deep scarlet. Oriole. Yüan Chěn. CrYelRi, *tr. by* Sam Hamill

Her drooping flowers dabble upon. Betty by the Sea. Ronald McCuaig. NOBAu

Her earliest settlers, in brief. Arthur Guiterman. AmWit *Fr.* Lyric Baedeker, The.

Her eighteen months shattered. Gadafi's Little Daughter. Einion Evans. BBMWP, *tr. by* Mike Jenkins

Her End. Gwyneth Lewis. MoWP, *tr. by* Richard Poole

Her even lines her steady temper show. On a Lady's Writing. Anna Laetitia Barbauld. PEW

Her exquisite yellow youth. (LL) Jessie Mitchell's Mother. Gwendolyn Brooks. ColAP; NALW; OxAAAP

Her eyebrows are arched willows. To the Tune: Southern Song. Wen T'ing-yün. CrYelRi, *tr. by* Sam Hamill

Her Eyes. Helen Hunt Jackson. PoBW; TCAPo

Her Eyes. Daniel Casper von Lohenstein. GePo, *tr. by* George C. Schoolfield

Her Eyes. Devulapalli Krishna Sastri. HotL, *tr. by* V. Narayana Rao

Her Eyes a Thousand Times Over. Chani DiPrima. HW

Her eyes and places his hand on her breast. (LL) In a Duplex Near the San Andreas Fault. Dionisio D. Martinez. NoP-4; NoP-5

Her eyes are bright as sparkling stars. Mine. Mary E. Tucker. CBWP-1

Her eyes are fixed; they seek the skies. Murillo's Magdalen. William Ellery Channing. APN-1

Her eyes flood lickes his feets faire staine. Bible, *N.T.* NOSC; SacPr *Fr.* St. Luke.

Her eyes have in them. Her Eyes. Devulapalli Krishna Sastri. HotL, *tr. by* V. Narayana Rao

Her eyes the glow-worm[e] lend thee. Night-Piece, to Julia, The. Robert Herrick. NAEL-6v1; NAEL-7v1; NoP-4; NoP-5; NOSC; OBEV; TFi

Her eyes were coins of porter and her West. Michael Hartnett. ModIr *Fr.* Farewell to English, A.

Her eyes were gentle; her voice was for soft singing. Old Woman Remembers, An. Sterling Allen Brown. ISC

Her face concealed in the shade of the apricot tree as she lies in the garden behind the hospital. Hospital. Yun Tongju. CAMKP, *tr. by* Kay Richards and Steffen Richards

Her Face, Her Tongue, Her Wit. Sir Arthur Gorges. WoPoe

Her face / Is a spotless moon. Rāmprasād Sen. SinGod, *tr. by* Rachel Fell McDermott

Her face was in a bed of hair. Emily Dickinson. PoBW

Her face was thrawed. Pieta. Alastair MacKie. EdScPo

Her Faith. Joseph Hilaire Pierre Belloc. SacPr

Her faltering hand upon the balustrade. John Keats. OxBEV *Fr.* Eve of St. Agnes, The.

Her fate seizes her and brings her. Her First Calf. Wendell Berry. GoPo

Her father blended truth and myth. Singing Down the Breadfruit. Pauline Stewart. NOxBChV

Her father is sick. He dozes most afternoons. Anastasia McLaughlin. Tom Paulin. PBCIP

Her father lessons me I at times am hard. Augusta Davies Webster. ViWPN *Fr.* Mother and Daughter.

Her father lov'd me; oft invited me. William Shakespeare. FaBoWar; OxAEP-1; WaAnP *Fr.* Othello.

Her father's brother rapes her! Fountain of Cyanë, The. Donald Davie. HarvBoo

Her Final Show. Rafael Campo. BloBone

Her finger an elephant trunk discoils. Dungle sublime. Ronaldo V. Wilson. BtF

Her fingers bore the winecup in. Two of Them, The. Hugo von Hofmannsthal. STV, *tr. by* John Frederick Nims

Her First Calf. Wendell Berry. GoPo

Her First Jew. Joan Logghe. ICANM

Her First Week. Sharon Olds. ExTi

Her foot sparkled like silver. Rufinus. ErotSp, *tr. by* Sam Hamill

Her for a mistress would I fain enjoy. How to Choose a Mistress. *Unknown.* NOSC

Her future, all in her, presented an avenue of gloom, as if to say Go on, do what you. Seeking Out His face in a Cup. Fanny Howe. FTOS

Her Garden. Donald Hall. BAP-01; OxBoAm

Her Gift. Annie Hindle. PoBW

Her glad hand. Erin Mouré. NLPA *Fr.* Wittgenstein Letters to Mel Gibson's Braveheart, The.

Her going through changes. Seth Bingham. William W. Cook. SpirFl

Her goodness leaves scores on the skin. Marian Hymn. Christiania Whitehead. NeBl

Her grandmother called her from the playground. Legacies. Nikki Giovanni. FuFl

Her Great Thighs. Pablo Picasso. YaTCFP, *tr. by* Mary Ann Caws

Her grieving parents cradled here. Epitaph. Sylvia Townsend Warner. MoBrPo

Her Habit. Lucie Brock-Broido. ExTi

Her Hair. Charles Baudelaire. NAWM-7v2, *tr. by* Dorren Bell

Her hair is long, very, very long. Country, A. Fawziyya Abu Khalid. PoArWo, *tr. by* Farouk Mustafa

Her hair was still tangled, her mouth still drunk. Night Visit, The (22). Khwaja Shams-ad-din Muhammad Hafiz. WED, *tr. by* Robert Bly and Leonard Lewisohn

Her handlers, dressed in vests and flannel pants. Electrocuting an Elephant. George Bradley. RaF

Her hands feed striped cloth into the machine. First Quilt. Ann Townsend. AmPoNex

Her hands lift and tend King Salmon. Hands of Mary Joe, The. Mary Tallmountain. LoL

Her hands were clasp'd, her dark eyes raised. Gertrude; or, Fidelity till Death. Felicia Dorothea Hemans. RWP

Her heart cried out,—"Come home, come home." Lee-Shore, The. Edwin John Pratt. IFF

Her Heart Is a Rose Petal and Her Skin Is Granite. Lorene Zarou-Zouzounis. PoArWo

Her heart so stricken, Helen. Alcaeus. WoPoe, *tr. by* Sam Hamill

Her heart that loved me once is rottenness. Two Thoughts of Death. Christina Georgina Rossetti. ViWPN

Her house loomed at the end of a Berkshire lane. Not at Home. Robert Graves. CABP

Her Husband. Ted Hughes. HarvBoo

Her husband is a gentleman and, despite all, she loves him. His image. ATM. Elizabeth Bachinsky. IFF

Her husband was regally draped in heavenly white. For Fatma and Her Co-Wives. Janeya K. Hisle. BtF

Her I was and her I drank. Gud Ber. *Unknown.* FaBoVe

Her imaginary playmate was a grown-up. Cinderella. Randall Jarrell. VCAP

Her islands. Quietness with a Happening. Gennady Aygi. WoBe, *tr. by* Peter France

Her job was to sort through the eyes. Perla at the Mexican Border Assembly Line of Dolls. Rigoberto González. AmPoNex

Her Kind. Anne Sexton. BrAP; CAP-8; HeIP-4; IJHIL; NALW; NAMCP V.2; PoPoPo; PtR; StAl; VCAP

Her Last Appeal to Phaon. Mary Robinson. CenSon; RWP

42. Her Last Appeal to Phaon. Mary Robinson. NPBRoP *Fr.* Sappho and Phaon.

Her last breath, disappointed. (LL) Martha Blake at Fifty-one. Austin Clarke. ModIr; NPeEn

Her—"last Poems." Emily Dickinson. InoFa; NALW

Her last words wandered across the ceiling. Death in the Evening. Miroslav Holub. PoSu, *tr. by* George Theiner

Her *'layin' down her burdens, bye and bye'.* (LL) Virginia Portrait. Sterling Allen Brown. GT; OxAAAP

Her Legs. Robert Herrick. NOSC

Her Life Runs Like a Red Silk Flag. Bruce Weigl. AF

Her Lips Are Copper Wire. Jean Toomer. APT-2; GT; NAAPv.2; NAMCP V.1; NoAM

Her lips disclosed to view. Solyman Brown. VerBaPo *Fr.* Dentologia; a Poem on the Diseases of the Teeth and Their Proper Remedies.

Her lips poised to open, to speak. (LL) Bellocq's Ophelia. Natasha Trethewey. FuFl; NeAmPo

Her List. Sharon Olds. BodElec

Her little boy weeping sought. (LL) William Blake. NoP-4; NoP-5; WaAnP *Fr.* Songs of Innocence.

Her Long Illness. Donald Hall. GoPo

Her look doth promise and her life assure. George Chapman. OxBSo *Fr.* Coronet for His Mistress Philosophy, A.

Her looks were inviting. Private Sorrow, A. George Oommen. PML

Her Losses make our Gains ashamed. Emily Dickinson. NALW

Her 'love,' for whose dear love I rise and fall. (LL) William Shakespeare. HeIP-4; NoSic; OxAEP-1; WaAnP *Fr.* Sonnets.

Her love in all her honor. (LL) Louis Zukofsky. APSN; APT-2; ColAP; GPTC; NAAPv.2; OxBoAm *Fr.* A.

Her magnificent eyes alone. Gustave Thibon, How Simone Weil Appeared to Me/2. Stephanie Strickland. ExTi

Her Majestie resembled to the crowned piller. Ye must read upward. George Puttenham. PBRV; WaAnP

Her Majesty. Arthur Waugh. ArBi

Her Man Described by Her Own[e] Dictamen. Ben Jonson. NAEL-7v1 *Fr.* Celebration of Charis in Ten Lyric[k] Pieces [*or* Peeces], A.

Her mascara makes butterfly patterns on my pillowcase. Lizzie. Cheryl Burke. WiU

Her mate devoured. Kikaku. SoOfWa, *tr. by* Sam Hamill

Her, Me, and Yochanan. Chava Pinchas-Cohen. DTA, *tr. by* Miriyam Glazer

Her melodious tongue lights up. Once Again, Anne Frank. Elina Wechsler. MirDau, *tr. by* Darrell Lockhart

Her memory fragmented like a necklace. Broken Necklace. Jill Bamber. Prnts

Her mind, adorned with virtues manifold. (LL) Edmund Spenser. HeIP-4; NIP-4; NoP-5 *Fr.* Amoretti.

Her mouth. First Kiss. Tim Seibles. NevBe

Her mouth: the tiger, the leap, the toll. Woman 12, A. Hugo Claus. TuT, *tr. by* Peter van de Kamp

Her Muffe. Richard Lovelace. PBRV

Her name, cut clear upon this marble cross. Dorothy Parker. AmWit *Fr.* Tombstones in the Starlight.

Her name I may or may not have made up. Men and Women. Frederick Seidel. BeAl

Her Name Is 'Dooti'. Mongane Wally Serote. TSAP

Her name is in the books I've bought at Oxfam. Fran. Christopher Pilling. NLP

Her Name like the Hours. Gloria Evans Davies. OBWVE

Her name tells of how. Quiet Until the Thaw. Jacob Nibenegenesabe. AmFaPo, *tr. by* Howard Norman

Her name was Lena. She was but a child. Albery Allson Whitman. NAAPv.1 *Fr.* Octoroon, The.

Her nipple. Milky Way, The. Sinan Anton. IrPoTo, *tr. by* the author

Her nose is like a satellite. Song. William Logan. PoDa

Her notebook declares, "If for you fathers." Corrido Blanco. Alfred Arteaga. ASA

Her orchids were meaty, purple organs. Cultivator. Judith Ortiz Cofer. PfSP

Her Other Language. Nancy Mattson. IFF

Her own clasped hands. (LL)   Preface to a Twenty Volume Suicide Note. Imamu Amiri Baraka. AmFaPo; BB; ESEAA

Her Passing. William Drummond of Hawthornden. OBEV

Her Passion Increases. Mary Robinson. CenSon; RWP

8. Her Passion Increases. Mary Robinson. NPBRoP *Fr.* Sappho and Phaon.

Her perfect naked breast. Argentarius. ErotSp, *tr. by* Sam Hamill

Her planted eye to-day controls. Ralph Waldo Emerson. APN-1; NoP-4; NoP-5 *Fr.* Quatrains.

Her pleasure—what gave her pleasure—was to be walked. Martha's Wall. Paul Durcan. IrLP

Her Presence Was a Roomful of Flowers. Li Po. CCL1

Her purple shoes know the way, and the metal band on her ankle knows it. Sacrifice, The. Gertrud Kolmar. AF, *tr. by* David Kipp

Her Purse, at the Winter Solstice. Susan Hahn. PoDa

Her purse. That courtesy. (LL)   Rosa. Rita Dove. ExTi; FuFl

Her reasons for snapping seem clear: barbed tip. Kelly, Ringling Bros. Oldest Elephant, Goes On Rampage. Joel Brouwer. LegDan

Her Reflections on the Leucadian Rock Before She Perishes. Mary Robinson. CenSon; RWP

43. Her Reflections on the Leucadian Rock Before She Perishes. Mary Robinson. NPBRoP *Fr.* Sappho and Phaon.

Her refusal to accept a room of solitude. Pieces. Duane Niatum. HATNAP

Her Reply. Sir Walter Ralegh. *See* Nymph's [*or* Nimphs] Reply to the [Passionate] Shepherd [*or* Sheepheard], The.

Her Reticence. Theodore Roethke. RACG

Her Retirement. Anne Rouse. BeAl; NeBl

Her ringlets glistened like the gold of morn. Picture, A. Henrietta Cordelia Ray. CBWP-3

Her Rose Tattoo. Gerry LaFemina. AmPoNex

Her row veering off. Issa. EH, *tr. by* Robert Hass

Her Scream Has Been Stolen. Samiya Adelle Bashir. BRtP

Her sight is short, she comes quite near. Jenny Wren. W. H. Davies. MoBrPo

Her sins to her Saviour! (LL)   Bridge of Sighs, The. Thomas Hood. BRP; OBEV; OxAEP-2; TreFP

Her skull is large and soft to touch. Mei-Mei Berssenbrugge. AWPTFC *Fr.* Four Year Old Girl.

Her sleeping head with its great gelid mass. Perseus. Robert Earl Hayden. NoAM

Her small feet walk a mossy path. Year's End. Chang K'o-chiu. CrYelRi, *tr. by* Sam Hamill

Her smile drains. Funeral, The. Tatamkulu Afrika. TSAP

Her smile durable as chrome. Friendly Skies. Bruce A. Jacobs. BtF

Her song to me across years. (LL)   Cousin Mary. Wanda Coleman. GT; OxAAAP

Her songs died on the air. (LL)   Song: "She sat and sang alway." Christina Georgina Rossetti. NAEL-6v2; NAEL-7v2

Her soul a well, an eye, an open door. (LL)   Woman Who Weeps. Ellen Bryant Voigt. CAP-8; OPRER

Her soul is like a little thrust-tailed dog that follows her, whimpering. Nora. Jean Toomer. MotU

Her Story. Leah Korican. HW

Her street is dark. The tall housetops now shade. Her Street Is Dark. Antonio Machado Ruiz. SpanPo, *tr. by* John Crow

Her Strong Enchantments Failing. A. E. Housman. OxBEV; WoPoe

Her / strong / white / legs. Romp. Dave Etter. WeW-3

Her Sweet turn to leave the Homestead. Emily Dickinson. SWaP

Her sweet Weight on my Heart at Night. Emily Dickinson. TCAPo

Her terrace was the sand. Infanta Marina. Wallace Stevens. APT-1

Her that I love, I hate! "How's that, do you know?" they wonder. Catullus. STV

Her thin night dress? (LL)   Toi Derricotte. GT; OxAAAP

Her Three Unborn Baby Boys. Menke Katz. Prolet, *tr. by* Amelia Glaser

Her Tiara Flowers. Shen Manyuan. CCL1, *tr. by* Anne Birrell

Her toes, bite her arch, trail my tongue along the inside of her leg and. I Suck. Chrystos. WiU

Her towel up, turban-style, about her hair. (LL)   Aubade, An: "As she is showering, I wake to see." Timothy Steele. PasH; RA

Her Triumph. Ben Jonson. BASC; NAEL-7v1; NoP-4; NoP-5; NOSC; NPeEn *Fr.* Celebration of Charis in Ten Lyric[k] Pieces [*or* Peeces], A.

Her unmown green. (LL)   Picture of J. T. in a Prospect of Stone, The. Charles Tomlinson. NoP-4; NoP-5; NPeEn; WaAnP

Her veil, his tie. Epithalamion for Sarah and Tony. Jeff Mock. PoDa

Her Voice. Barney Bush. HATNAP

Her voice forever match to dry wood. Dirge in Jazz Time. Vassar Miller. FFC

Her voice roosts in my memory. Route. Philippe Soupault. PFTM-1

Her water breaking in me like an anointing. (LL)   Anointing, An. Thylias Moss. GT; MotU; ReTh

Her ways were gentle while a babe. Sinless Child, The. Elizabeth Oakes-Smith.

Her white arms became my entire horizon. Rooster and the Pearl, The. Max Jacob. CuPo

Her window ringed by moonlight. To a Young Widow. Po Chü-i. CrYelRi, *tr. by* Sam Hamill

Her wings inferring. Mail from Right Here, The. Brendan Galvin. PoCoUp

Her Word of Reproach. Sarah Morgan Bryan Piatt. NCAP

Her words pour out as if her throat were a broken. Judy Grahn. ASA *Fr.* Common Woman, The.

Her work was to count linings. Charles Reznikoff. APT-2

Her wounds came from the same source as her power. (LL)   Power. Adrienne Rich. CAP-8; ColAP; NALW; NAMCP V.2; NIL-7

Her young employers, having got in late. Summer Morning, A. Richard Wilbur. NBLV; StAl

Heraclitus. William Johnson Cory. OBEV; OxAEP-2; UV

Heraclitus. Leslie Rondin. MotU

Herald came, The. Sappho. SaLy, *tr. by* Diane Rayor

Heraldic Decoration. Julio Herrera y Reissig. BLPSL, *tr. by* Rene de Costa, Rigas Kappatos and Eleni Paidoussi

Heraldic Decoration. Julio Herrera y Reissig. TCLAP, *tr. by* Andrew Rosing

Heralds of New Jerusalem. Ayin Tur-Malka. NRoS, *tr. by* Esther Raizen

Heralds of the hurricane. Sandy Baldwin. AnSo

Herba Santa. Herman Melville. NCAP

Herbario. Laura Solórzano. SPV

Herbarium. Laura Solórzano. SPV, *tr. by* Jen Hofer

Herbert Street Revisited. John Montague. ModIr; PBCIP; PNI *Fr.* Great Cloak, The.

Herbert's a hard and horrid man. One for the Anthologies. Gavin Ewart. OBCoV

Herbertson telephoned. For the Record. Roy McFadden. PNI

Herb-Garden, The. Charles Hubert Sisson. HarvBoo

Herbie. David Alpaugh. OPRER

Hercules Furens. Seneca. *tr. by* Jasper Heywood
  Chorus. NPeEn, *tr. by* Jasper Heywood
  "Let oken club now strike, and poast of might." OBVE, *tr. by* Jasper Heywood

Hercules Oetaeus [*or* Hercules Oetæus]. Seneca.
  "Let other mount aloft, let other sore." OBVE, *tr. by* John Studley

Herd, The. Peter Fallon. PBCIP

Herding cows by his side. (LL)   Wild woman of the forests, The. Mirabai. WoPoe; WPoS, *tr. by* Jane Hirshfield

Herdsmen crush under their feet. Sappho. SaLy, *tr. by* Diane Rayor

Here. Sandra Maria Esteves. PueRic

Here. Issa. EH, *tr. by* Robert Hass

Here. Lawrence Joseph. UrbNat

Here. Jane Kenyon. LoL

Here. Philip Larkin. NAMCP V.2; NPeEn

Here. Glenna Luschei. GeoHom

Here. Grace Paley. BAP-01; BeAl; GoPo

Here. Octavio Paz. STV, *tr. by* John Frederick Nims

Here. Octavio Paz. TCLAP, *tr. by* Charles Tomlinson

Here. Erica Pedretti. MotU, *tr. by* Stuart Friebert

Here. Ken Smith. StAl

Here: "Sun that silvers all the buildings here, The." Mark Strand. PfSP

Here. Ronald Stuart Thomas. NPeEn

Here, a botched cozy live-in. Camille Martin. AnSo *Fr.* No truck.

Here, / a child born. Written After Hearing About the Soviet Invasion of Afghanistan. Sujata Bhatt. FiBr

Here a little child I stand. Grace for a Child. Robert Herrick. NAEL-6v1; TFi

Here a mile down at Betarram. At Betarram. Robert Hedin. GifTon

Here a pretty Baby lies. Upon a Child. Robert Herrick. OBEV

Here, above, / cracks in the buildings are filled with battered moonlight. Man-Moth, The. Elizabeth Bishop. APT-2; MoAmPo; NALW; NAMCP V.2; NoAM

Here all alone in silence might I mourne. Mary Sidney Wroth, Countess of Montgomery. NAEL-7v1 *Fr.* Urania.

(Here Am I) Broken Hearted. Lew Brown. ReLy

Here am I, little jumping Joan. Little Jumping Joan. Mother Goose. NTCP

Here am I yet, another twelvemonth spent. Arthur Hugh Clough. CenSon *Fr.* Blank Misgivings of a Creature Moving About in Worlds Not Realized.

Here, Amanda, gently bending. Garden Window, The. Aaron Hill. OBGa

Here among them the americans this baffling. [American Journal]. Robert Earl Hayden. ESEAA; ISC

Here and hereafter, touch a Paradise. (LL)   To Ned. Herman Melville. APN-2; NAAL-3; TCAPo

Here and Now. Robert Patrick Dana. LiTh

Here and now I have to dilute myself into many things. Vicente Huidobro. TCLAP *Fr.* Altazor.

Here and now is clear so we. 20-200 on 737. Heather McHugh. NIP-4

Here and There ("Some days start already swung from rafters.") Ann Lauterbach. BodElec

Here and There ("Today I wake having swung, naked, in London.") Ann Lauterbach. PmAP

Here and there. Elephant Rocks. Kay Ryan. ExTi

Here and There. Max Winter. FreRad

Here and there little breezes stir the rushes. Woodcutter on His Way Home, A. *Unknown.* EaWin, *tr. by* W. S. Merwin and Nguyen Ngoc Bich

Here are no signs of festival. African Christmas. John Press. OBCP

Here are only cliffs and crags. Outpost Soldier, The. *Vietnamese Oral Tradition.* CaDao, *tr. by* John Balaban

Here are the brains here the hearts. One o'Clock. Philippe Soupault. AF, *tr. by* Eden Paul

Here are the fireworks. The men who conspired and labored. Pearl Harbor. Robinson Jeffers. PWW2

Here are the homeless black men begging small coins. Man Named Troy, A. Reginald Shepherd. IllVoic

Here are the smallest windows in the world. Light hovers. Windows of Sarajevo, The. David Grubb. RSaN

Here are those who are challenged by. Jewish Singles Event, The. Stewart Florsheim. UnSA

Here are two half-grown black cats perched on a. Walking beside the Kamogawa, Remembering Nansen and Fudo and Gary's Poem. Philip Whalen. BB

Here are two pictures from my father's head. Wounds. Michael Longley. ModIr; NAMCP V.2; NPeEn; PBCIP; PNI; PoAgWa

Here are words written down. Journey. Thich Nhat Hanh. WhBo

"Here are your magic glasses. Ballad of the Magic Glasses. Maura Stanton. FFC

Here, as one breathes, one writes. In the Mountains. Andrey Andreievich Voznesensky. RusPo, *tr. by* Robert Arthur Douglas Ford

Here at my right hand. (LL) Shimmer. James Schuyler. NoP-5; VCAP

Here at the seashore they use the clouds over & over. Rhode Island. William Meredith. NoP-4; NoP-5

Here at the Vespasian-Carlton, it's just one. Boom! Howard Nemerov. NBLV; NIL-7; NIP-4

Here, at this moment, everything ends. Accelerando. José Hierro. RaW, *tr. by* Rachel Benson

Here be dragons, and bitter. Bitter Wood. Martin Carter. WoPoe

Here, because of the shock, the sudden. Desmond O'Grady. PBCIP *Fr.* Hellas.

Here before the sunrise blue and in this solitude. Janine Pommy-Vega. CLPP

Here begin dreams of flight, the wallpaper. Fog. Michelle Boisseau. ExTi

Here, behind this attic door is Borges. In Praise of Darkness. Scott Cairns. UpMys

Here beside dwelleth. Jolly Jugger, The. *Unknown.* NPeEn

Here, beside the Latin sea. Eheu! Rubén Darío. SpanPo, *tr. by* Anita Volland

Here beside the threshing floor, O hardworking ant. Antipater of Sidon. HePo, *tr. by* Barbara Hughes Fowler

Here birds fly south. At the Lighthouse. Nikolai Nikolaevich Morshen. TCRusP, *tr. by* John Glad

Here blooms the legend fed by [*or* with] Time and Chance. Rouen, Place de la Pucelle. Maria White Lowell. APN-2

Here bounds the gaudy, gilded chair. Birth-Day, The. Mary Robinson. WoRP

Here, Bullet. Brian Turner. AmWaPo

Here by the ample river's argent sweep. Two Backgrounds. Edith Wharton. APN-2

Here by the gray north sea. Northern Vigil, A. Bliss Carman. BrAP; OBEV

Here by the moorway you returned. Your Last Drive. Thomas Hardy. NAMCP V.1

Here, by this brook, we parted; I to the East. Brook; An Idyl, The. Alfred Tennyson. OxAEP-2

Here by this crumbling wall. Butterfly Garden, The. Alfred Noyes. OBGa

Here, calling up to mind what then I saw. NAEL-6v2; NAEL-7v2 *Fr.* Prelude, The; Growth of a Poet's Mind [1850 version].

Here, Charmian, take my bracelets. Cleopatra. William Wetmore Story. APN-1

Here circling trees, which form a shade. Joseph Giles. OBGa *Fr.* Leasowes: Or, A Poetical Description of the Late Mr. Shenstone's Rural Retirement, The.

Here closed the Tenant of that lonely vale. William Wordsworth. *Fr.* Excursion, The.

Here come Charles and Madeleina my child. Pounds and Ounces. Michael Brownstein. AHA

Here come exploding waves. Bounty. Robert Pack. PfSP

Here come I to my own again. Rudyard Kipling. NoAM *Fr.* Kim.

Here come my night thoughts. Something, The. Charles Simic. BAP-97

Here come real stars to fill the upper skies. Fireflies in the Garden. Robert Frost. BLPJKO; SAmP

Here come the dashing riders. Girls of the Rodeo. Margie B. Boswell. TiP2

Here Come the Dreamers. Marshall Barer. ReLy

Here come those splendid Persians! House of Xerxes. Paul Violi. PA9/11

Here come two very old men of exquisite caution. Here Come Two Very Old Men. Kit Wright. PML

Here comes a new storm, roiling and black. Kerosene. Chase Twichell. ExTi

Here comes / Babel, Isaak. Elderblossom. Johannes Bobrowski. AF

Here comes one more looking pale. Man from the Death Institute. Novica Tadic. VCWP, *tr. by* Charles Simic

Here comes one who in silence. When Love's Perished. Dambudzo Marechera. NAfrP

Here comes someone soft as goose down. *Unknown.* PriapPo *Fr.* Priapus Poems, The.

Here comes the question. Prerogative of Lieder, The. Ray DiPalma. FTOS

Here comes the smoking Bouillabaisse! (LL) Ballad of Bouillabaisse, The. William Makepeace Thackeray. OBEV; OxAEP-2

Here comes the woman who wears the plastic prick. Bowlers Anonymous. Stephen Dobyns. CAP-8

Here costive many minutes did I strain. Privy-Love for My Landlady. George Farewell. OBCoV

Here dead lie we because we did not choose. Epitaph. A. E. Housman. HarvBoo; OxBEV; Spl

Here, decayed, an old. Harlech Castle. John Corben. Spl

Here did his fathers live and pass. Ploughman: In Welsh Uplands, The. A. G. Prys-Jones. AngWePo

Here dock and tare. In the Grave No Flower. Edna St. Vincent Millay. NAAL-5

Here doth Dionysia lie. Epitaph of Dionysia. *Unknown.* OBEV

Here down my wearied [*or* wearyed] limbs I'll [*or* Ile] lay. On Himself[e]. Robert Herrick. BASC

Here droops the muse! while from her glowing mind. [Sonnet] Conclusive. Mary Robinson. CenSon; RWP

Here droops the Muse! while from her glowing mind. Mary Robinson. NPBRoP *Fr.* Sappho and Phaon.

Here dwells the whole and scattered. Biancamaria Frabotta. CItWP *Fr.* Heloise.

Here earth and sky are reduced to an ultimate simplicity. Nullarbor. William Hart-Smith. BMAP

Here envying and lies. On Leaving Prison. Luís De León. SpanPo, *tr. by* Brenda M. Sackett

Here, everything gets eaten: drippings, marinade. Olesya Nikolayeva. ItGoST, *tr. by* Paul Graves and Carol Ueland

Here *exactly*—a little elbow room. Here, in this margin of poor housing. Exile. Scott Cairns. UpMys

Here, few signs distinguish dawns from nights. Prisoner's Dream, The. Eugenio Montale. PoetW, *tr. by* Jonathan Galassi

Here followeth the unfashionable fashion, or the too too homely Worshipping of God. John Taylor.

  "Gods *Houses,* almost like *Troyes Ilion,.*" PBRV

[Here Follows Some] Verses upon the Burning of Our House [July 10th, 1666]. Copied Out of a Loose Paper]. Anne Bradstreet. BASC; ColAP; EMWP; MakPoe; NAAL-3; NAAL-5; NAAPv.1; NALW; NoP-4; NoP-5; NOSC; PEW; SacPr; TCAPo

  (Upon the Burning of Our House July 10th, 1666.) BrAP

Here for a few short years. To a Young Writer. Yvor Winters. APT-2

Here for a little we pause. Benicasim. Sylvia Townsend Warner. OBWP

Here. Forget. Poem. Charles Bernstein. FTOS

Here free from riot's hated noise. William Cowper. OBGa

Here from his prominent but thankfully. Old Bachelor Brother. Brad Leithauser. NoP-4; NoP-5; RA

Here from the castle's terraced site. Scene on the Northern Shore of Sicily. Ann Radcliffe. RWP

Here from the start, from our first of days, look. Tally Stick, The. Jarold Ramsey. NIL-7; NIP-4

Here he comes! Mr. BOOM BOOM Man. Michele Serros. BRtP

Here he is whom you read and clamor for. Martial. WoPoe *Fr.* Epigrams.

Here, here are our enjoyments done. Lucasia, Rosania and Orinda Parting at a Fountain, July 1663. Katherine Philips. EMWP; PEW

Here, here I live with what my board. His Content in the Country. Robert Herrick. CavPo

Here, Home. John Powell Ward. TCAWP

Here I am. Ode on Arrival. Carl Rakosi. BodElec

Here I am again with my sickle, spade, hoe. Weeding. Michael Hamburger. OBGa

Here I am all alone, quarrelling with the age, both feet kicking the jugs of Being. Against Ibn Arabi. Abdel Kader El Janabi. Eno, *tr. by* Pierre Joris

Here I am, an old man in a dry month. Gerontion. T. S. Eliot. APT-1; ColAP; NAAL-5; NAAPv.2; NAMCP V.1; NoAM; NPeEn; OxAEP; TCAPo; TFi; WaAnP

Here I am and forth I must. Prayer for the Journey. *Unknown.* SacPr

Here I am, awakened by accident. Brother Body. Peter Cooley. OPRER

Here I am denuded of plumage. My Generation. Kabura Zakama. NeNiPo

Here I am in the garden laughing. Here. Grace Paley. BAP-01; BeAl; GoPo

Here I am, looking at you, my orphan. Your thick scarf. Your cold cigarette. Linor Goralik. CRWP, *tr. by* the author and Robert Reid

Here I am once more before the sea. Here I am Once More. Rachida Madani. CFP; HAWP; NAfrP, *tr. by* Eric Sellin

Here I am / The same old fervent plea. You May Not Love Me. Johnny Burke. ReLy

Here I am writing my first villanelle. Saturday at the Border. Hayden Carruth. MakPoe; WaAnP

Here I am writing you on old newspaper against a tide of print. Cow *Perseverance,*The. Frederick D'Aguiar. NeBrP

Here I come the invisible man, perhaps in the employ. December Evening, '72. Tomas Tranströmer. WED, *tr. by* Robert Bly

Here I find refuge, though the woman. In the Bookstore. Allison Joseph. IllVoic

Here I go again. Starting from San Francisco. Lawrence Ferlinghetti. GM

Here I have enough to eat. Thanks for Daisen Osho's Visit. Muso Soseki. EaWin, *tr. by* W. S. Merwin

Here i lie in chinatown. My Ship Does Not Need a Helmsman. Alan Chong Lau. OpBo

Here I read Biggles; in this chair, *Ulysses.* Latitudes of Home, The. Alistair Elliot. OxBSo

Here, I said, "Here. These parts." (LL) In My Country. Jackie Kay. MFPA; NeBl; NeBrP; StAl

Here, I Say. Joanna Fuhrman. AmPoNex

Here I say again: the heart of the city has not yet died. Love, Attributed City. Nancy Morejón. TCLAP, *tr. by* Kathleen Weaver

Here I sing / of the Hesperides. Hesperides, The. Burleigh Mutтén. HW

Here I sing of the Muses. Queen Medusa. Burleigh Mutтén. HW

Here I sing / of Urania. Urania. Burleigh Mutтén. HW

Here I sit on a rock. Campfire. Anna Lindtová. INSAB

Here I stand in my cell looking out to freedom, Lord, here I stand. Beginning at the End: Capital/Capitol Punishment. Richard Bartee. BRtP

Here I stand / Replacing another, who has been murdered. End or a Beginning, An. Bei Dao. AF, *tr. by* Bonnie S. McDougall

Here I stand with life ahead of me. Today Is the First Day of the Rest of My Life. Richard Maltby, Jr. ReLy

Here I work in the hollow of God's hand. Prayer. Alice Oswald. NeBrP

Here I'm perched on a sheer cliff. Ode. Attila József. IQMS, *tr. by* Susanne K. Walther

Here in a distant place I hold my tongue. Egan O Rahilly. *Unknown.* OBMV, *tr. by* James Stephens

Here in a summer full of dust. Still Life. Luljeta Lleshanaku. WoBe, *tr. by* Henry Israeli

Here in caterpillar country. Hornworm: Summer Reverie. Stanley Kunitz. BodElec

Here in his lamp-lit parable, he'll scan. Garden, The. Victoria Mary Sackville-West. OBGa

Here in Houston there's no stomach for misery. Texas Splendor. Janet Lowery. TiP2

Here in Kansas is a school. Haskell. Witter Bynner. NoP-4; NoP-5

Here in Katmandu. Donald Justice. HeIP-4

(Sestina: Here in Katmandu.) WaAnP

Here in my curving hands I cup. This Quiet Dust. John Hall Wheelock. MoAmPo

Here in my garden. *Unknown.* ArkPo, *tr. by* Edwin A. Cranston

Here in my head, the home that is left for you. Burning the Letters. Randall Jarrell. MoAmPo

Here in my heart I am Helen. Song of One of the Girls. Dorothy Parker. AmWit; NALW

Here in our moment of darkness. We'll Be Together Again. Frankie Laine. ReLy

Here in Shinano. Issa. SoOfWa, *tr. by* Sam Hamill

Here in the country's heart. Country Faith, The. Norman Gale. OBEV

Here in the dark, O heart. Second Best. Rupert Brooke. MoBrPo

Here, in the darkness, where this plaster saint. Madeleine in Church. Charlotte Mew. VWP

Here in the dry consump. Extravagage of Zoos, The. Craig Arnold. AmPoNex

Here, in the ear of the earth. Our Skin Is Paper. Hilary Booth. SurWo

Here in the electric dusk your naked lover. Heat. Denis Johnson. MakPoe; SwNoth

Here in the flux of flood and drought. Trusting steel. Bryce Milligan. TiP2

Here in the good old U. S. A. In the Good Old U. S. A. José Angel Sr. Villalongo. UnSA

Here in the green scooped valley I walk to and fro. Green Valley, The. Sylvia Townsend Warner. MoBrPo

Here, in the half-dark of the sauna. Bodies, The. Elizabeth Spires. NIL-7

Here, in the hollow caverns of the rocks. Wily Fox, The. Edward Davies. OBWVE, *tr. by* Joseph P. Clancy

Here, in the lather of sebum, of the decomposed, the misconstrued, the. Evolution of Lather, The. Michael Portnoy. HeMarv

Here, in the middle of all this Houston heat, the two. Boxers, The. Andrew Feld. LegDan

Here, in the most Unchristian basement. Men's Room in the College Chapel, The. W. D. Snodgrass. MoAmPo

Here in the new white neighborhood. Beloved Spic. Martín Espada. OPRER

Here in the North I chase an old despair. Trumbull Stickney. APN-2

Here in the poorest mine country. Mica Country. Robert Morgan. LPSFW

Here, / in the room of my life. Room of My Life, The. Anne Sexton. CAP-8; NAMCP V.2; VCAP

Here in the scuffled dust. W. D. Snodgrass. NoP-5 *Fr.* Heart's Needle.

Here in the slack of night. Camphor Laurel. Judith Wright. BMAP

Here, in the terraced. Aquarium du Trocadéro. Duncan Bush. AngWePo; TCAWP

Here in the uplands. Scotland. Sir Alexander Gray. EdScPo

Here in the warm counties. Mythology of Snow, A. Violette Newton. TiP2

Here, in the withered arbor, like the arrested wind. Statue and Birds. Louise Bogan. MoAmPo

Here in these fretted caverns whence the sea. Sir Lewis Morris. AngWePo *Fr.* Lydstep Caverns.

Here in this bleak city of Rochester. Sestina d'Inverno. Anthony Hecht. NoAM

Here in this carload. Written in Pencil in the Sealed Railway-Car. Dan Pagis. AF, *tr. by* Stephen Mitchell

Here in this great house in the barrack square. Hambone and the Heart, The. Dame Edith Sitwell. OBMV

Here in this homely cabinet. Matthew Stevenson. NOSC *Fr.* Elegy upon Old Freeman, An.

Here in this house, among photographs. From Room to Room. Jane Kenyon. LoL

Here in this narrow room there is no light. Prothalamium. Arthur James Marshall Smith. BrAP

Here in this sequestered close. Garden Song, A. Austin Dobson. OBEV; OBGa

Here in this transport. Scrawled in Pencil in a Sealed Car. Dan Pagis. PoSu, *tr. by* Robert Friend

Here in West Philadelphia. Black Man's Sonata, A. Afaa Michael Weaver. UnSA

Here is a child who presses his head to the ground. Windows, The. W. S. Merwin. PoChi

Here is a common town with 13,000 brains. Española Pantoum. Joan Logghe. ICANM

Here is a ditch of hopelessly dead water. Dead Water. Wen Yi-tuo [*or* Wen I-to]. PFTM-1; WoPoe, *tr. by* Arthur Sze

Here is a fable men tell. Archilochus. SaLy, *tr. by* Diane Rayor

Here is a glass of water from my well. Glass of Water, A. May Sarton. IJHIL; StAl

Here is a green Jew. Soap. Gerald Stern. CAP-8; TaR

Here is a heart-shaped leaf. Maple Leaf. "Shu Ting." VCWP

Here is a little book of instructions. It says care. Art, Love, Geology. Bin Ramke. RoV

Here is a man, his ticket stamped. Ballad of the Several Past. Wyatt Prunty. WaAnP

Here is a map of our country. Adrienne Rich. BeAl; NAAL-5; StAl; WaAnP *Fr.* Atlas of the Difficult World, An.

Here is a message for you—the whole world sent it. For You, Walt Whitman. William Stafford. ViWalt

Here is a Mudwall tent, whose Matters are. Edward Taylor. TCAPo *Fr.* Preparatory Meditations Before My Approach to the Lord's Supper.

Here is a painting on wood. Hazards of Imagery, The. Paul Violi. KGB

Here is a room to come to. Portinaio. Julie Agoos. YaYoPo

Here is a ship you made. Ship, The. J. F. Hendry. EdScPo

Here is a soul, accepting nothing. Red Onion, Cherries, Boiling Potatoes, Milk. Jane Hirshfield. BeAl

Here is a story. Tess's Torch Song (I Had a Man). Ted Koehler. ReLy

Here is a symbol in which. Rock and Hawk. Robinson Jeffers. APT-1; CalPo; ColAP; NAMCP V.1; NoAM; OxBoAm

Here is a tiny, hard-shelled thing. He is the length of a child's tooth.   Exhausted Bug, The.   Robert Bly.   BodElec

Here is an island. Here is a house on stilts.   Bella Abramovna Dizhur.   ItGoST, *tr. by* Sarah Bliumis

Here is another bone to pick with you.   Lucille Clifton.   BodElec

Here is another poem in a picture.   Daryl Hine.   GS; NoAM

Here is my gift, not roses on your grave.   In Memory of M. B.   Anna Andreyevna Akhmatova.   PoetW, *tr. by* Max Hayward and Stanley Kunitz

Here is my horse Abstraction.   Winged Horse, The.   Louise Glück.   BodElec

Here is my philosophy.   Ladies and Gentlemen in Outer Space.   Ron Padgett.   P180

Here is my soul, with its strange.   Way It Must Be, The.   Enrique Molina.   TCLAP, *tr. by* Naomi Lindstrom

Here is my uncle, a rice ball in his mouth.   Nisei Picnic: From an Album, A.   David Mura.   LoL

Here is Peter. Here is Jane. They like fun.   Reading Scheme.   Wendy Cope.   MakPoe; WaAnP

Here is poor Villon's final word.   Ballade to End With, A.   François Villon.   WoPoe, *tr. by* Richard Wilbur

Here is stillness, there is still more.   Still.   Andrew Greig.   EdScPo

Here is the ancient floor.   Self-Unseeing, The.   Thomas Hardy.   MoBrPo; NAMCP V.1; OxAEP-2; OxBEV; PtR; WeW-3

Here is the black sheep, master.   Black Sheep, The.   Gojko Djogo.   AF, *tr. by* Michael March *and* Dušan Puvaić

Here is the crossroads where the slain.   Dead Man's Corner.   Robert Silliman Hillyer.   APT-2

Here is the form of Gaveston's exile.   Christopher Marlowe.   CAGL *Fr.* Edward the Second.

Here is the handyman with black legs.   Coloring.   Ron Koertge.   SUP

Here is the lantern and the key.   Demeter's Blessing.   Burleigh Muttén.   HW

Here is the machine, the dynamizer.   Dynamizer and the Oscilloclast, The.   Jack Coulehan.   BloBone

Here is the mother all boobed and bodicey.   Victorian Family Photograph.   Kit Wright.   OBCoV

Here is the News.   Michael Rosen.   OBSP

Here is the phial; here I turn the key.   Minor Poet, A.   Amy Levy.   VWP

Here is the place, my lord; good my lord, enter.   William Shakespeare.   OxAEP-1 *Fr.* King Lear.

Here is the place; right over the hill.   Telling the Bees.   John Greenleaf Whittier.   APN-1; ColAP; NAAPv.1; NoP-4; NoP-5; OxBoAm; TCAPo

Here is the proposition that heals.   Snail River.   James Bertolino.   PoCoUp

Here is the queen.   Adrian Brooks.   CAGL

Here is the rain we saw. (LL)   Losing a Language.   W. S. Merwin.   BeAl; EMP; NoP-4; NoP-5

Here is the Scripture, for your mind.   Vanitatum Vanitas.   Ferenc Kölcsey.   IQMS, *tr. by* Watson Kirkconnell

Here is the shadow of its joy. (LL)   Monet's "Waterlilies."   Robert Earl Hayden.   AmFaPo; GT

Here is the sign: it trembles.   Eugenio Montale.   WoPoe *Fr.* Motets [Mottetti].

Here is the soundless cypress on the lawn.   Nightingale near the House, The.   Harold Monro.   MoBrPo

Here is the toil of silkworms.   Inscription on a Robe.   *Unknown.*   CCL1, *tr. by* James Legge

Here is the town with its spine broken.   Photograph of the Courthouse Square, 1950s.   Betty Adcock.   TiP2

Here is the wolf. The wind, the sound of rain.   Tundra's Edge.   John Burnside.   EdScPo

Here is why we listen.   Beethoven's Romance in G.   David Wright.   ACAMVP

Here is your wooden keg.   Chandlery.   Peter Didsbury.   NeBrP

Here it comes again, imagination of myself.   International Date Line, Monday/Monday 27:XI:67.   Philip Whalen.   BB

Here it comes again: vision bevel-edged.   Gillian Clarke.   Prnts *Fr.* Glass.

Here it is, at daybreak, again, one square foot.   Here It Is.   Hayan Charara.   PrTe

Here it is, near the house.   Right in the Trail.   Gary Snyder.   PmAP

Here it is night: I stay at the Summit Temple.   Summit Temple, The.   Li Po.   TAL

Here it is spring again.   Late Singer, The.   William Carlos Williams.   SAmP

Here it never rains.   Monangamba Estate.   Antonio Jacinto.   SonAtl, *tr. by* Michael Cruz, Mary Jay and Lisa Martin

Here, it's a carless highway.   Highway, The.   Pak Sôwôn.   EcSo, *tr. by* Julie C. Park

Here it's a fortnight to Carnival.   Divorce Referendum, The.   Sarah Maguire.   MFPA

Here it's the rainy season, but it still hasn't rained.   Democracy.   Derick Burleson.   PoA 2002

Here Johnson lies; what human can deny.   Epitaph for Thomas Johnson, Huntsman. Charlton, Sussex.   *Unknown.*   NPeEn

Here lay a fair fat land.   Culbin Sands.   Andrew Young.   EdScPo

Here lay dark Pittsburgh, from whose site there broke.   James Kirke Paulding.   APN-1 *Fr.* Backwoodsman, The.

Here let me rest me feet!   Reverie of a Mum.   Nancy Keesing.   NOBAu

Here let me sit, in this empty, cool, terraced hall.   Ernest Francisco Fenollosa.   APN-2 *Fr.* Ode on Reincarnation.

Here let my Lord hang up his conquering lance.   Giles Fletcher, the Younger.   ChIV-2; NOSC; SacPr *Fr.* Christ's Victory and Triumph.

Here let us pause:—the opening prospect view.   John Pierpont.   APN-1 *Fr.* Airs of Palestine.

Here let us rest, while with meridian blaze.   Written at the Eagle's Nest, Killarney. July 26, 1800.   Mary Tighe.   CenSon; OxBSo

Here let's jump rope together here.   Picnic to the Earth.   Shuntaro Tanikawa.   PoetW, *tr. by* Harold Wright

Here lie Ciardi's pearly bones.   Elegy Just in Case.   John Ciardi.   AmWaPo; PWW2

Here Lies.   Stevie Smith.   PoA 2002

Here lies a Bond under this tomb.   On Bond the Usurer.   *Unknown.*   NOSC

Here lies a clerk who half his life had spent.   Volunteer, The.   Herbert Asquith.   OBWP

(Here lies the clerk who half his life had spent.)   FaBoWar

Here lies a dog: may every dog that dies.   Epitaph on the Favourite Dog of a Politician.   Joseph Hilaire Pierre Belloc.   OBSV

Here lies a lady of beauty and high degree.   John Crowe Ransom.   APT-1; MoAmPo; NAAPv.2; NAMCP V.1; NoAM *Fr.* Sixteen Poems in Eight Pairings.

Here lies a man who was so bright.   Epitaph.   Robert Finch.   IFF

Here lies a most beautiful lady.   Epitaph, An.   Walter De la Mare.   MoBrPo; OBEV

Here lies a poor woman who always was tired.   Epitaph.   *Unknown.*   OBCoV

Here Lies a Prisoner.   Charlotte Mew.   MoBrPo

Here lies a shoe-maker whose knife and hammer.   At His Father's Grave.   John Ormond.   OBWVE

Here lies / A worthy matron of unspotted life.   Epitaph on My Dear and Ever Honored Mother Mrs. Dorothy Dudley.   Anne Bradstreet.   NAAPv.1

Here lies, and none to mourn him but the sea.   Edna St. Vincent Millay.   HeIP-4 *Fr.* Epitaph for the Race of Man.

Here Lies Archeanassa.   Asclepiades.   WoPoe, *tr. by* Frederick Morgan

Here lies Cock Robbin dead and cold.   Death and Burial of Cock Robbin, The.   *Unknown.*   OWoS

Here lies David Garrick, describe me who can.   Oliver Goldsmith.   NPeEn; OxBEV *Fr.* Retaliation.

Here lies John Bun.   John Bun.   *Unknown.*   NBLV

Here lies John Hughes and Sarah Drew.   Epitaph.   Lady Mary Wortley Montagu.   CABP

Here lies Jonson [*or* lyes Johnson] with the rest.   Upon Ben Jo[h]nson.   Robert Herrick.   NoP-4; NoP-5

Here lies Miss Havisham.   Miss Havisham.   Olga Orozco.   TCLAP, *tr. by* Stephen Tapscott

Here lies my wife. Eternal peace.   Epigram.   James Vincent Cunningham.   NIP-4

Here lies New Critic who would fox us.   Epigram.   James Vincent Cunningham.   APT-2; MoAmPo

Here lies Nolly Goldsmith, for shortness call'd Noll.   On Oliver Goldsmith.   David Garrick.   OxBEV

Here lies old *Hobson*, Death hath broke his girt.   On the University Carrier Who Sick'n'd [*or* Sickened] in the Time of His Vacancy [, Being Forbid to go to London, by Reason of the Plague].   John Milton.   NOSC; OxAEP-1

Here lies one sweet of heart.   For My Father's Grave.   Yvor Winters.   IllVoic

Here lies our good Edmund, whose genius was such.   Oliver Goldsmith.   NPeEn; OxBEV *Fr.* Retaliation.

Here lies our Sovereign Lord the King.   Epitaph on Charles II.   John Wilmot, 2d Earl of Rochester.   WoPoe

Here lies poor Johnson. Reader! have a care.   Doctor Johnson.   Soame Jenyns.   OBSV

Here lies poor Nick, an honest creature.   Exemplary Nick.   Sydney Smith.   DiBP

Here lies resting, out of breath.   Little Elegy.   X. J. Kennedy.   InoFa; WaAnP

Here lies Sir Tact, a diplomatic fellow.   Epitaph.   Timothy Steele.   NBLV

Here lies the clerk who half his life had spent.   Herbert Asquith.   *See* Here lies a clerk who half his life had spent.

Here lies the fairest flower, that stood.   David's Epitaph on Jonathan.   Francis Quarles.   ChIV-1

Here lies the man was born and cried.   Epitaph, An: On a Man for Doing Nothing.   John Hoskyns.   NOSC

Here lies the noble flesh of Spartacus the knave.   Daniel Casper von Lohenstein.   GePo *Fr.* Arminius.

Here lies the preacher, judge, and poet, Peter.   On Peter Robinson.   Francis, Lord Jeffrey Jeffrey.   NBLV

Here lies the pride of Queens, pattern of Kings.   Anne Bradstreet.   TCAPo *Fr.* In Honour of that High and Mighty Princess Queen Elizabeth of Happy Memory.

Here lies to each her parents' ruth.   On My First Daughter.   Ben Jonson.   BASC; NAEL-6v1; NAEL-7v1; NoP-4; NoP-5; NOSC; WaAnP

Here lies, whom hound did ne'er pursue.   Epitaph on a Hare.   William Cowper.   NoP-4; NoP-5; PoPoPo

Here lies Wise and Valiant Dust.   Epitaph on the Earl of Strafford.   John Cleveland.   BASC; NOSC; NPeEn; OxBEV

Here lies wrapped up in forty thousand towels.   On Queen Caroline's Deathbed.   Alexander Pope.   NPeEn

Here lies wrapped up tight in sod.   Epitaph for a Postal Clerk.   X. J. Kennedy.   NIL-7; NIP-4

Here, Love, whether we love or not.   Second Hand, The.   Phyllis Webb.   IFF

Here low tide and morning coincide.   Northwest Passages.   Daryl Hine.   BrAP

Here luxury's the common lot. The light.   Grasse: The Olive Trees.   Richard Wilbur.   NoAM

Here lyes a Boy the finest Child from me.   On My Boy Henry.   Elizabeth Egerton, Lady Brackley.   EMWP

Here make an end of singing? (LL)   If All the World Were Paper.   *Unknown.*   NOSC; NTCP; OBCoV

Here, Missy! dis way, Missy! come along.   Albery Allson Whitman.   NAAPv.1 *Fr.* Octoroon, The.

Here must we pause; this only let me add.   William Wordsworth.   NAEL-6v2; NAEL-7v2 *Fr.* Prelude, The; Growth of a Poet's Mind [1850 version].

Here my garden is growing, the flowers of Eros I tend here.   Johann Wolfgang von Goethe.   EroLit *Fr.* Roman Elegies, The.

Here none think of wealth or fame.   Daigu.   ZenPo, *tr. by* Takashi Ikemoto and Lucien Stryk

Here not the flags, the rhythmic.   Neutrality.   Sidney Keyes.   MoBrPo

Here, O my Lord, I see Thee face to face.   Horatius Bonar.   SacPr *Fr.* This Do in Remembrance of Me.

Here, O my lord, I see thee face to face.   This Do in Remembrance of Me.   Horatius Bonar.

Here often I am a little like still a.   Here Often I Am.   Michel Deguy.   YaTCFP, *tr. by* Clayton Eshleman

Here on Mondays, after the.   Anglo-Saxon Comedy.   Peter Rose.   BMAP

Here, on the farthest point of the peninsula.   Of Politics, & Art.   Norman Dubie.   AmAlph; P180

Here on the west edge, the town turned its back on the west.   City Limits.   Ted Kooser.   GM

Here on this patio, lonely as a mushroom, which way should I look.   Antonio Cisneros.   TCLAP *Fr.* Loneliness.

Here on this stretcher now he coldly lies.   Mort, Le.   Howard Buck.   YaYoPo

Here once flint walls.   Tale, A [Revised Version].   Edward Thomas.   OxBEV

Here once the endless wagon-trains.   Old Fort Griffin.   Berta Hart Nance.   TiP2

Here [*or* How] richly, with ridiculous display.   Epitaph on the Politician Himself.   Joseph Hilaire Pierre Belloc.   MoBrPo; NBLV; OBSV

Here Philip the father buried.   Callimachus.   HePo, *tr. by* Barbara Hughes Fowler

Here, Queen of the Mountains.   Kamalākānta Bhattācārya.   SinGod, *tr. by* Rachel Fell McDermott

Here, reader, turn your weeping eyes.   Orator's Epitaph, The.   Henry Peter Brougham, 1st Baron Brougham and Vaux.   NBLV

Here Reynolds is laid, and to tell you my mind.   Oliver Goldsmith.   OBCoV; OxBEV *Fr.* Retaliation.

Here room and kingly silence keep.   By the Pacific Ocean.   Joaquin Miller.   CalPo

Here, said my guide.   Mary Bryan.   NPBRoP *Fr.* Visit, The.

"Here," said the Cloud-gatherer Zeus, "that is a journey you may well postpone.   Homer.   EroLit *Fr.* Iliad, The.

Here shadow[e] lie.   Epitaph for Sir Lawrence Tanfield.   Lady Elizabeth Tanfield.   NOSC

Here she lies, a pretty bud.   Upon a Child That Died [*or* Dyed].   Robert Herrick.   NoP-4; NoP-5; WaAnP

Here, she said, is your deepest well in Madras.   Deepest Well in Madras, The.   N. V. M. Gonzalez.   ReBoTo

Here, she said, put this on your head.   Flounder.   Natasha Trethewey.   OxAAAP; TWW

Here shift the scene, to represent.   Jonathan Swift.   OxBEV *Fr.* Verses on the Death of Dr. Swift, D.S.P.D, Occasioned by Reading a Maxim in Rochefoucauld.

Here should my wonder dwell, and here my praise.   Sir John Denham.   NAEL-6v1; NOSC; NPeEn *Fr.* Cooper's Hill.

Here silken twines, there locks you see.   Ear-string, An.   William Strode.   NOSC

Here sits the Lord Mayor.   Forehead, Eyes, Cheeks, Nose, Mouth, and Chin.   Mother Goose.   FaBoVe

Here sleeps the Queen, this is the royall bed.   Anne Bradstreet.   OxBEV; TCAPo *Fr.* In Honour of that High and Mighty Princess Queen Elizabeth of Happy Memory.

Here something stubborn comes.   Seed Leaves.   Richard Wilbur.   VisFro

Here stands death, a bluish decoction in a cup with no saucer.   Death.   Rainer Maria Rilke.   PFTM-1

Here Stanford lies, who thought it odd.   Ambrose Bierce.   CalPo

Here, still sequestered, Penmon's sacred dome.   Richard Llwyd.   AngWePo *Fr.* Beaumaris Bay.

Here, stranger, pause, nor view with scornful eyes.   Shipwrecked Tippoo.   William Wyndham.   DiBP

Here, take again thy sackcloth! and thank heaven.   Henry Vaughan.   AngWePo *Fr.* Upon a Cloak [*or* Cloke] Lent Him by Mr. J. Ridsley.

Here, take again thy sack-cloth! and thank heaven.   Upon a Cloak [*or* Cloke] Lent Him by Mr. J. Ridsley.   Henry Vaughan.   BASC

Here, / Take it home and give it to your wife.   Wooden Handle, The.   Gojko Djogo.   AF, *tr. by* Michael March and Dušan Puvaić

Here take my Picture, though I bid farewell.   John Donne.   FSCP; OxAEP-1; PBRV *Fr.* Elegies.

Here take no care, take here no care, my Muse.   Discontent, The.   Anne Killigrew.   BASC

Here, take this gift.   To a Certain Cantatrice.   Walt Whitman.   AmFaPo

Here, the bones of the Geblites.   Israel Revisited.   Luisa Futuransky.   MirDau, *tr. by* Celeste Kostopulos-Cooperman

Here the crow starves, here the patient stag.   T. S. Eliot.   NAEL-6v2 *Fr.* Landscapes.

Here the delicate dance of silence.   Woodtown Manor.   John Montague.   PBCIP

Here the foot prints stop;.   After Twenty Years.   Fadwa Tuqan.   AF, *tr. by Unknown*

Here the frailest leaves of me and yet my strongest lasting.   Here the Frailest Leaves of Me.   Walt Whitman.   APN-1; CAGL; NAAL-3; NAAL-5; NAAPv.1

Here the green vein of life.   Places.   Luciana Frezza.   CItWP, *tr. by* Cinzia Sartini Blum and Lara Trubowitz

Here the hangman stops his cart.   A. E. Housman.   ChIV-2; MoBrPo; OxAEP-2; UV *Fr.* Shropshire Lad, A.

Here the hills are earth's bones.   Asian Desert.   Dorothy, Duchess of Wellington Wellesley.   OBMV

Here the horse-mushrooms make a fairy ring.   Fairy Ring, The.   Andrew Young.   Spl

Here the human past is dim and feeble and alien to us.   Haunted Country.   Robinson Jeffers.   APT-1

Here the image of a child on a hill.   Michael Palmer.   APSN

Here the jack-hammer jabs into the ocean.   Colloquy in Black Rock.   Robert Lowell.   MoAmPo; OxBoAm

Here the moutain joins the sea.   Brief Ectasy.   Luciana Notari.   CItWP, *tr. by* Cinzia Sartini Blum and Lara Trubowitz

Here the part played by color is the inconsistency.   Risk of Abstraction, The.   Adriano Spatola.   PFTM-2, *tr. by* Paul Vangelisti

Here the picture is less gloomy.   All That Glitters.   Maureen Owen.   PmAP

Here, the ribs end, they—divide, into.   Recumbent.   Carl Phillips.   NAPBL

Here the sky's all spreading belly.   Flatlanders.   Monica Youn.   LegDan

Here, the trees pay their respectds, mourn openly.   Yom HaShoah in Florida.   Rick Hilles.   RWB

Here the white-rayed anemone is born.   In a Spring Grove.   William Allingham.   OxBSo

Here then is the life-giving activity given to every man: the sexual / act, vivificator.   Stefan Brecht.   CLPP *Fr.* Sex.

Here there pheasants.   Yaba.   EMJL *Fr.* Plum Blossom Scent.

Here there was once a country.   Venus Khoury-Gata.   PoCho

Here, there were pilgrims.   Living Spring, The.   Moses Glyn Jones.   BBMWP, *tr. by* Mike Jenkins

Here they all come to die.   Country of a Thousand Years of Peace, The.   James Merrill.   NoP-4

Here they are. The soft eyes open.   Heaven of Animals, The.   James Dickey.   CAP-8; ColAP; EmeKit; HeIP-4; InGu; InoFa; NAMCP V.2; NoAM; StAl; TRP; VCAP; WaAnP; WoPoe

Here they caper all over the scarred bronze.   Grasshoppers on the Bell.   László Nagy.   IQMS, *tr. by* Júlia Kada and Kenneth McRobbie

Here they come past High Street station, everyone I've ever known.   Big Parade, The.   Stephen Knight.   NeBl; TCAWP

Here they have no time for the fine graces.   Poem of Lewis.   Iain Crichton Smith.   EdScPo

Here they stand, rotund, and undiluted by grief.   Ever So, Between.   Valerie Martínez.   NAPBL

Here they stood, whom the Kecoughtan first believed.   Elegy in an Abandoned Boatyard.   Dave Jeddie Smith.   VCAP

Here they went with smock and crook.   Forefathers.   Edmund Charles Blunden.   NoP-4; NoP-5; OBEV; OBMV

Here--they've all started moving at once. Edoardo Cacciatore. ItPo *Fr.* Full Powers: Five Warning Signs.

Here, thirteen high school students died. Columbine High School / Littleton, CO. Albert Goldbarth. LiTh

Here Time. Silvia Baron Supervielle. YaTCFP, *tr. by* Rosemary Lloyd

Here Today. Andrew Elliott. PNI

Here too are dreaming landscapes. In the Miscroscope. Miroslav Holub. PoSu; WoPoe, *tr. by* Ian Milner and Jarmila Milner

Here too, 'tis sung, of old Diana stray'd. Alexander Pope. OxAEP-1 *Fr.* Windsor-Forest [*or* Windsor Forest].

Here torture was an art like landscape painting. Paul Engle. PoA 2002 *Fr.* Images of China.

Here 2. Bob Perelman. BAP-04

Here, under Pear-trees. David Campbell. BMAP

Here Usually Comes the Bride. Ogden Nash. NIL-7

Here war is harmless like a monument. W. H. Auden. OBWP

Here was the sound of water falling only. Owl, The. Robert Penn Warren. MoAmPo

Here, watching T.V. Hunting the Dugong. Gladys Cardiff. HATNAP

Here we are all, by day; by night we are [*or* w'are] hurled. Dream[e]s. Robert Herrick. NAEL-6v1; NAEL-7v1; OPOU; Spl

Here we are, my son, aliens in this place. Time, Place, and Parenthood. Hayden Carruth. PoChi

Here we are, picking the first fern-shoots. Song of the Bowmen of Shu [1915]. Bunno [Wen Wang *or* King Wen]. FaBoWar; NDACCP; OBVE, *tr. by* Ezra Pound

Here we are, see? At the Well. Paul Blackburn. APSN; PFTM-2

Here we are together. Good Morning. Arthur Freed. ReLy

Here We Come A-wassailing. *Unknown.* ChrPo

Here we come looby loo. Lubin. *Unknown.* FaBoVe

Here we enact the opening of the world. Australian Garden, An. Peter Porter. BrAP; OBGa

Here we have the sea of children; here. Geography Lesson. Carol Rumens. BeAl; MoWP

Here we have thirst. Egyptian Pulled Glass Bottle in the Shape of a Fish, An. Marianne Moore. APT-1; NALW

Here we must rest; and where else should we rest? Sepulchrum Domus Mea Est. William Austin. NOSC

Here we must stop. He breathed, and opening wide. Albery Allson Whitman. NAAPv.1 *Fr.* Octoroon, The.

Here we raise the dead. Kalamu ya Salaam. SpirFl *Fr.* New Orleans Haiku.

Here We Stand before the Temporal World. Joan Murray. YaYoPo

Here we stand on the brink of tomorrow. Year After Year. Bart Howard. ReLy

Here We Will Stay. Tawfiq Zayyad. PML, *tr. by* Charles Doria and Sharif Elmusa

Here we're set upon the green grass. Green Grass. *Unknown.* FaBoVe

Here Where Coltrane Is. Michael S. Harper. CAP-8; ESEAA

Here where I live. Hsieh Ling-yün. NDACCP *Fr.* Dwelling in the Mountains.

Here, where the baby paddles in the gutter. Lean Street. George Sutherland Fraser. EdScPo

Here, where the creek culls sand and silt. Sandbar at Moore's Creek. Judy Jordan. AmPoNex

Here, where the Danube pours its tawny waters. Hungary. Dániel Berzsenyi. IQMS, *tr. by* Watson Kirkconnell

Here where the elm trees were. Elegy. Constance Carrier. APT-2

Here where the end of bone is no end of song. Poet's Corner, The. Laura Riding Jackson. FuPo

Here, where the hills slope before the sunset and the chasm of time. Ramallah—January, 2002. Mahmoud Darwish. Eno, *tr. by* Ramsis Amun

Here, where the noises of the busy town. In the Jewish Synagogue at Newport. Emma Lazarus. TaR

Here Where the Path. Gabriella Leto. CItWP, *tr. by* Cinzia Sartini Blum and Lara Trubowitz

Here where the sun burned. Tomas Tranströmer. WoBe *Fr.* Haiku.

Here where the wind is always north-north-east. New England. Edwin Arlington Robinson. HeIP-4; MoAmPo; PoPoPo

Here, where the world is quiet. Garden of Proserpine, The. Algernon Charles Swinburne. CABP; InoFa; NAEL-6v2; NAEL-7v2; NoP-4; NoP-5; OxBEV; TFi

Here, where Vespasian's legions struck the sands. Embarcation. Thomas Hardy. OBWP

Here with a Loaf of Bread beneath the Bough. Omar Khayyám. UV *Fr.* Rubáiyát of Omar Khayyám [of Naishápúr], The.

Here with roses in bloom, with woodbine twining the laurel. Anacreon's Grave. Johann Wolfgang von Goethe. STV, *tr. by* John Frederick Nims

Here with the desert so austere that only. Burial Flags. Ralph Nixon Currey. PoWW

Here you are alone again. Mouse, The. Sa'di Yusuf. BeAl, *tr. by* Khaled Mattawa

Here you are, grand old sensualist! Rubens. Harriet Monroe. IllVoic

Here you are near me once more. Guillaume Apollinaire. AF

Here you could pass your holidays. Kyoto Garden, A. Dennis Joseph Enright. OBGa

Here you have fruits and flowers and boughs with leaves. Green. Paul Verlaine. WoPoe, *tr. by* Yvor Winters

Here you see old Tom Moore. *Unknown.* APN-2

Here you've got time to think. In Line at the Supermarket. Greg Pape. PBCAP; SUP

Hereafter, shall smell of the lamp, not thee. (LL) His Farewell [*or* Fare-well] to Sack. Robert Herrick. NAEL-6v1; NAEL-7v1

Hereafter, The. Andrew Hudgins. RA

Heredity. Thomas Hardy. HarvBoo

Heredity. Tony Harrison. HarvBoo; NAEL-6v2; NAEL-7v2; NAMCP V.2 *Fr.* School of Eloquence, The.

Heredom. Kenneth Irby. FTOS

Here's a body—there's a bed! Good Night. Thomas Hood. Spl

Here's a bowl of batter. Joy, The. Harryette Mullen. OxAAAP

Here's a dark picture. Tomas Tranströmer. WoBe *Fr.* Haiku.

Here's a girl from a dangerous town. Belfast Tune. Joseph Brodsky. VCWP

Here's a good piece of cheese (I perhaps might have kept it). Cheese for the Archdeacon, A. Thomas Hughes. AngWePo

Here's a jolly couple! Oh the jolly jolly couple! *Unknown.* NOSC

Here's a live one. Evidence on Film, The. Ron Charach. BloBone

Here's a Match. Krissi Banzon. BeDoSh

Here's a picture of me. Photographs. Alec Wilder. ReLy

Here's a song. Season Song. *Unknown.* WoPoe, *tr. by* Flann O'Brien

Here's a song of praise for all those people. Those Who Make Paths. Catherine Fisher. TCAWP

Here's a song that I've created. Remember Me? Al Dubin. ReLy

Here's a story I never told you. Letter after a Year. Donald Hall. PoDa

Here's an example from / A Butterfly. Example, The. W. H. Davies. MoBrPo

Here's another Spaniard! Welcome! Antonio Machado Ruiz. STV

Here's another window. Marina Ivanovna Tsvetayeva. AWTN *Fr.* Insomnia.

Here's balance / delicate as baby industry at. Up Thru the Years. Anne Waldman. AHA

Here's bumper, brave boys, the the health of our king. Refugee Song, A. *Unknown.* NAAPv.1

Here's Cooper, who's written six volumes to show. James Russell Lowell. TCAPo *Fr.* Fable for Critics, A.

Here's fine rosemary, sage, and thyme. Cries of London, The. *Unknown.* OPOU

Here's how it was: I caught you by the throat. To Eros. Alfonsina Storni. TANSG, *tr. by* Mark McCaffrey

Here's Looking at You Francis Bacon. Joan Retallack. FTOS

Here's my dream of a final exam. Two Apes of Brueghel, The. Wisława Szymborska. WoPoe, *tr. by* Sharon Olds

Here's my mom and dad leaving. Roc, The. Mohja Kahf. PoArWo

Here's no more news, than virtue, I may as well. To Sir Henry Wotton. John Donne. OxAEP-1

Here's something folk tales tell. Remember Haiti, Cuba, Vietnam. Andrew Salkey. RSaN

Here's That Rainy Day. Johnny Burke. ReLy

Here's the little dressmaker. Epith. Carol Muske-Dukes. MakPoe; PoDa

Here's the long trough, covered by a screen. China Camp, California. Kim Addonizio. GeoHom

Here's the one where the sun. Portraits at the Epicenter. Pimone Triplett. LegDan

Here's the thing: you're coming out of the men's room. Nosebleed, Gold Digger, KGB, Henry James, Handshake. David Kirby. SUP

Here's to Life. Violeta Parra. TCLAP, *tr. by* Joan Baez and James Upton

Here's to my best romance. Hooray for Love. Leo Robin. ReLy

Here's to the building trade. To the Building Trade. Matthew Sweeney. ModIr

Here's to the ladies who lunch. Ladies Who Lunch, The. Stephen Sondheim. ReLy

Here's to the maiden [*or* maid] of Bashful fifteen. Richard Brinsley Sheridan. NPeEn; OxBEV *Fr.* School for Scandal, The.

Here's what I see. Dogs Gambol. Novica Tadic. VCWP, *tr. by* Charles Simic

Here's what we've come to see, a boy. Daredevil. Stuart Dybek. MAAN

Here's where I wanted to put the streetcars. Old Postcards. Günter Eich. AF, *tr. by* Stuart Friebert

Hereto I come to view a voiceless ghost. After a Journey. Thomas Hardy. HarvBoo; NPeEn; OxAEP-2; OxBEV

Herido, El. Miguel Hernández. RaW

Heriger and the False Prophet. *Unknown*. WoPoe *Fr.* Cambridge Songs.

Heriger the bishop of Mainz once encountered. *Unknown*. WoPoe *Fr.* Cambridge Songs.

Heritage. Mahdi Muhammad Ali. IrPoTo, *tr. by* Salaam Yousif

Heritage. Gwendolyn B. Bennett. ColAP; NAAPv.2

Heritage. Countee Cullen. APT-2; ColAP; HeIP-4; MoAmPo; NAAL-5; NAAPv.2; NAMCP V.1; NoAM; NoP-4; NoP-5; PoPoPo; SSLK

Heritage. Haim Guri. HP

Heritage. Linda Hogan. UnSA

Heritage. Dorothea MacKellar. NOBAu

Herman Melville. Conrad Potter Aiken. NoAM

Hermann Fegelein. W. D. Snodgrass. BodElec *Fr.* Führer Bunker, The.

Hermann Hesse / poet of the clouds, is gone. Bare Wind, A. Pak Mogwŏl [*or* Mokwŏl]. CAMKP, *tr. by* Kevin O'Rourke

Hermeneutical as memory. Brieves from the Book of Kells. R. T. Smith. PoA 2002

Hermes. André Marie de Chénier. *tr. by* Paul Schmidt

"When the Euxine goddess with astonished eyes." WoPoe, *tr. by* Paul Schmidt

Hermes, lord of the dead, look down and guard. Libation Bearers, The. Aeschylus. NAWM-5v1, *tr. by* Robert Fagles

Hermes of the Ways. "H. D." NAAPv.2

Hermes took his attribute. "H. D." NAAPv.2 *Fr.* Tribute to the Angels.

Hermes Trismegistus. "H. D." NALW *Fr.* Tribute to the Angels.

Hermit, The. Eloise Bibb. CBWP-4

Hermit, The. W. H. Davies. MoBrPo

Hermetic Definition. "H. D."

Red Rose and a Beggar. PFTM-2

Hermetic Diary. Bruce Beasley. AmAlph

Hermit and the Soul, The. Henrietta Cordelia Ray. CBWP-3

Hermit Crab, The. Mary Oliver. WaAnP

Hermit doesn't sleep at night, The. Night Sitting. Ching An. CSKM, *tr. by* Jerome P. Seaton

Hermit Hoar. Samuel Johnson. NBLV

Hermit in his cave beside the sea, The. Hermit and the Soul, The. Henrietta Cordelia Ray. CBWP-3

Hermit Thoughts. Thich Tue Sy. WhBo

Hermit thrush ,??;;&~ (having chosen the wrong female). Pre-Uplift of the Sierra. Brenda Hillman. RoV

Hermit with Landscape. Daniel Hall. YaYoPo

Hermitage. Donald Davidson.

Descending Chestnut Ridge. FuPo

Hermitage at Chung-nan Mountain. Wang Wei. CrYelRi, *tr. by* Sam Hamill

Hermitage of the Bamboos, The. Pei Di and Wang Wei. CCL1 *Fr.* Wheel River.

Hermitage Road, The. Anne-Marie Albiach. YaTCFP, *tr. by* Keith Waldrop

Hermit's Life, A. Chungji. BecRai, *tr. by* Kim Daljin, Kim Won-Chung and Christopher Merrill

Hermit-thrush, A. (LL) Dawn. Angelina Weld Grimké. APT-1; NAAPv.2

Hernando De Soto. Rosemary Benét *and* Stephen Vincent Benét. NBLV

Hernando's Hideaway. Richard Adler and Jerry Ross. ReLy

Hero. Anne Carson. NLPA *Fr.* Glass Essay, The.

Hero. Semezdin Mehmedinović. RaF, *tr. by* Ammiel Alcalay

Hero, The. Marianne Moore. PoA 2002 *Fr.* Part of a Novel, Part of a Poem, Part of a Play.

Hero, The. Pablo Neruda. GifTon, *tr. by* William O'Daly

Hero, The. Siegfried Sassoon. OBWP

Hero and Leander. John Donne. NoSic; SoSe-8

Hero and Leander. Christopher Marlowe. NAEL-6v1; NAEL-7v1; NoP-5; NoSic

"Amorous Leander, beautiful and young." CAGL

Amorous Neptune. WaAnP

"And as her silver body downeward went." OxBEV

Bridal Song. OBEV

"By this Leander being near the land." NPeEn

Epithalamion Teratos. NoSic

"His bodie was as straight as Circes wand." NPeEn; OxBEV

Love at First Sight. WaAnP

"Men of wealthy Sestos, every year, The." AEP

"New light gives new directions, Fortunes new." NoSic; PBRV

""O Hero, Hero!" thus he cried full oft." EroLit

"O none but gods have power their love to hide." OxAEP-1

Hero and the Hydra, The. James McAuley.

Tomb of Heracles, The. BMAP

Hero first thought it, The. Truth. George Russell. MoBrPo

Hero is a good lad, The. He causes no anxiety. On the Tomb of the Unknown Soldier. László Mécs. IQMS, *tr. by* Watson Kirkconnell

Hero/Lil. David Meltzer.

Third Shell, The. PFTM-2

(HERO)neck: Attempts at a Portrait. Mariiane Mays.

#2, In Alabaster. PoPra

#3, In Black Ink. PoPra

#4, In Red. PoPra

Hero of the Mirages, The. László Arany. *tr. by* John Gordon Nichols

"Albion, teach me (and not with loud, unsubtle)." IQMS, *tr. by* J. G. Nichols

Herod the King came sounding through. In Galilee. Jessie Mackay. SacPr

Herodotus, while gossiping. Behind the Headlines. Raymond Garlick. TCAWP

Herod's Palace. Gwyneth Lewis. HarvBoo

Heroes. Robert Creeley. NoP-4; NoP-5; OxBoAm

Heroes. Sorley MacLean. FaBoTC; FaBoWar

Heroes. Kathleen Jessie Raine. FaBoWar

Heroes, The. Louis Simpson. OBWP

Heroes, and Kings! your distance keep. Epitaph for One Who Would Not Be Buried in Westminster Abbey. Alexander Pope. NPeEn

Heroes are always alive. *Unknown*. SLW, *tr. by* Marjolijn De Jager, Sayd Bahodin Majrouh and André Velter

Héroes del Cinco de Mayo. Zaragoza Clubs. *tr. by* Luis A. Torres

"My heart tells me." SWaP, *tr. by* Luis A. Torres

Heroes paused upon the plain, The. Byrnies, The. Thom Gunn. NoAM

Heroic Epistle to Sir William Chambers, An. William Mason. OBGa *Fr.* Heroic Epistle to Sir William Chambers, An.

Heroic Simile. Robert Hass. VCAP

Heroides. Ovid.

"To Paris that was once her owne though now it be not so." OBVE

Heroides: Dedicated to the Muses. Ekaterina Urusova. *tr. by* Catriona Kelly

"O Muses! I beseech you, fire my heart with song." ARWW, *tr. by* Catriona Kelly

Heroin. Jim Carroll. OBCoV

Heroin. Bob Hicok. AmPoNex; BAP-97

Heroine. Paul Groves. AngWePo

Heroine. Carol Muske-Dukes. AmAlph

Heroine in ass-skin. WHITE FOOLSCAP / Book of Cordelia. Susan Howe. PmAP

Heroism wasn't possible any longer. Chaplin and Others. Alan Llwyd. BBMWP, *tr. by* Joseph P. Clancy

Heron. James King Annand. NOxBChV

Heron. Norman Alexander MacCaig. EdScPo

Heron. Peter Sanger. Coast

Heron. Charles Tomlinson. WoBe *Fr.* Zipangu.

Heron, The. Stuart Henson. StAl

Heron, The. Theodore Roethke. APT-2; OWoS

Heron, The. Vernon Watkins. AngWePo; TCAWP

Heron in the Alyn. Gladys Mary Coles. TCAWP

Heron is a Presbyterian minister, The. Calvinist, The. Kenneth Steven. EdScPo

Heron moonlight feathers the full air, The. Height. Rosalie Moore. APT-2

Heron stalks, The. Sunset at Twin Lake. Anita Endrezze. HATNAP

Heron-Woman. Marjorie M. Evasco. ReBoTo

Herostratos and Herostratos. Sergey Stratanovsky. ItGoST, *tr. by* J. Kates

Herr Bruckner often wandered into church. Lives of the Great Composers. Dana Gioia. RA

Herr Direktor, ich sent Sei ein cable. Ein Complaint. Virginia Graham. OBCoV

Herrick, thou art too coarse [*or* coorse] to love. (LL) Vision, The ("Sitting alone (as one forsook).") Robert Herrick. CavPo; PBRV

Herring Girls, The. Iain Crichton Smith. NePenScot

Herring Girls, The. Derick Thomson. NePenScot

Herring is beheaded and boned, The. The filets are as big as a face, though folded up. Packing Herring. Helga Novak. MotU, *tr. by* Ann Maria Celona

Herring-bone and fern, this coat. Inheritance. Alan Jenkins. NeBrP

Herrings and Birch Trees. Jude Stéfan. YaTCFP, *tr. by* Edward Lucie-Smith

Hers could not stay for sympathy. (LL) It Is Not Beauty I Demand. George Darley. IrLP; NAEL-6v2

Hers is the clean apron, good for fire. Farm Wife. Ronald Stuart Thomas. GoPo

Hers was the vacant seat by the door. Illness. David Scott. NLP

He's a Blockhead who wants a proof of what he Can't Perceive. William Blake. PtR

He's a Cousin of Mine. Cecil Mack. ReLy

He's a fool, and don't I know it. Lorenz Hart. *See* After one whole quart of brandy.

He's a hero, says the soldier in fatigues, pointing at the kid. Hero. Semezdin Mehmedinović. RaF, *tr. by* Ammiel Alcalay

He's a high clear forehead.   Robert Johnstone.   PNI *Fr.* Every Cache.

He's about 300 pounds and knows martial arts, boxing and wrestling.   I'm Dealing with My Pain.   Denise Duhamel.   NeAmPo; SUP

He's an awkward bedfellow and I love to keep.   Paul Verlaine.   EroLit, *tr. by* Alistair Elliot

He's at the window now.   V's Farmhouse.   Lisa Fishman.   AmPoNex

He's carrying on with a distracting song.   Redwing Sonnets.   Julia Alvarez. BodElec

He's Crossed the River.   Carol Cullar.   TiP2

He's dead / the dog won't have to.   Death.   William Carlos Williams.   InoFa; NAMCP V.1

He's diving off the front of the stage!   Performance Poem.   Bob Holman. KGB

He's down again, aswim in a dream.   Liam.   Mary Jo Salter.   ExTi

He's driving a truck, and we know.   Young Elvis.   Cornelius Eady.   AllShUp

He's dropped his heart!   Man in Petersham.   John A. Scott.   PML

He's filled himself with himself.   Vasco [*or* Vasko] Popa.   PoSu *Fr.* Quartz Pebble, The.

He's going around with your letter.   Ghazal 34.   Mirza Asadullah Khan Ghalib. EaWin, *tr. by* Aijaz Ahmad and W. S. Merwin

He's gone, and all our plans.   To His Love.   Ivor Gurney.   InoFa; MakPoe; NAEL-7v2; NAMCP V.1; NoP-4; NoP-5; NPeeN; OBWP; PoAgWa; PoWW

He's gone, and for his absence thus I mourn.   Christopher Marlowe.   CAGL *Fr.* Edward the Second.

He's got a radio on his shoulder.   Street Music.   Greg Pape.   PBCAP

He's had.   Hypochondriac.   Geoffrey Holloway.   NLP

He's had enough of the circle.   Vasco [*or* Vasko] Popa.   PoSu *Fr.* Quartz Pebble, The.

He's had the chest pains for weeks.   Death of Santa Claus, The.   Charles Webb.   P180

He's in there still, with Johnny Appleseed.   Peter and the Dyke.   Paul Farley. NeBrP

He's Jus' de Same Today.   *Unknown.*   InvLi

He's knelt to fish her face up from the sidewalk.   Rebirth of Venus, The.   Mary Jo Salter.   FFC

He's lost him completely. And he now tries to find.   In Despair.   Constantine P. Cavafy.   CAGL, *tr. by* Edmund Keeley and Philip Sherrard

He's lost / in the wilderness of his future, or his past. (LL)   Armenian Language Is the Home of the Armenian, The.   Moushegh Ishkhan.   BLT; WoPoe, *tr. by* Diana Der Hovanessian

He's lying in poor water, a yard or so depth of poor safety.   October Salmon[, An].   Ted Hughes.   EmeKit

He's mad, who lying half dead gets up to march again.   Forced March.   Miklós Radnóti.   IQMS, *tr. by* Peter Zollman

He's made of small tight circles.   Bubble.   Trebor Healey.   BeDoSh

He's / most definitely / (my father died meanwhile) / against parting. (LL) Against Parting.   Natan Zach.   HP; PoSu

He's now the ruler of the country which once exiled him.   Exile's Return, The. Slavko Mihalic.   PoSu, *tr. by* Peter Kastmiler and Charles Simic

He's obsessed with clocks, she with politics.   Small Lochs.   Norman Alexander MacCaig.   NePenScot

He's on the porch.   Buson.   EH, *tr. by* Robert Hass

He's only rich that cannot tell his store. (LL)   Against Fruition ("Stay here, fond youth, and ask no more.")   Sir John Suckling.   CavPo; NOSC

He's part of all, yet all's transcended.   Chikusen.   ZenPo, *tr. by* Takashi Ikemoto and Lucien Stryk

He's played hookey to see the flick again.   David Wojahn.   PBCAP *Fr.* Mystery Train: A Sequence.

He's polite looking over the polaroids.   Warhol at Wetlands.   John Kinsella. NeBl

He's still young—; thirty, but looks younger.   Self-Portrait [1969].   Frank Bidart.   PoCho

He's sunk forever. There's no doubt.   Dictator, The.   Lajos Kassák.   IQMS, *tr. by* Paul Tabori

He's talking about interpolations.   If You Don't Force It.   Michael S. Harper. FaoP

He's the man who climbs his barn.   Man in the Moon.   Linda Hogan. HATNAP

He's to the War.   *Unknown.*   CCL1 *Fr.* Jun-zi yu-yi [Translations].

He's working the alto saxophone.   Hamlet at the Paris Aerobleu.   Ryan Van Cleave.   IaFF

Hesiod's is the theme and his the style.   Callimachus.   HePo, *tr. by* Barbara Hughes Fowler

Hesitantly, / I say that you.   Your Ostrich Nature.   Elin Llwyd Morgan. BBMWP, *tr. by* the author and Richard Poole

Hesitate to Call.   Louise Glück.   LW; StAl

Hesitating Veteran, The.   Ambrose Bierce.   CBCWP; PCW

Hesitation.   "Lu Hsün."   WoPoe, *tr. by* William R. Schultz

Hesitation of Agros, fully developing "Deom the morn to the evening he strays", The.   August 2000.   Holley Blackwell.   AnSo

Hesperia.   Richard Henry Wilde.
  "Across the Prairie's silent waste I stray."   APN-1
  "Beyond Vermont's green hills, against the skies."   APN-1
  "Change blots out change,—their very memory dies."   APN-1
  "Father of Rivers! standing by thy side."   APN-1
  "If the romantic land whose soil I tread."   APN-1
  "Mount Auburn! loveliest city of the dead."   APN-1
  "Saint Augustine, thy praise was sung by one."   APN-1
  "Where dost thou lie, great Nimrod of the West!"   APN-1

Hesperides, The.   Burleigh Muttén.   HW

Hesperus.   Star of Evening.   Sappho.   WoPoe, *tr. by* Paul Roche

Hester.   Charles Lamb.   OBEV

Hester Prynne Recalls a Sunday in June.   Kathleen Norris.   UpMys

Hestia, / you who have received the highest honor.   *Unknown.*   HW *Fr.* Homeric Hymns.

Heu Quam Precipita.   Boethius.   OBMV *Fr.* Consolation of Philosophy, The ("De Consolacione Philosophie").

Heureux Qui, Comme Ulysse, A Fait un Beau Voyage.   Joachim Du Bellay. WoPoe, *tr. by* Anthony Hecht

He-who-came-forth was.   Son, The.   Denise Levertov.   NALW

Hewn Hands.   David Craig.   UpMys

Hewn out of faith and composite politics.   Towards Springtime.   Ágnes Nemes Nagy.   IQMS, *tr. by* Ila Egon

Hexameters[; Paraphrase of Psalm XLVI] [*see also* "God in our refuge and strength, a very present help in trouble"].   Samuel Taylor Coleridge. ChIV-1

Hey.   Allan Kaplan.   AHA

Hey boatman.   Hades.   Vegunta Mohana Prasad.   HotL, *tr. by* V. Narayana Rao

Hey, Boys! Up Go We!   *Unknown.*   NOBAu

Hey Cool Papa.   For Cool Papa Bell.   Tom Dent.   ISC

Hey diddle diddle.   *Unknown.*   OxBEV

Hey, don't swat the fly!   Issa.   EMJL

Hey, ey, hey, ey / Make we myrie as we may.   *Unknown.*   OHMEL

Hey Father Death, I'm flying home.   Allen Ginsberg.   CLPP *Fr.* don't Grow Old.

Hey, feller, with a million smackers.   Are You Havin' Any Fun?   Jack Yellen. ReLy

Hey, fog, go home.   Jacinta Gonzales and Maria Viviana Soto.   ASA, *tr. by* Alfred Kroeber

Hey girl, you like that tree?   While Communing with a Tree near My Home. M. Eliza Hamilton.   BtF

Hey, green! going down the road in Ripton.   On the Road to Homer Noble Farm.   Kim Waller.   VisFro

Hey, Hara, Ganges-Holder.   Kamalākānta Bhattācārya.   SinGod, *tr. by* Rachel Fell McDermott

Hey, here comes God.   Here Comes God.   Tenneti Suri.   HotL, *tr. by* V. Narayana Rao

Hey, it's not wine I drink.   Rāmprasād Sen.   SinGod, *tr. by* Rachel Fell McDermott

Hey, Jock, Are Ye Glad Ye 'Listed?   Neil Munro.   EdScPo

Hey, Johnnie Cope, are ye wauking yet.   Johnnie Cope.   Adam Skirving. NePenScot

Hey! listen to my story 'bout.   Daddy.   Bobby Troup.   ReLy

Hey, Look Me Over.   Carolyn Leigh.   ReLy

Hey, look me over.   Hey, Look Me Over.   Carolyn Leigh.   ReLy

Hey, miz lady. . .bring your fine ass over here and talk to me.   Nickel Wine and Deep Kisses.   Patricia Smith.   BRtP

Hey, Mountain King, Gauri is sulking.   Kamalākānta Bhattācārya.   SinGod, *tr. by* Rachel Fell McDermott

Hey Nellie, / how long you been here? did you.   Smokey's Getting Old. Jessica Tarahata Hagedorn.   OpBo

Hey Nonny No!   *Unknown.*   OBEV

Hey old flame I swam.   Dark torch.   Michele Leggott.   VaPo

Hey! [*or* Hay!] now [*or* nou] the day dawis [*or* daunss].   Night Is Near [*or* Neir] Gone, The.   Alexander Montgomerie.   OBEV

Hey, pop! / Re-bop! / Mop! / Y-e-a-h! (LL)   Dream Boogie.   Langston Hughes. APSN; NAMCP V.1; OxAAAP; OxBoAm; PFTM-1; SSLK

Hey Shabaka.   Gwendolyn Brooks.   ESEAA *Fr.* Winnie.

Hey, sparrow!   Issa.   EH, *tr. by* Robert Hass

Hey There.   Richard Adler and Jerry Ross.   ReLy

Hey There, Peacock.   *Hungarian Oral Tradition.*   IQMS, *tr. by* Dermot Spence

Hey there, peacock, peacock—peacock of the Empress!   Hey There, Peacock. *Hungarian Oral Tradition.*   IQMS, *tr. by* Dermot Spence

Hey there, soldier, from the stateless.   Kiss, A.   Malka Lee.   Prolet, *tr. by* Amelia Glaser

Hey there, taxi, do your stuff. My Cutey's Due at Two-to-Two Today. Leo Robin. ReLy

Hey there / You with the stars in your eyes. Hey There. Richard Adler and Jerry Ross. ReLy

Hey, this little kid gets roller skates. 74th Street. Myra Cohn Livingston. SSCS

Hey! Who is She, dark as clouds. Rāmprasād Sen. SinGod, *tr. by* Rachel Fell McDermott

Hey, Willie. What are you, man? Boricua? Moreno? Que? Nigger-Reecan Blues. Willie Perdomo. InTrad

Hey...y! Uh...hm!, covered with sweat. Velemir Khlebnikov. TCRusP, *tr. by* Kathy Lewis and Bob Perelman

Hey! / Yo! ¡Hey Yo / Yo Soy! Jesús Papoleto Meléndez. BRtP

Hey yo I'm a savage in fake braids who races. I Bring You Greetings: How. Chrystos. WiU

¡Hey Yo / Yo Soy! Jesús Papoleto Meléndez. BRtP

He'Yoho'Ho! He'Yoho'Ho! *Arapaho Oral Tradition.* NAAPv.2

Heysel. Robat Powell. BBMWP, *tr. by* the author

Heyyy mama. Black Queen Blues. Mari E. Evans. OxAAAP

Heyyyyyy yo! / you shoulda but. Conjugation of the Verb: To Blow. Fredrica Africa Payne. BRtP

Hezekiah. Thomas Parnell.

"From the black beach and broad expanse of sea." ChIV-1

Hezekiah's Display. John Keble. ChIV-1

Hi! Walter De la Mare. NOxBChV

Hi. William Kulik. BodElec

Hi! handsome hunting man. Hi! Walter De la Mare. NOxBChV

Hi Kali, come on in. Oh Kali. Janine Canan. HW

Hi, Kuh, / those / gold'n bees / are I's. I's (pronounced *Eyes*). Louis Zukofsky. NAAPv.2

Hi! shoo aller birds. Bird Starver's Cry. *Unknown.* FaBoVe

Hi there. My name is George. Notes on the Peanut. June Jordan. NAMCP V.2; NoAM

Hi, Torquemada! Dinna fash yersel! Adjustan Mysel tae the Situation. William J. Tait. EdScPo

Hiawatha: The White Man's Foot. Henry Wadsworth Longfellow. NCAP *Fr.* Song of Hiawatha, The.

Hiawatha's Childhood. Henry Wadsworth Longfellow. *Fr.* Song of Hiawatha, The.

Hiawatha's Departure. Henry Wadsworth Longfellow. *Fr.* Song of Hiawatha, The.

Hiawatha's Fasting. Henry Wadsworth Longfellow. NAAPv.1 *Fr.* Song of Hiawatha, The.

Hibakusha's Letter (1955), The. David Mura. AtGh; OpBo

Hibernation. Maurizio Cucchi. ItPo, *tr. by* Gayle Ridinger

Hibiscus grows lushly on the grave mounds, The. Juan Chi. ColAnChi *Fr.* Songs of My Soul.

Hibiscus on the Lake. Chavali Bangaramma. HotL, *tr. by* V. Narayana Rao

Hic Finis Rapto 1. Julia A. Moore. STuOW *Fr.* John Robinson.

Hic Finis Rapto 2. Julia A. Moore. STuOW *Fr.* William House and Family.

Hic Finis Rapto 3. Julia A. Moore. STuOW *Fr.* Little Henry.

Hic Finis Rapto 4. Julia A. Moore. STuOW *Fr.* Carrie Monro.

Hic Finis Rapto 5. Julia A. Moore. STuOW *Fr.* Maryette Myers.

Hic Finis Rapto 6. Julia A. Moore. STuOW *Fr.* Little Libbie.

Hic Jacet. Rosamund Marriott Watson. ViWPN

Hiccups. Léon Damas. PFTM-1, *tr. by* Ellen Conroy Kennedy

Hickamore hackamore. Riddle. *Unknown.* FaBoVe

Hickie, The. Liz Lochhead. LW; MoWP

Hid by the august foliage and fruit of the grape vine. To a Chameleon. Marianne Moore. APT-1; NoP-5

Hid! Hid! *Unknown.* CCL1 *Fr.* Guan-ju.

"Hid! Hid!" the fish-hawk saith [fr. *the Chinese of the* Confucian Odes]. Ezra Pound. APSN

"Hid! Hid!" the fish-hawk saith. *Unknown.* CCL1 *Fr.* Guan-ju.

Hid in a close and lowly nook. City Garden, A. William Stanley Braithwaite. GT

Hidden. Ron Silliman.

"Lucky my ears 'pop' at the hilltop." FTOS

Hidden behind a rustic gate. To My Cousin, Ching-yuan, Twelfth Month, 403. T'ao Ch'ien. CrYelRi, *tr. by* Sam Hamill

Hidden by a minstrel-smile. (LL) Heritage. Gwendolyn B. Bennett. ColAP; NAAPv.2

Hidden Essence. Henrietta Cordelia Ray. CBWP-3

Hidden Flame. John Dryden. OBEV

Hidden ground. Daphne Marlatt. NLPA *Fr.* Touch to My Tongue.

Hidden in a mother-of-pearl drawer. Legend. Anne Ethuin. SurWo, *tr. by* Guy Ducornet

Hidden in and under separate skin we make for each other though. (LL) Daphne Marlatt. BrAP; NLPA *Fr.* Touch to My Tongue.

Hidden in hidden rooms. Hide and Seek. Mudrooroo Narogin. BMAP

Hidden in the clouds. Oyake. ArkPo, *tr. by* Edwin A. Cranston

Hidden in wonder and snow, or sudden with summer. Laurentian Shield. Francis Reginald Scott. BrAP

Hidden language, not that of hands or eyes, a language beyond gesture. Desert, The. Edmond Jabès. AF, *tr. by* Rosmarie Waldrop

Hidden Meaning. Susan Musgrave. NIL-7

Hidden Name. Victor Segalen. BBASP, *tr. by* Nathaniel Tarn

Hidden, oh hidden. Song for the Rainy Season. Elizabeth Bishop. APT-2

Hidden Path, The. Chông Hwajin. EcSo, *tr. by* Julie C. Park

Hidden Pleasure. Fanny Carrión de Fierro. TANSG, *tr. by* Sally Cheney Bell

Hidden Tears. Wei Chuang. CCL1, *tr. by* Lois Fusek

Hidden-in-winter. *Unknown.* ArkPo, *tr. by* Edwin A. Cranston

Hide. Caitríona O'Reilly. NIrP

Hide, Absalom, thy gilte tresses clear. Geoffrey Chaucer. WoPoe *Fr.* Legend of Good Women, The.

Hide and Seek. Robert Graves. NTCP

Hide and Seek. Mudrooroo Narogin. BMAP

Hide and Seek. Vernon Scannell. NOxBChV

Hide [*or* Hyd], Absalon, thy gilte tresses clere. Geoffrey Chaucer. OBEV *Fr.* Legend of Good Women, The.

Hide your daughters, lock your doors! (LL) We Are Americans Now, We Live in the Tundra. Marilyn Chin. FiBr; NIL-7; OPRER; UnSA

Hideho Heights. Melvin B. Tolson. APT-2; NAMCP V.1; OxBoAm; PFTM-1 *Fr.* Harlem Gallery.

Hideho Heights, / a black Gigas. Melvin B. Tolson. NAMCP V.1 *Fr.* Harlem Gallery.

Hide-n-Seek. Scott Bailey. BeDoSh

Hideous hue which William is, The. Purple William or The Liar's Doom. A. E. Housman. NOxBChV

Hideous laughter, The. Because the Wind Remembers. Frank Mkalawile Chipasula. HBAPE

Hides. Diane Glancy. FTtHH

Hiding. Dorothy Aldis. ChAP

Hiding in a remote and quiet temple. Studying in the Temple. Daegak Euchon. BecRai, *tr. by* Kim Daljin, Kim Won-Chung and Christopher Merrill

Hiding in the. Vidya. EaWin, *tr. by* J. Moussaieff Masson and W. S. Merwin

Hiding Place. Richard Armour. NIL-7; NIP-4

Hiding Place, The. Jorie Graham. WaAnP

Hiding under the hill. Garden, The. Harriet Monroe. IllVoic

Hie Away, Hie Away. Sir Walter Scott. OxAEP-2 *Fr.* Waverley.

Hiedra. Elsa Cross. RMCMP

Hielo. Mónica Nepote. SPV

Hiems. William Shakespeare. *See* Winter: "When icicles hang by the wall."

Hierofant. Oswald de Andrade. TCLAP, *tr. by* Flavia Vidal

Hierusalem. *Unknown.* SacPr

(New Jerusalem, The.) OBEV

Hierusalem, my happy [*or* happie] home. Hierusalem. *Unknown.* SacPr

Hies him to bed. (LL) Winter's Day, A. Joanna Baillie. NAEL-7v2; WoRP

Higgledy-piggledy / Mme. de Maintenon. Firmness. Anthony Hecht. AmWit

Higgledy-piggledy. Emily Dickinson. Wendy Cope. NIL-7

Higgledy-piggledy / Anna Karenina. Russian Soul II, The. John Hollander. NBLV

Higgledy-piggledy / Archangel Raphael. Paradise Lost, Book V: An Epitome. Anthony Hecht. NBLV

Higgledy-piggledy / Benjamin Harrison. Historical Reflections. John Hollander. OBCoV

Higgledy-piggledy / Franklin D. Roosevelt. Danish Wit. John Hollander. NBLV

Higgledy-piggledy / Gustav von Aschenbach. Down There on a Visit. Anthony Hecht. AmWit

Higgledy-piggledy / Heliogabalus. Heliogabalus. John Hollander. NBLV

Higgledy-piggledy / Jacqueline Kennedy. Neo-Classic. James Merrill. AmWit

Higgledy-piggledy / John Simon Guggenheim. No Foundation. John Hollander. OBCoV

Higgledy-piggledy / Judas Iscariot. Handicap. Anthony Hecht. AmWit

Higgledy-piggledy / Ludwig van Beethoven. Double Dactyls. E. William Seaman. OBCoV; WeW-3

Higgledy-piggledy / Mary of Magdala. Above All That? James Merrill. AmWit

Higgledy-piggledy / President Jefferson. Twilight's Last Gleaming. Arthur W. Monks. NIP-4

Higgledy-piggledy / Ralph Waldo Emerson. From the Grove Press. Anthony Hecht. AmWit; OBCoV

Higgledy-Piggledy / Thomas Stearns Eliot. Double Dactyl. Chris Wallace-Crabbe. OBCoV

Higglety, Pigglety, Pop! Samuel Griswold Goodrich. NOxBChV

High. Philip Lamantia. CalPo

High above the lake a bomber flies. This Summer's Sky. Bertolt Brecht. PoSu, *tr. by* Michael Hamburger

High above themselves. Above everything, flux, ooze. Hayden Carruth. StAl *Fr.* Paragraphs.

High above you some fool. In the Aviary. Gerald Costanzo. UrbNat

High Adventure. A. W. Spalding. ITBLP

High Altitude Photo of Hiroshima (Circa 1944). Kent Johnson. AtGh

High and Dry. Justin Quinn. NIrP

High and solemn mountains guard Rioupéroux. Rioupéroux. James Elroy Flecker. OBEV

High as a star, yet lowly as a flower. Beauty. Madison Cawein. APN-2

High as the sky it flies. Riddle. *Unknown.* FaBoVe

High at the window in her cage. Caged Bird, A. Sarah Orne Jewett. APN-2; ColAP; NAAPv.1

High autumn days. Sad Birds, The. Harry Mathews. PmAP

High bare field, brown from the plough, and borne, A. Potato Harvest, The. Sir Charles G. D. Roberts. BrAP; NIL-7

High ceilinged and the double mirrors, the. Gary Snyder. CAP-8

High Cliffs lashed by icy polar winds. Aleutian Islands. Blaise Cendrars. BLT, *tr. by* Monique Chefdor

High Country. Tim Thorne. BMAP

High cries were felled and a pure change happened. (LL) Seamus Heaney. InoFa; NoP-5; PNI *Fr.* Clearances.

High diddle diddle. Mother Goose. NPeEn

High dome, The. Seamen's Mission. Gerald Dawe. PNI

High, dry eminence, Gran Quivera, A. It Is Not Golgotha—It Is. Judson Crews. ICANM

High Embrace, The. William Everson. GeoHom

High, far, within the allotted density. Veronica, a Double Life. Kim Chôngnan. EcSo, *tr. by* Peter H. Lee

High Fidelity. Thom Gunn. PoA 2002

High-Five for I-5, A. Lawson Fusao Inada. WANABP

High Flight. John Gillespie, Jr. Magee. ITBLP; OtW; PoWW

High Germany. Edward Richard Burton Shanks. OBMV

High hard one—up, The. Chin Music. Alan Soldofsky. MoASP

High Heels. Ron Padgett. NYP2

High heels fought a battle with long skirts. Without Guile. Paul Verlaine. SxFrPo, *tr. by* Martin Sorrell

High high azure peaks—a bundle of brush tips. On the River on a Spring Day. Yi Illo. CATKP, *tr. by* Peter H. Lee

High Hills, The. Ivor Gurney. NPeEn

High, hollowed in green. Quest, The. Denise Levertov. LW

High Holy Days. Jane Shore. NoP-4; NoP-5

High in the air exposed the slave is hung. Robert Southey. CenSon *Fr.* Poems Concerning the Slave Trade.

High in the clouds on this gray day. Hawk over Inwood Road, A. A. C. Greene. TiP2

High in the darkening heavens. Harriet Tubman aka Moses. Samuel Allen. ISC

High in the inner regions of my body. Woman in Heat Wiping Herself, A. Sharon Olds. CAP-8

High in the mountain mist, a world apart. English, The. Sándor Sík. IQMS, *tr. by* James Turner

High in the mountains. Magic City Monastery. Wang Yang-ming. CrYelRi, *tr. by* Sam Hamill

High is the dark clouds. Caught in the Swamp. Joseph Ceravolo. BodElec; NYP2

High King of Glory permit her to get the mange, The. (LL) Glass of Beer, A. James Stephens. NBLV; OBCoV; OBMV; OxBEV

High Modes: Vision as Ritual: Confirmation. Michael S. Harper. FuFl

High mountain, A. Poem on Dry Mountain (A Zen Garden). Muso Soseki. EaWin, *tr. by* W. S. Merwin

High mountains, a million feet, skyward. Sailing Back to the Capital. Chan Fang-sheng. ChinPo, *tr. by* Ye Weilian *or* Wai-lim Yip]

High Noon. Li Shang-yin. CCL1, *tr. by* James J. Y. Liu

High Noon. John Wieners. AHA

High Noon at Los Alamos. Eleanor Wilner. AtGh; NoP-4; NoP-5

High noon in Daghestan; a lonely valley. Dream. Mikhail Yuryevich Lermontov. WoPoe, *tr. by* W. K. Matthews

High on a mountain's highest ridge. William Wordsworth. STuOW *Fr.* Thorn, The.

High on a rock, coeval with the skies. Temple of Chastity, The. Mary Robinson. CenSon; RWP

High on a rock, coëval with the skies. Mary Robinson. NPBRoP; STuOW *Fr.* Sappho and Phaon.

High on a slope in New Guinea. Man in the Dead Machine, The. Donald Hall. OtW

High on a Throne of Royal State, which far. John Milton. NAEL-6v1; OxAEP-1 *Fr.* Paradise Lost.

High on, above the lake, the mute Nowgorod. Invocation. Johannes Bobrowski. GTCP, *tr. by* Reinhold Grimm

High on his stockroom ladder like a dunce. Playboy. Richard Wilbur. CAP-8; NAMCP V.2; NoAM

High on the Mount of Rama a yaksha dwelt, who for. Kalidasa. WoPoe *Fr.* Cloud Messenger, The.

High on tree-tips, the hibiscus. Hsin-I Village. Wang Wei. ChinPo, *tr. by* Ye Weilian [*or* Yeh Wei-lien *or* Wai-lim Yip]

High ones die, die, The. They die. You look up and who's there? John Berryman. PoA 2002 *Fr.* Four Dream Songs.

High pink wall; plaster in map shapes peeling, A. Blue Arm. Bernard Spencer. NoAM

High plane for whom the winds incline. Airman's Virtue. William Meredith. WaAnP

High propositions of barrenness. Creation. Eunice Odio. TCLAP, *tr. by* Martha Collins

High Renaissance. George Starbuck. AmWit; NBLV

High rolling cycler! pilgrim of the land. Highroller. Mary F. Nixon-Roulet. ArBi

High School. Toi Derricotte. BtF

High School Band, The. Reed Whittemore. P180

High Speed. Debra Gregerman. AmPoNex

High stretched upon the swinging yard. Disguises. Thomas Edward Brown. SacPr

High Talk. William Butler Yeats. FaBoVe; RaBo

High tensile wire, when strained. Fencing. Anthony Lawrence. NOBAu

High the Mount of Wu. Li Ho. ChinPo, *tr. by* Ye Weilian [*or* Yeh Wei-lien *or* Wai-lim Yip]

High Tide. Jean Starr Untermeyer. MoAmPo

High Tide at Gettysburg, The. Will Henry Thompson. CBCWP

High Tide on the Coast of Lincolnshire, 1571, The. Jean Ingelow. OxAEP-2

High to Low. Langston Hughes. APT-2; PoPoPo

High Treason. José Emilio Pacheco. TCLAP, *tr. by* Alastair Reid

High up here I live. My Room. Marceline Desbordes-Valmore. WoPoe, *tr. by* Edmund Charles Blunden

High Up the Thunder Gods, Downstairs the Hunger. Andrew Schelling. AmZen

High up there she saw what. Stuff. Linda Gregg. ExTi

High Water Everywhere. Charlie Patton. APT-1

High waving heather'neath stormy blasts bending. Emily Jane Brontë. PEW

High Way to the Spital House, The (Hye Way to the Spyttell Hous, The). Robert Copland.
    "To write of Sol in his exaltation." NoSic

High wind. . .They turn their backs to it, and push. Glasgow Schoolboys, Running Backwards. Douglas Dunn. BeAl; RSaN

High wind, cold moon. Shokaku. ZenPo, *tr. by* Takashi Ikemoto and Lucien Stryk

High Windows. Philip Larkin. HarvBoo; NAEL-6v2; NAEL-7v2; NAMCP V.2; NoAM; PoetW; PoPoPo

High Wood. Philip Johnstone. FaBoWar

High / yellow / black / girl. To Anita. Sonia Sanchez. ISC

High, yellow, coiled and weighting the branch like an odd piece of fruit, a snake slept. St. Louis Zoo, The. Carol Frost. CAP-8

High-born Helen, round your dwelling. Helen. Mary Lamb. NOBRP

High-Class Bananas, The. Gary Gildner. PBCAP

Higher Argument. John Milton. NOSC

Higher Empiricism, The. Francis C. Golffing. PoA 2002

Higher Living Away from the World. Hamhur Kiwha. BecRai, *tr. by* Kim Daljin, Kim Won-Chung and Christopher Merrill

Higher Pantheism in a Nutshell, The. Algernon Charles Swinburne. CABP *Fr.* Heptalogia, The.

Higher Pantheism, The. Alfred Tennyson. CABP; InvLi

Highest Bidder, The. Witter Bynner. TCAPo

Highest things are easiest to be shown, The. Demonstration, The. Thomas Traherne. BASC

Highflown: Love. Eugene B. Redmond. OxAAAP

High-hearted Surrey! I do love your ways. Salutation, A. Louise Imogen Guiney. APN-2

High-heeled shoes. Red High-heeled Shoes. Mihangel Morgan. BBMWP, *tr. by* Martin Davis

High-heels were struggling with a full-length dress. Young Fools, The. Paul Verlaine. WoPoe, *tr. by* Louis Simpson

Highland, 1955. Kevin Fitzpatrick. MiVo

Highland Glen near Loch Ericht, A.   Arthur Hugh Clough.   FaBoVe *Fr.* Bothie of Tober-na-Vuolich, The [A Long-Vacation Pastoral].

Highland Graveyard.   Kathleen Jessie Raine.   EdScPo *Fr.* Eileann Chanaidh.

Highland Mary.   Robert Burns.   NPBRoP; OBEV

Highland Mary.   Mary Weston Fordham.   CBWP-2

Highland Poor, The.   Anne Grant.   RWP *Fr.* Highlanders, The.

Highland Woman, A.   Sorley MacLean.   HarvBoo; NePenScot

Highlanders, The.   Anne Grant.
  Part 2.
    Highland Poor, The.   RWP

Highmindedness, a jealousy for good.   Addressed to Haydon.   John Keats.   CenSon

Highroller.   Mary F. Nixon-Roulet.   ArBi

High-Toned Old Christian Woman, A.   Wallace Stevens.   NAAL-5; NAAPv.2; NoAM; OxBoAm

Highway.   Glenna Luschei.   ICANM

Highway 6.   Timothy Liu.   AmPoNex

Highway Commissioner dreams of us, The.   From His Bed in the Capital City.   David Berman.   LegDan

Highway 5.   Fleda Brown Jackson.   PoDa

Highway I was walking on, The.   Charles Reznikoff.   FTOS *Fr.* By the Well of Living and Seeing.

Highway is full of big cars, The.   Come, and Be My Baby.   Maya Angelou.   OPOU

Highway is narrow, the curves dangerous, The.   Passing Piedras Blancas.   Abigail Albrecht.   GeoHom

Highway Poems.   Lisel Mueller.   IllVoic

Highway, The.   Pak Sôwôn.   EcSo, *tr. by* Julie C. Park

Highway, The.   Edwin John Pratt.   BrAP

Highway, The.   Sir Philip Sidney.   OBEV; OxAEP-1

Highwayman, The.   Alfred Noyes.   BRP; ChAP; ITBLP; NOxBChV; OBNV; OBSP

Highwaymen, The.   Maxine W. Kumin.   CAP-8

Highways of Antarctica blow constantly, The.   Octans the Octant.   Alan Robert Wilson.   Coast

Hijos de la Tierra.   Blas de Otero.   RaW

Hijrah [Migration] to God, The.   Nazik al-Mala'ika.   IrPoTo, *tr. by* Jenna Abdul Rahman and Saleh Alyafai

Hike on the Downs, A.   Sir John Betjeman.   OBCoV

Hike to the top of Vernal Falls.   Norman Fischer.   WANABP *Fr.* Success.

Hiking a levee through the salt marsh.   Wings and Seeds: For My Birth Mother.   Sandra McPherson.   LoL; PoA 2002

Hilbert's Program.   Milo De Angelis.   NeIt, *tr. by* Lawrence Venuti

Hildegard of Bingen.   Litany for the Living.   Maura Eichner.   UpMys

Hill, A.   Anthony Hecht.   NAMCP V.2; NIL-7; NoP-4; NoP-5; OxBoAm; VCAP

Hill, The.   Rupert Brooke.   BLPJKO; MoBrPo; OxBSo

Hill, The.   Robert Creeley.   BrAP; RaBo; TRP

Hill, The.   Edgar Lee Masters.   ColAP; IllVoic; NAMCP V.1; NoAM; OxBoAm *Fr.* Spoon River Anthology.

Hill beside the wood had dressed in green, The.   After the Battle.   Anton Malczewski.   WoPoe, *tr. by* Jerzy Peterkiewicz and Burns Singer

Hill County Rest Home.   Carol Coffee Reposa.   TiP2

Hill Farmer Speaks, The.   Ronald Stuart Thomas.   OBWVE

Hill Field, The.   Donald Davie.   NPeEn

Hill Figures.   Maggie O'Sullivan.   Oth

Hill Fort, Caerleon.   Sam Adams.   AngWePo

Hill of Huazi, The.   Pei Di and Wang Wei.   CCL1 *Fr.* Wheel River.

Hill of the Hatchet-Leaved Bamboos.   Pei Di and Wang Wei.   CCL1 *Fr.* Wheel River.

Hill of Truth, The.   John Donne.   OBSV *Fr.* Satires.

Hill Songs of Saint Orm, The.   B. P. Nichol.   PFTM-2 *Fr.* Martyrology 7, The.

70: The Hill Summit.   Dante Gabriel Rossetti.   NoP-4; NoP-5 *Fr.* House of Life, The.

Hill Wife, The.   Robert Frost.   NoP-4; NoP-5; RACG
  Impulse, The.   RaBo; TCAPo
  Oft-Repeated Dream, The.   TCAPo

Hill-billy, hill-billy come to buy.   *Unknown.*   OBVE *Fr.* Wei Wind.

Hillcrest.   Edwin Arlington Robinson.   APT-1

Hills, The.   Frances Darwin Cornford.   MoBrPo

Hills, The.   D. H. Lawrence.   ChIV-1

Hills, The: "Unrepeatable, ever-present mirage."   Ivan Teofilov.   CSCBP, *tr. by* Georgi Belev and Lisa Sapinkopf

Hills all glowed with a festive light, The.   Illuminated City, The.   Felicia Dorothea Hemans.   RWP

Hills and leafless forests slowly yield, The.   In November.   Archibald Lampman.   NIL-7

Hills and mountains come into view.   *Unknown.*   CCL1 *Fr.* Travels of Mu, Son of Heaven, The.

Hills are white with snow, The.   Lament.   Cho Wen-chun.   CrYelRi, *tr. by* Sam Hamill

Hills are wroth; the stones have scored you bitterly, The.   To a Young Girl Leaving the Hill Country.   Arna Bontemps.   GT

Hills fled from our sight; but left his golden load. (LL)   To Autumn.   William Blake.   NAEL-6v2; NAEL-7v2

Hills in emerald robes of richest dye, The.   Among the Berkshire Hills.   Henrietta Cordelia Ray.   CBWP-3

Hills lie quilted in snow.   First Thaw.   Tessa Ransford.   EdScPo

Hills lie, The.   Winter Night, Glencoe.   Anne B. Murray.   CFP

Hills like burnt pages, The.   Or Anything Resembling It.   Michael Palmer.   BodElec; CAP-8; WoBe

Hills of buttercups.   Steve Sanfield.   WhBo

Hills of Cualann, The.   Joseph Campbell.   IrV

Hills sink to plains, and man returns to dust.   Philip Freneau.   TCAPo *Fr.* House of Night, The.

Hills slide eastward into the desert, The.   Mount of Olives, The.   Shirley Kaufman.   DTA

Hills' soothing American voice muscle.   Horseshoe.   Merrill Gilfillan.   AHA

Hills step off into whiteness, The.   Sheep in Fog.   Sylvia Plath.   NPeEn

Hills, the bridge, the country, the squeaking wheelbarrow, The.   Bobbin Stops, The.   István Sinka.   IQMS, *tr. by* Adam Makkai

Hills turn hugely in their sleep, The.   Robert Silliman Hillyer.   MoAmPo *Fr.* Prothalamion.

Hills were lush, The.   Monterey.   David Schubert.   APT-2

Hills where I grew up had learned to hide, The.   Hughesville Scythe, The.   Henry Taylor.   LPSFW

Hill-Shade, The.   William Barnes.   OxBEV

Hill-Side Park, The.   W. H. Davies.   OBGa

Hillside Thaw, A.   Robert Frost.   AmFaPo

Hill-track, The.   Kathleen Jamie.   MoWP; NeBrP

Hilly Pavlovsk still I can see before me.   Pavlovsk.   Anna Andreyevna Akhmatova.   RusPo, *tr. by* Robert Arthur Douglas Ford

Hilo: First Night Back.   Garrett Kaoru Hongo.   LoL

Hilversum, Kalundborg, Brno, the loud world over.   Louis Aragon.   RWPCtW *Fr.* Little Suite for Loudspeaker.

Him.   Charles Wright.   CAP-8; WaAnP

Him again, the bard of bards, bard of the boards, he of the company and crew.   Shakespeare's Wages.   Marvin Bell.   IaFF

Him back up. "Isn't he awful?" she said. (LL)   Portrait from the Infantry.   Alan Dugan.   AF; AmWaPo; PWW2

Him, His Place.   Liam Rector.   BodElec

Him I'm thinking of.   *Unknown.*   ChinPo, *tr. by* Ye Weilian [*or* Yeh Wei-lien *or* Wai-lim Yip]

Him, on the Bicycle.   Bruce Weigl.   AmAlph

Him strong Genius urged to roam.   Ralph Waldo Emerson.   TCAPo *Fr.* Life.

Him the way we leave a porchlight on.   She Wants.   David Baratier.   AmPoNex

Himalayan Balsam.   Anne Stevenson.   OxAEP-2

Himare—black town.   Exiles.   *Unknown.*   SonAtl, *tr. by* Rita Kelly and Michael Portas

Himself.   Edwin John Ellis.
  "At Golgotha I stood alone."   OBMV

Himself.   Peter Fallon.   PBCIP

Himself it was who wrote.   Astræa.   Ralph Waldo Emerson.   APN-1

Himself with gas before he drills / archy. (LL)   Don Marquis.   AmWit; NBLV *Fr.* Archy and Mehitabel.

Hind and the Panther, The.   John Dryden.
  Churches of Rome and of England, The.   UV
  "Portly prince, and goodly to the sight, A."   OBSV
  Presbyterians, The.   NOSC

Hind of Morning, The.   George Campbell Hay.   EdScPo

Hindu to His Body, A.   A. K. Ramanujan.   PoetW

Hinglish.   Gerald Stern.   BodElec

Hinny / by / stallion, An.   Louis Zukofsky.   APSN *Fr.* A.

Hint of gold where the moon will be, A.   Want of You, The.   Angelina Weld Grimké.   NAAPv.2

Hinterland.   Margaret Stanley-Wrench.   OBGa

Hints.   Giancarlo Majorino.   ItPo, *tr. by* Gayle Ridinger

Hints at Distance.   Michael Portnoy.   HeMarv

Hip Hop Bop.   Jabari Asim.   InTrad

Hipotético espectador, El.   Coral Bracho.   RMCMP

Hippolytus Temporizes.   "H. D."   APT-1; HarvBoo; RACG

Hippopotamus.   Joanna Cole.   NTCP

Hippopotamus, The.   T. S. Eliot.   NAEL-6v2; OBMV; SacPr; TCAPo

Hir bowgy cheekes been as softe as clay.   Description of His Ugly Lady, A.   Thomas Hoccleve.   WaAnP

Hiraeth.   *Unknown*.   OBWVE, *tr. by* Aneirin Talfan Davies

Hiram Helsel.   Julia A. Moore.   VerBaPo

Hiram, I think the sump is backing up.   Mending Sump.   Kenneth Koch.   NAMCP V.2; NoAM; VisFro

Hiram Powers' "Greek Slave."   Elizabeth Barrett Browning.   GS; NALW; ViWPN

Hired Hand.   David Lee.   GifTon

Hirmophrodite in sense in Art a monster.   Railing Rimes Returned upon the Author by Mistress Mary Wrothe.   Mary Sidney Wroth, Countess of Montgomery.   EMWP

Hiroshima.   "Agyeya."   WoPoe, *tr. by* Agyeya *and* Leonard Nathan *and* Leonard Nathan

Hiroshima.   Marie Luise Kaschnitz.   GTCP, *tr. by* Lisel Mueller

Hiroshima Day at the Riviera Coffeeshop.   Andrea Collins.   AtGh

Hiroshima Maiden.   Lee Ann Roripaugh.   AmWaPo

Hirsute hell chimney-spouts, black thunderthroes.   To My First White Hairs.   Wole Soyinka.   OPOU

His.   Martha Rhodes.   LaCa

His absence is the knife that cuts your throat?   Abu Sa'id Abul Khayr.   WoPoe *Fr.* Four Poems on Death.

His acre. His arbour.   Alan Halsey.   Oth *Fr.* Robin Hood Book, A.

His all the mercy and the power. (LL)   Herman Melville.   APN-2; ChIV-1 *Fr.* Moby Dick.

His alliance was fragmented.   Petition for Langston Hughes, A.   Clarence Major.   EGAG

His Answer.   Clara Ann Thompson.   CBWP-2

His Anthem, to Christ on the Cross.   Robert Herrick.   CavPo

His arm grew heavy on me as he slept, the oaks'.   California Poem.   Chryss Yost.   GeoHom

His arrow was huge beyond compare.   *Various authors*.   CATKP *Fr.* Songs of Flying Dragons.

His art is eccentricity, his aim.   Pitcher, The.   Robert Francis.   MoASP; RaBo; WeW-3

His Ashes.   Sharon Olds.   InoFa

His attractive face a bit pale.   In the Street.   Constantine P. Cavafy.   CAGL, *tr. by* Edmund Keeley and Philip Sherrard

His back and clavicles are draped.   Antonio Banderas in His Underwear.   Regie Cabico.   WiU

His ball, beautiful leaved, and his noisy boxwood rattle.   Leonidas of Tarentum.   HePo, *tr. by* Barbara Hughes Fowler

His Ballad of Agincourt.   Michael Drayton.   WaAnP

His balls: it sure was pleasant to spend a day in the country. (LL)   Farm Implements and Rutabagas in a Landscape.   John Ashbery.   HarvBoo; NAMCP V.2; PmAP; WaAnP

His bare feet warmed by the thick black dust.   Shelly Beach.   Christopher Koch.   NOBAu

His beak could open a bottle.   Little Owl Who Lives in the Orchard.   Mary Oliver.   CAP-8

His best / were the two.   My Father's Fights.   Stuart Dybek.   PBCAP

His bicycle stood at the window-sill.   Seamus Heaney.   ArBi; EmeKit *Fr.* Singing School.

His blood will not be traced while I live. (LL)   Hallaig.   Sorley MacLean.   EdScPo; HarvBoo; NePenScot; NPeEn; WoPoe

His bodie was as straight as Circes wand.   Christopher Marlowe.   NPeEn; OxBEV *Fr.* Hero and Leander.

His Body.   Sandra McPherson.   LoL

His Body: a perfect shock absorber. (LL)   Passage.   Billy Marshall-Stoneking.   BMAP; NOBAu

His body doubled.   On the Swag.   Ronald Allison Kells Mason.   SacPr

His body is credits rising because.   As Western Culture Declined Without Its Knowing.   Steve Healey.   LegDan

His body washed up on the sands.   Ten Ways of Looking at P.B. Shelley.   Hugo Claus.   LWR, *tr. by* John M. Coetzee

His Books.   Robert Southey.   OBEV

His bride to the fair island. (LL)   Enchanted Island, The.   Letitia Elizabeth Landon.   CABP; NOBRP

His changing eyes. (LL)   Cat and the Moon, The.   William Butler Yeats.   CtM; HarvBoo; WHSW

His children are not there. (LL)   Footnote to the Amnesty Report on Torture.   Margaret Atwood.   NAMCP V.2; NoAM

His children tuckered out, tucked in (three girls).   Frost at Midnight.   Mary Jo Salter.   RA; VisFro

His clumsy body is a golden fruit.   Deaf-Mute in the Pear Tree.   Patricia K. Page.   NAMCP V.2; NoAM; NoP-4; NoP-5

His Confession.   The Archpoet.   NAWM-7v1, *tr. by* Helen Waddell

His conscience may remain unriven. (LL)   To His Importunate Mistress.   Peter De Vries.   NBLV; NIL-7; NIP-4

His Content in the Country.   Robert Herrick.   CavPo

His corpse owre a' the city lies.   Dead Liebknecht, The.   Hugh MacDiarmid.   OBVE

His Costume.   Sharon Olds.   BAP-01

His cycle kerbed, the peeler found.   Roy McFadden.   PNI *Fr.* Memories of Chinatown.

His daughter saw him first, hanging.   Coach in Effigy.   Jack Ridl.   LiTh

His daughter, / the visionary warrior, the silent man.   His Daughter.   Ursula K. Le Guin.   FiBr

His Dawn Vision.   Seamus Heaney.   PoetW

His day was not really complete until.   Letters from Baron Von Hügel to a Niece.   David Scott.   NLP

His Defence against the Idle Critic.   Michael Drayton.   NOSC

His dinner on the stove, Grandpa smirked at our jar.   Leftover Blessings.   Julia Kasdorf.   PBCAP

His drinking was different in sunshine.   Asked for a Happy Memory of Her Father, She Recalls Wrigley Field.   Beth Ann Fennelly.   RWB

His endeavors were disagreements.   Popeye's Last Words.   Tom Ahern.   OnScMo

His endless look. (LL)   This Lunar Beauty.   W. H. Auden.   MoBrPo; NAMCP V.1; NPeEn; OBMV

His Excuse for Loving.   Ben Jonson.   NAEL-7v1; NOSC; PtR *Fr.* Celebration of Charis in Ten Lyric[k] Pieces [or Peeces], A.

His Eye Is on the Sparrow.   C. D. Martin.   TCAPo

His eyes are mournful, but the long lined palm.   Creatures in the Zoo.   Babette Deutsch.   APT-2

His eyes are quickened so with grief.   Lost Love.   Robert Graves.   MoBrPo

His eyes burned shrewdly as emerging stars. (LL)   Star Watcher, The.   Peter Davison.   WaAnP; YaYoPo

His eyes were so distant.   Georg Trakl.   Else Lasker-Schüler.   PFTM-1

His face is trodden deeper in the mud. (LL)   Glory of Women.   Siegfried Sassoon.   FaBoWar; NAEL-6v2; NAEL-7v2; NoP-4; NoP-5; OBWP; OxAEP-2; OxBSo

His face severe in clouds above the waters of childhood.   Remembering My Father.   Zbigniew Herbert.   VCWP, *tr. by* John Carpenter and Bogdana Carpenter

His Farewell [or Fare-well] to Sack.   Robert Herrick.   NAEL-6v1; NAEL-7v1 (His Farewell to Sack.)   CavPo

His father and grandfather before him were coachmen.   Birth of a Coachman.   Paul Durcan.   PBCIP

His father answered: "Son, you are a Maury."   Albery Allson Whitman.   NAAPv.1 *Fr.* Octoroon, The.

His father did intend that Harry should.   John L. Thomas.   AngWePo *Fr.* Harry Vaughan.

His father gave him a box of truisms.   Truisms, The.   Louis MacNeice.   OBSV; PNI

His Father, Singing.   Leslie Norris.   TCAWP

His father's steel, piercing the wholesome fruit.   King Honour's Eldest Son.   Elinor Wylie.   SacPr

His Favourite Seat.   Deborah Randall.   NeBl

His Feet are shod with Gauze.   Emily Dickinson.   IPoFL; SAmP

His fingers are caterpillars balanced.   Blue Movies.   Maurya Simon.   GifTon

His fingers leaned.   Sun House.   Haki R. Madhubuti.   ESEAA

His Fingers Seem to Sing.   Sam Cornish.   GT

His fingers wake, and flutter; up the bed.   Conscious.   Wilfred Owen.   PoWW

His first bullet is a present, a mark of intelligence that will.   Knee, The.   Ciaran Carson.   PNI

His fists beating time. Then the hands giving way. (LL)   It's Only Rock and Roll but I Like It: The Fall of Saigon, 1975.   David Wojahn.   IllVoic; ReTh

His flames ar[e] joy[e]s, his bands true lovers' might. (LL)   Mary Sidney Wroth, Countess of Montgomery.   BASC; EMWP; NoP-5 *Fr.* Pamphilia to Amphilanthus.

His flames ar[e] joy[e]s, his bands true lovers' might.   Mary Sidney Wroth, Countess of Montgomery.   BASC *Fr.* Pamphilia to Amphilanthus.

His Flute, My Ears.   Gregory Scofield.   IFF

His footprints have failed us.   Dead in the Sierras.   Joaquin Miller.   CalPo

His frame slighter than friends remember. (LL)   David Walker (1785–1830).   Rita Dove.   OxAAAP; WaAnP

His Friend's Last Battle.   Theodore Nicholl.   AngWePo

His gaze has been so worn by the procession.   Panther, The.   Rainer Maria Rilke.   GTCP, *tr. by* Walter Arndt

His glory and his monuments are gone. (LL)   Meru.   William Butler Yeats.   GSo; NAMCP V.1; NoAM; OxBSo; PoPoPo

His golden ear-loops cover.   Calm in the Vegetable Beard of Time.   Hoa Nguyen.   WANABP

His golden locks time hath to silver turned [or turn'd].   George Peele.   NIP-4; NoP-4; NoP-5; NPeEn; OxBEV; TFi *Fr.* Polyhymnia.

His Grace! impossible! what dead! Satirical Elegy on the Death of a Late Famous General, A. Jonathan Swift. NBLV; NPeEn; OBSV; WaAnP

His grace is no longer called for. Missing God. Dennis O'Driscoll. BeAl

His Grange, or Private Wealth. Robert Herrick. BASC; CavPo

His guitar has a severed neck. Blues for Elliot Sharp. Ronny Someck. IrPoTo, *tr.* by Vivian Eden

His Hair. Mirabai. WED, *tr.* by Robert Bly

His hair was a crow fished out of a blocked chimney. Not the Furniture Game. Simon Armitage. BeAl

His hand came out of the east. Homer. OBVE *Fr.* Iliad, The.

His hands were moving like twin engines. Traveling Gospel. Cynthia Cruz. IAoNAP

His head appeared in the hand. Orpheus. John Kinsella. BMAP

His heart, synchronized with my steps. Portrait, A. Eman Mersaal. AnVo, *tr.* by Mohamed Enani

His heart, to me, was a place of palaces and pinnacles and shining towers. I Have Been through the Gates. Charlotte Mew. MoBrPo

His heart to the darkness and into the sadness of joy. (LL) First Song. Galway Kinnell. NAMCP V.2; NoP-4; NoP-5

His heart was in his garden; but his brain. Frederick Goddard Tuckerman. APN-2; NoP-4; TCAPo *Fr.* Sonnets: Second Series, 1854–1860.

His holy / slowly. Darwin. Lorine Niedecker. APSN; APT-2

His home address was inked inside his cap. Flood. Tony Harrison. InoFa

His hour being not yet come. (LL) William Wordsworth. NAEL-6v2; NAEL-7v2 *Fr.* Prelude, The; Growth of a Poet's Mind [1850 version].

His howls flow patient and slow. Deserted Angel, The. Anna Hajnal. IQMS, *tr.* by Jeannette Nichols

His Imperial Majesty, a slave to beauty. Everlasting Wrong, The. Po Chü-i. CCL1, *tr.* by H. A. Giles

His job is as regular. (LL) It brightens up into the branches. George Oppen. APT-2; PFTM-1

His journalist. Gaugin. Manuel Vázquez Montalbán. RaW, *tr.* by Robert Mezey

His khaki tie was perfectly knotted in wartime. Making Friends with Ties. Hugo Williams. PML

His kidney floats in a bowl. I Have Got to Stop Loving You. So I Have Killed My Black Goat. Ai. CAP-8

His kingdom is forever. (LL) Mighty Fortress Is Our God, A. Frederic Henry Hedge and Martin Luther. GePo; SacPr

His Lady's Cruelty. Sir Philip Sidney. *See* Sonnet 31: "With how sad steps, O Moon[e], thou climb'st the skies."

His Lamp Near Daybreak. Yannis Ritsos. AWTN, *tr.* by Martin McKinsey

His large ears hear. My Father at 85. Robert Bly. OxBoAm

His last days linger in that low attic. Old Jockey, The. Frederick Robert Higgins. OBMV

His last glimpse of the former wife. After Eden. James Simmons. PNI

His last prayer in the garden began, as most. More Earnest Prayer of Christ, The. Scott Cairns. UpMys

His last white eärms, an' they stood still. (LL) Turnstile, The. William Barnes. NPeEn; OxBEV

His Last Words. Yun Tongju. CAMKP, *tr.* by Kay Richards and Steffen Richards

His laugh. Spell of Blazing Trees, The. Sa'adyya Muffareh. PoArWo, *tr.* by Mona Fayad

His left hand, in heat of noonday. Ann Griffiths. WPoS

His Legs Strong and Lithe. Itaikkunrurkilar. WoPoe, *tr.* by George L. Hart III

His legs were long and thin, his knees bent and feet crossed. Fanny Howe. FaoP *Fr.* Passion, The.

His Letanie, to the Holy Spirit. Robert Herrick. *See* His Litany to the Holy Spirit.

His life, at the end, seemed—even the anguish—simple. Robert Penn Warren. NAAPv.2 *Fr.* Audubon: A Vision.

His life is in the body of the living. Soul and Body of John Brown, The. Muriel Rukeyser. CBCWP; MoAmPo

His life was the practice of forming a single. Stephen Dobyns. PoA 2002

His Litany to the Holy Spirit. Robert Herrick. BASC; NOSC
  (His Letanie, to the Holy Spirit.) SacPr
  (Litany to the Holy Spirit.) OBEV

His little fleet floated in a trio. Columbus. J. Slauerhoff. TuT, *tr.* by Desmond Egan

His little trills and chirpings were his best. Tombstones in the Starlight. Dorothy Parker.

His living name. (LL) Epilogue: "Those blessèd structures, plot and rhyme." Robert Lowell. HarvBoo; NAAL-5; NAMCP V.2; NoAM; NoP-4; NoP-5; OxBoAm; PoetW; PoPoPo; StAl; VCAP; WaAnP

His Long Home. Rosanna Warren. ExTi

His malice was a pimple down his good. John Berryman. NAMCP V.2 *Fr.* Dream Songs.

His merry Companions returned in a Throng. (LL) Butterfly's Ball [and the Grasshopper's Feast], The. William Caldwell Roscoe. NOBRP; OxBEV

His Metrical Prayer. James Graham, Marquess of Montrose. *See* On Himself, upon Hearing What Was His Sentence.

His mind is as high as a mountain. Han-shan (Cold Mountain). ColAnChi, *tr.* by Red Pine

His mind moves upon silence. (LL) Long-Legged Fly. William Butler Yeats. NAEL-6v2; NAEL-7v2; NAMCP V.1; NoAM; NoP-4; NoP-5; NPeEn; WaAnP

His Mistress' Dog. Wentworth Dillon, 4th Earl of Roscommon. DiBP

His mither sings to the bairnie Christ. O Jesu Parvule. Hugh MacDiarmid. EdScPo

His money-making properties come back like a beach. Epilogue. Gig Ryan. VaPo

His morning posture is sketched naked. Painting the Nude. Eric Dyer. BloBone

His mother, a petrol pump attendant, was said by those who knew her. Hard to Place. Elaine Randell. Oth

His Mother Drinks. Edwin Emanuel Bradford. VerBaPo

His mother sets the supper out. Peter De Vries. PoA 2002 *Fr.* Conscript.

His mother wept so bitterly. Mother of Judas, The. Yevgeny Mikhailovich Vinokurov. GI, *tr.* by Anthony Rudolf

His mouth to my mouth. (LL) My Grief on the Sea. Biddy Cussrooee. IrLP; OBEV, *tr.* by Douglas Hyde

His mustache was graying like my father's. For the Man I Met on Georgia Ave. Matthew Watley. BtF

His naked skin clothed in the torrid mist. Serf, The. Roy Campbell. MoBrPo; OBMV

His name is Mister Snow. Mister Snow. Oscar Hammerstein, II. ReLy

His name was / Mohammed Sceab. In Memoriam. Giuseppe Ungaretti. PoCho

His name was Yuba! When Yuba Plays the Rumba on the Tuba. Herman Hupfeld. ReLy

His name— *R. Frost* —write large in bold strokes on the mailbox. Making Love at the Frost Place. Michael Waters. VisFro

His nature being one with Heaven. *Various authors.* CATKP *Fr.* Songs of Flying Dragons.

His new-fangled rifle, his green new steel helmet. (LL) March 1, The. Robert Lowell. AmWaPo; PoetW; PoPoPo

His night job is insomnia. Dissecting Uncle Sorrow. Rick Alley. AmPoNex

His nights in the aunts' house, their talk and tea. Provincial Adolescence, A. Michael Foley. PNI

His nose is short and scrubby. My Dog. Marchette Chute. WHSW

His Offering, with the Rest, at the Sepulcher. Robert Herrick. ChIV-2

His old age fell on years of abundant harvest. Felicitous Life, A. Czeslaw Milosz. PoSu, *tr.* by the author and Lillian Vallee

His original way. Free Old Man. Muso Soseki. EaWin, *tr.* by W. S. Merwin

His pains so racked my heart. Sympathy. Viola Meynell. LW

His paper propped against the electric toaster. Daniel at Breakfast. Phyllis McGinley. OBSV

His parents. Causality and Chance in Love. Karen Press. TSAP

His parents are having tea. Chogyam Trungpa. WhBo

His parents would sit alone together. Dumka, The. B. H. Fairchild. GoPo

His pecker limp, he pats her ass and blindly back to business goes. (LL) Snatch. Lincoln Kirstein. AmWaPo; PWW2

His Pen did once meat from the eater fetch. Excellent Wigglesworth, Remembered by Some Good Tokens, The. Cotton Mather. SacPr

His penis rises before him, a compulsion. He would take hormones if. Barbie's Molester. Denise Duhamel. ReTh

His photograph, yellowed by the years. Big John. Norman J. Loftis. SpirFl

His Picture. John Donne. FSCP; OxAEP-1; PBRV *Fr.* Elegies.

His piercing pince-nez. Some dim frieze. Ted Berrigan. FTOS; NYP2 *Fr.* Sonnets, The.

His Pilgrimage. Sir Walter Ralegh. *See* Passionate Man[']s Pilgrimage, The.

His place, as he sat and as he thought, was not. Quiet Normal Life, A. Wallace Stevens. NAAL-5; NoAM

His Poetry His Pillar. Robert Herrick. NOSC

His Prayer for Absolution. Robert Herrick. SacPr

His Prayer to Ben Jonson. Robert Herrick. BASC; NAEL-6v1; NAEL-7v1; NoP-4; NoP-5; NOSC

His Promise. Aaron Shurin. FTOS

His Request to Julia. Robert Herrick. CavPo; NOSC

His Return to London. Robert Herrick. BASC; NAEL-6v1; NAEL-7v1

His Reward. Sir Thomas Wyatt. NoSic

His roads between the thunder and the sun. (LL) Black Vulture, The. George Sterling. APT-1; ASA; CalPo

His room, His room is a burning aquarium. Aden. J. D. McClatchy. WaAnP

His Rule of Behaviour: If You Are Civil, I Am Sober. James Carkesse. NOSC

His Saviour[']s Words, Going to the Cross[e]. Robert Herrick. ChIV-2; SacPr

His scarlet face lights up the room in which he stands, alone. Internal Travels. Pierre Reverdy. MotU, tr. by Michael Benedikt

His Shield. Marianne Moore. NALW

His shoulder did I hold. Any Saint. Francis Thompson. MoBrPo

His silence in the middle of stones. Chiedu Ezeanah. NeNiPo Fr. Song of Songs.

His simple is. Drive. Maggie Hannan. NeBl

His sins were scarlet, but his books were read. (LL) On His Books. Joseph Hilaire Pierre Belloc. MoBrPo; NBLV; WeW-3

His skin like cream is free of wrinkles. Rosa/Filí. Maria Arillaga. TANSG

His sleeping form. Issa. EMJL, tr. by Haruo Shirane

His Smell. Sharon Olds. MoWP

His snores / protect the sleeping hut. Wife of the Husband. Micere Githae Mugo. HAWP

His solid flesh had never been away. Alienation. Howard Phillips Lovecraft. APT-1

His son! His son! His son! (LL) Rundown Church (Ballad of the First World War). Federico García Lorca. RaBo; WED, tr. by Robert Bly

His Son's / A Jew. Unknown. OBCoV

His sorrow hangs like a heart in the star-flowered boundary tree. Him. Charles Wright. CAP-8; WaAnP

His spirit fled into the gloom below. (LL) Virgil. NAWM-5v1; NAWM-7v1 Fr. Aeneid [or Eneados or Aeneis], The.

His Spirit in smoke ascended to high heaven. Lynching, The. Claude McKay. APT-1; ColAP; GT; InoFa; NAAL-5; NAMCP V.1

(His spirit is smoke ascended to high heaven.) TCAPo

His stars eternally. (LL) Drummer Hodge. Thomas Hardy. BrAP; FaBoWar; HarvBoo; NAEL-6v2; NAEL-7v2; NAMCP V.1; NoAM; NoP-4; NoP-5; OBWP; OxAEP-2; WeW-3

His stature tall, his body long. Denis Florence MacCarthy. IrV

His stature was not very tall. Robert Greene. NoSic Fr. Greene's Vision.

HIS:STORY. Lee Ranaldo. HeMarv

His sullen kinsmen, by the winter sea. Santa Claus. Dom Moraes. NoAM

His sun's arms and grappling. Isaac: a Poise. Peter Cole. ChIV-1

His tale anoon, and saide as ye may heere. (LL) Geoffrey Chaucer. NAEL-6v1; NAEL-7v1; NoP-5; WaAnP Fr. Canterbury Tales, The.

His Tears to Thamesis [or Thamasis]. Robert Herrick. NOSC

His theme / over and over. Williams: An Essay. Denise Levertov. PmAP

His thing is singing. Elvis. Sam Cornish. AllShUp

His thought appalled us. It bore the mark of having strayed too deep into the company of others. Isn't It Romantic? Timothy Donnelly. IIR

His tongue out with its fork. (LL) Eve. Christina Georgina Rossetti. ChIV-1; NALW; NIL-7; NIP-4

His too-Good News would strip the Scripture. Two Evangelists. Robert A. West. PoA 2002

His Toys. Michael Dennis Browne. SUP

His Uncle came on Franklin Hyde. Franklin Hyde. Joseph Hilaire Pierre Belloc. NBLV

His vision, from the constantly passing bars. Panther, The. Rainer Maria Rilke. ASA; NAWM-7v2, tr. by Stephen Mitchell

His vision or not? Three "Dharma Poems." Diane Di Prima. WANABP; WhBo

His Visitor. Thomas Hardy. HarvBoo

His waiting becomes a time to hear thoughts, the sound. Picture of a Japanese Farmer, Woodland, California, May 20, 1942. James Masao Mitsui. OpBo

His was a chamber in the topmost tower. Prisoner, The. Charles Tennyson Turner. CenSon

His Waves. Rick Noguchi. AmPoNex

His way home to the mark. (LL) Boston Hymn. Ralph Waldo Emerson. CBCWP; InvLi; PCW; TCAPo

His weary eyes watch lanterns in the square. James Clarence Mangan in Trinity College Library. Timothy Brownlow. IFF

His wife and he enter. Labour and Delivery. Ron Charach. BloBone

His wife away from home. Karai Senryū. EMJL, tr. by Makoto Ueda

His wife. Forty years he painted her. Bonnard's Nudes. Raymond Carver. GoPo

His wife nods, and a secret smile. James Fenton. HP Fr. German Requiem, A.

His wife then composed a poem with the names of medicines its theme and. Poem of Medicine Puns. Unknown. ColAnChi; WoPoe, tr. by Victor H. Mair

His wild heart beats with painful sobs. Happy Warrior, The. Sir Herbert Read. FaBoWar

His Winding-Sheet. Robert Herrick. BASC; OBEV

His window frames our pictured, distanced city. Very Rich Hours, The. Nick Drake. BeAl; NeBl

His words were magic and his heart was true. Uncle Ananias. Edwin Arlington Robinson. MoAmPo; NIP-4

His work was done; his blessing lay. Frances Ellen Watkins Harper. Fr. Moses: A Story of the Nile.

Hispaniola. Amy Clampitt. NAMCP V.2

Hiss and flashing lights of a jet, The. Strategic Air Command. Gary Snyder. AtGh

Hiss and gone, A. (LL) Similes. Charles Reznikoff. APT-2; OxBoAm

Hiss, hiss. (LL) Holy Ghost. Larissa Szporluk. LegDan; NeAmPo

Hissing. Wine, urine and ashes. (LL) Geoffrey Hill. NAMCP V.2; NoAM; NoP-4 Fr. Mercian Hymns.

Hist whist / little ghostthings. E. E. Cummings. NOxBChV

Histoire. Harry Mathews. NIP-4; OxBoAm; PmAP

Historia. Brian Clements. TiP2

Historia / debe tener. Ana Belén López Pulido. SPV

Historia del laberinto, La. Veronica Volkow. RMCMP

Historians and newsmen and people who are just curious ask me, Who am I writing for? Who I Write For. Vicente Aleixandre. TAPaP, tr. by Lewis Hyde

Historic, side-long, implicating eyes. La Gioconda; Leonardo Da Vinci, The Louvre. Michael Field. CABP; ViWPN

Historical Judas, The. Howard Nemerov. NoP-4

Historical Reflections. John Hollander. OBCoV

Historical Site. Arthur Powers. RWB

Historically these people have been noted for a strange dish called. Okeydokey Tribe, The. Chrystos. WiU

Histories of Bodies. Mariko Nagai. PuP-23

Histories, The. Victoria Edwards Tester. ICANM

Historiography. Lorenzo Thomas. SeSe

History. Elin ap Hywel. ATSWP, tr. by Robert Minhinnick

History. Wendell Berry. LPSFW

History: "In Boston, a tongue of red paint traces the city's history, from Massacre to Tea Party to Faneuil Hall." Joel Brouwer. PoDa

History. John Burnside. BeAl; PoAgWa

History. Kelly Cherry. FFC

History. G. K. Chesterton. OBSV Fr. Songs of Education.

History. Carl Dennis. BAP-97; OxBoAm

History: "Everything's a metaphor, some wise." Rita Dove. ExTi; FFC; WaAnP

History. Maura Dooley. NeBl; StAl

History. Ralph Waldo Emerson. APN-1

History. Robert Fitzgerald. APT-2

History. Juan Gelman. TCLAP, tr. by Robert Marquez

History. Jorie Graham. HarvBoo

History. Jennifer Michael Hecht. PoDa

History. D. H. Lawrence. RaBo

History. Robert Lowell. ColAP; PoetW; VCAP

History. Paul Muldoon. StAl

History. Heberto Padilla. AF, tr. by Alastair Reid

History. Adrienne Rich. NIL-7 Fr. Inscriptions.

History. Tracy K. Smith. LegDan

History. Gary Soto. PBCAP

History. Lucien Stryk. Vesp

History. Alpay Ulku. AmPoNex

History. Yevgeny Mikhailovich Vinokurov. tr. by Daniel Weissbort Objects. TCRusP, tr. by Daniel Weissbort

History among the Rocks. Robert Penn Warren. CBCWP; MoAmPo Fr. Kentucky Mountain Farm.

History and Reality. Stephen Spender. HP

History As Trash. Michelle T. Clinton. SpirFl

History Classes. Tony Harrison. NAMCP V.2 Fr. School of Eloquence, The.

History Goes to Work. Elizabeth Garrett. MFPA; NeBl

History has to live with what was here. History. Robert Lowell. ColAP; PoetW; VCAP

History? Here's an end of that. Shame of Llanfaes, The. Gerallt Lloyd Owen. BBMWP, tr. by Ronald Stuart Thomas

History hibernates here. Maridunum. Douglas Phillips. AngWePo

History, Hollers, and Horn. Sterling Plumpp. FuFl

History Lesson. Natasha Trethewey. SUP

History Lesson, A. Miroslav Holub. PoSu, tr. by George Theiner

History Lessons. Seamus Deane. PBCIP; PNI

History Myth of the Coming of the A'shiwi as Narrated by 'Kiäklo. Zuni Oral Tradition.
"Following their road of exit, they stooped over and came out." APN-2

History Never Happened. Mr. Social Control. RSaN

History of a Face, The. İlhan Berk. tr. by Talat Sait Halman
3. Exile. NaPG, tr. by Talat Sait Halman

History of Air Travel, A. Anna Leahy. OtW

History of Costume, A. Michelle Cliff. OxWW

History of Dub Poetry, The. "Mbala." WaCA

History of Education. David McCord. AmWit; APT-2

History of France. Kenward Elmslie. NYP2

History of Ideas. James Vincent Cunningham. NIP-4; VCAP *Fr.* Epigrams: A Journal.

History of my country is, The. Horizon of Gunbutts. Patrick Sylvain. OGAHCP, *tr. by* Boadiba and Jack Hirschman

History of My Face. Khaled Mattawa. AmPoNex

History of My Father's House, The. Vona Groarke. MFPA

History of my feeling for you (or is it the way you change), The. History of My Feeling, The. Kathleen Fraser. CalPo

History of My Life, The. John Ashbery. OxBoAm

History of My Stupidity, The: Volume 3, Chapter 5. Edward Hirsch. RoV

History of Myself. Larry Goodell. ICANM

History of New Mexico. Gaspar Pérez De Villagrá. Canto 1. NAAPv.1

History of Photography, A. Mary Karr. PoA 2002

History of Poetry, The. Peter Cooley. P180

History of Rain, The. Conor O'Callaghan. NIrP

History of Sexual Preference, A. Robin Becker. BodElec; ExTi

History of the Airplane. Lawrence Ferlinghetti. OtW

History of the Caesars, A. Isidor Schneider. APT-2

History of the Flood, The. John Heath-Stubbs. NOxBChV

History of the Human Body, The. Edmund Berrigan. IIR

History of the Invisible. Rodger Kamenetz. TaR

History of the Lyre, A. Letitia Elizabeth Landon. VWP

History of the Quilt That Heaved Life into Stars Patched, Circled, Stitched and Square. Carletta Carrington Wilson. BtF

History of the world, The. My Government. Matthew Rohrer. LegDan

History of this moment lengthens in shadow, The. Ars Poetica at the Window. Marvin Bell. CAP-8

History of women sighs, The. History of Women, The. Leslie Ullman. SweBea

History of Women, The. Leslie Ullman. SweBea

History Set, The. Vincent Woods. NIrP

History Teacher, The. Billy Collins. SUP

History Teacher in the Warsaw Ghetto Rising. Evangeline Paterson. RSaN

History's / the cathedral. Ana Belén López Pulido. SPV, *tr. by* Jen Hofer

History's gilt and grandiose opulence. Poet of Our Climate, A. Katha Pollitt. PoA 2002

Hit and hit and hit and hit and fallen. Like Her Body The World. Martha Collins. ExTi

Hit Men, The. Philippa Lawrence. Prnts

Hit squad. Tatamkulu Afrika. TSAP

Hitchcock would have loved 136. Woman Hanging from Lightpole, Illinois Route 136. Lucia Cordell Getsi. IllVoic

Hitcher. Simon Armitage. EmeKit

Hitch-Haiku. Alan Jackson. EdScPo

Hitchhiker. Galway Kinnell. OxBoAm

Hitchhikers, The. Diane Wakoski. NoAM

Hitchhiker of the ivory smile. Letters to a Kenyan Friend. D. Cyril Jones. BBMWP, *tr. by* Peter Finch

Hither, Ardelia, I your steps pursue. Some Reflections. Anne Finch, Countess of Winchilsea. ChIV-1

Hither thou com'st: the busy [*or* busie] wind all night. Bird, The. Henry Vaughan. OBEV

Hither, where tangled thickets of the acacia. Babiaantje, The. Frank Templeton Prince. MoBrPo

Hits and Runs. Carl Sandburg. MoASP

Hitting Golfballs off the Bluff. Jeffrey Harrison. MoASP

Hive. Nick Flynn. LegDan

Hive is for where, The. Rest of Love, The. Carl Phillips. AmAlph

Hiver, L'. Pascalle Monnier. YaTCFP

Hlahla! Uthlofan, lauflings! Incantation by Laughter. Velemir Khlebnikov. PoCho, *tr. by* Paul Schmidt

HMS Glasshouse. Sean O'Brien. RSaN

HMS *Glory.* Charles Causley. FaBoWar

Ho, all you cats in all the street. Cat's Meat. Harold Monro. OBMV

Ho! brother [*or* broder] Teague, dost hear de decree. Lilli Burlero [A New Song]. Thomas Wharton, 1st Marquess of Wharton. BASC

Ho Chih-Chang. Ho Ch'e Ch'ang. NAAPv.2,

Ho! Cupid calls, come Lovers, come. Cupid's Call. James Shirley. NOSC

Ho, everyone that thirsteth. A. E. Housman. ChIV-1

Ho, for the Pirate Don Durk of Dowdee! Pirate Don Durk of Dowdee, The. Mildred Plew Meigs. ChAP

Ho, Giant! This is I! Bean-Stalk, The. Edna St. Vincent Millay. NOxBChV

Ho Ho Ho Caribou. Joseph Ceravolo. PmAP

Ho Hum. Edward Heyman. ReLy

'Ho!' said the child, 'how fine the horses go'. Mother, The. Dora Sigerson Shorter. VWP

Ho, why dost thou shiver and shake. Gaffer Gray. Thomas Holcroft. OxAEP-1

Ho, ye poor, who seek. John Dyer. STuOW *Fr.* Fleece, The.

Hoagie Scam, The. Jim Daniels. SUP

Hoar Frost. Morton Dauwen Zabel. PoA 2002

Hoar frost has congealed. Along the Grand Canal. Ch'in Kuan. BLT, *tr. by* Kenneth Rexroth

Hoar with salt-sleet and chalkings of the birds. (LL) Frederick Goddard Tuckerman. APN-2; OxBoAm *Fr.* Sonnets.

Hoarding the little mounds of sorrow laid up in our hearts. (LL) Homage to Paul Cézanne. Charles Wright. EMP; NAMCP V.2; VCAP

Hoardings screened the landscape from his sight. Copy-writer's Dream, The. Bruce Dawe. BMAP

Hoar-Frost. Amy Lowell. ColAP

Hoarfrost and Fog. Barton Sutter. UrbNat

Hoarse is the husky tickling's muffled chant. Pendulum, The. Árpád Tóth. IQMS, *tr. by* Watson Kirkconnell

Hoatchunk' Narwoanar, or Winnebago War Song. *Unknown.* APN-2, *tr. by* Caleb Atwater

Hobart Town, Van Diemen's Land (11th June, 1837). Hal Porter. NOBAu

Hobbyhorse, The. Sezai Karakoç. NaPG, *tr. by* Talat Sait Halman

Hobie [*or* Hobbie] Noble. *Unknown.* IBB

Hobson has supt, and's newly gon to bed. (LL) On the University Carrier Who Sick'n'd [*or* Sickened] in the Time of His Vacancy [, Being Forbid to go to London, by Reason of the Plague]. John Milton. NOSC; OxAEP-1

Hoccleve Remembers His Madness. Thomas Hoccleve. NPeEn *Fr.* My Compleinte.

Hock-Cart, or Harvest Home, The. Robert Herrick. BASC; NAEL-6v1; NAEL-7v1; NOSC; OxAEP-1

Hod Carrier, The. John Ashbery. AHA

Hoe too is an edged tool. Maternal Love. *Unknown.* CATKP, *tr. by* Peter H. Lee

Hoeing. Gary Soto. PBCAP

Hoes are careful how, The. August. Tade Ipadeola. NeNiPo

Hog Butcher for the World. Chicago. Carl Sandburg. AmFaPo; APT-1; BRP; ColAP; EMP; FaBoA; FTtHH; IllVoic; MoAmPo; NAAL-5; NAAPv.2; NAMCP V.1; NoAM; NoP-4; NoP-5; OxBoAm; PoA 2002; TCAPo; TFi; TRP; WaAnP

Hog Heaven. Robert Siegel. PoA 2002

Hogar del poeta es una silla, El. Metamorfosis de la silla. Alberto Blanco. RMCMP

Hogarcito de La Madrugada, El. Anthony R. Vigil. AmPoNex

Hogwash. Robert Francis. NIL-7; NIP-4; TRP

Hohenlinden. Thomas Campbell. CABP; NOBRP; NPBRoP; OBWP; TFi

Hoireann o. Blue Song. Mary Macleod. NePenScot, *tr. by* Robert Crawford

Hoist, The. David Constantine. BeAl

Hoist great blocks of language into place. Philip Whalen. WhBo

Hoist was strange, The. Going up, the nurse said. Hoist, The. David Constantine. BeAl

Hoist your burdens, get on down the road. (LL) Gravelly Run. A. R. Ammons. EMP; LPSFW; NAMCP V.2; NoAM; PoA 2002; PoDa; VCAP

Hokku: "Geese flew over, The." Toyo Suyemoto. NAAPv.2

Hokku: In the Falling Snow. Richard Wright. NoP-5 *Fr.* Hokku Poems.

Hokusai. Hokusai the Old Master, Who Painted a Wave Like Nobody Ever Painted a Wave Before Him. Jan Erik Vold. PML, *tr. by* the author

Holbain. Anne Batten Cristall. RWP

Hold a glass of pure water to the eye of the sun! Glass of Pure Water, The. Hugh MacDiarmid. PFTM-2

Hold a hand held out without a protective glove. Your Figure or the War Against Fat. Joyce Mansour. SurPaPo, *tr. by* Mary Ann Caws

Hold: and I grind your manhood bone and bone. (LL) Ghost, The. Propertius. PoA 2002; WoPoe, *tr. by* Robert Lowell

Hold, are you mad? you damned [*or* damn'd] confounded dog. John Dryden. OBCoV *Fr.* Tyrannic Love.

Hold back completely. Archilochus. SaLy, *tr. by* Diane Rayor

Hold fast to dreams. Dreams. Langston Hughes. PtR

Hold Fast Your Dreams. Louise Driscoll. ChAP; ITBLP

Hold hard then, heart. This way at least you live. (LL) Fist, The. Derek Walcott. BeAl; ESEAA

Hold high the woof, dear friends, that we may see. On a Piece of Tapestry. George Santayana. APN-2

Hold it Steady. Honorée Fanonne Jeffers. BRtP

Hold it up sternly—see this it sends back, (who is it? is it you?). Hand-Mirror, A. Walt Whitman. NAAL-3; NAAPv.1; NAMCP V.1; PoPoPo

Hold me close. Song of Surrender. Saleem Peeradina. Vesp

Hold me hard light, soft light hold me.   Twelve O'Clock Chant.   Leonard Cohen.   IFF

Hold me / let me lay my head.   Place Setting.   Johari M. Rashad.   PasH

Hold me tight and very close to you.   *Unknown.*   SLW, *tr. by* Marjolijn De Jager, Sayd Bahodin Majrouh and André Velter

Hold me tightly in your arms.   *Unknown.*   SLW, *tr. by* Marjolijn De Jager, Sayd Bahodin Majrouh and André Velter

Hold me / till only, these are my.   White Fish in Reeds.   Joseph Ceravolo.   BodElec; NYP2

Hold my Rooster.   *Unknown.*   FaBoVe

Hold my rooster, hold my hen.   Hold my Rooster.   *Unknown.*   FaBoVe

Hold not your lips so close; dispense.   Kiss, The 1656. To Mrs. C.   Thomas Shipman.   NOSC

Hold of the land. (LL)   Battle of Brunanburh.   *Unknown.*   CABP; FaBoWar; OBVE; OBWP, *tr. by* Alfred Tennyson

Hold on, nightingale!   Tomas Tranströmer.   WoBe *Fr.* Haiku.

Hold on or let go. (LL)   Variations on the Word *Love*.   Margaret Atwood.   LW; NoAM

Hold out a handful of snow.   Natalya Gorbanevskaya.   TCRusP, *tr. by* Daniel Weissbort

Hold Out to the End.   *Unknown.*   SSUS

Hold thou now, Earth, now hand of man cannot.   *Unknown.*   NAEL-6v1

Hold to the future. With firm hands. The future of each afterlife, of.   Textbook of Poetry, 21, A.   Jack Spicer.   ASA

Hold up the right corner of the sea.   When He Believed Himself to Be a Young Girl Lifting the Skin of the Water.   Juan Felipe Herrera.   TouFir

Hold up the universe, good girl. Hold up.   Good Girl.   Molly Peacock.   FFC

Hold your hand in your ear.   Polar.   Jacqueline Senard.   SurWo, *tr. by* Myrna Bell Rochester

Hold Your Light.   *Unknown.*   SSUS

Hold your mad hands! for ever on your plain.   Robert Southey.   CenSon

Hölderlin Hybrids.   Rosmarie Waldrop.

  At the Sea.   WoBe

  Unaccountable Lapses.   WoBe

Holdfast, The.   George Herbert.   NAEL-7v1

Holding a jug of wine among the flowers.   Drinking Alone under Moonlight.   Li Po.   TAL

Holding a keepsake of the wind in its hand.   On the Sand Dune.   Kawamura Yoichi.   GifTon, *tr. by* Naoshi Koriyama and Edward Lueders

Holding a knife, or imagining it holds a knife, my blood goes to sleep in my hand.   Knife.   Franz Wright.   MotU

Holding a varnished paper parasol.   Buddha and the Seven Tiger Cubs.   Henri Cole.   NAMCP V.2

Holding Hands.   Lenore M. Link.   NTCP

Holding her picture in his hands, he whispered:.   Eurydice.   Rosita Copioli.   CItWP, *tr. by* Cinzia Sartini Blum and Lara Trubowitz

Holding Mode, A.   John Ashbery.   VaPo

Holding My Beads.   Grace Nichols.   ItWoWo

Holding the feathered dancing string.   Koel (Rainbird) and Effigy.   *Unknown.*   NOBAu, *tr. by* Mungayana Nundhirribala

Holding the Holy Card.   J. Patrick Lewis.   IJHIL

Holding the last of his old-found toys, he subjects himself to grim inventory.   Iconoclast's Closet, The.   Oliver Pitcher.   EGAG

Holding the Line.   Tom French.   NIrP

Holding the Mirror Up to Nature.   Howard Nemerov.   PoA 2002

Holding the razorblade my arms became severed and fell off.   Yi Sang.   CAMKP *Fr.* Crow's-Eye View.

Holding the Sky.   William Stafford.   GM

Holding the Thought of Love.   Bernadette Mayer.   OxBoAm

Holding us all at once, I watch.   Spin.   Tracy Ryan.   NeBl

Holds steady in my right hand.   My Pen.   Tom Pickard.   Oth

Holds up the bodies which this Eden grows. (LL)   Australian Garden, An.   Peter Porter.   BrAP; OBGa

Hole.   Leonard Nathan.   CalPo; PBCAP

Hole in the ozone.   Garry Gay.   CalPo

Hole in the Sea, The.   Marvin Bell.   Vesp

Hole the day digs for your feeling is opening now, The. Let it go.   End Is an Animal, The.   Claudia Keelan.   RoV

Hole, then the strike, on a pin buzz, A.   There Is a Caterpillar That Makes a Very Complicated Hammock.   Clark Coolidge.   NYP2

Hole, Where Once in Passion We Swam.   Dave Jeddie Smith.   NoAM

Holes Commence Falling.   David Huddle.   PBCAP

Holes in maps look through to nowhere. (LL)   Map of Places, The.   Laura Riding Jackson.   APT-2; NAMCP V.1

Holes in the wall, The.   Issa.   EH, *tr. by* Robert Hass

Holes you made, The.   Coal Miners, The.   James Ballowe.   IllVoic

Holiday.   Susan Hahn.

  X: October 1 *(morning)*.   Vesp

Holiday Inside an Incubator.   Yi Yônju.   EcSo, *tr. by* Yung-Hee Kim

Holiday Present.   Ilya Abu Madi.   NAAPv.2, *tr. by* George Dimitri Selim

Holiday squeals, as if all were scrambling for their lives.   Platform One.   Ted Hughes.   NoP-5

Holiday, The.   Hans Magnus Enzensberger.   VCWP, *tr. by* the author and Michael Hamburger

Holiness[e] on the head.   Aaron.   George Herbert.   BASC; ChIV-1; FSCP; NOSC; SacPr

Holla, Approach.   William Shakespeare.   NPeEn *Fr.* Love's Labour's Lost.

Holland.   Hendrik Marsman.   TuT, *tr. by* Michael Longley

Holland Brick, A.   Wallace Bruce.   VerBaPo

Holland, that scarce deserves the name of land.   Character of Holland, The.   Andrew Marvell.   BASC

Hollanditis.   Simon Vinkenoog.   CLPP, *tr. by* Charles McGeehan

Hollis Street Square, Halifax.   John Steffler.   BeAl

Hollo! keep it up, boys—and push around the glass.   Drinking Song.   Robert Fergusson.   OxAEP-1

Hollow.   Susan Wood.   TiP2

Hollow, The.   Ricardo Pau-Llosa.   Vesp

Hollow eyes of shock remain, The.   Two Years Later.   John Wieners.   PmAP; RaBo

Hollow Men, The.   T. S. Eliot.   APT-1; BrAP; MoAmPo; NAAL-5; NAEL-7v2; NoP-5; OBMV; OxBoAm; WaAnP

Hollow or filamentary or silled.   Magma.   Norman Henry, II Pritchard.   EGAG

Hollow Thesaurus, The.   Roger McDonald.   BMAP

Hollow winds of night no more, The.   Poem on the Bill Lately Passed for Regulating the Slave-Trade, A.   Helen Maria Williams.   RWP

Hollow Wood, The.   Edward Thomas.   OWoS

Hollowness.   Mac Wellman.

  "Two hollow eyes follow a cat's crie."   FTOS

Holly and Hickory.   Robert Penn Warren.   LPSFW *Fr.* Some Quiet, Plain Poems.

Holly and Ivy.   *Unknown.*   NPeEn

Holly and the ivy, The.   Holly and the Ivy, The.   *Unknown.*   ChrPo

Holly Gone.   Gloria Evans Davies.   AngWePo

Holly gone I discover.   Holly Gone.   Gloria Evans Davies.   AngWePo

Holly leaves are glinting in the sun, The.   Mixed Weather.   Sydney Tremayne.   EdScPo

Hollyhocks, The.   Basho.   EH, *tr. by* Robert Hass

Hollywood Finch, The.   A. V. Christie.   NAPBL

Holm Oak, The.   Mariella Bettarini.   CItWP, *tr. by* Cinzia Sartini Blum and Lara Trubowitz

Holmes.   James Russell Lowell.   TCAPo *Fr.* Fable for Critics, A.

Holocaust.   Charles Reznikoff.

  Entertainment.   NAMCP V.1

  "Jewish women were lined up by German troops in charge of the territory."   NAAPv.2

  "When the Second World War began."   HP

Holy and hokey, Hallowe'en.   Trick or Treat.   John Frederick Nims.   IllVoic

Holy Baptism (2).   George Herbert.   ChIV-2

Holy Body.   Susan Griffin.   ASA

Holy Book like the Eighth Sphere, does shine, The.   Reason.   Abraham Cowley.   SacPr

Holy boy, The.   Children of Love.   Harold Monro.   MoBrPo

Holy Child Descends, The.   Gu Cheng.   WoBe, *tr. by* Joseph R. Allen

Holy [*or* H.] Communion, The ("Not in rich furniture, or fine array.")   George Herbert.   ChIV-1

Holy Days.   Larry Neal.   OxAAAP

Holy earth is overspread with leaves, The.   On Visiting Sokei, Where the Sixth Patriarch Lived.   Tesshu.   ZenPo, *tr. by* Takashi Ikemoto and Lucien Stryk

Holy Fair, The.   Robert Burns.   OBSV

Holy Family.   Muriel Rukeyser.   ChIV-2; MoAmPo

Holy Field, The.   Henry Hart Milman.   SacPr

Holy Ghost.   Larissa Szporluk.   LegDan; NeAmPo

Holy Ghost first knocks, so high extold, shews the end come, The.   Gatehouse Salutation, The.   Eleanor Touchet Davies.   EMWP

Holy Ghost Flies into Second Baptist on Airline Highway in Baton Rouge, The.   Kathleen Crown.   FiBr

Holy Goddess Tellus, / Mother of Living Nature.   Holy Goddess Tellus.   *Unknown.*   HW

Holy, Holy, Holy.   Reginald Heber.   SacPr

Holy! Holy! Holy! Holy! Holy! Holy! Holy! Holy! Holy! Holy! Holy! Holy! Holy! Holy! Holy!   Footnote to Howl.   Allen Ginsberg.   CLPP

"Holy, holy, holy!" the choir chants sweet and low.   Opening Service, An.   Clara Ann Thompson.   CBWP-2

Holy Innocents.   David Brendon Hopes.   UpMys

Holy Innocents, The.   Robert Lowell.   MoAmPo; OBCP

Holy Land, The. Maurice Riordan. NIrP

Holy life of music and of verse, The. (LL) William Wordsworth. NPBRoP; WaAnP *Fr.* Prelude, The; Growth of a Poet's Mind [1805 version].

Holy Longing, The. Johann Wolfgang von Goethe. ItP; RaBo; WoPoe, *tr. by* Robert Bly

Holy mirror, The. Basho. EMJL, *tr. by* Haruo Shirane

Holy Moses! Have a look! On Visiting Westminster Abbey. Amanda Ros. VerBaPo

Holy Night. Lucille Clifton. NALW

Holy of Holies, The. G. K. Chesterton. SacPr

Holy Office, The [*with music*]. James Joyce. NoAM

Holy Order. Gemino H. Abad. ReBoTo

Holy poets of antiquity tell us the foolish take the path, The. David McFadden. NLPA

Holy Pools Have Only Water, The. Kabir. *See* How Much Is Not True.

Holy Priestess of Heaven, The. *Unknown.* HW, *tr. by* Samuel Noah Kramer and Diane Wolkstein *and* Samuel Noah Kramer

Holy Russia. Maksimilian Aleksandrovich Voloshin. TCRusP, *tr. by* Bob Perelman

Holy Satyr. "H. D." MoAmPo

Holy Sepulchre, The. Rowland Watkyns. BASC

Holy Scripture, Writ Divine. From a London Bookshop. *Unknown.* NBLV

Holy Shechina, / are You that gentle female Voice. Poem for the Shechina. Cassia Berman. HW

Holy Skirts. Else Von Freytag-Loringhoven. PFTM-1

Holy Solitude, in the skies above you. Solitude. Dániel Berzsenyi. IQMS, *tr. by* Watson Kirkconnell

Holy Sonnet. Robert Kelly. WhBo

Holy Sonnets. John Donne.

Divine Meditations.

"At the round earth's imagined [*or* imagin'd] corners, blow." BASC; BrAP; ChIV-2; ClHu; CtM; HeIP-4; MakPoe; NAEL-6v1; NAEL-7v1; NAWM-5v1; NoP-5; NOSC; NPeEn; OxAEP-1; OxBEV; OxBSo; RSR; SacPr; TFi; WaAnP; WoPoe

"Batter my heart, three-personed [*or* three person'd] God; for you." BASC; BrAP; CABP; ClHu; FSCP; GSo; HeIP-4; InvLi; NAEL-6v1; NAEL-7v1; NIL-7; NIP-4; NoP-4; NoP-5; NOSC; NPeEn; OxAEP-1; OxBSo; PBRV; PoPoPo; SacPr; SoSe-8; TFi; WaAnP

"Death be not proud, though some have called thee." BASC; BLPJKO; BrAP; HeIP-4; InoFa; ITBLP; NAEL-6v1; NAEL-7v1; NAWM-5v1; NIL-7; NIP-4; NoP-5; NOSC; NPeEn; OPOU; OxAEP-1; OxBEV; OxBSo; PtR; RSR; SacPr; SoSe-8; TRP; WaAnP; WeW-3

"I am a little world made cunningly." BASC; ChIV-1; NAEL-6v1; NAEL-7v1; NIP-4; NoP-4; NoP-5; OxBSo

"If poisonous [*or* poysonous] mineral[l]s, and if that tree." BASC; FaBoVe; NAEL-6v1; NAEL-7v1; NoP-4; NoP-5; OxAEP-1

"O might those sigh[e]s and tear[e]s return[e] again[e]." SacPr

"Oh my black[e] soul[e]! now thou art summoned." OxAEP-1

"Oh, to vex me, contraries [*or* contraryes] meet in one." BASC; ChIV-2; NAEL-7v1; NOSC; WaAnP

"Show me dear[e] Christ, thy spouse, so bright and clear[e]." BASC; FSCP; NAEL-6v1; NAEL-7v1; NoP-4; NoP-5; NOSC; OxBSo; PBRV; WaAnP

"Since she whom[e] I loved [*or* lov'd *or* lovd] hath paid [*or* payd] her last debt." BASC; FSCP; NAEL-6v1; NAEL-7v1; NOSC; PBRV

"Spit in my face ye [*or* you] Jew[e]s, and pierce my side." BASC; WaAnP

"This is my play's [*or* playes] last scene, here heavens appoint." BASC; FaBoVe

"Thou hast made me, and shall thy work[e] decay?" GSo; InvLi; NAEL-6v1; NAEL-7v1; NoP-4; NoP-5; NOSC; OxAEP-1

"What if this present were the world's last night?" BASC; HeIP-4; NAEL-6v1; NAEL-7v1; NOSC; OxAEP-1

"Why are we[e] by all creatures waited on?" BASC

La Corona. ChIV-2

Nativity [*or* Nativitie]. ChrPo

Holy stond in the hall, fayre to behold. Holly and Ivy. *Unknown.* NPeEn

Holy the days of the old prune face junkie men. Holy Days. Larry Neal. OxAAAP

Holy Thursday. Geoffrey Hill. UpMys

Holy Thursday [1]. William Blake. BrAP; GoPo; NAEL-6v2; NAEL-7v2; NAWM-7v2; NOBRP; NoP-4; NoP-5; NPBRoP; NPeEn; TFi *Fr.* Songs of Innocence.

Holy Thursday [2]. William Blake. BrAP; NAEL-6v2; NAEL-7v2; NOBRP; NoP-4; NoP-5; NPBRoP *Fr.* Songs of Experience.

Holy Tide, The. Frederick Tennyson. OBEV; SacPr

Holy Water. Hayan Charara. AmPoNex

Holy Well. Padraic Fallon. BBASP

Holy Willie's Prayer. Robert Burns. BrAP; CABP; NAEL-6v2; NAEL-7v2; NOBRP; NoP-5; NPBRoP; OBCoV; OBSV; TFi

Holyhead. September 25, 1727. Jonathan Swift. IrLP

Holywell. John Jones.

"Now slowly winding from the mountain's head." AngWePo

Homage. Barbara Guest. AHA

Homage: Doo-Wop. Joseph Stroud. GoPo

Homage in dance, An. Robert Filliou. PFTM-2 *Fr.* 14 Songs and 1 Riddle.

Homage: Light from the Hall. David Wojahn. PBCAP *Fr.* Mystery Train: A Sequence.

Homage: Summer/Winter, Shay Creek. Joseph Stroud. GeoHom

Homage to a Bellhop. Yusef Komunyakaa. BodElec

Homage to a Government. Philip Larkin. NAMCP V.2; NoAM; OxBEV

Homage to a Tom-Cat. Thomas Parkinson. ASA

Homage to Bly and Lorca. In London. Robert Creeley. AHA

Homage To Charlotte Rampling. Todd Swift. OpeFie

Homage to Claude Lorrain. Charles Wright. NoP-5

Homage to Diana. Sir Walter Ralegh. NoSic; NPeEn

Homage to Elvis, Homage to the Fathers. Bruce Weigl. ReTh

Homage to Faiz Ahmed Faiz. Agha Shahid Ali. OpBo

Homage to Ferd. Holthausen. Gwen Harwood. NOBAu

Homage to Hieronymus Bosch. Thomas MacGreevy. ModIr

Homage to Issac Newton. János Pilinszky. IQMS; StAl, *tr. by* Peter Jay

Homage to Jack Yeats. Thomas MacGreevy. OBMV

Homage to Lester Flatt. David Bottoms. SwNoth

Homage to Life: Jules Supervielle. Joseph Stroud. PoDa; TAPaP

Homage to Literature. Muriel Rukeyser. SeSe

Homage to Mistress Bradstreet. John Berryman.

"Winters close, Springs open, no child stirs, The." NAAL-5; NoP-4; NoP-5

Homage to Mistress Bradstreet. John Berryman.

"So squeezed, wince you I scream? I love you & hate." PoCho

"When by me in the dusk my child sits down." ColAP

Homage to my hips [*with music*]. Lucille Clifton. CAP-8; NAMCP V.2; StAl; WaAnP

Homage to Paul Cézanne. Charles Wright. EMP; NAMCP V.2; VCAP

Homage to Robert Johnson. David St. John. SwNoth

Homage to Salvador Allende. Edward Palmer Thompson. RSaN

Homage to Sextus Propertius. Ezra Pound.

"Shades of Callimachus, Coan ghosts of Philetas." APT-1; OBVE; OxBoAm; WoPoe

"When, when, and whenever death closes our eyelids." APT-1; NPeEn; OBMV; PoA 2002

Homage to Sharon Stone. Lynn Emanuel. BodElec

Homage to Tara Our Mother. *Unknown.* HW

Homage to the British Museum [*with music*]. William Empson. MoBrPo; NPeEn; OxBEV

Homage to the Brown Bomber. Michael S. Harper. MoASP

Homage to the buddhas. Kyunyŏ, Great Master. CATKP *Fr.* Eleven Poems on the Ten Vows of the Universally Worthy Bodhisattva.

Homage to the Canal People. Andrew Sant. NOBAu

Homage to the Empress of the Blues. Robert Earl Hayden. APT-2; ESEAA; NAAL-5; NAMCP V.2; OxAAAP; OxBoAm

Homage to the Fox. Andrew Hudgins. UpMys *Fr.* Liar's Psalm, The.

Homage to the New World. Michael S. Harper. ESEAA

Homage to the Painter General Ts'ao. Tu Fu [*or* Du Fu]. CrYelRi, *tr. by* Sam Hamill

Homage to the *Word-Hoard*. Joseph Stroud. TAPaP

Hombre despojóse de sí mismo, El. Víspera, La. José Ángel Valente. RaW

Hombre gris avanza por la calle de niebla, Un. Remordimiento en Traje de Noche. Luis Cernuda. RaW

Hombre quiso ver el mundo, Un. Tierra prometida, La. Jorge Fernández Granados. RMCMP

Home. Franta Bass. INSAB

Home. Anne Brontë. VWP

Home: "These days whenever I stay away too long." Frederick D'Aguiar. NeBrP

Home. Calvin Forbes. GT

Home. Edgar Albert Guest. BRP; ITBLP

Home. Robinson Jeffers. BodElec

Home. Pauline Kaldas. PoArWo

Home. Dennis O'Driscoll. BeAl

Home. Frank Ormsby. ModIr; PBCIP; PNI

Home: "Like sapphire and terracotta mingling in the Ganga." Kavikondala Venkatarao. CFP

Home. David Walker. MotU

Home. Bruce Weigl. AmAlph

Home, A. Susan Coolidge. SWaP

Home address: galaxy and star number. End of the Questionnaire. Dan Pagis. PoSu, *tr.* by Robert Friend

Home: After a Poem by Frost. Steve Wilson. VisFro

Home after home after home. Sibling Rivalry. Kenward Elmslie. BAP-04

Home After Three Months Away. Robert Lowell. PoetW

Home Again. John Montague. *Fr.* Rough Field, The.

Home Again among Gardens and Fields. T'ao Ch'ien. NDACCP, *tr.* by David Hinton

Home again in dreams, I'm walking that foothill road. Sycamore Canyon Nocturne. Christopher Buckley. GeoHom; PfSP

Home at Grasmere [1800 version]. William Wordsworth. "Mine eyes did ne'er." NPBRoP

Home Avenue. C. S. Giscombe. RD

Home Burial. Robert Frost. APT-1; ColAP; NAAPv.2; NAMCP V.1; NoP-5; OxBoAm; SoSe-8; TRP; WaAnP

Home Coming. Lenrie Peters. HBAPE

Home Cookin. Estelle E. Farley. BtF

Home Farm. John Burnside. WaAnP

Home for a visit, you brought me. Bangkok Gang, The. Maxine W. Kumin. NAMCP V.2

Home for receiving those from whom God has withdrawn. On the Bell Frieze of a Roman Church. René Char. WoPoe, *tr.* by Mark Rudman

Home for Thanksgiving. W. S. Merwin. NoAM

Home for three days. Buson. EMJL *Fr.* Spring Breeze on the Kema Embankment.

Home for Winter. Marcia Falk. TaR

Home Free. Diana O'Hehir. ASA

Home from casino or fish fry. Upper Peninsula Landscape with Aunts. Pamela Gemin. SweBea

Home from school my daughter's curled. Moles in Spring. Dave Jeddie Smith. PfSP

Home furthest off grows dearer from the way. Soldier, The. John Clare. FaBoWar

Home Greeting, A [*with music*]. Priscilla Jane Thompson. CBWP-2

Home Guard. Craig Watson. "Then the old fruit-and-vegetable economy dried up and blew away but self-defense gave us a way." Eno

Home, home from the horizon far and clear. At Night. Alice Thompson Meynell. OxAEP-2

Home, home, though I come home. Home. Chŏng Chiyong. CAMKP, *tr.* by Kevin O'Rourke

Home in Three Days. Don't Wash. Linda Smukler. WiU

Home Industries First: The Song of Colin, a Discerning Shepherd, Lamenting the State of the Woollen Manufactory. William Shenstone. STuOW *Fr.* He Repeats the Song of Colin, a Discerning Shepherd [*or Elegy 18*].

Home Is So Sad. Philip Larkin. PoetW

Home is where one starts from. As we grow older. T. S. Eliot. BeAl *Fr.* Four Quartets.

Home is where the heart is. To drink its water. Ingrid de Kok. TSAP

Home Movie. Grace Schulman. WaAnP

Home Movies: A Sort of Ode. Mary Jo Salter. WaAnP

Home News. Ahmed Tidjani-Cissé. NAfrP; PML, *tr.* by Gerald Moore

Home no more home to me, whither must I wander? Robert Louis Stevenson. AmFaPo

Home of the Percys' high-born race. Alnwick Castle. Fitz-Greene Halleck. APN-1

Home on the Range. *Unknown.* GoPo

Home on the Range, A. *Unknown.* APN-2

Home Remedy. Paula McLain. SweBea

Home, Sweet Home! John Howard Payne. APN-1; BRP; TCAPo *Fr.* Clari, the Maid of Milan.

Home Team. James Applewhite. LPSFW

Home the dark prisoner in his shroud of coats. (LL) Blood Donor. Robert Morgan. AngWePo; TCAWP

Home, The Spare Room, The. Robert Adamson. BMAP

Home they brought her warrior dead. Alfred Tennyson. OxAEP-2 *Fr.* Princess, The.

H[ome], thou return'st from Thames, whose naiads long. Ode on the Popular Superstitions of the Highlands of Scotland, An. William Collins. OxAEP-1

Home Thoughts. Thomas D'Arcy Magee. IrV

Home Thoughts from Abroad. William Robert Rodgers. OBCoV

Home to Farm. *Unknown.* ChinPo, *tr.* by Ye Weilian [*or Yeh Wei-lien or Wai-lim Yip*]

Home to Roost. Kay Ryan. OxBoAm

Home, too, was out there. Lawson Fusao Inada. GeoHom *Fr.* Legends from Camp.

Home Town Elegy. George Sutherland Fraser. EdScPo

Home Truths from Abroad. *Unknown.* UV

Home-coming. Léonie Adams. MoAmPo

Homecoming. Anthony Caleshu. NIrP

Homecoming, The [*with music*]. James Keir Baxter. BrAP

Homecoming. Bruce Dawe. BMAP; EmeKit

Homecoming: "I was a boy when I left home." Ho Ch'e Ch'ang. NDACCP, *tr.* by Kenneth Rexroth

Homecoming. Langston Hughes. SAmP; TRP

Homecoming. Dorianne Laux. ExTi

Homecoming: "After the cries of gulls and the fogbound island." Thomas McGrath. PWW2

Homecoming. Joao Pedro. NAfrP, *tr.* by Don Burness

Homecoming. Linda Reuther. "And the Great Mother said." HW

Homecoming: "Lost in the vastness of the void Pacific." Karl Shapiro. APT-2; PWW2

Homecoming. Edith Södergran. WPoS

Homecoming. Wisława Szymborska. PoSu, *tr.* by Adam Czerniawski

Homecoming of Love Amongst Illustrious Ruins. Rafael Alberti. CLPP, *tr.* by Kenneth Rexroth

Homecoming Singer, The. Jay Wright. OxBoAm; VCAP

Homecomings. Pablo Neruda. GifTon, *tr.* by William O'Daly

Homeland. Mahdi Muhammad Ali. IrPoTo, *tr.* by Salaam Yousif

Homeland. Ogaga Ifowodo. NeNiPo

Homeless. Beatrix Gates. WiU *Fr.* Triptych.

Homeless. Michael Hannon. GeoHom

Homeless. Adelaide Anne Procter. VWP

Homeless Compleynt. Allen Ginsberg. BodElec

Homeless on Cold Food Festival Day. Moon on the Cold Flood Festival. Tu Fu [*or Du Fu*]. CrYelRi, *tr.* by Sam Hamill

Homeless people. En-vi-RON-ment. Lee Bennett Hopkins. HHAm

Homeless Vets. S. P. Shephard. BtF

Home-Loving Dog, The. Matthew Prior. DiBP *Fr.* Solomon on the Vanity of the World.

Homely Accommodation, Suit Gent. William Price Turner. EdScPo

Homely one, The. Feast Day Dog. Anne MacNaughton. ICANM

Homemade Smiles. Jose Angel Figueroa. PueRic

Homenajes de Gratitud. Zaragoza Clubs. *tr.* by Luis A. Torres "When the French, to their shame." SWaP, *tr.* by Luis A. Torres

Homeostasis finally. System oscillation over. All parameters at rest. Middle Manager in Paradise, The. Michael Foley. PNI

Homeowners unite. Firebombing, The. James Dickey. AmWaPo; OBWP; PWW2

Homeplace, The. Lenard D. Moore. GT

Homer. George Campbell Hay. EdScPo

Homer and the Brazen Head of Rumour. George Chapman. NOSC

Homer in Basic. Kenneth Rexroth. NAMCP V.1

Homer Travestie. Thomas Bridges. "Squabbling gods the fight forsake, The." FaBoWar

Homer was poor. His scholars live at ease. James Vincent Cunningham. WoPoe *Fr.* Epigrams.

Homer where born where buried of whom the son. Brian Coffey. ModIr *Fr.* Death of Hektor, The.

Homeric Hexameter, The. Samuel Taylor Coleridge. OxAEP-2

Homeric Hymns. *Unknown. tr.* by Charles Boer, Padraic Fallon, Patricia Monaghan, Thelma Sargent and Percy Bysshe Shelley

Homeric Hymn to Ares, The. *tr.* by Charles Boer "Hear me, / helper of mankind." RaBo, *tr.* by Charles Boer

Homeric Hymn to Hermes. *tr.* by Padraic Fallon Stealing of Apollo's Cattle, The. WoPoe, *tr.* by Padraic Fallon

Hymn to Aphrodite. HW, *tr.* by Patricia Monaghan

Hymn to Aphrodite [*or Venus*]. *tr.* by William Congreve Venus Goes After Anchises. OBVE, *tr.* by William Congreve Venus Tells Anchises the Story of Aurora and Tithonus. OBVE, *tr.* by William Congreve

Hymn to Hestia, The. *tr.* by Charles Boer "Hestia, / you who have received the highest honor." HW, *tr.* by Charles Boer

Hymn to Mercury [*or Hermes*]. *tr.* by Percy Bysshe Shelley "Seized with a sudden fancy for fresh meat." OBVE, *tr.* by Percy Bysshe Shelley

Hymn to the Earth, The. HW, *tr.* by Charles Boer

Hymn to the Moon, The. *tr.* by Charles Boer "Go on, / Muses, / and sing the Moon with her big wings." HW, *tr.* by Charles Boer

Homeric Interim. Reginald Shepherd. RD

Homeric Simile. William Meredith. *See* Simile: "As when a heavy bomber in the cloud."

Homer's Gift of Fame. Homer. NOSC *Fr.* Iliad, The.

Homer's Iliad, To the Reader. George Chapman.
  "And, for our tongue, that still is so empayr'd." PBRV

Homes. Charlotte Perkins Stetson Gilman. SWaP

Homes for All. Phoebe Cary. SWaP

Homes of England, The. Felicia Dorothea Hemans. NAEL-7v2; NOBRP; PEW; RWP; UV; ViWPN

Home's the place we head for in our sleep. Indian Boarding School: The Runaways. Louise Erdrich. CAP-8; HATNAP; NoAM; UnSA

Homesick. Helmut Heissenbüttel. CLPP, *tr.* by Jerome Rothenberg

Homesick. *Unknown, fr. Terezin Concentration Camp.* INSAB

Homesick Blues. Langston Hughes. GM; MoAmPo

Homesick Bride, The. *Vietnamese Oral Tradition.* CaDao, *tr.* by John Balaban

Homesickness. Chŏng Chiyong. CAMKP, *tr.* by Anthony, Brother of Taizé

Homesickness. Paul Muldoon. GPPA

Homestead. Tu Fu [*or* Du Fu]. CrYelRi, *tr.* by Sam Hamill

Homestead, USA. D. L. Crockett-Smith. OxAAAP

Homesteaders. Rosemary Catacalos. TiP2

Homesteaders. Debra Nystrom. RWB

Homesteading. Eva Salzman. MFPA

Homesteading. Eric Tretheway. Coast

Home-Study Course in Freedom. Radoi Ralin. CSCBP, *tr.* by Georgi Belev and Lisa Sapinkopf

Home-Thoughts, from Abroad. Robert Browning. CABP; ClHu; HeIP-4; NAEL-6v2; NAEL-7v2; NoP-4; NoP-5; OBEV; TFi; UV

Home-Thoughts, from the Sea. Robert Browning. NAEL-6v2; NAEL-7v2

Hometown. Salih Michael Fisher. CAGL

Hometown flophouse, The. Hotel Nights with My Mother. Linda McCarriston. TWF

"Hometown"; well, most admit an affection for a city. Return to Cardiff. Dannie Abse. AngWePo; TCAWP

Homeward. P'an Yüeh. CCL1, *tr.* by Anne Birrell

Homeward Bound. Ezekiel Mphahlele. AF

Homeward-Bound Passenger Ship, The. Edward Edwin Foot.
  "Captain scans the ruffled zone, The." VerBaPo

Disaster at Sea. STuOW

Homewards. Tomas Tranströmer. WoPoe, *tr.* by Robin Fulton

Homework. Allen Ginsberg. NoAM

Homework. Mona Van Duyn. FFC; VCAP

Homework Assignment on the Subject of Angels. Tadeusz Rózewicz. VCWP

Homework! Oh, Homework! Jack Prelutsky. ChAP

Homily. Dan Pagis. MotU, *tr.* by Stephen Mitchell

Homines qouque si taceant, vocem invenient libri. Steve McCaffery. FTOS *Fr.* Panopticon.

Homing crows drift in the air at nest time. Song for the Falling Kingdom. Li Po. NDACCP, *tr.* by Ezra Pound

Homing In. Lilace Mellin Guignard. LiTh

Homing Instinct. Mary Vanek. TiP2

Homme Moyen Sensuel, L'. Ezra Pound.
  "Alas, eheu, one question that sorely vexes." OBSV
  "'Tis of my country that I would endite." OBSV

Hommes not taillé dans leurs tourments une fleur, Les. An neuf. Aimé Césaire. YaTCFP

Homo called sapiens. (LL) Apostrophe to Man. Edna St. Vincent Millay. NAAL-5; NALW

Homo Erectus. Yusef Komunyakaa. PML

Homo Erectus, Cerne Abbas. Mercer Simpson. TCAWP

Homo Ludens. Anne Carson. MoWP *Fr.* Beauty of the Husband, The.

Homo Sapiens. Carol Frost. CAP-8

Homo Suburbiensis [for Craig McGregor]. Bruce Dawe. BMAP

Homo Will Not Inherit. Mark Doty. AmAlph; HarvBoo; NAMCP V.2; OPRER; WiU

Homocide [*for Ronald Gibson*]. Essex Hemphill. GT

Homosexuality. Frank O'Hara. CAGL; PFTM-2; PoA 2002; WaAnP

Homunculus et La Belle Etoile. Wallace Stevens. MoAmPo

Honest matrons, pray retire. *Unknown.* PriapPo *Fr.* Priapus Poems, The.

Honestly I'd as soon be dead! Sappho. STV

Honesty. Sir Thomas Wyatt. NoSic

Honesty; *lunaria*: satin seed, satin pod. the moon is two half-, four quarter. Syliva Legris. PoPra *Fr.* Negative Garden.

Honesty-Stones. J. S. Harry. NOBAu

Honey. Sterling Allen Brown. *See* Honey / When de man.

Honey. Diane Levy. WhBo

Honey. Robert Morgan. BLT

Honey [*with music*]. James Wright. MotU

Honey Fig. Nasri Hajjaj. Eno, *tr.* by Ibrahim Muhawi

Honey in the Honeycomb. John Latouche. ReLy

Honey Moon [*with music*]. Kathleen Leland Baker. NBLV

Honey of a Wild Bee. Abraham Sutskever. MotU, *tr.* by Ruth R. Wisse

Honey of peace in old poems, The. (LL) To the Stone-Cutters. Robinson Jeffers. ColAP; MoAmPo; NAAL-5; OxBoAm

Honey, pepper, leaf-green limes. Jamaica Market. Agnes Maxwell-Hall. WHSW

Honey, take yo' bressed time. (LL) Sister Lou. Sterling Allen Brown. APT-2; InoFa

Honey / When de man. Sister Lou. Sterling Allen Brown. APT-2; InoFa (Honey.) GM; ISC

Honeybee upon the Tundra. Joan Jobe Smith. SUP

Honeycomb, The. Pauline Stainer. NeBl; StAl

Honeymoon. Alice Friman. MPUn

Honeymoon, The. James Simmons. PNI

Honeymoon is Over, The. Judith Viorst. LW

Honeymoon Postcard. Paul Durcan. OBCoV

Honeymooning couples blithely hanging out. ITMA. Roddy Lumsden. NeBl

Honey-red hue of the picture, The. Christ Bearing the Cross by El Greco. David Craig. UpMys

Honeystain. . . / the rhetoricians of blackness. Anti-Semanticist, The. Everett Hoagland. OxAAAP

Honeysuckle. J. C. Bloem. TuT, *tr.* by Desmond Egan

Honeysuckle Rose. Andy Razaf. ReLy

Honeysuckles tap soil. Nocturne: My Sister Life. Erin Belieu. NeAmPo

Hong Kong Blues. Hoagy Carmichael. ReLy

Hong Kong 87, New York 84. Solstice Quipu. Arthur Sze. WANABP

Hongo Store 29 Miles Volcano Hilo, Hawaii, The. Garrett Kaoru Hongo. PoPoPo

Honky-Tonk Blues. Walter McDonald. SwNoth

Honnd by honnd we schulle ous take. Hand by Hand We Shall Us Take. *Unknown.* SacPr

Honor, The. Denis Johnson. LaCa

Honor be to Mudjekeewis! Henry Wadsworth Longfellow. UV *Fr.* Song of Hiawatha, The.

Honor Card. Betsy Colquitt. TiP2

Honor thy / To thine own. Vigil: Dwindle. Robin Behn. AmAlph

Honora, should that cruel time arrive. To Honora Sneyd. Anna Seward. CenSon; PoBW

Honorable woodland snake. Poem about Rain. Nikolai Alekseievich Zabolotsky. TCRusP, *tr.* by Daniel Weissbort

Honored Counselor, Ornament of Heaven, Joy of An! Lady of the Morning, The. *Unknown.* HW, *tr.* by Samuel Noah Kramer and Diane Wolkstein *and* Samuel Noah Kramer

Honour. Ceri Wyn Jones. BBMWP, *tr.* by Robert Minhinnick

Honour Dishonoured. Wilfrid Scawen Blunt. OBMV

Honour is flashed off exploit, so we say. Gerard Manley Hopkins. OxAEP-2

Honour Killing. Imtiaz Dharker. BeAl

Honour past all bens. Duncan Ban MacIntyre. NePenScot *Fr.* Last Farewell to the Hills.

Honour, that Guardian Angel, can alone. Martha Sansom. LW *Fr.* Clio.

Honour your hands, my comrade, scarred and worn. For a Working Woman. Frances Moore. RSaN

Honourable Entertainment Given to the Queen's Majesty in Progress at Elvetham, 1591, The. *Various authors.*
  Phillida and Coridon. NoSic; OBEV

Honoured I lived e'erwhile with honoured men. Honour Dishonoured. Wilfrid Scawen Blunt. OBMV

Hooded Crane Tower. Wang Chih-huan. CCL1, *tr.* by Stephen Owen

Hooded Legion, The. Gerald McCarthy. AmWaPo

Hoodoo numberman. For Etheridge Knight. Lamont B. Steptoe. OxAAAP

Hoodoo Scott Cooley Scalps John Wohrle. Steven Tye Culbert. TiP2

Hoodoo Whisper. Adrian Castro. BRtP

Hoofbeats pounded. Good Attitude to Horses, A. Vladimir Vladimirovich Mayakovsky. TCRusP, *tr.* by P. Lemke

Hook. Floyd Skloot. MoASP

Hook. James Wright. OxBoAm

Hook, The. Duncan Bush. TCAWP

Hook shot kisses the rim and, A. Fast Break. Edward Hirsch. MoASP; P180; VCAP

Hooker. Jean-Claude Martineau. OGAHCP, *tr.* by Boadiba and Jack Hirschman

Hooly and Fairly. Joanna Baillie. RACG; WoRP

Hoop Snake. Rebecca Wee. P180

Hoopla. Star Black. KGB

Hooray for Hollywood. Thomas M. Disch. PoA 2002

Hooray for Hollywood. Johnny Mercer. ReLy

Hooray for Love. Leo Robin. ReLy

Hooters. Meic Stephens. AngWePo; TCAWP

Hooting grossly, without explanation. (LL) Women Laughing. U. A. Fanthorpe. ItWoWo; MoWP

Hope. Emily Jane Brontë. NoP-4; NoP-5

Hope. Opus 2. Witter Bynner. APT-1, *tr. by* Emanuel Morgan

Hope: "It's hopeless, you told me." Aharon Shabtai. WoBe, *tr. by* Peter Cole

Hope. Josephine D. Henderson Heard. CBWP-4

Hope. George Herbert. ChIV-2; NPeEn; OxBEV; WeW-3

Hope ("He rose up on his dying bed.") Langston Hughes. APSN; OxBoAm; PFTM-1

Hope ("Sometimes when I'm lonely.") Langston Hughes. TRP

Hope. Dolores de Iruretagoyena de Humphrey. ReBoTo

Hope ("Week is dealt out like a hand, The.") Randall Jarrell. MoAmPo

Hope. Sydney E. Jerrold. SacPr

Hope. Sor Juana Inés de la Cruz. SpanPo, *tr. by* Kate Flores

Hope. Lisel Mueller. GoPo

Hope. F. D. Reeve. PoA 2002

Hope [*with music*]. Clara Ann Thompson. CBWP-2

Hope. Mary E. Tucker. CBWP-1

Hope: "She has a way of standing as if a belt of weights." Robyn Zappala. PfS

Hope and Despair. Lascelles Abercrombie. OBMV

Hope appears. Where Hope Lives. Carol Bell. GeoH

Hope Chest. Stephanie Williams. AnSo

Hope chewed and spit out, broken sleep. Anam Street 1. Yi Kyŏngnim. EcSo, *tr. by* Peter H. Lee

Hope Deferred [*with music*]. Clara Ann Thompson. CBWP-2

Hope for a Miracle. György Sárközi. IQMS, *tr. by* Roy Fuller

Hope for Her. W. S. Merwin. MotU

Hope for refugees. Karen Press. TSAP

Hope I handed Alfred, The. Azalea Poem, The. Jack Coulehan. BloBone

Hope is agony. Mikhail Naimy. NAAPv.2 *Fr.* Chord [*or* Cord] of Hope, The.

Hope is the thing with feathers. Emily Dickinson. AmFaPo; APN-2; BLPJKO; ChAP; MoAmPo; NoP-4; NoP-5; OxBoAm; SAmP; TCAPo

Hope like a wisp of straw shines in the stable. Paul Verlaine. SxFrPo, *tr. by* Martin Sorrell

Hope, of all ills that men endure. In Praise of Hope. Abraham Cowley. OxAEP-1

Hope of burning off at least the top layer of the time's uncleanness, from the acid-bottles. (LL) Prescription of Painful Ends. Robinson Jeffers. APT-1; MoAmPo

Hope Thou in God [*with music*]. Josephine D. Henderson Heard. CBWP-4

Hope! Thou vain, delusive maiden. Hope. Josephine D. Henderson Heard. CBWP-4

Hope was but a timid friend. Hope. Emily Jane Brontë. NoP-4; NoP-5

Hope, whose weak[e] being ruined [*or* ruin'd] is. NOSC *Fr.* Mistress, The.

Hopeful Spiritual Athlete, The. Kabir. RaBo, *tr. by* Robert Bly (Spiritual Athlete in an Orange Robe, The.) WED

Hopeless Desire Soon Withers and Dies. A. W. NoSic

Hopeless Eveningsong. Leonidas Malenis. SonAtl, *tr. by* George Emba, Maria Henson, Elpida Kyriakide and Eleftherios Papaleontiou

Hopelessness. Li Ch'ing-chao. BLT, *tr. by* Kenneth Rexroth

Hop-Garden, The. Christopher Smart.
  Book the First.
    Hops and Pops. STuOW
  Book the Second.
    Nail in the Grass, The. STuOW

Hopi Prophet Chooses a Pop. Heid E. Erdrich. AmPoNex

Hoping I could still save him. (LL) Flowers: "Right now I am the flower girl." Margaret Atwood. NoP-4; NoP-5

Hoping it might be so. (LL) Oxen, The. Thomas Hardy. CABP; ChAP; ChrPo; CtM; HarvBoo; MoBrPo; NAMCP V.1; NoAM; OBCP; OxAEP-2; PoCho; SoSe-8; TFi; TRP; WeW-3

Hoping It Might Be So. Kit Wright. StAl

Hoping publicly to humiliate her husband. Of Love, Death and the Sea-Squirt. Chris Greenhalgh. NeBl

Hopkins Enters the Roman Catholic Church. David Scott. NLP

Hopkins wrote, punning bird and verb. All Quail to the Wallowing. Lynne McMahon. ExTi

Hopper: In the Cafe. W.R. Elton. PoSol

Hopper never painted this, but here. American Solitude. Grace Schulman. PoSol

Hopper o'ditches, A. Riddle. *Unknown.* FaBoVe

Hopper painted this one empty of people. Cobb's Barns. Anne Babson Carter. PoSol

Hopper's "Nighthawks" (1942). Ira Sadoff. PoSol

Hopper's Women. Sue Standing. PoSol

Hopping frog, hop here and be seen. Christina Georgina Rossetti. VWP

Hopping Toad Blues. Raymond R. Patterson. SeSe

Hoppity. Alan Alexander Milne. NTCP

Hop-poles stand in cones, The. Midnight Skaters, The. Edmund Charles Blunden. MoBrPo; NPeEn; WoPoe

Hops and Pops. Christopher Smart. STuOW *Fr.* Hop-Garden, The.

Hops are a menace on the moon, a nuisance crop. Moon-Hops. Ted Hughes. CABP

Horace. Dániel Berzsenyi. IQMS, *tr. by* Peter Zollman

Horace Belisha was briefly Minister of Transport in the wartime Government of National Caligari. Horace Belisha. Geoff Ward. VaPo

Horace composed an ode about a certain boy. Marbod of Rennes. CAGL; EroLit *Fr.* Unyielding Youth, The.

Horace Kephart. Robert Morgan. LPSFW

Horae. Robert Fitzgerald. APT-2

Horae Canonicae. W. H. Auden.
  Lauds. BBASP
  Prime. NAMCP V.1
  Terce. GI

Horatian Ode. Joseph Warren Beach. PoA 2002

Horatian Ode upon Cromwell's Return from Ireland, An. Andrew Marvell. BASC; CABP; FSCP; NAEL-6v1; NAEL-7v1; NoP-4; NoP-5; NOSC; NPeEn; OBEV; OBWP; OxAEP-1; OxBEV; PBRV; PoPoPo; TFi; WaAnP

Horatio. Nan Cohen. IaFF

Horatio's Philosophy. R. S. Gwynn. IaFF

Horatius [*or* Horatius at the Bridge]. Thomas Babington Macaulay, 1st Baron Macaulay. CABP; FaBoWar; OBNV; OBWP; OxAEP-2 *Fr.* Lays of Ancient Rome.

Horeb's mountain top of old. Mountain Tops. Lizelia Augusta Jenkins Moorer. CBWP-3

Horestes. John Pickering.
  Haltersick's Song. NoSic
  Song Sung by Egistus and Clytemnestra. NoSic
  Vice's Song, The. NoSic

Horizon. David Emrys James. WoPoe, *tr. by* Anthony Conran

Horizon. Mac Lojowski. AmZen

Horizon. Laura Solórzano. SPV, *tr. by* Jen Hofer

Horizon. Philippe Soupault. YaTCFP, *tr. by* Mary Ann Caws and Patricia Terry

Horizon. Philippe Soupault. YaTCFP

Horizon, The. Kevin Hart. NOBAu

Horizon Blues. David Henderson. GT

Horizon Burns, The. Ernesto Lumbreras. RMCMP, *tr. by* Rebecca Seiferle

Horizon crawls, the. Rain Making. Dana Gilkes. BtF

Horizon line. Poem. Raymond Radiguet. CuPo

Horizon of Expectations, A. Only Indirectly. Giulia Niccolai. CItWP, *tr. by* Cinzia Sartini Blum and Lara Trubowitz

Horizon of Gunbutts. Patrick Sylvain. OGAHCP, *tr. by* Boadiba and Jack Hirschman

Horizon of islands shifting. Outer Banks, The. Muriel Rukeyser. APT-2

Horizon slopes away, The. Departure. Pierre Reverdy. CuPo

Horizons release skies. Rules and Ranges for Ian Tyson. Roy Fisher. Oth

Horizontal in a deckchair on the bleak ward [*or* Horizontal on a deckchair in the Ward]. Ezra Pound. Robert Lowell. NoAM

Horizonte. Laura Solórzano. SPV

Horn, The. Léonie Adams. MoAmPo

Horn hung on an oak, A. Bit of Brass, A. Padraic Fallon. ModIr; NPeEn

Horn of doom is blaring!, The. Sergey Aleksandrovich Yesenin. CAGL, *tr. by* Simon Karlinsky

Horn of Roland, The. Marina Ivanovna Tsvetayeva. TCRusP, *tr. by* William H Tjalsma

Horned Snake, The [*with music*]. Louis Oliver. HATNAP; NAAPv.2

Hornet holds on to the curtain, winter, The. Letter. Jean Valentine. CAP-8

Hornets collect on the side of the sun. Beetle Light. Madeline DeFrees. GifTon

Hornets occasionally build their nests near roads. Homer. OBVE *Fr.* Iliad, The.

Horns and cloven hoof are in the mire, The. Coronado at Rio Grande Del Norte. Arthur M. Sampley. TiP2

Horns [*or* Hornes] to bulls wise Nature lends. Beauty. Thomas Stanley. OBVE

Hornworm: Autumn Lamentation. Stanley Kunitz. AmFaPo; BodElec; ItP

Hornworm: Summer Reverie. Stanley Kunitz. BodElec

Horny or Harm seems an ordinary home. Various Readings of an Illegible Postcard. Christine Hume. AmPoNex

Horoscope. Colleen J. McElroy. GT

Horowitz debuted a Schumann piece. What I Heard on the Radio Today. Marc J. Straus. BloBone

Horrible Today, The. Max Jacob. AF, *tr. by* Ron Padgett

Horrid Voice of Science, The. Vachel Lindsay. PoA 2002

Horror. Gyula Illyés. IQMS, *tr.* by Anthony Edkins

Horror Movie. Kim Sŭnghŭi. CAMKP, *tr.* by Anthony, Brother of Taizé

Horse. Gloria Anzaldúa. UnSA

Horse. Louise Glück. NALW

Horse. John Thompson. Coast

Horse. Chase Twichell. ExTi; StAl

Horse: "First horse I ever saw, The." Michael Waters. NevBe; UrbNat

Horse, The. Marie Laurencin. CuPo

20 The Horse. Conor O'Callaghan. NIrP *Fr.* Loose Change.

Horse, The. Tristan Tzara. YaTCFP, *tr.* by Mary Ann Caws *and* Jean-Pierre Cauvin

Horse, The. James Wright. YaYoPo

Horse, The: "They spoke of the horse alive." Philip Levine. AtGh; VCAP

Horse, The: "Up the moss-grown." Georgi Borisov. CSCBP, *tr.* by Georgi Belev and Lisa Sapinkopf

Horse and a flea and three blind mice, A. Whoops! *Unknown.* NTCP

Horse and Tree. Rita Dove. TRP

Horse beneath me seemed, The. Ride, The. Richard Wilbur. CAP-8

Horse Boyle was called Horse Boyle because of his brother Mule. Dresden. Ciaran Carson. ModIr; NPeEn; PBCIP; PNI

Horse butcher, The. Pierre McOrlan. MFP, *tr.* by Martin Sorrell

Horse. *Caballo negro.* Black horse in my hair. H. Chic. Virgil Suárez. NevBe

Horse Calligram. Guillaume Apollinaire. PFTM-1

Horse Chestnut Tree, The. Richard Eberhart. MoAmPo

Horse comes out of the dark, A. Horse in Glasgow. Jenni Daiches. EdScPo

Horse Girls. Tammy Armstrong. Coast

Horse he sits on its saddless, The. Young Horseman. Lajos Kassák. IQMS, *tr.* by Edwin Morgan

Horse in Glasgow. Jenni Daiches. EdScPo

Horse in My Yard, The. Gene Shuford. TiP2

Horse is white, The. Or it. Saving the Appearances. Charles Tomlinson. OxBEV

Horse meadow quarters roots as large, The. Genius of Fog at Ecola Creek Mouth. Sandra McPherson. ExTi

Horse neighs, wants to gallop, A. *Unknown.* CATKP, *tr.* by Peter H. Lee

Horse on a Fence. George Evans. PmAP

Horse stands near a well whose rim is the edge of the world, The. Children's Book of Knowledge, The. Jesse Lee Kercheval. SUP

Horse Thief, The. William Rose Benét. MoAmPo

Horse with birds on its mane, doubt on its tail, The. Godhorse. Kojo Laing. HBAPE

Horseback [*with music*]. Carolyn Kizer. MoASP

Horseback he saw. Hoodoo Scott Cooley Scalps John Wohrle. Steven Tye Culbert. TiP2

Horseback on Sunday morning. Wild Geese, The. Wendell Berry. TRP

Horsehoe Crab in Flagrante Delicto. Richard Price. EdScPo

Horseman, pass by! (LL) Under Ben Bulben. William Butler Yeats. NAEL-6v2; NAEL-7v2; NAMCP V.1; NoAM; NoP-4; NoP-5

Horse-Mill, The. Robert Rendall. EdScPo

Horses. Witter Bynner. APT-1

Horses: "Setting out on my bicycle alone." Henri Cole. PoDa

Horses. Dylan Iorwerth. BBMWP *Fr.* Sand.

Horses. Pablo Neruda. BeAl, *tr.* by Stephen Mitchell

Horses [*with music*]. Gwyn Thomas. BBMWP; OBVVE, *tr.* by Joseph P. Clancy

Horses. Dorothy, Duchess of Wellington Wellesley. OBMV

Horses, The. Ted Hughes. BeAl; NAMCP V.2; NoAM; WaAnP

Horses, The. Michael Longley. StAl

Horses at a Breach in the Great Wall. Ch'en Lin. ChinPo, *tr.* by Ye Weilian [*or* Yeh Wei-lien *or* Wai-lim Yip]

Horses at Christmas. Henry Shukman. BeAl

Horses Before Troy. Melih Cevdet Anday. *tr.* by Talat Sait Halman

6. Love. NaPG, *tr.* by Talat Sait Halman

Horse's eyes, The. (LL) Switch. Sean O Riordain. ModIr; StAl, *tr.* by Patrick Crotty

Horses go down at dawn, The. Horses in the Lake. Pablo Antonio Cuadra. TCLAP, *tr.* by Ann McCarthy de Zavala and Grace Schulman

Horses in Flowers. Sappho. OBVE; WoPoe, *tr.* by Guy Davenport

Horses in Snow [*with music*]. Roberta Hill Whiteman. NoAM

Horses in the Lake. Pablo Antonio Cuadra. TCLAP, *tr.* by Ann McCarthy de Zavala and Grace Schulman

Horses in the Ocean. Boris Abramovich Slutsky. TCRusP, *tr.* by Daniel Weissbort

Horses know how to swim. Horses in the Ocean. Boris Abramovich Slutsky. TCRusP, *tr.* by Daniel Weissbort

Horse's mind, The. Unity. Fazil Hüsnü Daglarca. RaBo, *tr.* by Tâlat S. Halman

Horses nuzzle, The. Shared Life, A. Katherine Soniat. PfSP

Horses of Meaning, The. Eiléan Ní Chuilleanáin. BeAl

Horses of the Sea, The. Christina Georgina Rossetti. NTCP *Fr.* Sing-Song.

Horses of Yilderin, The. Kenneth Patchen. APT-2

Horses which Titan when discharged for the night, The. Catius As Conius Silius Italicus. RomPo *Fr.* Punica, The.

Horseshoe. Merrill Gilfillan. AHA

Horseshoes. David Bottoms. PoA 2002

Hortus Urbanus / Urban Garden. Colin Morton.
  "Twice now this morning I am wakened by full-throated geese." IFF

Hos Ego Versiculos. Francis Quarles. NOSC *Fr.* Argalus and Parthenia.

Hosanna. Thomas Traherne. ChIV-2

Hosannah! *Christus natus est.* (LL) Christus Natus Est. Countee Cullen. ChIV-2; ChrPo

Hosannah the home run! (LL) Dream of a Baseball Star. Gregory Corso. BB; PmAP

Hospital. Charles North. FTOS

Hospital. Yun Tongju. CAMKP, *tr.* by Kay Richards and Steffen Richards

Hospital, The. Patrick Kavanagh. CABP; EmeKit; ModIr; NPeEn

Hospital, The. Boris Abramovich Slutsky. TCRusP, *tr.* by Daniel Weissbort

Hospital Barge at Cérisy. Wilfred Owen. HarvBoo; TCAWP

Hospital Corners. Alison Townsend. SweBea

Hospital Duties. *Unknown.* CBCWP

Hospital Evening [*with music*]. Gwen Harwood. EmeKit

Hospital garden on Sunday, A. Frost. Fedya Filkova. CSCBP, *tr.* by Georgi Belev and Lisa Sapinkopf

Hospital Gypsy Song. Aleksandr Arkadevich Galich. TCRusP, *tr.* by Gerry Smith

Hospital Interiors. Giovanni Raboni. ItPo, *tr.* by Gayle Ridinger

Hospital: it wasn't her idea, The. John Ashbery. ColAP

Hospital Night. Francis Webb. BMAP

Hospital Soliloquy, A. Rose Terry Cooke. NAAPv.1; SWaP

Hospital State, The. Betsy Sholl. PBCAP

Hospital Window, The. James Dickey. CAP-8; EMP; NAMCP V.2; NoAM; VCAP

Host. Bruce Bond. Vesp

Host is riding from Knocknarea, The. Hosting of the Sidhe, The. William Butler Yeats. NAMCP V.1; NoAM

Host of peaks rear up into the color of cold, A. Spending the Night at a Mountain Temple. Chia Tao. CCL1, *tr.* by Stephen Owen

Host of the Air, The. William Butler Yeats. IrV

Host set forth, and pour'd his steel waves far out of the fleet, The. Homer. FaBoWar *Fr.* Iliad, The.

Host slices slice after slice of glistening sashimi, The. (LL) In Your Honor. Arthur Sze. GifTon; ICANM

Host tells his guest his dream, The. Song for Three Dreams. Chunghur Hyujung. BecRai, *tr.* by Kim Daljin, Kim Won-Chung and Christopher Merrill

Hostage. Dixie Partridge. LiTh

Hostage to the phalli. Queynt. Anne Rouse. NeBl

Hostages, The. Muriel Rukeyser. AF

Hostel, The. Herman Melville. APN-2 *Fr.* Clarel: A Poem and Pilgrimage in the Holy Land.

Hostess. Laura Kasischke. PoDa

Hostess of the Ferry Inn, The. Gwerfyl Mechain. OBVVE, *tr.* by H. Idris Bell

Hostilidad. Gerardo Diego. RaW

Hostilities Between France and England Extended to America. Braddock's Defeat. Joel Barlow. AmWaPo *Fr.* Columbiad, The.

Hostility. Gerardo Diego. RaW, *tr.* by Ralph Nelson and Hardie St. Martin

Hosting of the Sidhe, The. William Butler Yeats. NAMCP V.1; NoAM

Hot. Anne Carson. NLPA *Fr.* Glass Essay, The.

Hot air balloon convention floats, The. Looking Up. Sujata Bhatt. EmeKit

Hot and Cold. Silvio Giussani. ItPo, *tr.* by Gayle Ridinger

Hot Anger stirs the soup; Grief moves the dust. Sisters, The. Melissa Cannon. FFC

Hot blue moonlight down the steep sky. Anne Carson. NLPA *Fr.* Glass Essay, The.

Hot Comb. Natasha Trethewey. SpirFl

Hot day. Dying of thirst. Slake myself. Meleager. EroLit, *tr.* by Kenneth McLeish

Hot Day In Sydney, A. *Unknown.* NOBAu

Hot days of errands and badges, paper, shrill rage. Robert Pinsky. PfSP *Fr.* City Elegies.

Hot Dog. Gerald Stern.

8. ViWalt

Hot House. Rick Zand. MAAN

Hot, humid, the smell of sewage. Greenhalgh's Pub. Julian Croft. NOBAu

Hot ice shoots (it seems) through. Epiphany. Christine D'Haen. TuT, *tr. by* Dennis O'Driscoll

Hot in June a narrow winged. Nameless One, A. Margaret Avison. BrAP; HeIP-4

Hot night hangs on the roof. In Time. *Unknown.* SonAtl, *tr. by* El-Houssaine Baali, Colin Hobday and Ursula Hobday

Hot night makes us keep our bedroom windows open, The. To Speak of Woe That Is in Marriage. Robert Lowell. CAP-8; NAMCP V.2; NoAM; WaAnP

Hot night of the ramparts. Embrace the Blade. Joyce Mansour. HAWP, *tr. by* Carol Cosman

Hot Ports. Léon Laleau. SonAtl, *tr. by* Hannah Bourgein, Carrol F. Coates, Kurt Ganzl and Pierre Laleau

Hot Property, A. Ronald Wallace. SUP

Hot spray softens her neck muscles, The. Shower, The. Kimiko Hahn. CAP-8

Hot stink of skunk. Camino Real. Adrienne Rich. BodElec

Hot Sun, Cool Fire. George Peele. *See* Bethsabe's Song.

Hot sun[ne], cool[e] fire, temper[e]d with sweet air[e]. George Peele. ChIV-1; NoSic; NPeEn; OxBEV

Hot thumb, The. Just after Michael's Death, the Game of Pool. Richard Tipping. BMAP

Hot Wind, Provincetown Harbor. Cynthia Huntington. MAAN

Hotel. Alfonso D'Aquino. RMCMP

Hotel. Alfonso D'Aquino. RMCMP, *tr. by* Rebecca Seiferle

Hotel. Jane Rohrer. ACAMVP

Hotel again! My friend Paul is a prisoner of the Germans My, The. In Search of the Traitor. Max Jacob. AF, *tr. by* Michael Brownstein

Hotel d'Avignon. G. C. Waldrep. LegDan

Hotel de Dream. Jane Cooper. ExTi

Hotel de L'Etoile. Matthew Rohrer. AmPoNex

Hôtel de l'Univers et Portugal. James Merrill. PoA 2002

Hotel foyer empty, The. Except for. Sestri Levante / Liguria 2. Günter Kunert. GTCP, *tr. by* Reinhold Grimm

Hôtel Fraternité. Hans Magnus Enzensberger. CLPP, *tr. by* Jerome Rothenberg

Hotel Fresno. Dixie Salazar. GeoHom

Hotel Lautréamont. John Ashbery. FTOS; HarvBoo

Hotel Lullaby. Srikanth Reddy. IIR

Hotel Marine. David Campbell. BMAP

Hotel Nights with My Mother. Linda McCarriston. TWF

Hotel Normandie Pool, The. Derek Walcott. VCWP

Hotel Room. Blaga Dimitrova. CSCBP, *tr. by* Georgi Belev and Lisa Sapinkopf

Hotels 1970. John Wieners. AHA

Hotel—to begin, A/ again. (LL) Again. Robert Creeley. NAMCP V.2; VCAP

Hotgun on the Death of Yadeka Harjo. Alexander L. Posey. NAAPv.2

Hotpink crimplene petunias. Matching Flowers. Kate Foley. Prnts

Hots, The. Michael Sharkey. NOBAu

Hotwire. Leslie Ullman. PoA 2002

Hou Ji (Lord Millet), Progenitor of Zhou. *Unknown.* CCL1, *tr. by* William Jennings

Houdini. Moniza Alvi. EmeKit; MFPA

Houdini. Eli W. Mandel. NIP-4

Hound, The. Robert Francis. SoSe-8

Hound and Leper. Beckian Fritz Goldberg. PfS

Hound of Heaven, The. Francis Thompson. CABP; ChIV-2; InvLi; MoBrPo; NAEL-6v2; NAEL-7v2; OBMV; SacPr; TFi

    "I fled Him, down the nights and down the days." EroLit; ITBLP; WaAnP

Hound Song. Donald Finkel. P180

Hound that men the Tumbler name, The. Ludovico Ariosto. DiBP *Fr.* Orlando Furioso.

Hound that they had them among, A. Henry the Minstrel (Blind Harry). DiBP *Fr.* Sir William Wallace.

Hounds, The. John Freeman. OBMV

Hounds are either the work of wind, The. Dennis Phillips. FTOS *Fr.* Means.

Hounds Howl at the Moon. Y. Nokhem. Prolet, *tr. by* Amelia Glaser

Hour, The. Juana de Ibarbourou. TCLAP, *tr. by* Sophie Cabot Black

Hour, The. Call, The. Aaron Kurtz. Prolet, *tr. by* Amelia Glaser

Hour After Hour, Day After Day. Rosalía de Castro. SpanPo, *tr. by* Muriel Kittel

Hour at last come round, The. Dying Gaul, The. Desmond O'Grady. PBCIP

Hour farther witch art in Heaven. Hour Farther. Robert Desnos. MFP; YaTCFP, *tr. by* Martin Sorrell

Hour from night to day, The. Four in the Morning. Wisława Szymborska. BLT

Hour Glass, The. Edward Quillinan. NOBRP

Hour in a Studio, An. Richard Watson Gilder. APN-2

Hour is tired as if it were were time for bed, The. Uri Zvi Greenberg. FIT, *tr. by* Robert Friend

Hour of Death, The. Felicia Dorothea Hemans. NOBRP

Hour of Fear. J. Dyfnallt Owen. BBMWP, *tr. by* Gillian Clarke

Hour of Life, An. Jean-Paul Nyunai. SonAtl, *tr. by* Kurt Ganzl, Christophe Mirambeau, Aliko Songolo and Kenneth Wilburn

Hour of Magic, The. W. H. Davies. MoBrPo

Hour of Sleep, The. Robert Ellis. OBWVE, *tr. by* H. Idris Bell

Hour of the Angel, The. Rudyard Kipling. OxBSo *Fr.* Land and Sea Tales.

Hour of the Siesta, The. Judith Ortiz Cofer. PueRic

Hour ten he rose, ten-sworded, every finger. Timoshenko. Sidney Keyes. OBWP

Hour, the spot, are here at last, The. At Harper's Ferry Just before the Attack. Edward W. Williams. CBCWP

Hour upon hour I keep them hanging there like jellyfish. Drownproofing Lesson. Robin Behn. AmAlph

Hour when the moon mists over. Dawn. Philippe Jaccottet. VCWP

Hourglass. Josephine Jacobsen. NoP-4; NoP-5

4. Hourglass. Robert B. Shaw. PoA 2002 *Fr.* Chronometrics.

Hourglass, The. Joseph Beaumont. NOSC

Hour-Glass, The. Ben Jonson. NIP-4

Hourglass Lying Down. Alice Rahon. SurWo, *tr. by* Nancy Deffebach and Vanina Deler

Hour-glass whispers to the lion's paw, The. W. H. Auden. BrAP; OxAEP-2

Hours ago he woke up the sky. Bird on a Jaunt. T. Harri Jones. TCAWP

Hours before dawn we were woken by the quake. Aubade. William Empson. OxAEP-2; OxBEV

Hours between washing and the well, The. Soul Keeping Company. Lucie Brock-Broido. AWPTFC

Hours continuing long, sore and heavy-hearted. Hours Continuing Long. Walt Whitman. NAAPv.1; PoPoPo

Hours glide, The. Midnight. Vicente Huidobro. CuPo

Hour's Glory, The. Henrietta Cordelia Ray. CBWP-3

Hours Musicians Keep, The. Aleda Shirley. SwNoth

Hours of my youth spent dallying. Sand-time Measuring. Moses Glyn Jones. BBMWP, *tr. by* Mike Jenkins

Hours of Sleep [*with music*]. *Unknown.* NBLV

Hours of the Day, The. George Dillon. IllVoic

Hours pass / slowly as a snail. Clockface. Judith Thurman. Spl

Hours rise up putting off stars and it is, The. E. E. Cummings. MoAmPo

Hours that kept looking at us, The. Handless Clock. Raymond Radiguet. CuPo

House. Robert Browning. NAEL-6v2

House. Robert Hass. LoL

House. Selima Hill. BeAl

House. Laura Mullen. ExTi

House. Ellen Bryant Voigt. LPSFW

House, A. A car. Sweet things. Gold. Sister. Angela Agali. NeNiPo

House, The ("Mas-Soñer / Restaurat—Any.") Robert Creeley. FTOS

House, The. Dewi Stephen Jones. BBMWP, *tr. by* the author

House, The. Robert Minhinnick. AngWePo

House, The. Gabriela Mistral. TCLAP, *tr. by* Doris Dana

House, The. Gabriela Mistral. BBASP, *tr. by* Doris Dana

House, The. Mary Oliver. WaAnP

House, The. Vincent Woods. NIrP

House and Land [*with music*]. Allen Curnow. BrAP

House and the Road, The. Josephine Preston Peabody. ITBLP

House Beautiful, The. John Dyer. STuOW *Fr.* Fleece, The.

House Beside the Sea, The. Rachel Hadas. FFC

House Beyond, The. John Fitzgerald. BBMWP, *tr. by* Joseph P. Clancy

House Blessing. *Zuni Oral Tradition.* NAWM-7v2 *Fr.* Shalako.

House (Blown Apart). David Shapiro. BodElec

House built within men's reach, A. Drinking Wine. *Unknown.* ChinPo, *tr. by* Ye Weilian [*or* Yeh Wei-lien *or* Wai-lim Yip]

House by the *acequia*, The. Casa, La. Rosemary Catacalos. TiP2

House by the Sea. Johanna Kruit. TuT, *tr. by* Micheal O'Siadhail

House by the Sea, The. Elizabeth Stoddard. SWaP

House by the Side of the Road, The [*with music*]. Sam Walter Foss. BRP; ITBLP

House Call to a Man with Parkinson's Disease, A. Michael O'Reilly. BloBone

House can be haunted by those who were never there, A. Selva Oscura. Louis MacNeice. HarvBoo

House Cap. Bernadette Mayer. FTOS

House cat has never seen the sea, The. Woman asleep. Marie-Claire Bancquart. MFP, *tr. by* Martin Sorrell

House catch on fire and ain't no water 'round. Southern Blues. *Unknown*. APT-1

House Face. D. A. Powell. IAoNAP

House full, [a] yard full, [A]. Riddle. *Unknown*. NTCP

House, Garden, Madness. Cate Marvin. PoDa

House had gone to bring again, The. Need of Being Versed in Country Things, The. Robert Frost. APT-1; NAMCP V.1; NoAM; SAmP; TCAPo; TRP

House I once lived in now calls out to me, A. Haunting. Andrew Steeves. Coast

House in Broad Street, red brick, with nine rooms, The. Things, The. Conrad Potter Aiken. WeW-3

House in Krasnogruda. Czeslaw Milosz. BodElec, *tr. by* the author and Robert Hass

House in Rome. Snorri Hjartarson. PML, *tr. by* Alan Boucher

House in St. Petersburg. Stanley Burnshaw. WoPoe

House in Taos, A. Langston Hughes. APT-2

House in the Field. Gennady Aygi. WoBe, *tr. by* Peter France

House in the Green Well, The. John Hall Wheelock. MoAmPo

House in the long ago, The. House by the Sea. Johanna Kruit. TuT, *tr. by* Micheal O'Siadhail

House is crammed: tier beyond tier they grin, The. Blighters. Siegfried Sassoon. NAMCP V.1; NoAM; OxBEV; PoWW

House is empty now with my hand. House Is Empty Now. Juan Felipe Herrera. PfSP

House is haunted; when the little feet, The. Haunted. Edith Nesbit. VWP

House is so quiet now, The. Vacuum, The. Howard Nemerov. NIL-7; NIP-4; StAl

House is watched, the watchers only planets, The. Wages of Love. C. D. Wright. CAP-8

House knows this and the kitchen knows this, The. Nostalgia, Cheryl, Is the Best Heroin. Arielle Greenberg. LegDan

House my earthly parent left, The. Cottage, The. Jones Very. APN-1

House of Alvargonzález, The. Antonio Machado Ruiz. SpanPo, *tr. by* Denise Levertov

House of Breath. Ken Gerner. GifTon

House of Busyrane, The. Edmund Spenser. NoSic *Fr.* Faerie Queene, The.

House of Cards, The. Vern Rutsala. MotU

House of Changes. Jeni Couzyn. BrAP

House of Christmas, The. G. K. Chesterton. ChrPo; MoBrPo; SacPr

House of Dior. Robyn Schiff. LegDan

House of each sentence endlessly hinged, house of each phrase opened elegy. Dead House Sonnet. Brian Teare. LegDan

House of Falling Leaves, The. William Stanley Braithwaite. OxAAAP

House of five fires, you never raised me. In the Longhouse, Oneida Museum. Roberta Hill Whiteman. NoAM

House of God, The. Bishop Richard Mant. SacPr

House of Life, The. Dante Gabriel Rossetti.
    Part One—Youth and Change.
      4: Lovesight. NAEL-6v2
      6a: Nuptial Sleep. NAEL-6v2; NAEL-7v2
      19: Silent Noon. BrAP; GSo; NAEL-6v2; NAEL-7v2; NoP-4; NoP-5
      50: Willowwood ("And now Love sang: but his was such a song"). CABP; NAEL-6v2; OxBSo
      49: Willowwood ("I sat with Love upon a woodside well"). NAEL-6v2; OxBSo
      51: Willowwood ("O ye, all ye that walk in Willowwood"). NAEL-6v2; OxBSo
      52: Willowwood ("So sang he: and as meeting rose and rose"). NAEL-6v2; OxBSo
    Part Two—Change and Fate.
      83: Barren Spring. NoP-4
      78: Body's Beauty. NAEL-7v2
      71: The Choice ("Eat thou and drink; to-morrow thou shalt die"). ChIV-2
      73: The Choice ("Think thou and act; to-morrow thou shalt die"). ChIV-2; OBEV
      72: The Choice ("Watch thou and fear; to-morrow thou shalt die"). ChIV-2
      98: He and I. OxBSo
      66: The Heart of the Night. SacPr
      70: The Hill Summit. NoP-4; NoP-5
      63: Inclusiveness. NAEL-6v2
      86: Lost Days. SacPr
      91: Lost on Both Sides. NoP-4
      74: Old and New Art (St Luke the Painter). SacPr
      101: The One Hope. BrAP; GSo; NAEL-6v2; NAEL-7v2
      90: Retro me, Sathana! ChIV-2
      77: Soul's Beauty. NAEL-7v2; OBEV; OxAEP-2
      97: A Superscription. BrAP; GSo; NAEL-6v2; NAEL-7v2; NoP-4
    "Sonnet is a moment's monument, A." BrAP; GSo; NAEL-6v2; NAEL-7v2; NIL-7; NoP-4; NoP-5

House of Memories. Ch'oe Sûngja. EcSo, *tr. by* Mickey Hong

House of Mercy, A. Stevie Smith. HarvBoo; MoWP; NAMCP V.1

House of Night, The. Philip Freneau.
    "And by that light around the dome appear'd." NAAL-3; TCAPo
    "And from the woods the late resounding note." TCAPo
    "And from within the howls of Death I heard." TCAPo
    "And here and there with laurel shrubs between." NAAL-3
    "At distance far approaching to the tomb." NAAL-3; TCAPo
    "At last, by chance and guardian fancy led." NAAL-3; TCAPo
    "Before the hearse Death's chaplain seem'd to go." TCAPo
    "But now this man of hell toward me turned." NAAL-3
    "By some sad means, when reason holds no sway." TCAPo
    "Dark was the sky, and not one friendly star." TCAPo
    "Dim burnt the lamp, and now the phantom Death." TCAPo
    "Hills sink to plains, and man returns to dust." TCAPo
    "Meantime from an adjoining chamber came." NAAL-3
    "Much spoke he of the myrtle and the yew." NAAL-3
    "No pleasant fruit or blossom gaily smiled." NAAL-3
    "Nor look'd I back, till to a far off wood." TCAPo
    "O'er a dark field I held my dubious way." TCAPo
    "Pathetic were their words, and well they aimed." NAAL-3
    "Peace to this awful dome!"—when straight I heard." NAAL-3
    "Poppy there, companion to repose, The." NAAL-3
    "Primrose there, the violet darkly blue, The." NAAL-3
    "Rude, from the wide extended Chesapeke." TCAPo
    "Sad was his countenance, if we can call." NAAL-3
    "Then up three winding stairs my feet were brought." NAAL-3
    "There cedars dark, the osier, and the pine." NAAL-3
    "Too nearly join'd to sickness, toils, and pains." TCAPo
    "Towering Alps, the haughty Appenine, The." TCAPo
    "Trembling, across the plain my course I held." TCAPo
    "Trembling I write my dream, and recollect." NAAL-3; TCAPo
    "Up rushed a band, with compasses and scales." NAAL-3
    Vision of the Night, The. NAAL-3
    "What is this Death, ye deep read sophists, say?" TCAPo
    "When Nature bids thee from the world retire." TCAPo

House of Prayer, The. William Cowper. ChIV-2 *Fr.* Olney Hymns.

House of Rest. Sir John Betjeman. OxAEP-2 *Fr.* House of Rest.

House of Rest, The. Julia Ward Howe. SWaP

House of Spring. Muso Soseki. EaWin, *tr. by* W. S. Merwin

House of Teletubbies, The. Dylan Iorwerth. BBMWP *Fr.* Sand.

House of the Hare, The. Naomi Mitchison. MoWP

House of the Mouse, The. Lucy Sprague Mitchell. NTCP

House of Xerxes. Paul Violi. PA9/11

House on a Cliff. Louis MacNeice. HarvBoo; ModIr; NPeEn

House on a Red Cliff. Michael Ondaatje. NoP-5

House on Bentalou Street, The. Beginnings. Afaa Michael Weaver. PBCAP

House on fire my mom's. Hoa Nguyen. WANABP

House on Moscow Street, The. Marilyn Nelson Waniek. UnSA

House on the Hill, The. Edwin Arlington Robinson. APN-2; CtM; MakPoe; MoAmPo; NAAPv.1; NCAP; OxBoAm

House over the garden is a bouquet of evening windows, The. Mikhail Yeryomin. ItGoST, *tr. by* J. Kates

House persists, the permanent, The. House Remembered, The. Eiléan Ní Chuilleanáin. MoWP

House Poem. Laura Solórzano. SPV, *tr. by* Jen Hofer

House Remembered, The. Eiléan Ní Chuilleanáin. MoWP

House ringed round with trees and in the trees, A. Asylum. John Freeman. OBMV

House Slave, The. Rita Dove. AmAlph; NAMCP V.2; NoAM; OxAAAP

House Sparrows. Anthony Hecht. OWoS

House Style, The. Elizabeth Macklin. KGB

House That Fear Built: Warsaw, 1943, The. Jane Flanders. PBCAP

House That Jack Built, The. Mother Goose. OxBEV

House That Jack Built, The. *Unknown*. NBLV

House that shored my childhood up, The. Manse, The. Alastair Reid. EdScPo

House That Was, The. Laurence Binyon. MoBrPo

House, village, city, land, and empire harvest hurt. Women's Rule. Friedrich von Logau. GePo, *tr. by* George C. Schoolfield

House Was Quiet and the World Was Calm, The. Wallace Stevens. NoP-4; NoP-5; OxBoAm; PoCho; SAmP

House was shaken by a rising wind, The. Brainstorm. Howard Nemerov. OxBoAm; TRP

House we moved into has been landscaped, The. Buildings and Grounds. Henry Taylor. LPSFW

House, with blind unhappy face, The. Gray Folk, The. Edith Nesbit. PEW

House with Nobody in It, The.   Joyce Kilmer.   ChAP

House Without Walls.   Han-shan (Cold Mountain).   BB; CCL1; NDACCP; WoPoe, *tr. by* Gary Snyder

Houseboat Ferry.   Jessica Freeman.   AnSo

Housebound.   Amy Gerstler.   ExTi

Housefire.   Miranda Field.   LegDan

Household Cavalry, Llanstephan.   Sally Roberts Jones.   TCAWP

Household Gods.   Jim Elledge.   SwNoth

Household Muse.   Joyce Sutphen.   SweBea

Household of Eight.   Abraham Reisen.   WoPoe, *tr. by* Nathan Halper

Household of Ruth, The.   Mrs. Henry Linden.   CBWP-4

Household words, no more depart. (LL)   Seaweed.   Henry Wadsworth Longfellow.   APN-1; ColAP

Householder Departs from the City, The.   Nathan Alterman.   FIT, *tr. by* Robert Friend

House—In the Grove of the World.   Gennady Aygi.   WoBe, *tr. by* Peter France

Housekeeping.   Lucie Brock-Broido.   ExTi

Housekeeping.   Virginia Chase Sutton.   SweBea

Housekeeping.   Natasha Trethewey.   SweBea

Housekeeping in a Dream.   Laura Kasischke.   SweBea

Houseless.   Daphne Marlatt.   NLPA *Fr.* Touch to My Tongue.

Housemaid's Ballad, The.   Dōyaku Sensei, Master Artery.   EMJL, *tr. by* Haruo Shirane

House-Mates.   Leon Gellert.   NOBAu

House—or world.   House—In the Grove of the World.   Gennady Aygi. WoBe, *tr. by* Peter France

Houses.   Agha Shahid Ali.   NIP-4

Houses.   Aileen Fisher.   NTCP

Houses, The.   October.   Yvor Winters.   APT-2

Houses, an embassy, the hospital.   Days of 1964.   James Merrill.   NAMCP V.2; OxBoAm; VCAP

Houses and rooms are full of perfumes, the shelves are crowded with perfumes. Walt Whitman.   CAGL; ColAP *Fr.* Song of Myself.

Houses and the haystacks are on fire, The.   Razglednica (2).   Miklós Radnóti. IQMS, *tr. by* Peter Zollman

Houses are faces.   Houses.   Aileen Fisher.   NTCP

Houses are haunted, The.   Disillusionment of Ten O'Clock.   Wallace Stevens. APT-1; ItP; NAAPv.2; NAMCP V.1; NoAM; OxBoAm; SAmP; SoSe-8; TCAPo; TRP

Houses, churches, mixed together.   Description of London, A.   John Bancks. OBCoV

Houses die, and will not die, The.   Heartland.   Jim Barnes.   HATNAP

Houses, dim boards, daubed with a searing script.   Oskar Loerke.   GTCP *Fr.* At the Edge of the Great City.

Houses have their secrets. They signal back and forth by means of colors. Evening Walk.   Yannis Ritsos.   MotU, *tr. by* Martin McKinsey

Houses in country and city.   Requiem.   Wang Fan-chih.   CrYelRi, *tr. by* Sam Hamill

Houses Like Angels.   Jorge Luis Borges.   TCLAP, *tr. by* Robert Fitzgerald

Houses like piles of children's books.   Anna Gorenko.   CRWP, *tr. by* Peter France

Houses of Emily Dickinson, The.   Larry Rubin.   NIP-4

House-snake dwells here still, The.   Closed World, The.   Denise Levertov. NoP-4

House-Top, The.   Herman Melville.   APN-2; BrAP; CBCWP; NAAL-3; NAAPv.1; NCAP; OxBoAm; TCAPo

Housewife.   Josephine Miles.   APT-2

Housewife.   Anne Sexton.   NALW; WaAnP

Housewife, The.   Ginger Andrews.   SUP

Housewifery.   Edward Taylor. *See* Huswifery.

Housework.   Joan Larkin.   WiU

Housework.   William Matthews.   CAP-8

House-wreckers have left the door and a staircase, The.   House-wreckers, The. Charles Reznikoff.   APT-2

House-wreckers, The.   Charles Reznikoff.   APT-2

Housing Poem, The.   Dian Million.   ReEnLa

Hous-keping's dead, *Saturio:* wot'st thou where?   Joseph Hall.   PBRV *Fr.* Virgidemiarum Book 5.

Houston: An Ode.   Paul Christensen.
   Prolog.   TiP2

Houston Haiku.   Robert Phillips.   TiP2

Houston Heights.   Janet Lowery.   TiP2

Houston's adolescence was my adolescence.   Houston's Adolescence.   Robert Bonazzi.   TiP2

Hovering.   Jessica Lowenthal.   OnScMo

Hovering quietly by my window on this dark night.   Apparition.   Cho Chihun. CAMKP, *tr. by* Kyung-Ja Chun

How.   Joanne Burns.   BMAP

How?   Vladimir Holan.   PoSu, *tr. by* Ian Milner and Jarmila Milner

How?   Abraham Sutskever.   HP

How?   Tontongi.   OGAHCP, *tr. by* Boadiba and Jack Hirschman

How a Place Becomes Holy.   Yehoshua November.   IJHIL

How a single word.   Vocabulary of Dearness.   Naomi Shihab Nye.   CAP-8

How about that! (LL)   To Satch.   Samuel Allen.   FuFl; ISC; MoASP

How about the Mount of Mounts?   Looking at Mount T'ai-Shan.   Tu Fu [*or* Du Fu].   ChinPo, *tr. by* Ye Weilian [*or* Yeh Wei-lien *or* Wai-lim Yip]

How About You.   Ralph Freed.   ReLy

How absence becomes presence.   Presence, The.   Elder Olson.   IllVoic

How admirable!   Basho.   EH, *tr. by* Robert Hass

How admirable—the fine gentleman.   Ryokan.   EMJL, *tr. by* Burton Watson

How Am I To Tell You.   Carlos Bousoño.   RaW, *tr. by* Hardie St. Martin

How an Old Man Can Regain His Youth Through Sexual Potency.   Ibn Kamal. EroLit, *tr. by* Mary Jo Lakeland

How and where they met is cause for speculation.   At the Ritz.   Lynn Emanuel.   OxBoAm

How Annandale Went Out.   Edwin Arlington Robinson.   APT-1; GSo; MoAmPo; NAMCP V.1; NoAM; SoSe-8

How any face looks at itself.   Discredit.   Sianne Ngai.   OnScMo

How Apollo's laurel sapling shakes.   Callimachus.   HePo *Fr.* Hymns.

How are the mighty fallen, and the weapons of war perished! (LL)   Bible, *O.T.* NPeEn; OBVE; OBWP *Fr.* Second Samuel.

How Are Things in Glocca Morra?   E. Y. Harburg.   ReLy

How Are You?   Carole Satyamurti.   StAl

How are you faring, Uma.   Rām Basu.   SinGod, *tr. by* Rachel Fell McDermott

How are you? It's autumn.   Autumn Letter.   No Hyangnim.   EcSo, *tr. by* Aimee N. Kwon

How at my sheet goes the same crooked worm. (LL)   Force That through the Green Fuse Drives the Flower, The.   Dylan Thomas.   BrAP; CABP; HarvBoo; MoBrPo; NAEL-6v2; NAEL-7v2; NAMCP V.2; NoAM; NoP-4; NoP-5; NPeEn; OBWEV; OxAEP-2; OxBEV; PtR; TFi; WaAnP

How Awful.   Idea Vilariño.   TANSG, *tr. by* Louise B. Popkin

How awful, how sublime this view.   Written on the Sea-Shore.   Felicia Dorothea Hemans.   RWP

How awkward it looks.   Buson.   EH, *tr. by* Robert Hass

How Beastly the Bourgeois Is.   D. H. Lawrence.   BrAP; NAEL-6v2; NAEL-7v2; OBSV

How beauteous is the bond.   Peau de Chagrin of State Street, The.   Oliver Wendell Holmes.   TCAPo

How beautiful are thy feet with shoes.   Bible, *O.T.*   EroLit *Fr.* Song of Solomon, The [*or* The Song of Songs].

How beautiful, how beautiful you streamed upon my sight.   Corinne's Last Love-Song.   Lady Jane Francesca Wilde.   IrLP; VWP

How beautiful, I thought, as I was waking, the stars shining in my mother's hair. (LL)   Mi Mamá, the Playgirl.   Richard Garcia.   InoFa; SUP

How beautiful is the rain!   Rain in Summer.   Henry Wadsworth Longfellow. TreFP

How beautiful the pair of birds in the autumn sky.   At Moments Like This, I Always Blush.   Ch'ŏn Yanghŭi.   EcSo, *tr. by* Aimee N. Kwon

How beautiful the river is in spring.   Sunset.   Tu Fu [*or* Du Fu].   CrYelRi, *tr. by* Sam Hamill

How beautiful you are, my love.   Canticle for Abba Jacob, A.   Marilyn Nelson Waniek.   FFC

How beautifully they remembered beauty. (LL)   Silver Sands, The.   Richard Blanco.   AmPoNex; NAPBL

How bittersweet it is on winter nights.   Cracked Bell, The.   Charles Baudelaire.   SxFrPo, *tr. by* James McGowan

How blessed [*or* blest] was the created state.   Fall, The.   John Wilmot, 2d Earl of Rochester.   ChIV-1

How blest are lovers in disguise!   Song, A.   George Farquhar.   NOSC

How blest be[e] they then, who his favo[u]rs prove.   Mary Sidney Wroth, Countess of Montgomery.   BASC *Fr.* Pamphilia to Amphilanthus.

How blest is he, who for his country dies.   To the Earl of Oxford, Late Lord Treasurer.   Jonathan Swift.   FaBoWar; OBVE

How blest the land that counts among.   Statesmen, The.   Ambrose Bierce. APN-2

How brave is the hunter who nobly will dare.   Manly Sports.   Marion Bernstein.   NePenScot

How bright this weird autumnal eve.   Fires in Illinois.   John James Piatt. APN-2

How brightly glistening in the sun.   Home.   Anne Brontë.   VWP

How brittle are the Piers.   Emily Dickinson.   NCAP; SacPr

How Callum Innes Paints.   Peter Finch.   Oth

How calm the water flows!   River.   Jorge Guillén.   RaW, *tr. by* Charles Guenther

How calmly gliding through the dark-blue sky.   Robert Southey. *Fr.* Roderick, The Last of the Goths.

How Came What Came Alas.   HeidiLynn Nilsson.   NeAmPo; PoDa

How can a sock come to have so much importance? Sock, A. Sandra McPherson. MotU

How can anyone know that a whale. Shore, The. W. S. Merwin. ItP

How can I breathe? *You can't, you fool!.* (LL) Sanctuary. Elinor Wylie. MoAmPo; NAAPv.2

How can I describe anything when all these interruptions keep *arriving* and then. Hannah Weiner. PmAP *Fr.* Clairvoyant Journal.

How can I give right directions. Sadakichi. NAAPv.1 *Fr.* My Rubaiyat.

How can I give thee up, my child, my dearest, earliest born. Wail of the Divorced. Mary E. Tucker. CBWP-1

How can I help but admire the ever perseverant. Insider's View of the Garden, The. Maxine W. Kumin. IPoFL

How can I hope a wise heart to attain. Dietmar von Aist [*or* Eist]. GePo

How Can I See You, Love. David Vogel. HP, *tr. by* A. C. Jacobs

How Can I Sing. Odia Ofeimun. HBAPE

How can I speak your spirit. Earth Man. Lynne Wycherley. Prnts

How can I tell you of the terrible cries. Wars, The. Howard Moss. VCAP

How can I tell you what is in my heart. How Deep Is the Ocean? (How High Is the Sky?). Irving Berlin. ReLy

How can I thank you B, for your ear, your mind, your affection? Inn at Kirchstetten, The. James Laughlin. PmAP

How can I, that girl standing there. Politics. William Butler Yeats. AmFaPo; GoPo; HeIP-4; ItP; NAMCP V.1; PLBUT

How can I then return in happy plight. William Shakespeare. AWTN *Fr.* Sonnets.

How can I turn from Africa and live? (LL) Far Cry from Africa, A. Derek Walcott. AmFaPo; BrAP; ESEAA; HeIP-4; NAEL-6v2; NAEL-7v2; NAMCP V.2; NIL-7; NoAM; NoP-4; NoP-5

How Can I Turn Off This Engine Now? Christopher Davis. LiTh

How can I turn this wheel that turns my life. Wheel, The. Edwin Muir. NAMCP V.1; NoAM

How can I write about you. My True Love Hath My Heart. Naomi Mitchison. LW

How can one make an absence flower. John Montague. PBCIP *Fr.* Dead Kingdom, The.

How can she live till in her blood He live! (LL) Ribh Considers Christian Love Insufficient. William Butler Yeats. BBASP; RaBo

How can that black woman be so beautiful? Kamalākānta Bhattācārya. SinGod, *tr. by* Rachel Fell McDermott

How can the day arrest. Karen Weiser. IIR

How can they stand it, going out in the world with only $10 and a hydrogen bomb? (LL) Yiddishe Kopf. Allen Ginsberg. BodElec; TaR

How can we know the dancer from the dance? (LL) Among School Children. William Butler Yeats. BrAP; CABP; HarvBoo; MoBrPo; NAEL-6v2; NAEL-7v2; NAMCP V.1; NAWM-7v2; NIL-7; NIP-4; NoAM; NoP-4; NoP-5; NPeEn; OxBEV; PoPoPo; TFi; TRP; WaAnP

How can we live in harmony with each other. This mortal coil. Robert Fleming. BtF

How can we live without the unknown in front of us? Argument. René Char. AF

How / Can you. On South Africa. Kim C. Lee. InTrad

How can you be quite so uncouth? After sharing. Ode to the Diencephalon. W. H. Auden. OxAEP-2

How can you forget me? Low to High. Langston Hughes. APT-2

How! Canst thou see the basket, wherein lay. Moses in Infancy. Jones Very. ChIV-1

How certain the mule's step in the abyss. Rhapsody for the Mule. José Lezama Lima. TCLAP, *tr. by* Dudley Fitts, José Rodríguez Feo and Donald D. Walsh

How changed is here each spot man makes or fills! Thyrsis. Matthew Arnold. NAEL-6v2; NAEL-7v2; NoP-4; NoP-5; OBEV; WaAnP

How close the clouds press this October first. No Map. Stephen Dobyns. GoPo

How cold are thy baths, Apollo! Jugurtha. Henry Wadsworth Longfellow. TCAPo

How come a thickish tree. View, A. James Schuyler. BodElec

How come alle ye that ben i-broght. *Unknown.* OHMEL

How come, Henry dear. Mamma Goes Where Papa Goes. Jack Yellen. ReLy

How come / I wanna know. To the Latin Lover I Left at the Candy Store. Magdalena Gomez. PueRic

How come nobody is being bombed today? All Quiet. David Ignatow. PoCho

How come the inlaid lute has fifty strings? Inlaid Lute, The. Li Shang-yin. ChinPo, *tr. by* Ye Weilian [*or* Yeh Wei-lien *or* Wai-lim Yip]

How come you don't write more about eagles. Indian Things. Mark Turcotte. Vesp

How comes it, Flora, that, whenever we. Queen of Hearts, The. Christina Georgina Rossetti. NPeEn

How comest thou, O flower so fair. Snowdrop, The. Mary Weston Fordham. CBWP-2

How comforting. Day They Cleaned Up the Border, The: El Salvard, February, 1981. Wendy Rose. AmWaPo; HATNAP

How compare either of this grim twain? Thomas Hardy and A. E. Housman. Max Beerbohm. NBLV

How cool / forehead touched. Sono-Jo, Lady. ZenPo, *tr. by* Takashi Ikemoto and Lucien Stryk

How Could All That Have Happened Here? Everett Hoagland. FuFl

How could I have known. Rufinus. ErotSp, *tr. by* Sam Hamill

How could I seek the empty world again? (LL) Remembrance: "Cold in the earth—and the deep snow piled above thee!" Emily Jane Brontë. BrAP; CABP; MakPoe; NAEL-6v2; NAEL-7v2; NoP-4; NoP-5; NPeEn; OxAEP-2; OxBEV; PEW; PoPoPo; TFi; VWP; WeW-3

How could I wake from childhood. To Be. Marvin Bell. BodElec

How could she not take pride in him. On the Marriage at Cana. Rainer Maria Rilke. GI

How could they be anything but elegies, those stories. How Could They. John Smith. Coast

How could you have forgotten her. Kamalākānta Bhattācārya. SinGod, *tr. by* Rachel Fell McDermott

How Cruel Is the Story of Eve. Stevie Smith. NALW

How curious. I had no idea! Today has / ended. Short Talk on Gertrude Stein About 9:30. Anne Carson. OpeFie

How cut haft for an axe? *Unknown.* NDACCP, *tr. by* Ezra Pound

How dare I in thy courts appear. Hymn. Phoebe Cary. SacPr

How dare we now be anything but numb? (LL) Rejoinder to a Critic. Donald Davie. CABP; NoP-4

How dare you! To the Police Officer Who Refused to Sit in the Same Room as My Son because He's a "Gang Banger." Luis J. Rodriguez. IllVoic

How dare you say that still you love? Unfaithful Lover, The. Charlotte Dacre. RWP

How dark it is, how dark and miserable! Prometheus Pyrphoros. Trumbull Stickney.

How dark the veins of your temples. Final Vigil. Georg Heym. WoPoe, *tr. by* Peter Viereck

How dear to my heart are the grand politicians. Old Hokum Buncombe, The. Robert E. Sherwood. NBLV

How dear to this heart are the scenes of my childhood. Old Oaken Bucket, The. Samuel Woodworth. BRP; TCAPo

How Death Comes. *Unknown.* WaAnP

How decisively. Paavo Haavikko. WoPoe *Fr.* Fifteen Epigrams in Praise of the Tyrant.

How Deep Is the Ocean? (How High Is the Sky?). Irving Berlin. ReLy

How deep the woods are (ah) Jacklight. Louise Erdrich. CAP-8; HATNAP; NIL-7; WeW-3

How deep yon azure dyes the sky! Thomas Parnell. OxAEP-1 *Fr.* Night Piece on Death.

How delicious to walk into the stillness. To Go Through Life Is to Walk Across a Field. S. J. Marks. BodElec

How delightful to meet Mr. Hodgson! T. S. Eliot. NBLV *Fr.* Five-Finger Exercises.

How did a block of winter. Justin Quinn. NIrP *Fr.* Six Household Appliances.

How did decay work its way into the theater of water. Synchronized Swimming. Angela Sorby. AmPoNex

How did I get where I am today? God Almighty the First Garden Made. Kathleen Jamie. GPPA

How did it come to be. Soul in Space. Chase Twichell. AmZen

How did it happen that we quarreled? Words! Words! Jessie Redmond Fauset. NAAPv.1

How did money get into the soul; how did base dollars and cents ascend from the slime. Money. C. K. Williams. OxBoAm

How did the grapes come to know. Pablo Neruda. GifTon *Fr.* Book of Questions, The.

How did the stones vote. Election, The. Leonard Nathan. ASA; PBCAP

How Did They Kill My Grandmother? Boris Abramovich Slutsky. FaBoWar, *tr. by* Elaine Feinstein

How did they kill my grandmother? How They Killed My Grandmother. Boris Abramovich Slutsky. HP, *tr. by* Daniel Weissbort

How did they understand Livy my grandfather my great grandfather. Transformations of Livy. Zbigniew Herbert. PoetW, *tr. by* Bogdana Carpenter and John Carpenter *and* Bogdana Carpenter

How did you come here beneath the full moon. *Unknown.* SLW, *tr. by* Marjolijn De Jager, Sayd Bahodin Majrouh and André Velter

How did you feel, Mary. Calvary Way. May Miller. OxAAAP

How did you like it? she asked. After Forty Years of Marriage, She Tries a New Recipe for Hamburger Hot Dish. Leo Dangel. GoPo

How died my master, Strato? William Shakespeare. OxAEP-1 *Fr.* Julius Caesar.

How difficult for me is Hebrew. Charles Reznikoff. APT-2

How dimm'd is the glory that circled the Gael. Lament of O'Gnive, The. Fearflatha O'Gnive. IrV, *tr.* by Jeremiah Joseph Callanan

How disgusting. How disgusting. Idea Vilariño. TANSG, *tr.* by Louise B. Popkin

How dishonest the sun. Seeing through the Sun. Linda Hogan. HATNAP

How Do I Feel? Kenneth Fearing. APT-2

How do I feel about "There's a Moon Out Tonight." Ode: The Capris. Mark Halliday. P180

How do I find my soul's extremest anguish. Mary Sidney Wroth, Countess of Montgomery. OxBSo

How do I hate you? Let me count the ways. Sonnet. Stanley J. Sharpless. UV

How do I know the sound. Crows. Mariana Romo-Carmona. WiU

How do I know why you ask me, "How *are* you?" Cross Questions. John Wheelwright. APT-2

How do I love thee? Beyond Compare. Marshall Barer. ReLy

How do I love thee? Let me count the ways. Elizabeth Barrett Browning. AmFaPo; BrAP; CABP; CenSon; GSo; HeIP-4; ITBLP; MakPoe; NAEL-6v2; NAEL-7v2; NALW; NIL-7; NIP-4; NoP-4; NoP-5; OPOU; OxAEP-2; OxBSo; PoPoPo; TFi; UV; VWP; WaAnP *Fr.* Sonnets from the Portuguese.

How do I love thee thou inward old. My love is strung with the ancient. John MacKenzie. Coast

How do I pity that proud wealthy clown. My Estate. John Norris. NOSC

How do I spin my time away. On the Spirit Adulterated by the Flesh. Thomas Warton, the Elder. ChIV-1

How do I thank thee, death, and bless thy power. On the Lady Arabella. Richard Corbet. NOSC

How do owls find each other. Owls at the Shakespeare Festival. William Stafford. IaFF

How do people feel. Stolen Away. Joseph Ceravolo. FTOS

How do they do it, the ones who make love. Sex without Love. Sharon Olds. HeIP-4; NIL-7; NIP-4; TRP

How do they get so close to the window. Kiss Me Deadly. Karen Volkman. LegDan

How do we break the habit of big words. Anatoly Steiger. TCRusP, *tr.* by Paul Schmidt

How do you account for things: take night. Above the Fray Is Only Thin Air. A. R. Ammons. BodElec

How do you cut an ax-handle? *Unknown.* ColAnChi *Fr.* Classic of Odes.

How do you like to go up in a swing. Swing, The. Robert Louis Stevenson. BLPJKO; ChAP; NOxBChV; NTCP; TLR

How do you make a black man red. Plan of the Klan. Michelle T. Clinton. InTrad

How do you move? Conversation with Isadora Duncan. Molly Bendall. AmPoNex

How Do You Shape an Axe Handle? Gary Snyder. NoAM

How Do Your Eggs Want You (?). Pedro Juan Pietri. PueRic

How does a body do in the ground? Lazarus Standup: Shooting Script. Anne Carson. NAMCP V.2

How does a man live. How? Tontongi. OGAHCP, *tr.* by Boadiba and Jack Hirschman

How does a person get to be a capable liar? Golly, How Truth Will Out. Ogden Nash. MoAmPo

How does it feel to be. Nude Woman Spotted in Cappuccino Cup As Advertising Dollar Co-opts Another Life. Bahiyyih Maroon. SpirFl

How does it happen, tell me. Edgar Lee Masters. OBSV *Fr.* Spoon River Anthology.

How does my father. Eyes of Soon Children. Honorée Fanonne Jeffers. AnSo

How does one stand. American Sublime, The. Wallace Stevens. FaBoA; OxBoAm

How does the water / Come down at Ladore? Cataract of Lodore, The. Robert Southey. NPBRoP

How does thy mercies stil renew. Dec. 5th 1644 Upon Robin Austins Recovery of the Smal Pox and General Popams Son John Diing of Them. Katherine Austen. EMWP

How doth the city sit solitary that was full of people. *Unknown.* WoPoe *Fr.* Lamentations.

How Doth the Little Busy Bee. Isaac Watts. ChAP
  (Against Idleness and Mischief.) OxAEP-1; OxBEV; UV

How drunk I got tonight. Drinking Spree Beneath the Open Sky. Slavko Mihalic. PoSu, *tr.* by Peter Kastmiler

How early the autumn seemed to have come that year. Autumn, the Nightwalk, the City, the River. David Wheatley. NIrP

How easily happiness begins by. Onions. William Matthews. CAP-8; EmeKit

How easy is a bush supposed [*or* suppos'd] a bear! (LL) William Shakespeare. IJHIL; WaAnP *Fr.* Midsummer Night's Dream, A.

How Elizabeth Foole and Her Husband Parted by Means of Her Sister in Law. Elizabeth With. EMWP

How Europe Underdeveloped Africa. Edward Kamau Brathwaite. WoBe

How Everything Adores Being Alive. Mary Oliver. BeAl

How Everything Happens (Based on a Study of the Wave). May Swenson. APT-2

How fair they lie!—the circling hills. Noiseless Wheel, The. James Benjamin Kenyon. ArBi

How Far? Vassar Miller. FFC

How far apart are she and I! Proud Lady, The. Robin Ernest William Flower. IrLP

How far are they deceived, that hope in vain. In the Person of a Lady, to Bajazet, Her Unconstant Gallant. "Ephelia." PEW

How far far away. Star. Chŏng Chiyong. CAMKP, *tr.* by Anthony, Brother of Taizé

How far from enough. *Unknown.* ArkPo, *tr.* by Helen Craig McCullough

How far is it? Getting There. Sylvia Plath. GM

How far is it to you by foot? How Far? Vassar Miller. FFC

How far is St. Helena from a little child at play? St. Helena Lullaby, A. Rudyard Kipling. FaBoWar; OBMV

How far the unknown trancends the what we know. (LL) Nature. Henry Wadsworth Longfellow. ITBLP; NAAPv.1

How far, ye Nymphs and Dryads! must we stray. On the Rapid Extension of the Suburbs. John Thelwall. CenSon

How fared you when you mortal were? After. Ralph Hodgson. MoBrPo

How fashionably sad my early poems are! About My Poems. Donald Justice. PoA 2002

How Fast. Martha Rhodes. NAPBL

How fast thou fliest, O Time, on loves swift wings. Mary Sidney Wroth, Countess of Montgomery. NOSC *Fr.* Pamphilia to Amphilanthus.

How fickle's health! when sickness thus. Upon a Friend's Pet Cat, Being Sick. John Winstanley. TriCat

How fine a light on. May Song. Johann Wolfgang von Goethe. STV, *tr.* by John Frederick Nims

How Firm a Foundation. "K." SacPr

How forlorn and lost. Heart of the Matter. Susan Prospere. MakPoe

How found you him? William Shakespeare. OxAEP-1 *Fr.* Cymbeline.

How fragile the flesh. Millennium Cities. Lawrence Ferlinghetti. WhBo

How frail / Above the hole. Niagara. Adelaide Crapsey. APT-1; NAAPv.2

How fresh, O[h] Lord, how sweet and clean. Flower, The. George Herbert. AngWePo; BASC; BrAP; FSCP; NAEL-6v1; NAEL-7v1; NoP-4; NoP-5; NPeEn; OBGa; OxBEV; PBRV

How fresh the air, the birds how busy now! Birds' Nest. John Clare. OWoS

How funny you are today New York. Steps. Frank O'Hara. CAP-8; PmAP; PtR

How funny your name would be. Myrtle. John Ashbery. NAAL-5

How Garnett Mims and the Enchanters Came into Your Life. Bruce Smith. SwNoth

How gently slumber rests upon her face. Percy Bysshe Shelley. NPBRoP *Fr.* Cenci, The.

How gladly would I lay my aching head. Jane Alice Sargant. CenSon

How God Answers the Soul. Mechthild von Magdeburg. WPoS, *tr.* by Oliver Davies

How God Comes to the Soul. Mechthild von Magdeburg. WPoS, *tr.* by Oliver Davies

How God speeds the tax-bribed plough. Drone v. Worker. Ebenezer Elliott. OBSV

How good it would be. Oh Life. Yi Kyŏngnim. EcSo, *tr.* by Peter H. Lee

How good it would be if our surroundings always. Dinner at Le Caprice. Rachel Wetzsteon. RA

How good of Mrs. Metz! The blur. Snapshots. John Updike. NoP-4

How good the fur of a bear feels! Bear Fur. Takamura Kotaro. CAoMJL1, *tr.* by Leith Morton

How goodly are the tentes of Jacob and thine habitacions Israel. Bible, *O.T.* OBVE *Fr.* Numbers.

How goofy and horrible is life. Just. Frottage. Dean Young. BAP-97

How grace this hallowed day? Christmas. Henry Timrod. APN-2

How great the tale, that there should. Consecration. Murdoch O'Daly. IrV, *tr.* by Eleanor Hull

How green— / Flowering slopes. Naito Joso. ZenPo, *tr.* by Takashi Ikemoto and Lucien Stryk

How happy for us, that it is not at home! (LL) Place of the Damned [*or* Damn'd], The. Jonathan Swift. ChIV-2; OBSV

How happy I can be with my love away! Absence, The. Sylvia Townsend Warner. MoBrPo

How happy is he born and taught. Character of a Happy Life, The. Sir Henry Wotton. BASC; NOSC; OBEV; OxBEV; SacPr

How happy is the little Stone. Emily Dickinson. APN-2

How happy the animals seem just now. October, Yellowstone Park. Maxine W. Kumin. ExTi; PfSP

How hard for a dead man to pretend to be.   Dances of Death.   Aleksandr Aleksandrovich Blok.   *tr.* by Peter France and Jon Stallworthy

How hard is my fortune.   Convict of Clonmel, The.   *Irish Oral Tradition.*   IrV, *tr.* by Jeremiah Joseph Callanan

How hard it is for me, who live.   Marriage.   Wendell Berry.   WaAnP

How hard it is to take September.   Absolute September.   Mary Jo Salter.   ExTi

How hard it is, we say.   Clothes Maketh the Man.   Theodore Weiss.   NoAM

How hard this life is hallowed by the body.   Puritan Way of Death, The.   David Baker.   Vesp

How hard to control the route.   Orientation from Afar.   Silvana Colonna.   ItPo, *tr.* by Gayle Ridinger

How have I lived here so long? (LL)   Of the Finished World.   Lucie Brock-Broido.   MakPoe; WaAnP

How have I served you? I have let you waste.   John Hewitt.   IrLP; PNI *Fr.* Sonnets for Roberta (1954).

How He Saw Her.   Ben Jonson.   NAEL-7v1 *Fr.* Celebration of Charis in Ten Lyric[k] Pieces [*or* Peeces], A.

How He Should Like to Be Kissed.   Paul Fleming.   GePo, *tr.* by Harold B. Segel

How heal the phantom body of its phantom ill.   Tesshu.   ZenPo, *tr.* by Takashi Ikemoto and Lucien Stryk

How heavy do I journey on the way.   William Shakespeare.   OxAEP-1 *Fr.* Sonnets.

How heavy the days are.   How Heavy the Days.   Hermann Hesse.   IJHIL, *tr.* by James Wright

How! hey! It is non lees.   *Unknown.*   OHMEL

How High the Moon.   Nancy Hamilton.   ReLy

How High the Moon.   Lance Jeffers.   SeSe

How his body stood against a thicket. rich in hardwood gentry: ponderous and gloomy.   D. A. Powell.   NAPBL

How his own members bloat and shrink again. (LL)   Ogres and Pygmies.   Robert Graves.   NAMCP V.1; NoAM

How, how, he said. Friend Chang, I said.   Chinese Nightingale, The.   Vachel Lindsay.   MoAmPo

How I Brought the Good News from Aix to Ghent (or Vice Versa).   R. J. Yeatman *and* W. C. Sellar.   UV

How I Came to Have a Man's Name.   Emma Lee Warrior.   HATNAP

How I Changed My Name, Felice.   Felix Stefanile.   UnSA

How I Come to You.   Molly Peacock.   RA

How I cut the fresh branches of succulent rhyme.   Poet Grows Old, The.   Oliver Wendell Holmes.   TCAPo

How I Discovered Poetry.   Marilyn Nelson.   ExTi

How I Felt Pawning My Coat: Shown to Ch'oe Chongbon.   Yi Kyubo.   CATKP, *tr.* by Kevin O'Rourke

How I Got Born.   Cornelius Eady.   FuFl

How I Got That Name [An Essay on Assimilation].   Marilyn Chin.   CalPo; GeoHom; LoL; NAMCP V.2

How I Got the Word.   Marvin Bell.   BodElec

How I Had to Act.   Molly Peacock.   FFC

How I hate myself, this body which is me.   Eloi, Eloi, Lama Sabachthani?   D. H. Lawrence.   GI

How I Learned English.   Gregory Djanikian.   UnSA

How I Learned to Sweep.   Julia Alvarez.   FFC; RA; SweBea

How I love the natural Buddha.   Because of the Rain.   Jinkag Haesim.   BecRai, *tr.* by Kim Daljin, Kim Won-Chung and Christopher Merrill

How I love this girl who until.   It Is Sticky in the Subway.   David Schubert.   APT-2

How I See Things.   Yusef Komunyakaa.   ESEAA; OxAAAP

How I Shaded the Book.   Michael Burkard.   LaCa

How I tried to explain.   Kind of Blue.   A. Van Jordan.   LegDan

How I would have the poem rest.   Mahogany Ship, The.   Judith Rodriguez.   BMAP

How I Wrote It.   David Dooley.   TRP

How I'll Live Then.   Sibyl James.   FiBr

How in the sad depths of old centuries.   Song About Benedek Virág.   Dezső Kosztolányi.   IQMS, *tr.* by Watson Kirkconnell

How Infinite Are Thy Ways.   William Force Stead.   OBMV *Fr.* Uriel.

How innocent their lives look.   Photos of a Salt Mine.   Patricia K. Page.   NAMCP V.2; NIP-4; NoAM

How intelligent he looks!   Changing Diapers.   Gary Snyder.   RaBo

How interesting that in 12th century Japan Saigyo remark'd.   Haibun Flycatcher.   Andrew Schelling.   AmZen; WANABP

How intimate was the earth in days gone by.   Earth, The.   David Gwenallt Jones.   OBWVE, *tr.* by Dyfnallt Morgan

How Is He Coming Then.   Lucille Clifton.   NALW

How is it.   Wall, The.   Witter Bynner.   APT-1

How is it I was not raised.   In the Dark Backward.   Gloria Vando.   TouFir

How is it that Fortune now always ignores me?   Las, Où Est Maintenant Ce Mespris de Fortune.   Joachim Du Bellay.   WoPoe, *tr.* by Fred Beake

How is it with another woman?   Attempt at Jealousy, An.   Marina Ivanovna Tsvetayeva.   TCRusP, *tr.* by Bob Perelman, Aleksandar Petrov and Shirley Rihner

How is your life with the other one.   Attempt at Jealousy, An.   Marina Ivanovna Tsvetayeva.   GPTC; OxBEV; WoPoe, *tr.* by Elaine Feinstein

How It All Comes Back.   William Daniel Ehrhart.   AmWaPo

How It Begins / How It Ends.   Richard Blanco.   LegDan

How It Comes.   Dorothy Barresi.   SwNoth

How It Comes About.   Larry Eigner.   PmAP

How it goes.   Severance.   Kit Robinson.   FTOS

How It Happened.   Mark Smith-Soto.   RWB

How It Is.   Maxine W. Kumin.   InoFa; NALW; NAMCP V.2; NoAM

How it starts, how it ends: wild tuft in the sky, a cloud. This blue.   Möbius Strip.   Anne Simpson.   IFF

How It Strikes a Contemporary.   Robert Browning.   NPeEn

How It Will Always Seem.   David Rivard.   PBCAP

How keen the nights.   Fluteplayers from Finmarken.   Carl Rakosi.   FTOS

How lacking in permanence the minds of the sentient.   Hakuin.   ZenPo, *tr.* by Takashi Ikemoto and Lucien Stryk

How L'Akhdar Ben Youssef Wrote His Last Poem.   Sa'di Yusuf.   IrPoTo, *tr.* by Khaled Mattawa

How large a mouth has a good singer. He knows.   Gertrude Stein.   OxBoAm *Fr.* Book Concluding with As A Wife Has a Cow a Love Story, A.

How larger is remembrance than desire!   Ebbtide at Sundown.   Michael Field.   OxBSo; VWP

How Late Desire Looks.   Katrina Roberts.   NAPBL

How Lies Grow.   Maxine Chernoff.   IllVoic; PmAP; SUP

How life and death in Thee.   To Our Blessed Lord upon the Choice of His Sepulchre.   Richard Crashaw.   NOSC

How like a fire doth love increase in me[e].   Mary Sidney Wroth, Countess of Montgomery.   NOSC *Fr.* Pamphilia to Amphilanthus.

How like a man, is Man, who rises late.   Eye-Opener.   Malcolm Lowry.   NoP-4; NoP-5

How like a rich and gorgeous picture hung.   November Landscape, A.   Sarah Helen Whitman.   ColAP

How like a winter hath my absence been[e].   William Shakespeare.   AEP; HeIP-4; NAEL-6v1; NAEL-7v1; NoP-5; NoSic; OBEV; OxAEP-1; TFi *Fr.* Sonnets.

How like an angel came I down!   Wonder.   Thomas Traherne.   BASC; NAEL-6v1; NAEL-7v1; NoP-4; NoP-5; NPeEn; OxBEV; WaAnP

How like her! But 'tis she herself.   In the Mile End Road.   Amy Levy.   PEW; RACG; ViWPN

How like the leper, with his own sad cry.   Buoy-Bell, The.   Charles Tennyson Turner.   GSo

How like you this, what hath she now deserved? (LL)   Sir Thomas Wyatt.   *See* I would fain know[e] what she hath deserved.

How Lisa Loved the King.   "George Eliot."   LW *Fr.* How Lisa Loved the King.

How little does history manage to tell?   Lessons in History.   Robert Penn Warren.   BodElec

How little of the world had been left dry! (LL)   Loved, on a sudden thou didst come to me.   Michael Field.   ViWPN; VWP

How little the reach, what is *love* love? its.   Small print.   Daphne Marlatt.   OpeFie

How Little We Know.   Johnny Mercer.   ReLy

How Little We Know (How Little It Matters).   Carolyn Leigh.   ReLy

How Liu Chih-yüan Bade San-niang Good-bye and Joined the Army in T'ai-yüan.   *Chinese Oral Tradition.*   ColAnChi *Fr.* Ballad of the Hidden Dragon.

How Long?   Emma Lazarus.   SWaP

How Long.   Andrea Zanzotto.   VCWP

How long ago Hector took off his plume.   Parting in Wartime.   Frances Darwin Cornford.   NIP-4

How long ago we dreamed.   Carol of the Three Kings.   W. S. Merwin.   ChrPo

How long, and yet how long.   How Long?   Emma Lazarus.   SWaP

How long beneath water-spun sand, silt.   After the Shipwreck.   Corey Marks.   LegDan

How long between the grain and the wind.   How Long.   Andrea Zanzotto.   VCWP

How long can one man live.   Mourning for Yin Yao.   Wang Wei.   CrYelRi, *tr.* by Sam Hamill

How long can this floating life last?   Drinking Alone.   Wang Ji.   CCL1, *tr.* by Stephen Owen

How long, despondent birds, with silent throats.   Bird, to Its Young, The.   Mihály Tompa.   IQMS, *tr.* by Watson Kirkconnell

How long did we watch? How long did those.   Deer, The.   David Baker.   PfSP

How long did you wait.   Suicide, The.   Jennifer Rose.   PfS

How Long Does the Curator Dance For?   Edwin Torres.   HeMarv

How long for the small yellow flowers. Time. Robert Creeley. BodElec; ICANM

How long, great God, a wretched captive here. Expostulation, The. Elizabeth Singer Rowe. PEW

How long has our kind been marginalized. Potato Manifesto, The. Cynthia Hwang. FThHH

How long has she stood like this, not knowing. Contact Sheet. Michael Murphy. NIrP

How Long Has This Been Going On? Ira Gershwin. ReLy

How Long Has Trane Been Gone. Jayne Cortez. ISC

How Long Have We Forgotten How to Listen! Nelly Sachs. WPoS, *tr. by* Matthew Mead and Ruth Mead

How long in his damp trance young Juan lay. Lord Byron. NAEL-6v2; NAEL-7v2; NPBRoP *Fr.* Don Juan.

How long is has taken me to recall. First Snowfall: Intimations. Edward Hirsch. PfSP

How long it seems. Karai Senryū. EMJL, *tr. by* Makoto Ueda

How long, long ago. Kenneth Rexroth. APSN *Fr.* Love Poems of Marichiko, The.

How long, O lord, shall I forgotten be? Bible, *O.T.* NoSic; OBVE

How long she waited for her executioner! Head of Medusa. Marya Alexandrovna Zaturenska. MoAmPo

How long since I sat last? In the Cage of Doves. Mac Lojowski. AmZen

How Long the Lord. Attila József. IQMS, *tr. by* Anton N. Nyerges

How long the tree's been barren. Hoge. ZenPo, *tr. by* Takashi Ikemoto and Lucien Stryk

How long the winter has lasted—like a Mahler. Walking Alone in Late Winter. Jane Kenyon. MoW

How lovely are the tombs of the dead nymphs. Panope. Dame Edith Sitwell. MoBrPo

How lovely is a steak platter! Steak Platter, A. Takamura Kotaro. CAoMJL1, *tr. by* Leith Morton

How lovely is thy dwelling. Bible, *O.T.* CABP *Fr.* Psalms.

How lovely the Russian lady. Its Pliancy. Hans Lodeizen. TuT, *tr. by* Eamon Grennan

How lovely to remember you. Poems of Nine to Ten P.M. Nazim Hikmet. NaPG, *tr. by* Talat Sait Halman

How lucky that I ran into you. To My Twenties. Kenneth Koch. EMP; NoP-5

How lumpy and warlike you all looked. Land Army Photographs. Tony Curtis. TCAWP

How magnificant the war is! War Works Hard, The. Dunya Mikhail. WoBe, *tr. by* Liz Winslow

How many a day in various hues arrayed. To My Eldest Brother, With the British Army in Portugal. Felicia Dorothea Hemans. RWP

How many a throb of the young poet-heart. Early Aspirations. William Bell Scott. CenSon

How many apples grow on the tree? George Barker. NOxBChV

'How Many Bards Gild the Lapses of Time!'. John Keats. CenSon; OxAEP-2

How many children must have come to pass. Walter Parmer. Greg Williamson. RA

How many ciphers. Waste. David Chaloner. VaPo

How many constants *should* there be? Native. Rae Armantrout. PFTM-2

How many dawns, chill from his rippling rest. Hart Crane. AmFaPo; ChIV-1; ClHu; ColAP; EMP; FaBoA; HarvBoo; MakPoe; MoAmPo; NAAL-5; NAAPv.2; NoP-4; OxBoAm; PoPoPo; TFi; TRP *Fr.* Bridge, The.

How many dawns, chill from his rippling rest. Bridge, The. Hart Crane. APT-2; NAMCP V.1

How many days now, living in seclusion, in solitude? Chen Zi'ang. CCL1

How many days would it be. (LL) Gertrude Stein. MotU; OxBoAm *Fr.* Book Concluding with As A Wife Has a Cow a Love Story, A.

How many doors will this man open. Death. Roy Fuller. NoAM

How many drops has the ocean sea? Sándor Petőfi. IQMS *Fr.* Clouds, The.

How many empty hotel rooms. Sea Sprite, Hermosa Beach, The. Maurya Simon. GeoHom

How many engineers trained to hold back a million gallons of ocean *en El Malecón?*. Malecón, El. Harryette Mullen. RD

How many fields which like a sponge. Amelia Rosselli. ItPo, *tr. by* Gayle Ridinger

How many friends have I? Count them. Songs of Five Friends. Yun Sŏndo. CATKP *tr. by* Peter H. Lee *Fr.* Songs of Five Friends.

How many heads. Yum Yab. Anne Waldman. WhBo

How many lives ago. Kenneth Rexroth. APSN; APT-2 *Fr.* Love Poems of Marichiko, The.

How many loves had I. Doll. John Wieners. FTOS

How many men are killed by power, by power. Juvenal. OBVE *Fr.* Satires.

How many million years before wood turns to stone? Anita Barrows. WhBo

How many moments must(amazing each). E. E. Cummings. PoA 2002

How Many More Minutes Until We Can Devour Our Breached Contract? Joanna Fuhrman. PrTe

How many mountains. Wakayama Bokusui. CAoMJL1, *tr. by* Donald Keene

How Many Nights. Galway Kinnell. GoPo

How many notes written . . . . Suicide Note. Janice Mirikitani. OxWW

How many of you are there? Map. Raymond Radiguet. CuPo

How many pallid Christs, with painted blood. All Around Us. Constance Urdang. PBCAP

How Many Paltry, Foolish, Painted Things. Michael Drayton. HeIP-4; NAEL-7v1; NIP-4; NoP-5; NOSC *Fr.* Idea.

How many scenes, O sun. Ode to the Sun. Eloise Bibb. CBWP-4

How many shoelaces will they make of that! (LL) Mad Yak, The. Gregory Corso. BB; PFTM-2; PmAP; WaAnP

How many smiles for a tale, gypsy girl? Sonnet and Duet for Flapper and Poet. Alexander Pomerantz. Prolet, *tr. by* Amelia Glaser

How many thousand of my poorest subjects. William Shakespeare. AWTN *Fr.* King Henry IV, Pt. II.

How Many Times. Marie Howe. BeAl; LaCa; P180

How many times, Death. O All Down within the Pretty Meadow. Kenneth Patchen. WeW-3

How many times did the Church prevent war? Chimes of Neverwhere, The. Les A. Murray. UpMys

How many times do I love thee, dear? Thomas Lovell Beddoes. NAEL-6v2 *Fr.* Torrismond.

How many times God will remember. Silence, The. Robert Mezey. TaR

How many times has the moon shone full? Tune: "Water Mode Song." Su Tung-p'o. ColAnChi, *tr. by* James Robert Hightower

How many times have I traveled. Commuter. Lisel Mueller. GM

How many times have I—on entering the plaza. Contemporaries. Antonio Deltoro. RMCMP, *tr. by* Christian Viveros-Fauné

How many times night's silent queene her face. Sonnet. William Drummond of Hawthornden. NPeEn

How many times these low feet staggered. Emily Dickinson. NAAL-3; TCAPo; WeW-3

How many voices can I plum in this poem? Serpentine Voices. Diana García. TouFir

How many wise men and heroes. To the Tune "The River Is Red." Ch'iu Chin. ItWoWo, *tr. by* Chung Ling and Kenneth Rexroth

How many years can a man possess? Weeping for Ying Yao. Wang Wei. WoPoe, *tr. by* Tony Barnstone, Willis Barnstone and Xu Haixin

How many years, decades, since I'd even thought of Gary. Basement, The. Alan Shapiro. TaR

How many years I have loved your poems! This Night: For Walt Whitman. Robert Bly. ViWalt

How many years of suffering. Tea. Amy Uyematsu. WhBo

How many years past was it I burned out their nest. Yellowjackets. William Heyen. CAP-8

How many years since 1619 have I been singing Spirituals? Since 1619. Margaret Abigail Walker. NoP-4; NoP-5

How marvelous the man is. Basho. WED, *tr. by* Robert Bly

How memory cuts away the years. Autumn. Jean Starr Untermeyer. MoAmPo

How merciful it is. Scarlet Letter, The. Lee Upton. AmAlph

How Mother Courage Saves Desdemona. Jeanne Murray Walker. IaFF

How *much.* Issa. EH, *tr. by* Robert Hass

How Much a Word Could Help. "Zelda." NRoS, *tr. by* Esther Raizen

How much alike are the wise man. After Reading Han-Shan. Thomas Rain Crowe. AmZen

How much better it seems now. Next Poem, The. Dana Gioia. NoP-4; NoP-5

How much Christian, so to speak, can I get? Jacob Glatstein. GI

How much death works. Eyes Fastened with Pins. Charles Simic. VCAP

How much farther? Not much farther. Distance. N. Revathi Devi. HotL, *tr. by* V. Narayana Rao

How Much Is Not True. Kabir. RaBo, *tr. by* Robert Bly
(Holy Pools Have Only Water, The.) WED

How Much Is This One? Pak Nohae. CAMKP, *tr. by* Scott Swaner

How Much Is This Poem Going to Cost Me? Denise Duhamel. NeAmPo

How Much Longer? Robert Mezey. OBWP

How much longer can I get away. Miss July Grows Older. Margaret Atwood. NAMCP V.2

How Much Longer Will I Be Able to Inhabit the Divine Sepulcher. John Ashbery. FTOS; HarvBoo; OxBoAm; PmAP

How much of paper's spoiled! what floods of ink! Mary Jones. PEW

How much, Preventing God! how much I owe. Grace. Ralph Waldo Emerson. APN-1; InvLi; NCAP

How much wood would a woodchuck chuck? Wood-chuck. *Unknown.* TLR

How much work. Hating Jews. Tom Wayman. LTA

How My Mother-in-Law Instructed Me in Slaughter. Sarah Kennedy. SweBea

How my true love and I lay without touching. Leland Bardwell. StAl

How near me came the hand of Death. Widow's Hymn, A. George Wither. OBEV

How near to the borders can we venture. Map of the Kingdom, A. David Wright. ACAMVP

How Near Vietnam Came to Us. Paul Zarzyski. SwNoth

How neatly this world divides. Near Sheridan. Robin Becker. PoCoUp

How nice! How convenient! Marvelous Land of Indefinitions, The. Lorenzo Thomas. PmAP

How now! is he dead? William Shakespeare. OxAEP-1 Fr. Antony and Cleopatra.

How numbers make trails. Music at the Heart of Thinking 54. Fred Wah. OpeFie

How odd / Of God. Chosen People, The. W. N. Ewer. OBCoV

How odd this winter is. Chronic Appendicitis. Luljeta Lleshanaku. WoBe, tr. by Henry Israeli

How oft alas my brother have I warned thee to beware. Lines Written for a Friend on the Death of His Brother, Caused by a Railway Train Running Over Him Whilst He Was in a State of Inebriation. James Henry Powell. VerBaPo

How oft, ere morning lit the eastern steep. Richard Hall. AngWePo Fr. Venni-Vach Revisited.

How oft in schoolboy-days, from the school's sway. Frederick Goddard Tuckerman. APN-2; NoP-4; OxBoAm Fr. Sonnets.

How oft I've watch'd thee from the garden croft. Orion. Charles Tennyson Turner. GSo

How oft, when thou, my music, music play'st. William Shakespeare. NAEL-6v1; NAEL-7v1; OxAEP-1 Fr. Sonnets.

How often does a man need to see a woman? Word Made Flesh, The. Walter James Turner. OBMV

How often have I carried our family word. Quoof. Paul Muldoon. FaBoVe; NAMCP V.2; NPeEn; PBCIP; PNI; StAl

How often have I courteously uncrossed. Sonnet of a Gentleman. Alan Brownjohn. PML

How often have I started out. Inspiration. Robert W. Service. WeW-3

How often have you made love to someone. Return of the Prodigals. Kurt Brown. SUP

How often I turn round. Fear, The. Andrew Young. EdScPo

How often in the overflowing streets. William Wordsworth. NPBRoP; WaAnP Fr. Prelude, The; Growth of a Poet's Mind [1805 version].

How often in the years that close. Meditation, A. Herman Melville. PCW

How often my grandparents allude to death, now. Behind the Veil. Andrew Lansdown. NOBAu

How often our joy burns out. Melancholiacs, The. Mary Ruefle. AmAlph

How often, these hours, have I heard the monotonous crool of a dove. Dove, The. Walter De la Mare. OWoS

How often we forget all time, when lone. Stanzas. Edgar Allan Poe. APN-1

How old are these two, anyway? On a Portrait of Two Beauties. Hồ Xuân Hương. PoDa, tr. by John Balaban

How Old Is Pilar? Manuel González Prada. SpanPo, tr. by William M. Davis

How Old Is the Old Mole? Marie-Dominique Massoni. SurWo, tr. by Myrna Bell Rochester

How old was Mary out of whom you cast. Charlotte Mew. MoBrPo Fr. Madeleine in Church.

How, on a summer night. Music Like Water, The. Jane Hirshfield. PasH

How parched, how marrow-dust dry. Thirst of Turtles, The. Thomas Lux. AmAlph

How Passion Comes to Matter. Donald Revell. RoV

How People Do. Imamu Amiri Baraka. EGAG

How pitiful! Basho. EMJL, tr. by Haruo Shirane

How pitiful is her sleep. In Memory of Kathleen. Kenneth Patchen. MoAmPo

How pitiful, the feelings of the world. 157. Shih Shu. CSKM, tr. by James H. Sanford

How pleasant are the green. Lying in Bed on a Summer Morning. Carl Rakosi. APT-2; NAAPv.2

How pleasant it is to have money. (LL) Arthur Hugh Clough. NBLV; OBCoV Fr. Spectator ab Extra.

How pleasant it is to have money. (LL) Arthur Hugh Clough. OBCoV; OBSV Fr. Spectator ab Extra.

How Pleasant to Know Mr. Lear. Edward Lear. NAEL-6v2; NAEL-7v2; NoP-4; NoP-5; OxAEP-2; OxBEV; PoPoPo; UV

  (By Way of Preface.) NBLV

How Poetry Comes to Me. Gary Snyder. LoL; PoPoPo; WhBo

How pointless this straining. Patrizia Cavalli. ItPo, tr. by Gayle Ridinger

How poor was Jacob's motion, and how strange. On Jacob's Purchase. Francis Quarles. ChIV-1

How possibly could I. Cameo in Sudden Light. Lorenzo Thomas. FTOS

How precise it seems, like a doll house. Housework. William Matthews. CAP-8

How probable to the eye, this collation. Lakes, The. David Wright. NLP

How proudly Man usurps the power to reign. Martha Hanson. CenSon

How? Providence? and yet a Scottish crew? Rebel Scot, The. John Cleveland. BASC

How? 'Providence', and yet a Scottish crew? John Cleveland. NOSC Fr. Rebel Scot, The.

How pure at heart and sound in head. Alfred Tennyson. NAEL-6v2; NAEL-7v2 Fr. In Memoriam A. H. H.

How pure we were then, before Rimbaud, before Blake. Grace. Love. Take care of us. Please. (LL) Gas Station, The. C. K. Williams. CAP-8; VCAP

How quickly. Stanford M. Forrester. AmZen

How quickly the postures shift. On Your Own. Tess Gallagher. LaCa

How quiet and how still to-day old Bethel's corners 'round. Day after Conference, The. Josephine D. Henderson Heard. CBWP-4

How quiet it is. The sound of the mouths of trees rubbing in the midst of the day. Pure Talk. Yi Chinmyông. EcSo, tr. by Carolyn U. So

How Quiet under the Earth. Miguel de Unamuno. RaW, tr. by Robert Bly

How quietly in ruined state. Aix-La-Chappelle, 1945. Edgar Bowers. InGu

How rare is a mossy jetty. Yun Sôndo. CATKP Fr. Angler's Calendar, The.

How razor-clean was it supposed to become. Guardian Angel of Self-Knowledge, The. Jorie Graham. MoWP

How reluctantly. Basho. SoOfWa, tr. by Sam Hamill

How rich, O Lord! how fresh thy visits are! Unprofitablenes. Henry Vaughan. NAEL-7v1; NOSC

How Roses Came Red ("Roses at first were white.") Robert Herrick. NAEL-7v1

How Roses Came Red ("'Tis said, as Cupid danced [or danc't] among.") Robert Herrick. SoSe-8

How rough a sea. Basho. TAL

How sacred and how innocent. Country Life, A. Katherine Philips. BASC

How sad for my begging bowl. (LL) I've forgotten. Ryokan. EMJL; WoPoe, tr. by Burton Watson

How sad it must be. Poem for My Father, A. Sonia Sanchez. OxAAAP

How shall I address you, my Beloved Woman? Woman: The Eternal. Rafiq Azad. PML, tr. by Afia Dil

How shall I array my love? Question, The. Frederick Goddard Tuckerman. APN-2; ColAP

How shall I be a poet? Poeta Fit, Non Nascitur. Lewis Carroll. OBSV

How shall I begin my song. Frances Densmore and Tohono O'odham. NAAPv.1 Fr. Songs for Treating Sickness, Sung during the Four Parts of the Night.

How shall I begin my song. Songs for the Four Parts of the Night. Tohono O'odham. WPoS, tr. by Frances Densmore

How shall I hold my spirit, that it not. Love Song. Marilyn Nelson. ExTi

How shall I not love them, snoozing. Dogs in Dutch Paintings, The. David Graham. PoDa

How shall I paint thee?—Be this naked stone. William Wordsworth. CenSon Fr. River Duddon [A Series of Sonnets], The.

How shall the harp of poesy regain. Sonnets, Devotional and Memorial. Felicia Dorothea Hemans.

How shall we adorn. Angle of Geese. N. Scott Momaday. HATNAP

How shall we please this age? If in a song. To Nysus. Sir Charles Sedley. OBSV

How shall we praise the magnificence of the dead. Tetélestai. Conrad Potter Aiken. APT-1; MoAmPo

How Shall We Rise to Greet the Dawn? Sir Osbert Sitwell.

  "Continually they cackle thus." PoWW

How Shall We Sing the Lord's Song in a Strange Land? Andrew Hudgins. UpMys

How shall we speak of Canada. W. L. M. K. Francis Reginald Scott. BrAP

How shall your name go down in history. To Youth. Josephine D. Henderson Heard. CBWP-4

How she disapproves of walls. Wasp. Bobi Jones. ATSWP, tr. by Robert Minhinnick

How she let her long hair down over her shoulders, making a love. O Best of All Nights, Return and Return Again. James Laughlin. GifTon

How She Resolved to Act. Merrill Moore. MoAmPo

How she sat there. Rosa. Rita Dove. ExTi; FuFl

How she worked was this: Give me what I need, I am bending down. Hands of the Body Without the Body, and Nothing to Hold, The. Katie Ford. LegDan

How should I direct my steps to her now? Woman, A. Sa'di Yusuf. PML, tr. by Lena Jayyusi and W. S. Merwin and Naomi Shihab Nye

How should I leave my love alone! (LL) Juan-er: Curl-Grass. Unknown. APT-1; CCL1, tr. by Ezra Pound

How should I not be glad to contemplate. Everything Is Going to Be All Right. Derek Mahon. BeAl; PBCIP; PoCu

How should I praise thee, Lord! how should my r[h]ymes.   Temper (1), The.
   George Herbert.   NoP-4; NoP-5

How Should I Say This?   Robert Dow.   BAP-97

How should I your true love know.   William Shakespeare.   NoSic Fr. Hamlet.

How silent is the world.   In the Night.   Robert Ivanovich Rozhdestvensky.
   RusPo, tr. by Robert Arthur Douglas Ford

How silently the years have sped away.   To My Dead Brother.   Clara Ann
   Thompson.   CBWP-2

How silly and how dear, how very dear.   Gift.   Ian Hamilton Finlay.   EdScPo

How sits this city, late most populous.   Lamentations of Jeremy, for the Most
   Part According to Tremeullius.   John Donne.

How sleek it still looks to my '90s eyes.   On Seeing a '57 Chevy Cruising 16th
   and O.   Grace Bauer.   RWB

How sleep the brave who sink to rest.   How Sleep the Brave.   William Collins.
   CABP; OBEV; OxAEP-1; TFi

How slowly glide the hours by, the minutes hours seem.   Drunkard's Wife, The.
   Mary E. Tucker.   CBWP-1

How small, of all that human hearts endure.   Lines Contributed to Goldsmith's
   "The Traveller."   Samuel Johnson.   NPeEn

How smart is smart? thinks Heart. Is smart.   Why Fool Around?   Stephen
   Dobyns.   PML; PoDa

How so well a gardener be.   John Gardner.   OBGa Fr. Feat of Gardening, The.

How soft a Caterpillar steps—.   Caterpillar.   Emily Dickinson.   SAmP

How soft the pause! the notes melodious cease.   Written at Killarney. July 29,
   1800.   Mary Tighe.   CenSon

How Some of It Happened.   Marie Howe.   ExTi

How soon doth man decay!   Mortification.   George Herbert.   FSCP; NOSC

How Soon Hath Time.   John Milton.   BrAP; NoP-5

How soon hath Time the subtle [or suttle] thief [or theef] of youth.   John
   Milton.   HeIP-4; NAEL-6v1; NoP-4; NOSC

How soon shall I be stretched at yours! (LL)   La Belle Juive.   Henry Timrod.
   APN-2; TCAPo

How soon we come to road's end.   Apologia Pro Vita Sua.   Charles Wright.

How speak of the not-I without screaming? (LL)   Man Walks By with a Loaf of
   Bread on His Shoulder, A.   César Vallejo.   PoetW; TCLAP, tr. by Clayton
   Eshleman

How splendid in the morning glows.   James Elroy Flecker.   OBEV Fr. Hassan.

How Spring Comes.   Alice Notley.   PmAP

How Stars Start.   Al Young.   ESEAA

How stern you appear.   Dylan Thomas.   ArBi Fr. Me and My Bike.

How still he stands as mists begin to move.   Guard at the Binh Thuy Bridge,
   The.   John Balaban.   AF

How still, / How strangely still.   Sea Calm.   Langston Hughes.   APT-2

How still the Riddle lies! (LL)   Some things that fly there be.   Emily
   Dickinson.   NCAP; NoP-5

How strange a thing was friendship, long ago.   Friendship.   Florence Converse.
   PoBW

How strange are dreams! I dreamed the other night.   J. Gordon Coogler.
   VerBaPo Fr. How Strange Are Dreams.

How strange is this herald who arrives.   Tapestry of the Heart, The.   Jolanda
   Insana.   CItWP, tr. by Cinzia Sartini Blum and Lara Trubowitz

How strange it seems! These Hebrews in their graves.   Jewish Cemetery at
   Newport, The.   Henry Wadsworth Longfellow.   APN-1; ChIV-1; ColAP;
   FaBoA; HeIP-4; NAAL-5; NAAPv.1; NCAP; NoP-4; NoP-5; OxBoAm;
   PoPoPo; TCAPo; WaAnP

How strange to be gone in a minute? A man.   Ted Berrigan.   FTOS; PFTM-2;
   PmAP; WaAnP Fr. Sonnets, The.

How strange to think of giving up all ambition!   Watering the Horse.   Robert
   Bly.   StAl

How strangely beats my troubled heart.   Nostalgia.   Lajos Áprily.   IQMS, tr.
   by Watson Kirkconnell

How strangely blind is prejudice, the Negro's greatest foe!   Prejudice.   Lizelia
   Augusta Jenkins Moorer.   CBWP-3

How strong does my passion flow.   On Her Loving Two Equally.   Aphra Behn.
   NALW; NIL-7; NIP-4

How strongly does my Passion flow.   Song: On Her Loving Two Equally.
   Aphra Behn.   NoP-5

How subtle-secret is your smile! Did you love none then? Nay, I know.   Oscar
   Wilde.   MoBrPo Fr. Sphinx, The.

How suddenly she roused my ardor.   Close Call.   X. J. Kennedy.   PoDa

How sweet a Lord is mine? If any should.   Edward Taylor.   OxBoAm Fr.
   Preparatory Meditations: Part 1 (Complete).

How sweet and awful is the place.   Isaac Watts.   SacPr

How sweet and innocent are country sports.   James Thomson.   UV Fr. Of a
   Country Life.

How sweet and lovely dost thou make the shame.   William Shakespeare.
   HeIP-4 Fr. Sonnets.

How Sweet I Roamed [or Roam'd] from Field to Field.   William Blake.
   BrAP; TFi

   (Song.)   NAEL-6v2; NoP-4; NoP-5; NPBRoP

How sweet is harmless solitude!   Solitude.   Mary Mollineux.   NOSC

'How sweet is mortal Sovranty!' — think some.   Omar Khayyám.   UV Fr.
   Rubáiyát of Omar Khayyám [of Naishápúr], The.

How sweet is the season, the sky how serene.   Song for A Fishing Party.
   Jonathan Odell.   NAAPv.1

How sweet is the Shepherd's sweet lot!   William Blake.   ChAP; NPBRoP Fr.
   Songs of Innocence.

How sweet it is, when mother Fancy rocks.   William Wordsworth.   CenSon

How sweet the answer Echo makes.   Echo.   Thomas Moore.   NOBRP

How sweet the moonlight sleeps upon this bank!   William Shakespeare.
   OxAEP-1; TreFP Fr. Merchant of Venice, The.

How sweet the name of Jesus sounds.   Name of Jesus, The.   John Newton.
   SacPr

How sweet to weight the line with all these vowels!   Gaiety of Form, The.
   Robert Bly.   BodElec

How sweet now like a boy I dawdle by ditches.   Widespread Implications.
   A. R. Ammons.   BodElec

How swiftly time doth passe away.   To Her Husband, on New Year's Day 1651.
   Gertrude Aston Thimelby.   EMWP

How terrifying at night is the convex face of the black.   First Psalm
   (Posthumous).   Bertolt Brecht.   PFTM-1

How that girl can move.   Dog Star.   Gerry Gomez Pearlberg.   WiU

How that glory remains in remembrance.   Unknown.   NoP-4 Fr. Beowulf.

How that great work of Love enhances Nature's. (LL)   Elizabeth Barrett
   Browning.   CenSon; OxAEP-2 Fr. Sonnets from the Portuguese.

How the Big Thicket Got Smaller.   Jerry Bradley.   TiP2

How the Camel Got His Hump.   Rudyard Kipling.   Fr. Just-So Stories.

How the Cumberland Went Down.   Silas Weir Mitchell.   PCW

How the days went.   Now That I Am Forever with Child.   Audre Lorde.
   NALW; NAMCP V.2; OxAAAP

How the dead women destroy them in their minds, from negative space.   How
   the Dead Women May Operate from Negative Space.   Alice Notley.   Eno

How the Dead Women May Operate from Negative Space.   Alice Notley.   Eno

How the Demons Were Assimilated and Became Productive Citizens.   A. E.
   Stallings.   PoDa

How the Doughty Duke of Albany like a Coward Knight Ran Away Shamefully.
   John Skelton.

   "O ye wretched Scots."   OBSV

How the Earth Loves You.   David Waltner-Toews.   ACAMVP

How the Elderly Drive.   Erin Belieu.   AmPoNex

How the face changes, the cloud.   How the Healing Takes Place.   Joan Larkin.
   LaCa

How the First Hielandman of God Was Made.   Unknown.   OBSV

   (How the first Helandman of god was maid of Ane hors turd in argylle as is
   said.)   NePenScot

How the Healing Takes Place.   Joan Larkin.   LaCa

How the Heart Aches.   N. V. M. Gonzalez.   ReBoTo

How the Last Act Begins.   Chana Bloch.   ExTi

How the majestic stellar lights of Heav'n.   Compensation.   Henrietta Cordelia
   Ray.   CBWP-3

How the melody of a single ice cream truck.   Desire.   Kathy Fagan.   GeoHom

How the Mighty Have Fallen.   Norman Fischer.   WANABP

How the moon triumphs through the endless nights!   James Thomson.
   NePenScot Fr. City of Dreadful Night, The.

How the New Teacher Got Her Nickname.   Brian Patten.   NOxBChV

How the Pope is Chosen.   James Tate.   OxBoAm; SUP

How the Rainbow Works.   Al Young.   ESEAA

How the rain-day froze.   Child Christ at the Top of the Stairs.   James Ragan.
   TWW

How the Real Bible Is Written.   William Stafford.   CAP-8

How the river cools your blood is something you can't.   Autobiography,
   Chapter XVII: Floating the Big Piney.   Jim Barnes.   HATNAP

How the Sestina (Yawn) Works.   Anne Waldman.   AHA

How the Soul Speaks to God.   Mechthild von Magdeburg.   WPoS, tr. by
   Oliver Davies

How the splendour of these veils and of this dress.   Phaedra.   Osip Emilevich
   Mandelstam.   OBVE, tr. by James Greene

How the tenor warbles in April!   Madrigal.   Mary Leader.   NAPBL; PoDa

How the Tortoise Knew It Was Her Time.   Joan I. Siegel.   PoCoUp

How / the two people soaked.   Kim Namjo.   CAMKP Fr. Love's Cursive.

How the Wild South East Was Lost.   Kit Wright.   OBCoV

How the Women Will Stop War.   Aristophanes.   FaBoWar Fr. Lysistrata.

How the world changes! How I myself change!   Metamorphoses.   Nikolai
   Alekseievich Zabolotsky.   TCRusP, tr. by John Glad

How the young flutist smiles.   Bulat Shalvovich Okudzhava.   ItGoST, tr. by
   Ronnie Apter and Mark Herman

How these pieces of paper: lined unlined small large crinkled smooth.   How.
   Joanne Burns.   BMAP

How They Brought the Good News from Ghent to Aix. Robert Browning. NAEL-6v2; NAEL-7v2; OBSP; UV

How they kept their rendezvous. (LL) *Unknown.* NAEL-6v1; NAEL-7v1; NAWM-7v1 *Fr.* Sir Gawain and the Green Knight [Marie Borroff Translation].

How They Killed My Grandmother. Boris Abramovich Slutsky. HP, *tr. by* Daniel Weissbort

How They Loved. Jean Janzen. ACAMVP

How They Took the City. Virgil. NAWM-5v1; NAWM-7v1 *Fr.* Aeneid [*or* Eneados *or* Aeneis], The.

How thin and sharp is the moon tonight! Winter Moon. Langston Hughes. SAmP

How thin is the membrane between himself and the world. (LL) Robert Penn Warren. NAAL-5; NAMCP V.1 *Fr.* Audubon: A Vision.

How Things Bear Their Telling. Ann Lauterbach. ExTi

How Things Work. Gary Soto. NAMCP V.2; NoAM

How thought you that this thing could captivate! Alfred Tennyson. OxBSo

How Thubten Sang His Songs. Tsering Wangno Dhompa. WANABP

How time reverses. For My Contemporaries. James Vincent Cunningham. APT-2; OxBoAm; VCAP; WaAnP

How to accomplish this latest admonition. Drive Friendly. Robert Phillips. TiP2

How to Approach Your Lover's Wife. Amy Bottke. OPRER

How to Be a Street Poet. John Rodriguez. BRtP

How to Be Here? Tim Lilburn. OpeFie

How to Behave with the Ill. Julia Darling. PoCu

How to behold what cannot be held? Giovanni da Fiesole on the Sublime. Richard Howard. GS

How to Build a Prayer. S. Pearl Sharp. BtF

How to Catch a Ghost in a Jar. Cynthia Cruz. IAoNAP

How to Change a Flat. Leslie Anne McIlroy. AmPoNex

How to Choose a Mistress. Edmond Prestwich. NOSC

How to Choose a Mistress. *Unknown.* NOSC

How to Continue. John Ashbery. OxBoAm

How To Cook Women. Takagi Kyozo. PML, *tr. by* James Kirup and Michio Nakano

How to deal with these hours. Midnight Saving Time. Adrien Stoutenburg. AWTN

How to Disappear. Amanda Dalton. NeBl

How to Do. Cornelius Eady. BRtP

How to Do It. Martial. WoPoe, *tr. by* Fred Chappell

How to Drink the Sun. Vladimir Alekseievich Soloukhin. TCRusP, *tr. by* Daniel Weissbort

How to Eat a Poem. Eve Merriam. ChAP

How to explain my heroic courtesy? I feel. Elephant, The. Dan Chiasson. LegDan

How to fuck casually. What I've Learned in My Travels. Tom Clark and Lewis Warsh. AHA

How to Get a Baby. Judith Ortiz Cofer. NIL-7; PueRic

How to Get On in Society. Sir John Betjeman. OBSV; UV

How to Get There. Frank O'Hara. NoP-4; NoP-5

How to isolate the fragments of the night. Fragments of the Night, The. José Lezama Lima. TCLAP, *tr. by* Willis Barnstone

How to keep—is there ány any, is there none such, nowhere known. Leaden Echo and the Golden Echo, The. Gerard Manley Hopkins. MoBrPo; OBMV

How to Kill. Keith Douglas. HarvBoo; NPeEn; PLBUT; PoAgWa; PoWW

How to kill a living thing. Eibhlín Nic Eochaidh. StAl

How to Leave an Island. Carmelita McGrath. Coast

How to Like It. Stephen Dobyns. CAP-8; SUP

How to Listen. Major L. Jackson. PoDa

How to live as a single natural being. Plan for a Curriculum of the Soul, A. Charles Olson. PFTM-2

How to live? How be simple and literal? How? Vladimir Holan. PoSu, *tr. by* Ian Milner and Jarmila Milner

How to Live in the Elegy. Tracy Philpot. AmPoNex

How to Live Through This Night (A Dream). Nina Iskrenko. ItGoST, *tr. by* Patrick Henry, John High and Katya Olmsted

How to Look at Mexican Highways. Mónica de la Torre. LegDan

How to Make Good Baked Salmon from the River. Nora Dauenhauer. ReEnLa

How to Make It. Yvonne Jackson. BtF

How to Make Love to a Man. Sharon Doubiago. MAAN

How to Make Rhubarb Wine. Ted Kooser. PBCAP

How to make this impure. Empty Page, The. Sara de Ibáñez. TCLAP, *tr. by* Andrew Rosing

How to Meditate. Jack Kerouac. BB

How to Obtain Her. *Unknown.* NoSic

How to Paint a Perfect Christmas. Miroslav Holub. OBCP, *tr. by* Ian Milner and George Theiner

How to Play Night Baseball. Jonathan Holden. MoASP

How to put this exactly? I mean without. First Steps. J. D. McClatchy. WiU

How to qualify a pear tree without pointing at the sky. Roy Kiyooka. NLPA *Fr.* Pear Tree Pomes.

How to Reach the Sun . . . on a Piece of Paper. Wes Magee. NOxBChV

How to Regain Your Soul. William Stafford. EMP; PoA 2002

How to Ride Out a Storm. Mildmay Fane, 2d Earl of Westmorland. NOSC

How to say hate was in rancorous bloom. Upon Finding a Black Woman's Door Sprayed with Swastikas, I Tell Her This Story of Hands. Kevin Stein. SwNoth

How to say the distance, not the difference. Black English. Richard Katrovas. LTA

How to See Deer. Philip Booth. GoPo

How to serve you, and you trust me. (LL) To Lucasta, from Prison. Richard Lovelace. BASC; CavPo

How to shake a ripe pear down. Roy Kiyooka. NLPA *Fr.* Pear Tree Pomes.

How to shrug off. How to shrug off. Idea Vilariño. TANSG, *tr. by* Louise B. Popkin

How to Start a War. Phyllis McGinley. OBSV

How to stay here in evening the snow. Stopping By. Laura Mullen. IAoNAP

How to strip, clean and re-sight a bolt-action Martini-Henry. (LL) Fundamentals. Ian Duhig. NeBl; NeBrP

How to Stuff a Pepper. Nancy Willard. AFaM

How to Survive Nuclear War. Maxine W. Kumin. AtGh

How to Tell a Camel. J. Patrick Lewis. TLR

How to tell it all? Referring to what chronicles? Six Lectures in Verse. Czeslaw Milosz. *tr. by* the author and Leonard Nathan

How to Tell the Wild Animals. Carolyn Wells. NBLV

How to Thank God for Your Loneliness. Stephen Valentine. RWB

How to Wait. Kelly Cherry. LPSFW

How to Watch Your Brother Die. Michael Lassell. CAGL; WiU

How to Write a Poem after September 11th. Nikki Moustaki. PA9/11

How to Write a Villanelle. Elisavietta Ritchie. PoA 2002

How to Write Anglo-Welsh Poetry. John Davies. AngWePo; TCAWP

How to Write the Great American Indian Novel. Sherman Alexie. NAMCP V.2

How to Write the New Mennonite Poem. Jeff Gundy. ACAMVP

How tranquil is man's life. Life Withdrawn, The. Luís De León. SpanPo, *tr. by* Edwin Morgan

How ugly babies are! How heedless. Vikram Seth. OBCoV *Fr.* Golden Gate, The.

How unpleasant to meet Mr. Eliot! T. S. Eliot. NBLV; OBCoV; UV *Fr.* Five-Finger Exercises.

How vainly men themselves amaze. Garden, The. Andrew Marvell. BASC; BrAP; ClHu; FSCP; MakPoe; NAEL-6v1; NAEL-7v1; NIL-7; NIP-4; NoP-5; NOSC; NPeEn; OBGa; OxBEV; PBRV; PoPoPo; TFi; TRP; WaAnP

How vast a world is figured by a word! Word: Man, A. Washington Allston. APN-1

How vast, how dread, o'erwhelming is the thought. On a Falling Group in the Last Judgement of Michael Angelo, in the Cappella Sistina. Washington Allston. APN-1

How vast karma. Seigen-yuiin. ZenPo, *tr. by* Takashi Ikemoto and Lucien Stryk

How very noble! Basho. SoOfWa, *tr. by* Sam Hamill

How vigilant was Spenser. Edmund Clerihew Bentley. OBCoV *Fr.* Clerihews.

How warm this woodland wild Recess! Recollections of Love. Samuel Taylor Coleridge. NAEL-6v2

How was it? / Sweet. (LL) Came to me— / Who? Rudaki. OBVE; OxBEV; WoPoe, *tr. by* Basil Bunting

How was she, my God, how was she? Fleeting Return. Juan Ramón Jiménez. BLPSL, *tr. by* Rene de Costa, Rigas Kappatos and Eleni Paidoussi

How We Are Spared. W. S. Merwin. CAP-8

How We Carry Ourselves. Jimmy Santiago Baca. AF

How We Danced. Anne Sexton. NAAL-5; NAMCP V.2 *Fr.* Death of the Fathers, The.

How We Drove the Trotter. W. T. Goodge. NOBAu

How we go on. (LL) Axe Handles. Gary Snyder. CAP-8; ColAP; LoL; NAMCP V.2; NoAM; PmAP; PoPoPo; TWF; VCAP

How We Heard the Name. Alan Dugan. NoAM; PtR; YaYoPo

How we loved them. Bicycles and the Apex, The. George Oppen. CalPo

How We Made a New Art on Old Ground. Eavan Boland. PoA 2002

How We See. Edward Bond. HP

How we stare at objects they kept. Open-Air Museum. Michael Thorpe. Coast

How weak his will to resist has become. Gravity, Death. Agi Mishol. DTA, *tr. by* Tsipi Keller

How welcome it is, how sweet that the old stories do not always. Rhiannon. Christine Furnival. TCAWP

How well do I recall that walk in state. Frederick Goddard Tuckerman. APN-2; NoP-5 *Fr.* Sonnets.

How well he knows he must lift out. Sea Inside the Sea. Tess Gallagher. PasH

How well her name an *Army* doth present. Anagram. George Herbert. ChIV-2

How well the brittle boat doth personate. On the Same [Death of My Dear Brother, Mr. H.S., Drowned]: The Boat. William Hammond. NOSC

How well, you, you resemble! You or You. Laura Riding Jackson. MoWP

How wild the sea is. Basho. SoOfWa

How will I hide? (LL) Question: "Body my house." May Swenson. APT-2; GPTC; NAMCP V.2; OxBoAm; PtR

How will I think of you. December 21st. Jean Valentine. CAP-8

How will it be, the day death comes? Day Death Comes, The. Faiz Ahmad Faiz. PoetW, *tr. by* Naomi Lazard

How will it be with me in time of love? (LL) After Communion. Christina Georgina Rossetti. SacPr; WPoS

How will it go, crumbling earthquake, towering inferno, juggernaut, volcano, smashup. New Reality Is Better Than a New Movie!, A. Imamu Amiri Baraka. NAMCP V.2; NoAM; WaAnP

How will our unborn children scoff at us. Future Verdict, The. Ada Cambridge. NOBAu

How will the earth die? . . . will she freeze? will she burn? Sándor Petőfi. IQMS *Fr.* Clouds, The.

How will they look upon us wingless ones. Aeronauts, The. Rhoda Hero Dunn. OtW

How will we get used to joy. Rapture of Dry Ice Burning off Skin as the Moment of the Soul's Apotheosis, The. Thylias Moss. NAMCP V.2

How will you fill your goblet? How? Abraham Sutskever. HP

How will you know what my poem is like. My Ravine. Dan Chiasson. LegDan

How will You rescue me, Tara? Kamalākānta Bhattācārya. SinGod, *tr. by* Rachel Fell McDermott

How will you your Christmas keep? Keeping Christmas. Eleanor Farjeon. OBCP

How wisely Nature did decree. Eyes and Tears. Andrew Marvell. FSCP

How Woeful It Is For Me. Péter Bornemisza. IQMS, *tr. by* Paul Tabori

How woeful it is for me from thee to be parted. How Woeful It Is For Me. Péter Bornemisza. IQMS, *tr. by* Paul Tabori

How wonderful! Look what. Rāmprasād Sen. SinGod, *tr. by* Rachel Fell McDermott

How wonderful the courtesan clothes. Nothing but Curves. Menna Elfyn. BBMWP, *tr. by* Elin ap Hywel

How wonderful, Tomasito! Celebration. Thomas McGrath. GifTon; PoChi

How wonderfully it was all arranged that each. Dash It. Annie Dillard. UpMys

How would I know, America? (LL) America: "Please don't ask me, America." Dunya Mikhail. IrPoTo; WoBe, *tr. by* Liz Winslow

How would it be if you took yourself off. Landscape with Tractor. Henry Taylor. InGu

How would you. To the Far Corners of Fractured Worlds. Susan Griffin. GifTon

How would you have us, as we are? We To America. James Weldon Johnson. APT-1

How 'Ya Gonna Keep 'Em Down on the Farm? (After They've Seen Paree). Sam M. Lewis and Joe Young. ReLy

How yet resolves the Governor of the town? William Shakespeare. FaBoWar *Fr.* King Henry V.

How you became a poet's a mystery! Tony Harrison. HarvBoo; NAEL-6v2; NAEL-7v2; NAMCP V.2 *Fr.* School of Eloquence, The.

How you like these threads, said white spider. Spider. Paul Muldoon and Gerald Stern. GPPA

How, you said, you used to sleep—the way. At the Egyptian Exhibit. Daniel Tobin. NAPBL

How Zenists carry on. Gekko-Sojo. ZenPo, *tr. by* Takashi Ikemoto and Lucien Stryk

How-a! How-a! / O-ta-pa! / I am proud of being at home! *Unknown.* APN-2 *Fr.* War Dance.

"How'd I solve de Negro Problum?" Uncle Rube on the Race Problem. Clara Ann Thompson. CBWP-2

However. Jane Mead. NAPBL

However difficult the cliff. On Climbing the Mountain Where Buddha Trained. Mokusen. ZenPo, *tr. by* Takashi Ikemoto and Lucien Stryk

However, Eumolpus, our champion in time of trouble and the author of the present harmony. Petronius Arbiter. EroLit *Fr.* Satyricon.

However far. Feeling, A. Robert Creeley. PoDa

However heaped the fire. Fire Is Laid, The. *Hungarian Oral Tradition.* IQMS, *tr. by* Dermot Spence

However legendary. Diamond Cutters, The. Adrienne Rich. ItP

However the battle is ended. Inspiration, An. Ella Wheeler Wilcox. ITBLP

However the image enters. Afterimages. Audre Lorde. LTA; VCAP

However you look at it. Secular, The. Chris Wallace-Crabbe. NOBAu

Howl. Allen Ginsberg. HarvBoo; NAAL-5; NAMCP V.2

   "I saw the best minds of my generation destroyed by madness, starving hysterical naked." CAP-8; EMP; NoAM; NoP-4; NoP-5; PmAP; VCAP; WaAnP

   "What sphinx of cement and aluminum bashed open their skulls and ate up their brains and imagination?" BB; CLPP

Howl. Beau Sia. HeMarv

Howl, Howl. Christopher Reid. OBCoV

Howl, howl, howl! O! you are men of stones. William Shakespeare. OxAEP-1 *Fr.* King Lear.

Howling Babe, The. (LL) La Préface. Charles Olson. APT-2; PFTM-2

How's it going? Sure, You Can Ask Me a Personal Question. Iwan Llwyd. BBMWP, *tr. by* Grahame Davies

Hoy con el viento del Norte. Tiempo Mezquino. Claudio Rodríguez. RaW

Hoy estoy sin saber yo no sé como. Me Sobra el Corazón. Miguel Hernández. RaW

Hoy habito el día de la Virgen. País de los milagros, El. Dana Gelinas. SPV

Hoy voy a describir el campo. Campo de Batalla, El. Angel González. RaW

Hrothgar Answered. *Unknown.* WoPoe *Fr.* Beowulf.

Hrothgar answered helm of the Shield-Danes. *Unknown.* WoPoe *Fr.* Beowulf.

Hsin-I Village. Wang Wei. ChinPo, *tr. by* Ye Weilian [*or* Yeh Wei-lien *or* Wai-lim Yip]

Huadxí que ziyaba. Víctor Terán. RMCMP

Huai Nan Tzu, a Taoist book from the 2nd century B.C.E., The. Anecdotal Evidence. Eliot Weinberger. WANABP

Hubiera yo veloz por él el mundo. Con sólo dos o tres estambres revientan las flores masculinas. Ascienden desde el fondo de sí mismas, candentes y jugosas. A mano suelta se revuelcan, se crían bajo este cielo a medias entre luz y sombra. María Baranda. RMCMP

Hubris. Mary Karr. NIL-7

Huc omnes pariter. Boethius. OBMV *Fr.* Consolation of Philosophy, The ("De Consolacione Philosophie").

Huckster at Noontime. James Ragan. TWW

Hucksters haggle in the mart, The. For a War Memorial. G. K. Chesterton. PoWW

Huddie Ledbetter. Paul Foreman. TiP2

Hudibras. Samuel Butler.

   Agrippa's Pug. DiBP

   Argument, The. BASC; NAEL-6v1; NAEL-7v1

   Arms and the Man. NOSC

   Bear-Baiting. DiBP

   "For his religion it was fit." OBCoV; OBSV; OxBEV

   "Quoth he, My faith as adamantine." OBSV

   "There is a tall long-sided dame." OBSV

   "What makes a knave a child of God." OBSV

   "When civil fury [*or* dudgeon] first grew high." BASC; CABP; NAEL-6v1; NAEL-7v1

Hudney, Sutej IX, X, XI, 7, 9, 25, 58, 60, 61, 64. Index. Paul Violi. OxBoAm; PmAP

Hudor / HUDOR et Pax. Ezra Pound. *Fr.* Cantos.

Hudson is angry, white-capped, splashing, The. Three Poems. Michael Lassell. WiU

Hudson tells us of them. Hudson's Geese. Leslie Norris. TCAWP

Hudson's Geese. Leslie Norris. TCAWP

Hudson's not a river but an estuary, The. Palisades Park. Samba. Robert Pinsky. BAP-04

Hue and Cry after Fair Amoret, A. William Congreve. NPeEn; OBEV; OxBEV

   (Fair Amoret.) IrLP

Hue is as rich, The. Ki no Tsurayuki. WoPoe, *tr. by* Helen Craig McCullough

Huellas de los ojos que miraron estas líneas, Las. Libro de Segunda Mano. Antonio Deltoro. RMCMP

Huelsenbeck / janko, chant / tzara. L'amiral cherche une maison à louer. Richard Huelsenbeck, Marcel Janko and Tristan Tzara. PFTM-1

Huerfano Valley Seed Songs. Andrew Schelling. AmZen

Hues of Electric Blue. Felicia L. Morgenstern. BtF

Huevos puestos por un tigre. Antonio Deltoro. RMCMP

Huffing puffing upstairs downstairs telephone. Not Dead Yet. Allen Ginsberg. BodElec

Huffy Henry hid the day. John Berryman. ColAP; EMP; NAMCP V.2; NoP-4; NoP-5; VCAP *Fr.* Dream Songs.

Hug o' War. Shel Silverstein. NTCP

Hug, The. Tess Gallagher. StAl

Hug, The. Thom Gunn. HarvBoo; NPeEn; StAl

Huge baroque tower: behind the balcony railing a lighted lamp, A. Faenza. Dino Campana. MotU, *tr. by* Charles Wright

Huge birds flap through the toxin dark. Orpheus. Eurydice. Hermes. Joanna Klink. IAoNAP; LegDan

Huge brightly lit ship emerges from the harbor, says K, A. Brief History of the City. Robert Peterson. GeoHom

Huge Car with the Sad Voice, The. Kojo Laing. HBAPE

Huge cement truck turns the corner, A. Four about Heavy Machinery. David Young. MotU

Huge dog, Broderick, and, The. Messengers, The. Robert Creeley. NAAL-5

Huge doll of my body, The. My Life. Mark Strand. NoAM

Huge elm, with rifted trunk all notched and scarred. Shepherd's Tree, The. John Clare. CenSon

Huge frog and I, A. Issa. EH, *tr. by* Robert Hass

Huge frogs and curses. Gu Cheng. PFTM-2 *Fr.* Bulin File, The.

Huge Mouth. Hwang Insuk. EcSo, *tr. by* Peter H. Lee

Huge Person, The. Günter Eich. MotU, *tr. by* David Walker

Huge shards of glass and ice slash through the North Sea. North Sea. Duo Duo. PFTM-2, *tr. by* Tony Barnstone and Newton Liu

Huge shoe mounts up from the horizon, A. Wounded Breakfast, The. Russell Edson. MotU

Huge summer afternoon with no sign of rain, A. Basketball. Louis Jenkins. MoASP

Huge upon the hazy plain. Pastoral. Archibald MacLeish. GM

Huge vapo[u]rs brood above the clifted shore. Written near a Port on a Dark Evening. Charlotte Smith. CenSon; NoP-4; NoP-5

Huge with Time, a wombfruit lanced. Wole Soyinka. HBAPE

Huge wound in my head began to heal, The. Wound, The. Thom Gunn. NPeEn

Hugerl, for a decade now. W. H. Auden. CAGL *Fr.* Three Posthumous Poems.

Hugging the Shore. Mary E. Tucker. CBWP-1

Hugh Selwyn Mauberley (Life and Contacts). Ezra Pound. APT-1; NAMCP V.1; NoAM; NoP-5

    4. AmWaPo; HarvBoo; HeIP-4; InoFa; MoAmPo; NPeEn; OBWP; OxBoAm; PoAgWa; PoWW; TRP; WaAnP

    5. AmWaPo; HarvBoo; InoFa; MoAmPo; NPeEn; OxBoAm; PoAgWa; TRP; WaAnP

    "Age demanded an image, The." HarvBoo; MoAmPo; NPeEn

    "Beneath the sagging roof." MoAmPo; NAAPv.2

    Brennbaum. MoAmPo; NAAPv.2

    "Conservatrix of Milesien." NAAPv.2

    "Daphne with her thighs in bark." NAAPv.2

    (E. P. Ode Pour l'Election de Son Sepulchre.) MoAmPo; NAAPv.2; NoAM; TCAPo

    (Envoi: "Go, dumb-born book.") MoAmPo

    Envoi (1919). NAAPv.2; TCAPo

    Hugh Selwyn Mauberley. NAAPv.2

    Mauberly (1920).

        Age Demanded, The. TCAPo

        "For three years, diabolus in the scale." TCAPo

        Medallion. NoP-5; TCAPo

        "Scattered Moluccas." TCAPo

    Mr. Nixon. MoAmPo; NAAPv.2

    Siena Mi Fe'; Disfecemi Maremma. MoAmPo; NAAPv.2

    "Tea-rose tea-gown, etc., The." ColAP; HarvBoo; MoAmPo

    Yeux Glauques. MoAmPo; NAAPv.2

Hughesville Scythe, The. Henry Taylor. LPSFW

Hughie [the] Gra[e]me [Version from Scott's Minstrelsy]. *Unknown.* IBB

Huguenot, A. Mary Elizabeth Coleridge. SacPr

Huguenot Graveyard at the Heart of the City, The. Eavan Boland. HarvBoo

Hui-chu Temple, Mount K'un. Wang An-shih. CrYelRi, *tr. by* Sam Hamill

Hui-neng's Pond. Muso Soseki. EaWin, *tr. by* W. S. Merwin

Huître, de la grosseur d'un galet moyen, est d'une apparence plus rugueuse, L'. Huître, L'. Francis Ponge. YaTCFP

Hula Dancers Dance the Hula, Kilauea the Caldera, The. John Tarrant. WhBo

Hula Skirt, 1959, The. Kimiko Hahn. UnSA

Hullo! Sam Walter Foss. VerBaPo

Hullo hullo one more night stop guessing it's me the cave man there are cicadas which. Automatic Crystal, The. Aimé Césaire. SurPaPo, *tr. by* Clayton Eshleman and Annette Smith

Hullo, Inside. Max Fatchen. NOxBChV

Hullo, Lord! / A minor poet. Sound Letter. Marina Boroditskaya. CRWP, *tr. by* Ruth Fainlight

Hulls jut out of sand, sink, emerge as if from black holes. Heart with Little or No Bedrock for Anchor, A. Vivian Shipley. ExTi

Hully Gully. Rita Dove. SwNoth

Hum. Ann Lauterbach. OxBoAm

Human Abstract, The. William Blake. NAEL-6v2; NAEL-7v2; NOBRP; NPBRoP; OxAEP-2 *Fr.* Songs of Experience.

Human Affection. Stevie Smith. NALW

Human and Divine. Phoebe Cary. SacPr

Human being is but an act of generosity, The. Accuracy of the Scale, The. Alberto Blanco. RMCMP, *tr. by* Joan Lindgren

Human beings and spirits all take their sustenance. Night and Dawn. Khwaja Shams-ad-din Muhammad Hafiz. WED, *tr. by* Robert Bly and Leonard Lewisohn

Human beings are / soft and supple when alive. Lao Tzu. ColAnChi *Fr.* Tao Te Ching.

Human beings suffer. Seamus Heaney. PLBUT; TWF *Fr.* Cure at Troy, The.

Human body is a little universe, The. Enlightenment. Shih Shu. WoPoe, *tr. by* James H. Sanford

Human body is a little universe, The. 55. Shih Shu. CSKM, *tr. by* James H. Sanford

Human Cry, The. Alfred Tennyson. InvLi

Human cunt, like the eye, dilates, The. Tryst. Olga Broumas. WiU

Human emotions and cognition. Why We Ask You Not to Touch. Charles Bernstein. NoP-5

Human Excrement. Stanley Plumly. PfSP

Human eye, a sphere of waters and tissue, absorbs an energy that, The. Ronald Johnson. APSN *Fr.* Ark.

Human faces pile up in your sight, like heaps of flunky's smudged, undone paperwork. (LL) Bitter Angel. Amy Gerstler. MotU; PmAP

Human Heart its hungry Gorge, The. (LL) William Blake. ChIV-1; NAEL-6v2; NAEL-7v2; NoP-4; NoP-5 *Fr.* Songs of Experience.

Human House. VCWP, *tr. by* Christopher Drake

Human Life. Matthew Prior. OBCoV; OxBEV

Human Misery. Andreas Gryphius. GePo, *tr. by* George C. Schoolfield

Human Museum, The. Brenda Coultas. HeMarv

Human Non-Sequitur. Larry Goodell. ICANM

Human now, The. September 30. Sarah Menefee. Eno

Human race would die out all, The. Bondage. Gyula Illyés. IQMS, *tr. by* Dorren Bell

Human reason is beautiful and invincible. Incantation. Czeslaw Milosz. PtR; VCWP, *tr. by* the author and Robert Pinsky

Human shape is a ghost, The. Jelaluddin Rumi. LoL, *tr. by* Coleman Barks and John Moyne

Human sigh commuted to life imprisonment, The. Sonnet Against Nuclear Weapons. Jane Miller. ExTi

Human spirits saw I on a day, The. Questioning Spirit, The. Arthur Hugh Clough. SacPr

Human strength. Simonides. SaLy, *tr. by* Diane Rayor

Human torch / races through Prague, A. Ballad of Jan Palach, Student and Heretic. Ondra Lysohorsky. AF, *tr. by* Ewald Osers

Human Tragedy, The. Alfred Austin.

    "And do they wear that lubricating lie." VerBaPo

    "But the fleet hours pass pitilessly fleeter." VerBaPo

Human Universe, The. Valerie Martínez. TouFir

Humane chariot, most valuable. To the Bicycle. John Gibbens. ArBi

Humanist, The. Geoffrey Hill. UpMys

Humanities Lecture. William Stafford. NoAM

Humanity. Han Yü. CCL1, *tr. by* H. A. Giles

Humanity. T. Gwynn Jones. BBMWP, *tr. by* Gillian Clarke

Humanity raised three flags atop three mountains. Three Flags. Murad Mikha'il. IrPoTo, *tr. by* Christina Coyle and Sadok Masliyah

HUMANITY, the field of miseries. Exaltatio Humanae Naturae. William Alabaster. NoSic

Humankind has not declined! Sándor Petőfi. IQMS *Fr.* Clouds, The.

Humankind, that my broken mother, fooled. On Mankind. Attila József. IQMS, *tr. by* Adam Makkai

Humans. Attila József. IQMS, *tr. by* Vernon Watkins

Humans don't know how to communicate with each other. Human Non-Sequitur. Larry Goodell. ICANM

Humble Herb Is Rival to Prozac. Rachel Hadas. PoDa

Humble life of dull and easy work, The. Paul Verlaine. SxFrPo, *tr. by* Martin Sorrell

Humble Litany. Aida Cartagena de Portalatin. TANSG, *tr. by* Emma Jane Robinett

Humble Petition of a Beautiful Young Lady, The. *Unknown.* IrLP

Humble Petition of the British Jacobins to their Brethren of France, The. *Unknown.* NOBRP

Humble Wish, The. B–ll M–rt–n. LW

Humble-Bee, The. Ralph Waldo Emerson. APN-1; NAAPv.1; NCAP

Humbly, He Speaks to His Tools. Venus Khoury-Gata. PoArWo, *tr. by* Lucy McNair

Humbly showeth: / That I went to warm myself in Lady Betty's chamber, because I was cold. Jonathan Swift. CABP

Hume's Suicide of the External World. Christine Hume. LegDan

Humid July drive-in nights. River Road. Cyd Adams. TiP2

Humidity. C. D. Wright. AmAlph

Humiliating the Laser-Beam. Ödön Palasovszky. IQMS, tr. by Kenneth McRobbie

Humiliation in Its Disguises. Andrew Crozier. VaPo

Humility. George Herbert. NOSC

Humm Tee Dim Tay. Humpty Dumpty. Michael Rosen. NOxBChV

Humming bee purrs softly o'er his flower, The. Cricket, The. Frederick Goddard Tuckerman. APN-2; NAAPv.1; NCAP; TCAPo

Humming Eyelashes. Miguel Hernández. RaW, tr. by Hardie St. Martin

Humming in the mist. Tomas Tranströmer. WoBe Fr. Haiku.

Humming the deep security of life. (LL) Nests in Elms. Michael Field. NAEL-7v2; VWP

Humming wll put you to sleep, The. Your Death and Mine. János Pilinszky. IQMS, tr. by Adam Makkai

Hummingbird. X. J. Kennedy. NOxBChV

Humming-Bird. D. H. Lawrence. NAMCP V.1; NoAM; OWoS; OxBEV

Hummingbird, A. Emily Dickinson. APN-2; HeIP-4; NAAL-3; NAAL-5; NoP-4; NoP-5; SoSe-8; TCAPo

Humming-Bird, The. Mary E. Tucker. CBWP-1

Hummingbird at Dawn. Catharino James Elijio. OWABP

Hummingbird Light. Diane Wakoski. PmAP

Hummingbird looks up from his flower punchbowl with an expression of pure dazzlement, The. Send-Off, The. Michael Fried. PoCho

Hummingbird Pauses at the Trumpet Vine. Mary Oliver. NAAL-5

Hummingbirds. Norman Dubie. BodElec

Hummingbirds. Ruth Stone. ExTi

Hummock in the Malookas, A. Matthew Rohrer. AmPoNex

Humorless, hundreds of trunks gray in the blue expanse. Leafless Trees, Chickahominy Swamp. Dave Jeddie Smith. NAMCP V.2

Humours. John Marston. NoSic Fr. Satires.

Hump, The. Rudyard Kipling. NOxBChV Fr. Just-So Stories.

Hump-Backed Flute Player, The. Gary Snyder. APSN; PFTM-2 Fr. Mountains and Rivers without End: The Market.

Humphy-backit heron, A. Heron. James King Annand. NOxBChV

Humpty Dumpty. Michael Rosen. NOxBChV

Humpty Dumpty sat on a wall. Mother Goose. OxBEV

Humpty Dumpty's Poetic Recitation. Lewis Carroll. NPeEn Fr. Through the Looking-Glass.

Humpty Dumpty's Recitation. Lewis Carroll. OBSP See Humpty Dumpty's Poetic Recitation.

Humpty Dumpty's Song. Lewis Carroll. OBCOV See Humpty Dumpty's Poetic Recitation.

Humus. Karen Press. TSAP

Hun so loved the cry, one falling elephant's, The. Lenox Hill. Agha Shahid Ali. AmAlph; NAMCP V.2; NoP-5

Hunchback Girl: She Thinks of Heaven. Gwendolyn Brooks. ChAP Fr. Street in Bronzeville, A.

Hunchback in the Park, The. Dylan Thomas. AngWePo; MoBrPo; NAEL-6v2; NAEL-7v2; NAMCP V.2; NoAM; NoP-4; NoP-5; OxBEV; TCAWP

Hunchback of Dugbe, The. Wole Soyinka. VCWP

Hunchback on the corner, with gum and shoelaces, The. Pursuit. Robert Penn Warren. FuPo; MoAmPo

Hunchèd camels of the night, The. Arab Love-Song, An. Francis Thompson. MoBrPo

Hunched, hump-backed, gigantic. Blues. Edward Kamau Brathwaite. GT

Hunched I make my way, uncertainly. On the Back of a Photograph. János Pilinszky. PoSu; StAl, tr. by Peter Jay

Hunched in a corner seat, I'd watch him pass. Notes from Underground: W. H. Auden on the Lexington Avenue IRT. Grace Schulman. ExTi

Hunched in the squat sleeper box of a black semi hurtling toward Fresno. Wordsworth's Socks. Elliot Fried. SUP

Hunched like poker players at my kitchen table. Corpses, The. Lynn Emanuel. ExTi

Hunder pipers canna blaw, A. Calvinist Sang. Alexander Scott. EdScPo

Hundred and one butter lamps are offered to my uncle who is no more, A. Bardo. Tsering Wangno Dhompa. WANABP

Hundred black birds lifting back, The. Early Morning—Ucross, Wyoming. Christopher Buckley. PfSP

Hundred Headless Woman, The. Max Ernst. PFTM-1 Fr. Hundred Headless Woman, The.

Hundred Himalayas, A. Sydney Lea. VisFro

Hundred houses were in ruins, A. Jaroslav Seifert. AF Fr. Bombing of the Town of Kralupy, The.

Hundred hundred kisses, A. Johannes Secundus. EroLit Fr. Basia.

Hundred men shouting at once, helping to rattle the oars, A. Blue Rapids. Lu Yu. ColAnChi, tr. by Burton Watson

Hundred miles from the capital city of hope, A. Yevgeny Aleksandrovich Yevtushenko. TCRusP, tr. by Peter Levi and Robin Milner-Gulland

Hundred mountains and no bird, A. River-Snow. Liu Tsung-yüan. CCL1; ItP, tr. by Witter Bynner

Hundred spirits whisper "Peace", A. (LL) Alfred Tennyson. NAEL-6v2; NAEL-7v2 Fr. In Memoriam H. H.

Hundred steps in darkness, not the next, The. (LL) Night Operations, Coastal Command RAF. Howard Nemerov. AF; PWW2

Hundred thousand million mites we go, A. Hundred Thousand Million Mites, A. Charles Hamilton Sorley. PoWW

Hundred thousand sparrows descend on my empty courtyard, A. Cold Sparrows. Yang Wan-li. NDACCP, tr. by David Hinton

Hundred thousand worlds are flowers in the sky, A. Han-shan Te-ch'ing. CSKM, tr. by Red Pine

Hundred Worries, A. Tu Fu [or Du Fu]. CrYelRi, tr. by Sam Hamill

Hundred Years Ago, A. Sarah Morgan Bryan Piatt. NAAPv.1

Hundred years, and half have passed already, A. Sent to the Magistrate of P'eng-chou. Tu Fu [or Du Fu]. CrYelRi, tr. by Sam Hamill

Hundred years from now, dear heart, A. In a Rose Garden. John Bennett. ITBLP

Hundred Years from Today, A. Ned Washington and Joseph Young. ReLy

Hundred years the Ark in the building was, A. Michael Drayton. ChIV-1 Fr. Noah's Flood.

Hundreds of birds are singing in the square. Marché aux Oiseaux. Richard Wilbur. OWoS

Hundreds of millions of years ago, days were many hours shorter. Fog. Mei-Mei Berssenbrugge. ICANM

Hundreds of open flowers. House of Spring. Muso Soseki. EaWin, tr. by W. S. Merwin

Hundreds of starlings. Calligraphy of Birds. Larry Smith. AmZen

Hundreds of thousands dead this week in Bangladesh. Grace. William Heyen. PfSP

Hundred-sunned Phenix. George Darley. OWoS

Hundred-year men? Ghosts Clap Hands. Wang the Zealot. CCL1, tr. by C. H. Kwock and Vincent McHugh and Vincent McHugh

Hundred-year-old china doll's head the sea washes up on its gray beach, The. Hundred-Year-Old China Doll's Head, The. Charles Simic. MotU

Hung be the heavens with black, yield day to night. William Shakespeare. OxAEP-1 Fr. King Henry VI, Pt. I.

Hung clouded in the dragon-guarded shrine. (LL) Christopher Pearse Cranch. APN-1; GM Fr. Seven Wonders of the World.

Hung midsea / Like a boat mid-air. Michael McClure. BB

Hung outside the door to dry. (LL) Caravan. Michael Longley. ModIr; PNI

Hung there in the thermal. Vultures. Margaret Atwood. OWoS

Hungarian Summer [1918]. Gyula Juhász. IQMS, tr. by Adam Makkai

Hungarian Winter. Gyula Juhász. IQMS, tr. by Adam Makkai

Hungarian Writer, The. János Batsányi. IQMS, tr. by Adam Makkai

Hungary. Dániel Berzsenyi. IQMS, tr. by Watson Kirkconnell

Hungary. Sándor Petőfi. IQMS, tr. by Peter Zollman

Hunger. Jeffrey Renard Allen. RD

Hunger. Jack Gilbert. BeAl

Hunger. Attila József. IQMS, tr. by Watson Kirkconnell

Hunger. Mikhail Naimy. NAAPv.2

Hunger. Jerome Rothenberg. APSN

Hunger. Sharan Strange. FuFl

Hunger, A. Benjamin Saltman. P180

Hunger and Imagination. Teresa Whitman. MiVo

Hunger Camp at Jaso. Wisława Szymborska. AF

Hunger for Something. Chase Twichell. BeAl

Hunger of the Lemur, The. Matthew Rohrer. NeAmPo

Hungerdance, The. Menke Katz. Prolet, tr. by Amelia Glaser

Hungering on the gray plain of its birth. Lion Named Passion, A. John Hollander. NoAM

Hungrier than i / thot. (LL) Dualism in ralph ellison's invisible man. Ishmael Reed. EGAG; ESEAA

Hungry. Luis J. Rodriguez. FTtHH

Hungry and cold, under Ping City's walls. Under the Walls of Ping City. Li Ho. CCL1, tr. by John Frodsham

Hungry, and plucking / the fruit. (LL) O Taste and See. Denise Levertov. AFaM; BeAl; ChIV-1; IPoFL; NoP-4; NoP-5; PoPoPo

Hungry and thirsty for holiness. Vasco [or Vasko] Popa. PoSu Fr. St Sava's Spring.

Hungry as the Sea. Melanie Kenny. IaFF

Hungry Belly Kill Daley. Lorna Goodison. NAMCP V.2

Hungry bower of drolleries. Gavin Selerie. Oth Fr. Roxy.

Hungry enough to come home. (LL) All the Soups. Martha Rhodes. AFaM; ExTi; LaCa; SweBea

Hungry Form. Caroline Bergvall. VaPo

Hungry Gap-Time, The. Thomas Lux. AmAlph

Hungry Ghost Surrenders His Tackle Box, A. Maj Ragain. AmZen

Hungry, I eat a bowl of rice with greens. Mountain Life. Chungji. BecRai, tr. by Kim Daljin, Kim Won-Chung and Christopher Merrill

Hungry Knight, The. Barbara Guest. NYP2

Hungry Man's Wheel, The. César Vallejo. PFTM-1

Hungry Master and Hungry Cat. Abu Shamaqmaq. TriCat

Hungry Orange, A. Nasri Hajjaj. Eno, tr. by Ibrahim Muhawi

Hunner funnels bleezin', reekin', A. Oor Location. Janet Hamilton. NePenScot

Hunt by Night, The. Derek Mahon. HarvBoo

Hunt is up, the morn is bright and grey, The. William Shakespeare. DiBP Fr. Titus Andronicus.

Hunt, The: "To be in the way, belonging. To wait." Sophie Cabot Black. NevBe

Hunt the Thimble. Dannie Abse. TCAWP

Hunt till you find him. Hunting for the Lord. Unknown. SSUS

Hunt-Cup, The. Daniel Tobin. NAPBL

Hunter. Linda Bierds. AmAlph

Hunter, The. Yvor Winters. NAAPv.2 Fr. Magpie's Shadow, The.

Hunter friend of mine. Daydream of Ants, The. Tanure Ojaide. NAfrP

Hunter Home from the Hill, The. Kerry Hardie. BeAl; NIrP

Hunter to the husbandmand, The. Valentine, A. Robert Graves. FuPo

Hunters, The. Ruth Temple Lindsay. SacPr

Hunter Trials. Sir John Betjeman. OBCoV

Hunters are back, The. Audre Lorde. GT; NAAL-5

Hunters are sympathetic, The. Season for Hunting, A. Teresa D. Cader. PfSP

Hunters Ask God, The. Unknown. SonAtl, tr. by P. Gavanna

Hunter's Dance in Early Fall. Debra Haaland Toya. ReEnLa

Hunters in the Snow, The. William Carlos Williams. GS; OxBoAm Fr. Pictures from Brueghel.

Hunter's Song. Unknown. APN-2, tr. by Albert S. Gatschet

Hunter's Song at Nightfall, The. Johann Wolfgang von Goethe. STV, tr. by John Frederick Nims

Hunters went out with guns, The. Good Grease. Mary Tallmountain. UnSA

Hunting. Tymoteusz Karpowicz. PoSu, tr. by Jan Darowski

Hunting. Janet Kauffman. ACAMVP

Hunting. Gary Snyder. Fr. Myths and Texts.

Hunting Civil War Relics at Nimblewill Creek. James Dickey. LPSFW

Hunting for a City. Unknown. SSUS

Hunting for Cherubs. Jeffrey McDaniel. IIR

Hunting for the Lord. Unknown. SSUS

Hunting horn upon the plain, A. Mystery of the Three Horns, The. Jules Laforgue. WoPoe, tr. by William Jay Smith

Hunting in Twilight. David Scott Ward. AmPoNex

Hunting of a Stag, The. Margaret Lucas Cavendish, Duchess of Newcastle. EMWP

Hunting of the Hare, The. Margaret Lucas Cavendish, Duchess of Newcastle. BASC; FaBoVe; NAEL-7v1; NOSC

Hunting of the Snark, The. Lewis Carroll. OBNV

  Baker's Tale, The. NAEL-6v2; NAEL-7v2; OxAEP-2

  Fit the First: The Landing. WaAnP

  Fit the Second: The Bellman's Speech. OBCoV

  Vanishing, The. OxAEP-2

Hunting Pheasants in a Cornfield. Robert Bly. TRP

Hunting Rabbits. Peter Skrzynecki. BMAP

Hunting the dodder. Sang-zhong: Hunting the Dodder. Unknown. CCL1, tr. by V. W. X.

Hunting the Dugong. Gladys Cardiff. HATNAP

Hunting the Wren. Unknown. FaBoVe

Hunting with. Harry Gilonis. Oth Fr. Forty Fungi.

Hunting-Song of the Seeonee Pack. Rudyard Kipling. BLPJKO Fr. Jungle Book, The.

Huntington sleeps in a house six feet long. Southern Pacific. Carl Sandburg. GM

Huntsman, The. Helen Adam. APT-2

Huntsman, The. Edward Lowbury. OBSP

Huntsman, I charge thee, tender well my hounds. William Shakespeare. DiBP Fr. Taming of the Shrew, The.

Huntsman waits with watchful eye, The. Fair Ilonka. Mihály Vörösmarty. IQMS, tr. by Watson Kirkconnell

Hunts—through clear glass windows. Indoor Cat, The. Paul Petrie. PoCoUp

Hurakán: A Two Way Poem. Linda M. Rodriguez Guglielmoni. FTtHH

Hurdler Explains Her Reasons, A. Mary Kathleen Rayburn. PfS

Hurley High. Paul Zarzyski. SwNoth

Hurlygush and hallyoch o the watter, The. Hurlygush. Maurice Lindsay. EdScPo

Huron, The. Ruth Herschberger. OxBoAm

Huron Carol, The. Jesse Edgar Middleton. OBCP

Hurrah for Cooper and Cary. Julia A. Moore.

  Call, A (1876). STuOW

Hurra[h] for the pumpkin pie! (LL) Thanksgiving Day. Lydia Maria Child. NTCP; WHSW

Hurrah for Thunder. Christopher Okigbo. HBAPE

Hurrahing in Harvest. Gerard Manley Hopkins. MoBrPo; NAEL-6v2; NAEL-7v2; OxBSo; SacPr

Hurray, hurray, the jade's away. Witch o' Fife, The. James Hogg. NePenScot

Hurricane. John Balaban. UrbNat

Hurricane, The. Hart Crane. MoAmPo

Hurricane, The. Philip Freneau. TCAPo

Hurricane Doris. Lorenzo Thomas. FTtHH

Hurricane Season. Edwina Trentham. AtGh

Hurricane Sisters Work Regardless, The. Ginger Andrews. SweBea

Hurrier, The. Harold Monro. MoBrPo

Hurry, Hurry, Mary Dear! N. M. Bodecker. TLR

Hurry me Nymphs! O, hurry me. George Darley. NPeEn Fr. Nepenthe.

Hurry of bell-notes, A. Station Island. Seamus Heaney.

Hurry, take pleasure in the oblique caress of rain while the sun shines. Natalya Gorbanevskaya. TCRusP, tr. by Daniel Weissbort

Hurry up, Christendom, think about salvation. András Szkhárosi Horvát. IQMS Fr. About Two Kinds of Faith: That of Christ and That of the Pope's Ragged Patchwork.

Hurry up, my love, and quickly rise to the assault. Unknown. SLW, tr. by Marjolijn De Jager, Sayd Bahodin Majrouh and André Velter

Hurry up, my love, if you want to delight in me. Unknown. SLW, tr. by Marjolijn De Jager, Sayd Bahodin Majrouh and André Velter

Hurrying through the underworld, soundless. (LL) Second Glance at a Jaguar. Ted Hughes. BrAP; NAMCP V.2; NoAM

Hurt. Marcie Hans. CA

Hurt Hawks. Robinson Jeffers. APT-1; ChAP; ColAP; EMP; HarvBoo; MoAmPo; NAAPv.2; NAMCP V.1; NoAM; NoP-4; NoP-5; OWoS; OxBoAm; TFi; TRP; WaAnP

Hurt not the trees. (LL) Trees Are Down, The. Charlotte Mew. ChIV-2; MoBrPo; MoWP; OxAEP-2; VWP

Hurtled under the lover-sundering river. Traveling Boy. William Meredith. YaYoPo

Hurtling between hedges now, I see. Limerick Train, The. Brendan Kennelly. PBCIP

Hurtling past us in an old Volvo are women who speak with forked. Women who Speak with Steak Knives. Susan Hampton. BMAP

Husband and Wife. Edward Hirsch. IllVoic

Husband and Wife. Vietnamese Oral Tradition. CaDao, tr. by John Balaban

Husband and wife! No converse now ye hold. Husband's and Wife's Grave, The. Richard Henry Dana. APN-1

Husband, if you will be my dear. Wife to Husband. John Harington. NoSic

Husband, now you despise me. Okot P'Bitek. NAMCP V.2 Fr. Song of Lawino.

Husband of To-Day, The. Edith Nesbit. VWP

Husband or a lover has run this one out, A. People at the Pay Telephone, The. Victoria McCabe. OPRER

Husband, that man is ill and weak. Adam Lindsay Gordon. STuOW Fr. Ashtaroth: A Dramatic Lyric.

Husband to Wife. John Harington. NoSic

Husband, today could you and I behold. Wife Speaks, The. Elizabeth Stoddard. SWaP

Husbandman, The. George Wither. NOSC Fr. Collection of Emblemes, Ancient and Moderne, A.

Husband's and Wife's Grave, The. Richard Henry Dana. APN-1

Husbands and Wives. Miriam Hershenson. NTCP

Husband's Lament, The. Brian Merriman. OBVE Fr. Midnight Court, The.

Husband's Return, The. Priscilla Jane Thompson. CBWP-2

Hush. Mary Elizabeth Coleridge. PoBW

Hush. David St. John. CalPo; FaoP

Hush, Hush. John Bingham Morton. UV Fr. When We Were Very Silly.

Hush, hush, / Nobody cares! John Bingham Morton. UV Fr. When We Were Very Silly.

Hush! Hush! Whisper who dares! Alan Alexander Milne. UV Fr. Vespers.

Hush is over all the teeming lists, A. Frederick Douglass. Paul Laurence Dunbar. CBCWP

Hush, little baby, don't say a word. Unknown. TLR

Hush little Lily. Chillen Get Shoes. Sterling Allen Brown. APT-2; NoP-4; NoP-5

Hush, lullay. Lullaby. Léonie Adams. MoAmPo

Hush! my dear, lie still and slumber. Cradle Hymn, A. Isaac Watts. OBEV

Hush now. You cannot describe it. Hunt the Thimble. Dannie Abse. TCAWP

Hush of / the river, The. Canoer, The. Diane Wakoski. HeIP-4

Hush! Somebody's calling your name. Ambrosia. Dorothy Marie Rice. FuFl

Hush! 'tis a holy hour—the quiet room. Evening Prayer, at a Girls' School. Felicia Dorothea Hemans. VWP

Hush! 'tis the gap between two lightnings. Room. Non Pax—Expectatio. Francis Thompson. OxBSo

Hush ye, hush ye! honey, darlin'. Lullaby. Clara Ann Thompson. CBWP-2

Hush Yo Mouf. Thomas Sayers Ellis. InTrad

Hush-a-bye, baby, on the tree-top. Mother Goose. OxBEV

Hushaby baby, on a tree top. Broadcasting to the G.B.P. D. H. Lawrence. RWPCtW

Hushaby, hushaby, wee little coon. Negro Song. Sarah Barkan. Prolet, tr. by Amelia Glaser

Hush'd be the Camps To-Day. Walt Whitman. SAmP Fr. Memories of President Lincoln.

Hushed world o midnicht, The. Philomel. Sydney Goodsir Smith. EdScPo

Huswifery. Edward Taylor. ColAP; InvLi; ITBLP; NAAL-3; NAAL-5; NAAPv.1; NIP-4; OxBoAm; SacPr; TCAPo; TFi

(Housewifery.) NoP-4; NoP-5; WaAnP

Huszt. Ferenc Kölcsey. IQMS, tr. by Watson Kirkconnell

Hut in Harmony. Muso Soseki. EaWin, tr. by W. S. Merwin

Hut in the bush of bark or rusty tin, The. Hatters, The. Nan McDonald. NOBAu

Hut of the Phantom Dwelling, The. Basho. EMJL, tr. by Burton Watson

Hut Poem #1. Jonathan Greene. WhBo

Huxley Hall. Sir John Betjeman. CABP; OBSV

Huzza! Hodgson, we are going. Lines to Mr Hodgson. Lord Byron. OBCoV

Hyacinth. Louise Glück. NoAM

Hyaenas [or Hyenas], The. Rudyard Kipling. BrAP; NAEL-6v2; NAEL-7v2; OBSV

Hybrid Magnolias in Late April. Gibbons Ruark. PoDa

Hydra, The. W. S. Merwin. NAMCP V.2

Hydrangea. Paul Muldoon and Gerald Stern. GPPA

Hydrangeas. Joan Houlihan. IAoNAP

Hydriotaphia. Tony Kushner. ASA

"Happily I turn the earth." ASA

Hydrocarbons of flesh and stone. (LL) Lyell's Hypothesis Again. Kenneth Rexroth. APSN; APT-2; NAAPv.2

Hydrodamalis Gigas. John Glenday. NeBrP

Hydromaniac. Rosemary Tonks. EmeKit

Hyena, The. Cees Buddingh'. TuT, tr. by John Hughes

Hygiene. Toni Mirosevich. RaF

Hygiene. Reginald Shepherd. ReTh

Hygiene of the Soul, The. Zbigniew Herbert. MotU, tr. by Czeslaw Milosz

Hyla Brook. Robert Frost. APT-1; CtM; NAMCP V.1; TCAPo

Hylas. Bayard Taylor. CAGL Fr. Hylas.

Hymen, god of marriage bed. Epithalamium. Joseph Rutter. NOSC

Hymen hath together tied. Epithalamium. R. Hatton. NOSC

Hymen's Triumph. Samuel Daniel.

Love Is a Sickness. OBEV

Hymn. Joseph Addison. OxAEP-1

Hymn. Saint Francis Xavier. ChIV-2

Hymn. Jack Kerouac. CLPP

Hymn. John Greenleaf Whittier. NOxBChV

Hymn, The. Denise Levertov. BodElec

Hymn, The: "To the Almighty on his radiant throne." Anne Finch, Countess of Winchilsea. ChIV-1 Fr. Pindaric Poem, A.

Hymn 1. Faith. Christopher Smart. ChIV-1 Fr. Hymns for the Amusement of Children.

Hymn 2. Anna Laetitia Barbauld. SacPr

Hymn 2. Hope. Christopher Smart. ChIV-1 Fr. Hymns for the Amusement of Children.

Hymn 8. Fortitude. Christopher Smart. ChIV-2 Fr. Hymns for the Amusement of Children.

Hymn 10. William Cowper. See Future Peace and Glory of the Church, The.

Hymn 11. Beauty. Christopher Smart. SacPr Fr. Hymns for the Amusement of Children.

Hymn: "Blest are the moments, doubly blest." William Wordsworth. SacPr

Hymn: "Christians, awake, salute the happy morn." John Byrom.

"Christians, awake, salute the happy morn." SacPr

Hymn: "Drop, drop, slow tears, and bathe those beauteous feet." Phineas Fletcher. SacPr

Hymn: "Eternal gates lift up their heads, The." Cecil Frances Alexander. SacPr

Hymn 15. Taste. Christopher Smart. ChIV-1 Fr. Hymns for the Amusement of Children.

Hymn: "Hark what a sound, and too divine for hearing." Frederic William Henry Myers. SacPr

Hymn: "How dare I in thy courts appear." Phoebe Cary. SacPr

Hymn: "Hymn of glory let us sing, A." The Venerable Bede. SacPr, tr. by Elizabeth Charles

Hymn: "I know if I find you I will have to leave the earth." A. R. Ammons. WaAnP

Hymn: "If in my womb and mind You placed." Alda Merini. CItWP, tr. by Cinzia Sartini Blum and Lara Trubowitz

Hymn: "Inspirer and hearer of prayer." Augustus Montague Toplady. SacPr

Hymn: "Jesus these eyes have never seen." Ray Palmer. SacPr

Hymn: "Jesus, where'er thy people meet." William Cowper. SacPr Fr. Olney Hymns.

Hymn: "Lord, when the wise men came from far[r]." Sidney Godolphin. NPeEn; RSR; SacPr

(Lord when the wise men came from Farr.) OxBEV; PBRV

(Meditation on the Nativity.) NOSC

Hymn: "Lord, within thy fold I be." Priscilla Jane Thompson. CBWP-2

Hymn: "Now the day is over." Sabine Baring-Gould. SacPr; WHSW

Hymn: "Now the shadows flee and vanish." William Williams. AngWePo

Hymn: "O God of Hosts, thine Ear incline." Unknown. NOBRP

Hymn: "Splendid body is private, and calls for more, The." Rex Warner. RSaN

Hymn: "What conscience dictates to be done." Alexander Pope. SacPr

Hymn: "What is the world, and what is life." William Williams. AngWePo

Hymn: "When I survey the wondrous cross." Isaac Watts. OxAEP-1; SacPr

(Crucifixion to the World by the Cross of Christ.) NPeEn; OxBEV

(When I Survey the Wondrous Cross.) WaAnP

Hymn: "When our heads are bowed with woe." Henry Hart Milman. SacPr

Hymn: "When storms arise." Paul Laurence Dunbar. SacPr

Hymn: "Ye golden lamps of heaven, farewell." Philip Doddridge. SacPr

Hymn: "You, who gave colour to the dawn." T. Rowland Hughes. BBMWP, tr. by Sally Roberts Jones

Hymn, A: "Lead gently, Lord, and slow." Paul Laurence Dunbar. SacPr

Hymn, a snare, and an exceeding sun, A. (LL) Boy Breaking Glass. Gwendolyn Brooks. ESEAA; NAMCP V.2; NoAM; NoP-4; NoP-5; PtR

Hymn, An: "Wake, O my soul; awake, and raise." Phineas Fletcher. NOSC

Hymn Among the Ruins. Octavio Paz. PFTM-1; TCLAP, tr. by William Carlos Williams

Hymn before Action. Rudyard Kipling. FaBoWar

Hymn before Sunrise, in the Vale of Chamouni. Samuel Taylor Coleridge. SacPr

Hymn for Advent. Jeremy Taylor. SacPr

Hymn for All Seasons. László Nagy. IQMS, tr. by Adam Makkai

Hymn for Lanie Poo. Imamu Amiri Baraka. BB

Each Morning. ESEAA

Hymn for Portia White. George Elliott Clarke. IFF

Hymn for Seedtime and a Safe Harvest (Arval Hymn). Unknown. WoPoe, tr. by Janet Lembke

Hymn for the Boatmen, as They Approach the Rapids under the Castle of Heidelberg. William Wordsworth. SacPr Fr. Memorials of a Tour of the Continent; 1820.

Hymn for the Sound of Hymns. George Scarbrough. LPSFW

Hymn in Praise of Neptune, A. Thomas Campion. OBEV

Hymn of Empedocles. Matthew Arnold. OBEV Fr. Empedocles on Etna.

Hymn of Freedom. Michael J. Barry. IrV

Hymn of glory let us sing, A. Hymn. The Venerable Bede. SacPr, tr. by Elizabeth Charles

Hymn of Heavenly Love, An. Edmund Spenser. SacPr

Hymn of Love, The. György Sárközi. IQMS, tr. by Adam Makkai

Hymn of Pan. Percy Bysshe Shelley. OBEV

Hymn of the City. William Cullen Bryant. NAAPv.1

Hymn of the Earth. William Ellery Channing. APN-1

Hymn of the Fairest Fair, The. William Drummond of Hawthornden.

"In those vast fields of light, ethereal plains." NOSC

Hymn of the Patriotic War Veterans. Benjamin Péret. AF, tr. by Keith Hollaman

Hymn on the Morning of Christ's Nativity. John Milton. OBEV Fr. On the Morning of Christ's Nativity.

Hymn on the Seasons, A. James Thomson. CABP Fr. Seasons, The.

Hymn[:] Sung at the Completion of the Concord Monument, April 19, 1836. Ralph Waldo Emerson. See Concord Hymn.

Hymn To a Woman Under Interrogation. Reiner Kunze. PoSu, tr. by Ewald Osers

Hymn to Aphrodite. Unknown. HW Fr. Homeric Hymns.

Hymn to Aphrodite [or Venus]. Unknown. Fr. Homeric Hymns.

Hymn to Apollo. Callimachus. HePo Fr. Hymns.
Hymn to Artemis. Callimachus. HePo Fr. Hymns.
Hymn to Comus. Ben Jonson. NOSC
Hymn[e] to Cynthia. Ben Jonson. NOSC Fr. Cynthia's Revels.
Hymn to Demeter. Callimachus. HePo Fr. Hymns.
Hymn to Diana. Ben Jonson. See Hymn[e] to Cynthia.
Hymn to Earth. Elinor Wylie. MoAmPo
Hymn to Eros. Denise Levertov. LW
Hymn[e] to God My God, In My Sickness[e], A. John Donne. BASC; HeIP-4; NAEL-6v1; NAEL-7v1; NoP-4; NoP-5; NOSC; OxAEP-1; PBRV; SoSe-8; TFi
Hymn to Her Unknown. Walter James Turner. OBMV
Hymn to Hestia, The. Unknown. Fr. Homeric Hymns.
Hymn to Him, A. Alan Jay Lerner. ReLy
Hymn to Holy Women, A. Notker Balbulus. NAWM-7v1, tr. by Peter Dronke
Hymn to Hualien, A. Hung Hung. PML, tr. by Steve Bradbury
Hymn to Indra, A [ad. fr. Sanskrit]. Sir William Jones. NOBRP
Hymn to Intellectual Beauty. Percy Bysshe Shelley. HeIP-4; NAEL-6v2; NAEL-7v2; NOBRP; NoP-4; NoP-5; NPBRoP
Hymn to Ishtar. Ashur-Nasir-Pal, King of Assyria. HW
Hymn to Light. Abraham Cowley. OxAEP-1 Fr. Pindarique Odes.
Hymn to Love. Lascelles Abercrombie. OBEV Fr. Emblems of Love.
Hymn to Mercury [or Hermes]. Unknown. Fr. Homeric Hymns.
Hymn to My God in a Night of My Late Sickness[e], A. Sir Henry Wotton. NOSC; SacPr
Hymn to Na'a'yena, A [ad. fr. Sanskrit]. Sir William Jones. NOBRP
Hymn to Night. Melville Cane. MoAmPo
Hymn to Night. Unknown. WoPoe Fr. Rig Veda.
Hymn to Night. Unknown. WoPoe Fr. Vedic Hymns.
Hymn to Nut. Unknown. HW
Hymn to Pan. John Fletcher. OBEV Fr. Faithful Shepherdess, The.
Hymn to Priapus. D. H. Lawrence. OBMV
Hymn to Proserpine. Algernon Charles Swinburne. NAEL-6v2; NAEL-7v2
Hymn to Saint Geryon. Michael McClure. PmAP
Hymn to Sarira. Great Master Chajang. BecRai, tr. by Kim Daljin, Kim Won-Chung and Christopher Merrill
Hymn to St. Maximinus, A. Hildegard von Bingen. NAWM-7v1, tr. by Peter Dronke
Hymn to Su'rya, A [ad. fr. Sanskrit]. Sir William Jones. NOBRP
Hymn to the Earth, The. Unknown. HW Fr. Homeric Hymns.
Hymn to the Fairest Fair, A. William Drummond of Hawthornden.
"O king, whose greatness none can comprehend." SacPr
Hymn to the Fallen. Unknown. FaBoWar; OBWP, tr. by Arthur Waley
Hymn to the Graces, A. Robert Herrick. NOSC
Hymn to the Guilotine. "Peter Pindar." NOBRP
Hymn to the Moon, The. Unknown. Fr. Homeric Hymns.
Hymn to the Name and Hono[u]r of the Admirable Saint[e] Teresa, A. Richard Crashaw. BASC; FSCP; NoP-4; OBEV
"Love, thou art absolute sole lord." NOSC; OxBEV
"Thou art love's victim; and must die." EroLit
Hymn to the National Flag. Margaret Junkin Preston. PCW
Hymn to the Night. Henry Wadsworth Longfellow. APN-1; NAAPv.1; TCAPo
Hymn to the North Star. William Cullen Bryant. NCAP
Hymn to the Sacred Mushroom. Bob Cobbing. Oth
Hymn to the Saints, and to Marquis Hamilton, An. John Donne. NOSC
Hymn to the Sun. Akhenaton. WoPoe, tr. by John Perlman
Hymn to the Supreme Being. Christopher Smart. ChIV-1
Hymn to the Thousand Islands. Henrietta Cordelia Ray. CBWP-3
Hymn to the Thousand-Eyed Sound Observer. Hüimyŏng. CATKP, tr. by Peter H. Lee
Hymn to the Virgin. Unknown. NoSic
Hymn to the Virgin. Unknown. RSR
Hymn to the Virgin, The. Ieuan ap Hywel Swrdwal.
Hymn to the Virtue of Wine. Liu Ling. CCL1, tr. by Richard B. Mather
Hymn to Yellow. Genevieve Taggard. APT-2
Hymn upon St. Bartholomew's Day, An. Thomas Traherne. SacPr
Hymn Written at the Holy Sepulchre in Jerusalem. George Sandys. SacPr
Hymn[e] of Heavenly Beauty [or Beautie], An. Edmund Spenser.
"Cease then my tongue, and lend unto my mind." InvLi
Hymne of the Daie of Judgment, The. Lady Elizabeth Tyrwhit. EMWP
Hymne of the State of all Adams Posteritie, An. Lady Elizabeth Tyrwhit. EMWP
Hymn[e] on the Nativity [or Nativitie] of My Saviour, A. Ben Jonson. ChIV-2; SacPr
Hymn[e] to Christ, at the Author's Last Going into Germany, A. John Donne. BASC; NAEL-6v1; NAEL-7v1; NOSC; NPeEn; OxAEP-1; SacPr

Hymn[e] to God the Father, A. John Donne. BASC; FSCP; NAEL-6v1; NAEL-7v1; NoP-5; NOSC; NPeEn; OxBEV; SacPr; SoSe-8; TFi
Hymn[e] to God the Father, A. Ben Jonson. BrAP; InvLi; NoP-4; NoP-5; NOSC; OxAEP-1; SacPr
Hymne to Love, An. Robert Herrick. NOSC
Hymns. Callimachus. tr. by Barbara Hughes Fowler
Hymn to Apollo. HePo, tr. by Barbara Hughes Fowler
Hymn to Artemis. HePo, tr. by Barbara Hughes Fowler
Hymn to Demeter. HePo, tr. by Barbara Hughes Fowler
On the Bath of Pallas. HePo, tr. by Barbara Hughes Fowler
Hymns. Charles Wesley.
"My God! I know, I feel thee mine." NoP-5
Hymns and Fragments. Friedrich Hölderlin. tr. by Richard Sieburth
"But speech." WoPoe, tr. by Richard Sieburth
Hymns and Spiritual Songs for the Fasts and Festivals of the Church of England. Christopher Smart.
Crucifixion of Our Blessed Lord. ChIV-2
Nativity of Our Lord and Saviour Jesus Christ, The. ChrPo; NPeEn; OxBEV; SacPr
Christmas Day. OBCP
Nativity of St. John the Baptist, The. ChIV-2
New Year. ChrPo
St. Thomas. ChIV-2
Hymns for Saturday. Christopher Smart. NOxBChV
Hymns for the Amusement of Children. Christopher Smart.
Conclusion of the Matter, The. ChIV-1
Hymn 1. Faith. ChIV-1
Hymn 2. Hope. ChIV-1
Hymn 8. Fortitude. ChIV-2
Hymn 11. Beauty. SacPr
Hymn 15. Taste. ChIV-1
(Hymns for Saturday.) NOxBChV
Hymns in Darkness. Nissim Ezekiel.
"I met a man once." WoPoe
Hymns of Job. Maya Bejerano. tr. by Tsipi Keller
"From morning slumber a stir a shift a spinning motion of tossing." DTA, tr. by Tsipi Keller
"In a slick, black bodysuit Job stood before me." DTA, tr. by Tsipi Keller
"Interlude." DTA, tr. by Tsipi Keller
"It has all begun with still waters." DTA, tr. by Tsipi Keller
"Job: I was cast onto a new life cycle." DTA, tr. by Tsipi Keller
"Noon. 12:45 already." DTA, tr. by Tsipi Keller
"Oh spare me, spare me." DTA, tr. by Tsipi Keller
"Suddenly I was stabbed from behind." DTA, tr. by Tsipi Keller
Hymns of the Marshes. Sidney Lanier. APN-2
Marsh Song—At Sunset. TCAPo
Marshes of Glynn, The. NAAPv.1; NoP-5
Sunrise.
"In my sleep I was fain of their fellowship, fain." TCAPo
Hymns to Our Lady of Chartres. Geoffrey Hill.
"Eia ergo. For this is Sion's twin city."
"Love is at odds. Your beauty has gone out." UpMys
Hymns to the Night. "Novalis." tr. by Dick Higgins
Longing for Death. WoPoe, tr. by Dick Higgins
Hymnus Ad Patrem Sinensis. Philip Whalen. BB; WANABP
Hyped up on caffeine and Thorazine. Something to Say. Betsy Sholl. ExTi
Hyperbola, The. Footnote at "Figure of Speech." Tina Darragh. FTOS
Hyperbole. David Craig. UpMys
Hyperbole! Can't you smile. Prose for Des Esseintes. Donald Davie. OBVE
Hyperboreans, The. Pindar. WoPoe Fr. Pythian Odes.
Hyperion. Friedrich Hölderlin. tr. by M. L. Rosenthal
Schicksalslied. WoPoe, tr. by M. L. Rosenthal
Hyperion. John Keats.
Saturn. NOBRP; OxAEP-2; OxBEV
Hyperion. Leslie Norris. TCAWP
Hyperion's Bones. Tracey Herd. NeBl
Hyperion's Song of Fate. Friedrich Hölderlin. NAWM-7v2, tr. by Christopher Middleton
Hyphen's Hyphen. Susan Gevirtz. OnScMo
Hypochondriac. Geoffrey Holloway. NLP
Hypochondriasis. Ambrose Bierce. APN-2 Fr. Devil's Dictionary, The.
Hypocrite and the concubine, / Livin' among the swine. Hypocrite and the Concubine, The. Unknown. SSUS
Hypocrite Swift now takes an eldest daughter. Hypocrite Swift. Louise Bogan. PoA 2002
Hypocrite women, how seldom we speak. Hypocrite Women. Denise Levertov. NALW

Hypothesis. Ted Olson. YaYoPo

Hypothetical. John K. Samson. PoPra

Hypothetical Spectator, The. Coral Bracho. RMCMP, *tr. by* Suzanne Jill Levine

Hysteria. T. S. Eliot. IJHIL; OxBEV

Hysteria. Dionisio D. Martinez. NAMCP V.2

Hysteria of morning. A clearing, the half-gnawed. Aubade 2. Geoffrey O'Brien. PA9/11

Hyunsonja Asks for an Enlightenment Song. Master Naong. BecRai, *tr. by* Kim Daljin, Kim Won-Chung and Christopher Merrill

Hywel and Blodwen. Idris Davies. AngWePo

Hywel and Olwen are alone in the fern. Angry Summer 28, The. Idris Davies. TCAWP

I

I. Jan Arends. TuT, *tr. by* Peter van de Kamp

I. Anne Carson. NLPA *Fr.* Glass Essay, The.

I. Gabriella Sica. CItWP, *tr. by* Cinzia Sartini Blum and Lara Trubowitz

I abhor the slimy kiss. Robert Herrick. CavPo

I abide in a goodly museum. Ballad of the Ichthyosaurus. May Kendall. ViWPN

I accompanied you as far as the village of granaries. Nocturne (I Accompanied You). Léopold Sédar Senghor. WoPoe, *tr. by* Melvin Dixon

I add one further word to you, a question rather. Henri Michaux. GPTC *Fr.* I Am Writing to You from a Far-Off Country.

I admire Ben Jonson's statement: it is right. Past and Present. John Peale Bishop. InGu

I admire the quixotic display of your paramountcy. On His Royal Blindness Paramount Chief Kwangala. Jack A. Mapanje. AF

I admit I have always wanted. 10th Untitled Poem. Pedro Juan Pietri. PueRic

I advance for as long as forever is. (LL) Twenty-four Years. Dylan Thomas. NAMCP V.2; OxBEV

I advocate a semi-revolution. Semi-Revolution, A. Robert Frost. FTtHH

I agree with everything you say. He's a five-year-old boy, maybe six. Song of Krishna. Viswanatha Satyanarayana. HotL, *tr. by* V. Narayana Rao and David Shulman

I ain't going to hurry up for the white man no more. I ain't Going to Hurry No More. Jesse F. García. UnSA

I ain't got long to stay here. (LL) Steal Away to Jesus. *Unknown.* NoP-4; NoP-5

I Ain't Got Nothin' But the Blues. Don George. ReLy

I aint jokin people, I aint playin around. Concentration Camp Blues. Henry Dumas. SeSe

I ain't no baby making machine. Extremes Ain't My Thing As Salaam Alaikum. Tufara Waller Muhammad. UnSA

I ain't superstitious. Superstitions. Maggie Pogue Johnson. CBWP-4

I alone, writing, wanting, the winter sun false, furious, The. What I Want You to See Is She When Not Here As in Now. Rachel Zucker. IAoNAP

I, Alphonso, live and learn. Alphonso of Castile. Ralph Waldo Emerson.

I already knew the secrets of light. Someone Is Probably Dead. Marvin Bell. BodElec

I always bow down deep before a small tree and a great tyrant. Paavo Haavikko. WoPoe *Fr.* Fifteen Epigrams in Praise of the Tyrant.

I always choose the plainest food. Matthew Green. VerBaPo *Fr.* Spleen, The.

I always felt like a bird blown through the world. Stripping and Putting On. May Swenson. WeW-3

I always had such a good time, good time girl. Each and. Little Red Riding Hood. Ania Walwicz. BMAP

I always had to climb the long hill of Garrapata to get back to you. Long Hill of Garrapata, The. Renée Gregorio. FiBr; ICANM

I always knew. In Explanation to the Mother. Kiren Shoman. OWABP

I always knew / you were singing! Throat Song: The Whirling Earth. Wendy Rose. HATNAP

I always lay before my rushing heart. And Look for God. Else Lasker-Schüler. BBASP, *tr. by* Robert P. Newton

I always like summer. Knoxville, Tennessee. Nikki Giovanni. OxAAAP

I always remember your beautiful flowers. Pad, Pad. Stevie Smith. NPeEn; OxBEV

I always saw, I always said. Red Dress, The. Dorothy Parker. APT-1

I always say I won't go back to the mountains. Sourdough Mountain Lookout. Philip Whalen. BB

I always see, I don't know why. Knowledgeable Child, The. Leonard Alfred George Strong. OBMV

I always try to dislike my poets. It's Hard to Dislike Ewart. Gavin Ewart. OBCoV

I always was afraid of Somes's Pond. Atavism. Elinor Wylie. NALW; PoA 2002

I Am. Imamu Amiri Baraka. FuFl

I Am. John Clare. BBASP; CABP; NAEL-6v2; NAEL-7v2; NoP-4; NoP-5; NPeEn; OxBEV; PoPoPo; TFi; TRP; WoPoe
(Written in Northampton County Asylum.) OBEV; OxAEP-2

I am. (LL) Both Your Mothers. Jerzy Ficowski. HP; PoSu, *tr. by* Keith Bosley

I am. (LL) Manna. Joseph Stroud. CalPo; GeoHom

I am. Yevgeny Aleksandrovich Yevtushenko. HP

I am 1939 and cold air. Katyn Forest. Steven Sherrill. BAP-97

I am a babe of royalty. Royal Education. Winthrop Mackworth Praed. OBSV

I am a bairn. De. Robert Alan Jamieson. FaBoVe

I am a bold Coachman, and drive a good hack. Hackney Coachman, The; Or, The Way to Get a Good Fare. Hannah More. WoRP

I am a book with a cover of blue. Solo with Chorus. Rose Fyleman. NOxBChV

I am a broken-hearted milkman, in grief I'm arrayed. Polly Perkins. *Unknown.* OBCoV

I am a Camera. Bob Kaufman. PFTM-2

I am a camera. Good Man Talking to Himself, A. Guiguis Shoukry. AnVo, *tr. by* Mohamed Enani

I Am a Cameraman. Douglas Dunn. EmeKit; StAl

I am a child. Survivals. Ruth Behar. MirDau

I am a child of cosmic caresses across continents. You and I. Dinah Elena Consuegra. RWB

I am a child of the valley. Delta. Margaret Abigail Walker. YaYoPo

I am a clumsy painter. Artist, The. Han Yong'un [*or* Yongwun]. CAMKP, *tr. by* Sammy Solberg

I am a collection of landscapes. Sight. Pamela Alexander. AmAlph

I am a constand corner sitter, I. Corners. Kate Y. A. Bone. EdScPo

I Am a Cowboy in the Boat of Ra. Ishmael Reed. CalPo; ESEAA; NIL-7; NIP-4

I Am a Creature of the Obvious. Keith Antar Mason. BtF

I am a dangerous animal now. Prelude to a Poem. Kim Ch'unsu [*or* Chunsoo]. CAMKP, *tr. by* Kevin O'Rourke

I am a dark cypress driven in the wind. Neurosis. Elizabeth Bartlett. MoWP

I am a daughter of that land. Letitia Elizabeth Landon. RWP *Fr.* Improvisatrice, The.

I am a drowned man's tomb. There is a farmer's. Epitaph, An. Plato. PoCho, *tr. by* Burton Raffel

I am a false philosopher of this. Radiating Naïveté. Lucie Brock-Broido. OPRER

I Am A Finn. James Tate.
  I Am a Finn. EmeKit; OxBoAm; SUP
  I Am Still a Finn. EmeKit; OxBoAm

I am a flower. Ego Flos. Guido Gezelle. TuT, *tr. by* Peter van de Kamp

I am a gentle Anarchist. Gentle Anarchist, The. Brunton Stephens. NOBAu

I am a gentleman in a dustcoat trying. Piazza Piece. John Crowe Ransom. APT-1; ColAP; CtM; FuPo; HarvBoo; HeIP-4; InGu; MoAmPo; NAMCP V.1; NoAM; NoP-4; NoP-5; OxBoAm; TFi

I am a glider on time's thermals. John Hawkhead. NewEx

I am a God in the depths of my thought. Sonnet. Willem Kloos. TuT, *tr. by* Tony Curtis and Tony Curtis

I am a great inventor, did you but know it. Ernest Crosby. FaBoWar *Fr.* War and Hell.

I am a Jew. Franta Bass. INSAB

I am a Jew among sunflowers, a Jew. Insomnia Litany. Joan Logghe. OPRER

I am a Jew and will be a Jew forever. I am a Jew. Franta Bass. INSAB

I am a jovial miner. Miner's Ballad, The. Lewis Morris. AngWePo

I am a kindred spirit to death. Kinsman of Death, The. Endre Ady. IQMS, *tr. by* Peter Zollman

I am a lady young in beauty waiting. (LL) Piazza Piece. John Crowe Ransom. APT-1; ColAP; CtM; FuPo; HarvBoo; HeIP-4; InGu; MoAmPo; NAMCP V.1; NoAM; NoP-4; NoP-5; OxBoAm; TFi

I am a little orphan girl. Orphan Girl, An. Mrs. Henry Linden. CBWP-4

I am a little world made cunningly. John Donne. BASC; ChIV-1; NAEL-6v1; NAEL-7v1; NIP-4; NoP-4; NoP-5; OxBSo *Fr.* Holy Sonnets.

I am a lonely being, scarred by swords. Riddles. *Unknown.* NoP-4; NoP-5, *tr. by* Richard Hamer

I am a mad mother. Projected Scenario of a Performance to Be Given Before the UN. Lawson Fusao Inada. FaBoA

I am a male chauvinist pig. In a Pig's Eye. Ronald Wallace. SUP

I am a man: little do I last. Brotherhood. Octavio Paz. LoL, *tr. by* Eliot Weinberger

I am a man now. Here. Ronald Stuart Thomas. NPeEn

I am a man of war and might. Soldier, A. Sir John Suckling. WaAnP

I am a man, upo da land. *Unknown.* NePenScot

I am a martyr. I was killed in a small war for the sake of the homeland. Hungry Orange, A. Nasri Hajjaj. Eno, *tr. by* Ibrahim Muhawi

I am a miner. The light burns blue. Nick and the Candlestick. Sylvia Plath. ItP; NALW

I am a Mo Village Girl. Ke-Mo Village Girl. *Vietnamese Oral Tradition.* CaDao, *tr. by* John Balaban

I Am a Most Fleshly Man. Robert Duncan. CAGL

I am a Negro. Negro. Langston Hughes. NAAPv.2

I am a nervous young sailor on a huge ocean liner that is. Ocean Liner. Peter Schjeldahl. AHA

I am a night mute as my sorrow. Voice of Conscience, The. Murad Mikha'il. IrPoTo, *tr. by* Christina Coyle and Sadok Masliyah

I am a nightingale in the garden of grief. İzzet Molla. OLP, *tr. by* Walter Andrews, Najaat Black and Mehmet Kalpakli

I am a nude formalist poet, a sprung. Solidarity Is the Name We Give to What We Cannot Hold. Charles Bernstein. OxBoAm

I Am a Parcel of Vain Strivings Tied. Henry David Thoreau. APN-1; ColAP; NoP-4; NoP-5; OxBoAm; TCAPo

 (Sic Vita.) NAAPv.1; NCAP

I am a Peeping Tom Girl, and from my seat on the downtown bus. Peeping Tom Tom Girl. Marisela Norte. GeoHom

I am a person of inflexible habits. Anthony Hecht. PoA 2002 *Fr.* Venetian Vespers, The.

I am a pilgrim adrift upon ancient waters. Refugee. Gideon Ferebee. BtF

I am a poet. Uncertainty of the Poet, The. Wendy Cope. OPOU

I am a poet—so why should I care. Ars Poetica. Attila József. IQMS, *tr. by* Michael Beevor

I am a poor wayfaring stranger. Poor Wayfaring Stranger. *Unknown.* SacPr

 (I'm just a poor wayfaring stranger.) TCAPo

I am a raped poem. Raped Poem. Bhairavayya. HotL, *tr. by* V. Narayana Rao

I am a reaper whose muscles set at sundown. All my oats are cradled. Harvest Song. Jean Toomer. NoP-4; NoP-5; WaAnP

I am a sea-shell flung. Frutta di Mare. Geoffrey Scott. OBMV

I am a servant of the War Lord. Archilochus. SaLy, *tr. by* Diane Rayor

I am a service. Family Romance. Joshua Clover. AmPoNex

I am a solitary man, not a democracy. Yehuda Amichai. PoSu *Fr.* Travels of a Latter-Day Benjamin of Tudela.

I am a soul in the world: in. Invention of Comics, The. Imamu Amiri Baraka. GT

I am a tethered fuck-angel. Of My Nipple Ring Halos. Edwin Torres. HeMarv

I am a tree on the margin. Union. Annie Foster. NLP

I am a very old pussy. Old Cat's Confessions, An. Christopher Pearse Cranch. APN-1

I Am a Victim of Telephone. Allen Ginsberg. NBLV

I am a wandering child. Women at the Crossroad / (May Elegba Forever Guard the Right Doors). Opal Palmer Adisa. GT

I am a white, Episcopal-raised, almost. Work. David Huddle. AmWaPo

I am a white girl gone brown to the blood color of my mother. For the Color of My Mother. Cherríe Moraga. UnSA

I am a widow. could be charleville could be anywhere. Dream of Rimbaud. Patti Smith. OxBoAm

I am a winged creature, flightless. Su Jarwood. NewEx

I am a woman and my poems. Practice of Magical Evocation, The. Diane Di Prima. PmAP

I am a word hunter. Collective Search. Patrick Sylvain. InTrad

I am about to make my home. Thomas Merton. WhBo *Fr.* Cables to the Ace.

I am about to recite a psalm that I know. Corruption. Srikanth Reddy. LegDan

I am absent but deep in this absence. Poetry Is a Heavenly Crime. Vicente Huidobro. TCLAP, *tr. by* W. S. Merwin

I am accused of tending to the past. Lucille Clifton. ISC; NAMCP V.2

I am afraid. Wedding Day. Seamus Heaney. OxAEP-2

I Am Afraid of Fire. Anna Swirszczynska [*or* Swir]. AF, *tr. by* Czeslaw Milosz

I am afraid of losing the marvel of your eyes of a statue, and the accent the solitary rose of your breath lays on my cheek at night. Federico García Lorca. CAGL *Fr.* Sonetos del Amor Oscuro [Sonnets of Dark Love].

I am afraid of the unknown. You Called to Me, Prison Windows. Danièle Amrane. HAWP, *tr. by* Eric Sellin

I am afraid to lose the marvel. Sonnet of Sweet Complaint. Federico García Lorca. BLPSL, *tr. by* Rene de Costa, Rigas Kappatos and Eleni Paidoussi

I am afraid to own a Body. Emily Dickinson. NCAP

I Am Africa. Kimberly Ann Collins. InTrad

I am agog for foam. Tumultuous come. Basil Bunting. BrAP

I am Alfred Nobel, inventing dynamite. Dynamite. Peter Schjeldahl. MotU

I am Alice of Daphne, and my heart clogs for John Pounden. Alice of Daphne, 1799. John Ennis. PBCIP

I Am Alien in Africa and Everywhere. Dennis Brutus. PML

I am alive—I guess. Emily Dickinson. OxBoAm

I am all the time being pursued. Horror Movie. Kim Sŭnghŭi. CAMKP, *tr. by* Anthony, Brother of Taizé

I am almost afraid to write down. Old WPA Swimming Pool in Martins Ferry, Ohio, The. James Wright. CAP-8

I Am Alone. Léopold Sédar Senghor. PoetW; VCWP, *tr. by* Melvin Dixon

I am alone. / I lie next to stone. Does Poetry Matter? Christopher Bursk. PoA 2002

I am alone in the garden, separated. Perfect Heart, The. Shara McCallum. AmPoNex; P180

I am alone in the plains. I Am Alone. Léopold Sédar Senghor. PoetW; VCWP, *tr. by* Melvin Dixon

I am already a singing flower. Singing Flower, The. "Shu Ting." VCWP, *tr. by* Carolyn Kizer and Y. H. Zhao

I am already quite scarce. For years. Last Ones, The. Dan Pagis. PoSu, *tr. by* Stephen Mitchell

I am always behind. Jo Shapcott. NewEx

I am always sorry for the big ape falling. Goliath Poem. Terrance Hayes. AmPoNex

I am Ambassador of Otherwhere. Robert Graves. PoA 2002

I am America™. America™. Forrest Cole. RWB

I am an ancient reluctant conscript. Old Timers. Carl Sandburg. NoAM

I am an architect in Vienna. Michael Palmer. APSN

I Am an Atheist Who Says His Prayers. Karl Shapiro. APT-2

I am an entry in all kinds of books. Dezsö Kosztolányi. IQMS *Fr.* Laments of a Sad Man.

I am an ephemeral and none too discontented citizen of a metropolis thought to be modern. City. Arthur Rimbaud. SxFrPo, *tr. by* Martin Sorrell

I am an honest man. Sonnet. Octavio Armand. TCLAP, *tr. by* Jason Shinder

I am an honest man. José Martí. TCLAP *Fr.* Simple Verses.

I am an old gentleman who, in his bath. Old Gentleman, An. Alain Bosquet. PML, *tr. by* William Jay Smith

I am an orphan. Orphan, An. Malhas Thurayya. PoArWo, *tr. by* Nasser Farghaly

I Am Ardent, I Am Brunette. Gustavo Adolfo Bécquer. SpanPo, *tr. by* Kate Flores

I am as brisk. Three Undated Fragments. John Keats.

I Am As God and God As I. "Angelus Silesius." GePo *Fr.* Cherubical Wanderer, The.

I Am as Happy as a Queen on Her Throne [*with music*]. Mrs. Henry Linden. CBWP-4

I am as I am and so will I be. Sir Thomas Wyatt. NoSic

I am as large as God, and God as small as I. "Angelus Silesius." GePo *Fr.* Cherubical Wanderer, The.

I am as virtuous as a rabbinical student. Spiritual Morning. Robin Becker. TaR

I am asian america. Because I Am It's a Race Thing Trip. Chong Xiong. BRtP

I am asking about the way ahead. Lenrie Peters. HBAPE

I am asking for understanding / for the women who have not given. For the Barren Woman. Desanka Maksimovic. GI, *tr. by* Ivo Soljan

I Am Asking You to Come Back Home. Jo Carson. RaBo

I am astounded at their mouthful names. Building Nicole's Mama. Patricia Smith. SpirFl

I am at a retreat house, Still Point, not too far from Yaddo. From a Letter: About Snow. Toi Derricotte. SpirFl

I am at Deep Well where the spirit-trees. Roland Robinson. NOBAu *Fr.* Deep Well.

I am at last that thing, a stranger in my own life. Diary. Gerald Stern. OPRER

I am a-trouble in de mind. I'm A-Trouble in de Mind. *Unknown.* SSUS

I am attracted by the dust. In the House. Stephen Dunn. PoDa

I am awakened by a knock on the door. It's Tom Disch. He. Reading, The. Peter Schjeldahl. AHA

I am away from home. Faithful Wife, The. Patricia Beer. LW

I am bathing. All my greyness. El Curandero. Rafael Campo. BloBone

I am become a shell of delicate alleys. Airliner. Francis Webb. NOBAu

I Am Becoming My Mother. Lorna Goodison. OPOU

I am beginning to alter. Poem. Bernadette Mayer. NYP2

I am being carried on great winds across the sky. (LL) Sometimes I Go about Pitying Myself. *Unknown.* RaBo; WoPoe, *tr. by* Robert Bly and Frances Densmore

I am being followed by a table. Intermission from Thursday. Pedro Juan Pietri. PueRic

I am bent over a sink of heavenly suds. Sinking, The. Faith Shearin. SweBea

I Am Beset with a Dream of Fair Woman.   Maureen Duffy.   LW

I am beside you now.   Yvor Winters.   NAAPv.2 *Fr.* Magpie's Shadow, The.

I am black. (LL)   William Edward Burghardt DuBois. *See* Hail to the black!

I am black and I have seen black hands, millions and millions of them.   I Have Seen Black Hands.   Richard Wright.   AF; APT-2; GPTC

I am black-browed.   Pauline Stainer.   NewEx

I am Born and I Burn in My Love.   Abdul Wahab Al-Bayati.   IrPoTo, *tr. by* Farouk Abdel Wahab

I am born in a field.   One Body.   Margaret Gibson.   AmZen

I am bound, I am bound, for a distant shore.   Henry David Thoreau.   TCAPo

I am Brahman. But we're stuck for a maid.   I am Brahman.   J. Adwaita Dèr Mouw.   TuT, *tr. by* Peter van de Kamp

I am busy doing drawings.   David's Rumor.   Liam Rector.   OPRER

I am but a riverboat—hopelessly in touch.   Dear America.   Jeffrey McDaniel.   LegDan; RWB

"I am but clay," the sinner plead.   Distinction.   Paul Laurence Dunbar.   SacPr

I am but finite, yet thine infinitely. (LL)   Artillery [*or* Artillerie].   George Herbert.   NoP-4; NoP-5; WaAnP

I am Cap'tain Zombi.   René Depestre.   PFTM-2 *Fr.* Rainbow for the Christian West, A.

I am chained.   Lotte Kramer.   NewEx

I am Chango hurler of thunder.   René Depestre.   PFTM-2 *Fr.* Rainbow for the Christian West, A.

I Am Cherry Alive.   Delmore Schwartz.   NOxBChV

I am Chiang Liang.   Old Leaves from the Chinese Earth.   Sadanand Rege.   WoPoe, *tr. by* Dilip Chitre

I am Child of sand and sun.   Child of the Sun.   Lillian M. Fisher.   HHAm

I am child to no one, mother to a few.   Self-Portrait.   Linda Pastan.   ExTi

I am clothed.   Message from Inland.   Maura Eichner.   UpMys

I am come into my garden, my sister, my spouse.   Bible, *O.T.*   EroLit; OBVE *Fr.* Song of Solomon, The [*or* The Song of Songs].

I am come to the threshold of a spring.   In April.   Sylvia Townsend Warner.   MoWP

I Am Consecrated to the Coming One.   Wafaa' Lamrani.   PoArWo, *tr. by* Richard McKane and Tahia Abdel Nasser

I am constantly wounded.   *Unknown.*   WoPoe *Fr.* Carmina Burana.

I am content, I do not care.   Careless Content.   John Byrom.   OBCoV

I am content to live the patient day.   Tuckanuck.   George Cabot Lodge.   APN-2

I am convinced that finally.   Apple, The.   Vladimir Alekseievich Soloukhin.   TCRusP, *tr. by* Daniel Weissbort

I am crushed, burning.   To My Son, Abbas.   Khurshid-Banu.   SonAtl, *tr. by* Betty Blair, Azer H. Hasret and Mehmet Kara

I am cuddle-shaped and freckled.   James Berry.   NewEx

I am curiously stirred.   Courtship, The.   Ann Beresford.   LW

I am dancing and.   Heavy Headed Dance, The.   Jayne Cortez.   BAP-97; FuFl

I Am Dancing with My Mennonite Father.   Anna Ruth Ediger Baehr.   ACAMVP

I am dark, daughters of Jerusalem.   Bible, *O.T.*   WPoS *Fr.* Song of Solomon, The.

I am dating a woman whose brother is a Trotskyite.   Influencing Factors.   Karen, Helfrich.   PoDa

I am dead.   Larva, The.   Tadeusz Rózewicz.   PoSu, *tr. by* Magnus F. Krynski

I Am Dead But I Know the Dead Are Not Like This.   Charles Bukowski.   PmAP

I am dead, to be sure.   Small Fig Tree, A.   Donald Hall.   ChIV-2; GI

I Am Deaf.   Osip Emilevich Mandelstam.   TCRusP, *tr. by* John Glad

I am deceiving you: deceivers are what we are.   Two Poems.   T. H. Parry-Williams.   BBMWP, *tr. by* Richard Poole

I am deeply convinced that objects.   Yevgeny Mikhailovich Vinokurov.   TCRusP *Fr.* History.

I am Dekanawideh and with the chiefs of the Five Nations.   Tree of the Great Peace, The.   *Iroquois Oral Tradition.*   NAAPv.1

I am describing to Arlene an interview I've done with James Taylor.   Talking to Arlene.   Peter Schjeldahl.   MotU

I am describing to you on the phone.   Echoes.   Michael Longley.   BeAl

I am desolate.   Love's Despair.   George Sigerson.   IrLP

I am determined to continue this bond.   Act of Caution, An.   Mahe Jabeen.   HotL, *tr. by* V. Narayana Rao

I am dreaming.   Let Me Call You Sweetheart.   Beth Slater Whitson.   TCAPo (I am dreaming Dear of you.)   NAAPv.2

I am driving to you and I will drive all the way to New York.   Home in Three Days. Don't Wash.   Linda Smukler.   WiU

I am driving west in the afternoon.   Sphinx.   Van K. Brock.   AllShUp; SwNoth

I am dying now because I do not die.   James Keir Baxter.   HarvBoo *Fr.* Jerusalem Sonnets.

I am dying somehow strangely . . . Life is not killing me.   Ineffable, The.   Delmira Agustini.   TANSG, *tr. by* Mark McCaffrey

I am dying strangely . . . it is not life.   Ineffable, The.   Delmira Agustini.   TCLAP, *tr. by* Karl Kirchwey

I am dying under this heat.   Almost a God.   Emanuel Carnevali.   APT-2

I am earth and water, you will not pass me, will not ford me, my friend, my friend.   I Am Earth and Water.   Anne Hébert.   YaTCFP, *tr. by* Marilyn Hacker

I am egg-shell fragile and grapefruit sour.   Breakfast Poem.   Clare Pollard.   NeBl

I am everything you've heard I am.   Chant.   Ron Schreiber.   PrTe

I am exceedingly green: chillgreen.   Twelve Faces of the Emerald.   Dan Pagis.   WoPoe, *tr. by* Stephen Mitchell

I am falling in love.   Imperfection.   Elizabeth Carlson.   TWF

I am far from sentimental or romantic.   Very Soft Shoes.   Marshall Barer.   ReLy

I Am Fashion's Toy [*with music*].   Mary E. Tucker.   CBWP-1

I am fevered with the sunset.   Sea Gypsy, The.   Richard Hovey.   BRP; TCAPo
   (I am fever'd with the sunset.)   ChAP

I am filled with love like a melon.   Morning Love Song.   Marge Piercy.   PasH

I am filthy. Lice gnaw me. Swine, when they look at me, vomit. The scabs.   Comte de Lautréamont.   PFTM-1 *Fr.* Maldoror.

I am fire and water, honestly combined, on free terms. (LL)   Vierge Moderne.   Edith Södergran.   ItWoWo; PFTM-1, *tr. by* Stina Katchadourian

I am first mouth, then hand.   Edwyna Prior.   NewEx

I am five.   Venus's-flytraps.   Yusef Komunyakaa.   FaoP; PtR

I am floating in a thin cloud.   Among Goldfinches.   Bill Morgan.   ArBi

I am forbidden to stop to see. As if I were condemned to see while walking.   I Am Forbidden.   Jacques Dupin.   MotU; YaTCFP, *tr. by* Paul Auster

I am four in this photograph, standing.   History Lesson.   Natasha Trethewey.   SUP

I am four monkeys.   Tree, The.   Alfred Kreymborg.   APT-1

I am four years older than you but scarcely an unwobbling.   James Harrison.   BodElec *Fr.* Letters to Yesenin.

I am fourteen.   Hanging Fire.   Audre Lorde.   BrAP; NAMCP V.2; NIL-7; NIP-4; NoAM; NoP-4; PoPoPo; TRP

I Am from Ireland.   *Unknown. See* I Am of Ireland.

I am from Warsaw.   Oratorio for a Concentration Camp.   János Pilinszky.   IQMS, *tr. by* Adam Makkai

I am fully qualified to work as a doorkeeper, and for this reason.   Rabi'a al-Adawiyya.   WPoS

I am giving a lecture on poetry.   In English in a Poem.   Lynn Emanuel.   ExTi

I am glad daylong for the gift of song.   Rhapsody.   William Stanley Braithwaite.   TCAPo

I am glad that I am not one of those.   Side 32.   Víctor Hernández Cruz.   PueRic

I am going.   Road to Seoul, The.   Kim Chiha.   CAMKP, *tr. by* David R. McCann

I Am Going Because the Ear of Wheat and the Dawn Are Not Mine.   León Felipe.   RaW, *tr. by* W. S. Merwin

I am going far to see the land.   Tohono O'odham.   NAAPv.1 *Fr.* Songs for Treating Sickness, Sung during the Four Parts of the Night.

I am going to be your host tonight.   My Name Is Dimitri.   John Ashbery.   BodElec

I am going to carry my bed into New York City tonight.   96 Vandam.   Gerald Stern.   P180

I am going to cock my head tonight like a dog.   How to Listen.   Major L. Jackson.   PoDa

I am going to fail.   Strawberry.   Paisley Rekdal.   LegDan

I am going to keep things like this. (LL)   Hawk Roosting.   Ted Hughes.   BrAP; EMP; HeIP-4; OWoS; OxBEV; WaAnP

I am going to sing to you, gentlemen.   Deported.   *Unknown.*   NAAPv.2

I Am Going to Speak of Hope.   César Vallejo.   PoetW, *tr. by* Clayton Eshleman

I Am Going to Talk About Hope.   César Vallejo.   TCLAP; WED, *tr. by* Robert Bly

I am going with David Bennett to his house in the suburbs to.   David's Sister.   Peter Schjeldahl.   AHA

I Am Goya.   Andrey Andreievich Voznesensky.   OBWP; VCWP

I am green and replete like a song that has blown through the grass.   Song of the Strange Woman.   Leah Goldberg.   FIT, *tr. by* Robert Friend

"I am green under my cloud," the island said.   Pacific.   Robert Fitzgerald.   PWW2

I am greeted by a hand holding straws.   Hide-n-Seek.   Scott Bailey.   BeDoSh

I am growing old.   In the Shadow of Death.   Juan Chi.   CCL1, *tr. by* Michael Bullock and C. J. Chen

I am growing on a woman's corpse.   Origin.   Rosario Castellanos.   TANSG, *tr. by* Magda Bogin

I am Hajar the immigrant.   First Thing, The.   Mohja Kahf.   PoArWo

I am half, my children half again.   Half-.   Julia Park Rodrigues.   TWW

I am half Russian, 30, almost got my MA. Inconsistent Self-Portrait. Yuliya Kunina. CRWP, *tr. by* Richard McKane

I am happy. Utitia'q's Song. *Inuit Oral Tradition.* AWTN, *tr. by* Franz Boas and Brian Swann

I am happy in my love. Girl's Song. *Unknown.* WoPoe, *tr. by* Edwin Gladding Burrows

I am happy to live correctly and simply. Marina Ivanovna Tsvetayeva. BBASP, *tr. by* Mary Jane White

I am hating myself for the last time. Late Psalm. Betsy Sholl. ACAMVP; MAAN

I am haunted. . .every night. Death in Four Voices. Buland Al-Haidari. IrPoTo, *tr. by* Hussein Kadhim and Christopher Merrill

I Am He That Aches with Love. Walt Whitman. ErotSp

I am he who aches with amorous love. Pact, A. Robert Hass. BodElec

I am here. (LL) John Milton. OxBEV; WoPoe *Fr.* Comus; a Masque Presented at Ludlow Castle.

I am here, and shells are quaking over the cracked city. To a War Correspondent. Star Black. KGB

I am here, and there is nothing to say. Lecture on Nothing. John Cage. FTOS; PFTM-2

I am his Highness' dog at Kew. Epigram Engraved on the Collar of a Dog Given [*or* Which I Gave] to His Royal Highness. Alexander Pope. NTCP; OxBEV

I am holding this turquoise. Serenity in Stones, The. Simon J. Ortiz. ColAP

I am Homero Aridjis. Self-Portrait at Fifty-Four Years Old. Homero Aridjis. WoBe, *tr. by* George McWhirter

I am homesick now for middle age, as then. Listening to Collared Doves. Edith Jay Scovell. HarvBoo

I am huntin' for a city, to stay a while. Hunting for a City. *Unknown.* SSUS

I am. / I am from and of The Mother. Creed for Free Women, A. Elsa Gidlow. HW

I am I, but also the other. *Unknown.* WoPoe *Fr.* Upanishads, The.

I am immortal in Cheyenne! Norman Rosten. YaYoPo

I am in a daydream of my uncle. Thirteen Years. Erin Mouré. NIL-7

I Am in a Novel. D. H. Lawrence. OBCoV

I Am in Danger—Sir. Adrienne Rich. HarvBoo; NAAL-5; NALW

I am, in fact, the Madman of Chu. Lu Mountain Song For the Palace Censor Empty-Boat Lu, A. Li Po. CCL1, *tr. by* Elling O. Eide

I am in love, meantime, you think; no doubt you would think so. Arthur Hugh Clough. FaBoVe; NPeEn *Fr.* Amours de Voyage.

I am in love with the laughing sickness. Zizi's Lament. Gregory Corso. BB

I am in love, you say; I do not think so exactly. (LL) Arthur Hugh Clough. FaBoVe; NPeEn *Fr.* Amours de Voyage.

I am in Midtown to see a movie and, having an hour to kill. Adventures with Nick & Cindy. Peter Schjeldahl. AHA

I am in my Eskimo-hunting-song mood. Eskimo Occasion. Judith Rodriguez. BrAP; ItWoWo; NOBAu

I am in my room observing my record player covered with dust. Analysis. Syl Cheney-Coker. NAfrP

I am in need of music that would flow. Sonnet. Elizabeth Bishop. CtM; PoCu

I am in pain. Yury Timofeievich Galanskov. TCRusP, *tr. by* Olive Dehn

I am in prayer! I tell myself tonight. Incantation. Peter Cooley. LiTh

I am in the book. Dream Dream, The. Michael Davidson. FTOS

I am in the most exquisite distress. Laura H. Kennedy. PasH

I am in the rain, with black writing. Womb. Sonia Sekula. SurWo

I am inside someone. Agony, An. As Now. Imamu Amiri Baraka. NAAL-5; NAMCP V.2; NoP-4; NoP-5; UnSA

I am invited to enter these gardens. Welshman at St. James' Park, A. Ronald Stuart Thomas. AngWePo

I Am Ireland. Padraic Pearse. OBMV, *tr. by* Lady Augusta Gregory

I am irradiated by the room through which a tram runs. X-Rays. I. K. Bonset. TuT, *tr. by* Desmond Egan

I am isolated bourgeoisie. Isolated Bourgeoisie. Ed Friedman. PrTe

I am jealous! I am jealous! which I ne'er have been before. Lines / Suggested by the Song of a Nightingale. Eliza Cook. VWP

I am John Reed. John Reed's Monologue. Yevgeny Aleksandrovich Yevtushenko. RusPo, *tr. by* Robert Arthur Douglas Ford

I am Judas. William Butler Yeats. GI *Fr.* "Calvary."

I am just coming / Just going in. (LL) Wind Is Blowing West, The. Joseph Ceravolo. NYP2; OxBoAm

I am just going outside and may be some time. Antarctica. Derek Mahon. NPeEn; PBCIP; StAl

I am just the warm water. Obsessions Are Important. Primus St. John. BtF

I am just unlearning. Remigration. Hilde Domin. GTCP, *tr. by* Agnes Stein

I am king. Vicente Huidobro. TCLAP *Fr.* Altazor.

I am knotted in pain. Obeah Mama Dot. Frederick D'Aguiar. Oth

I Am Learning to Abandon the World. Linda Pastan. PoA 2002

I Am Like a Desert Owl, an Owl among the Ruins. Noelle Kocot. LegDan

I am like none of you. You must recognize. Not of This World. Sheri Hostetler. ACAMVP

I am Lilith, grandmother of Mary Magdalene. Liturgy for Lilith. Cosi Fabian. HW

I am listening for your footsteps death. Body Inside the Soul, The. Bell Hooks. ISC

I Am Listening to Istanbul. Orban Veli Kanik. WoPoe, *tr. by* Murat Nemet-Nejat

I am listening to Istanbul with my eyes closed. I Am Listening to Istanbul. Orban Veli Kanik. WoPoe, *tr. by* Murat Nemet-Nejat

I am living, I remember you. (LL) What the Living Do. Marie Howe. BeAl; ExTi; PoCho; PoDa

I am living more alone now than I did. Last Chapter, The. Walter De la Mare. MoBrPo

I am locked in a little cedar box. Satan Says. Sharon Olds. OxBoAm; PBCAP

I am / look / ing at. You Too? Me Too—Why Not? Soda Pop. Robert Hollander. NIL-7; NIP-4

I am looking for the photo that would make all the difference in my life. Lost and Found. Maxine Chernoff. PmAP

I am looking for the women of my house. Lineage. Daisy Zamora. LoL, *tr. by* Margaret Randall

I am looking out, the window. In Conference. Gordon Hodgeon. RSaN

I am lost. / I had swum before. May. Joseph Ceravolo. NYP2

I am lying down with a man in bed at the far end of a large room. Dream in Barcelona. Meret Oppenheim. YaTCFP, *tr. by* Mary Ann Caws

I am made all things to all men. At His Execution. Rudyard Kipling. ChIV-2

I am madly in love despite the angry behavior of one who finds fault [with me]! Abu Bakr ibn Abd al-Malik Ibn Quzman. HiArP, *tr. by* James T. Monroe

I am Marilyn Mei Ling Chin. How I Got That Name. Marilyn Chin. CalPo; GeoHom; LoL; NAMCP V.2

I am Masjid. Ideal Wife. Mahe Jabeen. HotL, *tr. by* V. Narayana Rao

I am Mawu of the Waters. Mawu of the Waters. Abena Busia. HAWP; NAfrP

I am mighty melancholy. Vandunk's Four Humours, in Quality and Quantity. Richard Brathwaite [*or* Brathwait]. NOSC

I am Minerva, the village poetess. Edgar Lee Masters. APT-1; IllVoic *Fr.* Spoon River Anthology.

I am Misanthropos, and hate mankind. William Shakespeare. DiBP *Fr.* Timon of Athens.

I am monarch of troubles a host. Verses. Maria Jane Jewsbury. VWP

I am more cursed at close a dent outside. Isidore Ducasse Comte de Lautréamont. Michelle Grangaud. YaTCFP, *tr. by* Paul Lloyd and Rosemary Lloyd

I am Moses awaiting. Video Victim. Luis H. Francia. ReBoTo

I am most honoured. Great Foreign Writer Visits Age-Old Temple, Greeted by Venerable Abbess, 1955. Anthony Thwaite. OBCoV

I am moved often, and easily. Few Facts about Me, A. Charles North. NYP2; PmAP

I Am My Beloved's, and His Desire Is towards Me. Francis Quarles. NPeEn; OxAEP-1; SacPr

I am my own. As I Am My Father's. Rose Drachler. TaR

I Am / Myself-Eclectic. Be Careful When You Go Looking for a Madonna Cuz You Just Might Find a Woman. Pat Russell. BtF

I am never alone in this world. Seduction. Cornelius Eady. OxAAAP

I Am New York City 2. Jayne Cortez. PrTe

I am no disciple of Audubon. Survivors. Sterling Plumpp. UrbNat

I am no heir, no proud ancestor. I Want to Be Loved. Endre Ady. IQMS, *tr. by* Peter Zollman

I am no longer sure of anything. To the Ocean. S. J. Marks. BodElec

I am no one: a man. León Felipe. RaW *Fr.* Black Dog Is Sleeping on Top of the Light, A.

I am no shepherd of a child's surmises. Montana Pastoral. James Vincent Cunningham. APT-2; MoAmPo; OxBoAm

I am no woman. I am a neuter. Vierge Moderne. Edith Södergran. ItWoWo; PFTM-1, *tr. by* Stina Katchadourian

I am nobody. Richard Wright. APT-2

I am none but king of repetition. King of Repetition. Marc Jaffee. BAP-04

I Am Not a Conspiracy Everything Is Not Paranoid the Drug Enforcement Administration Is Not Everywhere. Susan Musgrave. NIL-7; NoAM

I am not a flower of song. Ghazal 12. Mirza Asadullah Khan Ghalib. EaWin, *tr. by* Aijaz Ahmad and W. S. Merwin

I am not a handsome man. Eclipse. Ed Roberson. GT

I am not a mechanism, an assembly of various sections. Healing. D. H. Lawrence. RaBo

I am not a metaphor or symbol. Distant Drum, The. Calvin C. Hernton. GT

I am not a painter, I am a poet. Why I Am Not a Painter. Frank O'Hara. CAP-8; EMP; NAMCP V.2; NoAM; NoP-4; NoP-5; OxBoAm; PoPoPo; VCAP; WaAnP

I am not a person.　Waka.　Lindley Williams Hubbell.　APT-2

I am not a piñata, Rodney King insists. Now can't we all get along? (LL) Affirmative Action Blues (1993).　Elizabeth Alexander.　ExTi; FaoP

I am not afraid of loving, I am afraid of forgetting I loved.　Forgetting, Love. Nathalie Handal.　PoArWo

I Am Not an Amazon—a Warrior.　Bronislava Volková.　Vesp

I am not an Arab, I am not a Jew.　Palestine.　Marvin X.　BRtP

I am not any of the faces.　Failure of an Invention.　Safiya Henderson-Holmes. BRtP; UnSA

I am not born.　Lost Memory of Delhi, A.　Agha Shahid Ali.　FTtHH

I am not certain I love him.　Bluebeard.　Mark Bibbins.　WiU

I am not convinced we shall ever make that journey.　Clouded Skies.　Philippe Jaccottet.　YaTCFP, tr. by David Constantine and Mark Treharne

I am not done with my changes. (LL)　Layers, The.　Stanley Kunitz. BodElec; CAP-8; ItP

I am not eagle ey'd to face the Sun.　To the Reader.　Rowland Watkyns. BASC

I am not even my own ghost. (LL)　Luis de Góngora y Argote.　SpanPo; WoPoe Fr. Spectre of the Rose, The.

I am not gay by your definition.　Explanation.　William Barber.　CAGL

I am not going to invite you.　Blond.　Joseph De Roche.　HeIP-4

I am not here now.　7th Untitled Poem.　Pedro Juan Pietri.　PueRic

I Am Not I.　Juan Ramón Jiménez.　RaBo; WED, tr. by Robert Bly

I am not. I am.　Hot Property, A.　Ronald Wallace.　SUP

I am not I; pity the tale of me. (LL)　Sir Philip Sidney.　NAEL-6v1; NAEL-7v1; NoSic Fr. Astrophil and Stella.

I Am Not Just a Body for You.　Shakuntala Hawoldar.　HAWP

I am not making myself up for public consumption.　Determinate Inflorescence: Ephemera.　Liz Waldner.　PoDa

I am not moved (O Thou my God!) to love Thee.　To Christ Crucified.　Miguel de Guevara.　SpanPo, tr. by Ian Fletcher

I am not my body.　Madame X.　Margherita Guidacci.　CItWP, tr. by Cinzia Sartini Blum and Lara Trubowitz

I am not myself, I am my sisters.　Monologue of the Magdalene.　John Peck. HarvBoo

I am not nor mean to be.　"H. D."　WaAnP Fr. Helen in Egypt.

I am not one of those who believe that a city must not rise to catastrophe one more back.　Virgin Forest, The.　Aimé Césaire.　SurPaPo, tr. by Clayton Eshleman and Annette Smith

I am not resigned to the shutting away of loving hearts in the hard ground. Dirge Without Music.　Edna St. Vincent Millay.　AmFaPo; BrAP; GoPo; InoFa

I am not shaving, I'm writing about it.　Shaving.　Richard Blanco. AmPoNex; NAPBL

I am not striving with the tree that will not bend for me.　Ebb.　Sorley MacLean.　NePenScot

I am not such a clever one.　I'm Old-Fashioned.　Johnny Mercer.　ReLy

I am not sure if I knew the truth.　Youth.　Unknown.　WeW-3, tr. by Laurence Hope

I Am Not the Great Diver.　León Felipe.　RaW, tr. by Julio de la Torre

I am not the hero of this piece.　Composite.　Cornelius Eady.　FuFl

I am not the walrus.　Ishmael Reed.　SpirFl

I am not the wind, nor the sail.　Song of Pursuit.　Gabriel Zaid.　TCLAP, tr. by Mónica Hernández-Cancio

I am not thinking of Death, but Death is thinking of me.　2002.　Mark Strand. OxBoAm

I am not tired.　Am I the Only One.　Aydın Hatipoğlu.　NaPG, tr. by Talat Sait Halman

I am not to be trifled with.　Hoatchunk' Narwoanar, or Winnebago War Song. Unknown.　APN-2, tr. by Caleb Atwater

I am not what my lips explain.　Utterance.　Donald Davidson.　FuPo

I am not wiser for my age.　Ralph Waldo Emerson.　TCAPo Fr. Quatrains.

I am not yet born; O hear me.　Prayer Before Birth.　Louis MacNeice.　BeAl; FaBoVe; HarvBoo; PNI

I am not yet twenty-two and I am tired of living.　Asclepiades.　HePo, tr. by Barbara Hughes Fowler

I am not your lover and you will never know me.　Minutiae 3.　P. F. Widdows. FaBoWar

I am obnoxious to each carping tongue.　Anne Bradstreet.　WoPoe Fr. Prologue, The.

I Am of Ireland.　Unknown.　NAEL-6v1; NAEL-7v1; NoP-5
　(I Am from Ireland.)　WaAnP

I am of old and young, of the foolish as much as the wise.　Walt Whitman. NAWM-7v2 Fr. Song of Myself.

I Am of the Tribe of Yehuda.　Rosita Kalina.　MirDau, tr. by Maria Xirinachs

I am old and I am heavy.　Reinforcements [2].　Raymond Queneau.　YaTCFP, tr. by Keith Waldrop

I am old enough now for a tree.　Weathering.　Alastair Reid.　EdScPo

I am old, sick and lonely.　Verses.　Su Tung-p'o.　TAL

I am on my way running.　Song for a Young Girl's Puberty Ceremony. Unknown.　ChAP; ItWoWo, tr. by Frances Densmore

I Am on My Way to Oklahoma to Bury the Man I Nearly Left My Husband For. Sandra Cisneros.　TiP2

I am one anatomy and take turns. Sometimes after dinner I wrap them in a newspaper.　Hello.　Sabrina Orah Mark.　LegDan

I am one of passion's asses.　Girls of Llanbadarn, The.　Dafydd ap Gwilym. OBWVE, tr. by Rolfe Humphries

I am / one of them.　3 Old Men at Separate Tables.　Charles Bukowski.　PML

I am one of you, though you do not.　Buying Fish.　Susan Wicks.　MFPA

I am open.　Michael Datcher.　BtF

I am, outside. Incredible panic rules.　John Berryman.　VCAP Fr. Dream Songs.

I am outside of.　Dualism in Ralph Ellison's Invisible Man.　Ishmael Reed. EGAG; ESEAA

I am peasant.　Transfiguration.　Jack Hirschman.　CLPP

I am peeling four pink grapefruit.　Natasha Sajé.　PoDa

I am personally indebted to antiquity because if it were left.　Invention. Barbara Hamby.　SUP

I am pleased with a frame of four lights.　My Greenhouse.　Edwin Morgan. OBGa

I am plural. My intents are manifold.　Nondescript, The.　Peter Scupham. HarvBoo

I am poor and old and blind.　Belisarius.　Henry Wadsworth Longfellow. APN-1

I am poor brother Lippo, by your leave!　Fra Lippo Lippi.　Robert Browning. BrAP; NAEL-6v2; NAEL-7v2; NoP-4; NoP-5; OxAEP-2; WaAnP

I am poor once more! (LL)　I never lost as much but twice.　Emily Dickinson. HeIP-4; MoAmPo; NAAL-3; NAAL-5; NAAPv.1; NAMCP V.1; NCAP; NoAM; NoP-4; NoP-5; TCAPo

I am possessed by Eros.　Tattooing the Motherline.　Krista Franklin.　BRtP

I am powerless against the world. (LL)　Night in a Room by the River.　Tu Fu [or Du Fu].　AWTN; CrYelRi, tr. by Sam Hamill

I am prepared when you don't show up. For three days.　Memory Lapse. Judith Strasser.　CFP

I am quiet, like this, stubbornly quiet.　Attitude.　Magda Portal.　TANSG, tr. by Shaun Griffin and Emma Sepúlveda-Pulvirenti

I am quite mad and you are wholly sane.　Mad Woman.　Su'ad al-Mubarak Al-Sabah.　PoArWo, tr. by John Heath-Stubbs and May Jayyusi

I Am Raftery [or Raferty].　Anthony Raftery.　IrV; WoPoe, tr. by Douglas Hyde

I am reading a diary at night.　Discovering Lasseter.　Conal Fitzpatrick. NOBAu

I am restored in beauty. (LL)　Shootingway Ceremony Prayer.　Unknown. WoPoe; WPoS, tr. by Gladys A. Reichard

I am riding on a limited express, one of the crack trains of the nation.　Limited. Carl Sandburg.　BeAl; MoAmPo

I Am Root.　Claribel Alegría.　PoetW; VCWP, tr. by Carolyn Forché

I am Rose my eyes are blue.　Gertrude Stein.　APT-1

I am running down a street with a pistol and behind me is all of.　Bensonhurst. Jack Wiler.　BRtP

I Am Sad.　Le Ngoc Hiep.　WoPoe, tr. by John Balaban and T. L. Nguyen

I am sad / I better hurry up and finish this.　On Rachmaninoff's Birthday #158. Frank O'Hara.　AHA

I am sad this morning.　Kenneth Rexroth.　APSN Fr. Love Poems of Marichiko, The.

I am saying goodbye to the trees.　Going Home.　Derek Mahon.　HarvBoo

I am seeing this: two men are sitting on a pole.　Mitchells, The.　Les A. Murray.　PML

I am sending you this letter.　Line from St. David's, A.　Ronald Stuart Thomas. AngWePo

I am set off.　Luxembourg Garden.　Afaa Michael Weaver.　GT

I am shaking life a leaf in the orchard.　Orchard in the Spring.　Jane Rohrer. BodElec

I am sick of.　Autumnal Equinox.　Svetlana Dengina.　CRWP, tr. by Daniel Weissbort

I am silver and exact. I have no preconceptions.　Mirror.　Sylvia Plath. MoWP; NIL-7; NIP-4; OxBoAm; StAl

I am simple like the light.　Transmutation.　Julia de Burgos.　TANSG, tr. by Heather Rosario Sievert

I Am Singing Now.　Luci Tapahonso.　UnSA

I Am Singing the Cold Rain.　Lance Henson.　HATNAP

I am singing to the heavens above.　Incantations of Modoc Conjurers. Unknown.　APN-2, tr. by Albert S. Gatschet

I AM SINGLE AND I AM JUST.　Photo Genic.　Olga Broumas.　ExTi

I am sitting across the table.　Sunday at the State Hospital.　David Ignatow. RaBo

I am sitting again on the steps of the burned out barrack.　On the Far Edge of Kilmer.　Gerald Stern.　LoL

I am sitting alone among the silence of the animals. Sleep of Beasts, The. Peter Cooley. UrbNat

I am sitting here. Poor Girl's Meditation, The. *Unknown*. OBMV, *tr. by* Padraic Colum

I am sitting in a strange room listening. Baby-Sitting. Gillian Clarke. TCAWP

I am sitting sad and lonely. Lines to Florence. Mary Weston Fordham. CBWP-2

I am sitting thirty feet above the water. For Song. Gerald Stern. BBASP

I am sixteen you are my first love. Gail. Hugh Seidman. KGB

I am sleepless in the glow and shadow of the lamplight. Visiting Zan, Abbot of Dayun. Tu Fu [*or* Du Fu]. CCL1, *tr. by* Kenneth Rexroth

I am sleepy, and the oozy weeds about me twist. (LL) Herman Melville. APN-2; NCAP; WoPoe *Fr.* Billy Budd, Foretopman.

I am slow moving. After Bird Watching near the Mexican Border. Robert Burlingame. TiP2

I am so fair that wheresoe'er I wend. Beauty Accurst. Richard Le Gallienne. RACG

I am so happy. Can't You See? Segun Akinlolu. NeNiPo

I Am So in Love I Grow a New Hymen. Sandra Cisneros. IllVoic

I am so small walking on the beach. Whitman Leaves the Boardwalk. Edward Hirsch. ViWalt

I am so tired of having a body. Take Five of These. Julie Kalendek. OnScMo

I am sometimes the clarinet. Clarinet. Terrance Hayes. IIR

I am sorry, my little cat, I am sorry—. War Cat. Dorothy Leigh Sayers. TriCat

I am sorry you are. Roots. Charlotte Watson Sherman. ISC

I am southern hear me roar i am burning flags bearing crosses i. Cause I'm from Dixie Too. Evie Shockley. RD

I am space. On Reading the New Physics—Creation and Cosmology. Cosi Fabian. HW

I am speaking of that hollow-eyed race. They Never Grew Old. Judith Ortiz Cofer. PueRic

I am spectator actor and author. Of One and Two, of All. Paul Eluard. YaTCFP, *tr.* by Mary Ann Caws

I am standing above the noontide. Christopher Okigbo. NAMCP V.2 *Fr.* Heavensgate.

I am standing at the subway entrance on the northeast corner. Drugstore. Peter Schjeldahl. AHA

I am standing for peace and non-violence. Patriot, The. Nissim Ezekiel. EmeKit; FaBoVe

I am standing in the post office, about. James Tate. EmeKit; OxBoAm; SUP *Fr.* I Am A Finn.

I am standing tensely at the desk. Current "Now, Voyager" Fantasy. Remy Holzer. OPRER

I am staring out the window. African Sculpture. Christopher Gilbert. ESEAA

I Am Still a Finn. James Tate. EmeKit; OxBoAm *Fr.* I Am A Finn.

I am still completely happy. Evening in the Country. John Ashbery. PoDa

I am still on fire. Distance. Eugene B. Redmond. SeSe

I am still wandering. She-Ghost of Tiresias. Monica A. Hand. BtF

I am storing at heart a bundle of grass. Nightmare 3. Abdul Maqsoud Abdul Karim. NAfrP, *tr.* by Clarissa C. Burt

I am stuck. Everything I want to say. Goodbye in the Shape of a Knot. Bob Hicok. AmAlph

I am sure you would find it misty here. Mark Strand. CAP-8 *Fr.* Dark Harbor.

I am surrounded by parrots. Parrots. Selima Hill. MoWP

I Am Taliesin. I Sing Perfect Metre. *Unknown*. OBWVE, *tr.* by Ifor Williams

I am tempted by rumors, by history. Coming Off a Depression, She Prepares for Venice. A. V. Christie. NAPBL

I am that Dido which thou here do'st see. Ausonius. NoSic; OBVE

I am that Savior that vouchsafed to die. On the Inscription Over the Head of Christ on the Cross. Henry Colman. ChIV-2

I am that serpent-haunted cave. Pythoness, The. Kathleen Jessie Raine. MoBrPo

I am the acorn. Journey. Judith Nicholls. OBSP

I am the American heartbreak. American Heartbreak. Langston Hughes. APT-2

I am the ancient Apple-Queen. Pomona. William Morris. NPeEn; OxBEV; WoPoe

I Am the Babe of Joseph Stalin's Daughter. Rochelle Owens. PFTM-2

I am the bird that flutters against your window in the morning. Guardian Angel. Rolf Jacobsen. RaBo; WED, *tr.* by Robert Bly

I Am the Blood. Isaac Rosenberg. MoBrPo

I am the blossom pressed in a book. Briefly It Enters, and Briefly Speaks. Jane Kenyon. AFaM; HW

I am the blue! I come from the lower world. Helen. Paul Valéry. OBVE, *tr.* by Robert Lowell

I am the boy with his hands raised over his head. House That Fear Built: Warsaw, 1943, The. Jane Flanders. PBCAP

I am the broken reed in this deathly organ. How We Carry Ourselves. Jimmy Santiago Baca. AF

I am the captain of my soul. (LL) W. E. Henley. AmFaPo; BRP; CABP; CtM; MoBrPo; NAEL-6v2; NAEL-7v2; OBEV; OBMV *Fr.* Echoes.

I am the captain of my soul. Probably. Keith Preston. NBLV

I Am the Cat. Leila Usher. ITBLP

I am the cat of cats. I am. Cat of Cats, The. William Brighty Rands. NOxBChV

I am / the clear unmuffled. Bluesman. Charlie R. Braxton. BRtP

I am the dancer. Spirit of the Dancer. Lisa Elaine Johnson. BtF

I am the dark one,—the unconsoled. El Desdichado. Gérard de Nerval. WoPoe, *tr.* by Robert Duncan

I am the desert. Carthage. Najaat Al-Udwany. PoArWo, *tr.* by Moulouk Berry and Ali Farghaly

I am the difficult silk that slides from your grasp. Elizabeth Garrett. NewEx

I Am the Door [*or* Doore]. Richard Crashaw. NAEL-6v1; NAEL-7v1

I am the family face. Heredity. Thomas Hardy. HarvBoo

I am the farmer, stripped of love. Hill Farmer Speaks, The. Ronald Stuart Thomas. OBWVE

I am the feast-maker. W. E. Henley. FaBoWar *Fr.* Song of the Sword.

I am the ferryboat. Ferryboat and the Traveler. Han Yong'un [*or* Yongwun]. CAMKP, *tr.* by Sammy Solberg

I am the first. Paul Celan. VCWP, *tr.* by Michael Hamburger

I am the first and I am the last. Bible, *O.T.* InvLi *Fr.* Isaiah.

I am the first fruit of your loins. Olayimika. Toyin Adewale. NeNiPo

I am the first to drink of the blue that still looks for its eye. I am the first. Paul Celan. VCWP, *tr.* by Michael Hamburger

I am the fledgling Love—easily caught since I just left. Asclepiades. GPTC,

I am the free-thinker who reads Voltaire. Skeptic, The. Colette Inez. PA9/11

I Am the Freshly Dead Husband. Kojo Laing. HBAPE; NAfrP; PML

I am the fruit of Adams hands, through sin lockt in satans bands. Hymne of the State of all Adams Posteritie, An. Lady Elizabeth Tyrwhit. EMWP

I am the grandson of György Dózsa. Grandson of György Dózsa, The. Endre Ady. IQMS, *tr.* by Sir Maurice Bowra

I am the grass / Let me work. (LL) Grass. Carl Sandburg. AmWaPo; ColAP; FaBoWar; InoFa; MoAmPo; NAAL-5; NAAPv.2; NAMCP V.1; NoAM; NoP-4; NoP-5; OBWP; OxBoAm; PoAgWa; PoPoPo; StAl; TCAPo; TFi; WaAnP

I am the grave of Baucis the bride. Passing by. Erinna. HePo *Fr.* Epigrams.

I am the great Baron-Samedi. René Depestre. PFTM-2 *Fr.* Rainbow for the Christian West, A.

I am the Great Bassist. Great Bassist, The. Lawson Fusao Inada. OpBo

I am the great sun, but you do not see me. I Am the Great Sun. Charles Causley. OxBSo

I Am the Hazel-Nut. Karel Van de Woestijne. TuT, *tr.* by Michael Longley

I am the hazel-nut. An anaemic worm. I Am the Hazel-Nut. Karel Van de Woestijne. TuT, *tr.* by Michael Longley

I am the Hunt which rathe and early rise. Blazon Pronounced by the Huntsman, The. Jacques du Fouilloux. DiBP, *tr.* by George Turberville

I am the keeper of the earth and air. Keeper. Esther Iverem. GT

I am the keeper of the Elysian Garden. Elysian Garden. Carmen Boullosa. RMCMP, *tr.* by Geoff Hargreaves

I am the laughing woman who's afraid to go to sleep. (LL) Fragment. Angelina Weld Grimké. NAAPv.2; OxBoAm

I am the little man who smokes & smokes. John Berryman. IJHIL *Fr.* Dream Songs.

I am the living body of the Great Spirit above. Chants to the Deity. *Unknown*. APN-2, *tr.* by Henry Rowe Schoolcraft

I am the Living Quetzalcoatl. Living Quetzalcoatl, The. D. H. Lawrence. OWoS

I am the lover you have never seen. Wishing You. C. D. Grant. BRtP

I am the man who looked for peace and burial. War Poet. Sidney Keyes. FaBoWar; NoP-4; NoP-5; PoWW; WaAnP

I am the man you will never defeat. Mongane Wally Serote. TSAP *Fr.* No Baby Must Weep.

I am the month when roses. June. Mary Weston Fordham. CBWP-2

I am the mother of sorrows. Paradox, The. Paul Laurence Dunbar. TCAPo

I Am the Mountainy Singer. Joseph Campbell. MoBrPo

I am the mover of other eyes. Dirge for the Living. Rosalie Moore. YaYoPo

I am the new man. Djeni. Seitlhamo Motsapi. TSAP

I am the night watchman of rue de Flandre. Night Watchman of Pont-au-Change, The. Robert Desnos. AF, *tr.* by Carolyn Forché

I am the October lady. Horoscope. Colleen J. McElroy. GT

I am the old *shul* between the railroad and the glass factory. Religion. Judith W. Steinberg. PfS

I am the one / Uncomforted. (LL) Three Emily's, The. Dorothy Livesay. BrAP; NALW

I am the one who determined that the year must number 356 days and be divided into 12 months. Monologue, A. Mihai Ursachi. PML, *tr. by* the author and Adam J. Sorkin.

I am the one who gnawed the blanket through. Message from Outside. Gary Snyder. BodElec

I am the one who talks with the mountains. Dear Webster. Connie Fife. ReEnLa

I am the one whose praise. Hildegard von Bingen. HW, *tr. by* Gabriele Uhlein

I am the only being whose doom. Emily Jane Brontë. NALW

I am the only hero of my verses. Lyric Poet's Epilogue, The. Mihály Babits. IQMS, *tr. by* Peter Zollman

I am the only one, the only one left. *Unknown.* APN-2 *Fr.* Sacred Songs of the Konkau.

I am the orphan cloud. Dusk of Autumn: Writing What My Heart Embraces. Ching An. CSKM, *tr. by* Jerome P. Seaton

I Am the People, the Mob. Carl Sandburg. IllVoic

I am the people—the mob—the crowd—the mass. I Am the People, the Mob. Carl Sandburg. IllVoic

I Am the Poet. Walt Whitman. BLT

I am the poet of reality. I Am the Poet. Walt Whitman. BLT

I am the poet of the Body and I am the poet of the Soul. Walt Whitman. BrAP; CAGL; ColAP; NAWM-7v2; WaAnP; WeW-3 *Fr.* Song of Myself.

I am the poet of the spare room. Home, The Spare Room, The. Robert Adamson. BMAP

I am the pure red witch. Moi-Même. Carmen Bruna. SurWo, *tr. by* Natalie Kenvin

I Am the Reasonable One. Rosario Morales. PueRic

I am the reasonable one. I am the one you can say your spite to, the. I Am the Reasonable One. Rosario Morales. PueRic

I am the Red Cloud. *Unknown.* APN-2 *Fr.* Sacred Songs of the Konkau.

I am the room for all seasons. Waiting Room. U. A. Fanthorpe. PoCu

I am the rose of Sharon, and the lily of the valleys.I Am the Rose of Sharon. Bible, *O.T.* OBVE *Fr.* Song of Solomon, The [*or* The Song of Songs].

I am the ruined queen. Dido: Swarming. Kathleen Spivack. PoA 2002

I am the running man. Running Man. Cornelius Eady. FaoP

I am the self-appointed guardian of English literature. Souvenir de Monsieur Poop. Stevie Smith. MoWP; NALW; NAMCP V.1

I am the ship in which you sail. Freight. Maura Dooley. StAl

I am the Silver. Ride Me Baby, Ride Me. Felicia L. Morgenstern. BtF

I am the sister of him. Little. Dorothy Aldis. NTCP; WHSW

I am the Smoke King. Song of the Smoke, The. William Edward Burghardt DuBois. ISC; SSLK

I am the snake-woman kneeling at Knossos. Power of the Soul. Sheilah Glover. HW

I am the sole homosexual. Power of One. Walta Borawski. CAGL

I Am the Son of King Gog of Magog. Gyula Reviczky. IQMS, *tr. by* Adam Makkai

I am the song that sings the bird. I Am the Song. Charles Causley. NOxBChV; StAl

I am the spirit astir. Autochthon. Sir Charles G. D. Roberts. IFF

I am the still rain falling. Moods. Sara Teasdale. APT-1

I am the stone that kills me. (LL) Stone: "When the stone fall that morning out of the johncrow sky." Edward Kamau Brathwaite. NAMCP V.2; PFTM-2; WaCA; WoBe

I am the swift scribble. Patricia Hawkhead. NewEx

I am the teacher of athletes. Walt Whitman. CAGL; ColAP *Fr.* Song of Myself.

I am the thought on the bath in the room without mirrors. Blue Wind, The. Nadja. SurWo, *tr. by* Richard Howard

I am the thunder of my tribe. *Unknown.* APN-2 *Fr.* Songs of the Kwakiutl Indians.

I am the tongue. Second Tongue. Gearóid Mac Lochlainn. NIrP, *tr. by* the author and Séamas Mac Annaidh

I Am the Tropical Night's High Noon. Maria Martins. SurWo, *tr. by* Rachel Blackwell

I am the true vine, and my Father is the husbandman. Bible, *N.T.* OBVE *Fr.* St. John.

I am the used-arrow collector. Actor Speaks, An. Ben Scammell. NLP

I Am the Very Model [*or* Pattern] of a Modern Major-General. William Schwenck Gilbert. NoP-5 *Fr.* Pirates of Penzance, The.

I am the very pattern of a modern major-gineral. William Schwenck Gilbert. UV *Fr.* Pirates of Penzance, The.

I am the voice of Redwood Creek. River Meditation. Wendy Johnson. WhBo

I am the voice of the mountainside. I am the Voice. Jigerkhwen. IrPoTo, *tr. by* Muhamad Tawfiq Ali

I Am the Way. Alice Thompson Meynell. OBMV

I am the wealthy one. Demeter's Song. Starhawk. HW

I am the wee falorie man. Wee Falorie Man, The. *Unknown.* FaBoVe

I am the whistling of night. Second Portrait. Manuela Fingueret. MirDau, *tr.* by Roberta Gordenstein

I am the witness of the massacre. Mahmoud Darwish. PoAgWa *Fr.* Poem for the Land.

I am the woman always too young to be. I've Been Around: It Gets Me Nowhere. Marie Ponsot. ExTi

I am the woman, and about to enter. (LL) Meditation in Seven Days, A. Alicia Ostriker. PBCAP; TaR

I am the woman of the great expanse of the water. María Sabina. PFTM-1 *Fr.* Midnight Velada, The.

I am the woman with the black black skin. Fragment. Angelina Weld Grimké. NAAPv.2; OxBoAm

I am the word that speaks the man. (LL) I Am the Song. Charles Causley. NOxBChV; StAl

I Am Thine, O Lord. Fanny Crosby. SWaP

I am Thine, O Lord, I have heard Thy voice. I Am Thine, O Lord. Fanny Crosby. SWaP

I am thinking, as I break away from here. (LL) Goodbye to the Old Friends. Henry Taylor. InGu; LPSFW

I am thinking of a fairy tale. Fat Is Not a Fairy Tale. Jane Yolen. P180

I am thinking of hedges and orchards. Home Farm. John Burnside. WaAnP

I am thinking of that boy who bragged about the day he threw a dog over and watched it struggle to stay upright all the way down. Boy at the Paterson Falls. Toi Derricotte. BtF; PBCAP

I am thirty-three and working in an expensive clothier. Clerk's Tale, The. Spencer Reece. LegDan

I am thirty-two and wise. For My Birthday. Attila József. IQMS, *tr. by* Anton N. Nyerges

I am three letters. You are a new phenomenon. What is it. That discord. Neutrino (means little one). Jason Christie. PoPra

I Am Thy Charge, Thy Care! Michael Field. PoBW

I am thy fugitive, thy votary. To the Lord Love. Michael Field. OBMV

I am Thy grass, O Lord! Trust. Lizette Woodworth Reese. SWaP

I am thy other self, what thou wilt be. Thy Better Self. Jones Very. TCAPo

I am tired of civilization. (LL) Tired. Fenton Johnson. APT-1; OxAAAP; TCAPo

I am tired of this barn! said the colt. Barn, The. Elizabeth Jane Coatsworth. OBCP

I am tired of work; I am tired of building up somebody else's civilization. Tired. Fenton Johnson. APT-1; OxAAAP; TCAPo

I am to follow her. There is much grace. George Meredith. NAEL-6v2 *Fr.* Modern Love.

I am to see to it that I do not lose you. (LL) To a Stranger. Walt Whitman. APN-1; OxBoAm; SAmP

I am told. Ingredients of Glass. Margaret Speak. Prnts

I am told by many of you that I must forgive and so I shall. Powwow at the End of the World, The. Sherman Alexie. WaAnP

I am told, sir, you're keeping an eye on your wife. Careful Husband, The. The Earl of Longford. IrLP

I am told that the best people have begun saying. War Has Been Given a Bad Name. Bertolt Brecht. BeAl; HP; PoAgWa; PoSu, *tr. by* John Willett

I am too. Gale Nelson. OnScMo

I am too alone in the world, and not alone enough. I Am Too Alone in the World. Rainer Maria Rilke. WED, *tr. by* Robert Bly

I am too fond of the universe to live with just one being. Shady Soul. Max Jacob. YaTCFP, *tr. by* Mary Ann Caws

I am too near, too clear a thing for you. Flower of Mullein, A. Lizette Woodworth Reese. MoAmPo

I am too old to burn ships, even if I am a pirate don't mind me. Old Pirate in These Waters, An. Ali Püsküllüoğlu. WoPoe, *tr. by* Murat Nemet-Nejat

I am too young to grow a beard. Street Song. Thom Gunn. HeIP-4

I am transparent, she says. Transparent like the sounds of dawn. I am the mirror, I stand aside. In the Daylight. Marcelin Pleynet. YaTCFP, *tr. by* Mary Ann Caws

I am true in the land of ancient sounds. Susan Taylor. NewEx

I am trusting Thee, Lord Jesus. Trusting Jesus. Frances Ridley Havergal. SacPr

I am trying to decide to go swimming. Wind Is Blowing West, The. Joseph Ceravolo. NYP2; OxBoAm

I am trying to decipher the language of insects. After the Alphabets. W. S. Merwin. PoA 2002

I am trying to drain my mind. Prelude to Nothing. Sonia Sanchez. GT

I am trying to make sense of this butterfly's flight. Collaboration: Migration Patterns. Anthony Caleshu. NIrP

I am twelve years old, my hair in braids. Music Mother. Naomi Feigelson Chase. MiVo

I am twenty-four. Survivor, The. Tadeusz Różewicz. BeAl; HP; PoAgWa; PoSu, *tr. by* Adam Czerniawski

I am twenty-two years old. Chirst. Portrait. Miklós Radnóti. IQMS, *tr. by* Thomas Land

I asked if I got sick and died, would you.   Question, A.   John Millington Synge.   MoBrPo; OBMV

I asked if I should pray.   Mohini Chatterjee.   William Butler Yeats.   NoAM

I asked my dead to tea.   Tea Party, The.   Jean Earle.   TCAWP

I Asked My Love.   Abu Sa'id.   EroLit

I asked my love: "Why do you make yourself so beautiful?"   I Asked My Love. Abu Sa'id.   EroLit

I asked my parents.   Going to Norway.   Jack Anderson.   SUP

I asked no other thing.   Emily Dickinson.   APN-2

I asked [or askd] my Dear Friend, Orator Prigg.   Orator Prigg.   William Blake. OBSV

I asked professors who teach the meaning of life to tell me what is happiness. Happiness.   Carl Sandburg.   IllVoic

I asked the cuckoo of Zen Cloud Mountain.   Cuckoo and Skylark.   Sŏ Chŏngju.   CAMKP, tr. by David R. McCann

I asked the heaven of stars.   Night Song at Amalfi.   Sara Teasdale.   APT-1; MakPoe; MaMoMo

I asked the Lord: "Sire, is this true."   Dream Question, A.   Thomas Hardy. ChIV-1

I asked the maid in dulcet tone.   Scones.   Unknown.   OBCoV

I asked your mother for you.   Goodnight Irene.   Unknown.   NAAPv.2

I associate hours and days.   Monotomy.   Gabriella Sica.   CItWP, tr. by Cinzia Sartini Blum and Lara Trubowitz

I assume that we are talking about saving a few young men from suicide and a few others from becoming cops or firemen.   Rhetoric.   Francis Ponge. WoPoe, tr. by Serge Gavronsky

I assure them. But they will not have it. (LL)   Zoom!   Simon Armitage. HarvBoo; StAl

I, / at one time.   Self-Hatred of Don L. Lee, The.   Haki R. Madhubuti. ESEAA

I ate pancakes one night in a Pancake House.   Player Piano, The.   Randall Jarrell.   OxBoAm

I ate the tongue of the stag.   Sacrilege.   Nina Cassian.   StAl, tr. by William Jay Smith and Petre Solomon

I Attend a Poetry Reading.   Steve Kowit.   SUP

I awake light-hearted this morning of spring.   Spring Morning, A.   Meng Hao Jan.   CCL1, tr. by Witter Bynner

I awakened to dryness and the ferns were dead.   Tragedy of the Leaves, The. Charles Bukowski.   CalPo; SUP

I awoke, all of me embers, there's no homeland in my home.   Suns in the Night of the Massacre.   Aziz Samawi.   IrPoTo, tr. by Alex Bellem

I awoke happy, the house.   Revelation, The.   William Carlos Williams. SAmP

I awoke in the midsummer not-to-call night, in the white and the walk of the morning.   Moonrise.   Gerard Manley Hopkins.   MoBrPo

I awoke with the yellow bright morning.   Sunshine.   Macel Aguilar.   BeDoSh

I ax all dem brudder roun'.   Archangel Open the Door.   Unknown.   SSUS

I ax Fader Georgy for religion.   This Is the Trouble of the World.   Unknown. SSUS

I back the car over a soft, large object.   C. D. Wright.   AmAlph; CAP-8

I bathe at night. I dress in white. The sheets are clean.   Before Bed.   Mary Ruefle.   PoCho

I be a Goddess 'cause.   Why I Be a Goddess.   Rha Goddess.   BRtP

I bear the sucker-torch to the western tree-ridge.   Songs of Spirits.   Unknown. APN-2, tr. by Jeremiah Curtin

I beat like a deaf man on the door of the dead.   Son of the Bone Speaks, The. Roger Gilbert-Lecomte.   PFTM-1

I became a criminal when I fell in love.   Siren.   Louise Glück.   OxBoAm

I bed next to you, I feel your heartbeat.   Kenny Fries.   AmPoNex Fr. Healing Notebooks, The.

I / been runnin' wid.   Spookism.   Lamont B. Steptoe.   FuFl

I been to church, folks.   Swallow Wings.   Rosemary Catacalos.   TiP2

I Been Working on the Railroad.   Unknown.   TCAPo

I before e.   Exceptions.   Felice Belle.   BRtP

I beg death's pardon now. And mourn the dead. (LL)   Pardon, The.   Richard Wilbur.   BrAP; InoFa; NIL-7; NoAM

I beg God's grace, guardian of the parish.   In Praise of Tenby.   Unknown. OBWVE, tr. by Joseph P. Clancy

I beg of you, Chung Tzu.   Chung Tzu.   Unknown.   WoPoe, tr. by Arthur Waley

I beg to dicker with my silver-tongued companion.   Sleeping with the Dictionary.   Harryette Mullen.   AWPTFC

I beg you, beg you, mother.   Unknown.   WoPoe Fr. Mourning Songs of Greece.

I began losing the battles.   Domestic Blues.   Teresa Calderón.   TANSG, tr. by Celeste Kostopulos-Cooperman

I begged off. Eyes, eyes, the color of dogs, crosses. (LL)   Blue Kashmir, '74. Carol Muske-Dukes.   AmAlph; PuP-23

I begin each day.   Kikaku.   SoOfWa, tr. by Sam Hamill

I begin through the grass once again to be bound to the Lord.   Reconciliation. George Russell.   OBMV

I beheld her and was conquered at the start.   I Guess I'll Have to Change My Plan.   Howard Dietz.   ReLy

I beheld her, on a day.   Ben Jonson.   NAEL-7v1 Fr. Celebration of Charis in Ten Lyric[k] Pieces [or Peeces], A.

I behold her there.   Together Again.   Victor Vroomkoning.   TuT, tr. by Anne Kennedy

I, being born a woman and distressed.   I, Being Born A Woman [And Distressed].   Edna St. Vincent Millay.   APT-1; HarvBoo; LW; NAAPv.2; NALW; NAMCP V.1; NIL-7; NIP-4; NoP-4; NoP-5

I Believe.   Unknown.   HP

I believe a leaf of grass is no less than the journey-work of the stars.   Walt Whitman.   ColAP; SAmP; WaAnP Fr. Song of Myself.

I believe in.   Credo.   Fiona Farrell.   BeAl

I Believe in All That Has Never Yet Been Spoken.   Rainer Maria Rilke.   TWF, tr. by Anita Barrows and Joanna Macy

I believe in magic. I believe in the rights.   Credo.   Maxine W. Kumin.   ExTi

I believe in nothing, I collaborate, I assist.   Eduardo Milán.   RMCMP, tr. by Roberto Tejada

I believe in the chance behind which God smiles.   My Dear Little Fellow. László Mécs.   IQMS, tr. by Watson Kirkconnell

I believe in the heretical teachings of a degenerate age, the witchcraft of the Christian God.   Secret Song of the Heretics.   Kitahara Hakushū.   WoPoe, tr. by Donald Keene

I believe in the solitary person.   Gunnar Ekelof.   WED Fr. Variations.

I believe in the soul; so far.   Old World, The.   Charles Simic.   CAP-8; StAl

I believe in the sun.   I Believe.   Unknown.   HP

I Believe in You.   Frank Loesser.   ReLy

I believe in you my soul, the other I am must not abase itself to you.   Walt Whitman.   CAGL; ColAP; NoP-5 Fr. Song of Myself.

I believe it was a calm evening.   Widower.   Julia Copus.   NeBl

I believe that it is raining, but it is not.   It Is Raining.   Jacques Roubaud. YaTCFP, tr. by Françoise Gramet and Richard Sieburth

I believe the Blacks are bad.   Sun, The.   Benjamin Zephaniah.   Oth

I believe the dose will do. (LL)   Receipt to Cure the Vapours, A.   Lady Mary Wortley Montagu.   NoP-4; NoP-5; NPeEn; OxBEV; PEW

I believe / The greatest gift.   Making Contact.   Virginia Satir.   TWF

I believe there is a song that is stranger than wind, that sips the scald from the telling, toss, toss.   Karen Volkman.   IAoNAP

I believe there is no justice.   What I Believe.   Michael C. Blumenthal. PLBUT

I believe there is no one alive who weeps for my sorrow.   Heinrich von Morungen.   GePo

I believe there is something else.   Credo.   Matthew Rohrer.   IIR

I believe to have one dog is better than a hundred thousand cats.   Cats—A Retrospective.   Paula Cunningham.   NIrP

I belong here.   Legacy.   Sydney March.   BtF

I belt out "I feel pretty, oh, so pretty" in the best Ethel Merman I can muster. (LL)   Man I Love and I Shop at Jewel, The.   Jim Elledge.   IllVoic; ReTh

I bend over the woman.   Country Midwife, The: A Day.   Ai.   AmAlph

I bended unto me a bough of May.   I Bended unto Me.   Thomas Edward Brown.   NTCP

I, Bertolt Brecht, came out of the black forests.   Of Poor B.B.   Bertolt Brecht. GTCP; WoPoe, tr. by Michael Hamburger

I beseech God's favour, faultless your gift.   Petition for Reconciliation. Cynddelw Brydydd Mawr.   OBWVE, tr. by Joseph P. Clancy

"I bet I can hold my breath."   One-Upmanship.   Miriam Chaikin.   NTCP

I bet you don't wear shoulder pads in bed.   Wagers.   Marilyn Hacker.   RA

I bind unto myself to-day.   St Patrick's Breastplate.   Saint Patrick.   SacPr, tr. by Frances Alexander

I bite my nails. I prowl round, here—there.   Where?   France Preseren. SonAtl, tr. by Merica Delic, Ursula Hobday and Ziva Pecavar

I blame even clear-voiced.   Korinna [or Corinna].   SaLy, tr. by Diane Rayor

I Blame It On Him.   Len Roberts.   PML

I blame old women for buying paper roses.   Look, No Hands.   Pearse Hutchinson.   PBCIP

I Bless the Daily Labor.   Marina Ivanovna Tsvetayeva.   WPoS

I bless the daily labor of my hands.   I Bless the Daily Labor.   Marina Ivanovna Tsvetayeva.   WPoS

I bless the everyday labor.   Marina Ivanovna Tsvetayeva.   BBASP, tr. by Mary Jane White

I bless[e] thee, Lord, because I GROW.   Paradise.   George Herbert.   AngWePo; BASC; NOSC

I blink and half my life is over.   Pete Winslow.   CLPP

I Blinked My Eyes, Looked Up and Everyone Was 25 Years Older.   Joanne Kyger.   WANABP

I block out the midday brightness with a screen depicting dark woods. Impromptu on a Hangover.   P'i Jih-hsiu.   ColAnChi, tr. by Burton Watson

I blow tobacco smoke. Mushroom. Takahashi Shinkichi. ZenPo, *tr. by* Takashi Ikemoto and Lucien Stryk

I bought a dollar and a half's worth of small red potatoes. Simple Truth, The. Philip Levine. BeAl; CAP-8; NoP-4; NoP-5

I bought a great big hat. Would You Believe It? Bart Howard. ReLy

I Bought a New Red. Chrystos. WiU

I bought a red-brick villa. Song for Straphangers. George Buchanan. PNI

I bought a spray of blossoms from a vendor. To the Tune: Magnolia Blossoms. Li Ch'ing-chao. CrYelRi, *tr. by* Sam Hamill

I bow before the buddhas. Kyunyŏ, Great Master. CATKP *Fr.* Eleven Poems on the Ten Vows of the Universally Worthy Bodhisattva.

I bow to the wall I face, to the life I face. Bowing. Paul S. Piper. AmZen

I breathe the air of another country. Australia. Gary Catalano. NOBAu

I breathed my fill—and then breathed out. Tatiana Bek. ItGoST, *tr. by* Richard McKane

I breathed to myself, *"Hold on! I'm coming"*. (LL) Three Ways of Recovering a Body. Helen Dunmore. MoWP; StAl

I bring back the petticoat and the bottle of scent. (LL) Lent. William Robert Rodgers. ModIr; PNI

I bring Fae flowers. When I cross the street. Fae. Timothy Steele. VisFro

I bring fresh showers for the thirsting flowers. Cloud, The. Percy Bysshe Shelley. BrAP; CABP; NAEL-6v2; NAEL-7v2; NoP-4; NoP-5; NPBRoP

I bring myself back from the streets that open like long. Home for Thanksgiving. W. S. Merwin. NoAM

I bring you a bit of seaweed which was tangled with the sea. Obsession. Robert Desnos. SurPaPo, *tr. by* Mary Ann Caws

I bring you along with me. Theatre, The. Remco Campert. TuT, *tr. by* Desmond Egan

I bring you as offering. (LL) Orchard. "H. D." APT-1; MoAmPo

I Bring You Greetings: How. Chrystos. WiU

I bring you the offspring of an Idumæan night! Gift of the Poem. Stéphane Mallarmé. AWTN, *tr. by* Kate Flores

I bring you words freshly. Word Gifts for an Australian Critic. Merlinda Bobis. ReBoTo

I broke a glass, got bloodstains on the sheet. Eight Days in April. Marilyn Hacker. FFC

I broke bread. Under the Williamsburg Bridge. Galway Kinnell. UrbNat

I Brood about Some Concepts, for Example. Alicia Ostriker. PBCAP

I brood on the uselessness of letters. (LL) Snow Storm. Tu Fu [*or* Du Fu]. BLT; NDACCP, *tr. by* Kenneth Rexroth

I brought my children to the mound. Anniversaries of War. Yehuda Amichai. VCWP, *tr. by* Benjamin Harshav and Barbara Harshav

I brought my life this far. Anniversary. Odysseus Elytis. AF, *tr. by* Edmund Keeley and Philip Sherrard

I brought my love. Beloved. Iyamide Hazeley. NAfrP

I build my house up on de rock. Bound to Go. *Unknown*. SSUS

I build the perfect silence with my hands. Wavelength. Jane Holland. NeBl

I built her a tower when I was young. For Una. Robinson Jeffers. APT-1

I built my house near where others dwell. Written While Drunk. Ch'ien T'ao. WoPoe, *tr. by* William Acker and Cyril Birch

I built my hut beside a traveled road. Poems After Drinking Wine. Ch'ien T'ao. ColAnChi, *tr. by* James Robert Hightower

I built my soul a lordly pleasurehouse. Palace of Art, The. Alfred Tennyson. NOBRP

I built on the sand. Foundations. Leopold Staff. BLT, *tr. by* Czeslaw Milosz

I buried my father. Little Father. Li-Young Lee. BeAl; P180

I burned my life, that I might find. Alchemist, The. Louise Bogan. APT-2; MoAmPo; NAAPv.2; NAMCP V.1

I buy the dark with my last fifteen cents. Depression Days. Pat Mora. UnSA

I buy you coral. Coral. Katie Donovan. NIrP

I buzz in the dizzy fly, I crawl in the creeping things. Amergin. Susan Langstaff Mitchell. IrV

I buzz through two security doors. Visiting Father. Juan Delgado. TouFir

I by you put on. Lloyd Addison. EGAG

I Cain't Say No. Oscar Hammerstein, II. ReLy

I call my mother on her birthday, the way. April Elegy (Sam Selvon d.1994). Christopher Wiseman. IFF

I call on no saviour, there's no gleam in the night. Amen. Jacques Réda. YaTCFP, *tr. by* Stephen Romer

I call out crazed in fever in a room. With Whitman at the Friendship Hotel. Anthony Piccione. ViWalt

I call that parent rash and wild. Velvet Hand, The. Phyllis McGinley. OBCoV

I call up words that he may write them down. Demands of the Muse. Vernon Watkins. PoA 2002

I called for my carriage and went to look at strange rarities. Looking at Stone Drum Mountain. Yu Ch'an. CCL1, *tr. by* John Frodsham

I called my father long-distance last night. Storm, The. Richard Jones. PoChi

I called one day—on Eden's strand. Emily Dickinson in Southern California. X. J. Kennedy. NBLV; OBCoV

I called the white donkey who hurt my left shoulder. Calling the White Donkey. Ray Gonzalez. TouFir

I called today, Peter, and you were away. Thermal Stair, The. William Sydney Graham. HarvBoo

I called you because I could not stand alone. Burden. Peter Kane Dufault. NoP-4; NoP-5

I came a thousand miles to share your dream. To Yuan Chen. Po Chü-i. CrYelRi, *tr. by* Sam Hamill

I came at night to the dark house. Survivors, The. Tracey Herd. BeAl; NeBl

I came back from home yesterday, spent. Consolation. Tanure Ojaide. EmeKit

I came back from the National Library. Revelation, The. Max Jacob. YaTCFP, *tr. by* Moishe Black and Maria Green

I came before you with simple plaits. Theology of Hair, The. Menna Elfyn. BBMWP, *tr. by* Elin ap Hywel

I came, doctor, because my head hurts. Poems from the Erotic Left. Ana María Rodas. TANSG, *tr. by* Zoë Anglesey

I came east to pay a son's respects. Yen-chou City Wall Tower. Tu Fu [*or* Du Fu]. CrYelRi, *tr. by* Sam Hamill

I came [*or* come] from Alabama wid my Banjo on my knee. Oh! Susanna. Stephen Collins Foster. TCAPo

I came from Santa Barbara. California Colors: A Song. Charlotte Perkins Stetson Gilman. CalPo

I came from the banks of the Ganges. On the Tisza. Endre Ady. IQMS, *tr. by* Anton N. Nyerges

I Came from Under the Earth. *Unknown*. WoPoe, *tr. by* Jean Guiart

I came here as a wanderer. Listening to a Flute in Yellow Crane Pavilion. Li Po. CrYelRi, *tr. by* Sam Hamill

I came here. I don't know you here. Clark Coolidge. PmAP *Fr.* At Egypt.

I came home and found a lion in my living room. Lion for Real, The. Allen Ginsberg. EmeKit

I came in a dream to a mountain in the sea. Kuan Hsiu. CCL1, *tr. by* Edward H. Schafer

I came in tonight and my building sighed. Sleepless. Eileen Myles. WiU

I came into the City and none knew me. Upper Chamber, An. Frances Bannerman. OBEV

I came into the pasture-ground. Settlement. Ingeborg Bachmann. PoSu, *tr. by* Daniel Huws

I came late to the dharma. Meal for the Monks, A. Wang Wei. CrYelRi, *tr. by* Sam Hamill

I came out of the unmade. Kwaja Abdullah Ansari. SonAtl, *tr. by* Assadullah Aimal Jadder

I came to a place where buildings were going up. Errand. David Morley. NLP

I Came to a Valley in the Wilderness. Baldomero Garcilaso de la Vega. SpanPo, *tr. by* Edwin Morgan

I came to a valley in the wilderness. I Came to a Valley in the Wilderness. Baldomero Garcilaso de la Vega. SpanPo, *tr. by* Edwin Morgan

I came to the Cathedral because I had been told that I might find a certain Pedro there. Of Fiction and Things. Josué Ramírez. RMCMP, *tr. by* Margaret Sayers Peden

I came to the cities in a time of disorder. Bertolt Brecht. AF *Fr.* To Those Born Later.

I came to the end at an inappropriate midnight. Post Operative. Thomas William Shapcott. BMAP

I came to the lake and six cranes were there. Six Cranes at Dusk. Henri Faust. YaYoPo

I came to this world. Rāmprasād Sen. SinGod, *tr. by* Rachel Fell McDermott

I came to visit my friend. Birds of Detroit. Greg Pape. PBCAP

I / came upon an owl. Totems. Christine Ama Ata Aidoo. HAWP

I came, yes, dear, dear. Kore in Hades. Kathleen Jessie Raine. NALW

I came, you know, but your gate was locked. Old Friend. Dimitris Tsaloumas. BMAP

I camped one night in Lasca Land. I Dreamt of Lasca. Jack E. Murphy. TiP2

I can barely imagine my mother. Roses, The. Jennifer Snyder. BodElec

I can be. Anything. Brenda Brooks. PoBW

I can be no more than four or five. Auschwitz. János Pilinszky. IQMS, *tr. by* Peter Jay

I can break your heart. (LL) Kid, The. Ai. GT; NoAM

I can close my eyes one heartbeat. My Father's Country. Joyce Lee. NOBAu

I Can Cook, Too. Betty Comden and Adolph Green. ReLy

I Can Dream, Can't I? Irving Kahal. ReLy

I can feel she has got out of bed. Rapture. Galway Kinnell. FaoP

I can feel the tug. Punishment. Seamus Heaney. EmeKit; EMP; NAEL-6v2; NAEL-7v2; NAMCP V.2; NoAM; NoP-4; NoP-5; OxAEP-2; PBCIP; PoPoPo; WaAnP

I cannot live with You.　Emily Dickinson.　APN-2; MoAmPo; NAAL-3; NAAL-5; NAAPv.1; NCAP; NoP-4; OxBoAm; TCAPo; TRP; WaAnP

I cannot live without thee! (LL)　To His Coy Love, A Canzonet.　Michael Drayton.　NOSC; PBRV

I cannot observe myself unobserved.　Skip Fox.　AnSo

I cannot possibly think of you.　Critic, The.　Frank O'Hara.　OxBoAm

I cannot reach it; and my striving eye.　Childhood.　Henry Vaughan.　NOSC

I cannot reach my rose. (LL)　Che Sara Sara.　Rose Terry Cooke.　NAAPv.1; SWaP

I cannot recall you gentle.　Black Mother Woman.　Audre Lorde.　OxAAAP

I cannot say.　Lady Izumi.　WPoS

I cannot say that I am phenomena by model.　Will Alexander.　Eno Fr. Concerning the Henbane Bird.

I Cannot Say the Name of the City.　Slavko Mihalic.　PoSu, tr. by Peter Kastmiler

I cannot see beyond it! I cannot see beyond it! (LL)　True Love.　Sharon Olds.　BodElec; StAl

I cannot see him plain, that far-off sire.　Immigrant, The.　Donald Davidson.　FuPo

I cannot see the features right.　Alfred Tennyson.　NAEL-6v2; NAEL-7v2; WaAnP Fr. In Memoriam A. H. H.

I cannot see the short, white curls.　Dumb World, The.　W. H. Davies.　OBWVE

I cannot send you back my hart.　Answeare to my Lady Alice Edgertons Songe, Of I prethy send mee back my Hart, An.　Lady Jane Cavendish.　EMWP

I cannot sleep. The long, long.　Night Thoughts.　Lu Yu.　NDACCP; WoPoe, tr. by Kenneth Rexroth

I cannot spare water or wine.　Mithridates.　Ralph Waldo Emerson.　APN-1; NCAP

I cannot speak with my voice but with my voices.　Foundation Stone. Alejandra Pizarnik.　TANSG, tr. by Susan Bassnett

I cannot stand the man who wears.　Ringless.　Diane Wakoski.　FTtHH; NALW

I cannot stifle this gigantick woe.　Bible, O.T.　STuOW Fr. Paraphrase on the Book of Job, A.

I cannot stop thinking of that old hat.　My Grandfather's Hat.　Judith Ortiz Cofer.　TouFir

I cannot tell the sorrows that I feel.　He Was Acquainted with Grief.　Jones Very.　SacPr

I cannot tell what you and other men.　William Shakespeare.　WaAnP Fr. Julius Caesar.

I cannot tell who loves the skeleton.　La Bella Bona-Roba.　Richard Lovelace.　NOSC; OxBEV

I cannot tell you how it was.　May.　Christina Georgina Rossetti.　NPeEn; OxBEV; WaAnP

I cannot think the thing farewell. (LL)　Alfred Tennyson.　NAEL-6v2; NAEL-7v2; WaAnP Fr. In Memoriam A. H. H.

I can't be contained in this tiny body.　Suburban buddha, coffeehouse christ.　Mark S. Kuhar.　AmZen

I can't bear a journey to the village.　Listless.　Tu Fu [or Du Fu].　CrYelRi, tr. by Sam Hamill

I can't bear to watch your hips.　Argentarius.　ErotSp, tr. by Sam Hamill

I Can't Become a Buddhist.　Adrienne Su.　NAPBL

I can't begin to tell you.　On Going Without Saying.　Jean Bleakney.　NIrP

I can't believe it.　Against Cinderella.　Julia Alvarez.　FiBr

I Can't Believe That You're in Love with Me.　Clarence Gaskill.　ReLy

I can't believe there's not.　To John Ashbery.　Frank O'Hara.　AHA

I can't believe you've come back.　Rise.　Brenda Shaughnessy.　AmPoNex

I can't, Celinda, say I love.　To Celinda.　Elizabeth Singer Rowe.　BASC; PEW

I can't concentrate on poetry.　Kevin and Nicole.　Amanda Nazario.　HeMarv

I can't even remember the name of the one who fell.　Robert Penn Warren.　GM Fr. Ballad: Between the Boxcars [1923].

I can't even see my hands in front of my face.　Diver for the NYPD Talks to His Girlfriend, A.　Richard Garcia.　TouFir; UrbNat

I can't feel the sunshine.　Lesbia Harford.　PoBW

I can't forget / How she stood at the top of that long marble stair.　Piazza di Spagna, Early Morning.　Richard Wilbur.　NoP-4; NoP-5

I can't get him out of my mind, out of my mind.　John Berryman.　BeAl; NoP-4 Fr. Dream Songs.

I can't get out of this city.　To Marthe.　Bill Bathurst.　AHA

I Can't Get Started.　Ai.　GT

I Can't Get Started.　Ira Gershwin.　APT-2; ReLy

I can't get started with you. (LL)　I Can't Get Started.　Ira Gershwin.　APT-2; ReLy

I Can't Give You Anything but Love.　Dorothy Fields.　APT-2; ReLy

I can't help it, The.　Knock Knock.　Michael Dennis Browne.　SUP

I Can't Help You.　Ryszard Krynicki.　BLT

I can't just sit here.　Today Is Not the Day.　Audre Lorde.　AfrBLW

I can't keep my eyes off the poet's.　At the Poetry Reading.　John Brehm.　PoA 2002

I can't keep my hands from stones.　Archeology.　Lorna Dee Cervantes.　TouFir

I can't keep my verbs straight. That's part of.　Part of What I Mean.　Frank Gaspar.　UrbNat

I can't lend it to you. I am not the same as last year.　Journal Encounter, The.　Kim Suyŏng.　CAMKP, tr. by Young-Jun Lee

I can't look at all at these lush fields of Hoho.　Walking the Plateau.　Lupenga Mphande.　NAfrP

I can't really remember now. The soundless foamed.　Thinking.　Jorie Graham.　BAP-97; ExTi

I can't remember.　Biology Teacher.　Zbigniew Herbert.　PoSu, tr. by John Carpenter and Bogdana Carpenter

I can't remember how it happened.　Father and Son.　Robert Greacen.　PNI

I can't remember really envying them.　Fatherhood.　Joan Waddleton.　Prnts

I can't remember the name of the gaunt monk.　Deep Shit.　Daniel Tobin.　NAPBL

I can't remember what the class trip was.　Samaritans.　Gerald Stern.　GPPA

I can't remember why I stepped outside.　Pepper.　Joe Osterhaus.　NAPBL

I can't say I'm of the bear clan or the elk people.　Hides.　Diane Glancy.　FTtHH

I can't say much about Richie Savalo.　Motorcycle Ward.　David Moolten.　BloBone

I can't say our garden is a delight.　Louisiana.　Steve Crow.　HATNAP

I can't say words like kiss, cuss, miss, or bless.　Unknown.　PriapPo Fr. Priapus Poems, The.

I can't see anymore.　Cloud of Dusk, A.　Michael Burkard.　BAP-04

I can't show my face.　It's the Talk of the Town.　A. J. Neiburg and Marty Symes.　ReLy

I can't sleep at night.　Crazy Blues.　Perry Bradford.　NAAPv.2

I can't sleep Georgia.　Georgia.　Philippe Soupault.　SurPaPo, tr. by Mary Ann Caws and Patricia Terry

(I'm not sleeping Georgia.)　YaTCFP

I can't sleep; no light burns.　Lines Written at Night During Insomnia. Alexander Sergeyevich Pushkin.　AWTN, tr. by D. M. Thomas

I can't sleep on the pavilion.　Revisiting Kumkang Pavilion.　Jungkwan Ilson.　BecRai, tr. by Kim Daljin, Kim Won-Chung and Christopher Merrill

I can't solve this.　How Callum Innes Paints.　Peter Finch.　Oth

I Can't Speak.　Alicia Ostriker.　PoA 2002

I can't speak of.　Moving Camp Too Far.　Nila NorthSun.　TWF

I can't stall any longer. I have to buy an outfit for.　Carol Dine.　PfS Fr. Fugue.

I Can't Stand the Fire.　Unknown.　SSUS

I can't stand the wily magpie and all his extravagant stories!　Unknown.　ColAnChi Fr. Four Tz'u from Tun-huang.

I can't stand these bird-songs.　Han-shan (Cold Mountain).　BB; NDACCP, tr. by Gary Snyder

I can't stay behind, my Lord, I can't stay behind!　I Can't Stay Behind.　Unknown.　SSUS

I can't stop eating sweets!　Candy Man, The.　Leslie Bricusse.　ReLy

I can't stuff myself anymore! (arguments in the form of noble people).　Not-France.　Carla Harryman.　PFTM-2

I can't talk to you now.　Failure.　Lina Tibi.　PoArWo, tr. by Subhi Hadidi and Nathalie Handal

I can't turn a smell.　Jo Shapcott.　MoWP Fr. Roses, The.

I can't understand myself.　New Year's Card, A.　Hwang Insuk.　EcSo, tr. by Peter H. Lee

I Can't Write a Poem about Class Rage.　Erin Belieu.　TAPaP

I Care and I'm Willing to Serve.　Marian Wright Edelman.　TWF

I care little for people's suspicions.　James Gleashure.　IrLP Fr. Mary Hogan's Quatrains.

I care not for my Lady's soul.　Lust of the Eyes, The.　Elizabeth Siddal.　VWP

I Care Not for These Ladies.　Thomas Campion.　NAEL-7v1; NoP-4; NoP-5; NoSic

I caressed your face with my fingers.　Faithful Mirror.　Gyula Illyés.　IQMS, tr. by Adam Makkai and Donald E. Morse

I carouse all night.　Song.　Cho-yong.　WoPoe, tr. by Okhee Yoo and Michael Stephens

I carried my wife inside me.　Carrying My Wife.　Moniza Alvi.　NeBl

I Carried Statues.　Ágnes Nemes Nagy.　PoSu

I carried you to an island.　Sea-bundle.　Jennifer Rankin.　BMAP

I carry a dead relationship around everywhere with me.　This Dead Relationship.　Katherine Pierpoint.　EmeKit; StAl

I carry in the vases the yearning.　Yearning of Karakashian, The.　Chava Pinchas-Cohen.　DTA, tr. by Miriyam Glazer

I carry it on my keychain, which itself.　Ring, The.　Diane Wakoski.　PoA 2002

I carry me on my fingertips. Love Me. Amal Moussa. PoArWo, *tr. by* Khaled Mattawa

I carry my lantern at noon. Diogenes. Lamiah Abbas Imara. IrPoTo, *tr. by* Basima Qattan Bezirgan and Elizabeth Fernea

I carry your heart with me(i carry it in). E. E. Cummings. ItP

I cartwheel like a knife. These Last Days. Katie Donovan. NeBl

I carve a small rooster from wood. Yi Chehyŏn. CATKP *Fr.* Contemporary Folk Songs.

I carve a small rooster from wood. Contemporary Folk Songs. Yi Chehyŏn. CATKP, *tr. by* Peter H. Lee

I carve my defiant, raging pulse. Judas and Jesus. Endre Ady. IQMS, *tr. by* Peter Zollman

I carved your name on my watchband. Letters from a Man in Solitary. Nazim Hikmet. AF

I catch myself trying. Untitled Blues; After a Photograph by Yevgeni Yevtushenko. Yusef Komunyakaa. ESEAA; GT; UnSA

I catch sight of the promised land. (LL) Ars Poetica. Claribel Alegría. LoL; TANSG, *tr. by* Darwin Flakoll

I catch the smell of beans. Sveta Litvak. CRWP, *tr. by* Daniel Weissbort

I caught a chameleon lizard. Chameleon, The. Judith Ortiz Cofer. PfSP

I caught a fella last night in the South Pacific. Radio. Harriet Monroe. APT-1

I Caught a Glimpse. Philip Levine. GeoHom

I caught a little ladybird. Christina Georgina Rossetti. FaBoVe; NPeEn

I caught a tremendous fish. Fish, The. Elizabeth Bishop. APT-2; BeAl; BrAP; CAP-8; ChAP; HarvBoo; HeIP-4; MoAmPo; MoASP; NAAL-5; NALW; NAMCP V.2; NoAM; NoP-4; NoP-5; PoetW; PoPoPo; TFi; TRP; WaAnP

I caught it. Radioactive Ball, The. Carole Oles. PfSP

I caught the cold flash of the blue / unappeasable sky. (LL) Robin Redbreast. Stanley Kunitz. CAP-8; NoP-4; NoP-5

I caught the last of a great caravan of clouds. 4AM. Tim Seibles. RD

I caught this morning morning's minion, King. Windhover, The. Gerard Manley Hopkins. AmFaPo; BrAP; CABP; ClHu; MoBrPo; NAEL-6v2; NAEL-7v2; NAMCP V.1; NIL-7; NoAM; NoP-4; NoP-5; NPeEn; OWoS; OxAEP-2; OxBEV; OxBSo; PoPoPo; SacPr; TFi; TRP; WaAnP

I caught you by the neck. To Eros. Alfonsina Storni. PoCho, *tr. by* Kay Short

I caught you, sir, having a look at her. Once in Love with Amy. Frank Loesser. ReLy

I cause great many worries to my mother. Spoons with Realistic Dead Flies on Them. Charles Simic. NAMCP V.2

I cease not from desire till my desire. Khwaja Shams-ad-din Muhammad Hafiz. TAL *Fr.* Odes.

I celebrate a bush that belongs. Bush, The. James Nicholas. BBMWP, *tr. by* Joseph P. Clancy

I celebrate myself. Lecturing on Walt Whitman and Emily Dickinson in China. Jesse Glass. ViWalt

I celebrate myself, and sing myself. Walt Whitman. ColAP; FaBoVe; MoAmPo; NAAL-3; NAAL-5; NAAPv.1; NAMCP V.1; NAWM-7v2; NCAP; NIL-7; NoAM; NoP-5; PoPoPo; RaBo; SAmP; TCAPo; WaAnP *Fr.* Song of Myself.

I celebrate myself, / And what I assume you shall assume. Walt Whitman. APN-1; HeIP-4; OxBoAm *Fr.* Leaves of Grass [1855 Version].

I celebrate racquetball and sing racquetball. Song of Racquetball. David Allan Evans. MoASP

I certainly have lost something. Kenneth Koch. NoAM *Fr.* Days and Nights.

I chanced upon a new book yesterday. To Edward FitzGerald. Robert Browning. NAEL-6v2

I Chant of the Miracle Stag (Christian Version). *Hungarian Oral Tradition.* IQMS, *tr. by* Adam Makkai

I Chant of the "Miracle Stag" (Shamanistic Version). *Hungarian Oral Tradition.* IQMS, *tr. by* Adam Makkai

I chant the pickled alewife, I wallow in surfeit. Song of the Cook. Natasha Sajé. SweBea

I charm thy life. Robert Southey. NOBRP *Fr.* Curse of Kehama, The.

I check for gestapo agents. I Eat Lunch with a Schizophrenic. Laurel Ann Bogen. SUP

I Cherish That Love. Kabir. WoPoe, *tr. by* Pritish Nandy

I chew a bitter cud, lying. Green Nostalgia. Thế Lữ'. WoPoe, *tr. by* Nguyen Ngoc Bich

I Ching. Diane Di Prima. SeSe

I Ching [*or* The Book of Changes *or* The Classic of Changes]. *Unknown.*

  Chi-chi (Already across the stream). ColAnChi, *tr. by* Richard A. Kunst

  Ch'ien (Heaven). ColAnChi, *tr. by* Richard A. Kunst

  K'un (Earth). ColAnChi, *tr. by* Richard A. Kunst

  "Marrying maiden, The / Undertakings bring misfortune." PFTM-1, *tr. by* Cary F. Baynes and Richard Wilhelm

  Wei-chi (Not yet across the stream). ColAnChi, *tr. by* Richard A. Kunst

I choose a place that is unfrequented by men. (LL) Madly Singing in the Mountains. Po Chü-i. BLT; WoPoe, *tr. by* Arthur Waley

I choose back lanes for the pace they will impose. Sunday Morning. Robert Minhinnick. TCAWP

I choose to come every noon. Sauna 2. Karina Africa-Bolasco. ReBoTo

I chopped down the house that you had been saving to live in next summer. Variations on a Theme by William Carlos Williams. Kenneth Koch. AmWit; NAMCP V.2; NBLV; NIL-7; NIP-4; NoAM; NoP-4; NoP-5; OxBoAm; PmAP; PoPoPo; WaAnP

I chose the bed down-stairs by the sea-window for a good death-bed. Bed by the Window, The. Robinson Jeffers. APT-1

I chose the blonde from the chemist's, thirty-six. Happening at Sordid Creek. Peter Porter. NoAM

I chose this. To be this. Meteor. Larissa Szporluk. BAP-01; LegDan

I chuck my Bible in the parlour fire. Song. Peter Redgrove. EmeKit

I chuck their chins. Anne Born. NewEx

I circled on leather paws. Return, The. Theodore Roethke. PoA 2002

I claim in the last hour of this known hysterical breathing. Wind in a Box. Terrance Hayes. LegDan

I classed, appraising once. Loved Once. Elizabeth Barrett Browning. ViWPN

I clean my teeth in water drawn from a cold well. Reading Buddhist Classics with Chao at His Temple in the Early Morning. Liu Tsung-yüan. CCL1, *tr. by* Witter Bynner

I cleared mother's apartment of her urine-soaked rags today, while she wept. When the Gods Put on Meter. Cal Bedient. BAP-01

I clearly hear the crowing of a rooster. I Don't Know That Man. Jan Polkowski. AF, *tr. by* Michael March *and* Jaroslaw Anders

I climb a barren hill and ponder. Zhi-hu: Young Soldier Thinks of Home. *Unknown.* CCL1, *tr. by* Rewi Alley

I climb high to look at Luotang city. I Climb High to Look at Spring. Shen Yüeh. CCL1, *tr. by* Anne Birrell

I Climb High to Look at Spring. Shen Yüeh. CCL1, *tr. by* Anne Birrell

I climb high to look out upon the world. Ancient Airs. Li Po. CrYelRi, *tr. by* Sam Hamill

I climb the black rock mountain. Where Mountain Lion Lay [*or* Laid] Down with Deer. Leslie Marmon Silko. TRP

I climb the C scale on the old piano. In C. W.'s Closet. Afaa Michael Weaver. OxAAAP

I climb these hills as if walking on air. After Shih-te. Shih Shu. CSKM, *tr. by* James H. Sanford

I climb'd [*or* climbed] the dark brow of the mighty Hellvellyn. Hellvellyn. Sir Walter Scott. ItP

I climbed a hill as light fell short. Song of Honor [*or* Honour], The. Ralph Hodgson. MoBrPo

I climbed Lotus Mountain in the west. Old Style Poem. Li Po. CrYelRi, *tr. by* Sam Hamill

I climbed the apple tree in my friend's garden. Apples. Maurice Riordan. NIrP

I climbed the dark brow of the mighty Helvellyn. Wanderer's Dog, The. Sir Walter Scott. DiBP

I climbed the hillside to the lady's house. Visiting Father and Friends. Allen Ginsberg. TaR

I climbed the Taihang mountain. Sikong Tu. CCL1 *Fr.* Twenty-Four Modes of Poetry.

I climbed these crags to build a secluded cabin. All Around My New House at Stone Gate. Hsieh Ling-yün. CCL1, *tr. by* John Frodsham

I climbed through woods in the hour-before-dawn dark. Horses, The. Ted Hughes. BeAl; NAMCP V.2; NoAM; WaAnP

I cling to the funk. Funk. Mary Weems. SpirFl

I cling to this crippled tree. Rivers, The. Giuseppe Ungaretti. PFTM-1

I close my door and trace the transformations of nature. Chang Chiu-ling. ColAnChi *Fr.* Poems of Reflection on the Vicissitudes of Life.

I close my eye on its red haze. I Can Talk to Them. Hoda Hussein. AnVo, *tr. by* Mohamed Enani

I close my eyes. 49th Birthday Trip (What Are You On?). Samuel Menashe. P180

I close my eyes. Self in Variation, The: Scenes From Meditation. Harvena Richter. ICANM

I close my eyes, and think of water. (LL) Trying to Pray. James Wright. BBASP; WaAnP

I close my eyes; waves blow against the pillow. Moored for the Night at the Lan-chi Riverside Courier Station. Yang Wan-li. GifTon, *tr. by* Paul Hansen

I close the book on *Crime and Punishment*. Crime and Punishment. Paul Lake. RA

I closed my book to listen. Church Bells. Clara Ann Thompson. CBWP-2

I Closed My Eyes To-Day and Saw. William Force Stead. OBMV

I collected the ears in my apron. Ruth. Elizaveta Kuzmina-Karavayeva. ARWW, *tr. by* Catriona Kelly

I come. Wopko Jensma. TSAP

I come across from Mellstock while the moon wastes weaker. His Visitor. Thomas Hardy. HarvBoo

I come across your old letters. Not for Burning. Joyce Sutphen. PoDa

I come back to the geography of it. Charles Olson. NAMCP V.2 *Fr.* Maximus Poems, The.

I come down from the heights of the green hill in a state of suspicion and absence. In the Burning Wood. Nasri Hajjaj. Eno, *tr. by* Ibrahim Muhawi

I come from a family of businessmen, teachers, priests. Origins. Leonard Nolens. TuT, *tr. by* Michael O'Loughlin

I come from a long line hollowed out on a dry night. Blue Terrance, The. Terrance Hayes. LegDan

I come from alcohol. Genealogy. Joan Larkin. LaCa

I come from nothing; but from where. Song of Derivations, A. Alice Thompson Meynell. CABP

I come from shadows. Look. Song of Taking Leave. Emilio Prados. RaW, *tr. by* Robert Mezey

I come from the city of Boston. Boston. John Collins Bossidy. NBLV; OBCoV

I come home at all hours; all hours she receives. Street Life. Alan Jenkins. PML

I come home early, feel the pale house close. IVF. Kona Macphee. StAl

I come home in the evening. Nissim Ezekiel. OBCoV *Fr.* Songs for Nandu Bhende.

I come, I come! ye have called me long. Voice of Spring, The. Felicia Dorothea Hemans. RWP

I come, I said, to be useful and to entertain. Pleasure. Delmore Schwartz. OxBoAm

I come in from the canal. I don't know anything. Ignorant Lust After Knowledge, The. William Bronk. OxBoAm

I come in self-annihilation and the grandeur of inspiration. William Blake. NPBRoP *Fr.* Milton.

I come off a little bit ventilated. Wings. John Godfrey. PmAP

I come quietly. Tree Stillness. Karen L. Mitchell. GT

I come the rushing wind that shook the place. Promise, The. Jones Very. NCAP

I come to, knocking on the door of the cellar. Moonshine Sonata. John Tranter. KGB

I come to read them poems. In White America. Lucille Clifton. LTA

I come to represent the case. Annie Pengelly. Lorna Goodison. NAMCP V.2

I come to speak through your dead mouth. Pablo Neruda. PoCho *Fr.* Heights of Macchu Picchu, The.

I come to tell you that my son is dead. Prince, The. Edgar Bowers. InGu

I come to town de udder night. Daniel Decatur Emmett. TCAPo

I come to you. Prayer of a Woman in Charge of Berry Picking in Knights Inlet. *Unknown.* WPoS

I come to you / with the semen. Pregnant, I Come. Joseph Ceravolo. NYP2

I come upon it suddenly, alone. James Whitcomb Riley. CA *Fr.* Country Pathway, A.

I compare the awesome flight of Nungesser to the limitless work of Picasso. Painting. André Salmon. CuPo

I Concentrate on You. Cole Porter. ReLy

I concentrated my attention with careful subtlety to this end. (LL) Hysteria. T. S. Eliot. IJHIL; OxBEV

I concluded years ago. Plain Ole Brother Blues. Jarvis Q. DeBerry. BRtP

I confess. Banners of the Heart. Fawziyya Al-Sindi. PoArWo, *tr. by* Joseph T. Zeidan

I confess. Russell Leong. FTtHH *Fr.* Aerogrammes.

I confess I was walking towards [you]. Write like one walks. Juliana Spahr. IIR

I confess that I am not. Translation of Raimundo Luz, The: My Amusing Despair. Scott Cairns. UpMys

I consecrate to thee. (LL) Rose Aylmer. Walter Savage Landor. CABP; NAEL-6v2; NAEL-7v2; NOBRP; NoP-4; NoP-5; OBEV; OxAEP-2; TFi; WeW-3

I Consent That Everything Vanishes. Robert Marteau. YaTCFP, *tr. by* John Montague

I consider myself a poet but im not reading poetry as you see. Private Occasion in a Public Place, A. David Antin. PmAP

I Considered Myself. Youssri Hassaan. AnVo, *tr. by* Mohamed Enani

I consoled myself for not being able to describe. No Consolation. Norman Alexander MacCaig. HarvBoo

I consumed nights inside books. Readings. Armanda Guiducci. CItWP, *tr. by* Cinzia Sartini Blum and Lara Trubowitz

I converse with my uncle. Middle Age. Luis Omar Salinas. GeoHom

I cop a squat on a squared-off log. Ballplayer. Evie Schockley. P180

I cough a lot (sinus?) so I. Getting Up Ahead of Someone (Sun). Frank O'Hara. CAP-8

I could be a heart patient in my forties, waiting out winter. Bad Karma. Mary Crockett Hill. AmPoNex

I could be a hole. Where Spring Is. Steve Healey. LegDan

I could be stone. Man Wearing Bird. Denise Levertov. UpMys

I could be the waitress. On Not Flying to Hawaii. Alison Luterman. P180

I could become a great grinning host. Poem. Jack Kerouac. CLPP

I could do wid one o' dem boogie tonight. Antonette's Boogie. Kendel Hippolyte. WaCA

I could eat you. (LL) Dove-Love. Judith Wright. NAMCP V.2; NIL-7; NIP-4; NoAM

I could get up from this kitchen table, I think. Hayfork, The. Henry Taylor. PoDa

I could go seeking some secret part of nature, the bulbous tumor. Abomination. Mary Crockett Hill. AmPoNex

I could have a job, but am too lazy to choose it. Lazy Man's Song. Po Chü-i. CCL1; OBVE *tr. by* Arthur Waley

I could have been Lord Dacre or a balalaika-maker. Peter Norman. UV

I could have brought you. Just Like Eve. Magi Gibson. EdScPo

I Could Have Danced All Night. Alan Jay Lerner. ReLy

I could have said obscurely: Cast about. *Unknown.* PriapPo *Fr.* Priapus Poems, The.

I could have taught the actor a thing or two. For Gloucester on Being Newly Blind. Michelle LaBarre. IaFF

I could hear the music as I waited to be born. Aragon Ballroom, The. John Dickson. IllVoic

I could imagine a biblical presence. Parousia. John Burnside. NeBrP

I could just as easily be nine years old. Night Beach. Vic Coccimiglio. InvLad

I could lie down in all that blue. Dreaming Horse. Silvia Curbelo. TouFir

I could look even at God with grave forgiving eyes. (LL) Sanctuary, The. Sara Teasdale. APT-1; NAAPv.2

I could love thee till I die. Platonic Lady, The. John Wilmot, 2d Earl of Rochester. NOSC

I could never reach this place. Mennonite Funeral in the Shenandoah Valley. Jane Rohrer. ACAMVP

I could no deeper love. (LL) Song: "Love still has something of the sea." Sir Charles Sedley. OxAEP-1; OxBEV

I could not dig: I dared not rob. Rudyard Kipling. FaBoWar; NBLV; OPOU; PoWW; WoPoe *Fr.* Epitaphs of the War [1914–1918].

I could not look on Death, which being known. Rudyard Kipling. HarvBoo; InoFa; NPeEn; WoPoe *Fr.* Epitaphs of the War [1914–1918].

I could not see to see. (LL) I heard a Fly buzz—when I died. Emily Dickinson. APN-2; BrAP; ClHu; ColAP; HeIP-4; MoAmPo; NAAL-3; NAAL-5; NAAPv.1; NALW; NAMCP V.1; NAWM-7v2; NoAM; NoP-4; NoP-5; OxBoAm; PoPoPo; PtR; SAmP; SoSe-8; TCAPo; TFi; TRP; WaAnP; WeW-3

I could not swallow the lake. (LL) Swallow the Lake. Clarence Major. ESEAA; FTOS; GT; OxAAAP; PmAP

I could rather be rather be here. (LL) Gertrude Stein. NoP-4; NoP-5 *Fr.* Stanzas in Meditation.

I could resign that eye of blue. To Cloe. Martial. NBLV, *tr. by* Thomas Moore

I could say other things if I really wanted to wound. (LL) Henri Michaux. GPTC; MotU *Fr.* I Am Writing to You from a Far-Off Country.

I could see, far above my head, a black speck. Victor Hugo. SxFrPo, *tr. by* A. M. and E. H. Blackmore

I could see the black wings glistening on either side. Mythology of Heavenly Messengers, The. Rebecca Seiferle. ICANM

I could simply die, Priapus. *Unknown.* PriapPo *Fr.* Priapus Poems, The.

I could sit in this hot bath for hours. Meditation. Roberta Spear. PoCho

I could smell the river in. Sotère Torregian. AHA *Fr.* Golden Palomino Bites the Clock, The.

I could stop writing. Visions of Arthur. René Ricard. AHA

I could take the Harlem night. Juke Box Love Song. Langston Hughes. OxBoAm; SAmP

I could take you by the orchards. On the Way to the Sitter's. Gary Margolis. PfSP

I could tell. One Ran Before. Yvor Winters. CalPo

I could tell our chances were slim. Gone for some time. Martin Mooney. NIrP

I could use a dove in my heart. Arch of Sanctification, The. Bob Hicok. Vesp

I could wish to be dead! Tragic Mary Queen of Scots, II, The. Michael Field. OBMV

I couldn't do it again. Garden, The. Louise Glück. NoP-4; NoP-5

I couldn't have liked it more. (LL) I've Been to a Marvelous Party. Noël Coward. NBLV; ReLy

I couldn't stand still watching them forever. Chinaberry, The. Andrew Hudgins. CAP-8

I couldn't touch a stop and turn a screw. Thirty Bob a Week. John Davidson. CABP; NePenScot; NPeEn; OxBEV

I Counsel You Beware. A. E. Housman. StAl

I Count the Days Until I See You, Dear. Lesbia Harford. PoBW

I count the rays of the jellyfish. Mansion Beach. Elizabeth Spires. PoDa

I count your quick life by the minute, day, and year. Xenia: Stranger/Guest. David Gewanter. NAPBL

I Cover the Waterfront. Edward Heyman. ReLy

I crave an ampler, worthier sphere. Anno 1829. Heinrich Heine. OBVE, tr. by Charles Stuart Calverley

I crawl, I creep; my Christ, I come. Robert Herrick. CavPo

I crawled. Into a Dead Zone. Mati Katz. NRoS, tr. by Esther Raizen

I crawled out of the wreckage whistling. Witness. Rachel Wetzsteon. AmPoNex

I cremated Sam McGee! (LL) Cremation of Sam McGee, The. Robert W. Service. BRP; IFF; OBCoV; OBNV; TCAPo; WaAnP

I cried all night, my little shtetl. My Shtetl on the Dnestr. Ber Grin. Prolet, tr. by Amelia Glaser

I Cried for You. Arthur Freed. ReLy

I cried on my mother's breast, cried sore. Lament. Cathal Ó Searcaigh. ModIr, tr. by Seamus Heaney

I crisscrossed with Monk. Jazz Fan Looks Back. Jayne Cortez. ESEAA

I crossed. Thomas Bolt. YaYoPo Fr. Way Out of the Wood, The.

I crossed the deep sea. Unknown. WoPoe Fr. Egil's Saga.

I crouch over my radio. Speech. Henry Taylor. NBLV

I crouch over the bare. Bicycle Sprint. Pamela Alexander. ArBi

I crowd all earth into a traveller's eye. Shillong. Bernard Gutteridge. PoWW

I cry. Woman's Mourning Song, The. Bell Hooks. ISC

I cry I cry. No Categories! Stevie Smith. NoP-4; NoP-5

I cry, in the vernacular, this plain manifesto. Monologue for Selah Bringing Spring to Whylah Falls. George Elliott Clarke. OpeFie

I Cry Your Mercy, Pity, Love—Ay, Love! John Keats. CenSon
  (I Cry Your Mercy.) NPBRoP

I cupboard these pickled peaches in Time's despite. (LL) Homework. Mona Van Duyn. FFC; VCAP

I Curse in the Highest Sky. Violeta Parra. TANSG, tr. by Shaun Griffin and Emma Sepúlveda-Pulvirenti

I curse in the highest sky. I Curse in the Highest Sky. Violeta Parra. TANSG, tr. by Shaun Griffin and Emma Sepúlveda-Pulvirenti

I curse the optimistic views of Haig. Scribbled at a Cabinet Meeting. Sir Edward Carlson. FaBoVe

I cut the deck. Valentine for Ben Franklin Who Drives a Truck in California, A. Diane Wakoski. NoAM

I damn such fools!—Go, go you're bit. (LL) Day of Judgement, The. Jonathan Swift. ChIV-1; NPeEn; OBSV; OxBEV

I dance amid the miracles. Partial. Louis Aragon. YaTCFP, tr. by Mary Ann Caws

I dance on all the mountains. Gary Snyder. GeoHom Fr. Myths and Texts.

I danced on "Shop Around." Boppin' Is Safer Than Grindin'. Thulani Davis. GT

I Danced with You Once Only Onliest One. Ivan Arguelles. ASA

I dare not ask a kiss[e]. To Electra. Robert Herrick. OBEV

I daren't inscribe my name. (LL) Throwing Out My Father's Dictionary. Moniza Alvi. MoWP; Prnts

I dashed around on a Dragon-Steed. Dragon-Steed, The. Sándor Weöres. IQMS, tr. by Adam Makkai and Donald E. Morse

I daydream, melancholy at the windowsill. Remembering. Yüan Chên. CrYelRi; ErotSp, tr. by Sam Hamill

I didn't know what estrangement. In Emily's Manner. Armanda Guiducci. CItWP, tr. by Cinzia Sartini Blum and Lara Trubowitz

I Decide Not to Have Children. Marilyn Nelson. InoFa

I decide to do it free, without a rope or net. Climbing My Grandfather. Andrew Waterhouse. BeAl

I decided to stop. Eros in His Striped Shirt. Beckian Fritz Goldberg. PfS

I declare myself. Nu-plastik Fanfare Red. Judith Rodriguez. BMAP

I declared, and immediately rejected this. For instance. What Was There to Bring Me to Delight But to Love and Be Loved? Paisley Rekdal. LegDan

I decorated the house. Why Didn't They Apologize. . .? Buland Al-Haidari. IrPoTo, tr. by Hussein Kadhim and Christopher Merrill

I defended Genet on the subject of terror in London. Edoardo Sanguineti. ItPo Fr. Reisebilder.

I defy you Wallace Stevens. I Defy You. Shirley Lim. UnSA

I delve deep into the place distrusting, my touch clumsy—as if I were detaching my spine. Place, The. Mónica Nepote. SPV, tr. by Jen Hofer

I demand that the human race. Poem. Jack Kerouac. CLPP

I depend on the stars. For Sleep. Larry Eigner. FTOS

I derive endless satisfaction from thinking, saying, and singing the follow. Of of Titmouse. Michael Portnoy. HeMarv

I descend into the whiteness of this hand, this table. Descent. David Huerta. RMCMP, tr. by Mark Schafer

I descend on my love. How God Comes to the Soul. Mechthild von Magdeburg. WPoS, tr. by Oliver Davies

I Despair Because I Don't Have Words. Patrizia Valduga. CItWP, tr. by Cinzia Sartini Blum and Lara Trubowitz

I detest innocent women. Thoughts on Innocence. Olga Nolla. TANSG, tr. by Paula Vega

I did but look and love awhile. Enchantment, The. Thomas Otway. OBEV

I Did But Prompt the Age. John Milton. See On the Detraction Which Followed upon My Writing Certain Treatises.

I did but prompt the age to quit their [or thir] clogs. On the Detraction Which Followed upon My Writing Certain Treatises. John Milton. NoP-4

I did expect a ring. (LL) Hope. George Herbert. ChIV-2; NPeEn; OxBEV; WeW-3

I did it. Viking. Brett Rutherford. OtW

I did it. I killed my mother tongue. Poet's Confession, A. Gwyneth Lewis. BeAl

I did not choose Arabia; it chose me. The shabby money. Gwendolyn MacEwen. StAl Fr. T. E. Lawrence Poems, The.

I did not climb the apple trees in Sussex. Apple Trees in Sussex, The. Samuel Allen. FuFl

I did not fall from the sky. Women of Dan Dance with Swords in Their Hands to Mark the Time When They Were Warriors, The. Audre Lorde. MoWP; NALW; NoAM

I did not imagine being bald. Chemotherapy. Julia Darling. BeAl

I did not know death was so strange. (LL) Child Dying, The. Edwin Muir. PoWW; WoPoe

I did not live until this time. To My Excellent Lucasia, On Our Friendship. Katherine Philips. BASC; LW; NALW; NoP-4; NoP-5; NOSC; NPeEn; OxBEV; PBRV; PEW; PoBW

I did not love him for myself alone. Trinity. Michael Field. VWP

I did not love you anymore, yet I never stopped. Sadistic Love. Julio Herrera y Reissig. BLPSL, tr. by Rene de Costa, Rigas Kappatos and Eleni Paidoussi

I Did Not Manage To Save. Jerzy Ficowski. HP; PoSu, tr. by Keith Bosley and Krystyna Wandycz Bosley

I did not see Lannes at Ratisbon. Heroes. Sorley MacLean. FaBoTC; FaBoWar

I did not stand at the altar, I stood. Wedding Vow, The. Sharon Olds. MPUn

I did not think that I should find them there. Clerks, The. Edwin Arlington Robinson. APN-2; MoAmPo

I did not touch your night, or your air, or dawn. Pablo Neruda. TCLAP, tr. by Stephen Tapscott

I did not want to kiss the famous writer. Woman in the Red House. Michael Burkard. LaCa

I didn't come out my mummy's tummy. What Jenny Knows. Jackie Kay. NOxBChV

I didn't die. Dateline Hyderabad. Ajanta. HotL, tr. by V. Narayana Rao

I didn't get much sleep last night. Underwear. Lawrence Ferlinghetti. EmeKit

I didn't have anything to think about. (LL) Kenneth Rexroth. APSN; APT-2; NAMCP V.1 Fr. Love Poems of Marichiko, The.

I didn't have this face then. Portrait. Cecília Meireles. TCLAP, tr. by Luiz Fernández García

I didn't just read the Bible, I lived it. Charisma. Ai. ExTi

I Didn't Know About You. Bob Russell. ReLy

I didn't know him. Suicide on Pentwyn Bridge. Gillian Clarke. AngWePo

I didn't know how to save you then. Song to Myself at Seventeen. Gerard Wozek. BeDoSh

I didn't know I was grateful. Home. Bruce Weigl. AmAlph

I didn't know my own face. On a Portrait of the Poet. Po Chü-i. CrYelRi, tr. by Sam Hamill

I Didn't Know What Time It Was. Lorenz Hart. ReLy

I didn't know whether from Phoenician sands. Glass, The. Esther Ettinger. DTA, tr. by Mariana Barr

I didn't let the blue ship run aground a wreck. Noah. Margit Szécsi. IQMS, tr. by Agnes Arany-Makkai

I didn't listen to one stone this year. Bitter Thoughts. Gerald Stern. PfSP

I didn't think about the house much. Honeysuckle. J. C. Bloem. TuT, tr. by Desmond Egan

I didn't think there was room in the world for yet. Elinor White Frost Speaks. N. M. Brewka. VisFro

I didn't want this, not. Marina Ivanovna Tsvetaeva. OBVE Fr. Poem of the End.

I didn't want to be. High School. Toi Derricotte. BtF

I die I die the Mother said. Grey Monk, The. William Blake. PtR

I Die of Thirst While at the Fountain Side.   François Villon.   WoPoe, tr. by David Curzon and Jeffrey Fiskin

I died & went to Hell & it was nothing like L.A.   Hell.   Steve Kowit.   CalPo; SUP

I died for Beauty—but was scarce.   Emily Dickinson.   APN-2; BrAP; MakPoe; MoAmPo; NAAL-3; NAAL-5; NAAPv.1; NAWM-7v2; OxBoAm; SAmP

I died with [or at] the first blow and was buried.   Autobiography.   Dan Pagis.   PoSu

  (I died with the first blow and was buried.)   AF; VCWP

I died with the first blow and was buried.   Autobiography.   Dan Pagis.   FIT, tr. by Robert Friend

I dig into your city; piece together your shattered pottery of desire.   Me As an Archaeologist.   John MacKenzie.   Coast

I dig my teeth into the crust of this land.   Leave in Mid-Winter.   John Short.   FaBoWar

I dip a brush in tar.   Resurrections of Layla Al-Attar, The.   Jawad Yaqoob.   IrPoTo, tr. by Chuck Miller and Saadi A. Simawe

I discover I have nothing to hide.   Criminal Justice System.   Rebecca Wolff.   RWB

I discover in every equation an error.   Crumbled Paper for Future Poems.   Fawzi Karim.   IrPoTo, tr. by Chuck Miller and Saadi A. Simawe

I discovered the evidence.   Crazy Horse Speaks.   Sherman Alexie.   UnSA

I discovered the sweet lovely lady.   Albrecht von Johannsdorf.   GePo

I discuss with my heart.   Song Sun.   CATKP, tr. by Peter H. Lee

I disgraced myself in my lover's eyes.   Unknown.   SLW, tr. by Marjolijn De Jager, Sayd Bahodin Majrouh and André Velter

I dismount and ask, "Anybody home?"   Mountain Folk.   Kim Ch'anghyŏp.   CATKP, tr. by Peter H. Lee

I dismount from my horse and I offer you wine.   At Parting.   Wang Wei.   CCL1, tr. by Witter Bynner

I do confess thou'rt smooth and fair.   To His Forsaken Mistress.   Sir Robert Aytoun.   OBEV

I do direct the night.   Portrait of Myself with Arshile Gorky and Gertrude Stein.   Jerome Rothenberg.   FTOS

I do errands early.   Siesta.   Leslie Anne McIlroy.   AmPoNex

I Do Like To Be Beside the Seaside.   Dame Edith Sitwell.   PFTM-1 Fr. Façade.

I do my best to smile at spring, small flowers.   White Days.   Reginald Shepherd.   GT

I Do Not.   Michael Palmer.   BodElec; CAP-8; NoP-5; OxBoAm; WoBe

I do not ask, O Lord, that life may be.   Adelaide Anne Procter.   SacPr

I Do Not Believe That David Killed Goliath.   Charles Reznikoff.   ChIV-1

I do not belong here.   Belonging.   Jay Parini.   PfSP

I do not call it his sign.   Mahadevi.   WoPoe; WPoS, tr. by Jane Hirshfield

I do not care; some day I shall not think; I shall not be.   (LL)   Quiet House, The.   Charlotte Mew.   HarvBoo; NALW; NPeEn

I do not catch these subtle shades of feeling.   Wife of All Ages, The.   Edith Nesbit.   VWP

I do not complain of suffering for Love.   Knowing Love in Herself.   Hadewijch.   WPoS, tr. by Oliver Davies

I do not count the hours I spend.   Waldeinsamkeit.   Ralph Waldo Emerson.   APN-1

I do not do nature.   Manifesto.   Peter E. Murphy.   UrbNat

I do not doubt you would have liked.   Mother's Day.   Daisy Zamora.   LoL, tr. by Margaret Randall

I do not feel this suffering as César Vallejo.   I Am Going to Talk About Hope.   César Vallejo.   TCLAP; WED, tr. by Robert Bly

I do not have a body.   Bill Herbert.   NewEx

I do not hold a mirage in my hand—.   What's Not in the Heart.   Abba Kovner.   AF, tr. by Shirley Kaufman

I do not know.   (LL)   Echoes.   Audre Lorde.   NoP-4; NoP-5

I do not know.   Anne Ranasinghe.   HP

I do not know English.   I Do Not.   Michael Palmer.   BodElec; CAP-8; NoP-5; OxBoAm; WoBe

I do not know if, climbing some steep hill.   Opportunity.   Helen Hunt Jackson.   SWaP

I do not know if the color of the day.   Poem of Attrition, A.   Etheridge Knight.   GT; OxAAAP

I Do Not Know It for Sure.   Jaime Sabines.   TCLAP, tr. by Isabel Bize

I do not know it for sure, but I suppose.   I Do Not Know It for Sure.   Jaime Sabines.   TCLAP, tr. by Isabel Bize

I do not know more than the Sea tells me.   Achilles' Song.   Robert Duncan.   FTOS

I do not know much about gods; but I think that the river.   T. S. Eliot.   NoP-4 Fr. Four Quartets.

I do not know the date.   Letter from Santa Cruz.   Maura Eichner.   UpMys

I do not know the power of my hand.   When I Know the Power of my Black Hand.   Lance Jeffers.   ISC

I do not know what has destroyed you.   Destruction.   Shakuntala Hawoldar.   CFP; HAWP

I do not know what promise it makes to him.   (LL)   Birth of Love.   Robert Penn Warren.   APT-2; VCAP

I do not know where I have been.   Hell, well, heaven.   Mongane Wally Serote.   TSAP

I do not know which god sent me.   Kofi Awoonor.   VCWP Fr. Night of My Blood (1971).

I do not know whose woods those are. I do not care.   David Waltner-Toews.   IFF Fr. Coming Up for Air.

I do not know your name, I have never seen.   Lyrical Letter to the Other Woman.   Alfonsina Storni.   TCLAP, tr. by Dana Stangel

I do not like my state of mind.   Symptom Recital.   Dorothy Parker.   APT-1

I do not like the circus.   Yevgeny Mikhailovich Vinokurov.   TCRusP, tr. by Anthony Rudolf

I do not like the way you slide.   Egg Thoughts.   Russell Hoban.   NTCP

I do not live in the depthless cool.   Turning of the Year, The.   Delaina Thomas.   OpBo

I do not love my country. Its abstract splendour.   High Treason.   José Emilio Pacheco.   TCLAP, tr. by Alastair Reid

I do not love [or like] thee, Doctor Fell.   Doctor Fell.   Martial.   NBLV; OBCoV; OBVE; OxBEV, tr. by Thomas Brown

I Do Not Love Thee.   Caroline Elizabeth Norton.   OBEV

I do not love thee, Doctor Fell.   (LL)   Doctor Fell.   Martial.   NBLV; OBCoV; OBVE; OxBEV, tr. by Thomas Brown

I do not love thee, Dr. Fell.   Truth at Last, The.   Fred Chappell.   WoPoe

I do not love thee!—no! I do not love thee!   I Do Not Love Thee.   Caroline Elizabeth Norton.   OBEV

I do not love you as I loved.   Dechtire.   Thomas MacGreevy.   IrLP

I do not love you as if you were salt-rose, or topaz.   Pablo Neruda.   BeAl Fr. 100 Love Sonnets.

I do not mean to speak harshly of her.   Song of a Foolish Wife.   Unknown.   CATKP, tr. by Carolyn So

I do not mind the embrace.   55.   Taban lo Liyong.   PML

I do not need thy food, but thou dost mine.   My Meat and Drink.   Jones Very.   InvLi

I do not suffer this pain as Vallejo.   I Am Going to Speak of Hope.   César Vallejo.   PoetW, tr. by Clayton Eshleman

I do not think of thee—I am too near thee.   (LL)   Elizabeth Barrett Browning.   CenSon; PEW Fr. Sonnets from the Portuguese.

I do not think of you lying in the wet clay.   In Memory of My Mother.   Patrick Kavanagh.   NAMCP V.1; NoAM; RaBo

I do not think that skies and meadows are.   Reciprocity.   John Drinkwater.   PoA 2002

I do not think the ending can be right.   But That Is Another Story.   Donald Justice.   NoP-4; OxBoAm

I do not think you will.   Challenge to the Reader, A.   Tad Richards.   SwNoth

I do not travel with Joad eyes.   To California Where Rhymes Fail.   Margaret Rozga.   RWB

I do not trust math.   For my 27th birthday: a poem longer than 10 lines in which pronouns appear.   Giovanni Singleton.   BtF

I do not understand.   In the Synagogue.   Cynthia Ozick.   TaR

I do not understand the world, Father.   On the Subject of Poetry.   W. S. Merwin.   TAPaP

I do not visit his grave. He is not there.   Peachstone.   Dannie Abse.   AngWePo; WeW-3

I do not want a plain box, I want a sarcophagus.   Last Words.   Sylvia Plath.   BrAP

I Do Not Want the Ceiling of the Sistine Chapel.   Felicity Napier.   Prnts

I do not want to be a border-guard, said the border-guard.   Lamentation of the Border-Guard.   Gali-Danah Zinger.   CRWP, tr. by the author and Ashraf Noor

I do not want to be reflective any more.   Wolves.   Louis MacNeice.   NoAM

I do not want to belabor invisibility.   Summer after Last, The.   Michael Burkard.   LaCa

I do not waste what is wild.   Empty Kettle.   Louis Oliver.   HATNAP; NAAPv.2

I do not wear white as a general rule.   Trousseau.   Vona Groarke.   MFPA

I do not weep over this hooted blood.   Refusal to Inter.   Mohammed Khaïr-Eddine.   PFTM-2, tr. by Pierre Joris

I do not wish, in spite of all.   Fabio Morabito.   RMCMP, tr. by Geoff Hargreaves

I do not wish that anyone were here.   Postcard from a Travel Snob.   Sophie Hannah.   MFPA

I do not witness myself.   Fifth Amendment, The.   Susan Hahn.   ExTi

I do remember some things.   Manna.   James Tate.   GM

I do something consciously.   Jackson Mac Low.   PmAP Fr. Pronouns, The—A Collection of 40 Dances—For the Dancers.

I do the hole hole.   Stripping Leaves from Sugarcane.   Hawaiian Oral Tradition.   NAAPv.1

I do want to be a famous poet. Fourth Rome, The. Nikolai Alekseievich Klyuyev. CAGL, *tr.* by Simon Karlinsky

I dock the dead, the damaged and diseased. Pruning. Jim Wilson. EdScPo

I done been 'roun' to evvy spot. Belle Layotte. George Washington Cable. APN-2

I done try go to church, I done go for court. One Wife for One Man. Frank Aig-Imoukhuede. PML

I don't always go alone to the bottom of my self. Poet, A. Jules Supervielle. YaTCFP, *tr.* by Patricia Terry

I don't ask to be forgiven. How Stars Start. Al Young. ESEAA

I don't believe in anything. California Dreaming. Rochelle Nameroff. SwNoth

I don't believe in ashes; some of the others do. Veteran. Fanny Howe. OxBoAm

I don't believe in God but gravity. Theology. Richard Newman. Vesp

I don't believe the sleepers in this house. Cabin in the Clearing, A. Robert Frost. APT-1

I don't blow the trumpet or step up to the speaker's platform. Revolution. Enrique Lihn. TCLAP, *tr.* by Jonathan Cohen

I don't care for this artificial layer any more. Mei-Mei Berssenbrugge. AWPTFC *Fr.* Kali.

I don't care if there's powder on my nose. It Never Entered My Mind. Lorenz Hart. ReLy

I don't care what the weatherman says. Jeepers Creepers. Johnny Mercer. ReLy

I don't care who. I Gotta Right to Sing the Blues. Ted Koehler. ReLy

I don't dare start thinking in the morning. Blues at Dawn. Langston Hughes. SAmP

I don't even know. Saigyō. WoPoe, *tr.* by Steven D. Carter

I don't expect to touch heaven. Sappho. SaLy, *tr.* by Diane Rayor

I don't feel at home where I am. Regina Derieva. CRWP, *tr.* by Alan Shaw

I don't feel like reading another book. Yang Wan-li. ColAnChi *Fr.* Songs of Depression.

I don't feel weary and noways tired. I Don't Feel Weary. *Unknown.* SSUS

I don't for example consider that poets are. Iain Sinclair. Oth *Fr.* Ebbing of Kraft, The.

I don't get. Untitled. Christopher Nickelson. BtF

I don't give a damn. Croon. Langston Hughes. PFTM-1

I don't give a damn if some Thracian ape strut. Archilochus. WoPoe, *tr.* by Stuart Silverman

I don't give a duck. (LL) Poem in Time of Winter. Ray Mathew. NOBAu; OBCoV

I don't go out. Reply to Reizan Osho. Muso Soseki. EaWin, *tr.* by W. S. Merwin

I don't have any medals. I feel their lack. James Harrison. BodElec *Fr.* Letters to Yesenin.

I don't have any seed to cast about the world. Patrizia Cavalli. ItPo, *tr.* by Gayle Ridinger

I don't have golden hair to toss around. Not Ophelia. Allison Joseph. IaFF

I don't have to live large to know I'm in charge. I'm the Man. Lindamichellebaron. BRtP

I don't imagine I'll manage to express Sunyata. I Fail as a Dharma Teacher. Diane Di Prima. BB; WhBo

I don't kiss the guy who guzzles wine beside the brimming bowl and talks battles and tearful war. Elegy 2. Anacreon. CAGL, *tr.* by Peter Bing and Rip Cohen

I don't know. Basho. EH, *tr.* by Robert Hass

I don't know. After Seeing Paintings in a Small Book by T. C. Cannon (1946-1978). Alice Sadongei. HATNAP

I don't know anymore the night terrible anonymity of death. Sun the First. Odysseus Elytis. GifTon, *tr.* by Olga Broumas

I don't know anything about God but what the human record tells. Even on Sunday. Robin Blaser. FTOS

I don't know as I get what D. H. Lawrence is driving at. Poem. Frank O'Hara. CAP-8

I don't Know Enough About You. Peggy Lee. ReLy

I don't Know Exactly. Eva Svankmajerová. SurWo, *tr.* by Katerina Pinosová

I don't know exactly how it started. You're Getting to Be a Habit with Me. Al Dubin. ReLy

I don't know how I lost my amulets. Nujoum Al-Ghanim. PoArWo *Fr.* Trespasses.

I don't know. I wonder how long this life of mine. I Don't Know. Daria Menicanti. CItWP, *tr.* by Cinzia Sartini Blum and Lara Trubowitz

I don't know if the old people will return one day. Legacies. Heberto Padilla. TCLAP, *tr.* by Andrew Hurley and Alastair Reid

I don't know just why. Summer Birds and Flowers (2). Margaret Gibson. AmZen

I don't know now if it was kindness—we do. Fresh Stain. Tess Gallagher. ExTi

I don't know politics but I know the names. Introduction. Kamala Das. NALW

I don't know somehow it seems sufficient. Gravelly Run. A. R. Ammons. EMP; LPSFW; NAMCP V.2; NoAM; PoA 2002; PoDa; VCAP

I Don't Know That Man. Jan Polkowski. AF, *tr.* by Michael March and Jaroslaw Anders

I don't know the Baltic marshes. And Never Did. Tedi López Mills. RMCMP, *tr.* by Esther Allen

I don't know what came first, poets or festivals. Meeting Ezra Pound. Miroslav Holub. MotU, *tr.* by Stuart Friebert and Dana Hábová

I don't know what day it is. Ship Without a Sail, A. Lorenz Hart. ReLy

I don't know what I should do—I'm of two minds. Sappho. SaLy, *tr.* by Diane Rayor

I don't know what it is. It's Raining in Love. Richard Brautigan. P180

I don't know what it was you gave my husband to eat. Horse butcher, The. Pierre McOrlan. MFP, *tr.* by Martin Sorrell

I don't know what the final buzzer means. Triple Overtime. Lucinda Roy. GT

I don't know what to do with his body. Nude on a Horsehair Sofa by the Sea. Matthea Harvey. IAoNAP

I don't know what to say to you, neighbor. Winter. Marie Ponsot. ExTi

I don't know what you think you're doing. To an Adolescent Weeping Willow. Marvin Bell. CAP-8

I don't know where my mother got him. Pittsburgh, 1948, The Music Teacher. Gerald William Barrax. PoDa

I don't know where the owls go when they leave this place, or if. Four Poems. Gary Young. GeoHom; PfSP *Fr.* Days.

I don't know where you come from. Letter to a Roving Poet. Amadou Lamine Sall. NAfrP

I don't know whether it's possible. Streetwalker Trying to Speak to Sojourner Truth, A. Elaine Maria Upton. BtF

I don't know who I am or was I know only my chaos. Eyes. Juan Gelman. TCLAP, *tr.* by Robert Marquez and Elinore Randall

I don't know who that man is. Pilate's Wife. Nina Kossman. GI

I Don't Know Why (I Just Do). Roy Turk. ReLy

I don't know why I'm so crazy. Why? Myra Cohn Livingston. CA

I don't know why it is. Cocked Finger, The. Stephen Dunn. AtGh

I don't know why the horned lizard wants to live. Justification of the Horned Lizard. Pattiann Rogers. SUP

I don't know your stories. This one here. Feud, The. Sydney Lea. RA

I don't like a tall general, swaggering. Archilochus. SaLy, *tr.* by Diane Rayor

I don't like foreign languages; I won't study them. Chiao-jan. CCL1, *tr.* by Stephen Owen

I don't like it here, I want to go back. Edge of the Roof, The. Jelaluddin Rumi. WED, *tr.* by Robert Bly

I don't like my teeth. I feel they are too small. They give the wrong impression. First Impression. Joe Wenderoth. NAPBL

I don't like poems about philosophy. Moore's Paradox. John Koethe. OxBoAm

I don't like this, being carried sideways. Sleeping Compartment. Norman Alexander MacCaig. EmeKit

I don't like to eat outside. (LL) Appeal to the Grammarians. Paul Violi. BAP-04; OxBoAm

I don't like weddings. Wedding in the Courthouse, The. Kathleen Norris. MPUn

I don't love flowers / I love women. Lilac by the Museum on St. Wenceslas Square, The. Vitězslav Nezval. AF, *tr.* by Ewald Osers

I don't mean the place where. Terra Incognita. Joyce Sutphen. RWB

I don't mean to make you cry. Monologue for an Onion. Suji Kwock Kim. LegDan

I don't mind dying. As Befits a Man. Langston Hughes. GoPo

I don't mind eels. Eel, The. Ogden Nash. NTCP

I don't mind taking a hike in the woods. Take a Hike. Jim Simmerman. PoA 2002

I don't need. Fire Ants. Joseph Somoza. ICANM

I don't need to know any more about death. White Crane. Dean Young. IllVoic

I don't need to see *Shane* to know. I Learned about Being Tough from a Stetson Ad. Adam Houle. RWB

I don't need to tell you what you've done. No Fairy Story. Kona Macphee. BeAl

I don't need your photograph. Very Thought of You, The. Ray Noble. ReLy

I don't recall his name. Contra, The. Sandra M. Castillo. TouFir

I don't remember. Ode to Walt Whitman. Pablo Neruda. ViWalt, *tr.* by Willis Barnstone

I don't remember being very, very good or horrid. But I do. "C" ing in Colors: Red. Safiya Henderson-Holmes. SpirFl

I don't Remember Christmas. Richard Maltby, Jr. ReLy

I don't remember him. Yevgeny Mikhailovich Vinokurov. TCRusP, *tr. by* Daniel Weissbort

I don't remember how it began. Singing Back the World. Dorianne Laux. P180

I don't remember seeing it at night. It would look like. Remembering the Pacific. Diane Wakoski. GeoHom

I don't remember the last time. Beggar's Song. A. Van Jordan. LegDan

I don't remember the name of the bar, at the end. Short history of vodka, A. Ronny Someck. IrPoTo, *tr. by* Vivian Eden

I don't remember train whistles. Narrative of the Life and Times of John Coltrane: Played by Himself, A. Michael S. Harper. SeSe

I don't remember where he was taking us. Chase, The. Richard Tayson. AmPoNex

I Don't See You, Yet I Know. Pedro Salinas. RaW, *tr. by* Donald Hall

I don't sell for nothing less. (LL) Lady in the Pink Mustang, The. Louise Erdrich. HATNAP; OPRER; ReTh

I don't / share my recipes with them. Only the Hand That Stirs Knows What's in the Pot. Luz Maria Umpierre. PueRic

I don't speak for myself. I Don't Speak. Eugène Guillevic. YaTCFP, *tr. by* Denise Levertov

I don't take your words. Words. Takahashi Shinkichi. WhBo

I don't think I could have done other than I did. (LL) Douglass, a Last Letter. Tim Seibles. MAAN; RD

I don't think it's been done, but it's been said. Curious Experiments. Pamela White Hadas. PfSP

I don't travel on planes. Unwinged Ones, The. Ogden Nash. OtW

I don't understand how Janis Joplin did it, how she made her voice. Penalty for Bigamy Is Two Wives, The. William Matthews. SwNoth

I don't understand the conflict of the winds. Alcaeus. SaLy, *tr. by* Diane Rayor

I don't understand why the stream. Enfield Falls. A. R. Ammons. LPSFW

I don't want a bag of bread. To Mani Leyb. Shifre Vays. Prolet, *tr. by* Amelia Glaser

I Don't Want Any More Visitors. Ingrid Jonker. HAWP, *tr. by* Ingrid Jonker

I Don't Want to be a Soldier. *Unknown.* PoWW *Fr.* Soldiers' Songs of the First World War.

I don't want to return a sad spirit. Luis Cernuda. CAGL, *tr. by* Rick Lipinski

I don't want to see you. Erosion. Claribel Alegría. TANSG, *tr. by* Darwin Flakoll

I don't Want to Walk Without You. Frank Loesser. ReLy

I don't wish you were. Never Land. Yusef Komunyakaa. ReTh

I don't wonder where you are anymore. Vespers. Louise Glück. HarvBoo

I don't write haiku. I'm no good at silence. Phantom Haiku/Silent Film. Jacqueline Osherow. ExTi

I don't yearn for their steep excursion. Ode for Orville and Wilbur Wright. David Moolten. OtW

I doubt not God is good, well-meaning, kind. Yet Do I Marvel. Countee Cullen. AmFaPo; APT-2; BrAP; InvLi; NAAL-5; NAAPv.2; NAMCP V.1; NIL-7; NoAM; NoP-5; SSLK; WaAnP

I drag a boat over the ocean. Lal Ded. WPoS

I drag my heavy heart. From the Heights. Li Shang-yin. CrYelRi, *tr. by* Sam Hamill

I drank at night on East Slope, sobered up, got drunk again. Tune: "Immortal by the River." Su Tung-p'o. ColAnChi, *tr. by* James Robert Hightower

I draw a window. Table in the Wilderness, A. Li-Young Lee. Vesp

I draw aside flowery bedside curtains. To the Tune: Sands of the Washing Stream. Li Ch'ing-chao. CrYelRi, *tr. by* Sam Hamill

I draw my sight in when I sleep. Evening Song. Elizabeth Madox Roberts. APT-1

I draw these letters. Writing. Octavio Paz. PoCho, *tr. by* Eliot Weinberger

I dreaded that first Robin, so. Emily Dickinson. APN-2; MoAmPo; NAAL-3; NAAL-5

I Dream. Valentine Penrose. SurWo, *tr. by* Roy Edwards

I dream a world where man. I Dream a World. Langston Hughes. OxAAAP

I dream all the time of women. If I Were a God. Osama El-Dinasouri. AnVo, *tr. by* Mohamed Enani

I Dream Awake. José Martí. TCLAP, *tr. by* Elinore Randall

I Dream I'm the Death of Orpheus. Adrienne Rich. NALW

I dream no ill of Death. (LL) Confession of Faith. Elinor Wylie. APT-1; MoAmPo

I dream of. Memory of a Dream From the Year 1963. Tadeusz Rózewicz. PoSu

I dream of a red-rose tree. Women and Roses. Robert Browning. NAEL-6v2

I dream of coupling. Dream of Pairing. Ntozake Shange. GT

I dream of dancing naked under stars. Surviving. Gail Tremblay. FiBr

I dream of Jeanie with the light brown hair. Jeanie with the Light Brown Hair. Stephen Collins Foster. APN-2

I dream of journeys repeatedly. Theodore Roethke. ColAP; NAMCP V.1; NoAM *Fr.* North American Sequence.

I Dream of St. Francis. Peter Orlovsky. BB

I dream of you. Maria Viviana Soto. ASA, *tr. by* Alfred Kroeber and Jacinta Gonzales

I dream of you to wake: would that I might. Christina Georgina Rossetti. OxBSo *Fr.* Monna Innominata.

I dream with open eyes. I Dream Awake. José Martí. TCLAP, *tr. by* Elinore Randall

I dream. Youth is beyond the rain she arrives. I Dream. Valentine Penrose. SurWo, *tr. by* Roy Edwards

I dream'd a morning dream—a torrent brought. Dream, A. Charles Tennyson Turner. OxBSo

I dream'd I lost a pearl, and so it prov'd. On the Death of My Dear Friend and Play-Fellow Mrs. E. D. Having Dream'd the Night Before I Heard Thereof That I Had Lost a Pearl. Jane Barker. EMWP; PoBW

I dream'd I walk'd, in raptures high. Thomas Baker. STuOW *Fr.* Steam Engine; or, The Power of the Flame, The.

I dream'd in a dream I saw a city invincible to the attacks of the whole of the rest of the earth. I Dream'd in a Dream. Walt Whitman. APN-1

I dream'd that, as I wander'd by the way. Question, The. Percy Bysshe Shelley. OBEV; OxBEV

I dream'd that I walk'd in Italy. Going Back Again. Edward Robert Bulwer-Lytton. VerBaPo

I dreamed a man unknown to me in a city no. 30th Year Dream. Gregory Corso. BodElec

I dreamed all my dreams. If I Had You. Jimmy Campbell and Reginald Connelly. ReLy

I dreamed, and saw a modern Hell, more dread. Pessimist's Vision, The. Constance Naden. ViWPN; VWP

I dreamed I dwelled in a homeless place. New Stanzas for *Amazing Grace*. Allen Ginsberg. WhBo

I dreamed I met you beside the wall. Heraldic Decoration. Julio Herrera y Reissig. TCLAP, *tr. by* Andrew Rosing

I Dreamed I Moved among the Elysian Fields. Edna St. Vincent Millay. NoP-4; NoP-5

I dreamed I stood upon a little hill. Two Loves. Lord Alfred Bruce Douglas. CAGL

I dreamed I was a dog in a dog show. Dog Show. Laurie Anderson. OxWW

I dreamed I was the spade. Spade. Dan Chiasson. PoCho

I dreamed it rose. Black Buoy. Robert H. Davis. HATNAP

I dreamed last night. Sit Down, You're Rockin' the Boat. Frank Loesser. ReLy

I dreamed last night. Journey Away, A. Carl Rakosi. PFTM-1

I dreamed my voice was an Anasazi pot. Song. Demetria Martinez. ICANM

I dreamed of him last night, I saw his face. Dead Poet, The. Lord Alfred Bruce Douglas. GSo

I dreamed of touching the world's grief. I Dreamed of Touching. Georges Bataille. YaTCFP, *tr. by* Rosemary Lloyd

I dreamed of war-heroes, of wounded war-heroes. Heroes, The. Louis Simpson. OBWP

I dreamed [*or* dream'd] this mortal part of mine. Vine, The. Robert Herrick. CavPo; EroLit; NAEL-6v1; NAEL-7v1; NoP-4; NoP-5

I dreamed Ted Williams. Dream of a Baseball Star. Gregory Corso. BB; PmAP

I dreamed that a score of us were sitting in a large room with open windows. Insect, The. Ivan Turgeniev. MotU, *tr. by* Isabel Florence Hapgood

I dreamed that you were standing. Heraldic Decoration. Julio Herrera y Reissig. BLPSL, *tr. by* Rene de Costa, Rigas Kappatos and Eleni Paidoussi

I dreamed the heavy sky suddenly opened a gate. Dream. Vahan Tekeyan. AF, *tr. by* Diana Der Hovanessian and Marzbed Margossian

I dreamed the nymph that o'er my fancy reigns. Sir William Alexander, Earl of Stirling. NOSC *Fr.* Aurora.

I dreamed there was a bird. Bird, The. Susan M. Whitmore. AmPoNex

I dreampt a dreame to night. William Shakespeare. OxBEV

I Dreamt a Dream. Arthur Hugh Clough. NAEL-6v2 *Fr.* Dipsychus [and the Spirit].

I dreamt a dream; till morning light. Arthur Hugh Clough. NAEL-6v2 *Fr.* Dipsychus [and the Spirit].

I Dreamt a Dream—What can it mean? William Blake. RACG *Fr.* Songs of Experience.

I Dreamt a Pig. Dacia Maraini. CItWP, *tr. by* Cinzia Sartini Blum and Lara Trubowitz

I dreamt ane dreame, o that my dreame wer trew! Dreame, Ane. Alexander Montgomerie. NePenScot

I dreamt I climbed to a high, high plain. Pitcher, The. Yüan Chên. CCL1, *tr. by* Arthur Waley

I dreamt I drank too much lemonade. Cruising. Gig Ryan. BMAP

I dreamt last night of you, John-John. John-John. Thomas Macdonagh. IrLP

I dreamt last night you. Week after Your Death, A. Robert Bly. NAMCP V.2

I dreamt of cooking roast pig. I Dreamt a Pig. Dacia Maraini. CItWP, *tr.* by Cinzia Sartini Blum and Lara Trubowitz

I Dreamt of Lasca. Jack E. Murphy. TiP2

I dreamt of the old house. To My Sister. Olga Fiodorovna Berggolts. TCRusP, *tr.* by Daniel Weissbort

I Dreamt of Visiting Relatives. Amelia Rosselli. CItWP, *tr.* by Cinzia Sartini Blum and Lara Trubowitz

I dreamt you stood upon the trap of the world. On the Death of Ronald Ryan. Bruce Dawe. BMAP

I dreamt your suicide note. Bag of Mice. Nick Flynn. AmPoNex; NAPBL

I Drift in the Wind. Ingrid Jonker. HAWP, *tr.* by Jack Cope

I drifted into sleep. Dermot Bolger. IrLP *Fr.* Lament for Arthur Cleary, The.

I drink but don't get drunk. Drunkenness. "Anvari." WoPoe, *tr.* by Geoffrey Squires

I drink champagne early in the morning. Cordon Negro. Essex Hemphill. CAGL

I Drink to the Asters of War. Osip Emilevich Mandelstam. TCRusP, *tr.* by John Glad

I drink to the asters of war, to everything for which I stand accused. I Drink to the Asters of War. Osip Emilevich Mandelstam. TCRusP, *tr.* by John Glad

I drink, wherever I go, to the charms. Gracey Nugent. Turlough Carolan. IrLP; OxBEV, *tr.* by Austin Clarke

I drive Eastward. The ethics of return. James Vincent Cunningham. APT-2

I drive fast, uphill. Coming Over Coldwater. Carol Muske-Dukes. GeoHom

I drive home with the books that I will read. Edgar Bowers. VCAP *Fr.* Autumn Road.

I drive my chariot up to the Eastern Gate. *Unknown.* CCL1,

I drive round the dirty streets of Freetown. Poet Among Those Who Are Also Poets. Syl Cheney-Coker. NAfrP

I drive toward distant clouds and my mother's dying. Not Swans. Susan Bartels Ludvigson. P180

I drive Westward. Tumble and loco weed. James Vincent Cunningham. APT-2; NoAM

I drop the torch of rags in a bucket of water. New Crops for a Free Man. Ai. BodElec

I dropp'd here three weeks ago, yes—I know. Mad Soldier, The. Edward Wyndham Tennant. FaBoWar

I dropped beside him. Taut as is the cord. Razglednica (4). Miklós Radnóti. IQMS, *tr.* by Iain MacLeod

I dropped my sail and dried my dropping seines. Mass at Dawn. Roy Campbell. OxAEP-2

I dropped something. I picked it up. Mariane Baggers Eriksen. WhBo

I drops in to see young Ben. Chorus of a Song That Might Have Been Written by Albert Chevalier. Max Beerbohm. OBCoV; UV

I drove all night from the red light. Homing Instinct. Mary Vanek. TiP2

I drove my chariot through the Northern Suburbs Gate. Driving My Chariot Through the Northern Suburbs Gate. Ruan Yu. CCL1, *tr.* by John Frodsham

I drove my father for lettuce on the day his wife. Small Purchase. Bob Hicok. AmAlph

I drove three thousand miles to ask a question. No answer, naturally. Karl Shapiro. BodElec *Fr.* Bourgeois Poet, The.

I drove today along the foothills. Los Angeles. James Harms. GeoHom

I drown in the drumming ploughland, I drag up. Hawk in the Rain, The. Ted Hughes. WaAnP

I du believe in Freedom's cause. James Russell Lowell. APN-1; NCAP *Fr.* Biglow Papers, The.

I dug, beneath the cypress shade. Grave of Love, The. Thomas Love Peacock. OxAEP-2

I dug you artless, I dug you out. Did you re-do? You dug me less, art. Music for Homemade Instruments. Harryette Mullen. AWPTFC; BAP-01

I dug your bull. Saturday Night Decades. Sterling Plumpp. IllVoic

I dwell alone—I dwell alone, alone. Autumn. Christina Georgina Rossetti. VWP

I dwell in Grace's court[e]. Content and Ri[t]ch[e]. Robert Southwell. ChIV-2; NoSic

I dwell in Possibility. Emily Dickinson. APN-2; HeIP-4; NAAPv.1; NALW; NAMCP V.1; NAWM-7v2; NCAP; NIL-7; NoAM; OxBoAm; TCAPo; WaAnP

I dwell in seclusion and observe the creative process. Ch'en Tzu-ang. ColAnChi *Fr.* Poems of Reflection on the Vicissitudes of Life.

I dwell in the forest nursing a long illness. Ch'en Tzu-ang. ColAnChi *Fr.* Poems of Reflection on the Vicissitudes of Life.

I dwell in this leaky Western castle. Dowager. John Montague. ModIr

I dwelt alone. Eulalie—A Song. Edgar Allan Poe. STuOW

I Dye Alive. Robert Southwell. SacPr

I.E. Claude Royet-Journoud. OnScMo, *tr.* by Keith Waldrop

I. EAST TEXAS. Travels in the South. Simon J. Ortiz. UnSA

I eat a persimmon. Masaoka Shiki. CAoMJL1, *tr.* by Burton Watson

I Eat Kids Yum Yum! Dennis Lee. TLR

I Eat Lunch with a Schizophrenic. Laurel Ann Bogen. SUP

I eat my peas with honey. Peas. *Unknown.* NTCP

I eat oatmeal for breakfast. Oatmeal. Galway Kinnell. EmeKit; FaoP; StAl

I eat steak and live on the big neon avenue and fear strangers. New Life, The. Lisa Jarnot. LegDan

I eat up, the hundred feelings vanish. Old, and a Fever. Po Chü-i. NDACCP, *tr.* by David Hinton

I eat with them at table. From the Viking Museum. John Peck. HarvBoo

I edged back against the night. High Tide. Jean Starr Untermeyer. MoAmPo

I emerge from you like your shadow. Shakti. Elsa Cross. RMCMP, *tr.* by Margaret Sayers Peden

I enjoy dancing. Clare Pollard. NeBl *Fr.* Friday Night at the End of a Millennium, A.

I enter Ruth Flowers' School of Cosmetology. Saturday before Easter, The. Beverlyjean Smith. PfS

I enter the orchard at nightfall. Snow in Condoland. Chase Twichell. PfSP

I enter this moment in retrospect, already. Narcissus Learning the Words to This Song. Reginald Shepherd. WiU

I enter through the open mirror. Memories of the Day I Gave Birth to a Daughter. Kim Hyesun. EcSo, *tr.* by Youngju Ryu

I entered it before I understood it. Spring at Nant Dywelan. Bobi Jones. OBWVE, *tr.* by Joseph P. Clancy

I entered my parlor one bright summer morn. Humming-Bird, The. Mary E. Tucker. CBWP-1

I entered the streetcar of poetry. Streetcar Named Poetry, A. Yevgeny Aleksandrovich Yevtushenko. RusPo, *tr.* by Robert Arthur Douglas Ford

I entered their space in appearance. now I need another device. Back. Alice Notley. Eno

I Entered Where I Did Not Know. San Juan de la Cruz. SpanPo, *tr.* by Willis Barnstone

I entered with a torch before me. Fleance. Michael Longley. PNI

I envied my wife her nightly visions. Fish. Moniza Alvi. NeBl

I envy. Issa. EH, *tr.* by Robert Hass

I envy not in any moods. Alfred Tennyson. BrAP; CABP; CAGL; NAEL-6v2; NAEL-7v2; NAWM-7v2 *Fr.* In Memoriam A. H. H.

I envy not the dead that rest. Mary Elizabeth Coleridge. VWP

I Envy the Cracked, Black Basalt. Katrina Porteous. NeBl

I envy those. Where we are. Gerald Locklin. GoPo

I envy you your chance of death. Fragment 68. "H. D." NAAPv.2; NAMCP V.1

I, Erica Jong, in the midst of my life. Testamant (Or, Homage to Walt Whitman). Erica Jong. ViWalt

I, E—S—J—, poet by vocation, now make my first will and. Owl of Minerva Takes Flight in the Evening, The. E. San Juan, Jr. ReBoTo

I escort. Praises of the Bantu Kings (1–10). Jerome Rothenberg. FTOS

I establish relations of familiarity. Personal Portrait, A. Guiguis Shoukry. AnVo, *tr.* by Mohamed Enani

I etch ephemeral sketches in flat, black water. Night Haul. Joe Denham. OpeFie

I even embrace the pain. (LL) Remembering. Yüan Chěn. CrYelRi; ErotSp, *tr.* by Sam Hamill

I even feel sure you will assist me again, Master of insight and beauty. (LL) John Berryman. InvLi; PLBUT *Fr.* Eleven Addresses to the Lord.

I / even I. Announcement, An. Sri Sri. HotL, *tr.* by V. Narayana Rao

I, even I, am he who knoweth the roads. De Aegypto. Ezra Pound. APT-1

I exchange eyes with the Mad Queen. Vision. Harry Crosby. APT-2

I exist as water stained with tea. Mary Rockwell, 1950. Juliana Baggott. RWB

I expand my heart so that. Dawn. Gabriela Mistral. TANSG, *tr.* by Maria Giachetti [*or* Jacketti] and Maria Jacketti

I expect every one. Wonderful Guy, A. Oscar Hammerstein, II. ReLy

I expect him any minute now although. Glimpse of Starlings, A. Brendan Kennelly. PoCu; StAl

I expect to be praised. Intermission from Wednesday. Pedro Juan Pietri. PueRic

I expected him to look dead in the casket. Elegy. Richard Hugo. GM

I Explain a Few Things. Pablo Neruda. PoetW, *tr.* by Nathaniel Tarn

I explain the silvered passing of a ship at night. Stephen Crane. APN-2; TCAPo

I explained the reason. I opened the mouth of words and the snuffling expressed the knife. House Poem. Laura Solórzano. SPV, *tr.* by Jen Hofer

I explore you, my flesh, my gold, my body, that I spy on you, my raw naked paper. Last Stroll, The: Homage to Pascoli. Edoardo Sanguineti. PFTM-2, *tr.* by Richard Collins

I explored the grounds with monks this evening. Visiting the Monastery at Lung-men. Tu Fu [*or* Du Fu]. CrYelRi, *tr.* by Sam Hamill

I Fail as a Dharma Teacher. Diane Di Prima. BB; WhBo

I fail to cut your hands. Matisse: Blue Nude, 1952. Dionisio D. Martinez. TouFir

I failed my exam, which is difficult. James Tate. EmeKit; OxBoAm *Fr.* I Am A Finn.

I fain would kiss my Julia's dainty leg. Robert Herrick. *See* Fain would I kiss my Julia's dainty leg.

I fain would know what she hath deserved. (LL) Sir Thomas Wyatt. *See* I would fain know[e] what she hath deserved.

I Fall in Love Too Easily. Sammy Cahn. ReLy

I fancied that I could paint. Hungry Belly Kill Daley. Lorna Goodison. NAMCP V.2

"I favor your enterprise," the soup ladle says. You Know What I'm Saying? Irving Feldman. BAP-97

I fear I shall. And the Birds Sing of Life. Stephen Caldwell Wright. BtF

I fear I shall begin to grow in love. Ben Jonson. NAEL-7v1; OxBEV *Fr.* Volpone.

I fear that appearances are worshipped throughout France. Rat and the Elephant, The. Jean de La Fontaine. OBVE, *tr. by* Marianne Moore

I fear the night, the ruthless night. Robber, The. Louis Untermeyer. STuOW

I fear thee, ancient Mariner! Samuel Taylor Coleridge. NPeEn *Fr.* Rime of the Ancient Mariner, The (1798 version).

I fear to love thee, Sweet, because. To Olivia. Francis Thompson. MoBrPo

I fear what I shall find. (LL) On a Return from Egypt. Keith Douglas. NoP-4; NoP-5

I fear[e] no Earthly Powers. On Himself[e]. Robert Herrick. CavPo

I fear[e] no more. (LL) Hymn[e] to God the Father, A. John Donne. BASC; FSCP; NAEL-6v1; NAEL-7v1; NoP-5; NOSC; NPeEn; OxBEV; SacPr; SoSe-8; TFi

I feared bacchantic rages in that house. Bronx Park. Richard Foerster. UrbNat

I feel a regret, Steve Biko. Music for Martyrs. Gwendolyn Brooks. OxAAAP

I feel a sudden urge to sing. It's De-Lovely. Cole Porter. ReLy

I feel alone, like a finger without a hand. Sunday. Antonio Deltoro. RMCMP, *tr. by* Christian Viveros-Fauné

I feel an apparition. Instant of Clearness. Jean Le Roy. OBVE, *tr. by* Wallace Stevens

I feel as if I ne'er could sing again! (LL) To Elizabeth Barrett Browning, in 1851. Dora Greenwell. PoBW; VWP

I feel groggy and weary and tragic. But Alive. Lee Adams. ReLy

I Feel I Am. John Clare. OxBSo

I feel I am alone tonight. City a Wrecked Ship, The. Amal Dunqul. NAfrP, *tr. by* Sharif Elmusa and Thomas G. Ezzy

I feel I should go to Norfolk Virginia and drink. Reality U.S.A. Mark Halliday. StAl

I feel it when the game is done. Footnote to Tennyson. Gerald Bullett. UV

I feel like a mango. Mango, A. Joyce Mansour. SurWo, *tr. by* Mary Beach

I feel like a stranger. Return to the Homeland. Adelina da Silva. NAfrP, *tr. by* Don Burness

I feel like dancin', baby. Sunday by the Combination. Langston Hughes. APT-2

I feel like I've buried somebody inside of me. Death Asphodel. Jean Valentine. ExTi

I feel like the Emperor Nero. Crazy Rhythm. Irving Caesar. ReLy

I feel like your umbilical cord. Umbilical Cord. Ellyn Maybe. AmPoNex

I feel my heart melt. Dusk. Gabriela Mistral. TANSG, *tr. by* Maria Giachetti [*or* Jacketti]

I feel my life added to theirs. (LL) Finding a Long Gray Hair. Jane Kenyon. ItP; LoL

I feel on my crossed arms the short. Metro Taxqueña. Carla Faesler Bremer. SPV, *tr. by* Jen Hofer

I feel raped by being robbed until. Monique. Cynthia Hogue. LiTh

I feel ridiculous. On Sale. Léon Damas. YaTCFP, *tr. by* Mary Ann Caws

I feel sick. Unspent. *Unknown.* SonAtl, *tr. by* Abdul Kalam Azad and Eric Howarth

I feel strongly about sanctity & wash. Wu Gambinos. Jeni Olin. FreRad

I feel that God is traveling. God. César Vallejo. WED, *tr. by* Robert Bly

I feel the coming glory of the Light. (LL) Credo: "I cannot find my way." Edwin Arlington Robinson. ITBLP; MoAmPo; OxBoAm

I Feel the Dead. Sophia De Mello Breyner. VCWP, *tr. by* Ruth Fainlight

I feel the dead in the cold of violets. I Feel the Dead. Sophia De Mello Breyner. VCWP, *tr. by* Ruth Fainlight

I feel the flames of hottest summer day. (LL) Sir Philip Sidney. NAEL-6v1; NAEL-7v1 *Fr.* Astrophil and Stella.

I feel the truth; so let the world surmise. (LL) George Meredith. NAEL-6v2; NoP-4; NoP-5 *Fr.* Modern Love.

I feel their absence and I burn. (LL) Warming Her Pearls. Carol Ann Duffy. BeAl; EdScPo; MakPoe; MoWP; NAMCP V.2; NeBrP; NePenScot; NoP-4; NoP-5; PoBW

I feel their entire histories ravish me. (LL) Winter: "Ten o'clock train to New York, The." Ruth Stone. InoFa; OxBoAm

I Feel Unattractive during Mating Season. Cindy Goff. LaCa

I feel unexpectedly. Fragrance. Kay Sage. SurWo

I feel warm. Jubilee. Sabah As-Sabah. InTrad

I feel within myself a life. Mother, The. Caroline Clive. VWP

I feel your legs touching. Lines. Afaa Michael Weaver. BtF

I fell. Makeda (Queen of Sheba). WPoS

I fell asleep, and had a dream. Unromantic Awakening, An. Priscilla Jane Thompson. CBWP-2

I fell beside him and his corpse turned over. Razglednica (4). Miklós Radnóti. IQMS, *tr. by* Zsuzsanna Ozsváth and Frederick Turner

I fell beside him. His body—which was taut. Razglednica (4). Miklós Radnóti. IQMS, *tr. by* Geroge Gömöri and Clive Wilmer

I fell in love with Demo of Paphos. No big surprise. Philodemus. HePo *Fr.* Epigrams.

I fell in the battle in Ashdod. Since Then. Yehuda Amichai. NRoS, *tr. by* Esther Raizen

I fell next to him. His body rolled over. Postcard (Found on His body after He Was Killed by the Nazis). Miklós Radnóti. RaBo, *tr. by* Stephen Berg, S. J. Marks and Steven Polgar

(Nine miles from here.) HP

I felt a Cleaving in my Mind. Emily Dickinson. APN-2

(I felt a cleavage in my mind.) TRP

I Felt a Funeral in My Brain. Emily Dickinson. APN-2; HeIP-4; NAAL-3; NAAPv.1; NALW; NAMCP V.1; NoP-4; NoP-5; OxBoAm; RaBo; SoSe-8; TCAPo; TFi

I felt awakening in me at night. Ivan Davidkov. CSCBP *Fr.* Clay and Star.

I felt no tremor and I caught no sounds. White Dust, The. Wilfrid Wilson Gibson. MoBrPo

I felt some folded paper in my pocket. Solo Palabras. Magdalena Gomez. PueRic

I felt the absence of perspective. Orphic Night. James Longenbach. NevBe

I felt the empty cabin wasn't abandoned. Living Alone. Richard Hugo. CAP-8

I felt / the foetus stir. L'Chayim. Carl Rakosi. NAAPv.2

I felt the lurch and halt of her heart. Lightning. D. H. Lawrence. MoBrPo

I felt the season changing in the yard today. Man and the Tree, The. Philip Mead. NOBAu

I fight and fight. / I wake up. Grow. Joseph Ceravolo. BodElec; NYP2

I fight in red for the same reasons. Why I Choose Red. Hugh MacDiarmid. RSaN

I fight—it's time, it's right—and am torn to pieces fighting. (LL) Kneeling Down to Look [*or* Peer] into a Culvert. Robert Bly. NAMCP V.2; NoAM

I fill my pockets with pine cones and empty them. Bowl with Pine Cones. Kinereth Gensler. PfS

I fill this cup to one made up. Health, A. Edward Coote Pinkney. APN-1

I fill'd [*or* filld] with woes the passing Wind. (LL) Crystal Cabinet, The. William Blake. NPBRoP; NPeEn

I finally finished the rough draft of my treatise. Pledge. Great Master Wonhyo. BecRai, *tr. by* Kim Daljin, Kim Won-Chung and Christopher Merrill

I Finally Managed to Speak to Her. Hal Sirowitz. P180

I find his feet. He is what is left of my life. (LL) "Dreadful Has Already Happened, The." Mark Strand. NoAM; VCAP

I find it difficult to not see the women. Women at the Pit-head, The. Bobi Jones. BBMWP, *tr. by* Joseph P. Clancy

I find it necessary to breathe the morning air, to smell the potatoes frying. Northern Sun, The. Sherwin Bitsui. LegDan

I find it scarcely. Fire After Fire, The. Ken Harris. AnSo

I find no fault in this just man. (LL) Eighth Air Force. Randall Jarrell. NAMCP V.2; NoAM; NoP-4; NoP-5; OBWP; PoWW; PWW2; TRP; VCAP; WaAnP

I find no peace and all my war[r] is done. Petrarch. OBVE *Fr.* Sonnets to Laura.

I find you in all these things of the world. I Find You. Rainer Maria Rilke. WED, *tr. by* Robert Bly

I Find You, Lord, All Things and In All. Rainer Maria Rilke. BBASP, *tr. by* Stephen Mitchell

I finde hou whilom ther was on. John Gower. NPeEn; OxBEV *Fr.* Confessio Amantis.

I fired the brush pile by the creek. Third Possibility, A. Wendell Berry. UpMys

I first discovered what was killing these men. Absalom. Muriel Rukeyser. NAMCP V.2

I first fell in love with Dena, and hey. Seduced and Abandoned. Radoi Ralin. CSCBP, *tr. by* Georgi Belev and Lisa Sapinkopf

I first learnt to swim at home in my father's study. Swim Right Up to Me. Katherine Pierpoint. MFPA

I first saw her in the zendo. For Carole. Gary Snyder. WANABP

I first tasted under Apollo's lips. Evadne. "H. D." LW

I fish for minnows in the lake. Epigram. Su Tung-p'o. NDACCP, *tr. by* Kenneth Rexroth

I fish until the clouds turn blue. Shifting Colors. Robert Lowell. BodElec

I fit storm windows, hammer odd. Protest Poem, A. David Wright. ACAMVP

I flash for megabucks. Diana Gittins. NewEx

I fled him, down the nights and down the days. Francis Thompson. EroLit; ITBLP; WaAnP *Fr.* Hound of Heaven, The.

I fled Him, down the nights and down the days. Hound of Heaven, The. Francis Thompson. CABP; ChIV-2; InvLi; MoBrPo; NAEL-6v2; NAEL-7v2; OBMV; SacPr; TFi

I flee the city, temples, and each place. Sonnet 17. Louise Labé. WoPoe, *tr. by* Willis Barnstone

I flew into New York. Milk. Eileen Myles. KGB

I flinched at the handshake of a woman in labour. Handshakes, The. Robert Crawford. NeBrP

I floated on a cloud one day. Cloud Fantasy. Henrietta Cordelia Ray. CBWP-3

I flourish between pleasure and pain. Michael Longley. NewEx

I fly a black kite on a long string. Dangerous Games. Carolyn Kizer. ASA

I fly the flag of the menstruating black dog. Dog, The. Stanley Moss. BodElec

I fly, to seek my lover, or my grave! (LL) Bids Farewell to Lesbos. Mary Robinson. CenSon; RWP

I folded myself and sent me to you. Long Distance. Laila Halaby. PoArWo

I follow her down the night, begging her not to depart. (LL) Aware. D. H. Lawrence. MoBrPo; NAMCP V.1; NoAM

I follow her into the front room. Bill Griffiths. Oth *Fr.* Building: The New London Hospital.

I follow my impulsive feet wherever they might go. Han-shan Te-ch'ing. CSKM, *tr. by* Red Pine

I follow my mother in from the car. In Chapel. John Pook. AngWePo

I follow quickly, I ascend to the nest in the fissure of the cliff. (LL) Walt Whitman. ColAP; SAmP; WaAnP *Fr.* Song of Myself.

I follow the gurgle to the fall *all fall*. Ghost of Me. Andy Young. AnSo

I Follow the Jinzhu Torrent. Hsieh Ling-yün. CCL1, *tr. by* John Frodsham

I follow the river, heron-seeking. Heron in the Alyn. Gladys Mary Coles. TCAWP

I followed and breathed in silence. God. Samuel Greenberg. APT-1

I followed deadpan rivers down and down. Drunken Boat. Arthur Rimbaud. SxFrPo, *tr. by* Martin Sorrell

I followed, o splendid season. Poem to Show the Trouble That Befell Him When He Was at Sea, A. Thomas Prys. OBWVE, *tr. by* Gwyn Williams

I followed the narrow cliffside trail half way up the mountain. Deer Lay Down Their Bones, The. Robinson Jeffers. APT-1; GPTC; NoAM

I followed the winding path. Cutting, A. Ou-yang Hsiu. CrYelRi, *tr. by* Sam Hamill

I followed this vision to Boston. (LL) Woolworth's. Donald Hall. ItP; OBCoV

I followed Whitman. Gerald Stern. ViWalt *Fr.* Hot Dog.

I Forgot for a Moment. Edna St. Vincent Millay. NAAL-5

I forgot for a moment France! I forgot England; I forgot my care. I Forgot for a Moment. Edna St. Vincent Millay. NAAL-5

I forgot I forgot the other heritage the other strain refrain. Other Heritage, The. Aurora Levins Morales. PueRic

I forgot to tell you about the red sheets my sister bought for us that were. Sign. Linda Smukler. WiU

I foster a Love fond of playing ball. It throws. Meleager. HePo

I found a ball of grass among the hay. Mouse's Nest. John Clare. NAEL-6v2; NAEL-7v2; NPeEn

I found a corpse, with golden hair. Edward Robert Bulwer-Lytton. VerBaPo *Fr.* Vampyre, The.

I found a dimpled spider, fat and white. Design. Robert Frost. APT-1; BrAP; ColAP; HeIP-4; NAAL-5; NAAP:n.2; NAMCP V.1; NIL-7; NoAM; NoP-4; NoP-5; OxBoAm; OxBSo; PoPoPo; RaBo; SAmP; SoSe-8; TFi; TRP; WaAnP

I found a fox, caught by the leg. Fellow Mortal, A. John Masefield. OxAEP-2

I found a golden seashell on the beach. Seashell, The. Rubén Darío. TCLAP, *tr. by* Lysander Kemp

I found a guidebook to the port he knew. Laws of Gravity. Paul Farley. BeAl

I found a lamb. Lamb. Kenneth Steven. EdScPo

I Found a Million Dollar Baby (In a Five and Ten Cent Store). Mort Dixon and Billy Rose. ReLy

I found a pigeon's skull on the machair. Perfect. Hugh MacDiarmid. NePenScot; NoP-4; OxBEV; WoPoe

I found a torrent falling in a glen. Torrent, The. Edwin Arlington Robinson. APN-2

I found a / weed. Reflective. A. R. Ammons. OxBoAm; VCAP

I found again in the heart of a friend. (LL) Arrow and the Song, The. Henry Wadsworth Longfellow. BRP; ColAP; TCAPo; UV

I found her deep in the forest. Enchanted Princess, An. Rosamund Marriott Watson. ViWPN

I found her in the shade of spring. Rose Wreaths, The. Friedrich Gottlieb Klopstock. GePo, *tr. by* J. W. Thomas

I Found Her Out There. Thomas Hardy. NAMCP V.1; NoAM; OxAEP-2

I found him in the guard-room at the Base. Lamentations. Siegfried Sassoon. OBSV; OxAEP-2

I found him stumbling about when the mother. Burying. Paul Ruffin. TiP2

I found his wool face, I went away. Reading Walt Whitman. Calvin Forbes. ESEAA; ViWalt

I found it in the woods, moss-mottled. Skull of a Snowshoe Hare, The. Robert Wrigley. RoV

I found it on a radiant day. I Found It. Fadwa Tuqan. BBASP; CFP, *tr. by* Patricia Alanah Byrne, Salma Khadra Jayyusi and Naomi Shihab Nye

I found my father. Cockfighter's Daughter, The. Ai. BeAl

I Found My Love by the Secret Canal. *Unknown.* WoPoe, *tr. by* John L. Foster

I found one word. Thérèse 'Awwad. PoArWo, *tr. by* Kamal Boullata

I Found Orpheus Levitating. Nick Carbó. NAPBL; ReBoTo

I found out why people murder. Why People Murder. Ellen Bass. RaF

I found the hummingbird. Sah Sin. Tess Gallagher. AmZen

I found the land above the river, where. In Memory of H. F. Peter Klappert. YaYoPo

I found the letter in a book I bought at an outdoor theatre turned flea market every weekend. Letter, The. Morton Marcus. GeoHom

I found the letter with old bills and papers in the drawer. Letter, The. Otto Orban. MotU, *tr. by* George Szirtes

I found the packets of seed in a cobwebbed drawer. Lost Seed. Patrick Williams. PNI

I found the words to every thought. Emily Dickinson. APN-2

I found them between far hills, by a frozen lake. God of Love, The. George MacBeth. EmeKit

I found this jawbone at the sea's edge. Relic. Ted Hughes. EMP; NAEL-6v2; NAEL-7v2; NoP-4

I found you on a rainy morning. Nansen. Gary Snyder. BB

I, from my chamber window, mark. Autumn Thoughts. Mary E. Tucker. CBWP-1

I from my window looked at early dawning. Bereft. Josephine D. Henderson Heard. CBWP-4

I funnel up. *Unknown.* SonAtl, *tr. by* K. Thosi

I gave birth to life. Maternity. Anna Swirszczynska [*or* Swir]. PoChi, *tr. by* Czeslaw Milosz and Leonard Nathan

I gave birth to two babies, aborted two, she grumbled for thirty-three years. Song of a Balloon in Search of Her Mom's Balloon. Yi Hyangji. EcSo, *tr. by* Catherine J. Kim

I gave chase. Evidence, The. Tom Leonard. Oth

I gave myself to Him—. Emily Dickinson. APN-2

I gave the surge of myself to the dawn. Alejandra Pizarnik. TANSG *Fr.* Tree of Diana.

I gave to Hope a watch of mine: but he. Hope. George Herbert. ChIV-2; NPeEn; OxBEV; WeW-3

I gave you wings. Black stone, blue heave shall take. Captive. Theognis. WoPoe, *tr. by* Richmond Lattimore

I Gaze across the Distant Hills. William Williams. OBWVE, *tr. by* H. Idris Bell

I gaze at you. Tattooed Man, The. Robert Earl Hayden. NoAM

I gaze at you in your portrait. Ice. Mónica Nepote. SPV, *tr. by* Jen Hofer

I gaze over the landscape, clouded and dark. Shepherd's Wife's Farewell to the Old Pasture, The. István Sinka. IQMS, *tr. by* Gavin Ewart

I gaze through a telescope at the Orion Nebula. Before Completion. Arthur Sze. ICANM

I Gaze upon My Country's Walls. Francisco de Quevedo y Villegas. SpanPo, *tr. by* Kate Flores

I gaze upon the roast. Pot Roast. Mark Strand. AmFaPo

I gazed upon thy face—and beating life. Beauty. Jones Very. SacPr

I genuinely wanted them to come. What Song the Syrens Sang. Eleanor Brown. MFPA

I Get a Kick Out of You. Cole Porter. APT-1

I Get Along Without You Very Well. Hoagy Carmichael. ReLy

I get her up on the curb, two wheels off the street. Changing the Oil. Eloise Klein Healy. WiU

I get my degree. Lawd, Dese Colored Chillum. Ruby C. Saunders. LTA

I get numb and go in. W. D. Snodgrass. CAP-8 *Fr.* Heart's Needle.

I get off my horse, offer you wine. Parting. Wang Wei. CCL1, *tr. by* Stephen Owen

I get off the bus ride. Getting Off the Ride. Mafika Pascal Gwala. TSAP

I get them in range and shoot. Photo Safari. Bruce Berger. PoCoUp

I get up. I am sick of. Chu Shu-chen. BLT,

I give my word on it. There is no way. Still and All. Burns Singer. HarvBoo

I give thee all, I can no more. Sum, A. Lewis Carroll. Spl

I give you a house of snow. Dove of New Snow, The. Vachel Lindsay. MoAmPo

I Give You Back. Joy Harjo. AmWaPo; HATNAP; LoL

I give you now Professor Twist. Purist, The. Ogden Nash. MoAmPo; NBLV

I Give You Thanks My God. Bernard Dadié. PoetW, *tr. by* Donatus Ibe Nwoga

I give you the end of a golden string. William Blake. Spl *Fr.* Jerusalem.

I give you the unhinged sleeve. If So, Tell Me [1999]. Barbara Guest. AWPTFC

I glance down at my shoe and—there's the lace! To Be Said Over and Over Again. György Petri. VCWP, *tr. by* Geroge Gömöri and Clive Wilmer

I go. Buson. ChAP; EH, *tr. by* Robert Hass

I go a road / among the upturned. In the Underworld. Muriel Rukeyser. APSN

I go along chanting the wayhouse poem. Inscribed on the Wall of Hsü Hsüan-Ping's Retreat. Li Po. WoPoe, *tr. by* Elling O. Eide

I Go Back to May 1937. Sharon Olds. BLT; EmeKit; FaoP; GoPo; LoL; MoWP; NIL-7; WaAnP

I go before, my darling. *Unknown.* NoSic

I Go, but Where? Oh Gods! Patrizia Cavalli. CItWP, *tr. by* Cinzia Sartini Blum and Lara Trubowitz

I go down step by step. Midnight Flowers. Eavan Boland. ModIr

I go for voting clean. (LL) Frances Ellen Watkins Harper. NAAPv.1; NALW *Fr.* Aunt Chloe.

I go. I go. I go. Ngungalari. Archie Weller. RACG

I go in under foliage. In Rain. Wendell Berry. LPSFW

I go North to cold, to home, to Kinnaird. Kinnaird Head. George Bruce. EdScPo

I go on dreaming. Antonio Machado Ruiz. BLPSL, *tr. by* Rene de Costa, Rigas Kappatos and Eleni Paidoussi

I go on in the dark, lit from within; does day exist? I Go on in the Dark, Lit from Within. Miguel Hernández. AF, *tr. by* Timothy Baland

I go out. Top of the World, The. Yves Bonnefoy. VCWP, *tr. by* John Naughton

I go out alone. Buson. SoOfWa, *tr. by* Sam Hamill

I go out / in search of a bathroom. Holy Child Descends, The. Gu Cheng. WoBe, *tr. by* Joseph R. Allen

I go out to find whatever comes. Slow. Marvin Bell. MoASP

I go see *The Bicycle Thief.* Bicycle Thief, The. Bill Berkson. AHA

I go separately. Santa Fe Trail. Barbara Guest. FTOS

I Go, the Wind Pushing Me Along. Fanny Beznos. SurWo, *tr. by* Myrna Bell Rochester

I go through hollyhocks. Las Trampas U.S.A. Charles Tomlinson. ICANM

I go through the wood in silence. Kit Wright. NewEx

I go to great troubles. Elders, The. Charles Simic. FTtHH

I go to say goodbye to the *cailleach.* John Montague. PBCIP *Fr.* Rough Field, The.

I go to sleep on one beach. Quiet Nights. Raymond Carver. EmeKit

I go to the mountain side. Choices. Tess Gallagher. AmZen

I go to the Turkish shop, buy a bun. Turkish Bakery, The. O Cham. CATKP, *tr. by* Peter H. Lee

I go to work. Workday. Linda Hogan. HATNAP

I go where I love and where I am loved. "H. D." APT-1; HarvBoo *Fr.* Flowering of the Rod, The.

I go, with your good grace, lords and kinsmen. Hartmann von Aue. GePo

I got a call from the White House, from the. Bounden Duty. James Tate. BAP-04; OxBoAm

I got a gal at the head of the creek. Cripple Creek. *Unknown.* APN-2

I got a one-eyed wife, a headless child. Guess Who. Fred Chappell. NBLV

I got an island in the Pacific. Occasional Man, An. Ralph Blane and Hugh Martin. ReLy

I Got Beat Up A Lot in High School. Christopher Murray. BeDoSh

I got caught staring out the window when the bells were ringing. Once When I Was in the Eighth Grade. Maurice Kilwein Guevara. AmPoNex

I got fucked and it wasn't no thang. Black Rape. Michelle T. Clinton. InTrad

I got hallelujah watermelons!—virginal pears!—virtuous corn! Haligonian Market Cry. George Elliott Clarke. Coast

I got home, very late, and parked the. Here, Home. John Powell Ward. TCAWP

I got in the shower. Trouble with Spain. Charles Bukowski. SUP

I Got It Bad and That Ain't Good. Paul Francis Webster. ReLy

I Got Lost in His Arms. Irving Berlin. ReLy

I got me dressed for going down. Country Fair. Fay M. Yauger. TiP2

I got me flowers to straw [*or* strew *or* strow] Thy [*or* the] way. Easter. George Herbert. OBEV; OxBEV

I got myself a military man. My Man o' War. Andy Razaf. ReLy

I got out of bed. Otherwise. Jane Kenyon. AmFaPo; BeAl; GoPo; LoL; OxBoAm; P180; PLBUT; PoCu; StAl

I Got Plenty o' Nuthin'. Ira Gershwin. ReLy

I Got Rhythm. Ira Gershwin. ReLy

I got so I could take his name. Emily Dickinson. APN-2

I got some news from Kailasa! Īśvarcandra Gupta. SinGod, *tr. by* Rachel Fell McDermott

I got stones in my passway. Stones in My Passway. Robert Johnson. APT-2

I got the horse right here. Fugue for Tinhorns. Frank Loesser. ReLy

I Got the Sun in the Morning. Irving Berlin. ReLy

I got to keep on dancing. Alvin Cash/Keep on Dancin'. David Henderson. GT

I got up early and faced the east. Early. Jean-Baptiste Tati-Loutard. WoPoe, *tr. by* Eric Sellin

I got up early Sunday morning. Who and Each. Ron Padgett. PmAP

I got up. My legs too. Was I here? Yes. In the Library. Hamutal Bar Yosef. DTA, *tr. by* Shirley Kaufman

I Gotta Right to Sing the Blues. Ted Koehler. ReLy

I grant you there is much excuse. Flowers of Rhetoric. Morris Gilbert Bishop. AmWit

I Greet You. J. Greshoff. TuT, *tr. by* Dennis O'Driscoll

I greet you, friend and neighbour. I Greet You. J. Greshoff. TuT, *tr. by* Dennis O'Driscoll

I greet you, son, with joy and winter rue. Muse in Late November. Jonathan Henderson Brooks. ChIV-1

I grew. Strong Bond, The. Juana de Ibarbourou. TCLAP, *tr. by* Sophie Cabot Black, Linda Scheer and Maria Negroni

I Grew Up. Lenore Keeshig-Tobias. FFC

I grew up bent over. Prodigy. Charles Simic. AF; AmWaPo; EMP; NAMCP V.2; NoP-5; VCAP

I grew up in a big house with leaky rafters. Slippery Ground. Daniel Simidor. OGAHCP, *tr. by* Boadiba and Jack Hirschman

I grew up on the reserve. I Grew Up. Lenore Keeshig-Tobias. FFC

I grew up with the language of electrics. My Father Makes a Lightbox for Vivienne Westwood. Nicolette Golding. Prnts

I grieve and dare not show my discontent. On Monsieur's Departure. Queen of England Elizabeth I. CABP; NAEL-6v1; NAEL-7v1; NALW; WaAnP

I grieve for my second daughter. Written on Seeing the Flowers, and Remembering My Daughter. Kao Ch'i. ColAnChi, *tr. by* F. W. Mote

I grieved for Buonaparté, with a vain. 1801. William Wordsworth. CenSon (I grieved for Bonaparté with a vain.) NPBRoP

I GROPE for your cold trail. God in Hiding, God of Faith. John Fitzgerald. BBMWP, *tr. by* Joseph P. Clancy

I / groped. Edge Guide for Impression. Clarence Major. EGAG

I grow a white rose. José Martí. SonAtl, *tr. by* Paul Estevin, C. Vale and Eva Asensio Vicente

I grow accustomed to a new disguise. Journal. John Ciardi. PoA 2002

I grow crazier with each passing day. *Unknown.* SLW, *tr. by* Marjolijn De Jager, Sayd Bahodin Majrouh and André Velter

I grow old under an intensity. Mirror. James Merrill. BeAl; PoA 2002

I Guard Your Eyes. Endre Ady. IQMS, *tr. by* Adam Makkai

I guess all I'm trying to say is I saw Crazy Horse die for. You Can Start the Poetry Now, Or: News from Crazy Horse. Thomas McGrath. TAPaP

I guess an' fear! (LL) To a Mouse; On Turning Her up in Her Nest, with the Plough, November, 1785. Robert Burns. BRP; CABP; FaBoVe; HeIP-4; NAEL-6v2; NAEL-7v2; NePenScot; NoP-4; NoP-5; NPBRoP; NPeEn; OxAEP-2; OxBEV; TFi; UV; WaAnP

I guess Black men fall. Just Say No Blues. Tracie Morris. BtF

I guess I'll be back late. Human House. VCWP, *tr. by* Christopher Drake

I Guess I'll Have to Change My Plan. Howard Dietz. ReLy

I guess I'm sick, because this is the third day. Chills. Bella Akhatovna Akhmadulina. ItGoST, *tr. by* F. D. Reeve

I guess it was because it was the first time I had been anyplace. Wo/man's Voice Must Be Heard, A. Lorena M. Craighead. InTrad

I guess it was the summer of nineteen. Six Families of Puerto Ricans. Terence Winch. FTtHH

I guess we haven't got a sense. Two Sleepy People. Frank Loesser. ReLy

I guess you were the winter, a din that hid. Fractal Audition. Pimone Triplett. NAPBL

I gulp down seven drinks of water. Hiccups. Léon Damas. PFTM-1, *tr. by* Ellen Conroy Kennedy

I gurgled straight out of my. In Gurgle Veritas. Luis H. Francia. ReBoTo

I had a bear that danced. Song in Sligo. Jean Garrigue. APT-2; OxBoAm

I had a chair at every hearth. Lamentation of the Old Pensioner, The (1890 version). William Butler Yeats. NoAM; TRP; WeW-3

I had a child who delighted me. Two, Hers and Mine. Susan Griffin. PoChi

I had a conversation with a goat. Goat, The. Umberto Saba. WoPoe, *tr. by* Stephen Sartarelli

I had a crisis at the supermarket, yesterday. My Androgynous Years. James Harms. NeAmPo

I had a dream. Nightmare Boogie. Langston Hughes. APSN; APT-2; NAMCP V.1; OxBoAm

I had a dream / A dream about you, Baby! Everything's Coming Up Roses. Stephen Sondheim. ReLy

I had a dream: Columbia the Great. Albery Allson Whitman. APN-2 *Fr.* Idyll of the South, An.

I had a dream in my mother's womb three days before I was born. Reader of This Page. Maurice Kilwein Guevara. NAPBL

I had a dream in the day. Dream, The. Marie Howe. LaCa

I had a dream one winter's night. Dream, A. Maggie Pogue Johnson. CBWP-4

I had a dream, which was not all a dream. Darkness. Lord Byron. CABP; NAEL-6v2; NAEL-7v2; NPBRoP; TreFP

I Had a Duck-billed Platypus. Patrick Barrington. OBCoV

I Had a Future. Patrick Kavanagh. NoAM

I had a good dream last night. Rām Basu. SinGod, *tr. by* Rachel Fell McDermott

I Had a Hippopotamus. Patrick Barrington. ITBLP

I had a hippopotamus; I loved him as a friend. I Had a Hippopotamus. Patrick Barrington. ITBLP

I had a house; I had a yard. Fog. Lizette Woodworth Reese. APT-1

I had a little desert, I kept it in the study. Bathtub Panopticon. Joshua Clover. CalPo

I had a little dog, and my dog was very small. Child's Dream, A. Frances Darwin Cornford. NOxBChV

I had a most marvellous piece of luck. I died. (LL) John Berryman. CAP-8; HarvBoo *Fr.* Dream Songs.

I had a picture by him—a print, I think—on my bedroom wall. Homage to Claude Lorrain. Charles Wright. NoP-5

I Had a Really Good Idea for a Poem in Cynwil Elfed. Elinor Wyn Reynolds. BBMWP, *tr. by* Grahame Davies

I had a silver penny. Nursery Rhyme of Innocence and Experience. Charles Causley. NOxBChV

I had a small, nonspeaking part. Cameo Appearance. Charles Simic. NAMCP V.2; NoP-5; OxBoAm

I had a son and his name was John. Rundown Church (Ballad of the First World War). Federico García Lorca. RaBo; WED, *tr. by* Robert Bly

I had a strange dream last night. I Had a Strange Dream. Irina Ratushinskaya. CFP, *tr. by* David McDuff

I had almost forgotten the singing in the streets. Singing in the Streets. Leonard Clark. NOxBChV

I had almost lost. Eugenio Montale. WoPoe *Fr.* Motets [Mottetti].

I had already looked at the coco-palms, the tamarinds. Manuscript in a Bottle. Pablo Antonio Cuadra. BLPSL, *tr. by* Rene de Costa, Rigas Kappatos and Eleni Paidoussi

I had always thought perhaps there would be no poets at all in New York. Author's Club. Juan Ramón Jiménez. WED, *tr. by* Robert Bly

I had ambition, by which sin. Ambition. W. H. Davies. MoBrPo

I had as lief be embraced by the porter at the hotel. Two Figures in Dense Violet Night. Wallace Stevens. MoAmPo

I had been bothered by a secret weariness. Charles Reznikoff. APT-2 *Fr.* Early History of a Writer.

I had been hungry, all the Years. Emily Dickinson. AFaM; MoAmPo; NAAPv.1; NALW; SAmP; TCAPo; WPoS

I had been thinking of Gabriel,. "H. D." MoWP; NAAPv.2; NALW; NAMCP V.1 *Fr.* Tribute to the Angels.

I had been trying to get through all day. Diaries. Ben Scammell. NLP

I had been vexed, if vexed I had not been. (LL) Sir Philip Sidney. NAEL-6v1; NAEL-7v1 *Fr.* Astrophil and Stella.

I had been watching them drift up and down. North. Roger Mitchell. PoCoUp

I Had But Fifty Cents. *Unknown.* NBLV; WHSW

I Had Climbed the Long Slope. John Barnie. TCAWP

I had climbed the long slope of the spur from Capel Madog to Banc-y-Darren. I Had Climbed the Long Slope. John Barnie. TCAWP

I had come all the way here from the sea. And Bees of Paradise. Hart Crane. OxBoAm

I had come from a dying man's room. Line Drive. Arthur Ginsberg. BloBone

I had come to the edge of the water. Seamus Heaney. NPeEn; PBCIP *Fr.* Station Island.

I had come to the house, in a cave of trees. Medusa. Louise Bogan. APT-2; MoAmPo; NAAPv.2; NALW; NAMCP V.1; NoAM; NoP-4; NoP-5; PtR

I had eight birds hatcht [*or* hatched] in one nest. In Reference to Her Children, 23 June, 1659 [*or* 1659]. Anne Bradstreet. NAAL-3; NAAPv.1

I had everything and luck: Rings of smoke. Autobiographia. G. E. Patterson. P180

I had everything arranged. Rushes, The. Kevin Young. LegDan

I had fallen asleep, my hand on your belly. Perfection of Wisdom Suite, A: Hymns for the Perfection of Wisdom in Paradise. Andrew Schelling. WANABP

I had for my winter evening walk. Good Hours. Robert Frost. MoW

I had found out a gift for my fair. Constance Naden. VWP *Fr.* Evolutional Erotics.

I had gone broke, and got set to come back. Epigram. James Vincent Cunningham. MoAmPo; VCAP

I had grieved. I had wept for a night and a day. Mrs Lazarus. Carol Ann Duffy. NAMCP V.2

I had heard / before, of an. Mr. Brodsky. Charles Tomlinson. NAMCP V.2; NoAM; NoP-4; NoP-5

I had heard the bird's name, and searched with intent. Oyster-Eaters, The. John Blight. NOBAu

I had him sit next me at table, my fire-lock lean'd in the corner. (LL) Walt Whitman. SAmP; WaAnP *Fr.* Song of Myself.

I had it all wrong from the start. Place for Four-Letter Words. Peter Sears. ArBi

I had just arrived on the advanced slope and I. Lines in Recollection. Russell Atkins. EGAG

I had just turned the classic page. To A. H. James M. Whitfield. APN-2

I had learnt from your words. Decline of Gaelic, The. Meg Bateman. MoWP

I had located the reflecting pines in the dark glass. Dementia. Norman Dubie. AmAlph

I had made a mistake. Anne Carson. PLBUT *Fr.* Life of Towns, The.

I had meant to write about a pear tree i knew as a child. Roy Kiyooka. NLPA *Fr.* Pear Tree Pomes.

I had my eyes shut the whole time. Kate Clanchy. PoCu

I had my faults. Confession. Suzanne Wise. LegDan

I had never seen a cornfield in my life. In the Elementary School Choir. Gregory Djanikian. OPRER; UnSA

I had never seen her so angry, and her rage revealed a measure of love I had missed. Gary Young. RaF

I Had No Books. Noberto James. PML, *tr. by* Beth Wellington

I had no gift for it. Padraic Fallon. ModLr *Fr.* Three Houses.

I had no thought of violets of late. Sonnet. Alice Moore Dunbar-Nelson. InGu

I had no time to Hate. Emily Dickinson. SWaP

I had no witnesses. Disappeared Woman V. Marjorie Agosin. TANSG, *tr. by* Cola Franzen

I had not an evil end in view. True Dream, A. Elizabeth Barrett Browning. NALW

I had not fastened my sash over my gown. Tzu Yeh. EroLit; WoPoe, *tr. by* Chung Ling and Kenneth Rexroth

I had not known of Hsiang-chi Monastery. Visiting Hsiang-Chi Monastery. Wang Wei. WoPoe, *tr. by* Eva Shan Chou

I had not thought that it would be like this. (LL) Eden Rock. Charles Causley. NoP-4; NoP-5; NPeEn; StAl

I Had Occasion to Tell a Visitor about an Old Trip I Took. Lu Yu. WoPoe, *tr. by* Burton Watson

I had often, cowled in the slumberous heavy air. Dürer: Innsbruck, 1495. "Ern Malley." BMAP

I had pelted the robot with all. Space Parable. Max Winter. NeAmPo

I had seen, as dawn was breaking. Nuit Blanche, La. Rudyard Kipling. MoBrPo; UV

I had seen coconut trees and tamarinds. Manuscript in a Bottle. Pablo Antonio Cuadra. TCLAP, *tr. by* Ann McCarthy de Zavala and Grace Schulman

I had sex with a famous poet last night. Sex with a Famous Poet. Denise Duhamel. KGB; NeAmPo

I had so long been troubled by official hat and robe. Dwelling by a Stream. Liu Tsung-yüan. CCL1, *tr. by* Witter Bynner

I had some cards printed. Madam's Calling Cards. Langston Hughes. SAmP

I had some romantic. Don Marquis. AmWit *Fr.* Mehitabel's Extensive Past.

I had the lab science, the ecology of texts. Other Syllabus, The. Chenjerai Hove. HBAPE

I had thought I could say these words. That Is the Way. Max Winter. FreRad

I had thought so little, really, of *her*. First Birth. Sharon Olds. StAl

I had time to think about things. After I Was Dead. Laura Mullen. ExTi

I had to get an operation to get some peace. I didn't.   Give Peace a Chance.   Judith W. Steinbergh.   PfS

I had to give a great speech to a filled hall, beginning.   Impossible, The.   Jane Miller.   BodElec

I had to kick their law into their teeth in order to save them.   Negro Hero.   Gwendolyn Brooks.   AmWaPo; ColAP; OxBoAm; PWW2; RACG; WaAnP

I had to let my cutman go. (LL)   Moorer Denies Holyfield in Twelve.   Olena Kalytiak Davis.   AmPoNex; MoASP

I had to see *La Bohème* again just to.   Mimi.   Paul Muldoon and Gerald Stern.   GPPA

I had to step outside, having just finished.   Redbud.   Betsy Sholl.   ACAMVP

I had to write my.   Spofford Hall.   Alison Stone.   SwNoth

I had two pillows and one was England.   Laughing Moon, The.   Moniza Alvi.   MFPA

I had vanished at least a dozen times / into something better. (LL)   Sleeping in the Forest.   Mary Oliver.   CAP-8; PLBUT

I had walked since dawn and lay down to rest on a bare hillside.   Vulture.   Robinson Jeffers.   APT-1; NAMCP V.1; NoAM

I had wanted to go hunt.   H. C. ten Berge.   TuT *Fr.* Lusitanian Variant, The.

I had written to Aunt Maud.   Waste.   Harry Graham.   OBCoV; UV

I Hadn't Anyone Till You.   Ray Noble.   ReLy

I hadn't been that ashamed since.   Sleeping with Artemis.   Josh Bell.   LegDan; PoDa

I hadn't met his kind before.   Love.   Kate Clanchy.   BeAl; MoWP

I hadn't said the *kaddish* prayer.   Kaddish.   Herschel Miller.   Prolet, *tr. by* Amelia Glaser

I hang from a thin green rope.   Elizabeth Rapp.   NewEx

I hang on to the hem of her dress like a child hanging.   Two Little Girls.   Fawziyya Abu Khalid.   PoArWo, *tr. by* Farouk Mustafa

I hang the window inside out.   Watching the Mayan Women.   Luisa Villani.   P180

I happy am if well with you. (LL)   In Reference to Her Children, 23 June, 1659 [*or* 1659].   Anne Bradstreet.   NAAL-3; NAAPv.1

I hardly ever tire of love or rhyme.   *Variation on Belloc's "Fatigue"*.   Wendy Cope.   UV

I hardly saw His Face.   John in Prison.   Sydney E. Jerrold.   SacPr

I hate & love. And if you should ask how I can do both.   Catullus.   NAWM-7v1 *Fr.* Carmina [Charles Martin Translation].

I hate and love. Ignorant fish, who even.   Odi et Amo.   Catullus.   WoPoe, *tr. by* Frank Bidart

I hate and love, wouldst thou the reason know?   De Amore Suo.   Catullus.   OBVE, *tr. by* Richard Lovelace

I hate artifice. All these.   Autonomy Is Jeopardy.   Charles Bernstein.   NAMCP V.2

I hate feeling.   Taxing.   Eileen Myles.   BodElec

I hate hole hole work.   *Hawaiian Oral Tradition.*   NAAPv.2

I Hate My Moaning.   Gerald Stern.   IJHIL

I hate my staring. I hate my moaning. Sometimes.   I Hate My Moaning.   Gerald Stern.   IJHIL

I hate my verses, every line, every word.   Love the Wild Swan.   Robinson Jeffers.   APT-1; MoAmPo; NoAM

I hate that drum's discordant sound.   Ode.   John Scott of Amwell.   NIP-4; OxAEP-1

I hate that particular dream.   My Own Little Piece of Hollywood.   James Harms.   AmPoNex

I hate the cyclic poem, nor do I rejoice.   Callimachus.   HePo, *tr. by* Barbara Hughes Fowler

I Hate the Light.   Osip Emilevich Mandelstam.   TCRusP, *tr. by* John Glad

I hate the Spring in parti-coloured vest.   Sonnet.   Mary Locke.   CenSon

I hate the tardy elegiac lay.   Off Duty [*or* To Della Crusca].   Hannah Cowley.   STuOW

I hate the travel logs that tell you.   Thoughts While Walking.   Rachel Wetzsteon.   ExTi

I hate this shadow of a ghost.   Kenneth Rexroth.   APT-2; NAAPv.2; NAMCP V.1 *Fr.* Love Poems of Marichiko, The.

I hate to see de evenin' sun go down.   St. Louis Blues.   William Christopher Handy.   APT-1; NAAPv.2; ReLy; TCAPo

I hate war. I'm worried, of course.   Worried.   Nguyen Binh Khiem.   WoPoe, *tr. by* Nguyen Ngoc Bich

I hate wide mouth black girls.   Illusion.   Colleen J. McElroy.   ISC; OxAAAP

I hated moving furniture.   Moving Furniture.   Josie Kearns.   SweBea

I hated the Road Runner.   Memory.   Bob Hicok.   SUP

I hated thee, fallen tyrant! I did groan.   Feelings of a Republican on the Fall of Bonaparte.   Percy Bysshe Shelley.   CenSon

I hated you; I confess I hated you.   I Do Not Want the Ceiling of the Sistine Chapel.   Felicity Napier.   Prnts

I Have.   Jan Arends.   TuT, *tr. by* Peter van de Kamp

I have.   Robert Duncan.   WhBo

I have a beautiful child, her form.   Sappho.   SaLy, *tr. by* Diane Rayor

I have a bird in my head and a pig in my stomach.   Alive for an Instant.   Kenneth Koch.   PmAP

I have a blue piano at home.   My Blue Piano.   Else Lasker-Schüler.   GTCP, *tr. by* Irmgard Hunt

I have a bowl of paper whites.   Window Ledge in the Atom Age.   Elwyn Brooks White.   NBLV

I have a boy of five years old.   Anecdote for Fathers [Showing How the Art of Lying May Be Taught].   William Wordsworth.   NoP-5

I have a brain populated by women.   Valerio Magrelli.   ItPo, *tr. by* Gayle Ridinger

I have a comrade who's sleeping.   I Have a Comrade.   Georges Castera.   OGAHCP, *tr. by* Boadiba and Jack Hirschman

I have a couple acres of land.   Wang Fan-chih.   ColAnChi, *tr. by* Victor H. Mair

I have a daughter/ mozambique.   Bocas: A Daughter's Geography.   Ntozake Shange.   WaAnP

I have a delicious problem.   Giant Red Woman.   Clarence Major.   GT

I Have a Dream.   Patricia Parker.   OxAAAP

I have a dream of bicycles.   Bicycle Dream.   Lauris Edmond.   ArBi

I have a fading flower in my hand.   *Unknown.*   SLW, *tr. by* Marjolijn De Jager, Sayd Bahodin Majrouh and André Velter

I have a feeling.   Let's Fall in Love.   Ted Koehler.   ReLy

I have a feeling that beneath the little halo on your noble head.   You Fascinate Me So.   Carolyn Leigh.   ReLy

I have a feeling that my boat.   Oceans.   Juan Ramón Jiménez.   RaW; WED, *tr. by* Robert Bly

I have a fifth of therapy.   Interview with Doctor Drink.   James Vincent Cunningham.   WoPoe

I have a fish's tail, so I'm not qualified to love you.   Siren.   Amy Gerstler.   ExTi

I have a friend.   Black March.   Stevie Smith.   EmeKit

I have a friend who.   Haiku #3.   Kim C. Lee.   InTrad

I have a friend who is red hot with pain.   Anne Carson.   BodElec *Fr.* Truth About God, The.

I have a friend who still believes in heaven.   Celestial Music.   Louise Glück.   BBASP; CAP-8; OxBoAm

I have a garden of my own.   Child's Song.   Sir Thomas More.   ChAP

I Have a Gentle Cock [*or* Gentil Cok].   *Unknown.*   NoP-4; NoP-5; OPOU; WaAnP

I have a goblet. I will share it with you.   Feast, The.   Mary Ruefle.   AmAlph

I have a grief.   John Crowe Ransom.   OxBoAm *Fr.* Sixteen Poems in Eight Pairings.

I have a lean, long-boned spite in me.   She Goes with Her Brother to the Place of Their Forebears.   Kerry Hardie.   NIrP

I have a life. I stand abandoned.   Unmarked Stop in Front of Westmond General Store, Westmond, Idaho.   Jonathan Johnson.   AmPoNex

I have a life that did not become.   Easter Morning.   A. R. Ammons.   NAAL-5; NAMCP V.2; NoAM; OxBoAm; PoA 2002; PoetW

I have a little budgie.   Fat Budgie, The.   John Lennon.   NBLV

I have a little dog.   Please Pass the Biscuit.   Ogden Nash.   AmWit

I have a little pipe that I.   Last Will and Testament.   Géza Páskándi.   IQMS, *tr. by* J. G. Nichols

I have a little shadow that goes in and out with me.   My Shadow.   Robert Louis Stevenson.   ChAP; ITBLP; ItP; UV

I have a little shadow that goes out sometimes with me.   My Shadow.   W. Hodgson Burnett.   UV

I have a love in ghostland.   Christina Georgina Rossetti.   EroLit

I have a lover.   Tuesday Night Affair.   Sandra Turner Bond.   ISC

I have a mistress, for perfections rare.   Devout Lover, A.   Thomas Randolph.   OBEV

I have a mobile phone in my mouth.   Games.   Admiel Kosman.   PML, *tr. by* Lisa Katz

I have a name of my own.   Gruoch.   Gruoch.   Marion Lomax.   NeBl

I have a neighbor.   Brown Rosellen.   FFC

I have a new garden.   *Unknown.*   OBGa

I Have a Rendezvous with Death.   Alan Seeger.   AmWaPo; APT-1; BRP; FaBoWar; TCAPo

I have a rotten memory began.   Forget How to Remember How to Forget.   John Hollander.   PoDa

I have a silence in the rain.   Michael Burkard.   BodElec

I have a sister, little sister, living in Zhongli.   Tu Fu [*or* Du Fu].   CCL1 *Fr.* Seven Songs Written During the Qianyuan Era While Staying at Tonggu District.

I have a slight thrumming aura of backache.   Parable of a Marriage (Chi Gong).   Mark Doty.   MAAN

I have a smiling face, she said.   Mask, The.   Elizabeth Barrett Browning.

VWP

I have a sorrow not wholly mine, but another's. (LL)   On a Certain Engagement South of Seoul.   Hayden Carruth.   AmWaPo; PWW2; WaAnP

I Have a Stage in My Head.   Yona Volach.   DTA, *tr. by* Miriyam Glazer

I have a theory about motion.   Jazz Dancer.   Cornelius Eady.   SeSe

I have a vision.   High Heels.   Ron Padgett.   NYP2

I have a voice in my head that talks backwards.   Lemn Sissay.   NewEx

I have a word to say to you as men and as a man speaking to.   David Jones.   TCAWP *Fr.* Tribune's Visitation, The.

I have a word with you, and your' to wait.   Albery Allson Whitman.   NAAPv.1 *Fr.* Octoroon, The.

I have a yong suster.   I Have a Young Sister.   *Unknown.*   FaBoVe   (I have a yong sister.)   NoP-4; NoP-5; WaAnP

I have a young love.   Sailor, The.   Sylvia Townsend Warner.   OBMV

I Have a Young Sister.   *Unknown.*   FaBoVe

I have abandoned the dream kitchens for a low fire.   Mayo Tao, The.   Derek Mahon.   BeAl

I have almost ev'rything.   Something to Live For.   Billy Strayhorn.   ReLy

I have already come to the verge of.   Unborn Child, An.   Derek Mahon.   BeAl; CABP; PNI; WoPoe

I have already lost the style and maze of language.   Sabah Al-Kharrat Zwein.   PoArWo *Fr.* Inclined House, The.

I have always been lucky.   Bicycle, The.   James Brown.   ArBi

I have always been remarkably impressed.   Dull Sonnet.   Henry Reed.   OxBEV

I have always found Mark Twain to be a rather depressing character.   Second Why.   Ron Padgett.   NYP2

I have always laughed.   Voice.   Ron Padgett.   OxBoAm

I have always longed to.   Riding Bike with No Hands.   Julia Kasdorf.   ArBi

I have always loved particulars: the angels.   On Muranowska Street.   Myra Sklarew.   TaR

I have always loved the word *guitar*.   Guitar.   David St. John.   InvLad

I have always regretted the shallowness of words.   Looking at My Knife-Hilt, a Song.   Liu Yu Hsi.   CCL1, *tr. by* Daniel Bryant

I have an appointment with elsewhere.   Wedding Day.   Mark Levine.   AmPoNex; BAP-01

I have an arrow that will find its mark.   Ralph Waldo Emerson.   TCAPo

I have an ear for music.   Pretty Girl Is Like a Melody, A.   Irving Berlin.   ReLy

I have (and long shall have) a white great nimble cat.   White Great Nimble Cat, A.   Sir Philip Sidney.   TriCat

I have assumed a conscious sociability.   Garden Party.   Sir Herbert Read.   OBGa

I have at times seen all the eastern sky.   Dante Alighieri.   NAWM-7v1 *Fr.* Divine Comedy, The (Mandelbaum Translation).

I have avoided your wide English eyes.   Sweet William.   "Ern Malley."   BMAP

I have beaten out my exile. (LL)   Ezra Pound.   MoAmPo; NAMCP V.1; NoAM; PoA 2002 *Fr.* Lustra.

I have become overcrowded here. Like the layers of stone inside a mountain.   Earth Remembers, The.   Ágnes Nemes Nagy.   MotU, *tr. by* Hugh Maxton

I have been a day boarder, Lord. I have preferred the table to the Bed.   Unbosoming, The.   Olena Kalytiak Davis.   LegDan

I have been a movie fan.   He Never Did That to Me.   Noël Coward.   NBLV

I have been a privileged spectator at innumerable acts of vandalism.   Drummer, The.   Bruce Beaver.   BMAP

I have been a rover.   Breezin' Along with the Breeze.   Haven Gillespie.   ReLy

I have been all men known to history.   Taliesin 1952.   Ronald Stuart Thomas.   HarvBoo

I have been all my lovers.   Desire 1.   Thulani Davis.   ISC

I have been bitter with you, my brother.   Colloquy with John Keats.   "Ern Malley."   BMAP

I have been brought into darkness.   *Unknown.*   WoPoe *Fr.* Lamentations.

I have been cruel to a fat pigeon.   Fly.   W. S. Merwin.   ChAP; OWoS

I have been dreaming half the night.   Night Piece.   Robin Skelton.   IFF

I have been dying a long time.   Earth, Take Me Back.   John Hall Wheelock.   APT-1

I have been encouraged to wait.   Yet Still.   Rashidah Ismaili.   HAWP; ItWoWo

I have been faithful to thee, Cynara! in my fashion. (LL)   Non Sum Qualis Eram Bonae sub Regno Cynarae.   Ernest Dowson.   CABP; ClHu; HeIP-4; MoBrPo; NoP-4; NoP-5; OBEV; OBMV; TFi

I have been having an affair.   Affair of the Heart.   Peter Porter.   BMAP

I have been heavy and had much selecting. I saw a star which.   Lifting Belly.   Gertrude Stein.

I have been her kind. (LL)   Her Kind.   Anne Sexton.   BrAP; CAP-8; HeIP-4; IJHIL; NALW; NAMCP V.2; PoPoPo; PtR; StAl; VCAP

I have been here before.   Sudden Light.   Dante Gabriel Rossetti.   CABP; NoP-4; NoP-5; NPeEn; OxBEV

I have been in great distress.   Lover's Prize, A.   Countess de Die Beatrice.   EroLit; NAWM-7v1, *tr. by* Peter Dronke

I have been in this bar.   Man Who Married Magdalene, The.   Anthony Hecht.   ChIV-2

I have been kissed before, she added, blushing slightly.   Arthur Hugh Clough.   FaBoVe *Fr.* Bothie of Tober-na-Vuolich, The [A Long-Vacation Pastoral].

I have been lazy.   Thanks Sent to Taihei Osho.   Muso Soseki.   EaWin, *tr. by* W. S. Merwin

I have been looking all over for a place to start from.   Places.   PfS

I have been looking these pages over, my dearest wife.   Ovid.   WoPoe *Fr.* Tristia.

I have been losing you.   To Love That Well.   Janice Townley Moore.   IaFF

I have been noting events for forty years.   Basil Bunting.   NPeEn *Fr.* Chomei at Toyama.

I have been one acquainted with the night.   Acquainted with the Night.   Robert Frost.   AmFaPo; APT-1; AWTN; BLPJKO; BrAP; GSo; HarvBoo; MoAmPo; NAAPv.2; NAMCP V.1; NoAM; NoP-4; NoP-5; OxBoAm; SAmP; TFi; TRP; WeW-3

I have been profligate of happiness.   To Olive.   Lord Alfred Bruce Douglas.   OBEV

I have been proud and said, 'My love, my own'. (LL)   Elizabeth Barrett Browning.   CenSon; ITBLP; LW *Fr.* Sonnets from the Portuguese.

I have been reading about Paul Eluard tonight.   Paul Eluard.   Anne Waldman.   AHA

I have been sent for. It has happened before in our country. (LL)   I Was Sent For.   Lupenga Mphande.   NAfrP; PML

I have been so enchanted by the girls.   My Turn.   Glyn Maxwell.   NeBrP

I have been so great a lover: filled my days.   Great Lover, The.   Rupert Brooke.   MoBrPo

I have been staring at a sentence.   Riverside Drive.   Louis Simpson.   CAP-8

I have been studying how I may compare.   William Shakespeare.   OxAEP-1; WoPoe *Fr.* King Richard III.

I have been studying the difference.   White Towels.   Richard Jones.   P180

I have been teaching poetry too long.   Great Pat Smith American Dreampoem, The.   Patricia Smith.   ICANM

I have been tempted to rush the job.   Chairmaker, The.   Siobhan Campbell.   IrLP; MFPA

I have been the woman on the subway.   Release.   Lisa Sewell.   AmPoNex

I have been thinking.   Lilies.   Mary Oliver.   BBASP; WaAnP

I Have Been through the Gates.   Charlotte Mew.   MoBrPo

I have been to Paris since we parted. (LL)   As Children Together.   Carolyn Forché.   NoAM; OxWW

I have been treading on leaves all day until I am autumn-tired.   Leaf-Treader, A.   Robert Frost.   MoAmPo

I have been urged by earnest violins.   Music.   Wilfred Owen.   CAGL

I have been waiting to speak to you.   Eve (Rachel).   Michael S. Harper.   ESEAA

I have been walking above Cwmchwefri.   Cwmchwefri.   T. Harri Jones.   AngWePo

I have been walking by the harbour.   Folderol.   Vona Groarke.   StAl

I have been wanton, and too bold I fear.   Robert Herrick.   CavPo

I have been warned. It is more than thirty years since I wrote.   But I Am Growing Old and Indolent.   Robinson Jeffers.   APT-1; ColAP

I have been watching her for a long time. I have been watching.   Public Place (After Olga Broumas), The.   Achy Obejas.   WiU

I have been watching slow things the long afternoon.   Slow.   Robert Francis.   APT-2

I have been watching the war map slammed up for advertising in front of the newspaper office.   Buttons.   Carl Sandburg.   AmWaPo

I have been with you, and I have thought of you.   Chinese Villanelle.   John Yau.   PmAP; WaAnP

I have been young, and now am not too old.   Report on Experience.   Edmund Charles Blunden.   NPeEn; OBMV; OBWP; OxBEV; PoAgWa

I have begged the angels.   Good-Bye, Valentine.   Leslie Anne McIlroy.   AmPoNex

I have beginning and end.   Monument, A.   Vladislav Felitsianovich Khodasevich.   TCRusP, *tr. by* John Glad

I have begun to die.   Sentry, The.   Alun Lewis.   AngWePo; PoWW; TCAWP

I have braided my hair but it has come undone.   *Unknown.*   SLW, *tr. by* Marjolijn De Jager, Sayd Bahodin Majrouh and André Velter

I have braved, for want of wild beasts, steel cages.   May 24, 1980.   Joseph Brodsky.   PoCho, *tr. by* the author and Joseph Brodsky

I have broken the sound barrier of morality.   Gay Poet, The.   William Barber.   CAGL

I have brothers, younger brothers in a place far away.   Tu Fu [*or* Du Fu].   CCL1 *Fr.* Seven Songs Written During the Qianyuan Era While Staying at Tonggu District.

I have brought the twittering flags old bear-hug.   With Walt Whitman at Fredericksburg.   Dave Jeddie Smith.   ViWalt

I have burned ten thousand volumes.   On the Day of Washing the Buddha in the Year Ting-wei (1607), I Dreamed That My Late Son Shih-ch'ü Was Holding a Book, and Appeared To Be Quite Happy. He Said That He Had Earned His Chin-shih Degree in the Underworld. After We Sighed and La. T'ang Hsien-tsu.   ColAnChi, *tr. by* Jonathan Chaves

I have but four, the treasures of my soul.   Slave Mother, The: A Tale of the Ohio.   Frances Ellen Watkins Harper.   ColAP; NAAPv.1

I have but one chance left,—and that is going to Florence.   Arthur Hugh Clough.   FaBoVe *Fr.* Amours de Voyage.

I have carried it with me each day: that morning I took.   Morning, A.   Mark Strand.   CAP-8

I have cast in here a soul.   War Songs.   *Unknown.*   APN-2, *tr. by* Alfred Longley Riggs

I have changed my mind; or my mind is changed in me.   Philoctetes.   Henry Reed.   HarvBoo

I have chosen to live near the rebuilt walls of my memory.   Porte Dorée. Léopold Sédar Senghor.   PoetW, *tr. by* Melvin Dixon

I have cleared this space of you, for you, for you. (LL)   Sweet Reader, Flanneled and Tulled.   Olena Kalytiak Davis.   BAP-01; NAPBL

I have climbed all the way to the summit.   Auditor Thinks about Female Nature, An.   Jamie Grant.   NOBAu

I have come at last to the short.   Great Canzon, The.   Dante Alighieri.   ItP, *tr. by* Kenneth Rexroth

I have come down.   Prologue.   Odia Ofeimun.   HBAPE; NAfrP

I have come far enough.   Form of Women, A.   Robert Creeley.   ErotSp

I have come in my own time.   California Light.   Sherley Anne Williams.   CalPo; GeoHom

I have come out to smell the hyacinths which again in this.   For and Against the Environment.   D. M. Black.   EmeKit

I have come to believe this fickleness.   Theology of Doubt, The.   Scott Cairns.   UpMys

I have come to claim.   I Have Come to Claim Marilyn Monroe's Body.   Judy Grahn.   ReTh

I Have Come to Claim Marilyn Monroe's Body.   Judy Grahn.   ReTh

I have come to my end, but you.   Wind, The.   Boris Leonidovich Pasternak.   RusPo, *tr. by* Robert Arthur Douglas Ford

I have come to the borders of sleep.   Lights Out.   Edward Thomas.   HarvBoo; OxAEP-2; PoWW; WoPoe

I have come to this land.   Saw-Mill Shack, The.   Thomas Rain Crowe.   AmZen

I have come to you tonite out of the depths.   Reflections After the June 12th March for Disarmament.   Sonia Sanchez.   ESEAA

I have committed errors.   Kyunyŏ, Great Master.   CATKP *Fr.* Eleven Poems on the Ten Vows of the Universally Worthy Bodhisattva.

I have confidence, Peacock, and my eyes are soft.   Lincoln Bedroom, The.   Donald Berger.   NAPBL

I have constructed a labyrinth without a Minotaur.   In My Labyrinth (The Minotaur's Game).   Carlota Caulfield.   TANSG, *tr. by* Chris Allen

I have counted the chemical for a hundred reasons.   Harbour.   Frank Lima.   AHA

I have crossed an ocean.   Epilogue.   Grace Nichols.   NAMCP V.2

I have cultivated.   Jewel Field.   Muso Soseki.   EaWin, *tr. by* W. S. Merwin

I have cut the plaintain grove.   Witch, The.   Santal.   RaBo

I have decided I will not be like John Hu anymore.   Edge of Something, The.   Linda Gregg.   BodElec

I have decided I'm divine.   Ballade of the New God.   Thomas M. Disch.   RA

I have decided not to forget these little houses.   Houston Heights.   Janet Lowery.   TiP2

I have desired to go.   Heaven-Haven.   Gerard Manley Hopkins.   HeIP-4; MoBrPo; NoAM; OBEV; OxAEP-2; SoSe-8; TFi

I have destroyed your home. You have destroyed my home. (LL)   Jerusalem.   James Fenton.   BeAl; HarvBoo

I have discovered that I'm like Raquel.   Like Raquel.   Maria Arrillaga.   TANSG

I have discovered that most of.   January Morning.   William Carlos Williams.   APT-1

I have done all I could.   Tree and the Lady, The.   Thomas Hardy.   MoBrPo

I have done it again.   Lady Lazarus.   Sylvia Plath.   AmFaPo; CAP-8; ChIV-2; ColAP; EMP; FTtHH; HarvBoo; IJHIL; MoWP; NAAL-5; NALW; NAMCP V.2; NIL-7; NIP-4; NoAM; NoP-4; NoP-5; OxBoAm; OxWW; PoetW; PoPoPo; TRP; VCAP; WaAnP

I Have Done My Reckoning.   Attila József.   IQMS, *tr. by* Michael Hatwell

I have done one braver thing.   Undertaking, The.   John Donne.   NAEL-6v1; NAEL-7v1

I have done the deed. Didst thou not hear a noise?   William Shakespeare.   OxAEP-1 *Fr.* Macbeth.

I have done this with a loving heart for my father Amun.   Queen Hatshepsut.   HAWP *Fr.* Obelisk Inscriptions.

I have done what I could but you avoid me.   My Life by Somebody Else.   Mark Strand.   CAP-8

I have dreamt a dream of fulfillment, of freedom.   Disciples Asleep at Gethsemane.   Paul Kane.   GI

I have dreamt it again: standing suddenly still.   Wormwood.   Thomas Kinsella.   PBCIP

I have drunk up nights and spent the days.   Sonnet two.   Arthur Nortje.   TSAP

I have eaten.   This Is Just to Say.   William Carlos Williams.   APT-1; BrAP; ChAP; GoPo; HarvBoo; HeIP-4; NAAL-5; NAAPv.2; NAMCP V.1; NIL-7; NIP-4; NoAM; NoP-4; NoP-5; OPOU; OxBoAm; PoPoPo; TRP; WaAnP

I have electricity in me.   Intimate Mixture.   Elena Georgiou.   WiU

I have embraced the summer dawn.   Dawn.   Arthur Rimbaud.   SxFrPo, *tr. by* Martin Sorrell

I have encountered a valley, in ragged bast matting.   Elena Ignatova.   ItGoST, *tr. by* Sibelan Forrester

I have entered into the Desert.   Charles Erskine Scott Wood.   APT-1 *Fr.* Poet in the Desert, The.

I have examin'd and do find.   To Mrs M. A. at Parting.   Katherine Philips.   NAEL-6v1; NAEL-7v1

I Have Exhausted the Delighted Range.   Michael Hartnett.   ModIr

I Have Faith.   Rainer Maria Rilke.   BBASP, *tr. by* Robert Bly

I have faith in all those things that are not yet said.   I Have Faith.   Rainer Maria Rilke.   BBASP, *tr. by* Robert Bly

I have fallen in love with American names.   American Names.   Stephen Vincent Benét.   APT-2; FaBoA; OxBoAm

I have fallen to the ground.   Birthday.   Dianne Edenfield Edwards.   ICANM

I have felt the Gulf churn butter.   I Have Felt the Gulf: Mississippi.   Jerry W., Jr. Ward.   FuFl

I Have Felt the Gulf: Mississippi.   Jerry W., Jr. Ward.   FuFl

I have felt the swaying of the elephant's shoulders; and now you want me to climb on a jackass? Try to be serious. (LL)   Why Mira Can't Go Back to Her Old House.   Mirabai.   WED; WPoS, *tr. by* Robert Bly

I have finally learned.   Valerio Magrelli.   NeIt

"I have finished another year," said God.   New Year's Eve.   Thomas Hardy.   MoBrPo; NAMCP V.1; NoAM

I have finished making your clothes.   Embroidery's Secret, The.   Han Yong'un [*or* Yongwun].   CAMKP, *tr. by* Sammy Solberg

I Have Folded My Sorrows.   Bob Kaufman.   EGAG

I Have Folded This Letter in Ten Places.   Tim Griffin.   FreRad

I have forgotten all about fishing. (LL)   Yun Sŏndo.   CATKP; WoPoe *Fr.* Angler's Calendar, The.

I have forgotten my skin, misplaced my body.   Proximity.   C. Dale Young.   LegDan

I have forgotten whatever.   Wall, A.   Andrew Motion.   NeBrP

I have found God.   Discovery.   Hilda Schiff.   HP

I Have Found My Lover.   Frances Densmore.   APT-1 *Fr.* Chippewa Music.

I have found myself.   DC Nocturne.   Kenneth Carroll.   AmPoNex

I have found out a gift for my Erin.   Pastoral Ballad by John Bull, A.   Thomas Moore.   OBSV

I have freed myself at last.   From the Bridge.   Claribel Alegría.   AF

I have from you this red.   Valerio Magrelli.   NeIt

I have given birth to a see-through child.   Lines.   Colette Bryce.   NIrP

I have given you my true love.   I'm Through with Love.   Gustave Kahn.   ReLy

I have gone into my eyes.   Depression.   Sonia Sanchez.   ESEAA

I Have Gone into My Prison Cell.   Shakuntala Hawoldar.   CFP; HAWP

I have gone out, a possessed witch.   Her Kind.   Anne Sexton.   BrAP; CAP-8; HeIP-4; IJHIL; NALW; NAMCP V.2; PoPoPo; PtR; StAl; VCAP

I have got into the slow train.   In the Stopping Train.   Donald Davie.   NPeEn

I Have Got My Leave.   Rabindranath Tagore.   OBMV *Fr.* Gitanjali.

I Have Got to Stop Loving You. So I Have Killed My Black Goat.   Ai.   CAP-8

I have got wine, but am not well enough to drink.   Sitting Quietly: Written During My Illness.   Po Chü-i.   CCL1, *tr. by* Arthur Waley

I have gret wonder, be this lyght.   Book of the Duchesse, The.   Geoffrey Chaucer.

I have had a companion on the road.   Daio.   EaWin, *tr. by* W. S. Merwin

I have had a strange dream: I see a young woman wearing a white dress.   Brugge.   Franz Wright.   MotU

I have had asthma for a.   Visitors.   Tu Fu [*or* Du Fu].   BLT, *tr. by* Kenneth Rexroth

I have had enough.   Sheltered Garden.   "H. D."   NAAPv.2

I have had my dream—like others.   Thursday.   William Carlos Williams.   APT-1

I have had my ups and downs.   Song of Mehitabel, The.   Don Marquis.   TriCat

I have had playmates, I have had companions.   Old Familiar Faces, The.   Charles Lamb.   OBEV; OxAEP-2; OxBEV
(Where are they gone, the old familiar faces?)   NOBRP; NPBRoP

I have had to learn the simplest things.   Charles Olson.   APT-2; NAAL-5; NAMCP V.2; PmAP *Fr.* Maximus Poems, The.

I have halted my horse by the tree of the doves. Song. "St.-John Perse." YaTCFP, *tr. by* T. S. Eliot

I have heard it said. To the Muse. Denise Levertov. APSN

I have heard of a crannog cut off from the sun. Corpsebeach. Snorri Sturluson. SonAtl

I have heard that hysterical women say. Lapis Lazuli. William Butler Yeats. BrAP; CABP; HeIP-4; NAEL-6v2; NAEL-7v2; NAMCP V.1; NAWM-7v2; NoAM; NoP-4; NoP-5; TFi

I have heard the pigeons of the Seven Woods. In the Seven Woods. William Butler Yeats. NoAM

I have heard the silvery note. Song. Sándor Kisfaludy. IQMS, *tr. by* Anthony Edkins

I have heard what the talkers were talking, the talk of the beginning and the end. Walt Whitman. CAGL *Fr.* Song of Myself.

I have held the man in my mouth. Rendered Dog. Sarah Messer. LegDan

I have hopped, when properly wound up. Tin Frog, The. Russell Hoban. Spl (I have hopped, when properly wound up, the whole length.) Spl

I have horns, but am not beast. Gordon Wardman. NewEx

I have in my possession. Fetish. Christopher Reid. NeBrP

I have in my throat one word. One Word. Gabriela Mistral. TCLAP, *tr. by* Doris Dana

I have inherited another woman's flowers. In-Patient. Carole Satyamurti. PoCu

I have invented a new species of poetry, "verse without words" or sound-. Hugo Ball. PFTM-1 *Fr.* Flight out of Time.

I have invented new worlds. I have dreamed. Birth of the Sun, The. Pablo Antonio Cuadra. TCLAP, *tr. by* Thomas Merton

I have it, looking to my left, the cars of this. Not Much Singing. Charles Bukowski. BodElec

I have it now. Stone, The. Henry Vaughan. ChIV-1

I have just / asked you to. This Is Just to Say. Erica-Lynn Gambino. GoPo

I have just come down from my father. Hospital Window, The. James Dickey. CAP-8; EMP; NAMCP V.2; NoAM; VCAP

I have just realized that the stakes are myself. Revolutionary Letter #1. Diane Di Prima. CLPP

I have just seen a beautiful thing. Angelina Weld Grimké. *See* I have just seen a most beautiful thing.

I have just seen a most beautiful thing. Black Finger, The. Angelina Weld Grimké. NAAPv.2

(I have just seen a beautiful thing.) OxBoAm

I have just seen you go down the mountain. Departure. Wang Wei. TAL

I have killed a virgin by being born. Géza Páskándi. IQMS *Fr.* Language Memory.

I have kissed your son's feet. Flora's Plea to Mary. Juan Delgado. TouFir

I have known the inexorable sadness of pencils. Dolor. Theodore Roethke. BrAP; GPTC; HeIP-4; NAMCP V.1; NoAM; OPOU; OxBoAm; PoA 2002; StAl; TRP

I have known the silence of the stars and of the sea. Silence. Edgar Lee Masters. MoAmPo

I have laborede sore and suffered deyyth. *Unknown. See* I have labored sore and suffered deth.

I have lain awake in the darkness many nights. Darkness, The. Charles E. Butler. YaYoPo

I have lain on my back. Introit. Mongane Wally Serote. TSAP

I have learn'd. William Shakespeare. OxAEP-1 *Fr.* King Henry IV, Pt. I.

I have learned. Rāmprasād Sen. SinGod, *tr. by* Rachel Fell McDermott

I have learned about dying by looking at two pictures. Björn Olinder's Pictures. Michael Longley. StAl

I have learned that love is not a picnic. Blue Again. Dorothy Fields. ReLy

I have learnt by heart the lesson of goodbyes. Tristia. Osip Emilevich Mandelstam. WoPoe, *tr. by* James Greene

I have learnt the Hebrew blessing before eating bread. Charles Reznikoff. APT-2

I have led her home, my love, my only friend. Alfred Tennyson. NAEL-6v2 *Fr.* Maud [A Monodrama].

I have left my wife at the airport. Following the Road. Larry Smith. AmZen

I have liv'd long enough: my way of life. William Shakespeare. WaAnP *Fr.* Macbeth.

I have lived. Remembering the Past. Al Robles. ReBoTo

I have lived anxious and hurt. *Unknown.* CATKP, *tr. by* Peter H. Lee

I have lived between my two hands. Hands. Edvard Kocbek. PoSu, *tr. by* Michael Scammell and Veno Taufer

I have lived in circles of solitude. Consultation. Jayne Cortez. SurWo

I have lived in important places, times. Epic. Patrick Kavanagh. CABP; HarvBoo; MakPoe; ModIr; NAMCP V.1; NoP-4; NoP-5; NPeEn; OxBSo

I have lived it, and lived it. Sofas, Fogs, and Cinemas, The. Rosemary Tonks. MoWP

I have lived long enough, having seen one thing, that love hath an end. Hymn to Proserpine. Algernon Charles Swinburne. NAEL-6v2; NAEL-7v2

I have located it, my ghost town. Ghost Town. Michael Longley. ModIr

I Have Longed to Move Away. Dylan Thomas. OxBEV

I Have Longings for My Dead. Devorah Amir. DTA, *tr. by* Miriyam Glazer

I have looked at you as Christ, imagine, Veronica and they separated. To Forget the Image. Michel Deguy. PFTM-2, *tr. by* Clayton Eshleman

I Have Lost A Verse. Julia de Burgos. TANSG, *tr. by* Heather Rosario Sievert

I have lost all regret of evil with the years gone by. Three Stars. Robert Desnos. SurPaPo, *tr. by* Mary Ann Caws

I have lost, and lately, these. Upon the Loss[e] of His Mistresses. Robert Herrick. BASC; CavPo; NAEL-6v1; NAEL-7v1; NOSC

I have lost my friend. The semi trucks out there. Stubble Burning, The. Sarah Ruden. AmPoNex

I Have Loved Flowers. Robert Bridges. MoBrPo

I Have Loved My Horrible Self, Lord. Six Apologies, Lord. Olena Kalytiak Davis. PLBUT

I have loved so many violent loves. Declaration at Forty. Judson Crews. ICANM

I have loved the air outside Shop-Rite Liquor. Poetics. August Kleinzahler. PmAP; WaAnP

I have loved your hands. Gardener, The. Ellen Kort. IPoFL

I have made a footprint, a sacred one. Planting Initiation Song. *Unknown.* WoPoe; WPoS, *tr. by* Francis La Flesche

I have made a footprint, I live in the light of day. (LL) Planting Initiation Song. *Unknown.* WoPoe; WPoS, *tr. by* Francis La Flesche

I have made a mistake, someone tells me. Beaten Track, The. Steve Benson. FTOS

I have made myself beautiful in my worn clothes. *Unknown.* SLW, *tr. by* Marjolijn De Jager, Sayd Bahodin Majrouh and André Velter

I have made silken verses. Re-Conversion. Novella Nikolaevna Matveyeva. TCRusP, *tr. by* Nigel Stott

I have (may I always keep!) blonde Minerva's protection: my vessel. Ovid. RomPo *Fr.* Tristia.

I have met them at close of day. Easter 1916. William Butler Yeats. BrAP; HarvBoo; HeIP-4; IrV; NAEL-6v2; NAEL-7v2; NAMCP V.1; NAWM-7v2; NIL-7; NIP-4; NoAM; NoP-4; NoP-5; NPeEn; OBWP; OxAEP-2; PoPoPo; TFi; WaAnP

I have moved to Dublin to have it out with you. John Berryman. InoFa; NAMCP V.2; NoAM; TRP *Fr.* Dream Songs.

I have moved to the house by the sea. One Year Later. Robyn Zappala. PfS

I have moved to this home of Immortals. Living in the Summer Mountains. Yü Hsüan-chi. WoPoe, *tr. by* Chung Ling and Kenneth Rexroth

I have my reasons. Alphabetizer Speaks, The. Patty Seyburn. LegDan

I have my statues. The ages have bequeathed them to me. My Statues. Henri Michaux. YaTCFP, *tr. by* Mary Ann Caws and Patricia Terry

I have neither Plummes nor Cherries. Nicholas Breton. NPeEn *Fr.* Solemne Long Enduring Passion, A.

I have never battled to buy a fine house. Inscription Written by Me in My Small Garden. Po Chü-i. CCL1, *tr. by* Arthur Waley

I have never been at the top of wind-played Olympus. Uri Zvi Greenberg. FIT, *tr. by* Robert Friend

I have never churned buttermilk. What does it require? Taste of Life Going On, The. Opal Moore. FuFl

I have never had my fill even of poor food. Elegy to Myself. Ch'oe Kinam. CATKP, *tr. by* Chi-gyu Kim [*or* Kim Chonggil]

I have never opened a book in my life. White Lie, The. Don Paterson. NeBrP

I have never seen him, this invisible member of the panel, this thirteenth juror. People vs. the People, The. Kenneth Fearing. MoAmPo

I have never understood. Lockerbie. Charles Muñoz. OtW

I Have Never Wanted Fame. Antonio Machado Ruiz. RaW, *tr. by* Robert Bly

I have nine principal talents. Kali Kolsson. SonAtl

I have no bowl. Ozaki Hosai. CAoMJL1, *tr. by* Janine Beichman

I have no Brother—they who meet me now. Thy Brother's Blood. Jones Very. APN-1

I have no care for systematic theology. Eschatology. Morris Gilbert Bishop. AmWit

I have no daughter. I desire none. (LL) For My Daughter. Weldon Kees. OxBoAm; OxBSo; WaAnP

I have no dog, but it must be. My Dog. John Kendrick Bangs. ITBLP

I have no doubt you will accomplish. Your Going. Carol Baker. PfS

I have no ears or eyes. Tugged Hand, The. W. H. Davies. TCAWP

I have no God, I have no land. Songs of Innocence. Attila József. IQMS, *tr. by* Thomas Kabdebo and Anton N. Nyerges

I have no illusions. Visibility. Maura Stanton. BodElec

I have no Life but this. Emily Dickinson. FaBoVe

I have no memories or photograph of my father. O-Bon: Dance for the Dead. Garrett Kaoru Hongo. LoL

I have no mockings or arguments, I witness and wait. (LL) Walt Whitman. CAGL; ColAP; NAWM-7v2 *Fr.* Song of Myself.

I have no name. William Blake. NPBRoP; OxAEP-2; PoPoPo *Fr.* Songs of Innocence.

I have no name for the nameless thing. Nameless Thing. Robert Penn Warren. BodElec

I have no opinion. Opinion of Hagar, The. Alicia Ostriker. TaR

I have no pain, dear mother, now. *Unknown*. OBCoV *Fr.* Soldiers' Songs of the First World War.

I have no seed to spread over the world. I Have No Seed to Scatter through the World. Patrizia Cavalli. NeIt, *tr. by* Muriel Kittel Robert McCracken

I have no shame, no regret. Cosmopolitan Poetry. János Arany. IQMS, *tr. by* Madeline Mason

I have no substance and no form. Nigel Cameron. NewEx

I have no wine other than sorrows mixed in the cup with flowing tears. Abū Bakr Yahya ibn Muhammad ibn 'Abd ar-Rahmān al-Qaisī Ibn Baqī. HiArP, *tr. by* James T. Monroe

I have no wit, no words, no tears. Better Resurrection, A. Christina Georgina Rossetti. ViWPN; VWP

I have not been nailed to the most absurd of rocks. Laughable. Aimé Césaire. ConPit, *tr. by* Clayton Eshleman and Annette Smith

I have not come to sing, you can put away your guitar. I Have Not Come to Sing. León Felipe. RaW, *tr. by* W. S. Merwin

I have not come within their frozen. Twilight in the Library. John Tripp. TCAWP

I have not even been in the fields. Charles Reznikoff. NAAPv.2

I have not ever seen my father's grave. Father Son and Holy Ghost. Audre Lorde. ESEAA; NoAM

I Have Not Lingered in European Monasteries. Leonard Cohen. BrAP

I have not missed the irony of this magnetism, my being. Flowers. Raylene Hinz-Penner. ACAMVP

I Have Not Signed a Treaty with the United States Government. Chrystos. UnSA

I have not slept for a week. Death of the Race Car Driver, The. Norman Dubie. MoASP

I have not stood at this grave nor have I. After a Time. Elizabeth Jennings. HarvBoo

I have not stood back to back with friends now fallen. Only 20 Years Old. Gideon Rosenthal. NRoS, *tr. by* Esther Raizen

I have not woken from a dream nor arrived by express train. Prague in the Midday Sun. Vitězslav Nezval. AF, *tr. by* Ewald Osers

I have not won. Farewell, A. Eithne Strong. IrLP

I Have Not Woven My Poems. Sarah Barkan. Prolet, *tr. by* Amelia Glaser

I have not written a new poem. Apple. Aleida Rodríguez. FaoP

I have nothing to give you, but my anger. Love Poem for My Country, A. Frank Mkalawile Chipasula. HBAPE; NAfrP

I have nothing to say about the war. Yehuda Amichai. PoSu *Fr.* Patriotic Songs.

I have nothing to say about this garden. Unexpected Visit. Fleur Adcock. BrAP

I have nothing to say on a white afternoon. Snow Day. Rosanna Warren. MoW

I have nothing to say to you, Billie Holiday. Billie in Silk. Angela Jackson. ReTh; SeSe

I have noticed that the hostess in peasant dress. For the Jim Crow Mexican Restaurant in Cambridge, Massachusetts, Where My Cousin Esteban was Forbidden to Wait Tables Because He Wears Dreadlocks. Martín Espada. PrTe

I have observed the learned astronomer. For Whitman. Diane Wakoski. ViWalt

I Have of Sorwe So Grete Woon. Geoffrey Chaucer. PtR *Fr.* Book of the Duchesse, The.

I have often imagined that glances. Valerio Magrelli. NeIt

I have only seen my mother in photographs. Goodnight, Goodbye. Meg Kearney. NevBe

I have only yielded you the privilege of my mouth. *Unknown*. SLW, *tr. by* Marjolijn De Jager, Sayd Bahodin Majrouh and André Velter

I have painted them in the same mild tones of grayish green. Orchid and Rock. Stephen Mitchell. WhBo

I have perceiv'd that to be with those I like is enough. Walt Whitman. SAmP *Fr.* I Sing the Body Electric.

I have pined for the sight of the sea for years. Beautiful Sea, The. Mary E. Tucker. CBWP-1

I have plans for you. Jesus Speaks to the Church at Eastertime. Elizabeth Burns. EdScPo

I have planted a cedar in my garden. Cedar, The. Han G. Hoekstra. TuT, *tr. by* Peter van de Kamp

I have played with her when a child. Alfred Tennyson. NAEL-6v2 *Fr.* Maud [A Monodrama].

I Have Plenty of Heart. Miguel Hernández. RaW; WED, *tr. by* Robert Bly

I have *poetic* licence, i WriTe thE way i waNt. According to My Mood. Benjamin Zephaniah. NOxBChV

I have pondered. Prayer #3. Jeff Tweedy. IIR

I have portrayed temptation as amusing. Good Loser, The. Sophie Hannah. HarvBoo

I have prayed for the end of his breath. Fay Zwicky. BMAP *Fr.* Three Songs of Love and Hate.

I have problems. Division of Labor. Feyyaz Kayacan. WoPoe, *tr. by* Feyyaz Fergar

I have put a blockade on high-mindedness. After Laforgue. Sean O'Brien. NeBrP

I have put on a grotesque mask. Last Poem. Hugo Williams. NPeEn

I have put upon my wall. For the Intellectuals. Jeremy Ingalls. YaYoPo

I have raged for thousands of years. Pear's Complaint. Greg Youmans. FTtHH

I have reached, alas, the long shadow. Sestina. Dante Alighieri. WoPoe, *tr. by* James Schuyler

I have read *seed catalogue* and *the wind our enemy* and *fielding* and still i will fail to present you. Prairie Long Poem. Jon Paul Fiorentino. PoPra

I have repainted my beauty mark and blackened my eyelids. *Unknown*. SLW, *tr. by* Marjolijn De Jager, Sayd Bahodin Majrouh and André Velter

I have risen from your body. Onion, The. John Thompson. Coast

I have said / She 's adulteress; I have said with whom. William Shakespeare. OxAEP-1 *Fr.* Winter's Tale, The.

I have said that the soul is not more than the body. Walt Whitman. ColAP *Fr.* Song of Myself.

I have sailed the south rivers of China and prayed to the hillside Buddhas. In Search of Aunt Jemima. Crystal Williams. AmPoNex; BtF

I have seen a court, and a dozen courts. Christmas Revel, A. Dafydd Bach ap Madog Wladaidd. OBWVE

I have seen / A curious child, who dwelt upon a tract. William Wordsworth. ITBLP *Fr.* Excursion, The.

I have seen a lovely thing. Blight. Arna Bontemps. ColAP

I have seen a robin cock his head so. Botticelli's St. Sebastian. Brigit Pegeen Kelly. ExTi

I have seen angels. Dancing with Demons. Christine de Luca. EdScPo

I Have Seen Black Hands. Richard Wright. APT-2; GPTC

I have seen come on. Death. John A. Stone. InoFa

I have seen flowers come in stony places. Epilogue. John Masefield. OxBEV

I have seen her, wonderful! This Version of Love. Dorothy Hewett. BMAP

I / have seen it. Texas Chainsaw Massacre. Sherman Alexie. LiTh

I have seen lines on a paper. Borders. Afaa Michael Weaver. GT

I have seen many horrible headlines. Oprah Out of Control. R. S. Gwynn. PoDa

I have seen myself and others. Before We Drown. Adrien Stoutenburg. CalPo

I have seen, O desolate one, the voice has its tower. Bell Tower. Léonie Adams. MoAmPo; OxBoAm

I have seen old ships sail like swans asleep. Old Ships, The. James Elroy Flecker. MoBrPo; OBMV

I have seen rare sunshine held in the first birch leaves. Annunciation. Ken Etheridge. AngWePo

I have seen the black Vedas. One Book, The. Velemir Khlebnikov. TCRusP, *tr. by* Kathy Lewis and Bob Perelman

I have seen the dazzling beauty of the swiftly flying wheel. Bicycle Glee Song, A. Glory Anna. ArBi

I have seen the high. Cave of Night, The. John Montague.

I have seen the rain speak. New Dream, A (Wuski A-Baw-Tan). Jennifer Pierce Eyen. ReEnLa

I have seen the soft light flicker. Message from Ohanapecosh Glacier. W. M. Ransom. GifTon

I have seen the sun break through. Bright Field, The. Ronald Stuart Thomas. AngWePo; TCAWP

I have seen this picture before. From Homegrown: An Asian-American Anthology of Writers. Colleen J. McElroy. LTA

I have seen your feet gilded by morning. Metamorphoses of M. John Peale Bishop. APT-1

I have serious doubts the people around me. Good Morning Coffee Makes Vivid of the Vague; Suddenly You Have Hands and Eyes and Legs! Peter Sears. NevBe

I have shut my balcony door. Casida of Sobbing. Federico García Lorca. AF, *tr. by* Robert Bly

I have slept and I awaken . . . Or I haven't awakened. Dulce Maria Loynaz. TANSG *Fr.* Last Days of Home.

I have slept by the cold window. Snow at Rohatsu Sesshin. Muso Soseki. EaWin, *tr. by* W. S. Merwin

I have slipped. Cycles in Flight: The Racing Bike. Allison A. deFreese. ArBi

I have so fiercely dreamed of you. Last Poem. Robert Desnos. AmFaPo, *tr. by* X. J. Kennedy

I have so little sorrow. Song. Patricia Jones. ISC

I have so often dreamed of you that you have become unreal.   I Have So Often
   Dreamed of You.   Robert Desnos.   SurPaPo, *tr.* by Mary Ann Caws

I have sown beside all waters in my day.   Black Man Talks of Reaping, A.
   Arna Bontemps.   APT-2; ColAP; NAAPv.2; SSLK; WaAnP

I have spent ten years.   Song Sun.   CATKP, *tr.* by Peter H. Lee

I have staked out my ground.   My Ground.   Marie Luise Kaschnitz.   PFTM-2,
   tr. by Lisel Mueller

I have stood in forests, so old and vast.   Forests and Caverns.   Eleanor Percy
   Lee and Catherine Anne Warfield.   SWaP

I have studied the tight curls.   Movement Song.   Audre Lorde.   VCAP

I have supposed my past is a part of myself.   Past, The.   Ha Jin.   NIL-7

I have swallowed a mighty gulp of poison.   Night in Hell.   Arthur Rimbaud.
   SxFrPo, *tr.* by Martin Sorrell

I have swum too far.   Waves.   Robin Robertson.   P180

I have syllables that need to be performed.   Can We Talk?   Laini Mataka.
   BtF

I have taken scales from off.   Fishmonger.   Marsden Hartley.   APT-1

I have taken that vow.   Red-haired Man's Wife, The.   James Stephens.
   MoBrPo

I Have Taken the Suits and Shoes to Oxfam.   Felicity Napier.   Prnts

I have the address exactly. I know her name.   At the Exhibition of Parables.
   Donald Revell.   BodElec

I have the blues.   Left All Alone Again Blues.   Anne Caldwell.   ReLy

I have the itch on my nape.   Pain.   Lupenga Mphande.   NAfrP

I have the net into which all fishes go.   Net, The.   Edith Södergran.   WoPoe,
   tr. by David McDuff

I have the same.   December 9th.   Eileen Myles.   PmAP

I have the white-blue eye of my Gallic ancestors.   Bad Blood.   Arthur
   Rimbaud.   MotU, *tr.* by Louise Varese

I have thee, thou hast me.   *Unknown.*   GePo, *tr.* by Alexander Gode

I have these poisons we must choose. (LL)   Song in Sligo.   Jean Garrigue.
   APT-2; OxBoAm

I have this feeling you were beautiful.   Emine and Hamide.   Hettie Jones.
   PrTe

I have this large tattoo on my chest. It is like a dream I have.   Confessional
   Poem.   Louis Jenkins.   RaBo

I have this need to feel you.   Love/a Many Splintered Thing.   Kevin Powell.
   InTrad

I have this thing, and only this, to do. (LL)   Parabola.   Alec Derwent Hope.
   BrAP; NOBAu; PoA 2002

I Have This Vision of Madness.   Perry Brass.   CAGL

I have thought of beaches, fields.   Bundles.   Carl Sandburg.   MoAmPo

I have thought so much about the girl.   Muliebrity.   Sujata Bhatt.   HarvBoo;
   MoWP; NeBrP

I Have Thoughts That Are Fed by the Sun.   William Wordsworth.   NPBRoP
   Fr. Fragments from Dove Cottage Manuscript.

I have thoughts that are fed by the sun.   William Wordsworth.   NPBRoP

I have thrown wide my window.   Midnight.   Michael Roberts.   OBMV

I have to confess that *Bon appétit* never strikes me as an appropriate invitation.
   Landscape and Chardin.   Charles North.   NYP2

I have to find it again, an extreme music. Inspired by voicings.   After C (3):
   Tayloriana.   John Keene.   FuFl

I have to go.   *Unknown.*   SonAtl, *tr.* by Alan Brierly

I Have to Go Now.   Maggie Estep.   HeMav

I have to remember.   Thirteen.   Jimmy Santiago Baca.   FaoP

I have to say poetry and is that nothing and am I saying it.   Opening the Cage.
   Edwin Morgan.   NIL-7

I have to sing.   Orpingalik's My Breath: Eskimo Song.   Stephen Berg.
   GifTon

I have to step.   Signatures.   Tomas Tranströmer.   WoBe, *tr.* by Robin Fulton

I have to thank God I'm a woman.   Affinity, The.   Anna Wickham.   NALW

I have torn down my peace.   Endings.   Bill Pearlman.   ICANM

I have tossed hours upon the tides of fever.   Bout with Burning.   Vassar Miller.
   MoAmPo

I Have Touched.   Patti Tana.   PasH

I have traveled, I have traveled.   Consumptive, The.   Priscilla Jane Thompson.
   CBWP-2

I have tried.   Soledad.   Brother Yao.   BtF

I have tried earnestly to express.   Gertrude Stein.   APT-1 *Fr.* Stanzas in
   Meditation.

I Have Tried Hard.   Zindzi Mandela.   HAWP; NAfrP

I have tried to shift the stars.   Juniper Moon Pulls at My Bones, The.   Earle
   Thompson.   HATNAP

I have turned into a little shrine, a favorite.   Favorite Little Shrine, A.   Enrique
   Lihn.   VCWP

I have turned to the landscape because men disappoint me.   Ram's Horn, The.
   John Hewitt.   ModIr; PNI

I have two countries: Cuba and the night.   Two Countries.   José Martí.
   TCLAP, *tr.* by Elinore Randall

I have two daughters.   Lost Land, The.   Eavan Boland.   NAEL-7v2

I Have Two Sons and the One I Love Best Is Robert.   Paula Tatarunis.
   BloBone

I have walked a great while over the snow.   Witch, The.   Mary Elizabeth
   Coleridge.   CABP; NAEL-7v2; NALW; PoBW; ViWPN; VWP

I Have Walked Down Many Roads.   Antonio Machado Ruiz.   RaW, *tr.* by
   Robert Bly

I have walked here before.   Stand Still.   Jim Peterson.   PoCoUp

I have walked, lost, over the world, asking for bread and light.   I Am Going
   Because the Ear of Wheat and the Dawn Are Not Mine.   León Felipe.
   RaW, *tr.* by W. S. Merwin

I have walked the distance of the earth.   Names and sorrows.   D. Rubin Green.
   CAGL

I have walked through many lives.   Layers, The.   Stanley Kunitz.   BodElec;
   CAP-8; ItP

I have walked to the very ends of the earth.   *Unknown.*   NAAPv.2

I have wandered for seventy years in the sea of illusion.   Deathbed Song.
   Buhyu Sunsoo.   BecRai, *tr.* by Kim Daljin, Kim Won-Chung and
   Christopher Merrill

I have wanted excellence in the knife-throw.   Language of the Brag, The.
   Sharon Olds.   FiBr; MakPoe; PBCAP

I have wanted other things more than lovers.   Monody to the Sound of Zithers.
   Kay Boyle.   PoA 2002

I have wanted to swim.   Why Women Become Water.   Annette Spaulding-
   Convy.   RWB

I have washed the mountain.   Mountain, The.   Hashim Shafiq.   IrPoTo, *tr.* by
   Ralph Saverese and Saadi A. Simawe

I have wasted my life. (LL)   Lying in a Hammock at William Duffy's Farm in
   Pine Island, Minnesota.   James Wright.   CAP-8; ColAP; ItP; MakPoe;
   NAMCP V.2; OxBoAm; StAl; TRP; VCAP; WaAnP

I have wasted so much.   Burned in the Test.   Wilma Elizabeth McDaniel.
   CalPo

I have watched the summer day come up from the top of a pier of the
   Williamsburgh Bridge.   John Reed.   APT-1; FTtHH *Fr.* America in 1918.

I have wept with the spring storm.   After the Persian.   Louise Bogan.   PoA
   2002

I have wished a bird would fly away.   Minor Bird, A.   Robert Frost.   APT-1;
   OWoS; SAmP

I have worked since daylight in the hayfields.   Day's End.   Alden Nowlan.
   Coast

I have wrapped my dreams in a silken cloth.   For a Poet.   Countee Cullen.
   BLPJKO; ItP

I have written.   Woman Who Wrote Too Much, The.   Kay Ryan.   ExTi

I have your name: wholly holy, Hebrew.   Water from the Well.   Duriel Harris.
   BRtP

I haven't.   Apparition.   Sherwin Bitsui.   LegDan

I Haven't Done Playing with Words.   Edvard Kocbek.   PoCho, *tr.* by Michael
   Scammell

I haven't learned to live abandonedly yet, Mother.   Scenes for an Elegy.
   Michael Klein.   WiU

I haven't remembered anything, only that the names.   Obvious Tradition, The.
   Bill Berkson.   NYP2

I haven't seen him, yeah.   Conscience.   Meirion MacIntyre Huws.   BBMWP,
   tr. by Geriant Løvgreen

I haven't the heart to poke poor Billy. (LL)   Harry Graham.   NBLV;
   NOxBChV *Fr.* Some Ruthless Rhymes.

I haven't the heart to say.   To an Unknown Poet.   Carolyn Kizer.   OPRER

I haveta turn my television down sometimes cuz.   Ntozake Shange.   UnSA *Fr.*
   Okra to Greens /.

I heal the ramparts of the deponent tense.   Global Rewards Redemption Centre,
   The.   Gig Ryan.   VaPo

I hear a bird.   How Are Things in Glocca Morra?   E. Y. Harburg.   ReLy

I hear a clock strike a hammer.   This Catching of Breath at the Top.   Robert J.
   Gibbs.   Coast

I hear a river thro' the valley wander.   Variations on a Fragment by Trumbull
   Stickney.   John Hollander.   NAMCP V.2; NoP-4; NoP-5

I hear a river thro' the valley wander.   Trumbull Stickney.   APN-2; NoP-4;
   NoP-5; OxBoAm

I hear a sound, like music through the gale.   Last Longhorn's Farewell, The.
   John P. Sjolander.   TiP2

I Hear a Step.   Ted Greenwald.   FTOS

I hear a whistling.   Emmett Till.   James A. Emanuel.   NIL-7; NIP-4

I hear again the tread of war go thundering through the land.   Albert Sidney
   Johnston.   Kate Brownlee Sherwood.   CBCWP

I hear America singing, the varied carols I hear.   I Hear America Singing.
   Walt Whitman.   BLPJKO; HHAm; ITBLP; MoAmPo; NIL-7; SAmP; TFi;
   WeW-3

I hear an army charging upon the land.   James Joyce.   CtM; IrLP

I hear an outcry in art.   Scream, The: Edvard Munch (1893).   Alan Llwyd.
   BBMWP, *tr.* by Joseph P. Clancy

I hear and is my heart not badly shaken? (LL) Shancoduff. Patrick Kavanagh. HarvBoo; WoPoe

I hear eating. Night Fun. Judith Viorst. TLR

I hear footsteps over my head all night. Walker, The. Arturo Giovannitti. APT-1

I hear her voice like. Her Voice. Barney Bush. HATNAP

I hear in my heart, I hear in its ominous pulses. Wild Ride, The. Louise Imogen Guiney. ColAP; RACG; TCAPo

I hear in the deep heart's core. (LL) Lake-Isle of Innisfree, The. William Butler Yeats. BLPJKO; CABP; ChAP; ClHu; HeIP-4; IPoFL; MoBrPo; NAEL-6v2; NAEL-7v2; NAMCP V.1; NoAM; NoP-4; NoP-5; OBEV; OxAEP-2; PoPoPo; TFi; UV; WaAnP

I hear it was charged against me that I sought to destroy institutions. I Hear It Was Charged against Me. Walt Whitman. APN-1; CAGL; MoAmPo

I Hear Music. Frank Loesser. ReLy

I hear music when I look at you. Song Is You, The. Oscar Hammerstein, II. ReLy

I hear my children come. They trample with their feet. Sick Queen, The. Frances Darwin Cornford. MoWP

I hear my neighbor's bees. (LL) By the Road to the Air-Base. Yvor Winters. NAAPv.2; NAMCP V.1

I hear myself / drought caught pleading. Echo. Audre Lorde. OxAAAP

I hear [or heare] the whistling ploughman [or plough-man] all day long. On the Ploughman [or Plough-Man]. Francis Quarles. NOSC; SacPr

I hear singing and there's no one there. You're Just in Love. Irving Berlin. ReLy

I hear tapping in your silence. Looking Deep. Magdalena Gomez. PueRic

I hear tell there's a stranger in the Jones household. F.D.R. Jones. Harold Rome. ReLy

I hear that since you left me. My Version. Kit Wright. NoP-5

I HEAR THAT THE AXE HAS FLOWERED. Paul Celan. PoSu

I hear the apes howl sadly. Written for Old Friends in Yang-Jou City While Spending the Night on the Tung-Lu River. Meng Hao Jan. WoPoe, tr. by Greg Whincup

I hear the halting footsteps of a lass. Harlem Shadows. Claude McKay. APT-1; ColAP; NAAL-5; NAAPv.2; TCAPo

I hear the man downstairs slapping the hell out of his stupid wife again. .38, The. Ted Joans. WeW-3

I hear the noise about thy keel. Alfred Tennyson. NAEL-6v2; NAEL-7v2; NAWM-7v2 Fr. In Memoriam A. H. H.

I hear the Shadowy Horses, their long manes a-shake. Michael Robartes Bids His Beloved Be at Peace. William Butler Yeats. NoAM

I hear the trumpets of flying angels. Trumpets, The. Jorge de Lima. TCLAP, tr. by Luiz Fernández García

I hear the voice. Israel. Carl Rakosi. ChIV-1

I hear the wood slats wince on the back porch. After the Wedding. David Biespiel. NAPBL

I hear they're hoping to run trips. 'Do You Think We'll Ever Get to See Earth, Sir?' Sheenagh Pugh. TCAWP

I hear voices in the next room. In the Bluemist Motel. Greg Pape. ReTh

I Hear You Call, Pine Tree. Yonejiro (Yone) Noguchi. CalPo

I hear you call, pine tree, I hear you upon the hill, by the silent pond where the lotus flowers bloom, I hear you call, pine tree. I Hear You Call, Pine Tree. Yonejiro (Yone) Noguchi. CalPo

I hear you have gone to live among the village mounds. Visiting the Hermit Cheng. Po Chü-i. TAL

I hear you, I will come. (LL) A. E. Housman. MoBrPo; NAEL-6v2; OxAEP-2; SoSe-8; UV Fr. Shropshire Lad, A.

I hear you Trane. Afreeka Brass. Mwatabu Okantah. SeSe

I hear you were. How I See Things. Yusef Komunyakaa. ESEAA; OxAAAP

I hear your familiar footsteps all about me. Second Life of My Mother. Jorge Carrera Andrade. TCLAP, tr. by Muna Lee

I hear your friends in the street. For My Daughter. Reginald Gibbons. LiTh

I heard a bird at dawn. Rivals, The. James Stephens. OBEV; OBMV

I Heard a Bird Sing. Oliver Herford. NTCP

I heard a Fly buzz—when I died. Emily Dickinson. APN-2; BrAP; ClHu; ColAP; HeIP-4; MoAmPo; NAAL-3; NAAL-5; NAAPv.1; NALW; NAMCP V.1; NAWM-7v2; NoAM; NoP-4; NoP-5; OxBoAm; PoPoPo; PtR; SAmP; SoSe-8; TCAPo; TFi; TRP; WaAnP; WeW-3

I heard a gentle maiden, in the spring. Time, Hope, and Memory. Thomas Hood. TreFP

I heard a great humming. Memory of Wings. Jabari Asim. BtF

I heard a herald's note announce the coming of a king. Rex Mundi. David Gascoyne. NoP-4

I Heard a Linnet Courting. Robert Bridges. OBMV
  (Linnet, The.) OBEV

I heard a mouse. Mouse, The. Elizabeth Jane Coatsworth. NOxBChV

I heard a puir deleerit loon. Newsboy. Albert D. Mackie. EdScPo

I heard a thousand blended notes. Lines Written in Early Spring. William Wordsworth. NAEL-6v2; NAEL-7v2; NOBRP; NPBRoP; SacPr

I heard a winter tree in song. Conceit. Mervyn Laurence Peake. Spl

I heard a woman. Butterflies under Persimmon. Mark Jarman. MAAN

I heard a woman's lips. Harrison Street Court. Carl Sandburg. APT-1

I heard a wood thrush in the dusk. Wood Song. Sara Teasdale. APT-1

I heard an angel speak last night. Curse for a Nation, A. Elizabeth Barrett Browning. NALW; ViWPN

I heard an elderly gentleman on the street say to his friend. David McFadden. NLPA

I heard an elf go whistling by. Behind Stowe. Elizabeth Bishop. BLPJKO

I heard an old farm-wife. Son, The. Frederic Ridgely Torrence. TCAPo

I heard an owl at midday. Como lo Siento. Lorna Dee Cervantes. NoAM

I Heard Christ Sing. Hugh MacDiarmid. ChIV-2

I heard Christ sing quhile roond him dar. I Heard Christ Sing. Hugh MacDiarmid. ChIV-2

I heard from Pablo Neruda. Pablo Neruda. Jose Angel Figueroa. PueRic

I heard hasty steps. Christmas. Gerardo Deniz. RMCMP, tr. by Mónica de la Torre

I heard her tell the story another way. Lighthouse, The. Vona Groarke. NIrP

I heard in the night the pigeons. No Child. Padraic Colum. OBMV

I heard it. Voice from the Dead, A. Mbuyiseni Oswald Mtshali. PML

I heard it on the radio today. BLS. G. E. Patterson. BRtP

I heard last night a little child go singing. Elizabeth Barrett Browning. PEW; VWP Fr. Casa Guidi Windows.

I heard last night a lovely lute. Summer Eve's Vision, A. Maria Jane Jewsbury. VWP

I heard my mother say it once. Lesson of the Teeth, The. Judith Ortiz Cofer. TouFir

I heard my name, the day rose and disappear over the beach. City of Men. Aaron Shurin. FTOS

I heard my son burst out of his room. Rightful One, The. David Ignatow. TaR

I heard new words prayed at cows. Seamus Heaney. ModIr Fr. Sweeney Redivivus.

I heard on the meadow. Heinrich von Morungen. GePo

I heard once. Sent to Yuan Chen at White Cabin Peak. Pao Hsien. CSKM, tr. by Paul Hansen

I heard one who said: "Verily." Cassandra. Edwin Arlington Robinson. APT-1; NoAM; OxBoAm

I heard or seemed to hear the chiding Sea. Sea-Shore. Ralph Waldo Emerson. APN-1; ColAP

I heard that many temples were destroyed. Lament. Hamhur Kiwha. BecRai, tr. by Kim Daljin, Kim Won-Chung and Christopher Merrill

I heard that when birds without feet get tired. To Single Women. Ch'ôn Yanghûi. EcSo, tr. by Aimee N. Kwon

I heard the bullet's hiss. John William DeForest. PCW Fr. Campaigning.

I Heard the Byrd. Oliver Lagrone. SeSe

I heard the dead men singing in the sun. (LL) Supremacy. Edwin Arlington Robinson. APN-2; NoAM

I heard the dogs howl in the moonlight night. Dream, A [or The]. William Allingham. IrV

I heard the dust falling between the walls. (LL) Redeployment. Howard Nemerov. AmWaPo; OBWP; PoWW

I heard the Indian Agent say. Old man's lazy, The. Peter Blue Cloud. HATNAP; LTA

I heard the jerk. Bicycle Days. Robin Becker. ArBi

I heard the man. Forgiveness. Morton Marcus. RaF

I heard the Master preach. Master's Sermon, The. Han Yong'un [or Yongwun]. CAMKP, tr. by Sammy Solberg

I heard the pulse of the besieging sea. To S.C. Robert Louis Stevenson. NePenScot

I heard the summer sea. World Voice, The. Bliss Carman. BrAP

I heard the terrible laughter of termites. Pest. Major L. Jackson. LegDan

I heard the trailing garments of the Night. Hymn to the Night. Henry Wadsworth Longfellow. APN-1; NAAPv.1; TCAPo

I heard them say I'm ugly. Ugly Child, The. Elizabeth Jennings. NOxBChV

I heard those voices again. Voices. Frances Bellerby. MoWP

I heard wild geese over the hospital grounds. Gunnar Ekelof. WED Fr. Swan, The.

I Heard You Solemn-Sweet Pipes of the Organ. Walt Whitman. APN-1; SAmP

I heard your heartbeat. Heartsong. Jeni Couzyn. BeAl; HAWP

I heave my morning like a sack. Norbert Dentressangle Van, The. Sophie Hannah. HarvBoo

I heed the warning not to "sit beneath the eaves." Passing Seven-League Rapids. Meng Hao Jan. ColAnChi, tr. by Daniel Bryant

I Held a Shelley Manuscript. Gregory Corso. BB; PmAP

I Held His Name. Alberto A. Ríos. NoAM

I held it truth, with him who sings. Alfred Tennyson. BrAP; CAGL; HeIP-4; NAEL-6v2; NAEL-7v2; NAWM-7v2; NoP-5 Fr. In Memoriam A. H. H.

I held out the shot mallard, she took it from me.   Daniel's Duck.   Kerry Hardie.   NIrP

I held the briefcase at arm's length from me.   Briefcase, The.   Paul Muldoon.   CABP; NAMCP V.2

I held the man for nothing in my arms. (LL)   Saint Judas.   James Wright.   GI; NAMCP V.2

I Held the Vein, But Death.   Dennis Phillips.   FTOS

I held your sins against you for so long.   Confession.   Eli Goodwin.   BtF

I helped to take them. (LL)   Confederate Flags, The.   Ambrose Bierce.   AmWaPo; CBCWP

I here, thou there, yet both but one. (LL)   Letter to Her Husband, Absent upon Public[k] Employment, A.   Anne Bradstreet.   BrAP; HeIP-4; NAAL-3; NAAL-5; NAAPv.1; NALW; NoP-4; NoP-5; PEW; PoPoPo; WaAnP

I, Hermes, have been set up.   Anyte.   OBVE; WoPoe, tr. by Kenneth Rexroth

I, Hermes, stand here by the windy tree-lined.   Anyte.   SaLy, tr. by Diane Rayor

I hid in its wet hollowed trunk.   Baobab Tree 1996, The.   Susan Hahn.   PoA 2002

I hide behind simple things that you may find me.   Meaning of Simplicity, The.   Yannis Ritsos.   PFTM-2, tr. by Kimon Friar

I hide my heart and not my deeds.   Chiao-jan.   CCL1, tr. by Stephen Owen

I hit the road as if it were a linear place to shake my fist.   Lisa Gill.   ICANM Fr. Letters to a Dead Trappist.

I hoard the sky a setting sun leaves.   Wandering Ch'ing-Ling Strea in Nan-Yang.   Li Po.   NDACCP, tr. by David Hinton

I hoed and trenched and weeded.   A. E. Housman.   MoBrPo; WeW-3 Fr. Shropshire Lad, A.

I hold a chipped bowl in my hands.   Game, The.   Edvard Kocbek.   PoSu, tr. by Michael Scammell and Veno Taufer

I Hold A Lust To See People.   Out of the Wailing.   Stephen Caldwell Wright.   ISC

I hold a newspaper, reading.   Fish.   Takahashi Shinkichi.   ZenPo, tr. by Takashi Ikemoto and Lucien Stryk

I hold after its bath, it looks. (LL)   Out of Bronx subway June forest.   Edwin Denby.   AHA; NYP2

I hold it towards you. (LL)   This Living Hand, Now Warm and Capable.   John Keats.   AmFaPo; NoP-5; TRP

I hold it true, whate're befall.   Alfred Tennyson.   UV Fr. In Memoriam A. H. H.

I hold my bet for the clouds.   Fete on the Lake.   Molly Bendall.   NAPBL

I hold my breath and balance on a cliff.   Prognosis.   Debra Bruce.   IllVoic

I hold my brudder wid a tremblin' han'.   Wrestle on, Jacob.   Unknown.   SSUS

I hold my honey and I store my bread.   My Dreams, My Works Must Wait Till after Hell.   Gwendolyn Brooks.   NoP-4; NoP-5; WaAnP

I hold my honey and I store my bread.   Gwendolyn Brooks.   IllVoic Fr. Gay Chaps at the Bar.

I hold that Christian grace abounds.   My Creed.   Alice Cary.   TreFP

I hold up my chin.   Little Red Riding Hood and the Wolf.   Gillie Bolton.   Prnts

I hold your head tight between.   Kenneth Rexroth.   APSN; APT-2; NAAPv.2; NAMCP V.1 Love Poems of Marichiko, The.

I hood my eyes against the savage light.   Nina Gabrielian.   CRWP Fr. Erebuni.

I hope I do not sound boasting.   Rubai.   Nazim Hikmet.   WoPoe, tr. by Taner Baybars

I hope my child'll [or ma chile'll].   Lament over Love.   Langston Hughes.   NAMCP V.1

I hope my good old asshole holds out.   Sphincter.   Allen Ginsberg.   NAMCP V.2

I hope that we will meet again.   Friend and Beloved.   Tim Seibles.   RD

I hope there will be someone.   Seven Days.   Gu Cheng.   WoBe, tr. by Joseph R. Allen

I hope they never get a rope on you, weather.   Weather.   May Swenson.   FTtHH

I hope to meet again. (LL)   There's a Meeting Here To-Night.   Unknown.   NAAPv.1; SSUS

I hope you'll make sense of the notes. (LL)   Waste Land Limericks.   Wendy Cope.   HarvBoo; PoCho

I hoped that with the brave and strong.   He Doeth All Things Well.   Anne Brontë.   SacPr

I hung foxfur on the door.   Mother, and Given Girl.   Unknown.   SonAtl, tr. by Alec Sett, A. Valderin and Tamer Yazircioglu

I hungered so for life! (LL)   Edgar Lee Masters.   APT-1; IllVoic Fr. Spoon River Anthology.

I hunt among stones. (LL)   Kingfishers, The.   Charles Olson.   APSN; HarvBoo; OxBoAm; VCAP

I / i look at your face my mama.   Mongane Wally Serote.   TSAP Fr. No Baby Must Weep.

I? / I walk alone.   Soliloquy of the Solipsist.   Sylvia Plath.   HarvBoo

I, Icarus.   Alden Nowlan.   BrAP; NOxBChV

I idle at the window.   On Spring.   Li Ch'ing-chao.   NDACCP, tr. by Kenneth Rexroth

I idly cut a parsley stalk.   On a Midsummer Eve.   Thomas Hardy.   FaBoVe

"I, if I perish, perish"—Esther spake.   Christina Georgina Rossetti.   OxBSo Fr. Monna Innominata.

I ignore their mouth smells voices touch.   To the Readers Who Write to Me.   Daria Menicanti.   CItWP, tr. by Cinzia Sartini Blum and Lara Trubowitz

I, Ikey Faa, being of whole and sound mind, (nobody thinks it but me).   Ikey: His Will in Winter Written.   George Mackay Brown.   EdScPo

I imagine her couplings and uncouplings.   Foxfire.   Dominique Parker.   SpirFl

I imagine it, a land.   Sir Gelli Meurig.   Ronald Stuart Thomas.   AngWePo

I imagine that these thousand.   Descent, The.   James Tate.   YaYoPo

I imagine this is a movement the owl loves!   Hearing Music Through Dark Trees.   Ethan Paquin.   LegDan

I imagine this [or the] midnight moment's forest.   Thought-Fox, The.   Ted Hughes.   BrAP; HeIP-4; MakPoe; NAMCP V.2; NoAM; NoP-5; NPeEn; StAl; WaAnP

I imagine you a virgin.   Haiti.   Chiqui Vicioso.   TANSG, tr. by Daisy Cocco De Filippis

I imagine you sitting on the doorstep.   These Words Are for You, Grandmother.   Jean Janzen.   ACAMVP

I imagined the atmosphere would be clear.   Writing in the Afterlife.   Billy Collins.   CAP-8

I implore Neptune to claim his child to-day! (LL)   At the Carnival.   Anne Spencer.   APT-1; NAAPv.2

I implore you, deer-shooter.   Anacreon.   SaLy, tr. by Diane Rayor

I impose on myself the costly punishment.   Purple Spot, The.   Ramón López Velarde.   BLPSL, tr. by Rene de Costa, Rigas Kappatos and Eleni Paidoussi

I in a new understanding of my confusion. (LL)   In Broken Images.   Robert Graves.   HarvBoo; NoP-4; NoP-5; TRP

I in My Bed of Thistles.   Rosalía de Castro.   SpanPo, tr. by Edwin Morgan

I, in your frutefull woomb conceyved, born was.   Nicholas Grimald.   PBRV Fr. Funeral Song, Upon the Decease of Annes His Mother, A.

I inhabit a sacred wound.   Lagoonal Calendar.   Aimé Césaire.   VCWP

I inhale my baby's.   Inhaling His Hair.   Gillian Ferguson.   NeBl

I insert the blue and silver.   Chembank Card.   David S. Mills.   InTrad

I insult the bourgeois! The money-grabbing bourgeois.   Ode to the Bourgeois Gentleman.   Mário de Andrade.   GPTC, tr. by Jack E. Tomlins

I intended an ode.   Austin Dobson.   OBEV Fr. Rose-Leaves.

I investigate / the sun. Let it do me.   I Investigate the Sun.   Imamu Amiri Baraka.   EGAG

I is the ghost of Stevey Fizzlegig.   Ghost, The.   Fitz-James O'Brien.   FaBoVe

I / is the total black.   Coal.   Audre Lorde.   ESEAA; NAAL-5; NALW; NAMCP V.2; NoAM; NoP-4; NoP-5; VCAP

(I is the total black.)   MoWP

I itched inside and caught my lover's eye.   Fēng Mĕng-lung.   ColAnChi; WoPoe Fr. Mountain Songs.

I jiggled it.   This Tooth.   Lee Bennett Hopkins.   TLR

I John saw. I testify.   "H. D."   NALW Fr. Tribute to the Angels.

I Join the Sparrows.   Ira Sadoff.   PfSP

I, José Hierro, a man.   Any Afternoon.   José Hierro.   RaW, tr. by Robert Mezey

I journey / And the highway journeys too.   Vasco [or Vasko] Popa.   PoSu Fr. Besieged Serenity.

I journeyed to the suburbs, and there I was told.   T. S. Eliot.   UV Fr. Choruses from "The Rock."

I joy, dear[e] Mother, when I view.   British Church, The.   George Herbert.   AngWePo

I joy not in no earthly bliss.   Quiet Mind, The.   Unknown.   NoSic

I joy to see how in your drawen work.   Edmund Spenser.   NoP-4; NoP-5; PBRV; WaAnP Fr. Amoretti.

I jump, as I pass myself in a window.   I'm the Guy with the Gut.   Ifor Ap Glyn.   BBMWP, tr. by the author

I just came back from a lovely trip.   Santa Claus Is Comin' to Town.   Haven Gillespie.   ReLy

I just can't seem to get that campus bloom.   Lonely Coed, A.   Billy Strayhorn.   ReLy

I just didn't get it.   Ego.   Denise Duhamel.   NeAmPo; SUP

I just fell / Hook, line and sinker.   What a Perfect Combination.   Irving Caesar, Bert Kalmar and Harry Ruby.   ReLy

I Just Found Out About Love.   Harold Adamson.   ReLy

I just got an invitation through the mails.   Top Hat, White Tie, and Tails.   Irving Berlin.   ReLy

I just have a sad look sometimes.   Chicana.   Edward H. Garcia.   TiP2

I Just Heard John Buffington Died.   Kalamu ya Salaam.   SpirFl

I Just Missed the Bus and I'll Be Late for Work.   Ariel Dorfman.   AF, tr. by Ariel Dorfman and Edith Grossman

I just said I didn't know.   Parachutes, My Love, Could Carry Us Higher.   Barbara Guest.   ASA; NYP2; OxBoAm

I just saw a maniac.   Five Foot Two, Eyes of Blue (Has Anybody Seen My girl?).   Sam M. Lewis and Joe Young.   ReLy

I just think it will happen, soon. (LL)   Going, Going.   Philip Larkin.   NAMCP V.2; NoAM; OxAEP-2

I just want to say a few words about the other.   Other Day, The.   Richard Jackson.   PfSP

I just wanted to tell what I saw.   don't Explain.   Betsy Sholl.   ACAMVP

I just woke up from a start afternoon nap. I.   Little Bad Dream Charm.   Kathy Fagan.   PoCho

I keep a blue bottle.   Melancholy inside Families.   Pablo Neruda.   RaBo; WED, *tr.* by Robert Bly and James Wright

I keep a blue vial.   Melancholy in the Families.   Pablo Neruda.   ConPit, *tr.* by Clayton Eshleman

I keep a TV monitor on my chest.   Shorts / Excerpts.   Bill Knott.   PBCAP

I keep a wall of rock or trees.   River Journal.   Bruce Weigl.   AmAlph

I keep asking.   Masaoka Shiki.   CAoMJL1, *tr.* by Burton Watson

I keep falling in love.   Jack Kerouac.   PmAP *Fr.* Mexico City Blues.

I Keep Forgetting.   Lily Brett.   HP

I Keep Going Back to Joe's.   Jack Segal.   ReLy

I keep him waiting, tuck in the curtains.   Rita Dove.   GT *Fr.* Suite for Augustus, A.

I keep looking for my face to appear on a milk carton.   Missing.   Joseph Stroud.   CalPo

I keep meaning to tell you.   Zohar.   Tom Carey.   KGB

I keep reminding my husband that we both ride.   Ellen Craft.   Honorée Fanonne Jeffers.   AnSo

I keep seeing your car in the streets.   Little Brother Poem, The.   Naomi Shihab Nye.   TiP2

I keep the custom of the Ferry.   Hostess of the Ferry Inn, The.   Gwerfyl Mechain.   OBWVE, *tr.* by H. Idris Bell

I keep the rustic gate closed.   Idleness.   Lu Yu.   NDACCP, *tr.* by Kenneth Rexroth

I keep thinking.   Paranoid Egotist, A.   Dan Nielsen.   SUP

I Keep to Myself Such Measures.   Robert Creeley.   NAMCP V.2; NoAM; OxBoAm; PmAP

I keep you locked up in a black display cabinet.   Ultimate Luxury Woman, The.   Virgil Mihaiu.   PML, *tr.* by Liviu Bleoca and Adam J. Sorkin

I keep your old snaps in my bottom drawer.   Old Snaps, The.   Derek Mahon.   IrLP

I kenning [*or* kening] through astronomy divine.   Edward Taylor.   ChIV-2; ColAP; NAAL-3; NAAL-5; NAAPv.1; NoP-4; NoP-5; TCAPo *Fr.* Preparatory Meditations Before My Approach to the Lord's Supper.

I kept brushing the cloth over the pouch of her stomach.   Night Strategies.   David Bottoms.   PoChi

I kept it hidden, it was easy.   Fragment (Found Inside My Mother).   Nick Flynn.   AmPoNex

I kept the house on the corner of Linden and Pineapple Streets.   Birdie McReynolds.   Samuel Hoffenstein.   NBLV

I kick the earth.   Windy Day/Slayton, Texas.   Charles Behlen.   TiP2

I kick through a forest of hands.   Annie Dillard.   UpMys *Fr.* Feast Days.

I kicked an Edinbro dug-luver's dug.   Nemo Canem Impune Lacessit.   Robert Garioch.   EdScPo

I killed a bee on the Street of Scissors.   Michael Palmer.   APSN

I killed a snake this morning in the grass.   Snake, The.   Vance Palmer.   NOBAu

I kiss my Russian Revolution.   Eduard Veniaminovich Limonov.   TCRusP *Fr.* Secret Notebook.

I kiss your lips.   Spring in This World of Poor Mutts.   Joseph Ceravolo.   AHA; FTOS; NYP2

I kissed I thanked juliette récamier.   Emma Zola at Wimbledon Let's Say.   Jude Stéfan.   YaTCFP, *tr.* by Marilyn Hacker

I kissed my father. (LL)   Gift, The: "To pull the metal splinter from my palm."   Li-Young Lee.   BodElec; CAP-8; LoL; NAMCP V.2; OpBo; RaBo; RoV; TWF; UnSA

I Kissed Pa Twice after His Death.   Mattie J. Peterson.   VerBaPo

I kissed the cold earth that is heaven.   Mea Shearim.   Tamara Kamenszain.   MirDau, *tr.* by Roberta Gordenstein

I kissed the warm live hand that held the thing. (LL)   Maundy Thursday.   Wilfred Owen.   NPeEn; OxBSo

I kissed you, bride and lost, and went.   Loser, The.   Adrienne Rich.   RACG

I kneel down to peer into a culvert.   Kneeling Down to Look [*or* Peer] into a Culvert.   Robert Bly.   NAMCP V.2; NoAM

I knew a cuckold once. I grieve for him.   My Friend the Cuckold.   Morris Gilbert Bishop.   OBCoV

I knew a guerilla fighter.   Guerilla Fighter.   Jofre Rocha.   NAfrP, *tr.* by Don Burness

I knew a man, a common farmer, the father of five sons.   Walt Whitman.   BLT *Fr.* I Sing the Body Electric.

I knew a man, he was my chum.   Trench Poets.   Edgell Rickword.   FaBoWar

I knew a man who could only love.   War Memoir, A.   Arnold Rattenbury.   RSaN

I knew a simple soldier boy.   Suicide in the Trenches.   Siegfried Sassoon.   FaBoWar; PoAgWa; PoWW

I knew a woman, lovely in her bones.   I Knew a Woman.   Theodore Roethke.   APT-2; BrAP; HeIP-4; ItP; MoAmPo; NAAL-5; NAMCP V.1; NIL-7; NoAM; NoP-4; NoP-5; OxBoAm; RaBo; SoSe-8; TFi; TRP; VCAP; WaAnP

I knew a young hooker / called Jade.   Janice Mirikitani.   UnSA

I knew, all the rest of my life.   To Get Clear.   J. P. Ward.   AngWePo

I knew her for a little ghost.   Little Ghost, The.   Edna St. Vincent Millay.   NAAPv.2

I knew her self was not in that strange place. (LL)   Harlem Dancer, The.   Claude McKay.   APT-1; ISC; NAAL-5; NAAPv.2; NAMCP V.1; NIL-7; NIP-4; NoAM; OxBoAm; TCAPo; WaAnP

I knew him as a friend: married. She was older.   Rowing in Familiar January.   Milo De Angelis.   NeIt, *tr.* by Lawrence Venuti

I knew how to make myself feel.   Warmness.   Anabel Torres.   TANSG, *tr.* by Celeste Kostopulos-Cooperman

I Knew I'd Sing.   Heather McHugh.   OxBoAm

I knew it was love, and I felt it was glory. (LL)   Stanzas Written on the Road between Florence and Pisa.   Lord Byron.   BrAP; NAEL-6v2; NAEL-7v2

I knew not grief.   Lament of Mary, The.   *Unknown.*   IQMS, *tr.* by Michael Beevor

I knew not who had wrought with skill so fine.   Before a Painting.   James Weldon Johnson.   GT

I knew that in winter it would snow.   Plumbers.   Susan Miles.   NOxBChV

I knew the artifice would finally come to this.   To an Audience.   John Koethe.   BAP-04

I knew the dick size of every boy in my class.   Sixth Grade.   Melanie Hope.   WiU

I knew the length of an average penis.   Size of It, The.   Timothy Liu.   WiU

I knew the names of all the cows before.   Girl on a Tractor.   Joyce Sutphen.   GoPo; IPoFL

I knew the time had come.   Nevertheless (I'm in Love with You).   Bert Kalmar and Harry Ruby.   ReLy

I knew too that through them I knew too that he was through, I knew.   Valentine to Sherwood Anderson, A.   Gertrude Stein.   NoAM; PFTM-1

I knew you.   Name, Many Names, A.   Anne Simpson.   Coast

I knew you forever and you were always old.   Some Foreign Letters.   Anne Sexton.   MoAmPo

I knew you in the passion of my prayers at night.   Hijrah [Migration] to God, The.   Nazik al-Mala'ika.   IrPoTo, *tr.* by Jenna Abdul Rahman and Saleh Alyafai

I knew your brother many years ago, but not that well, I said.   David McFadden.   NLPA

I knit a way through the traffic.   Morning Radio.   Deirdre Shanahan.   RWPCtW

I know.   Male Grownups.   Hoda Hussein.   PoArWo, *tr.* by Cornelia Al-Khaled

I Know.   David St. John.   CalPo

I know a bundle of humanity.   Young and Healthy.   Al Dubin.   ReLy

I know a couple of newlyweds.   Okay, Toots.   Gustave Kahn.   ReLy

I know a dark secluded place.   Hernando's Hideaway.   Richard Adler and Jerry Ross.   ReLy

I know a funny little man.   Mr Nobody.   *Unknown.*   ITBLP
   (I know a funny little man.)   ChAP

I know a green grass path that leaves the field.   Green River, The.   Lord Alfred Bruce Douglas.   OBEV

I know a little bit about a lot of things.   I Don't Know Enough About You.   Peggy Lee.   ReLy

I know a little cupboard.   Cupboard, The.   Walter De la Mare.   NTCP

I know a little language of my cat, though Dante says.   Robert Duncan.   FTOS; NAMCP V.2

I Know a Man.   Robert Creeley.   AmFaPo; CAP-8; ICANM; NAMCP V.2; NIP-4; NoP-4; NoP-5; OxBoAm; StAl; VCAP

I know a man who put together an ideal woman.   Ideal Woman, An.   Yehuda Amichai.   PoDa, *tr.* by Chana Bloch and Chana Kronfeld

I know a man who put together an ideal woman.   Ideal Woman, An.   Yehuda Amichai.   PML, *tr.* by Chana Bloch and Stephen Mitchell

I know a place where the sun is like gold.   Four-Leaf Clover.   Ella Higginson.   SWaP

I know a private mountain range with a big bowl in its center.   Geo-Bestiary #X.   James Harrison.   TAPaP

I Know a Strange, Gigantic Hymn.   Gustavo Adolfo Bécquer.   NAWM-7v2, *tr.* by Bruce Phenix

I Know a Village.   Phyllis McGinley.
   5:32, The.   APT-2

I know all about boys, I do.   All about Boys and Girls.   John Ciardi.   NOxBChV

I know all the notes of your voice. You. Gillian Coote. WhBo

I know at least some of my upper teeth could have been saved. Romeo, Grown Old. James Wright. BodElec

I know better. Family Tree. Yusef Komunyakaa. FaoP

I know. But I do not approve. And I am not resigned. (LL) Dirge Without Music. Edna St. Vincent Millay. AmFaPo; BrAP; GoPo; InoFa

I know but will not tell. Elegy. Alan Dugan. NIL-7; NIP-4

I know death is not where you end. (LL) Long Hill of Garrapata, The. Renée Gregorio. FiBr; ICANM

I know everyone. Jeep Driver, The. Martín Espada. PueRic

I know Exactly the Sort of Woman I'd Like to Fall in Love With. Deryn Rees-Jones. MFPA

I know exactly what I want to say. For J. W. Rafael Campo. RA

I know exactly what I want to say. Two Hundred and Sixty-Five Words. Sophie Hannah. HarvBoo

I know: from flesh. José Martí. TCLAP Fr. Simple Verses.

I Know Full Well the Water's Flowing Power. San Juan de la Cruz. SpanPo, tr. by James Edward Tobin

I know her children. Goddam Street, The. Robert Coles. BloBone

I know her not! Her hand has been in mine. Lady in the White Dress, Whom I Helped into the Omnibus, The. Nathaniel Parker Willis. APN-1

I Know How Every Poet. James Laughlin. TAPaP

I know how it happened and it has been a long time. Memorization. Adisa Vera Beatty. FuFl

I know how these things go. Small Power. Lynne Hugo. PfS

I know how to make a bed. Making a Bed. Howard Moss. OxBoAm

I know how worthless this poem will be. Shuntaro Tanikawa. PFTM-2 Fr. With Silence My Companion.

I Know I Aint Hip No More. Peter Harris. BtF

I know I am but summer to your heart. Edna St. Vincent Millay. HeIP-4

I know I am / The Negro Problem. Dinner Guest: Me. Langston Hughes. LTA; NoP-5; SSLK

I know I can only speak for myself. Glass Bracelets, The. Kimiko Hahn. PrTe

I know I change / have changed. Daguerreotype Taken in Old Age. Margaret Atwood. NoAM

I know I dreamed again last night. At Dawn. Michael Patrick Hearn. CA

I know I have the best of time and space, and was never measured and never will be measured. Walt Whitman. See I know I have the best of time and space, and was never measured and will never be measured.

I know I have the best of time and space, and was never measured and will never be measured. Walt Whitman. ColAP; NAWM-7v2; NoAM Fr. Song of Myself.

I know I have the best of time and space—and that I was never measured, and never will be measured. Walt Whitman. See I know I have the best of time and space, and was never measured and will never be measured.

I know, I know, Mother. Kamalākānta Bhattācārya. SinGod, tr. by Rachel Fell McDermott

I know I know short conviction. Silence Wager Stories. Susan Howe. BodElec; FTOS; WoBe

I know, I know—though the evidence. Blow, West Wind. Robert Penn Warren. ColAP; WaAnP

I Know I Ought to Love You. Selima Hill. NeBrP

I know I should pity me. I Should Care. Sammy Cahn. ReLy

I know if I find you I will have to leave the earth. Hymn. A. R. Ammons. WaAnP

I know in time there will be hell to pay. (LL) Hell to Pay. Susanne Doyle. CalPo; FFC

I know it by thy song! (LL) To a Wandering Female Singer. Felicia Dorothea Hemans. ViWPN; VWP

I know it's not playing Gaelic, it's simply not good enough. East. Conor O'Callaghan. NIrP

I know just how you feel. Young Don't Want to Be Born. James Wright. BodElec

I know member, know Lord. Bell da Ring. Unknown. SSUS

I know monks masturbate at night. Earnest Liberal's Lament, The. Ernest Hemingway. OBSV

I Know Moon-Rise [or Moonrise] [see also I Know de Moonlight and I Knoyw Moonlight]. Unknown. APN-2

I know my foolishness, a mere art trying to shake a tree. Yüan Hao-wen. ColAnChi Fr. Poems on Poetry.

I know my soul hath power to know all things. Sir John Davies. OBEV Fr. Nosce Teipsum.

I know my upper arms will grow. Life I Led, The. Nikki Giovanni. GT

I know no couple better can agree! (LL) On Giles and Joan. Ben Jonson. NAEL-6v1; NAEL-7v1

I know no paint of poetry. On Fairford Windows. William Strode. NOSC

I know no safe depository of the ultimate powers of the. Passage from a Letter to William Charles Jarvis, September 28, 1820. Thomas Jefferson. TWF

I know not how, dear heart, I came to love you as I do. Nathaniel to Ruth. Emily Jane Pfeiffer. ViWPN

I know not if it was a dream. I viewed. Passing Show, The. Ambrose Bierce. APN-2

I know not that the men of old. Men of Old, The. Richard Monckton, 1st Baron Houghton Milnes. OBEV; TreFP

I know / Not these my hands. Amaze. Adelaide Crapsey. APT-1; NAAPv.2; OxBoAm

I know not what awaits me. Last Hymn. Philip Paul Bliss. SacPr

I know not what I am, and what I know, I'm not. "Angelus Silesius." GePo Fr. Cherubical Wanderer, The.

I Know Not What I Seek Eternally. Rosalía de Castro. SpanPo, tr. by Muriel Kittel

I know not what my merit may have been, that I returned at dawn. Hagomel. Uriel Ofek. NRoS, tr. by Esther Raizen

I know not what to do. Fragment 36 [or Thirty-Six]. "H. D." BrAP; NALW; PoBW

I know not why, but all this weary day. Henry Timrod. APN-2

I know now I always wanted to write, to. Douglas Barbour. IFF Fr. Flame on the Spanish Stairs, A: John Keats in Rome.

I know now that once I longed to be white. When I Was Growing Up. Nellie Wong. OxWW; UnSA

I know of course. I, the Survivor. Bertolt Brecht. HP; PoSu

I know of your body: the reefs. In This Warm Dark Mosque. Coral Bracho. RMCMP, tr. by Suzanne Jill Levine

I know salt marshes that move along like one big. Audacity of the Lower Gods. Yusef Komunyakaa. CAP-8

I know some lonely Houses off the Road. Emily Dickinson. APN-2; MoAmPo

I know someone from another world is trying to get through to me. I Know Someone from Another World. James Tate. MotU

I know something / But I can't express it. S'posin'. Andy Razaf. ReLy

I Know That All Beneath the Moon Decays. William Drummond of Hawthornden. GSo

I know that He exists. Emily Dickinson. APN-2; NCAP

I know that he told that I snared his soul. Edgar Lee Masters. APT-1 Fr. Spoon River Anthology.

I know that his eyes look into mine. Assurance. Josephine D. Henderson Heard. CBWP-4

I Know That I Am a Great Sinner. Swami Purohit. OBMV

I know that I shall meet my fate. Irish Airman Foresees His Death, An. William Butler Yeats. BrAP; ChAP; FaBoWar; HarvBoo; HeIP-4; IrV; MoBrPo; NAMCP V.1; NoAM; NoP-4; NoP-5; OBMV; OBWP; PoAgWa; PoPoPo; PoWW; TFi; WaAnP; WeW-3

I know that life is Jason. Golden Fleece, The. Oscar Williams. PoA 2002

I know that peace is soon coming, and love of common object. Geranium. Edward Dorn. PmAP

I know that things are getting tougher. Knowledge. Tim Armstrong and Jesse Michaels. ASA

I know that this was Life—the track. Alfred Tennyson. CAGL; NAEL-6v2; NAEL-7v2 Fr. In Memoriam A. H. H.

I know that what our neighbours call longueurs. Lord Byron. OBSV Fr. Don Juan.

I Know That You Know. Anne Caldwell. ReLy

I know the bottom, she says. I know it with my great tap root. Elm. Sylvia Plath. NAMCP V.2; NoAM; NoP-4; NoP-5; OxBoAm

I know the colour rose, and it is lovely. Pathology of Colours. Dannie Abse. BloBone; NIP-4; NoAM; TCAWP

I know the incapacity of dream. Compassion's Bird. Jay Wright. ESEAA

I know the language just turns you into metaphor, rock of ages like. Fred Wah. NLPA Fr. This Dendrite Map: Father / Mother Haibun.

I know the man who eavesdrops. Last Call. Silvia Curbelo. TouFir

I know the moon is troubling. I Know. David St. John. CalPo

I know the [or a] thing that's most uncommon. On a Certain Lady at Court. Alexander Pope. OBEV

I know the rituals, the spells of grapes. Garrett Kaoru Hongo. GeoHom Fr. Cruising 99.

I know, the sadness. Spoonful of Cocoa, A. Ishikawa Takuboku. CAoMJL1, tr. by Leith Morton

I know the sound of the ecstatic flute. Lamp without Oil, The. Kabir. WED, tr. by Robert Bly

I know the spring that spurts and flows. Spring. Margherita Guidacci. CItWP, tr. by Cinzia Sartini Blum and Lara Trubowitz

I know the sun shines, and the lilacs are blowing. Enlisted Today. Unknown. CBCWP

I know the things I've lost are so many that I could not begin to count them. Possession of Yesterday. Jorge Luis Borges. WoPoe, tr. by Nicomedes Suarez Arauz

I know the truth—give up all other truths! Marina Ivanovna Tsvetayeva. OPOU; PLBUT, *tr.* by Elaine Feinstein

(I Know the Truth.) WPoS

I know the value of water. Thanksgiving. Tracy Philpot. IAoNAP

I know the way. Phyllis Webb. NLPA *Fr.* Naked Poems.

I know the ways of learning; both the head. Pearl, The. Matth. 13:45. George Herbert. BASC; ChIV-2; FSCP; NOSC; OxBEV

I know the wind. Leaves of Grass. Kang Ŭn'gyo. EcSo, *tr.* by Ann Y. Choi

I know thee not, bright creature, ne'er shall know. Charles Johnston. CenSon

I know them, their shapes & movements, their differing attitudes. Reprise. Pamela Alexander. AmAlph

I know there are pigeons smaller than we are. Evolving Similarities. Ralph Angel. BodElec

I know there is a person. Poem to Be Read and Sung. César Vallejo. TCLAP, *tr.* by Clayton Eshleman

I know there is someone. Poem to Be Read and Sung. César Vallejo. WED, *tr.* by Robert Bly and James Wright

I know these trees. Upper Marlboro. Kenneth Carroll. SpirFl

I know this chapter of misery—must bring. Lamentation. Dic Jones. BBMWP, *tr.* by Anthony Conran

I know this ground. I walked here once before. Whitman: The Wall. Philip Dacey. ViWalt

I know thou art a senseless thing. Old Crib, The. Mary E. Tucker. CBWP-1

I know 'tis vain ye mountains, and ye woods. Painter, A. Thomas Cole. APN-1

I know to whom I write. Here, I am sure. Epistle to Master John Selden, An. Ben Jonson. BASC

I Know Too Well and Sadly Enough. Luis Rosales. RaW, *tr.* by Ralph Nelson and Rita García Nelson

I know very well I could not. (LL) I Saw in Louisiana a Live-Oak Growing. Walt Whitman. APN-1; ColAP; NAAL-3; NAAPv.1; NAMCP V.1; NCAP; NIP-4; NoAM; NoP-4; OxBoAm; PoPoPo; PtR; SAmP; TCAPo; WaAnP

I know what I see. I Think That I Shall Never See. Jim Heynen. UrbNat

I know what it's like to be looked at. Kids on Television Imagine Me, The. Jordan Davis. HeMarv

I know what should be out. Ismail. HotL,

I know what the caged bird feels, alas! Sympathy. Paul Laurence Dunbar. APN-2; GT; IJHIL; NAAPv.1; NIL-7; NoP-4; NoP-5; SSLK; TCAPo

I know what's happening, see what's coming. Thursday Afternoon: Life Is Sweet. Holly Iglesias. SweBea

I Know When I'm Going Home. *Unknown.* SSUS

I know where I'm goin'. I Know Where I'm Going. *Unknown.* IrLP

I know where the timid fawn abides. Indian Story, An. William Cullen Bryant. NAAPv.1

I know why the caged bird sings! (LL) Sympathy: "I know what the caged bird feels, alas!" Paul Laurence Dunbar. APN-2; GT; IJHIL; NAAPv.1; NIL-7; NoP-4; NoP-5; SSLK; TCAPo

I know winter's here. Fe de vida. José Hierro. ConPit, *tr.* by Clayton Eshleman

I Know You Are, But What Am I? Paul Beatty. InTrad

I know you are reading this poem. Adrienne Rich. NAAL-5 *Fr.* Atlas of the Difficult World, An.

I know you don't know what. Argent, L'. Lorenzo Thomas. FuFl

I know you have a world I cannot share. Other Woman, The. Eavan Boland. IrLP

I know you. I recognise the stumbling sway. From the Moment I Picked Up Your Book. Ann Sansom. MFPA

I know you Lawyers can, with ease. Fables: Second Series. John Gay.

I know you little, I love you lots. My Love For You. *Unknown.* Spl

I know you: solitary griefs. Precept of Silence, The. Lionel Pigot Johnson. MoBrPo; SacPr

I know you think of me when you are lonely. Plea for My Heart's Sake. Naomi Long Madgett. SeSe

I know you think that things. Dear Superman. Ron Koertge. SUP

I know, you told me. Death and the Good Citizen. A. K. Ramanujan. PoetW

I know you wonder why I wear. Green Hair. Elinor Wylie. APT-1

I know—and yet I cannot share, as once. August the First; Court Martial. The Mother Speaks. Marjorie Oludhe Macgoye. HBAPE

I know—the Mongol yoke, the years of famine. Lev Vladimir Loseff. TCRusP, *tr.* by Henry Pickford

I lack the braver mind. Confession of Faith. Elinor Wylie. APT-1; MoAmPo

I laid down my long net in the big tide. Net Breaker, The. Brewster Ghiselin. APT-2

I laks yo' kin' of lovin'. Long Gone. Sterling Allen Brown. APT-2

I lament the abandoned. Chant of Lamentation. Haunani-Kay Trask. FiBr

I landed on Iona's holy isle. Iona. Frederick Tennyson. SacPr

I language want, to dress[e] my fancies in. Imagination. Margaret Lucas Cavendish, Duchess of Newcastle. BASC; NOSC

I lately lost a preposition. Naughty Preposition, The. Morris Gilbert Bishop. NBLV

I laugh till my jaw unhinges. Skin Full. Lavinia Greenlaw. NoP-5

I laugh when I hear that the fish in the water is thirsty. Thirsty Fish, The. Kabir. WED, *tr.* by Robert Bly

I laughed at sweethearts I met at schools. My Heart Stood Still. Lorenz Hart. ReLy

I laughed at that boy. Stuck. Cheryl Clarke. WiU

I launched a boat frail as a butterfly. (LL) Ted Berrigan. NYP2; PFTM-2 *Fr.* Sonnets, The.

I lay and listened to the long lisping sigh. Voice of the Wheat, The. Jack Lindsay. RSaN

I lay at rest in the violet-fragrant. Persephone's Journey. Patricia Monaghan. HW

I Lay Awake, Wandering in that Limbo. Gustavo Adolfo Bécquer. SpanPo, *tr.* by John Haines

I lay dear treasure for you. Pack, The. Frank Prewett. HATNAP

I lay down by the side of the road. Bluebonnets. Gail Mazur. CFP

I lay down in the empty street and parked. Advice from the Experts. Bill Knott. P180

I lay down singing, down. Ophelia in Utah. Kathleen Lynch. IaFF

I lay face-downward on the grass. Barrier, The. Louis Lavater. NOBAu

I lay in the dark, with him by my side. Bullet Hole Man. Nancy D. Tolson. BRtP

I lay in the Holy Cross. Reginald Pugh, The Man Who Came from the Army. Emma Lee Warrior. HATNAP

I lay my harp on the curved table. Harp, The. Po Chü-i. TAL

I lay on her bed. Loft, The. Richard Jones. GoPo

I lay on that rock where the storms have their dwelling. Rock of Cader Idris, The. Felicia Dorothea Hemans. RWP

I lay out the sheet. Dr. Wasserman. Brenda Coultas. HeMarv

I lay the suitcase on Father's bed. Strait-Jackets, The. Pascale Petit. BeAl

I lay waiting. Bog Queen. Seamus Heaney. NAMCP V.2; NoAM; RACG

I lay with an acupuncture needle. Even the Eagles Must Gather. Alma Villanueva. FFC

I lay with my heart under me. Cicada. Adrien Stoutenburg. CalPo

I lean on my staff, gaze at the sunlit snow. Evening View as the Snow Clears. Chia Tao. CCL1, *tr.* by Stephen Owen

I leaned out of window, I smelt the white clover. Jean Ingelow. TreFP *Fr.* Songs of Seven.

I leant [*or* leaned] upon a coppice gate. Darkling Thrush, The. Thomas Hardy. AmFaPo; BrAP; CABP; ClHu; CtM; HarvBoo; MoBrPo; NAEL-6v2; NAEL-7v2; NAMCP V.1; NIL-7; NIP-4; NoAM; NoP-4; NoP-5; NPeEn; OBEV; OWoS; OxBEV; PoPoPo; SoSe-8; TFi; WaAnP; WoPoe

I leap into the river, the current doesn't carry me away. *Unknown.* SLW, *tr.* by Marjolijn De Jager, Sayd Bahodin Majrouh and André Velter

I leapt out of bed as if stung. Telling Myself. Kay Ekevall. RSaN

I Learn a Lesson about Our Society. Janice Gould. GeoHom

I learn by going where I have to go. (LL) Waking, The ("I wake to sleep, and take my waking slow.") Theodore Roethke. AmFaPo; APT-2; BrAP; HeIP-4; IJHIL; ITBLP; MakPoe; MoAmPo; NAAL-5; NAMCP V.1; NIL-7; NIP-4; NoAM; NoP-4; NoP-5; OxBoAm; PoPoPo; RaBo; StAl; TFi; VCAP; WaAnP; WeW-3; WoPoe

I learn to live by guile, to do without love. Book of Routh. Carolyn Beard Whitlow. FFC

I Learned about Being Tough from a Stetson Ad. Adam Houle. RWB

I learned about love on a Templetouhy bog. Striking Distance. Tom French. NIrP

I learned from my mother how to love. What I Learned from My Mother. Julia Kasdorf. ACAMVP; AmPoNex; GoPo; PBCAP; SweBea

I learned harmony in mama's wails. She Kneels at the Wailing Wall. Cheryl "Blue." Floyd-Miller. BtF

I learned in my credulous youth. Why, Some of My Best Friends Are Women. Phyllis McGinley. AmWit

I learned it from my teacher way back in Sunday School. Reciprocity. Kim Gannon. ReLy

I learned of your death over spiced tea. For Etheridge Knight. Jackie Warren-Moore. SpirFl

I Learned That Her Name Was Proverb. Denise Levertov. UpMys

I learned / the interminable list. In Memoriam. Manuel Vázquez Montalbán. RaW, *tr.* by Robert Mezey

I learned the spoons from. Musician Talks about "Process," The. Rita Dove. ESEAA; PoDa

I learned three virtues from my teacher. Taking Pleasure in Myself. Hueung Powoo. BecRai, *tr.* by Kim Daljin, Kim Won-Chung and Christopher Merrill

I learned to be honest. Question of Climate, A. Audre Lorde. NAMCP V.2; NoAM

I learned to fuck one summer in a burgeoning subdivision. Development. Joel Brouwer. NevBe

I learned to name them—brown-nut-warm, wide. Afterwards: Caliban. Ansel Talvikki. AmPoNex

I learned to read in the dark. Song of the Third Generation. Julia Lisella. UnSA

I learned to shoot. Casting. Kevin Young. GT

I learned two things. Riding Lesson. Henry Taylor. GoPo; NBLV

I learned yesterday. Antonin Artaud. PFTM-2 *Fr.* To Have Done with the Judgment of God.

I leave Don Juan for the present, safe. Lord Byron. NOBRP *Fr.* Don Juan.

I leave him pleading. There's too much to do. (LL) Towards Curing AIDS. Rafael Campo. BloBone; NeAmPo

I leave it for you to say why it is. Pietà. Allen Afterman. NOBAu

I leave me people, me land, me home. Wherever I Hang. Grace Nichols. NAMCP V.2

I leave my empty house at dawn. Empty House. Yüan Chĕn. CrYelRi; ErotSp, *tr. by* Sam Hamill

I leave my property to my two daughters. Language's Will and Testament, The. Gwyneth Lewis. ATSWP, *tr. by* Robert Minhinnick

I leave myself about, slatternly. Slattern. Kate Clanchy. MoWP

I leave no tracks so my live loves. Death of thelma sayles, The. Lucille Clifton. OxAAAP

I leave the English Department for my second life. Her Rose Tattoo. Gerry LaFemina. AmPoNex

I leave the window open. Buffalo Dreams. Bart Edelman. RWB

I leave thy praises unexpressed. Alfred Tennyson. NAEL-6v2; NAEL-7v2 *Fr.* In Memoriam A. H. H.

I leave to the highborn. Reizan Osho Visits Me. Muso Soseki. EaWin, *tr. by* W. S. Merwin

I Leave You These Imprints on the Earth. Alda Merini. CItWP, *tr. by* Cinzia Sartini Blum and Lara Trubowitz

I led my Silvia to a grove. Song. Aphra Behn. BASC

I left a piece of my head in that smoky-smelling house, there. Visitor's Memories, The. Sandor Csoori. ConPit, *tr. by* Clayton Eshleman and Gyula Kodolanyi

I left by the front door. Difference, The. Jackie Hardy. NeBl

I left Cornell / with half a wit; six mismated socks. Prayer. Daniel Berrigan. AF

I left home as a youth and am returning an old man. Written Impromptu upon Returning to My Hometown. Ho Ch'e Ch'ang. ColAnChi, *tr. by* Victor H. Mair

I left it, precious, balanced. Silver Creature. Maxwell Boyle. ArBi

I Left My Hat in Haiti. Alan Jay Lerner. ReLy

I Left My Home. *Hungarian Oral Tradition.* IQMS, *tr. by* Dermot Spence

I left my home in a fair land. I Left My Home. *Hungarian Oral Tradition.* IQMS, *tr. by* Dermot Spence

I left my locked mouth. No-Word Hut. Muso Soseki. EaWin, *tr. by* W. S. Merwin

I Left My Low amd Humble Home. Nathaniel Hawthorne. APN-1

I left nothing behind me. Engraving Twenty-Nine. Fadhila Chabbi. PoArWo, *tr. by* Yaseen Noorani

I left parts of myself everywhere. St. Thomas Aquinas. Charles Simic. OxBoAm

I left thee when the midnight bell had tolled. Dream of Blue Eyes, A. Frederick William Faber. CenSon

I Left Those Walls. Nina Cassian. PoSu, *tr. by* Nina Cassian and Naomi Lazard

I left untilled by the force of gravity and passing especially quickly into. Transit. Prageeta Sharma. HeMarv

I let her garden go. Her Garden. Donald Hall. BAP-01; OxBoAm

I let him go. Angling. Elise Paschen. PoA 2002

I let mind and body go and gained a life of freedom. Han-shan Te-ch'ing. CSKM, *tr. by* Red Pine

I let my life keep on going every day. (LL) I Have Plenty of Heart. Miguel Hernández. RaW; WED, *tr. by* Robert Bly

I let my plummet sink and sink. Plummet, The. Edward Dowden. IrLP

I let myself be led because I let loose. Eduardo Milán. RMCMP, *tr. by* Roberto Tejada

I lie across the rafters of the loft. House, The. Robert Minhinnick. AngWePo

I lie alone in my grass hut. Ryokan. EMJL, *tr. by* Burton Watson

I lie and imagine a first light gleam in the bay. Achill. Derek Mahon. PBCIP; PNI

I lie at ease where cassia blossoms fall. Birdsong Valley. Wang Wei. CrYelRi, *tr. by* Sam Hamill

I lie in bed. Awakening. John G. de la Parra, Jr. BeDoSh

I lie in bed smelling the scent of cork. Old Woman Reclining. Claudia Buckholts. PfS

I lie in my crib midday this is. Baby's Pantoum. Anne Waldman. FFC

I lie in the palm of its hand. I wake in the quiet. Unknowing, The. Linda Gregg. ExTi

I lie in you, my space of love. Brevity of Embraces. Armanda Guiducci. CItWP, *tr. by* Cinzia Sartini Blum and Lara Trubowitz

I lie like a stone on the hill. In the Jerusalem Hills. Leah Goldberg. FIT, *tr. by* Robert Friend

I lie on my back in the cemetery, elbows tight. Mt. Auburn Owl. Pamela Alexander. AmAlph

I lie out flat on the river pavilion. River Pavilion. Tu Fu [*or* Du Fu]. CrYelRi, *tr. by* Sam Hamill

I lie under the crust of the night singing. Pregnant Woman. Ingrid Jonker. HAWP, *tr. by* Jack Cope and William Plomer

I lie under your hand—a cur. Dog. Ingrid Jonker. HAWP, *tr. by* Jack Cope and William Plomer

I lied about the shortcut, the high road. More Fun in the New World. Karen Solie. OpeFie; PoPra

I lied when I said I'd get back to entertaining myself. Will Run Like Rabbits for Food. Chris O. Cook. FreRad

I lift my head and watch. Thoughts in Exile. Su Tung-p'o. NDACCP, *tr. by* Kenneth Rexroth

I lift my heavy heart up solemnly. Elizabeth Barrett Browning. CenSon; LW; NALW; PEW; VWP *Fr.* Sonnets from the Portuguese.

I lift my lamp beside the golden door! (LL) New Colossus, The. Emma Lazarus. AmFaPo; APN-2; CA; CtM; FaBoA; GS; GSo; HHAm; NAAPv.1; NIL-7; NoP-4; NoP-5; OxBoAm; SWaP; TCAPo

I lift the boy's body. Good Shepherd, The: Atlanta, 1981. Ai. RACG

I lift up mine eyes unto the hills. Hills, The. D. H. Lawrence. ChIV-1

I light my candles. Ritual. Rosita Kalina. MirDau, *tr. by* Roberta Gordenstein

I Light My Lamp. Luis Cano. OWABP

I like a church; I like a cowl. Problem, The. Ralph Waldo Emerson. APN-1; NAAL-3

I like a look of Agony. Emily Dickinson. APN-2; BrAP; HeIP-4; NAAL-3; NAAL-5; NoP-4; NoP-5; PoPoPo; TCAPo

I like a pinto bean now and then. Brightness. Maggie Nelson. HeMarv

I like a ship in storms was tossed. John Gay. NoP-5 *Fr.* Beggar's Opera, The.

I like being in a city crowd where no one. Encounter. Marianne Poloskey. RWB

I like being in your apartment, and not disturbing anything. Staying at Ed's Place. May Swenson. VCAP

I like divorce. I love to compose. No Return. William Matthews. P180

I like hanbok because it's roomy. Hanbok. Pak Mogwŏl [*or* Mokwŏl]. CAMKP, *tr. by* Kevin O'Rourke

I like it here. Under the Apple Tree. Diana Rivera. InvLad

I like it when my friend has lovers, their happy moans. For Every Heart. Olga Broumas. ErotSp

I like lazy weather. Lazy River. Sidney Arodin and Hoagy Carmichael. ReLy

I like learning useless things. Learning. Michael Casey. YaYoPo

I like mine overripe. Bittermelon. Alan Chong Lau. WhBo

I like my anger my grouchy furious love. Ikkyu Sojun. IJHIL, *tr. by* Stephen Berg

I like my body when it is with your. E. E. Cummings. PasH

I like my body when you hover over me. Moonburn. Laura H. Kennedy. PasH

I Like My Own Poems. Jack Grapes. SUP

I like my poems short. Steve Sanfield. WhBo

I like people. Trombone Solo. Stoddard King. NBLV

I like poems that resemble a tram. Imitation of Boileau. Yelena Shwarts. TCRusP, *tr. by* Anna Barker and Daniel Weissbort

I like "short grass" and the way we sang once—James Hamilton and I sang once. Ballad Values (2). C. S. Giscombe. RD

I like sitting alone when the moon is shining. Song of the pines. Po Chü-i. TAL

I like sleeping with somebody. *Unknown.* EaWin, *tr. by* J. Moussaieff Masson and W. S. Merwin

I like Sunday evenings after you're here. To H. John Wieners. FTOS

I like the articulate crack. Pool Is a Godless Sport. James Haug. MoASP

I like the backs of houses. Fronts are smug. Hinterland. Margaret Stanley-Wrench. OBGa

I like the clattering of hoof on street. Metrics. Rhina P. Espaillat. FFC

I like the cold rooms of autumn, sitting. Morning Coffee. György Petri. VCWP, *tr. by* Geroge Gömöri and Clive Wilmer

I like the cool and heft of it, dull metal on the palm. Smoking. Elton Glaser. BAP-97; P180

I like the fact that our most important conversations are held in the sea. Conversations with Louis. Jane Duran. MoWP

I like the fox shall grieve. John Gay. NoP-5 *Fr.* Beggar's Opera, The.

I like the generosity of numbers. Numbers. Mary. P180; PoDa

I like the hunting of the hare. Old Squire, The. Wilfrid Scawen Blunt. OBEV

I like the idea that nothing. For Jose Mercado Vasquez and Frances Roman Vasquez. Robert Vasquez. GeoHom

I Like the Likes of You. E. Y. Harburg. ReLy

I like the things with roots that know the earth. Things That Grow. Hazel Hall. NAAPv.2

I like the way they look together. Photograph of My Parents. Silvia Curbelo. TouFir

I Like Them Fluffy. Sir Alan Patrick Herbert. NBLV

I like these men and women who have to do with death. Common and Particular. David Constantine. PoCu

I like this secret walking. Charles Reznikoff. APT-2

I like to be alone. In My Leisure. Chungji. BecRai, tr. by Kim Daljin, Kim Won-Chung and Christopher Merrill

I Like to Collapse. Joseph Ceravolo. NYP2

I like to find. Pleasures. Denise Levertov. NAMCP V.2; NoAM

I like to get off with people. Conviction (iv). Stevie Smith. LW

I like to hear of wealth and gold. Common Things. Paul Laurence Dunbar. GT

I like to lay. Why I Dont Leave the Apartment Until After Ten Some Mornings. Kalamu ya Salaam. BtF

I like to look at you. You Touch Me. Andrena Zawinski. PasH

I like to smell the pillows, you say to me. Pillows. Antonio Deltoro. RMCMP, tr. by Christian Viveros-Fauné

I like to think (and). All Watched Over by Machines of Loving Grace. Richard Brautigan. CalPo

I like to think of a day for all those. Coming into Their Own. Sheenagh Pugh. AngWePo

I Like to Think of Harriet Tubman. Susan Griffin. NALW

I like to think the first one. After the Neutron. Terrance Keenan. AtGh

I like to touch your tattoos in complete. First Poem for You. Kim Addonizio. CalPo

I like to walk / And hear the black crows talk. Crows. David McCord. MoAmPo

I like to walk down Fisher Street. Fisher Street. Thylias Moss. GT

I like to watch. Bath, The. Robin Becker. PBCAP

I like you when you are silent and you look as if you are absent. Poem 15. Pablo Neruda. BLPSL, tr. by Rene de Costa, Rigas Kappatos and Eleni Paidoussi

I like you with nothing. Are you. Sky. William Stafford. PoDa

I like your handsome drugs. Your pleasant. Joshua Beckman. LegDan

I like your thin nose. Larry Fagin. AHA Fr. Parade of the Caterpillars, The.

I liked rainy days. My Life Before I Knew It. Lawrence Raab. GoPo

I liked that, said Offa, "sing it again." (LL) Geoffrey Hill. NAMCP V.2; NoAM; NPeEn; WoPoe Fr. Mercian Hymns.

I liked the way. Power of Prayer, The. Rita Ann Higgins. MoWP

I likes a woman. Preference. Langston Hughes. APSN

I likes to take it real slow. (LL) Reactionary Poet, The. Ishmael Reed. ESEAA; GT

I limp along, looking for feathers. Stuffy Turkey. Dave Etter. SeSe

I 'listed at home for a lancer. Lancer. A. E. Housman. MoBrPo; OBWP

I listen, and the mountain lakes. Maybe Alone on My Bike. William Stafford. ArBi

I listen through underground walls like prisoners signaling. Gloria Gervitz. MirDau Fr. Yiskor.

I Listen to Alice Walker on a Pocket Radio. Paulann Petersen. FiBr

I listened, heartwise, for the knock. (LL) Sweep Me through Your Many-Chambered Heart. Diane Ackerman. NIL-7; NIP-4

I listened to the Phantom by Ontario's shore. Walt Whitman. MoAmPo Fr. By Blue Ontario's Shore.

I listened to the voices that shattered. Enmeshment. Lewis Warsh. FTOS

I little thought (my Damon) once, that you. Irreconcilable, The. Damaris, Lady Masham. EMWP

I live alone, like pith in a tree. "Michaelangelo" the Elder. Bob Kaufman. OxAAAP

I live alone where echoes roost. Charles Bennett. NewEx

I live amidst hills of desolate buildings. For South Bronx. Sandra Maria Esteves. PueRic

I Live and Do Not Live in Myself. San Juan de la Cruz. SpanPo, tr. by Stephen Stepanchev

I live at the foot of the mountain. Unknown. CATKP, tr. by Kevin O'Rourke

I live at the head of the Long River. Tune: "The Diviner." Li Chih-yi. ColAnChi, tr. by Victor H. Mair

I live between. I stalk space of these authors shunt. This Garden Being: The Hanging of Books. Clark Coolidge. FTOS

I live for books. Light. Diane Wakoski. OPOU

I Live for My Car. Wanda Coleman. SUP

I live in a doorway. Sonrisas. Pat Mora. NIL-7; NIP-4

I live in a little country village. Han-shan (Cold Mountain). WoPoe, tr. by Robert Henricks

I live in a room named East. Suddenly. Robin Blaser. FTOS

I live in a town. Family Jewels. Essex Hemphill. GT

I live in an orchard. Confetti of bruised petals. Postcard from the Garden. Marge Piercy. NoAM

I Live in Music. Ntozake Shange. ISC

I live in peace and quiet, confining myself to home. My Way. Kim Koengp'il. CATKP, tr. by Chi-gyu Kim [or Kim Chonggil]

I live in sin, and dying to myself I live. Michelangelo Buonarroti. CAGL, tr. by James M. Saslow

I Live in the Mouth of History. Kalamu ya Salaam. SpirFl

I live in the town of Cahir. Haulier's Wife Meets Jesus on the Road Near Moone, The. Paul Durcan. ModIr

I live in town without all that racket. T'ao Ch'ien. NDACCP Fr. Drinking Wine.

I live inside of a machine. On Being a Householder. Alan Dugan. NAMCP V.2; NoAM

I live my life day today as if. To My Bones. Zoltán Jékely. IQMS, tr. by George Szirtes

I live on my farm in a beautiful vale. Edward Williams. AngWePo Fr. Happy Farmer, The.

I live on the water. Winding Up. Derek Walcott. NoAM

I live quietly and go nowhere. My Father's House. Calvin Forbes. ESEAA

I live / with a bullet in my heart. Margarita Iosifovna Aliger. ItWoWo, tr. by Daniel Weissbort

I live with love encompassed round. Love's Mirror. Constance Naden. ViWPN; VWP

I live without inhabiting/ Myself. San Juan de la Cruz. OBVE Fr. Coplas about the Soul Which Suffers with Impatience to See God.

I live; yet 'tis not I. He lives in me. Devotion. Paul Fleming. GePo, tr. by F. Warnke

I lived alone as happy as Larry. Brian Merriman. OBVE Fr. Midnight Court, The.

I lived behind a window. Idyll. Peter Balakian. PfSP

I lived between my heart and my head. Self-Portrait. Edward Hirsch. RoV

I lived for many years in the bush—far out—and I starved for lack of rain. Gravy Train, The. R. R. Davidson. NOBAu

I lived for thousands and thousands of years as a mineral and then I died and became a plant. Tell Me, What Have I Lost? Jelaluddin Rumi. WED, tr. by Robert Bly

I lived here nearly 5 years before I could. Chicago Poem. Lew Welch. BB

I lived here, too. On prison fare and water. On the Wall of My Age. Lajos Áprily. IQMS, tr. by Paul Tabori

I lived in a house. Painted Windows. Gloria Fuertes. RaW, tr. by Philip Levine

I lived in a ruin called The Lion. Pentti Saarikoski. PML, tr. by Herbert Lomas

I lived in a tree. The dream specified. Condo. Louise Glück. BodElec

I lived in the first century of world wars. (LL) Poem: "I lived in the first century of world wars." Muriel Rukeyser. FTtHH; NAMCP V.2; RaF; WaAnP

I lived in the first century of world wars. Poem. Muriel Rukeyser. FTtHH; NAMCP V.2; RaF; WaAnP

I lived in those times. For a thousand years. Epitaph. Robert Desnos. PFTM-1

I lived inside myself until I loved. Psalm (Traherne). Dan Beachy-Quick. LegDan

I lived on an alley where every cat and dog. Ambassador, The. Pablo Neruda. TAPaP, tr. by William O'Daly

I lived on drugs and understood the pushers. Passing Through Experiences. Robert Adamson. BMAP

I lived on this earth in an age. Fragment. Miklós Radnóti. IQMS, tr. by Geroge Gömöri and Clive Wilmer

I lived with Mr. Punch, they said my name was Judy. Variations. Randall Jarrell. WoPoe

I lived with my old man full nigh ten year. How Elizabeth Foole and Her Husband Parted by Means of Her Sister in Law. Elizabeth With. EMWP

I lived with visions for my company. Elizabeth Barrett Browning. CenSon Fr. Sonnets from the Portuguese.

I loathe a boy who won't be hugged and kissed. Strato. CAGL, tr. by Daryl Hine

I loathe [or lothe] that I did love. Aged Lover Renounceth Love, The. Thomas, 2d Baron Vaux of Harrowden Vaux. NoSic

I loathe them, I loathe them. Unknown. CATKP, tr. by Wen Hsia-min

I loathe you: keep your distance, you lowly crowd! Against Horace. Mihály Babits. IQMS, tr. by Adam Makkai and J. G. Nichols

I loathed you, Spoon River. I tried to rise above you. Edgar Lee Masters. APT-1; OxBoAm Fr. Spoon River Anthology.

I Locked the World Out. Emilio Prados. RaW, tr. by Hardie St. Martin

I long for critical acclaim. Starlette. Chioma Okereke. BRtP

I long for him most. Ono no Komachi. ErotSp, *tr. by* Sam Hamill

I long for my voice that found you. Now. Cengiz Bektaş. NaPG, *tr. by* Talat Sait Halman

I long for the call to council. Alcaeus. WoPoe, *tr. by* Sam Hamill

I long to talk[e] with some old lover's ghost. Love's Deity [*or* Deitie]. John Donne. SoSe-8

I longed for your lips, dreamed of their roses. We Who Were Executed. Faiz Ahmad Faiz. PoetW, *tr. by* Agha Shahid Ali

I look. Catharina Regina von Greiffenberg. WPoS *Fr.* On the Sweet Comfort Brought by Grace.

I look. Daughter. Susan Griffin. PoChi

I look after you as you go. Weingarten Travel Blessing, The. *Unknown.* GePo, *tr. by* Carroll Hightower

I look at a gaunt face. Face. Yi Sang. CAMKP, *tr. by* Edward Mack

I look at girls as an act of escapism. Why I Look at Girls. Christian Langworthy. IIR

I look at my mother's photograph on the wall. Depression. János Pilinszky. IQMS, *tr. by* Peter Jay

I look at my shadow over and over in the lake. Looking in the Lake. Po Chü-i. TAL

I look at the mountain from the window. In Hiding. Miklós Radnóti. TAPaP, *tr. by* Stephen Berg, S. J. Marks and Steven Polgar

I look at the night through the window. Candlelight Dinner. Oscar Hahn. PML, *tr. by* James Hoggard

I look at the sky and [its] stars scattered everywhere. Bare Rocks and Stars. *Vietnamese Oral Tradition.* CaDao, *tr. by* John Balaban

I look at the swaling sunset. In Trouble and Shame. D. H. Lawrence. OBMV

I look at the tree. Just Made It. Lawson Fusao Inada. WhBo

I look at you. Empty Streets. Hilmi Yavuz. NaPG, *tr. by* Talat Sait Halman

I / Look at you and suddenly. Old Devil Moon. E. Y. Harburg. ReLy

I look at you so old and unaccomplished. I Look at You So Old. Armanda Guiducci. CItWP, *tr. by* Cinzia Sartini Blum and Lara Trubowitz

I look at you this way. Song for Saint Ein. B. P. Nichol. OpeFie

I look at you woman. Letter to a Black Woman. Sharron K. Williams. OWABP

I look back—I do not see the ancients. Song on Youzhou Terrace. Chen Zi'ang. CCL1, *tr. by* Stephen Owen

I look down at my husband leaving me. Turning into an Oak Tree. Cindy Goff. LaCa

I look for a way of writing. Valerio Magrelli. NeIt

I look hard at the eyes that are real. Clown, The. Renée Gregorio. ICANM

I look, I look. Home. Franta Bass. INSAB

I look in that one kind of dwindled. And in this. Album—A Runthru. Clark Coolidge. AHA; FTOS; NYP2

I Look into My Glass. Thomas Hardy. HarvBoo; NAEL-6v2; NAEL-7v2; NAMCP V.1; NoP-4; NoP-5; OxAEP-2; WeW-3

I look into the eyes of loved women. Savior. Ray Gonzalez. TouFir

I look into the lake (the lacquered water). From a Boat at Coniston. Norman Nicholson. NLP

I Look into the Sky. Emilio Prados. RaW, *tr. by* María Isabel Chipman Prados

I look now within myself. Poem for Mankind and Its Hope. Clementina Suárez. TANSG, *tr. by* Janet N. Gold

I look onto an alley here. Day for Anne Frank, A. C. K. Williams. TaR

I look out of the window at the retreating back. Jealousy. Inna L'vovna Lisnyanskaya. CRWP, *tr. by* Daniel Weissbort

I look out the window: spring is coming. To Robert Lowell and Osip Mandelstam. Frederick Seidel. BodElec

I look over my own shoulder. Zen of Housework, The. Al Zolynas. BLT

I look over the old photos. Camp Story. Michael S. Harper. OxAAAP

I looked across the rollers of the deep. Frederick Goddard Tuckerman. NoP-5 *Fr.* Sonnets.

I looked across the water. Loon upon the Lake, The. *Ojibwa Oral Tradition.* APN-2; OWoS, *tr. by* Charles Fenno Hoffman

I looked at my days and saw that. Purpose. Desmond O'Grady. PBCIP

I looked at my horoscope. It's a Good Day. Dave Barbour and Peggy Lee. ReLy

I looked at that face, dumbfounded. The lights of *métro* stations flew by. Esse. Czeslaw Milosz. MotU, *tr. by* the author and Robert Pinsky

I looked down on a child today, not becuse he or she was smaller than me. I Looked Down on a Child Today. Barry MacSweeney. VaPo

I looked for Beauty:—on a throne. Beauty and Her Visitors. Winthrop Mackworth Praed. NOBRP

I looked for my love's long-home. Suliko. *Unknown.* SonAtl, *tr. by* Dorli Meek and Tamara Romanyk

I looked for you all my life. To Papaji. Nina Wise. WhBo

I looked for you everywhere yet nowhere. Cloak of Dawn. Amadou Lamine Sall. NAfrP

I looked in my heart while the wild swans went over. Wild Swans. Edna St. Vincent Millay. HarvBoo; MoAmPo; MoWP; OWoS

I looked in the first glass. Three Mirrors, The. Edwin Muir. NoAM

I looked into my heart to write. Summer Song I. George Barker. HarvBoo

I looked into the eyes of Robert Frost. Worldly Failure. Richard Eberhart. VisFro

I looked on that prophetic land. Presences Perfected. Siegfried Sassoon. MoBrPo

I looked out toward the pasture at the cows. Africa. Michael Heffernan. VisFro

I looked to find a man who walked with God. Enoch. Jones Very. ChIV-1; TCAPo

I looked to find Spring's early flowers. Lament of the Flowers, The. Jones Very. APN-1; ColAP

I Looked Up from My Writing. Thomas Hardy. NAMCP V.1; NoAM; WaAnP

I Looked You in the Face Last Night. Aneirin Talfan Davies. BBMWP, *tr. by* Joseph P. Clancy

I loosened my cap strings and put on serge clothes again. Poem about my Study at the Back of the House. Chan Fang-sheng. CCL1, *tr. by* John Frodsham

I lose faith in my left hand. Heart's Graveyard Shift, The. Yusef Komunyakaa. InGu

I lose myself within thy mind—from room. To Elizabeth Barrett Browning, in 1851. Dora Greenwell. PoBW; VWP

I lost my friend. Talin of the Pasta Factory. Rossana Ombres. CItWP, *tr. by* Cinzia Sartini Blum and Lara Trubowitz

I lost: my Joy turn'd to a Blaze. (LL) Apostacy, The. Thomas Traherne. OxBEV; SacPr

I lost the love, of heaven above. Vision, A. John Clare. NAEL-6v2; NAEL-7v2; OxBEV

I lov'd thee from the earliest dawn. Early Affection. George Moses Horton. TCAPo

I lovd thee living and lament thee dead. Mrs. Winchcombe. EMWP

I love a girl named Madelin'. Paddlin' Madelin' Home. Harry Woods. ReLy

I love a lady's bottom. The family objects. The family says this love will mean the end of them. January 11, 1997. Joe Wenderoth. IIR

I love a man who is not worth. Did This Happen to Your Mother? Did Your Sister Throw Up a Lot? Alice Walker. ISC

I love a still conservatory. Magic. Walter James Turner. OBGa

I love Adam. He is brave of heart. Eve. Jacob Fichman. FIT, *tr. by* Robert Friend

I Love All Beauteous Things. Robert Bridges. OxAEP-2

I love all sights of earth and skies. Flaneur [*or* Flâneur], The. Oliver Wendell Holmes. APN-1; NAAPv.1

I love America. Ham bones and shoes. In the New Country. Barbara Ras. OPRER

I love and fear him. Lady Kasa. WoPoe, *tr. by* Kenneth Rexroth

I love and hate. Ah! never asky why so! Catullus. OBVE

I love, and must: So far[e]well liberty. (LL) Mary Sidney Wroth, Countess of Montgomery. BASC; CABP; NAEL-6v1; NAEL-7v1; NOSC *Fr.* Pamphilia to Amphilanthus.

I love and serve my lady with a will. François Villon. EroLit *Fr.* Grand Testament.

I love being a woman. Manifest, The. Olga Nolla. TANSG, *tr. by* Paula Vega

I Love Being Here with You. Peggy Lee. ReLy

I love breasts, hard. Breasts. Charles Simic. RaBo; WaAnP

I love desire, the state of want and thought. Why I Am Not a Buddhist. Molly Peacock. ExTi

I love hanging out laundry, bright linens. Past, The. Betsy Sholl. ExTi

I love her with the seasons, with the winds. Constancy. Michael Field. ViWPN; VWP

I love how it swells. Anodyne. Yusef Komunyakaa. AmAlph

I Love How Your Eyes Close Every Time You Kiss Me. Erica Bernheim. LegDan

I love! I love! I shall not hide it. I'll not deny it. *Unknown.* SLW, *tr. by* Marjolijn De Jager, Sayd Bahodin Majrouh and André Velter

I Love in White Ink. Siham Da'oud. PoArWo, *tr. by* Helen Knox and Smadar Lavie

I love it, I love it; and who shall dare. Old Arm-Chair, The. Eliza Cook. VWP

I love it, I love it, and who shall dare. Old Bike, The. *Unknown.* ArBi

I love it when he rides standing. Riding Their Bikes. Ellen Kirvin Dudis. ArBi

I love Jesus, who said to us. Antonio Machado Ruiz. WED *Fr.* Moral Proverbs and Folk Songs.

I love jukeboxes in dark, middle aged bars. Lucky 7. Katharine Harer. MiVo

I Love, Love. Gabriela Mistral. BLPSL, *tr. by* Rene de Costa, Rigas Kappatos and Eleni Paidoussi

I love / love's delicacy. Sappho. ErotSp, *tr. by* Sam Hamill

I love Master Meng. For Meng Hao-Jan. Li Po. WoPoe, *tr. by* Greg Whincup

I Love My Enemies. Leonid Andreievich Zavalnyuk. GI, *tr. by* Magda Bogin

I love my friend's. My Friend's Dog. Meret Oppenheim. SurPaPo, *tr. by* Catherine Schelbert

I Love My Jean. Robert Burns. *See* Of A' the Airts [the Wind Can Blaw].

I Love My Love. Helen Adam. EdScPo

I love my Love, and my Love loves me! (LL) Answer to a Child's Question. Samuel Taylor Coleridge. ITBLP; NOxBChV; NPBRoP

I love my neighbour. Love Thy Neighbour. D. H. Lawrence. ChIV-2

I love my work and my children. God. Ovid in the Third Reich. Geoffrey Hill. CABP; HarvBoo; HP; NAMCP V.2; NoAM; NPeEn; OxBEV

I love not thy perfections. When I hear. Wilfrid Scawen Blunt. OBMV *Fr.* Love Sonnets of Proteus, The.

I Love Old Whitman So. Allen Ginsberg. ViWalt

I Love Passover. Aharon Shabtai. PoCho, *tr. by* Peter Cole

I love roads. Roads. Edward Thomas. HarvBoo

I LOVE SEAHORSES, TEDDYBEARS, AFRICAN VIOLETS. Mad Sonnet: Grace. Michael McClure. BB

I love Sir Bamboo Tree. Bamboo Tree. Jinkag Haesim. BecRai, *tr. by* Kim Daljin, Kim Won-Chung and Christopher Merrill

I love sweets. Ellen West. Frank Bidart. NAMCP V.2; RACG

I love the Autumn. Thoughts. Jacqueline Kennedy Onassis. BLPJKO

I love the bars and taverns. Bars. Nicolás Guillén. TCLAP, *tr. by* Eric Orozco

I love the bronze, the crystal and the porcelains. My Loves. Julián de Casal. BLPSL, *tr. by* Rene de Costa, Rigas Kappatos and Eleni Paidoussi

I love the cows best when they are a few feet away. Cow Worship. Gerald Stern. LoL

I love the deep quiet—all buried in leaves. Contradiction. Alice Cary. NAAPv.1

I love the east, I love the west. I Love Being Here with You. Peggy Lee. ReLy

I love the Fall, I love the endless tumbling. Eve Falling. Jane McVeigh. HW

I love the fog. It's not one hundred degrees. Cotton in a Pill Bottle. Dean Young. ASA

I love the handful of the earth you are. Pablo Neruda. TCLAP, *tr. by* Stephen Tapscott

I love the hour before takeoff. Vacation. Rita Dove. OtW; SpirFl

I love the indolence of lying on the grass. Ballad of Indolence. Herman De Coninck. TuT, *tr. by* Eamon Grennan

I love the joyful time of Easter. In Praise of War. Bertrans de Born. NAWM-7v1, *tr. by* Frederick Goldin

I love the lit corners of your kerosine smile. Senior Lady Sells Garden Eggs. Kojo Laing. HBAPE

I love the master, Meng Hao-jan. To Meng Hao-jan. Li Po. ColAnChi, *tr. by* Stephen Owen

I love the names o Scotland. Scottish Names. Raymond Vettese. EdScPo

I love the old melodious lays. Proem. John Greenleaf Whittier. APN-1

I love the quality of the. Essay on William Carlos Williams, An. Víctor Hernández Cruz. PmAP

I love the silent hour of night. Night. Anne Brontë. VWP

I love the small hours of the night. Pleasant Joys of Brotherhood, The. James Simmons. OBCoV; PBCIP; PML

I love the sound of the bone against the plate. Osso Buco. Billy Collins. CAP-8

I love the thought of his anger. Seamus Heaney. PoetW *Fr.* Sweeney Redivivus.

I love Thee. (LL) "Why do I love" You, Sir? Emily Dickinson. APN-2; LW

I Love Thee. Josephine D. Henderson Heard. CBWP-4

I love thee for thy fickleness. *Unknown.* NOSC

I love thee, I love thee, and life will depart. Mother's Love, A. Ellen Johnston. VWP

I love thee, mournful, sober-suited Night! To Night. Charlotte Smith. NAEL-6v2; NAEL-7v2

I love thee; never dream that I am dumb. Penetration. Michael Field. VWP

I love them, I listen to them. Bells, The. Rosalía de Castro. SpanPo, *tr. by* Edwin Morgan

I love these hands, designed by God to end my wrists. Hands, The. Marco Antonio Montes de Oca. MotU, *tr. by* Brian Swann

I love this body of mine that has lived a life. Celebration of the Body. Daisy Zamora. LoL, *tr. by* Dinah Livingston

I love this byre. Shadows are kindly here. Innkeeper's Wife, The. Clive Sansom. OBCP

I Love Thy Kingdom, Lord [*with music*]. Timothy Dwight. TCAPo

I love to drive women's cars. Eclipse. Jonathan Johnson. AmPoNex

I love to find a door. Like the spinal tap. Tap. Alice Jones. BloBone

I love to go out in late September. Blackberry Eating. Galway Kinnell. BeAl; CAP-8; InvLad; NIL-7; NIP-4; SoSe-8; WaAnP

I love to hear the cock crow in. Cock-a-Doo. Stevie Smith. OWoS

I love to lick English the way I licked the hard. English Flavors. Laure-Anne Bosselaar. SUP

I love to ride the D train just to emerge from the tunnel. East Seventh Street. Mark Wunderlich. WiU

I love to rise ere gleams the tardy light. December Morning. Anna Seward. CenSon

I love to rise in a summer morn. William Blake. OxAEP-2 *Fr.* Songs of Experience.

I Love to See a Lady Nice and Natural at Any Price. Amanda Ros. VerBaPo

I love to see boards lying on the ground in early spring. Old Boards. Robert Bly. GoPo

I love to see the starry flag. Our Flag. *Unknown.* CA

I love to see, when leaves depart. Autumn. Roy Campbell. MoBrPo; OBMV

I love to stay in bed. Summer Morning. Charles Simic. GoPo; WaAnP

I love to tell the story. Katherine Hankey. SacPr

I love to walk. Discharged Soldier, The. William Wordsworth. NPBRoP

I love to walk under trees at midday. Midday. Irmgard Hunt. GTCP, *tr. by* Sam McLean

I love to watch, while you are lazing. Snake that Dances, The. Charles Baudelaire. EroLit

I love uncertain gestures. Valerio Magrelli. NeIt

I love when you take over. Lumens. Olga Broumas. ExTi

I love *you*. (LL) Dance of the Infidels. Al Young. ESEAA; SeSe

I love you and it makes me rather dull. Villanelle: Late Summer. Marilyn Hacker. WaAnP

I love you, / and you. On, Off, Over. Richard Price. EdScPo

I love you as a sheriff searches for a walnut. To You. Kenneth Koch. P180

I love you at ten in the morning, at eleven, at twelve noon. I love you with my. I Love You at Ten in the Morning. Jaime Sabines. PML, *tr. by* W. S. Merwin

I love you beyond the depths of my own soul. Yunus Emre. NaPG, *tr. by* Talat Sait Halman

I love you first because your face is fair. V-Letter. Karl Shapiro. IllVoic; NoAM

I love you for your brownness. To a Dark Girl. Gwendolyn B. Bennett. ColAP; WaAnP

I love you, great new Titan! Soldier: Twentieth Century. Isaac Rosenberg. PoWW

I love you he said but saying it took twenty years. Sources of the Delaware. Dean Young. BAP-01

I love you, I love you, is my song. Love Song. Pablo Neruda. ErotSp; GifTon, *tr. by* William O'Daly

I love you in the newly born. Finger-nails. Paolo Buzzi. PFTM-1

I love you like the grain of wheat loves the sun rising above its blackbird head. (LL) Where Are You. Benjamin Péret. SurPaPo; YaTCFP, *tr. by* Rachel Stella

I Love, You Love. Rubén Darío. BLPSL, *tr. by* Rene de Costa, Rigas Kappatos and Eleni Paidoussi

I love you, / Not only for what you are. Love. Roy Croft. ITBLP

I love you, rotten. Medlars and Sorb-Apples. D. H. Lawrence. FaBoVe; NAMCP V.1; NoAM; NPeEn

I love you said the locust to the leaf. Companions. Tade Ipadeola. NeNiPo

I Love You So. Ahmet Ada. NaPG, *tr. by* Talat Sait Halman

I love you so much. To My Son. David Shapiro. OxBoAm

I Love You Sweatheart. Thomas Lux. SUP

I love you / though, possibly, we haven't met. Ave Atque Vale. Pennar Davies. BBMWP, *tr. by* Joseph P. Clancy

I Love You, Though You're Unemployed. Dawn L. Hannaham. BtF

I love you, which is easy to see. You're Laughing at Me. Irving Berlin. ReLy

I Love You . . . Why Do You Hate Me? Rosalía de Castro. SpanPo, *tr. by* Edwin Morgan

I love you with a love that knows no waning, whereas some of men's loves are midday mirages. Ibn Hazm al-Andalusi. HiArP, *tr. by* James T. Monroe

I love you with my life—'tis so I love you. I Love You with My Life. Michael Field. VWP

I love you would have no application for the moment. Strophe. "H. D." MotU

I love your eyes. It's Got to Be Love. Lorenz Hart. ReLy

I love your plumpness. Sally Young. NewEx

I loved a lass, a fair one. I Loved a Lass. George Wither. OBEV; VerBaPo

I loved a red-haired girl. For My Dead Red-Haired Mother. Ruth Stone. OxBoAm

I loved him not; and yet, now he is gone. Walter Savage Landor. OBEV; TreFP *Fr.* Citation and Examination of William Shakespeare, The.

I loved my friend. Poem [2]. Langston Hughes. NAAPv.2; NTCP

I loved my lord, my black-haired lord, my young love. Magnet, The. Ruth Stone. MoAmPo

I Loved Ophelia. Catherine Imbriglio. IAoNAP

I loved the light of course. Memories of Italy (Broken Sestina). John Ash. NeBrP

I loved the rain. Shorter Life, The. Peter Didsbury. NeBrP

I loved the Supremes as much as baseball. Allegiance. Forrest Hamer. MoASP

I loved the way it felt once, practically invincible. Outside the Depot. Betsy Sholl. LTA

I loved thee long and dearly. Florence Vane. Philip Pendleton Cooke. APN-1

I loved them until they loved me. (LL) Ballade at Thirty-Five. Dorothy Parker. AmWit; APT-1

I loved Theotormon. Visions of the Daughters of Albion. William Blake. CABP; NAEL-6v2; NAEL-7v2; NPBRoP

I Loved You. Alexander Sergeyevich Pushkin. AmFaPo, *tr.* by D. M. Thomas

I loved you; and perhaps I love you still. I Loved You. Alexander Sergeyevich Pushkin. AmFaPo, *tr.* by D. M. Thomas

I loved you Atthis once long ago. Sappho. SaLy, *tr.* by Diane Rayor

I loved you first: but afterwards your love. Christina Georgina Rossetti. OxBSo *Fr.* Monna Innominata.

I loved you first the time I saw you last. Letting Go. Daryl Hine. NoP-4; NoP-5

I loved—who hasn't? I worshipped—hasn't. I Loved—Who Hasn't? Philodemus. WoPoe, *tr.* by George Economou

I luikit up unto that Castell fair. Elizabeth Melville, Lady Culross. EMWP *Fr.* Ane Godly Dream.

I lu-love you very well. Stuttering Lover, The. Fred Emerson Brooks. VerBaPo

I lurk on the floor of silence. Hunting. Tymoteusz Karpowicz. PoSu, *tr.* by Jan Darowski

I. M. Margaritae Sorori. W. E. Henley. *See* Margaritae Sororis.

I Made a House of Houselessness. Rose Cecil O'Neill. LW

I Made a New Memory for You. Maya Bejerano. DTA, *tr.* by Miriyam Glazer

I made a posy for my love. Posies. Agnes Mary Frances Robinson. VWP

I made a posy [*or* posie], while the day ran by. Life. George Herbert. BASC; FSCP; NoP-4; NoP-5; NOSC

I made another garden, yea. Song. Arthur William Edgar O'Shaughnessy. OBEV

I made car batteries new. Awakened in a Field. Juan Delgado. GeoHom

I made her tell me of the affair. First Person Omniscient. Jeffrey McDaniel. LaCa

I made it that cold winter when. Rebecca Baggett. FiBr *Fr.* Art of the Amish: A Quilt Exhibition.

I made love with a man—hugely muscled, lean— the body. Trick, The. Mark Wunderlich. WiU

I made my song a coat. Coat, A. William Butler Yeats. NAEL-6v2; NAEL-7v2; NAMCP V.1; NoAM; OxAEP-2; PtR

I Made Myself a Path. N. V. M. Gonzalez. ReBoTo

I made myself a path on the side of a hill. I Made Myself a Path. N. V. M. Gonzalez. ReBoTo

I made myself as a tree. March Hares. Andrew Young. SAmP

I made myself into armored concrete against the worms that graw us and suck us dry. Season of Anger. René Depestre. PFTM-2, *tr.* by Pierre Joris

I made no choice / I decided nothing. Margaret Atwood. NALW *Fr.* Circe / Mud Poems.

I made the pilgrimage again. Derailment: A Delirium. Steve Chimombo. HBAPE

I made these mountains. Drainlayer. Duncan Bush. AngWePo

I make a little mother out of mud, sticks. Matter. Joan Houlihan. IAoNAP

I make a pact with you, Walt Whitman. Pact, A. Ezra Pound. APT-1; ColAP; NAAL-5; NAAPv.2; NAMCP V.1; NoAM; NoP-5; RaF; ViWalt; WaAnP

I make a simple assertion. Working with Tools. A. R. Ammons. TRP

I make a trip to each clock in the apartment. Paris, 7 A.M. Elizabeth Bishop. PoA 2002

I make an elephant. Elephant, The. Carlos Drummond de Andrade. ItP, *tr.* by Mark Strand

I make eye contact with babies on the street. I Know I Aint Hip No More. Peter Harris. BtF

I make my shroud but no one knows. Song. Adelaide Crapsey. APT-1; NAAPv.2

I make my way alone through the hand-to-hand fighting. On. Paul Muldoon. GPPA

I make no moan or outcry, just don't sleep. For Paul. Eve Triem. APT-2

I make tiny, tiny huts. Miniaturist, The. Maurice Kilwein Guevara. AmPoNex; TouFir

I make up things to say. I've Told Ev'ry Little Star. Oscar Hammerstein, II. ReLy

I making de Queen's English accessory / to my offence. (LL) Listen Mr Oxford Don. John Agard. NPeEn; Oth

I Mandate Ridges Raving. David Thomas Roberts. AnSo

I many times thought Peace had come. Emily Dickinson. SAmP

I, Mariya, burn your fingers. Kseniya Marennikova. CRWP, *tr.* by Daniel Weissbort

I marked where lovely Venus and her court. Venus's Looking-Glass. Christina Georgina Rossetti. NALW

I married. Lorine Niedecker. APT-2; FTOS; NAAPv.2; OxBoAm

I married a man from County Roscommon. Overheard in County Sligo. Gillian Clarke. HarvBoo; StAl; TCAWP

I married a man of the Croydon class. Nervous Prostration. Anna Wickham. MoWP

I married an emancipated woman. *Unknown.* NAAPv.2

I married in my youth a wife. James Vincent Cunningham. MoAmPo

I married my cousin after all. (LL) Dearest Love. Salma Khadra Jayyusi. CFP; PoArWo, *tr.* by Charles Doria

I married my Lord, and meant to live with him. My First Marriage. Kabir. WED, *tr.* by Robert Bly

I marveled at the sight of you who without knowing. Whole Two Weeks After The Million Man March; and Still, If You'd Ask Me, This Is All I Could Say about It, A. Richard Rykard. SpirFl

I mastered pastoral theology, the Greek of the Apostles. Minister, The. Fenton Johnson. APT-1

I maun feed frae common trough ana'. Vision of Myself, A. Hugh MacDiarmid. OxBEV

I, Maximus of Gloucester, to You ("Off-shore, by islands hidden in the blood.") Charles Olson. NAMCP V.2; NoAM; PmAP *Fr.* Maximus Poems, The.

I may be a boxer. On the Declaration of Joy. Fathi Abdullah. AnVo, *tr.* by Mohamed Enani

I may be smelly and I may be old. River God, The. Stevie Smith. BrAP; MoWP

I may be too old to run a mile. It's Never Too Late to Fall in Love. Sandy Wilson. ReLy

I May Be Wrong (But I Think You're Wonderful). Harry Ruskin. ReLy

I May, I Might, I Must. Marianne Moore. AmFaPo; ChAP

I may picture her there. (LL) Thoughts of Phena. Thomas Hardy. HarvBoo; NoP-4; NPeEn

I may practice divination with the bones. Axolotl. Arthur Sze. AmAlph

I may wear a dawning smile for shirt. Coat. Meirion MacIntyre Huws. BBMWP, *tr.* by Grahame Davies

I may wel sike for grevous is my peyne. *Unknown.* OHMEL

I mean that too, but yet a hidden strength. John Milton. NOSC *Fr.* Comus; a Masque Presented at Ludlow Castle.

I mean to go down into the valley. Widow Opening Her Heart, The. Mary McGinnis. ICANM

I mean *you* as though referring to two furies because. Eduardo Milán. RMCMP, *tr.* by Roberto Tejada

I measure every Grief I meet. Emily Dickinson. MoAmPo

I measure time by how a body sways. (LL) I Knew a Woman. Theodore Roethke. APT-2; BrAP; HeIP-4; ItP; MoAmPo; NAAL-5; NAMCP V.1; NIL-7; NoAM; NoP-4; NoP-5; OxBoAm; RaBo; SoSe-8; TFi; TRP; VCAP; WaAnP

I meditate upon a swallow's flight. Coole Park, 1929. William Butler Yeats. CABP; OBMV

I meet little Rosa early in de mornin'. Early in the Morning. *Unknown.* SSUS

I meet myself each and every day. Olga Ivanova. CRWP, *tr.* by Jenefer Coates

I meet two soldiers sometimes here in Hell. That Exploit of Yours. Ford Madox Ford. PoWW

I meet you again in public. I. Blues. Honor Moore. PfS

I meet you in an evil time. Eclogue for Christmas, An. Louis MacNeice. NAMCP V.1; NoAM; OBMV

I met a fair maiden so sweet and so fair. Girl by the River, The. Alton Delmore. APT-2

I met a girl from Derrygarve. New Song, A. Seamus Heaney. CABP

I met a King this afternoon! Emily Dickinson. ChAP

I met a lady / on a lazy street. From the Hazel Bough. Earle Birney. BrAP; IFF; NIP-4

(He met a lady.) HeIP-4

I met a little cottage Girl. William Wordsworth. UV *Fr.* We Are Seven.

I met a little cottage-girl. Wordsworth on Lloyd George. Mary Visick. UV

I met a little Elf-man, once. Little Elf, The. John Kendrick Bangs. NTCP

I met a man my age running a greenhouse. Scarlet Crown. Marc J. Straus. BloBone

I met a man once. Nissim Ezekiel. WoPoe *Fr.* Hymns in Darkness.

I met a seer. Stephen Crane. MoAmPo

I met a seer. Eidólons. Walt Whitman. APN-1

I met a tall broadchest. Murmuring. Kofi Anyidoho. NAfrP

I met a traveler [*or* traveller] from an antique land. Ozymandias. Percy Bysshe Shelley. BLPJKO; BrAP; BRP; CABP; CenSon; ChAP; ClHu; CtM; GSo; HeIP-4; MakPoe; NAEL-6v2; NAEL-7v2; NIL-7; NIP-4; NoP-4; NoP-5; NPBRoP; NPeEn; OPOU; OxBEV; OxBSo; PoPoPo; PtR; SoSe-8; TFi; UV; WaAnP

I met a traveller from an antique land. Ozymandias Revisited. Morris Gilbert Bishop. NBLV; UV

I met a woman, weeping by the sea. Cavour. Menella Bute Smedley. VWP

I met ayont the cairney. Empty Vessel. Hugh MacDiarmid. EdScPo; NePenScot; NPeEn; OxBEV

I met brightness of brightness upon the path of loneliness. Enchanted Mistress, The. Egan O'Rahilly. IrLP, *tr. by* Augusta, Lady Gregory

I met her as a blossom on a stem. Dream, The. Theodore Roethke. NIL-7

I met her in a dream. Better Than Crying. Ishikawa Takuboku. CAoMJL1, *tr. by* Leith Morton

I met her, not by chance. Flower of Air, The. Gabriela Mistral. TCLAP, *tr. by* Doris Dana

I met her on the first of August. Nessa. Paul Durcan. IrLP

I met him at a party just a couple of years ago. Mad About the Boy. Noël Coward. ReLy

I met in a merchant's place. Charles Reznikoff. APT-2

I met in Mesilla. Edward Dorn. PFTM-2 *Fr.* Gunslinger.

I met Jack on a Friday night. Tip for Saturday, A. Francis Webb. BMAP

I met Ted at two parties at the same house. April Not an Inventory but a Blizzard. Alice Notley. OxBoAm

I met the Angel Sus on the Skin Bridge. Kenneth Irby. PFTM-2

I met the Bishop on the road. Crazy Jane Talks with the Bishop. William Butler Yeats. CABP; NAEL-6v2; NAEL-7v2; NAMCP V.1; NoAM; NoP-4; NoP-5; OxAEP-2; PoPoPo; TRP

I met the Buddha in a dream. Buddha and I, The. Atanu Dey. WhBo

I met the thieving miss magpie, number 123. I Met the Thieving Miss Magpie. Patrizia Vicinelli. ItPo, *tr. by* Gayle Ridinger

I met this girl who was visiting Atlanta. She looked. Tradition/Abstraction. Mendi Lewis Obadike. RD

I met Tu Fu on a mountaintop. About Tu Fu. Li Po. CrYelRi, *tr. by* Sam Hamill

I met up with him on a corner of Florida Street. Encounter. Alfonsina Storni. TANSG, *tr. by* Mark McCaffrey

I met wizened wood-woman. Old Woman and the Sandwiches, The. Libby Houston. OBSP

I might as well be king of rainy lands. Spleen LXXVII. Charles Baudelaire. SxFrPo, *tr. by* James McGowan

I might as well begin by saying how much I like the title. Workshop. Billy Collins. OxBoAm

I might have been born in Beirut. Curriculum Vitae. Lawrence Joseph. PBCAP

I might have died when I was young. Song of the Old Man. Richard Jones. IllVoic

I might not have known his voice. Last Letter. Gerald William Barrax. ESEAA

I might suvive. Pedaling Paranoia. Jane Mayes. ArBi

I might, unhappy word, O me, I might. Sir Philip Sidney. NPeEn *Fr.* Astrophil and Stella.

I milked the cows, I churned the butter, I stored the cheese. Letter from Home, The. Jamaica Kincaid. MotU

I mind o' the Ponnage Pule. Ponnage Pool, The. Helen B. Cruickshank. NePenScot

I mind them or the show or resonance of them—I come and I depart. (LL) Walt Whitman. ColAP; SAmP; WaAnP *Fr.* Song of Myself.

I mind ye when your hair was straucht. Schoolquine. Alastair MacKie. EdScPo

I mingle with the young and gay. I Smile, but Oh! My Heart Is Breaking. Mary E. Tucker. CBWP-1

I mingle with your bones. One Lost, The. Isaac Rosenberg. MoBrPo

I miss being a kid, but barely recall those parts. Tenant of Wildfeld Hall, The. Todd Swift. OpeFie

I miss my grandmother. Dream Poem. Mary Jo Bona. UnSA

I miss our lizards. The one who watched us. Lizards in Sardinia. Eamon Grennan. WaAnP

I miss the polished brass, the powerful black horses. On the Road to Woodlawn. Theodore Roethke. InoFa

I missed. Empty Cage, The. Lise Deharme. SurWo, *tr. by* Franklin Rosemont

I missed him when the sun began to bend. Lost and Found. George Macdonald. SacPr

I Missed His Book, but I Read His Name. John Updike. NoP-4; NoP-5

I missed it. So much did they make of this news. In Memory. Tony Lopez. VaPo

I missed sharing your birthday by hours. Daughter-to-Father Talk. Kamilah Aisha Moon. BRtP

I missed / the last transport. Abandoned, The. Zbigniew Herbert. PoSu, *tr. by* Michael March and Jaroslaw Anders

I mock thee not, though I by thee am mocked. To Flaxman. William Blake. PtR

I moot go walke the wode so wilde. Sir Thomas Wyatt. OHMEL

I mope the new spring away in a white coat. Spring Rain. Li Shang-yin. ChinPo, *tr. by* Ye Weilian [*or* Yeh Wei-lien *or* Wai-lim Yip]

I most remember the class where we lie. Acting. Suzanne Cleary. BeAl; P180

I mounted, to escape the empty blankness, the inevitable misery of rain puddles at night. Well, Is it Going to Budge, the Beast? Elke Erb. OnScMo, *tr. by* Rosmarie Waldrop

I mourn maiden Antibia: desiring her, many. Anyte. SaLy, *tr. by* Diane Rayor

I mourn with thee, and yet rejoice. Penitent, The. Anne Brontë. SacPr

I mouth. Hickie, The. Liz Lochhead. LW; MoWP

I Move the Meeting Be Adjourned. Nicanor Parra. TCLAP, *tr. by* Allen Ginsberg

I move to the window. Threading the Miles. Alfred Encarnacion. OpBo

I moved across the Dharma-nature. Getsudo. ZenPo, *tr. by* Takashi Ikemoto and Lucien Stryk

I moved into my house one day. Moving In. May Sarton. APT-2

I moved with the morning. (LL) Field of Light, A. Theodore Roethke. PtR; WaAnP

I must admit to this outright theft. Robo. Nick Carbó. NAPBL

I must be. (LL) All but Blind. Walter De la Mare. MoBrPo; WeW-3

I Must Be Able to Protect You. 'Marnia. LW

I must be careful about such things as these. Sonnet. Ed Roberson. GT

I must be mad, or very tired. Meeting-House Hill. Amy Lowell. APT-1; ColAP; MoAmPo; TCAPo

I must become a child again. (LL) Innocence. Thomas Traherne. BASC; CABP; ChIV-2; NOSC

I must become small and hide where he cannot reach. Fooling God. Louise Erdrich. ReEnLa; UpMys; WaAnP

I must feel this soil again. Digging Soil. Peter Gruffydd. AngWePo

I must get up early in the morning. Coming Forth By Day. Philip Whalen. AHA

I must go down to the seas again, to the lonely sea and the sky. Sea Fever. John Masefield. BLPJKO; BRP; CABP; ChAP; ITBLP; MoBrPo; OxAEP-2; UV; WaAnP

I must go down to the seas again, where the billows romp and reel. Sea-Chill. Arthur Guiterman. UV

I must go on, till in my tearful line. Cross, The. Jones Very. NCAP

I must have back this breath. Dealing Scraps. Ruth Garnett. ISC

I must have been dozing in the tub. Soap-Pig, The. Paul Muldoon. PBCIP

I must have passed the crest a while ago. Long Hill, The. Sara Teasdale. MoAmPo; TCAPo

I must hide him down in my deepest veins. Totem. Léopold Sédar Senghor. PML; PoetW, *tr. by* Melvin Dixon

I must look funny. Reasons to Commute by Bicycle. Frederic William Kirchner. ArBi

I must love the questions. Reassurance. Alice Walker. ASA

I must make nude statues. Now's the Time for Love. Sait Faik. NaPG, *tr. by* Talat Sait Halman

I must not dare to sleep. (LL) Coora Flower, The. Gwendolyn Brooks. IllVoic; NAAL-5; NIL-7; NoP-4

I must not grieve my love, whose eyes would read [*or* reede]. Samuel Daniel. OBEV *Fr.* Sonnets to Delia.

I must not think of thee; and, tired yet strong. Renouncement. Alice Thompson Meynell. GSo; LW; MoBrPo; OBEV; OBMV; OxBSo; PEW; VWP

I must possess you utterly. Possession. Richard Aldington. MoBrPo

I must remember. Spreading Wings on Wind. Simon J. Ortiz. HATNAP

I must see the lighthouse keeper. Pious One, The. Gabriela Mistral. BBASP, *tr. by* Doris Dana

I must tell you. Young Sycamore. William Carlos Williams. APT-1

I must tell you, my dear. Love in Mayfair. May Probyn. VWP

I Mustn't Ask. Mao Wen-hsi. CCL1, *tr. by* Burton Watson

I mustn't ask about him [Tune: "Drunk among the Flowers"]. I Mustn't Ask. Mao Wen-hsi. CCL1, *tr. by* Burton Watson

I, my dear, was born to-day. On My Birthday, July 21. Matthew Prior. OBEV

I, my mother, my two brothers. Segregation #1. Carlos German Belli. TCLAP, *tr. by* Isabel Bize

I myself. (Invocation for Storing Corn). *Unknown.* WPoS, *tr. by* Francisco X. Alarcón

I myself like the climate of New York. Climate, The. Edwin Denby. NYP2

I myself saw furious with blood. Aeneas at Washington. Allen Tate. APT-2; FuPo; NoAM

I myself was that man splitting wood in the daybreak. (LL) Man Splitting Wood in the Daybreak, The. Galway Kinnell. OxBoAm; VCAP

I name you Evening, O ambiguous Evening, you fluttering leaf. Man and Beast. Léopold Sédar Senghor. PFTM-1

I named it sickle. But he. Hook, The. Duncan Bush. TCAWP

I need a ritual to perform, / clean and sane, for this perfect washday. Domestic Tranquility. Gerald William Barrax. GT

I need huge trees to grow within me. Secrecy of Mirrors, The. Al-Zahra Al-Mansouri. PoArWo, tr. by Nathalie Handal, Richard McKane and Tahia Abdel Nasser

I need kai kai ah. For the Poets. Jayne Cortez. InoFa; PmAP

I need me a house like that. Where the Heart Is. Ntozake Shange. GT

I need not die to go. Where, O, Where? Elinor Wylie. NAAPv.2

I Need Not Go. Thomas Hardy. OBEV

I need nothing but God's mercy. Question. Edith Södergran. WPoS

I need something easy. Honey Moon. Kathleen Leland Baker. NBLV

I need the walls on either end. Kicking and Breathing. Gary Margolis. PfSP

I need to know their names. Lost Women, The. Lucille Clifton. BodElec

I need to learn a language but not english. Language. Jennifer Maiden. BMAP

I need to whoop it up some. Stomping with Pettit on the Battenkill. Garrett Kaoru Hongo. PfSP

I needed fox Badly I needed. Fox. Adrienne Rich. NAMCP V.2

I needed some familiar thing to ease. Prairie Friend. Maude E. Cole. TiP2

I needed to point to the buildings, as if they all stood. Thirty Years Rising. Olena Kalytiak Davis. AmPoNex; LegDan

I needlessly mapped an occasion, splitting my support. Interface. Jeff Derksen. NLPA

I ne'er was struck before that hour. First Love. John Clare. GoPo; NoP-4; NoP-5; PoPoPo

I never asked you for your hand. Strand of Hair, A. Justin Quinn. NIrP

I never cared much for moonlit skies. I'm Beginning to See the Light. Don George. ReLy

I never could qualify as a saint. Maybe I Should Change My Ways. John Latouche. ReLy

I never dared be radical when young. Ten Mills. Robert Frost.

I never deny my past. Love Me. Badr Shakir al-Sayyab. IrPoTo, tr. by Mustapha Kamal and Ralph Saverese

I Never Do Anything Twice (Madam's Song). Stephen Sondheim. ReLy

I never drank of Aganippe well. Sir Philip Sidney. NAEL-6v1; NAEL-7v1; NoSic Fr. Astrophil and Stella.

I Never Dream of My Father. Eva Hung. ArBi

I never feel a thing is real. It's Only a Paper Moon. E. Y. Harburg and Billy Rose. ReLy

I Never Felt Better. Ralph Blane and Hugh Martin. ReLy

I never follow an inferior way. (LL) George Wither. NOSC; SacPr Fr. Collection of Emblemes, Ancient and Moderne, A.

I never forgave that night its steep descent. Identity Crisis. Sam Gardiner. NIrP

I never gave a lock of hair away. Elizabeth Barrett Browning. CenSon; OxBSo Fr. Sonnets from the Portuguese.

I never gave a thought to them at first. Field Mushrooms. W. S. Merwin. CAP-8

I never go anywhere. Will You Marry Me? Taeko Tomioka. CFP, tr. by Aoyami Miyuki and Leza Lowitz

I never had a toothache, but the desire to have one crossed my mind constantly. Toothache. Maxine Chernoff. SUP

I never hear the word "escape." Emily Dickinson. NCAP; SAmP

I never intended to have this life, believe me. Resemblance between Your Life and a Dog, The. Robert Bly. CAP-8; OxBoAm

I never knew that by August. Losing My Sight. Lisel Mueller. ExTi

I never knew the worth of him / Until he died. (LL) Old Story, An. Edwin Arlington Robinson. MoAmPo; OxBoAm

I never knew them all, just hummed. All the Old Songs. Walter McDonald. TiP2

I never knew, then, why it was named that. Hollow. Susan Wood. TiP2

I never knew you were a magician. Morisseau-Leroy. Max Manigat. OGAHCP, tr. by Boadiba and Jack Hirschman

I never liked the World Trade Center. World Trade Center, The. David Lehman. PA9/11

I never lost as much but twice. Emily Dickinson. HeIP-4; MoAmPo; NAAL-3; NAAL-5; NAAPv.1; NAMCP V.1; NCAP; NoAM; NoP-4; NoP-5; TCAPo

I never made friends faster. Learning the War. Wendy Wilder Larsen. OPRER

I never played for you. You'd have thrown. For the Death of Vince Lombardi. James Dickey. MoASP

I never rear'd a young gazelle. Henry Sambrooke Leigh. UV

I Never rested on the Muses bed. To William Drummond of Hawthornden. Mary, of Morpeth Oxlie. EMWP

I never said I loved you, John. No, Thank You, John. Christina Georgina Rossetti. NAEL-6v2; NAEL-7v2; PtR

I Never Saw a Goddess Go. Austin Hummell. AmPoNex

I never saw a man in all my days—. Rural Scenes. John Clare. CenSon

I never saw a Moor. Emily Dickinson. AmFaPo; HeIP-4; ITBLP; MoAmPo; SAmP; TFi; WPoS

I never saw a Purple Cow. Purple Cow, The. Frank Gelett Burgess. ASA; BRP; CalPo; NBLV; NTCP; OBCoV; TCAPo; TFi; TLR

I Never Saw Great Lakes. Nancy Morejón. TANSG, tr. by Joy Renjilian-Burgy

I never saw my mother's body. My Mother's Body. Enid Shomer. NevBe

I never saw such a place as this. Estes' Backyard, The. Pamela Stewart. UrbNat

I never saw that land before. Edward Thomas. HarvBoo

I never set my two eyes on a head was so fine as your head. Translation from Walter von der Vogelweide, A. Walther von der Vogelweide. MoBrPo, tr. by John Millington Synge

I never shall forget thee—'tis a word. To Mrs. Norton. Frances Anne Kemble. VWP

I never soared, and never did I soar. Bulat Shalvovich Okudzhava. TCRusP, tr. by Denis Johnson, Aleksandar Petrov and Shirley Rihner

I never spoke. Indian Boy Love Song (#2). Sherman Alexie. WaAnP

I never stoop'd so low, as they. John Donne. FSCP

I never thought for a moment. Emily Dickinson, Bismarck and the Roadrunner's Inquiry. Ray A. Young Bear. HATNAP

I never thought frogs. One Morning beside a Pond. Rofel G. Brion. ReBoTo

I never thought that you could mourn. Mistaken. Mary Elizabeth Coleridge. PoBW

I never throw away a piece of paper. Paper Boat—Sent to Mother. Bingxin. CFP, tr. by Michelle Yeh

I never told you. What They Do to You in Distant Places. Marvin Bell. MoASP

I never touched thy royal hand, dead queen. Lost Light, The. Emily Jane Pfeiffer. VWP

I never travel'd further north. Let's Take a Walk Around the Block. Ira Gershwin and E. Y. Harburg. ReLy

I never turned anyone into a pig. Circe's Power. Louise Glück. OxBoAm

I never wanted the red of fire, the black at midnight. Miracle. Wen Yi-tuo [or Wen I-to]. PFTM-1

I never went to Yasnaya Polyana. Yasnaya Polyana. R. Gerallt Jones. BBMWP, tr. by Robert Minhinnick

I never wish to sing again as I used to, when two new eyes could always. Karen Volkman. IAoNAP

As he takes from you, I engraft you new. (LL) William Shakespeare. AEP; CABP; ClHu; GSo; HeIP-4; NAEL-6v1; NAEL-7v1; NIL-7; NIP-4; NoP-5; NoSic; NPeEn; OBEV; OxAEP-1; OxBEV; OxBSo; PoPoPo; SoSe-8; TFi; TRP; WeW-3 Fr. Sonnets.

I never writ, nor no man ever loved [or lov'd]. (LL) William Shakespeare. AEP; BLPJKO; BrAP; CABP; ClHu; GSo; HeIP-4; NAEL-6v1; NAEL-7v1; NIL-7; NIP-4; NoP-5; NoSic; NPeEn; OBEV; OxAEP-1; OxBEV; OxBSo; PoPoPo; PtR; SoSe-8; TFi; TRP; WaAnP; WeW-3 Fr. Sonnets.

I, Nezahualcóyotl ask it. Nezahualcóyotl. PoCho

I no longer have to choose between. Ismailia Eclipse. Khaled Mattawa. NAPBL

I no longer live on Linnaen Street. Tenant at Will, A. Stuart Dischell. PoCho

I no longer wonder. After Reading Poems to Einhir. Gwyn Williams. TCAWP

I nod and nod to my own shadow and thrust. Climbing Suilven. Norman Alexander MacCaig. HarvBoo

I nostril you I hair you. End of the World, The: To Embody. Gherasim Luca. YaTCFP, tr. by Mary Ann Caws and Jean-Pierre Cauvin

I not only was burned by love. Put 'Em in a Box, Tie 'Em with a Ribbon (And Throw 'Em in the Deep Blue Sea). Sammy Cahn. ReLy

I notice my child is missing in the Choôon Dynasty Wing. National Museum Hallway. Kim Hyesun. EcSo, tr. by Youngju Ryu

I, now at Carthage. He, shot dead at Rome. Vale from Carthage. Peter Viereck. MoAmPo; PWW2; WoPoe

I now think, Love is rather deaf, than blind. My Picture Left in Scotland. Ben Jonson. NAEL-6v1; NAEL-7v1; NPeEn; PtR

(I now thinke, Love is rather deafe, then blind.) PBRV

I Object, Said the Object. Mairi MacInnes. MoWP

I observe certain eyes gazing steadily at me as if speckled snakes [issuing from them] were attacking me from both sides. Abū Āmir Ahmad Ibn Shuhayd. HiArP, tr. by James T. Monroe

I observe: "Our sentimental friend the moon!" Conversation Galante. T. S. Eliot. TCAPo

I offer myself to everyone as a reward. Gift of Oneself, The. Valery Larbaud. YaTCFP, *tr.* by Mary Ann Caws and Patricia Terry

I offer these verses to you, Claudia, because you are their mistress. Ernesto Cardenal. BLPSL, *tr.* by Rene de Costa, Rigas Kappatos and Eleni Paidoussi

I offer you four things. Roselle Angwin. NewEx

I often drift, on fancy's wondrous stream. Cyclolotry. *Unknown.* ArBi

I often go to Melano. Geographical History, The. Giulia Niccolai. CItWP, *tr.* by Cinzia Sartini Blum and Lara Trubowitz

I often kept his suitors at bay. Book of Style, The. Molly Bendall. PoDa

I often think of my old age. Fragments 1920–1921. Nikolai Stepanovich Gumilyov. TCRusP, *tr.* by Mary Jane White

I often wonder who will find. Sándor Petőfi. IQMS *Fr.* Clouds, The.

I, Olga Orozco, tell everyone, from your heart, that I am dying. Olga Orozco. Olga Orozco. TCLAP, *tr.* by Stephen Tapscott

I on my horse, and Love on me doth try. Sir Philip Sidney. NAEL-6v1; NAEL-7v1; NoP-4; NoP-5 *Fr.* Astrophil and Stella.

I once broke evening bread with the brown-faced, white-smiled Prince of Siam. Words of Oblivion and Peace. Gabriel Preil. FIT, *tr.* by Robert Friend

I once drove to Atlantic City. Zoom (The Commodores). Thulani Davis. ISC

I once had. Wings, The. Delmira Agustini. TCLAP, *tr.* by Elizabeth Gordon

I once had a gown, it was almost new. Alice Blue Gown. Joseph McCarthy. ReLy

I once heard the survivors. Don Marquis. NBLV *Fr.* Certain Maxims of Archy.

I once hitched a lift in a pick-up. Conor O'Callaghan. NIrP *Fr.* Loose Change.

I once knew a woman named Benedicta, who infused everything. Which One Is Genuine? Charles Baudelaire. RaBo, *tr.* by Robert Bly

I once pledged. Hazing (for Tony New and Albee). Brian G. Gilmore. BtF

I once saw my grandma with her hair undone. Katherine's Hair. David Marlatt. AmPoNex

I Once Was a Maid. Robert Burns. NBLV

I once was happy, when while yet a child. Charlotte Smith. PEW *Fr.* Beachy Head.

I Only Am Escaped Alone to Tell Thee. Howard Nemerov. HeIP-4; NoAM

I only chant painfully in the autumn wind. On a Rainy Autumn Night. Ch'oe Ch'iwŏn. CATKP, *tr.* by Peter H. Lee

I only did it for a laugh. My Way. Liz Lochhead. BeAl

I Only Have Eyes for You. Al Dubin. ReLy

I only knew one poet in my life. How It Strikes a Contemporary. Robert Browning. NPeEn

I only saw my father's face in butchery. Bull-roarer, The. Gerald Stern. CAP-8

I Open the Cigarette. Alda Merini. CItWP, *tr.* by Cinzia Sartini Blum and Lara Trubowitz

I open the door. Exaggeration of Despair, The. Sherman Alexie. BAP-97; NeAmPo; PrTe

I open the first door. Elegy. Tomas Tranströmer. WoPoe, *tr.* by Robert Bly

I open the top. Walking at Night. Brian Swann. PoCoUp

I open the wrong door. Kiss, The. Angela Ball. ExTi

I opened a stone volume—but only. Quarry. T. Arfon Williams. BBMWP, *tr.* by Emyr Lewis

I opened my eyes from sleep, and suddenly. Mihri Hatun. OLP, *tr.* by Walter Andrews, Najaat Black and Mehmet Kalpakli

I opened my veins. Unstoppably. Marina Ivanovna Tsvetayeva. MoWP, *tr.* by Elaine Feinstein

I opened the door so my last look. One More Brevity. Robert Frost. APT-1

I opened this poem with a yawn. How the Sestina (Yawn) Works. Anne Waldman. AHA

I Opened Your Head. Joyce Mansour. NAWM-7v2, *tr.* by Serge Gavronsky

I opens ma mouth an' laughs. (LL) Homesick Blues. Langston Hughes. GM; MoAmPo

I ordered this, this clean wood box. Arrival of the Bee Box, The. Sylvia Plath. NALW; NAMCP V.2; NPeEn; OxBoAm

I ought to be glad. Louis MacNeice. OBCoV *Fr.* Autumn Journal.

I ought to hurry up in order to save what can be saved. My Poetry. Lajos Kassák. IQMS, *tr.* by Adam Makkai

I overheard the other night / standing by the window. Imamu Amiri Baraka. BB *Fr.* Wise/Whys.

I, Ovid, poet of my wantonness. Ovid. OBVE *Fr.* Elegies.

I owe my living to the abattoir. My father, the manager, sat in the office. Abattoir, The. Ania Walwicz. BMAP

I owed my second birth. My Father's Workshop. Anna Swirszczynska [*or* Swir]. GifTon, *tr.* by Czeslaw Milosz and Leonard Nathan

I own a print of cows on a green hill. City Beneath the City, The. Eloise Klein Healy. GeoHom

I own nigger, I purchased it with the blood of my fathers. I stole it. In Exchange for Forty Acres. Bruce Jackson. AmPoNex

I own Pandora's box. For Albert, the Terrible. Carlota Caulfield. TANSG, *tr.* by Chris Allen

I pace the sounding sea-beach and behold. Milton. Henry Wadsworth Longfellow. GSo; NAAPv.1

I paced the length of it—one hundred and forty-three. On Seeing the Reformation Memorial in Geneva. Gyula Illyés. IQMS, *tr.* by John Wilkinson

I packed my bags in dawn moonlight. Departing from Yiyang in the Early Morning. Wang Po. CCL1, *tr.* by Stephen Owen

I packed some provisions and took up my light staff. On Cimbing Mount Green Crag in Yongjia. Hsieh Ling-yün. CCL1, *tr.* by John Frodsham

I paid a spring-time visit to your country. Jean West. NewEx

I paid for the blooding of Hobson's hide. Account, An. Mick North. NLP

I paid my becoming well not to become. On the Calligraphy of Black Chant. Ed Roberson. EGAG

I Paint What I See. Elwyn Brooks White. AmWit; NBLV

I painted my eyes with black antimony. Love Song. *Unknown.* WoPoe, *tr.* by Ulli Beier and H. Gaden

I painted rouge on my lips. One Who's in Love with Love, The. Hagiwara Sakutaro. CAoMJL1; PFTM-1, *tr.* by Hiroaki Sato

I painted the mailbox. That was fun. Painting the Gate. May Swenson. TLR; WeW-3

I painted the roof of a skyscraper. Carl Sandburg. CA

I park the car because I'm happy. Now. Christopher Gilbert. GT; OxAAAP

I part the curtain of my back room. Twilight. Yi Yuksa. CAMKP, *tr.* by David R. McCann

I pass a / door. Daily Task. Belinda Zubicueta Carmona. TANSG, *tr.* by Celeste Kostopulos-Cooperman

I pass a sign, ATF FBI KNOW HOW TO LIE. Battery. Diane Glancy. LiTh

I pass the day tense, day-. Kenneth Rexroth. APSN *Fr.* Love Poems of Marichiko, The.

I Pass the Night at General Headquarters. Tu Fu [*or* Du Fu]. NDACCP, *tr.* by Kenneth Rexroth

I pass the swamp borders. Raul Bopp. TCLAP *Fr.* Black Snake.

I pass two women in the hall. Pilgrimage. Yoshioka Minoru. PFTM-2, *tr.* by Eric Selland

I passed along the water's edge below the humid trees. Indian upon God, The [*or* An]. William Butler Yeats. MoBrPo

I passed beside the reverend walls. Alfred Tennyson. NAEL-6v2; NAEL-7v2 *Fr.* In Memoriam A. H. H.

I passed Slimgullion, Morgan Mine. Sierra Kid. Philip Levine. GeoHom

I passed the window and saw their lovely flash of wings. Regret for the Mourning Doves Who Failed to Mate. Bruce Weigl. UrbNat

I passed thurgh a gardyn grene. *Unknown.* OHMEL

I pastori (The Shepherds). Gabriele D'Annunzio. TWF

I patched my coat with sunlight. Coat, The. Dennis Lee. TLR

I peeled bits of straw and I got switches too. Song. John Clare. NAEL-6v2; NAEL-7v2

I peer adown a shining group. Tribute. Eloise Bibb. CBWP-4

I, peregrine of noon. Yvor Winters. NAAPv.2 *Fr.* Magpie's Shadow, The.

I persist in mingling fictions with the most fearful realities. Shared Nights. Paul Eluard. YaTCFP, *tr.* by Mary Ann Caws

I pick a daimen icker from the thrave. Sir James Murray. Edwin Morgan. HarvBoo

I picked this fragile sprig of heather. Farewell, The. Guillaume Apollinaire. YaTCFP, *tr.* by Roger Shattuck

I picnicked with you on Pugak Mountain. Returning to Dupawon. Jungkwan Ilson. BecRai, *tr.* by Kim Daljin, Kim Won-Chung and Christopher Merrill

I picture you profiled in Film Noir tones. Algren. Donny O'Rourke. PML

I pitched my day's leazings in Crimmercrock Lane. Dark-Eyed Gentleman, The. Thomas Hardy. MoBrPo; NBLV

I pity you, my feathers. Tohono O'odham. NAAPv.1 *Fr.* Songs for Treating Sickness, Sung durring the Four Parts of the Night.

I place a dead butterfly on the page. Instead of You. Stephen Dunn. CAP-8

I place my hope on the water. Language Issue, The. Nuala Ni Dhomhnaill. ModIr; MoWP; NPeEn, *tr.* by Paul Muldoon

I place these numbed wrists to the pane. Nightmare Begins Responsibility. Michael S. Harper. ESEAA; GT; LoL; NAMCP V.2; OxAAAP; PoPoPo; VCAP

I placed a jar in Tennessee. Anecdote of the Jar. Wallace Stevens. BrAP; ColAP; EMP; FaBoA; HeIP-4; MoAmPo; NAAL-5; NAAPv.2; NAMCP V.1; NAWM-7v2; NIL-7; NoAM; NoP-4; NoP-5; OxBoAm; PoA 2002; PoPoPo; SAmP; TCAPo; TFi; WaAnP

I placed my hand cupped. Return of an Ikon. Dimitris Tsaloumas. BMAP

I planned to have a border of lavender. Paul Goodman. OxBoAm

I plant beans below the southern hill. Returning to Fields and Gardens (2). T'ao Ch'ien. WaAnP, *tr.* by Arthur Sze

I planted for you. Three Gifts. Vincent Woods. NIrP

I planted him in this country / like a flag. (LL) Death of a Young Son by Drowning. Margaret Atwood. BrAP; NIL-7

I planted rice before Spring Festival. Su Tung-p'o. ColAnChi *Fr.* Eastern Slope.

I plaster myself with ashes. Giríscandra Ghos. SinGod, *tr.* by Rachel Fell McDermott

I play a spade:—Such strange new faces. Arrivals at a Watering-Place. Winthrop Mackworth Praed. NOBRP; NPeEn

I play it cool / And dig all jive. Motto. Langston Hughes. ItP; NAMCP V.1

I play marimba on your rib cage. Los Amantes. Richard Garcia. TouFir

I Play My Zither. Hsiao Kang. CCL1, *tr.* by Anne Birrell

I play my zither by the northern window. I Play My Zither. Hsiao Kang. CCL1, *tr.* by Anne Birrell

I play tennis with the shells. Poem. Paul Dermée. CuPo

I play your furies back to me at night. High Fidelity. Thom Gunn. PoA 2002

I played piano while my daddy knelt. Southern Crescent Was on Time, The. Andrew Hudgins. GM

I played with you 'mid cowslips blowing. Thomas Love Peacock. OBEV *Fr.* Gryll Grange.

I pledge allegiance to the Earth. Pledge of Allegiance to the Family of Earth, A. Mim Kelber. HW

I pledge myself through thick and thin. Tory Pledges. Thomas Moore. OBSV

I pluck the grass. Cai-bin: I Pluck the Grass. *Unknown.* CCL1

I plucked pink blossoms from mine apple tree. Apple Gathering, An. Christina Georgina Rossetti. CtM; NAEL-6v2; NAEL-7v2

I plunged my beak in the marbling cheek. Eliza Cook. VerBaPo *Fr.* Carrion Crow, The.

I, / poet by trade. Ars Poetica. Claribel Alegría. LoL; TANSG, *tr.* by Darwin Flakoll

I point to where the pain is, the ache. Here. Ken Smith. StAl

I ponder you in clamor and in silence. Psalm. Tudor Arghezi. AF, *tr.* by Andrei Bantas and Thomas Amherst Perry

I practiced the piano all afternoon. Involuntary Music. D. Nurske. MiVo

I praise a patron high-hearted in strife. In Praise of Owain Gwynedd. Cynddelw Brydydd Mawr. OBWVE, *tr.* by Joseph P. Clancy

I praise a prince, lord of king's country. Spoils of Annwn, The. *Unknown.* WoPoe, *tr.* by Anthony Conran

I praise the country women. Grit. Geoff Page. NOBAu

I praise the speech, but cannot now abide it. Of the Wars in Ireland. John Harington. NoSic

I praise the tortilla in honor of El Panzón. Praise the Tortilla, Praise the Menudo, Praise the Chorizo. Ray Gonzales. UnSA

I praise those ancient Chinamen. Hymnus Ad Patrem Sinensis. Philip Whalen. BB; WANABP

I praised the daisies on my lawn. J Is for Jealousy. W. H. Davies. TCAWP

I praised thee not while living; what to thee. To Elizabeth Barrett Browning, in 1861. Dora Greenwell. PoBW; VWP

I pray and weep in my bed at night (craving sleep). Praise Poem to Christ, A. Catrin Ferch Gruffydd ab Ieuan ap Llywelyn Fychan. EMWP

I pray that the great world's flowering stay as it is. Gardener to His God, The. Mona Van Duyn. RACG

I pray the Lord my soul to take. Ogden Nash. NBLV *Fr.* One from One Leaves Two.

I pray thee, Antonio, be comforted. Leigh Hunt. *Fr.* Legend of Florence, A.

I pray thee by the soul of her that bore thee. Iris, Her Book. Oliver Wendell Holmes. NCAP

I pray thee leave, love me no more. To His Coy Love, A Canzonet. Michael Drayton. NOSC; PBRV

I pray thee Nymph Penaeis stay, I chase not as a fo. Ovid. OBVE *Fr.* Metamorphoses.

I pray you all give [*or* gyve] your audience [*or* audyence]. Everyman. *Unknown.* NAWM-5v1

I pray you, be mery and synge with me. *Unknown.* SacPr

I pray yow all with on thoght. *Unknown.* SacPr

I prayed for Halabcha and my palms were lit by fiery sweat. Mountain of Dreams. Aziz Samawi. IrPoTo, *tr.* by Alex Bellem

I prayed to the ghost of Carrie. Ian Duhig. NeBl

I prefer a young man for coition, and him only. How an Old Man Can Regain His Youth Through Sexual Potency. Ibn Kamal. EroLit, *tr.* by Mary Jo Lakeland

I prefer red chile over my eggs. Green Chile. Jimmy Santiago Baca. NIL-7

I prefer to come from silence to talk. Valerio Magrelli. ItPo, *tr.* by Gayle Ridinger

I Prefer Your Uneasiness Like a Dark Lantern. Laurence Iché. SurWo, *tr.* by Myrna Bell Rochester

I prepare for you the way I plan. Simplest and the Hardest, The. Margaret Lloyd. OPRER

I prepare the last meal. Capital Punishment. Sherman Alexie. PrTe

I prepared a lamb for him (a sacrifice floating). Cayenne. Angela Jackson. SweBea

I Present Myself to the World. Amina Saïd. PoArWo, *tr.* by Lucy McNair

I press'd my Julia's lips, and in the kiss. Robert Herrick. CavPo

I pretend to wait for you to enlarge the minutes. Patrizia Cavalli. NeIt

I pretend you're stroking my hair. Post-operative. Helen Kitson. PoCu

I prithee, daughter, do not make me mad. William Shakespeare. OxAEP-1 *Fr.* King Lear.

I prithee spare me, gentle boy. Song. Sir John Suckling. CavPo

I promised I'd be good that day. Calling, The. Ai. MAAN

I prove a theorem and the house expands. Geometry. Rita Dove. HeIP-4; NAMCP V.2; PtR

I puked and cried—that's what Mom said. Seven Ages of Man. J. D. Smith. IaFF

I pull opposites together. Guida Swan. NewEx

I pull the huge book down from the bookcase. *Automobiles of the Asylum.* Philip Hammial. BMAP

I pulled a hummingbird out of the sky one day but let it go. Wind. Dionne Brand. NOxBChV

I pulled on a suit of mail. Precautions. Martin Sorescu. VCWP, *tr.* by Joana Russell-Gebbett and Paul Muldoon

I Pulled on the Reins. Juan Ramón Jiménez. RaW, *tr.* by Robert Bly

I pulled the street up as you suggested. Something for Easter. Robert Creeley. InvLad

I Pursue a Form. Rubén Darío. SpanPo, *tr.* by Dorren Bell

I pursue a form that does not fit my style. I Pursue a Form. Rubén Darío. SpanPo, *tr.* by Dorren Bell

I push out of Customs, stumble, almost fall, legs numb from. Restroom. Chitra Divakaruni. UnSA

I put a lot of stock in the old. Old Age. Rolf Jacobsen. WED, *tr.* by Robert Bly

I put all the woolen blankets, both saddle. Fever. Jana Harris. FiBr

I put aside the swim team ribbons. Belongings. A. V. Christie. AmPoNex

I put back the rifle on a steel rack. After the Rains of Saigon. Walter McDonald. TiP2

I put my cameleer off two thousand and one times. Sand in Flames. Nujoum Al-Ghanim. PoArWo, *tr.* by Clarissa C. Burt

I put my cap in the cage. Quartier Libre. Jacques Prévert. CLPP, *tr.* by Lawrence Ferlinghetti

I put my hand to the cloth. History of the Quilt That Heaved Life into Stars Patched, Circled, Stitched and Square. Carletta Carrington Wilson. BtF

I put my hands through your head. White Paintings V. Laura Mullen. RoV

I put my hat upon my head. Ballad. Samuel Johnson. OxAEP-1; UV

I put my hat upon my head. Peter Veale. NBLV

I put on a diving mask and went down / A few feet below the. Ecolog. Lawrence Ferlinghetti. WhBo

I put on a pair of overshoes. Around My Room. William Jay Smith. TLR

I put on La Pathétique. La Pathétique. Lily Brett. HP

I put on my socks: the men in the next room put on their socks. Ninth Symphony. Michael Brownstein. MotU

I put the peas in Galileo's telescope. Confessio. Alan Jackson. EdScPo

I put the pyracantha in a blue vase. December 1, 1994. Gerald Stern. PoDa

I put your leaves aside. Weather-Cock Points South, The. Amy Lowell. APT-1; NALW; NoP-4; NoP-5; OxBoAm

I quail, lean to beginnings, sheath-wet. (LL) Cuttings (later) ("This urge, wrestle, resurrection of dry sticks.") Theodore Roethke. APT-2; CAP-8; NAAL-5; NAMCP V.1; NoAM; OBGa; TRP; VCAP; WaAnP

I quake like Satan. Herbert Lomas. NewEx

I quit med school when I found out the stiff they gave me. Dangerous Life. Lucia Maria Perillo. IllVoic

I quitted and betook myself to France. William Wordsworth. OxAEP-2 *Fr.* Prelude, The; Growth of a Poet's Mind [1805 version; Selections from Anthologies].

I rage, I melt, I burn. John Gay. NAEL-6v1 *Fr.* Acis and Galatea: An English Pastoral Opera.

I raise my brush to write a poem to tell my dear wife. *Unknown.* NAAPv.2

I raise my hat. John Mole. OBCoV *Fr.* Penny Toys.

I raised my glass, and—solid, pungent, like the soot-encrusted. Calvin Klein's Obsession. Ciaran Carson. EmeKit

I ran. Whipping, The. Samuel F. Reynolds. SpirFl

I ran across. New York Notebooks, The. Howard Moss. BodElec

I ran away wanting you to follow and then catch up. Motive. Catherine Imbriglio. IAoNAP

I ran into Tu Fu by a Rice Grain Mountain. To Send to Tu Fu as a Joke. Li Po. ColAnChi, *tr.* by Elling O. Eide

I ran to the brook to do my hair. Warpath Song. *Unknown*. AmWaPo, *tr.* by Maurice Boyd

I ran to the church. Journey Back to Christmas. Gwen Dunn. OBCP

I ran up and grabbed your arm, the way a man. At the Washing of My Son. David Ray. RaBo

I ran up six flights of stairs. Whole Mess . . . Almost, The . . Almost, The. Gregory Corso. BB

I rang them up, while touring Timbuctoo. To Someone Who Insisted I Look up Someone. X. J. Kennedy. OBCoV

I ransack her room. Loot and pillage. Looking for Mother. Dorothy Molloy. NIrP

I reach from pain. Reuben, Reuben. Michael S. Harper. CAP-8; LoL; NAMCP V.2

I reached heaven and it was syrupy. Transformation and Escape. Gregory Corso. PFTM-2

I reached the harbor on foot. Port of Call. Hwang Tonggyu. CAMKP, *tr.* by Kevin O'Rourke

I reached the highest place in Spoon River. Edgar Lee Masters. *Fr.* Spoon River Anthology.

I reached the middle of the mount. Dirge. Ralph Waldo Emerson. TCAPo

I read a book. Poems from Prison. Nazim Hikmet. NaPG, *tr.* by Talat Sait Halman

I read a boy's poem called. Every Morning After Killing Thousands of Angels. VCWP, *tr.* by Christopher Drake

I read a novel by a friend of mine. I Am in a Novel. D. H. Lawrence. OBCoV

I read a sad poem / on the wall. Graffiti. Jane Yolen. SSCS

I read, before my eyelids dropt their shade. Dream of Fair Women, A. Alfred Tennyson.

I read by the afternoon light then hope. Like Ulysses. Bin Ramke. RoV

I read for wolftooth and bearclaw. *Unknown*. WoPoe *Fr.* Three Swedish Spells.

I read how Quixote in his random ride. Parable. Richard Wilbur. HarvBoo

I read in the papers about the / Freedom Train. Freedom Train. Langston Hughes. GM

I read in unforgettable books. Constant Memories. Patrick Sylvain. InTrad

I read in *Webster's New World Dictionary for Young Readers*. To Become Unconscious. Ebony Page. BRtP

I read last night of the Grand Review. Second Review of the Grand Army, A. Bret Harte. CBCWP; PCW

I read my face on smooth stones. Moraine Lake. Brian Henry. PoCoUp

I read of a Confessor, and a King. Upon the mournful death of our late Soveraign Lord Charles the first, King of England, etc. Rowland Watkyns. BASC

I read of a thousand killed. Thousand Killed, A. Bernard Spencer. FaBoWar; OBWP

I read once of a valley. After Babel. Peter Goldsworthy. NOBAu

I read over my lines. New York. Hugh Seidman. PA9/11

I read / Sand Creek massacre. Brief Wyoming Meditation. Diane Di Prima. BB

I Read That It Was All a Chain. Marianne Vitale. HeMarv

I read the marble-lettered name. Grave in Hollywood Cemetery, Richmond, A. Margaret Junkin Preston. CBCWP; PCW

I read the poems of the dead. Blood of Others, The. Gioconda Belli. TANSG, *tr.* by Steven F. White

I read them, letters of lovers, the mad ones. Agha Shahid Ali. BeAl *Fr.* Country Without a Post Office, The.

I read to the entire plebe class. Poetry Reading at West Point, A. William Matthews. P180

I read you the soft verses of antiquity. 19 January 1944. Salvatore Quasimodo. AF, *tr.* by Jack Bevan

I realize the horse seen from an airplane looks like a violin. Art of a Cold Sun. G. E. Murray. IllVoic

I really can't stay! Baby, It's Cold Outside. Frank Loesser. ReLy

I really hate to say it but I need a lady's room. (LL) Motorcyclists, The. James Tate. NAMCP V.2; NoAM; ReTh

I really love you, / believe me. It is something I inherited. Attila József. Attila József. AF, *tr.* by John Batki

I really thought that drinking here would. Knocking Around. John Ashbery. NoAM

I reap no gains but trouble at your place when I come near. Fuzuli. NaPG, *tr.* by Talat Sait Halman

I reason, Earth is short. Emily Dickinson. APN-2; BeAl; NCAP; TCAPo

I recall days of burnishings. Sax. Robert Minhinnick. ATSWP

I recall their way of hanging back. Making the Middle Be. Brent MacLaine. Coast

I reckon—when I count at all. Emily Dickinson. APN-2; MoAmPo; NIL-7; NIP-4; NoP-4; NoP-5; OxBoAm; TCAPo

I Recognize You. Rosario Morales. PueRic

I recognize you. Spitting out four, five, six-syllable English words. I Recognize You. Rosario Morales. PueRic

I recollect a nurse call'd Ann. Terrible Infant, A. Frederick Locker-Lampson. OBCoV

(I recollect a nurse called Ann.) NOxBChV

I recommend herbs for you. Conversation in Front of a Helicopter. Rosario Murillo. CLPP, *tr.* by Alejandro Murguía

I redden to the roots when Jacqueline Dupont zuts. Conversation Class. Dorothy Molloy. NIrP

I rediscovered Frost at thirty-three. Robert Frost. David Keplinger. VisFro

I Reel Off. "Lucebert." TuT, *tr.* by Mary E. O'Donnell

I reel off a little revolution. I Reel Off. "Lucebert." TuT, *tr.* by Mary E. O'Donnell

I refuted it all. Therapy. Giovanna. SurWo, *tr.* by Myrna Bell Rochester

I regret nothing. Prayer for My Children. Kate Daniels. PoCho

I Regret Nothing. Sergey Aleksandrovich Yesenin. TCRusP, *tr.* by Nigel Stott

I regret nothing, neither do I complain nor weep. I Regret Nothing. Sergey Aleksandrovich Yesenin. TCRusP, *tr.* by Nigel Stott

I regret the passing, the dying, of the vague dream. Return to Shaoshan. Mao Tse-tung. WoPoe, *tr.* by Willis Barnstone and Ko Ching-po

I Rejoice. Kofi Awoonor. BrAP

I rejoiced when from Wales once again. Hugh MacDiarmid. BrAP *Fr.* World of Words, The.

I release you, my beautiful and terrible. I Give You Back. Joy Harjo. AmWaPo; HATNAP; LoL

I rememba. Rayboy Blk & Bluz. Shirley Bradley LeFlore. SpirFl

I remember. Birth. Gioconda Belli. TANSG, *tr.* by Steven F. White

I Remember. Ted Berrigan. NYP2

I Remember. Eavan Boland. PBCIP

I Remember. Joe Brainard. CAGL

I Remember. Joe Brainard.
  "I remember the first time I got a letter that said "After Five Days Return To" on the envelope." AHA

I Remember: "I remember kindergarten." Lydia Cortéz. TWF

I Remember. Anne Sexton. LW

I Remember. Stevie Smith. NIL-7; PoAgWa

I Remember. Wei Chuang. CCL1, *tr.* by John Minford

I Remember. Fay M. Yauger. TiP2

I remember a certain brook that offered the impiety of drunkenness to the topers [sitting] along its course, with [its] cups of golden [wine]. Abd al-Jabbār ibn Abī Bakr Ibn Hamdīs. HiArP, *tr.* by James T. Monroe

I remember a dim evening in Kishinyov [or Kishinev]. Woman from the Book of Genesis, A. Dovid Knut. TCRusP, *tr.* by John Glad

I remember a house where all were good. In the Valley of the Elwy. Gerard Manley Hopkins. OxAEP-2

I remember a waterfall at the bottom of grottoes. Someone I knew, a. Trance Event. Robert Desnos. PFTM-1

I remember an ancient Chinese picture kept over there in Daitokuji. Ernest Francisco Fenollosa. APN-2 *Fr.* Ode on Reincarnation.

I remember being ashamed of my father. Fathers and Sons. Tom Leonard. CABP; NePenScot

I remember being late. At the final minute. With My Mother, Missing the Train. Helena Nelson. Prnts

I remember biting on a little piece of flesh inside my mouth until a very sweet sort of pain came. Joe Brainard. AHA *Fr.* More I Remember More.

I remember coming up. Breath. Reginald Gibbons. BodElec

I remember conversations. Lookin Good. StacyLynn. BtF

I remember dancing in July on the banks of the Hudson in the City. Journal of the Plague Years, A. Walter Holland. CAGL

I remember despotic times. Gaffer Speaks. Ghulam-Reza Ruhani. WoPoe, *tr.* by Omar S. Pound

I Remember Dexedrine. 1970. Pamela Brown. BMAP

I remember fleeing the rebels. P'eng-ya Road. Tu Fu [or Du Fu]. CrYelRi, *tr.* by Sam Hamill

I remember Galileo describing the mind. I Remember Galileo. Gerald Stern. CAP-8

I remember God as an eccentric millionaire. Quite Apart from the Holy Ghost. Adrian Mitchell. OBSV

I Remember Haifa Being Lovely But. Lyn Lifshin. CFP; UnSA

I remember how. Our Land. Aharon Shabtai. WoBe, *tr.* by Peter Cole

I remember how, at that time, in this meadow. When We Were Children. Alexander the Wild. WoPoe, *tr.* by David Ferry

I remember how in Spain. Musica. Philip Dacey. MiVo

I remember how, long ago, I found. Crystals like Blood. Hugh MacDiarmid. HarvBoo

I remember how the child was tugging his mother. Raising of Icarus, The. Envoi. Guy Goffette. YaTCFP, *tr.* by Marilyn Hacker

I Remember, I Remember. Thomas Hood. ITBLP; NPBRoP; OxAEP-2; OxBEV; TFi; TreFP

I Remember, I Remember. Philip Larkin. HarvBoo

I Remember It Well. Alan Jay Lerner. ReLy

I remember kicking the bales down. Zoo. Polly Clark. NeBl

I remember kindergarten. I Remember. Lydia Cortéz. TWF

I remember Kitty saying we shared a deep longing for. Classic Water. David Berman. IIR

I remember little of myself. Patrizia Cavalli. ItPo, *tr.* by Gayle Ridinger

I remember living on the Lower East Side. Joe Brainard. AHA *Fr.* I Remember More.

I remember long ago slipping away. P'eng-Ya Song. Tu Fu [*or* Du Fu]. NDACCP, *tr.* by David Hinton

I remember long veils of green rain. Green Rain. Dorothy Livesay. NALW; NIP-4; NoP-4

I remember lying awake. Endangered Roots of a Person. Wendy Rose. ReEnLa

I remember Malcolm. Ras Baraka. InTrad

I Remember More. Joe Brainard.
"I remember living on the Lower East Side." AHA

I remember my childhood bedroom. Little Poem. Max Jacob. CuPo

I remember / my first confession. Confession. Alice Lee. ReEnLa

I remember now, in my forties. Tree, A. Fadhil Assultani. IrPoTo, *tr.* by Saadi A. Simawe

I remember once hearing. One Day We'll Be Able to Talk to the Dead. Jackie Wills. PoCu

I remember one death in my boyhood. Of John Davidson. Hugh MacDiarmid. HarvBoo; NePenScot; OxBEV

I remember other days. I Cried for You. Arthur Freed. ReLy

I remember painting "I HATE TED BERRIGAN" in big black letters all over my white wall. I Remember. Ted Berrigan. NYP2

I remember rooms that have had their part. Rooms. Charlotte Mew. HarvBoo; MoWP; PoBW; PoCho

I Remember Sharpeville. Sipho Sepamla. AF

I remember / Sitting on his lap. Grandfather Grandfather. Marlon D. Satchell. InTrad

I remember sitting together in parks. Love's Advocate. Phoebe Hesketh. LW

I remember Sulayma when the passion. In Battle. Abu-l-Hasan Ibn Al-Qabturnuh. NAWM-7v1, *tr.* by Lysander Kemp

I remember sun. Penance. Sherman Alexie. MoASP

I remember that he wrote them backwards. My Grandfather's Poems. Edward Hirsch. TaR

I remember that once. Reply to Bukko Zenji's Poem at Seiken-ji. Muso Soseki. EaWin, *tr.* by W. S. Merwin

I remember / That year among the flowers. I Remember. Wei Chuang. CCL1, *tr.* by John Minford

I remember the Arabic numerals on the dashboards. Necking. Sharon Olds. FaoP

I remember the birth. Birth, 1975. Cheryl Van Dyke. GifTon

I remember the bliss. Do, Do, Do. Ira Gershwin. ReLy

I Remember the Blue River. Mei Yao Ch'en. NDACCP, *tr.* by Kenneth Rexroth

I remember the Chillicothe ball players grappling the Rock. Hits and Runs. Carl Sandburg. MoASP

I remember the cities I have never seen. Tomorrow, Tomorrow. Derek Walcott. PoetW

I remember the clumsy surgery: the face. For H. V. (1901–1927). Weldon Kees. NoP-5

I remember the day when we first met among the flowers. Offering Congratulations to the Enlightened Reign. Ou-yang Chiung. ColAnChi, *tr.* by Lois Fusek

I remember the dread with which I at a quarter past four. False Security. Sir John Betjeman. NoAM; NoP-4; NoP-5

I remember the first time I got a letter that said "After Five Days Return To" on the envelope. Joe Brainard. AHA *Fr.* I Remember.

I remember the fragrance of. Snaps of Immigration. Víctor Hernández Cruz. TouFir

I remember the last red rose. 3 A.M. Lauris Edmond. BeAl

I remember the log of Pi, the battle. Log of Pi, The. Marc J. Straus. BloBone

I remember the long corridors. Jeannette Miller. TANSG, *tr.* by Paula Vega

I remember the long corridors where the shadow was continuous. I Remember the Long Corridors. Jeannette Miller. TANSG, *tr.* by Paula Vega

I remember the neckcurls, limp and damp as tendrils. Elegy for Jane. Theodore Roethke. APT-2; BrAP; ColAP; InoFa; MoAmPo; NAMCP V.1; NoP-4; NoP-5; PoPoPo; PtR; TFi; TRP; WaAnP; WeW-3

I remember the night. Aleksandr Vertinsky. TCRusP, *tr.* by John Glad

I remember the night my mother. Night of the Scorpion. Nissim Ezekiel. BrAP

I remember the nights, and the sounds of the nights. What It's Like To Be Alive. Deryn Rees-Jones. BeAl

I remember the old joke. Cliff, The. David Rowbotham. NOBAu

I remember the rain as the feathery fringe of her shawl. (LL) Green Rain. Dorothy Livesay. NALW; NIP-4; NoP-4

I remember the Roman Emperor, one of the cruellest of them. Exeat. Stevie Smith. NAEL-6v2; NAMCP V.1; NoAM

I remember the room in which he held. My Father with Cigarette Twelve Years Before the Nazis Could Break His Heart. Philip Levine. TaR

I remember the smell of cut grass. New Blue Bike, A. C. J. Stevens. ArBi

I remember the time I was called. Civilizing the Filipino. Nick Carbó. AmPoNex

I remember the United States of America. Box Comes Home, A. John Ciardi. AmWaPo; PWW2

I remember the way the big windows washed. I Remember. Eavan Boland. PBCIP

I remember the way the cows stood. Childhood in the Country, A. Maisha Baton. ICANM

I remember them. Ones Forgotten, The. Haim Guri. NRoS, *tr.* by Esther Raizen

I remember this as her kitchen. Kitchen. Allison Joseph. SweBea

I remember those carpenter's hands. Pa Poem 4: Naked and Nailed. Patrick Friesen. ACAMVP

I remember today a Quebec roadside, the crucifix. Crucifix, The. Daniel Berrigan. UpMys

I remember two dwarfs, back there in our country home. Nicaraguan Triptych. Rubén Darío. TCLAP, *tr.* by Lysander Kemp

I remember when I met Joe Brainard. For Joe Brainard. David Trinidad. WiU

I remember when I wrote The Circus. Circus, The. Kenneth Koch. OxBoAm; PmAP

I remember when, in high school if you wore green and yellow on Thursday it meant that you were queer. I Remember. Joe Brainard. CAGL

I remember when they opened the Gaza Strip Club. Carson Cistulli. FreRad *Fr.* Twenty-Six Friends, That's the Same as Your Age.

I remember when we first fled the rebels. Song of Pengya. Tu Fu [*or* Du Fu]. CCL1, *tr.* by Burton Watson

I remember when you shared my insomnia. Broken Lampstand, The. Wu Wei-yeh. ColAnChi, *tr.* by Jonathan Chaves

I Remember You. Johnny Mercer. ReLy

I remember you as you were that last autumn—. Poem. Pablo Neruda. CLPP, *tr.* by Kenneth Rexroth

I remember you as you were that ultimate autumn. Pablo Neruda. WED, *tr.* by Robert Bly

I remember you, Comrade N. N. N. N. Miryana Basheva. CSCBP, *tr.* by Georgi Belev and Lisa Sapinkopf

I remember you were. Marisel. Juan Gonzalo Rose. BLPSL, *tr.* by Rene de Costa, Rigas Kappatos and Eleni Paidoussi

I remember your neck, its strength. Night. Mary Dorcey. PoBW

I remember your strut. Toward Guinea: For Larry Neal, 1937–1981. Houston A., Jr. Baker. ISC

I remembered Tung Tsao-chiu of Lo-yang. Remembering Our Excursion in the Past. Li Po. ChinPo, *tr.* by Ye Weilian [*or* Yeh Wei-lien *or* Wai-lim Yip]

I removed the rains and motored. Head at the Covers, A. Bill Berkson. NYP2

I repeat. Vsevolod Nekrasov. ItGoST, *tr.* by Gerald Janecek

I repeat I'm ready, but ready for what? Eugenio Montale. ItPo, *tr.* by Gayle Ridinger

I repent the actual. It has never got me anywhere. Andrew Hudgins. UpMys *Fr.* Liar's Psalm, The.

I resemble everyone. Self-Portrait. A. K. Ramanujan. NAMCP V.2; NoP-4; NoP-5; PML; PoetW

I reside at Table Mountain and my name is Truthful James. Society upon the Stanislaus, The. Bret Harte. CalPo

I respect the dumb bastards. Billy's Famous Lounge. Joe Wenderoth. NAPBL

I rest in the grace of the world, and am free. (LL) Peace of Wild Things, The. Wendell Berry. BeAl; GoPo; InGu; IPoFL; PLBUT

I return on horseback. Kil Chae. CATKP, *tr.* by Peter H. Lee

I Return to the Place I Was Born. T'ao Ch'ien. NDACCP; WaAnP, *tr.* by Kenneth Rexroth

I returned to the church. Of All There Is. C. Mikal Oness. GeoHom

I returned to the village. Return to the Village. Na'im Araidi. PLBUT, *tr.* by Jay Shir

I returned with a bottle of wine, with a deck of cards, with flowers. Return, The. Dalia Hertz. FIT, *tr.* by Robert Friend

I returned your book of poetry to the store. Saints. Arielle Greenberg. BAP-04; LegDan

I. RICE CHILD. Mama. Claire Kageyama. UnSA

I, Richard Kent, beneath these stones. Epitaph. Sylvia Townsend Warner. MoBrPo

I ride in a red painted carriage. Song of Xiling Lake, A. Su Hsiao-hsiao. CCL1, *tr. by* Chung Ling and Kenneth Rexroth

I ride my bicycle to work each day. Bicycle. Livingston Taylor. ArBi

I ride / the "A" train. Riding the "A." May Swenson. APT-2; GM; OxBoAm

I ride the heathen sea to my ache crouching in the heights; some of. Wail of Heights, The. Wafaa' Lamrani. PoArWo, *tr. by* Richard McKane and Tahia Abdel Nasser

I ride through Queens. Invitation to Madison County, An. Jay Wright. ESEAA

I, rimmeled, awake before the dressing sun. Lynnette Roberts. MoWP *Fr.* Gods with Stainless Ears.

I rise at dawn, and stumble up steep, crumbling. At Summer's End. Charles Harper Webb. GeoHom

I rise from the depths of my resemblance. I Rise from the Depths. Jean Daive. MFP, *tr. by* Martin Sorrell

I rise in the dawn, and I kneel and blow. Song of the Old Mother, The. William Butler Yeats. MoBrPo

I rise in the morning and close my shutter. John Wheelwright. AmWit

I rise like a red balloon, untethered and vacant. Myths of the Disappearance. Monica Ferrell. LegDan

I rise up above my self. Good Friday. Lucille Clifton. OxAAAP

I Rise with an Effort. Philippe Jaccottet. VCWP, *tr. by* Derek Mahon

I rise with an effort and look out. I Rise with an Effort. Philippe Jaccottet. VCWP, *tr. by* Derek Mahon

I rock my son. (LL) Rocking. Gabriela Mistral. BBASP; CFP, *tr. by* Doris Dana

I rode one evening with Count Maddalo. Percy Bysshe Shelley. NPBRoP; NPeEn *Fr.* Julian and Maddalo; A Conversation.

I rode to Streatham Common on a tram. Mind Reborn in Streatham Common, A. Richard Percival Lister. OBCoV

I roll awake on the carpet over. In Directions. John Rybicki. AmPoNex

I / roll my eyes because you. And All the Sisters Said. Janeya K. Hisle. BtF

I romp with joy in the bookish dark. (LL) Eating Poetry. Mark Strand. NAMCP V.2; NoAM; PtR; StAl; WaAnP

I rose at the dead of night. Chilly Night, A. Christina Georgina Rossetti. VWP

I rose from daylong desk at last. Vision. James Devaney. NOBAu

I rose from marsh mud. Lorine Niedecker. APT-2; FTOS

I rose while yet the cattle, heat-opprest [*or* oppressed]. William Wordsworth. CenSon *Fr.* River Duddon [A Series of Sonnets], The.

I run, I run, I am gathered to thy heart. (LL) Renouncement. Alice Thompson Meynell. GSo; LW; MoBrPo; OBEV; OBMV; OxBSo; PEW; VWP

I sagh Him with flesh al bi-spred: He cam from Est. *Unknown.* SacPr

I said a while back. Acknowledgement. Keorapetse Kgositsile. SeSe

I said, Ah! what shall I write? A, a, a, Domine Deus. David Jones. HarvBoo

I said, "Be mine." Archilochus. EroLit *Fr.* Seduction, The.

I said bismillah in your name, Singer. Standing Worship. Dhabya Khamees. PoArWo, *tr. by* Clarissa C. Burt

I said fate plays a game without a score. I Sit by the Window. Joseph Brodsky. VCWP, *tr. by* Howard Moss

I said I will find what is lowly. Still. A. R. Ammons. OxBoAm

I said: I will go into the garden and consider roses. Discipline. Mary Ursula Bethell. PoBW

I said: "I will, then, be a toad." (LL) Think as I think, said a man. Stephen Crane. IJHIL; WeW-3

I said I would always live for her. Hartmann von Aue. GePo

I said in my youth. Primer, The. Josephine Jacobsen. NoP-4; NoP-5

I said, Jim, let me see that thing. Jim's Hairball. Lee Upton. AmAlph

I said: On all these, Death, with gentleness, come down. (LL) Judge Not. Theodore Roethke. ChIV-2; GI

I said petals from an appletree. (LL) Portrait of a Lady. William Carlos Williams. HarvBoo; NAAL-5; NAAPv.2; NAMCP V.1; NoAM; NoP-5; OxBoAm; WaAnP

I said, / take my belly. Madonna of the Peaches. Joan Logghe. HW

I said to him, you melt me. Melt me. Amanda Nazario. HeMarv

I said to him—Just don't throw me into that briar patch. Mariya Galina. CRWP, *tr. by* Daniel Weissbort

I said to my baby. Langston Hughes. APSN; APT-2; OxBoAm; SSLK *Fr.* Lenox Avenue Mural.

I said to my companion, this is walking. Victoria Market. Francis Brabazon. NOBAu

I Said to My Heart. Charles, Earl of Peterborough Mordaunt. OxBEV

I said: "Your Christian name?" Lovers, The. Alain Bosquet. PML, *tr. by* William Jay Smith

I said—Then, dearest, since 'tis so. Last Ride Together, The. Robert Browning. EroLit; ITBLP; NAEL-6v2; NAEL-7v2; OBEV

I sall goe intill ane haire. Shapeshifting. Isabel Gowdie. EMWP

I salute God, asylum's gift. Poem on His Death-Bed. Cynddelw Brydydd Mawr. OBWVE, *tr. by* Joseph P. Clancy

I salute the most high lord. Poet's Loves, The. Hywel ab Owain Gwynedd. OBWVE, *tr. by* Gwyn Williams

I salute you. Cedars. Nadia Tuéni. PoArWo

I salvaged one photograph form the general clear-out, plucked. Hazel Goodwin Morrissey Brown. Sinéad Morrissey. MFPA; NIrP

I sang as one. Conflict, The. Cecil Day Lewis. MoBrPo; NoP-4

I sang in the sun. Race Relations. Carolyn Kizer. LTA

I sang of quiet Achille, Afolabe's son. Derek Walcott. NAMCP V.2 *Fr.* Omeros.

I sat. At the Door of Anticipation. Hala Mohammad. PoArWo, *tr. by* Cornelia Al-Khaled

I sat across, behind my desk. Two Suffering Men. Eugene Hirsch. BloBone

I sat all morning in the college sick bay. Mid-Term Break. Seamus Heaney. AmFaPo; BeAl; NIL-7; PoPoPo; WaAnP

I sat alone at my window. Retrospect. Josephine D. Henderson Heard. CBWP-4

I sat before my glass one day. Other Side of a Mirror, The. Mary Elizabeth Coleridge. NAEL-7v2; NALW; ViWPN; VWP

I sat beside the glassy evening sea. Departure, The. William Vaughn Moody. APN-2

I sat beside the glowing grate, fresh heaped. William Cullen Bryant. NCAP

I sat by the edge of the field. Kim Roberts. AmPoNex *Fr.* Constellation Frigidaire, The.

I sat down in the colored section. Segregated Railway Diner—1946. Robert Winner. LTA

I sat down on a rock. Walther von der Vogelweide. GePo

I sat down to remember. Sediment of Lukewarm and Radiant Rain. Coral Bracho. TANSG, *tr. by* Celeste Kostopulos-Cooperman

I sat in the door of our cottage. Autumn Day, An. Clara Ann Thompson. CBWP-2

I sat in the Mercado Modelo. My Last Night in Bahia. Carolyne Wright. RoV

I sat me down upon a green bank-side. Bronx. Joseph Rodman Drake. APN-1

I sat next to the Duchess at tea. Limerick. *Unknown.* SoSe-8

I sat on cushioned otter-skin. Madness of King Goll, The. William Butler Yeats. NAEL-6v2; NAEL-7v2

I sat on my stool. Father. Ralph Dickey. ESEAA

I sat on the couch. Sullen, young. Cup of Coffee, The. Carole Bernstein. AmPoNex

I sat on the steel stile the other day. T. Glynne Davies. BBMWP *Fr.* Ruins.

I sat there on the quayside by the landing. By the Danube. Attila József. IQMS, *tr. by* Peter Zollman

I sat there singing her. Songs. Langston Hughes. APT-2

I sat transfixed. Sunset on the River. Corinth Morter-Lewis. OWABP

I sat under my father's clothesline. Con Los Pájaros. Juan Delgado. AmPoNex

I sat up all night and watched you sleep. I did. To Beth On Her Forty-Second Birthday. Jane Chambers. PoBW

I sat upon the ground, and the ground was fire. Abba Kovner. NRoS, *tr. by* Esther Raizen

I sat with John Brown. That night moonlight framed. Narrative. Russell Atkins. EGAG; GT

I sat with Love upon a woodside well. Dante Gabriel Rossetti. NAEL-6v2; OxBSo *Fr.* House of Life, The.

I sat within a window, looking west. East or West? Charles Tennyson Turner. OxBSo

I save your grace inside. Fire Keeper. Bahiyyih Maroon. SpirFl

I saved a life once. Lipsticktion. Edwin Torres. HeMarv

I saved seventy dollars to buy Jan a present. Jan's Birthday. David Lee. GifTon

I savour on my own. (LL) Pleasant Joys of Brotherhood, The. James Simmons. OBCoV; PBCIP; PML

I saw a band of warriors coming on. War Dance. Miidhu. NOBAu, *tr. by* George von Brandenstein

I saw a boy with eager eye. Two Boys, The. Mary Lamb. WoRP

I Saw a Cave of Sable Depth Profound. Thomas Cole. APN-1

I saw a famous man eating soup. Soup. Carl Sandburg. HHAm

I saw a film once. Celia de Fréine. NIrP *Fr.* Price on My Head, A.

I saw a fishpond all on fire. *Unknown.* OxBEV

I saw a flat space. Frozen Field, The. Sheenagh Pugh. TCAWP

I saw a garden with a thousand rills. Education in Wales. Goronva Camlan. AngWePo

I saw a gold pillar from earth to heaven. Message of King Sakis and the Legend of the Twelve Dreams He Had in One Night, The. *Unknown.* WoPoe, *tr. by* Charles Simic

I saw a great building with many storeys piled high. Tony Charles. NewEx

I saw a gull that slipped on the ice. Town a Bird Sanctuary, The. Jan Eijkelboom. TuT, *tr. by* Peter van de Kamp

I saw a headless she-mule. Good Friday: For Lack of an Orchestra. Jack Spicer. APSN

I Saw a Jolly Hunter. Charles Causley. NOxBChV; OPOU

I saw a little girl. Heart's Fine Gold, The. W. O. Bourne. TreFP

I saw a maiden, fairest of the fair. Charity. Henrietta Cordelia Ray. CBWP-3

I saw a man pursuing the horizon. Stephen Crane. APN-2; ChAP; IJHIL; MoAmPo; NAAPv.1; NoP-4; OxBoAm; TCAPo

I saw a mesa. Leaving Port Authority for the St. Regis Rezz. Wendy Rose. HATNAP

I saw a mouth jeering. A smile of melted red iron ran over it. Its laugh was full of nails rattling. It was a child's dream of a mouth. Gargoyle. Carl Sandburg. NAMCP V.1; NoAM

I Saw a Peacock [with a Fiery Tail]. *Unknown.* OPOU; OWoS

I saw a rose come loupin' oot. Ballad of the General Strike. Hugh MacDiarmid. RSaN

I saw a shadow on the ground. Sky, The. Elizabeth Madox Roberts. MoAmPo

I saw a ship a-sailing. Mother Goose. NTCP

I saw a Ship of martial build. Berg, The. Herman Melville. ColAP; NCAP; NoP-4; NoP-5; PoPoPo; TCAPo

I saw a sky of stars that rolled in grime. Sidney Lanier. APN-2; NCAP *Fr.* Street Cries.

I saw / a specialist a cook. To the Heart. Tadeusz Różewicz. PoSu, *tr. by* Victor Contoski

I saw a stable, low and very bare. Mary Elizabeth Coleridge. ChIV-2; OBCP; SacPr

I saw a star slide down the sky. Falling Star, The. Sara Teasdale. ChAP

I saw a staring virgin stand. William Butler Yeats. *Fr.* Resurrection, The.

I saw a strange creature. Cynewulf. WoPoe *Fr.* Riddles (Exeter Book).

I saw a tree. Piece of Bone, The. Katerina Pinosová. SurWo

I saw a vision. Gwyneth Lewis. NeBl *Fr.* Parables & Faxes.

I saw a woman, a certain woman, or the woman, or another woman. Woman I Carelessly Killed, The. Kim Chŏngnan. EcSo, *tr. by* Peter H. Lee

I saw a woman sitting on a beast. Sonnet 13. Edmund Spenser. ChIV-2

I saw a word in the air. Cecilia Vicuña. TANSG *Fr.* Palabrarmás.

I saw a young deer standing. Moment. Hildegarde Flanner. APT-2; ASA

I saw among the clouds a monstrous trumpet. Trumpet of Judgement, The. Victor Hugo. SxFrPo, *tr. by* A. M. and E. H. Blackmore

I saw an eagle sweep to the sky. Sun-Struck Eagle, The. Eleanor Percy Lee and Catherine Anne Warfield. SWaP

I saw an infant—health, and joy, and light. Infant, The. Agnes Strickland. CenSon

I saw an ugly beast come from the sea. Sonnet 12. Edmund Spenser. ChIV-2

I Saw as a Child. Zindzi Mandela. NAfrP

I saw Aurora bouncing down the street. Wish Fulfillment. Maggie Nelson. HeMarv

I saw before me a stormy condition. I'm Livin' in a Great Big Way. Dorothy Fields. ReLy

I saw Budapest burning. Horror. Gyula Illyés. IQMS, *tr. by* Anthony Edkins

I saw children at Christmas in 1945. Children at Christmas in 1945. Vladimir Holan. AF, *tr. by* C. G. Hanzlicek and Dana Habova

I saw dawn creep across the sky. Summer Morning, A. Rachel Lyman Field. ChAP

I saw de beam in my sister's eye. *Unknown.* SSUS

I saw Esau sawing wood. *Unknown.* Spl

I Saw Eternity the other night. World, The (1). Henry Vaughan. ChIV-2; FSCP; NAEL-6v1; NAEL-7v1; NoP-5; NOSC; NPeEn; OxAEP-1; OxBEV; PBRV; SacPr; TFi; WaAnP

I saw fair[e] Chloris [*or* Cloris] walk alone. On Chloris Walking in the Snow. William Strode. NPeEn

I saw ferlies in thon mountain pule. Mountain Pule. James King Annand. EdScPo

I saw God! Do you doubt it? What Thomas an Buile Said in a Pub. James Stephens. MoBrPo

I saw her amid the dunghill debris. Tinker's Wife. Patrick Kavanagh. NoAM

I saw her coming through the flowery grass. Spring Love. Francis Ledwidge. IrLP

I saw her first in Cabbage time. I Saw Her in Cabbage Time. Slocum Slugs. VerBaPo

I saw her in a cluttered basement store. Note, The. Melvin B. Tolson. GT

I Saw Her in Cabbage Time. Slocum Slugs. VerBaPo

I saw her in the fleeting wind. To Echo. Anna Maria Jones. CenSon

I saw her near Anaheim by the fence. Orphan, The. Glover Davis. GeoHom

I saw him. When I Passed in the Afternoon. Laura Riesco. TANSG, *tr. by* Shaun Griffin and Emma Sepúlveda-Pulvirenti

I saw him a squat man with red hair. Off Brighton Pier. Alan Ross. OBWP

I saw him dead; I saw his Body fall. Francis Quarles. PBRV *Fr.* Divine Fancies.

I saw him in the Airstrip Gardens. Betjeman, 1984. Charles Causley. UV

I saw him in the Café Royal. On Seeing an Old Poet in the Café Royal. Sir John Betjeman. OxBEV; UV

I saw him once before. Last Leaf, The. Oliver Wendell Holmes. BRP; ITBLP; NAAL-3; TCAPo

I saw him the other day as I went to Nanteos. Hedgehog, The. David Gwenallt Jones. BBMWP, *tr. by* Joseph P. Clancy

I saw him yesterday. Quarrel, The. Josephine D. Henderson Heard. CBWP-4

I saw Hsiao-lien by the river. Lute Player, The. Li Ho. CrYelRi, *tr. by* Sam Hamill

I Saw in Louisiana a Live-Oak Growing. Walt Whitman. APN-1; ColAP; NAAL-3; NAAPv.1; NAMCP V.1; NCAP; NIP-4; NoAM; NoP-4; OxBoAm; PoPoPo; PtR; SAmP; TCAPo; WaAnP

I Saw It! Ilya L'vovich Selvinsky. TCRusP, *tr. by* Denis Johnson

I saw it by chance. Plantain. Pak Sŏwŏn. EcSo, *tr. by* Julie C. Park

I saw it coming. Death of Adam, The. Elma Mitchell. EdScPo

I saw its periscope in the tide. Mangrove. John Blight. NOBAu

I saw Julian Bond in 1965 at a SNCC rally. Glad All Over. Patricia Spears Jones. BRtP

I saw little tracks in the snow. Invisible Tree. Tamura Ryuichi. WoPoe, *tr. by* Naoshi Koriyama and Edward Lueders

I saw magic on a green country road. Michael Hartnett. PBCIP *Fr.* Thirteen Sonnets.

I Saw My Father Drowning. David Vogel. HP, *tr. by* A. C. Jacobs

I saw my father naked, once, I. Once. Sharon Olds. NAMCP V.2

I saw my grandad late last evening. Gathering in the Days. Gareth Owen. NOxBChV

I saw my grandmother grow weak. First Death. Donald Justice. CAP-8

I Saw My Lady Weep. *Unknown.* NoSic

(My Lady's Tears.) OBEV

I saw my own children leaning. To the Dregs. Betsy Sholl. ExTi

I saw my soul at rest upon a day. Sestina. Algernon Charles Swinburne. MakPoe

I saw my soul become flesh breaking open. Annunciation. Jean Valentine. CAP-8

I saw my toes the other day. In Extremis. John Updike. OBCoV

I saw myself. Lew Welch. WhBo

I saw new Earth, new Heaven, said Saint John. Sonnet 15. Edmund Spenser. ChIV-2

I saw no temple. (LL) "H. D." NAAPv.2; NALW; NAMCP V.1 *Fr.* Tribute to the Angels.

I saw no Way. The Heavens were stitched. Emily Dickinson. TCAPo

I saw nobody coming, so I went instead. (LL) 76: Henry's Confession. John Berryman. EMP; NAMCP V.2; NoAM; VCAP *Fr.* Dream Songs.

I saw not they were strange, the ways I roam. After Music. Josephine Preston Peabody. TCAPo

I saw old Autumn in the misty morn. Autumn. Thomas Hood. OBEV; OxAEP-2

I saw on the slant hill a putrid lamb. For a Lamb. Richard Eberhart. ColAP; SoSe-8

I saw one whom I love more than my life. Noonday Vision, A. Frances Anne Kemble. PoBW

I saw our golden years on a black gale. Sonnet for Christmas. Judith Wright. LW

I saw prophets tearing at their pasted-on beards. What I Saw. Zbigniew Herbert. AF, *tr. by* John Carpenter and Bogdana Carpenter

I saw streaming up out of the sidewalk the homeless women and men. Under Voice, The. Jean Valentine. BodElec; CAP-8; ExTi

I saw, sweet Licia, when the spider ran. Giles Fletcher, the Elder. OxBSo *Fr.* Licia.

I saw that the shanty town had grown over the graves and that the crowd lived among the memorials. Lines for Translation into Any Language. James Fenton. AF

I saw the best minds of my generation destroyed by madness, starving hysterical naked. Allen Ginsberg. CAP-8; EMP; HarvBoo; NAAL-5; NAMCP V.2; NoAM; NoP-4; NoP-5; PmAP; VCAP; WaAnP *Fr.* Howl.

I saw the blood. I was sixteen. Mack Charles Parker Lynching, The. Sybil Pittman Estess. LiTh

I saw the bodies of earth's men. Navigators, The. Walter James Turner. OBMV

I saw the daughter of the sun; she stood. I Saw the Daughter of the Sun. Elizabeth Daryush. StAl

I saw the / dead bird on the sidewalk. Maze, The. Joanne Kyger. BB

I saw the dog in a dream. Huge white. Orchard, The. Brigit Pegeen Kelly. FaoP

I saw the early morning mist. Dead Horse, The. Cecília Meireles. TCLAP, *tr. by* James Merrill

I saw the first pear. Orchard. "H. D." APT-1; MoAmPo

I saw the garden where my aunt had died. Entertainment of War, The. Roy Fisher. BeAl

I saw the hawk ride updraft in the sunset over Wyoming. Mortal Limit. Robert Penn Warren. InGu

I saw the humble relation that tended the peevishness of wealth. Poor Relation, The; or, Pious Hope Frustrated. Martin Farquhar Tupper. STuOW

I saw the Man that saw this wondrous sight. (LL) I Saw a Peacock [with a Fiery Tail]. *Unknown.* OPOU; OWoS

I saw the midlands. Kisses in the Train. D. H. Lawrence. MoBrPo

I saw the old god of war stand in a bog between chasm and rockface. God of War, The. Bertolt Brecht. AF, *tr. by* Michael Hamburger

I saw the picture in *Newsweek* or *Time.* Mary Magdalene's Left Foot. Andrew Hudgins. UpMys

I saw the ramparts of my native land. Sonnet: Death Warnings. Francisco de Quevedo y Villegas. OxBEV; WoPoe, *tr. by* John Masefield

I Saw the Red Electric. Joyce Mansour. HAWP, *tr. by* Albert Herzing

I saw the salt. Ode to Salt. Pablo Neruda. WED, *tr. by* Robert Bly

I saw the shapes that stood upon the clouds. London Nightfall. John Gould Fletcher. MoAmPo

I saw the sky descending, black and white. Where the Rainbow Ends. Robert Lowell. MoAmPo; PoetW

I saw the spiders marching through the air. Mr. Edwards and the Spider. Robert Lowell. ColAM; HarvBoo; HeIP-4; NAAL-5; NoP-4; NoP-5; TFi

I saw the spot where our first parents dwelt. Garden, The. Jones Very. APN-1; OxBoAm

I saw the sun set yesterday. Sunset Reverie. Edney Cain. OWABP

I saw the virtues sitting hand in hand. Humility. George Herbert. NOSC

I saw thee once—once only—years ago. To Helen. Edgar Allan Poe. NAAPv.1

I saw these waves. Dread. Frederick D'Aguiar. WaCA

I saw / three little black boys. Rehearsal. Baba Lukata. BtF

I Saw Three Ships Come Sailing In. *Unknown.* ChrPo

I saw two hares in the corn. Dance, The. Gareth Alban Davies. OBWVE, *tr. by* Gwyn Jones

I saw where in the shroud did lurk. On an Infant Dying as Soon as Born. Charles Lamb. OBEV

I saw white pelicans rise. Riding on the Coast Starlight. Ursula K. Le Guin. PoCoUp

I saw with open eyes. Stupidity Street. Ralph Hodgson. MoBrPo

I saw you going into Sax's Steak Sandwiches. Sax's and Selves. Mark Halliday. P180

I saw you in the street, head lowered, stumbling. Co-alcoholic. Joan Larkin. LaCa

I saw you naked, gazing past me. One Night When We Paused Half-way. Kate Clanchy. MFPA

I saw you once, Medusa; we were alone. Muse as Medusa, The. May Sarton. HW; NALW

I saw you perform. Count Ossie. Opal Palmer Adisa. WaCA

I saw you smoldering. To an Old Friend. Nadia Hazboun Reimer. PoArWo

I saw you strolling by your solitary. Would You Like to Take a Walk? Mort Dixon and Billy Rose. ReLy

I saw you there, at the end. In the Spring of Hjalmar Calrson: The Real Story. Christopher Howell. RoV

I Saw You through My Closed Eye. Joyce Mansour. NAWM-7v2, *tr. by* Serge Gavronsky

I saw you walking through Newark Penn Station. I Saw You Walking. Deborah Garrison. PoCho

I saw you. / You were like scarred stones scattered on the green. Yekhi'el Khazak. NRoS, *tr. by* Esther Raizen

I saw your eyes like bumps of flint. Ogun's Friend. Jayne Cortez. FTtHH

I saw your gaping eyes. Renegade. Andrée Chedid. PoArWo, *tr. by* Lucy McNair

I saw your manager fight. He was. Elegy for Lyn James. Leslie Norris. OBWVE; TCAWP

I say. all you young girls waiting to live. Song No. 2. Sonia Sanchez. FFC

I say *alligator* and a slab breaks off the boulder. Intermezzo with Five Crocodiles. Efraín Bartolomé. RMCMP, *tr. by* Asa Zatz

I say although the fire were wondrous hot. Sir John Harington. NPeEn *Fr.* Orlando Furioso.

I say Down with all candidates. Down with All Candidates. Felix Morisseau-Leroy. OGAHCP, *tr. by* Boadiba and Jack Hirschman

I say, "Hail!" to the Holy One who appears in the heavens! Holy Priestess of Heaven, The. *Unknown.* HW, *tr. by* Samuel Noah Kramer and Diane Wolkstein

I say, I am quite done. Let Zeus Record. "H. D."

I say "I love" and that's enough. Simple Life, The. Philip Whalen. WANABP

I say I'll move the mountains. Crazy She Calls Me. Bob Russell. ReLy

I Say, Mr. A. Samuel Allen. SeSe

I say serenity. I already knew that words pulled me here but didn't truly understand. Women's Language. Kim Chôngnan. EcSo, *tr. by* Peter H. Lee

I say someone in another time will remember us. Sappho. SaLy, *tr. by* Diane Rayor

I say that my sweetly prattling Heliodora will someday. Meleager. HePo, *tr. by* Barbara Hughes Fowler

I Say That the Cricket the Scorpion the Grasshopper. Mariella Bettarini. CItWP, *tr. by* Cinzia Sartini Blum and Lara Trubowitz

I say that words are men and when we spell. Anna Hempstead Branch. APT-1; NALW *Fr.* Sonnets from a Lock Box.

I say things to myself. Phraseology. Jayne Cortez. EGAG

I say to myself, they're. They're Family Men. Ellen Bass. AtGh

I say to the lead. Poem without a Title. Charles Simic. CAP-8

I say to You Halt. Shadow. Patricia Goedicke. AtGh

I say you shall not speak to him of war. (LL) Twelfth Night. Elinor Wylie. ChrPo; SacPr

I says oh Jesus, can't I count on you people? New. Gillian Conoley. RoV

I scarce believe [*or* beleeve] my love to be so pure. Love's Growth. John Donne. NoP-4; NoP-5; NOSC; NPeEn; PBRV

I scarcely know my worthless picture. Any Husband to Many a Wife. Emily Jane Pfeiffer. ViWPN; VWP

I scissor the stem of the red carnation. Salome. Ai. NoAM

I scoop up fine sand with the plastic shovel. On the Anniversary of My Father's Death. Michael Lieberman. BloBone

I scorn the doubts and cares that hurt. Garden Song, A. George R. Sims. OBCoV; OBGa

I scraped off your smile with nails. Capital Punishment. Nina Cassian. PoSu, *tr. by* Nina Cassian

I scream as you bite. Kenneth Rexroth. APSN; APT-2; NAAPv.2 *Fr.* Love Poems of Marichiko, The.

I scrub the long floorboards. Finding a Long Gray Hair. Jane Kenyon. ItP; LoL

I sdrive to dddeflect at a blow the blow. César Vallejo. PFTM-1 *Fr.* Trilce.

I / search. Dubbed Out. Jean Binta Breeze. WaCA

I search for not knowing in the middle of what I know best. Evening of the Sixth Day, The. Rose Drachler. APT-2

I search for phrases. Too Marvelous for Words. Johnny Mercer. ReLy

I search for your hair like gold in the rain. Roots. Arthur Ade Amaker. BRtP

I search the chemistry of specific emotions. At the Electronic Frontier. Miguel Algarin. UnSA

I searched for my Self. Lal Ded. WPoS

I See a Bear. Ted Hughes. NOxBChV

I see a farmer walking by himself. Farmer, The. Fredegond Maitland Shove. SacPr

I see a mild emanation of light. Mozart in a Classroom of Children. Daniel Bachhuber. MiVo

I see a Soldiers service is forgot. Peter Woodhouse. FaBoWar

I see a wall; but unwhole. Wall, The. Karol Wojtyla. SonAtl, *tr. by* Massimo Ceresa, Favorita '68 and Pyotr Vincent

I see again and again in my eyes. Tendril Love of Africa. Molara Ogundipe-Leslie. HAWP

I see all human wits. Ralph Waldo Emerson. TCAPo *Fr.* Quatrains.

I see as through a skylight in my brain. Persephone. Michael Longley. NPeEn; PBCIP

I see before me now a traveling army halting. Bivouac on a Mountain Side. Walt Whitman. CBCWP; NAAPv.1; PCW

I See Chano Pozo. Jayne Cortez. PmAP

I See Chile in My Rearview Mirror. Agha Shahid Ali. AmAlph; NAMCP V.2; NoP-4

I see during the night guard. Bizerta. George Campbell Hay. NePenScot

I see her close beside me with silent lips sad and tremulous. (LL) Once I Pass'd through a Populous City. Walt Whitman. NAAL-3; NAAL-5; NAAPv.1; RaBo; SAmP

I see her seventeen. Arizona Highways. James Welch. NoAM

I see her yet, that dark-eyed one. Memory, A. Adah Isaacs Menken. CBWP-1; NAAPv.1; ViWPN

"I see herrin'."—I hear the glad cry. With the Herring Fishers. Hugh MacDiarmid. CABP

I see him in a sense as strapped to his chair. Francis Webb. BMAP *Fr.* Around Costessey.

I see how the slanting sunlight upon the windows. Window Washing. Phyllis Thompson. ICANM

I see in my mind, surrounding God. Vittoria da Colonna, Marchesa di Pescara. WPoS

I see in you the estuary that enlarges and spreads itself grandly as it pours in the great sea. To Old Age. Walt Whitman. Spl

I see in your beautiful face, my lord. Michelangelo Buonarroti. CAGL, *tr. by* James M. Saslow

I see it as it looked one afternoon. Long Island Sound. Emma Lazarus. APN-2; NAAPv.1; OxBoAm; SWaP

I see it in terms of images: humans and angels. Armageddon. William Dickey. AtGh

I see its waters crossing at the bone. (LL) Sexual Water. Pablo Neruda. ConPit; PFTM-1, *tr. by* Clayton Eshleman

I See Madmen. Tadeusz Rózewicz. PoSu, *tr. by* Adam Czerniawski

I see madmen who. I See Madmen. Tadeusz Rózewicz. PoSu, *tr. by* Adam Czerniawski

I see Mike's painting, called SARDINES. (LL) Why I Am Not a Painter. Frank O'Hara. CAP-8; EMP; NAMCP V.2; NoAM; NoP-4; NoP-5; OxBoAm; PoPoPo; VCAP; WaAnP

I see my mother waving—her unfussed. Distances. Katherine Gallagher. Prnts

I see no equivalents. Poet at Night-Fall, The. Glenway Wescott. PoA 2002

I see no plans ahead of me. Where is Tomorrow? Yasser Musa. OWABP

I see now you were rehearsing death. Room 703. Jane Rohrer. ACAMVP

I see pictures of the dead. Huge Mouth. Hwang Insuk. EcSo, *tr. by* Peter H. Lee

I see roses in December. Crazy in the Heart. William Engvick. ReLy

I see straight through myself. Academic. John Skoyles. PoA 2002

I see that there it is on the beach. It is. Memorial Service for the Invasion Beach Where the Vacation in the Flesh Is Over. Alan Dugan. AF; PWW2

I see the blue, the green, the golden and the red. Angelus. Kathleen Jessie Raine. BBASP

I see the children running out of school. Poet Laments the Coming of Old Age, The. Dame Edith Sitwell. BrAP; NAEL-6v2; NAMCP V.1; NoAM

I see the elephants in the yard. Elephants Are in the Yard, The. Indran Amirthanayagam. OpBo

I see the fields the sea. Identities. Paul Eluard. SurPaPo, *tr. by* Mary Ann Caws

I see the Four-fold Man. The Humanity in deadly sleep. William Blake. NOBRP *Fr.* Jerusalem.

I see the ginnnnn of resurrection glass to glass! (LL) I Am the Freshly Dead Husband. Kojo Laing. HBAPE; NAfrP; PML

I see the millet combing gold. Midsummer. Alexander L. Posey. APN-2

I See the Moon. *Unknown.* NTCP

I see the mountain every day, but I'm never satisfied. Leisurely Enjoyment. Chungji. BecRai, *tr. by* Kim Daljin, Kim Won-Chung and Christopher Merrill

I see the music of Robert Schumann. On How Robert Schumann Was Defeated by Demons. Francisco Hernandez. RMCMP, *tr. by* Christian Viveros-Fauné

I see the Sunday sun beating. Memory of Sunday. Mairtin O Direain. ModIr, *tr. by* Patrick Crotty

I see the temple in thy pillar reared. Jacob's Pillow, and Pillar. Henry Vaughan. ChIV-1

I see the white / light / And the night / Flies. (LL) *Unknown.* APT-1; OBVE; OxBoAm; WeW-3 *Fr.* Langue d'Oc.

I see thee pine like her in golden story. Coleridge. Theodore Watts-Dunton. GSo

I see them coming up the road. Happy Pair, A. Priscilla Jane Thompson. CBWP-2

I see them in summer. Riddle. Tom Dawe. Coast

I see them standing at the formal gates of their colleges. I Go Back to May 1937. Sharon Olds. BLT; EmeKit; FaoP; GoPo; LoL; MoWP; NIL-7; WaAnP

I see them[—]crowd on crowd they walk the earth. Dead, The. Jones Very. APN-1; NoP-4; NoP-5; OxBoAm; SacPr; TCAPo

I see thine image through my tears tonight. Elizabeth Barrett Browning. CenSon *Fr.* Sonnets from the Portuguese.

I see, under the canopy of death. Funeral, The. Ward Abbott. ICANM

I SEE words on my forehead IN THE AIR. Hannah Weiner. AHA *Fr.* Clairvoyant Journal.

I see you as victim of your own virtue. You have given your life to humanity. Fallen. Samira Vijghen. FTtHH

I See You Dancing, Father. Brendan Kennelly. BeAl

I see you dart into the world. Transformation. Jeni Couzyn. HAWP

I see you displaced, condensed, within my dream. Dream. Josephine Miles. PoA 2002

I see you every morning with a poet's eyes. Merci Bien, Monsieur. Carlota Caulfield. TANSG, *tr. by* Chris Allen

I see you in a hundred places. Now. Where and What You Are. Robert McDowell. CalPo

I see you Mama Goldie, Perdido. Wisdom Is. Quo Vadis Gex-Breaux. FuFl

I see you my brother. Song for Serpents, A. Kysha N. Brown. BtF

I see you, not as you stand before me. Letter to Yeni on Peering into Her Life. Sandra M. Castillo. TouFir

I see you now, my mother and father. Beachy Head. Hilary Davies. Prnts

I see you sitting. Matmiya. Mary Tallmountain. HATNAP; IPoFL; LoL

I see you what you are: you are too proud. William Shakespeare. OxAEP-1 *Fr.* Twelfth Night.

I See Your Face Before Me. Howard Dietz. ReLy

I see / your hands in my nightmares. Ekaterina Vlasova. CRWP, *tr. by* Peter France

I Seek a Form. Rubén Darío. TCLAP, *tr. by* Lysander Kemp

I seek a form that my style cannot discover. I Seek a Form. Rubén Darío. TCLAP, *tr. by* Lysander Kemp

I seek it in the steamy odor. Prayer to the Muse of Ordinary Life. Kate Daniels. ExTi; PoDa

I seem to be the victim of a cruel jest. And Her Mother Came Too. Dion Titherage. OBCoV; ReLy

I seem to have woken up in the pot-shed. My Father Speaks to Me from the Dead. Sharon Olds. NAMCP V.2

I seemed to be nowhere at all. (LL) Migratory. Mark Doty. AmAlph; BeAl

I seen't dis papuh cup dancin' across the street 2day. Dancin' Our Lives Away. Lorena M. Craighead. InTrad

I seent you. Apology to Pangea. Tracie Morris. RD

I send a message, my worthy chief. Message to a Loved One Dead, A. Josephine D. Henderson Heard. CBWP-4

I send, I send here my supremest kiss. His Tears to Thamesis [*or* Thamasis]. Robert Herrick. NOSC

I send my heart up to thee, all my heart. In a Gondola. Robert Browning.

I send my messages ahead of me. Poet and Person. Denise Levertov. GifTon

I send my needle. Stitching. Katie Donovan. NIrP

I send you here a sort of allegory. To —. With the Following Poem. Alfred Tennyson. NOBRP

I send you, my love. Hongnang. CATKP, *tr. by* Peter H. Lee

I sent my body to Bollywood. Ménage à Trois. Gwyneth Lewis. MoWP

I Sent Thee Late. Louis Zukofsky. APT-2

I sente a ringe, a little bande. To Helene. George Darley. NOBRP

I set a loom in the street. Shadow of a Loom, The. Cecilia Vicuña. WANABP

I set aside to tell the restless toil. George Gascoigne. FaBoWar *Fr.* Fruits of War, The.

I set down the emerald lamp. Gekkutsu-Sei. ZenPo, *tr. by* Takashi Ikemoto and Lucien Stryk

I set my bag on the table that is also a toilet. Sit in my chair that is also. Sleeper. Amy Fusselman. HeMarv

I set my table with metaphor. Passover. Linda Pastan. TaR

I set out from my village three springs ago. Buson. EMJL *Fr.* Spring Breeze on the Kema Embankment.

I set the bowl of raw vegetables on the table. Before You Leave. Ai. GT

I settled at Cold Mountain long ago. Settled at Cold Mountain. Han-shan (Cold Mountain). CCL1; NDACCP, *tr. by* Gary Snyder

I shadow the pond. Black Bean Soup. Lucien Stryk. BodElec

I shake my hair in the wind of morning. Triumph of Love. John Hall Wheelock. MoAmPo

"I shall be careful to say nothing at all." How She Resolved to Act. Merrill Moore. MoAmPo

I shall be glad to be silent, Mother, and hear you speak. White Thought, The. Stevie Smith. Spl

I shall be gone, and you may whistle for me. (LL) Oh, Oh, You Will Be Sorry for That Word! Edna St. Vincent Millay. HeIP-4; NALW

I shall be mad if you get smashed about. Soldier Addresses His Body, The. Edgell Rickword. PoWW

I shall be still stronger. I Want to Sleep. Jorge Guillén. RaW; WoPoe, *tr. by* James Wright

I shall begin with a rose for courage. Poem of Flight, The. Philip Levine. OtW

I shall bend toward you with my entire body. *Unknown.* SLW, *tr. by* Marjolijn De Jager, Sayd Bahodin Majrouh and André Velter

I shall but love thee better after death. (LL) Elizabeth Barrett Browning. AmFaPo; BrAP; CABP; CenSon; GSo; HeIP-4; ITBLP; MakPoe; NAEL-6v2; NAEL-7v2; NALW; NIL-7; NIP-4; NoP-4; NoP-5; OPOU; OxAEP-2; OxBSo; PoPoPo; TFi; UV; VWP; WaAnP *Fr.* Sonnets from the Portuguese.

I shall come back to die. In This Dark House. Edward Davison. OBMV

I shall cry God to give me a broken foot. Flash Crimson. Carl Sandburg. MoAmPo

I shall die, but that is all that I shall do for Death.   Conscientious Objector.   Edna St. Vincent Millay.   FaBoWar

I shall die soon, I know.   Soon.   Vikram Seth.   PML

I shall draw a broken tower.   9/15/01.   David Lehman.   PA9/11

I shall ebb out with them, who homeward go. (LL)   John Donne.   BASC; FSCP; NOSC *Fr.* Elegies.

I shall empty my hand.   Neutrality.   Eman Mersaal.   AnVo, *tr. by* Mohamed Enani

I shall find in paradise that emaciated rose shoot.   Maria Luisa Spaziani.   NeIt *Fr.* Star of Free Will, The.

I Shall Forget.   Laurence Hope.   OxBSo

I shall forget you presently, my dear.   Edna St. Vincent Millay.   APT-1; HeIP-4; NAAPv.2

I shall gather myself into myself again.   Crystal Gazer, The.   Sara Teasdale.   MoAmPo

I shall give them all to my elder daughter. (LL)   If I Should Ever by Chance.   Edward Thomas.   MoBrPo; OBMV; OBWVE

I shall go among red faces and virile voices.   Cattle Show.   Hugh MacDiarmid.   MoBrPo; OBMV; OxBEV

I Shall Go Back.   Edna St. Vincent Millay.   MoAmPo

I shall go back again to the bleak shore.   I Shall Go Back.   Edna St. Vincent Millay.   MoAmPo

I shall go back to my mother's grave after this war.   Louis Zukofsky.   PWW2 *Fr.* Song for the Year's End, A.

I shall hate you.   Hatred.   Gwendolyn B. Bennett.   RaBo

I shall hear that grand Amen. (LL)   Lost Chord, A.   Adelaide Anne Procter.   ITBLP; SacPr; UV; VWP

I shall keep singing!   Emily Dickinson.   APN-2; GoPo

I shall know why—when Time is over.   Emily Dickinson.   SAmP

I shall leave you my snores.   Relic, A.   Alaa Khalid.   AnVo, *tr. by* Mohamed Enani

I shall lie hidden in a hut.   Prophecy.   Elinor Wylie.   ItWoWo

I shall lie like this when I am dead.   Going to Sleep.   Dorothy Livesay.   IFF

I Shall Live To Be Old.   Sara Teasdale.   APT-1

I shall live to be old, who feared I should die young.   I Shall Live To Be Old.   Sara Teasdale.   APT-1

I shall look at the grass.   Perseverance.   Martin Sorescu.   VCWP, *tr. by* D. J Enright and Joana Russell-Gebbett

I shall look for loving crops from the birth, life, death, immortality, I plant so lovingly now. (LL)   Woman Waits for Me, A.   Walt Whitman.   ErotSp; HeIP-4

I shall make rings around you.   Fortresses.   Night-Piece.   Joy Davidman.   YaYoPo

I shall marry the very next man who asks me.   (I'll Marry) the Very Next Man.   Sheldon Harnick.   ReLy

I shall never forget his blue eye.   Dylan Thomas.   UV *Fr.* Parachutist.

I shall never get out of this! There are two of me now.   In Plaster.   Sylvia Plath.   NAMCP V.2

I shall never get you put together entirely.   Colossus, The.   Sylvia Plath.   BrAP; MoWP; NALW; NAMCP V.2; NoAM; NoP-4; NoP-5; VCAP; WoPoe

I shall not be myself, death.   Zenith.   Juan Ramón Jiménez.   SpanPo, *tr. by* Kate Flores

I Shall Not Care.   Sara Teasdale.   APT-1; MoAmPo; TCAPo

I Shall Not Die for Thee.   *Irish Oral Tradition.*   IrV, *tr. by* Douglas Hyde

I shall not fail that rendezvous. (LL)   I Have a Rendezvous with Death.   Alan Seeger.   AmWaPo; APT-1; BRP; FaBoWar; TCAPo

I shall not lie to find a lurid rhyme.   Sofiya Parnok.   ARWW, *tr. by* Catriona Kelly

I shall not lose thee though [*or* tho'] I die. (LL)   Alfred Tennyson.   CAGL; HeIP-4; NAEL-6v2; NAEL-7v2; NoP-5 *Fr.* In Memoriam A. H. H.

I Shall Not Pass This Way Again.   *Unknown.*   ChAP

I shall not repeat others' comments about me. (LL)   Wet Casements.   John Ashbery.   NAMCP V.2; OxBoAm

I shall not say how long and late she heard.   Albery Allson Whitman.   NAAPv.1 *Fr.* Octoroon, The.

I shall not say to you, "don't go!"   Lavinia.   Özdemir Asaf.   NaPG, *tr. by* Talat Sait Halman

I shall not see thee. Dare I say.   Alfred Tennyson.   NAEL-6v2; NAEL-7v2 *Fr.* In Memoriam A. H. H.

I shall not sing a May song.   Crazy Woman, The.   Gwendolyn Brooks.   ItWoWo; NALW

I shall not soon forget.   Still Life.   Thom Gunn.   NAMCP V.2; PoCho

I Shall Paint My Nails Red.   Carole Satyamurti.   StAl

I shall rejoice, and my prediction's true. (LL)   Vote, The.   Ralph Knevet.   FaBoWar; NOSC

I Shall Run through the Shadow.   Juan Ramón Jiménez.   RaW, *tr. by* W. S. Merwin

I shall say, Lord, "Is it music, is it morning."   Resurgam.   Marjorie Lowry Christie Pickthall.   SacPr

I shall sleep calm beneath its wave! (LL)   Letitia Elizabeth Landon.   NPBRoP; RWP; VWP *Fr.* Improvisatrice, The.

I shall sleep in white calico.   Song of War.   Kofi Awoonor.   PoetW

I shall stop weeping.   Sleep soundly, dear poet.   Evelina Shats.   CRWP, *tr. by* Daniel Weissbort

I Shall Take You in Rough Weather.   Frank Prewett.   HATNAP

I shall think of you.   Lady Kasa.   ArkPo, *tr. by* Edwin A. Cranston

I Shall Vote Centre.   Roger Woddis.   UV

I shall vote Centre because.   I Shall Vote Centre.   Roger Woddis.   UV

I shall vote Labour because.   I Shall Vote Labour.   Christopher Logue.   UV

I shall write of the old men I knew.   In These Dissenting Times.   Alice Walker.

I shan't be gone long—You come too. (LL)   Pasture, The.   Robert Frost.   APT-1; BLPJKO; ItP; MoAmPo; NAAL-5; NAAPv.2; SAmP; TLR; TRP; WHSW

I shaved my legs a second time.   Love Song.   Frederick Seidel.   BAP-04; OxBoAm

I shot a kit fox, a tapir, an an ibex.   Killing the Animals.   Charles Harper Webb.   LiTh

I shot an arrow into the air.   Shot at Random, A.   Dominic Bevan Wyndham Lewis.   UV

I shot an arrow into the air.   Arrow and the Song, The.   Henry Wadsworth Longfellow.   BRP; ColAP; PCo; UV

I shot my man, 'cause he done me wrong. (LL)   Frankie and Johnny [*or* Johnnie *or* Albert].   *Unknown.*   FaBoA; NAAPv.2; NIP-4; TCAPo

I should be able to give up tea, I think. And wine. (LL)   Women.   Trần Tế Xu'o'ng.   EaWin; WoPoe, *tr. by* W. S. Merwin and Nguyen Ngoc Bich

I should be glad I didn't get the clap.   Parting Roundel.   Jemal Sharah.   NOBAu

I should be glad of another death. (LL)   Journey of the Magi.   T. S. Eliot.   BrAP; ChrPo; GI; HeIP-4; ItP; MoAmPo; NAAL-5; NAEL-6v2; NAEL-7v2; NAMCP V.1; NIL-7; NIP-4; NoP-4; NoP-5; OBCP; OBMV; OxBoAm; StAl; TFi; TRP

I should be happy with my lot.   Nameless Pain.   Elizabeth Stoddard.   SWaP

I Should Care.   Sammy Cahn.   ReLy

I should have been too glad, I see.   Emily Dickinson.   APN-2; SacPr

I should have learned to do this years ago.   Learning to Drive at 32.   Allison Joseph.   BRtP

I should have thought.   At Baia.   "H. D."   APT-1; ColAP; PoBW

I should know what God and man is. (LL)   Flower in the Crannied Wall.   Alfred Tennyson.   BBASP; BRP; ITBLP; NAEL-6v2; NAEL-7v2; TFi

'I should like,' said the vase from the china-store.   Toys Talk of the World, The.   Katharine Pyle.   NOxBChV

I should like to creep.   Mona Lisa, A.   Angelina Weld Grimké.   APT-1; NAAPv.2

I should like to see that country's tiles, bedrooms.   Keeping Their World Large.   Marianne Moore.   PWW2; WaAnP

(I should like to see that country's tiled bedrooms.)   RaBo

I should like you all to know.   I'm a Gigolo.   Cole Porter.   OBCoV; ReLy

I should not feel it to be strange. (LL)   Alfred Tennyson.   NAEL-6v2; NAEL-7v2 *Fr.* In Memoriam A. H. H.

I should not presume to express any view.   Triangular Legs.   Sir Alan Patrick Herbert.   NBLV

I should retire at half-past eight? (LL)   Grown-up.   Edna St. Vincent Millay.   AmWit; NAAPv.2; NAMCP V.1; NoAM

I Should Run for Cover But I'm Right Here.   Harris Schiff.   AHA

I should see that in my hands glittered a gem beyond counting. (LL)   Aubade: "As I would free the white almond from the green husk."   Amy Lowell.   NAAPv.2; NIL-7

I shoulder my axe and set off home through the stillness. (LL)   Noonday Axeman.   Les A. Murray.   NAEL-7v2; NoP-4; NoP-5

I shouldered a kind of manhood.   Funeral Rites.   Seamus Heaney.   ModIr; PBCIP; PoetW

I shouldn't write this.   No.   Idea Vilariño.   TANSG, *tr. by* Louise B. Popkin

I shouted at Him.   At the Mosque.   Chairil Anwar.   PML; PoetW, *tr. by* Burton Raffel

I showed her Heights she never saw.   Emily Dickinson.   PoBW

I Shut My Eyes Tight.   Nazim Hikmet.   NaPG, *tr. by* Talat Sait Halman

I shut the door on the racket.   Shoe Shop.   Barton Sutter.   SoSe-8

I sicken of myself, my members all are shaking.   To Himself.   Andreas Gryphius.   GePo, *tr. by* George C. Schoolfield

I sigh at day-dawn, and I sigh.   Sappho.   Christina Georgina Rossetti.   VWP

I sigh for the land of the Cypress and Pine.   Song—Written at the North.   Samuel Henry Dickson.   APN-1

I sighed for a world left desolate without you.   Love Song in Absence.   Judith Wright.   RSR

I simply wish to die.   Sappho.   SaLy, *tr. by* Diane Rayor

I sing. (LL)   Empty Kettle.   Louis Oliver.   HATNAP; NAAPv.2

I sing a place called Newborn.   Thermal Signatures.   Sam Witt.   IAoNAP

I sing America, in its wild and autochthonous state. Manifesto, A. José Santos Chocano. TCLAP, *tr. by* Andrew Rosing

I sing divine Astræa's praise. Dialogue between two shepherds, Thenot and Piers, in praise of ASTRÆA. Mary Sidney Herbert, Countess of Pembroke. EMWP; NAEL-6v1

I Sing for the Animals. *Teton Sioux Oral Tradition.* TCAPo

I sing for the similarity and I moan for. Dog That I Am. Gerald Stern. BAP-04

I sing her praises. (LL) Woman. Ina Coolbrith. FTtHH; NAAPv.1

I sing, I sing, I sing. Incantation Songs of the Klamath Lake People. *Unknown.* APN-2, *tr. by* Albert S. Gatschet

I sing my own true story, tell my travels. Seafarer, The. *Unknown.* NoP-4

I Sing of a Maiden. *Unknown.* CABP; ChIV-2; ChrPo; NAEL-7v1; NoP-4; NoP-5; TFi; WaAnP

I sing of Aphrodite, the lover's goddess. *Unknown.* HW *Fr.* Homeric Hymns.

I sing of arms and the heroic man. Gaspar Pérez De Villagrá. NAAPv.1 *Fr.* History of New Mexico.

I sing of brooks, of blossom[e]s, birds, and bowers. Argument of His Book, The. Robert Herrick. BASC; CavPo; NAEL-6v1; NAEL-7v1; NoP-4; NoP-5; NOSC; NPeEn; OxAEP-1; PoPoPo; SacPr; TFi; WaAnP; WoPoe

I Sing of Change. Niyi Osundare. NAfrP

I sing of pilchards, caught on a rod. Pilchard-Curing Song, The. Alice Oswald. MFPA

I sing of simple people and the harder virtues, by Associated Stuffed Shirts & Company, Incorporated, 358 West 42d Street, New York, brochure enclosed. Literary. Kenneth Fearing. APT-2

I sing / of the beauty of Athens. I Sing of Change. Niyi Osundare. NAfrP

I sing of warfare and a man at war. Virgil. NAWM-5v1; NAWM-7v1 *Fr.* Aeneid [*or* Eneados *or* Aeneis], The.

I sing the birth was born to-night. Carol. Ben Jonson. ChrPo

I sing the birth, was born[e] to-night. Hymn[e] on the Nativity [*or* Nativitie] of My Saviour, A. Ben Jonson. ChIV-2; SacPr

I Sing the Body Electric. Philip Levine. ViWalt

I Sing the Body Electric. Walt Whitman. APN-1 *Fr.* Leaves of Grass [1855 Version].

"I have perceiv'd that to be with those I like is enough." SAmP

"I knew a man, a common farmer, the father of five sons." BLT

"Male is not less the soul nor more, he too is in his place, The." ErotSp

"Man's body at auction, A." SAmP

"This is the female form." ErotSp

I sing the civill Warres, tumultous Broyles. Civil Wars, The. Samuel Daniel.

I sing the man that never equal knew. Alexandreis. Anne Killigrew. NoP-4; NoP-5

I sing the olive oil, I who lately sang. Year of the Olive Oil, The. Charles North. FTOS; NYP2

I sing the quality of bamboo. Bamboo. Eric Rolls. NOBAu

I sing the Sofa. I, who lately sang. William Cowper. *Fr.* Task, The.

I sing the steir, strabush, and strife. William Tennant. NePenScot *Fr.* Papistry Storm'd.

I sing the town. Town and Country. Arthur Waugh. ArBi

I sing the tree is a heron. Merce of Egypt. Charles Olson. APT-2; NoP-4; NoP-5

I sing thee with the stock-dove's throat. Michael Field. VWP

I sing this song about myself, full sad. Wife's Lament, The. *Unknown.* NoP-4; NoP-5, *tr. by* Richard Hamer

I sing to a breeze that runs through the rafters. Vox Angelica. Timothy Liu. NeAmPo; WiU

I sing to him that rests below. Alfred Tennyson. NAEL-6v2; NAEL-7v2; NAWM-7v2 *Fr.* In Memoriam A. H. H.

I sing *tree*, making green. Last Night's Dream. Denise Levertov. NoAM

I sing what I saw. Gorcheanu: The Three Laments. Aneirin. WoPoe, *tr. by* Desmond O'Grady

I sink in the falling snow. Monstrance. János Pilinszky. PoSu, *tr. by* Peter Jay

I sink into bed. My Imperialism. Tamura Ryuichi. AF; PFTM-2; VCWP, *tr. by* Christopher Drake

I sink into my mother's arms. Appalachia Novena. Kyle Thompson. RWB

I, sinner, poet of sin. Last Judgement. Blas de Otero. RaW, *tr. by* Hardie St. Martin

I sit. Everything I Need to Know I Learned in Kindergarten. Martin Jude Farewell. OPRER

I Sit. Susan Griffin. PoChi

I sit alone among dark bamboos. Bamboo Grove. Wang Wei. ChinPo, *tr. by* Ye Weilian [*or* Yeh Wei-lien *or* Wai-lim Yip]

I sit alone in quiet leisure. Sitting Alone. Mookam Choinul. BecRai, *tr. by* Kim Daljin, Kim Won-Chung and Christopher Merrill

I sit alone in the bamboo dark. At a House in the Bamboo Grove. Wang Wei. CrYelRi, *tr. by* Sam Hamill

I sit alone on the rocks trying to prepare. In the Wilderness. James Simmons. GI

I sit anchored on my stoop bereft of all things glimmering. Lisa Gill. ICANM *Fr.* Letters to a Dead Trappist.

I sit and beat the wizard's magic drum. Wizard's Chant, The. *Unknown.* APN-2, *tr. by* Charles Godfrey Leland

I sit and look out upon all the sorrows of the world, and upon all oppression and shame. I Sit and Look Out. Walt Whitman. NAAL-3; NAAPv.1; SAmP

I sit and sew—a useless task it seems. I Sit and Sew. Alice Moore Dunbar-Nelson. InGu; NAAPv.2; NALW; WaAnP

I sit, astonished by the pink kite. Affair of Kites. Robin Robertson. EdScPo

I sit at my desk. Love Poems of Marichiko, The. Kenneth Rexroth.

I sit at the foot of snow-capped mountains. Keeping Watch. Sojourner Kincaid Rolle. GeoHom

I sit beside my peaceful hearth. Due of the Dead, The. William Makepeace Thackeray. FaBoWar; OBWP

I sit by the mossy fountain; on the top of the hill of winds. James Macpherson. NePenScot *Fr.* Fragments of Ancient Poetry, Collected in the Highlands of Scotland.

I sit by the roadside. Changing the Wheel. Bertolt Brecht. PoSu, *tr. by* Michael Hamburger

I sit by the shed. Winter Billet. Peter Huchel. PoSu, *tr. by* Michael Hamburger

I Sit by the Window. Joseph Brodsky. VCWP, *tr. by* Howard Moss

I sit by the window all morning. At a Motel near O'Hare Airport. Jane Kenyon. OtW

I sit crotch high. Under the Oak Table. Colleen J. McElroy. GT; OxAAAP

I sit down at a table and open a book of poems. Library. Louis Jenkins. RaBo

I sit down beside my brass lamp. Peeling Pippins. Mary Tallmountain. HATNAP

I sit down on the floor of a school for the retarded. He Sits Down on the Floor of a School for the Retarded. Alden Nowlan. StAl

I sit drinking wine and, for a long time, don't notice the dusk. Losing Myself. S. J. Marks. BodElec

I sit here at your edge, in your embankment's screen. Shepherd-Song. Sigmund von Birken. GePo, *tr. by* George C. Schoolfield

I sit here with all my words intact. Silence around an Ancient Stone. Rosario Castellanos. TANSG, *tr. by* Magda Bogin

I sit here with the wind is in my hair. To Helen of Troy (N.Y.). Peter Viereck. WeW-3

I sit in a glass submarine. New York Seizures. Eugene B. Redmond. BRtP; FuFl

I sit in a wind-driven place. Deathbed Song. Jungkwan Haean. BecRai, *tr. by* Kim Daljin, Kim Won-Chung and Christopher Merrill

I sit in an office at 244 Madison Avenue. Spring Comes to Murray Hill. Ogden Nash. AmWit; APT-2

I sit in autumn sunlight. John Montague. IrLP *Fr.* Great Cloak, The.

I sit in front of our Zenith TV, eat. Marlo Thomas in Seven Parts and Epilogue. Jeffery Conway. WiU

I sit in Lees. At 11:40 PM with. Poem for vipers, A. John Wieners. BB

I Sit in My Lofty Study. Hsieh T'iao. CCL1, *tr. by* John Frodsham

I sit in my moulded black chair. Twa Warlds. Duncan Glen. EdScPo

I Sit in My Room. Jean Toomer. GT

I sit in my sorrow a-weary, alone. Window Just Over the Street, The. Alice Cary. PoBW; SWaP

I sit in my woody house. Green Noise of Ohio Hardwoods, The. Kathe Davis. AmZen

I sit in one of the dives. September 1, 1939. W. H. Auden. AF; BrAP; HarvBoo; MoBrPo; NAMCP V.1; NoP-5; OxAEP-2; OxBoAm; PoAgWa; PWW2; StAl; WaAnP

I sit in the dark, not brooding. New York Poem, The. Sam Hamill. WANABP

I sit in the top of the wood, my eyes closed. Hawk Roosting. Ted Hughes. BrAP; EMP; HeIP-4; OWoS; OxBEV; WaAnP

I sit, in treatment, at the movies, devoted. Valerio Magrelli. NeIt

I sit in wonder. Wes "Scoop" Nisker. WhBo

I sit on the lemon. More than love. *Unknown.* SonAtl, *tr. by* Mohammed Attiyah and Lubna Khader

I sit on the lonely headland. On the Headland. Bayard Taylor. CAGL

I sit once more at the glory hole. Back on the Job. John G. Fisher. IFF

I sit over grief. Rea Nikonova. CRWP, *tr. by* Gerald Janecek

I sit too still and think about five years. August 1990. C. Mikal Oness. GeoHom

I sit under Rand MacNally's. Westering. Seamus Heaney. HarvBoo

I sit with Joseph Conrad in Monet's garden. Zimmer Imagines Heaven. Paul Zimmer. PBCAP

I sit with my back to the engine, watching. Crossing the Border. Norman Alexander MacCaig. HarvBoo

I sit / with my sleeping husband. My Sleeping Husband. Nzadi Z. Keita. BtF

I slap on latex gloves before I put. Towards Curing AIDS. Rafael Campo. BloBone; NeAmPo

I slap on the buttonwood tree with the palm of my hand. Walk, A. Hwang Insuk. EcSo, tr. by Peter H. Lee

I sleep now with the Lord, by the Lord's strength will I rise up. Lady Katherine Killigrew Wrote This Poem about Her Own Death, The. Katherine Killigrew. EMWP

I slept the sleep of the just. New Life, The. Louise Glück. BodElec

I slide into his life. I Have Taken the Suits and Shoes to Oxfam. Felicity Napier. Prnts

I slouch in bed. James Wright. EmeKit Fr. Two Hangovers.

I slow down the waterfall to a chandelier. Frozen Rain. Michael Longley. PBCIP

I slowly crack my joints to ready and steady myself. Sharpen my mind on. Mimi Goese. HeMarv

I smell dry snuffy turf smoke clouding the cottages. Irish Scullery Maid, The. Joyce Herbert. TCAWP

I Smile, but Oh! My Heart Is Breaking. Mary E. Tucker. CBWP-1

I smoothed and blocked my hands like a shirt in a gift box. Home Remedy. Paula McLain. SweBea

I sniff for hot coals. Bridal Rites. Rebecca McClanahan. MPUn

I so liked Spring last year. Charlotte Mew. OxAEP-2; OxBEV

I so love the flame. Memorial Candle. Yelena Shwarts. CRWP, tr. by Stephanie Sandler

I sold my possessions, even the colorful pencils. Translation of Raimundo Luz, The: My Imitation. Scott Cairns. UpMys

I, Solomon, David's son, King of Jerusalem. Henry Howard, Earl of Surrey. ChIV-1 Fr. Paraphrase of Part of the Book of Ecclesiates, A.

I sometimes alligators heard. Mattie J. Peterson. VerBaPo Fr. Old Homestead, The.

I sometimes hold it half a sin. Alfred Tennyson. CAGL; NAEL-6v2; NAEL-7v2; NAWM-7v2 Fr. In Memoriam A. H. H.

I sometimes sleep with other girls. Cavalier Lyric. James Simmons. UV

I Sometimes Think. Unknown. EroLit

I sometimes think that I should like. I Sometimes Think. Unknown. EroLit

I sometimes think that never blows so red. Omar Khayyám. CABP; CtM; TRP Fr. Rubáiyát of Omar Khayyám [of Naishápúr], The.

I sometimes think the crone I will become. Crone I Will Become, The. Jean Hegland. FiBr

I sought a theme and sought for it in vain. Circus Animals' Desertion, The. William Butler Yeats. BeAl; BrAP; HarvBoo; MakPoe; NAEL-6v2; NAEL-7v2; NAMCP V.1; NAWM-7v2; NIP-4; NoAM; NoP-4; NoP-5; TFi

I sought for Peace, but could not find. Peace. Samuel Speed. SacPr

I sought my Lord in de wilderness, in de wilderness, in de wilderness. I'm Going Home. Unknown. SSUS

I sought my lover at twilight. Tsangyang Gyatso. WoPoe Fr. Love-Poems of the Sixth Dalai Lama.

I sought of bishop and priest and judges. On Christians, Mercy Will Fall. Unknown. OBWVE, tr. by D. Myrddin Lloyd

I sought to share. Passage, The. Adonis. VCWP, tr. by Samuel Hazo

I span and Eve span. Eve-Song. Mary Gilmore. LW

I speak, and I don't want to lie. Life Story. Paul Zweig. BodElec

I speak directly. Rifle, The. Tymoteusz Karpowicz. PoSu, tr. by Jan Darowski

I speak for none of your kind. End of the Owls, The. Hans Magnus Enzensberger. BeAl, tr. by Jerome Rothenberg

'I speak for the world of scholarship'. Happy Arabia. Tom Matthews. PNI

I Speak in All Ages. René Daumal. YaTCFP, tr. by Mary Ann Caws

I speak like a green girl. Ophelia's Rant before She's Heavy with Drink. Leilani R. Hall. IaFF

I speak like Plath after the oven did its job. African Beneath the American, The. Wanda Coleman. RD

I speak no polite. Turf Song. Sterling Plumpp. GT

I Speak of the City. Octavio Paz. VCWP, tr. by Eliot Weinberger

I speak this poem now with grave and level voice. Immortal Autumn. Archibald MacLeish. MoAmPo

I speak to my Lord though I am dust and ashes. Oaks and Squirrels. Anne Porter. ChIV-1

I speak to the unbeautiful of this bird. Peacock, The. James Merrill. OWoS

I speak with the mouth of Qeqertuanaq. Aua. IFF Fr. Magic Words.

I spell out my house in newly dead tree. I spell out Sunday of clear omissions. Mute Poem. Laura Solórzano. SPV, tr. by Jen Hofer

I spend all day in my office, reading a poem. Perfect Reader. Mary Ruefle. AmAlph

I spend my days knitting booties. After the Miscarriage. Diane Gilliam Fisher. SweBea

I spent a nicht amang the cognoscenti. I Was Fair Beat. Robert Garioch. EdScPo; OBCoV

I spent a night turning in bed. Whip, The. Robert Creeley. ICANM; PFTM-2

I spent all morning in the café talking. Beyond. Jamie McKendrick. PoCu

I spent my mysterious childhood. West Texas Mid-Century. Roxy Gordon. TiP2

I spent the afternoon rummaging through. Black Tulips. Martha Vertreace. IllVoic

I spent the entire day in official details. At the Desk. Theodor Storm. WoPoe, tr. by Robert Bly

I spent the entire night leading a blind man. Uncertain Oneiromancy. Denise Levertov. MakPoe

I Spent the Night. Dacia Maraini. CItWP, tr. by Cinzia Sartini Blum and Lara Trubowitz

I spent the night after my mother died. Autumn 1980. Marilyn Hacker. InoFa

I spent the summer singing for you. Tanana Valley. Janice Gould. FiBr

I spin through time. Planet Earth Speaks, The. Alma Villanueva. HW

I Spit on the Innate Christ. Antonin Artaud. ConPit, tr. by Clayton Eshleman

I spoiled the day. Wasted Day, A. Frances Darwin Cornford. MoBrPo

I spot him at the water's edge with his daughter. Incarnate. Robin Becker. PfS

I sprang to the rollocks and Jorrocks and me. How I Brought the Good News from Aix to Ghent (or Vice Versa). R. J. Yeatman and W. C. Sellar. UV

I sprang to the stirrup, and Joris, and he. How They Brought the Good News from Ghent to Aix. Robert Browning. NAEL-6v2; NAEL-7v2; OBSP; UV

I spur my horse through the wrecked town. Wrecked Town, The. Han-shan (Cold Mountain). CCL1, tr. by Gary Snyder

I spy on the building. Piazza Gimma. Fabio Morabito. RMCMP, tr. by Geoff Hargreaves

I Spy the Three-Colored Peach Blossom. Kim Ku. WoPoe, tr. by Kevin O'Rourke

I staggered on through darkness. Edgar Lee Masters. APT-1 Fr. Spoon River Anthology.

I / stand alone. Another Moment. Sim Kombem. NAfrP

I Stand Alone. Tu Fu [or Du Fu]. CrYelRi, tr. by Sam Hamill

I stand alone in the cold autumn. Mao Tse-tung. WoPoe, tr. by David Lattimore

I stand and inspect the phenomena drawn up. Elena Lazutkina. CRWP, tr. by Robert Reid

I stand and watch the rain. Rain and the Tyrants. Jules Supervielle. GPTC; WoPoe, tr. by David Gascoyne

I stand at the cistern in front of the old barn. Wendell Berry. UpMys Fr. Three Elegiac Poems.

I stand at the field's edge. Earth Movers, The. Christopher Cokinos. UrbNat

I Stand at the Window and Wave My Arms About. Angela Cooke. ArBi

I stand before the calendar and count the days. Menstrual Irregularities. Pak Sôwôn. EcSo, tr. by Julie C. Park

I Stand Beneath the Mountain with an Illiterate Heart. Chard DeNiord. PfSP

I stand beside my window in the night. From Soul to Soul. Árpád Tóth. IQMS, tr. by Watson Kirkconnell

I stand beside the gate, alone, deep. Ritual. Anna Ruth Ediger Baehr. ACAMVP

I Stand Here, Do You Understand. Olav H. Hauge. RaBo, tr. by Robert Bly (I Stand Here, D'Ya Understand.) WED

I stand here in the sight of everyone a man full of sense. Pretty Redhead, The. Guillaume Apollinaire. GPTC, tr. by James Wright

I stand in full armor. Poem. Paul Klee. PFTM-1

I stand like some country crow across the street. Romania, Romania. Gerald Stern. MiVo

I stand on slenderness all fresh and fair. Cut Flower, A. Karl Shapiro. WeW-3

I stand on the mark beside the shore. Runaway Slave at Pilgrim's Point, The. Elizabeth Barrett Browning. NALW; ViWPN; VWP

I stand on tiptoe to reach the window that's open a crack. Window, The. Boris Hristov. CSCBP, tr. by Georgi Belev and Lisa Sapinkopf

I stand to-day on this historic ground. National Cemetery, Beaufort, South Carolina, The. Josephine D. Henderson Heard. CBWP-4

I stand under a leafless tree. Rain—Birdoswald. Frances Horovitz. StAl

I stand upon a hill and see. Map of the City, A. Thom Gunn. NAEL-6v2; NAEL-7v2; NoP-4; NoP-5

I stand with standing stones. All the Earth, All the Air. Theodore Roethke. HarvBoo

I stand with you braced against the wind. (LL) Yoko. Thom Gunn. NoAM; PtR

I stand within the stony, arid town. City Tree, The. Isabella Valancy Crawford. BrAP

I stared at the ruin, the powder of the dead. Colosseum. Katie Ford. LegDan

I starred last night, I shone. Performance. Les A. Murray. PML

I start out for a walk at last after weeks at the desk. After Long Busyness. Robert Bly. CAP-8; OxBoAm

I start with a straight back and two points. Peter Dale. NewEx

I started a fire with Kali's name. Āśutos Deb. SinGod, *tr. by* Rachel Fell McDermott

I started by reading the banner headline. Story of Abraham, The. Alicia Ostriker. InvLi

I Started Early, Took My Dog. Emily Dickinson. *See* By the Sea.

I started the day with a jog/fast walk. Present Moments. David McElroy. TiP2

I started to translate in seventy-three. Gwyneth Lewis. BBMWP *Fr.* Language Murderer, The.

I started to write a song about love, then I decided, No. Difficult Music, The. Reginald Shepherd. NeAmPo

I Starve My Belly for a Sublime Purpose. Anna Swirszczynska [*or* Swir]. BLT

I stay and go: I am a pause. (LL) Between Going and Staying. Octavio Paz. PoCho; TCLAP, *tr. by* Eliot Weinberger

I stayed home and watched it on television. (LL) Funeral of Poetry, The. Karl Shapiro. APT-2; OxBoAm

I stayed [*or* staid] the night for shelter at a farm. Robert Frost. APT-1; NoAM; PoA 2002 *Fr.* Two Witches.

I stayed overnight at a motel by the E3. Gallery, The. Tomas Tranströmer. PFTM-2, *tr. by* Robin Fulton

I stayed still a while. Love in an Empty Lot. Hô Sugyông. EcSo, *tr. by* Youngju Ryu

I stayed under the moon too long. Moonburn. Marge Piercy. NAMCP V.2

I step across the white dust of the runway. Selima Hill. MoWP *Fr.* Accumulation of Small Acts of Kindness, The.

I step from Jordan without you. (LL) Killing Floor. Ai. NAMCP V.2; NoAM; WaAnP

I step out into the snow, my eyes shut. Summer Again. Yves Bonnefoy. VCWP, *tr. by* Lisa Sapinkopf

I step out of the car and stare. Blessing the House. Jim Daniels. SUP

I stepped from black to black. Black Power. Raymond R. Patterson. OxAAAP

I stepped from Plank to Plank. Emily Dickinson. SAmP; TCAPo

I stepped off the Cuzco-Machu. Sierra Walk. Carolyne Wright. RoV

I Still Can't Say the Word. Walter McDonald. LiTh

I still don't know how to use the chopsticks as right or as natural. Fred Wah. NLPA *Fr.* This Dendrite Map: Father / Mother Haibun.

I still got hope Tang says. Frank Stanford. FTtHH

I Still Have Everything You Gave Me. Naomi Shihab Nye. ExTi

I still live somewhat behind. Thinker between the Bronze Shield and the Human Flesh, The. Salah Niyazi. IrPoTo, *tr. by* Melissa Brown and Saadi A. Simawe

I still remember that first day. We got off with our splintered. Murdered Luggage. Jose Angel Figueroa. PueRic

I still shall smile and go my careless way. Sonnet. Mamie A. Richardson. LW

I still would take a day for your demise. First Birthday After Death, The. John Collin Murphey. TiP2

I stink to make you bitch. Pathology of Proximity, The. Mark Bibbins. AmPoNex

I stirred wet sand and gathered myself. Seamus Heaney. NoAM *Fr.* Sweeney Redivivus.

I stitched *Queen Charlotte's Crown.* Rebecca Baggett. FiBr *Fr.* Art of the Amish: A Quilt Exhibition.

I stoke it again, and crouch closer. (LL) Hearth, The. C. K. Williams. BeAl; WaAnP

I stole forth dimly in the dripping pause. Moon Compasses. Robert Frost. ITBLP

I stole from you, my coy Juventius honey. To Juventius. Catullus. CAGL, *tr. by* Frank O. Copley

I stole through the dungeons, while everyone slept. Alternative Endings to an Unwritten Ballad. Paul Dehn. OBCoV

I stomp about these rooms in an old overcoat. Sketch for an Aesthetic Project. Jay Wright. GT

I stood and watched the still, mysterious Night. Night. Augusta Cooper Bristol. APN-2

I stood as one enchanted. Entangled. Mathilde Blind. VWP

I stood at the back of the shop, my dear. Thomas Hardy. MoBrPo *Fr.* Satires of Circumstance in Fifteen Glimpses.

I stood at the modern knothole. Still Life w/Influences. Joyelle McSweeney. LegDan

I stood before it for hours in wintertime. (LL) Hill, A. Anthony Hecht. NAMCP V.2; NIL-7; NoP-4; NoP-5; OxBoAm; VCAP

I stood beside thy lowly grave. Grave of a Poetess, The. Felicia Dorothea Hemans. NPBRoP; RWP; VWP

I stood in the cold. Guard, A. John Alexander Frazier, Jr. BtF

I stood in the doorway. Spring Storm. Johanna Rayl. PasH

I stood in the ruins of Dowlais. Idris Davies. AngWePo *Fr.* Gwalia Deserta.

I stood in the tunnel warehouse. Gifts. Murray Jackson. OxAAAP

I stood in Venice, on the Bridge of Sighs. Lord Byron. CtM; NAEL-6v2; NAEL-7v2 *Fr.* Childe Harold's Pilgrimage.

I stood, like a god, on the corner where. Conviction. T. H. Parry-Williams. BBMWP, *tr. by* Richard Poole

I stood naked in the icy brook. All of It, The. Chase Twichell. AmZen

I stood on the bridge at midnight. Bridge, The. Henry Wadsworth Longfellow. APN-1; ITBLP; NAAPv.1; OxBoAm

I stood once more in that garden. Dream 1: the Bush Garden. Margaret Atwood. BrAP

I stood over her. On Reporting the Murder of a Young Prostitute. Judith Vollmer. LiTh

I stood still and was a tree amid the wood. Tree, The. Ezra Pound. HarvBoo

I stood upon a high place. Stephen Crane. APN-2; NAAPv.1

I stood with three comrades in Parliament Square. Armistice Day. Charles Causley. NAEL-6v2; NAEL-7v2; NoP-4; NoP-5; OBWP

I stoompled oud ov a dafern. Wein Geist. Charles Godfrey Leland. APN-2

I stop for breath at height of land—not much. Hundred Himalayas, A. Sydney Lea. VisFro

I stop some where waiting for you. (LL) Walt Whitman. APN-1; HeIP-4; OxBoAm *Fr.* Leaves of Grass [1855 Version].

I stop somewhere waiting for you. (LL) Song of Myself. Walt Whitman. MoAmPo; NAAL-3; NAAL-5; NAAPv.1

I stop somewhere waiting for you. (LL) Walt Whitman. AmFaPo; CAGL; ColAP; ItP; NAWM-7v2; NoP-5; SAmP; WaAnP *Fr.* Song of Myself.

I stop to consult my diary and think how queer. Rogation Day: Portrush. James Simmons. PBCIP

I stop worrying about anything. Old Man in Retirement. Muso Soseki. EaWin, *tr. by* W. S. Merwin

I Stop Writing the Poem. Tess Gallagher. GoPo

I stopped home at lunch because I left my cock on the bathroom sink. Trash. Linda Smukler. WiU

I stopped in the open under an apple bough. Field, The. Christopher Pilling. NLP

I Stopped in Tupelo, Elvis. Van K. Brock. AllShUp

I stopped the car and stepped out onto gravel. Tracey Herd. NeBl *Fr.* Mystery of the Missing Century, The.

I stopped to pick up the bagel. Bagel, The. David Ignatow. P180

I stopped writing poetry. Bernard Welt. BAP-01

I stored you against my eyelids. Heart's Hunger. Karen Press. TSAP

I stow this moment with all the other baggage. Objects in Mirror Are Closer Than They Appear. Reginald Shepherd. RD

I straightened the true fruit. Early Poem. Laura Solórzano. SPV, *tr. by* Jen Hofer

I stretch my arms like a swan flying. I Stretch My Arms. James Harpur. StAl

I stretch my hand. Hand. Takahashi Shinkichi. ZenPo, *tr. by* Takashi Ikemoto and Lucien Stryk

I stretched out my hand to you. Thomas Kinsella. HarvBoo *Fr.* Notes.

I strike the keys. Window Box. Thomas Scott Fisken. IJHIL

I stripped your soul down, part after part. I Stripped Your Soul Down. Gerardo Diego. RaW, *tr. by* Hardie St. Martin

I stroll backward through the garden's maze. Addiction. Cindy Goff. LaCa

I stroll on Madison in expensive clothes, sour. Summer. Edwin Denby. NYP2; OxBoAm

I strolled across. Waking, The. Theodore Roethke. OxBoAm

I strolled upon the Brooklyn Bridge one day. It Was All for Him. Amin Al-Rihani. NAAPv.2

I Strove with None. Edward Morgan Forster. UV

I strove with none for none was worth my strife. I Strove with None. Edward Morgan Forster. UV

I strove with none, for none was worth my strife. Walter Savage Landor. NPeEn; OxBEV; TFi; TRP; UV *Fr.* Last Fruit Off an Old Tree, The.

I struck the board, and cried, "No more." Collar, The. George Herbert. BASC; BrAP; CABP; ClHu; FaBoVe; FSCP; HeIP-4; InvLi; ItP; NAEL-6v1; NAEL-7v1; NIL-7; NIP-4; NoP-4; NoP-5; NOSC; NPeEn; OBWVE; PBRV; PoPoPo; SacPr; TFi; WeW-3

I struggled to read Homer in translation. God Shed His Grace. Philip Stephens. AmPoNex

I studied in the hedge school. Herd, The. Peter Fallon. PBCIP

I Study Rocks. Jeannette Armstrong. ReEnLa

I study rocks / strewn into the distance. I Study Rocks. Jeannette Armstrong. ReEnLa

I study the board like the rules of a dead language. Prince. Ann Sansom.

NeBl

I study the lives on a leaf: the little. Minimal, The. Theodore Roethke. NAMCP V.1; NoAM; OxBoAm

I Substitute for the Dead Lecturer. Imamu Amiri Baraka. BrAP

I subtract the days one by one, seal them. Before Our Encounter. Margherita Guidacci. CItWP, tr. by Cinzia Sartini Blum and Lara Trubowitz

I succumbed to all the visions. Nicole Brossard. PFTM-2 Fr. Barbizon, The.

I Suck. Chrystos. WiU

I suck at. Ogiwara Seisensui. CAoMJL1, tr. by Donald Keene

I suck your breasts. Bringing Back the Draft. E. Ethelbert Miller. FuFl

I Suddenly. George Buchanan. PNI

I suddenly have come to love. I Suddenly. George Buchanan. PNI

I suddenly understand: I'm watching you chop away. Life Is Happy. Albert Goldbarth. SUP

I suffer when I sit next to Joe Brainard's painting "Bingo." Joe Brainard's Painting "Bingo." Ron Padgett. NYP2

I suggested the opera because he said he had never been. Ditches. Karen Kipp. BodElec

I summon to the winding ancient stair. Dialogue of Self and Soul, A. William Butler Yeats. MoBrPo; NAEL-6v2; NAEL-7v2; NAMCP V.1; NoAM

I summoned my best skill, and toiled, intent. William Wordsworth. NAEL-6v2; NAEL-7v2 Fr. Prelude, The; Growth of a Poet's Mind [1850 version].

I support the animal's urge to survive. On the Job. Ira Sadoff. PfSP

I suppose France this morning is as white as here. Behind the Line. Ivor Gurney. HarvBoo

I suppose it hasn't been easy living with me either. Poem in Praise of My Husband (Taos). Diane Di Prima. BB

I suppose it's myself that you're making allusion to. At the "Atlantic" Dinner, December 15, 1874. Oliver Wendell Holmes. OBCoV

I suppose the time will come. Emily Dickinson. FaBoVe

I suppose we might do away with words like sin. Recuperation of Sin, A. Scott Cairns. UpMys

I surprise the women. In the Locker Room. Madeline DeFrees. ExTi

I surrender to Roget's Pocket Thesaurus. Written in Blood. Tiffany Midge. ReEnLa

I survived. (LL) Survivor, The. Tadeusz Rózewicz. BeAl; HP; PoAgWg; PoSu, tr. by Adam Czerniawski

I suspect he knew that trunks are metaphors. Houdini. Eli W. Mandel. NIP-4

I swam the Huron of love, and am not ashamed. Huron, The. Ruth Herschberger. OxBoAm

I swan! it's pleasant now we've beaten. Hospital Soliloquy, A. Rose Terry Cooke. NAAPv.1; SWaP

I swear a dim yellow light settled around the head. Mute Trout. Terrance Hayes. RD

I swear I know not how, but as fleeting as. Jaques Lured by Audrey. Leon Stokesbury. IaFF

I Swear to You, That Ship Never Sunk in Middle-Passage! Lawrence S. Cumberbatch. EGAG

I sweep the sidewalk, over and over again, in the summer afternoons. Eve in Eden. Manuela Fingueret. MirDau, tr. by Roberta Gordenstein

I sweep the street and lift me hat. Old Man at the Crossing, The. Leonard Alfred George Strong. OBMV

I swing the spirit like a child. Imploration for Clear Weather. Unknown. APN-2, tr. by W. J. Hoffman

I swing / the thin tin. Compass. Elizabeth Alexander. NAPBL

I swive as well as others do. Mock Song, The. John Wilmot, 2d Earl of Rochester. NoP-5

I syng of a mayden that is makeles. I Sing of a Maiden. Unknown. ChIV-2; TFi

  (I sing of a maiden.) CABP; ChrPo; NAEL-7v1; NoP-4; NoP-5; WaAnP

I take a bath in the mountain stream. Bath, A. Mookam Choinul. BecRai, tr. by Kim Daljin, Kim Won-Chung and Christopher Merrill

I take as my theme "The Independent Woman." Carolyn Kizer. FFC; VCAP Fr. Pro Femina.

I Take Back Everything I've Said. Nicanor Parra. PoCho, tr. by Miller Williams

I take Douglas to visit his grandfather. He's 13 and he. Carol Dine. PfS Fr. Fugue.

I take heart, breaking in. Mud Dauber Wasp, The. Peter Kane Dufault. NoP-4

I take him outside. Speaking. Simon J. Ortiz. NIL-7

I take my bike. Oregon Landscape with Lost Lover. Olga Broumas. GifTon

I take my endless way. (LL) A. E. Housman. HeIP-4; MoBrPo; NoP-4; NoP-5 Fr. Shropshire Lad, A.

I take my orders form the whiff. My Gospel Is. Chris Forhan. PoDa

I take my pen in hand. Letter, The. Elizabeth Riddell. LW; NOBAu

I take my son outside. What I Tell Him. Simon J. Ortiz. ChAP

I take my text in Matthew, and by de Revelation. There's a Meeting Here To-Night. Unknown. NAAPv.1; SSUS

I take my wine jug out among flowers. Drinking Alone with the Moon. Li Po. CrYelRi, tr. by Sam Hamill

I take off my shirt, I show you. Taking Off My Clothes. Carolyn Forché. NAMCP V.2; NIL-7; NoAM

I take on / her legacy. Jacqueline Goldberg. MirDau Fr. Luba.

I take the baby for a stroll in the pre-storm. Three Strolls. Alice Notley. AHA

I take the clue divine. (LL) My Cocoon tightens—Colors tease. Emily Dickinson. APN-2; NAAL-3

I take the long way home, knowing. Subway in March, 5:45 P.M. Maggie Nelson. IIR

I take the path, that leads to the garden of error. I Take the Path. Abdelwahab Meddeb. YaTCFP, tr. by Charlotte Mandell

I take the pressure of thine hand. (LL) Alfred Tennyson. NAEL-6v2; NAEL-7v2; NoP-5 Fr. In Memoriam A. H. H.

I take the snap from center, fake to the right, fade back. Football. Louis Jenkins. MoASP; P180; RaBo

I Take Thee Life. Margot Ruddock. OBMV

I take to the open road. Walt Whitman. ArBi Fr. Song of the Open Road.

I Take Two of These Tablets Tonight and in the Morning Go on Living. Denise Riley. Oth Fr. Seven Strangely Exciting Lies.

I take up my belly and go. Wanting To. Jan G. Elburg. TuT, tr. by Peter van de Kamp

I take you with me. Theatre. Remco Campert. TuT, tr. by Theo Dorgan

I takin' our comparative mis-saying. Fuck All Departments. Lionel Fogarty. VaPo

I Talk to My Body. Anna Swirszczynska [or Swir]. BLT

I talk to your photograph each day. If I Had a Talking Picture of you. Lew Brown, B. G. DeSylva and Ray Henderson. ReLy

I talked one midnight with the jolly ghost. W. E. Henley. OBMV Fr. Hawthorn and Lavender.

I talked to a farmer one day in Iowa. Iowa Farmer. Margaret Walker Alexander. GT

I talked to old Lem. Old Lem. Sterling Allen Brown. APT-2; NAMCP V.1

I Taste a Liquor Never Brewed. Emily Dickinson. APN-2; BLPJKO; HeIP-4; ITBLP; MoAmPo; NAAL-3; NAAL-5; NAMCP V.1; NoAM; OxBoAm; SoSe-8; TCAPo; TFi

I taste the unfamiliar. Occasional Loquats. Gus Blaisdell. ICANM

I taught myself poetry for a few pennies. Coppers. Boris Abramovich Slutsky. TCRusP, tr. by Daniel Weissbort

I taught myself to live simply and wisely. Anna Andreyevna Akhmatova. ItWoWo, tr. by Richard McKane

I teach German literature, and this is how it goes. Teaching German Literature. Vincent Buckley. OBCoV

I tell a wanderer's tale, the same. Encounter at St. Martin's. Ken Smith. OPOU

I tell an easy story, all lies. Round Lake. Janet Kauffman. ACAMVP

I tell her about the pool. Speaking about My Cracked Sump. Andrew Waterhouse. BeAl; PoCu

I tell her she has outlived her usefulness. Altar. Marilyn Chin. NAMCP V.2; PoPoPo

I tell it the way it is. Letters from the Poet Who Sleeps in a Chair. Nicanor Parra. AF, tr. by Miller Williams

I tell my closest friend, Carolyn, on the phone. Fungus Considered. Monica Berlin. MAAN

I tell my mother my girlfriend is a good Catholic girl—. Votive Candles. Nick Carbó. NeAmPo

I tell my secret? No indeed, not I. Winter: My Secret. Christina Georgina Rossetti. NAEL-6v2; NAEL-7v2; NPeEn; VWP

I tell myself, I'm through with you. Foolin' Myself. Jack Lawrence. ReLy

I tell the truck. Ruts. Jonathan Greene. WhBo

I tell thee, Charmion, could I time retrieve. Song. William Congreve. IrLP

I tell thee, Dick, where I have been. Ballad[e] [upon a Wedding], A. Sir John Suckling. BASC; NAEL-7v1; NoP-4; NoP-5; WaAnP

I tell you. Blood. Viki Radden. BtF

I tell you, hopeless grief is passionless. Grief. Elizabeth Barrett Browning. HeIP-4; NALW; NPeEn; OBEV; VWP

I tell you I am angry. Friendship, The. Toi Derricotte. PBCAP

I tell you it was a hard punch to my brain. Edoardo Sanguineti. ItPo Fr. Reisebilder.

I tell you that I see her still. I Only Am Escaped Alone to Tell Thee. Howard Nemerov. HeIP-4; NoAM

I terminated with the color red. Scarlet Skirt. Víctor Hernández Cruz. TouFir

I test my bath before I sit. Samson Agonistes. Ogden Nash. APT-2; OBCoV

I' th' isle of Britain, long since famous grown. Satire on Charles II, A. John Wilmot, 2d Earl of Rochester. NOSC

I thank all who have loved me in their hearts. Elizabeth Barrett Browning. CenSon Fr. Sonnets from the Portuguese.

I Thank Life for So Many Gifts. Violeta Parra. TANSG, *tr.* by Bonnie Shepard

I thank thee, Father, that the night is near. Night. Jones Very. InvLi

I thank You God for most this amazing. I Thank You God. E. E. Cummings. StAl

I that all through my early days. Lament for the Makers. W. S. Merwin. InoFa; PoA 2002

I that erstwhile the world's sweet air did draw. George Wither. NOSC *Fr.* Shephe[a]rd's Hunting, The.

I that have been[e] a lover, and could show [*or* shew] it. Sonnet to the Noble Lady, the Lady Mary Wroth, A. Ben Jonson. NAEL-7v1; NoP-4; NoP-5

I that in heill [*or* health] wes [*or* was] and gladnes[s] [*or* glaidness]. Lament for the Makaris [*or* Makars *or* Makers]. William Dunbar. InoFa; MakPoe; NePenScot; NoP-4; NoP-5; OBEV; OxBEV; WaAnP

I that lived ever about you. English Girl. *Unknown.* OBMV, *tr.* by E. Powys Mathers

I, the dog they call Spot, was about to sing. Autumn. Five Dogs. Mark Strand. PtR

I, the Emperor, will have my burial place as I desire. Funerary Edict. Victor Segalen. YaTCFP, *tr.* by Mary Ann Caws and Patricia Terry

I' the how-dumb-deid o' the cauld hairst nicht. Eemis-Stane, The. Hugh MacDiarmid. EdScPo; NAEL-6v2; NePenScot; NPeEn

I the late madonna of barren lands. (LL) Jamaica 1980. Lorna Goodison. GT; WaAnP

I, the marble statue with fiery head, while. Marble Beads. Delmira Agustini. TANSG, *tr.* by Mark McCaffrey

I, the Neighbor Mr. Uskovich, Watch Every Morning Kenji Takezo Hold His Breath. Rick Noguchi. NeAmPo

I, the old woman of Beare. Old Woman of Beare Regrets Lost Youth, The. *Unknown.* OBMV, *tr.* by Frank O'Connor

I, the poet William Yeats. To Be Carved on a Stone at Thoor Ballylee. William Butler Yeats. NAMCP V.1; NoAM; NoP-4; NoP-5

I the roses love in the gardens of Adonis. Fernando Pessoa. WoPoe, *tr.* by Susan M. Brown and Edwin Honig

I, the Survivor. Bertolt Brecht. HP; PoSu

I, therefore, will begin. Soul of the age! Ben Jonson. WaAnP *Fr.* To the Memory of My Beloved, the Author Mr [*or* Master] William Shakespeare: And What He Hath Left Us.

I thi hovie an thi howd o sleep. Socialist Manifesto for East Balgillo, The. W. N. Herbert. NePenScot

I think a man's seventy years are few! Seventy Years Are Few. Lu Chih. WoPoe, *tr.* by Bruce Carpenter

I think about it. Sex. David C. Yates. TiP2

I think about the mornings it saved me. Reading Plato. Rick Barot. LegDan

I think about you. No Choice. Norman Alexander MacCaig. EdScPo

I think all day about how terrible. Purpose. Diane Seuss. SweBea

I think Archie Shepp played hambone hambone where you been in our. Suite Repose. Carl Hancock Rux. SpirFl

I think at a distance I hear a loud voice. Missionary, The. Mrs. Henry Linden. CBWP-4

I think at some point I looked at my father. Waste Sonata. Sharon Olds. BeAl

I Think Continually of Those Who Were Truly Great. Stephen Spender. BLPJKO; HarvBoo; HeIP-4; MoBrPo; NoP-4; NoP-5; PLBUT; RaBo; TFi (Truly Great, The.) CABP; NAMCP V.1

I think crowbar Bay Rum Dominica. Call Me 'Shortchange'. Joel Dailey. AnSo

I think he was behind me. Behind Me. Martha Rhodes. ExTi

I Think I Am Going to Call My Wife Paraguay. David Kirby. SUP

I think I came close to being insane a few months ago. Poem. C. K. Williams. BodElec

I think I could turn and live with animals, they are so placid and self-contained. Walt Whitman. NAWM-7v2; SAmP; WeW-3 *Fr.* Song of Myself.

I think I grow tensions. Flower, The. Robert Creeley. CAP-8; PmAP

I Think I Know No Finer Things than Dogs. Hally Carrington Brent. ITBLP

I think I must have lived. Fox, The. Philip Levine. SoSe-8

I think I remember this moorland. We Have Been Here Before. Morris Gilbert Bishop. AmWit

I think I see her sitting bowed and black. Oriflamme. Jessie Redmond Fauset. NAAPv.2

I think I see my father's sister stand. Elizabeth Barrett Browning. NALW *Fr.* Aurora Leigh.

I think I should have loved you presently. Edna St. Vincent Millay. APT-1; NAAL-5; NAAPv.2

I think I was enchanted. Emily Dickinson. APN-2; NALW

I think I was three. Once upon a Seesaw with Charlie Chan. Cyn Zarco. ReBoTo

I think I will not hang myself to-day. (LL) Ballade of Suicide, A. G. K. Chesterton. NBLV; OBCoV

I think I wrote a poem today but I don't know well. Noon Point. Clark Coolidge. PmAP

I Think I'll Call It Morning. Gil Scott-Heron. IJHIL

I think I'll die. Masaoka Shiki. CAoMJL1 *Fr.* Thirty-nine Haiku.

I think it better that in times like these. On Being Asked for a War Poem. William Butler Yeats. FaBoWar; NIP-4; OBWP; OxAEP-2; PoAgWa; PoWW

I think it happened. Anyway. Barbara Jagger. Prnts

I think it mercy if thou wilt forget. (LL) John Donne. BASC; FaBoVe; NAEL-6v1; NAEL-7v1; NoP-4; NoP-5; OxAEP-1 *Fr.* Holy Sonnets.

I think it must be lonely to be God. Gwendolyn Brooks. InvLi *Fr.* Street in Bronzeville, A.

I think it must be spring. Quartet of Daffodils, A. Lorna Goodison. CFP

I Think It Rains. Wole Soyinka. AF

I think it's good the squirrel lives with us. Red Squirrel. Bruce Weigl. BodElec

I think mice. (Mice). Rose Fyleman. NTCP

I think my friend's mother. Kali. Leslie Simon. HW

I think naught great: I am the highest thing of all. "Angelus Silesius." GePo *Fr.* Cherubical Wanderer, The.

I think no woman of such skill. Sappho. SaLy, *tr.* by Diane Rayor

I think not on the state, nor am concerned. Upon the Double Murther of King Charles I. Katherine Philips. BASC; NAEL-7v1

I think now how we biked toward the sand. Way a Child Might Believe, The. Olga Broumas. ArBi

I think of a flower that no eye has ever seen. Beauty. Laurence Binyon. MoBrPo

I think of a man in a forest. Old Man in Meditation. Henrik Nordbrandt. PML, *tr.* by Anne Born

I think of a tiger. The fading light [*or* half-light] enhances. Other Tiger, The. Jorge Luis Borges. PoetW, *tr.* by Alastair Reid

I think of a wineglass. Dedicatory (to My Wife). Antonio Cisneros. PML, *tr.* by Carol A. Klee

I think of all the toughs through history. Lines for a Book. Thom Gunn. CABP

I think of corner shots, the ball. Day and Night Handball. Stephen Dunn. MoASP

I think of difficulty, of geometry. Dinner on an April 10th. Carla Faesler Bremer. SPV, *tr.* by Jen Hofer

I think of her sometimes when I lie in bed. Marged. Gillian Clarke. MoWP

I think of Issa, a man of few words. Night Journal. Charles Wright. CAP-8; InGu

I think of Issa often these days, his poems about the loneliness. Comice. Joseph Stroud. PoChi

I think of it with wonder now. Glass, The. Sharon Olds. NIL-7; NIP-4

I think of my brother and his routine. Lithium. Marcus Cafagña. LiTh

I think of Oedipus, old, led by a boy. (LL) Terminal. Thom Gunn. CAGL; OxBEV

I think of our anonymous boys. Nocturnal Visits. Claribel Alegría. CFP; TANSG; VCWP, *tr.* by Darwin Flakoll

I think of that meadow off down in Coyne's. Coyne's. John Ennis. PBCIP

I think of the Celts as rather a whining lady. Celts, The. Stevie Smith. NoP-4; NoP-5

I think of the land and the wheat. Nadia Tueni. CFP, *tr.* by Elaine Gardiner

I think of the Martian landscape late delivered. Martian Landscape. Abbie Huston Evans. APT-1

I think of the ones like the poet John Haines. Working in Darkness. Thomas McGrath. BodElec

I think of the razor-sharp knife. Talking of Sharp Things. Frank Mkalawile Chipasula. HBAPE

I think of the twenty thousand poems of Li Po. Word Drunk. James Harrison. TAPaP

I think of thee!—my thoughts do twine and bud. Elizabeth Barrett Browning. CenSon; PEW *Fr.* Sonnets from the Portuguese.

I think of things we used to do. It's Been So Long. Harold Adamson. ReLy

I Think of Those Mornings. Morton Marcus. GeoHom

I think of those mornings before dawn. I Think of Those Mornings. Morton Marcus. GeoHom

I think of what it's like to team with Lance. Tour de France. Michael Cantor. ArBi

I think of you. Well, The. Ted Sexauer. WhBo

I Think of You as of a Good Life-boat. Emily Hickey. PoBW

I think of you in this warmer century. To a friend with osteoporosis. Elizabeth Smither. PoCu

I think of you when I am dead, the way rocks. Also Love You. Reginald Shepherd. IIR

I think of your quiet grave now and again. Night Call. Annie Finch. VisFro

I think on the whole I would rather read. Frank O'Hara Five, Geoffrey Chaucer Nil. Geoff Hattersley. NeBl

I Think Over Again My Small Adventures. *Unknown.* WoPoe

I think she sleeps: it must be sleep, when low. George Meredith. NAEL-6v2 *Fr.* Modern Love.

I think sometimes about. Friedrich von Hausen. GePo

I think somewhere there is a room. Circle Drawn in Water. Franz Wright. AmAlph

I think 'Sorry Missus' was what he said. (LL) Wounds. Michael Longley. ModIr; NAMCP V.2; NPeEn; PBCIP; PNI; PoAgWa

I think that I shall never read. Poems. Thomas M. Disch. PoA 2002; UV

I Think That I Shall Never See. Jim Heynen. UrbNat

I think that I shall never see. Easy Puddings. Bernadette Mayer. AHA

I think that I shall never see. Song of the Open Road. Ogden Nash. APT-2

I think that I shall never see / A poem lovely as a tree. Trees. Joyce Kilmer. APT-1; BRP; ChAP; ITBLP; PoA 2002; TCAPo; UV

I think that look of Christ might seem to say. Meaning of the Look, The. Elizabeth Barrett Browning. SacPr

I think that Sadness is an idiot born. Sadness. Mary Elizabeth Coleridge. ViWPN

I think that someone will remember us in another time. Yard Work. Charles Wright. WaAnP

I think the day draws near when I could stay. Day Draws Near, The. Augusta, Lady Gregory. IrLP

I think the dead are tender. Shall we kiss? She. Theodore Roethke. NIL-7; StAl

I think the deaths of domestic animals. Animals. Miller Williams. BeAl; P180

I think the Hemlock likes to stand. Emily Dickinson. NCAP

I think the thing you call Renown. Winthrop Mackworth Praed. OBSV *Fr.* Chaunt of the Brazen Head, The.

I think the train is headed this way. Airports of the World. Eugene Richie. KGB

I think then I live in a world of silence. Note, A. Clark Coolidge. AHA

I think there are most tigers in the wood. (LL) Ceremony. Richard Wilbur. NAAL-5; NAMCP V.2; NoAM

I think there is in this the stuff for many lyrics:—the. Harlem Happiness. Sterling Allen Brown. OxBoAm

I think therefore I am not. Cogito Ergo. Jerzy Ficowski. PoSu, *tr. by* Frank J. Corliss, Jr. and Grazyna Sandel

I think these days of the wind in your hair. Savage Memories. Yehuda Amichai. FIT, *tr. by* Robert Friend

I think things in the mirror. Meet Me at the St Francis. Iwan Llwyd. ATSWP, *tr. by* Robert Minhinnick

I think this house's mouth is full of dirt. Independence Day, 1956: A Fairy Tale. James Galvin. PoPoPo

I think this night is cold for Hugh; the heaviness of its downpour is a cause. On Maguire's Winter Campaign. Eochaidh Ó Heóghusa. PBRV

I think to Live—may be a Bliss. Emily Dickinson. SWaP

I think to make love to a nurse would be perfect. Angel. Andrew Elliott. PNI

I think to say this / wrongly. (LL) Whip, The. Robert Creeley. ICANM; PFTM-2

I think, too late for me now. Another Easter Poem. Honorée Fanonne Jeffers. RD

I think too often of funeral ceremonies. Night in the Shape of a Bison. Joyce Mansour. SurWo, *tr. by* Mary Beach

I think very well of Susan but I do not know her name. Gertrude Stein. NoP-4; NoP-5 *Fr.* Stanzas in Meditation.

I think, whatever mortals crave. Chaunt of the Brazen Head, The. Winthrop Mackworth Praed.

I think you are most yourself when you're swimming. Not Bad, Dad, Not Bad. Jan Heller Levi. P180

I think you are ready. (LL) Tract. William Carlos Williams. InoFa; MoAmPo; NAAPv.2; NAMCP V.1; NoAM; SAmP

I Think You Got Me Confused. Timothy Anderson. BeDoSh

I think you would like this seaside town—it makes me dream of whales. Anchorage, The. Mark Wunderlich. NeAmPo

I thirst for water; wine is my need no longer. Uri Zvi Greenberg. FIT, *tr. by* Robert Friend

I though from condemnation free. Ralph Erskine. SacPr *Fr.* Believer's Riddle, The.

I Thought About You. Johnny Mercer. ReLy

I thought: all this is only preparation. Mistake, A. Czeslaw Milosz. BeAl, *tr. by* Renata Gorczynski and Robert Hass

I thought all your walled cities. Tumbling Dice. Rachel Loden. SwNoth

I thought, as I wiped my eyes on the corner of my apron. Ancient Gesture, An. Edna St. Vincent Millay. NALW; NIL-7

I Thought Back and. Ann Stanford. PoChi

I thought because I had looked into your eyes. Star, The. Kathleen Jessie Raine. MoWP

I thought / but I know her so well. Rosy Ear. Zbigniew Herbert. BeAl; PML, *tr. by* Czeslaw Milosz

I thought for ten years, then I made my house. *Unknown.* SonAtl, *tr. by* Anthony, Brother of Taizé, Kim Fulton and Sunyoung Yi

I thought he was bankrupt. Max Jacob. PFTM-1 *Fr.* Cock and the Pearl, The.

I thought he was dumb. Tortoise Shout. D. H. Lawrence. NAEL-6v2; NAMCP-7v2; PFTM-1

I thought I saw an angel flying low. Nocturne at Bethesda. Arna Bontemps. ChIV-2; NAAPv.2; OxAAAP

I thought I saw him look my way and crossed. Portrait of the Town Leonard. Louise Erdrich. UpMys

I thought I wanted to wear. My Tattoo. Mark Doty. WiU

I thought I was a boy. Of Riches. Stephanie Williams. AnSo

I thought I was growing wings. Seeing for a Moment. Denise Levertov. VCAP

I thought I was so tough. Tamer and Hawk. Thom Gunn. HarvBoo

I thought I'd end up a Hippie American Gothic. No, No Nostalgia! Stephanie Brown. BodElec

I thought if only I could marry. Unfair to Women. *Unknown.* OBWVE, *tr. by* Gwyn Jones

I thought it made me look more "working class." Tony Harrison. NAEL-6v2; NAEL-7v2; NAMCP V.2 *Fr.* School of Eloquence, The.

I Thought It Was Harry. William Bronk. APSN; OxBoAm

I thought it was high time. Letter to My Mother, Sixteen Years after the Fact. Todd Davis. ACAMVP

I thought it was spring—lazy sun, soft breeze. To the Tune: Bodhisattva's Headdress. Li Ch'ing-chao. CrYelRi, *tr. by* Sam Hamill

I thought it would last my time. Going, Going. Philip Larkin. NAMCP V.2; NoAM; OxAEP-2

I thought love's game was over. Taking a Chance on Love. Ted Fetter and John Latouche. ReLy

I thought my all was given before. Wretten by Me at the Death of My 4th Sonne and 5th Child Perigrene Payler. Mary Carey. EMWP

I thought of a house where the stones seemed suddenly changed. Lo! A Child Is Born. Hugh MacDiarmid. EdScPo

I thought of leaving her for a day. Second Thoughts. Michael Field. LW; ViWPN

I thought of other significant hearts. Heart. David Scott. BeAl; PoCu

I thought of Thee, my partner and my guide. William Wordsworth. CenSon; NPBRoP *Fr.* River Duddon [A Series of Sonnets], The.

I thought of thee—I thought of thee. Confessional, The. Nathaniel Parker Willis. APN-1

I thought of them mingling with the others. Liliane Giraudon. SCFWP *Fr.* Poem with Incense Paper.

I thought of Troy, what we had built her for. (LL) Aeneas at Washington. Allen Tate. APT-2; FuPo; NoAM

I thought of walking round and round a space. Seamus Heaney. NoP-5 *Fr.* Clearances.

I thought of you. Lament. Gregory Orr. ArBi

I thought once how Theocritus had sung. Elizabeth Barrett Browning. CenSon; NoP-4; NoP-5; OBEV; OxAEP-2; PoPoPo *Fr.* Sonnets from the Portuguese.

I thought Silver must have snaked logs. Silver. A. R. Ammons. NoP-4

I thought so once; but now I know it. (LL) My Own Epitaph. John Gay. InoFa; NIL-7; NIP-4; NPeEn; OxBEV

I thought someone had said Olmsted brought them. Hollywood Finch, The. A. V. Christie. NAPBL

I thought that I was ravished to a height. Unum est Necessarium. Agnes Mary Frances Robinson. VWP

I thought that you were an anchor in the drift of the world. World, The. William Bronk. APSN

I thought the earth / remembered me, she. Sleeping in the Forest. Mary Oliver. CAP-8; PLBUT

I thought the night without a sound was falling. William Force Stead. OBMV *Fr.* Uriel.

I thought the war was. In the Casbah. Salma Khadra Jayyusi. CFP; PoArWo, *tr. by* Charles Doria

I thought thee wondrous when thy soul portrayed. To Charlotte Cushman. Eliza Cook. VWP

I thought to view the comeliness. Pine. Kimiko Hahn. PoDa

I thought wearing an evergreen dress. Pine. Kimiko Hahn. PoDa

I thought when he hadn't been there for two or three days—. In the Chung Mode, to the Tune of "P'u T'ien Lo." *Unknown.* ColAnChi, *tr. by* Wayne Schlepp

I thought you were my victory. Victory, The. Anne Stevenson. BeAl

I thought you were without genitals, that nothing cracked you open and made you insatiable. For Sister Sue Ellen and Her Special Messenger. Toi Derricotte. ExTi

I thought Zen poems. Misunderstanding, A. Maggie Nelson. PoDa

I threat'ned [or threatened] to observe the strict decree. Holdfast, The. George Herbert. NAEL-7v1

I threw a snowball across the backyard. Listen. Miller Williams. P180

I threw it out. To Philip Whalen, 1999. Diane Di Prima. WANABP

I threw the inside of my gizzard out, splashing. Zimmer Drunk and Alone, Dreaming of Old Football Games. Paul Zimmer. PBCAP

I throw back the teepee flap. Women Fell like Beautiful Horses, The. Gloria Bird. FiBr

I throw myself here at your feet, sinful. To My Lady of Poetry. Alfonsina Storni. PoCho, tr. by Kay Short

I throw the line in from this little island. Lake of the Ten Thousand Mountains, The. Meng Hao Jan. EaWin, tr. by W. S. Merwin

I thumped on you the best I could. W. D. Snodgrass. NAMCP V.2; NoAM Fr. Heart's Needle.

I tie eight sticks together. Cabato. Ray Gonzalez. TouFir

I Time of What. Danielle Collobert. YaTCFP, tr. by Michael Tweed

I tink I hear my brudder say. Stars Begin to Fall. Unknown. SacPr; SSUS

I to My Brothers. Judith Wright. BMAP Fr. For a Pastoral Family.

I to the hills lift up mine eyes. Unknown. GoPo Fr. Bay Psalm Book, The.

I told everyone / your name was Arthur. Arturo. Maria Gillan. UnSA

I told my brothers I heard. Yusef Komunyakaa. InoFa Fr. Songs for My Father.

I told my brothers I heard. Songs for My Father. Yusef Komunyakaa. FuFl

I told my love I told my love [see also "Never seek to tell thy love"]. William Blake. OxBEV

I told the Sun that I was glad. Sun, The. John Drinkwater. NTCP

I Told Them I Should Be Here. Kate Schmitt. IJHIL

I told you, sir, it was a plot; you see. Ben Jonson. NAEL-7v1 Fr. Volpone.

I, too, am America. (LL) I, Too. Langston Hughes. APT-2; HarvBoo; HeIP-4; MakPoe; NAAL-5; NOxBChV; PoPoPo; SSLK; StAl

I Too am changed—I scarce know why. Ten Years Ago. Alaric Alexander Watts. TreFP

I, too, am not an exception but a person born into this world. Song of the Pure Land. Master Naong. CATKP, tr. by Pori Park

I too am waiting. Pablo. Dieter Weslowski. InvLad

I too beneath your moon, almighty Sex. Edna St. Vincent Millay. APT-1; NAAL-5; NALW

I, too, bless the cradle that rocked me. To János Arany in Answer to His Poem "Cosmopolitan Poetry." Gyula Reviczky. IQMS, tr. by Madeline Mason

I too could give my heart to history. History. Carl Dennis. BAP-97; OxBoAm

I, too, dislike it. Poetry [1967 Version]. Marianne Moore. BrAP; HarvBoo; NIL-7; OxBoAm

I too, dislike it. Poetry [1925 Version]. Marianne Moore. NIL-7

I, too, dislike it: there are things that are important beyond all this fiddle. Poetry [1921 Version]. Marianne Moore. AmFaPo; APT-1; ColAP; HeIP-4; MoAmPo; NAAL-5; NAAPv.2; NALW; NAMCP V.1; NIP-4; NoAM; NoP-4; NoP-5; OxBoAm; PoPoPo; TCAPo; TFi; WaAnP

I, too, have been a Wanderer; but, alas! William Wordsworth. OxAEP-2 Fr. Prelude, The; Growth of a Poet's Mind [1805 version].

I, too, have declared war. War. Aharon Shabtai. PoCho, tr. by Peter Cole

I, too, have faked the glamor of gray towers. Disloyal Lines to an Alumnus. Edmund Wilson. OBCoV

I too love jeans and jazz and Treasure Island. Sa'di Yusuf. PoAgWa; PoCho Fr. America, America.

I, too, saw God through mud. Apologia Pro Poemate Meo. Wilfred Owen. MoBrPo; NAEL-6v2; NAEL-7v2; NAMCP V.1

I, too, sing America. I, Too. Langston Hughes. APT-2; HarvBoo; HeIP-4; MakPoe; NAAL-5; NOxBChV; PoPoPo; SSLK; StAl

I too speak of the rose. Rose Nocturnal. Xavier Villaurrutia. GPTC, tr. by Donald Justice

I, too, want to be. Self-Portrait. Milán Füst. IQMS, tr. by Paul Tabori

I, too, was born for happiness. Philosophy of Life. Dániel Berzsenyi. IQMS, tr. by Watson Kirkconnell

I too was born out of a lion's mouth. Let Heroes Account to Love. Alan Dugan. NoAM

I took a day to search for God. Vestigia. Bliss Carman. BrAP

I took a piece of the rare cloth of Ch'i. Present from the Emperor's New Concubine, A. Pan Chieh-yü. NDACCP; WoPoe, tr. by Kenneth Rexroth

I took a shortcut through blood. Back in the World. Ai. BAP-97

I took a walk on the railroad track. Walk, A. Raymond Carver. GM

I took another day. Postponement of Self. Laura Riding Jackson. OxBoAm

I Took by the Throat the Circumcised Dog. Chad Davidson. IaFF

I took each word he said as gospel truth. Can't We Be Friends? Paul James. ReLy

I took for emblem the upland moors and the rocky. Llanafan Unrevisited. T. Harri Jones. AngWePo

I took God with me to the sheep fair. I said, 'Look'. Sheep Fair Day. Kerry Hardie. BeAl; MoWP; NIrP

I took her dainty eyes, as well. Villanelle of His Lady's Treasures. Ernest Dowson. MakPoe

I took her to the river. Unfaithful Married Woman, The. Federico García Lorca. GPTC, tr. by Rolfe Humphries

I took him by the arm and said. F. Mullen. UV

I took love home with me. Act #2. John Wieners. BB

I took money and bought flowering trees. Planting Flowers on the Eastern Embankment. Po Chü-i. OBGa, tr. by Arthur Waley

I took my cousin to Prettyboy Dam. Poems for My Cousin. Josephine Jacobsen. APT-2

I took my girl to a fancy ball. I Had But Fifty Cents. Unknown. NBLV; WHSW

I took my heart in my hand. Twice. Christina Georgina Rossetti. OBEV; VWP

I took my life and threw it on the skip. Skip, The. James Fenton. HarvBoo

I took my oath I would inquire. Inquest, The. W. H. Davies. AngWePo

I took my Power in my Hand. Emily Dickinson. ChIV-1; SAmP

I took off petal after petal, as if you were a rose. I Took Off Petal After Petal. Juan Ramón Jiménez. WED, tr. by Robert Bly

I took one Draught of Life. Emily Dickinson. APN-2

I took out my rib. My Little Woman. Asaf Halet Çelebi. NaPG, tr. by Talat Sait Halman

I took / the kings' yawl. Night 9. Salim Hatubou. SonAtl, tr. by Carole Beckett, Kurt Ganzl, Eva Mallenby, Eric Milan, Christophe Mirambeau, Martin Ottenheimer and Simon Young

I took the road from Brighton-town. Search. Eleanor Slater. YaYoPo

I took the scroll: I could not brook. Lines Written Under a Picture of a Girl Burning a Love-Letter. Letitia Elizabeth Landon. NOBRP

I took the thought. Carillonneur. Ricardo M. de Ungria. ReBoTo

I took the train to Rome. Celebrities. Alain Bosquet. PML, tr. by William Jay Smith

I took up the burden of life anew. To My Mother. Mary Weston Fordham. CBWP-2

I took wild honey from the plants. Distribution of Poetry. Jorge de Lima. PFTM-1

I took your mother's hand and the PLANE. Postcard from London, A. Cathal McCabe. NIrP

I tossed my friend a wreath of roses, wet. Gifts. Mary Elizabeth Coleridge. VWP

I touch the cornerstone of the year. Vertigo. Pedro Serrano. RMCMP, tr. by Geoff Hargreaves

I touch the night sleeping in your leaf. Its alchemy of dying next to a white stone. Regression of the Willow. Ernesto Lumbreras. RMCMP, tr. by Rebecca Seiferle

I touch you in the night, whose gift was you. Science of the Night, The. Stanley Kunitz. APT-2; ColAP; MoAmPo

I touch your hand. Younger Than Springtime. Oscar Hammerstein, II. ReLy

I touched life. Roses and Thorns. Kim Sŭnghŭi. CAMKP, tr. by Anthony, Brother of Taizé

I towered far, and lo! I stood within. God-Forgotten. Thomas Hardy. InvLi

I train my train into this city of mud and brick and collide. This Sun. John Rybicki. AmPoNex

I trained me a falcon, for more than a year. Unknown. GePo

I travel along broad paved roads. On Roads. Ber Grin. Prolet, tr. by Amelia Glaser

I travel your body as I would travel the world. Octavio Paz. BLPSL Fr. Sunstone.

I traveled to the ocean. Prayer to the Pacific. Leslie Marmon Silko. NAMCP V.2; NoP-4; PoPoPo; WeW-3

I Travelled among Unknown Men. William Wordsworth. BrAP; NAEL-6v2; NAEL-7v2 Fr. Lucy.

I travelled [or travel'd] thro' a land of men. Mental Traveller, The. William Blake. ChIV-2; NAEL-6v2; WoPoe

(I travelled through a land of men.) NPBRoP

I travelled [or travell'd or traveled] on, seeing the hill, where lay. Pilgrimage, The. George Herbert. BASC; NAEL-6v1; NAEL-7v1; NOSC

I travelled through a land of men. William Blake. See I travelled [or travel'd] thro' a land of men.

I trespass by the harsh, welling canal. April 19, 19—: A Sonnet. George Elliott Clarke. BtF

I tried each thing, only some were immortal and free. As One Put Drunk into the Packet-Boat. John Ashbery. NAMCP V.2; VCAP

I tried repeating, which feels now. Foolish Thing. Michael Burkard. BodElec

I tried this play one day. My father leaves his medicines open. I take. Daredevil. Ania Walwicz. BMAP

I tried to complete a life circumstance like a building I aspired to, loose in space on used land. Mei-Mei Berssenbrugge. AWPTFC Fr. Retired Architect, The.

I tried to imagine the Vilna ghetto. After the Survivors Are Gone. Peter Balakian. WaAnP

I tried to tell her. Offspring. Naomi Long Madgett. GT; OxAAAP; SoSe-8

I tried to tell the doctor. Oh, I'm 10 Months Pregnant. Ntozake Shange. GT

I trudged along a road. All Dreams Are Sexual. Hwang Insuk. EcSo, tr. by Peter H. Lee

I trust every animal. Dogalypse. Andrey Andreievich Voznesensky. CLPP

I trust I have not wasted breath. Alfred Tennyson. NAEL-6v2; NAEL-7v2 Fr. In Memoriam A. H. H.

I try impressing you from a barstool. I Feel Unattractive during Mating Season. Cindy Goff. LaCa

I try not to get fancy or fussy. Third Maisie Poem. Daniel Nester. IIR

I try talking to you in this near-September air after I water the dry spots. Fred Wah. NLPA Fr. This Dendrite Map: Father / Mother Haibun.

I try to forget, but it is in vain. To the Distant One. Po Chü-i. TAL

I try to hide in Proust. No-Good Blues. Yusef Komunyakaa. OxBoAm

I try to hold my lie in mind. In/Silence. Jorie Graham. AWPTFC

I try to hold your face in my mind's million eyes. Bride's Hours, A. Jean Valentine. MPUn

I try to imagine the lid closing but it won't. Piano, The. Sarah Manguso. IIR

I try to listen for the abstract shape. Ode to Mozart. Maura Stanton. MiVo

I try to make myself afraid. Ovation. Carol Muske-Dukes. AmAlph

I try to make wishes right. Jacob Nibenegenesabe. WoPoe Fr. Wishing Bone Cycle, The.

I try to tune in, but Europe's blurred voice. Short Wave. Hilary Llewellyn-Williams. RWPCtW; TCAWP

I Try to Turn in My Jock. David Hilton. MoASP

I Try to Waken and Greet the World Once Again. James Wright. EmeKit Fr. Two Hangovers.

I tumbled next to him, his body turned. Razglednica (4). Miklós Radnóti. IQMS, tr. by Peter Zollman

I turn my head and say, Ah, grasshopper. Grasshopper. Danielle Legros Georges. BRtP

I turn out the driveway, point down the street. Artemis in Echo Park. Eloise Klein Healy. CalPo; GeoHom

I turn the page and read. At the British Museum. Richard Aldington. MoBrPo

I turn this green hexagonal tile with. In the Living Room. Arthur Sze. WANABP

I turn to you high priests. Lament. Tadeusz Rózewicz. PoSu, tr. by Magnus J. Krynski

I turned and gave my strength to woman. Two Generations. Leonard Alfred George Strong. OBMV

I turned aside and bowed my head and wept. (LL) Tropics in New York, The. Claude McKay. APT-1; GT; MakPoe; NAAPv.2; NAMCP V.1; NoAM; OxBoAm

I turned on the TV. Tube Time. Eve Merriam. TLR

I twist the dial and you are everywhere. (LL) Elegy for Elvis. Richard Blessing. AllShUp; InoFa; SwNoth

I understand. In the Restaurant. Gerald William Barrax. GT

I understand her well because I too practice love. Etymology. Olga Broumas. WiU

I understand now, Tara, I understand. Rāmdulāl Nandī. SinGod, tr. by Rachel Fell McDermott

I understand the large hearts of heroes. Walt Whitman. SAmP Fr. Song of Myself.

I understand you well enough, John Donne. Letter to John Donne, A. Charles Hubert Sisson. HarvBoo

I understood it as you did: indifference. (LL) Elegy for N. N. Czeslaw Milosz. BodElec; GPTC, tr. by the author and Lawrence Davis

I undress and lie down next to you in bed. On This Side of the River. Stephen Berg. GifTon; TAPaP

I Undressed Myself. Thérèse 'Awwad. PoArWo, tr. by Kamal Boullata

I unplug. Lightning and Thunder. Janice Finney. PfS

I urge you. Sappho. SaLy, tr. by Diane Rayor

I urge you, milord, not to cherish your robe of golden thread. Robe of Golden Thread, The. Autumn Maid Tu (Tu Ch'iu-niang). ColAnChi, tr. by Victor H. Mair

I urgency, I begged. Give me your dish, I said, icy. Hélène Cixous. VCAP Fr. Vivre L'Orange.

I used the table as a reference and just did things from there. Texas. Mei-Mei Berssenbrugge. PmAP

I used to be a sprinter, running. Hurdler Explains Her Reasons, A. Mary Kathleen Rayburn. PfS

I used to be / an admissions counselor. Skin Color from the Sun. Daryl Ngee Chinn. LTA

I used to be, at one time, a red. Wintery Music. Sarah Kirsch. GTCP, tr. by Reinhold Grimm

I used to be my mother's baby. I'm Nobody's Baby. Benny Davis and Lester Santly. ReLy

I used to be your echo. Elena Vasileva. CRWP, tr. by Max Nemtsov

I used to dream of your wake. For My Mother. Duriel Harris. BtF

I used to dream that I would discover. Bill (Original Version). P. G. Wodehouse. ReLy

I used to dream that I would discover. Bill. P. G. Wodehouse. ReLy

I used to fall. My Heart Belongs to Daddy. Cole Porter. ReLy

I Used to Go to Church. G. E. Patterson. PoDa

I used to have bracelets, I do not wear them now. Unknown. SLW, tr. by Marjolijn De Jager, Sayd Bahodin Majrouh and André Velter

I used to imagine we were a fine two-headed. Alive. Hayden Carruth. BeAl

I used to know when mango ripe. Plenty Time Pass Fast, Fas Dey So. Cheryl Boyce Taylor. WiU

I used to lead a lovely life of sin. Fings Ain't Wot They Used t'Be. Lionel Bart. ReLy

I used to lie on the floor for hours after. Cord, The. Leanne O'Sullivan. P180

I used to live in a big house by the Church of St. Francis. León. Ernesto Cardenal. TCLAP, tr. by Jonathan Cohen

I used to peer inside. Posthuman. Maura Stanton. BodElec

I used to ride around in the hole. By the Skin of Our Luck. Mark Bibbins. IIR

I used to sit under trees and meditate. Buddha. Jack Kerouac. BB

I used to sleep in a bed my father made. Bed. Kendra Borgmann. PoDa

I Used to Tell You, "Frances, We Grow Old." Ausonius. WoPoe, tr. by Kenneth Rexroth

I used to think. Dramatic Fragments. Trumbull Stickney.

I used to think all poets were Byronic. Triolet. Wendy Cope. OBCoV

I used to think it might be fun to be. Lucky to Be Me. Betty Comden and Adolph Green. ReLy

I used to think . . . number was fixed and still. Anna Hempstead Branch. APT-1 Fr. Sonnets from a Lock Box.

I used to think that grown-up people chose. Childhood. Frances Darwin Cornford. OxBEV

I used to think that immortality. Superman Is Dead. Rafael Campo. ReTh

I used to tow targets. Flight as a Way of Life. Ann Darr. PWW2

I used to visit all the very gay places. Lush Life. Billy Strayhorn. ReLy

I used to wait for the flowers. What's Left. Kerry Hardie. BeAl; NIrP

I used to walk on solid gr'und. To a Sea Eagle. Hugh MacDiarmid. MoBrPo

I used to watch the roses loosen. Boy Crazy. Maurya Simon. GeoHom

I Usually Look Around Me. Iman Mirsal. NAfrP, tr. by Clarissa C. Burt

I veer from Beaver Valley onto Swansonville Road. Swansonville. Mary Lou Sanelli. IPoFL

I Visit the Twenty-four Coin-op Church of Elvis. Fleda Brown Jackson. AllShUp

I visited Jesus today. Visiting Jesus. Martin Birnbaum. Prolet, tr. by Amelia Glaser

I visited Père Lachaise to look for the remains of Apollinaire. At Apollinaire's Grave. Allen Ginsberg. BB

I wad ha'e gi'en him my lips tae kiss. Mary's Song. Marion Angus. EdScPo; LW

I waded, deepening, into the dark water. River, The. Raymond Carver. PoDa

I wage not any feud with Death. Alfred Tennyson. NAEL-6v2; NAEL-7v2 Fr. In Memoriam A. H. H.

I wait for a guest who does not come. Written on the Wall of Ch'ŏnsu Monastery. Yi Illo. CATKP, tr. by Peter H. Lee

I wait for him by the subway exit. It's night, the. Leslie Kaplan. SCFWP Fr. Livre des ciels, Le.

I wait for the mailman. Crystal Chandeliers. David Ignatow. BodElec

I wait for the owl. Bruja: Witch. Pat Mora. FiBr

I wait in the next room, watching how she struggles. Erato. Phyllis Thompson. ICANM

I wait upon de Lord. Go in the Wilderness. Unknown. SSUS

I waited all night. Kenneth Rexroth. NAAPv.2 Fr. Love Poems of Marichiko, The.

I waited and worked / To win myself leisure. Koheleth. Louis Untermeyer. ChIV-1

I waited eighteen years to become a man. Basket Case. Basil T. Paquet. AmWaPo; FaBoWar

I Waited for You Last Night. Zindzi Mandela. HAWP; NAfrP

I waited full two hours, or more. Tryst, The. Mary E. Tucker. CBWP-1

I waited, heavy-hearted; then went on. After the Voices. Victor Hugo. SxFrPo, tr. by A. M. and E. H. Blackmore

I waited too long. In a Boat Shed. Robert Creeley. InvLad

I wak'd, she fled, and day brought back my night. (LL) John Milton. See I waked [or wak'd], she fled, and day brought back my night.

I Wake and Feel the Fell of Dark, Not Day. Gerard Manley Hopkins. AWTN; BrAP; CABP; FaBoVe; NAEL-6v2; NAEL-7v2; NAMCP V.1; NoP-4; NoP-5; NPeEn; OxAEP-2; OxBSo; RSR; TRP; WaAnP

I wake and my bed is gleaming with moonlight. Quiet Night Thoughts. Li Po. EaWin, tr. by W. S. Merwin

I wake because the phone is really ringing. Fucking. Frederick Seidel. BodElec

I wake, but before I know it it is done. Aging. Randall Jarrell. PoA 2002

I wake! delusive phantoms hence, away! Reaches Sicily. Mary Robinson. CenSon; RWP

I wake early into. Justin Quinn. NIrP

I wake from my noon nap. Muso Soseki. EaWin, tr. by W. S. Merwin

I wake! I feel the day is near. Chanticleer. Celia Laighton Thaxter. NOxBChV

I wake in a dark flat. Afterlives. Derek Mahon. NAMCP V.2

I wake in the dark and remember. Rain Travel. W. S. Merwin. ColAP; GoPo

I wake in the dark. My face is a stunned. Persephone (Unplugged). Stephen Burt. LegDan

I wake in the morning. Lilith. Suzanne Benton. HW

I wake to sleep, and take my waking slow. Waking, The. Theodore Roethke. AmFaPo; APT-2; BrAP; HeIP-4; IJHIL; ITBLP; MakPoe; MoAmPo; NAAL-5; NAMCP V.1; NIL-7; NIP-4; NoAM; NoP-4; NoP-5; OxBoAm; PoPoPo; RaBo; StAl; TFi; VCAP; WaAnP; WeW-3; WoPoe

I wake to strangled voices. Stepping in the Same River. Karen Chamberlain. GeoH

I wake to the radio's *today found two bound hands*. I walk to the corner market. September 18. Pat Reed. Eno

I wake to the sound of a soft, low patter. Night Rain. Countee Cullen. GT

I wake up. Raul Bopp. TCLAP Fr. Black Snake.

I wake up a novice and ask him to make tea. Han-shan Te-ch'ing. CSKM, tr. by Red Pine

I wake up and say: I'm through. Morning Exercises. Nina Cassian. CFP; PoSu, tr. by Andrea Deletant and Brenda Walker

I wake up back aching from soft bed Pat. Ted Berrigan. NYP2 Fr. Sonnets, The.

I wake up cold, I who. Man With Night Sweats, The. Thom Gunn. CABP; CalPo; HarvBoo; PoPoPo

I wake up dreaming I'm forty years in. Winged Abyss. Nathaniel Mackey. ESEAA

I wake up growling apples and dirt. Shiner. Maggie Nelson. AmPoNex

I wake up in your bed. I know I have been dreaming. Adrienne Rich. ErotSp; NoAM; TRP Fr. Twenty-one Love Poems.

I wake up my car. Morning Bird Songs. Tomas Tranströmer. WED, tr. by Robert Bly

I wake up on my left side. Kukutis's Consciousness Becomes Alienated. Marcelijus Martinaitis. TWW, tr. by Laima Sruoginis

I wake up standing before a scene I stood. Phantom Light of All Our Day, The. Nathaniel Mackey. GT

I waked [or wak'd], she fled, and day brought back my night. (LL) On His Deceased Wife. John Milton. NPeEn; OBEV; OxBSo; SacPr; TFi

(I wak'd, she fled, and day brought back my night.) (LL) CABP; PBRV

(I waked, she fled, and day brought back my night.) (LL) GSo; NoP-4

I wakened on my hot, hard bed. Watch, The. Frances Darwin Cornford. MoBrPo; PtR

I wakened, still a child. Life Ahead, The. Philip Levine. NoAM

I Walk a Little Faster. Carolyn Leigh. ReLy

I walk again in the night. Magic Song. *Unknown*. APN-2, tr. by Henry Rowe Schoolcraft

I walk among dark shapes. Hunting in Twilight. David Scott Ward. AmPoNex

I walk and I rest while the eyes of my dead. Choir, The. Olga Broumas. CAP-8

I walk around the city. Infections. Miguel Algarin. PueRic

I walk [or walked] beside the prisoners to the road. Camp in the Prussian Forest, A. Randall Jarrell. FaBoWar; HP; MoAmPo; OBWP; PoWW; PWW2

I walk down a long / passage way. Poem for museum goers, A. John Wieners. BB

I walk down the garden paths. Patterns. Amy Lowell. AmFaPo; AmWaPo; APT-1; MoAmPo; NoP-4; NoP-5; WHSW

I Walk in the History of My People. Chrystos. UnSA

I Walk in the Solitude of Books. Marie-Claire Bancquart. YaTCFP, tr. by Mary Ann Caws

I walk into the vineyard at night, into acres of cordoned vines. Revelation in the Mother Lode. George Evans. AF; PmAP

I walk naked and. Alone in Your House. Kim Addonizio. PasH

I walk on meadows run to weed. Magyar Fallow, The. Endre Ady. IQMS, tr. by Anton N. Nyerges

I walk on the sea-shore. Voice. Zbigniew Herbert. PoSu, tr. by Czeslaw Milosz

I walk on tiptoes, so as not to disturb. Opposites Attack. Jeffrey McDaniel. LegDan

I walk out the kitchen door. Other Side of the House, The. Rita Dove. AmAlph

I walk six blocks to the park. Hoarfrost and Fog. Barton Sutter. UrbNat

I walk some hundred paces from the old house. Depths of Fields. Luis Cabalquinto. ReBoTo

I walk the coasts of Ibeju Lekki. New Testament, The. Nike Adesuyi. NeNiPo

I walk the forest in the moonlight. In Front of Good Prince Silence. Endre Ady. IQMS, tr. by Alan Dixon

I walk the land of Anahuac which is the land of my dead. Return, The. Rosario Castellanos. TANSG; TCLAP, tr. by Magda Bogin

I walk the streets and though not meanly drest. Poor, The. Jones Very. SacPr

I walk through the long schoolroom questioning. Among School Children. William Butler Yeats. BrAP; CABP; HarvBoo; MoBrPo; NAEL-6v2; NAEL-7v2; NAMCP V.1; NAWM-7v2; NIL-7; NIP-4; NoAM; NoP-4; NoP-5; NPeEn; OxBEV; PoPoPo; TFi; TRP; WaAnP

I walk through the polders. Polderland. Hendrik Marsman. TuT, tr. by Michael Longley

I walk to the river in deep snow. The ice is thick. Patrick Lane. IFF Fr. Linen Crow, a Caftan Magpie, A.

I walked abroad in [or on] a snowy day. Soft Snow. William Blake. SoSe-8

I walked along the streets of Hong Kong town. Love Is a Many-Splendored Thing. Paul Francis Webster. ReLy

I walked around in my mother's high heels. Cobwebs. Melinda Goodman. WiU

I walked around New York half-dazed, and what. Mengele Shitting. Jason Sommer. NAPBL

I walked beside the stone. My Grandmother's Burial Ground. Elizabeth Cook-Lynn. HATNAP

I walked down the street. Listeners, The. Louis Simpson. BodElec

I walked, gritting my teeth, past charred. In Those Years. Sergey Sergeievich Narovchatov. TCRusP, tr. by Bob Perelman and Shirley Rihner

I walked in a desert. Stephen Crane. OxBoAm

I walked into the garden afterwards. September 1939. Alan Brownjohn. RWPCtW

I walked into the room. To My Father. John Berryman. PoPoPo

I walked on the banks of the tincan banana dock and sat down under the huge shade of a Southern Pacific locomotive. Sunflower Sutra. Allen Ginsberg. GM; NAMCP V.2; PoPoPo; VCAP

I walked out of my dress. Like the Magic Glow of Paradise. Clementina Suárez. TANSG, tr. by Janet N. Gold

I walked out on the lamp shadowed concrete at midnight May Day passing a dark'd barfront. Manhattan May Day Midnight. Allen Ginsberg. WhBo

I Walked over the Grave of Henry James. Richard Eberhart. APT-2

I walked slowly along the river. One Hundred and Fifty Years. Jack Davis. BMAP

I Walked [or Walkt or Walk'd] the Other Day to Spend My Hour. Henry Vaughan. BASC; FSCP; NAEL-6v1

I walked the two blocks from the subway down. Going Home Madly. Brooke Wiese. UrbNat

I walked through Ballinderry in the spring-time. Lament for the Death of Thomas Davis. Sir Samuel Ferguson. IrV

I walked through the lonely marsh. Charles Reznikoff. NAMCP V.1

I walked where in their talking graves. At the British War Cemetery, Bayeux. Charles Causley. NAEL-6v2; NAEL-7v2; NoP-4; NoP-5; OBWP; PoWW

I walked with him one melancholy night. Lycidas. Thomas Bailey Aldrich. TreFP

I Wan Bi President. Ezenwa-Ohaeto. NAfrP

I wander all night in my vision. Sleepers, The. Walt Whitman. NAAL-3

I wander all night in my vision. Walt Whitman. AWTN Fr. Sleepers, The.

I wander all night in my vision. Walt Whitman. APN-1 Fr. Leaves of Grass [1855 Version].

I wander thro' each charter'd street. William Blake. RSaN

I wander through a crowd of women. At Piccadilly Circus. Vivian de Sola Pinto. OBMV

I wander through [or thro'] each chartered [or charter'd] street. William Blake. BrAP; CABP; ClHu; HeIP-4; IJHIL; NAEL-6v2; NAEL-7v2; NAWM-7v2; NIL-7; NIP-4; NOBRP; NoP-4; NoP-5; NPBRoP; NPeEn; OxAEP-2; OxBEV; PoPoPo; TFi; TRP; WeW-3 Fr. Songs of Experience.

I wandered away from my early childhood, framed by her massive hair. Officials rob. Material's Daughter. Aaron Shurin. FTOS

I wandered for many years after leaving the dusty world. Reply to a Poem by Songgyedang. Buhyu Sunsoo. BecRai, tr. by Kim Daljin, Kim Won-Chung and Christopher Merrill

I wandered lonely as a cloud. En Famille. Robert Creeley. BAP-01

I Wandered Lonely as a Cloud. William Wordsworth. BRP; CABP; ChAP; ClHu; NAEL-6v2; NAEL-7v2; NOBRP; NoP-4; NoP-5; PoPoPo; SoSe-8; TFi; WaAnP

(Daffodils.) ChAP; ITBLP; NPBRoP

(Daffodils, The.) OBEV; TreFP

I wandered lonely as a cloud in Foyles. Upon Finding Dying: An Introduction, by L. E. Sissman, Remaindered at IS. Louis Edward Sissman. NoP-4

I wandered lonely by the sea. Goose-Girl, The. Edith Nesbit. VWP

I wandered [or / wander'd] today to the hill, Maggie. When You and I Were Young, Maggie. George W. Johnson. TCAPo

I wandered out a while agone. George Wither. NOSC Fr. Fair Virtue, the Mistress of Philarete [Selections from anthologies].

I wandered out through the steeples of rust, the gate that was a broken bed. (LL) Dresden. Ciaran Carson. ModIr; NPeEn; PBCIP; PNI

I wandered through the ancient wood. Cataract Isle, The. Christopher Pearse Cranch. APN-1

I wandered through the pills of light. Molino. Maggie Nelson. HeMarv

I wanna. . .wanna a blues poem. To Aretha Franklin from Sparkle. Amina Baraka. BRtP

I Wanna Be Black. Michelle T. Clinton. InTrad

I Wanna Be Loved. Edward Heyman and Billy Rose. ReLy

I wanna be the leader. Leader, The. Roger McGough. OPOU

I Wannabe Your Queen. Susan Swartwout. SwNoth

I want a god. Prayer. Francisco X. Alarcón. RaF

I want a heart that fits me. Unknown. SonAtl, tr. by Rob Fikki and Ginger Thornton

I want a hero: an uncommon want. Lord Byron. NAEL-6v2; NAEL-7v2 Fr. Don Juan.

I want a hero: an uncommon want. Lord Byron. NoP-5 Fr. Don Juan.

I want a little breeze. What Do I Want? Madduri Nageshbabu. HotL, tr. by V. Narayana Rao

I want a love. Cinema Yosemite. Del Ray Cross. FreRad

I want / a love to hold. Defense Rests. Vassar Miller. MoAmPo

I want a red dress. What Do Women Want? Kim Addonizio. BeAl

I Want a Solid Piece of Sunlight and a Yardstick to Measure it With. Tom Postell. EGAG

I want free life and I want fresh air. Lasca. Frank Desprez. TiP2

I want him to have another living summer. 14-Year-Old Convalescent Cat in the Winter, A. Gavin Ewart. OPOU

I want his doughnut. He was eating that fucking doughnut the first. Riot at Winchell's. Bruce Jackson. AmPoNex

I want, in the shade of a wing. José Martí. BLPSL, tr. by Rene de Costa, Rigas Kappatos and Eleni Paidoussi

I want men that I can squeeze. Nobody Makes a Pass at Me. Harold Rome. ReLy

I want my body bathed again by southern suns, my soul reclaimed again from southern land. Southern Song. Margaret Abigail Walker. InGu

I want my funeral to include this detour. Detour. Michael Longley. BeAl; NAMCP V.2

I want my soul to find its proper body. (LL) Piano Solo. Nicanor Parra. PoetW; TCLAP, tr. by William Carlos Williams

I want no paradise only to be. Kiwi Bird in the Kiwi Tree, The. Charles Bernstein. FTOS; NAMCP V.2

I want nothing but your fire-side now. Hearthstone. Harold Monro. OBMV

I want [or wanted] to sniff the glue that holds families together. Logic in the House of Sawed-Off Telescopes. Jeffrey McDaniel. AmPoNex; LegDan; NeAmPo

I want some valiant soldier here. Hail, Mary. Unknown. SSUS

I want something suited to my special needs. Needs. A. R. Ammons. NIL-7; NIP-4

I want that picture, the perfect view. Immortal Picture, The. Richard Eberhart. BodElec

I want the phone to ring. Talkin' Trash. Elena Georgiou. WiU

I want the robes, the skins of the game animals, the meat of the game animals. Bring them to me. Let us enjoy ourselves. Unknown. APN-2 Fr. Minnetare Songs.

I want the sign to read, never come back again. Message, The. Jeffrey Hillard. AtGh

I want the water to go on without its bed. Ghazal of the Terrifying Presence. Federico García Lorca. WED, tr. by Robert Bly

I Want the Words Back. Margaret Randall. FiBr

I want things. On the Corner. Kit Robinson. FTOS

I want to admire the dawn moon. Yun Sŏndo. CATKP Fr. Angler's Calendar, The.

I want to be. Last of the Fire Kings, The. Derek Mahon. BeAl; NAMCP V.2; PNI

I want to be a cow. Cow. Selima Hill. StAl

I want to be a force for real good. John Coltrane (1926–1967). Imamu Amiri Baraka. FuFl

I want to be an angel and really think. Mad Cow in Love, The. Jo Shapcott. NeBrP

I Want to Be Bad. Lew Brown, B. G. DeSylva and Ray Henderson. ReLy

I want to be carried, heavily sedated. Dream of a Slave. Gavin Ewart. EmeKit

I want to be / famous. Dilemma. David Budbill. GoPo

I Want to Be Happy. Irving Caesar. ReLy

I want to be in the Bay Area. Temperate. Joseph Somoza. ICANM

I want to be known. Claim to Fame. Beau Sia. HeMarv

I Want to Be Loved. Endre Ady. IQMS, tr. by Peter Zollman

I want to be my Fader's chil'en. Trouble of the World, The. Unknown. SSUS

I want to be near this mild unforgiving man. Father. Paul Zweig. BodElec

I want to be remembered. Cover Photograph. Marilyn Nelson. InvLi

I want to be simple. Dark Star, Black Star. Rikki Ducornet. SurWo

I want to belong to the third sex. Third Sex, The. Patricia Young. BrAP

I want to check. After the Anti-Semitic Calls on a Local Talk Station. Lyn Lifshin. UnSA

I want to climb up Jacob's ladder, Jacob's ladder. Jacob's Ladder. Unknown. SSUS

I want to cry my pain and I am telling you so you will love me and cry for me in a nightfall of nightingales with a dagger, with kisses and with you. Federico García Lorca. CAGL Fr. Sonetos del Amor Oscuro [Sonnets of Dark Love].

I want to die in the wintertime. Things My Grandfather Must Have Said. Mark Cox. SUP

I Want to Die Like-A Lazarus Die. Unknown. SSUS

I Want to Die While You Love Me. Georgia Douglas Johnson. APT-1; ISC; TCAPo

I want to drown in good-salt water. Miss Millay Says Something Too. Samuel Hoffenstein. NBLV

I want to enter death. Desire. Claribel Alegría. LoL

I want to fiddle with a pipe and look profound. Why I Want to Be the Next Poet Laureate. Elliot Fried. SUP

I want to find your texture under water. Touching You Underwater. Stephen J. Lyons. PasH

I want to gather your darkness. To Drink. Jane Hirshfield. PasH

I want to get the screams in here. Elvis Presley. Rochelle Nameroff. SwNoth

I want to get up early one more morning. At Least. Raymond Carver. GoPo

I Want to Go Home. Unknown. SSUS

I Want to Go to Keta. Kobena Eyi Acquah. NAfrP

I Want to Hear a Yankee Doodle Tune. George M. Cohan. ReLy

I Want To Join the Band. Unknown. SSUS

I want to kill myself. Dezső Kosztolányi. IQMS Fr. Laments of a Poor Little Child.

I want to know the unity in all things and the difference. Ballad. A. R. Ammons. OxBoAm

I want to know too. Belief and disbelief. God and the G-Spot. Ellen Bass. NevBe

I want to live in the shade of your face. Tinfoil. Joyce Mansour. MFP; YaTCFP, tr. by Martin Sorrell

I want to look at what happened. Ofay-watcher Looks Back. Mongane Wally Serote. NAfrP; TSAP

I want to love my real father so he can see me. Range of It, The. Michael Klein. WiU

I Want to Love You Very Much. 'Marnia. LW

I want to make a toast to some victory. Childhood. Hoda Hussein. PoArWo, tr. by Cornelia Al-Khaled

I want to make you. Haiku. Sonia Sanchez. ISC

I want to mow while riding. (LL) Needs. A. R. Ammons. NIL-7; NIP-4

I want to praise bodies. To Praise. Ellen Bass. FiBr

I want to return to the first urges, those urges that seemed so unconscious of their beginnings. To Return to the Urges Unconscious of their Beginnings. Pham Tien Duat. AmFaPo, tr. by Kevin Bowen and Ngo Vinh Hai

I Want to Revise This Sequence. Nicole Brossard. YaTCFP, tr. by Marilyn Hacker

I want to ride the currents. Riding the Currents. Susan Bright. TiP2

I want to scream into the pink hearing aid nestled in his hairy ear, Where is your fist?. Finding His Fist. Patricia Smith. SpirFl

I want to see the slim palm-trees. Heritage. Gwendolyn B. Bennett. ColAP; NAAPv.2

I want to sing: to be a flower. Song. Rafael Alberti. RaW, tr. by Charles Guenther and Hardie St. Martin

I Want to Sleep. Jorge Guillén. RaW; WoPoe, tr. by James Wright

I want to sleep the sleep of the apples. Ghazal of the Dark Death. Federico García Lorca. WED, tr. by Robert Bly

I want to sleep with you side by side. I Want to Sleep with You. Joyce Mansour. YaTCFP, tr. by Mary Ann Caws

I Want to Speak with the Blood That Lies Down.   James Tipton.   GeoH

I want to study philosophy in Paris.   Frontier.   Oswald de Andrade.   TCLAP, tr. by Flavia Vidal

I want to take the word back into my body, back.   Cajun.   Sheryl St. Germain.   OPRER

I want to tell jokes.   Tenderitis.   Maxine Chernoff.   IllVoic

I want to tell what happens.   Washing Your Hair.   Lucia Cordell Getsi.   IllVoic

I want to tell you.   All the Trees.   Ellen Bass.   PfS

I want to tell you about the emptiness of Presque Isle.   Presque Isle, Maine.   Tammy Armstrong.   Coast

I want to tell you the story of that winter.   Provenance.   Joseph Stroud.   PoChi

I want to travel the common road.   Common Road, The.   Silas H. Perkins.   ITBLP

I want to understand light years.   Brown Rosellen.   FFC

I want to understand the steep thing.   Climbing You.   Erica Jong.   PoA 2002

I want to wash my father's face.   Last Acts.   Sharon Olds.   NIP-4

I want to write a love poem for the girls I kissed in seventh grade.   Practicing.   Marie Howe.   FaoP

I want to write a poem.   N-word, The.   Evie Shockley.   BRtP

I want to write, but out comes foam.   Intensity and Height.   César Vallejo.   PoetW, tr. by Clayton Eshleman

I Want to Write like a Postcard.   Rebecca Radner.   WhBo

I want to write you.   Love Poem.   Linda Pastan.   NIL-7; NIP-4

I want you for my bodyguard.   On Guard.   Marge Piercy.   PoDa

I want you to feel.   Yearn On.   Katie Donovan.   NIrP

I want you to have some of what I'm having.   Labor Day Picnic Poem.   Todd Colby.   HeMarv

I Want You to Know.   Micere Githae Mugo.   HAWP

I want you to plunge into my life.   Deep Pool, The.   James Laughlin.   PoDa

I want your body.   When You Call Again.   Francine Witte.   PfS

I wanta say just gotta say something.   Beautiful Black Men.   Nikki Giovanni.   WaAnP

I wanted.   Retrospect.   Erich Fried.   GTCP, tr. by Stuart Hood

I wanted a good place to settle.   Cold Mountain.   Han-shan (Cold Mountain).   CCL1, tr. by Gary Snyder

I wanted a rib sandwich.   Rib Sandwich.   William J. Harris.   UnSA

I wanted a stamp for the parcel of figs.   Encounter at the Post Office Counter.   Christopher Pilling.   NLP

I wanted an older brother to show me.   My Mysterious Body.   Rane Arroyo.   BeDoSh

I wanted my name.   Poem for Ed "Whitey" Ford, A.   Jonathan Holden.   MoASP

I wanted so ably.   World, The.   Robert Creeley.   NoP-4; NoP-5; PmAP; VCAP

I wanted the heart to scream.   Song of the Burning.   David Wojahn.   SwNoth

I wanted them over.   Say Ja.   Tom Mandel.   PmAP

I wanted to be a priestess of love.   Priestess of Love.   Ann Elizabeth Hostetler.   ACAMVP

I wanted to be sure to reach you.   To the Harbormaster.   Frank O'Hara.   OxBoAm; VCAP

I wanted to be touched, so I went walking.   Who Owns the Night and Lease Stars.   Reginald Shepherd.   AmPoNex

I wanted to describe the wild iris.   Wild Iris.   Patricia Y. Ikeda.   WhBo

I Wanted to Dream the Mailman.   Vivian Lamarque.   CItWP, tr. by Cinzia Sartini Blum and Lara Trubowitz

I wanted to feel exalted so I picked up.   James Harrison.   BodElec Fr. Letters to Yesenin.

I wanted to find you inside me.   Death of the Kiss.   Pura López Colomé.   RMCMP, tr. by Forrest Gander

I wanted to get into the feathers alright.   Seven Dwarfs, Each on His Deathbed, Remember Snow White, The.   Ron Koertge.   SUP

I wanted to go down to where the roots begin.   Origins.   Eric Ormsby.   NoP-4; NoP-5

I wanted to have a wedding.   Wedding Party.   Allison Joseph.   AmPoNex; ExTi; MPUn

I wanted to hear.   Static.   Mary Barnard.   APT-2

I Wanted to Kill My King.   Sarah Kirsch.   GTCP, tr. by Irmgard Hunt

I wanted to know my mother when she sat.   Leroy.   Imamu Amiri Baraka.   PmAP

I wanted to know what it was like before we.   Waving Good-Bye.   Gerald Stern.   GoPo; PoA 2002

I wanted to see the self, so I looked at the mulberry.   Self and the Mulberry, The.   Marvin Bell.   BodElec; CAP-8

I wanted to shoot the jerk.   At 4:00 A.M. Asleep.   John Balaban.   SUP

I wanted to stand on the sea.   Seer, The.   Abd al-Karim Kassid.   IrPoTo, tr. by Chuck Miller and Saadi A. Simawe

I wanted to start the story.   We Are Going to Be Here Now.   Primus St. John.   GT

I wanted to stay with my dog.   May.   Bruce Weigl.   P180

I wanted to teach him the names of flowers.   Michael Longley.   ModIr Fr. Mayo Monologues.

I wanted to tell you about it.   I Wanted to Tell You.   Martine Broda.   YaTCFP, tr. by Mary Ann Caws

I wanted to write you a letter.   Letter from a Contract Worker.   Antonio Jacinto.   PoetW, tr. by Margaret Dickinson and Michael Wolfers

I wanted to write you a letter.   Letter From a Contract Worker.   Antonio Jacinto.   PML, tr. by Margaret Dickinson

I wanted you here in the wards, where I am the doctor! (LL)   Variations on a Theme by William Carlos Williams.   Kenneth Koch.   AmWit; NAMCP V.2; NBLV; NIL-7; NIP-4; NoAM; NoP-4; NoP-5; OxBoAm; PmAP; PoPoPo; WaAnP

I Wanted You in the Kitchen of My Heart.   James Tipton.   GeoH

I wanted you to listen to the bells.   Swarm, The.   Jorie Graham.   NAMCP V.2

I warn you to remain velvet and motionless on whatever.   Wildlife.   Tracy Philpot.   AmPoNex

I was a blue night.   Van Gogh.   Yi Sanghûi.   EcSo, tr. by Jennifer M. Lee

I was a body. I was a laboratory. I was okay with that.   Saltbox Brothel.   Danielle Pafunda.   BeDoSh

I was a boy when I left home.   Homecoming.   Ho Ch'e Ch'ang.   NDACCP, tr. by Kenneth Rexroth

I was a child when first I read your books.   To Elizabeth Barrett Browning.   Bessie Rayner Parkes.   VWP

I was a clockwork doll that night.   Clockwork Doll.   Dahlia Ravikovitch.   FIT, tr. by Robert Friend

I was a cottage maiden.   Cousin Kate.   Christina Georgina Rossetti.   VWP

I was a diver then.   Reprieve, The.   Elizabeth Garrett.   NeBl

I was a dog in my former life, a very good.   Promotion, The.   James Tate.   OxBoAm

I was a girl waiting by the roadside for my boyfriend to come.   Elwha River, The.   Gary Snyder.   NoAM

I was a glutton. (LL)   Epitaphs: "Drowning / I felt for a moment reaching towards me."   Charles Reznikoff.   APT-2; NAMCP V.1

I was a humdrum person.   What Is This Thing Called Love?   Cole Porter.   ReLy

I was a mere boy in a stone-cutter's shop.   Abraham.   Delmore Schwartz.   ChIV-1; TaR

I was a murderer ninety times a day. (LL)   Fire, the lamp, and I, were alone together, The.   Mary Elizabeth Coleridge.   ViWPN; VWP

I was a pawn when we began this. I bowed to your black majesty.   Lament of the White Queen.   Ann Drysdale.   TCAWP

I was a peasant girl from Germany.   Edgar Lee Masters.   NAAPv.1; NAMCP V.1; NoAM Fr. Spoon River Anthology.

I Was a Phony Baloney!   Stephanie Brown.   AmPoNex; BodElec

I was a quick-footed, long-eared hare, just snatched from my mother's.   Meleager.   HePo, tr. by Barbara Hughes Fowler

I was a real phony baloney.   I Was a Phony Baloney!   Stephanie Brown.   AmPoNex; BodElec

I was a rebel, if you please.   Address by an Ex-Confederate Soldier to the Grand Army of the Republic, An.   Maurice Thompson.   CBCWP

I was a ripe fig.   Paranoia.   Salwa Al-Neimi.   PoArWo, tr. by Subhi Hadidi and Nathalie Handal

I was a seven-year-old taken by the current.   Once near the Border.   David Mura.   MAAN

I was a shepherd to fools.   Rudyard Kipling.   WoPoe Fr. Epitaphs of the War [1914–1918].

I was a sorry, sorry. (Baloney.). (LL)   I Was a Phony Baloney!   Stephanie Brown.   AmPoNex; BodElec

"I Was a Stranger and Ye Took Me In."   Mary E. Tucker.   CBWP-1

I was a stranger in the city.   Foggy Day (in London Town), A.   Ira Gershwin.   ReLy

I was a stricken deer, that left the herd.   William Cowper.   NAEL-6v1; NAEL-7v1 Fr. Task, The.

I was a voice. (LL)   Anna Liffey.   Eavan Boland.   BodElec; ModIr

I was a week away from the red chip when they outed me.   Rounding the Horn.   L. S. Asekoff.   BAP-97

I was a youth of studious mind.   Evolutional Erotics.   Constance Naden.   ViWPN

I was a youth of studious mind.   Constance Naden.   VWP Fr. Evolutional Erotics.

I was about five years old, and Gamal Abdul-Nasser could lift a whole building.   Child Hunting Tales, A.   Magdy El-Gabry.   AnVo, tr. by Mohamed Enani

I Was About Three Years of Age.   Hanny Michaelis.   TuT, tr. by Peter van de Kamp

I was again beside my Love in a dream.   Mathilde Blind.   ViWPN Fr. Love in Exile.

I was alone on a sunny shore.   Forest Lake.   Edith Södergran.   WPoS, tr. by Stina Katchadourian

I was already.   In China.   Terry Wolverton.   WiU

I was always called in early for dinner. don't Forget. Stephen Berg. PoChi

I was an Arab. Fantasy, A. Mathilde Blind. PoBW; ViWPN; VWP

I was an ice baby. Anne Sexton. NAMCP V.2 *Fr.* Death Baby, The.

I was angry with my friend. William Blake. NAEL-6v2; NAEL-7v2; NoP-4; NoP-5; NPBRoP; NPeEn; OxAEP-2; OxBEV; SoSe-8; TFi; WaAnP; WeW-3 *Fr.* Songs of Experience.

I was as dark and slim as a Polynesian girl. Sketch. Cecília Meireles. TCLAP, *tr.* by Luiz Fernández García

I was asking for something specific and perfect for my city. Mannahatta. Walt Whitman. MoAmPo

I was asleep but my heart stayed awake. Song. Bible, *O.T.* WPoS

I was asleep when the guest came. Look-Alike, The. Valerie Gillies. EdScPo

I was back in Buffalo when you died and when I came out for your. Fred Wah. NLPA *Fr.* This Dendrite Map: Father / Mother Haibun.

I was bee-belly setting out from the island of the first morning. Songs of Good Hope, The. Michele Leggott. VaPo

I was blue / Just as blue as I could be. Blue Skies. Irving Berlin. ReLy

I was born 26 july 1939 in ventersdorp. Spanner in the what? works. Wopko Jensma. TSAP

I was born a country boy on Sundays. Empty Place at the Celebration, An. José Ángel Valente. RaW, *tr.* by Ralph Nelson and Hardie St. Martin

I was born a foreigner. Minority. Imtiaz Dharker. NeBl

I was born a white boy. Balthazar's Poem. Chris Searle. RSaN

I Was Born Almost Ten Thousand Years Ago. *Unknown.* OBCoV

I Was Born at Birth of Blossoms. Rosalía de Castro. STV, *tr.* by John Frederick Nims

I was born downtown on a wintry day. Recapitulations. Karl Shapiro. TaR

I was born for poetry. Born for Poetry. Chellapilla Venkata Sastri. HotL, *tr.* by V. Narayana Rao and David Shulman

I was born in a dough trough. Kukutis's Fruitless Bread. Marcelijus Martinaitis. TWW, *tr.* by Laima Sruoginis

I was born in a Free City, near the North Sea. Curriculum Vitae. Lisel Mueller. IllVoic

I was born in a state. Politics of Memory, The. Kevin Hearle. CalPo

I was born in Belfast between the mountain and the gantries. Carrickfergus. Louis MacNeice. NAEL-6v2; NAMCP V.1; NoAM; PNI

I was born in Belgium, I am Belgian. Place and Date. Leonard Nolens. TuT, *tr.* by Michael O'Loughlin

I was born in Boston in. American Poem, An. Eileen Myles. WiU

I was born in Kansas. Sunflower. Mack David. ReLy

I Was Born in Lucerne. Philip Levine. CAP-8

I was born in Mississippi. Poem for Myself (Or Blues for a Mississippi Black Boy), A. Etheridge Knight. InGu; PoPoPo

I was born in the Congo. Ego Tripping (There May Be a Reason Why). Nikki Giovanni. GT; InGu; ISC; RaBo; TWF

I was born on an Irish sea of eggs and porter. HMS *Glory.* Charles Causley. FaBoWar

I Was Born on the Twenty-First in Spring. Alda Merini. CItWP, *tr.* by Cinzia Sartini Blum and Lara Trubowitz

I was born out of sun-rays. Iris. Jacques Perk. TuT, *tr.* by Peter van de Kamp

I was born tearing fabrics from dawn. Cielo Min. Natalia Toledo. RMCMP, *tr.* by Alberto A. Ríos

I was born the year of the loon. Chronicle. Mei-Mei Berssenbrugge. OpBo

I was born to the god's disappointment. Under an Impure Star. Armanda Guiducci. CItWP, *tr.* by Cinzia Sartini Blum and Lara Trubowitz

I was born to this snowy-red earth. Song Taught to Joseph, The. Ray A. Young Bear. AF

I was born with a stone in my hand. In My Other Life. Shara McCallum. AmPoNex

I was born with twelve fingers. Lucille Clifton. CAP-8

I Was Buried in Janzoor. Khaled Mattawa. LegDan

I was buried near this dyke [*or* Dike]. Epitaph, An. William Blake. OBCoV

I was calling airspeed. Where We Crashed. Richard Hugo. PWW2

I was Capulet, he Romeo. Romeo Is Dead. H. Palmer Hall. IaFF

I was coming back from. Truck, The. John A. Stone. BloBone

I was coming to that. (LL) Welsh Incident. Robert Graves. OBSP; OxBEV; WaAnP

I was created for one man alone. Don't Ever Leave Me. Oscar Hammerstein, II. ReLy

I was deformed like an angel fallen among cottons in a courtyard. Chap. 10 Book 2. Blas de Otero. RaW, *tr.* by Hardie St. Martin

I was descending from the mountains of sleep. Afternoon Sleep. Robert Bly. WoPoe

I was doing nothing in particular. Pain. Charles Simic. BodElec

I was driving into the wind. Penitence. John Burnside. StAl

I was drowsy, but my heart was awake. Listen! *Unknown.* WoPoe *Fr.* Song of Solomon, The [*or* The Song of Songs].

I was eating a chicken sandwich with mayonnaise. Frenchie. Stephen Dobyns. BodElec

I was eleven the first time I saw it. Hail. Debra Kang Dean. NevBe

I was empty as a new car, and. Reading *Bonjour, Tristesse* at the Florence Crittenden Home for Unwed Mothers. Diane Wakoski. GeoHom

I was enriched, not casting after marvels. Magnificat in Little. Léonie Adams. OxBoAm

I Was Fair Beat. Robert Garioch. EdScPo; OBCoV

I was familiar with the word. April in Houston. Dolores de Iruretagoyena de Humphrey. ReBoTo

I was feeling low. I tried to make a sandwich but all I could find were two. Ecstasy Notebook. Thomas Lux. MotU

I was fishing in the abandoned reservoir. Quinnapoxet. Stanley Kunitz. LoL

I was flying over sydney. Flying. Michael Dransfield. BMAP

I was following a man. Following a Man. John Ash. HarvBoo

I was foretold, your rebel[l] sex. Deposition from Love, A. Thomas Carew. BASC; CavPo

I was four in this photograph fishing. Fifth Grade Autobiography. Rita Dove. ISC; NIL-7; NIP-4

I was four months gone. Ringing Chamber, The. Pauline Stainer. BeAl

I was given the Silver Star. Ace. Mark Pawlak. PrTe

I was glad to sit down. Kinaxixi. Agostinho Neto. PoetW; WoPoe, *tr.* by W. S. Merwin

I was going along a dusty highroad. Mountain Talk. A. R. Ammons. LPSFW; OxBoAm

I was going to ardently pursue this day. Topophilia. Mary Ruefle. BAP-97

I was going to be a radio man. I Was Going to Be. Larry Goodell. ICANM

I was going to say something. Ancestor. Thomas Kinsella. ModIr; NPeEn; OxBEV; PBCIP

(I was going up to say something.) NoP-4; NoP-5

I was going to the river for water. Mirabai. WPoS

I was going up to say something. Thomas Kinsella. *See* I was going to say something.

I was hanging out my wash. Red Wool Shirt, The. Alden Nowlan. Coast

I was helping my mother. Fifteen. Patricia Pogson. NLP

I was here before, a long time ago. Lines Composed Over Three Thousand Miles from Tintern Abbey. Billy Collins. OxBoAm; WaAnP

I was hoping to be happy by seventeen. Saturday at the Canal. Gary Soto. P180; TWF

I was ill, lying on my bed of old papers. Secret Garden, The. Rita Dove. NoAM

I was in blossom when I was a child. Ballade. Charles, Duc d' Orléans. WoPoe, *tr.* by Tony Barnstone and Willis Barnstone

I was in deep, through. Arrival. Debra Kang Dean. UrbNat

I was in Hawaii, but the letter. How I Got the Word. Marvin Bell. BodElec

I was in Princeton of all. Where I Was. Dan Brown. P180

I was in the bookstore, reading the ends of mysteries. Three Songs. Rachel Wetzsteon. RA

I was in town before my end. I knew more deeply. How I Shaded the Book. Michael Burkard. LaCa

I was in Viareggio relatively often, seven or eight times. Viareggio. Günter Eich. MotU, *tr.* by David Walker

I was innocent of grief. Lament of Mary, The. *Unknown.* IQMS, *tr.* by Adam Makkai

I was inside Coltrane's blue chords. Set Piece. Houston A., Jr. Baker. BtF

I was invested in mother-earth, the crypt of roots. Geoffrey Hill. NAMCP V.2; NoAM *Fr.* Mercian Hymns.

I was joyful when I was told. House Beyond, The. John Fitzgerald. BBMWP, *tr.* by Joseph P. Clancy

I was just beginning to feel in the mood. Old Husband Suspects Adultery, An. Gavin Ewart. NoAM

I was just setting on the porch. This Is How It Comes. R. T. Smith. LiTh

I was just / shoving off. To Wang Lun. Li Po. CCL1, *tr.* by David Young

I was just turned twenty-one. Edgar Lee Masters. AmWaPo; APT-1 *Fr.* Spoon River Anthology.

I was kissed once. Kiss, The. Alice Walker. GT

I was kneeling in the willow when. Praying. Cynthia Cruz. IAoNAP

I was late in understanding the meaning of humility. Odysseus Elytis. GifTon *Fr.* Anoint the Ariston.

I was leaning across your chest. Hydromaniac. Rosemary Tonks. EmeKit

I was leaving my fifty-eighth year. 1994. Lucille Clifton. FuFl

I was like Beirut. Like Beirut. Haim Guri. NRoS, *tr.* by Esther Raizen

I was listening to Gregorian chants. Quick Poem, A. Adam Zagajewski. PoCho, *tr.* by Clare Cavanagh

I was living in New York. Mary's Dream. Van K. Brock. AllShUp; SwNoth

I Was Looking for the University. Clarence Major. GT

I was looking for your hair. A un Desconocido. Lorna Dee Cervantes.

TouFir

I was making a fire in my hands. (LL) Oranges. Gary Soto. CAP-8; NAMCP V.2; NoAM; WeW-3

I was making for the village inn. Conscription, The. Tu Fu [or Du Fu]. CCL1, tr. by E. H. Parker

I was making my way home late one night. Aisling. Paul Muldoon. PNI

I was mindless. Potter's Wheel, The. Calvin Forbes. GT

I was miserable, of course, for I was seventeen. Mingus at the Showplace. William Matthews. OxBoAm; PoA 2002; SeSe

I was most interested in what they looked like dead. Lilacs for Ginsberg. Gerald Stern. CAP-8

I was my own ghost that walked among the hills. About Scotland, &C. Ruthven Todd. EdScPo

I was never able to recite a fable. You Were Never Lovelier. Johnny Mercer. ReLy

I was nine years old. Luck. Raymond Carver. LaCa

I was not a good daughter. Persephone. Kathleen Norris. HW

I was not allowed to live my life. Essential, The. Aleksandar Ristovic. BeAl, tr. by Charles Simic

I was not born from your womb. Angola. Amélia Veiga. HAWP, tr. by Julia Kirst

I was not born to Helicon, nor dare. Gratulatory to Mr. Ben Johnson for His Adopting of Him to Be His Son, A. Thomas Randolph. NPeEn

I was not in safety, neither had I rest, neither was I quiet; yet trouble came. (LL) Bible, O.T. NPeEn; OBVE Fr. Job.

I was not more than five. A girl in the fields. Nudes. Rodney Jones. MAAN

I was not; now I am—a few days hence. Mystery, The. Paul Laurence Dunbar. APN-2; NAAPv.1

I was not ready for your form to be cold. Periodic Table of Ethereal Elements. Lucie Brock-Broido. AWPTFC

I was not sorrowful, I could not weep. Spleen. Ernest Dowson. MoBrPo

I Was Not There. Karen Gershon. HP

I was not useful? So. Fidelity Rewarded. Dora Greenwell. VWP

I was of delicate mind. I stepped aside for my needs. Rudyard Kipling. NPeEn Fr. Epitaphs of the War [1914–1918].

I was on a tractor in the rain. Pragmatist. Ken Babstock. OpeFie

I was on a white coast once. Canticle. David Shapiro. OxBoAm

I was on an English boat going from Siracusa in Sicily to Tunis in North Africa. What Else (Part 2). Walter Abish. OnScMo

I was on my high. Thorn Merchant's Mistress, The. Yusef Komunyakaa. RACG

I was on my way to see my woman. Blink Your Eyes. Sekou Sundiata. FaoP

I was on the couch when the jehova's witnesses came. Patrick Pardo. ReBoTo

I was one of maybe 20 people sitting in a dark theater on Fourth Stree. Puffy Jacket. Amy Fusselman. HeMarv

I was one of the saved. As a Child. Robert Bly. InvLad

I Was One of Them. Gurram Jashuva. HotL, tr. by V. Narayana Rao

I was one out of a hundred, out of thousands. When They Robbed Me of My Name. Nora Strejilevich. MirDau, tr. by Celeste Kostopulos-Cooperman

I was only a young man. Hook. James Wright. OxBoAm

I was our brother / Iscariot. (LL) Peter and John. Elinor Wylie. MakPoe; MoAmPo

I was out in the early evening, taking a walk in the fields to think about this. Strange Fruit. Joy Harjo. SeSe

I was out with lanterns. Self Portrait in Froehlichia. Cynthia Cruz. IAoNAP

I was parading the Côte d'Azur. My Father's Geography. Afaa Michael Weaver. GT; OxAAAP; PBCAP

I was passionate. Lal Ded. WPoS

I was playing hopscotch on the slate. Our Sharpeville. Ingrid de Kok. HAWP

I was playing, I suppose. When It Happened. Hilda Schiff. HP

I was pleased by blue hydrangea because at. Hydrangea. Paul Muldoon and Gerald Stern. GPPA

I was proud of the Coca-Cola stitched in red. Coke. Philip Dacey. SUP

I was pulling veronica out of the lawn when this hornet came. A. R. Ammons. NoAM Fr. Sphere.

I was reading about rationalism. Bat, The. Jane Kenyon. LoL

I was resting comfortably. Just in Time. Betty Comden and Adolph Green. ReLy

I was riding around Albany. Night Robert Frost Died, The. Lyn Lifshin. VisFro

I was riding one of the best-loved horses in the world. Out West. Bill Manhire. EmeKit

I was run over by the truth one day. To Whom It May Concern (Tell Me Lies about Vietnam). Adrian Mitchell. BeAl; FaBoWar; OBWP; RSaN

I Was Sent For. Lupenga Mphande. NAfrP; PML

I was sent forth from the power. Unknown. PFTM-1 Fr. Thunder, Perfect Mind, The.

I was sent in to see her. Tear. Thomas Kinsella. ModIr; NoP-4; NoP-5; OxBEV

I was sent into the woods for nuts. Eaten by the Wolf. Alexei Remizov. MotU, tr. by Nancy Condee

I was sent to fetch an eye. Naked Vision. Gwen Harwood. EmeKit; StAl

I was seven. 321738. Kiren Shoman. OWABP

I was seventy-seven, come August. Little Old Lady in Lavender Silk, The. Dorothy Parker. NBLV

I was sewing a seam one day. Seams. Hazel Hall. APT-1

I Was Sick and in Prison. Jones Very. ColAP; SacPr

I was sitting behind a somewhat neat old person. Concert. Josephine Miles. NALW

I was sitting in mcsoreley's. outside it was New York and beauti- / fully snowing. E. E. Cummings. NAMCP V.1; NoAM

I was sitting in my study. Papa's Letter. Unknown. WeW-3

I was sitting on the roof with my grandmother. Coming of Age. Michael Palma. UnSA

I Was Sleeping Where the Black Oaks Move. Louise Erdrich. CAP-8; HATNAP; NoP-4; NoP-5; PoPoPo

I was small and half-believed I could disappear. Blink. Cecilia Woloch. RaF

I was so assailed by the memory. Quant Souvenir Me Ramentoit. Charles, Duc d' Orléans. WoPoe, tr. by Fred Chappell

I was so buoyant. Bella Akhatovna Akhmadulina. TCRusP, tr. by Daniel Weissbort

I was so chill, and overworn, and sad. Song. Anna Wickham. MoBrPo

I was so sick last night I. Morning After. Langston Hughes. NAMCP V.1; NBLV; NoAM; OBCoV

I was somewhere in Utah or Wyoming. When My Car Broke Down. John Brehm. PoDa

I Was Speaking of Oranges to a Lady. José Garcia Villa. WoPoe

I was squatting beside Carmel's lilies of the valley. Rain in April. Kerry Hardie. NIrP

I was standing at the pond, in my posh fly fishing class, when a squeal. Mother Nature. Amy Fusselman. HeMarv

I was standing in front of The Magic Mirror. Magic Mirror, The. Edward Hirsch. PoDa

I was standing in the bedroom. I Don't Remember Christmas. Richard Maltby, Jr. ReLy

I was standing in the frozen garden. Dirt. Chase Twichell. PfSP

I was standing outside the killing shed. Goanna. Anthony Lawrence. PML

I was standing there. Oral Tradition, The. Eavan Boland. PBCIP

I was standing there. Saitō Mokichi. CAoMJL1, tr. by Amy Vladek Heinrich

I was sticking my hands into his pockets. Inside Father's Pockets. Martha Rhodes. ExTi

I was stolen by the gypsies. My parents stole me right back. I Was Stolen by the Gypsies. Charles Simic. MotU

I Was Suffering Exile. Nahabed Kouchag. WoPoe, tr. by Desmond O'Grady

I was suffering exile like a rambling. I Was Suffering Exile. Nahabed Kouchag. WoPoe, tr. by Desmond O'Grady

I was summoned to the porter's lodge for an overseas call from California. Scrabble. David Starkey. ReTh

I was swimming. First Exercise. Michael Ryan. NevBe

I was takin' off my bonnet. Darwinism in the Kitchen. Unknown. NBLV

I was teaching my little sister how to fly when she broke her. Station (2). James Galvin. GiftCon

I was that lonely. (LL) Geranium, The. Theodore Roethke. EmeKit; WeW-3

I was The Gateway. Here they came and passed. Nacogdoches Speaks. Karle Wilson Baker. TiP2

I was the last passenger of the day. Bus, The. Leonard Cohen. HeIP-4

I was the one who waited in the garden. Resurrection, The. Elizabeth Jennings. HarvBoo

I was the only child of Frances Harris of Virginia. Edgar Lee Masters. NAAPv.1; NAMCP V.1; NoAM Fr. Spoon River Anthology.

I was the only girl under the stairs. Paul Muldoon. NoAM

I was the patriarch of the shining land. John Sutter. Yvor Winters. MoAmPo; NAMCP V.1; NoAM

I was the reflection of malevolence. Ugly Heart, The. Martha Anthony. InTrad

I was the rock. Child of Adam. Viola C. White. YaYoPo

I was the slightest in the House. Emily Dickinson. NAAPv.1

I was the staunchest of our fleet. Derelict, The. Rudyard Kipling. NoAM

I was the type who would laugh at romance. It's Love Again. Sam Coslow. ReLy

I was the west. Vermont. Dan Chiasson. LegDan

I was thinking of the rotten candybar I bit into. La Jolla. In 3 Acts. J. Cody Peterson. FTtHH

I was thrashing on the couch. That Great Wingless Bird. Adrian C. Louis. UnSA

I was three-ish. Right Arm, The. Paul Muldoon. NoAM

I was thy Neighbour once, thou rugged Pile! Elegiac Stanzas: Suggested by a Picture of Peele Castle, in a Storm, Painted by Sir George Beaumont. William Wordsworth. NAEL-6v2; NAEL-7v2; NOBRP; NoP-4; NPBRoP; NPeEn; WaAnP

(I was thy neighbor once, thou rugged Pile!) GS; NoP-4

I was tired of being a woman. Consorting with Angels. Anne Sexton. MoWP; NALW

I was tired. So I lay down. Mnemonic. Li-Young Lee. UnSA

I was told look for blue. (LL) Blue: "As through marble or the lining of." Carl Phillips. BtF; OxAAAP

I was too late for the most important. Longing for Jail, A. Edvard Kocbek. PoSu, tr. by Michael Scammell and Veno Taufer

I was twelve, and did not. Lesson on Braces. Jean Valerie. SpirFl

I was upon my way to seek him there. (LL) Henry Wadsworth Longfellow. APN-1; TCAPo Fr. Tales of a Wayside Inn.

I Was Very Prolific. Suzanne Wise. AmPoNex

I was very prolific in my generating qualities. I Was Very Prolific. Suzanne Wise. AmPoNex

I was walking. Ode to Bicycles. Pablo Neruda. ArBi, tr. by Margaret Sayers Peden

I was walking along the Sea of Galilee. Walking along the Sea of Galilee. Dovid Knut. TCRusP, tr. by John Glad

I was walking behind Elliot Carter. Poem for Elliot Carter on His 90th Birthday. Alan Dugan. BodElec

I was walking home down a hill near our house on a balmy afternoon under the blossoms. Singing, The. C. K. Williams. CAP-8

I was walking in a government warehouse. Fifteen Million Plastic Bags. Adrian Mitchell. EmeKit; OBSV

I was walking near the hotel in the evening. Southern Dawn. Pier Paolo Pasolini. VCWP, tr. by Norman MacAfee and Luciano Martinengo

I was washing my daughter's hair. Name of God, The. Imtiaz Dharker. NeBl

I Was Washing Outside in the Darkness. Osip Emilevich Mandelstam. AF

I was watching a robin fly after a finch—the smaller bird. Detail. Eamon Grennan. StAl

I was watching for it, everytime watching, for the neck that was. Karen Volkman. AmPoNex

I was Willie Metcalf. Edgar Lee Masters. APT-1 Fr. Spoon River Anthology.

I was with Special Force, blue-X-ing raids. Trial. Ruth Padel. MFPA

I was with Ulysses, Odysseus son of Laertes. I Was with Ulysses. Pennar Davies. BBMWP, tr. by Joseph P. Clancy

I was wondering, did I write that I would get through this. Women. Kim Hyesun. CAMKP, tr. by Jiwon Shin

I was wrapped in black. Us. Anne Sexton. MPUn

I was wrong when I compared the mask of my own face. Gift, The. Rebecca Seiferle. ICANM; PoChi

I was your rebellious son. To My Mother. Wendell Berry. GoPo; PoA 2002

I Wash. Martine Broda. YaTCFP, tr. by Mary Ann Caws

I Wash the Shirt. Anna Swirszczynska [or Swir]. BLT

I wash your ankles. Mary Magdalene. Louise Erdrich. CAP-8

I washed a load of clothes. Alone for a Week. Dolores Kendrick. FFC

I wasn't driving. Bus Driver Poem, The. Khaled Mattawa. AmPoNex

I wasn't the first one. Wine and Wooing. Donny O'Rourke. EdScPo

I wasn't with you when death came. When Death Came. Adam Zagajewski. VCWP, tr. by Renata Gorczynski

I wasted so much time. Face in the Depths of the Desert, The. Rebecca Seiferle. ICANM

I watch a handsome young female. Interlude. Sarah Cortez. TiP2

I watch a man in the schoolyard. Speech Against Stone. Charles Martin. RA

I watch a streak of red that might have issued from Christ's breast. (LL) Soldiers Bathing. Frank Templeton Prince. MoBrPo; OBWP

I watch, and long have watched, with calm regret. William Wordsworth. OxBSo

I watch her in the corner there. Arachne. Rose Terry Cooke. APN-2; NAAPv.1

I watch her silhouette. Her Back to Me. Ed Stever. PasH

I watch me until I disappear and we. Analogue. Marie Ponsot. CLPP

I watch, O youths, this farmhouse and this place. Unknown. PriapPo Fr. Priapus Poems, The.

I watch Tai Chi per / forating my mind. I am the Babe of Joseph Stalin's Daughter. Rochelle Owens. PFTM-2

I watch the Beast as it licks itself. War. André Breton. AF, tr. by Mary Ann Caws and Jean-Pierre Cauvin

I watch the foam, its delicacy nothing. Foam. Claudio Rodríguez. RaW, tr. by Robert Mezey

I watch the happier people of the house. Neurasthenia. Agnes Mary Frances Robinson. NPeEn

I watch the Indians dancing to help the young corn at Taos pueblo. The old men squat in a ring. New Mexican Mountain. Robinson Jeffers. NoAM

I watch the limitless distance of autumn. Watching the Distances. Tu Fu [or Du Fu]. CrYelRi, tr. by Sam Hamill

I watch the sanitary state. Unknown. VerBaPo

I watch them killing my husband. Last Take. Carol Muske-Dukes. GeoHom

I watch through walls of windows where the rain. Bad Weather at the Airport. Kurt J. Fickert. OtW

I watch you. Watching You. Simon J. Ortiz. HATNAP

I watch you through my small window. Voyeur. Sandra M. Castillo. LiTh

I Watched. Kimmika L. H. Williams. BtF

I watched a rosebud very long. Symbols. Christina Georgina Rossetti. NALW

I watched her. Marina's Daughters, 1964. Rebecca Spears. TiP2

I watched him breathe. (LL) Race, The. Sharon Olds. InvLad; OxBoAm; RaBo

I watched its first green push. Tulip. Penny Harter. TWW

I watched my mother at the microphone. Nostalgia. Darryl Holmes. InTrad

I watched Odysseus go on board the flagship. Choice, The. Theo Dorgan. PML

I watched old squatting chimpanzee: he traced. Sporting Acquaintances. Siegfried Sassoon. OxBSo

I watched the hills drink the last color of light. Thought's End. Léonie Adams. MoAmPo

I watched the long road of the River of Stars. (LL) Drinking Alone with the Moon. Li Po. APT-1; ASA, tr. by Witter Bynner and Kang-hu Kiang

I watched the Moon around the House. Emily Dickinson. APN-2; NCAP

I watched the turtle dwindle day by day. Death and the Turtle. May Sarton. GoPo

I watched thee when the foe was at our side. Love and Death. Lord Byron. CAGL

I watched them float up the dark chimney. (LL) Sorrow. D. H. Lawrence. InoFa; NAMCP V.1; NPeEn; OBMV

I watched them once, at dusk, on television, run. Salmon. Jorie Graham. FaoP; StAl

I watched you roll it out. (LL) Bamboo Mat. Yüan Chĕn. CrYelRi; ErotSp, tr. by Sam Hamill

I watched you walk across the street. Dangerous World, The. Naomi Replansky. PoBW

I watches me climb. First Flight. Daniel Gerard Hoffman. OtW

I watered my horse at the Long Wall caves. Song. Ch'en Lin. ColAnChi, tr. by Burton Watson

I waved a gun last night. Self-Portrait as the Letter Y. Tracy K. Smith. LegDan

I wear a warning bloodcoat. Elba. Gerrit Kouwenaar. PFTM-2, tr. by Peter Nijmeijer

I wear America like Hendrix. Battle of Johnny Freedom, The. Damon McLaughlin. RWB

I wear bright colours. Elma Mitchell. NewEx

I wear the scaly skin of frequent fevers. Genius. Margit Szécsi. IQMS, tr. by Agnes Arany-Makkai

I weave with brightly colored strings. Falling in Love with Love. Lorenz Hart. ReLy

I Wed a Toy Bride. Yi Sang. CAMKP, tr. by Walter Lew

I weep and weep a tear. Tear, The. Martin Sorescu. VCWP, tr. by Seamus Heaney and Joana Russell-Gebbett

I weep for Adonais—he is dead! Adonais; An Elegy on the Death of John Keats. Percy Bysshe Shelley. CABP; InoFa; NAEL-6v2; NAEL-7v2; NOBRP; NoP-4; NoP-5; OxAEP-2; TFi; WaAnP

I weep for Adonis, "The lovely Adonis is dead." Lament for Adonis. Bion. HePo, tr. by Barbara Hughes Fowler

I weep. It is not yet daylight. (LL) House Slave, The. Rita Dove. AmAlph; NAMCP V.2; NoAM; OxAAAP

I welcome you, silvery moon. Early Graves, The. Friedrich Gottlieb Klopstock. GePo, tr. by J. W. Thomas

I well remember how some threescore years. Very Old Man. James Henry. OxBEV

I wend to the sea. Consolation. Micheál Fanning. IrLP

I wende to deeth, knight stith in stour. Unknown. OHMEL

I went along the slope of the days. Zacoalco or Landscape. Laura Solórzano. SPV, tr. by Jen Hofer

I went away from the lights of Fourteenth Street. Hello, Dolly! Jerry Herman. ReLy

I Went Back. A. R. Ammons. LPSFW

I went back in the alley. Homecoming. Langston Hughes. SAmP; TRP

I went before God, and he said. Love's Compensation. Voltairine de Cleyre. SWaP

I went by this building. Red Flower. Ann Turner. SSCS

I went down by Cascadilla. Cascadilla Falls. A. R. Ammons. OxBoAm

I went down ole Jamaica way. Lock and Key, The. Vicki-Ann Asservero. BtF

I went down the bank to pick fragrant plants. Buson. EMJL *Fr.* Spring Breeze on the Kema Embankment.

I went down to my garden patch. *Unknown.* TLR

I went down to the railway. Willow Song. Anne Stevenson. NoP-4

I went down to the river. Life Is Fine. Langston Hughes. NAMCP V.1; NBLV; PtR; SAmP

I Went Downtown. *Unknown.* TLR

I went east to Asia; I went west to Europe. *Unknown.* NAAPv.2

I went fishing for a lost word. Meaning of a Word, The. Vincent Woods. NIrP

I went for a walk over the dunes again this morning. Corsons Inlet. A. R. Ammons. ColAP; InGu; NAAL-5; NAMCP V.2; NoAM; NoP-4; NoP-5; OxBoAm; VCAP; WaAnP

I went in twilight, while the sun was lost. Abandoned House, The. César Dávila Andrade. SonAtl, *tr. by* Jenny Boarder, Thomas Boarder, Lisa Martin and Lisandro Pena

I went into a public-'ouse to get a pint o' beer. Tommy. Rudyard Kipling. CABP; FaBoWar; MoBrPo; NoP-4; NoP-5; OBWP; OxAEP-2; UV

I went into the kitchen just now to stir the black beans and rice. Kitchens. Aurora Levins Morales. PueRic

I Went Into the Maverick Bar. Gary Snyder. VCAP

I went into the wood one day. Fairy Story. Stevie Smith. NOxBChV; OBSP

I went on Friday afternoons. Au Tombeau de Mon Père. Ronald McCuaig. NOBAu

I Went Out. Velemir Khlebnikov. TCRusP, *tr. by* Kathy Lewis and Bob Perelman

I went out in the night. I Went Out. Velemir Khlebnikov. TCRusP, *tr. by* Kathy Lewis and Bob Perelman

I went out of the conf'rence to get a pint of beer. Mary Wilson. UV *Fr.* Harold Wilson's Selected Poems.

I went out one night with people from work. Matthew Rohrer. LegDan *Fr.* World at Night, The.

I went out to the hazel wood. Song of Wandering Aengus, The. William Butler Yeats. BLPJKO; ChAP; CtM; IrLP; IrV; MoBrPo; NAMCP V.1; PtR; RaBo; TFi; WaAnP

I went to a party. Rose on My Cake, The. Karla Kuskin. TLR

I went to a psychiatrist to cure my anxiety. Korean Women. Yi Kyŏngnim. EcSo, *tr. by* Peter H. Lee

I went to Anton Fransch's funeral. Funeral of Anton Fransch, The. Tatamkulu Afrika. TSAP

I went to Chartres for windows; angled my neck. Chacun à son goût. Dorothy Molloy. NIrP

I went to ch'ch, 'tother night. Sister Johnson's Speech. Maggie Pogue Johnson. CBWP-4

I went to Cuba on a raft I made. Belonging. Rafael Campo. AmPoNex; WiU

I went to Hsun-yang River to see a friend off at night. Song of the P'i-P'a. Po Chü-i. ChinPo, *tr. by* Ye Weilian [*or* Yeh Wei-lien *or* Wai-lim Yip]

I went to ma daddy. Hard Daddy. Langston Hughes. NAMCP V.1

I went to play with Billy. He. What Johnny Told Me. John Ciardi. TLR

I went to river last night. Voz de la Gente. Jimmy Santiago Baca. PmAP

I went to the animal fair. Animal Fair. *Unknown.* NTCP

I went to the church and walked by niggas dealin. Sundays. Seitu J. Hart. BRtP

I went to the dances at Chandlerville. Edgar Lee Masters. IllVoic; MoAmPo; NoAM *Fr.* Spoon River Anthology.

I went to the field to break. Unsteady Yellow. Tess Gallagher. InvLad

I went to the Garden of Love. William Blake. ItP; NAEL-6v2; NAEL-7v2; NoP-4; NoP-5; NPBRoP; NPeEn; OBGa; OxAEP-2; OxBEV; PoPoPo; TFi; TRP *Fr.* Songs of Experience.

I went to the Victory Burlesk twice, or maybe it was only once. Victory Burlesk, The. Margaret Atwood. MotU

I went to this party and all the ones who had disappeared. Bermuda Triangle. Joel Long. AmPoNex

I went to turn the grass once after one. Tuft of Flowers, The. Robert Frost. APT-1; MoAmPo; NAAPv.2

I went under cover of night. Nicodemus. Howard Nemerov. GI; TaR

I went up to the roof garden which was above the third floor. Motion. Yi Sang. CAMKP, *tr. by* Edward Mack

I went walkin' / By the blue bayou. Blue Bayou. Langston Hughes. NAMCP V.1

I went walking in the Rose Gardens. Washington Park. Gerald Costanzo. UrbNat

"I wept it! Ha ha!" (LL) Crying. Galway Kinnell. ChAP; NTCP

I were unkind unless that I did shed. Lines on His Companions Who Died in the Northern Seas. Thomas James. NOSC

I whisk the litter from my mother's tomb. Sweeping. Leslie Monsour. FFC

I whistled to companions, sang "Chopping Wood." Entering Quiao Gorge and Anju Creek. Chen Zi'ang. CCL1, *tr. by* Stephen Owen

I who am dead a thousand years / And wrote this sweet archaic song. To a Poet a Thousand Years Hence. James Elroy Flecker. MoBrPo

I, who am Nature, the mother of all things, the mistress of all the elements. I Who Am Nature, Mother of All. Lucius Apuleius. HW

I who am singing these lines today. Enigmas, The. Jorge Luis Borges. PoCho, *tr. by* John Updike

I who am the beauty of the green earth and the white moon. Charge of the Goddess, The. Doreen Valiente. HW, *tr. by* Starhawk

I who by day am function of the light. James Vincent Cunningham. APT-2 *Fr.* Epigrams: A Journal.

I who employ a poet's tongue. Timid Lover. Countee Cullen. ColAP

I who have always believed too much in words. (LL) Fly. W. S. Merwin. ChAP; OWoS

I Who Have Nothing. Bĕkes. IrPoTo, *tr. by* Abdul Kadir Said Ferhadi

I who have yearned for you and wept. Regret. Chŏng Sŏ. CATKP, *tr. by* Peter H. Lee

I, who in times before, with youthful mind. Miklós Zrínyi. IQMS *Fr.* Zrinyiad, The.

I, who leapt beneath the Mtskhetian white moon. Lines Written During a Sleepless Night in Tbilisi. Bella Akhatovna Akhmadulina. ARWW, *tr. by* Catriona Kelly

I who live here, it is I. Karen Press. TSAP

I who picked up the neat. Eleanor's Letters. Donald Hall. GoPo

I, who used to ward off the starlings and that snatcher. Antipater of Sidon. HePo, *tr. by* Barbara Hughes Fowler

I who wait for myself. Poetry Calendar, A. Chimako Tada. VCWP, *tr. by* Naoshi Koriyama and Edward Lueders

I Who Was Born. Adriann Roland Holst. TuT, *tr. by* Desmond Egan

I, who was lower than any worm. Seven. Natan Zach. FIT, *tr. by* Robert Friend

I whole in body, and in mind. Isabella Whitney. NoP-5 *Fr.* Manner of Her Will and What She Left to London and to All Those in It, at Her Departing, The.

I will accept thy will to do and be. Bruised Reed Shall He Not Break, A. Christina Georgina Rossetti. OxAEP-2

I will arise and go now, and go to Innisfree. Lake-Isle of Innisfree, The. William Butler Yeats. BLPJKO; CABP; ChAP; ClHu; HeIP-4; IPoFL; MoBrPo; NAEL-6v2; NAEL-7v2; NAMCP V.1; NoAM; NoP-4; NoP-5; OBEV; OxAEP-2; PoPoPo; TFi; UV; WaAnP

I will arise and go now, and go to Inverness. Cockney of the North, The. Harry Graham. UV

I will arise with my tomahawk in my hand. I Will Arise with My Tomahawk. *Unknown.* AmWaPo, *tr. by* Jesse Walter Fewkes

I will at once follow the vows. Kyunyŏ, Great Master. CATKP *Fr.* Eleven Poems on the Ten Vows of the Universally Worthy Bodhisattva.

I Will Be Arriving Next Thursday in My Wedding-Dress. Selima Hill. NeBrP

I will be born in one week. June 20. Lucille Clifton. PoChi

I will be in Ostia. Ostia Will Receive You. Friederike Mayröcker. PFTM-2, *tr. by* Beth Bjorklund

I will be sorry for their childishness. (LL) Coventry Patmore. OBEV; OxAEP-2; SoSe-8 *Fr.* Unknown Eros, The.

I will be the gladdest thing. Afternoon on a Hill. Edna St. Vincent Millay. APT-1; ChAP; NTCP

I will be your lover. Bush Speaks, The. Ernest G. Moll. NOBAu

I will begin by mentioning the word. Phase Four. John Berryman. BodElec

I will blame him. After Listening to Jack Teagarden .... James McKean. SeSe

I Will Bow and Be Simple. *Unknown.* TCAPo

I will break the back. Hwang Chini. CATKP, *tr. by* David R. McCann

I Will Bring You Twin Grays. Marla Big Boy. ReEnLa

I will build a house of rest. House of Rest, The. Julia Ward Howe. SWaP

I will build you a house. Tou Wan Speaks to Her Husband Liu Sheng. Rita Dove. ESEAA

I will build you a house of windows to let. Song of a Thousand Empty Hands. Adele Ne Jame. PoArWo

I will choose a place where the snakes feel safe. Ideal Retreat, The. Khong Lo. EaWin, *tr. by* W. S. Merwin and Nguyen Ngoc Bich

I will confesse. Hymne to Love, An. Robert Herrick. NOSC

I will consider my son William. Arrival. Jeffrey Harrison. NevBe

I will consider the outnumbering dead. Merlin. Geoffrey Hill. TRP

I Will Cut Out the Middle Watch. Hwang Chini. WoPoe, *tr. by* John S. Major

I will die in Miami in the sun. Variations on a Text by Vallejo. Donald Justice. CAP-8; NAMCP V.2; NoAM; VCAP

I will die in Paris, on a rainy day. Black Stone Lying on a White Stone. César Vallejo. PoCho; TCLAP; WED, *tr. by* Robert Bly and John Knoepfle

I will enjoy thee now my Celia, come. Rapture, A. Thomas Carew. BASC; CABP; NAEL-6v1; NAEL-7v1; OxAEP-1

I will enjoy thee now my Celia, come. Thomas Carew. PBRV *Fr.* Rapture, A.

I will find that it's still there. (LL) Mementos, 1. W. D. Snodgrass. MoAmPo; NoP-4; NoP-5; OxBoAm; VCAP

I will get me to the wood. After Ch'u Yuan. Ch'u Yüan. NDACCP

I will gladly give you my mouth. *Unknown*. SLW, *tr.* by Marjolijn De Jager, Sayd Bahodin Majrouh and André Velter

I will go and plough in the Palace Yard. King's Courtyard, The. *Hungarian Oral Tradition*. IQMS, *tr.* by Dermot Spence

I will go back to that silent evening. That Silent Evening. Galway Kinnell. StAl

I Will Go Back to the Great Sweet Mother. Algernon Charles Swinburne. NAEL-6v2 *Fr.* Triumph of Time, The.

I will go home to my children. (LL) Fathers and Sons. Tom Leonard. CABP; NePenScot

I will go up the mountain after the Moon. Fannie Stearns Gifford. RACG *Fr.* Songs of Conn the Fool, The.

I will go with the first air of morning. Fishing. Dorothy, Duchess of Wellington Wellesley. OBMV

I will grieve alone. In Response to a Rumor that the Oldest Whorehouse in Wheeling, West Virginia, Has Been Condemned. James Wright. CAP-8; NAMCP V.2; NoAM; OxBoAm; VCAP

I will haunt these States. Vow, A. Allen Ginsberg. CLPP; OBWP

I will have all my beds blown[e] up, not stuft. Ben Jonson. OxBEV *Fr.* Alchemist, The.

I will have few cooking-pots. Domestic Economy. Anna Wickham. ItWoWo

I will have to accept women. This Form of Life Needs Sex. Allen Ginsberg. CLPP

I will have to forget. To Ms. Ann. Lucille Clifton. ESEAA

I will have / you meet. Slick. Víctor Hernández Cruz. PueRic

I will in Cassio's lodging lose this napkin. William Shakespeare. OxAEP-1 *Fr.* Othello.

I will leave less than this behind me. (LL) Difficult Body. Mark Wunderlich. NAPBL; Vesp

I will let loose against you the fleet-footed vines. Rudyard Kipling. NOxBChV *Fr.* Second Jungle Book, The.

I will lie on the bed of the river. (LL) Riverbed, The. Vona Groarke. MFPA; NIrP

I will lift up mine eyes unto the hills, from whence cometh my help. Bible, O.T. WaAnP *Fr.* Psalms.

I will live and survive and be asked. I Will Live and Survive. Irina Ratushinskaya. CFP; ItGoST, *tr.* by David McDuff

I will live in Ringsend. Ringsend. Oliver St. John Gogarty. OBMV

I will look this land over. Master of an Expanse. Fabio Morabito. PML, *tr.* by E. Bell

I Will Look Up. Josephine D. Henderson Heard. CBWP-4

I will look with detachment. On Being Head of the English Department. Pinkie Gordon Lane. GT

I will lose you. It is written. Sweater, The. Gregory Orr. TRP

I will make you brooches and toys for your delight. Song of a Traveller, The. Robert Louis Stevenson. MoBrPo; OBEV

I will miss you. Do not expect applause. (LL) Johann Joachim Quantz's Five Lessons. William Sydney Graham. EmeKit; HarvBoo

I will my collection of hats. Exchange of Hats, An. Stanley Moss. BodElec

I will never again. Promise, The. Toi Derricotte. GT

I will never be this beautiful again. On the Death of Nizar Qabbani. Mohja Kahf. PoArWo

I will never leave here. (LL) Prisoner of Los Angeles (2). Wanda Coleman. CalPo; GeoHom

I will no longer kiss. On Himself[e]. Robert Herrick. CavPo

I will not be able to explain why. Natalya Gorbanevskaya. CRWP, *tr.* by Elizabeth Krizenesky

I Will Not Be Your Sickness. Marge Piercy. BrAP

I Will Not Crush the World's Corolla of Wonders. Lucian Blaga. PFTM-1

I will not die completely, my dear friend! Non Omnis Moriar. Manuel Gutiérrez Nájera. BLPSL, *tr.* by Rene de Costa, Rigas Kappatos and Eleni Paidoussi

I will not expose. Not My Knees. Stazja McFayden. ArBi

I Will Not Give Thee All My Heart. Grace Hazard Conkling. LW

I will not go down like an old rag. Worker Dies, A. Clementina Suárez. TANSG, *tr.* by Janet N. Gold

I will not have or value a man. I. Gabriella Sica. CItWP, *tr.* by Cinzia Sartini Blum and Lara Trubowitz

I will not let you say a Woman's part. Woman's Answer, A. Adelaide Anne Procter. VWP

I will not pare my nails. No Second Deirdre. Máire Mhac an tSaoi. IrLP

I will not play at tug o' war. Hug o' War. Shel Silverstein. NTCP

I Will Not Pretend. Anna Ruth Ediger Baehr. ACAMVP

I will not rest in my questions. Questions. Marjorie Agosin. FiBr

I will not shut me from my kind. Alfred Tennyson. CABP; NAEL-6v2; NAEL-7v2 *Fr.* In Memoriam A. H. H.

I will not speak. No. Patti Tana. PasH

I will not toy with it nor bend an inch. White City, The. Claude McKay. APT-1; NAMCP V.1; NoAM; OxBoAm; RaBo

I will not try to reach again. Evenlode, The. Joseph Hilaire Pierre Belloc. OxAEP-2

I will not write about our bodies in the gray dawn, calm and awake as trees. Ugly Poem. Carmen Horst. ACAMVP

I will now sing this beautifully. Sappho. SaLy, *tr.* by Diane Rayor

I will obey you to my utmost power. To a Lady, Who Desired Me Not To Be in Love with Her. John, Baron Cutts Cutts. NOSC

I will only mention the taking root of people and animals. Cities Have Been Cut Off at the Feet, The. Hans Arp. MotU, *tr.* by Bethany Schneider

I will pluck from my tree a cherry-blossom wand. Cherry-Blossom Wand, The. Anna Wickham. MoBrPo

I will praise darkness now, but then the leaf. (LL) Room, The. Conrad Potter Aiken. APT-1; InGu; MoAmPo

I will put my best heart forward and hope. After Eighteen Years of This Sort of Thing. Mark Robinson. RSaN

I will read a few of these to see if they exist. Theory of the Flower, The. Michael Palmer. HarvBoo

I will remember. Courage. Boris Leonidovich Pasternak. FaBoWar, *tr.* by Unknown

I will remember rainbows as I wander. (LL) Variations on a Fragment by Trumbull Stickney. John Hollander. NAMCP V.2; NoP-4; NoP-5

I will rise / from my troth. Wine Bowl. "H. D." NoP-4; NoP-5

I will roar and squander. Folly's Song. Thomas Dekker *and others*. NOSC

I will sew you a self. Big White Dress, The. Lisa Rosenberg. PoDa

I will sing in the rising. Song Poem, The. Lenard D. Moore. SpirFl

I will speak about women of letters, for I'm in the racket. Carolyn Kizer. BrAP; FTtHH; NALW *Fr.* Pro Femina.

I Will Still Sing. Amelia Blossom Pegram. HAWP

I will stop dreaming now. Success. Cornelius Eady. ISC

I will strike down wooden houses; I will burn aluminum. Prophecy. Donald Hall. NoP-5; OxBoAm

I will take that ancestral one. (LL) Two Standards. Elise Paschen. OPRER; ReEnLa

I will take the orange and toss it as high as I can. (LL) Kiss of the Sun. Mary Ruefle. AmAlph; FaoP

I will take this chair apart and build a tree with it. Tree. Stratis Haviaras. MotU

I will teach you my townspeople. Tract. William Carlos Williams. InoFa; MoAmPo; NAAPv.2; NAMCP V.1; NoAM; SAmP

I Will Tell You During the Walk. Isabel Meyrelles. SurWo, *tr.* by Guy Ducornet

I will tell you during the walk to Fomalhaut. I Will Tell You During the Walk. Isabel Meyrelles. SurWo, *tr.* by Guy Ducornet

I will tell you. Maybe. David St. John. GeoHom *Fr.* Of the Remembered.

I will tell you, / The barge she sat in, like a burnisht throne. William Shakespeare. OxBEV *Fr.* Antony and Cleopatra.

I will tell you what he told me. Berryman. W. S. Merwin. GifTon

I will tell your what lies under this hill. Under the Drumlin. David Brendon Hopes. UpMys

I will tell you words which you will. Vanessa's Bower. Medbh McGuckian. MoWP

I will the devil kiss. (LL) Small Fig Tree, A. Donald Hall. ChIV-2; GI

I will throw this bridge across. (LL) This Bridge Across. Christopher Gilbert. ESEAA; GT

I will try to remember. It was light. Ending With a Line From *Lear*. Marvin Bell. PoChi

I will turn on nothing. Promise. Joe Wenderoth. BodElec

I will turn out bad. (LL) My Wicked Wicked Ways. Sandra Cisneros. ItWoWo; WaAnP

I will wait here in the fields. Stay Home. Wendell Berry. LPSFW

I will walk into some one's dwelling. Love Song. *Unknown*. APN-2, *tr.* by Henry Rowe Schoolcraft

I will walk with a lover of wisdom. Little Elegy. Denis Devlin. ModIr

I will whisper your name. Eshu. Adesanya Alakoye. ISC

I will write a sketch of my early life. Author's Early Life, The. Julia A. Moore.

I will write songs against you. Charles Reznikoff. RaF

I will write you a rollicking, nonsense rhyme. Versicle, A. James Clarence Harvey. ArBi

I will you allë swalewë withouten any bot. Dragon Speaks, The. *Unknown*. NPeEn

I will—of You—. (LL) Alter! When the Hills do—. Emily Dickinson. SoSe-8; TCAPo

I wince in self-revelation. Sincerity. Ágnes Nemes Nagy. VCWP, *tr.* by Hugh Maxton

I wind the thick twine around my body and drop down into the well. Psychotherapy. Nasri Hajjaj. Eno, *tr.* by Ibrahim Muhawi

I. WINEMAKING. Elegy. Arthur L. Clements. UnSA

I Winna Let On. James King Annand. NOxBChV

I wis a student at King's. Professor's Wife, The. Flora Garry. EdScPo

I wish a greater knowledge, then t'attaine. Francis Quarles. PBRV *Fr.* Divine Fancies.

I wish for no cars, coalfires, clang. Millenary. Richard Kenney. PfSP

I wish he wouldn't sulk, it's unbecoming. Queen Gertrude's Soliloquy. Gail White. IaFF

I Wish I Been Dere. *Unknown.* SSUS

I wish I could be. Kenneth Rexroth. APSN; APT-2 *Fr.* Love Poems of Marichiko, The.

I wish I could look. Elena Vasileva. CRWP, *tr. by* Max Nemtsov

I wish I could remember the [*or* that] first day. Christina Georgina Rossetti. LW; OxBSo *Fr.* Monna Innominata.

I Wish I Didn't Love You So. Frank Loesser. ReLy

I wish I knew the names of flowers. Naming of Flowers, The. Jennie Osborne. Prnts

I wish I loved the human race. Wishes of an Elderly Man[, Wished at a Garden Party, June 1914]. Sir Walter Alexander Raleigh. NBLV; OBCoV

I wish I owned a Dior dress. Reflections at Dawn. Phyllis McGinley. NBLV

I wish I thought *What Jolly Fun*! (LL) Wishes of an Elderly Man[, Wished at a Garden Party, June 1914]. Sir Walter Alexander Raleigh. NBLV; OBCoV

I wish I was. *Unknown.* SonAtl, *tr. by* Allison Jordan, Mike Jordan and Milly Orpen

I Wish I Was a Grown Up Man. Maggie Pogue Johnson. CBWP-4

I wish I was in de land ob cotton. Dixie [*or* Dixie's Land]. Daniel Decatur Emmett. APN-1; CBCWP; TCAPo

I wish i were. Poem For My Nephew. Nikki Giovanni. NOxBChV

I Wish I Were in Love Again. Lorenz Hart. OBCoV

I wish I were spring water. Gabriella Sica. CItWP *Fr.* Poems for a Little Boy.

I wish I were where Helen lies. Helen of Kirconnell. *Unknown.* OBEV; OxBEV

I wish I'd had a normal everyday life. Bacon and eggs. Seared to the Echo. Barry MacSweeney. VaPo

I wish I'd never been born. (LL) Po' Boy Blues. Langston Hughes. ColAP; NAMCP V.1

I Wish in the City of Your Heart. Robley, Jr. Wilson. InvLad; P180

I wish it soon may have a better. (LL) Verses on the Death of Dr. Swift, D.S.P.D, Occasioned by Reading a Maxim in Rochefoucauld. Jonathan Swift. NAEL-6v1; NAEL-7v1; NoP-5

I wish it were over the terrible pain. Introspective. Christina Georgina Rossetti. VWP

I Wish My Love Was a Block of Wood. *Unknown.* IrLP

I wish my soul was an unmoved boulder. Bridge. Katri Vala. SonAtl, *tr. by* Marja Heininen, Ursula Hobday and Phoebe Ravenhall

I wish, O Son of the Living God, O Ancient Eternal King. Song of Manchan the Hermit, The. *Unknown.* IrV, *tr. by* Eleanor Hull

I wish she were here. Issa. SoOfWa, *tr. by* Sam Hamill

I wish that all my poems. Juan Ramón Jiménez. MiVo, *tr. by* Dennis Maloney

I wish that I had spoken only of it all. (LL) Gertrude Stein. NoP-4; NoP-5 *Fr.* Stanzas in Meditation.

I wish that I had spoken only of it all. Gertrude Stein. NoP-4; NoP-5 *Fr.* Stanzas in Meditation.

I wish that there were some wonderful place. Land of Beginning Again, The. Louisa Fletcher. ITBLP

I wish the bell saved you. Once the Dream Begins. Yusef Komunyakaa. RoV

I wish the rent. Little Lyric (*Of Great Importance*). Langston Hughes. APT-2; NBLV; OBCoV

I wish them cramps. Wishes for Sons. Lucille Clifton. CAP-8; SUP

I wish there were a touch of these boats about my life. Boat Poem. Bernard Spencer. EmeKit

I wish to be a nameless woman. Nameless Woman, A. No Ch'ŏnmyŏng. WoPoe, *tr. by* Ko Won

"I wish to buy a dog," she said. On Buying a Dog. Edgar Klauber. NTCP

I wish to God I could forget the Frenchman. French Prisoner, The. János Pilinszky. IQMS, *tr. by* Peter Zollman

I wish to God I never saw you, Mag. Mag. Carl Sandburg. APT-1

I wish to make this preaching short. Charms of Small Women. Juan, Archpriest of Hita Ruiz. BLPSL, *tr. by* Rene de Costa, Rigas Kappatos and Eleni Paidoussi

I wish to say something to you, but shame. Sappho. SaLy, *tr. by* Diane Rayor

I wish to state in the first place that. SURcenSURE. Marcel Duchamp. PFTM-1

I wish we had broken up five years ago. Hearts. Melvin E. Lewis. BtF

I wish you Alfred now a good night. To Alfred Gwyer. Joseph Gwyer. VerBaPo

I wish you knew September. If You Knew September. John Nelson. GeoH

I Wish You Love (Que Reste-t-il de Nos Amours?). Charles Trenet. ReLy, *tr. by* Albert A. Beach

I wish you were alive here in my life so we could share the ease of our. Fred Wah. NLPA *Fr.* This Dendrite Map: Father / Mother Haibun.

I with the mind then of a child squandering. On the Shores of Szántód. Ferenc Jankovich. IQMS, *tr. by* Madeline Mason

I with time to life ascend. Musical Pumpkin-Hut. Heinrich Albert. GePo, *tr. by* George C. Schoolfield

I, with whose colors [*or* colours] Myra dressed [*or* dress'd *or* drest] her head. Fulke, 1st Baron Brooke Greville. NoSic; OBEV; OxBEV; PBRV *Fr.* Caelica.

I woke. A tiny knot of skin on a silver table. Geburt des Monicakinds. Monica Ferrell. LegDan

I woke as mist licked the pavement. Climbing. C. Mikal Oness. GeoHom

I woke at dawn—and you were lying there. Morn's Recompense. Clement Andrews. CAGL

I Woke, This Meant a Love in the World. İlhan Berk. NaPG, *tr. by* Talat Sait Halman

I woke to a shout: 'I am Alpha and Omega'. Gog. Ted Hughes. NAMCP V.2

I woke to your face not looking at me. Saint's First Wife Said, The. G. E. Patterson. IIR

I woke up about 2:30 this morning and thought about Philip's / hat. Philip Whalen's Hat. Joanne Kyger. BB

I woke up and found you above me. Husband and Wife. Edward Hirsch. IllVoic

I woke up dreaming. Knockout, The. Sydney March. BtF

I woke up early. Ngodup Paljor. WhBo

I woke up in the dark. After *The Little Mariner*. Olga Broumas. BodElec

I woke up singing this morning. It's a Most Unusual Day. Harold Adamson. ReLy

I woke up this mornin'. Sylvester's Dying Bed. Langston Hughes. NAMCP V.1; NoAM; SAmP

I woke up this mornin' [/] with an awful achin' head. Empty Bed Blues. Bessie Smith. APT-2; OxBoAm

I Woke Up This Morning. Karla Kuskin. TLR

I woke up this morning feeling. Diagnosis. Terence Winch. PoDa

I woke up to the bleating of a lamb. ChrisEaster. Molly Peacock. FFC

I woke up with purple hair and Paul. Rocket to Russia. Alison Stone. SwNoth

I won apples out of season for her. Take Me, Loneliness. Gzar Hantoosh. IrPoTo, *tr. by* Saadi A. Simawe and Ellen Doré Watson

I wonder. Sterling Plumpp. FuFl *Fr.* Mary.

I wonder about the trees. Sound of Trees, The. Robert Frost. APT-1; NoAM

I wonder, by my troth, what thou and I. Good-Morrow, The. John Donne. BASC; BrAP; CABP; ClHu; FaBoVe; FSCP; ItP; NAEL-6v1; NAEL-7v1; NAWM-5v1; NIL-7; NoP-4; NoP-5; NOSC; OxAEP-1; OxBEV; SoSe-8; TFi; WaAnP

I wonder do you feel today. Two in the Campagna. Robert Browning. ItP; NAEL-6v2; NAEL-7v2; NoP-4; NoP-5; NPeEn; OxAEP-2; OxBEV; TFi

I wonder, Duddon, if you still remember. To the River Duddon. Norman Nicholson. NLP; NoP-4; NoP-5

I wonder how many old men last winter. Minneapolis Poem, The. James Wright. CAP-8; NAMCP V.2; NoAM

I wonder if I could find it. Searching for *Melinda's Magic Moment*. Allison Joseph. NAPBL

I wonder if the dust collecting here. Dust on the Mantel: Sonnet. Jacqueline Osherow. InoFa

I wonder if the elephant. Pete at the Zoo. Gwendolyn Brooks. TLR

I wonder if the sap is stirring yet. First Spring Day, The. Christina Georgina Rossetti. FaBoVe

I wonder now only when it will happen. When. Sharon Olds. AtGh

I wonder, since we are both traveling out. Traveling Out, The. Lucile Adler. ICANM

I wonder sometimes if the soldiers lying. Song for the Heroes. Alex Comfort. MoBrPo

I Wonder What Became of Me. Johnny Mercer. ReLy

I Wonder What Happened to Him. Noël Coward. ReLy

I wonder what happened to those old dears from my childhood? Useful. Elin ap Hywel. ATSWP, *tr. by* Robert Minhinnick

I wonder what he'll think of me! Soliloquy. Oscar Hammerstein, II. ReLy

I wonder what I ought to do today. Anne Hathaway Composes Her 18th Sonnet. Neil Curry. NLP

I Wonder What It Feels Like to Be Drowned? Robert Graves. MoBrPo

I wonder what Spanish poets would say about this. Cicada Blue. Charles Wright. KGB

I wonder what to mean by *sanctuary,* if a real or. Triphammer Bridge. A. R. Ammons. ColAP; OxBoAm

I wonder what Wright and Baldwin. Mental Terrorism. Kevin Powell. InTrad

I wonder where it is, now. Covered Dish. Kristin Kovacic. SweBea

I wonder where it is we belong. Should I Stay or Should I Go? Sarah Rosenblatt. AmPoNex

I wonder where julia found that strange, rather common little boy? (LL) False Security. Sir John Betjeman. NoAM; NoP-4; NoP-5

I wonder whether. Dieback. Elizabeth Dodd. UrbNat

I wonder who she was and how she got there. Questions about the Sphinx. Celia Gilbert. PfS

I Wonder Why She Kept on Saying "Si-Si-Si-Si-Senor." Sam M. Lewis and Joe Young. ReLy

I wonder why that scene comes back tonight. Pilate Remembers. William E. Brooks. ChIV-2

I wonder why you came to me last night. I Wonder Why. Katharine Tynan Hinkson. IrLP

I wonder will he still be gentle. Rhoda Coghill. IrLP

I wondered always where. Hunchback of Dugbe, The. Wole Soyinka. VCWP

I won't abandon you, though you cause me. Şeyh Galib. OLP, tr. by Walter Andrews, Najaat Black and Mehmet Kalpakli

I won't be in the same room with this poem. First Lady Challenges a Loa-as-Poem. James Richardson. RD

I won't be reconstructed / And I don't give a damn. (LL) Rebel, The. Innes Randolph. AmWaPo; NBLV

I won't be sitting shiva. Today. Shifre Vays. Prolet, tr. by Amelia Glaser

I won't care / if you desert me. Chinook Oral Tradition. ErotSp, tr. by Sam Hamill

I Won't Dance. Dorothy Fields. ReLy

I won't go back to it. Mise Eire. Eavan Boland. NAMCP V.2

I won't go in today, I'll stay out today. Karen Volkman. NeAmPo

I won't go with you. I want to stay with Grandpa! My Last Afternoon with Uncle Devereux Winslow. Robert Lowell. GPTC; NoP-4; NoP-5

I won't kiss your hand, madam. My Romance. Lorenz Hart. ReLy

I won't let even. For Taihei Osho. Muso Soseki. EaWin, tr. by W. S. Merwin

I won't look at her. Work. Yusef Komunyakaa. CAP-8; LPSFW

I won't say much about it now, except that she got. Reading the Elephant. Andrew Motion. HarvBoo

I won't say much for the sea. On the Coast near Sausalito. Robert Hass. OxBoAm

I Won't Sell His Love. Fadwa Tuqan. AF, tr. by Mounah Aikhouri and Hamid Algar

I Won't Send Roses. Jerry Herman. ReLy

I work. Tanka. Ishikawa Takuboku. CAoMJL1, tr. by Makoto Ueda

I work all day, and get half-drunk at night. Aubade. Philip Larkin. AWTN; BodElec; BrAP; CABP; EMP; NAEL-6v2; NAEL-7v2; NAMCP V.2; NoP-4; NoP-5; PoetW; SoSe-8; StAl; TRP; WaAnP

I work all day and hardly drink at all. Corniche. Les A. Murray. NAMCP V.2

I work and I remember. I conceive. That's All. Lawrence Joseph. PBCAP

I work at night, surrounded by city. Burial in the East. Pablo Neruda. TRP

I work at night, the city all around me. Funeral in the East. Pablo Neruda. TRP, tr. by Robert Bly

I work at the Palace Ballroom. Ten Cents a Dance. Lorenz Hart. ReLy

I work for the C.I.A. It's Miller Time. Víctor Hernández Cruz. PueRic; TouFir

I work in the evening, alone and in silence. James Harpur. NewEx

I work nights, in the ring of the city. Burial in the East. Pablo Neruda. TRP, tr. by Ben Belitt

I Work with the shape. Song. Michael McClure. ASA

I worked all the winter. Tired as I Can Be. Bessie Jackson. FaBoVe; GoPo

I worked for a woman. Madam and Her Madam. Langston Hughes. NAMCP V.1; RACG; SAmP

I worked on race at the factory. Kim Hunter. RD

I Worry. Wendy Cope. HarvBoo

I worry about you. I Worry. Wendy Cope. HarvBoo

I worry for the broccoli's sake. Consider the Garden. Michael Collier. PfSP

I worship the greatest first. Hippolytus Temporizes. "H. D." APT-1; HarvBoo; RACG

I worshipped—did not "pray." (LL) My period had come for Prayer. Emily Dickinson. APN-2; BBASP

I wot a burde in boure bright. Unknown. OHMEL

I would ask of you, my darling. Will You Love Me When I'm Old? Unknown. ITBLP

I Would Be Clad in Christis Skin. Unknown. SacPr

I would be ignorant as the dawn. Dawn, The. William Butler Yeats. BLPJKO

I Would Be True. Howard Arnold Walter. ITBLP

I would choose to be a doorkeeper. Katharine Tynan Hinkson. SacPr

I would draw her face with blood. Sin Hŭm. CATKP, tr. by Peter H. Lee

I would fain know[e] what she hath deserved. (LL) Lover Showeth How He Is Forsaken of Such as He Sometime Enjoyed, The. Sir Thomas Wyatt. CABP; ClHu; HeIP-4; MakPoe; NoSic; NPeEn; OxBEV; TFi; TRP

(How like you this, what hath she now deserved?) (LL) NAEL-6v1; NAEL-7v1; NoP-4

(I fain would know what she hath deserved.) (LL) NIL-7; PoPoPo

I would give my father in ransom for a gazelle of imā guarded by a lion of the thicket. Abū 'Abdillāh Muhammad Ibn 'Ubāda al-Qazzāz. HiArP, tr. by James T. Monroe

I would give my father in ransom for a precious possession that clings to [my] soul! Abū 'Abdillāh Muhammad Ibn 'Ubāda al-Qazzāz. HiArP, tr. by James T. Monroe

I would have been as great as George Eliot. Edgar Lee Masters. APT-1; IllVoic; RACG Fr. Spoon River Anthology.

I would have cut away the crescent moon. (LL) Perfect Heart, The. Shara McCallum. AmPoNex; P180

I Would Have Loved You. Fernando Charry Lara. BLPSL, tr. by Rene de Costa, Rigas Kappatos and Eleni Paidoussi

I would have loved you. I Would Have Loved You. Fernando Charry Lara. BLPSL, tr. by Rene de Costa, Rigas Kappatos and Eleni Paidoussi

I would have wept if weeping. Marilyn Bowering. IFF Fr. Autobiography.

I would hear Spanish first. If I Were Rita Hayworth. Patricia Jones. ReTh

I would I were Actaeon, whom Diana did disguise. I Would I Were Actaeon. Bewe. NoSic

I would I were the glow-worm, thou the flower. Mathilde Blind. ViWPN Fr. Love in Exile.

I would lie low, the ground on which men tread. Earth, The. Jones Very. APN-1

I would like all things to be free of me. Proof. Brendan Kennelly. PBCIP

I would like for ebony and ivory. Harmony. Andrea M. Wren. InTrad

I would like just to be silent. Jerzy Ficowski. HP

I would like kindness, assurance. Children Imagining a Hospital. U. A. Fanthorpe. PoCu

I would like to ask that dumb ox, Thomas. Prospect Park. David Schubert. APT-2

I Would Like to Be a Dot in a Painting by Miró. Moniza Alvi. MoWP

I would like to be that elderly Chinese gentleman. Dreaming in the Shanghai Restaurant. Dennis Joseph Enright. EmeKit

I would like to believe that in the darkness. Burning Bush. Alison Apotheker. PoCoUp

I Would Like to Describe. Zbigniew Herbert. PoSu, tr. by Czeslaw Milosz

I would like to describe the simplest emotion. I Would Like to Describe. Zbigniew Herbert. PoSu, tr. by Czeslaw Milosz

I would like to let things be. Facts of Life, Ballymoney. Eamon Grennan. PBCIP

I would like to live long enough to see the State Quarters Program. Prospects. Tony Towle. PA9/11

I would like to say something for things as they are, in themselves. Things of the World, The. Robert Sargent. PoA 2002

I would like to tell about an enduring sorrow I have not forgotten. Ode to a Long Sorrow. Ricardo Molinari. TCLAP, tr. by Inés Probert

I would like to undo it, to take back. Lament. G. E. Patterson. AmPoNex

I would like to use. Basho. SoOfWa, tr. by Sam Hamill

I would like to watch you sleeping. Variation on the Word Sleep. Margaret Atwood. AmFaPo; BeAl

I would like to write a poem. Like Riding a Bicycle. George Bilgere. ArBi

I Would Like You for a Comrade. Edward Abbott Parry. NOxBChV

I would live all my life in nonchalance and insouciance. Introspective Reflection. Ogden Nash. NBLV; OBCoV

I would live for a day and a night. Song-Maker, The. Anna Wickham. MoBrPo

I Would Live in Your Love. Sara Teasdale. LW

I would live in your love as the sea-grasses live in the sea. I Would Live in Your Love. Sara Teasdale. LW

I would make a crown / Of all the cities I have known. Express. Vicente Huidobro. PFTM-1

I would not alter thy cold eyes. Flos Lunae. Ernest Dowson. OBMV

I would not always reason. The straight path. Conjunction of Jupiter and Venus, The. William Cullen Bryant. APN-1

I would not argue with you tonight. No Argument Tonight. Tijan M. Sallah. NAfrP

I would not be the Moon, the sickly thing. In Dispraise of the Moon. Mary Elizabeth Coleridge. PEW; ViWPN

I would not breathe, when blows thy mighty wind. Spirit, The. Jones Very. NCAP

I would not, could I, make thy life as mine. Vain Wish, A. Philip Bourke Marston. GSoI

I would not do by thee as thou hast done! (LL) Lines on Hearing That Lady Byron Was Ill. Lord Byron. NPeEn; OxAEP-2

I would not go to old Joe's house. Old Joe Clark. Unknown. APN-2

I would not have the risk diminished. (LL) Map of the City, A. Thom Gunn. NAEL-6v2; NAEL-7v2; NoP-4; NoP-5

I would not leave that land, if I were thou. To Charles Roux, of Switzerland. Nathaniel Parker Willis. APN-1

I would not paint—a picture. Emily Dickinson. APN-2; NAAL-3; NAAL-5; NoP-4; NoP-5; OxBoAm; TCAPo; TRP

I Would Not Recommend Love. Harold Norse. CLPP

I would not sail again with sheep. (LL) Sheep. W. H. Davies. MoBrPo; NPeEn

I would not sing you to sleep. Lullaby. Reetika Vazirani. PoCho

I would not tell you. Aria from X. Thulani Davis. WhBo

I would not the good bishop be. (LL) Problem, The. Ralph Waldo Emerson. APN-1; NAAL-3

I would not want, I think, a higher intelligence, one. Erosion. Jorie Graham. FaoP

I would not work elsewhere but on a farm. Miscellaneous Poem. T'ao Ch'ien. CCL1, tr. by Gladys Yang and Yang Xianyi

I would prefer. Counterfeiter, The. Michael Davitt. PBCIP, tr. by Philip Casey

I would rather show you the nothing in my sky-blue eyes. Monomaniacal Possessor of the Firmament. Hans Arp. MotU, tr. by Bethany Schneider

I would sleep until the mottled jaguar dawn. Auditory Hallucinations. Joyce Mansour. HAWP, tr. by Carol Cosman

I would speak to you cracked crystal howling like a dog on a night of flailing sheets. Where Are You. Benjamin Péret. SurPaPo; YaTCFP, tr. by Rachel Stella

I Would Steal Horses. Sherman Alexie. NeAmPo

I would that all men my hard case would know. Behold the Deeds! Henry Cuyler Bunner. NBLV

I would that folk forgot me quite. Tess's Lament. Thomas Hardy. FaBoVe

I would the gift I offer here. Dedication. John Greenleaf Whittier. APN-1

I would to heaven that I were so much clay. Lord Byron. NAEL-6v2; NAEL-7v2; NoP-5; OxBEV Fr. Don Juan.

I Wouldn't. John Ciardi. TLR

I wouldn't coax the plant if I were you. Woman with Flower. Naomi Long Madgett. GT; OxAAAP

I Wouldn't Even Bleed. Benjamin Alire Sáenz. TiP2

I wouldn't have known if I didn't stay home. Night in a World, A. Heather McHugh. InvLad

I wouldn't know what it's like to be a pawn. Maurizio Cucchi. ItPo, tr. by Gayle Ridinger

I wouldn't like to be one. In Praise of the Great Bull Walrus. Alden Nowlan. BeAl

I wouldn't marry a farmer. Railroad Man for Me, A. Unknown. CA

I Wouldn't Thank You for a Valentine. Liz Lochhead. BeAl

I would've intervened. As Zeus. Ron Drummond. PA9/11

I wound my heart. I give my poetry its blood to drink. Shiraz Moon. Abdul Wahab Al-Bayati. IrPoTo, tr. by Farouk Abdel Wahab

I wove myself of many delicious strands. Einstein's Bathrobe. Howard Moss. VCAP

I wove this basket. Pozo Basket, The. Glenna Luschei. GeoHom

I wrap the blue towel. White Porch, The. Cathy Song. BeAl; NAAL-5; YaYoPo

I write a scenario for moving pictures. Samuel Hoffenstein. AmWit Fr. Notebook of a Schnook, The.

I Write For. John Hewitt. PNI

I write from the denser enclave of the stricken. From a Clinic Waiting Room. Amy Clampitt. WaAnP

I write in praise of the solitary act. Against Coupling. Fleur Adcock. EmeKit; MoWP; NALW

I write my God in blue. Jay Wright. ESEAU; TRP Fr. Logbook of Judgments.

I write now in English and now in Scots. Caledonian Antisyzygy, The. Hugh MacDiarmid. OxBEV

I write of Jam, a subject stiff. On Jam. Joseph Hilaire Pierre Belloc. NBLV

I write only to say this. James Vincent Cunningham. APT-2

I write that in order to write this. What is written. Emmanuel Hocquard. OnScMo; YaTCFP Fr. At Christmas.

I write the poetry of degenerate youth. Handicraft—After Marina Tsvetaeva. Duo Duo. PoetW, tr. by Michelle Yeh

I write this swishing poem for you. For the Seventh Day. Sandor Csoori. TAPaP, tr. by Len Roberts

I write to make people anxious and miserable and to worsen their indigestion. (LL) Serious Concerns. Wendy Cope. NoP-5; OBCoV

I write to you beneath this tent. Post Card. Guillaume Apollinaire. AF; FaBoWar, tr. by Oliver Bernard

I write you from Wordsworth's cottage. For a Portrait of Annette Vallon. Andrey Andreievich Voznesensky. RusPo, tr. by Robert Arthur Douglas Ford

I wrote a book, thank the Lord. Fluency. Adelia Prado. TCLAP, tr. by Marcia Kirinus

I wrote a new poem. Like That. Rebecca Radner. WhBo

I wrote a panegyric on you—and I'm sorry. Composing. "Anvari." WoPoe, tr. by Dick Davis

I wrote a poem. Untitled One. Kwan Booth. BtF

I wrote: In the dark cavern of our birth. Strange Type. Malcolm Lowry. NoP-4; NoP-5; NPeEn

I wrote my IOU onna flapjack. City of No Reprieve. Willard Gellis. RWB

I wrote so meagerly to you. But what I couldn't write. To Friends Behind a Frontier. Tomas Transtromer. WoPoe, tr. by Robin Fulton

I wrote stubbornly into the evening. Nexus. Rita Dove. OxAAAP

I wrote them with my nail on the plaster. Flowers of Mildew. Tudor Arghezi. WoPoe, tr. by Michael Impey and Brian Swann

I wrote this when the sky was still serene. Prologue. Mihály Vörösmarty. IQMS, tr. by Peter Zollman

I wrote to you to say that I'd be there. One's Correspondence. Connie Bensley. OBCoV

I wrung my hands under my dark veil. Anna Andreyevna Akhmatova. PoetW; RaBo, tr. by Max Hayward and Stanley Kunitz

I wuz goin' wif Puddin. Interlude. Sibby Anderson-Thompkins. InTrad

I Years had been from Home. Emily Dickinson. SAmP

I yet SUPERIOR am to you. (LL) Forsaken Wife, The. Elizabeth Thomas. GoPo; LW

I, Yi, Yi, Yi, Yi (I Like You Very Much). Mack Gordon. ReLy

I Yield Thee Praise. Philip Jerome Cleveland. SacPr

I yielded myself to the perfect whole. (LL) Each and All. Ralph Waldo Emerson. APN-1; ColAP; NAAL-3; NAAL-5; NAAPv.1; NCAP; OxBoAm; TCAPo; TreFP

I, you, he, she, we. Jelaluddin Rumi. LoL

I, Zhang Pingzi, had traversed the Nine Wilds and seen their wonders. Bones of Zhuangzi, The. Chang Heng. CCL1, tr. by Arthur Waley

I-5 Incident. Juan Delgado. AmPoNex; GeoHom

Iago. Julian Bernick. IaFF

Iago. Arthur Powers. IaFF

Iago had his reasons. Literature 100. Carmen Germain. IaFF

Iago Prytherch his name, though, be it allowed. Peasant, A. Ronald Stuart Thomas. AngWePo; OBWVE; OxBEV

Iago, the Poet. J. P. Dancing Bear. IaFF

Iago to His Torturers. R. S. Gwynn. IaFF

Iambicum Trimetrum. Edmund Spenser. NPeEn; OBEV

Ianthe. Walter Savage Landor.
  (Ianthe.) OBEV
  Ianthe. NOBRP; NPeEn; OxBEV; TFi; WeW-3
  (Ianthe's Question.) OBEV
  (Past Ruined Ilion Helen Lives.) NAEL-6v2; NAEL-7v2; NoP-4; NoP-5
  "Proud word you never spoke, but you will speak." OBEV
  (Verse: "Past ruin'd Ilion.") OBEV
  Well I Remember How You Smiled. NAEL-6v2

Íbamos once amigos a tu entierro. Julio Campal. Gerardo Diego. RaW

Ibn Gabirol. Yehuda Amichai. AF, tr. by Assia Gutmann

Icarium Mare. Richard Wilbur. UpMys

Icarus. Edward Field. OtW

Icarus. Valentin Iremonger. ModIr

Icarus. Unknown. OBEV

Icarus drowning. (LL) William Carlos Williams. BrAP; NAAL-5; NAAPv.2; NAMCP V.1; NoAM; NoP-5; OtW; OxBoAm; PoPoPo Fr. Pictures from Brueghel.

Icarus in November. Alec Brock Stevenson. FuPo

Icarus Schmicarus. Adrian Mitchell. OBCoV

Ice. Alan Gould. NOBAu

Ice. Ágnes Nemes Nagy. IQMS, tr. by Ila Egon

Ice. Mónica Nepote. SPV, tr. by Jen Hofer

Ice. Maureen Seaton. IllVoic

Ice ages exist, ice ages exist. Inger Christensen. PFTM-2 Fr. Alphabet.

Ice and fires. Ice and Fires Contend with My Child. Félix Lope de Vega Carpio. SpanPo, tr. by W. S. Merwin

Ice and Fires Contend with My Child. Félix Lope de Vega Carpio. SpanPo, tr. by W. S. Merwin

Ice and the scotch, the fable, The. Tacit. Thom Ward. AmPoNex

Ice Cream. Ronny Someck. IrPoTo, tr. by Vivian Eden

Ice Cube. Kit Robinson. ASA

Ice Eagle, The. Diane Wakoski. PFTM-2

Ice Floe. Arthur Sze. WhBo

Ice Hadn't Cracked, The. Stingy Ground: Frozen with its Hoard of Bulbs. D. A. Powell. IAoNAP

Ice honed by wind. Tracking the Siuslaw Man. Jim Barnes. HATNAP

Ice In. Jacques Roubaud. YaTCFP, tr. by the author

Ice in the school-room, listen. Schooling, A. Seamus Deane. PNI

Ice in the trees. Queen Herod. Carol Ann Duffy. P180

Ice inside the window seems forever, The. Whistling in January. David J. Rothman. GeoH

Ice on eaves, sparrow melts in my head. Eternity. Takahashi Shinkichi. ZenPo, tr. by Takashi Ikemoto and Lucien Stryk

Ice plates the tarn in its hollow. Pinder. Mick North. NLP

Ice rain coats berries. Tanka. Henry Beissel. IFF

Ice Skating. Greg Kuzma. InvLad

Ice Storm. Robert Earl Hayden. APT-2; ESEAA

Iceberg Theory, The. Gerald Locklin. BeAl; GoPo

2. Icebox. Justin Quinn. NIrP Fr. Six Household Appliances.

Ice-capers! Time cannot stale. Curling: Old Murrayfield Ice Rink. Angus Calder. EdScPo

Ice-Cream Sandwich, The. Karen Swenson. NevBe

Ice-Cream Wars, The. John Ashbery. PoA 2002

Icehouse in Summer, The. Howard Nemerov. NAMCP V.2; NoAM

Ice-jammed hard-clasped branches in the blocks a whole river of them. Seasons, The. Susan Stewart. PoCho

Icelandic Language, The. Bill Holm. GoPo

Ich am of Irlonde. William Butler Yeats. NAEL-7v1

Ich sterbe . . . Life ebbs with an easy flow. End of a War, The. Sir Herbert Read. OBMV

Ich stieg vom Pferd und reichte ihm den Trunk. Abschied des Freundes, Der. Wang Wei. CCL1, tr. by Hans Bethge

Ich was ein chint so wolgetan. Unknown. EroLit Fr. Carmina Burana.

Ich was not yet. Calypso. Ernst Jandl. PFTM-2

Ichabod[!]. John Greenleaf Whittier. APN-1; NAAL-3; NAAL-5; NAAPv.1; PoCho; TCAPo

Ichot a burde in boure bryht. Unknown. OBEV

Ici l'heure. Silvia Baron Supervielle. YaTCFP

Ici souvent je suis un peu comme encore un. Ici souvent je suis. Michel Deguy. YaTCFP

Icicles Round a Tree in Dumfriesshire. Ruth Padel. MoWP

Icicles upon the pane, The. February. Henrietta Cordelia Ray. CBWP-3

Iconoclast. Ann Elizabeth Hostetler. ACAMVP

Iconoclast's Closet, The. Oliver Pitcher. EGAG

Iconography of Childhood, The. Sherley Anne Williams.
"Buildings of the, The." GeoHom
"Summer mornings we." GeoHom
"Town less, A." GeoHom

Icy evil that struck his father down, The. El-Hajj Malik El-Shabazz. Robert Earl Hayden. ESEAA

Icy Rose. Anne Waldman. AHA

Icy wind bites, An. What Maks Makems. Tom Pickard. Oth

Id. Harry Clifton. PBCIP

ID. Heather McHugh. OxBoAm

I'd 20/20 the dogs. Happy Hour. Walid Bitar. KGB

I'd a dream to-night. Mater Dolorosa. William Barnes. OBEV

I'd already lost my hair. Now my sun. Corn, The. Daniel David Moses. HATNAP

I'd be a Butterfly born in a bower. I'd Be a Butterfly. Thomas Haynes Bayly. STuOW

I'd be a dainty contained cool. If I Were a Bird. Lorine Niedecker. FTOS; OxBoAm

I'd been awakened before by hammers cracking across the pond. Armored Hearts. David Bottoms. PoA 2002

I'd been browsing the poetry section at Cody's. Berkeley, Late Spring. Forrest Hamer. GeoHom

I'd been tired, under. Hitcher. Simon Armitage. EmeKit

I'd been / trying. Other Contexts. Ted Berrigan. AHA

ID bracelet I never did give, The. How Near Vietnam Came to Us. Paul Zarzyski. SwNoth

I'd Buy You, Wisdom. Jan Kochanowski. WoPoe Fr. Laments, The.

I'd buy you, Wisdom, with all of the world's gold. Jan Kochanowski. WoPoe Fr. Laments, The.

I'd decided I initiate most. Sonnet 37. Phyllis Koestenbaum. FFC

I'd dislocated my life, so I went to the zoo. In Houston. Gail Mazur. PtR

I'd Give a Dollar for a Dime. Andy Razaf. ReLy

I'd give everything I own for that gazelle. Gazelle, The. Shmuel HaNagid. WoPoe, tr. by Peter Cole

I'd give it five stars. Revelation: The Movie. Elton Glaser. PBCAP

I'd happily survey the world. Natalya Belchenko. CRWP, tr. by Robert Reid

I'd have to ask the grass to let me sleep. (LL) To Dorothy. Marvin Bell. CAP-8; InvLad; VCAP

I'd have to piss through my eyes to cry for you. I Just Missed the Bus and I'll Be Late for Work. Ariel Dorfman. AF, tr. by Ariel Dorfman and Edith Grossman

I'd have walked straight past if you hadn't said. Night We Stole a Full-Length Mirror, The. Greta Stoddart. MoWP

I'd heard so much good. Desert Reservation. Barry Lopez. GifTon

I'd known he was enrolled, but still. Prayer of Miss Budd, The. Marilyn Nelson. BtF

I'd lie there with a book, until the lights went out. Emergency Services. Jonathan Wonham. RWPCtW

I'd like a different dog. Dogs and Weather. Winifred Welles. BLPJKO

I'd like to be a tree. My father clinked. Tree. Andrew Hudgins. InvLad

I'd like to be nothing. Iwan Goll. GTCP, tr. by Reinhold Grimm

I'd like to be rich. No not casually but positively streaming with weatlh. Hard. On Being Reproaced by Saintly Mediators for Bad Budgeting. Anna Mendelssohn. VaPo

I'd like to get away, Junior. There's a Small Hotel. Lorenz Hart. ReLy

I'd Like to Go Alone. Alena Synková. INSAB

I'd like to go away alone. I'd Like to Go Alone. Alena Synková. INSAB

I'd like to go home. Summer Nostalgia. Virginia E. Escandor. ReBoTo

I'd like to have a wild bird. Five Wishes. Anne Porter. KGB

I'd like to have a word. Book of Lies, The. James Tate. YaYoPo

I'd like to know everything. Jazz. Angela Ball. BAP-01

I'd like to paint monkey-eaters. Monkey-eaters. Takahashi Mutsuo. PFTM-2, tr. by Hiroaki Sato

I'd like to remove one thing. Larry Fagin. AHA Fr. Parade of the Caterpillars, The.

I'd like to taste my life again in little. Return to Paris. Jules Supervielle. MFP, tr. by Martin Sorrell

I'd Like to Try Telling You of Spring. Elena Clementelli. CItWP, tr. by Cinzia Sartini Blum and Lara Trubowitz

I'd like to turn my eyes. Cat and Mirror. Chase Twichell. BeAl

I'd like to walk out on ignorance like this. On the Pier. Brenda Hillman. PoA 2002

I'd like to write one poem but darkness is down. In the Red Book. Kelvin Corcoran. Oth

I'd live like that low vineyard. Like the Vineyard. Na Hûidôk. EcSo, tr. by Peter H. Lee

I'd Love to Be a Fairy's Child. Robert Graves. ChAP

I'd love to make a coumbite. Coumbite. Hilario Batista Felix. OGAHCP, tr. by Boadiba and Jack Hirschman

I'd love to make them linger on, those nymphs. Favn in the Afternoon, A. Stéphane Mallarmé. SxFrPo, tr. by A. M. and E. H. Blackmore

I'd make a bed for you. Labasheedy (The Silken Bed). Nuala Ni Dhomhnaill. CABP, tr. by the author

I'd never killed one before. I guess the best way. First Turtle. David Lee. NevBe

I'd never seen pain so bland. Bud Powell, Paris, 1959. William Matthews. OxBoAm

I'd rather be at the beach. I'd rather beat each ache. Bumber to Bumper. Harryette Mullen. RD

I'd rather be taken for brave than anything else. (LL) Frost at Midnight. Mary Jo Salter. RA; VisFro

I'd rather have fingers than toes. On Digital Extremities. Frank Gelett Burgess. CalPo

I'd rather have no name, no name for my man to call. N-e-m-e-s-i-s Blues. A. Van Jordan. PoCho

I'd rather my fist be made of steel. Last Word, The. Imamu Amiri Baraka. UnSA

I'd rather see than be one! (LL) Purple Cow, The. Frank Gelett Burgess. ASA; BRP; CalPo; NBLV; NTCP; OBCoV; TCAPo; TFi; TLR

I'd really love to become a flower, or clouds. Clinic in a Dangerous Season 1, A. Yi Yônju. EcSo, tr. by Yung-Hee Kim

I'd say he'd had too much. Runaway Cow, A. Cathal Ó Searcaigh. ModIr, tr. by Patrick Crotty

I'd say that's a "proud" or swollen wound on my finger, body's pride. Fred Wah. NLPA Fr. This Dendrite Map: Father / Mother Haibun.

I'd seen a head or two a club had done with. Benefit Picnic, Cigar Makers' Strike, August 1884. Kevin Stein. PoDa

I'd sell my soul for that fawn. Shmuel HaNagid. ErotSp, tr. by Harris Lenowitz and Jerome Rothenberg

I'd shoot the man who pulled up slowly in his hot car this morning. If I Had a Gun. Gig Ryan. BMAP

I'd smoke in the freezer. Shoplifters. Maura Stanton. ReTh

I'd swear blind it's June, 1962. My Flu. Michael Donaghy. StAl

I'd toddle safely home and die—in bed. (LL) Base Details. Siegfried Sassoon. BrAP; FaBoWar; MoBrPo; NPeEn; OxBEV; PLBUT

I'd wake up starved on the day of the match. Reflections on Hillsborough in Memoriam. T. H. Naisby. NOBAu

I'd watch her each evening. Longliner at Sunset. Enos D. Watts. Coast

I'd wed you without herds, without money, or rich array. Cashel of Munster. William English. IrLP; IrV; OBEV, tr. by Sir Samuel Ferguson

Idanre and Other Poems (1967). Wole Soyinka.
  Death in the Dawn. NAMCP V.2
  Night. WaAnP; WoPoe
Idbury bells are ringing. Country Thought. Sylvia Townsend Warner.
  MoBrPo
Idea. Michael Drayton.
  25. PBRV
  Another to the River Ankor. NOSC
  As Love And I. NoSic
  "As other men, so I myself do muse." NOSC; NoSic
  ("Dear, why should you command me to my rest.") GSo
  "Evil [or Evill] spirit, your beauty, haunts me still, An." NoSic
  (Farewell to Love.) MakPoe; NOSC
  How Many Paltry, Foolish, Painted Things. HeIP-4; NAEL-7v1; NIP-4;
    NoP-5; NOSC
  (Idea 6.) WaAnP
  "If he, from heaven that filched the living fire." NoP-4; NoP-5
  Like an Adventurous Seafarer Am I. NOSC
  "Love, in a humour, played the prodigal." NoSic
  (Parting, The.) OBEV
  (Since There's No Help.) CABP; PoPoPo
  "Since there's no help, come let us kiss and part." AEP; BASC; ClHu; GSo;
    HeIP-4; NAEL-6v1; NAEL-7v1; NoP-5; OPOU; OxBSo; SoSe-8; TFi;
    WaAnP
  (Sonnet 1.) WaAnP
  Sonnet 8. NOSC; WaAnP
  Sonnet 35: Some, misbelieving and profane. AEP
  (Sonnet 6: 'How many paltry, foolish, painted things'.) AEP; NAEL-6v1
  Three Sorts of Serpents Do Resemble Thee. PtR
  (To the Critic.) NOSC
  To the Reader of These Sonnets. NAEL-6v1; NAEL-7v1; NOSC
  "Truce, gentle love, a parley now I crave." NoSic
  "You not alone, when you are still alone." OxBSo
Idea, The. Agnes Mary Frances Robinson. VWP
Idea, The. Mark Strand. CAP-8; NAMCP V.2; OxBoAm
Idea 6. Michael Drayton. See How Many Paltry, Foolish, Painted Things.
Idea came from prairie dogs, The. Living Life as a Living Target. Roxy
  Gordon. TiP2
Idea danced before us as a flag, The. Many Soldiers. Edgar Lee Masters.
  TCAPo
Idea!: Four-word poems! Maxine Hong Kingston. FaoP
Idea is, the marriage still exists, The. Arguing Bartusiak. Albert Goldbarth.
  CAP-8
Idea of an infinite number of stars brought Newton to his knees, The.
  Presocratic, Surfing, Breathing Cosmology Blues, The. Christopher
  Buckley. BodElec
Idea of Ancestry, The. Etheridge Knight. AF; ESEAA; InGu; ISC; NIP-4;
  OxAAAP; PBCAP; RaBo; StAl
Idea of Detroit, The. Jim Gustafson. FTtHH
Idea of Housework, The. Dorianne Laux. SweBea
Idea of Islands, The. Judith Ortiz Cofer. PueRic
Idea of Love Between Us, The. Kate Light. AmPoNex
Idea of making love as sticking out your tongue, The. Idea of Making Love,
  The. Alicia Ostriker. FiBr
Idea of Order at Key West, The. Wallace Stevens. AmFaPo; APT-1; BrAP;
  ColAP; HarvBoo; HeIP-4; MakPoe; MoAmPo; NAAL-5; NAAPv.2;
  NAMCP V.1; NAWM-7v2; NIL-7; NIP-4; NoAM; NoP-4; NoP-5;
  OxBoAm; PoPoPo; SAmP; TFi; WaAnP
Idea of Russia, The. Viktor Krivulin. TCRusP, tr. by Anna Barker and Daniel
  Weissbort
Idea of trust, or, The. Idea of Trust, The. Thom Gunn. HarvBoo; ItP; NPeEn
Idea that freezes me this time, The. Theory and Practice in Poetry. Eleanor
  Wilner. TAPaP
Ideal. Carol Muske-Dukes. AmAlph
Ideal, An. Henrietta Cordelia Ray. CBWP-3
Ideal, The. James Fenton. BeAl
Ideal, The. T. R. Hummer. LTA
Ideal Bar, The. Frank O'Hara. BodElec
Ideal General, The. Archilochus. FaBoWar, tr. by A. Watson Bain
Ideal Retreat, The. Khong Lo. EaWin, tr. by W. S. Merwin and Nguyen Ngoc
  Bich
Ideal Wife. Mahe Jabeen. HotL, tr. by V. Narayana Rao
Ideal Woman, An. Yehuda Amichai. PoDa, tr. by Chana Bloch and Chana
  Kronfeld
Ideal Woman, An. Yehuda Amichai. PML, tr. by Chana Bloch and Stephen
  Mitchell
Idealism [limerick]. Ronald Arbuthnott Knox. NBLV; OxBEV

Ideally, you should be in your own. American Living Room, The: A Tract.
  William Meredith. BodElec
Ideas Go Only So Far. Matthea Harvey. LegDan
Ideas Gray Suits Bowler Hats Baal. Ed Roberson. BAP-04
Idea's Mirror. Michael Drayton.
  "Golden sun upon his fiery wheels, The." NoSic
Idem the Same. Gertrude Stein. See Valentine to Sherwood Anderson, A.
Identifying with the Buddha. Charles Harper Webb. Vesp
Identikit. Jim Brodey.
  "Spoor bank, The." AHA
Identities. Paul Eluard. SurPaPo, tr. by Mary Ann Caws
Identity. Thomas Bailey Aldrich. TCAPo
Identity. Elizabeth Jennings. MoWP
Identity. Margit Mikes. IQMS, tr. by Susanne K. Walther
Identity A Poem. Gertrude Stein. PFTM-1
Identity Card. Mahmoud Darwish. VCWP, tr. by Denys Johnson-Davies
Identity Crisis. Sam Gardiner. NIrP
Ideological Tango. Radoi Ralin. CSCBP, tr. by Georgi Belev and Lisa
  Sapinkopf
Idiocy of the hemp family. Eros Poesis. Tatiana Shcherbina. ItGoST, tr. by
  J. Kates
Idiot, The. Dudley Randall. LTA
Idiot, The. Charles Reznikoff. APT-2
Idiot bêle du regard, L'. Malcolm de Chazal. YaTCFP Fr. Sens plastique
  (1947).
Idiot bleats with his gaze. Plastic Sense (1947 version). Malcolm de Chazal.
  YaTCFP, tr. by Mary Ann Caws
Idiot Boy, The. William Wordsworth. NOBRP; NPBRoP; OBNV
Idiot Girl, The. Mary F. Johnson. CenSon
Idiot in the Bath, The. M. Vasalis. TuT, tr. by Peter van de Kamp
Idiot neutre n'est pas toujours un artiste, Un. Mon Pouchkine. Nathalie
  Quintane. YaTCFP
Idiot-Born, The. Eliza Cook. VWP
Idiotic silence of state holidays, The. Gratitude. György Petri. VCWP, tr. by
  Geroge Gömöri and Clive Wilmer
Idle. . .nothing to do. Voicing Deepest Thoughts. Yu Xuanji. CCL1, tr. by
  Genevieve Wimsatt
Idle as trout in light Colonel Jones. Famine Road, The. Eavan Boland.
  MoWP
Idle Pursuits. Alexander Pope. OBSV Fr. Dunciad, The.
Idle Song. Po Chü-i. NDACCP, tr. by David Hinton
Idle Visitation, An. Edward Dorn. PmAP Fr. Gunslinger.
Idle Words. Walter Savage Landor. OBSV
Idleness. Lu Yu. NDACCP, tr. by Kenneth Rexroth
Idler Listening to Socrates Discussing Philosophy with His Boy-Friends, An.
  Edward Cracroft Lefroy. CAGL
Idler with a wand for a walking stick, An. Batyushkov. Osip Emilevich
  Mandelstam. OBVE
Idols. Witter Bynner. APT-1
Idonean lemur, sport with me. Invitation. Orrick Johns. APT-1
Idyl. Henrietta Cordelia Ray. CBWP-3
Idyl: "Tiny fish." John James. Oth
Idyl of Harvest Time, An. John Townsend Trowbridge. APN-2
Idyl of Spring, An. Henrietta Cordelia Ray. CBWP-3
Idyll. Miklós Zrínyi. tr. by René Bonnerjea
  "Early in the spring-time a huntsman full of sorrow." IQMS, tr. by René
    Bonnerjea
Idyll: "He was a selfish shellfish." Stoddard King. NBLV
Idyll: "I lived behind a window." Peter Balakian. PfSP
Idyll: "Lord, forgive me if I do not look for you." Henriqueta Lisboa.
  TCLAP, tr. by Hélcio Veiga Costa
Idyll of the South, An. Albery Allson Whitman.
  "I had a dream: Columbia the Great." APN-2
Idylls. Theocritus. tr. by Charles Stuart Calverley, Barbara Hughes Fowler, W.
  Douglas P. Hill, Unknown and William Carlos Williams
Idyll 1: Thyrsis. HePo, tr. by Barbara Hughes Fowler
Idyll 1. WoPoe, tr. by William Carlos Williams
Idyll 2: The Enchantment. tr. by Thomas Creech
  Enchantment, The. OBVE, tr. by Thomas Creech
Idyll 2: The Sorceress. HePo, tr. by Barbara Hughes Fowler
Idyll 21: The Fishermen. OBVE, tr. by Charles Stuart Calverley
Idyll 27: Daphnis. OBVE, tr. by John Dryden
Idyll 6: Damoetas and Daphnis. HePo, tr. by Barbara Hughes Fowler
Idyll 7: Harvest Home. HePo, tr. by Barbara Hughes Fowler
Idyll 11: Cyclops. HePo, tr. by Barbara Hughes Fowler
Idyll 11: The Cyclops. OBVE, tr. by Elizabeth Barrett Browning
Idyll 13: Hylas. HePo, tr. by Barbara Hughes Fowler

Idyll 15: Gorgo and Praxinoa. HePo, *tr.* by Barbara Hughes Fowler

Idyll 20: Neteheard [*or* Neatherd]. NoSic; OBVE, *tr.* by *Unknown*

Idyll 24: Little Heracles. HePo, *tr.* by Barbara Hughes Fowler

Idyll 29. CAGL, *tr.* by W. Douglas P. Hill

Idylls of the King. Geoffrey Hill. NoAM *Fr.* Apology for the Revival of Christian Architecture in England, An.

Idylls of the King. Alfred Tennyson.

    Coming of Arthur, The. NAEL-7v2

    Passing of Arthur, The. NAEL-6v2; NAEL-7v2

       Prayer. SacPr

    Pelleas and Ettarre. NAEL-6v2

Iersche brybour baird, vyle beggar with thy brattis. William Dunbar. NePenScot *Fr.* Flyting of Dumbar [*or* Dunbar] and Kennedie [*or* Kennedy], The.

Iesu. George Herbert. SacPr

IESU is in my heart, his sacred name. Iesu. George Herbert. SacPr

Iesu, swete son dere! Our Lady's Song. *Unknown.* OBEV

If. Franklin Pierce Adams. APT-1

If. Edward Bond. HP

If. Mortimer Collins. OBCoV

If. Daria Menicanti. CItWP, *tr.* by Cinzia Sartini Blum and Lara Trubowitz

If. Robert Penn Warren. BodElec

If a body is what you want. Here, Bullet. Brian Turner. AmWaPo

If a clear fountain still keeping a sad course. Mary Sidney Wroth, Countess of Montgomery. RACG

If a custom-tailored vet. Cole Porter. NBLV *Fr.* Always True to You in My Fashion.

If a daughter bent on pleasing. Prodigal Daughter, The. Dorothy Barresi. SweBea

If a fir tree had a foot or two like a turtle, or a wing. That Journeys Are Good. Jelaluddin Rumi. RaBo; WED, *tr.* by Robert Bly

If a Fish Fell in a Forest. John Nelson. GeoH

If a good man were ever housed in Hell. Good Man in Hell, The. Edwin Muir. MoBrPo

If a large hart: Joyned with a Noble minde. M. S. Sir Will: Dyer, Kt: Who Put on Immortality Aprill the 29th Anno Domini 1621. Lady Catherine Dyer. EMWP

If a man and a woman happen down streets that no one else notices. Man and a Woman, A. Roberto Fernández Retamar. PML, *tr.* by Mark Weiss

If a man finds it necessary to eat garbage. Wendell Berry. UpMys *Fr.* Prayers and Sayings of the Mad Farmer.

If a mistake as to the other if in mistake as to the brother, if by mistake. Gertrude Stein. MotU *Fr.* Book Concluding with As A Wife Has a Cow a Love Story, A.

If a monkey drives a car. Poems We Can Understand. Paul Hoover. PmAP; WaAnP

If a peacock ever passes. Disillusion for Rubén Darío. Nancy Morejón. TCLAP, *tr.* by Kathleen Weaver

If a Pig Wore a Wig. Christina Georgina Rossetti. NPeEn; VWP

If a Privileged Light. Gabriella Leto. CItWP, *tr.* by Cinzia Sartini Blum and Lara Trubowitz

If a song flies to me from the garden. Tatiana Bek. ItGoST, *tr.* by Richard McKane

If a straight horizontal thread one meter long falls from a height of one. 1914 Box, The. Marcel Duchamp. PFTM-1

If a Suite in Praise of the Yoruba Oracle. Awotunde Aworinde. PFTM-1 *Fr.* If a Suite in Praise of the Yoruba Oracle.

If a swan / sang. (LL) Swan and Shadow. John Hollander. NoP-4; NoP-5; OxBoAm; PoA 2002; VCAP

If a train departs at 10:20 P.M.. Word Problems. Kate Rushin. PfS

If a two-headed goat pisses its. What's Your Take. Jayne Cortez. PrTe

If aa the bluid shed at thy Tron. Capernaum. Lewis Spence. EdScPo

If, after the bombardment is over. Discourse on Method, The. Heberto Padilla. VCWP

If all be true that I do think. Catch, A. Henry Aldrich. NOSC

If all but one deny me, I am not. Riddle, A. Daniel Hoffman. PoCho

If all happy families are alike. Happy and Unhappy Families 1. Lisel Mueller. ExTi

If all the answer's to be the Sinai sort. Golden Calf. Norman Alexander MacCaig. ChIV-1

If all the grief and woe and bitterness. Planh for the Young English King. Bertrans de Born. APT-1, *tr.* by Ezra Pound

If all the hearts that shrivelled in their graves. Sándor Petőfi. IQMS *Fr.* Clouds, The.

If all the trees in all the woods were men. Cacoëthes Scribendi. Oliver Wendell Holmes. NBLV; OBCoV

If all the world and love were young. Nymph's [*or* Nimphs] Reply to the [Passionate] Shepherd [*or* Sheepheard], The. Sir Walter Ralegh. AEP; AmFaPo; BrAP; CABP; ClHu; HeIP-4; NAEL-6v1; NAEL-7v1; NBLV; NIL-7; NIP-4; NoP-4; NoP-5; NoSic; NPeEn; PoPoPo; RACG; TFi; TRP; UV; WaAnP; WeW-3

If all the world were cake. To Drink. Philippe Soupault. SurPaPo, *tr.* by Mary Ann Caws and Patricia Terry

If All the World Were Paper. *Unknown.* NOSC; NTCP; OBCoV (Interrogativa Cantilena.) OxBEV

If all transgressions here should have their pay. Gods Providence. Robert Herrick. SacPr

If all you boast of your great art be true. To Alchemists. Ben Jonson. BASC

If all you need, my sister sweet. Alfred de Musset. WoPoe *Fr.* Night in May, A.

If along the highroad. Zun-da-lu: If Along the Highroad. *Unknown.* CCL1, *tr.* by Arthur Waley

If an eagle be imprisoned. America. Henry Dumas. ChAP; OxAAAP

If an inaudible whistle. What the Dog Perhaps Hears. Lisel Mueller. MiVo

If and when I did look up, the sky over the Moy was the very same gray blue. Misfits, The. Paul Muldoon. GPPA

If any ask why there's no great She-Poet. Dedication of the Cook. Anna Wickham. MoBrPo; NALW

If any have a stone to shy. Pebble, The. Elinor Wylie. ChIV-1; MoAmPo

If any mourn us in the workshop, say. Rudyard Kipling. InoFa; WoPoe *Fr.* Epitaphs of the War [1914–1918].

If any pleasure can come to a man through recalling. Catullus. NAWM-7v1 *Fr.* Carmina [Charles Martin Translation].

If any question why we died. Rudyard Kipling. HarvBoo; InoFa; NPeEn; PoAgWa; WoPoe *Fr.* Epitaphs of the War [1914–1918].

If any sink, assure that this, now standing. Emily Dickinson. PCW

If any thing delight me for to print. To God. Robert Herrick. SacPr

If any woman of us all. Magdalen. Harriet Prescott Spofford. SWaP

If anyone asks you. Like This. Jelaluddin Rumi. ErotSp, *tr.* by Coleman Barks

If anything's to be praised, it's most likely how. Joseph Brodsky. StAl *Fr.* Part of Speech, A.

If art were a series of arbitrary digs. On Geoffrey Grigson. Cyril Connolly. OBCoV

If, as they always claim upon returning. Soul. Alan Shapiro. PoA 2002

If, as they say, poetry is a sign of something. Kiss of the Sun. Mary Ruefle. AmAlph; FaoP

If / at the last minute. Repenting. Sarah Klassen. ACAMVP

If, at the pharmacy, I say to the woman. Pharmacy. Aaron Anstett. AmPoNex

If, at your desk, you push aside your work. Spell. Kate Clanchy. StAl

If aught can teach us aught, Affliction's looks. Sir John Davies. WoPoe *Fr.* Nosce Teipsum.

If aught of oaten stop, or pastoral song. Ode to Evening. William Collins. CABP; NAEL-6v1; NAEL-7v1; NoP-4; NoP-5; OBEV; OxAEP-1; TFi (If ought of oaten stop, or pastoral song.) NPeEn; OxBEV

If aught of simple song have power to touch. Birthday Crown, The. William, Archbishop of Armagh Alexander. SacPr

If Auschwitz had been in Hampshire. If. Edward Bond. HP

If bathing were a virtue, not a lust. Opus 118. Arthur Davison Ficke. APT-1, *tr.* by Anne Knish

If bees are few. (LL) To make a prairie it takes a clover and one bee. Emily Dickinson. HeIP-4; NBLV; TCAPo

If Bethlehem were here today. Christmas Morning. Elizabeth Madox Roberts. MoAmPo (If Bethlehem were here to-day.) NOxBChV

If between basin and range you wake. Waking at the Middle of Nowhere. Reg Saner. PoCoUp

If boy, or man, or woman steals I hump. *Unknown.* PriapPo *Fr.* Priapus Poems, The.

If but some vengeful god would call to me. Hap. Thomas Hardy. BrAP; CABP; GSo; MoBrPo; NAEL-6v2; NAEL-7v2; NAMCP V.1; NoAM; NoP-4; NoP-5; OxBSo; WaAnP

If by chance, Flaccus, someone could offer me for the asking. Martial. CAGL *Fr.* Epigrams.

If by chance you were simply to miss a step. Liliane Giraudon. SCFWP *Fr.* Poem with Incense Paper.

If by Dull Rhymes Our English Must Be Chained. John Keats. BrAP; CenSon (On the Sonnet.) NIL-7; NIP-4; NoP-4; NoP-5

If by his torturing, savage foes untraced. Captive Escaped in the Wilds of America, The. Addressed to the Hon. Mrs. O'Neill. Charlotte Smith. CenSon

If by mischance the people in the street. George Wither. PBRV *Fr.* Britain's Remembrancer Canto 4.

"If Candlemas be fine and clear." At Candlemas. Charles Causley. OBCP

If casual concourse did the world compose. Sir Richard Blackmore. STuOW *Fr.* Creation.

If Chickens Could Talk. Víctor Hernández Cruz. PueRic

If China. Stanislaw Baranczak. AF

If china, then only the kind. Stanislaw Baranczak. AF

If Christians threaten to start a pogrom. Christmas Eve. Marina Boroditskaya. CRWP, *tr. by* Ruth Fainlight

If come into this world again I must. Dew on a Dusty Heart. Jean Starr Untermeyer. MoAmPo

If "compression is the first grace of style." To a Snail. Marianne Moore. APT-1; NALW; NAMCP V.1; OxBoAm; PoPoPo

If constancy in love, if a brave heart. Petrarch. ErotSp, *tr. by* Sam Hamill

If Cynthia Be a Queen, a Princess, and Supreme. Sir Walter Ralegh. NoP-4; NoP-5

If design govern in a thing so small. (LL) Design. Robert Frost. APT-1; BrAP; ColAP; HeIP-4; NAAL-5; NAAPv.2; NAMCP V.1; NIL-7; NoAM; NoP-4; NoP-5; OxBoAm; OxBSo; PoPoPo; RaBo; SAmP; SoSe-8; TFi; TRP; WaAnP

If doughty [*or* daughty] deeds my lady please[s]. Robert Graham. OBEV

If, driving home from the Russian poet's. Poetry Bug, The. Barry Spacks. PoA 2002

If, dumb too long, the drooping Muse hath stayed. To the Earl of Warwick, on the Death of Mr. Addison. Thomas Tickell. OxAEP-1

If duty, wife, lead thee to deem. Husband to Wife. John Harington. NoSic

If Each Day Falls. Pablo Neruda. WoPoe, *tr. by* William O'Daly

If e'er in thy sight I found favour, Apollo. Poet's Prayer, The. *Unknown*. OBSV

If Elvis Presley / is. In the Funk World. Imamu Amiri Baraka. FuFl; NAMCP V.2

If ever a garden was Gethsemane. Anne Spencer. InGu

If Ever Hapless Woman Had a Cause. Mary Sidney Herbert, Countess of Pembroke. MakPoe

If ever I had dreamed of my dead name. To My Friend (With an Identity Disc). Wilfred Owen. CAGL

If Ever I Would Leave You. Alan Jay Lerner. ReLy

If ever love had force in huma[i]ne bre[a]st? Mary Sidney Wroth, Countess of Montgomery. BASC *Fr.* Pamphilia to Amphilanthus.

If ever mercy move you murder me. To the Mercy Killers. Dudley Randall. SoSe-8

If ever there was a beginning. Let There Be Light! D. H. Lawrence. ChIV-1

If ever there was a vehicle for nostalgia. Trains. William Scammell. NLP

If ever two were one, then surely we. To My Dear and Loving Husband. Anne Bradstreet. AmFaPo; BASC; BrAP; ColAP; ErotSp; HeIP-4; ITBLP; LW; NAAL-3; NAAL-5; NAAPv.1; NIL-7; NIP-4; NoP-4; NoP-5; NOSC; OxBEV; OxBoAm; OxWW; PEW; SacPr; TCAPo; TFi; WaAnP; WeW-3

If ever you should go by chance. How To Tell the Wild Animals. Carolyn Wells. NBLV

If every name is (as the Greek maintains). Golem, The. Jorge Luis Borges. PoetW, *tr. by* John Hollander

If everyone decided to be flowers. Flowers. Leo Vroman. TuT, *tr. by* James Liddy

If everything happens that can't be done. E. E. Cummings. SoSe-8; WeW-3

If evil could be safer, on the whole. (LL) Election Day, 1984. Carolyn Kizer. ExTi; GifTon

If external action is effete. Past Is the Present, The. Marianne Moore. APT-1; OxBoAm

If famous Apelles with his hand of art. Pietro Aretino. GS

If fictive music fails your lyre, confess. Richard Wilbur. NBLV *Fr.* Flippancies.

If, finding it, he fails to find / Its master. (LL) Snail, The. Vincent Bourne. NPeEn; OBVE, *tr. by* William Cowper

If flowers bloom, I think of the moon. Yi Chŏngbo. CATKP, *tr. by* Peter H. Lee

If, flying south, gas, cylinders, and wings uphold you. Mathematician's Dream, The. Reuel Denney. YaYoPo

If for all the promises you regard so lightly. Horace. STV *Fr.* Odes.

If for the King I should forsake my God, should I doo well? (LL) Anne Dowriche. PBRV; WaAnP *Fr.* French Historie, The.

If Fortune Smiles. Rofel G. Brion. ReBoTo

If Fred Astaire had been really smart. Johnny Laces Up His Red Shoes. Cornelius Eady. InvLad

If friends, you would but now this place accost. Invitation to my Friends at Cambridge, An. Jane Barker. BASC

If From My Lips Some Angry Accents Fell. Charles Lamb. CenSon (To Mary Ann Lamb, the Author's Best Friend and Sister.) NPBRoP

If from the public way you turn your steps. Michael [A Pastoral Poem]. William Wordsworth. NAEL-6v2; NAEL-7v2; NOBRP; OxAEP-2; WaAnP

If God as a scribe were to write. They Who Are Poor. Attila József. IQMS, *tr. by* Vernon Watkins

If God compel thee to this destiny. Thought for a Lonely Death-Bed, A. Elizabeth Barrett Browning. ViWPN

If God had a wife, she'd be a doozy. Coward. Maurya Simon. ExTi

If God had stopped work after the fifth [*or* third] day. Linda Pastan. InvLi; SoSe-8 *Fr.* Imperfect Paradise, The.

If gold in a glimpse din. Arctic Sun. Christine Hume. IAoNAP

If half my heart is here, doctor. Angina Pectoris. Nazim Hikmet. VCWP

If Harriet Tubman. If Harriet Tubman Were Alive Today. Verneda Sagay-Lights. BtF

If Hart Crane played trumpet. Almost Blue. Mark Doty. SeSe

If he asks about me, trace on the ground. Nocturne and Elegy. Emilio Ballagas. CAGL, *tr. by* Fanny Arango-Ramos and William Keeth

If he could have kept. Sam. Lucille Clifton. UnSA

If he could solve the riddle. Sphinx. Robert Earl Hayden. GT

If he could speak he would deny it. (LL) Epigram: "Here lies New Critic who would fox us." James Vincent Cunningham. APT-2; MoAmPo

If he did not come apart in her hands, he fell. Diane Di Prima. PFTM-1 *Fr.* Loba.

If he, from heaven that filched the living fire. Michael Drayton. NoP-4; NoP-5 *Fr.* Idea.

If He Had. Gary Young.

"Fog descends over the tidal surge and the shallow lagoons." GeoHom

"Owl drifts slowly through the canyon where three flickers worry a pitted oak for grubs, An." GeoHom

If he had loved me he would not have designed. Man-Torpedo-Boat. Tessa Rumsey. LegDan

If he had only been a more inspiring Leader. On the Death of Ludwig Erhard. Hal Colebatch. NOBAu

If he have feeling, is[,] to cry! (LL) When Lovely Woman. Phoebe Cary. APN-2; UV

If He Let Us Go Now. Sherley Anne Williams. OxAAAP

If he turns them, they are purple, black from head to heel. Pathologist. Ellen Dudley. OPRER

If He Walked into My Life. Jerry Herman. ReLy

If he were I, he would do what I did. (LL) Hanging Man, The. Sylvia Plath. OxBoAm; VCAP

If Heaven had no love for wine. Drinking Alone in Moonlight. Li Po. TAL

If Heaven has into being deigned to call. Slavery. Hannah More. RWP; WoRP

If heaven were to do again. Peaceful Shepherd, The. Robert Frost. MoAmPo

If Hercules' tall stature might be guessed. On a Good Leg and Foot. William Strode. NOSC

If homely virtues draw from me a tune. Envoy. James Weldon Johnson. SacPr

If hono[u]r to an ancient name be due. On the Welsh Language. Katherine Philips. EMWP; NoP-5; NOSC

If Hot Flowers Come to the Street. R. Meenakshi. WoPoe, *tr. by* Martha Ann Selby

If I am as cute as a button. Domestic Bliss. John Yau. OxBoAm

If I am first in the ground, visit me. Lynx. Alan Robert Wilson. Coast

'If I am Jesse's son,' said he. Goliath and David. Robert Graves. FaBoWar

If I Am Too Brown or Too White for You. Wendy Rose. HATNAP

If I became. If I Became a Stone. Sŏ Chŏngju. VCWP, *tr. by* David R. McCann

If I Blindfold You. Marjorie Welish. FTOS

If I but stretch out my hand, someone grips it. I feel this is certain. Unknown World, The. György Sárközi. IQMS, *tr. by* Watson Kirkconnell

If I can let you go as trees let go. May Sarton. PoBW *Fr.* Autumn Sonnets, The.

If I can stop one Heart from breaking. Emily Dickinson. BRP

If I comb out my hair. Spell for a Daughter. Theresa Kishkan. IFF

If I could be still / there would be a beach. Truro. Rose Solari. AmPoNex

If I Could Be with You. Henry Creamer. ReLy

If I could but see the white cap. *Unknown*. CCL1 *Fr.* Su-guan [Translations].

If I could catch the green lantern of the firefly. Lover, A. Amy Lowell. OxBoAm

If I could chop wood. Karate. Stanley Plumly. MoASP

If I could come back from the dead, I would come back. Apple. Susan Stewart. AmAlph; BAP-01

If I could cry from fear in a lonely house. Ode to Federico García Lorca. Pablo Neruda. ConPit, *tr. by* Clayton Eshleman

If I could just touch your ankle, he whispers, *there.* Persephone Underground. Rita Dove. FFC

If I could keep my innermost me. Sanctuary, The. Sara Teasdale. APT-1; NAAPv.2

If I Could Mourn Like a Mourning Dove. Frank Bidart. NAMCP V.2

If I could only get all of you. Trying Again. Dahlia Ravikovitch. VCWP

If I could only hear. Speak to Me. Fanny Carrión de Fierro. TANSG, *tr. by* Sally Cheney Bell

If I could [*or* co'd], I would [*or* wo'd] not so. (LL) Bracelet to Julia, The. Robert Herrick. BASC; OBEV

If I could read Schemhammphorasch? (LL) Schemhammphorasch. Rose Terry Cooke. NAAPv.1; SWaP

If I could send him only. Her Reticence. Theodore Roethke. RACG

If I could speak with you. . .but that's all gone. Hamlet to Ophelia. Peter Cummings. IaFF

If I Could Tell You. W. H. Auden. HarvBoo; OxBoAm; WaAnP

If I could tell you I would let you know. (LL) If I Could Tell You. W. H. Auden. HarvBoo; OxBoAm; WaAnP

If I could track you down to have you taste. Patterns. Roberta Hill Whiteman. HATNAP

If i cud ever write a. To P. J. (2 Yrs Old Who Sed Write a Poem for Me in Portland, Oregon). Sonia Sanchez. CA

If I desire something, I know it not. Hadewijch II. WPoS

If I did complain, who among my friends. George Bowering. OpeFie *Fr.* Kerrisdale Elegies.

If I did tell she. English Girl Eats Her First Mango. John Agard. BeAl

If I didn't cry all the time, my house would still be desolate. My Head and My Knees. Mirza Asadullah Khan Ghalib. WED, *tr. by* Robert Bly and Sunil Dutta

If I Died Tonight. Idea Vilariño. TANSG, *tr. by* Louise B. Popkin

If I do take somebody's word on. Toward a Personal Semantics. June Jordan. EGAG

If I don't believe in me. Boundary. Pedro Serrano. RMCMP, *tr. by* Geoff Hargreaves

If I don't drive around the park. Observation. Dorothy Parker. APT-1; NAMCP V.1; OxBoAm

If I drink water while this doth last. Thomas Love Peacock. NBLV *Fr.* Crotchet Castle.

If I found you wandering round the edge. On Ballycastle Beach. Medbh McGuckian. PBCIP

If I gave 5 birds. Red Shirt, The. Philip Levine. BodElec

If I get up one more time in the dark. Mentioning of Souls. Gerald Stern. PLBUT

If I Go All the Way Without You Where Would I Go! Ntozake Shange. FaoP

If I grow bitterly. Scrub. Edna St. Vincent Millay. APT-1

If I had a beau. Dashing White Sergeant, The. John Burgoyne. FaBoWar

If I had a Green Automobile. Green Automobile, The. Allen Ginsberg. BB

If I Had a Gun. Gig Ryan. BMAP

If I had a nickel. .05. Ishmael Reed. ESEAA

If I had a shiny gun. Frustration. Dorothy Parker. AmWit

If I Had a Talking Picture of you. Lew Brown, B. G. DeSylva and Ray Henderson. ReLy

If I had always known what I've learnt. Private Truce. Lőrinc Szabó. IQMS, *tr. by* Peter Zollman

If I had been careful last December. Ashtray in the Snow. Robert Wrigley. RoV

If I had chosen thee, thou shouldst have been. Wilfrid Scawen Blunt. GSo *Fr.* Love Sonnets of Proteus, The.

If I had died that Friday in Paris. Izet Sarajlić. PML, *tr. by* Charles Simic

If I had done the right thing, never run away. Right Thing, The. Pesha Gertler. FiBr

If I had given you that love and care. John Hewitt. PNI *Fr.* Sonnets for Roberta (1954).

If I had known, if I had known, would I ever. Old Water. Jeff Gundy. ACAMVP

If i had known the number of hours i would find myself mute. Roy Kiyooka. NLPA *Fr.* Pear Tree Pomes.

If I had known this burden on my tongue. Mama. Timothy Liu. WiU

If I Had Made the World. Sarah Morgan Bryan Piatt. NCAP

If I had no memory. Bad Truth. Jane Rohrer. BodElec

If I had not met the red-haired boy whose father. One of the Lives. W. S. Merwin. OxBoAm

If I had peace to sit and sing. Singer, The. Anna Wickham. MoBrPo

If I had thought. Robert Creeley. WoBe *Fr.* Life and Death.

If I had thought thou couldst have died. To Mary. Charles Wolfe. IrLP; OBEV

If I Had You. Jimmy Campbell and Reginald Connelly. ReLy

If I had your smile awaiting me. Tracks of Longing. Sion Aled. BBMWP, *tr. by* Grahame Davies

If I have but one life, let me live it. Gospel According to Clairol, The. Rachel Loden. CalPo

If I have created a world for you, in your place. Name Drawn from the Names, The. Juan Ramón Jiménez. RaW, *tr. by* Robert Bly

If I have faltered more or less. Celestial Surgeon, The. Robert Louis Stevenson. MoBrPo

If I have sinned in act, I may repent. Sonnet 27. Hartley Coleridge. CenSon

If I have to be a playmate. Miss October. Rachel Loden. RWB

If I Have to Yield My Bones. Milán Füst. IQMS, *tr. by* Paul Tabori

If I held back each word, perhaps. Poem. Timothy Liu. AmPoNex

If I hide out at Cold Mountain. Happy Among These Cliffs. Han-shan (Cold Mountain). CCL1; NDACCP, *tr. by* Gary Snyder

If I journeyed to a suburb of a Sunday. Marbled Chuckle in the Savannahs. Kenward Elmslie. FTOS

If I just had a piano. Testimonial. Langston Hughes. APT-2

If I leave all for thee, wilt thou exchange. Elizabeth Barrett Browning. CenSon *Fr.* Sonnets from the Portuguese.

If I Leave You. Alberto A. Ríos. PoChi

If I lie naked. Confession. Pearl Cleage. ISC

If I, like Solomon. O To Be A Dragon. Marianne Moore. APT-1; ChIV-1; NAAL-5; NALW

If I live [*or* grow] to be old, for I find I go down. Old Man's Wish, The. Walter Pope. NOSC

If I lived in this place for a thousand years. Cuchulainn. Michael O'Loughlin. PBCIP

If I look at his hand on the gearshift. Gearshift Poem, The. Jane Rohrer. ACAMVP

If I look up from here. When Suzy Was. Kelvin Corcoran. Oth

If I love you. Thread. Catherine Lucy Czerkawska. LW

If I love you! (LL) Madam and Her Madam. Langston Hughes. NAMCP V.1; RACG; SAmP

If I Love You. Frank Prewett. HATNAP

If I loved the moon I would not praise. Shall I Compare Thee? T. Alan Broughton. PoDa

If I Loved You. Oscar Hammerstein, II. ReLy

If I make it over the pass. Hauling Over Wolf Creek Pass in Winter. Walter McDonald. AmWaPo

If I may have it, when it's dead. Emily Dickinson. NCAP

If I might guess, then guess I would. Dorcas. George Macdonald. SacPr

If I might offer. *Unknown*. ArkPo, *tr. by* Helen Craig McCullough

If I might only love my God and die! If Only. Christina Georgina Rossetti. SacPr

If I might where I pleased compose my nest. Golden Grove, Carmarthen. Rowland Watkyns. AngWePo

If I must dial a number to call you. Valerio Magrelli. NeIt

If I never again saw your eyes. Russia. Svetlana Dengina. CRWP, *tr. by* Daniel Weissbort

If I offered up my bell and bones to you, Boy. Amanda. Lisa Glatt. AmPoNex

If I offered you my geographic tongue. Sestina of the Geographic Tongue. Rachel Rose. IFF

If I once got free of this net. Mary Hogan's Quatrains. Máire Mhac an tSaoi. ModIr, *tr. by* Patrick Crotty

If I Only Had a Brain (If I Only Had a Heart) (If I Only Had the Nerve). E. Y. Harburg. ReLy

If I only had time! To Vera, Who Asked a Song. Edith Nesbit. PoBW

If I Only Knew. Nelly Sachs. PoAgWa; PoSu, *tr. by* Matthew Mead and Ruth Mead

If I open this flask of jade, in which is enclosed a. Vase of Perfume, The. Chang Wu-chien. BLPJKO, *tr. by* Gertrude Laughlin Joerissen

If I popped in at Downing Street. Prayer, A. Max Beerbohm. UV

If I profane with my unworthiest hand. William Shakespeare. OxAEP-1; SoSe-8 *Fr.* Romeo and Juliet.

If I pull off these woollen mitts of mine. Kate Braid. IFF *Fr.* Glenn Gould Poems.

If I remember right, his first letter. Letter, The. Andrew Motion. EmeKit; NeBrP

If I remember you, Oh Jerusalem. Psalms (Chapter 137, Verse 5-6). Manuela Fingueret. MirDau, *tr. by* Roberta Gordenstein

If I said I once loved a girl who stacked. Working Girl. David Marlatt. AmPoNex

If I say Thy name, art Thou there ? It may be so. John Berryman. ItP *Fr.* Eleven Addresses to the Lord.

If I shall enterprise to make. Praise of Faith, The. John Hall. ChIV-2

If I should cast off this tattered coat. Stephen Crane. APN-2

If I Should Die. Ben King. NBLV

If I should die, think only this of me. Rupert Brooke. AmFaPo; CABP; EMP; FaBoWar; GSo; HeIP-4; InoFa; MoBrPo; NAEL-6v2; NAEL-7v2; NoP-4; NoP-5; OBEV; OBWP; PoA 2002; PoWW; TFi; UV; WaAnP

If I Should Ever by Chance. Edward Thomas. MoBrPo; OBMV; OBWVE

If I should go away. Post-Script: for Gweno. Alun Lewis. AngWePo

If I should learn, in some quite casual way. Edna St. Vincent Millay. APT-1; HeIP-4; NAAPv.2; OxBoAm

If I should lose, think only this of me. Doctor, The. Roger Woddis. UV

If I should now forget, or not remember thee. To Spencer. George Turberville. NoSic

If I should pass the tomb of Jonah. Losers. Carl Sandburg. MoAmPo; NoAM

If I should see your eyes again. Jewels. Sara Teasdale. APT-1

If I should suddenly start to sing. Things Are Looking Up. Ira Gershwin. ReLy

If I shriek. Questions. Marc Kaminsky. AtGh

If I sit out all night alone. Nights in Siuna. Rebecca Gordon. FiBr

If I speak for the dead, I must leave. Author's Prayer. Ilya Kaminsky. LegDan

If I speak this slowly your arthritis. Nostrum. Christopher Pilling. PoCu

If I stare at you with such great insistence. *Unknown.* SLW, *tr. by* Marjolijn De Jager, Sayd Bahodin Majrouh and André Velter

If I still had the use of my mind I'd call it insane. Gasmask, The. David Wheatley. NIrP

If I stretch my neck all the way. Goree. Harriet Jacobs. SpirFl

If I switched off the light. Variation on a Theme of Wallace Stevens. John Burnside. WaAnP

If I think you'll think I'm brainwashed. Looking Up My Balance. Anselm Berrigan. HeMarv

If I thought I could get away. Kenneth Rexroth. APSN *Fr.* Love Poems of Marichiko, The.

If I Told Him: A Completed Portrait of Picasso. Gertrude Stein. OxBoAm

If I told him would he like it. If I Told Him: A Completed Portrait of Picasso. Gertrude Stein. OxBoAm

If I told you I used to know the circular truth. Eagles. James Dickey. BodElec

If I told you we could see nail polish stopping. Small Patch of Ice, A. Betsy Sholl. PBCAP

If I use my forbidden hand. Bond, The. Nuala Ni Dhomhnaill. PBCIP, *tr. by* Medbh McGuckian

If I Walked Straight Slap. Ivor Gurney. Spl

If I was not myself, I would be somebody else. Somebody Else. Jackie Kay. BeAl; NeBl

If I was you. (LL) Bad Luck Card. Langston Hughes. NoP-4; NoP-5; SAmP; TRP

If I went there a second time. First Sunset at Outler's Ranch. Enid Shomer. NevBe

If I Were a Bell. Frank Loesser. ReLy

If I Were a Bird. Lorine Niedecker. FTOS; OxBoAm

If I were a cassowary. Impromptu. Samuel Wilberforce. NBLV; OWoS

If I were a cinnamon peeler. Cinnamon Peeler, The. Michael Ondaatje. StAl

If I Were a God. Osama El-Dinasouri. AnVo, *tr. by* Mohamed Enani

If I were a man. I Know Exactly the Sort of Woman I'd Like to Fall in Love With. Deryn Rees-Jones. MFPA

If I were a man, I'd have all the moonlight. Woman. Juana de Ibarbourou. TCLAP, *tr. by* Sophie Cabot Black

If I were a poet / of love, I would make. Antonio Machado Ruiz. ErotSp, *tr. by* Robert Bly

If I Were a Rich Man. Sheldon Harnick. ReLy

If I were but a bird. *Unknown.* GePo

If I were called in. Water. Philip Larkin. EmeKit; NAMCP V.2

If I were dead, and in my place. Song to Amoret, A. Henry Vaughan. NAEL-7v1

If I were doing my Laundry I'd wash my dirty Iran. Homework. Allen Ginsberg. NoAM

If I Were Earth. Henry Dumas. OxAAAP

If I were fierce, and bald, and short of breath. Base Details. Siegfried Sassoon. BrAP; FaBoWar; MoBrPo; NPeEn; OxBEV; PLBUT

If I were French, I'd write. Breasts. Maxine Chernoff. PmAP; ReTh

If I were from Timbuktu, perhaps. Dark Mirror. Calvin Forbes. GT

If I were giv'n to mirthe 'twowld [or 'twould] be more cross. Mary Sidney Wroth, Countess of Montgomery. NoP-5 *Fr.* Pamphilia to Amphilanthus.

If I were God, up in the sky. Child's Thought, A. Bertha Moore. VerBaPo

If I were home right now. Good Friday. Rofel G. Brion. ReBoTo

If I were in China this minute. Foreign Ways. Diana Chang. UnSA

If I were King of France, that noble fine land. Heather, The. Neil Munro. EdScPo

If I were loved, as I desire to be. Alfred Tennyson. GSo; OxBSo

If I were only dafter. Witter Bynner. TCAPo *Fr.* Spectra.

If I were Pablo Neruda. My Name. Daniel Berrigan. AF

If I Were Rita Hayworth. Patricia Jones. ReTh

If I were sitting. Midnight Song. Pinkie Gordon Lane. GT

If I were stone dead and buried under. Felo de Se. Richard Hughes. OBMV

If I were the spreading tide sheets I would overwhelm your insteps. Spray. Biddy Jenkinson. ModIr, *tr. by* Alex Osborne

If I were the type to play around. Sleigh Ride in July. Johnny Burke. ReLy

If I Were Tickled by the Rub of Love. Dylan Thomas. ItP

If I were to paint myself for you. Make-Up. Cheryl Clarke. WiU

If I were to tell of our labours, our hard lodging. Aeschylus. FaBoWar *Fr.* Agamemnon.

If I were to walk this way. Wood Road, The. Edna St. Vincent Millay. APT-1

If I were to write with my blood. Nok Lady in Terracotta. Ifi Amadiume. HAWP

If I were tortur'd with greensickness. Song. Elizabeth Polwhele. EMWP

If I were used to writing verse. First Attempt in Rhyme, A. Thomas Hood. OBCoV

If I were writing on rock. Mesa Blanca. Víctor Hernández Cruz. PFTM-2

If I were young again. In the Garden of Apples. Colette Ni Ghallchóir. NIrP, *tr. by* the author

If I when my wife is sleeping. William Carlos Williams. *See* If when my wife is sleeping.

If I wis a thoosan, I cudna mind mair nor whit I mind nou. Melt Twa. James Logie Robertson. EdScPo

If I Write a Poem. A. Van Jordan. SpirFl

If I Yes. Olga Broumas. GifTon

If I'm Going to Die I'm Going to Have Some Fun. George M. Cohan. ReLy

If, in a fisherman's hut, you poke. Hand-Rolled Cigarettes. Yevgeny Aleksandrovich Yevtushenko. VCWP

If, in an odd angle of the hutment. Eighth Air Force. Randall Jarrell. NAMCP V.2; NoAM; NoP-4; NoP-5; OBWP; PoWW; PWW2; TRP; VCAP; WaAnP

If in his study he hath so much care. Antiquary. John Donne. NOSC

If in me anger, or disdain. Richard Lovelace. CavPo

If in my womb and mind You placed. Hymn. Alda Merini. CItWP, *tr. by* Cinzia Sartini Blum and Lara Trubowitz

If in place of a nose she had a horse. Gertrude Stein. MotU; OxBoAm *Fr.* Book Concluding with As A Wife Has a Cow a Love Story, A.

If in that Syrian garden, ages slain. Easter Hymn. A. E. Housman. GI

If, in the month of dark December. Written After Swimming from Sestos to Abydos. Lord Byron. NAEL-6v2; NAEL-7v2; NBLV; NoP-4; NoP-5

If in the years to come you should recall. Edna St. Vincent Millay. HeIP-4; NAAPv.2

If instead of being this way. Of Another Fashion. Emilio Ballagas. CAGL, *tr. by* Fanny Arango-Ramos and William Keeth

If I's layin' 'mong de t'ings I's allus knowed. (LL) Death Song, A. Paul Laurence Dunbar. InoFa; OxAAAP

If it ain't simply this, what is it? Keep Talking. Philip Levine. WeW-3

If it be event, I go towards and not back. I go tower, not floor. Karen Volkman. NAPBL

(If it be event, I go toward and not back. I go tower, not floor.) LegDan

If it be night then, when the screech-owl's call. Sonnet: "If it be night . . . ." Alec Brock Stevenson. FuPo

If it but herald death, the vision is divine! (LL) Emily Jane Brontë. IJHIL; NoP-4; OBEV *Fr.* Prisoner, The. A Fragment.

If it chance your eye offend you. A. E. Housman. ChIV-2 *Fr.* Shropshire Lad, A.

If it comes down to choosing sides. Judy. Paul Allen. PoDa

If it could weep, it could arise and go. (LL) Grief. Elizabeth Barrett Browning. HeIP-4; NALW; NPeEn; OBEV; VWP

If it doesn't come bursting out of you. So you want to be a writer? Charles Bukowski. OxBoAm

If it ever is. Invitation, The. Robert Creeley. FTOS

If it ever occurs to her to be kind to me. Ghazal 25. Mirza Asadullah Khan Ghalib. EaWin, *tr. by* Aijaz Ahmad and W. S. Merwin

If it form the one landscape that we the inconstant ones. In Praise of Limestone. W. H. Auden. HarvBoo; NAEL-6v2; NAEL-7v2; NAMCP V.1; NoAM; NoP-4; NoP-5; OxBoAm; WaAnP

If it grew and the ocean depths were filled in by large cubes of salts. Map. Gerardo Deniz. RMCMP, *tr. by* Mónica de la Torre

If it had been possible. Cesare Greppi. ItPo, *tr. by* Gayle Ridinger

If it is but sleep. *Unknown.* ArkPo, *tr. by* Edwin A. Cranston

If It Is Not My Portion. Rabindranath Tagore. OBMV *Fr.* Gitanjali.

If it is real the white. Certainty. Octavio Paz. TCLAP, *tr. by* Charles Tomlinson

If it is true. Georg Heym—The Almost Metaphysical Adventure. Zbigniew Herbert. PoetW, *tr. by* Bogdana Carpenter and John Carpenter

If It Is True What Is Said of the Work. Heather Ramsdell. IAoNAP

If it is you, there / in the light boat on the pond. Lady Ise. WoPoe, *tr. by* Irma Brandeis and Etsuko Teraski

If it please God. Blandeur. Kay Ryan. CalPo; OxBoAm

If it was not death? (LL) Night Toad. Susan Wicks. MoWP; StAl

If it were a sea, this immense wind. Maria Luisa Spaziani. NeIt

If it were done when 'tis done, then 'twere well. William Shakespeare. OxAEP-1 *Fr.* Macbeth.

If it were inconsequence my being. Sketches for 13 Sonnets. Ebbe Borregaard. AHA

If it / Were lighter touch. Guarded Wound, The. Adelaide Crapsey. APT-1; NAAPv.2

If It Were Not. Andrea Zanzotto. VCWP

If it were not your face that melts. If It Were Not. Andrea Zanzotto. VCWP

If its spiritual offense does it as wrongdoing take place more in more in the second. Where Leftover Misery Goes. Alice Notley. BAP-01

If it's appendicitis, you're in trouble. Coast of Texas, The. Isabel Nathaniel. TiP2

If it's good to live. Antonio Machado Ruiz. WED Fr. Moral Proverbs and Folk Songs.

If it's hard to climb the greased pole. Life in the Provinces. Carlos Sahagún. RaW, tr. by Robert Mezey

If it's like a river, the current is too much for us. Defining Time. Carl Dennis. PoA 2002

If It's Only Rhythm. Dennis Phillips. FTOS Fr. Etudes.

If it's over, let it be over. In Memoriam. Jean Bleakney. NIrP

If it's true you made light. Creed. Belkis Cuza Malé. TANSG, tr. by Pamela Carmell

If it's Tuesday. Moulton Transformations. Dixie Salazar. GeoHom

If I've been dead for twenty years or so. Abu Sa'id Abul Khayr. WoPoe Fr. Four Poems on Death.

If I've done this right. This Message Will Self-Destruct in Sixty Seconds. Martin Ross. PA9/11

If Japan is. Rate of Exchange, The. Nakano Shigeharu. CAoMJL1, tr. by Miriam Silverberg

If just for once for just one day I could be a hippopotamus. If Just For Once. Toon Tellegen. TuT, tr. by Peter van de Kamp

If just for once the swing of cause and effect. Variation and Reflection on a Theme by Rilke (The Book of Hours, Book 1, Poem 7). Denise Levertov. UpMys

If just one moment anywhere on this earth. (LL) Prison Evening, A. Faiz Ahmad Faiz. BeAl; VCWP, tr. by Agha Shahid Ali

If keir hardie was the man on the moon. Paul Summers. RSaN

If King Jamshid's diamond cup breaks, that's it. Clay Cup, The. Mirza Asadullah Khan Ghalib. WED, tr. by Robert Bly and Sunil Dutta

If life is but a blot on a living day. Lamarck. Osip Emilevich Mandelstam. TCRusP, tr. by John Glad

If life were never bitter. If. Mortimer Collins. OBCoV

If Light can thus deceive, wherefore not Life? (LL) To Night. Joseph Blanco White. GSo; OBEV; OxAEP-2

If light, then, could part the carbon lattices. Caisson. Maurice Riordan. NIrP

If, like winds. Robert Desnos. MFP, tr. by Martin Sorrell

If, like winds semaphored by a rose. If, Like Winds. Robert Desnos. MFP, tr. by Martin Sorrell

If Loup Garou means change into. Loup Garou Means Change Into. Ishmael Reed. FaoP

If love is chaste, what bears adultery? Sonnet. Sibylla Schwarz. GePo, tr. by George C. Schoolfield

If love is the greatest reality. Into Their True Gentleness. Pearse Hutchinson. IrLP

If Love Was Jazz. Linda France. BeAl

If Lucy should be dead! (LL) Strange Fits of Passion Have I Known. William Wordsworth. BrAP; NAEL-6v2; NAEL-7v2; NOBRP; OBEV Fr. Lucy.

If Luther's day expand to Darwin's year. Herman Melville. APN-2; NCAP; TCAPo Fr. Clarel: A Poem and Pilgrimage in the Holy Land.

If maiden is your soul, like Mary undefiled. "Angelus Silesius." GePo Fr. Cherubical Wanderer, The.

If Man Could Name. Luis Cernuda. BLPSL, tr. by Rene de Costa, Rigas Kappatos and Eleni Paidoussi

If man could name what he loves. If Man Could Name. Luis Cernuda. BLPSL, tr. by Rene de Costa, Rigas Kappatos and Eleni Paidoussi

If Marilyn Monroe. Leo Romero. LTA

If Martin Van Buren ever swam in water. Jackson Mac Low. APSN Fr. Presidents of the United States of America, The.

If Mary came would Mary. Penitent Considers Another Coming of Mary, A. Gwendolyn Brooks. NoAM

If medals were ordained for drinks. To a Boon Companion. Oliver St. John Gogarty. OBMV

If memory is written in pencil. Still Burn. M. S. C. Okolo. NeNiPo

If money grew on trees. Annual Returns. Greg Williamson. RA

If more than once, as annals tell. Timoleon. Herman Melville. APN-2

If muscles are the currency of dreams. Lifting. Dorothy Barresi. MoASP

If Music be the food of love, play on. William Shakespeare. OxBEV; WaAnP Fr. Twelfth Night.

If [or Yf] my dear[e] might me the child[e] of state. William Shakespeare. NoSiC; NPeEn; PBRV Fr. Sonnets.

If my disciple thou wilt be. Lady Hungerford's Meditacions upon the Beades, The. Anne Dormer, Lady Hungerford. EMWP

If my fat / was too much for me. Invitation. Grace Nichols. MoWP; NAMCP V.2

If my feet will arrive again, at my home. Lyric in Exile, A. Hussein Elhami. AmFaPo, tr. by Shmuel Shoshani

If my heart were a wild bird, it would nest. Fuzuli. OLP, tr. by Walter Andrews, Najaat Black and Mehmet Kalpakli

If my lips shred to pieces—oh, courage! Before Easter. Mihály Babits. IQMS, tr. by Peter Zollman

If my Love came down from the Mourne hills. Roving Lover, The. Frederick Robert Higgins. IrLP

If my lover dies, let me be his shroud! Unknown. SLW, tr. by Marjolijn De Jager, Sayd Bahodin Majrouh and André Velter

If my lovesick dream. Pak Hyogwan. CATKP, tr. by Peter H. Lee

If my mother had never been the protected child. House in St. Petersburg. Stanley Burnshaw. WoPoe

If my next wish you cannot guess. (LL) You've told me, Maro. Martial. NIL-7; NIP-4, tr. by F. Lewis

If my parents and your parents. Almost a Love Poem. Yehuda Amichai. HP, tr. by Glenda Abramson

If my poor Harp has ever poured. To the Late William Jerdan. Eliza Cook. VWP

If, my religion safe, I durst embrace. To Sir Henry Savile [upon His Translation of Tacitus]. Ben Jonson. BASC

If My Voice Dies While on Land. Rafael Alberti. RaW, tr. by Robert Bly

If my wife were to have an affair. What I Would Do. Marc Petersen. P180

If Myra counts fifteen cows and Alfredo counts nine. Baltazar Beats His Tutor at Scrabble. Belle Waring. ExTi

If Nancy Hanks / Came back as a ghost. Nancy Hanks. Rosemary Benét and Stephen Vincent Benét. NTCP

If Nature Bellows. Mariella Bettarini. CItWP, tr. by Cinzia Sartini Blum and Lara Trubowitz

If nature prompts you, or if friends persuade. William Whitehead. OBSV Fr. Charge to the Poets, A.

If no love is, O God, what fe[e]le I so. Geoffrey Chaucer. NoP-4 Fr. Troilus and Criseyde [or Criseide].

If no one has misjudged himself. Or lied. (LL) Reasons for Attendance. Philip Larkin. NAMCP V.2; PoPoPo

If not famous ourselves, oh let us. Vanna White's Bread Pudding. Michael Pettit. ReTh

If not for Uncle Li. X. Daniel Hall. YaYoPo

If not the case then what is! Jena Osman. OnScMo Fr. Twelve Parts of Her.

If not you? (LL) Speed of Darkness, The. Muriel Rukeyser. APSN; APT-2; PFTM-2

If now you hate me as you say. Forgetfulness. The Earl of Longford. IrLP

If Now You Knocked on My Door. Patrizia Cavalli. CItWP, tr. by Cinzia Sartini Blum and Lara Trubowitz

If, O Maecenas, versed in lore antique. Horace. OBVE

If, O my Lesbia, I should commit. Second Philosopher's Song. Aldous Leonard Huxley. OBCoV

If of the dead save good nought should be said. William Drummond of Hawthornden. NOSC

If "oh" knows us, dear ache of windward time. Erin Mouré. NLPA Fr. Wittgenstein Letters to Mel Gibson's Braveheart, The.

If old Satchmo had never been born! (LL) Melvin B. Tolson. NAAPv.2; NAMCP V.1 Fr. Harlem Gallery.

If on a cold winter morning you. Roy Kiyooka. NLPA Fr. Pear Tree Pomes.

If on your walks you have moved some stones. Word to the Wise, A. Octavio Armand. TCLAP, tr. by Carol Maier

If on your way you see. Heart and the Severed Head, The. Rosita Copioli. CItWP, tr. by Cinzia Sartini Blum and Lara Trubowitz

If once again a flood fell from the spheres. Couplets. Yehuda Amichai. FIT, tr. by Robert Friend

If once we efface the joys of the chase. Adam Lindsay Gordon. STuOW Fr. Ye Wearie Wayfarer.

If One Always Denies. Luciana Notari. CItWP, tr. by Cinzia Sartini Blum and Lara Trubowitz

If one reflects well on slate. Slate. Francis Ponge. YaTCFP, tr. by Simon Watson Taylor

If one should bring me this report. Alfred Tennyson. NAEL-6v2; NAEL-7v2 Fr. In Memoriam A. H. H.

If Only. Herman De Coninck. TuT, tr. by Theo Dorgan

If Only. Christina Georgina Rossetti. SacPP

If Only. Lina Tibi. PoArWo, tr. by Subhi Hadidi and Nathalie Handal

If only a small miracle. Small Miracle, A. Anabel Torres. TANSG, tr. by Celeste Kostopulos-Cooperman

If only daffodils had caught the light. It Would Have Been Enough. Robert Pack. PfSP

If Only for One Night. Gordon Chambers. InTrad

If only God were a violet. If Only. Lina Tibi. PoArWo, tr. by Subhi Hadidi and Nathalie Handal

If only I could be, just a little, sick again.   If Only.   Herman De Coninck.   TuT, *tr. by* Theo Dorgan

If only I could forget that Frenchman.   French Prisoner, The.   János Pilinszky.   PoSu, *tr. by* Janos Csokits and Ted Hughes

If only I could write in the first person.   In the First Person.   Yosano Akiko.   CAoMJL1, *tr. by* Janine Beichman

If only I could write you a summer-poem.   Let the Wind Recite.   Yang Mu.   PML, *tr. by* Zhang Cuo

If only I might touch Neobule's hand.   Archilochus.   SaLy, *tr. by* Diane Rayor

If only I'd known then what I was reaching for.   Shame.   Tom Sleigh.   PfSP

If only Life-and-Death.   *Unknown.*   TAL

If only now you were to emerge from.   Lingua Franca.   Chris Stroffolino.   BodElec

If only she could make herself.   Security.   Shirley Kaufman.   DTA

If only somebody would drill with a finger-long rig down.   *Ancestored-Back* Is the Overpresiding Spirit of This Poem.   Albert Goldbarth.   CAP-8; PoDa

If only that so many dead lie round. (LL)   Church Going.   Philip Larkin.   BrAP; CABP; EMP; HarvBoo; HeIP-4; MoBrPo; NAEL-6v2; NAEL-7v2; NAMCP V.2; NIL-7; NIP-4; NoAM; NoP-4; NoP-5; SoSe-8; TFi; WaAnP

If only the bell keeps him alive though that is.   Night.   Gerald Stern.   BodElec

If only the bud would open like the beloved's ruby lips.   Baqi.   OLP, *tr. by* Walter Andrews, Najaat Black and Mehmet Kalpakli

If only the earth.   What Does One Write When the World Starts to Disappear?   Sujata Bhatt.   FiBr

If Only the Horse Was Left to Its Solitude.   Abdel Kader El Janabi.   Eno, *tr. by* Pierre Joris

If only the light might last.   At an Island Farm.   Brad Leithauser.   PoA 2002

If only we could forgive ourselves, and didn't.   Few and Far Between.   Dick Barnes.   CalPo

If ought of oaten stop, or pastoral song.   William Collins.   *See* If aught of oaten stop, or pastoral song.

If our antagonists take me.   [Last Poems].   Osip Emilevich Mandelstam.   PFTM-1

If our love were not.   Our Love.   Xavier Villaurrutia.   TCLAP, *tr. by* Michael Surman

If out of a dire suspicion.   Robert Penn Warren.   NoAM *Fr.* Penological Study: Southern Exposure.

If patience true could termine passions warr.   Joshua Sylvester.   OxBSo *Fr.* Du Bartas: His Divine Weeks and Works.

If petals are falling.   Falling Petals.   Cho Chihun.   CAMKP, *tr. by* Kyung-Ja Chun

If pleasures be mine.   Sadakichi.   NAAPv.1 *Fr.* Tanka.

If poems are eternal occasions, then.   Marginalization of Poetry, The.   Bob Perelman.   FTOS

If poetry wells up from some true source.   David Wheatley.   NIrP *Fr.* Sonnets to James Clarence Mangan.

If poisonous [*or* poysonous] mineral[l]s, and if that tree.   John Donne.   BASC; FaBoVe; NAEL-6v1; NAEL-7v1; NoP-4; NoP-5; OxAEP-1 *Fr.* Holy Sonnets.

If poor (you say) she drains her husband's purse.   Geoffrey Chaucer.   OBSV *Fr.* Canterbury Tales, The.

If Praxiteles had been an animator, this form.   Louganis.   Eloise Klein Healy.   WiU

If *puce* were sound not color.   First Performance of the Rock 'n Roll Band *Puce Exit.*   Kevin Stein.   SwNoth

If right in front of me.   Flowering Quince.   Winfield Townley Scott.   APT-2

If rightly tuneful bards decide.   Amoret.   Mark Akenside.   OBEV

If Rome so great, and in her wisest age.   To Edward Alleyn.   Ben Jonson.   NOSC

If safety can be had from hollow men.   Kate Light.   AmPoNex *Fr.* Five Urban Love Songs.

If saying No / to the world to the present.   Solo for Two Voices.   Octavio Paz.   STV, *tr. by* John Frederick Nims

If she be not as kind as fair.   Song.   Sir George Etherege.   NOSC

If she come to it. (LL)   Girl, A.   Michael Field.   NAEL-7v2; ViWPN; VWP

If she could see it, she would never let him see. (LL)   Lovers, The.   Dorianne Laux.   BodElec; ErotSp

If she forgets, though, and glances back again, it will still be in there, furtively watching, crying. (LL)   Alzheimer's: The Wife.   C. K. Williams.   EMP; VCAP

If She Only Had One Minute.   Kay Ryan.   ExTi

If she should give me all I ask of her.   George Henry Boker.   APN-2 *Fr.* Sonnets: A Sequence on Profane Love.

If she was beautiful is uncertain the more.   Legend of Lilja.   Sarah Kirsch.   AF, *tr. by* Wayne Kvam

If she wishes to go I will not forgive her. (LL)   River God, The.   Stevie Smith.   BrAP; MoWP

If so, Peace. (LL)   Living with Chris.   Ted Berrigan.   NYP2; OxBoAm

If So, Tell Me [1999].   Barbara Guest.   AWPTFC

If So the Man You Are.   Dominic Bevan Wyndham Lewis.   OBSV

If, some morning, you go out.   Regarding Music.   Siv Cedering.   MiVo

If some nosey body asks "well."   Poem for a "Divorced" Daughter.   Horace Coleman.   ISC

If someone barefoot stood in a saloon.   Saloon with Birds.   Christopher Middleton.   HarvBoo

If someone came what would I do.   Lazy Cloud's Nest 2.   Ali Hsiying.   ColAnChi, *tr. by* Jerome P. Seaton

If someone somewhere exists.   Someone Who Knows My Heart.   Kim Yöngnang.   CAMKP, *tr. by* Anthony, Brother of Taizé

If Someone Tells You It's Not for Sure.   Jaime Sabines.   PoetW; TCLAP, *tr. by* Philip Levine

If Someone Would Come.   Lady Izumi.   WoPoe, *tr. by* Steven D. Carter

If something is not done.   And in the U.S.A.   Miguel Algarin.   FTtHH

If Sometimes in the Haunts of Men.   Lord Byron.   CAGL

If Sonnets Were in Fashion.   Tom Dawe.   Coast

If stars catch sight of your beauty in me.   You Will Come to Me.   Celâl Sılay.   NaPG, *tr. by* Talat Sait Halman

If such there were—with *you*, the moral of his strain! (LL)   Lord Byron.   NAEL-6v2; NAEL-7v2 *Fr.* Childe Harold's Pilgrimage.

If Suddenly a Clod of Earth.   Harold Monro.   MoBrPo *Fr.* Strange Meetings.

If suddenly you do not exist.   Dead Woman.   Pablo Neruda.   StAl, *tr. by* Brian Cole

If sunlight fell like snowflakes.   Sunflakes.   Frank Asch.   NTCP

If that a sinner's sighs are angels' food.   Madrigal.   *Unknown.*   SacPr

If that exact Appelles now did live.   Contemplation on Bassets Down-Hill by the Most Sacred Adorer of the Muses Mrs. A. K., A.   Anne Kemp.   EMWP

If That—indeed—redeem. (LL)   Prison gets to be a friend, A.   Emily Dickinson.   APN-2; NCAP

If the Birds Knew.   John Ashbery.   PoA 2002

If the blues would let me.   Miss Blues'es Child.   Langston Hughes.   ChAP; SAmP

If the car has stalled by the mall in the shape of a star.   Ocean State.   Stephen Burt.   LegDan

If the clouds come good, our tobacco will grow. We will be happy.   *Unknown.*   APN-2 *Fr.* Minnetare Songs.

If the cricket sings and I lower my eyelashes.   Unfinished Life Story.   Gerardo Diego.   RaW, *tr. by* Ralph Nelson

If the egg had one spot of blood on it.   White Petticoats.   Chana Bloch.   MPUn

If the flies did not hurry themselves to the window.   Theology.   Jane Hirshfield.   WANABP

If the flowers could ask me.   David Brendon Hopes.   UpMys *Fr.* Something of the Flowers.

If the following day is slow to arrive. (LL)   Saturday Night in the Village.   Giacomo Leopardi.   OBVE; WoPoe, *tr. by* Robert Lowell

If the gods bring to you.   Each Moment a White Bull Steps Shining into the World.   Jane Hirshfield.   PoDa

If the green lizard darts.   Eugenio Montale.   WoPoe *Fr.* Motets [Mottetti].

If the heart is a house my parents.   Pulse, The.   Martha Kapos.   Prnts

If the heart of a man is deprest [*or* depressed] with cares.   John Gay.   NAEL-6v1 *Fr.* Beggar's Opera, The.

If the heat of one body resting.   What Does the Body Dream at Rest?   Russell Leong.   WhBo

If the hour has not rung, death will not be coming.   *Unknown.*   SLW, *tr. by* Marjolijn De Jager, Sayd Bahodin Majrouh and André Velter

If the lady hath any loveliness, let it die.   Blackberry Winter.   John Crowe Ransom.   APT-1

If the land of the Flowery Flag is occupied by us in turn.   *Unknown.*   NAAPv.2

If the Led Striker call it a strike.   American, An.   Rudyard Kipling.   FaBoA

If the lost word is lost, if the spent word is spent.   T. S. Eliot.   UV *Fr.* Ash Wednesday [*or* Ash-Wednesday].

If the man who turnips cries.   Ballad.   Samuel Johnson.   OxAEP-1

If the mind has wealth and rank.   Sikong Tu.   CCL1 *Fr.* Twenty-Four Modes of Poetry.

If the money's between your legs can you be a dead woman?   Destroy.   Alice Notley.   Eno

If the muse were mine to tempt it.   Colored Soldiers, The.   Paul Laurence Dunbar.   APN-2; CBCWP

If the opening were forever.   Hans Faverey.   WoBe *Fr.* Eighteen Poems.

If the Owl Calls Again.   John Haines.   GifTon; HeIP-4

If the path of my dreams.   Yi Myŏnghan.   CATKP, *tr. by* Peter H. Lee

If the post came at night.   Correspondence.   Ilse Aichinger.   GTCP, *tr. by* Michael Hamburger

If the Prophets Broke in.   Nelly Sachs.   BBASP, *tr. by* Matthew Mead and Ruth Mead

If the red slayer think he slays. Brahma. Ralph Waldo Emerson. APN-1; ColAP; CtM; NAAPv.1; NoP-4; NoP-5; OBEV; OxBoAm; TCAPo; TFi; UV

If the restroom door had been unlocked. If he had one less beer. Hygiene. Toni Mirosevich. RaF

If the romantic land whose soil I tread. Richard Henry Wilde. APN-1 *Fr.* Hesperia.

If the Sage, making light of alabaster. In Praise of Jade. Victor Segalen. YaTCFP, *tr. by* Timothy Billings and Christopher Bush

If the ship you are traveling on is wrecked. Charles Reznikoff. NAAPv.2

If the Silence Should Suddenly Return. Ekaterina Iosifova. CSCBP, *tr. by* Georgi Belev and Lisa Sapinkopf

If the Soul Loses Its Gift Then It Loses Ground, If Hell. Amelia Rosselli. CItWP, *tr. by* Cinzia Sartini Blum and Lara Trubowitz

If the Soul was Born with Pinions. Marina Ivanovna Tsvetayeva. WPoS

If the stars fell; night's nameless dreams. Joseph. G. K. Chesterton. ChIV-2; ChrPo

If the stuffed gray cat stares facedown. Boy Removes All Traces from His Room, The. Naomi Shihab Nye. MAAN

If the times were good. Issa. EH, *tr. by* Robert Hass

If the Tomb Is Not Oblivion. Manuel González Prada. SpanPo, *tr. by* William M. Davis

If the tombstone placed over me is small to see and close. Leonidas of Tarentum. HePo, *tr. by* Barbara Hughes Fowler

If the touching memory of broken glass in his eye does not sound the hour. If the Touching Memory. Dora Maar. YaTCFP, *tr. by* Mary Ann Caws

If the voice spoke Venetian blind. Jena Osman. OnScMo *Fr. Twelve Parts of Her.*

If the water were clear enough. King of the River. Stanley Kunitz. PtR

If the wild bowler thinks he bowls. Brahma. Andrew Lang. UV

If the year is meditating a suitable gift. Request to a Year. Judith Wright. BrAP; ItWoWo; NALW; NAMCP V.2; NoAM; NoP-4; NoP-5

If, then, the State will but assistance lend. George Eveleigh. STuOW *Fr. Science Revealed.*

If there are any heavens my mother will (all by herself) have. E. E. Cummings. MoAmPo

If there are wing-shaped stones in the water. Papalote Creek. Stephen Harrigan. TiP2

If there be a rainbow in the eve. *Unknown.* FaBoVe

If there be any one can take my place. Christina Georgina Rossetti. OxBSo *Fr. Monna Innominata.*

If there be nothing new, but that which is. William Shakespeare. TreFP *Fr. Sonnets.*

If there exists a hell—the case is clear. To Sir Toby. Philip Freneau. NAAL-3; NAAPv.1; NoP-4; NoP-5; WaAnP

If there had been only. Buddha in the Woodpile, A. Lawrence Ferlinghetti. WANABP

If There Is a God. Eli Alon. NRoS, *tr. by* Esther Raizen

If there is a god. To the Six Million. Irving Feldman. TaR

If there is a God, he has a lot to answer for. If There Is a. Laura Fargas. CFP

If there is a god in war. If There Is a God. Eli Alon. NRoS, *tr. by* Esther Raizen

If there is a Pure Land. Death Sunyata Chant: A Rite for Passing Over. Diane Di Prima. BB; WANABP

If there is a scheme. Charles Reznikoff. WoPoe

If there is any life when death is over. On the Dunes. Sara Teasdale. TCAPo

If there is anyone. Open Letter to the Entertainment Industry, An. Beau Sia. BRtP

If there is no connection between the wild. Discoveries, Trade Names, Genitals, and Ancient Instruments. Carl Rakosi. APT-2

If there is no heaven and you are in it. Elegy for a Bad Example. Rodney Jones. InGu

If there is no Laura, there is still her name. Lauras. Günter Eich. MotU, *tr. by* David Walker

If there is one monkey it plays one violin. Wild Pigs of Kalimantan, The. Kazuko Shiraishi. WoBe, *tr. by* Samuel Grolmes and Yumiko Tsumura

If there is only one world, it is this one. Decrescendo. Larry Levis. SwNoth

If There Is Someone Lovelier Than You. Howard Dietz. ReLy

If there is something that takes you. Conjuring Against Alien Spirits. Quincy Troupe. ISC

If there is still some room left in your heart. To a Hooligan Girl. Lajos Kassák. IQMS, *tr. by* Michael Kitka

If there must be a god in the house, must be. Less and Less Human, O Savage Spirit. Wallace Stevens. BBASP

If there was a house with three girls in it. Céilí. Ciaran Carson. PBCIP

If there wasn't a full moon over Naples when. Noodling. Narda Bush. MAAN

If there were a road to the horizon. Shadow Grammar. Terence Winch. BAP-97

If there were another. Songs of an Other. Robert Duncan. PmAP

If there were any power in human love. Sonnet. Frances Anne Kemble. VWP

If there were dreams to sell. Dream-Pedlary. Thomas Lovell Beddoes. OBEV; OxAEP-2

If there were locomotives to ride home on. Connoisseur of Jews, The. Jerome Rothenberg. TaR

If there were nothing in the desert but. Blank to Fill in on the Visa of Pollen. Aimé Césaire. WoPoe, *tr. by* Gregson Davis

If there were, oh! an Hellespont of cream. John Davies of Hereford. NPeEn; OBCoV *Fr. Scourge of Folly, The.*

If there were time for everything. Lights at Newport Beach, The. Joe Bolton. AmPoNex

If There's No Sugar. Dawn L. Hannaham. BtF

If they are mine or no. (LL) Tell Me Not Here [It Needs Not Saying]. A. E. Housman. NoAM; NPeEn; OxBEV

If they can get across our garden they have eaten it. Negotium Perambulans. Peter Redgrove. OBGa

If They Honoured Me, Giving Me Their Gifts. Michael Field. OBMV

If they let me go into the temple. Stupidity. Vegunta Mohana Prasad. HotL, *tr. by* V. Narayana Rao

If they remove the flower. Separation. Bekes Jr. IrPoTo, *tr. by* Muhamad Tawfiq Ali

If they say that grace is gone. Yi Hwang. CATKP *Fr. Twelve Songs of Tosan.*

If they should ask what makes the stuff of us. Edinburgh. Robert Adamson. EdScPo

If they would ask me I would say. I Didn't Know About You. Bob Russell. ReLy

If they'd had a spark of wit or vision. Florida. Campbell McGrath. NAPBL

If this [*or* thys] be love, to draw[e] a weary [*or* wearie] breath. Samuel Daniel. GSo *Fr. Sonnets to Delia.*

If this brain's over-tempered. I've Tasted My Blood. Milton Acorn. Coast

If This Is Paradise. Dorianne Laux. GeoHom

If this is paradise: trees, beehives. If This Is Paradise. Dorianne Laux. GeoHom

If this is the way it is, we must live through it. If. Robert Penn Warren. BodElec

If This Isn't Love. E. Y. Harburg. ReLy

If this myth is alive. Parvati. Sujata Bhatt. MoWP

If this prime ass is with his brother worms. Monody on Doctor Olmsted. Edgar Allan Poe. TCAPo

If This Room Is Our World. Weldon Kees. AWTN

If this room is our world, then let. If This Room Is Our World. Weldon Kees. AWTN

If this were a movie, the sound of sizzling would foretell disaster. Schadenfreude. Stephanie Brown. BodElec

If this were a world. *Unknown.* WoPoe *Fr. Kokin Shu.*

If this world's friends might see but once. Seed Growing Secretly, The. Henry Vaughan. ChIV-2

If those paint sorrow best—who feel it most! (LL) Partial Muse, has from my earliest hours, The. Charlotte Smith. CenSon; RWP

If thou but suffer God to guide thee. Georg Neumark. SacPr, *tr. by* Catherine Winkworth

If thou could'st empty all thy self of self. Indwelling. Thomas Edward Brown. SacPr

If Thou Couldst Know What 'Tis to Weep. Lady Caroline Lamb. RWP

If thou didst feed on western plains of yore. To a Goose [*or* Gosse]. Robert Southey. CenSon

If thou dislik'st the piece thou light'st on first. To the Sour[e] Reader. Robert Herrick. NBLV; NoP-4; NoP-5

If thou hast squander'd years to grave a gem. Charge, A. Herbert Trench. OBEV

If thou kiss not me? (LL) Love's Philosophy. Percy Bysshe Shelley. ItP; OxAEP-2

If thou must love me, let it be for nought. Elizabeth Barrett Browning. CenSon; GSo; HeIP-4; LW; OBEV; OxAEP-2; OxBSo *Fr. Sonnets from the Portuguese.*

If thou shouldst ever come by choice or chance. Samuel Rogers. OxAEP-2 *Fr. Italy.*

If Thou Shouldst Return. Clara Ann Thompson. CBWP-2

If thou wilt come and dwell with me at home. Richard Barnfield. CAGL *Fr. Affectionate Shepherd [or Shephearde], The.*

If thou wilt come with me to the County of Leitrim. Flower of Nut-Brown Maids, The. Eleanor Hull. IrLP

If Thou Wilt Ease Thine Heart. Thomas Lovell Beddoes. WaAnP

If thou would'st view fair Melrose aright. Sir Walter Scott. NPBRoP; OxAEP-2 *Fr. Lay of the Last Minstrel, The.*

If thought can reach to Heaven. Rabbi's Song, The. Rudyard Kipling. ChIV-1

If thus we needs must go. Heart, The. Michael Drayton. NOSC

If thy sad heart, pining for human love. Sarah Helen Whitman. NAAPv.1 *Fr.* Sonnets from the Series Relating to Edgar Allan Poe.

If Time Waits. Fanny Carrión de Fierro. TANSG, *tr. by* Sally Cheney Bell

If to be absent were to be. To Lucasta, [on] Going beyond the Seas. Richard Lovelace. OBEV; OxAEP-1

(To *Lucasta, Going Beyond the Seas.*) CavPo

If to your ear it wonder bring. Ben Jonson. OxBEV *Fr.* Key Keeper, The.

If(touched by love's own secret)we,like homing. E. E. Cummings. PoA 2002

If trees could talk. Alabama Poem. Nikki Giovanni. OxAAAP

If truth in hearts that perish. A. E. Housman. CAGL *Fr.* Shropshire Lad, A.

If two sides of "therefore" are a mete descend. Erin Mouré. NLPA *Fr.* Wittgenstein Letters to Mel Gibson's Braveheart, The.

If waker care, if sudden [or sodayne] pale colo[u]r. Sir Thomas Wyatt. NoSic

If Washington Should Come to Life. George M. Cohan. ReLy

If Washington should come to life and see how matters stand. If Washington Should Come to Life. George M. Cohan. ReLy

If we all come to the net together. (LL) Coming to the Net (for Arthur Ashe). Brian G. Gilmore. BtF; SpirFl

If we all knew where. Rainbow, The. Opal Palmer Adisa. GT

If we are dying, let's do it slowly, together. Well-Known Elizabethan Double Entendre, A. Pamela Alexander. YaYoPo

If we are lucky. Starwork. L. S. Asekoff. EleElec

If we are to cross the barriers of snow. Ark for Lawrence Durrell, An. Robert Duncan. RaBo

If we, as we are, are dust, and dust, as it will, rises. Snow. Charles Wright. CAP-8; ColAP; OxBoAm

If we be fools of chance, indeed, and tend. Emily Jane Pfeiffer. ViWPN *Fr.* To Nature.

If we became water and met. Becoming Water. Kang Ŭn'gyo. EcSo, *tr. by* Ann Y. Choi

If we can get married. *Hawaiian Oral Tradition.* NAAPv.2

If we can truly remember, they will not forget. (LL) Of History and Hope. Miller Williams. InGu; RWB

If we could get the hang of it entirely. Entirely. Louis MacNeice. StAl

If we could know the mystery. Our Task. Henrietta Cordelia Ray. CBWP-3

If we could only push these walls. Maze Without a Minotaur. Dana Gioia. RA

If we do not lift quickly the dead bodies from the beaches. Memorial. William Bronk. PWW2

If we eat, we choke. Bread wedges in our throats. Publick Fast on Account of the Afflicted: March 31, 1692. Nicole Cooley. NeAmPo

If we forget where we come from. My Class Draws a Blank on Robbie Burns. Richard Lemm. Coast

If we live all our lives under lies. Cuba Libre. Imamu Amiri Baraka. BB

If we live well, in heaven with Christ our souls shall dwell. (LL) For Soldiers. Humphrey Gifford. FaBoWar; NoSic

If we must die. On the Night of the Day the Worlds Ends. Lucile Adler. ICANM

If we must die— [or ,]let it not be like hogs. If We Must Die. Claude McKay. APT-1; ColAP; ISC; NAAL-5; NAAPv.2; NAMCP V.1; NoAM; OxAAAP; OxBoAm; SSLK; TFi

If we no old historian's name. Enquiry, The. Katherine Philips. OxBEV

If we place across a level surface a certain number of passageways and galleries which crisscross and communicate. Sponge. Fabio Morabito. RMCMP, *tr. by* Geoff Hargreaves

If we talk, we're too tired to make love; if we. Marilyn Hacker. VCAP *Fr.* Taking Notice.

If we tell, gently, gently. Vanity. Birago Diop. WoPoe, *tr. by* Ulli Beier and Gerald Moore

IF we those generous sons deservedly praise. Upon My Lord Winchilsea's Converting the Mount in His Garden to a Terrace. Anne Finch, Countess of Winchilsea. OBGa

If we throw our eyes way out to sea. Across the Bay. Naomi Shihab Nye. ExTi

If We Were in a Gregg Araki Movie. Douglas A. Martin. BeDoSh

If we were in Talisker on the shore. Shores. Sorley MacLean. EdScPo, *tr. by* Iain Crichton Smith

If well thou viewst us with no squinted eye. Against a Rich Man Despising Poverty. Phineas Fletcher. NOSC

If we've promised them aught, let us keep our promise! (LL) Pied Piper of Hamelin, The. Robert Browning. NOxBChV; OBNV; OBSP

If what heals can bless. Come Green Again. Winfield Townley Scott. ICANM

If what she heard is true. Maybe Desdemona. Dan Johnson. IaFF

If what the *Curious* have observ'd be true. Cameleon Lover, The. *Unknown.* TCAPo

If, what this said, I dared repeat at last! (LL) Elizabeth Barrett Browning. CenSon; OxAEP-2 *Fr.* Sonnets from the Portuguese.

If What we could—were what we would. Emily Dickinson. TCAPo

If whatever is, is right. Pope. Manuel González Prada. SpanPo, *tr. by* William M. Davis

If, when a blind moth. Meteor Showers—Yosemite. Dixie Salazar. GeoHom

If when Don Cupid's dart. Love's Offence. Sir John Suckling. NOSC

If, when I die, I must be buried, let. My Grave. Ella Wheeler Wilcox. SWaP

If when my wife is sleeping. Danse Russe. William Carlos Williams. AmFaPo; NAAPv.2; NAMCP V.1; NoP-4; NoP-5; OxBoAm; RaBo; SAmP

(If I when my wife is sleeping.) WoPoe

If when the sun at noon displays. Beautiful Mistress, A. Thomas Carew. CavPo

If when the wind blows. Daniel Webster's Horses. Elizabeth Jane Coatsworth. MoAmPo

If where we hunt defines us. After the Noise of Saigon. Walter McDonald. OPRER

If, whittler and dumper, gross carver. Arc Inside and Out, The. A. R. Ammons. NoAM; NoP-4; NoP-5

If Will had wings. Home Thoughts. Thomas D'Arcy Magee. IrV

If wind that wastes its time among the trees. Vertigo. Andrew Zawacki. IIR; LegDan

If Winter comes, can Spring be far behind? (LL) Ode to the West Wind. Percy Bysshe Shelley. BrAP; CenSon; ClHu; HeIP-4; MakPoe; NAEL-6v2; NAEL-7v2; NAWM-7v2; NIL-7; NIP-4; NOBRP; NoP-4; NoP-5; NPeEn; OBEV; OxAEP-2; OxBEV; OxBSo; PoPoPo; TFi; TRP; WaAnP; WeW-3

If, with the literate, I am. Dorothy Parker. NALW; NAMCP V.1 *Fr.* Pig's-Eye View of Literature, A.

If within the cruel Southland you have chanced to take a ride. Jim Crow Cars. Lizelia Augusta Jenkins Moorer. CBWP-3

If witt may be the Childe of chance and rise. On the Returne of King Charles 2nd. Ann Lee. EMWP

If Women Could Be Fair. Edward, 17th Earl of Oxford De Vere. NoSic

If Words. Sinéad Morrissey. NIrP

If words became things. If Words. Sinéad Morrissey. NIrP

"If words could speak words should have told . . . ." Out There. Breyten Breytenbach. VCWP

If Ye Hivni. I. W. King. EdScPo

If ye hivni ate a cauld pie along. If Ye Hivni. I. W. King. EdScPo

If ye'll only gimme RUM! (LL) Convicts' Rum Song. *Unknown.* FaBoVe; NOBAu

If yet I have not all thy love. Lovers' Infiniteness[e]. John Donne. NOSC

If You. Robert Creeley. NoAM

If you are a revolutionary. Reactionary Poet, The. Ishmael Reed. ESEAA; GT

If you are always kind. (LL) Mary's Lamb [or Mary and Her Lamb]. Sarah Josepha Buell Hale. BRP; SWaP

If you are an Apostle, whose name is engraved on the Tablet of Martyrs. Lion and the Apostle, The. Fadil Azzawi. IrPoTo, *tr. by* Ralph Saverese and Saadi A. Simawe

If You Are Asked. Olena Kalytiak Davis. LegDan

If you are bound for the sun's empty plum. There Are Many Pathways to the Garden. Philip Lamantia. ASA

If you are cold, this poem will not warm you. This Poem. Constance Urdang. PBCAP

If you are living, remember. Farewell to Maria. Tadeusz Borowski. HP, *tr. by* Tadeuszt Pióro

If you are looking for the warmth of my arms, you will have to risk your life. *Unknown.* SLW, *tr. by* Marjolijn De Jager, Sayd Bahodin Majrouh and André Velter

If you are lucky in this life. Lucky. Tony Hoagland. BeAl

If you are not to become a monster. Enemies. Wendell Berry. RaF

If You Ask Me. Gunnar Ekelof. PFTM-1, *tr. by* Muriel Rukeyser and Leif Sjöberg

If you ask me where I am. If You Ask Me. Gunnar Ekelof. PFTM-1, *tr. by* Muriel Rukeyser and Leif Sjöberg

If you ask me where I have been. There Is No Forgetting (Sonata). Pablo Neruda. ConPit, *tr. by* Clayton Eshleman

If You Ask Me Where I Live. Gunnar Ekelof. WED, *tr. by* Robert Bly

If you ask what my favourite programme is. Video Box: 25, The. Edwin Morgan. EmeKit

If you breach the daycare's twelve-hour limit. Daycare in a Doublewide. Janet Norman Knox. RWB

If you burn my scorched soul too often, Love, she'll fly. Meleager. HePo, *tr. by* Barbara Hughes Fowler

If You Came. Ruth Pitter. PoBW

If you came dancing back. For Edward Thomas Killed at Arras. Geoffrey Matthews. RSaN

If you came to my secret glade. If You Came. Ruth Pitter. PoBW

If you can keep your head when all about you. Recruiting Song. Michael Foster. UV

If you can keep your head when all about you. If. Rudyard Kipling. BRP; ChAP; CtM; ITBLP; UV

If you can see why she feels that she kneels if you can see why he knows that he shows what he bestows. On Her Way. Gertrude Stein. PFTM-1

If you can sleep when those who write about you. Rewards and Fairies. Roger Woddis. UV

If You Cannot Find the Truth Right Where You Are, Where Do You Expect to Find It? Maj Ragain. AmZen

If you cannot look at the sun. Charles Reznikoff. NAAPv.2

If you can't accept the fact that. Grandmothers, The. Amy Lingafelter. FreRad

If you can't be free, be a mystery. (LL) Canary. Rita Dove. ESEAA; LoL; OxAAAP; SeSe; VCAP

If you can't say what you mean. Bad Days. Harvey Shapiro. PA9/11

If you choose to believe me, good. Now I will tell how Octavia, the spider-web city, is made. Italo Calvino. MotU Fr. Invisible Cities.

If you come as softly. Memorial 1. Audre Lorde. WaAnP

If you come at all. Yourself and Myself. Unknown. IrLP, tr. by Thomas Kinsella

If You Come Close to Me. Suchart Sawadsri. PML, tr. by the author and Kathryn Rhett

If you come early to one of these little churches. Our Speaker This Morning. Chris Willerton. TiP2

If you come here in summer. Edge. Kenneth Steven. EdScPo

If you come my way that is. Poem from Llanybri. Lynnette Roberts. AngWePo; TCAWP

If you come to a land with no ancestors. Riding into California. Shirley Lim. GeoHom

If you complain your flames are hot. To Her Lover's Complaint. Jane Barker. NPeEn

If you could come on the late train for. Young Ionia, The. John Frederick Nims. IllVoic

If you could crowd them into forty lines! Limitations. Siegfried Sassoon. MoBrPo

If you could have wings would you want them? Wings. Susan Stewart. AmAlph

If you could see, fair brother, how dead beat. Prolonged Sonnet: When the Troops Were Returning from Milan. Niccolò degli Albizzi. FaBoWar; OBVE; PoAgWa, tr. by Dante Gabriel Rossetti

If you could shuck your skin and watch. Wrong Street, The. Cornelius Eady. OxAAAP

If you could sit with me beside the sea to-day. Longing. Paul Laurence Dunbar. ErotSp

If you could turn graffiti into gold. Unknown. PriapPo Fr. Priapus Poems, The.

If You Could Write One Great Poem, What Would You Want It to Be About? Robert Pinsky. PoCho

If you dare breathe out in Verkhoyansk. Star Whisper. Carol Rumens. StAl

If you, dear Celia, cannot bear. Sacrifice: An Epistle to Celia, The. Mary Leapor. PEW

If you did not know how to love. Unknown. SLW, tr. by Marjolijn De Jager, Sayd Bahodin Majrouh and André Velter

If you didn't see the six-legged dog. Country Fair. Charles Simic. EmeKit; OxBoAm; P180

If you do love, as well as I. Thought, The. Edward Herbert, 1st Baron Herbert of Cherbury. AngWePo

If you do not have a towel. Camp. Janet Fisher. MFPA

If you do not have a wound in the center of your chest. Unknown. SLW, tr. by Marjolijn De Jager, Sayd Bahodin Majrouh and André Velter

If you do not shake the bottle. On Tomato Ketchup. Unknown. NBLV; Spl

If you doan mind, would you please Mind moving over, please. Gloria. Lincoln Kirstein. APT-2

If you don't blink, nothing is funny or so. Evidence. Joanna Fuhrman. AmPoNex

If You Don't Force It. Michael S. Harper. FaoP

If you don't have a woman that lives with you. Strange Business. Jelaluddin Rumi. LoL, tr. by Coleman Barks

If you don't know boys, you can't follow them. Berlin Series. Arielle Greenberg. LegDan

If you don't know the kind of person I am. Ritual to Read to Each Other, A. William Stafford. GoPo; RaBo; RaF

If you dream of scissors. Book of Dreams, The. Richard Garcia. TouFir

If you dropped me on the table. Cesare Greppi. ItPo, tr. by Gayle Ridinger

If you evah go to Houston. Midnight Special. Unknown. APT-1

If you ever, ever, ever meet a grizzly bear. Grizzly Bear. Mary Austin. BLPJKO

If you ever find. Imamu Amiri Baraka. NAMCP V.2; PFTM-1 Fr. Why's / Wise.

If you ever plan to motor west. (Get Your Kicks On) Route 66! Bobby Troup. ReLy

If you ever see Pedro. Poet Pedro Pietri. Jose Angel Figueroa. PueRic

If you exist; and if, furthermore. Boy Leading a Horse. Geoffrey Nutter. IAoNAP

If you for orders, and a gown design. John Oldham. Fr. Satyr Address'd to a Friend That Is About to Leave the University, and Come Abroad in the World, A.

If you found my heart's scroll in the dust. Hayyim Nahman Bialik. FIT, tr. by Robert Friend

If you go down to the woods today. Teddy Bear's Picnic. Jimmy Kennedy. BLPJKO

If you grow your hair you save on heating bills. Empty Shrine Buddha, The. Joanne Kyger. WhBo

If you had a lot of money. It Follows. Ruth Stone. BodElec

If you had fallen from sleep. Eurydice. Luciana Frezza. CItWP, tr. by Cinzia Sartini Blum and Lara Trubowitz

If You Hadn't—But You Did. Betty Comden and Adolph Green. ReLy

If you have a bike, get on it at night. Instructions for How to Get Ahead of Yourself While the Light Still Shines. Jenny Bornholdt. ArBi

If you have a daughter. Toishan Song, A. Unknown. WoPoe, tr. by Gary Gach and C. H. Kwock and Vincent McHugh

If you have a sickness. Back to the Blues. S. Brandi Barnes. BtF

If you have a word of cheer. Tell Her So. Mrs. Henry Linden. CBWP-4

If you have conquered. Only You. Fanny Carrión de Fierro. TANSG, tr. by Sally Cheney Bell

If you have forgotten water-lilies floating. Water-Lilies. Sara Teasdale. MoAmPo

If you have lost the radio beam, then guide yourself by the sun or the stars. Any Man's Advice to His Son. Kenneth Fearing. IllVoic

If you have revisited the town, thin Shade. To a Shade. William Butler Yeats. NAEL-6v2; NAEL-7v2

If you have taken this rubble for my past. Delta. Adrienne Rich. HarvBoo; LoL; NIL-7; NIP-4

If you have tears, prepare to shed them now. William Shakespeare. OxAEP-1 Fr. Julius Caesar.

If you have time to chatter. Nanao Sakaki. WhBo

If you have to choose. Monk's Misterioso. Sydney March. BtF

If you have to choose between economy and democracy, choose economy. Folk Form. Rick London. Eno

If you haven't made noise enough to warn him, singing, shouting. Meeting a Bear. David Wagoner. WeW-3

If you hear a song in blue. Prelude to a Kiss. Irving Gordon and Irving Mills. ReLy

If you heard your lover scream in the next room, and you ran in and saw his pinkie. Hunting for Cherubs. Jeffrey McDaniel. IIR

If You Imagine. Raymond Queneau. GPTC, tr. by Michael Benedikt

If you in the village think that my work was a good one. Edgar Lee Masters. APT-1 Fr. Spoon River Anthology.

If you kiss my mouth, you must give me your heart. Unknown. SLW, tr. by Marjolijn De Jager, Sayd Bahodin Majrouh and André Velter

If You Knew. Robert Desnos. SurPaPo; YaTCFP, tr. by Mary Ann Caws

If You Knew September. John Nelson. GeoH

If You Knew Susie (Like I Know Susie). B. G. DeSylva. ReLy

If you laid out all the limbs from the Civil War hospital. Ghazal 39. James Harrison. ViWalt

If you lay for Iago at the stage door with a brick. Colloquial Reply, A: To Any Newsboy. Vachel Lindsay. AmWit

If You Leave at Daybreak. Félix Lope de Vega Carpio. SpanPo, tr. by Kate Flores

If you like Chance. Lamb, Willow: An Arch Dolefulness Has Taken Me This Far. Rebecca Wolff. LegDan

If you like I'll take you back. Willingness. Chairil Anwar. PoetW, tr. by Burton Raffel

If You Listen. Rosemerry Wahtola Trommer. GeoH

If you live along with all the other people. Worm Either Way. D. H. Lawrence. NoAM

If you look up de road you see fader Mosey. Join the Angel Band. Unknown. SSUS

If you love it not, of night. (LL) Out in the Dark. Edward Thomas. MoBrPo; OBWVE; OxBEV

If you love me. Lady Izumi. WoPoe, tr. by Willis Barnstone

If you love me, as I love you. Samuel Hoffenstein. AmWit Fr. Love-songs, at Once Tender and Informative.

If you melt some lead. Valerio Magrelli. NeIt

If you must lie. Keep a Good Thought. Bernard Keller. BtF

If you must, then touch it. But only with a long pole of exhaustion. Sleep. Beth Tornes. MotU

If you / my lover / want to drop a penny from the top of the. 12 Second Poem. Trasi Johnson. InTrad

If you name your daughter *vision*. Tempest, The. Stephen Corey. IaFF

If You Need a Reason. Silvia Curbelo. BodElec

If you never spend your money. Icarus Schmicarus. Adrian Mitchell. OBCoV

If you once. Orlanda Blues: 24th Chorus. Jack Kerouac. WhBo

If you plow foul furrows filling up fine paper. To The Poets. Ábrahám Barcsay. IQMS, *tr. by* Adam Makkai

If you really think about it, nothing so childish or nice in those vanished years. The. Little Boy, I'm Not Sure Anymore, A. James Sacré. PML, *tr. by* David Ball

If you refuse me once, and think again. Ditty. Edward Herbert, 1st Baron Herbert of Cherbury. NOSC

If you return to the Truth, to the emptiness of delusion. To an Outstanding Elder. Buhyu Sunsoo. BecRai, *tr. by* Kim Daljin, Kim Won-Chung and Christopher Merrill

If You Saw a Negro Lady. June Jordan. GT

If you saw my little backyard, "Wot a pretty spot!" you'd cry. Cockney's Garden, The. Edgar Bateman. OBGa

If You Say the Right Word, I Can Sing. Meret Oppenheim. SurWo, *tr. by* Catherine Schelbert

If you see me, keep to one side. (LL) Self-Portrait of the Other. Heberto Padilla. TCLAP; VCWP, *tr. by* Andrew Hurley and Alastair Reid

If you seek for Eldorado. (LL) Eldorado. Edgar Allan Poe. APN-1; ChAP; ColAP; NAAPv.1; NCAP; NoP-4; NoP-5; NOxBChV; TCAPo

If you seek me on some day long after. Day Long After, A. Kim Sowŏl. CAMKP, *tr. by* David R. McCann

If you set out in this world. Seventh, The. Attila József. AF; PtR, *tr. by* John Batki

If you sheltered me like a maybug in a cupboard. Listen. Benjamin Péret. SurPaPo, *tr. by* Rachel Stella

If you should come to our silent. Father. John Tripp. TCAWP

If you should look for this place after a handful of lifetimes. Tor House. Robinson Jeffers. APT-1

If you should say to me don't mention love. Sadi. WoPoe, *tr. by* Dick Davis

If you should see me. Mother. . .Sister. . .Daughter. Jean Binta Breeze. RSaN

If you should see unchaste obscenities. *Unknown*. PriapPo *Fr.* Priapus Poems, The.

If you sleep you will have nothing but dust. *Unknown*. SLW, *tr. by* Marjolijn De Jager, Sayd Bahodin Majrouh and André Velter

If you start to write a poem. Poem, The. Clementina Suárez. TANSG, *tr. by* Janet N. Gold

If you stay in comfort too long. You Will Forget. Chenjerai Hove. HBAPE; NAfrP; PLBUT

If you take a clock from which the hours have flown. On These Conditions. Gerardo Diego. RaW, *tr. by* Ralph Nelson

If you take the moon in your hands. "H. D." APT-1; OxBoAm *Fr.* Sigil.

If you tenderly love me. Qian-shang: Gird Your Loins. *Unknown*. CCL1, *tr. by* Arthur Waley

If you think Odysseus too strong and brave to cry. Argos. Michael Collier. WaAnP

If You Think With Fire. "Hsiung Hung." CFP, *tr. by* Chung Ling and Kenneth Rexroth

If you think your town's a warm place. Antarctica. Clive Holden. PoPra

If you threw her in the water. Middle Daughter, The. Barbara Kingsolver. FiBr

If you truly love me, my love, go off and liberate our land! *Unknown*. SLW, *tr. by* Marjolijn De Jager, Sayd Bahodin Majrouh and André Velter

If you try to do what's right. Lines Suggested by an Edition of Blake's Poems. Sir Walter Alexander Raleigh. OBCoV

If you turn out the bathroom lights. How to Make It. Yvonne Jackson. BtF

If you understand. Beauty and Mind. Fazil Hüsnü Daglarca. NaPG, *tr. by* Talat Sait Halman

If you upon a woman. Bitter Cup, A. Mihály Vörösmarty. IQMS, *tr. by* Watson Kirkconnell

If you wander far enough. Oh No. Robert Creeley. HeIP-4

If You Want. Lenous Surprice. OGAHCP, *tr. by* Boadiba and Jack Hirschman

If you want a game to tame you and to take your measure in. Trucker, The. Will Dyson. NOBAu

If you want my apartment, sleep in it. Rent. Jane Cooper. StAl

If you want to die you will have to pay for it. (LL) Charon. Louis MacNeice. NAMCP V.1; OxBEV; PNI

If you want to get to the heaven. Litany of the Little Bourgeois. Nicanor Parra. TCLAP, *tr. by* James Laughlin

If you want to go to God, go without. Going to God with the Shepherds. L. William Countryman. RSR

If you want to make good in a Broadway show. Down by the Erie Canal. George M. Cohan. ReLy

If you watch me. Cleaning Indian Dahl. Jane O. Wayne. InvLad

If You Weep, I Think That. Larry Eigner. FTOS

If you were an alley violinist. Alley Violinist. Robert Lax. GoPo

If you were coming in the Fall. Emily Dickinson. PtR; SoSe-8; TCAPo

If you were drowning, I'd come to the rescue. Love Song. Joseph Brodsky. BAP-97

If you were exchanged in the cradle and. Story That Could Be True, A. William Stafford. NTCP; RaBo

"If you were me . . ." the lad began. Agreement of Predicate Pronouns, The. Thomas M. Disch. KGB

If you were not what I know you to be. Forbidden Love. Elizabeth Daryush. PoBW

If You Were the Only Girl in the World. Clifford Grey. ReLy

If you were the very last one on the line. Crack the Whip. Carol Muske-Dukes. AmAlph

If you were to ask me why I dwell among green mountains. Conversations in the Mountains. Li Po. RaBo; TAL, *tr. by* Robert Payne

If you were to hear me imitating Pavarotti. Changed Man, The. Robert Phillips. GoPo

If you were to read my poems, all of them, I mean. Waterfall, The. Michael Longley. BeAl

If you were to squeeze me and wash. Bitter. Ifi Amadiume. HAWP; NAfrP

If you will come on such a day. Gardener, The. Sidney Keyes. MoBrPo

If you will tell me why the fen. I May, I Might, I Must. Marianne Moore. AmFaPo; ChAP

If you wish I'll give you. Present, The. Marie Laurencin. CuPo

If you wish in this world to advance. William Schwenck Gilbert. OBCoV *Fr.* Ruddigore.

If you wish to move your reader. In Praise of Coldness. Jane Hirshfield. BAP-01

If you wish to sell your kisses. Balade. Charles, Duc d' Orléans. NAWM-7v1, *tr. by* Sarah Spence

If you wonder why. No Offense. Kevin Young. LTA

If you won't be my Valentine. Angry Valentine, An. Myra Cohn Livingston. CalPo

If you would give as I do. Mother Lakshmi's Poem. Cassia Berman. HW

If you would give me. Story of Keys, The. Richard Garcia. TouFir

If you would let me leave. Dedication. *Unknown*. CATKP, *tr. by* Peter H. Lee

If you would only stop to count your blessings. Count Your Blessings. Mrs. Henry Linden. CBWP-4

If you would scan the beauties of a pup. Martial. DiBP *Fr.* Epigrams.

If you would seek us. William Shakespeare. OxAEP-1 *Fr.* Winter's Tale, The.

If you would write a villanelle. How to Write a Villanelle. Elisavietta Ritchie. PoA 2002

If you wound my hide it bleeds to enrich your crops. Words of an Old Woman. Howard Phelps Putnam. APT-2

If you'll listen for a moment, I will tell you now, my friends. What We Teach at Claflin. Lizelia Augusta Jenkins Moorer. CBWP-3

If your child has a trunk on its nose, be not afraid of elephants. Henri Michaux. YaTCFP *Fr.* Slices of Knowledge.

If your first memory was the arms of your father. Reprieve on the Stoop. Belle Waring. PBCAP

If your friendship to take I must take too your clack. To a Lady, Who Was a Great Talker. Elizabeth Moody. PoBW

If your husband owns a rifle company, you must face facts. This Contradiction of Passion. Susan Goyette. OpeFie

If your mother is a Jew, you are a Jew. Meditation in Seven Days, A. Alicia Ostriker. PBCAP; TaR

If your mouth's all set for fig fruit. *Unknown*. PriapPo *Fr.* Priapus Poems, The.

If your right brain causes you to sin. Hemispheres. Jessica Smucker Falcón. ACAMVP

If your soul is called. Kim Namjo. CAMKP *Fr.* Love's Cursive.

If your wharf is washed away. Cedar Cove. John Steffler. Coast

If You're Anxious for to Shine in the High Aesthetic Line. William Schwenck Gilbert. NAEL-6v2; NAEL-7v2; NBLV *Fr.* Patience.

If you're anxious to shine in the high aesthetic line as a man of culture rare. William Schwenck Gilbert. CABP *Fr.* Patience.

"If you're aristocratic," said Nietzsche. Limerick. Gerry Hamill. OBCoV

If you're ever in a jam, here I am. Friendship. Cole Porter. ReLy

If you're going to be a street poet. How to Be a Street Poet. John Rodriguez. BRtP

If you're great enough. Shame on You. Langston Hughes. APT-2

If you're in a communicative mood, call us up. Traveler's Companion. Bill Berkson. AHA

If you're looking for water. Tinker Mather. NewEx

If you're not going to sleep. Jelaluddin Rumi. EaWin, *tr. by* Talat Sait Halman and W. S. Merwin

If you're not home, where. Numbers, Letters. Imamu Amiri Baraka. PFTM-2

If you're one of seven. Seven Deadly Sins. Yusef Komunyakaa. BAP-01

If you're one who keeps a bust made in my likeness. Ovid. RomPo *Fr.* Tristia.

If you're so out of love with happiness. John Oldham. OBSV *Fr.* Satyr Address'd to a Friend That Is About to Leave the University, and Come Abroad in the World, A.

If you're still and never speak. Han-shan (Cold Mountain). TAPaP, *tr. by* Red Pine

If youth would refuse to obey. Sadakichi. NAAPv.1 *Fr.* My Rubaiyat.

If you've ever owned. On Slow Learning. Scott Cairns. UpMys

If you've ever stole a pheasant-egg be'ind the keeper's back. Loot. Rudyard Kipling.

If you've given your heart away. Ghazal. Mirza Asadullah Khan Ghalib. WoPoe, *tr. by* Frances W. Pritchett

If you've got but fifty cents! (LL) I Had But Fifty Cents. *Unknown.* NBLV; WHSW

I-Feel-Like-I'm Fixin'-To-Die Rag. Joe McDonald. ASA

IFF. Howard Nemerov. AmWaPo; BodElec; PWW2

Ifor Hael's hall, poorly it looks. Hall of Ifor Hael, The. Evan Evans. OBWVE, *tr. by* Gwyn Williams

If-you-don't-go-down-with ME! (LL) Disobedience. Alan Alexander Milne. NOxBChV; NTCP; TLR; UV

Igloo! Igloo! Yi Sanghûi. EcSo, *tr. by* Jennifer M. Lee

Ignatius, Bishop and Martyr. David Citino. UpMys

Ignis Fatuus. Yusef Komunyakaa. BAP-04

Ignoramuses. How to Drink the Sun. Vladimir Alekseievich Soloukhin. TCRusP, *tr. by* Daniel Weissbort

Ignorance. Gerardo Deniz. RMCMP, *tr. by* Mónica de la Torre

Ignorance, error, cupidity, and sin. To the Reader. Charles Baudelaire. WoPoe, *tr. by* Stanley Kunitz

Ignorance of Death. William Empson. NAMCP V.1; NoAM

Ignorancia. Gerardo Deniz. RMCMP

Ignorant, in the sense. Death of an Irishwoman. Michael Hartnett. EmeKit; PBCIP; StAl

Ignorant Lust After Knowledge, The. William Bronk. OxBoAm

Ignorant people so that. Brief Curriculum. Reiner Kunze. PoSu, *tr. by* Michael Hamburger

Ignore dull days; forget the showers. Lesson from a Sundial [Sun-Dial]. *Unknown.* Spl

Ignore that last one I sent you. Message: Bottle #32. J. Allyn Rosser. P180

Ignore the men, start sleeping with the wives. (LL) Gwyneth Lewis. MFPA; NeBrP *Fr.* Welsh Espionage.

Ignored what needed to be ignored—though can one? Laureate. Hugh Seidman. BodElec

Ignoring lash and rope. Ox Turned Loose. Muso Soseki. EaWin, *tr. by* W. S. Merwin

Igual / a empezar a morder la puerta de allá enfrente. Hotel. Alfonso D'Aquino. RMCMP

Iguana láctea. Dolores Dorantes. SPV

Ihesus woundes so wide. Wounds, as Wells of Life, The. *Unknown.* SacPr

Ikebana. Cathy Song. YaYoPo

Ikeja, Friday, Four O'Clock. Wole Soyinka. PoetW

Ikey: His Will in Winter Written. George Mackay Brown. EdScPo

Ikhnaton looked like. Why I Often Allude to Osiris. Ishmael Reed. GT

Ikon. Timothy Liu. ReTh

Ikon: The Harrowing of Hell. Denise Levertov. BodElec

Ikonostasis. The Sound of the Sea Filling a Faraway Room. Sam Witt. IAoNAP

Ikons, The. James Keir Baxter. BeAl

Ikoyi / The moon here. Niyi Osundare. NAfrP *Fr.* Moonsongs.

Il est Rosa moins Rosa. Source. Benjamin Péret. YaTCFP

Il est une conception dans la joie, je le veux, il est une vision dans le rire. Tristesse de l'Eau. Paul Claudel. YaTCFP

Il faut croire qu'il méprise les femmes, et ne s'en cache point. Sadique Judith, La. Claude Cahun. YaTCFP

Il faut laisser maison, et vergers et jardins. Il Faut Laisser. Miklós Radnóti. IQMS, *tr. by* Neville Masterman

Il faut l'escargot il faut le liseron. Jardin de l'un, Le. Salah Stétié. YaTCFP

Il la défiait, s'avançait vers son coeur, comme un boxeur ourlé ailé et puissant. Mortel Partenaire, Le. René Char. YaTCFP

Il mange une glace de couleur. Glace de, Une. Jacques Roubaud. YaTCFP

Il m'est interdit de m'arrêter pour voir. Il m'est interdit. Jacques Dupin. YaTCFP

Il naissait un poulain sous les feuilles de bronze. Chanson. "St.-John Perse." YaTCFP

Il neige sur mon toit et sur les arbres. Souffle. Pierre Reverdy. YaTCFP

Il n'est que temps de remonter au soleil. Il n'est que temps. Louis-René des Forêts. YaTCFP

Il n'y a de salut pour l'homme. Romancero d'une petite lampe. René Depestre. YaTCFP

Il Pastor Fido. Sir Richard Fanshawe. *tr. by* Sir Richard Fanshawe

Fall, The. NOSC, *tr. by* Sir Richard Fanshawe

Golden Age, The. NOSC; OBVE

(Great Favorit Beheaded, A.) NPeEn; OBVE; OxBEV; WoPoe, *tr. by* Sir Richard Fanshawe

"Learn women all from this housewifery." OBVE

"Our beauty is to us that which to men." OBVE

Rose, A. OBEV

"Well may that kisse be sweet that's giv'n t' a sleek." OBVE

Il Penseroso. John Milton. BASC; NAEL-6v1; NAEL-7v1; NoP-4; NoP-5; NOSC; OBEV; TFi

Il pleut. Jacques Roubaud. YaTCFP

Il respire avant d'écrire. Jacques Dupin. YaTCFP

Il s'est éloigné des villages. Désert à l'essai. Jean Grosjean. YaTCFP

1. Il Vecchio Is Our Love. David McFadden. NLPA

Il y a. Jacques Dupin. YaTCFP

Il y a la Guerre ou la Paix. Claire Malroux. YaTCFP

Il y a longtemps que tu n'existes pas. Qui quoi. Michel Deguy. YaTCFP

Il y a quelque part, pour un lecteur absent, mais impatiemment attendu. Il y a. Jacques Dupin. YaTCFP

Ilahi. Pir Sultan Abdal. WoPoe, *tr. by* Murat Nemet-Nejat

Ilaria, thou that wert so fair and dear. Tomb of Ilaria Giunigi, The. Edith Wharton. APN-2

Ildrich mitzdonja—astatootch. Klink—Hratzvenga (Deathwail). Else Von Freytag-Loringhoven. APT-1

Ile Au Haut is way down there in the distance. Chart Indent. Richard Eberhart. BodElec

I'le be at lest a Martyr in desire. (LL) In Emulation of Mr Cowleys Poem Call'd The Motto. Mary Astell. EMWP; NOSC

Iliad. Humbert Wolfe. MoBrPo

Iliad of peace began, The. Animal Nativity. Les A. Murray. UpMys

Iliad, The. Homer. *tr. by* George Chapman, William Congreve, William Cowper, Sir John Denham, John Dryden, Edward Earl of Derby, Robert Fagles, Robert Fitzgerald, Richmond Lattimore, Christopher Logue, Robert Lowell, George Meredith, John Ogilby, Alexander Pope, Emile Victor Rieu, Alfred Tennyson and Thomas Yalden

Achilles and Priam. NAWM-7v1, *tr. by* Robert Fagles

Achilles' Dream. CAGL, *tr. by* Emile Victor Rieu

Achilles' Lament and the Funeral of Patroclus. CAGL, *tr. by* Emile Victor Rieu

Achilles Over the Trench. OBVE, *tr. by* Alfred Tennyson

"Achilles with wild fury in his heart." OBWP

Ajax and his Brother. OBVE

"Ajax the swift swerv'd never from the side." OBVE

"All grave old men, and souldiers they had bene, but for age." OBVE

"All silent stood; at last stood forth one dolon, that did dare." FaBoWar, *tr. by* George Chapman

"And as in winter time when Jove his cold-sharpe javelines throwes." NPeEn; OBVE

"And as when with the West-wind's flawes the sea thrusts up her waves." OBVE

"And now was Paris come / From his high towres." OBVE

Andromache's Lamentation. OBVE

Apollo Defeats Patroclus. OBVE, *tr. by* Christopher Logue

(Apollo Strikes Patroclus.) NPeEn, *tr. by* Christopher Logue

"As when an architect some palace wall." OBVE

"As when devouring flames some forest seize." OBVE

"As when of frequent bees." OBVE

"As when the winds, ascending by degrees." OBVE

"At her departure his disdain return'd." OBVE

"Atrides summon'd all to arms, to arms himself dispos'd." FaBoWar, *tr. by* George Chapman

Battle. OBVE, *tr. by* Alfred Tennyson

"Big with great purposes and proud, they sat." OBVE

"Bright-footed Thetis did the sphere aspire." NoSic

"But ere sterne conflict mixt both strengths, faire Paris stept before." OBVE

"But Jove against the Greeks sent forth his son." FaBoWar, *tr. by* Edward Earl of Derby

"But now, no longer deaf to honour's call." OBVE

"Dardanus...was son of Zeus the Lord of the clouds." CAGL, *tr. by* Emile Victor Rieu

Death of Hector, The. NAWM-7v1, *tr. by* Robert Fagles

Destruction of the Grecian Fort, The. OBVE

Embassy to Achilles, The. NAWM-7v1, *tr. by* Robert Fagles

"Embodied close, the lab'ring Grecian train." OBVE

"Fierce they drove on, impatient to destroy." OBVE

"Frail as the leaves that quiver on the sprays." OBVE

Goddess intervenes between Achilles and Agamemnon, The. OBVE, *tr. by* John Dryden

Greeks Like Clouds, The. OBVE

Hector Arms. NOSC

Hector Flees before Achilles. OBVE

Hector Returns to Troy. NAWM-7v1, *tr. by* Robert Fagles

Hector's Child and the Plume. OBVE

Hector's Defiance. NOSC

Helen and the Elders. NPeEn, *tr. by* George Chapman

Helen's Lamentation. OBVE

""Here," said the Cloud-gatherer Zeus, "that is a journey you may well postpone." EroLit, *tr. by* Emile Victor Rieu

Homer's Gift of Fame. NOSC

"Host set forth, and pour'd his steel waves far out of the fleet, The." FaBoWar, *tr. by* George Chapman

Invocation, The. OBVE, *tr. by* John Dryden

"Like Leaves on Trees the Race of Man is found." OBVE

Neptune Goes to the Greeks. NOSC

Night Piece: the Trojans outside Troy. OBVE *tr. by* George Chapman

"Nor lingered Paris in the lofty house." OBVE

"Now Here of the Golden Throne, looking out from where she stood on the summit of Olympus, was quick to observe two things." EroLit, *tr. by* Emile Victor Rieu

Old Trojan Chiefs See Helen, The. OBVE

Paris and Menelaus. OBVE

Patroclus Fights and Dies. NAWM-7v1, *tr. by* Robert Fagles

Patroclus Spears Thestor. OBVE

Priam and Achilles. NOSC, *tr. by* George Chapman

Proposition and Invocation. NOSC, *tr. by* George Chapman

Rage of Achilles, The. NAWM-7v1, *tr. by* Robert Fagles

River Scamander Attacks Achilles. OBVE

"Rude Mars had th' ordering of their spirits; of Greeks, the learned Maid." FaBoWar, *tr. by* George Chapman

Sacrifice to Apollo, The. OBVE

Sarpedon's Speech to Glaucus. NPeEn; OBVE, *tr. by* Sir John Denham

Shield of Achilles, The. NOSC

Shield of Achilles, The. NAWM-7v1, *tr. by* Robert Fagles

"So mourn'd Pelides his late loss, so weighty were his moans." FaBoWar, *tr. by* George Chapman

Stones and Snow. OBVE

"Then Achilles." WoPoe, *tr. by* Christopher Logue

"Then rash Patroclus with new fury glows." FaBoWar, *tr. by* Alexander Pope

"Then tall Hektor of the shining helm answered her: "All these."" AmFaPo, *tr. by* Richmond Lattimore

"Then to th' extremest heat of fight he did his valour turn." FaBoWar, *tr. by* George Chapman

"This said, divine Talthybius he call'd, and bad him haste." FaBoWar, *tr. by* George Chapman

"Through the host with this the goddess ran." FaBoWar, *tr. by* George Chapman

"Thus Neptune rous'd these men." FaBoWar, *tr. by* George Chapman

Tide of Battle Turns, The. NAWM-7v1, *tr. by* Robert Fagles

"To this, great hector said." FaBoWar, *tr. by* George Chapman

Two Ajaxes Compared to Oxen, The. OBVE

Vulcan Forges the Shield of Achilles. OBVE, *tr. by* Alexander Pope

Wasps, The. OBVE

Watch and the Dogs, The. OBVE

Wearing Achilles' Armour, Patroclus, along with the Myrmidons, Attacks the Trojans. OBVE

"Why dost thou so explore." OBVE

I'll admit an occasional affair. I Hadn't Anyone Till You. Ray Noble. ReLy

I'll always be the dish you're stuck with when. Always Secondary. Deena November. IJHIL

I'll always love you. Staring. Zhang Shuai. CCL1, *tr. by* Anne Birrell

I'll always love you. Pining. Zhang Shuai. CCL1, *tr. by* Anne Birrell

I'll always remember my town by the sea. (LL) Block City. Robert Louis Stevenson. AmFaPo; NTCP

Ill am I, paralyzed, whom God did hurt. From Catullus Poem LI. B. P. Nichol. OpeFie

I'll away, I'll away, I'll away, I'll no longer stay. (LL) Song Bewailing the Time of Christmas, So Much Decayed in England, A. *Unknown.* NoP-4; NoP-5

I'll bark against the Dog-star. Loving Mad Tom. *Unknown.* NOSC

I'll be a small brown bird. Lavinia. Kathleen Kirk. IaFF

I'll be a tree, if you are its flower. I'll Be a Tree. Sándor Petőfi. IQMS, *tr. by* Egon F. Kunz

I'll Be a Wicked Old Woman. Radmila Lazić. BeAl, *tr. by* Charles Simic

I'll Be Around. Alec Wilder. ReLy

I'll be around / No matter how. I'll Be Around. Alec Wilder. ReLy

I'll be in Ostia. Ostia Will Receive You. Friederike Mayröcker. GTCP, *tr. by* Reinhold Grimm

I'll Be Seeing You. Irving Kahal. ReLy

I'll be the first. Dream of the Ring: The Great Jack Johnson, A. George Barlow. ESEAA; MoASP

I'll be the Vicar of Bray, Sir. (LL) Vicar of Bray, The. *Unknown.* OBSV; OxBEV

I'll be tired of you. Then I'll Be Tired of You. E. Y. Harburg. ReLy

I'll be your Gigadibs,—despise. To Mr. Maunder Maunder, Professional Poet. Genevieve Taggard. APT-2

I'll bequeath no goods to you when I am dead. Testament. Tudor Arghezi. AF, *tr. by* Andrei Bantas and Thomas Amherst Perry

Ill blows the wind that profits nobody. William Shakespeare. FaBoWar *Fr.* King Henry VI, Pt. III.

I'll bugger you and fuck you in the mouth. To Aurelius and Furius. Catullus. CAGL, *tr. by* Eugene O'Connor

I'll burn my books!—Ah, Mephistophilis! (LL) Christopher Marlowe. FaBoVe; HeIP-4 *Fr.* Doctor Faustus.

I'll check "other." (LL) Check One. Regie Cabico. ReBoTo; WiU

I'll come for you. (LL) Passage. Elizabeth Alexander. FuFl; ISC

I'll die in Paris on a rainy day. Black Stone on a White Stone. César Vallejo. WoPoe, *tr. by* Willis Barnstone

I'll die of mental anguish. Rāmprasād Sen. SinGod, *tr. by* Rachel Fell McDermott

I'll dig with it. (LL) Digging. Seamus Heaney. BeAl; NAEL-6v2; NAEL-7v2; NAMCP V.2; NoP-4; NoP-5; WaAnP

I'll dress you. Love Poem for Three for Kaye & Me. Gregory Corso. PmAP

I'll drown my book. (LL) William Shakespeare. OxAEP-1; WaAnP *Fr.* Tempest, The.

I'll faint no more beneath the burden. Submission. Clara Ann Thompson. CBWP-2

Ill fares the land to giddy lust of power. Vanity of National Grandeur, The. John Thelwall. CenSon

Ill fares the land, to hastening ills a prey. Oliver Goldsmith. OBSV; UV *Fr.* Deserted Village, The.

I'll find the stable and pull out the bolt. (LL) Fascination of What's Difficult, The. William Butler Yeats. NAEL-6v2; NAEL-7v2; NAMCP V.1; OxAEP-2

I'll follow and bring you back by force. I *will*! (LL) Home Burial. Robert Frost. APT-1; ColAP; NAAPv.2; NAMCP V.1; NoP-5; OxBoAm; SoSe-8; TRP; WaAnP

I'll Follow Thee. Clara Ann Thompson. CBWP-2

I'll gather some by spells, and incantation. (LL) To ———: "Had I a man's fair form, then might my sighs." John Keats. CenSon; OxAEP-2

I'll Get By (As Long As I Have You). Roy Turk. ReLy

I'll give a candle. Fair Exchange. Aileen Fisher. NOxBChV

I'll give you a silver dollar. Why Didnt He Tell Me the Whole Truth. Imamu Amiri Baraka. OxAAAP

I'll go among the dead to see my friend. Afternoon at the Beach, An. Edgar Bowers. CalPo; VCAP

I'll go down to my grave unbroken. Workwoman's Death, A. Clementina Suárez. SonAtl, *tr. by* Carole Gibson, Anne Swann and Lee Weingast

I'll go, said I, to the woods and hills. Apostate, The. Alfred Edgar Coppard. OBMV

I'll go to Santiago. (LL) Song of the Cuban Blacks. Federico García Lorca. RaBo; WED, *tr. by* Robert Bly

Ill Government. Robert Herrick. CavPo

I'll grant thee *mine* with all the powers I know. (LL) Female Philosopher, The. Charlotte Dacre. NOBRP; RWP

I'll have a drink, you take a bite. Conversation with a Cat. Yelena Shwarts. CRWP, *tr. by* Stephanie Sandler

Ill Humor. Johann Wolfgang von Goethe. STV, *tr. by* John Frederick Nims

I'll Kill you if you Quote it! (LL) Cinq Ans Après. Frank Gelett Burgess. OBCoV; TFi

I'll lay me doun an' dee. (LL) Siller Croun, The. Susanna Blamire. LW; NPBRoP

I'll lay this halfway me, which we the body name. Martin Opitz. GePo

I'll live, and as he pulls me down mount higher. (LL) Ovid. CABP; NoSic *Fr.* Elegies.

I'll make you one, he said, "and balance it." Suit, The. Seamus Heaney. PoA 2002

(I'll Marry) the Very Next Man. Sheldon Harnick. ReLy

I'll meet thee, Pyramus, at Ninny's tomb. Ninny's Tomb. Patricia Beer. HarvBoo

I'll never be able to tell you why it's funny. Poem on the Limits for My Writing Group: Atlantic Center for the Arts, New Smyrna Beach, Florida. Diane Di Prima. AmZen

I'll never forget the boy. Memory, A. Yi Chŏngbo. CATKP; WoPoe, tr. by Kevin O'Rourke

I'll Never Know No Sunday in This Weekday Room. Sabah As-Sabah. InTrad

I'll Never Love Thee More. James Graham, Marquess of Montrose. See My Dear and Only Love.

I'll no be had for naething. Heiress, The. Carolina Oliphant, Baroness Nairne. NePenScot

I'll not be silent, though you put your finger. Francisco de Quevedo y Villegas. SpanPo Fr. Satiric and Censorious Epistle.

I'll only show your lines, and say, 'Tis this. (LL) Ode: Of Wit. Abraham Cowley. NAEL-6v1; NAEL-7v1; NOSC

I'll only tell the story once. Bitter Mangoes, The. George Scurfield. FaBoWar

I'll pass as a man today and take up public space with my urges in. Passing. Cheryl Clarke. WiU

I'll put a trinket on. (LL) Morns are meeker than they were, The. Emily Dickinson. ChAP; SAmP

I'll Remember April. Patricia Johnston and Don Raye. ReLy

I'll remember how in 6th-grade English class, always. Mrs. Frye and the Pencilsharpener. Bill Knott. BodElec

I'll sacrifice in flames of love to Thee. (LL) Edward Taylor. NAAL-3; NAAL-5; NAAPv.1 Fr. Preparatory Meditations Before My Approach to the Lord's Supper.

I'll Say She Does. B. G. DeSylva, Al Jolson and Gustave Kahn. ReLy

I'll say. So no more now, from your loving husband, Wilfred. (LL) Jungle Husband, The. Stevie Smith. HarvBoo; NBLV; NIL-7; NIP-4

I'll See You Again. Noël Coward. ReLy

I'll See You Down the Lane. Alison Pryde. Prnts

I'll See You in My Dreams. Gustave Kahn. ReLy

I'll settle for the 6 horse. No. 6. Charles Bukowski. P180

I'll sing you a new ballad, and I'll warrant it first-rate. Fine Old English Gentleman, The; New Version. Charles Dickens. OBSV; RSaN

I'll sing you a song. Bar on the Piccola Marina, A. Noël Coward. NBLV (In a "bijou" abode.) ReLy

I'll sink my roots far down. Returning Spring. Pauli Murray. GT

I'll sleep by the creek and purify my ears. (LL) Back at Cold Mountain. Hanshan (Cold Mountain). BB; CCL1; NDACCP, tr. by Gary Snyder

I'll speak of a bird remembering how it was once a bird. Peace on Earth. No Hyegyŏng. EcSo, tr. by Ann Y. Choi

I'll still follow you, primordial. Tortoise and Badger. Cheryl Clarke. FFC

I'll String Along with You. Al Dubin. ReLy

I'll Take Romance. Oscar Hammerstein, II. ReLy

I'll Take You Home Again, Kathleen. Thomas P. Westendorf. NAAPv.1

I'll tell as briefly as I can. Wild Dreams, The. Unknown. NAWM-7v1, tr. by Ned Dubin

I'll tell thee everything I can. Lewis Carroll. BrAP; NAEL-6v2; NAEL-7v2; NoAM; NoP-4; NoP-5; TFi; UV Fr. Through the Looking-Glass.

I'll tell ye of ane great occasioun. Did Ye See Me? Robert Garioch. OBCoV

I'll tell you. Way it is now, The. Charles Bukowski. GoPo

I'll tell you how I speak a piece. Way To Do It, The. Mary Mapes Dodge. SWaP

I'll tell you how the Sun rose. Emily Dickinson. APN-2; ITBLP

I'll Tell You How You Were Born. Luis Cernuda. CAGL, tr. by Rick Lipinski

I'll tell you how you were born, forbidden pleasures. I'll Tell You How You Were Born. Luis Cernuda. CAGL, tr. by Rick Lipinski

I'll tell you something: every day. Fantasy, A. Louise Glück. NAMCP V.2

I'll tell you something for. Love War, The. Desmond O'Grady. IrLP

I'll tell you the story of Jimmy Jet. Jimmy Jet and His TV Set. Shel Silverstein. OBCoV

I'll tell you two fortunes, my fine little lad. Telling Fortunes. Alice Cary. SWaP

I'll think of the Leech-gatherer on the lonely moor! (LL) Resolution and Independence. William Wordsworth. NAEL-6v2; NAEL-7v2; NOBRP; NoP-4; NoP-5; OxAEP-2; TFi

I'll think of thee, mine own, dear one. To a Loved One. Mary Weston Fordham. CBWP-2

I'll throw parties where death blindfolded is spun: won't someone be stuck. and won't I be missed. (LL) Sleek mechanical dart: the syringe noses into the blue vein marking the target of me. D. A. Powell. LegDan; NeAmPo

I'll try / the whole / cause, / and / condemn / you / to / death. (LL) Lewis Carroll. NoAM; OBCoV Fr. Alice's Adventures in Wonderland.

I'll try to hide my smile. (LL) Smile, A. Tzu Yeh. CrYelRi; ErotSp, tr. by Sam Hamill

I'll Twine White Violets. Meleager. NIP-4

I'll Walk Alone. Sammy Cahn. ReLy

I'll weave in the white violet. I'll weave in. Meleager. HePo, tr. by Barbara Hughes Fowler

Ill Wind. Ted Koehler. ReLy

Ill wind with a Samsonite suitcase, An. Chance. Ai. ExTi

I'll worship You with tears, Ma. Ganapti Pāthak. SinGod, tr. by Rachel Fell McDermott

Illa mala rulidala. Mater Dolorosa. Eugene Jolas. APT-2

Illegibility. Franz Wright. AmAlph

Illegitimate Poem. Vivian Lamarque. CItWP, tr. by Cinzia Sartini Blum and Lara Trubowitz

Illegitimate Things. William Carlos Williams. MoAmPo

Illettrée. Je n'ai jamais pu lire qu'entre les lignes. Illettrée. Claire Lejeune. YaTCFP

Ill-fated Bard! she cried, "whose lengthening grief." Tiff, The [or The Interview]. Robert Merry. STuOW

Ill-fated Water, The. Efraín Bartolomé. RMCMP, tr. by Asa Zatz

Illicit. D. H. Lawrence. PoA 2002

Illicit Passion. Abena Busia. NAfrP

Illinois: At Night, Black Hawk's Statue Broods. James W. Rivers. PoA 2002

Illinois Farmer. Carl Sandburg. HHAm

Illiterate, The. William Meredith. EMP; NoP-4; NoP-5; OxBSo; PoA 2002; VCAP

Illiterate. I could not read except between the lines. Illiterate. Claire Lejeune. YaTCFP, tr. by Mary Ann Caws

Illness. Franta Bass. INSAB

Illness. Boris Leonidovich Pasternak. tr. by Theodore Weiss "At dusk you appear, a school-girl still." WoPoe, tr. by Theodore Weiss

Illness. David Scott. NLP

Illogical logic of life is exactly, The. 1 x 2. Hedva Harechavi. DTA, tr. by Miriyam Glazer

Ills of all the human race, The. Misunderstood. Lizelia Augusta Jenkins Moorer. CBWP-3

Illuminated City, The. Felicia Dorothea Hemans. RWP

Illumination. Anthony Hecht. ChrPo

Illumination. R. T. Smith. PoDa; Vesp

Illuminations. Louise Glück. HarvBoo; NALW

Illuminations. Arthur Rimbaud. tr. by Enid Rhodes Peschal and T. Sturge Moore

Illumined. Sikong Tu. CCL1 Fr. Twenty-Four Modes of Poetry.

Illumined bright now shines the splendid dome. Mary Tighe. NOBRP Fr. Psyche.

Illusion. Colleen J. McElroy. ISC; OxAAAP

Illusion. George Russell. IrLP

Illusion, The. F. D. Reeve. VisFro

Illusion Collector, Age 37, The. Keith Abbott. WhBo

Illusion is one of the flatness: the sky, The. Winter, Never Mind Where. Hyam Plutzik. APT-2

Illusion works impenetrable. Maia. Ralph Waldo Emerson. APN-1

Illusions. Ralph Waldo Emerson. APN-1 (Motto to "Illusions.") NCAP

Illusions. Llion Jones. BBMWP, tr. by Geraint Løvgreen

Illusions. Sally Roberts Jones. AngWePo

Illusions. Tzu Yeh. CrYelRi, tr. by Sam Hamill

Illusions she didn't know she had were shattered when. Scholar, The. Vijay Seshadri. KGB

Illusory Hermitage. Master Naong. BecRai, tr. by Kim Daljin, Kim Won-Chung and Christopher Merrill

Illustration. John Ashbery. NAAL-5

Illustration, The [—a Footnote]. Denise Levertov. PoA 2002

Illustration, The / is nothing to you without the application. To a Steam Roller. Marianne Moore. APT-1; MoAmPo; NAMCP V.1; NoP-5; OxBoAm; PoPoPo

Illustration of a Picture. Oliver Wendell Holmes. TreFP

Illustrious Ancestors. Denise Levertov. OxBoAm; PmAP; TaR

Illustrious Holland! hard would be his lot. Lord Byron. OBSV Fr. English Bards and Scotch Reviewers [1812 version].

Ill-Wishing Him. Dorothy Nimmo. BeAl

Ilmarinen struck. Unknown. WoPoe Fr. Kalevala, The.

Ilona Budai, The Cruel Mother. Hungarian Oral Tradition. IQMS, tr. by Adam Makkai

Ilona Karmel, born in Cracow in 1925, was sixteen when she was deported to a German labor camp. White Lines. Fanny Howe. Eno

Ilonam Budai leaned out through her window. Ilona Budai, The Cruel Mother. Hungarian Oral Tradition. IQMS, tr. by Adam Makkai

I'm 41st in line for Plisetskaya. Chorus of Nymphs, A. Andrey Andreievich Voznesensky. VCWP, tr. by Vera Dunham and H. W. Tjalsma

I'm a backward. Backward Sound. Nina Kossman. CRWP, tr. by the author

I'm a bad, bad man. Bad Man. Langston Hughes. NAMCP V.1

I'm a boy with my cousin. Boy Girl Game, The. Jody Helfand. BeDoSh

I'm a broken-hearted miner, who loves his cup to drain. Stringybark Cockatoo, The. Unknown. NOBAu

I'm a Coffee Rancher. Coffee Rancher, The. *Unknown.* SonAtl, *tr. by* Alan Brierly

I'm a Dragonfly Caught in a Net. Chŏng Hwajin. EcSo, *tr. by* Julie C. Park

I'm a Fool to Love You. Cornelius Eady. P180

I'm a Gigolo. Cole Porter. OBCoV; ReLy

I'm a glum one; it's explainable. I Can't Get Started. Ira Gershwin. APT-2; ReLy

I'm a Hip Hop Cheerleader. Jessica Care Moore. BRtP

I'm a lean dog, a keen dog, a wild dog and lone. Lone Dog. Irene McLeod. NOxBChV

I'm a little bit off. Little Bit Off, A. Richard Maltby, Jr. ReLy

I'm a little gentleman. One Little Boy. *Unknown.* NOxBChV

I'm a little husbandman. Another Little Boy. *Unknown.* NOxBChV

I'm a man. Transition #2. Sabah As-Sabah. InTrad

I'm a penny fallen from heaven's. Motive. Reginald Shepherd. NeAmPo

I'm a person who is difficult. If You Come Close to Me. Suchart Sawadsri. PML, *tr. by* the author and Kathryn Rhett

I'm a riddle in nine syllables. Metaphors. Sylvia Plath. HeIP-4; NAMCP V.2; SoSe-8

I'm a Stranger Here Myself. Ogden Nash. ReLy

I'm a tough true-hearted sailor. Every Bullet Has Its Billet. *Unknown.* FaBoWar

I'm a true Canadian but it's not my fault if I can't stand Canadian beer. David McFadden. NLPA

I'm a vane that wants to turn to the west./I'm a van that wants to. Acromatic Dawn. Yi Hyangji. EcSo, *tr. by* Catherine J. Kim

I'm a very ordinary man. I Want to Be Happy. Irving Caesar. ReLy

I'm a wanderer. Basho. SoOfWa, *tr. by* Sam Hamill

(I'm Afraid) The Masquerade Is Over. Herb Magidson. ReLy

I'm afraid, you say, are you? out in the wintry air. Daphne Marlatt. NLPA *Fr.* Touch to My Tongue.

I'm all afire and from bright blaze annealed. Concerning Himself. Paul Fleming. GePo, *tr. by* George C. Schoolfield

I'm all alone in this world, she said. 50–50. Langston Hughes. NoAM

I'm all lost in Fabric World. Plenty. Allison Joseph. SweBea

I'm alone here, but. Clinic in a Dangerous Season 7, A. Yi Yŏnju. EcSo, *tr. by* Yung-Hee Kim

I'm Always Chasing Rainbows. Joseph McCarthy. ReLy

I'm an African, that's what he said. He was standing on the corner. Another Impostor. Bruce Jackson. AmPoNex

I'm an ol' king bee, honey. King Bee Blues. George Elliott Clarke. IFF

I'm an unthinking dog. Explosion. Takahashi Shinkichi. AtGh; ZenPo, *tr. by* Takashi Ikemoto and Lucien Stryk

I'm angry because I hate to be angry and because I hate to be angry. It's Called Kings. Suzana Cabañas. BRtP

I'm ashamed of my cheap rodeo. My Rodeo. Jack Grapes. SUP

I'm at the point of hurting myself and listening to myself. Eunice Odio. TANSG *Fr.* Creation.

I'm A-Trouble in de Mind. *Unknown.* SSUS

I'm awake, I'm away! Black Runner, The. Angelina Weld Grimké. NAAPv.2

I'm back after twenty years of baiting the trap of the past. At the House of Ghosts. Adrian C. Louis. MoASP

I'm back again scrutinising the Milky Way. Alien, The. Greg Delanty. WaAnP

I'm back in my town—excruciatingly familiar. Leningrad. Osip Emilevich Mandelstam. TCRusP, *tr. by* John Glad

I'm Beginning to See the Light. Don George. ReLy

I'm beginning to talk to myself. But My Blood. Rose Romano. UnSA

I'm being stalked by a bird. Dina Gatina. CRWP, *tr. by* Chris Jones

I'm Bert, p'rhaps you've heard of me, Bert, you've had word of me. Burlington Bertie from Bow. William Hargreaves. OBCoV

I'm big for ten years old. Dumb Insolence. Adrian Mitchell. NOxBChV

I'm bound to the hills. (LL) Lonesome Water. Roy Helton. APT-1; MoAmPo

I'm building a nest in the garden. Amanda Dalton. NeBl *Fr.* Room of Leaves.

I'm burned by love. Loveburn. *Unknown.* SonAtl, *tr. by* Jenny Ako, Micha Graham, Ursula Hobday and S. Lundberg

I'm busy! / I am building. New Heart, The. Semyon Isaakovich Kirsanov. CLPP, *tr. by* Anselm Hollo

I'm careful of the words I say. Be Careful. *Unknown.* NBLV

I'm ceded—I've stopped being Theirs. Emily Dickinson. APN-2; NAAPv.1; NALW; SacPr; TRP; WPoS

I'm certain you saw these ample breasts lift and catch in a sigh. Mata Hari Blues or Why I Will Never Be a Spy. Jewell M. Handy. BRtP

I'm cheerful, whatever happens. Cloud. Takahashi Shinkichi. ZenPo, *tr. by* Takashi Ikemoto and Lucien Stryk

I'm coming back on All Saints' Day. When I Died. Jo Shapcott. StAl

I'm coming, coming out of space. Three Octets. Osip Emilevich Mandelstam. RusPo, *tr. by* Robert Arthur Douglas Ford

I'm Craving for That Kind of Love. Noble Sissle. ReLy

I'm cross with god who has wrecked this generation. John Berryman. NAMCP V.2 *Fr.* Dream Songs.

I'm curled into a ball. Poetry Reading. Anna Swirszczynska [*or* Swir]. BLT; TAPaP, *tr. by* Czeslaw Milosz and Leonard Nathan

I'm dead, but waiting for you, and you'll wait for someone. Message to the Living. *Unknown.* PoCho, *tr. by* Burton Raffel

I'm deaf? (LL) Mosquito at my ear. Issa. ChAP; EH, *tr. by* Robert Hass

I'm Dealing with My Pain. Denise Duhamel. NeAmPo; SUP

I'm delighted by the velocity of money as it whistles. Velocity of Money. Allen Ginsberg. NIL-7

I'm discontented with homes that are rented. Tea for Two. Irving Caesar. ReLy

I'm dizzy from hunger. Three Pieces of Candy. Anna Swirszczynska [*or* Swir]. PoChi, *tr. by* Czeslaw Milosz and Leonard Nathan

I'm doing it again. Reading, The. Gabriel Gbadamosi. HBAPE

I'm doing this poetry reading with Simone. Dream. Joanne Kyger. WhBo

I'm down. Step on my neck, you savage god, with your heel. Meleager. HePo, *tr. by* Barbara Hughes Fowler

I'm drawing a picture of a chicken. New Joke, The. Deborah Bacharach. FiBr

I'm drawn to the happiness of birds. Translating Birdsong. Jean Sprackland. MoWP

I'm drawn to the ineffable, yet cathedrals leave me empty. Enigma of the Stigma, or Vice Versa. Peter Johnson. Vesp

I'm dreaming geographically these days. Rafael Campo. WiU *Fr.* Song for My Lover.

I'm Dreaming of Your Body All Nude. Lyonel Trouillot. OGAHCP, *tr. by* Boadiba and Jack Hirschman

I'm driving down the highway in the dark. Poem for a New Girlfriend. Joseph Millar. NevBe

I'm driving tonight into November. Birthday, The. Elizabeth Morgan. P180

I'm dropping out. (LL) Marks. Linda Pastan. NIL-7; NIP-4

I'm drunk—my joy is boundless. Composition in Drunkenness. Chang Yüeh. CCL1, *tr. by* Stephen Owen

I'm dumb / but I'm honest. Why I Am a Whore. Donna Brook. PrTe

I'm engaged to New Mexico. I've been engaged for eighteen years. Something Like Marriage. Joan Logghe. ICANM

I'm Explaining a Few Things. Pablo Neruda. TCLAP, *tr. by* Nathaniel Tarn

I'm fat, look, *fat.* Philip Gross. StAl *Fr.* Wasting Game, The.

I'm feelin' mighty lonesome. Black Coffee. Sonny Burke and Paul Francis Webster. ReLy

I'm flying home. Flying over America. Kalamu ya Salaam. BRtP

I'm flying to South Carolina. Long Distance Moan. Blind Lemon Jefferson. APT-2

I'm fond, nereids and nymphs, unlike some, of the pig. Circe. Carol Ann Duffy. NeBrP

I'm Fond of Doctors. Samuel Hoffenstein. OBCoV

I'm for it, as the last leaves shred. Function of Winter, The. Jay Parini. WaAnP

I'm forty-four now. Thoughts on Eyes Growing Dim: Presented to Chŏn Iji. Yi Kyubo. CATKP, *tr. by* Kevin O'Rourke

I'm forty-one. I was twenty-three then. Vermont. David Huddle. AmWaPo

I'm from Latin America. Latter-day Mother Courage. Maria del Rosario. CFP, *tr. by* Gail Wronsky

I'm full of blackbirds and their flight tonight. That's Good, That's Enough. Judyth Hill. ICANM

I'm glad I'm not getting old like that. Staying Young. Bob Merrill. ReLy

I'm Glad I'm Not Young Any More. Alan Jay Lerner. ReLy

I'm Glad There Is You (In This World of Ordinary People). Paul Madeira. ReLy

I'm goin' to buy a paper doll that I can call my own. Paper Doll. Johnny S. Black. ReLy

I'm goin' to whoop you, Sammy Taylor. Domestic Storm, A. Priscilla Jane Thompson. CBWP-2

I'm going, all along. (LL) Some keep the Sabbath going to Church. Emily Dickinson. BLPJKO; HeIP-4; MoAmPo; TCAPo

I'm Going Home. *Unknown.* SSUS

I'm going out. Issa. EH, *tr. by* Robert Hass

I'm going out and get something. Riot Act, April 29, 1992. Ai. CAP-8; ESEAA; NIL-7

I'm going out to clean the pasture spring. Pasture, The. Robert Frost. APT-1; BLPJKO; ItP; MoAmPo; NAAL-5; NAAPv.2; SAmP; TLR; TRP; WHSW

I'm going out to dine at Gray's. Ballade of Hell and of Mrs. Roebeck. Joseph Hilaire Pierre Belloc. NPeEn

I'm going stark, staring mad because of the guns. (LL)   Repression of War Experience. Siegfried Sassoon. AF; NAMCP V.1; NoAM

I'm going to ask you to transition into a new theme about. United States of America, The. Lisa Jarnot. Eno

(I'm going to ask you to transition into a new theme.) LegDan

I'm going to die, he says. Heaven Is Just Another Country. Jaime Jacinto. ReBoTo

I'm going to England. And France. Going to Europe. Michael Lassell. WiU

I'm going to have to leave you, he said. Ill-Wishing Him. Dorothy Nimmo. BeAl

I'm going to make a seawall. Seawall. Julia de Burgos. PoCho, *tr. by* Jack Agüeros

I'm going to move ahead. Border. Taslima Nasrin. VCWP

I'm going to murder you with love. Food of Love. Carolyn Kizer. RaBo

I'm going to push it. (LL)   Precision German Craftsmanship. Matthew Rohrer. NAPBL; NeAmPo

I'm going to put Johnny Dominguez right here. Photograph: Migrant Worker, Parlier, California, 1967. Larry Levis. CalPo; GeoHom

I'm going to roll over. Issa. EH, *tr. by* Robert Hass

I'm going to slap my anger onto a wet slab. Release. Myra Schneider. PoCu

I'm Going to Sleep. Alfonsina Storni. TCLAP, *tr. by* Andrew Rosing

I'm going to tell You something that is true. Abu Sa'id Abul Khayr. WoPoe *Fr.* Four Poems on Death.

I'm going to throw open my windows and yell: 'halleluiah'. When It's All Over. Myra Schneider. PoCu

I'm going to try and overcome my limitation. Serious Concerns. Wendy Cope. NoP-5; OBCoV

I'm going to your fair. March. Ekaterina Iosifova. CSCBP, *tr. by* Georgi Belev and Lisa Sapinkopf

I'm going under were the last words. Teen Drowns in Rehabilitation Camp Days Before 17th Birthday, Questions Persist. Gaylord Brewer. AmPoNex

I'm Gonna Go Fishin'. Peggy Lee. ReLy

I'm Gonna Laugh You Right Out of My Life. Joseph McCarthy, Jr. ReLy

I'm gonna lay down my sword and shield. Down by the Riverside. *Unknown.* NAAPv.2

I'm gonna love you. Come Rain or Come Shine. Johnny Mercer. ReLy

I'm Gonna Sit Right Down and Write Myself a Letter. Joe Young. ReLy

I'm Gonna Slap Those Doctors. Jack Coulehan. BloBone

I'm gonna stay on the battlefield. For Sweet Honey in the Rock. Sonia Sanchez. FuFl

I'm gonna take myself a piece of sunshine. I Think I'll Call It Morning. Gil Scott-Heron. IJHIL

I'm growing my beard from the turret room. Haymakers. Deborah Randall. NeBl

I'm Gwine to Alabamy. *Unknown.* SSUS

I'm happiest when most away. Emily Jane Brontë. NAEL-6v2; NAEL-7v2

I'm happy. I've got. Why I Think About Hiroshima and Nagasaki. Edward A. Dougherty. AtGh

I'm happy, Kerouac, your madman Allen's. Malest Cornifici Tuo Catullo. Allen Ginsberg. BB

I'm happy to sit among these cliffs. (LL)   Happy Among These Cliffs. Hanshan (Cold Mountain). CCL1; NDACCP, *tr. by* Gary Snyder

I'm having a sunbath on the rug. Last Day. May Swenson. NAMCP V.2

"I'm having five minutes," he said. Five Minutes. Norman Nicholson. NLP

I'm heading off to Pasárgada. Off to Pasárgada. Manuel Bandeira. TCLAP, *tr. by* Candace Slater

I'm here alone for the weekend, get fires going and burn all that junk. Fred Wah. NLPA *Fr.* This Dendrite Map: Father / Mother Haibun.

I'm here, on the dark porch, restyled in my mother's chair. Sitting at Night on the Front Porch. Charles Wright. ColAP; GeoHom

I'm hiding, I'm hiding. Hiding. Dorothy Aldis. ChAP

I'm Hip. Dave Frishberg. ReLy

I'm hip / I'm no square. I'm Hip. Dave Frishberg. ReLy

I'm holding my cigarette out the car window. Smoking. Ronald Wallace. SwNoth

I'm in a car marked blueberry. Poetry Detective. Edwin Torres. HeMarv

I'm in a mirrorless room. Yi Sang. CAMKP; PFTM-1 *Fr.* Crow's-Eye View.

I'm in black leather, the guns are wrapped in string, tape, wire, and cloth. Evidence of Death's Voodoo—Inside and Outside the "Gun As Art Exhibit." Wendy Bishop. LiTh

I'm in love with a man. Party's Over, The. Betty Comden and Adolph Green. ReLy

(I'm In Love With) The Honorable Mr. So and So. Sam Coslow. ReLy

I'm in Paris with you. (LL)   In Paris with You. James Fenton. NoP-4; NoP-5; StAl

I'm in the mix, and the mix is in me. Ode to DJ. Trebor Healey. BeDoSh

I'm in the Mood for Love. Dorothy Fields. ReLy

I'm in trouble, Lord, I'm in trouble. I'm in Trouble. *Unknown.* SSUS

I'm in trouble, she said. It's Good To Be Here. Alden Nowlan. StAl

I'm Japanese. Love. Ayukawa Nobuo. PML, *tr. by* Leza Lowitz and Oketani Shogo

I'm Jewish because love my family matzoh ball soup. Yiddishe Kopf. Allen Ginsberg. BodElec; TaR

I'm just a big old rusty wok. Tenzo's Song. Gillian Coote. WhBo

I'm just a little "Jackie Horner." When I Take My Sugar to Tea. Irving Kahal and Pierre Norman. ReLy

I'm Just a Lucky So-and-So. Mack David. ReLy

I'm just a poor wayfaring stranger. *Unknown. See* I am a poor wayfaring stranger.

I'm just a woman. Am I Blue? Grant Clarke. ReLy

I'm just about as solitary. No Love, No Nothin'. Leo Robin. ReLy

I'm just going to school. (LL)   Soul Make a Path Through Shouting. Cyrus Cassells. GifTon; GT; OPRER; UnSA

I'm just jotting this note so you won't forget. He Writes to the Soul. Christopher Howell. RoV

I'm just Miss Blues'es child! (LL)   Miss Blues'es Child. Langston Hughes. ChAP; SAmP

I'm just saying that I'm damn sick of ape every night, cried father. (LL)   Ape. Russell Edson. PmAP; RaBo; SUP

I'm Just Wild about Harry. Noble Sissle. ReLy

I'm keeping to myself on my little porch. Soundtracks. Timothy Geiger. AmPoNex

I'm laying across a leather couch with Maria. Thursday Poem. DJ Renegade. FuFl

I'm learning how to read the rocks. Indian Ruins Along Rio de Flag. Greg Pape. PBCAP

I'm leaving / Now you can make love. Issa. ZenPo, *tr. by* Takashi Ikemoto and Lucien Stryk

I'm like all lovers, wanting love to be. Poem. Lesbia Harford. NOBAu

I'm like / rock candy baby. Rock Candy. A. Wanjiku H. Reynolds. BRtP

I'm Livin' in a Great Big Way. Dorothy Fields. ReLy

I'm living in one place so long. Birds. Maxine Hong Kingston. FaoP

I'm lookin' far in mind, b'lieve I'm fixin' to die, b'lieve I'm fixin' to die. Fixin' to Die. Bukka White. APT-2

I'm looking for a blue door. Sleep. Mary Crockett Hill. AmPoNex

I'm looking forward to my death, she said. As a Child in the Temple. Andrew Hudgins. UpMys

I'm looking out of the window. Invention of a Garden, The. Jay Wright. GT

I'm lost in the middle of my birthday. Rabindranath Tagore. PoCho *Fr.* Final Poems.

I'm mad, and I don't mean deranged, rabid, foolish, impudent, infatuated. Top Stories. Brigitte Byrd. LiTh

I'm made in sport by Nature, when. On an Indian Tomineois, the Least of Birds. Thomas Heyrick. NOSC

(I'me made in sport by Nature, when.) NPeEn

I'm makin' a road. Florida Road Workers. Langston Hughes. MoAmPo

I'm Mighty Glad I'm Living and That's All. George M. Cohan. ReLy

I'm mother. Woman as Artist. Eleanor Ross Taylor. InGu

I'm My Own Mother, Now. Stella P. Chipasula. HAWP

I'm naebody noo, though in days that are gane. I'm Naebody Noo. William Anderson. NePenScot

1: I'm Naked, Bruised, and I Smell of You. Jaime Sabines. MotU *Fr.* Adam and Eve.

I'm Neither the Loosening of Song nor the Close-Drawn Tent of Music. Mirza Asadullah Khan Ghalib. WoPoe, *tr. by* Adrienne Rich

I'm nervous and upset. Tonight at Eight. Sheldon Harnick. ReLy

I'm no artist but in bed. Artist, The. Han Yong'un [*or* Yongwun]. WoPoe, *tr. by* Bruce Taylor

I'm no fighting man, he says. Novella Nikolaevna Matveyeva. TCRusP, *tr. by* Daniel Weissbort

I'm no matron, mother of warriors, Cornelia. Heart's Desire. Adelia Prado. TANSG, *tr. by* Ellen Doré Watson

I'm Nobody! Who are you? Emily Dickinson. AmFaPo; APN-2; ChAP; HeIP-4; ItP; NAAPv.1; NALW; NBLV; NoP-5; OBCoV; OxBoAm; PoPoPo; SAmP; TCAPo

I'm Nobody's Baby. Benny Davis and Lester Santly. ReLy

I'm not a child any more, Syama. Bhadreśvar Mandal. SinGod, *tr. by* Rachel Fell McDermott

I'm Not a Man. Harold Norse. CAGL

I'm not a poet. Excuse and Explanation. Yevgeny Bunimovich. PML, *tr. by* Patrick Henry

I'm not a poet / How well I know it. You're the Cream in My Coffee. Lew Brown, B. G. DeSylva and Ray Henderson. ReLy

I'm not afraid of love. Creation Story, The. Joy Harjo. WaAnP

I'm not at all afraid. Grass. Blaga Dimitrova. CSCBP, *tr. by* Georgi Belev and Lisa Sapinkopf

I'm not at home if people call. (LL)   Arrivals at a Watering-Place.   Winthrop Mackworth Praed.   NOBRP; NPeEn

I'm Not Complaining.   Philip Schultz.   SoSe-8

I'm not going down into that cave anymore.   Melissa Quits School.   Lucile Burt.   TWF

I'm not going to cry all the time.   My Heart.   Frank O'Hara.   OxBoAm

I'm not going to tell you everything.   Closed Mill.   Maggie Anderson.   PBCAP

I'm not here.   "H. D."   MoAmPo *Fr.* Halcyon.

I'm not in court to be judged.   Jenny Lewis.   NewEx

I'm not interested in.   Jerusalem.   Naomi Shihab Nye.   CFP; RaF

I'm not looking at you, though it might seem that I am.   Dreamt Up.   Dennis Cooper.   WiU

I'm not Myself at All!   Samuel Lover.   IrV

I'm not planning to turn into gold. Somebody else.   Bassus.   HePo *Fr.* Epigrams.

I'm not right. I'm interfered with.   Truth about Northern Lights, The.   Christine Hume.   IAoNAP

I'm not sleeping Georgia.   Philippe Soupault. *See* I can't sleep Georgia.

I'm not sleeping now.   Maysoun Saqr Al-Qasimi.   PoArWo *Fr.* Morning of Every Sin, The.

I'm not so deep in it.   Muso Soseki.   EaWin, *tr. by* W. S. Merwin

I'm not sure it happened. Through the branches.   Canto Eleven.   Tomas Venclova.   WoPoe, *tr. by* Vyt Bakaitis

I'm not sure of my age; descending pale.   Fourteenth Ode.   Sekeena Shaben.   PoArWo

I'm nothing / I'll always be nothing.   Tobacco Shop, The.   Álvaro de Campos.   GPTC, *tr. by* Richard Zenith

I'm of no interest to myself.   Dissolving Presence, A.   Sándor Weöres.   IQMS, *tr. by* Adam Makkai and Donald E. Morse

I'm Old-Fashioned.   Johnny Mercer.   ReLy

I'm on a straight path with the sun gone down.   Luigi Fontanella.   NeIt

I'm on my way to Canada.   Away to Canada.   Joshua McCarter Simpson.

I'm on the ledge / outside your hotel bedroom.   Paparazzi, The.   Ai.   ExTi

I'm on the phone with Jade.   Jade's Iguanas Are Dead.   Gregory Razran.   IJHIL

I'm on the way.   Prose of the Trans-Siberian and Little Jean of France.   Blaise Cendrars.   CuPo

I'm out here for trouble / and I've got the Black Mountain Blues. (LL)   Black Mountain Blues.   Bessie Smith.   FTtHH; PFTM-1

I'm out of touch with stars. The bar's.   For Jack Spicer.   David Meltzer.   ASA

I'm outside sun-bathing on Kenward Elmslie's lawn in Calais.   Aug. 29, 1967.   Joe Brainard.   AHA

I'm over seventy now.   Poetry: A Chronic Disease.   Yi Kyubo.   CATKP, *tr. by* Kevin O'Rourke

I'm painting my wife's toes.   At Twenty-Three Weeks She Can No Longer See Anything South of Her Belly.   Thom Ward.   GoPo

I'm pedaling in to work.   Old Man on a Bike.   Peter Sizer.   ArBi

I'm persistent as the pink locust.   Pink Locust, The.   William Carlos Williams.   SAmP

I'm pondering the question.   Rain in Ivy.   Chase Twichell.   AmZen

I'm pretending not to see him so I can eat my lunch.   Poets on Poets.   Nin Andrews.   KGB

I'm pushing off.   Outside the Door.   Marie Luise Kaschnitz.   GTCP, *tr. by* Reinhold Grimm

I'm recallin' / Times when I was small, in.   Hallelujah!   Clifford Grey and Leo Robin.   ReLy

I'm Rooted.   René Philoctete.   OGAHCP, *tr. by* Boadiba and Jack Hirschman

I'm Saddest When I Sing.   Thomas Haynes Bayly.   STuOW

I'm Sayin Though.   Marco Villalobos.   BRtP

I'm saying / I have outgrown promises.   Magnetic Charms.   Lorenzo Thomas.   AnSo

I'm scared a lonely. Never see my son.   John Berryman.   NoP-4; NoP-5 *Fr.* Dream Songs.

I'm scrambling an egg for my daughter.   Egg.   C. G. Hanzlicek.   GoPo

I'm Sending You Saint Francis Preaching to the Birds.   Karen Kipp.   BodElec

I'm sentimental, so I walk in the rain.   Why Try to Change Me Now?   Joseph McCarthy, Jr.   ReLy

I'm serious. In your eyes the sea was two children, spying on me.   Angel of Sand, The.   Rafael Alberti.   RaW, *tr. by* Rachel Benson

I'm sewing on new buttons.   Invisible Mender, The.   Sarah Maguire.   MFPA

I'm sick. I hear the cranes.   1915.   Anna Andreyevna Akhmatova.   WoPoe, *tr. by* Stephen Berg

I'm sick of cautious lyricism.   Poetics.   Manuel Bandeira.   TCLAP, *tr. by* Candace Slater

I'm sick of celestial whodunits, wherein God.   Search, The.   Maurya Simon.   ExTi

I'm sick of embarking in dories.   Pour Prendre Congé.   Dorothy Parker.   AmWit

I'm sick of love songs.   Happy As the Day Is Long.   Ted Koehler.   ReLy

I'm sick. They didn't stop coming.   January-May 1951 Slaughter, The.   Rolando Hinojosa.   AmWaPo

I'm silent now. A stillness to carry my heart away.   Greetings from My Shtetl (A Letter from Poland).   Chaim Plotkin.   Prolet, *tr. by* Amelia Glaser

I'm sittin' on the stile, Mary.   Lament of the Irish Emigrant.   Helen Selina Blackwood, Countess of Dufferin and Clandeboye.   IrV

I'm sitting at the same table again, in the hopes.   Ten Questions for Mona.   Matthew Zapruder.   IIR

I'm sitting by the hearthstone now.   Twilight Musings.   Mary Weston Fordham.   CBWP-2

I'm sitting by the pool at the Mondrian.   Sunset Stripping: Visiting L.A.   Michael Lassell.   WiU

I'm sitting here alone. It's the middle of the night, with memories.   Jimmy Santiago Baca.   ICANM *Fr.* Healing Earthquakes.

I'm sitting home, I feel lonesome.   Samuel Hoffenstein.   AmWit *Fr.* Notebook of a Schnook, The.

I'm sitting in the kitchen and.   Gallery, The.   Sally Keith.   LegDan

I'm sitting in the sunshine.   Postponed Nightmare.   Sandor Csoori.   VCWP, *tr. by* Len Roberts and László Vértes

I'm sitting on a bench on a warm Sunday evening watching the.   David McFadden.   NLPA

I'm Sitting on Top of the World.   Sam M. Lewis and Joe Young.   ReLy

I'm sitting with my mother.   Dr Hanagan.   Ann O'Neill.   PoCu

I'm 68 now, feeble and frail, besieged.   Wind Sickness Strikes.   Po Chü-i.   NDACCP, *tr. by* David Hinton

I'm sixty, this autumn.   *Unknown.*   NAAPv.2

I'm skiving off again, this time pasting down old family photographs.   Physics.   Eva Salzman.   MoWP

I'm skulking by the scandal and the handle on the door.   John Hegley.   NewEx

I'm Smith of Stoke, aged sixty-odd.   Epitaph on a Pessimist.   Thomas Hardy.   TRP

I'm so blue I don't know what to do.   If I Could Be with You.   Henry Creamer.   ReLy

I'm so happy since the day.   My Baby Just Cares for Me.   Gustave Kahn.   ReLy

I'm so in love.   At Long Last Love.   Cole Porter.   ReLy

I'm so out of it I can't remember.   Apiary.   B. H. Boston.   GeoHom

I'm so sad to / Think that I have had to.   Till the Clouds Roll By.   P. G. Wodehouse.   NAAPv.2; ReLy

I'm so tired of this dull routine.   Let's Get Away from It All.   Tom Adair.   ReLy

(I'm So) Weary of It All.   Noël Coward.   ReLy

I'm sorry for the Dead—Today.   Emily Dickinson.   SAmP

I'm sorry I done it, Major.   Deserter, The.   Gilbert Frankau.   FaBoWar

I'm sorry. I have a hard time not laughing.   Coming Forth.   Scott Cairns.   UpMys

I'm sorry I'm late.   Apology and Explanation.   John Sparrow.   OBCoV

I'm sorry, officer. I didn't see the sign.   First Offense.   David Lehman.   PmAP

I'm sorry to say it, but fucking.   Merengue.   Mary Ruefle.   FaoP

I'm speaking again.   Speaking.   Michael Ryan.   SoSe-8

I'm speaking, of course, on the mirror, the shadow, the other.   Brother, The.   Franz Wright.   MotU

I'm speaking to make you silent.   Gali-Danah Zinger.   CRWP, *tr. by* the author and Ashraf Noor

I'm spending my nights in the doss house.   Soup Kitchen Song.   *Unknown.*   NOBAu

I'm standing here in the church.   A Capella.   Robert Patrick Dana.   Vesp

I'm standing here inside my skin.   Phrase Book.   Jo Shapcott.   MoWP; NeBrP; PoAgWa; StAl

I'm standing in elm shadow.   Bread.   William Heyen.   ViWalt

I'm Standing, Lord.   Stand Still, and See.   Betty Scott Stam.   SacPr

I'm Still Here.   Stephen Sondheim.   ReLy

I'm still struck (as when I saw my first Pasque-flower).   Black Train, The.   Thomas McGrath.   GM

I'm sure we should all be as happy as kings. (LL)   Happy Thought.   Robert Louis Stevenson.   BRP; Spl

I'm Surplus.   Hwang Insuk.   EcSo, *tr. by* Peter H. Lee

I'm surprised, you could say a little shocked.   Southpaw.   Maurice Riordan.   NIrP

I'm swimming in vast stretches of dry ocean.   Ackermann Steppe, The.   Adam Mickiewicz.   WoPoe, *tr. by* Vyt Bakaitis

I'm tackling this particularly chewy piece of sushi and.   Moderation Kills (Excusez-Moi, je suis Sick as a Dog).   David Kirby.   P180

I'm taught P-l-o-u-g-h.   O-U-G-H.   Charles Battell Loomis.   NBLV

I'm tellt the auncient Celts collectit heids.   Celtic History, A.   William Neill.   EdScPo

I'm the Guy with the Gut.   Ifor Ap Glyn.   BBMWP, *tr. by* the author

I'm the individual. Individual's Soliloquy, The. Nicanor Parra. PFTM-2, *tr. by* Lawrence Ferlinghetti and Allen Ginsberg

I'm the kid that's all the candy. Yankee Doodle Boy, The. George M. Cohan. ReLy

I'm the Kilfenora teaboy. Kilfenora Teaboy, The. Paul Durcan. PBCIP

I'm the kind of guy who finds himself past midnight. Bottom's Dream. Leon Stokesbury. IaFF

I'm the Man. Lindamichellebaron. BRtP

I'm the man when. Trash Talker, The. Howard Rambsy II. BRtP

"I'm the naked power-grab!" yodel the latecomers. Confessional. Tom Breidenbach. KGB

I'm the Slim Lady the real Slim Lady. Owed to Eminem. June Jordan. BRtP

I'm the son of a buccaneer. Super High. Evan X. Hyde. OWABP; PML

I'm the tomb of Baukis, a bride; passing the deeply lamented. Erinna. SaLy, *tr. by* Diane Rayor

I'm the Way I Am. Jacques Prévert. STV, *tr. by* John Frederick Nims

I'm thinking about you. What else can I say? Postcard. Margaret Atwood. NoAM

I'm thinking of your sex. César Vallejo. TCLAP, *tr. by* Sandy McKinney

I'm thist a little crippled boy, an' never goin' to grow. James Whitcomb Riley. VerBaPo *Fr.* Happy Little Cripple, The.

I'm Through with Love. Gustave Kahn. ReLy

I'm tired of Love: I'm still more tired of Rhyme. Fatigue. Joseph Hilaire Pierre Belloc. NBLV; UV

I'm tired of murdering children. Two Vietnam Poems: (1966). Bill Knott. PBCAP

I'm tired of these grim wastes of snow and ice. Imre Madách. IQMS *Fr.* Tragedy of Man.

I'm told beneath her ribs. Beneath Her Ribs. Hwang Insuk. EcSo, *tr. by* Peter H. Lee

I'm troubled by one thought—to die. I'm Troubled By One Thought. Sándor Petőfi. IQMS, *tr. by* Adam Makkai

I'm trying to fit my destiny into. Yuliya Kunina. CRWP, *tr. by* Max Nemtsov

I'm trying to pray; one of the voices of my mind says, "God, please help me do this." Vessel, The. C. K. Williams. TaR

I'm ugly but I don't know why. Sandra Tappenden. NewEx

I'm unhappy / So unhappy. One I Love (Belongs to Someone Else), The. Gustave Kahn. ReLy

I'm using my plain brain to imagine her fancy cortex. Fancy Cortex. Harryette Mullen. AWPTFC

I'm using the saw again. Carpenter's Song, A. Im Yŏngjo. CAMKP, *tr. by* Edward W. Poitras

I'm Very Happy Where I Am: A Peasant Woman's Song, 1864. Dion Boucicault. IrV

I'm waiting for sleep, but it won't come. Svidrigailov's Last Night. László Kálnoky. IQMS, *tr. by* Kenneth McRobbie and Zita McRobbie

I'm walking out on Rome. Antonio Porta. CLPP

I'm watching a space invasion movie in which a wife. Mr. Pillow. Barbara Hamby. SUP

I'm watching and waiting. Thanks a Lot, but No Thanks. Betty Comden and Adolph Green. ReLy

I'm watching old films. Adolescent Experiences. Sion Eirian. BBMWP, *tr. by* Robert Minhinnick

I'm watching the news and the workers. Restricting Gate, The. Alan Dent. RSaN

I'm wearin' [*or* wearing] awa', John [*or* Jean]. Land o' the Leal, The. Carolina Oliphant, Baroness Nairne. NePenScot; NOBRP; NPeEn; OBEV; OxBEV

I'm what is missing. Valerio Magrelli. ItPo, *tr. by* Gayle Ridinger

I'm what you might call a two-track Hamster. Hambone Two Tongue. David Chapman Berry. IaFF

I'm wiser now. So what? It's like the rack. Youth. David J. Rothman. GeoH

I'm wishing and fishing. I'm Craving for That Kind of Love. Noble Sissle. ReLy

I'm Writing a Poem. Emile Célestin-Mégie. OGAHCP, *tr. by* Boadiba and Jack Hirschman

I'm writing from the Botanic Garden at Tilden Park. Tilden Park. Alison Deming. UrbNat

I'm writing this for love. Lovepoem Writing Me. Madeline J. Tiger. MiVo

I'm writing this just after an encounter. Whatever You Say Say Nothing. Seamus Heaney. OBWP

I'm your momma, and I could always tell when. Eyes in the Back of Her Head. Harryette Mullen. OxAAAP

Image. Thomas Ernest Hulme. NPeEn

Image, The. Robert Hass. BLT; CAP-8

Image, The. Richard Hughes. OBMV

Image Cast by a Body Intercepting Light. Matthea Harvey. IAoNAP

Image comes, An. Laser. A. R. Ammons. NAMCP V.2; NoAM

Image dance of change, An. Conclusion. Siegfried Sassoon. MoBrPo

Image from Beckett, An. Derek Mahon. ModIr; NPeEn

Image in Lava, The. Felicia Dorothea Hemans. CABP; NOBRP

Image o' God, The. Joe Corrie. ChIV-1; RSaN

Image of Lethe, An. Coming of War, The; Actaeon. Ezra Pound. PoA 2002

Image of the Engine. George Oppen. APT-2

Image of the Engineer's model, An. Birdland. Allen Fisher. Oth

Image of the Fish. Mónica Nepote. SPV, *tr. by* Jen Hofer

Image of the frozen lake, The. Luigi Fontanella. NeIt

Image of thee is written in my soul, The. Sonnet 5. Baldomero Garcilaso de la Vega. BLPSL, *tr. by* Rene de Costa, Rigas Kappatos and Eleni Paidoussi

Image / of truth is fire: it mounts, The. Day Without Night. Louise Glück. TaR

Image, The / (the rim) / and going 'round. Poem for the Sefirot as a Wheel of Light, A. Naftali Bacharach. PFTM-1

Image Was of Me Flowing through You, The. David Steinberg. PasH

Image-Maker, The. Oliver St. John Gogarty. OBEV; OBMV

Imagen del Pez. Mónica Nepote. SPV, *tr. by* Jen Hofer

Image-Nation. Robin Blaser.
  Image-Nation 21 (territory). NLPA
  Image-Nation 22 (in memoriam). NLPA; PFTM-2
  Image-Nation 23 (imago-mundi). NLPA
  Image-Nation 24 ('oh pshaw'). NLPA

Imagerie d'Epinal. Aleksander Wat. AF

Imageries of dreams reveal a gracious age. Age of a Dream, The. Lionel Pigot Johnson. OBMV

Images. Richard Aldington. MoBrPo

Images. Valery Larbaud. BLT, *tr. by* William Jay Smith

Images. Naomi Long Madgett. LTA

Images. Miklós Radnóti. IQMS, *tr. by* Peter Zollman

Images distilled from the dream. Postwar. Bei Dao. WoBe, *tr. by* Iona Man-Cheong and Eliot Weinberger

Images from the Arcadian Dream Garden. Ian Hamilton Finlay.
  "Ruined stone temple by the side of a lake, A." PFTM-2

Images of Angels. Patricia K. Page. NoAM

Images of China. Paul Engle.
  Chinese Courtesy. PoA 2002
  Torture. PoA 2002

Images of John (1967–92). Danton R. Remoto. ReBoTo

Images of San Luis. Luis Lopez. GeoH

Images of the San Francisco Disaster. Larry Kramer. GeoHom

Images: "Scene 1. Front angle, dark sky, or the middle of the universe." Kim Chŏngnan. EcSo, *tr. by* Peter H. Lee

Images That Hurt, The. Anne Ridler. MoWP

Imaginary Career. Rainer Maria Rilke. BBASP, *tr. by* Stephen Mitchell

Imaginary Crimes in a Real Garden. Russell Atkins. EGAG

Imaginary Elegies. Jack Spicer.
  "God must have a big eye to see everything." PmAP
  "God's other eye is good and acid. So bright." PmAP
  "Poetry, almost blind like a camera." PmAP

Imaginary hats, real plastic. Charm for What Looks Like. Kathy Fagan. RWB

Imaginary Iceberg, The. Elizabeth Bishop. MoAmPo

Imaginary man, go. Here is your passport. Instructions for Crossing the Border. Dan Pagis. PoSu, *tr. by* Stephen Mitchell

Imagination. Johnny Burke. ReLy

Imagination. Margaret Lucas Cavendish, Duchess of Newcastle. BASC; NOSC

Imagination. John Davidson. MoBrPo *Fr.* New Year's Eve.

Imagination all walled up. Crime and Punishment. János Pilinszky. IQMS, *tr. by* Adam Makkai

Imagination and Taste, How Impaired and Restored. William Wordsworth. NAEL-6v2; NAEL-7v2 *Fr.* Prelude, The; Growth of a Poet's Mind [1850 version].

Imagination Dead Imagine. Samuel Beckett. PFTM-2

Imagination in flight: an improvisational duet. Harriet Jacobs. SpirFl

Imagination of Flowers, The. Lee Upton. AmAlph

Imagination that we spurned and crave, The. (LL) To the One of Fictive Music. Wallace Stevens. APT-1; MoAmPo; NoP-4; TCAPo

Imaginative Life, The. Geoffrey Hill. NoAM

Imagine. Andrée Chedid. HAWP, *tr. by* Mirène Ghossein and Samuel Hazo

Imagine a city where nothing's. Rusted Legacy. Adrienne Rich. PoDa

Imagine a Forest. William Sydney Graham. HarvBoo

Imagine a girl from Poland. Polish Girl Standing on a Chair, A. J. B. Charles. TuT, *tr. by* Gregory O'Donoghue

Imagine a long brown poem. Sunset Along U.S. Highway 90 Between Langtry and Sanderson. David C. Yates. TiP2

Imagine a poem that starts with a couple. Reading in Place. Mark Strand. OxBoAm

Imagine a Revolution. Yasser Musa. OWABP

Imagine a surface. Test. Kay Ryan. PoA 2002

Imagine a town where no one walks the streets. Hopper's "Nighthawks" (1942). Ira Sadoff. PoSol

Imagine a woman who honors the face of the Goddess in her own changing face. Patricia Lynn Reilly. HW *Fr.* Imagine a Woman.

"Imagine being the first to say: *surveillance*." Inventors. Michael C. Blumenthal. NoAM

Imagine corn new-discovered, tassels. Goddess Corn Finds Her Dress in Disarray,The. Terese Svoboda. ExTi

Imagine dinin car. Negotiation. Leroy McLucas. EGAG

Imagine father that you had a brother were. Landscape with Next of Kin. Olga Broumas. WiU

Imagine for yourself what was in my heart. Piazza San Marco. Jean-Pierre Rosnay. PML, *tr. by* J. Kates

Imagine hailing a taxi. Hidden Meaning. Susan Musgrave. NIL-7

Imagine how much I hope, imagine. Famous Poems of the Past Explained. Bin Ramke. PoDa; RoV

Imagine it, a Sophocles complete. Fire at Alexandria, The. Theodore Weiss. NoAM; PoA 2002; SAmP

Imagine living in a strange, dark city for twenty years. Foreign. Carol Ann Duffy. HarvBoo

Imagine me elsewhere and kneeling. Post-Communion Striptease. Jill Alexander Essbaum. NAPBL

Imagine my offense to see "witch," "hag." Kindness of Abishag, The. Davi Walders. VisFro

Imagine now, an affection the same size. Disappointments of Childhood, The. Michael C. Blumenthal. PoA 2002

Imagine or remember how the road at last led us. Nocturne Militaire. Thomas McGrath. AF

Imagine spring's thaw, your brother said. Heroin. Bob Hicok. AmPoNex; BAP-97

Imagine that any mind ever *thought* a red geranium! Red Geranium and Godly Mignonette. D. H. Lawrence. NoAM

Imagine that July morning: Cape Henry and Virginia. Tempest, The. William Jay Smith. MoAmPo

Imagine that motion, the turning and pressing. Elinor Frost's Marble-Topped Kneading Table. Pattiann Rogers. VisFro

Imagine the Angels of Bread. Martín Espada. PrTe; TouFir

Imagine the bridge launched, its one foot. Bridges. Leslie Norris. TCAWP

Imagine / The monk took off. Masaoka Shiki. ZenPo, *tr. by* Takashi Ikemoto and Lucien Stryk

Imagine the ocean. Imagine. Andrée Chedid. HAWP, *tr. by* Mirène Ghossein and Samuel Hazo

Imagine the sound of words. Between Language and Desire. Silvia Curbelo. TouFir

Imagine them as they were first conceived. Images of Angels. Patricia K. Page. NoAM

Imagine this: a mighty giant asleep. Dmitry Aleksandrovich Prigov. ItGoST, *tr. by* Robert Reid

Imagine this man as a lonely boy. Men From the Boys. Kate Clanchy. EdScPo

Imagine this scene in a desolate place. Bardo of Perception. Janet Rodney. WANABP

Imagine waking. Agoraphobia. Linda Pastan. ExTi

Imagine we worshipped water. Praise the Daughter. Melanie Hope. BtF

Imagine you are having a dream. Workingman's Wife: *Who She Is, Who She Is Not, What She Buys—And Why.* Chuck Wachtel. PrTe

Imagine. You come easily to me. Genesis. Ali Smith. PoBW

Imagining Point Dume. Diane Wakoski. GeoHom

Imagining / the grassy ground not shown. Tanka. Shaku Chōkū. CAoMJL1, *tr. by* Makoto Ueda

Imagining Their Own Hymns. Brigit Pegeen Kelly. IllVoic

Imagist at Coney Island. Maura Eichner. UpMys

Imago. Amy Clampitt. VCAP

Imam stands above your grave to pray with open hands, The. Ghazal for Open Hands. Martín Espada. PrTe

Imani in Sunburst Summer: A Chant. Askia Muhammad Touré. SpirFl

Imani's Song. Alison Morris. BtF

Imbolc. Jeanne Shannon. ICANM

I'me made in sport by Nature, when. Thomas Heyrick. *See* I'm made in sport by Nature, when.

Imelda. Felicia Dorothea Hemans. RWP

I—merely a moon-mimer. Pierrot Says. Jules Laforgue. SonAtl, *tr. by* Gregory Beaven and Kurt Ganzl

Imitating an Ode by Sapho. Gertrudis Gomez de Avellaneda. BLPSL, *tr. by* Rene de Costa, Rigas Kappatos and Eleni Paidoussi

Imitating the Old Poems. Pao Chao. CCL1, *tr. by* Burton Watson

Imitation. Joseph Hilaire Pierre Belloc. OBCoV

Imitation. Tim Griffin. FreRad

Imitation of Boileau. Yelena Shwarts. TCRusP, *tr. by* Anna Barker and Daniel Weissbort

Imitation of Chaucer. Alexander Pope. OBCoV

Imitation of Life. Afaa Michael Weaver. UnSA

Imitation of Pope A Compliment to the Ladies. William Blake. OBCoV

Imitation of the Arabic. Alexander Sergeyevich Pushkin. CAGL, *tr. by* Michael Green

Immaculate Conception. Louise Erdrich. BBASP

Immaculate Conception, The. Paul Eluard and Andre Breton. 32 Positions of Love, The. PFTM-1

Immaculate Lives. Cathy Song. SweBea

Immaculate Perception, The. Christopher Dewdney. OpeFie

Immaculate white bed. (LL) Nantucket. William Carlos Williams. HarvBoo; OxBoAm; TRP; WeW-3

Immanent. Walter De la Mare. PoA 2002

Immanuel Kant. Miroslav Holub. VCWP

Immaterial Nocturnes: Hudson and Worth. Tony Towle. PA9/11

Immeasurable haze. To the Holy Spirit. Yvor Winters. MoAmPo

Immeasurable Pain. Li Yu [*or* Li Hou-Chu]. CCL1, *tr. by* Arthur Waley

Immediate Content Recognition. Diane Ward. PmAP

Immemorial, / And after us. 29 Poems. Louis Zukofsky.

Immense acreage of solitude, An. Utopia. Richard Greene. Coast

Immense architecture / building in air. Journal of the Laguna de San Ignacio. Nathaniel Tarn. APSN

Immense, august, like some Titanic bloom. Chartres. Edith Wharton. APN-2

Immense coldness from the Longobards, An. Longobards, The. Zbigniew Herbert. PoSu, *tr. by* Czeslaw Milosz

Immense hope, and forbearance, The. Spring Day. John Ashbery. ColAP

Immense Hour. Juan Ramón Jiménez. SpanPo, *tr. by* Edward F. Gahan

Immense plain, The. Ruined City, The. Pao Chao. WoPoe, *tr. by* Michael Bullock and C. J. Chen

Immensity. Morning. Giuseppe Ungaretti. PFTM-1

Immensity cloistered [*or* Immensitie cloysterd] in thy dear[e] womb[e]. John Donne. ChrPo *Fr.* Holy Sonnets.

IMMERITO. (LL) Edmund Spenser. NAEL-6v1; NAEL-7v1 *Fr.* Shepherd's Calender, The.

Immigrant. Fleur Adcock. OPOU

Immigrant. Arthur Nortje. BrAP; TSAP

Immigrant, The. Donald Davidson. FuPo

Immigrant Picnic. Gregory Djanikian. PoA 2002; PoDa

Immigrants. Debra Kang Dean. NAPBL

Immigrants. Robert Frost. AmFaPo

Immigrants. Lotte Kramer. RSaN

Immigrants. Pat Mora. UnSA

Immigrants. Aurora Levins Morales. PueRic

3. The Immigrants. Charles Reznikoff. NAAPv.2 *Fr.* Testimony.

Immigrants in Our Own Land. Jimmy Santiago Baca. AF; UnSA

Immobile, but fearless. Hares, The. Susan Miles. LW

Immolated. Herman Melville. NCAP

Immoralist, The. Robin Robertson. NeBrP

Immorality, An. Ezra Pound. AmWit; MoAmPo; TCAPo *Fr.* Ripostes of Ezra Pound.

Immortal. Mark Van Doren. MoAmPo

Immortal, An. Les A. Murray. UpMys

Immortal, The. Charles Simic. PoA 2002

Immortal. And will wash itself of all deaths. (LL) River. Ted Hughes. NAEL-6v2; NoP-4

Immortal as our Soul. (LL) To My Excellent Lucasia, On Our Friendship. Katherine Philips. BASC; LW; NALW; NoP-4; NoP-5; NOSC; NPeEn; OxBEV; PBRV; PEW; PoBW

Immortal Autumn. Archibald MacLeish. MoAmPo

Immortal babe, who this dear day. For Christmas Day. Joseph Hall. SacPr

Immortal Bard! thou fav'rite of the Nine! Womans Labour, an epistle, The. Mary Collier. PEW

Immortal, invisible, God only wise. Walter Chalmers Smith. SacPr

Immortal Part, The. A. E. Housman. MoBrPo; SoSe-8 *Fr.* Shropshire Lad, A.

Immortal Picture, The. Richard Eberhart. BodElec

Immortal Pilots, The. Chase Twichell. PfSP

Immortal substance scintillating bright. Grave Wedding of Lu Chong. Gan Bao. CCL1, *tr. by* Kenneth DeWoskin

Immortality. Samuel Marshak. RusPo, *tr. by* Robert Arthur Douglas Ford

Immortality. Lizelia Augusta Jenkins Moorer. CBWP-3

Immortality. George Russell. OBMV

Immortality Ode, The. William Wordsworth. *See* Ode: Intimations of Immortality from Recollections of Early Childhood.

Immortals' Paduk Game. Pak Chaesam. CAMKP, *tr. by* David R. McCann and Jiwon Shin

Imogene. Eloise Bibb. CBWP-4

Impact of a dollar upon the heart, The. Stephen Crane. OxBoAm

Impartial Law enrolled a name, The. My Name and I. Robert Graves. NoAM

Impassion'd strains my trembling lips rehearse. Anne Batten Cristall. RWP *Fr.* Enthusiast, The. Songs of Arla.

Impatient Heart, The. Bruce Andrews. FTOS

Impatient Man Kills with His Piano-playing, The. John Wilkinson. VaPo

Impatient with spring's incendiary budding. Lighthouse, The. Jocelyn Emerson. IAoNAP

Impediment. Stephen Dunn. PoSol

Impenitent, we meet again. To Levine on the Day of Atonement. Robert Mezey. TaR

Imperative. Scott Cairns. UpMys

Imperceptively the world became haunted by her white dress. White Dress, The. Marya Alexandrovna Zaturenska. MoAmPo

Impercipient, The. Thomas Hardy. NAEL-6v2; NAEL-7v2

Imperfect Enjoyment, The. John Wilmot, 2d Earl of Rochester. BASC; NAEL-7v1; NoP-5

Imperfect Enjoyment, The. William Walsh and Sir George Etherege. NOSC

Imperfect Is Our Paradise, The. Joy Katz. NeAmPo

Imperfect Paradise, The. Linda Pastan. InvLi; SoSe-8 *Fr.* Imperfect Paradise, The.

Imperfect Poetry and Meaningless Poetry. Iijima Koichi. TAPaP, *tr. by* Naoshi Koriyama and Edward Lueders

Imperfect Sonnet, The. Philip Whalen. WANABP

Imperfection. Elizabeth Carlson. TWF

Imperial. Don Paterson. NeBrP

Imperial Adam, naked in the dew. Imperial Adam. Alec Derwent Hope. BMAP; BrAP; ChIV-1; HarvBoo; NIP-4; NoAM; NoP-4; NoP-5

Imperial Airways. Louis Untermeyer. OtW

Imperial Eloquence. Samuel Daniel. *See* Poetry in England.

Imperial host before proud Gloucester lay, The. Powers of Darkness. Abraham Cowley. NOSC

Imperial Hotel. Nakano Shigeharu. CAoMJL1, *tr. by* Miriam Silverberg

Imperial Measure. Vona Groarke. BeAl; MoWP; NIrP

Imperialism—The Dancing Do Not Die. Thomas Stanley. BtF

Imperious Fool! think not because you're fair. To a Proud Beauty. "Ephelia." PEW

Imperium Pelagi, or, The Merchant. Edward Young.

   Final Paean. STuOW

   Sting Her Up! STuOW

   To a Solemn Musick. STuOW

Impermanence. Ko Ŭn. CAMKP, *tr. by* Anthony, Brother of Taizé

Impersonal the aim. Night of Battle. Yvor Winters. PoA 2002; PWW2

Impertinence at first is born. John Gay. *Fr.* Fables: First Series.

Imperturbable wader, The. Rondeau Tempo. Rossana Ombres. CItWP, *tr. by* Cinzia Sartini Blum and Lara Trubowitz

Impetuous purple success, The. Painter's Son, The. Frank O'Hara. BodElec

Impetus. Mary Leader. NAPBL

Implications of One Plus One. Marge Piercy. PasH

Implicit Faith. Aubrey Thomas De Vere. SacPr

Implies that some therefore. All Do Not All Things Well. Thom Gunn. NoP-5

Imploration for Clear Weather. *Unknown.* APN-2, *tr. by* W. J. Hoffman

Imploring Mecca / to achieve. Be-Bop Boys. Langston Hughes. APSN; APT-2

Implosions. Adrienne Rich. PoA 2002

Imponderable the dinosaur. Hart Crane. MoAmPo *Fr.* Bridge, The.

Importune me no more! (LL) When I Was Fair and Young. Queen of England Elizabeth I. NIP-4; NoSic

   (Go! go! go! seek some other where, importune me no more.) (LL) LW; NoP-5

Impose the letters *CD* on a staff. *Unknown.* PriapPo *Fr.* Priapus Poems, The.

Impossible, The. Jane Miller. BodElec

Impossible, The. Bruce Weigl. BodElec

Impossible blossom, to sweet impossible blossom. (LL) From Blossoms. Li-Young Lee. BeAl; GoPo; IPoFL; RoV; StAl; TRP

Impossible Indispensability of the Ars Poetica, The. Hayden Carruth. TAPaP

Impossible it is fully to sense—the artist's. One-day Snow. T. Arfon Williams. BBMWP, *tr. by* Emyr Lewis

Impossible Marriage, The. Donald Hall. OxBoAm

Impossible Pictures, The. Tom Paulin. CABP

Impossible Poem, The. George Oppen. ASA *Fr.* Some San Francisco Poems.

Impossible Tasks. *Vietnamese Oral Tradition.* CaDao, *tr. by* John Balaban

Impossible, the way one black walnut, fallen. Man Who Knew the Words to "Louie, Louie", The. David Keller. SwNoth

Impossible to be silent, impossible to speak. Travel Notes. John Riley. Oth

Impossible to call a lamb a lambkin. Gone Are the Days. Norman Alexander MacCaig. CABP

Impossible to Tell. Robert Pinsky. InoFa

Impossible truth: I asked God, The. Above the Timberline. Alan Michael Parker. AmPoNex

Impresión de Destierro. Luis Cernuda. RaW

Impression de Nuit; London. Lord Alfred Bruce Douglas. OBEV

Impression du Matin. Oscar Wilde. MoBrPo; NAEL-6v2; NAEL-7v2; NoAM

Impression of Exile. Luis Cernuda. RaW, *tr. by* Hardie St. Martin

Impressionist. Paul Foreman. TiP2

Imprimis—My departed Shade I trust. Mira's Will. Mary Leapor. CABP; NoP-4; NPeEn; OxBEV; PEW

Imprimis, there's a table blotted. Inventory of the Furniture of a Collegian's Chamber, An. John Winstanley. OBSV

Imprint of Microscopic Life Found in Arctic Stones. Patricia Goedicke. GifTon

Imprisoned. Celia Laighton Thaxter. TCAPo

Imprisoned God, The. Murad Mikha'il. IrPoTo, *tr. by* Christina Coyle and Sadok Masliyah

Imprisoned Recusant Writes to His Wife, An. Francis Tregian. NoSic

Imprisoned Soul, The. Walt Whitman. *See* Last Invocation, The.

Imprisoned Souls. János Arany. IQMS, *tr. by* Peter Zollman

Imprisoned souls of soldiers and of me, The. (LL) Homecoming: "Lost in the vastness of the void Pacific." Karl Shapiro. APT-2; PWW2

Impromptu. Mary Elizabeth Coleridge. VWP

Impromptu. Frances Anne Kemble. APN-1

Impromptu. Tu Fu [*or* Du Fu]. CrYelRi, *tr. by* Sam Hamill

Impromptu. Samuel Wilberforce. NBLV; OWoS

Impromptu on a Hangover. P'i Jih-hsiu. ColAnChi, *tr. by* Burton Watson

Impromptu on Charles II. John Wilmot, 2d Earl of Rochester. BASC; NBLV; OBSV; OxAEP-1

Impromptu: To Lady Winchelsea Occasioned by Four Satirical Verses on Women Wits, in *The Rape of the Lock.* Alexander Pope. NAEL-7v1; NoP-4; NoP-5; WaAnP

Improper Disposal. John Bradley. LiTh

Improvement, The. John Ashbery. AmFaPo

Improvisation. Alfred Kreymborg. APT-1

Improvisation for Jerald Bullis, An. A. R. Ammons. BodElec

Improvisation for Piano [*after Mood Indigo*]. Afaa Michael Weaver. UnSA

Improvisation for the Stately Dwelling, An. A. R. Ammons. BodElec

Improvisations on a Sentence by Poe. Jack Spicer. APSN; CalPo; OxBoAm

Improvisatrice, The. Letitia Elizabeth Landon.

   Indian Bride, The. NPBRoP

   Introduction. RWP

   Lorenzo. RWP

   Sappho's Song. NPBRoP; RWP; VWP

Improvised Song of Joy. Takomaq. WoPoe, *tr. by* Knud Rasmussen

Impulse among us is to throw eyes, The. Dark Underfoot. Thom Ward. AmPoNex

Impulse, The. Robert Frost. RaBo; TCAPo *Fr.* Hill Wife, The.

Impulse to Call & Spring Upon, The. Lee Ann Brown. VaPo

In. Andrew Hudgins. CAP-8

In 1845 Dr. James Marion Sims had seen it many times. Crystals. Thylias Moss. NAMCP V.2

In 1900. Borinkins in Hawaii. Víctor Hernández Cruz. PueRic

In 1940. Anna Andreyevna Akhmatova. FaBoWar; PoetW *Fr.* In 1940.

In 1940. Anna Andreyevna Akhmatova.

   In 1940. FaBoWar; PoetW, *tr. by* Max Hayward

In 1944. Statistic. Michelle Parkerson. ISC

In 1956 I was the shepherd boy. Conversion of Saint Paul, The. Michael Waters. Vesp

In 1965 my parents broke two laws of Mississippi. Miscegenation. Natasha Trethewey. LegDan

In 1966, / when I started down the trail. Porter on the Trail, A. Larry Rottman. ViWalt

In 1969. Katharyn Howd Machan. SwNoth

In 1969 I was angry. Song Embodying What I've learned in Thirty-Five Years. Dick Lourie. PrTe

In 1978 I write something about how. Get It Again. Mark Halliday. PtR

In 1985 / the Lone Ranger. Confessions from the Last Cloud. Jose Angel Figueroa. PueRic

In a back room. Resonance. Christopher Gilbert. ESEAA

In a bare cup. (LL) Henry David Thoreau. *See* While I droop here.

In a Beautiful Glass. Dewi Stephen Jones. BBMWP, *tr. by* Joseph P. Clancy

In a beautiful time. Sugar Loaf Hill. Nanao Sakaki. WhBo

In a Bed-Sitter. Hal Porter. NOBAu

In a / big. Self-Portrait in the Supermarket. Rolf Dieter Brinkmann. GTCP, tr. by Reinhold Grimm

In a "bijou" abode. Noël Coward. See I'll sing you a song.

In a bitter wind. Buson. SoOfWa, tr. by Sam Hamill

In a Blind Garden. David Shapiro. ChIV-1

In a blue series towards his sleepy eyes. John Berryman. CAP-8 Fr. Dream Songs.

In a Boat Shed. Robert Creeley. InvLad

In a boat without oars we rowed for land. Song of Lies, A. Vincent Woods. BeAl; NIrP

In a Book-store. Francis Saltus Saltus.
"Sad, on Broadway next afternoon." VerBaPo

In a brief symphony of candied light. (LL) Winnings. Garrett Kaoru Hongo. FTtHH; GeoHom; OpBo

In a broad and many-peopled land. Sleepless Night, A. Pak Inhwan. CAMKP, tr. by Scott Swaner

In a Burger King kills. Reading Whitman's Democratic Vistas. Terry Savoie. ViWalt

In a Bye-Canal. Herman Melville. APN-2; NCAP

In a cabin, in a canyon. My Darling Clementine. Percy Montrose. ASA

In a Calendar of Saints. Neil Curry. NLP

In a Castilian Graveyard. Miguel de Unamuno. RaW, tr. by Donald Hall

In a cavern, in a canyon. Clementine. Unknown. NAAPv.1

In a certain sense, they are not serious. Robert Pinsky. NoAM Fr. Essay on Psychiatrists.

In a cerulean ruckus. Yellow Dog Café. Yusef Komunyakaa. LPSFW

In a chain reaction. Atomic Pantoum. Peter Meinke. WeW-3

In a Chain-Store Cafeteria. Paul Grano. NOBAu

In a chariot of light from the regions of day. Liberty Tree. Thomas Paine. AmWaPo

In a Charleston, South Carolina gift store. 1994 Inventory. Toi Derricotte. SpirFl

In a childhood of hats. Hat Lady, The. Linda Pastan. SoSe-8

In a Church of Padua. Herman Melville. APN-2

In a Churchyard. Richard Wilbur. HeIP-4; UpMys

In a City. Zbigniew Herbert. PoDa, tr. by Bogdana Carpenter and John Carpenter

In a city of darkness caught up in time. Days. Jean Tardieu. YaTCFP, tr. by David Kelley

In a city, Trieste or Udine. Day of My Death, The. Pier Paolo Pasolini. VCWP, tr. by Max Hayward

In a Classroom. Adrienne Rich. LoL

In a clearing. Traveling Valise. Marjorie Agosin. MirDau, tr. by Laura Nakazawa

In a cleft that's christened Alt. Man and the Echo. William Butler Yeats. NAMCP V.1

In a closed room. Music For Two Players 2. Mieko Shiomi. WhBo

In a cloud bones of steel. Bridge, The. Charles Reznikoff. OxBoAm

In a coign of the cliff between lowland and highland. Forsaken Garden, A. Algernon Charles Swinburne. NoP-4; NoP-5; NPeEn; OBGa; OxAEP-2

In a collection of sun. Lock City. David Henderson. EGAG

In a comma. Dolores Dorantes. SPV, tr. by Jen Hofer

In a common pit, without a headstone. Few Autobiographical Facts, A. Anna Barkova. ARWW, tr. by Catriona Kelly

In a Convent Garden. Alan Brownjohn. OBGa

In a Copy of More's (or Shaw's or Wells's or Plato's or Anybody's) Utopia. Max Beerbohm. OBCoV

In a Copy of Omar Khayyám. James Russell Lowell. NCAP

In a corn field. Nature. No Hyangnim. EcSo, tr. by Aimee N. Kwon

In a corner of the barn where juice oozes out of rotten fruit. Clinic in a Dangerous Season 8, A. Yi Yŏnju. EcSo, tr. by Yung-Hee Kim

In a Corner of the Sky. Federico García Lorca. PFTM-1 Fr. Night (Suite for Piano and Poet's Voice).

In a cottage by the mountain. Aphra Behn. EroLit

In a Country Church. Ronald Stuart Thomas. HarvBoo

In a curtain of powdered snow launched like a waterfall. (LL) Octopus, An. Marianne Moore. NAMCP V.1; OxBoAm

In a dark and trying hour. Cornelius Whur. VerBaPo Fr. Unfortunate Gentleman, The.

In a dark bar corner we talk for about an hour. Hangover. Jeffery Conway. WiU

In a dark, dark wood, there was a dark, dark house. Dark House, The. Unknown. NTCP

In a dark night, when the light. Dark Night. San Juan de la Cruz. WoPoe, tr. by Frank Bidart

In a dark room a candle is lit. Set Theory. Alberto Blanco. RMCMP, tr. by Gustavo V. Segade

In a dark time, the eye begins to see. In a Dark Time. Theodore Roethke. APT-2; CAP-8; HeIP-4; ItP; MoAmPo; NAAL-5; NAMCP V.1; NoAM; NoP-4; NoP-5; OxBoAm; PLBUT; RaBo; TFi; VCAP

In a darkening house we sat. Sunday the Power Went Off, The. Duncan Bush. TCAWP

In a day or two the chairs will fall to pieces. Little House, Big House. Medbh McGuckian. PNI

In a decrepit part of town. My Children Visit the Zendo. Tom Greening. WhBo

In a deep sleep. One the Morening the King Was Taken Ill My Dreame of Him. Frances Feilding. EMWP

In a diary found beside a skeleton. Oink as Taunt. Roger Fanning. NAPBL

In a dim corner of my room for longer than my fancy thinks. Oscar Wilde. TriCat Fr. Sphinx, The.

In a dim room above the freightyards, next to an old brass bed, an angel is taking off his wings. Poem Against the Horizon, The. David Young. MotU

In a dingy kitchen. Lamentations. Alter Brody. APT-2

In a disingenuous letter. Oranges Returned, The. Gilbert Sorrentino. FTOS

In a dismal air; a light of breaking summer. Lament. George Sutherland Fraser. PoWW

In a dream. Issa. EH, tr. by Robert Hass

In a dream he fled the house. Coleridge. Medbh McGuckian. MoWP

In a dream I bought a. Dream May 18, 1958. Peter Orlovsky. BB

In a dream I cried out. Forsaken. Kim Sowŏl. CAMKP, tr. by David R. McCann

In a dream I never exactly dreamed. Another Life. Frank Bidart. OxBoAm; VCAP

In a dream I returned to the river of bees. River of Bees, The. W. S. Merwin. HeIP-4; VCAP

In a dream I see the moon. 137. Shih Shu. CSKM, tr. by James H. Sanford

In a dream I wasn't having yet. Night Is out of Sight, The. Pedro Juan Pietri. PueRic

In a dreamlike fall, the long. Apis Mellifica. Roger McDonald. NOBAu

In [a] drear-nighted December. In [a] Drear-nighted December. John Keats. PoPoPo

In a drugstore north of Ft. Lauderdale. Story I Like to Tell, The. Robin Becker. PBCAP

In a Dublin Museum. Sheila Wingfield. MoWP

In a Duplex Near the San Andreas Fault. Dionisio D. Martinez. NoP-4; NoP-5

In a fairytale rainforest. Discovered the freedom of the last resort. (LL) Hazel Goodwin Morrissey Brown. Sinéad Morrissey. MFPA; NIrP

In a far off hamlet near the sea. Uranne. Mary Weston Fordham. CBWP-2

In a few days now when two memories meet. James Vincent Cunningham. APT-2; OxBoAm

In a field / I am the absence. Keeping Things Whole. Mark Strand. CAP-8; HeIP-4; ItP; NAMCP V.2; OxBoAm; PoPoPo; VCAP

In a flurry of zeal. Régime. Karel Soudijn. TuT, tr. by Ruth Hooley

In a forest of frost, in a dawn of cornflowers. (LL) Poppies in October. Sylvia Plath. NAMCP V.2; NoAM; OxBoAm; StAl

In a form we have no words for, and you live on it. (LL) Simple Truth, The. Philip Levine. BeAl; CAP-8; NoP-4; NoP-5

In a fountain at the harbor, children. Charleston. Afaa Michael Weaver. RWB

In a Garden in the Grounds of Coleorton, Leicestershire. William Wordsworth. OBGa

In a garden shed two tea-chests. Hyperion's Bones. Tracey Herd. NeBl

In a garden that I know. Ownership. Ina Coolbrith. SWaP

In a Glazed-Over World. Carl Mayfield. ICANM

In a Gondola. Robert Browning.
Song: "Moth's kiss, first, The!" OBEV

In a good mood. Ness. Lawson Fusao Inada. WhBo

In a great. . .big. . .night. (LL) Sylvester's Dying Bed. Langston Hughes. NAMCP V.1; NoAM; SAmP

In a grove most rich of shade. Sir Philip Sidney. NoSic; PBRV Fr. Astrophil and Stella.

In a Hand Not My Own. Bill Berkson. NYP2

In a heart that bears the image. Fitnet Khanim. OLP, tr. by Walter Andrews, Najaat Black and Mehmet Kalpakli

In a heavy light like yellow onions. (LL) Yellow Light. Garrett Kaoru Hongo. GeoHom; OpBo; WaAnP

In a herber [or a harbour or an arbour] green [or grene], asleep [or aslepe] whereas [or where as or where] I lay. Robert Wever. OBEV Fr. Lusty Juventus.

In a high wind, on a rock in the back paddock. Laurie Duggan. BMAP Fr. Ash Range, The.

In a highly classified report smuggled. Wings. Maureen Seaton. FFC

In a hollow of the forest. Bomber, The. Brian Vrepont. NOBAu

In a thousandth of a second. Asymmetry of the Universe. Fabio Doplicher. NeIt, tr. by Stephen Sartarelli

In a Time of Pestilence. Thomas Nashe. See Adieu, Farewell, Earth's Bliss[e].

In a tissue-thin monotone of blue-grey buds. Spring Strains. William Carlos Williams. APT-1; TCAPo

In a Train. Robert Bly. InvLad

In a train station in winter. Film in a railway station, A. Fadil Azzawi. IrPoTo, tr. by Ralph Saverese and Saadi A. Simawe

In a tree standing. Saigyō. WoPoe, tr. by Donald Keene

In a U-Haul North of Damascus. David Bottoms. ReTh

In a vacant lot behind a body shop. Child in the City, A. Lucien Stryk. UrbNat

In a valley in Wisconsin there is a graveyard where the graves are flooded by a spring. Voluntary Servitude. Mark Wunderlich. LegDan

In a valley of leafless scrub oaks. On the Road Home. C. G. Hanzlicek. GeoHom

In a valley [or the vale or the vaile] of this restless [or restles] mind. Quia Amore Langueo. Unknown. OBEV, tr. by Helen Gardner

In a vase of gold. Irises. Michael Field. ViWPN

In a villa in a little old Italian town. Mona Lisa. Ray Evans and Jay Livingston. ReLy

In a Village by the River. Li Po. CrYelRi, tr. by Sam Hamill

In a Village by the River. Tu Fu [or Du Fu]. CrYelRi, tr. by Sam Hamill

In a voice the color of sleep. In the Color of Sleep. Rose Ausländer. GTCP, tr. by Irmgard Hunt

In a warm bar one fine morn. Drivel. Emyr Lewis. BBMWP, tr. by the author

In a way i would not. Way I, A. Jacques Roubaud. YaTCFP, tr. by the author

In a wee, twee cul-de-sac. Fruit of Knowledge, The. Robert Johnstone. PNI

In a wheat field. Conversation, A. Gisèle Prassinos. PFTM-1

In a wood box. Morning's Journey, The. Mahmoud al-Braikan. IrPoTo, tr. by Ralph Saverese and Saadi A. Simawe

In a wooden barrel. (LL) Salt. Yusef Komunyakaa. OPRER; UnSA

In a word of glitter and glow. I See Your Face Before Me. Howard Dietz. ReLy

In a world alive in imitation. Imitation. Tim Griffin. FreRad

In a world of souls, I set out to find them. Worldling. Elizabeth Spires. ExTi

In a world where kapok on a sidewalk looks like an "accident." Shirley Temple Surrounded by Lions. Kenward Elmslie. NYP2

In a year the nightingales were said to be so loud. Kingfisher, The. Amy Clampitt. OWoS

In / ability to love, The. Ghost Song. Jack Spicer. APSN

In Abyrdeyn he gert a consaill cry. Henry the Minstrel (Blind Harry). NePenScot Fr. Actis and Deidis of the Illustere and Vailyeand Campioun Schir William Wallace, Knicht of Ellerslie, The.

In Acknowledgment of the Praises of European Writers. Sor Juana Inés de la Cruz. SpanPo, tr. by Constance Urdang

In adolescence I knew travellers. Muriel Rukeyser. AmWaPo Fr. Poem out of Childhood.

In Æsop's tales an honest wretch we find. Fable, A. Matthew Prior. NoP-4; NoP-5

In aeternum I was once determed. Sir Thomas Wyatt. NoSic

In Africa. Roy Fuller. PoWW

In Africa, the saying is. No, Women Don't Cry. Opal Palmer Adisa. WaCA

In After Days. Austin Dobson. OBEV

In Age-Old Lakes. Iwan Goll. GTCP, tr. by Reinhold Grimm

In ages past [animals] lived and died. James Milligan. VerBaPo Fr. Science of Geology, The.

In agony saying: "The last night of his life." Double Dialogue: Homage to Robert Frost. Muriel Rukeyser. VisFro

In Agypt's land contaygious to the Nile. Pharao's Daughter. Michael Moran. ChIV-1

In air hard as sand. Mary Kinzie. FFC

In Aku Aku is there double. Oh, Noa, Noa! William Cole. NBLV

In al this world nis a murier lyf. Unknown. OHMEL

#2, In Alabaster. Mariiane Mays. PoPra Fr. (HERO)neck: Attempts at a Portrait.

In Alaska an Eskimo girl. Eskimo Girl, The. David Ray. LTA

In Alesia, our last town, our final stronghold. In Alesia. Andrew Hudgins. PoDa

In Alicante they bowl the barrels. Alicante Lullaby. Sylvia Plath. PtR

In all dying things. (LL) Saint Rose of Lima. Judith Ortiz Cofer. PueRic; TouFir

In all earnestness, I speak to all my sisters. Unknown. NAAPv.2

In all the country. Another Spring. Tu Fu [or Du Fu]. CrYelRi, tr. by Sam Hamill

In all the good Greek of Plato. Survey of Literature. John Crowe Ransom. AmWit; NBLV

In all the land no women found so fair. (LL) Beauty of Job's Daughters, The. Jay Macpherson. ChIV-1; IFF

In all the old paintings. Annunciation. Kay Smith. NIL-7; NIP-4

In all the space of space. Chauvinist. Norman Alexander MacCaig. NPeEn

In all their passionate anonymity. (LL) Old Bachelor Brother. Brad Leithauser. NoP-4; NoP-5; RA

In all these rotten shops, in all this broken furniture. Dancing, The. Gerald Stern. CAP-8; LoL; UnSA

In all things there are veritable atoms. Sikong Tu. CCL1 Fr. Twenty-Four Modes of Poetry.

In all those stories the hero. Heroes. Robert Creeley. NoP-4; NoP-5; OxBoAm

In Alsace. Distant Howling. Miroslav Holub. StAl, tr. by Ewald Osers

In Amagansett, for crying out loud, setting the arm of his French helpmeet. Last Time I Saw Chris, The. Paul Muldoon. BAP-04

In america. Bow to Allah. Brian G. Gilmore. ISC

In America, began / the lecturer, "everyone must have a." Student, The. Marianne Moore. OxBoAm

In America, or now this silence between songs. (LL) Cures. David Rivard. AllShUp; SwNoth

In America, television is a special god. Television as God. Tijan M. Sallah. NAfrP

In America, there is an answer for everything. Tomorrow, We'll Dance in America. James Harms. AmPoNex

In Ampezzo ("In days of summer let me go.") Trumbull Stickney. ColAP

In Ampezzo ("Only once more and not again—the larches.") Trumbull Stickney. APN-2

In amusements he was so cagey and in his caginess amusing. On the Death of My Tomcat Murr. Vladislav Felitsianovich Khodasevich. TCRusP, tr. by Mary Jane White

[In an Age of Fops and Toys]. Ralph Waldo Emerson. NAAPv.1 Fr. Voluntaries.

In an Airplane I'm Supposed To. Sarah Kirsch. PFTM-2, tr. by Wayne Kvam

In an ancient overgrown park. Duckweed. Leopold Staff. PoSu, tr. by Adam Czerniawski

In an apothecary's chest of drawers. Sharping Stone, The. Seamus Heaney. NAEL-7v2

In an Artist's Studio. Christina Georgina Rossetti. NAEL-6v2; NAEL-7v2; NALW; NoP-4; NoP-5; PEW; ViWPN; VWP

In an astonished O. (LL) Still Life: "I shall not soon forget." Thom Gunn. NAMCP V.2; PoCho

In an early childhood day. Too Many Rings Around Rosie. Irving Caesar. ReLy

In an eastern city where I won't return. In a City. Zbigniew Herbert. PoDa, tr. by Bogdana Carpenter and John Carpenter

In an effort to get people to look. Quiet World, The. Jeffrey McDaniel. SUP

In an elegy for a musician. Elegy for Bob Marley, An. William Matthews. SwNoth; WaAnP

In an Emergency. (LL) Faith is a fine invention. Emily Dickinson. APN-2; NAAL-3; NAAL-5; NAAPv.1; NCAP; NoP-4; NoP-5; OxBoAm; TCAPo

In an eternal night. (LL) Garden of Proserpine, The. Algernon Charles Swinburne. CABP; InoFa; NAEL-6v2; NAEL-7v2; NoP-4; NoP-5; OxBEV; TFi

In an envelope of skin. Envelope of Skin. Dorothy Molloy. NIrP

In an Iridescent Time. Ruth Stone. MoAmPo; NALW; OxWW

In an Irish Churchyard. Violet Fane. VWP

In an old book. Saying, The. Ernst Stadler. PoCho

In an orchard soft with rot. (LL) Never May the Fruit Be Plucked. Edna St. Vincent Millay. AFaM; APT-1

In an oxygen tent / the war in Spain has ended long ago / Aunt Rose. (LL) To Aunt Rose. Allen Ginsberg. CLPP; ColAP; NAMCP V.2; NoAM; NoP-4; NoP-5; OxBoAm; PmAP; TaR; WaAnP

In an unmarked pit, that were harvested by their own light. (LL) Cauliflowers. Paul Muldoon. ModIr; NAMCP V.2

In an upper room at midnight. Love Feast, The. W. H. Auden. OBCoV

In an Urban School. Toi Derricotte. PBCAP

In ancient Japan, to travel. Leaving the October Palace. Jane Hirshfield. CalPo

In Ancient Rome There Stood. Filomena Ibarra. NAAPv.1, tr. by Unknown

In and Out. Jane Kenyon. LoL Fr. Having It Out with Melancholy.

In and out, behind, across. Mending. Ingrid de Kok. TSAP

In and Out of Check Points. Ye Weilian [or Yeh Wei-lien or Wai-lim Yip]. OPRER

In Andrea's Garden. Susan Hampton. BMAP

In Anguish, the Heart Finally Prays. Andy Young. AnSo

In Annapolis Royal, we stepped on a soldier. Valley, After Blossoms, The. Jeanette Lynes. Coast

In another poem about the vandals, the vandals. Another Poem about the Vandals. Alan Michael Parker. NeAmPo

In Answer to a Question from P. W. Lew Welch. BB

In Answer to Amy's Question What's a Pickerel. Stanley Plumly. PfSP

In Answer to the Question: Have You Ever Considered Suicide. Kate Rushin. PfS

In Answer to Their Questions. Giovanna (Janet) Capone. UnSA

In answer to what was being insisted upon. (LL) Falling in Love at Sixty-Five. Mona Van Duyn. NoP-4; NoP-5

In Answer to Your Query. Naomi Lazard. NBLV

In antipoetry, it is poetry that is sought, not eloquence. Note on the Lessons of Antipoetry. Nicanor Parra. WoBe, *tr. by* Liz Werner

In Antwerp, Bruges, Ostend and Ghent. Ballade 2. Eustache Deschamps. WoPoe, *tr. by* David Curzon and Jeffrey Fiskin

In any case / we're setting the world on fire. In Any Case. Yosl Grinshpan. Prolet, *tr. by* Amelia Glaser

In any group there are the beautiful and. Noreen. Peter Meinke. IaFF

In April. Richard Kenney. WaAnP; YaYoPo

In April. Sylvia Townsend Warner. MoWP

In April, in New England, the earth ball yields. In April. Richard Kenney. WaAnP; YaYoPo

In April one seldom feels cheerful. Waste Land Limericks. Wendy Cope. HarvBoo; PoCho

In April the carnival came. Distance Between Zero and One, The. David Keplinger. AmPoNex

In April the lake water is clear. Late Spring. Meng Hao Jan. NDACCP, *tr. by* William Carlos Williams

In April when the flowers spring. Heinrich von Veldeke. GePo

In Arabic. Agha Shahid Ali. FaoP

In Arcadia. Lawrence Durrell. MoBrPo

In Arctic latitudes, almost another. In the Shadow of the Poisoned Wind. Jack Marshall. AtGh

In Arizona. Louis Zukofsky. TRP *Fr.* 29 Songs.

In Arizona coming across the border with dope in my tires. Itinerary. Doug Anderson. OPRER

In Arizona / (how many years in the mountains). Louis Zukofsky. TRP *Fr.* 29 Songs.

In Armorik, that called is Britaine [*or* Britayne]. Geoffrey Chaucer. NAEL-6v1 *Fr.* Canterbury Tales, The.

In Atlanta, Gee A. (LL) Slim in Atlanta. Sterling Allen Brown. APT-2; NAMCP V.1; NoP-4; NoP-5

In Auckland it was the twelve days' garland. James Keir Baxter. HarvBoo *Fr.* Jerusalem Sonnets.

In August. Hamlin Garland. APN-2

In August he boarded the bus / for southern Mexico and saw. Mexican World Mural / 5 x 25. Juan Felipe Herrera. TouFir

In Austin Reigns a Bald-Headed Queen. Pat LittleDog. TiP2

In autumn. Absentia Animi. Gunnar Ekelof. PFTM-1

In Autumn. Ma Chih-yüan. CryYelRi, *tr. by* Sam Hamill

"In autumn moonlight, when the white air wan." Robert Bridges. GSo

In autumn, when the son *in Virgine*. Bouge of Court, The. John Skelton.

In back of our town. Gasco. Günter Grass. CLPP, *tr. by* Jerome Rothenberg

In back of the real. Allen Ginsberg. HeIP-4; PtR

In balance with this life, this death. (LL) Irish Airman Foresees His Death, An. William Butler Yeats. BrAP; ChAP; FaBoWar; HarvBoo; HeIP-4; IrV; MoBrPo; NAMCP V.1; NoAM; NoP-4; NoP-5; OBMV; OBWP; PoAgWa; PoPoPo; PoWW; TFi; WaAnP; WeW-3

In ballet the foot disappears. Fetish. Beckian Fritz Goldberg. AmAlph

In Ball's Market after surfing till noon. Supremes, The. Mark Jarman. GeoHom; SwNoth

In *Bath* a wanton wife did dwell. *Unknown.* PBRV *Fr.* Wanton Wife of Bath, The.

In Battle. Abu-l-Hasan Ibn Al-Qabturnuh. NAWM-7v1, *tr. by* Lysander Kemp

In battle today my lover turned his back to the enemy. *Unknown.* SLW, *tr. by* Marjolijn De Jager, Sayd Bahodin Majrouh and André Velter

In Bayreuth once. Mary Desti's Ass. Frank O'Hara. FTOS

In Beatle light. For Craig Who Leapt Off a Cliff in to Hummingbird Light. Diane Wakoski. PmAP

In beauty. (LL) Eagle Poem. Joy Harjo. HATNAP; NAAL-5; WeW-3

In bed I muse on Tenier's [*or* Teniers'] boors. Bench of Boors, The. Herman Melville. APN-2; AWTN; NAAL-3; SoSe-8

(In bed I muse on Tenier's boors.) NoP-4

In Bed this Morning. Teresa Blagg. PasH

In bed we laugh, in bed we cry. Translation of Lines by Benserade. Isaac de Benserade. WoPoe, *tr. by* Samuel Johnson

In Bed with a Book. Mona Van Duyn. PoA 2002

In Bed with James Tate. Regie Cabico. BRtP

In Bed with Joan & Alex. Ted Berrigan. AHA

In bed with our bodies so completely intertwined. Love Poem, The. Andrew Elliott. PNI

In Belfast, Europe, your man. British Connection, The. Padraic Fiacc. PNI

In Berkeley. Robert Pinsky. PfSP

In Berlin, August 1945: Lehrte Bahnhof. Alun Llywelyn-Williams. BBMWP; OBWVE, *tr. by* Joseph P. Clancy

In Bethlehem. Christus Natus Est. Countee Cullen. ChIV-2; ChrPo

In between incarnations. Robert Kelly. WhBo *Fr.* Flowers of Unceasing Coincidence, The.

In Bible times heavenly messengers disguised as beggars were everywhere. Unforeseen, The. Amy Gerstler. MotU

In Bikini when as sudden. Fish Dream, The. John Engels. AtGh

In Black Churches. Lamont B. Steptoe. BRtP

In black core of night, it explodes. African Dream. Bob Kaufman. GT; OxAAAP

#3, In Black Ink. Mariiane Mays. PoPra *Fr.* (HERO)neck: Attempts at a Portrait.

In Blackwater Woods. Mary Oliver. CAP-8; NAAL-5

In Blanco County, near Floydada. Coronado Points. Alan Birkelbach. TiP2

In Blood's Domaine. Robert Duncan. PFTM-2 *Fr.* Passages.

In blossom today, then scattered. Blossoms in the Wind. Takajiro Ohnishi. FaBoWar

In Blue-Stocking Hollow. Donald Davidson. FuPo

In body healthy, and composed in mind. (LL) Mira's Will. Mary Leapor. CABP; NoP-4; NPeEn; OxBEV; PEW

In bold letters. (LL) Can't Tell. Nellie Wong. ItWoWo; LTA; OpBo

In Bonds. Alice Cary. SWaP

In Boston, a tongue of red paint traces the city's history, from Massacre to Tea Party to Faneuil Hall. History. Joel Brouwer. PoDa

In both stirrups. (LL) Tethered horse, A. Buson. ChAP; EH, *tr. by* Robert Hass

In boxcars displaced persons howl hymns of home like wolves at bay. DP's. Lincoln Kirstein. AmWaPo

In boyhood's days we read with keen delight. Christopher Pearse Cranch. APN-1 *Fr.* Seven Wonders of the World.

In Brief. Angel Cuadra. AF, *tr. by* Katherine Rodriguez Nieto

In bright succession raise, her *Ornament* and *Guard*! (LL) Cotter's Saturday Night [nscribed to Robert Aiken [*or* R. A****], Esq.], The. Robert Burns. NOBRP; TreFP

In brilliant gas light. Good Night. William Carlos Williams. SAmP

In Britain. Peter Didsbury. StAl

In broad daylight I dream I. Dream at Night, A. Mei Yao Ch'en. BLT, *tr. by* Kenneth Rexroth

In Broken Images. Robert Graves. HarvBoo; NoP-4; NoP-5; TRP

In Brueghel's great picture, The Kermess. Dance, The. William Carlos Williams. APT-1; BrAP; HarvBoo; HeIP-4; NAAL-5; NAAPv.2; NAMCP V.1; NIL-7; NIP-4; NoAM; NoP-4; PoPoPo; SAmP; SoSe-8; TFi; WaAnP

In bubbles to the elbow, on my knees. Story after the Story, The. Marie Ponsot. ExTi

In Buddy's Eyes. Stephen Sondheim. ReLy

In bunches bright as marigolds. Duckling, Swan. Jim Elledge. SwNoth

In Burning Thirst. Kim Chiha. CAMKP, *tr. by* David R. McCann

In bygone days, you surely know. Nighingale, The. János Arany. IQMS, *tr. by* Peter Zollman

In Byzantine profile, looking about. One sees pictures of Dante. Carl Phillips. OxAAAP

In C. W.'s Closet. Afaa Michael Weaver. OxAAAP

In cabinets of amethyst and frost. (LL) Geoffrey Hill. NAEL-6v2; NAEL-7v2; NoAM; NoP-4; NoP-5; NPeEn *Fr.* Apology for the Revival of Christian Architecture in England, An.

In California. Donald Davie. NAMCP V.2; NoAM

In California. Kathy Fagan. GeoHom

In California. Nov 22, 1988. Ishmael Reed. ESEAA

In California During the Gulf War. Denise Levertov. PrTe

In California, north of the Golden Gate. Mendocino Rose. Garrett Kaoru Hongo. WeW-3

In California, she'd be a surfer girl. Deb at the Ham Slicer. Cynthia Gallaher. SUP

In California there are one hundred and eighty-seven reasons. 187. Leroy V. Quintana. LiTh

In California with Neruda. Shirley Lim. GeoHom

In calm and cool and silence, once again. First-Day Thoughts. John Greenleaf Whittier. APN-1

In calm of sleep. White Solitude. Leopoldo Lugones. TCLAP, *tr. by* Julie Schumacher

In candent ire the solar splendor flames. Oliver Wendell Holmes. TCAPo *Fr.* Autocrat of the Breakfast Table, The.

In candy kitchens so many days. Blackman in the Desecrated Synagogue—Living in the Last Days. David Henderson. EGAG

In Carmen County. Corrido of "Gregorio Cortez." *Unknown.* NAAPv.2

In Carrowdore Churchyard. Derek Mahon. NoP-4; NoP-5; PBCIP; PNI

In Case. James Sherry.
  "What should be the title of a king. Too, how also to include. What happened
  when." FTOS

In case nobody ever told you. Travel Note. Albert Huffstickler. TiP2

In Case of Monsters. Stephen Knight. NeBl

In case you fancy coloring books. My Coloring Book. Fred Ebb. ReLy

In catholic school. For Talking. Denise Nico Leto. UnSA

In ceaseless Rosemary. (LL) Essential oils—are wrung. Emily Dickinson.
  APN-2; SWaP; TCAPo

In Celebration. Mark Strand. NAMCP V.2; NoAM

In Celebration of My Uterus. Anne Sexton. CAP-8; NALW

In celebration of surviving. Chuck Miller. GoPo

In Celia's face a question did arise. Lips and Eyes. Thomas Carew. OBVE,
  tr. by Thomas Carew

In Central Park. Moyshe-Leyb Halpern. WoPoe, tr. by John Hollander

In certain places, still, surprisingly, you come. Footnote on Monasticism, A:
  Dingle Peninsula. John Montague. BBASP

In Cesario's breeches, I fell in love. Viola, to Olivia. Mary Makofske. IaFF

In Cézanne's studio, we're dappled with joy. Liliane Welch. Coast

In chamber low and scored by time. Herman Melville. APN-2 Fr. Clarel: A
  Poem and Pilgrimage in the Holy Land.

In Chandler Country. Dana Gioia. GeoHom

In Chapel. John Pook. AngWePo

In Charon's palm it pay the toll to Death. (LL) Dante Gabriel Rossetti. BrAP;
  GSo; NAEL-6v2; NAEL-7v2; NIL-7; NoP-4; NoP-5 Fr. House of Life,
  The.

In Chartres. Euros Bowen. BBMWP, tr. by the author

In Cheever Country. Dana Gioia. GM

In Chicago, it is snowing softly. Legend, The. Garrett Kaoru Hongo. LoL;
  MakPoe; OpBo; TRP

In Chicago near the lake, on the North Shore. That Winter. Ruth Stone.
  GPTC

In childhood once I saw a mouser spring. Albery Allson Whitman. NAAPv.1
  Fr. Octoroon, The.

In childhood's sunny day my heart was taught to love. To Whittier. Josephine
  D. Henderson Heard. CBWP-4

In China. Lost Sister. Cathy Song. NAMCP V.2; NoAM

In China. Terry Wolverton. WiU

In China, / even the peasants. Lost Sister. Cathy Song. NAAL-5

In China swings the mandarin. Encouraging. Attila József. WoPoe, tr. by
  John Batki

In Choate Road. Inchoate Road. B. P. Nichol. NLPA

In Choker's Lane, the doors appear. Choker's Lane. Kenneth Slessor.
  BMAP

In Christ Church, Bristol, on Thomas Turner, Twice Master of the Company of
  Bakers. Francis, Lord Jeffrey Jeffrey. NBLV

In Christ there is no East or [or nor] West. All One in Christ. John Oxenham.
  SacPr

In Church. Thomas Hardy. MoBrPo Fr. Satires of Circumstance in Fifteen
  Glimpses.

In Cineam. Sir John Davies. DiBP Fr. Epigrams.

In cinemas we sought. Sing, Brothers, Sing! William Robert Rodgers.
  MoBrPo

In cities I'm as rare as I'm unwelcome. James Turner. NewEx

In city [or cittie], nor on hill, but al[l] the night must sleep[e] alone. (LL)
  Theocritus. NoSic; OBVE Fr. Idylls.

In Clarke County, the story goes, the family name. Virginia Reel. Charles
  Wright. LPSFW

In classic beauty, cold, immaculate. Mnemosyne. Madison Cawein. APN-2

In classical environs. Goliardic Song. Anthony Hecht. OBCoV

In climes beyond the solar road. Thomas Gray. OxAEP-1 Fr. Progress of
  Poesy, The.

In clouds drew on the evening's close. Evening. Gertrude. Anne Batten
  Cristall. RWP

In cock-wattle sunset or grey. Nostalgia. Louis MacNeice. OxAEP-2

In Cold February Twilight. Frederic William Kirchner. ArBi

In cold grey morning. Prisoner of Los Angeles (2). Wanda Coleman. CalPo;
  GeoHom

In Cold Hell, in Thicket. Charles Olson. APT-2; PmAP

In cold stiff soils the bleaters oft complain. John Dyer. STuOW Fr. Fleece,
  The.

In Cold Storm Light. Leslie Marmon Silko. NoAM

In cold weather on a. At Seven a Son. Elaine Feinstein. HarvBoo

In colour, with their eyelids shut. (LL) Martian Sends a Postcard Home, A.
  Craig Raine. NAEL-6v2; NAEL-7v2; NAMCP V.2; NoAM; NoP-4; NoP-
  5; NPeEn; WaAnP

In coming to the feast I found. Horn, The. Léonie Adams. MoAmPo
  (While coming to the feast I found.) APT-2; OxBoAm

In Commendation of Music. William Strode. OBEV

In Communication with a UFO. Helen Chasin. YaYoPo

In Conference. Gordon Hodgeon. RSaN

In confirmation, I hear sevenfold lark-songs pealing. (LL) Wild Common, The.
  D. H. Lawrence. NAMCP V.1; NoAM

In contact, lo! the flint and steel. Ambrose Bierce. APN-2 Fr. Devil's
  Dictionary, The.

In Containing a Thought Satisfied with Chaste Love. Sor Juana Inés de la
  Cruz. BLPSL, tr. by Rene de Costa, Rigas Kappatos and Eleni Paidoussi

In Contemplation of My Wretched Life. Catherine Parr, Lady Borough.
  "Christ was obedient unto his father." EMWP

In converse with the mountains, moors, and fens. (LL) Prelude: "Still south I
  went and west and south again." John Millington Synge. MoBrPo;
  OBMV

In Cool, Green Haunts. Mahlon Leonard Fisher. WeW-3

In cool seas of September click the stones. Reculver Bay. Vicki Raymond.
  NOBAu

In Cosmum. Sir John Davies. NPeEn

In coughing too. Ozaki Hosai. CAoMJL1, tr. by Janine Beichman

In countless upward-striving waves. Nominalist and Realist. Ralph Waldo
  Emerson. APN-1

In court to serve, decked with fresh array. Courtier's Life, The. Sir Thomas
  Wyatt. NoSic

In Creve Coeur, Missouri. Rosanna Warren. PoPoPo

In crisis you may know me. October Poem. Tamura Ryuichi. AF, tr. by
  Christopher Drake

In crisp italic, meticulous and signed. Man Who Wrote Yeats, the Man Who
  Wrote Mozart, The. Michael Hartnett. ModIr

In crystal. Autumn Rose. Amal Moussa. PoArWo, tr. by Khaled Mattawa

In danger of which. Poem. Ray DiPalma. FTOS

In Dante's Hell. Geoff Page. OBCoV

In dark fens of the Dismal Swamp. Slave in the Dismal Swamp, The. Henry
  Wadsworth Longfellow. TCAPo

In Dark Times. Bertolt Brecht. PoAgWa, tr. by Humphrey Milnes

In darkness, crabs are believed to rest. Duressor. Larissa Szporluk.
  AmPoNex

In daylight, there is life and living speech. Early Morning Landing. Charles
  Bruce. Coast

In days, my Lord, when mother Time. Soame Jenyns. OBSV Fr. Epistle
  Written in the Country to the Right Honourable the Lord Lovelace, An.

In days of old beside the Nile. Cleopatterer. P. G. Wodehouse. ReLy

In days of old, certain patriots beid. Independence Day. Unknown. VerBaPo

In days of summer let me go. In Ampezzo. Trumbull Stickney. ColAP

In daytime hours. Better Days. Essex Hemphill. CAGL

In de glory of the Lord. (LL) Edward Kamau Brathwaite. BrAP; NAMCP V.2
  Fr. Arrivants: A New World Trilogy, The.

In de mornin' when I rise. Tell My Jesus "Morning." Unknown. SSUS

In dearth of faith, and scarcitie of friendes. Samuel Daniel. Fr. Civil Wars, The.

In death I know well enough all things end in emptiness. To Show to My Sons.
  Lu Yu. ColAnChi, tr. by Burton Watson

In Death Valley. Edwin Markham. APN-2

In death we will share one coffin. (LL) Married Love. Kuan Tao Shēng.
  PasH; WoPoe, tr. by Chung Ling and Kenneth Rexroth

In Debtor's Yard the stones are hard. Oscar Wilde. WaAnP Fr. Ballad of
  Reading Gaol, The.

In December, snow. Why We Play Basketball. Sherman Alexie. MoASP

In Defence of Adultery. Julia Copus. StAl

In Defence of Drunkards. Jan Kochanowski. WoPoe, tr. by Jerzy Peterkiewicz
  and Burns Singer

In Defence of Metaphysics. Charles Tomlinson. MoBrPo

In Defense of Our Overgrown Garden. Matthea Harvey. IIR

In delicate beach-grass, a slight breeze. Thoughts, Traveling at Night. Tu Fu
  [or Du Fu]. NDACCP, tr. by David Hinton

In delight, at the moment of conception. Marin Georgiev. CSCBP Fr.
  Memory.

In delivering my son from me, I bury a second husband. All's Well That Ends
  Well. William Shakespeare.

In Derision of a Country Life. Edward Ravenscroft. NOSC

In Desolation. John Beaumont. SacPr

In Despair. Constantine P. Cavafy. CAGL, tr. by Edmund Keeley and Philip
  Sherrard

In despair at not being able to rival the creations of God. Hymn to Her
  Unknown. Walter James Turner. OBMV

In different shades of blue ink. Approaching the Equinox. John Tritica.
  ICANM

In dim green depths rot ingot-laden ships. Sunken Gold. Eugene Lee-
  Hamilton. GSo

In Directions. John Rybicki. AmPoNex

In discord this incipience, disregard. Well, You Needn't. Karen Volkman.
  PoDa

In Dispraise of the Moon. Mary Elizabeth Coleridge. PEW; ViWPN

In Distrust of Merits. Marianne Moore. AmWaPo; APT-1; ColAP; MoAmPo; NAAL-5; NAAPv.2; OBWP

In Divés' Dive. Robert Frost. AmWit; GI *Fr.* Ten Mills.

In doggerel and stout let me honour this country. Western Landscape. Louis MacNeice. ModIr

In-doors and out,—summer and winter—Mirth. (LL) To the Grasshopper and the Cricket. Leigh Hunt. CenSon; GSo; OxBSo

In dread, all that the clergy teach the young. (LL) Straying Student, The. Austin Clarke. ModIr; NPeEn

In dream / the beavers come to. Seneca Journal 1: "A Poem of Beavers." Jerome Rothenberg. APSN

In dreaming down to Morden, via Bank. (LL) Her Retirement. Anne Rouse. BeAl; NeBl

In Dreams. Patricia Pogson. NLP

In / dreams / diving deeper / than my disbelief. Keith Cartwright. AmPoNex

In dreams I crossed a barren land. Ballade of Broken Flutes. Edwin Arlington Robinson. APN-2

In drugstores across America. Gia. Tracey Herd. MFPA

In Dublin. Weather Forecast. Sion Aled. BBMWP, *tr. by* Grahame Davies

In Duc Ninh a village of 1,654 households. Two Villages. Grace Paley. FaBoWar

In due course of course you will all be issued with. Henry Reed. BrAP; NAEL-6v2 *Fr.* Lessons of the War.

In due course one admits the sex was magnificent. Break It on Down. Brian Henry. WaAnP

In Duffryn Woods. John Stuart Williams. AngWePo

In Earliest Spring. William Dean Howells. *See* Earliest Spring.

In early autumn, there's a concerto. Music One Looks Back On, The. Stephen Dobyns. GoPo

In early March, I watch you sleep, your mouth. Sonnet to the Imagination. Robin Becker. BodElec

In early spring talk still young and highflown. Welcome. Micheal O'Siadhail. IrLP

In early spring, when the ice on the snowy mountain. Virgil. IPoFL *Fr.* Georgics.

In early summer when the grasses grow. On Reading the Seas and Mountains Classic. Ch'ien T'ao and James Robert Hightower. ColAnChi

In early youth's unclouded scene. Thirty-eight: Addressed to Mrs H—y. Charlotte Smith. NALW; PEW

In eastern village and western village. Silkworm Song of Torchlit Fields. Kao Ch'i. ColAnChi, *tr. by* Jonathan Chaves

In Easton a certain citizen. Tune: "Wu Yeh-erh" Twitting the Teller of Tall Tales. *Unknown.* ColAnChi, *tr. by* James I. Crump

In eaves sole sparrow[e] sit[t]s not more alone. David's Peccavi. Robert Southwell. ChIV-1

In Ecclesiastes I Read. J. P. White. ChIV-1

In Ecclesiastes I read, "That which is far off and exceeding deep." In Ecclesiastes I Read. J. P. White. ChIV-1

In effect, the nucleus of a cell without living cell substance. Virus, The. Britton Wilkie. AHA

In Egypt of her dead. (LL) Birds in Snow. "H. D." APT-1; PoA 2002; WaAnP

In Egypt they worshiped me. I Am the Cat. Leila Usher. ITBLP

In Egypt's sandy silence, all alone. Ozymandias. Horace Smith. CenSon

In eighteen hundred and forty-one. Working on the Railway. *Unknown.* APN-2

In eighteen months she has grown. Nicola. William Scammell. NLP

In 1861, George Hew sailed in a rowboat. Network, The. Arthur Sze. OpBo

In either hand the hast'ning angel caught. John Milton. OPOU *Fr.* Paradise Lost.

In Emily's Manner. Armanda Guiducci. CItWP, *tr. by* Cinzia Sartini Blum and Lara Trubowitz

In Emmanuel's Land. Anne R. Cousin. SacPr

In Emulation of Mr Cowleys Poem Call'd The Motto. Mary Astell. EMWP; NOSC

In England. Duo Duo. PoetW, *tr. by* Maghiel van Crevel

In England's green & pleasant Land. (LL) William Blake. BrAP; CABP; ChIV-1; ClHu; CtM; HeIP-4; NAEL-7v2; NAWM-7v2; NOBRP; NoP-4; NPeEn; OxBEV; TFi; WoPoe *Fr.* Milton.

In English. Gertrude Stein. OxBoAm *Fr.* Book Concluding with As A Wife Has a Cow a Love Story, A.

In English in a Poem. Lynn Emanuel. ExTi

In ethics class so many years ago. Ethics. Linda Pastan. WaAnP

In Eudoxia, which spreads both upward and down, with winding alleys. Italo Calvino. MotU *Fr.* Invisible Cities.

In Europe, you can't move without going down into history. In the Yukon. Ralph Gustafson. NoP-4

In even Will Hunter's hands. (LL) Weepies, The. Paul Muldoon. NoAM; PNI

In every breast affection fires, there dwells. Anna Seward. CenSon

In every half-filled glass a river. Drinking Song. Silvia Curbelo. TouFir

In every hotel. Avignon. Remco Campert. PoetW, *tr. by* Jeffery Paine

In every language and opened its doors. (LL) Arabic. Naomi Shihab Nye. CAP-8; PoArWo

In every old lady I chance to meet. Old Ladies. Will Allen Dromgoole. WeW-3

In every one be her great glory famed. (LL) In Honour of that High and Mighty Princess Queen Elizabeth of Happy Memory. Anne Bradstreet. NAAL-5; NALW

In every part of every living thing. Lake Superior. Lorine Niedecker. OxBoAm

In every photo in your album the women workers huddle. What Seeps In. Devorah Amir. DTA, *tr. by* Miriyam Glazer

In every place, on every shore, I will be waiting for you. Portrait of the Beautiful Unknown Woman. Juan Sánchez Peláez. BLPSL, *tr. by* Rene de Costa, Rigas Kappatos and Eleni Paidoussi

In Every Pot and Closet. Marilyn Zuckerman. PfS

In every week. (LL) Planter's Daughter, The. Austin Clarke. IrLP; ModIr; NAMCP V.1; NPeEn; OxBEV

In evil hour, and with unhallow'd voice. William Crowe. NOBRP

In evil hour did Pope's declining age. On the Edition of Mr. Pope's Works with a Commentary and Notes. Thomas Edwards. OxBSo

"In Evil Long I Took Delight." John Newton. SacPr

In ev'ry race, in ev'ry clime. Lines to a Graduate. Lizelia Augusta Jenkins Moorer. CBWP-3

In Exchange for Forty Acres. Bruce Jackson. AmPoNex

In Exile. Emma Lazarus. APN-2; NAAPv.1

In Explanation to the Mother. Kiren Shoman. OWABP

In Extremis. John Updike. OBCoV

In Eyemouth Harbour. Gordon Meade. EdScPo

In fact Adam and Eve are not their names. (LL) Names. William Matthews. PfSP; PoCoUp

In fair London city I was born. Deserter, The. *Unknown.* FaBoWar

In fair Provence, the land of lute and rose. Sestina. Sir Edmund William Gosse. MakPoe

In faith, I do[e] not love thee with mine eyes. William Shakespeare. HeIP-4; OxAEP-1 *Fr.* Sonnets.

In faith, Squier, thou hast thee wel yquit. Geoffrey Chaucer. NAEL-6v1 *Fr.* Canterbury Tales, The.

In fall, when afternoons begin. Near-Sightedness. Edmond Yi-teh Chang. OpBo

In farming country you are sure to find them. Old Yellow Shop, The. Abbie Huston Evans. APT-1

In far-off England, years ago. Destiny. Eloise Bibb. CBWP-4

In fascination of her brightness. (LL) Dome of Sunday, The [*or* A]. Karl Shapiro. MoAmPo; NoAM

In Favor of One's Time. Frank O'Hara. PoA 2002

In fear and trembling, I think I would fulfill my life. Task, A. Czeslaw Milosz. AF, *tr. by* the author and Czeslaw Milosz

In February, digging his garden, planting potatoes. Letters from Yorkshire. Maura Dooley. NeBl

In feeling I was but a child. One Year Ago. Adah Isaacs Menken. CBWP-1

In Ferrara. Ken Bolton and John Jenkins. BMAP

In Festubert. Edmund Charles Blunden. OBMV

In Fields of Buffalo. Walter McDonald. TiP2

In Fields of Sleepdreaming. Delmira Agustini. TANSG, *tr. by* Mark McCaffrey

In fields where roses fade. (LL) A. E. Housman. HeIP-4; InoFa; MoBrPo; NAEL-6v2; NAEL-7v2; NAMCP V.1; NoAM; NoP-4; NoP-5; PoPoPo; TFi *Fr.* Shropshire Lad, A.

In 15 minutes. California Peninsula: El Camino Real. Al Young. GeoHom; GT

In 5th grade social studies class we. In 5th Grade. Valerie Caesar. BRtP

In 'Fifty Congress Passed a Bill. Elymas Payson Rogers. CBCWP *Fr.* Poem on the Fugitive Slave Law, A.

In fifty-nine. Oxford Gardens. Charles McDonald. NLP

In filthy Puerto Rico lives a bird with no. Hayden Carruth. BodElec *Fr.* Paragraphs.

In flame and a clamorous breath known to the eye-pecking gulls. (LL) Rudyard Kipling. PoWW; WoPoe *Fr.* Epitaphs of the War [1914–1918].

In Flanders fields the poppies blow. In Flanders Fields. John McCrae. BRP; ChAP; FaBoWar; IFF; ITBLP; NoP-4; NoP-5; OBWP; PoWW

In Fla[u]ndres whilom [*or* whylom] was a compa[ig]nye. Geoffrey Chaucer. NAEL-6v1; NAEL-7v1; WaAnP *Fr.* Canterbury Tales, The.

In Flight. Jennifer Regan. OtW

In Flood. Charles Hubert Sisson. HarvBoo

In Florida, where these things can happen.   Prince of the Powers of the Air. Debora Greger.   PoDa

In flowering willows.   Memento on the Departure of a Friend, from Yeh, Last Day of the Second Moon.   Chia Tao.   CSKM, tr. by Mike O'Connor

In '42. In Czechoslovakia. Trains. (LL)   Villanelle from a Sentence in a Poet's Brief Biography.   Jacqueline Osherow.   ExTi; WaAnP

In '42 he was conscripted to work on trains.   Villanelle from a Sentence in a Poet's Brief Biography.   Jacqueline Osherow.   ExTi; WaAnP

In Fragments, In Streams.   Talvikki Ansel.
   "Along the road, the bright painted crosses."   YaYoPo
   "At night, coolness like water lapping."   YaYoPo
   "Before first light, we would open the nets."   YaYoPo
   "Halley's Comet crossed the jungle sky."   YaYoPo
   "Teatro Amazonas, remnant, the."   YaYoPo
   "Waking, months after I leave the jungle."   YaYoPo

In from the fields they come.   Harvesters, The.   Mary Gilmore.   NOBAu

In from the night.   Answer Me.   Adah Isaacs Menken.   CBWP-1; PoBW; ViWPN

In Front of a Large Number of People.   John Godfrey.   FTOS

In front of everybody.   Boy Exploded on the Corner Today, A.   Seth Tucker. LiTh

In front of everyone. (LL)   Crows in a Strong Wind.   Cornelius Eady. ESEAA; InvLad

In Front of Good Prince Silence.   Endre Ady.   IQMS, tr. by Alan Dixon

In front of my house there's a vineyard.   Unknown Also Attracts Cowards, The. Gloria Fuertes.   RaW, tr. by Philip Levine

In front of the building where the florist.   On the Galloping Cusp of the New Now.   Mark S. Kuhar.   AmZen

In Front of the House.   Aliyah Abdul-Salaam.   AnVo, tr. by Mohamed Enani

In front of the hut, she scavenges for dates: let her be.   Second Letter to My Nephew Wulang.   Tu Fu [or Du Fu].   CCL1, tr. by Jerome P. Seaton

In front of the inn we saw a sailor.   Sailor, A.   Ivan Slamnig.   PML, tr. by Vasa D. Mihailovich and Charles David Wright

In Front of the Mirror.   Vicente Aleixandre.   RaW, tr. by Herbert Baird and William Stafford

In front of the mirror in my parents' bedroom lay a pink conch.   Conch. Zbigniew Herbert.   StAl, tr. by Bogdana Carpenter and John Carpenter

In front of the sombre mountains, a faint, lost ribbon of rainbow.   D. H. Lawrence.   PoA 2002

In front of the throb.   Before John and Maria's Wedding.   Hilda Raz.   ExTi

In front of us the road's turned misty-grey.   Evening Halo of Light, An.   Árpád Tóth.   IQMS, tr. by Thomas Kabdebo

In front of you I go.   I Am With You.   Lajos Kassák.   IQMS, tr. by Edwin Morgan

In full glare [or flare] I came here, man-tall but thin.   Roundhouse Voices, The. Dave Jeddie Smith.   ColAP; GM; NoAM; VCAP; WaAnP

In full voice sent.   Continental Walk.   Allen Fisher.   PFTM-2

In full-blown Dignity, see Wolsey stand.   Juvenal.   OxBEV Fr. Vanity of Human Wishes, The; The Tenth Satire of Juvenal [Imitated].

In futurity / I prophetic see.   William Blake.   NOBRP Fr. Songs of Experience.

In futurity / I prophetic see.   William Blake.   NOBRP Fr. Songs of Innocence.

In Fuzhou, far away, my wife is watching.   Moonlit Night.   Tu Fu [or Du Fu]. WoPoe, tr. by Vikram Seth

In Galilee.   Jessie Mackay.   SacPr

In gardening I continued to sit on my side of the car: to.   Song of the Gourd. C. D. Wright.   GPPA

In Gardens in the Rhondda.   Idris Davies.   AngWePo

In gayer hours, when high my fancy ran.   Richard Savage.   OBSV Fr. Bastard, The.

In Geneva I pawned my pocket watch and passport.   Sam Truitt.   AmPoNex Fr. Anamorphosis Eisenhower.

In ghostlier demarcations, keener sounds. (LL)   Idea of Order at Key West, The.   Wallace Stevens.   AmFaPo; APT-1; BrAP; ColAP; HarvBoo; HeIP-4; MakPoe; MoAmPo; NAAL-5; NAAPv.2; NAMCP V.1; NAWM-7v2; NIL-7; NIP-4; NoAM; NoP-4; NoP-5; OxBoAm; PoPoPo; SAmP; TFi; WaAnP

In Glass.   Catherine Tufariello.   PoA 2002

In Glencullen.   John Millington Synge.   OBMV

In God's name, mam, don't mention.   To a Blind Mother.   Gilbert Ruddock. BBMWP, tr. by Mike Jenkins

In Golden Gate Park that day.   Lawrence Ferlinghetti.   PmAP

In good King Charles's golden days.   Vicar of Bray, The.   Unknown.   OBSV; OxBEV

In gorgeous reticence. (LL)   Brancusi's Golden Bird.   Mina Loy.   APT-1; HarvBoo; MoWP; NAAPv.2; NAMCP V.1

In Gothic times, when feudal laws obtained.   Triumph of Superstition, The. Raphael and Ianthe.   Anne Batten Cristall.   RWP

In Goya's greatest scenes we seem to see.   Lawrence Ferlinghetti.   CalPo; HeIP-4; NAMCP V.2; NoAM; PmAP

In goyng to my naked bedde, as one that would have slept.   Richard Edwards. OxBEV

In grade school I wondered.   Zimmer in Grade School.   Paul Zimmer. PBCAP

In grandfather's house I ran up and down.   Doris Hulme.   NewEx

In graves where drips the winter rain.   Unknown.   OBMV Fr. Black Book of Carmarthen, The.

In Greece in 1939, these kids had this little snake trapped in a corner, kicking it and laughing.   Art of the Snake Story, The.   Amy England.   BAP-01

In grief and anguish of my heart, my voice I did extend.   Song of Jonah in the Whale's Belly, The.   Michael Drayton.   ChIV-1

In grief the flood is bursting home. (LL)   Low Tide on Grand Pré.   Bliss Carman.   BrAP; IFF

In grievous deity my cat.   Startled into Life Like Fire.   Charles Bukowski. PmAP

In Gurgle Veritas.   Luis H. Francia.   ReBoTo

In haiku there are various sorts of.   Short Talk on Trout.   Anne Carson. OpeFie

In halls fine silken women.   Candle, The.   Hsiao Yen [or Emperor Wu of Liang].   CCL1, tr. by Anne Birrell

In happy climes, the seat of innocence.   George Berkeley. See Muse, disgusted at an age and clime, The.

In happy hours, when the imagination.   Henry Wadsworth Longfellow. TCAPo Fr. Michael Angelo: A Fragment.

In Harlem wandering from street to street. (LL)   Harlem Shadows.   Claude McKay.   APT-1; ColAP; NAAL-5; NAAPv.2; TCAPo

In harmony.   What Was Not Conceivable.   Fatima Mahmoud.   PoArWo, tr. by Khaled Mattawa

In harmony the ospreys cry.   Unknown.   CCL1 Fr. Guan-ju.

In Harmony with Nature.   Matthew Arnold.   CABP

In haste poste haste, when first my wandering [or wandring] mind[e].   George Gascoigne.   NoSic Fr. Gascoigne's Memories.

In Hayden's Collage.   Michael S. Harper.   ESEAA

In hearts all rocky now the late remorse of love. (LL)   Lord Byron.   NAEL-6v2; NAEL-7v2 Fr. Childe Harold's Pilgrimage.

In hearts at peace, under an English heaven.   Rupert Brooke.   AmFaPo; CABP; EMP; FaBoWar; GSo; HeIP-4; InoFa; MoBrPo; NAEL-6v2; NAEL-7v2; NoP-4; NoP-5; OBEV; OBWP; PoA 2002; PoWW; TFi; UV; WaAnP

In Heaven.   Robert Patrick Dana.   RWB

In Heaven a spirit doth dwell.   Israfel.   Edgar Allan Poe.   APN-1; NAAL-3; NAAPv.1; TCAPo

In heaven I will find the words not said.   To the Victims of Mauthausen. Maria Luisa Spaziani.   CItWP, tr. by Cinzia Sartini Blum and Lara Trubowitz

In heaven it is always autumn. The leaves are always near.   In Heaven It Is Always Autumn.   Elizabeth Spires.   CAP-8

In Heaven [or Heav'n], their earthy [or earthly] bodies left behind. (LL)   To Lucasta, [on] Going beyond the Seas.   Richard Lovelace.   OBEV; OxAEP-1

In Heaven, Queen Juno saw. She's trapped.   Virgil.   EroLit Fr. Aeneid [or Eneados or Aeneis], The.

In heaven soaring up, I dropped [or dropt] an ear[e].   Edward Taylor.   NAAL-3 Fr. God's Determinations [touching his Elect].

In Heaven, / Some little blades of grass.   Stephen Crane.   MoAmPo

In heavenly realms of hellas dwelt.   E. E. Cummings.   OBSV

In heavy drink and in love.   Atlantis.   Slavko Mihalic.   PoSu, tr. by Charles Simic

In Heavy Mind.   James Agee.   MoAmPo

In Hecate's Garden.   Ziporah Hildebrandt.   HW

In hell, maximum use.   Fresco.   Martin Sorescu.   VCWP, tr. by D. J Enright and Joana Russell-Gebbett

In Hellbrunn.   Georg Trakl.   WED, tr. by Robert Bly

In Henry Carlile's Writing 213.   Martha Silano.   AmPoNex

In her best gingham dress, teased hair.   God of Pepper, The.   Alan Michael Parker.   NeAmPo

In her boudoir, the young lady—unacquainted with grief.   Unknown.   OBVE; OxBEV, tr. by Arthur Waley

In her cloak and hat.   Elizabeth Anna Hart.   NOxBChV

In her ear he whispers gaily.   Lord of Burleigh, The.   Alfred Tennyson. STuOW

In her early age the mother's toenails curl over her toes.   Mother, The.   Marie Howe.   LaCa

In her golden chamber.   Alice.   Isa Blagden.   PoBW

In her hand the knife, brisk, brilliant as moon-claw.   Cleaning a Fish.   Dave Jeddie Smith.   NoAM

In her hands she holds.   Man She Called Honey, and Married, The.   Alberto A. Ríos.   ReTh

In her lap woman gathers all labors.   Fragment for the Mother.   Mariella Bettarini.   CItWP, tr. by Cinzia Sartini Blum and Lara Trubowitz

In her last sickness, my mother took my hand in hers. Kaddish. Charles Reznikoff. NAAPv.2; TaR

In her living room. Goggles and Helmet. Donald Hall. PoA 2002

In her lover's studio, the walls. Artist's Daughter, The. Kimiko Hahn. CAP-8

In Her Moonlit Chamber. Wen T'ing-yün. CCL1, *tr. by* Glen Baxter

In Her Own Image. Eavan Boland. PBCIP

In Her Prison. Sarah Morgan Bryan Piatt. NCAP

In her room at the prow of the house. Writer, The. Richard Wilbur. CAP-8; NAMCP V.2; NoAM; PoPoPo; SoSe-8

In her storefront living room. Palm Reader, The. Nicholas Christopher. NoP-4; NoP-5

In her tomb by the sounding sea. (LL) Annabel Lee. Edgar Allan Poe. BLPJKO; BRP; ChAP; HeIP-4; ITBLP; NAAL-3; NAAL-5; NAAPv.1; NCAP; NoP-5; OBSP; OxBoAm; TCAPo; TFi

(In her tomb by the side of the sea.) (LL) APN-1; ColAP; NoP-4; PoPoPo; WaAnP

In her very name is a ripple of applause. Portrait of Plisetskaya. Andrey Andreievich Voznesensky. RusPo, *tr. by* Robert Arthur Douglas Ford

In her youth she was muffled in a veil of longing. Mirror of the Battle. Ayin Tur-Malka. NRoS, *tr. by* Esther Raizen

In here it's deliberately dark so one may sigh. Rooms Are Never Finished. Agha Shahid Ali. AmAlph

'In here,' our teacher said. Owl. Ted Walker. NOxBChV

In Hexameter sings serenely a Harvard Professor. Couplet: February 24, 1847. Henry Wadsworth Longfellow. APN-1

In Heytesbury Wood. Siegfried Sassoon. OBGa

In hidden ease. (LL) Locusts a-wing, multiply. *Unknown*. APSN; NDACCP, *tr. by* Ezra Pound

In Hiding. Miklós Radnóti. TAPaP, *tr. by* Stephen Berg, S. J. Marks and Steven Polgar

In High Places. Harriet Monroe. PoA 2002

In high school I had a friend. Domingo Limón. Alberto A. Ríos. NAAL-5

In Hilo Hospital. Joan Swift. PoDa

In him inexplicably mixed appeared. Lord Byron. NOBRP *Fr.* Lara.

In Him We Live [and Move and Have Our Being]. Jones Very. APN-1

In his blackest suit. Funeral Mass. Patricia K. Page. GPPA

In his blue suit, an Oxford Standard Authors. Study in Blue. Evan Jones. NOBAu

In his book *The Theory of Religion* (Zone Books, New York, 1992, trans. Robert Hurley) George Bataille analyzes the arising of human consciousness. Violence of Oneness, The. Norman Fischer. Eno

In his clean vegetation. Henri Rousseau and Friends. Michael Ondaatje. BrAP

In his darkroom he is finally alone. War Photographer. Carol Ann Duffy. EdScPo

In his father's cupped hands. Pheasant Plucker's Son, The. Mick North. NLP

In his fluttering winding-sheet. (LL) Elegy: "Do not look for him." Leonard Cohen. BrAP; HeIP-4

In his lambskin coat. Gao-yang: In His Lambskin Coat. *Unknown*. CCL1, *tr. by* V. W. X.

In his last year, he was all but blind. In Memory of William Carlos Williams. Hans Magnus Enzensberger. GTCP, *tr. by* Reinhold Grimm and Felix Pollak

In his life. Abd El-Hadi Fights a Superpower. Taha Muhammad Ali. PoCho, *tr. by* Peter Cole

In his lodge beside a river. Henry Wadsworth Longfellow. *Fr.* Song of Hiawatha, The.

In his malodorous brain what slugs and mire. God. Isaac Rosenberg. OxBEV

In his narrow, gleaming eyes. Leader, The. Yunna Petrovna Moritz. TCRusP, *tr. by* Daniel Weissbort

In his own age, Democritus could find. Juvenal. BASC *Fr.* Satires.

In his own world. This morning. Visibility of Spirits, The. Laura Kasischke. SweBea

In his place. Vanzetti's Ghost. Yosl Grinshpan. Prolet, *tr. by* Amelia Glaser

In his songs and poems. Dead Chrysanthemums. Ber Grin. Prolet, *tr. by* Amelia Glaser

In his struggle against pragmatism and the horrible tendency of reaching useful ends. Loss and Recovery of the Hair, The. Julio Cortázar. MotU, *tr. by* Paul Blackburn

In his unsteady box at last into the earth. (LL) Cinquevalli. Edwin Morgan. HarvBoo; NePenScot

In his unweeting way. (LL) New Year's Eve. Thomas Hardy. MoBrPo; NAMCP V.1; NoAM

In his winged collar. Japanese Jokes. Peter Porter. OBCoV

In Honor of David Anderson Brooks, My Father. Gwendolyn Brooks. OxAAAP

In Honor of that High and Mighty Princess, Queen Elizabeth, of Most Happy Memory. Anne Bradstreet. *See* In Honour of that High and Mighty Princess Queen Elizabeth of Happy Memory.

In honor of the dumb the blind the deaf. Second Nature. Paul Eluard. SurPaPo, *tr. by* Samuel Beckett

In Honor of the Sardana and the Tenora. Max Jacob. CuPo

In honour of something or other—poor. Sign Illuminated, A. Roy Fisher. EmeKit

In Honour of St. David's Day. *Unknown*. OBWVE

In Honour of Taffy Topaz. Christopher Darlington Morley. WHSW

In Honour of that High and Mighty Princess Queen Elizabeth of Happy Memory. Anne Bradstreet. NAAL-5; NALW

  "Here lies the pride of Queens, pattern of Kings." TCAPo

  "Here sleeps the Queen, this is the royall bed." OxBEV; TCAPo

In Hospital. W. E. Henley.

  Before. MoBrPo

  Interior. NPeEn

  Waiting. NAEL-6v2; NAEL-7v2; NPeEn

In Hospital: Poona (1). Alun Lewis. AngWePo; OBWVE; TCAWP

In hospital where windows meet. Lady of Quality, A. Thomas Kinsella. PBCIP

In Hospital-land. Gillian Ferguson. MFPA

In Houston. Gail Mazur. PtR

In Humenne, in this time of drought. Huckster at Noontime. James Ragan. TWW

In hurly burly Broadway. Broadway Morning. Menna Elfyn. BBMWP, *tr. by* Gillian Clarke

In Hus, a land which near the sun's uprise. Paraphrase upon Job, A. Bible, O.T.

In idle August, while the sea soft. Schooner Flight, The. Derek Walcott. ESEAA; HarvBoo; NAEL-7v2; NAMCP V.2; NoP-4

In Ignorant Cadence. Maura Stanton. YaYoPo

In Illness, Dismissing My Singing Girl. Ssu-k'ung Shu. ColAnChi, *tr. by* Burton Watson

In Imitation. Larry Eigner. FTOS

In Imitation of Anacreon. Matthew Prior. OxBEV

In Imitation of Horace. Aphra Behn. NOSC

In India. Nissim Ezekiel. BrAP

In Intensive Care. Olivia Byard. PoCu

In Irlonde. (LL) I Am of Ireland. *Unknown*. NAEL-6v1; NAEL-7v1; NoP-5

In it there is a dream. Girl's Head, A. Katherine Gallagher. NOBAu

In Italian They Call the Bird *Civetta*. Robert Penn Warren. LPSFW *Fr.* Some Quiet, Plain Poems.

In Italy a man's name, here a woman's. How I Changed My Name, Felice. Felix Stefanile. UnSA

In Italy, a scholar is giving an after-dinner talk on her study of Dante and the. Paradiso. Cornelius Eady. OxAAAP

In Italy, where this sort of thing can occur. Hill, A. Anthony Hecht. NAMCP V.2; NIL-7; NoP-4; NoP-5; OxBoAm; VCAP

In its first dumb form. Susan Howe. FTOS *Fr.* Secret History of the Dividing Line.

In its streets my visions multiply. Blind City. Mona Saudi. PoArWo, *tr. by* Kamal Boullata

In its travels, the phoenix stopped at Phoenix Tower. On Phoenix Tower in Chin-Ling. Li Po. NDACCP, *tr. by* David Hinton

In Japan. Michael Burn. TCAWP

In Japan Beyond. Yonejiro (Yone) Noguchi. NAAPv.2

In Japan the poets write to each other. In Japan. Michael Burn. TCAWP

In Japan, they are called play women. Standing with Chiyo-Ni. Pesha Gertler. FiBr

In Jetavana Park I found a place to rest. Han-shan Te-ch'ing. CSKM, *tr. by* Red Pine

In Jiaozhi the weather is strange. Lodging in Annam. Du Shenyan. CCL1, *tr. by* Stephen Owen

In Jimmy's Garden [*for James Baldwin (1924–1987)*]. Quincy Troupe. GT

In Joe Brainard's collage its white arrow. Ted Berrigan. NYP2; OxBoAm *Fr.* Sonnets, The.

In Josef Koudelka's photograph, untitled & with no date. Sensationalism. Larry Levis. AmAlph

In joy, that our lives / are so familiar. (LL) Return of the Native. Imamu Amiri Baraka. APSN; OxAAAP

In joyous Summer, when the exulting earth. Lament of the Forest, The. Thomas Cole. APN-1

In Juarez. Susan Wheeler. IFF

In Juda desert. Aleksandra Petrova. CRWP, *tr. by* Dennis Silk

In June. Robert Kelly. FTOS

In June, amid the golden fields. Groundhog, The. Richard Eberhart. APT-2; BrAP; InoFa; MoAmPo; NAAPv.2; NAMCP V.1; NoAM; RaBo; TFi; TRP; WaAnP

In June and Gentle Oven.   Anne Wilkinson.   BrAP

In June, examiners.   Grand Central Hotel, The.   Roy McFadden.   PNI

In June the sun is a bonnet of light.   Sun.   Gary Soto.   TRP

In June was a jar had.   In June.   Robert Kelly.   FTOS

In June, which is still June here, but once removed.   June: Dutch Harbor.   William Meredith.   YaYoPo

In just a Country Town. (LL)   There's been a Death, in the Opposite House.   Emily Dickinson.   APN-2; InoFa; SAmP; SoSe-8

In Just- / spring when the world is mud.   In Just.   E. E. Cummings.   BLPJKO; ChAP; FaBoVe; HarvBoo; HeIP-4; MoAmPo; NAAL-5; NAAPv.2; NAMCP V.1; NIL-7; NIP-4; NoP-4; NOxBChV; PoPoPo; SoSe-8; WaAnP; WeW-3

In Kansas.   Carter Revard.   HATNAP

In Kenscoff Market the breeze brought spices.   Kenscoff.   Lorna Goodison.   GT

In Kerry.   John Millington Synge.   IrLP; MoBrPo

In Key West, our world spilled gleaming quarters. 1962.   Green Room, The.   Sydney Lea.   MAAN

In Killian Village, midnight.   Trailer Trash.   Alison Pelegrin.   RWB

In Kind.   Linda France.   NeBl

In Köhln [Köln], a town of monks and bones.   Cologne.   Samuel Taylor Coleridge.   NBLV

In Korea they say.   They Say.   TAPaP

In La Mancha he mopeth.   Rusty Man, The.   Herman Melville.   NCAP

In Lakeview Cemetery.   Christian Wiman.   AmPoNex

In Language.   Eugene Gloria.   OpBo

In Las Vegas.   Katherine Lederer.   IIR; LegDan

In late autumn, folding screen pictures look cold in the dim candlelight.   Sitting at Night at an Old Inn in Silla.   Yujŏng.   BecRai, tr. by Kim Daljin, Kim Won-Chung and Christopher Merrill

In late sun, the beauty of river and hill.   Quatrain: In Late Sun.   Tu Fu [or Du Fu].   CCL1, tr. by Burton Watson

In late winter / I sometimes glimpse bits of steam.   Bear, The.   Galway Kinnell.   CAP-8; MakPoe; StAl; TRP; VCAP; WaAnP

In later life, quietude my only care.   Answer to Vice-Prefect Chang.   Wang Wei.   ChinPo, tr. by Ye Weilian [or Yeh Wei-lien or Wai-lim Yip]

In later years, my daughter said to me.   Muse.   Rebecca Seiferle.   PoChi

In leaden slippers I laugh at the fountain of night, and scorn a solitary swan.   Kitasono Katsue.   CAoMJL1

In letters of gold on T'ang's bathtub.   Confucius.   PFTM-1 Fr. Great Digest, The.

In Lidda, in Ramla, in the Galilee.   Here We Will Stay.   Tawfiq Zayyad.   PML, tr. by Charles Doria and Sharif Elmusa

In lieu of the ring, a carbon fiber frame.   Dragonfly.   Tania Pryputniewicz.   ArBi

In life three ghostly friars were we.   Ghosts, The.   Thomas Love Peacock.   OBCoV

In life we could seldom meet.   Visit.   Tu Fu [or Du Fu].   NDACCP, tr. by William Carlos Williams

In light, and nothing else, awake. (LL)   At the San Francisco Airport.   Yvor Winters.   CalPo; HeIP-4; NIL-7; NIP-4; OxBoAm

In light metal coverings the moon falls on my face.   Remembering the Night Fountains.   I. K. Bonset.   TuT, tr. by Desmond Egan

In Line at Pancho's Tacos.   Bill Mohr.   SUP

In Line at the Supermarket.   Greg Pape.   PBCAP; SUP

In little time I stake my claim.   Ann Griffiths.   Sally Roberts Jones.   AngWePo

In living Streams that Spring.   Some Account of Anne Whitehead's Early Experience, as Written by Her Near Thirty Years Ago.   Anne Greenwell.   EMWP

In London.   Robert Creeley.   AHA

In London.   Harris Khalique.   PML

In London / every now and then.   Like a Beacon.   Grace Nichols.   OPOU

In London stands a famous pile.   South Sea Ballad, A.   Edward Ward.   OBCoV

In London there I was bent.   London Lickpenny.   Unknown.   OBSV

In London Town.   Mary Elizabeth Coleridge.   VWP

In long trains ever increasing grow the gourds.   Mian: The House of Zhou.   Unknown.   CCL1, tr. by James Legge

In looking o'er the prospects.   Prospect of the Future, The.   Mrs. Henry Linden.   CBWP-4

In Los Angeles / while the mountains cleared of smog.   Tongue-tied in Black and White.   Michael S. Harper.   ESEAA

In Louisiana.   John William DeForest.   AmWaPo

In Love.   Amanda Dalton.   NeBl Fr. Room of Leaves.

In love and grief in Eve's encircling arms. (LL)   Adam's Dream.   Edwin Muir.   NoP-4; NoP-5

In love are we made visible.   In Love Made Visible.   May Swenson.   NAMCP V.2

In Love For Long.   Edwin Muir.   MoBrPo

In Love In Vain.   Leo Robin.   ReLy

In Love Made Visible.   May Swenson.   NAMCP V.2

In love with mountains, I go out my gate.   Evening View from Grass Hill.   Gensei.   WoPoe, tr. by Burton Watson

In Love with You.   Kenneth Koch.   PoDa

In love's name, Your emissary. (LL)   Gift, The.   Louise Glück.   CFP; TaR

In loving thee thou know'st I am forsworn.   William Shakespeare.   HeIP-4 Fr. Sonnets.

In lurid cartoon colors, the big baby.   Eden.   Emily Grosholz.   FFC; RA

In Manchester today a man was seen.   Here is the News.   Michael Rosen.   OBSP

In many a village churchyard's simple grave.   Obscurity of Woman's Worth.   Caroline Elizabeth Norton.   VWP

In March begin to think.   In March.   John Engels.   PfSP

In March I dreamed of mud.   From the Journals of the Frog Prince.   Susan Mitchell.   PtR

In martial sports I had my cunning tried.   Sir Philip Sidney.   NAEL-6v1; NAEL-7v1; NoSic Fr. Astrophil and Stella.

In mass graves the bodies of plants.   Mikhail Grobman.   TCRusP, tr. by John Glad

In math I was the whiz kid, keeper.   Flash Cards.   Rita Dove.   ESEAA; LoL; PoPoPo

In matter's smallest.   Pamela Alexander.   AmAlph Fr. Foxlight.

In May.   John Millington Synge.   MoBrPo

In May my heart was breaking.   Autumn Valentine.   Dorothy Parker.   IJHIL

In May of nineteen-hundred forty-two.   Fathering the Map.   Robert Pack.   PfSP

In May, when sea-winds pierced our solitudes.   Rhodora, The [On Being Asked Whence Is the Flower].   Ralph Waldo Emerson.   AmFaPo; APN-1; ITBLP; NAAL-3; NAAL-5; NAAPv.1; NoP-4; NoP-5; OxBoAm; TCAPo; TFi

In Mayo.   Michael Longley.   IrLP

In May's gaud gown and ruby reckoning.   May.   Karen Volkman.   LegDan

In McDonalds, a light-skin boy is crying.   Mother's Day at McDonald's.   Patricia Elam.   BtF

In McNeil Island Prison for bad checks, my father worked to pay off his debts.   Father and Farther.   Sherman Alexie.   AmPoNex

In me a moonscape of organs.   Scan.   Gillian Ferguson.   NeBl

In me is a little painted square.   Old Age.   Maxwell Bodenheim.   TaR

In Me, Past, Present, Future Meet.   Siegfried Sassoon.   OBEV

In me something glimpsed its occasion.   Passing Through.   Patrick Williams.   PNI

In me the sleeping wound of stupor. (LL)   This time I won't permit the blue.   Patrizia Cavalli.   Nelt; VCWP, tr. by Judith Baumel

In me, the sound something numb come alive makes. (LL)   Purr, The.   Molly Peacock.   ExTi; PasH

In me (the worm) clearly.   "H. D."   APT-1; NAMCP V.1 Fr. Walls Do Not Fall, The.

In me they dump their cans, their toilet paper.   River's Answer, The.   Ben Howard.   PoCoUp

In Memoriam: "If it's over, let it be over."   Jean Bleakney.   NIrP

In memoriam. (LL)   Robin Blaser.   NLPA; PFTM-2 Fr. Image-Nation.

In Memoriam.   W. J. Gruffydd.   OBWVE, tr. by R. Gerallt Jones

In Memoriam.   Martin Johnston.   BMAP; NOBAu

In Memoriam.   Michael Longley.   ModIr; PNI

In Memoriam: "On this coast where they once arrived destined."   Samuel Maio.   CalPo

In Memoriam ("Aprendí / la interminable lista.")   Manuel Vázquez Montalbán.   RaW

In Memoriam ("I learned / the interminable list.")   Manuel Vázquez Montalbán.   RaW, tr. by Robert Mezey

In Memoriam.   M. R. Peacocke.   NLP

In Memoriam.   Léopold Sédar Senghor.   PoetW, tr. by Melvin Dixon

In Memoriam (2): "Young priest, dead suddenly, A."   Daniel Berrigan.   UpMys

In Memoriam: "His name was / Mohammed Sceab."   Giuseppe Ungaretti.   PoCho

In Memoriam A. H. H.   Alfred Tennyson.

"Again at Christmas did we weave."   NAEL-6v2; NAEL-7v2; NAWM-7v2

"And all is well, though [or tho'] faith and form."   NAEL-6v2; NAEL-7v2

"And was the day of my delight."   NAEL-6v2; NAEL-7v2

"Be near me when my light is low."   BrAP; CABP; HeIP-4; NAEL-7v2; NAWM-7v2; NoP-5; WaAnP

"By night we lingered [or linger'd] on the lawn."   NAEL-6v2; NAEL-7v2; NAWM-7v2; NoP-5; WaAnP

"Calm is the morn without a sound."   BrAP; HeIP-4; NAEL-6v2; NAEL-7v2; NAWM-7v2; NoP-5; NPeEn; OxBEV; WaAnP

"Contemplate all this work of Time."   BrAP; NAEL-6v2; NAEL-7v2; NAWM-7v2

"Danube to the Severn gave, The."   NAEL-6v2; NAEL-7v2; NAWM-7v2; NoP-5

"Dark house, by which once more I stand."   BrAP; HeIP-4; InoFa; NAEL-6v2; NAEL-7v2; NAWM-7v2; NoP-5; NPeEn; OxBEV; SoSe-8; WaAnP

"Dear friend, far off, my lost desire."   CAGL; NAEL-6v2; NAEL-7v2

"Dip down upon the northern shore."   NAEL-6v2; NAEL-7v2; WaAnP

"Doors, where my heart was used to beat."   NAEL-6v2; NAEL-7v2; NoP-5

"Dost thou look back on what hath been."   NAEL-6v2; NAEL-7v2

Epilogue.
  "And rise, O moon, from yonder down."   NAEL-6v2; NAEL-7v2
  "Today the grave is bright for me."   NAWM-7v2

"Fair ship, that from the Italian shore."   CAGL; NAEL-6v2; NAEL-7v2

"Happy lover who has come, A."   InoFa; NAEL-6v2; NAEL-7v2

"Heart-affluence in discursive talk."   NAEL-6v2; NAEL-7v2

"How pure at heart and sound in head."   NAEL-6v2; NAEL-7v2

"I cannot see the features right."   NAEL-6v2; NAEL-7v2; WaAnP

"I envy not in any moods."   BrAP; CABP; CAGL; NAEL-6v2; NAEL-7v2; NAWM-7v2
  "I hold it true, whate're befall."   UV

"I hear the noise about thy keel."   NAEL-6v2; NAEL-7v2; NAWM-7v2

"I held it truth, with him who sings."   BrAP; CAGL; HeIP-4; NAEL-6v2; NAEL-7v2; NAWM-7v2; NoP-5

"I know that this was Life—the track."   CAGL; NAEL-6v2; NAEL-7v2

"I leave thy praises unexpressed."   NAEL-6v2; NAEL-7v2

"I passed beside the reverend walls."   NAEL-6v2; NAEL-7v2

"I shall not see thee. Dare I say."   NAEL-6v2; NAEL-7v2

"I sing to him that rests below."   NAEL-6v2; NAEL-7v2; NAWM-7v2

"I sometimes hold it half a sin."   CAGL; NAEL-6v2; NAEL-7v2; NAWM-7v2

"I trust I have not wasted breath."   NAEL-6v2; NAEL-7v2

"I wage not any feud with Death."   NAEL-6v2; NAEL-7v2

"I will not shut me from my kind."   CABP; NAEL-6v2; NAEL-7v2

"If one should bring me this report."   NAEL-6v2; NAEL-7v2

"In those sad words I took farewell."   NAEL-6v2; NAEL-7v2

"It is the day when he was born."   NAEL-6v2; NAEL-7v2

"Lo, as a dove when up she springs."   NAEL-6v2; NAEL-7v2

"Love is and was my Lord and King."   CAGL; NAEL-6v2; NAEL-7v2; OBEV

"My own dim life should teach me this."   NAEL-6v2; NAEL-7v2

"Now fades the last long streak of snow."   NAEL-6v2; NAEL-7v2; NPeEn; WaAnP

"Now, sometimes in my sorrow shut."   CAGL; NAEL-6v2; NAEL-7v2; NAWM-7v2

"O living will that shalt endure."   NAEL-6v2; NAEL-7v2

"O Sorrow, cruel fellowship."   NAEL-6v2; NAEL-7v2; NAWM-7v2

"O Sorrow, wilt thou live with me."   NAEL-6v2; NAEL-7v2

"O[h], yet we trust that somehow good."   BrAP; CABP; ItP; NAEL-6v2; NAEL-7v2; NoP-5; WaAnP

"Old warder of these buried bones."   NAEL-6v2; NAEL-7v2

"Old yew, which graspest at the stones."   NAEL-6v2; NAEL-7v2; NAWM-7v2; NoP-5; NPeEn; WaAnP

"On that last night before we went."   NAEL-6v2; NAEL-7v2

"One writes, that "Other friends remain.""   NAEL-6v2; NAEL-7v2

"Path by which we twain did go, The."   CAGL; NAEL-6v2; NAEL-7v2; NAWM-7v2

"Peace; come away: the song of woe."   NAEL-6v2; NAEL-7v2

"Ring out, wild bells, to the wild sky."   BrAP; ChrPo; CtM; NAEL-6v2; NAEL-7v2; NAWM-7v2; OxAEP-2; RSR; TreFP

"Risest thou thus, dim dawn, again."   NAEL-6v2; NAEL-7v2

"Risest thou thus, dim dawn, again."   NAEL-6v2; NAEL-7v2

"Sad Hesper o'er the buried sun."   NAEL-6v2; NAEL-7v2; NoP-5

"Sleep, kinsman thou to death and trance."   NAEL-6v2; NAEL-7v2

"So careful of the type? but no."   BrAP; NAEL-6v2; NAEL-7v2; NAWM-7v2; NoP-5; NPeEn; WaAnP

"Still onward winds the dreary way."   NAEL-6v2; NAEL-7v2

"Strong Son of God, immortal Love."   NAEL-6v2; NAEL-7v2; NAWM-7v2; SacPr

"Sweet after showers, ambrosial air."   NAEL-6v2; NAEL-7v2

"Tears of the widower, when he sees."   CAGL; NAEL-6v2; NAEL-7v2

"That each, who seems a separate whole."   NAEL-6v2; NAEL-7v2

"That which we dare invoke to bless."   CABP; NAEL-6v2; NAEL-7v2; NAWM-7v2
  "That which we dare invoke to bless."   SacPr

"There rolls the deep where grew the tree."   NAEL-6v2; NAEL-7v2; WaAnP

"Thy spirit ere our fatal loss."   CAGL

"Thy voice is on the rolling air."   CAGL; HeIP-4; NAEL-6v2; NAEL-7v2; NoP-5

"Time draws near the birth of Christ, The."   NAEL-6v2; NAEL-7v2; NAWM-7v2; RSR; SoSe-8

"Time draws near the birth of Christ, The."   ChrPo; NAEL-6v2; NAEL-7v2

"To Sleep I give my powers away."   CtM; NAEL-6v2; NAEL-7v2

"Tonight the winds begin to rise."   NAEL-6v2; NAEL-7v2; NAWM-7v2

"Tonight ungathered let us leave."   ChrPo; NAEL-6v2; NAEL-7v2

"Unwatched, the garden bough shall sway."   OBGa

"We leave the well-beloved place."   TreFP

"What words are these have fallen from me?"   NAWM-7v2

"When I contemplate all alone."   NAEL-6v2; NAEL-7v2

"When on my bed the moonlight falls."   InoFa; NAEL-6v2; NAEL-7v2; NoP-5

"When rosy plumelets tuft the larch."   NAEL-6v2; NAEL-7v2

"Wild bird, whose warble, liquid sweet."   NAEL-6v2; NAEL-7v2; NoP-5

"Wish, that of the living whole, The."   BrAP; NAEL-6v2; NAEL-7v2; NAWM-7v2; NoP-5; SacPr; WaAnP

"Witch-elms that counterchange the floor."   NAEL-6v2; NAEL-7v2; OBGa

"With such compelling cause to grieve."   NAEL-6v2; NAEL-7v2

"With trembling fingers did we weave."   NAEL-6v2; NAEL-7v2

"Yet if some voice that man could trust."   NAEL-6v2; NAEL-7v2

"You say, but with no touch of scorn."   NAEL-6v2; NAEL-7v2

In Memoriam Akbar Babool.   Wopko Jensma.   TSAP

In Memoriam. Alphonse Campbell Fordham.   Mary Weston Fordham.   CBWP-2

In Memoriam Ben Zwane.   Wopko Jensma.   TSAP

In Memoriam Charles Reznikoff.   George Oppen.   APT-2

In Memoriam: Dedicated to My Father.   Wang Xiaolong.   PML, *tr. by* Michelle Yeh

In Memoriam Dylan Thomas.   Hugh MacDiarmid.   BrAP *Fr.* World of Words, The.

In Memoriam (Easter, 1915).   Edward Thomas.   NoP-4; NoP-5; OBWP; OBWVE; PoAgWa; Spl

In Memoriam Francis Ledwidge.   Seamus Heaney.   NAMCP V.2; NoAM

In Memoriam Frederick Douglass.   Eloise Bibb.   CBWP-4

In Memoriam Frederick Douglass.   Henrietta Cordelia Ray.   CBWP-3

In Memoriam Gyula Juhász.   Sándor Weöres.   IQMS, *tr. by* Edwin Morgan

In Memoriam James Joyce.   Hugh MacDiarmid.
  "We must look at the harebell as if."   BrAP; NAEL-6v2; NAEL-7v2; NoP-4; NoP-5

In Memoriam John Coltrane.   Michael Stillman.   CalPo

In Memoriam Krishna Menon.   E. J. Thribb.   OBCoV

In Memoriam Larry Parnes ("Mr Parnes Shillings and Pence").   E. J. Thribb.   OBCoV

In Memoriam Mae Noblitt.   A. R. Ammons.   ItP

In Memoriam of E. B. Clark.   Lizelia Augusta Jenkins Moorer.   CBWP-3

In Memoriam Paul Celan.   Edward Hirsch.   MakPoe

In Memoriam Paul Laurence Dunbar.   Henrietta Cordelia Ray.   CBWP-3

In Memoriam, Private D. Sutherland.   Ewart Alan Mackintosh.   PoWW

In Memoriam Salvador Dali.   E. J. Thribb.   OBCoV

In Memoriam. Susan Eugenia Bennett.   Mary Weston Fordham.   CBWP-2

In Memorium: Robert Hayden.   Norman J. Loftis.   SpirFl

In Memory.   Bei Dao.   WoBe, *tr. by* Iona Man-Cheong and Eliot Weinberger

In Memory.   Tony Lopez.   VaPo

In Memory of a Black Union Leader.   Aimé Césaire.   VCWP

In Memory of a Poet.   Olga Sedakova.   CRWP, *tr. by* Robert Reid

In Memory of Arthur Clement Williams.   Eloise Bibb.   CBWP-4

In Memory of Basil, Marquess of Dufferin and Ava.   Sir John Betjeman.   OBWP

In Memory of Bryan Lathrop.   Edgar Lee Masters.   PoA 2002

In Memory of Colonel Charles Young.   Countee Cullen.   WaAnP

In Memory of Eva Gore-Booth and Con Markievicz.   William Butler Yeats.   GPTC; NAMCP V.1; NoAM; NPeEn; OBMV

In Memory of Gerard Dillon.   Michael Longley.   PBCIP

In Memory of H. F.   Peter Klappert.   YaYoPo

In memory of Harriet Tubman.   Harriet Tubman.   *Unknown.*   HHAm

In Memory of His Father.   Publius Papinius Statius.   RomPo *Fr.* Sylvae [*or* Silvae].

In Memory of Ho Chi-chen.   Li Po.   CrYelRi, *tr. by* Sam Hamill

In Memory of Idris Davies.   John Tripp.   AngWePo

In Memory of James M. Rathel.   Josephine D. Henderson Heard.   CBWP-4

In Memory of Jane Fraser [*or* Frazer].   Geoffrey Hill.   NAEL-6v2; NAEL-7v2; NAMCP V.2; NIL-7; NoAM; UpMys

In Memory of John Keats.   Yury Mikhailovich Kublanovsky.   TCRusP

In Memory of Joseph Brodsky.   Mark Strand.   WaAnP

In Memory of Kathleen.   Kenneth Patchen.   MoAmPo

In Memory of M. B. Anna Andreyevna Akhmatova. PoetW, *tr.* by Max Hayward and Stanley Kunitz

In Memory of Major Robert Gregory. William Butler Yeats. IrV; NAEL-6v2; NAEL-7v2; NAMCP V.1; WaAnP

In Memory of Music. William Wordsworth. DiBP

In Memory of My Dear Grandchild Anne Bradstreet Who Deceased June 20, 1669, Being Three Years and Seven Months Old. Anne Bradstreet. InoFa; NAAL-3

In Memory of My Dear Grandchild Elizabeth Bradstreet Who Deceased August, 1665, Being a Year and Half Old. Anne Bradstreet. BASC; ColAP; NAAL-3; NAAL-5; NAAPv.1

In Memory of My Feelings. Frank O'Hara. APSN; ColAP; HarvBoo

In Memory of My Friend the Bassoonist John Lenox. Donald Justice. BodElec

In Memory of My Mother. Patrick Kavanagh. NAMCP V.1; NoAM; RaBo

In Memory of My Mother. Cathal McCabe. NIrP

In Memory of Radio. Imamu Amiri Baraka. BB; NoP-4; NoP-5; RWPCtW

In Memory of Robert Frost. William Meredith. VisFro

In Memory of Sigmund Freud. W. H. Auden. NAMCP V.1; NoAM; OxBoAm

In Memory of Sir Hiram Maxim (1840–1916). Hans Magnus Enzensberger. GTCP, *tr.* by Reinhold Grimm

In Memory of Stevie Smith. Patricia Beer. MoWP

In Memory of the Boys of Dexter, Kentucky. Joe Bolton. AmPoNex

In Memory of the Funeral Horses. Zoltán Jékely. IQMS, *tr.* by Geroge Gömöri and Adam Makkai

In Memory of the Unknown Poet, Robert Boardman Vaughn. Donald Justice. CAP-8; NAMCP V.2; NoAM; WaAnP

In Memory of the Utah Stars. William Matthews. CAP-8; MoASP

In Memory of the Vertuous and Learned Lady Madre de Teresa That Sought an Early Martyrdome. Richard Crashaw.

"Love thou art absolute, sole Lord." SacPr

In Memory of W. B. Yeats. W. H. Auden. AmFaPo; BrAP; CABP; GPTC; HeIP-4; MakPoe; MoBrPo; NAEL-6v2; NAEL-7v2; NAMCP V.1; NIL-7; NoAM; NoP-4; NoP-5; NPeEn; OxAEP-2; OxBoAm; TFi; TRP; WaAnP; WeW-3

In Memory of William Carlos Williams. Hans Magnus Enzensberger. GTCP, *tr.* by Reinhold Grimm and Felix Pollak

In Memory: The Miami Showband—Massacred 31 July 1975. Paul Durcan. BeAl

In Memory We Are Walking. Maria Gillan. UnSA

In memory where sleep is perfect. Proscenium Moon. Dave Brinks. AnSo

In Mem'ry's fairest court a shrine is set. To Laura. Henrietta Cordelia Ray. CBWP-3

In Mexico. Mariposa. Rigoberto González. BeDoSh

In Mexico? (LL) I Am Not a Conspiracy Everything Is Not Paranoid the Drug Enforcement Administration Is Not Everywhere. Susan Musgrave. NIL-7; NoAM

In Mexico, I met myself one day. El Día de los Muertos. Rafael Campo. RA

In Mexico I'll finish the novel I'll write. In Answer to a Question From P. W. Lew Welch. BB

In midair, he hesitates at the moment. From Rooftops, Kenji Takezo Throws Himself. Rick Noguchi. NeAmPo

In Millais' painting, Ophelia dies face up. Bellocq's Ophelia. Natasha Trethewey. FuFl; NeAmPo

(In Millais's painting, Ophelia dies faceup.) RD

In Minako Wada's House. Brad Leithauser. NoP-4; NoP-5

In Mind. Denise Levertov. NAAL-5; NALW

In mine ladye's chaumber. (LL) *Unknown. See* In my lady's chamber.

In mining Wales at Aberfan. Aberfan. Kirkpatrick Dobie. EdScPo

In Mississippi. Stanley Crouch. GT

In Modern Dress. Craig Raine. NoAM

In mole-blue indolence the sun. Jungle, The. Alun Lewis. AngWePo; OBWVE

In moments of anguish. Old Wharf Canto. Jared Angira. NAfrP

In Moncur Street. Dorothy Hewett. NOBAu

In Monet's landscape, this woman fades away. Portraits of the Ladies. Elizabeth Crowell. PfS

In Montana, claws skim through the dawn. Experts at Veneers. Kenward Elmslie. NYP2

In Moonlight, Somewhere, They Are Singing. Robert Penn Warren. LPSFW

Fr. Some Quiet, Plain Poems.

In Morfudd's Arms. Dafydd ap Gwilym. OBWVE, *tr.* by Rolfe Humphries

In morning light my damson show'd [*or* showed]. Plum Tree by the House, The. Oliver St. John Gogarty. OBEV

In Mournful Praise and Memory of the French Song. Jaime Gil de Biedma. RaW, *tr.* by Timothy Baland

In Mourning for His Dead Wife. P'an Yüeh. CCL1, *tr.* by Kenneth Rexroth

In mourning wise since daily I increase. Sir Thomas Wyatt. NoSic

In moving-slow he has no Peer. Sloth, The. Theodore Roethke. ChAP; ItP; TRP

In Mr. Turner's Fields. Sam Cornish. OxAAAP

In mud. Eating what is here. Fish, bread, tea, rice. (LL) Fish Tea Rice. Linda Gregg. BeAl; ExTi

In Muddy Waters. Larry Smith. AmZen

In Murasaki's time. Tale of Genji. Hugh Seidman. YaYoPo

In musty light, in the thin brown air. In the Basement of the Goodwill Store. Ted Kooser. OPRER

In my begging bowl. Ryokan. WoPoe, *tr.* by Burton Watson

In my beginning is my end. In succession. T. S. Eliot. *Fr.* Four Quartets.

In my book of sacral nomenclature. Roy Kiyooka. NLPA *Fr.* Pear Tree Pomes.

In my broken heart's disdain! (LL) Runaway Slave at Pilgrim's Point, The. Elizabeth Barrett Browning. NALW; ViWPN; VWP

In my calling. Saitō Mokichi. CAoMJL1, *tr.* by Amy Vladek Heinrich

In my chest a cave. Last Bullet, The. Nidaa Khoury. PoArWo, *tr.* by Roger Tavor and Linda Zisquit

In my childhood trees were green. Autobiography. Louis MacNeice. ModIr; NPeEn; PNI

In my country. Jackie Kay. MFPA; NeBl; NeBrP; StAl

In my country. Result of an Observation. Lenous Surprice. OGAHCP, *tr.* by Boadiba and Jack Hirschman

In My Craft or Sullen Art. Dylan Thomas. AmFaPo; BrAP; HeIP-4; NAMCP V.2; NIL-7; NIP-4; NoAM; NoP-4; NoP-5; OPOU; PoPoPo; RaBo; TCAWP; WaAnP; WeW-3; WoPoe

In my criminal stage I fell in love with Bert. Blow, Blow, Thou Winter Wind. Peter Meinke. IaFF

In my dark cell, low prostrate on the ground. Abelard to Eloisa. Judith Madan. RACG

In my day-break dream. Roy Kiyooka. NLPA *Fr.* Pear Tree Pomes.

In My Days. Giovanna Pollarolo. TANSG, *tr.* by Marjorie Agosin

In my days it seems like a dream, like fiction. In My Days. Giovanna Pollarolo. TANSG, *tr.* by Marjorie Agosin

In my declining years, in a land beyond the ocean. Joseph Brodsky. TCRusP *Fr.* Sonnets on the Statue of Mary, Queen of Scots, in the Luxembourg Gardens, Paris.

In My Dream. A. V. Christie. AmPoNex

In my dream. Author of the Jesus Papers Speaks, The. Anne Sexton. PFTM-2

In my dream, children. Jerusalem. Adrienne Rich. TaR

In my dream dark wings. Bird of Death. Sharon Olinka. TWW

In my dream I take. Kemo Sabe. Diane Glancy. LTA

In my dream, my car is an aquarium. Wish. William Heyen. PfSP

In my dream of the hydroplane. Sailing to Bien Hoa. Bruce Weigl. MotU

In my dream Pinocchio is six feet tall. Here, I Say. Joanna Fuhrman. AmPoNex

In my dream, sweaters are referred to as "vulvas." Vulva Operetta. Jessica Tarahata Hagedorn. ReBoTo

In my dream you are a mendicant. Dream of a Trophy. Ingrid de Kok. TSAP

In my dreams a strange sun, a leaf in an autumn. Sun of Death. José Luis Hidalgo. RaW, *tr.* by Hardie St. Martin

In my dreams you walk dripping from a sea-journey on the highway across America in tears to the door of my cottage in the Western night. (LL) Howl. Allen Ginsberg. HarvBoo; NAAL-5; NAMCP V.2

In my dry cell. Riven Quarry, The. Gloria C. Oden. GT

In my enormous city it is—night. Marina Ivanovna Tsvetayeva. OxBEV *Fr.* Insomnia.

In my eye I've no apple; every object. Instrument and Agent. Norman Alexander MacCaig. NePenScot

In my eyes he matches the gods, that man who. Sappho. ASA; PoCho, *tr.* by Jim Powell

In my family. People in My Family. Grace Paley. TaR

In my family, decisions are made by the lama. Autonomy of the Mind. Tsering Wangno Dhompa. WANABP

In my fantasy I am the leader. Leader of the Pack, The. Gerald Locklin. SUP

In My Father's House. George Barlow. ESEAA; OxAAAP

In my father's house. My Father's House. Narlan Matos-Teixera. PML, *tr.* by the author and Al Zolynas

In my father's house are many cobwebs. Portrait of the Artist as an Old Man. Michael Dransfield. BMAP

In my father's house when dusk had fallen. In My Father's House. Samuel Allen. OxAAAP

In my 56th year. Tinnitus. Karen McCosker. NevBe

In my first dream the world appeared. Seven Ages, The. Louise Glück. PoCho

In my first thirty years of life [*after* Han-shan]. Back at Cold Mountain. Han-shan (Cold Mountain). BB; CCL1; NDACCP, *tr. by* Gary Snyder

In my garden, the leaves that float in the air. Leaves. Abd al-Karim Kassid. IrPoTo, *tr. by* Chuck Miller and Saadi A. Simawe

In my grandfather's house. And He Wept Aloud, So That the Egyptians Heard It. Alden Nowlan. Coast

In my grandmother's house there was always chicken soup. Story About Chicken Soup, A. Louis Simpson. PoWW; UnSA

In my great loneliness. "Rachel." FIT, *tr. by* Robert Friend

In my hand. (LL) Eve. Dorothy Livesay. ItWoWo; NALW

In my hands your. Praise. Anne K. Smith. PasH

In my hidden house. Issa. SoOfWa, *tr. by* Sam Hamill

In my home town we called them the loonies. Touched. Elizabeth Dodd. AmPoNex

In my hometown, there is rust. Elders Are Gods, The. Tijan M. Sallah. BRtP; NAfrP

In my hospital dream. Dreaming My Dad. John Hegley. PoCu

In my house at the edge of the lake. Islands. Vona Groarke. NIrP

In my house / Mice and fireflies. Issa. ZenPo, *tr. by* Takashi Ikemoto and Lucien Stryk

In my house we had an elephant named Italy. Autobiography. Robert Viscusi. UnSA

In My Idleness. Lady Izumi. WoPoe, *tr. by* Steven D. Carter

In My Labyrinth (The Minotaur's Game). Carlota Caulfield. TANSG, *tr. by* Chris Allen

In my lady's chamber. (LL) I Have a Gentle Cock [*or* Gentil Cok]. *Unknown.* NoP-4; NoP-5; OPOU; WaAnP

  (In mine ladye's chaumber.) (LL) EroLit; OBCoV

In my land there are no distinctions. Poem for the Young White Man Who Asked Me How I, An Intelligent, Well-Read Person Could Believe in the War Between Races. Lorna Dee Cervantes. FTtHH; PBCAP; PoPoPo

In my left pocket a Chickasaw hand. Truth Is, The. Linda Hogan. HATNAP; ItWoWo; LTA

In My Leisure. Chungji. BecRai, *tr. by* Kim Daljin, Kim Won-Chung and Christopher Merrill

In my leisure, I open the door and sit in the wind. To a Monk Asking About Zen. Chimi Sucho. BecRai, *tr. by* Kim Daljin, Kim Won-Chung and Christopher Merrill

In my lonely house, I'm drunk with passion again. (LL) One Night. Constantine P. Cavafy. CAGL; EroLit, *tr. by* Edmund Keeley and Philip Sherrard

In my medicine cabinet. Jack Kerouac. WhBo

. . . In my melodious city cupolas burn. Marina Ivanovna Tsvetayeva. AF *Fr.* Cycle Akhmatova, The.

In my mind's eye fields be burning bloody rags. 1691. Tituba of Salem. Gale Jackson. BtF

In my mother's house I had many homes. In My Mother's House. Elin ap Hywel. ATSWP, *tr. by* Robert Minhinnick

In my mother's house there are many mansions. In My Mother's House. Elin ap Hywel. BBMWP, *tr. by the author*

In My Mother's Room [*(for Vanessa)*]. Colleen J. McElroy. GT

In my mouth I taste sacrilege. Salomé. Silvia Grénier. SurWo, *tr. by* Natalie Kenvin

In my movie it would all spring from the mind of some Futurist. On Speed, or How We Murdered Nostalgia. James Stewart. ICANM

In my movie the boat goes under. Sailor, The. Geof Hewitt. GoPo

In my native province when I was young. From the Tibetan. John Hewitt. PNI

In my neighborhood I saw two swans take a taxi. Swans' Book, The. Víctor Hernández Cruz. PueRic

In my office, where you sat years ago and talked. Elegy for John, My Student Dead of AIDS. Robert Cording. PoA 2002

In My Other Life. Shara McCallum. AmPoNex

In My Own Album. Charles Lamb. NPBRoP

  (Verses for an Album.) NOBRP

In my Park Avenue penthouse. Little Girl from Little Rock. Leo Robin. ReLy

In my quiet grass hut. Kim Sujang. CATKP, *tr. by* Peter H. Lee

In my remote springtime. (LL) Far Away and Long Ago. Rubén Darío. PFTM-1; SpanPo, *tr. by* Denise Levertov

In my room. Father's Poem, A. Sarah Arsone. WhBo

In my room, on the whitewashed wall. Fishing-Tackle, The. Bertolt Brecht. PoSu, *tr. by* Lee Baxendall

In my rose-wet cave—whatever happens, this is. (LL) Adrienne Rich. EroLit; NALW; NoAM; WaAnP *Fr.* Twenty-one Love Poems.

In my season as red as the red-breasted. Reality of Autumn, The. Duane Niatum. HATNAP

In my shadow world, no one. Adulterer, The. Scott Cairns. UpMys

In my sixty-eighth year drought stopped the song of the rivers. Judith Wright. HarvBoo *Fr.* Shadow of Fire: Ghazals, The.

In my sleep I return here. I who live here, it is I. Karen Press. TSAP

In my sleep I saw. Three Ruba'iyat. Abdul Wahab Al-Bayati. IrPoTo, *tr. by* Carolina Hotchandani and Najat Rahman

In my sleep I was fain of their fellowship, fain. Sidney Lanier. TCAPo *Fr.* Hymns of the Marshes.

In my sleeve the colored ball worth a thousand in gold. Ryokan. EMJL, *tr. by* Burton Watson

In my solitude. Antonio Machado Ruiz. WED *Fr.* Moral Proverbs and Folk Songs.

In my solitude, you'll haunt me. Solitude. Eddie DeLange and Irving Mills. ReLy

In my story the sisters forecast bad weather. Resurrection. Nicole Cooley. Vesp

In my sweet and sad song. Mary Stuart, Queen of Scots. EMWP

In My Thirtieth Year. Archibald MacLeish. MoAmPo

In my two hands. Poem for You, A. Paul Laraque. BRtP

In My View. Tukaram. WoPoe, *tr. by* Dilip Chitre

In my wicker basket. (LL) Wicker Basket, A. Robert Creeley. NAMCP V.2; NoAM

In my young days I never. To an Old Tune. Hsin Ch'i-chi. NDACCP, *tr. by* Kenneth Rexroth

In My Youth. Juan Chi. CCL1, *tr. by* Michael Bullock and C. J. Chen

In my youth I lived for a time in the house of some aunts. Tunnel, The. Nicanor Parra. GPTC; TCLAP, *tr. by* W. S. Merwin

In my youth I used to write songs. Burning My Manuscripts. Yi Kyubo. CATKP, *tr. by* Kevin O'Rourke

In my youth's summer I did sing of One. Lord Byron. NOBRP *Fr.* Childe Harold's Pilgrimage.

In nameless warmth, sun light in every corner. Edgar Bowers. VCAP *Fr.* Autumn Shade.

In narrow room nature's whole wealth, yea more. John Milton. NOSC; WaAnP *Fr.* Paradise Lost.

In narrowest girdle, O reluctant Muse. After-Dinner Poem (Terpsichore), An. Oliver Wendell Holmes. TCAPo

In nature apt to like when I did see. Sir Philip Sidney. NAEL-6v1; NAEL-7v1 *Fr.* Astrophil and Stella.

In nature there are only two kinds of beings. Theory of Fractals. Gustavo V. Segade. RMCMP

In Nature's pieces still I see. Divine Mistress, A. Thomas Carew. CavPo

In New Jersey Once. Maria Gillan. InvLad

In New Jersey once, marigolds grew wild. In New Jersey Once. Maria Gillan. InvLad

In new romance with blackness. Again the Summoning. Lawrence S. Cumberbatch. EGAG

In New York. Dennis Cooper. ReTh *Fr.* Some Adventures of John Kennedy Jr.

In / New York. My Father's Girlfriend. E. Ethelbert Miller. SpirFl

In New York they have banned smoking. Afternoon Train. Afaa Michael Weaver. BRtP

In Nick Ray's "Bigger Than Life." 1956. Maxine Scates. PBCAP

In Night when colours all to blacke are cast. Fulke, 1st Baron Brooke Greville. NAEL-7v1; NPeEn *Fr.* Caelica.

In 1915 my grandfather's. Grandfather. Michael S. Harper. ESEAA; VCAP; WaAnP

In nineteen hundred they preferred. Upper Family. Maxwell Bodenheim. AmWit

In 1935 Hitler said / "The Third Reich." Distances. Otto René Castillo. AF, *tr. by* Margaret Randall

In 1935, the year I was born. Chinese Journal. Charles Wright. NoP-5

In 1937, Robert Johnson. Man Who Beat Hemingway, The. Martín Espada. MoASP

In 1936. Reforma Agraria. Ian Duhig. ModIr

In No Strange Land. Francis Thompson. *See* Kingdom of God, The.

In no wise is the pillar-of-fire. "H. D." WPoS *Fr.* Walls Do Not Fall, The.

In Nomine. Catherine Imbriglio. IAoNAP

In northern climes there liv'd a chief of fame. Otagamiad. Jane Johnston Schoolcraft. SWaP

In November: "Hills and leafless forests slowly yield, The." Archibald Lampman. NIL-7

In number, weight, and measure, needs not rhyme [*or* rhime]. (LL) On Mr Milton's "Paradise Lost." Andrew Marvell. BASC; CABP; FSCP; NOSC

In Numbers, and but these few. Ode on the Birth of Our Saviour, An. Robert Herrick. ChrPo

In Nunhead Cemetery. Charlotte Mew. NoP-4; NoP-5

In Oak. Marianne Bluger. IFF

In Obitum Ben Johnson Poetae Eximii. Mildmay Fane, 2d Earl of Westmorland. NOSC

In Ocean's wide domains. Witnesses, The. Henry Wadsworth Longfellow. PCW

In October. Claire Malroux. VCWP, *tr.* by Marilyn Hacker

In October marching, taking the sweet air. Towards Lillers. Ivor Gurney. NAEL-6v2; NoP-4

In October of the year. Ox Cart Man. Donald Hall. GoPo; IPoFL; LoL

In o'er-strict calyx lingering. To Beethoven. Sidney Lanier. NCAP

In Ojinaga-across-the-river. West Texas Rain Journal. Candice Favilla. ExTi

In Oklahoma. Toni Asante Lightfoot. BtF

In Oklahoma, / Bonnie and Josie. Life Is Motion. Wallace Stevens. SAmP

In old Barcelona I met sweet Romona. I Wonder Why She Kept on Saying "Si-Si-Si-Si-Senor." Sam M. Lewis and Joe Young. ReLy

In old Savannah. Hard-Hearted Hannah (The Vamp of Savannah). Charles Bates, Bob Bigelow and Jack Yellen. ReLy

In old stories the jungle was busy. Sun-Hunters, The. Mark O'Connor. NOBAu

In one image of the camps, the snow sifts down. Failure of Similes, The. Richard Foerster. PoA 2002

In one late dart. Late Flight of The Love God. Mona Van Duyn. ExTi

In one night. Reply to Suzan Osho's Snow Poem. Muso Soseki. EaWin, *tr.* by W. S. Merwin

In one of its cornices are the two boots of a man. 8 Little Theatres of the Cornices. Erin Mouré. BAP-04

In one of my travels. Empty City, An. Mahmoud al-Braikan. IrPoTo, *tr.* by Ralph Saverese and Saadi A. Simawe

In one of these excursions, travelling then. William Wordsworth. OxAEP-2 *Fr.* Prelude, The; Growth of a Poet's Mind [1805 version].

In one of those excursions (may they ne'er). William Wordsworth. NAEL-6v2; NAEL-7v2 *Fr.* Prelude, The; Growth of a Poet's Mind [1850 version].

In one of your earliest letters, the one you wrote in response to. Nathaniel Mackey. FTOS *Fr.* Song of the Andoumboulou.

In one version of the legend the sirens couldn't sing. Envy of Other People's Poems. Robert Hass. RoV

In order that this reality exist you must stretch a yellow vault over the black. Toscanità. Dino Campana. MotU, *tr.* by Charles Wright

In order to blow what it's like being born. (LL) Lester Leaps In. Al Young. ESEAA; SeSe

In order to play one needs magic and Rousseau and must remember play. Magic (or Rousseau). Carla Harryman. FTOS

In order to reach you. Reencounter with the Goddess. Olga Nolla. TANSG, *tr.* by Paula Simawe

In order to revitalize the roaring of phosphenes. In Order to Speak. Aimé Césaire. VCWP

In Order to Speak. Aimé Césaire. VCWP

In order to understand how Mary was at that. Rainer Maria Rilke. WED *Fr.* Life of the Virgin Mary, The.

In other days. (LL) Fare Well. Walter De la Mare. NoP-4; NoP-5; OBEV; OxBEV

In other days, I was poor enough to suit. Cold Mountain Poem No. 158. Han-shan (Cold Mountain). WoPoe, *tr.* by E. Bruce Brooks

In other years I watched the sky for birds. Waiting for the Invasion. Barbara Kingsolver. AtGh

In our backyard, the agama. Mr. Agama. Tijan M. Sallah. NAfrP

In our community everything was kept quiet. Kiss in the Dark, A. Thomas Sayers Ellis. GT

In our content, before the autumn came. Elinor Wylie. NALW *Fr.* Nineteen Sonnets.

In our family goodness is a guest. Humans. Attila József. IQMS, *tr.* by Vernon Watkins

In our game of lfight, half-way down. Spirit of the Staircase, The. Lavinia Greenlaw. NeBrP

In our hands is a fresh yearning for you. Prayer to the New Year, A. Fadwa Tuqan. PoArWo, *tr.* by Samira Kawar

In our idleness, cinnamon blossoms fall. Bird-Cry Creek. Wang Wei. NDACCP, *tr.* by David Hinton

In our kitchen. Truth About Karen, The. Kenneth Carroll. ISC

In our little house Creedence were singing. Horses at Christmas. Henry Shukman. BeAl

In our monotonous sublime. (LL) Waking Early Sunday Morning. Robert Lowell. HarvBoo; NAMCP V.2; OxBoAm; VCAP

In our neighborhood of run-down houses. Good Humor. Allison Joseph. SUP

In our old shipwrecked days there was an hour. George Meredith. NAEL-6v2 *Fr.* Modern Love.

In Our Only Time. C. D. Wright. AmAlph

In our parks. (LL) Civil war photo. George Oppen. APT-2; PFTM-1

In our present state of knowledge only false tears are suitable for treatment and regular production. From the Technology of Tears. Zbigniew Herbert. BeAl, *tr.* by Peter Dale Scott

In Our Tenth Year. Simon Armitage. OxBSo

In our time men die before they are dead. Ferry of Lead, The. Iwan Goll. WoPoe, *tr.* by Galway Kinnell

In our town, people live in rows. Fired Pot, The. Anna Wickham. LW; NPeEn

In our very own little civil war. Brendan Kennelly. ModIr *Fr.* Cromwell.

In our world it's unusual. Nikolay Novikov. TCRusP *Fr.* Stone and Sky.

In pain, in poverty, at night. Relentlessly Lovelorn, the Non-Sleeper Whispers and Re-Whispers a Magic Charm Against His Wound's Roar. Stephen Margulies. AWTN

In pairs / as if to illustrate their sisterhood. For the Sisters of the Hôtel Dieu. Abraham Moses Klein. BrAP; NoP-4

In pale moonlight. Buson. SoOfWa, *tr.* by Sam Hamill

In Parenthesis. David Jones.
  "And the deepened stillness as a calm, cast over us." NPeEn
  "And to Private Ball it came as if a rigid beam of great weight." OBWVE
  "But sweet sister death has gone debauched today and stalks." NPeEn; OBWP; OxAEP-2
  Five Unmistakable Marks, The.
    "Across upon this undulated board of verdure chequered bright." NAMCP V.1; NoAM
    "Gentle slopes are green to remind you, The." NAEL-6v2; NAEL-7v2
  King Pellam's Launde.
    "So thus he sorrowed till it was day and heard the foules sing, then somewhat he was comforted." NAMCP V.1; NoAM
  Private John Ball Wounded in the Wood. TCAWP
  "This Dai adjusts his slipping shoulder-straps." AngWePo
  "You can hear the silence of it." FaBoWar

In Paris one night the doorbell rings. Search for Baby Combover, The. David Kirby. PoDa

In Paris the Tour Saint-Jacques swaying. Vigilance. André Breton. SurPaPo, *tr.* by Jean-Pierre Cauvin and Mary Ann Caws
  (In Paris, the Tour Saint-Jacques.) YaTCFP
  (In Paris the tower of Saint-Jacques swaying.) NAWM-7v2

In Paris with You. James Fenton. NoP-4; NoP-5; StAl

In Particular. Elena Karina Byrne. PoDa

In paschall feast, the end of a[u]ncient rite. Of the Blessed Sacrament of the Altar [*or* Aulter]. Robert Southwell. OBEV

In Passing an Old Friend's Farm. Meng Hao Jan. CCL1, *tr.* by Soame Jenyns

In passing with my mind. Right of Way, The. William Carlos Williams. APT-1

In past years I lived in an age of peace. After the Raiders Have Gone: To Clerks and Officials. Yüan Chieh. CCL1, *tr.* by Stephen Owen

In Paths Untrodden. Walt Whitman. APN-1; CAGL; NAAPv.1; TCAPo

In pause, in. Where Things of a Kind. Heather Ramsdell. IAoNAP

In peace. Louis Zukofsky. APT-2 *Fr.* A.

In peace the aleph. Aleph Poem. Jerome Rothenberg. FTOS

In Peking to a Woman with a Veil. Cho Hwi. CATKP, *tr.* by Peter H. Lee

In Pencil. Moishe Nadir. Prolet, *tr.* by Amelia Glaser

In Père La Chaise. Joaquin Miller. APN-2

In Pereira and Armenia rescue workers use listening devices. After the Colombian Earthquake. Maurice Kilwein Guevara. NAPBL

In Pericles' city, cold marble nights. Euripides' Cave. Elizabeth Morgan. PoDa

In Petrograd. Yury Mikhailovich Kublanovsky.
  "Armor of the Petrograd oak is rusty, but, The." TCRusP

In Pilgrim Life Our Rest [*with music*]. Edwin Sandys. ChIV-1

In Pilsen. Five Minutes after the Air Raid. Miroslav Holub. PoAgWa, *tr.* by George Theiner

In pinup ruffles now she flaunts. Mundus Muliebris. Mary Evelyn. NOSC

In pious times ere [*or* e'r] priest-craft did begin. John Dryden. MakPoe; NoP-5; NOSC *Fr.* Absalom and Achitophel.

In pious times ere priest-craft did begin. Absalom and Achitophel. John Dryden. BASC; NAEL-6v1; NAEL-7v1; NOSC

In Piranesi's rarer prints. Herman Melville. TCAPo *Fr.* Clarel: A Poem and Pilgrimage in the Holy Land.

In placid hours well-pleased we dream. Art. Herman Melville. AmFaPo; APN-2; BrAP; ColAP; NAAL-3; NAAPv.1; NCAP

In Plaster. Sylvia Plath. NAMCP V.2

In plazas calcined pure white, builds charge. Interludes. Fabio Doplicher. NeIt, *tr.* by Stephen Sartarelli

In Pliny, *Phoenice*. Phoenicians. Island of Summer. Robert Penn Warren.

In poems free and helpless and unjust. (LL) Cottage Street, 1953. Richard Wilbur. BodElec; CAP-8; NoP-5; PoPoPo

In police procedurals they are dying all over town. In Bed with a Book. Mona Van Duyn. PoA 2002

In Pompano Beach, Florida. Robin Becker. PBCAP

In Port Talbot. John Davies. TCAWP

In Porthcawl. Will Ifan. BBMWP, *tr.* by Robert Minhinnick

In Portuguese. Adelia Prado. TCLAP, *tr.* by Marcia Kirinus

In powdery blue dark. Kiss Her That She Don't Know How. Carletta Carrington Wilson. BtF

In Prague. Paul Celan. VCWP, *tr. by* Michael Hamburger

In Prague, or perhaps Budapest. Statues. Lisel Mueller. ExTi

In Praise of a Contented Mind. Sir Edward Dyer. *See* My Mind to Me a Kingdom Is.

In Praise of a Girl. Huw Morus. OBWVE, *tr. by* Gwyn Williams

In Praise of a Gold and Silver Painted Scene of the Buddha Manifestation in the Pure Land of the West, with a Preface. Li Po. CCL1; WoPoe, *tr. by* Elling O. Eide

In Praise of a Sword Given Him by His Prince. Colman mac Lenini. WoPoe, *tr. by* Richard O'Connell

In Praise of Bic Pens. David Hilton. P180

In Praise of Bungey. Sir John Harington. DiBP *Fr.* Epigrams.

In Praise of California Wines. Yvor Winters. APT-2

In Praise of Ch'an Master Wang You Who Cares for the Bonnet Monkeys around His Mountain Studio. Shi Zhiyuan. CSKM, *tr. by* Paul Hansen

In Praise of Ching K'o. Ch'ien T'ao. ColAnChi, *tr. by* James Robert Hightower

In Praise of Cocoa, Cupid's Nightcap. Stanley J. Sharpless. NBLV

In Praise of Coldness. Jane Hirshfield. BAP-01

In Praise of Darkness. Jorge Luis Borges. GPTC, *tr. by* Hoyt Rogers

In Praise of Darkness. Scott Cairns. UpMys

In Praise of Fidelia. Mildmay Fane, 2d Earl of Westmorland. NOSC

In praise of God. (LL) Pope's Penis, The. Sharon Olds. CAP-8; NAMCP V.2; OxBoAm

In Praise of Han Shan. Charles Wright. BAP-04; OxBoAm

In Praise of His Mistress. Thomas Carew. BASC

In Praise of Hope. Abraham Cowley. OxAEP-1

In Praise of Jade. Victor Segalen. YaTCFP, *tr. by* Timothy Billings and Christopher Bush

In Praise of Krishna. Ruskhan. WoPoe, *tr. by* Stephen Schaffer and Allen Shapiro

In Praise of Limestone. W. H. Auden. HarvBoo; NAEL-6v2; NAEL-7v2; NAMCP V.1; NoAM; NoP-4; NoP-5; OxBoAm; WaAnP

In Praise of May. *Unknown.* IrV, *tr. by* Thomas William Hazen Rolleston

In Praise of My Sister. Wisława Szymborska. PoSu

In Praise of Owain Gwynedd. Cynddelw Brydydd Mawr. OBWVE, *tr. by* Joseph P. Clancy

In Praise of Rain. Tu Fu [*or* Du Fu]. CrYelRi, *tr. by* Sam Hamill

In Praise of Robert Desnos. Franck Venaille. YaTCFP, *tr. by* Mary Ann Caws

In Praise of Self-Deprecation. Wisława Szymborska. BLT

In Praise of Spring. Chŏng Kŭgin. CATKP, *tr. by* Peter H. Lee

In Praise of Tenby. *Unknown.* OBWVE, *tr. by* Joseph P. Clancy

In Praise of the Body. Anna Hajnal. IQMS, *tr. by* Kenneth McRobbie

In Praise of the Great Bull Walrus. Alden Nowlan. BeAl

In Praise of the Portrait of My Former Master. Sŏsan, Great Master. CATKP, *tr. by* Peter H. Lee

In Praise of the Puffball. Nancy Willard. PfSP

In Praise of the Seattle Coalition. Eliot Katz. BRtP

In Praise of War. Bertrans de Born. NAWM-7v1, *tr. by* Frederick Goldin

In Prais[e] of Women [*or* Wemen]. William Dunbar. CABP; NoP-4; WaAnP

In Praise of Women in General. Thomas Randolph. NOSC

In Praise of Zigzags. Jane O. Wayne. InvLad

In print you told the world, the first imprint. Kinda Blue Miles Davis Died Today. Everett Hoagland. BodElec

In Prison. William Morris. FaBoWar

In Prison. Paul Verlaine. EdScPo, *tr. by* Neil Munro

In prison cell I sadly sit—. Last Rhyme and Testament of Tony Lumpkin. Harry Morant. FaBoWar

In prison you put on your clothes. Rehabilitative Report: We Can Still Laugh. Daniel Berrigan. AF

In program notes. Program Notes. Ruth Roston. MiVo

In Progress. Christina Georgina Rossetti. NAEL-6v2; NAEL-7v2

In Queen St., Cardiff, I halt to watch in a choice. Living in Real Times. Duncan Bush. TCAWP

In Question. Gertrude Stein. OxBoAm *Fr.* Book Concluding with As A Wife Has a Cow a Love Story, A.

In Raglan Lane, in the gentle rain, I saw dark love again. Raglan Lane. Brendan Kennelly. BeAl

In Rain. Wendell Berry. LPSFW

In rain, two hundred runners streaming. Marathon. John Powell Ward. TCAWP

In Ramallah. Ramallah. Bei Dao. WoBe, *tr. by* Iona Man-Cheong and Eliot Weinberger

In rancid dives with gaudy fronts. On Coahuila Street. Heriberto Yépez. RMCMP, *tr. by* Mark Weiss

In reality, sheep are brave, enlightened. Lies. Jo Shapcott. StAl

In reality the barn wasn't clean, ninety men. Trakl. Norman Dubie. BodElec

In Recompense. Eda Lou Walton. LW

In rectangular vertigo the balepress. Making Hay. Philip Hodgins. NOBAu

#4, In Red. Mariiane Mays. PoPra *Fr.* (HERO)neck: Attempts at a Portrait.

In red weather. (LL) Wallace Stevens. *See* Catches tigers / In red weather.

In Reference to Her Children, 23 June, 1659 [*or* 1659]. Anne Bradstreet. NAAL-3; NAAPv.1

In Referring to What Does Not Exist. Skip Fox. AnSo

In repetition, minor violences grew more blunt and less precise. Heather Ramsdell. IAoNAP *Fr.* Vague Swimmers.

In Reply to a Poem by Liu Chaisang. T'ao Ch'ien. CCL1, *tr. by* William Acker

In Reply to Vice-Magistrate Chang. Wang Wei. NDACCP, *tr. by* David Hinton

In Reply to Wei Dan. Lingche. CCL1, *tr. by* Stephen Owen

In Residence: A Worst Case View. Sean O'Brien. OBCoV

In respect of riches, then, just or unjust. Unrighteous Mammon (Luke 16:9). Ernesto Cardenal. GI, *tr. by* Robert Pring-Mill

In Respectful Memory of Mr. Yarker. John Close. Mentem Mortalia Tangunt. STuOW

In Response to a Rumor that the Oldest Whorehouse in Wheeling, West Virginia, Has Been Condemned. James Wright. CAP-8; NAMCP V.2; NoAM; OxBoAm; VCAP

In restaurants we argue. They Eat Out. Margaret Atwood. NAMCP V.2; NoAM

In resurrection, there is confusion. "H. D." APT-1 *Fr.* Flowering of the Rod, The.

In Retirement at Zhongnan. Wang Wei. CCL1, *tr. by* Jerome P. Seaton

In return can't you see that the only. Anne Portugal. SCFWP *Fr.* Bath, The.

In Reverie. Harriet McEwen Kimball. TreFP

In rhythmic beat I respond to the tune of that song, having forgotten the words. Thermometer of Happiness. Shehata El-Iryaan. AnVo, *tr. by* Mohamed Enani

In rich old Ranger, a synonym for danger. Justice in Old Ranger. Boyce House. TiP2

In roaring he shall rise and on the surface die. (LL) Kraken, The. Alfred Tennyson. CtM; NAEL-6v2; NAEL-7v2; NoP-4; NoP-5

In Robert Johnson's blue song. Hell Hound Blues. D. L. Crockett-Smith. OxAAAP

In Rome, at 26. Scirocco. Jorie Graham. FaoP

In Rome, on Campo dei Fiori. Czeslaw Milosz. HP

In Rome or in Paris. Millares 1965. Rafael Alberti. RaW, *tr. by* Hardie St. Martin

In rooms whose lights. Way We Live, The. Vicki Feaver. BeAl

In rose and gold declining light. Young Oaks, The. Andrew Hudgins. LPSFW

In rosy morn I saw Aurora red. Shortness of Life. Thomas Fairfax, Baron Fairfax of Cameron. NOSC

In Rough Weather. Paul Lake. RA

In ruling well what guerdon? Life runs low. Two Old Kings, The. John Byrne Leicester Warren, 3d Baron De Tabley. OBEV

In run-out ground in coveys. Fringed Gentians. Abbie Huston Evans. APT-1

In Russia fear is dying now. Fear (Extracts). Yevgeny Aleksandrovich Yevtushenko. RusPo, *tr. by* Robert Arthur Douglas Ford

In Saba, as by one consent. Herman Melville. APN-2 *Fr.* Clarel: A Poem and Pilgrimage in the Holy Land.

In sable clad, Urania come. Ode on the Passion. Thomas Warton, the Elder. ChIV-2

In sad and ashy weeds. Anne, Duchess of Arundel Howard. NOSC; WaAnP *Fr.* Good Shepherd's Sorrow for the Death of His Beloved Son, The.

In Saginaw, in Saginaw. Saginaw Song, The. Theodore Roethke. NBLV

In Salem. Lucille Clifton. ESEAA

In Salem Dwelt a Glorious King. Thomas Traherne. ChIV-1

In sand. Poem. Chimalum Nwankwo. NAfrP

In Santa Maria del Popolo. Thom Gunn. HarvBoo; NPeEn

In Santiago. Félix Lope de Vega Carpio. WoPoe, *tr. by* W. S. Merwin

In Santiago the green. In Santiago. Félix Lope de Vega Carpio. WoPoe, *tr. by* W. S. Merwin

In Sarajevo. Luck in Sarajevo. Izet Sarajlić. StAl

In Saturn's reign, at Nature's early birth. Juvenal. NPeEn; OBSV; OBVE; OxBEV *Fr.* Satires.

In Scarlet Town where I was born. Bonny Barbara Allan. *Unknown.* HeIP-4; NAEL-6v1; NAEL-7v1; NePenScot; NoP-5

In School. Dennis Cooper. ReTh; WiU *Fr.* Some Adventures of John Kennedy Jr.

In School House. Henry Cuyler Bunner. Real Romance, A. VerBaPo

In school I was taught the names. Columbus Day. Jimmie Durham. HATNAP; LTA

In sealed box cars travel. Still. Wisława Szymborska. AF, *tr. by* Robert A. Maguire

In search of a sheep. (LL) How the Pope Is Chosen. James Tate. OxBoAm; SUP

In Search of Aunt Jemima. Crystal Williams. AmPoNex; BtF

In Search of Krishna. Devulapalli Krishna Sastri. HotL, *tr. by* V. Narayana Rao

In Search of the Traitor. Max Jacob. AF, *tr. by* Michael Brownstein

In search of them—the aliens we don't. X Files, The. Rafael Campo. PoDa

In search of treasure near the Pyramids. Stanzas in Bloomsbury. Richard Howard. MakPoe

In search of wisdom, far from wit I fly. Wit and Wisdom. Ambrose Philips. OxAEP-1

In Season. Lisa Suhair Majaj. PoArWo

In seasonal rain. Buson. SoOfWa, *tr. by* Sam Hamill

In Seclusion. Tu Fu [*or* Du Fu]. CrYelRi, *tr. by* Sam Hamill

In second grade I felt about him and. Ice-Cream Sandwich, The. Karen Swenson. NevBe

In secret I burn, in secret I weep. *Unknown.* SLW, *tr. by* Marjolijn De Jager, Sayd Bahodin Majrouh and André Velter

In secret I come back to Luino. Each Time That Almost. Vittorio Sereni. PML, *tr. by* Marcus Perryman and Peter Robinson

In secret, Lois Lane wore coins and jewels. No, Superman Was Not the Only One. Katharyn Howd Machan. ReTh

In secret place where once I stood. Flesh and the Spirit, The. Anne Bradstreet. BASC; ChIV-2; NAAL-3; NAAPv.1; OxWW

In secret were freed. (LL) Family Secrets. Toi Derricotte. OxAAAP; SpirFl

In seed time learn, in harvest teach, in winter enjoy. William Blake. Fr. Marriage of Heaven and Hell, The.

In September. John Ormond. TCAWP

In September, at falling of the leaf. The Lady of the Assembly. OBGa Fr. Assembly of Ladies, The.

In September 1939. Bernard Gutteridge. PoWW

In serving, serve. Jinzu. ZenPo, *tr. by* Takashi Ikemoto and Lucien Stryk

In seventh grade Larry Saclarides had a gym locker next to mine, and dark skin, and dark hair. Corporeal. Robert Ayres. OPRER

In Shadow. Hart Crane. NAAPv.2

In *Shall We Dance*, the thirties musical. Shall We Dance. Joe Osterhaus. NAPBL

In Shanty Malone's, hot night one day after. September 5. Robert Peterson. GeoHom

In shapes that grow organic and bizarre. Air Show. John Updike. OtW

In Shards the Sylvan Vases Lie. Herman Melville. *See* Ravaged Villa, The.

In Siberia's wastes. Siberia. James Clarence Mangan. NPeEn

In Sickness. Written Soon after the Author's Coming to Live in Ireland, upon the Queen's Death, October 1714. Jonathan Swift. CABP

In/Silence. Jorie Graham. AWPTFC

In silence, O Silent God. / *Selah!*. (LL) Litany of [*or* at] Atlanta, A. William Edward Burghardt DuBois. APT-1; NAAPv.1; OxAAAP; TCAPo

In silent night when rest I took. [Here Follows Some] Verses upon the Burning of Our House [July 10th, 1666. Copied Out of a Loose Paper]. Anne Bradstreet. BASC; ColAP; EMWP; MakPoe; NAAL-3; NAAL-5; NAAPv.1; NALW; NoP-4; NoP-5; NOSC; PEW; SacPr; TCAPo

In Simili Materia. Timothy Russell. P180

In- / Sincerity. L. B. J. Tapes, The. Ben Friedlander. Eno

In Singapore, in the airport. Singapore. Mary Oliver. CAP-8; NIL-7

In sixteen-hundred-and-sixteen. Ballad for Apothecaries, A. Anne Stevenson. RSaN

In sixth grade Mrs. Walker. Persimmons. Li-Young Lee. CAP-8; NAAL-5; NAMCP V.2; NIL-7; NIP-4; NoP-4; NoP-5; OPRER

In sleep a king, but, waking, no such matter. (LL) William Shakespeare. CAGL; NAEL-6v1; NAEL-7v1; NoP-5; NoSic; OBEV; OxAEP-1; TFi Fr. Sonnets.

In sleep I saw my mother scrubbing stairs. Mother. Daphne Rock. Prnts

In Slumber Late. *Unknown.* SacPr

In small lawns of home. (LL) From Disaster. George Oppen. APT-2; NAMCP V.1

In Snow. William Allingham. OxBSo

In snow, all tracks. Animal Languages. Chase Twichell. StAl

In So Doing. Lawson Fusao Inada. WhBo

In sober mornings, do[e] not thou rehe[a]rse. When He Would Have His Verses Read. Robert Herrick. BASC; CavPo; NOSC

In solitary. Wopko Jensma. TSAP

In solitude. Pei Di and Wang Wei. CCL1 Fr. Wheel River.

In somber eyes no tears of grieving. Silesian Weavers, The. Heinrich Heine. NAWM-7v2, *tr. by* Hal Draper

In sombre forest, when the sun was low. Mayflies. Richard Wilbur. CAP-8

In some cool room in college after. We Could Have Met. Lee Cataldi. BMAP

In some dim sense he sees. Hog Heaven. Robert Siegel. PoA 2002

In some location. Inventing Fables about the Stone. Julia Galemire. MirDau, *tr. by* Roberta Gordenstein

In some of the stores they sell a cheese rinse. Operators Are Standing By. John Ashbery. BodElec

In some old Split park. Green branch with a sadness of yellow fruit. Tin Ujević. SonAtl, *tr. by* Merica Delic, Ursula Hobday and Ziva Pecavar

In some small town, one indifferent summer. (LL) Syringa. John Ashbery. APSN; GPTC; NoAM; VCAP

In some unused lagoon, some nameless bay. Dismantled Ship, The. Walt Whitman. TCAPo

In somer when the shawes be sheyne. May in the Green-Wood. *Unknown.* OBEV

In somer, when the shawes be sheyne. Robin Hood and the Monk. *Unknown.* OBNV

In something you have written in school, you say. Robert Pinsky. ColAP Fr. Explanation of America, An.

In songs of triumph, to proclaim him mine! (LL) Phaon Awakes. Mary Robinson. CenSon; RWP

In sooth, I know not why I am so sad. William Shakespeare. OxAEP-1 Fr. Merchant of Venice, The.

In sophiatown / can themba. Till no one. Wopko Jensma. TSAP

In sorrow deepe, I wake, I sleepe with griefe my Hart opprest. Dittie to the Same Subject, A. Dame Gertrude More. EMWP

In Spain. Emily Lawless. IrV

In Spain, where the courtly Castilian hidalgo twangs lightly each night his romantic guitar. Carmen. Newman Levy. AmWit

In Spanish he whispers there is no time left. Visitor, The. Carolyn Forché. OPOU

In Spanishburg there are boys in tight jeans. Spitting in the Leaves. Maggie Anderson. PBCAP

In Sparkhill buried lies that man of mark. Local Note. Arthur Guiterman. NBLV

In Spayn. Sir Thomas Wyatt. NoSic; OPOU

In spite of all. Her Body Is Private. Eleanor Wilner. ExTi

In spite of all the learned have said. Indian Burying Ground, The. Philip Freneau. ColAP; NAAL-3; NAAPv.1; NoP-4; NoP-5; OxBoAm; TCAPo; TFi

In Spite of Everything, the Stars. Edward Hirsch. BeAl

In Spite of How. Heather Ramsdell. IAoNAP

In spite of ice, in spite of snow. On Observing a Large Red-Streak Apple. Philip Freneau. NAAL-3

In spite of stillness. Vista Vert. David Chaloner. VaPo

In spite of what the quarrymen said. Clearsightedness. Andrew Salkey. RSaN

In splintering shallows at the local pool. Swimming Pool Ghost, The. Gillian Ferguson. MFPA

In spotted globes, that have resembled all. Greatness in Little. Richard Leigh. NOSC

In Spring. Ibycus. SaLy, *tr. by* Diane Rayor

In spring, I dream through dawn. Spring Dreams. Meng Hao Jan. CrYelRi, *tr. by* Sam Hamill

In spring mountains, alone, I set out to find you. Written on the Wall at Chang's Recluse Home. Tu Fu [*or* Du Fu]. NDACCP, *tr. by* David Hinton

In spring of youth it was my lot. Lake, The: To———. Edgar Allan Poe. APN-1

(In youth's spring, it was my lot.) NAAL-3

In Spring one sleeps. Abandon. Li Po. CCL1, *tr. by* Arthur Cooper

In spring rain. Issa. EH, *tr. by* Robert Hass

In spring the blue azures bow down. Spring Azures. Mary Oliver. CAP-8

In spring you sleep and never know the morn comes. Meng Hao Jan. NDACCP, *tr. by* William Carlos Williams

In springtime the violets. Springtime. Nikki Giovanni. TLR

In Squire Park with M., Esquire. Julianne Buchsbaum. LegDan

In stained barn drenched. Paysagesque. Norman Henry, II Pritchard. GT

In State, Part 1. Forceythe Willson. APN-2

In steel clouds. [Winter Sketches II: Subway]. Charles Reznikoff. PoA 2002; WoPoe

In still transparency, the water pools. Waterfall. Greg Williamson. RA

In streets east, streets west, they expound the Buddhist canon. Girl of Mount Hua, The. Han Yü. ColAnChi, *tr. by* Burton Watson

In strenuous hope I wrought. Vesica Piscis. Coventry Patmore. SacPr

In subsequent waves. Sleeplessness. Luigi Fontanella. NeIt, *tr. by* W. S. Di Piero

In such a fix to be so fertile. (LL) Turtle, The. Ogden Nash. NAAPv.2; NoP-4; NoP-5; SoSe-8

In such a night, when every louder wind. Nocturnal Reverie, A. Anne Finch, Countess of Winchilsea. BrAP; NAEL-6v1; NAEL-7v1; NALW; NoP-4; NoP-5; OxAEP-1; OxBEV

In sudden flare / Of the mosquito wick. Buson. ZenPo, tr. by Takashi Ikemoto and Lucien Stryk

In sullen silence. Tanka. Toki Zenmaro. CAoMJL1, tr. by Makoto Ueda

In summer. Lesbian Corn. Elaine Equi. IllVoic

In Summer at the South Pavilion Thinking of Xing. Meng Hao Jan. CCL1, tr. by Witter Bynner

In summer elms are made for me. Dilemma of the Elm. Genevieve Taggard. MoAmPo

In summer let's buy blue lampshades. Words. Kitasono Katsue. CAoMJL1, tr. by John Solt

In summer, like the theaters, I close up. Valerio Magrelli. NeIt

In summer, the house seemed ever so beautiful, timeless. Record of a Certain Summer. Yi Chinmyŏng. EcSo, tr. by Carolyn U. So

In summer the Jews of my childhood sit on chairs. Rue de Rosiers: To My Brother Fred. Liliane Richman. TWW

In summer's heat[e] and mid-time of the day. Ovid. CABP; ErotSp; NoSic; NPeEn; OBVE; OxAEP-1; OxBEV Fr. Elegies.

In summer's mellow midnight. Emily Jane Brontë. See Night Wind, The.

In summertime on Bredon. A. E. Housman. MoBrPo; NAEL-6v2; OxAEP-2; SoSe-8; UV Fr. Shropshire Lad, A.

In summer-time, when all the sky was blue. Song Out of Season, A. May Probyn. VWP

In sun or cold the weather picks scarecrow bones clean. Long Blues, The. Calvin C. Hernton. GT

In Sung China. Heart's Counting Knows Only One, The. Jane Hirshfield. WhBo

In sunlight suffused. Pak Chaesam. CAMKP, tr. by David R. McCann and Jiwon Shin

In superstitious panic. Nikolai Nikolaevich Morshen. TCRusP, tr. by John Glad

In Switzerland lang syne befell. Ballant o' the Laird's Bath, The. Douglas Young. EdScPo

In Syros' harbor abandoned merchant ships lay idle. Syros. Tomas Tranströmer. BLT, tr. by Leif Sjöberg and May Swenson

In Szetejnie. Czeslaw Milosz. BodElec, tr. by the author and Robert Hass

In Tagalog Ibon Means Bird. Nick Carbó. AmPoNex

In Taiwan, a child washes me in a tub. Purification. Doug Anderson. AmWaPo

In Tall Grass. Carl Sandburg. PoA 2002

In ten years, not once have these colours shown. Queen's Tears. Tony Curtis. TCAWP

In tender May when the sweet laugh of Christ. Puritan, The. Karl Shapiro. MoAmPo

In Tenebris. Thomas Hardy.
  "When the clouds' swoln bosoms echo back the shouts of the many and strong." ChIV-1; NAMCP V.1; NoAM

In Teos and in Samos. Anacreon. Friedrich von Hagedorn. GePo, tr. by George C. Schoolfield

In Terezin in the so-called park. Yes, That's the Way Things Are. Bachner, Miroslav Košek and Hanuš Löwy. INSAB

In Thai Binh (Peace) Province. Denise Levertov. AF

In that building, long and low. Ropewalk, The. Henry Wadsworth Longfellow. NCAP

In that corner where we slept together. César Vallejo. BLPSL, tr. by Rene de Costa, Rigas Kappatos and Eleni Paidoussi

In That Corner Where We Slept Together. César Vallejo. WoPoe, tr. by Tony Barnstone, Willis Barnstone and Haixin Xu and Willis Barnstone

In that corner where we slept together. In That Corner Where We Slept Together. César Vallejo. WoPoe, tr. by Tony Barnstone and Willis Barnstone

In that country the animals. Animals in That Country, The. Margaret Atwood. NALW; NoAM

In that dark, the tongue moved. "For some folks," it said. (LL) Robert Penn Warren. AmWaPo; CBCWP Fr. Day Dr. Knox Did It, The.

In that fair form, and fairer soul of thine. (LL) Stanzas: "Ah! think'st thou, Laura, then, that wealth." Charlotte Smith. NoP-4; NoP-5

In that gesture toward signing the stages to fullness. Velocity Among the Ruins of Angel Republic. Andrew Zawacki. LegDan

In that great day / People, in that great day. Judgment Day, The. James Weldon Johnson. APT-1; ChIV-2

In that great day when God's a-going to rain down fire? (LL) Judgment Day, The. James Weldon Johnson. APT-1; ChIV-2

In that I have so greatly failed thee, Lord. So Little and So Much. John Oxenham. SacPr

In that I loved you, Love, I worshipped you. To Eros. Wilfred Owen. CAGL

In that instant. Image from Beckett, An. Derek Mahon. ModIr; NPeEn

In that land all is and nothing's ought. Neither Here nor There. William Robert Rodgers. MoBrPo

In that land, in that land. Southern Paiute Poetry. Unknown. APN-2, tr. by John Wesley Powell

In That Moment When the Body Drowns. Mariella Bettarini. CItWP, tr. by Cinzia Sartini Blum and Lara Trubowitz

In that moment you sailed for all of death. Elegy for Your Absence. Eugenio Florit. TCLAP, tr. by Hoffman Reynolds Hays

In that novel you bought at the chain, a young woman looks back on her life. Fictions. William Kulik. BodElec

In that November off Tehuantepec. Sea Surface Full of Clouds. Wallace Stevens. APT-1; MoAmPo

In that, O Queen of queens, thy birth was free. To Our Blessed Lady. Henry Constable. NoSic

In That Place Was Another House. Ernst Meister. GTCP, tr. by Michael Hamburger

In that repository of auction pots and post-Ark. Homely Accommodation, Suit Gent. William Price Turner. EdScPo

In that same gardin all the goodly flowres. Edmund Spenser. NPeEn Fr. Faerie Queene, The.

In that shop which deals exclusively in forests sawn into. Wood merchant's parlour, The. Pierre McOrlan. MFP, tr. by Martin Sorrell

In that small dark fever of every reawakening. Patrizia Cavalli. ItPo, tr. by Gayle Ridinger

In that so sudden summer storm they tried. Summer Storm. Louis Simpson. OxBSo

In that state I came return. (LL) Retreat[e], The. Henry Vaughan. BASC; CABP; ClHu; FSCP; NAEL-6v1; NAEL-7v1; NIP-4; NoP-4; NoP-5; NOSC; NPeEn; OBEV; OBWVE; OxBEV; PBRV; RSR; TFi

In that this happening. Louis Zukofsky. APT-2 Fr. 29 Songs.

In that world as it may be, newborn and haunted, what will solitude mean? (LL) Yom Kippur 1984. Adrienne Rich. NoAM; PfS; TaR

In the 19th Century, clever mediums. Veiled Lady, The. Maura Stanton. BodElec

In the 19th century concert hall. Re-Emergence of the Trombone, The. Fred Muratori. MiVo

In the Absence of Bliss. Maxine W. Kumin. NAMCP V.2; NoAM; TaR

In the absence of progress. Where To? Ernesto Lumbreras. RMCMP, tr. by Rebecca Seiferle

In the afternoon. Back Porch Fundamentalist. Maura Eichner. UpMys

In the afternoon hours of autumn heading home. Silence. Marin Georgiev. CSCBP, tr. by Georgi Belev and Lisa Sapinkopf

In the afternoon sun. Beams. Audre Lorde. ESEAA; NoAM

In the Age of Postcapitalism. Lawrence Joseph. PBCAP

In the Age of the Radio Telescope. James Scruton. PoA 2002

In the air. (LL) Bolt / In the frame. George Oppen. APT-2; PFTM-1

In the air cuddling with the wildest regions. Reproducing one trauma after another. Carla Harryman. BAP-04 Fr. Baby.

In the air, in the empty air. (LL) War in the Air, The. Howard Nemerov. ColAP; EMP; OtW; PWW2; VCAP

In the air to aggravate the truly menacing. (LL) Chez Jane. Frank O'Hara. ColAP; NoAM; PoA 2002

In the airconditioned drone. Monsoon Girl. Harry Clifton. PBCIP

In the almond—what dwells in the almond? Mandorla. Paul Celan. PoSu, tr. by Michael Hamburger

In the Ambulance. Wilfrid Wilson Gibson. FaBoWar

In the ankle. Unnamed. David Chaloner. VaPo

In the annals saints. Holy Well. Padraic Fallon. BBASP

In the antique forest dreary. Rhyme of the Antique Forest. Henrietta Cordelia Ray. CBWP-3

In the apartment above me. No, No, Nora. Gustave Kahn. ReLy

In the April rain I climbed up to drink. Meditation in the Spring Rain. Wendell Berry. UpMys

In the arms of the sea. (LL) Response to Rimbaud's Later Manner. Thomas Sturge Moore. CABP; OBMV

In the Ashtray. Vasco [or Vasko] Popa. VCWP, tr. by Anne Pennington

In the Attic. Donald Justice. OxBoAm

In the Autumn, on Retreat at a Mountain Temple. Lady Izumi. WPoS
  (Autumn, On Retreat at a Mountain Temple.) WoPoe

In the Autumn, when the geese honk overhead going south, I spread my feathers and follow the sun. Dust of Mexico, The. David Johnson. ICANM

In the autumn wind? (LL) What voice. Basho. ASA; EH, tr. by Robert Hass

In the autumn-come-winter park. David Kherdian. UrbNat Fr. Taking the Soundings on Third Avenue.

In the Aviary. Gerald Costanzo. UrbNat

In the back bedroom, laughing when you pull. First Time: 1950. Honor Moore. FFC

In the back of the dark Chinese store. Thrashing Doves, The. Jack Kerouac. PmAP

In the back they are collecting. Abandoned Conversation with the Senses. Matthea Harvey. LegDan

In the Background of Silence. Yusef Komunyakaa. CAP-8

In the Backyard. Julio Marzán. PueRic

In the backyard of our house on Norwood. Minks, The. Toi Derricotte. FuFl; UrbNat

In the balmy night, in the night. Song of the Silent Night. Aurelio Arturo. BLPSL, tr. by Rene de Costa, Rigas Kappatos and Eleni Paidoussi

In the banana zone, in the poinciana tropics. Louvres. Les A. Murray. BMAP

In the bar. Paso del Norte. Ray Gonzales. TiP2

In the Barn. Roger Fanning. OPRER

In the baroque style of coral, India. Coral Reef, The. John Blight. NOBAu

In the Basement of the Goodwill Store. Ted Kooser. OPRER

In the basement of the museum finery is on display; a history of costume. History of Costume, A. Michelle Cliff. OxWW

In the Bath. Jo Shapcott. MoWP

In the Bathtub, to Mnemosyne. John Wheelwright. APT-2

In The Battle of the Somme, the uncut version. No Man's Land. Tom French. NIrP

In the Bavarian steeple, on the hour. Spire, The. Ellen Bryant Voigt. NoAM

In the beauty shop, the saleswoman dabs. Bergamot. Justin Chin. AmPoNex

In the bed are two, submissive. Strato. CAGL, tr. by Byrne Fone

In the bedroom. Madame Secretary. Michael McClure. Eno

In the Bedroom of Fear. David Citino. LiTh

In the Beeyard. Linda Bierds. AmAlph

In the beggar's tin. Issa. SoOfWa, tr. by Sam Hamill

In the beginner's mind there are many possibilities. Beginner's Mind. Shunryu Suzuki. WhBo

In the beginnin o aa things the Wurd wis there ense. Bible, N.T. FaBoVe Fr. St. John.

In the Beginning. Jill Alexander Essbaum. NAPBL

In the Beginning. Sandra Maria Esteves. PueRic

In the Beginning. Shara McCallum. NAPBL

In the Beginning. Howard Nemerov. BodElec

In the Beginning. Dylan Thomas. ChIV-2

In the beginning. Birth of the Bike, The. Unknown. ArBi

In the Beginning. Miriam Therese Winter. HW

In the beginning, all flight attendants were nurses. History of Air Travel, A. Anna Leahy. OtW

In the beginning God created the heaven and the earth. Bible, O.T. NAWM-5v1 Fr. Genesis.

In the beginning God created the heavens and. REcreation. Askhari. InTrad

In the beginning God made thee. Aholibah. Algernon Charles Swinburne. ChIV-1

In the beginning, God, the great schoolmaster. Autograph on the Soul, The. Adah Isaacs Menken. CBWP-1

In the beginning he merely marked. West Coast Indian. George Clutesi. HATNAP

In the beginning He put man's parts. Sister Mary Appassionata Lectures the Eighth Grade Boys and Girls: The Family Jewels. David Citino. UpMys

In the beginning hope for her was a large white cloth thickly covered with embroidery. Hope for Her. W. S. Merwin. MotU

In the beginning / It was easy to forget them. Apparition (ca. 1896). Teresa Palma Acosta. TiP2

In the beginning / it was hard. And then night fell. Unknown. SonAtl, tr. by Albert Mahera, Ralph Regenvanu and Nick Thieberger

In the beginning Love satisfies us. Love's Maturity. Hadewijch. WPoS, tr. by Oliver Davies

In the beginning of old. Ch'u Yüan. WoPoe Fr. Heaven Questions, The.

In the beginning the desert. Desert, The. Al-Munsif Al-Wahaybi. PML, tr. by Salma Khadra Jayyusi and Naomi Shihab Nye

In the beginning / The horses said, we need plains. Ibrahim Nasrallah. Eno Fr. Salvos of Mercy.

In the beginning, the water. In the Beginning. Carlos Sahagún. RaW, tr. by Hardie St. Martin

In the beginning, the word. You Bet Your Life. Nancy Vieira Couto. PBCAP

In the beginning there were days set aside for various tasks. Anne Carson. OxBoAm; WoBe Fr. Truth About God, The.

In the Beginning Was a Word. Robert Graves. PoA 2002

In the beginning was the dark. Mississippi. Rita Dove. AmAlph; StAl

In the beginning was the highway. Knitting needles and variegated. In the Beginning. Lynn Davies. Coast

In the beginning was the number cruncher. Computer Aided Design: Creation. Jackie Hardy. NeBl

In the beginning was the sound. In the Beginning. Sandra Maria Esteves. PueRic

In the beginning was the three-pointed star,. In the Beginning. Dylan Thomas. ChIV-2

In the beginning was the who, and the world was with who, and the world was who. Gospel According to the Middle. Catherine Imbriglio. IAoNAP

In the Beginning Was the Word. Anna Hempstead Branch. APT-1

In the beginning was the Word. Gail Holst-Warhaft. GI Fr. St. John.

In the beginning, / Wisdom. In the Beginning. Miriam Therese Winter. HW

In the belly of a ship. Schrimshaw Sailor, The. Gordon Meade. EdScPo

In the biographies of Rilke, you get the feeling. Letter to a Young Poet. Robert Wrigley. RoV

In the Bitter Country. Mary Ruefle. AmAlph

In the Black Camaro. David Bottoms. ReTh

In the black moon. Song of the Rider. Federico García Lorca. WoPoe, tr. by Edwin Honig

In the black winter morning. Bereft. Thomas Hardy. NAMCP V.1; NoAM

In the black winter of 1909. Uprising of the 20,000, The. Unknown. NAAPv.2

In the blackberry. Otogami. ArkPo, tr. by Edwin A. Cranston

In the bleak mid-winter. Christmas Carol, A. Christina Georgina Rossetti. OxBEV; RSR; SacPr; VWP

In the blizzard. From the Spotted Night. Ray A. Young Bear. HATNAP
(In the blizzard / while chopping wood.) AF

In the blood, Winnowing. Carl Phillips. WiU

In the Blooming Time o'th' year. Silvio's Complaint: A Song, to a Fine Scotch Tune. Aphra Behn. EMWP; RACG

In the blue air. Bats. Mary Oliver. HeIP-4

In the Blue Distance. Nelly Sachs. GTCP, tr. by Michael Hamburger

In the blue hubbub of the same-through-wealth sky. Geography. Kenneth Koch. NAMCP V.2; NoAM

In the blue velvet gown nobody else could wear. Party She Outdid Herself, The. Craig Arnold. NAPBL

In the Bluemist Motel. Greg Pape. ReTh

In the bluish climate of a stony city, they are. Theory of a Good Death. Maria Negroni. PoCho, tr. by Anne Twitty

In the boat / Crescent moon's light. Tan Taigi. ZenPo, tr. by Takashi Ikemoto and Lucien Stryk

In the Body. Ferreira Gullar. TCLAP, tr. by Renato Rezende

In the body of the town I'm a pupil. Evgeniya Lavut. CRWP, tr. by Yury Drobyshev and Carol Rumens

In the Bog behind My House. Ira Sadoff. PfSP

In the Boobiehatch. Das Lanzilloti. IJHIL

In the Bookstore. Allison Joseph. IllVoic

In the Borghese, Caravaggio, painter of boy whores, street punk. Caravaggio: Swirl and Vortex. Larry Levis. GeoHom

In the Borghese Gardens. Charles Tomlinson. OBGa

In the Boston Public Library on Boylston Street, where all the bums come in stinking from the cold. Critic, The. C. K. Williams. OPRER

In the Boston Sunday Herald just three lines. To an American Poet Just Dead. Richard Wilbur. NBLV

In the Botkin Hospital. Bella Akhatovna Akhmadulina. CRWP, tr. by Catriona Kelly

In the Box. John Powell Ward. PML

In the Bramble Stream, white stones stick out. In the Mountain. Wang Wei. ChinPo, tr. by Ye Weilian [or Yeh Wei-lien or Wai-lim Yip]

In the branches' shade. Marina Khagen. CRWP, tr. by Linor Goralik

In the brave days of old. (LL) Thomas Babington Macaulay, 1st Baron Macaulay. CABP; FaBoWar; OBNV; OBWP; OxAEP-2 Fr. Lays of Ancient Rome.

In the brave days of old. (LL) Thomas Babington Macaulay, 1st Baron Macaulay. CABP; TreFP Fr. Lays of Ancient Rome.

In the breath of the tent. Night, Hornby Island. Danielle Janess. IFF

In the bright broad Swiss glare I stand listening. Recessional. Thomas MacGreevy. ModIr

In the brown grasses slanting with the wind. William Ellery Leonard. APT-1 Fr. Two Lives.

In the brown water. Pike, The. Amy Lowell. APT-1; NAMCP V.1

In the brutal nights we used to dream. Reveille. Primo Levi. HP, tr. by Ruth Feldman and Brian Swann

In the burned house I am eating breakfast. Morning in the Burned House. Margaret Atwood. NAMCP V.2

In the Burning Air. Jean Valentine. PA9/11

In the Burning Wood. Nasri Hajjaj. Eno, tr. by Ibrahim Muhawi

In the burnt-out courtyard. Well, The. Rose Ausländer. GTCP, tr. by Irmgard Hunt

In the bus café drinking tea, I watch. Connection in Bridgend. John Tripp. TCAWP

In the bush outside my window. Cricket. Seido Ray Ronci. AmZen

In the cab of a truck bound straight across Ohio. Poet at Eighteen, The. Dick Allen. PoA 2002

In the cabinet with the lattice. Confession. Susan Hahn. IllVoic

In the Cage of Doves. Mac Lojowski. AmZen

In the callows of my intern year of. Venipuncture. John Graham-Pole. BloBone

In the Camp There Was One Alive. Randall Jarrell. HP

In the capital Spring comes late. Buying Flowers. Po Chü-i. TAL

In the cards and at the bend in the road. To Luck. W. S. Merwin. PoA 2002

In the Carolinas. Wallace Stevens. SAmP

In the Casbah. Salma Khadra Jayyusi. CFP; PoArWo, tr. by Charles Doria

In the casket of the Hours. Unknown. TAL Fr. Meditations, The.

In the cave with a long-ago flare. Painters. Muriel Rukeyser. NAAL-5

In the cedar canoe gliding and paddling. Geese Gone Beyond. Gary Snyder. NoAM

In the cedar-limbs. (LL) Thirteen Ways of Looking at a Blackbird. Wallace Stevens. APT-1; BrAP; ChAP; ColAP; HeIP-4; NAAL-5; NAAPv.2; NAMCP V.1; NoAM; NoP-4; NoP-5; OWoS; OxBoAm; PoPoPo; PtR; SAmP; TCAPo; TFi

In the cemetery of the whales. Cemetery of the Whales, The. Yevgeny Aleksandrovich Yevtushenko. RusPo, tr. by Robert Arthur Douglas Ford

In the cemetery on North Hill. Mourning. Kuan P'an-p'an. CCL1, tr. by Chung Ling and Kenneth Rexroth

In the center of a harsh and spectrumed city. Outside. Audre Lorde. BrAP

In the center of Fedora, that gray stone metropolis, stands a metal building with a crystal globe in every room. Italo Calvino. MotU Fr. Invisible Cities.

In the center of the bloodvein. My Uncle Is My Honor and a Guest in My House. Etheridge Knight. BodElec

In the center of town, on the small square facing the mosque. Archaelogical Site, An. Ivan Tsanev. CSCBP, tr. by Georgi Belev and Lisa Sapinkopf

In the centre of the poster, Napoleon. Arthur Rimbaud. OBWP Fr. Eighteen-Seventy.

In the centre of the sheep-field. Pipistrelles. Kathleen Jamie. NeBrP

In the chamber the lady knows no sadness. Complaint from a Lady's Chamber. Wang Ch'ang-ling. ChinPo, tr. by Ye Weilian [or Yeh Wei-lien or Wai-lim Yip]

In the changeling air before morning. Night Work. Sharan Strange. FuFl

In the Chariot Drawn by Dragons. Michael Van Walleghen. IllVoic

In the childhood of April, while purple woods. Dead to the Living, The. Edith Nesbit. VWP

In the Children's Hospital. Hugh MacDiarmid. BrAP; NAEL-6v2; NAEL-7v2

In the Chinhae Camp. Yi Sunsin. CATKP, tr. by Peter H. Lee

In the Chung Mode, to the Tune of "P'u T'ien Lo." Unknown. ColAnChi, tr. by Wayne Schlepp

In the church fallen like dancers. Enfidaville. Keith Douglas. PoWW

In the Church of I AM she hears there is a time to heal. Do What You Can. Lawrence Joseph. PBCAP

In the Church of Marosszentimre. Zoltán Jékely. IQMS, tr. by J. G. Nichols

In the Churchyard at Cambridge. Henry Wadsworth Longfellow. BrAP

In the city, under the saw-toothed leaves of an oak. Rita Dove. MAAN; NAAL-5 Fr. Thomas and Beulah.

In the classroom, the furious boy—a heavy star. Furious Boy, The. Toi Derricotte. OxAAAP

In the Clear Long After. Olena Kalytiak Davis. NAPBL; PoDa

In the closed house. Eclogue. Jean Follain. YaTCFP, tr. by Stephen Romer

In the cloud-grey [or -gray] mornings. Hoar-Frost. Amy Lowell. ColAP

In the clutch of blind embryo. Jake Berry. AnSo Fr. Brambu Drezi.

In the clutter and clatter of the Bronx. Providence Journal V: Israel of Puerto Rico. Afaa Michael Weaver. SpirFl

In the coffins. (LL) War. Miguel Hernández. AF; RaBo

In the cold Campèa, where ridges. Campèa. Andrea Zanzotto. VCWP

In the cold change, which time hath wrought on love. Caroline Elizabeth Norton. CenSon

In the cold, cold parlor. First Death in Nova Scotia. Elizabeth Bishop. HarvBoo; InoFa

In the cold dome of the college observatory. Conjunctions. Eamon Grennan. PBCIP

In the cold I will rise, I will bathe. Lonely Death, The. Adelaide Crapsey. APT-1

In the cold under the Grand Street / arcade. (LL) 16 Year-Old Girl Who's Standing, A. Rudolph Muller. OGAHCP; PoCho, tr. by Boadiba and Jack Hirschman

In the Coliseum. Henry Wadsworth Longfellow. TCAPo Fr. Michael Angelo: A Fragment.

In the Color of Sleep. Rose Ausländer. GTCP, tr. by Irmgard Hunt

In the colors of the useful. Useful, The. Jean Follain. TAPaP, tr. by W. S. Merwin

In the coming heat. Frances Densmore. APT-1 Fr. Chippewa Music.

In the Compound. Albert Huffstickler. TiP2

In the convent vegetable garden the nuns. In a Convent Garden. Alan Brownjohn. OBGa

In the cool dark behind the blinds. Siesta. Carmen Horst. ACAMVP

In the cool of dawn I sought a strange seclusion. Poem on Stone House Mountain, A. Hsieh Ling-yün. CCL1, tr. by John Frodsham

In the cool of morning Andrew Jackson came. Twilight on Union Street. Donald Davidson. FuPo

In the coolness of black suns. Bad Days Will End, The. Penelope Rosemont. SurWo

In the corner of a flower-shop. Twelve. Rossana Ombres. NeIt

In the corner of the living room was an album of unbearable photos. Dead in Frock Coats, The. Carlos Drummond de Andrade. PFTM-1

In the corner where she crouched. On the Threshold. Pierre Reverdy. CuPo

In the country of confusion my father. Bicycle Ride, The. Henry Israeli. ArBi

In the country of Guatemala. Is This Man, Martin Bormann? Roderick Watson. EdScPo

In the Country of the Black Pig. Christopher Hope. EmeKit

In the Country of the Dead. Habib Tengour. YaTCFP, tr. by Marilyn Hacker

In the country saying, she was only. Prague: Old Woman in the Street. Daniel Berrigan. UpMys

In the County Tyrone, in [or near] the town of Dungannon. Old [or Ould] Orange Flute, The. Unknown. OBCoV

In the course of his life, her husband determined with unprecedented precision. Mrs. Charles Sanders Peirce, Or The Solution to the Universe. Nancy Condee. OnScMo

In the course of travel: strychnine every few hours. some italian art. D. A. Powell. FaoP

In the Courtyard of the Servants. Ferenc Jankovich. IQMS, tr. by Madeline Mason

In the courtyard where the cooing of pigeons. Courtyard, The. Eddy Van Vliet. VCWP, tr. by John Van Tiel

In the cowslip's peeps I lie. Clock-A-Clay. John Clare. NAEL-6v2; NAEL-7v2

(In the cowslips peeps I lye.) NOxBChV

In the cream gilded cabin of his steam yacht. Ezra Pound. MoAmPo; NAAPv.2 Fr. Hugh Selwyn Mauberley (Life and Contacts).

In the Crevices of Night. Gloria Vando. TouFir

In the Crockett Hotel dining room. Other Alamo, The. Martín Espada. AmWaPo

In the Cross of Christ I Glory. Sir John Bowring. SacPr

In the Cubano diner, tiny cups. Glass-Bottom Boat. Elizabeth Spires. CAP-8

In the curious phenomenon of your occipital horn. (LL) To a Snail. Marianne Moore. APT-1; NALW; NAMCP V.1; OxBoAm; PoPoPo

In the daily space. Daily Space. João Cabral de Melo Neto. VCWP

In the Damp Places. Nijole Miliauskaite. VCWP, tr. by Jonas Zdanys

In the dampness of my tongue the serpent's coil. Rosary. Pedro Serrano. RMCMP, tr. by Geoff Hargreaves

In the Dark. Patrick Williams. PNI

In the dark, a child might ask, What is the world?. Nativity. Li-Young Lee. Vesp

In the Dark Backward. Gloria Vando. TouFir

In the dark blue night. Mirror, The. "Shu Ting." PFTM-2, tr. by Dennis Ding, Fang Dai and Edward Morin

In the Dark Body of Metamorphosis. Mario Luzi. tr. by Gayle Ridinger

"But then an even greater sense of the inexpressible." ItPo, tr. by Gayle Ridinger

"Reflective life separates us from the sources of reflection." ItPo, tr. by Gayle Ridinger

In the dark cave of Slovenia. Neanderthal, with Help from Cave and Bear, Invents the Flute. David Citino. PoDa

In the dark dungeons of the mind. Praying-Mantis, The. Annie Charlotte Dalton. IFF

In the dark night that keeps us apart. Unknown. SLW, tr. by Marjolijn De Jager, Sayd Bahodin Majrouh and André Velter

In the dark of the coast. Daphne Marlatt. BrAP; NLPA Fr. Touch to My Tongue.

In the dark room, lit only by the stray light. Why a Boy. Justin Chin. WiU

In the dark sky there. Lyn Hejinian. FTOS Fr. Cell, The.

In the dark, there, our eyes. Landscapes and home. Landscapes and Home / Ghazal 22. Yvonne Blomer. IFF

In the dark we disappear, pure being. Wight. Stanley Plumly. PoA 2002

In the dark womb where I began. C. L. M. John Masefield. InoFa; MoBrPo

In the Dark Word, Khurbn. Jerome Rothenberg. TaR

In the Dark World. Haniel Long. APT-1

In the darkening church. Rufus Prays. Leonard Alfred George Strong. MoBrPo

In the Darkness of the Other. Clara Silva. TANSG, tr. by Celeste Kostopulos-Cooperman

In the dawn-dirty light, in the biggest snow of the year. Roe-Deer. Ted Hughes. NAMCP V.2; NoAM; NOxBChV; OxAEP-2

In the day / sand rains. Road from Khartoum, The. Sheree Renée Thomas. BRtP

In the Daylight. Marcelin Pleynet. YaTCFP, *tr. by* Mary Ann Caws

In the dayroom crooked mouths open and close. Strange Beasts. Beda Higgins. PoCu

In the days before. For Mordecai Richler's Shalinsky Who Said "A Jew Is An Idea." Joseph Sherman. Coast

In the days of Caesar Augustus. Christmas Day; the Family Sitting. John Meade Falkner. ChIV-2

In the days of lace-ruffles, perukes and brocade. Brown Bess. Rudyard Kipling. FaBoWar

In the days of my youth, in the days of my youth. Village Revisited. Elwyn Brooks White. AmWit

In the days of old. Thomas Love Peacock. NOBRP

In the Days of Old Rameses. *Unknown.* OBCoV

In the Days of Prismatic Color. Marianne Moore. NAMCP V.1

In the Days of Rin-Tin-Tin. Daniel Gerard Hoffman. ReTh

In the Days of Socrates. Friedrich Hölderlin. PFTM-1

In the days of the broken cubes of Picasso. Cubes. Langston Hughes. APT-2

In the days when moles still held their general meetings. Brief Thoughts on Cats Growing on Trees. Miroslav Holub. PoSu, *tr. by* Ian Milner and Jarmila Milner

In the days when tights were worn. Celia de Fréine. NIrP *Fr.* Price on My Head, A.

In the dead hour of night. Silent Night, The. Mrs. Henry Linden. CBWP-4

In the dead night we walk behind a hearse. Abel. John Wheelwright. ChIV-1

In the dead of the night. Moon and Spectator, The. Léonie Adams. APT-2

In the december of my springs. December of My Springs, The. Nikki Giovanni. GT

In the deep cave. Dolores Dorantes. SPV, *tr. by* Jen Hofer

In the Deep Museum. Anne Sexton. BrAP; MoAmPo; WaAnP

In the deep night, that all is well. (LL) Alfred Tennyson. CAGL; NAEL-6v2; NAEL-7v2; OBEV *Fr.* In Memoriam A. H. H.

In the deep of night, vacantly. Growing Pearl 1. Kim Sŭnghŭi. EcSo, *tr. by* K. Kim Richards and Steffen Richards

In the deep silence of nights. Thought. Ahmad Nadeem Qasmi. WoPoe, *tr. by* Raja Changez Sultan

In the deepening autumn of a mountain fastness in Aso. Song of the Faithful Daughter Shiragiku. Ochiai Naobumi. CAoMJL1, *tr. by* Leith Morton

In the deepest night and a full moon. Under a Full Moon. Merle Woo. FiBr

In the deeps are the violence and terror of which psychology has warned us. Annie Dillard. TWF *Fr.* Teaching a Stone to Talk.

In the deepsea reaches you can not. Reflections in a passing mirror. Arthur Nortje. TSAP

In the Defences. Elizabeth Akers Allen. SWaP

In the Defense Department there is a shop. Heaven as Anus. Maxine W. Kumin. CAP-8

In the dense scopes. Figures in an Ancient Ink. Carl Rakosi. APT-2

In the Deposits of the Heart. Anna Cascella. CItWP, *tr. by* Cinzia Sartini Blum and Lara Trubowitz

In the depths of the courtyard. Submarine. Antonio Deltoro. PML, *tr. by* John Oliver Simon

In the depths of the parasol I see the marvelous prostitutes. Man and Woman Absolutely White, A. André Breton. PFTM-1

In the depths of the parasol I see the marvelous prostitutes. Man and a Woman Absolutely White, A. André Breton. ConPit, *tr. by* Clayton Eshleman

In the desert. Stephen Crane. APN-2; ColAP; IJHIL; MoAmPo; NAAPv.1; NoP-4; NoP-5; OxBoAm; TCAPo

In the desert. Desert Has Many Teachings, The. Mechthild von Magdeburg. WPoS, *tr. by* Jane Hirshfield

In the Desert. Herman Melville. NCAP

In the Desert. Dmitry Aleksandrovich Prigov. ItGoST, *tr. by* Robert Reid

In the desert of Itabira. Traveling as a Family. Carlos Drummond de Andrade. TCLAP, *tr. by* Virginia de Araújo

In the deutzia. Sora. EMJL, *tr. by* Haruo Shirane

In the diamond. Robert Creeley. WoBe *Fr.* Life and Death.

In the difficulty of what it is to be. (LL) Wallace Stevens. ColAP; NAMCP V.1 *Fr.* Notes toward a Supreme Fiction.

In the dimly lit room. Vision of Your Body. Daisy Zamora. LoL, *tr. by* Dinah Livingston

In the Distance. Silvio Giussani. ItPo, *tr. by* Gayle Ridinger

In the docile light of Pinehurst. Boy I Never Met, The. Lesley-Anne Bourne. Coast

In the Dordogne. John Peale Bishop. APT-1; OBWP; PoWW

In the Doria Pamphili garden. Folly. Henri Cole. NAMCP V.2

In the drained fields. Buson. EH, *tr. by* Yoel Hoffmann

In the drained reflecting pool in the small park. Bringing Zeus to His Knees. Antler. AtGh

In the dream, I am burning the rice. Offering. Sharan Strange. FuFl; GT

In the dream, I am Koresh. In the Compound. Albert Huffstickler. TiP2

In the dream I became 2 men my age. 1980. C. S. Giscombe. GT

In the dream I enter the house. Bone-Flower Elegy. Robert Earl Hayden. APT-2; NAMCP V.2; NoAM

In the dream I had when he came back, not sick. Promise, The. Marie Howe. LaCa

In the dream I travel by sea. Incognito. Nancy Mitchell. LaCa

In the dream, N. is singing "a white city." A teacher he had is wearing a girdle. White City, A. Michael Burkard. IJHIL

In the dream vultures circle above my mother's cousin. Chasm, The. Suji Kwock Kim. AmWaPo

In the dreamy silence. Autumn. Alexander L. Posey. APN-2

In the dreamy silence after bath. Mother, The. Sharon Olds. PBCAP

In the dull ache that is midnight for a boy. American Manhood. Robert Wrigley. PoDa

In the dungeon-crypts, idly did I stray. Prisoner, The. A Fragment. Emily Jane Brontë. NAEL-6v2; NAEL-7v2; NALW; NoP-5

In the dust . . . in the cool / tombs. (LL) Carl Sandburg. *See* Tell me if any get more than the lovers. . .in the dust. . .in the cool tombs.

In the dust-covered street. Crossing the Border. Gu Cheng. WoBe, *tr. by* Joseph R. Allen

In the dustless. This Atomising of Things. Pauline Stainer. MoWP

In the Dying Afternoon. Ramón López Velarde. BLPSL, *tr. by* Rene de Costa, Rigas Kappatos and Eleni Paidoussi

In the early crystal morning. In the Early Morning Breeze. Lawrence S. Cumberbatch. EGAG

In the early days of marriage. Before these Wars. Carol Rumens. Prnts

In the early evening. Reading by Mechanic Light. Thomas McGrath. BodElec; GifTon

In the early evening, as now, a man is bending. Poem. Louise Glück. MoWP

In the early hours of the next morning dawning. *Unknown.* WoPoe *Fr.* Epic of Gilgamesh, The.

In the early morning before the shop. Drum: *Leo's Tool & Die, 1950.* Philip Levine. NAMCP V.2

In the Early Morning Breeze. Lawrence S. Cumberbatch. EGAG

In the early mornings. May Song. Félix Lope de Vega Carpio. SpanPo, *tr. by* Kate Flores

In the early springtime, after their tea. Dame Edith Sitwell. NALW *Fr.* Façade.

In the early winter dusk the broken city dark. City Dark, The. Robert Pinsky. PfSP

In the East Central State of Nigeria, four years. Epilogue to Casualties. John Pepper Clark Bekedermo. HBAPE

In the ebony of an ancient cupboard. (LL) My Cousin Agueda [*or* Agatha]. Ramón López Velarde. OBVE; TCLAP, *tr. by* Samuel Beckett

In the Echoey Tunnel. Christopher Reid. NeBrP

In the Egg. Günter Grass. AF

In the eggs. John Corben. Spl

In the Elementary School Choir. Gregory Djanikian. OPRER; UnSA

In the Emperor's bed. Kikaku. SoOfWa, *tr. by* Sam Hamill

In the empty mountains after the new rain. Autumn Twilight in the Mountains. Wang Wei. NDACCP; WaAnP, *tr. by* Kenneth Rexroth

In the end. Hairbrush, The. Sandra Hochman. YaYoPo

In the end. Dario Villa. ItPo, *tr. by* Gayle Ridinger

In the End Is the Body. Gail Holst-Warhaft. GI

In the end is the body—what we know. In the End Is the Body. Gail Holst-Warhaft. GI

In the end of the sabbath, as it began to dawn toward the first day of the week. Bible, *N.T.* NAWM-5v1 *Fr.* St. Matthew.

In the end when the doctors circle around. Advantages of Being a World Class Athlete, The. Anthony Lacavaro. MoASP

In the end you are weary of this ancient world. Zone. Guillaume Apollinaire. WoPoe, *tr. by* Samuel Beckett

In the end you want the clean dimensions of it mentioned. Death, A. Thomas Lynch. PoA 2002

In the Enola Gay. August 6, 1945. Alison Fell. PoAgWa; RSaN

In the Evening. Siv Cedering Fox. CA

In the evening. Another Night in the Ruins. Galway Kinnell. InvLad

(In the evening / haze darkening on the hills.) AF

In the Evening. Adrienne Rich. WaAnP

In the evening, an animated salesman, a cartoon version of a man. Persuasion. Patty Seyburn. AmPoNex

In the evening at the palace, she lowers her pearl screen. Complaint Near the Jade Stairs. Hsieh T'iao. CrYelRi, *tr. by* Sam Hamill

In the evening came the order. Susie's Lament for Johnny. Mihály Csokonai Vitéz. IQMS, *tr. by* Anthony Edkins

In the evening dusk when earth. Interpretation of Dinner by the Uninvited Guest, An. Lorna Dee Cervantes. TouFir

In the evening / haze darkening on the hills. Galway Kinnell. *See* In the evening.

In the Evening ("Music rang out in the garden, The.") Anna Andreyevna Akhmatova. FiBr, *tr. by* Judith Hemschemeyer

In the evening the autumn woods ring. Grodek. Georg Trakl. AF, *tr. by* Daniel S. Simko

In the evening the dusk. Poet Is Dead, The. William Everson. NoAM

In the evening / The mists trail. *Unknown.* TAL

In the Evening the Sky Roams, a Meaager. Amelia Rosselli. CItWP, *tr. by* Cinzia Sartini Blum and Lara Trubowitz

In the evening we came back. Light Left On, A. May Sarton. GoPo

In the evening when the light is dim. Valerio Magrelli. NeIt

In the Evening Your Vision Widens. Nelly Sachs. WPoS, *tr. by* Michael Roloff

In the evenings. When did she know, when did she know it. Lucille Clifton. ExTi

In the Evening's Gentle Sunshine. Franz Kafka. GTCP, *tr. by* Reinhold Grimm

In the evil time. A. Velichansky. TCRusP, *tr. by* Daniel Weissbort

In the Eyes of the Gods. André Breton. WoPoe, *tr. by* Jack Rogow and Bill Zavatsky

In the face before he ran out into the street. (LL) I Found Orpheus Levitating. Nick Carbó. NAPBL; ReBoTo

In the faint blue light. Vincent Buckley. BMAP *Fr.* Stroke.

In the fall of the year *jen-hsü* in the seventh month on the day after the full moon. Red Cliff Rhapsodies. Su Tung-p'o. ColAnChi, *tr. by* Richard Strassberg

In the falling snow. Richard Wright. NIL-7; NoP-5 *Fr.* Hokku Poems.

In the family I eat. Family man. Lionel Abrahams. TSAP

In the family of things. (LL) Wild Geese: "You do not have to be good." Mary Oliver. BLT; GoPo; PoCu; TWF

In the far corner. Blackbird, The. Humbert Wolfe. NOxBChV

In the Far West. Cow Boy. Vicente Huidobro. PFTM-1

In the farther sky rain gathers. Squall Line. Joan Houlihan. IAoNAP

In the fat, green greenery. Mango. *Unknown.* SonAtl, *tr. by* Martha Belton, Kurt Ganzl, F. Silai and Jim Yarris

In the Field. David Miller. OnScMo

In the field-furrow. "H. D." APT-1 *Fr.* Tribute to the Angels.

In the Fields. Antonio Machado Ruiz. RaW, *tr. by* Robert Bly

In the Fields. Charlotte Mew. MoBrPo; OxAEP-2

In the Fields or on the Hill. Pierre Reverdy. YaTCFP, *tr. by* Patricia Terry

In the fifteenth she was painted. Beatrice. J. Bernlef. TuT, *tr. by* Peter van de Kamp

In the 5th century B.C. Buddhist Barbie. Denise Duhamel. SUP

In the 50s, we drove each month to my uncle's house. Gambling. Vince Gotera. OpBo

In the final hour, our lady,—Of. Our Lady. Carl Phillips. CAP-8

In the final years of the twelfth century. Inferno 1, 32. Jorge Luis Borges. PoetW, *tr. by* Anthony Kerrigan

In the fine land, the west land, the land where I belong. (LL) West Wind, The. John Masefield. CABP; MoBrPo

In the fine print of her face. My Beloved. Charles Simic. OxBoAm

In the first cage. Aisle of Dogs. Chase Twichell. EmeKit

In the First Circle of Limbo. Carl Rakosi. BAP-04

In the first country. Bright after Dark. Pearse Hutchinson. PBCIP

In the first month I think. Tempo. Lauris Edmond. BeAl

In the first negative, a shape presages. Sound Waves. Mary Kinzie. FFC

In the First Person. Yosano Akiko. CAoMJL1, *tr. by* Janine Beichman

In the first snowflake imprinting the kitchen window by the sink. Poem on My Birthday. Peter Cooley. NevBe

In the first taxi he was alone tra-la. Taxis, The. Louis MacNeice. EmeKit; NPeEn; PNI

In the fish shop. Basho. EH, *tr. by* Robert Hass

In the Fist of Your Hatred. Shakuntala Hawoldar. CFP

In the Fist of Your Hatred. Gwendoline C. Konie. HAWP

In the flatlands. Fall, The. John Kinsella. NeBl

In the flower of fury, the folded poppy, / Night. (LL) Sentry, The. Alun Lewis. AngWePo; PoWW; TCAWP

In the flower-time of youth. Love of Boys, The. Solon. CAGL, *tr. by* John Addington Symonds

In the Fog. Lilian Moore. TLR

In the fog lit. Visit to Turk's Head Pub. Manuel Ulacia. RMCMP, *tr. by* Indran Amirthanayagam

In the fog / there are men and women waiting. In the Fog. Kang Ŭn'gyo. EcSo, *tr. by* Ann Y. Choi

In the fog we drift hither. Rain on the River [1956]. Lu Yu. NDACCP, *tr. by* Kenneth Rexroth

In the Forest. Heather Allen. GifTon

In the forest of noyous hevynesse. Lost. Charles, Duc d' Orléans. NPeEn

In the Forest of Vaal. János Vajda. IQMS, *tr. by* Watson Kirkconnell

In the forest overhead. Les Grottes. Gillian Clarke. HarvBoo

In the Forests of Sleep. Habiba Muhammadi. PoArWo, *tr. by* Ibrahim Muhawi

In the Formal Garden. Peter Jones. OBGa

In the Forties. Jaime Gil de Biedma. RaW, *tr. by* Timothy Baland

In the forties the populace was sucking on barb. New/Aguas Buenas/Jersey. Víctor Hernández Cruz. TouFir

In the foul rag-and-bone shop of the heart. (LL) Circus Animals' Desertion, The. William Butler Yeats. BeAl; BrAP; HarvBoo; MakPoe; NAEL-6v2; NAEL-7v2; NAMCP V.1; NAWM-7v2; NIP-4; NoAM; NoP-4; NoP-5; TFi

In the frayed apple leaves a grin of copper. Child Is Revenant to the Man, The. Vincent Buckley. BMAP

In the fresh snow. (LL) Born into a World Knowing. Susan Griffin. PoChi; WhBo

In the frondescence. Essence. Bernard Bador. ConPit, *tr. by* Clayton Eshleman

In the frozen ground under my feet. Wild Hyacinth. Joan I. Siegel. PoCoUp

In the fruit bowl shutters half-closed. Josée Lapeyrère. SCFWP *Fr.* Apples.

In the Funk World. Imamu Amiri Baraka. FuFl; NAMCP V.2

In the gale, in the field's bright stubble. Beacon. Vladimir Levchev. CSCBP, *tr. by* Georgi Belev and Lisa Sapinkopf

In the garden. Garden. Michael Bullock. OBGa

In the Garden. Edward Dowden.

Singer, The. OxBSo

In the Garden. *Unknown.* SoSe-8

In the Garden: "It seemed to me so much like you." Nissim Ezekiel. BrAP

In the Garden at Swainston. Alfred Tennyson. OBEV

In the Garden by the Sea: Easter. Kelly Cherry. LPSFW

In the Garden City Café with its murals on the wall. Huxley Hall. Sir John Betjeman. CABP; OBSV

In the gardens, I followed your eye. Perennial Garden. Marianne Boruch. AmAlph

In the Garden of Apples. Colette Ni Ghallchóir. NIrP, *tr. by* the author

In the garden of dusk. In the Beginning. Shara McCallum. NAPBL

In the Garden of Shut-Eye Town. (LL) Sugar-Plum Tree, The. Eugene Field. ITBLP; NBLV

In the Garden of the Lord. Helen Keller. SacPr

In the garden of time and destiny, we have seen. In the Garden of Time and Destiny. Nâbî. OLP; WoPoe, *tr. by* Walter Andrews, Najaat Black and Mehmet Kalpakli

In the garden shed, among flower-pots. Voice. Susan Wicks. MFPA

In the garden there strayed. In the Garden. *Unknown.* SoSe-8

In the Garden: Villa Cleobolus. Lawrence Durrell. OBGa

In the gardens. Flower-sellers, Budapest. Kathleen Jamie. NePenScot

In the gathering dusk. (LL) White Oxen. Louis Simpson. NAMCP V.2; NoAM

In the General Area of North Texas. Scott Cairns. TiP2

In the gilded abyss, crimson, frozen, gilded, the abyss where sorrow shelters. Head Filled with Beauty, The. Pierre Reverdy. YaTCFP, *tr. by* Mary Ann Caws

In the girdered dark. Drink of Milk, A. John Montague. ModIr; PNI

In the glare the gannets dive. Another Name for the Cassiterides. Rod Mengham. VaPo

In the glass something glimmers, cold and sad. Windowpane I. Chŏng Chiyong. CAMKP, *tr. by* Anthony, Brother of Taizé

In the glassed-in jazz club acres above. Night above the Town. Thomas Lux. SeSe

In the Gloaming. Charles Stuart Calverley. OBCoV

In the Gloaming. Jennifer Maiden. BMAP

In the gloom of whiteness. Snow. Edward Thomas. OPOU

In the Gloom on the Left. Joyce Mansour. PFTM-2, *tr. by* Molly Bendall

In the glorious reign of Silla, calm and bright. Song of Ch'ŏyong. *Unknown.* CATKP, *tr. by* Peter H. Lee

In the Gloriovs Epiphanie of Ovr Lord God, A Hymn. Svng as by the Three Kings. Richard Crashaw. FSCP

In "The Gold Bug," the overt finding of the treasure. Poe: An Assay (1). Jane Hirshfield. BAP-04

In the golden reign of Charlemaign the king. Rhotruda. Frederick Goddard Tuckerman. NCAP

In the golden twilight the rain. Terrace in the Snow, The. Su Tung-p'o. NDACCP, *tr. by* Kenneth Rexroth

In the Good Old Summer Time. Ren Shields. NAAPv.2

In the Good Old U. S. A. José Angel Sr. Villalongo. UnSA

In the gorge where bells resound. Return to Wang River. Wang Wei. CrYelRi, *tr. by* Sam Hamill

In the grass of the twilight: the seventh day is God. Géza Páskándi. IQMS *Fr.* Language Memory.

In the Grave No Flower. Edna St. Vincent Millay. NAAL-5

In the great nave of the church. Musician, The. Philip Dacey. MiVo

In the great night my heart will go out. Tohono O'odham. NAAPv.1 *Fr.* Songs for Treating Sickness, Sung during the Four Parts of the Night.

In the great white tent lit by floodlight. Mostly Mozart at Planting Fields Arboretum. David Zeiger. MiVo

In the green and yellow grass of the broad field. Sabbath Morning. Marcia Falk. TaR

In the green escape of my palace, over a bridge, under a. Etel Adnan. PoArWo *Fr.* There.

In the green fleece shorts is taking off. That Man. Reginald Shepherd. WiU

In the green light of water, like the day. Swans, The. Dame Edith Sitwell. BrAP

In the green meadow stood a cow. Did I say it was a blush? Titled. Tom Ahern. OnScMo

In the greenest of our valleys. Haunted Palace, The. Edgar Allan Poe. APN-1; BrAP; NAAL-3; NAAPv.1; OxBoAm; TCAPo; TFi

In the Greenhouse. Eugenio Montale. PoetW, *tr. by* Jonathan Galassi

In the Greenwood. Desmond O'Grady. IrLP

In the grey evening. Garden Hose, The. Beatrice Janosco. NTCP

In the Grounds. Douglas Dunn. NoP-4; NoP-5

In the Grove. Rachel Hadas. KGB

In the groves of Africa from their natural wonder. African Elegy, An. Robert Duncan. NoAM

In the *gui-mao* year of Zhong-he, in the third month of spring. Lament of the Lady of Qin. Wei Chuang. CCL1, *tr. by* Lionel Giles

In the gutter / boys who try. Up-Beat. Langston Hughes. APT-2

In the gymnasium the balls spun. Poets, The. Afaa Michael Weaver. FuFl

In the Hairy Arms of Whitman. Bill Kushner. PA9/11

In the hall of mirrors nobody speaks. Roman Baths at Nîmes, The. Henri Cole. MakPoe

In the hall of The Mountain King. Real Estate. Michael Hannon. GeoHom

In the hallway above the pit of the stairwell. Indictment of Senior Officers. Sharon Olds. PBCAP

In the harbour, in the island, in the Spanish Seas. Trade Winds. John Masefield. OBMV

In the harvest too. And Then the Water. Milo De Angelis. NeIt, *tr. by* Lawrence Venuti

In the heart of little old New York. Forty-second Street. Al Dubin. ReLy

In the heart of night, in winter, there was this hour. Rain at Night. Jakov Steinberg. FIT, *tr. by* Robert Friend

In the heart of the heart. Missing Jew, The. Rodger Kamenetz. TaR

In the heart of the Indian territory of Oklahoma. Go For Broke. André Breton. PFTM-1

In the heart of winter and a boy running. (LL) History Lessons. Seamus Deane. PBCIP; PNI

In the heat ruddy circles. Sunstroke. Blaga Dimitrova. CSCBP, *tr. by* Georgi Belev and Lisa Sapinkopf

In the hickory scent. Smokehouse, The. Yusef Komunyakaa. NoP-4; NoP-5

In the high autumn skies of September. My Thatched Roof Is Ruined by the Autumn Wind. Tu Fu [*or* Du Fu]. CCL1, *tr. by* Stephen Owen

In the high seat, before-dawn dark. Why Log Truck Drivers Rise Earlier Than Students of Zen. Gary Snyder. GeoHom; LoL

In the high wilderness. Coplas. AF, *tr. by* Robert Bly

In the highflown language. Highflown: Love. Eugene B. Redmond. OxAAAP

In the highlands, in the country places. Robert Louis Stevenson. OBEV

In the Hill Country. Max Jacob. MotU, *tr. by* John Ashbery

In the Hills. Wang Wei. TAL

In the hills where the hoop. Death of Crazy Horse, The. Lucille Clifton. ESEAA

In the hole we found beside the road. Construction of the Museum. Michael Palmer. BodElec; WoBe

In the hollow below the hill vaults. Recording the Spirit Voices. David Bottoms. TAPaP

In the Holy Nativity of Our Lord God. Richard Crashaw. NAEL-6v1; NAEL-7v1

(Verses from the Shepherd's Hymn.) OBEV

In the Holy Nativity of Ovr Lord God A Hymn Svng as by the Shepheards. Richard Crashaw. *See* In the Holy Nativity of Our Lord God.

In the home of mysterious life I lie. Songs of the Sacred Mysteries. *Unknown.* APN-2, *tr. by* Alfred Longley Riggs

In the hometown tonight. Castle in Lynn, A. Linda McCarriston. LoL

In the Hospital, Near the End. Sharon Olds. *See also* Lifting, The.

In the Hospital Near the End. Sharon Olds. NIP-4

In the hot dark they dug a hole. Crucifixion (Montgomery, Alabama). Andrew Hudgins. UpMys

In the hot white dome of air. Happiness. Lee Upton. AmAlph

In the hotel bar Brank ignores his shrimp rotini. Questmale. Mark Halliday. MAAN

In the hottest time, when all is still and windless. *Unknown.* CCL1 *Fr.* Tzu Yeh Songs.

In the hour between wolf and dog the sacred cow of hardship. Sacred Cow of Hardship, The. Agi Mishol. DTA, *tr. by* Tsipi Keller

In the hour of death, after this life's whim. Dominus Illuminatio Mea. Richard Doddridge Blackmore. OBEV; SacPr

In the hour[e] of my distress[e]. His Litany to the Holy Spirit. Robert Herrick. BASC; NOSC

In the House. Stephen Dunn. PoDa

In the house are all her years. Inheritance. Kathleen Norris. UpMys

In the house in Detroit. Sand Nigger. Lawrence Joseph. OPRER

In the house of the man with no hands. Probable Cause. Thomas McGrath. GifTon

In the house of those who serve the Muses, a dirge. Sappho. SaLy, *tr. by* Diane Rayor

In the house that has died. Water Song. Afaa Michael Weaver. ISC

In the humming dawn. (LL) Honeycomb, The. Pauline Stainer. NeBl; StAl

In the hummingbird house. Hummingbird Light. Diane Wakoski. PmAP

In the ideal. Harvest Home. Bettye T. Spinner. TWF

In the imperfect time when we have the right. Emyr Lewis. BBMWP *Fr.* Freedom.

In the Inner City. Lucille Clifton. HeIP-4; SSCS; UnSA

In the Interest of Possibility. Thom Ward. AmPoNex

In the intoxicating moonlight. Intoxicating Moonlight. Kim Yŏngnang. CAMKP, *tr. by* Anthony, Brother of Taizé

In the Italian quarter of London I found a group of clerks, waiters and idealistic barbers. Sentences. Thornton Wilder. MotU

In the Jerusalem Hills. Leah Goldberg. FIT, *tr. by* Robert Friend

In the Jewish Synagogue at Newport. Emma Lazarus. TaR

In the Jury Room, in Pain. Paul Goodman. BodElec

In the Just Dampened Park. Patrizia Cavalli. CItWP, *tr. by* Cinzia Sartini Blum and Lara Trubowitz

In the Key of Farewell. Pao Ling-hui. CCL1, *tr. by* Anne Birrell

In the key of life. (LL) Wedding Party. Allison Joseph. AmPoNex; ExTi; MPUn

In the Kingdom of Perpetual Repair. Kevin Stein. IllVoic

In the King's Rooms. Timothy Steele. RA

In the kitchen a tanged fetid forest. Cemetery in the Mind, The. Dambudzo Marechera. NAfrP

In the kitchen as the toast browns. At My Father's House. Nancy Travis. ISC

In the Kitchen before Dinner. Jane Rohrer. ACAMVP; BodElec

In the Kitchen Dancing to Kitty Wells. Heather Sellers. SweBea

In the Kitchen of the Old House. Donald Hall. CAP-8

In the Laboratory. Dan Pagis. PoSu, *tr. by* Robert Friend

In the Labyrinth of Elements. Duane Niatum. PoCoUp

In the Lake District. Joseph Brodsky. BLT, *tr. by* George L. Kline

In the land o' the leal. (LL) Land o' the Leal, The. Carolina Oliphant, Baroness Nairne. NePenScot; NOBRP; NPeEn; OBEV; OxBEV

In the land of Haiti. Ernst Mirville. OGAHCP, *tr. by* Boadiba and Jack Hirschman

In the land of milk and honey. People of Figs. Nidaa Khoury. DTA, *tr. by* Karen Alkalay-Gut

In the land of mutual rivers. Mappa Mundi. Philip Gross. BeAl

In the land of Schlaraffenland. Igor Vladimirovich Chinnov. TCRusP, *tr. by* John Glad

In the land of turkeys in turkey weather. Dance of the Macabre Mice. Wallace Stevens. PFTM-1

In the language of the spirit. Leap Year. Charles North. FTOS

In the Last Circle. Edgar Bowers. CalPo

In the last days of my father's life. His Smell. Sharon Olds. MoWP

In the last, far field [half-buried in barberry bushes, red-fruited]. Dead Horse in Field. Robert Penn Warren. BodElec

In the last light I drove. After Supper. David Keller. SwNoth

In the last low cottage in Blackthorn Lane. Wise-Woman, The. Agnes Mary Frances Robinson. VWP

In the last minutes he said more to her. Seamus Heaney. InoFa; NoP-5; PNI *Fr.* Clearances.

In the last place of refuge, my own soul. (LL) William Wordsworth. NAEL-6v2; NAEL-7v2 *Fr.* Prelude, The; Growth of a Poet's Mind [1850 version].

In the late autumn's dusky-golden prime. Vespertilia. Rosamund Marriott Watson. ViWPN

In the latitude of the Balearic Islands. Letter from a Cattleboat. Harry Edmund Martinson. WED, *tr. by* Robert Bly

In the Lebanese Mountains.   Nadia Tuéni.   PoArWo, *tr. by* Samuel Hazo

In the lens of memory, that smudged bungler.   Spectral Dues.   Pimone Triplett.   AmPoNex

In the lethargy which follows the machinations of the.   Amelia Rosselli.   PFTM-2 *Fr.* Martial Variations.

In the Library.   Michael Patrick Hearn.   NTCP

In the Library.   Hamutal Bar Yosef.   DTA, *tr. by* Shirley Kaufman

In the Life and Death of Rosamel Del Valle.   Eunice Odio.   tr. by Arthur Natella
     "It is not true that you are far from "the light that can find you.""   TANSG, *tr. by* Arthur Natella
     "It is the dawn."   TANSG, *tr. by* Arthur Natella

In the life we live [*or* lead] together every paradise is lost.   Against Botticelli.   Robert Hass.   OxBoAm

In the life you lead.   Life Beside This One, The.   John N. Morris.   PoA 2002

In the Limpid Air.   Michel Houellebecq.   YaTCFP, *tr. by* Mary Ann Caws

In the Line of Duty.   Jayne Cortez.   SurWo

In the line of duty. (LL)   Don Juan (After He'd Consumed Tons of Lipstick).   Martin Sorescu.   PML; PoDa, *tr. by* Adam J. Sorkin and Irina Grigorescu Pan

In the lion's eye.   Michael McClure.   WANABP *Fr.* Haiku Rows.

In the little red house by the river.   Wilderspin.   Mary Elizabeth Coleridge.   ViWPN; VWP

In the little town out of which death sprawled over the classroom map.   Joseph Brodsky.   StAl *Fr.* Part of Speech, A.

In the Living Room.   Arthur Sze.   WANABP

In the living room sit the men.   Untitled.   Phillina Sun.   FTtHH

In the lobby, three old women, in deep armchairs, sit.   Lagoon.   Joseph Brodsky.   TCRusP, *tr. by* Daniel Weissbort

In the Locker Room.   Madeline DeFrees.   ExTi

In the loco.   3D.   José Craveirinha.   SonAtl, *tr. by* Martin Balas and Sophia Balas

In the long journey out of the self.   Journey to the Interior.   Theodore Roethke.   TRP

In the long open Vancouver Island room.   Agatha Christie Books By The Window, The.   Michael Ondaatje.   BrAP

In the long river, [the] fish swim off without a trace.   Replies.   *Vietnamese Oral Tradition.*   CaDao, *tr. by* John Balaban

In the long run we must fix our compass.   Respected, Feared, and Somehow Loved.   Marjorie Welish.   OnScMo; PmAP

In the long run you're tired of this ancient world.   Zone.   Guillaume Apollinaire.   CuPo

In the long, sleepless watches of the night.   Cross of Snow, The.   Henry Wadsworth Longfellow.   APN-1; AWTN; ColAP; GSo; HeIP-4; NAAPv.1; NoP-4; NoP-5; TCAPo

In the Longhouse, Oneida Museum.   Roberta Hill Whiteman.   NoAM

In the Lord's eyes. (LL)   This Place Rumord to Have Been Sodom.   Robert Duncan.   CAGL; CalPo

In the lost portrait by Siqueiros.   Shadow Portrait.   Paul Mariani.   PfSP

In the Lost Province.   Tom Paulin.   PBCIP

In the love of home and country and the flag of Uncle Sam.   Loyalty to the Flag.   Lizelia Augusta Jenkins Moorer.   CBWP-3

In the lowlands is the goat's-peach.   Shi-you chang-chu: In the Lowlands.   *Unknown.*   CCL1, *tr. by* Arthur Waley

In the Lungs.   Milo De Angelis.   NeIt, *tr. by* Lawrence Venuti

In the Lybian desert I.   Modo and Alciphron.   Sylvia Townsend Warner.   MoBrPo

In the Madonna Dell' Orto.   Peter Rafferty.   NLP

In the manger of course were crows and the Child Himself / Was like unto a lamb.   Anthony Hecht.   GI

In the Mansions Above.   *Unknown.*   SSUS

In the Marble Quarry.   James Dickey.   LPSFW; NoP-4

In the margins, in the white spaces around words. (LL)   Elegy: "Pages of history open, The. The dead enter."   Sandra M. Gilbert.   PoA 2002; WaAnP

In the market, car horns, alarms, the barking of dogs. (LL)   Diver for the NYPD Talks to His Girlfriend, A.   Richard Garcia.   TouFir; UrbNat

In the market of Totora.   Letter to Ko.   Dennis Nurkse.   PoDa

In the marketplace where St Florian.   She Looked At the Sun.   Tadeusz Rózewicz.   PoSu, *tr. by* Magnus F. Krynski

In the marriage, not able to anticipate how they would feel.   Short Narrative of Hand and Face in Service of PLOT, Entitled, A.   Claudia Rankine.   NAPBL

In the mazes of loitering people, the watchful and furtive.   Chance Meetings.   Conrad Potter Aiken.   TCAPo

In the meal-bin. (LL)   Seamus Heaney.   BeAl; ModIr; WaAnP *Fr.* Mossbawn.

In the melon-patch / Thief, fox.   Tan Taigi.   ZenPo, *tr. by* Takashi Ikemoto and Lucien Stryk

In the men's room(s).   Marge Piercy.   BeAl

In the merry month of May.   Nicholas Breton.   NoSic; OBEV *Fr.* Honourable Entertainment Given to the Queen's Majesty in Progress at Elvetham, 1591, The.

In the mid-1800s.   Island of Women, The.   June McGlashan.   ReEnLa

In the mid-dark if early night.   Children.   Pinkie Gordon Lane.   FuFl

In the mid-days of autumn, on their eves.   John Keats.   NPBRoP *Fr.* Isabella, or The Pot of Basil.

In the middle.   Black Love Black Hope.   Doughtry Long.   SeSe

In the middle of a canefield near Higuey.   Viejo.   Jean-Claude Martineau.   OGAHCP, *tr. by* Boadiba and Jack Hirschman

In the middle / of a dimly lit room.   3rd Untitled Poem.   Pedro Juan Pietri.   PueRic

In the middle of a tiny spot and nearly bare there is a nice thing to say that.   Leave, A.   Gertrude Stein.   PFTM-1

In the Middle of Life.   Tadeusz Rózewicz.   GPTC, *tr. by* Joanna Trzeciak

In the middle of our times.   Middle.   Jimmie Durham.   HATNAP

In the middle of Priest Lake.   Madeline DeFrees.   ExTi

In the middle of the canyon.   Quarrel.   Federico García Lorca.   RaW, *tr. by* Herbert Baird and William Stafford

In the middle of the day.   To B. P.   Aleksandr Semionovich Kushner.   TCRusP, *tr. by* Daniel Weissbort

In the middle of the forest there's an unexpected clearing.   Clearing, The.   Tomas Tranströmer.   MotU, *tr. by* Robert Bly

In the middle of the night.   Praying.   Cynthia Cruz.   IAoNAP

In the middle of the night.   Tryst.   Duvvuri Ramireddy.   HotL, *tr. by* V. Narayana Rao

In the middle of the night I sit up, remembering.   Lost Photograph.   Luisa Igloria.   RWB

In the middle of the night I slipped away from my husband.   Philodemus.   HePo *Fr.* Epigrams.

In the middle of the night, when we get up.   True Love.   Sharon Olds.   BodElec; StAl

In the middle of the poem my daughter reminds me.   Finding What's Lost.   Dorianne Laux.   GeoHom

In the Middle of the Road.   Carlos Drummond de Andrade.   TCLAP, *tr. by* John Nist

In the middle of the road there was a stone.   In the Middle of the Road.   Carlos Drummond de Andrade.   BLT; PoetW, *tr. by* Elizabeth Bishop

In the middle of the road was a stone.   In the Middle of the Road.   Carlos Drummond de Andrade.   TCLAP, *tr. by* John Nist

In the middle of the wood I set sail.   Amhrán na mBréag.   Pearse Hutchinson.   PBCIP

In the middle silences of this night's course the blackthorn.   David Jones.   OxAEP-2 *Fr.* Mabinog's Liturgy.

In the mid-sixties.   TV in Black and White.   Gary Soto.   ReTh; RWB

In the Midst of Life.   Tadeusz Rózewicz.   PoSu

In the Midst of Possibility.   Gabriel Fitzmaurice.   IrLP

In the midst of the Great Sadovaya.   Secret Agent, A.   Yevgeny Borisovich Rein.   ItGoST, *tr. by* Judith Hemschemeyer

In the midst of this world.   Issa.   SoOfWa, *tr. by* Sam Hamill

In the Midwest.   Edward Hirsch.   PfSP

In the mild west dissolv'd the blaze of day.   Anne Batten Cristall.   RWP *Fr.* Thelmon and Carmel; An Irregular Poem.

In the Mile End Road.   Amy Levy.   PEW; RACG; ViWPN

In the mirror in front of me.   Your Body Glistens From the Bath.   Charles Rossiter.   PasH

In the mirror it's plain to see.   Bald.   Bill Zavatsky.   FaoP

In the mirror of the open window the mirror-cloud drifts.   Clouds.   Sándor Weöres.   IQMS, *tr. by* Edwin Morgan

In the mirror of time.   Upon It They Gently Reflect.   Coral Bracho.   RMCMP, *tr. by* Suzanne Jill Levine

In the mirror there is no sound.   Mirror.   Yi Sang.   CAMKP, *tr. by* Walter Lew

In the Miscroscope.   Miroslav Holub.   PoSu; WoPoe, *tr. by* Ian Milner and Jarmila Milner

In the misty night humming to themselves like morons.   Louis MacNeice.   AF

In the Moment.   César Vallejo.   WED, *tr. by* Robert Bly

In the moment before it disappears. (LL)   Garden, The.   Mark Strand.   ColAP; NoAM

In the moment the tennis player majestically launches.   In the Moment.   César Vallejo.   WED, *tr. by* Robert Bly

In the monsoon when the heat dropped to ninety.   Papasan.   Doug Anderson.   AmWaPo

In the month of Averil.   Cuckoo, The.   *Unknown.*   FaBoVe

In the month of her death, she is standing by the windowframe.   Ein Leben.   Dan Pagis.   GPTC, *tr. by* Stephen Mitchell

In the Moonlight.   Thomas Hardy.   NAMCP V.1; NoAM *Fr.* Satires of Circumstance in Fifteen Glimpses.

In the moonlight / I met Berserk. Anecdote of the Prince of Peacocks. Wallace Stevens. AWTN

In the moonlit garden paulownia leaves fall. Taking Leave of Minister So Seyang. Hwang Chini. CATKP, tr. by Peter H. Lee

In the Morning. Steve Kowit. BLT

In the morning after the great chaos concert the faces emptied. Sign of the Bite, The. Ronny Someck. IrPoTo, tr. by Vivian Eden

In the morning, as he was returning to the city. Donald Hall. GI Fr. St. Matthew.

In the morning, before breakfast, I save my own life. Man Saves Own Life. Aaron Anstett. AmPoNex

In the morning God pulled me onto the porch. As If There Were Only One. Martha Serpas. Vesp

In the morning gone again and only body, presence but not is—is this. Avoid. Rachel Zucker. IAoNAP

In the morning I set out from the sun-lit shore. What I Saw When I Had Crossed the Lake. Hsieh Ling-yün. CCL1, tr. by John Frodsham

In the morning in the blue snow. Annual Gaiety. Wallace Stevens. MoAmPo

In the morning of my manswarmed days. Horse in My Yard, The. Gene Shuford. TiP2

In the morning of the tribe this name Ancapagari was given to these mountains. Ancapagari. Carolyn Forché. YaYoPo

In the morning or at any time, in the morning. Morning. Duo Duo. PoetW, tr. by Maghiel van Crevel

In the morning part. Did John's Music Kill Him? Alfred B. Spellman. EGAG; SeSe

In the morning she thinks. Learning to Live with the Piano. Ann Lundberg Grunke. MiVo

In the morning the languid rhythm. Morning Set. Joe Denham. OpeFie

In the morning, the water fed the sky. Commentary Text Commentary Text Commentary Text. David Shapiro. PmAP

In the morning / Very bright the. In Bed with Joan & Alex. Ted Berrigan. AHA

In the morning when I leave my hogan. Mother's Lace. Shonto Begay. NOxBChV

In the morning, when the sun. David Craig. UpMys Fr. Marian Sector.

In the morning with my staff I sought the topmost crag. On Climbing the Highest Peak of Stone Gate Mountain. Hsieh Ling-yün. ColAnChi, tr. by Richard W. Bodman

In the morning with the journey all before us on the road. One Step at a Time. Joseph Morris. ITBLP

In the most obscure of streets in the shadow of architectural ribs, where. Zurich Chronicle February 1916. Tristan Tzara. PFTM-1

In the Mount of Final Repose there is no repose. In the Mount of Final Repose. Eli Alon. NRoS, tr. by Esther Raizen

In the Mountain. Wang Wei. ChinPo, tr. by Ye Weilian [or Yeh Wei-lien or Wai-lim Yip]

In the mountain rain. Death Poems in September. Diane Di Prima. BB

In the mountain village. Basho. EMJL, tr. by Haruo Shirane

In the mountains? (LL) Three "Dharma Poems." Diane Di Prima. WANABP; WhBo

In the Mountains. Andrey Andreievich Voznesensky. RusPo, tr. by Robert Arthur Douglas Ford

In the Mountains. Wang Po. CrYelRi, tr. by Sam Hamill

In the Mountains as Autumn Begins. Wen T'ing-yün. CCL1, tr. by Kenneth Rexroth

In the mountains it's cold. In the Mountains. Han-shan (Cold Mountain). CCL1; NDACCP, tr. by Gary Snyder

In the Mountains of the Moon, Uganda. Lorna Goodison. WaAnP

In the Mountains on a Summer Day. Li Po. TAL

In the movie plays. Cup of Coffee, a Sandwich, and You. Al Dubin and Billy Rose. ReLy

In the MR waiting room, gown pants and booties. MRI. Ron Charach. BloBone

In the multitude of counsellors. Kyrielle: Party Politics. Frederick Thomas Bennett Macartney. NOBAu

In the Museum. Isabella Gardner. SoSe-8

In the Museum of the Word (Henri Matisse). Ann Lauterbach. AWPTFC

In the museum of translucent. Exhibits, The. Tracey Herd. MFPA

In the music of the morns. Call, A. Thomas Holley Chivers. STuOW

In the Naked Bed, in Plato's Cave. Delmore Schwartz. APT-2; MoAmPo; NAMCP V.2; NoAM; PoA 2002; WaAnP

In the nation of rainy days. Pluvia. Donald Hall. PfSP

In the nativity of time. Love Made in the First Age[: To Chloris]. Richard Lovelace. NAEL-6v1; NAEL-7v1

In the nearby mountains, a green mountain haze. 82. Shih Shu. CSKM, tr. by James H. Sanford

In the network, in the ruin. Trope Market. Jackson Mac Low. PmAP

In the never truly ever. Song Beside a Sippy Cup. Jenny Factor. P180; PoDa

In the New Country. Barbara Ras. OPRER

In the New World. Florence Elon. ASA

'In the New World Happiness Is Allowed'. Peter Porter. BMAP

In the Next Galaxy. Ruth Stone. BeAl; StAl

In the Next Life in an absinthe slip. Self Portrait in Horse Hair Wig. Cynthia Cruz. IIR

In the next seat the young man from Bangalore sleeps. Carpe Diem: Time Piece. Marilyn Krysl. PuP-23

In the Night. Ch'oe Ch'ung. WoPoe, tr. by Peter H. Lee

In the Night. Kim Hyesun. CAMKP, tr. by Jiwon Shin

In the Night. Carmela Raàm-Lachish. NRoS, tr. by Esther Raizen

In the Night. Robert Ivanovich Rozhdestvensky. RusPo, tr. by Robert Arthur Douglas Ford

In the night. Blues. Sonia Sanchez. GT

In the Night. James Stephens. OBMV

In the Night. Unknown. NBLV

In the Night. Ella Wheeler Wilcox. SWaP

In the night, awash with symbols. Night. Duo Duo. PoetW, tr. by Donald Finkel and Li Guohua

In the night each one of us is alone. House, The. Dewi Stephen Jones. BBMWP, tr. by the author

In the night, in the wind, at the edge of the rain. Irises. Li-Young Lee. BLT

In the night of the beginning. Alice Rahon. SurWo, tr. by Nancy Deffebach and Vanina Deler

In the night she told a story. Story, A. Jean Ingelow. VWP

In the night that lasted a lifetime. Dream of a Snow Flower, The. Shakir Samawi. IrPoTo, tr. by Chuck Miller and Saadi A. Simawe

In the night there are naturally the seven marvels of the world. Sleep Spaces. Robert Desnos. SurPaPo, tr. by Mary Ann Caws

In the night / Though we're apart. Haunted Heart. Howard Dietz. ReLy

In the night woods, any stir is sudden. Panic. Austin Hummell. LiTh

In the nightmare scenarios of a Jewish grandmother. Grandmother Living in Fear of Free Verse. Nina Corwin. VisFro

In the nights of insomnia I read. Anne. Alice Derry. FiBr

In the nighttime someone in my place. In The Nighttime Someone. Luigi Fontanella. NeIt, tr. by Michael Palma

In the north birds feather a long wind. Portrait of a Lady Walking. Djuna Barnes. APT-1

In the north there is a lovely woman. Song, A. Li Yen-nien. ColAnChi, tr. by Anne Birrell

In the northwest there is a Weaving-lady. Ts'ao Chih. CCL1

In the numb, numberless days. Burning, The. N. Scott Momaday. HATNAP

In the Nursing Home. Jane Kenyon. BeAl

In the office is Mrs. Apostolacos; the bus driver is Ray. (LL) Questions, The: "What about the people who came to my father's office." Robert Pinsky. ColAP; NAMCP V.2; NoAM

In the offing scattereth foam, thy white sails crowding. (LL) Passer-by, A. Robert Bridges. MoBrPo; OBEV

In the old accents I will sing, my Glory, my Delight. Fellowship. Michael Field. VWP

In the old age black was not counted fair. William Shakespeare. NAEL-6v1; NAEL-7v1; OxAEP-1 Fr. Sonnets.

In the Old Capital. Sǒ Chǒngju. CAMKP, tr. by David R. McCann

In the Old Days. C. D. Wright. InGu Fr. Just Whistle.

In the old days (a custom laid aside). Abraham Davenport. John Greenleaf Whittier. NoP-4; TCAPo

In the old days, before the war, things were different. You could walk out to the end of the dock. Before the War. Margaret Atwood. MotU

'In the old days,' she explained to a grandchild bred in England. Stone of Patience. Mimi Khalvati. MFPA

In the old days with married women's stockings. Libertine, The. Louis MacNeice. ModIr; NAMCP V.1; NoAM

In the old house. Formal Poem, A. Amal Moussa. PoArWo, tr. by Khaled Mattawa

In the Old Neighborhood. Rita Dove. SpirFl

In the old neighborhood, each funeral parlor. Teach Us to Number Our Days. Rita Dove. ESEAA; NoAM

In the old olive wood box. Snake Dress, The. Pascale Petit. MoWP

In the old park frozen and alone. Exchange of Feelings. Paul Verlaine. SxFrPo, tr. by Martin Sorrell

In the old picture. Picture, The. Einir Jones. BBMWP, tr. by Joseph P. Clancy

In the old, scratched, cheap wood of the typing stand. Dreamwood. Adrienne Rich. PoA 2002

In the old sense. De son eage; the case presents. H. S. Mauberley (Life and Contacts) Part 1 by Ezra Pound. Alex Rawls. AnSo

In the old testament. Bible Study. Gloria C. Oden. ESEAA; GT

In the old way and raise our heritage. (LL) Poem from Llanybri. Lynnette Roberts. AngWePo; TCAWP

In the old way the old wood. Fanny Howe. FaoP *Fr.* Passion, The.

In the olive darkness of the sally-trees. Bull, The. Judith Wright. BrAP

In the one cool room in the house. Andrew Taylor. BMAP

In the only moment of ecstasy I have. Peaches. Anne-Marie Oomen. NevBe

In the Open Air. Gwyneth Lewis. ATSWP, *tr.* by Robert Minhinnick

In the orchard. Warmth, The. Petar Alipiev. CSCBP, *tr.* by Georgi Belev and Lisa Sapinkopf

In the orchard. Plume. Richard Kenney. NoP-4

In the Orchard. Anne Stevenson. ColAP; WaAnP

In the orchard grass, through the daisies and clover. Blossom. May Probyn. VWP

In the orchard rooms. Fruit. Philippe Jaccottet. MFP, *tr.* by Martin Sorrell

In the other gardens. Autumn Fires. Robert Louis Stevenson. NOxBChV

In the outer suburbs the coalmen race their carts. Coalmen, The. László Nagy. IQMS, *tr.* by Tony Connor

In the Outhouse. Katherine Pierpoint. MFPA

In the painting above your bed a woman pauses. Thirst. Mark Wunderlich. AmPoNex

In the palace at dusk the blinds of pearl are unfurled. Complaint of the Jade Staircase. Hsieh T'iao. CCL1, *tr.* by John Frodsham

In the Palace of the President this morning. Easter Sunday, 1985. Charles Martin. RA

In The Palace of the slums. Welsh Valley Cinema, 1930s. Dannie Abse. TCAWP

In the Palais Royal Garden. Christopher Pearse Cranch. APN-1

In the pale light of the half moon, she sees him. Somnambulist. Adele Ne Jame. PoArWo

In the pale moonlight. World's First Face, The. W. S. Rendra. WoPoe, *tr.* by Burton Raffel

In the Palm of My Hand. Víctor Terán. RMCMP, *tr.* by Donald Frischmann

In the Pantry. Hugh MacDiarmid. NAMCP V.1; NoAM

In the parched word, unformulated, it shrinks. On the Facets: The Flashing. Coral Bracho. PFTM-2, *tr.* by Thomas Hoeksema

In the Park. Judith Beveridge. BMAP

In the Park. Gwen Harwood. BMAP; NIL-7

In the Park. Peter Jones. OBGa

In the Park. Maxine W. Kumin. CAP-8

In the Park. Tom Sleigh. MAAN

In the park a crow awakes. Kenneth Rexroth. APSN *Fr.* Love Poems of Marichiko, The.

In the park behind the battlements where my men's group meets. Displaced Person. Christopher Davis. RWB

In the park the peacocks. Sun King Sulking. Peter Porter. PoA 2002

In the parking lot where the path to the sea begins. Homeless. Michael Hannon. GeoHom

In the Parlour. Martin Mooney. NIrP

In the Past. Trumbull Stickney. ColAP

In the past the warring nations. Civilisation. János Arany. IQMS, *tr.* by Peter Zollman

In the pathway of the sun. Penelope. Dorothy Parker. FaBoWar; PoAgWa

In the patient world, be an instant. Ian Patterson. VaPo *Fr.* Hardihood.

In the Paul Guillaume Gallery. Pierre Albert-Birot. CuPo

In the Pea Patch. Maxine W. Kumin. AFaM; CAP-8

In the penetrating damp. Restless Night in Camp, A. Tu Fu [*or* Du Fu]. NDACCP, *tr.* by Kenneth Rexroth

In the Person of a Lady, to Bajazet, Her Unconstant Gallant. "Ephelia." PEW

In the Person of Womankind (In Defense of Their Inconstancy). Ben Jonson. NAEL-6v1

In the photo, if I am disheveled, hanging onto the blank fence spikes, where were your arms? Emily. Catherine Imbriglio. IAoNAP

In the Picture. Elke Erb. MotU, *tr.* by Craig Federhen

In the Pines. Bill Monroe. GM

In the place that is my own place, whose earth. Sycamore, The. Wendell Berry. LPSFW; UpMys

In the place where. Judy Grahn. NALW *Fr.* Edward the Dyke and Other Poems.

In the plain stands a plum tree. *Unknown.* NaPG, *tr.* by Talat Sait Halman

In the play about the first telescope, a man notes. To Janet, on Galileo. Honor Moore. PfS

In the plum blossom scent. Basho. EMJL *Fr.* Plum Blossom Scent.

In the pocket. Winona Baker. IFF *Fr.* Spring.

In the poem about the vandals, the vandals. Vandals, The. Alan Michael Parker. LegDan; NeAmPo

In the poem about their dying. Vandals Dying, The. Alan Michael Parker. LegDan

In the poem he learns to turn and turn, and prose seems always a sentence long. (LL) Notes for Echo Lake 3. Michael Palmer. PmAP; WaAnP

In the poem that comes just before sleep. Just Before Sleep. Peter Everwine. GeoHom

In "The Poems," in my eyes, in the line, "Guillaume Apollinaire is dead." (LL) Ted Berrigan. NYP2; PFTM-2 *Fr.* Sonnets, The.

In the polyglot. Cupid. Clare Rossini. MAAN

In the pond of our new garden. Visiting Hour. Stewart Conn. StAl

In the poor man's house. Teiga. SoOfWa, *tr.* by Sam Hamill

In the Poppy Field. James Stephens. IrV

In the Post Office. Thom Gunn. CAGL

In the postmodern world. Being Sick Together. Elaine Equi. IllVoic

In the Potting Shed. Sir Osbert Sitwell. OBGa

In the Praise of Music. Humphrey Gifford. NoSic

In the prelight. Monday Morning. Audrey Shafer. BloBone

In the presence of blue, it's the eye. Past Midnight, My Daughter Awakened by Miles Davis' *Kind of Blue.* Kevin Stein. IllVoic

In the prison's visitors room, I'm waiting for my. Utah Jazz, The. Rick Higgerson. MAAN

In the *Proceedings of the Royal Institute of Anthropophagy.* Perversion, A. Christopher Reid. OBCoV

In the prose version. Helen Paints a Room (1984). John A. Scott. BMAP

In the Proximity of Andy Warhol. Jürgen Becker. GTCP, *tr.* by Reinhold Grimm

In the public square. Mysterious. Sadiq al-Saygh. IrPoTo, *tr.* by Ralph Saverese and Saadi A. Simawe

In the Public Theater lobby, I wait for Marie. Marilyn Hacker. VCAP *Fr.* Taking Notice.

In the puffing gusty nights. Lighthouse Keeper. Harry Edmund Martinson. WED, *tr.* by Robert Bly

In the pure morning, near the old temple. Buddhist Retreat Behind Broken-Mountain Temple, A. Ch'ang Chien. CCL1, *tr.* by Witter Bynner

In the Purple Bar. Gig Ryan. BMAP

In the purple light, heavy with redwood, the slopes drop seaward. Apology for Bad Dreams. Robinson Jeffers. APT-1; MoAmPo

In the quarries should you toil. Make Your Mark. David Barker. TreFP

In the quiet of the barn loft study I've read the poem again. Reading "Crossing Brooklyn Ferry" on a Summer Morning. Howard Nelson. ViWalt

In the railroad yards, leaving the city of darkness. And as for Man. Loren C. Eiseley. GM

In the rain, in Baltimore. Woman Is Waiting for a Bus, A. Maura Eichner. UpMys

In the rain, the lonesome. Banner Bearer, The. William Carlos Williams. PoCho

In the ranks of the Austrian you found him. Forced Recruit, The. Elizabeth Barrett Browning. FaBoWar

In the Reading-Room of the Brtish Museum. Louise Imogen Guiney. APN-2

In the Realm of Emptiness. (LL) Saying Good-bye to a Singing Girl Who Has Decided to Become a Nun. Mo Shih-lung. ColAnChi; WoPoe, *tr.* by Jonathan Chaves

In the Rearview Mirror. Karl Krolow. GTCP, *tr.* by Reinhold Grimm

In the rear-view mirror suddenly. Auto Mirror. Adam Zagajewski. BLT

In the recessed tomb of eyelids. Transparent Man, The. Bernard Bador. ConPit, *tr.* by Clayton Eshleman

In the Red Book. Kevin Corcoran. Oth

In the region of rain and cloud. Desire's Persistence. Jay Wright. ESEAA

In the Restaurant. Gerald William Barrax. GT

In the Restaurant. Thomas Hardy. MoBrPo *Fr.* Satires of Circumstance in Fifteen Glimpses.

In the retelling. At the Commission. Ingrid de Kok. TSAP

In the Ringwood. Thomas Kinsella. PBCIP

In the ripest days of August, sunflowers. Whisper, The. Eugene Gloria. OpBo

In the Ritz at Meknes. Manuel Ulacia. RMCMP, *tr.* by Indran Amirthanayagam

In the river bank, an empty sandpit. Frankfurt. János Pilinszky. PoSu

In the Roman Forum. István Vas. IQMS, *tr.* by Bruce Berlind

In the Room. James Thomson. NePenScot; OxBEV

In the room awash with light. His Last Words. Yun Tongju. CAMKP, *tr.* by Kay Richards and Steffen Richards

In the Room I. Prnts

In the Room of Never Grieve. Anne Waldman. AmZen

In the room the women come and go. Mother Dawning. Janine Canan. HW

In the room where we lie, light. This Close. Dorianne Laux. ExTi

In the room's corner the shadow played its little flute. Flute, The. Sophia De Mello Breyner. VCWP, *tr.* by Ruth Fainlight

In the rose creeping into the tower of exiles. Winter Day, A. Philip Lamantia. CLPP

In the Rosy Bowers of Aiden. Thomas Holley Chivers. STuOW *Fr.* Vigil of Aiden, The.

In the Royal City spring is almost over. Flower Market, The. Po Chü-i. CCL1, *tr. by* Arthur Waley

In the Rubble. Judson Crews. ICANM

In the ruins, in the tavern. Esrâr Dede. OLP, *tr. by* Walter Andrews, Najaat Black and Mehmet Kalpakli

In the rush at pau hana. *Hawaiian Oral Tradition.* NAAPv.2

In the rush odour of Danish meadows. Peter Huchel. PoSu

In the sacred city of Benares. (LL) Courtesy, a Trenchant Grace, A. Cyrus Cassells. GT; WiU

In the salt warp. Origins. Carl Rakosi. FTOS

In the same mud in the terrible ground. (LL) Survival: Infantry. George Oppen. AmWaPo; FTOS; NAMCP V.1; PWW2

In the same way. (LL) Apology. William Carlos Williams. NAAPv.2; SAmP

In the same way that the mindless diamond keeps. Poetry. Don Paterson. P180

In the satin shade of an olive tree. Achilles and the Tortoise. Miroslav Holub. PoSu, *tr. by* Stuart Friebert and Dana Hábová

In the scattered light. EMJL *Fr.* Mad Verse.

In the school auditorium. Bully. Martín Espada. LTA

In the schoolyard / girls with fat legs. Self-Portrait at Age Ten. Homero Aridjis. WoBe, *tr. by* George McWhirter

In the sea, Biscayne, there prinks. Homunculus et La Belle Etoile. Wallace Stevens. MoAmPo

In the seacoast alley. Na Aurea. Natalia Toledo. RMCMP, *tr. by* Alberto A. Ríos

In the season of brightness. Twelfth Man, The. Iftiqar Arif. PML, *tr. by* Brenda Walker and Andrea Deletant

In the season of late August star-fall. Amazing Grace in the Back Country. Robert Penn Warren. ColAP

In the Season of Suicides. Lisa D. Chavez. LiTh

In the season of this ripening. Elemental. Marjorie M. Evasco. ReBoTo

In the second circle—the level of perpetual dysfunction. Walt Whitman in Hell. T. R. Hummer. ViWalt

In the second month, sleeping a lot, all sleepy and dazed. Daytime Dream. Tu Fu [*or* Du Fu]. WoPoe, *tr. by* Eva Shan Chou

In the second reign year of Haamfung, a trip to Gold Mountain was made. Song of the Wife of a Gold Mountain Man. *Chinese Oral Tradition.* NAAPv.1

In the Secret House of Night. Jorge Teillier. BLPSL, *tr. by* Rene de Costa, Rigas Kappatos and Eleni Paidoussi

In the secret of night. Liana, The. Gabriela Mistral. BBASP, *tr. by* Doris Dana

In the separate histories. Pretty Blue Apron. James McMichael. PtR

In the sequestered court quiet reigns. Tune: "Beating Silk Floss." Li Yü. ColAnChi, *tr. by* Jiaosheng Wang

In the Servants' Quarters. Thomas Hardy. FaBoVe; MoBrPo

In the Service of the Wheel. Hans Faverey. TuT, *tr. by* Peter van de Kamp

In the Sevan Mountains. Silva Kaputikyan. SonAtl, *tr. by* Dorli Meek

In the Seven Woods. William Butler Yeats. NoAM

In the seventh month, declining is the Fire Star. *Unknown.* ColAnChi *Fr.* Classic of Odes.

In the seventh month the Fire ebbs. Qui-yue: In the Seventh Month. *Unknown.* CCL1, *tr. by* Arthur Waley

In the shabby train no seat is vacant. Refugees, The. Randall Jarrell. MoAmPo

In the shade of a metaphor. Patrizia Cavalli. NeIt

In the shade of a plane tree with our shopping. City Park. Christine Crow. SSCS

In the shade of a wall. New Sweater. Kees Ouwens. TuT, *tr. by* Peter van de Kamp

In the shadow of a wing. José Martí. TCLAP *Fr.* Simple Verses.

In the Shadow of Death. Juan Chi. CCL1, *tr. by* Michael Bullock and C. J. Chen

In the Shadow of Fire. Frieda Hughes. NeBl

In the shadow of floodlights. 911. Jim Daniels. LiTh

In the shadow of the gleaming carpet. Loving Poem. Gisèle Prassinos. YaTCFP, *tr. by* Mary Ann Caws

In the Shadow of the Poisoned Wind. Jack Marshall. AtGh

In the Shadows of the Wu-t'ung Tree. *Unknown.* CrYelRi, *tr. by* Sam Hamill

In the Shakespeare Garden at Northwestern University. Paul Carroll. IllVoic

In the shallows. Basho. EMJL, *tr. by* Haruo Shirane

In the shambles of love, they kill only the best,. Jelaluddin Rumi. RaBo *Fr.* Four Quatrains.

In the shape of this night, in the still fall. Kenneth Patchen. ItP *Fr.* Eight Early Poems.

In the shimmer of distance. At Lushan Temple. Ching An. CSKM, *tr. by* Jerome P. Seaton

In the shimmering countries that exude the summer. Manuscript Found in a Book of Joseph Conrad. Jorge Luis Borges. PoetW, *tr. by* Alastair Reid

In the shimmering heat every plant grows jealous. Diana Hartog. NLPA *Fr.* Oasis.

In the shop, she, her mother, and grandmother. Charles Reznikoff. APT-2; NAAPv.2

In the shop-window of a small city a white, yellow and green plaster. Dragon Carries the Inscription "Kunigundula" and Is Led on a Leash, The. Hans Arp. MotU, *tr. by* Bethany Schneider

In the shower, at the shaving mirror or beach. My Mammogram. J. D. McClatchy. WiU

In the shower naked. Breast Examination. Wanda Coleman. GT

In the Shreve High football stadium. Autumn Begins in Martins Ferry, Ohio. James Wright. CAP-8; ColAP; EMP; HeIP-4; IJHIL; MoASP; NAAL-5; NAMCP V.2; NoAM; OxBoAm; StAl; VCAP; WaAnP; WeW-3

In the Sierras. Al Young. CalPo

In the sightless air I dwell. Song of a Spirit. Ann Radcliffe. RWP

In the sights of the iron bee, the rose opened in tears. (LL) At the Gates of Aerea. René Char. BAP-04; MotU, *tr. by* Franz Wright

In the silence and the gloom. (LL) Aftermath. Henry Wadsworth Longfellow. APN-1; NAAL-3; NAAPv.1; PoPoPo

In the silence that prolongs the span. Black Jackets. Thom Gunn. HeIP-4; NAEL-6v2; NAEL-7v2; NoP-4; NoP-5

In the silent halls of Hades, down the windless halls of Hades. Danaïds, The. Mihály Babits. IQMS, *tr. by* Peter Zollman

In the Silurian seas! (LL) Lay of the Trilobite. May Kendall. NPeEn; ViWPN; VWP

In the sister's garden it is still winter. Family History, The. Nicole Cooley. AmPoNex

In the 60's, there was emotion to go around. Courageousness. Imamu Amiri Baraka. EGAG

In the sixty-eight years. Accounting. Claribel Alegría. TANSG, *tr. by* Darwin Flakoll

In the sixty-three years. Summing Up. Claribel Alegría. LoL

In the sky. Last Hour, The. Tudor Arghezi. WoPoe, *tr. by* Michael Impey and Brian Swann

In the sky, I've seen. Woman and Beauty. Goran. IrPoTo, *tr. by* Abdul Kadir Said Ferhadi

In the sky of men the bread of stars seemed to me shadowy and hardened. Fighters. René Char. YaTCFP, *tr. by* Thomas Merton

In the sky the eagle, there is his place, there far above us. Eagle Above Us, The. *Unknown.* WoPoe, *tr. by* Willard Trask

In the sky there is nobody asleep. Nobody, nobody. City That Does Not Sleep. Federico García Lorca. RaW, *tr. by* Robert Bly

In the sleeping ward, night-nurses. Immoralist, The. Robin Robertson. NeBrP

In the slight ripple, the fishes dart. In the Slight Ripple, the Mind Perceives the Heart. Delmore Schwartz. APT-2

In the Slight Ripple, the Mind Perceives the Heart. Delmore Schwartz. APT-2

In the sludge drawer of animals in arms. Rules of Sleep. Howard Moss. VCAP

In the small beauty of the forest. Psalm. George Oppen. APT-2; CalPo; HarvBoo; ItP; NAMCP V.1; OxBoAm; PFTM-2; PoCho; WoPoe

In the small old barn. Eternal Landscape, The. Lenard D. Moore. GT

In the small town where the hero was born. Pietà. Wisława Szymborska. VCWP

In the Smoking-Car. Richard Wilbur. GM; MoAmPo

In the snowy yard a baroque thermometer. Comatas. Harry Mathews. NYP2

In the snug harbors, helicopter and electric eel. Spring Street Girl Friend (#8). C. D. Wright. GPPA

In the South. His Fingers Seem to Sing. Sam Cornish. GT

In the south aisle of the abbey at Hexham. Musician, The. David Wright. NLP

In the south country there lives a lovely lady. Ts'ao Chih. CCL1, *tr. by* John Frodsham

In the South Courtyard. Wen T'ing-yün. CCL1, *tr. by* Glen Baxter

In the south courtyard everywhere willow floss covers the ground. In the South Courtyard. Wen T'ing-yün. CCL1, *tr. by* Glen Baxter

In the South lies a lonesome, hungry Land. Laughter in the Senate. Sidney Lanier. AmWaPo

In the south, sleeping against. Legacy. Imamu Amiri Baraka. ColAP; NAMCP V.2; NoAM

In the southern land many birds sing;. South, The. Wang Chien. BLT, *tr. by* Arthur Waley

In the Southern Mode, to the Tune "A Sprig of Flowers" The Refusal to Get Old. Kuan Han-ch'ing. ColAnChi, *tr. by* Wayne Schlepp

In the spring. Shingle Flies. Hugh MacDonald. Coast

In the spring, by the big shuck-pile. Burning the Cat. W. S. Merwin. NIP-4

In the Spring Garden. Geoffrey Grigson. OBGa

In the Spring of Hjalmar Calrson: The Real Story. Christopher Howell. RoV

In the Spring of No Letters. Marlene Cookshaw. IFF
In the Spring the quince and the. Ibycus. WoPoe, tr. by Kenneth Rexroth
In the Spring when the feeling was chronic. You Took Advantage of Me.
   Lorenz Hart. ReLy
In the spring, when winds blew and farmers were plowing fields. American
   Spring Song. Sherwood Anderson. APT-1
In the Springtime I am always. Old Age. Ou-yang Hsiu. NDACCP, tr. by
   Kenneth Rexroth
In the State of "Old Palmetto," from the town of Eutawville. Eutawville
   Lynching, The. Lizelia Augusta Jenkins Moorer. CBWP-3
In the Stealth of Stillness. Thurayya Al-Urayyid. PoArWo, tr. by Farouk
   Mustafa
In the Steam Bath. Manuel Ulacia. RMCMP, tr. by Indran Amirthanayagam
In the steamer is the trout. Eating Together. Li-Young Lee. CAP-8; IllVoic;
   InvLad; NAAL-5; NAMCP V.2
In the Steps of the Moon. Philippe Jaccottet. YaTCFP, tr. by Edward Lucie-
   Smith
In the still of night. Mothers. Kay Boyle. PoChi
In the Still of the Night. Cole Porter. ReLy
In the still pond. Summer's End. Eve Merriam. WhBo
In the still world. War Ending, The. Medbh McGuckian. NAMCP V.2
In the still-blistering late afternoon. Farmer, The. Ellen Bryant Voigt.
   WeW-3
In the stillness after dawn we two. Equinox 1980. Peter Davison. NoP-4;
   NoP-5
In the Stopping Train. Donald Davie. NPeEn
   "Things he has been spared, The." NAMCP V.2
In the Storm of Roses. Ingeborg Bachmann. AF, tr. by Mark Anderson
   (Aria 1.) WoPoe
In the story of Patroclus. Triumph of Achilles, The. Louise Glück.
   OxBoAm
In the strange early morning half light we sit. In the World. Brigid Lowry.
   WhBo
In the strange quiet, I realise. Forty-one, Alone, No Gerbil. Sharon Olds.
   BeAl
In the Street. Constantine P. Cavafy. CAGL, tr. by Edmund Keeley and Philip
   Sherrard
In the street young men play ball, else in fresh shirts. People on Sunday.
   Edwin Denby. NYP2
In the Studio. Charles Tomlinson. RWPCtW
In the Style of Han Shan and Shih Te. Wang An-shih. tr. by Jan W. Walls
   "Had I been an ox or horse." WoPoe, tr. by Jan W. Walls
In the subtropics it must be spring. Psyche and Eros in Florida. Debora
   Greger. PoA 2002
In the Suburbs. Louis Simpson. CAP-8; TRP
In the suburbs our lives were separated. Walls, The. Douglas Goetsch.
   AmPoNex
In the Subway—Getting Used to Ugliness 3. Kim Chŏngnan. EcSo, tr. by
   Peter H. Lee
In the Sulphur Garden. David St. John. AmAlph
In the summer I walked a trail, trying to accept things as they are. Figure and
   Ground. Christine Garren. PoDa
In the summer months on every crossing to Piraeus. Watching for Dolphins.
   David Constantine. HarvBoo; StAl
In the summer rain. Buson. EH, tr. by Robert Hass
In the sun, it is hot. Office Geraniums. Laura Newburn. UrbNat
In the sun-drenched. City of Salt, The. Gregory Orr. BodElec
In the survey 57 percent responded that yes. Minnesota Farmers Blame Bad
   Crop on Jews. Robert Hershon. PrTe
In the sweet shire of Cardigan. Simon Lee, the Old Huntsman; with an Incident
   in which He Was Concerned. William Wordsworth. NAEL-6v2; NAEL-
   7v2
In the sweet shire of Cardigan. William Wordsworth. STuOW Fr. Simon Lee
   [Original Version].
In the sweetness of new spring. Spring Song. William of Aquitaine.
   NAWM-7v1, tr. by Peter Dronke
In the swollen head of the nation. (LL) Robert Duncan. APSN; NAMCP V.2
   Fr. Passages.
In the Synagogue. Cynthia Ozick. TaR
In the tall orange marigolds, some bees. August. Pamela Stewart. ExTi
In the Tank. Thom Gunn. NoAM
In the tattered wallpaper I see a butterfly dying. Yi Sang. CAMKP; PFTM-1
   Fr. Crow's-Eye View.
In the tavern where I slept last night. Dead Eyes. Syl Cheney-Coker. NAfrP
In the teacher's lounge, the tall, pretty. Art. Susan Aizenberg. ExTi
In the temple of my soul, demons pray. Beggar, The. Murad Mikha'il.
   IrPoTo, tr. by Christina Coyle and Sadok Masliyah
In the terrible years of Yezhovism I spent seventeen months standing in.
   Instead of a Preface. Anna Andreyevna Akhmatova. PFTM-1

In the Theatre. Dannie Abse. BloBone; NoAM; TCAWP
In the Theatre. Paulette Roeske. Vesp
In the thicket's shade. Issa. EH, tr. by Robert Hass
In the Thiergarten, on a bench, I'm sitting and smoking. Arno Holz. GTCP
   Fr. Phantasus.
In the third decade of March. Where Art Is a Midwife. Tom Paulin. ModIr;
   NPeEn
In the Third Month. David Ray. RaBo
In the third month, a sudden flow of blood. Vow, The. Anthony Hecht. TaR
In the third month her laughter sounds strained. On the Metamorphoses
   Brought About By Emotion: The Rebellion of the Eyes. Andrey
   Andreievich Voznesensky. PFTM-2, tr. by Anselm Hollo
In the third-class seat sat the journeying boy. Midnight on the Great Western.
   Thomas Hardy. OxAEP-2; WoPoe
In the Tibetan map of the world, the world is a circle and at the center. Wild
   White Horses. Laurie Anderson. WhBo
In the tombs orgies go on by themselves. Letter to Her Brother. Amelia
   Rosselli. PFTM-2, tr. by Lucia Re and Paul Vangelisti
In the torment of its burnt body? (LL) If I Only Knew. Nelly Sachs.
   PoAgWa; PoSu, tr. by Matthew Mead and Ruth Mead
In the Torrent. Johannes Bobrowski. WoPoe, tr. by Mark Rudman
In the torrential downpours, Lorca arrives one night at our house. Duende.
   Virgil Suarez. PML
In the tower the bell. Bell, The. Richard Jones. P180
In the Town. Unknown. OBCP, tr. by Eleanor Farjeon
In the town of Bardez where Armenians. Dance, The. Siamanto. AF, tr. by
   Peter Balakian and Nevart Yaghlian
In the town streets. Sparrow. Reginald Gibbons. IllVoic
In the town where every man is king. Josephine Miles. NALW
In the Toy Shop. May Kendall. ViWPN
In the Tradition of Bobbitt. Saundra Sharp. SpirFl
In the Tradition Too. Ras Baraka. InTrad
In the train. Only in Poetry. Ajip Rosidi. WoPoe, tr. by Harry Aveling
In the Train. James Thomson. OBEV
In the tranced dancing of men. (LL) Bear on the Delhi Road, The. Earle
   Birney. BrAP; HeIP-4; NoAM; NoP-4; NoP-5
In the transatlantic fury. Cyrus Cassells. TAPaP Fr. Magician-Made Tree,
   The.
In the tree—several stars, miscellaneous images, and telephone wires patterning
   lightning. Behind Eyelids. Pierre Reverdy. MotU, tr. by Michael
   Benedikt
In the tunnel of woods, as the road. Last Things. William Meredith.
   NAMCP V.2; NoAM
In the turgid silence the hammers rumble. Symphony of the Hammers.
   Evaristo Ribera Chevremont. NAAPv.2
In the twenties, I would visit Dachau often with my brother. Aubade of the
   Singer and Saboteur, Marie Triste: 1941. Norman Dubie. AmWaPo
In the Twentieth Century. James Philip McAuley. ChIV-2
In the Twenty-Fifth Year of Marriage, It Goes On. Alicia Ostriker. PBCAP
In the twenty-fifth year of my age. Petit Testament. "Ern Malley." BMAP
In the twilight of the nineteenth century. Fin de Siècle. Joe Bolton.
   AmPoNex
In the twinkling of an eye. Bone Scan. Gwen Harwood. HarvBoo
In the Underworld. Muriel Rukeyser. APSN
In the universal Sun. (LL) To Jane: The Invitation. Percy Bysshe Shelley.
   NAEL-6v2; NPBRoP; NPeEn
In the unmade light I can see the world. West Wall. W. S. Merwin. RaBo
In the unmannered madhouse. Asylum. Star Black. PA9/11
In the Upstairs Window. Carol Potter. PfS
In the usual iconography of the temple or the local Wok. Shoveling Snow with
   Buddha. Billy Collins. OxBoAm
In the vale of resteles mynde. Unknown. OHMEL
In the Valley. Priscilla Jane Thompson. CBWP-2
In the Valley of Cauteretz. Alfred Tennyson. NAEL-6v2
In the Valley of the Elwy. Gerard Manley Hopkins. OxAEP-2
In the Valley of the Jerte. Time of Cherries, A. Suzanne Burrows. Prnts
In the valley there is an order to these things. Preparations. Tony Curtis.
   TCAWP
In the valley where the stream leaps. Unknown. CATKP, tr. by Peter H. Lee
In the valleys of the future we shall walk. Desmond O'Grady. PBCIP Fr.
   Lines in a Roman Schoolbook.
In the version of the Tree Little Pigs. Wolf Soup. Vijay Seshadri. LiTh
In the very earliest time. Magic Words. Eskimo Oral Tradition. BLT, tr. by
   Edward Field
In the very earliest time. Magic Words. Unknown. RaBo, tr. by Edward
   Field
In the Very Midst of Life. Martin Luther. GePo, tr. by F. Samuel Janow
In the Vices. Donald Evans. APT-1

In the village churchyard she lies. In the Churchyard at Cambridge. Henry Wadsworth Longfellow. BrAP

In the Village of My Forefathers. Vasco [or Vasko] Popa. PoSu Fr. Raw Flesh.

In the village of the dead. Gary Snyder. PFTM-2 Fr. Myths and Texts.

In the vine-shadows on the veranda. Sisters, The. Judith Wright. NALW

In the vortex of class warfare. Poem, A. Luis Rogelio Nogueras. PML, tr. by Mark Weiss

In the Waiting Room. Elizabeth Bishop. APT-2; BrAP; CAP-8; FTtHH; GPTC; HeIP-4; NAAL-5; NALW; NAMCP V.2; NoAM; NoP-4; NoP-5; OxBoAm; PoetW; VCAP

In the Waiting Room: "Consult your tongue like a weather forecast." Linda France. PoCu

In the waiting room, she releases. First Payment. Jon Mukand. BloBone

In the waiting room we'd stared. Perfect Example of a Paralysed Larynx, A. Stephanie Norgate. PoCu

In the waking jungle / pepsinated. Mullhaven. Judson Crews. ICANM

In the wall I heard the crack. Crack, The. Carla Faesler Bremer. SPV, tr. by Jen Hofer

In the War they made a celestial cave. Robert Duncan. APSN Fr. Passages.

In the warm, humid night, noiseless and dead, a boy cries. Boy Crying in the Night. Carlos Drummond de Andrade. PML, tr. by Mark Strand

In the watchtower of fantasy. Peregrin, Wandering Hunter of Faces. José María Eguren. TCLAP, tr. by Iver Lofving

In the waters, blue and permanent. (LL) Drowned Children, The. Louise Glück. NAMCP V.2; OxBoAm; VCAP

In the Way Back. Debra Kang Dean. UnSA

In the way that the most of the wind. Wind and Tree. Paul Muldoon. NPeEn

In the Wee Small Hours of the Morning. Bob Hilliard. ReLy

In the welfare waiting room. Institutional Blue. Ann Townsend. NAPBL

In the Well. Andrew Hudgins. P180

In the well-bucket / A morning glory. Chiyojo. ZenPo, tr. by Takashi Ikemoto and Lucien Stryk

In the west, the weary Day. In Reverie. Harriet McEwen Kimball. TreFP

In the west you're still asleep. You Who Sleep. Philippe Soupault. AF, tr. by Eden Paul

In the white egg. Yannis Ritsos. PFTM-2 Fr. Second Series.

In the white of my thought. For Robert Desnos. Tristan Tzara. AF

In the white plum blossoms. Buson. EH, tr. by Robert Hass

In the wide and rocky pasture where the cedar trees are gray. Connecticut Road Song. Anna Hempstead Branch. TCAPo

In the wide womb of possibility. Sir Richard Blackmore. STuOW Fr. Creation.

In the wild October night-time, when the wind raved round the land. Thomas Hardy. MoBrPo; OBMV Fr. Dynasts, The.

In the wild soft summer darkness. Summer Night, Riverside. Sara Teasdale. APT-1

In the wild zone, we wait and watch and pray. Zoning. Joanne M. Braxton. BtF

In the Wilderness. Robert Graves. ChIV-2; MoBrPo

In the Wilderness. James Simmons. GI

In the Wilderness. Colville N. Young. OWABP

In the wilds, a dead doe. Unknown. ChinPo, tr. by Ye Weilian [or Yeh Wei-lien or Wai-lim Yip]

In the willows along the river at Pleasure Bay. At Pleasure Bay. Robert Pinsky. NAAL-5

In the wind. (LL) Moment: "I saw a young deer standing." Hildegarde Flanner. APT-2; ASA

In the wind that blows. Dead, The. René Arcos. FaBoWar, tr. by Christopher Middleton

In the wind that ripples over them. Last Scene in the First Act. Marge Piercy. NoAM

In the wind. This is the wind in a field of corn. (LL) Wind: "This is the wind, the wind in a field of corn." James Fenton. BeAl; NAEL-6v2; NAEL-7v2; NeBrP

In the Window. Carla Faesler Bremer. SPV, tr. by Jen Hofer

In the window of the drawing-room. Family Photograph, The. Vona Groarke. MFPA

In the wine as it waits in the glass. (LL) Mark Strand. NoP-4; NoP-5 Fr. Dark Harbor.

In the Winter. Sir Osbert Sitwell. OBGa

In the winter dusk. Surveillances. Tom Paulin. PNI

In the winter river. Prince Shiki. SoOfWa, tr. by Sam Hamill

In the winter stadium, picturing. What You Can't See. Karen Chase. SeSe

In the wintertime. Toe'osh; a Laguna Coyote Story. Leslie Marmon Silko. NAMCP V.2; NoAM

In the withering gusts. Basho. EMJL Fr. Mad Verse.

In the withering gusts. Basho, Kakei and Yasui. EMJL

In the wonder of the Sea. (LL) Sea Gypsy, The. Richard Hovey. BRP; TCAPo

In the wondrous light of a pair of brown eyes. Admiration. Josephine D. Henderson Heard. CBWP-4

In the Woods. Heinz Piontek. CLPP, tr. by Jerome Rothenberg

In the Woods. Unknown. SonAtl, tr. by Lester Browne, J.P. Coyne and Meagan Pfelz

In the woods are filaments of light. Signs. Mariana Romo-Carmona. WiU

In the woodyard were green and dry. Rick of Green Wood, The. Edward Dorn. PmAP

In the Workhouse. George R. Sims. OBCP

In the world. (LL) World, The. Robert Creeley. NoP-4; NoP-5; PmAP; VCAP

In the World. Brigid Lowry. WhBo

In the world are many roads I haven't walked, and I have pain. Song. Yi Kyŏngnim. EcSo, tr. by Peter H. Lee

In the world of friends, in the world of long-distance travel. From the Window of a Plane. Andrey Andreievich Voznesensky. TCRusP, tr. by Daniel Weissbort

In the world of the high jump, if something can go wrong. Learning from the Movies. Rachel Wetzsteon. ExTi

In the world we've made. Kiev, the Ukraine, Nuclear Accident. David Romtvedt. GifTon

In the wracles of walsingam. Unknown. PBRV

In the wracks of Walshingham. Unknown. NoP-4

In the yard. Morning Buddhism. E. Ethelbert Miller. BtF

In the yard. Yard. No Hyangnim. EcSo, tr. by Aimee N. Kwon

In the yard across the street we saw a snowman holding a garbage can lid smashed into a likeness of the mad English king, George the Third. (LL) You Were Wearing. Kenneth Koch. NIP-4; NoP-4; NoP-5; OxBoAm; PtR

In the Yard of the Policlinic. Vladimir Holan. AF, tr. by C. G. Hanzlicek

In the yard, peonies burst their white hearts. Peonies. Mark Wunderlich. PoDa

In the year dan-e. Owl, The. Chia Yi. CCL1, tr. by Burton Watson

In the year eighteen seventy-six. Julia A. Moore. STuOW Fr. Centennial Celebration, The.

In the year nineteen-hundred-fourteen, in his pink and white diamond-patterned costume. Marshmallow Man, The. Jean Follain. MotU, tr. by Louise Imogen Guiney

In the year since Jesus died for men. Siege of Corinth, The. Lord Byron.

In the years of her age the most beautiful. Petrarch. OBMV Fr. Sonnets to Laura.

In the yellow of butter. Afternoon in Pangasinan with No Electricity, An. Regie Cabico. ReBoTo

In the yellow pickup. Weekend Equestrian, The. Afaa Michael Weaver. GT

In the yellow room among the grey furniture I sit sorrowfully. Corner Boy's Farewell. Burns Singer. HarvBoo

In the yellow-cloud dusk, the crows. Crows at Dusk. Li Po. CrYelRi, tr. by Sam Hamill

In the Yiddish song a goat danced under. Under Her Crib. Marcia Pelletiere. OPRER

In the young spring evening. Sappho. HW, tr. by Charoula

In the young spring evening. In the young spring evening. Sappho. HW, tr. by Charoula

In the youth of summer. Hills of Cualann, The. Joseph Campbell. IrV

In the Yukon. Ralph Gustafson. NoP-4

In the Yukon the other day. Foundlings in the Yukon. A. K. Ramanujan. NAMCP V.2; PoetW

In the zero of the night, in the lipping hour. Approach to Thebes, The. Stanley Kunitz. PoA 2002

In the Zoo. A. K. Ramanujan. VCWP

In the zoo's glass room, two dozen warblers. Maintaining the Species. Deborah Burnham. UrbNat

In Thee! (LL) Wild Nights—Wild Nights! Emily Dickinson. APN-2; EroLit; ErotSp; HeIP-4; NAAL-3; NAAL-5; NAAPv.1; NALW; NAMCP V.1; NCAP; NIL-7; NIP-4; NoAM; NoP-4; NoP-5; OxBoAm; PoBW; PoPoPo; PtR; RaBo; TCAPo; WaAnP; WPoS

In their bridal-white feathers the egrets. Metamorphosis. Richard Lemm. Coast

In their cage, the lion mounts the lioness. Zoo. Georgi Belev. CSCBP, tr. by the author and Lisa Sapinkopf

In their dark, Mexican eyes. (LL) Sonrisas. Pat Mora. NIL-7; NIP-4

In their depths? (LL) Mona Lisa, A. Angelina Weld Grimké. APT-1; NAAPv.2

In their direction. (LL) Death of a Soldier, The. Wallace Stevens. AmWaPo; APT-1; NAAPv.2; NAMCP V.1; OBWP; OxBoAm; SAmP; SoSe-8

In Their House. Leah Aini. DTA, tr. by Miriyam Glazer

In their house some door is always. In Their House. Leah Aini. DTA, tr. by Miriyam Glazer

In their / limousines the. Educators, The. D. M. Black. EdScPo

In their long hair they lie. Tombs of the Hetaerae. Rainer Maria Rilke. PFTM-1

In their own order. 1. at nagasaki. Lucille Clifton. ESEAA

In their purple hearts. (LL) Pear Tree. "H. D." ColAP; MoAmPo; PtR; TCAPo

In their religion they are so unev'n. Daniel Defoe. OBSV *Fr.* True-born Englishman, The.

In their territory there lived. Letter from the Shaman: The Tribe with No Myth. David Citino. UpMys

In Thelmon's breast contending passions rise. Anne Batten Cristall. RWP *Fr.* Thelmon and Carmel; An Irregular Poem.

In there these short hairs. All Shook Up. Dan Sicoli. AllShUp; SwNoth

In these all-white courtyards where the south wind blows. Mad Pomegranate Tree, The. Odysseus Elytis. GPTC; WoPoe, *tr. by* Edmund Keeley and Philip Sherrard

In these cold evenings, when the rain. Fear of the Earth. Alex Comfort. MoBrPo

In These Dark Times. Julia Vinograd. ASA

In these days. Longing. Thomas McGrath. BodElec

IN these deep solitudes and awful cells. Eloisa to Abelard. Alexander Pope. NAEL-6v1; NAEL-7v1; RACG

In These Dissenting Times. Alice Walker. Women. CFP

In these few years. Mother's Voice. Robert Creeley. NAMCP V.2

In these high places we are melting out. Interlude on Mustagh Tower. Andrew Greig. EdScPo

In these I find my calling. North Point North. John Koethe. PoDa

In these last three hours of the world. (LL) Allegory of the Supermarket. Stephanie Brown. AFaM; SUP

In these mountain villages and harbor towns. Muso Soseki. EaWin, *tr. by* W. S. Merwin

In these neat boxes. New World. Sally Roberts Jones. AngWePo

In these screes, I cannot see. Influence. Ceri Wyn Jones. BBMWP, *tr. by* Elin ap Hywel

In these twilight years, I love tranquility. In Reply to Vice-Magistrate Chang. Wang Wei. NDACCP, *tr. by* David Hinton

In these wrinkles, bared. Strata. Roger Jones. TiP2

In Thessaly there is a deep-set valley. Ovid. NAWM-7v1 *Fr.* Metamorphoses.

In thin sun that lifted its hands. Dog's Grave, A. Ted Kooser. PoDa

In this and whatever days to come. Et Quidquid Aspiciebam Mors Erat. Robert Fitzgerald. APT-2

In this big house—. Saturn. Günter Grass. AF

In this blue light. San Sepolcro. Jorie Graham. MoWP; VCAP

In this café they have solved the problem of names. Martin Johnston. BMAP *Fr.* In Transit: A Sonnet Square.

In this chill morning of a wintry spring. Sonnet Written from an Eastern Apartment in the Bishop's Palace at Lichfield, Which Commands a View of Stowe Valley. Anna Seward. RWP

In this church full of objections not one voice. Church Full of Objections. Anthony Caleshu. NIrP

In this city where it's perfectly ordinary. Oh, the Gingkos. Edward Field. BodElec

In this climate of storms. Thresholds of tolerance. Lionel Abrahams. TSAP

In this cloudy sky overhead now. Cabin in the Sky. John Latouche. ReLy

In this cold monument lies one. Epitaph on M. H., An. Charles Cotton. NPeEn

In This Cool Transparent Spring. Osip Emilevich Mandelstam. TCRusP, *tr. by* John Glad

In this country. October Falls in Black and White. Joe Lothamer. GeoH

In this country lightning quickens stone. Mineral Kingdom. Jacques Dupin. VCWP, *tr. by* Paul Auster

In this country you may not. Small passing. Ingrid de Kok. HAWP; TSAP

In this damned country, what haven't you apportioned like / your own farms? Fratricide. Abdula Peshew. IrPoTo, *tr. by* Muhamad Tawfiq Ali

In This Dark House. Edward Davison. OBMV

In this dark I rest. Eye Mask. Denise Levertov. BLT

In this day and age. Bruce George. BRtP

In this day and age Lord. Loss. C. K. Williams. MakPoe

In this deep solitude of wastes more than forlorn. Solitude. Andreas Gryphius. GePo, *tr. by* George C. Schoolfield

In this dingy café. Lola Ridge. APT-1 *Fr.* Ghetto, The.

In this dream I walked. You Can't Escape Your Life Record. Manila Koordada. WoPoe

In this earthly configuration. Concentration Constellation. Lawson Fusao Inada. GeoHom

In this empty room we gather. Colin Morton. IFF *Fr.* Three Small Rooms.

In this garden, after a day of rain. Where Are You? Carole Satyamurti. Prnts

In this gay village hangs a wondrous sign. North Country Village, A. Susanna Blamire. RWP

In this green month when resurrected flowers. Memorial Wreath. Dudley Randall. CBCWP

In This House. Veronica Forrest-Thomson. EdScPo

In this house without walls on a hill. Smile, A. Tzu Yeh. CrYelRi; ErotSp, *tr. by* Sam Hamill

In this image. MRI of a Poet's Brain. Vernon Rowe. BloBone

In this imperfect, gloomy scene. Female Friend, The. Cornelius Whur. STuOW

In this incremental darkening. Moles, The. Mark Cox. MAAN

In This January. Susan Goyette. OpeFie

In this kingdom. Egg. Linda Pastan. InvLad

In This Land. Mahmoud Darwish. BeAl, *tr. by* Sabri Hafiz and Sarah Maguire

In this land the rivers carve furrows and canyons as sudden to the eye. Daphne Marlatt. NLPA *Fr.* Touch to My Tongue.

In this land vague malevolence. Van Diemen's Land. Allen Afterman. NOBAu

In This Landscape. Diane Di Prima. WANABP

In this landscape conspicuous for nothing but dust. In This Landscape. Diane Di Prima. WANABP

In this language, no industrial revolution. Icelandic Language, The. Bill Holm. GoPo

In this little corner, you have ruined it in the entire world. (LL) City, The. Constantine P. Cavafy. PLBUT; WoPoe, *tr. by* Rae Dalven

In this little room. Slave Cabin, Sotterly Plantation, Maryland, 1989. Lucille Clifton. LoL

In this little Urn[e] is laid. Upon Prue [or Prew], His Maid. Robert Herrick. NAEL-6v1; NAEL-7v1; NoP-4; NoP-5; NPeEn

In this lone, open glade I lie. Lines Written in Kensington Gardens. Matthew Arnold. NAEL-6v2; NAEL-7v2

In this lonely, varying light of dawn with the residue of desire. Homo Sapiens. Carol Frost. CAP-8

In this meantime the Trachin king sore vexed in his thought. Ovid. NoSic *Fr.* Metamorphoses.

In this mind. Nod. Christopher Davis. AmPoNex

In this mirror I am enclosed. Guillaume Apollinaire. YaTCFP *Fr.* Heart, Crown, and Mirror.

In this moment I am sitting contented and alone. Handsome Is as Handsome Does. James Wright. BodElec

In this mountain village. Issa. SoOfWa, *tr. by* Sam Hamill

In this mouth I gather darkness, an aria. Elegy for the Unsaid. Simone Muench. RWB

In this old house. (LL) Gwendolyn Brooks. BeAl; ESEAA; NAMCP V.2; NoAM; StAl; WaAnP *Fr.* Street in Bronzeville, A.

In this old neighborhood. Man Who Didn't Sign, The. Radoi Ralin. CSCBP, *tr. by* Georgi Belev and Lisa Sapinkopf

In this old village now, at night. Village. Jean Earle. AngWePo

In this our. Roy Kiyooka. NLPA *Fr.* Pear Tree Pomes.

In this parable of vengeance. Impossible Pictures, The. Tom Paulin. CABP

In this picture, a well-read young mother ponders a paragraph. Seesaw. Amy Gerstler. MotU

In this place years ago. At the Door of the Native Studies Director. Robert H. Davis. HATNAP

In this poem my mother is not dead. Sounding the Name. Robert Kroetsch. BeAl

In this poetry. (LL) Homage to Life: Jules Supervielle. Joseph Stroud. PoDa; TAPaP

In this quiet alley, Ch'ien-ming Temple. Mural, Ch'ien-ming Temple. Lu Yu. CrYelRi, *tr. by* Sam Hamill

In this river the heart is like a ruined waterwheel; in whichever direction it turns, there is water before it. Jelaluddin Rumi. BBASP, *tr. by* A. J. Arberry

In this room. No One. Lilian Moore. TLR

In this season, through the clear tears. August, on the Rented Farm. Dave Jeddie Smith. ColAP

In this short interval to tear. Ejaculation. Elinor Wylie. APT-1

In this short Life. Emily Dickinson. SAmP

In this small fort, besieged with snow. Lines Written on a Window at The Leasowes. William Shenstone. NPeEn

In this small hut. Muso Soseki. EaWin, *tr. by* W. S. Merwin

In this soft age, in my soft. Rock Climbers, The. Robert Francis. MoASP

In this splendor of white sky. White Claw, The. Alfonsina Storni. TCLAP, *tr. by* Andrew Rosing

In this squalid, dirty dooryard. Pear Tree, The. Edna St. Vincent Millay. MoAmPo

In this strang[e] labyrinth [or labourinth] how shall I turn[e]? Mary Sidney Wroth, Countess of Montgomery. BASC; CABP; EMWP; NAEL-6v1; NAEL-7v1; NoP-4; NoP-5; NPeEn; PBRV *Fr.* Pamphilia to Amphilanthus.

In This, the Fifth World. Jennifer Lisa Vest. BtF

In this the moment of departure. Departure. Mai Sayigh. PoArWo, *tr. by* Lena Jayyusi and Naomi Shihab Nye

In this Theayter they has plays. Old Woman, Outside the Abbey Theater, An. Leonard Alfred George Strong. MoBrPo

In this third year of Reagan, my 27th year. Peter Oresick. AtGh *Fr.* American Peace, An.

In This Tree. Jacques Roubaud. YaTCFP, *tr. by* Rosmarie Waldrop

In this vain, busy world, where the good and the gay. Stanzas. Mary Robinson. WoRP

In This Warm Dark Mosque. Coral Bracho. RMCMP, *tr. by* Suzanne Jill Levine

In This Way. Gertrude Stein. PFTM-1

In this white room in Mojácar. Verso Libre. Nick Carbó. NAPBL

In this wide moorland fringed with dirty haze. Covenanting Country. Sir Alec Cairncross. EdScPo

In this wind, the sharp blue cut of the San Gabriels flattens against the neon east. Killarney Clary. GeoHom

In this world. Trials of the Poet. Andrée Chédid. YaTCFP, *tr. by* Rosemary Lloyd

In this world. Issa. EH, *tr. by* Robert Hass

In this world / Even butterflies. Issa. ZenPo, *tr. by* Takashi Ikemoto and Lucien Stryk

In this world it is noblest. Yana Tokareva. CRWP *Fr.* On Russian Poetry (1996-2000).

In this world, shadows do not speak to us. Skin. Anthony Butts. AmPoNex

In this world, (the *Isle of Dream[e]s*). White Island, The: or Place of the Blest. Robert Herrick. NoP-4; NoP-5; NOSC; NPeEn

In this world there lives a Mighty One. Mighty One, The. Ssu-ma Hsiang-ju. CCL1, *tr. by* Burton Watson

In this year of cataclysm pre-predicted. Heartease 3. Lorna Goodison. WaCA

In this year of executioners' songs. Let the Midnight Special. Joseph Bruchac. GM

In th'olde [*or* tholde] dayes of the king Arthour. Geoffrey Chaucer. NAEL-6v1; NAEL-7v1; NoP-5 *Fr.* Canterbury Tales, The.

In those days a decree went out. Peregrine. Barton Sutter. UrbNat

In those days, I couldn't tell if I was strong. Working Construction. Eric Chock. OpBo

In those days, in a place where dentists thrive. In the Lake District. Joseph Brodsky. BLT, *tr. by* George L. Kline

In those days said Hiawatha. Henry Wadsworth Longfellow. APN-1; NAAPv.1 *Fr.* Song of Hiawatha, The.

In those days the oatfields. Stacking the Straw. Amy Clampitt. VCAP

In those days, those days which exist for me only as the most elusive memory now. Dress, The. C. K. Williams. BeAl; StAl

In those days, wasy of feinting and of tenderness. Ballad, The. Michel Deguy. YaTCFP, *tr. by* Clayton Eshleman

In those days, we accepted the spindrift. Catechism of the Sea. Christopher Buckley. MAAN

In those days / When civilization kicked us in the face. Vultures, The. David Diop. WoPoe, *tr. by* Ulli Beier and Gerald Moore

In those days when my father was still big. Johnson Brothers Ltd. Rutger Kopland. BeAl; VCWP, *tr. by* James Brockway

In those days you were still in love. From the Lake. David St. John. MAAN

In Those Old Wars. Alden Nowlan. BrAP

In those painful days, we knew. Yesterday's Illusion *or* Remembering the Thirties. Alun Llywelyn-Williams. OBWVE, *tr. by* R. Gerallt Jones

In Those Rooms. Marianne van Hirtum. SurWo, *tr. by* Guy Flandre and Peter Wood

In those rooms. In Those Rooms. Marianne van Hirtum. SurWo, *tr. by* Guy Flandre and Peter Wood

In those sad words I took farewell. Alfred Tennyson. NAEL-6v2; NAEL-7v2 *Fr.* In Memoriam A. H. H.

In those vast fields of light, ethereal plains. William Drummond of Hawthornden. NOSC *Fr.* Hymn of the Fairest Fair, The.

In Those Years. Sergey Sergeievich Narovchatov. TCRusP, *tr. by* Bob Perelman and Shirley Rihner

In Those Years. Adrienne Rich. ExTi; LoL

In those years, people will say, we lost track. In Those Years. Adrienne Rich. ExTi; LoL

In three weeks he will be back down talking. Called Up: Tinker to Evers to Chance. Dorothy Barresi. MoASP

In thrice 10,000 seasons, I will come back to this world. Domestic Mysticism. Lucie Brock-Broido. PoPoPo

In through the porch and up the silent stair. Old House, The. Amy Levy. PEW; ViWPN; VWP

In thy own self's perennial masterdom. (LL) At Sainte-Marguerite. Trumbull Stickney. APN-2; TCAPo

In Time. *Unknown.* SonAtl, *tr. by* El-Houssaine Baali, Colin Hobday and Ursula Hobday

In time it came round, the time. Christmas Ballad. San Juan de la Cruz. STV, *tr. by* John Frederick Nims

In Time like Glass. Walter James Turner. MoBrPo; OBMV

In Time of Gold. "H. D." PoA 2002

In Time of Grief. Lizette Woodworth Reese. APN-2

In Time of Pestilence. Thomas Nashe. *See* Adieu, Farewell, Earth's Bliss[e].

In Time of Silver Rain. Langston Hughes. SAmP

In Time of "The Breaking of Nations." Thomas Hardy. BrAP; ChIV-1; HarvBoo; MoBrPo; NAEL-6v2; NAEL-7v2; NAMCP V.1; NoAM; NoP-4; NoP-5; OBEV; OBWP; OPOU; OxAEP-2; PoWW; TFi; WeW-3

In Time of War. W. H. Auden. NAMCP V.1

In Time of War. Amy Lowell. NAAPv.2

In time of yore when shepherds dwelt. Olden Love-making. Nicholas Breton. NoSic

In time the Princess playing with the child. Michael Drayton. ChIV-1 *Fr.* Moses His Birth and Miracles.

In Times and Places. Umberto Piersanti. NeIt, *tr. by* Stephen Sartarelli

In time's assembly line. Assembly Line. "Shu Ting." VCWP

In times of stormy weather. Strange Hurt. Langston Hughes. APT-2

In to thir dirk and drublie day[i]s. William Dunbar. NPeEn

In Tooting, the tomato. Love Song of Tooting, A. Kit Wright. NoP-5

In Topaz. Toyo Suyemoto. ASA; NAAPv.2

In Tornado Weather. Judith Kerman. P180

In Torrett, Minorca. Norman Kreitman. EdScPo

In Tortuous Ways. Sikong Tu. CCL1 *Fr.* Twenty-Four Modes of Poetry.

In Town. Austin Dobson. MakPoe

In town, the news grows. On the Sixth Day of the War. Mac Lojowski. AmZen

In trackless woods, it puzzled me to find. In Trackless Woods. Richard Wilbur. CAP-8

In Transit: A Sonnet Square. Martin Johnston.
  Café of Situations, The. BMAP
  Drinking Sappho Brand Ouzo. BMAP

In Trauma 1, a gay Latino kid. Rafael Campo. WiU *Fr.* Ten Patients, and Another.

In tropical climes there are certain times of day. Mad Dogs and Englishmen. Noël Coward. NBLV; ReLy

In Trouble and Shame. D. H. Lawrence. OBMV

In truth, / Cordelia was a scorpion in blue. Souvenir of the Manassah Ball. Lorenzo Thomas. RD

In truth it was a landscape wildly gay. James Kirke Paulding. APN-1 *Fr.* Backwoodsman, The.

In truth, O Love, with what a boyish kind. Sir Philip Sidney. OxBSo *Fr.* Astrophil and Stella.

In Trying Times. Heberto Padilla. AF; PoetW, *tr. by* Andrew Hurley and Alastair Reid

In Tsegihi. Arthur Rimbaud. PFTM-1 *Fr.* Night Chant, The.

In Tse'gíhi, / In the house made of the dawn. *Navajo Oral Tradition.* NAAPv.1 *Fr.* Night Chant, The.

In turns therefrom sipped lovers' wine. (LL) Under the Waterfall. Thomas Hardy. NAEL-6v2; NAEL-7v2; NoP-4; NoP-5

In Two Fields. Waldo Williams. OBWVE, *tr. by* Gwyn Jones

In Two Fields. Waldo Williams. BBMWP, *tr. by* Anthony Conran

In undetected trains we left our land. Embarkation, 1942. John Jarmain. PoWW

In unexperienc'd infancy. Thomas Traherne. *See* In unexperienced infancy.

In unexperienced infancy. Shadows in the Water. Thomas Traherne. NoP-4; NoP-5; WoPoe

  (In unexperienc'd infancy.) CABP; NPeEn

In unknown country, the burning car. Night Driving. Jane Draycott. MoWP

In Vain. Adah Isaacs Menken. CBWP-1

In vain against the formless wolves of air. John Gneisenau Neihardt. APT-1 *Fr.* Song of the Messiah, The.

In vain by various griefs oppressed. Swansea Bay. Julia Ann Hatton. AngWePo

In vain, dear Madam, yes, in vain you strive. Epistle to a Lady, An. Mary Leapor. CABP

In vain do I see that the trees are still green. October. Paul Claudel. YaTCFP, *tr. by* James Lawler

In vain I gather up these stars from the ground. Meng Chiao. CCL1 *Fr.* Apricots Die Young.

In vain I see the morning rise. Poet's Delay, The. Henry David Thoreau. TCAPo

In vain, in vain it is, I find. Necessity of Fate, The. Jane Barker. EMWP

In vain! In vain! My pleading all in vain! Arria to Poetus. Mary E. Tucker. CBWP-1

In vain, in vain—the all-composing Hour.   Alexander Pope.   NoP-4; NoP-5 *Fr.* Dunciad, The.

In vain, search in the dust.   Milan, August 1943.   Salvatore Quasimodo. WoPoe, *tr.* by Peter Russell

In vain to me the smiling [*or* smileing] Mornings shine.   Sonnet [on the Death of Mr. Richard West].   Thomas Gray.   BrAP; CenSon; NoP-4; OxBSo; GSo; InoFa; NoP-4; NoP-5

In vain to Woods and Deserts I retire.   Verses Design'd by Mrs. A. Behn to be Sent to a Fair Lady.   Aphra Behn.   PoBW

In vain you boast poetic names of yore.   Impromptu: To Lady Winchelsea Occasioned by four Satirical Verses on Women Wits, In *The Rape of the Lock.*   Alexander Pope.   NAEL-7v1; NoP-4; NoP-5; WaAnP

In vain your bangles cast.   Abiku.   Wole Soyinka.   PoetW

In vain[e], fair[e] sorceress[e], thy eyes speak[e] charms.   William Habington. NOSC *Fr.* Castara.

In vaulted place where shadows flit.   In a Church of Padua.   Herman Melville. APN-2

In Verona, my late cousin Romeo.   This Can't Be Love.   Lorenz Hart.   ReLy

In Vietnam I was always afraid of mines.   Mines.   Bruce Weigl.   PoAgWa

In View of the Fact.   A. R. Ammons.   OxBoAm

In Virgyne the sweltrie sun gan sheene.   Excelente Balade of Charitie, An. Thomas Chatterton.   OxAEP-1

In/Vocation.   Lawson Fusao Inada.   WhBo

In Vorkuta no disciple of the Lord.   Vorkuta.   Horst Bienek.   AF

In *Wakefield* there lives a jolly Pinder.   Jolly Pinder of Wakefield, The. *Unknown.*   PBRV

In Waking Words.   Dorothy Barresi.   SweBea

IN Wales there is a borough town.   Tale of a Friar and A Shoemaker's Wife, a. Thomas Churchyard.   NoSic

In walking naked. (LL)   Coat, A.   William Butler Yeats.   NAEL-6v2; NAEL-7v2; NAMCP V.1; NoAM; OxAEP-2; PtR

In wanting to silence any song. (LL)   Minor Bird, A.   Robert Frost.   APT-1; OWoS; SAmP

In Waste Places.   James Stephens.   MoBrPo

In water nothing is mean. The fugitive.   Patience.   Elaine Feinstein.   MoWP

In water shadows.   Earth Dream.   Esther Shumyatsher.   Prolet, *tr.* by Amelia Glaser

In water-heavy nights behind grandmother's porch.   Adolescence—1.   Rita Dove.   ISC; NAAL-5; NoAM

In waters where no charts avail.   Island, The.   Herman Melville.   NCAP

In waves of untraveled seas.   To a Lady Combing Her Hair.   Juan de Tassis y Peralta, Count of Villamediana.   BLPSL, *tr.* by Rene de Costa, Rigas Kappatos and Eleni Paidoussi

In waves still as the skillful yachts pass over. (LL)   Yachts, The.   William Carlos Williams.   APT-1; BrAP; HeIP-4; MoAmPo; NAAPv.2; NAMCP V.1; NoAM; NoP-4; NoP-5; SAmP; TFi

In Westminster Abbey.   Sir John Betjeman.   FaBoWar; HarvBoo; NAMCP V.1; NBLV; NIL-7; NIP-4; NoAM; OBSV; OxAEP-2

In wet May, in the months of change.   Exequy, An.   Peter Porter.   NoAM; NoP-4; NoP-5

In what darke silent grove.   William Habington.   ChIV-1 *Fr.* Castara.

In What Disappears.   John Brandi.   ICANM

In what dynasty, under what emperor.   Against Conscription.   Wei Chuang. CrYelRi, *tr.* by Sam Hamill

In what estate so ever I be.   Timor Mortis.   *Unknown.*   NoP-4; NoP-5; SacPr (In what estat so evere I be.)   OHMEL

In what fond flight, how many ways and days! (LL)   Dante Gabriel Rossetti. NAEL-7v2; OBEV; OxAEP-2 *Fr.* House of Life, The.

In what happened, nothing.   Small Bodies That Cannot Be Healed.   Fathi Abdullah.   AnVo, *tr.* by Mohamed Enani

In what house, the jade flute that sends these dark notes drifting.   Spring Night in Luoyang—Hearing a Flute.   Li Po.   CCL1, *tr.* by Burton Watson

In what language do I pray?   Two Voices.   Diana Der Hovanessian.   TWW

In what place is one most free of bonds?   To Patriarch Sun at Hua-yang Grotto. Li Te-yü.   ColAnChi, *tr.* by Edward H. Schafer

In What Region, in What Part of the World.   Gutierre de Cetina.   SpanPo, *tr.* by Kate Flores

In what region, in what part of the world.   In What Region, in What Part of the World.   Gutierre de Cetina.   SpanPo, *tr.* by Kate Flores

In what rich harmony, what polished lays.   John Pierpont.   APN-1; TreFP *Fr.* Airs of Palestine.

In what torn[e] ship soever I embark[e].   Hymn[e] to Christ, at the Author's Last Going into Germany, A.   John Donne.   BASC; NAEL-6v1; NAEL-7v1; NOSC; NPeEn; OxAEP-1; SacPr

In which being there together is enough. (LL)   Final Soliloquy of the Interior Paramour.   Wallace Stevens.   APT-1; BBASP; ColAP; HarvBoo; NAAPv.2; WaAnP

In Which He Rejoices Over Having Discarded Love.   Bálint Balassi.   IQMS, *tr.* by Joseph Leftwich

In which I had been reading, at my side. (LL)   William Wordsworth.   NAEL-6v2; NAEL-7v2 *Fr.* Prelude, The; Growth of a Poet's Mind [1850 version].

In which if they turn and twist, it is neither with volition nor consciousness. (LL)   Grave, A.   Marianne Moore.   APT-1; HeIP-4; NAAPv.2; NAMCP V.1; NoAM; NoP-4; NoP-5; TFi; TRP; WeW-3

In Which Names.   Ilse Aichinger.   AF, *tr.* by Allen H. Chappel

In which people burn. (LL)   George Oppen.   AmWaPo; NAMCP V.1 *Fr.* Of Being Numerous.

In Which Roosevelt Is Compared to Saul.   Vachel Lindsay.   ChIV-1

In White.   Robert Frost.   TRP

In White America.   Lucille Clifton.   LTA

In white clouds, in green mountains.   Taoist Song.   Teng Yu-pin.   CrYelRi, *tr.* by Sam Hamill

In white pleated trousers, peering through green.   Stravinsky in L.A.   Elizabeth Alexander.   AmPoNex

In white, / the unpainted statue of the young girl.   Our Lady of the Snows. Robert Hass.   CAP-8; GoPo

In Wild Iris Time.   Jerry Martien.   GeoHom

In williams / i would drink all 1100 springs of texas.   In Williams.   David Henderson.   EGAG

In wind from Asia and a wanton rain. (LL)   Way a Ghost Dissolves, The. Richard Hugo.   NoAM; NoP-4; NoP-5

In wind or water streame do require to be writ. (LL)   Unto no body my woman saith she had rather a wife be [*or* bee].   Catullus.   OBVE; WoPoe, *tr.* by Sir Philip Sidney

In winter. (LL)   Ode to My Socks.   Pablo Neruda.   RaBo; TCLAP; TRP; WED, *tr.* by Robert Bly

In winter evenings.   March.   Rosemerry Wahtola Trommer.   GeoH

In winter I get up at night.   Bed in Summer.   Robert Louis Stevenson. BLPJKO; BRP; NBLV

In Winter in my Room.   Emily Dickinson.   APN-2; NAAL-3; NALW; NCAP; NoAM

In winter in the woods alone.   Robert Frost.   HeIP-4

In winter my loved one.   Land of Fog.   Ingeborg Bachmann.   GTCP, *tr.* by Irmgard Hunt

In winter my loved one retires.   Fog Land.   Ingeborg Bachmann.   WoPoe, *tr.* by Michael Hamburger

In winter, sprawled on soft cushions.   War Memories.   Xenophanes.   WoPoe, *tr.* by Theodore Blanchard

In winter, those first mornings after my father died.   Pier, The.   Garrett Kaoru Hongo.   OpBo

In winter, when he was out of work and it was too cold outside to.   Shooting Crows.   Peter Markus.   AmPoNex

In winter, when the fields are white.   Lewis Carroll.   NPeEn *Fr.* Through the Looking-Glass.

In winter, with dusk enshrouding the town.   Rejected Gift, The.   Ida G. M. Gerhardt.   TuT, *tr.* by Ruth Hooley

In winter you were tender.   Do You Remember Ch'ôongp'a Street?   Ch'oe Sûngja.   EcSo, *tr.* by Mickey Hong

In winter / your streets.   Winterdirge.   Charles S. Taylor.   TiP2

In with the child.   Dusk and the Wife.   A. V. Christie.   PoDa

In with them, and tore down the slaughterhouse [*or* slaughter-house *or* slaughter house]. (LL)   Reuben Bright.   Edwin Arlington Robinson.   APN-2; GSo; MoAmPo; NAMCP V.1; NCAP; NoP-4; NoP-5; OxBoAm

In Worcester, Massachusetts.   In the Waiting Room.   Elizabeth Bishop.   APT-2; BrAP; CAP-8; FTtHH; GPTC; HeIP-4; NAAL-5; NALW; NAMCP V.2; NoAM; NoP-4; NoP-5; OxBoAm; PoetW; VCAP

In wrath and grief away the Paynims fly.   *Unknown.*   OBWP *Fr.* Song of Roland, The.

In wreck, in dearth, in necksong.   Dennis Lee.   OpeFie *Fr.* Un.

In Wyoming, at the confluence.   Dreaming at the Rexall Drug.   Robin Becker. ReTh

In Xanadu did Kubla Khan.   Kubla Khan: or, A Vision in a Dream.   Samuel Taylor Coleridge.   BLPJKO; BrAP; BRP; CABP; CtM; HeIP-4; NAEL-6v2; NAEL-7v2; NAWM-7v2; NIL-7; NIP-4; NOBRP; NoP-4; NoP-5; NPBRoP; NPeEn; OBEV; OBGa; OxAEP-2; OxBEV; PoPoPo; SoSe-8; TFi; TRP; WaAnP; WeW-3; WoPoe

In Xóchitl in Cuícatl.   Ernesto Cardenal.   PFTM-2, *tr.* by Carlos Altschul and Monique Altschul

In years of old.   John Addington Symonds.   CAGL *Fr.* Eudiades.

In years to come, I ask, be kind.   Strato.   CAGL, *tr.* by Byrne Fone

In yellow towns against a stormy sky.   In Yellow Towns.   Léon-Paul Fargue. MotU, *tr.* by Lydia Davis

In yesterday's Monthly Meeting, with its dry, financial theme.   Monastîr. Cynan.   BBMWP, *tr.* by Sally Roberts Jones

"In yonder fields" (with that directs her eye.   William Chamberlayne.   NOSC *Fr.* Pharonnida.

In Yoshiwara.   Yomono Akara.   EMJL, *tr.* by Steven D. Carter

In your absence, I come.   Intensive Care.   Helen Lamb.   PoCu

In your astral palace, I. Hsüeh T'ao [or Xue Tao]. WoPoe *Fr.* Trying on New-Made Clothes: Three Poems.

In your bosom. Great Little One. John Fitzgerald. BBMWP, *tr. by* Joseph P. Clancy

In Your Dream after Falling in Love. Richard Hugo. BodElec

In your dream you met Demeter. Demeter. Genevieve Taggard. HW

In your extended absence, you permit me. Vespers. Louise Glück. CAP-8; OxBoAm

In Your Eyes. Dora Teitelboim. Prolet, *tr. by* Amelia Glaser

In your frail loft. Last Window. Dewi Stephen Jones. BBMWP, *tr. by the* author

In your hands. Your Hands. Marjorie Agosin. PoDa, *tr. by* Mary C. Berg

In your honor, a man presents a sea bass. In Your Honor. Arthur Sze. GifTon; ICANM

In your honor, Lord Priapus. *Unknown.* PriapPo *Fr.* Priapus Poems, The.

In Your Mind. Carol Ann Duffy. EmeKit; StAl

In your mystery. For Larry Levis in Memory. Luis Omar Salinas. GeoHom

In your next letter I wish you'd say. Letter to N.Y. Elizabeth Bishop. GoPo

In your old age. Mourning for the Layman Named Cloud Peak. Muso Soseki. EaWin, *tr. by* W. S. Merwin

In Your Own Sweet Time. Alane Rollings. IllVoic

In your palm, the ripe weight. (LL) Persimmons. Li-Young Lee. CAP-8; NAAL-5; NAMCP V.2; NIL-7; NIP-4; NoP-4; NoP-5; OPRER

In your quest or request God is remote. Love Poem. Huda Na'mani. BBASP, *tr. by* Samuel Hazo and Lena Jayyusi

In Your Racing Dream. Richard Hugo. BodElec

In your sight. Spinal Cord. 'Aisha Arnaout. PoArWo, *tr. by* Mona Fayad

In your super-logical. You Are Right. Cathryn Essinger. PoA 2002; PoDa

In your thigh caressing my cheek. Quiet. (LL) Quietly. Kenneth Rexroth. ErotSp; GoPo

In your think tank you're Olympia. Siren. Jonathan Galassi. PoDa

In your three-piece suit and your tuxedo shoes. Zombie. Thomas Heise. LegDan

In your truck without a notion, fighting a lot of feeling. Press Play. Rebecca Wolff. LegDan

In your twenties you knew with elegiac certainty. Lifetime devoted to literature, A. Judith Rodriguez. BrAP; NOBAu

In your version of heaven I am blond, thinner. In Your Version of Heaven I am Younger. Rachel Zucker. BAP-01

In Your Version of Heaven I am Younger. Rachel Zucker. BAP-01

In your wide-brimmed, black. Moscow Station, The. Yevgeny Borisovich Rein. ItGoST, *tr. by* Judith Hemschemeyer

In youth, gay scenes attract our eyes. Vanity of Existence, The. Philip Freneau. TCAPo

In youth I had nothing. Poem on Returning to Dwell in the Country. T'ao Ch'ien. WoPoe, *tr. by* William Acker

In youth I had nothing. Five Poems on Returning to Dwell in the Country. T'ao Ch'ien. CCL1, *tr. by* William Acker

In Youth Is Pleasure. Robert Wever. OBEV *Fr.* Lusty Juventus.

In youth, it was a way I had. Indian Summer. Dorothy Parker. NIL-7; NIP-4

In youth thou enteredst [or enter'dst] on glass-bottled wall. (LL) To a Cat. John Keats. CenSon; OxBSo; TriCat

In youth's spring, it was my lot. Edgar Allan Poe. *See* In spring of youth it was my lot.

In yr absence / i. Max Factor Pink. Nigel Roberts. BMAP

Inadvertently I passed the border of her teeth and swallowed her agile tongue. Tongue, The. Zbigniew Herbert. BeAl, *tr. by* Czeslaw Milosz

INAMORATAS, with an approbation. Sundays of Satin-Legs Smith, The. Gwendolyn Brooks. SeSe

Inanna, Astarte, Ishtar and Isis. Prayer of Dedication. Cosi Fabian. HW

Inanna spoke. *Unknown.* WoPoe *Fr.* Cycle of Inanna: The Courtship of Inanna and Dumazi, The.

Inanna's Chant. Janine Canan. HW

Inattentive, suborned, betrayed, and shiftless. Young Prince of Tyre. "Ern Malley." BMAP

Inauguration. Road to the Presidency. Oneca Hitchman-Britton. BRtP

Inauguration. Lorenzo Thomas. EGAG

Inauguration Day: January 1953. Robert Lowell. OxBSo

Inauguration of Fukusan Dormitory. Muso Soseki. EaWin, *tr. by* W. S. Merwin

InaUniqueTracethatRemovesBeforeandAfterLeftandRight. Yi Sang. CAMKP; PFTM-1 *Fr.* Crow's-Eye View.

Inca had three arrows in his hand, The. Inca's Arrows, The. Manuel González Prada. SpanPo, *tr. by* Kate Flores

Inca Tupac Upanqui, The. William Hart-Smith. NOBAu

Incamos a sonidos recreidos. Sonido Ink(quieto). Brenda Cárdenas and Aidé Rodriguez. BRtP

Incantation. Peter Cooley. LiTh

Incantation. Zinaida Nikolayevna Gippius. ARWW, *tr. by* Catriona Kelly

Incantation. Czeslaw Milosz. PtR; VCWP, *tr. by* the author and Robert Pinsky

Incantation: "Let all poems speak and address themselves." E. Ethelbert Miller. OxAAAP

Incantation: "She / impregnates my face. Her hair taken, and in the veins addicted blood." Anne-Marie Albiach. OnScMo, *tr. by* Keith Waldrop

Incantation by Laughter. Velemir Khlebnikov. PoCho, *tr. by* Paul Schmidt

Incantation Songs of the Klamath Lake People. *Unknown.* APN-2, *tr. by* Albert S. Gatschet

Incantation: "White well, A." Elinor Wylie. APT-1; NAMCP V.1

Incantations of Modoc Conjurers. *Unknown.* APN-2, *tr. by* Albert S. Gatschet

Incantations of the Sea: Moando Coast. Mukula Kadima-Nzuji. NAfrP, *tr. by* Gerald Moore

Incarnate. Robin Becker. PfS

Incarnate for our marriage you appeared. Marriage, The. Yvor Winters. NAAPv.2

Incarnatio Est Maximum Dei Donum [or Donum Dei]. William Alabaster. NoSic

Incarnation. Joan Houlihan. IAoNAP

Incarnation, The. William Langland. OBEV *Fr.* Vision of Piers Plowman, The.

Incarnation and Passion, The. Henry Vaughan. SacPr

Inca's Arrows, The. Manuel González Prada. SpanPo, *tr. by* Kate Flores

Incautious youth, why do'st thou so misplace. To My Young Lover. Jane Barker. BASC; LW

Incense burned to ash in a bronze bowl. Night Watch. Wang An-shih. CrYelRi, *tr. by* Sam Hamill

Incense burns to embers in the burner. To the Tune: The Water Clock. Wen T'ing-yün. CrYelRi, *tr. by* Sam Hamill

Incessant Poem. Laura Solórzano. SPV, *tr. by* Jen Hofer

Inch by inch along the bed. Home Free. Diana O'Hehir. ASA

Inch to the left, An. Sniper. Lucien Stryk. PWW2

Inchcape Rock, The. Robert Southey. NPBRoP; OBNV; OBSP; OxAEP-2

Inching / From dark to dark—. Gyodai. ZenPo, *tr. by* Takashi Ikemoto and Lucien Stryk

Inchoate Road. B. P. Nichol. NLPA

Inchworm, The. David McFadden. NLPA

Incidence. Rae Armantrout. FTOS

Incident. Imamu Amiri Baraka. AF; NoAM

Incident. Countee Cullen. APT-2; ChAP; NAAL-5; NAAPv.2; NAMCP V.1; NoAM; NoP-4; NoP-5; NOxBChV; NTCP; PoPoPo; PtR; SSLK

Incident, An. Douglas Le Pan. BrAP; NoP-4

Incident, An. Frederick Tennyson. SacPr

Incident at Imuris. Alberto A. Ríos. NIP-4

Incident in a Filing Cupboard. Roddy Lumsden. PoDa

Incident in Italy. Samuel Carter. STuOW *Fr.* Avenger, The.

Incident in the Early Life of Ebenezer Jones, Poet, 1828, An. Sir John Betjeman. NAMCP V.1; NoAM

Incident in Transylvania. Roger McDonald. BMAP

Incident of the French Camp. Robert Browning. OBWP

Incident to murder. (LL) John Berryman. HarvBoo; OxBoAm *Fr.* Dream Songs.

Incidental among staves of branches. Villa Fidelia. Michael Murphy. NIrP

Incidentals in the Day World. Alice Notley. AHA

Incidentes Domésticos. Miguel de Unamuno.

3. RaW

Incidents. Daniil Kharms. MotU, *tr. by* George Gibian

Incidents in the Life of My Uncle Arly. Edward Lear. OBCoV

Incitement for Rowing to Sailing-place. Alexander MacDonald. NePenScot *Fr.* Clanranald's Galley.

Inclined House, The. Sabah Al-Kharrat Zwein. *tr. by* Kaissar Afif

"I have already lost the style and maze of language." PoArWo, *tr. by* Kaissar Afif

63: Inclusiveness. Dante Gabriel Rossetti. NAEL-6v2 *Fr.* House of Life, The.

Incognito. Nancy Mitchell. LaCa

Incognito Lounge, The. Denis Johnson. ReTh

Incomers. Gareth Alban Davies. BBMWP, *tr. by* the author and Mike Jenkins

Incommunicado. Sylvia Plath. BodElec

Incomparable-Verse Valley. Muso Soseki. EaWin, *tr. by* W. S. Merwin

Incomplete Anthem. Fadhil Assultani. IrPoTo, *tr. by* the author and Richard McKane

Incomplete History of Rock Music in the Hebrides, An. Donald S. Murray. EdScPo

Incomplete Scenario Involving What the Voice Said. Jane Mead. NAPBL

Incompleteness. Adelaide Anne Procter. TreFP

Incompleteness. Henrietta Cordelia Ray. CBWP-3

Incomprehensible, The. Isaac Watts. SacPr

Inconsistent Self-Portrait. Yuliya Kunina. CRWP, *tr. by* Richard McKane

Inconstancy. James Harrington. PBRV

Incontinence. Susan Hahn. IllVoic

Incorporation of Sophia's Cereal, The. Bernadette Mayer. NYP2

Incorrigible, false coquette. Kiss, The. Francis Saltus Saltus. VerBaPo

Incorrigible state of bewilderment. Snow Fell Twice, the Sun Always Shone. Sakyong Mipham. WhBo

Increasing moonlight drifts across my bed, The. Fredericksburg. Thomas Bailey Aldrich. AmWaPo; PCW; TCAPo

Incredible happens, he knows, The. Wendell Berry. UpMys *Fr.* Handing Down, The.

Incredible splendour—ethereal, delicate! Hayim Lenski. FIT, *tr. by* Robert Friend

Incredibly bright blue almost white open sky, An. I Just Heard John Buffington Died. Kalamu ya Salaam. SpirFl

Indecent Exposure (A True Story). Linwood M. Ross. InTrad

Indecent, self-soiled, bilious. Geocentric. Pattiann Rogers. SUP

Indecision. Víctor Terán. RMCMP, *tr. by* Donald Frischmann

Indeed, child, the little pimpernel, most modest. Letter from the Grass, A. Conrad Potter Aiken. InGu

Indeed I have sought thee too long, O Apollo. Search for Apollo, A. Agnes Mary Frances Robinson. VWP

Indeed I must confess. Abraham Cowley. NoP-5 *Fr.* Mistress, The.

Indeed Indeed, I Cannot Tell. Henry David Thoreau. RaBo

Indeed, it will soon be over, I shall be done. Intimations of Mortality. Stanley Kunitz. MoAmPo

Indeed (my Dear) you wrong my Dog in this. Love Me, Love My Dog. George Turberville. DiBP

Indeed, the enemy. *Zuni Oral Tradition.* NAWM-7v2 *Fr.* Scalp Dance, The.

Indeed this very love which is my boast. Elizabeth Barrett Browning. CenSon *Fr.* Sonnets from the Portuguese.

Indeed You Came Home Too Late. Gabriella Leto. CItWP, *tr. by* Cinzia Sartini Blum and Lara Trubowitz

Indefiniteness is an element of the true music. Improvisations on a Sentence by Poe. Jack Spicer. APSN; CalPo; OxBoAm

Indelible. Jayne Cortez. EGAG

Independance wid a vengeance. Independance. Louise Bennett. FaBoVe; NAMCP V.2

Independence Bell—July 4, 1776. *Unknown.* HHAm

Independence Day. Wendell Berry. UpMys

Independence Day. *Unknown.* VerBaPo

Independence Day, 1956: A Fairy Tale. James Galvin. PoPoPo

Independence Day Letter. Donald Hall. NoP-5

Independence Dignity. Louise Bennett. NAMCP V.2

Independent Study. Paul Beatty. AmPoNex

Index. Bernadette Mayer. NYP2

Index. Paul Violi. OxBoAm; PmAP

India. Walter James Turner. MoBrPo

India that one read about, The. I Wonder What Happened to Him. Noël Coward. ReLy

Indian. Feroza F. Jussawalla. RWB

Indian, The. Eliza Kirkham Mathews. CenSon

Indian at the Burial-Place [*or* Burying-Place] of His Fathers, An. William Cullen Bryant. APN-1

Indian Bagman's Toast. *Unknown.* FaBoVe

Indian Blood. Mary Tallmountain. FiBr; UnSA

Indian Boarding School: The Runaways. Louise Erdrich. CAP-8; HATNAP; NoAM; UnSA

Indian Boy Love Song (#2). Sherman Alexie. WaAnP

Indian Bride, The. Letitia Elizabeth Landon. NPBRoP *Fr.* Improvisatrice, The.

Indian Burying Ground, The. Philip Freneau. ColAP; NAAL-3; NAAPv.1; NoP-4; NoP-5; OxBoAm; TCAPo; TFi

Indian Car. Catron Grieves. ReTh

Indian Cave Jerry Ramsey Found, The. William Stafford. NoAM

Indian City, The. Felicia Dorothea Hemans. RWP

Indian Corn. William W. Cook.
    "Corn, corn, sweet Indian corn." VerBaPo

Indian Counsel. Edwin Ford Piper. APT-1

Indian Emperor, The. John Dryden.
    (Song from The Indian Emperor.) NoP-4; NoP-5

Indian Girl. Lenard D. Moore. GT

Indian Gone!, The. Josiah D. Canning. APN-1

Indian Hero's Creed, The. *Unknown.* DiBP

Indian Locks. Jessica Smucker Falcón. ACAMVP

Indian Movie, New Jersey. Chitra Divakaruni. NIL-7; UnSA

Indian Names. Lydia Huntley Sigourney. APN-1; ColAP; SWaP

Indian Never Had a Horse, The. Etel Adnan.
    "There is a word that never." PoArWo

Indian Peaks, Colorado. Reg Saner. PoCoUp

Indian Reservation: Caughnawaga. Abraham Moses Klein. NoP-4

Indian Rope Trick. Geoffrey Holloway. NLP

Indian Ruins Along Rio de Flag. Greg Pape. PBCAP

Indian Serenade, The. Percy Bysshe Shelley. OBEV; RaBo; TreFP
    (Indian Girl's Song, The.) NAEL-6v2; NAEL-7v2

Indian Singing in 20th Century America. Gail Tremblay. HATNAP; LTA; ReEnLa

Indian Song. Major L. Jackson. FuFl; WaAnP

Indian Song: Survival. Leslie Marmon Silko. WaAnP

Indian Story, An. William Cullen Bryant. NAAPv.1

Indian Suffering. Joseph Ceravolo. NYP2

Indian Summer. Olga Fiodorovna Berggolts. TCRusP, *tr. by* Daniel Weissbort

Indian Summer. Cristina Campo. CItWP, *tr. by* Cinzia Sartini Blum and Lara Trubowitz

Indian Summer. Karen Chamberlain. GeoH

Indian Summer. Emily Dickinson. APN-2; MoAmPo; NAAL-3; NAAL-5; TCAPo
    (These Are The Days When Birds Come Back.) BLPJKO; NAAPv.1

Indian Summer. Hamlin Garland. APN-2

Indian Summer. William Ellery Leonard. APT-1 *Fr.* Two Lives.

Indian Summer. Dorothy Parker. NIL-7; NIP-4

Indian Summer. Boris Leonidovich Pasternak. RusPo, *tr. by* Robert Arthur Douglas Ford

Indian Summer. Lizette Woodworth Reese. SWaP

Indian Summer Day on the Prairie, An. Vachel Lindsay. IllVoic

Indian summer / Dragonfly shadows seldom. Masaoka Shiki. ZenPo, *tr. by* Takashi Ikemoto and Lucien Stryk

Indian Things. Mark Turcotte. Vesp

Indian upon God, The [*or* An]. William Butler Yeats. MoBrPo

Indian weed [now] withered quite, The. Religious Use of [Taking] Tobacco, A. Robert Wisdome. OBCoV

Indian Woman's Death-Song, The. Felicia Dorothea Hemans. NoP-4; NoP-5; NPBRoP; PEW; RWP

Indiana. Reed Bye. AHA

Indianapolis on the q.t.: camp sites, no consequences. Negromania, Negrophilia, Negrophobia. C. S. Giscombe. RD

Indians are ignorant of Europe's Coyne yet call it Monéash and notice. Rosmarie Waldrop. PFTM-2 *Fr.* Key into the Language of America, A.

Indians found the best places, The. Texas: Sesquicentennial. William Virgil Davis. TiP2

Indians in the Woods, The. Janet Lewis. IllVoic

Indians must be the loneliest people on Earth—. Janice Gould. UnSA

Indian's Retort, The. Jones Very. NCAP

Indian's Welcome to the Pilgrim Fathers, The. Lydia Huntley Sigourney. TCAPo

Indictment of Senior Officers. Sharon Olds. PBCAP

Indifference. Dmitry Vasil'evich Bobyshev. TCRusP, *tr. by* Daniel Weissbort

Indifference. Indifference. Dmitry Vasil'evich Bobyshev. TCRusP, *tr. by* Daniel Weissbort

Indifference. Harry Graham. NBLV

Indifference, The / of rain. Death. Joe Wenderoth. AmPoNex

Indifferent as a statue. Similes. Charles Reznikoff. APT-2; OxBoAm

Indifferent glimmer of distant stars, The. Garden of Gethsemane, The. Boris Leonidovich Pasternak. GI, *tr. by* Nina Kossman

Indifferent, he condescends to glide. (LL) Swan, The. Rainer Maria Rilke. NAWM-7v2; OWoS, *tr. by* Stephen Mitchell

Indifferent, The. John Donne. BASC; NAEL-6v1; NAEL-7v1; NAWM-5v1; NOSC; SoSe-8

Indifferent to heaven and hell. (LL) It was deep April, and the morn. Michael Field. NAEL-7v2; ViWPN; VWP

Indignation. José Santos Chocano. TCLAP, *tr. by* Andrew Rosing

Indignation Jones. Edgar Lee Masters. APT-1 *Fr.* Spoon River Anthology.

Indigo. Chitra Divakaruni. OpBo

Indigo Glass in the Grass, The. Wallace Stevens. PoA 2002

Indigolava Kirri-Amma. Hunters Ask God, The. *Unknown.* SonAtl, *tr. by* P. Gavanna

Indirective. James Galvin. VisFro

Indirectly kind fire is glowing over forgotten reasons. Strictly personal. Anna Mendelssohn. VaPo

Indiscriminate Venus grasps at any remedy, The. *Unknown.* CAGL *Fr.* Leiden Manuscript, The.

Individualist Speaks, The. Louis MacNeice. OBMV

Individual's Soliloquy, The. Nicanor Parra. PFTM-2, *tr. by* Lawrence Ferlinghetti and Allen Ginsberg

Indolent Housewife—in Daisies—lain! (LL) How many times these low feet staggered. Emily Dickinson. NAAL-3; TCAPo; WeW-3

Indoor Cat, The. Paul Petrie. PoCoUp

Indoors. Vona Groarke. NIrP

Indoors I sat, with my two sons. Night Song. Lajos Áprily. IQMS, *tr. by* Watson Kirkconnell

Indoors the tang of a tiny oil lamp. Outdoors. House on a Cliff. Louis MacNeice. HarvBoo; ModIr; NPeEn

Induction, The. Thomas, 1st Earl of Dorset Sackville. NoSic *Fr.* Mirror for Magistrates.

Indulgence. Leopoldo Lugones. TCLAP, *tr. by* Julie Schumacher

Indulgence in the flowing bowl. To a Kill-Joy. Wang Ji. CCL1, *tr. by* H. A. Giles

Industrial City. Antigone Kefala. BMAP

Industrial Teflon Comes Into Domestic Use. Fleda Brown Jackson. PoA 2002

Industry undressing in front of Agriculture. Eclogue. Michael Hofmann. HarvBoo

Indwelling. Thomas Edward Brown. SacPr

Inedible. Elke Erb. MotU, *tr. by* Craig Federhen

Ineffable, The. Delmira Agustini. TANSG, *tr. by* Mark McCaffrey

Ineffable, The. Delmira Agustini. TCLAP, *tr. by* Karl Kirchwey

Inescapable: to start with the history. Seq. Maggie Hannan. NLP

Iness. (LL) L(a. E. E. Cummings. NIL-7; NIP-4; TRP

Inevitable. Sir John Betjeman. MoBrPo

Inexhaustibly is boys. (LL) Careless Love. Stanley Kunitz. FaBoWar; PWW2

Inexorable. William Drummond of Hawthornden. *See* Madrigal: "Like the Idalian Queen[e]."

Inexorable. William Drummond of Hawthornden. *See* Madrigal: "My thoughts hold mortal[l] strife."

Infallible Doussiekie. Alexander Geddes. DiBP

Infancy. Carlos Drummond de Andrade. BeAl; TCLAP, *tr. by* Elizabeth Bishop

Infancy! fearless, lustful, happy, nestling for delight. William Blake. OxAEP-2 *Fr.* Visions of the Daughters of Albion.

Infancy—*lluv luve yur broder Jacob.* (LL) What We Need Words For. Rebecca Seiferle. PoChi; TAPaP

Infant, The. Oliver Pitcher. EGAG

Infant, The. Agnes Strickland. CenSon

Infant Boy at Midcentury. Robert Penn Warren. *Fr.* Promises.

Infant Innocence. A. E. Housman. Spl

Infant is white, like down, The. And the youth dark-complexioned, like shingle. A. Velichansky. TCRusP, *tr. by* Daniel Weissbort

Infant Joy. William Blake. NPBRoP; OxAEP-2; PoPoPo *Fr.* Songs of Innocence.

Infant quirk of a pine, An. *Navidad,* St. Nicholas Ave. Alfred Corn. NoP-4; NoP-5

Infant Song. Charles Causley. NOxBChV

Infant Sorrow. William Blake. IJHIL; NAEL-6v2; NAEL-7v2; NPBRoP; OxAEP-2; OxBEV; PoPoPo *Fr.* Songs of Experience.

Infant Spouse, The. Joan Houlihan. IAoNAP

Infanta Marina. Wallace Stevens. APT-1

Infanticide. Pattiann Rogers. CFP

Infantry. Alun Lewis. PoWW

Infantry Assault. Doug Anderson. AmWaPo

Infatuation. Frederick Goddard Tuckerman. NCAP

Infatuation. But it would not do. Albery Allson Whitman. NAAPv.1 *Fr.* Octoroon, The.

Infatuation, sadism, lust, avarice. To the Reader. Charles Baudelaire. NAWM-7v2, *tr. by* Robert Lowell

Infections. Miguel Algarin. PueRic

Infelice. Stevie Smith. LW

Infelix. Adah Isaacs Menken. CBWP-1; NAAPv.1; TCAPo

Infernal. Karen Volkman. BAP-97

Inferno. Dante Alighieri. NAWM-7v1 *Fr.* Divine Comedy, The (Mandelbaum Translation).

Inferno 1, 32. Jorge Luis Borges. PoetW, *tr. by* Anthony Kerrigan

Inferno: Canto 1. Dante Alighieri. NAWM-5v1 *Fr.* Divina Commedia (Selections from Anthologies, in English).

Infidelities. Elaine Feinstein. MoWP

Infidelities. James McCorkle. PoDa

Infidelity. C. Dale Young. LegDan

Infinite a sudden Guest, The. Emily Dickinson. WPoS

Infinite consanguinity it bears. Hart Crane. AmFaPo; ColAP *Fr.* Voyages.

Infinite gentleness, infinite irony. Effigy of a Nun. Sara Teasdale. NAAPv.2

Infinite in the Skies, The. Alphonse Marie Louis de Lamartine. SxFrPo, *tr. by* A. M. and E. H. Blackmore

Infinite peach-blossom shades. Peach Blossoms. Yüan Chên. CrYelRi, *tr. by* Sam Hamill

Infinite, The. Giacomo Leopardi. NAWM-7v2, *tr. by* Ottavio M. Casale

Infinite We Count the Dead! The Dance is Almost Finished! Death. Amelia Rosselli. CItWP, *tr. by* Cinzia Sartini Blum and Lara Trubowitz

Infinite weariness comes into the faces of the old tenements, An. Ghetto Twilight. Alter Brody. TaR

Infinity shows the ever-awakening of space in sign, as a sign. Law of Trichotomy. Holley Blackwell. AnSo

Infinity, when all things it beheld. Edward Taylor. NAAL-3; NAAPv.1; NOSC; OxBEV; OxBoAm; TCAPo; WaAnP *Fr.* God's Determinations [touching his Elect].

Infirm and aged, doth he sit. Old Year, The. Priscilla Jane Thompson. CBWP-2

Inflation. Nicanor Parra. AF, *tr. by* Miller Williams

Inflight. Gary Gach. WhBo

In-flight Note. Judith Rodriguez. BMAP

Inflorescence. Arthur Sze. WANABP

Influence. Ceri Wyn Jones. BBMWP, *tr. by* Elin ap Hywel

Influence of Anxiety at the Seaside with Tea, The. Todd Swift. OpeFie

Influence of Natural Objects [in Calling Forth and Strengthening the Imagination in Boyhood and Early Youth]. William Wordsworth. OxBEV *Fr.* Prelude, The; Growth of a Poet's Mind [1850 version].

Influence of Natural Objects, The. James Simmons. PNI

Influencing Factors. Karen, Helfrich. PoDa

Informant, The. Eiléan Ní Chuilleanáin. ModIr

Infra-Red. Diana Hartog. NLPA *Fr.* Oasis.

Ing. Walter Conrad Arensberg. APT-1; NAAPv.2

Ing. Clark Coolidge.

  Ad. AHA

  Nothing at Newbegins. AHA

Ing? Is it possible to mean *ing*? Ing. Walter Conrad Arensberg. APT-1; NAAPv.2

Ingathering. Carolyn Kizer. ExTi

Ingenious insect, but of ruthless mould. To the Spider. Thomas Russell. CenSon

Ingenuity too astonishing, An. Sun Underfoot Among the Sundews, The. Amy Clampitt. NoP-4; NoP-5; OxBoAm; StAl

Inglorious Milton, The. Francis Letters. NOBAu

Ingoldsby Legends, The. Thomas Ingoldsby.

  Jackdaw of Rheims, The. OBCoV; OBNV; OBSP

Ingrateful[l] Beauty Threatened. Thomas Carew. CavPo; OBEV; PBRV

Ingratitude, how deadly is thy smart. Sonnet: Ingratitude. Anna Seward. CenSon

  (Ingratitude, how deadly is the smart.) WaAnP

Ingredients of Glass. Margaret Speak. Prnts

Inhabitants of Old Jerusalem, The. John Dryden. BrAP *Fr.* Absalom and Achitophel.

Inhaling His Hair. Gillian Ferguson. NeBl

Inheritance. George Bruce. EdScPo

Inheritance. Michael Donaghy. PML

Inheritance. Alan Jenkins. NeBrP

Inheritance. Kathleen Norris. UpMys

Inheritance, The. James Aitchison. EdScPo

Inheritance: "We had a country to keep." Gerallt Lloyd Owen. BBMWP, *tr. by* Gillian Clarke

Inheritors, The. William Peskett. PNI

Inhuman Henry. A. E. Housman. NBLV

Inhumation. Kathleen Jamie. GPPA

Inimitably quick. Static Autumn. Yvor Winters. PoA 2002

Iniquity of the Fathers upon the Children, The. Christina Georgina Rossetti. FaBoVe

Inis Fal. Egan O'Rahilly. OBMV, *tr. by* James Stephens

Inishbofin on a Sunday morning. Seamus Heaney. HarvBoo *Fr.* Seeing Things.

Initial, Dæmonic, and Celestial Love. Ralph Waldo Emerson. Dæmonic and the Celestial Love, The. APN-1

Initially, an unbecoming enthusiasm. Science and the Single Girl. Karen Solie. PoPra

Initiation. Monifa Atungaye Love. ISC

Initiation. Rainer Maria Rilke. ItP, *tr. by* C. F. MacIntyre

Initiation, The. Shuja Nawaz. PML

Injian Ocean sets an' smiles, The. For to Admire. Rudyard Kipling. MoBrPo

Injured by iron I am a loner. Riddle, A. *Unknown.* PoCho, *tr. by* John Hollander

Injured Prince Vindicated, or, A Scurrilous and Detracting Pamphlet Answered, An. Elinor James. BASC

Injustice of the Courts. Lizelia Augusta Jenkins Moorer. CBWP-3

Ink. Abdel Kader El Janabi. Eno, *tr. by* Pierre Joris

Ink ain't spewed from this pen. And Now Yu. David S. Mills. InTrad

Ink characters have a free touch, The. Execution Poster, The. Mary Ruefle. AmAlph

Ink runs from the corners of my mouth. Eating Poetry. Mark Strand. NAMCP V.2; NoAM; PtR; StAl; WaAnP

Ink-black, but moving independently. Fable of the Ant and the Word. Mary Barnard. PoA 2002

Inks of all colours are filling my dreams. Dezső Kosztolányi. IQMS *Fr.* Laments of a Poor Little Child.

Inkspot, The. Paul Muldoon and Gerald Stern. GPPA

Inlaid Lute, The. Li Shang-yin. ChinPo, *tr. by* Ye Weilian [*or* Yeh Wei-lien *or* Wai-lim Yip]

Inland. Edna St. Vincent Millay. HarvBoo

Inland far though and away. Salt Longing. Austin Hummell. AmPoNex

Inland, inland, inland, inland. Oxaitoq's Song. *Unknown.* APN-2, *tr. by* Franz Boas

Inland sea, The. Jenny Joseph. MoWP

Inland sea—blue as a sapphire—set, An. Opal Sea, The. Ella Higginson. SWaP

Inmate, An. Peter Kocan. NOBAu

Inmates. Maggie Hannan. NLP

Inn at Kirchstetten, The. James Laughlin. PmAP

Inn of Angels, The. Giampiero Neri. ItPo, *tr. by* Gayle Ridinger

Innard. Silvia Eugenia Castillero. SPV, *tr. by* Jen Hofer

Innately reserved. Tanka. Kanoko Okamoto. CAoMJL1, *tr. by* Makoto Ueda

Inner Bloke. Joanne Limburg. NeBl

Inner greet. Greenberg said it. Columbus. Muriel Rukeyser. AF

Inner Man, The. Charles Simic. OPRER

Inner note. Ingrid de Kok. TSAP

Inner Part, The. Louis Simpson. PLBUT; RaBo

Inner Realm, The. Priscilla Jane Thompson. CBWP-2

Inner Temple Masque, The. William Browne.
Sirens' Song, The. OBEV

Inner Tube. Michael Ondaatje. NAMCP V.2; NoAM

Inner urge I cannot kill, An. I Light My Lamp. Luis Cano. OWABP

Inner Workings. Kuan Chung. ColAnChi *Fr.* Kuan Tzu.

Inniskeen Road: July Evening. Patrick Kavanagh. NAMCP V.1; NoAM; NPeEn; OxBSo; StAl

Innkeeper's Wife, The. Clive Sansom. OBCP

Innocence [*(to Tony White)*]. Thom Gunn. HP

Innocence. Patrick Kavanagh. ModIr

Innocence. Wisława Szymborska. PoSu, *tr. by* Jan Darowski

Innocence. Thomas Traherne. BASC; CABP; ChIV-2; NOSC

Innocence? / In a sense. Life, A. Howard Nemerov. OBCoV

Innocence of the world. Prikaz. André Salmon. CuPo

Innocence? Soon as you try putting your finger on it. 1966. David Rivard. PBCAP

Innocency or Not Song X. Gerald Early. BodElec

Innocent decision: to enjoy. Triple Feature. Denise Levertov. NoP-4; NoP-5

Innocent England. D. H. Lawrence. NPeEn; OBCoV

Innocent Ill, The. Abraham Cowley. BASC

Innocent to innocent. James Vincent Cunningham. APT-2

Innocents have come to make their cast, The. Kites: Ars Poetica. Ben Belitt. APT-2

Innocent's Song. Charles Causley. OBCP

Innominatus. Sir Walter Scott. OBEV

Inns are not residences. (LL) Silence. Marianne Moore. APT-1; HarvBoo; NAAPv.2; NALW; OxBoAm; PtR; TRP; WoPoe

Innsbruck, now I must depart. *Unknown.* GePo

Innumerable Christ, The. Hugh MacDiarmid. HarvBoo; OxAEP-2

Innumerable the images. Documentary Film. "Ern Malley." BMAP

Innumerable toads are croaking in the enormous silence. (LL) Walt Whitman: "But do you really want to see Whitman's house instead of Roosevelt's?" Juan Ramón Jiménez. ViWalt; WED, *tr. by* Robert Bly

Inpatient. Dolores Kendrick. FFC

In-Patient. Carole Satyamurti. PoCu

Inquest, By Hand. Jim Schley. NevBe

Inquest, The. W. H. Davies. AngWePo

Inquiry into Gifts, or the Indigo Bunting. Jeff Gundy. ACAMVP

Inquisition. Gloria Wade-Gayles. ISC

Inquisition, The. Victor Hugo. SxFrPo, *tr. by* A. M. and E. H. Blackmore

Inquisition, The: A Romance. Roger Weingarten. MAAN

Inquisitors, The. Robinson Jeffers. MoAmPo

INRI. Melanie Hope. WiU

Insatiableness. Thomas Traherne. BBASP; NOSC

Inscribe on Your Heart. Juan Chi. CCL1, *tr. by* Michael Bullock and C. J. Chen

Inscribe on your heart. Inscribe on Your Heart. Juan Chi. CCL1, *tr. by* Michael Bullock and C. J. Chen

Inscribed at Summit Temple. Li Po. CCL1; WoPoe, *tr. by* Elling O. Eide

Inscribed on a Painting by Myself. Ni Tsan. ColAnChi, *tr. by* Jonathan Chaves

Inscribed on the Doors of My Bookshelves. Yang Hsün-chi. ColAnChi, *tr. by* John Timothy Wixted

Inscribed on the Wall of Hsü Hsüan-Ping's Retreat. Li Po. WoPoe, *tr. by* Elling O. Eide

Inscription. William Cowper. OBGa

Inscription. Sophia De Mello Breyner. StAl, *tr. by* Richard Zenith

Inscription. Stephen Rodefer. OnScMo

Inscription at Mount Vernon. *Unknown.* HHAm

Inscription at Villers-Bretonneux. Geoff Page. NOBAu

Inscription Etched by Water. Pak Tujin. CAMKP, *tr. by* Edward W. Poitras

Inscription for a Mirror in a Deserted Dwelling. William Rose Benét. MoAmPo

Inscription for a Portrait. T'ang Yin. WoPoe, *tr. by* Graham Martin and John A. Scott

Inscription for a War [*'Stranger, go tell the Spartans we died here obedient to their commands.' Simonides of Keos,* for the Spartan Dead at Thermopylae]. Alec Derwent Hope. BMAP; NoP-4; NoP-5; WaAnP

Inscription for an Old Bed. William Morris. OBEV

Inscription for the Ceiling of a Bedroom. Dorothy Parker. AmWit

Inscription for the Entrance to a Wood. William Cullen Bryant. APN-1

Inscription for the Moss-Hut at Dove Cottage. William Wordsworth. OBGa

Inscription in a Beautiful Retreat Called Fairy Bower. Hannah More. NoP-4; NoP-5

Inscription in Osmington Church, Dorset. *Unknown.* NPeEn

Inscription in St Mary Magdalene Church, Milk Street, London. *Unknown.* NPeEn

Inscription on a Bathing Vessel. *Unknown.* CCL1, *tr. by* James Legge

Inscription on a Robe. *Unknown.* CCL1, *tr. by* James Legge

Inscription on a Staff. *Unknown.* CCL1, *tr. by* James Legge

Inscription on an Old Tomb at Guangling. Li Po. CCL1, *tr. by* Elling O. Eide

Inscription on the Liberty Bell. Bible, *O.T.* CA

Inscription on the Tomb of the Lady Mary Wentworth, The. Thomas Carew. *See* Maria Wentworth.

Inscription over His Door. Gido. ZenPo, *tr. by* Takashi Ikemoto and Lucien Stryk

Inscription, The: "While yet Rolfe's foot in stirrup stood." Herman Melville. APN-2 *Fr.* Clarel: A Poem and Pilgrimage in the Holy Land.

Inscription: "To them who crossed the flood." Herman Melville. PCW

Inscription Written by Me in My Small Garden. Po Chü-i. CCL1, *tr. by* Arthur Waley

Inscriptions. Mark Akenside.
For a Grotto. OBGa

Inscriptions. Adrienne Rich.
History. NIL-7

Inscrutable question, The. Simon Williams. NewEx

Insect. Sándor Weöres. IQMS, *tr. by* Peter Zollman

Insect, The. Ivan Turgeniev. MotU, *tr. by* Isabel Florence Hapgood

Insect Affection. Elizabeth Oakes-Smith. STuOW *Fr.* Sinless Child, The.

Insect born of royalty has Marx, The. Why Fortune Is the Empress of the World. Turner Cassity. PoA 2002

Insect or blossom? Fragile, fairy thing. Mariposa Lily, The. Ina Coolbrith. NAAPv.1

Insect song. (LL) From the bough. Issa. BLT; ZenPo, *tr. by* Takashi Ikemoto and Lucien Stryk

Insects. Issa. WED; WoPoe, *tr. by* Robert Bly

Insects. Isidor Schneider. APT-2

Insects are neat in death. Bee. Patricia Pogson. NLP

Insects chirp outside the four walls, The. *Unknown.* NAAPv.2

Insects hung in the air, frozen invisible pouches, contorted parodies of medieval fate, The. Privacy. Carla Harryman. MotU

Insects on a bough. Issa. EH; NIL-7, *tr. by* Robert Hass

Insects, why cry? Insects. Issa. WED; WoPoe, *tr. by* Robert Bly

Insensibility. Wilfred Owen. BrAP; FaBoWar; NoP-4; NoP-5; OBWP; OxAEP-2; PoWW

Insensibility. William Wordsworth. STuOW *Fr.* Liberty [*sequel to* Gold and Silver Fishes in a Vase].

Insensible Hottentot, The. John Dyer. STuOW *Fr.* Fleece, The.

Inserting the Mirror. Rosmarie Waldrop.
"To explore the nature of rain I opened the door because inside the workings of language clear vision is impossible." PmAP

Inside. Celia de Fréine. NIrP *Fr.* Price on My Head, A.

Inside a cave in a narrow canyon near Tassajara. Hands. Robinson Jeffers. CalPo

Inside Diameter. Clarence Major. PmAP

Inside each of us lies the secret. How They Loved. Jean Janzen. ACAMVP

Inside each one. Wintermelon. Alan Chong Lau. WhBo

Inside Father's Pockets. Martha Rhodes. ExTi

Inside: George Gaines at Graterford Prison, 1981. David Keplinger. AmPoNex

Inside Green Eyes, Black Eyes. Diana Der Hovanessian. TWW

Inside his head he heard the stormy crows. (LL) Brainstorm. Howard Nemerov. OxBoAm; TRP

Inside it. And that thing / screams. (LL) Agony, An. As Now. Imamu Amiri Baraka. NAAL-5; NAMCP V.2; NoP-4; NoP-5; UnSA

Inside / (jittery / burned language). Re:searches (Fragments, after Anakreon, for Emily Dickinson). Kathleen Fraser. PmAP

Inside Job, An. Brendan Galvin. PoCoUp

Inside Long Treks. Lewis Warsh. AHA

Inside my ears. P Word Poem, The. Leticia R. Benson. InTrad

Inside my eye. Inside Green Eyes, Black Eyes. Diana Der Hovanessian. TWW

Inside my heart I hear. Bible, O.T. AHA Fr. Psalms [David Rosenberg Adaption].

Inside my mother. Sari, The. Moniza Alvi. BeAl

Inside of my inspection house there are. Specific Incendiaries of Springtime, The. Lisa Jarnot. VaPo

Inside of the spine of *Macbeth* is ditch-dark, The. Ditch, The. Lee Upton. IaFF

Inside of which careen. Kingdom of Heaven, The. Pattiann Rogers. PoCoUp

Inside Our Dreams. Jeanne Willis. StAl

Inside Out. Jenna Johnson. MAAN

Inside, The. David Wojahn. YaYoPo

Inside the aircraft, I take off my necktie, unfasten my seat belt, and stand up. From Athens to Cairo. Sunil Gangopadhyay. PML, tr. by Nandini Gupta

Inside the Amish health food store. Papaya: Lancaster County. Juanita Brunk. ACAMVP

Inside the Apple. Yehuda Amichai. ItP, tr. by Chana Bloch

Inside the Bouquet. Max Dauthendey. GTCP, tr. by Reinhold Grimm

Inside the box, her heels escape the air. Vanishing. Roddy Lumsden. EdScPo

Inside, the church lights up today's rain. Fernando Pessoa. PFTM-1 Fr. Oblique Rain.

Inside the empty chamber of a wave is the same. Not Surfing Some Days. Rick Noguchi. AmPoNex

Inside the Fence: Tule Lake Internment Camp. Kim R. Stafford. GifTon

Inside the fog that encloses the trees, they undergo a stripping. Francis Ponge. WED,

Inside the Great Pyramid. Gwendolyn MacEwen. BrAP

Inside the home fashioned of tin and mud. Open Kitchen, The. Kimiko Hahn. PrTe

Inside the Horizon. New Song. Vincente Huidobro. CuPo

Inside the Hummingbird Aviary. David Huddle. PfSP

Inside the Iris. Kim Hyesun. EcSo, tr. by Youngju Ryu

Inside the lunchroom the travelling nuns wove. Feathered Dancers. Kenward Elmslie. AHA; NYP2; PmAP

Inside the mask her eyes are very dark. Face Mask. Patricia Pogson. NLP

Inside the nighttime of the storm. Enormous Hand, The. Jorge de Lima. PFTM-1

Inside the Pass. Farewell to Wei Feng, Going to Far-South Mountain. Hsi Chou. CSKM, tr. by Paul Hansen

Inside the River. James Dickey. PoA 2002

Inside the rock on which we live, another rock. Lazarus (1st draft). Anne Carson. WaAnP

Inside the shed, he'd rigged. Division. Michael Chitwood. PoDa

Inside the strict pine coffin. Shards. Enid Shomer. TaR

Inside the temple enclosure. Hall of the Guardian God. Muso Soseki. EaWin, tr. by W. S. Merwin

Inside, the turned liver. Gertrude to Hamlet. Lee Upton. IaFF

Inside the veins there are navies setting forth. Waking from Sleep. Robert Bly. NoP-4; NoP-5

Inside the vessels of too many women I've hid from myself far too many times when I lacked the courage to be alone. Cocaine Mad-Scream Article #33 LoveSong. Gylan Kain. BRtP

Inside the White Star it was warm, tumbled clothes. White Star, The. Minnie Bruce Pratt. ExTi

Inside / The wireless is irritable with static. Dog Fight. Eric Rolls. NOBAu

Inside the Wolf's fang, the mountain of heather. Amulet. Ted Hughes. NOxBChV

Inside the womb-like darkness. Wedding. No Hyegyông. EcSo, tr. by Ann Y. Choi

Inside this clay jug there are canyons and pine mountains, and the maker of canyons and pine mountains! Clay Jug, The. Kabir. WED, tr. by Robert Bly

Inside this new love, die. Quietness. Jelaluddin Rumi. PtR, tr. by Coleman Barks

Inside those caves, grottos of shame, full of mud, a child is still taking shelter, hopping. Geranium and the Child. Ece Ayhan. PFTM-2, tr. by Murat Nemet-Nejat

Inside water, a waterwheel turns. Jelaluddin Rumi. WoPoe, tr. by Coleman Barks and John Moyne

Inside Your Sea My Boat Was Sailing. Patrizia Cavalli. CItWP, tr. by Cinzia Sartini Blum and Lara Trubowitz

Insider's View of the Garden, The. Maxine W. Kumin. IPoFL

Insides of Alfred Hitchcock, The. Alejandrino Hufana. ReBoTo

Inside—the laughter of friends. Birthday Poem. Steve Sanfield. WhBo

Insight into private affairs. . .raises certain barristers and magistrates to such great heights. Richard Murray Vaughan. Coast

Insincere Wish Addressed to a Beggar, An [with music]. Mary Elizabeth Coleridge. NPeEn; PEW; VWP

Insistence of Beauty, The. Stephen Dunn. CAP-8

Insistent as a whistle, her voice up. Claiming Kin. Ellen Bryant Voigt. WaAnP

Insistently through sleep—a tide of voices. Hart Crane. MoAmPo; NoAM; OxBoAm Fr. Bridge, The.

Insomnia. Elizabeth Bishop. AWTN

Insomnia. Tristan Corbière. AWTN, tr. by Georges Guy and Kenneth Koch

Insomnia. Cornelius Eady. AWTN; ESEAA

Insomnia. Dana Gioia. AWTN

Insomnia. Abu Amir ibn al-Hammarah. WoPoe, tr. by Cola Franzen

Insomnia. Osip Emilevich Mandelstam. TCRusP, tr. by John Glad

Insomnia. Debra Nystrom. AWTN

Insomnia. Joyce Carol Oates. AWTN

Insomnia. Wyatt Prunty. RA

Insomnia. Salvatore Quasimodo. AWTN, tr. by Allen Mandelbaum

Insomnia. Justin Quinn. NIrP

Insomnia. Dante Gabriel Rossetti. AWTN

Insomnia. Tiziano Rossi. ItPo, tr. by Gayle Ridinger

Insomnia. Marina Ivanovna Tsvetayeva. tr. by Elaine Feinstein
    "Black as an iris, as an iris sucking up the." PoCho, tr. by Nina Kossman
    "Here's another window." AWTN, tr. by Elaine Feinstein
    "In my enormous city it is—night." OxBEV, tr. by Elaine Feinstein
    "Tonight—I am alone in the night." AWTN, tr. by Elaine Feinstein
    "Who sleeps at night? No one is sleeping." AWTN, tr. by Elaine Feinstein

Insomnia and the Seven Steps to Grace. Joy Harjo. NAMCP V.2

Insomnia at the Solstice. Jane Kenyon. AWTN

Insomnia: "Even when I fall asleep early." Lu Yu. NDACCP, tr. by Kenneth Rexroth

Insomnia. Homer. Taut Sails. Osip Emilevich Mandelstam. AWTN; PoCho, tr. by Clarence Brown and W. S. Merwin and W. S. Merwin

Insomnia. Homer. Taut sails. Insomnia. Osip Emilevich Mandelstam. TCRusP, tr. by John Glad

Insomnia, impalpable Creature! Insomnia. Tristan Corbière. AWTN, tr. by Georges Guy and Kenneth Koch

Insomnia Litany. Joan Logghe. OPRER

Insomnia of Tremayne, The. Donald Justice. AWTN

Insomnia on a Summer Night. Umberto Saba. AWTN, tr. by Christopher Millis

Insomnia Song. Gregory Orr. AWTN

Insomnia: The Distances. Sydney Lea. RA

Insomnia the Gem of the Ocean. John Updike. NBLV

Insomnia thinks and pronounces syllables. Insomnia. Tiziano Rossi. ItPo, tr. by Gayle Ridinger

Insomniac. M. Loncar. AmPoNex

Insomniac. Sylvia Plath. AWTN

Insomniac trees rattle silken little. Unholy Spring. John Godfrey. FTOS

Inspection, The. Fred Voss. BeAl

Inspiration. Mário de Andrade. TCLAP, tr. by Jack E. Tomlins

Inspiration. Robert W. Service. WeW-3

Inspiration. Stephen Stepanchev. PoA 2002

Inspiration. James Tate. BodElec; OxBoAm

Inspiration, An. Ella Wheeler Wilcox. ITBLP

Inspiration: "Rumpled, torpid, bored, too tasteful to rhyme." William Matthews. OxBoAm

Inspiration: "Think of those Chinese monks' tales." Jane Hirshfield. WANABP

Inspiration ("Whate'er we leave to God, God does.") Henry David Thoreau. APN-1; ColAP; NCAP; OxBoAm

Inspire us now with one accord. Forward to Nationhood. Reginal Faber. OWABP

Inspirer and hearer of prayer. Hymn. Augustus Montague Toplady. SacPr

Instability. Henrietta Cordelia Ray. CBWP-3

Instance of fore-ordained harmony, An. Igor Vladimirovich Chinnov. TCRusP, *tr. by* John Glad

Instant Control. Michael Portnoy. HeMarv

Instant he boarded the plane, The. Toad. Takahashi Shinkichi. ZenPo, *tr. by* Takashi Ikemoto and Lucien Stryk

Instant of Clearness. Jean Le Roy. OBVE, *tr. by* Wallace Stevens

Instant of white roses, An. Phyllis Webb. NLPA *Fr.* Naked Poems.

Instant sprang at me, a winter instant, An. At Fourth and Main in Liberal, Kansas, 1932. William Stafford. CAP-8

Instants 1. Jacqueline Risset. SCFWP, *tr. by* Serge Gavronsky

Instead of a cup of tea, instead of milk. Crepuscule with Muriel. Marilyn Hacker. AFaM

Instead of a dream we want a definate hand. Instead of a Dream. Ch'oe Sûngja. EcSo, *tr. by* Mickey Hong

Instead of a Preface. Anna Andreyevna Akhmatova. PFTM-1

Instead of an Animal. Leslie Scalapino. PFTM-2

Instead of becoming the empress of joined kingdoms. End of the Game. Artur Miedzyrzecki. PoSu, *tr. by* John Batki and Artur Miedzyrzecki

Instead of being confined on Madison Avenue I could soar in a Jiffy to Second or Third. (LL) Spring Comes to Murray Hill. Ogden Nash. AmWit; APT-2

Instead of bridal bed and holy wedding songs. Anyte. SaLy, *tr. by* Diane Rayor

Instead of burning the book or getting its value. Secret, The. Eiléan Ní Chuilleanáin. MoWP

Instead of Clements' Ferry, it is now Sunset Retreat. (LL) To Clements' Ferry. Josephine D. Henderson Heard. CBWP-4; SWaP

Instead of coin and money. John Skelton. NoSic *Fr.* Tunning of Elinour Rumming, The.

Instead of his leash. Karen Alkalay-Gut. DTA *Fr.* Between Bombardments: A Journal.

Instead of icepacks. Dancing in Menopause. Dorothy Perry Thompson. SpirFl

Instead of Lent I have been feasting. God and the Holy Stones. Annie Foster. NLP

Instead of Reading Marcus Aurelius. Claudia Keelan. RWB

Instead of You. Stephen Dunn. CAP-8

Instinct. Bill Berkson. NYP2

Instinct. Edith Södergran. PFTM-1

Instinct, The. Jack Myers. BodElec

Instinct of Self-Preservation, The. Nanni Balestrini. *tr. by* Lawrence R. Smith "What matters here is (can a fish live." PFTM-2, *tr. by* Lawrence R. Smith

Institute for Social Change, The. Joshua Clover. AmPoNex

Institution of the dear love of comrades, The. (LL) I Hear It Was Charged against Me. Walt Whitman. APN-1; CAGL; MoAmPo

Institutional Blue. Ann Townsend. NAPBL

Institutions. Kim Sünghûi. EcSo, *tr. by* K. Kim Richards and Steffen Richards

Instructed by the fiery dead. (LL) Cross, The. Allen Tate. ChIV-2; MoAmPo

Instructing Clarity in a Confusion. Arkadii Dragomoschenko. ItGoST, *tr. by* Elena Balashova and Lyn Hejinian

Instructing Fellow Buddhists after Picking Brackens. Chungji. BecRai, *tr. by* Kim Daljin, Kim Won-Chung and Christopher Merrill

Instruction. Hazel Hall. NAAPv.2

Instruction Manual, The. John Ashbery. NAMCP V.2; NoAM; OxBoAm; YaYoPo

Instruction, The. Thomas Traherne. BASC

Instructions. Sheri Hostetler. ACAMVP

Instructions. Gary Snyder. NoP-5

Instructions for a Waitress. Yehuda Amichai. PoSu, *tr. by* Harold Schimmel

Instructions for Academic Poets Who Talk to God. Honorée Fanonne Jeffers. RD

Instructions for Building Straw Huts. Yusef Komunyakaa. GT

Instructions for Crossing the Border. Dan Pagis. PoSu, *tr. by* Stephen Mitchell

Instructions for How to Get Ahead of Yourself While the Light Still Shines. Jenny Bornholdt. ArBi

Instructions for Your New Osiris. Lorenzo Thomas. PmAP

Instructions on How to Cry. Julio Cortázar. MotU, *tr. by* Paul Blackburn

Instructions on Landscaping. Richard Jago. OBGa *Fr.* Edge-Hill.

Instructions to a Seed. David Curzon. GI

Instructions to Be Left Behind. Marvin Bell. TAPaP

Instructions to Her Next Husband. Judith Taylor. SUP

Instructions to the Player. Carl Rakosi. APT-2; MiVo

Instructor said, The / *Go home and write.* Theme for English B. Langston Hughes. APT-2; ColAP; FaBoA; NAMCP V.1; NIL-7; NIP-4; NoAM; NoP-4; NoP-5; PoPoPo; PtR; SSLK; WaAnP

Instrument. Gerrit Achterberg. TuT, *tr. by* Peter van de Kamp

Instrument, The. Kathleen Jessie Raine. PoA 2002

Instrument and Agent. Norman Alexander MacCaig. NePenScot

Instrument of Choice. Robert Phillips. GoPo

Insufficient, like all apologies. Knob Pines. David Swanger. GeoHom

Insular firebird, The. Cages, The. James Tate. YaYoPo

Insular Prejudice. Christopher Smart. DiBP *Fr.* English Bull Dog, Dutch Mastiff, and Quail, The.

Insulin Receptor. H. J. Van Peenen. BloBone

Insulted. Priscilla Jane Thompson. CBWP-2

Insusceptibles, The. Adrienne Rich. HeIP-4

Intact. Stephanie Strickland. ExTi

Intact Pitcher. Yolanda Bedregal. TANSG, *tr. by* Carolyne Wright

Integrating the Strawberry Swimming Pool in 1998. Cecil Brown. FTtHH

Integration. Angela Shannon. BtF

Integrity. Adrienne Rich. ColAP; StAl

Intelijencia, Dame. Juan Ramón Jiménez. RaW

Intellect. Ralph Waldo Emerson. APN-1; NoP-4; NoP-5

Intellect of man is forced to choose, The. Choice, The. William Butler Yeats. NoAM; WaAnP

Intellect of woman must not choose, The. Intellect of Woman, The. Annie Finch. WaAnP

Intellect so ravenous to know, The. Wendell Berry. UpMys *Fr.* Sabbaths.

Intellectual Life, The. Damon Krukowski. OnScMo

Intellectual Powers of the Soul, The. John Davies. SacPr

Intellectual, The. Yury Timofeievich Galanskov. TCRusP, *tr. by* Olive Dehn

Intellectual, The. Janet Paisley. EdScPo

Intelligence, Give Me. Juan Ramón Jiménez. RaW, *tr. by* Robert Bly

Intelligence of the stars, The. (LL) Flight of Apollo, The. Stanley Kunitz. OPRER; OtW; TaR

Intelligence Quotient, The. Deborah Harding. SUP

Intelligence Quotients. Dorothy Perry Thompson. SpirFl

Intelligence / That's whit ah'm luikin fur in a fella. Intellectual, The. Janet Paisley. EdScPo

Intemperate torch grazed, The. Night-piece. "Ern Malley." BMAP

Intended for Sir Isaac Newton. Alexander Pope. WeW-3
(Epitaph Intended for Sir Isaac Newton, in Westminster Abbey.) NPeEn; OxBEV

Intended, The. Mary Ruefle. AmAlph

Intense and terrible beauty, how has our race with the frail naked nerves. Gale in April. Robinson Jeffers. MoAmPo

Intensely exciting montage of Macchu Picchu, erupting volcanos, An. Cinema Vérité: Jacques Derrida and God's *Tsimtsum.* Tom Andrews. MotU

Intensities, The. Cups #5. Robin Blaser. ASA

Intensity and Height. César Vallejo. PoetW, *tr. by* Clayton Eshleman

Intensive Care. Helen Lamb. PoCu

Intensive Care. Carol Muske-Dukes. PBCAP

Intent ear hears the silence hears silence and then the pen, The. Pen Vine and Scroll. John Taggart. FTOS

Intent to consider. Kit Robinson. FTOS *Fr.* Up Early.

Intent upon meaning, we mean. Reading the Signs. Eric Tretheway. PfSP

Inter, mitzy, titzy, tool. *Unknown.* FaBoVe

Interborough Rapid Transit Co. (LL) Rapid Transit. William Carlos Williams. APT-1; OxBoAm

Intercede for us dear saint we beseech thee. Prayer to Saint Grobianus. Roger McGough. NOxBChV

Interchange. Ted Kooser. UrbNat

Intercity Dub. Jane King. WaCA

Intercity, Swansea-London. Jon Dressel. TCAWP

Interest points for. Bleecker Street. Hugh Seidman. BodElec

Interesting case, the progress of a bird. When, An. Will to Will. Keith Waldrop. PmAP

Interesting how we fall in love. Unwritten Law. Louise Glück. BodElec

Interesting People of Newfoundland. John Ashbery. VaPo

Interests of a black man in a cellar, The. Black Tambourine. Hart Crane. NAMCP V.1; NoAM

Interface. Jeff Derksen. NLPA

Interference Song. Liz Lochhead. RSaN

Interior. Padraic Colum. MoBrPo

Interior. W. E. Henley. NPeEn *Fr.* In Hospital.

Interior. Gilberto Owen. MotU, *tr. by* Mark Strand

Interior, An. Paul Farley. NeBrP

Interior at Petworth: From Turner. Rosanna Warren. NoAM

Interior Music, The. Patricia Goedicke. MiVo

Interior Scroll. Carolee Schneemann. PFTM-2

Interior with a Violin. Marianne Boruch. AmAlph

Interior with Faded Colors. Blaga Dimitrova. CSCBP, *tr. by* Georgi Belev and Lisa Sapinkopf

Interlaced Lines for the Same Moment. Ghada El-Shafa'i. PoArWo, *tr. by* Atef Abu-Seif and Nathalie Handal

Interlinked is truth to duty, have you had the precious thought. Duty, or Truth at Work. Lizelia Augusta Jenkins Moorer. CBWP-3

Interlude. Sibby Anderson-Thompkins. InTrad

Interlude. Maya Bejerano. DTA *Fr.* Hymns of Job.

Interlude. Maxwell Bodenheim. APT-1

Interlude. Keidrych Rhys. AngWePo

Interlude. Dame Edith Sitwell. MoBrPo

Interlude: "I watch a handsome young female." Sarah Cortez. TiP2

Interlude of Joy. George Seferis. PoetW, *tr. by* Edmund Keeley and Philip Sherrard

Interlude on Mustagh Tower. Andrew Greig. EdScPo

Interlude: "Sing together." Rachel Beck. IaFF

Interludes. Fabio Doplicher. NeIt, *tr.* by Stephen Sartarelli

Intermedio con cinco cocodrilos. Efraín Bartolomé. RMCMP

Intermezzo with Five Crocodiles. Efraín Bartolomé. RMCMP, *tr. by* Asa Zatz

Interminable heat of summer lies over, The. Heat. Carol Cullar. TiP2

Intermission. Andrew Feld. LegDan

Intermission from Friday. Pedro Juan Pietri. PueRic

Intermission from Monday. Pedro Juan Pietri. PueRic

Intermission from Saturday. Pedro Juan Pietri. PueRic

Intermission from Sunday. Pedro Juan Pietri. PueRic

Intermission from Thursday. Pedro Juan Pietri. PueRic

Intermission from Wednesday. Pedro Juan Pietri. PueRic

Intermittent. Yousif al-Sa'igh. IrPoTo, *tr. by* Chuck Miller and Saadi A. Simawe

Intermittent Dream of a Sad Night. Marceline Desbordes-Valmore. WoPoe, *tr. by* Louis Simpson

Internal Migration: On Being on Tour. Alan Dugan. NAMCP V.2; NoAM

Internal Travels. Pierre Reverdy. MotU, *tr. by* Michael Benedikt

International blossoms shrivel. They Do Not Have to Nest in Your Hair: A Tribute to Ron Brown. Carolyn Joyner. BtF

International Date Line lies motionless between Samoa and Tonga, The. For Mats and Laila. Tomas Tranströmer. MotU, *tr. by* Robert Bly

International Date Line, Monday/Monday 27:XI:67. Philip Whalen. BB

International Ode. Oliver Wendell Holmes. TreFP

Inter-Office Memorandum. Ogden Nash. APT-2

Interplay. Xue Di. OnScMo, *tr. by* Wang Ping and Keith Waldrop

Interpretation of a Poem by Frost. Thylias Moss. NAMCP V.2; VisFro

Interpretation of Dinner by the Uninvited Guest, An. Lorna Dee Cervantes. TouFir

Interpretations. Baba Lukata. BtF

Interpreter. Carmen Horst. ACAMVP

Interr'd [*or* Interred] beneath this marble stone. Epitaph, An. Matthew Prior. NAEL-6v1; NAEL-7v1; OBCoV; OBSV

Interrogation, The. Li-Young Lee. PoPoPo

Interrogation, The. Edwin Muir. NPeEn; PoWW

Interrogations of the Sparrow. Elizabeth Spires. FFC

Interrogativa Cantilena. *Unknown. See* If All the World Were Paper.

Interrupt this Ground. (LL) Ample make this Bed. Emily Dickinson. ItP; MoAmPo; NAAL-3; WoPoe

Interrupted Meditation. Robert Hass. BAP-97; FaoP

Interrupted Reproof, The. Priscilla Jane Thompson. CBWP-2

Interruption. Sarah Fox. PfS

Interruption of Flight. Lisa Williams. AmPoNex

Intersection, The. Charles Bernstein. PFTM-2 *Fr.* Artifice of Absorption.

Interstate 80. Michael Anania. IllVoic

I-35, South of Waco. William Virgil Davis. TiP2

Interval, An. June 30th. Vera Gheraducci. CItWP

Interval of Five Tones Being the Dominant, An. Brooks Haxton. PoDa

Interview. Manuel Bandeira. TCLAP, *tr. by* Candace Slater

Interview from the Belly of a Whale. Konstantin Pavlov. CSCBP, *tr. by* Georgi Belev and Lisa Sapinkopf

Interview with a Combat Photographer. Chivas Sandage. MAAN

Interview with a Piece of Smoke. Steve Healey. IIR

Interview with an Alchemist in the New Age. Stephanie Brown. BodElec

Interview with Doctor Drink. James Vincent Cunningham. WoPoe

Interview with the Poet. Gwyneth Lewis. ATSWP, *tr. by* Robert Minhinnick

Interview with the Poet. Gwyneth Lewis. BBMWP *Fr.* Language Murderer, The.

Intery, mintery, cutery corn. Mother Goose. FaBoVe

Intil the pit-mirk nicht we northwart sail. Arctic Convoy. James King Annand. EdScPo

Intimacy if we can [intimate] an. Dark Continent, The. Sean Manzano Labrador. BAP-04

Intimate. Gabriela Mistral. SpanPo, *tr. by* Kate Flores

Intimate Associations. Charles Baudelaire. WoPoe, *tr. by* Robert Bly

Intimate Conversations with God. Kwaja Abdullah Ansari. *tr. by* Wheeler M. Thackston

"O God, / I have bound myself to you to the exclusion of all else." BBASP, *tr. by* Wheeler M. Thackston

Intimate evenings, times long past, refined to remembrance. A La Recherche. Miklós Radnóti. IQMS, *tr. by* Peter Zollman

Intimate Letter 1973. Padraic Fiacc. PNI

Intimate Mixture. Elena Georgiou. WiU

Intimate Parnassus. Patrick Kavanagh. MoBrPo

Intimates. D. H. Lawrence. NBLV; RaBo

Intimations. Howard Nemerov. BodElec

Intimations of Anxiety. Laila Al-Saih. PoArWo, *tr. by* May Jayyusi and Naomi Shihab Nye

Intimations of Mortality. Stanley Kunitz. MoAmPo

Intimidations of an Autobiography. James Tate. NoAM

Into a dark and lonely wood. (LL) Villain, The. W. H. Davies. AngWePo; MoBrPo

Into a Dead Zone. Mati Katz. NRoS, *tr. by* Esther Raizen

Into a simple gift I could give in friendship? (LL) Wedding-Ring. Denise Levertov. CAP-8; NIL-7

Into a swirl of scuttling leaves. (LL) Windy City. Stuart Dybek. IllVoic; PoCho

Into Battle. Julian Grenfell. FaBoWar; OBEV; OBMV; OBWP

Into blossom. (LL) Blessing, A: "Just off the highway to Rochester, Minnesota." James Wright. AmFaPo; CAP-8; ChAP; GoPo; MoAmPo; NAAL-5; NAMCP V.2; NoAM; NoP-4; NoP-5; OxBoAm; PoA 2002; PoPoPo; RaBo; StAl; TRP; VCAP

Into Concrete Mixer Throw. Barbara Roe. UV

Into each other's gaze.. (LL) Judas Iscariot. Stephen Spender. MoBrPo; NIP-4

Into exile with only a few shirts. Cloak, The. Robert Graves. HarvBoo

Into First. Ron Egatz. NevBe

Into Her Eyes a Tear Crept. Gustavo Adolfo Bécquer. SpanPo, *tr. by* Kate Flores

Into her eyes a tear crept. Into Her Eyes a Tear Crept. Gustavo Adolfo Bécquer. SpanPo, *tr. by* Kate Flores

Into her mother's bedroom to wash the ballooning body. Jessie Mitchell's Mother. Gwendolyn Brooks. ColAP; NALW; OxAAAP

Into hey nony nony. (LL) William Shakespeare. NoSic; UV Fr. Much Ado about Nothing.

Into his rosy chamber stepped the Sun. At Sunset. Henrietta Cordelia Ray. CBWP-3

Into it his unbearable story. (LL) On This Side of the River. Stephen Berg. GifTon; TAPaP

Into it they rush, frantic from the seasonal muzak. Calm, The. John McAuliffe. NIrP

Into Mexico. Mona Van Duyn. VCAP

Into my bosom and be lost in me. (LL) Alfred Tennyson. NAEL-6v2; NAEL-7v2; NoP-4; NoP-5; NPeEn; OxAEP-2; TFi; WoPoe Fr. Princess, The.

Into my empty head there come. Morning Swim. Maxine W. Kumin. CAP-8

Into my heart a seed was cast. Hunger. Mikhail Naimy. NAAPv.2

Into my heart an air that kills. Yon Far Country. A. E. Housman. HarvBoo; MoBrPo; NoAM; NPeEn; OPOU; OxAEP-2; OxBEV; TFi; WaAnP

Into my heart an air that kills. A. E. Housman. HarvBoo; MoBrPo; NoAM; NPeEn; OPOU; OxAEP-2; OxBEV; TFi; WaAnP Fr. Shropshire Lad, A.

Into Perfect Spheres Such Holes Are Pierced. Catherine Barnett. PoCho

Into space-time walks bass strings of charlie mingus. One for Charlie Mingus. Quincy Troupe. SpirFl

Into Still Air. Larry Smith. AmZen

Into that dark permanence of ancient forms. (LL) John Montague. ModIr; NoP-4; NoP-5; PBCIP; PNI Fr. Rough Field, The.

Into that peace all history must feed. (LL) At Vshchizh. Fyodor Ivanovich Tyutchev. OBWP; OxBEV; WoPoe, *tr. by* Henry Gifford and Charles Tomlinson

Into that pit. Burning Shit at An Khe. Bruce Weigl. AF; AmWaPo

Into the Ark. John Blight. BMAP

Into the aubade. Fit Für Gaing Farth. Barbara Guest. AHA

Into the Beautiful. (LL) As imperceptibly as Grief. Emily Dickinson. APN-2; NoP-4; NoP-5; SoSe-8

Into the blue river hills. Sunset from Omaha Hotel Window. Carl Sandburg. APT-1

Into the changes of autumn brush. To Kill a Deer. Carol Frost. CAP-8; MoASP

Into the closed air of the slow. Ted Berrigan. NYP2 Fr. Sonnets, The.

Into the clouds, and never more return! (LL) Ode on Indolence. John Keats. NAEL-6v2; NAEL-7v2; NPBRoP

Into the common bowl. Salad Days. Bruce Berger. SwNoth

Into the darkness and the hush of night. Night. Henry Wadsworth Longfellow. APN-1

Into the Depths. Adah Isaacs Menken. CBWP-1

Into the Dusk-Charged Air. John Ashbery. APSN

Into the flame Godmother put her hand. David's Night in Veliès. James Merrill. HarvBoo

Into the Foghorn. Paul Celan. BBASP, *tr. by* Michael Hamburger

Into the furnace let me go alone. Baptism. Claude McKay. NAAPv.2

Into the gloom of the deep, dark night. Engine, The. Ella Wheeler Wilcox. APN-2

Into the glories of the [*or* th'] almighty sun. (LL) On a Drop of Dew. Andrew Marvell. BASC; FSCP; NIL-7; NOSC

Into the grave. (LL) To Blossoms. Robert Herrick. BrAP; NAEL-6v1; NOSC; OBEV; TreFP

Into the grip of another. (LL) Driving with Dominic in the Southern Province We See Hints of the Circus. Michael Ondaatje. NAMCP V.2; NoP-5

Into the Hearth They Are Tossing Logs. Manuel González Prada. SpanPo, *tr. by* Kate Flores

Into the hearth they are tossing logs. Into the Hearth They Are Tossing Logs. Manuel González Prada. SpanPo, *tr.* by Kate Flores

Into the house. Issa. IllVoic *Fr.* Issa: A Suite of Haiku.

Into the ice ravaged rag-weed and phlox. Praying. Cynthia Cruz. IAoNAP

Into the last dream of Offa the King. (LL) Geoffrey Hill. NAMCP V.2; NoAM; WoPoe *Fr.* Mercian Hymns.

Into the Light. Pattiann Rogers. PoCoUp

Into the Next One. Valerie Martínez. AmPoNex

Into the pause, while peppermints were passed. Dylan Thomas at Tenby. Raymond Garlick. TCAWP

Into the quiet of this room. Room, The. William Soutar. NePenScot

Into the Red Velvet. Joyce Mansour. SurWo, *tr. by* Guy Flandre and Peter Wood

Into the red velvet of your belly. Into the Red Velvet. Joyce Mansour. SurWo, *tr.* by Guy Flandre and Peter Wood

Into the rescued world newcomer. Beyond Knowledge. Alice Thompson Meynell. ChIV-1

Into the ring of the dance. (LL) Caedmon. Denise Levertov. BrAP; ItP; NAMCP V.2; NoAM; NoP-4; NoP-5; PoCho

Into the silver night. Revelation. Sir Edmund William Gosse. OBEV

Into the sixties. Don't Cry, Scream. Haki R. Madhubuti. SeSe

Into the skies, one summer's day. Thought, The. William Brighty Rands. OBEV

Into the soil a seed is sown. Mors et Vita. James Edwin Campbell. TCAPo

Into the soil of England. (LL) How Beastly the Bourgeois Is. D. H. Lawrence. BrAP; NAEL-6v2; NAEL-7v2; OBSV

Into the street the Piper stept. Robert Browning. OxAEP-2 *Fr.* Pied Piper of Hamelin, The.

Into the sunshine. Fountain, The. James Russell Lowell. TreFP

Into the towering gulfs of air. (LL) Veni Coronaberis. Geoffrey Hill. NoP-4; NoP-5

Into the underneath—. Recessional. Robert Kelly. FTOS

Into the unforgiving new day. (LL) Man with the Saxophone, The. Ai. CFP; SeSe

Into the void behold my shuddering flight,. Anna Hempstead Branch. NALW *Fr.* Sonnets from a Lock Box.

Into the Woods. Ko Ŭn. CAMKP, *tr. by* David R. McCann

Into the woods my Master went. Ballad of Trees and the Master, A. Sidney Lanier. APN-2; ChIV-2; ColAP; ITBLP; TCAPo

Into the world where they are. (LL) Hearing Loss. Christian Wiman. AmPoNex; PoDa

Into Their True Gentleness. Pearse Hutchinson. IrLP

Into these loves, who but for passion look[e]s. Michael Drayton. NAEL-6v1; NAEL-7v1; NOSC *Fr.* Idea.

Into this other world he cannot build without you. (LL) Thief, The. Dorianne Laux. ErotSp; ExTi; PasH

Into this pleasant Shadow all the weak & weary. William Blake. NOBRP *Fr.* Milton.

Into This Time. Jayne Cortez. EGAG

Into this wild abyss. John Milton. NOSC *Fr.* Paradise Lost.

Into whose ear the deeds are spoken. The only. History. Jorie Graham. HarvBoo

Into your trunk. Her Story. Leah Korican. HW

Intolerably sad, profound. Before the Anæsthetic; or, A Real Fright. Sir John Betjeman. HarvBoo

Intoothed constrict. Giant Yellow. Maggie O'Sullivan. Oth

Intoxicated just because I smiled at you. *Unknown.* SLW, *tr. by* Marjolijn De Jager, Sayd Bahodin Majrouh and André Velter

Intoxicating draughts he never does drink. Joseph Gwyer. VerBaPo *Fr.* Ode on the Visit of the Shah of Persia.

Intoxicating Moonlight. Kim Yŏngnang. CAMKP, *tr. by* Anthony, Brother of Taizé

Intoxication of final loneliness. (LL) Medlars and Sorb-Apples. D. H. Lawrence. FaBoVe; NAMCP V.1; NoAM; NPeEn

Intoxication of Love. Li Po. CCL1, *tr. by* Judith Gautier and James Whitall [*or*Whittal]

Intractable between them grows. Metal and the Flower, The. Patricia K. Page. GPPA

Intractable two no longer among, The. Nathaniel Mackey. Eno; RD *Fr.* Song of the Andoumboulou.

Intrepid Ricardo, The. Edmund Clerihew Bentley. OBCoV *Fr.* Clerihews.

Intricate ship. Alice Notley. FTOS

Intricate songs' lost measure. (LL) Epitaph: "So I may say." "H. D." APT-1; NAAPv.2; NAMCP V.1; OxBoAm

Intricately vast process has produced, The. Prospero Listens to the Night. Jack Gilbert. BodElec

Introducing *New Year's SOLUTIONS*, from Saint Terri's Inc. Joe-Anne McLaughlin-Carruth. NevBe

Introduction. Anna Andreyevna Akhmatova. PFTM-1

Introduction. William Blake. *See* Piping Down the Valleys Wild.

Introduction. Letitia Elizabeth Landon. RWP *Fr.* Improvisatrice, The.

Introduction. James Russell Lowell. *Fr.* Biglow Papers, The.

Introduction. Edgar Allan Poe. *See* Romance.

Introduction: "Hear the voice of the Bard!" William Blake. ChIV-1; NAEL-6v2; NAEL-7v2; NAWM-7v2; NOBRP; NoP-4; NoP-5; NPBRoP; NPeEn; OxBEV; TFi *Fr.* Songs of Experience.

Introduction: "I don't know politics but I know the names." Kamala Das. NALW

Introduction: "Should you ask me, whence these stories?" Henry Wadsworth Longfellow. ColAP *Fr.* Song of Hiawatha, The.

Introduction, The: "Did I, my lines intend for public[k] view." Anne Finch, Countess of Winchilsea. BrAP; EMWP; NAEL-6v1; NAEL-7v1; NALW; NoP-4; NoP-5; WaAnP

Introduction, The: "They were introduced in a grave glade." Louis MacNeice. IrLP; PNI

Introduction: History and Praise of the Danes; Account of Grendel's Attacks on Heorot. *Unknown.* NoP-5 *Fr.* Beowulf [Heaney Translation].

Introduction: My Themes. Pablo Neruda. GifTon, *tr. by* William O'Daly

Introduction of a refrain, The. 'Twixt Cup and Lip. Mark Hollis. NBLV

Introduction to a Prayer. Fritzi Harmsen van Beek. WoPoe, *tr. by* Claire Nicholas White

Introduction to Eden. Matthea Harvey. IAoNAP

Introduction to Methods of Mathematical Physics. Lisa Rosenberg. PoA 2002

Introduction to My Anthology, An. Marvin Bell. TAPaP

Introduction to Poetry. Billy Collins. BeAl; OxBoAm; P180

Introduction to Poetry. Paul Lake. RA

Introduction to the Fables. The Shepherd and the Philosopher. John Gay. *Fr.* Fables: First Series.

Introduction—Childhood and School-Time. William Wordsworth. NAEL-6v2; NAEL-7v2 *Fr.* Prelude, The; Growth of a Poet's Mind [1850 version].

Introduction—Childhood and School-Time. William Wordsworth. *Fr.* Prelude, The; Growth of a Poet's Mind [1805 version].

Introductory Poem to the Penitential Psalms. Sir Thomas Wyatt. SacPr

Introit. Paul Murray. BBASP

Introit. Mongane Wally Serote. TSAP

Introitus. János Pilinszky. IQMS, *tr. by* Ted Hughes

Introspective. Christina Georgina Rossetti. VWP

Introspective Reflection. Ogden Nash. NBLV; OBCoV

Intruder. Alison Bielski. AngWePo

Intruder, The. Carolyn Kizer. CAP-8

Intruder in a Set Scene. Norman Alexander MacCaig. NePenScot

Intruder, The. Delmira Agustini. BLPSL, *tr. by* Rene de Costa, Rigas Kappatos and Eleni Paidoussi

Intruder, uprooter. Since Akkad, Since Elam, Since Sumer. Aimé Césaire. WoPoe, *tr. by* Gregson Davis

Intrusion. Denise Levertov. VCAP

Intrusion, The. Biljana Dragoslav Obradović. LiTh

Intrusion of Ovid, The. Paul Guest. PoDa

Intuition, An. Britton Wilkie. AHA

Intuition of reciprocal knowledge, An. Nicole Brossard. PFTM-2 *Fr.* Barbizon, The.

Inupiat Christmas Pageant, The. Peggy Shumaker. PBCAP

Invaders from Mars. Robert Glück. WiU

Invaders from South of the Border Imperil Native Population. Charles Harper Webb. GeoHom

Invaders, The. Bernard Spencer. FaBoWar

Invades, and drowns them all in tears. (LL) Foreign Ruler, A. Walter Savage Landor. OBSV; OxBEV

Invalid girl asked, An. Those Who Do Not Dance. Gabriela Mistral. WPoS, *tr. by* Maria Giachetti [*or* Jacketti]

Invalid of Park Street, The. David Brendon Hopes. UpMys

Invaluable is the Soto Way.   Gasan.   ZenPo, *tr. by* Takashi Ikemoto and Lucien Stryk

Invariably pure and austere, poets mostly.   Meng Chiao.   NDACCP *Fr.* Mourning Lu Yin.

Invariably when wine redeems the sight.   Wine Menagerie, The.   Hart Crane.   APT-2; NoAM

Invasion.   Anna Enquist.   TuT, *tr. by* Peter van de Kamp

Invective Against Denise, a Witch.   Pierre de Ronsard.   WoPoe, *tr. by* Anthony Hecht

Invective against Ibis.   Ovid.
   "While Thracians shal with arrowes war, Iaziges with bowe."   OBVE

Inventario.   Pedro Serrano.   RMCMP

Inventing Fables about the Stone.   Julia Galemire.   MirDau, *tr. by* Roberta Gordenstein

Inventing My Parents.   Susan Bartels Ludvigson.   PoSol

Inventing Stasis.   Bernadette Mayer.   AHA

Inventing the Hawk.   Lorna Crozier.   BeAl

Invention.   Barbara Hamby.   SUP

Invention.   Robert Clarkson Tongue.   ArBi

Invention of a Garden, The.   Jay Wright.   GT

Invention of Comics, The.   Imamu Amiri Baraka.   GT

Invention of Heaven, The.   Dean Young.   P180

Invention of Pittsburgh, The.   Maggie Anderson.   PBCAP

Invention of Secrecy, The.   David Citino.   PoA 2002

Inventions.   Miroslav Holub.   PoSu, *tr. by* George Theiner

Inventions.   William Scammell.   NLP

Inventors.   Michael C. Blumenthal.   NoAM

Inventory.   Günter Eich.   GTCP, *tr. by* Charlotte Melin and David Young

Inventory.   Günter Eich.   AF, *tr. by* David Young

Inventory.   Joan Larkin.   WiU

Inventory.   Dorothy Parker.   NBLV

Inventory.   Jacques Prévert.   STV, *tr. by* John Frederick Nims

Inventory.   Pedro Serrano.   RMCMP, *tr. by* Geoff Hargreaves

Inventory. Journal.   Pamela Alexander.   AmAlph

Inventory of Places Propitious for Love.   Angel González.   VCWP, *tr. by* Steven Ford Brown

Inventory of the Furniture of a Collegian's Chamber, An.   John Winstanley.   OBSV

Inverse Proportion.   Han Yong'un [*or* Yongwun].   CAMKP, *tr. by* Sammy Solberg

Inverse Proportions.   Jack Matthews.   PoA 2002

Inverse Square Law of the Propagation of Light, The.   Christopher Buckley.   PoA 2002

Inversnaid.   Gerard Manley Hopkins.   FaBoVe; MoBrPo; NoAM; NPeEn; SacPr; TFi

Inverso, suspendido.   Arcano 12: El Colgado.   Veronica Volkow.   RMCMP

Inverted, suspended.   Arcana 12: The Hanged Man.   Veronica Volkow.   RMCMP, *tr. by* Margaret Sayers Peden

Investigative Poetry.   Edward Sanders.
   "Content of History Will be Poetry, The."   PFTM-2

Investment, The.   Robert Frost.   APT-1; GoPo

Invictus.   W. E. Henley.   AmFaPo; BRP; CABP; CtM; MoBrPo; NAEL-6v2; NAEL-7v2; OBEV; OBMV *Fr.* Echoes.

Invisible ancestors.   Letter from Mexico.   Homero Aridjis.   TCLAP, *tr. by* Eliot Weinberger

Invisible and frozen imprinted in the rock. (LL)   Jerome Rothenberg.   AmWaPo; PFTM-2 *Fr.* Khurbn.

Invisible Atoms of the Air, The.   Gustavo Adolfo Bécquer.   SpanPo, *tr. by* Kate Flores

Invisible atoms of the air, The.   Invisible Atoms of the Air, The.   Gustavo Adolfo Bécquer.   SpanPo, *tr. by* Kate Flores

Invisible Autumn.   Joseph Ceravolo.   FTOS

Invisible cargo arrived.   Contraband.   Lamont B. Steptoe.   FuFl

Invisible catches and secret hooks, bone.   Chastity Belt.   Yusef Komunyakaa.   KGB

Invisible, chimerical.   Riddle.   Daryl Hine.   NoP-4; NoP-5

Invisible Cities.   Italo Calvino.   *tr. by* William Weaver

Invisible dikes for words.   Cartography.   Antonio Deltoro.   RMCMP, *tr. by* Christian Viveros-Fauné

Invisible Dreams.   Toi Derricotte.   PuP-23

Invisible Element, The.   István Vas.   IQMS, *tr. by* George Szirtes

Invisible flower—invisible flower, The. (LL)   Yi Sang.   CAMKP; PFTM-1 *Fr.* Critical Condition.

Invisible Hand.   L. S. Asekoff.   BodElec

Invisible in vernal pools.   Sonnet.   Michele Glazer.   IAoNAP

Invisible, indivisible Spirit.   "H. D."   APT-1 *Fr.* Tribute to the Angels.

Invisible is stronger than the visible, The.   History of the Invisible.   Rodger Kamenetz.   TaR

Invisible King, The.   Johann Wolfgang von Goethe.   RaBo, *tr. by* Robert Bly

Invisible Men, The.   Nakasuk.   RaBo, *tr. by* Edward Field

Invisible Mender, The.   Sarah Maguire.   MFPA

Invisible Tree.   Tamura Ryuichi.   WoPoe, *tr. by* Naoshi Koriyama and Edward Lueders

Invisible wall, The.   Luis Cernuda.   CAGL, *tr. by* Rick Lipinski

Invisibles.   Joanne M. Braxton.   BtF

Invitation.   Marion Angus.   LW

Invitation.   Orrick Johns.   APT-1

Invitation.   Myra Cohn Livingston.   TLR

Invitation.   Grace Nichols.   MoWP; NAMCP V.2

Invitation.   Grace Nichols.
   "Come up and see me sometime."   EroLit

Invitation, The.   Robert Creeley.   FTOS

Invitation, The.   Ruth Fainlight.   MoWP *Fr.* Sheba and Solomon.

Invitation, The.   George Herbert.   ChIV-1

Invitation, The.   Goronwy Owen.   OBWVE, *tr. by* George Burrow

Invitation, The.   Percy Bysshe Shelley. *See* To Jane: The Invitation.

Invitation au Voyage 2.   John Wieners.   AHA

Invitation au Voyage, L'.   Charles Baudelaire.   ItP; WoPoe, *tr. by* Richard Wilbur
   (Invitation to the Voyage.)   NAWM-7v2

Invitation Into the Country, In Imitation of Horace, An.   Jane Colman Turell.
   "Though my small incomes never can afford."   TCAPo

Invitation to a Ghost.   Donald Justice.   InGu; PfSP

Invitation to a Sabbath.   Harry Mathews.   NYP2

Invitation to a Voyage.   Max Jacob.   CuPo

Invitation to Brecknock, An.   Henry Vaughan.
   "Since last we met, thou and thy horse, my dear."   AngWePo

Invitation to Forget.   Erich Fried.   GTCP, *tr. by* Stuart Hood

Invitation to Hsiao Ch'u-shih.   Po Chü-i.   OBVE, *tr. by* Arthur Waley

Invitation to Madison County, An.   Jay Wright.   ESEAA

Invitation to Miss Marianne Moore.   Elizabeth Bishop.   NALW

Invitation to my Friends at Cambridge, An.   Jane Barker.   BASC

Invitation to the Cricket.   Holly Hughes.   AmZen

Invitation to the Dance.   Pentti Saarikoski.
   "No, Quetzalcoatl, don't come back."   VCWP

Invitation to the Voyage.   Charles Baudelaire.   SxFrPo, *tr. by* James McGowan

Invitation to the Voyage.   Charles Baudelaire. *See* Invitation au Voyage, L'.

Invitation to the Waltz.   George Crabbe.   STuOW *Fr.* Tales of the Hall.

Invite to Eternity, An.   John Clare.   NAEL-6v2; NAEL-7v2

Invited onto the grounds of the god.   Poetry.   Jane Miller.   GifTon; TAPaP

Inviting a Friend to Supper.   Ben Jonson.   BASC; BrAP; ItP; NAEL-6v1; NAEL-7v1; NoP-4; NoP-5; NOSC; NPeEn; PBRV; WaAnP

Inviting a Tiger for the Weekend.   José Garcia Villa.   WoPoe

Inviting a tiger for the weekend.   Inviting a Tiger for the Weekend.   José Garcia Villa.   WoPoe

Invocation.   Maria Elena Cruz Varela.   VCWP, *tr. by* Mairym Cruz-Bernal *and* Deborah Digges

Invocation.   N. Revathi Devi.   HotL, *tr. by* V. Narayana Rao

Invocation.   Samuel Hoffenstein.
   "Come, live with me and be my love."   NBLV

Invocation.   Ann Lauterbach.   OxBoAm

Invocation.   Sana'i.   BBASP, *tr. by* Nasrollah Pourjavady and Peter Lamborn Wilson

Invocation: "American muse, whose strong and diverse heart."   Stephen Vincent Benét.   APT-2 *Fr.* John Brown's Body.

Invocation: "Come down from heaven to meet me when my breath."   Siegfried Sassoon.   MoBrPo

Invocation: "High on, above the lake, the mute Nowgorod."   Johannes Bobrowski.   GTCP, *tr. by* Reinhold Grimm

Invocation: "I, who in times before, with youthful mind."   Miklós Zrínyi.   IQMS *Fr.* Zrinyiad, The.

Invocation: "It's crazy to think one could describe them."   Robert Pinsky.   NoAM *Fr.* Essay on Psychiatrists.

Invocation: "O holy Justice! Hiding your puissance."   Benedek Virág.   IQMS, *tr. by* Watson Kirkconnell

Invocation: "Pheobus, arise! / And paint the sable skies."   William Drummond of Hawthornden.   OBEV

Invocation: "Silent, about-to-be-parted-from house."   Denise Levertov.   PoA 2002

Invocation, The: "Wrath of *Peleus* Son, O Muse, resound, The."   Homer.   OBEV *Fr.* Iliad, The.

Invocation: "This August night, raccoons."   Jane Hirshfield.   BodElec; GeoHom

Invocation: "This is for Elsa, also known as Liz."   Marilyn Hacker.   ExTi; PuP-23; WiU

(Invocation for Storing Corn).   *Unknown.*   WPoS, *tr. by* Francisco X. Alarcón

Invocation of Silence. Richard Flecknoe. NOSC

Invocation of the Creator. *Yoruba Oral Tradition*. BLT

Invocation of the Great Bear. Ingeborg Bachmann. VCWP, *tr. by* Mark Anderson

Invocation To Dsilyi N'Eyani. *Unknown*. APN-2; TCAPo *Fr.* Mountain Chant, The.

Invocation. To Horror. Hannah Cowley. NOBRP

Invocation to Kali, The. May Sarton.
"It is time for the invocation." HW

Invocation to the Conference of the Birds. Farid-uddin Attar. BBASP, *tr. by* C.S. Nott

Invocation, To the Genius of Slumber Written Oct. 1787. Anna Seward. PEW

Invocation to the Muse. Richard Hughes. MoBrPo

Invocation to the Muse. Henrietta Cordelia Ray. CBWP-3

Invocation to the Social Muse. Archibald MacLeish. OxBoAm

Invocation to the Spirit Said to Haunt Wroxall Down. Mary F. Johnson. CenSon

Invocation to the U' wannami. *Unknown*. APN-2, *tr. by* Matilda Coxe Stevenson

Invocation to Urania. John Milton. NAEL-6v1; NOSC *Fr.* Paradise Lost.

Invocation to Youth. Laurence Binyon. OBEV

Invokes Reason. Mary Robinson. CenSon; RWP

7. Invokes Reason. Mary Robinson. NPBRoP *Fr.* Sappho and Phaon.

Involuntary Music. D. Nurske. MiVo

Involves / the breaking of solid ground. Digging of Deep Wells, The. Hugh MacDonald. Coast

Io and Jove. Ovid. NAWM-7v1 *Fr.* Metamorphoses.

Io! Paean! Io! sing. Charles Lamb. OxAEP-2 *Fr.* Triumph of the Whale, The.

Iolanthe. William Schwenck Gilbert.
Nightmare, [A *or* The]. OBCoV
"When Britain really ruled the waves." NAEL-6v2

Iona. Frederick Tennyson. SacPr

Iovis XIX: Why That's a Blade Can Float. Anne Waldman. PFTM-2

Iowa Blues Bar Spiritual. Juan Felipe Herrera. ReTh

Iowa Farmer. Margaret Walker Alexander. GT

Iphigenia [*or* Iphigeneia] in Aulis. Euripides.
"And Pergamos, / City of the Phrygians." OBVE, *tr. by* "H. D."

Iphigenia in Extremis. Alfred Tennyson. STuOW *Fr.* Dream of Fair Women, A.

Iphis and Ianthe. Ovid. NAWM-7v1 *Fr.* Metamorphoses.

Ipsithilla, my pet, my favorite dish. Catullus. WoPoe, *tr. by* Robert Mezey

1. Ipswich. Pamela Alexander. AmAlph *Fr.* Foxlight.

I'r Hen Iaith a'i Chaneuon. Ian Duhig. ModIr

Irae. Edward Kamau Brathwaite. NAMCP V.2

Iram indeed is gone with all his Rose. Omar Khayyám. OBEV *Fr.* Rubáiyát of Omar Khayyám [of Naishápúr], The.

Iranian Song. Velemir Khlebnikov. TCRusP, *tr. by* Kathy Lewis and Bob Perelman

Iranian whirling girl, Iranian whirling girl—. Iranian Whirling Girls. Po Chü-i. ColAnChi, *tr. by* Victor H. Mair

Iranian Whirling Girls. Po Chü-i. ColAnChi, *tr. by* Victor H. Mair

Iranian Whirling Girls. Yüan Chên. ColAnChi, *tr. by* Victor H. Mair

Irapuato. Earle Birney. NIL-7

Iraqi Evening, An. Yousif al-Sa'igh. IrPoTo, *tr. by* Chuck Miller and Saadi A. Simawe

Iraqi Sorrows. Aziz Samawi. IrPoTo, *tr. by* Alex Bellem

Ireland. Walter Savage Landor. OBCoV

Ireland. Paul Muldoon. PBCIP

Ireland. Dora Sigerson Shorter. OBEV

Ireland 1972. Paul Durcan. PBCIP; PoAgWa

Irene loves a man. One Secret That Has Carried, The. Jason Shinder. OPRER

Iri and Toshi Maruki are "painting the bomb." Hell Mural, The: Panel I. Ronald Wallace. AtGh

Iridescent exhausted finch, An. Flight. Miranda Beeson. PA9/11

Iridescent vibrations of midsummer light, The. John Gould Fletcher. PoA 2002 *Fr.* Irradiations.

Iris. Ok-Ku Kang. WhBo

Iris. Herman Melville. NCAP

Iris. Jacques Perk. TuT, *tr. by* Peter van de Kamp

Iris. Muriel Rukeyser. APSN; ColAP

Iris. David St. John. AmAlph; MakPoe

Iris. William Carlos Williams. WeW-3

Iris, An. Buson. EH, *tr. by* Robert Hass

Iris, Her Book. Oliver Wendell Holmes. NCAP

Irises. Michael Field. ViWPN

Irises. Li-Young Lee. BLT

Irises. Gustaf Sobin. APSN

Irish. Paul Celan. OBVE, *tr. by* Michael Hamburger

Irish Airman Foresees His Death, An. William Butler Yeats. BrAP; ChAP; FaBoWar; HarvBoo; HeIP-4; IrV; MoBrPo; NAMCP V.1; NoAM; NoP-4; NoP-5; OBMV; OBWP; PoAgWa; PoPoPo; PoWW; TFi; WaAnP; WeW-3

Irish Cliffs of Moher, The. Wallace Stevens. RaBo

Irish Emigrant, The. Helen Selina Blackwood, Countess of Dufferin and Clandeboye. *See* Lament of the Irish Emigrant.

Irish Fairy lost her way, An. Irish Fairy, The. Menella Bute Smedley. VWP

Irish Fairy, The. Menella Bute Smedley. VWP

Irish for No, The. Ciaran Carson. PNI

Irish Greyhound, The. Katherine Philips. DiBP

Irish Hierarchy Bans Colour Photography. Paul Durcan. PBCIP

Irish lady can say, that to-day is every day, The. Cézanne. Gertrude Stein. OxBoAm

Irish Patriarch, The. Ruth Pitter. NALW

Irish Peasant Girl, The. Charles Joseph Kickham. IrV

Irish Poetry. Eavan Boland. PoDa

Irish poets, learn your trade. William Butler Yeats. OxAEP-2 *Fr.* Under Ben Bulben.

Irish Requiem, An. Michael O'Loughlin. PBCIP

Irish Sailor, The. *Irish Oral Tradition*. IrV

Irish Scullery Maid, The. Joyce Herbert. TCAWP

Irish Sheep, The. Job Degenaar. TuT, *tr. by* Aidan Sharkey

Irish Song [Rosie O'Grady]. Noël Coward. NBLV; OBCoV

Irish soul walks away from Paddy's, An. Day Lily and the Fox, The. Emily Hiestand. OPRER

Irish Spinning-Wheel, The. Alfred Perceval Graves. IrV

Irish Woman Washing. Laima Sruoginis. PoDa

Irishman in Coventry, An. John Hewitt. ModIr; PNI

Irishman's Epistle to the Officers and Troops at Boston, The. *Unknown*. NAAPv.1

Irish-speaking Mynah, The. Gearóid Mac Lochlainn. NIrP, *tr. by* Ciaran Carson

Iron bug, through the Spring. (LL) Spring in This World of Poor Mutts. Joseph Ceravolo. AHA; FTOS; NYP2

Iron cannons from the Revolution. Ghost music. Common, The. Gail Mazur. UrbNat

Iron Horse. Allen Ginsberg.
"Who's the enemy, year after year?" AmWaPo

Iron Horse is rusting, The. End of the Line, The. Thomas McGrath. GM

Iron in her roar. (LL) Meteor. Larissa Szporluk. BAP-01; LegDan

Iron Lung. Lavinia Greenlaw. MFPA

Iron Man of the Hoh. Nelson Bentley. GifTon

"Iron Man" sat with gone eyes / a witnessing body, The. Rogue and Jar: 4/27/77. Thulani Davis. SeSe

Iron Spike. Seamus Heaney. BodElec; TRP

Iron tree blooms. Wakuan-Shitai. ZenPo, *tr. by* Takashi Ikemoto and Lucien Stryk

Iron waves, rising to mesh with an iron sky. (LL) Far from Home. Nicholas Christopher. NoP-5

Iron-blue lie of hills, An. Near the Rio Grand. Del Marie Rogers. TiP2

Ironical Elegy, Composed in Those Terribly Sad Moments When I Cannot Write. Andrey Andreievich Voznesensky. RusPo, *tr. by* Robert Arthur Douglas Ford

Ironing. Nellie Wong. FFC

Ironing Goatskin. Víctor Hernández Cruz. PueRic

Irradia / la coraza de ceniza. Dolores Dorantes. SPV

Irradiates / the ash carapace. Dolores Dorantes. SPV, *tr. by* Jen Hofer

Irradiations. John Gould Fletcher. MoAmPo
"Flag let loose for a day of festivity, The." PoA 2002
"Iridescent vibrations of midsummer light, The." PoA 2002
"Not noisily, but solemnly and pale." PoA 2002
"Over the roof-tops race the shadows of clouds." PoA 2002
"Slowly along the lamp-emblazoned street." PoA 2002
"Trees, like great jade elephants, The." MoAmPo

Irrational Gigantic Anger. John Hookham Frere. NPBRoP *Fr.* Whistlecraft.

Irrationale. László Szabédi. IQMS, *tr. by* J. G. Nichols

Irreconcilable, The. Damaris, Lady Masham. EMWP

Irregular continuity of discrete particles blasted into the atmosphere: writing, The. Radiant. James Sherry. FTOS

Irregular rattle (shutters) and, An. Master of the Golden Glow, The. James Schuyler. FTOS

Irregular Verses. Dorothy Wordsworth. PoBW

Irrelevant and Useless. David Budbill. AmZen

Irresistible. Kenneth Koch. AHA

Irresistible Light, An. Dorothy Phaire. BtF

Irresolute the down upon your cheek. Martial. RomPo, *tr. by* Peter Whigham

Irresponsive silence of the land, The. Christina Georgina Rossetti. OBEV *Fr.* Thread of Life, The.

Irreverent Epistle to Jesus Christ. Romelia Alarcón de Folgar. TANSG, *tr. by* Alison Ridley

Irreversible? Is time—were it as itself—reading underneath the influence of palindromitis. Oskar Pastior. OnScMo, *tr. by* Harry Mathews

Irritable Songs. Russell Atkins. EGAG

Irving Katzenstein told me a poem once. Beer Bottles. Lindley Williams Hubbell. APT-2

Is. Fazil Hüsnü Daglarca. NaPG, *tr. by* Talat Sait Halman

Is a black shambling bear. Earth Is a Living Thing, The. Lucille Clifton. HW

Is a cave, there are bones at the hearth. (LL) Abel's Bride. Denise Levertov. NALW; OxBoAm

Is a grave, where was once lonely naked squab in every glance. Most Notoriously Absent North American Bird in Her Face, The. Skip Fox. AnSo

Is a haunting, haunted moon. (LL) Far Rockaway. Delmore Schwartz. APT-2; OxBoAm

Is a little wind. Four Bird Songs. Simon J. Ortiz. HATNAP

Is a mildewed tent. Under the center pole. Despair. Maxine W. Kumin. FFC

Is a monstrance / the blue dogs bay. Moon Is the Number 18, The. Charles Olson. APT-2; HarvBoo; PFTM-2

Is a plantigrade-gaited and prowly inquisitor. This Grizzly. Reg Saner. PoCoUp

Is a question of strength. Oppression. Jimmy Santiago Baca. AF

Is a secret one infers. Landscapes with Set-Screws. X. J. Kennedy. UrbNat

Is a shoe in the refrigerator. Male in the Women's Locker Room, A. Natasha Saje. MAAN

Is a short life of trouble. (LL) Other Side of the River, The. Charles Wright. InGu; OxBoAm; VCAP

Is a son born into this world of woe? Charles Churchill. OBSV *Fr.* Times, The.

Is a special speech to me. (LL) Boy Died in My Alley, The. Gwendolyn Brooks. NAMCP V.2; NoAM

Is a / Spring / Loaded / Sperm. Twin Barrel Bucky: A Kingston 12 Dub, The. Brian Meeks. WaCA

Is a strange brooch in this all-hating world. (LL) William Shakespeare. OxAEP-1; WoPoe *Fr.* King Richard III.

Is a trifle too gay. (LL) Don Marquis. AmWit; APT-1; OBCoV *Fr.* Archy and Mehitabel.

Is a word you must grow. Brave. Jeanette Lynes. Coast

Is About. Allen Ginsberg. BAP-97

Is about five years. Half-Life of Sorrow, The. Roger Greenwald. AtGh

Is Ajar. Pierre Reverdy. YaTCFP, *tr. by* John Ashbery

Is all laze and boudoir. She reclines, wigless. April. Angela Shaw. NeAmPo

Is all this sorrow? I don't know. Yehuda Amichai. PoSu *Fr.* Laments on the War Dead.

Is *also* Stewart Granger. (LL) Prisoner of Zenda, The. Richard Wilbur. NBLV; OBCoV

Is always towards the furthest, and. Sixth Ode: The Grottoes. Gustaf Sobin. WoBe

Is an assemblage. Le passage (Morbihan). Tony Baker. Oth

Is an astonishingly slim. Chris Wallace-Crabbe. BMAP *Fr.* Bits and Pieces, The.

Is an enchanted thing. Mind Is an Enchanting Thing, The. Marianne Moore. APT-1; HeIP-4; MoAmPo; NAAL-5; NAAPv.2; NoP-4; NoP-5

Is an unnatural act. (LL) Phenomenology of Anger, The. Adrienne Rich. PFTM-2; WaAnP

Is anybody here in favor of a redistribution of wealth? Song of Songs, The. Ogden Nash. AmWit

Is anything central? One Thing That Can Save America, The. John Ashbery. FaBoA; NoAM; OxBoAm; PmAP

Is as a future. (LL) Africa of the Statue, The. Amina Saïd. HAWP; NAfrP, *tr. by* Eric Sellin

Is as it had not been. (LL) Visitor in Marl, A. Emily Dickinson. APN-2; TCAPo

Is back upon your mouth these thousand years. (LL) To Jesus on His Birthday. Edna St. Vincent Millay. ChIV-2; HeIP-4

Is Beautiful. Kiren Shoman. OWABP

Is best from age to age. (LL) John Bunyan. OBEV; SacPr *Fr.* Pilgrim's Progress, The.

Is blisse with immortalitie. Her Majestie resembled to the crowned piller. Ye must read upward. George Puttenham. PBRV

   (Her Majestie resembled to the crowned pillar. Ye must read upword.) WaAnP

Is breaking in despair. (LL) Slave Mother, The. Frances Ellen Watkins Harper. NAAPv.1; WaAnP

Is broken, be admitted in. (LL) Shadows in the Water. Thomas Traherne. NoP-4; NoP-5; WoPoe

Is buried with the pole. (LL) Astronomy. A. E. Housman. NoP-4; NoP-5; OBWP

Is by His hand alone that guides nature and fate. (LL) In Memory of My Dear Grandchild Elizabeth Bradstreet Who Deceased August, 1665, Being a Year and Half Old. Anne Bradstreet. BASC; ColAP; NAAL-3; NAAL-5; NAAPv.1

Is come close and touch me. (LL) Fast Gas. Dorianne Laux. GeoHom; SUP

Is come, my love is come to me. (LL) Birthday, A. Christina Georgina Rossetti. CABP; LW; NAEL-6v2; NAEL-7v2; NALW; OBEV; PEW; TFi; UV; ViWPN; VWP

Is coming, and makes noise. (LL) Approach of the Storm, The. *Chippewa Oral Tradition.* NAAL-5; NAAPv.2; OBVE, *tr. by* Frances Densmore

Is Culcha Weapon? Brian Meeks. WaCA

Is dead, or thinks he's dead. (LL) Philosophic Taed, The. William Soutar. EdScPo; NePenScot

Is deathless and eternal there. (LL) City of the End of Things, The. Archibald Lampman. BrAP; IFF

Is different now. The body. What's It For. Pamela Stewart. ExTi

Is distance. If she knows it. Under Flag. Myung Mi Kim. AmWaPo

Is each neat niplet of her breast. (LL) Upon the Nipples of Julia's Breast. Robert Herrick. ErotSp; NAEL-6v1; NAEL-7v1; NOSC

Is even more fun than going to San Sebastian, Irún, Hendaye, Biarritz, Bayonne. Having a Coke with You. Frank O'Hara. VCAP

Is everything made of dry ice? January, Anchorage. Linda McCarriston. UrbNat

Is given in outline and no more. (LL) Alfred Tennyson. CAGL; NAEL-6v2; NAEL-7v2; NAWM-7v2 *Fr.* In Memoriam A. H. H.

Is giv'n thee till the break of day. (LL) William Blake. ChIV-1; NAEL-6v2; NAEL-7v2; NAWM-7v2; NOBRP; NoP-4; NoP-5; NPBRoP; NPeEn; OxBEV; TFi *Fr.* Songs of Experience.

Is grace delivered. Streetcorner Church. Sharan Strange. InTrad

Is harder than having let you go. (LL) Family Reunion. Maxine W. Kumin. AFaM; GoPo

Is hovering in the air, there, in the highest. All the Wide Grin of Him. Eleanor Wilner. ExTi

Is hows to hump a cows. (LL) Way to hump a cow is not, The. E. E. Cummings. AmWit; NoAM

Is I. (LL) Napoleon. Walter De la Mare. NPeEn; OxBEV; Spl; WoPoe

Is idle, biologically speaking. (LL) I shall forget you presently, my dear. Edna St. Vincent Millay. APT-1; HeIP-4; NAAPv.2

Is immortal diamond. (LL) That Nature Is a Heraclitean Fire and of the Comfort of the Resurrection. Gerard Manley Hopkins. FaBoVe; NAEL-7v2; NoP-4; NoP-5; PFTM-1

Is in love with someone. Someone. Ruth Forman. AmPoNex

Is is a legend already: a wide wide stubble. Victory Bonfire. Ruth Pitter. RSaN

Is It? Else Von Freytag-Loringhoven. NAAPv.2

Is it a cuckoo that cries? Yun Söndo. CATKP; WoPoe *Fr.* Angler's Calendar, The.

Is it a plane in the sky. Poem. Paul Dermée. CuPo

Is it an idle fantasy. Mist Maiden, The. Henrietta Cordelia Ray. CBWP-3

Is it anxiety, nausea. Self-Portrait of the Other. Heberto Padilla. TCLAP; VCWP, *tr. by* Andrew Hurley and Alastair Reid

Is it any better in Heaven, my friend Ford. To Ford Madox Ford in Heaven. William Carlos Williams. ColAP

Is it bad to have come here. Gallant Chateau. Wallace Stevens. MoAmPo

Is It Because I Am Black? Joseph Seamon, Jr. Cotter. OxAAAP

Is it because your sable hair. La Belle Juive. Henry Timrod. APN-2; TCAPo

Is it better to die by the hand of an intimate. Infernal. Karen Volkman. BAP-97

Is it clouds? Or mountains? Is it Wu? Or Yue? Stopping at Amakusa Sea. Rai San'yo. EMJL, *tr. by* Haruo Shirane

Is it for me to eat what food I have. War Song. *Unknown.* AmWaPo, *tr. by* Ruth Underhill

Is it illusion? or does there a spirit from perfecter ages. Arthur Hugh Clough. OxAEP-2 *Fr.* Amours de Voyage.

Is it in cold hard cash? the kind. Wendy Rose. AmWaPo

Is it indeed so? If I lay here dead. Elizabeth Barrett Browning. CenSon *Fr.* Sonnets from the Portuguese.

Is it me tossing. Insomnia Song. Gregory Orr. AWTN

Is it normal to get this wet? Baby, I'm frightened. Imperial. Don Paterson. NeBrP

Is it not lovely, while the day flows on. By the Swanannoa. William Gilmore Simms. APN-1

Is It Not Strange? Elizabeth Delmore. NLP

Is it not strange that men can die. Reflection. Walter James Turner. OBMV

"Is It Nothing to You?" May Probyn. OBEV; SacPr

Is it possible. Varium et Mutabile. Sir Thomas Wyatt. NoSic

Is It Possible. Sir Thomas Wyatt. *See also* Varium et Mutabile.

Is it raining. Mary, can you see? Wildflowers. Richard Howard. NoAM

Is it really a revolution, though? Lunch with Pancho Villa. Paul Muldoon. ModIr; NAMCP V.2

Is it showering? Natsume Soseki. CAoMJL1, *tr.* by Makoto Ueda

Is It Snowing in Guangzhou? Marilyn Chin. FaoP

Is it some party, in a parlour. William Wordsworth. NPBRoP *Fr.* Peter Bell.

Is it the bed? (LL) Caught in the Swamp. Joseph Ceravolo. BodElec; NYP2

Is it the boy in me who's looking out. Boy, The. Marilyn Hacker. ExTi; WiU

Is it the long dry grass that is so erotic. Prelude. Fleur Adcock. MoWP

Is it the motion of the stabbing knife, and. Stone Wall and Fiesta. János Pilinszky. IQMS, *tr.* by Adam Makkai

Is it the palm, the cocoa-palm. Palm-Tree, The. John Greenleaf Whittier. NCAP

Is it the plenitude of seasons, then, the number. John Hollander. OxBoAm *Fr.* Powers of Thirteen.

Is it, then, your opinion. Poet Ridiculed by Hysterical Academics, The. W. D. Snodgrass. BrAP

Is it thy will thy image should keep open. William Shakespeare. AWTN; CAGL *Fr.* Sonnets.

Is it time now to go away? Death of a Vermont Farm Woman. Barbara Howes. MoAmPo

Is it time to change the record? But I'm dreaming again. Sergey Gandlevsky. ItGoST, *tr.* by Philip Metres

Is it to love, to fix the tender gaze. Describes the Characteristics of Love. Mary Robinson. CenSon; RWP

Is it to love, to fix the tender gaze. Mary Robinson. NPBRoP *Fr.* Sappho and Phaon.

Is it true that after this life of ours we shall one day be awakened. Resurrection. Vladimir Holan. PoSu; StAl, *tr.* by George Theiner

(After this life here, we're to be awakened one day.) AF

Is It True What They Say About Dixie? Irving Caesar and Sammy Lerner. ReLy

Is it Ulysses that approaches from the east. World as Meditation, The. Wallace Stevens. HeIP-4

Is It Wise? Stevie Smith. NAEL-6v2; NAEL-7v2

Is it you standing among the olive trees. Mark Strand. NAMCP V.2; NoP-4; NoP-5 *Fr.* Dark Harbor.

Is its head. (LL) Arrow Song. *Chippewa Oral Tradition.* NAAPv.2; TCAPo

Is Joy's insuring quality. (LL) Go not too near a House of Rose. Emily Dickinson. MoAmPo; NIL-7; NIP-4

Is lang time. Red Rebel Song. Jean Binta Breeze. RSaN

Is large, bald, beakless, and blind. (LL) Fork. Charles Simic. CAP-8; ChAP; ColAP; NAMCP V.2; PoPoPo; TRP; WaAnP; WeW-3

Is learned. In this poem they're right. Cruelty, the Vandals Say. Alan Michael Parker. NeAmPo

Is less ta'en up wi't. (LL) Empty Vessel. Hugh MacDiarmid. EdScPo; NePenScot; NPeEn; OxBEV

Is life. Allan Graham. ICANM

Is like a tin cup toppled in the straw. (LL) Desert of Love, The. János Pilinszky. IQMS; OBVE, *tr.* by Ted Hughes

Is like swimming alone. Singing Alone. Nancy Cox. MiVo

Is Lisle and Lucas slaine? Oh say not soe. On Those Two Unparalleled Friends, Sr: G: Lisle and Sr: C: Lucas, Who Were Shott to Death at Colechester. Hester Lee Pulter. EMWP

Is love a fancy, or a feeling? No. Hartley Coleridge. CenSon

Is love a light for me? A steady light. Secret Flowers. Katherine Mansfield. LW

Is love so prone to change and rot. Bed of Forget-Me-Nots, A. Christina Georgina Rossetti. VWP

Is made up of reservoirs. Hard Structure of the World, The. Richard Eberhart. NoAM

Is manhood less because man's face is black? Albery Allson Whitman. APN-2 *Fr.* Twasinta's Seminoles; Or Rape of Florida.

Is master of all I am. (LL) Sphinx, The. Ralph Waldo Emerson. APN-1; TCAPo

Is "merchant" an inglorious name? Edward Young. STuOW *Fr.* Imperium Pelagi, or, The Merchant.

Is merry glory. Langston Hughes. Gwendolyn Brooks. ColAP

Is music is men. Eddie Priest's Barbershop and Notary. Kevin Young. AmPoNex; ISC; SpirFl

Is my all-time favorite song. (LL) Play It Again, Salmonella. Jeffrey McDaniel. AmPoNex; SUP

Is my black Mother Syama really black? Kamalākānta Bhattācārya. SinGod, *tr.* by Rachel Fell McDermott

Is my favourite. Who flies. Owl. George MacBeth. EmeKit

Is my shit correct? Puttin' on the Dog. Everett Hoagland. OxAAAP

Is My Soul Asleep? Antonio Machado Ruiz. WED, *tr.* by Robert Bly

Is my team ploughing. A. E. Housman. BrAP; MoBrPo; NAMCP V.1; NoAM; NoP-4; NoP-5; OBEV *Fr.* Shropshire Lad, A.

Is / Not. Margaret Atwood. BrAP

Is not a cloud at all. Cloud of Unknowing, The. Christopher Edgar. BAP-01

Is not one of the seven deadly sins. Self-Pity. Philip Hodgins. NOBAu

Is not the woman moulded by your wish. Pastiche. Elinor Wylie. NALW

Is not thilke the mery moneth of May. Edmund Spenser. PBRV *Fr.* Shepherd's Calender, The.

Is not unlike building a poem: the pure. Building an Outhouse. Ronald Wallace. PBCAP

Is nothing real but when I was fifteen. Ground Swell. Mark Jarman. GeoHom; MoASP

Is nothing to the Dead. (LL) My Triumph lasted till the Drums. Emily Dickinson. APN-2; BrAP; OBWP; PoAgWa

Is now as weak as ever. (LL) Time I've Lost in Wooing, The. Thomas Moore. AmFaPo; NAEL-6v2; NAEL-7v2; NOBRP

Is of the slightest bondage made aware. (LL) Silken Tent, The. Robert Frost. APT-1; BrAP; ColAP; NAMCP V.1; NoP-4; NoP-5; OxBSo; TRP; WaAnP; WeW-3

Is only a love song. A god without power to unlock. (LL) Cell Angel. Menna Elfyn. BBMWP; MoWP, *tr.* by Gillian Clarke

Is only a plateful of mince. (LL) Bitcherel. Eleanor Brown. MFPA; NeBl; StAl

Is only Monday in the world. (LL) King of the Cats is Dead, The. Peter Porter. EmeKit; NoAM

Is only not to be disgraced. (LL) Northern Suburb, A. John Davidson. NePenScot; NPeEn

Is only there. (LL) Peace. George Herbert. NOSC; TreFP

Is oppression as old as the moss around ponds? World's One Hope, The. Bertolt Brecht. AF

Is peopled with many surfaces. My Rival's House. Liz Lochhead. CFP; EdScPo; EmeKit

Is powerless to our Western Cotton! (LL) Haschish, The. John Greenleaf Whittier. APN-1; NCAP

I's (pronounced *Eyes*). Louis Zukofsky. NAAPv.2

Is proud, and makes the breath of glory real! (LL) Sonnet to Lake Leman. Lord Byron. CenSon; NPBRoP

Is quicker. (LL) Reflections on Ice-breaking. Ogden Nash. APT-2; NAAPv.2; NBLV; NIL-7; NoP-4; NoP-5

Is / red beans. Energy. Víctor Hernández Cruz. PueRic

Is round. For days we sail, for months. Passionate World, The. Anne Michaels. BeAl; PoDa

Is rounded with a sleep. (LL) William Shakespeare. ASA; UV *Fr.* Tempest, The.

Is scarcely right; this red should have been much duller. (LL) Vlamertinghe. Edmund Charles Blunden. NoP-4; OBWP

Is she mine,—and for life. Mésalliance, A. May Probyn. NPeEn

Is Sin, then, fair? Sting of Death, The. Frederick George Scott. SacPr

Is slender and her red hair lights the wall. (LL) Degrees of Gray in Philipsburg. Richard Hugo. CAP-8; ItP; NAMCP V.2; NoAM; OxBoAm; TRP; VCAP; WaAnP

Is slow. Tedious. Like midnight mass on Christmas Eve. Unlearning English. Michael Melo. ReBoTo

Is so frigid upon the fundament. (LL) Samson Agonistes. Ogden Nash. APT-2; OBCoV

Is speaking it pelts. Then and Now. James Laughlin. PmAP

Is still warm. (LL) Lament for the Dorsets. Alfred Wellington Purdy. BrAP; NoAM

Is sung, but breaks off in the middle. (LL) Samuel Butler. BASC; NAEL-6v1; NAEL-7v1 *Fr.* Hudibras.

Is taken by surprise. Sometimes the Mind. Jane Mead. NAPBL

Is that an attitude for a flower, to stand. Hyacinth. Louise Glück. NoAM

Is that dance slowing in the mind of man. Theodore Roethke. APT-2; MoAmPo; NoAM

Is that foolish youth still sawing. Ancient Autumn. Charles Simic. ColAP

Is that not the moon? Narihira. WoPoe *Fr.* Ise Monogatari, The.

Is that one day they'll win. My Worst Fear. Cyn Zarco. ReBoTo

Is that the flesh made word. Music At The Heart Of Thinking 42. Fred Wah. OpeFie

Is that the moon, nearing its final quarter. Pogrom. Ed. Hoornik. TuT, *tr.* by Mary E. O'Donnell

Is that the same moon. Narihira. ErotSp, *tr.* by Sam Hamill

Is that to me? (LL) Thursday. Edna St. Vincent Millay. AmWit; PoA 2002

Is that where it happens? Improvement, The. John Ashbery. AmFaPo

Is that you, Barnes? Now see here, friend. From. Crab-Apple Crisis, The. George MacBeth. AtGh

Is that you sistah Harris? Afternoon Gossip, An. Priscilla Jane Thompson. CBWP-2

Is the alphabet responsible. Learning to Write. Audre Lorde. GT

Is the bell to awaken God that we've heard ringing. (LL) Garden Shukkei-en, The. Carolyn Forché. AtGh; ExTi; WaAnP

(It is the bell to awaken God that we've heard ringing.) (LL) AtGh; WaAnP

Is the body's way. Coming. Heather McHugh. EmeKit

Is the bright light of shipwreck. (LL) George Oppen. AmWaPo; NAMCP V.1 Fr. Of Being Numerous.

Is the burden of my song. (LL) Love Me Little, Love Me Long. Unknown. NoP-4; NoP-5; WaAnP

Is the child coming to receive it? (LL) Wanderer's Bouquet. Sŏ Chŏngju. CAMKP; WoPoe, tr. by David R. McCann

Is the fish ready? You're a tedious while. Edward Ward. WaAnP Fr. Nuptial Dialogues.

Is the man bigger than a fly's wing? what pleasure! Tablet V. Armand Schwerner. PFTM-1

Is the man here, they said. Margaret Atwood. PoetW Fr. Four Small Elegies.

Is the mother of earth, moon, and stars. Hogarcito de La Madrugada, El. Anthony R. Vigil. AmPoNex

Is the one gift you cannot give. (LL) At the British War Cemetery, Bayeux. Charles Causley. NAEL-6v2; NAEL-7v2; NoP-4; NoP-5; OBWP; PoWW

Is the poem at the end of the world. (LL) Shapeshifter Poems. Lucille Clifton. BodElec; LoL

Is the province of cats. Living by accident. Propinquity. Alastair Reid. EdScPo

Is the reader leaning late and reading there. (LL) House Was Quiet and the World Was Calm, The. Wallace Stevens. NoP-4; NoP-5; OxBoAm; PoCho; SAmP

Is the river a boundary line? In and Out of Check Points. Ye Weilian [or Yeh Wei-lien or Wai-lim Yip]. OPRER

Is the skeleton flashing. Nicotine. Art Beck. CalPo

Is the snow on Kurakake mountain. (LL) Snow on Saddle Mountain, The. Miyazawa Kenji. ColAP; NoAM; OxBoAm; WaAnP, tr. by Gary Snyder

Is the soul solid, like iron? Some Questions You Might Ask. Mary Oliver. BeAl; ColAP; NoAM; StAl

Is the sparrow-camel. (LL) He "Digesteth Harde Yron." Marianne Moore. APT-1; NAAPv.2; NAMCP V.1; NoAM; OWoS

Is the spirit the true lover of the flesh? Sándor Petőfi. IQMS Fr. Clouds, The.

Is the sun a miner, a thief, a gambler. June Ghazal. Arthur Sze. GifTon

Is the wheel that brings it round. (LL) Wheel. Wendell Berry. RSR; UpMys

Is the woman in the pool of light. Lake Echo, Dear. C. D. Wright. AmAlph

Is then no nook of English ground secure. On the Projected Kendal and Windermere Railway. William Wordsworth. CenSon

Is there a god of the gulf between a man. On God. Maurice Manning. LegDan

Is there a great green commonwealth of Thought. John Masefield. MoBrPo Fr. Sonnets.

Is there a mind in you, universe? Urban Tree. Alexander Gerov. CSCBP, tr. by Georgi Belev and Lisa Sapinkopf

Is there a solitary wretch who hies. On Being Cautioned against Walking on an Headland Overlooking the Sea, Because It Was Frequented by a Lunatic. Charlotte Smith. CenSon; NAEL-7v2; NPeEn; WoRP

Is there any heart not bleeding. Ahmed Pasha. OLP, tr. by Walter Andrews, Najaat Black and Mehmet Kalpakli

Is there any reward? Joseph Hilaire Pierre Belloc. OBCoV

Is there any treasure like the Mother's name? Kalyānkumār Mukhopādhyāy. SinGod, tr. by Rachel Fell McDermott

Is there anybody there? said the Traveler. Listeners, The. Walter De la Mare. ClHu; HeIP-4; MoBrPo; NoAM; NoP-4; NoP-5; NOxBChV; OBEV; OBMV; OBSP; OxAEP-2; SoSe-8; TFi

Is there anyone around who cannot see. Between the Devil and the Deep Blue Sea. Ted Koehler. ReLy

Is there anything as I can do ashore for you. Valediction, A (Liverpool Docks). John Masefield. OBMV

Is there anything sweeter than this hour? Unknown, fr. Egyptian hieroglyphics. EroLit, tr. by Joseph Kaster

Is there, for honest Poverty. For A' That and A' That ["Is there, for honest poverty"]. Robert Burns. BRP; NAEL-6v2; NePenScot; NPBRoP; OxAEP-2; OxBEV; TFi; TreFP; UV

Is There For Honest Poverty. Robert Burns. See also For A' That and A' That ["Is there, for honest poverty"].

Is there no heart capable of love. Sheyhülislâm Yahya Efendi. OLP, tr. by Walter Andrews, Najaat Black and Mehmet Kalpakli

Is there not a single madman in this village? Unknown. SLW, tr. by Marjolijn De Jager, Sayd Bahodin Majrouh and André Velter

Is there not something in the pleading eye. Oliver Wendell Holmes. DiBP Fr. Wind-Clouds and Star-Drifts.

Is there peace? (LL) Caernarfon, 2 July [or July 2] 1969. T. Glynne Davies. BBMWP; OBWVE, tr. by Joseph P. Clancy

Is there There. Is there There in dying. Luis H. Francia. ReBoTo

Is there There in dying. Luis H. Francia. ReBoTo

Is this a fast, to keep. To Keep a True Lent. Robert Herrick. SacPr

Is this a holy thing to see. William Blake. BrAP; NAEL-6v2; NAEL-7v2; NOBRP; NoP-4; NoP-5; NPBRoP Fr. Songs of Experience.

Is This All! Nanduri Subbarao. HotL, tr. by V. Narayana Rao

Is this, baby, what you were born to feel, and do, and be? (LL) American Rhapsody. Kenneth Fearing. APT-2; MoAmPo

Is this darkness the night of Power, or the black falling of your hair? Bibi Hayati. WPoS

Is this happening. Ronald Johnson. FTOS Fr. Ark.

Is this how it will end? Final Curtain. Gerwyn Williams. BBMWP, tr. by the author and Richard Poole

Is This Man, Martin Bormann? Roderick Watson. EdScPo

Is this man turning angel as he stares. Messenger, The. Thom Gunn. PoA 2002

Is this my father's skin. My Father's Caul. Susan Wicks. MoWP

Is this my tomb, this humble stone. Charlotte Brontë. VWP

Is this only fear of radiation? Radiophobia. Lyubov Sirota. AtGh, tr. by Leonid Levin and Elisavietta Ritchie

Is this peace? Kayaking through. Peace #3. Alma Villanueva. FFC

'Is this, saith one, the Nation that we read'. Andrew Marvell. PBRV Fr. First Anniversary of the Government under O.C., The.

Is this the little girl I carried? Sunrise, Sunset. Sheldon Harnick. ReLy

Is this the monument of Leonato? William Shakespeare. OxAEP-1 Fr. Much Ado about Nothing.

Is this the river East I heard? East River's Charm. Samuel Greenberg. OxBoAm

Is this the street? Never a sign of life. Stormy Night. William Robert Rodgers. ModIr; PNI

Is this the way my Father. Matin Hymn. Josephine D. Henderson Heard. CBWP-4

Is this then a touch? . . . quivering me to a new identity. Walt Whitman. CAGL Fr. Song of Myself.

Is this, then, the star of freedom? Imprisoned Souls. János Arany. IQMS, tr. by Peter Zollman

Is this to be? Rokaku. NAAPv.2

Is this too dark? Is It Snowing in Guangzhou? Marilyn Chin. FaoP

Is this what. Saitō Mokichi. CAoMJL1, tr. by Amy Vladek Heinrich

Is this where Tasso walked? Old Sant'Onofrio. Pure Dust. Maria Luisa Spaziani. NeIt, tr. by Beverly Allen

Is this where we unhook the brief self, inot a denatured light. Camille Martin. AnSo Fr. No truck.

Is this your special light. Six Nations Museum Onchiota, New York—January. Wendy Rose. HATNAP

Is this—the way? (LL) Title divine—is mine! Emily Dickinson. APN-2; NAAPv.1; NALW; OxBoAm; TCAPo

Is thy face like thy mother's, my fair child! Lord Byron. NAEL-6v2; NAEL-7v2 Fr. Childe Harold's Pilgrimage.

Is thy sun obscured to-day. My Grace Is Sufficient. Josephine D. Henderson Heard. CBWP-4

Is to become a footnote. My Ambition. James Laughlin. GifTon; PoA 2002

Is to leave all and take the thread of love. (LL) Mary Sidney Wroth, Countess of Montgomery. BASC; CABP; EMWP; NAEL-6v1; NAEL-7v1; NoP-4; NoP-5; NPeEn; PBRV Fr. Pamphilia to Amphilanthus.

Is to leave all, and take the thread of love. Mary Sidney Wroth, Countess of Montgomery. BASC; EMWP; NoP-5 Fr. Pamphilia to Amphilanthus.

Is too good to be true, in all its definitions. Purple Loosestrife. Ann Townsend. ExTi; NeAmPo

Is too precise in every part. (LL) Delight in Disorder. Robert Herrick. BASC; BrAP; CABP; CavPo; ClHu; ErotSp; HeIP-4; NAEL-6v1; NAEL-7v1; NIL-7; NIP-4; NoP-4; NoP-5; NOSC; NPeEn; OBEV; OxAEP-1; OxBEV; PBRV; TFi; TRP; TWF; WaAnP; WeW-3

Is waiting for his Old Dutch? (LL) Fat White Woman Speaks, The. G. K. Chesterton. OBCoV; UV

Is water deep enough to drown. (LL) Muse of Water, A. Carolyn Kizer. FFC; VCAP

Is what he's found in his first villanelle. (LL) Saturday at the Border. Hayden Carruth. MakPoe; WaAnP

Is what I keep telling them, but they hook me. I Was Buried in Janzoor. Khaled Mattawa. LegDan

Is what remained or what they thought. Fever. Eavan Boland. NAMCP V.2

Is what to make of a diminished thing. (LL) Oven Bird, The. Robert Frost. APT-1; GSo; HeIP-4; ItP; NAAL-5; NAAPv.2; NAMCP V.1; NoAM; NoP-4; NoP-5; OWoS; OxBoAm; TCAPo; WaAnP

Is what we called her. The story was. Crater Face. Denise Duhamel. BRtP; LiTh

Is what you first see, stepping off the train. Welcome to Hiroshima. Mary Jo Salter. AmWaPo; AtGh; NIL-7; NIP-4; RA

Is where God learns. (LL) Just as the Winged Energy of Delight. Rainer Maria Rilke. RaBo; WED, tr. by Robert Bly

Is where we turned around, surrendered to fate. Delphos, Ohio. Campbell McGrath. NeAmPo

Is wired within for this, in every room. (LL) Children of Wealth. Elizabeth Daryush. MoWP; NPeEn; OxBEV; OxBSo; RSaN

Is womanly, past question. (LL) Elizabeth Barrett Browning. NAEL-6v2; NAEL-7v2 *Fr.* Aurora Leigh.

Is wrought with tumult of acclaim. (LL) Alfred Tennyson. NAEL-6v2; NAEL-7v2 *Fr.* In Memoriam A. H. H.

Is you got a goddamn naura. "Ok," I said. "Ok." (LL) Sonnet: "Well, she told me I had an aura. "What?" I said." Hayden Carruth. GifTon; StAl

Is your icebox full of food? Straw Hat in the Rain. Harry Akst and Lew Brown. ReLy

Is Your Town Nineveh? Marianne Moore. APT-1

Is your voice "silence?" Inverse Proportion. Han Yong'un [*or* Yongwun]. CAMKP, *tr. by* Sammy Solberg

Isaac: a Poise. Peter Cole. ChIV-1

Isaac and Archibald. Edwin Arlington Robinson. APT-1

Isaac's Marriage. Henry Vaughan. ChIV-1

Isabel met an enormous bear. Adventures of Isabel. Ogden Nash. ChAP; MoAmPo; NOxBChV; NTCP; PtR

Isabella, or The Pot of Basil. John Keats.
    "In the mid-days of autumn, on their eves." NPBRoP

Isabella spits at Spain. Bourbons. Walter Savage Landor. OBSV

Isabelle. James Hogg. NPBRoP

Isaiah. Bible, *O.T. tr. by* New Revised Standard Version
    "Comfort ye, comfort ye my people." OBVE
    "I am the first and I am the last." InvLi, *tr. by* New Revised Standard Version
    Rod of Jesse, The. OBVE
    Song of The Suffering Servant, The. NAWM-5v1
    "Wilderness and the solitarie place shall be glad for them, The." OBVE

Isaiah ate the blood-red ember. Andrew Hudgins. UpMys *Fr.* Psalm Against Psalms.

Isaiah by Kerosene Lantern Light. Robert Harris. ChIV-1; NOBAu

Isaiah: Chapter 66. David Rosenberg. ChIV-1

Isaiah said would be the serpent's meat. (LL) On Falling Asleep by Firelight. William Meredith. ChIV-1; NoAM

Isaiah 66.11. Francis Quarles. ChIV-1

Isalutu. Askhari. InTrad

Isandula. Hume Nisbet. FaBoWar

Isatou Died. Lenrie Peters. HBAPE; PoetW

Is—Bury me not in a land of slaves!. (LL) Bury Me in a Free Land. Frances Ellen Watkins Harper. ColAP; ISC; NAAPv.1; TCAPo; WaAnP

I'se been upon de karpet. Old Maid's Soliloquy. Maggie Pogue Johnson. CBWP-4

Ise Monogatari, The. Narihira. *tr. by* F. Vos
    Facing His Own Death. WoPoe, *tr. by* F. Vos
    Regretting the Past. WoPoe, *tr. by* F. Vos

Iseult stands at Tintagel. Rückenfigur. Susan Howe. NAMCP V.2

Ishmael. Herbert Edward Palmer. OBEV

Ishtar. Judith Wright. NALW; NAMCP V.2; NoAM

Isidore Ducasse comte de Lautréamont. Michelle Grangaud. YaTCFP, *tr. by* Paul Lloyd and Rosemary Lloyd

Isipingo. Douglas Livingstone. TSAP

Isis in the Heart. Rudolfo Anaya. ICANM

Isis (Lady of Petals). Jonathan Cott. HW

Isis Wanderer. Kathleen Jessie Raine. NALW

Isk. (LL) Narrative. Russell Atkins. EGAG; GT

Isla Mujeres. Lorna Dee Cervantes. TouFir

Islamic Army, The. Caught, April 2002—A Prayer for Peace. Hettie Jones. PrTe

Island. Corsino Fortes. SonAtl, *tr. by* Jose Barros, Gunga Tavares and Krystyna Ziemba

Island, The. Milton Acorn. Coast

Island, The. Randall Jarrell. HarvBoo

Island, The. Brendan Kennelly. PBCIP

Island, The. Herman Melville. NCAP

Island, The. Ronald Stuart Thomas. InvLi

Island and Europe, The. Luis Andrade Silva. NAfrP, *tr. by* Don Burness

Island ("Between two rivers.") Langston Hughes. APT-2 *Fr.* Lenox Avenue Mural.

Island Celebration. Kenward Elmslie. FTOS

Island eyes. 23 October 1992. Virginia Cerenio. ReBoTo

Island in the Earth. Sara de Ibáñez. TCLAP, *tr. by* Inés Probert

Island in the Evening, The. Fairfield Porter. PoA 2002

Island in the Light. Sara de Ibáñez. TCLAP, *tr. by* Inés Probert

Island in the Moon, An. William Blake.
    Chapter Six.
    (Old Corruption.) NPBRoP
    (Lo, the Bat.) NPBRoP
    "Hail Matrimony, made of Love!" OxBEV
    "O I say you Joe."
    Village Cricket. NPBRoP

Island Mary. Lucille Clifton. NALW

Island of Lost Tears, The. Sky Gilbert. PML

Island of Miracles. Catherine Phil MacCarthy. ArBi

Island of Puerto Rico. Caribbean Sea. Gabriela Mistral. TANSG, *tr. by* Maria Giachetti [*or* Jacketti]

Island of Summer. Robert Penn Warren.
    Masts at Dawn. NoP-4; NoP-5; VCAP
    Riddle in the Garden. NoAM
    Where the Slow Fig's Purple Sloth. APT-2; NAMCP V.1

Island of the Three Marias. Alberto A. Ríos. NoAM

Island of Women, The. June McGlashan. ReEnLa

Island Rose. Hamish Maclaren. EdScPo

Island within Island. Henry Dumas. GT

Island Women of Paris, The. Rita Dove. LoL

Islandis. Víctor Hernández Cruz. TouFir

Islandman. Brenda Chamberlain. AngWePo; OBWVE

Islands. Vona Groarke. NIrP

Islands. Nicholas Hasluck. NOBAu

Islands, The. "H. D." MoAmPo; TCAPo

Islands, The. Robert Earl Hayden. ESEAA

Islands, The. Randall Jarrell. ItP

Islands are green. Alaskan Fragments June 1981—Summer Solstice. Wendy Rose. HATNAP

Islands scars of the water. Aimé Césaire. PFTM-1 *Fr.* Notebook of a Return to the Native Land.

Islands, we got lost. Minimal Ulysses. Jorge Fernández Granados. RMCMP, *tr. by* John Oliver Simon

Islands which have. Islands. Nicholas Hasluck. NOBAu

Islas, nos perdemos. Mínimos Ulises. Jorge Fernández Granados. RMCMP

Isle of Portland, The. A. E. Housman. MoBrPo *Fr.* Shropshire Lad, A.

"Isle of the Hares" confessed to me, The. Saint Margaret's Legend. Endre Ady. IQMS, *tr. by* Anton N. Nyerges

Isles of Greece, The. Lord Byron. NPBRoP

Isles of Greece, the isles of Greece!, The. Lord Byron. BLPJKO; OBEV; OxAEP-2 *Fr.* Don Juan.

Islet the Dachs. George Meredith. DiBP

ISM, The. Wanda Coleman. OxAAAP; PmAP

Ismailia Eclipse. Khaled Mattawa. NAPBL

Isn't It a Pity? Ira Gershwin. ReLy

Isn't it good she asked (as). Rhyme. James Laughlin. WeW-3

Isn't it nice that everyone has a grocery list. Population. Mark Halliday. ItP

Isn't it plain the sheets of moss, except that. Landscape. Mary Oliver. HeIP-4

Isn't it rich? Send in the Clowns. Stephen Sondheim. ReLy

Isn't It Romantic? Timothy Donnelly. IIR

Isn't it strange some people make. Some People. Rachel Lyman Field. ChAP; NTCP

Isn't it sweet to hear one's language lift. Upon Overhearing Tagalog. Fatima Lim-Wilson. AmPoNex

Isn't one of your prissy richpeoples' swans. Swan at Edgewater Park, The. Ruth L. Schwartz. P180

Isn't She Not a Bird. Nina Iskrenko. PFTM-2, *tr. by* Forrest Gander and Mala Kotamraju

Isn't there a man. Storm, The. Mun Chônghui. EcSo, *tr. by* Catherine J. Kim

Isn't there a word for it? The fine wet. Veil of If, The. Molly Peacock. FiBr

Isn't This a Lovely Day (To Be Caught in the Rain?). Irving Berlin. ReLy

Isn't with her family or anyone. Lady on the Cover of *Family Circle*, The. Ingrid Wendt. SweBea

Isolate. Clarence Major. PmAP

Isolate *and.* Barrett Watten. FTOS *Fr.* Progress.

Isolated Bourgeoisie. Ed Friedman. PrTe

Isolated here in the South, fiddling with British Rail. Explaining Magnetism. Maura Dooley. MoWP

Isolation. Alphonse Marie Louis de Lamartine. SxFrPo, *tr. by* A. M. and E. H. Blackmore

Isolation of exile is a gutted, The. Waiting. Arthur Nortje. HBAPE; TSAP

Isolation: To Marguerite. Matthew Arnold. BrAP; NAEL-6v2; NAEL-7v2 *Fr.* Switzerland.

Isosceles Lighthouse, The. Alfred Goldsworthy Bailey. Coast

Isosceles of knees. Junior Life Saving. Maxine W. Kumin. TWF

Israeal in ancient days. William Cowper. ChIV-2 *Fr.* Olney Hymns.

Israel. Carl Rakosi. ChIV-1

Israel. Charles Reznikoff.
   "Our eldest son is like Ishmael, Jacob is like you." ChIV-1

Israel II. Charles Reznikoff. ChIV-1

Israel Revisited. Luisa Futuransky. MirDau, *tr.* by Celeste Kostopulos-Cooperman

Israeli Navy, The. Marvin Bell. TaR

Israfel. Edgar Allan Poe. APN-1; NAAL-3; NAAPv.1; TCAPo

Issa: A Suite of Haiku. Issa. *tr.* by Lucien Stryk
   "After night in." IllVoic, *tr.* by Lucien Stryk
   "Charcoal fire." IllVoic, *tr.* by Lucien Stryk
   "Cherry blossoms." IllVoic, *tr.* by Lucien Stryk
   "Frog and I." IllVoic, *tr.* by Lucien Stryk
   "Into the house." IllVoic, *tr.* by Lucien Stryk
   "Morning glory." IllVoic, *tr.* by Lucien Stryk
   "My empty face." IllVoic, *tr.* by Lucien Stryk
   "My thinning hair." IllVoic, *tr.* by Lucien Stryk
   "New Year's Day." IllVoic, *tr.* by Lucien Stryk
   "Plum in bloom." IllVoic, *tr.* by Lucien Stryk
   "Snail—baring." IllVoic, *tr.* by Lucien Stryk
   "Song of skylark." IllVoic, *tr.* by Lucien Stryk
   "What a moon." IllVoic, *tr.* by Lucien Stryk
   "Winter moon." IllVoic, *tr.* by Lucien Stryk
   "Wonderful— / under cherry blossoms." IllVoic, *tr.* by Lucien Stryk
   "Woodpecker on." IllVoic, *tr.* by Lucien Stryk

Issa, perter than the sparrow. Martial. DiBP *Fr.* Epigrams.

Issa's Portrait. Martial. DiBP *Fr.* Epigrams.

Issei's history. *Unknown.* NAAPv.2

Issue for me, The. Note to My Liberal Feminist Sister, A. Nanna Banyiwa Horne. NAfrP

Issue is to divide into two, duplicate, derive language which is a, The. Fred Wah. NLPA *Fr.* This Dendrite Map: Father / Mother Haibun.

Issue, with cold feet, jumped in bed with us, An. All-Night Issue, The. Jackie Warren-Moore. SpirFl

Issues. Christine Ama Ata Aidoo. HAWP

Is't here the fairies haunt the place. On a Nook Called Fairyland. Henrietta Cordelia Ray. CBWP-3

It. Linda Bierds. AmAlph

It. Roger Mitchell. PoCoUp

It. Muso Soseki. EaWin, *tr.* by W. S. Merwin

It. Sharon Olds. MoWP

It absently through her ring. (LL) Dacca Gauzes, The. Agha Shahid Ali. BeAl; NAMCP V.2; NIL-7; NoP-4; NoP-5

It, after all, a place for the genuine. (LL) Poetry [1967 Version]. Marianne Moore. BrAP; HarvBoo; NIL-7; OxBoAm

It ain't Necessarily So. Ira Gershwin. ReLy

It ain't so much a question of not knowin' whut to do. I Cain't Say No. Oscar Hammerstein, II. ReLy

It all came down to nothing. Resounding Zero, A. Nicanor Parra. WoBe, *tr.* by Liz Werner

It All Depends on How You Look at It. Miroslav Košek. INSAB

It All Depends on You. Lew Brown, B. G. DeSylva and Ray Henderson. ReLy

It all returns. (LL) For Love. Robert Creeley. NAMCP V.2; PmAP; VCAP

It all went well from the very start. Rainer Maria Rilke. WED *Fr.* Life of the Virgin Mary, The.

It Allows a Portrait in Line Scan at Fifteen. Les A. Murray. HarvBoo

It always falls most heavily on the person least able to deal with it. Lonely Tylenol. Sharon Mesmer. HeMarv

It always felt to me—a wrong. Emily Dickinson. ChIV-1

It always made me feel better. Sun Worshiper. Fred Voss. SUP

It amazed me that the shapes of penises. Early Images of Heaven. Sharon Olds. CAP-8

It Amazes Me! Carolyn Leigh. ReLy

It appears / a drama of exacting dimension. Blurred Edge. Barbara Guest. NYP2

It approaches from behind. Behind the Nationalist's Flag. F. Richard Thomas. RWB

It arches like a rainbow. Bridge Where the Moon Crosses, The. Muso Soseki. EaWin, *tr.* by W. S. Merwin

It Arrives Suddenly and Carries Us Off As Usual. Marge Piercy. PasH

It asked a crumb—of Me. (LL) Hope is the thing with feathers. Emily Dickinson. AmFaPo; APN-2; BLPJKO; ChAP; MoAmPo; NoP-4; NoP-5; OxBoAm; SAmP; TCAPo

It asked for bread and butter first. Perfect Child, The. Adrian Porter. NBLV

It be as short as yours. (LL) Life. George Herbert. BASC; FSCP; NoP-4; NoP-5; NOSC

It be the last time I'm snuffin' candles in cold dark. Sadie Snuffs a Candle. Dolores Kendrick. ESEAA

It becomes apparent that I miss great occasions. Dates. Michael Ondaatje. BrAP

It becomes your soul: that sucking, itch that. Pride. V. B. Price. ICANM

It began as an item on a questionaire. Greenhouses and Gardens. David Lehman. PfSP

It began as truth, as fact. Lawson Fusao Inada. GeoHom *Fr.* Legends from Camp.

It began to snow at midnight. And certainly. Snow. Vladimir Holan. StAl, *tr.* by Ian Milner and Jarmila Milner

It began well didn't it, all that euphoria. Alice's Cat, New Year's Eve 1990. Anne Grimes. Prnts

It began / When God popped His head. Noah's Ark. Roger McGough. OBSP

It began with division. He knows this. He can read: "God was." Genesis: A Retrospective. Peter Johnson. Vesp

It begins again, the nocturnal pulse. Assassination, The. Donald Justice. VCAP

It begins as a house, an end terrace. Zoom! Simon Armitage. HarvBoo; StAl

It begins in a small room. Short Story. Ruth Buchman. PfS

It begins in the vestry. Story of Sound. Peter Makuck. NevBe

It begins like this. Ringlet, The. Jean Sprackland. MoWP

It begins to boil. The smoke's gullet, and the automobile's, they find their prey. Incessant Poem. Laura Solórzano. SPV, *tr.* by Jen Hofer

It begins to tell 'round midnight, 'round midnight. 'Round Midnight. Bernie Hanighen. ReLy

It begins with my dog, now dead, who all his long life. Retrieval System, The. Maxine W. Kumin. InvLad; WeW-3

It begins with one or two soldiers. Truce. Paul Muldoon. FaBoWar; PBCIP; PNI

It Being Forbidden. Martha Rhodes. KGB; NAPBL

It being my almost invariable habit. Frank Kuppner. EdScPo *Fr.* Old Guidebook to Prague, An.

It bends the trees and floats them. After Life. Anna Hajnal. IQMS, *tr.* by Jeannette Nichols

It bothers me: the genital smell of the bay. Rondeau at the Train Stop. Erin Belieu. GifTon; NeAmPo

It breaks apart as water will not do. Indoors. Vona Groarke. NIrP

It brightens up into the branches. George Oppen. APT-2; PFTM-1

It bulked large above my sandcastles. Ailsa Craig. Gerald Mangan. EdScPo

It burns, then weeps like a berry, toughens. Sore Thumb. Mara Bergman. PoCu

It came into her mind, seeing how the snow. Edna St. Vincent Millay. NALW *Fr.* Sonnets from an Ungrafted Tree.

It came one day like a thunderbolt. Why don't I? O. F. Diaz-Duque. ReTh

It came to me that all this time. Days and Nights. Kenneth Koch.

It came to me that many devout Jews who perished in them German concentration camps. Intuition, An. Britton Wilkie. AHA

It came to mind but by chance, suggested by the. Main Idea, The. Milo De Angelis. ItPo, *tr.* by Gayle Ridinger

It came to pass—. Adonis. PFTM-2 *Fr.* Desire Moving Through the Maps of the Material.

It Came upon the Midnight Clear. Edmund Hamilton Sears. APN-1; ChrPo; SacPr; TCAPo

It came upon the noontide air. Bishop James A. Shorter. Josephine D. Henderson Heard. CBWP-4

It can be known that he changed from Friday to Sunday. Gertrude Stein. MotU *Fr.* Book Concluding with As A Wife Has a Cow a Love Story, A.

It can be said poets. Bardo of Writing. Janet Rodney. WANABP

It can begin almost anywhere. How to Thank God for Your Loneliness. Stephen Valentine. RWB

It can kill a man. (LL) Poetry Is a Destructive Force. Wallace Stevens. APT-1; RaBo

It can rain, it can snow, it can sleet, it can blow. My Special Friend (Is Back in Town). Andy Razaf. ReLy

It cannot come. Balboa, the Entertainer. Imamu Amiri Baraka. AF; NoAM

It cannot keep. (LL) After Minor Surgery. Linda Pastan. EMP; PoA 2002

It can't be called back. (LL) Long Time Ago. Leslie Marmon Silko. NAMCP V.2; NoAM

It ceased to hurt me, though so slow. Emily Dickinson. SAmP

It Certainly Was Divine Running into You. Joanne Kyger. WANABP

It certainly won't be heaven, in fact. Castro Street. Art Beck. CalPo

It chanced his lips did meet her forehead cool. George Meredith. WaAnP *Fr.* Modern Love.

It chaunced me on day beside the shore.   Ruines of Time, The.   Edmund Spenser.   OxAEP-1

It churns.   To Derek Walcott.   R. Gerallt Jones.   BBMWP, *tr. by* the author

It comes about that the drifting of these curtains.   Curtains in the House of the Metaphysician, The.   Wallace Stevens.   PoA 2002

It comes as a surprise once more.   Autopsy.   James L. Foy.   BloBone

It comes blundering over the.   How Poetry Comes to Me.   Gary Snyder.   LoL; PoPoPo; WhBo

It comes from out of the blue.   (All of a Sudden) My Heart Sings.   Jean-Marie Blanvillain and Harold Rome.   ReLy

It comes of really cold.   .22.   Joy Lahey.   AnSo

It comes to mind.   Likenesses.   Norman Alexander MacCaig.   NePenScot

It comes to my shoulder.   Natsume Soseki.   CAoMJL1, *tr. by* Makoto Ueda

It comes up out of the ocean.   August.   William Stafford.   BodElec

It comes with the force of a body blow.   Clair de Lune.   Jules Laforgue.   WoPoe, *tr. by* William Jay Smith

It contains nothing.   Museum Vase.   Robert Francis.   APT-2

It continues to the edge of the mirror.   Reversal of Worlds.   Georgi Rupchev.   CSCBP, *tr. by* Georgi Belev and Lisa Sapinkopf

It costs $1.50 for my van to enter.   Taos Pueblo Indians: 700 strong according to Bobby's last census.   Miguel Algarin.   PueRic

It could be said, even here, that what remains of the self.   In Memory of Joseph Brodsky.   Mark Strand.   WaAnP

It Could Happen to You.   Johnny Burke.   ReLy

It could have been the way the Southern.   Sunday.   Angela Shannon.   BtF

It could have burned to the ground. (LL)   World Where News Travelled Slowly, A.   Lavinia Greenlaw.   MFPA; MoWP; NoP-5

It could have happened.   There But for the Grace.   Wisława Szymborska.   TWF, *tr. by* Magnus J. Krynski and Robert A. Maguire

It could take from Monday to Thursday.   World Where News Travelled Slowly, A.   Lavinia Greenlaw.   MFPA; MoWP; NoP-5

It Couldn't Be Done.   Edgar Albert Guest.   BRP; ITBLP

It creeps up behind you on all fours.   Mess With It.   Linda France.   MFPA

It cried three times.   Buson.   EH, *tr. by* Robert Hass

It crumbles.   Border.   Gillian Clarke.   HarvBoo; MoWP

It darted across the pond.   Catch, The.   Stanley Kunitz.   APT-2; NAMCP V.1; PtR

It descended one schoolday.   Eclipse, Kenwick, 1974.   Tracy Ryan.   NeBl

It descends rapidly under the twistable vine in the sky.   Ivano Fermini.   ItPo, *tr. by* Gayle Ridinger

It Did.   Robert Lowell.   NoAM

It did no good to think, or to stop thinking. It did no good.   Responsibility.   Lisa Lewis.   BodElec

It did not condemn. (LL)   Bible is an antique Volume, The.   Emily Dickinson.   APN-2; ChIV-1; NAAL-3; NoP-4; NoP-5

It didn't begin in Death Valley.   Scatological History.   Lisa Rye.   MAAN

It Didn't Begin with Horned Owls Hooting at Noon.   Kevin Stein.   IllVoic

It didn't matter where we lived.   To All Us Sansei Who Wanted to Be Westside.   Amy Uyematsu.   GeoHom

It didn't require great character at all.   Power of Taste, The.   Zbigniew Herbert.   PoetW; PoSu, *tr. by* Bogdana Carpenter and John Carpenter

It didn't take much to write, must've come from the heart.   Night I Won the Crown in the National Eisteddfod of My Dreams, The.   Elinor Wyn Reynolds.   BBMWP, *tr. by* the author

It discovers by night.   Poem, The.   Donald Hall.   BeAl

It dissipated suspected.   Epitaph.   Marie-Claire Bancquart.   MFP, *tr. by* Martin Sorrell

It dissipates day.   Mirror of a Moment, The.   Paul Éluard.   NAWM-7v2, *tr. by* Lloyd Alexander

It does help to know.   Poster.   Ferreira Gullar.   TCLAP, *tr. by* Renato Rezende

It does look.   Sad Night of October 1959.   Jaime Gil de Biedma.   RaW, *tr. by* Robert Mezey and Hardie St. Martin

It does not matter.   After Theresienstadt.   Myra Sklarew.   TaR

It doesn't exist, I know, but I love.   Buddy Bolden Cylinder, The.   William Matthews.   SeSe

It doesn't matter how deep you dig in.   Dancing on Beethoven's Birthday.   Edith Rylander.   MiVo

It doesn't matter if you can't see.   Some Kind of Crazy.   Major L. Jackson.   FuFl; SpirFl

It doesn't matter now if the golden wine.   It Doesn't Matter Now.   Antonio Machado Ruiz.   RaW, *tr. by* Robert Bly

It doesn't matter where I knew her.   Vibration Society.   Bill Berkson.   AHA

It doesn't matter / whether / a tree falls.   Lyric.   Elizabeth Dodd.   AmPoNex

It doesn't really matter if I met him in a bar, picked him up or was.   Future.   Vicki Viidikas.   BMAP

It doesn't speak and it isn't schooled.   Desire.   Molly Peacock.   RA

It Don't Mean a Thing (If It Ain't Got That Swing).   Duke Ellington.   NAAPv.2

It drizzled, but didn't bend.   Sultry Night, A.   Boris Leonidovich Pasternak.   TCRusP, *tr. by* Bogdan Boychuk and Mark Rudman

It Dropped So Low in My Regard.   Emily Dickinson.   HeIP-4

It dwells in quietude, speechless.   Sikong Tu.   CCL1 *Fr.* Twenty-Four Modes of Poetry.

It embarrasses my niece to think of her mother.   How to Do.   Cornelius Eady.   BRtP

It ended, and the morrow brought the task.   George Meredith.   NAEL-6v2; NAEL-7v2 *Fr.* Modern Love.

It faces west, and round the back and sides.   Domicilium.   Thomas Hardy.   OBGa

It falles me here to write of Chastity.   Edmund Spenser.   NAEL-6v1; NAEL-7v1 *Fr.* Faerie Queene, The.

It falls into the water with a gurgle. Bubbles rise to the top and burst.   Sunlight Showers Down in Sheets.   Chông Hwajin.   EcSo, *tr. by* Julie C. Park

It feels a shame to be Alive.   Emily Dickinson.   AmWaPo; FaBoWar; PCW

It feels good as it is without the giant.   Wallace Stevens.   ColAP *Fr.* Notes toward a Supreme Fiction.

It feels like creation.   Death Stayed.   Terese Svoboda.   PoDa

It feels like, gay! (LL)   Sonnet: "Caught—the bubble."   Elizabeth Bishop.   APT-2; WaAnP

It feels so good to be by myself.   Deceiving Words.   Leonor Scliar-Cabral.   MirDau, *tr. by* Regina Igel

It feels so neat to be a fish again.   Ode on a Bicycle on Halsted Street in a Sudden Summer Thunderstorm.   Paul Carroll.   IllVoic

It fell about the Lammas tide.   [Battle of Otterburn, The] [Version from Minstrelsy of the Scottish Border].   *Unknown.*   IBB; NePenScot

It fell about the Martinmas.   Jamie Telfer of [*or* in] the Fair Dodhead.   *Unknown.*   IBB

It fell about the Martinmas time.   Get Up and Bar the Door.   *Unknown.*   HeIP-4; NePenScot; NoP-4; NoP-5

It fell about the Martinmas[s].   Edom o' Gordon [Foulis Version].   *Unknown.*   NePenScot

It fell in the ancient periods.   Uriel.   Ralph Waldo Emerson.   APN-1; NAAL-3

It fell like a stone from the sky.   Wounded Angel, The.   Robert Phillips.   Vesp

It fell on a day, and a bonnie simmer [*or* bonny summer] day.   Bonnie House o' Airlie, The.   *Unknown.*   OBEV

It fell when I was sleeping. In my dream.   Land-Mine, The.   George MacBeth.   OBWP

It felt like the zero in brook ice.   Funeral, The.   Norman Dubie.   NAMCP V.2; NoAM

It fill the sky to beat on an airy shell. (LL)   Bell Tower.   Léonie Adams.   MoAmPo; OxBoAm

It fills my hand.   Losing My Hair.   Dzvinia Orlowsky.   NevBe

It first began when sitting in the huge auditorium.   On Having Been an Experimental Sacred Cow for Four Years, and a Token African on Faculty.   Kofi Awoonor.   HBAPE

It floats about, that boat of cypress wood.   Bo-zhou: That Boat of Cypress Wood.   *Unknown.*   CCL1, *tr. by* James Legge

It flows through old hushed Egypt and its sands.   Nile, The.   Leigh Hunt.   CenSon; GSo

It Follows.   Ruth Stone.   BodElec

It fortifies my soul to know.   With Whom Is No Variableness, Neither Shadow of Turning.   Arthur Hugh Clough.   SacPr

It foundered, our boat, my shipmates.   Thalassa.   José Luis Rivas.   RMCMP, *tr. by* Alastair Reid

It frightens us to see that the forest.   Clarity of Silence.   Francisco Segovia.   RMCMP, *tr. by* Michael Wiegers

It gathers where the moody sky is bending.   Ave Atque Vale.   Nora May French.   CalPo

It gives a lovely light! (LL)   First Fig.   Edna St. Vincent Millay.   AmWit; APT-1; BLPJKO; BRP; ChAP; NAAPv.2; NALW; NAMCP V.1; NIL-7; NoAM; NoP-4; NoP-5; OxBoAm; PoA 2002

It gives our nights sorrow and pain.   Five Hymns to Pain.   Nazik al-Mala'ika.   PoArWo, *tr. by* Husain Haddawy

It gives such divine materials to men, and accepts such leavings from them at last. (LL)   This Compost.   Walt Whitman.   MoAmPo; NAAL-3; OBGa; PFTM-1

It glimmers like a wakeful lake in the dusk narrowing room.   Mirror, The.   Isaac Rosenberg.   NAMCP V.1; NoAM

It glitters like the smashed beer bottle in the sun.   War, Like.   Hans Magnus Enzensberger.   GTCP, *tr. by* Reinhold Grimm

It Goes Against My Interest to Confess It.   Gustavo Adolfo Bécquer.   SpanPo, *tr. by* Dorren Bell

It goes against my interest to confess it.   It Goes Against My Interest to Confess It.   Gustavo Adolfo Bécquer.   SpanPo, *tr. by* Dorren Bell

It goes away from you suddenly, doesn't it surely first?   Saturday Night.   Clark Coolidge.   FTOS

It got me up.   Monster, The.   Karen L. Mitchell.   GT

It got so bad I never saw. Arsonist Tells His Story to the Attorney, The. Charles Rafferty. AmPoNex

It gradually became a different country. Morning in America. John Koethe. OxBoAm

It grew in the black mud. Rice. Mary Oliver. PoCoUp

It had been badly shot. Widgeon. Seamus Heaney. NPeEn

It had, he thought, a totemic resonance, that image of the woman suffering. Prose for Two Voices. Jack Foley. CalPo

It had long been dark, though still an hour before supper-time. Charles Reznikoff. NAAPv.2; NAMCP V.1

It had no voice, or anything like that. At South Fork Cemetery. Henry Taylor. LPSFW

It had taken this to notice. Colour of the Old Man's Eyes, The. Judy Gahagan. Prnts

It Had to Be You. Gustave Kahn. ReLy

It hangs deep in his robes, a delicate. Pope's Penis, The. Sharon Olds. CAP-8; NAMCP V.2; OxBoAm

It hangs from heaven to earth. Tapestry. Charles Simic. VCAP

It hap'd a gentle youth—a lordly heir. Edward Edwin Foot. STuOW Fr. Jane Hollybrand; or, Virtue Rewarded.

It happened at midnight. Enough Rain for Agnes Walquist. Allen Grossman. BAP-01

It happened before my eyes. Love's Fool. Margit Szécsi. IQMS, tr. by Kenneth McRobbie

It happened in an instant. Blueness of the Day, The. David Mura. OPRER

It happened in Paris. My Night with Frederico García Lorca (As Told by Edouard Roditi). Jaime Manrique. WiU

It happened that a fama was dancing respite and dancing. Normal Behavior of the Famas. Julio Cortázar. TCLAP, tr. by Paul Blackburn

It happened that a gentleman dropped his glasses on the. Very Real Story, A. Julio Cortázar. TCLAP, tr. by Paul Blackburn

It happened—I felt it happen. Have You Met Miss Jones? Lorenz Hart. ReLy

It happens inevitably. Rough Guide. Grahame Davies. BBMWP, tr. by the author

It happens that I am tired of being a man. Walking Around. Pablo Neruda. PoetW; VCWP, tr. by W. S. Merwin

It happens that I am tired of being a man. Walking Around. Pablo Neruda. ConPit, tr. by Clayton Eshleman

It happens that one pronounces. Speech Alone. Jean Follain. TAPaP, tr. by W. S. Merwin

It happens through the blond window, the trees. Ascension. Denis Devlin. ChIV-2

It happens / we are half-naked. Chelsea. Eric Johnson. NevBe

It happens when I've been driving. I Caught a Glimpse. Philip Levine. GeoHom

It hardly mattered what time of year. No Tool or Rope or Pail. Bob Arnold. GoPo; IPoFL; OPRER

It has a head like a cat, feet like a cat. Riddle. Unknown. NTCP

It has a hole in it. Not only where I. Surface, The. Jorie Graham. HarvBoo; NAMCP V.2; NoP-5

It has all. From Gloucester Out. Edward Dorn. PmAP

It has all begun with still waters. Maya Bejerano. DTA Fr. Hymns of Job.

It has always been King Herod that I feared. Twelfth Night. Elinor Wylie. ChrPo; SacPr

It has been a long time now. Marriage and Midsummer's Night. Linda Gregg. OxBoAm

It has been a long walk to Cootehill. Walking to Cootehill. John Engels. PfSP

It has been long since first my fears grew light. Jakov Steinberg. FIT, tr. by Robert Friend

It has been proposed that the stars should be removed from sight. Paavo Haavikko. WoPoe Fr. Fifteen Epigrams in Praise of the Tyrant.

It has been raining for three days. Rainy Season. Charles Reznikoff. APT-2

It has been raining now since. Rain Downriver. Philip Levine. VCAP

It has been said that I sometimes lie, or bend the truth. Gwendolyn MacEwen. StAl Fr. T. E. Lawrence Poems, The.

It has been snowing. Past midnight, drunk on purple wine. Winter Night, A. Georg Trakl. MotU, tr. by Robert Bly

It has brought its flute it is a long way. (LL) Dusk in Winter. W. S. Merwin. BLT; OxBoAm

It has come from further than the roads. Snow, The. Yves Bonnefoy. YaTCFP, tr. by John Naughton

It has done its work—I toss it carelessly to fall where it may. (LL) Spontaneous Me. Walt Whitman. NAAL-3; NAAL-5

It has for ages been observed. Vladimir Uflyand. TCRusP, tr. by Daniel Weissbort

It has gone with me as with a child. Heinrich von Morungen. GePo

It has happened. What Happens. Erich Fried. BeAl, tr. by Stuart Hood

It has happened all before, and yet. It Has Happened. Jack Lindsay. RSaN

It has happened / and it goes on happening. What Happens. Tadeusz Różewicz. AF, tr. by Robert A. Maguire

It has something to do with final words. Gladys Cardiff. ReEnLa

It has stayed stuck in my eyes. Wild Root. Juana de Ibarbourou. TCLAP, tr. by Sophie Cabot Black and Maria Negroni

It has taken me. Leaving You. Lily Brett. HP

It Has the Unassuming Face of a Burnt-out Candle. Velemir Khlebnikov. AF, tr. by Paul Schmidt

It has to be a hill. Michael Hartnett. PBCIP Fr. Notes on My Contemporaries.

It has to be loved the way a laundress loves her linens. Planet Earth. Patricia K. Page. BeAl; IFF

It has to do with my body being less than human, a heavy load of sponge surrounding my bones. Water. Mary Anne Cartelli. MotU

It held its head still. Gray Heron, The. Galway Kinnell. OWoS

It hovers in dark corners. Hope. Lisel Mueller. GoPo

It huddled there. Laventille. Derek Walcott. NAMCP V.2

It is. Dario Villa. ItPo, tr. by Gayle Ridinger

It is 5:15 a.m. Dear Chris, hello. (LL) Ted Berrigan. FTOS; PFTM-2; PmAP; WaAnP Fr. Sonnets, The.

It is 6:25 in Washington. One More Once. Reuben Jackson. BtF

It is 7:53 Friday morning in the Universe. Personal Poem # 7. Ted Berrigan. NYP2

It is 12:20 in New York a Friday. Day Lady Died, The. Frank O'Hara. CAP-8; EMP; InoFa; ItP; NAMCP V.2; NoAM; NoP-4; NoP-5; OxBoAm; PFTM-2; PmAP; RaBo; SwNoth; TRP; VCAP; WaAnP

It is 19—. / X years have passed. Backgrounds. Justin Quinn. NIrP

It is 1904 or 1905—we don't know the time of year. After the American Wake. Vincent Woods. NIrP

It is 1974 and out the institutional open windows. Panty Raid. Terri Ford. PoDa

It is 3:17 a.m. in New York city, yes, it is. Ted Berrigan. FTOS

It is a beauteous evening, calm and free. It Is a Beauteous Evening. William Wordsworth. BrAP; BRP; CenSon; GSo; HeIP-4; NAEL-6v2; NAEL-7v2; NIP-4; NOBRP; NoP-4; NoP-5; NPBRoP; OxAEP-2; TFi

It is a beautiful summer night. Summer Night. Antonio Machado Ruiz. WoPoe, tr. by Willis Barnstone

It is a broken country. Wild Orchard. William Carlos Williams. PoA 2002

It is a child of a subjected land. To Lord Byron. Gyula Juhász. IQMS, tr. by J. G. Nichols

It is a Christmas rite that. Nativity Play, The. Gwyn Thomas. BBMWP, tr. by the author

It is a clearing deep in a forest: overhanging boughs. Johnson's Cabinet Watched by Ants. Robert Bly. NAMCP V.2; NoP-5; OxBoAm

It is a cold and snowy night. The main street is deserted. Driving to Town Late to Mail a Letter. Robert Bly. CAP-8; HeIP-4

It is a cramped little state with no foreign policy. Shame. Richard Wilbur. EmeKit; OBCoV; OxBoAm

It is a dim April. Swan at Sheffield Park, The. David St. John. CAP-8

It is a dreadful cry that rises up. Mark Strand. PoCho Fr. Dark Harbor.

It is a dreary evening. My Journal. Adelaide Anne Procter. VWP

It is a fearful thing to be. Pope, The. A. E. Housman. NPeEn; OBCoV

It is a fearful thing to be / Me. (LL) Pope, The. A. E. Housman. NPeEn; OBCoV

It is a fearful thing to fall into the hands of the living God. Hands of God, The. D. H. Lawrence. ChIV-2; InvLi

It is a flaw. John Keats. NPBRoP Fr. To J. H. Reynolds, Esq.

It is a flower. On this mountainside it is dying. (LL) Flower Herding on Mount Monadnock. Galway Kinnell. HeIP-4; NoAM

It Is a German Honeymoon. Kenneth Rexroth. APT-2

It is a ghost posed on my lips. Here: never. (LL) Prayer: "Over a dock railing, I watch the minnows, thousands, swirl." Jorie Graham. AWPTFC; PtR

It is a God-damned lie to say that these. Another Epitaph on an Army of Mercenaries. Hugh MacDiarmid. FaBoWar; NAEL-6v2; NAEL-7v2; NAMCP V.1; NoAM; NoP-4; NoP-5; OBWP; WaAnP

It is a good thing. Baskets. Louise Glück. AFaM

It is a great day. (LL) Today Is a Day of Great Joy. Víctor Hernández Cruz. LoL; PueRic

It is a great half world. Tooms 4. Donald Revell. RoV

It is a great pity we don't know. Going Without Saying. Bernard O'Donoghue. BeAl; PoCu

It is a great sundial in the desert. Meditations on a World of Stones. Mahmoud al-Braikan. IrPoTo, tr. by Ralph Saverese and Saadi A. Simawe

It is a hollow garden, under the cloud. Winter Swan. Louise Bogan. APT-2; ColAP; OWoS; OxBoAm

It is a huge spider, which can no longer move. Spider, The. César Vallejo. RaBo; WED, tr. by Robert Bly

It is a human universe: & I. Ted Berrigan. PFTM-2 Fr. Sonnets, The.

It is a kind of triage, a setting. Triage. Margot Schilpp. AmPoNex; PoDa

"It is a kynde knowyng," quod she, "that kenneth in thine herte." William Langland. OxBEV *Fr.* Vision of Piers Plowman, The.

It is a land with neither night nor day. Cobwebs. Christina Georgina Rossetti. CABP; NAEL-6v2; NAEL-7v2; NALW; VWP

It is a late twentieth-century cliché that we must turn off. These Current Events. Kimiko Hahn. PrTe

It is a new America. Jean Toomer. BLPJKO *Fr.* Blue Meridian, The.

It is a night of summer: overhead. John Addington Symonds. CAGL *Fr.* Three Visions of Imperial Rome.

It is a part of the policy. Schedule of Benefits, A. John N. Morris. PoA 2002

It is a place where poets crowned may feel the heart's decaying. Cowper's Grave. Elizabeth Barrett Browning. OxAEP-2

It is a puzzle for the insane. Different Ones #6—Future Possibilities (An Aids Soliloquy). Viki Akiwumi. InTrad

It is a sigh of climbing feet. My Name's Not Rodriguez. Luis J. Rodriguez. BRtP; FaoP

It Is a Small Plant. William Carlos Williams. ColAP

It is a strange bird. Strange Bird, A. Michael Dransfield. BMAP

It is a stubble field, where a black rain is falling. De Profundis. Georg Trakl. WoPoe, *tr. by* James Wright

It is a sultry day; the sun has drank [*or* drunk]. Summer Wind. William Cullen Bryant. APN-1

It is a terror. Perspectives on the Second World War. Irena Klepfisz. TaR

It is a tide pool, shallow, water coming in. Looking into a Tide Pool. Robert Bly. CAP-8

It is a wicked world of toil without much mirth, and the multitude. Conversation between Two Sisters, One Choosing an Aged Man, and the Other Choosing Youth, A. Angharad Pritchard. EMWP

It is a willow when summer is over. Willow Poem. William Carlos Williams. WaAnP

It is a winter afternoon. What We Lost. Eavan Boland. HarvBoo

It is again ourselves whom we defeat. (LL) Defeat. Witter Bynner. APT-1; PWW2

It is All Souls' Day, then, a reverential day in Portugal. Lisbon. Russell Atkins. GT

It is all space, 13,000 square feet, they say. Opening in Santa Fe, The. Raylene Hinz-Penner. ACAMVP

IT IS ALMOST BEAUTIFUL when fraud and hypocrisy. Senate Hearings. Michael McClure. BB

It is almost polio season. The girls. Ars Poetica. Norman Dubie. TAPaP

It is almost time to grow up. Movin' with Nancy. David Trinidad. PmAP

It is already a murder mystery. Josée Lapeyrère. SCFWP *Fr.* Apples.

It is always a shock when they take off their caps. Callers. Christine Evans. TCAWP

It is always difficult to measure. Our World Is Less Full Now That Mr. Fuller Is Gone. Kalamu ya Salaam. ISC

It is always easy to sentimentalize old lovers. They are distant. To H.N. David Mura. UnSA

It is always embarrassing for a German to order. Harry's Bar Ballad. Giulia Niccolai. CItWP, *tr. by* Cinzia Sartini Blum and Lara Trubowitz

It is always late at night and always the night in mist. Zeno's Progress. Thomas Centolella. ArBi

It is always November, the driveway lined with gold. Where My Mother Cries. Juanita Brunk. ACAMVP

It is an ancient custom. Ancient Custom, An. Anatoly Steiger. TCRusP, *tr. by* John Glad

It is an ancient Mariner. Rime of the Ancient Mariner, The (1798 version). Samuel Taylor Coleridge. AmFaPo; CABP; HeIP-4; NAEL-6v2; NAEL-7v2; NoP-4; OBEV; OBNV; OxAEP-2; OxBEV; PoPoPo; TFi

It is an ancient Mariner. Rime of the Ancient Mariner, The (1817 version). Samuel Taylor Coleridge. NoP-5; WaAnP

It is an ancyent Marinere. Samuel Taylor Coleridge. *See* It is an ancient Mariner.

It is an antique carcass eaten up by rust. Frisco-City. Blaise Cendrars. BLT, *tr. by* Monique Chefdor

It is an August evening, in Wicklow. Thomas Kinsella. ModIr *Fr.* Messenger, The.

It is an auncient waggonere. Rime of the Aunciente Waggonere, The. William Maginn. ClHu

It is an illusion that we were ever alive. Rock, The. Wallace Stevens. APT-1

It is an old established hotel. Latest Hotel Guest Walks Over Particles That Revolve in Seven Other Dimensions Controlling Latticed Space, The. Ruth Stone. OxBoAm

It is an old story: the oppressed. Seven Horizons. Stephen Stepanchev. PoDa

It is as if infancy were the whole of incarnation. Luci Shaw. SacPr

It is as if they are ashamed. Elephants Dying, The. Michael C. Blumenthal. NoAM

It is as old as it thinks itself to be. Parmenides Machine, A. Charles Stein. PFTM-2

It is as true as strange, else trial feigns. John Davies of Hereford. OxBSo *Fr.* Wit's Pilgrimage.

It is Ash Wednesday and Christ is waiting. Campesino's Lament, The. Judith Ortiz Cofer. PueRic; TouFir

It is at every moment different water. (LL) Childhood Around 1950, A. Alan Williamson. ASA; FaoP

It Is August 24th. Cortney Davis. FiBr

It is autumn at the grass hut on Jade Peak. At the Thatched Hall of the Ts'ui Family. Tu Fu [*or* Du Fu]. CrYelRi, *tr. by* Sam Hamill

It is beautiful and still. Moorland. Ronald Stuart Thomas. StAl

It is because of exile I am here. Tristia. Charles Hubert Sisson. HarvBoo

It is because you were my friend. Mortal Combat. Mary Elizabeth Coleridge. VWP

It is best. At Night. Jane Hirshfield. BodElec

It is best to enter the political life of a nation with a suntan. Cultivation. Ed Friedman. PrTe

It is better. Abandoning Your Car in a Snowstorm: Rosslyn, Virginia. Michael C. Blumenthal. NoAM

It is better not to go back to the village. Baleful Return. Ramón López Velarde. TCLAP, *tr. by* Victor Tulli

It is better this year. If the Birds Knew. John Ashbery. PoA 2002

It is better to appear. My Twentieth Century. RoV

It is big sky and its changes. Orkeny / This Life. Andrew Greig. StAl

It is bitter cold, and late, and falling. Outside the City. Tu Fu [*or* Du Fu]. NDACCP, *tr. by* David Hinton

It is blood. It is not hail, battering my temples. July 18, 1936–July 18, 1938. Miguel Hernández. AF, *tr. by* Timothy Baland

It is blue. (LL) Blue Monday. Diane Wakoski. NALW; PmAP

It is burning ice, it is a cold fire. Amorous Sonnet Defining Love. Francisco de Quevedo y Villegas. BLPSL, *tr. by* Rene de Costa, Rigas Kappatos and Eleni Paidoussi

It is chill and dark in my small room. Thin. Caitríona O'Reilly. NIrP

It Is Clear Why the Angels Come No More. Jack Gilbert. YaYoPo

It is clear why the angels come no more. It Is Clear Why the Angels Come No More. Jack Gilbert. YaYoPo

It is close to a quarter of a century since then. Christmas Carol, A. T. H. Parry-Williams. BBMWP, *tr. by* Joseph P. Clancy

It is cold, bitter as a penny. Who Will Know Us? Gary Soto. GM

It is cold dark midnight, yet listen. Homeless. Adelaide Anne Procter. VWP

It is cold here. Moths, The. W. S. Merwin. HeIP-4

It is cold, the snow is deep. Poor North. Mark Strand. NAMCP V.2

It is colder now. Epistle to Be Left in the Earth. Archibald MacLeish. APT-1; MoAmPo

It is common knowledge to every schoolboy and even every Bachelor of Arts. Portrait of the Artist as a Prematurely Old Man. Ogden Nash. APT-2

It is dangerous for a woman to defy the gods. Letter to My Sister. Anne Spencer. InGu; TCAPo

It is dangerous to leave written that which is badly written. William Carlos Williams. PFTM-2 *Fr.* Paterson.

It Is Dangerous to Read Newspapers. Margaret Atwood. HeIP-4; ItP; OBWP

It is dark inside the body, and wet. OneThousand Bullfrogs Rejoice. Larissa Szporluk. LegDan

It is dawn. Has this lamp, then, finished. Task of Hope, The. Yves Bonnefoy. YaTCFP, *tr. by* John Naughton

It is December. Morning Songs. Robert E. Penn. WiU

It is December in Wicklow. Seamus Heaney. NPeEn; PBCIP; PNI; WaAnP *Fr.* Singing School.

It Is Deep. Carolyn M. Rodgers. SSLK

It is difficult to describe what we felt. Centrifuge, The. Billy Collins. BAP-04

It Is Difficult to Exaggerate the Importance of Mushrooms as Food. Chris Torrance. Oth

It is difficult to keep sane in it. Rain Forest. Eric Rolls. NOBAu

It is difficult to know what to do with so much happiness. So Much Happiness. Naomi Shihab Nye. BeAl; PLBUT

It is difficult to read. The page is dark. Phosphor Reading by His Own Light. Wallace Stevens. APT-1

It is done! Laus Deo! John Greenleaf Whittier. CBCWP; PCW

It is done by us all, as God disposes, from. Excrement Poem, The. Maxine W. Kumin. GoPo

It is done in beauty. (LL) *Unknown.* APN-2; TCAPo *Fr.* Mountain Chant, The.

It is dusty on the edges. I Still Have Everything You Gave Me. Naomi Shihab Nye. ExTi

It is duty and not hospitality that has diverted the ancient guest. Dream of Mimesis, A. Katherine Lederer. BodElec

It is early evening, still, in Honolulu, and in London, now, it must be well past dawn. 4 A.M. Kenneth Fearing. APT-2

It is early morning. Aubade, An. Irving Layton. WoPoe

It is early morning within this room: without. Winter Sunrise. Laurence Binyon. NPeEn

It is earnest. Scenes from the Door. Gertrude Stein. AF

It is easily forgotten, year to. Memorial Day. Michael Anania. NoAM

It is Easter / The last flurries. Three-Card Monte. Malena Mörling. AmPoNex

It is easy for the mind. Point and Counter-Point in All Things. Jane Mead. NAPBL

It is easy to proclaim yourself. Marginalization of Poetry, The. Mitch Highfill. HeMarv

It is eighteen years ago, almost to the day. Walking Away. Cecil Day Lewis. BeAl

It is enough for me by day. Enough. Sara Teasdale. APT-1

It is enough! I saw you vanish into air. (LL) Butterfly. D. H. Lawrence. BLT; NAMCP V.1; NoAM

It is enough! My feeble sense. Dying Song. Anton Ulrich. GePo, tr. by George C. Schoolfield

It is enough to listen now. Ceasefire. Jane Bailey. FiBr

It is equal to living in a tragic land. Dry Loaf. Wallace Stevens. RaBo

It is essential that Summer be grafted to. Poem for July 4, 1994. Sonia Sanchez. SpirFl

It is essential that the U. S. A. standard of hygiene and inspection. Laurie Duggan. BMAP Fr. Three Found Poems.

It is evening before I rise. In Seclusion. Tu Fu [or Du Fu]. CrYelRi, tr. by Sam Hamill

It is evening in the town of X. 2032. Mark Strand. OxBoAm

It is ever so that the vital essence of things is what gives them life. Kuan Chung. ColAnChi Fr. Kuan Tzu.

It is Everywhere. Jean Toomer. GT

It is exactly a year today since you slapped me in public. Sea Stone. Sinéad Morrissey. NIrP

It is fall again, October rains. Bam Chi Chi Lala. Lorna Goodison. NAMCP V.2

It is Fate [alone] that causes us distress, first by the blow itself and then by the traces it leaves; so what is the use of weeping over illusions and vain imagings? Abd al-Majīd ibn Abd Allāh Ibn Abdūn. HiArP, tr. by James T. Monroe

It is first that angle at which you sleep. Milkflowers. Robert Wrigley. PasH

It is foolish. Tree. Jane Hirshfield. CalPo

It is for me poetry. Rochelle Owens. PFTM-2 Fr. W.C. Fields in French Light.

It is forbidden to write about a certain class of violence. With Your Permission. Mario Benedetti. TCLAP, tr. by David Arthur McMurray

It is four in the afternoon. Time still for a poem. Public Journal. Phyllis McGinley. NBLV

It is friday / the eagle has flown. Coming of John, The. Amus Mor. SeSe

It is ghosts that kill you without a drop of blood. Purple Thought, The. Houda Al-Na'mani. PoArWo, tr. by Richard McKane

It is glorious. Old Song of the Musk Ox People. Brian Swann. PoCoUp

It is God body and no mo. (LL) Sacrament of the Altar, The. Unknown. NoP-4; NoP-5

It is going to rain. She Thinks of Her Beloved. Lu Chi. NDACCP, tr. by Kenneth Rexroth

It is good in May, in marvelous wet May, to be the chairman of the All-Russian Extraordinary Committee in the city of Odessa. Eduard Veniaminovich Limonov. TCRusP Fr. Secret Notebook.

It is good knowing that glasses. Antonio Machado Ruiz. WED Fr. Moral Proverbs and Folk Songs.

It is good to come out after driving and walk on the bare grass. Les A. Murray. NAMCP V.2 Fr. Buladelah-Taree Holiday Song Cycle, The.

It is good to have chosen. Homage to Life: Jules Supervielle. Joseph Stroud. PoDa; TAPaP

It is hard as diamonds; it wants to destroy us all. (LL) Unbeliever, The. Elizabeth Bishop. NAAL-5; NoAM

It is hard for those who have never known persecution. T. S. Eliot. SacPr Fr. Rock, The.

It is hard going to the door. Door, The. Robert Creeley. BrAP; NAAL-5; NAMCP V.2; NoAM

It is hard to become a truly good. Simonides. SaLy, tr. by Diane Rayor

It is hard / To make a poem in prison. To Make a Poem in Prison. Etheridge Knight. AF

It is hard to want a thing you know will hurt another. From a Vacant House. Mark Wunderlich. NeAmPo

It is hardly enough to stir and mix. Secrets of the Landscape, The. Jacob Fichman. FIT, tr. by Robert Friend

It is harm to me and anguish. Dirge. Mary Macleod. EMWP

It is her eyes. In Her Own Image. Eavan Boland. PBCIP

It is her right, to bind with warmest ties. Woman's Rights. Rebekah Gumpert Hyneman. SWaP

It is high time to go back to the sun. It Is High Time. Louis-René des Forêts. YaTCFP, tr. by John Naughton

It is hot today, dry enough for cutting grain. August from My Desk. Roland Flint. OtW

It is I, O Azure, come from the caves below. Helen. Paul Valéry. WoPoe, tr. by Richard Wilbur

It Is I Who Must Begin. Vaclav Havel. TWF

It is I who travel in the winds. George Copway's Dream Song. Unknown. APN-2, tr. by George Copway

It Is Important. Gail Tremblay. WeW-3

It is important to do something meaningless. First Thing. Kit Robinson. FTOS

It is important work. Interpreter. Carmen Horst. ACAMVP

It is in slow choking. Man, That Is Born of a Woman. Rosanna Warren. ExTi; PfSP

It is in the small things we see it. Courage. Anne Sexton. GoPo; PLBUT; TWF

It Is in Vain, the Sorrow. Paul Fleming. GePo, tr. by J. W. Thomas

It is incessantly. Sui Veneris/The Poet of No Return. Ricardo M. de Ungria. ReBoTo

It is——is it——? Is It? Else Von Freytag-Loringhoven. NAAPv.2

It is January, and there are the crows. Crows. Mary Oliver. MoW

It is June, it is June. Andraitx—Pomegranate Flowers. D. H. Lawrence. NAMCP V.1; NoP-4; NoP-5

It is late at night. Pavese Said Death Will Come Bearing Your Eyes. Erica Bernheim. LegDan

It is late at night and still I am losing. Robert Frost. AmWit; GI Fr. Ten Mills.

It is Leviathan, mountain and world. History. Robert Fitzgerald. APT-2

It Is like a Shortness of Breath. Margherita Guidacci. CItWP, tr. by Cinzia Sartini Blum and Lara Trubowitz

It is / like/making a cake. Loving. Angela Jackson. BtF

It is like smoke escaping through a screened. In a Room. William Virgil Davis. YaYoPo

It is like the first and last time I tried a Coleman. Falling in Love at Sixty-Five. Mona Van Duyn. NoP-4; NoP-5

It is likely enough that lions and scorpions. Ante Mortem. Robinson Jeffers. MoAmPo

It is little I repair to the matches of the Southron folk. At Lord's. Francis Thompson. OPOU

It is made of finest linen. Baby's Dress, A. Hazel Hall. FiBr

It is Margaret you mourn for. (LL) Spring and Fall [To a Young Child]. Gerard Manley Hopkins. BrAP; CABP; ClHu; CtM; HeIP-4; InoFa; NAEL-6v2; NAEL-7v2; NAMCP V.1; NIL-7; NIP-4; NoAM; NoP-4; NoP-5; OPOU; PoPoPo; PtR; TFi; TRP; WaAnP

It is May on every hand. Bird Song. William Carlos Williams. SAmP

It is milkweed smells so sweet Peter and Joan tell me. From the Porch of the Frost Place. Gray Jacobik. VisFro

It is Monday and the children are laughing. Children Are Laughing, The. Gwendolyn MacEwen. IFF

It Is Monsoon at Last. Basil T. Paquet. AmWaPo

It is more onerous. Obligation to Be Happy, The. Linda Pastan. PoA 2002

It is morning because the sun has risen. Concerning the Afterlife, the Indians of Central California Had Only the Dimmest Notions. Robert Hass. LoL

It is morning, Senlin says, and in the morning. Conrad Potter Aiken. NoAM; NoP-5 Fr. Senlin; a Biography.

It is most curious to see what a power a few calm words. Arthur Hugh Clough. NPeEn Fr. Amours de Voyage.

It is most true that eyes are formed to serve. Sir Philip Sidney. NAEL-6v1; NAEL-7v1; NoSic Fr. Astrophil and Stella.

It is most true that God to Israel. Bible, O.T. NoSic

It is my celebration. I Will Still Sing. Amelia Blossom Pegram. HAWP

It is my desire, it is my wish. Elias Lönnrot. PFTM-1 Fr. Kalevala, The.

It is my desire moving. Adonis. PFTM-2 Fr. Desire Moving Through the Maps of the Material.

It is my house, and yet one room is locked. Room, The. Kevin Hart. StAl

It is my joy at evening to be gazing. Soul Woven of Shadows. Árpád Tóth. IQMS, tr. by Edmund Charles Blunden and J. G. Nichols

It is my last night in Havana. Apagón, El. Sandra M. Castillo. TouFir

It is my last winter, and all. Verlaine Dying. David Wheatley. NIrP

It is my nature that makes me love you often. How God Answers the Soul. Mechthild von Magdeburg. WPoS, tr. by Oliver Davies

It is my only description. (LL) I Keep to Myself Such Measures. Robert Creeley. NAMCP V.2; NoAM; OxBoAm; PmAP

It is myself. To a Dog Injured in the Street. William Carlos Williams. SAmP

It is nearly always an excuse, never to have done this. Civilization Day. Noelle Kocot. LegDan

It is never enough to know what you want. Wish to Be Believed, The. Mona Van Duyn. PoA 2002

It is next to my flesh. Raspberry Sweater, A. Frank O'Hara. AHA

It is night. Cholera. Nazik al-Mala'ika. PoArWo, tr. by Husain Haddawy and Nathalie Handal

It is night. Existence. Thich Nhat Hanh. WhBo

It is night again. Tzu Yeh. EroLit; WoPoe, tr. by Chung Ling and Kenneth Rexroth

It is night and the barbarians have not come. Poem Beginning with a Line by Cavafy. Derek Mahon. PNI

It is night for the last time. Letters, The. Louise Glück. HarvBoo

It Is Night, in My Study. Miguel de Unamuno. RaW, tr. by Lillian Jean Stafford and William Stafford

It is night like a red rag. Moment of War, A. Laurie Lee. OBWP

It is night. You are asleep. And beautiful tears. Ted Berrigan. NYP2; PFTM-2 Fr. Sonnets, The.

It is no vulgar nature I have wived. George Meredith. NAEL-6v2 Fr. Modern Love.

It Is Not. Valerie Martínez. TouFir

It is not a fissure. Archipelago. Dafydd Rowlands. BBMWP, tr. by Meic Stephens

It is not a range of a mountain. Gertrude Stein. NoP-4; NoP-5 Fr. Stanzas in Meditation.

It is not as though you come. All the Same. Clarence Major. BodElec

It is not at all surprising. Gertrude Stein. OxBoAm Fr. Book Concluding with As A Wife Has a Cow a Love Story, A.

It is not bad. Let them play. Bloody Sire, The. Robinson Jeffers. PoA 2002; PWW2

It Is Not Beauty I Demand. George Darley. IrLP; NAEL-6v2

(Loveliness of Love, The.) OxAEP-2

(Song, A.) NOBRP

It is not, Celia, in our power. To a Lady Asking Him How Long He Would Love Her. Sir George Etherege. OBEV

It is not chaos or death—it is form, union, plan—it is eternal life—it is Happiness. (LL) Walt Whitman. CAGL; ColAP; ItP Fr. Song of Myself.

It is not clear how he entered me. Houdini. Moniza Alvi. EmeKit; MFPA

It is not cosy to live. From the Chinese. Michael Smith. PBCIP

It is not far beyond the Village church. Walden. William Ellery Channing. APN-1

It is not for you, finally, that I write these lines. Madrigal 3. Aurelio Arturo. BLPSL, tr. by Rene de Costa, Rigas Kappatos and Eleni Paidoussi

It Is Not Golgotha—It Is. Judson Crews. ICANM

It is not grief or pain;. After Soufrière. Michael Field. VWP

It Is Not Growing Like a Tree. Ben Jonson. WaAnP Fr. To the Immortal Memory and Friendship of That Noble Pair, Sir Lucius Cary and Sir H. [or Henry] Morison.

It is not gunfire I hear, but a hunting horn. (LL) Aristocrats. Keith Douglas. FaBoWar; NAEL-6v2; NAEL-7v2; NAMCP V.1; NoAM; NoP-4; NoP-5; OBWP

It is not happiness. Not the man standing. Ariel Singing. Timothy Liu. NeAmPo

It is not I, ever or now. (LL) Pebble, The. Elinor Wylie. ChIV-1; MoAmPo

It is not in yr service that I wear myself out. Loba Addresses the Goddess, The / or The Poet as Priestess Addresses the Loba-Goddess. Diane Di Prima. HW; PmAP

It Is Not Just. Shakuntala Hawoldar. HAWP

It Is Not Just. Harriet Jacobs. ISC

It is not just that I am looking. It Is Not Just. Shakuntala Hawoldar. HAWP

It is not known. Ana Belén López Pulido. SPV, tr. by Jen Hofer

It is not necessarily a zone of understanding. Ikonostasis. The Sound of the Sea Filling a Faraway Room. Sam Witt. IAoNAP

It is not now I learn. Song. Louise Bogan. APT-2

It is not often. Grace. Imtiaz Dharker. MoWP

It is not poetry you fear, but poets. For Micha's Mother, Who Signs. Robert A. Fink. PoA 2002

It is not so easy to live on the earth. For a Long Time I Have Wanted to Write a Happy Poem. Richard Jackson. PfSP

It is not so easy to shoot a man. Of Violence. G. Travis Regier. LiTh

It is not spoken to him. Truth You Carry Is Very Dark, The. Alfred B. Spellman. EGAG

It is not that the sea lanes. Stone and Fern. Leslie Norris. AngWePo

It is not that there is beginning is there. Work, The. Armand Schwerner. BodElec

It is not / the Afro. I Am Africa. Kimberly Ann Collins. InTrad

It is not the clay road. Romanticism. Claudia Keelan. RoV

It is not the moon, I tell you. Mock Orange. Louise Glück. CAP-8; MakPoe; NAMCP V.2; NoAM; OxBoAm; PoPoPo; VCAP

It is not true. Death's Secret. Gösta Ågren. StAl, tr. by David McDuff

It is not true that the shortest path between two points is the. Lover of Blue Writing above the Sea, The. Ghada al-Samman. PoArWo, tr. by Saad Ahmed and Miriam Cooke

It is not true that you are far from "the light that can find you." Eunice Odio. TANSG Fr. In the Life and Death of Rosamel Del Valle.

It is not what they built. It is what they knocked down. German Requiem, A. James Fenton. HarvBoo; NAEL-6v2; NAEL-7v2; NAMCP V.2; NoAM; NoP-5; NPeEn

It is not—I swear it by every fiery omen to be seen these nights. Readings, Forecasts, Personal Guidance. Kenneth Fearing. MoAmPo

It is now nearly forty years, I guess. Mother's Lament, The. Helen Selina Blackwood, Countess of Dufferin and Clandeboye. VWP

It is now one hundred years. Julia A. Moore. STuOW Fr. Hurrah for Cooper and Cary.

It is—Occasionally. (LL) We do not play on Graves. Emily Dickinson. NIL-7; NIP-4

It is of absolutely no importance how often they add it. (LL) Gertrude Stein. NoP-4; NoP-5 Fr. Stanzas in Meditation.

It is, of course, the wrong house. Houses of Emily Dickinson, The. Larry Rubin. NIP-4

It is on the Earth that all things transpire. Fish Tea Rice. Linda Gregg. BeAl; ExTi

It is one that most people should be prepared to be blank upon. (LL) Ignorance of Death. William Empson. NAMCP V.1; NoAM

It is only the men who are hungry. The pigeons are fed. (LL) Trinity Place. Phyllis McGinley. AmWit; MoAmPo; SoSe-8

It is other people who have separated. Lady Otomo no Sakanoé. TAL

It is our only friend. (LL) Earth Dweller. William Stafford. BeAl; IPoFL

It is over now, but they will not let it be over. Stephen Vincent Benét. Fr. John Brown's Body.

It is over. What is over? Amen. Christina Georgina Rossetti. WPoS

It is perfectly natural for the Sun to shine initially in the upper / lefthand corner of the first page of this book. Sun as a Spinning Top (I), The. Francis Ponge. AF, tr. by Serge Gavronsky

It is pleasant in October. Nights in Fresno. Luis Omar Salinas. GeoHom

It is portentous, and a thing of state. Abraham Lincoln Walks at Midnight. Vachel Lindsay. APT-1; CBCWP; IllVoic; MoAmPo; NAAPv.2; TCAPo; TFi

It is possible the heights of this view are a museum. Les A. Murray. BMAP Fr. Sydney Highrise Variations, The.

It is presumptuous and irresponsible to pray for other people. Wendell Berry. UpMys Fr. Prayers and Sayings of the Mad Farmer.

It Is Raining. Jacques Roubaud. YaTCFP, tr. by Françoise Gramet and Richard Sieburth

It is raining on Crocodiles. Cuba, Crocodiles, Rain. Keith Armstrong. RSaN

It is raining softly. Front Window, The. Rae Desmond Jones. BMAP

It Is Raining Today. Sandra Maria Esteves. PueRic

It is raining—a rain. Quality of Mercy, The. Lee Upton. AmAlph

It is Ramadan. The butcher's children come from the mosque. Eid Al-Fitr. Kerry Krause. AFaM

It is right. Planting Onions. Jane Flanders. IPoFL

It is Said by Some Sailors, the Old. Maria Luisa Spaziani. CItWP, tr. by Cinzia Sartini Blum and Lara Trubowitz

It is said that a lover seen in dreams. Dreams. Myŏngok. WoPoe, tr. by Okhee Yoo and Michael Stephens

It is said that writing serves to keep one at a distance; to. Love of Poetry. Jacqueline Risset. SCFWP, tr. by Serge Gavronsky

It is said that you came from China. Rose Beetle, The. W. S. Merwin. CAP-8

It is scribbled along the body. Eighth Sky. Michael Palmer. FTOS

It is she alone that matters. Bouquet of Belle Scavoir. Wallace Stevens. MoAmPo

It is snowing in Athens tonight & Apollo with ice in his beard. Weather Seems Different, The. Eliot Katz. PA9/11

It is snowing on my roof and on the trees. Breath. Pierre Reverdy. YaTCFP, tr. by Mary Ann Caws and Patricia Terry

It is so clear. Domino Theory (or Snoop Dogg rules the world), The. Kenneth Carroll. SpirFl

It is so hard to be earth bound. Ornithology. Laini Mataka. ISC

It is so long gone by, and yet. Reminiscence, A. Amy Levy. VWP

It is so old, the date is dim. My House Not Made with Hands. Helen Hunt Jackson. SWaP

It is so peaceful on the ceiling! Sleeping on the Ceiling. Elizabeth Bishop. APT-2; OBGa

It is so sad. Loneliness, The. John Wieners. PmAP

It is so small a thing. Matthew Arnold. OBEV Fr. Empedocles on Etna.

It is so still in the house. Mother's Song, The. Unknown. OBCP, tr. by Peter Freuchen

It is so thin a splinter of singing. (LL) Splinter. Carl Sandburg. SoSe-8; Spl

It is some time since I have been. Hill, The. Robert Creeley. BrAP; RaBo; TRP

It is Soul Brother Number One, James Brown. David Wojahn. PBCAP *Fr.* Mystery Train: A Sequence.

It is spring, almost dawn when the crowds gather. Leaving Government Offices. Tu Fu [*or* Du Fu]. CrYelRi, *tr.* by Sam Hamill

It is Spring in the mountains. Written on the Wall at Zhang's Hermitage. Tu Fu [*or* Du Fu]. CCL1, *tr.* by Kenneth Rexroth

It is spring today. Visitation. Jaime Jacinto. ReBoTo

It is spring when the storks return. Reading. Ruth Stone. ExTi

It is springtime, here the leaves are sprouting on the trees. *Unknown.* SLW, *tr.* by Marjolijn De Jager, Sayd Bahodin Majrouh and André Velter

It is springtime out here in Kansas. Kansas. J. P. Dunn. VerBaPo

It Is Sticky in the Subway. David Schubert. APT-2

It Is Still Early. Elvira Levy. MirDau, *tr.* by Roberta Gordenstein

It is still spring, it is still meant tenderly. (LL) Vita Nova. Louise Glück. NAMCP V.2; NoP-5

It is still warm enough to slip from the weeds into the lake's edge. William Carlos Williams. MotU *Fr.* Kora in Hell.

It is strenuous to mentally encompass. Poem Wrapped Around Quotation from Samantha Power. Donna Brook. PrTe

It is subtle, and weary, and wide. Doubt, A. Sarah Morgan Bryan Piatt. NCAP

It is such a beautiful day I had to write you a letter. Thoughts of a Young Girl. John Ashbery. WaAnP

It is summer, and treachery blurs with the sounds of midnight. June 1940. Weldon Kees. PWW2

It is summer, and we are in a house. Modern Love. Douglas Dunn. NPeEn

It is Sunday afternoon. At the End of the Weekend. Ted Kooser. PBCAP

It is Sunday, day of rest. My daughter is out, her pet rat. Burial. Judith W. Steinbergh. PfS

It is ten years since I have seen these shirts. Shirt Poem, The. Gerald Stern. ItP

It is terrible, I admit that. All for Nothing. Lőrinc Szabó. IQMS, *tr.* by Edwin Morgan

It Is That Dream. Olav H. Hauge. WED, *tr.* by Robert Bly

It is that hour when listening ones will weep. John Neal. APN-1 *Fr.* Battle of Niagara, The.

It is that they spend so much time in the sky. Birthday. Gerald Stern. PfSP

It is that time. Andif. Seitlhamo Motsapi. TSAP

It is the air of atrocity. George Oppen. AmWaPo; NAMCP V.1 *Fr.* Of Being Numerous.

It is the bell to awaken God that we've heard ringing. (LL) Carolyn Forché. *See* Is the bell to awaken God that we've heard ringing.

It is the best thing. Pregnancy. Sandra McPherson. LoL

It is the breast I remember seeing. Possible. Ruth L. Schwartz. WiU

It is the cause, it is the cause, my soul [*or* (my soule)]. William Shakespeare. OxBEV *Fr.* Othello.

It is the clay that makes the earth stick to his spade. In Nunhead Cemetery. Charlotte Mew. NoP-4; NoP-5

It is the cloudy morning. Father of the Bride. Robin Metz. MAAN

It is the color of light. Lyric: I Am Looking at Music. Pinkie Gordon Lane. FuFl

It is the cry of women, my good Lord. William Shakespeare. OxBEV *Fr.* Macbeth.

It is the dawn. Eunice Odio. TANSG *Fr.* In the Life and Death of Rosamel Del Valle.

It is the day when all the sons of God. Hellas. Percy Bysshe Shelley.

It is the day when he was born. Alfred Tennyson. NAEL-6v2; NAEL-7v2 *Fr.* In Memoriam A. H. H.

It is the deep spring of my life, this love for men. Wellspring, The. Sharon Olds. BodElec

It is the earth that snarls and slashes with black jaguar. Earth Chorus. Juan Felipe Herrera. FTtHH

It is the evening. Nativity Poem. Louise Glück. GI; HarvBoo

It is the fashion now to wave aside. Edna St. Vincent Millay. HeIP-4

It is the first mild day of March. To My Sister. William Wordsworth. MakPoe; NPBRoP

It is the grass that moves, not the quails. Quails. Takahashi Shinkichi. ZenPo, *tr.* by Takashi Ikemoto and Lucien Stryk

It is the Harvest Moon! On gilded vanes. Harvest Moon, The. Henry Wadsworth Longfellow. APN-1

It is the heart of the night. Curfew. Teresa de Jesús. AF, *tr.* by Maria Proser

It is the hour of lamps. Harvard Classics. Henri Cole. NAMCP V.2

It is the immodesty we bring to these. Huguenot Graveyard at the Heart of the City, The. Eavan Boland. HarvBoo

It is the kindness of the rabbi I remember now, nine months. Grief. Robin Becker. TaR

It is the little girl. Franz Wright. BLT *Fr.* After Picasso.

It is the little stone of unhappiness. What I Have Written I Have Written. Peter Porter. BMAP; NOBAu

It is the middle of October. First Dimension of Skunk, The. Ray A. Young Bear. HATNAP

It is the middle of the night—I cannot sleep. Juan Chi. ColAnChi *Fr.* Songs of My Soul.

It is the miller's daughter. Miller's Daughter, The. Alfred Tennyson. OBEV

It is the movement that incites the form. Like Most Revelations. Richard Howard. OxBoAm

It is the nature of poets. Poets. James Laughlin. TAPaP

It is the old show, but the young son can fly. Father Knows Best. David Shapiro. OxBoAm

It is the old-time weights. Big Scales, The. Olav H. Hauge. WED, *tr.* by Robert Bly

It is the pain, it is the pain, endures. Villanelle. William Empson. HarvBoo; NAMCP V.1; NoAM; TRP; UV; WaAnP

It is the past that maketh my despair. Experience Too Late. Letitia Elizabeth Landon. RWP

It is the picnic with Ruth in the spring. Picnic, The. John Logan. NevBe; TRP

It is the rain, now unleashed, that you watch unravel through the bars of the wood-framed window. Knack for Slipping Away, A. José Luis Rivas. RMCMP, *tr.* by Susan Briante

It is the road to God. Road Home, The. Gillian Allnutt. NeBrP; StAl

It is the roots from all the trees that have died. Across the Swamp. Olav H. Hauge. RaBo; WED; WoPoe, *tr.* by Robert Bly

It is the Sabbath land, which calls to prayer. House of God, The. Bishop Richard Mant. SacPr

It is the saddest part of a sad story. Wiglaf. Marisa De Los Santos. NAPBL

It is the same as war, our sensations and words replaced in it (elation). Slaves' Outside Evening or Evening, Pal Mal Comic. Leslie Scalapino. Eno

It is the same each time. Daylight a broad blade. Milagros Mourns the Queen of Scat. Marisa De Los Santos. NAPBL

It is the season of meat. Cruising a Hungry World. Scott Hightower. BeDoSh

It is the sense, it is the sense, controls. Not Pastoral Enough. Veronica Forrest-Thomson. EdScPo

It is the soul that sees; the outward eyes. George Crabbe. OxAEP-1 *Fr.* Lover's Journey, The.

It is the sound of lions lapping. Bush. Josephine Jacobsen. NoP-4; NoP-5

It is the spot I came to seek. Indian at the Burial-Place [*or* Burying-Place] of His Fathers, An. William Cullen Bryant. APN-1

It is the stress that holds the structure up. Castle, The. Patricia K. Page. IFF

It is the sun's doing. River Song. Roberta Spear. GeoHom

It is the thing you do open a book. Dedicated to You. Reetika Vazirani. TAPaP

It Is the Third Watch. *Unknown.* WoPoe, *tr.* by Kevin O'Rourke

It is the third watch. The girl. It Is the Third Watch. *Unknown.* WoPoe, *tr.* by Kevin O'Rourke

It is the thunder is. Eden, Eden. Gwendolyn MacEwen. BrAP

It is the time of illusion and reality. January 30, 1976: Message to Myself. Bob Kaufman. PFTM-2

It is the time when. Kenneth Rexroth. APSN *Fr.* Love Poems of Marichiko, The.

It is the voice of my husband that calls. (LL) Flower of Gold. Pedro Pérez Conde. PoCho; RMCMP, *tr.* by Michael Wiegers

It is the wish of the general. Paragraph from English Speaking World. Clarence Major. EGAG

It is the writer's object. Lyn Hejinian. NAMCP V.2 *Fr.* Cell, The.

It is the year's end, the winds are blasting, and I. December 30th. Ivor Gurney. NAEL-6v2

It is these crisp November days. Gale Sayers. Ta-Nehisi Coates. BtF

It is this deep blankness is the real thing strange. Let It Go. William Empson. HarvBoo; NPeEn; OxBEV

It Is This Way with Men. C. K. Williams. RaBo; VCAP

It is 3:00 A.M. Shabbat. At the Wall. Vernice Wineera Pere. CFP

It is three o'clock in the morning. Trials of a Tourist. Anne Tibble. NBLV

It is Thursday, October 23rd. Ocean of the Streams of Story. Primus St. John. GT

It is time for the invocation. May Sarton. HW *Fr.* Invocation to Kali, The.

It is time for the others to come. Magus, The. James Dickey. GI

It is time for you to stop trying to be so smart. Advice. Suzanne Wise. LegDan

It is time to be old. Terminus. Ralph Waldo Emerson. APN-1; BrAP; GoPo; NCAP; TCAPo

It is time to think. Natalya Gorbanevskaya. TCRusP, *tr.* by Daniel Weissbort

It is to be without the staple references of male heterosexual poets. After Hearing Heterosexual Poets in October 1974: What It Seems Like To Write a Male Homosexual Love Poem Now. Joseph Cady. CAGL

It is to my people as a gift in their lap. Wulf and Eadwacer: A Woman's Lament. *Unknown*. WoPoe, *tr. by* Jonathan McKeage

It is to thee, my Derest Lord, that I. Sepr. ye 6th 1666 Thursday A Thanks Geving for the Stoping of the Fire in London. Elizabeth, Viscountess Mordaunt. EMWP

It is today you will come. Día de Los Muerto. Cynthia Harper. TiP2

It is too early for white boughs, too late. Mid-March. Lizette Woodworth Reese. SWaP

It is true, as someone has said, that in. Mark Strand. NoP-4; NoP-5 *Fr.* Dark Harbor.

It is true, fellow citizens. Edgar Lee Masters. APT-1 *Fr.* Spoon River Anthology.

It Is True. I Am Not a Poet the Way You Are. Biancamaria Frabotta. CItWP, *tr. by* Cinzia Sartini Blum and Lara Trubowitz

It is true; many cities conserve. More Chagall than Chagall. Luisa Futuransky. MirDau, *tr. by* Celeste Kostopulos-Cooperman

It is true, Martin Heidegger, as you have written. Envelope, The. Maxine W. Kumin. CFP; NALW

It is true that I believed in the immense privilege of living. Horse, The. Tristan Tzara. YaTCFP, *tr. by* Mary Ann Caws

It is twelve years since I have been there. Kartúshkiya-Beróza. Alter Brody. TaR

It is waking in the night. Fix. Michael Dransfield. NOBAu

It Is Well with My Soul. Horatio G. Spafford. SacPr

It is well—it is well with the child! (LL) Nativity, A. Rudyard Kipling. ChrPo; GI

It is what grammarians call a difference of tense and aspect. (LL) Anne Carson. OxBoAm; WoBe *Fr.* Truth About God, The.

It is what he does not know. On a Squirrel Crossing the Road in Autumn, in New England. Richard Eberhart. APT-2; HeIP-4

It is what recurs that we believe. If I Could Mourn Like a Mourning Dove. Frank Bidart. NAMCP V.2

It is what the river-merchant's wife writes her water-bound husband. Cho-Fu-Sa. Tanya Larkin. FreRad; IIR

It is what they do not say. (LL) German Requiem, A. James Fenton. HarvBoo; NAEL-6v2; NAEL-7v2; NAMCP V.2; NoAM; NoP-5; NPeEn

It is what, to tell the truth, you sometimes feel. History. Kelly Cherry. FFC

It is when gulfs and bays of blood. Punishments. Rafael Alberti. AF, *tr. by* Geoffrey Connell

It is when I hear Mozart. Deafness. Richard Ryan. PBCIP

It is windy today. A wall of wind crashes against. Cloudy Day. Jimmy Santiago Baca. LoL

It is wine-harvest, summer, the year's heart. Poem for Maurice O'Shea, A. Geoffrey Lehmann. NOBAu

It is winter again. Stopping to Take Notes. Michael Smith. PBCIP

It is winter and the new year. Mark Strand. NAMCP V.2 *Fr.* Elegy for My Father.

It Is Winter, I Know. Merrill Moore. MoAmPo

It is with sadness and hopelessness. Discrimination. *Unknown*. NAAPv.2

It is with the poet as with a guinea worm. To a Friend and Fellow Poet. Hugh MacDiarmid. NePenScot

It is world of the back hune wone it is. Emilio Villa. ItPo *Fr.* Words.

It is worthless to write a line. Chantars No Pot Gaire Valer. Bernard [*or* Bernart] de Ventadour *or* Ventadorn. APSN, *tr. by* Paul Blackburn

It is written in the Book of Usable Minutes. Train Rising Out of the Sea. John Ashbery. ColAP

It is wrong to stay here and talk forever, the sack of thunder. Money. Beckian Fritz Goldberg. AmAlph

It is your own soul you destroy, / not ours. (LL) Weeping Woman. Denise Levertov. AF; AmWaPo

It is yourself you seek. Man Alone. Louise Bogan. NoP-4; NoP-5

"It isn't a game for girls." Reaching Yellow River. Roberta Hill Whiteman. HATNAP

It isn't any of this. Nanni Cagnone. ItPo, *tr. by* Gayle Ridinger

It isn't Aphrodite, but wild Eros. Alcman. SaLy, *tr. by* Diane Rayor

It isn't as if I never enjoyed good wine. I'm Not Complaining. Philip Schultz. SoSe-8

It Isn't Gentleness. Francisco Segovia. RMCMP, *tr. by* Michael Wiegers

It isn't hard to see. We've Come This Far. Mona Lisa Saloy. FuFl

It isn't raining for me. Robert Loveman. ITBLP

It isn't that you were ignorant. From the Meadow. Peter Everwine. GeoHom

It isn't the body. Inner Man, The. Charles Simic. OPRER

It isn't the young men sprawling in chairs I mind. Old Professor, The. John Holmes. APT-2

It isn't very far as highways lie. Going to Walden. Mary Oliver. WhBo

It jangles in a mild breeze. Sean Dunne. ModIr *Fr.* Sydney Place.

It Just Doesn't Matter. Rodney M. McNeil. InTrad

It just so happens that I'm tired of being a man. Walkin' Around. Pablo Neruda. PFTM-1, *tr. by* Jerome Rothenberg

It keeps eternal whisperings around. On the Sea. John Keats. NoP-4

It keeps us awake. Fiasco, The. Walter Helmut Fritz. GTCP, *tr. by* Reinhold Grimm

It lay in my palm soft and trembled. Lorena. Lucille Clifton. CAP-8

It lies in our hands in crystals. Love Like Salt. Lisel Mueller. P180

It lies--when urged to, it lies. Nanni Cagnone. ItPo, *tr. by* Gayle Ridinger

It lieth, gazing on the midnight sky. On the Medusa of Leonardo da Vinci in the Florentine Gallery. Percy Bysshe Shelley. GS

It little profits that an idle king. Ulysses. Alfred Tennyson. AmFaPo; BLPJKO; BrAP; CABP; ClHu; CtM; HeIP-4; MakPoe; NAEL-6v2; NAEL-7v2; NAWM-7v2; NIL-7; NIP-4; NoP-4; NoP-5; NPeEn; OxAEP-2; OxBEV; PoPoPo; SoSe-8; TFi; TRP; WaAnP; WeW-3

It lives in the damps of rejection. Silverfish. Robert Siegel. PfSP

It looked extremely rocky for the Mudville nine that day. Casey at the Bat. Ernest Lawrence Thayer. ChAP; ITBLP

(Outlook wasn't brilliant for the Mudville nine that day, The.) AmFaPo; APN-2; BRP; CtM; FaBoA; ItP; OBCoV; OxBoAm; TCAPo

It looks like she's drowning. Gwyneth Lewis. NeBl

It looks to me like a hero's welcome. Anna Akhmatova's Funeral. Martin Mooney. ModIr

It makes me feel lonely when I realize the past simply does not exist. David McFadden. NLPA

It makes me grin to recall my innocence. Split. George Held. ArBi

It Makes Me Sad. Gary Daniel. OGAHCP, *tr. by* Boadiba and Jack Hirschman

It may be a little different. Blood to Blood. Alvin Aubert. OxAAAP

It may be that she wields a pen. Note. Mary Abigail Dodge (Gail Hamilton). SWaP

It may be true that she has passed her spring. Beauty of Ilona Zrínyi, The. István Gyöngyösi. IQMS, *tr. by* Watson Kirkconnell

It may indeed be phantasy [*or* fantasy], when I. To Nature. Samuel Taylor Coleridge. NPBRoP; OxBSo

It may of course be John his father-in-law. Stone Face, The. Harri Webb. AngWePo

It means / no madcap delight will intrude. What Her Absence Means. Christy Brown. IrLP

It means the place where the revelation. Oracle. Gale Renée Walden. RWB

It Might As Well Be Spring. Oscar Hammerstein, II. ReLy

It might be lonelier. Emily Dickinson. APN-2; SAmP; TCAPo

It might be so. (LL) Slice of Wedding Cake, A. Robert Graves. BrAP; NAEL-6v2; NAEL-7v2

It might have been a neurotic's paradise. Cana. Peter Steele. GI

It might mean immersion, that sign. Alice Fulton. ExTi

It might seem matter for regret. Lower Life, The. May Kendall. VWP

It mounts at sea, a concave wall. From the Wave. Thom Gunn. NAEL-6v2; NAEL-7v2; NoP-4; NoP-5

It moves out through the room. Polka. Diane Jarvenpa. MiVo

It must acknowledge the spiritual forces which have made it. (LL) When I Buy Pictures. Marianne Moore. APT-1; ColAP

It Must Be Abstract. Wallace Stevens. *Fr.* Notes toward a Supreme Fiction.

It must be done, my soul, but 'tis a strange. Meditation, The. John Norris. NOSC

It must be so--Plato, thou reason'st well. Joseph Addison. *Fr.* Cato.

It must be some disease I have. Like This (1). Stevie Smith. PtR

It must be that in the midst. Ed Roberson. EGAG

It must be there. In the ancient storeroom. Cost of Truth, The. Carlos Bousoño. RaW, *tr. by* Lewis Hyde

It must be troubling for the god who loves you. God Who Loves You, The. Carl Dennis. BeAl; PoDa

It must have been 1988. For Whom the Bells Toll and Toll and Toll. John Nelson. GeoH

It must have been after a. Present From Ted. Margaret Avison. GPPA

It must have been one o'clock at night. Comes to Rest. Constantine P. Cavafy. CAGL, *tr. by* Edmund Keeley and Philip Sherrard

It must have been Tom Stoppard. Film Version, The. Barry Spacks. IaFF

It must, it must be so! (LL) Image in Lava, The. Felicia Dorothea Hemans. CABP; NOBRP

It nearly cancels my fear of death, my dearest said. Cremation. Robinson Jeffers. BLT

It neither was the words nor yet the tune. Two Girls Singing. Iain Crichton Smith. EdScPo; NePenScot

It Never Entered My Mind. Lorenz Hart. ReLy

It Never Rains. Anthony Hecht. AmWit

It Never Was You. Maxwell Anderson. ReLy

It no longer overlooks the river. Jewel, The. Dunya Mikhail. IrPoTo, *tr. by* Salaam Yousif

It nods and curtseys and recovers. A. E. Housman. OxBEV *Fr.* Shropshire Lad, A.

It occurred on the evening before Waterloo. Old Sam. Stanley Holloway. OBCoV

It occurred to me there are no. Grassy Sound. A. R. Ammons. WaAnP

It occurs to me now. Lesson, The. Charles Simic. AF

It occurs to me that I would like to write a poem about Naples. Ungrateful Citizens, The. John Ash. NeBrP

It once happened. Issa. EH, tr. by Robert Hass

It once might have been, once only. Youth and Art. Robert Browning. NAEL-6v2; NPeEn

It only takes one night with the wind on its knees. Hysteria. Dionisio D. Martinez. NAMCP V.2

It out, run with it. (LL) Pet Panther. A. R. Ammons. NoP-4; NoP-5

It Out-Herods Herod. Pray You, Avoid It. Anthony Hecht. AF; NAMCP V.2; NIP-4; NoAM

It pales. As if a look. Horae. Robert Fitzgerald. APT-2

It passes, you'll remember, through lead. Passes through. Workmen Photographed inside the Reactor. David Wojahn. IllVoic

It pierces through me. Buson. WoPoe, tr. by Tony Barnstone

It Pleases. Gary Snyder. FaoP

It pours. Night Rain. Karen L. Mitchell. GT

It preens on a root at the edge of the igarapo. Conversation with the Sun Bittern. Ansel Talvikki. PoDa

It puzzles much the sages' brains. On Lord Cobham's Garden. Nathaniel Cotton. OBGa

It rained from dawn. The fire died in the night. Northern Morning, A. Alistair Elliot. StAl

It rained in my sleep. September. Linda Pastan. InvLad

It rained quite a lot, that spring. You woke in the morning. Metropolitan Nightmare. Stephen Vincent Benét. APT-2

It Rains. Edward Thomas. OxBEV

It rains above the sea in gentle murmurs. Gray Waves. Leopoldo Lugones. TCLAP, tr. by Julie Schumacher

It rains across the country I remember. (LL) Mnemosyne. Trumbull Stickney. APN-2; CtM; NAAPv.2; TCAPo

It rains, and nothing stirs within the fence. It Rains. Edward Thomas. OxBEV

It rains as I write this. Mad heart, be brave. (LL) Country Without a Post Office, The. Agha Shahid Ali. AmAlph; NAMCP V.2

It rains on the roofs. Sottoportico San Zaccaria. Kenneth Rexroth. ErotSp

It rattles dully on the roof. Rain. Konstantin Iakovlevich Vanshenkin. TCRusP, tr. by Daniel Weissbort

It really irks me to think I'm afraid of heights. Abyss. Diane Di Prima. BB

It rests in me, unmindful. A, B, C's, The. Imamu Amiri Baraka. EGAG

It rests me to be among beautiful women. Tame Cat. Ezra Pound. APT-1

It rises over the lake, the farms. Kite, The. Mark Strand. ColAP

It rises to self-awareness. Omoide no Tsukimi. Gus Blaisdell. ICANM

It rose dark as a stack of peat. Suilven. Andrew Young. EdScPo

It said on his report card, five years old, the boy. Can Tie Shoes but Won't. Thomas Lux. AmAlph

It says here. Adelaide's Lament. Frank Loesser. ReLy

It Says, I Did So. Mary Jo Bang. KGB

It scares me, the genius we have. Business of Love is Cruelty, The. Dean Young. SUP

It seconds the crickets of the province. Rocking Chair, The. Abraham Moses Klein. HeIP-4

(It seconds the crickets of the province. Heard.) BrAP; NoP-4

It seemed a dream of God—and now a memory. During a Friend's Illness. Gennady Aygi. WoBe, tr. by Peter France

It seemed a simple case of opulence. Herod's Palace. Gwyneth Lewis. HarvBoo

It seemed as if the enormous journey. Non-Stop. James Tate. BodElec

It seemed, at the time, so indifferent an age that I recall nothing of it except an infinite tedium to be endured. Poet Grows Older, The. Charles Wright. MotU

It seemed corrival of the world's great prime. Fallen Yew, A. Francis Thompson. MoBrPo

It seemed each morning he would never find the right words for the story. Post Script. Bret Lott. MAAN

It seemed that out of battle I escaped. Strange Meeting. Wilfred Owen. BrAP; FaBoWar; HarvBoo; HeIP-4; MakPoe; MoBrPo; NAEL-6v2; NAEL-7v2; NAMCP V.1; NoAM; NoP-4; NoP-5; OBWP; OxAEP-2; OxBEV; PoWW; TCAWP; TFi; WaAnP

It seemed the kind of life we wanted. Clouds Gathering. Charles Simic. ColAP

It seemed the obvious place to go, the sea. Cricketer's Retirement Day, The. Julia Copus. NeBl

It seemed / the sky was a harbor, into which rode. Casualty. Edwin Rolfe. APT-2

It seemed to me so much like you. In the Garden. Nissim Ezekiel. BrAP

It seemed to Pliny, stationed at Misenum. Pompeii: Plaster Casts. Peter Scupham. HarvBoo

It seems a certain time ago: a-maybe. One Time. Douglas Livingstone. NoP-4

It seems a day / (I speak of one from many singled out). Nutting. William Wordsworth. NAEL-6v2; NAEL-7v2; NOBRP; WaAnP

It seems a flower, but not a flower. Flower, A. Po Chü-i. TAL

It seems a stage. Gypsy's Window, The. Denise Levertov. CLPP

It seems as every ship their sovereign knows. John Dryden. STuOW Fr. Annus Mirabilis.

It seems everlasting, this mild delusive fall. Wishful Fall. Michael Thorpe. Coast

It seems I have no tears left. They should have fallen. Tears. Edward Thomas. NAEL-6v2; NAEL-7v2

It seems important to behave. Outbursts. In Intensive Care. Olivia Byard. PoCu

It seems me speaking all the lonely time. Soliloquy: South Africa. Arthur Nortje. TSAP

It seems my life now is surplus. I'm Surplus. Hwang Insuk. EcSo, tr. by Peter H. Lee

It seems my life will be spent. For Five Minutes. Na Hûidôk. EcSo, tr. by Peter H. Lee

It seems no day passes now. Family Procession, A. John Pepper Clark Bekedermo. HBAPE

It seems nothing can provoke. Eyes. Edip Cansever. NaPG, tr. by Talat Sait Halman

It seems our days are shaped by conflagration. Fire. Luis J. Rodriguez. UnSA

It seems that Aphrodite took with joy. Nossis. SaLy, tr. by Diane Rayor

It seems to be. (LL) Twice Times Then Is Now. Ibn Hazm al-Andalusi. OBVE; WoPoe, tr. by Omar S. Pound

It seems to be DARK all the time. Despair. John Berryman. ViWalt

It seems to be the time of bad gigs. Written in Bracing, Gray L.A. Rainlight. Al Young. SpirFl

"It seems to me," said Booker T. Booker T. and W. E. B. Dudley Randall. NoAM

It seems wrong that out of this bird. Blackbird Singing, A. Ronald Stuart Thomas. OBWVE

It semes white and is red. Sacrament of the Altar, The. Unknown. NoP-4; NoP-5

It shall suffice that they were breathed [or breath'd], and died [or dyed] for her delight. (LL) Follow your saint, follow with accents sweet. Thomas Campion. BASC; NOSC; NoSic; OxAEP-1

It shames one to look. Yury Timofeievich Galanskov. TCRusP, tr. by Daniel Weissbort

It shines in the garden. Garden, The. Mark Strand. ColAP; NoAM

It shines through clouds and rain. Echo and Elixir 1. Khaled Mattawa. LegDan

It should alarm no one that the horizon gathers up behind the leaves. Meditate. Gerardo Deniz. RMCMP, tr. by Mónica de la Torre

It should be in your nature to instantly trivialize anything. Advice to a Young Philosopher. Anselm Berrigan. HeMarv

It should have a woman's name. Lake in Central Park, The. Jay Wright. ESEAA; GT

It Shouldn't Happen to a Dream. Don George. ReLy

It sifts from Leaden Sieves. Snow, The. Emily Dickinson. MoW; SoSe-8; WHSW

It silvers the lawn. Moonlight. Michael Ryan. BodElec

It sinks; and I am ready to depart. (LL) Walter Savage Landor. NPeEn; OxBEV; TFi; TRP; UV Fr. Last Fruit Off an Old Tree, The.

It smells of sea and earth, of things dying and newly born. Hanoi Market, The. Yusef Komunyakaa. AmAlph

It snowed. Marmalade. Elizabeth Delmore. NLP

It snowed. It snowed comfortably. No, that's not it. In the beginning, it snowed violently. Snow. Yi Chinmyông. EcSo, tr. by Carolyn U. So

It snowed so much, a lady loved a gentleman so dearly. Lady of the Snow, The. Vivian Lamarque. CItWP, tr. by Cinzia Sartini Blum and Lara Trubowitz

It snows. December. Charles Simic. OxBoAm

It snows and stops, now it is January. Alicia Ostriker. ExTi Fr. Mastectomy Poems, The.

It so happens I am sick of being a man. Walking Around. Pablo Neruda. RaBo; WED, tr. by Robert Bly

It so happens I'm tired of just being a man. Walking Around. Pablo Neruda. TCLAP, tr. by Ben Belitt

It soars alone. Another Summit. Muso Soseki. EaWin, tr. by W. S. Merwin

It sometimes happens. Curse of the Cat Woman. Edward Field. WeW-3

It sometimes is very amusing. At least freer, the tulip-colored venom of the snow snake. Tompkins Sq. Branches With Snowy Arms. Lewis Ellingham. AHA

It soothes the savage doubts. Apocalypse. Dennis Joseph Enright. OBSV

It Sounded. Larry Eigner. FTOS

It sounded as if the Streets were running. Storm. Emily Dickinson. NAAL-3

It sounds like something that's been. Men There Were Then, The. Howard White. PML

It Speaks. Kang Ŭn'gyo. EcSo, *tr. by* Ann Y. Choi

It speaks, now and then. Phantom Pain. Linda Bierds. AmAlph

It stands in water, wrapper in heron. It makes. Heron. Norman Alexander MacCaig. EdScPo

It stands to reason. Wax crafted by bees. Sister Mary Appassionata Lectures the Eighth Grade Boys and Girls on the Nature of the Candle. David Citino. UpMys

It stands where northern willows weep. Queen of Prussia's Tomb, The. Felicia Dorothea Hemans. RWP

It Started. Jimmy Santiago Baca. LoL

It started about noon. On top of Mount Batte. Seeing the Eclipse in Maine. Robert Bly. InvLad

It started before Christmas. Now our son. Red Hat, The. Rachel Hadas. OxBoAm; RA; WaAnP

It started. First the salts. Geyser, The. Ágnes Nemes Nagy. PoSu, *tr. by* Bruce Berlind

It started with lapis lazuli. Glasshouse, The. Vona Groarke. NIrP

It started with the Greatest Hits album. On the Elvis Mailing List. Neal Bowers. AllShUp; SwNoth

It starts in the morning. Foreplay. Natasha Josefowitz. PasH

It starts in the park near Brentwood Primary School. Bright Cigar-Shaped Object Hovers Over Mount Pleasant, A. John Kinsella. NeBl

It starts in the pub, in the back room. Explaining the Declaration. Hans Magnus Enzensberger. BeAl, *tr. by* David Constantine

It starts in the small hours. An interlude. James Merrill. NoAM *Fr.* Mirabell: Books of Number.

It starts / inevitably / as something. Insomniac. M. Loncar. AmPoNex

It starts on the Lower East Side. Lower East Side: The George Bernstein Story. Edward Field. OBCoV

It starts to rain, and my blue. Moon Landing, 1969. Mary Jane Nealon. ArBi

It starts with the picture of my grandfather. Cloud Unfolding, The. Ernesto Trejo. FTtHH; LTA

It steals in through her screen. (LL) To the Tune: The Wine Spring: "Eternal autumn rain—evening sounds." Li Hsun. CrYelRi; ErotSp, *tr. by* Sam Hamill

It stifles me—God, must I sit and sew? (LL) I Sit and Sew. Alice Moore Dunbar-Nelson. InGu; NAAPv.2; NALW; WaAnP

It stood in the sunset sky. Barn and the Down, The. Edward Thomas. OxBEV

It stops the town we come through. Workers raise. Troop Train. Karl Shapiro. AmWaPo; APT-2; OxBoAm; PWW2; WaAnP

It strayed about her head and neck like a. Scarf, The. Brendan Kennelly. IrLP

It sushes. Cynthia in the Snow. Gwendolyn Brooks. TLR

It sweeps, as sweeps an army. Scale Force, Cumberland. Letitia Elizabeth Landon. NPBRoP; RWP

It takes a fast car. Lost Parents. Lawrence Ferlinghetti. ReTh

It takes a heap o' livin' in a house t' make it home. Home. Edgar Albert Guest. BRP; ITBLP

It takes a long time to make a meadow. Natural History. Chana Bloch. ASA

It takes a lot to get you there, but it won't. Beer. Gerald Locklin. SUP

It takes a mighty fire. H. D. Carberry. CA

It takes a very stupid dolt. *Unknown.* ColAnChi *Fr.* Classic of Odes.

It takes all sorts of in- and outdoor schooling. Robert Frost. SoSe-8

It takes life to love Life. (LL) Edgar Lee Masters. IllVoic; MoAmPo; NoAM *Fr.* Spoon River Anthology.

It takes so little. Midday. Cees Nooteboom. PML, *tr. by* Leonard Nathan and Herlinde Spahr

It takes two hands to turn the key. Locking the Church. David Scott. NLP

It taunts me. Desire's a Desire. Selima Hill. StAl

It / tears us whole. Tale That's Not a Tale, A. Binyo Ivanov. CSCBP, *tr. by* Georgi Belev and Lisa Sapinkopf

It terrifies me to go round with all my blood lodges between flesh and heart. Beacon. Pedro Serrano. RMCMP, *tr. by* Geoff Hargreaves

It Took a Village. Stephanie Brown. AmPoNex

It took generations to mature. Liberace. Jonathan Holden. ReTh

It took me ten days. In the Beginning Was the Word. Anna Hempstead Branch. APT-1

It Took One Hundred Years. Malika O'Lahsen. HAWP; WoPoe, *tr. by* Eric Sellin

It took 27 years to write this poem. Ruth. Colleen J. McElroy. OxAAAP

It took us both to water the new lawn. Watering the New Lawn. Michael S. Smith. PasH

It took Without to make Within a heaven. Within and Without. Elizabeth Jessup Blake. YaYoPo

It towers. Gem Mountain. Muso Soseki. EaWin, *tr. by* W. S. Merwin

It traces the irregularities of pavement. Gradually. Stuart Dybek. LiTh

It trails always behind me. Jamaica 1980. Lorna Goodison. GT; WaAnP

It trembled so the wind swept it away. Poplar Leaf, The. George Seferis. PFTM-1

It tried to get from out the cage. Cage, The. James Stephens. OxBEV

It turns out. Little Dantesque. James Galvin. BAP-01

It turns out you can have a daughter selling. Mama Loves Janis Joplin. Richard Speakes. SwNoth

It used to be at the bottom of the hill. Sea, The. E. A. Markham. EmeKit

It used to be that the rat was a cynic. Rat, The. Karen Kipp. BodElec

It walks the sky, cloudless. Ogiwara Seisensui. CAoMJL1, *tr. by* Janine Beichman

It wants to be dark, lavish. Love Poem. Barbara J. Orton. NeAmPo

It wants to say something. Why the Stone Remains Silent. William Kloefkorn. GifTon

It was 3.30 in the afternoon, mid-November. Soup and Sherry. George Bruce. EdScPo

It was 1945. Confessions of an Old Believer. Jim Burns. RSaN

It was 1945, and it was May. When I Was Conceived. Michael Ryan. NevBe

It was 1963 or 4, summer. Lesson. Forrest Hamer. P180

It was a bash! I Heard the Byrd. Oliver Lagrone. SeSe

It was a beautiful and silent day. William Wordsworth. OxAEP-2 *Fr.* Prelude, The; Growth of a Poet's Mind [1805 version].

It was a beauty that I saw. Ben Jonson. ItP *Fr.* New Inn, The.

It was a bird of Paradise. In London Town. Mary Elizabeth Coleridge. VWP

It was a bowl of roses. W. E. Henley. MoBrPo *Fr.* Hawthorn and Lavender.

It Was a Boy. Tracy Philpot. IAoNAP

It was a brave attempt! adventurous he. Launching Into Eternity. Isaac Watts. SacPr

It was a bright and cheerful afternoon. Summer and Winter. Percy Bysshe Shelley. OxAEP-2

It was a bright day and all the trees were still. Silence. Walter James Turner. MoBrPo

It was a chilly winter's night. Winter Night, A. William Barnes. WoPoe

It was a chosen plot of fertile land. Edmund Spenser. *See* Lo I the man, whose Muse whilome [*or* whylome] did maske.

It was a cool evening. Freeman Field. Marilyn Nelson Waniek. ESEAA

It was a dark, dank, dreadful night. Malfeasance, The. Alan Bold. OBSP

It was a day of slow fever. Someone else's life. Kapka Kassabova. BeAl

It was a day peculiar to this piece of the planet. Scotland. Alastair Reid. EdScPo; NePenScot

It was a dismal, and a fearful night. On the Death of Mr. William Hervey [*or* Harvey]. Abraham Cowley. OxAEP-1 *Fr.* On the Death of Mr. William Hervey [*or* Harvey].

It was a dismal and a fearful night. Abraham Cowley. OxAEP-1 *Fr.* On the Death of Mr. William Hervey [*or* Harvey].

It was a divine hour for the human race. Swan, The. Rubén Darío. TCLAP, *tr. by* Lysander Kemp

It was a dream and shouldn't I bother about a dream? Songe d'Athalie. Stevie Smith. OxBEV

It was a dream and you were walking through a field of hosannas. Abstract. Sam Hamill. BodElec

It was a dreary morning when the wheels. William Wordsworth. NAEL-6v2; NAEL-7v2 *Fr.* Prelude, The; Growth of a Poet's Mind [1850 version].

It Was a Gentle Air. Rubén Darío. TCLAP, *tr. by* Lysander Kemp

It was a gentle air, with turns and pauses. It Was a Gentle Air. Rubén Darío. TCLAP, *tr. by* Lysander Kemp

It was a glorious May morning. Victor Garibaldi. Melvin B. Tolson. GT

It was a good day and I was about to do something important. Precision German Craftsmanship. Matthew Rohrer. NAPBL; NeAmPo

It was a good word once, a little sparkler. Protest Poem. Vernon Scannell. OBCoV

It was a good year, he says at the top of the new hotel. As If I Knew. Max Winter. FreRad

It was a graveyard scene. The crescent moon. Great Unaffected Vampires and the Moon. Stevie Smith. NoAM

It was a heartfelt game, when it began. Portrait. Judith Wright. SoSe-8

It was a honey time there in the valley. Honey. Diane Levy. WhBo

It was a house of female habitation. House of Mercy, A. Stevie Smith. HarvBoo; MoWP; NAMCP V.1

It was a kind and northern face. Praise for an Urn. Hart Crane. MoAmPo; NAAPv.2; NoAM; WeW-3

It Was a Long Time Before. Leslie Marmon Silko. NoAM

It was a long way round from. For Norman Nicholson. David Scott. NLP

It was a lovely night. William Robert Rodgers. PNI *Fr.* Resurrection: An Easter Sequence.

It was a lover and his lass. William Shakespeare. NoSic; OBEV; TFi *Fr.* As You Like It.

It Was a Lover and His Lass. William Shakespeare. *See* Country Song.

It was a Maine lobster town. Water. Robert Lowell. HeIP-4; NoP-4; NoP-5

It was a mild Christmas, the small fine rain kept washing over. She Replies to Carmel's Letter. Kerry Hardie. BeAl; NIrP

It was a mild spring. Kitchen Beast. Amanda Dalton. NeBl

It was a misunderstanding. Man of the House. Bob Hicok. SUP

It was a night like this, at the end of summer. Balcony, The. Louise Glück. CAP-8

It was a night of early spring. Wisdom. Sara Teasdale. MoAmPo

It was a night when the planets. Perspective Lovesong. "Ern Malley." BMAP

It was a November night of wind. Anne Carson. OxBoAm; WoBe *Fr.* Truth About God, The.

It was a party; I had on my party dress. Origins. Joan Larkin. WiU

It was a picture I had after the war. Lamb, The. Linda Gregg. CFP

It was a place where apples sprouted teeth. Childhood. Chitra Divakaruni. OpBo

It was a poignant moment. Howl, Howl. Christopher Reid. OBCoV

It was a polo match played by royal order. *Various authors.* CATKP *Fr.* Songs of Flying Dragons.

It was a quiet way—. Emily Dickinson. NCAP

It was a real well, real. Old Wives' Tales. Constance Urdang. PBCAP

It was a ritual. Rosa's Beauty. Jane Alberdeston Coralin. BRtP

It was a school where all the children wore darned worsted. Fond Memory. Eavan Boland. ModIr; NAMCP V.2

It Was a Season Tattooed on the Forehead of the Earth. Venus Khoury-Gata. PoArWo, *tr. by* Lucy McNair

It was a small, private school and the walls told. Elegy for a Professor. Nicholas Samaras. TWW

It was a summer evening. Sentences While Remembering Hiraethog. T. Glynne Davies. OBWVE, *tr. by* R. Gerallt Jones

It was a summer [*or* summer's] evening. Battle of Blenheim, The. Robert Southey. BRP; CABP; FaBoWar; NPBRoP; OBWP; TFi; WaAnP ('Twas a summer evening.) UV

It was a Summer's night, a close warm night. William Wordsworth. MakPoe *Fr.* Prelude, The; Growth of a Poet's Mind [1805 version; Selections from Anthologies].

It was a tall young oysterman lived by the river-side. Ballad of the Oysterman, The. Oliver Wendell Holmes. TCAPo

It was a testimony. Gregory's House. David Huddle. PBCAP

It was a time of lies and infamy. All Spain. Young Spain, A. Antonio Machado Ruiz. RaW, *tr. by* Charles Guenther

It was a time, that summer '66. I Wanna Be Black. Michelle T. Clinton. InTrad

It was a time when wise men. Period. Ronald Stuart Thomas. HarvBoo

It was a trance: thieves, clowns, and the blind girl. Clamor. Ann Lauterbach. PmAP

It was a useless thing to do with the morning. Buffalo Clouds over the Maestro Hoon. Norman Dubie. AmAlph

It Was a Very Good Year. Ervin Drake. ReLy

It was a village built in a green rent. Brothers, and a Sermon. Jean Ingelow.

It was a vision he had, a candle he lit. Idea of Love Between Us, The. Kate Light. AmPoNex

It was a waning crescent. July Dawn. Louise Bogan. AWTN

It was a way a day, this made some sum. Gertrude Stein. NAMCP V.1 *Fr.* Tender Buttons.

It was a way of punishing the house, setting it a blaze. Interior at Petworth: From Turner. Rosanna Warren. NoAM

It was a wing, it was a kiss. Fall. Silvia Curbelo. NevBe

It was a winter's morning. Harry Graham. UV *Fr.* Battue of Berlin, The.

It was about the deep of night. Ballad of Christmas, A. Walter De la Mare. OBCP

It was about the Martinmas time. Barbara Allan. *Unknown.* BrAP (It was in and about the Martinmas time.) NoP-4; WaAnP

It was after vespers one evening. Low Church. Stanley J. Sharpless. NBLV; OBCoV

It was after war; Edward Thomas had fallen at Arras. Mangel-Bury, The. Ivor Gurney. HarvBoo

It was after we laid the infant. Leaf. Cathy Song. ExTi

It was afternoon tea, with tea foods spread out. Coffee in the Afternoon. Alberto A. Ríos. P180

It was afterwards. Another Love Affair/Another Poem. E. Ethelbert Miller. ISC

It was agreed we would not mount by those. Jacob's Ladder. Donald Davie. OxBSo

It Was All for Him. Amin Al-Rihani. NAAPv.2

It was all go with the jazz-band and all go with the dance. Cynan. BBMWP *Fr.* Prodigal Son, The.

It was all like a childhood picture. Cuckoo. Robert Desnos. PFTM-1

It was all so different from what she'd expected. At Thirty-Three. Hans Magnus Enzensberger. VCWP, *tr. by* the author, Hans Magnus Enzensberger and Michael Hamburger

It was all the clods at once become. Earth Dweller. William Stafford. BeAl; IPoFL

It Was All Very Tidy. Robert Graves. NPeEn

It was already too late. Lightning Spreads Out across the Water. Patricia Fargnoli. PoDa

It was an adventure much could be made of: a walk. Orpheus Alone. Mark Strand. OxBoAm

It was an Artless Poster Girl pinned up against my wall. Poster Girl's Defence, The. Carolyn Wells. SWaP

It was an evening in November. Pig, The. *Unknown.* OBCoV

It was an icy day. Complete Destruction. William Carlos Williams. SAmP

It was an open-air market in full swing midday February 1994. It was an open-air market. Adrian Oktenberg. AmWaPo

It was and on was so. Story, The. Carly Sachs. BAP-04

It was announced in the *Daily Times*, the *New Nigerian.* Launching Our Community Developement Fund. Tanure Ojaide. HBAPE

It was as if. Spring Song. Peter Fallon. PBCIP

It was as if God had taken a pen of fire. American Apocalypse. Edward Hirsch. IllVoic

It was as if she couldn't know herself. Only other persons could do that. Transmutation. Gael Turnbull. BeAl

It was astonishing to walk into room 233 at the Days Inn. Days Inn. Linda Smukler. WiU

It was at My Lai or Sonmy or something. Women, Children, Babies, Cows, Cats. Robert Lowell. PoAgWa

It was at the far edge of the far edge. Third World. Christina Rivera-Garza. SPV, *tr. by* Jen Hofer

It was at the Noon Bridge we were drinking—. Tune: "Immortal at the Riverbank." Ch'en Yü-yi. ColAnChi, *tr. by* Jiaosheng Wang

It was at the roadside pavilion that we were to bid adieu. Tune: "Bells Ringing in the Rain." Liu Yung. ColAnChi, *tr. by* Jiaosheng Wang

It was august, i was inner city. Friendly Town #1. Safiya Henderson-Holmes. UnSA

It was beautiful as God. White Tiger, The. Ronald Stuart Thomas. AngWePo

It was before the white wicker basket fell. Bicycle, The. Risa Lichtman. ArBi

It was beloved old man Clay who used to say. State's Claim That It Seeks in No Way to Deprive Indians of Their Rightful Share of Water, The. Simon J. Ortiz. ICANM

It was better. Sin, 1969. Afaa Michael Weaver. BtF

It was bleak december just last night or the night. New Philosophy of Composition, or, How to Ignore the Non-Reasoning Creature Capable of *Speeech* Perched Outside Your Bathroom Window, A. Olena Kalytiak Davis. NAPBL

It was blood ice and a kind of fog. Making Love in the Meat Locker. Robert Masterson. ICANM

It was booze made my boss talk of Stalin's days. Hospital Gypsy Song. Aleksandr Arkadevich Galich. TCRusP, *tr. by* Gerry Smith

It was boss cook's fault. He left. Tip, The. Belle Waring. PBCAP

It was by such a state of logical perpendiculars. Thinking the Alps. Michael Davidson. PmAP

It was clear when I left the party. Old Man Leaves Party. Mark Strand. PoDa

It was cold and windy, scarcely the day. End of March, The. Elizabeth Bishop. NAMCP V.2

It was cold in that room, after the cold hours. My Grandmother Died in the Early Hours of the Morning. T. Harri Jones. AngWePo; TCAWP

It was cropping time the night. Brent MacLaine. Coast *Fr.* Story of My Land, The.

It was dark / coming into Pittsburgh. We Want More Say. John Beecher. InGu

It was dawn when the wolf turned away from me. Wolf, The. Jennifer Grotz. LegDan

It was day. I felt I had to leave the village. I did. Before long. Farmer, The. Kees Ouwens. TuT, *tr. by* Peter van de Kamp

It was deep April, and the morn. Michael Field. NAEL-7v2; ViWPN; VWP

It was déjà vu all over again. Proverbs from Purgatory. Lloyd Schwartz. PtR

It was Delilah who mercilessly. Doré V. José Manuel del Pino. PML, *tr. by* G. F. Racz

It was early, early all in the Spring. My Boy Willie. *Unknown.* MakPoe

It Was Early Evening. Víctor Terán. RMCMP, *tr. by* Donald Frischmann

It was early in the morning. Goodhousekeeping #17. Safiya Henderson-Holmes. ISC

It was Easter as I walked in the public gardens. 1929. W. H. Auden. OxAEP-2

It was $8,000 with a GI loan. Floor Plans. Maxine Scates. PBCAP

It was evening. We went to sleep, Laila and I. We were lovers. Laila's Face. Nasri Hajjaj. Eno, tr. by Ibrahim Muhawi

It was everywhere, in the streets and houses. Sadness. Stephen Dunn. StAl

It was exactly eleven. Pawiak 1943. Jerzy Ficowski. PoSu, tr. by Frank J. Corliss, Jr. and Grazyna Sandel

It was exhausting. To Love a Stranger. Sibby Anderson-Thompkins. InTrad

It was extraordinarily clear. River 1. José Luis Rivas. RMCMP, tr. by Alastair Reid

It was fabulous, what the body told. (LL) What the Body Told. Rafael Campo. AmPoNex; BloBone; NeAmPo; WiU

It Was Fever That Made the World. Jim Powell. NIP-4; SwNoth

It was first marching, hardly we had settled yet. First March. Ivor Gurney. OxBEV

It was for this that man came into the world, to fight. Chapter and Verse. Gonzalo Rojas. TCLAP, tr. by Christopher Maurer

It was four days before the Chongyang Festival. Unknown. NAAPv.2

It was fuck this, fuck that. Men's Talk. Len Roberts. PML

It was general conflagration. (LL) Devil's Thoughts, The. Samuel Taylor Coleridge and Robert Southey. NPBRoP; OBSV

It was genuine—real fox. Cross Country. Ann Sansom. MFPA

It was gonna be his ticket home just a flesh wound you know like. Just squeeze. Terry Hertzler. SUP

It was good. Love Song, A. Lindiwe Mabuza. HAWP

It was good when you were here. Paul Goodman. BodElec

It was here, in the long red meadow. Two Rivers. Hilary Llewellyn-Williams. AngWePo; TCAWP

It was high summer. Please the Carrots. Dave Brinks. AnSo

It was him, Elvis, sheepishly. Elvis at the End of History. Fleda Brown Jackson. AllShUp

It was his story. It would always be his story. In Memory of the Unknown Poet, Robert Boardman Vaughn. Donald Justice. CAP-8; NAMCP V.2; NoAM; WaAnP

It was hot. A size too large. High Holy Days. Jane Shore. NoP-4; NoP-5

It was hot. The forest burnt. Time. Monkey. Vladislav Felitsianovich Khodasevich. TCRusP, tr. by Daniel Weissbort

It was iMpossible. 25 Mesostics Re and Not Re Mark Tobey. John Cage. PmAP

It was in Abomey that I felt. Dahomey. Audre Lorde. PfS

It was in an empty lot. How I Learned English. Gregory Djanikian. UnSA

It was in and about the Martinmas time. Unknown. See It was about the Martinmas time.

It was in Berlin you mixed up John and J. J. Cale. Early to Bed, Early to Rise. Mark Ford. NeBrP

It was in June the eight and thirtieth day. John Taylor. NOSC Fr. Sir Gregory Nonsense's News from No Place.

It was in the Spring of 1825. Noel Petty. UV

It was in the transept of the church, winter in. Haunted Importantly. Jack Gilbert. WaAnP

It was in winter. Steeples, spires. Fortunate Traveller, The. Derek Walcott. NAMCP V.2; NoAM

It was insane. I thought it myself. The winter. First Reader Santee Training School, 1873, The. Diane Glancy. LTA

It was just a gas station. It was not spectacular carnage. World, The. Gillian Conoley. BodElec; RoV

It was just across the border. Ensenada Wedding. Robert Thomas. FaoP

It was just this summer I began to forgive. I was six, all cow-. Martin. Pamela Stewart. ExTi

It was last spring. Impression of Exile. Luis Cernuda. RaW, tr. by Hardie St. Martin

It was late last night when my lord came home. Cyril Connolly. OBCoV Fr. Where Engels Fears to Tread.

It was late on a winter's evening. Autobiography. John Burnside. NePenScot

It was late September. I'd just poured a glass of wine, begun. Mrs Midas. Carol Ann Duffy. BeAl; P180

It was light. Whoever it was. Evening with Stars. Srikanth Reddy. LegDan

It was like a church to me. Moor, The. Ronald Stuart Thomas. OBWVE; WaAnP

It was like a stream. Mahadevi. WPoS

It was like keeping a puppy in your underpants. Puppy Called Puberty, A. Adrian Mitchell. StAl

It was like soul-kissing, the way the words. How I Discovered Poetry. Marilyn Nelson. ExTi

It was like the moment when a bird decides not to eat from your hand. Part of Eve's Discussion. Marie Howe. P180

It was like this: / you were happy, then you were sad. It Was Like This : You Were Happy. Jane Hirshfield. AmZen

It was lit at the bride's hearth while she played. Take: A Roman Wedding. Alice Fulton. ExTi

It was love at first sight, on the Staten Island ferry. Bare Bones. Kenward Elmslie. NYP2

It was lying near my back porch. Traveling Through the Yard. Rae Armantrout. OxBoAm

It was many and many a year ago. Samuel Brown. Phoebe Cary. APN-2; NAAPv.1

It was many and many a year ago. Annabel Lee. Edgar Allan Poe. BLPJKO; BRP; ChAP; HeIP-4; ITBLP; NAAL-3; NAAL-5; NAAPv.1; NCAP; NoP-5; OBSP; OxBoAm; TCAPo; TFi

It was Montmartre. Mam'selle. Mack Gordon. ReLy

It was my birthday. I was half child, sensing by their feel which scenes I would remember. Pretty. Jayne Anne Phillips. MotU

It was my bridal night I remember. I Remember. Stevie Smith. NIL-7; PoAgWa

It was my desire that fashioned you. Fabulation. Elsa Cross. RMCMP, tr. by Margaret Sayers Peden

It was my fate to help Billy Redanz learn how to read. Story of My Life, The. Liz Rosenberg. PBCAP

It was my fifth year to heaven. Christopher Robin Changes Guard with Dylan Thomas. Bill Greenwell. UV

It was (my love told me) my sister. For C., Who Died of Childbirth at the Age of One Year and Eleven Months. Giovanni Raboni. ItPo, tr. by Gayle Ridinger

It was my thirtieth year to heaven. Poem in October. Dylan Thomas. AngWePo; NAEL-6v2; NAEL-7v2; NAMCP V.2; NoAM; NPeEn; OxAEP-2; PoA 2002; SoSe-8; TCAWP; UV

It was near a thicky shade. Description of the Shepherd and His Wife, The. Robert Greene. NoSic

It was near evening, the room was cold. Oath, The. Allen Tate. InGu

It was near the Coliseum, RKO, / in the Bronx. Laughing Gas. Ruth Whitman. UnSA

It was nearly seven thousand years ago. Lady of Pazardzik. Starr Goode. HW

It was never too strong for us. Arabic Coffee. Naomi Shihab Nye. AFaM

It was night I met you. Two Beautiful Creatures. Promise Ogochukwu Okekwe. NeNiPo

It was night in one of the old cities. Humanity. T. Gwynn Jones. BBMWP, tr. by Gillian Clarke

It was no vast dynastic fate. Father's Death, A. John Hewitt. PNI

It was not all right when we got to your car and I saw the boxes. In the Upstairs Window. Carol Potter. PfS

It was not always so. The shaping hand. Birth of the Smile, The. Rainer Maria Rilke. EroLit, tr. by J. B. Leishman

It was not Death, for I stood up. Emily Dickinson. APN-2; NAAL-3; NAAL-5; NAAPv.1; OxBoAm; SAmP; TCAPo

It was not dying: everybody died. Losses. Randall Jarrell. AmFaPo; AmWaPo; BrAP; OtW; PoA 2002

It was not evil, though it looked that way. Anniversary Trip. James Hoggard. TiP2

It was not I who began it. Eve to Her Daughters. Judith Wright. NALW; NoP-4; NoP-5

It was not like your great and gracious ways. Coventry Patmore. OBEV Fr. Unknown Eros, The.

It was not love. No flowers or ripened figs. Immaculate Conception. Louise Erdrich. BBASP

It was not meant for human eyes. Combat, The. Edwin Muir. MoBrPo

It was not that you were pure. Possibiliites: Remembering Malcolm X. Haki R. Madhubuti. SpirFl

It was not to them I wanted to speak. Love. Sarah Arvio. PoCho

It was not warm. Innocency or Not Song X. Gerald Early. BodElec

It was nothing more than a Neapolitan Christmas creche. The light. Horrible Today, The. Max Jacob. AF, tr. by Ron Padgett

It was October. It was the Depression. Money. Tale of Time. Robert Penn Warren. NAAPv.2

It was October once, fragile as. In the Beginning. Jill Alexander Essbaum. NAPBL

It was official, in an American sort of way. Homesteading. Eva Salzman. MFPA

It was on one Monday morning just about one o'clock. Titanic, The. Unknown. APT-3

It was on the floor, being X-ed out by her long. Marianne Faithfull's Cigarette. Gerry Gomez Pearlberg. WiU

It was only a coincidence / The tree rows in orchards are capable of patterns. It Was Only a Coincidence. Lyn Hejinian. CalPo

It was only a small place and they had cheered us too much. St. Aubin d'Aubigne. Paul Dehn. OBWP

It was only important. Moss of His Skin, The. Anne Sexton. NALW

It was only yesterday. Singer Has Aged, The. Badr Shakir al-Sayyab. IrPoTo, *tr. by* Ibtisam Barakat

It was only yesterday. Gone with the Wind. Herb Magidson. ReLy

It was over at Isândula, the bloody work was done. Fight at Rorke's Drift, The. Emily Jane Pfeiffer. ViWPN

It was over here that my love, in his mercy. Michelangelo Buonarroti. CAGL, *tr. by* James M. Saslow

It was over Target Berlin the flak shot up our plane. World War II. Edward Field. PWW2

It was perfect. He could do. Other. Ronald Stuart Thomas. AngWePo

It was pneumonia. Lament of the Virtues and Verses on Account of the Death of Don Guido. Antonio Machado Ruiz. OBVE

It was probably raining. Calgary Bay. Margaret Gillies Brown. EdScPo

It was Puerto Rico waking up inside her. Puerto Rico waking her. Puertoricanness. Aurora Levins Morales. PueRic

It Was Raining in Delft. Peter Gizzi. IIR

It was really me who came up with that. Fourth Supreme, The. Allison Joseph. BtF

It was reasonable. Last Days. Donald Hall. InoFa

It was rumored on the block. Figure Motioned with Its Mangled Hand Toward the Wall Behind It, The. Kenneth Patchen. APT-2

It was seven or eight years ago. Secret Love. Behçet Necatigil. NaPG, *tr. by* Talat Sait Halman

It was shattered. Battle of Maldon, The. *Unknown.* OBWP, *tr. by* Kevin Crossley-Holland

It was shattered. *Unknown.* OBWP

It was Sir Christopher Gardiner. Rhyme of Sir Christopher, The. Henry Wadsworth Longfellow. NCAP

It was six men of Hindostan. Blind Men and the Elephant, The. John Godfrey Saxe. ITBLP

  (It was six men of Indostan.) BRP

It was six men of Indostan. John Godfrey Saxe. *See* It was six men of Hindostan.

It was snowing. For the first time, conquered. Victor Hugo. WoPoe *Fr.* Expiation.

It was / so hot. Malcolm de Chazal. SonAtl, *tr. by* Gregory Beaven and Kurt Ganzl

It was solitary and serene. Birds' Refuge, The. Sojourner Kincaid Rolle. GeoHom

It was something I'd overheard. Lucifer in Starlight. David St. John. CAP-8

It was spring, saturday. To Hell and Back, with Cake. Safiya Henderson-Holmes. UnSA

It was strange. Taino. Jose Angel Figueroa. PueRic

It was such a pearly, pink season. Tatyana Rizdvenko. CRWP

It was such a pretty little donkey. Donkey, The. Stevie Smith. HarvBoo

It was summer. Summer or Its Ending. Yehuda Amichai. PoSu, *tr. by* Dennis Silk

It was Summer, all the time. When Mark Deloach Ruled the World. Dominique Parker. SpirFl

It was Sunday in the fair ears of my burro. César Vallejo. TCLAP, *tr. by* Clayton Eshleman

It was taken some time ago. This Is a Photograph of Me. Margaret Atwood. BrAP; NALW; NAMCP V.2; NoAM; NoP-5

It was that fierce contested field when Chickamauga lay. Thomas at Chickamauga. Kate Brownlee Sherwood. PCW

It was that rainy summer night. Love Jam. Everett Hoagland. BRtP

It was the Age of Reason. Swallows and Tortoises. Neil Curry. NLP

It was the arrival of the kings. Adoration of the Magi, The. Christopher Pilling. OBCP

It was the Bastot Maulion. Orthone. Philip Pendleton Cooke. APN-1

It was the colour of incense. Womanhood, The. Elizabeth Garrett. MFPA

It was the day when the sun's rays turned pale with grief for his. Petrarch. NAWM-7v1 *Fr.* Sonnets to Laura.

It was the dead who groaned within! (LL) Sleeper, The. Edgar Allan Poe. BrAP; NAAL-3; NCAP

It was the dingiest bird. Robin Redbreast. Stanley Kunitz. CAP-8; NoP-4; NoP-5

It was the first day of the war. Silence. Bella Abramovna Dizhur. ItGoST, *tr. by* Sarah Bliumis

It was the first gift he ever gave her. Black Lace Fan My Mother Gave Me, The. Eavan Boland. HarvBoo; ModIr; MoWP; NPeEn

It was the first week of the falling year. Young Man of Galway's Lament, The. James Harpur. IrLP

It was the flowery season of the year. Luis de Góngora y Argote. SpanPo *Fr.* Solitudes, The.

It was the frosty early hours when finally. Weakness, The. Bernard O'Donoghue. ModIr; NoP-4

It was the garden of the golden apples. Long Garden, The. Patrick Kavanagh. HarvBoo; OBGa

It was the middle of the night and I had lived. Mt. Pisgah. James Kimbrell. NAPBL

It was the morning of that blessed day. Petrarch. NAWM-5v1 *Fr.* Sonnets to Laura.

It was the New Year's Eve explosion: chaos of mud and snow, crisscrossed by a thousand carriages. Joker, A. Charles Baudelaire. MotU, *tr. by* Edward K. Kaplan

It was the Rainbow gave thee birth. Kingfisher, The. W. H. Davies. AngWePo; OBEV; OBWVE

It was the saints drove him out. Departures. David Helwig. Coast

It was the schooner *Hesperus.* Wreck of the Hesperus, The. Henry Wadsworth Longfellow. APN-1; BRP; NAAPv.1; OBNV; TCAPo; TreFP

It was the shortest night of the year. I'd been drinking. Stealing the Genre. Carol Rumens. MoWP

It was the sound mostly. Tassajara, Early 1970's. Diane Di Prima. WANABP

It was the sound of darkness, mother said. Dark Angel. Kevin Hart. StAl

It was the Southern drifting over the flats on a hundred low trestles. Recent Past, The. C. S. Giscombe. GT; OxAAAP

It was the spring after my sister died that I began to notice the moths. From a Paris Hotel Room. Jennifer Bartlett. ICANM

It was the time before. Tear. Linda Hogan. ExTi

It was the time that Rigby. Rigby. Mark Todd. GeoH

It was the twilight of the iguana. Some Beasts. Pablo Neruda. TCLAP, *tr. by* James Wright

It was the winter I had to get away. Men Talk. Stephen P. Dunn. NIP-4

It was the winter wild[e]. John Milton. OBEV *Fr.* On the Morning of Christ's Nativity.

It was the winter wild[e]. John Milton. NPeEn; OxBEV *Fr.* On the Morning of Christ's Nativity.

It was their fate to live in a strange time. Juan Lopez and John Ward. Jorge Luis Borges. FaBoWar, *tr. by* Rodolfo Torragno

It was then night: the sound[e] and quiet sleep [*or* slepe]. Virgil. MakPoe *Fr.* Aeneid [*or* Eneados *or* Aeneis], The.

It was then that destiny decided to take me by the hand. Destiny. Maria Luisa Spaziani. NeIt, *tr. by* Beverly Allen

It was three slim does and a ten-tined buck in the bracken lay. Revenge of Hamish, The. Sidney Lanier. APN-2; NCAP

It was time for the screaming to stop. 3 Poems for Benedetta Barzini. Gerard Malanga. AHA

It was time when children bound to meet. Switzer's Wife, The. Felicia Dorothea Hemans. RWP

It was Tiny's habit. Sketches of Harlem. David Henderson. EGAG

It was too late for Man. Emily Dickinson. BBASP

It was too late; we were tragically hip. (LL) Blunts. Major L. Jackson. LegDan; SpirFl

It was too lonely for her there. Robert Frost. RaBo; TCAPo *Fr.* Hill Wife, The.

It was too soon. Water and Light. Noah Blaustein. MoASP

It Was upon a Lammas Night. Robert Burns. NPBRoP

It was upon the twilight of that day. Samuel Daniel. OBWP *Fr.* Civil Wars, The.

It was very funny, Grypus. Publius Papinius Statius. RomPo *Fr.* Sylvae [*or* Silvae].

It Was War. Miryana Basheva. CSCBP, *tr. by* Georgi Belev and Lisa Sapinkopf

It was wet and white and swift and where I am. Snow Line. John Berryman. PoA 2002

It was what you might as well wish for. Moon in a Mason Jar. Robert Wrigley. RoV

It was when we were living. When My Grandmother Said "Pussy." Carole Bernstein. AmPoNex; UnSA

It was when you were dying and you. Cave of AIDS, The. Mark Scott. PoA 2002

It was where the wooden bridge. Dora Markus. Eugenio Montale. PoetW, *tr. by* William Arrowsmith

It was wild. Assassination. Haki R. Madhubuti. GT

It was winter. We Were Three. Claribel Alegría. AF; TCLAP, *tr. by* Carolyn Forché

It was winter. Boris Leonidovich Pasternak. GI

It was winter and already dusky in town. Rejected Gift, The. Ida G. M. Gerhardt. TuT, *tr. by* Peter van de Kamp

It was Winter in Manhattan. Violets for Your Furs. Tom Adair. ReLy

It was winter. The wind. Christmas Star, The. Boris Leonidovich Pasternak. WoPoe, *tr. by* Nina Kossman

It was with resolution that she gave up the. Ice Eagle, The. Diane Wakoski. PFTM-2

It was yesterday morning. Little Old Letter. Langston Hughes. SAmP

It was your birthday, we had drunk and dined. Hug, The. Thom Gunn. HarvBoo; NPeEn; StAl

It was your lightness that drew me. Lightness. Meg Bateman. EdScPo; NePenScot; StAl, tr. by the author

It was your resting-place. (LL) Ah, Are You Digging on My Grave? Thomas Hardy. MoBrPo; NAEL-6v2; NAEL-7v2

It wasn't about no woman. He Was a Man. Sterling Allen Brown. InGu

It wasn't by chance that Marpessa preferred Idas over Apollo. Marpessa's Choice. Yannis Ritsos. VCWP, tr. by Edmund Keeley

It wasn't easy. I had to get him. Moving God. Pattiann Rogers. TiP2

It wasn't Ernest; it wasn't Scott. Song for the Squeeze-Box. Theodore Roethke. NBLV

It wasn't just about sex, but about. Longing. Rane Arroyo. BeDoSh

It wasn't on Crete, but in the hills of Berkeley. Night Blooming Jasmine. Diane Wakoski. GeoHom

It wasn't only envy but also a vague desire. Christmas Story, A. Alan Shapiro. TaR

It wasn't Oscar Wilde who said, "Die, my dear." Last Words. William Matthews. PoA 2002

It wasn't our battalion, but we lay alongside it. Sergeant-Major Money. Robert Graves. FaBoWar; OBWP

It wasn't so long ago, i tell you in a stream. See No Indian, Hear No Indian. Victoria Lena Manyarrows. TWW

It wasn't that she didn't recognize him in the light from the. Yannis Ritsos. VCWP

It wasn't the leaves that descended upon you. Chrysalis. Sherwin Bitsui. LegDan

It Wasn't the Love of Others or Mine. Gabriella Leto. CItWP, tr. by Cinzia Sartini Blum and Lara Trubowitz

It wasn't the rooster's familiar cry. Birds That Woke Us: An Urban Pastoral, The. Jeffrey Harrison. UrbNat

It waved not through an Eastern sky. Palm Tree, The. Felicia Dorothea Hemans. ViWPN

It well may be. I do not think I would. (LL) Love is not all: it is not meat nor drink. Edna St. Vincent Millay. APT-1; GSo; HeIP-4; NAAPv.2; NAMCP V.1; NoAM; OxBoAm; WaAnP

It went many years. Lockless Door, The. Robert Frost. TCAPo

It were my soul's desire. Soul's Desire, The. Unknown. SacPr, tr. by Eleanor Hull

It wes upon a shere thorsday that our lord aros. Unknown. NAEL-6v1

It will all go backward. Leaves. After My Death. David Young. InoFa

It will always happen—the death of a friend. Genesis Text for Larry Levis, Who Died Alone, A. Norman Dubie. MAAN

It Will Be a New World. Ko Chŏnghŭi. EcSo, tr. by Catherine J. Kim

It will be cold now in Crete. Time Zones. Jane Duran. MFPA

It will be looked for, book, when some but see. To My Book. Ben Jonson. FaBoVe; NAEL-6v1; NAEL-7v1

It will be otherwise. (LL) Otherwise: "I got out of bed." Jane Kenyon. AmFaPo; BeAl; GoPo; LoL; OxBoAm; P180; PLBUT; PoCu; StAl

It will be strange. When the Vacation Is Over for Good. Mark Strand. AtGh

It will be word enough of praise. (LL) Poet, A. Thomas Hardy. NAMCP V.1; NoAM

It will look as though I am flying into myself. (LL) Death: "Going to sleep, I cross my hands on my chest." Bill Knott. PBCAP; PoCho

It will make the muslins drop. May—1941. Valentine Penrose. SurPaPo, tr. by Mary Ann Caws

It Will Not Apprehend the Object. Patrizia Cavalli. CItWP, tr. by Cinzia Sartini Blum

It will not be / any more. No More. Idea Vilariño. BLPSL, tr. by Rene de Costa, Rigas Kappatos and Eleni Paidoussi

It will not be simple, it will become your will. (LL) Final Notations. Adrienne Rich. BeAl; BrAP; PoA 2002; PoCu

It will not be simple, it will not be long. Final Notations. Adrienne Rich. BeAl; BrAP; PoA 2002; PoCu

It will not bring me knowledge of my hunger. (LL) Harvest Song. Jean Toomer. NoP-4; NoP-5; WaAnP

It Will Not Do. Deryn Rees-Jones. MFPA

It will not do how stupidly you love her. It Will Not Do. Deryn Rees-Jones. MFPA

It will probably not be our lot to return to the pellucid Straits of Tiran. Without the Boy. Nathan Yonathan. NRoS, tr. by Esther Raizen

It will resound finely. Frances Densmore. APT-1 Fr. Chippewa Music.

It will snow fiercely enough to fill all these open graves. (LL) Retrieval System, The. Maxine W. Kumin. InvLad; WeW-3

It won't. Keep Quiet. Lawson Fusao Inada. WhBo

It would be. Phone Call to Rutherford. Paul Blackburn. PFTM-2

It would be easier. Albuquerque Graveyard, The. Jay Wright. ESEAA

It would be easier if they were on. Lovers, The. Geoffrey Holloway. NLP

It would be nice, I think. What She Said. Kallatanar. WoPoe, tr. by A. K. Ramanujan

It would be worth it to go ninety miles out of your way. Royal Manor Road. Gerald Stern. InvLad

It would have been a dragon, this monstrous jet. Dragon-Watching in St. Louis. Carter Revard. OtW; UrbNat

It would have been a kind of action replay. Wound Man, The. Sinéad Morrissey. BeAl; NIrP

It would have been better than this. (LL) Waiting for Icarus. Muriel Rukeyser. OtW; OxBoAm

It Would Have Been Enough. Robert Pack. PfSP

It would have starved a Gnat. Emily Dickinson. NCAP

It would have to be a dream. Twilight Time. Floyd Skloot. MiVo

It would melt. Basho. ChAP; EH, tr. by Robert Hass

It would never be Common—more—I said. Emily Dickinson. APN-2

It would never be morning, always evening. Memory of Brother Michael. Patrick Kavanagh. HarvBoo

It would only be from the other world. (LL) Meeting in a Lift. Vladimir Holan. PML; StAl, tr. by Ian Milner and Jarmila Milner

It would surely be known for years after as the day I shot. James Harrison. BodElec Fr. Letters to Yesenin.

Italia, Io Ti Saluto! Christina Georgina Rossetti. VWP

Italian. In Answer to Their Questions. Giovanna (Janet) Capone. UnSA

Italian Eclogues. Derek Walcott. BAP-97

Italian Garden, The. William Carlos Williams. OBGa

Italian in England, The. Robert Browning. OBNV

Italian Marcello, you breathe a much sweeter air. Elena Ignatova. ItGoST Fr. Verses about Music.

Italian Masons. Sarah Barkan. Prolet, tr. by Amelia Glaser

Italian Music in Dakota. Walt Whitman. APN-1

Italian soldier shook my hand, The. George Orwell. OBWP; OxAEP-2

Italians Are Excited, The. Freda Downie. EmeKit

Italians are excited, The. Italians Are Excited, The. Freda Downie. EmeKit

Italic. Roger McGough. OBCoV

Italics. Anselm Hollo. PmAP

Italics, Mine. Greg Williamson. LegDan

Italist Chant. Rohan B. Preston. WaCA

Italy. Edward Coote Pinkney. APN-1

Italy. Samuel Rogers. Ginevra. OxAEP-2

Italy 1942. Franco Fortini. ItPo, tr. by Gayle Ridinger

Italy. Samuel Rogers. Barry, the St. Barnard. DiBP

Itchin, when I behold thy banks again. To the River Itchin, near Winton. William Lisle Bowles. CenSon; NAEL-6v2; OxBSo

Itching, soft, becalmed, asleep like snails. Sloth. V. B. Price. ICANM

Ité. Ezra Pound. MoAmPo

Item. E. E. Cummings. MoAmPo

Item in Science Tuesday happens to catch my eye, An. Humble Herb is Rival to Prozac. Rachel Hadas. PoDa

Items in an envelope. What he'd kept. Father's Things. R. V. Bailey. Prnts

Iterating Sonnet. Leigh Hunt. OxBSo

Iteration. Piera Oppezzo. CItWP, tr. by Cinzia Sartini Blum and Lara Trubowitz

Ithaca. Constantine P. Cavafy. BLPJKO, tr. by Rae Dalven

Ithaca last night, Syracuse at noon, Cedar Rapids tonight. Seeing Auden Off. Philip Booth. PoA 2002

Ithaca-Liverpool. Gladys Mary Coles. Prnts

Ithaka. Constantine P. Cavafy. WoPoe, tr. by Edmund Keeley and Philip Sherrard

Ithaka. Constantine P. Cavafy. BeAl; PtR, tr. by Edmund Keeley and Philip Sherrard

Itherness. Ellie McDonald. CABP

'Ithin the woodlands, flow'ry gleåded. My Orcha'd in Lindèn Lea. William Barnes. FaBoVe; NPeEn; OxBEV

Itinerary. Doug Anderson. OPRER

Itinerary. Edwin Morgan. HarvBoo; OBCoV

Itinerary. Reginald Shepherd. RD

ITMA. Roddy Lumsden. NeBl

Žito the Magician. Miroslav Holub. PoSu; WoPoe, tr. by Ian Milner and George Theiner

I—Towards a Definition. Alice Notley. ExTi

It's 5:03 a.m. on the 11th of July this morning. Personal Poem # 8. Ted Berrigan. NYP2

It's 8:54 a.m. in Brooklyn it's the 28th [or 26th] of July [and]. Ted Berrigan. NYP2; OxBoAm; PmAP Fr. Sonnets, The.

It's 9/11/2001. I Am New York City 2. Jayne Cortez. PrTe

It's 1667. Reason is everywhere, saving. Even Ornaments of Speech Are Forms of Deceit. Ron Koertge. PoDa

It's 1962 March 28th. Things I Didn't Know I Loved. Nazim Hikmet. AF; AmFaPo; GPTC; VCWP, *tr.* by Randy Blasing and Mutlu Konuk

It's 1990. 1990. Bob Holman. FTtHH

It's 2157. Two adventuring spacemen rocketing home. Counterfeit Earth!, The. Albert Goldbarth. ReTh

It's '66 and Keaton's playing. Buster's Last Hand. Jennifer O'Grady. AmPoNex

It's 7 a.m. mother, the walking. Election Day. R. Zamora-Linmark. ReBoTo

It's a beating. Dolores Dorantes. SPV, *tr.* by Jen Hofer

It's a beautiful day: sunny, crisp, cloudless. Flexible. William Kulik. BodElec

It's a bit like looking through the big window. Poetry. Nick Laird. NIrP

It's a Blue World. George Forrest and Robert Wright. ReLy

It's a classic American scene. American Classic. Louis Simpson. StAl

It's a crime story she's in. Femme Fatale. Suzanne Lummis. PoDa

It's a Dog's Life. Bruce A. Jacobs. BtF

"It's a '49," Rhinehardt said, and slammed. Making Money: Drought Year in Minkler, California. Gary Soto. NoAM

It's a funny thing. Poem for Sigmund. Lorna Crozier. LW

It's a Good Day. Dave Barbour and Peggy Lee. ReLy

It's a good harvest this year. "Mang Ke." PFTM-2 *Fr.* Apeherd.

It's a good thing Dad deserted Mom. How I Came to Have a Man's Name. Emma Lee Warrior. HATNAP

(Before a January dawn, under a moondog sky.) ReEnLa

It's a good way to live and. Sky Diving. Ishmael Reed. FaoP

It's a grand thing when you're old, love. Life's Golden Sunset. Mrs. Henry Linden. CBWP-4

It's a grand view of valley and farm. From the High Ground. Thomas Lux. AmAlph

It's a Great Big Shame. Edgar Bateman. OBCoV

It's a great day. Last night I visited my old. Joanne Kyger. WhBo

It's a great pleasure to / wake "up." Many Happy Returns. Ted Berrigan. AHA

It's a Hard, Hard World for a Man. P. G. Wodehouse. ReLy

It's a hot summer day outside. At the Machine. Kalman Hayzler. Prolet, *tr.* by Amelia Glaser

It's a kind of flower. Queen Anne's Lace. Raymond Souster. BrAP

It's a lazy afternoon. Lazy Afternoon. John Latouche. ReLy

It's a lean car...a long-legged dog of a car...a gray-ghost eagle. Portrait of a Motorcar. Carl Sandburg. APT-1

It's a lie. Wooden Horse. Nagnamuni. HotL, *tr.* by V. Narayana Rao

It's a limited edition given out by the Gideons. Bill, Posted, A. BAP-97

It's a list of what I cannot touch. Elegy with a Thimbleful of Water in the Cage. Larry Levis. AmAlph

It's a long autumn day. Dance of Death. Hwang Insuk. EcSo, *tr.* by Peter H. Lee

It's a long time since the dawn chase over shires. Hunt-Cup, The. Daniel Tobin. NAPBL

It's a long walk in the dark. John's Song. Joan Aiken. TLR

It's a Lovely Day Today. Irving Berlin. ReLy

It's a lovely day today. It's a Lovely Day Today. Irving Berlin. ReLy

It's a miracle, waking every morning. Nurse, The. R. Gerallt Jones. BBMWP, *tr.* by Robert Minhinnick

It's a Most Unusual Day. Harold Adamson. ReLy

It's a Party (1959). Baron Wormser. SeSe

It's a pity we have to suffer. Elegy. Tom Clark. OxBoAm

It's a Queer Time. Robert Graves. MoBrPo

It's a question of altitude, or latitude. Brute Image. John Ashbery. NoP-4; NoP-5

It's a real old-fashioned butcher's shop. Crafty Butcher, The. Susan Hampton. BMAP; NOBAu

It's a ribbon tied to the rain's hair. Rainbow. Paul Laraque. OGAHCP, *tr.* by Boadiba and Jack Hirschman

It's a scientific toy for children. Battery woman. Pierre McOrlan. MFP, *tr.* by Martin Sorrell

It's a scorching May morning in Memphis. Automobiles. Iwan Llwyd. ATSWP, *tr.* by Robert Minhinnick

It's a sheroot, that's what. To Jerusalem, 1990. Myra Shapiro. OPRER

It's a slow warmth I find once more. Luigi Fontanella. NeIt

It's a spring morning; sun pours in the window. Carolyn Kizer. NoP-5; OxBoAm *Fr.* Pro Femina.

It's a story as famous as the three little pigs. Going Out for Cigarettes. Billy Collins. MAAN; OPRER

It's a strange courage. El Hombre. William Carlos Williams. NAAPv.2; SAmP; StAl

It's a strange season. Song of a Middle-Aged Woman. Mun Chônghui. EcSo, *tr.* by Catherine J. Kim

It's a sudden hue. Resolve. Leslie Ullman. ExTi

It's a sunny pleasant anchorage, is Kingdom Come. Port of Many Ships. John Masefield. OBMV

It's a tall order that expects pain to crystallize into beauty. And we must. Rosmarie Waldrop. PfS *Fr.* Lawn of Excluded Middle.

It's a thrill to love a boy: even Kronos' son, king of immortals, once longed for Ganymede. Theognis. CAGL *Fr.* Second Book of Theognis, The.

It's a Thursday, getting late. Barbells of the Gods, The. Mark Cox. OPRER

It's a town house built between the wars. Aerial, The. Robert Minhinnick. TCAWP

It's a very odd thing. Miss T. Walter De la Mare. NTCP

It's a wandering kind of crazy way I'm taken. Visiting New York. Sarah Rosenblatt. AmPoNex

It's a warm wind, the west wind, full of birds' cries. West Wind, The. John Masefield. CABP; MoBrPo

It's a weary life, it is. From the Antique. Christina Georgina Rossetti. OxBEV; PEW

It's a Woman's World. Eavan Boland. ItWoWo

It's a Wonder. Monique Charbonel. SurWo, *tr.* by Myrna Bell Rochester

It's a wonder. It's a Wonder. Monique Charbonel. SurWo, *tr.* by Myrna Bell Rochester

It's aborbed, perceived, partially picked up. The brighness envelops. Alicia Kozameh. MirDau *Fr.* Saltos Sobre El Exilio.

It's about style. Place Where He Arose, The. George Barlow. GT

It's after one. Last Statement. Vladimir Vladimirovich Mayakovsky. PBCIP, *tr.* by Tom Paulin

It's all. Young Girl Peeling Apples. Mary Jo Salter. FFC

It's All Aboard for THIS IS IT. (LL) P.O.E. Lincoln Kirstein. APT-2; PoWW; PWW2

It's all go to Claridges, it's all go to the champers. More Bagpipe Music. E. O. Parrott. UV

It's all love and loss and what was never said. Pop. Vona Groarke. NIrP

It's all ordinary experience. Dream and Poetry. Hu Shih. WoPoe, *tr.* by Kai-yu Hsu

It's All Right with Me. Cole Porter. ReLy

It's all the same to me what time it is. Paradise Lost, Book IV, lines 639—654. Leslie Johnson. UV

It's all the same to morning what it dawns on. Aubade. Nuala Ni Dhomhnaill. PBCIP, *tr.* by Michael Longley

It's all very well to dream of a dove that saves. Birdwatchers of America. Anthony Hecht. NAMCP V.2; NoAM

It's All Yours. Dorothy Fields. ReLy

It's almost Biblical driving this midnight burning highway. Red Velvet Jacket. Lynda Hull. ExTi

It's altogether something else with shrapnel. Proverbs. Teresa de Jesús. AF, *tr.* by Maria Proser, Arlene Scully *and* James Scully

It's always. Dark, The. Myra Cohn Livingston. TLR

It's always been nineteen something for me. 2000. Dave Jeddie Smith. CAP-8

It's always been that way. Dead Never Fight against Anything, The. Pattiann Rogers. SUP

It's always ourselves we find in the sea. (LL) Maggie and milly and molly and may. E. E. Cummings. ChAP; NoAM; NOxBChV; WaAnP

It's Always Waiting. José Luis Hidalgo. RaW, *tr.* by Hardie St. Martin

It's an awful feeling to watch the moon and stars above. Shake Down the Stars. Eddie DeLange. ReLy

It's an easy game, this reviewin'—the editor sends yer a book. Ballad of George R. Sims, The. Sir John Betjeman. OBCoV; UV

It's an experience everyone has that nobody else will know. Prayer at the End. Saunders Lewis. BBMWP, *tr.* by Joseph P. Clancy

It's an ordinary rock. From the Wailing Wall. Enid Shomer. TaR

It's an owercome sooth for age an' youth. Robert Louis Stevenson. OxBEV

It's an unhappy fate. Song of the Alaskero. *Unknown.* NAAPv.2

It's another warm night. Eating Dinner at My Sister's. David Romtvedt. AtGh

It's any kid's most exquisite fantasy. David Wojahn. AllShUp; PBCAP *Fr.* Mystery Train: A Sequence.

It's as if our heads were on fire, the way. Kando. ZenPo, *tr.* by Takashi Ikemoto and Lucien Stryk

It's as if the world were taking great steps backward. Children of the Planet. Blas de Otero. RaW, *tr.* by Hardie St. Martin

It's as if you are given the sky to carry. Thelonius. Afaa Michael Weaver. BtF; FuFl

It's August and I have not. Drinking While Driving. Raymond Carver. LaCa

It's autumn in the country I remember. Mnemosyne. Trumbull Stickney. APN-2; CtM; NAAPv.2; TCAPo

It's awf'lly bad luck on Diana. Hunter Trials. Sir John Betjeman. OBCoV

It's awf'ly nice of all you girls to see me to the train. So Long, Mary. George M. Cohan. ReLy

Its back was leaves that mimed the leaves in back of us, but. Station (1). James Galvin. GifTon

It's Barbie you mourn for. (LL) Barbie's Ferrari. Lynne McMahon. P180; RWB

Its beak is red and it has a battlefield-look. Valentine Delivered by a Raven. Tess Gallagher. ExTi

It's been 50 years since. My Father's Retirement. A. Van Jordan. SpirFl

It's been a hard winter, but summer is here and the fields. Tomas Tranströmer. RaBo Fr. Standing Up.

It's been a long day's drive through a landscape. Cinema Point. Philip Mead. BMAP

It's been a long time. Joanne Kyger. BB

It's been almost thirty-five years. Valentino's Hair. Yvonne Sapia. TRP

It's been forever since I returned to walk. Remembering East Mountain. Li Po. CrYelRi, tr. by Sam Hamill

It's been going on a long time. Way of Life, A. Howard Nemerov. NIL-7; NIP-4

It's been pelting down. Sheltering Places. Gerald Dawe. PNI

It's Been So Long. Harold Adamson. ReLy

It's been this way for some time. New Jersey Turnpike. Richard Cumbie. NBLV

It's been twenty-seven years. Meteor. C. M. Mayo. RWB

It's been years since we left Ethiopia. Mother of Andromeda, The. Julie Fay. NAPBL

It's best made in dry-fish camp. How To Make Good Baked Salmon from the River. Nora Dauenhauer. ReEnLa

It's best to be best. Best? Siv Widerberg. NTCP, tr. by Verne Moberg

It's better not to live in Moscow. Dmitry Aleksandrovich Prigov. ItGoST, tr. by Robert Reid

It's better to know her name. Anne Portugal. SCFWP Fr. Bath, The.

Its birth and rebirth and decay. (LL) Semele Recycled. Carolyn Kizer. CAP-8; NALW

It's black as ink. What Have We Done. Gary Daniel. OGAHCP, tr. by Boadiba and Jack Hirschman

Its black wings vibrated in and out. (LL) Anne Carson. OxBoAm; WoBe Fr. Truth About God, The.

Its body brevity, and wit its soul. (LL) What Is an Epigram? Samuel Taylor Coleridge. NIL-7; NIP-4

Its body in a rag-tag army. (LL) Louis MacNeice. OBWP; OxAEP-2 Fr. Autumn Journal.

It's boring looking at the same old contents. Natalya Belchenko. CRWP, tr. by Robert Reid

Its boundary is wider than the world. Regarding the Heart. Haewŏn. BecRai, tr. by Kim Daljin, Kim Won-Chung and Christopher Merrill

It's bright as the sun in a bright place. May Day. Jinkag Haesim. BecRai, tr. by Kim Daljin, Kim Won-Chung and Christopher Merrill

It's bright the icy foam as it flows. From Exile. Dafydd Benfras. OBWVE, tr. by Anthony Conran

Its bright, unequivocal eye. (LL) Having It Out with Melancholy. Jane Kenyon. EMP; ExTi; IJHIL; PoA 2002

It's brilliant. It's a tear you can stand a car. Prince Rupert's Drop, The. Jane Draycott. OxBSo

It's Called Kings. Suzana Cabañas. BRtP

Its called, "We Want it All. . .The Whole World!" (LL) New Reality Is Better Than a New Movie!, A. Imamu Amiri Baraka. NAMCP.V2; NoAM; WaAnP

It's calm today. I sit outside, or inside by the window. Light as Air. Ron Padgett. NYP2

Its casual Hesperides. (LL) Burden. Peter Kane Dufault. NoP-4; NoP-5

"Its claws have struck through the clouds." Wolfram von Eschenbach. GePo

It's cold at last and cautious winds creep. Grandfather at the Indian Health Clinic. Elizabeth Cook-Lynn. HATNAP; UnSA

It's cold, you say, the house. From a Conversation During Divorce. Carol Rumens. EmeKit

It's coming along, the assimilation. Assimilation, The. Barry Spacks. RWB

Its country and its God! (LL) Homes of England, The. Felicia Dorothea Hemans. NAEL-7v2; NOBRP; PEW; RWP; UV; ViWPN

It's crazy to think one could describe them. Robert Pinsky. NoAM Fr. Essay on Psychiatrists.

It's dangerous to be too comfortable. In Every Pot and Closet. Marilyn Zuckerman. PfS

It's dark in this wood, soft mocker. Praise to the End! Theodore Roethke.

It's darker and cooler. Cloud, The. Ekaterina Iosifova. CSCBP, tr. by Georgi Belev and Lisa Sapinkopf

It's darker than the dark bottom. Doing the Reactionary. Harold Rome. ReLy

It's darker tonight than when those shepherds watched. Christmas in Europe: 1945. J. M. Edwards. BBMWP, tr. by Robert Minhinnick

It's daybreak and I wish I could believe. Paul Celan: A Grave and Mysterious Sentence. Edward Hirsch. TaR

Its decline was gradual. Casualty. Michael Longley. NAMCP V.2

It's De-Lovely. Cole Porter. ReLy

It's devilishly hot. Poem Seen in a Motel Fan. Alberto Blanco. CLPP, tr. by John Oliver Simon

It's difficult to say what it all meant. Jack, Afterwards. Philip Dacey. ReTh

It's dinner time once more. Pantoum: In a Texas Farm-House Kitchen. Edyth Renshaw. TiP2

It's disturbing that it's not a surprise. Undertakers. Robert Johnstone. PNI

It's done phonetically, of course, at great. Francis Ford Coppola and Anthropologist Interpreter Teaching Gartewienna Tribesmen to Sing "Light My Fire," Philippine Jungle, 1978. David Wojahn. ReTh

It's driving into all that goldness makes. California, She Replied. Kathy Fagan. GeoHom

It's dull in the huge palace where I live. Warm to the Cuddly-toy Charm of a Koala Bear. Gavin Ewart. EmeKit

It's early evening here in the small world, where gods gamble for good. Mourning Song. Joy Harjo. NAMCP V.2

It's early morning and across the street. Homage to Sharon Stone. Lynn Emanuel. BodElec

It's early when we set out on the Ch'en-ts'ang Road. Ch'ai-kuan Mountain Pass. Wang Shih-chieng. ColAnChi, tr. by Richard John Lynn

It's earthquake weather in California. Earthquake Weather. Janice Gould. GeoHom

It's Easy. Lee Cataldi. BMAP

It's easy for me to believe. On Inheriting Departure. HeidiLynn Nilsson. NeAmPo

It's easy to be witty in French. For the Common Market. Michael Burn. OBCoV

It's easy to die. Peter Levitt. WhBo

It's easy to invent a Life. Emily Dickinson. APN-2; TCAPo

It's easy to talk, and writing words on the page. Philippe Jaccottet. StAl Fr. Songs from Below.

It's easy to throw away if you've always. Re:composition. Martha Collins. PfS

Its edge is a very fine mouth, a sharp and brilliant division—the black like a form of light that marks shores. Fish of Fleeting Skin. Coral Bracho. RMCMP, tr. by Suzanne Jill Levine

Its edges foamed with amethyst and rose. Great Breath, The. George Russell. MoBrPo; OBEV; OBMV

It's either the Prize or a terminal worry. Memory, A. Heinrich Heine. WoPoe, tr. by Francis C. Golffing

It's evening. There's time. Leslie Kaplan. SCFWP Fr. L'Excès-L'usine.

Its expanse is gigantic. Factory, The. Lajos Kassák. IQMS, tr. by Michael Kitka

Its expression resigned, humble even, as if it knows. Death of a Horse. Michael Longley. NAMCP V.2

It's extant only on official forms. Letter From My Father, A. Donny O'Rourke. EdScPo

Its eyes falling back against the interior of their cylinders, opened—thus laying—. Forward or Back. Aaron Shurin. FTOS

It's fading. By an Unknown Poet from Eastern Europe, 1955. György Petri. VCWP, tr. by Geroge Gömöri and Clive Wilmer

It's fall and a full moon. Basho. WED, tr. by Robert Bly

It's fall and dusk. Basho. WED, tr. by Robert Bly

It's February But. Janet Fisher. MFPA

It's filthy. Drop it. Drop it! Drop it! Drop it! (LL) Bone. C. K. Williams. CAP-8; UrbNat

It's five o'clock. Someone's taped my name out. Threnody for Sunset. Richard Cecil. BodElec

It's flying in the wind. Phoenix, The. Yi Hyangji. EcSo, tr. by Catherine J. Kim

Its foliage: the compassion of whoever sleeps a heart among bees. Overflowing Willow. Ernesto Lumbreras. RMCMP, tr. by Rebecca Seiferle

It's forever since I faced East Mountain. Thinking of East Mountain. Li Po. NDACCP, tr. by David Hinton

It's Fourth of July and for this one day to celebrate. Birthday Party on Old Orchard Road, A. Vivian Shipley. LiTh

It's freezing and you try to remember June. Against Numerology. Richard Caddel. Oth

It's Friday night and I've just had. 6/20/97. Harvey Shapiro. KGB

It's from before the spin of human fire. Chambered Nautilus. Linda Hogan. BodElec

It's full as Opera. (LL) I cannot dance upon my Toes. Emily Dickinson. APN-2; NCAP; TCAPo

It's fun to take speed. Speed, a Pastoral. John Forbes. BMAP

It's funny, but I don't remember much. Depressive Episode. Janet Holmes. ExTi

It's Gardena, late Saturday afternoon. Winnings. Garrett Kaoru Hongo. FTtHH; GeoHom; OpBo

(It's Gardena, late Saturday afternoon / on Vermont Avenue.) UnSA

Its gaze filled my abyss, its gaze melted. Pain. Enrique Gonzáles Martínez. TCLAP, *tr.* by Samuel Beckett

It's getting dark, little thief of starlight! Tristan Corbière. WoPoe *Fr.* Afterwards.

Its glory and its kingdom and its power! (LL) To ———: "Vainly my heart had with thy sorceries striven." Sarah Helen Whitman. APN-1; NAAPv.1; TCAPo

It's Go In / Quiet Illumined Grass / Land. Leslie Scalapino. "Silver half freezing in day." WANABP

It's going to be a thick night tonight. Officers' Mess. Gavin Ewart. FaBoWar

It's gonna rain any minute. Good for Nothin' Joe. Ted Koehler. ReLy

It's good, isn't it? Nowadays. Fred Ebb. ReLy

It's good, my child, you often wash your hair. Pope Alexander VI. Geoffrey Lehmann. NOBAu

It's good to be back, they say, lifting up the trap door and peeking in. Transylvania, 1919. Sabrina Orah Mark. LegDan

It's Good To Be Here. Alden Nowlan. StAl

It's good to be neuter. Stanzas, Sexes, Seductions. Anne Carson. NAMCP V.2

It's Got to Be Love. Lorenz Hart. ReLy

Its grandest lesson: "On! sail on!" (LL) Columbus: "Behind him lay the gray Azores." Joaquin Miller. APN-2; BRP; CalPo

Its hair is a fine weed. Grace. C. D. Wright. CAP-8

It's Halloween. Jack Prelutsky. NTCP

It's happening: the full fell fall. Bliss. Jay Parini. PfSP

It's Hard to Dislike Ewart. Gavin Ewart. OBCoV

It's hard to get away from hay these days. Thistle. Vona Groarke. NIrP

It's hard to know how well a town is when you only swing. Endurance of Poth, Texas, The. Naomi Shihab Nye. TiP2

It's hard to know if you're alive or dead. It's a Queer Time. Robert Graves. MoBrPo

It's hard to say, John, but I need some money. Imre Madách. IQMS *Fr.* Tragedy of Man.

It's hard to see but think of a sea. Louis Zukofsky. APT-2

It's hawk teaching song to swim. Landscape Over Zero. Bei Dao. PoDa, *tr.* by David Hinton and Yanbing Chen

It's he, it's sea. the sea is continuous; a continuous body. Sea. Bernadette Mayer. NYP2

It's her durability that astounds. Village Woman. Margaret Gillies Brown. EdScPo

It's here at last. Eyes in the know. Comet Come. Norman Nicholson. NLP

Its highways built up like new loves, raw and speedy. (LL) And One for My Dame. Anne Sexton. NoP-4; NoP-5

It's ho! for a ride in the open. Queen of Girlhood, The. Margaret Elizabeth Sangster. ArBi

It's hopeless. Our heads are full of television. I Can't Speak. Alicia Ostriker. PoA 2002

It's hopeless, you told me. Hope. Aharon Shabtai. WoBe, *tr.* by Peter Cole

It's hot, an smoggy as Mars outside. Dennis Cooper. ReTh *Fr.* Some Adventures of John Kennedy Jr.

It's important to join the crowds of those traveling. Walking with Others. Jelaluddin Rumi. WED, *tr.* by Robert Bly

It's impossible to live. Hierofant. Oswald de Andrade. TCLAP, *tr.* by Flavia Vidal

It's in the Blood. Nellie Wong. FTtHH

It's in the featureless. Son et Lumière. Mark Todd. GeoH

It's in the perilous boughs of the tree. Childhood's Retreat. Robert Duncan. NAMCP V.2; NoAM

Its islands of England. Level Cambridgeshire. Anne Stevenson. PfSP

It's joy to be up in the morning when the dew's on the grass and clover. Joy. Eben Eugene Rexford. ArBi

It's Just As Well About Heather. Chris O. Cook. FreRad

It's Kind of Lonesome Out Tonight. Don George. ReLy

It's kind of you to let me come alone. Imre Madách. IQMS *Fr.* Tragedy of Man.

It's Lamkin was a mason good. Lamkin. *Unknown.* NPeEn

It's languor and ecstasy. Paul Verlaine. SxFrPo, *tr.* by Martin Sorrell

It's late but everything comes next. (LL) Jerusalem. Naomi Shihab Nye. CFP; RaF

It's late fall. Basho. WED, *tr.* by Robert Bly

It's late in the city and I'm asleep. It's Me, I'm Not Home. Reetika Vazirani. PoCho

It's late. I've come. My Indigo. Li-Young Lee. CAP-8

It's late summer weather, time bitter. At Flowering-Brightness Monastery in Yung-Ch'ung District. Po Chü-i. NDACCP, *tr.* by David Hinton

Its leaves flutter, they thrive or wither, its outspread. Book. Robert Pinsky. PoDa

It's leaving thee, my bonnie [*or* bony] Mary! (LL) Silver Tassie, The. Robert Burns. OBEV; WoPoe

Its lettered pleats and crevices. Letters from the Concertina File 1939–1940. Sue MacIntyre. Prnts

Its life is longer. Refrigerator, The. Sue Sinclair. Coast

It's light gray and made of zinc. Freezing Pan, The. Helga Novak. MotU, *tr.* by Ann Maria Celona

It's like a story. Alive or Not. Alfred Wellington Purdy. BeAl

It's like a tap-dance. Yes. Muriel Rukeyser. MakPoe; StAl

It's like a terrible dream designed to make you scream. Drama, The. Suliaman El-Hadi. SpirFl

It's like coming through a chrysanthemum forest. Large Pots. Gerald Stern. GPPA

It's like escaping a hot, bright room. Friends and High Places. Jeffrey McDaniel. LaCa

It's like God calling me out. Dancing after Sanchez. Staci Lightburn. BRtP

It's like rediscovering point by point. Liliane Giraudon. SCFWP *Fr.* Poem with Incense Paper.

It's like snow. Statue, The. Ivano Fermini. ItPo, *tr.* by Gayle Ridinger

It's like the Light. Emily Dickinson. FaBoVe

It's like the riddle Tolstoy. Slow Dance. David St. John. AmAlph

It's like the sweet must that wasps. When Slow October Changes Color. Umberto Piersanti. NeIt, *tr.* by Stephen Sartarelli

It's Like This. WhBo

It's like this. There are quantities. There's on- / goingness. Philosopher's Stone. Jorie Graham. AWPTFC

It's little I care what path I take. Departure. Edna St. Vincent Millay. MoAmPo

It's long pest midnight, there's no one in the street. West End Perk, The. James Bridie. EdScPo

It's long way from Keats' Corner to Sandburg Ave. All Around the Town. Genevieve Taggard. APT-2

It's Love Again. Sam Coslow. ReLy

Its lower jaw scissors. Eight-Legged Colt, Chernobyl. Jerah Chadwick. AtGh

It's Magic. Sammy Cahn. ReLy

It's marvellous in winter to dance on the ice. No Name for It. Harry Edmund Martinson. WED, *tr.* by Robert Bly

It's me, Artaud, Antonin. Civil Status. Antonin Artaud. ConPit, *tr.* by Albert James Arnold and Clayton Eshleman

It's me, Cassandra. Monologue for Cassandra. Wisława Szymborska. PoSu, *tr.* by Grazyna Drabik *and* Sharon Olds

It's me, child. Goodbye to a Spaceman. Ojars Vacietis. SonAtl, *tr.* by Tamara Romanyk and Sharon Strauch

It's Me, I'm Not Home. Reetika Vazirani. PoCho

It's me, O passerby, the poplar tree. *Unknown.* PriapPo *Fr.* Priapus Poems, The.

It's me, the pregnant Puerto Rican girls, short Mexicans. Me and Baby. Ana Castillo. IllVoic

It's me—I am a War Eagle! *Unknown.* APN-2 *Fr.* War Dance.

Its "mild wild head doth lie." (LL) Sea Unicorns and Land Unicorns. Marianne Moore. NALW; PFTM-1

It's Miller Time. Víctor Hernández Cruz. PueRic; TouFir

Its mind is on something among lotus leaves. Kingfisher with Fish in Beak. Ch'ien Ch'i. CCL1, *tr.* by Stephen Owen

Its mother on guard. Issa. EH, *tr.* by Robert Hass

It's much cushier when it's raining rabbits. Experimental Animals. Dennis O'Driscoll. StAl

It's much too cold to travel. Going and Coming of Sequins. Joyce Mansour. PFTM-2, *tr.* by Molly Bendall

It's my birtday I've got an empty. June 11. David Lehman. P180

It's my lunch hour, so I go. Step Away from Them, A. Frank O'Hara. NAMCP V.2; OxBoAm; PtR; VCAP; WoPoe

It's my safe world, moving through the dark. Bus Driver, The. Netta Gillespie. AmZen

It's natural the Boys should whoop it up for. Moon Landing. W. H. Auden. EmeKit; OxAEP-2

It's nearly ten o'clock in the morning and I have work to do. Walking the Baby to the Liquor Store. Michael Van Walleghen. IllVoic

It's Never Too Late to Fall in Love. Sandy Wilson. ReLy

It's night, an extra quilt. Steve Sims. NewEx

It's nightfall and between two grey facades. Souvenir. Paul Van Ostaijen. TuT, *tr.* by Tony Curtis

It's no coincidence / this is a used. Tricks With Mirrors. Margaret Atwood. BrAP; NIP-4

It's no go the merry-go-round [*or* merrygoround], it's no go the rickshaw. Bagpipe Music. Louis MacNeice. BeAl; BrAP; CABP; EMP; HarvBoo; MakPoe; NAEL-6v2; NAEL-7v2; NAMCP V.1; NBLV; NoAM; NoP-4; NoP-5; OBSV; OxBEV; TFi; UV

It's no great matter what men deem. Resolution, The. Richard Baxter. SacPr

It's no labour of love, this document. Mapmaker's Song, The. Gwyneth Lewis. BBMWP, *tr. by* the author and Richard Poole

It's no one else's fault, Syama Ma. Dāśarathi Rāy. SinGod, *tr. by* Rachel Fell McDermott

It's no use. Fortnight. Pak Inhwan. CAMKP, *tr. by* Scott Swaner

It's no use. Sappho. HW, *tr. by* Mary Barnard

It's no use. It's no use. Sappho. HW, *tr. by* Mary Barnard

"It's no use," he says, "she's left me." This is after several. In a Tavern. Louis Jenkins. RaBo

It's No Use Raising a Shout. W. H. Auden. OBMV; OxBoAm

It's no worse than say Odessa or Post or Snyder. Atmosphere for Poetry in Abilene, The. Robert A. Fink. TiP2

It's Nostalgia Week at Frank 'n' Helen's. At Frank 'n' Helen's. Constance Urdang. PBCaP

Its nostrils black, the horse plunges. Battle. Aleksandr Petrovich Tkachenko. ItGoST, *tr. by* Maia Tekses

It's not a dress, and he hasn't got the lips. Girl in a Fur-Trimmed Dress. Honor Moore. WiU

It's not a fancy restaurant, nor is it. Tenderly. Stephen Dobyns. CAP-8

It's not a good sign. Bulletin. Binyo Ivanov. CSCBP, *tr. by* Georgi Belev and Lisa Sapinkopf

It's not a sheltered world. The noise begins over there, on the other side of the wall. Vermeer. Tomas Tranströmer. WED, *tr. by* Robert Bly

It's not all as evil as you think. (LL) Sunflower. Rolf Jacobsen. RaBo; WED, *tr. by* Robert Bly

It's not always easy. Face the Animal. Jean Follain. BLT, *tr. by* Heather McHugh

It's not always easy. Footprints. Esther Louise. BRtP

It's not as if I'm intending on spending the rest of my life doing this. Bearhug, The. Nick Laird. NIrP

It's not bad news, it's no news at all that this night. City Life. Alvin Greenberg. UrbNat

It's not because I loved a man. Female Buddha. Kim Sŭnghŭi. EcSo, *tr. by* K. Kim Richards and Steffen Richards

It's not easy. Leaving Scotland by Train. Hugh McMillan. EdScPo

It's not exciting to have a bar of soap. Living with Chris. Ted Berrigan. NYP2; OxBoAm

It's not for nothing that I love you. Love's Reasons. Han Yong'un [*or* Yongwun]. CAMKP, *tr. by* Sammy Solberg

It's not good or bad it's how you get around these. By Bicycle. Matthea Harvey. ArBi

It's not greed I feel in me, the silver in my pocket. Kiss of Judas. Jennifer Grotz. LegDan

It's not like anything. Basho. EH, *tr. by* Robert Hass

It's not much of a choice. Troth. Michael Davidson. FTOS

It's not much of a fall with. Improvisatin for Jerald Bullis, An. A. R. Ammons. BodElec

It's not my. Have Pen, Will Travel. Charles Bernstein. NAMCP V.2

It's not my world, I grant, but I made it. Ride. Josephine Miles. OxBoAm

It's not nature that upholds utility. Gudo. ZenPo, *tr. by* Takashi Ikemoto and Lucien Stryk

It's not necessary for someone to die. Claudia Hernández de Valle-Arizpe. RMCMP *Fr.* Hemicránea.

It's not only the accumulation of small slights. Keep Going. Gail Mazur. ExTi

It's not Siva. Rāmprasād Sen. SinGod, *tr. by* Rachel Fell McDermott

It's not so easy to die. Problem, A. Alexander Gerov. CSCBP, *tr. by* Georgi Belev and Lisa Sapinkopf

It's Not So Good to be Born a Girl/ Sometimes. Ntozake Shange. SSLK

It's not so much the partis pris as. Philosophical Songs. Charles North. KGB

It's not something I like to burden my readers with as a rule. How Much Is This Poem Going to Cost Me? Denise Duhamel. NeAmPo

It's not surprising. Pan Cogito on Virtue. Zbigniew Herbert. PoSu, *tr. by* Adam Czerniawski

It's not that I don't like the hospital. Lost in the Hospital. Rafael Campo. AmPoNex

It's not that I harbor a weeping willow. Salvation. James Kimbrell. LegDan

It's not that I'm worried. Concern. Steve Sanfield. WhBo

It's not that it's really a very interesting shoe when you come right down to it but you learn a lot from his explanations. (LL) Dachau Shoe, The. W. S. Merwin. AmWaPo; MotU

It's not that you were present. Mourning. Daniel Weissbort. GI

It's not the crutches we decry. Crutches. Nikki Giovanni. PfS

It's not the hens that matter. Tray of Eggs, A. Michael Laskey. BeAl

It's not the year two-thousand, my poor love. Towards the New Millennium. Zoltán Jékely. IQMS, *tr. by* George Szirtes

It's not too late I suppose. How to Write Anglo-Welsh Poetry. John Davies. AngWePo; TCAWP

It's not true that the sky and its way of holding out. Setting Sail. Gerardo Diego. RaW, *tr. by* Ralph Nelson

It's not when they leave. Maya Borisova. TCRusP, *tr. by* Daniel Weissbort

It's nothing really, and really, it could have been worse, and of course, he's. Grandfather-in-law. David Mura. LoL

It's November the thirty-third. Ninth Symmetrical Poem. Michael Palmer. HarvBoo

It's nuthatch on the box elder outside the window. October. David Brendon Hopes. UpMys

It's odd how snow fails at totality. Of Art & Memory. Norman Dubie. AmAlph

It's odd to have a separate month. It. October. Bill Berkson. NYP2

It's one a.m. and I am. Real Devotion of Events, The. Judith Goldman. Eno

It's 110 in Atascadero. Arrangement. Glenna Luschei. GeoHom

It's one of those days when everything is half-off. Diogenes Tries to Forget. Mary Karr. PoA 2002

It's Only a Paper Moon. E. Y. Harburg and Billy Rose. ReLy

It's only a trickle. Laocoon/Serpent. Novica Tadic. VCWP, *tr. by* Charles Simic

It's only a week but already you are slipping. History. Maura Dooley. NeBl; StAl

It's only at Christmas and New Year. Fitzroy. Andrew Taylor. BMAP

Its only riddle: *how.* Hans Faverey. WoBe *Fr.* Eighteen Poems.

It's Only Rock and Roll but I Like It: The Fall of Saigon, 1975. David Wojahn. IllVoic; ReTh

It's only the attic I miss. Anorexic, The. Ruth Anderson Barnett. OPRER

It's over / and that is all. It's Over. Víctor Terán. RMCMP, *tr. by* Donald Frischmann

It's over, love. Look at me pushing fifty now. Late Night Ode. Horace. PfSP; WaAnP; WiU; WoPoe, *tr. by* J. D. McClatchy

It's over now, the time for observation, for. Maurizio Cucchi. ItPo, *tr. by* Gayle Ridinger

It's over. Or it is for me, anyway. Vale. Rolando Hinojosa. TiP2

Its own identity. (LL) This Consciousness that is aware. Emily Dickinson. InoFa; NAAL-3; NAAPv.1

Its pale tendrilous horn. (LL) Cuttings. Theodore Roethke. APT-2; IPoFL; NAAL-5; NAMCP V.1; NoAM; OBGa; WaAnP

Its pecked-at ripeness that scans you, then moves on. (LL) Haw Lantern, The. Seamus Heaney. HarvBoo; MakPoe; NoAM; PNI

It's pleasant to board the ferry in the sunscape. Déjeuner sur l'herbe. Tu Fu [*or* Du Fu]. BLT, *tr. by* Carolyn Kizer

Its Pliancy. Hans Lodeizen. TuT, *tr. by* Eamon Grennan

It's Possible That While We Were Dreaming. Antonio Machado Ruiz. WED, *tr. by* Robert Bly

Its pristine bloom. (LL) On Receiving News of the War. Isaac Rosenberg. HarvBoo; MoBrPo; OBWP; OxAEP-2; PoWW

It's probably like the excitement of your first cigarette, but it lasts. Hell. Peter Johnson. Vesp

It's probably the year her marriage. Satin Doll. David Wojahn. PBCAP

It's quarter to three. One for My Baby (And One More for the Road). Harold Arlen and Johnny Mercer. ReLy

"It's queer," she said, "I see the light." Maid-Servant at the Inn, The. Dorothy Parker. ChrPo

Its quick soft silver bell beating, beating. Auto Wreck. Karl Shapiro. APT-2; NIL-7; NIP-4

It's quiet, all right. Basho. WED, *tr. by* Robert Bly

It's quiet here among the haunted tenses. Last of England, The. Peter Porter. GS

It's quiet in the house so quiet. Mother's Song. *Unknown.* WoPoe, *tr. by* Stephen Berg

Its rails and the Main Chance gone to scrap. Rights of Way. Thomas Reiter. GM

It's Raining. Vicente Aleixandre. RaW, *tr. by* Robert Bly

It's raining, / and still people say there's no God! Rain. Olga Sedakova. CRWP, *tr. by* Catriona Kelly

It's raining as if for the first time. Feeling. Nikolai Kanchev. CSCBP, *tr. by* Georgi Belev and Lisa Sapinkopf

It's raining... don't sleep yet. Rainy Night. Juana de Ibarbourou. TCLAP, *tr. by* Sophie Cabot Black

It's Raining in Love. Richard Brautigan. P180

It's raining on black coal and warm wet ashes. Two Lorries. Seamus Heaney. EMP; NoP-5

It's raining stair-rods and chairlegs. Black Wet, The. W. N. Herbert. NeBl

It's really something, the onion. Onion. Wisława Szymborska. PoSu, *tr. by* Grazyna Drabik *and* Sharon Olds

Its reign. (LL) Take Yourself to the Rose-Garden. Nedîm. OLP; WoPoe, *tr. by* Walter Andrews, Najaat Black and Mehmet Kalpakli

Its retributions work like clockwork. Under the Eyes. Tom Paulin. PNI

It's right to call you son. That cursing alcoholic. Letter to an Absent Son. Madeline DeFrees. PoChi

It's rumored no longer to exist. (LL) Alzheimer's. Bob Hicok. AmPoNex; BeAl; P180; PoCu

It's run an' jump an' hop an' skip. Owdham Footbo'. Ammon Wrigley. FaBoVe

It's sad that it rains in the Autumn. Fever Tune. Karel Van de Woestijne. TuT, tr. by Tony Curtis and Tony Curtis

It's sad / To be the Mayor of Jerusalem. Mayor. Yehuda Amichai. PoSu, tr. by Assia Gutmann

It's said you spoke once and then chose silence. Refusing the Call. Enid Shomer. TaR

It's Saturday afternoon at the edge of the world. Laguna Blues. Charles Wright. NAMCP V.2; PoPoPo; WaAnP

It's Saturday night, and I'm feeling reckless. Saturday Night. Sir Alan Patrick Herbert. NBLV

It's Saturday night and Lisa. Bachelor Song. Douglas Goetsch. PML; PoDa

Its senile pleasure. (LL) University. Karl Shapiro. APT-2; PoA 2002

It's silly of you tho think the rich. Unless You Are a Horse. Robert Hershon. PrTe

It's silly to hope for Father's wealth. Rāmprasād Sen. SinGod, tr. by Rachel Fell McDermott

Its skirt of rain and wind and snow. Second Rondeau. Johann Nikolaus Götz. GePo, tr. by George C. Schoolfield

It's smoke, the star, a broom. Smoke. Rubén Bonitaz Nuño. STV, tr. by John Frederick Nims

It's / snowing defective. Self-Pity Is a Kind of Lying, Too. James Schuyler. BodElec

It's snowing hard enough that the taxis aren't running. Rites of Manhood, The. Alden Nowlan. RaBo

It's snowing in Plouda. / It's snowing in Blauda too. It's Snowing in Plouda. Erica Pedretti. MotU, tr. by Franz Wright

It's snowing this afternoon and there are no flowers. Absences. Donald Justice. CAP-8

It's so barren down there. Down the Bay. Mary Dalton. OpeFie

It's so beautiful, life, goddamn death. Thing Was Moving, The. Charles Olson. NAMCP V.2

It's so cold my cock is furled. Pissing off the Back of the Boat into the Nivernais Canal. William Matthews. CAP-8

It's so easy. Buddy Holly Poem, The. Maurice Kilwein Guevara. TouFir

It's so easy to lose track of things. A screwdriver, for instance. Place for Everything, A. Louis Jenkins. GoPo; IJHIL

It's so hard to say in a son's words. Prayer to My Mother. Pier Paolo Pasolini. VCWP, tr. by Norman MacAfee

It's so much easier to get further from home than nearer that all men become travelers. Vectors: Forty-five Aphorisms and Ten-second Essays. James Richardson. BAP-01

It's so much easier to get further from home than nearer that all men become travelers. James Richardson. PoDa Fr. Vectors: Aphorisms and Ten-Second Essays.

It's So Peaceful in the Country. Alec Wilder. ReLy

It's so pure in the cemetery. Not Like That. Adrienne Rich. EmeKit

It's spring, all right. Basho. WED, tr. by Robert Bly

It's spring and Jake toddles to the garden. Jake Addresses the World from the Garden. Jack Myers. SUP

It's spring, moisture's. Walt Whitman in New Orleans, 1848. David Citino. ViWalt

It's springtime and young boys. Young Boys, The. Linda Hogan. ArBi

It's still here. It's still here-er. Be ready. Be ready. Mothering. Carla Harryman. FTOS

Its story told, what was. Vigil. Ken Harris. AnSo

It's strange / I know exactly what killed phyllis hyman. Phyllis. Jacqueline Johnson. BRtP

Its strength, and struck. (LL) Eight O'Clock. A. E. Housman. MoBrPo; NAMCP V.1; NoAM; SoSe-8

It's such a little thing to weep. Life's Trades. Emily Dickinson. TCAPo

It's suffocation time again. Teachable Texts. Steve McCaffery. NLPA

It's summer, 1956, in Maine, a camp resort. Poem for Adlai Stevenson and Yellow Jackets. David Young. P180

It's Sunday. Sunday. Kathleen Spivack. PfS

It's Sunday evening. Pomp holds the receipts. Chopin. Marilyn Nelson. RA

It's Sunday, October ninth, and the earth here is barren after harvest. Gary Young. GeoHom Fr. Braver Deeds.

It's sweaty work, the getting ready part. Early Thoughts of Winter. Maxine W. Kumin. ExTi

Its teeth worked doubtfully. Key, The. John Ormond. AngWePo; TCAWP

It's that dream we carry with us. It Is That Dream. Olav H. Hauge. WED, tr. by Robert Bly

It's that hour when I empty my dreams of my existence in order. Hot and Cold. Silvio Giussani. ItPo, tr. by Gayle Ridinger

It's that old devil called love again. That Old Devil Called Love. Doris Fisher and Allan Roberts. ReLy

It's that time when grass begins growing its hair. Tree of Life, The. Margaret Holley. PoA 2002

It's the aftermath of surrender. Request Radio. Carol Muske-Dukes. AmAlph

It's the anarchy of poverty. Poor, The. William Carlos Williams. MoAmPo

It's the boom of ice. When She Laughs. Judith Sornberger. HW

It's the broken phrases, the fury inside him. Art Pepper. Edward Hirsch. SeSe

It's the ceaseless wind. Insomnia. Debra Nystrom. AWTN

It's the country of childhood. Jardin des Colombières. Lauris Edmond. OBGa

It's the cup of blood. Rose, The. Kelly Cherry. LPSFW

It's the darkest morning of the year. St. Thomas's Day. Gillian Clarke. HarvBoo

It's the first night, I suppose. First Night, A. Peter Kane Dufault. NoP-4; NoP-5

It's the Fourth of July, the flags. Immigrant Picnic. Gregory Djanikian. PoA 2002; PoDa

It's the hot air, the dare, the heat of sway. Blames, for Rane and Diane. Glenn Sheldon. MiVo

It's the kind of cooking where before you begin. Furious Cooking. Maureen Seaton. SUP; SweBea

It's the kind of place where. American Standard. David Baratier. AmPoNex

It's the last snow of the season. All, the Nothing, The. Yves Bonnefoy. VCWP, tr. by Lisa Sapinkopf

It's the misunderstanding of ashes at the airport. Columbarium. Judi Benson. InoFa

It's the old rule that drunks have to argue. New Rule, The. Jelaluddin Rumi. RaBo, tr. by Coleman Barks and Robert Bly

It's the only thing Kenji Takezo does. Breath He Holds, The. Rick Noguchi. NeAmPo

It's the poor first light of morning. Obscure, The. Norman Dubie. NoAM

It's the ragged source of memory. House on Moscow Street, The. Marilyn Nelson Waniek. UnSA

It's the same face, again and again, hovering near the window. Face, The. Mahmoud al-Braikan. IrPoTo, tr. by Ralph Saverese and Saadi A. Simawe

It's the season of birdsong. Summer. Xuan Quynh. PoCho, tr. by Nguyen Ba Chung and Carolyn Forché

It's the season of spring, let us be. Sheykhi. OLP, tr. by Walter Andrews, Najaat Black and Mehmet Kalpakli

It's the story of a very unfortunate Memphis man. Hong Kong Blues. Hoagy Carmichael. ReLy

It's the story that counts. Margaret Atwood. NALW Fr. Circe / Mud Poems.

It's the sun with its single eye, the fire-spitting mouth that never tires of charring eternity. From Some Time to This Place. José Emilio Pacheco. MotU, tr. by Philip Levine

It's the Talk of the Town. A. J. Neiburg and Marty Symes. ReLy

It's the tone, not the harp. Song, The. L. Tureski. Prolet, tr. by Amelia Glaser

It's the torque of a spring Sunday. Blues in "C." Ron Overton. SeSe

It's the wine, this ache, this longing. Song. Liu Yung. CrYelRi, tr. by Sam Hamill

It's the wreath you don't come upon. Apprentice Prophecies, The. David Craig. UpMys

It's the wrong place and the wrong time. It's All Right with Me. Cole Porter. ReLy

It's their otherness I admire. Can Pigeons Be Heroes? Ruth L. Schwartz. WiU

It's there / in the hole of the sea. Hole in the Sea, The. Marvin Bell. Vesp

It's there, somewhere in the Platonic cold store. Peter Porter. OxBSo Fr. Sanitized Sonnets, The.

It's thirty years ago. Free Throw. Mark Kraushaar. MoASP

It's this crazy weather we've been having. Crazy Weather. John Ashbery. ColAP

Its this familiar black line from the tops. Elaine Randell. Oth Fr. Snoad Hill Poems, The.

It's this one, the smell. This flying of metallic particles between the teeth. Street Country. Laura Solórzano. SPV, tr. by Jen Hofer

"It's Three No Trumps," the Soldier Said. Guy Innes. UV

It's thus he does it of a winter night. (LL) Old Man's Winter Night, An. Robert Frost. APT-1; GPTC; ItP; MoAmPo; NAMCP V.1; NoAM; OxBoAm

It's time again. James Schuyler. FTOS

It's time again not to push a metaphor too far. Rising. Sam Hamill. AmZen

It's time for me to go. I know a pine-tree that overhangs the sea.   It's Time for Me to Go.   George Seferis.   MotU, tr. by Edmund Keeley and Philip Sherrard

It's time. The air is ready. The sky has an opening. (LL)   Piece of the Storm, A.   Mark Strand.   BeAl; CAP-8; WaAnP

It's time to end my lonely holiday.   Autumn in New York.   Vernon Duke.   ReLy

It's time to get back to the car. Already, at half-past three.   Sunday in Great Tew.   Peter McDonald.   ModIr; PNI

It's time to make love. Douse the glim.   Limerick.   Conrad Potter Aiken.   NBLV

It's to possess more than the skin.   Cutting the Jewish Bride's Hair.   Ruth Whitman.   TaR

It's to the other man, to Borges, that things happen.   Borges and Myself.   Jorge Luis Borges.   PoetW, tr. by Norman Thomas Di Giovanni

It's to you I come in my hours of thirsting, as to.   Life.   Delmira Agustini.   TANSG, tr. by Mark McCaffrey

It's too darn hot.   Too Darn Hot.   Cole Porter.   ReLy

"It's too easy."   Malaria.   Paolo Ruffilli.   NeIt, tr. by Felix Stefanile

It's too good for them.   Sex and the Over Forties.   Peter Porter.   BMAP

It's too late to hear a nightingale.   Yonejiro (Yone) Noguchi.   CalPo

It's too much, B writing to A's wife.   Institute for Social Change, The.   Joshua Clover.   AmPoNex

It's true.   Bitter Poem, A.   Sri Sri.   HotL, tr. by V. Narayana Rao

It's true, here we are all blonde.   Shangri-la.   Suzanne Lummis.   CalPo

It's true, I could hold you.   Red River.   Molly Fisk.   PasH

It's true I got caught in / the world.   After Lalon.   Allen Ginsberg.   BB

It's True I Went to the Market.   Mirabai.   WED; WPoS, tr. by Robert Bly

It's true! It's true! The crown has made it clear.   Camelot.   Alan Jay Lerner.   ReLy

It's true she liked it.   Small Pain, A.   Martha Rhodes.   LaCa

It's true such reckless grace should never die.   Elegy.   David St. John.   RoV

It's true that anyone can fall.   Shantung.   Denise Riley.   MoWP

It's true that billboard silhouettes and power.   Parking Lot.   Leslie Monsour.   CalPo

It's true that my soul mea culpa is empty.   Anthills.   Peter Meinke.   Vesp

It's true: you wake up one morning and they're gone.   Highwaymen, The.   Maxine W. Kumin.   CAP-8

It's TV Newstime.   Interference Song.   Liz Lochhead.   RSaN

It's twenty years ago and more.   In Moncur Street.   Dorothy Hewett.   NOBAu

It's unlikely that a decent poem is in me.   Not So Good Night in the San Pedro of the World, A.   Charles Bukowski.   PoA 2002

It's up the spout and Charley Wag.   Moral, The.   W. E. Henley.   OxAEP-2

It's useless.   Panorama.   Romelia Alarcón de Folgar.   TANSG, tr. by Alison Ridley

It's very cold, Catherine is bundled in a coat, a poncho on the top of that, high boots, gloves.   Snow: II.   C. K. Williams.   NoP-4; NoP-5

It's Walt Whitman's birthday.   May 31, 1989.   Joe Benevento.   ViWalt

It's wind, not rain, dry cattle need.   Wind and Hardscrabble.   Walter McDonald.   TiP2

It's winter again, you said. It was April.   Two Thousand and Two.   Catherine Hunter.   PoPra

It's winter. Humid and cold. White or grey.   Winter.   Pascalle Monnier.   YaTCFP, tr. by Serge Gavronsky

It's winter. The city sleeps in its yellow mist.   Capitol, The.   Innokenty Fiodorovich Annensky.   WoPoe, tr. by Stephen Berg

It's wonderful how I jog.   Animals Are Passing from Our Lives.   Philip Levine.   CalPo; CAP-8; ColAP; RaBo; WaAnP

Its work is memory.   Pen, The.   Galway Kinnell.   BodElec

It's you puts the green sprig in my hatband.   Unknown.   WoPoe Fr. Three Gypsy Songs.

It's your best friend's 16th birthday party.   Heavy-Petting Zoo, The.   Clare Pollard.   NeBl

It's your father.   Therapist's Comment, The.   Jenny Hamlett.   Prnts

Its youth. The sea grows old in it. (LL)   Fish, The: "Wade / through black jade."   Marianne Moore.   APT-1; BrAP; ColAP; EMP; GPTC; MoAmPo; NAAPv.2; NAMCP V.1; NoAM; NoP-4; NoP-5; OxBoAm; WaAnP

It's Yoyo who says Tonguing, a form of kissing.   Elegant Tongue, The.   Terrance Hayes.   LegDan

Itself ornament the weave of presence. (LL)   Mollusc.   Les A. Murray.   NAMCP V.2; UpMys

Itylus.   Algernon Charles Swinburne.   NPeEn; UV

Ityopia phase-in.   Seitlhamo Motsapi.   TSAP

Ivanhoe.   Sir Walter Scott.
   (When Israel, of the Lord Beloved.)   ChIV-1

I've a beau, his name is Jim.   Laziest Gal in Town, The.   Cole Porter.   ReLy

I've a head like a concertina, I've a tongue like a buttonstick.   Cells.   Rudyard Kipling.   FaBoWar

I've a mouth like a parrot's cage.   Tripoli.   Peter A. Sanders.   FaBoWar

I've a pile of memories on my other.   Frequently unasked questions.   Charles Bernstein.   NoP-5

I've a proposal here from Mr Murray.   John Hookham Frere.   NPBRoP Fr. Whistlecraft.

I've a Shooting Box in Scotland.   Cole Porter.   NAAPv.2

I've always been afraid of death by fire.   Ten Million Flames of Los Angeles, The.   Amy Uyematsu.   CalPo; GeoHom

I've always been going somewhere—Vancouver.   Madwoman on the Train, The.   Alfred Wellington Purdy.   NoAM

I've always hated.   I Want to Hear a Yankee Doodle Tune.   George M. Cohan.   ReLy

I've always liked the view from my mother-in-law's house at night.   Looking West from Laguna Beach at Night.   Charles Wright.   MakPoe

I've always loved the autumn. Trees bleed amber.   Riverside Park.   Rachel Hadas.   OxBoAm

I've always loved (your) Grace in 14 lines, sometimes.   Birthday Sonnet for Grace.   Bernadette Mayer.   PmAP

I've always wanted to play the part.   Little Brown Brother.   Nick Carbó.   AmPoNex; ReBoTo

I've an empty stomach.   Ballad of Biddy Early, The.   Nancy Willard.   FFC

I've been a pris'ner, locked in a jail.   Over My Shoulder.   Harry Woods.   ReLy

I've Been Around: It Gets Me Nowhere.   Marie Ponsot.   ExTi

I've been blues travelin/ through mississippi streets.   13th Letter, The.   Jolivette Anderson.   BRtP

I've been booed in the shower.   Singing in the Toyota.   Dave Etter.   IllVoic

I've been eating.   Minnesota Fats Describes His Youth.   Elizabeth Alexander.   AmPoNex

I've been given these hot delicious muffins.   How Long Does the Curator Dance For?   Edwin Torres.   HeMarv

I've been hunting through woods.   It Never Was You.   Maxwell Anderson.   ReLy

I've been in an open field.   Day in the Life of . . . , A.   Conyus.   GT

I've been in love for long.   In Love For Long.   Edwin Muir.   MoBrPo

I've been in love. Who hasn't? I went out and got drunk.   Philodemus.   HePo Fr. Epigrams.

I've been in that place.   Tomas Tranströmer.   WoBe Fr. Haiku.

I've been loveless all my life.   On Love.   Hsü Tsai-ssu.   CrYelRi; ErotSp, tr. by Sam Hamill

I've been married and married.   To Keep My Love Alive.   Lorenz Hart.   ReLy

I've been named Poosie, and.   Confession.   Paul Gallico.   TriCat

I've [or I] been scar[r]ed and battered.   Still Here.   Langston Hughes.   SAmP

I've been sleeping out, Miriam.   Poem to Ma Ferguson.   Charles S. Taylor.   TiP2

I've been smoking steadily all morning.   Mathios Paskalis among the Roses.   George Seferis.   PFTM-1; PoetW, tr. by Edmund Keeley and Philip Sherrard

I've been thinking about what love is for.   Love, with Trees and Lightning.   Catie Rosemurgy.   IIR

I've been thinking of your father.   From Then to Now.   Kim Addonizio.   LiTh

I've Been to a Marvelous Party.   Noël Coward.   NBLV; ReLy

I've been to Palestine.   Vachel Lindsay.   MoAmPo Fr. Booker Washington Trilogy, The.

I've been told that a storm front.   Biblical Winnipeg.   Clive Holden.   PoPra

I've been walking in circles for what seems like days.   Moto Perpetuo.   Dionisio D. Martinez.   NAMCP V.2

I've been worried all day long.   You Made Me Love You (I Didn't Want to Do It).   Joseph McCarthy.   ReLy

I've begun to love the cold, the slick, bitter seed.   Outlook.   Crystal Bacon.   UrbNat

I've brewed myself a whole bunch of trouble.   To the Tune "Moon Over West River."   Yang Shen.   ColAnChi, tr. by Jonathan Chaves

I've changed / Shrunk probably.   I've Changed.   Norman Fischer.   WANABP

I've chosen this title because not only do I like it.   Statue of a Libertine, The.   Ron Padgett.   AHA

I've cleaned house.   Saturday Afternoon, When Chores Are Done.   Harryette Mullen.   ISC; OxAAAP

I've come back all skin and bone.   Diggins-Oh, The.   Unknown.   NOBAu

I've come back to my city. These are my own old tears.   Leningrad.   Osip Emilevich Mandelstam.   AF

I've come back to the country where I was happy.   Adult.   Linda Gregg.   BLT

I've come to give you fruit from out my orchard.   Crossed Apple, The.   Louise Bogan.   HeIP-4; NALW
   (I've come to give you fruit from out of my orchard.)   RACG

I've come to kneel before you, while you're falling down.   Church.   Nikolai Kanchev.   CSCBP, tr. by Georgi Belev and Lisa Sapinkopf

I've come to tell you of things dear to me.   Skin / Meat / BONES.   Anne Waldman.   PmAP

I've come to the back of the house where the kitchen and the bathroom are. I've Come to the Back of the House. Luis Rosales. RaW, tr. by Ralph Nelson and Rita García Nelson

I've come to the house of the Immortals. At Home in the Summer Mountains. Yu Xuanji. WPoS, tr. by Jane Hirshfield

I've cracked the blue bowl! China Maniacs. May Probyn. VWP

I've cropped the black hair Diego loves. Painting / (Frida Kahlo). Elizabeth Alexander. GT

I've decided to return to the emperor's court. Return of the Proconsul, The. Zbigniew Herbert. PoSu

I've dimmed the lights low. Pleasure. Allison Joseph. PasH

I've discovered a way to stay friends forever. Friendship. Shel Silverstein. NTCP

"I've done my bits of mindless aggro too." Tony Harrison. FaBoVe

I've Dreamed of You So Much. Robert Desnos. WoPoe, tr. by Michael Benedikt and William Kulik

I've dreamed such dreams of you. Robert Desnos. MFP, tr. by Martin Sorrell

I've dreamed such dreams of you that you're losing / your reality. I've dreamed such dreams of you. Robert Desnos. MFP, tr. by Martin Sorrell

I've dreamt of you so often that you become unreal. I've Dreamt of You So Often. Robert Desnos. YaTCFP, tr. by Mary Ann Caws and Jean-Pierre Cauvin

I've dropped me swag in many camps. Search, The. Charles Shaw. NOBAu

I've eaten handfuls of fire. Back Then. Yusef Komunyakaa. GT

I've expanded like the swollen door in summer. Yom Kippur, Taos, New Mexico. Robin Becker. TaR

I've fallen down the finest steps in Europe. Modern Day Sisphus. Jeffrey McDaniel. LaCa

I've forgotten. Ryokan. EMJL; WoPoe, tr. by Burton Watson

I've forgotten everything but the Good Two. Casino. S. L. Wisenberg. PfS

I've forgotten the net and rod. Yun Sŏndo. CATKP Fr. Angler's Calendar, The.

I've forgotten the words. Fabio Morabito. RMCMP, tr. by Geoff Hargreaves

I've gathered the women like talismans, one. Calypso. Olga Broumas. CAP-8

I've given this world the best years of my life. Bindweed. J. B. Bryan. ICANM

I've given up wanting. Dīnrām. SinGod, tr. by Rachel Fell McDermott

I've given you the farewell kiss. Man is Dumb, A. Franz Werfel. GTCP, tr. by Irmgard Hunt

I've gone and done. (LL) Hay for the Horses. Gary Snyder. BB; CAP-8; GoPo; LoL; TRP

I've gone mad drinking nectar. Mahendranāth Bhattācārya. SinGod, tr. by Rachel Fell McDermott

I've got a brand new sweetie. I'll Say She Does. B. G. DeSylva, Al Jolson and Gustave Kahn. ReLy

I've got a creed. Spread a Little Happiness. Clifford Grey. ReLy

I've got a disposition and a way of my own. Ida Cox. NAAPv.2

I've got a Feelin' You're Foolin'. Arthur Freed. ReLy

I've Got a Gal in Kalamazoo. Mack Gordon. ReLy

I've got a home in a-that Rock. Got a Home in That Rock. Unknown. APN-2

I've got a mule, her name is Sal. Erie Canal, The. William S. Allen. HHAm (I've got an old mule and her name is Sal.) APN-2

I've Got a Pocketful of Dreams. Johnny Burke. ReLy

I've got a stubborn goose whose gut's. Rhyme. Sylvia Plath. BodElec

I've got a talking chair. Conversation. Mihangel Morgan. BBMWP; BeAl, tr. by Martin Davis

I've got a taste for trashy thrillers. My Taste for Trash. Chase Twichell. ExTi

I've Got an Apple Ready. John Walsh. NOxBChV

I've got an old mule and her name is Sal. William S. Allen. See I've got a mule, her name is Sal.

I've Got Five Dollars. Lorenz Hart. ReLy

I've got my chair and a good book and I'm sitting. Homage: Summer/Winter, Shay Creek. Joseph Stroud. GeoHom

I've Got My Love to Keep Me Warm. Irving Berlin. ReLy

I've Got Rings on My Fingers. F. J. Barnes and R. P. Weston. ReLy

I've got some good news, honey. Darktown Strutter's Ball, The. Shelton Brooks. ReLy

I've Got the World on a String. Ted Koehler. ReLy

I've got to keep moving. Hellhound on My Trail. Robert Johnson. APT-2; PFTM-2

I've Got You Under My Skin. Cole Porter. ReLy

I've got you under my skin. I've Got You Under My Skin. Cole Porter. ReLy

I've Got Your Number. Carolyn Leigh. ReLy

I've gotten used to this window. Glimpse from the Past. Ilse Aichinger. AF, tr. by Allen H. Chappel

I've Grown Accustomed to Her Face. Alan Jay Lerner. ReLy

I've grown accustomed to her face! I've Grown Accustomed to Her Face. Alan Jay Lerner. ReLy

I've grown old since our farewell, bitterly cultivating the Tao. Dreaming of Long Ago. Po Chü-i. NDACCP, tr. by David Hinton

I've had a mighty busy day. When the Midnight Choo-Choo Leaves for Alabam'. Irving Berlin. ReLy

I've had a million dreams. You Stepped Out of a Dream. Gustave Kahn. ReLy

I've had enough. Bridge Poem, The. Kate Rushin. TWF

I've had enough of your baseness and I haven't killed myself. To the Enemies. Vladimir Holan. AF tr. by C. G. Hanzlicek

I've had my eye on you. San Francisco Streets. Thom Gunn. CalPo

I've heard about Houdini and the rest of them. It's Magic. Sammy Cahn. ReLy

I've heard all about musicians. Saxophonetyx. Cyn Zarco. WaAnP

I've heard from strangers you may be living. To My Younger Brother. Tu Fu [or Du Fu]. CrYelRi, tr. by Sam Hamill

I've heard her thin cry, where the rivers meet. (LL) Two Rivers. Hilary Llewellyn-Williams. AngWePo; TCAWP

I've heard it said about this valley. Owl's Landscape, An. Jon Veinberg. GeoHom

I've heard it sung—it may be true or no. Sebestyén Tinódi. IQMS Fr. Chronicle of Sigismund, The.

I've heard the[m] lilting at our [or the] ewe-milking [or yowe-milking or yewe-milking]. Flowers of the Forest, The. Jane Elliot. NePenScot; NoP-4; NoP-5; OxBEV

I've heard them lilting at loom and belting. Two Songs. Cecil Day Lewis. NAMCP V.1; NoP-4; NoP-5

I've heard them lilting at loom and belting. Cecil Day Lewis. OBMV Fr. Two Songs.

I've hunched so long above this puzzle. Big Jigsaw. Chris Forhan. NAPBL

I've included this letter in the group. Instructions to Be Left Behind. Marvin Bell. TAPaP

I've intended to be harder, to refuse your body in the storms. Spare Tire (the atheist's unmailed letter to god). Ivan Urquiza-Vicente. Vesp

I've interviewed Leslie Howard. Zip. Lorenz Hart. ReLy

I've jouked into a pub. Paula Cunningham. NIrP Fr. Dog Called Chance, A.

I've just found joy. Sweet Lorraine. Mitchell Parish. ReLy

I've just had an astounding dream as I lay in the straw. Minstrel's Song. Ted Hughes. OBCP

I've known a Heaven, like a Tent. Emily Dickinson. GoPo; NCAP

I've known fancies turn into dreaming. Describing a Dream for Someone. Wang Seng-ju. ColAnChi, tr. by Anne Birrell

I've known him so long I've almost forgotten the first photo he showed. Man Struck Twenty Times by Lightning, The. Maxine Chernoff. PmAP

I've known rivers. Negro Speaks of Rivers, The. Langston Hughes. APT-2; BLPJKO; ColAP; CtM; HarvBoo; HeIP-4; ISC; NAAL-5; NAAPv.2; NAMCP V.1; NIL-7; NIP-4; NoAM; NoP-4; NoP-5; OxAAAP; RaBo; SSLK; TCAPo; TFi; WaAnP; WeW-3

I've learned how. Buson. EMJL Fr. Spring Breeze on the Kema Embankment.

I've learnt to wash in petrol tins, and shave myself in tea. Lament of a Desert Rat. N. J. Trapnell. FaBoWar

I've left my own old home of homes. Flitting, The. John Clare. OxAEP-2

I've left on this dreary boat once too often. Sealink. Brendan Cleary. NeBl

I've lived at Cold Mountain—how many autumns [after Han-shan]. Han-shan (Cold Mountain). NDACCP, tr. by Gary Snyder

I've lived in the ghetto here for more than a/ year. Homesick. Unknown, fr. Terezin Concentration Camp. INSAB

I've long desired dawn. Wishes. Philippe Jaccottet. MFP, tr. by Martin Sorrell

I've Looked Everywhere. J. B. Bryan. ICANM

I've lost a sense. Why should I care? On Going Deaf. Anne Stevenson. PoCu

I've lost her, I thought, and called for the bill. (LL) Bistro Styx, The. Rita Dove. NoP-4; NoP-5

I've lost her now, my turtle-dove. Villanelle. Jean Passerat. WaAnP, tr. by Jay Parini

I've lost my Love, I know not where. Madness. Robert Merry. NOBRP

I've lost my rifle and bayonet. Unknown. PoWW

I've lost pal, 'e's the best in all the tahn. It's a Great Big Shame. Edgar Bateman. OBCoV

I've made this alarming discovery. Cucumbers of Wolverhampton, The. Ifor Ap Glyn. BBMWP, tr. by Nigel Jenkins

I've met enough people. Alena Synková. INSAB

I've neither wealth nor power. I'll Get By (As Long As I Have You). Roy Turk. ReLy

I've never applauded "The Star-Spangled Banner." Anthems. Irena Praitis. RWB

I've never been able to bear. (LL) Failure of an Invention. Safiya Henderson-Holmes. BRtP; UnSA

I've never been in love enough. Fabio Morabito. RMCMP, tr. by Geoff Hargreaves

I've never been to Prague, and the last time. Letter to Jorge Luis Borges: Apropos of the Golem. John Hollander. TaR

I've never been too keen on lions and. At the Zoo. John Davies. AngWePo

I've never bothered with the names of flowers. My Field Guide. Erin Belieu. NAPBL

I've Never Feared. Antipater of Thessalonica. WoPoe, tr. by Sam Hamill

I've never feared the setting of the Pleiades. I've Never Feared. Antipater of Thessalonica. WoPoe, tr. by Sam Hamill

I've never scaled the heights of Macchu Picchu with a backpack. Road Less Travelled, The. Alan Jenkins. WaAnP

I've never seen a soul detached from its gender. Horse. Chase Twichell. ExTi; StAl

I've no idea whose woods these are. Traveling with Cats on a Snowy Evening. Gail White. VisFro

I've often wish'd that I could write a book. John Hookham Frere. NOBRP Fr. Prospectus and Specimen of an Intended National Work by William and Robert Whistlecraft...Relating to King Arthur and His Round Table.

I've overslept my stop. . .the train will spit me out. Tatyana Milova. CRWP, tr. by Robert Reid

I've paid for too many degrees. Theory My Natural Brown Ass. Sonnet L'Abbé. OpeFie

I've paid thee what I promised; that's not all:. To His Peculiar Friend Master Thomas Shapcott, Lawyer. Robert Herrick. NOSC

I've plucked every bud hanging over the wall. To the Tune "A Spray of Flowers" (Not Giving In to Old Age). Kuan Han-ch'ing. WoPoe, tr. by Stephen Owen

I've plucked every flower that grows over the wall. In the Southern Mode, to the Tune "A Sprig of Flowers" The Refusal to Get Old. Kuan Han-ch'ing. ColAnChi, tr. by Wayne Schlepp

I've Plucked the Berry. William Motherwell. OxAEP-2

I've positioned myself to relax. Insomnia on a Summer Night. Umberto Saba. AWTN, tr. by Christopher Millis

I've pulled the last of the year's young onions. Eating Alone. Li-Young Lee. CAP-8; NAAL-5; NAMCP V.2; TRP; WeW-3

I've quenched my lamp, I struck it in that start. Pilate's Wife's Dream. Charlotte Brontë. VWP

I've returned to Hong Kong from America. Unknown. NAAPv.2

I've rushed down past the churning. Transparent Woman. Donna Henderson. FiBr

I've said good-bye many times. To My Mother. Simeon Dumdum. ReBoTo

I've sailed several of the world's oceans. First Canzone. Nikolai Stepanovich Gumilyov. TCRusP, tr. by Mary Jane White

I've Seen a Dead Man. Juan Sobalvarro. PML, tr. by John Oliver Simon

I've seen a Dying Eye. Emily Dickinson. APN-2; NAAL-3; NAAPv.1; NCAP

I've seen black masses on their knees. Scottsboro. Y. A. Rontsh. Prolet, tr. by Amelia Glaser

I've seen the famous Rembrandts. You Leave Me Breathless. Ralph Freed. ReLy

I've seen the lights of gay Broadway. Beale Street Blues. William Christopher Handy. APT-1

I've / seen the Mississippi River. Mississippi Blues. Lamont B. Steptoe. SpirFl

I've seen the sea—how could I settle for a river? When We Are Apart. Yüan Chên. CrYelRi, tr. by Sam Hamill

I've sensed ghosts more than once. Father, Mother, Robert Henley, who hanged himself in the ninth grade, et al. Stephen Dunn. StAl

I've set six stones in a row near the eastern. Ghost of Santo Domingo, The. Suzanne Gardinier. NeAmPo

I've slept three centuries on a bed of rocks. Paths of Light. Amina Saïd. YaTCFP, tr. by Mary Ann Caws

I've solved the riddles of the planets. Galileo. János Székely. IQMS, tr. by Geroge Gömöri and Adam Makkai

I've sought out corner bars, lived in corner houses. Corners. Stephen Dunn. PoA 2002

I've spent my life in nothing. (LL) What horror to awake at night. Lorine Niedecker. APT-2; NAAPv.2; NAMCP V.1

I've stayed in the front yard all my life. Gwendolyn Brooks. CAP-8; ESEAA; NAMCP V.2; NoAM; NOxBChV; OxBoAm Fr. Street in Bronzeville, A.

I've stripped the bed. Man in My Bed Like Cracker Crumbs, A. Sandra Cisneros. SweBea

I've taken my fun where I've found it. Ladies, The. Rudyard Kipling. FaBoWar; MoBrPo; NAEL-6v2; NAEL-7v2

I've taken the last drag. City, Evening, and an Old Man: Me, The. "Dhoomil." WoPoe, tr. by Vinay Dharwadker

I've talked (remember). Alba. Imamu Amiri Baraka. FTOS

I've Tasted My Blood. Milton Acorn. Coast

I've Thirty Months, and that's my pride. I've Thirty Months. John Millington Synge. OBMV

I've thrown away my toys. On the Good Ship Lollipop. Sidney Clare. ReLy

I've Told Ev'ry Little Star. Oscar Hammerstein, II. ReLy

I've told you for the clouds. I've Told You. Paul Eluard and Andre Breton. YaTCFP, tr. by Mary Ann Caws

I've tossed an apple at you; if you can love me. Apple, The. Plato. WeW-3

I've touched each string, each muse I have invoked. Pindaric, to the Athenian Society, A. Elizabeth Singer Rowe. BASC

I've traveled eight thousand miles. Untitled. Baekoon Kyunghan. BecRai, tr. by Kim Daljin, Kim Won-Chung and Christopher Merrill

I've tried the new moon tilted in the air. Freedom of the Moon, The. Robert Frost. APT-1

I've tried to explain that you are my Heaven on earth. Until the Real Thing Comes. Sammy Cahn and Mann Holiner. ReLy

I've tried to store away. Palace of Mourners, A. Patrick Sylvain. BRtP

I've two teenage daughters, a decent. Fear of Shoplifting. Maureen Seaton. FFC

I've used up all my film on bombed hospitals. In Thai Binh (Peace) Province. Denise Levertov. AF

I've ventured it of purpose free. Ulrich von Hutten's Song. Ulrich von Hutten. GePo, tr. by Catherine Winkworth

I've visited the place. Unwittingly. John Burnside. StAl

I've waited a long time. Naturalist, A. William O'Daly. PoChi

I've wandered east, I've wandered west. Jeanie Morrison. William Motherwell. TreFP

I've warned you of the bloodbath. Cassandra to Agamemnon. Nina Kossman. CRWP, tr. by the author

I've watched a young woman fondling three strands of her own hair. Jealousy. Elaine Restifo. IJHIL

I've watched thee, Scarab! Yea, an hour in vain. Scarabaeus Sisyphus. Mathilde Blind. ViWPN

I've watched you now a full half-hour. To a Butterfly. William Wordsworth. NPBRoP

I've wined and dined on Mulligan stew. Lady Is a Tramp, The. Lorenz Hart. ReLy

I've wished ill to the searing warplanes. Jet Planes. Gwyn Williams. TCAWP

I've won (lost) my day. Elegy. Carlos Drummond de Andrade. TCLAP, tr. by Virginia de Araújo

I've worked, I've worked so hard; reading, reading. Abulqâsem Ferdowsi. SonAtl, tr. by Hafiz Boboyorov, Darius Irandust, Esfandiar Kiani and Dave Straub

I've written love notes all my life. Ars Poetica. Kevin Prufer. IIR

I've written you a song. Blah, Blah, Blah. Ira Gershwin. ReLy

I've yoked together my large silence and my small outcry. And That Is Your Glory. Yehuda Amichai. BBASP, tr. by Stephen Mitchell

IVF. Kona Macphee. StAl

Ivory Tower, The. Allen Tate. APT-2; OxBoAm

Ivresse d'Amour. Li Po. CCL1, tr. by Judith Gautier

Ivy. Elsa Cross. RMCMP, tr. by Margaret Sayers Peden

Ivy Crown, The. William Carlos Williams. ItP; NAAPv.2; NAMCP V.1; NoAM

Ivy on my window sill, The. Last Poem. Mihály Tompa. IQMS, tr. by Madeline Mason

Ivy ties the cellar door in autumn. Dreaming of Hair. Li-Young Lee. BodElec

I. W. To her unconstant Lover. Isabella Whitney. EMWP; PBRV

Wáchale! She's a black lace bra. Black Lace Bra Kind of Woman. Sandra Cisneros. TiP2

Iwapele, release me. Release. Femi Osofisan. NAfrP

I'yehe! my children—Uhi'yeye'heye! Arapaho Oral Tradition. NAAPv.2 Fr. Ghost-Dance Songs.

Izu Dancer, The. Kimiko Hahn. CAP-8

Izzy. Ira Sadoff. BodElec

J

J. Alfred Prufrock to. Said. George Starbuck. AmWit

J. C. Lawson / my great-grandfather. Town History, 1917. David Huddle. PBCAP

J Car, The. Thom Gunn. MakPoe

J. Edgar Hoover. Said. George Starbuck. AmWit

J is for Jealousy. W. H. Davies. TCAWP

J o l l y m e r r y. Computer's First Christmas Card, The. Edwin Morgan. NOxBChV; OxBEV

J S L. R. Williams Parry. BBMWP, tr. by Emyr Humphreys

J unsubtle serif H or gemini a fish or eternity in(terrupt)completed, A.   Jill Hartman.   PoPra

Ja Da, Ja Da.   Ja Da.   Bob Carleton.   NAAPv.2

Ja Nul Homs Pris Ne Ira a Raison.   Richard I, Coeur de Lion.   WoPoe, *tr. by* Frank Templeton Prince
  (Coeur de Lion.)   HarvBoo

JA ZZ : (The "Say What?") IS IS JA LIVES.   Imamu Amiri Baraka.   SpirFl

János Kemény.   István Gyöngyösi. *tr. by* Watson Kirkconnell
  "Day is done; the twilight grows more dark, The."   IQMS, *tr. by* Watson Kirkconnell

Jabberwocky.   Lewis Carroll.   AmFaPo; BrAP; BRP; CABP; ChAP; ClHu; CtM; HeIP-4; ITBLP; NAEL-6v2; NAEL-7v2; NBLV; NoAM; NoP-4; NoP-5; NOxBChV; NTCP; OBSP; OxAEP-2; OxBEV; TFi; TRP; UV *Fr.* Through the Looking-Glass.

Jacaranda.   Carol Muske-Dukes.   AmAlph

Jacaranda blindings.   Progress.   Bernard Bador.   ConPit, *tr. by* Clayton Eshleman

Jacaranda purple lends.   After winter '76.   Lionel Abrahams.   TSAP

Jack.   Máire Mhac an tSaoi.   IrLP

Jack.   Charles Henry Ross.   NOxBChV; Spl

Jack, Afterwards.   Philip Dacey.   ReTh

Jack and I got see-double drunk. (LL)   Rank.   Lincoln Kirstein.   FaBoA; OBWP; OxBoAm; PWW2

Jack and Jill.   James Vincent Cunningham.   OxBoAm

Jack and Jill.   A. E. Housman.   UV

Jack and Jill went up the hill.   *Unknown.*   OxBEV

Jack at Jack in the Box.   Jack in the Box.   Ko Won.   Vesp

Jack Barrett went to Quetta.   Story of Uriah, The.   Rudyard Kipling.   OxBEV

Jack, dear, at last we are free!—But her mother came to! (LL)   And Her Mother Came Too.   Dion Titherage.   OBCoV; ReLy

"Jack fell as he'd have wished," the Mother said.   Hero, The.   Siegfried Sassoon.   OBWP

Jack finds his wife a perfect beauty. (LL)   Double Transformation, The.   Oliver Goldsmith.   OBCoV; OBNV

Jack Frost.   Fay Zwicky.   BMAP

Jack Gilbert.   Campbell McGrath.   NAPBL

Jack Hall.   Thomas Hood.   NOBRP

Jack hammer! brain chiseller! come out!   Men at Work.   Richard Tipping.   NOBAu

Jack, if you got to be a rounder.   Street Song.   Langston Hughes.   APT-2

Jack in the Box.   Ko Won.   Vesp

Jack Johnson Does the Eagle Rock.   Cornelius Eady.   ESEAA; MoASP

Jack johnson licked.   White Hope.   Ishmael Reed.   ISC

Jack of the North.   *Unknown.*
  "Now for that slawnders sake."   PBRV

Jack Rhymer.   David Brendon Hopes.   UpMys

Jack the Giant-Killer.   James Whitcomb Riley.   NOxBChV

Jack Would Speak Through the Imperfect Medium of Alice.   Alice Notley.   PmAP

Jack, you are quiet now among the dead.   To John Reed.   Max Eastman.   APT-1

Jackals prowl, the serpents hiss, The.   Elegy.   Arthur Guiterman.   AmWit

Jackdaw of Rheims, The.   Thomas Ingoldsby.   CABP

Jackdaw of Rheims, The.   Thomas Ingoldsby.   OBCoV; OBNV; OBSP *Fr.* Ingoldsby Legends, The.

Jackdaw sat on the Cardinal's chair!, The.   Jackdaw of Rheims, The.   Thomas Ingoldsby.   CABP

Jackdaw sat on the Cardinal's chair, The.   Thomas Ingoldsby.   OBCoV; OBNV; OBSP *Fr.* Ingoldsby Legends, The.

Jacked.   Lola Haskins.   LiTh

Jacket Notes.   Ishmael Reed.   UnSA

Jacket of Gray, The.   Caroline Augusta Ball.   CBCWP

Jackey Jackey gallops on a horse like a swallow.   Bushranger, A.   Kenneth Slessor.   NOBAu

Jackfish and walleye circle like clouds as he strains.   Sturgeon.   Karen Solie.   PoPra

Jackie and I cross-legged.   Brown Girl, Blonde Okie.   Gary Soto.   NOxBChV

Jackie in Cambodia.   Catherine Bowman.   ReTh

Jack-in-the-Box.   John Mole.   NOxBChV

Jack-in-the-Box is Jack-in-the-Box.   Jack-in-the-Box.   John Mole.   NOxBChV

Jacklight [*with music*].   Louise Erdrich.   CAP-8; HATNAP; NIL-7; WeW-3

Jack's Last Words.   Stephen Kessler.   GeoHom

Jack's Letter.   John Crowe Ransom.   BrAP

Jack's Pigeon.   R. F. Langley.   HarvBoo

Jackson, Mississippi.   Margaret Abigail Walker.   InGu

Jackson Pollock had a quaint.   Phyllis McGinley.   OBCoV; OBSV *Fr.* Spectator's Guide to Contemporary Art.

Jacob.   Phoebe Cary.   APN-2

Jacob.   Delmore Schwartz.   ChIV-1; TaR

Jacob Mosqueda Wrestles with the Angels.   Rolando Hinojosa.   AmWaPo

Jacob Wrestling with the Angel.   Jones Very.   ChIV-1

Jacobite's Epitaph, A.   Thomas Babington Macaulay, 1st Baron Macaulay.   OBEV
  (Epitaph on a Jacobite.)   OxAEP-2

Jacob's Ladder.   Donald Davie.   OxBSo

Jacob's Ladder.   *Unknown.*   SSUS

Jacob's Ladder, The.   Denise Levertov.   APSN; BrAP; ChIV-1; NAAL-5; PFTM-2

Jacob's Pillow, and Pillar.   Henry Vaughan.   ChIV-1

Jacques s'apprête.   Luis d'Antin Van Rooten.   OBCoV *Fr.* Mots d'Heures: Gousses, Rames.

1. Jade.   Mark Doty.   AmAlph *Fr.* Fog Argument.

Jade.   Phyllis Thompson.   ICANM

JADE a sign on the road announces, *ijada, piedra de.*   Daphne Marlatt.   NLPA *Fr.* Touch to My Tongue.

Jade faces of the girls on Yueh Stream, The.   Girls of Yueh, The.   Li Po.   TAL

Jade Flower Palace ("Stream swirls, The. The wind moans in.")   Tu Fu [*or* Du Fu].   CCL1, *tr. by* Kenneth Rexroth

Jade Flower Palace ("Where the stream winds pine winds linger.")   Tu Fu [*or* Du Fu].   ColAnChi, *tr. by* David Lattimore

Jade kettle with a purchase of spring, A.   Sikong Tu.   CCL1 *Fr.* Twenty-Four Modes of Poetry.

Jade river: birds are dazzling white and whiter.   Wu-Chuen.   Tu Fu [*or* Du Fu].   ChinPo, *tr. by* Ye Weilian [*or* Yeh Wei-lien *or* Wai-lim Yip]

Jade slipped from my wrist, The.   Spaces We Leave Empty.   Cathy Song.   YaYoPo

Jade Tree Blossoms in the Back Garden, A.   Emperor Chen Shubao.   CCL1, *tr. by* John Frodsham

Jade water runs.   Poem Fifty.   Nancy Morejón.   TANSG, *tr. by* Joy Renjilian-Burgy

Jade whips, gold stirrups, hooves of a thoroughbred.   Song of the Insolent Air.   Ch'i-chi.   CSKM, *tr. by* Burton Watson

Jade's Iguanas Are Dead.   Gregory Razran.   IJHIL

Jade-Staircase Grievance.   Li Po.   NDACCP, *tr. by* David Hinton

Jaffa Gate.   Notes in Jerusalem.   Nicholas Samaras.   TWW

Jaffa, July 1948.   Hamutal Bar Yosef.   DTA, *tr. by* Shirley Kaufman

Jagged head.   King & Queen.   John Montague.   PBCIP

Jagged mouth.   Woodland God.   Johannes Bobrowski.   WoPoe, *tr. by* Rich Ives

Jaguar, The.   Ted Hughes.   BrAP

Jaguar's Dream, The.   Charles Marie René Leconte de Lisle.   WoPoe, *tr. by* James Lasdun

Jah Brown si-down.   Ethiopia Unda a Jamaican Mango Tree.   Opal Palmer Adisa.   WaCA

Jah Music.   Lorna Goodison.   WaCA

Jah Son / Another Way.   Kendel Hippolyte.   WaCA

Jaham Sings of the Fear of the Moon.   Eric Ormsby.   IFF

J'ai cru rejoindre par instants une réalité plus profonde comme un fleuve la mer.   J'ai cru rejoindre.   Jacques Dupin.   YaTCFP

J'ai cueilli ce brin de bruyère.   Adieu, L'.   Guillaume Apollinaire.   YaTCFP

J'ai dormi trois siècles sur un lit de rochers.   Amina Saïd.   YaTCFP *Fr.* Sentiers de lumière.

J'ai embrassé j'ai remercié juliette récamier.   Emma Zola à Wimbledon supposons.   Jude Stéfan.   YaTCFP

J'ai l'impression d'être ridicule.   Solde.   Léon Damas.   YaTCFP

J'ai mes statues. Les siècles me les ont léguées: les siècles de mon attente.   Mes statues.   Henri Michaux.   YaTCFP

J'ai tant rêvé de toi que tu perds ta réalité.   J'ai tant rêvé de toi.   Robert Desnos.   YaTCFP

J'aime trop l'univers pour vivre avec un seul être.   Mauvais caractère.   Max Jacob.   YaTCFP

Jain Bird Hospital in Delhi, The.   William Meredith.   VCAP

Jair son of Manasseh went and seized the encampments.   Thomas Merton.   ChIV-1 *Fr.* Geography of Lograire, The.

Jake Addresses the World from the Garden.   Jack Myers.   SUP

Jam Session.   Langston Hughes.   APT-2

Jam Trap, The.   Charles Tomlinson.   MoBrPo

Jamaica 1980.   Lorna Goodison.   GT; WaAnP

Jamaica Market.   Agnes Maxwell-Hall.   WHSW

Jamaica, October 18, 1972.   Shara McCallum.   AmPoNex; BtF

Jamaica oman cunny sah!   Jamaica Oman.   Louise Bennett.   NAMCP V.2

Jamais d'autre que toi en dépit des étoiles et des solitudes.   Jamais d'autre que toi.   Robert Desnos.   YaTCFP

Jamal; Nineteen Cows In a Slow Line Walking.   Gwendolyn Brooks.   ESEAA *Fr.* Children Going Home.

Jamal's Lamentation.   Reuben Jackson.   GT

James Baldwin, 1924–1987.   Alvin Aubert.   FuFl

James Brown.   Linwood M. Ross.   InTrad

James Cagney was the one up both our streets.   Continuous.   Tony Harrison.   NPeEn

James Clarence Mangan in Trinity College Library.   Timothy Brownlow.   IFF

James Dean.   Rae Desmond Jones.   BMAP

James Dean and the Pig.   Joseph Like.   ReTh

James Hugo Johnston.   Maggie Pogue Johnson.   CBWP-4

James James.   Disobedience.   Alan Alexander Milne.   NOxBChV; NTCP; TLR; UV

James Madison's hand cd lead an ox to water.   Jackson Mac Low.   APSN Fr. Presidents of the United States of America, The.

James Monroe / laid a hand.   Jackson Mac Low.   APSN Fr. Presidents of the United States of America, The.

James Rigg.   James Hogg.   NPBRoP

[James Russell] Lowell.   James Russell Lowell.   NAAPv.1; TCAPo Fr. Fable for Critics, A.

James went first because James always went first. The year I was six.   Licking Wounds.   Alice Anderson.   AmPoNex

James Wetherell.   Edwin Arlington Robinson.   MoAmPo

Jameson's Ride.   Alfred Austin.   UV

   "Wrong! Is it wrong? Well, may be."   UV

Jamie Telfer of [or in] the Fair Dodhead.   Unknown.   IBB

Jamilah and Us.   Nazik al-Mala'ika.   IrPoTo, tr. by Basima Qattan Bezirgan and Elizabeth Fernea

Jamilah! Beyond the horizon, far beyond the borders of nations, you weep.   Jamilah and Us.   Nazik al-Mala'ika.   IrPoTo, tr. by Basima Qattan Bezirgan and Elizabeth Fernea

Jammed into denim, grinning in Polaroid.   Ballad of the Bright Angel.   Bruce Berger.   GeoH

Jan van Hogspeuw staggers to the door.   Card-Players, The.   Philip Larkin.   BLT

Jane.   Philip Hammial.   BMAP

Jane Austen.   Patricia Beer.   CABP

Jane Doe #2.   Rafael Campo.   AmPoNex; WiU Fr. Ten Patients, and Another.

Jane Hollybrand; or, Virtue Rewarded.   Edward Edwin Foot.   VerBaPo

   Good Young Squire, The.   STuOW

   Graceful Divine, A.   STuOW

   "Lord Arnold delicately sought to name."   VerBaPo

Jane is big.   Elegy for Jane Kenyon (2).   Jean Valentine.   PoDa

Jane, Jane, / Tall as a crane.   Aubade.   Dame Edith Sitwell.   MoBrPo; NALW; NAMCP V.1; NoAM

Janet Waking.   John Crowe Ransom.   APT-1; ColAP; FuPo; InGu; MoAmPo; NoAM; PtR; WaAnP

Jan's Birthday.   David Lee.   GifTon

Januaries, Nature greets our eyes.   Brazil, January 1, 1502.   Elizabeth Bishop.   BLT; NAMCP V.2; NoAM; PoetW; PoPoPo; VCAP

January.   Douglas Gibson.   OBCP

January.   John Heath-Stubbs.   OBCP

January.   Issa.   EH, tr. by Robert Hass

January.   Henrietta Cordelia Ray.   CBWP-3

January: "After days of putting down my poem."   Ellen Bryant Voigt.   CAP-8

January.   William Carlos Williams.   MoAmPo

January.   Baron Wormser.   GoPo

January 1, 1829.   Nathaniel Parker Willis.   APN-1

January 1, 1999.   Alex Rawls.   AnSo Fr. What's Your Sign?

January 8, 1996.   Kimmika L. H. Williams.   BRtP

January 11, 1997.   Joe Wenderoth.   IIR

January 18, 1979.   John Yau.   OxBoAm

January 20.   David Lehman.   VisFro

January 28, 2003.   Juliana Spahr.   LegDan

January 30, 1976: Message to Myself.   Bob Kaufman.   PFTM-2

January 1965, Looking on.   Kenneth Irby.   FTOS

January, 1795.   Mary Robinson.   NAEL-7v2; NPBRoP; OxBEV; WoRP

January, Anchorage.   Linda McCarriston.   UrbNat

January and February were never so empty and gray.   Spring Will Be a Little Late This Year.   Frank Loesser.   ReLy

January brings the snow.   Garden Year, The.   Sara Coleridge.   ChAP

January first isn't New Year's.   Happy New Year, Anyway.   Joanna Cole.   NTCP

January Hangover.   Pedro Pietri.   BRtP

January in Kyoto.   Nishiwaki Junzaburo.   WoPoe

January, Love, and the Galician.   Jay Wright.   ICANM

January Morning.   William Carlos Williams.   APT-1

January of a Gnat, The.   Carl Rakosi.   APT-2; FTOS

January Ovaries.   Susan Hahn.   ExTi

January played.   One Year.   N. M. Bodecker.   TLR

January-May 1951 Slaughter, The.   Rolando Hinojosa.   AmWaPo

January's Janus wind.   Hayes, The.   Emyr Lewis.   ATSWP, tr. by Robert Minhinnick

Janus.   Laurence Perrine.   PoA 2002

Janus am I; oldest of potentates.   Poet's Calendar, The.   Henry Wadsworth Longfellow.   APN-1

Janus, old man.   January in Kyoto.   Nishiwaki Junzaburo.   WoPoe

Japan.   Maxine Chernoff.   PmAP

   Amble.   PmAP

   Black.   PmAP

Japan.   Billy Collins.   CAP-8; FaoP; NoP-5

Japanese Beetles [2003].   X. J. Kennedy.   AmWit

Japanese City.   Kenward Elmslie.   NYP2; PmAP

Japanese Figures 1.   Unknown.   EaWin, tr. by W. S. Merwin

Japanese Figures 2.   Unknown.   EaWin, tr. by W. S. Merwin

Japanese Hokkus.   Yonejiro (Yone) Noguchi.

Japanese Jokes.   Peter Porter.   OBCoV

Japanese paragraph, The.   Annotations Tropes and Lacunae of the Itoku Master.   Ray DiPalma.   FTOS

Japanese Presentation I and II.   Joan Retallack.   FTOS

Japanese restaurant is good in autumn—in dank weather—the hot napkins, the warm sake, The.   Eduard Veniaminovich Limonov.   TCRusP Fr. Secret Notebook.

Japanese soldier, A.   Narrow Road to the Deep North, The.   Paul Muldoon.   HarvBoo

Japanese yen's gone, The.   Here and Now.   Robert Patrick Dana.   LiTh

Japs.   Lawson Fusao Inada.   FTtHH

Jaques Lured by Audrey.   Leon Stokesbury.   IaFF

Jar of cider and my pipe, A.   Sluggard, The.   W. H. Davies.   OBMV

Jar of Honey, A.   Jacob Polley.   BeAl

Jar of Pens.   Robert Pinsky.   FaoP

Jardin de l'un, Le.   Salah Stétié.   YaTCFP

Jardín de madera.   Dana Gelinas.   SPV

Jardin des Colombières.   Lauris Edmond.   OBGa

Jardín Elíseo.   Carmen Boullosa.   RMCMP

Jargon is like J.'s new language.   Comic.   Heather Fuller.   Eno

Jarrangulli.   Roland Robinson.   NOxBChV

Jarrow.   Carol Rumens.   RSaN; StAl

Jars of octopus, The.   Basho.   EH, tr. by Robert Hass

Jasbo Brown.   DuBose Heyward.   SeSe

Jasmine.   Claude McKay.   APT-1; GT

Jasmine.   E. Ethelbert Miller.   GT; OxAAAP

Jasmine blinker of your breath, The.   Ideal Bar, The.   Frank O'Hara.   BodElec

Jason.   Anthony Hecht.   ColAP

Jastrzebia Góra.   Cathal McCabe.   NIrP

Jaunty crop-haired graying, The.   Poem about People.   Robert Pinsky.   VCAP

Jaunty traveller that comes to peer, The.   Llyn y Gadair.   T. H. Parry-Williams.   BBMWP; OBWVE, tr. by Anthony Conran

J'avais installé sous l'arbre une sorte d'auvent fait de planches.   Pourquoi je deviens un saint.   Oliver Cadiot.   YaTCFP

Jawing gum. (LL)   Gum.   Jean Toomer.   APT-2; NAMCP V.1

Jaya / don't wake up Hara's wife.   Harināth Majumdār.   SinGod, tr. by Rachel Fell McDermott

Jaya, tell him that Uma will not be sent.   Kamalākānta Bhattācārya.   SinGod, tr. by Rachel Fell McDermott

Jayhawkers, an army, and fire are the reasons.   Kaiser's Burnout.   Betty Adcock.   TiP2

Jays, The.   John Heath-Stubbs.   NOxBChV

Jazz.   Angela Ball.   BAP-01

Jazz as Was.   Al Young.   ESEAA

Jazz at the Intergalactic Nightclub.   Michael McClure.   SeSe

Jazz Band.   Frank Marshall Davis.   SeSe

Jazz Band in a Parisian Cabaret.   Langston Hughes.   MoAmPo

Jazz Dancer.   Cornelius Eady.   SeSe

Jazz Fan Looks Back.   Jayne Cortez.   ESEAA

Jazz Fantasia.   Carl Sandburg.   MoAmPo

Jazz of This Hotel, The.   Vachel Lindsay.   SeSe

Jazz radio on a midnight kick.   Round About Midnight.   Bob Kaufman.   CalPo

Jazz Rain.   Quo Vadis Gex-Breaux.   FuFl

Jazz Station.   Michael S. Harper.   NoAM

Jazzonia.   Langston Hughes.   ColAP; NAAPv.2

Je chante ma femme de l'autre rive.   Je chante ma femme.   André Velter.   YaTCFP

Je consens que tout s'efface.   Robert Marteau.   YaTCFP

Je crains pas ça tellment la mort de mes entrailles.   Je crains pas ça tellment.   Raymond Queneau.   YaTCFP

Je crois qu'il pleut, mais il ne pleut pas. Il pleut. Jacques Roubaud. YaTCFP

Je danse au milieu des miracles. Parti Pris. Louis Aragon. YaTCFP

Je lave. Martine Broda. YaTCFP

Je marche dans la solitude des livres. Marie-Claire Bancquart. YaTCFP

Je me redresse avec effort et je regarde. Je me redresse avec effort. Philippe Jaccottet. YaTCFP

Je me souviens comme l'enfant tire sa mère. Relèvement d'Icare, L': Envoi. Guy Goffette. YaTCFP

Je m'obstine à mêler des fictions aux redoutables réalités. Paul Éluard. YaTCFP *Fr.* Nuits partagées.

Je m'offre à chacun comme sa récompense. Don de soi-mème, Le. Valery Larbaud. YaTCFP

Je ne crois pas décidément que nous ferons ce voyage. Pensées sous les nuages. Philippe Jaccottet. YaTCFP

Je ne dors pas Georgia. Georgia. Philippe Soupault. YaTCFP

Je ne parle pas pour moi. Je ne parle pas. Eugène Guillevic. YaTCFP

Je ne vais pas toujours seul au fond de moi-mème. Poète, Un. Jules Supervielle. YaTCFP

Je parle dans tous les âges. René Daumal. YaTCFP

Je prends le chemin, qui mène au jardin de l'erreur, je joue avec les noms. Je prends le chemin. Abdelwahab Meddeb. YaTCFP

Je rêvais de toucher la tristesse du monde. Je rêvais de toucher. Georges Bataille. YaTCFP

Je suis ce cours de sable qui glisse [*Author's own French vers. of his* "My way is in the sand flowing"]. Samuel Beckett. YaTCFP

Je suis claire dit-elle. Je suis claire comme les rumeurs de l'aube. Dans la lumière du jour. Marcelin Pleynet. YaTCFP

Je suis couchée avec un homme dans un lit qui est à l'extrémité d'une grande salle. Rêve à Barcelone. Meret Oppenheim. YaTCFP

Je suis la terre et l'eau, tu ne me passeras pas à gué, mon ami, mon ami. Je suis la terre et l'eau. Anne Hébert. YaTCFP

Je suis le spectateur et l'acteur et l'auteur. D'un et de deux, de tous. Paul Éluard. YaTCFP

Je suis revenu de la Bibliothèque Nationale. Révélation, La. Max Jacob. YaTCFP

Je suis vieux et je suis lourd. Renfort [2]. Raymond Queneau. YaTCFP

Je t'adore. Thomas Kinsella. NAMCP V.2; NoAM

Je te l'ai dit pour les nuages. Je te l'ai dit. Paul Éluard. YaTCFP

Je te narine je te chevelure. Fin du monde, La: Prendre corps. Gherasim Luca. YaTCFP

Je temps de quoi. Danielle Collobert. YaTCFP

Je veux dormir avec toi coude à coude. Je veux dormir avec toi. Joyce Mansour. YaTCFP

Je veux revoir cette séquence. Nicole Brossard. YaTCFP

Je veux vivre à l'ombre de ton visage. Papier d'argent. Joyce Mansour. YaTCFP

Je voudrais te parler cristal fêlé hurlant comme un chien dans une nuit de draps battants. Où Es-Tu. Benjamin Péret. YaTCFP

Je voulais te l'avouer. Martine Broda. YaTCFP

Je vous dis adieu monsieur mon sergent. Renfort [1]. Raymond Queneau. YaTCFP

Je ziet hoe het gebeurt. Afdaling op klaarlichte dag. Rutger Kopland. LWR

Jealous Twain, The. Sir Walter Scott. DiBP *Fr.* Marmion.

Jealousy. Mei-Mei Berssenbrugge. OpBo; PmAP

Jealousy. Mary Elizabeth Coleridge. LW

Jealousy: "I look out of the window at the retreating back." Inna L'vovna Lisnyanskaya. CRWP, *tr. by* Daniel Weissbort

Jealousy: "I've watched a young woman fondling three strands of her own hair." Elaine Restifo. IJHIL

Jean. Robert Burns. *See* Of A' the Airts [the Wind Can Blaw].

Jean Rhys. William Scammell. NLP

Jean Richepin's Song. Herbert Trench. OBMV

Jean tells me that the Senator. Chateau de Soupir, 1917. Malcolm Cowley. AmWaPo

Jean-Baptiste Chardin. Self-Portrait on a Summer Evening. Eavan Boland. NPeEn

Jeane Dixon's America. Gerald Costanzo. ReTh

Jeanie Morrison. William Motherwell. TreFP

Jeanie with the Light Brown Hair. Stephen Collins Foster. APN-2

Jeanne Duval's Confession. Yusef Komunyakaa. BAP-97

Jeanne was holed up (pitch darkness; bread and water). Victor Hugo. SxFrPo, *tr. by* A. M. and E. H. Blackmore

Jeare your Benefactress, that's but Just. To; Oxon. Marey Waller. EMWP

J'écris cela pour écrire ceci. Ce qui est écrit l'est. Emmanuel Hocquard. YaTCFP *Fr.* À Noël.

Jeelie Piece Song, The. Adam McNaughtan. EdScPo

Jeep Cherokee. Bruce A. Jacobs. PoDa

Jeep Driver, The. Martín Espada. PueRic

Jeepers Creepers. Johnny Mercer. ReLy

Jeepney. Gemino H. Abad. ReBoTo

Jeepneyfying. Noel Mateo. ReBoTo

Jeffers Country. Sherod Santos. GeoHom

Jefferson Company, The. Clarence Major. BodElec

Jefferson Highway. Billy. Oktavi Allison. BRtP

Jeffery, or, the Soldier's Progress. Philip Freneau. AmWaPo

Jeffrey Lee Pierce. Campbell McGrath. NAPBL

Jeffrey Lee Pierce is dead, at age 37, Salt Lake City, Utah. Jeffrey Lee Pierce. Campbell McGrath. NAPBL

Jehovah evokes the promised signs. Tovu-Vavohu. Manuela Fingueret. MirDau, *tr. by* Roberta Gordenstein

Jehoviah, Hallelujah, / De Lord is perwide. Jehovah, Hallelujah. *Unknown.* SSUS

Jelly Bean Policy, The. Jose Angel Figueroa. RWB

Jellyfish, A. Marianne Moore. ItP; NAAPv.2

(Jelly-Fish, A.) ChAP

Jemez Mountains Meditation. Jim Cohn. WhBo

Jemez Pueblo: December 26. Patricia Smith. ICANM

Jemmy Ball, a lucky digger. Moggy's Wedding. Charles Robert Thatcher. NOBAu

Jenkins, all too clearly it is time. Four of the Belt. Tom Leonard. BeAl

Jennie McGrew. Edgar Lee Masters. RACG

Jenny come ower the hill. Doors of Sleep, The. Marion Angus. EdScPo; NePenScot

Jenny Hit Me. John Clarke. UV

Jenny hit me when we met. Jenny Hit Me. John Clarke. UV

Jenny in Love. Dolores Kendrick. ESEAA

Jenny in Sleep. Dolores Kendrick. ESEAA

Jenny Kissed Me. Leigh Hunt. *See* Rondeau: "Jenny kissed [*or* kiss'd] me when we met."

Jenny kissed [*or* kiss'd] me when we met. Rondeau. Leigh Hunt. CABP; NBLV; NIL-7; NTCP; OBEV; OxAEP-2; OxBEV

Jenny Nettles. Allan Ramsay and *Unknown.* NePenScot

Jenny Wren. W. H. Davies. MoBrPo

Jenny Wren. Walter De la Mare. OWoS

Jeopard, The. Silvia Eugenia Castillero. SPV, *tr. by* Jen Hofer

Jeopardo, El. Silvia Eugenia Castillero. SPV

Jephtha's Daughter. Lord Byron. ChIV-1

Jerboa, The. Marianne Moore. NALW

Jerdan's mills agrinding, Jerdan's ahay. Jordan's Mills. *Unknown.* SSUS

Jeremiah. Bible, *O.T.*

"For Thus saith The Lord to the men of Judah and Jerusalem." OBVE

Jeremie 17. Bible, Apocrypha. ChIV-1

Jerked from meditation. One Golgotha. Douglas Livingstone. TSAP

Jerking and twitching as he walks. Mightier than the Pen. Kingsley Amis. OBCoV

Jerome in His Study. Clark Coolidge. FTOS

JERRY'S HOME TOLD YOU not to move the couch, hurt hip *leg tonight* why. Hannah Weiner. PFTM-2 *Fr.* Clairvoyant Journal.

Jerry's Plains, 1848. Geoff Page. BMAP

Jersey Rain. Robert Pinsky. BAP-01

Jerusalem. Yehuda Amichai. BeAl, *tr. by* Chana Bloch and Stephen Mitchell

Jerusalem. William Blake. *See* Preface: "And did those feet in ancient time."

Jerusalem. William Blake.

(England! Awake! Awake! Awake!) NoP-4; NoP-5

Epigraph. Spl

Fields from Islington to Marybone, The. OBNV

"Hampstead Highgate Finchley Hendon Muswell hill: rage loud." NOBRP

"I see the Four-fold Man. The Humanity in deadly sleep." NOBRP

"Trembling I sit day and night. My friends are astonished at me." NPBRoP; WaAnP

Jerusalem. Sara Riwka Erlich. MirDau, *tr. by* J. M. Deisler and Auristela Xavier

Jerusalem. James Fenton. BeAl; HarvBoo

Jerusalem. Jacob Fichman. FIT, *tr. by* Robert Friend

Jerusalem. Manuela Fingueret. MirDau, *tr. by* Roberta Gordenstein

Jerusalem. David Morley. NLP

Jerusalem. Naomi Shihab Nye. CFP; RaF

Jerusalem. Adrienne Rich. TaR

Jerusalem a child reborn every day. Jerusalem. Sara Riwka Erlich. MirDau, *tr. by* J. M. Deisler and Auristela Xavier

Jerusalem, a Whirling Glass. Luisa Futuransky. MirDau, *tr. by* Celeste Kostopulos-Cooperman

Jerusalem! Cry of the hungry heart, oblivion's. Jerusalem. Jacob Fichman. FIT, *tr. by* Robert Friend

Jerusalem Delivered. Torquato Tasso. *tr.* by G. Grinnell-Milne

"Who first of Christian warriors now did chance." FaBoWar, *tr.* by G. Grinnell-Milne

Jerusalem, I am a pilgrim. Olga Klein Weisz. MirDau, *tr.* by Leslie MacIntosh

Jerusalem roses are complicated. Jerusalem, a Whirling Glass. Luisa Futuransky. MirDau, *tr.* by Celeste Kostopulos-Cooperman

Jerusalem sits on her mountains, a woman. Bride, The. Alicia Ostriker. TaR

Jerusalem Song. Lisa Suhair Majaj. PoArWo

Jerusalem Sonnets. James Keir Baxter.

"Brother Ass, Brother Ass, you are full of fancies." HarvBoo

"Colin, you can tell my words are crippled now." HarvBoo

"I am dying now because I do not die." HarvBoo

"In Auckland it was the twelve days' garland." HarvBoo

Jerusalem, Timeless. Luisa Futuransky. MirDau, *tr.* by Celeste Kostopulos-Cooperman

Jerusalem, ungoverned city. Stratis the Sailor by the Dead Sea. George Seferis. WoPoe, *tr.* by Rex Warner

Jerusalem Walked thru War. Julia Vinograd. FTtHH

Jervis Bay, The. Michael Thwaites.

"On either side the *Jervis Bay* the convoy was dipping." FaBoWar

Jesse James. William Rose Benét. MoAmPo

Jesse James. *Unknown.* APN-2

Jesse James was a lad who [*or* that] killed many a man. Jesse James. *Unknown.* APN-2

Jesse James was a two-gun man. Jesse James. William Rose Benét. MoAmPo

Jessie Mitchell's Mother. Gwendolyn Brooks. ColAP; NALW; OxAAAP

Jest 'fore Christmas. Eugene Field. ChrPo

Jester walked in the garden, The. Cap and Bells, The. William Butler Yeats. MoBrPo; NAMCP V.1; NoAM

Jesu. George Herbert. RSR

Jesu! bless our slender Boat. William Wordsworth. SacPr *Fr.* Memorials of a Tour of the Continent; 1820.

Jesu Christ, my Leman Swete. *Unknown.* SacPr

Jesu Crist, myn leman swete. Jesu Christ, my Leman Swete. *Unknown.* SacPr

JESU is in my heart, his sacred name. Jesu. George Herbert. RSR

Jesu, Lord, that madist me. Richard of Caistre. SacPr

Jesu, Lover of my Soul. Charles Wesley. SacPr

JESU, thy love within me is so main. Divine Sonnet, A. William Alabaster. NoSic

Jesus. James Philip McAuley. ChIV-2

Jesus. Novica Tadic. VCWP, *tr.* by Charles Simic

Jesus Asleep. Anne Sexton. PFTM-2

Jesus before Pilate said nothing. Jesus Before Pilate. René Daumal. GI; MotU, *tr.* by Katharine Washburn

Jesus calls us! O'er the tumult. Cecil Frances Alexander. SacPr

Jesus Dies. Anne Sexton. PFTM-2; RACG

Jesús, Estrella, Esperanza, Mercy: / Sails flashing to the wind like weapons. Middle Passage. Robert Earl Hayden. APT-2; CAP-8; ColAP; NAAL-5; NAMCP V.2; NoAM; OxAAAP; OxBoAm; TRP; VCAP; WaAnP

Jesus / Good Friday blood on the teeth night a. Gospel Poem #2. David Craig. UpMys

Jesus, Hayden, it's hard to believe you're. To Hayden Carruth on His Eightieth Birthday. Sam Hamill. WANABP

Jesus, I am cruelly lonely. Concerning That Prayer I Cannot Make. Jane Mead. LaCa; PLBUT

Jesus I am resting, resting. Jean Sophia Pigott. SacPr

Jesus in the water does not look clean or fish-like or marine at all but. Post card (central park). Rachel Zucker. IAoNAP

Jesus Is Condemned to Death. Pamela Mordecai. WaCA

Jesus / Loaded Jowl Cakes Mother of seismic dreams. Gospel Poem #1. David Craig. UpMys

Jesus' mother never had no man. Conception. Waring Cuney. APT-2

Jesus, my Light. They Shall Look on Him. Michael Field. VWP

Jesus Never Sleeps. David Graham. SwNoth

Jesus Praying. Hartley Coleridge. ChIV-2

Jesus / Risen / past the amphibial claws. Gospel Poem #3. David Craig. UpMys

Jesus shall reign where'er the sun. Isaac Watts. SacPr

Jesus slept as still as a toy. Jesus Asleep. Anne Sexton. PFTM-2

Jesus' Song. Esther Louise. BtF

Jesus Speaks to the Church at Eastertime. Elizabeth Burns. EdScPo

Jesus Suckles. Anne Sexton. PFTM-2

Jesus, the very thought of thee With sweetness fills my breast. *Unknown.* SacPr, *tr.* by Edward Caswell

Jesus these eyes have never seen. Hymn. Ray Palmer. SacPr

Jesus, they run into millions. (LL) Soldiers. *Unknown.* FaBoWar; PoAgWa

Jesus, Thou Joy of Loving Hearts. Bernard of Clairvaux. SacPr, *tr.* by Ray Palmer

Jesus, thy blood and righteousness. Nikolaus Ludwig, Graf von Zinzendorf. SacPr, *tr.* by John Wesley

Jesus tucked with cousins into mirrors. Wake. Kevin Young. OxAAAP

Jesus Unborn. Anne Sexton. PFTM-2

Jesus was not the Son of God. He was a yogi. What We Believe. Charles Harper Webb. Vesp

Jesus Wept. William Michael Rossetti. CenSon

Jesus! What a friend for sinners! J. Wilbur Chapman. SacPr

Jesus, where'er thy people meet. William Cowper. SacPr *Fr.* Olney Hymns.

Jesus will always be there. He's waiting. It's true. Gospel. Andrew Hudgins. UpMys

Jesus, Won't You Come By-And-Bye! *Unknown.* SSUS

Jet black, once pretty. Paralyzed. Willie Abraham Howard Jr. BtF

Jet Lag. Peter Makuck. OtW

Jet Plane. Aloysius Michael Sullivan. OtW

Jet Planes. Gwyn Williams. TCAWP

Jet Set Melodrama. Michael Brownstein. AHA; FTOS

Jethro Somes' Apostrophe to His Former Comrades. John Pauker. PWW2

Jets. Christopher Meredith. AngWePo

Jetty, The. Henri Michaux. MotU, *tr.* by Richard Ellmann

Jetty, The. Elaine Randell. Oth *Fr.* Snoad Hill Poems, The.

Jeune Fille Endormie. Jean Cocteau. YaTCFP

Jew answers every question with another question, The. Edmond Jabès. PFTM-2 *Fr.* Book of Questions, The.

Jew, The. Isaac Rosenberg. ChIV-1; MoBrPo

Jewel and jetsam, wanted and unforgiven. (LL) Thelonius. Afaa Michael Weaver. BtF; FuFl

Jewel Cliff. Muso Soseki. EaWin, *tr.* by W. S. Merwin

Jewel Field. Muso Soseki. EaWin, *tr.* by W. S. Merwin

Jewel of the almost islands and the isles. Catullus. *See* Apple of islands, Sirmio, & bright peninsulas, set.

Jewel Stairs' Grievance, The. Li Po. NDACCP; OBVE, *tr.* by Ezra Pound

Jewel, The. Dunya Mikhail. IrPoTo, *tr.* by Salaam Yousif

Jewel, The. Mary Ruefle. AmAlph

Jewelled steps are already quite white with dew, The. Jewel Stairs' Grievance, The. Li Po. NDACCP; OBVE, *tr.* by Ezra Pound

Jewels. Sara Teasdale. APT-1

Jewels wherever we look. *Unknown.* GifTon, *tr.* by David Ray

Jewish. Dick Lourie. PrTe

Jewish. Harvey M. Plotnick. OPRER

Jewish Cemetery at Berlin-Weissensee, The. Günter Kunert. GTCP, *tr.* by Reinhold Grimm

Jewish Cemetery at Newport, The. Henry Wadsworth Longfellow. APN-1; ChIV-1; ColAP; FaBoA; HeIP-4; NAAL-5; NAAPv.1; NCAP; NoP-4; NoP-5; OxBoAm; PoPoPo; TCAPo; WaAnP

Jewish Cemetery at Olsany, Kafka's Grave, April, Sunny Weather, The. Miroslav Holub. PoSu

Jewish Cemetery, Frankfurt. Jenni Daiches. EdScPo

Jewish Cemetery in Guanabacoa, The. Ruth Behar. MirDau

Jewish King Lear is getting ready, The. Adler. Gerald Stern. TaR

Jewish Singles Event, The. Stewart Florsheim. UnSA

Jewish Time Bomb, The. Yehuda Amichai. RaF, *tr.* by Chana Bloch and Chana Kronfeld

Jewish women were lined up by German troops in charge of the territory. Charles Reznikoff. NAAPv.2 *Fr.* Holocaust.

Jews at Haifa. Randall Jarrell. MoAmPo

Jews from Holland, France, and Hungary, and later from. Charles Reznikoff. HP

Jew's hands, translucent in the dusk, The. Spinoza. Jorge Luis Borges. TCLAP, *tr.* by Richard Howard and César Renert

Jews in Babylonia. Charles Reznikoff.

I. FTOS

Jews in Hell. Tom Mandel. PmAP

Jews in the Land of Israel. Yehuda Amichai. PoSu

Jews Speak in Heaven, The. Gary Catalano. NOBAu

Jezebel to the Eunuchs. Eleanor Brown. MFPA

Jhesu, since thou me made and bought. Prayer to Jesus 1. Richard Rolle of Hampole. SacPr

Ji Gate. Kao Shih. CCL1, *tr.* by Stephen Owen

Jiang Yuying, Famous Professor at Beijing University, Who Daringly Rendered into Chinese the First Complete Walt Whitman. Willis Barnstone. ViWalt

Jiang Zhong-zi: Hep-Cat Chung. *Unknown.* CCL1, *tr.* by Ezra Pound

Jiangnan. Po Chü-i. CCL1, *tr.* by Marsha Wagner

Jiangnan is wonderful! Jiangnan. Po Chü-i. CCL1, *tr.* by Marsha Wagner

Jig. Cecil Day Lewis. IrLP

Jig fades to silence, except it doesn't, The. (LL) Notations of Ten Summer Minutes. Norman Alexander MacCaig. EmeKit; NPeEn

Jig! Let's dance!, A. Streets 1. Paul Verlaine. SxFrPo, *tr. by* Martin Sorrell

Jigsaw Puzzle. Deborah Boe. PfS

Jigsaw Puzzle. Russell Hoban. NTCP

Jihad. J. D. McClatchy. AmWaPo

Jihad. Thelma Seto. TWW

Jill's a good kid who's had some tough luck. But that's another story. Politics of Narrative, The: Why I Am a Poet. Lynn Emanuel. SUP

Jill's Death. George Buchanan. PNI

Jilted Queen, The. NAEL-7v1 *Fr.* Aeneid [*or* Eneados *or* Aeneis], The.

Jim. Joseph Hilaire Pierre Belloc. *See* Jim Who Ran Away from His Nurse, and Was Eaten by a Lion.

Jim Bludso of the Prairie Belle. John Milton Hay. APN-2

Jim Crack Corn; or The Blue Tali Fly. *Unknown.* APN-2

Jim Crow Car. Langston Hughes. GM

Jim Crow Cars [*with music*]. Lizelia Augusta Jenkins Moorer. CBWP-3

Jim Dumps was a most unfriendly man. Force. *Unknown.* OBCoV

Jim Dumps was a most unfriendly man. *Unknown.* OBCoV *Fr.* Advertising Rhymes.

Jim Hall's guitar walking around. From Rich Uneasy America to My Friend Christopher Logue. Adrian Mitchell. SeSe

Jim Jackson caught a cold. If I'm Going to Die I'm going to Have Some Fun. George M. Cohan. ReLy

Jim O'Shea was cast away upon an Indian isle. I've Got Rings on My Fingers. F. J. Barnes and R. P. Weston. ReLy

Jim Silversmith stands tall over me. Indian. Feroza F. Jussawalla. RWB

Jim the Janitor Is Dead. Dora Teitelboim. Prolet, *tr. by* Amelia Glaser

Jim went north to Maine. West Texas Suicide. Lillian Wright. TiP2

Jim Who Ran Away from His Nurse, and Was Eaten by a Lion. Joseph Hilaire Pierre Belloc. NOxBChV; OBSP; OxAEP-2

(Jim.) NoAM

Jimeen Connor, the butcher, is coming round. Brendan Kennelly. ModIr *Fr.* Cromwell.

Jimi and Tony. Mark Doty. InoFa; WiU *Fr.* Atlantis.

Jimmy. . . / said he never tasted. Roots 2: the conjure woman replies. Cherryl "Blue." Floyd-Miller. BtF

Jimmy C. Courthouse Graffiti for Two Voices. Martín Espada. InvLad

Jimmy Jet and His TV Set. Shel Silverstein. OBCoV

Jimmy was soldier brave and bold. K-K-K-Katy. Geoffrey O'Hara. ReLy

Jim's Hairball. Lee Upton. AmAlph

Jine 'Em. *Unknown.* SSUS

Jing gorge: white rocks jut. On the Mountain. Wang Wei. CCL1, *tr. by* Jerome P. Seaton

Jingle Bells. James S. Pierpont. TCAPo

Jingle in a broken tongue, A. (LL) Poet, The. Paul Laurence Dunbar. NAAPv.1; TCAPo

Jingling her moon of parchment. Preciosa and the Wind. Federico García Lorca. STV, *tr. by* John Frederick Nims

Jings! but it's laughable, tae. (LL) Image o' God, The. Joe Corrie. ChIV-1; RSaN

Jinny. *Unknown.* NOSC

Jinny the Just. Matthew Prior. OBEV

Jist Ti Let Yi No. Tom Leonard. NePenScot

Jiu-mu: South, Droops a Tree. *Unknown.* CCL1, *tr. by* V. W. X.

Jive, The. Mafika Pascal Gwala. TSAP

Jo Gravis in His Metal Garden. Sinéad Morrissey. NIrP

Joachaim est sans doute au fond du jardin. Aïeul, L'. Jean Grosjean. YaTCFP

Joachim must be in the garden. Ancestor, The. Jean Grosjean. YaTCFP, *tr. by* Mary Ann Caws *and* Jean-Pierre Cauvin and Patricia Terry

Joan of Arc. Benjamin Péret. PFTM-1

Joan of Arc. Robert Southey.
  "These are the Daemons that pervert the power." NAEL-7v2

Joan of Arc, in Rheims. Felicia Dorothea Hemans. RWP; ViWPN

Joanne. Joanne Kyger. AHA

Joan's kiss. Watching the Planes Come In at La Guardia. John Frederick Nims. OtW

Joan's one-eighth. I'm a quarter. Two Standards. Elise Paschen. OPRER; ReEnLa

Job. Bible, *O.T.* NAWM-5v1, *tr. by* King James Version, New Revised Standard Version and R. P. Scheindlin
  "As a servant earnestly desireth the shadow, and as an hireling looketh for the reward of his work." AWTN, *tr. by* King James Version
  Job Cries Out. OBVE
  Let the Day Perish [Wherein I Was Born]. NPeEn; OBVE
  Leviathan. OBVE

"Moreover the Lord answered Job, and said." OBVE

"Then Job spoke and cursed his day and chanted and said." WoPoe, *tr. by* R. P. Scheindlin

"Who is this that darkeneth counsel by words without knowledge?"
  "Knowest thou the time when the wild goates of the rocke bring forth?" OBVE

"Then the Lord answered Job out of the whirlwind, and sayd." OBVE; WoPoe

"Then the Lord answered Job out of the whirlwind." InvLi, *tr. by* New Revised Standard Version

"Wing of the ostrich rejoiceth, The." OWoS

Job. Elizabeth Sewell. ChIV-1

Job 18, 2. José Emilio Pacheco. TCLAP, *tr. by* Alastair Reid

Job came to the rabbi. Grant of death, The. Anna Glazova. CRWP, *tr. by* Max Nemtsov

Job Cries Out. Bible, *O.T.* OBVE *Fr.* Job.

Job Davies, eighty-five. Lore. Ronald Stuart Thomas. BeAl; NoP-4; NoP-5

Job from His Mountain. David Brendon Hopes.
  "And Job from his mountain sees." UpMys

Job Hunting. Brian Patten. RSaN

Job: I was cast onto a new life cycle. Maya Bejerano. DTA *Fr.* Hymns of Job.

Job in certain lives has been to find **A**, The. Spell, The. Molly Peacock. FFC

Job Interview, The. Richard Howard. OxBoAm

Job Militant. Francis Quarles.
  Meditatio Tertia Decima. ChIV-1

Job: "My mother sold life insurance." Erika Meitner. NevBe

Job No. 75-14. Clemens Starck. PoDa

Job. I. John Hall. ChIV-1

Job sat in a corner of the dump eating asparagus. Cæsura. John Ashbery. ChIV-1

2. The Job. Charles Reznikoff. ColAP; NAAPv.2 *Fr.* Testimony.

Job the Father. Richard Shelton. PBCAP

Job's Epitaph. Joshua Sylvester. ChIV-1

Job's Wife. Shirley Kaufman. DTA

Job-seeker, talk time hoping. Mr. Bezuidenthout's Dogs. Musaemura Bonus Zimunya. NAfrP

Jo'burg City, Johannesburg, Jo'burg City. (LL) City Johannesburg. Mongane Wally Serote. NAfrP; TSAP

Jock o' the Side [Version from Poetical Museum; Albyn's Anthology 2]. *Unknown.* IBB

Jock of Hazeldean. Sir Walter Scott. NAEL-6v2; NAEL-7v2; NOBRP

Jockeyed by fleas and led, as we say. Dogs of Montone, The. William Matthews. PfSP

Jocular Lines to Plotius Grypus. Publius Papinius Statius. RomPo *Fr.* Sylvae [*or* Silvae].

Joe. Emily Pauline Johnson. SWaP

Joe and Ned. Susanna Blamire. RWP

Joe Gargery's Epitaph on His Father. Charles Dickens. FaBoVe *Fr.* Great Expectations.

Joe insisted that life is extreme. Conversation in Woodside. Kim Addonizio. GeoHom

Joe Williams at the Blue Note/Chicago, 1955; March 30 1999. Sam Hamod. FTtHH

Joe, you Big Shot! You Big Man! Pidgin Pinch. William Jay Smith. PWW2

Joey, the head lifeguard. All the Pools in Queens. Erika Meitner. NevBe

Jog On, jog on, the footpath way. William Shakespeare. NoSic *Fr.* Winter's Tale, The.

Jogger on Riverside Drive, 5:00 A.M., The. Agha Shahid Ali. MoASP

Johann Joachim Quantz's Five Lessons. William Sydney Graham. EmeKit; HarvBoo

Johannes Agricola in Meditation. Robert Browning. SacPr

John. Jones Very. ChIV-2

John 1:1 and 14. Gail Holst-Warhaft. GI *Fr.* St. John.

John 11:30–44; Now Jesus had not yet come to the village. Rainer Maria Rilke. GI *Fr.* St. John.

John 1:14 (1964). Jorge Luis Borges. GI

John 1:14 (1969). Jorge Luis Borges. GI, *tr. by* Norman Thomas Di Giovanni

John 1:14; And the Word became flesh and dwelt among us. Jorge Luis Borges. GI *Fr.* St. John.

John 12:24–25; Truly, truly, I say to you. Pier Paolo Pasolini. GI *Fr.* St. John.

John 13:21–30; When Jesus had thus said, he was troubled. Nina Kossman. GI *Fr.* St. John.

John 14:1–2. Mary Elizabeth Fullerton. GI *Fr.* St. John.

John 20:11–18; But Mary stood weeping outside the tomb. Rainer Maria Rilke. GI *Fr.* St. John.

John 2:1–12; On the third day there was a marriage. Rainer Maria Rilke. GI *Fr.* St. John.

John 3; But Men Loved Darknesse Rather than Light. Bible, *N.T.* ChIV-2 *Fr.* St. John.

John 3:1–15; Now there was a man. Howard Nemerov. GI *Fr.* St. John.

John Adams knew the hand. Jackson Mac Low. APSN *Fr.* Presidents of the United States of America, The.

John Adams lies here, of the parish of Southwell. On a Carrier Who Died of Drunkenness. Lord Byron. NBLV

John and Anne. William Meredith. BodElec

John Anderson, My Jo ("John Anderson, my jo, John, / I wonder what ye mean.") Robert Burns. FaBoVe

John Anderson, My Jo ("John Anderson my jo, John / When we were first acquent.") Robert Burns. HeIP-4; ItP; NePenScot; NOBRP; NoP-5; OBEV; OxBEV; TFi; TreFP; TRP; WoPoe

John Anderson, my jo, John, / I wonder what ye mean. John Anderson, My Jo. Robert Burns. FaBoVe

John Anderson my jo, John / When we were first acquent. John Anderson, My Jo. Robert Burns. HeIP-4; ItP; NePenScot; NOBRP; NoP-5; OBEV; OxBEV; TFi; TreFP; TRP; WoPoe

John Arm—strongs last good night. *Unknown.* PBRV

John Berryman Listening to Robert Johnson's "King of the Delta Blues," January 1972. David Wojahn. SeSe

John Bird, a laborer, lies here. Epitaph. Sylvia Townsend Warner. MoBrPo

John Birks Gillespie: An Appreciation and Reflection. Everett Goodwin. BtF

John Brown. Vachel Lindsay. MoAmPo *Fr.* Booker Washington Trilogy, The.

John Brown, glowing far and down. Smell of Coal Smoke, The. Les A. Murray. NOBAu

John Brown's Body. Henry Howard Brownell. HHAm

John Brown's Body. Stephen Vincent Benét.
 Book One.
  John Brown's Prayer. CBCWP
 Book Two.
  Congressmen Came Out To See Bull Run. CBCWP
 Book Five.
  Love Came By From the Riversmoke. MoAmPo
 Book Eight.
  "John Brown's body lies a-mouldering in the grave." APT-2
  Song of the Riders. MoAmPo
 Invocation. APT-2

John Brown's Prayer. Stephen Vincent Benét. CBCWP *Fr.* John Brown's Body.

John Bun. *Unknown.* NBLV

John Burns of Gettysburg. Bret Harte. CBCWP; PCW

John Cabot, out of Wilma, once a Wycliffe. Riot. Gwendolyn Brooks. NALW; SSLK

John Charles Fremont waited for Jupiter. Jupiter at Beer Springs. Thomas Hornsby Ferril. YaYoPo

John Coltrane. Alfred B. Spellman. *See* John Coltrane: An Impartial Review.

John Coltrane (1926–1967). Imamu Amiri Baraka. FuFl

John Coltrane: An Impartial Review. Alfred B. Spellman. EGAG
 (John Coltrane.) SeSe

John Doe. Rafael Campo. InoFa *Fr.* Ten Patients, and Another.

John Donne would think of an island. Another Poem in English. Lorenzo Thomas. EGAG

John Donne, You Were Wrong. Janet Caird. EdScPo

John Evereldown. Edwin Arlington Robinson. APN-2; NAAPv.1; NCAP

John Fane Dingle. Glaucopis. Richard Hughes. OBMV

John, founder of towns,—dweller in none. Bread-Word Giver. John Wheelwright. ChIV-2

John Gilbert Was a Bushranger. *Unknown.* NOBAu

John Gorham. Edwin Arlington Robinson. MoAmPo

John had. Happiness. Alan Alexander Milne. AmFaPo; NOxBChV

John had eight hundred men and mo'. John Barbour. DiBP *Fr.* Bruce, The.

John Hancock. Lee Bennett Hopkins. HHAm

John Hardy. *Unknown.* APN-2

John he comes to my house. For Jan, with Love. David Lee. GifTon

John Henry. *Unknown.* NAAPv.2

John Henry tol' his cap'n. *Unknown.* TCAPo

John in Prison. Sydney E. Jerrold. SacPr

John, John, of the Holy Order. *Unknown.* SSUS

John, John, wid de holy order. John, John, of the Holy Order. *Unknown.* SSUS

John Keats. Lord Byron. UV

John Keats, keep revel with me, too. (LL) To John Keats, Poet, at Springtime [*or* Spring Time]. Countee Cullen. BrAP; OxBoAm; PtR

John Knox. Iain Crichton Smith. EdScPo

John lifts the bread. John Says Mass on All Souls' Day. David Craig. UpMys

John, look what Mis' Nelson give me. Easter Bonnet, The. Clara Ann Thompson. CBWP-2

John Marr. Herman Melville. APN-2

John Masefield Relates the Story of Tom, Tom, the Piper's Son. Louis Untermeyer. MoAmPo *Fr.* Mother Goose Up-to-Date.

John Maydew or The Allotment. Charles Tomlinson. OBGa

John McGoldrick's Trial for the Quaker's Daughter. *Irish Oral Tradition.* IrV

John Milton. W. H. Auden. AmWit *Fr.* Academic Graffiti.

John Milton and My Father. Patricia Beer. HarvBoo

John Percy. John Bingham Morton. UV

John Percy / Said to his nursy. John Percy. John Bingham Morton. UV

John Quincy Adam's right hand. Jackson Mac Low. APSN *Fr.* Presidents of the United States of America, The.

John Rabbit, by Dame Eagle chased. Eagle and the Beetle, The. Jean de La Fontaine. OBVE, *tr. by* Elizur Wright

John Reed's Monologue. Yevgeny Aleksandrovich Yevtushenko. RusPo, *tr. by* Robert Arthur Douglas Ford

John Robinson. Julia A. Moore.
 Hic Finis Rapto 1. STuOW

John saw-r-O, John saw-r-O. . .John saw de holy number settin' on de golden altar. Golden Altar, The. *Unknown.* SSUS

John Says Mass on All Souls' Day. David Craig. UpMys

John Smith and His Son, John Smith. Wallace Stevens. TLR

John Smith and his son, John Smith. Wallace Stevens. TLR *Fr.* Lettres d'un Soldat.

John Sutter. Yvor Winters. MoAmPo; NAMCP V.1; NoAM

John Thompson. Douglas Lochhead. Coast

John, Tom, and James [*with music*]. Charles Henry Ross. NBLV

John was a bad boy, and beat a poor cat. John, Tom, and James. Charles Henry Ross. NBLV

John while swimming in the ocean. Brats. X. J. Kennedy. NBLV

John Winthrop, "Reasons to be Considered for...the Intended Plantation in New England," 1629. Nicole Cooley. NeAmPo

John-John. Thomas Macdonagh. IrLP

Johnnie Cope. Adam Skirving. NePenScot

Johnnie get your gun, get your gun, get your gun. Over There. George M. Cohan. FaBoA; ReLy

Johnny and Jane and Jack and Lou. Children's Ball-Bouncing Song. *Unknown.* NOBAu

Johnny B. Goode. James Seay. SwNoth

Johnny come down de hollow. *Unknown.* APN-2

Johnny could only sing one note. Johnny One-Note. Lorenz Hart. ReLy

Johnny Crow. Johnny Crow's Garden. L. Leslie Brooke. NOxBChV

Johnny Crow's Garden. L. Leslie Brooke. NOxBChV

Johnny Guitar is watching Duncan Renaldo. Kinescope. Dionisio D. Martinez. TouFir

Johnny, I Hardly Knew Ye. *Unknown.* FaBoWar; IrV; NPeEn; PoAgWa

Johnny Laces Up His Red Shoes. Cornelius Eady. InvLad

Johnny One-Note. Lorenz Hart. ReLy

Johnny, the kitchen sink has been clogged for days, some utensil probably fell down there. What the Living Do. Marie Howe. BeAl; ExTi; PoCho; PoDa

Johnny was bashful and shy. You'd Be Surprised. Irving Berlin. ReLy

Johnny Weissmuller Dead in Acapulco. Clive James. NOBAu

Johnny's Pet Superstition [*with music*]. Clara Ann Thompson. CBWP-2

John's Song. Joan Aiken. TLR

Johnson Brothers Ltd. Rutger Kopland. BeAl; VCWP, *tr. by* James Brockway

Johnson City, Texas. Albert Huffstickler. TiP2

Johnson's Cabinet Watched by Ants. Robert Bly. NAMCP V.2; NoP-5; OxBoAm

Join Me in Celebrating. James Simmons. PNI

Join the Angel Band. *Unknown.* SSUS

Joining the Circus. David Keller. NevBe

Joint is Jumpin', The. A. R. Johnson, J. C. Johnson and Andy Razaf. ReLy

Joint is jumpin', The. Joint is Jumpin', The. A. R. Johnson, J. C. Johnson and o Andy Razaf. ReLy

Jojopan. Art Goodtimes. GeoH

Jojo's. Christopher Davis. LiTh

Joke, A. Aleksander Wat. BLT

Joke, A? Tell me. Stupid. Paisley Rekdal. LegDan

Joke the size of a small moon headed, A. For Stuart Porter, Who Asked for a Poem That Would Not Depress Him Further. Jeffrey Skinner. PBCAP

Joker, A. Charles Baudelaire. MotU, *tr. by* Edward K. Kaplan

Joker who haunts Monticello, A. Morris Gilbert Bishop. AmWit

Joke's on me!, The. (LL) Sarah. Delmore Schwartz. ChIV-1; TaR

La Jolla. In 3 Acts. J. Cody Peterson. FTtHH

Jolly Fat Widows, The.   Julia Fields.   GT

Jolly fat widows, The.   Jolly Fat Widows, The.   Julia Fields.   GT

Jolly Good Ale and Old.   William Stevenson *and* John Still.   OBEV *Fr.* Gammer Gurton's Needle.

Jolly good, I said. (LL)   I Saw a Jolly Hunter.   Charles Causley.   NOxBChV; OPOU

Jolly Jugger, The.   *Unknown.*   NPeEn

(Juggler and the Baron's Daughter, The.)   NoSic

Jolly Pinder of Wakefield, The.   *Unknown.*   PBRV

Jolly Young Waterman, The.   Charles Dibdin.   OxAEP-1

Jonah.   Randall Jarrell.   ChIV-1

Jonah and the Whale.   Gareth Owen.   OBSP

Jonah and the Whale.   *Unknown.*   NPeEn *Fr.* Patience.

Jonah had his whale but we had sedans.   Big Cars.   Jane Flanders.   PBCAP

Jonah wept within the whale.   To a Song of Sappho Discovered in Egypt. Leonora Speyer.   APT-1

Jonah's Prayer.   Mihály Babits.   IQMS, *tr. by* Peter Zollman

Jone o' Grinfilt.   Joseph Lees.   NOBRP

JoNelle.   Angela Shannon.   BtF

JoNelle don't believe in nakedness.   JoNelle.   Angela Shannon.   BtF

Joni Mitchell.   Joseph Hutchison.   SwNoth

Joplin's voice, edged like a crack.   People Are Dropping Out of Our Lives. Albert Goldbarth.   SwNoth

Jordan (1).   George Herbert.   BASC; BrAP; FSCP; NAEL-6v1; NAEL-7v1; NoP-4; NoP-5; NOSC; OxBEV; TFi; WoPoe

Jordan (2).   George Herbert.   BASC; CABP; FSCP; NAEL-6v1; NAEL-7v1; NOSC; OBWVE; PBRV; SacPr

Jordan's Mills.   *Unknown.*   SSUS

Joseph.   G. K. Chesterton.   ChIV-2; ChrPo

Joseph.   Timothy Steele.   RA

Joseph, being seventeen years old, was feeding the flock with his brethren. Bible, *O.T.*   NAWM-5v1 *Fr.* Genesis.

Joseph Conrad.   Malcolm Lowry.   CLPP

Joseph Conrad's *Heart of Darkness.*   Liliane Giraudon.   SCFWP *Fr.* Poem with Incense Paper.

Joseph, i afraid of stars.   Holy Night.   Lucille Clifton.   NALW

Joseph in Carcere.   Sir Francis Hubert.   ChIV-1 *Fr.* Egypt's Favorite.

Joseph is without doubt rent in pieces an evil beast hath devoured him. Friends.   Nathan Yonathan.   NRoS, *tr. by* Esther Raizen

Joseph Joseph breathed slower.   Then.   Lawrence Joseph.   PBCAP

Joseph speaks to gericault in the studio.   Michael Datcher.   BRtP

Joseph the lost will return, Jacob should not.   Sitting in the Grief House (250). Khwaja Shams-ad-din Muhammad Hafiz.   WED, *tr. by* Robert Bly and Leonard Lewisohn

Joseph was an old man.   Cherry-Tree Carol, The.   *Unknown.*   ChrPo; HeIP-4; MakPoe; TFi

Josephine Baker Museum, The.   Elizabeth Alexander.   FuFl

Joseph's Coat.   George Herbert.   ChIV-1

José's Japanese Sword.   Ray Gonzalez.   LiTh

Joshu exclaimed, "Dog's no Buddha."   Ichigen.   ZenPo, *tr. by* Takashi Ikemoto and Lucien Stryk

Joshua.   X. J. Kennedy.   ChIV-1

Joshua at Shechem.   Charles Reznikoff.   ChIV-1

Joshua Clark.   Maurice Kenny.   FTtHH

Joshua Fit de Battle of Jericho [*or* ob Jerico].   *Unknown.*   APN-2

Joshua Reynolds.   Oliver Goldsmith. *See* Sir Joshua Reynolds.

Joshu's "Oak in the courtyard."   Eian.   ZenPo, *tr. by* Takashi Ikemoto and Lucien Stryk

Joshu's "Oak in the courtyard."   Monju-Shindo.   ZenPo, *tr. by* Takashi Ikemoto and Lucien Stryk

Joshu's word—Nothingness.   Kuchu.   ZenPo, *tr. by* Takashi Ikemoto and Lucien Stryk

Joue splendide émerge des mousselines d'aubépine, La.   Lever de Soleil. Saint-Pol Roux.   YaTCFP

Joueur de flûte, j'ai tant erré dans les terres d'ombre.   Joueur de flûte.   Lorand Gaspar.   YaTCFP

Jour de Pritemps Le Poète Exprime Ses Sentiments au Sortir de l'Ivresse, Un. Li Po.   CCL1, *tr. by* Marie-Jean-Léon, Marquis d'Hervey de Saint-Denys

Jour, par-dessus le feuillage et les fleurs embaumées, le vent, Un.   Flûte Mystérieuse, La.   Li Po.   CCL1, *tr. by* Judith Gautier

Jour, quand nous dirons: C'était le temps du soleil, Un.   Regret de la terre, Le. Jules Supervielle.   YaTCFP

Jour, Un.   Boris Vian.   YaTCFP

Journal.   Blaise Cendrars.   YaTCFP

Journal.   John Ciardi.   PoA 2002

Journal.   Amy Fusselman.   HeMarv

Journal *Encounter*, The.   Kim Suyŏng.   CAMKP, *tr. by* Young-Jun Lee

Journal of the Laguna de San Ignacio.   Nathaniel Tarn.   APSN

Journal of the Plague Years, A.   Walter Holland.   CAGL

Journalist, The.   Cornelius Mathews.   APN-1 *Fr.* Poems on Man in His Various Aspects under the American Republic.

Journalists.   Rudyard Kipling.   HarvBoo *Fr.* Epitaphs of the War [1914–1918].

Journalist's Convention 1987.   Esther Iverem.   InTrad

Journals, The.   Gaylord Brewer.   AmPoNex

Journaux Quotidiens.   Marguerite Yourcenar.   YaTCFP

Journey.   Breyten Breytenbach.   AF, *tr. by* Denis Hirson

Journey.   Elizabeth Cook-Lynn.   HATNAP

Journey.   Rodney Hall.   NOBAu

Journey: "Ah, could I lay me down in this long grass."   Edna St. Vincent Millay.   BrAP

Journey.   Judith Nicholls.   OBSP

Journey: "Get the word and go."   Eamon Grennan.   PoDa

Journey: "Here are words written down."   Thich Nhat Hanh.   WhBo

Journey.   Vasco [*or* Vasko] Popa.   PoSu *Fr.* Besieged Serenity.

Journey.   Cathy Song.   ExTi

Journey 55.   Jerry W., Jr. Ward.   FuFl

Journey, A.   Edward Field.   BLT

Journey, The.   Emmy Bridgwater.   SurWo

Journey, The.   Chikamatsu Monzaemon.   WoPoe *Fr.* Love Suicides at Sonezaki, The.

Journey, The.   Mary Oliver.   StAl; TWF

Journey, The.   Leanne O'Sullivan.   NIrP

Journey, The.   James Wright.   CAP-8; GPTC; NAAL-5; NoAM

Journey, The: "I am wearing my gray wool pants, and my brown boots." Howard Nelson.   IJHIL

Journey, and the struggles of the moon, The. (LL)   Ajanta.   Muriel Rukeyser. APT-2; MoAmPo

Journey Away, A.   Carl Rakosi.   PFTM-1

Journey Back to Christmas.   Gwen Dunn.   OBCP

Journey back was a nightmare, The.   Epilogue.   Colette Bryce.   NIrP

Journey ends between the black spiders and the white spiders, The.   Mondo Henbane.   Charles Wright.   PfSP

Journey in Winter.   Johann Wolfgang von Goethe. *tr. by* James Wright Three Stanzas.   WoPoe, *tr. by* James Wright

Journey into Misery.   Iwan Goll.   GTCP, *tr. by* Christopher Middleton

Journey it went. (LL)   John Keats.   NAEL-6v2; NAEL-7v2; NPBRoP *Fr.* Sleep and Poetry.

Journey, 1966.   Anselm Hollo.   PmAP

Journey North.   Tu Fu [*or* Du Fu].   ColAnChi, *tr. by* Hugh M. Stimson

Journey North, The.   Tu Fu [*or* Du Fu].   CrYelRi, *tr. by* Sam Hamill

Journey of a Doe.   Chava Pinchas-Cohen.   DTA, *tr. by* Miriyam Glazer

Journey of the Magi.   T. S. Eliot.   BrAP; ChrPo; GI; HeIP-4; ItP; MoAmPo; NAAL-5; NAEL-6v2; NAEL-7v2; NAMCP V.1; NIL-7; NIP-4; NoP-4; NoP-5; OBCP; OBMV; OxBoAm; StAl; TFi; TRP

Journey of the Shadow, The.   Nada El-Hage.   PoArWo, *tr. by* Nathalie El-Hani

Journey Onwards, The.   Thomas Moore.   OxAEP-2

Journey Out.   Rachel Hadas.   RA

Journey Renewed.   William Wordsworth.   CenSon *Fr.* River Duddon [A Series of Sonnets], The.

Journey: the North Coast.   Robert Gray.   BMAP

Journey Through Hell.   Nicanor Parra.   WoPoe, *tr. by* Miller Williams

Journey to Iceland.   W. H. Auden.   PoA 2002

Journey to Italy began in your youth, The.   To the South.   Christine Casson. NevBe

Journey to the End of Night.   Bernard Bador.   ConPit, *tr. by* Clayton Eshleman

Journey to the Interior.   Margaret Atwood.   BrAP

Journey to the Interior.   Theodore Roethke.   TRP

Journey to the Place of Ghosts [*Wölbe dich, Welt: / Wenn die Totenmuschel heranschwimmt, / will es hier läuten. / Vault over, world: / when the seashell of death washes up / there will be a knelling.*].   Jay Wright.   GT; VCAP

Journey with Basho, A.   David Ray.   AmZen

Journey's end / Still alive.   Basho.   ZenPo, *tr. by* Takashi Ikemoto and Lucien Stryk

Journeys, The.   Edward Kamau Brathwaite.   HarvBoo

Jours, Les.   Jean Tardieu.   YaTCFP

Jove, for Europa[e]s love took[e] shape of bull.   Barnabe Barnes.   OxBSo *Fr.* Parthenophil and Parthenophe.

Jove send me more such afternoon[e]s as this. (LL)   Ovid.   CABP; ErotSp; NoSic; NPeEn; OBVE; OxAEP-1; OxBEV *Fr.* Elegies.

Jove wields the lightning, Neptune's trident-lord.   *Unknown.*   PriapPo *Fr.* Priapus Poems, The.

Jove, you hold Dodona sacred.   *Unknown.*   PriapPo *Fr.* Priapus Poems, The.

Jovencita across the street sinks into the dark mouth of her bus, Una.   As the Beer Trucks Eclipse the Light of Morning.   Anthony R. Vigil.   AmPoNex

Joy.   Thomas Centolella.   GifTon

Joy. Sydney, Lady Morgan Owenson. NOBRP

J-O-Y. James Richardson. RD

Joy: "It's joy to be up in the morning when the dew's on the grass and clover." Eben Eugene Rexford. ArBi

Joy. Susan Wicks. MFPA

Joy, The. Harryette Mullen. OxAAAP

Joy a fix'd state—a tenure, not a start! Joy. Sydney, Lady Morgan Owenson. NOBRP

Joy! a heart so overflowing. Bernard [or Bernart] de Ventadour or Ventadorn. STV

Joy Addict, The. James Harms. NAPBL; NeAmPo

Joy and anger are not caused by outside things. Miscellaneous Feelings in the Sui Garden. Yüan Mei. ColAnChi, tr. by Jonathan Chaves

Joy and Pleasure. W. H. Davies. OBMV

Joy, did I [or I did] lock thee up; but some bad man. Bunch of Grapes, The. George Herbert. ChIV-1; NAEL-6v1; NAEL-7v1; NOSC

Joy-fulfiller / fruit provider / many-skilled cook of the whole year. On the Fruit-Providing Autumn Season. Catharina Regina von Greiffenberg. WPoS, tr. by Michael Hamburger

Joy is a trick in the air. Birth-Dues. Robinson Jeffers. MoAmPo

Joy Island. Marianne Vitale. HeMarv

Joy Mountain. Muso Soseki. EaWin, tr. by W. S. Merwin

Joy of Church Fellowship Rightly Attended, The. Edward Taylor. NAAL-3 Fr. God's Determinations [touching his Elect].

Joy of Love, The. Yi Hyangji. EcSo, tr. by Catherine J. Kim

Joy of my life, full oft for loving you. Edmund Spenser. HeIP-4 Fr. Amoretti.

Joy of My Life! While Left Me Here. Henry Vaughan. BASC

Joy of Union, The [with music]. Yang Fang. CCL1, tr. by Burton Watson

Joy, Shipmate, Joy! Walt Whitman. MoAmPo

Joy Sonnet in a Random Universe. Helen Chasin. NIL-7

Joy to the World. Isaac Watts. SacPr

Joying in flowers without let. Sikong Tu. CCL1 Fr. Twenty-Four Modes of Poetry.

Joyous birds, hid under greenewood shade, The. Torquato Tasso. OBVE Fr. Godfrey of Bulloigne; or, The Recoverie of Jerusalem [Gerusalemme Liberata].

Joyous, who can help but sing? Bitter Harvest. Tzu Yeh. CrYelRi, tr. by Sam Hamill

Joyous you should be. Lines to a Depressed Friend. Frank O'Hara. AHA

Joze was born in the village of Loski Potok. Yugoslav Story. Susan Hampton. BMAP

J's the Jumping Jay-Walker. Phyllis McGinley. SSCS Fr. All around the Town.

Juan and Julia. Lord Byron. NPBRoP Fr. Don Juan.

Juan de Juni the priest said. Aodh Ruadh O'Domhnaill. Thomas MacGreevy. OBMV

Juan in England. Lord Byron. FaBoVe Fr. Don Juan.

Juan Lopez and John Ward. Jorge Luis Borges. FaBoWar, tr. by Rodolfo Torragno

Juan Martínez, Juan Nadie, Juan Todos. Heriberto Yépez. RMCMP

Juan Martínez, Juan Nobody, Juan All. Heriberto Yépez. RMCMP, tr. by Mónica de la Torre

Juana. Felicia Dorothea Hemans. RWP

Juan-er: Curl-Grass. Unknown. APT-1; CCL1, tr. by Ezra Pound

Juanita, Wife of Manuelito. Simon J. Ortiz. WaAnP

Juan's Puberty. Lord Byron. NPeEn Fr. Don Juan.

Juan's Song. Louise Bogan. NoP-4; NoP-5; OxBoAm

Jubilate Agno. Christopher Smart.
  "For I pray God to bless Polly in the the blessing of Naomi." WaAnP
  "For the word of God is a sword on my side—no matter what other weapon a stick or a straw." BBASP
  Fragment A.
    "Let Anaiah bless with the Dragon-fly, who sails over the pond by the wood-side and feedeth on the cresses." FaBoVe
  Fragment B.
    (For I will consider my Cat Jeoffry.) ChAP; OxBEV
    "For man is between the pinchers while his soul is shaping and purifying." ChIV-1
    "For the doubling of flowers is the improvement of the gard'ner's talent." ChIV-2; NPeEn
    "Let Peter rejoice with the Moon Fish who keeps up the life in the waters by night." ChIV-2
    My Cat Jeoffry. BrAP; CABP; HeIP-4; NAEL-6v1; NAEL-7v1; NoP-4; NoP-5; NPeEn; OBWVE; OxAEP-1; PoPoPo; TriCat; TRP; WaAnP; WeW-3
  Fragment C.
    "For I prophesy that we shall have our horns again." ChIV-1
Jubilate Canis. Erica Jong. WaAnP

Jubilate Matteo. Gavin Ewart. UV

Jubilation T. Cornpone. Johnny Mercer. OBCoV

Jubilee. Sabah As-Sabah. InTrad

Jubilee for the Bomb. Maureen Seaton. MAAN

Judah in Exile Wanders [with music]. George Sandys. ChIV-1

Judas. Vassar Miller. ChIV-2; MoAmPo

Judas and Jesus. Endre Ady. IQMS, tr. by Peter Zollman

Judas and the Profiteer. Sir Osbert Sitwell. FaBoWar

Judas descended to this lower Hell. Judas and the Profiteer. Sir Osbert Sitwell. FaBoWar

Judas Iscariot. Ronald Allison Kells Mason. SacPr

Judas Iscariot. Stephen Spender. MoBrPo; NIP-4

Judas Iscariot / sat in the upper. Judas Iscariot. Ronald Allison Kells Mason. SacPr

Judas Maccabaeus. Henry Wadsworth Longfellow.
  Act 1: The Citadel of Antiochus at Jerusalem. AWPTFC

Judas' Reproach. Nina Kossman. GI

Judas says the dead man's alibi had collapsed and. Alibi of a Dead Man. Giovanni Raboni. ItPo, tr. by Gayle Ridinger

Judas Touch, The [for J.M.]. David Malouf. BMAP

Judas? You want Judas? Look. Woodcarver of Stendal, The. Sheenagh Pugh. TCAWP

Judenrein. This Is the Map. Rodger Kamenetz. TaR

Judge eternal, throned in splendours. Henry Scott Holland. SacPr

Judge Not [with music]. Josephine D. Henderson Heard. CBWP-4

Judge Not. Theodore Roethke. ChIV-2; GI

Judge not a Princess' worth impeached hereby. Michael Drayton. NoSic Fr. England's Heroical Epistles.

Judge not, that you be not judged. Theodore Roethke. GI Fr. St. Matthew.

Judge Not the Preacher; for He is Thy Judge. George Herbert. OxAEP-1

Judge not; the workings of his brain. Adelaide Anne Procter. SacPr

Judge of an abnormal stone. Narrator, The. Milo De Angelis. NeIt, tr. by Lawrence Venuti

Judge Somers. Edgar Lee Masters. OBSV Fr. Spoon River Anthology.

Judge tenderly—of Me! (LL) This Is My Letter to the World. Emily Dickinson. APN-2; HeIP-4; NAAL-3; NAAL-5; NAAPv.1; NALW; NoAM; OxWW; SAmP; TCAPo; WaAnP

Judge, The. Claire Ottenstein Ross. TiP2

Judged by the Company One Keeps. Unknown. NBLV

Judgement. Ciaran Carson. PBCIP

Judgement. Meiling Jin. CFP

Judgement Day. Odia Ofeimun. HBAPE

Judgement doth execute. (LL) Psalm 58: "Do ye, o congregation." Bible, O.T. NoP-4; NoP-5, tr. by Unknown

Judgement / is coming. Something Terrible Something. Sam Cornish. BtF

Judges, who rule the world by laws. Psalm 58. Bible, O.T. NoP-4; NoP-5, tr. by Isaac Watts

Judging by the pictures. Karai Senryū. EMJL, tr. by Makoto Ueda

Judging Distances. Henry Reed. BrAP; NAEL-6v2; NAEL-7v2; NIL-7; NIP-4; NoP-4; NoP-5; NPeEn; OxBEV; PoWW Fr. Lessons of the War.

Judgment. Eleanor Wilner. ExTi

Judgment Day. Robert Garioch. OBVE

Judgment Day, The. James Weldon Johnson. APT-1; ChIV-2

Judgment in Heaven, A. Francis Thompson.
  Epilogue. MoBrPo

Judith. Lascelles Abercrombie.
  Song. MoBrPo

Judith. Eloise Bibb. CBWP-4

Judith. Vicki Feaver. MoWP

Judith. Gertrud Kolmar. AF, tr. by David Kipp

Judith. Félix Lope de Vega Carpio. WoPoe, tr. by Brian Soper
  (On the Triumph of Judith.) SpanPo

Judith. Adah Isaacs Menken. APN-2; CBWP-1; SWaP; ViWPN

Judith dances on my wall. Dance She Does, The. Harryette Mullen. ISC

Judith of Bethulia. John Crowe Ransom. APT-1; NoAM

Judith Recalls Holofernes. Maura Stanton. YaYoPo

Judy. Paul Allen. PoDa

Judy asks, "You." Judy Comes to Visit. "Alta." ASA

Judy Comes to Visit. "Alta." ASA

Judy likens the day with Elly. Girls Sitting Together Like Dolls. Christiania Whitehead. NeBl

Judy Sugden! Judy, I made you caper. Barnsley and District. Donald Davie. NoAM

Judy Travaillo Variations, The. Michael Anania. IllVoic

Juegan los dos con una piedra. Piedra en la arena. Coral Bracho. RMCMP

Jugged Hare. Jean Earle. TCAWP

Juggler. Richard Wilbur. UpMys

Juggler and the Baron's Daughter, The. *Unknown. See* Jolly Jugger, The.

Jugs, The. Paul Celan. HP; OBVE, *tr. by* Christopher Middleton

Jugurtha. Henry Wadsworth Longfellow. TCAPo

Juice. Vera Pavlova. CRWP *Fr.* Signs of Life.

Juice of bitter herbs has, The. Chŏng Ch'ŏl. CATKP, *tr. by* Peter H. Lee

Juicio Final. Blas de Otero. RaW

JuJu. Askia Muhammad Touré. SeSe

Juke Box Love Song. Langston Hughes. OxBoAm; SAmP

Jukebox Saturday Night. Al Stillman. ReLy

Jules Pascin. Mina Loy. HarvBoo

Julia Disdainful: or, The Frozen Zone. Robert Herrick. CavPo

Julia, if I chance to die. His Request to Julia. Robert Herrick. CavPo; NOSC

Julia, when thy Herrick dies. To Julia. Robert Herrick. NOSC

Julian. David Brendon Hopes.
  "*Witch* the lakemen call her, this wind." UpMys

Julian and Maddalo; A Conversation. Percy Bysshe Shelley.
  "I rode one evening with Count Maddalo." NPBRoP; NPeEn

Julian and Mia. Estrellitas. Carlos Cumpian. IllVoic

Julian laughing aloud, glad. Denise Levertov. *Fr.* Showings, The: Lady Julian of Norwich, 1342-1416.

Julian, there are vast gaps we call black holes. Showings, The: Lady Julian of Norwich, 1342-1416. Denise Levertov.

Juliet's Garden. Charles Tomlinson. OBGa

Julio Campal. Gerardo Diego. RaW

Julio Campal ("We were walking to your funeral, eleven friends.") Gerardo Diego. RaW, *tr. by* Robert Mezey

Julito used to shine the soul. Song 1 from "Three Songs from the 50's." Víctor Hernández Cruz. FTtHH

Julius Caesar and the Honey-Bee. Charles Tennyson Turner. OxBSo

Julius Caesar. William Shakespeare.
  Antony's Oration [over Caesar's Body]. MakPoe; OxAEP-1; OxBEV; WaAnP
  "How died my master, Strato?" OxAEP-1
  "I cannot tell what you and other men." WaAnP
  "If you have tears, prepare to shed them now." OxAEP-1
  "O mighty Cæsar! dost thou lie so low?" OxAEP-1
  "O, pardon me, thou bleeding piece of earth." OxAEP-1
  "Since Cassius first did whet me against Cæsar." OxAEP-1
  "There is a tide in the affairs of men." ITBLP
  "Who ever knew the heavens menace so?" OxAEP-1

July. Daniel Gray-Kontar. SpirFl

July. Julio Herrera y Reissig. TCLAP, *tr. by* Andrew Rosing

July. Marion Lomax. NeBl

July. Alexander L. Posey. APN-2

July [*with music*]. Henrietta Cordelia Ray. CBWP-3

July. Sonia Sanchez. GT

July. Margit Szécsi. IQMS, *tr. by* Agnes Arany-Makkai

July 4th. May Swenson. PoA 2002

July 4, 1984: For Buck [*with music*]. June Jordan. NAMCP V.2; NoAM

July 6, 2001 (2). Tom Montag. AmZen *Fr.* Plain Poems: A Fairwater Daybook.

July 10, 1999. Alex Rawls. AnSo *Fr.* What's Your Sign?

7-30-96. Erren Geraud Kelly. BtF

July 18, 1936–July 18, 1938. Miguel Hernández. AF, *tr. by* Timothy Baland

July, 1949. Ron Rash. RWB

July Dawn. Louise Bogan. AWTN

July Has Come for the Dead. Milo De Angelis. ItPo, *tr. by* Gayle Ridinger

July in my hometown. Blue Grapes. Yi Yuksa. CAMKP, *tr. by* David R. McCann

July: "Loud is the Summer's busy song." John Clare. NPBRoP; WaAnP *Fr.* Shepherd's [*or* Shepheards] Calendar, The.

July Thirteenth. Jeanne Wells. PfS

July, when white waves pounce upon our heads. Eye. Nishiwaki Junzaburo. CAoMJL1, *tr. by* Hosea Hirata

July's contour of green. (LL) Successful Summer, A. David Schubert. APT-2; ChIV-1

Jumbled in the Common Box. W. H. Auden. OxBoAm

Jumblies, The [*with music*]. Edward Lear. CABP; NAEL-6v2; NAEL-7v2; NOxBChV; TFi; UV

Jump back, honey, jump back. (LL) Negro Love Song, A. Paul Laurence Dunbar. APN-2; ColAP; SSLK

Jump Black Honey Jump Black. Malkia Amala Cyril. InTrad

Jump for Joy. Paul Francis Webster. ReLy

Jump Rope Rhyme of the 49er Daughters. Wayde Compton. IFF

Jump Shooter, The [*with music*]. Dennis Trudell. MoASP

Jump stone hand leaf shadow sun. Robert Duncan. APSN *Fr.* Passages.

Jump stop shake. (LL) Blackberry Sweet. Dudley Randall. ISC; SoSe-8; WeW-3

Jumping out of the straw. Supposed Dancer, The. Roy Fisher. HarvBoo

Jumping rope. Jerry Kilbride. WhBo

Jump-Rope Rhyme. *Unknown.* NTCP

Juncos. William Stafford. OWoS

Juncos flotan en el riachuelo, Los. Riachuelo con Lavanderas. Jorge Guillén. RaW

June: "Wind at the ear says *June.*" Bei Dao. WoBe, *tr. by* Iona Man-Cheong and Eliot Weinberger

June: "You can't hang a heavy mirror." Monica Raymond. PfS

June. William Cullen Bryant. TreFP

June. Mary Weston Fordham. CBWP-2

June [*with music*]. Henrietta Cordelia Ray. CBWP-3

June 9, 1999. Alex Rawls. AnSo *Fr.* What's Your Sign?

June 11. David Lehman. P180

June 15, 1992: Widow's Walk, Harpswell, Maine. Sandra M. Gilbert. InoFa

June 20. Lucille Clifton. PoChi

June 1940. Weldon Kees. PWW2

June 22. I have finished here. Inventory. Journal. Pamela Alexander. AmAlph

June 30th. Vera Gheraducci. CItWP

June at Truro Beach the joyous bathers. Kite-Flying. Christopher Gilbert. GT

June, but the morning's cold, the wind. Porth Cwyfan. Roland Mathias. AngWePo; TCAWP

June: Dutch Harbor. William Meredith. YaYoPo

June Fourth. Gerald Stern. PoA 2002

June Fugue. Thomas William Shapcott. NOBAu

June Ghazal. Arthur Sze. GifTon

June heat exiles our real needs, The. Without Villages. Ray Gonzalez. TouFir

June in her eyes, in her heart *January.* (LL) Spring, The: "Now that the Winter's gone, the earth hath lost." Thomas Carew. CavPo; NoP-4; NoP-5; PBRV

June Is Bustin' Out All Over. Oscar Hammerstein, II. ReLy

June means weddings in everyone's lexicon. Here Usually Comes the Bride. Ogden Nash. NIL-7

June, 1915. Charlotte Mew. OxAEP-2

June rain drizzles through the heavy boughs. Reply to T'ao Ch'ien. Sam Hamill. WANABP

June rain / hollyhocks turning. Basho. ZenPo, *tr. by* Takashi Ikemoto and Lucien Stryk

June sun in an orchard. My Mother's Burial. Sean O Riordain. ModIr, *tr. by* Patrick Crotty

Juneteenth. Marilyn Nelson. ExTi

Jungle, The. Alun Lewis. AngWePo; OBWVE
  "Grey monkeys gibber, ignorant and wise." FaBoWar

Jungle Book. Tom Raworth. PFTM-2

Jungle Book, The. Rudyard Kipling.
  Kaa's Hunting.
  Mowgli's Brothers.
  Hunting-Song of the Seeonee Pack. BLPJKO

Jungle Café, The [*with music*]. Gary Soto. NoAM

Jungle Husband, The. Stevie Smith. HarvBoo; NBLV; NIL-7; NIP-4

Jungle Music. Warren Woessner. MiVo; SwNoth

Jungle Night. "K." FaBoWar

Jungle Night, A. Nguyễn Chí Thiện. VCWP, *tr. by* Huynh Sanh Thông

Jungle night—it rains and rains, roofs leak, A. Jungle Night, A. Nguyễn Chí Thiện. VCWP, *tr. by* Huynh Sanh Thông

Jungle Warfare. Jack Spicer. APSN

Junior High Dance. Allison Joseph. UnSA

Junior League woman in blue, A. Chitchat with the Junior League Women. Gary Soto. PoDa

Junior Life Saving. Maxine W. Kumin. TWF

Juniper. Abbie Huston Evans. APT-1

Juniper, aspen, blue spruce, just thawing snow. Call of Nature, The. Tony Harrison. NoAM

Juniper Moon Pulls at My Bones, The. Earle Thompson. HATNAP

Juniper pure land quiver. (LL) Haibun Flycatcher. Andrew Schelling. AmZen; WANABP

Junk. Richard Wilbur. NoP-4; NoP-5; WaAnP; WeW-3

Junkies loved Charles Parker and the sports, The. Historiography. Lorenzo Thomas. SeSe

Junkyard. Greg Williamson. LegDan

Juno still jealous[e] of her husband Jove. Mary Sidney Wroth, Countess of Montgomery. OxBSo *Fr.* Pamphilia to Amphilanthus.

Junt. Norman Henry, II Pritchard. EGAG

Junto a la Laguna del Cristo, en la Aldehuela de Yeltes, una Noche de Luna Llena. Miguel de Unamuno. RaW *Fr.* En Casa Ya.

Junto a las catorce buenas razones. Sueño de los justos, El. Dana Gelinas. SPV

Junto a los condominios de los vivos. Fabio Morabito. RMCMP

Jun-zi yang-yang: The Gudeman's Come Hame (scoticè). *Unknown.* CCL1, *tr. by* James Legge

Jun-zi yu-yi [Translations]. *Unknown.* CCL1
  He's to the War. CCL1, *tr. by* Ezra Pound
  Ode (scoticè). CCL1, *tr. by* James Legge

Jupiter at Beer Springs. Thomas Hornsby Ferril. YaYoPo

Jusqu'aux bords de ta vie. Regarder l'enfance. Andrée Chédid. YaTCFP

Just a few car lengths from his front door. Five Verses for Shariputra Mugged Outside His Building. Tony Trigilio. AmZen

Just a few of us here at midday. My Train. Barbara Ras. NAPBL

Just a few years ago, when everything was permanent. Tesoro. Valerie Martínez. TouFir

Just a Gigolo. Julius Brammer. ReLy, *tr. by* Irving Caesar and Leonello Casucci

Just a herd of Negroes. Share-Croppers. Langston Hughes. SAmP

Just a hunch, really. Quickening. Lee Miriam Whitman-Raymond. PfS

Just a little party, nothing swank. Her Retirement. Anne Rouse. NeBl

Just a little white with the dust. (LL) Break of Day in the Trenches. Isaac Rosenberg. CABP; EMP; HarvBoo; MoBrPo; NAEL-6v2; NAEL-7v2; NAMCP V.1; NIL-7; NoAM; NoP-4; NoP-5; NPeEn; OBWP; OxAEP-2; OxBEV; PoA 2002; PoAgWa; PoWW; TFi; WaAnP

Just a Product of a Certain Situation. Steve Griffiths. AngWePo

Just a Smack at Auden. William Empson. MoBrPo; OBCoV

Just above where my house sits on the slope. Thomas Müntzer. Jeffrey Wainwright. HarvBoo

Just across the street from the Instituto Dante Allighieri. And Yet I Know. James Wright. BodElec

Just after me. Weasel. Lyubomir Levchev. CSCBP, *tr. by* Georgi Belev and Lisa Sapinkopf

Just after Michael's Death, the Game of Pool. Richard Tipping. BMAP

Just after midnight, Andrew woke. Son. Richard Jones. PoChi

Just after the tanker sank I sat eight hundred fifty miles away. News of the Cranes. Rodney Jones. InGu

Just an hour before the hump of last night, when—not with an old. Their Hats Is Always White. Jim Elledge. SwNoth

Just an instant the sun hung. Williamsbridge. Jana Beranová. TuT, *tr. by* Aidan Sharkey

Just an Ordinary Joe. John Wieners. AHA

Just and fit actions, Ptolemy (he saith). Lucan. OBVE *Fr.* Civil War [Bellum Civile] *or* Pharsalia.

Just Another Gig. Baron James Ashanti. SeSe

Just another joint. Closing Time. Eric Muirhead. TiP2

Just are the ways of God. John Milton. InvLi *Fr.* Samson Agonistes.

Just around twenty. Looking at Winter Trees. Pak Chaesam. CAMKP, *tr. by* David R. McCann and Jiwon Shin

Just as a child, already by sleep possessed. Welcome to Thomas Mann. Attila József. IQMS, *tr. by* Vernon Watkins

Just as beyond the sky is the sky, beyond life, life. Céanne. Jean Tardieu. YaTCFP, *tr. by* David Kelley

Just as he reach'd this stirring close. Cornelius Whur. STuOW *Fr.* Liberality of Sentiment.

Just as He spoke it from his Hands. Emily Dickinson. APN-2

Just as I Am. Charlotte Elliott. SacPr

Just as I wonder. Orchid Flower, The. Sam Hamill. AmZen; WANABP

Just as my fingers on these keys. Peter Quince at the Clavier. Wallace Stevens. APT-1; HeIP-4; MoAmPo; NAAL-5; NAMCP V.1; NAWM-7v2; NoAM; NoP-4; NoP-5; OxBoAm; SAmP; TCAPo; TFi

Just as she did on earth. (LL) Thomas Lux. *See* On earth.

Just as sun. This River. Annette Allen. MPUn

Just as, surely, sweat is consommé. Piquant. Roddy Lumsden. NeBrP

Just as the shady grove delights all with its whispering breezes. Anna Dering on Bartolomeo Silva, Doctor of Turin. Anne Lok. EMWP

Just as the twilight's holy hour. To an Infant. Mary Weston Fordham. CBWP-2

Just as The Watchman. Rainer Maria Rilke. BBASP, *tr. by* Robert Bly

Just as the watchman in the wine fields. Just as The Watchman. Rainer Maria Rilke. BBASP, *tr. by* Robert Bly

Just as the white ibis runs. Eye of Creation, The. Angelina Muñiz Huberman. MirDau, *tr. by* Aurora Camacho

Just as the Winged Energy of Delight. Rainer Maria Rilke. RaBo; WED, *tr. by* Robert Bly

Just as we were amazed to learn. Psychopathology of Everyday Life, The. William Matthews. NIP-4

Just as you think you've gained great wealth. Caroline Gilman. SWaP *Fr.* Oracles for Youth.

Just as you walk out of the Japanese garden. Carp. Dionisio D. Martinez. TouFir

Just Asking. Carl Hancock Rux. BtF

Just at the most exciting part. Full Supporting Programme. William Price Turner. EdScPo

Just autumn. Burnt lawns. Go-Summer. Mary O'Donoghue. NIrP

Just back from a beach of sand and shells. Old Lobsterman, The. John Townsend Trowbridge. APN-2

Just Because I Am. Malkia Amala Cyril. InTrad

Just because I forget. Letter for Duncan. Larry Eigner. FTOS

Just because of you. *Unknown.* ArkPo, *tr. by* Helen Craig McCullough

Just because there is music. Maybe I'm Amazed. Jim Carroll. PmAP

Just because you don't know what work is. (LL) What Work Is. Philip Levine. BeAl; CAP-8; EmeKit; ItP

Just before dawn the women are washing. Sketch from the Campaign in the North, A. Vijay Seshadri. PoDa

Just Before Sleep. Peter Everwine. GeoHom

Just before the tunnel, the train. City Animals. Chase Twichell. UrbNat

Just before winter. Pushing Forty. Alison Fell. EdScPo

Just below street level, the little door. Gypsy Hand. Miriam Sagan. ICANM

Just below the cottage door. Ground wave. Ingrid de Kok. TSAP

Just beyond that big sign for Ebenezer Church? Cash or Turtle or Heaven. Reginald Gibbons. Vesp

Just beyond the gate. Issa. SoOfWa, *tr. by* Sam Hamill

Just broke from school, pert, impudent, and raw. Soame Jenyns. OBSV *Fr.* Modern Fine Gentleman, The.

Just by being different. (LL) Summer Storm. Dana Gioia. GoPo; OxBoAm; RA

Just by being / I'm here. Issa. ZenPo, *tr. by* Takashi Ikemoto and Lucien Stryk

Just came home from a disturbing appointment with my new primary. Ticker. Amy Fusselman. HeMarv

Just chew it and rub it on. (LL) Anne Carson. BodElec; WoBe *Fr.* Truth About God, The.

Just controls their operations: the Napoleon of Crime! (LL) Macavity: The Mystery Cat. T. S. Eliot. AmWit; ChAP; NBLV; UV

Just days after the vet came. Healing the Mare. Linda McCarriston. LoL

Just dead. (LL) Triad. Adelaide Crapsey. APT-1; InoFa; OxBoAm; TCAPo

Just don't get caught. I won't exact a tithe. *Unknown.* PriapPo *Fr.* Priapus Poems, The.

Just Dump Me on the Palace Steps. Ange Mlinko. IIR

Just enough of rain. Haiku. Richard Wright. APT-2

Just flew inside my chest. Some. Panic Bird, The. Robert Phillips. BeAl; P180; PoCu

Just Folks. Edgar Albert Guest. ITBLP

Just for a handful of silver he left us. Lost Leader, The. Robert Browning. NAEL-6v2; NAEL-7v2

Just for a quarter of a day, I'd have you. Garden, The. John Glenday. NeBrP

Just for a while. *Unknown.* NAAPv.2

Just for fun. Tanka. Ishikawa Takuboku. CAoMJL1, *tr. by* Makoto Ueda

Just for me, my dad sweeps the entire. Learning to Ride My Bike. George Held. ArBi

Just for the sake of recovering. Loch Thom. William Sydney Graham. EdScPo; NePenScot

Just for Today. Ervin Drake. ReLy

Just forty years ago. (LL) Sawmill. Richard Kenney. NoP-4; NoP-5

Just four miles to go and the frontier ahead. German Frontier at Basel: 1942 and 1992, The. Hilda Schiff. HP

Just Friends. Sam M. Lewis. ReLy

Just give me a minute to get myself. So You Want to Hear the Blues. Grace Bauer. MiVo

Just half our three score years and ten. Martial. RomPo, *tr. by* Peter Whigham

Just how fucking good I look. (LL) For Desire. Kim Addonizio. BeAl; SUP

Just how it came to rest where it rested. Tyre, The. Simon Armitage. NeBrP

Just How It Happened. Priscilla Jane Thompson. CBWP-2

Just How Low Can a Highbrow Go When a Highbrow Lowers His Brow? Ogden Nash. OxBoAm

Just in the dawn of blushing womanhood. Albery Allson Whitman. NAAPv.1 *Fr.* Octoroon, The.

Just in Time. Betty Comden and Adolph Green. ReLy

Just keeping on drinking till your head fell off. History of Myself. Larry Goodell. ICANM

Just last friday. Jamal's Lamentation. Reuben Jackson. GT

Just like as in a nest of boxes round. Margaret Lucas Cavendish, Duchess of Newcastle. *See* Just like unto a nest of boxes round.

Just Like Eve. Magi Gibson. EdScPo

Just like that—suddenly, in a single movement!—a barrier falls and disappears. Time and the Response, The. Nathan Alterman. NRoS, *tr. by* Esther Raizen

Just Like the Legend. Léon Damas. PFTM-1

Just like unto a nest of boxes round. Of Many Worlds in This World. Margaret Lucas Cavendish, Duchess of Newcastle. NOSC; NPeEn

(Just like as in a nest of boxes round.) NoP-5; WaAnP

Just look 'ee here Mr. Preacher, you're a-goin' a bit too fur. Told to the Missionary. George R. Sims. DiBP

Just look, 'tis a quarter past six, love. Coming Woman, The. Mary Weston Fordham. CBWP-2; SWaP

Just lost, when I was saved! Called Back. Emily Dickinson. MoAmPo

Just Made It. Lawson Fusao Inada. WhBo

Just man into barren climes, The. Marriage of Heaven and Hell by William Blake, The. Alex Rawls. AnSo

Just missed him! (LL) On a Squirrel Crossing the Road in Autumn, in New England. Richard Eberhart. APT-2; HeIP-4

Just my luck. I gave up smoking last month. Luck. Marc J. Straus. BloBone

Just no comb/toe rings/titty rings/rings for the clitoris too/unfinished. Beauty Rituals 2000. Nwenna Kai. BRtP

Just Now. *Unknown.* SSUS

Just now I found a young boy. Catullus. EroLit, *tr. by* Peter Whigham

Just now in wild, free mood I yearn. Chen Zi'ang. CCL1,

Just now / Out of the strange. Warning, The. Adelaide Crapsey. APT-1; NAAPv.2; Spl; TCAPo

Just now the lilac is in bloom. Old Vicarage, Grantchester, The. Rupert Brooke. MoBrPo; NoP-4; NoP-5

Just off his motorbike. Going to Mass after Fifteen Years. Maxine Scates. PBCAP

Just off the highway to Rochester, Minnesota. Blessing, A. James Wright. AmFaPo; CAP-8; ChAP; GoPo; MoAmPo; NAAL-5; NAMCP V.2; NoAM; NoP-4; NoP-5; OxBoAm; PoA 2002; PoPoPo; RaBo; StAl; TRP; VCAP

Just off the Santa Monica Pier. Dolphin, The. Maurya Simon. GeoHom

Just once. For the White Poets Who Would Be Indian. Wendy Rose. CalPo

Just once, / As I looked. Iago. Julian Bernick. IaFF

Just once before I die. Lower East Side Poem, A. Miguel Piñero. PueRic

Just once to say 'i love you' all the feeling felt. Love song 2. B. P. Nichol. OpeFie

Just one clock dings. . .the shy bell. Siesta. Julio Herrera y Reissig. SonAtl, *tr. by* Carole Gibson and Lisa Martin

Just One of Those Things. Cole Porter. APT-1; ReLy

Just only alive. Friederike Roth. GTCP *Fr.* Meadow and Might.

Just quartering a Tree. (LL) Thunder-Storm, A. Emily Dickinson. APN-2; NCAP; WeW-3

Just Quartering a Tree. (LL) Wind begun to knead the Grass, The. Emily Dickinson. NIL-7; WeW-3

Just relax just relax. (LL) Girl Machine. Kenward Elmslie. AHA; NYP2

Just rises and floats away. (LL) Lilies. Mary Oliver. BBASP; WaAnP

Just say, "He's out." Absence. Takahashi Shinkichi. ZenPo, *tr. by* Takashi Ikemoto and Lucien Stryk

Just Say No Blues. Tracie Morris. BtF

Just short of the pass—juniper and spruce. Beyond Freedom. Michael Hannon. GeoHom

Just sitting around smoking, drinking and telling stories. And with March a Decade in Bolinas. Joanne Kyger. BLT

Just squeeze. Terry Hertzler. SUP

Just the luck of the draw. Our 17th Street Years. Bruce Weigl. BodElec

Just the other day i ate up the last bowlful of. Roy Kiyooka. NLPA *Fr.* Pear Tree Pomes.

Just the place for a Snark! the Bellman cried. Lewis Carroll. WaAnP *Fr.* Hunting of the Snark, The.

Just the right number of letters—half the alphabet. John Hollander. OxBoAm *Fr.* Powers of Thirteen.

Just the Two of Us. Kate Jennings. BMAP

Just then, forgetful of the strict command. Homer. OBVE *Fr.* Odyssey.

Just then the squeaky camera caught. Home Movie. Grace Schulman. WaAnP

Just there, in a corner of the whin-field. Our Lady of Ardboe. Paul Muldoon. PBCIP

Just think how amazing! someone getting up and walking on the water. (LL) Galilee Shore. Allen Ginsberg. ChIV-2; FTOS

Just this one day in all the year. Skeleton in the Cupboard, The. Dora Sigerson Shorter. VWP

Just this side of the reservation. 2 Ways of Crossing the Creek. Red Hawk. PoDa

Just to say the word. Issa. SoOfWa, *tr. by* Sam Hamill

Just to see you I invent circuitous walks. *Unknown.* SLW, *tr. by* Marjolijn De Jager, Sayd Bahodin Majrouh and André Velter

Just too late to save the stamp. (LL) Waste. Harry Graham. OBCoV; UV

Just us. / In our little house. Kenneth Rexroth. APSN *Fr.* Love Poems of Marichiko, The.

Just Walk On, Condemned to Die. Miklós Radnóti. IQMS, *tr. by* Zsuzsanna Ozsváth and Frederick Turner

Just Walking Around. John Ashbery. PtR

Just watch. Temple of Your Familiar. Felicia L. Morgenstern. BtF

Just when hope withers, a reprieve is granted. Exit. Rita Dove. AmAlph; ExTi

Just when I think the Buddhists. Not a Sparrow. Tess Gallagher. AmZen

Just when I thought there wasn't room enough. My Philosophy of Life. John Ashbery. BodElec; OxBoAm

Just when it has seemed I couldn't bear one more friend. Sweetness. Stephen Dunn. StAl

Just when our drawing-rooms begin to blaze. William Cowper. NoP-4; NoP-5; NPBRoP; NPeEn *Fr.* Task, The.

Just when the sermon. Prince Shiki. SoOfWa, *tr. by* Sam Hamill

Just When Thou Wilt. Frances Ridley Havergal. VWP

Just when Thou wilt, O Master, call! Just When Thou Wilt. Frances Ridley Havergal. VWP

Just when you thought it safe enough. Androgyny. Steve Orlen. OPRER

Just Whistle. C. D. Wright.

   In the Old Days. InGu

Just who was Miss Mary Mack. On Sidewalks, on Streetcorners, as Girls. Allison Joseph. IllVoic

Just within my reach the lightning bug turns off. Stanford M. Forrester. AmZen

Just Word Wranglin'. John Nelson. GeoH

Just Yesterday. Mark Bibbins. LegDan

Just you walk out from that hospital air into the rasp edge of winter. You Could Have Been Me. Belle Waring. PoDa

Justice. George Chapman. NOSC *Fr.* Tears of Peace, The or Euthymia Raptus.

Justice. Langston Hughes. NAAPv.2

Justice. Ben Marcus. HeMarv

Justice Arnett. Edgar Lee Masters. APT-1 *Fr.* Spoon River Anthology.

Justice Denied in Massachusetts. Edna St. Vincent Millay. MoAmPo; NAAPv.2

Justice in Old Ranger. Boyce House. TiP2

Justice is bright; the State is luminous. South, Southwest. William Burford. TiP2

Justice of Men! I Go in Search of You. Rosalía de Castro. SpanPo, *tr. by* Edwin Morgan

Justice of men! I go in search of you. Justice of Men! I Go in Search of You. Rosalía de Castro. SpanPo, *tr. by* Edwin Morgan

Justice of the Peace, The. Joseph Hilaire Pierre Belloc. OBSV

Justice of the Peace, The. Alison Luterman. MPUn

Justice to Scotland [*at. to* Robert Burns (1759–96)]. *Unknown.* NBLV

Justification. William Strode. NOSC

Justification of the Horned Lizard. Pattiann Rogers. SUP

Justified—through Calvaries of Love. (LL) Renunciation. Emily Dickinson. APN-2; MoAmPo; NAAL-3

Justiniano Lamé Has Been Killed. Jimmie Durham. HATNAP

Justly might Female *Tortoises* complain. Oppian [of Corycus]. NPeEn *Fr.* Halieutica.

Just-So Stories. Rudyard Kipling.

   How the Camel Got His Hump.

    Hump, The. NOxBChV

   Merrow Down. NOxBChV

Justus Quidem Tu Es, Domine. Gerard Manley Hopkins. *See* Thou Art Indeed Just, Lord.

Jutacalla Rock. Robert Morgan. LPSFW

Juxtapositions. David Wright. NLP

K

K for the Klondyke, a country of gold. Joseph Hilaire Pierre Belloc. NoAM *Fr.* Moral Alphabet, A.

K was burn at the bend of the ear in the mouth of Remember. Kirstenography. Harryette Mullen. FaoP

Ka 'Ba. Imamu Amiri Baraka. ISC; PmAP

Ka Hale / The Nurturing Place. Kalehua Parrilla Kim. FiBr

Ka Waiapo Lani. Queen Lili'u-o-ka-lani. SWaP

Kaa's Hunting. Rudyard Kipling. *Fr.* Jungle Book, The.

Kabuki. Yvonne Cullen. NIrP

Kaczynski. Jeffrey Clapp. LiTh

Kadavu: / sandbay. Kadavu. *Unknown.* SonAtl, *tr. by* Martin Barwood and Samuel Kila

Kaddish. Allen Ginsberg. OxBoAm; PmAP
"O mother / what have I left out." BB; CLPP
"Your last night in the darkness of the Bronx—I phonecalled—thru hospital to secret police." NAMCP V.2
Kaddish. David Ignatow. GoPo; RaBo; TaR
Kaddish. Herschel Miller. Prolet, tr. by Amelia Glaser
Kaddish. Charles Reznikoff. TaR
Kaddish. Charles Reznikoff. NAAPv.2; TaR
Kagwa hunted the lion. Huntsman, The. Edward Lowbury. OBSP
Kaiser Dead. Matthew Arnold. DiBP
Kaiser's Burnout. Betty Adcock. TiP2
Kalaloch. Carolyn Forché. NoAM; YaYoPo
Kalamazoo. Vachel Lindsay. AmWit
Kaleidoscope. Maria Elena Cruz Varela. VCWP, tr. by Mairym Cruz-Bernal
Kaleidoscope. G. K. Page. NoAM
Kaleidoscope, The. Douglas Dunn. OxBSo
Kalevala, The. Elias Lönnrot.
"It is my desire, it is my wish." PFTM-1
Kalevala, The. Unknown. tr. by Keith Bosley
Fire. WoPoe, tr. by Keith Bosley
Kali. Mei-Mei Berssenbrugge. AWPTFC
Kali. Lucille Clifton. HW
Kali. Elsa Cross. TANSG, tr. by Patricia Dubrava
Kali. Ziporah Hildebrandt. HW
Kali. Leslie Simon. HW
Kali / Is everything You do misleading? Kamalākānta Bhattācārya. SinGod, tr. by Rachel Fell McDermott
Kali, Ma. Rāmprasād Sen. SinGod, tr. by Rachel Fell McDermott
Kali Ma tottering up steps to shelter tin roof, feeling her way to curb. Describe: The Rain on Dasaswamedh Ghat. Allen Ginsberg. BB; FTOS
Kali / my toes strike lightning. Kali. Ziporah Hildebrandt. HW
Kali! / Today in the dark grove. Kamalākānta Bhattācārya. SinGod, tr. by Rachel Fell McDermott
Kali, what family are You from? Kamalākānta Bhattācārya. SinGod, tr. by Rachel Fell McDermott
Kali, you have removed all my difficulties. Kamalākānta Bhattācārya. SinGod, tr. by Rachel Fell McDermott
Kallo dedicated her portrait in the house of golden. Nossis. SaLy, tr. by Diane Rayor
Kalmyk poppies, horde of pan-Mongol tulips. A. Velichansky. TCRusP, tr. by Daniel Weissbort
Kamasutra Sutra. Harryette Mullen. WANABP
Kan (observe). Six Characters from the Heart Sutra. Kazuaki Tanahashi. WhBo
Kangaroo. Mary Jo Salter. WaAnP
Kangaroo, The. Barron Field. NOBAu
Kangaroo is standing up, and dwindling like a plant, A. Dusk, The. Robert Gray. BMAP
Kangaroo, Kangaroo! Kangaroo, The. Barron Field. NOBAu
Kanheri Caves. Dom Moraes. NoP-4; NoP-5
Kannon's tiled temple. Basho. SoOfWa, tr. by Sam Hamill
Kansas. J. P. Dunn. VerBaPo
Kansas 1. Unknown. NAAPv.1 Fr. Ballad of Kansas, The [El corrido de Kiansis].
Kansas Boy. Ruth Lechlitner. PoA 2002
Kansas City Kitty. Edgar Leslie. ReLy
Kansas City West Bottoms. Edward Dahlberg. PoA 2002
Kansas one million centuries ago, a tropical sea. Sea of Kansas, Ohio Tundra, Time Still Running Out, The. David Citino. UpMys
Kanteletar, The. Unknown. tr. by Keith Bosley
Lullabies, 2:174. WoPoe, tr. by Keith Bosley
Kanyariri, Village of Toil. Village, The. Marina Gashe. CFP; HAWP
Karanje Village. Alun Lewis. TCAWP
Karate. Stanley Plumly. MoASP
Karazah to Karl. Adah Isaacs Menken. CBWP-1
Karl Marx Died 1883 Aged 65. Antonio Cisneros. TCLAP, tr. by Maureen Ahern and David Tipton
Karma. Edwin Arlington Robinson. APT-1; HeIP-4; MoAmPo
Karshish, the picker-up of learning's crumbs. Epistle Containing the Strange Medical Experience of Karshish, the Arab Physician, An. Robert Browning. ChIV-2; NAEL-6v2; NAEL-7v2
Kartúshkiya-Beróza. Alter Brody. TaR
Kashmir shrinks into my mailbox. Postcard from Kashmir. Agha Shahid Ali. NAMCP V.2; NIL-7
Kaspar Is Dead. Hans Arp. PFTM-1
Kaspar Is Dead. Hans Arp. GTCP, tr. by Christopher Middleton
Kassacks. Annette M'Baye d'Erneville. HAWP, tr. by Brian Baer

Katakalos. Rosemary Catacalos. TiP2
Katemir's muse, next the world's cant immured. Lomonosov. Anna Semionovna Prismanova. ARWW, tr. by Catriona Kelly
Kath Walker. Lionel Fogarty. VaPo
Käthe Kollwitz. Muriel Rukeyser. NALW
Katherine's Hair. David Marlatt. AmPoNex
Katie Casey was base-ball mad. Take Me Out to the Ball Game. Jack Norworth. NAAPv.2; TCAPo
Katie Kádár. Hungarian Oral Tradition. IQMS, tr. by Adam Makkai
Katie Went to Haiti. Cole Porter. ReLy
Katie went to Haiti. Katie Went to Haiti. Cole Porter. ReLy
Katori Maru, October 1920. James Masao Mitsui. OpBo
Katrina on the Porch. Alice Cary. APN-2
Katya's proud she has a much-admired husband. Party on Women's Day, A. Olesya Nikolayeva. ItGoST, tr. by Paul Graves and Carol Ueland
Katydids scraped in the dim trees. Katydids. Amy Lowell. APT-1
Katyn Forest. Steven Sherrill. BAP-97
Kaunas 1941. Johannes Bobrowski. AF
Kavikanthabharana. Kshemendra. tr. by J. Moussaieff Masson and W. S. Merwin
"Poet should learn with his eyes, A." EaWin; WoPoe, tr. by J. Moussaieff Masson and W. S. Merwin
Kaya-Magan am I! the first person. Kaya-Magan, The. Léopold Sédar Senghor. PFTM-1
Kaya-Magan, The. Léopold Sédar Senghor. PFTM-1
Kayenta Times Yet Dreaming On. Nia Francisco. HATNAP
[Kazak]. David Schloss. PoA 2002 Fr. Figures in the Carpets.
K-Doe Codas. Brett Evans. AnSo
Keen as the blade of the guillotine, grey as its steel. Execution of Madame du Barry, The. J. J. Bray. NOBAu
Keen, Fitful Gusts are Whisp'ring. John Keats. CenSon
Keen stars were twinkling, The. To Jane: The keen stars were twinkling. Percy Bysshe Shelley. NAEL-6v2; NAEL-7v2
Keener tempests come: and fuming dun, The. James Thomson. NoP-5 Fr. Seasons, The.
Keep a Good Thought. Bernard Keller. BtF
Keep a Hand on Your Dream. X. J. Kennedy. CA
Keep a red heart of memories. Haze. Carl Sandburg. TCAPo
Keep away. Song of Repulse to a Vain Lover. Makah Oral Tradition. NAAPv.1
Keep away from sharp words. Admonitions of the Boudoir. Anne Waldman. AmZen
Keep back the one word more. Reserve. Lizette Woodworth Reese. SWaP
Keep bees and. Advice to the Young. Miriam Waddington. NIP-4
Keep Going. Gail Mazur. ExTi
Keep It Simple. Ray Evans and Jay Livingston. ReLy
Keep it simple / don't make too much of love. Keep It Simple. Ray Evans and Jay Livingston. ReLy
Keep love and he wings. Fragment 40. "H. D." BrAP
Keep love for youth, and violets for the spring. Autumn Violets. Christina Georgina Rossetti. ViWPN
Keep Me. Malka Heifetz-Tussman. ASA, tr. by Kathryn Hellerstein
Keep on walkin and walkin talkin to mysel. Hard Road Blues. Unknown. FaBoVe
Keep Quiet. Lawson Fusao Inada. WhBo
Keep Talking. Philip Levine. WeW-3
Keep the Home Fires Burning (Till the Boys Come Home). Lena Guilbert Ford. NAAPv.2
Keep the Season. James McAuley. BMAP
Keep thou. Anguish. Adelaide Crapsey. APT-1
Keep walking intently. Theater Music. Takehisa Kosugi. WhBo
Keep walking, though there's no place to get to. Jelaluddin Rumi. LoL, tr. by Coleman Barks
Keep watch over the orchard, attentive Priapus! Unknown. PriapPo Fr. Priapus Poems, The.
Keep you trouble to youself. Rules, The. Philip Dacey. SUP
Keep your eye on the grand old flag. (LL) You're a Grand Old Flag. George M. Cohan. NAAPv.2; ReLy
Keeper [(for Washington, D.C.)]. Esther Iverem. GT
Keepin' Out of Mischief Now. Andy Razaf. ReLy
Keeping. Richard Howard. MAAN
Keeping Christmas. Eleanor Farjeon. OBCP
Keeping Going. Seamus Heaney. ModIr
Keeping my head above the millions. Thirty Years On. Charles Hobday. RSaN
Keeping on and on. Spring Travel. Chia Tao. CSKM, tr. by Mike O'Connor
Keeping Quiet. Pablo Neruda. TWF, tr. by Alastair Reid

Keeping their difficult balance. (LL) Love Calls Us to the Things of This World. Richard Wilbur. AmFaPo; BrAP; CAP-8; ColAP; EMP; HeIP-4; MoAmPo; NAAL-5; NAMCP V.2; NIL-7; NIP-4; NoAM; NoP-4; NoP-5; OxBoAm; TFi; UpMys; VCAP; WaAnP

Keeping Their World Large. Marianne Moore. PWW2; WaAnP

Keeping Things Whole. Mark Strand. CAP-8; HeIP-4; ItP; NAMCP V.2; OxBoAm; PoPoPo; VCAP

Keeping Track. Maurya Simon. GeoHom

Keeping Track of the Serpents. Víctor Hernández Cruz. TouFir

Keeping vigil for minimum wage. Undergoing: Jewish General Hospital, Montreal 6:35 a.m. Fraser Sutherland. Coast

Keeping Watch. Sojourner Kincaid Rolle. GeoHom

Keeps a different time. Across the street, Lake Michigan folds. Edgewater Hospital. Albert Goldbarth. PoA 2002

Keepsake, The. Samuel Taylor Coleridge. NPBRoP

Keepsake to treasure?, A. Poughkeepsie. Emyr Humphreys. BBMWP, tr. by Elin ap Hywel

Kehama's Curse. Robert Southey. NOBRP Fr. Curse of Kehama, The.

Keine Kadish wird man sagen. (LL) Louis Zukofsky. NAMCP V.1; PFTM-1; TaR Fr. Poem Beginning "The."

Keine Lazarovitch, 1870-1959. Irving Layton. NIP-4

Kelly. Rafael Campo. WiU Fr. Ten Patients, and Another.

Kelly on a Mountain. Man from Strathbogie, The. Olive Mary Finnin. NOBAu

Kelly, Ringling Bros. Oldest Elephant, Goes On Rampage. Joel Brouwer. LegDan

Kelly sharpened is powerful, asexual and yawns. Anorexia. Jennifer Maiden. BMAP

Kelly's kept an unlicensed bull, well away. Outlaw, The. Seamus Heaney. NIL-7

Kelp. Nora Dauenhauer. HATNAP

Kemo Sabe. Diane Glancy. LTA

Ke-Mo Village Girl. Vietnamese Oral Tradition. CaDao, tr. by John Balaban

Ken. Charlotte Mew. VWP

Kendall Gulls. Ricardo Pau-Llosa. UrbNat

Kenji Takezo Becomes Water. Rick Noguchi. NeAmPo

Kenji Takezo does not have the gift of vision. Really Long Ride, The. Rick Noguchi. NeAmPo

Kenji Takezo feels everybody. Turn of Privacy, The. Rick Noguchi. AmPoNex; NeAmPo

Kenless Strand, The. Sydney Goodsir Smith. WoPoe

Kennedy Airport. Aaron Kramer. OtW

Kenscoff. Lorna Goodison. GT

Kensington Gardens. Muriel Spark. OBGa

Kentish Independent of 1843, The. Late Richard Dadd, 1817–1886, The. Michael Hofmann. NeBrP

Kentucky. M. Loncar. NAPBL

Kentucky Belle. Constance Fenimore Woolson. CBCWP

Kentucky Mountain Farm. Robert Penn Warren.
  History among the Rocks. CBCWP; MoAmPo
  Watershed. OxBoAm; PoA 2002

Kentucky water, clear springs: a boy fleeing. Swimmers, The. Allen Tate. APT-2; FuPo; MoAmPo; NAAPv.2; NAMCP V.1; NoAM; NoP-5

Kenyatta Listening to Mozart. Imamu Amiri Baraka. PmAP

Kepler Considers the Dimensions of a Sheep. Linden Ontjes. PoDa

Kept. Louise Bogan. APT-2

Kéramos. Henry Wadsworth Longfellow. APN-1

Kerensky. Lola Ridge. APT-1

Kerf, The. Sam Truitt. AmPoNex Fr. Anamorphosis Eisenhower.

Kerosene. Chase Twichell. ExTi

Kerosene lamp burns deep within an inner courtyard, A. Sewing Box, The. Chŏng Hwajin. EcSo, tr. by Julie C. Park

Kerouac and. Future Martyr of Supersonic Waves. Juan Felipe Herrera. TouFir

Kerouac Creek Work Tune. Hoa Nguyen. WANABP

Kerouac, we knock. Ray McNiece. AmZen

Kerrisdale Elegies. George Bowering.
  "If I did complain, who among my friends." OpeFie

Kerr's Ass. Patrick Kavanagh. ModIr

Kestrel. Peter Sanger. Coast

Ketjak. Ron Silliman.
  "Revolving door." PFTM-2

Kettle hisses, The. One small boy longs for summer. Mafika Pascal Gwala. TSAP

Kettle Rooted to the Void. Anabel Torres. TANSG, tr. by Celeste Kostopulos-Cooperman

Kevin and Nicole. Amanda Nazario. HeMarv

Kevin of the N.E. Crew. Elizabeth Alexander. FFC

Kew. Erasmus Darwin. OBGa Fr. Botanic Garden, The.

Key, The. Richard Jones. GifTon

Key, The. John Ormond. AngWePo; TCAWP

Key, The. Peter Scupham. HarvBoo

Key and the Tree, The. Alessandro Ceni. ItPo, tr. by Gayle Ridinger

Key Episodes from an Earthly Life. C. D. Wright. AmAlph

Key into the Language of America, A. Rosmarie Waldrop.
  Chapter XXIII: Of Marriage. PFTM-2
  Chapter XXIV: Concerning Their Coyne. PFTM-2

Key is always nomadic, The. Role Reversal. Maria Luisa Spaziani. CItWP, tr. by Cinzia Sartini Blum and Lara Trubowitz

Key Keeper, The. Ben Jonson.
  Song. OxBEV

Key: nnnn N N gahn. 13th Horse Song of Frank Mitchell, The. María Sabina. PFTM-1

Key of Water, The. Octavio Paz. VCWP; WoPoe, tr. by Elizabeth Bishop

Key, the shifting is, The. Andy Weaver. PoPra Fr. Were the Bees.

Key to Closet. Gertrude Stein. MotU; OxBoAm Fr. Book Concluding with As A Wife Has a Cow a Love Story, A.

Key to Dreams. Georg Nikolic. IllVoic

Keys. Barbara J. Garshman. PasH

Keys of the Saint. Ernesto Lumbreras. RMCMP, tr. by Rebecca Seiferle

Keys please. In This Way. Gertrude Stein. PFTM-1

Keys that open doors, The. Thorny Gaps Suddenly Moving. Fatma Kandil. PoArWo, tr. by Khaled Mattawa

Khentei, Khangai, Soyon—awe-rearing ranges. My Country. D. Natsagdorzh. SonAtl, tr. by Bat-Erdene Baabar, Susie Drost, Clare Eaton and S. Erdenebat

Kh'hob dikh lib. Yuri Suhl. Prolet, tr. by Amelia Glaser

Khobayza. Zulaykha Abu-Risha. PoArWo, tr. by Clarissa C. Burt and Nathalie Handal

Khurbn. Jerome Rothenberg.
  Dibbukim (Dibbiks). PFTM-2
  Dos Geshray (The Scream). FTOS; PFTM-2
  Dos Oysleydikn (The Emptying). AmWaPo; PFTM-2

Kiche Manitou. Nathaniel Mackey. FTOS

Kick a Little Stone. Dorothy Aldis. TLR

Kick at the rock, Sam Johnson, break your bones. Epistemology. Richard Wilbur. NoAM

Kicking and Breathing. Gary Margolis. PfSP

Kicking his mother until she let go of his soul. Mundus et Infans. W. H. Auden. MoBrPo; NoAM

Kid. Simon Armitage. BeAl

Kid, The. Ai. GT; NoAM

Kid had walked these streets before, The. African Burial Ground called Tribeca, The. David Henderson. BRtP

Kid kid kid kootje. Scaring Hens. Peter Finch. Oth

Kid Stuff. Frank Horne. NOxBChV

Kid was already noxious carrion, The. Song at the End of a Meal. John Hollander. TaR

Kidnap[p]er. Tess Gallagher. LaCa

Kids! Lee Adams. ReLy

Kids and her, The. 2 Months Rent Due and 1 Bag of Rice. Luci Beach. ReEnLa

Kids are good at this, The. Their nimble fingers. Origami. Greg Williamson. NAPBL

Kids! / I don't know what's wrong with these kids today! Kids! Lee Adams. ReLy

'Kids make a home,' he said, the family man. Family Man, The. Bruce Dawe. BMAP

Kids on Television Imagine Me, The. Jordan Davis. HeMarv

Kids / Playing Stick Ball. Snapshot: West Philly. Kimmika L. H. Williams. BtF

Kids shoot out of the car roaring. St Bees in Winter. William Scammell. NLP

Kiev, the Ukraine, Nuclear Accident. David Romtvedt. GifTon

Kilaben Bay Song. Unknown. NOBAu, tr. by Perce Haslam

Kilbarchan now may say alas! Life and Death of [Habbie Simson] the Piper of Kilbarchan, The. Robert Sempill. NPeEn

Kilcash. Unknown. OBMV, tr. by Frank O'Connor

Kildan women had never seen trees, The. Kildan Women, The. Kenneth Rosen. NevBe

Kildan Women, The. Kenneth Rosen. NevBe

Kilfenora Teaboy, The. Paul Durcan. PBCIP

Kilgore Rangerette Whose Life Was Ruined, The. Cynthia MacDonald. TiP2

Kilimanjaro. Hélène d'Oettingen. CuPo

Kilimanjaro Sunrise. Sŏ Chŏngju. CAMKP, tr. by David R. McCann

Kill me not every [or ev'ry] day. Affliction (2). George Herbert. NOSC

Kill me with spite; yet we must not be foes. (LL)   William Shakespeare. HeIP-4; OxAEP-1 *Fr.* Sonnets.

Kill That Crowing Cock.   *Unknown.*   NDACCP, *tr. by* Kenneth Rexroth

Kill, The.   Carl Phillips.   WiU

Kill the DJ.   Reg E. Gaines.   BRtP

Kill the others is a theory.   Why I Hate Theory.   Bruce Weigl.   AmAlph

Killary.   Herbert Trench.   IrV

Killdeer screaming over the flowering acres.   Prairie Spring.   Loren C. Eiseley. PoCho

Killed.   Lee Ranaldo.   HeMarv

Killed at the Ford.   Henry Wadsworth Longfellow.   CBCWP; PCW

Killed / by a white woman.   Clay.   Imamu Amiri Baraka.   ESEAA

Killed by the Elevator, C—e Factory, Dundee.   Nelly's Lament for the Pirnhouse Cat.   Ellen Johnston.   VWP

Killed, The.   Douglas Burnet Smith. "Returning, near morning."   Coast

Killer Blues.   Calvin Forbes.   IllVoic

Killer Dog.   Gwyn Thomas.   BBMWP, *tr. by* Joseph P. Clancy

Killer, The.   Judith Wright.   BMAP

Killers.   Cordelia Candelaria.   FTtHH

Killers said.   Synagogue in Prague.   Alan Sillitoe.   HP

Killing Floor.   Ai.   NAMCP V.2; NoAM; WaAnP

Killing Memory.   Haki R. Madhubuti.   IllVoic

Killing No Murder.   Sylvia Townsend Warner.   MoBrPo

Killing oneself.   Epistle on Suicide.   Bertolt Brecht.   StAl, *tr. by* John Willett

Killing, The.   Edwin Muir.   GI

Killing the Animals.   Wesley McNair.   P180

Killing the Animals.   Charles Harper Webb.   LiTh

Killing Time.   Simon Armitage. "Meanwhile, somewhere in the state of Colorado, armed to the teeth." NoP-5

Killing Time #2.   Simon Armitage.   BeAl

Kilmeny.   James Hogg.   OBEV; OxAEP-2 *Fr.* Queen's Wake, The.

Kiln-charred children in the yard, The.   Sculpture Garden.   Austin Hummell. AmPoNex

Kilroy.   Peter Viereck.   MoAmPo; PWW2

Kiltartan Legend.   Padraic Fallon.   ModIr

Kim.   Rudyard Kipling. Prodigal Son, The.   NoAM

Kimchee in Worcester (Mass.).   Alfred Corn.   WiU

1. Kimiko Ozawa.   Lee Ann Roripaugh.   AmWaPo *Fr.* Heart Mountain, 1943.

Kimono, The.   James Merrill.   CAP-8; ColAP; WaAnP

Kin.   Ruth Forman.   AmPoNex

Kin.   Michael S. Harper.   OxAAAP

Kinaxixi.   Agostinho Neto.   PoetW; WoPoe, *tr. by* W. S. Merwin

Kind, almost courtly, a "good listener," he kept lovers.   One-Page Novel. David Gewanter.   NAPBL

Kind and selfless to his brothers.   *Various authors.*   CATKP *Fr.* Songs of Flying Dragons.

Kind are my stars indeed but that so late.   To Mrs B. from a Lady Who Had a Desire to See Her, and Who Complains on the Ingratitude of Her Fugitive Lover.   *Unknown.*   EMWP

Kind height, kind in the right stomach with a little sudden mill.   Gertrude Stein. NAMCP V.1 *Fr.* Tender Buttons.

Kind in glass and a cousin, a spectacle and nothing strange, A.   Gertrude Stein. MoWP; NAAPv.2; NAMCP V.1 *Fr.* Tender Buttons.

Kind of an Ode to Duty.   Ogden Nash.   AmWit

Kind of blindness, that's what's needed now, A.   Way Light Bends, The. William Daniel Ehrhart.   AtGh

Kind of Blue.   A. Van Jordan.   LegDan

Kind of Catastrophe, A.   Rachel Zucker.   IIR

Kind of Culture, A.   Mihály Babits.   IQMS, *tr. by* Peter Zollman

Kind of empty in the way it sees everything, the earth gets to its feet and salutes the sky.   For John Clare.   John Ashbery.   HarvBoo; MotU

Kind of grace it is to slay with speed, A. (LL)   Sir Philip Sidney.   NoP-4; NoP-5 *Fr.* Astrophil and Stella.

Kind of Loss, A.   Ingeborg Bachmann.   PoetW, *tr. by* Mark Anderson

Kind of malignant mind creeps through earth, A.   Excursions.   Ray Ragosta. OnScMo

Kind of mountain pond or lake, A.   Dusk Coming on outside ———, New York.   Stanley Plumly.   PfSP

Kind of Ransom.   Marla Jernigan.   AnSo

Kind of Shadow That Calls Out Fate, The.   Tony Hoagland.   AmWaPo

Kind of Wakefulness, A.   Robert J. Gibbs.   Coast

Kind pity [*or* Kinde pitty] chokes my spleen[e]; brave scorn forbids.   John Donne.   BASC; FSCP; NAEL-6v1; NAEL-7v1; NoP-4; NoP-5; OxAEP-1; SacPr *Fr.* Satires.

Kind sir, do listen.   From the Spirit of Phillis Wheatley to the Spirit of Thomas Jefferson (A Note 212 Years Later).   Karen Williams.   BtF

Kind Valentine.   David Schubert.   OxBoAm

Kinda Blue Miles Davis Died Today.   Everett Hoagland.   BodElec

Kinde are her answeres.   Thomas Campion.   OxBEV

Kindertotenlieder.   Timothy Liu.   NeAmPo

Kindled moons are moving on the road.   Military Funeral in the Heat of Day. T. Carmi.   NRoS, *tr. by* Esther Raizen

Kindly Deed, A.   Priscilla Jane Thompson.   CBWP-2

Kindly people of Vancouver, B.C., The.   Parable of the Boy and the Polar Bear. Roger Fanning.   NAPBL

Kindly rain its proper season knows, The.   Kindly Rain, The.   Tu Fu [*or* Du Fu].   CCL1, *tr. by* W. J. B. Fletcher

Kindly Rain, The.   Tu Fu [*or* Du Fu].   CCL1, *tr. by* W. J. B. Fletcher

Kindly watcher by my bed, lift no voice in prayer.   Music.   George Du Maurier.   OBEV

Kindness.   Thomas Sturge Moore.   OBMV

Kindness.   Sylvia Plath.   MoWP

Kindness.   Mary E. Tucker.   CBWP-1

Kindness: "Before you know what kindness really is."   Naomi Shihab Nye. BeAl; IJHIL

Kindness, an Irish lilt in her voice.   Bath.   Myra Schneider.   PoCu

Kindness and Generosity.   Tiruvalluvar.   WoPoe *Fr.* Kural, The.

Kindness glides about my house.   Kindness.   Sylvia Plath.   MoWP

Kindness of Abishag, The.   Davi Walders.   VisFro

Kindness to Animals.   Laura Elizabeth Richards.   NTCP

Kindness to Animals.   *Unknown.*   WHSW

Kinds of Blue #41 Far Hills.   Don McKay.   OpeFie

Kinescope.   Dionisio D. Martinez.   TouFir

King, The.   Skipwith Cannell.   APT-1

King, The.   Rudyard Kipling.   CABP

King and Hermit.   *Unknown.*   IrV, *tr. by* Kuno Meyer

King and No King, A.   Robert Herrick.   PBRV

King and Queen of Dumfriesshire sit, The.   King and Queen of Dumfriesshire, The.   W. N. Herbert.   EdScPo; NeBrP

King and Queen of the Pelicans we.   Pelican Chorus, The.   Edward Lear. OBSP

King: April 4, 1968 [*For Eva Ray*].   Gerald William Barrax.   ESEAA; GT

King Arthur made new knights to fill the gap.   Alfred Tennyson.   NAEL-6v2 *Fr.* Idylls of the King.

King Arthur rode in another world.   Blue from Heaven, The.   Stevie Smith. BrAP

King Arthur's Waes-hael.   Robert Stephen Hawker.   OBEV

King asked, The.   King's Breakfast, The.   Alan Alexander Milne.   UV

King Bee Blues.   George Elliott Clarke.   IFF

King Billy.   Edwin Morgan.   EdScPo; NePenScot; NoP-4; NoP-5

King Billy on the Walls.   Sheenagh Pugh.   AngWePo

King Ch'in Drinks Wine.   Li Ho.   ChinPo, *tr. by* Ye Weilian [*or* Yeh Wei-lien *or* Wai-lim Yip]

King Ch'in rides a tiger to roam the Eight Poles.   King Ch'in Drinks Wine.   Li Ho.   ChinPo, *tr. by* Ye Weilian [*or* Yeh Wei-lien *or* Wai-lim Yip]

King Claudius.   Kirkpatrick Dobie.   EdScPo

King Cobra as Political Assassin, The.   Ray A. Young Bear.   HATNAP

King David.   Stephen Vincent Benét.   ChIV-1

King David and King Solomon.   Authorship.   James Ball Naylor.   GoPo; NBLV

King David Dances.   John Berryman.   ChIV-1

King Don Luis.   O. V. de L. Milosz.   WoPoe, *tr. by* John Peck

King Edward scales the hills of Wales.   Bards of Wales, The.   János Arany. IQMS, *tr. by* Peter Zollman

King Emanuel.   *Unknown.*   SSUS

King Estmere.   *Unknown.*   OBNV

King. Father. Mother. Husband. Wife.   Testing the Confucian Ideal. *Vietnamese Oral Tradition.*   CaDao, *tr. by* John Balaban

King for the night! the rabbi cried.   Bar Mitzvah, The.   Philip Schultz.   TaR

King George V.   Charles W. Hayward.   NOBAu

King he reigns on a throne of gold, The.   Leveller, The.   Barry Cornwall. OxAEP-2

King Henry V.   William Shakespeare. "But if the cause be not good, the King himself hath a."   RaF "Doth Fortune play the huswife with me now?"   FaBoWar "Fortune is Bardolph's foe, and frowns on him."   FaBoWar Henry V at the Siege of Harfleur.   OxAEP-1; WaAnP Henry V before Agincourt.   BLPJKO "How yet resolves the Governor of the town?"   FaBoWar "King is full of grace and fair regard, The."   OxAEP-1 Muse of Fire, A.   OxAEP-1

"Now entertain conjecture of a time." FaBoWar; OxAEP-1

"O! that we now had here." FaBoWar; OxAEP-1

(Speech Before Harfleur, The.) ITBLP

"Thus with imagin'd wing our swift scene flies." OxAEP-1

"We are but warriors for the working-day." FaBoWar

King Henry IV, Pt. I. William Shakespeare.

"I have learn'd." OxAEP-1

"My liege, I did deny no prisoners." FaBoWar

"O, Harry! thou hast robb'd me of my youth." OxAEP-1

"So shaken as we are, so wan with care." OxAEP-1

King Henry IV, Pt. II. William Shakespeare.

"But wherefore did he take away the crown?" OxAEP-1

"How many thousand of my poorest subjects." AWTN

"This new and gorgeous garment, majesty." OxAEP-1

King Henry VI, Pt. I. William Shakespeare.

King Is Dead, A. OxAEP-1

King Henry VI, Pt. II. William Shakespeare.

Bear-Baiting Cur, The. DiBP

King Henry VI, Pt. III. William Shakespeare.

"Great lords, wise men ne'er sit and wail their loss." FaBoWar

"Ill blows the wind that profits nobody." FaBoWar

"Owl shriek'd at thy birth, an evil sign, The." OxAEP-1

King Henry VIII. John Fletcher and William Shakespeare.

Music. NOSC

(Orpheus.) OBEV

King Henry's Song. Joseph Addison. STuOW Fr. Rosamond.

King Honour's Eldest Son. Elinor Wylie. SacPr

King in Thule, The. Johann Wolfgang von Goethe. STV, tr. by John Frederick Nims

King Is Dead, A. William Shakespeare. OxAEP-1 Fr. King Henry VI, Pt. I.

King is father, The. Statesmanship. Ch'ungdam, Master. CATKP, tr. by Peter H. Lee

King is full of grace and fair regard, The. William Shakespeare. OxAEP-1 Fr. King Henry V.

King is thinking Tricia's got nice tits, The. Nixon Names Elvis Honorary Federal Narcotics Agent at Oval Office Ceremony, 1973. David Wojahn. AllShUp

King John. William Shakespeare.

"Must you with hot irons burn out both mine eyes?" OxAEP-1

"This England never did, nor never shall." OxAEP-1

King Kong Meets Wallace Stevens. Michael Ondaatje. BrAP; NIL-7

King Lear. Peter Huchel. PoSu, tr. by Michael Hamburger

King Lear Bewildered. Patricia Storace. FFC

King lear in a mr. whippy van. Revisionism. Joanne Burns. BMAP

King Lear. William Shakespeare.

Blow, Winds. OxAEP-1

"Come on, sir; he[e]re's the place: stand still." OxAEP-1; OxBEV

"Here is the place, my lord; good my lord, enter." OxAEP-1

"Howl, howl, howl! O! you are men of stones." OxAEP-1

"I prithee, daughter, do not make me mad." OxAEP-1

Lear and the Dogs. DiBP

"O my dear father! Restoration, hang." OxAEP-1

King Matthias in Gömör. János Garay. IQMS, tr. by James Turner

King Midas. Howard Moss. OxBoAm

King Midas. Howard Moss.

King's Speech, The. PoA 2002

King of Brentford's Testament abr, The. William Makepeace Thackeray. OBNV

King of Ch'in Drinks Wine, The. Li Ho. WoPoe, tr. by A. C. Graham

King of Ch'in rides out on his tiger and roams to the Eight Bounds, The. King of Ch'in Drinks Wine, The. Li Ho. WoPoe, tr. by A. C. Graham

King of China's Daughter, The. Dame Edith Sitwell. MoBrPo

King of depth. Bridge of Old Wonders. Muzaffar Nawwab. IrPoTo, tr. by Carol Bardenstein

King of Glory [or Glorie], King of Peace, / I will love thee. Praise (2). George Herbert. ChIV-1

King of Glory [or Glorie], King of Peace, / With the one make war[re] to cease. L'Envoy. George Herbert. BASC

King of honour, louder than of England, The. Lament for the Country Soldiers. Les A. Murray. BMAP

King of Huainan, The. Magic Cinnabar. Pao Chao. ColAnChi, tr. by Anne Birrell

King of my freedom here, with every prop. My Study. Edward Palmer Thompson. RSaN

King of Nowhere said to me, The. Two Songs of Queen Anne Boleyn. Dame Edith Sitwell. BrAP

King of Oo-Rinktum-Jing, The. James Whitcomb Riley. NOxBChV

King of Owls, The. Louise Erdrich. NoAM

King of Repetition. Marc Jaffee. BAP-04

King of rock 'n' roll, The. Painkillers. Thom Gunn. AllShUp; SwNoth

King of Spain. Tiger, The. Marie Laurencin. CuPo

King of the Beasts, deep in the wood, The. Lion and the Echo, The. Brian Patten. OBSP

King of the bodhi tree, The. Kyunyŏ, Great Master. CATKP Fr. Eleven Poems on the Ten Vows of the Universally Worthy Bodhisattva.

King of the Cats is Dead, The. Peter Porter. EmeKit; NoAM

King of the gods once loved a Trojan boy, The. Ovid. CAGL Fr. Metamorphoses.

King of the Mountains is on his way to Hara's abode, The. Kamalākānta Bhattācārya. SinGod, tr. by Rachel Fell McDermott

King of the perennial holly-groves, the riven sandstone. Geoffrey Hill. NAMCP V.2; NoAM; NPeEn; WoPoe Fr. Mercian Hymns.

King of the River. Stanley Kunitz. PtR

King of the three worlds, lord of laws. Hymn to Sarira. Great Master Chajang. BecRai, tr. by Kim Daljin, Kim Won-Chung and Christopher Merrill

King of waters, the sea shouldering whale, The. Sea's Abundant Progeny, The. William Wood. NOSC

King, once summoned his favorites, A. King's Favorites, The. Priscilla Jane Thompson. CBWP-2

King Pellam's Launde. David Jones. Fr. In Parenthesis.

King & Queen. John Montague. PBCIP

King Richard II. William Shakespeare.

"Draw near, / And list what with our council we have done." OxAEP-1

"Go bind thou up young dangling apricots." OBGa

Let's Talk of Graves.

Death of Kings, The. TRP

King Richard III. William Shakespeare.

"I have been studying how I may compare." OxAEP-1; WoPoe

"Now is the winter of our discontent." OxBEV

"Where is the duke my father with his power?" OxAEP-1

"Why looks your Grace so heavily today?" OxAEP-1

King Saul and I. Yehuda Amichai. PoSu, tr. by Assia Gutmann

King Saul was disconcerted. David and Goliath. Priscilla Jane Thompson. CBWP-2

King sent for his wise men all, The. W. James Reeves. NOxBChV; NTCP

King shall come when morning dawns, The. Unknown. RSR

King sits in Dumferline [or Dumferling orDumfermline or Dumfermlin] town [or toune], The. Sir Patrick Spens [or Spence]. Unknown. BrAP; ClHu; GoPo; MakPoe; NAEL-6v1; NAEL-7v1; NePenScot; NIL-7; NIP-4; NoP-4; NoP-5; NPeEn; OBEV; OBSP; OxBEV; PoPoPo; TFi; WaAnP; WeW-3

King Solomon, before his palace gate. Henry Wadsworth Longfellow. APN-1; TCAPo Fr. Tales of a Wayside Inn.

King Solomon's Camel. Natan Zach. PoSu, tr. by Jon Silkin

King Solomon's Camel is a hypocritical creature. King Solomon's Camel. Natan Zach. PoSu, tr. by Jon Silkin

King Solomon's Magnetic Quiz. John Wieners. FTOS

King Star trails nine lesser stars, The. King Star, The. Vietnamese Oral Tradition. CaDao, tr. by John Balaban

King surveying, with judicious Eyes, The. Joseph Trapp. OxBEV

King then left his coach, The. Homer. NOSC Fr. Iliad, The.

King to Oxford sent a troop of horse, The. Epigram. Sir William Browne. OxBEV

King Tommy's Rise and Fall. Ella Wheeler Wilcox. ArBi

King Tut in America. Kwadwo Opoku-Agyemang. NAfrP

King upon whose bosom let me lie, The. (LL) Torso, The / Passages 18. Robert Duncan. CAGL; HarvBoo; OxBoAm; PmAP

King was being chased by the Queen, The. Windows of the Castle, The. Russell Edson. MotU

King Wen's Epithalamium. Unknown. CCL1 Fr. Guan-ju.

King with His Queen, The. Monica Ferrell. IIR

Kingcups. Sacheverell Sitwell. MoBrPo

Kingdom. Leopold Staff. PoSu, tr. by Adam Czerniawski

Kingdom Coming. Henry Clay Work. APN-2

Kingdom of God, The. Francis Thompson. SacPr

(In No Strange Land.) ITBLP; MoBrPo; OBEV

Kingdom of Heaven. Léonie Adams. MoAmPo

Kingdom of Heaven Compared to a Grain of Mustard-Seed, The. Henry Vaughan. ChIV-1

Kingdom of Heaven, The. Pattiann Rogers. PoCoUp

Kingdom, The. Barry Silesky. IllVoic

Kingdome 1974, The. George Bowering. BrAP

Kinged. Shalin Hai-Jew. UnSA

Kingfisher, The. Amy Clampitt. OWoS

Kingfisher, The. W. H. Davies. AngWePo; OBEV; OBWVE

Kingfisher, The.   John Heath-Stubbs.   NOxBChV

Kingfisher, The.   John Lloyd.   AngWePo

Kingfisher, The.   Mary Oliver.   BLT

Kingfisher.   Norman Alexander MacCaig.   NoP-4; NoP-5

Kingfisher in highest cypress green.   Sic transit.   Skip Fox.   AnSo

Kingfisher is a glorious thing, The.   Kingfisher, The.   John Lloyd.   AngWePo

Kingfisher rises out of the black wave, The.   Kingfisher, The.   Mary Oliver. BLT

Kingfisher with Fish in Beak.   Ch'ien Ch'i.   CCL1, *tr.* by Stephen Owen

Kingfisher's Boxing Gloves, The.   James Fenton.   NoAM

Kingfishers frolic among the orchid blossoms.   Poem on the Wandering Immortal.   Kuo P'o.   ColAnChi, *tr.* by Burton Watson

Kingfishers sport among orchids and begonias.   Kuo P'o.   ChinPo, *tr.* by Ye Weilian [*or* Yeh Wei-lien *or* Wai-lim Yip]

Kingfishers, The.   Charles Olson.   APSN; HarvBoo; OxBoAm; VCAP

Kingis Quair, The.   James I, King of Scotland.
"Heigh in the hevynnis figure circulere."   NePenScot

Kings, The.   Louise Imogen Guiney.   SacPr

King's Breakfast, The.   Alan Alexander Milne.   UV

Kings Came Riding.   Charles Williams.   OBCP

King's Courtyard, The.   *Hungarian Oral Tradition.*   IQMS, *tr.* by Dermot Spence

Kings' Daughters, Home for Unwed Mothers, 1948.   C. D. Wright.   InGu

King's Disguise, The.   John Cleveland.   BASC

Kings do not touch doors.   Pleasures of the Door, The.   Francis Ponge. WoPoe, *tr.* by Raymond Federman

Kings do not touch doors.   Pleasures of the Door, The.   Francis Ponge. MotU, *tr.* by Lane Dunlop

Kings don't touch doors.   Delights of the Door, The.   Francis Ponge.   RaBo; WED, *tr.* by Robert Bly

King's Favorites, The.   Priscilla Jane Thompson.   CBWP-2

Kings go by with jeweled crowns, The.   John Masefield.   MoBrPo *Fr.* Lollingdon Downs.

King's Highway to the Dare-Not-Know, The.   Dreams Are the Royal Road to the Unconscious.   Paul Goodman.   PoA 2002

King's Last Farewell to the World, The.   *Unknown.*   BASC

Kings / like golden gleams.   History Lesson, A.   Miroslav Holub.   PoSu, *tr.* by George Theiner

King's Men, The.   William Heyen.   PoA 2002

Kings never touch a door.   Pleasures of a Door.   Francis Ponge.   YaTCFP, *tr.* by Lee Fahnestock

Kings of the sea, The. (LL)   Forsaken Merman, The.   Matthew Arnold. NAEL-6v2; NAEL-7v2; OBNV; OBSP

King's Own Regulars, The [And Their Triumphs Over the Irregulars]. *Unknown.*   NAAPv.1

Kings passed in the dark barge, which Merlin dreamed. (LL)   Hospital Barge at Cérisy.   Wilfred Owen.   HarvBoo; TCAWP

King's Sabbath, The.   Archibald Lampman.   IFF

Kings shall go, so will their pretty queens, The.   Eternity.   Kabir.   WoPoe, *tr.* by Arvind Krishna Mehrotra

King's Son, The.   Thomas Boyd.   OBMV

King's Speech, The.   Howard Moss.   PoA 2002 *Fr.* King Midas.

Kinky.   Denise Duhamel.   AmPoNex

Kinky Hair Blues.   Una Marson.   MoWP

Kinloch Ainort.   Sorley MacLean.   HarvBoo

Kinmont Willie.   *Unknown.*   IBB

Kinnaird Head.   George Bruce.   EdScPo

Kinshasa, Lumbumbasha.   Bajji.   Rashidah Ismaili.   HAWP

Kinsman of Death, The.   Endre Ady.   IQMS, *tr.* by Peter Zollman

KIRK OF ULPHA to the pilgrim's eye, The.   William Wordsworth.   CenSon *Fr.* River Duddon [A Series of Sonnets], The.

Kirkintilloch Revisited.   Gerald Mangan.   EdScPo

Kirkwall Auction Mart.   David Scott.   NLP

Kirkyaird by the Sea, The.   Douglas Young.
"Steikit, consecrat, fou o fire but fuel."   OBVE

Kirkyard.   George Mackay Brown.   NePenScot; NPeEn

Kirstenography.   Harryette Mullen.   FaoP

Kisagata.   Basho.   EMJL, *tr.* by Haruo Shirane

Kisimiso.   Musaemura Bonus Zimunya.   HBAPE; NAfrP

Kiss.   Susan Aizenberg.   ExTi

Kiss.   Emanuel Carnevali.   APT-2

Kiss.   Kitahara Hakushū.   CAoMJL1, *tr.* by Leith Morton

Kiss.   Shuntaro Tanikawa.   PML, *tr.* by Harold Wright

Kiss, A.   Malka Lee.   Prolet, *tr.* by Amelia Glaser

Kiss, A.   Mary E. Tucker.   CBWP-1

Kiss, The.   Angela Ball.   ExTi

Kiss, The.   Chana Bloch.   FaoP

Kiss, The.   Marie Howe.   ExTi; FaoP

Kiss, The.   Thomas Moore.   NOBRP

Kiss, The.   Edith Nesbit.   LW

Kiss, The.   Plato.   STV, *tr.* by John Frederick Nims

Kiss, The.   Francis Saltus Saltus.   VerBaPo

Kiss, The.   Alice Walker.   GT

Kiss, The: "Greatest bliss, The."   Charlotte Dacre.   CABP; NOBRP; WaAnP

Kiss the past until it's bitter, his.   Boy, Allegorically Deployed.   Reginald Shepherd.   RD

Kiss, The: "She had imagined the kiss."   Paul Hoover.   SUP

Kiss, The 1656. To Mrs. C.   Thomas Shipman.   NOSC

Kiss? A. Pray tell me, what is in a kiss.   Kiss, A.   Mary E. Tucker.   CBWP-1

Kiss from Her, A.   Rufinus.   STV, *tr.* by John Frederick Nims

Kiss from her, A! Her mouth, coming even close to your own, how.   Kiss from Her, A.   Rufinus.   STV, *tr.* by John Frederick Nims

Kiss her that she don't know how.   Carletta Carrington Wilson.   BtF

Kiss I begged; but, smiling, she, A.   Weeping and Kissing.   Sir Edward Sherburne.   NOSC

Kiss I didn't give you, The.   Time.   Dulce Maria Loynaz.   TANSG, *tr.* by Alan West

Kiss in the Dark, A.   Thomas Sayers Ellis.   GT

Kiss me again, and kiss me still, and kiss.   Louise Labé.   EroLit, *tr.* by Frances Webb

Kiss Me Deadly.   Karen Volkman.   LegDan

Kiss me in the moon's sparkling glow.   *Unknown.*   SLW, *tr.* by Marjolijn De Jager, Sayd Bahodin Majrouh and André Velter

Kiss Me, Then Give Birth to Me.   Cemal Süreya.   NaPG, *tr.* by Talat Sait Halman

Kiss my lips. She did.   Gertrude Stein.   APT-1; PFTM-1; PoBW *Fr.* Lifting Belly.

Kiss my mother left here when she died, The. (LL)   Elizabeth Barrett Browning.   CenSon; OxBSo *Fr.* Sonnets from the Portuguese.

Kiss of Betrothal, The.   Charles Tennyson Turner.   CenSon

Kiss of Caiaphas, The. (LL)   Oscar Wilde.   NPeEn; OxBEV *Fr.* Ballad of Reading Gaol, The.

Kiss of Judas.   Jennifer Grotz.   LegDan

Kiss of the Sun.   Mary Ruefle.   AmAlph; FaoP

Kiss that's on thy lip impressed, The.   Duet.   Lady Caroline Lamb.   RWP

Kiss Tomorrow Goodbye.   Marjorie Welish.   FTOS

Kiss[e] me, sweet: the wary [*or* warie] lover.   Ben Jonson.   EroLit; NOSC *Fr.* Volpone.

Kisses.   Giancarlo Majorino.   ItPo, *tr.* by Gayle Ridinger

Kisses.   William Strode.   NOSC

Kisses and embraces disgusted her.   Gustave Thibon, How Simone Weil Appeared to Me/3.   Stephanie Strickland.   ExTi

Kisses in the Train.   D. H. Lawrence.   MoBrPo

Kisses Loathsome.   Robert Herrick.   CavPo

Kisses not for our mouths,—light the dark summer, The. (LL)   Dark Summer. Louise Bogan.   APT-2; ItP

Kisses, The.   Johannes Secundus.   EroLit *Fr.* Basia.

Kisses upon the doors! The houses fall.   Poeta Fui.   Julia Budenz.   FFC

Kissie Lee.   Margaret Abigail Walker.   NALW; RaF

Kissing.   Fleur Adcock.   StAl

Kissing.   Edward Herbert, 1st Baron Herbert of Cherbury.   NOSC

Kissing Helena.   Plato.   OBVE, *tr.* by Percy Bysshe Shelley

Kissing Ramén.   Michael Lassell.   WiU

Kissing, still unable to speak. (LL)   John Montague.   NoP-4; NoP-5; PBCIP; PNI *Fr.* All Legendary Obstacles.

Kissing the ground. (LL)   We Never Know.   Yusef Komunyakaa.   AmAlph; OxBoAm; WhBo

Kitchen.   Anne Carson.   AFaM

Kitchen.   Anne Carson.   NLPA *Fr.* Glass Essay, The.

Kitchen.   Robert Creeley.   OxBoAm

Kitchen.   Allison Joseph.   SweBea

Kitchen Beast.   Amanda Dalton.   NeBl

Kitchen: "Everywhere I go it's the same old thing."   Twain Dooley.   IJHIL

Kitchen is quiet as a bone when I come in.   Kitchen.   Anne Carson.   AFaM

Kitchen is quiet as a bone when I come in.   Anne Carson.   NLPA *Fr.* Glass Essay, The.

Kitchen party voices hesitated, The.   Mother's Winter Guests.   Tammy Armstrong.   Coast

Kitchen Terrarium.   Linda McCarriston.   PfS

Kitchenette building.   Gwendolyn Brooks.   GT; NAAL-5; NoP-4; NoP-5; OxAAAP; PoPoPo *Fr.* Street in Bronzeville, A.

Kitchens.   Aurora Levins Morales.   PueRic

Kitchens: 1959.   Juliana Baggott.   SweBea

Kitchens of the Metropole and Imperial hotels yielded up to the Irish Republic, The.   Imperial Measure.   Vona Groarke.   BeAl; MoWP; NIrP

Kitchen's old-fashioned planter's clock portrays, The. Nightfishing. Gjertrud Schnackenberg. WeW-3

Kite. Brian McCabe. EdScPo

Kite, The. Adelaide O'Keeffe. NOxBChV

Kite, The. Ōkuma Kotomichi. EMJL, tr. by Haruo Shirane

Kite, The. Mark Strand. ColAP

Kite, The. Olga Sulchinskaya. CRWP, tr. by Richard McKane

Kite is a victim you are sure of, A. Kite Is a Victim, A. Leonard Cohen. BrAP

Kite!/ Summon not me to enter: there's no doubt. For a Lady's Summons of Non-Entry. William Drummond of Hawthornden. NOSC

Kite, The. Aleksandr Aleksandrovich Blok. FaBoWar, tr. by Frances Cornford and Esther Polinowsky Salaman

Kite-Flying. Christopher Gilbert. GT

Kite-Flying. Sarah Kirsch. tr. by Wayne Kvam
   Call. PFTM-2, tr. by Wayne Kvam
   Mornings. PFTM-2, tr. by Wayne Kvam
   Renting a Room. PFTM-2, tr. by Wayne Kvam

Kites: Ars Poetica. Ben Belitt. APT-2

Kites at the Washington Monument. Greg Williamson. NAPBL

Kites shriek / Together—. Issa. ZenPo, tr. by Takashi Ikemoto and Lucien Stryk

Kith. Marion Lomax. NeBl

Kitten and [the] Falling Leaves, The. William Wordsworth.
   Kitten at Play, The. ChAP

Kitten at Play, The. William Wordsworth. ChAP Fr. Kitten and [the] Falling Leaves, The.

Kitten, writes the mousy boy in his neat. In-flight Note. Judith Rodriguez. BMAP

Kitty of Coleraine. Edward Lysaght. IrLP

Kitty's Atalantis for the year 1766. Unknown.
   "What's that in which good housewives take delight." EroLit

Kitzbuhl Church. Karen Alkalay-Gut. DTA

Ki-u-nad'-dis-si's Song. Unknown. APN-2 Fr. Sacred Songs of the Konkau.

Kiwi at four a.m. among the sheets green slice of cool going down easy, A. Daphne Marlatt. NLPA Fr. Touch to My Tongue.

Kiwi Bird in the Kiwi Tree, The. Charles Bernstein. FTOS; NAMCP V.2

K-K-K-Katy. Geoffrey O'Hara. ReLy

Kleptomaniac. Polly Clark. NeBl

Kleptomaniac, The. Roger McGough. NOxBChV

Klink—Hratzvenga (Deathwail). Else Von Freytag-Loringhoven. APT-1

Kluane, the Yukon. Nathaniel Tarn. WANABP

Klupzy Girl, The. Charles Bernstein. PmAP

Klytemnestra. Emily Jane Pfeiffer. ViWPN

Knack for Slipping Away, A. José Luis Rivas. RMCMP, tr. by Susan Briante

Knedneuch land. In the Pantry. Hugh MacDiarmid. NAMCP V.1; NoAM

Knee, The. Ciaran Carson. PNI

Kneel, and let us pray for the departed. Lost Property. Elizabeth Garrett. MFPA; MoWP

Kneeling. Gertrude Stein. PFTM-1

Kneeling. Ronald Stuart Thomas. WaAnP

Kneeling Down to Look [or Peer] into a Culvert. Robert Bly. NAMCP V.2; NoAM

Kneeling Here, I Feel Good. Marge Piercy. IPoFL

Kneeling, I'm staring at the soil. Nazim Hikmet. NaPG, tr. by Talat Sait Halman

Kneeling / in this store window. Smash Your Fist. Anabel Torres. TANSG, tr. by Celeste Kostopulos-Cooperman

Knees garnished with impetigo. (LL) Geoffrey Hill. NAEL-6v2; NAEL-7v2; NAMCP.V.2; NoAM; NoP-4; NoP-5; NPeEn; WoPoe Fr. Mercian Hymns.

Knees of a Natural Man [(for Jay Wright)]. Henry Dumas. GT; OxAAAP

Knees on off fists and hello lute's. armillaria mellea. Tony Baker. Oth

Knees trembled but she touched the veins, The. Fanny Howe. FaoP Fr. Passion, The.

Knew her themselves, through all her veils [or vailes]. (LL) Ingrateful[l] Beauty Threatened. Thomas Carew. CavPo; OBEV; PBRV

Knew nothing of the coming rain. (LL) Rain: "Teacher asked Paul, A." Naomi Shihab Nye. CFP; P180

Knew you upon the one true time. I by you put on. Lloyd Addison. EGAG

Knickerbocker Knockabout. Clyde Watson. NOxBChV

Knickerbocker Knockabout. Knickerbocker Knockabout. Clyde Watson. NOxBChV

Knife. Gloria Vando. LiTh; TouFir

Knife. Franz Wright. MotU

Knife All Blade, A. João Cabral de Melo Neto. VCWP, tr. by Galway Kinnell

Knife blade of cold air keeps prying, A. Upstate. Derek Walcott. GT; OPRER

Knife Gets Bigger, A. Chông Hwajin. EcSo, tr. by Julie C. Park

Knife like a precious bond, The. Journey. Rodney Hall. NOBAu

Knife on the fruit dish, The. Obsession. Pak Sŏwŏn. EcSo, tr. by Julie C. Park

Knife reduces a polished oval, The. Anne Cluysenaar. Prnts Fr. Poems of Memory.

Knife That Is All Blade, The. João Cabral de Melo Neto. tr. by Elizabeth Gordon
   "Like a bullet." TCLAP, tr. by Elizabeth Gordon

Knife, The. Keith Douglas. NoAM

Knife was much sharper than I thought, The. Accuser, The. Shirley Kaufman. GifTon

Knife-thrower's wife stands, The. Knife-Thrower's Wife, The. Mekeel McBride. OPRER

Knife-Thrower's Wife, The. Mekeel McBride. OPRER

Knight and Shepherd's Daughter, The. Unknown. NoP-4; NoP-5

Knight, Death, and the Devil, The. Randall Jarrell. GS; WeW-3

Knight Errant, The. Louise Imogen Guiney. RACG
   Donatello's Saint George.
   "Oh, give my youth, my faith, my sword." TCAPo

Knight Fallen on Evil Days, The. Elinor Wylie. MoAmPo

Knight of My Maiden Love. Priscilla Jane Thompson. CBWP-2

Knight of "silver tongue" and stately grace, A. Wendell Phillips. Henrietta Cordelia Ray. CBWP-3

Knight of the Grail, The. Unknown. OBEV

Knight [or Knyght] ther[e] was, and that a worthy man, A. Geoffrey Chaucer. UV Fr. Canterbury Tales, The.

Knight went down to the river's rim, A. Ballad. Gerda Mayer. OBSP

Knight who came was Launcelot at good need, The. (LL) Defense of Guenevere, The. William Morris. NAEL-6v2; NAEL-7v2

Knightliest of the knightly race, The. Virginians of the Valley, The. Francis Orrery Ticknor. PCW

Knights Errant. Yu Hsin. CCL1, tr. by John Minford

Knights of the Joyous Venture, The. Rudyard Kipling. Fr. Puck of Pook's Hill.

Knights of the White Camellia and Deacons of Defense. Yusef Komunyakaa. LPSFW

Knights! / Posse on the move, bit to bridle, bridle to bit. Knights Errant. Yu Hsin. CCL1, tr. by John Minford

Knight's Prayer, The. Unknown. InvLi

Knight's Tomb, The. Samuel Taylor Coleridge. NPeEn

Knitting. Mary E. Tucker. CBWP-1

Knitting is a bore but Elizabeth. Robert Watches Elizabeth Knitting. Jo Shapcott. MoWP

Knob Pines. David Swanger. GeoHom

Knock at a star with my exalted head. (LL) Bad Season Makes the Poet Sad, The. Robert Herrick. BASC; CavPo; NAEL-6v1; NAEL-7v1

Knock Knock. Michael Dennis Browne. SUP

Knock on the forehead. Strawberry Blond. Bill Berkson. NYP2

Knock the zoo out of your eye, the sand dollar with dried. American Avalon. Connie Deanovich. AmPoNex

Knocker, A. Zbigniew Herbert. PoSu, tr. by Czeslaw Milosz

Knocking Around. John Ashbery. NoAM

Knocking Donkey Fleas off a Poet from the Southside of Chi. Haki R. Madhubuti. SeSe

Knocking on the door. Mimi Khalvati. Prnts Fr. Entries on Light.

Knockout, The. Sydney March. BtF

Knot. Susan Wicks. EmeKit

Knot, The. Henry Vaughan. BASC; RSR

Knot Hole Gang, The. Brendan Galvin. MoASP

Knot of military officers, A. William Wordsworth. NPBRoP Fr. Prelude, The; Growth of a Poet's Mind [1805 version; Selections from Anthologies].

Know Celia, (since thou art so proud.). Ingrateful[l] Beauty Threatened. Thomas Carew. CavPo; OBEV; PBRV

Know I must and think I will. Ballad of the Life and Times of Joe Louis, A. Calvin C. Hernton. FTtHH

Know, I said, feeling better. (LL) Bounden Duty. James Tate. BAP-04; OxBoAm

Know masculinity, / Maintain femininity. Lao Tzu. ColAnChi Fr. Tao Te Ching.

Know me? I am the ghost of Ganesvoort Pier. Among the Missing. Richard Howard. OxBoAm

Know, that I would accounted be. To Ireland in the Coming Times. William Butler Yeats. IrV; NAMCP V.1; NoAM

Know that more than white is missing. (LL) Lessons from a Mirror. Thylias Moss. ESEAA; LTA; OxAAAP

Know, The. Christine Qunta. NAfrP

Know, The. Know, The. Christine Qunta. NAfrP

Know then, the only joy of an anchor—to be strong. Anchor, The. John Blight. BMAP

Know then thyself, presume not God to scan. Alexander Pope. NAEL-6v1; NAEL-7v1; SacPr; TFi *Fr.* Essay on Man, An.

Know then: / Toward summer when the sun is in Hyades. Ezra Pound. OBVE

Know this light, they prey, "touch me with this light." (LL) Moon on Friday Night, The. Susan Goyette. Coast; OpeFie

Know this wind as. Prophetissa. Diane Di Prima. PFTM-2

Know Thy Enemy. Christopher Logue. RSaN

Know 'tis but a loom of land. Land, Ho! Thomas Edward Brown. SacPr

Know what I'm like? Some captain moors his ship. Ausiàs March. STV

Know ye the man whom God has blessed. Lines to the Hon. George L. Knox. Eloise Bibb. CBWP-4

Know you fair, on what you look? Richard Crashaw. CABP

Know you faire, on what you looke. Richard Crashaw. FSCP

Know you that land where forest shadows fold. Mignon. Johann Wolfgang von Goethe. WoPoe, *tr. by* Anthony Hecht

Knowes what was first, and what shall be the end. (LL) Fulke, 1st Baron Brooke Greville. NOSC; NoSic *Fr.* Caelica.

Knowest thou the time when the wild goates of the rocke bring forth? Bible, *O.T.* OBVE *Fr.* Job.

Knowing barely enough to know it was not theirs. (LL) Brief History of Light, A. Caitríona O'Reilly. MoWP; NIrP

Knowing her schedule you're half. Stealing from Your Mother. Dan Chiasson. LegDan

Knowing hot is always ended. Sending Men Back to the Sea. Mary McGinnis. ICANM

Knowing I would never be. Stilt-walker. Susan Wicks. Prnts

Knowing, in a sense, there is no such thing / as the wrong man. (LL) On Hearing the Airlines Will Use a Psychological Profile to Catch Potential Skyjackers. Stephen Dunn. OtW; SUP

Knowing Love in Herself. Hadewijch. WPoS, *tr. by* Oliver Davies

Knowing Nothing. Jane Hirshfield. BeAl

Knowing Nothing Shuts the Iron Gates. Kabir. RaBo, *tr. by* Robert Bly

Knowing nothing shuts the iron gates; the new love opens them. Knowing Nothing Shuts the Iron Gates. Kabir. RaBo, *tr. by* Robert Bly

Knowing of the world it. Nathaniel Mackey. WoBe *Fr.* Song of the Andoumboulou.

Knowing Our Place. Carole Satyamurti. StAl

Knowing that someday it would have to halt in a yellow wildflower, the flower's pollen. Tamburā. Anuradha Mahapatra. FiBr, *tr. by* Paramita Banerjee and Carolyne Wright

Knowing, The. Sharon Olds. PasH

Knowing the dead, and how some are disposed. Two Formal Elegies. Geoffrey Hill. NAMCP V.2

Knowing the volume of our trade in kisses. (LL) Catullus. NAWM-7v1; WoPoe *Fr.* Carmina [Charles Martin Translation].

Knowing those cared for whom they love. (LL) Due of the Dead, The. William Makepeace Thackeray. FaBoWar; OBWP

Knowingness. John Hughes. PNI

Knowledge. Louise Bogan. APT-2; NAMCP V.1; PoA 2002

Knowledge. Tim Armstrong and Jesse Michaels. ASA

Knowledge, Acquaintance, Resort, Favour, with Grace. John Skelton. CABP

Knowledge after Death. Henry Charles Beeching. SacPr

Knowledge falls down, and slogans fall down. Half a Lemon, Half a Cigarette, and Half a Desire to Have It Off. Haytham El-Shawwaf. AnVo, *tr. by* Mohamed Enani

Knowledge is an old error remembering its youth. Aphorisms. Francis Picabia. SurPaPo, *tr. by* Marcel Jean

Knowledge ("Knowledge was being processed. It was in the argument machine.") Carla Harryman. BAP-04 *Fr.* Baby.

Knowledge not of sorrow, you were, The. George Oppen. APT-2; PFTM-1

Knowledge of God. John Frederick Nims. InvLi

Knowledge was being processed. It was in the argument machine. Carla Harryman. BAP-04 *Fr.* Baby.

Knowledge ("White fuzz in the air froze on a screen. Baby danced the cancan.") Carla Harryman. BAP-04 *Fr.* Baby.

Knowledgeable Child, The. Leonard Alfred George Strong. OBMV

Known to the boys in his Latin class as "Sir." Mysteries of Caesar, The. Anthony Hecht. NoP-4

Knows as I make for her white side, shivering. (LL) Hooters. Meic Stephens. AngWePo; TCAWP

Knows for certain who salvaged that load. (LL) Ship of Death, A. Seamus Heaney. NAEL-6v2; NoP-4

Knows the new maid steals, and forgives her. (LL) Difference Between Pepsi and Coke, The. David Lehman. PmAP; ReTh

Know'st thou the land which lovers ought to choose? Italy. Edward Coote Pinkney. APN-1

Knoxville, San Diego, Winnipeg, Buffalo, Granby, Toronto: a list. David McFadden. NLPA

Knoxville, Tennessee. Nikki Giovanni. OxAAAP

Köcsey. Ferenc Kölcsey. IQMS, *tr. by* Watson Kirkconnell

Koel (Rainbird) and Effigy. *Unknown.* NOBAu, *tr. by* Mungayana Nundhirribala

Koheleth. Louis Untermeyer. ChIV-1

Ko-Ishin-Mit Goes Fishing. George Clutesi. HATNAP

Ko-jin goes west from Ko-kaku-ro [*or* Ko-keku-to]. Separation on the River Kiang. Li Po. CCL1; NDACCP, *tr. by* Ezra Pound

Kojo: I Am A Black. Gwendolyn Brooks. ESEAA *Fr.* Children Going Home.

Kokin Shu. *Various authors. tr. by* Helen Craig McCullough
  "Beloved person must I think, The." TAL, *tr. by* Arthur Waley
  "If this were a world." WoPoe, *tr. by* Helen Craig McCullough
  "My love / Is like the grasses." TAL, *tr. by* Arthur Waley
  "Though you made me think." WoPoe, *tr. by* Helen Craig McCullough

Koko Taylor sang. Blues at 1. Dorothy Perry Thompson. SpirFl

Kolob Canyon. William Stafford. PfSP

Konchu Kazu Aru Yube Ako Iyo-Iyo Seicho Shitari. Violet Kazue De Cristoforo. CalPo

Kong Breaks a Leg at the William Morris Agency. William Trowbridge. ReTh

Kookaburra. Frieda Hughes. NeBl

"Kookoorookoo! kookoorookoo!" / Crows the cock before the morn. Christina Georgina Rossetti. FaBoVe

Kopis'taya. Paula Gunn Allen. HATNAP

Koprivshtitsa. Ivan Tsanev. CSCBP, *tr. by* Georgi Belev and Lisa Sapinkopf

Kora in Hell. William Carlos Williams.
  "For what it's worth: Jacob Louslinger, white haired, stinking, dirty bearded." MotU
  "It is still warm enough to slip from the weeds into the lake's edge." MotU
  "Pathology literally speaking is a flower garden." TCAPo
  "Some fools once were listening to a poet reading his poem." TCAPo
  "There is neither beginning nor end to the imagination." CLPP
  "There's force to this cold sun, makes beard stubble stand shinily." TCAPo
  "Why go further? One might conceivably rectify the rhythm." TCAPo

Kore. Robert Creeley. NAAL-5; OxBoAm; RaBo

Kore. Daphne Marlatt. NLPA *Fr.* Touch to My Tongue.

Kore in Hades. Kathleen Jessie Raine. NALW

Korean Figures. *Unknown.* EaWin, *tr. by* W. S. Merwin

Korean grass. EMJL *Fr.* Mad Verse.

Korean Mums. James Schuyler. OxBoAm; PmAP; VCAP

Korean ship, The. Buson. EMJL, *tr. by* Haruo Shirane

Korean Woman Seated by a Wall, A. William Meredith. AmWaPo

Korean Women. Yi Kyŏngnim. EcSo, *tr. by* Peter H. Lee

Korea's six dragons flew in the sky. *Various authors.* CATKP *Fr.* Songs of Flying Dragons.

Korf receives one day from the coppers. Summons. Christian Morgenstern. WoPoe, *tr. by* David R. Slavitt

Korf, whom worry easily attacks. Anxiety for the Future. Christian Morgenstern. WoPoe, *tr. by* W. D. Snodgrass

Kőrös was our river, we would go, The. Black Kőrös. József Erdélyi. IQMS, *tr. by* Alan Dixon

Koskiusko. Samuel Taylor Coleridge. OxBSo *Fr.* Effusions.

Kosmos. Julia Ward Howe. ColAP

Kosmos [2003]. Yusef Komunyakaa. ViWalt

Kouretes hid the goddess's, The. Korinna [*or* Corinna]. SaLy, *tr. by* Diane Rayor

Kraken, The. Alfred Tennyson. CtM; NAEL-6v2; NAEL-7v2; NoP-4; NoP-5

Kral Majales. Allen Ginsberg. BB; PFTM-2

Kralupy is not a pretty town. Bombing of the Town of Kralupy, The. Jaroslav Seifert. *tr. by* Ewald Osers

Krishna played on the charmingly juicy flute. Song, The. Balakrishna Sama. PoetW

Krismas Dinnah [*with music*]. Maggie Pogue Johnson. CBWP-4

Kruger sets his feet. Brass Knuckles. Stuart Dybek. PBCAP

Ku Feng (After the Style of Ancient Poems). Li Po. ChinPo, *tr. by* Ye Weilian [*or* Yeh Wei-lien *or* Wai-lim Yip]

Kuan Chü, The. *Unknown.* CCL1 *Fr.* Guan-ju.

Kuan Kuan. *Unknown.* CCL1 *Fr.* Guan-ju.

"Kuan Kuan" the chü's. *Unknown.* CCL1 *Fr.* Guan-ju.

Kuan ts'ü. *Unknown.* CCL1 *Fr.* Guan-ju.

Kuan Tzu. Kuan Chung.
  Duties of the Student. ColAnChi, *tr. by* W. Allyn Rickett
  Inner Workings. ColAnChi, *tr. by* W. Allyn Rickett

Kuan-kuan call the ospreys. *Unknown.* ColAnChi *Fr.* Classic of Odes.

Kuan-kuan, the ospreys. *Unknown.* ChinPo, *tr. by* Ye Weilian [*or* Yeh Wei-lien *or* Wai-lim Yip]

Kuan-kuan, the Ospreys. *Unknown.* CCL1 *Fr.* Guan-ju.

Kuan-Yin Shan: Mother-of-Mercy Mountain. Mike O'Connor. WANABP

Kubla Khan: or, A Vision in a Dream. Samuel Taylor Coleridge. BLPJKO; BrAP; BRP; CABP; CtM; HeIP-4; NAEL-6v2; NAEL-7v2; NAWM-7v2; NIL-7; NIP-4; NOBRP; NoP-4; NoP-5; NPBRoP; NPeEn; OBEV; OBGa; OxAEP-2; OxBEV; PoPoPo; SoSe-8; TFi; TRP; WaAnP; WeW-3; WoPoe

Kudzu has crossed. Ray McNiece. AmZen

Kukutis broke into song: How fortunate I am. Kukutis's Song. Marcelijus Martinaitis. TWW, *tr. by* Laima Sruoginis

Kukutis Describes His Hut. Marcelijus Martinaitis. TWW, *tr. by* Laima Sruoginis

Kukutis in the Reich's Guard House. Marcelijus Martinaitis. TWW, *tr. by* Laima Sruoginis

Kukutis, Kukutis, you good soul. Kukutis's Lament under the Heavens. Marcelijus Martinaitis. TWW, *tr. by* Laima Sruoginis

Kukutis's Consciousness Becomes Alienated. Marcelijus Martinaitis. TWW, *tr. by* Laima Sruoginis

Kukutis's Fruitless Bread. Marcelijus Martinaitis. TWW, *tr. by* Laima Sruoginis

Kukutis's Lament under the Heavens. Marcelijus Martinaitis. TWW, *tr. by* Laima Sruoginis

Kukutis's Sermon to the Pigs. Marcelijus Martinaitis. TWW, *tr. by* Laima Sruoginis

Kukutis's Sinful Spirit. Marcelijus Martinaitis. TWW, *tr. by* Laima Sruoginis

Kukutis's Song. Marcelijus Martinaitis. TWW, *tr. by* Laima Sruoginis

Kukutis's Swallow's Hymn. Marcelijus Martinaitis. TWW, *tr. by* Laima Sruoginis

Kukutis's Trip on the Samogitian Highway. Marcelijus Martinaitis. TWW, *tr. by* Laima Sruoginis

Kulakundalini, Goddess Full of Brahman, Tara. Rāmprasād Sen. SinGod, *tr. by* Rachel Fell McDermott

Kultur spurns Ubu—thus Ubu pulls stunts. Ubu shuns. Christian Bök. OpeFie *Fr.* Chapter U.

Kulu. Seitlhamo Motsapi. TSAP

Kŭm River. Shin Tongyŏp. *tr. by* Anthony, Brother of Taizé

"Back when we were children." CAMKP, *tr. by* Anthony, Brother of Taizé

Scene 8. CAMKP, *tr. by* Anthony, Brother of Taizé

Scene 9. CAMKP, *tr. by* Anthony, Brother of Taizé

"We have seen heaven." CAMKP, *tr. by* Anthony, Brother of Taizé

Kumara / Nich, nich, pasalam, bada. Bald Mountain Zaum-Poems. *Unknown.* PFTM-1

Kumquat for John Keats, A. Tony Harrison. BeAl; NoP-4; NoP-5; WaAnP

Kumuhea the night-caterpillar loves the woman. Woman Who Married a Caterpillar, The. *Unknown.* WoPoe, *tr. by* Armand Schwerner

K'un (Earth). *Unknown.* ColAnChi *Fr.* I Ching [*or* The Book of Changes *or* The Classic of Changes].

Kundiman. Bataan Faigao. ReBoTo

Kundry was Wagner's creation. And they brought Tefnut back, from her wilderness. Structure of Rime XVIII. Robert Duncan. FTOS

Kung walked / by the dynastic temple. Ezra Pound. APT-1; NAAPv.2; OxBoAm; WaAnP *Fr.* Cantos.

Kun-shih, my pride, my son. Boasting of My Son. Li Shang-yin. ColAnChi, *tr. by* James J. Y. Liu

Kural, The. Tiruvalluvar. *tr. by* Emmons E. White

Gift of Children, The. WoPoe, *tr. by* Emmons E. White

Kindness and Generosity. WoPoe, *tr. by* Emmons E. White

Learning. WoPoe, *tr. by* Emmons E. White

Ku-ring-gai Rock Carvings. David Campbell.

Lovers, The. BMAP

Kurt, last night Dwight Evans put it all. Fifth Inning, The. Donald Hall. MoASP

Kurt, terror is merely the thesis. Eighth Inning, The. Donald Hall. MoASP

Kŭ' siut Song. *Unknown.* APN-2, *tr. by* Franz Boas

Ku'u Pua I Paoakalani. Queen Lili'u-o-ka-lani. SWaP

(My Flower at Paoa-ka-lani.) NAAPv.1

Kwaakwaa. Gynae One. Christine Ama Ata Aidoo. HAWP

"*Kwakwha.*" / "*Askwali.*" Parallax. Arthur Sze. GifTon

Kwan Ts'eu. *Unknown.* CCL1 *Fr.* Guan-ju.

Kwang-kwang cry the mallards. *Unknown.* CCL1 *Fr.* Guan-ju.

Kwan-kwan cries the *ts'ü-kiu* bird. *Unknown.* CCL1 *Fr.* Guan-ju.

Kwan-kwan go the ospreys. *Unknown.* CCL1 *Fr.* Guan-ju.

KYE HO! Wonderful! Kambala. WPoS

KYE HO! Wonderful! Dakini Lion-Face. WPoS

Kylemore Castle. Richard Murphy. ModIr *Fr.* Price of Stone, The.

Kyoto 1—Kinkaku-ji. William Kistler. WhBo

Kyoto 2—Ryoanji. William Kistler. WhBo

Kyoto Garden, A. Dennis Joseph Enright. OBGa

Kyoto Minor Retainer. Dōyaku Sensei, Master Artery. EMJL, *tr. by* Haruo Shirane

Kypris and Nereids, let that brother. Sappho. SaLy, *tr. by* Diane Rayor

Kypris, / May she find you very bitter. Sappho. SaLy, *tr. by* Diane Rayor

Kyrie. Ellen Bryant Voigt.

"All ears, nose, tongue and gut." ExTi

Kyrielle. May Probyn. VWP

Kyrielle: Party Politics. Frederick Thomas Bennett Macartney. NOBAu

KZ. Carolyne Wright. RoV

L

L(a. E. E. Cummings. NIL-7; NIP-4; TRP

(Poem.) OxBoAm

L. B. J. Tapes, The. Ben Friedlander. Eno

L.E.L.'s Last Question. Elizabeth Barrett Browning. VWP

L L L, The. Russell Atkins. EGAG

L.R.D.G. J. G. Meddemmen. FaBoWar

L Y L Y T. David Meltzer. PFTM-2 *Fr.* Hero/Lil.

La balala ika. Balalaïka. Pierre Albert-Birot. CuPo

La Bella Bona-Roba. Richard Lovelace. NOSC; OxBEV

La Belle Juive. Henry Timrod. APN-2; TCAPo

La Berline Arrêtée Dans la Nuit. O. V. de L. Milosz. GifTon, *tr. by* Kenneth Rexroth

La Bodega Sold Dreams. Miguel Piñero. PueRic

La Chapelle. 92nd Division. Ted. Rita Dove. AmAlph

La Corona. John Donne. ChIV-2 *Fr.* Holy Sonnets.

La Crosse at Ninety Miles an Hour. Richard Eberhart. APT-2

La Dame Jaune. Oscar Wilde. IrLP

La Dulce Culpa. Cherríe Moraga. FiBr

La Fabrique de Tabac (Tobacco Harvest). Beverly Matherne. TWW

La Fayette. Samuel Taylor Coleridge. CenSon *Fr.* Effusions.

La Figlia Che Piange. T. S. Eliot. APT-1; HarvBoo; HeIP-4; OxBEV; OxBoAm; PoA 2002; TCAPo

La Gialletta Gallante, or the Sunburned Exotic Beauty. Edward Herbert, 1st Baron Herbert of Cherbury. NOSC

La Gioconda; Leonardo Da Vinci, The Louvre. Michael Field. CABP; ViWPN

La Gorgue. Ivor Gurney. OxBEV

La Guardia, the Story. Jane Mead. BodElec

La, La, La! [*with music*]. Thomas M. Disch. NBLV

La, la, la. To live with, to be like, to be. Hymn to Yellow. Genevieve Taggard. APT-2

La Llorona. Juan Delgado. GeoHom

La Migra. Pat Mora. NIL-7; UnSA

La muerte es una tormenta. La tormenta. Martín Espada. PueRic

La narrativa says you must paint a flower. Untitled (April '91). Michael Palmer. BodElec

La Naval De Manila: Selim Sot as a Modern Political Observer. Eric Gamalinda. ReBoTo

La Pathétique. Lily Brett. HP

La Plata, Missouri: Clear November Night [*with music*]. Jim Barnes. HATNAP

La Pologne? La Pologne? It's awfully cold there, isn't it? she asked. Words. Wisława Szymborska. MotU, *tr. by* Krystyna Piorkowski

La Pologne? La Pologne? It's very cold over there, isn't it? the lady. Words. Wisława Szymborska. PoSu, *tr. by* Krystof Zarzecki

La Préface. Charles Olson. APT-2; PFTM-2

la Promenade, A. Paul Verlaine. OBVE, *tr. by* Arthur Symons

La Puente. Elsa Rediva E'der. ReBoTo

La Querida. Bino A. Realuyo. ReBoTo

La Route Jackman. Alfred Goldsworthy Bailey. Coast

La Sombra of Who I Am. Michaela Raen. PoArWo

L.A. spring, our boulevard of flowering jaca. Blue Kashmir, '74. Carol Muske-Dukes. AmAlph; PuP-23

La tormenta. Martín Espada. PueRic

La Tormenta. Geraldine Monk. Oth

10. La Traviata. David McFadden. NLPA

La Vie C'est la Vie. Jessie Redmond Fauset. NAAPv.2

Labane. Annette M'Baye d'Erneville. HAWP, *tr. by* Brian Baer

Labasheedy (The Silken Bed) [*with music*]. Nuala Ni Dhomhnaill. CABP, *tr. by* the author

Label, the labor, the color, the shade, The. The shirt. (LL) Shirt. Robert Pinsky. ColAP; FaoP; HarvBoo; NAAL-5; OxBoAm; StAl

Labeled bins on the California hillside, The. Recycling Center. Brenda Hillman. CalPo

Labeur du jour. Paul De Roux. YaTCFP

Labor and Rest. Dinah Maria Mulock. TreFP

Labor Day. David Cope. ViWalt

Labor Day. Louise Glück. NIL-7; NoAM

Labor Day in Dillon, MT. Montana's Biggest Weekend. Whitney Ward. FTtHH

Labor Day Picnic Poem. Todd Colby. HeMarv

Labor raises honest sweat. Dignity of Labor, The. Robert Bersohn. NBLV

Laboratory: long low building wide windows, The. Laboratory, The. Gordon Rodgers. Coast

Laboratory Poem. James Merrill. CAP-8

Laboratory, The. Gordon Rodgers. Coast

Laboratory, The (Ancien Régime). Robert Browning. NAEL-6v2; NAEL-7v2; OBEV

Laborers keep on coming, The. *Hawaiian Oral Tradition.* NAAPv.2

Laborers, The. Jones Very. SacPr

Laborie, Choiseul, Vieuxfort, Dennery. Sainte Lucie. Derek Walcott.

Laborious, stumpy, droopy, askew. Complete Semen Study. Michael Ryan. BodElec

Labour. Kristina Rungano. HAWP

Labour and Delivery. Ron Charach. BloBone

Labour Pantoum. Kirsten Emmott. IFF

Labourer, The [*with music*]. Iolo Goch. OBWVE, *tr. by* Gwyn Williams

Labouring man, that tills the fertile soil, The. Pains and Gains. Edward, 17th Earl of Oxford De Vere. NoSic

Labrador coastline is a spill of islands, The. What's Lost. Michael Crummey. Coast

Laburnum. Paula Meehan. ModIr

Labyrinth. Walter Helmut Fritz. GTCP, *tr. by* Reinhold Grimm

Labyrinth. Jaime Torres Bodet. TCLAP, *tr. by* Sonja Karsen

Labyrinth, The. Jorge Luis Borges. PoetW; WoPoe, *tr. by* John Updike

Labyrinth, The. Edwin Muir. MoBrPo

Labyrinth, A. A pencil shaft of light. Forms of Forts. Susan Stewart. AmAlph

Labyrinth of byways, A. Forever Parted: Graveyard. Gu Cheng. VCWP, *tr. by* Jerome P. Seaton

Lace Makers, The. Stanley Moss. PoA 2002

Lace woven and rewoven with every wave. Siv, With Ocean (Pacific). Ron Loewinsohn. ASA

Lacedemonian Instruction. William Blake. WoPoe

Lachin y Gair. Lord Byron. NePenScot

Lachon has brought home the bacon. Ode 6. Bacchylides. PoCho, *tr. by* David R. Slavitt

Lachrimae Amantis. Félix Lope de Vega Carpio. OxBSo; UpMys; WoPoe *Fr.* Lachrimae; or Seven Tears Figured in Seven Passionate Pavans.

Lachrimae; or Seven Tears Figured in Seven Passionate Pavans. Geoffrey Hill. *tr. by* Geoffrey Hill

Lachrimae Amantis. OxBSo; UpMys; WoPoe, *tr. by* Geoffrey Hill

Lachrimae Verae. NAEL-6v2; NoAM; NoP-5

Masque of Blackness, The. NoAM

Lachrimae Verae. Geoffrey Hill. NAEL-6v2; NoAM; NoP-5 *Fr.* Lachrimae; or Seven Tears Figured in Seven Passionate Pavans.

Lack of Balance but not Fatal, A. Jackson Mac Low. FTOS

Lackawanna. Galway Kinnell. GM

Lackawanna Elegy. Iwan Goll. AF, *tr. by* Galway Kinnell

lackblockblackb. Ian Hamilton Finlay. TRP

Lacking my love, I go from place to place. Edmund Spenser. NoSic *Fr.* Amoretti.

Laconicum (sweating room). Matthea Harvey. IAoNAP *Fr.* Thermae.

Lacquer dust and powdered bone and red cinnabar grains. Arrowhead from the Ancient Battlefield of Ch'ang-p'ing, An. Li Ho. FaBoWar, *tr. by* A. C. Graham

Lacrimae Rerum. Patricia Goedicke. ExTi

Lacrosse. Gary Margolis. MAAN

Lacteal iguana. Dolores Dorantes. SPV, *tr. by* Jen Hofer

Lad, come kiss me. Invitation. Marion Angus. LW

Lad, glancing like a virgin. Anacreon. SaLy, *tr. by* Diane Rayor

Lad, of all-sufficient merit, The. John Gay. *Fr.* Fables: First Series.

Ladder horned against moonlight. Days of 1935. James Merrill. OxBoAm

Ladder of success is an image I abhor. Forever Afternoon. Adam David Miller. FuFl

Ladder stretching up to heaven, A. Hymn to Holy Women, A. Notker Balbulus. NAWM-7v1, *tr. by* Peter Dronke

Ladders. Elizabeth Alexander. FFC

Ladders. Deanna Ortiz. ICANM

Laddie still, The / Was seated on my knee, when at the door. Robert Williams Buchanan. DiBP *Fr.* Willie Baird.

Lade xneza benda. Na Aurea. Natalia Toledo. RMCMP

Laden with snow. Elk in Winter. Robert Pack. WaAnP

Ladie [*or* Lady], that in the prime of earliest youth. Sonnet 9. John Milton. OxBSo

Ladies and gentlemen. Complaint on the Oblivion of the Dead. Jules Laforgue. WoPoe, *tr. by* William Jay Smith

Ladies and gentlemen. I Move the Meeting Be Adjourned. Nicanor Parra. TCLAP, *tr. by* Allen Ginsberg

Ladies and gentlemen, allow me to introduce to you Breyten Breytenbach. Threat of the Sick. Breyten Breytenbach. PoetW, *tr. by* Denis Hirson

Ladies and Gentlemen in Outer Space. Ron Padgett. P180

Ladies and gentlemen, this is High Wood. High Wood. Philip Johnstone. FaBoWar

Ladies bow, and partners set, The. Soliloquy of a Maiden Aunt. Dollie Radford. OxBEV

Ladies Defence, The: Or, The Bride-Woman's Counsellor Answer'd: A Poem in Dialogue Between Sir John Brute, Sir William Loveall, Melissa, and a Parson. Mary Lee, Lady Chudleigh.

"Unhappy they, who by their duty led." PEW

Ladies' Home Journal, The [*sonnet*]. Sandra M. Gilbert. NIP-4

(Sonnet: The Ladies' Home Journal.) NIL-7

Ladies, I crave your indulgence for. Young Laundryman, The. William Carlos Williams. SAmP

Ladies, I do here present you. Hannah Wolley. EMWP *Fr.* Queen-Like Closet, The.

Ladies of Dimbaza, The. Carole Boston Weatherford. FiBr

Ladies Prayer to Cupid, A. Thomas Carew. OBVE

Ladies that guild the glittering noon. General Eclipse, The. John Cleveland. BASC

Ladies, The. Rudyard Kipling. FaBoWar; MoBrPo; NAEL-6v2; NAEL-7v2

Ladies, to this advice give heed. Maxim Revised, A. *Unknown.* NBLV

Ladies Who Lunch, The. Stephen Sondheim. ReLy

Ladies Who Sing with a Band, The. George Marion, Jr. ReLy

Ladies, why don't you lift a stone. Sea, The. Yi Hyangji. EcSo, *tr. by* Catherine J. Kim

Ladies, you see time flieth. *Unknown.* NoSic

Lads and maidens rinsed their wounds. End of Mythology, The. Konstantin Pavlov. CSCBP, *tr. by* Georgi Belev and Lisa Sapinkopf

Lads in their hundreds to Ludlow come in for the fair, The. A. E. Housman. MoBrPo *Fr.* Shropshire Lad, A.

Lads of Wamphray, The. *Unknown.* IBB

Lads, The. Dennis O'Driscoll. PML

Lady, A [*with music*]. Amy Lowell. MoAmPo; TCAPo

Lady A. L, The. Richard Lovelace. CavPo

Lady, accept this garland. Dancing Girl. Walther von der Vogelweide. NAWM-7v1, *tr. by* Peter Dronke

Lady and Gentleman. Richard Weber. IrLP

Lady and the Bear, The. Theodore Roethke. ChAP; NBLV

Lady and the Doctor, The. Helen Leigh. WoRP

Lady asks me, A. Ezra Pound. APT-1; OBVE *Fr.* Cantos.

Lady at the Castle, The [*with music*]. John Hollander. NoAM

Lady behind the desk, The. Looking for W.E.B. Kate Rushin. PfS

Lady Blessington! cried the glad usher aloud. Leigh Hunt. STuOW *Fr.* Blue-Stocking Revels; or, The Feast of the Violets.

Lady came to a Bear by a Stream, A. Lady and the Bear, The. Theodore Roethke. ChAP; NBLV

Lady Charlotte Guest. Goronva Camlan. AngWePo

Lady Cicely Wemyss. James I, King of England. NOSC

Lady Comes to an Inn, A. Elizabeth Jane Coatsworth. MoAmPo

Lady down at the end of the bar keeps looking at, The. Freaky time. Charles Bukowski. OxBoAm

Lady Fortune is both friend and foe, The. Fortune. *Unknown.* HeIP-4

(Lady Fortune is bothe frend and fo, The.) OHMEL

Lady Freedom Among Us. Rita Dove. LoL

Lady Geraldine's Courtship. Elizabeth Barrett Browning.

Snoblesse Oblige. STuOW

Lady herself would come instead?, The. (LL) "H. D." MoWP; NAAPv.2; NALW; NAMCP V.1 *Fr.* Tribute to the Angels.

Lady Hungerford's Meditacions upon the Beades, The. Anne Dormer, Lady Hungerford. EMWP

Lady I Know, A. Countee Cullen. *See* For a Lady I Know.

Lady! I would that verse of mine. Stanzas. Edgar Allan Poe. NCAP

Lady in Kicking Horse Reservoir, The. Richard Hugo. CAP-8; NAMCP V.2; NoAM; NoP-4; NoP-5; VCAP

Lady in Red, The. Mort Dixon. ReLy

Lady in the Pink Mustang, The. Louise Erdrich. HATNAP; OPRER; ReTh

Lady in the unbecoming bonnet, The. All Hallow. Josephine Miles. APT-2

Lady in the White Dress, Whom I Helped into the Omnibus, The. Nathaniel Parker Willis. APN-1

Lady Is a Tramp, The. Lorenz Hart. ReLy

Lady Katherine Killigrew Wrote This Poem about Her Own Death, The. Katherine Killigrew. EMWP

Lady known as Paris, A.   Last Time I Saw Paris, The.   Oscar Hammerstein, II. ReLy

Lady, Lady.   Anne Spencer.   NAAPv.2

Lady, Lady, I saw your face.   Lady, Lady.   Anne Spencer.   NAAPv.2

Lady, lady, should you meet.   Social Note.   Dorothy Parker.   LW

Lady, last Saturday.   I Like the Likes of You.   E. Y. Harburg.   ReLy

Lady Lazarus.   Sylvia Plath.   AmFaPo; CAP-8; ChIV-2; ColAP; EMP; FTtHH; HarvBoo; IJHIL; MoWP; NAAL-5; NALW; NAMCP V.2; NIL-7; NIP-4; NoAM; NoP-4; NoP-5; OxBoAm; OxWW; PoetW; PoPoPo; TRP; VCAP; WaAnP

Lady leans over the table writing.   Damachi.   Philip Whalen.   AHA

Lady Lost.   John Crowe Ransom.   MoAmPo

Lady Love.   Paul Éluard.   OBVE; SurPaPo; WoPoe, tr. by Samuel Beckett

Lady, lovely lady.   Vain and Careless.   Robert Graves.   NOxBChV

Lady Macbeth, Afterward.   Edwin Romond.   IaFF

Lady Mary Villiers lies, The.   Epitaph on the Lady Mary Villiers.   Thomas Carew.   OBEV

(Lady Mary Villers lies, The.)   CavPo

(Lady Mary Villers lyes, The.)   NPeEn; OxBEV; PBRV

Lady Moon.   Richard Monckton, 1st Baron Houghton Milnes.   NOxBChV

Lady Moon, Lady Moon, where are you roving?   Lady Moon.   Richard Monckton, 1st Baron Houghton Milnes.   NOxBChV

Lady of all powers.   From The Hymn to Inanna.   Enheduanna.   WPoS

Lady of Largest Heart.   Enheduanna.   HW, tr. by Betty De Shong Meador

Lady of Miracles.   Nina Cassian.   StAl, tr. by Laura Schiff

Lady of Pazardzik.   Starr Goode.   HW

Lady of Petals, / gone into Underworld.   Isis (Lady of Petals).   Jonathan Cott. HW

Lady of Quality, A.   Thomas Kinsella.   PBCIP

Lady of Shalott, The.   Alfred Tennyson.   BrAP; NAEL-6v2; NAEL-7v2; NOBRP; NoP-4; NoP-5; OBEV; OBNV; OBSP; OxAEP-2; TFi; WaAnP

Lady of the Lake, The.   Sir Walter Scott.

(Ballad: Alice Brand.)   OxAEP-2

(Boat Song.)   OxAEP-2

Chase, The.   NePenScot

Baffled Staghounds, The.   DiBP

Combat, The.

Lufra Avenged.   DiBP

Coronach.

Flowers and Trees.   OxAEP-2

(Harp of the North, Farewell!)   OxAEP-2

Lady of the lake, what does all our weeping lead to? A pair of keys, paucity of summer—just because.   Karen Volkman.   IAoNAP

Lady of the Lambs, The.   Alice Thompson Meynell. See Shepherdess, The.

Lady of the Morning, The.   Unknown.   HW, tr. by Samuel Noah Kramer and Diane Wolkstein

Lady of the Night star-breathed.   Night-Blooming Jasmine, The.   Audre Lorde. ColAP

Lady of the Snow, The.   Vivian Lamarque.   CItWP, tr. by Cinzia Sartini Blum and Lara Trubowitz

Lady of the White Castle, The.   Endre Ady.   IQMS, tr. by Dermot Spence and Paul Tabori

Lady of the winds.   Palm Tree, A.   Rosario Castellanos.   TCLAP, tr. by Myralyn F. Allgood

Lady of Trees, The.   Mary Elizabeth Coleridge.   VWP

Lady on Streetcar.   Sandro Penna.   STV, tr. by John Frederick Nims

Lady on the Cover of Family Circle, The.   Ingrid Wendt.   SweBea

Lady Poets With Foot Notes, The.   Ernest Hemingway.   IllVoic

Lady Poverty, The.   Alice Thompson Meynell.   OBMV

Lady Poverty was fair, The.   Lady Poverty, The.   Alice Thompson Meynell. OBMV

Lady "Rogue" Singleton.   Stevie Smith.   OPOU

Lady Selecting Her Christmas Cards.   Phyllis McGinley.   ChrPo

Lady she sat in her bower alone, The.   Faithless Knight, The.   Caroline Elizabeth Norton.   NPBRoP

Lady Spring / is exquisitely dressed.   Lady Spring.   Gabriela Mistral.   CFP, tr. by Maria Giachetti [or Jacketti]

Lady Stood Alone, A.   Dietmar von Aist [or Eist].   GePo, tr. by J. W. Thomas

"Lady, take this garland."   Walther von der Vogelweide.   GePo

Lady, tell me, will you, pray.   Found—Who Lost?   Mary E. Tucker.   CBWP-1

Lady, the shepherds have all gone.   Ya Se Van Los Pastores.   Dudley Fitts. APT-2

Lady, this alabaster.   Soap.   M. R. Peacocke.   NLP

Lady, this is my sonnet to your eyes. (LL)   George Meredith.   CABP; NoP-4; NoP-5 Fr. Modern Love.

Lady, those cherries plenty.   Unknown.   NoSic

Lady, thy face is very beautiful.   Letitia Elizabeth Landon.   NOBRP

Lady T-rc----l's Ring.   Unknown.   NOBRP

Lady was her name and she was sniffing up the horseflies on the hill.   Sterling Park.   Del Ray Cross.   FreRad

Lady, we would behold thee moving bright.   To Christina Rossetti.   Michael Field.   NAEL-7v2; VWP

Lady weare those bayes, you may.   Eleanora Wyatt Finch.   EMWP

Lady weeps at a dark window, A.   Moonless Night.   Louise Glück.   AWTN

Lady / when ya purple heels hit concrete.   You So Woman.   Ruth Forman. SpirFl

Lady, when you were alive.   Mortician's Twelve-year-old Son, The.   Ai. CAP-8

Lady whines, then dines; is slapped and killed, The.   Mosquito, A.   Brad Leithauser.   StAl

Lady Who Ascends into the Heavens, The.   Unknown.   HW, tr. by Samuel Noah Kramer and Diane Wolkstein

Lady, who goes there?   Continued Song of Longing.   Chŏng Ch'ŏl.   CATKP, tr. by Peter H. Lee

Lady Who Offers Her Looking-Glass to Venus, The [with music].   Matthew Prior.   NPeEn; OBEV; OxBEV

Lady, whom my belovéd loves so well!   Petition, A.   Frances Anne Kemble. LW

Lady with thine eyes of beauty.   Valentine, The.   Mary Weston Fordham. CBWP-2

Lady, you think too much of speeds.   Statistics.   Stephen Spender.   MoBrPo

LADY, you think you spite me.   Unknown.   NoSic

Ladybird.   Unknown.   FaBoVe

Ladybird has left, A.   Summer in Killowen.   Cathal McCabe.   NIrP

Ladybird, Ladybird fly away home.   Mother Goose.   FaBoVe

Ladybirds. (LL)   August 6, 1945.   Alison Fell.   PoAgWa; RSaN

Lady's Boogie.   Langston Hughes.   APT-2

Lady's Days.   Larry Neal.   SeSe

Lady's Dressing Room, The.   Jonathan Swift.   NAEL-7v1; NoP-4; NoP-5; WaAnP

Lady's Farewell, The.   Nuño Fernández Torneol.   WoPoe, tr. by Yvor Winters

Lady's hound, restore the hound, Sir Knight, The.   Edward Robert Bulwer-Lytton.   DiBP Fr. Arthur.

Lady's in Love with You, The.   Frank Loesser.   ReLy

Lady's love is gained, A.   Price of Disrespect, The.   Lizelia Augusta Jenkins Moorer.   CBWP-3

Lady's Way.   Reuben Jackson.   GT

Lady's "Yes," The.   Elizabeth Barrett Browning.   ViWPN

Lady's-Maid's Song, The.   John Hollander.   OxBoAm

Laertes.   Homer.   ModIr Fr. Odyssey.

Laertes has groupies, proof he has taste.   Hamlet Off-stage: Laertes Cool. David Chapman Berry.   P180

Lago Maggiore.   Thomas Cole.   APN-1

Lagoon.   Joseph Brodsky.   TCRusP, tr. by Daniel Weissbort

Lagoonal Calendar.   Aimé Césaire.   VCWP

Lagoons, Hanlan's Point.   Raymond Souster.   BrAP

Lagos.   Rashidah Ismaili.   HAWP

Lagos you are dirty.   Lagos.   Rashidah Ismaili.   HAWP

Laguna Blues.   Charles Wright.   NAMCP V.2; PoPoPo; WaAnP

Laguna de los muertos no tiene fin, La.   Dolor de corazón.   Pura López Colomé.   RMCMP

Laguna man said.   Wind and Glacier Voices.   Simon J. Ortiz.   HATNAP

Lai.   May Probyn.   VWP

Lai with Sounds of Skin.   Chryss Yost.   CalPo

Laid in My Quiet Bed.   Henry Howard, Earl of Surrey.   CABP

Laid in my quiet bed, in study as I were.   Laid in My Quiet Bed.   Henry Howard, Earl of Surrey.   CABP

Laid Off.   Francis Webb.   BMAP

Laila's Face.   Nasri Hajjaj.   Eno, tr. by Ibrahim Muhawi

Laïque, says the Frenchman to the Frenchman, and the.   Like.   Robert Desnos. MFP, tr. by Martin Sorrell

Laïque, says the Frenchman to the Frenchman, and the Frenchman is civil. Like.   Robert Desnos.   YaTCFP, tr. by Martin Sorrell

Lair, The.   Rachel Hadas.   FFC

Laird o' Cockpen, he's proud an' he's great, The.   Laird o' Cockpen, The. Carolina Oliphant, Baroness Nairne.   NOBRP; NPeEn; OxBEV

Lais.   "H. D."   MoAmPo

Lake.   Georgi Belev.   CSCBP, tr. by the author and Lisa Sapinkopf

Lake.   Octavio Paz.   TCLAP, tr. by Rachel Benson

Lake, A.   Thomas Lovell Beddoes.   NPeEn Fr. Last Man, The.

Lake, The.   Tom Clark.   AHA

Lake, The.   Alphonse Marie Louis de Lamartine.   NAWM-7v2, tr. by Andrea Moorhead

Lake, The.   Alphonse Marie Louis de Lamartine.   SxFrPo, tr. by A. M. and E. H. Blackmore

Lake, The.   Geoffrey O'Brien.   KGB

Lake, The. Gertrude Pape. SurWo, *tr.* by Her de Vries

Lake, The. Edgar Allan Poe. *See* Lake: To———, The.

Lake, The. James Stephens. MoBrPo

Lake and when to hold to the swell of it, The. (LL) Learning to Swim at Forty-Five. Colleen J. McElroy. FiBr; GT

Lake Austin Diorama. John Collin Murphey. TiP2

Lake Balaton. Ágnes Nemes Nagy. IQMS, *tr.* by Hugh Maxton

Lake Baskunchak. Andrey Alekseievich Amalrik. TCRusP, *tr.* by John Glad

Lake Drummond Dream. Dave Jeddie Smith. VCAP

Lake Echo, Dear. C. D. Wright. AmAlph

Lake Has Swallowed the Whole Sky, The. Silvia Curbelo. TouFir

Lake in Central Park, The. Jay Wright. ESEAA; GT

Lake is sharp along the shore, The. Lakeshore. Francis Reginald Scott. BrAP

Lake Isle, The. Ezra Pound. OBCoV; OxBoAm; PoA 2002

Lake lay blue below the hill, The. Mary Elizabeth Coleridge. VWP

Lake Leman. Lord Byron. BrAP *Fr.* Childe Harold's Pilgrimage.

Lake Leman woos me with its crystal face. Lord Byron. NAEL-6v2; NAEL-7v2; NOBRP; NPBRoP; WaAnP *Fr.* Childe Harold's Pilgrimage.

Lake Leman woos me with its crystal face. Lord Byron. BrAP *Fr.* Childe Harold's Pilgrimage.

Lake marsh grass like two eels who were caught, The. (LL) Twilight Polka Dots. Barbara Guest. NoP-4; NoP-5; NYP2; PmAP

Lake Morning in Autumn. Douglas Livingstone. NoP-4

Lake Murry. Pinkie Gordon Lane. GT

Lake of Gaube, The. Algernon Charles Swinburne. CABP; NAEL-6v2

Lake of night is still in the valley, The. Pine, The. Saunders Lewis. OBWVE, *tr.* by Gwyn Morgan

Lake of the dead has no shore, The. Heartache. Pura López Colomé. RMCMP, *tr.* by Forrest Gander

Lake of the Ten Thousand Mountains, The. Meng Hao Jan. EaWin, *tr.* by W. S. Merwin

Lake of the Woods, The. Richard Ryan. PBCIP

Lake of Zurich, The. Friedrich Gottlieb Klopstock. GePo, *tr.* by George C. Schoolfield

Lake Song. Colette Inez. PLBUT

Lake Superior. Lorine Niedecker. OxBoAm

  "And at the blue ice superior spot." FTOS

Long, The / Canoes. FTOS

  "Schoolcraft left the Soo—canoes." FTOS

  "Through all this granite land." FTOS

Lake, The; Or, Modern Improvement in Landscape. Anna Seward. OBGa

Lake: To———, The. Edgar Allan Poe. APN-1

  (Lake, The.) NAAL-3

Lake was covered with gloom, The. Enna plunged into it screaming. (LL) Geography. Kenneth Koch. NAMCP V.2; NoAM

Lake was filled with distinguished fish purchased, The. Twilight Polka Dots. Barbara Guest. NoP-4; NoP-5; NYP2; PmAP

Lake Yi. Pei Di and Wang Wei. CCL1 *Fr.* Wheel River.

Lakefront, Cleveland. Russell Atkins. GT

Lake-Isle of Innisfree, The. William Butler Yeats. BLPJKO; CABP; ChAP; ClHu; HeIP-4; IPoFL; MoBrPo; NAEL-6v2; NAEL-7v2; NAMCP V.1; NoAM; NoP-4; NoP-5; OBEV; OxAEP-2; PoPoPo; TFi; UV; WaAnP

Lakelse Avenue. George Stanley. NLPA *Fr.* Mountains and Air.

Lakes [*with music*]. David Donnell. NoAM

Lakes, The. David Wright. NLP

Lakeshore. Francis Reginald Scott. BrAP

Lakeside. Edmund Wilson. OBCoV *Fr.* Easy Exercises in the Use of Difficult Words.

Lakeside Identification, A. Robert Pinsky. NoP-4; NoP-5 *Fr.* Essay on Psychiatrists.

Lakeward. Trumbull Stickney. APN-2

Lakota Sister/Cherokee Mother. Victoria Lena Manyarrows. UnSA

Lalai (Dreamtime). Sam Woolagoodjah. NOBAu

Lalla Rookh. Thomas Moore.

  Fire-Worshippers, The. NPBRoP

  "Oh! ever thus from childhood's hour." UV

L'Allée. Paul Verlaine. OBGa,

L'Allegro. John Milton. BASC; NAEL-6v1; NAEL-7v1; NoP-4; NoP-5; NOSC; OBEV; PBRV; PoPoPo; TFi

Lamarck. Osip Emilevich Mandelstam. TCRusP, *tr.* by John Glad

Lamb. Michael Dennis Browne. RaBo

Lamb. Kenneth Steven. EdScPo

Lamb, The. William Blake. BrAP; ChIV-2; HeIP-4; ITBLP; NAEL-6v2; NAEL-7v2; NAWM-7v2; NIL-7; NIP-4; NOBRP; NoP-4; NoP-5; NPBRoP; OxAEP-2; PoPoPo; SoSe-8; TFi; TRP; WaAnP *Fr.* Songs of Innocence.

Lamb, The. Linda Gregg. CFP

Lamb and the Wolves, The. Ignacy Krasicki. WoPoe, *tr.* by Jerzy Peterkiewicz and Burns Singer

Lamb could not get born, A. Ice wind. February 17th. Ted Hughes. NPeEn

Lamb of Peace, the Ram of War, The. William Witherup. AtGh

Lamb of the shepherds, Child, how still you lie. (LL) Holy Innocents, The. Robert Lowell. MoAmPo; OBCP

Lamb Was Bleating Softly, The. Juan Ramón Jiménez. WED, *tr.* by Robert Bly

Lamb, Willow: An Arch Dolefulness Has Taken Me This Far. Rebecca Wolff. LegDan

Lambda. Melvin B. Tolson. NAAPv.2; NAMCP V.1 *Fr.* Harlem Gallery.

Lambent cobblestones refract the blue, The. Next to the *Café Chaos*. Olga Broumas. BodElec

Lambeth Walk. Douglas Furber and Noel Gay. ReLy

Lambeth you've never seen. Lambeth Walk. Douglas Furber and Noel Gay. ReLy

Lambs that learn to walk in snow. First Sight. Philip Larkin. NTCP; PtR

Lamda. Melvin B. Tolson. OxAAAP

Lame Beggar, A. John Donne. NoSic

Lame Boy Returns, The. Juan Delgado. TouFir

Lame Goat, The. Jelaluddin Rumi. TWF, *tr.* by Coleman Barks

Lament. Liu Chi-hsün. WoPoe, *tr.* by Tony Barnstone

Lament: "For the green turtle with her pulsing burden." Gillian Clarke. HarvBoo; TCAWP

Lament. Máire Mhac an tSaoi. ModIr, *tr.* by Patrick Crotty

Lament. G. E. Patterson. AmPoNex

Lament: "Hills are white with snow, The." Cho Wen-chun. CrYelRi, *tr.* by Sam Hamill

Lament: "I cried on my mother's breast, cried sore." Cathal Ó Searcaigh. ModIr, *tr.* by Seamus Heaney

Lament: "I heard that many temples were destroyed." Hamhur Kiwha. BecRai, *tr.* by Kim Daljin, Kim Won-Chung and Christopher Merrill

Lament: "I thought of you." Gregory Orr. ArBi

Lament: "I turn to you high priests." Tadeusz Rózewicz. PoSu, *tr.* by Magnus J. Krynski

Lament: "In a dismal air; a light of breaking summer." George Sutherland Fraser. PoWW

Lament: "Late autumn, a brief shower." Liu Yung. CrYelRi, *tr.* by Sam Hamill

Lament: "Those we love die like birds." Mai Sayigh. CFP, *tr.* by Charles Doria and Salma Khadra Jayyusi

Lament: "Ways of heaven are mysterious, The." T'ao Ch'ien. CrYelRi, *tr.* by Sam Hamill

Lament: "What moved me, was the way your hand." Dorothy Livesay. BrAP

Lament: "While my city gently sleeps." Harold Carrington. EGAG

Lament: "Your dying was a difficult enterprise." Thom Gunn. CAGL; GPTC; InoFa

Lament at Night. H. Leivick. AWTN, *tr.* by Marie Syrkin

Lament Beginning w/a Line after Cavafy. Eric Gamalinda. ReBoTo

Lament: "Cheek by cheek on our pillow[s]." *Unknown.* ErotSp, *tr.* by Sam Hamill

  (Elegy.) CrYelRi

Lament for a Courtesan. Li Ho. CrYelRi, *tr.* by Sam Hamill

Lament for a Leg. John Ormond. AngWePo; NoP-4; NoP-5; OBWVE

Lament for Adonis. Bion. HePo, *tr.* by Barbara Hughes Fowler

Lament for Adonis. Bion. WaAnP, *tr.* by John Addington Symonds

Lament for Arthur Cleary, The. Dermot Bolger.

  "I drifted into sleep." IrLP

Lament for Bion. Moschus. HePo, *tr.* by Barbara Hughes Fowler

Lament for Chaucer. Thomas Hoccleve. OBEV *Fr.* De Regimine Principum.

Lament for Ch'en T'ao. Tu Fu [*or* Du Fu]. CrYelRi, *tr.* by Sam Hamill

Lament for Crassus. Michael Hofmann. NeBrP

Lament for Culloden. Robert Burns. FaBoWar; OBEV

Lament for Evolution. Joy Davidman. YaYoPo

Lament for Five Sons Lost in a Plague. Abu Dhu'ayb al-Hudhali. WoPoe, *tr.* by Omar S. Pound

Lament for Flodden, The. Jane Elliot. *See* Flowers of the Forest, The.

Lament for Fortune's Frailty, A. Chiu Tsz-yung. ColAnChi *Fr.* Cantonese Love-Songs.

Lament for Ignacio Sánchez Mejías. Federico García Lorca. OBVE, *tr.* by Arthur Lloyd

Lament for Ignacio Sánchez Mejías. Federico García Lorca. NAWM-7v2, *tr.* by J. L. Gili and Stephen Spender

Lament for Ignacio Sanchez Mejias. Federico García Lorca. *tr.* by Alan S. Trueblood

  Absence of the Soul. WoPoe, *tr.* by Alan S. Trueblood

  Goring and the Death, The. WoPoe, *tr.* by Alan S. Trueblood

Lament for Ignacio Sánchez Mejías. Federico García Lorca. *tr.* by Galway Kinnell

Lament for Lleucu Llwyd. Llywelyn Goch ap Meurig Hen. OBWVE, *tr.* by Joseph P. Clancy

Lament for Llywelyn ap Gruffudd. Gruffudd ab yr Ynad Coch. OBWVE, *tr.* by Joseph P. Clancy

Lament for Lu Yin. Meng Chiao. CCL1, *tr.* by Stephen Owen

Lament for MacGregor of Glenstrae. Mrs. MacGregor of Glanstrae. NePenScot, *tr.* by Iain Crichton Smith

Lament for Our Lady's Shrine at Walsingham, A. *Unknown.* NoP-4; NPeEn; PBRV

Lament for Passenger Pigeons. Judith Wright. HarvBoo

Lament for Prince Chagoo. *Unknown.* WoPoe, *tr.* by Jean S. Grigsby

Lament for Siôn y Glyn [*with music*]. Lewis Glyn Cothi. OBWVE, *tr.* by Joseph P. Clancy

Lament for Tadhg Cronin's Children. Egan O'Rahilly. ModIr; PBCIP; WoPoe, *tr.* by Michael Hartnett

Lament for the Country Soldiers. Les A. Murray. BMAP

Lament for the Cuckoo. Alcuin. NAWM-5v1

Lament for the Death of a Bullfighter. Joshua Beckman. AmPoNex

Lament for the Death of Guillén Peraza. *Unknown.* WoPoe, *tr.* by W. S. Merwin

Lament for the Death of Thomas Davis. Sir Samuel Ferguson. IrV

Lament for the Dorsets. Alfred Wellington Purdy. BrAP; NoAM

Lament for the Drowned Country. Mary Durack. NOBAu

Lament for the Evanescence of Life, A. Yamanoé no Okura. WoPoe, *tr.* by Helen Craig McCullough

Lament for the Great Music. Hugh MacDiarmid.
    "Yet there is no great problem in the world today." NoP-5

Lament for the Makaris [*or* Makars *or* Makers]. William Dunbar. InoFa; MakPoe; NePenScot; NoP-4; NoP-5; OBEV; OxBEV; WaAnP
    (Lament: When He Wes Se[i]k.) NPeEn

Lament for the Makers. Frank Bidart. PtR

Lament for the Makers. W. S. Merwin. InoFa; PoA 2002

Lament for the Makers: "No call upon anyone but the timber drifting in the waves." Jack Spicer. FTOS

Lament for the Stag. Pierre Jean Jouve. YaTCFP, *tr.* by Keith Waldrop

Lament for the State of the Country, A. Iain Lom. NePenScot, *tr.* by Meg Bateman

Lament for Urien, The. *Unknown.* OBMV *Fr.* Red Book of Hergest, The.

Lament in Good Weather. Lucia Maria Perillo. ExTi

Lament of a Desert Rat. N. J. Trapnell. FaBoWar

Lament of a Graying Woman. Cho Wen-chun. NDACCP, *tr.* by William Carlos Williams

Lament of a Poor Blind. Thomas Hood. DiBP

Lament of a Subwayite. Eugene O'Neill. UV

Lament of Edward Blastock, The. Dame Edith Sitwell. OBMV

Lament of Gilgamesh for Enkidu, The. *Unknown.* CAGL *Fr.* Epic of Gilgamesh, The.

Lament of Maev Leith-Dherg, The. *Unknown.* OBWP, *tr.* by Thomas William Hazen Rolleston

Lament of Mary, The. *Unknown.* IQMS, *tr.* by Michael Beevor

Lament of Mary, The. *Unknown.* IQMS, *tr.* by Adam Makkai

Lament of Mary, The. *Unknown.* IQMS, *tr.* by Watson Kirkconnell

Lament of O'Gnive, The. Fearflatha O'Gnive. IrV, *tr.* by Jeremiah Joseph Callanan

Lament of Swordy Well, The. John Clare. FaBoVe

Lament of the Banana Man, The. Evan Jones. PML

Lament of the Captive, The. Richard Henry Wilde. APN-1; ColAP; TCAPo

Lament of the Farm Wife of Wu. Su Tung-p'o. ColAnChi, *tr.* by Burton Watson

Lament of the Flowers, The. Jones Very. APN-1; ColAP

Lament of the Forest, The. Thomas Cole. APN-1

Lament of the Frontier Guard. Li Po. APT-1; NAMCP V.1; NDACCP; NPeEn; OBVE; OBWP; PoAgWa, *tr.* by Ezra Pound

Lament of the Irish Emigrant. Helen Selina Blackwood, Countess of Dufferin and Clandeboye. IrV
    (Irish Emigrant, The.) IrLP; OxAEP-2

Lament of the Lady of Qin. Wei Chuang. CCL1, *tr.* by Lionel Giles

Lament of the Unmarried Girl, The. Brian Merriman. OBVE *Fr.* Midnight Court, The.

Lament of the Virgin. *Unknown.* NAWM-7v1

Lament of the Virtues and Verses on Account of the Death of Don Guido. Antonio Machado Ruiz. OBVE

Lament of the White Queen. Ann Drysdale. TCAWP

Lament on the Water. Pak Illo. CATKP, *tr.* by Peter H. Lee

Lament over Love. Langston Hughes. NAMCP V.1

Lament the harp that in its casement broods. Trapped Wind. Geoff Ward. VaPo

Lamentation. Dic Jones. BBMWP, *tr.* by Anthony Conran

Lamentation during His Most Painful Illness. Simon Dach. GePo, *tr.* by Ingrid Waløe-Engel

Lamentation of Queen Elizabeth, A. Sir Thomas More. NoSic

Lamentation of the Border-Guard. Gali-Danah Zinger. CRWP, *tr.* by the author and Ashraf Noor

Lamentation of the Old Pensioner, The (1890 version). William Butler Yeats. NoAM; TRP; WeW-3

Lamentation of the Old Pensioner, The (1925 version). William Butler Yeats. TRP; WeW-3

Lamentation on Ur. Tom Sleigh. PoCho

Lamentation, The. John Marckant. SacPr

Lamentations. Bible, *O.T. tr.* by Susan Stewart
    "How doth the city sit solitary that was full of people." WoPoe, *tr.* by Susan Stewart
    "I have been brought into darkness." WoPoe, *tr.* by Susan Stewart
    "Scribes have cast the blame, The." WoPoe, *tr.* by Susan Stewart

Lamentations. Alter Brody. APT-2

Lamentations [*with music*]. Norman Dubie. NoAM

Lamentations. Louise Glück. VCAP

Lamentations. Siegfried Sassoon. OBSV; OxAEP-2

Lamentations au cerf. Pierre Jean Jouve. YaTCFP

Lamentations of Jeremy, for the Most Part According to Tremeullius. John Donne.

Lamentations of Round-Oak Waters. John Clare.
    "Look backward on the days of yore." NPBRoP

Lamenting the Civil War. Muso Soseki. EaWin, *tr.* by W. S. Merwin

Lamenting the Inevitable. Alicia Ostriker. UnSA

Lamenting thru gipsies his fast suicide. (LL) Political Poem. Imamu Amiri Baraka. AF; NoAM; PmAP

Laments for the Afghan Women. Hettie Jones. PrTe

Laments her Early Misfortunes. Mary Robinson. CenSon; RWP

Laments of a Poor Little Child. Dezső Kosztolányi. *tr.* by Leslie A. Kery, Egon F. Kunz and Peter Zollman
    "Dear mum's old picture." IQMS, *tr.* by Peter Zollman
    "I want to kill myself." IQMS, *tr.* by Peter Zollman
    "Inks of all colours are filling my dreams." IQMS, *tr.* by Leslie A. Kery
    "Like someone who has fallen between the rails." IQMS, *tr.* by Egon F. Kunz

Laments of a Sad Man. Dezső Kosztolányi. *tr.* by Leslie A. Kery
    "I am an entry in all kinds of books." IQMS, *tr.* by Leslie A. Kery

Laments of the Gorges. Meng Chiao.
    1. CCL1, *tr.* by Stephen Owen
    2. CCL1, *tr.* by Stephen Owen

Laments of the Gorges ("Long ago, everyone laughed together.") Meng Chiao. NDACCP, *tr.* by David Hinton

Laments on the War Dead. Yehuda Amichai.
    "Is all this sorrow? I don't know." PoSu

Laments, The. Jan Kochanowski. *tr.* by Stanislaw Barańczak and Seamus Heaney
    I'd Buy You, Wisdom. WoPoe, *tr.* by Stanislaw Barańczak and Seamus Heaney
    Where Is That Gate for Grief. WoPoe, *tr.* by Stanislaw Barańczak and Seamus Heaney

Laments the Volatility of Phaon. Mary Robinson. CenSon; RWP

9. Laments the Volatility of Phaon. Mary Robinson. NPBRoP *Fr.* Sappho and Phaon.

Lamia. John Keats. NAEL-6v2; NAEL-7v2; NoP-5
    "Upon a time, before the faery broods." NOBRP

L'amiral cherche une maison à louer. Richard Huelsenbeck. PFTM-1

Lamisca, who breathed her last in lamentable pangs of labor. Dioscorides. HePo *Fr.* Epigrams.

L'Amitié: To Mrs M Awbrey. Katherine Philips. BrAP

Lamium. Louise Glück. HarvBoo; StAl

Lamkin. *Unknown.* NPeEn

Lammas Hireling, The. Ian Duhig. NeBrP

Lamp, The. Paul Farley. NeBrP

Lamp, The. Charles Whitehead. OBEV

Lamp are you, above all stars of night, A. Pole Star, The. Coslett Coslett. OBWVE, *tr.* by Kenneth Hurlstone Jackson

Lamp burns blue, everyone asleep, The. Sharing Lodging with Hsieh Shih-hou. Mei Yao Ch'en. ColAnChi, *tr.* by Burton Watson

Lamp lit, A. Roberto Juarroz. VCWP *Fr.* Thrid Vertical Poetry.

Lamp lost its master at home, The. Elegy. Great Master Hyecho. BecRai, *tr.* by Kim Daljin, Kim Won-Chung and Christopher Merrill

Lamp must be replenish'd [*or* replenished], but even then, The. Manfred. Lord Byron. NAEL-6v2; NAEL-7v2; NOBRP

Lamp without Oil, The. Kabir. WED, *tr. by* Robert Bly

Lamp[e], The. Henry Vaughan. ChIV-2

Lamper, The. Maggie Hannan. NLP

Lamplight from our kitchen window-pane. Again. Glyn Jones. OBWVE; TCAWP

Lamplighter, The. Robert Louis Stevenson. ITBLP; NePenScot

Lamplighter, if you can't set two equally. Rufinus. HePo, *tr. by* Barbara Hughes Fowler

Lamprey, glowing with uncommon fires, The. William Diaper. OBVE *Fr.* Halieutica.

Lampriskos, the dear Muses allow you. Schoolmaster, The. Herodas. HePo, *tr. by* Barbara Hughes Fowler

Lamps Are Brought In, The. George Kalamaras. Vesp

Lamps have been left burning in a fish, The. Unbruised. Tom Ahern. OnScMo

Lamps hung like a lynching, The. All the Way Home. Primus St. John. EGAG

Lana Turner has collapsed! Poem. Frank O'Hara. CAP-8; CLPP; FTOS; ItP; OxBoAm; PmAP

Lancer. A. E. Housman. MoBrPo; OBWP

Land. Agha Shahid Ali. PoA 2002

Land, A / That never existed. Atlantis. Walter Helmut Fritz. GTCP, *tr. by* Reinhold Grimm

Land, The. Rudyard Kipling. MoBrPo

Land, The. Victoria Mary Sackville-West. OBGa

Land, The / Of sun and sucking pigs. Cokaigne Fantasy. Arthur Leslie Morton. RSaN

Land and Sea Tales. Rudyard Kipling.
  Hour of the Angel, The. OxBSo
  Nurses, The. NoAM

Land Army Photographs. Tony Curtis. TCAWP

Land at the World's End, The. Brian Swann. PoCoUp

Land Beneath the Sea, The. Thomas Jeffrey Llewelyn Prichard.
  "What can you see in yonder bay." AngWePo

Land between us, The. Honesty-Stones. J. S. Harry. NOBAu

Land breaks yellow south below, pale squares. View from Cortona, A. Richard Hugo. AF

Land has been dead in its pores all the war long, The. Great Odor of Summer, The. `Nathaniel Tarn. ICANM

Land here, little birdie, come across the green woods! Rare Is the Wheat-Field in Which There's No Blemish. *Hungarian Oral Tradition*. IQMS, *tr. by* Adam Makkai

Land, Ho! Thomas Edward Brown. SacPr

Land is hushed, a reddening sun, The. Silver Platter, The. Nathan Alterman. NRoS, *tr. by* Esther Raizen

Land lies in water; it is shadowed green. Map, The. Elizabeth Bishop. APT-2; ColAP; NAMCP V.2

Land lies open: summer fallow, hayfield, pasture, The. Mysteries of The Incarnation: "She Said Yeah." Kathleen Norris. UpMys

Land Love. Douglas Dunn. NePenScot

Land not mine, still, A. Anna Andreyevna Akhmatova. WPoS

Land o' the Leal, The. Carolina Oliphant, Baroness Nairne. NePenScot; NOBRP; NPeEn; OBEV; OxBEV

Land of Beginning Again, The. Louisa Fletcher. ITBLP

Land of Cotton. Gilbert Sorrentino. FTOS

Land of Counterpane, The. Robert Louis Stevenson. BLPJKO; ChAP; NBLV; NTCP; PtR; TLR; WHSW

Land of fandangoes. Spanish Jake. Irving Caesar and Sammy Lerner. ReLy

Land of Fog. Ingeborg Bachmann. GTCP, *tr. by* Irmgard Hunt

Land of Heart's Desire, The. William Butler Yeats.
  (Fairy Song.) MoBrPo

Land of Lincoln. Angela Sorby. AmPoNex

Land of Little Sticks, 1945. James Tate. AtGh; BodElec

Land of Mirrors, The. Amira El-Zein. PoArWo, *tr. by* Husain Haddawy

Land of old codgers after the summer, A. Autumn. Maurice Gilliams. TuT, *tr. by* Sean Dunne

Land of our fathers where at eventide. Intermittent Dream of a Sad Night. Marceline Desbordes-Valmore. WoPoe, *tr. by* Louis Simpson

Land of pure water and cloud trembles at the flicking whip, The. Riding a Horse in the Rain. Daegak Euchon. BecRai, *tr. by* Kim Daljin, Kim Won-Chung and Christopher Merrill

Land of Song. Nigel Jenkins. AngWePo

Land of spices; something understood, The. (LL) Prayer (1): "Prayer the Church's banquet, Angels' age." George Herbert. AngWePo; BASC; GSo; NAEL-6v1; NAEL-7v1; NoP-4; NoP-5; NOSC; OBWVE; OxAEP-1; OxBSo; PoPoPo; TFi

Land of Story-Books, The. Robert Louis Stevenson. ChAP; ITBLP; NePenScot

Land of the Discount Price, Home of the Brand Name. Harryette Mullen. Eno

Land of the Lost. Charles Porter. BtF

Land of the Shí, The. Molly Peacock. PA9/11

Land O'Lakes, Wisconsin: Vajrayana Seminary. Allen Ginsberg. BBASP

Land recieved the hollowest of sleep. Earth at Its Origin. Anne Hébert. YaTCFP, *tr. by* Mary Ann Caws

Land Stretching Up to the Sky, A. Nada El-Hage. PoArWo, *tr. by* Nathalie El-Hani

Land that answers best the farmer's care, The. Christopher Smart. *Fr.* Hop-Garden, The.

Land up here hasn't been worked in years, The. Eternity's Woods. Paul Zweig. BodElec

Land was ours before we were the land's, The. Gift Outright, The. Robert Frost. BLPJKO; ColAP; FaBoA; HarvBoo; HHAm; MoAmPo; NAAL-5; NAMCP V.1; NoAM; NoP-4; NoP-5; OxBoAm; PoPoPo; TFi; TRP; WaAnP

Land was theirs after we were the land's, The. Big Rock-Candy Mountain, The. Louis Edward Sissman. GM

Land was there before us, The. Inauguration. Lorenzo Thomas. EGAG

Land was white, The. Riddle. *Unknown*. FaBoVe

Land Where the Good Songs Go, The. P. G. Wodehouse. ReLy

Landcrab I. Margaret Atwood. NIP-4

Landcrab II. Margaret Atwood. NIP-4

Landed: A Valentine. Richard Howard. PoA 2002

Landfall. Randolph Stow. BMAP

Landfall, The. John Blight. BMAP

Landfall in Unknown Seas [*with music*]. Allen Curnow. NoP-4; NoP-5

Landfill west of the lake. Arc Welder. Martha Vertreace. MAAN

Landing. James P. Lenfestey. OtW

Landing. Sandy Shreve. IFF

Landing Area. J. H. Prynne. PFTM-2

Landing in the summer shade. Struggle for the Border, The. Dick Gallup. AHA

Landing of Rochambeau, The. Michael Davidson. FTOS; OnScMo

Landing of the Pilgrim Fathers [in New England], The. Felicia Dorothea Hemans. BRP; HHAm; ITBLP; NAEL-6v2; NAEL-7v2; NoP-4; NoP-5

Landing on the Moon. Odia Ofeimun. EmeKit

Landing Pattern. Philip Appleman. GoPo

Landing, The. J. D. McClatchy. OxBoAm

Landing under Water, I See Roots. Annie Finch. PoDa

Landlady in Bangkok, The. Karen Swenson. GifTon

Landlady, The. Margaret Atwood. NALW

Landlady, The. Patricia K. Page. BrAP

Landlord is wringing our lives dry, The. (LL) Drinking Art, The. Robert Minhinnick. AngWePo; TCAWP

Landlord, landlord, / My roof has sprung a leak. Ballad of the Landlord. Langston Hughes. WaAnP

Landlord's coat is tulip red, The. Wild Sports of the West. John Montague. CABP

Landlord's Tale: Paul Revere's Ride, The. Henry Wadsworth Longfellow. *See* Paul Revere's Ride [The Landlord's Tale].

Landmarks. Claude Wilkinson. BtF

Land-Mine, The. George MacBeth. OBWP

Lands around my dwelling, The. Improvised Song of Joy. Takomaq. WoPoe, *tr. by* Knud Rasmussen

Land's end. And sound and river come. Point, The. Robert Earl Hayden. ESEAA

Lands which leap very high. On the Islands of All Winds. Aimé Césaire. VCWP

Landscape. Larry Fagin and George Schneeman. AHA

Landscape. Johanna Kruit. TuT, *tr. by* Micheal O'Siadhail

Landscape. Maria Manuela Margarido. HAWP, *tr. by* Julia Kirst

Landscape. Hendrik Marsman. TuT, *tr. by* Michael Longley

Landscape. Mary Oliver. HeIP-4

Landscape. Octavio Paz. OBVE, *tr. by* Charles Tomlinson

Landscape. Hannie Rouweler. TuT, *tr. by* Aidan Sharkey

Landscape. Eunice De Souza. NAMCP V.2

Landscape. Paul Van Ostaijen. TuT, *tr. by* Tony Curtis

Landscape: "Clear autumn opens endlessly away." Tu Fu [*or* Du Fu]. NDACCP, *tr. by* David Hinton

Landscape: "Dimensions are dizzying; peaks, The." Marguerite Bouvard. PfS

Landscape: "Stupid. But each of us took turns." Michael Collier. PfSP

Landscape, The. George Daniel. NOSC

Landscape, The. Richard Payne Knight. OBGa *Fr.* Landscape, The.

Landscape, The. Richard Payne Knight.
  Landscape, The. OBGa

Landscape: 1. B. P. Nichol. OpeFie

Landscape, A. Margaret Lucas Cavendish, Duchess of Newcastle. NOSC

Landscape and Chardin. Charles North. NYP2

Landscape as it stood, The. Landscape. Hannie Rouweler. TuT, tr. by Aidan Sharkey

Landscape, as the events of a prior discontinuity. Aphrodite of Economy. Mark McMorris. IAoNAP

Landscape at the End of the Century. Stephen Dunn. CAP-8

Landscape Beyond Warsaw. Peter Huchel. PoSu

Landscape Described, A. William Cowper. NAEL-6v1; NAEL-7v1 Fr. Task, The.

Landscape Gardeners, The. Geoffrey Grigson. OBGa

Landscape Heard, A. Filippo Tommaso Marinetti. PFTM-1

Landscape near an Aerodrome, The. Stephen Spender. MoBrPo; NAMCP V.1; NoAM

Landscape of return is drawn, A. Mercedes Roffé. TANSG, tr. by Kathryn Kopple

Landscape of return is sketched, A. Scene of Return is Sketched, A. Mercedes Roffé. MirDau

Landscape of the Capibaribe River. João Cabral de Melo Neto. VCWP, tr. by Richard Zenith

Landscape Over Zero. Bei Dao. PoDa, tr. by David Hinton and Yanbing Chen

Landscape Painting. Diane Glancy. TWW

Landscape (the landscape!) again: Gloucester, The. Librarian, The. Charles Olson. PmAP

Landscape Winter. Anne Sexton. MoW

Landscape with a Calm. T. J. Clark. BAP-04

Landscape with Boat. Wallace Stevens. APT-1

Landscape with Dog. Paul Mariani. PfSP

Landscape with Figures. Frank Ormsby. PBCIP

Landscape with Next of Kin. Olga Broumas. WiU

Landscape with Nymphs and Satyrs. Norman Henry, II Pritchard. GT

Landscape with One Figure. Douglas Dunn. NePenScot

Landscape with Saxophonist. Thylias Moss. ESEAA

Landscape with the Fall of Icarus. William Carlos Williams. BrAP; NAAL-5; NAAPv.2; NAMCP V.1; NoAM; NoP-5; OtW; OxBoAm; PoPoPo Fr. Pictures from Brueghel.

Landscape with 3 People. Lee Harwood. AHA

Landscape with Tractor. Henry Taylor. InGu

Landscape with Yellow Birds. Shuntaro Tanikawa. PoetW, tr. by Harold Wright

Landscape without a Hat. Bobi Jones. ATSWP, tr. by Robert Minhinnick

Landscapes. T. S. Eliot.
  Cape Ann. NAEL-6v2; NoAM
  New Hampshire. NoAM; WeW-3
  Rannoch, by Glencoe. NAEL-6v2
  Virginia. FaBoA

Landscapes. Duriel Harris. SpirFl

Landscapes. Pauline Kaldas. PoArWo

Landscapes. Heberto Padilla. VCWP

Landscapes and Home / Ghazal 22. Yvonne Blomer. IFF

Landscapes they walk through unseeing measure their lives, The. Landscapes They Walk Through, The. Jean Follain. MotU, tr. by Mary Feeney and William Matthews

Landscapes with Set-Screws. X. J. Kennedy. UrbNat

Landslide. John Engels. PfSP

Landwind: a gale at dawn scooping down from the hills. Gale at Dawn. William Everson. APT-2

Langaig. Richard Hugo. CAP-8

Langston. Frederick D'Aguiar. Oth

Langston Blues. Dudley Randall. SeSe

Langston Hughes. Gwendolyn Brooks. ColAP

Langston Hughes. Kevin Young. NeAmPo

Langston Hughes. Langston Hughes. Kevin Young. NeAmPo

Language. Marjorie Agosin. TANSG, tr. by Cola Franzen

Language. Jennifer Maiden. BMAP

Language. Marc Matthews. WaCA

Language. Jack Spicer.
  Thing Language. APSN; FTOS; OxBoAm

Language, The. Robert Creeley. CAP-8; PmAP

Language Animal, The. Thomas Lux. AmAlph

Language / created the landscape, The. In a Monotonous Dream. Elaine Equi. PmAP

Language Difficulty. Ann Drysdale. TCAWP

Language Event Two. Robert Desnos. PFTM-1

Language is impossible. Motherland. Jo Shapcott. NeBrP

Language is only an instrument for the attainment of science. Taxonomy. Joy Katz. NeAmPo

Language Is Only Words, A. Myrddin ap Dafydd. BBMWP, tr. by Anthony Conran

Language is the house with lamplight in its windows. Anne Michaels. StAl Fr. What the Light Teaches.

Language Issue, The. Nuala Ni Dhomhnaill. ModIr; NPeEn, tr. by Paul Muldoon

Language Issue, The. Nuala Ni Dhomhnaill. MoWP

Language Lesson 1976. Heather McHugh. ItP

Language Memory. Géza Páskándi. tr. by Agnes Arany-Makkai
  "Close your eyes over my sins." IQMS, tr. by Agnes Arany-Makkai
  "I have killed a virgin by being born." IQMS, tr. by Agnes Arany-Makkai
  "In the grass of the twilight: the seventh day is God." IQMS, tr. by Agnes Arany-Makkai
  "Mother of God, you tired Mary." IQMS, tr. by Agnes Arany-Makkai
  "My shirt got torn to rags." IQMS, tr. by Agnes Arany-Makkai
  "You don't even have any sins!" IQMS, tr. by Agnes Arany-Makkai

Language Mesh. Paul Celan. VCWP, tr. by Michael Hamburger

Language Murderer, The. Gwyneth Lewis. tr. by the author
  Final Minutes, The. BBMWP, tr. by the author and Richard Poole
  Forgetting Begins, The. BBMWP, tr. by Geriant Løvgreen
  Interview with the Poet. BBMWP, tr. by the author

Language of Departure. Peter Cooley. PML

Language of Fossils, The [with music]. Anita Endrezze. HATNAP

Language of Great-Aunts, The. Alberto A. Ríos. UnSA

Language of loss, A? I have some business in Arabic. In Arabic. Agha Shahid Ali. FaoP

Language of Love. Rae Armantrout. PmAP

Language of the Brag, The. Sharon Olds. FiBr; MakPoe; PBCAP

Language of the Dead, The. Thomas McGrath. BodElec

Language of Weather, The. Ray A. Young Bear. HATNAP

Language Pile, The. Donald Berger. NAPBL

Language sovereign secret incompatible submerged in the universal wound. Mohammed Dib. PFTM-2 Fr. Formulaires.

Language that but sparely floo'ers, The. Hugh MacDiarmid. NePenScot Fr. Drunk Man Looks at the Thistle, A.

Languages. Carl Sandburg. APT-1; ColAP

Language's Will and Testament, The. Gwyneth Lewis. ATSWP, tr. by Robert Minhinnick

Langue d'Oc. Various authors. tr. by Ezra Pound
  Alba ("When the nightingale to his mate"). APT-1; OBVE; OxBoAm; WeW-3, tr. by Ezra Pound

Languid African nights. Nights. Alda Lara. HAWP, tr. by Julia Kirst

Languid, and sad, and slow. William Lisle Bowles. CenSon; NAEL-6v2

Languid, and sad, and slow, from day to day. Languid, and sad, and slow. William Lisle Bowles. CenSon; NAEL-6v2

Languid lady next appears in state, The. Edward Young. NPeEn Fr. Love of Fame, the Universal Passion.

Languid, lethargic, listless and slow. Complacent Tortoise, The. Brian Patten. OBSP

Languid stomach curses even the pure, The. John Armstrong. STuOW Fr. Art of Preserving Health, The.

Languidez de las cosas subalternas. Estío en Bidonville. Angel González. RaW

Languish. Allan Graham. ICANM

Languor After Pain. Adelaide Crapsey. NAAPv.2

Lank poverty, dank poverty. Tin Wash Dish, The. Les A. Murray. BMAP

Lanky frog, hold. Issa. WED, tr. by Robert Bly

Lanky hank of a she in the inn over there, The. Glass of Beer, A. James Stephens. NBLV; OBCoV; OBMV; OxBEV

Lantern Out of Doors, The. Gerard Manley Hopkins. SacPr

Lantern sways from the Banner Pole, A. Pole at the Village Pagoda, The. Vietnamese Oral Tradition. CaDao, tr. by John Balaban

Lantern-ceiling and quiet, A. Presbyterian Study. Tom Paulin. PBCIP

Lanterns—swinging slowly in narrow arcs. (LL) Art of Measuring Light, The. Ellen Hinsey. AmPoNex; YaYoPo

Lanval. Marie de France. NAEL-7v1

Lanza 51. Filippo Scarlatti. CAGL, tr. by James J. Wilhelm

Lao Figures. Unknown. EaWin, tr. by W. S. Merwin

Laocoön. Virgil. OBVE Fr. Aeneid [or Eneados or Aeneis], The.

Laocoon/Serpent. Novica Tadic. VCWP, tr. by Charles Simic

Laocöon! thou great embodiment. Josiah Gilbert Holland. APN-1 Fr. Marble Prophecy, The.

Laon and Cythna [Earlier version of The Revolt of Islam]. Percy Bysshe Shelley.
  "So now my summer task is ended, Mary." NPBRoP

Laozi. Po Chü-i. CCL1, tr. by Arthur Waley

Lap Dog. Takahashi Shinkichi. ZenPo, tr. by Takashi Ikemoto and Lucien Stryk

Lap dog in a cloth-wrapped box. Lap Dog. Takahashi Shinkichi. ZenPo, tr. by Takashi Ikemoto and Lucien Stryk

Lapiade, Opus 3. Ödön Palasovszky. IQMS, tr. by Kenneth McRobbie

Lapis Lazuli. William Butler Yeats. BrAP; CABP; HeIP-4; NAEL-6v2; NAEL-7v2; NAMCP V.1; NAWM-7v2; NoAM; NoP-4; NoP-5; TFi

Lapping of waters / thick, upon razorblade. Marsden Hartley. APT-1

Lapsus Linguae. Keith Preston. NBLV; OBCoV

Lara. Lord Byron.
   "In him inexplicably mixed appeared." NOBRP

Lara awakes in my memory, a Tatarian cat, lying in wait for me. I am Born and I Burn in My Love. Abdul Wahab Al-Bayati. IrPoTo, tr. by Farouk Abdel Wahab

Larga carretera, Una. Amancer de Otoño. Antonio Machado Ruiz. RaW

Large box is handily made of what is necessary to replace any substance, A. Gertrude Stein. MoWP Fr. Tender Buttons.

Large Branch Splintering Off a Tree in a Storm, A. Thomas Lux. LaCa

Large Grieving Women. Slavko Mihalic. PoSu, tr. by Charles Simic

Large kitchen is almost dark, The. Acolyte, The. Denise Levertov. CAP-8

Large Little Circle. Lew Welch. WhBo

Large, low, whirring block of perfectly white, perfectly flat marble, on chrome legs. Hospital. Charles North. FTOS

Large plate from the eighteenth century, The. Solitude. Michael Cuddihy. GifTon

Large Pots. Gerald Stern. GPPA

Large Red Man Reading. Wallace Stevens. APT-1; NAAPv.2; NAMCP V.1

Large rock balanced upon a small rock. (LL) Reading Lao Tzu Again in the New Year. Charles Wright. PfSP; PoA 2002

Large Room with Wood Floor. Clarence Major. GT

Large slug slides, A. Ransetsu. SoOfWa, tr. by Sam Hamill

Large state is like a low-lying estuary, A. Lao Tzu. ColAnChi Fr. Tao Te Ching.

Large transparent baby like a skeleton in a red tree, A. Visible Baby, The. Peter Redgrove. EmeKit

Large U.S. flag flaps loudly outside our dining room, suspended on a pole, A. Gloria. Bill Berkson. Eno

Large, yellow sky. A mountain ridge. Pinetree. Ágnes Nemes Nagy. PoSu, tr. by Bruce Berlind

Large yellow wings, black-fringed, The. Butterfly on Rock. Irving Layton. BrAP; NoAM

Large-headed beauty, head so alluring, The. Unknown. ColAnChi Fr. Classic of Odes.

Larger Loneliness, A. Eli Bosnick. IJHIL

Largest bud in creation travels, The. Sweet Time. Molly Peacock. FiBr

Largo. Paul Celan. PoSu, tr. by Michael Hamburger

Largo. Deryn Rees-Jones. TCAWP

Largo. Sydney Goodsir Smith. EdScPo

Lark. Tom Earley. AngWePo

Lark. William Neill. EdScPo

Lark in the Clear Air, The. Sir Samuel Ferguson. IrLP

Lark Now Leaves His Watery [or Wat'ry] Nest. Sir William Davenant. OxBEV; TFi
   (Aubade: "Lark now leaves his watery [or wat'ry] nest, The.") OBEV
   (Song: "Lark now leaves his wat'ry [or watery] nest, The.") NOSC

Lark sings as she has always done. Lark. William Neill. EdScPo

Lark, The. Mother's Mark. Jana Beranová. TuT, tr. by Aidan Sharkey

Lark, The. Unknown. OWoS

Lark, The. Unknown. NOSC

Larkin Automatic Car Wash, The. Gavin Ewart. NoAM

Larking. Karen Solie. OpeFie

Larkspur; delphinium (D. consolida). moving closer: her hands, a prayer. Syliva Legris. PoPra Fr. Negative Garden.

Larkspur—bluemoss—his deciduous hands. Science. Michele Glazer. IAoNAP

Larry Kept Saying Primo Levi Was an Accident. Jeni Olin. FreRad

Lars Porsena of Clusium. Thomas Babington Macaulay, 1st Baron Macaulay. CABP; FaBoWar; OBNV; OBWP; OxAEP-2 Fr. Lays of Ancient Rome.

Larson Arson. Margaret Benbow. PoDa

L'Art, 1910. Ezra Pound. HeIP-4; TCAPo

Larva, The. Tadeusz Rózewicz. PoSu, tr. by Magnus F. Krynski

Las calles lloran / Streets Are Crying. Francisco X. Alarcón. GeoHom

Las casitas near the gray cannery. Freeway 280. Lorna Dee Cervantes. NoAM; WeW-3

Las Flores para una Niña Negra. Demetrice A. Worley. SpirFl

Las Girlfriends. Sandra Cisneros. TiP2

'Las, how long shall I. John Lyly. NoSic Fr. Midas.

Las Magdalenas. Judith Ortiz Cofer. TouFir

Las manos abiertas de Mongo. Dándole la mano a Mongo. Martín Espada. SeSe

Las Marías, our Indian mothers, have. Marías, Old Indian Mothers. Rigoberto González. GeoHom

Las! Mort Qui T'a Fait Si Hardie. Charles, Duc d' Orléans. WoPoe, tr. by Fred Chappell

Las, Où Est Maintenant Ce Mespris de Fortune. Joachim Du Bellay. WoPoe, tr. by Fred Beake

¿Las Oyes Cómo Piden Realidades. . .? Pedro Salinas. RaW

Las Trampas U.S.A. Charles Tomlinson. ICANM

Lasca. Frank Desprez. TiP2

Lascars, The. Peter Thomas. AngWePo

Lascivious shivers. Early bloom. As if. Subway Train. Gottfried Benn. GTCP, tr. by Michael Hamburger

Laser. A. R. Ammons. NAMCP V.2; NoAM

Lash like mine no honest man shall dread, A. Alexander Pope. NPeEn Fr. Epistle to Dr. Arbuthnot.

Lashed by the brute season's whip. Summit, The. Yi Yuksa. CAMKP, tr. by Kyung-Ja Chun

Lashed to black parachutes. (LL) On Finding a Swastika Carved on a Tree in the Hills above Heidelberg. Kevin Prufer. AmPoNex; LegDan

Lashed to the wheel of night. Paris. Ingeborg Bachmann. VCWP, tr. by Mark Anderson

Lasithi. David Constantine. HarvBoo

Lasithi: notable for windmills. Summits are. Lasithi. David Constantine. HarvBoo

Lass A-Laundering. Unknown. STV, tr. by John Frederick Nims

Lass cam' sabbin', A. Wishin' Well, The. Helen B. Cruickshank. EdScPo

Lass in the Female Factory, The. Unknown. NOBAu

Lass of Aughrim, The [with music]. Paul Muldoon. NoAM; PBCIP

Lass of Fair Wone, The. Gottfried August Bürger. NPBRoP, tr. by William Taylor

Lass of Patie's Mill, The. Allan Ramsay. OxAEP-1

Lass of Richmond Hill, The [with music]. Leonard McNally. IrLP

Lass with a Lump of Land. Allan Ramsay. OxBEV

Lassie, can ye say. For a Wife in Jizzen. Douglas Young. EdScPo

Lassitude of a summer's day wrapped in the sadness, The. Sway. Henry Israeli. IIR

Last. Donald Revell. RoV

Last Acts. Sharon Olds. NIP-4

Last Affair: Bessie's Blues Song. Michael S. Harper. ESEAA; FuFl

Last American of the season, The. Bemidji. John Redmond. NIrP

Last and greatest herald of Heaven's King, The. Saint John Baptist. William Drummond of Hawthornden. OBEV; OxAEP-1

Last and greatest Herauld of Heavens King, The. For the Baptiste. William Drummond of Hawthornden. NPeEn; OxBEV; PBRV

Last Apple, The. Carol Coiffait. Prnts

Last at Lucy's, The. John Tripp. TCAWP

Last Banquet of Antony and Cleopatra, The. Felicia Dorothea Hemans. RWP

Last Battle and Death of Chingis Khan, The. Unknown. WoPoe Fr. Secret History of the Mongols, The.

Last bell is ringing, The. Czech Dream. Lee Harwood. Oth

Last bridge I won't. Marina Ivanovna Tsvetaeva. EroLit Fr. Poem of the End.

Last Bullet, The. Nidaa Khoury. PoArWo, tr. by Roger Tavor and Linda Zisquit

Last Call. Silvia Curbelo. TouFir

Last carpenter feelie pocket guru. Twenties 27. Jackson Mac Low. PmAP

Last Chance for the Tarzan Holler. Thylias Moss. ExTi

Last Chantey, The. Rudyard Kipling. MoBrPo

Last Chapter, The. Walter De la Mare. MoBrPo

Last chord of a bolero, The. (LL) Two Guitars. Víctor Hernández Cruz. PueRic; TouFir

Last Chorus, The. Percy Bysshe Shelley. See World's Great Age, The.

Last Cigar. Peter Gizzi. VaPo

Last cold lilies cringed, The. Hoar Frost. Morton Dauwen Zabel. PoA 2002

Last Confession, A [fr. A Woman Young and Old]. William Butler Yeats. NIP-4

Last Cry of the Damp Fly, The. Dennis Lee. NTCP

Last Day. Martinus Nijhoff. TuT, tr. by Desmond Egan

Last Day. May Swenson. NAMCP V.2

Last Day, The. Lucile Adler. ICANM

Last Day, The. Kevin Hart. BMAP

Last Day, The. George Seferis. PoetW, tr. by Edmund Keeley and Philip Sherrard
   "Day was cloudy, The. No one could come to a decision." AF

Last Day, The. Edward Young.
   Submarine Jaunt, A. STuOW

Last day in the month of March. Child is Not a Knife, A. Göran Sonnevi. PFTM-2, *tr. by* Rika Lesser

Last Day of August, The. Naomi Shihab Nye. CAP-8

Last Day of the Year; or, New Year's Eve, The [*with music*]. Mrs. Henry Linden. CBWP-4

Last day of your sweet companionship, The. Dizains, Les. Maurice Scève. WoPoe, *tr. by* Phillip Lopate

Last Daybreak Song. *Unknown.* APN-2 *Fr.* Mountain Chant, The.

Last Days. Donald Hall. InoFa

Last Days. Richard Hugo. PoA 2002

Last Days. Betsy Struthers. IFF

Last Days at Teddington. Thom Gunn. OBGa

Last Days in Camden. Robert B. Shaw. ViWalt

Last Days of a Slow Cooker. Mursalata Muhammad. FTtHH

Last Days of Alice. Allen Tate. APT-2; FuPo

Last Days of Home. Dulce Maria Loynaz. *tr. by* Alan West

  "I have slept and I awaken . . . Or I haven't awakened." TANSG, *tr. by* Alan West

Last days of the summer: bright and clear, The. Harvest Gathering. Phoebe Cary. SWaP

Last Days, The: "Russet leaves of the sycamore, The." George Sterling. CalPo

Last Ditch. Jason Schneiderman. BeDoSh

Last Drunkard, The. William Bingham Tappan.

  "He stood, the last—the last of all." VerBaPo

Last enchanted white deer come to drink, The. (LL) Sanctuary. Donald Davidson. APT-1; FuPo

Last Evening. Rainer Maria Rilke. OBWP

Last Evening, The. Rainer Maria Rilke. FaBoWar, *tr. by* C. F. MacIntyre and Carlyle Ferren MacIntyre

Last Farewell to Kukutis. Marcelijus Martinaitis. TWW, *tr. by* Laima Sruoginis

Last Farewell to the Hills. Duncan Ban MacIntyre. *tr. by* Iain Crichton Smith On Ben Dorain.

  To the Air of a Pibroch. NePenScot, *tr. by* Iain Crichton Smith

Last Fire Feast, The. Daniela Gioseffi.

  "These are the word wounds." AtGh

Last Flower, The. Nova Ray. WhBo

Last freezing rain of winter. Seasonal, 1991. Roland Flint. PoCho

Last Friday, in the big light of last Friday night. Reality Is an Activity of the Most August Imagination. Wallace Stevens. APT-1; NAMCP V.1; NoAM; OxBoAm

Last Fruit Off an Old Tree, The. Walter Savage Landor.

  (Dying Speech of an Old Philosopher.) NoP-4; NoP-5

  (Finis.) OBEV

  "I strove with none, for none was worth my strife." NPeEn; OxBEV; TFi; TRP; UV

  (On His Seventy-Fifth Birthday.) CtM; OxAEP-2

Last Galway Hooker, The. Richard Murphy. PBCIP

Last Giustiniani, The. Edith Wharton. APN-2

Last Gods. Galway Kinnell. PasH; RaBo

Last Good War—and Afterward, The. Isabel Joshlin Glaser. HHAm

Last Happy Day, The. Naomi Long Madgett. FuFl

Last heard in a country church, in a prayer. Obsolescence of *Thou*, The. Rodney Jones. PoA 2002

Last Hellos, The. Les A. Murray. HarvBoo; PoCu

Last Hill in a Vista. Louise Bogan. OxBoAm

Last Hour, The. Tudor Arghezi. WoPoe, *tr. by* Michael Impey and Brian Swann

Last Hymn. Philip Paul Bliss. SacPr

Last I heard of Paul Hanson he was dead, The. Four Dead Sons. James Wright. BodElec

Last I Heard, The. Ayukawa Nobuo. PML, *tr. by* Leza Lowitz and Oketani Shogo

Last in a line of English teachers, failure's sour breath. Reading the Names. Elizabeth McLagan. FiBr

Last in before Dark. Jason Sommer. PoDa

Last Instructions. Garth Tate. ISC

Last Instructions to a Painter, The. Andrew Marvell.

  "After two sittings, now our Lady State." OBSV

  Charles II. OBSV

  "Paint Castlemaine in colours that will hold." OBSV

Last Instrument, The. Johannes Göransson. FreRad

Last Invocation, The. Walt Whitman. MoAmPo

  (Imprisoned Soul, The.) OBEV

Last Iraq, The. Fadil Azzawi. IrPoTo, *tr. by* Salaam Yousif

Last January. Last I Heard, The. Ayukawa Nobuo. PML, *tr. by* Leza Lowitz and Oketani Shogo

Last Journey. Enrique Gonzáles Martínez. TCLAP, *tr. by* Samuel Beckett

Last Journey. John Montague. ModIr; PBCIP; PNI *Fr.* Dead Kingdom, The.

Last Judgement. Blas de Otero. RaW, *tr. by* Hardie St. Martin

Last Land of Exile. Jorge Guillén. RaW, *tr. by* Charles Guenther

Last Lauch. Douglas Young. EdScPo; NBLV

Last leaf that is going to fall has fallen. Wallace Stevens. NAMCP V.1 *Fr.* Ordinary Evening in New Haven, An.

Last Leaf, The. Oliver Wendell Holmes. BRP; ITBLP; NAAL-3; TCAPo

Last Lesson of the Afternoon. D. H. Lawrence. NoAM

Last Letter. Gerald William Barrax. ESEAA

Last Letter, The. Bertus Aafjes. TuT, *tr. by* Tony Curtis and Tony Curtis

Last Lie, The. Bruce Weigl. AF; AmWaPo

Last light falls across your pictured face, The. Letter, A. Sophie Jewett. PoBW

Last light of a July evening drained, The. Cloister, The. William Matthews. CAP-8

Last lighted torch of the century, The. (LL) Come Thunder. Christopher Okigbo. HBAPE; NAMCP V.2; VCWP; WaAnP

Last Living Castrato, The. Jennifer Grotz. LegDan

Last Longhorn's Farewell, The. John P. Sjolander. TiP2

Last Look at the Mutineers, A. Matthew Rohrer. AmPoNex

Last Look in the Sambre Canal, A. John Bensko. YaYoPo

Last Love. Fyodor Ivanovich Tyutchev. WoPoe, *tr. by* Vladimir Vladimirovich Nabokov

Last Man, The. Thomas Lovell Beddoes.

  Crocodile, A. NPeEn; OxBEV

  Lake, A. NPeEn

Last Man, The. Thomas Campbell. NOBRP; NPBRoP

Last Man, The. Thom Gunn. OxAEP-2

Last Man, The. Thom Gunn. OxAEP-2 *Fr.* Misanthropos.

Last Man, The. Thomas Hood. NPBRoP

Last Marriage, A. Virginia Hamilton Adair. BeAl; StAl

Last Minutes, The. Gwyneth Lewis. ATSWP, *tr. by* Robert Minhinnick

Last night. Grand Get Together, The. Grace Birabwa Isharaza. CFP

Last night. Hazel Tells LaVerne. Katharyn Howd Machan. ReTh; SUP

Last Night. Sharon Olds. StAl

Last night. Loving Again. Gloria Wade-Gayles. ISC

Last Night: "When the sun sets, and he isn't home, she walks." Chryss Yost. CalPo; PoDa

Last night a baby gargled in the throes. Widow in Wintertime, A. Carolyn Kizer. CAP-8

Last night a bomb exploded on the veranda. Garden Fragrance. Lam Thi My Da. PoCho, *tr. by* Martha Collins and Thuy Dinh

Last night a few years ago my sister. Sky. James Harms. NAPBL

Last night a jar was emptied. Written on the Tavern Wall. Wang Ji. CCL1, *tr. by* Stephen Owen

Last night a plum branch blossomed by my door. (LL) Rebirth. Man Giac. EaWin; WoPoe, *tr. by* W. S. Merwin and Nguyen Ngoc Bich

Last night, after everybody in the neighborhood had gone to sleep. Breaking and Entering: A Very Short Novel in Verse. Bobby Byrd. ICANM

Last night, again, I dreamed. Waking in March. Philip Levine. CalPo

Last night, ah, yesternight, betwixt her lips and mine. Non Sum Qualis Eram Bonae sub Regno Cynarae. Ernest Dowson. CABP; ClHu; HeIP-4; MoBrPo; NoP-4; NoP-5; OBEV; OBMV; TFi

Last night, among his fellow roughs. Private of the Buffs; or, The British Soldier in China. Sir Francis Hastings Doyle. FaBoWar; OBEV

Last night as I was returning home alone. Cronies. Lyubomir Levchev. PML, *tr. by* Theodore Weiss

Last night, as I was sleeping. Last Night. Antonio Machado Ruiz. RaBo, *tr. by* Robert Bly

Last night at black midnight I woke with a cry. Ghosts of the Buffaloes, The. Vachel Lindsay. MoAmPo

Last night, at sunset. Vespers. Amy Lowell. NAAPv.2

Last Night at the Flamingo. John Iozia. CAGL

Last night, before I came to bear. Angel, The. James Wright. YaYoPo

Last night blonde spitfire Angie Dickinson beat steel-eyed. Brute Strength. Wanda Coleman. PmAP

Last night, dead drunk, I dawdled. Tune: "Airing Inmost Feelings." Li Ch'ing-chao. ColAnChi, *tr. by* Jiaosheng Wang

Last night, driving west along the parkway. Moonrise as Abstraction. Paul Mariani. PfSP

Last night during your reading. Andy Weaver. PoPra *Fr.* Were the Bees.

Last night for the first time since you were dead. To L. H. B. Katherine Mansfield. FaBoWar

Last night his clumsy love. Music. David Huddle. MiVo

Last night I did not fight for sleep. In Hospital: Poona (1). Alun Lewis. AngWePo; OBWVE; TCAWP

Last night, I dreamed of America. More. Ai. GT

Last night I dreamed we parted once again. Frederick Goddard Tuckerman. GSo *Fr.* Sonnets.

Last night I dreamed you drank coffee. One More Sign. Roberta Hill Whiteman. HATNAP

Last night I dreamt in Chinese. Modern Secrets. Shirley Lim. OPOU; StAl; UnSA

Last night I dreamt my father called to us. When My Dead Father Called. Robert Bly. GoPo; MAAN

Last night I flew a helicopter. Short Story. Maura Stanton. BodElec

Last night I had a dream. *Unknown.* SLW, *tr. by* Marjolijn De Jager, Sayd Bahodin Majrouh and André Velter

Last night I had a dream that has come true. *Unknown.* SLW, *tr. by* Marjolijn De Jager, Sayd Bahodin Majrouh and André Velter

Last night I had a drink with an old friend who told me that people. David McFadden. NLPA

Last night I heard your long-drawn sighs. Seeing the Beloved in a Dream. Shen Yüeh. ColAnChi, *tr. by* Richard Mather and Richard B. Mather

Last night, I heard your mother. Apology to Andrew. Richard Jones. AWTN

Last night I lay beside you, unable to sleep. Loving the Flesh. Todd Davis. ACAMVP

Last night I saw the savage world. Song for a Birth or a Death. Elizabeth Jennings. HarvBoo

Last night I saw your corpse. Joyce Mansour. HAWP, *tr. by* Willis Barnstone

Last night I spent beside my lover. Fěng Měng-lung. ColAnChi *Fr.* Mountain Songs.

Last night I started out happy. That Old Feeling. Lew Brown. ReLy

Last night / I stood in the cold dark. Coward, The. Kate Rushin. BRtP

Last night I talked to a woman. Dance Pianist, The. Angela Ball. ExTi

Last night I walked sleep-stained to the door. Stain of the Sea, The (414). Khwaja Shams-ad-din Muhammad Hafiz. WED, *tr. by* Robert Bly and Leonard Lewisohn

Last night I was close to my lover, oh evening of love not to return again! *Unknown.* SLW, *tr. by* Marjolijn De Jager, Sayd Bahodin Majrouh and André Velter

Last night I was reading the Chronicle of the Three Kingdoms. Tune: "Trimming the Silver Lamp." Fan Chung-yen. ColAnChi, *tr. by* James Robert Hightower

Last night I watched my brothers play. Brothers, The. Edwin Muir. HeIP-4

Last Night in Calcutta. Allen Ginsberg. FTOS; NAMCP V.2; NoAM

Last night in Fall River in Lafayette Park. How It Will Always Seem. David Rivard. PBCAP

Last Night in Havana. Richard Blanco. NAPBL

Last night in La Plata an avalanche of stars. La Plata, Missouri: Clear November Night. Jim Barnes. HATNAP

Last night in sleep. Dream. Jean R. Désiré. OGAHCP, *tr. by* Boadiba and Jack Hirschman

Last night in the open shippen. Christmas Day. Andrew Young. OBCP

Last night it was already half past eleven. Do You Wonder Why I Am Sleepy. James Purdy. CAGL

Last night, just as the tints of autumn's sky. Fruit-Gift, The. John Greenleaf Whittier. TCAPo

Last night my kisses drowned in the softness of black hair. Black Hair. *Unknown.* EroLit

Last night no comb held back my hair. Was I Not Made for Love? *Unknown.* CCL1, *tr. by* John Frodsham

Last night rain fell. Recollections. Lita Hunter Krohn. OWABP

Last night Ryokan. There is no ripple on the world. Paul S. Piper. AmZen

Last night, scattering rains, sudden winds. Tune: "Dream Song." Li Ch'ing-chao. ChinPo, *tr. by* Ye Weilian [*or* Yeh Wei-lien *or* Wai-lim Yip]

Last night she ran out barefoot over. Infidelities. Elaine Feinstein. MoWP

Last Night that She Lived, The. Emily Dickinson. HeIP-4; NAAL-3

Last night, The. Leaving, The. Nancy Mitchell. LaCa

Last night the apple trees shook and gave each lettuce a heart. In Defense of Our Overgrown Garden. Matthea Harvey. IIR

Last night the cherry-apple. Inscription for a Portrait. T'ang Yin. WoPoe, *tr. by* Graham Martin and John A. Scott

Last night the stars seemed not themselves. Atomic Psalm. Maurya Simon. GifTon

Last night there was rain with a soughing wind. Tune: "The Crow's Nocturnal Cry." Li Yü. ColAnChi, *tr. by* Jiaosheng Wang

Last night they took our drainpipe for the bonfire. Little Night Music, A. Paul Grattan. NIrP

Last night was the strangest night. *Unknown.* SLW, *tr. by* Marjolijn De Jager, Sayd Bahodin Majrouh and André Velter

Last night watching the Pleiades. Gary Snyder. WeW-3 *Fr.* Four Poems for Robin.

Last night we had a thunderstorm in style. Robert Louis Stevenson. NPeEn

Last night we sailed, my love and I. Barcarolle. May Probyn. VWP

Last night went walking with a woman that I know. Trap Door. Vítězslav Nezval. PFTM-1

Last night when the yellow moon. Wadasa Nakamoon, Vietnam Memorial. Ray A. Young Bear. HATNAP

Last Night When We Were Young. E. Y. Harburg. ReLy

Last night when we were young. Last Night When We Were Young. E. Y. Harburg. ReLy

Last night while I was sleeping. Antonio Machado Ruiz. BeAl, *tr. by* Willis Barnstone

Last night with hair unbrushed. *Unknown.* ChinPo, *tr. by* Ye Weilian [*or* Yeh Wei-lien *or* Wai-lim Yip]

Last Night with Rafaella. David St. John. CAP-8

Last night without sight of you my brain was ablaze. Sadi. WoPoe, *tr. by* Basil Bunting

Last night you laid it (Madam) in our dish. Sir John Harington. DiBP *Fr.* Epigrams.

Last night you were a river. Conquest. Pauli Murray. GT

Last night you were sleeping in my arms. *Unknown.* SLW, *tr. by* Marjolijn De Jager, Sayd Bahodin Majrouh and André Velter

Last night your ghost walked in at two. Deadman's Shoes. Kate Clanchy. MFPA

Last Night's Dream. Denise Levertov. NoAM

Last night's stars, last night's winds. Without Title (1). Li Shang-yin. ChinPo, *tr. by* Ye Weilian [*or* Yeh Wei-lien *or* Wai-lim Yip]

Last night's winter gale. North Shore Park. Brent MacLaine. Coast

Last of April, The. John Clare. CenSon

Last of England! O'er the sea, my dear, The. Last of England, The. Ford Madox Brown. GS

Last of England, The. Ford Madox Brown. GS

Last of England, The. Peter Porter. GS

Last of his toothpaste, last of his Wheat Chex, last. Crazy Menu. Tess Gallagher. InoFa

Last of His Tribe. Oodgeroo of the tribe Noonuccal. BMAP

Last of the Courtyard, The. Emily Grosholz. FFC

Last of the Fire Kings, The. Derek Mahon. BeAl; NAMCP V.2; PNI

Last of the shadows may close my eyes. Love Constant Beyond Death. Francisco de Quevedo y Villegas. WoPoe, *tr. by* W. S. Merwin

Last of the wheat is drought-bruised, bending, The. Walking Fields at Night South of Hampton, Iowa. Steve Gehrke. AmPoNex

Last of thy unhappy Mother's Verse, The. (LL) On the Death of My First and Dearest Child, Hector Philips. Katherine Philips. InoFa; NAEL-6v1; NAEL-7v1

Last One, The [*with music*]. W. S. Merwin. NoAM

Last Ones, The. Dan Pagis. PoSu, *tr. by* Stephen Mitchell

Last Oracle from Delphi. *Unknown.* WoPoe, *tr. by* Katherine Washburn

Last Page of the Civil War. Vladimir Vladimirovich Mayakovsky. RusPo, *tr. by* Robert Arthur Douglas Ford

Last peach in the water—full of fish and eyes, The. (LL) Leaving, The. Brigit Pegeen Kelly. IllVoic; YaYoPo

Last Performance, The. May Kendall. ViWPN

Last Picnic, The. Stanley Kunitz. AF

Last Picture, The. Philip Dacey. PoDa

Last Platform, The. Yury Timofeievich Galanskov. TCRusP, *tr. by* Olive Dehn

Last Poem. Ted Berrigan. NYP2

Last Poem. Robert Desnos. AmFaPo, *tr. by* X. J. Kennedy

Last Poem. Hsieh Ling-yün. CCL1, *tr. by* John Frodsham

Last Poem [*with music*]. Po Chü-i. CCL1, *tr. by* Arthur Waley

Last Poem. Mihály Tompa. IQMS, *tr. by* Madeline Mason

Last Poem. Hugo Williams. NPeEn

Last Poem: Goodbye to My Garden. Yuan Mei. GifTon, *tr. by* Jerome P. Seaton

Last Poem in the World, The. Hayden Carruth. TAPaP

Last Poem, Snow Tree. Norman Dubie. NAMCP V.2

Last Poem, The. Jiri Orten. AF, *tr. by* Lyn Coffin

[Last Poems]. Osip Emilevich Mandelstam. PFTM-1

Last Poems 10. Rabindranath Tagore. PoCho *Fr.* Final Poems.

Last Poems 13. Rabindranath Tagore. PoCho *Fr.* Final Poems.

Last pose flickered, failed, The. Rain after a Vaudeville Show. Stephen Vincent Benét. MoAmPo

Last Quatrain of the Ballad of Emmett Till, The. Gwendolyn Brooks. ESEAA; NAAL-5; NAMCP V.2

Last quatrain, The. (LL) Bronzeville Mother Loiters in Mississippi, A. Meanwhile, a Mississippi Mother Burns Bacon. Gwendolyn Brooks. ESEAA; FuFl; IllVoic

Last rays of the setting sun, The. Last Rays of the Sun. Juan Chi. CCL1, *tr. by* Michael Bullock and C. J. Chen

Last Rays of the Sun. Juan Chi. CCL1, *tr. by* Michael Bullock and C. J. Chen

Last Rhyme and Testament of Tony Lumpkin. Harry Morant. FaBoWar

Last Ride Together, The. Robert Browning. EroLit; ITBLP; NAEL-6v2; NAEL-7v2; OBEV

Last Rites. David Citino. UpMys

Last Rites. Christina Georgina Rossetti. FaBoVe; NPeEn

Last Rites. Francis Reginald Scott. BrAP

Last river leaves for desolation, The. Last River, The. Iwan Goll. AF, *tr. by* Galway Kinnell

Last River, The. Iwan Goll. AF, *tr. by* Galway Kinnell

Last Round, The. Anna Wickham. MoBrPo

Last Running, The. Jerry Craven. TiP2

Last Sark, The. Ellen Johnston. NePenScot

Last Scene in the First Act. Marge Piercy. NoAM

Last settlement scraggled out with a barbed wire fence, The. Flight in the Desert, The. William Everson. ChIV-2

Last Shot. Jon Veinberg. PoDa

Last Simplicity, The. Francis Ponge. MotU, *tr. by* Cid Corman

Last small credits fade, The. After a Movie. Henry Taylor. GoPo

Last Solo: Charlie Parker, Hotel Stanhope, March 12, 1955. David Jauss. MiVo

Last Song in the Rock. *Navajo Oral Tradition.* NAAPv.1

Last Song of Sappho, The. Felicia Dorothea Hemans. VWP

Last Song of Sitting Bull. *Unknown.* AmWaPo

Last Song of the Exploding Stick. *Unknown.* APN-2; NAAPv.1 *Fr.* Mountain Chant, The.

Last Song, The. Charles Bukowski. GoPo

Last Songs. Galway Kinnell. VCAP

Last Spell Cast, The. Michael Brownstein. FTOS

Last Statement [*with music*]. Vladimir Vladimirovich Mayakovsky. PBCIP, *tr. by* Tom Paulin

Last Statement for a Last Oracle. Alan Dugan. NoAM

Last Still Days in a Bunker, The. Walter McDonald. AF

Last Stop. George Seferis. AF

Last Stroll, The: Homage to Pascoli. Edoardo Sanguineti. PFTM-2, *tr. by* Richard Collins

Last summer. Eleanor Schick. CA

Last sunbeam, The. Dirge for Two Veterans. Walt Whitman. APN-1; BLT; CBCWP; ItP; MoAmPo

Last Supper, The [*with music*]. Jacques Prévert. CLPP, *tr. by* Lawrence Ferlinghetti

Last suppers, I fancy, are always wide-screen. Gwyneth Lewis. NeBl; StAl

[Last Survivor's Speech in Old English, The]. *Unknown.* NoP-5 *Fr.* Beowulf [The Complete Text in Anglo-Saxon].

Last Survivor's Speech, The. *Unknown.* NoP-5 *Fr.* Beowulf [Heaney Translation].

Last Take. Carol Muske-Dukes. GeoHom

(Unsent Letter 4: Last Take.) AmAlph

Last Testaments. Lorna Crozier.

"Before she walked into the river." LW

Last, the last, the. (LL) Company, The. Robert Creeley. FTOS; OnScMo

Last, the very last, The. Butterfly, The. Pavel Friedmann. INSAB

Last thin acre of stalks that stood, The. Immortal. Mark Van Doren. MoAmPo

Last Thing I Say, The. Marvin Bell. PoChi

Last Things. William Meredith. NAMCP V.2; NoAM

Last Things, The. Gwyn Thomas. BBMWP, *tr. by* the author

Last time he saw her he did not know that it was the, The. Lady of the Last Time, The. Vivian Lamarque. CItWP, *tr. by* Cinzia Sartini Blum and Lara Trubowitz

Last time here I suffered through ten days of flood, The. Returning to Dongrae. Chimi Sucho. BecRai, *tr. by* Kim Daljin, Kim Won-Chung and Christopher Merrill

Last time I gave my body up, The. Kill, The. Carl Phillips. WiU

Last time I saw Charlie. Bird. James E. Cherry. BtF

Last Time I Saw Chris, The. Paul Muldoon. BAP-04

Last time I saw Donald Armstrong, The. Performance, The. James Dickey. FaBoWar; InGu

Last time I saw it was 1968, The. Hiding Place, The. Jorie Graham. WaAnP

Last Time I Saw Paris, The. Oscar Hammerstein, II. ReLy

Last time I saw Paul Castle, The. At the Vietnam Memorial. George Bilgere. PoA 2002

Last time, I think. Issa. EH, *tr. by* Robert Hass

Last time i was home, The. Mothers. Nikki Giovanni. OxAAAP

Last time it was shearwaters, The. Feeding Frenzies. C. G. Hanzlicek. GeoHom

Last time the curtain arises, The. Last Performance, The. May Kendall. ViWPN

Last time you left. Greeting to Lu Yu, A. Li Yeh. CCL1, *tr. by* Chung Ling and Kenneth Rexroth

Last Train, The. Linda Pastan. GM

Last trainees are climbing the diving tower, The. Naval Trainees Learn How to Jump Overboard, The. David Wagoner. VCAP

Last Trains, The. C. G. Hanzlicek. GM

Last Trams. Kenneth Slessor. BMAP

Last Utterance of the Delphic Oracle, The. *Unknown.* OBVE, *tr. by* Kenneth Rexroth

Last Vision of Eoghan Rua Ó Súilleabháin, The. Michael Hartnett. PBCIP

Last Visit to Chestnut Middle School. Jaime Shaggy Flores. BRtP

Last, walking with stiff legs as if they carried bundles. At Last the Women are Moving. Genevieve Taggard. BeAl

Last Waltz in Santiago. Ariel Dorfman. AF, *tr. by the author*

Last War, The. Kingsley Amis. OBSV

Last war was my favourite picture story, The. In September 1939. Bernard Gutteridge. PoWW

Last Warm Day, A. Katherine Soniat. PfSP

Last watch has sounded in K'uei-chou, The. Dawn Landscape. Tu Fu [*or* Du Fu]. NDACCP, *tr. by* David Hinton

Last week a half-crazed Mormon woman in blue-white. Pharaoh's Palace. David Wojahn. AllShUp

Last week, the old men drove out from the winery. Why I Make the Best Barrels. Eliza Garza. IPoFL

Last week you gathered armfuls of apple blossoms. Apple Shrine, The. Linda Pastan. Vesp

Last white sawdust on the floor was grown, The. Edna St. Vincent Millay. NALW *Fr.* Sonnets from an Ungrafted Tree.

Last Will and Testament. Hans Magnus Enzensberger. PoSu

Last Will and Testament. Thomas McGrath. PoChi

Last Will and Testament. Géza Páskándi. IQMS, *tr. by* J. G. Nichols

Last Will and Testament, A. John Winstanley. FaBoVe; OBSV

Last Window. Dewi Stephen Jones. BBMWP, *tr. by* the author

Last winter, there was this one time when I was just talking with some of my juniors who want to be writers. Memo on Composition. Hwang Jiwoo. CAMKP, *tr. by* Young-Jun Lee and Scott Swaner

Last Wolf, The. Mary Tallmountain. ReEnLa

Last Word, A. Ernest Dowson. GSo; MoBrPo

Last word I can picture you saying to me, The. Mains du Bon Dieu, Les. Jack Bedell. Vesp

Last Word of a Bluebird, The. Robert Frost. NOxBChV

Last Word, The. Imamu Amiri Baraka. UnSA

Last Word, The. Gaylord Brewer. RWB

Last Words. William Matthews. PoA 2002

Last Words before Winter. Louis Untermeyer. MoAmPo

Last Words: "I do not want a plain box, I want a sarcophagus." Sylvia Plath. BrAP

Last Words of My English Grandmother, The. William Carlos Williams. APT-1; InoFa; NAMCP V.1; PtR; RaBo; SAmP

Last Words of the Prophet. *Unknown.* APN-2 *Fr.* Mountain Chant, The.

Last Words on Greece. Lord Byron. CAGL

Last words 184, 185, 186, 187, 188, 189, 190. (LL) Index. Paul Violi. OxBoAm; PmAP

Last year a molar fell out. Losing a Tooth. Han Yü. CCL1, *tr. by* Stephen Owen

Last year fighting at the source of the Sang-kan. Fighting South of the Wall. Li Po. WoPoe, *tr. by* Elling O. Eide

Last year I lost an. Poem on Losing One's Teeth. Han Yü. GifTon, *tr. by* Kenneth O. Hanson

Last year I made up a baby. I made her in the shape of a hatbox or a cake. Ideas Go Only So Far. Matthea Harvey. LegDan

Last year I used to ride the J CHURCH Line. J Car, The. Thom Gunn. MakPoe

Last year in a lovely temple in Hirosawa. Hakugai. ZenPo, *tr. by* Takashi Ikemoto and Lucien Stryk

Last year the magnolias flared. On Commonwealth Avenue and Brattle Street. Diana Der Hovanessian. UrbNat

Last year we fought by the springs of Sankan river. Fighting on the South Frontier. Li Po. TAL

Last year when I accompanied you. To a Traveler. Su Tung-p'o. NDACCP, *tr. by* Kenneth Rexroth

Lasting Things, The. Franz Werfel. GTCP, *tr. by* Reinhold Grimm

Lasting visage in a lasting bush, A. Wallace Stevens. NAMCP V.1 *Fr.* Notes toward a Supreme Fiction.

Lastly, Marvelous, I wanted to be rich. E-Mail. Reetika Vazirani. NAPBL

Lastness. Galway Kinnell.

"Black bear sits alone, A." RaBo

Laszlo. Frieda Hughes. NeBl

Lat no man come into this halle. *Unknown.* OHMEL

Lat take a cat, and fostre him [*or* hym] wel[l] with milk. Geoffrey Chaucer. TriCat *Fr.* Canterbury Tales, The.

Latching On, Falling Off. Beth Ann Fennelly. NevBe

Late. Benjamin Paul Blood. APN-2

Late. Louise Bogan. APT-2

Late Afternoon. Molly Fisk. PasH

Late afternoon and the man finds himself. Language of Departure. Peter Cooley. PML

Late Afternoon at the Arboretum. Kelly Cherry. SwNoth

Late afternoon, autumn equinox. Natural History. Sam Hamill. PoChi

Late afternoon. Huancayo. We'd made the long haul down. Trick, A. Steve Kowit. SUP

Late afternoon in July, too early to begin, A. Gypsy, The. Susan Stewart. CFP

Late Afternoon, Late in the Twentieth Century. Jeffrey Skinner. PBCAP

Late afternoon rain of a postponed summer. Dusk: July. Marilyn Hacker. FFC

Late Apollo. Carl Phillips. AmAlph

Late Apostasy, A. V. Penelope Pelizzon. AmPoNex

Late April and you are three; today. W. D. Snodgrass. NoP-5; VCAP Fr. Heart's Needle.

Late Arrivals. Sybil Kollar. FFC

Late arrivals at Mass, in lace. Sunday. Mário de Andrade. TCLAP, tr. by Jack E. Tomlins

Late as last summer. Thou Didst Say Me. Miriam Waddington. BrAP

Late at een, drinkin' the wine. Dowie Houms o' Yarrow, The [Hogg Version from Scotch Ballads, Materials for Border Minstrelsy; Scott's Minstrelsy]. Unknown. OBEV

Late at night I sit alone and work on deadwood zen. Han-shan Te-ch'ing. CSKM, tr. by Red Pine

"Late at night I stood on a battlement." Der von Kürenberg. GePo

Late at night, listening to the winter rain. Ryokan. AWTN Fr. Winter.

Late at night, when you're so lonely. Pure Loneliness, The. Michael Ryan. BodElec

Late Aubade, A. Richard Wilbur. BrAP; SoSe-8

Late August, before the harvest, every one of us worn down. Hungry Gap-Time, The. Thomas Lux. AmAlph

Late August, given heavy rain and sun. Blackberry-Picking. Seamus Heaney. ChAP; PtR

Late August on the Lido. John Hollander. YaYoPo

Late August, say the records, when the gowk-storm. Chartres of Gowrie, The. Don Paterson. NePenScot

Late Author: Snapshot in the Rain, The. Dan Pagis. FIT, tr. by Robert Friend

Late autumn, a brief shower. Lament. Liu Yung. CrYelRi, tr. by Sam Hamill

Late autumn labyrinth. Out in the Open. Tomas Tranströmer. WED, tr. by Robert Bly

Late autumn strips the distant hills. To a Friend. Li Po. CrYelRi, tr. by Sam Hamill

Late Bloomer at the Front of My Garden. Li Po. ColAnChi, tr. by Elling O. Eide

Late Bus (After a Series of Hold-Ups). Russell Atkins. LTA

Late butterflies gliding through the air. Poem. Timothy Liu. NeAmPo; TAPaP

Late day flames. Evening Song. Ralph J., Jr. Mills. IllVoic

Late December noon, near freezing. Parthenon at Nashville, The. Joe Bolton. AmPoNex

Late December, Where Are You, Robert Frost? Willis Barnstone. VisFro

Late Echo. John Ashbery. PoA 2002; WaAnP

Late evening cow, The. Buson. SoOfWa, tr. by Sam Hamill

Late evening finally comes. Yakamochi. ErotSp, tr. by Sam Hamill

Late evening, July, and no one at home. California Twilight. Charles Wright. GeoHom

Late Flight of The Love God. Mona Van Duyn. ExTi

Late for Breakfast. Mary Dawson. TLR

Late Fragment. Raymond Carver. IJHIL; StAl

Late Friday / we watched Eddie blow the blues. With Thanks to Eddie Shaw. Janet Lowe. PasH

Late Ghazal. Adrienne Rich. HarvBoo

Late Hour, The. Mark Strand. AWTN

Late Hours. Lisel Mueller. GoPo

Late, I love but quietness. To Magistrate Zhang. Wang Wei. CCL1, tr. by Jerome P. Seaton

Late in an evening as I walk'd alone. Complaint of Thames 1647 When the Best of Kings Was Imprisoned by the Worst of Rebels at Holmbie, The. Hester Lee Pulter. EMWP

Late in Han. Tune: "Happily Flitting Oriole." Wu Li. ColAnChi, tr. by Jonathan Chaves

Late in life, I care for ease alone. Reply to a Magistrate. Wang Wei. CrYelRi, tr. by Sam Hamill

Late in November. Thaw, The. Marianne Wolfe. GifTon

Late in the afternoon of Halloween. Wall between Us, The. Mark Vinz. VisFro

Late in the Day, Gazing Out from a River Pavilion. Chia Tao. CSKM, tr. by Mike O'Connor

Late in the day, the sun. Midsummer. Sherod Santos. GeoHom

Late in the Forest I did Cupid See. Mary Sidney Wroth, Countess of Montgomery. NPeEn; OxBSo; PBRV Fr. Pamphilia to Amphilanthus.

Late in the morning, on the side balcony. Breakfast on the Balcony. Yevgeny Borisovich Rein. TCRusP, tr. by Daniel Weissbort

Late in the season the world digs in, the fat blossoms. Over and Over Stitch. Jorie Graham. VCAP

Late Indian summer's. Sun Bu-er. WoPoe; WPoS, tr. by Jane Hirshfield

Late into every night, Penelope carefully undid almost that whole day's work. Room with a view. Robert John Moore. Coast

Late, just past midnight. Off from Swing Shift. Garrett Kaoru Hongo. GeoHom; ReTh

Late Lamented Fame of the Giant City of New York. Bertolt Brecht. FaBoA Fr. Late Lamented Fame of the Giant City of New York.

Late Lamented Fame of the Giant City of New York. Bertolt Brecht. tr. by Frank Jellinek

Late Lamented Fame of the Giant City of New York. FaBoA

Late Lamented Wind, Burned in Indignation, The. Bob Kaufman. EGAG

Late lark twitters from the quiet skies, A. W. E. Henley. MoBrPo; OBEV Fr. Echoes.

Late, Last Rook, The. Ralph Hodgson. MoBrPo

Late, late in a gloamin' Kilmeny came hame! (LL) James Hogg. OBEV; OxAEP-2 Fr. Queen's Wake, The.

Late, late, so late! and dark the night and chill! Alfred Tennyson. SacPr

Late lies the wintry sun a-bed. Winter Time [or Winter-Time]. Robert Louis Stevenson. MoBrPo

Late Light. Joseph Somoza. ICANM

Late light allows us to begin. 59th Light Poem: for La Monte Young and Marian Zazeela—6 November 1982. Jackson Mac Low. PmAP

Late light, uneven mole-gnawed meadow. Afternoon Walk: The Sea Ranch. Sandra M. Gilbert. ASA

Late Lights in Minnesota. Ted Kooser. BLT

Late March mist is an angry Cerberus, The. Persephone, 1978. Thomas McCarthy. ModIr

Late Minoan I: (Ewers of Hagia Triada). Lorand Gaspar. YaTCFP, tr. by Ronnie Scharfman

Late Mr Charles Lynch Digresses, The. Paul Durcan. ModIr

Late night fog. Holy Body. Susan Griffin. ASA

Late Night Movies I. John Yau. OnScMo

Late Night Ode. Horace. PfSP; WaAnP; WiU; WoPoe, tr. by J. D. McClatchy

Late Night Radio. Geoff Page. BMAP

Late Night Radio. Aleda Shirley. ExTi

Late night, you and the dog. At Twelve. Elizabeth McLagan. FiBr

Late nights without hope. Nights Without Hope (Rebetiko Song). Yannis Papaionnou. WoPoe, tr. by Gail Holst-Warhaft

Late November on our way to work. I Learn a Lesson About Our Society. Janice Gould. GeoHom

Late October Camping in the Sawtooths. Gary Snyder. BLT

Late October sun. White Earth. Gerald Vizenor. HATNAP

Late on another winter day in Indiana, lake water. Envying the Art of the Cartographer. Edward Byrne. RWB

Late one night, alone in bed, the book. J. D. McClatchy. PoA 2002 Fr. Essay on Friendship, An.

Late one night I hear his breath. Coltrane and My Father. Ralph Sneeden. SeSe

Late Passenger, The. Clive Staples Lewis. P180

Late Psalm. Betsy Sholl. ACAMVP; MAAN

Late repentance, and the long despair, The. To George Sand on her Interview with Elizabeth Barrett Browning. Isa Blagden. VWP

Late Richard Dadd, 1817–1886, The. Michael Hofmann. NeBrP

Late Round. Kim Addonizio. MoASP

Late Sabbath afternoon, remembering. Home for Winter. Marcia Falk. TaR

Late Season. Sydney Lea. WaAnP

Late Show, The. Rachel Wetzsteon. NeAmPo

Late Singer, The. William Carlos Williams. SAmP

Late Sir John Ogilvy, The. William McGonagall. VerBaPo

Late Snow. M. R. Peacocke. BeAl

Late Spring. Robert Hass. BLT

Late Spring. Meng Hao Jan. NDACCP, tr. by William Carlos Williams

Late Spring. Tzu Yeh. CrYelRi, tr. by Sam Hamill

Late Spring in the Nuclear Age. Andrew Hudgins. AtGh

Late spring / Paling rose. Sodo. ZenPo, tr. by Takashi Ikemoto and Lucien Stryk

Late Summer. Ruth L. Schwartz. AmPoNex

Late summer, and at midnight. Guttural Muse, The. Seamus Heaney. HarvBoo

Late Summer Litany. Julie Moulds. AmPoNex

Late Summer News. Dorothy Barresi. SwNoth

Late summer rain crashes, The. La Fabrique de Tabac (Tobacco Harvest). Beverly Matherne. TWW

Late summers, early autumns, you can see something that binds. Adrienne Rich. NAAL-5; WaAnP *Fr.* Atlas of the Difficult World, An.

Late sun opening the book. Siesta in Xbalba. Allen Ginsberg.

Late that summer. Surrendered Names. Gerald Vizenor. HATNAP

Late that summer my girlfriend's boyfriend. Fifteen. Richard Frost. NevBe

Late tonight, when Sears or Penney's. What We Could Do. William Trowbridge. SUP

Late 20th Century: Spring. Jerry Martien. GeoHom

Late Twentieth-Century Prayer, A. Ernest Sandeen. WeW-3

Late Wasp, The. Edwin Muir. HarvBoo

Late Winter. James McAuley. BMAP

Late Winter. Ice cold and drained of color. GWB in the Rain, The. Mary Stewart Hammond. KGB

Late Winter in Menard County. John Knoepfle. IllVoic

Late Winter in West Texas. Robert Burlingame. TiP2

Late winter, sky darkening after school. Euphoria. Major L. Jackson. LegDan

Late Wisdom. George Crabbe. OBEV *Fr.* Reflections.

Late Words for My Sister. Robin Becker. ExTi

Late-born and woman-souled I dare not hope. Echoes. Emma Lazarus. APN-2; GSo; NAAPv.1

Late-born daughters of famous fathers, The. Late-Born Daughters, The. Lisel Mueller. ExTi

Late-Born Daughters, The. Lisel Mueller. ExTi

Late-Flowering Lust. Sir John Betjeman. BrAP

Lately, alas, I knew a gentle boy. Sympathy. Henry David Thoreau. CAGL

Lately, I've become accustomed to the way. Preface to a Twenty Volume Suicide Note. Imamu Amiri Baraka. AmFaPo; BB; ESEAA

Lately, I've been watching them, pecking. Some Sparrows. Ernesto Trejo. PoCho

Lately, I've begun to look. Trip to Delphi. Alice Friman. RWB

Lately my neighbor wheezes. Running. Leslie Ullman. PBCAP

Lately on yonder swelling bush. Budd, The. Edmund Waller. PBRV

Lately she thinks. Other Tongues. Lynne Weiss. PfS

Lately, too much disturbed, you stay breathing in me. Apology. Joanna Klink. IIR

Later, a cormorant. Cormorant. Peter Preece. AngWePo

Later, back in my cell, back in the thick stench. Between the Lines. Michael Hamburger. HP

Later he must have watched. Swimming in the Flood. John Burnside. EmeKit

Later Life: A Double Sonnet of Sonnets. Christina Georgina Rossetti.
  Later Life: A Double Sonnet of Sonnets. WPoS
  "Something this foggy day, a something which." NAEL-6v2 (Sonnet 26.) VWP

Later, on the Neckar's oil-slick banks. On Finding a Swastika Carved on a Tree in the Hills above Heidelberg. Kevin Prufer. AmPoNex; LegDan

Later Still. Philip Levine. ColAP; WaAnP

Later that night you find yourself in someone else's house. Athens. Vladimir Levchev. CSCBP, *tr. by* Georgi Belev and Lisa Sapinkopf

Later, the doctor called Shiva Kincaid will send me home. Third Stair, Seventh Stair, Landing. Jane Mead. SweBea

Later, when you climb the stairs. (LL) Onions. William Matthews. CAP-8; EmeKit

Lateral Disregard. Harry Mathews. BAP-04; NYP2

Late-rising moon. (LL) Night Song of the Los Angeles Basin. Gary Snyder. PfSP; UrbNat

Latest Decalogue, The. Arthur Hugh Clough. BrAP; CABP; ChIV-1; NAEL-6v2; NAEL-7v2; NoP-4; NoP-5; NPeEn; OBSV; OxBEV; SacPr; TFi; WeW-3; WoPoe

Latest Hotel Guest Walks Over Particles That Revolve in Seven Other Dimensions Controlling Latticed Space, The. Ruth Stone. OxBoAm

Latest News. David Craig. RSaN

Latest once-more-with-feeling-please, The. Summer, A. Carl Phillips. AmAlph

Latet Anguis. William Cornish. OBEV

Lathe we were at, The. Metal-work. David Morley. NLP

Latin and Soul for Joe Bataan. Víctor Hernández Cruz. PueRic

Latin Lesson, The. Eavan Boland. ModIr

Latin Music in New York. Jessica Tarahata Hagedorn. FTtHH; PmAP

Latin Night at the Pawnshop. Martín Espada. TRP

Latitudes of Home, The. Alistair Elliot. OxBSo

Latte, Il. Edward Jerningham. STuOW

Latter rain, it falls in anxious haste, The. Latter Rain, The. Jones Very. APN-1; TCAPo

Latter Rain, The ("Latter rain, it falls in anxious haste, The.") Jones Very. APN-1; TCAPo

Latter-day Mother Courage. Maria del Rosario. CFP, *tr. by* Gail Wronsky

Latter-Day Warnings. Oliver Wendell Holmes. NCAP

Lattice at/of (Com)pare (Dis)pair. Tina Darragh. FTOS

Lattice at "Split." Tina Darragh. FTOS

Latticed Culotte and Starry Blouse. Alice Notley. AHA

Latvian Autumn, The. Johannes Bobrowski. PoSu

Latvian Songs. Johannes Bobrowski. AF

Laud and Praise Made For Our Sovereign Lord the King. John Skelton. PBRV *Fr.* Lawde and Prayse Made for Our Sovereigne Lord the Kyng, A.

Laudare. Constance Carrier. APT-2

Lauds. W. H. Auden. BBASP *Fr.* Horae Canonicae.

Laugh and Be Merry. John Masefield. MoBrPo

Laugh, and the world laughs with you. Solitude. Ella Wheeler Wilcox. BRP; GoPo; SWaP; TCAPo

Laugh / talk / joke. Let's Just Tell It. Jabari Asim. FuFl

Laugh that ate the snake and, The. Laugh, The. Don McKay. OpeFie

Laugh, The. Don McKay. OpeFie

Laughable. Aimé Césaire. ConPit, *tr. by* Clayton Eshleman and Annette Smith

Laughin at Cha. Kenneth Carroll. BRtP

Laughing All the Way. Liz Cashdan. Prnts

Laughing at Myself. Chŏng Yagyong. CATKP, *tr. by* Chi-gyu Kim [*or* Kim Chonggil]

Laughing at Myself 1. Ching An. CSKM, *tr. by* Jerome P. Seaton

Laughing at Myself 2. Ching An. CSKM, *tr. by* Jerome P. Seaton

Laughing at that. (LL) Reality Demands. Wisława Szymborska. BeAl; VCWP, *tr. by* Stanisław Barańczak and Clare Cavanagh

Laughing Gas. Ruth Whitman. UnSA

Laughing, merry, childish voices, woke us in their eager glee. Christmas, South, 1866. Mary E. Tucker. CBWP-1

Laughing Moon, The. Moniza Alvi. MFPA

Laughing Mountain. Muso Soseki. EaWin, *tr. by* W. S. Merwin

Laughing out of pearls, / A full moon appears. Abū l-'Abbās Al-A'mā at-Tuṭīlī. HiArP, *tr. by* James T. Monroe

Laughing Song. William Blake. *See* When the Green Woods Laugh.

Laughing the stormy, husky, brawling laughter of Youth, half-naked, sweating, proud to be Hog Butcher, Tool Maker, Stacker of Wheat, Player with Railroads and Freight Handler to the Nation. (LL) Chicago. Carl Sandburg. AmFaPo; APT-1; BRP; ColAP; EMP; FaBoA; FTtHH; IllVoic; MoAmPo; NAAL-5; NAAPv.2; NAMCP V.1; NoAM; NoP-4; NoP-5; OxBoAm; PoA 2002; TCAPo; TFi; TRP; WaAnP

Laughing through clouds, his milk-teeth still unshed. Rudyard Kipling. PoWW *Fr.* Epitaphs of the War [1914–1918].

Laughing, with a TV's blue-static figures. When Loneliness Is a Man. Yusef Komunyakaa. AWTN; OxAAAP

Laughing youngsters, The. Spring Song. Federico García Lorca. SpanPo, *tr. by* Rachel Benson and Robert O'Brien

Laughs gayly o'er their burial place. (LL) Unknown Dead, The. Henry Timrod. AmWaPo; PCW

Laughter. Wisława Szymborska. PoSu, *tr. by* Magnus F. Krynski

Laughter in the Senate. Sidney Lanier. AmWaPo

Laughter our first noun, and our long verb, howl. (LL) Nurture. Maxine W. Kumin. CAP-8; PoA 2002

Laughter out of dead bellies. (LL) Ezra Pound. AmWaPo; HarvBoo; HeIP-4; InoFa; MoAmPo; NPeEn; OBWP; OxBoAm; PoAgWa; PoWW; TRP; WaAnP *Fr.* Hugh Selwyn Mauberley (Life and Contacts).

Launch into writing and you launch into the unnamed future, with language as a cutting edge. Provisionally. Ken Edwards. Oth

Launch thy bark, mariner. Mariner's Hymn. Caroline Anne Bowles Southey. TreFP

Launching Into Eternity. Isaac Watts. SacPr

Launching Our Community Developement Fund. Tanure Ojaide. HBAPE

Laundress, The. Velemir Khlebnikov. *tr. by* Kathy Lewis and Bob Perelman Burning Field, The. TCRusP, *tr. by* Kathy Lewis and Bob Perelman

Laundress, The. Thomas Kinsella. HarvBoo

Laundromat, The. Dorianne Laux. SUP

Laundry so near the ocean bothered Frank. Duo-Tang. Kenward Elmslie. AHA; FTOS

Laundry Song, The. Wen Yi-tuo [*or* Wen I-to]. NAAPv.2

Laundry spread out, clothing and house-linens held by clothespins. Alberto Giacometti. René Char. MotU, *tr. by* Charles Guenther

Laundryman, The. Karai Senryū. EMJL, *tr. by* Makoto Ueda

Laura. Thomas Campion. *See* Rose-cheeked Laura[, Come].

Laura. Johnny Mercer. ReLy

Laura Cashdollars. Bernadette Mayer. NYP2

Laura to Petrarch.　Mary Robinson.　CenSon

Laura Waits for Him in Heaven.　Petrarch.　OBMV *Fr.* Sonnets to Laura.

Laura was lightsome, gay, and free from guile.　Caroline Elizabeth Norton.　VWP *Fr.* Marriage and Love.

Lauras.　Günter Eich.　MotU, *tr.* by David Walker

Laureate.　Hugh Seidman.　BodElec

Laureate, The.　William Edmonstoune Aytoun.　UV

Laureate, The.　Robert Graves.　OBSV

Laurel Axe, The.　Geoffrey Hill.　NAEL-6v2; NAEL-7v2; NoAM; NoP-4; NoP-5; NPeEn *Fr.* Apology for the Revival of Christian Architecture in England, An.

Laurel in the Berkshires.　Adelaide Crapsey.　NAAPv.2

Laurel of Liberty. A Poem, The.　Robert Merry.
　"Genius, or Muse, whate'er thou art! whose thrill."　NOBRP

Laurel Street, 1950.　Dorothy Perry Thompson.　SpirFl

Laurence Olivier's Hamlet.　David Oliveira.　IaFF

Laurentian Shield.　Francis Reginald Scott.　BrAP

Laus Deo.　Roland Mathias.　AngWePo *Fr.* Tide-Reach.

Laus Deo!　John Greenleaf Whittier.　CBCWP; PCW

Lavatory Attendant, The.　Wendy Cope.　MoWP; UV

Lavender light laces through fretwork.　Air like stained glass cuts me, The.　Marge Piercy.　FiBr

Lavender Windowpanes and White Curtains.　Juan Ramón Jiménez.　WED, *tr.* by Robert Bly

Lavender windowpanes! They are like a pedigree of nobility.　Lavender Windowpanes and White Curtains.　Juan Ramón Jiménez.　WED, *tr.* by Robert Bly

Lavender Woman, The.　Lizette Woodworth Reese.　APN-2

Laventie.　Ivor Gurney.　NAMCP V.1

Laventille.　Derek Walcott.　NAMCP V.2

Lavinia.　Özdemir Asaf.　NaPG, *tr.* by Talat Sait Halman

Lavinia.　Kathleen Kirk.　IaFF

Law.　Tiziano Rossi.　ItPo, *tr.* by Gayle Ridinger

Law, The.　Samuel Butler.　NBLV

Law against Lovers, The.　Sir William Davenant.
　(Viola's Song.)　NOSC

Law and order isn't easy.　Rotten fish.　Karen Press.　TSAP

Law can take a purse in open court, The.　Law, The.　Samuel Butler.　NBLV

Law Given at Sinai, The.　Isaac Watts.　ChIV-1

Law. I dedicate my awakening to this matter. (LL)　Geoffrey Hill.　NoP-4; NoP-5 *Fr.* Mercian Hymns.

Law is plain, The.　First Stone, The.　Vievee Francis.　NevBe

Law is rootless and thus grows out of itself, The.　On Arriving at Oeo Temple.　Jinkag Haesim.　BecRai, *tr.* by Kim Daljin, Kim Won-Chung and Christopher Merrill

Law like Love.　W. H. Auden.　OxBoAm

Law makes long spokes of the short stakes of men.　Legal Fiction.　William Empson.　HarvBoo; NoAM; NoP-4; NoP-5

Law of Trichotomy.　Holley Blackwell.　AnSo

Law, say the gardeners, is the sun.　Law like Love.　W. H. Auden.　OxBoAm

Law That Says, The.　Sipho Sepamla.　AF

Law was ever above kings, The.　Morgan Llwyd.　AngWePo *Fr.* Charles, the last king of Britain.

Law which (as they say) Priapus coined, The.　*Unknown.*　PriapPo *Fr.* Priapus Poems, The.

Law, which each citizen knows well.　Boris Abramovich Slutsky.　TCRusP, *tr.* by Daniel Weissbort

Lawd, Dese Colored Chillum.　Ruby C. Saunders.　LTA

Lawd Zambesi!　For Singing In Good Mood.　Lebert Bethune.　GT

Lawde and Prayse Made for Our Sovereigne Lord the Kyng, A.　John Skelton.　Laud and Praise Made For Our Sovereign Lord the King.　PBRV

Lawn as white as driven snow.　William Shakespeare.　NoSic; NPeEn *Fr.* Winter's Tale, The.

Lawn of Excluded Middle.　Rosmarie Waldrop.　FTOS
　"It's a tall order that expects pain to crystallize into beauty. And we must."　PfS

Lawn Roller, The.　Robert Layzer.　OBGa

Lawn Sprinkler, The.　Queen Lili'u-o-ka-lani.　WoPoe, *tr.* by Alfons L. Korn and Mary Kawena Pukui

Lawrence.　Tony Hoagland.　SUP

Lawrence and Edison in New Jersey: 1923.　Linda Bierds.　ExTi

Lawrence of virtuous [*or* vertuous] Father virtuous [*or* vertuous] Son.　To Mr. Lawrence.　John Milton.　OBEV
　(*Lawrence* of vertuous Father vertuous Son.)　PBRV

Laws.　Carol Frost.　CAP-8

Laws are the secret avengers, The.　Avengers, The.　Edwin Markham.　MoAmPo

Laws of blind unrest, not art, The.　Prayer.　Kathleen Jessie Raine.　BBASP

Laws of God, the Laws of Man, The.　A. E. Housman.　CAGL; MoBrPo; NPeEn; OBSV

Laws of Gravity.　Paul Farley.　BeAl

Lawyer and the critic but behold, The.　Lord Byron.　NePenScot *Fr.* Don Juan.

Lawyer had a legal mouse, A.　Legal Mouse, A.　Lizelia Augusta Jenkins Moorer.　CBWP-3

Lawyer says, The.　Deposed.　John Alexander Frazier, Jr.　BtF

Lawyers.　*Unknown.*　OBCoV

Lawyers themselves uphold the commonweal.　Lawyers.　*Unknown.*　OBCoV

Lay a garland on my hearse.　Francis Beaumont *and* John Fletcher.　OBEV *Fr.* Maid's Tragedy, The.

Lay aside phrases; speak as in the night.　This Is Not Death.　Humbert Wolfe.　MoBrPo

Lay down, boys, and take a little nap / Lay down, boys, and take a little nap.　Cumberland Gap.　*Unknown.*　APN-2

Lay down the red carpet—My dowry is death. (LL)　Streets of Laredo, The.　Louis MacNeice.　FaBoWar; OBWP

Lay down their life; they do not hate. (LL)　At a Calvary near the Ancre.　Wilfred Owen.　ChIV-2; GI

Lay down these words.　Riprap.　Gary Snyder.　CalPo; NAAL-5; NAMCP V.2; NoAM; OxBoAm; PmAP; PoCho; PoPoPo; VCAP

Lay me down beneaf de willers in de grass.　Death Song, A.　Paul Laurence Dunbar.　InoFa; OxAAAP

Lay me on an anvil, O God.　Prayers of Steel.　Carl Sandburg.　BeAl; MoAmPo; SSCS

Lay of a Golden Goose, The.　Louisa May Alcott.　SWaP

Lay of an Irish Harp, or Metrical Fragments, The.　Sydney, Lady Morgan Owenson.
　Fragment 10. The Boudoir.　RWP
　Fragment 19. L'Amant Mutin.　RWP
　Fragment 35. The Irish Jig.　RWP

Lay of Ike, The.　John Berryman.　OxBoAm *Fr.* Dream Songs.

Lay of King Saint Ladislas, The.　*Unknown.*　IQMS, *tr.* by Anthony Edkins

Lay of the Lash, The.　*Unknown.*　FaBoWar

Lay of the Last Minstrel, The.　Sir Walter Scott.
　Branksome's Heir and the Hound.　DiBP
　"Breathes there the [*or* a] Man with soul so dead."　ITBLP; NePenScot; OxBEV; SoSe-8; TFi
　(Innominatus.)　OBEV
　Love.　OxAEP-2
　Melrose Abbey.　NPBRoP; OxAEP-2
　Minstrel, The.　OxAEP-2
　(Nature's Sympathy with the Poet.)　OxAEP-2
　"O Caledonia! stern and wild."　NePenScot
　(Patriotism.)　OxAEP-2
　(Poet, The.)　TreFP

Lay of the Rover.　Aimé Césaire.　WoPoe, *tr.* by Gregson Davis

Lay of the Trilobite.　May Kendall.　NPeEn; ViWPN; VWP

Lay [*or* Short Lay] of Sigurd, The.　*Unknown. Fr.* Elder Edda, The.

Lay these words into the dead man's grave.　In Memoriam Paul Celan.　Edward Hirsch.　MakPoe

Lay This Body Down.　*Unknown.*　SSUS

Lay your head in my lap.　Olga Popova.　ItGoST, *tr.* by J. Kates

Lay your head on a block of butter and chop.　Lakshminkara.　WPoS

Lay your sleeping head, my love.　Lullaby.　W. H. Auden.　EMP; HarvBoo; ItP; NAEL-6v2; NAEL-7v2; NAMCP V.1; NoAM; NoP-4; NoP-5; OxAEP-2; OxBEV; StAl; TFi; WaAnP; WeW-3

Lay Your Sleeping Head, My Love.　W. H. Auden. *See* Lullaby: "Lay your sleeping head, my love."

Layered, The.　Nick Laird.　NIrP

Layers, The.　Stanley Kunitz.　BodElec; CAP-8; ItP

Laying a fart.　Karai Senryū.　EMJL, *tr.* by Burton Watson

Laying Down the Tower.　Marge Piercy.
　Seven of Pentacles, The.　IPoFL; TWF

Laying the Dust.　Denise Levertov.　BrAP; MoWP

Laying the foundations of community, she labors all alone.　Regret for a Spider Web.　James Wright.　MotU

Laying the pen aside, when he had signed.　Faustus.　Alec Derwent Hope.　NOBAu

Layla, / promise that you will be my salvation.　Dread.　Sadiq al-Saygh.　IrPoTo, *tr.* by Ralph Saverese and Saadi A. Simawe

Layman's Lament, The.　Judyth Collin.　WhBo

Layoffs and ransacked apartments, the, The.　May 1988.　Susan Stewart.　AmAlph

Lays of Ancient Rome. Thomas Babington Macaulay, 1st Baron Macaulay. Horatius [*or* Horatius at the Bridge]. CABP; FaBoWar; OBNV; OBWP; OxAEP-2

"But hark! the cry is Astur." OBWP

"Then out spake brave Horatius." CABP; TreFP

Lazarus. James Keir Baxter. HarvBoo

Lazarus. Anne Carson. WaAnP *Fr.* TV Men.

Lazarus. Ron Koertge. OPRER

Lazarus. Ágnes Nemes Nagy. IQMS, *tr. by* Adam Makkai

Lazarus. Ágnes Nemes Nagy. IQMS, *tr. by* Hugh Maxton

Lazarus. Ágnes Nemes Nagy. IQMS, *tr. by* Ila Egon

Lazarus. Ágnes Nemes Nagy. PoSu, *tr. by* Frederic Will

Lazarus / don't come forth from the grave. Anti-Lazarus, The. Nicanor Parra. GI, *tr. by* Edith Grossman

Lazarus (1st draft). Anne Carson. WaAnP

Lazarus, of course. Translation of Raimundo Luz, The: My Incredulity. Scott Cairns. UpMys

Lazarus' Sister. Elaine Feinstein. HarvBoo

Lazarus Standup: Shooting Script. Anne Carson. NAMCP V.2

Laziest Gal in Town, The. Cole Porter. ReLy

Laziest man ever was Floyd Scott. Lazy. David Lee. GoPo

Lazily I stir a white feather fan. In the Mountains on a Summer Day. Li Po. TAL

Lazy. David Lee. GoPo

Lazy. Lu Yu. NDACCP, *tr. by* Kenneth Rexroth

Lazy Afternoon. John Latouche. ReLy

Lazy are slaughtered, The. Measures Taken, The. Erich Fried. WoPoe, *tr. by* Michael Hamburger

Lazy cattails and the rain, The. (LL) Day after Chasing Porcupines. James Welch. NoAM; WaAnP

Lazy Cloud's Nest 1. Ali Hsiying. ColAnChi, *tr. by* Jerome P. Seaton

Lazy Cloud's Nest 2. Ali Hsiying. ColAnChi, *tr. by* Jerome P. Seaton

Lazy dog (a bomb containing ten), The. John Cage. APSN *Fr.* Diary: How to Improve the World (You Will Only Make Matters Worse).

Lazy eternity. J unsubtle serif H or gemini a fish or eternity in(terrupt)completed, A. Jill Hartman. PoPra

Lazy flowers brew honey for the bees. Love Song. Hu Chih-yu. CrYelRi, *tr. by* Sam Hamill

Lazy Man, The. *Unknown.* WoPoe, *tr. by* Ulli Beier and Bakare Gbadamosi

Lazy Man's Haiku, The. John Ridland. CalPo

Lazy Man's Song. Po Chü-i. OBVE, *tr. by* Arthur Waley

Lazy Man's Song. Po Chü-i. CCL1, *tr. by* Arthur Waley

Lazy People, The. Shel Silverstein. NTCP

Lazy River. Sidney Arodin and Hoagy Carmichael. ReLy

Lazy Thought, A. Eve Merriam. SSCS

Lazy Witch. Myra Cohn Livingston. NOxBChV

Lazy-bones, lazy-bones, wake up and peep! Nonsense Verses. Charles Lamb. OBCoV

L'Chayim. Carl Rakosi. NAAPv.2

LD Ansure, The. Lady Dorothy Shirley. EMWP

Le Diner. Arthur Hugh Clough. OBCoV; OBSV *Fr.* Spectator ab Extra.

Le Jazz Hot. Anselm Hollo. SeSe

Le Livre. Stéphane Mallarmé.

"End / conscience." PFTM-1

Le Loupgarou. Derek Walcott. OxBSo

Le Médecin Malgré Lui. William Carlos Williams. PoA 2002

Le Monocle de Mon Oncle. Wallace Stevens. TCAPo

Le passage (Morbihan). Tony Baker. Oth

Leaba Shíoda. Nuala Ni Dhomhnaill. CABP

Lead. Ambrose Bierce. APN-2 *Fr.* Devil's Dictionary, The.

Lead & zinc company, The. Holes Commence Falling. David Huddle. PBCAP

Lead drains from your heart on the left side, The. Poem. Tony Towle. AHA

Lead gently, Lord, and slow. Hymn, A. Paul Laurence Dunbar. SacPr

Lead her there. (LL) Flight: "Series of white squares, each, A." Pamela Alexander. AmAlph; OtW

Lead, Kindly Light, amid the encircling gloom. Pillar of the Cloud, The. John Henry, Cardinal Newman. ChiV-1; InvLi; NPeEn; SacPr

Lead me along the hills. For Erwin Smith, Cowboy Photographer. Larry McMurtry. TiP2

Lead me home. (LL) Take My Hand, Precious Lord. Thomas A. Dorsey. APT-2; ISC; NAAPv.2

Lead me like a lost sheep. Poems for Rasmia. Gzar Hantoosh. IrPoTo, *tr. by* Saadi A. Simawe and Ellen Doré Watson

Lead me, Sicilian Maids, to haunted bowers. Her Confirmed Despair. Mary Robinson. CenSon; RWP

Lead me, Sicilian maids, to haunted bowers. Mary Robinson. NPBRoP *Fr.* Sappho and Phaon.

Lead me with your cold, sure hand. To Virgil. Helen Dunmore. BeAl

Lead my pony. Basho. SoOfWa, *tr. by* Sam Hamill

Leadbelly. Cornelius Eady. ESEAA

Leadbelly Gives an Autograph. Imamu Amiri Baraka. PmAP

Leaden Echo and the Golden Echo, The. Gerard Manley Hopkins. MoBrPo; OBMV

Leaden eyelids of wan twilight close, The. George Henry Boker. APN-2 *Fr.* Sonnets: A Sequence on Profane Love.

Leaden-eyed, The. Vachel Lindsay. StAl; TCAPo

Leader of the pack, long seasoned in the saddle, The. Bicycle Race in *Beowulf*, The. David Galef. ArBi

Leader of the Pack, The. Gerald Locklin. SUP

Leader, The. Roger McGough. OPOU

Leader, The. Yunna Petrovna Moritz. TCRusP, *tr. by* Daniel Weissbort

Leaders of the Crowd, The. William Butler Yeats. OxBoAm

Leading / me now? (LL) Kore. Robert Creeley. NAAL-5; OxBoAm; RaBo

Leading to the underworld. (LL) Tu Do Street. Yusef Komunyakaa. AmAlph; AmWaPo; CAP-8; LTA; NAMCP V.2; OxBoAm; SwNoth

Leading with his chin, though bristling. Blue Is the Hero. Bill Berkson. AHA; NYP2

Leaf. Cathy Song. ExTi

Leaf: "Your gaze stays awake in the night." Fazil Hüsnü Daglarca. NaPG, *tr. by* Talat Sait Halman

Leaf, A / left. Aram Saroyan. AHA

Leaf for Hand in Hand, A. Walt Whitman. APN-1

Leaf from a Log Book, A. H. Babcock. OtW

Leaf from freedom's golden chaplet fair, A. To My Father. Henrietta Cordelia Ray. CBWP-3

Leaf from the Devil's Jest-Book, A. Edwin Markham. APN-2

Leaf[e] gold, Lord of thy golden wedge o'erlaid. Edward Taylor. NAAL-3; NAAL-5; NAAPv.1 *Fr.* Preparatory Meditations Before My Approach to the Lord's Supper.

Leaf Huts and Snow Houses. Olav H. Hauge. WED, *tr. by* Robert Bly

Leaf / Of the yam. Kikaku. ZenPo, *tr. by* Takashi Ikemoto and Lucien Stryk

Leaf on the gray sand-path, A. Unreturning Spring, The. Laurence Binyon. CABP

Leaf Struck by Bird Droppings. Yi Hyangji. EcSo, *tr. by* Catherine J. Kim

Leaf, treeless, A. Paul Celan. PoSu

Leaf, Treeless for Bertolt Brecht, A. Paul Celan. AF, *tr. by* Michael Hamburger

Leaf will wrinkle to decay, The. Crest Jewel, The. James Stephens. MoBrPo

Leafage of years is brown, your hair is not brown, The. (LL) Your Hand Full of Hours. Paul Celan. OBVE; PoetW, *tr. by* Michael Hamburger

Leafbud straggles forth, The. Upper Broadway. Adrienne Rich. ItWoWo

Leafless are the trees; their purple branches. Golden Mile-Stone, The. Henry Wadsworth Longfellow. NCAP

Leafless buoyancy. Sukhanovo. Natalya Gorbanevskaya. AF, *tr. by* Daniel Weissbort

Leafless Trees, Chickahominy Swamp. Dave Jeddie Smith. NAMCP V.2

Leafshade stirring on lichened bark. Culture and Anarchy. Adrienne Rich. NALW

Leafsmoke. Marianne Bluger. IFF

Leaf-Treader, A. Robert Frost. MoAmPo

Leafy Plant of Wisdom, A. Kim Chôngnan. EcSo, *tr. by* Peter H. Lee

Leafy the boughs—they also hide big fruit. (LL) Do Not Expect Again a Phoenix Hour. Cecil Day Lewis. MoBrPo; NoAM

Leafy-with-love banks and the green waters of the canal. Canal Bank Walk. Patrick Kavanagh. MoBrPo; NAMCP V.1; NoAM; NoP-4; NoP-5

Leaguered in fire. Autumn Sunset, An. Edith Wharton. APN-2

Leak in the Dike, The. Phoebe Cary. ITBLP

Leaking Roof. Gahlia Gwangwa'a. NAfrP

Lean and hungry and tired of my dry bones and years? (LL) Since 1619. Margaret Abigail Walker. NoP-4; NoP-5

Lean Gaius, who was thinner than a straw. Lucilius. OBVE; WoPoe, *tr. by* Peter Porter

Lean on the Lord's Side. *Unknown.* SSUS

Lean Street. George Sutherland Fraser. EdScPo

Leaned on their automobile horns as he toppled. (LL) Bull Moose, The. Alden Nowlan. BeAl; BrAP

Leaning across a fence and munching grass. (LL) Todd. Stewart Conn. EdScPo; NePenScot

Leaning against a strong river, my infinite stroke. Oarsman, The. Paul Valéry. YaTCFP, *tr. by* Mary Ann Caws and Patricia Terry

From Manzanilla come! (LL) Emily Dickinson. BrAP; NAAPv.1

Leaning all by himself. Dry Tree. Muso Soseki. EaWin, *tr. by* W. S. Merwin

Leaning back like a lover against this beech tree's. Beech Tree, The. Michael Longley. NAMCP V.2

Leaning dark away, The. (LL) Light Sleep. Hazel Hall. APT-1; NAAPv.2

Leaning into the Afternoons. Pablo Neruda. TCLAP, *tr. by* W. S. Merwin

Leaning into the afternoons I cast my sad nets. Leaning into the Afternoons. Pablo Neruda. TCLAP, *tr. by* W. S. Merwin

Leaning into the Tilt. Virginia McGuire. FiBr

Leaning on a lamp. Leaning on a Lamppost. Noel Gay. ReLy

Leaning on a Lamppost. Noel Gay. ReLy

Leaning on my staff. Watching the Late Day Clear after Snowfall. Chia Tao. CSKM, *tr. by* Mike O'Connor

Leaning on my staff, I summon the recluse. Summoning the Recluse. Tso Ssu. CCL1, *tr. by* John Frodsham

Leaning over the wall at Trafalgar Square. Cosmos in London. Arthur Nortje. HBAPE

Leans listening on the gate, in all respect. (LL) Middle of the World. D. H. Lawrence. NoAM; WoPoe

Leap Before You Look. W. H. Auden. NoAM; PLBUT

Leap into the light, ye living Forms! Cornelius Mathews. APN-1 *Fr.* Poems on Man in His Various Aspects under the American Republic.

Leap out, chill water, over reeds and brakes. River God, The. Sacheverell Sitwell. MoBrPo

Leap, plashless as they swim. (LL) Bird came down the Walk, A. Emily Dickinson. AmFaPo; APN-2; ColAP; HeIP-4; ITBLP; MoAmPo; NAAL-3; NAAL-5; NAAPv.1; NAMCP V.1; NAWM-7v2; NCAP; NoAM; NoP-4; NoP-5; NTCP; OxBoAm; SAmP; TFi

Leap, The. James Dickey. NIL-7; NIP-4

Leap Yeah Party, De. Maggie Pogue Johnson. CBWP-4

Leap Year. Charles North. FTOS

Leap-Centuries. Paul Celan. OBVE, *tr. by* Michael Hamburger

Leaped at the caribou. Ho Ho Ho Caribou. Joseph Ceravolo. PmAP

Leaping for the river, the frog. Issa. WED, *tr. by* Robert Bly

Leaping from the eucalyptus branch, the wild desert pigs. Border, The. Joanna Rawson. AmPoNex

Leaping Laughers, The. George Barker. OBMV

Leaping trout sees, The. Onitsura. SoOfWa, *tr. by* Sam Hamill

Lear. William Carlos Williams. NAAL-5; PoA 2002

Lear and the Dogs. William Shakespeare. DiBP *Fr.* King Lear.

Lear Drives His Rambler across Laurel Mountain. Charles Clifton. IaFF

Lear Expands His Last Words to Cordelia. Sheryl Cornett. IaFF

Lear Of Whylah Falls. George Elliott Clarke. OpeFie

Learn, flowers, from me, what parts we play. Luis de Góngora y Argote. SpanPo; WoPoe *Fr.* Spectre of the Rose, The.

Learn how to consume my mouth! *Unknown.* SLW, *tr. by* Marjolijn De Jager, Sayd Bahodin Majrouh and André Velter

Learn now, dear Prince! how, if thy soul be set. *Unknown.* TAL *Fr.* Bhagavad-Gita, The.

Learn. The winter trees. Winter Trees. Ágnes Nemes Nagy. IQMS, *tr. by* Hugh Maxton

Learn to labor and to wait. (LL) Psalm of Life, A. Henry Wadsworth Longfellow. AmFaPo; APN-1; BRP; ITBLP; ItP; NAAL-3; NAAL-5; NAAPv.1; TCAPo

Learn to live. Cid Corman. WhBo

Learn women all from this housewifery. Sir Richard Fanshawe. OBVE *Fr.* Il Pastor Fido.

Learned and a happy ignorance, A. Eden. Thomas Traherne. ChIV-1

Learned, full of inward pride, The. Two Monkeys, The. John Gay. OBCoV

Learned man came to me once, A. Stephen Crane. MoAmPo

Learned Mistress, A. Frank O'Connor. IrLP

Learned Mistress, A. *Unknown.* OBMV, *tr. by* Frank O'Connor

Learned Wife, The. Juvenal. BASC *Fr.* Satires.

Learning. Michael Casey. YaYoPo

Learning. Sion Eirian. BBMWP *Fr.* Adolescent Experiences.

Learning. Juan Chi. CCL1, *tr. by* Graeme Wilson

Learning. Tiruvalluvar. WoPoe *Fr.* Kural, The.

Learning a Dead Language. W. S. Merwin. TAPaP

Learning and a ladder. Karai Senryū. EMJL, *tr. by* Makoto Ueda

Learning by Doing. Howard Nemerov. WeW-3

Learning Experience. Marge Piercy. NAMCP V.2; NoAM

Learning from the Movies. Rachel Wetzsteon. ExTi

Learning from the tale of Admetos, my friend, love the brave. Praxilla. SaLy, *tr. by* Diane Rayor

Learning on a stick, I entered a deep forest. Enjoying Spring. Hwansung Jian. BecRai, *tr. by* Kim Daljin, Kim Won-Chung and Christopher Merrill

Learning ("So Learned Men in Controversies Spend"). George Chapman. NOSC *Fr.* Tears of Peace, The, or Euthymia Raptus.

Learning the Angels. Rennie McQuilkin. PoDa

Learning the Bicycle. Wyatt Prunty. NeBr

Learning the Language. Brewster Ghiselin. APT-2

Learning the Trees. Howard Nemerov. VCAP

Learning the War. Wendy Wilder Larsen. OPRER

Learning to Drive at 32. Allison Joseph. BRtP

Learning to Laugh. Allison Joseph. PasH

Learning to live alone, learning alone. George Stanley. NLPA *Fr.* Mountains and Air.

Learning to Live with the Piano. Ann Lundberg Grunke. MiVo

Learning to Love America. Shirley Lim. GeoHom

Learning to love differently is hard. To Have without Holding. Marge Piercy. NIL-7; NIP-4

Learning to Read. Frances Ellen Watkins Harper. NAAPv.1; NALW *Fr.* Aunt Chloe.

Learning to Ride My Bike. George Held. ArBi

Learning to See Crooked. Gerald Locklin. SUP

Learning to Sing in Parts. Jean Janzen. ACAMVP

Learning to Smile. Art Goodtimes. GeoH

Learning to Speak. Eli Clare. PfS

Learning to Swim at Forty-Five [*I could not whistle and walk in storms along Lake Michigan's shore . . . I could not swallow the lake.*]. Colleen J. McElroy. FiBr; GT

Learning to Swim at Poverty Beach. Peter E. Murphy. NevBe

Learning to talk over and over. Camille Martin. AnSo

Learning to Walk Alone. Judith Ortiz Cofer. PueRic

Learning to Write. Audre Lorde. GT

Learning Window. James Longenbach. NAPBL

Lease of my leaving, heartfelt lack, what does. Sonnet. Karen Volkman. IAoNAP

Leash. Lisa Glatt. SUP

Leasowes: Or, A Poetical Description of the Late Mr. Shenstone's Rural Retirement, The. Joseph Giles. OBGa *Fr.* Leasowes: Or, A Poetical Description of the Late Mr. Shenstone's Rural Retirement, The.

Least Corpse, The. Angel González. RaW, *tr. by* Robert Mezey

Least, The. Roy Fisher. HarvBoo

Least, the meanest, The. Least, The. Roy Fisher. HarvBoo

Leather-helmed locust, The. (LL) Fortunate Traveller, The. Derek Walcott. NAMCP V.2; NoAM

Leave, A. Gertrude Stein. PFTM-1

Leave eye lessons I. Leave I. Lessons. I. Leave I lessons, I. (LL) Guillaume Apollinaire. Gertrude Stein. NAAPv.2; NAMCP V.1; OxBoAm

Leave him: he's quiet enough: and what matter. Here Lies a Prisoner. Charlotte Mew. MoBrPo

Leave in Mid-Winter. John Short. FaBoWar

Leave, leave, thy gadding thoughts. Henry Vaughan. SacPr *Fr.* Search, The.

Leave me alone! my mirth would make you weep. (LL) Solo. Mary Elizabeth Coleridge. ViWPN; VWP

Leave me alone! my tears would make you laugh. Solo. Mary Elizabeth Coleridge. ViWPN; VWP

Leave me, love, and never come back. Love Turned the Light Out. John Latouche. ReLy

Leave Me O Love. Sir Philip Sidney. AEP; GSo; HeIP-4; NIP-4; NPeEn; OxAEP-1; SacPr; TFi

(Leave me ô Love, which reachest but to dust.) BrAP

Leave me: oh! leave me. Dying. Adah Isaacs Menken. CBWP-1

Leave me to the night. Voice, A. Lina Tibi. PoArWo, *tr. by* Subhi Hadidi and Nathalie Handal

Leave the Doors Standing Open. Juan Ramón Jiménez. RaW, *tr. by* Ralph Nelson

Leave the earth behind you! What are you looking for here in a planet overcrowded with corpses. Leave the earth behind you! Fadil Azzawi. IrPoTo, *tr. by* Ralph Saverese and Saadi A. Simawe

Leave the service of your master and be my loyal follower. *Unknown.* SLW, *tr. by* Marjolijn De Jager, Sayd Bahodin Majrouh and André Velter

Leave what is white for whiter use. Stone For A Statue. Sarah Morgan Bryan Piatt. NCAP

Leaves. Frank Asch. NTCP

Leaves. Countee Cullen. GT

Leaves. W. H. Davies. MoBrPo

Leaves. Michael Field. VWP

Leaves. Sam Hamod. UnSA

Leaves. Abd al-Karim Kassid. IrPoTo, *tr. by* Chuck Miller and Saadi A. Simawe

Leaves. Frederic Manning. NOBAu

Leaves. Lloyd Schwartz. UrbNat

Leaves are coming down in huge bunches now, The. Natural. Ellen Doré Watson. PoDa

Leaves are falling, falling from trees, The. Fall. Robin Robertson. NeBrP

Leaves are sere, The. November. Henrietta Cordelia Ray. CBWP-3

Leaves are splitting free in the invisible. Inverse Square Law of the Propagation of Light, The. Christopher Buckley. PoA 2002

Leaves are storm-rattled jester's bells, The. King Lear Bewildered. Patricia Storace. FFC

Leaves a-Vallen [*with music*]. William Barnes. NPeEn

Leaves blown. Yonejiro (Yone) Noguchi. CalPo

Leaves fall turning turning to the ground. Han Yü. CCL1; WoPoe *Fr.* Autumn Thoughts.

Leaves fall with rain in these vacant mountains. Kwŏn P'il. CATKP, *tr. by* Chi-gyu Kim [*or* Kim Chonggil]

Leaves flick past the windows of the train, The. Smirr. W. N. Herbert. NeBrP

Leaves flipping green and silver in the wind, The. Leaves Flipping. George Bowering. BrAP

Leaves fritter. Single Most. Rae Armantrout. OnScMo

Leaves have a sense of, The. Elegy. Lewis Warsh. BodElec

Leaves have their time to fall. Hour of Death, The. Felicia Dorothea Hemans. NOBRP

Leaves / Murmuring by myriads in the shimmering trees. From My Diary, July 1914. Wilfred Owen. MoBrPo

Leaves must be green in Spring.. (LL) Malvern Hill. Herman Melville. APN-2; CBCWP; ColAP; PCW

Leaves of a Dream Are the Leaves of an Onion, The. Arthur Sze. OpBo

Leaves of Grass. Kang Ŭn'gyo. EcSo, *tr. by* Ann Y. Choi

Leaves of Grass [1855 Version, Complete Text]. Walt Whitman.

   Boston Ballad, A. APN-1

   Europe the 72nd and 73rd Years of These States. APN-1

   Faces. APN-1

   Great Are the Myths. APN-1

   I Sing the Body Electric. APN-1

   Sleepers, The. APN-1

   Song for Occupations, A. APN-1

   Song of Myself. APN-1; HeIP-4; OxBoAm

   Song of the Answerer. APN-1

   There Was a Child Went Forth. APN-1

   To Think of Time. APN-1

   Who Learns My Lesson Complete. APN-1

Leaves of Heaven, The. Edward Sanders. RaBo

Leaves of Hypnos. René Char.

   "Poet, conserver of the infinite faces of the living, The." PFTM-1

Leaves of Hypnos No. 128. René Char. AF, *tr. by* Cid Corman

Leaves of the mountain pear are red, The. Yi Kyubo. CATKP *Fr.* Farmhouse: Three Poems.

Leaves some trout. Buson. EH, *tr. by* Robert Hass

Leaves spread like hands. Political Life of Palm Trees, The. Sandra Del Valle. RWB

Leaves, that whisper, whisper ever. Rosabel. Angelina Weld Grimké. PoBW

Leaves, though little time they have to live, The. October Maples, Portland. Richard Wilbur. UpMys

Leaves though thick are falling; one by one, The. Autumn Leaves. Jones Very. APN-1

Leaves very still as they are carried, The. (LL) Surface, The. Jorie Graham. HarvBoo; NAMCP V.2; NoP-5

Leaves were already on the trees, the fruit blossoms, The. With Janice. Kenneth Koch. PmAP

Leaves will fall again sometime and fill, The. Sunday Morning Apples. Hart Crane. HarvBoo; ItP

Leave-Taking. Frank Gelett Burgess. OBCoV

Leavetaking. Ingrid de Kok. TSAP

Leavetaking. Gunnar Ekelof. PFTM-2 *Fr.* Mölna Elegy.

Leavetaking. Veronica Rospigliosi. Prnts

Leavetaking. Rita Wong. IFF

Leave-taking, A. Algernon Charles Swinburne. OxBEV

Leave-Taking ("Death in a war.") Eli Alon. NRoS, *tr. by* Esther Raizen

Leave-taking Near Shoku. Li Po. NDACCP, *tr. by* Ezra Pound

Leaving. Rae Armantrout. FTOS

Leaving. Pamela Brown. BMAP

Leaving. T. Crunk. YaYoPo

Leaving. Tiziano Rossi. ItPo, *tr. by* Gayle Ridinger

Leaving [*with music*]. Cathy Song. NoAM

Leaving. Richard Wilbur. HarvBoo

Leaving all his wisdom standing. Hots, The. Michael Sharkey. NOBAu

Leaving behind my writing brush and. *Unknown.* NAAPv.2

Leaving behind us the alien, foreign city of Dublin. Going Home to Mayo, Winter, 1949. Paul Durcan. PBCIP

Leaving by West Gate. West Gate Ballad. *Unknown.* CCL1, *tr. by* Anne Birrell

Leaving Ch'in-chou. Tu Fu [*or* Du Fu]. CrYelRi, *tr. by* Sam Hamill

Leaving colour; leaving breath. Syliva Legris. PoPra *Fr.* Negative Garden.

Leaving Crete, come visit again our temple. Sappho. STV; WeW-3

Leaving Eden. Nadya Aisenberg. OPRER

Leaving Eden. Ralph Dickey. ESEAA

Leaving Government Offices. Tu Fu [*or* Du Fu]. CrYelRi, *tr. by* Sam Hamill

Leaving Home. Bei Dao. WoBe, *tr. by* Iona Man-Cheong and Eliot Weinberger

Leaving Home. Sarah Rosenblatt. AmPoNex

Leaving Home. Yi Hyangji. EcSo, *tr. by* Catherine J. Kim

Leaving home I left behind on the table. Glossy Mail. Norman Kreitman. EdScPo

Leaving lower earth the long thorn hedgerow. Ascending Strathbraan. Tom Pow. EdScPo

Leaving Mother, 1954. John Graham-Pole. BloBone

Leaving my footprints. From My Hut in Miura. Muso Soseki. EaWin, *tr. by* W. S. Merwin

Leaving my house in the morning. Mikhail Alekseievich Kuzmin. CAGL, *tr. by* Michael Green

Leaving my old mother in the seaside town. Looking Homeward from a Mountain Pass. Sin Saimdang, Lady. CATKP, *tr. by* Chi-gyu Kim [*or* Kim Chonggil]

Leaving on a ten day trip. Travel Poem. Diane Di Prima. WANABP

Leaving one's boy favorite in a priest's charge. Dangerous Things. *Unknown.* EMJL, *tr. by* Edward Putzar

Leaving Paris. Todd Swift. OpeFie

Leaving Port Authority for the St. Regis Rezz [*with music*]. Wendy Rose. HATNAP

Leaving Rattle Bar. Clark Coolidge. FTOS

Leaving San Francisco. Marilyn Chin. CalPo; GeoHom

Leaving Scotland by Train. Hugh McMillan. EdScPo

Leaving Sonora. Agha Shahid Ali. NAMCP V.2

Leaving Syracuse. Al Young. ESEAA

Leaving, The. Brigit Pegeen Kelly. IllVoic; YaYoPo

Leaving, The. Nancy Mitchell. LaCa

Leaving the Atocha Station. John Ashbery. PmAP

Leaving the capital. Goddess of the Luo, The. Ts'ao Chih. CCL1, *tr. by* Burton Watson

Leaving the Chapala RV Park south of Guadalajara, I drive into the small village of Ajijic and a supermarket. Road-Kill. David Johnson. ICANM

Leaving the Country. Wyn Cooper. OPRER

Leaving the Motel. W. D. Snodgrass. NIL-7; NIP-4

Leaving the Mountain. Baggok Choneung. BecRai, *tr. by* Kim Daljin, Kim Won-Chung and Christopher Merrill

Leaving the October Palace. Jane Hirshfield. CalPo

Leaving the Old Gods. Janet McAdams. OPRER

Leaving the [streams] of Ocean. Korinna [*or* Corinna]. SaLy, *tr. by* Diane Rayor

Leaving the Tate. Fleur Adcock. BrAP

Leaving the university, preoccupied. Winter Night. Chandra Mayor. PoPra

Leaving the Village. *Vietnamese Oral Tradition.* CaDao, *tr. by* John Balaban

Leaving the West Coast. Christopher Buckley. CalPo

Leaving the white glow of filling stations. Strand at Lough Beg, The. Seamus Heaney. NAMCP V.2; NoAM; NPeEn; OBWP

Leaving their murderous tribute on the sand. (LL) Figurehead, The. Léonie Adams. APT-2; OxBoAm

Leaving their villages, men on fire. Men on Fire. Kriapur (Kristianto Agus Purnomo). PML, *tr. by* Harry Aveling

Leaving thine outgrown shell by life's unresting sea! (LL) Oliver Wendell Holmes. APN-1; ColAP; CtM; ITBLP; NAAL-3; NAAPv.1; NCAP; NoP-4; NoP-5; OxBoAm; TCAPo; TFi; WaAnP *Fr.* Autocrat of the Breakfast Table, The.

Leaving this world must be the flower. Blossom at the End of the Body. Beckian Fritz Goldberg. AmAlph

Leaving Winston-Salem. Toneka Nathene Bonitto-Burwell. BtF

Leaving You. Lily Brett. HP

Leaving you. Courtesy, A Trenchant Grace, A. Cyrus Cassells. GT; WiU

Leaving Yuba City. Chitra Divakaruni. GeoHom

Lebanon. Frank O'Hara. CAGL

Lecture 5. Czeslaw Milosz. GI *Fr.* Six Lectures in Verse.

Lecture #1. Brenda Coultas. HeMarv

Lecture on Nothing. John Cage. FTOS; PFTM-2

Lecture Upon the Bat, A. Caitríona O'Reilly. MoWP; NIrP

Lecture upon the Shadow, A. John Donne. NAEL-6v1; NAEL-7v1; NoSic

Lectures on Love, The. Edward Hirsch. PuP-23

Lecturing on Walt Whitman and Emily Dickinson in China. Jesse Glass. ViWalt

Led by the pow'r [*or* powre] of grief[e], to wailings [*or* waylings] brought. Mary Sidney Wroth, Countess of Montgomery. PEW *Fr.* Pamphilia to Amphilanthus.

Leda. Rubén Darío. SpanPo, *tr. by* Dorren Bell

Leda. "H. D." BrAP

Leda. Rainer Maria Rilke. RaBo, *tr.* by Robert Bly

Leda 3. Lucille Clifton. NAMCP V.2

Leda and the Swan. Oliver St. John Gogarty. IrLP

Leda and the Swan. William Butler Yeats. BrAP; CABP; ClHu; EMP; EroLit; GSo; HarvBoo; HeIP-4; MoBrPo; NAEL-6v2; NAEL-7v2; NAMCP V.1; NAWM-7v2; NIL-7; NIP-4; NoAM; NoP-4; NoP-5; NPeEn; OWoS; OxAEP-2; OxBEV; OxBSo; PoPoPo; SoSe-8; TFi; TRP; WaAnP; WeW-3

Leda's Sister and the Geese. Katharyn Machan Aal. SoSe-8

Leda's Version. James Harrison. NIP-4

Ledde I the daunce a mydsomer day. *Unknown.* OHMEL

Lede guiterriste was a craftie ladde, The. Probatioun Officeres Tale, The. Gerard Benson. NBLV

Ledge, The. Harry Mathews. NYP2

Ledger, The. Robert Kroetsch. NLPA

Lee in the Mountains. Donald Davidson. CBCWP; FuPo

Lee Morgan. David Henderson. SeSe

Lee to the Rear. John Randolph Thompson. CBCWP

Leech-Gatherer, The. William Wordsworth. *See* Resolution and Independence.

Leeds for Pleasure. John Dyer. STuOW *Fr.* Fleece, The.

Lee's Lunch / Spaghetti. Brilliant Sad Sun. William Carlos Williams. HarvBoo; NAAPv.2

Lee-Shore, The. Edwin John Pratt. IFF

Leeward of the house is nothing but the tip. Lilacs. David Biespiel. AmPoNex

Left All Alone Again Blues. Anne Caldwell. ReLy

Left Bank Jazz Society, The. Afaa Michael Weaver. UnSA

Left but this. (LL) Victims, The. Sharon Olds. NIL-7; SoSe-8

Left by his friend to breakfast alone on the white. Edward Lear. W. H. Auden. OxAEP-2; OxBSo

Left Eye. Brenda Hillman. ASA

Left Eye of Odin, The. Regina DeCormier-Shekejian. TWW

Left for myself. This World, Poor Thing. N. Revathi Devi. HotL, *tr.* by V. Narayana Rao and A. K. Ramanujan

Left for us to assume what purpose. Skiddaw House. David Scott. NLP

Left hand holding distaff and wool retained on it (ah mixture). Catullus. APSN

Left hand leading a yellow hound. Tune: "A Riverside Town." Su Tung-p'o. ColAnChi, *tr.* by Jiaosheng Wang

Left Henry to live on. (LL) John Berryman. NAMCP V.2; NoP-4; NoP-5 *Fr.* Dream Songs.

Left in the field / among big-bellied ewes. Naayawva Taawi. Wendy Rose. UnSA

Left in the ground. (LL) Wilfred Owen. *See* Lost in the ground.

Left leg flung out, head cocked to the right. Poet. Karl Shapiro. MoAmPo; NoAM

Left like an unknown's breath on mirrors. Lawrence Durrell. MoBrPo *Fr.* Eight Aspects of Melissa.

Left line says, The. Natural Functions. Jonathan Cott. AHA

Left off the highway and. Waiting. Raymond Carver. GoPo

Left Rites. Hylda Sims. Prnts

Left the opium and myopia outside. Larissa Lai. PoPra

Left to itself, they say, every foetus. From the Dressing-room. Medbh McGuckian. MoWP

Leftover Blessings. Julia Kasdorf. PBCAP

Leftover talk in your head. (LL) And, Yes, Those Spiritual Matters. Christopher Gilbert. ESEAA; InoFa

Leftovers in the Cup. Mirza Asadullah Khan Ghalib. WED, *tr.* by Robert Bly and Sunil Dutta

Lefty. Imamu Amiri Baraka. EGAG

Leg in a Plaster Cast, A. Muriel Rukeyser. MoAmPo

Leg, The. Karl Shapiro. MoAmPo; WeW-3

Legacies. Nikki Giovanni. FuFl

Legacies. Emily Grosholz. FFC

Legacies. Heberto Padilla. TCLAP, *tr.* by Andrew Hurley and Alastair Reid

Legacy. Imamu Amiri Baraka. ColAP; NAMCP V.2; NoAM

Legacy. Siobhan Campbell. MFPA

Legacy. Ludwig Heinrich Christoph Hölty. SonAtl, *tr.* by Kurt Ganzl and Markus Jaigirder

Legacy. Ceri Wyn Jones. BBMWP, *tr.* by Dafydd Wyn Jones

Legacy [*with music*]. Maurice Kenny. HATNAP

Legacy. Joan Larkin. WiU

Legacy. Sydney March. BtF

Legacy, The. Heinrich von Morungen. GePo, *tr.* by F. C. Nicholson

Legal children of a literary man, The. Relationships. Mona Van Duyn. OxBoAm

Legal Fiction [*with music*]. William Empson. HarvBoo; NoAM; NoP-4; NoP-5

Legal Mouse, A [*with music*]. Lizelia Augusta Jenkins Moorer. CBWP-3

Legend. W. H. Auden. CAGL

Legend: "Old black man was stood on the block, The." Sterling Allen Brown. OxBoAm

Legend. Anne Ethuin. SurWo, *tr.* by Guy Ducornet

Legend. Louise Glück. TaR

Legend. Shin Kyŏngnim. CAMKP, *tr.* by Kevin O'Rourke

Legend. Judith Wright. NOBAu

Legend, A. Adelaide Anne Procter. SacPr

Legend, The. Garrett Kaoru Hongo. LoL; MakPoe; OpBo; TRP

Legend had it Woody Guthrie hitched. Backyards of America. Leonard Kress. RWB

Legend is whispered, The. Shapeshifter Poems. Lucille Clifton. BodElec; LoL

Legend lives on from the Chippewa on down, The. Wreck of the Edmund Fitzgerald, The. Gordon Lightfoot. NoP-4

Legend of Captain Jones, The. David Lloyd.

Legend of Florence, A. Leigh Hunt.

    Act 2.

    Domestic Chat. STuOW

Legend of Good Women, The. Geoffrey Chaucer. *tr.* by Burton Raffel and Selden Rodman

    "And as for me, though that I konne [*or* can] but [*or* my wit be] lyte." HeIP-4

    Balade. OBEV

    Ballade. WoPoe, *tr.* by Burton Raffel and Selden Rodman

Legend of Home, The. Lawson Fusao Inada. GeoHom *Fr.* Legends from Camp.

Legend of Lilja. Sarah Kirsch. AF, *tr.* by Wayne Kvam

4. The Legend of Lost Boy. Lawson Fusao Inada. CalPo *Fr.* Legends from Camp.

Legend of Manor Hall, The. Thomas Love Peacock. NPBRoP

Legend of Provence, A. Adelaide Anne Procter. VWP

Legend of the Albino Farm. Erin Belieu. NeAmPo

Legend of the Baker and Her Daughter, The. Mihangel Morgan. BBMWP, *tr.* by Martin Davis

Legend of the Crossing-Sweeper. May Kendall. VWP

15. The Legend of the Full Moon over Amache. Lawson Fusao Inada. AmWaPo *Fr.* Legends from Camp.

6. The Legend of the Great Escape. Lawson Fusao Inada. AmWaPo *Fr.* Legends from Camp.

Legend of the Knight of the Red Crosse, or of Holinesse, The. Edmund Spenser. NAEL-7v1; NoP-5 *Fr.* Faerie Queene, The.

10. The Legend of the Magic Marbles. Lawson Fusao Inada. AmWaPo *Fr.* Legends from Camp.

Legend of the Northland, A. Phoebe Cary. OBSP

Legendary. James McAuley. BMAP

Legendary muscle that wants and grieves, The. Hearts, The. Robert Pinsky. VCAP

Legends from Camp. Lawson Fusao Inada.

    "F.B.I. swooped in early, The." GeoHom

    "It began as truth, as fact." GeoHom

    Legend of Home, The. GeoHom

    4. The Legend of Lost Boy. CalPo

    15. The Legend of the Full Moon over Amache. AmWaPo

    6. The Legend of the Great Escape. AmWaPo

    10. The Legend of the Magic Marbles. AmWaPo

Legging Behind. Ramy Ditzanny. NRoS, *tr.* by the author

Legion hall in Atherton contains, The. By-Products. Baron Wormser. ReTh

"Legion" to "Lent" for "R." Tina Darragh. FTOS

Legs of the elk punctured the snow's crust, The. To Christ Our Lord. Galway Kinnell. HeIP-4

Leiden Manuscript, The. *Unknown. tr.* by John Boswell

    Wise Rejoice with Ganymede, The. CAGL, *tr.* by John Boswell

Leir. Ann Lauinger. IaFF *Fr.* Three Songs for *King Leir.*

Leisure. W. H. Davies. AngWePo; GoPo; MoBrPo; OBEV; OBMV; TFi

Leisurely Enjoyment. Chungji. BecRai, *tr.* by Kim Daljin, Kim Won-Chung and Christopher Merrill

L. E. L. Christina Georgina Rossetti. VWP

Lela's Charms. Lizelia Augusta Jenkins Moorer. CBWP-3

"Lem" cuts a figure eight around "le ma" and "le me." "Legion" to "Lent" for "R." Tina Darragh. FTOS

Lemme be wid Casey Jones. Odyssey of Big Boy. Sterling Allen Brown. NAMCP V.1

Lemmings. Patricia Beer. CABP

Lemmings die every year. Over the cliff. Lemmings. Patricia Beer. CABP

Lemmy knows two. Wopko Jensma. TSAP

Lemon and Rosemary. Veronica Forrest-Thomson. Oth

Lemon for Me, A. No Ch'ŏnmyŏng. CAMKP, *tr.* by Mickey Hong

Lemon, Hot Water and a Blood Clot. Dacia Maraini. CItWP, *tr.* by Cinzia Sartini Blum and Lara Trubowitz

Lemon rind rubbed on the rim. Espresso. Carol Lee Saffoti. UnSA

Lemon ship floats by between tugs, A. Pockets of Haze. Lewis MacAdams. AHA

Lemon trees. Texas Memoranda. Lexie Dean Robertson. TiP2

Lemon Trees, The. Eugenio Montale. PoetW; WoPoe, *tr.* by William Arrowsmith

Lemon Trees, The. Eugenio Montale. PFTM-1

Lemon: / we could never. Three Trees. Wanda Coleman. BrAP

Lemonade Stand. Myra Cohn Livingston. TLR

Lemon-house was being over-, The. In the Greenhouse. Eugenio Montale. PoetW, *tr.* by Jonathan Galassi

Lemons. Gail Martin. SweBea

Lemurs somehow, at that lilt of the road. Slow Animals Crossing. W. N. Herbert. NeBrP; StAl

Lena Lovelace. Melvin B. Tolson. GT

Leñador. Federico García Lorca. RaW *Fr.* Canciones para Terminar.

Lenaia. Susan M. Whitmore. AmPoNex

Lend me a battle of unavoidable suggestions. Emilio Villa. ItPo *Fr.* Words.

Lend me, a little while, the key. Pedlar, The. Charlotte Mew. NOxBChV

Lend me your arm. Little Song of the Maimed. Benjamin Péret. OBWP, *tr.* by David Gascoyne

Lend me your great sound, your fine smooth speed. Ode. Valery Larbaud. YaTCFP, *tr.* by Mary Ann Caws and Patricia Terry

Lend me your precious toys. To W.S.—On his Wonderful Toys. Walter Davies. NOxBChV

Lend me your presence, and I will lend you mine. (LL) Little Citizen, Little Survivor. Hayden Carruth. GoPo; OPRER

Lending Out Books. Hal Sirowitz. GoPo

L'Enfant Glacé. Harry Graham. NBLV; OBCoV

Length of a Wave, The. Nick Laird. NIrP

Lenin. Dorothy, Duchess of Wellington Wellesley. "So I came down the steps to Lenin." OBMV

Leningrad. Osip Emilevich Mandelstam. AF

Leningrad. Osip Emilevich Mandelstam. TCRusP, *tr.* by John Glad

Leningrad Cemetery, Winter of 1941. Sharon Olds. NIL-7; NIP-4

Leningrad stairwell, A. Sergey Stratanovsky. ItGoST, *tr.* by J. Kates

Lenora. Gottfried August Bürger. NPBRoP, *tr.* by William Taylor (Ellenore.) NOBRP

Lenore. Edgar Allan Poe. APN-1; TCAPo

Lenox Avenue / by daylight. Dive. Langston Hughes. APT-2

Lenox Avenue Mural. Langston Hughes.
  Comment on Curb. APSN; APT-2; OxBoAm
  (Dream Deferred.) SoSe-8; TWF
  "Good morning, daddy!" APSN; APT-2; OxBoAm
  Harlem. APSN; APT-2; BrAP; GT; HeIP-4; NAMCP V.1; NIL-7; NIP-4; NoP-4; NoP-5; OxBoAm; RaBo; SAmP; SSLK; WaAnP
  Island. APT-2
  Letter. APT-2
  Same in Blues. APSN; APT-2; OxBoAm; SSLK

Lenox Hill. Agha Shahid Ali. AmAlph; NAMCP V.2; NoP-5

Lens. Steve Jonas. EGAG

Lens. Richard Kenney. PfSP

Lens. Anne Wilkinson. BrAP

Lens of crystal whose transparence calms, A. Self-portrait. Elinor Wylie. APT-1; NAAPv.2

Lent. William Robert Rodgers. ModIr; PNI

Lenten is comen wyth love to toun. *Unknown.* OHMEL

Lentil, a lentil, a lentil, a stone, A. Woman Cleaning Lentils, The. Zehrd [*or* Zahrad]. PML, *tr.* by Diana Der Hovanessian and Marzbed Margossian

Lentinus! thou dost nought but fume, and fret. Martial. OBVE

L'Envoi. Rudyard Kipling. BRP
  (When Earth's Last Picture Is Painted.) UV

L'Envoi. Edwin Arlington Robinson. ITBLP

L'Envoi: "What is the moral? Who rides may read." Rudyard Kipling. MoBrPo

L'Envoy. George Herbert. BASC

Leoda þearfe; ne mæg ic her leng wesan. *Unknown. Fr.* Beowulf [The Complete Text in Anglo-Saxon].

Leodogran, the King of Cameliard. Alfred Tennyson. NAEL-7v2 *Fr.* Idylls of the King.

León. Ernesto Cardenal. TCLAP, *tr.* by Jonathan Cohen

Leona, dear, twelve months ago. Eloise Bibb. CBWP-4

Leonard. Jeffrey McDaniel. AmPoNex

Leonard Commits Redeeming Adulteries with All the Women in Town. Louise Erdrich. UpMys

Leonard Refuses to Atone. Louise Erdrich. UpMys

Leonardo's Bicycle. Cal Bedient. ArBi

Leonardo's "Mona Lisa." Edward Dowden. GSo

Leopard in Eden, The. Gail White. FFC

Leopard Lives in a Muu Tree, A. Jonathan Kariara. PML

Leopard seemed harmless, The. Leopard, The. Cindy Day Roberts. LaCa

Leopard Skin. Douglas Stewart. NOBAu

Leopard, The. Cindy Day Roberts. LaCa

Leopardi. Mark Strand. CAP-8

Leopards break into the temple and drink to the dregs what is in the sacrificial pitchers. Leopards in the Temple. Franz Kafka. MotU, *tr.* by Clement Greenberg

Leopards in the Temple. Franz Kafka. MotU, *tr.* by Clement Greenberg

Lepanto. G. K. Chesterton. FaBoWar; MoBrPo; OBMV; OBNV

Leper. Sŏ Chŏngju. CAMKP, *tr.* by David R. McCann

Leper, The. Algernon Charles Swinburne. OxBEV

Leper opens the hydrant, drinks water, A. Nowadays. Tushar Roy. WoPoe, *tr.* by Ron D. K. Banerjee

Leper-House and the Impenitents, The. James Thomson. NePenScot *Fr.* Castle of Indolence, The.

Lepers. Aloysius Bertrand. MotU, *tr.* by James Weeks

Lepers grew excited, The. Apprentice Sees Himself in the Sunset, The. David Craig. UpMys

Lepidoptery. James Sherry. FTOS

Leron-leron sinta, umakyat sa papaya. When the Grain Is Golden and the Wind Is Chilly, Then It Is the Time to Harvest. Nick Carbó. NeAmPo

Leroy. Imamu Amiri Baraka. PmAP

Les Americains. Diane Di Prima. Eno

Les Anges Sont Blancs. George Seferis. PFTM-1

Les Congés du Lépreux. Jean Bodel. WoPoe, *tr.* by Frank Templeton Prince

Les Fils (Sons). Beverly Matherne. TWW

Les Grottes. Gillian Clarke. HarvBoo

Les Luths. Frank O'Hara. NAMCP V.2; NoAM

Les Manèges de la Mer (1964). Edouard J. Maunick.

Les Millwin. Ezra Pound. APT-1; OBCoV

Les Planches-en-Montagnes. Michael Roberts. OBMV

Lesbia. Catullus. EroLit, *tr.* by Peter Whigham

Lesbia, Caelius—yes, our darling. Catullus. NAWM-7v1 *Fr.* Carmina [Charles Martin Translation].

Lesbia forever on me rails. Catullus. OBVE

Lesbia hurls abuse at me in front of her husband. Catullus. NAWM-7v1 *Fr.* Carmina [Charles Martin Translation].

Lesbia, let us live only for loving. Catullus. NAWM-7v1; WoPoe *Fr.* Carmina [Charles Martin Translation].

Lesbia / live with me. Catullus. EroLit *Fr.* Carmina.

Lesbian Corn. Elaine Equi. IllVoic

Lesbian couple, A. Neighbors. Yi Cha. PML, *tr.* by Wang Ping and Richard Sieburth

Lesbian youths are all abroad today, The. Erinna's Spinning. Margaret Junkin Preston. SWaP

Lesbia's sparrow! Catullus. EroLit, *tr.* by Peter Whigham

Lesion. Robert Budde. PoPra

Lesley Gore got her rival good. Answer Song. David Trinidad. WiU

Less afraid the better thou shalt speed, The. (LL) Ah silly pug wert thou so sore afraid. Queen of England Elizabeth I. NoP-4; NoP-5

Less and Less Human, O Savage Spirit. Wallace Stevens. BBASP

Less than a day in paradise. Stones Where the Haft Rotted, The. Meng Chiao. CCL1, *tr.* by A. C. Graham

Less than a golden one it cannot be. (LL) Abraham Cowley. NOSC; OxAEP-1 *Fr.* Sylva.

Less than the wind that runs to the flamy call! (LL) Enkindled Spring, The. D. H. Lawrence. NAMCP V.1; NoAM

Less to improve her body than to trick. Winter Swim. Pimone Triplett. NAPBL

Less we paid, the more we climbed, The. Tendrils. Cheap Seats, the Cincinnati Gardens, Professional Basketball, 1959. William Matthews. MoASP; PML

Less[e] loss[e] to let her go[e]. (LL) Content and Ri[t]ch[e]. Robert Southwell. ChIV-2; NoSic

Lesser proof than old Voltaire's, yet greater, A. Orange Buds by Mail from Florida. Walt Whitman. NAAL-3

Lesson. Forrest Hamer. P180

Lesson. Barbara Winder. MiVo

Lesson, The. Kevin Hearle. PoCu

Lesson, The. Miroslav Holub. PoSu, *tr.* by Ian Milner and Jarmila Milner

Lesson, The. Charles Simic. AF

Lesson, The: "Cleaned, lubed and wiped." James Brown. ArBi

Lesson, The: "Stand next to your bike, like that." Claudia M. Reder. ArBi

Lesson 3. Helmut Heissenbüttel. PFTM-2 *Fr.* Textbook 10.

Lesson for the Proud, A. Thomas Baker. STuOW *Fr.* Steam Engine; or, The Power of the Flame, The.

Lesson From a Sundial [Sun-Dial]. *Unknown.* Spl

Lesson from the Cockerel. Maggie O'Sullivan. Oth

Lesson in a Picture, A. Sarah Morgan Bryan Piatt. NCAP

Lesson in Anatomy, A. Liz Rosenberg. NIL-7

Lesson in Music, A. Alastair Reid. WaAnP

Lesson in Natural History, A. Vyacheslav Kupriyanov. TCRusP, *tr. by* Pamela Davidson

Lesson in Observation, A. Dan Pagis. AF, *tr. by* Stephen Mitchell

Lesson in Translation, A. Gabriel Preil. FIT, *tr. by* Robert Friend

Lesson of Night, A. Charles Ghigna. MiVo

Lesson of Silence, A [*with music*]. Tymoteusz Karpowicz. PoSu, *tr. by* Czeslaw Milosz

Lesson of the Sugarcane, The. Judith Ortiz Cofer. TouFir

Lesson of the Teeth, The. Judith Ortiz Cofer. TouFir

Lesson on Braces. Jean Valerie. SpirFl

Lessons. Philippe Jaccottet.
    "Between us and the farthest star." StAl, *tr. by* Derek Mahon

Lessons. Cleopatra Mathis.
    Given What Manages. ExTi

Lessons. Graham Thomas. AngWePo

Lessons from a Mirror. Thylias Moss. ESEAA; LTA; OxAAAP

Lessons in History. Robert Penn Warren. BodElec

Lessons in lying. Nzadi Z. Keita. BtF

Lessons of the War. Henry Reed. HeIP-4; OBWP
    Judging Distances. BrAP; NAEL-6v2; NAEL-7v2; NIL-7; NIP-4; NoP-4; NoP-5; NPeEn; OxBEV; PoWW
    Naming of Parts. AmFaPo; BrAP; FaBoWar; MoBrPo; NAEL-6v2; NAEL-7v2; NoP-4; NoP-5; OxBEV; PoPoPo; RaBo; SoSe-8; TFi; UV; WaAnP
    Unarmed Combat. BrAP; NAEL-6v2

Lesssons in Survival. Peter Scupham. PoCu

Lest her own captive else should her subdue. (LL) On the Welsh Language. Katherine Philips. EMWP; NoP-5; NOSC

Lest I forget. Lost Friend, The. Marjorie Lowry Christie Pickthall. PoBW

Lest it may more quarrels breed. Twelve Articles. Jonathan Swift. NBLV; OBCoV

Lest men suspect your tale to be untrue. Devil's Advice to Story-Tellers, The. Robert Graves. NAEL-6v2; NoAM

Lest one touch of this heart convey its grief. (LL) Elizabeth Barrett Browning. CABP; CenSon; VWP; WaAnP *Fr.* Sonnets from the Portuguese.

Lest Poets paint each Jewish saint. Battles of Joshua. *Unknown.* VerBaPo

Lest the fair cheeks begin their shrivelling. Homework. Mona Van Duyn. FFC; VCAP

Lest the world, flesh[e], yea Devil[l] put[t] thee out. (LL) John Donne. BASC; FSCP; NAEL-6v1; NAEL-7v1; NOSC; PBRV *Fr.* Holy Sonnets.

Lest We Forget. Patricia A. Holt Abner. BRtP

Lestenyt, lordynges, both elde and yinge. Of a Rose, a Lovely Rose. *Unknown.* OBEV

Lester Leaps In. Al Young. ESEAA; SeSe

Lester Tells of Wanda and the Big Snow. Paul Zimmer. GoPo

Let *a* be taken as. Project of Linear Inquiry, The. Michael Palmer. PmAP

Let a race of men now rise and take control. (LL) For My People. Margaret Abigail Walker. InGu; ISC; ItP; OxAAAP; SSLK; TWF; WaAnP

Let a stalk of wheat. Wheat. Ishihara Yoshiro. IPoFL

Let "A" stand for the belovèd, "B." Making a Love Poem. Leonard Nathan. IaFF

Let age approve of youth, and death complete the same! (LL) Rabbi Ben Ezra. Robert Browning. NAEL-6v2; NAEL-7v2

Let air discover who you are, deliver. Entering a Wilderness Area. William Stafford. PfSP

Let all mortal flesh keep silence, And with fear and trembling stand. *Unknown.* SacPr, *tr. by* Gerard Moultrie

Let all poems speak and address themselves. Incantation. E. Ethelbert Miller. OxAAAP

Let all the family gather. Light Another Candle. Miriam Chaikin. NTCP

Let all the multitudes of light. F. B. MacNutt. SacPr

Let America Be America Again. Langston Hughes. AF; BLPJKO

Let Anaiah bless with the Dragon-fly, who sails over the pond by the wood-side and feedeth on the cresses. Christopher Smart. FaBoVe *Fr.* Jubilate Agno.

Let any thief whom we carelessly suffer to pass. *Unknown.* PriapPo *Fr.* Priapus Poems, The.

Let Archimedes loud his glasses' glory roar. Her Eyes. Daniel Casper von Lohenstein. GePo, *tr. by* George C. Schoolfield

Let beasts whine at your grave my father. In Memoriam Gyula Juhász. Sándor Weöres. IQMS, *tr. by* Edwin Morgan

Let by Rain. Edward Taylor. ColAP; NAAL-3; OxBEV

Let dainty wits cry on the sisters nine. Sir Philip Sidney. NoSic *Fr.* Astrophil and Stella.

Let each his discontent reveal. John Gay. DiBP *Fr.* Fables: First Series.

Let earth and heaven combine. Charles Wesley. NPeEn

Let Elizur[e] rejoice with the Partridge, who is a prisoner of state and is proud of his keepers. Christopher Smart. *Fr.* Jubilate Agno.

Let 'em censure: what care I? In Imitation of Anacreon. Matthew Prior. OxBEV

Let England close. Let the green sea-anemone close. (LL) Out. Ted Hughes. FaBoWar; NAMCP V.2

Let Evening Come. Jane Kenyon. BeAl; GoPo; MakPoe; OxBoAm; PoCu; PtR

Let every prudish reader use his feet. Martial. RomPo, *tr. by* Anthony Reid

Let foreign [*or* forrain] nations of their language boast. Son[ne], The. George Herbert. AngWePo

Let forty thousand pecks of pearls. Chŏng Ch'ŏl. CATKP, *tr. by* Peter H. Lee

Let gleaming motes of hayseed in the barn. Moments of Summer. Rachel Hadas. RA

Let Go of It. Cindy Day Roberts. LaCa

Let Go the Whore of Babylon. Miles Coverdale. ChIV-2

Let God's Saints Come In. *Unknown.* SSUS

Let Happiness smile, as she wings their sweet dreams. (LL) Stolen White Girl, The. John Rollin Ridge. APN-2; NAAPv.1

Let heaven and earth go about their changes. (LL) Settled at Cold Mountain. Han-shan (Cold Mountain). CCL1; NDACCP, *tr. by* Gary Snyder

Let her be courtesan, scholar or saint. Beirut. Nadia Tuéni. PoArWo

Let her who walks in Paphos. Lais. "H. D." MoAmPo

Let Heroes Account to Love. Alan Dugan. NoAM

Let him answer as he will. Companion, The. Edwin Arlington Robinson. NoAM

Let him hate you through the glass, And. (LL) Midnight Skaters, The. Edmund Charles Blunden. MoBrPo; NPeEn; WoPoe

Let Him have his sleep! (LL) Sor Juana Inés de la Cruz. WoPoe; WPoS *Fr.* Fifth Villancico, in Alternating Voices, Written for the Feast of the Nativity in Puebla, 1689, The.

Let him have his spats and cane. (LL) Sporting Beasley. Sterling Allen Brown. APT-2; NAMCP V.1

Let Him Not Grow Up. Gabriela Mistral. BeAl, *tr. by* Ursula K. Le Guin

Let him that will, ascend the tottering seat. Seneca. OBVE *Fr.* Thyestes.

Let Him with Kisses of His Mouth [*with music*]. *Unknown.* ChIV-1

Let innocence remain. Prayer. Pierre Albert Jourdan. YaTCFP, *tr. by* Mary Ann Caws *and* Jean-Pierre Cauvin

Let it all be seen in your light, blushing drops. (LL) Trickle Drops. Walt Whitman. APN-1; NAAL-3; NAAL-5; NAAPv.1

Let It Be. Musaemura Bonus Zimunya. NAfrP

Let it be alleys. Let it be a hall. Lovely Love, A. Gwendolyn Brooks. CAP-8

Let it be forgotten, as a flower is forgotten. Song. Sara Teasdale. MoAmPo; PoA 2002; TCAPo

Let It Be Known. Joette Harland-Watts. InTrad

Let it be known that. Let It Be Known. Joette Harland-Watts. InTrad

Let it come. Last Day, The. Lucile Adler. ICANM

Let it end here where the blueprint. Making Chicago. Dennis Schmitz. IllVoic

Let It Go. William Empson. HarvBoo; NPeEn; OxBEV

Let it go. (LL) Man, That Is Born of a Woman. Rosanna Warren. ExTi; PfSP

Let it live and grow. (LL) Love Letters. Josephine D. Henderson Heard. CBWP-4; SWaP

Let it no longer be a forlorn[e] hope. On the Baptized Ethiopian. Richard Crashaw. ChIV-2; NoP-4; NoP-5, *tr. by* Richard Crashaw

Let it not your wonder move. Ben Jonson. NAEL-7v1; NOSC; PtR *Fr.* Celebration of Charis in Ten Lyric[k] Pieces [*or* Peeces], A.

Let it rain and thunder! Who Cares? Ira Gershwin. ReLy

Let it snow. Let blue skies fade to steel. Let It Snow. David J. Rothman. GeoH

Let It Snow! Let It Snow! Let It Snow! Sammy Cahn. ReLy

Let kings command, and do[e] the best they may. Power in the People, The. Robert Herrick. BASC

Let life not be a litany. Oh, It's You Again. Carl Mayfield. ICANM

Let Man toil to win his living. Song for the Workers, A. Eliza Cook. VWP

Let man's soul[e] be a sphe[a]re, and then, in this. Good Friday [*or* Goodfriday], 1613. Riding Westward. John Donne. BASC; BBASP; BrAP; ChIV-2; FSCP; NAEL-6v1; NAEL-7v1; NoP-4; NoP-5; NOSC; PBRV; SacPr; TFi; WaAnP

Let Mary Live long. Loyal English Man's Wish for the Preservation of the King and Queen, The. Anne Morcott. EMWP

Let me be the great nail holding a skyscraper through blue nights into white stars. (LL) Prayers of Steel. Carl Sandburg. BeAl; MoAmPo; SSCS

Let me be the man who. Way He'd Like It, The. Al Zolynas. SUP

Let me be to Thee as the circling bird. Gerard Manley Hopkins. SacPr

Let me borrow her corpse a little. Death of a Grandmother. Harvey Shapiro. TaR

Let me but do my work from day to day. Work. Henry Van Dyke. SacPr

Let Me Call You Sweetheart. Beth Slater Whitson. TCAPo

Let me confess. I'm sick of these sestinas. My Confessional Sestina. Dana Gioia. PoA 2002; RA

Let me confess[e] that we two must be twain[e]. William Shakespeare. HeIP-4; PBRV *Fr.* Sonnets.

Let Me Die on the Prairie. Fanny Crosby. SWaP

Let me die on the prairie! and o'er my rude grave. Let Me Die on the Prairie. Fanny Crosby. SWaP

Let me dive to the bottom of the hotel pool. New Year. Jason Shinder. NevBe

Let me do to you what they do. Knot. Susan Wicks. EmeKit

Let Me Enjoy. Thomas Hardy. NoAM

Let me enter my chamber and sing my songs of love. (LL) Carolyn Kizer. NoP-5; OxBoAm *Fr.* Pro Femina.

Let me feed full, till that I fart, say[e]s Jill. (LL) Upon Jack and Jill: Epigram. Robert Herrick. NAEL-6v1; NAEL-7v1

Let me find Roland, I won't stop till I kill him! (LL) *Unknown.* NAWM-5v1; NAWM-7v1 *Fr.* Song of Roland, The.

Let Me Gather from the Earth. Margaret Fuller. TCAPo

Let me gather from the Earth, one full grown fragrant flower. Let Me Gather from the Earth. Margaret Fuller. TCAPo

Let me get. Nice Sister-Scholars Need Loving, Too. David Earl Jackson. BtF

Let me give something!—as the years unfold. Frederick Goddard Tuckerman. APN-2 *Fr.* Sonnets.

Let me give something!—though my spring be done. Frederick Goddard Tuckerman. APN-2 *Fr.* Sonnets.

Let me go forth, and share. Ode in May. Sir William Watson. OBEV

Let Me In. Judith Baumel. TaR

Let me move slowly through the street. Crowded Street, The. William Cullen Bryant. NCAP

Let me never have her father. Prayer to Be with Mercurial Women. Roddy Lumsden. BeAl; EdScPo; NeBl

Let me never know myself apart from the living God! (LL) Hands of God, The. D. H. Lawrence. ChIV-2; InvLi

Let me not love thee, if I love thee not. (LL) Affliction (1). George Herbert. BASC; FSCP; NAEL-6v1; NAEL-7v1; NoP-4; NoP-5; NOSC

Let me not thirst with this Hock at my Lip. Emily Dickinson. WPoS

Let me not to the marriage of true minds. William Shakespeare. AEP; BLPJKO; BrAP; CABP; ClHu; GSo; HeIP-4; NAEL-6v1; NAEL-7v1; NIL-7; NIP-4; NoP-5; NoSic; NPeEn; OBEV; OxAEP-1; OxBEV; OxBSo; PoPoPo; PtR; SoSe-8; TFi; TRP; WaAnP; WeW-3 *Fr.* Sonnets.

Let me not to the marriage of true swine. Wendy Cope. WaAnP *Fr.* Strugnell's Sonnets.

Let me out in the dark, let me go, let me go! (LL) Divorce. Anna Wickham. MoBrPo; NALW

Let me pour [or powre] forth. Valediction, A: of Weeping. John Donne. BASC; FSCP; HeIP-4; NAEL-6v1; NAEL-7v1; NoP-4; NoP-5; NOSC; WeW-3

Let me propose to you this way. Eclipsed. Richard Meier. IIR

Let me recall my Fathers' (names). Sacrifice of Isaac, The. Rabbi Ephraim ben Jacob. NAWM-7v1, *tr. by* Judah Goldin

Let Me Remind You You Are Still under Oath. Nance Van Winckel. RWB

Let Me Sing and I'm Happy. Irving Berlin. ReLy

Let me sing of ten comrades. Squad in the Land, A. Hillel Omer. NRoS, *tr. by* Esther Raizen

Let me sleep this night away. Upon Himselfe Being Buried. Robert Herrick. PBRV

Let me speak for the gray-green lichen. Grist for Grace. Judyth Hill. ICANM

Let me speak one word, muzzle. Farewell, The. Rosario Castellanos. TANSG, *tr. by* Magda Bogin

Let me strap / the baby in the seat, just don't say. If He Let Us Go Now. Sherley Anne Williams. OxAAAP

Let me take my leave, my mother. My Mother Dear. *Hawaiian Oral Tradition.* NAAPv.1

Let me take this other glove off. In Westminster Abbey. Sir John Betjeman. FaBoWar; HarvBoo; NAMCP V.1; NBLV; NIL-7; NIP-4; NoAM; OBSV; OxAEP-2

Let me tell you a little story. Miss Gee. W. H. Auden. UV; WaAnP

Let me tell you a little story / About Miss Edith Gee. Moral Tale, A. Roger Woddis. UV

Let me tell You a thing or two, Tara. Rāmprasād Sen. SinGod, *tr. by* Rachel Fell McDermott

Let me tell you the shortest story. You're Not a Man If You don't Die. Husein Tahmiscic. PML, *tr. by* John Hartley Williams

Let me tell you the shortest story. You're Not a Man If You don't Die. Ülkü Tamer. PML, *tr. by* Talat Sait Halman

Let me tell you the story of how I began. Song: Lift-Boy. Robert Graves. OxAEP-2

Let me tell you what is nat'rally de fac'. Who Is on the Lord's Side. *Unknown.* SSUS

Let me thy Angel[l] be[e], be[e] thou my Lord. (LL) Edward Taylor. NOSC; TCAPo; WaAnP *Fr.* Preparatory Meditations Before My Approach to the Lord's Supper.

Let me wake in the night. Wendell Berry. UpMys *Fr.* Prayers and Sayings of the Mad Farmer.

Let mee thinke no more on thee. Nicholas Breton. NPeEn *Fr.* Solemne Long Enduring Passion, A.

Let men pay for their. Yosano Akiko. CAoMJL1, *tr. by* Janine Beichman

Let mind be more precious than soul; it will not. Geoffrey Hill. UpMys *Fr.* Funeral Music.

Let Mother Earth now deck herself in flowers. Sir Philip Sidney. OxAEP-1 *Fr.* Countesse of Pembroke's Arcadia, The.

Let My Country Awake. Rabindranath Tagore. ItP; PtR; TWF *Fr.* Gitanjali.

Let my first Knowing be of thee. Emily Dickinson. TCAPo

Let my fond lips but drink thy golden wine. Go into the Highways and Hedges, And Compel Them to Come In. Aleister Crowley. CAGL

Let my house be mist and haze. Yi Hwang. CATKP *Fr.* Twelve Songs of Tosan.

Let My People Go. Noémia da Sousa. HAWP, *tr. by* Jacques-Noël Gouat

Let my people go! (LL) Go Down, Moses. *Unknown.* NAAPv.1; NoP-4; NoP-5

Let My People Go [*see also* Go Down, Moses]. *Unknown.* APN-2

Let my words. Prayer. Joseph Bruchac. UnSA

Let nature take a turn at saying what love is! (LL) Self and the Mulberry, The. Marvin Bell. BodElec; CAP-8

Let No Charitable Hope. Elinor Wylie. APT-1; ColAP; IJHIL; MoAmPo; NAAPv.2; NALW; NAMCP V.1; OxBoAm

Let no man boste of cunning nor vertu. Like a Midsummer Rose. John Lydgate. SacPr

Let no one impute to self-pity or censure. Poem of the Gifts. Jorge Luis Borges. TCLAP, *tr. by* Ben Belitt

Let no tempest subside no rock stagger. In Memory of a Black Union Leader. Aimé Césaire. VCWP

Let no word with its thinking threat. A La Une. Marie Ponsot. CLPP

Let Noah build an ark out of the old lady's shoe and. Anne Sexton. NALW *Fr.* O Ye Tongues.

Let none look at *me!*. (LL) Mother and Poet. Elizabeth Barrett Browning. InoFa; NAEL-6v2; NALW; ViWPN; VWP

Let not a star suspect the mystery! Embalmment. Michael Field. VWP

Let not Death boast his conquering power. On Eleanor Freeman, Who Died 1650, Aged 21. *Unknown.* OBEV

Let not my titles, crowns, and worldly honors. (To the Virgin). Maria De' Medici. WPoS, *tr. by* Laura Anna Stortoni *and* Mary Prentice Lillie

Let not our naive labours have been in vain! (LL) Disused Shed in Co. Wexford, A. Derek Mahon. CABP; EmeKit; ModIr; NAMCP V.2; NoP-4; NoP-5; NPeEn; PBCIP; PNI; StAl

Let not the rugged brow the rhymes accuse. Mary Tighe. NoP-4; RWP *Fr.* Psyche.

Let not the sluggish sleep. Song. William Byrd. SacPr

Let not the title of my verse offend. Natural Child, The. Helen Leigh. WoRP

Let not this plunder be misconstrued. Dennis Brutus. EroLit

Let not thy beauty make thee proud. Aurelian Townshend. NOSC

Let not young souls be smothered out before. Leaden-eyed, The. Vachel Lindsay. StAl; TCAPo

Let not your heart be troubled. Mary Elizabeth Fullerton. GI *Fr.* St. John.

Let nothing disturb thee. Lines Written in Her Breviary. Saint, of Avila Theresa. WPoS, *tr. by* Henry Wadsworth Longfellow

Let now thy power be great O Lord. Numeri XIII. John Hall. ChIV-1

Let Observation, Shuddering the While. F. Mullen. UV

Let Observation with extensive view. Vanity of Human Wishes, The; The Tenth Satire of Juvenal [Imitated]. Juvenal. CABP; MakPoe; NAEL-6v1; NAEL-7v1; NoP-4; NoP-5; OxAEP-1; OxBEV; TFi; UV; WaAnP; WoPoe, *tr. by* Samuel Johnson

Let oken club now strike, and poast of might. Seneca. OBVE *Fr.* Hercules Furens.

Let one bird sing. (LL) When Autumn Came. Faiz Ahmad Faiz. PLBUT; PoetW, *tr. by* Naomi Lazard

Let other mount aloft, let other sore. Seneca. OBVE *Fr.* Hercules Oetaeus [*or* Hercules Oetæus].

Let other poets raise a fracas. Scotch Drink. Robert Burns. ChIV-1

Let others cope with governing. Roistering I'll Chaff. Luis de Góngora y Argote. SpanPo, *tr.* by William M. Davis

Let others draw from smiling skies their theme. Philip Freneau. NAAL-3 *Fr.* House of Night, The.

Let others hail the holidays with laughter. Ausiàs March. STV

Let others speak. Canticle. Joseph Bruchac. ViWalt

Let others to the Printing Presse run fast. Robert Herrick. PBRV

Let others write of battles fought. True Heroism. *Unknown.* ITBLP

Let Peter rejoice with the Moon Fish who keeps up the life in the waters by night. Christopher Smart. ChIV-2 *Fr.* Jubilate Agno.

Let poetry be like a key. Ars Poetica. Vincente Huidobro. PFTM-1; TCLAP, *tr.* by David Guss

Let poets praise the blossom of wild Spring. Spring in London. John Bingham Morton. OBCoV

Let Ramah rejoice with Cochineal. Christopher Smart. *Fr.* Jubilate Agno.

Let rigid Cato read these lines of mine. (LL) When He Would Have His Verses Read. Robert Herrick. BASC; CavPo; NOSC

Let some sad trumpeter stand. 'Back on Times Square, Dreaming of Times Square'. Allen Ginsberg. CLPP

Let Sporus tremble—"What? That thing of silk." Alexander Pope. OBSV; OxBEV *Fr.* Epistle to Dr. Arbuthnot.

Let the bird of loudest [*or* lowdest] lay. Phoenix and the Turtle, The. William Shakespeare. NoP-5; NoSic; OBEV; OxAEP-1; OxBEV
  (Let the bird of loudest lay.) CABP; NoP-4
  (Let the bird of lowdest lay.) PBRV

Let the boy try along this bayonet-blade. Arms and the Boy. Wilfred Owen. BrAP; MoBrPo; OxBEV; WeW-3

Let / the / child / be / born. Song for Bringing a Child into the World. *Seminole Oral Tradition.* NAAPv.1

Let the city sleep on undisturbed. David Wheatley. NIrP *Fr.* Sonnets to James Clarence Mangan.

Let the crocus air invoke spring. Crocus Air. Winfield Townley Scott. APT-2

Let the cruel spring begin, Sweeney. Epithalamion. Nancy Schoenberger. SwNoth

Let the day grow on you upward. Earth. Derek Walcott. StAl

Let the Day Perish [Wherein I Was Born]. Bible, *O.T.* NPeEn; OBVE *Fr.* Job.

Let the day perish, wherein I was borne, and the night in which it was said, There is a man-childe conceived. Bible, *O.T.* NPeEn; OBVE *Fr.* Job.

Let the earth last. Ayocuan Cuetzpaltzin. PoCho

Let the first syllable of PEnelope be followed by the first of DIdo, the first of CAnus by that of REmus. *Unknown.* EroLit

Let the form be a garden in wild wilderness. This Poem. Barbara Leslie Jordan. ExTi; PoDa

Let the four-clustered ivy flourish about you, Anacreon. Antipater of Sidon. HePo, *tr.* by Barbara Hughes Fowler

Let the harp be mute for ever. Lady Caroline Lamb. RWP *Fr.* Fugitive Pieces and Reminiscences of Lord Byron with Some Original Poetry, Letters and Recollections of Lady Caroline Lamb, ed. I. Nathan.

Let the hypocrites practice their way. Sheyhülislâm Yahya Efendi. OLP, *tr.* by Walter Andrews, Najaat Black and Mehmet Kalpakli

Let the light of late afternoon. Let Evening Come. Jane Kenyon. BeAl; GoPo; MakPoe; OxBoAm; PoCu; PtR

Let the lover be disgraceful, crazy. Jelaluddin Rumi. RaBo *Fr.* Three Quatrains.

Let the male Poets their male Phoebus choose [*or* chuse]. To the Excellent Orinda. "Philo-Philippa." BASC

Let the memorial hill remember, instead of me. Yehuda Amichai. PoSu *Fr.* Patriotic Songs.

Let the Midnight Special. Joseph Bruchac. GM

Let the mullah raise his prayer to the dawn. *Unknown.* SLW, *tr.* by Marjolijn De Jager, Sayd Bahodin Majrouh and André Velter

Let the night keep. Night. William Rose Benét. MoAmPo

Let the number be learnt like a verse from Scripture. Schutzstaffeln 45326. Dafydd Rowlands. BBMWP, *tr.* by Meic Stephens

Let the older accompany the younger. Poem for the Purchase of a First Bra. Allison Joseph. BtF

Let the pines rock in torment of the storm. Horatian Ode. Joseph Warren Beach. PoA 2002

Let the Poet Come. León Felipe. RaW, *tr.* by W. S. Merwin

Let the rain kiss you. April Rain Song. Langston Hughes. NOxBChV; NTCP

Let the Raspberry Jam in the Crystal Jar Stand for It. Patricia Dienstfrey. AFaM

Let the snake wait under. Sort of a Song, A. William Carlos Williams. APT-1; NAAL-5; NoP-4; NoP-5; WoPoe

Let the speckled hens praise her. Speckled Hen's Morning Song to Biddy Early, The. Nancy Willard. FFC

Let the springs squeak. Squeak. Philip Dacey. SUP

Let the storm wash the plates. (LL) Strawberries. Edwin Morgan. EdScPo; NoP-4; NoP-5

Let the throbs commence. Throbs for the Instructress. Pedro López-Adorno. BRtP

Let the white blossoms blow. Love Song in Summer's Furnace Heat. James Schevill. ASA

Let the Wind Recite. Yang Mu. PML, *tr.* by Zhang Cuo

Let the Words. Boris Leonidovich Pasternak. TCRusP, *tr.* by Bogdan Boychuk and Bob Perelman

Let the words be shed like amber. Let the Words. Boris Leonidovich Pasternak. TCRusP, *tr.* by Bogdan Boychuk and Bob Perelman

Let the world under marital law be smashed to bits, startled fingernail covered in grime, silent path, and last conflagration. Bolero at Armageddon. David Huerta. RMCMP, *tr.* by Mark Schafer

Let the world's sharpness, like a clasping knife. Elizabeth Barrett Browning. CenSon *Fr.* Sonnets from the Portuguese.

Let the young people. Soldiers. Sutardji Calzoum Bachri. WoPoe, *tr.* by Harry Aveling

Let their hooves print the next bit of the story. Horses of Meaning, The. Eiléan Ní Chuilleanáin. BeAl

Let them be! Get out! Imre Madách. IQMS *Fr.* Tragedy of Man.

Let them bestow on every airt[h] a limb. On Himself, upon Hearing What Was His Sentence. James Graham, Marquess of Montrose. NePenScot; NOSC; NPeEn

Let them bury your big eyes. Edna St. Vincent Millay. APT-1; InoFa; MoAmPo *Fr.* Memorial to D. C..

Let Them Call It Jazz. Stewart Brown. WaCA

Let Them Choose Paths. Odia Ofeimun. HBAPE

Let them identify you to the future in these songs. (LL) Spirit Whose Work Is Done. Walt Whitman. CBCWP; NAAL-3; PCW

Let them lie perilous and beautiful. (LL) Equilibrists, The. John Crowe Ransom. APT-1; FuPo; InGu; NoAM

Let them lie—their day is over. Refrigerium. Frederick Goddard Tuckerman. TCAPo

Let Them Mock! Xuanjue. CCL1 *Fr.* Canticle of the Way.

Let them mock! Let them laugh! Xuanjue. CCL1 *Fr.* Canticle of the Way.

Let them return, saying you blush again for the great Great-grandmother. Hart Crane. PFTM-1

Let them serve you champagne in bed. Words. Tomaz Salamun. PoCho, *tr.* by the author and Christopher Merrill

Let there be a small state with few people. Lao Tzu. ColAnChi *Fr.* Tao Te Ching.

Let there be braziers, holophotal lenses. Fiat Lux. Robert Crawford. NeBrP

Let there be commerce between us. (LL) Pact, A. Ezra Pound. APT-1; ColAP; NAAL-5; NAAPv.2; NAMCP V.1; NoAM; NoP-5; RaF; ViWalt; WaAnP

Let there be *lamps* of whatever variety. Twenty-seven Props for a Production of *Eine Lebenszeit.* Timothy Donnelly. LegDan

Let there be life, said God. And what He wrought. Power and the Glory, The. Siegfried Sassoon. OBMV

Let there be light! Colley Cibber. STuOW *Fr.* Birthday Ode, 1732.

Let There Be Light! D. H. Lawrence. ChIV-4

"Let there be light!" said God, and there was light! Lord Byron. OBWP *Fr.* Don Juan.

Let There Be New Flowering. Lucille Clifton. RaF

Let there be time for the fields to redeem. Time Once Again. Mark McMorris. IAoNAP

Let there be treaties, bridges. Against Extremity. Charles Tomlinson. HarvBoo

Let this one clear square of thought be just. Your Name on It. Brenda Shaughnessy. LegDan

Let this rock crush me with its weight. *Unknown.* SLW, *tr.* by Marjolijn De Jager, Sayd Bahodin Majrouh and André Velter

Let those who are in favour with their stars. William Shakespeare. FaBoWar; GoPo; OxAEP-1 *Fr.* Sonnets.

Let those who hear this voice become aware. David Gascoyne. RWPCtW *Fr.* Night Thoughts.

Let Tyrants Shake Their Iron Rod [*with music*]. William Billings. TCAPo
  (Chester.) NAAPv.1

Let us abandon then our gardens and go home. Justice Denied in Massachusetts. Edna St. Vincent Millay. MoAmPo; NAAPv.2

Let us all point an accusing finger at Mr. Latour. Long Time No See, 'Bye Now. Ogden Nash. OxBoAm

Let us be guests in one another's house. Any Wife or Husband. Carol Haynes. ITBLP

Let Us Be Midwives! Kurihara Sadako. ItWoWo, *tr.* by Richard H. Minear

Let us be tender to each other, dear. Beggar Love. Adriann Roland Holst. TuT, *tr.* by Desmond Egan

Let us begin and carry up this corpse. Grammarian's Funeral, A. Robert Browning. NAEL-6v2; NAEL-7v2

Let us begin to understand the argument. Ivory Tower, The. Allen Tate. APT-2; OxBoAm

Let us begin with a simple line. Art Class. James Galvin. TAPaP

Let us build a little house. Samuel Hoffenstein. AmWit *Fr.* Love-songs, at Once Tender and Informative.

Let us call her footnote, oddity, heart tug. Woman Who Died in Line, The. Patricia Smith. SpirFl

Let us celebrate the single-cloaked beings. Psalm to the Creatures. Gwilym R. Jones. OBWVE, *tr.* by Joseph P. Clancy

Let Us Consider Where the Great Men Are. Delmore Schwartz. MoAmPo *Fr.* Shenandoah.

Let Us Describe. Gertrude Stein. PFTM-1

Let us describe how they went. It was a very windy night and the road. Let Us Describe. Gertrude Stein. PFTM-1

Let us each day enure our selves to dye. Blessednesse of Faithfull Soules by Death, The. William Drummond of Hawthornden. SacPr

Let us effect a moratorium on things. Scalpel in Hand. Marjorie Welish. FTOS

Let us forgive Ty Kendricks. Southern Cop. Sterling Allen Brown. OxBoAm; SoSe-8

Let us give thanks to God above. Thanksgiving. Lizelia Augusta Jenkins Moorer. CBWP-3

Let Us Go and Find a Place of Worship. Carmelita McGrath. Coast

Let us go hence, my songs; she will not hear. Leave-taking, A. Algernon Charles Swinburne. OxBEV

Let us go hence: the night is now at hand. Last Word, A. Ernest Dowson. GSo; MoBrPo

Let us go on then. Free Radicals. James Sherry. FTOS

Let us go then, you and I. Love Song of J. Alfred Prufrock, The. T. S. Eliot. AmFaPo; APT-1; BrAP; ClHu; ColAP; EMP; GPTC; HarvBoo; HeIP-4; IJHIL; MakPoe; MoAmPo; NAAL-5; NAAPv.2; NAEL-6v2; NAEL-7v2; NAMCP V.1; NAWM-7v2; NIL-7; NoAM; NoP-4; NoP-5; NPeEn; OxAEP-2; OxBEV; OxBoAm; PoA 2002; PoPoPo; SoSe-8; TCAPo; TFi; TRP; WaAnP; WeW-3; WoPoe

Let us have deities, he said, but not as indulgence. Near House, The. Mark Van Doren. APT-2

Let us honor the offerings. Beneath Winter's Roof. Ekaterina Iosifova. CSCBP, *tr.* by Georgi Belev and Lisa Sapinkopf

Let us, however, recover the Sceptre. "H. D." HarvBoo *Fr.* Walls Do Not Fall, The.

Let us, in this time of bittersweet lament. Attending, The. Fred Chappell. RWB

Let us live in a lull of the long winter-winds. For C.W.B. Elizabeth Bishop. GoPo

Let us live the slow way. On the Porch—Denton, Texas. Martha Elizabeth. TiP2

Let Us Love As We Choose: Water. Mariella Bettarini. CItWP, *tr.* by Cinzia Sartini Blum and Lara Trubowitz

Let us make homage to the fox, for his tail is as lush. Andrew Hudgins. UpMys *Fr.* Liar's Psalm, The.

Let us now consider the ocean. Beginner's Guide to the Ocean, A. Ogden Nash. AmWit

Let us now drink, I imagine patriot cry to patriot. Aftermath. Paul Muldoon. NAMCP V.2

Let us now praise famous men. Bible, Apocrypha. OBVE *Fr.* Ecclesiasticus.

Let us now praise women. Ourstory. Carole Satyamurti. BeAl; MoWP

Let Us Pledge. Wendell Berry. PoCoUp

Let us pledge allegiance to the flag. Let Us Pledge. Wendell Berry. PoCoUp

Let us preserve. Three Written Poems, Unconnected. Marianne Vitale. HeMarv

Let us recall the illusion. Will Alexander. WANABP *Fr.* Asia.

Let us remember Spring will come again. May, 1915. Charlotte Mew. PLBUT

Let us salute what delivers us, the flame yellow bulldozer, the giant beetle. Let Us Salute. Jacques Dupin. MotU, *tr.* by Paul Auster

Let us say I was sitting in this place. Kitzbuhl Church. Karen Alkalay-Gut. DTA

Let us see, is this real. Pawnee War-Song. *Unknown*. APN-2, *tr.* by Daniel Garrison Brinton

Let us sing of Federation. Federation. W. T. Goodge. NOBAu

Let us sing the sacred songs. (LL) Carriers of the Dream Wheel. N. Scott Momaday. ColAP; WaAnP

Let us sleep now. (LL) Strange Meeting. Wilfred Owen. BrAP; FaBoWar; HarvBoo; HeIP-4; MakPoe; MoBrPo; NAEL-6v2; NAEL-7v2; NAMCP V.1; NoAM; NoP-4; NoP-5; OBWP; OxAEP-2; OxBEV; PoWW; TCAWP; TFi; WaAnP

Let us sleep together here tonight. Kenneth Rexroth. APSN *Fr.* Love Poems of Marichiko, The.

Let us slip into. Dream, The. Olav H. Hauge. WED, *tr.* by Robert Bly

Let Us Strive to Do Something. Mrs. Henry Linden. CBWP-4

Let us suppose it a California day. Founding of Yuba City, The. Chitra Divakaruni. GeoHom

Let us synge unto the Lorde, for he is become glorious. Bible, *O.T.* OBVE *Fr.* Exodus.

Let us take to our heart a lesson, no braver lesson can be. Tapestry Weaver, The. Anson G. Chester. ITBLP

Let us thank Almighty God. Creatrix. Anna Wickham. MoBrPo

Let us the fruit of Love's pursuit. Round of Life. Richard Outram. IFF

Let us walk in the white snow. Velvet Shoes. Elinor Wylie. MoAmPo; NAAPv.2; WHSW

Let us walk where reeds are growing. Walk by the Water, A. Charlotte Smith. NPBRoP

Let us walk with this cone of light. Clair de Lune. Gwen Harwood. BMAP

Let what declines find a level of its own. Approach, The. Daniel Halpern. PfSP

Let who so lyst with mighty mace to raygne. Seneca. OBVE *Fr.* Thyestes.

Let Wisdom Wear the Crown: Hymn for Gaia. Elsa Gidlow. HW

Let wits contest. Posy [*or* Posie], The. George Herbert. ChIV-1; NOSC

Let you drag me here, without demurring. To Belinda. Johann Wolfgang von Goethe. STV, *tr.* by John Frederick Nims

Let your permanency under the brilliance of the stars be long. Jaime Saenz. BLPSL, *tr.* by Rene de Costa, Rigas Kappatos and Eleni Paidoussi

Let Zeus Record. "H. D."
"Stars wheel in purple, yours is not so rare." APT-1; MoAmPo

Lethargic vs violence as alternatives of each other for los americanos, The. Anecdotes of the Late War. Charles Olson. CBCWP

Lethargy of evil in her eyes—The The. Dying Viper, A. Michael Field. CABP

Lethe. Mary Barnard. APT-2

Lethe. "H. D." APT-1; MoAmPo; TCAPo

Lethe had passed those lips, and he knew all. (LL) George Meredith. NAEL-6v2; NAEL-7v2; NoP-4; NoP-5 *Fr.* Modern Love.

Leticia, no sé como decir lo que estoy pensando. Oda para Leticia. Oscar Bermeo. IJHIL

Let's be brave when the laughter dies. Let's Be Brave. Edgar Albert Guest. ITBLP

Let's be girls, Ma. Najrul Islām. SinGod, *tr.* by Rachel Fell McDermott

Let's Be Merry. Christina Georgina Rossetti. TLR

Let's Be Merry. Christina Georgina Rossetti. TLR *Fr.* Sing-Song.

Let's Begin. Otto Harbach. ReLy

Let's begin with dinner, the menu. Dinner Guest, The. Ann Townsend. SweBea

Let's build a ferry boat. Sile Na gCioch. Pat Parnell. HW

Let's call him *Jim Crow*. Reconsideration of the Blackbird, A. Thylias Moss. ESEAA

LET'S CALL IT THE / COLLECTIVE CONSCIOUSNESS (WE'VE GOT. John Cage. APSN *Fr.* Diary: How to Improve the World (You Will Only Make Matters Worse).

Let's call it the first protocol. Disarmed. Elin ap Hywel. ATSWP, *tr.* by Robert Minhinnick

Let's Call the Whole Thing Off. Ira Gershwin. ReLy

Let's contend no more, Love. Woman's Last Word, A. Robert Browning. NAEL-6v2; RACG

Let's count the bodies over again. Counting Small-Boned Bodies. Robert Bly. AmWaPo

Let's Do It. Noël Coward. ReLy

Let's do it, let's fall in love. (LL) Let's Do It, Let's Fall in Love. Cole Porter. ReLy; UV

Let's Do It, Let's Fall in Love. Cole Porter. ReLy; UV

Let's Do This Poem (1.26). Horace. WED, *tr.* by Robert Bly

Let's Dress Up. Mary Ann Hoberman. TLR

Let's dress up in grown-up clothes. Let's Dress Up. Mary Ann Hoberman. TLR

Let's drink a cup of wine; let's drink another! Chŏng Ch'ŏl. CATKP, *tr.* by Kevin O'Rourke

Let's Eat Stars. Nanao Sakaki. WhBo

Let's erase your pupose: policy geek-ozoa, lock 'n' rote a limbo *chi minh* chingaling. Bruce Andrews. BAP-04 *Fr.* Dang Me.

Let's Face the Music and Dance. Irving Berlin. ReLy

Let's Fall in Love. Ted Koehler. ReLy

Let's fill in the form: date of birth. Larisa Miller. CRWP, *tr.* by Richard McKane

Let's fly off to Finland, far. My Test Market. Rachel Loden. CalPo; PoDa; VisFro

Let's Get Away from It All. Tom Adair. ReLy

Let's get married. "That's False." Macbeth in Battle. Marjorie Welish. VaPo

Let's get our dreams unstuck. Cape of Good Hope, The. Jean Cocteau. CuPo

Let's go. Basho. EMJL

Let's go and live in Accra! Accra. Alexander Gerov. CSCBP, *tr. by* Georgi Belev and Lisa Sapinkopf

Let's go back to the rooms where we once walked. Sister. Magali Alabaú. TANSG, *tr. by* Mary Jane Treacy

Let's go—much as that dog goes. Overland to the Islands. Denise Levertov. PmAP

Let's Go Over It All Again. James Fenton. BeAl

Let's go rolling, rolling. Getting Dirty. Dorthi Charles. TLR

Let's go see blood flow. Blood. Georges Castera. OGAHCP, *tr. by* Boadiba and Jack Hirschman

Let's go see old Abe. Lincoln Monument: Washington. Langston Hughes. CBCWP

Let's Go to Hell. Srirangam Narayana Babu. HotL, *tr. by* V. Narayana Rao

Let's go to the park where. Ramsden. Margaret Avison. GPPA

Let's have a look at another five. (LL) Robert Frost. AmWit; GI *Fr.* Ten Mills.

Let's Have Another Cup of Coffee. Irving Berlin. ReLy

Let's hear it for Dwayne Coburn, who was small. Body Bags. R. S. Gwynn. RA

Let's Hear It for Goliath. Jon Dressel. AngWePo; TCAWP

Let's hear the music first and foremost. Art of Poetry, The. Paul Verlaine. SxFrPo, *tr. by* Martin Sorrell

Lets his glass / set there. (LL) Neighbor. Langston Hughes. APSN; OxBoAm; PFTM-1

Let's just say that every time you fall you never hit the ground. Let's Just Say. Charles Bernstein. Eno

Let's just say you slap me. Hard. Parable of the Cheek. J. Allyn Rosser. MAAN

Let's Just Tell It. Jabari Asim. FuFl

Let's Live Cheerfully. Takahashi Shinkichi. ZenPo, *tr. by* Takashi Ikemoto and Lucien Stryk

Let's live, let's live. Song of Green Mountain. *Unknown.* CATKP, *tr. by* Peter H. Lee

Let's look around ourselves. Three Moral Tales. Emmanuel Hocquard. YaTCFP, *tr. by* Michael Palmer

Let's look for the kids. One Two or Three. Philippe Soupault. SurPaPo, *tr. by* Mary Ann Caws and Patricia Terry

Let's make a bureaucracy. On The Empress's Mind. John Ashbery. RACG

Let's meet on the road to Morocco. Road to Morocco, The. Johnny Burke. ReLy

Let's mill grain with a rattle *hiyae.* Song of the Pestle. *Unknown.* CATKP, *tr. by* Peter H. Lee

Let's not fool ourselves. Sentences. Nicanor Parra. AF, *tr. by* Miller Williams

Let's Not Get Ahead of Ourselves. John Redmond. NIrP

Let's not have tea. White wine. Artemis. Olga Broumas. YaYoPo

Let's not talk. Spring. Tracy K. Smith. PoDa

Let's Not Talk About Love. Cole Porter. ReLy

Let's not talk of subway series. Puente. Americo Casiano. BRtP

Let's Open the Dam: "Let's open the dam." Ko Chônghûi. EcSo, *tr. by* Catherine J. Kim

Let's play Houston We Have a Problem in which Houston. Analogies. Arielle Greenberg. LegDan

Let's play *La Migra.* La Migra. Pat Mora. NIL-7; UnSA

Let's put aside. Gaelic is alive. Aonghas MacNeacail. NePenScot

Let's Put Out the Lights and Go to Sleep. Herman Hupfeld. ReLy

Let's radio opinions, koorie side effects in death. No Grudge. Lionel Fogarty. BMAP

Let's return to the shore. Yun Sôndo. CATKP *Fr.* Angler's Calendar, The.

Let's Say. Yusef Komunyakaa. RoV

Let's Say. Bob Perelman. PmAP

Let's say I give this everything I've got. Perfect Work. Bill Berkson. AHA

Let's say it was Jesus. Who is Jesus? Why should Jesus be the name. Visions of Jesus. Jerome Rothenberg. APSN

Let's say you are a man (some of you are). Allegorical Matters. Stephen Dobyns. BodElec

Let's see first afros I saw were on these girls from. Southern University, 1962. Kevin Young. SpirFl

Let's see the world. Are you coming with me. What's for dinner. (LL) World, The: "It was just a gas station. It was not spectacular carnage." Gillian Conoley. BodElec; RoV

Let's spin the bottle. Game, The. Stanley Kunitz. PoA 2002

Let's spit the two of us let's spit. Poem to Shout in the Ruins. Louis Aragon. PFTM-1

Let's spread our net out on the sand. Yun Sôndo. CATKP *Fr.* Angler's Calendar, The.

Let's start at the beginning. Maps. Alberto Blanco. RMCMP, *tr. by* Michael Wiegers

Let's stay asleep, out in the open. Four. Ofelia Perez Sepúlveda. SPV, *tr. by* Jen Hofer

Let's stop angling and see. Yun Sôndo. CATKP *Fr.* Angler's Calendar, The.

Let's take a look at the moon as a beautiful woman—half-angry. Diana Hartog. NLPA *Fr.* Oasis.

Let's Take a Walk Around the Block. Ira Gershwin and E. Y. Harburg. ReLy

Let's take / The duckweed way. Issa. ZenPo, *tr. by* Takashi Ikemoto and Lucien Stryk

Let's take the train. E. E. Cummings. GM

Let's Talk. Chase Twichell. WANABP

Let's talk about his death. Let's Talk. Chase Twichell. WANABP

Let's talk of graves, of worms, and epitaphs. William Shakespeare. TRP *Fr.* King Richard II.

Let's tell the other story about Pitzeem and his horse. Pitzeem and the Mare. Robert Bly. CAP-8

Let's tread on fragrant grasses. Yun Sôndo. CATKP *Fr.* Angler's Calendar, The.

Let's try another hand, let's redo the count. Edoardo Cacciatore. ItPo *Fr.* Full Powers: Five Warning Signs.

Let's try something. Del Ray Cross. FreRad

Let's try the present hour. Francis Picabia. PFTM-1 *Fr.* Eunuch Unique.

Let's write a poem about lazy people. Lazy People, The. Shel Silverstein. NTCP

Let[t] folly praise that fancy [*or* phancy] loves, I praise and love that Child[e]. Child[e] My Choice [*or* Choyse], A. Robert Southwell. OxBEV; SacPr

Letter. Yehuda Amichai. VCWP

Letter. Blaise Cendrars. YaTCFP, *tr. by* Ron Padgett

Letter. Keith Gilyard. SpirFl

Letter. Sue Hubbard. Prnts

Letter. Dhabya Khamees. PoArWo, *tr. by* Clarissa C. Burt

Letter. Sarah Ruden. AmPoNex

Letter. Mark Strand. NoAM

Letter. Margit Szécsi. IQMS, *tr. by* Kenneth McRobbie

Letter: "Dear Antigone." Leonard Nathan. CalPo; PBCAP

Letter ("Dear Mama, / Time I pay rent and get my food.") Langston Hughes. APT-2 *Fr.* Lenox Avenue Mural.

Letter: "Endings always erase the traces of their plot." Tedi López Mills. RMCMP, *tr. by* C. M. Mayo

Letter, The. W. H. Auden. NoAM

Letter, The. Amy Lowell. NAAPv.2; NALW; PoBW

Letter, The. Morton Marcus. GeoHom

Letter, The. Mun Chônghui. EcSo, *tr. by* Catherine J. Kim

Letter, The. Otto Orban. MotU, *tr. by* George Szirtes

Letter, The. Po Chü-i. CCL1, *tr. by* Arthur Waley

Letter, The. Elizabeth Riddell. LW; NOBAu

Letter, The. Mary Ruefle. AmAlph

Letter, The: "Few broken things linger in my palm, A." Feriha Aktan. NaPG, *tr. by* Talat Sait Halman

Letter, The: "If I remember right, his first letter." Andrew Motion. EmeKit; NeBrP

Letter 3. Charles Olson. APT-2; PmAP *Fr.* Maximus Poems, The.

Letter 1. George Crabbe. CABP *Fr.* Borough, The.

Letter 1. From Miss Biddy Fudge to Miss Dorothy———. Thomas Moore. NOBRP *Fr.* Fudge Family in Paris, The.

Letter 5. Michael Palmer. FTOS *Fr.* Letters to Zanzotto.

Letter, A. Ralph Waldo Emerson. *See* Dear Brother, Would You Know the Life.

Letter, A. Sophie Jewett. PoBW

Letter, A. Viktor Aleksandrovich Sosnora. ItGoST, *tr. by* Maia Tekses

Letter, A: "Mail runner carries the bag of mail, The." Kavikondala Venkatarao. HotL, *tr. by* V. Narayana Rao

Letter, A: "My love, / When you were here there was." Li Po. NDACCP, *tr. by* William Carlos Williams

Letter, A ("Thrash away, you'll hev to rattle"). James Russell Lowell. AmWaPo *Fr.* Biglow Papers, The.

Letter about Horror, A. Milán Füst. IQMS, *tr. by* Jess Perlman

Letter after a Year. Donald Hall. PoDa

Letter: Blues. Elizabeth Alexander. RA

Letter by letter. Boleros #21. Jay Wright. ICANM

Letter Following. Aidan Carl Mathews. PBCIP

Letter for All-Hallows (1949), A. Peter Kane Dufault. NoP-4; NoP-5

Letter for Duncan. Larry Eigner. FTOS

Letter from a Cattleboat. Harry Edmund Martinson. WED, *tr. by* Robert Bly

Letter from a Contract Worker. Antonio Jacinto. PoetW, *tr. by* Margaret Dickinson and Michael Wolfers

Letter From a Contract Worker. Antonio Jacinto. PML, *tr. by* Margaret Dickinson

Letter from a Coward to a Hero. Robert Penn Warren. MoAmPo

Letter from a Girl to Her Own Old Age, A. Alice Thompson Meynell. MoBrPo; VWP

Letter, From a Lady in London to a Lady at Lausanne, A. Winthrop Mackworth Praed. *See* Talented Man, The.

Letter from Aragon, A. John Cornford. OBWP

Letter from Artemisa in the Town, to Chloe [*or* Cloe], in the Country, A. John Wilmot, 2d Earl of Rochester. NPeEn

Letter from Berlin, A. Jon Stallworthy. OBWP

Letter from Brazil, A. Louis Simpson. BodElec

Letter from Brooklyn, A. Derek Walcott. BrAP

Letter from Chicago. May Sarton. NALW

Letter from Home. G. E. Patterson. AmPoNex

Letter from Home in Spanish. Judith Ortiz Cofer. ExTi

Letter from Home, The. Jamaica Kincaid. MotU

Letter from Kuwait. Lenard D. Moore. BtF

Letter from McCarty's Farm. Ellen Kort. IPoFL

Letter from Memory. Vera Pavlova. *tr. by* Daniel Weissbort
   9. CRWP, *tr. by* Daniel Weissbort
  12. CRWP, *tr. by* Daniel Weissbort
  17. CRWP, *tr. by* Daniel Weissbort

Letter from Mexico. Homero Aridjis. TCLAP, *tr. by* Eliot Weinberger

Letter from Mr Crashaw to the Countess of Denbigh, Against Irresolution and Delay in Matters of Religion, A. Richard Crashaw. *See* To the Noblest and Best of Ladies, the Countess of Denbigh.

Letter From My Father, A. Donny O'Rourke. EdScPo

Letter from my love to-day!, A. Ballad of Hell, A. John Davidson. MoBrPo

Letter from my mother was waiting, A. Poem in Which I Refuse Contemplation. Rita Dove. NAAL-5

Letter from Phillis Wheatley, A. Robert Earl Hayden. ESEAA; NoAM

Letter from Pretoria Central Prison. Arthur Nortje. BrAP; HBAPE

Letter from Santa Cruz. Maura Eichner. UpMys

Letter from Spain. Langston Hughes. NAAPv.2

Letter from the Coast, A. Mark Doty. HarvBoo

Letter from the Grass, A. Conrad Potter Aiken. InGu

Letter from the Shaman: The Tribe with No Myth. David Citino. UpMys

Letter Home. Natasha Trethewey. RD

Letter Home from Brooklyn. Enid Shomer. UrbNat

Letter: "Hornet holds on to the curtain, winter, The." Jean Valentine. CAP-8

Letter Left On the Porch of the Kerouac House. Ray McNiece. AmZen

Letter lies unanswered, thus free of lies, The. Correspondence. Henri Coulette. PoA 2002

Letter like pink thrift breaks up the rock-slate, a. Nevrazumitelny. Wendy Mulford. Oth

Letter of a Mother. Robert Penn Warren. MoAmPo

Letter of Recommendation. Yehuda Amichai. PoCho, *tr. by* the author and Ted Hughes

Letter of the 26th June. Philippe Jaccottet. MFP, *tr. by* Martin Sorrell

Letter: "Pigeon-house of letters, The." Miguel Hernández. WED, *tr. by* Robert Bly

Letter S. Anne Waldman. AHA

Letter VI. William Sydney Graham. EdScPo

Letter Six—The Pious Editors' Creed. James Russell Lowell. APN-1; NCAP *Fr.* Biglow Papers, The.

Letter Smuggled in a Fish. Yüan Chěn. CrYelRi, *tr. by* Sam Hamill

Letter to a Benedictine Monk. Marilyn Nelson Waniek. GT

Letter to a Black Woman. Sharron K. Williams. OWABP

Letter to a Boy at School. Anna Wickham. NOxBChV

Letter to a Brother in Exile. Rosemary Catacalos. TiP2

Letter to a Cretan Flute-Maker. Justin Vitiello. UnSA

Letter to a Dead Father. Richard Shelton. PBCAP

Letter to a Friend. Marjorie Oludhe Macgoye. HAWP

Letter to a Friend. Jon Stallworthy. NoAM

Letter to a Friend. Robert Penn Warren. MoAmPo

Letter to a Friend: Who Is Nancy Daum? James Schuyler. PmAP

Letter to a Future Generation. Gwendolyn MacEwen. BrAP

Letter to a Poet. Robert Hass. YaYoPo

Letter to a Roving Poet. Amadou Lamine Sall. NAfrP

Letter to a Tormented Playwright [*(for Yulisa Amadu Maddy)*]. Syl Cheney-Coker. HBAPE

Letter to a Young Poet. Robert Wrigley. RoV

Letter to a Zen Master. Han Wo. CCL1, *tr. by* Graeme Wilson

Letter to an Absent Son. Madeline DeFrees. PoChi

Letter to an American Visitor. Alex Comfort. FaBoWar

Letter to an Exile. Claribel Alegría. TANSG, *tr. by* Louise B. Popkin

Letter to an Imaginary Friend. Thomas McGrath.
  Part One.
    "From here it is necessary to ship all bodies east." GifTon
  Part Three.
    "And we, of the damned poor, trot our frost-furred horses." GifTon

Letter to an Unconceived Son. Tyehimba Jess. BRtP

Letter to André Breton. Antonin Artaud. ConPit, *tr. by* Clayton Eshleman

Letter to Bee. Emily Dickinson. OxBoAm; SAmP; TLR

Letter to Birch from Deer Lodge. Richard Hugo. BodElec

Letter to Blessing from Missoula. Richard Hugo. BodElec

Letter to Carlos Pellicer. Eunice Odio. TCLAP, *tr. by* Martha Collins

Letter to Daddy, A. *Unknown, fr. Terezin Concentration Camp.* INSAB

Letter to Daphnis, A. Anne Finch, Countess of Winchilsea. EMWP; LW; MakPoe; NALW; PEW
  (Letter to Daphnis, April 2, 1685, A.) NOSC

Letter to Daphnis, April 2, 1685, A. Anne Finch, Countess of Winchilsea. *See* Letter to Daphnis, A.

Letter to David James Duncan, February 16, 2003. Mandy L. Smoker. PrTe

Letter to Einstein Beginning Dear Albert. Paul Hoover. IllVoic

Letter to El Flaco on His Birthday. Richard Blanco. NAPBL

Letter to Eve. Alan Dugan. YaYoPo

Letter to Ezekiel Mphahlele. Sonia Sanchez. FuFl

Letter to Friends East and West. Albert Goldbarth. IllVoic

Letter to Gale from Ovando. Richard Hugo. BodElec

Letter to Goldbarth from Big Fork. Richard Hugo. BodElec

Letter to Haislip from Hot Springs. Richard Hugo. BodElec

Letter to Her Brother. Amelia Rosselli. PFTM-2, *tr. by* Lucia Re and Paul Vangelisti

Letter to Her Husband, Absent upon Public[k] Employment, A. Anne Bradstreet. BrAP; HeIP-4; NAAL-3; NAAL-5; NAAPv.1; NALW; NoP-4; NoP-5; PEW; PoPoPo; WaAnP

Letter to Hill from St. Ignatius. Richard Hugo. BodElec

Letter to Hugo from Later. Jane Hirshfield. GeoHom

Letter to Ibrahim. Khaled Mattawa. AmPoNex

Letter to Jeanne (at Tassajara). Diane Di Prima. BB

Letter to John Donne, A. Charles Hubert Sisson. HarvBoo

Letter to Jorge Luis Borges: Apropos of the Golem. John Hollander. TaR

Letter to Julia, in Rhyme. Henry Luttrell.
  "Have you not seen (you must remember)." NOBRP
  "London, within thy ample verge." NOBRP

Letter to Ko. Dennis Nurkse. PoDa

Letter to Lady Margaret Cavendish Holles-Harley, When a Child, A. Matthew Prior. *See* Letter to the Honourable Lady Margaret Cavendish Holles-Harley, A.

Letter to Libbey from St. Regis. Richard Hugo. BodElec

Letter to Lord Byron. W. H. Auden.
  "England, my England--you have been my tutrix." OBSV
  "You lived and moved among the best society." OBSV

Letter to Mantsch from Havre. Richard Hugo. MoASP

Letter to Medea. Helga Novak. GTCP, *tr. by* Susan L Cocalis

Letter to Miguel Otero Silva, in Caracas. Pablo Neruda. AF, *tr. by* Robert Bly
  "When I was writing my love poems, which sprouted from me." WED, *tr. by* Robert Bly

Letter to Miss E. B. on Marriage. Mary Savage. LW *Fr.* Letter to Miss E.B. on Marriage.

Letter to My Assailant. Suzanne Lummis. SUP

Letter to My Mother. Suzanne Gardinier. NeAmPo

Letter to My Mother. Mary McGinnis. ICANM

Letter to My Mother. Sergey Aleksandrovich Yesenin. RusPo, *tr. by* Robert Arthur Douglas Ford

Letter to My Mother, Sixteen Years after the Fact. Todd Davis. ACAMVP

Letter to My Sister. Anne Spencer. InGu; TCAPo

Letter to My Spouse. Miklós Radnóti. IQMS, *tr. by* Peter Zollman

Letter to My Wife. Miklós Radnóti. AF

Letter to Myself as a Child. Juanita Brunk. ACAMVP

Letter to N.Y. Elizabeth Bishop. GoPo

Letter to Oberg from Pony. Richard Hugo. BodElec

Letter to Peter Levi, A. Elizabeth Jennings. OxAEP-2

Letter to Robert Frost, A. Robert Silliman Hillyer. MoAmPo

Letter to Russel Barron. Robert Gibb. SwNoth

Letter to Sara Hutchinson. Samuel Taylor Coleridge. NPBRoP

Letter to Spencer. George Scarbrough. LPSFW

Letter to the Academy. Langston Hughes. AF

Letter to the Actor Charles Laughton concerning the Work on the Play "The Life of Galileo." Bertolt Brecht. PoSu, *tr. by* Michael Hamburger

Letter to the Countess of Denbigh. Richard Crashaw. *See* To the Noblest and Best of Ladies, the Countess of Denbigh.

Letter to the Front. Muriel Rukeyser.
  Sestina. AmWaPo
  To be a Jew in the Twentieth Century. NALW; PoCho; TaR
Letter to the Honourable Lady Margaret Cavendish Holles-Harley, A. Matthew Prior. NoAM
  (Letter to Lady Margaret Cavendish Holles-Harley, When a Child, A.) OBEV
Letter to the Survivors. Charles E. Butler. YaYoPo
Letter to Thelonius. Wopko Jensma. TSAP
Letter to Walt Whitman. Mark Doty. ViWalt
Letter to William Carlos Williams, A. George Young. BloBone
Letter to Yeni on Peering into Her Life. Sandra M. Castillo. TouFir
Letter to Youki. Robert Desnos. AF, tr. by Carolyn Forché
Letter which can wither, a learning which can suffer and an outrage which is simultaneous is principal, A. Gertrude Stein. NAMCP V.1 Fr. Tender Buttons.
Letter with No Address. Donald Hall. InoFa
Letter Written With the Left Hand, A. Ko Chônghûi. EcSo, tr. by Catherine J. Kim
Letters. Maxine W. Kumin.
  "Your laugh, your scarves, the gloss of your makeup." NAMCP V.2
Letters and bookishness. (LL) Troubles of a Book, The. Laura Riding Jackson. HarvBoo; MoWP; NAMCP V.1
Letters & Other Worlds. Michael Ondaatje. BrAP; NAMCP V.2; NoAM; NoP-4; NoP-5
Letters for a Document. Lee Bartlett. ICANM
Letters from a Father. Mona Van Duyn. NoP-4; NoP-5
Letters from a Man in Solitary. Nazim Hikmet. AF
Letters from a New England Negro. Sherley Anne Williams. ESEAA
Letters from an Exile. Valerie Duff. OPRER
Letters from Baron Von Hügel to a Niece. David Scott. NLP
Letters from Camp. Arielle Greenberg. IIR
Letters from Chankiri Prison. Nazim Hikmet. PFTM-1
Letters from Home. Elmaz Abinader. PoArWo
Letters from Poston Relocation Camp (1942–45). David Mura. LTA
Letters from School, The. Juan Delgado. TouFir
Letters from the Concertina File 1939–1940. Sue MacIntyre. Prnts
Letters from the Earth. Rodney Jones. InGu
Letters from the Front. Michael Klein. WiU
Letters from the Ming Dynasty. Joseph Brodsky. PoetW, tr. by Derek Walcott
Letters from the North Star. Kevin Young. NeAmPo
Letters from the Poet Who Sleeps in a Chair. Nicanor Parra. AF, tr. by Miller Williams
Letters from Yorkshire. Maura Dooley. NeBl
Letters I, your lone friend, write in sorrow, The. From William Tyndale to John Frith. Edgar Bowers. InGu
Letters in the Family. Adrienne Rich. NIL-7
Letters of the Jews as strict as flames, The. Alphabet, The. Karl Shapiro. APT-2; EMP; NoAM; PoA 2002; TaR
Letters Richard in a morning read, The. George Crabbe. Fr. Tales of the Hall.
Letters, The. Louise Glück. HarvBoo
Letters, The / holding what they can, hold. A. R. Ammons. NAMCP V.2 Fr. Tombstones.
Letters to a Dead Trappist. Lisa Gill. ICANM
  19. ICANM
  35. ICANM
  37. ICANM
  40. ICANM
  65. ICANM
Letters to a Kenyan Friend. D. Cyril Jones. BBMWP, tr. by Peter Finch
Letters to a Vanishing Fiancée. James Kimbrell. LegDan
Letters to a Young Poet. Adrienne Rich. ExTi
Letters to an Unknown Woman. Nicanor Parra. BLPSL, tr. by Rene de Costa, Rigas Kappatos and Eleni Paidoussi
Letters to Childhood. Mohammed Shehadeh. PoCho, tr. by Aziz Shibab
Letters to Edward Thomas. Glyn Maxwell.
  "Poem to Mr Thomas and Mr Frost." NoP-5
Letters to Live Poets. Bruce Beaver.
  "Three images of dying stick in my mind like morbid transfers." NOBAu
Letters to My Brother. Jamal Juma'h. tr. by Emily Howard and Salaam Yousif
  "Thus my brother." IrPoTo, tr. by Emily Howard and Salaam Yousif
Letters to Taranta Babu. Nazim Hikmet. tr. by Talat Sait Halman
  Fifth Letter. NaPG, tr. by Talat Sait Halman
Letters to the Dead: Denise Levertov. Dick Lourie. PrTe

Letters to Yesenin. James Harrison.
  "I am four years older than you but scarcely an unwobbling." BodElec
  "I don't have any medals. I feel their lack." BodElec
  "I wanted to feel exalted so I picked up." BodElec
  "It would surely be known for years after as the day I shot." BodElec
  "Lustra. Officially the cold comes from Manitoba." BodElec
  "This matted and glossy photo of Yesenin." BodElec
  "What if I own more paper clips than I'll ever use in this." BodElec
Letters to Zanzotto. Michael Palmer.
  Letter 5. FTOS
Letting down the isinglass curtains. Parent. Josephine Miles. NALW
Letting Go. Daryl Hine. NoP-4; NoP-5
Letting his wisdom be the whole of love. World and the Child, The. James Merrill. MakPoe
Letting in the Jungle. Rudyard Kipling. Fr. Second Jungle Book, The.
Letting it soften. (LL) Soup Kitchen. Betsy Sholl. ACAMVP; PBCAP
Letting midnight / out on bail. Jam Session. Langston Hughes. APT-2
Letting the Beat Go. Robert Duncan. FTOS
Lettre. Blaise Cendrars. YaTCFP
Lettre Sende by on Yonge Woman to A-noder, Whiche Aforetyme Were Felowes To-geder, A. Unknown. EMWP
Lettres d'un Soldat. Wallace Stevens.
  "John Smith and his son, John Smith." TLR
Lettuce devours its leaves, The. Passage. Penelope Rosemont. SurWo
Letty's Globe. Charles Tennyson Turner. NPeEn; OBEV; OxBEV; OxBSo
Levantado por varias alas de amor. Vuelo. Pedro Serrano. RMCMP
Levantine, A. William Plomer. OBMV
Levedy, ic thonke thee. Thanks and a Plea to Mary. Unknown. FaBoVe
Levee: Letter to No One, The. Lorna Dee Cervantes. TouFir
Level Cambridgeshire. Anne Stevenson. PfSP
Level slope of colored sea, The. Metaphysical. Robert Fitzgerald. PoA 2002
Leveller, The. Barry Cornwall. OxAEP-2
Leveller, The. Robert Graves. FaBoWar
Leveller's Rant, The. Alexander Brome. BASC
Lever de Soleil. Saint-Pol Roux. YaTCFP
Leviathan. Bible, O.T. OBVE Fr. Job.
Leviathan. W. S. Merwin. ChIV-1; NoAM
Leviathan. Peter Quennell.
  "Music met Leviathan returning, A." MoBrPo
Levis Exsurgit Zephirus. Unknown. WoPoe Fr. Cambridge Songs.
Levitation. Carl Phillips. OxAAAP
Levite and His Concubine at Gibeah, The. Paul Durcan. ModIr
Leviticus (Chapter 7, Verse 2-5). Manuela Fingueret. MirDau, tr. by Roberta Gordenstein
Lewis. Derick Thomson. EdScPo
Lewis Mumford. George Buchanan. PNI
L'Excès-L'usine. Leslie Kaplan. tr. by Serge Gavronsky
  "Cables are made near the window. The cables have." SCFWP, tr. by Serge Gavronsky
  "Factory, one goes there, The. Everything is there." SCFWP, tr. by Serge Gavronsky
  "Factory, the factory universe, the one, The." SCFWP, tr. by Serge Gavronsky
  "It's evening. There's time." SCFWP, tr. by Serge Gavronsky
  "One parks the bike. The yard is full of rounded." SCFWP, tr. by Serge Gavronsky
  "When one gets there, the frigidaire in a corner is." SCFWP
  "Yard, one's got to cross it, The. Total nostalgia." SCFWP, tr. by Serge Gavronsky
Lexically. Ken Edwards. Oth Fr. 3600 Weekends.
Lexicon of Exile. Aleida Rodríguez. CalPo
Lexington Avenue Express. Percy Johnston. EGAG
Leyendo a Virgilio. Tedi López Mills. RMCMP
Li Bo put it in a poem, this West-of-the-Waters Abbey. Tu Mu. CCL1 Fr. Recalling Former Travels.
Li Furen. Emperor Wu of Han. CCL1, tr. by Arthur Waley
Li Hung-yi ripped Chih-yüan's fine clothes to rags and gave him a cotton gown and trousers to wear. Chinese Oral Tradition. ColAnChi Fr. Ballad of the Hidden Dragon.
Li Po. Undressing for Li Po. Carl Phillips. WiU
Li Po drowned when he stepped into a pond. Li Pos of the Polis. Simeon Dumdum. ReBoTo
Li Pos of the Polis. Simeon Dumdum. ReBoTo
Li Po's poetry: no match anywhere. Spring Day: Thinking of Li Po. Tu Fu [or Du Fu]. ChinPo, tr. by Ye Weilian [or Yeh Wei-lien or Wai-lim Yip]
Liadan and Curithir. Kuno Meyer. IrLP
Liam. Mary Jo Salter. ExTi

Liana, The.   Gabriela Mistral.   BBASP, *tr. by* Doris Dana

Lianas in bright bloom hang from mahogany shade.   Jaguar's Dream, The.   Charles Marie René Leconte de Lisle.   WoPoe, *tr. by* James Lasdun

Liar, I thought, kneeling with the others.   White Spine.   Henri Cole.   NAMCP V.2

Liar! You tell our children of freedom.   Scottsboro.   Betsalel Friedman.   Prolet, *tr. by* Amelia Glaser

Liar's Psalm, The.   Andrew Hudgins.
    Homage to the Fox.   UpMys
    Repentance.   UpMys

Lilb. 2. Metrum 4.   Boethius.   FSCP *Fr.* De Consolatione Philosophiae [Trans. Henry Vaughan].

Lib. 2. Metrum 5.   Boethius.   NOSC; OBVE *Fr.* Consolation of Philosophy, The ("De Consolacione Philosophie").

Libation.   Palorine Williams.   Prnts

Libation Bearers, The.   Aeschylus.   NAWM-5v1, *tr. by* Robert Fagles

Libations.   Ferenc Kölcsey.   IQMS, *tr. by* Adam Makkai

Libera nos, Domine—Deliver Us, O Lord.   Philip Freneau.   OxBEV

Liberace.   Jonathan Holden.   ReTh

Liberación.   E. A. Mares.   ICANM

Liberal, or Innocent by Definition.   James Philip McAuley.   NOBAu

Liberality of Sentiment.   Cornelius Whur.
    And So Home.   STuOW

Liberate me.   In the First Circle of Limbo.   Carl Rakosi.   BAP-04

Liberation.   Abena Busia.   HAWP; PoetW

Liberation.   Vegunta Mohana Prasad.   HotL, *tr. by* V. Narayana Rao

Liberators.   Dennis Nurkse.   PrTe

Liberia?   Libretto for the Republic of Liberia.   Melvin B. Tolson.

Libertine, The.   Louis MacNeice.   ModIr; NAMCP V.1; NoAM

Liberty.   Ernst Mirville.   OGAHCP, *tr. by* Boadiba and Jack Hirschman

Liberty [*sequel to* Gold and Silver Fishes in a Vase].   William Wordsworth.
    Insensibility.   STuOW

Liberty: "Liberty means different things to different people."   Anne Carson.   NLPA *Fr.* Glass Essay, The.

Liberty means different things to different people.   Anne Carson.   NLPA *Fr.* Glass Essay, The.

Liberty Song, The.   John Dickinson.   NAAPv.1

Liberty [*or* Libertie], that we[e]'ll enjoy tonight, The. (LL)   Inviting a Friend to Supper.   Ben Jonson.   BASC; BrAP; ItP; NAEL-6v1; NAEL-7v1; NoP-4; NoP-5; NOSC; NPeEn; PBRV; WaAnP

Liberty, The.   Sarah Fyge Egerton.   EMWP

Liberty to M. le Diplomate.   Sydney Thompson Dobell.   OxBSo

Liberty Tree.   Thomas Paine.   AmWaPo

Libido.   Larissa Szporluk.   AmPoNex

Libido portion goes haywire, The.   Century of Hands.   Michael Davidson.   FTOS

Libra, September.   John Taylor.   NOSC

Librarian, The.   Charles Olson.   PmAP

Library.   Pierre Alféri.   YaTCFP, *tr. by* Cole Swensen

Library.   Louis Jenkins.   RaBo

Library in a Garden, A.   Richard Le Gallienne.   OBGa

Library, The.   Timothy Steele.   RA

Libre como el que más.   Temporada de Paraíso, Una.   José Luis Rivas.   RMCMP

Libretto for the Republic of Liberia.   Melvin B. Tolson.
    Ti.   APT-2

Libro de Segunda Mano.   Antonio Deltoro.   RMCMP

Libyan Airliner/Egyptian Acrobats/Israeli Air Circus [2004 version].   Sam Hamod.   OtW

Lice, The.   Mei Yao Ch'en.   CrYelRi, *tr. by* Sam Hamill

Lice-Seekers.   Arthur Rimbaud.   SxFrPo, *tr. by* Martin Sorrell

Lich Gate, The.   Clayton Eshleman.   PmAP

Licia.   Giles, the Elder Fletcher.
    "I saw, sweet Licia, when the spider ran."   OxBSo

Licit tremendous unjust oxidized fancified notions tremulously.   Tactics.   Jen Hofer.   Eno

Licked the blood off his fists. (LL)   Revolt in the Mirror, A.   Wolfgang Bächler.   GTCP; PML, *tr. by* Reinhold Grimm

Licking Wounds.   Alice Anderson.   AmPoNex

Licorice.   Laini Mataka.   BtF

Licorice Chronicles.   Ted Greenwald.
    "Coordinating cities gulls still gull, and, arms binged with wine, as wine."   FTOS

Licorice Fields at Pontefract, The.   Sir John Betjeman.   CABP

Licorice lips noosed around Her neck as he drooled in Her ear that he always did like.   Yellah.   Lisa Pegram.   BRtP

Lid of the Chevy trunk couldn't close, The.   First TV in a Mennonite Family.   Julia Kasdorf.   AmPoNex

Liddell and Scott.   Thomas Hardy.   OBCoV

Lidice.   Ernst Waldinger.   FaBoWar, *tr. by Unknown*

Lidice sounds like marriage bells in June.   Lidice.   Ernst Waldinger.   FaBoWar, *tr. by Unknown*

Lie back, daughter, let your head.   First Lesson.   Philip Booth.   GoPo

Lie doon, my dear, and in your ear.   Coorie Doon.   Matt McGinn.   EdScPo

Lie down beside me if it's good for you.   Coming Downtown.   Marilyn Hacker.   PoBW

Lie down in sleep but suddenly.   Insomnia.   Joyce Carol Oates.   AWTN

Lie down on the bright hill.   Dress, The.   Mark Strand.   CAP-8

Lie down with us and wait. (LL)   Gathering Mushrooms.   Paul Muldoon.   HarvBoo; ModIr; NAEL-7v2; NoP-4; PBCIP; PNI

Lie in my arms until the kids get up. (LL)   Almost Aubade.   Marilyn Hacker.   NAMCP V.2; NoAM

Lie / stand up.   Practice.   Peter Bailey.   WhBo

"Lie still, my newly married wife."   Griesly Wife, The.   John Streeter Manifold.   MoBrPo

Lie still now.   This Room and Everything in It.   Li-Young Lee.   CAP-8; IllVoic; NAAL-5; OpBo; RoV

Lie, that we come from water, A.   Landcrab I.   Margaret Atwood.   NIP-4

Lie, The.   Sir Walter Ralegh.   NAEL-6v1; NAEL-7v1; NoP-4; NoP-5; NoSic; NPeEn; OxBEV; PBRV; PoPoPo; TFi; WaAnP

Liebre, La.   Silvia Eugenia Castillero.   SPV

Lied du figuier.   René Char.   YaTCFP

Lied of the Fig Tree.   René Char.   YaTCFP, *tr. by* Gustaf Sobin

Lies.   Martha Collins.   ExTi; PuP-23

Lies.   Jo Shapcott.   StAl

Lies: "Little bitch!"   Pak Sôwôn.   EcSo, *tr. by* Julie C. Park

Lies a dead deer on yonder plain.   Ye-you si-jun: Lies a Dead Deer.   *Unknown*.   APSN; CCL1; NDACCP, *tr. by* Ezra Pound

Lies are as at home.   After the Report from Iron Mountain.   Jerry W., Jr. Ward.   FuFl

Lies Concerning Speed.   Christine Hume.   IAoNAP

Lies I could tell, The.   White Lies.   Natasha Trethewey.   TWW

Lies in flawed words and stubborn sounds. (LL)   Poems of Our Climate, The.   Wallace Stevens.   APT-1; NAMCP V.1; NoP-4; NoP-5; OxBoAm; SoSe-8

Lies in the full, soft rain. (LL)   Lo, my loved is dying, and the call.   Michael Field.   ViWPN; VWP

Lies like a rod of rippled jade. (LL)   Symphony in Yellow.   Oscar Wilde.   MoBrPo; NoAM; OPOU

Lies lost in a strength of jasmine down a summer beach. (LL)   Málaga.   Pearse Hutchinson.   ModIr; PBCIP

Lies We Tell Ourselves.   Marj Hahne.   BRtP

Lieth there so cold? [*or* cold!]. (LL)   What the Bullet Sang.   Bret Harte.   APN-2; CalPo; OBEV

Lieu et la formule reculent avec l'écho à la reconquête des territoires en friche, Le.   Des rites.   Annie Le Brun.   YaTCFP

Life.   Delmira Agustini.   TANSG, *tr. by* Mark McCaffrey

Life.   Francis Bacon. *See* Life of Man, The.

Life.   Anna Laetitia Barbauld.   NAEL-6v2; NAEL-7v2; NoP-4; NoP-5; OBEV; OxAEP-1

Life.   Anna Laetitia Barbauld.
    Life's "Good-Morning."   TreFP

Life.   Ralph Waldo Emerson.
    "Him strong Genius urged to roam."   TCAPo

Life.   George Herbert.   BASC; FSCP; NoP-4; NoP-5; NOSC

Life.   Dennis O'Driscoll.   BeAl

Life: "O the blessedness of life! It's lucky, no doubt."   T. H. Parry-Williams.   BBMWP, *tr. by* Richard Poole

Life.   Henrietta Cordelia Ray.   CBWP-3

Life.   Jo Shapcott.   StAl

Life.   Mary E. Tucker.   CBWP-1

Life.   Edith Wharton.   APN-2

Life, A.   Janet Fisher.   MFPA

Life, A.   Howard Nemerov.   OBCoV

Life: a cloud crossing the peak.   Mumon Gensen.   ZenPo, *tr. by* Takashi Ikemoto and Lucien Stryk

Life, A / of collecting pollen.   Poem.   Shin Yu Pai.   AmZen

Life Ahead, The.   Philip Levine.   NoAM

Life ain't never been promised to nobody.   For Aunt Cathy.   Kevin Powell.   InTrad

Life and Death.   Robert Creeley.
    "If I had thought."   WoBe
    "In the diamond."   WoBe
    "Long road of it all, The."   NAMCP V.2; WoBe
    "*Oh my god*—you."   WoBe
    "Out here there."   WoBe
    "Sear at the center."   WoBe
    "When it comes."   NAMCP V.2; WoBe

Life and death. Allan Graham. ICANM

Life and Death of Edward II, The. Sir Francis Hubert. "This highest scholar in the school of sin." NOSC

Life and Death of [Habbie Simson] the Piper of Kilbarchan, The. Robert Sempill. NPeEn

Life and Death of Jason, The. William Morris. (Nymph's Song to Hylas, The.) OBEV

Life, are you keeping something in reserve? Gift, The. Amado Nervo. TCLAP, tr. by Sue Standing

Life As a Book That Has Been Put Down. John Ashbery. FTOS

Life at last I know is terrible. What Is Terrible. Roy Fuller. PoWW

Life at the Capital. Li Ho. CrYelRi, tr. by Sam Hamill

Life at War. Denise Levertov. CAP-8; WaAnP

Life Beside This One, The. John N. Morris. PoA 2002

Life calls us, and we go, massing our courage. Karolina Pavlova. ARWW, tr. by Catriona Kelly

Life contracts and death is expected. Death of a Soldier, The. Wallace Stevens. AmWaPo; APT-1; NAAPv.2; NAMCP V.1; OBWP; OxBoAm; SAmP; SoSe-8

Life Cycle of Common Man. Howard Nemerov. NBLV

Life, Death. Chu Yohan. CAMKP, tr. by Kyung-Ja Chun

Life death does end and each day dies with sleep. (LL) No Worst, There Is None. Pitched Past Pitch of Grief. Gerard Manley Hopkins. GSo; HeIP-4; MoBrPo; NAEL-6v2; NAEL-7v2; NAMCP V.1; NoAM; NoP-4; NoP-5; OxAEP-2; PoPoPo; TFi; WoPoe

Life Doesn't Frighten Me. Maya Angelou. ChAP

Life Draws a Tree. Roberto Juarroz. GPTC; TCLAP, tr. by W. S. Merwin

Life Everlasting, The. Reginald Gibbons. Vesp

Life flows to death as rivers to the sea. James Vincent Cunningham. APT-2

Life for a Life. Mary E. Tucker. CBWP-1

Life Forms. Robin Becker. BodElec

Life, friends, is boring. We must not say so. John Berryman. BrAP; CAP-8; ColAP; EMP; HarvBoo; HeIP-4; NAMCP V.2; NoAM; NoP-4; NoP-5; OxBoAm; PoetW; PtR; TRP; VCAP; WaAnP Fr. Dream Songs.

Life gives / us something. Life. Dennis O'Driscoll. BeAl

Life grows so clear, beneath the dreaming lamp. Vision of Niamh, The. Eva Gore-Booth. PoBW

Life has dark secrets; and the hearts are few. Letitia Elizabeth Landon. VWP Fr. Fragments.

Life has just begun. 'S Wonderful. Ira Gershwin. ReLy

Life has loveliness to sell. Barter. Sara Teasdale. ITBLP; SoSe-8

Life, Having Become Still. Brenda Brooks. IFF

Life, hope, they conquer death, generally, always. After the Convention. Robert Lowell. NoAM

Life I could have lived, the. My Two Lives. Ernest Sandeen. PoA 2002

Life! I know not what thou art. Life. Anna Laetitia Barbauld. NAEL-6v2; NAEL-7v2; NoP-4; NoP-5; OBEV; OxAEP-1

Life! I know not what thou art. Life. Anna Laetitia Barbauld.

Life I Led, The. Nikki Giovanni. GT

Life in the Comics. Jenny Mueller. IAoNAP

Life in the Egg 3. Kim Sŭnghŭi. CAMKP, tr. by Anthony, Brother of Taizé

Life in the Provinces. Carlos Sahagún. RaW, tr. by Robert Mezey

Life in this world. Basho. EH, tr. by Robert Hass

Life in this world. Iio Sogi. SoOfWa, tr. by Sam Hamill

Life in us is like the water in the river, The. Henry David Thoreau. GoPo Fr. Walden [prose work].

Life Is a Dream. Pedro Calderón de la Barca. NAWM-5v1

Life is a glass wherein we dimly see. Life's Boundary. Henrietta Cordelia Ray. CBWP-3

Life is a house in ruins. And we mean to fix it up. Couplings. Menna Elfyn. BBMWP, tr. by Joseph P. Clancy

Life is a jest. John Gay. See Life is a jest; and all things show it.

Life is a jest; and all things show it. My Own Epitaph. John Gay. InoFa; NIL-7; NIP-4; NPeEn; OxBEV

(Life is a jest.) CABP

Life Is a Killer. John Giorno. PmAP

Life is a sinking sun, a sea of blood. Life, Death. Chu Yohan. CAMKP, tr. by Kyung-Ja Chun

Life Is a Song, Let's Sing It Together. Joe Young. ReLy

Life Is Fine. Langston Hughes. NAMCP V.1; NBLV; PtR; SAmP

Life is full of mirth and pleasure. Adieu. Mary E. Tucker. CBWP-1

Life Is Happy. Albert Goldbarth. SUP

Life is (I think) a blunder and a shame. (LL) W. E. Henley. NAEL-6v2; NAEL-7v2; NPeEn Fr. In Hospital.

Life is in the rice-field, wealth in the wheat. Grace before Meat. Robert David Fitzgerald. NOBAu

Life Is Just a Bowl of Cherries. Lew Brown. ReLy

Life is just a journey, someone told me long ago. Life's Dovey Junctions. Geriant Løvgreen. BBMWP, tr. by the author

Life is like a bubble. On a Deathbed. T'aego, National Preceptor. CATKP, tr. by Peter H. Lee

Life is Long, the. John Harington. ChIV-2

Life is lovely in seclusion. Retirement. Yüan Chěn. CrYelRi, tr. by Sam Hamill

Life is made. Veronique Tadjo. NAfrP, tr. by Faustine Boateng Gyima

Life is made up of vanities—so small. Stern Truth. Letitia Elizabeth Landon. VWP

Life is more wearisome than. Do Not Get Up. Ishikawa Takuboku. CAoMJL1, tr. by Leith Morton

Life Is Motion. Wallace Stevens. SAmP

Life is not a highway strewn with flowers. April Showers. B. G. DeSylva. ReLy

Life is not made for meetings. Presented to Wei Ba, Gentleman in Retirement. Tu Fu [or Du Fu]. CCL1, tr. by Burton Watson

Life is nothing but time. Gloria Gervitz. CFP; MirDau, tr. by Stephen Tapscott

Life . . . is remembering waking up. Sandro Penna. CAGL, tr. by John McRae

Life is slow, but it seems exciting. In Buddy's Eyes. Stephen Sondheim. ReLy

Life is such a great adventure. Hundred Years from Today, A. Ned Washington and Joseph Young. ReLy

Life Is the Body's Light. Robert Herrick. CavPo

Life is too black as he paints it and "Reading's nastiness sometimes." Peter Reading. StAl Fr. Ukulele Music.

Life it asks of us is a dog's life, The. (LL) Victor Dog, The. James Merrill. NAMCP V.2; NoAM; NoP-4; NoP-5

Life keeps me alive: all its tubes. Life Supports. William Bronk. APSN

"Life! length of life!" for this, with earnest cries. Juvenal. OBVE Fr. Satires.

Life, like a marble block, is given to all. Life. Edith Wharton. APN-2

Life, looking out attentive from the eyes of the doe. (LL) Buck in the Snow, The. Edna St. Vincent Millay. ColAP; MoWP; NALW; NoP-4; NoP-5; WaAnP

Life Model. Maggie Hannan. NeBl

Life moves slowly, with a warm, oozing tread. Meaning of Soup, The. Gabriel Celaya. RaW, tr. by Robert Mezey and Hardie St. Martin

Life never knows the return of spring. (LL) John Gay. NoP-4; NoP-5 Fr. Beggar's Opera, The.

Life of a Beetle, The. Franck André Jamme. YaTCFP, tr. by Michael Tweed

Life of a Cucapá Woman, The. Heriberto Yépez. RMCMP, tr. by Harry Polkinhorn

Life of a Day, The. Tom Hennen. GoPo

Life of a Dead Dog. David Avidan. FIT, tr. by Robert Friend

Life of a Salesman. Emily Grosholz. RA

Life of an Echo, The. Judith Ortiz Cofer. PueRic

Life of an orphan boy, The. Ballad of the Orphan Boy, The. Unknown. CCL1, tr. by Anne Birrell

Life of Art, The. Denise Levertov. BodElec

Life of Eternity, The. Gene Frumkin. ICANM

Life of Ideas, The. Chris Wallace-Crabbe. OBGa

Life of Intimate Fleeing, A. Robert Kelly. FTOS

Life of Lincoln West, The. Gwendolyn Brooks. NoAM

Life of Man, The. Francis Bacon. NoSic (Life.) OxAEP-1

Life of my life, take not so soon thy flight. To His Dying Brother, Master William Herrick. Robert Herrick. CavPo; NOSC

Life of St Sava, The. Vasco [or Vasko] Popa. PoSu Fr. St Sava's Spring.

Life of the Body, The. Diane Bonds. PoSol

Life of the roebuck was mine, The. To Lady Elizabeth Foster, from Georgiana, Duchess of Devonshire, When She Was Apprehensive of Losing Her Eyesight–1796. Georgiana Cavendish, Duchess of Devonshire. PoBW

Life of the Virgin Mary, The. Rainer Maria Rilke. tr. by Robert Bly
1. The Birth of Mary. WED, tr. by Robert Bly
2. Mary Presented at the Temple. WED, tr. by Robert Bly
4. Mary's Visit with Elizabeth. WED, tr. by Robert Bly
12. The Quiet Mary Knew with the Risen Christ. WED, tr. by Robert Bly
5. The Suspicions of Joseph. WED, tr. by Robert Bly

Life of Towns, The. Anne Carson.
Town of Finding Out About the Love of God. PLBUT

Life of water. Pavilion. Elsa Cross. RMCMP, tr. by Margaret Sayers Peden

Life of wealth does not appeal to me at all, A. Room in Bloomsbury, A. Sandy Wilson. ReLy

Life of yon trim Shakspere [or Shakespeare] on the tree?, The. (LL) Mocking Bird, The. Sidney Lanier. APN-2; TCAPo

Life on this earth as I know it is incredibly difficult and depressing a great deal of time. After-Life, The. Anne Waldman. AHA

Life One Leads, The. Gabriel Celaya. RaW, *tr.* by Robert Mezey and Hardie St. Martin

Life: "Paper bird I have in my chest, A." Vicente Aleixandre. RaW, *tr. by* Robert Bly

Life Plastic. Michael Field. VWP

Life pours out images, the accidental. Rokeby Venus, The. Robert Conquest. GS

Life (priest and poet say) is but a dream. Dragon-Fly, The. Walter Savage Landor. OBEV

Life roars on, of course. Longing. Femi Osofisan. NAfrP

Life says, "If I never knew pleasure, man would live like a beast." Talk. Murad Mikha'il. IrPoTo, *tr.* by Christina Coyle and Sadok Masliyah

Life scums the cream of Beauty with Time's spoon. Posset for Nature's Breakfast, A. Margaret Lucas Cavendish, Duchess of Newcastle. STuOW

Life Sentence. János Pilinszky. IQMS, *tr.* by Peter Jay

Life sometimes held such sweetness for him. My Grandfather and His Apple-Tree. John Ormond. AngWePo; TCAWP

Life Story. *Unknown.* OBSP

Life Story. Paul Zweig. BodElec

Life stretches to one hundred years. Sikong Tu. CCL1 *Fr.* Twenty-Four Modes of Poetry.

Life Supports. William Bronk. APSN

Life that dies and that subsists. Interview. Manuel Bandeira. TCLAP, *tr. by* Candace Slater

Life the hound. Hound, The. Robert Francis. SoSe-8

Life, the story goes. Anna Liffey. Eavan Boland. BodElec; ModIr

Life, they said. Myths. Nazik al-Mala'ika. IrPoTo, *tr.* by Ferial J. Ghazoul

Life today is hectic. What's Going to Happen to the Tots? Noël Coward. NBLV

Life turns us beneath the scorching sun. Evening Trumpet. Boris Hristov. CSCBP, *tr. by* Georgi Belev and Lisa Sapinkopf

Life up to now had been no mistake. Elvis Acts as His Own Pallbearer. Fleda Brown Jackson. AllShUp

Life wants to carry me off. Hatching Thunder. Jacqueline Scott. OGAHCP, *tr. by* Boadiba and Jack Hirschman

Life was a song. You Were Meant for Me. Arthur Freed. ReLy

Life was back lanes, therefore out of bounds. Alan Wearne. BMAP *Fr.* Nightmarkets, The.

Life was so peaceful at the drive-in. Arthur Murray Taught Me Dancing in a Hurry. Johnny Mercer. ReLy

Life we find is nevermore. Deception. Josephine D. Henderson Heard. CBWP-4

Life! We've been long together. Anna Laetitia Barbauld. TreFP *Fr.* Life.

Life which now I lead is as a perfect death, The. Love Is Life and Death. Georg Rudolph Weckherlin. GePo, *tr.* by George C. Schoolfield

Life with the graveyard. (LL) Familial. Jacques Prévert. CLPP; FaBoWar; PoAgWa, *tr. by* Lawrence Ferlinghetti

Life Withdrawn, The. Luís De León. SpanPo, *tr.* by Edwin Morgan

Life Within an Egg. Kim Sŭnghŭi. EcSo, *tr.* by K. Kim Richards and Steffen Richards

Life yet of his lines shall never out, The. (LL) Upon the Lines and Life of the Famous Scenic Poet, Master William Shakespeare. Hugh Holland. AngWePo; OBWVE

Life You Have, The. Yona Volach. DTA, *tr.* by Miriyam Glazer

Life you have, The. Life You Have, The. Yona Volach. DTA, *tr.* by Miriyam Glazer

Lifeguard, The. James Dickey. NoP-4; NoP-5; SoSe-8

Life-Hook. Juana de Ibarbourou. TCLAP, *tr.* by Sophie Cabot Black and Maria Negroni

Lifeless, floating, drowned. Something Remembered. Emilio Prados. RaW, *tr. by* Hardie St. Martin

Lifeless plains at the foot of. Wanderings on a Heavenly Body. László Kálnoky. IQMS, *tr.* by Kenneth McRobbie and Zita McRobbie

Lifeless son—the mother's agony, The. Three Marys at Castle Howard, in 1812 and 1837, The. Ebenezer Elliott. SacPr

Lifeline. Vijay Seshadri. BAP-97

Lifelong. Sharon Olds. ExTi

Lifelong farewell. Idea Vilariño. TANSG, *tr.* by Louise B. Popkin

Lifenet Intense feeling Burroughs; face. Tapa Kearney. AHA *Fr.* Cuba.

Life-Parting. *Unknown.* CCL1,

Lifes. Achy Obejas. WiU

Life's a dream, and I'm over sixty. Mountain Life. Baekoon Kyunghan. BecRai, *tr. by* Kim Daljin, Kim Won-Chung and Christopher Merrill

Life's a Funny Proposition after All. George M. Cohan. ReLy

Life's a game. I Know That You Know. Anne Caldwell. ReLy

Life's an empty thing. Me and My Girl. Douglas Furber and Noel Gay. ReLy

Life's as we / Find it—death too. Daie-Soko. ZenPo, *tr. by* Takashi Ikemoto and Lucien Stryk

Life's Boundary. Henrietta Cordelia Ray. CBWP-3

Life's Dovey Junctions. Geriant Løvgreen. BBMWP, *tr. by* the author

Life's dreary for me. Body and Soul. Frank Eyton, Edward Heyman and Robert Sour. ReLy

Life's Golden Sunset. Mrs. Henry Linden. CBWP-4

Life's "Good-Morning." Anna Laetitia Barbauld. TreFP *Fr.* Life.

Life's Morning. Howell Elvet Lewis. OBWVE, *tr. by* H. Idris Bell

Life's Parallels, A. Christina Georgina Rossetti. NAEL-6v2; NAEL-7v2

Life's pathway to me is dreary. Opium-Eater, The. Mary E. Tucker. CBWP-1

Life's smallest miseries are, perhaps, its worst. Small Miseries. Letitia Elizabeth Landon. VWP

Life's spent guarding. What there is to guard, A. August the First: The Watchman Speaks. Marjorie Oludhe Macgoye. HBAPE

Life's stormy surge had scarcely touched. Grafted Bud, The. Mary Weston Fordham. CBWP-2

Life's Success. James Martineau. OWABP

Life's Trades. Emily Dickinson. TCAPo

Life-Saving Medal. Philippe Soupault. PFTM-1

Lifetime devoted to literature, A. Judith Rodriguez. BrAP; NOBAu

Lifetime mirrored: Chang and Eng, A. Siamese Twins in Love. Susan Swartwout. ReTh

Lift Every Fist and Swing. Rohan B. Preston. BRtP

Lift Every [*or* Ev'ry] Voice and Sing. James Weldon Johnson. APT-1; InGu; ISC; TCAPo

Lift latch, step in, be welcome, Sir. Luncheon, A. Max Beerbohm. OBSV

Lift Me Higher. Mary E. Tucker. CBWP-1

Lift me, O you, whose arms are young! *Unknown.* RWP *Fr.* Aged Bard's Wish, The.

Lift not the painted veil which those who live. Sonnet: Lift Not the Painted Veil. Percy Bysshe Shelley. CenSon; GSo; NOBRP

Lift up the turf / and slip in beside you. (LL) Temporarily in Oxford. Anne Stevenson. NoP-4; NoP-5

Lift up thine eyes, sweet Psyche! What is she. Psyche, Before the Tribunal of Venus. Nathaniel Parker Willis. APN-1

Lift up your heads, ye Gates; and ye everlasting Portals. Robert Southey. STuOW *Fr.* Vision of Judgement, A.

Lift your arms to the stars. Love and Liberation. John Hall Wheelock. MoAmPo

Lift your flowers. Chicory and Daisies. William Carlos Williams. APT-1

Lift your heads, all you peoples, to the wet heat rising in the airshaft. Praise Psalm of the City-Dweller. April Bernard. NIL-7

Lifting. Dorothy Barresi. MoASP

Lifting Belly. Gertrude Stein.

  "Kiss my lips. She did." APT-1; PFTM-1; PoBW

  "Lifting belly. Are you. Lifting." OxWW

Lifting belly. Are you. Lifting. Gertrude Stein. OxWW *Fr.* Lifting Belly.

Lifting his slowly trickling jaws. Tête-à-Tête. Edwin Honig. NoAM

Lifting, The. Sharon Olds. CAP-8; InoFa; MoWP; NIL-7

  (In the Hospital, Near the End.) NIP-4; PoCu

Lifting whither, cycle of the sift. Sonnet. Karen Volkman. IAoNAP

Lifts a spare shadow. Valorous Vine. Barbara Guest. AWPTFC

Lifts up his voice and shouts: "Strike! you are warriors!" AOI. (LL) *Unknown.* NAWM-5v1; NAWM-7v1 *Fr.* Song of Roland, The.

Light. Marianne Boruch. PoSol

Light. Fireflies. Paul Fleischman. NOxBChV

Light. Peter Markus. AmPoNex

Light. Martinus Nijhoff. TuT, *tr. by* Desmond Egan

Light. Michael Ondaatje. NIP-4

Light. Diane Wakoski. OPOU

Light, A / in darkness. Night 1. Salim Hatubou. SonAtl, *tr. by* Carole Beckett, Kurt Ganzl, Eva Mallenby, Eric Milan, Christophe Mirambeau, Martin Ottenheimer and Simon Young

Light, The. Nude by Edward Hopper, A. Lisel Mueller. PoSol

Light, The. Martinus Nijhoff. WoPoe, *tr. by* Raphael Rudnik

Light after darkness, gain after loss. Afterwards. Frances Ridley Havergal. SacPr

Light among the leaves, The. Return to the City. Manuel Ulacia. RMCMP, *tr. by* Indran Amirthanayagam

Light and air, The? They are mountain-perfect, here in Taos, near. Hopi Prophet Chooses a Pop. Heid E. Erdrich. AmPoNex

Light and Dark, East and West. Robert Hershon. PrTe

Light and dark, when hurt is all I can do. (LL) Paso Robles, San Luis Obispo, San Luis Obispo. David Oliveira. CalPo; GeoHom

Light and dry. Locust Wood Mallet for Papermaking, A. Lin Pu. ColAnChi, *tr. by* Paul Hansen

Light and joyous figure, one that seems, A. Dancing Girl, The. Letitia Elizabeth Landon. CenSon

9. Light and Laughter. David McFadden. NLPA

Light, and light's duplicity. Crabapple Blossoms. Peter Sanger. Coast

Light & Love. Cathal McCabe. NIrP

Light and Shadow. Hugh MacDiarmid. HarvBoo

Light Another Candle. Miriam Chaikin. NTCP

Light as Air. Ron Padgett. NYP2

Light at Equinox. Léonie Adams. ColAP

Light beats upon me, The. Mid-day. "H. D." APT-1; NAAL-5; NAAPv.2; NAMCP V.1

Light begins. Snow begins. Un Extraño. Tess Gallagher. ExTi

Light Breaks Where No Sun Shines. Dylan Thomas. MoBrPo; OxAEP-2; OxBEV

Light breeze rustles the reeds, A. Night Thoughts While Travelling. Tu Fu [or Du Fu]. NDACCP, tr. by Kenneth Rexroth

Light, Bright, Etc. C. S. Giscombe. RD

Light brush of dawn, A. Louise Herlin. MFP, tr. by Martin Sorrell

Light brush of dawn, A. Light brush of dawn, A. Louise Herlin. MFP, tr. by Martin Sorrell

Light by the barn that shines all night, The. Light by the Barn, The. William Stafford. CAP-8

Light canvas or any finished painting. Smoke Painting. Yoko Ono. WhBo

Light clarity avocado salad in the morning. Poem. Frank O'Hara. OxBoAm

Light comes back. Silent Promise, A. Jay Emerson Johnson. RSR

Light cross of lonely strolls, The. Larisa Miller. CRWP, tr. by Richard McKane

Light drifts from the stalled. Out of My Own Pocket. Martha Collins. ExTi

Light drizzle falling off, A. Taking a Captive / 1984. Barney Bush. HATNAP

Light, drunk with insult. You and me. (LL) Postfeminism. Brenda Shaughnessy. AmPoNex; LegDan

Light exists in Spring, A. Emily Dickinson. APN-2; ITBLP; NCAP

Light Exists In The Fire, The. "Angelus Silesius." GePo Fr. Cherubical Wanderer, The.

Light Falls Obliquely. Eric Gamalinda. ReBoTo

Light fills the great spaces. Selective Memory. Robin Becker. PfS

Light flashes red, The. Market day. Mwatabu Okantah. BtF

Light flows our war of mocking words, and yet. Buried Life, The. Matthew Arnold. BrAP; NAEL-6v2; NAEL-7v2

Light foot hears you and the brightness begins, The. Poem Beginning with a Line by Pindar, A. Robert Duncan. PmAP; VCAP

Light, for example, black. Light, for Example. Jacques Roubaud. YaTCFP, tr. by Rosmarie Waldrop

Light Forms. Robert Trammell. TiP2

Light from a dead star—even at the beginning. Torch. Aleida Rodríguez. FaoP

Light from Parallel Worlds. David Huerta. RMCMP, tr. by Mark Schafer

Light from the clouds is dazzling my eyes, The. Offered in Thanks for a Present of Wine and a Goose. Yu Hsin. CCL1, tr. by John Frodsham

Light from the planet Venus, soon to set. Evening-Star. Louise Bogan. APT-2

Light from the street lamp shines, The. Night. Justin Chin. AmPoNex

Light, God's white light breaks and must bedizen, The. Light, The. Martinus Nijhoff. WoPoe, tr. by Raphael Rudnik

Light, God's white light, breaks up into colours. Light. Martinus Nijhoff. TuT, tr. by Desmond Egan

Light goes out, The. Texas Sunrise, A. Jay Brannan. BeDoSh

Light going out in the forehead, A. Swimming By Night. James Merrill. ColAP; HarvBoo

Light here has begun to pass and as it passes, The. Art of Measuring Light, The. Ellen Hinsey. AmPoNex; YaYoPo

Light hosann'd in the mirrors. Timing. Anne Rouse. NeBl

Light I don't have slanting through broken walls. Air. John Godfrey. FTOS

Light in Darkness. Mary E. Tucker. CBWP-1

Light, in its daylong play, refuses, the. Above the Rio Grande. Charles Tomlinson. ICANM

Light, in light breezes and a favoring sun. Watching Tennis. John Heath-Stubbs. OxBSo

Light in One's Blood, The. Gemino H. Abad. ReBoTo

Light in the moon the only light is on Sunday, A. Gertrude Stein. TCAPo Fr. Rooms.

Light in the morning, The. Kitchen. Robert Creeley. OxBoAm

Light in the shipyards is so long in coming. Astrelegy. Andrew Zawacki. IAoNAP

Light in the skull of the bird, The. Nathaniel Tarn. APSN Fr. Lyrics for the Bride of God.

Light into the olive entered. After Greece. James Merrill. BrAP; ColAP; TRP

Light Invested. Carlos A. Angeles. ReBoTo

Light is burning late, A. John Montague. ModIr; PBCIP; PNI Fr. Great Cloak, The.

Light is different here, The. Prelude to the Fall. Kate Schmitt. IJHIL

Light is falling on the wild philodendrons. (LL) Old Liberators, The. Robert Hedin. GoPo; P180

Light is laying waste the heavens. Native Stone. Octavio Paz. TCLAP, tr. by Muriel Rukeyser

Light is on in my father's study, A. Working late. Louis Simpson. CAP-8

Light is the inside, The. Girl Powdering Her Neck. Cathy Song. NoP-4

Light Leaving a Small Harbour. Chairil Anwar. SonAtl, tr. by Peter Lennon and Tracey Yuan

Light Left On, A. May Sarton. GoPo

Light Listened. Theodore Roethke. MoAmPo

Light. Love. Freedom. Like a Blessing. Stanley Crouch. GT

Light, my light, who commanded, 'Disappear! Hayim Lenski. FIT, tr. by Robert Friend

Light of awakening, The. Moon Mountain. Muso Soseki. EaWin, tr. by W. S. Merwin

Light of evening, Lissadell, The. In Memory of Eva Gore-Booth and Con Markievicz. William Butler Yeats. GPTC; NAMCP V.1; NoAM; NPeEn; OBMV

Light of my eyes, there is something to be said. Khwaja Shams-ad-din Muhammad Hafiz. WoPoe, tr. by Basil Bunting

Light of Other Days, The. Thomas Moore. See Oft In the Stilly Night.

Light of Our Souls. Kata Szidónia Petröczy. IQMS, tr. by Marie B. Jaffe

Light of our souls, to you we call. Light of Our Souls. Kata Szidónia Petröczy. IQMS, tr. by Marie B. Jaffe

Light of the Blade, The. André Du Bouchet. YaTCFP, tr. by Paul Auster

Light of the lake and the autumn moon, The. Gazing on Lake Dongting. Liu Yu Hsi. CCL1, tr. by Stephen Owen

Light of the moon. Buson. EH, tr. by Robert Hass

Light of the silver torch that has no smoke. In the Night. Ch'oe Ch'ung. WoPoe, tr. by Jean S. Grigsby

Light on his thigh was like, The. King of the Cats is Dead, The. Peter Porter. EmeKit; NoAM

Light / on my mother's tongue. Lucille Clifton. ESEAA

Light painted the sky, some months ago, The. Painting the Eaves. Tony Towle. PmAP

Light passes, The. Evening. "H. D." APT-1; HarvBoo

Light Pole. Rolf Jacobsen. WED, tr. by Robert Bly

Light projected lifetimes ago. Telescope. Sydney Lea. RA

Light pulling away from trees, The. Distance. Peter Everwine. GeoHom; PoCho

Light rain is on the light dust. Wang Wei. NDACCP, tr. by Ezra Pound

Light rain makes me long for you, The. San Diego (On a rainy day). Lamea Abbas Amara. PoArWo, tr. by Nathalie Handal and Mike Maggio

Light rain settles this white dust. White Dress. Yüan Chěn. CrYelRi, tr. by Sam Hamill

Light Reading. Vassar Miller. FFC

Light says hurry and the woman, The. Sky-Blue Dress, The. Cathy Song. SweBea

Light screams, it backs me up, The. Noise Will Start Tomorrow, The. Jeanne Megnen. SurWo, tr. by Guy Ducornet

Light Shining out of Darkness. William Cowper. CABP; NoP-4; NoP-5; NPeEn; OxBEV; SacPr; TFi Fr. Olney Hymns.

Light silently shifts even as three kittens leap, The. Patio. Manuel A. Viray. ReBoTo

Light Sleep. Hazel Hall. APT-1; NAAPv.2

Light Snow-Fall after Frost, A. Thomas Hardy. WaAnP

Light so intensifies the ghost holds off. Grace. John Wilkinson. VaPo

Light splashed this morning. Round, The. Stanley Kunitz. BeAl; BodElec; NAMCP V.1

Light starts in a promising street, The. Capriccio of Roman Ruins and Sculpture with Figures, A. J. D. McClatchy. GS

Light that seemed to join parallel worlds, A. Light from Parallel Worlds. David Huerta. RMCMP, tr. by Mark Schafer

Light that shone when Hope was born, The. (LL) Alfred Tennyson. NAEL-6v2; NAEL-7v2 Fr. In Memoriam A. H. H.

Light the fire when night is near. Light the Fire. Edith Jay Scovell. MoWP

Light the first light of evening, as in a room. Final Soliloquy of the Interior Paramour. Wallace Stevens. APT-1; BBASP; ColAP; HarvBoo; NAAPv.2; WaAnP

("The Light They Make"). Debra Bruce.
   Sonnet 2. FFC
   Sonnet 4. FFC

Light Throws Shadows. Drahomira Vandas. SurWo, tr. by Guy Ducornet

Light throws shadows, The. Light Throws Shadows. Drahomira Vandas. SurWo, tr. by Guy Ducornet

Light, / unbearable.   Sailors Shielding Their Eyes During Atomic Bomb Test, Bikini, 1947.   John Bradley.   AtGh

Light Up the World With Your Faith.   George Stanley.   NLPA *Fr.* Mountains and Air.

Light up thy halls! 'Tis closing day.   F. de Samara to A. G. A.   Emily Jane Brontë.   NALW

Light was out; the sky was down, The.   Gnostic Prelude.   James McAuley.   BMAP

Light weed, whose poisoned scent with sickly power.   Poppy, The.   Sarah Hamilton.   CenSon

Light went out in the Cairo skies, The.   Streets of Black and White.   Ahmed Yamani.   AnVo, *tr. by* Mohamed Enani

Light winter rain.   Buson.   SoOfWa, *tr. by* Sam Hamill

Light would pass over her face, A. (LL)   Those Who Love.   Sara Teasdale.   GoPo; LW

Light Years and the Love Lost in the Oleanders.   Alane Rollings.   WeW-3

Light You Give Off, The.   Jelaluddin Rumi.   RaBo, *tr. by* Coleman Barks and John Moyne

Light-Bearer of Liberty, The.   J. W. Scholl.
   "Gooing babies, helpless pygmies."   VerBaPo

Lighted brazier.   Winter.   Ngo Chi Lan.   EaWin, *tr. by* W. S. Merwin and Nguyen Ngoc Bich

Lighten me.   Miserly.   Michel Leiris.   YaTCFP, *tr. by* Cole Swensen

Lightening, The.   Gabriella Sica.   CItWP, *tr. by* Cinzia Sartini Blum and Lara Trubowitz

Lighter.   Again: Air in the Tops—Of Birches.   Gennady Aygi.   WoBe, *tr. by* Peter France

Lighter Fluid.   Rodger Kamenetz.   LiTh

Lightfall.   Pamela Alexander.   AmAlph

Lightheartedly Take from the Palms of My Hands.   Osip Emilevich Mandelstam.   WoPoe, *tr. by* James Greene

Lightheartedly take from the palms of my hands.   Lightheartedly Take from the Palms of My Hands.   Osip Emilevich Mandelstam.   WoPoe, *tr. by* James Greene

Lighthouse.   Joseph Ceravolo.   NYP2

Lighthouse.   Jane Hirshfield.   WANABP

Lighthouse.   Gerard Woodward.   EmeKit

Lighthouse, The.   Jocelyn Emerson.   IAoNAP

Lighthouse, The.   Vona Groarke.   NIrP

Lighthouse as an image, The.   February: Pemaquid Point.   Ira Sadoff.   PoSol

Lighthouse beam briefly illuminates, The.   Wave Falling on the Beach, A.   Lawrence Goeckel.   ICANM

Lighthouse Keeper.   Harry Edmund Martinson.   WED, *tr. by* Robert Bly

Lighthouse of Alexandria, The.   Mercedes Roffé.   TANSG, *tr. by* Kathryn Kopple

Lighthouse the slick line.   Ballad of Echolocation, The.   Ryan Knighton.   IFF

Lighting a Fire.   X. J. Kennedy.   NOxBChV

Lighting her thin French cigarette.   Bathing Girls, The.   Tracey Herd.   NeBl

Lighting one candle.   Buson.   EH, *tr. by* Robert Hass

Lighting the lantern.   Buson.   EH, *tr. by* Robert Hass

Lighting up, lest all our hearts should break.   Words for Jazz Perhaps.   Michael Longley.   SeSe

Lighting Up Time.   Dennis O'Driscoll.   PoDa

Light-Keeper, The.   Robert Louis Stevenson.   NePenScot

Lightless, unholy, eldritch thing.   Bat, The.   Ruth Pitter.   MoWP

Lightly a slight shadow floats on the March snows.   Hayim Lenski.   FIT, *tr. by* Robert Friend

Lightly Bound.   Stevie Smith.   NALW

Lightly forsaking / the Spring mist as it rises.   Seeing the Returning Geese.   Lady Ise.   WoPoe, *tr. by* Irma Brandeis and Etsuko Teraski

Lightly he laughed, as one that read my thought.   Alfred Tennyson.   OBGa *Fr.* Gardener's Daughter, The.

Lightly she fell where the vets' hands held her.   On the Euthanasia of a Pet Dog.   Elizabeth Smither.   BeAl

Lightly she lifts the large, pure, luminous shell.   Imprisoned.   Celia Laighton Thaxter.   TCAPo

Lightly stepped a yellow star.   Emily Dickinson.   MoAmPo; SAmP

Lightness.   Meg Bateman.   EdScPo; NePenScot; StAl, *tr. by* the author

Lightning.   Basho.   EH, *tr. by* Robert Hass

Lightning.   Witter Bynner.   APT-1

Lightning.   D. H. Lawrence.   MoBrPo

Lightning.   Haniel Long.   APT-1

Lightning, The.   Judah Al-Harizi.   BLT, *tr. by* T. Carmi

Lightning, The.   James ("Jim.") Grabill.   AtGh

Lightning and the gale!, The. (LL)   Old Ironsides.   Oliver Wendell Holmes.   AmWaPo; APN-1; BRP; NAAL-3; NAAPv.1; NCAP; OxBoAm; TCAPo; TFi

Lightning. And the mile between. Thunder. Pulse. Wink. The moon is bright and full above the desert.   Lightning. And the Mile Between.   Killarney Clary.   MotU

Lightning and Thunder.   Janice Finney.   PfS

Lightning and thunder, The.   Baby-Sermon, A.   George Macdonald.   NOxBChV; Spl

Lightning bug has wings of gold, The.   Bugs.   *Unknown.*   HHAm

Lightning flash.   Basho.   EH, *tr. by* Robert Hass

Lightning flash—,A.   Buson.   SoOfWa, *tr. by* Sam Hamill

Lightning flashes, The!   Haiku.   Basho.   SoSe-8, *tr. by* Earl Miner

Lightning gleam, A.   Haiku.   Basho.   SoSe-8, *tr. by* Harold G. Henderson

Lightning hits the roof.   Woman to Man.   Ai.   NoAM

Lightning in the clouds!   Basho.   WeW-3

Lightning is a yellow Fork, The.   Emily Dickinson.   NCAP

Lightning is angry in the night.   Michael Is Afraid of the Storm.   Gwendolyn Brooks.   NOxBChV

Lightning / is the future brightening.   Mabrak.   Bongo Jerry.   WaCA

Lightning Spreads Out across the Water.   Patricia Fargnoli.   PoDa

Lightning struck directly in the center, The.   Death on Village Creek, A.   H. Palmer Hall.   TiP2

Lightning-gleam, A.   Basho.   TAL

Lightning's shaft, but dazzles to destroy!, The. (LL)   Dreams of a Rival.   Mary Robinson.   CenSon; RWP

Lights.   Ernesto Cardenal.   TCLAP, *tr. by* Jonathan Cohen

Lights are bright.   I Wonder What Became of Me.   Johnny Mercer.   ReLy

Lights are going out, The.   Buson.   EH, *tr. by* Robert Hass

Lights are out in the street, and a cool wind swings, The.   Aubade.   Rosamund Marriott Watson.   ViWPN

Lights at Newport Beach, The.   Joe Bolton.   AmPoNex

Lights dimmed, the scraper scraped, and I could feel.   Surgical Moves.   Rachel Wetzsteon.   AmPoNex; ExTi

Lights extinguished, by the hearth I leant, The.   Legend of Provence, A.   Adelaide Anne Procter.   VWP

Lights from the Cambucí district on nights of crime.   Nocturne.   Mário de Andrade.   TCLAP, *tr. by* Jack E. Tomlins

Lights in the Sky are Stars, The.   Kenneth Rexroth.
   Heart of Herakles, The.   BLT
   Sword in a Cloud of Light, A.   StAl

Lights. Not the histrionic reds and golds.   Port Phillip Night.   Francis Webb.   BMAP

Lights of London, The.   Louise Imogen Guiney.   APN-2

Lights of the Bigtop.   Garrett McDowell.   BtF

Lights of the city come on for further exploits, The. (LL)   Rain is Falling, The.   Homero Aridjis.   STV; TCLAP, *tr. by* John Frederick Nims

Lights off, the clock glowing 2:10, The.   Soup, The.   Gary Soto.   NoP-4; NoP-5

Lights Out.   John Gilgun.   AmZen

Lights out.   How to Meditate.   Jack Kerouac.   BB
   (—lights out—/ fall, hands a-clasped, into instantaneous.)   CLPP

Lights Out.   Edward Thomas.   HarvBoo; OxAEP-2; PoWW; WoPoe

Lights out. Shades up.   Girl in a Nightgown.   Wallace Stevens.   AmFaPo

Lights, paving—, The.   George Oppen.   APT-2; PFTM-1

Light's Reading, The.   Alan Williamson.   PoSol

Light's rosary, blood-bright spheres.   Ribes rubrum.   Elizabeth Garrett.   NeBl

Lights shine all the way to the horizon.   Aegean Sea.   Manuel Ulacia.   RMCMP, *tr. by* Indran Amirthanayagam

Lights went out, The.   Nuclear Peril.   Pinkie Gordon Lane.   BtF

Light-spring, oh sun, in light our wedding joys immure.   Daniel Casper von Lohenstein.   GePo *Fr.* Arminius.

Lightweight.   Jack Myers.   SUP

Light-winged smoke, Icarian bird.   Henry David Thoreau.   APN-1; ColAP; TCAPo

Ligne droite, rang de nageurs, cent pieds par ligne.   Perpétuel *voyez* physique, 17/5.   Bernard Collin.   YaTCFP

Ligurra's fearful I'll contrive.   Martial.   RomPo, *tr. by* Peter Whigham

Liidxi na Olga.   Natalia Toledo.   RMCMP

Like.   Cathleen Calbert.   PoDa

Like.   Robert Desnos.   MFP, *tr. by* Martin Sorrell

Like.   Robert Desnos.   YaTCFP, *tr. by* Martin Sorrell

Like a Beacon.   Grace Nichols.   OPOU

Like a bird.   Poem.   Philip Whalen.   AHA

Like a bird in the sky. (LL)   Ego Tripping (There May Be a Reason Why).   Nikki Giovanni.   GT; InGu; ISC; RaBo; TWF

Like a Blessing.   Stanley Crouch.   GT

Like a branch of *jacaranda*. (LL)   You Called Me *Corazón*.   Sandra Cisneros.   AmFaPo; RaF

Like a brightly lit after-hour bus.   Saturday Night, Arriving in Seoul.   Kim Hyesun.   CAMKP, *tr. by* Jiwon Shin

Like a bullet. Knife All Blade, A. João Cabral de Melo Neto. VCWP, tr. by Galway Kinnell

Like a bullet. João Cabral de Melo Neto. TCLAP Fr. Knife That Is All Blade, The.

Like a Bulrush. Marianne Moore. APT-1

Like a bulwark against fate. At Rest in the Blast. Marianne Moore. MoAmPo

Like a bunch of flowers the evening sky is glowing. Inside the Bouquet. Max Dauthendey. GTCP, tr. by Reinhold Grimm

Like a car stuck in gear. Getting Through. Deborah Pope. PoA 2002

Like a child playing peek-a-boo with me. I Had a Really Good Idea for a Poem in Cynwil Elfed. Elinor Wyn Reynolds. BBMWP, tr. by Grahame Davies

Like a child's cut-out, she holds her weight. Dark Horse. Phillis Levin. FFC

Like a clothesline of whites. Slow Fade to Black. Thomas Sayers Ellis. LegDan

Like a cloud, like a shroud. This Year. Abubakar Othman. NeNiPo

Like a cobweb hung upon the tree. Rick Noguchi. NAAPv.2 Fr. Japanese Hokkus.

Like a cobweb hung upon the tree. Yonejiro (Yone) Noguchi. CalPo

Like a convalescent, I took the hand. Seamus Heaney. NAEL-6v2; NAEL-7v2; NAMCP V.2; NoAM; NoP-5 Fr. Station Island.

Like a disk, a trembling coin spinning on its own diameter. Edoardo Sanguineti. ItPo Fr. Scartabello.

Like a Dog. Mihály Babits. IQMS, tr. by Peter Zollman

Like a Dog. Cheryl Boyce Taylor. BRtP

Like a dog howling endlessly. Idea Vilariño. TANSG, tr. by Louise B. Popkin

Like a dog howling endlessly. Like a dog howling endlessly. Idea Vilariño. TANSG, tr. by Louise B. Popkin

Like a dog in his lowly corner. Like a Dog. Mihály Babits. IQMS, tr. by Peter Zollman

Like a dowry like a razzle-dazzle. Shoreless bath a fabulous boast, A. Bronislava Volková. Vesp

Like a dragged gem, floating. Night of Fathers. Valerie Martínez. TouFir

Like a Drifting Boat. Han-shan (Cold Mountain). CCL1, tr. by Gary Snyder

Like a drop of water is my heart. Youth and Maidenhood. Sarah Williams. LW

Like a drunk treading on his trouser cuffs. Convalescing in London. Thomas M. Disch. RA

Like a Face. Erica Bernheim. LegDan

Like a faded painting. Mara Malanova. CRWP, tr. by Nika Skandiaka

Like a fastball, or a perfect pass. (LL) Dennis Cooper. ReTh; WiU Fr. Some Adventures of John Kennedy Jr.

Like a fawn from the arrow, startled and wild. Eliza Harris. Frances Ellen Watkins Harper. WaAnP

Like a fine what shirt I put it on. House Beside the Sea, The. Rachel Hadas. FFC

Like a Fire in a Fire. Mary Jo Bang. NAPBL

Like a first coat of whitewash when it's wet. Twelfth Morning; or What You Will. Elizabeth Bishop. APT-2

Like a fist of black dust pitched in the wind. (LL) Glimpse of Starlings, A. Brendan Kennelly. PoCu; StAl

Like a flash of light that bewitches the word. Desert 1. Monica Mansour [or Mansur]. MirDau, tr. by Celeste Kostopulos-Cooperman

Like a flat sea. Population. George Oppen. PoA 2002

Like a Floating Jasmine. Idea Vilariño. TANSG, tr. by Louise B. Popkin

Like a floating jasmine. Like a Floating Jasmine. Idea Vilariño. TANSG, tr. by Louise B. Popkin

Like a funeral bell. (LL) Afternoon in February. Henry Wadsworth Longfellow. APN-1; ColAP

Like a gaunt, scraggly pine. Lincoln. John Gould Fletcher. CBCWP; MoAmPo

Like a ghost that suddenly confronts us. In Front of the Mirror. Vicente Aleixandre. RaW, tr. by Herbert Baird and William Stafford

Like a gondola of green scented fruits. Images. Richard Aldington. MoBrPo

Like a green turtle on the dusty highway. Sky in Daduza Township, The. Bruce Weigl. AmAlph

Like a handful of leaves. Cesare Greppi. ItPo, tr. by Gayle Ridinger

Like a hen pheasant. Unknown. CATKP, tr. by Peter H. Lee

Like a hippopotamus in a river's sultriness you wallow. Pregnant Woman. Bobi Jones. BBMWP, tr. by Joseph P. Clancy

Like a Horse. Robin Behn. AmAlph

Like a hound with nose to the trail. Michaelmas. Norman Nicholson. MoBrPo

Like a huntsman after weary chase. Edmund Spenser. HeIP-4; NoP-5 Fr. Amoretti.

Like a kinsman. Tollund Man, The. Hugo Claus. PFTM-2, tr. by Theo Hermans

Like a lizard in the sun, though not scuttling. Laureate, The. Robert Graves. OBSV

Like a lonely bark. Bo-zhou: Like a Lonely Bark. Unknown. CCL1, tr. by V. W. X.

Like a love-letter, full of sweet surprise. (LL) Still-Life. Elizabeth Daryush. MoWP; NPeEn; OxBEV

Like a mad lion, like a wild bull. Race, The. Nuala Ni Dhomhnaill. PBCIP, tr. by Michael Hartnett

Like a mauve carnation puckered up and dim. Sonnet to the Asshole. Paul Verlaine. CAGL, tr. by Alan Stone

Like a memory beyond death. Deeper Than a Dream. Peter Blue Cloud. AtGh

Like a Midsummer Rose. John Lydgate. SacPr

Like a minaret. Abode of Arrival. Ahmed Taha. NAfrP, tr. by Clarissa C. Burt

Like a mirror comes the afternoon. Bullfight. Pedro Serrano. RMCMP, tr. by Geoff Hargreaves

Like a model's smile. (LL) Mantle. William Heyen. MoASP; ReTh

Like a mountain bristled. CXXX. Pita Amor. TANSG, tr. by Shaun Griffin and Emma Sepúlveda-Pulvirenti

Like a Mourningless Child. Kenneth Patchen. MoAmPo

Like a Naked Light. Emilio Prados. RaW, tr. by Hardie St. Martin

Like a nigger is what my white friend, M. Talk. Terrance Hayes. LegDan

Like a painting it is set before one. View from the Window, The. Ronald Stuart Thomas. NoP-4; NoP-5

Like a painting we will be erased, no one can remain. Anne Carson. WoBe Fr. Truth About God, The.

"Like a plum!" Lawrence says. "Frieda in anger." Lawrence and Edison in New Jersey: 1923. Linda Bierds. ExTi

Like a poisonous snake in my blood. Love. Samar Sen. WoPoe, tr. by Pritish Nandy

Like a poor buffoon, of his deformity. Horn of Roland, The. Marina Ivanovna Tsvetayeva. TCRusP, tr. by William Tjalsma

Like a pot turned on the straw. How Is He Coming Then. Lucille Clifton. NALW

Like a prowling wolf, I padded from door to door. Return, The. Evan J. Thomas. AngWePo

Like a relative. Tollund Man. Hugo Claus. TuT, tr. by Peter van de Kamp

Like a relentless milkman up the stairs. (LL) Living in Sin. Adrienne Rich. NIL-7; NIP-4; NoP-4; OxBoAm; SoSe-8; WaAnP

Like a river glorious. Perfect Peace. Frances Ridley Havergal. SacPr

Like a rope that has been snapped. Irrationale. László Szabédi. IQMS, tr. by J. G. Nichols

Like a rubber tire another. Strong Winds Below the Canyons. Larry Kramer. GeoHom

Like a ruddy child you fall asleep in september. Aleksey Petrovich Tsvetkov. TCRusP

Like a sailor in the ship's rigging he slid over the tropic of Cancer and the / tropic of Capricorn. George Seferis. PFTM-1

Like a seesaw, like a rainbow, the colored. Patrizia Vicinelli. ItPo Fr. Foundations of Being, The.

Like a shadow or a friend. (LL) Kindness: "Before you know what kindness really is." Naomi Shihab Nye. BeAl; IJHIL

Like a silent, solemn, wire-haired choir. Coyotes at Eyebrow Lake, Saskatchewan. David Waltner-Toews. ACAMVP

Like a silhouette furred in a dark brown fire from across the room Mark puts. From the Mark Prejsnar Playbook. James Sanders. AnSo

Like a sister who borrows. Burial. Rebecca McClanahan. PoDa

Like a skein of loose silk blown against a wall. Garden, The. Ezra Pound. APT-1; BrAP; HeIP-4; MoAmPo; NIL-7; NIP-4; NoP-4; NoP-5; OxBoAm; PoPoPo

Like a sleeping swine upon the skyline. Muckish Mountain (The Pig's Back). Sir Shane Leslie. IrV

Like a small gray / coffee-pot. Gray Squirrel, The. Humbert Wolfe. MoBrPo

Like a soldier's ribbon on a tunic tacked. (LL) Pathology of Colours. Dannie Abse. BloBone; NIP-4; NoAM; TCAWP

Like a solider on leave from the front. (LL) Women don't Die on the Front Lines. Belkis Cuza Malé. CFP; TANSG, tr. by Pamela Carmell

Like a spear afterwards / cut out. Autumn-Time, Wind and the Planet Pluto. Joseph Ceravolo. NYP2

Like a spooky shadow. Shadow, A. Abd al-Rahim Salih al-Rahim. IrPoTo, tr. by Ralph Saverese and Saadi A. Simawe

Like a sprinter in a long-awaited race. If Only for One Night. Gordon Chambers. InTrad

Like a star or a stick suddenly given. Nights in the Constellation of the Tree Stepping from its Robe. Beckian Fritz Goldberg. AmAlph

Like a stone without a hand, chance. Arcana 10: Fortune. Veronica Volkow. RMCMP, tr. by Margaret Sayers Peden

Like a Stranger. Melisa Gürpinar. NaPG, tr. by Talat Sait Halman

Like a stunned piano, like a bucket. In Spite of Everything, the Stars. Edward Hirsch. BeAl

Like a sweet orange sucked by a boy. Creation. Ifi Amadiume. HAWP

Like a thick horse's mane. Marina Ivanovna Tsvetaeva. WoPoe *Fr.* Poem of the End.

Like a vein of hard coal, it was the strike. Gate City Breakdown. Charles Wright. LPSFW

Like a well-trained soldier. Wind. Ok-Ku Kang. WhBo

Like a whirling water-wheel. Sikong Tu. CCL1 *Fr.* Twenty-Four Modes of Poetry.

Like a whistled song. (LL) Bachelor Song. Douglas Goetsch. PML; PoDa

Like a white candle through a shuttered hand. (LL) Sisters, The. Roy Campbell. NoP-4; NoP-5; OBMV

Like a white lotus. Tanka. Ishikawa Takuboku. CAoMJL1, *tr. by* Makoto Ueda

Like a Wind from Lotus Blossoms. Sŏ Chŏngju. CAMKP, *tr. by* David R. McCann

Like a wishbone. Inner note. Ingrid de Kok. TSAP

Like a worm I writhe in your tight fist. In the Fist of Your Hatred. Shakuntala Hawoldar. CFP

Like a worm I writhe in your tight fist. In the Fist of Your Hatred. Gwendoline C. Konie. HAWP

Like a worn book of lore the crumpled sky opens. Thatched House. Yi Yuksa. CAMKP, *tr. by* Kyung-Ja Chun

Like air on skin, coolness of yachts at mooring. Yachts on the Nile. Bernard Spencer. NoAM

Like all children, you were a de facto. Unsubscriber, The. Bill Knott. PoCho

Like all fools, I believed. You Are Too Beautiful. Lorenz Hart. ReLy

Like all guests my son got in the way. Speaking of Gabriel. Rosario Castellanos. TANSG, *tr. by* Magda Bogin

Like all his people he felt at home in the forest. Bearer, The. Hayden Carruth. PoA 2002

Like all the apes in the neighborhood. Ready. Dan Pagis. FIT, *tr. by* Robert Friend

Like always / like forever. *Paiute Oral Tradition.* SonAtl, *tr. by* Walter Andeis, Harmon Jenkin and Donald Luskett

Like an accident or an insistence, without model or precedent. Earliest Known Representation of a Storm in Western Art, The. Lavinia Greenlaw. MFPA

Like an Adventurous Seafarer Am I. Michael Drayton. NOSC *Fr.* Idea.

Like an Animal. Jimmy Santiago Baca. AF

Like an animal, I scavenge. Raptor in the Kitchen. Joyce Peseroff. PoDa

Like an elephant. Mahadevi. WoPoe, *tr. by* A. K. Ramanujan

Like an enfranchised bird, who wildly springs. Sonnet 7. Caroline Elizabeth Norton. CenSon; VWP

Like an extinguished star. Abandonment. Al-Zahra Al-Mansouri. PoArWo, *tr. by* Richard McKane and Tahia Abdel Nasser

Like an home-reared animal in a quiet nook. David Jones. *Fr.* In Parenthesis.

Like an idiot before God. (LL) What's Left. Kerry Hardie. BeAl; NIrP

Like an imperialist, it has changed the landscape forever. (LL) Purple Loosestrife. Ann Townsend. ExTi; NeAmPo

Like an object whose loss has begun to be felt. Lost and Found and Lost Again. John Ashbery. BodElec

Like an old, wrecked sponge-diver leaking. Sometimes Feel. Pearse Hutchinson. ModIr

Like an ox. Jules Supervielle. MFP, *tr. by* Martin Sorrell

Like an ox streaming saliva, yoked to the plough. Like an ox. Jules Supervielle. MFP, *tr. by* Martin Sorrell

Like an urn for sacred relics. Perfumist, The. Jorge Fernández Granados. RMCMP, *tr. by* John Oliver Simon

Like Ana. Nina Cassian. PoSu, *tr. by* Nina Cassian

Like Ankle-Rings, This Music. Gunnar Ekelof. PFTM-1

Like ankle-rings, this music. Like Ankle-Rings, This Music. Gunnar Ekelof. PFTM-1

Like any seagull in old tales I left...alone...while friends clung to. Veins All Dried Up. Fatma Kandil. PoArWo, *tr. by* Khaled Mattawa

Like as a huntsman after weary chase. Edmund Spenser. *See* Like a huntsman after weary chase.

Like as the armèd knight. Ballad Which Anne Askew[e] Made and Sang When She Was in Newgate, The. Anne Askew. CABP; EMWP; NoP-4; NoP-5; NoSic; SacPr; WaAnP

  (Lyke as the armed knyght.) NPeEn; PBRV

Like as the Damaske Rose you see. Simon Wastell. SacPr

Like as the fountain[e] of all light created. Incarnatio Est Maximum Dei Donum [*or* Donum Dei]. William Alabaster. NoSic

Like as the waves made toward[s] the pebbled [*or* pibled] shore. William Shakespeare. CABP; NAEL-6v1; NAEL-7v1; NIL-7; NIP-4; NoP-5; NoSic; NPeEn; OxAEP-1; OxBEV; OxBSo; PoPoPo; TFi; TreFP *Fr.* Sonnets.

Like ashes, like oceans swarming. Dead Gallop. Pablo Neruda. TCLAP, *tr. by* John Felstiner

Like Attracts Like. Emmett Williams. WeW-3

Like battered old millhands, they stand in the orchard. Old Apple Trees. W. D. Snodgrass. CAP-8

Like Beatrix Potter. Jeni Olin. FreRad

Like bees after being out in the world, gathering and sucking up their lot. Sadness of Memory, The. Barbara Ras. NAPBL

Like being. Ishikawa Takuboku. CAoMJL1, *tr. by* Carl Sesar

Like Beirut. Haim Guri. NRoS, *tr. by* Esther Raizen

Like blue smoke. (LL) Serenity. Philippe Jaccottet. MFP; YaTCFP, *tr. by* Martin Sorrell

Like bodiless water passing in a sigh. Fog. Louise Imogen Guiney. APN-2

Like brides behind veils, my people peep from drawn curtains. Sun Storm. Tsering Wangno Dhompa. WANABP

Like cancer cells, ivy, arthritis. Carol Rumens. NewEx

Like Ceres trying to free her daughter. Leonardo's Bicycle. Cal Bedient. ArBi

Like certain histories, this painting rewards. On a Painting by a Member of the Northwest Visionary School. Averill Curdy. RWB

Like chopping wood in dreams lightning blazed our post oak trail. Toward Mena. David Thomas Roberts. AnSo

Like city's rain, my heart. Paul Verlaine. ItP, *tr. by* Norman R. Shapiro

Like Clouds. Sándor Petőfi. IQMS, *tr. by* George F. Cushing

Like clouds that sail in summer skies. Like Clouds. Sándor Petőfi. IQMS, *tr. by* George F. Cushing

Like Coleridge, I waltz. Under the Ice. Stewart Conn. NePenScot

Like crazy. (LL) Vietnam. Clarence Major. HHAm; PoAgWa

Like Crusoe with the bootless gold we stand. Experience. Edith Wharton. APN-2

Like Deity—to keep. (LL) I think I was enchanted. Emily Dickinson. APN-2; NALW

Like Dolmens Round My Childhood. John Montague. ModIr; NoP-4; NoP-5; PBCIP; PNI *Fr.* Rough Field, The.

Like dolmens round my childhood, the old people. John Montague. ModIr; NoP-4; NoP-5; PBCIP; PNI *Fr.* Rough Field, The.

Like dolphins they narrow toward the end. Descriptions (of Living Elsewhere). Tracy Philpot. IAoNAP

Like dry wood in a burning fire. Michelangelo Buonarroti. CAGL, *tr. by* James M. Saslow

Like dust cloud over a bombed-out city, my father's. My Father's Hurricane. Fred Chappell. InGu

Like Empty Beer Cans. Ernesto Cardenal. TCLAP *Fr.* Gethsemani, KY.

Like empty beer cans, like empty. Ernesto Cardenal. TCLAP *Fr.* Gethsemani, KY.

Like every other place. Denton. Dave Oliphant. TiP2

Like falling fruit. Piao-you-mei: Like Falling Fruit. *Unknown.* CCL1, *tr. by* V. W. X.

Like Father. Herbert Williams. AngWePo

Like flustered actors. Kangaroo. Mary Jo Salter. WaAnP

Like foxgloves in the school of the grass moon. Flower Master, The. Medbh McGuckian. ModIr; PNI

Like fragments of an uncompleted world. Sierras. Joaquin Miller. APN-2

Like giant with a dwarf who thwarts him. Lóci Becomes a Giant. Lőrinc Szabó. IQMS, *tr. by* Egon F. Kunz

Like gnats after rain. Maqabane. Tatamkulu Afrika. TSAP

Like God. Lynn Emanuel. PuP-23

Like good unprocessed. Spiritual: "How did you feel when you come out the wilderness?" William W. Cook. SpirFl

Like Grandpa Paul / The water is all of my mind. Louis Zukofsky. ChIV-1 *Fr.* A.

Like gray moths tasting the scented world. Bicyclers, The. Harriet Monroe. ArBi

Like gript stick. Sermon, The. Richard Hughes. OBMV

Like ground that's been walked over, it echoes. Valerio Magrelli. ItPo, *tr. by* Gayle Ridinger

Like Grumbling Roman Plebs. Osip Emilevich Mandelstam. TCRusP, *tr. by* John Glad

Like Gulliver in Brobdingnag. Like Gulliver. György Sárközi. IQMS, *tr. by* Roy Fuller

Like gulls they are still calling. After Visiting Hours. U. A. Fanthorpe. PoCu

Like Hebe, ever fair and young. (LL) Evan Lloyd. AngWePo; OBWVE *Fr.* Powers of the Pen, The.

Like Her Body The World. Martha Collins. ExTi

Like his own sweat or the insults of the sea. (LL) Second Voyage, The. Eiléan Ní Chuilleanáin. EmeKit; ModIr; NPeEn

Like inky sponges that walk away in the deep water. (LL)   Drawn by Stones, by Earth, by Things That Have Been in the Fire.   Marvin Bell.   CAP-8; VCAP

Like intentions among suggestions. (LL)   Mountains.   Alice Oswald.   MFPA; StAl

Like it used to be, not even the future. (LL)   Ö.   Rita Dove.   StAl; WeW-3

Like jigsaw pieces to an unfound puzzle.   Fallen Maple Leaves.   Gerry Cambridge.   EdScPo

Like John Lee Hooker, like Lightnin Hopkins.   Who Am I in Twilight.   Al Young.   ASA

Like John on Patmos, brooding on the Four.   Commination, A.   Alec Derwent Hope.   ChIV-2

Like last year's autumn leaves. (LL)   Retired Ballerinas, Central Park West.   Lawrence Ferlinghetti.   NAMCP V.2; NoAM

Like Leaves on Trees the Race of Man is found.   Homer.   OBVE *Fr.* Iliad, The.

Like Leaving an Umbrella Somewhere.   Chŏng Hyŏnjong.   CAMKP, *tr. by* John M. Frankl

Like Leonardo's idea.   Map of Europe, A.   Derek Walcott.   BrAP

Like lust in the chill of the grave. (LL)   Hamatreya.   Ralph Waldo Emerson.   APN-1; NAAL-3; NCAP

Like lust in the chill of the grave. (LL)   Hamatreya.   Ralph Waldo Emerson.   NAAPv.1; OxBoAm; TCAPo

Like Mandelstam's swallow.   Irina Ratushinskaya.   ItGoST, *tr. by* David McDuff

Like many folk, when first I saddled a rucksack.   Furthest Distances I've Travelled, The.   Leontia Flynn.   NIrP

Like many of us, born too late.   Shut In.   Robert B. Shaw.   SoSe-8

Like many stories, this one begins with Jesus.   Urban Legend.   Lucia Maria Perillo.   RoV

Like Memory, Caverns.   Elizabeth Dodd.   AmPoNex

"Like men riding."   Nelly Trim.   Sylvia Townsend Warner.   MoBrPo

Like mist in the holy morning, the thin veil of love.   Love and the Child.   Ruth Pitter.   MoWP

Like mist on the lees.   Sadakichi.   NAAPv.1 *Fr.* Tanka.

Like misty moonlight.   Issa.   SoOfWa, *tr. by* Sam Hamill

Like molten bronze and iron shed blood.   Lamentation on Ur.   Tom Sleigh.   PoCho

Like Moses on top of the mountain.   Vicente Aleixandre.   *See* Every man can be like that.

Like Most Revelations.   Richard Howard.   OxBoAm

Like music come back to life—.   Small Variation.   Octavio Paz.   VCWP, *tr. by* Mark Strand

"Like Musical Instruments.."   Tom Clark.   TRP

Like my mother always did I hold the spare clothespins three at a time in my mouth. I.   Clothesline.   Laurie Kutchins.   SweBea

Like my mother, and my grandmother too.   Heaven.   Chairil Anwar.   PML; PoetW, *tr. by* Burton Raffel

Like my own boke. (LL)   Off the Back of a Lorry.   Tom Paulin.   ModIr; PBCIP

Like nervous birds in the sky. (LL)   Enemy Dead, The.   Bernard Gutteridge.   FaBoWar; PoWW

Like nomads we came.   Claiming the Dust.   Jean Janzen.   ACAMVP; GeoHom

Like nothing else in Tennessee. (LL)   Anecdote of the Jar.   Wallace Stevens.   BrAP; ColAP; EMP; FaBoA; HeIP-4; MoAmPo; NAAL-5; NAAPv.2; NAMCP V.1; NAWM-7v2; NIL-7; NoAM; NoP-4; NoP-5; OxBoAm; PoA 2002; PoPoPo; SAmP; TCAPo; TFi; WaAnP

Like Odysseus under the ram.   Archilochus.   OBVE

Like oil lamps, we put them out the back.   Emigrant Irish, The.   Eavan Boland.   AmFaPo; EmeKit; MoWP

Like one of those old sulphur matches.   Spanish Dancer.   Oliver Reynolds.   TCAWP

Like One Who.   Ágnes Nemes Nagy.   VCWP, *tr. by* Hugh Maxton

Like one who brings an important letter to the counter after office hours: the counter is already closed.   When Evil-Doing Comes Like Falling Rain.   Bertolt Brecht.   AF, *tr. by* John Willett

Like one who brought news from far.   Like One Who.   Ágnes Nemes Nagy.   VCWP, *tr. by* Hugh Maxton

Like other things.   Girl in the Kitchen.   "Vaidehi."   CFP, *tr. by* A. K. Ramanujan

Like Our Bodies' Imprint.   Yehuda Amichai.   AF, *tr. by* Assia Gutmann

Like our bodies' imprint.   Like Our Bodies' Imprint.   Yehuda Amichai.   AF, *tr. by* Assia Gutmann

Like Oxford colledg[e] bells, to supp. (LL)   On Westwall Downes [*or* On Westwell Downs].   William Strode.   NOSC; NPeEn

Like pain of fire runs down my body my love to you, my dear!   *Unknown.*   APN-2 *Fr.* Songs of the Kwakiutl Indians.

Like people or dogs, each day is unique.   Life of a Day, The.   Tom Hennen.   GoPo

Like Pornography.   Rob MacKenzie.   Oth

Like priceless treasures sinking in the sand. (LL)   America: "Although she feeds me bread of bitterness."   Claude McKay.   NAAL-5; NAAPv.2; NAMCP V.1; NIL-7; NIP-4; NoAM; OxBoAm; PLBUT; WaAnP

Like, pussy cat, pussy cat, where is you was?   Cool Cat.   Michael Myer.   TriCat

Like Rain it sounded till it curved.   Emily Dickinson.   NCAP

Like Raquel.   Maria Arrillaga.   TANSG

Like Riding a Bicycle.   George Bilgere.   ArBi

Like roadside grasses, feathered into bloom.   Summer love was ever thus.   Jean Bleakney.   NIrP

Like Rousseau.   Imamu Amiri Baraka.   PoA 2002

Like royalty, a life of lonely privilege, mounted high on the garage wall. (LL)   Place for Everything, A.   Louis Jenkins.   GoPo; IJHIL

Like sapphire and terracotta mingling in the Ganga.   Home.   Kavikondala Venkatarao.   CFP

Like Seals from Sleep.   Kevin Faller.   IrLP

Like shabby ghosts down dried-up river beds.   Prisoners of War.   John Jarmain.   FaBoWar

Like shifting forms in the world.   Lu Chi.   WoPoe *Fr.* Art of Writing, The.

Like silver dew are the tears of love.   Epitaph.   Alfred Edgar Coppard.   OBMV

Like Sister and Brother.   Enrique Gonzáles Martínez.   TCLAP, *tr. by* Nancy Christoph

Like sister and brother.   Like Sister and Brother.   Enrique Gonzáles Martínez.   TCLAP, *tr. by* Nancy Christoph

Like slime.   Failure.   Kay Ryan.   OxBoAm

Like sluggish electrons.   Amateur God, The.   Sean O'Brien.   NeBrP

Like Smoke from Our Campfire.   David Budbill.   AmZen

Like snows the camps on Southern hills.   Armies of the Wilderness, The.   Herman Melville.   PCW

Like some England some France.   Translated from the European.   Anna Gorenko.   CRWP, *tr. by* Peter France

Like some ill-fated butterfly, the literalists.   John Hollander.   VCAP *Fr.* Powers of Thirteen.

Like some seraglio of an Eastern king.   Curtain, The.   Darl Macleod Boyle.   YaYoPo

Like some winter animal the moon licks the salt of your hand.   Salt Lake, The.   Iwan Goll.   WoPoe, *tr. by* George Hitchcock

Like Someone in Love.   Johnny Burke.   ReLy

Like someone newly dead.   Familiar.   Maria Luisa B. Aguilar-Cariño.   ReBoTo

Like someone who has fallen between the rails.   Dezső Kosztolányi.   IQMS *Fr.* Laments of a Poor Little Child.

Like something broken of wing.   Chamber Music.   Carl Phillips.   NAPBL

Like stitches in a gown, holding sleeve to bodice.   Invalid of Park Street, The.   David Brendon Hopes.   UpMys

Like summer silk its denier.   On Removing Spiderweb.   Les A. Murray.   NAMCP V.2

Like Tapers cleare without number. (LL)   Famous Poems of the Past Explained.   Bin Ramke.   PoDa; RoV

Like That.   Rebecca Radner.   WhBo

Like that man who kicks off his shoes.   Idea Vilariño.   TANSG, *tr. by* Louise B. Popkin

Like that man who kicks off his shoes.   Like that man who kicks off his shoes.   Idea Vilariño.   TANSG, *tr. by* Louise B. Popkin

Like the beat beat beat of the tom-tom.   Night and Day.   Cole Porter.   ReLy

Like the best of worst nightmares.   Pins.   Menna Elfyn.   ATSWP, *tr. by* Robert Minhinnick

Like the briliance of an eye in darkness.   Your Anger.   Paz Molina.   TANSG, *tr. by* Steven F. White

Like the cadence of an old love song.   Child Life.   Mary E. Tucker.   CBWP-1

Like the Chinese, I too am going to.   Maurizio Cucchi.   ItPo, *tr. by* Gayle Ridinger

Like the city skyline they.   Commuters.   Betsy Hearne.   SSCS

Like the dogs of Nile be wise.   Dogs of Nile, The.   Jonathan Swift.   DiBP

Like the earth turning, I creak, and dream.   Inna L'vovna Lisnyanskaya.   CRWP, *tr. by* Ruth Fainlight

Like the eyes of a mild savior. (LL)   Blue Booby, The.   James Tate.   NAMCP V.2; NoAM

Like the fish of the bright and twittering fin.   Song from *Mardi*.   Herman Melville.   APN-2

Like the foghorn that's all lung.   Syrinx.   Amy Clampitt.   NAMCP V.2; NoP-4; NoP-5

Like the golden hub of an ancient.   Roy Kiyooka.   NLPA *Fr.* Pear Tree Pomes.

Like the golden scale that emerges.   Personae Separatae.   Eugenio Montale.   AF, *tr. by* William Arrowsmith

Like the hills under dusk you.   Love Song.   A. R. Ammons.   NAMCP V.2

Like the holy ghost that it is. (LL)   Migration.   Tony Hoagland.   BeAl; PoCho

Like the Idalian Queen[e]. Madrigal. William Drummond of Hawthornden. NOSC

Like the inflatable palm tree I gave to my lover. In Pompano Beach, Florida. Robin Becker. PBCAP

Like the inside of a picnic box. Mount Fuji. Kaneko Mitsuharu. WoPoe, *tr. by* James Kirkup and Akiko Takemoto

Like the leaves already blazing and falling farther north. (LL) Children Walking Home from School through Good Neighborhood. Donald Justice. CAP-8; NIL-7; NIP-8

Like the Magic Glow of Paradise. Clementina Suárez. TANSG, *tr. by* Janet N. Gold

Like the memory of the Angel of Death the moon moves quickly. Between Chimneys. Abraham Sutskever. MotU, *tr. by* Ruth R. Wisse

Like the only thing. Like you. (LL) On the Line. Ruth Padel. MFPA; NeBrP

Like the pale moon in the dawn. (LL) Kenneth Rexroth. APT-2; NAAPv.2; NAMCP V.1 *Fr.* Love Poems of Marichiko, The.

Like the poor, they are with us always. Sparrows. Christopher Buckley. CalPo

Like the radios, the songs, the poem and the stars. (LL) Poem Beginning with a Line by Frank Lima. Lisa Jarnot. LegDan; VaPo

Like the roofs of buildings. Zombie Jet. Connie Deanovich. AmPoNex

Like the rose I am laughing with all my body, not only with. Jelaluddin Rumi. BBASP, *tr. by* A. J. Arberry

Like the slender peach. Tao-yao: Like the Slender Peach. *Unknown.* CCL1, *tr. by* V. W. X.

Like the small sound. How It Comes. Dorothy Barresi. SwNoth

Like the stars of the sky many stars. Are You a Star? Chŏng Hyŏnjong. CAMKP, *tr. by* John M. Frankl

Like the sun, blowing out these evil stars. (LL) Love Poem for My Country, A. Frank Mkalawile Chipasula. HBAPE; NAfrP

Like the sun on February ice dazzling. Snow, Snow. Marge Piercy. MoW

Like the sweet-apple. Sappho. EroLit, *tr. by* Josephine Balmer

Like the swell of Summer's ocean. (LL) Stanzas for Music ("There be none of Beauty's daughters.") Lord Byron. NAEL-6v2; NAEL-7v2; NPBRoP

Like the tides I rise and fall. Patricia Bishop. NewEx

Like the time of her birth away from the world's face. On Seeing a Dead Lamb. Dic Jones. BBMWP, *tr. by* Gillian Clarke

Like the Trails of Ndakinna. Cheryl Savageau. TWW

Like the turning of things. Prostitute's Notebook, The. Leslie Burgess. PfS

Like the unbridled wind he winds after us. Lover River, The. Nazik al-Mala'ika. IrPoTo, *tr. by* Ibtisam Barakat

Like the undulant lark. Where the Light. Giuseppe Ungaretti. WoPoe, *tr. by* Denis Devlin

Like the vain curlings of the watery [*or* wat'ry] maze. First Anniversary of the Government under His Highness the Lord Protector, 1655, The. Andrew Marvell. BASC

Like the very gods in my sight is he who. Sappho. NAWM-7v1, *tr. by* Richmond Lattimore

Like the Vineyard. Na Hûidôk. EcSo, *tr. by* Peter H. Lee

Like the water's outflow, the dream continues to bleed. Friends. May Muzaffar. PoArWo, *tr. by* Tahia Abdel Nasser

Like thee I once have stemm'd the sea of life. Epitaph, An. James Beattie. OBEV

Like these. (LL) Amaze. Adelaide Crapsey. APT-1; NAAPv.2; OxBoAm

Like they had never been. (LL) Tryst [*or* Trysting Place], The. William Soutar. EdScPo; NePenScot; NPeEn

Like They Say. Robert Creeley. OxBoAm

Like This. Lajos Kassák. IQMS, *tr. by* Edwin Morgan

Like This. Carol Muske-Dukes. ExTi

Like This. Jelaluddin Rumi. ErotSp, *tr. by* Coleman Barks

Like this. . .You wouldn't hang me? I thought not. (LL) How Annandale Went Out. Edwin Arlington Robinson. APT-1; GSo; MoAmPo; NAMCP V.1; NoAM; SoSe-8

Like This (1). Stevie Smith. PtR

Like This (2). Stevie Smith. PtR

Like this boat on this spring ocean. En Route to America. Soyen Shaku. WhBo

Like this it happened. Day the Audience Walked Out on Me, and Why, The. Denise Levertov. BrAP

Like this one. (LL) Flower, The: "I think I grow tensions." Robert Creeley. CAP-8; PmAP

Like those jars that women put out to catch the dew of night. Gabriela Mistral. WPoS *Fr.* Prayer.

Like thousands, I took just pride and more than just. Reading Myself. Robert Lowell. NAMCP V.2; VCAP; WaAnP

Like Thousands of Others. Aleksandr Petrovich Tkachenko. ItGoST, *tr. by* Maia Tekses

Like to a baker's oven is the grave. In Christ Church, Bristol, on Thomas Turner, Twice Master of the Company of Bakers. Francis, Lord Jeffrey Jeffrey. NBLV

Like to a Feavers pulse my heart doth beat. Poetresses Petition, The. Margaret Lucas Cavendish, Duchess of Newcastle. BrAP
  (Like to a fever's pulse my heart doth beat.) CABP

LIKE to a ring without a finger. *Unknown.* NoSic

Like to *Diana* in her Summer weede. Robert Greene. PBRV

Like to the Artick needle, that doth guide. Francis Quarles. SacPr

Like to the clear [*or* cleere] in highest sphere [*or* spheare]. Thomas Lodge. OBEV *Fr.* Rosalynde; or Euphues' Golden Legacy.

Like to the damaske rose you see. Francis Quarles. NOSC *Fr.* Argalus and Parthenia.

Like to the falling of a star. Sic Vita. Henry King, Bishop of Chichester. BASC; NOSC

Like to the Indians, scorched with the sun[ne]. Mary Sidney Wroth, Countess of Montgomery. BASC; EMWP; NoP-5; NOSC *Fr.* Pamphilia to Amphilanthus.

Like to the marigold, I blushing close. Edward Taylor. ChIV-2 *Fr.* Preparatory Meditations Before My Approach to the Lord's Supper.

Like to the sentinel stars, I watch all night. To Lucasta. Richard Lovelace. NOSC

Like to thee [*or* the], faire cruell [*orcruel*] May. (LL) Song: "Shephard loveth thow me vell?" Jean Passerat. NPeEn; OBVE, *tr. by* William Drummond of Hawthornden

Like Trains of Cars on Tracks of Plush. Bee, The. Emily Dickinson. MoAmPo

Like tree shadows into the polished windscreen. (LL) From the Frontier of Writing. Seamus Heaney. BrAP; CABP; ModIr; PoetW; PoPoPo

Like truthles[s] dream[e]s, so are my joys expired. Farewell to the Court. Sir Walter Ralegh. NoSic

Like trying to blow a feather. Mouth to Mouth. Steve Gehrke. AmPoNex

Like two lonely swans. (LL) Anne Sexton. NAAL-5; NAMCP V.2 *Fr.* Death of the Fathers, The.

Like two proud armies marching in the field. Your Beauty and My Reason. *Unknown.* NoSic

Like Ulysses. Bin Ramke. RoV

Like unrequited love. Sub Umbra Floreo. Sharron K. Williams. OWABP

Like us he had his. Ulumbo, a Cat. Rutger Kopland. VCWP, *tr. by* James Brockway

Like vapour, the titanic scheme. Ultima Ratio. Friedrich Georg Jünger. UpMys; WoPoe, *tr. by* Les A. Murray

Like we call it / home. (LL) In the Inner City. Lucille Clifton. HeIP-4; SSCS; UnSA

Like well-played-up-to service at a net, mark left and right the forcing of the groves. (LL) David Jones. NAMCP V.1; NoAM *Fr.* In Parenthesis.

Like wet cornstarch, I slide. Refugee Ship. Lorna Dee Cervantes. NAMCP V.2; PoPoPo

Like wild tea blossoms. Who Stops the Dance? "Hsiung Hung." CFP, *tr. by* Chung Ling and Kenneth Rexroth

Like winds my eyelids close. Yvor Winters. NAAPv.2 *Fr.* Magpie's Shadow, The.

Like winter fog, the coal dust climbs her stockings. Vespertilio. Linda Bierds. AmAlph; ExTi

Like wolf—and black bull or goblin hound. Charlotte Brontë. VWP

Like you, I have looked off the cliff. Lightning, The. James ("Jim.") Grabill. AtGh

Like you, I too. RS Thomas. Fadhil Assultani. IrPoTo, *tr. by* Melissa Brown and Saadi A. Simawe

Like yours may sweeten and perfume my death.. (LL) Contemplation upon Flowers, A. Henry King, Bishop of Chichester. OBEV; PtR

Likelihood of Snow, The/ The Danger of Fire. Gerald Dawe. PNI

Likely. Lisa Coffman. AmPoNex

Likely as not a ruined head gasket. Image of the Engine. George Oppen. APT-2

Likely last nostalgic warmth of autumn, The. Mountain Ash without Cedar Waxwings. Robert Pack. PfSP

Like-minded people gather. Dooshi Sorou Soshite Matsu No Me Futori Shoka No Sora. Violet Kazue De Cristoforo. CalPo

Likeness has made them animal and shy. Twins, The. Karl Shapiro. MoAmPo

Likenesses. Norman Alexander MacCaig. NePenScot

Lil' Pito. Sandra Maria Esteves. PueRic

Lilac. Brad Daugherty. BeDoSh

Lilac. Jeanne Shannon. ICANM

Lilac. Mary Ellen Solt. NIL-7

Lilac by the Museum on St. Wenceslas Square, The. Vitězslau Nezval. AF, *tr. by* Ewald Osers

Lilac Petals. Kim Ch'unsu [*or* Chun-soo]. CAMKP, *tr. by* Anthony, Brother of Taizé

Lilac ribbon is unbound, A. Country of No Lack. Jean Starr Untermeyer. MoAmPo

Lilacs. David Biespiel. AmPoNex

Lilacs. Amy Lowell. APT-1; MoAmPo

Lilacs. Sue Sinclair. Coast

Lilacs. Karen Solie. OpeFie

Lilacs, The. Anne Simpson. Coast

Lilacs, The. Richard Wilbur. CAP-8

Lilacs and the Roses, The. Louis Aragon. OBWP, tr. by Louis MacNeice

Lilacs are in bloom, The. Late Afternoon at the Arboretum. Kelly Cherry. SwNoth

Lilacs blowing across his face glad he brought you. (LL) Tennis Court Oath, The. John Ashbery. NAMCP V.2; NoAM

Lilacs for Ginsberg. Gerald Stern. CAP-8

Lilacs in NYC. Mark Doty. WiU

Lilacs lift in generous bloom, The. At Home from Church. Sarah Orne Jewett. APN-2

Lilacs wither in the Carolinas, The. In the Carolinas. Wallace Stevens. SAmP

Lilatu Laili. Amin Al-Rihani. NAAPv.2

Lili Brik, stretched on a bridge. Mayakovsky in Paris. Andrey Andreievich Voznesensky. TCRusP, tr. by Daniel Weissbort

Lilian's Second Letter. Bessie Rayner Parkes. VWP Fr. Summer Sketches.

Lilies. Erica Funkhouser. PfS

Lilies. Mary Oliver. BBASP; WaAnP

Lilies, The. Richard Emil Braun. NoAM

Lilies, are you come! Tiger-Lilies. Michael Field. ViWPN

Lilies at Night. Beckian Fritz Goldberg. AmAlph

Lilies clustered fair and tall, The. Alone. Celia Laighton Thaxter. TCAPo

Lilies of the Field. Anne Rouse. MFPA; NeBl

Lilies of the Valley. Jon Silkin. NoAM

Lilies swinging censers fair. Easter Carol. Henrietta Cordelia Ray. CBWP-3

Lilies [or Lillies] that fester smell far worse than [or then] weeds. (LL) William Shakespeare. CABP; NAEL-6v1; NAEL-7v1; NIL-7; NoP-4; NoP-5; NoSic; NPeEn; OBEV; OxAEP-1; OxBEV; OxBSo; PBRV; TRP; WoPoe Fr. Sonnets.

Lilith. Suzanne Benton. HW

Lilith. Ron Koertge. CalPo

Lilith, Adam's First Companion. Elina Wechsler. MirDau, tr. by Darrell Lockhart

Lilith and the Doctor. Kathleen Norris. HW

Lilith is our daughter. Medusa and Perseus III: Lilith. Pat Parnell. HW

Lilli Burlero [A New Song]. Thomas Wharton, 1st Marquess of Wharton. BASC

Lilliputian Ode on Their Majesties' Accession, A. Henry Carey. FaBoVe; NPeEn; OBCoV

Lily Adair. Thomas Holley Chivers. APN-1

Lily bud floating, yellow as sorrow. Unknown. NDACCP, tr. by Ezra Pound

Lily Events. Unknown. PFTM-1

Lily in a Crystal, The. Robert Herrick. NAEL-6v1; NOSC

Lily on liquid roses floating. Champagne Rosée. John Kenyon. OBEV

Lily Pond. Vicki Feaver. EmeKit

Lily St. Cyr is dead. Class Dress. Dorothy Barresi. SUP

Lily, The. William Blake. NOBRP Fr. Songs of Experience.

Limb snaps, the hive is smashed, and the survivors, A. Crumbling Infrastructure, The. Thomas M. Disch. OxBoAm

Limblike to his own snout, projecting there. On a Chaplain's Nose. Francisco de Quevedo y Villegas. WoPoe, tr. by Roy Campbell

Limbo. Seamus Heaney. NoAM

Limbo Dancer, The. Josephine Jacobsen. FFC

Lime. Frank Lima. AHA

Lime, calcium, silica, pyrites. Memory Table 1, The. Christopher Dewdney. OpeFie

Limejuice Tub, The. Unknown. NOBAu

Limen. Natasha Trethewey. FuFl

Limerick: "Decrepit old gas man named Peter, A." Unknown. SoSe-8

Limerick: "Epicure, Dining at Crewe, An." Unknown. NTCP

(Waiter, Please.) NBLV

Limerick: "From Number Nine, Penwiper Mews." Edward Gorey. OBCoV

Limerick: "From the bathing machine came a din." Edward Gorey. AmWit; OBCoV

Limerick: "I sat next to the Duchess at tea." Unknown. SoSe-8

Limerick: ""If you're aristocratic," said Nietzsche." Gerry Hamill. OBCoV

Limerick Is Furtive and Mean, The. Limerick. Morris Gilbert Bishop. NBLV

Limerick: "It's time to make love. Douse the glim." Conrad Potter Aiken. NBLV

Limerick: "Limerick Is Furtive and Mean, The." Morris Gilbert Bishop. NBLV

Limerick: "Said an erudite sinologue: "How."" R. J. P. Hewison. OBCoV

Limerick: "Sex-life her husband dreamed of, The." Laurence Perrine. PoA 2002

Limerick: "Some Harvard men, stalwart and hairy." Edward Gorey. OBCoV

Limerick: "Staid schizophrenic named Struther, A." Unknown. NIP-4

Limerick: "There once was a bard of Hong Kong." Gerard Benson. OBCoV

Limerick: "There once was a girl from St. Paul." Unknown. NIP-4

Limerick: "There was a Young Lady of Parma." Edward Lear. OBCoV

Limerick: "There was a young lady of Portugal." Edward Lear. OBCoV

Limerick: "There was a young lady of Riga." Cosmo Monkhouse. NIL-7

Limerick: "There was a young lady of Tottenham." Unknown. WeW-3

Limerick: "There was a young maid who said, "Why."" Unknown. SoSe-8

Limerick: "There was a young person whose history." Edward Lear. OBCoV

Limerick: "There was an archdeacon who said." Unknown. OBCoV

Limerick: "There was an old fellow of Kaber." Philip Larkin. OBCoV

Limerick: "There was an old lady of Chertsey." Edward Lear. OBCoV

Limerick: "There was an old Lady of Winchelsea." Edward Lear. OBCoV

Limerick: "There was an old man of [or from] Peru / Who dreamt [or dreamed] he was eating his shoe." Unknown. SoSe-8

(Old Man from Peru, An.) NTCP

Limerick: "There was an old man of Thermopylae." Edward Lear. OxAEP-2

Limerick: "There was an old man of Toulouse." Edward Lear. OBCoV

Limerick: "There was an Old Man of Whitehaven." Edward Lear. NPeEn; OxAEP-2

Limerick: "There was an Old Man on some rocks." Edward Lear. OxBEV

Limerick: "There was an old man who screamed out." Edward Lear. NPeEn; OxAEP-2; OxBEV

Limerick: "There was an Old Man who supposed." Edward Lear. NAEL-6v2; NAEL-7v2

(There Was an Old man Who Supposed.) NoP-4; NoP-5

Limerick: "There was an old man whose despair." Edward Lear. OBCoV

Limerick: "There was an Old Person of Basing." Edward Lear. NPeEn; OxAEP-2

(Limericks, I (iii).) OBCoV

Limerick: "There was an old person of Bow." Edward Lear. OxAEP-2

Limerick: "To his club-footed child said Lord Stipple." Edward Gorey. OBCoV

Limerick: "Tutor who tooted a flute, A." Carolyn Wells. SoSe-8

Limerick: "Well, it's partly the shape of the thing." Unknown. SoSe-8

Limerick Train, The. Brendan Kennelly. PBCIP

Limericks, I (i). Edward Lear. OBCoV

Limericks, I (iii). Edward Lear. See Limerick: "There was an Old Person of Basing."

Limericks, I (iv). Edward Lear. OBCoV

Limestone pavement, The. Maen Madoc. Chris Torrance. AngWePo

Liminal. Sarah Maguire. MoWP

Liminal Highway. John K. Samson. PoPra

Limit. Diane Ward. FTOS

Limitations. Henrietta Cordelia Ray. CBWP-3

Limitations. Siegfried Sassoon. MoBrPo

Limited. Carl Sandburg. BeAl; MoAmPo

Limited Liability. John Ashbery. BodElec

Limits. Jorge Luis Borges. PoetW, tr. by Alastair Reid

Limits. Ralph Waldo Emerson. APN-1

Limits of Desire, The. Linda Gregg. ExTi

Limits of our language are the limits, The. Never Mororcco. Tessa Rumsey. LegDan

Limits (or Good-byes). Jorge Luis Borges. PoetW, tr. by Alan Dugan

Limits (or Good-byes). Jorge Luis Borges. TCLAP, tr. by Alan Dugan

Limped out of the hot sky a hurt plane. Navy Field. William Meredith. PWW2

Limpid Autumn; I gaze, no limit. Wasteland—Gazing Far Away. Tu Fu [or Du Fu]. CCL1, tr. by Florence Ayscough and Amy Lowell

Limpopo and Tugela churned. Scorpion, The. William Plomer. OBMV

Lincoln. John Gould Fletcher. CBCWP; MoAmPo

Lincoln. Henrietta Cordelia Ray. CBWP-3

Lincoln. Delmore Schwartz. APT-2

Lincoln Bedroom, The. Donald Berger. NAPBL

Lincoln Monument: Washington. Langston Hughes. CBCWP

Lincoln, the Man of the People. Edwin Markham. MoAmPo

Lincoln was sixty years old when the doctor told him he only had forty more years to live. Diagnosis, The. James Tate. BAP-01

Lincoln's Grave. Maurice Thompson. CBCWP

Linda. Jack Lawrence. ReLy

Linda June put your white dress on. P.W.T. Tom Weatherly. EGAG

Lindie, chile, fo' Lawd sake, tell me. After the Quarrel. Priscilla Jane Thompson. CBWP-2

L'indifférent. Michael Field. ViWPN

Line. Milo De Angelis. NeIt, *tr.* by Lawrence Venuti

Line: "You were drawn in the voice of my mother." Colette Bryce. NIrP

Line Drive. Arthur Ginsberg. BloBone

Line Drive Caught by the Grace of God. Linda Gregerson. ExTi; MoASP

Line from St. David's, A. Ronald Stuart Thomas. AngWePo

Line in long array where they wind betwixt green islands, A. Cavalry Crossing a Ford. Walt Whitman. AmWaPo; BLT; BrAP; CBCWP; FaBoA; HeIP-4; NAAL-3; NAAL-5; NAAPv.1; NAMCP V.1; NCAP; NoAM; NoP-4; NoP-5; PCW; SAmP; TCAPo; TFi; TRP; WaAnP

Line of a Poem. Zali Gurevitch. FIT, *tr.* by Robert Friend

Line of ants, The. Issa. EMJL, *tr.* by Haruo Shirane

Line of martins, A. Martins. Mike Jenkins. AngWePo

Line of the willows is old, The. For Jurij Koch. Robat Powell. BBMWP, *tr.* by the author

Line through the hold in the dank, The. Bellrope. Robert Morgan. BLT

Line Up. Forrest Hamer. OPRER

Lineage. Jeffrey McDaniel. LegDan

Lineage. Margaret Abigail Walker. ItP; ItWoWo; NALW; OxWW

Lineage. Daisy Zamora. LoL, *tr.* by Margaret Randall

Lineaments of a plummet-measured face, The. (LL) Statues, The. William Butler Yeats. NoAM; WeW-3

Lineaments of Gratified Desire, The. (LL) William Blake. ErotSp; NoP-4; NoP-5; OxBEV; WoPoe *Fr.* Several Questions Answered.

Lined coat, warm cap and easy felt slippers. Ease. Po Chü-i. Spl, *tr.* by Arthur Waley

Linen Crow, a Caftan Magpie, A. Patrick Lane.
"I walk to the river in deep snow. The ice is thick." IFF

Linen Industry, The. Michael Longley. IrLP; ModIr; NoP-4; NoP-5; PBCIP; PNI; StAl

Linen Workers, The. Michael Longley. ModIr; NPeEn *Fr.* Wreaths.

Lines. Ina Coolbrith. SWaP

Lines. Frances Anne Kemble. VWP

Lines. Sara Teasdale. APT-1

Lines. Henry Timrod. *See* Ode: "Sleep sweetly in your humble graves."

Lines: "At the Portals of the Future." Frances Ellen Watkins Harper. APN-2; NAAPv.1

Lines: Composed at the Old Temples of Maralipoor. Charles Timothy Brooks. APN-1

Lines: "Draw a line. Write a line. There." Martha Collins. P180

Lines: "Empty foolscap, The." Barbara Nickel. ACAMVP

Lines: "Gather the sacred dust." Abram Joseph Ryan. APN-2

Lines: "I Am." John Clare. *See* I Am.

Lines: "I feel your legs touching." Afaa Michael Weaver. BtF

Lines: "I have given birth to a see-through child." Colette Bryce. NIrP

Lines: "Oh, ye who in those Houses hold." Frances Sargent Osgood. NAAPv.1

Lines: "Repressive desublimation." David Bromige. FTOS

Lines: "Sun I worship, The." Yonejiro (Yone) Noguchi. NAAPv.2

Lines, The: "November, and the Sunday twilight fallen." Andrew Motion. NeBrP

Lines: To a Young Gentleman of Surpassing Beauty. Ellen Johnston. VWP

Lines: "When the lamp is shattered [or shatter'd]." Percy Bysshe Shelley. NAEL-7v2; OBEV; OxBEV

Lines: "When youthful faith hath fled." John Gibson Lockhart. OBEV

Lines Among the Leaves. Eliza Cook.
"Varied theme it utters, A." VerBaPo

Lines are straight and swift between the stars, The. Stars at Tallapoosa. Wallace Stevens. WoPoe

Lines by a Lady on the Loss of her Trunk. Richard Brinsley Sheridan. OBCoV

Lines Composed a Few Miles above Tintern Abbey on Revisiting the Banks of the Wye During a Tour, July 13, 1798. William Wordsworth. AmFaPo; BrAP; CABP; HeIP-4; NAEL-6v2; NAEL-7v2; NAWM-7v2; NIL-7; NoP-4; NoP-5; NPeEn; OxAEP-2; OxBEV; PoPoPo; TFi

Lines Composed Over Three Thousand Miles From Tintern Abbey. Billy Collins. OxBoAm; WaAnP

Lines Contributed to Goldsmith's "The Traveller." Samuel Johnson. NPeEn

Lines Contributed to Hawkesworth's "The Rival." Samuel Johnson. NPeEn

Lines for a Book. Thom Gunn. CABP

Lines for a Hindi Poet. Bahadur Tejani. PML

Lines for a Painter. Anthony Cronin. PBCIP

Lines for a Tomb. Donald Davidson. FuPo

Lines for an Old Man. T. S. Eliot. RaBo

Lines for Cuscuscaraway and Mirza Murad Ali Beg. T. S. Eliot. NBLV; OBCoV; UV *Fr.* Five-Finger Exercises.

Lines for Roethke Twenty Years after His Death. Duane Niatum. HATNAP

Lines for Translation into Any Language. James Fenton. AF

Lines from Love Letters. *Unknown.* OBEV

Lines from Love Letters, I. *Unknown.* OBEV

Lines from terrain are attractive trilling & deeply rolling theodolite. Franked. Anna Mendelssohn. VaPo

Lines from the Testament. Pier Paolo Pasolini. VCWP, *tr.* by Norman MacAfee

Lines I fashioned yesterday, The. Sacrifice. Gyula Illyés. IQMS, *tr.* by Marie B. Jaffe

Lines in a Roman Schoolbook. Desmond O'Grady.
"In the valleys of the future we shall walk." PBCIP
"This introspective exile here today." PBCIP

Lines in Dejection. Jean Valentine. YaYoPo

Lines in Praise of a Self-Chiming Clock. Hsüan-yeh. ColAnChi, *tr.* by Jonathan D. Spence

Lines In Prison. Anne Askew. *See* Ballad Which Anne Askew[e] Made and Sang When She Was in Newgate, The.

Lines in Recollection. Russell Atkins. EGAG

Lines in the Corner of a Manuscript. *Unknown.* FaBoVe

Lines in the hands of old people, The. Memories of Horses. Rolf Jacobsen. WED, *tr.* by Robert Bly

Lines in the Sand. Richard Sanger. IFF

Lines Left at Mr Theodore Hook's House in June, 1834. Thomas Ingoldsby. OBCoV

Lines Lost among Trees. Billy Collins. BAP-97

Lines of Life. Letitia Elizabeth Landon. NOBRP; NPBRoP; NPeEn

Lines of the Hand, The. Julio Cortázar. MotU; TCLAP, *tr.* by Paul Blackburn

Lines of this new song are nothing, The. Anew 20. Louis Zukofsky. APT-2; NAAPv.2

Lines of your arteries, The. Robert. Wendy Rose. HATNAP

Lines on a Carp. Gary Snyder. WaAnP

Lines on a Dead Girl. Priscilla Jane Thompson. CBWP-2

Lines on a Platonic Friendship. Daryl Hine. IllVoic

Lines on a Van's Dereliction. Douglas Houston. TCAWP

Lines on a Young Lady's Photograph Album. Philip Larkin. BrAP

Lines on Cambridge of 1830. Alfred Tennyson. OxBSo

Lines on Hearing That Lady Byron Was Ill. Lord Byron. NPeEn; OxAEP-2

Lines on His Companions Who Died in the Northern Seas. Thomas James. NOSC

Lines on Nonsense. Eliza Lee Cabot Follen. SWaP

Lines on Retirement, after Reading *Lear.* David Wright. IaFF

Lines on Roger Hilton's Watch. William Sydney Graham. NPeEn

Lines on the Award "Pipe Man of the Year" to Magnus Magnusson. E. J. Thribb. OBCoV

Lines on the Death of the Rev. S. K. Talmage. Mary E. Tucker. CBWP-1

Lines on the Tombs in Westminster. Francis Beaumont. OBEV *Fr.* On the Tombs in Westminster Abbey.

Lines Printed under the Engraved Portrait of Milton [In Tonson's Folio of the "Paradise Lost"]. John Dryden. OxAEP-1
(Epigram on Milton.) NAEL-6v1; NAEL-7v1

Lines Rhymed in a Letter from Oxford. John Keats. OBCoV

Lines Scribbled on an Envelope. Madeleine L'Engle. SacPr

Lines Started Outside Filene's Basement. James R. Scrimgeour. OPRER

Lines Suggested by an Edition of Blake's Poems. Sir Walter Alexander Raleigh. OBCoV

Lines Suggested by Hearing Music on the Boston Common at Night. Thomas Cole. APN-1

Lines / Suggested by the Song of a Nightingale. Eliza Cook. VWP

Lines through these words, The. Michael Palmer. PFTM-2 *Fr.* Sun.

Lines to———. Mary Weston Fordham. CBWP-2

Lines to a Depressed Friend. Frank O'Hara. AHA

Lines to a Don. Joseph Hilaire Pierre Belloc. MoBrPo; OBSV

Lines to a Graduate. Lizelia Augusta Jenkins Moorer. CBWP-3

Lines to a Movement in Mozart's E-Flat Symphony. Thomas Hardy. NoAM

Lines to a Nasturtium. Anne Spencer. APT-1; InGu

Lines to an Old Dress. Mary E. Tucker. CBWP-1

Lines to an Old School-House. Priscilla Jane Thompson. CBWP-2

Lines to Do with Youth. Witter Bynner. PoA 2002

Lines to Ellen, the Factory Girl. Ellen Johnston. VWP

Lines to Emma. Priscilla Jane Thompson. CBWP-2

Lines to Florence. Mary Weston Fordham. CBWP-2

Lines to His New Instructress. Maurice Riordan. NIrP

Lines to Mr Hodgson. Lord Byron. OBCoV
(Lisbon Packet, The.) NBLV

Lines to Mrs. Isabel Peace. Mary Weston Fordham. CBWP-2

Lines to Mrs. M. C. Turner. Eloise Bibb. CBWP-4

Lines to Ralph Hodgson Esqre. T. S. Eliot. NBLV *Fr.* Five-Finger Exercises.

Lines to the Hon. George L. Knox. Eloise Bibb. CBWP-4

Lines Where Beauty Lingers. Franklin Pierce Adams. AmWit

Lines Written at Night During Insomnia. Alexander Sergeyevich Pushkin. AWTN, *tr.* by D. M. Thomas

Lines Written During a Period of Insanity. William Cowper. IJHIL; NoP-4; NoP-5; NPeEn

(Lines Written Under the Influence of Delerium.) ChIV-1

Lines Written During a Sleepless Night in Tbilisi. Bella Akhatovna Akhmadulina. ARWW, *tr.* by Catriona Kelly

Lines Written for a Friend on the Death of His Brother, Caused by a Railway Train Running Over Him Whilst He Was in a State of Inebriation. James Henry Powell. VerBaPo

Lines Written for Allen Tate on His Sixtieth Anniversary. Donald Davidson. FuPo

Lines Written in Boston on a Beautiful Autumnal Day. Margaret Fuller. SWaP

Lines Written in Early Spring. William Wordsworth. NAEL-6v2; NAEL-7v2; NOBRP; NPBRoP; SacPr

Lines Written in Her Breviary. Saint, of Avila Theresa. WPoS, *tr.* by Henry Wadsworth Longfellow

Lines Written in Kensington Gardens. Matthew Arnold. OBGa

Lines Written in Kensington Gardens. Matthew Arnold. NAEL-6v2; NAEL-7v2

(Lines Written in Kensington Gardens.) OBGa

Lines Written in the Bay of Lerici. Percy Bysshe Shelley. NAEL-6v2; NAEL-7v2

Lines Written in the Church Yard of Richmond, Yorkshire. Herbert Knowles. SacPr

Lines Written in the Dark Illegible Next Day. Franz Wright. AmAlph

Lines Written on a Farewell View of the Franconia Mountains at Twilight. Henrietta Cordelia Ray. CBWP-3

Lines Written on a Window at The Leasowes. William Shenstone. NPeEn

Lines, / Written on Seeing My Husband's Picture, painted when he was young: "Those are the features, those the smiles." Anna Sawyer. LW

Lines Written on Visiting a Scene in Argyleshire. Thomas Campbell. NPBRoP

Lines Written Under a Picture of a Girl Burning a Love-Letter. Letitia Elizabeth Landon. NOBRP

Lines Written Under the Influence of Delerium. William Cowper. *See* Lines Written During a Period of Insanity.

Lines Written Under the Portrait of Robert Fergussson, the Poet, in a Copy of That Author's Works Presented to a Young Lady in Edinburgh, March 19th, 1787. Robert Burns. NePenScot

Lingam and the Yoni, The. Alec Derwent Hope. NoAM

Lingard and the Stars. Edwin Arlington Robinson. OxBSo

Linger not, stranger; shed no tear. Inscription for a War. Alec Derwent Hope. BMAP; NoP-4; NoP-5; WaAnP

Linger, tag, let go. Justin Quinn. NIrP

Lingerie shopping with Mom, I braced myself. Eve's Striptease. Julia Kasdorf. ACAMVP; NeAmPo

Lingering at the door of the bathhouse. Sakura. Mike O'Connor. WANABP

Lingering Doubt, The. Samuel Allen. FuFl

Lingering fade the rays of daylight, and the listening air is chilly. Philip and Mildred. Adelaide Anne Procter. VWP

Lingering sun: rivers and mountains brighten. Wu-Chueh. Tu Fu [*or* Du Fu]. ChinPo, *tr.* by Ye Weilian [*or* Yeh Wei-lien *or* Wai-lim Yip]

Ling-tai: He Measured Out His Spirit Tower. *Unknown.* CCL1, *tr.* by Heng Kuan

Lingua Franca. Chris Stroffolino. BodElec

Link. Mehmet Yardımcı. NaPG, *tr.* by Talat Sait Halman

Link Between Reader and Writer, The. Diana Hartog. NLPA *Fr.* Oasis.

Linked Verses. *Vietnamese Oral Tradition.* CaDao, *tr.* by John Balaban

Linked-Verse Sequence Throughout the Town, The. Basho, Boncho and Mukai Kyorai. *tr.* by Earl Miner

"Each year it is but a peck of rice." WoPoe, *tr.* by Earl Miner

Linnet in the rocky dells, The. Song. Emily Jane Brontë. RACG

Linnet, The. Robert Bridges. *See* I Heard a Linnet Courting.

Linnet who had lost her way, A. Tenebris Interlucentem. James Elroy Flecker. MoBrPo

Linstead Market. *Unknown.* FaBoVe

Lint. Rita Dove. AmAlph; TRP

Lion. John Wheelwright. AmWit

Lion, The. Joseph Hilaire Pierre Belloc. MoBrPo; NBLV; WHSW

Lion, The. Ogden Nash. TLR; WHSW

Lion, The. Walter James Turner. MoBrPo

Lion, The. István Vas. IQMS, *tr.* by Peter Zollman

Lion and Albert, The. Marriott Edgar. OBNV

Lion and lioness are intractable, The. Letter to Eve. Alan Dugan. YaYoPo

Lion and the Apostle, The. Fadil Azzawi. IrPoTo, *tr.* by Ralph Saverese and Saadi A. Simawe

Lion and the Echo, The. Brian Patten. OBSP

Lion ane his tamer, The. Crunch, The. Gerda Mayer. OBSP

Lion for Real, The. Allen Ginsberg. EmeKit

Lion has been frequenting this area, A. Big Bend: Lion Warning. Jane Epton Seale. TiP2

Lion, he prowleth far and near, The. Hunters, The. Ruth Temple Lindsay. SacPr

Lion is the [*or* a] beast to fight, The. Sage Counsel. Sir Arthur Thomas Quiller-Couch. NBLV

Lion Lion. Tom Raworth. PFTM-2

Lion Named Passion, A. John Hollander. NoAM

Lion of God in Vermont in May. Pamela White Hadas. PfSP

Lion of Judah, The. Jan Emmens. WoPoe, *tr.* by Adrienne Rich

Lion of the stars is losing power, The. Lion, The. István Vas. IQMS, *tr.* by Peter Zollman

Lion of waking roars, The. In the Forests of Sleep. Habiba Muhammadi. PoArWo, *tr.* by Ibrahim Muhawi

Lion remembers the forest, The. Captivity. Amy Levy. ViWPN

Lion stretched like a sandstone lion on the sandstone slab, The. Homesickness. Paul Muldoon. GPPA

Lion Tamer Remembers, The. Tristan Tzara. YaTCFP, *tr.* by Mary Ann Caws

Lion tamers wrestle with the lions in a cage, The. Apex. Nate Salsbury. NBLV

Lion, the Lion, he dwells in the waste, The. Lion, The. Joseph Hilaire Pierre Belloc. MoBrPo; NBLV; WHSW

Lion with peony eyes, A. Peony and a Lion, A. Ani Ilkov. CSCBP, *tr.* by Georgi Belev and Lisa Sapinkopf

Lionel, do you remember "Dark Shadows." After the Children Have Gone to Bed. Nicholas Samaras. TWW

Lìonmhorachd anns na speuran. Sorley MacLean. EdScPo, *tr.* by Iain Crichton Smith

Lions of fire, The. Kenneth Patchen. APT-2

Lions of the hill are gone, The. Deirdre's [*or* Deidre's] Lament for the Sons of Usnach. *Unknown.* IrLP, *tr.* by Sir Samuel Ferguson

Lion's Teeth. Rebecca Hoogs. PoDa

Lions who ate the Christians on the sands of the arena, The. Sunt Leones. Stevie Smith. GoPo; NAMCP V.1; NoAM

Lip. James Vincent Cunningham. OxBoAm *Fr.* Five Epigrams.

Lip they called him when he, The. Recondite war on women, The. Douglas Livingstone. TSAP

Lip was a man who used his head. James Vincent Cunningham. OxBoAm *Fr.* Five Epigrams.

Lips. Lance Larsen. AmPoNex

Lips and Eyes. Thomas Carew. OBVE, *tr.* by Thomas Carew

Lips! bold, frenzied utterance, shape to the thoughts that are. Dawn Behind Night. Isaac Rosenberg. RSaN

Lips of the dead once thoughtlessly. Yehuda Amichai. FIT, *tr.* by Robert Friend

Lips pressed against my heart. (LL) Evening Song. Jean Toomer. APT-2; GT

Lips reddened. Hooker. Jean-Claude Martineau. OGAHCP, *tr.* by Boadiba and Jack Hirschman

Lips That Touch Liquor. George W. Young. NBLV

Lips to the already dead Ayler. Migration of Drummond's Organs (After Death), The. Norman Weinstein. WaCA

Lipsticktion. Edwin Torres. HeMarv

Liquid brain solidifies in thought, The. In Anguish, the Heart Finally Prays. Andy Young. AnSo

Liquid City. Lorenzo Thomas. TiP2

Liquid Mercury. Gu Cheng. *tr.* by Joseph R. Allen

Aluminum Oxide. WoBe, *tr.* by Joseph R. Allen

Cord. WoBe, *tr.* by Joseph R. Allen

Dee dee da dee da. WoBe, *tr.* by Joseph R. Allen

Feel of the Wind, The. WoBe, *tr.* by Joseph R. Allen

Minor God, A. WoBe, *tr.* by Joseph R. Allen

Red Wheat. WoBe, *tr.* by Joseph R. Allen

Solar Flare. WoBe, *tr.* by Joseph R. Allen

There're Not Many Birds in the Village Now. WoBe, *tr.* by Joseph R. Allen

Willow Jar. WoBe, *tr.* by Joseph R. Allen

Writing Brush. WoBe, *tr.* by Joseph R. Allen

Liquidation. Leah Aini. DTA, *tr.* by Miriyam Glazer

Liquidity's a mystery; it's very rarely seen. Accounting Cat, The. John Clarke. UV

Liquor, wages, automobiles, women, dope. Elegy for Llywelyn Humphries. Meic Stephens. TCAWP

Lire et chanter est une chose propre tandis que parler c'est des minutes. Qualités d'apôtre. Gisèle Prassinos. YaTCFP

Lisa, Leona, Loretta? Salt. Yusef Komunyakaa. OPRER; UnSA

Lisboa / boa / woman with coal-black hair. Maria 1. Asaf Halet Çelebi. NaPG, *tr.* by Talat Sait Halman

Lisbon. Russell Atkins. GT

Lisbon Packet, The. Lord Byron. *See* Lines to Mr Hodgson.

Lisos al extremo cuando voltearon diurnos. Angélica Tornero. SPV

Lisp in Numbers, A. Edward Edwin Foot. STuOW; VerBaPo

List, The. Lawson Fusao Inada. WhBo

List, I hear the church bells ring. Church Bells, The. Mrs. Henry Linden. CBWP-4

List! list! the sleigh bells peal across the snow. December. Henrietta Cordelia Ray. CBWP-3

List of the Delusions of the Insane / What They Are Afraid Of, A. David Antin. APSN

List the harp in window wailing. Aeolian Harp, The. Herman Melville. NCAP

List to a Tale of Love in Acadie, home of the happy. (LL) Henry Wadsworth Longfellow. APN-1; NAAPv.1; NoP-4; TCAPo; UV *Fr.* Evangeline: A Tale of Acadie.

List to me while I tell you. Spaniard That Blighted My Life, The. Billy Merson. OBCoV

List to the sad wind, drearily moaning. Autumn. Priscilla Jane Thompson. CBWP-2

Listed into the cause of sin. True Use of Music, The. Charles Wesley. SacPr

Listen. Jack Grapes. SUP

Listen. Vladimir Vladimirovich Mayakovsky. PFTM-1

Listen. Listen. Vladimir Vladimirovich Mayakovsky. PFTM-1

Listen! Vladimir Vladimirovich Mayakovsky. CLPP, *tr. by* Maria Enzensberger

Listen! Lilian Moore. NTCP

Listen. Benjamin Péret. SurPaPo, *tr. by* Rachel Stella

Listen. Iain Crichton Smith. HarvBoo

Listen! To Olga. Alena Synková. INSAB

Listen. Yeshe Tsogyel. WPoS

Listen. Miller Williams. P180

Listen. . . / With faint dry sound. November Night. Adelaide Crapsey. APT-1; NAAPv.2; Spl; TCAPo

Listen / All creeping things. Issa. ZenPo, *tr. by* Takashi Ikemoto and Lucien Stryk

Listen, and when thy hand this paper presses. Letter from a Girl to Her Own Old Age, A. Alice Thompson Meynell. MoBrPo; VWP

Listen, Big Boy! Button Up Your Overcoat. Lew Brown, B. G. DeSylva and Ray Henderson. ReLy

Listen but once to the words written out by my hand. Short Summary. Louise Bogan. APT-2

Listen Carefully. Philip Levine. EmeKit

Listen Children. Lucille Clifton. ISC; NOxBChV

Listen, Christ, / You did alright in your day, I reckon. Goodbye Christ. Langston Hughes. NAAPv.2

Listen Galaxea. Alvaro Cardona-Hine. ICANM

Listen, good people, and you shall hear. W. H. Auden. OBNV *Fr.* Six Commissioned Texts.

Listen! Hear how I dreamed a great dream. Dream of the Rood, The. *Unknown.* NePenScot, *tr. by* Robert Crawford

Listen, I am holy. (LL) Concerning That Prayer I Cannot Make. Jane Mead. LaCa; PLBUT

Listen i have a complaint to make. Indelible. Jayne Cortez. EGAG

Listen, I stole Wagner's. "New World" Interview. Bruce Sweet. MiVo

Listen, / if stars are lit. Listen! Vladimir Vladimirovich Mayakovsky. CLPP, *tr. by* Maria Enzensberger

Listen I'll write a poem but don't laugh. Cosmic Realities Vanilla Tobacco Wakings. Tristan Tzara. YaTCFP, *tr. by* Mary Ann Caws *and* Jean-Pierre Cauvin

Listen, I'm coming to get you. Sion Eirian. BBMWP *Fr.* Adolescent Experiences.

Listen: it means "The Belovéd" in Persian, "witness" in Arabic. (LL) Ghazal: "Only language of loss left in the world is Arabic, The." Agha Shahid Ali. AmAlph; PML

Listen! I've a big surprise! Invitation. Myra Cohn Livingston. TLR

Listen! listen! for I enter now your thought. (LL) Two Songs of Advent. Yvor Winters. APT-2; NAAPv.2

Listen. Listen here, all about birds and beasts. Talking about Birds. *Vietnamese Oral Tradition.* CaDao, *tr. by* John Balaban

Listen! / Listen to the witch! Listen! Lilian Moore. NTCP

Listen Mr Oxford Don. John Agard. NPeEn; Oth

Listen my children, and you shall hear. Henry Wadsworth Longfellow. AmWaPo; BLPJKO; BRP; ChAP; ColAP; HHAm; ITBLP; NAAPv.1; NOxBChV; OBNV; OxBoAm; TCAPo; TFi; WaAnP *Fr.* Tales of a Wayside Inn.

Listen, my dearest, once this flesh of mine. Two Hearts Divided. R. Williams Parry. OBWVE, *tr. by* Joseph P. Clancy

Listen, my friend, this road is the heart opening. Heat of Midnight Tears, The. Mirabai. WED; WPoS, *tr. by* Robert Bly

Listen, nephew / When I opened the cantina. Tale of Sunlight, The. Gary Soto. CAP-8; NoAM

Listen not to the rain piercing the woods, pelting the leaves! Tune: "Calming Windswept Waves." Su Tung-p'o. ColAnChi, *tr. by* Jiaosheng Wang

Listen! Now I have come to step over your soul. Formula to Cause Death. *Cherokee Oral Tradition.* NAAPv.1

Listen, Saint Peter, to this little story. Keys of the Saint. Ernesto Lumbreras. RMCMP, *tr. by* Rebecca Seiferle

Listen, Sanoe. Sanoe. Queen Lili'u-o-ka-lani. SWaP

Listen! The fame of Danish kings. Beowulf. *Unknown. tr. by* Charles W. Kennedy, Gerald Benson, Michael O'Brien and Frederick Rebsamen

Listen, the hay-bells tinkle as the cart. Holy Innocents, The. Robert Lowell. MoAmPo; OBCP

Listen: the laureled poets. Lemon Trees, The. Eugenio Montale. PoetW; WoPoe, *tr. by* William Arrowsmith

Listen; the poets laureate. Lemon Trees, The. Eugenio Montale. PFTM-1

Listen. / The rejoicing of waters fills my ears this evening. Rhydwen Williams. BBMWP *Fr.* Mountain Streams.

Listen: there was a goat's head hanging by ropes in a tree. Brigit Pegeen Kelly. ExTi; IllVoic *Fr.* Southern Review, The.

Listen. This is the Noise of Myth. Eavan Boland. ModIr

Listen, this is the trinity, he said, tramping the wet road. Avatar, The. Kerry Hardie. NIrP; StAl

Listen to me and you shall hear. World is Turned Upside Down, The. *Unknown.* NOSC

Listen to me as one listens to the rain. As One Listens to the Rain. Octavio Paz. GPTC, *tr. by* Eliot Weinberger

Listen to me, as when ye heard our father. Canadian Boat Song. *Unknown.* OBEV

Listen to me, you wench! *Unknown.* CATKP, *tr. by* Wen Hsia-min

Listen to my tale of woe. Oh, Lady, Be Good! Ira Gershwin. ReLy

Listen to the coal. In Memoriam John Coltrane. Michael Stillman. CalPo

Listen to the cry going on at the marketplace. Lost Daughter, The (19). Khwaja Shams-ad-din Muhammad Hafiz. WED, *tr. by* Robert Bly and Leonard Lewisohn

Listen to the Mocking Bird. Septimus Winner. TCAPo

Listen to the reed-flute telling its tales. Jelaluddin Rumi. NaPG, *tr. by* Talat Sait Halman

Listen to the Rock Island train. Riding the Rock Island Through Kansas. Dave Etter. GM

Listen to the sea. Guillaume Apollinaire. PFTM-1 *Fr.* Victoire.

Listen to the Sound of My Horn. Rita Dove. SeSe

Listen to the sound of my horn . . . . Listen to the Sound of My Horn. Rita Dove. SeSe

Listen to the sound of their boots. Paper 43. Dominique Batraville. OGAHCP, *tr. by* Boadiba and Jack Hirschman

Listen to the tale. Slim Greer. Sterling Allen Brown. NAAPv.2; NAMCP V.1

Listen, what are you reading this for? Listen. Jack Grapes. SUP

Listen, / when i found there was no safety. To my Friend, Jerina. Lucille Clifton. ESEAA

Listen: when the summer sun began. Acoustics. William H. New. IFF

Listen, you chattering society that roosts by night. Bargain, The. Caradog Prichard. BBMWP, *tr. by* Joseph P. Clancy

Listen, you rhythm rounders. Truckin'. Ted Koehler. ReLy

Listene / secting. Clark Coolidge. WhBo

Listener of Bats. Laure-Anne Bosselaar. PoDa

Listener's Guide to the Birds, A. Elwyn Brooks White. OWoS

Listeners, The. Walter De la Mare. ClHu; HeIP-4; MoBrPo; NoAM; NoP-4; NoP-5; NOxBChV; OBEV; OBMV; OBSP; OxAEP-2; SoSe-8; TFi

Listeners, The. Louis Simpson. BodElec

Listenin' to that. Trio. Kimberly Ann Collins. InTrad

Listening. Aileen Fisher. NTCP

Listening in heaven. (LL) To Mark Anthony in Heaven. William Carlos Williams. SAmP; TCAPo

Listening into their black satin night. (LL) Listening Macaws, The. Hazel Hall. APT-1; NAAPv.2

Listening, listening; it is never still. Märchen, The. Randall Jarrell. HarvBoo

Listening Macaws, The. Hazel Hall. APT-1; NAAPv.2

Listening Nydia. Henrietta Cordelia Ray. CBWP-3

Listening to a Cricket in the Wainscoting. Robert Bly. InvLad

Listening to a Flute at Night near the City Wall. Li Yi. CrYelRi, *tr. by* Sam Hamill

Listening to a Flute in Yellow Crane Pavilion. Li Po. CrYelRi, *tr. by* Sam Hamill

Listening to a Flute on a Spring Night in Lo-yang. Li Po. CrYelRi, *tr. by* Sam Hamill

Listening to a Monk from Shu Playing the Lute. Li Po. WoPoe, *tr. by* Vikram Seth

Listening to a Monk Play the Reed Pipes. Hsüeh T'ao [*or* Xue Tao]. ColAnChi, *tr. by* Jeanne Larsen

Listening to a White Man Play the Blues. Silvia Curbelo. TouFir

Listening to Aunt Sue's stories. (LL) Aunt Sue's Stories. Langston Hughes. APT-2; SAmP

Listening to Collared Doves. Edith Jay Scovell. HarvBoo

Listening to Dvorak's Serenade in E. Colette Inez. MiVo

Listening to Gibbons at Rock-Pool Creek. Shen Yüeh. ColAnChi, *tr. by* Richard W. Bodman

Listening to Grownups Quarreling. Ruth Whitman. NTCP

Listening to Master Yu Chao Play the Lute. Heng Chao. CSKM, *tr. by* Paul Hansen

Listening to Mozart at Meadow Brook. Patricia Hooper. MiVo

Listening to Siôn Onwy. Creation. Donald Evans. BBMWP, *tr. by* Gillian Clarke

Listening to the Köln Concert. Robert Bly. RaBo

Listening to the Lute Played by Monk Chun from Shu. Li Po. ChinPo, *tr. by* Ye Weilian [*or* Yeh Wei-lien *or* Wai-lim Yip]

Listening to the moon. Buson. NIL-7, *tr. by* Robert Hass

Listening to the moon. Buson. EH, *tr. by* Robert Hass

Listening to the newsreel today. Newscast. Jared Angira. NAfrP

Listening to the plovers. Buson. EH, *tr. by* Robert Hass

Listening to the River. Su Tung-p'o. TAL

Listen—listen. Richard Ntiru. EroLit *Fr.* Rhythm of the Pestle.

Listless. Tu Fu [*or* Du Fu]. CrYelRi, *tr. by* Sam Hamill

Listless beauty of the hour, The. History. D. H. Lawrence. RaBo

Listless, still, they seem to weep. Muses. Ani Ilkov. CSCBP, *tr. by* Georgi Belev and Lisa Sapinkopf

Listlessly I hear the rain. Kim Sangyong. CATKP, *tr. by* Peter H. Lee

Listn the male chauvinist in mi dad. Girls Can We Educate We Dads? James Berry. NOxBChV

Lists became shorter, The. Making Lists. Gladys Cardiff. HATNAP

Lit up. Fumi Saito. CFP, *tr. by* Leza Lowitz, Otomo Miyuki and Akemi Tomioka

Litanies of Julia Pastrana (1832-1860), The. Thomas William Shapcott. NOBAu

Litany. Carolyn Creedon. BodElec

Litany. Elise Paschen. FFC

Litany: "Dirt grows up, The." Kevin Young. IIR

Litany: "From a ruler that's a curse." Charles Cotton. OBSV

Litany: "Mother of Sorrow." David Craig. UpMys

Litany: "My sweet, beloved companion." Margit Kaffka. IQMS, *tr. by* Paul Tabori

Litany: "You are the bread and the knife." Billy Collins. BeAl; CAP-8; NoP-5; OxBoAm; SUP

Litany, A. Frank O'Hara. BodElec

Litany for the Living. Maura Eichner. UpMys

Litany in Time of Plague, A. Thomas Nashe. *See* Adieu, Farewell, Earth's Bliss[e].

Litany of [*or* at] Atlanta, A. William Edward Burghardt DuBois. APT-1; NAAPv.1; OxAAAP; TCAPo

Litany of Sleep. Tristan Corbière.
  "You who snore with your sleeping wife so near." OBVE

Litany of the Dark People, The. Countee Cullen. ChiV-2

Litany of the Little Bourgeois. Nicanor Parra. TCLAP, *tr. by* James Laughlin

Litany, The. Dana Gioia. BAP-97; Vesp

Litany to Our Lady. Eugene O'Curry and *Unknown.* HW

Litany to the Holy Spirit. Robert Herrick. *See* His Litany to the Holy Spirit.

Litel wot it any man. *Unknown.* OHMEL

Lit-elle messe, moffette. Luis d'Antin Van Rooten. OBCoV *Fr.* Mots d'Heures: Gousses, Rames.

Literally thin-skinned, I suppose, my face. Weathering. Fleur Adcock. BeAl

Literary. Kenneth Fearing. APT-2

Literary art of Tu Fu is, The. Upon Reading Tu Fu's Poetry. Kwŏn P'il. CATKP, *tr. by* Richard John Lynn

Literary Excellence. Robert Harris. BMAP

Literary Reminiscences. Thomas Hood. OxBSo

Literature 100. Carmen Germain. IaFF

Literature and Action. Goronva Camlan. AngWePo

Literature: The God, Its Ritual. Merrill Moore. FuPo

Lithium. Marcus Cafagña. LiTh

Lithuania. Myra Sklarew.
  "At three-thirty in the morning in America." TaR

Lithuania, After Fifty-two Years. Czeslaw Milosz. *tr. by* the author and Robert Hass
  Goddess, A. BodElec, *tr. by* the author and Robert Hass
  Who? BodElec, *tr. by* the author and Robert Hass

Litrajure of Everyday Life, The. Michael C. Blumenthal. NoAM

Little. Dorothy Aldis. NTCP; WHSW

Little ash, a painted rose, a name, A. After a Death. Charles Tomlinson. HarvBoo

Little Aster. Gottfried Benn. PFTM-1

Little babe, while burns the west. Jean Ingelow. VWP

Little babe, while burns the west. Little babe, while burns the west. Jean Ingelow. VWP

Little Bad Dream Charm. Kathy Fagan. PoCho

Little Ballad of the Three Rivers. Federico García Lorca. BLPSL, *tr. by* Rene de Costa, Rigas Kappatos and Eleni Paidoussi

Little, barb'rous, cruel fly! Walsingham; or, the Pupil of Nature. Mary Robinson. RWP

Little before midnight down by the docks, A. In the Eyes of the Gods. André Breton. WoPoe, *tr. by* Jack Rogow and Bill Zavatsky

Little Belgian Orphan, A. Amanda Ros. VerBaPo

Little Bell. Mary E. Tucker. CBWP-1

Little Billee. William Makepeace Thackeray. OxAEP-2

Little bird, a tender bird, A. Siren Bird, The. Henrietta Cordelia Ray. CBWP-3

Little bird with tuneful throat. My Canary. Josephine D. Henderson Heard. CBWP-4

Little Birds Are Playing. Lewis Carroll. OWoS

Little birds aren't on rollers, The. Joan of Arc. Benjamin Péret. PFTM-1

Little birds of the night. Stephen Crane. APN-2

Little birds sit in their nest and beg, The. Little Birds, The. *Unknown.* NTCP

Little Birds, The. *Unknown.* NTCP

Little birds warble their song in the tree, The. Bird Song, The. Mrs. Henry Linden. CBWP-4

Little Bit in Love, A. Betty Comden and Adolph Green. ReLy

Little Bit Independent, A. Edgar Leslie. ReLy

Little bit independent, A. Little Bit Independent, A. Edgar Leslie. ReLy

Little bit, more or less each day, A. Beethoven's Sixth Symphony. Steve Benson. FTOS

Little Bit of Tumbler, A. Gertrude Stein. NAMCP V.1 *Fr.* Tender Buttons.

Little Bit Off, A. Richard Maltby, Jr. ReLy

Little bitch! Lies. Pak Sôwôn. EcSo, *tr. by* Julie C. Park

Little Black Boy, The. William Blake. AmFaPo; CABP; ChAP; HeIP-4; NAEL-6v2; NAEL-7v2; NAWM-7v2; NOBRP; NoP-4; NoP-5; OBEV; PoPoPo; TFi *Fr.* Songs of Innocence.

Little Black Bug. Margaret Wise Brown. NTCP

Little black thing among the snow, A. William Blake. BrAP; NAEL-6v2; NAEL-7v2; NAWM-7v2; NPBRoP *Fr.* Songs of Experience.

Little Black Train Is A-Comin'. *Unknown.* GM

Little Blessing, A. Nancy Willard. PfSP

Little boat on the great river, A. Crossing the Yellow River. Wang Wei. CrYelRi, *tr. by* Sam Hamill

Little boats were patchwork on the bay, The. Three Years from Sorrento. Dorothy Belle Flanagan. YaYoPo

Little bones of. Poem. Michael O'Brien. KGB

Little book—no, I don't begrudge you—you're off to the City. Ovid. RomPo *Fr.* Tristia.

Little Books / 137 / Silence Mar 22 79. Hannah Weiner. FTOS

Little Books 137 Silence Mar 22 79. Hannah Weiner. FTOS *Fr.* Little Books / Indians.

Little Books / Indians. Hannah Weiner.
  Little Books 137 Silence Mar 22 79. FTOS

Little Boots, The. Dafydd Rowlands. BBMWP, *tr. by* Meic Stephens

Little Bo-Peep. Mother Goose. WHSW

Little Bo-Peep has lost her sheep. Little Bo-Peep. Mother Goose. WHSW

Little Box from Olinalá, The. Gabriela Mistral. TANSG, *tr. by* Maria Giachetti [*or* Jacketti]

Little box gets her first teeth, The. Little Box, The. Vasco [*or* Vasko] Popa. GPTC, *tr. by* Charles Simic

Little boy a / Was wild about. Gimme a Little Kiss (Will Ya, Huh?). Jack Smith and Roy Turk. ReLy

Little boy asked me, colouring book in hand, A. What Colour's a Man. Zelma Jex. OWABP

Little Boy Blue. Eugene Field. BRP; ChAP; ITBLP; SoSe-8

Little Boy Found, The. William Blake. NoP-4; NoP-5; WaAnP *Fr.* Songs of Innocence.

Little Boy, I'm Not Sure Anymore, A. James Sacré. PML, *tr. by* David Ball

Little boy lost in the lonely fen, The.   William Blake.   NoP-4; NoP-5; WaAnP *Fr.* Songs of Innocence.

Little boy was looking for his voice, The.   Little Mute Boy, The.   Federico García Lorca.   RaW, *tr. by* W. S. Merwin

Little boy's hand, his hand full of trust, The.   But till that morning, ain't no one gonna harm you.   Susan Glickman.   BeAl

Little boys ride their bikes.   Father's Day.   Aarian Pope.   BRtP

Little breast.   Pierre Reverdy.   PFTM-1

Little Brother Poem, The.   Naomi Shihab Nye.   TiP2

Little brother, would I could.   On a 3 1/2 Oz. Lesser Yellowlegs, Departed Boston August 28, Shot Martinique September 3.   Eamon Grennan.   P180

Little brown baby wif spa'klin' eyes.   Little Brown Baby.   Paul Laurence Dunbar.   APN-2; NoP-4; NoP-5; PtR

Little Brown Brother.   Nick Carbó.   AmPoNex; ReBoTo

Little by little it becomes clear to me.   Unusual Autumn, An.   Dahlia Ravikovitch.   DTA, *tr. by* Chana Bloch

Little by little the first union. (LL)   Anne Carson.   BodElec; OxBoAm; WoBe *Fr.* Truth About God, The.

Little by little, wean yourself.   Jelaluddin Rumi.   BLT

Little called anything shows shudders, A.   Gertrude Stein.   NAMCP V.1 *Fr.* Tender Buttons.

Little called Pauline, A.   Gertrude Stein.   NAMCP V.1 *Fr.* Tender Buttons.

Little Cape Cod Landscape.   Charles North.   FTOS

Little Car, The.   Guillaume Apollinaire.   YaTCFP, *tr. by* Ron Padgett

Little cares that fretted me, The.   Out in the Fields [with God].   Elizabeth Barrett Browning.   ITBLP

Little Carol of the Virgin, A.   Félix Lope de Vega Carpio.   SpanPo, *tr. by* Denise Levertov

Little Cavalier, A.   Lucy Larcom.   SWaP

Little child sat on the floor, A.   Where Do School Days End?   Josephine D. Henderson Heard.   CBWP-4

Little child she, half defiant came, A.   Augusta Davies Webster.   VWP *Fr.* Mother and Daughter.

Little children full of joy.   Come and See My Little Toys.   BtF

Little children, never give.   Kindness to Animals.   *Unknown.*   WHSW

Little Children, Then Won't You Be Glad!   *Unknown.*   SSUS

Little churches wake up in the half light, The.   Nuns Go Walking.   Aldo Palazzeschi.   PFTM-1

Little Citizen, Little Survivor.   Hayden Carruth.   GoPo; OPRER

Little City.   Robert Horan.   YaYoPo

Little Clan, The.   Frederick Robert Higgins.   OBMV

Little Cloth, The.   Hilary Llewellyn-Williams.   TCAWP

Little cousin is dead, by foul subtraction, The.   Dead Boy.   John Crowe Ransom.   FuPo; HarvBoo; NAMCP V.1; NoAM; NoP-4

Little cramped words scrawling all over the paper.   Letter, The.   Amy Lowell.   NAAPv.2; NALW; PoBW

Little Crisis Framed in My Window.   Christopher Davis.   AmPoNex

Little crooked, A. (LL)   [Winter Sketches II: Subway].   Charles Reznikoff.   PoA 2002; WoPoe

Little crystal globe.   Earth.   Jules Supervielle.   MFP, *tr. by* Martin Sorrell

Little cullud boys / with fears.   Tag.   Langston Hughes.   APT-2

Little Dance Outside the Ruins of Unreason.   Carl Phillips.   NAPBL

Little Dancers, The.   Laurence Binyon.   MoBrPo

Little Dantesque.   James Galvin.   BAP-01

Little daunting, these periodic, A.   Prospect of the Interior.   Scott Cairns.   UpMys

Little Death.   Gwyn Thomas.   OBWVE, *tr. by* Joseph P. Clancy

Little Dog that wags his tail, A.   Emily Dickinson.   NOxBChV

Little dogs and all, The.   William Shakespeare.   DiBP *Fr.* King Lear.

Little drink enjoyed in the east of town, A.   Evening Stroll.   Ema Saikō.   WoPoe, *tr. by* Conrad Totman

Little ears of corn are parched, The.   Rain.   Ber Grin.   Prolet, *tr. by* Amelia Glaser

Little East of Jordan, A.   Emily Dickinson.   ChIV-1; NoP-4; NoP-5

Little Elegy.   Keith Althaus.   PoDa

Little Elegy.   Denis Devlin.   ModIr

Little Elegy [*for a child who skipped rope*].   X. J. Kennedy.   InoFa; WaAnP

Little elf is dressed in a floppy cap, The.   Fairy Tale.   Ron Padgett.   NYP2

Little Elf, The.   John Kendrick Bangs.   NTCP

Little Ellie sits alone.   Romance of the Swan's Nest, The.   Elizabeth Barrett Browning.   VWP

Little Essay on Communication.   Stephen Dunn.   PoA 2002

Little Exercise.   Elizabeth Bishop.   ColAP; MoAmPo

Little Father.   Li-Young Lee.   BeAl; P180

Little father I ransom with my life. (LL)   Little Father.   Li-Young Lee.   BeAl; P180

Little Fay's Thanksgiving.   Henrietta Cordelia Ray.   CBWP-3

Little feet of children.   Piececitos.   Gabriela Mistral.   ItP, *tr. by* Doris Dana

Little fevered island, blued to closing.   Foundered Star.   Jane Miller.   ExTi

Little firefly.   Spark.   Richard Lemm.   Coast

Little Fish.   D. H. Lawrence.   Spl

Little fleece of my flesh.   Close to Me.   Gabriela Mistral.   TCLAP, *tr. by* Doris Dana

Little Fly.   William Blake.   NAEL-6v2; NAEL-7v2; NBLV *Fr.* Songs of Experience.

Little fox hiding in the garden.   Fox's Trick, The.   Shimazaki Toson.   CAoMJL1, *tr. by* Leith Morton

Little French Lawyer, The.   John Fletcher.
    Song in the Wood.   NOSC

Little Friend.   *Unknown.*   WoPoe

Little Furnace.   Brenda Hillman.   BodElec

Little garden, A.   Garden, The.   Franta Bass.   INSAB

Little Ghost, The.   Edna St. Vincent Millay.   NAAPv.2

Little Gidding.   T. S. Eliot.   CABP; NAAPv.2; NAEL-6v2; NAEL-7v2; NAMCP V.1; NAWM-7v2; NoAM; NoP-5; OxAEP-2; OxBoAm; TFi *Fr.* Four Quartets.

Little Giffen.   Francis Orrery Ticknor.   CBCWP; PCW

Little girl.   Another Rhythm.   Akasha (Gloria) Hull.   ISC

Little Girl.   Vivian Lamarque.   CItWP, *tr. by* Cinzia Sartini Blum and Lara Trubowitz

Little Girl, Be Careful What You Say.   Carl Sandburg.   NOxBChV

Little Girl Blue.   Lorenz Hart.   APT-2

Little girl called Silé Javotte.   Christmas 1970.   Spike Milligan.   OBCP

Little Girl Found, The.   William Blake.   NOBRP *Fr.* Songs of Experience.

Little Girl Found, The.   William Blake.   NOBRP *Fr.* Songs of Innocence.

Little Girl from Little Rock.   Leo Robin.   ReLy

Little girl I was, The.   Laughter.   Wisława Szymborska.   PoSu, *tr. by* Magnus F. Krynski

Little girl is shy, The.   Dream Come True.   Molly Peacock.   RA

Little Girl Lost, The.   William Blake.   NOBRP *Fr.* Songs of Experience.

Little Girl Lost, The.   William Blake.   NOBRP *Fr.* Songs of Innocence.

Little Girl, My String Bean, My Lovely Woman.   Anne Sexton.   AFaM; NAAL-5

Little Girl of the Black Forest.   Lise Deharme.   SurWo, *tr. by* Franklin Rosemont

Little girl saw her first troop parade and asked, "What are those?", The.   Carl Sandburg.   HHAm *Fr.* People, Yes, The.

Little girl squealing, The.   In the Echoey Tunnel.   Christopher Reid.   NeBrP

Little Girl Talk.   Delores S. Williams.   OxAAAP

Little girl that a good family adopted, taken, The.   Daughter.   Olesya Nikolayeva.   ItGoST, *tr. by* Paul Graves and Carol Ueland

Little girl under a peach tree, A.   Peach, The.   Takahashi Shinkichi.   ZenPo, *tr. by* Takashi Ikemoto and Lucien Stryk

Little girl with scarlet enameled fingernails, A.   Melodic Trains.   John Ashbery.   FaoP; GM; NoP-4

Little Girls.   Laurence Alma-Tadema.   WHSW

Little Girls Posing All Dressed Up.   Clarence Major.   BodElec

Little girls smearing.   Schoolyard in April.   Kenneth Koch.   PoA 2002

Little Good Fellows, The.   Herman Melville.   NCAP

Little green involute fronds of fern at creekside.   Interrupted Meditation.   Robert Hass.   BAP-97; FaoP

Little green men play a samba in my mind.   Soulgroovin Ditty #7.   Hannah Howard.   BRtP

Little Grey Dreams.   Angelina Weld Grimké.   NAAPv.2

Little grey hill-glade, close-turfed, withdrawn, A.   Marsyas.   Sir Charles G. D. Roberts.   NoP-4

Little Hand.   Larry Fagin.   AHA

Little Hans.   Steve McCaffery.   FTOS

Little has come down to me of hers.   Pattern, The.   Paula Meehan.   ModIr

Little Heart to Heart with the Horizon, A.   Alice Fulton.   PfSP

Little Hearts, where light-wing'd Passion raignes, The.   Fulke, 1st Baron Brooke Greville.   PBRV *Fr.* Caelica.

Little hedge-row birds, The.   Old Man Travelling [Animal Tranquillity and Decay, a Sketch].   William Wordsworth.   NPeEn; OBWP

Little hedgerow birds, The.   Animal Tranquillity and Decay.   William Wordsworth.   OxBEV

Little Henry.   Julia A. Moore.
    Hic Finis Rapto 3.   STuOW

Little hints of reality march across the back.   Backing into the Future.   Dick Gallup.   BAP-97

Little hollows in the pavements shine, The.   Dream of Sappho, A.   Ella Higginson.   SWaP

Little horror does nothing—does not make love, does not make war, The.   *Unknown.*   SLW, *tr. by* Marjolijn De Jager, Sayd Bahodin Majrouh and André Velter

Little horror, oblivious to combat, sleeps quietly beside me, The. *Unknown.* SLW, *tr.* by Marjolijn De Jager, Sayd Bahodin Majrouh and André Velter

Little horror, take your rifle and kill me now. *Unknown.* SLW, *tr.* by Marjolijn De Jager, Sayd Bahodin Majrouh and André Velter

Little horror will not die of his own fever, The. *Unknown.* SLW, *tr.* by Marjolijn De Jager, Sayd Bahodin Majrouh and André Velter

Little horses fleeing, The. Rondeau of the Little Horses. Manuel Bandeira. TCLAP, *tr.* by Candace Slater

Little hours: two lovers herd upstairs, The. Almost Aubade. Marilyn Hacker. NAMCP V.2; NoAM

Little House, Big House. Medbh McGuckian. PNI

Little I ask; my wants are few. Oliver Wendell Holmes. APN-1; OxBoAm *Fr.* Autocrat of the Breakfast Table, The.

Little Infinite Poem. Federico García Lorca. RaBo; WED, *tr.* by Robert Bly

Little ink more or less!, A. Stephen Crane. APN-2

Little interrogation of the sky, A. Concerning Paradise. Christopher Buckley. GeoHom

Little Invitation in a Hushed Voice. Tess Gallagher. PasH

Little Jack Horner/ Sat in a corner. Mother Goose. SoSe-8

Little Jo wakes me up. Bill Griffiths. Oth *Fr.* Building: The New London Hospital.

Little Jock Elliot. *Unknown.* IBB

Little joe gould has lost his teeth and doesn't know where. E. E. Cummings. NoAM

Little Josie buried under the bright moon. Half-Caste Girl. Judith Wright. NALW

Little Jumping Joan. Mother Goose. NTCP

Little Kitchen Song, A. Mun Chônghui. EcSo, *tr.* by Catherine J. Kim

Little knife, The. Masaoka Shiki. CAoMJL1, *tr.* by Burton Watson

Little lady coyly shy. Caprichosa. Angelina Weld Grimké. PoBW

Little Lamb, A. *Unknown.* OBCoV

Little Lamb God bless thee! (LL) William Blake. BrAP; ChIV-2; HeIP-4; ITBLP; NAEL-6v2; NAEL-7v2; NAWM-7v2; NIL-7; NIP-4; NOBRP; NoP-4; NoP-5; NPBRoP; OxAEP-2; PoPoPo; SoSe-8; TFi; TRP; WaAnP *Fr.* Songs of Innocence.

Little Lamb, who made thee? William Blake. BrAP; ChIV-2; HeIP-4; ITBLP; NAEL-6v2; NAEL-7v2; NAWM-7v2; NIL-7; NIP-4; NOBRP; NoP-4; NoP-5; NPBRoP; OxAEP-2; PoPoPo; SoSe-8; TFi; TRP; WaAnP *Fr.* Songs of Innocence.

Little late rain, A. Sarah's Choice. Eleanor Wilner. TaR

Little learning is a dangerous [or dang'rous] thing, A. Alexander Pope. OxBEV *Fr.* Essay on Criticism, An.

Little less returned for him each spring, A. Anglais Mort à Florence. Wallace Stevens. SAmP

Little Libbie. Julia A. Moore.
Hic Finis Rapto 6. STuOW
"One morning in April, a short time ago." VerBaPo

Little light is going by, A. Firefly. Elizabeth Madox Roberts. NTCP

Little Lost Pup. Arthur Guiterman. ITBLP

Little Love Kiss. Lenous Surprice. OGAHCP, *tr.* by Boadiba and Jack Hirschman

Little loving / in between, A. (LL) Advice. Langston Hughes. NBLV; SAmP

Little Lyric (*Of Great Importance*). Langston Hughes. APT-2; NBLV; OBCoV

Little Madness in the Spring, A. Emily Dickinson. AmFaPo; TCAPo

Little Magic, A. Steve Jonas. EGAG

Little Man around the House. Yusef Komunyakaa. OxAAAP

Little Man, The. David Connolly. AmWaPo

Little Man, The. Hughes Mearns. NOxBChV

Little man, whom I love so much. Ode to Chaplin. Zoltán Jékely. IQMS, *tr.* by Joseph Leftwich

Little Mary Cassidy. Francis A. Fahy. IrV

Little Mary / she's a buried cargo. Hewn Hands. David Craig. UpMys

Little Millwins attend the Russian Ballet, The. Les Millwin. Ezra Pound. APT-1; OBCoV

Little Miracle. Molly Peacock. IFF

Little Miss Muffet discovered a tuffet. Embarrassing Episode of Little Miss Muffet, The. Guy Wetmore Carryl. AmWit

Little monkey goes like a donkey that means to say that more sighs last goes, A. Gertrude Stein. NAMCP V.1 *Fr.* Tender Buttons.

Little months little smokes. Comrade. Philippe Soupault. PFTM-1

Little more of his love, A. (LL) From Father to Son. Emyr Humphreys. AngWePo; OBWVE; TCAWP

Little moth round candle turning, The. Similie. Charlotte Dacre. NOBRP

Little Mother. Guido Gezelle. TuT, *tr.* by Mary E. O'Donnell

Little moths are creeping, The. Interior. Padraic Colum. MoBrPo

Little Mouse, The. Bachner, Miroslav Košek and Hanuš Löwy. INSAB

Little Mute Boy, The. Federico García Lorca. RaW, *tr.* by W. S. Merwin

Little nearer please, A. And a little nearer. Photograph and White Tulips. Dannie Abse. TCAWP

Little night. Paul Celan. VCWP, *tr.* by Michael Hamburger

Little Night, A. Douglas Oliver. Oth

Little Night Music, A. Paul Grattan. NIrP

Little night: when you. Little night. Paul Celan. VCWP, *tr.* by Michael Hamburger

Little Ode. Paul Goodman. PoA 2002

Little Ode for X. Maura Stanton. IllVoic

Little Ode to Melancholy. Ricardo Molinari. TCLAP, *tr.* by Inés Probert

Little Odes on Mount Star. Chŏng Ch'ŏl. CATKP, *tr.* by Peter H. Lee

Little of Distinction. Ruth Bidgood. TCAWP

Little of distinction, guide-books had said. Little of Distinction. Ruth Bidgood. TCAWP

Little of myself do I remember. Patrizia Cavalli. NeIt

Little Old Lady in Lavender Silk, The. Dorothy Parker. NBLV

Little Old Letter. Langston Hughes. SAmP

Little one, black angel. Diana Brandt. ACAMVP

Little one, go to sleep. Sleep soundly. Lullaby. *Vietnamese Oral Tradition.* CaDao, *tr.* by John Balaban

Little one sleeps in its cradle, The. Walt Whitman. ColAP; SAmP; WaAnP *Fr.* Song of Myself.

Little Ones' A. B. C, The. Noël Coward.
"A. Stands for Absolutely Anything." NBLV

Little onward lend thy guiding hand, A. John Milton. OxAEP-1; WoPoe *Fr.* Samson Agonistes.

Little onward lend thy guiding hand, A. Samson Agonistes. John Milton. BASC; NAEL-6v1

Little Orphant Annie's come to our house to stay. Little Orphant Annie. James Whitcomb Riley. APN-2; BRP; ChAP; ITBLP; NBLV; TCAPo

Little Overture. David Barber. AmPoNex

Little owl flew through the night, The. On the Adequacy of Landscape. Wallace Stevens. SAmP

Little Owl Who Lives in the Orchard. Mary Oliver. CAP-8

Little painted lady with your lovely clothes. Glad Rag Doll. Jack Yellen. ReLy

Little, passionately, not at all?, A. Villanelle of Marguerites. Ernest Dowson. MoBrPo

Little Phantoms. Oscar Hahn. PML, *tr.* by James Hoggard

Little picks of the roosters, The. Ballad of Black Grief. Federico García Lorca. STV, *tr.* by John Frederick Nims

Little Pilot Knob. David Thomas Roberts. AnSo

Little Pines. Ch'i-chi. CSKM, *tr.* by Burton Watson

Little Poem. Max Jacob. CuPo

Little poem, the two of us know too much. Envoy. George Garrett. InGu

Little Prayers. Paul Goodman. PLBUT

Little purple flowers under out feet. Site of the Indian Fights of 1871, Abilene. Naomi Shihab Nye. TiP2

Little ragged girl, our ball-boy, A. Game at Salzburg, A. Randall Jarrell. NoAM

Little Red Riding Hood. Ania Walwicz. BMAP

Little Red Riding Hood and the Wolf. Gillie Bolton. Prnts

Little Red-Cap. Carol Ann Duffy. MoWP; NeBrP; NoP-5

Little Research in Snow, A. Gabriel Preil. FIT, *tr.* by Robert Friend

Little Road says, Go, The. House and the Road, The. Josephine Preston Peabody. ITBLP

Little Road—not made of Man, A. Emily Dickinson. SWaP

Little Rose. *Unknown.* TreFP

Little rose bloomed in the way, A. Rose by the Wayside, The. D.A. Drown. TreFP

Little Round. Li-Young Lee. Vesp

Little Ruth. Yehuda Amichai. VCWP, *tr.* by Benjamin Harshav

Little shaikh from the land of Meknès sings in the middle of the marketplaces, A. Alī ibn Abd Allāh Shushtarī. HiArP, *tr.* by James T. Monroe

Little Shoes That Died, The. Mary Gilmore. NOBAu

Little Shroud, The. Letitia Elizabeth Landon. NAEL-7v2

Little snow blew in where we stood, A. Shift. Aaron Anstett. AmPoNex

Little snow people are hurrying down, The. Putting the World to Bed. Esther W. Buxton. NOxBChV

Little socks fly, pink. To the Station. Carla Willard. PfS

Little song, A. B. P. Nichol. OpeFie

Little Song ("Carmencita loves Patrick.") Langston Hughes. TLR

Little Song of the Maimed. Benjamin Péret. OBWP, *tr.* by David Gascoyne

Little Soul. Valérie-Catherine Richez. YaTCFP, *tr.* by Michael Tweed

Little soul, little perpetually undresed one. Penelope's Song. Louise Glück. NAMCP V.2

Little sparrows. Issa. EMJL, *tr.* by Haruo Shirane

Little sparrows, The. Pastoral. William Carlos Williams. SAmP

Little spit on the heart-mirror, A. Heart-Mirror. Tess Gallagher. AmZen

Little state-funded barrack, A. It Started. Jimmy Santiago Baca. LoL

Little stream used to cross my land, A. Su Tung-p'o. ColAnChi *Fr.* Eastern Slope.

Little Suite for Loudspeaker. Louis Aragon.
  "Hilversum, Kalundborg, Brno, the loud world over." RWPCtW, *tr. by* Rolfe Humphries

Little Sunlight, A. Takahashi Shinkichi. ZenPo, *tr. by* Takashi Ikemoto and Lucien Stryk

Little sycamore she planted, The. *Unknown, fr. Egyptian hieroglyphics.* ErotSp, *tr. by* Sam Hamill

Little sympathy, A. Ekaterina Vlasova. CRWP, *tr. by* Peter France

Little sympathy, who kicks beneath my ribs. Eighteenth-Century Medical Illustration: The Infant in its Little Room. Ann Townsend. AmPoNex

Little Tales. Zakiyya Malallah. PoArWo, *tr. by* Wen Chin Ouyang

Little Testament. Eugenio Montale. PoetW, *tr. by* Robert Lowell

Little Things. James Stephens. MoBrPo

Little Things. *Unknown.* ArBi

Little Things in Life, The. Irving Berlin. ReLy

Little things that no one needs. Bric-à-Brac. Dorothy Parker. APT-1

Little things, that run, and quail. Little Things. James Stephens. MoBrPo

Little thinkest thou, poor ant, who there. Ant, The. Richard Flecknoe. NOSC

Little thinks, in the field, yon red-cloaked clown. Each and All. Ralph Waldo Emerson. APN-1; ColAP; NAAL-3; NAAL-5; NAAPv.1; NCAP; OxBoAm; TCAPo; TreFP

Little think'st thou, poor[e] flower. Blossom[e], The. John Donne. NAEL-6v1; NAEL-7v1

Little Tin Box. Jerry Bock. ReLy

Little Tokyo bar. Iowa Blues Bar Spiritual. Juan Felipe Herrera. ReTh

Little too abstract, a little too wise, A. Return. Robinson Jeffers. HarvBoo

Little Tooth, A. Thomas Lux. BodElec; GoPo

Little Towns of Texas, The. Clyde Walton Hill. TiP2

Little toy dog is covered with dust, The. Little Boy Blue. Eugene Field. BRP; ChAP; ITBLP; SoSe-8

Little Travel Story, A. David Oliveira. GeoHom

Little tree / little silent Christmas tree. E. E. Cummings. NTCP; OBCP

Little trotty hetty coat. Riddle. *Unknown.* FaBoVe

Little Trotty Wagtail. John Clare. BLPJKO; NOxBChV

Little Turtle, The. Vachel Lindsay. BLPJKO; NOxBChV; NTCP; OBSP

Little Vagabond, The. William Blake. NBLV; OBSV *Fr.* Songs of Experience.

Little verses seek their meal, The. Salon de Vers. Orrick Johns. APT-1

Little water, A. It would lie on the thick dust, gleaming. (LL) Water. Leslie Norris. AngWePo; OBWVE

Little While, A. Sara Teasdale. APT-1

Little while, a little while, A. Emily Jane Brontë. VWP

Little while spring will claim its own, A. My Heart has Known its Winter. Arna Bontemps. GT

Little while, that in me sings no more, A. (LL) Sonnet 43: "What lips my lips have kissed, and where, and why." Edna St. Vincent Millay. APT-1; GoPo; HeIP-4; MakPoe; MoAmPo; NIP-4; OPOU; OxBoAm; WaAnP

Little while when I am gone, A. Little While, A. Sara Teasdale. APT-1

Little white clouds are racing over the sky, The. Magdalen Walks. Oscar Wilde. MoBrPo

Little white dog wags his tail, The. Landscape. Larry Fagin and George Schneeman. AHA

Little White Lies. Walter Donaldson. ReLy

Little White Rose, The. Hugh MacDiarmid. NePenScot

Little Woman with Medusa Eyes, A. Dacia Maraini. CItWP, *tr. by* Cinzia Sartini Blum and Lara Trubowitz

Little Wren, A. Priscilla Jane Thompson. CBWP-2

Little Wrongs. Fanny Howe. Eno

Littleton. Michael Bugeja. LiTh

Littoral space between there and here, The. Shoreline, The. Joe Denham. IFF

Liturgy for Lilith. Cosi Fabian. HW

Liturgy for Trinity, A. Barbara La Morticella. AtGh

Liu Ch'e. Emperor Wu of Han. APT-1; NDACCP; OBVE, *tr. by* Ezra Pound

Liv lying on the floor looking at. Short Narrative of Breasts and Wombs in Service of Plot Entitled, A. Claudia Rankine. BAP-01

Live, alterable cry against my breast. (LL) Filling the Gap. Lawson Fusao Inada. FTtHH; OpBo

Live and Let Live. Eliza Cook. STuOW

Live at Club Mozambique. Charles Simic. BodElec

Live at the Village Vanguard. Bill Zavatsky. FaoP

Live /, Bird Which. Larry Eigner. FTOS

Live blindly and upon the hour. The Lord. Live Blindly. Trumbull Stickney. APN-2; OxBoAm; TCAPo; WoPoe

Live, Evil Veil. John Wheelwright. ChIV-1

Live for tonight, and then the lights come. (LL) Gods at Three A.M., The. Reginald Shepherd. NeAmPo; WiU

Live in these conquering leaves; live all the same. Richard Crashaw. OxAEP-1 *Fr.* Flaming Heart, The.

Live, lads, and I will die. (LL) A. E. Housman. ChIV-2; MoBrPo; OxAEP-2; UV *Fr.* Shropshire Lad, A.

Live large, man, and dream small.. (LL) Lore. Ronald Stuart Thomas. BeAl; NoP-4; NoP-5

"Live like the wind," he said, "unfettered." Wind Bloweth Where It Listeth, The. Countee Cullen. GT

Live Oak. David Tokuyu Reid-Marr. WhBo

Live Oak, with Moss. Walt Whitman. NAAL-5

Live storm went through last night, The. Glad at the Cold (1955). Alan Dugan. NoAM

Live Walls. Mahe Jabeen. HotL, *tr. by* V. Narayana Rao

Live While You Live. Philip Doddridge. SacPr

Lived to see you throwing. Hesitate to Call. Louise Glück. LW; StAl

Lived unwedded. (LL) Edgar Lee Masters. APT-1; IllVoic *Fr.* Spoon River Anthology.

Livelier than elsewhere, Stella's image see. (LL) Sir Philip Sidney. GSo; NAEL-6v1; NAEL-7v1; NoSic; OxAEP-1; OxBSo; TFi; WaAnP *Fr.* Astrophil and Stella.

Lively lark stretched forth her wing, The. Edward, 17th Earl of Oxford De Vere. NoSic

Liverpool. Grahame Davies. BBMWP, *tr. by* the author

Lives. Derek Mahon. BeAl; EmeKit; ModIr; PBCIP

Lives ago, years past generations. Being the Third Song of Urias. Ken Smith. StAl

Lives and Times of John Keats, Percy Bysshe Shelley, and George Gordon Noel, Lord Byron, The. Dorothy Parker. NALW *Fr.* Pig's-Eye View of Literature, A.

Lives in Dreadful Wanting. Alex Kuo.
  "Then they are young and on vacation, their camera." FTtHH

Lives in eternity's sun rise. (LL) William Blake. AmFaPo; NoP-4; NoP-5; SoSe-8; Spl *Fr.* Several Questions Answered.

Lives in winter. Riddle. *Unknown.* NTCP

Lives of Alchemists, The. Charles Simic. KGB

Lives of many men are, The. To Wei Pa, a Retired Scholar. Tu Fu [*or* Du Fu]. NDACCP, *tr. by* Kenneth Rexroth

Lives of my mother fit in one name, The. Lifes. Achy Obejas. WiU

Lives of the Great Composers. Dana Gioia. RA

Lives of the Heart,The. Jane Hirshfield. ExTi; GoPo

Lives of the Saints. Debora Greger.
  "Notre Dame, Sainte Chapelle, Sacré Coeur by foot—." NoP-4

Lives of the Toll Takers, The. Charles Bernstein.
  "Our new / service orientation." NAMCP V.2

Lives two people live drift without. For the Recluse Wei Pa. Tu Fu [*or* Du Fu]. NDACCP, *tr. by* David Hinton

Livid lightnings flashed in the clouds, The. Stephen Crane. InvLi

Living. Denise Levertov. BLT; GoPo; OPOU; StAl

Living. Jaime Torres Bodet. TCLAP, *tr. by* Sonja Karsen

Living a little seems like dying slow. Diet, The. Bruce Meyer. IFF

Living Alone. Richard Hugo. CAP-8

Living alone in a sad-looking house. Jerry's Plains, 1848. Geoff Page. BMAP

Living Alone with Jesus. Maxine W. Kumin. UnSA

Living along the path. North Corridor. Michael Collier. GM

Living and dying. (LL) Grammarian's Funeral, A. Robert Browning. NAEL-6v2; NAEL-7v2

Living and Dying. Manuel González Prada. SpanPo, *tr. by* Kate Flores

Living at a Monastery, Sent to Chien Chang. Huai Ku. CSKM, *tr. by* Paul Hansen

Living at Eunjok Hermitage. Mookam Choinul. BecRai, *tr. by* Kim Daljin, Kim Won-Chung and Christopher Merrill

Living at the edges, I grow stranger. In Heaven. Robert Patrick Dana. RWB

Living at the Frost Place. Sue Ellen Thompson. VisFro

Living by your words. Rituals, Yours—and Mine. Kimberly M. Blaeser. ReEnLa

Living creatures are not welcome here. (LL) Ancestral Messengers / Composition 13. Ntozake Shange. AFaM; GT; IPoFL

Living for you is easy living. Easy Living. Leo Robin. ReLy

Living Heaven thy prayers respect, The. Spiritual Laws. Ralph Waldo Emerson. APN-1

Living in a wide landscape are the flowers. Desert Flowers. Keith Douglas. HarvBoo; NPeEn

Living in at Least Two Worlds. C. L. Rawlins. OPRER

Living in Cheston. Cynthia Rylant. HHAm *Fr.* Soda Jerk.

Living in Poverty. Shi Zhiyuan. CSKM, *tr. by* Paul Hansen

Living in Real Times. Duncan Bush. TCAWP

Living in seclusion far from the dizzying world. Hermit's Life, A. Chungji. BecRai, *tr. by* Kim Daljin, Kim Won-Chung and Christopher Merrill

Living in Sin. Adrienne Rich. NIL-7; NIP-4; NoP-4; OxBoAm; SoSe-8; WaAnP

Living in the Body. Joyce Sutphen. GoPo

Living in the earth-deposits of our history. Power. Adrienne Rich. CAP-8; ColAP; NALW; NAMCP V.2; NIL-7

Living in the La Brea Tar Pits. Nancy Vieira Couto. PBCAP

Living in the Summer Mountains. Yü Hsüan-chi. WoPoe, *tr. by* Chung Ling and Kenneth Rexroth

Living in this land of exile is ravaging my heart. *Unknown.* SLW, *tr. by* Marjolijn De Jager, Sayd Bahodin Majrouh and André Velter

Living is no laughing matter. On Living. Nazim Hikmet. PoetW, *tr. by* Randy Blasing and Mutlu Konuk

Living Life as a Living Target. Roxy Gordon. TiP2

Living long is containing. Rosina Alcona to Julius Brenzaida. Judith Wright. InoFa; NALW

Living man is blind and drinks his drop, A. William Butler Yeats. RaBo *Fr.* Dialogue of Self and Soul, A.

Living Memory. Adrienne Rich. OxBoAm; TRP

Living mother-of-pearl of a salmon, The. Hazel Stick for Catherine Ann, A. Seamus Heaney. NoAM

Living Near the Plaza of Thieves. Leslie Ullman. PBCAP

Living on the Plain in Early Autumn. Huai Ku. CSKM, *tr. by* Paul Hansen

Living or having lived. Flush / a Play. Leslie Scalapino. PmAP

Living paradise of flowers, land of honey. Merioneth. John Machreth Rees. OBWVE, *tr. by* Kenneth Hurlstone Jackson

Living quality of, The. William Carlos Williams. NAMCP V.1; NoAM *Fr.* Pictures from Brueghel.

Living Quetzalcoatl, The. D. H. Lawrence. OWoS

Living secluded. Cloud Mountain. Muso Soseki. EaWin, *tr. by* W. S. Merwin

Living Space. Imtiaz Dharker. NeBl

Living Spring, The. Moses Glyn Jones. BBMWP, *tr. by* Mike Jenkins

Living Temple, The. Oliver Wendell Holmes. APN-1 *Fr.* Autocrat of the Breakfast Table, The.

Living, The [*with music*]. Robert Pinsky. NoAM

Living, The. Interplay. Xue Di. OnScMo, *tr. by* Wang Ping and Keith Waldrop

Living Together. Edgar Bowers. PoDa

Living Voice. Kawai Suimei. CAoMJL1, *tr. by* Leith Morton

Living with Chris. Ted Berrigan. NYP2; OxBoAm

Living with Others. Al Zolynas. SUP

Livings. Philip Larkin.
    Seventy Feet Down. NPeEn

Livre des ciels, Le. Leslie Kaplan. *tr. by* Serge Gavronsky
    "He takes me to see his mother. She lives in the." SCFWP, *tr. by* Serge Gavronsky
    "I wait for him by the subway exit. It's night, the." SCFWP, *tr. by* Serge Gavronsky
    "Small house, the room, The. I walk in." SCFWP, *tr. by* Serge Gavronsky

Livre, pour vieillir, Le. Yves Bonnefoy. YaTCFP

Li-Young, don't feel lonely. Night Mirror. Li-Young Lee. WaAnP

Liza! call dat chile. Meal Time. Maggie Pogue Johnson. CBWP-4

Liza, go steep your long white hands. Spring Pastoral. Elinor Wylie. TCAPo

Lizard. Norman Kreitman. EdScPo

Lizard, The. Alphonse Marie Louis de Lamartine. SxFrPo, *tr. by* A. M. and E. H. Blackmore

Lizard, The. Hilda Morley. PmAP

Lizard, The. Lydia Pender. NOxBChV

Lizard, The ("Time to Tickle a Lizard, The.") Theodore Roethke. NOxBChV

Lizard on the wall, engrossed, The. Possibility, The. James Fenton. HarvBoo

Lizard's heart throbs, The. Lizard, The. Hilda Morley. PmAP

Lizards in Sardinia. Eamon Grennan. WaAnP

Lizie Wan sits at her father's bower door. *Unknown.* FaBoVe

Lizzie. Cheryl Burke. WiU

Lizzie. Nancy Vieira Couto. PBCAP

Llamaron posguerra a este troze de río, Le. Río. Carlos Sahagún. RaW

Llanafan Unrevisited. T. Harri Jones. AngWePo

Llanbadarn Baptism 1843. Gwyneth Lewis. BBMWP *Fr.* Wholeness.

Llangollen Vale. Anna Seward.
    To Time Past. RWP

Llanrhaeadr Ym Mochnant. Ronald Stuart Thomas. AngWePo

Llanto por Ignacio Sánchez Mejías. Federico García Lorca.
    3, Cuerpo Presente. RaW

Llaves de santo. Ernesto Lumbreras. RMCMP

Llévense a sus niños, llévenselos. Pueril. Gerardo Deniz. RMCMP

Llueve. Vicente Aleixandre. RaW

Lluvia, pie danzante y largo pelo, La. Relieves. Octavio Paz. IPoFL

Llyn y Gadair [*with music*]. T. H. Parry-Williams. BBMWP; OBWVE, *tr. by* Anthony Conran

Lo! A Child Is Born. Hugh MacDiarmid. EdScPo

Lo! an old song, yellow with centuries! Love, Weeping, Laid This Song. Lizette Woodworth Reese. APN-2

Lo, as a dove when up she springs. Alfred Tennyson. NAEL-6v2; NAEL-7v2 *Fr.* In Memoriam A. H. H.

Lo as I pause in the alien vale of the airport. Twenty-third Flight. Earle Birney. HeIP-4

Lo, between the Myrtles Standing [*with music*]. Ann Griffiths. OBWVE, *tr. by* H. Idris Bell

Lo, Colin, here the place whose pleasant site. Edmund Spenser. AEP

Lo! Death has reared himself a throne. City in the Sea, The. Edgar Allan Poe. APN-1; BrAP; NAAL-3; NAAPv.1; NCAP; NoP-4; NoP-5; OxBoAm; TCAPo; TFi; TRP

Lo, Della Crusca! In his closet pent. William Gifford. NOBRP *Fr.* Baviad, The.

Lo! down yon steep of vales proud Deva borne. Speech of the Nymph. Anna Seward. NOBRP

Lo! dreary Winter, howling o'er the waste. To———. Ann Yearsley. CenSon

Lo! fourscore years have passed; and where. John Greenleaf Whittier. TCAPo

Lo, haply walking in some clattering street. Haunted Streets. Mathilde Blind. ViWPN

Lo here I am lord, whither wilt thou send me? To Christ. William Alabaster. NoSic; OxBSo

Lo here I sit at Holyhead. Holyhead. September 25, 1727. Jonathan Swift. IrLP

Lo! here my hert. (LL) See! Here, My Heart. *Unknown.* NoP-4; NoP-5

Lo, here the state of every mortal wight. Respice Finem. Thomas Proctor. NoSic

Lo here, within the waters liquid womb. Thomas Traherne. ChIV-1 *Fr.* Meditations on the Six Days of the Creation.

Lo, How a Rose E'er Blooming. *Unknown.* ChrPo

Lo, how a rose is growing. *Unknown.* GePo

Lo how the sailor in a stormy night. Sonnet: On The Loss Of His Mistress. Sir Robert Aytoun. NOSC

Lo I the man, whose muse whilome did maske. Edmund Spenser. NAEL-6v1; NAEL-7v1; WaAnP *Fr.* Faerie Queene, The.

Lo I the man, whose Muse whilome [*or* whylome] did maske. Edmund Spenser. NAEL-7v1; NoP-5 *Fr.* Faerie Queene, The.

Lo! in the painted oriel of the West. Evening Star, The. Henry Wadsworth Longfellow. APN-1

Lo! in the west, fast fades the lingering light. Clifton Grove. Henry Kirke White.

Lo, Lord, Thou ridest! Hurricane, The. Hart Crane. MoAmPo

Lo, my good son, lo, my dear son, hey. I Chant of the "Miracle Stag" (Shamanistic Version). *Hungarian Oral Tradition.* IQMS, *tr. by* Adam Makkai

Lo, my loved is dying, and the call. Michael Field. ViWPN; VWP

'Lo, on her dying couch, the sufferer lies. Jane Alice Sargant. CenSon

Lo, Peter in Hell's Grosvenor Square. Percy Bysshe Shelley. NPBRoP *Fr.* Peter Bell the Third.

Lo que penetró tu vida—acedo espectáculo incrustado en el sitio del espasmo. Angélica Tornero. SPV

Lo! suddenly, with a sound which rang through heaven and earth. Indian Hero's Creed, The. *Unknown.* DiBP

Lo, the Bat. William Blake. NPBRoP

Lo! the glorious dawn is breaking. Easter Morn. Josephine D. Henderson Heard. CBWP-4

Lo the Immortal, borne by spirituality. Sikong Tu. CCL1 *Fr.* Twenty-Four Modes of Poetry.

Lo, the poor Indian! whose untutor'd mind. Alexander Pope. DiBP *Fr.* Essay on Man, An.

Lo, the unbounded sea. Ship Starting, The. Walt Whitman. TCAPo

Lo! this the land, where Freedom's sacred rage. Thomas, the Younger Warton. STuOW *Fr.* On the Marriage of the King.

Lo thus in breife (most sacred Majestye). To Queen Elizabeth. Jane Seager. EMWP

Lo! 'tis a gala night. Conqueror Worm, The. Edgar Allan Poe. APN-1; NCAP; TCAPo

Lo! what [*or* quhat] it is to love [*or* lufe]. Rondel of Luve [*or* Love], A. Alexander Scott. OBEV; OxBEV

Lo, when two dogs are fighting in the streets. Henry Fielding. DiBP *Fr.* Tom Thumb the Great.

Lo, where he shineth yonder. Hugh Holland. AngWePo

Lo, where left 'mid the sheaves, cut down by the iron-fanged reaper. On a Forsaken Lark's Nest. Mathilde Blind. ViWPN; VWP

LO, where with flowery head and hair all brightsome. *Unknown.* NoSic

Lo! ye children of men and the Mother. *Unknown.* APN-2 *Fr.* Generation of the Seeds, or the Origin of Corn, The.

Loaded like spoons. Slaveship[s]. Lucille Clifton. ESEAA; OPRER

Loaded on an oxcart [*or* ox cart]. (LL) Starlight Scope Myopia. Yusef Komunyakaa. AF; AmAlph; AmWaPo; MakPoe; NAMCP V.2; RoV

Loaded with mail of linked lies. Basil Bunting. FaBoWar *Fr.* Briggflatts [An Autobiography].

Loading a Boar. David Lee. TAPaP

Loadstone beckons to the long needle, The. Joy of Union, The. Yang Fang. CCL1, *tr. by* Burton Watson

Loaf, The. Paul Muldoon. BeAl

Loathesome life away, A. (LL) Haunted Beach, The. Mary Robinson. NPBRoP; RWP

Loba. Diane Di Prima.

Loba. Diane Di Prima.

   "If he did not come apart in her hands, he fell." PFTM-1

Loba Addresses the Goddess, The / or The Poet as Priestess Addresses the Loba-Goddess. Diane Di Prima. HW; PmAP

Loba as Eve. Diane Di Prima. HW

Loba's acid breast. San Fransisco. Miguel Algarin. PmAP

Lobe of opalescent glass. Heredom. Kenneth Irby. FTOS

Lobengula: Having a son at 38. Nikky Finney. SpirFl

Lobstee. Aram Saroyan. AHA

Lobster. Anne Sexton. ChAP

Lobster, The. Cynthia MacDonald. AFaM

Lobster, The. Carl Rakosi. APT-2

Lobster Quadrille, A. Lewis Carroll. NoAM; OxAEP-2; UV *Fr.* Alice's Adventures in Wonderland.

Lobsterpot Labyrinths. Daniel Gerard Hoffman. YaYoPo

Lobsterpot labyrinths wait. A porridge. Lobsterpot Labyrinths. Daniel Gerard Hoffman. YaYoPo

Lobsters in the Brain Coral. Laurence Lieberman. IllVoic

Lobsters in the Window. W. D. Snodgrass. TRP

Local groceries are all out of broccoli, The. Against Broccoli. Roy, Jr. Blount. NBLV

Local Note. Arthur Guiterman. NBLV

Local Ogres Are Against Me Here, The. Burns Singer. EdScPo

Local peddler of geographies, The. Executive Geochrone. Daniel Anderson. AmPoNex

Local Poet, A. John Hewitt. ModIr; PNI

Local row, A. Gods make their own importance. (LL) Epic. Patrick Kavanagh. CABP; HarvBoo; MakPoe; ModIr; NAMCP V.1; NoP-4; NoP-5; NPeEn; OxBSo

Local scandal, The. He's Crossed the River. Carol Cullar. TiP2

Localism or t/here. Juliana Spahr. LegDan

Localité. Claude Royet-Journoud. YaTCFP

Locality. Claude Royet-Journoud. YaTCFP, *tr. by* Keith Waldron

Locate *I / love you*some- / where in. Language, The. Robert Creeley. CAP-8; PmAP

   (Locate *I / love you* somewhere in.) FTOS

Loch Ness Monster's Song, The. Edwin Morgan. NePenScot; OPOU; StAl

Loch Thom. William Sydney Graham. EdScPo; NePenScot

Lochiel, Lochiel! beware of the day. Thomas Campbell. NePenSco. *Fr.* Lochiel's Warning.

Lochiel's Warning. Thomas Campbell.

   Wizard. NePenScot

Lochinvar. Sir Walter Scott. ChAP; NAEL-6v2; NAEL-7v2; NePenScot; NPBRoP; OxAEP-2; TFi *Fr.* Marmion.

Lóci Becomes a Giant. Lőrinc Szabó. IQMS, *tr. by* Egon F. Kunz

Lock and Key, The. Vicki-Ann Asservero. BtF

Lock City. David Henderson. EGAG

Lock me up. I am a. No Immunity. Dolores de Iruretagoyena de Humphrey. ReBoTo

Lock the door. In the dark journey of our night. Close. Carol Ann Duffy. EdScPo

Lock the Door, Lariston. James Hogg. IBB

Lock the door, Lariston, lion of Liddesdale. Lock the Door, Lariston. James Hogg. IBB

Lock the Place in Your Heart. Zindzi Mandela. HAWP

Locke sank into a swoon. Fragments. William Butler Yeats. NoAM

Locked arm in arm they cross the way. Tableau. Countee Cullen. BLPJKO; NAAPv.2

Locked House, A. W. D. Snodgrass. VCAP

Locked in bathrooms for hours. Hully Gully. Rita Dove. SwNoth

Locked up until next season's harvest. Death of the Farm Workers' Cat. Rigoberto González. AmPoNex

Locked with a Tear. Luis Rosales. RaW, *tr. by* Ralph Nelson and Rita García Nelson

Locker Room Etiquette. Craig Arnold. MoASP

Lockerbie. Charles Muñoz. OtW

Locket, The. John Montague. PBCIP *Fr.* Dead Kingdom, The.

Locking the Church. David Scott. NLP

Lockless Door, The. Robert Frost. TCAPo

Locks. Joy Dawson. BtF

Locksley Hall. Alfred Tennyson. NAEL-6v2; NAEL-7v2

Loco. Jane Holland. MFPA

Locomotive, The. Christopher Pearse Cranch. APN-1; GM *Fr.* Seven Wonders of the World.

Locomotive / What is a portrait? Textile 13. Marjorie Welish. VaPo

Locust Shell. Jody Gladding. YaYoPo

Locust Songs. Geoffrey Hill.

   Shiloh Church, 1862: Twenty-Three Thousand. UpMys

Locust thought, The. Locust Shell. Jody Gladding. YaYoPo

Locust Tree in Flower, The. William Carlos Williams. NAAPv.2; OxBoAm; Spl

Locust Wood Mallet for Papermaking, A. Lin Pu. ColAnChi, *tr. by* Paul Hansen

Locusts a-wing, multiply [fr. *the Chinese of the* Confucian Odes]. *Unknown.* APSN; NDACCP, *tr. by* Ezra Pound

Locusts, or Appolyonists, The. Phineas Fletcher.

   "Say Muses, say; who now in those rich fields." ChIV-1

   Sin, Despair, and Lucifer. NOSC

Lodestar. Joanna Klink. IAoNAP

Lodestar held lightly in the sky above a gray, A. Lodestar. Joanna Klink. IAoNAP

Lodging House in Town, A. Muso Soseki. EaWin, *tr. by* W. S. Merwin

Lodging in Annam. Du Shenyan. CCL1, *tr. by* Stephen Owen

Lodging, The. George Mackay Brown. EdScPo

Lodging with the Old Man of the Stream. Po Chü-i. BLT, *tr. by* Arthur Waley

Loe! formest of a rout that followd him. Virgil. OBVE *Fr.* Aeneid [*or* Eneados *or* Aeneis], The.

Loft, The. Richard Jones. GoPo

Lofty trees of the south, The. *Unknown.* ColAnChi *Fr.* Classic of Odes.

Log. David Bromige. FTOS

Log gets up yet again, goes rolling and bouncing down the beach, plunges as thought for good into the water, The. (LL) On the Oregon Coast. Galway Kinnell. NAMCP V.2; NoAM

Log of Pi, The. Marc J. Straus. BloBone

Log, The. Camp Fire. Alfonsina Storni. TANSG, *tr. by* Mark McCaffrey

Log Written by an Unknown Hand in the. Christine Hume. IAoNAP

Logbook of a Lost Caravan [*with music*]. Gyula Illyés. PFTM-1

Logbook of Judgments. Jay Wright.

   Meta-A and the A of Absolutes. ESEAA; TRP

Logging Trestle. Mary Barnard. APT-2

Logic. Malcolm de Chazal. YaTCFP, *tr. by* Mary Ann Caws

Logic does well at school. Scholars. Walter De la Mare. NoAM

Logic in the House of Sawed-Off Telescopes. Jeffrey McDaniel. AmPoNex; LegDan; NeAmPo

Logic is logic. That's all I say. (LL) Oliver Wendell Holmes. APN-1; BRP; ITBLP; NAAL-3; NAAPv.1; TCAPo; TFi *Fr.* Autocrat of the Breakfast Table, The.

Logic / Never / Thought. Logic. Malcolm de Chazal. YaTCFP, *tr. by* Mary Ann Caws

Logic of Queerness, The: (Releasing Your Ivy Evening Within). Ron Palmer. BeDoSh

Logical Positivist, The. David Bromige. FTOS

Logical principle is said to be an empty, A. Michael Palmer. HarvBoo *Fr.* Series.

Logique, La. Malcolm de Chazal. YaTCFP

Logocyclegram. Audrey Hughes. ArBi

Logos. Erich Fried. GTCP, *tr. by* Reinhold Grimm

Loin de moi et semblable aux étoiles, à la mer et à tous les accessoires de la mythologie poétique. Si Tu Savais. Robert Desnos. YaTCFP

Lointain est moins distant que le sol, le lit mordant, Le. Fraction. André Du Bouchet. YaTCFP

Lois at the Hair Salon. Lesley Dauer. AmPoNex

Loitered, you might say. On the Conditions of Place. Michael Anania. IllVoic

Loíza Aldea. Víctor Hernández Cruz. PueRic

Loíza / Who is there in you took. Loíza Aldea. Víctor Hernández Cruz. PueRic

Lok and bowe downe thyne eare o Lorde. Songe Made by Her Majestie and Songe before Her at Her Cominge from White Hall to Powles through Fleete Streete in Anno Domini 1588, A. Queen of England Elizabeth I. EMWP

Loke that none of you departe. The Peniarth Poet. AngWePo *Fr.* Drinking Song, A.

Loki tongue does not lend itself, The. Word from the Loki, A. Maurice Riordan. ModIr; NIrP

Lola the Elder. AKA. Bruce Andrews. PFTM-2

Lolita. Vladimir Vladimirovich Nabokov. APT-2 *Fr.* Lolita.

Lolita. Vladimir Vladimirovich Nabokov.
    Lolita. APT-2

Lolled in / meditation halls. Recalling Former Travels. Anne Waldman. AmZen

Lollies Noir. Dorothy Porter. BMAP

Lollingdon Downs. John Masefield.
    Choice, The. MoBrPo

Lolotte. *Unknown.* SSUS

Lombard Stag-Hunt, The. Sir William Davenant. DiBP *Fr.* Gondibert.

Lomonosov. Anna Semionovna Prismanova. ARWW, *tr. by* Catriona Kelly

London. William Blake. RSaN

London. Samuel Carter.
    Paean. STuOW

London. John Oldham. NOSC *Fr.* Satyr, A.

London, 1792. Emyr Lewis. ATSWP, *tr. by* Robert Minhinnick

London: A Poem in Imitation of the Third Satire of Juvenal. Samuel Johnson.
    Poverty in London. NPeEn; OBSV; OxAEP-1
    "Tho' grief and fondness in my breast rebel." NPeEn

London Air. Ted Berrigan. AHA

London, at the end of December, in the dark and fog. (LL) Smoking. Elton Glaser. BAP-97; P180

London Beggar, The. William Wordsworth. NPBRoP; WaAnP *Fr.* Prelude, The; Growth of a Poet's Mind [1805 version; Selections from Anthologies].

London Bells [*see also* The Bells of London *and* London Bells: "Gay go up and gay go down"]. *Unknown.* OPOU

London Bridge. Mother Goose. FaBoVe; NPeEn

London Bridge is broken down. London Bridge. Mother Goose. FaBoVe; NPeEn

London Despair. Frances Darwin Cornford. OBMV

London 1802 ("Milton! thou shouldst be living at this hour.") William Wordsworth. BrAP; CenSon; HeIP-4; InoFa; NAEL-6v2; NAEL-7v2; NIL-7; NIP-4; NOBRP; NoP-4; NoP-5; OxAEP-2; TFi; UV
    (England, 1802, II.) OBEV
    (Milton, Thou Shouldst Be Living at this Hour.) NPBRoP

London, Greater London (After *Satire III*). John Holloway. WoPoe

London: "I wander through [*or* thro'] each chartered [*or* charter'd] street." William Blake. BrAP; CABP; ClHu; HeIP-4; IJHIL; NAEL-6v2; NAEL-7v2; NAWM-7v2; NIL-7; NIP-4; NOBRP; NoP-4; NoP-5; NPBRoP; NPeEn; OxAEP-2; OxBEV; PoPoPo; TFi; TRP; WeW-3 *Fr.* Songs of Experience.

London Images. William Wordsworth. WaAnP *Fr.* Prelude, The; Growth of a Poet's Mind [1805 version; Selections from Anthologies].

London in July. Amy Levy. PoBW

London: John Lane, The Bodley Head. On the Imprint of the First English Edition of "The Works of Max Beerbohm." Max Beerbohm. OBCoV

London Lickpenny. *Unknown.* OBSV

London Lickpenny. *Unknown.* OBSV

London Nightfall. John Gould Fletcher. MoAmPo

London Plane-Tree, A. Amy Levy. PEW; ViWPN

London Poets. Amy Levy. PEW; ViWPN

London Pride. Noël Coward. ReLy

London Pride has been handed down to us. London Pride. Noël Coward. ReLy

London Rain. Louis MacNeice. NoP-4; NoP-5

London Rurality. George, the Younger Colman. OBGa *Fr.* London Rurality.

London Snow. Robert Bridges. MoBrPo; NoAM; OxAEP-2; TFi

London Subverted by the Furies. Abraham Cowley. NOSC

London Summer Morning, A. Mary Robinson. *See* London's Summer Morning.

London, thou art of townes *A per se.* To [*or* In Honour of] the City of London. William Dunbar. OBEV

London Welsh v. Bridgend. John Powell Ward. TCAWP

London, within thy ample verge. Henry Luttrell. NOBRP *Fr.* Letter to Julia, in Rhyme.

Londonderry Air, The. Nicolas Bentley. OBCoV

London's Resurrection. Simon Ford.
    "Hail, glorious day; mayst thou be writ in gold." NOSC

London's Summer Morning. Mary Robinson. NAEL-7v2; RWP; WoRP
    (London Summer Morning, A.) NPBRoP

Lone and level sands stretch far away, The. (LL) Ozymandias. Percy Bysshe Shelley. BLPJKO; BrAP; BRP; CABP; CenSon; ChAP; ClHu; CtM; GSo; HeIP-4; MakPoe; NAEL-6v2; NAEL-7v2; NIL-7; NIP-4; NoP-4; NoP-5; NPBRoP; NPeEn; OPOU; OxBEV; OxBSo; PoPoPo; PtR; SoSe-8; TFi; UV; WaAnP

Lone Bather [*with music*]. Abraham Moses Klein. HeIP-4

Lone Buck. *Unknown.* WoPoe *Fr.* Gathasaptasati, The.

Lone Dog. Irene McLeod. NOxBChV

Lone drake, upended, The. Solitary, The. Mary Barnard. APT-2

Lone figure is waving, A. Postcard from North Antrim, A. Seamus Heaney. PBCIP; PNI

Lone goose flying alone, A. Seeing Wonsunja Off to Kwandong Province. Chunghur Hyujung. BecRai, *tr. by* Kim Daljin, Kim Won-Chung and Christopher Merrill

Lone Pine. Amy Uyematsu. WhBo

Lone temple bell tolls at dusk, A. Returning Late to Lu-men Shan. Meng Hao Jan. CrYelRi, *tr. by* Sam Hamill

Lone tern turns in the blowsy wind, A. Because You Mentioned the Spiritual Life. Stephen Dunn. BodElec; Vesp

Lone Theudotos placed this gift beneath the mountain. Anyte. SaLy, *tr. by* Diane Rayor

Lone Tree. Lismaco Chavarría. SonAtl, *tr. by* Carole Gibson and Anne Swann

Lone Wild Goose. Tu Fu [*or* Du Fu]. CrYelRi, *tr. by* Sam Hamill

Loneliness. Basho. EMJL, *tr. by* Haruo Shirane

Loneliness. Antonio Cisneros. *tr. by* Maureen Ahern, William Rowe and David Tipton
    Hampton Court. TCLAP, *tr. by* William Rowe
    Paris Cinquième. TCLAP, *tr. by* Maureen Ahern and David Tipton

Loneliness. Dhabya Khamees. PoArWo, *tr. by* Clarissa C. Burt

Loneliness. Amjad Nasir. BBASP, *tr. by* Charles Doria and May Jayyusi

Loneliness. Tu Fu [*or* Du Fu]. CCL1, *tr. by* Kenneth Rexroth

Loneliness. Telly Wong. WhBo

Loneliness. Franz Wright. AmAlph

Loneliness, A. Haki R. Madhubuti. GT

Loneliness, The. John Wieners. PmAP

Loneliness, The / of the piles in the brackish water. Aristeas 2. Peter Huchel. GTCP, *tr. by* Reinhold Grimm

Loneliness comes out of his mattress face. Elegy for 6 So Far. Gig Ryan. BMAP

Loneliness is a laboratory; its territory is forever defined; for reasons beyond our conviction. More Important Than the Design of Cities Will Be the Design of Their Decay. Tessa Rumsey. LegDan

Loneliness leapt in the mirrors, but all week. Departure's Girl-Friend. W. S. Merwin. OxBoAm

Loneliness of a Wayfarer, The. Great Master Hyecho. BecRai, *tr. by* Kim Daljin, Kim Won-Chung and Christopher Merrill

Loneliness of Lincoln, The. X. J. Kennedy. HHAm

Loneliness of the Military Historian, The. Margaret Atwood. OpeFie

Loneliness One dare not sound, The. Emily Dickinson. TCAPo

Loneliness without rest! Ballad of One Doomed to Die. Federico García Lorca. AWTN, *tr. by* Langston Hughes

Lonely. Vasyl Symonenko. SonAtl, *tr. by* Dmytro Romanyk, Iryna Romanyk and Tamara Romanyk

Lonely Affair, A. Reuben Jackson. GT

Lonely and dreary was the day. Heart's Ease. Mary E. Tucker. CBWP-1

Lonely birds who cross out the sun. Ravens. Georgi Borisov. CSCBP, *tr. by* Georgi Belev and Lisa Sapinkopf

Lonely Coed, A. Billy Strayhorn. ReLy

Lonely Death, The. Adelaide Crapsey. APT-1

Lonely, desolate, the new literary scene. Hesitation. "Lu Hsün." WoPoe, *tr. by* William R. Schultz

Lonely Eagles. Marilyn Nelson Waniek. ESEAA

Lonely Farmer, The. Ronald Stuart Thomas. NoP-4

Lonely fox roams far abroad, The. Matthew Prior. DiBP *Fr.* Solomon on the Vanity of the World.

Lonely Heart, The. John Hewitt. *Fr.* Freehold.

Lonely Hearts. Wendy Cope. OBCoV; WaAnP

Lonely hermit does not yearn for tea, The. Cup of Clear Water, A. Thich Tue Sy. WhBo

Lonely Hermitage. Master Naong. BecRai, *tr. by* Kim Daljin, Kim Won-Chung and Christopher Merrill

Lonely Impulse of Delight, A—W.B. Yeats. David Kirk Vaughan. OtW

Lonely Journey, A. Kim Suyông. CAMKP, *tr. by* Anthony, Brother of Taizé

Lonely Lady, The. Charlotte Brontë. VWP

Lonely Land, The. Arthur James Marshall Smith. BrAP

Lonely man, The. Gas. Sidney Wade. PoSol

Lonely man, his head among the stars, A. Merlin. Thomas Caldecot Chubb. YaYoPo

Lonely man—leads a dog's life, A. Life of a Dead Dog. David Avidan. FIT, *tr. by* Robert Friend

Lonely Masquerader. Velemir Khlebnikov. TCRusP, *tr. by* Kathy Lewis and Bob Perelman

Lonely Night. P. C. Boutens. TuT, *tr. by* Tony Curtis and Tony Curtis

Lonely Night in Early Autumn. Po Chü-i. TAL

Lonely pity in your lifted eyes, The. (LL) John Hewitt. IrLP; PNI *Fr.* Sonnets for Roberta (1954).

Lonely poem is nothing, A. Not About Poems. Carolyn M. Rodgers. OxAAAP

Lonely, save for a few faint stars, the sky. Little Dancers, The. Laurence Binyon. MoBrPo

Lonely silence. Basho. SoOfWa, *tr. by* Sam Hamill

Lonely Street, The. William Carlos Williams. APT-1

Lonely stretch, in the bind of poor fishing and drouth, A. Daydreaming on the Trail. Miyazawa Kenji. PFTM-1

Lonely task it is to plow, A. Plowing: A Memory. Hamlin Garland. ChAP

Lonely Tower, The. Tom Paulin. ModIr

Lonely Town. Betty Comden and Adolph Green. ReLy

Lonely trembling soul can ache, The. José Martí. TCLAP *Fr.* Simple Verses.

Lonely Tylenol. Peter Gizzi. ReTh; VaPo

Lonely Tylenol. Sharon Mesmer. HeMarv

Lonely way, and as I went my eyes, a. Two Infinities. Edward Dowden. GSo

Lonely Wife, The. Li Po. NAAPv.2; NIL-7, *tr. by* Florence Ayscough and Amy Lowell

Lonely Women. Kysha N. Brown. BRtP

Lonely World [*with music*]. Mrs. Henry Linden. CBWP-4

Lonely world, A. Adam's Cry. Nengi Ilagha. NeNiPo

Lonesome Boy Blues. Kenneth Patchen. APT-2

Lonesome Death of Hattie Carroll, The. Bob Dylan. WaAnP

Lonesome Texas. Bettye Hammer Givens. TiP2

Lonesome Valley. *Unknown.* APN-2

Lonesome Valley, The. *Unknown.* SSUS

Lonesome Water. Roy Helton. APT-1; MoAmPo

Long, The / Canoes. Lorine Niedecker. FTOS *Fr.* Lake Superior.

Long After Heine. Gwen Harwood. HarvBoo

Long after hours. (LL) Hamlet. Ciaran Carson. FaBoVe; ModIr; PNI

Long after it was heard no more. (LL) Solitary Reaper, The. William Wordsworth. CABP; ClHu; HeIP-4; NAEL-6v2; NAEL-7v2; NOBRP; NoP-4; NoP-5; NPBRoP; OBEV; OxAEP-2; OxBEV; PoPoPo; SoSe-8; TFi; WaAnP; WeW-3

Long after life has fled. (LL) Lines of Life. Letitia Elizabeth Landon. NOBRP; NPBRoP; NPeEn

Long after rainfall, Sorceress Hills grow dark. Clear after Rain. Tu Fu [*or* Du Fu]. CrYelRi, *tr. by* Sam Hamill

Long after the pear tree's final surge of sap. Roy Kiyooka. NLPA *Fr.* Pear Tree Pomes.

Long after the time we were supposed to arrive. 20th Century, The. Lesley Dauer. NAPBL

Long after you have swung back. Losing Track. Denise Levertov. HeIP-4

Long Afternoon, The. Louis Simpson. BodElec

Long afterward, Oedipus, old and blinded, walked the. Myth. Muriel Rukeyser. APT-2; NAAL-5; NALW; NIL-7; OxBoAm

Long ago a brown alighted story was told. Remember Something Like This. Lionel Fogarty. BMAP

Long Ago (And Far Away). Ira Gershwin. ReLy

Long ago and far away I met the right love. There's a Man in My Life. George Marion, Jr. ReLy

Long ago black bears. William Oandasan. FTtHH *Fr.* Past, The.

Long ago, everyone laughed together. Laments of the Gorges. Meng Chiao. NDACCP, *tr. by* David Hinton

Long ago, his skin itches as men enter his pores. Mudrooroo Narogin. BMAP *Fr.* Song Cycle of Jacky, The.

Long ago, I burnt all those books. Remembering the invasion of Grenada by the USA. Bob Dixon. RSaN

Long ago I learned how to sleep. Wind Song. Carl Sandburg. MoAmPo

Long ago I made that journey, fall rain coming down lightly. I Had Occasion to Tell a Visitor about an Old Trip I Took. Lu Yu. WoPoe, *tr. by* Burton Watson

Long ago, I was wounded. I lived. First Memory. Louise Glück. RaF

Long ago in a poultry yard. Lay of a Golden Goose, The. Louisa May Alcott. SWaP

Long ago, in Kentucky, I, a boy stood. Robert Penn Warren. FuPo; ItP; NAAL-5; NAAPv.2 *Fr.* Audubon: A Vision.

Long ago in Silla, Venerable Ch'öyong. Yi Chehyön. CATKP *Fr.* Contemporary Folk Songs.

Long ago, in the forests of southern Europe. Stillness, the Dancing, The. Linda Bierds. RoV

Long ago my heart and mind. My Ideal. Leo Robin. ReLy

Long ago sweet songs were sung. For a Birthday. Sophie Jewett. PoBW

Long ago the ancient flutes sang. Secret Melodies. Debra Taub. SurWo

Long ago there was a mighty snake, and beings evil to men. *Unknown.* APN-2 *Fr.* Walam Olum; or, Red Score [of the Lenâpé], The [*or* The Wallam Olum; The Red Score or Painted History of the Lenni Lenape].

Long ago, when the Sultan sat. Muiveyo Cow, The. *Unknown.* SonAtl, *tr. by* Majid Rasheed and Ed Roplin

Long ago, when we were children. Strawberry Picking. Alexander the Wild. NAWM-7v1, *tr. by* Peter Dronke

Long ago when you wanted to marry me. To the Singing Girl Named Luu. Nguyễn Khuyến. WoPoe, *tr. by* Nguyen Ngoc Bich

Long and narrow, our land remained secluded. Song of Peace. Pak Illo. CATKP, *tr. by* Peter H. Lee

Long Banister Lane. Li Po. NDACCP, *tr. by* William Carlos Williams

Long Barren. Christina Georgina Rossetti. ViWPN

Long Beach Suite. Tom Wayman. BrAP

Long before dawn, anxiety has me. Dark Prayer. Gregory Orr. PfSP

Long before dawn your light. Chinese Nightingale. William Carlos Williams. NAAPv.2

Long before daylight they left their beds. *Unknown.* NAEL-6v1; NAEL-7v1; NAWM-7v1 *Fr.* Sir Gawain and the Green Knight [Marie Borroff Translation].

Long before he thought of his own death. My Dad's Wallet. Raymond Carver. GoPo

Long before I hear it, Naples bright. Napoli Again. Richard Hugo. AF

Long before morning glories perched upon opening day. Hometown. Salih Michael Fisher. CAGL

Long before the father died. Himself. Peter Fallon. PBCIP

Long before the Spaniards came. Cuando el tecolote canta, el Indio muere. Consuelo de Aerenlund. OPRER

Long before the wars. Queen Hera. Burleigh Muttén. HW

Long black night, The. Dusk in My Backyard. Keith Wilson. BLT; ICANM

Long Blues, The. Calvin C. Hernton. GT

Long Boat, The [*with music*]. Stanley Kunitz. CAP-8

Long body of the water fills its hollow, The. Staring at the Sea on the Day of the Death of Another. May Swenson. APT-2; NAMCP V.2; OxBoAm

Long bound in ice and horrid hills of snow. After a Storm, Going a Hawking. George Daniel. NOSC

Long Branch Song, A. Robert Pinsky. NoP-4; NoP-5

Long Coats with Deep Pockets. Sean Thomas Dougherty. AmPoNex

Long conversations. Basho. SoOfWa, *tr. by* Sam Hamill

Long corridor. Woman Mopping With a Rag Mop. Yi Chinmyông. EcSo, *tr. by* Carolyn U. So

Long day of pining, A. To the Tune: Drunk in Flower Shadows. Li Ch'ing-chao. CrYelRi, *tr. by* Sam Hamill

Long day spent listening, The. Papi Working. Julia Alvarez. WaAnP

Long day was bright, The. Nocturne. Frances Wynne. IrLP

Long days together I'd lie there on my back. Vale of My Youth, The. Will Ifan. BBMWP, *tr. by* Elin ap Hywel

Long desired, the dead return. Jay Macpherson. PoA 2002 *Fr.* Way Down, The.

Long did I toil and knew no earthly rest. At Home. John Quarles. SacPr

Long, Disconsolate Lines. Jane Cooper. InoFa

Long Distance. Maurice Kilwein Guevara. TouFir

Long Distance. Laila Halaby. PoArWo

Long Distance. Tony Harrison. NAEL-6v2; NAEL-7v2 *Fr.* School of Eloquence, The.

Long Distance II. Tony Harrison. PoCu; StAl

Long Distance. Aleda Shirley. ExTi

Long Distance. Max Winter. NeAmPo

Long Distance Moan. Blind Lemon Jefferson. APT-2

Long Division; a Tribal History. Wendy Rose. OPRER

Long Dress, A. Gertrude Stein. MoWP *Fr.* Tender Buttons.

Long Dress, A. Gertrude Stein. NAAPv.2 *Fr.* Tender Buttons.

Long Enough. Long Enough. Muriel Rukeyser. NAAL-5

Long Feud. Louis Untermeyer. MoAmPo

Long Finish. Paul Muldoon. HarvBoo

Long for Home. Moyshe-Leyb Halpern. WoPoe, *tr. by* Meyer Schapiro

Long for home and hate your homeland. Long for Home. Moyshe-Leyb Halpern. WoPoe, *tr. by* Meyer Schapiro

Long Garden, The [*with music*]. Patrick Kavanagh. HarvBoo; OBGa

Long Gone. Sterling Allen Brown. APT-2

Long gone the smoke-and-pepper childhood smell. Sarabande on Attaining the Age of Seventy-Seven. Anthony Hecht. BAP-01

Long Gone to Texas. William D. Barney. TiP2

Long Goodbye. Carrie St. George Comer. LegDan

Long goodbyes, the whistles in the dark, The. Eugenio Montale. WoPoe *Fr.* Motets [Mottetti].

Long grass of summer held back by wire fence. Cemetery at Loch End, Catalone, Cape Breton, The. Douglas Lochhead. Coast

Long green grasses of my island, The. Socope. Maria Manuela Margarido. HAWP, *tr. by* Julia Kirst

Long had I grieved at what I deemed abuse. Resignation. Paul Laurence Dunbar. SacPr

Long had this nation been amused in vain. Spanish Descent, The. Daniel Defoe.

Long hair, and curls woven not by Nature but by Art. Strato. CAGL, *tr. by* Daryl Hine

Long hard journey, A. Buson. SoOfWa, *tr. by* Sam Hamill

Long has it been my fate to hear. Sylphs of the Seasons, The. Washington Allston.

Long hast thou, friend! been absent from thy soil. Mr. Pope's Welcome from Greece. John Gay. OxAEP-1

Long have I beat with timid hands upon life's leaden door. Suppliant, The. Georgia Douglas Johnson. NAAPv.2

Long have I framed weak phantasies of Thee. Agnosto Theo [To an Unknown God]. Thomas Hardy. InvLi

Long have I lov'd this bonny Lasse. Thomas Deloney. PBRV

Long highway, A. Autumn Sunrise. Antonio Machado Ruiz. RaW, *tr. by* Robert Bly

Long Hill, The. Sara Teasdale. MoAmPo; TCAPo

Long Hill of Garrapata, The. Renée Gregorio. FiBr; ICANM

Long hoe, long hoe, handle of white wood. Tu Fu [*or* Du Fu]. CCL1 *Fr.* Seven Songs Written During the Qianyuan Era While Staying at Tonggu District.

Long I followed [*or* follow'd] happy guides. Forerunners. Ralph Waldo Emerson. APN-1; OBEV

Long in thy shackles [*or* shackels], liberty. To Lucasta, from Prison. Richard Lovelace. BASC; CavPo

Long is the night. Curriculum Vitae. Ingeborg Bachmann. PFTM-2, *tr. by* Jerome Rothenberg

Long Island Night, The. Howard Moss. OxBoAm

Long Island Sound. Emma Lazarus. APN-2; NAAPv.1; OxBoAm; SWaP

Long Island sound, the pitiless clamor, The. Penitential Cries of Jupiter Hammond, The. Gary Smith. GT

Long Kiang, reaching heaven, The. (LL) Separation on the River Kiang. Li Po. CCL1; NDACCP, *tr. by* Ezra Pound

Long lake in a swan-throated bed, longer, A. Meeting Walter Benjamin. Karen Solie. OpeFie

Long late train hoots under the freeway. South Texas Boxcar Blues. Chip Dameron. TiP2

Long lifetime, A. Kenneth Rexroth. BLT *Fr.* Earth Sky Sea Trees Birds House Beasts Flowers.

Long line of bohunks and hunyaks, A: we settled in podunk. thirteen consonants. D. A. Powell. AmPoNex

Long lines of cliff breaking have left a chasm. Enoch Arden. Alfred Tennyson.

Long Lines Sent to Ling Hu-Ch'u before He Comes to Visit My Tumbledown Home. Po Chü-i. NDACCP, *tr. by* David Hinton

Long live the people! How they lived! and boiled. Part II. Elizabeth Barrett Browning. PEW

Long live the weeds and the wilderness yet. (LL) Inversnaid. Gerard Manley Hopkins. FaBoVe; MoBrPo; NoAM; NPeEn; SacPr; TFi

Long live the weeds that overwhelm. Long Live the Weeds. Theodore Roethke. NoAM; PoA 2002

Long, long ago. Buson. EMJL *Fr.* Spring Breeze on the Kema Embankment.

Long long ago when the world was a wild place. Bedtime Story. George MacBeth. EmeKit; SoSe-8

Long, long Autumn Nights. Oguma Hideo. CAoMJL1, *tr. by* David G. Goodman

Long, long legs, The. From the Country to the City. Elizabeth Bishop. PoA 2002

Long, long night is o'er at last, The. Beasts of England, The. Andy Croft. RSaN

Long love that in my thought doth harbo[u]r, The. Sir Thomas Wyatt. GSo; NAEL-6v1; NAEL-7v1; NoP-5

  (Longe Love, That in My Thought Doeth Harbar, The.) BrAP

  (Sonnet: "The long love.") AEP

Long lustrous tiger, the flowered leopard, The. Felines. Daria Menicanti. CItWP, *tr. by* Cinzia Sartini Blum and Lara Trubowitz

Long Man, The. Mark Ford. NeBrP

Long Marriage, The. Maxine W. Kumin. PoDa

Long may our hearts, Nealce, guard that night. Petronius Arbiter. RomPo, *tr. by* J. P. Sullivan

Long Melancholy Tune, A. Li Ch'ing-chao. ColAnChi, *tr. by* Jiaosheng Wang

Long neglect has worn away. Long Neglect Has Worn Away. Emily Jane Brontë. NoP-4; NoP-5

Long night is deep, deep as water, The. Sleepless. Ch'in Kuan. CrYelRi, *tr. by* Sam Hamill

Long night, no inclination to sleep. Not Sleeping. Ch'i-chi. CSKM, *tr. by* Burton Watson

Long night of linden trees, your honey hands. Figurehead, The. Maria Luisa Spaziani. NeIt, *tr. by* Beverly Allen

Long night, the short sleep, and La Gorgue to wander, The. La Gorgue. Ivor Gurney. OxBEV

Long night: unable to sleep. *Unknown.* ChinPo, *tr. by* Ye Weilian [*or* Yeh Wei-lien *or* Wai-lim Yip]

Long Nook. John Wieners. FTOS

Long over whatever edge. Edge, The. Robert Creeley. FTOS

Long, perfect loveliness of sow, The. (LL) Saint Francis and the Sow. Galway Kinnell. AmFaPo; BeAl; ChAP; NAAL-5; OxBoAm; P180; TWF

Long rains, The. Basho. EH, *tr. by* Robert Hass

Long rain falls on the empty forest. Smoke rises, The. After Long Rain. Wang Wei. TAL

Long Road, The. Mongane Wally Serote. TSAP

Long road and a village, A. Holy Family. Muriel Rukeyser. ChIV-2; MoAmPo

Long road dreams. Drifter's Brand, A. Art Coelho. RWB

Long road of it all, The. Robert Creeley. NAMCP V.2; WoBe *Fr.* Life and Death.

Long rolling, The. Main-Deep, The. James Stephens. MoBrPo; OBMV

Long rubber mat sprawled across the field, A. Message No. 57. Holley Blackwell. AnSo

Long sea, how short-lasting, The. There Is No Land Yet. Laura Riding Jackson. ChIV-1

Long Shadow of Lincoln: A Litany, The. Carl Sandburg. CBCWP

Long shadows. Gem Forest. Muso Soseki. EaWin, *tr. by* W. S. Merwin

Long silence, A. All the shoes are shined and the cotton is picked. Sharrif Simmons. BRtP

Long Silence, The. Kenneth Steven. EdScPo

Long since I'd ceased to care. Parrot, The. Wilfrid Wilson Gibson. OBMV

Long, sleek cars rasp softly on the kerb, The. Luxury. Edgell Rickword. RSaN

Long slick black feller. Riddle. *Unknown.* FaBoVe

Long, slow days of spring, The. Buson. EMJL, *tr. by* Haruo Shirane

Long sobs of, The. Autumn Song. Paul Verlaine. SxFrPo, *tr. by* Martin Sorrell

Long steel grass. Dame Edith Sitwell. NAEL-6v2 *Fr.* Façade.

Long Story. Stephen Dobyns. CAP-8

Long summer rains / Barley's tasteless. Mokusetsu. ZenPo, *tr. by* Takashi Ikemoto and Lucien Stryk

Long Tale, A. Lewis Carroll. OBCoV

Long the proud Spaniards had vaunted to conquer us. Thomas Deloney. FaBoWar

Long thin window to the stars holds up the tenement, The. Hotel de L'Etoile. Matthew Rohrer. AmPoNex

Long time a child, and still a child, when years. Long Time a Child. Hartley Coleridge. CenSon; NPBRoP; NPeEn; OxBSo

Long Time Ago [*with music*]. Leslie Marmon Silko. NAMCP V.2; NoAM

Long time ago, A / A million years B.C. Pennies from Heaven. Johnny Burke. ReLy

Long time ago, I think, A. Hypothesis. Ted Olson. YaYoPo

Long time ago, twelve hours from here, A. Winged Snake Found on a Path. Matthew Rohrer. NevBe; PoDa

Long time ago, when I was a child, A. Snow Globe, The. Howard Nemerov. ItP

Long Time Back, A. *Unknown.* EaWin; WoPoe, *tr. by* J. Moussaieff Masson and W. S. Merwin

Long time back, A. Long Time Back, A. *Unknown.* EaWin; WoPoe, *tr. by* J. Moussaieff Masson and W. S. Merwin

Long time had Israel been disus'd from rest. Foreigners, The. John Tutchin. BASC

Long time hath Christ, long time I must confess. Of the Reed That the Jews Set in Our Saviour's Hand. William Alabaster. NoSic; NPeEn

Long time have human ignorance and guilt. William Wordsworth. NAEL-6v2; NAEL-7v2 *Fr.* Prelude, The; Growth of a Poet's Mind [1850 version].

Long time he lay upon the sunny hill. Childhood. Edwin Muir. HeIP-4; NePenScot; NoP-4; NoP-5; NPeEn

Long time in some forgotten churchyard earth of Warwickshire. Who Were before Me. John Drinkwater. OBMV

Long time, many years, we've had these wars, A. On a Certain Engagement South of Seoul. Hayden Carruth. AmWaPo; PWW2; WaAnP

Long Time No See, 'Bye Now. Ogden Nash. OxBoAm

Long time Plain Dealing in the haughty town. Plain Dealing's Downfall. *Unknown*. OBSV

(Long time plain dealing in the Hauty Town.) OxBEV

Long time since it seems today, A. W. H. Auden. FaBoA

Long time since the last scream cut short, A. Rathlin. Derek Mahon. ModIr

Long time's gone, A. On a Phrase from Southern Ohio. James Wright. LTA

Long Track Blues. Sterling Allen Brown. GM

Long Voyage, The. Malcolm Cowley. SoSe-8

Long Walk Home, The. Robert Fleming. BtF

Long war had ended, The. Next War, The. Sir Osbert Sitwell. PoWW

Long was Society o'er-run. Hannah More. PEW *Fr.* Bas Bleu; Or, Conversation, The.

Long was the night of error, nor dispelled. William Mason. OBGa *Fr.* English Garden, The.

Long Way After Ronsard, A. James Simmons. PBCIP

Long way from the whorehouse. Solo: The Good Blues. Dolores Kendrick. FFC

Long white banners flutter on the breeze, The. White Banners. Söng [*or* Sung] Sammun. WoPoe, *tr. by* Jean S. Grigsby

Long White Seam, The. Jean Ingelow. OxBEV

Long Wind, the Dawn Wind. Ezra Pound. APT-1

Long winter, but in every snow, A. Why I'm Different in Wyoming. Suellen Wedmore. RWB

Long Woman Bathing, The. Maurice Kilwein Guevara. TouFir

Long years ago, at fifteen, maybe less. Learning. Juan Chi. CCL1, *tr. by* Graeme Wilson

Long years have passed since first a merry child. To One Who Sleepeth. Mary E. Tucker. CBWP-1

Long-ago, still guiltless generations, The. New Stars, The. Martinus Nijhoff. WoPoe, *tr. by* Raphael Rudnik

Long-Barrow Princess 2. Elizaveta Kuzmina-Karavayeva. ARWW, *tr. by* Catriona Kelly

Long-Distance Call to Gregg, Who Lived with AIDS as Long as He Could. Alfred Corn. WiU

Long[e] love that in my thought do[e]th [*or* I] harbour [*or* harber *or* harbar], The. Petrarch. NPeEn *Fr.* Sonnets to Laura.

Longer. Gertrude Stein. MotU *Fr.* Book Concluding with As A Wife Has a Cow a Love Story, A.

Longer we are together, The. Ripening. Wendell Berry. RaBo

Longest train I ever saw, The. In the Pines. Bill Monroe. GM

Long-expected one and twenty. Short Song of Congratulation, A [*or* To a Young Heir]. Samuel Johnson. NAEL-6v1; NPeEn; OBCoV; OBSV; OxAEP-1; OxBEV; TFi; WoPoe

Longfellow [*with music*]. Henrietta Cordelia Ray. CBWP-3

Longfellow's Visit to Venice. Sir John Betjeman. OBCoV

Long-Felt Desires. Louise Labé. WoPoe, *tr. by* Annie Finch

Long-felt desires, hopes as long as vain. Long-Felt Desires. Louise Labé. WoPoe, *tr. by* Annie Finch

Long-haired preachers come out every [*or* ev'ry] night. Preacher and the Slave, The. Joe Hill. APT-1

Longing. Matthew Arnold. SoSe-8

Longing: "It wasn't just about sex, but about." Rane Arroyo. BeDoSh

Longing. Ina Coolbrith. SWaP

Longing. Paul Laurence Dunbar. ErotSp

Longing. George Herbert. FSCP; UV

Longing. Li Po. CCL1, *tr. by* Arthur Cooper

Longing. Thomas McGrath. BodElec

Longing. Femi Osofisan. NAfrP

Longing, A. Abburi Ramakrishna Rao. HotL, *tr. by* V. Narayana Rao and David Shulman

Longing, a Documentary. Anne Carson. BAP-01

Longing achieves nothing. Gamelia. Susan M. Whitmore. AmPoNex

Longing for a Man Faraway. Jaewol Kyunghun. BecRai, *tr. by* Kim Daljin, Kim Won-Chung and Christopher Merrill

Longing for Death. "Novalis." WoPoe *Fr.* Hymns to the Night.

Longing for Eternal Life, The. Liz Rosenberg. PBCAP

Longing for His Son, Furuhi. Yamanoé no Okura. WoPoe, *tr. by* Helen Craig McCullough

Longing for Jail, A. Edvard Kocbek. PoSu, *tr. by* Michael Scammell and Veno Taufer

Longing for My Hometown. Yujŏng. BecRai, *tr. by* Kim Daljin, Kim Won-Chung and Christopher Merrill

Longing for Someone. Li Po. CrYelRi; ErotSp, *tr. by* Sam Hamill

Longing for someone in Ch'ang-an. Longing for Someone. Li Po. CrYelRi; ErotSp, *tr. by* Sam Hamill

Longing for the plum blossoms. Basho. EMJL, *tr. by* Haruo Shirane

Longing for the sun on flat roofs, A. Art of Poetry, The. Jaime Gil de Biedma. RaW, *tr. by* Timothy Baland

Longing, I watch out the open window. Song. Tzu Yeh. CrYelRi, *tr. by* Sam Hamill

Longing to Return: A Lament. Shi Chong. CCL1, *tr. by* Hellmut Wilhelm

Longingly homeward the crane out of regions afar is returning. Szondi. Ferenc Kölcsey. IQMS, *tr. by* Watson Kirkconnell

Long-Legged Fly. William Butler Yeats. NAEL-6v2; NAEL-7v2; NAMCP V.1; NoAM; NoP-4; NoP-5; NPeEn; WaAnP

Longliner at Sunset. Enos D. Watts. Coast

Long-Man. Grace Nichols. Oth

Longobards, The. Zbigniew Herbert. PoSu, *tr. by* Czeslaw Milosz

Longon lights are far abeam, The. Old Australian Ways. Andrew Barton Paterson. NOBAu

Long-unlooked-for mansions of our tribe. (LL) Geoffrey Hill. NAMCP V.2; NoAM *Fr.* Mercian Hymns.

Longview, Texas. Cyd Adams. TiP2

Lonnie up and moved away. Teed Off. John Nelson. GeoH

Loo! loo! Lulu! lulu! Loo! loo! Loot! loot! Rudyard Kipling. UV *Fr.* Loot.

Look. Sarah Messer. LegDan

Look. Belle Waring. ExTi

Look, a man is flying and. Svetlana Kekova. CRWP, *tr. by* Ruth Fainlight

Look, a mirage, father and a strange, a strange. Horizon. David Emrys James. WoPoe, *tr. by* Anthony Conran

Look after in the street. (LL) Martha Blake. Austin Clarke. ModIr; OxBEV

Look again. . .the fence glistening in overcast light, the grass at its brightest. Images of no one. Of one's own family, burying itself. Vigil, The. Ralph Angel. MAAN

Look, ah, dry / streets, still. Indian Suffering. Joseph Ceravolo. NYP2

Look, all those pockes of mine. Pockets. Ernst Jandl. GTCP, *tr. by* Michael Hamburger

Look, among the boughs. Those stars are men. Star-Tribes, The. *Aborigine Oral Tradition*. NOBAu, *tr. by* Fred Biggs

Look and hold your breath. Vermeer's Paint. Bobi Jones. ATSWP, *tr. by* Robert Minhinnick

Look and remember. Look upon this sky. Travelogue for Exiles. Karl Shapiro. MoAmPo

Look and See. Mary Oliver. BeAl

Look Around. Brian Henry. IIR

Look as they rise, rise. Song of the Pleiades. *Pawnee Oral Tradition*. TCAPo

Look at all these waves. Mahendranāth Bhattācārya. SinGod, *tr. by* Rachel Fell McDermott

Look at him there in his stovepipe hat. American Primitive. William Jay Smith. MoAmPo; RaBo

Look at how upset you've got me. *Unknown*. PriapPo *Fr.* Priapus Poems, The.

Look at it, the season's shifting. On Opening. Mark Wunderlich. NAPBL

Look at Jonah embarking from Joppa, deterred by. Tom Fool at Jamaica. Marianne Moore. APT-1

Look at Me. Kim Ly Bui-Burton. PasH

Look at me / I'm as helpless as a kitten up a tree. Misty. Johnny Burke. ReLy

Look at me. I'm standing on a deck. Trying to Raise the Dead. Dorianne Laux. RoV

Look at me now, mother. Amanda Dalton. NeBl *Fr.* Room of Leaves.

Look at my knees. I Wonder What It Feels Like to Be Drowned? Robert Graves. MoBrPo

Look at Peter: sad and glum. Young Pete. Mihály Vörösmarty. IQMS, *tr. by* Yakov Hornstein

Look at that girl in blouse and patterned skirt. Deception. Kim Sujang. WoPoe, *tr. by* Kevin O'Rourke

Look at the bears. Berne. Bryan Martin Davies. BBMWP, *tr. by* Elin ap Hywel

Look at the faces of these sleeping ones. For the Fighters—A Lament. Ayin Tur-Malka. NRoS, *tr. by* Esther Raizen

Look at the ripe wheat. Grainfield. Ibn 'Iyad. WoPoe, *tr. by* Cola Franzen

Look at the sky: two doves are chasing. Impossible Tasks. *Vietnamese Oral Tradition*. CaDao, *tr. by* John Balaban

Look at the stars! look, look up at the skies! Starlight Night, The. Gerard Manley Hopkins. MoBrPo; NAEL-6v2; NAEL-7v2

Look at the valleys down there in the darkness. Angry Summer 20, The. Idris Davies. TCAWP

Look at them. / Asleep, with a country village air. Soldiers Sleep, The. Rafael Alberti. RaW, *tr. by* Rachel Benson

Look at These. Helen Farish. BeAl

Look at this Champagne factory. New Guide, A. Kenneth Koch. BodElec

Look at this keepsake. Lady Kasa. ArkPo, *tr. by* Edwin A. Cranston

Look at yourself. Glad to Be Unhappy. Lorenz Hart. ReLy

Look away! Look away! Look away! Dixie Land. (LL)   Dixie [*or* Dixie's Land].   Daniel Decatur Emmett.   APN-1; CBCWP; TCAPo

Look, Bach, I'm sorry to switch you off.   Radio 3.   Brian M. Waltham.   RWPCtW

Look Back into the Future.   Andrey Andreievich Voznesensky.   PFTM-2, *tr. by* Anselm Hollo

Look back with longing eyes and know that I will follow.   Flight, The.   Sara Teasdale.   LW

Look backward on the days of yore.   John Clare.   NPBRoP *Fr.* Lamentations of Round-Oak Waters.

Look, child, I should have mentioned this before.   Mother to Son.   Jenny Factor.   PoChi

Look closely at the letters. Can you see.   Body [*or* B o d y].   James Merrill.   CAP-8; NAMCP V.2; OxBoAm

Look, dear daughter.   Mother's Feet.   Kim Sŭnghŭi.   EcSo, *tr. by* K. Kim Richards and Steffen Richards

Look[e], Delia, how we[e] [e]steem[e] the half-blown[e] rose.   Samuel Daniel.   NoP-4; NoSic *Fr.* Sonnets to Delia.

Look! Do all the ripples move.   Ripples.   Ko Un.   WhBo

Look down. Heavier now. Onus of observable spectrums.   Fait Accompli.   Anne Waldman.   BodElec

Look First at the Air and Its Black Element Which Never Stops.   Roberto Juarroz.   TCLAP, *tr. by* W. S. Merwin

Look first at the air and its black element which never stops.   Look First at the Air and Its Black Element Which Never Stops.   Roberto Juarroz.   TCLAP, *tr. by* W. S. Merwin

Look, five blue eggs are gleaming there!   William Wordsworth.   NPBRoP

Look for color everywhere. (LL)   Today's News.   Elizabeth Alexander.   InTrad; ISC; OxAAAP

Look for the address.   Survival 1.   Chiqui Vicioso.   TANSG, *tr. by* Emma Jane Robinett

Look for the Silver Lining.   B. G. DeSylva.   ReLy; TCAPo

Look for You Yesterday, Here You Come Today.   Imamu Amiri Baraka.   SSLK

Look for your other half.   Antonio Machado Ruiz.   RaBo *Fr.* Moral Proverbs and Folk Songs.

Look hard at the world, they said.   What I Remember the Writers Telling Me When I Was Young.   William Meredith.   PoDa

Look he trusts again It's good.   Warning.   Tadeusz Rózewicz.   PoSu, *tr. by* Magnus F. Krynski

Look Here.   Pamela Alexander.   ExTi

Look here.   Rāmprasād Sen.   SinGod, *tr. by* Rachel Fell McDermott

Look here Boy.   Scout.   Wendell Ricketts.   BRtP

Look here, Petah! whut's dis here.   Examination, The.   Priscilla Jane Thompson.   CBWP-2

Look here, upon this picture, and on this.   William Shakespeare.   OxAEP-1 *Fr.* Hamlet.

Look, here's another bread-crumb for your piping.   To a Sparrow.   T. E. Nicholas.   BBMWP, *tr. by* Joseph P. Clancy

Look how evening descends and around us the barbed-wire-hemmed, wild.   Miklós Radnóti.   AF

Look how handsome I am.   Hymn of the Patriotic War Veterans.   Benjamin Péret.   AF, *tr. by* Keith Hollaman

Look How Rich We are Together.   Micere Githae Mugo.   HAWP

Look how the faithful struggle with the body.   Deposition, The.   Colette Bryce.   MoWP

Look how the lark soars upward and is gone.   False Poets and True.   Thomas Hood.   CenSon; NPBRoP

Look, how the rain fallen through the night.   Invitation au Voyage 2.   John Wieners.   AHA

Look how the table's becoming.   Trompe l'oeil.   Tracy Ryan.   NeBl

Look how they love themselves.   Sunworshippers.   Cathy Song.   NAMCP V.2

Look how we're wedded.   New Song of Solomon.   Cyrus Cassells.   WiU

Look how yon lecher's legs are worn away.   Epigram.   John Taylor.   NOSC

Look, I don't speak the language.   Message About the Times.   Remco Campert.   TuT, *tr. by* Theo Dorgan

Look, I don't speak the language.   Sign of the Times.   Remco Campert.   TuT, *tr. by* Desmond Egan

Look / I was lifted up.   Thomas Kinsella.   ModIr *Fr.* One.

Look, I'm not singing about soup.   Song about Soup, A.   Elin ap Hywel.   ATSWP, *tr. by* Robert Minhinnick

Look in my face; my name is Might-have-been.   Dante Gabriel Rossetti.   BrAP; GSo; NAEL-6v2; NAEL-7v2; NoP-4 *Fr.* House of Life, The.

Look in the dark alcove under the stairs.   Under the Stairs.   Frank Ormsby.   PBCIP

Look in thy glass, and tell the face thou viewest.   William Shakespeare.   NAEL-6v1; NAEL-7v1; NoP-4; NoP-5 *Fr.* Sonnets.

Look in thy glass and tell the face thou viewest.   Ellen McGrath Smith.   IaFF *Fr.* Shaken.

Look into thought and say what thou dost see.   Diving.   Charlotte Brontë.   PEW

Look it up.   There Is No Word for Sex in Taglog.   Noel Mateo.   ReBoTo

"Look! It's a wedding!" At the ice cream shop's.   What Do Women Want?   Mary Jo Salter.   FFC; RA

Look, Jane, look! Look at the dog! See him run! (LL)   Reading Scheme.   Wendy Cope.   MakPoe; WaAnP

Look, life has been constructed this way to make sure.   Paavo Haavikko.   WoPoe *Fr.* Fifteen Epigrams in Praise of the Tyrant.

Look. Listen. They are lighting.   Kenneth Rexroth.   CalPo *Fr.* Air and Angels.

Look, look at yourself in the mirror.   Glance.   Belkis Cuza Malé.   TANSG, *tr. by* Pamela Carmell

Look! My snail-shell hut.   Yun Sŏndo.   CATKP *Fr.* Angler's Calendar, The.

Look. New sprouts push through the fields.   Prayer on the Threshold of Tomorrow.   Vahan Tekeyan.   AF, *tr. by* Diana Der Hovanessian and Marzbed Margossian

Look, No Hands.   Pearse Hutchinson.   PBCIP

Look north if you like:.   Map Reading.   Raymond Garlick.   AngWePo

Look not in my eyes, for fear.   A. E. Housman.   CAGL *Fr.* Shropshire Lad, A.

Look not thou on beauty's charming.   Sir Walter Scott.   NAEL-6v2; NPeEn; OBEV; OxAEP-2; OxBEV; WoPoe *Fr.* Bride of Lammermoor, The.

Look, / O heartless ones.   We Have Even Lost our Tongues!   Ifi Amadiume.   HAWP

Look of day with last night's rid of moths, The. (LL)   Nothing So Far.   Laura Riding Jackson.   APT-2; ColAP

Look of love alarms, The.   William Blake.   WoPoe *Fr.* Several Questions Answered.

Look of shock on an old friend's face after years of not meeting, The.   Karl Shapiro.   BodElec *Fr.* Bourgeois Poet, The.

Look of thee, what is it like, The.   Emily Dickinson.   InvLi

Look on that form, once fit for the sculptor!   Working and Waiting.   Adah Isaacs Menken.   CBWP-1

Look on these waters, with how soft a kiss.   Aestuary, An.   George Croly.   NOBRP

Look once more ere we leave this specular Mount.   John Milton.   NOSC *Fr.* Paradise Regained [*or* Regain'd].

Look one way and the sun is going down.   Mockingbird, The.   Randall Jarrell.   OWoS

Look, our Spaniard's yawning.   Antonio Machado Ruiz.   STV

Look out how you use proud words.   Primer Lesson.   Carl Sandburg.   MoAmPo

Look out, Slim, these girls are trouble.   Bacchae, The.   Michael Donaghy.   NeBrP

Look out upon the stars, my love.   Serenade.   Edward Coote Pinkney.   APN-1

Look: rat has skin.   Rat, The.   *Unknown.*   WoPoe, *tr. by* John S. Major

Look round, brown moon, brown bird, as you rise to fly.   God is Good. It Is a Beautiful Night.   Wallace Stevens.   APT-1; SAmP

Look round: You see a little supper room.   De Cœnatione Micae.   Martial.   RomPo, *tr. by* Robert Louis Stevenson

Look! See what Vanity Fair says about the new Waldorf-Astoria: "All the luxuries of private home."   Come to the Waldorf-Astoria.   Langston Hughes.   NAAPv.2

Look! she said you can see.   Kris Hemensley.   BMAP *Fr.* Mile from Poetry, A.

Look skywards, but not always.   Stride On.   Iswar Ballav.   SonAtl, *tr. by* Binil Aryal, Sunita Khadgi, Pallav Ranjan, Phoebe Ravenhall and Karuna Shashi

Look sour, and hum a tune—as you may now. (LL)   Epistle to Miss [*or* Miss Teresa] Blount, on Her Leaving the Town after the Coronation.   Alexander Pope.   NAEL-6v1; NAEL-7v1; NoP-4; NoP-5

Look, stranger, on this island now.   On This Island.   W. H. Auden.   HarvBoo; NAEL-6v2; NAEL-7v2; NAMCP V.1; OxBEV

Look that is that uninvited.   Vasco [*or* Vasko] Popa.   PoSu *Fr.* Far Within Us.

Look, The.   Sara Teasdale.   APT-1; LW

Look! The air shudders when you breathe it in.   Paul Engle.   OxBSo

Look the builders of ruins are working.   November 1936.   Paul Éluard.   AF, *tr. by* Gilbert Bowen

Look. The land ends up.   Some Grand River Blues.   Daniel David Moses.   HATNAP

Look: the lute sounds in the girl's arms.   Lute, The.   Judah Al-Harizi.   BLT, *tr. by* T. Carmi

"Look," the ocean said (it was tumbled, like our sheets), "look in my eyes." (LL)   Crystal Lithium, The.   James Schuyler.   PmAP; VCAP

Look: the sun has spread its wings.   Sun, The.   Judah Al-Harizi.   BLT, *tr. by* T. Carmi

Look, the trees / are turning / their own bodies.   In Blackwater Woods.   Mary Oliver.   CAP-8; NAAL-5

Look there at the star!   Shepherd's Song at Christmas.   Langston Hughes.   ChrPo

Look, there goes the young lady across the street.   Peerless Lady, The.   Wang Wei.   NDACCP, *tr. by* William Carlos Williams

Look there! What a wheaten.   Hill Field, The.   Donald Davie.   NPeEn

Look, this is a high-class house—polished.   Countess P———'s Advice for New Girls.   Natasha Trethewey.   LegDan

Look, this string of words. So Be It. Ruth Stone. ExTi

Look: / three sweet blue riot policemen. This is not a riot policeman. Karen Press. TSAP

Look to the Mountain. Simon J. Ortiz. PoCoUp

Look to your words, old man. Good Grey Poet, The. Theodore Weiss. ViWalt

Look up, and swear by the slain of the War that you'll never forget! (LL) Aftermath. Siegfried Sassoon. BLPJKO; MoBrPo; PoWW

Look up, dear one, nor be cast down. Truth. Josephine D. Henderson Heard. CBWP-4

Look up . . . / From bleakening hills. Snow. Adelaide Crapsey. APT-1

Look upon me. Nag Hammadi Library. HW Fr. Thunder, The: Perfect Mind.

Look wha' happen las' week at de Oval! Edward Kamau Brathwaite. FaBoVe Fr. Rites.

Look what I did for you. (LL) Emptying Town. Nick Flynn. AmPoNex; LegDan; NAPBL

Look what your love has done to me. Unknown. SLW, tr. by Marjolijn De Jager, Sayd Bahodin Majrouh and André Velter

Look what's come to light. Mikhail Aizenberg. ItGoST, tr. by J. Kates

Look where she sits in languid loveliness. On a Beautiful Woman. Mary Russell Mitford. CenSon

Look where the Great Bear glows: he beats his son to teach him silence. Winegrower, The. Milán Füst. IQMS, tr. by Jess Perlman

Look, where the lawn's pocket lolls. Crocus (after snow), The. Patrick Warner. Coast

Look within / these words to the rough. Red Reed. Bruce Beasley. AmAlph

Look, ye saints! The sight is glorious. Second Advent, The. Thomas Kelly. SacPr

Looka here. (LL) Song No. 3: "Cain't nobody tell me any different." Sonia Sanchez. FFC; NOxBChV

Look-Alike, The. Valerie Gillies. EdScPo

Look'd up in perfect silence at the stars. (LL) When I Heard the Learn'd Astronomer. Walt Whitman. BrAP; BRP; ChAP; ColAP; MoAmPo; NAAL-3; NAAL-5; NAAPv.1; NoP-4; NoP-5; OxBoAm; PoPoPo; SoSe-8; WaAnP; WeW-3

Look[e] Home. Robert Southwell. NoSic

Looke how the woods, where enterlaced trees. Bible, O.T. OBVE

Looked after him thro' happy tears. (LL) Athenian Garden, An. Trumbull Stickney. APN-2; NoP-4; NoP-5

Lookin Good. StacyLynn. BtF

Looking. Robert Kelly. FTOS

Looking at a Portrait Sculpture of the Indian Holy Man, Asanga, (Japanese, Mujaku, Flowered about 350 C.E.—Stands in the Kofukuji Treasure Hall of Nara Japan. C. Robert Lloyd. ICANM

Looking at an Old Mirror. Olav H. Hauge. WED, tr. by Robert Bly

Looking at Childhood. Andrée Chédid. YaTCFP, tr. by Rosemary Lloyd

Looking at Her. Alan Brownjohn. OxBSo

Looking at Mount T'ai. Tu Fu [or Du Fu]. CrYelRi, tr. by Sam Hamill

Looking at Mount T'ai-Shan. Tu Fu [or Du Fu]. ChinPo, tr. by Ye Weilian [or Yeh Wei-lien or Wai-lim Yip]

Looking at My Knife-Hilt, a Song. Liu Yu Hsi. CCL1, tr. by Daniel Bryant

Looking at New-Fallen Snow from a Train. Robert Bly. GM

Looking at Stone Drum Mountain. Yu Ch'an. CCL1, tr. by John Frodsham

Looking at the Moon. Vivian Lamarque. CItWP, tr. by Cinzia Sartini Blum and Lara Trubowitz

Looking at the Morning Rain. Hsieh T'iao. CCL1, tr. by John Frodsham

Looking at the photograph is somehow not. At the Beach. Elizabeth Alexander. FuFl

Looking at the post love world. Immediate Content Recognition. Diane Ward. PmAP

Looking at Winter Trees. Pak Chaesam. CAMKP, tr. by David R. McCann and Jiwon Shin

Looking at you. Ashes in Oxford. Francisco Brines. RaW, tr. by Hardie St. Martin

Looking Back. Joanna Kadi. PoArWo

Looking back. Walking Down a Mountain. Ko Un. WhBo

Looking back. Boy, The. David Trinidad. BeDoSh

Looking Back at My Shadow. Chunghur Hyujung. BecRai, tr. by Kim Daljin, Kim Won-Chung and Christopher Merrill

Looking back, I blame translation. Interview with the Poet. Gwyneth Lewis. ATSWP, tr. by Robert Minhinnick

Looking back upon. Kagawa Kageki. EMJL, tr. by Haruo Shirane

Looking Before and After [with music]. Carter Revard. HATNAP

Looking by chance in at the open window. Foreboding, The. Robert Graves. PoA 2002

Looking Deep. Magdalena Gomez. PueRic

Looking down into my father's. Good Night, Willie Lee, I'll See You in the Morning. Alice Walker. InoFa; ISC; WeW-3

Looking down on the open-cast pit. Truant, A. Mike Jenkins. TCAWP

Looking for a Recluse but Failing to Find Him [with music]. Chia Tao. ColAnChi, tr. by Burton Watson

Looking for Another Version. Kathleen Aguero. PfS

Looking for binder-twine. Or so she says. (LL) Melon Grower, The. Alice Oswald. MFPA; MoWP

Looking for Choctaw. Yusef Komunyakaa. LPSFW

Looking for distinctive stones, I found the dead otter. One Morning. Eamon Grennan. P180

Looking for Indians. Cheryl Savageau. TWW

Looking for Master Yung Ts'un near His Hermitage. Li Po. CrYelRi, tr. by Sam Hamill

Looking for Mother. Dorothy Molloy. NIrP

Looking for Poetry. Carlos Drummond de Andrade. ChAP, tr. by Mark Strand

Looking for 78's in the 40's. Hugh Macpherson. EdScPo

Looking for something I had lost. 1st Untitled Poem. Pedro Juan Pietri. PueRic

Looking for something in the Sunday paper. Sunday News, The. Dana Gioia. WeW-3

Looking for the Recluse and Not Finding Him. Chia Tao. CCL1, tr. by Stephen Owen

Looking for Trouble. Roque Dalton. TCLAP, tr. by Richard Schaaf

Looking for W.E.B. Kate Rushin. PfS

Looking for you and me, my dear, looking for you and me. (LL) W. H. Auden. AmFaPo; BeAl; HP; OxAEP-2 Fr. Ten Songs.

Looking for your light. For the Lord of Caves. Allama Prabhu. PFTM-1

Looking Forward. Robert Louis Stevenson. NBLV

Looking Glass, The. Rudyard Kipling. OBMV

Looking Homeward from a Mountain Pass. Sin Saimdang, Lady. CATKP, tr. by Chi-gyu Kim [or Kim Chonggil]

Looking in the Lake. Po Chü-i. TAL

Looking in the mirror part of the future appears. Dancing There. Thomas Meyer. AnSo

Looking into a Tide Pool [with music]. Robert Bly. CAP-8

Looking into History. Richard Wilbur. VCAP

Looking into my daughter's eyes I read. For My Daughter. Weldon Kees. OxBoAm; OxBSo; WaAnP

Looking into the blue. Horizon Blues. David Henderson. GT

Looking North. Pamela Gillilan. Prnts

Looking now one way, now the other. (LL) Milk. Maurice Riordan. ModIr; NIrP

Looking out from death you will always see. Looking Out from Death. Duo Duo. AF; PML, tr. by Gregory Lee and Fred Moramarco

Looking Out in All Directions. Vietnamese Oral Tradition. CaDao, tr. by John Balaban

Looking Out to Sea Again on the Uptown Express. Sanford Fraser. UrbNat

Looking Outside the Cabin Window, I Remember a Line by Li Po. Charles Wright. PfSP

Looking over my shoulder. Allen Ginsberg. NIL-7

Looking Through a French Photographer's Portrayal of Rajasthan with Extensive Use of Orange Filters. Sujata Bhatt. MoWP

Looking through the window. Unknown. WhBo

9 (Looking through the Window: Psalm 121). Jacqueline Osherow. PoDa Fr. Scattered Psalms.

Looking thru the commercial. Loneliness, A. Haki R. Madhubuti. GT

Looking Thru Those Eyeholes. Russell Soaba. PML

Looking toward the west where the sun sinks away. In Praise of a Gold and Silver Painted Scene of the Buddha Manifestation in the Pure Land of the West, with a Preface. Li Po. CCL1; WoPoe, tr. by Elling O. Eide

Looking Up. Sujata Bhatt. EmeKit

Looking up at the sky. Looking Out in All Directions. Vietnamese Oral Tradition. CaDao, tr. by John Balaban

Looking up at the stars, I know quite well. More Loving One, The. W. H. Auden. ItP; OxBoAm

Looking up: blue sky's end. Orchid Pavilion. Wang Hsi-chih. ChinPo, tr. by Ye Weilian [or Yeh Wei-lien or Wai-lim Yip]

Looking Up from Aeroplanes. W. N. Herbert. EdScPo

Looking up into Leviathan. Shylock. J. B. Mulligan. IaFF

Looking Up My Balance. Anselm Berrigan. HeMarv

Looking Way Off. A. R. Ammons. PfSP

Looking West from Laguna Beach at Night. Charles Wright. MakPoe

Looking-Glass for Men and Maids, A. Unknown. BASC

Look—on the topmost branches of the world. Sunday Evening in the Common. John Hall Wheelock. MoAmPo

Looks, as dusk is falling, like a gun. (LL) Man in the Blue Smock, The. Günter Eich. GTCP; PML, tr. by Reinhold Grimm

Looks at me and be color. Lion Tamer Remembers, The. Tristan Tzara. YaTCFP, tr. by Mary Ann Caws

Looks like what drives me crazy. Evil. Langston Hughes. APT-2

Looks that weren't. Homage to a Bellhop. Yusef Komunyakaa. BodElec

Looks thy fair face and makes it still. (LL) Alfred Tennyson. NAEL-6v2; NAEL-7v2; WaAnP Fr. In Memoriam A. H. H.

Look—the moon is a perfect circle. II:II. Geoffrey Nutter. IIR

Look—up and tangle. Life Model. Maggie Hannan. NeBl

Looky here, America. Beaumont to Detroit: 1943. Langston Hughes. AmWaPo

Loom: Burnt Woods Cemetery, Western Bay, Newfoundland. Michael Crummey. Coast

Loom importunes, The. Yi Kyubo. CATKP Fr. Farmhouse: Three Poems.

Loom of Time, The. Unknown. ITBLP

Looming and almost molten and slowly moving its gold down hill. Sirmione. James Wright. BodElec

Looming bastion fringed with fire, A. (LL) Alfred Tennyson. NAEL-6v2; NAEL-7v2; NAWM-7v2 Fr. In Memoriam A. H. H.

Looming up. Strange Peak. Muso Soseki. EaWin, tr. by W. S. Merwin

Loon, A. Frances Densmore. APT-1 Fr. Chippewa Music.

Loon, The. Michael S. Harper. ESEAA

Loon Call, A. Richard Eberhart. ColAP

Loon house woke up, The. That Evening Pierre Insisted That I Had Two Roast Pigeons at Dinner. Lee Harwood. AHA

Loon / I thought it was, A. My Love Has Departed. Chippewa Oral Tradition. NAAL-5; OBVE, tr. by Frances Densmore

Loon upon the Lake, The. Ojibwa Oral Tradition. APN-2; OWoS, tr. by Charles Fenno Hoffman

Loons Mating. David Wagoner. BLT

Loop. Fiona Tinwei Lam. IFF

Loop Canal, The. Nikolai Alekseievich Zabolotsky. TCRusP, tr. by Denis Johnson and Kathy Lewis

Loop, Fleck, Sound and So On. Marianne Vitale. HeMarv

Looping the Loop. Mark Ford. NeBrP

Loops on bold fonts now form lots of words for books. Christian Bök. OpeFie Fr. Chapter O.

Loop-the-Loop in Prospect Park (1905). Gerry Gomez Pearlberg. WiU

Loopy Dupes. Andrew Crozier. Oth

Loose Change. Andrew Hudgins. UpMys

Loose Change. Conor O'Callaghan.

  5 The Bull. NIrP

  20 The Horse. NIrP

  1 The Peacock. NIrP

  10 The Salmon. NIrP

  100 The Stag. NIrP

Loose hands and part: I am not she you sought. Renunciation. Lizette Woodworth Reese. TCAPo

Loose heady laughter shook the humid night. Jasbo Brown. DuBose Heyward. SeSe

Loose Hinge. Carl Phillips. FaoP

Loose in the brush pines. Tango. Ntozake Shange. GT

Loose in the world. And out of proportion. (LL) Wound Man, The. Sinéad Morrissey. BeAl; NIrP

Loose process moving, A. Extraction. Anthony Barnett. OnScMo

Loose Shoes. Charles Bernstein. FTOS

Loose to the wind her golden tresses streamed. Petrarch. CenSon; RWP Fr. Sonnets to Laura.

Loose Woman. X. J. Kennedy. WeW-3

Loose Women. Sandra Cisneros. IllVoic

Loosed from Winter's prison. Unknown. TAL

Loosening Water. Luis Rosales. RaW, tr. by Ralph Nelson and Rita García Nelson

Loosing their feverish clutch. His Friend's Last Battle. Theodore Nicholl. AngWePo

Loot. Rudyard Kipling.

  "Loo! loo! Lulu! lulu! Loo! loo! Loot! loot!" UV

Loot the legions sent embraced these three, The. Victor, The. Lajos Áprily. IQMS, tr. by Watson Kirkconnell

Looters, The. Robert Minhinnick. TCAWP

Loo-wit. Wendy Rose. HATNAP

Loping silhouettes ahead of me. In Cold February Twilight. Frederic William Kirchner. ArBi

Loppèd tree in time may grow again [or againe or agayne], The. Times [or Tymes] Go[e] By Turn[e]s. Robert Southwell. ChIV-1; NoSic

Lopped tree in time may grow again, The. Times Go by Turns. Richard Verstegan. SacPr

Lop-sided from a shrapnel wound. Arthur. Geoffrey Adkins. FaBoWar

L'Orangerie. Frank Ormsby. ModIr Fr. Paris Honeymoon, A.

Lorca. Bob Kaufman. EGAG

Lorca Variations (XXVIII), The. Jerome Rothenberg. PFTM-2

Lord! Executioner of Flowers. Muhammad Al-Maghut. PFTM-2, tr. by May Jayyusi and Naomi Shihab Nye

Lord. Prayer for Marilyn Monroe. Ernesto Cardenal. TCLAP, tr. by Robert Pring-Mill

Lord. Troparion. Kassiane. WPoS, tr. by Liana Sakelliou

Lord. Awakening, The. Alejandra Pizarnik. TCLAP, tr. by Frank Graziano and María Rosa Fort

Lord, all I am and hope to be. Offering, An. Eloise Bibb. CBWP-4

Lord Apollo, who has never died, The. Many Are Called. Edwin Arlington Robinson. GI

Lord Arnold delicately sought to name. Edward Edwin Foot. VerBaPo Fr. Jane Hollybrand; or, Virtue Rewarded.

Lord, art thou at the table head above. Edward Taylor. ChIV-1; TCAPo Fr. Preparatory Meditations Before My Approach to the Lord's Supper.

Lord, at thy voice, my heart for fear hath trembled. Song of the Faithful, A. Michael Drayton. ChIV-1

Lord Barrenstock. Stevie Smith. NALW; NBLV; OBSV

Lord, bless us Hungarians. National Anthem. Ferenc Kölcsey. IQMS, tr. by Earl M. Herrick, Watson Kirkconnell and Adam Makkai

Lord Brain. Bruce Beasley. AmAlph

Lord, can a crumb of dust the earth outweigh. Edward Taylor. NAAL-3; NAAL-5; NAAPv.1; TCAPo Fr. Preparatory Meditations Before My Approach to the Lord's Supper.

Lord Chancellors were cheap as sprats. Gilbertian Cats. William Schwenck Gilbert. TriCat

Lord, come away! Hymn for Advent. Jeremy Taylor. SacPr

Lord, confound this surly sister. Curse, The. John Millington Synge. OBCoV

Lord De La Warr never saw this flat land. Delaware. David G. W. Scott. RWB

Lord Elderley, Lord Borrowmere, Lord Sickert and Lord Camp. Noël Coward. See Stately Homes of England, The.

Lord Elderley, Lord Borrowmere, Lord Sickert and Lord Camp. Stately Homes of England, The. Noël Coward. OBCoV

Lord feeds some of His prisoners better than others, The. Psalm. Reed Whittemore. GoPo

Lord Finchley [with music]. Joseph Hilaire Pierre Belloc. NBLV; NoAM; OxAEP-2

Lord Finchley tried to mend the Electric Light. Lord Finchley. Joseph Hilaire Pierre Belloc. NBLV; NoAM; OxAEP-2

Lord, forgive me if I do not look for you. Idyll. Henriqueta Lisboa. TCLAP, tr. by Hélcio Veiga Costa

Lord gie you chile de spirit. Gettin[g] de Spirit. Una Marson. MoWP

Lord, give me Love! give me the silent bliss. Love, Death, and Art. Agnes Mary Frances Robinson. VWP

Lord God of every race and every land. Prayer for Texas, A. Grace Noll Crowell. TiP2

Lord God of Heaven, who only are. Prayer of Nehemiah, The. George Wither. ChIV-1

Lord God said to Wu Yang, The. Summons of the Soul, The. Ch'u Yüan. WoPoe, tr. by David Hawkes

Lord God! this was a stone. Stone, The. Thomas Vaughan. OBWVE

Lord, Grant Us Calm. Christina Georgina Rossetti. SacPr

Lord Harry has written a novel. Novel of High Life, A. Thomas Haynes Bayly. OxAEP-2

Lord has shown me, The. Prayer in Four Verses. Pak Mogwŏl [or Mokwŏl]. WoPoe, tr. by Chi-gyu Kim [or Kim Chonggil]

Lord, have mercy on us! (LL) Thomas Nashe. HeIP-4; NoP-4; NoP-5; NoSic; NPeEn; OxBEV; TFi; TRP Fr. Summer's Last Will and Testament.

Lord Have Mercy rises up. Oh! Mercy Mercy Me! A Family Gathers to Marvin Gaye. Laura Soul Brown. FTtHH

Lord, Hear My Prayer. John Clare. BBASP; ChIV-1

Lord, hear my prayer when trouble glooms. Lord, Hear My Prayer. John Clare. BBASP; ChIV-1

Lord hear [or here] my prayer [or prayre] and let my cry[e] pass[e]. Bible, O.T. OBVE

Lord help me but my mind's a blank today, only a few words. Homage to the Word-Hoard. Joseph Stroud. TAPaP

Lord Heygate. Joseph Hilaire Pierre Belloc. OBCoV

Lord Hippo [with music]. Joseph Hilaire Pierre Belloc. NoAM

Lord, how can man preach thy eternal[l] word? Windows, The. George Herbert. BASC; NAEL-6v1; NAEL-7v1; NoP-4; NoP-5

Lord, how I wish he was judgin' yet. (LL) Unknown. CCL1; NDACCP Fr. Gan-tang [Translations].

Lord how many are my foes. Bible, O.T. OBVE

Lord I am here, O give me thy commission. (LL) To Christ. William Alabaster. NoSic; OxBSo

Lord, I can't preach like Dr. Martin Luther King Jr. or Jesse Jackson or turn a poetic phrase like Maya Angelou. I Care and I'm Willing to Serve. Marian Wright Edelman. TWF

Lord, I confesse, that Thou alone art able. To His Saviour. Robert Herrick. SacPr

Lord, / I dreamt it was the year 3001. Psalm for the Next Millennium. Jack Agüeros. PrTe

Lord, I have seen too much for one who sat. Lord, I Have Seen Too Much. Karl Shapiro. PWW2

Lord I know, and I know you know I know. Margin Prayer from an Ancient Psalter. Ian Duhig. EmeKit; NeBl

Lord I Sleep and I Sleep. David Shapiro. ChIV-1

Lord, I wish I were in Hallsboro, over by the tracks. Alligator Holes Down Along About Old Dock. A. R. Ammons. LPSFW

Lord, I'm done for: now Margot. Rondeau. Vincent Voiture. WoPoe, tr. by William Jay Smith.

Lord, I'm Just a worm. Bible, O.T. AHA Fr. Psalms [David Rosenberg Adaption].

Lord in the matter of your ninety-second element. To Whom it may concern. Judith Johnson Sherwin. YaYoPo

Lord is my herd, nae want sal fa' me, The. King James Version. See Lord is my shepherd; I shall not want, The.

Lord is my Shepherd, I have all I need, The. 23rd Psalm, The. Bobby McFerrin. HW

Lord is my shepherd, I shall not want, The. Bible, O.T. InvLi Fr. Psalms.

Lord is my shepherd; I shall not want, The. King James Version. BLPJKO; NAWM-5v1; NIL-7; NIP-4; TFi; WaAnP Fr. Psalms.

Lord: it is time. The summer was immense. Autumn Day. Rainer Maria Rilke. WoPoe, tr. by John Felsteiner

Lord let me all I can wild cherry. Photovoltaic. T. Begley and Olga Broumas. TAPaP

Lord let me suffer much. Prayer That Will Be Answered, A. Anna Kamienska. BLT

Lord Lord Lord caw caw caw Lord Lord Lord caw caw caw Lord. (LL) Kaddish. Allen Ginsberg. OxBoAm; PmAP

Lord Lucky [with music]. Joseph Hilaire Pierre Belloc. NBLV

Lord Lundy. Joseph Hilaire Pierre Belloc. OBSV

Lord Lundy from his earliest years. Lord Lundy. Joseph Hilaire Pierre Belloc. OBSV

Lord, make me an instrument of Thy [or Your] Peace. Prayer of St. Francis of Assisi for Peace. Saint Francis of Assisi. BLPJKO

Lord, make me coy and tender to offend. Unkindness. George Herbert. NOSC

Lord, Make Me More Patient. Unknown. SSUS

Lord, make me worthy of this number. To Anne Frank. Rosita Kalina. MirDau, tr. by Roberta Gordenstein

Lord, many times I am aweary quite. Lord, Many Times. Richard Chenevix Trench. SacPr

Lord, not you. Flickering Mind. Denise Levertov. UpMys

Lord of all worlds, let thanks and praise. John Quincy Adams. SacPr

Lord of Burleigh, The. Alfred Tennyson. STuOW

Lord of Gododdin will be praised in song, A. Aneirin. NePenScot Fr. Gododdin, The.

Lord of Heaven and Earth has made a feast, The. On a Feast. Francis Quarles. ChIV-2

Lord of Hosts, and God of Israel! Prayer of Hezekiah, The. George Wither. ChIV-1

Lord of the winds, I cry to Thee. Mary Elizabeth Coleridge. SacPr

Lord of the worlds. Viswanatha Satyanarayana. CFP Fr. Ramayana.

Lord of them that hurt his Saints, doth say, The. Mary Mollineux. EMWP, tr. by Henry Mollineux

Lord, / on 8th Street. Psalm for Distribution. Jack Agüeros. PrTe

Lord Orrery's Hector. Unknown. DiBP

Lord Quicksilver, god of erections, come down. To Hermes. Alfred Corn. CAGL; WiU

Lord Randal[l]. Unknown. CtM; HeIP-4; InoFa; NAEL-6v1; NAEL-7v1; NIL-7; NoP-4; NoP-5; NPeEn; OxBEV; PoPoPo; TFi; TRP; WaAnP; WeW-3

(Lord Rendal.) BrAP

Lord, receive my prayer / Sweet as incense smoke. Evening Prayer. Thomas Merton. ChIV-1

Lord, Remember Me! Unknown. APN-2

Lord, Remember Me. Unknown. SSUS

Lord Rendal. Unknown. See Lord Randal[l].

Lord said unto Jonah: "Rise, go down", The. Book of Jonah, The. Mihály Babits. IQMS, tr. by István Tótfalusi

Lord she's gone done left me done packed/up and split. Feeling Fucked/Up Up. Etheridge Knight. GT; PBCAP; RaBo

Lord speaks / this way, The. Isaiah: Chapter 66. David Rosenberg. ChIV-1

Lord Stanhope hit upon a novel plan. Thomas Baker. STuOW; VerBaPo Fr. Steam Engine; or, The Power of the Flame, The.

Lord Stanhope's Steamer. Thomas Baker. STuOW; VerBaPo Fr. Steam Engine; or, The Power of the Flame, The.

Lord summons Elijah-like, The. On Elijah's Chariot. Endre Ady. IQMS, tr. by Anton N. Nyerges

Lord, surely you took the position designed to infuriate. Strength. Helen Chasin. YaYoPo

Lord survives the rainbow of His will, The. (LL) Quaker Graveyard in Nantucket, The. Robert Lowell. ColAP; MakPoe; NAAL-5; NAMCP V.2; NoAM; NoP-5; VCAP; WaAnP

Lord, the Roman hyacinths are blooming in bowls and. Song for Simeon, A. T. S. Eliot. ChIV-2

(Lord, the Roman hyacinths are blooming in bowls.) GI

Lord, the snowful sky. Sailor's Carol. Charles Causley. OBCP

Lord, the time has come. The summer was immense. Day in October. Rainer Maria Rilke. WED, tr. by Robert Bly

Lord Thomas and Fair Annet. Unknown. NPeEn

Lord Thomas and Fair Annet. Lord Thomas and Fair Annet. Unknown. NPeEn

Lord, Thou hast crushed Thy tender ones, o'erthrown. Messina, 1908. Alice Thompson Meynell. SacPr

Lord, Thou hast given me a cell. Thanksgiving to God for His House, A. Robert Herrick. BASC; CavPo; NOSC

Lord thou hast told us that there be. God's Two Dwellings. Thomas Washbourne. SacPr

Lord to me a shepherd is, The. King James Version. See Lord is my shepherd; I shall not want, The.

Lord to me [or mee] a shepherd is, The. Unknown. TCAPo Fr. Bay Psalm Book, The.

Lord to your honour. Prayer to God. Esther Kello. EMWP

Lord took a staw at mankind, The. Deluge, The. William Dixon Cocker. EdScPo

Lord Ullin's Daughter. Thomas Campbell. NOBRP; NPBRoP

Lord Walter's Wife. Elizabeth Barrett Browning. NPeEn

Lord Wang / So virtuous he could commune with the spirits. Stele for Wang Ziqiao. Ts'ai Yung. CCL1, tr. by Donald Holzman

Lord wants me to go to Florida, The. Pentecost. Gwyneth Lewis. MFPA; NeBrP

Lord! what a busy [or busie], restles[s] thing. Pursuit[e], The. Henry Vaughan. AngWePo; NOSC; SacPr

Lord! what a goodly thing is want of shirts. John Cleveland. OBSV Fr. Rebel Scot, The.

Lord, what am I? A worm, dust, vapour, nothing! Anthem for the Cathedral of Exeter. Joseph Hall. SacPr

Lord, what are the sins. In a U-Haul North of Damascus. David Bottoms. ReTh

Lord, What is Man? Carl Rakosi. FTOS

Lord, what is man? why should he cost[e] thee [or you]. C[h]aritas Nimia; or, The Dear[e] Bargain. Richard Crashaw. NOSC

Lord, what these weders ar cold. Second Shepherd's Play, The. Unknown. NAEL-7v1

Lord, when I look at lovely things which pass. In the Fields. Charlotte Mew. MoBrPo; OxAEP-2

Lord, when the meadow has gone cold. Rooks, The. Arthur Rimbaud. FaBoWar, tr. by Norman Cameron

Lord, when the sense of Thy sweet grace. Song. Richard Crashaw. InvLi

Lord when the wise men came from Farr. Sidney Godolphin. See Hymn: "Lord, when the wise men came from far[r]."

Lord, when the wise men came from far[r]. Hymn. Sidney Godolphin. NPeEn; RSR; SacPr

Lord, when they kill me, let the job be thorough. Merthyr. Glyn Jones. AngWePo

Lord! when thou didst thy self undress. Incarnation and Passion, The. Henry Vaughan. SacPr

Lord, when will it be? Takahashi Mutsuo. PFTM-2 Fr. Self-Portraits.

Lord, while I sow earth or song. Harriet Tubman. Sam Cornish. OxAAAP

Lord, who createdst man in wealth and store. Easter Wings. George Herbert. AngWePo; BASC; BrAP; CABP; ChIV-1; FSCP; HeIP-4; MakPoe; NAEL-6v1; NAEL-7v1; NIL-7; NIP-4; NoP-4; NoP-5; NOSC; PBRV; PoPoPo; SacPr; TFi; TRP; WaAnP; WeW-3; WoPoe

Lord, who hast made me free. G. W. Briggs. SacPr

Lord Whoever, thank you for this air. Poem in Thanks. Thomas Lux. GoPo

Lord / whose face is this. Riddle. Gharib Nawaz. BBASP, tr. by Nasrollah Pourjavady and Peter Lamborn Wilson

Lord with glowing heart I'd praise thee. Francis Scott Key. SacPr

Lord with thine Altars Fire, mine Inward man. Edward Taylor. TCAPo Fr. Preparatory Meditations Before My Approach to the Lord's Supper.

Lord, with what care hast thou begirt us round! Sin (1). George Herbert. NoP-4; NoP-5; OxAEP-1; WaAnP

Lord, with what glory [or glorie] wast thou served [or serv'd] of old. Sion. George Herbert. ChIV-1

Lord, within thy fold I be.   Hymn.   Priscilla Jane Thompson.   CBWP-2

Lord, you are my lover.   How the Soul Speaks to God.   Mechthild von Magdeburg.   WPoS, *tr. by* Oliver Davies

Lord, you are our home.   David Rosenberg.   AHA *Fr.* Psalms [David Rosenberg Adaption].

Lord, You Have Ripped Away.   Antonio Machado Ruiz.   GI, *tr. by* Robert Bly

Lord, You may not recognize me.   Gift, The.   Louise Glück.   CFP; TaR

Lord / your chariot sped along.   Your Chariot.   Viswanatha Satyanarayana.   HotL, *tr. by* V. Narayana Rao

Lorde blesse the and kepe the, The,.   Bible, *O.T.*   OBVE

Lorde is my shepherde, The; therefore can I lack nothing.   King James Version.   *See* Lord is my shepherd; I shall not want, The.

Lording[e]s [*or* Lordynges]—quod he—in chirches whan I preche.   Geoffrey Chaucer.   NAEL-6v1; NAEL-7v1; WaAnP *Fr.* Canterbury Tales, The.

Lordly Hudson, The.   Paul Goodman.   APT-2; OxBoAm; PoCho

Lord's Arrival, The.   Endre Ady.   IQMS, *tr. by* Anton N. Nyerges

Lords, knights, and 'squires, the numerous band.   To a Child of Quality, Five Years Old, the Author Suppos'd Forty.   Matthew Prior.   OBEV; OxBEV

Lord's lost Him His mockingbird.   Mourning Poem for the Queen of Sunday.   Robert Earl Hayden.   InoFa; NAMCP V.2; NoAM; NoP-4; NoP-5; PoPoPo

Lord's my shepherd, I'll not want, The.   King James Version. *See* Lord is my shepherd; I shall not want, The.

Lord's name be praised, The.   Litanies of Julia Pastrana (1832-1860), The.   Thomas William Shapcott.   NOBAu

Lords of life, the lords of life, The.   Experience.   Ralph Waldo Emerson.   APN-1; TCAPo

Lord's Prayer.   Nicanor Parra.   GI, *tr. by* Miller Williams

Lord's Prayer, The.   Elizabeth Jennings.   MoWP

Lore.   Ronald Stuart Thomas.   BeAl; NoP-4; NoP-5

Lorena.   Lucille Clifton.   CAP-8

Lorenzo.   Letitia Elizabeth Landon.   RWP *Fr.* Improvisatrice, The.

Lorine, Lorine.   For Lorine Niedecker in Heaven.   Ralph J., Jr. Mills.   IllVoic

Lorne, Nova Scotia.   Geoffrey Cook.   Coast

Lorrayne / before you hit me with that object.   X Files, The: Bonnybridge, October '95.   Hugh McMillan.   EdScPo

Los árboles / Around here.   Los árboles son poetas / Trees Are Poets.   Francisco X. Alarcón.   GeoHom

Los árboles son poetas / Trees Are Poets.   Francisco X. Alarcón.   GeoHom

Los Amantes.   Richard Garcia.   TouFir

Los Angeles.   Nick Van Brunt.   FTtHH

Los Angeles.   James Harms.   GeoHom

Los Angeles after the Rain.   Dana Gioia.   UrbNat

Los Angeles Nocturne.   Xavier Villaurrutia.   TCLAP, *tr. by* Rachel Benson

Los Angeles, The Angels.   James Harms.   NeAmPo; PuP-23

Los Olivos.   Michael Lieberman.   BloBone

"Lose and love" is love's first art.   Song by the Shore, A.   Richard Hovey.   APN-2

Lose themselves eyes open. (LL)   Parable: "There was a saint once."   Carl Phillips.   AmAlph; CAP-8

Loser, The.   Adrienne Rich.   RACG

Losers.   Carl Sandburg.   MoAmPo; NoAM

Losing a Boat on the Brazos.   Walter McDonald.   TiP2

Losing a Language.   W. S. Merwin.   BeAl; EMP; NoP-4; NoP-5

Losing a Tooth.   Han Yü.   CCL1, *tr. by* Stephen Owen

Losing altitude, you can see below you the flames.   Death of Thomas Merton.   Harry Clifton.   PBCIP

Losing My Hair.   Dzvinia Orlowsky.   NevBe

Losing My Mind.   Stephen Sondheim.   ReLy

Losing My Sight.   Lisel Mueller.   ExTi

Losing Myself.   S. J. Marks.   BodElec

Losing myself in the swaying gray.   Ecologue.   Eugenio Montale.   WoPoe, *tr. by* William Arrowsmith

Losing Track.   Denise Levertov.   HeIP-4

Loss.   Judith Herzberg.   TuT, *tr. by* Joan McBreen

Loss.   C. K. Williams.   MakPoe

Loss and Recovery of the Hair, The.   Julio Cortázar.   MotU, *tr. by* Paul Blackburn

Loss is an unintentional decline in or disappearance of.   Definitions for Mendy.   David Antin.   APSN

Loss, my molester, at last patient be.   Mary Sidney Wroth, Countess of Montgomery.   PEW

Loss of Control.   Pat Mora.   FiBr

Loss of My Twins, The.   U Sam Oeur.   PML, *tr. by* Ken McCullough

Loss of something ever felt I, A.   Emily Dickinson.   ChIV-2; NALW; NCAP

Loss of the Royal George.   William Cowper.   OxAEP-1

Loss[e] in Delay[e].   Robert Southwell.   NoSic

Losses.   Randall Jarrell.   AmFaPo; AmWaPo; BrAP; OtW; PoA 2002

Losses.   Yusef Komunyakaa.   OxAAAP

Lost.   James Godden.   OBSP

Lost.   Bruce A. Jacobs.   BtF

Lost: "African drumbeat."   Corinth Morter-Lewis.   OWABP

Lost [*with music*].   Orkhan Muyassar.   BBASP, *tr. by* Samuel Hazo and Lena Jayyusi *and* W. S. Merwin

Lost.   Charles, Duc d' Orléans.   NPeEn

Lost.   Richard Henry Stoddard.   TreFP

Lost Acres.   Robert Graves.   NoAM

Lost: "Fog walks down the hill and finds our yard, The."   John Burnside.   EdScPo

Lost: "Stand still. The trees ahead and bushes beside you."   David Wagoner.   GoPo; PoA 2002; TWF

Lost: The Original, Its Reason and Its Rhyme.   Translation.   Rika Lesser.   KGB; PoA 2002

Lost. Again. I chase a piece of.   Angel.   Benjamin Alire Sáenz.   LiTh

Lost / amidst Caloplaca.   3 Pictograms From The Interior of BC.   Fred Wah.   OpeFie

Lost among flowers, the boat returns late.   Boating at Dusk.   Song Ikp'il.   CATKP, *tr. by* Chi-gyu Kim [*or* Kim Chonggil]

Lost and Found.   Maxine Chernoff.   PmAP

Lost and Found.   Jane Griffiths.   NeBl

Lost and Found.   George Macdonald.   SacPr

Lost and Found and Lost Again.   John Ashbery.   BodElec

Lost baby poem, The.   Lucille Clifton.   AmFaPo; BeAl; CAP-8; ESEAA; InoFa; ISC; OxAAAP; WaAnP

Lost Bee, The.   Phillis Levin.   RA

Lost Behind the Back of God.   Gyula Juhász.   IQMS, *tr. by* Adam Makkai

Lost Bird.   Chenjerai Hove.   HBAPE

Lost Body.   Terry Ehret.   GifTon

Lost Boy was not his name.   Lawson Fusao Inada.   CalPo *Fr.* Legends from Camp.

Lost Caress, The.   Alfonsina Storni.   BLPSL, *tr. by* Rene de Costa, Rigas Kappatos and Eleni Paidoussi

Lost. children have been known to.   Jill Hartman.   PoPra

Lost Children, The.   Randall Jarrell.   OxBoAm

Lost Chord, A.   Adelaide Anne Procter.   ITBLP; SacPr; UV; VWP   (Lost Chord, The.)   BRP

Lost Chord, The.   Dominic Bevan Wyndham Lewis.   UV

Lost Cranes.   Shi Zhiyuan.   CSKM

Lost Daughter.   Magdalena Gomez.   PueRic

Lost Daughter, The (19).   Khwaja Shams-ad-din Muhammad Hafiz.   WED, *tr. by* Robert Bly and Leonard Lewisohn

86: Lost Days.   Dante Gabriel Rossetti.   SacPr *Fr.* House of Life, The.

Lost days of my life until to-day, The.   Dante Gabriel Rossetti.   SacPr *Fr.* House of Life, The.

Lost, drifting, on the current, as the sun pours down.   After the Shipwreck.   Alicia Ostriker.   PLBUT

Lost Friend, A.   Henry Charles Leonard.   DiBP

Lost Friend, The.   Marjorie Lowry Christie Pickthall.   PoBW

Lost from an airy.   Mac Wellman.   HeMarv *Fr.* Rat Minaret: Miniaturist-Divan, The.

Lost Fugue for Chet.   Lynda Hull.   LaCa; SeSe

Lost Heifer, The.   Austin Clarke.   ModIr; WoPoe

Lost Horizon.   Hsi-chün.   ColAnChi, *tr. by* Anne Birrell

Lost Horseman, The.   Endre Ady.   IQMS, *tr. by* Anton N. Nyerges

Lost in bamboo.   Issa.   ZenPo, *tr. by* Takashi Ikemoto and Lucien Stryk

Lost in contemplation.   Jean Daive.   MFP, *tr. by* Martin Sorrell

Lost in contemplation of its end.   Lost in contemplation.   Jean Daive.   MFP, *tr. by* Martin Sorrell

Lost in glass gullies, searching for a suitcase.   Hotel Marine.   David Campbell.   BMAP

Lost in God, in Godhead found. (LL)   Threnody: "South-wind brings, The."   Ralph Waldo Emerson.   APN-1; TCAPo

Lost in Heaven.   Robert Frost.   MoAmPo

Lost in rivers of Mars Bars and more coffee to spill on the bus.   100 Times.   Arnold J. Kemp.   BtF

Lost in the Desert.   Clarence Major.   FTOS

Lost in the ground. (LL)   Miners.   Wilfred Owen.   MoBrPo; OBWVE; OxAEP-2   (Left in the ground.) (LL)   NAEL-6v2; NAEL-7v2; NAMCP V.1

Lost in the heart's worship and the body's sleep. (LL)   Love-Poem: "Yours is the face that the earth turns to me."   Kathleen Jessie Raine.   LW; MoBrPo

Lost in the Hospital.   Rafael Campo.   AmPoNex

Lost in the Stars.   Maxwell Anderson.   ReLy

Lost in the vastness of the void Pacific.   Homecoming.   Karl Shapiro.   APT-2; PWW2

Lost in Translation.   James Merrill.   NAMCP V.2; NoAM; NoP-4; NoP-5; OxBoAm; VCAP *Fr.* Book of Ephraim, The.

Lost Jewel, The. Julia Ward Howe. SWaP *Fr.* Lyrics of the Street.

Lost Land, The. Eavan Boland. NAEL-7v2

Lost Leader, The. Robert Browning. NAEL-6v2; NAEL-7v2

Lost Light, The. Emily Jane Pfeiffer. VWP

Lost! lost! lost! Anne Boleyn. Eloise Bibb. CBWP-4

Lost! lost! lost! Advertisement of a Lost Day. Lydia Huntley Sigourney. TreFP

Lost, lost too soon in yonder house or hall. (LL) Alexander Pope. NAEL-6v1; NAEL-7v1 *Fr.* Dunciad, The.

Lost Love. Dick Allen. NIP-4

Lost Love. Robert Graves. MoBrPo

Lost Love: "She keeps singing a song." Cahit Külebi. NaPG, *tr. by* Talat Sait Halman

Lost Lover, The. Delariviere Manley.
  Prologue [Spoken by Mr. Horden]. EMWP

Lost manor where I walk continually. Pier-Glass, The. Robert Graves. NoAM

Lost Masterpiece, The. Vincent Woods. NIrP

Lost Memory of Delhi, A. Agha Shahid Ali. FTtHH

Lost Mistress, The. Robert Browning. OBEV

Lost Name Woman. Shirley Lim. UnSA

91: Lost on Both Sides. Dante Gabriel Rossetti. NoP-4 *Fr.* House of Life, The.

Lost Opportunities. Henrietta Cordelia Ray. CBWP-3

Lost Orchard, The. Edgar Lee Masters. ColAP

Lost Parasol, The. Sándor Weöres.
  "Where metalled road invades light thinning air." OBVE

Lost Parents. Lawrence Ferlinghetti. ReTh

Lost Parrot, The. Naomi Shihab Nye. TiP2

Lost Photograph. Luisa Igloria. RWB

Lost Pilot, The. James Tate. AmWaPo; EmeKit; InoFa; NAMCP V.2; NoAM; OBWP; OtW; OxBoAm; PWW2; WaAnP

Lost Plaza Is Everywhere, The. Rafael Campo. AmPoNex

Lost Pleiad, The. Felicia Dorothea Hemans. NOBRP

Lost Pleiad, The. William Gilmore Simms. APN-1

Lost Property. Elizabeth Garrett. MFPA; MoWP

Lost Rules of Usage. Susan Stewart. AmAlph

Lost Seed. Patrick Williams. PNI

Lost Sister ("In China.") Cathy Song. NAMCP V.2; NoAM

Lost Sister ("In China, / even the peasants.") Cathy Song. NAAL-5

Lost Son, The. Theodore Roethke. APT-2; CAP-8; NAMCP V.1; NoP-4; NoP-5; OxBoAm; TRP

Lost Soul, A. Jay Macpherson. BrAP; NoP-4; NoP-5

Lost Teddy Bear, The [*with music*]. Maggie Pogue Johnson. CBWP-4

Lost, The ("Fairest day that ever yet has shone, The.") Jones Very. APN-1; NoP-4; NoP-5

Lost to a short pencil, words like *milk*. Think of the Words. Marianne Boruch. AmAlph

Lost to one another, the living and the dead, these ten years. Tune: "River Town." Su Tung-p'o. ColAnChi, *tr. by* James Robert Hightower

Lost to the world; lost to my selfe [*or* myself]; alone. On Himself[e]. Robert Herrick. NPeEn

Lost Tradition, A. John Montague. PBCIP *Fr.* Rough Field, The.

Lost Wife, The. Sean Dunne. ModIr *Fr.* Sydney Place.

Lost without you, though sun accompanies me. Daphne Marlatt. NLPA *Fr.* Touch to My Tongue.

Lost Woman, The. Patricia Beer. MoWP

Lost Women, The. Lucille Clifton. BodElec

Lost Wood, The. Renée Weiss and Theodore Weiss. PoCoUp

Lost World, The. Randall Jarrell.
  Night with Lions, A. StAl

Lost—lost—lost! Into the Depths. Adah Isaacs Menken. CBWP-1

Lot. David Helwig. NIP-4

Lot and His Daughters I. Alec Derwent Hope. ChIV-1

Lot and His Daughters II. Alec Derwent Hope. ChIV-1

Lot of Texas tales are told, A. Judge, The. Claire Ottenstein Ross. TiP2

Lotos-Eaters, The. Alfred Tennyson. BrAP; NAEL-6v2; NAEL-7v2; NoP-4; NoP-5

Lots of fish this time in the net of the heart. (LL) Fishing in the Keep of Silence. Linda Gregg. BodElec; GoPo

Lots of stripes. Automatic Text for Anne Ethuin. Elisabeth Lenk. SurWo, *tr. by* Gisela Baumhauer and Greta Wenziger

Lot's Wife. Abraham Cowley. NPeEn *Fr.* Davideis.

Lotus Flowers, The. Ellen Bryant Voigt. CAP-8; WaAnP

Lotus Lover, The. Tzu Yeh. CrYelRi, *tr. by* Sam Hamill

Lotus Sutra. Norman Fischer. WANABP

Lotus Sūtra. *Unknown.*
  Chapter 3: Parable. ColAnChi, *tr. by* Leon Hurvitz

Lotus-Gathering Boat. Hsüeh T'ao [*or* Xue Tao]. ColAnChi, *tr. by* Jeanne Larsen

Lotus-laden. Lotus-Gathering Boat. Hsüeh T'ao [*or* Xue Tao]. ColAnChi, *tr. by* Jeanne Larsen

Lou cierra el párpado. Dolores Dorantes. SPV

Loud complaints being made, in these quick-reading times. Announcement of a New Grand Acceleration Company for the Promotion of the Speed of Literature. Thomas Moore. OBCoV

Loud in my ear: screams. Tōge Sankichi. PFTM-2 *Fr.* Poems of the Atomic Bomb.

Loud is the Summer's busy song. John Clare. NPBRoP; WaAnP *Fr.* Shepherd's [*or* Shepheards] Calendar, The.

Loud, louder still, resounds the thundering peal. Thunder Storm. Mary F. Johnson. CenSon

Loud midnight-soothing melancholy bird. Edward Moxon. CenSon

Loud Music. Stephen Dobyns. P180

Loud Report through Lybian Cities goes, The. Virgil. NPeEn; OBVE *Fr.* Aeneid [*or* Eneados *or* Aeneis], The.

Loud, she whispers, "common, like me." My Mother, Listening to Flowers. Naomi Feigelson Chase. PfS

Loud talk in the overlighted house. Ends. Robert Frost. TRP

Loud the storm is howling. Song of the Dogs, The. Sándor Petőfi. IQMS, *tr. by* George Sutherland Fraser

Loud the storm is howling. Song of the Wolves,The. Sándor Petőfi. IQMS, *tr. by* George Sutherland Fraser

Loud thunder. Muso Soseki. EaWin, *tr. by* W. S. Merwin

Loud Thundering Storm. *Unknown. tr. by* Samuel Noah Kramer and Diane Wolkstein
  "Proud Queen of the Earth Gods, Supreme Among the Heaven Gods." HW, *tr. by* Samuel Noah Kramer and Diane Wolkstein *and* Samuel Noah Kramer

Loud waves up and down. *Unknown.* NAAPv.2

Loudens the sea-wind, downward plunge the bows. To D'Annunzio: Lines from the Sea. Robert Malise Bowyer Nichols. OBMV

Loudmouth Soup. Thomas Lux. LaCa

Loudspeaker repeating the same message, The. Demonstration. Hugh Seidman. PoA 2002

Loudspeakers saturate the world with christmas, The. December 1982/Detroit. Alvin Aubert. FuFl

Louganis. Eloise Klein Healy. WiU

Louis. Maurice Frederick Fitzhardinge Berkeley, 1st Baron Fitzhardinge. DiBP

Louis Armstrong. Ernst Moerman. SeSe

Louis, Louis, Louis, Louis. For Louis Armstrong, A Ju-Ju. Sarah Webster Fabio. SeSe

Louisa, serious grown and mild. To Louisa M[artin], Whom I Used to Call "Monkey." Charles Lamb. NPBRoP

Louisa's Wedding. Tracy Philpot. AmPoNex

Louise. Leo Robin. ReLy

Louise in Love. Mary Jo Bang. NAPBL

Louise peered into the corner of the cabinet. Dog Bark, The. Mary Jo Bang. NAPBL

Louisiana. Steve Crow. HATNAP

Louisiana Perch [*with music*]. Ron Padgett. FTOS; NYP2

Louisiana Sea of Faith, The. Dave Jeddie Smith. LPSFW

Louisville Lou (The Vampin' Lady). Milton Ager and Jack Yellen. ReLy

Lou's eyelid closing. Dolores Dorantes. SPV, *tr. by* Jen Hofer

Louse Hunting [*with music*]. Isaac Rosenberg. FaBoWar; NAEL-6v2; NAEL-7v2; NAMCP V.1; NoAM; NoP-4; NoP-5; OxAEP-2; OxBEV

Lousy in Center Field. James Tate. MoASP

Louvres. Les A. Murray. BMAP

Love. "Angelus Silesius." GePo *Fr.* Cherubical Wanderer, The.

Love. Samuel Butler. TreFP

Love. Kate Clanchy. BeAl; MoWP

Love. Roy Croft. ITBLP

Love. Joan Gordon. Prnts

Love. Juan Ramón Jiménez. SpanPo, *tr. by* Angel Flores

Love. Czeslaw Milosz. BeAl *Fr.* World, The.

Love. Blues. B. P. Nichol. IFF

Love. Sir Walter Scott. OxAEP-2 *Fr.* Lay of the Last Minstrel, The.

Love. Samar Sen. WoPoe, *tr. by* Pritish Nandy

Love. William Shakespeare. *See* Casket Song, A.

Love. *Unknown.* SoSe-8

Love: "Afternoon is offered to us, The." Oscar Cerruto. BLPSL, *tr. by* Rene de Costa, Rigas Kappatos and Eleni Paidoussi

Love: "All thoughts, all passions, all delights." Samuel Taylor Coleridge. NPBRoP; OBEV

Love: "Dark falls on this mid-western town." Eavan Boland. HarvBoo

Love: "Everything is out today." Larry Fagin. AHA *Fr.* Parade of the Caterpillars, The.

6. Love: "Forest would start when you held my hand, The." Melih Cevdet Anday. NaPG *Fr.* Horses Before Troy.

Love: "Fragile as a spider's web." May Sarton. PoBW

Love: if I die don't take me to the cemetery. Life-Hook. Juana de Ibarbourou. TCLAP, *tr.* by Sophie Cabot Black and Maria Negroni

Love: "I'm Japanese." Ayukawa Nobuo. PML, *tr.* by Leza Lowitz and Oketani Shogo

Love: "It was not to them I wanted to speak." Sarah Arvio. PoCho

Love: "Love can be a moment's madness." Ralph Blane and Hugh Martin. ReLy

Love: "Only the voice, the skin, the polished." Rosario Castellanos. FiBr, *tr.* by Carolyne Wright

Love: "There is many a country." Bekes Jr. IrPoTo, *tr.* by Muhamad Tawfiq Ali

Love: "What do you scrawl." Georgi Belev. CSCBP, *tr.* by the author and Lisa Sapinkopf

Love: "When you were here we never knew such a thing as evil." Ilhan Berk. NaPG, *tr.* by Talat Sait Halman

Love (3): "Love bade me welcome: yet my soul drew back." George Herbert. BASC; BBASP; CABP; ChIV-2; ClHu; CtM; FaBoVe; FSCP; HeIP-4; InvLi; NAEL-6v1; NAEL-7v1; NoP-4; NoP-5; NOSC; NPeEn; OBEV; OBWVE; OxAEP-1; OxBEV; PBRV; PoPoPo; PtR; RaF; TFi; WeW-3

Love a child is ever criing. Mary Sidney Wroth, Countess of Montgomery. *See* Song: "Love a child is ever crying [*or* criing]."

Love a child is ever crying [*or* criing]. Mary Sidney Wroth, Countess of Montgomery. BASC; LW; NAEL-6v1; NAEL-7v1; NoP-4; NoP-5; NOSC; OxBEV *Fr.* Pamphilia to Amphilanthus.

Love/a Many Splintered Thing. Kevin Powell. InTrad

Love a woman? You're [*or* Y'are] an ass. Song. John Wilmot, 2d Earl of Rochester. NBLV; NOSC; WoPoe

Love Affair 36. Jennifer Rankin. BMAP

Love after Love. Derek Walcott. BeAl; PML; PtR; RaF; TWF; WhBo

Love Again. Philip Larkin. PoetW

Love, again sweetly streaming down. Alcman. SaLy, *tr.* by Diane Rayor

Love always repairs to the noble heart. Love and Nobility. Guido Guinicelli. NAWM-7v1, *tr.* by James J. Wilhelm

Love Among Lepers. Richard Ronan. BodElec

Love among the Ruins. Robert Browning. NAEL-6v2; NAEL-7v2; OBEV

Love and Age. Thomas Love Peacock. OBEV *Fr.* Gryll Grange.

Love and Death. Lord Byron. CAGL
  (I Watched Thee.) NPBRoP

Love and Death: A Symphony. John Addington Symonds. CAGL
  "Thou dost establish—and our hearts receive—." CAGL

Love and Debt Alike Troublesome. Sir John Suckling. CavPo

Love and Discipline. Henry Vaughan. SacPr

Love and forgetting might have carried them. Two Look at Two. Robert Frost. MoAmPo

Love and Friendship. Emily Jane Brontë. LW; PoBW

Love and Honour. Joseph Hilaire Pierre Belloc. SacPr

Love and How It Becomes Important in Our Day to Day Lives. Miller Williams. PoA 2002

Love and Knowledge. Robert Penn Warren. NAAL-5; NAAPv.2 *Fr.* Audubon: A Vision.

Love and Liberation. John Hall Wheelock. MoAmPo

Love and Liberty—A Cantata. Robert Burns. NOBRP

Love And Life. John Wilmot, 2d Earl of Rochester. NPeEn; OBEV; OxBEV
  (Love and Life: A Song.) NOSC; WaAnP

Love and Life. Grace Buchanan Sherwood. NoP-4

Love and Life: A Song. John Wilmot, 2d Earl of Rochester. *See* Love And Life.

Love and Life of Women, The. Night Café. Gottfried Benn. PFTM-1

Love and Marriage. Sammy Cahn. ReLy

Love and marriage, love and marriage. Love and Marriage. Sammy Cahn. ReLy

Love and Nobility. Guido Guinicelli. NAWM-7v1, *tr.* by James J. Wilhelm

Love and Poetry. Dante Alighieri. NAWM-7v1, *tr.* by James J. Wilhelm

Love and Silence. Jelaluddin Rumi. WED, *tr.* by Robert Bly

Love and Sleep. Algernon Charles Swinburne. GSo; OxBSo

Love and the Child. Ruth Pitter. MoWP

Love and the Forest. Gülseli İnal. NaPG, *tr.* by Talat Sait Halman

Love and the gentle heart are one thing. Dante Alighieri. NAWM-7v1 *Fr.* Vita Nuova, La.

Love, and the Gout invade the idle Brain. Remedia Amoris. Elizabeth Thomas. LW

Love and the Years. Alfred Allen. IrLP

Love as Fear of Love in Laughter. Chris Stroffolino. IIR

Love / as it ought to be made. River Otters at Play. Harry Thurston. Coast

Love at eight is dust powdering the air. First Kill. M. L. Williams. NevBe

Love at First Sight. Christopher Marlowe. WaAnP *Fr.* Hero and Leander.

Love at First Sight. Wisława Szymborska. BeAl, *tr.* by Stanislaw Barańczak and Clare Cavanagh

Love at the closing of our days. Last Love. Fyodor Ivanovich Tyutchev. WoPoe, *tr.* by Vladimir Vladimirovich Nabokov

Love at the lips was touch. To Earthward. Robert Frost. APT-1; MoAmPo; NAMCP V.1; NoAM; NoP-4; OxBoAM; PtR; RaBo; TRP; WaAnP

Love, at what distance mine! Fear. James Vincent Cunningham. APT-2

Love, Attributed City. Nancy Morejón. TCLAP, *tr.* by Kathleen Weaver

Love bade me welcome: yet my soul drew back. Love (3). George Herbert. BASC; BBASP; CABP; ChIV-2; ClHu; CtM; FaBoVe; FSCP; HeIP-4; InvLi; NAEL-6v1; NAEL-7v1; NoP-4; NoP-5; NOSC; NPeEn; OBEV; OBWVE; OxAEP-1; OxBEV; PBRV; PoPoPo; PtR; RaF; TFi; WeW-3

Love Before Dinner. Alfred A. Yuson. ReBoTo

Love: Beginnnings. C. K. Williams. OxBoAM; StAl

Love begins with a question. Final Question, The. Yousif al-Sa'igh. IrPoTo, *tr.* by Chuck Miller and Saadi A. Simawe

Love, being in love with being in love. (LL) Being in Love. Marvin Bell. InvLad; StAl

Love between women. Ordinary, as Love. Susan Griffin. GifTon

Love Beyond Death. Francisco de Quevedo y Villegas. BLPSL, *tr.* by Rene de Costa, Rigas Kappatos and Eleni Paidoussi

Love Birds. Paul Henry. TCAWP

Love built a stately house; where *Fortune* came. World, The. George Herbert. CtM; NOSC

Love buries itself in me, up to the hilt. (LL) Renewal, A. James Merrill. CAP-8; VCAP

Love Burned Out the Light. Hala Mohammad. PoArWo, *tr.* by Cornelia Al-Khaled

Love Calls Us to the Things of This World. Richard Wilbur. AmFaPo; BrAP; CAP-8; ColAP; EMP; HeIP-4; MoAmPo; NAAL-5; NAMCP V.2; NIL-7; NIP-4; NoAM; NoP-4; NoP-5; OxBoAM; TFi; UpMys; VCAP; WaAnP

Love came along and said, "I know." Limits of Desire, The. Linda Gregg. ExTi

Love Came By From the Riversmoke. Stephen Vincent Benét. MoAmPo *Fr.* John Brown's Body.

Love Came By From the Riversmoke. Stephen Vincent Benét. MoAmPo *Fr.* John Brown's Body.

Love can be a blessing. In Love In Vain. Leo Robin. ReLy

Love can be a moment's madness. Love. Ralph Blane and Hugh Martin. ReLy

Love comes along like a popular song. I Found a Million Dollar Baby (In a Five and Ten Cent Store). Mort Dixon and Billy Rose. ReLy

Love comes hungry to anyone's hand. Love Song. Carol Muske-Dukes. BeAl

Love Constant Beyond Death. Francisco de Quevedo y Villegas. WoPoe, *tr.* by W. S. Merwin

Love Constant Beyond Death. Francisco de Quevedo y Villegas. AmFaPo, *tr.* by Willis Barnstone

Love cuts a lot of arguments short. Love and Silence. Jelaluddin Rumi. WED, *tr.* by Robert Bly

Love Cycle. Chinua Achebe. PML

Love, Death, and Art. Agnes Mary Frances Robinson. VWP

Love, Death and the Changing of the Seasons. Marilyn Hacker.
  (Aubade 2.) FiBr

Love delivers to me its sweetest thoughts. Petrarch. ErotSp, *tr.* by Sam Hamill

Love Deposed. Thomas Stanley. NOSC

Love Divine, All Loves Excelling. Charles Wesley. SacPr

Love Dream Verse. Gabriella Leto. CItWP, *tr.* by Cinzia Sartini Blum and Lara Trubowitz

Love Equals Swift and Slow. Henry David Thoreau. TCAPo

Love Feast, The. W. H. Auden. OBCoV

Love fed Heliodora's fingernail and made. Meleager. HePo

Love fed Heliodora's fingernail and made. Meleager. HePo, *tr.* by Barbara Hughes Fowler

Love flows not from my liver but her living. George Chapman. OxBSo *Fr.* Coronet for His Mistress Philosophy, A.

Love for Sale. Cole Porter. ReLy

Love from a Foreign City. Lavinia Greenlaw. EmeKit; MFPA; MoWP

Love. *Fucked in the ass*, Proust's heroine says, so he knows what she thinks of him. Series of Failures So That I'm Sick of the Word, A. Laura Mullen. IAoNAP

Love Ghost. Mimi Goese. HeMarv

Love, give me leave to serve thee, and be wise. Elegy, An: "Love, give me leave to serve thee, and be wise." Thomas Randolph. NOSC

Love gives away again to Fear. (LL)   Master and Guest.   Mary Elizabeth Coleridge.   ViWPN; VWP

Love God and keep his commandments. (LL)   Edgar Lee Masters.   APT-1; IllVoic Fr. Spoon River Anthology.

Love grows alone (though I my brain for counsel harrow).   He Loves in Vain. Christian Hofmann von Hofmannswaldau.   GePo, tr. by George C. Schoolfield

Love Guards [or Guides] the Roses of Thy Lips.   Thomas Lodge.   NoSic Fr. Phyllis.

Love had socked me.   Ridin' High.   Cole Porter.   ReLy

Love has earth to which she clings.   Bond and Free.   Robert Frost.   APT-1

Love has fooled us.   Easy Come, Easy Go.   Edward Heyman.   ReLy

Love has found its awakening. (LL)   This Morning.   Kristina Rungano. HAWP; NAfrP

Love has made me tender.   Never Swat a Fly.   Lew Brown, B. G. DeSylva and Ray Henderson.   ReLy

Love has pierced my heart with its flame.   Alcuin.   EroLit, tr. by John Boswell

Love has seven names.   Hadewijch.   WoPoe, tr. by Willis Barnstone and Elene Kolb

Love has subjugated me.   Hadewijch.   WPoS

Love, he is nearer though the moralist.   Love's Varlets.   Francis Thompson. SacPr

Love he to morrow, who lov'd never.   Unknown.   OBVE Fr. Vigil of Venus, The.

Love held a harp between his hands, and, lo!   Love's Music.   Philip Bourke Marston.   GSo

Love Her, Mind.   Rāmprasād Sen.   SinGod, tr. by Rachel Fell McDermott

Love holds my thoughts and feelings.   Continues in the Same State of Feeling. Francisco de Quevedo y Villegas.   BLPSL, tr. by Rene de Costa, Rigas Kappatos and Eleni Paidoussi

Love I Gave You Once, The.   Faiz Ahmad Faiz.   PtR, tr. by Mahbub-ul-Haq

Love. I, in mine, celebrate the love-choir. (LL)   Ovid in the Third Reich. Geoffrey Hill.   CABP; HarvBoo; HP; NAMCP V.2; NoAM; NPeEn; OxBEV

Love, if I could give you the eternal summer sun.   Beijing Spring.   Marilyn Chin.   ExTi

Love If This Is Love.   Dacia Maraini.   CItWP, tr. by Cinzia Sartini Blum and Lara Trubowitz

Love in a bungalow high on a hill.   Cottage for Sale, A.   Larry Conley. ReLy

Love, in a humour, played the prodigal.   Michael Drayton.   NoSic Fr. Idea.

Love in a Life.   Robert Browning.   NPeEn; OxBEV

Love in Age.   George Bruce.   EdScPo

Love in America.   Marianne Moore.   NIL-7

Love in an Empty Lot.   Hô Sugyông.   EcSo, tr. by Youngju Ryu

Love in Exile.   Mathilde Blind.
   1. ViWPN
   2. ViWPN
   4. ViWPN

Love in fantastick Triumph sat.   Aphra Behn.   See Song. Love Arm'd [or Armed].

Love in Fantastique [or fantastic] Triumph satt [or sat or sate].   Song. Love Arm'd [or Armed].   Aphra Behn.   BASC; LW; NALW; NoP-4; NoP-5; NOSC; NPeEn; OBEV; OxAEP-1; OxBEV; PEW; WeW-3

   (Love in fantastick Triumph sat.)   BrAP

Love in his heart, his empty hands, his eyes. (LL)   Coffin Worm, The.   Ruth Pitter.   MoBrPo; MoWP

Love in Mayfair.   May Probyn.   VWP

Love in my bosom like a bee.   Thomas Lodge.   See Love in my bosom[e] like a bee.

Love in my bosom[e] like a bee.   Thomas Lodge.   NoSic; OBEV Fr. Rosalynde; or Euphues' Golden Legacy.

Love in the Abstract.   Robert R. Calder.   EdScPo

Love in the Classroom.   Al Zolynas.   BLT; LTA; TWF

Love in the peaceful u.s.a.   Love U.S.A.   Kathleen Spivack.   LW

Love in the Time of Cholera.   Gzar Hantoosh.   IrPoTo, tr. by Saadi A. Simawe and Ellen Doré Watson

Love in the Valley.   George Meredith.   OBEV

Love in the Weather's Bells.   Jay Wright.   ESEAA Fr. Love's Dozen.

Love, in these, the darkest days.   Heel of Bernadette, The.   Colette Bryce. NIrP

Love interest, A.   Alex Rawls.   AnSo Fr. What's Your Sign?

Love is a babe as you know and when you.   Sonnet.   Bernadette Mayer. OxBoAm

Love is a deceit.   Kim Sangyong.   CATKP, tr. by Peter H. Lee

Love is a green girl.   Song.   Michael Stillman.   TLR

Love is a hovering, a deafening.   Rear Window.   Angela Shaw.   NeAmPo

Love Is a Keeper of Swans.   Humbert Wolfe.   MoBrPo

Love Is a Many-Splendored Thing.   Paul Francis Webster.   ReLy

Love Is a Mortal Disease.   Unknown.   IrV, tr. by Eleanor Hull

Love Is a Random Thing.   George Marion, Jr.   ReLy

Love is a region full of fires.   Description of Love, A.   Sir John Beaumont. NOSC

Love Is a Sickness.   Samuel Daniel.   OBEV Fr. Hymen's Triumph.

Love is a strange and powerful thing.   Darn That Dream.   Eddie DeLange. ReLy

Love is a twelve o'clock notion.   Morning After, The.   Dory Langdon Previn. ReLy

Love is a twin to death; it makes my senses dead.   "Angelus Silesius."   GePo Fr. Cherubical Wanderer, The.

Love is all. I tremble with it.   Robert Frost to Ezra Pound's Daughter from His Deathbed.   Gibbons Ruark.   VisFro

Love is and was my Lord and King.   Alfred Tennyson.   CAGL; NAEL-6v2; NAEL-7v2; OBEV Fr. In Memoriam A. H. H.

Love is apart from all things.   Great Fires, The.   Jack Gilbert.   BeAl

Love is at odds. Your beauty has gone out.   Geoffrey Hill.   UpMys Fr. Hymns to Our Lady of Chartres.

Love is best. (LL)   Love among the Ruins.   Robert Browning.   NAEL-6v2; NAEL-7v2; OBEV

Love is boring and passé, all the old baggage.   Blond Bombshell.   Lynn Emanuel.   OxBoAm

Love is / customary sight.   Kim Namjo.   CAMKP Fr. Love's Cursive.

Love Is Enough.   William Morris.   OBEV Fr. Love Is Enough.

Love is enough: though the World be a-waning.   William Morris.   OBEV Fr. Love Is Enough.

Love is False.   Kim Sangyong.   WoPoe, tr. by Chung Chong-wha

Love is false, that he loves me is a lie.   Love Is False.   Kim Sangyong. WoPoe, tr. by Chung Chong-wha

Love is foolish which studies the skin.   Wrinkling Together.   Leo Vroman. TuT, tr. by Anne Kennedy

Love is God, and sex conversion. (LL)   James Vincent Cunningham.   NIP-4; VCAP Fr. Epigrams: A Journal.

Love Is Here to Stay.   Ira Gershwin.   ReLy

Love is honest farming.   Kim Namjo.   CAMKP Fr. Love's Cursive.

Love Is Just Around the Corner.   Leo Robin.   ReLy

Love Is Life.   Richard Rolle of Hampole.   SacPr

Love Is Life and Death.   Georg Rudolph Weckherlin.   GePo, tr. by George C. Schoolfield

Love is life that lasteth ay, ther it in Crist is fest.   Love Is Life.   Richard Rolle of Hampole.   SacPr

Love / is like something heavy.   Six Variations on Love.   Víctor Terán. RMCMP, tr. by Donald Frischmann

Love is like the wild rose-briar.   Love and Friendship.   Emily Jane Brontë. LW; PoBW

Love is lovelier.   Second Time Around, The.   Sammy Cahn.   ReLy

Love is minister to us, our flock is the inmost soul.   Yunus Emre.   NaPG, tr. by Talat Sait Halman

Love is no more.   Amor Vincit Omnia.   Edgar Bowers.   VCAP

Love is not a profession.   Is / Not.   Margaret Atwood.   BrAP

Love Is Not a Word.   Eugene B. Redmond.   FTtHH

Love Is Not All.   Edna St. Vincent Millay.   BrAP

Love is not all: it is not meat nor drink.   Edna St. Vincent Millay.   APT-1; GSo; HeIP-4; NAAPv.2; NAMCP V.1; NoAM; OxBoAm; WaAnP

Love is not blind. I see with single eye.   Edna St. Vincent Millay. NAAPv.2

Love is not the reason.   Knowing Nothing.   Jane Hirshfield.   BeAl

Love Is Not Will But Destiny.   Juan de Tassis y Peralta, Count of Villamediana. BLPSL, tr. by Rene de Costa, Rigas Kappatos and Eleni Paidoussi

Love is not will, it is fate.   Love Is Not Will But Destiny.   Juan de Tassis y Peralta, Count of Villamediana.   BLPSL, tr. by Rene de Costa, Rigas Kappatos and Eleni Paidoussi

Love is progressing one can see precisely.   Love is Progressing.   Meir Wieseltier.   NRoS, tr. by Esther Raizen

Love is Round.   Alicia Galaz Vivar.   TANSG, tr. by Oliver Welden

Love is round like a seed or an egg.   Love is Round.   Alicia Galaz Vivar. TANSG, tr. by Oliver Welden

Love Is Sweeping the Country.   Ira Gershwin.   ReLy

Love is the blossom where there blows.   Giles, the Younger Fletcher.   OBEV Fr. Christ's Victory and Triumph.

Love is the lesson which the Lord us taught. (LL)   Edmund Spenser.   ChIV-2; NoSic; SacPr; WaAnP Fr. Amoretti.

Love is the Peace, whereto all thoughts doe strive.   Fulke, 1st Baron Brooke Greville.   NoSic; NPeEn Fr. Caelica.

Love is the plant of peace and most precious of virtues.   William Langland. SacPr Fr. Vision of Piers Plowman, The.

(Love Is) The Tender Trap.   Sammy Cahn.   ReLy

Love Is the Thing.   Ned Washington.   ReLy

Love is the water of eternal life, cures every woe.   Jelaluddin Rumi.   NaPG, tr. by Talat Sait Halman

Love is the whole and more than all. (LL)   My father moved through dooms of love.   E. E. Cummings.   ColAP; NAAL-5; NAMCP V.1; NoAM; NoP-4; OxBoAm; WaAnP; WoPoe

Love is too great a happiness.   Love.   Samuel Butler.   TreFP

Love is too young to know what conscience is.   William Shakespeare.   HeIP-4; NoSic; OxAEP-1; WaAnP *Fr.* Sonnets.

Love is unjust: justice is loveless. (LL)   Jacob.   Delmore Schwartz.   ChIV-1; TaR

Love, it is night. The orb of day.   Passionate Professor, The.   Bert Leston Taylor.   NBLV

Love. It was good. (LL)   Rondeau after a Transatlantic Telephone Call.   Marilyn Hacker.   ColAP; NAMCP V.2; NoAM

Love, it was good to talk to you tonight.   Rondeau after a Transatlantic Telephone Call.   Marilyn Hacker.   ColAP; NAMCP V.2; NoAM

Love itself shall slumber on. (LL)   To —: "Music, when soft voices die."   Percy Bysshe Shelley.   HeIP-4; NAEL-6v2; NAEL-7v2; OBEV; OxAEP-2; OxBEV; TFi

Love Jam.   Everett Hoagland.   BRtP

Love Lament.   *Vietnamese Oral Tradition.*   CaDao, *tr.* by John Balaban

Love Lamp.   W. D. Snodgrass.   CAP-8

Love leave to urge, thou know'st thou hast the hand.   Mary Sidney Wroth, Countess of Montgomery.   BASC *Fr.* Pamphilia to Amphilanthus.

Love Letter.   Sylvia Plath.   LW; PtR

Love Letter.   Katayoon Zandvakili.   AmPoNex

Love Letter from an Impossible Land.   William Meredith.   PWW2

Love Letter Sent South.   Pat LittleDog.   TiP2

Love Letters.   Josephine D. Henderson Heard.   CBWP-4; SWaP

Love Letters.   Lotte Kramer.   Prnts

Love Letters of the Dead.   Douglas Street.   FaBoWar

("Love Letters to Her Who Lives [Alas!] Away").   Nell Altizer.   Sonnet 2.   FFC

Love like a jugler, comes to play his prize [*or* prise].   Mary Sidney Wroth, Countess of Montgomery.   EMWP *Fr.* Pamphilia to Amphilanthus.

Love Like Salt.   Lisel Mueller.   P180

Love, Like Water.   Julia Copus.   BeAl; MoWP

Love long dormant showing itself.   Palais des Arts.   Louise Glück.   VCAP

Love, love, love, love.   That's My Weakness Now.   Bud Green and Sam H. Stept.   ReLy

Love, love today, my dear.   Song.   Charlotte Mew.   MoBrPo

Love, lust, longing: reasons, but not the reason, The. (LL)   Beauty of Things, The.   Robinson Jeffers.   APT-1; PoA 2002

Love Made in the First Age[: To Chloris].   Richard Lovelace.   NAEL-6v1; NAEL-7v1

Love Me.   Badr Shakir al-Sayyab.   IrPoTo, *tr.* by Mustapha Kamal and Ralph Saverese

Love Me.   Amal Moussa.   PoArWo, *tr.* by Khaled Mattawa

Love me at last, or if you will not.   Love Me At Last.   Alice Corbin.   LW

"Love me, for I love you"—and answer me.   Christina Georgina Rossetti.   OxBSo *Fr.* Monna Innominata.

Love Me Little, Love Me Long.   *Unknown.*   NoP-4; NoP-5; WaAnP

Love Me, Love My Dog.   George Turberville.   DiBP

Love me no more, now let the god depart.   Edna St. Vincent Millay.   HeIP-4

Love Me Not [for Comely Grace].   *Unknown.*   OBEV

Love Me or Leave Me.   Gustave Kahn.   ReLy

Love me, Sweet, with all thou art.   Man's Requirements, A.   Elizabeth Barrett Browning.   RACG; ViWPN

Love means to learn to look at yourself.   Czeslaw Milosz.   BeAl *Fr.* World, The.

Love Medicine, A [*with music*].   Louise Erdrich.   HATNAP

Love Medley: Patrice Cuchulain.   Michael S. Harper.   CAP-8

Love / Mother. (LL)   My Mother.   Robert Mezey.   GoPo; TaR

Love much-enduring through a year is my love, A.   What Is Love?   Eleanor Hull.   IrLP

Love Necessitates.   Eugene B. Redmond.   ISC

Love Nest, The.   Otto Harbach.   ReLy

Love never lets you go. (LL)   Ever-Fixed Mark, An.   Kingsley Amis.   NAMCP V.2; NoAM

Love not a loveliness too much.   Ownership.   Lizette Woodworth Reese.   MoAmPo

Love Notes.   Jennifer Strauss.   BMAP

Love now no fire hath left him.   Out of the Italian.   Giovanni Giambattista.   OBVE, *tr.* by Richard Crashaw

Love # 49: "This is how I felt."   Reuben Jackson.   BtF

Love of a woman, The.   Air: "The Love of a Woman."   Robert Creeley.   VCAP

Love of Boys, The.   Solon.   CAGL, *tr.* by John Addington Symonds

Love of Christ, The.   John Austin.   SacPr

Love of Fame, the Universal Passion.   Edward Young.   OBSV   "Languid lady next appears in state, The."   NPeEn

Love of form is a love of endings, The. (LL)   Celestial Music.   Louise Glück.   BBASP; CAP-8; OxBoAm

Love of King David and Fair Bethsabe.   George Peele.   ChIV-1

Love of my heart, living death, I await in vain your written word and I think with the dying flower, that if I live without myself I want to lose you.   Federico García Lorca.   CAGL *Fr.* Sonetos del Amor Oscuro [Sonnets of Dark Love].

Love of my life came not, The.   Deep-Sea Pearl, The.   Edith Matilda Thomas.   PoBW

Love of Our Country, The.   Evan Evans.   "Whatever clime we travel or explore."   AngWePo

Love of Poetry.   Jacqueline Risset.   SCFWP, *tr.* by Serge Gavronsky

Love of the Quartz Pebble, The.   Vasco [*or* Vasko] Popa.   PoSu *Fr.* Quartz Pebble, The.

Love of Travellers, The.   Angela Jackson.   BtF

Love of women leaves me cold; desire, The.   *Unknown.*   CAGL, *tr.* by Daryl Hine

Love On the Farm.   D. H. Lawrence.   CABP; MoBrPo; NAEL-6v2; NAEL-7v2; NAMCP V.1; NoAM; NoP-4; NoP-5

Love only one.   Letter, The.   Mun Chônghui.   EcSo, *tr.* by Catherine J. Kim

Love only reading unto me this art. (LL)   Sir Philip Sidney.   NAEL-7v1; NoSic *Fr.* Astrophil and Stella.

Love opened a vista rare with stars.   Love's Vista.   Henrietta Cordelia Ray.   CBWP-3

Love or Fame.   Caroline Lindsay.   VWP

Love plays a lute, and Thought an organ grand.   Two Musicians, The.   Henrietta Cordelia Ray.   CBWP-3

Love Poem.   Roque Dalton.   AF

Love Poem.   John Forbes.   BMAP

Love Poem.   Barbara J. Orton.   NeAmPo

Love Poem.   Linda Pastan.   NIL-7; NIP-4

Love Poem.   Norman Henry, II Pritchard.   GT

Love Poem (2): "Because you turn."   Walter Helmut Fritz.   GTCP, *tr.* by Reinhold Grimm

Love Poem 1990.   Peter Meinke.   P180

Love Poem: "First line of this poem, The."   Sabahattin Kudret Aksal.   NaPG, *tr.* by Talat Sait Halman

Love Poem: "Flowers upon your lips and hands."   Maurice James Craig.   IrLP

Love Poem for Three for Kaye & Me.   Gregory Corso.   PmAP

Love Poem: "In your quest or request God is remote."   Huda Na'mani.   BBASP, *tr.* by Samuel Hazo and Lena Jayyusi *and* W. S. Merwin

Love Poem: "My clumsiest dear, whose hands shipwreck vases."   John Frederick Nims.   IllVoic; PoA 2002

Love Poem: "No nightfall in June."   John Purser.   EdScPo

Love Poem: "Olfactory paradise."   E. K. Caldwell.   PasH

Love Poem / Song Regarding Weymouth Falls.   George Elliott Clarke.   Coast

Love Poem: "Speak earth and bless me with what is richest."   Audre Lorde.   NAMCP V.2; NoAM; PoBW

Love Poem: "There are too many similes for bed."   Erin Belieu.   TAPaP

Love Poem: "We have plenty of matches in our house." [*with music*].   Ron Padgett.   NYP2

Love Poem: "What you give me is."   Denise Levertov.   NIL-7

Love Poem: "When you think of me."   Ziya Osman Saba.   NaPG, *tr.* by Talat Sait Halman

Love Poem: "Your silver hair, a galaxy."   Carol Merrill.   ICANM

Love Poem, A.   Vagura.   WoPoe, *tr.* by Peter Dent and Edwin Gerow

Love Poem, A.   Vidya.   WoPoe, *tr.* by Peter Dent and Edwin Gerow

Love Poem for a Wife, 2.   A. K. Ramanujan.   WoPoe

Love Poem for My Country, A.   Frank Mkalawile Chipasula.   HBAPE; NAfrP

Love Poem, Later.   Judith McCombs.   FiBr

Love Poem, The.   Andrew Elliott.   PNI

Love Poem to an Avocado from a Tomato.   Yumi Thomas.   FTtHH

Love Poem with Toast.   Miller Williams.   PoDa

Love Poems.   Jack Spicer.   6.   FTOS

Love poems, The.   Wild Hooves.   Gary Rosenthal.   WhBo

Love Poems of Marichiko, The.   Kenneth Rexroth.   "As I came from the."   APSN; NAMCP V.1   "As the wheel follows the hoof."   APSN   "Chilled through, I wake up."   APT-2; NAAPv.2; NAMCP V.1   "Come to me, as you come."   APSN   "Did you take me because you loved me?"   APSN; APT-2   "Every morning, I."   APSN; APT-2; NAAPv.2; NAMCP V.1   "Fires / Burn in my heart."   APSN; NAAPv.2   "Frost covers the reeds of the marsh."   APSN   "Half in a dream."   APSN; APT-2; NAMCP V.1

"How long, long ago." APSN

"How many lives ago." APSN; APT-2

"I am sad this morning." APSN

"I cannot forget." APSN; APT-2; NAAPv.2; NAMCP V.1

"I hate this shadow of a ghost." APT-2; NAAPv.2; NAMCP V.1

"I hold your head tight between." APSN; APT-2; NAAPv.2; NAMCP V.1

"I pass the day tense, day-." APSN

"I scream as you bite." APSN; APT-2; NAAPv.2

"I waited all night." NAAPv.2

"I wish I could be." APSN; APT-2

"If I thought I could get away." APSN

"In the park a crow awakes." APSN

"It is the time when." APSN

"Just us. / In our little house." APSN

"Let us sleep together here tonight." APSN

"Lying in the meadow, open to you." APSN

"Making love with you." NAMCP V.1; PoCho

"Night is too long to the sleepless, The." APT-2

"Night without end. Loneliness." APSN; APT-2

"Now the fireflies of our youth." APSN

"Oh the anguish of these secret meetings." APSN; APT-2; NAAPv.2

"On the bridges." APSN

"On the mountain." NAAPv.2

"Once again I hear." NAAPv.2

"Once I shone afar like a." APSN

"Scorched with love, the cicada." APSN; NAAPv.2

"Some day in six inches of." APSN; APT-2; NAAPv.2; NAMCP V.1

"Spring is early this year." APSN

"This flesh you have loved." APSN; APT-2

"Two flowers in a letter." APSN

"Uguisu sing in the blossoming trees." APT-2

"Uguisu sleeps in the bamboo grove, The." APSN

"Who is there? Me." APSN

"Without me you can only." APSN; APT-2

"You ask me what I thought about." APSN; APT-2; NAMCP V.1

"You wake me." APSN; NAMCP V.1

"Your tongue thrums and moves." APSN; APT-2; NAAPv.2; NAMCP V.1

Love poems they read. Uses of Poetry. Winfield Townley Scott. PoA 2002

Love Rats. Cheryl Follon. BeAl

Love, Reason, Hate, did once bespeak. Barley-Break , A. Sir John Suckling. BASC; CavPo

Love Returned. Bayard Taylor. CAGL

Love rises up some days. Michael Field. VWP

Love rises up some days. Love rises up some days. Michael Field. VWP

Love Rockets. Jim Carroll. AHA

Love Says. Daria Menicanti. CItWP, *tr. by* Cinzia Sartini Blum and Lara Trubowitz

Love seeketh not Itself to please. William Blake. NAEL-6v1; NAEL-7v2; NoP-4; NoP-5; NPBRoP; NPeEn; OxAEP-2; OxBEV; TFi *Fr.* Songs of Experience.

Love set them going, our mothers. Sunday. Achy Obejas. WiU

Love set you going like a fat gold watch. Morning Song. Sylvia Plath. BeAl; ColAP; HarvBoo; HeIP-4; ItWoWo; NAAL-5; NAMCP V.2; NIL-7; NIP-4; NoP-4; NoP-5; PoPoPo; VCAP; WaAnP

Love shook my senses. Sappho. SaLy, *tr. by* Diane Rayor

Love should intend realities. Goodbye. John Ciardi. WeW-3

Love so alike, that none do slacken, none can die. (LL) Good-Morrow, The. John Donne. BASC; BrAP; CABP; ClHu; FaBoVe; FSCP; ItP; NAEL-6v1; NAEL-7v1; NAWM-5v1; NIL-7; NoP-4; NoP-5; NOSC; OxAEP-1; OxBEV; SoSe-8; TFi; WaAnP

Love Song. Jaufré Rudel. NAWM-7v1, *tr. by* Roy Rosenstein and George Wolf

Love Song. Marilyn Nelson. ExTi

Love Song. *Unknown.* WoPoe, *tr. by* Ulli Beier and H. Gaden

Love Song. *Unknown.* WoPoe,

Love Song 2. B. P. Nichol. OpeFie

Love Song, A: "It was good." Lindiwe Mabuza. HAWP

Love Song: "Clouds circle the moon." Ma Chih-yüan. CrYelRi, *tr. by* Sam Hamill

Love Song: "Fondling and snuggling." Kuan Yün-shih. CrYelRi, *tr. by* Sam Hamill

Love Song: I and Thou [*with music*]. Alan Dugan. AmFaPo; NAMCP V.2; NoAM

Love Song: "I cannot bear it, I cannot bear it at all." *Eskimo Oral Tradition.* NAAPv.1

Love Song: "I love you, I love you, is my song." Pablo Neruda. ErotSp; GifTon, *tr. by* William O'Daly

Love Song: "I shaved my legs a second time." Frederick Seidel. BAP-04; OxBoAm

Love Song: "I will walk into some one's dwelling." *Unknown.* APN-2, *tr. by* Henry Rowe Schoolcraft

Love Song: "If you were drowning, I'd come to the rescue." Joseph Brodsky. BAP-97

Love Song: "Lazy flowers brew honey for the bees." Hu Chih-yu. CrYelRi, *tr. by* Sam Hamill

Love Song: "Like pain of fire runs down my body my love to you, my dear!" *Unknown.* APN-2 *Fr.* Songs of the Kwakiutl Indians.

Love Song: "Like the hills under dusk you." A. R. Ammons. NAMCP V.2

Love Song: "Love comes hungry to anyone's hand." Carol Muske-Dukes. BeAl

Love Song: "New pier is concrete, the streets are paved, The." Samuel Maio. CalPo

Love Song: "One long and humid afternoon." Rofel G. Brion. PML; ReBoTo

Love Song: "Orioles and orioles." Ch'iao Chi. CrYelRi, *tr. by* Sam Hamill

Love Song: "She is a reed swaying in blue." Earle Thompson. HATNAP

Love Song: "Sweep the house clean." William Carlos Williams. MoAmPo; SAmP

Love Song: "There is a strong wall about me to protect me." Mary Carolyn Davies. LW

Love Song: "Though to think / Rejoiceth me." Margot Ruddock. OBMV

Love Song: "Your beauty, which I lost sight of once." Denise Levertov. PtR

Love Song for Chrysokomos (Goldenlocks). Angelo Poliziano. CAGL *Fr.* Greek Epigrams.

Love Song for Difficult Times. Maria Elena Cruz Varela. VCWP, *tr. by* Mairym Cruz-Bernal *and* Deborah Digges

Love Song for Marcus, A. Pacifico Massimi. CAGL *Fr.* Hecateleguim.

Love Song for the Belly Button 1. Kim Sŭnghŭi. EcSo, *tr. by* K. Kim Richards and Steffen Richards

Love Song in Absence. Judith Wright. RSR

Love Song in Summer's Furnace Heat. James Schevill. ASA

Love Song of a Red Cap. Sam Cornish. BtF

Love Song of J. Alfred Prufrock, The. T. S. Eliot. AmFaPo; APT-1; BrAP; ClHu; ColAP; EMP; GPTC; HarvBoo; HeIP-4; IJHIL; MakPoe; MoAmPo; NAAL-5; NAAPv.2; NAEL-6v2; NAEL-7v2; NAMCP V.1; NAWM-7v2; NIL-7; NoAM; NoP-4; NoP-5; NPeEn; OxAEP-2; OxBEV; OxBoAm; PoA 2002; PoPoPo; SoSe-8; TCAPo; TFi; TRP; WaAnP; WeW-3; WoPoe

Love Song of Tommo Frogley. Roger Crawford. UV

Love Song of Tooting, A. Kit Wright. NoP-5

Love Song to Eohippus. Peter Viereck. MoAmPo

Love Song to the Foal-Hide Flask. Mihály Csokonai Vitéz. IQMS, *tr. by* Thomas Kabdebo and Valerie Becker Makkai

Love Songs in Age. Philip Larkin. OxBEV

Love Songs to Joannes. Mina Loy. NAAPv.2

   1. NAMCP V.1

   2. NAMCP V.1

   3. NAMCP V.1

  13. NAMCP V.1

  14. NAMCP V.1

  26. NAMCP V.1

  29. NAMCP V.1

Love Sonnet, A. George Wither. *See* I Loved a Lass.

Love Sonnets of Proteus, The. Wilfrid Scawen Blunt.

As To His Choice of Her. GSo

Depreciating Her Beauty. OBMV

Love steals unheeded o'er the tranquil mind. Tyranny of Love, The. Mary Robinson. CenSon; RWP

Love still has something of the sea. Song. Sir Charles Sedley. OxAEP-1; OxBEV

Love Story, A. Robert Graves. NAEL-6v2

Love Story in Subtitles. Nancy Mitchell. LaCa

Love Suicides at Sonezaki, The. Chikamatsu Monzaemon. *tr. by* Donald Keene Journey, The. WoPoe, *tr. by* Donald Keene

Love that a reign of terror struck dumb. Poem for a New Year. Rachel Wetzsteon. NeAmPo

Love that breeds. Unbosoming. Michael Field. NAEL-7v2; VWP

Love, That Doth Reign and Live Within My Thought. Petrarch. *See* Complaint of a Lover Rebuked.

Love, That Doth Reign [*or* Raine] and Live Within My Thought. Petrarch. HeIP-4; OBVE *Fr.* Sonnets to Laura.

Love, that drained her, drained him she'd loved, though each. Turtle Dove, The. Geoffrey Hill. OxBEV

Love that never dies. (LL) Parable of the Four-Poster. Erica Jong. GoPo; LW

Love the aurora of these late september nights. Roy Kiyooka. NLPA *Fr.* Pear Tree Pomes.

Love the drill, confound the dentist. Saint's Logic. Linda Gregerson. ExTi; PoDa

Love the earth and sun and the animals, despise riches, gives alms to everyone that asks. Preface to *Leaves of Grass* [1855]. Walt Whitman. TWF

Love the earth like a mole. Starting with Little Things. William Stafford. IPoFL

Love the Human. Lucille Clifton. GT

Love the quick profit, the annual raise. Manifesto: The Mad Farmer Liberation Front. Wendell Berry. GoPo; IPoFL

Love the subtle ways the weather occurs and reoccurs. Roy Kiyooka. NLPA *Fr.* Pear Tree Pomes.

Love the Wild Swan. Robinson Jeffers. APT-1; MoAmPo; NoAM

Love Thee, Dearest? Love Thee? Thomas Moore. IrLP

Love thee? Yes, I'm sure I love thee. City by the Sea, The. Josephine D. Henderson Heard. CBWP-4

Love, thou art absolute sole lord. Hymn to the Name and Hono[u]r of the Admirable Saint[e] Teresa, A. Richard Crashaw. BASC; FSCP; NoP-4; OBEV

Love, thou art absolute sole lord. Richard Crashaw. NOSC; OxBEV *Fr.* Hymn to the Name and Hono[u]r of the Admirable Saint[e] Teresa, A.

Love thou art absolute, sole Lord. Richard Crashaw. SacPr *Fr.* In Memory of the Vertuous and Learned Lady Madre de Teresa that Sought an Early Martyrdome.

Love thy God and love Him only. Reality. Sir Aubrey De Vere. SacPr

Love Thy Neighbor. Mack Gordon. ReLy

Love Thy Neighbour. D. H. Lawrence. ChIV-2

Love, to give law unto his subject hearts. Sir Thomas Wyatt. ChIV-1 *Fr.* Penitential Psalms.

Love to gyve law unto his subject hertes. Introductory Poem to the Penitential Psalms. Sir Thomas Wyatt. SacPr

Love to *Hermes, Aphrodite* the friend, The. (LL) To the Fair Clarinda [*or* Clorinda], Who Made Love to Me, Imagin'd [*or* Imagined] More than Woman. Aphra Behn. BASC; CABP; EMWP; NALW; NIL-7; NoP-4; NoP-5; PEW; PoBW; WaAnP

Love, Today My Lip. Cristina Campo. CItWP, *tr. by* Cinzia Sartini Blum and Lara Trubowitz

Love Tomorrow. Talat Sait Halman. NaPG, *tr. by* Talat Sait Halman

Love Triumphant. John Dryden.
  "As, when some treasurer lays down the stick." NOSC

Love Turned the Light Out. John Latouche. ReLy

Love Turns You into a Rosebush. Gloria Fuertes. RaW, *tr. by* Philip Levine

Love, 20c the First Quarter Mile. Kenneth Fearing. WoPoe

Love U.S.A. Kathleen Spivack. LW

Love Under the Rain. Abdul Wahab Al-Bayati. IrPoTo, *tr. by* Farouk Abdel Wahab

Love Unexpressed. Constance Fenimore Woolson. APN-2

Love Unfeigned. Geoffrey Chaucer. OBEV *Fr.* Troilus and Criseyde [*or* Criseide].

Love Unfeigned, The. Geoffrey Chaucer. OBEV

Love Unknown. George Herbert. WaAnP

Love unreturn[e]d, howe'er [how ere] the flame. Constancy[e]. Sidney Godolphin. NOSC

Love Versus Learning. Constance Naden. ViWPN; VWP

Love War, The. Desmond O'Grady. IrLP

Love was alone with love. And there was nothing I could do about it. Love was. Matter. Carla Harryman. FTOS

Love was late in coming, and coming. "Rachel." FIT, *tr. by* Robert Friend

Love? We should smother it. Ruth Miller. LW *Fr.* Aspects of Love.

Love we thought would never stop, The. Ending. Gavin Ewart. NBLV; SoSe-8

Love, Weeping, Laid This Song. Lizette Woodworth Reese. APN-2

Love what art thou? A vain thought. Mary Sidney Wroth, Countess of Montgomery. NAEL-6v1; NAEL-7v1; NoP-4; NoP-5; WaAnP *Fr.* Urania.

Love Who Will, for I'll Love None. William Browne. NOSC

Love, Why don't You Come. *Unknown.* WoPoe, *tr. by* Kevin O'Rourke

Love, why don't you come! Love, Why don't You Come. *Unknown.* WoPoe, *tr. by* Kevin O'Rourke

Love will expire, the gay, the happy dream. George Crabbe. NOBRP; NPBRoP *Fr.* Tales.

Love Will Find Out the Way. *Unknown.* OBEV

Love winged my hopes and taught me how to fly. Icarus. *Unknown.* OBEV

Love with No Letup. Antonin Artaud. YaTCFP, *tr. by* Mary Ann Caws

Love, with Trees and Lightning. Catie Rosemurgy. IIR

Love without hope, as when the young bird-catcher. Love Without Hope. Robert Graves. NAEL-6v2; NAEL-7v2; NoP-4; NoP-5; NOxBChV; NPeEn; OPOU; OxBEV; Spl

Love without Hope is like Breath without Air. To Colindra. Elizabeth Thomas. LW

Love wooing Honour, Honour's love did win. Love and Honour. Joseph Hilaire Pierre Belloc. SacPr

Love you alone have been with us. Jelaluddin Rumi. EaWin, *tr. by* Talat Sait Halman and W. S. Merwin

Love, you ever want me, don't. (LL) Hesitate to Call. Louise Glück. LW; StAl

Love, You have struck me straight, my Lord! Resolution. Charles Leo O'Donnell. SacPr

Love, you were dying and one came and drew. Picture, A. Michael Field. VWP

Love Your Enemy. Yusef Iman. GI

Love-Poem: "Yours is the face that the earth turns to me." Kathleen Jessie Raine. LW; MoBrPo

Lovebirds. Jo Shapcott. BeAl

Loveburn. *Unknown.* SonAtl, *tr. by* Jenny Ako, Micha Graham, Ursula Hobday and S. Lundberg

Love-Charm Song. *Chippewa Oral Tradition.* NAAL-5; NAAPv.2

Love-Cry. Brendan Kennelly. IrLP

Loved and loving, God her trust. Fellowship in Grief. Thomas Aird. DiBP

Loved being takes place, The. Presence and Process. Michael Thorpe. Coast

Loved by thee. (LL) Woman's Last Word, A. Robert Browning. NAEL-6v2; RACG

Loved, on a sudden thou didst come to me. Michael Field. ViWPN; VWP

Loved Once. Elizabeth Barrett Browning. ViWPN

Loved one is not only the beloved; it is also everything yearned for, The. Preface. Han Yong'un [*or* Yongwun]. CAMKP, *tr. by* Sammy Solberg

Loved One, The. Evelyn Waugh.
  "They told me, Francis Hinsley, they told me you were hung." OBCoV

Loved One: "You were not gone." Sam White. IIR

Loved [*or* Lov'd] I not Hono[u]r more. (LL) To Lucasta, [on] Going to the War[re]s. Richard Lovelace. BASC; CABP; CavPo; ClHu; FaBoWar; NAEL-6v1; NAEL-7v1; NIL-7; NIP-4; NoP-4; NoP-5; NOSC; NPeEn; OBEV; OBWP; OxAEP-1; OxBEV; PBRV; PoPoPo; TFi; UV; WaAnP; WeW-3

Loveless and sleepless the sea. (LL) Silence Wager Stories. Susan Howe. BodElec; FTOS; WoBe

Love-letter, A [*with music*]. Mary E. Tucker. CBWP-1

Love-Letter-Burning. Daniel Hall. NoP-4; NoP-5

Loveliest flowers, though crooked in their border. Gardener. Robert Graves. OBGa

Loveliest girl in Vienna, The. Alma. Tom Lehrer. NBLV

Loveliest of trees, the cherry now. A. E. Housman. BrAP; ChAP; ClHu; MakPoe; MoBrPo; NAEL-6v2; NAEL-7v2; NAMCP V.1; NoAM; NoP-4; NoP-5; PoPoPo; SoSe-8; TFi; WaAnP; WeW-3 *Fr.* Shropshire Lad, A.

Lovelight. Gysbert Japicx. WoPoe, *tr. by* Rod Jellema

Loveliness beyond words. Bihari. ErotSp, *tr. by* Sam Hamill

Loveliness of Love, The. George Darley. *See* It Is Not Beauty I Demand.

Love-lorn Maid, at some far distant time, A. William Wordsworth. CenSon *Fr.* River Duddon [A Series of Sonnets], The.

Lovely. Erin Belieu. ExTi

Lovely afternoon. The firing squad. Sleep Writer, The. Maggie Anderson. PLBUT

Lovely Childhood. Gottfried Benn. PFTM-1

Lovely hill-torrents are. Song. Walter James Turner. MoBrPo

Lovely interlude. I'm in the Mood for Love. Dorothy Fields. ReLy

Lovely is the pine-grove. Sikong Tu. CCL1 *Fr.* Twenty-Four Modes of Poetry.

Lovely Lady [*with music*]. Tu Fu [*or* Du Fu]. CCL1, *tr. by* Burton Watson

Lovely Love, A. Gwendolyn Brooks. CAP-8

Lovely Mary Donnelly. William Allingham. IrV

Lovely Maya, Hermes' mother. Barnabe Barnes. NoSic *Fr.* Parthenophil and Parthenophe.

Lovely Monster. Joyce Mansour. SurWo, *tr. by* Guy Flandre and Peter Wood

Lovely Morning Thought. Arthur Rimbaud. SxFrPo, *tr. by* Martin Sorrell

Lovely Pamela, who found. Epitaph on a Party Girl. Richard Usborne. OBCoV

Lovely Shall Be Choosers, The. Robert Frost. MoAmPo

Lovely spring night, A. Basho. SoOfWa, *tr. by* Sam Hamill

Lovely Stuff. Diane Ward. PmAP

Lovely to be. Bouquet of Objects, A. Elaine Equi. PmAP

Lovely to Look At. Dorothy Fields and Jimmy McHugh. ReLy

Lovely visions of repose, The. (LL) On Esthwaite Water. Isabella Lickbarrow. NPBRoP; RWP; WaAnP

Lovely world of cottages. Victory at Guernica, The. Paul Eluard. SurPaPo, *tr. by* Mary Ann Caws

Lovepoem Writing Me. Madeline J. Tiger. MiVo

Love-Poems of the Sixth Dalai Lama. Tsangyang Gyatso. *tr.* by Brian Cutillo and Rick Fields

"I sought my lover at twilight." WoPoe, *tr.* by Brian Cutillo and Rick Fields

"Lover met by chance on the road." WoPoe, *tr.* by Brian Cutillo and Rick Fields

"White teeth smiling." WoPoe, *tr.* by Brian Cutillo and Rick Fields

"Wild horses running in the hills." WoPoe, *tr.* by Brian Cutillo and Rick Fields

Love-prone Asclepias with eyes like a summer's day. Meleager. HePo

Love-prone Asclepias with eyes like a summer's day. Meleager. HePo, *tr.* by Barbara Hughes Fowler

Lover. Catherine Wagner. IIR

Lover, A. Amy Lowell. OxBoAm

Lover, The. Coventry Patmore. OxAEP-2 *Fr.* Angel in the House, The.

Lover, The. C. K. Williams. OxBoAm

Lover, The; a Ballad. Lady Mary Wortley Montagu. NAEL-6v1; NAEL-7v1; NoP-4; NoP-5; OxBEV; PEW

Lover and Philosopher. Sir William Davenant. OBEV

(Philosopher and the Lover; To a Mistress Dying, The.) NPeEn

(To a Mistress Dying.) SacPr

Lover, Come Back to Me! Oscar Hammerstein, II. ReLy

Lover Compareth Himself to the Painful Falconer, The. *Unknown.* NoSic

Lover Digresses, The. Luis Cernuda. CAGL, *tr.* by Rick Lipinski

Lover in Winter Plaineth for the Spring, The. *Unknown. See* Western Wind.

Lover Man. James Cushing. SeSe

Lover met by chance on the road. Tsangyang Gyatso. WoPoe *Fr.* Love-Poems of the Sixth Dalai Lama.

Lover Mourns for the Loss of Love, The. William Butler Yeats. IrLP; WeW-3

Lover nudges, A. Sex. Yona Harvey. BRtP

Lover of Blue Writing above the Sea, The. Ghada al-Samman. PoArWo, *tr.* by Saad Ahmed and Miriam Cooke

Lover of Mountains. Muso Soseki. EaWin, *tr.* by W. S. Merwin

Lover of Rain in an Inkwell, The. Ghada al-Samman. PoArWo, *tr.* by Miriam Cooke and Richard McKane

Lover Release Agreement. J. Allyn Rosser. PoA 2002

Lover River, The. Nazik al-Mala'ika. IrPoTo, *tr.* by Ibtisam Barakat

Lover Showeth How He Is Forsaken of Such as He Sometime Enjoyed, The. Sir Thomas Wyatt. CABP; ClHu; HeIP-4; MakPoe; NoSic; NPeEn; OxBEV; TFi; TRP

(Remembrance.) WoPoe

(They Fle from Me That Sometyme Did Me Seke.) BrAP

(They Flee From Me.) CtM; NAEL-6v1; NAEL-7v1; NIL-7; NoP-4; NoP-5; PoPoPo; WaAnP

(Vixi Puellis Nuper Idoneus.) OBEV

Lover that Durst Not Speak to His M[istress], A. James Shirley. NOSC

Lover to His Lady, The [*with music*]. Plato. NoSic, *tr.* by George Turberville

Lover Under Suspicion. Ádám Pálóczi Horváth. IQMS, *tr.* by J. G. Nichols

Lover, Whose Mistress Feared a Mouse, Declareth That He Would Become a Cat if He Might Have His Desire, The. George Turberville. TriCat

Lovers. Michael Field. PoBW; ViWPN

Lovers, The. David Campbell. BMAP *Fr.* Ku-ring-gai Rock Carvings.

Lovers, The. Geoffrey Holloway. NLP

Lovers, The. Dorianne Laux. BodElec; ErotSp

Lovers, The. William Robert Rodgers. IrLP; PNI

Lovers, The. Jaime Sabines. TCLAP, *tr.* by Claudine-Marie D'Angelo

Lovers, The. William Jay Smith. MoAmPo

Lovers, The. Marya Alexandrovna Zaturenska. MoAmPo

Lovers, The: "I said: "Your Christian name?"" Alain Bosquet. PML, *tr.* by William Jay Smith

Lovers: "As a blind man." Meirion Pennar. BBMWP, *tr.* by Martin Davis

Lovers: "From somewhere over the houses, through the silence." Witter Bynner. APT-1; ASA

Lovers and madmen have such seething brains. William Shakespeare. IJHIL; WaAnP *Fr.* Midsummer Night's Dream, A.

Lover's Appeal, The. Sir Thomas Wyatt. NoSic

[And wilt thou leave me thus?) NAEL-6v1; NAEL-7v1

Lovers become quiet. Lovers, The. Jaime Sabines. TCLAP, *tr.* by Claudine-Marie D'Angelo

Lovers, continual lovers, only repay me. (LL) City of Orgies. Walt Whitman. APN-1; CAGL; ErotSp; NAAPv.1

Lover's death, how regular, The. Stark Major. Hart Crane. FuPo

Lovers depend on moonlight. It All Depends on You. Lew Brown, B. G. DeSylva and Ray Henderson. ReLy

Lovers' Duet. Wendy Lee. PasH

Lover's Exchange. Leigh Hunt. STuOW *Fr.* Story of Rimini, The.

Lover's Farewell, The. James Clarence Mangan. IrLP

Lovers, forget your love. Wind and Window Flower. Robert Frost. MoW

Lovers, fresh plighting lovers in our age. Lovers. Michael Field. PoBW; ViWPN

Lovers hold hands in never-opened novels. Used Book Store. Charles Simic. CAP-8

Lovers holding pits in their mouths. Moon Festival. Bei Dao. WoBe, *tr.* by Iona Man-Cheong and Eliot Weinberger

Lovers in the rain and flowers in the stall. Another Song About Paris. Dave Frishberg. ReLy

Lovers' Infiniteness[e]. John Donne. NOSC

Lover's Journey, The. George Crabbe.

"It is the soul that sees; the outward eyes." OxAEP-1

Lover's Logic. Allan Ramsay. DiBP *Fr.* Gentle Shepherd, The.

Lovers loitered on the deck talking, The. Feast, The. Robert Hass. GoPo

Lover's Lullaby, A. George Gascoigne. *See* Lullaby [*or* Lullabie] of a Lover, The.

Lover's Melancholy, The. John Ford.

Dawn. OBEV

Lovers of Achilles, The. Sophocles. *tr.* by Anne Carson

"This disease is an evil bound upon the day." EroLit, *tr.* by Anne Carson

Lovers of the Poor, The. Gwendolyn Brooks. CAP-8; ESEAA; IllVoic; LTA; NoAM

Lover's Prize, A. Countess de Die Beatrice. EroLit; NAWM-7v1, *tr.* by Peter Dronke

Lover's Progress, The. John Fletcher.

Dead Host's Welcome, The. OxAEP-1

Lover's quarrel hah. Reading the Facts about Frost in *The Norton Anthology*. George Starbuck. PoA 2002

Lover's Reply to Good Advice. Richard Hughes. MoBrPo

Lover's Return. Langston Hughes. SAmP

Lover's Return on a Bicycle, The. J. Gordon Coogler.

"Her charming steel-horse could not miss." VerBaPo

Lovers' Sestina, The. Bruce Meyer. IFF

Lover's Song, A. Goran. IrPoTo, *tr.* by Abdul Kadir Said Ferhadi

Lovers Total Recall. Tracie Morris. BtF

Lovers whose lifted hands are candles in winter. For a Child Expected. Anne Ridler. SacPr

Love's a baby dat grows up wild. Dat's Love (Habanera). Oscar Hammerstein, II. ReLy

Love's Advocate. Phoebe Hesketh. LW

Love's Alchemy [*or* Alchemie]. John Donne. BASC; NAEL-6v1; NAEL-7v1; NoP-4; NoP-5

Loves and sorrows of those who lose an orchard. Lost Orchard, The. Edgar Lee Masters. ColAP

Love's Chord. Edward Dowden. IrLP

Love's Clock. Sir John Suckling. NOSC

Love's Compensation. Voltairine de Cleyre. SWaP

Love's Constancy. Hadewijch. WPoS, *tr.* by Oliver Davies

Love's Cure. Francis Beaumont and John Fletcher.

Song. NOSC

Love's Cursive. Kim Namjo. CAMKP, *tr.* by David R. McCann and Hyunjae Yee Sallee

"As the spring." CAMKP, *tr.* by David R. McCann and Hyunjae Yee Sallee

"Do not let your blood." CAMKP, *tr.* by David R. McCann and Hyunjae Yee Sallee

"Even love dies of starvation." CAMKP, *tr.* by David R. McCann and Hyunjae Yee Sallee

"Even to the end of the earth." CAMKP, *tr.* by David R. McCann and Hyunjae Yee Sallee

"Heart that answers heart." CAMKP, *tr.* by David R. McCann and Hyunjae Yee Sallee

"How / the two people soaked." CAMKP, *tr.* by David R. McCann and Hyunjae Yee Sallee

"If your soul is called." CAMKP, *tr.* by David R. McCann and Hyunjae Yee Sallee

"Love is / customary sight." CAMKP, *tr.* by David R. McCann and Hyunjae Yee Sallee

"Love is honest farming." CAMKP, *tr.* by David R. McCann and Hyunjae Yee Sallee

"Love's half moon." CAMKP, *tr.* by David R. McCann and Hyunjae Yee Sallee

"Loving is precious." CAMKP, *tr.* by David R. McCann and Hyunjae Yee Sallee

"More painful, love is, The." CAMKP, *tr.* by David R. McCann and Hyunjae Yee Sallee

"Person who feeds me." CAMKP, *tr.* by David R. McCann and Hyunjae Yee Sallee

"Rather than deserting someone." CAMKP, *tr.* by David R. McCann and Hyunjae Yee Sallee

"This day so lonely." CAMKP, tr. by David R. McCann and Hyunjae Yee Sallee

"Though I am an ugly clay pot." CAMKP, tr. by David R. McCann and Hyunjae Yee Sallee

"Today, / love compromised my character." CAMKP, tr. by David R. McCann and Hyunjae Yee Sallee

"Uninvited woman, An." CAMKP, tr. by David R. McCann and Hyunjae Yee Sallee

"When a woman is without love." CAMKP, tr. by David R. McCann and Hyunjae Yee Sallee

"Words are sand." CAMKP, tr. by David R. McCann and Hyunjae Yee Sallee

"You already know." CAMKP, tr. by David R. McCann and Hyunjae Yee Sallee

Love's Deity [or Deitie]. John Donne. SoSe-8

Love's Despair. George Sigerson. IrLP

Love's Dozen. Jay Wright.

    Love in the Weather's Bells. ESEAA

Love's Emblem. John Clare. NIL-7; NIP-4

Love's Emblems. John Fletcher. NOSC

Love's Ending. Unknown. NoSic

Love's Farewell. Edmund Waller. OxBSo

Love's Fidelity. Petrarch. NoSic; OxBSo Fr. Sonnets to Laura.

Love's Fool [with music]. Margit Szécsi. IQMS, tr. by Kenneth McRobbie

Love's footprints. Unknown. SonAtl, tr. by P. Barsten, Billy Saan and Tracey Yuan

Love's Growth. John Donne. NoP-4; NoP-5; NOSC; NPeEn; PBRV

Love's half moon. Kim Namjo. CAMKP Fr. Love's Cursive.

Love's in the daily doings. Here. Glenna Luschei. GeoHom

Love's Justification. Michelangelo Buonarroti. OBVE, tr. by William Wordsworth

Love's Labour's Lost. William Shakespeare.

    Blossom, The. OBEV

    (Hiems.) NoSic

    "Holla, Approach." NPeEn

    "O! And I forsooth in love!" OBCoV

    ('On a day—alack the day!'.) AEP

    Spring. NAEL-6v1; NBLV; NIL-7; NIP-4; NoP-5; NoSic; OBEV; TFi

    (When Daisies Pied.) NoP-4; WaAnP

    Winter. ClHu; MakPoe; NAEL-6v1; NIL-7; NIP-4; NoP-5; OBEV; OxBEV; TFi; TRP; WaAnP; WeW-3

Love's Last Lesson. Letitia Elizabeth Landon. NAEL-7v2; RWP

3. Love's Like Milk. David McFadden. NLPA

Love's Martyrs. John Ford. NOSC Fr. Broken Heart, The.

Love's Matrimony. William Cavendish, Duke of Newcastle. NOSC

Love's Maturity. Hadewijch. WPoS, tr. by Oliver Davies

Love's Mirror. Constance Naden. ViWPN; VWP

Love's Mourner. Augusta Davies Webster. ViWPN; VWP Fr. Mother and Daughter.

Love's Music. Philip Bourke Marston. GSo

Love's Mystery. Joseph Beaumont. NOSC

Love's night and a lamp. Meleager. WoPoe, tr. by Peter Whigham

Love's Not Time's Fool. William Shakespeare. See Sonnet 116: "Let me not to the marriage of true minds."

Loves of the Eel [or Fishes], The. Oppian [of Corycus]. NPeEn Fr. Halieutica.

Loves of the Plants, The. Erasmus Darwin. Fr. Botanic Garden, The.

Loves of the Puppets. Richard Wilbur. UpMys

Loves of the Tortoise, The. Oppian [of Corycus]. NPeEn Fr. Halieutica.

Love's Offence. Sir John Suckling. NOSC

Love's Parallel. Elizabeth Garrett. MFPA

Love's Philosophy. Percy Bysshe Shelley. ItP; OxAEP-2

Love's Progress. James Vincent Cunningham. APT-2

Love's Progress. John Donne. BASC Fr. Elegies.

Love's Reasons. Han Yong'un [or Yongwun]. CAMKP, tr. by Sammy Solberg

Love's Secret. William Blake. ITBLP; NPeEn; OxBEV

    (Never Pain to Tell Thy Love.) NAEL-6v2; NAEL-7v2

Love's Siege. Sir John Suckling. NPeEn

    ("'Tis Now, Since I Sate Down Before.") CavPo

Love's Sun. William Cavendish, Duke of Newcastle. NOSC

Loves that ended long ago. Streets. Henrik Nordbrandt. VCWP, tr. by Henrik Norbrandt and Alexander Taylor

Love's the boy stood on the burning deck. Casabianca. Elizabeth Bishop. NIL-7; NoP-5; WoPoe

Love's thrice a robber, however you take it. On Love. Diophanes of Myrina. WoPoe, tr. by Dudley Fitts

Love's Triumph must be Honour's Funeral. (LL) Loving and Beloved. Sir John Suckling. CavPo; NAEL-6v1; NAEL-7v1

4. Love's Two Hemispheres. David McFadden. NLPA

Love's Varlets. Francis Thompson. SacPr

Love's Vista [with music]. Henrietta Cordelia Ray. CBWP-3

Love's Way. Kang Ŭn'gyo. CAMKP, tr. by Tae Yang Kwak

Love's Witness. Aphra Behn. LW

Loveshock. Unknown. SonAtl, tr. by Alan Brierly

Love-Sick Maid, The. Sir Richard Steele. IrLP Fr. Conscious Lovers, The.

Lovesickness: A Medieval Text. Jack Coulehan. BloBone

4: Lovesight. Dante Gabriel Rossetti. NAEL-6v2 Fr. House of Life, The.

Love-song: "Beautiful, delicate bright gazelle, The." Walter James Turner. OBMV

Love-Song, A: "Such a heart!" Unknown. IrLP, tr. by Brendan Kennelly

Love-songs, at Once Tender and Informative. Samuel Hoffenstein.

    "Had we but parted at the start." AmWit

    "If you love me, as I love you." AmWit

    "Let us build a little house." AmWit

    "Maid of Gotham, ere we part." AmWit

    "My sanguine and adventurous dear." AmWit

    "Your little hands." AmWit; NBLV; OBCoV

Lovest Thou Me? William Cowper. ChIV-2 Fr. Olney Hymns.

Lovey Joe, a boy I know, an expert judge of gals. Magnolia. Lew Brown, B. G. DeSylva and Ray Henderson. ReLy

Loving. Paul Eluard and Andre Breton. YaTCFP, tr. by Mary Ann Caws

Loving. Angela Jackson. BtF

Loving Again. Gloria Wade-Gayles. ISC

Loving Along Western Rivers. Stephen J. Lyons. PasH

Loving and Beloved. Sir John Suckling. CavPo; NAEL-6v1; NAEL-7v1

Loving and Liking [Irregular Verses Addressed to A Child]. Dorothy Wordsworth. SacPr; WoRP

Loving came her way. Violence of Pronoun, The. Primus St. John. EGAG

Loving friend, the gift of one. To Flush, My Dog. Elizabeth Barrett Browning. DiBP

Loving hard is easy. To stand on the gallows and to swear. Ailing. Sennur Sezer. NaPG, tr. by Talat Sait Halman

Loving in truth, and fain[e] in verse my love to show. Sir Philip Sidney. BrAP; CABP; GSo; NAEL-6v1; NAEL-7v1; NoP-4; NoP-5; NoSic; NPeEn; OxAEP-1; OxBEV; OxBSo; PBRV; TFi Fr. Astrophil and Stella.

Loving is precious. Kim Namjo. CAMKP Fr. Love's Cursive.

Loving Mad Tom. Unknown. See Tom o' Bedlam's Song.

Loving Mad Tom. Unknown. NOSC

Loving old priceless things. Makusho, Layman. ZenPo, tr. by Takashi Ikemoto and Lucien Stryk

Loving Poem. Gisèle Prassinos. YaTCFP, tr. by Mary Ann Caws

Loving the Flesh. Todd Davis. ACAMVP

Loving the rituals that keep men close. Palladas. OBVE, tr. by Tony Harrison

Loving You. Frances Horovitz. LW

Loving you was all that really mattered. Where Are You? Harold Adamson. ReLy

Low and mournful be the strain. Voluntaries. Ralph Waldo Emerson. APN-1; CBCWP

Low Barometer. Robert Bridges. CABP; NoAM

Low beating of the tom-toms, The. Danse Africaine. Langston Hughes. NAAPv.2

Low beginnings of content, The. (LL) Alfred Tennyson. NAEL-6v2; NAEL-7v2 Fr. In Memoriam A. H. H.

Low Bridge, Everybody Down. William S. Allen. See Erie Canal, The.

Low building with three beams merely shelters the body, The. Unknown. NAAPv.2

Low Church. Stanley J. Sharpless. NBLV; OBCoV

Low clouds, the shreds of dry grass, The. Tatyana Voltskaya. CRWP, tr. by Catriona Kelly

Low clouds yellow in a mist wind. First Movement. Padraic Fiacc. PNI

Low End, The. Tomás Riley. BRtP

Low gray skies over. Ray McNiece. AmZen

Low hang the eaves of the thatched hut. Tune: "Pure Serene Music" Rural Life. Hsin Ch'i-chi. ColAnChi, tr. by Jiaosheng Wang

Low huts, groans muffled. Midwives, The. Celia Gilbert. ChIV-1

Low in the grave he lay—Jesus, my Saviour. Up from the Grave He Arose. Robert Lowry. SacPr

Low in thy grave with thee. David's Lament for Jonathan. Peter Abelard. NAWM-5v1

Low murmurs creep along the woody vale. Written at Bignor Park in Sussex, in August, 1799. Charlotte Smith. CenSon

Low river flows like smoked glass, The. Prayer for My Son. James Applewhite. BLT

Low Road, The. Marge Piercy. BeAl; TWF

Low sandy beach and the thin scrub pine, The. Cape Cod. George Santayana. APN-2

Low Temple, A.   Jejuri Arun Kolatkar.   EmeKit

Low temple keeps its gods in the dark, A.   Low Temple, A.   Jejuri Arun Kolatkar.   EmeKit

Low Tide on Grand Pré.   Bliss Carman.   BrAP; IFF

Low to High.   Langston Hughes.   APT-2

Low to the water's edge.   Elegy on a Young Airedale Bitch Lost Two Years Since in the Salt-Marsh.   Yvor Winters.   APT-2

Low Volume.   Reiner Kunze.   PoSu, tr. by Michael Hamburger

Low ye hills in ocean lie.   My Heart Is in Merioneth.   Unknown.   OBWVE, tr. by Richard Llwyd

Low-anchored cloud.   Henry David Thoreau.   NCAP

Lower East Side Poem, A.   Miguel Piñero.   PueRic

Lower East Side: The George Bernstein Story.   Edward Field.   OBCoV

Lower leaves of the trees, The.   Sone no Yoshitada.   AmFaPo; ItP, tr. by Kenneth Rexroth

Lower Life, The.   May Kendall.   VWP

Lower New York.   George Cabot Lodge.   APN-2

Lower the Standard: That's My Motto [with music].   Karl Shapiro.   NoAM

Lower them and dream of home. (LL)   Still Night Thoughts.   Li Po.   ColAnChi; ItP, tr. by Burton Watson

Lower World, The.   Samuel Jackson Pratt.
   Blind Man's Dog, The.   DiBP

Lowering their slings and litters. (LL)   Family Reunion.   Louise Erdrich.   HATNAP; NAMCP V.2; NoAM; WaAnP

Lowery Cot.   Leonard Alfred George Strong.   MoBrPo

Lowest circle of hell, The. Contrary to prevailing opinion it is inhabited neither by despots nor matricides.   What Mr. Cogito Thinks About Hell.   Zbigniew Herbert.   GPTC; VCWP; WoPoe, tr. by Bogdana Carpenter and John Carpenter

Lowest circle of hell, The. Contrary to general opinion, neither mother.   What Mr. Cogito Thinks About Hell.   Zbigniew Herbert.   MotU, tr. by Stuart Friebert

Lowest trees have top[p]s, the ant[e] her gall, The.   Sir Edward Dyer.   NoSic; NPeEn

Lowlands.   William Reed Huntington.   APN-2

Low-Level Cross-Country.   Howard Nemerov.   GM

Lowliest duties on herself [or itself] did lay, The. (LL)   London 1802 ("Milton! thou shouldst be living at this hour.")   William Wordsworth.   BrAP; CenSon; HeIP-4; InoFa; NAEL-6v2; NAEL-7v2; NIL-7; NIP-4; NOBRP; NoP-4; NoP-5; OxAEP-2; TFi; UV

Low-tide shoals flat-lit.   Apophatic.   Jocelyn Emerson.   IAoNAP

Loyal English Man's Wish for the Preservation of the King and Queen, The.   Anne Morcott.   EMWP

Loyal hearts that saved your king.   Dirge for Two Generals.   Yejong, King of Koryŏ.   CATKP, tr. by Peter H. Lee

Loyal Housewife.   Daisy Zamora.   LoL, tr. by Margaret Randall

Loyalty.   Harvey Shapiro.   TaR

Loyalty to the Flag.   Lizelia Augusta Jenkins Moorer.   CBWP-3

Lozenge.   Hoa Nguyen.   WANABP

Lu Chi speaks of the heavenly arrow.   Meditation on the Wen-Fu.   Eleanor Wilner.   GifTon

Lu Mountain Song For the Palace Censor Empty-Boat Lu, A.   Li Po.   CCL1, tr. by Elling O. Eide

Lu ti nagana.   Víctor Terán.   RMCMP

Lu ti neza.   Lu ti nagana.   Víctor Terán.   RMCMP

Luba.   Jacqueline Goldberg. tr. by Joanne Friedman
   Luba 1.   MirDau, tr. by Joanne Friedman
   Luba 3.   MirDau, tr. by Joanne Friedman
   Luba 2.   MirDau, tr. by Joanne Friedman

Luba / conversation.   Jacqueline Goldberg.   MirDau Fr. Luba.

Luba 1.   Jacqueline Goldberg.   MirDau Fr. Luba.

Luba 3.   Jacqueline Goldberg.   MirDau Fr. Luba.

Luba 2.   Jacqueline Goldberg.   MirDau Fr. Luba.

Lubbock night is glittering, the shake roofs, The.   Triangulation.   Daryl E. Jones.   TiP2

Lubin.   Unknown.   FaBoVe

Lucan's Pharsalia Book 1.   Christopher Marlowe.
   "This said, the restles generall through the darke."   PBRV

Lucasia, Rosania and Orinda Parting at a Fountain, July 1663.   Katherine Philips.   EMWP; PEW

Lucasia's and Orinda's Name. (LL)   Friendship in Emblem[e], or the Seal[e], to my dearest Lucasia.   Katherine Philips.   CABP; EMWP; PBRV

Lucasta Replies to Lovelace.   G. K. Chesterton.   UV

Lucasta's Fan.   Richard Lovelace.   CavPo

Lucent dew congeals into frost, The.   Juan Chi.   ColAnChi Fr. Songs of My Soul.

Lucent lake was lit with sheen, The.   Thought of Lake Ontario, A.   Henrietta Cordelia Ray.   CBWP-3

Lucero de la Tarde.   Francisco Segovia.   RMCMP

Lucid at dusk the city lies revealed.   Night Flight : New York.   Muriel Rukeyser and Leif Sjoberg.

Lucifer, a student once wrote "fell."   Closer.   Albert Goldbarth.   PoA 2002

Lucifer blazing in superb effigies.   Bibliographers, The.   Geoffrey Hill.   UpMys

Lucifer in Starlight.   George Meredith.   CABP; ChIV-1; CtM; GSo; NAEL-6v2; NAEL-7v2; NoP-4; NoP-5; OBEV; OxBEV; OxBSo; TFi

Lucifer in Starlight.   David St. John.   CAP-8

Lucifer in the Train.   Adrienne Rich.   GM

Lucifer, Son of the Morning, Pretty Boy.   Lucifer's Epistle to the Fallen.   Scott Cairns.   UpMys

Lucifer's Epistle to the Fallen.   Scott Cairns.   UpMys

Lucinda Matlock.   Edgar Lee Masters.   IllVoic; MoAmPo; NoAM Fr. Spoon River Anthology.

Lucindy, who you 'spose I seed.   Common Occurrence, A.   Priscilla Jane Thompson.   CBWP-2

Lucio.   Frisbees on Light.   Giulia Niccolai.   CItWP, tr. by Cinzia Sartini Blum and Lara Trubowitz

Luck.   Raymond Carver.   LaCa

Luck.   Wilfrid Wilson Gibson.   OBMV

Luck ("Sometimes a crumb falls.")   Langston Hughes.   APT-2; OxBoAm; SAmP

Luck.   Carl Phillips.   AmAlph

Luck.   Marc J. Straus.   BloBone

Luck, Be a Lady.   Frank Loesser.   APT-2; ReLy

Luck, be a lady tonight. (LL)   Luck, Be a Lady.   Frank Loesser.   APT-2; ReLy

Luck in Sarajevo.   Izet Sarajlić.   StAl

Luck is yours that you can talk about, The.   Love Poem, A.   Vidya.   WoPoe, tr. by Peter Dent and Edwin Gerow

Luck to the craft that bears this name of mine.   To a Cape Ann Schooner.   John Greenleaf Whittier.   OxBSo

Luck, we've had it; our character the public's.   It Did.   Robert Lowell.   NoAM

Luck[e]s, my fair[e] falcon, and your fellow[e]s all.   Sir Thomas Wyatt.   NoP-5

"Luckies."   Reginald Gibbons.   IllVoic

Luckily for us. (LL)   Humming-Bird.   D. H. Lawrence.   NAMCP V.1; NoAM; OWoS; OxBEV

Luckily my lover put out the fire in my stern. (LL)   Fěng Mĕng-lung.   ColAnChi; WoPoe Fr. Mountain Songs.

Lucks, my Fair Falcon.   Sir Thomas Wyatt.   NoP-5

Luck's Shining Child.   George Garrett.   InGu

Lucky.   Tony Hoagland.   BeAl

Lucky 7.   Katharine Harer.   MiVo

Lucky Chance, The.   Aphra Behn.

Lucky Eugene.   Michael Foley.   PNI

Lucky Life.   Gerald Stern.   BodElec
   "Dear waves, what will you do for me this year?"   InvLad

Lucky life isn't one long string of horrors.   Lucky Life.   Gerald Stern.   BodElec

Lucky my ears 'pop' at the hilltop.   Ron Silliman.   FTOS Fr. Hidden.

Lucky One, The.   Reginald Shepherd.   GT

Lucky Smile.   Michele Wolf.   LiTh

Lucky Spence's Last Advice.   Allan Ramsay.   NePenScot

Lucky Strikes.   Ron Padgett.   FTOS

Lucky the husband.   Mabel Kelly.   Turlough Carolan.   OxBEV, tr. by Austin Clarke

Lucky to Be Me.   Betty Comden and Adolph Green.   ReLy

Lucky with day approaching, with leaning dawn. (LL)   Wanderer, The.   W. H. Auden.   HarvBoo; NAMCP V.1; NoAM; WaAnP; WeW-3; WoPoe

Lucrece and Nara.   Laura Riding Jackson.   APT-2

Lucrece's Death.   William Shakespeare.   NoSic Fr. Rape of Lucrece, The.

Lucretius felt the change of the world in his time, the great republic riding to the height.   Prescription of Painful Ends.   Robinson Jeffers.   APT-1; MoAmPo

Lucretius knew.   De Natura Rerum.   Yves Bonnefoy.   VCWP, tr. by Lisa Sapinkopf

Lucretius versus the Lake Poets.   Robert Frost.   OBCoV

Lucy.   William Wordsworth.   OBEV; TFi
   I Travelled among Unknown Men.   BrAP; NAEL-6v2; NAEL-7v2
   Lucy Gray.   NPBRoP
   She Dwelt among the Untrodden Ways.   BrAP; HeIP-4; InoFa; NAEL-6v2; NAEL-7v2; NIL-7; NIP-4; NoP-5; NPBRoP; NPeEn; OxAEP-2; UV; WeW-3
   Slumber Did My Spirit Seal, A.   BrAP; CtM; HeIP-4; InoFa; NAEL-6v2; NAEL-7v2; NOBRP; NoP-4; NoP-5; NPBRoP; NPeEn; OxBEV; PoPoPo; WeW-3

(Song.) NOBRP

Strange Fits of Passion Have I Known. BrAP; NOBRP; OBEV

(Strange Fits of Passion I Have Known.) NPBRoP; WaAnP

Three Years She Grew [in Sun and Shower]. BrAP; NAEL-6v2; NAEL-7v2; NoP-5; NPBRoP

Lucy Ashton's Song. Sir Walter Scott. NAEL-6v2; NPeEn; OBEV; OxAEP-2; OxBEV; WoPoe Fr. Bride of Lammermoor, The.

Lucy Gray. William Wordsworth. NPBRoP Fr. Lucy.

Lucy Gray; or, Solitude. William Wordsworth. NAEL-6v2; NAEL-7v2; NOBRP; OxAEP-2; WaAnP

Lucy Lipschutz, Lucy Lipschutz. Girl Refugee, The. Matilde Salganicoff. MirDau, tr. by Celeste Kostopulos-Cooperman

Lucy, Lucie. Peter Garner. IFF

Lucy, you brightness of our sphere, who are. To Lucy, Countess of Bedford, with Mr. Donne's Satires. Ben Jonson. NAEL-6v1; NAEL-7v1

(LUCY, you brightnesse of our spheare, who are.) PBRV

Lucy's Bones. Christine Evans. TCAWP

Lucy's Letter. James Berry. FaBoVe

Lud! what a group the motley scene discloses! Oliver Goldsmith. OBSV Fr. Epilogue to "The Sister."

Lufra Avenged. Sir Walter Scott. DiBP Fr. Lady of the Lake, The.

Lufthansa. John Tranter. BMAP; NOBAu

Lugar, El. Mónica Nepote. SPV

Lugar Vacío en la Celebración. José Ángel Valente. RaW

Lugs Benedict on the Coast, 1934. Tom Rea. GifTon

Lugubrious days pass with the amplitude of manatees. Florida, La. Virgil Suárez. BAP-04

Lui et Elle. D. H. Lawrence. NAMCP V.1; NoAM

Luini in porcelain! Ezra Pound. NoP-5; TCAPo Fr. Hugh Selwyn Mauberley (Life and Contacts).

Luis de Camões. Roy Campbell. OxAEP-2

Luke 14: A Commentary. Kathleen Norris. UpMys

Luke XXIII. Jorge Luis Borges. GI

Luke 10. Richard Crashaw. SacPr

Luke 10:25–37; And behold, a lawyer. Stephen Mitchell. GI Fr. St. Luke.

Luke 10:38–42; Now as they went on their way. Anna Kamienska. GI Fr. St. Luke.

Luke 11: Blessed Be the Paps Which Thou Hast Sucked. Richard Crashaw. NAEL-7v1

Luke 1:26–38; In the sixth month the angel Gabriel. Anna Kamienska. GI Fr. St. Luke.

Luke 1:39–56: In those days Mary arose. Rainer Maria Rilke. GI Fr. St. Luke.

Luke 15:11–19; And he said, "There was a man." Rainer Maria Rilke. GI Fr. St. Luke.

Luke 15:20–32; And he arose and came. Edwin Arlington Robinson. GI Fr. St. Luke.

Luke 16:1–9; He also said to the disciples. Ernesto Cardenal. GI Fr. St. Luke.

Luke 16:19–26; "There was a rich man." Robert Frost. GI Fr. St. Luke.

Luke 2:1–7; In those days a decree went out from Caesar Augustus. Louise Glück. GI Fr. St. Luke.

Luke 2:21–40; And at the end of eight days, when he was circumcised. T. S. Eliot. GI Fr. St. Luke.

Luke 23:26–38; And as they led him away. W. H. Auden. GI Fr. St. Luke.

Luke 23:26–38; And as they led him away. W. H. Auden. GI Fr. St. Luke.

Luke 23:39–43; One of the criminals. Jorge Luis Borges. GI Fr. St. Luke.

Luke: 24:13–32; That very day two of them. Eric Pankey. GI Fr. St. Luke.

Luke 24:36–49; As they were saying this, Jesus. Alec Derwent Hope. GI Fr. St. Luke.

Luke 2:8–20; And in that region there were shepherds. Bertolt Brecht. GI Fr. St. Luke.

Luke 5:1–11; While the people pressed upon him. Czeslaw Milosz. GI Fr. St. Luke.

Luke 6:39. William Carlos Williams. GI Fr. St. Matthew; He also told them a parable.

Luke 7; She Began To Wash His Feet with Teares and Wipe Them with the Haires of Her Head. Bible, N.T. NOSC; SacPr Fr. St. Luke.

Luke Havergal. Edwin Arlington Robinson. APN-2; MoAmPo; NAAL-5; NAAPv.1; NAMCP V.1; NoAM; OxBoAm; TCAPo; TFi

Luke 6.25. Francis Quarles. ChIV-2

Lull, The. Molly Peacock. OxBoAm

Lulla Lullaby. William Byrd. ChIV-2

Lullabies, 2:174. Unknown. WoPoe Fr. Kanteletar, The.

Lullabies of the Onion. Miguel Hernández. RaW, tr. by Philip Levine

Lullaby. Breyten Breytenbach. VCWP, tr. by Breyten Breytenbach

Lullaby. Debra Gregerman. AmPoNex

Lullaby. Jon Mukand. BloBone

Lullaby: "Beloved, may your sleep be sound." [fr. Words for Music Perhaps]. William Butler Yeats. OBMV

Lullaby: "Big as a down duvet the night." Molly Peacock. PasH

Lullaby: "Hush, lullay." Léonie Adams. MoAmPo

Lullaby: "Hush ye, hush ye! honey, darlin'." Clara Ann Thompson. CBWP-2

Lullaby: "I would not sing you to sleep." Reetika Vazirani. PoCho

Lullaby: "Lay your sleeping head, my love." W. H. Auden. EMP; HarvBoo; ItP; NAEL-6v2; NAEL-7v2; NAMCP V.1; NoAM; NoP-4; NoP-5; OxAEP-2; OxBEV; StAl; TFi; WaAnP; WeW-3

(Lay Your Sleeping Head, My Love.) BrAP; CtM

Lullaby: "Little one, go to sleep. Sleep soundly." Vietnamese Oral Tradition. CaDao, tr. by John Balaban

Lullaby: "My mother's an expert at one thing." Louise Glück. MoWP

Lullaby: "On the moon's round cay." Unknown. SonAtl, tr. by S. L. Lee, Wendy North and Colin Wilberts

Lullaby: "Say to me: out there are only streets, and cars." Constance Merritt. AmPoNex

Lullaby: "Sky is letting its blue eyes close, The." Attila József. IQMS, tr. by Vernon Watkins

Lullaby: "Sleep and rain, two gangsters." Alan Michael Parker. AmPoNex

Lullaby: "Sleep, little architect. It is your mother's wish." Joan Murray. OxBoAm; YaYoPo

Lullaby: "Someone would like to have you for her child." Unknown. WoPoe, tr. by Kwabenia Nketia

Lullaby: "Though the world has slipped and gone." Dame Edith Sitwell. NALW

Lullaby: "Upon my lap my sovereign sits." Richard Verstegan. OBEV

(Our Lady's Lullaby.) SacPr

Lullaby: "You are safe / You are lying in a hammock." Alpay Ulku. AmPoNex

Lullaby, A. Lewis Carroll. See Duchess's Lullaby, The.

Lullaby, A: "Din of work is subdued, The." W. H. Auden. NAMCP V.1; NoAM

Lullaby for Odysseus. Irina Ermakova. CRWP, tr. by Daniel Weissbort

Lullaby for Rachael. James Simmons. PNI

Lullaby for Suzanne. Michael Stillman. TLR

Lullaby for the Hungry, A. Muhammad Mahdi Al-Jawahiri. IrPoTo, tr. by Terri DeYoung

Lullaby, lullaby. / It is daybreak. Lullaby. Unknown. APN-2 Fr. Mountain Chant, The.

Lullaby: Moonlight Lingers. Robert Penn Warren. GPTC Fr. Promises.

Lullaby, O, lullaby! Thomas Hood. NBLV Fr. Domestic Poems.

Lullaby of Birdland. George David Weiss. ReLy

Lullaby of birdland. Lullaby of Birdland. George David Weiss. ReLy

Lullaby of Broadway. Al Dubin. ReLy

Lullaby of Donald Gorm, by his Nurse. Unknown. EMWP

Lullaby of the Onion. Miguel Hernández. AF; WED, tr. by Robert Bly

Lullaby [or Lullabie] of a Lover, The. George Gascoigne. NAEL-6v1; PtR

(Gascoigne's Lullaby [or Lullabie].) NoP-4; NoP-5; NoSic; WaAnP

(Lover's Lullaby, A.) OBEV

Lullaby "Purple." Eve Merriam. NOxBChV

Lullaby Town. John Irving Diller. ITBLP

Lullabye for a Butch. Melinda Goodman. WiU

Lullay, Lullay, Like a Child. John Skelton. See With Lullay, Lullay, Like a Child.

Lullay, lullay, litel child, child rest thee a throwe. Unknown. OHMEL

Lullay, lullay, litel child, why wepest thou so sore? Unknown. OHMEL

Lulled, at silence, the spent attack. Baggot Street Deserta. Thomas Kinsella. NAMCP V.2; NoAM

Lulled by rumble, babble, beep. (LL) Manhattan Lullaby. Norma Farber. SSCS; TLR

Lulled by rumble, babble, beep. Manhattan Lullaby. Norma Farber. SSCS; TLR

Lu-lung Village, Autumn. Hsu Hsuan. CrYelRi, tr. by Sam Hamill

Lulu's Back in Town. Al Dubin. ReLy

Lumber of a London-going dray, The. Incident in the Early Life of Ebenezer Jones, Poet, 1828, An. Sir John Betjeman. NAMCP V.1; NoAM

Lumber wagons are already there, The. Lumber Wagons, The. Juan Ramón Jiménez. WED, tr. by Robert Bly

Lumbers the wain; and day fades out like smoke. (LL) Potato Harvest, The. Sir Charles G. D. Roberts. BrAP; NIL-7

Lumens. Olga Broumas. ExTi

Lumière de la lame, La. André Du Bouchet. YaTCFP

Lumière, par exemple. noir. Lumière, par exemple. Jacques Roubaud. YaTCFP

Lu-ming: Salt Lick! Unknown. CCL1, tr. by Ezra Pound

Luminous new leaf. For Rita's Daughter, Just Born. Eunice De Souza. NAMCP V.2

Luminous rays penetrate the tarnished green of an eye that looks like a dead cenote. Chimera. Silvia Eugenia Castillero. SPV, *tr. by* Jen Hofer

Luminous, tranquil eyes. Madrigal 1. Gutierre de Cetina. BLPSL, *tr. by* Rene de Costa, Rigas Kappatos and Eleni Paidoussi

Lumpectomy Eve. Lucille Clifton. CAP-8

"Lumpish trollop, The !" Pastoral. Dominic Bevan Wyndham Lewis. UV

Lumumba Blues. Raymond R. Patterson. BRtP

Luna al norte de la estrella Aldebarán alumbra en el estuario, La. Marea roja. José Luis Rivas. RMCMP

Luna Moth. Carl Phillips. CAP-8; PoDa

Lunar Baedeker. Mina Loy. APT-1; OxBoAm

Lunar Eclipse. Tracy Ryan. NeBl

Lunar eclipse, and your solos spread, A. Blues Villanelle for Sonny Criss. Sascha Feinstein. AmPoNex

Lunar Eclipse, July 6, 1982. Diane Glancy. FiBr

Lunar Frost. Mary Kinzie. IllVoic

Lunar Paraphrase. Wallace Stevens. SAmP

Lunatic of Lindley Meadow, The. August Kleinzahler. PmAP

Lunatic, the Lover, and the Poet, The. William Shakespeare. IJHIL; WaAnP *Fr.* Midsummer Night's Dream, A.

Lunatics. Bella Akhatovna Akhmadulina. TCRusP, *tr. by* Daniel Weissbort

Lunch and Afterwards. Dannie Abse. BloBone

Lunch at The Mars. Question of Vitamins, A. Ron Charach. BloBone

Lunch in Nablus City Park. Naomi Shihab Nye. CFP

Lunch with Girl Scouts. Sharon Bryan. ReTh

Lunch with Pancho Villa. Paul Muldoon. ModIr; NAMCP V.2

Luncheon, A. Max Beerbohm. OBSV
  (Luncheon (Thomas Hardy Entertains the Prince of Wales), A.) UV

Luncheon on the Grass. Carl Phillips. AmFaPo

Lunching. Lori Tsang. BtF

Lune diminue, divin septembre, La. Après le déluge. Pierre Jean Jouve. YaTCFP

Lungi Crossing. Iyamide Hazeley. NAfrP

Lungs draw in the air and rattle it out again, The. Remorse. Sir John Betjeman. MoBrPo

Lungs have countless globules, you know, like bunches of grapes. Our Old Home. Yi Yônju. EcSo, *tr. by* Yung-Hee Kim

Lungs of the wrinkled gray-eyed man, The. Refugee. Laila Halaby. PoArWo

Lupines. Al Pittman. Coast

Lurching from gloomy limousines we slip. My Father's Funeral. Karl Shapiro. TaR

Lure. Susan Musgrave. BrAP

Lure, 1963. Denise Riley. Oth

Lure of the night's dædalina sea-born breath. On an Æolian Harp. George Cabot Lodge. APN-2

Lured by a summons he does not. Possessed, The. Mahmoud al-Braikan. IrPoTo, *tr. by* Ralph Saverese and Saadi A. Simawe

Lured by some corporal's smooth address. Jeffery, or, the Soldier's Progress. Philip Freneau. AmWaPo

Lurid Confessions. Steve Kowit. SUP

Lurking under the maple trees. Jewish Cemetery at Olsany, Kafka's Grave, April, Sunny Weather, The. Miroslav Holub. PoSu

Lush Life. Billy Strayhorn. ReLy

Lushly I walk, like flowers under the bitter orange. Happiest Man in the World, The. Gzar Hantoosh. IrPoTo, *tr. by* Saadi A. Simawe and Ellen Doré Watson

Lusiads, The. Luis de Camões [*or* Camões *or* Camoëns]. *tr. by* Richard Francis Burton and Sir Richard Fanshawe
  "Battle's uncertain work begins; and move." FaBoWar, *tr. by* Richard Francis Burton
  "Feats of Arms, and famed heroick Host, The." FaBoWar, *tr. by* Richard Francis Burton
  "Now through the ocean in great haste they flunder." OBVE
  "Shores are crown'd with people, The." OBVE
  "With glad reception our Commander meets." FaBoWar, *tr. by* Richard Francis Burton

Lusitanian Song. János Vajda. IQMS, *tr. by* Jean Overton Fuller

Lusitanian Variant, The. H. C. ten Berge.
  Dança Mortal. TuT
  Duel. TuT
  "Fortunes in knee breeches." TuT

Lust. Star Black. KGB

Lust in the long run spins a kingdom of lull. Spider of Doubt. Pimone Triplett. AmPoNex

Lust it comes out, that gluttony went in. (LL) On Gut. Ben Jonson. NoP-4; NoP-5; NPeEn; PoPoPo

Lust of the Eyes, The. Elizabeth Siddal. VWP

Lustra. Ezra Pound.
  Further Instructions. PoA 2002
  Rest, The. MoAmPo; NAMCP V.1; NoAM; PoA 2002

Lustra. Officially the cold comes from Manitoba. James Harrison. BodElec *Fr.* Letters to Yesenin.

Lust's too genteel to let the weather in. In a Bed-Sitter. Hal Porter. NOBAu

Lusty Juventus. Robert Wever.
  In Youth Is Pleasure. OBEV
  (Of Youth He Singeth.) NPeEn

Lusty May. *Unknown*. OBEV

Lusty wench as nimble as an eel, A. Epigram. John Taylor. NOSC

Lute, The. Judah Al-Harizi. BLT, *tr. by* T. Carmi

Lute, The: A Rhapsody. Hsi K'ang.
  Extracts. CCL1, *tr. by* Robert Hans van Gulik

Lute of Afric's Tribe, The. Albery Allson Whitman. APN-2

Lute Player, The. Li Ho. CrYelRi, *tr. by* Sam Hamill

Lute trills the most wondrous melodies, The. Singing Lute, The. Ibn Arfa' Ra'suh. HiArP; NAWM-7v1, *tr. by* James T. Monroe

"Luteous" to "Lymph" for "F." Tina Darragh. FTOS

Luther, they say, was unwise; he didn't see how things were going. Arthur Hugh Clough. FaBoVe *Fr.* Amours de Voyage.

Lutheran, Popish, Calvinistic, all of these confessions three. Faith. Friedrich von Logau. GePo, *tr. by* George C. Schoolfield

Lutra, the Fisher. James McMichael. CalPo

Lutteurs. René Char. YaTCFP

Luttrell. Richard Murphy. PBCIP *Fr.* Battle of Aughrim, The.

Luttrell, Master of Luttrellstown. Richard Murphy. PBCIP *Fr.* Battle of Aughrim, The.

Luwani Dangriga. Zoila Ellis. OWABP

Lux Est Umbra Dei. John Addington Symonds. GSo

Lux in Tenebris. Katharine Tynan Hinkson. SacPr

Luxembourg Garden. Afaa Michael Weaver. GT

Luxuriant, clustered round your cottage door! (LL) Jasmine. Claude McKay. APT-1; GT

Luxurious Man, to bring his Vice in use. Mower Against Gardens, The. Andrew Marvell. BASC; CABP; NAEL-6v1; NAEL-7v1; NIL-7; NoP-4; NoP-5; NOSC; NPeEn; OBGa; OxAEP-1; PBRV

Luxurious room, evening.—A large lighted chandelier. Open French win. They are Coming. Filippo Tommaso Marinetti. PFTM-1

Luxury. Yehuda Amichai. PoSu, *tr. by* Assia Gutmann

Luxury. Donald Justice. HeIP-4

Luxury. Edgell Rickword. RSaN

Luxury, then, is a way of. Political Poem. Imamu Amiri Baraka. AF; NoAM; PmAP

Lü-yi: Green Robe. *Unknown*. APSN; CCL1; NDACCP, *tr. by* Ezra Pound

Luz de los mundos paralelos. David Huerta. RMCMP

Luz entre las hojas, La. Regreso a la ciudad. Manuel Ulacia. RMCMP

Luz lo Malo que Tiene, La. Pedro Salinas. RaW

Luz que parecía unir mundos paralelos, Una. Luz de los mundos paralelos. David Huerta. RMCMP

Luzzato. Charles Reznikoff. BBASP
  (Padua 1717.) WaAnP

Lwonesomeness. William Barnes. OxBEV

Lybica. Jane Seager. EMWP

Lychees. Medbh McGuckian. PBCIP

Lycidas. Thomas Bailey Aldrich. TreFP

Lycidas. John Milton. AmFaPo; BASC; BrAP; CABP; ClHu; InoFa; MakPoe; NAEL-6v1; NAEL-7v1; NIL-7; NoP-4; NoP-5; NOSC; NPeEn; OBEV; OxAEP-1; OxBEV; PBRV; PoPoPo; TFi; WaAnP

Lycidas, in this valley have you maybe seen. Titus Calpurnius Siculus. RomPo *Fr.* Eclogues.

Lycurgus' Alauns. Geoffrey Chaucer. DiBP *Fr.* Canterbury Tales, The.

Lydia, in Heavens Name. Horace. OBVE *Fr.* Odes.

Lydia is as wide and slack. Martial. RomPo, *tr. by* Olive Pitt-Kethley

Lydia, oh, Lydia. Lydia, the Tattooed Lady. E. Y. Harburg. ReLy

Lydia Pinkham. *Unknown*. OBCoV

Lydia, the Tattooed Lady. E. Y. Harburg. ReLy

Lydia's Phantasmagoria. Gloria Vando. TouFir

Lydstep Caverns. Sir Lewis Morris.
  "Here in these fretted caverns whence the sea." AngWePo

Lyell's Hypothesis Again. Kenneth Rexroth. APSN; APT-2; NAAPv.2

The lyf so short, the craft so long to lerne. Parlement of Foules, The. Geoffrey Chaucer.

Lying [*with music*]. Richard Wilbur. MakPoe; OxBoAm

Lying above. Air. Charlotte Gardelle. CuPo

Lying apart now, each in a separate bed. One Flesh. Elizabeth Jennings. LW; NoP-4; NoP-5; OxAEP-2; Prnts

Lying asleep between the strokes of night. Love And Sleep. Algernon Charles Swinburne. GSo; OxBSo

Lying Awake. Thomas Hardy. FaBoVe; NPeEn

Lying Awake. W. D. Snodgrass. MoAmPo

Lying awake in a provincial town. Stretchmarks. Elizabeth Bartlett. MoWP

Lying back on a pile of leaves. White Soil. Joy Lahey. AnSo

Lying down alone. Lady Izumi. ArkPo, tr. by Earl Miner

Lying down by night I hear night's bells. Hearing Bells at Night in the Mountains. Chang Yüeh. CCL1, tr. by Stephen Owen

Lying down I lift my legs. Troubles with the Soul at Morning Calisthenics. Anna Swirszczynska [or Swir]. BLT

Lying full length. George Oppen. APSN Fr. Some San Francisco Poems.

Lying here alone. Lady Izumi. WeW-3

Lying here quietly beside you. Quietly. Kenneth Rexroth. ErotSp; GoPo

Lying in a Hammock at William Duffy's Farm in Pine Island, Minnesota. James Wright. CAP-8; ColAP; ItP; MakPoe; NAMCP V.2; OxBoAm; StAl; TRP; VCAP; WaAnP

Lying in Bed. Amaru. WoPoe, tr. by Henry Heifetz

Lying in bed in the pitch black, a little breathing underlies my own. Night Light. Kate Barnes. GoPo

Lying in bed late, you read to me. Anniversary. Judith Ortiz Cofer. PueRic; TouFir

Lying in Bed on a Summer Morning. Carl Rakosi. APT-2; NAAPv.2

Lying in bed turned away from each other, holding their. Lying in Bed. Amaru. WoPoe, tr. by Henry Heifetz

Lying in Small Pieces. Carol Bell. GeoH

Lying in the meadow, open to you. Kenneth Rexroth. APSN Fr. Love Poems of Marichiko, The.

Lying in their lowly state. Rispond Miser, The. Robert MacKay. NePenScot, tr. by Derick Thomson

Lying is an occupation. Song, A. Laetitia Pilkington. PEW

Lying low. (LL) Flower-fed Buffaloes, The. Vachel Lindsay. GM; ItP; MoAmPo; TRP

Lying next to you. Grand Canyon. Estelle E. Farley. BtF

Lying so primly propped. (LL) Bells for John Whiteside's Daughter. John Crowe Ransom. APT-1; BrAP; ColAP; FuPo; HarvBoo; HeIP-4; InGu; MakPoe; MoAmPo; NAAPv.2; NAMCP V.1; NIL-7; NIP-4; NoAM; NoP-4; NoP-5; OxBoAm; TFi; WaAnP; WeW-3

Lying under the olive tree[s], O world, O death? (LL) Ultima Ratio Regum. Stephen Spender. AF; FaBoWar; NoP-4; NoP-5; OBWP; PoWW

Lying under the stars. Kenneth Rexroth. BLT Fr. Lights in the Sky are Stars, The.

Lyke as a huntsman after weary chace. Edmund Spenser. See Like a huntsman after weary chase.

Lyke as a ship that through the ocean wyde. Edmund Spenser. NAEL-6v1; NAEL-7v1

Lyke as the armed knyght. Anne Askew. See Like as the armèd knight.

Lyke as the Culver on the barèd bough. Edmund Spenser. NoP-4; NoP-5

Lyke-Wake Dirge, A. Unknown. See Lyke-Wake Dirge, The [or A].

Lyke-Wake Dirge, The [or A]. Unknown. EMWP; NPeEn; OBEV; OxBEV; TFi; WeW-3; WoPoe

(Lyke-Wake Dirge, A.) NoP-4

Lyle Donaghy, Poet, 1902-1949. George Buchanan. PNI

Lynch 1. Aimé Césaire. ConPit, tr. by Clayton Eshleman

Lynched / the lakes. Our Earth Will Not Die. Niyi Osundare. HBAPE

Lynching. Lizelia Augusta Jenkins Moorer. CBWP-3

Lynching and Burning. Primus St. John. ISC; PoChi

Lynching for Skip James, A. Rudy Bee Graham. EGAG

Lynching, The. Claude McKay. APT-1; ColAP; GT; InoFa; NAAL-5; NAMCP V.1

Lynching, The. Thylias Moss. GT

Lynch—strip of unplowed land. "Luteous" to "Lymph" for "F." Tina Darragh. FTOS

Lyndon lay down among the / wildflowers. Johnson City, Texas. Albert Huffstickler. TiP2

Lynmouth Widow, A. Amelia Josephine Burr. LW

Lynn Schmidt says. Epiphany. Pem Kremer. HW

Lynx. Alan Robert Wilson. Coast

Lynx prowls past in the shade of the porch, her tufted ears pricked to the, A. Diana Hartog. NLPA Fr. Oasis.

Lynx-eyed, cat-quiet, sleepy mild. Tintype of a Private in the Fifteenth Georgia Infantry. Paul Horgan. CBCWP

Lyra Apostolica. John Keble.
United States. SacPr

Lyra Innocentium. John Keble. SacPr Fr. Waterfall, The.

Lyre. Donald Revell. RoV

Lyre of the sonnet, that fully [or full] many a time. Written December 1790. Anna Seward. CenSon

Lyric: "It doesn't matter / whether / a tree falls." Elizabeth Dodd. AmPoNex

Lyric: "Stammering it fights to get." Denise Riley. MoWP

Lyric Afterwards, A. Tom Paulin. PNI

Lyric Baedeker, The. Arthur Guiterman.
Philadelphia. AmWit
Seattle. AmWit

Lyric elixir of death, A. Poe. Mina Loy. APT-1

Lyric: I Am Looking at Music. Pinkie Gordon Lane. FuFl

Lyric in Exile, A. Hussein Elhami. AmFaPo, tr. by Shmuel Shoshani

Lyric on the Lyric, A. Lizette Woodworth Reese. APN-2

Lyric Poet's Epilogue, The. Mihály Babits. IQMS, tr. by Peter Zollman

Lyric to the Tune "Immortal by the River." Li Ch'ing-chao. WoPoe, tr. by Julie Landau

Lyrical Letter to the Other Woman. Alfonsina Storni. TCLAP, tr. by Dana Stangel

Lyrics. James Agee. MoAmPo
"Not met and marred with the year's whole turn of grief." APT-2

Lyrics for the Bride of God. Nathaniel Tarn.
(Section: America: Seen as a Bird.) PFTM-2
Section: America (2): Seen as a Bird. APSN

Lyrics of the Street. Julia Ward Howe.
Lost Jewel, The. SWaP
Outside the Party. SWaP
Soul-Hunter, The. SWaP
Street Yarn. SWaP

Lyrics to the Tune "Fairy Grotto." Su Tung-p'o. WoPoe, tr. by Greg Whincup

Lyrics to the Tune "The Charms of Niennu": At the Red Cliff I Ponder Over Antiquity. Su Tung-p'o. WoPoe, tr. by David Lattimore

Lysidice dedicated to you, Cypris. Asclepiades. HePo, tr. by Barbara Hughes Fowler

Lysistrata. Aristophanes. tr. by B. B. Rogers
How the Women Will Stop War. FaBoWar, tr. by B. B. Rogers

Lystrata. Aristophanes. NAWM-7v1, tr. by Douglass Parker

Lythe and listin, gentilmen. Unknown. NAEL-6v1 Fr. Gest of Robyn Hode.

Lythe and listin, gentilmen. Gest of Robyn Hode. Unknown.

LZ Gator Body Collector, The. Michael Casey. YaYoPo

M

M4. Emyr Lewis. ATSWP, tr. by Robert Minhinnick

M. assures me she'll be back. Landscape. Eunice De Souza. NAMCP V.2

M is for Marx. Cyril Connolly. OBCoV Fr. Where Engels Fears to Tread.

M. l'Épicier in his white hat. Soissons. Keith Douglas. NAMCP V.1; NoAM

M. [or Mr.] Crashaw's Answer for Hope. Richard Crashaw. NOSC

M. S. 1544. Jacqueline Risset. YaTCFP, tr. by Jennifer Moxley

M. S. 1544 [Maurice Scève]. Jacqueline Risset. YaTCFP

M. S. Sir Will: Dyer, Kt: Who Put on Immortality Aprill the 29th Anno Domini 1621. Lady Catherine Dyer. EMWP

M., Singing. Louise Bogan. ColAP; NoAM; WaAnP

Ma. Paul Muldoon. PNI

Ma, are you really dead? Mahendranāth Bhattācārya. SinGod, tr. by Rachel Fell McDermott

Ma chambre est au fond d'une cour et derrière des boutiques. Visitation. Max Jacob. YaTCFP

Ma Danse. Blaise Cendrars. YaTCFP

Ma déraison d'être. Gherasim Luca. YaTCFP

Ma femme à la chevelure de feu de bois. Union libre, L'. André Breton. YaTCFP

Ma god, 't aint goin so good. Letter to Thelonius. Wopko Jensma. TSAP

Ma, Hara's Beloved, Tara. Nīlmani Pātunī. SinGod, tr. by Rachel Fell McDermott

Ma, if You wore a Benarasi sari. Mā Bāsantī Cakrabarttī. SinGod, tr. by Rachel Fell McDermott

Ma, I've drunk Your poisoned nectar. Dīnrām. SinGod, tr. by Rachel Fell McDermott

Ma Ma Ma Malcolm. I Remember Malcolm. Ras Baraka. InTrad

Ma mammy bot me oot a shop. Telling Part, The. Jackie Kay. Prnts

Ma, my heart must be made of rice straw. Nellie Wong. UnSA Fr. Heart of Rice Straw, A.

Ma people, come an get ready. In memoriam Ben Zwane. Wopko Jensma. TSAP

Ma Rainey. Sterling Allen Brown. APT-2; NAAPv.2; NAMCP V.1; OxAAAP

Ma Ramon. R. Erica Doyle. BAP-01

Ma Ramon would fall upon the floor. Ma Ramon. R. Erica Doyle. BAP-01

Ma, the mail train is leaving now. Kalyānkumār Mukhopādhyāy. SinGod, tr. by Rachel Fell McDermott

Ma, You are Brahmani in the world of Brahma.   Śāradā Bhāndārī.   SinGod, tr. by Rachel Fell McDermott

Ma, You're inside me.   Rāmprasād Sen.   SinGod, tr. by Rachel Fell McDermott

Málaga.   Pearse Hutchinson.   ModIr; PBCIP

Más fuerto, más claro, más puro.   Quiero Dormir.   Jorge Guillén.   RaW

Mabel Kelly.   Turlough Carolan.   OxBEV, tr. by Austin Clarke

Mabel was married last week.   Emily Writes Such a Good Letter.   Stevie Smith.   OBCoV

Mabinog's Liturgy.   David Jones.
   "In the middle silences of this night's course the blackthorn."   OxAEP-2

Mabrak.   Bongo Jerry.   WaCA

Mac Flecknoe [or, A Satire upon the True-Blue Protestant Poet T. S.].   John Dryden.   BASC; CABP; NAEL-6v1; NAEL-7v1; NoP-4; NoP-5; OBSV; OxAEP-1; TFi
   Crown Prince of Dullness, The.   NOSC; OBCoV; OxBEV

Macadam, gun-grey as the tunny's belt.   Hart Crane.   MoAmPo; NAAPv.2 Fr. Bridge, The.

MacArthur High School.   Lacey A. Dalby.   BeDoSh

Macavity: The Mystery Cat.   T. S. Eliot.   AmWit; ChAP; NBLV; UV

Macavity's a Mystery Cat: he's called the Hidden Paw.   Macavity: The Mystery Cat.   T. S. Eliot.   AmWit; ChAP; NBLV; UV

Macaw preens upon a branch outspread, A.   Decoration.   Louise Bogan.   MoAmPo

Macbeth Does Murder Sleep.   William Shakespeare.   OxAEP-1 Fr. Macbeth.

Macbeth in Battle.   Marjorie Welish.   VaPo

Macbeth.   William Shakespeare.
   Differences in Dogs.   DiBP
   "Glamis thou art, andd Cawdor; and shalt be."   OxAEP-1
   "I have liv'd long enough: my way of life."   WaAnP
   "It is the cry of women, my good Lord."   OxBEV
   Macbeth Does Murder Sleep.   OxAEP-1
   "Now o'er the one half-world."   OxAEP-1
   "Scale of dragon, tooth of wolf."   UV
   "Seyton!—I am sick at heart."   OxAEP-1
   "To-morrow, and to-morrow, and to-morrow."   WaAnP
   Tomorrow, and Tomorrow, and Tomorrow.   SoSe-8
   Vaulting Ambition.   OxAEP-1
   "What bloody man is that? He can report."   FaBoWar

Macbeth was never Thane of Cawdor.   Shakespeare No More.   Anne MacLeod.   EdScPo

Machete.   Rikki Ducornet.   SurWo

Machine gun, A.   Saitō Sanki.   CAoMJL1, tr. by Masaya Saito

Machine gun soars, A.   Saitō Sanki.   CAoMJL1, tr. by Masaya Saito

Machine gunner aims, A.   El Alamein.   Steve Crow.   HATNAP

Machine That Cried, The.   Michael Hofmann.   NeBrP

Machine, The.   Kalman Hayzler.   Prolet, tr. by Amelia Glaser

Machinery.   David Huerta.   RMCMP, tr. by Mark Schafer

Machines.   Michael Donaghy.   NeBrP; StAl

Machines keep quiet, The.   Muffled might.   Strike.   Aaron Rapoport.   Prolet, tr. by Amelia Glaser

Machines waited for me, The.   "Antler."   CLPP Fr. Factory.

Machinist, Teaching His Daughter to Play the Piano, The.   B. H. Fairchild.   PoDa

Machynlleth.   Allen Fisher.   Oth Fr. Emergent Manner.

Mack Charles Parker Lynching, The.   Sybil Pittman Estess.   LiTh

Mackintosh— / And that / (Said John) / Is / That. (LL)   Happiness.   Alan Alexander Milne.   AmFaPo; NOxBCHV

Macon Prairie [(Nebraska)].   Willa Sibert Cather.   NAAPv.2

Macula of Light, A.   Forrest Gander.   OnScMo

Maculate Beauty.   Karl Kirchwey.   PoDa

Macumba Word.   Aimé Césaire.   PFTM-1

Mad About the Boy.   Noël Coward.   ReLy

Mad angel hammered with raging might, A.   Memories of a Summer Night.   Endre Ady.   IQMS, tr. by Peter Zollman

Mad are predators, The.   Too often lately they harbour.   Geoffrey Hill.   NoP-4; NoP-5 Fr. Mercian Hymns.

Mad as the Mist and Snow [fr. Words for Music Perhaps].   William Butler Yeats.   RaBo

Mad barber wants to cut my hair, The.   Theology.   Sherman Alexie.   NeAmPo

Mad Cow in Love, The.   Jo Shapcott.   NeBrP

Mad Cow Tries to Write the Good Poem, The.   Jo Shapcott.   MoWP

Mad daddy like mule.   Enclosure.   Christopher Gilbert.   SwNoth

Mad Dog, The.   Oliver Goldsmith.   See Elegy on the Death of a Mad Dog, An.

Mad Dogs and Englishmen.   Noël Coward.   NBLV; ReLy

Mad Farmer, Flying the Flag of Rough Branch, Secedes from the Union, The.   Wendell Berry.   PoCoUp

Mad Farmer Revolution, The.   Wendell Berry.   UpMys

Mad farmer, the thirsty one, The.   Mad Farmer Revolution, The.   Wendell Berry.   UpMys

Mad Fight Song for William S. Carpenter, 1966, A.   James Wright.   NoAM

Mad flight of a butterfly, The.   Nazi Song.   Paul Éluard.   AF, tr. by Lloyd Alexander

Mad Gardener's Song, The.   Lewis Carroll.   WoPoe Fr. Sylvie and Bruno.

Mad girl, The.   Buson.   EH, tr. by Robert Hass

Mad girl with the staring eyes and long white fingers, The.   Cassandra.   Robinson Jeffers.   APT-1; HeIP-4

Mad Hatter's Song, The.   Lewis Carroll.   UV Fr. Alice's Adventures in Wonderland.

Mad is mad.   Mad Talk.   Karel Appel.   PFTM-2

Mad is the poet men call Kit.   Christopher Smart.   Stanley Shaw.   UV

Mad Magnet of a Wild Wind.   Emyr Lewis.   BBMWP Fr. Dawn.

Mad Maid's Song, The.   Robert Herrick.   OBEV; RACG

Mad Man.   Steve Wilson.   LiTh

Mad Moll And Crazy Betty.   Mary Dalton.   OpeFie

Mad Mother, The.   William Wordsworth.   NPBRoP

Mad Murray Kadish.   Boots and Saddles.   Louis Simpson.   BodElec

Mad old maid of Amherst, The.   Emily Dickinson.   Yury Ivask.   TCRusP, tr. by William Tjalsma

Mad Patsy said, he said to me.   In the Poppy Field.   James Stephens.   IrV

Mad Pomegranate Tree, The.   Odysseus Elytis.   GPTC; WoPoe, tr. by Edmund Keeley and Philip Sherrard

Mad Potter, The.   John Hollander.   ColAP; VCAP

Mad Professor shouts, taps the blackboard with a stick, The.   Diana Hartog.   NLPA Fr. Oasis.

Mad reprisal for their loyalty, A. (LL)   Douglas Dunn.   InoFa; NoP-4; NoP-5 Fr. Elegies.

Mad Rout of the Rat, The.   Yi Kyubo.   CATKP, tr. by Kevin O'Rourke

Mad Scene, The.   James Merrill.   CAP-8; ItP; PoA 2002

Mad sculptor in our park, A.   Helen.   Peter Meinke.   PBCAP

Mad Soldier, The.   Edward Wyndham Tennant.   FaBoWar

Mad Song.   William Blake.   IJHIL; NAEL-6v2

Mad Sonnet: Fame.   Michael McClure.   BB

Mad Sonnet: Grace.   Michael McClure.   BB

Mad Talk.   Karel Appel.   PFTM-2

Mad, The.   Robert Pinsky.   NoAM Fr. Essay on Psychiatrists.

Mad to be had, to be felt and smelled. My lips.   W. H. Auden.   EroLit Fr. Platonic Blow, The.

Mad Tom's Song.   Unknown. See Tom o' Bedlam's Song.

Mad Verse.   Basho, Jūgo, Kakei, Shōhei, Tokoku and Yasui.   EMJL, tr. by Haruo Shirane
   "Asking the Second Nun."   EMJL, tr. by Haruo Shirane
   "At dusk."   EMJL, tr. by Haruo Shirane
   "By an unfaded stupa."   EMJL, tr. by Haruo Shirane
   "Empty house, An."   EMJL, tr. by Haruo Shirane
   "Having to Hide."   EMJL, tr. by Haruo Shirane
   "In a rice field."   EMJL, tr. by Haruo Shirane
   "In the scattered light."   EMJL, tr. by Haruo Shirane
   "In the withering gusts."   EMJL, tr. by Haruo Shirane
   "Korean grass."   EMJL, tr. by Haruo Shirane
   "Making / the Master of Early Dawn."   EMJL, tr. by Haruo Shirane
   "Man pulling the boat, A."   EMJL, tr. by Haruo Shirane
   "My grass hut."   EMJL, tr. by Haruo Shirane
   "Pain of deception, The."   EMJL, tr. by Haruo Shirane
   "Red-haired horse, A."   EMJL, tr. by Haruo Shirane
   "Retiring from court."   EMJL, tr. by Haruo Shirane
   "Silhouette, A."   EMJL, tr. by Haruo Shirane
   "Who's that?"   EMJL, tr. by Haruo Shirane

Mad Wolf in Lunar Web, Mad Crow on the Beach.   Mac Wellman.   FTOS

Mad Woman.   Su'ad al-Mubarak Al-Sabah.   PoArWo, tr. by John Heath-Stubbs and May Jayyusi

Mad Woman of Punnet's Town, The.   Leonard Alfred George Strong.   MoBrPo

Mad Yak, The.   Gregory Corso.   BB; PFTM-2; PmAP; WaAnP

Madalena.   Maria Eugénia Lima.   HAWP, tr. by Julia Kirst

Madalena / black freckled mulatto.   Madalena.   Maria Eugénia Lima.   HAWP, tr. by Julia Kirst

Madam and Her Madam.   Langston Hughes.   NAMCP V.1; RACG; SAmP

Madam and the Census Man.   Langston Hughes.   SAmP

Madam and the Minister.   Langston Hughes.   OxAAAP

Madam and the Rent Man.   Langston Hughes.   SAmP

Madam and the Wrong Visitor.   Langston Hughes.   SAmP

Madam[e], had all antiquity [or antiquitie] been lost.   To Mary, Lady Wroth.   Ben Jonson.   NOSC

Madam, / I cannot but congratulate. Advice to Virgins. Katherine Philips. EMWP

Madam, / I hope you'll think it's true. Strephon to Celia. A modern Love-Letter. Mary Leapor. BrAP; RACG

Madam Life. W. E. Henley. *See* Madam Life's A Piece in Bloom.

Madam Life's A Piece in Bloom. W. E. Henley. NAEL-6v2; OxBEV
(Madam Life.) MoBrPo
(To W. R.) NPeEn

Madam! permit a Muse, that has been long. To Madam Behn. "Ephelia." EMWP

Madam President. Boadiba. OGAHCP, *tr. by* the author and Jack Hirschman

Madam, / Reason is our soul's left hand, Faith her right. To the Countess of Bedford. John Donne. NOSC

Madam, the Lady Valeria is come to visit you. William Shakespeare. OxAEP-1 *Fr.* Coriolanus.

Madam to a Young Courtesan, The. Sarangapani. WoPoe, *tr. by* V. Narayana Rao, A. K. Ramanujan and David Shulman

Madam to you. (LL) Madam's Past History. Langston Hughes. HHAm; NAMCP V.1; NoAM; SAmP

Madam, Withouten Many Words. Sir Thomas Wyatt. *See* Madame, withouten Many Wordes.

Madam would speak with me. So, now it comes. George Meredith. NPeEn; OxBEV *Fr.* Modern Love.

Madam, you are right, the fight was a great pity. To the Woman in Bond Street Station. Edward Weismiller. PWW2

Madam / You were the very Magazine of rich. On my honorable Grandmother, Elizabeth Countess of Shrewbury. Lady Jane Cavendish. EMWP

Madam, your beauty and your lovely parts. Platonic Love. Edward Herbert, 1st Baron Herbert of Cherbury. NOSC

Madame Butterfly. David Moolten. BloBone

Madame Secretary. Michael McClure. Eno

Madame, withouten Many Wordes. Sir Thomas Wyatt. OBVE
(Madam, withouten Many Words.) NAEL-6v1; NAEL-7v1; NoP-4; NoSic

Madame X. Margherita Guidacci. CItWP, *tr. by* Cinzia Sartini Blum and Lara Trubowitz

Madam's Calling Cards. Langston Hughes. SAmP

Madam's Past History. Langston Hughes. HHAm; NAMCP V.1; NoAM; SAmP

Madarika. Vince Gotera. OpBo; ReBoTo

Madboy's Song. Muriel Rukeyser. MoAmPo

Madding moon, A. Niyi Osundare. HBAPE *Fr.* Moonsongs.

Made hair? The girls here. Naola Beauty Academy, New Orleans, Louisiana, 1943. Natasha Trethewey. NeAmPo; SpirFl; SUP

Made his hut in the vale, a tall man stretched out. *Unknown.* NDACCP, *tr. by* Ezra Pound

Made me dance with you. Latin Music in New York. Jessica Tarahata Hagedorn. FTtHH; PmAP

Made merry because it is so. (LL) Gertrude Stein. NoP-4; NoP-5 *Fr.* Stanzas in Meditation.

Made of Crêpe de Chine. Hazel Hall. FiBr

Made Out of Links. Hilda Morley. PmAP

Made Shine. Josephine Miles. NoAM

Made to Order Smile, The. Paul Laurence Dunbar. GT

Madeja. Silvia Eugenia Castillero. SPV

Madeleine, A. George Bilgere. PoDa

Madeleine in Church. Charlotte Mew. VWP

Madeleine in Church. Charlotte Mew.
"'Find rest in Him!' One knows the parsons' tags." ChIV-2
"How old was Mary out of whom you cast." MoBrPo

Madeline, A Domestic Tale. Felicia Dorothea Hemans. RWP

Madem you say I am sad I ansure noe. Upon the LD Saying KT Could Be Sad in Her Company. Katherine Thimelby Aston. EMWP

Madge Wildfire Sings. Sir Walter Scott. *See* Proud Maisie.

Maditation on the Nativity. Sidney Godolphin. *See* Hymn: "Lord, when the wise men came from far[r]."

Madly Singing in the Mountains. Po Chü-i. BLT; WoPoe, *tr. by* Arthur Waley

Madman (Prologue), The. Kahlil Gibran. TCAPo

Madman saith He said so: it is strange, The. (LL) Epistle Containing the Strange Medical Experience of Karshish, the Arab Physician, An. Robert Browning. ChIV-2; NAEL-6v2; NAEL-7v2

Madman, The. Tu Fu [*or* Du Fu]. CrYelRi, *tr. by* Sam Hamill

Madman's Song. Elinor Wylie. MoAmPo

Madness. Adelaide Crapsey. NAAPv.2

Madness. Robert Merry. NOBRP

Madness...madness. Five Nights of Bleeding. Linton Kwesi Johnson. WaCA

Madness of King Goll, The. William Butler Yeats. NAEL-6v2; NAEL-7v2

Madness of Love, The. Hadewijch. WPoS, *tr. by* Oliver Davies

Madness of love, The. Madness of Love, The. Hadewijch. WPoS, *tr. by* Oliver Davies

Madness of my tongue, The. (LL) Poems: "When you come back to me." Ruth Stone. BeAl; PoCho; StAl; TAPaP

Madness, the way they gallop off to foreign shores! Tanzan. ZenPo, *tr. by* Takashi Ikemoto and Lucien Stryk

Madonna. Blanca Varela. MotU, *tr. by* Martha Moody

Madonna del Parto: Our Lady of Birth-Giving. Jennifer Richter. FiBr

Madonna for the Damned—a 1980s Heroine. Corie Rosen. FTtHH

Madonna of the Angels in the skies. Song to the Virgin Mary. András Vásárhelyi. IQMS, *tr. by* René Bonnerjea

Madonna of the Evening Flowers. Amy Lowell. NAAL-5; NALW

Madonna of the Peaches. Joan Logghe. HW

Mador of the Moor. James Hogg.
Deep-Toned Jowler, The. DiBP

Madre Sofía. Alberto A. Ríos. NAAL-5; NAMCP V.2; NoAM

Madrid [—1937]. Langston Hughes. AF

Madrid. Frank O'Hara. FTOS

Madrid. Jay Wright. ESEAA

Madrid, 1937, / in the Plaza del Angel the women. Octavio Paz. BLPSL *Fr.* Sunstone.

Madrigal. Edmund Bolton. SacPr

Madrigal. Nicolás Guillén. CLPP, *tr. by* Kenneth Rexroth

Madrigal. Giovanni Raboni. ItPo, *tr. by* Gayle Ridinger

Madrigal. Sir Philip Sidney. NoSic *Fr.* Countesse of Pembroke's Arcadia, The.

Madrigal: "Ah! silly soul, what wilt thou say." William Drummond of Hawthornden. SacPr

Madrigal: "Ay me, alas, heigh ho, heigh ho!" Thomas Weelkes. NPeEn

Madrigal: "Daedal of my death, A." William Drummond of Hawthornden. NOSC

Madrigal: Eyes of Clear Serenity. Gutierre de Cetina. SpanPo, *tr. by* Kate Flores

Madrigal: "How the tenor warbles in April!" Mary Leader. NAPBL; PoDa

Madrigal: "If that a sinner's sighs be angels' food." *Unknown.* SacPr

Madrigal: "Like the Idalian Queen[e]." William Drummond of Hawthornden. NOSC
(Inexorable.) OBEV

Madrigal: "My Love in her attire doth show her wit." *Unknown.* HeIP-6; NAEL-6v1; NIP-4; OBEV; TFi

Madrigal: "My thoughts hold mortal[l] strife." William Drummond of Hawthornden. NOSC
(Inexorable.) OBEV

Madrigal: "This life, which seems so fair." William Drummond of Hawthornden. NOSC

Madrigal: "Unhappie [*or* Unhappy] Light." William Drummond of Hawthornden. NOSC

Madrigal 1. Gutierre de Cetina. BLPSL, *tr. by* Rene de Costa, Rigas Kappatos and Eleni Paidoussi

Madrigal 3. Aurelio Arturo. BLPSL, *tr. by* Rene de Costa, Rigas Kappatos and Eleni Paidoussi

Madrigal, a Lullaby for Xan. Marilyn Bowering. IFF

Madwoman in gloves, The. Hound and Leper. Beckian Fritz Goldberg. PfS

Madwoman in the Park, The. Dame Edith Sitwell. PFTM-1

Madwoman on the Train, The. Alfred Wellington Purdy. NoAM
(Sestina on a Train.) IFF

Mae Marsh, Motion Picture Actress. Vachel Lindsay.
"Arts are old, old as the stones, The." APT-1
"She is madonna in an art." APT-1

Mae West. Edward Field. GoPo

Mae West Chats It Up with Bessie Smith. Colleen J. McElroy. BAP-01

Maecenas, you, beneath the myrtle shade. To Maecenas. Phillis Wheatley. NAAL-5; WaAnP

Mæg ic be me sylfum soðgied wrecan. Seafarer (c. 10th century), The. *Unknown.*

Maen Madoc. Chris Torrance. AngWePo

Maestro. Ilya Kaminsky. LegDan

Mafioso. Sandra M. Gilbert. UnSA

Mag. Carl Sandburg. APT-1

Magalu. Helene Johnson. APT-2

Magazine jury of twelve rounds, A. U.S.A. Court of No Appeal, The. George Edward Tait. BRtP

Magdalen. Amy Levy. ViWPN; VWP

Magdalen. Harriet Prescott Spofford. SWaP

Magdalen Walks. Oscar Wilde. MoBrPo

Magdalene. Marina Ivanovna Tsvetaeva. GI, *tr. by* Michael M. Naydan

Magdalene at Michael's gate. Henry Kingsley. SacPr

Magdalene (I). Boris Leonidovich Pasternak. GI, *tr. by* Nina Kossman

Magellan Street, 1974. Maxine W. Kumin. GoPo
Maggid. Marge Piercy. TaR
Maggie. Duane Niatum. HATNAP
Maggie and milly and molly and may. E. E. Cummings. ChAP; NoAM; NOxBChV; WaAnP
Maggie Lauder. Francis Sempill. NePenScot
Maggie's taking care of a man. Brilliance. Mark Doty. BeAl; PoCu
Maggot Song. *Unknown.* NOBAu
Magi. Sylvia Plath. GI
Magi, The. Jeffrey Fiskin. GI
Magi, The. Louise Glück. GI; HarvBoo; PoA 2002
Magi, The. Ramon Guthrie. GI
Magi, The. William Butler Yeats. ChIV-2; GI; HarvBoo; NAMCP V.1; NoAM; NPeEn; OxAEP-2; PoA 2002; TRP
Magic: "You went by my house." Glenna Luschei. ICANM
Magic. Ovid. *Fr.* Metamorphoses.
Magic. William Shakespeare. OxAEP-1; WaAnP *Fr.* Tempest, The.
Magic. Walter James Turner. OBGa
Magic and mystery, spells Circæan. Thomas Love Peacock. NOBRP *Fr.* Rhododaphne.
Magic Apple Tree, The. Elaine Feinstein. HarvBoo
Magic bed, The. Bed in the Wilderness, The. Geoffrey O'Brien. PA9/11
Magic Broom, The. Marcia Southwick. PfS
Magic Carpet, The. Maurice Kilwein Guevara. TouFir
Magic Cinnabar. Pao Chao. ColAnChi, *tr. by* Anne Birrell
Magic City Monastery. Wang Yang-ming. CrYelRi, *tr. by* Sam Hamill
Magic Composer. Gilbert Sorrentino. FTOS
Magic Curtain, The. Stanley Kunitz. NAMCP V.1
Magic Formula. *Unknown.* CA
Magic Fox. James Welch. HATNAP; NoAM
Magic Glass, The. Felicia Dorothea Hemans. NOBRP
Magic, like the sho-nuff spaceman, you am. (LL) Poem for "Magic," A. Quincy Troupe. FTtHH; ISC
Magic Mirror, The. Edward Hirsch. PoDa
Magic of that name is fled, The. Wraith of the Rose, The. Frances Sargent Osgood. NAAPv.1
Magic (or Rousseau). Carla Harryman. FTOS
Magic Song. *Unknown.* APN-2, *tr. by* Henry Rowe Schoolcraft
Magic Strings. Li Ho. CCL1, *tr. by* John Frodsham
Magic Words. Aua.
  To Lighten Heavy Loads. IFF
Magic Words. *Eskimo Oral Tradition.* BLT, *tr. by* Edward Field
Magic Words. *Unknown.* RaBo, *tr. by* Edward Field
Magic Words to Cure a Sick Child. *Eskimo Oral Tradition.* PoChi
Magical Devices. Clara Silva. TANSG, *tr. by* Celeste Kostopulos-Cooperman
Magician was in the habit of amusing his public with the following little trick, A. Poetry and Thought. René Daumal. MotU; YaTCFP, *tr. by* Michael Wood
Magician-Made Tree, The. Cyrus Cassells.
  Bargain, The. TAPaP
Magicien avait coutume de divertir son monde du petit tour que voici, Un. Mot et la mouche, Le. René Daumal. YaTCFP
Magistrate. Chŏng Ch'ŏl. WoPoe, *tr. by* Graeme Wilson
Magma. Norman Henry, II Pritchard. EGAG
Magna Est Veritas. Coventry Patmore. NPeEn; OBEV; OxBEV
Magna Est Veritas. Stevie Smith. NPeEn; OxBEV
Magnet, The. Mario Benedetti. PML, *tr. by* Richard Zenith
Magnet, The. Ruth Stone. MoAmPo
Magnetic Charms. Lorenzo Thomas. AnSo
Magnetic Fields, The. André Breton.
  "Factory." PFTM-1
Magnetic Mountain, The. Cecil Day Lewis.
  (Condemned.) PoA 2002
  Nearing Again the Legendary Isle. MoBrPo
  "Tempt me no more; for I." MoBrPo; OBMV
Magnetic winds from the sun pour in. Augury. Caitríona O'Reilly. NIrP
Magnificat! Michael S. Glaser. OPRER
Magnificat. Michele Roberts. PoBW
Magnificat in Little. Léonie Adams. OxBoAm
Magnificence. John Skelton.
  "Stow, birde, stow, stow!" NoSic
  "Unto this process briefly compiled." NoSic
Magnificence. James Wright. BodElec
Magnificent! Magnificent! Fumon. ZenPo, *tr. by* Takashi Ikemoto and Lucien Stryk
Magnificent Peak. Muso Soseki. EaWin, *tr. by* W. S. Merwin
Magnificent Tomorrows. Haki R. Madhubuti. SpirFl

Magnificent, too, is the system of drains. Samuel Carter. STuOW *Fr.* London.
Magnolia. Lew Brown, B. G. DeSylva and Ray Henderson. ReLy
Magnolia. Mary Weston Fordham. CBWP-2
Magnolia bloom can sex the air. Likely. Lisa Coffman. AmPoNex
Magnolia buds, The. Pink magnolias, the punishment. Lee Varon. PfS
Magnolia Enclosure, The. Pei Di and Wang Wei. CCL1 *Fr.* Wheel River.
Magnolia oars; a boat of spice-wood. River Song. Li Po. ChinPo, *tr. by* Ye Weilian [*or* Yeh Wei-lien *or* Wai-lim Yip]
Magnum Vectigal Parsimonia. George Gascoigne. NoSic
Magpie. Alan Michael Parker. AmPoNex
Magpie chatters in a flowering bough by the hedge, A. Yi Chehyŏn. CATKP *Fr.* Contemporary Folk Songs.
Magpie has a nest, The. *Unknown.* CCL1 *Fr.* Que-chao [Translations].
Magpies. *Unknown.* OWoS
Magpies, The. Denis Glover. BeAl
Magpies in Picardy. T. P. Cameron Wilson. BLPJKO; FaBoWar
Magpie's Shadow, The. Yvor Winters. APT-2
  Cool Nights. NAAPv.2
  God of Roads. NAAPv.2
  Hunter, The. NAAPv.2
  Shadow's Song, The. NAAPv.2
  Sleep. NAAPv.2
Magryme, The. William Dunbar. FaBoVe
Magus, The. James Dickey. GI
Magyar Fallow, The. Endre Ady. IQMS, *tr. by* Anton N. Nyerges
Magyar Messiahs, The. Endre Ady. IQMS, *tr. by* Anton N. Nyerges
Magyar Scene Through Magyar Eyes, A. Gyula Juhász. IQMS, *tr. by* Godfrey Turton
Magyars, they say, are not fit for the art of dancing. Dance of the Magyars, The. Ádám Pálóczi Horváth. IQMS, *tr. by* J. G. Nichols
Mahabharata, The. *Unknown.*
  Sâvitrî; or, Love and Death. TAL
Mahlathini blues. Jive, The. Mafika Pascal Gwala. TSAP
Mahogany men. Uncles. Nikky Finney. ISC
Mahogany Ship, The. Judith Rodriguez. BMAP
Mahogany Tree, The. William Makepeace Thackeray. ChrPo
Mahratta Ghats, The. Alun Lewis. AngWePo; OBWVE; PoWW; TCAWP
Maia. Ralph Waldo Emerson. APN-1
Maïakovsky. Etel Adnan. Eno
Maïakovsky, where are you? Maïakovsky. Etel Adnan. Eno
Maid. Sarah Kennedy. SweBea
Maid Maia shook her head, here is, The. *Unknown.* WoPoe *Fr.* Homeric Hymns.
Maid Marian. Thomas Love Peacock.
  Over, Over. OxAEP-2
  Robin Hood and the Grey Friars. OxAEP-2
Maid of dark eyes, that glow with shy sweet fire. Rondels. Aleister Crowley. CAGL
Maid of Ehrenthal, The. Henrietta Cordelia Ray. CBWP-3
Maid of Gotham, ere we part. Samuel Hoffenstein. AmWit *Fr.* Love-songs, at Once Tender and Informative.
Maid of Need, A. Stephanie Williams. AnSo
Maid, where's my Lawrel? Oh my rageing Soul! Theocritus. OBVE *Fr.* Idylls.
Maid, where's my Lawrel? Oh my rageing Soul! Theocritus. *Fr.* Idylls.
Maid Who Becomes a Bear sought the gods and found them. *Unknown.* APN-2; NAAPv.1 *Fr.* Mountain Chant, The.
Maid Who Becomes a Bear walks far around, The. *Unknown.* APN-2; NAAPv.1 *Fr.* Mountain Chant, The.
Maida. Sir Walter Scott. DiBP
Maiden, The. *Unknown.* ArBi
Maiden and River. Mary Weston Fordham. CBWP-2
Maiden Called Love, The. Takeshima Hagaromo. CAoMJL1, *tr. by* Leith Morton
Maiden Castle. Dorothy, Duchess of Wellington Wellesley. PoBW
Maiden caught me in the wild, The. Crystal Cabinet, The. William Blake. NPBRoP; NPeEn
Maiden in the morë lay. *Unknown.* NPeEn
Maiden of Witch Mountain now departs, The. Farewell Song of Magic Strings. Li Ho. CCL1, *tr. by* John Frodsham
Maiden, there is something more. To Hersa. Forceythe Willson. APN-2
Maiden, thou wert thoughtless once. Fragment, A. Anne Brontë. VWP
Maiden to the Delphic temple came, A. Love or Fame. Caroline Lindsay. VWP
Maiden Truffle, The. Erasmus Darwin. STuOW *Fr.* Temple of Nature; or, The Origin of Society, The.
Maiden wept and, as a comforter, A. Passion and Love. Paul Laurence Dunbar. ErotSp

Maiden with her wheel of old, The. Maiden, The. *Unknown.* ArBi

Maidenhair. Michael Field. OxBSo

Maidenhead Written at the Request of a Friend. "Ephelia." NOSC; PEW

Maidens Blush, The. Joshua Sylvester.
  "But, fair Iëmpsar (wife of Potiphar)." ChIV-1

Maidens, kilt your skirts and go. Celia's Home-Coming. Agnes Mary Frances Robinson. OBEV; VWP

Maiden's Mistake, The. Frances Sargent Osgood. NAAPv.1

Maidens of London's Brave Adventures, Or, a Boon Voyage Intended for the Sea, The. Laurence Price. NOSC

Maides to bed, and cover coale. Belmans Song, A. Thomas Ravenscroft. NPeEn; PBRV

Maid's Complaint for Want of a Dil Doul, The. *Unknown.* EroLit

Maid's Lament, The. Walter Savage Landor. OBEV; TreFP *Fr.* Citation and Examination of William Shakespeare, The.

Maids, not to you my mind doth change. Michael Field. NAEL-7v2; ViWPN; VWP

Maid's Thanks for a Mirror, A. HSü Ling. CCL1, *tr. by* Anne Birrell

Maid's Tragedy, The. Francis Beaumont and John Fletcher.
  Aspatia's Song. OBEV
  Bridal Song. OBEV

Maid-Servant at the Inn, The. Dorothy Parker. ChrPo

Ma'ii was trotting along like he's always done. Coyote, Skunk, and the Prairie Dogs. *Navajo Oral Tradition.* NAAL-5

Mail. Sarah Kirsch. AF, *tr. by* Wayne Kvam

Mail. Sarah Kirsch. MotU, *tr. by* Peter Spycher

Mail from Right Here, The. Brendan Galvin. PoCoUp

Mail Has Come, The [*with music*]. Mary E. Tucker. CBWP-1

Mail King. Paul B. Janeczko. HHAm

Mail Order Catalogs. William Matthews. ReTh

Mail runner carries the bag of mail, The. Letter, A. Kavikondala Venkatarao. HotL, *tr. by* V. Narayana Rao

Mailman passes by, The. I'm Gonna Sit Right Down and Write Myself a Letter. Joe Young. ReLy

Main bridge of Constitution, The. Matthew XXV:30. Jorge Luis Borges. GI, *tr. by* David Curzon

Main cook lies sick on a banquette, and his assistant, The. Restaurant. Maxine Hong Kingston. OpBo

Main, d'un mouvement rythmique, Une. Trame, La. Pierre Reverdy. YaTCFP

Main Idea, The. Milo De Angelis. ItPo, *tr. by* Gayle Ridinger

Main street flanked by shabby storefronts, dust, The. Hempstead, 1923. Carol Coffee Reposa. TiP2

Main Temple Street, Puri. Jayanta Mahapatra. VCWP

Main thing is not to oversleep, so as later not to have to run for dear life, The. Morning. Mara Malanova. CRWP, *tr. by* Nika Skandiaka

Main-Deep, The. James Stephens. MoBrPo; OBMV

Mainly I liked walking through the water. Stations of the Crux. Michael Savitz. FreRad

Mains du Bon Dieu, Les. Jack Bedell. Vesp

Maintaining the Species. Deborah Burnham. UrbNat

Maintenant. Franck Venaille. YaTCFP

Maintenant ils me disent que je ressemble aux enfants du mois d'août. Maintenant. Franck Venaille. YaTCFP

Maire Macrae's Song. Kathleen Jessie Raine. EdScPo

Mais quand au but. M. S. 1544 [Maurice Scève]. Jacqueline Risset. YaTCFP

Mais quand j'aurai fermé les yeux. Mais quand j'aurai. Claude De Burine. YaTCFP

Mais qui ça qui rivait-'ous, Philoctete? Derek Walcott. NAMCP V.2 *Fr.* Omeros.

Maisie. James Merrill. HeIP-4

Maison Aragon. Tristan Tzara. PFTM-1

Majeski Plays the Saxophone. Martín Espada. SeSe

Majestic and brilliant. Forever Martial. *Unknown.* WoPoe, *tr. by* John S. Major

Major, The. Bernard Keller. BtF

Major abstraction is the idea of man, The. Wallace Stevens. ColAP *Fr.* Notes toward a Supreme Fiction.

Major Macroo [*with music*]. Stevie Smith. NBLV

Major moved to lift her from her seat, The. Albery Allson Whitman. NAAPv.1 *Fr.* Octoroon, The.

Make a joyful noise unto the Lord, all ye lands. Bible, *O.T.* WaAnP *Fr.* Psalms.

Make a Miracle. Frank Loesser. ReLy

Make a wide dreaming pansy of an old pond in the night. (LL) Nocturne in a Deserted Brickyard. Carl Sandburg. APT-1; MoAmPo

Make a wish, Tom, make a wish. (LL) Drifters. Bruce Dawe. BMAP; NoAM

Make Believe. Oscar Hammerstein, II. ReLy

Make Believe. Gerda Mayer. Prnts

Make Bright the Arrows. Edna St. Vincent Millay. ChIV-1

Make company break. Thomas Tusser. NoSic *Fr.* Five Hundred Points of Good Husbandry.

Make friendship with the stars. Stars, The. Lydia Huntley Sigourney. ColAP; TCAPo

Make haste away, and let one be. To His Book[e]. Robert Herrick. NOSC

Make haste slowly, my friend, make haste slowly. József Kiss. IQMS *Fr.* About My Grandfather.

Make heathens at your doors! (LL) Bible Defence of Slavery. Frances Ellen Watkins Harper. APN-2; NAAPv.1

Make Ifa. Jayne Cortez. SurWo

Make Ifa make Ifa make Ifa Ifa Ifa. Make Ifa. Jayne Cortez. SurWo

Make me a captive, Lord. Christian Freedom. George Matheson. SacPr

Make me a grave where'er you will. Bury Me in a Free Land. Frances Ellen Watkins Harper. ColAP; ISC; NAAPv.1; TCAPo; WaAnP

Make Me Loathe Earthly Likings. *Unknown.* SacPr

Make me, O Lord, thy spin[n]ing wheel[e] comple[a]te. Huswifery. Edward Taylor. ColAP; InvLi; ITBLP; NAAL-3; NAAL-5; NAAPv.1; NIP-4; OxBoAm; SacPr; TCAPo; TFi

Make Music with Your Life. Bob O'Meally. TWF

Make my grave shape of heart so like a flower be free aired. Snail Poem. Peter Orlovsky. BB

Make my heart as powerful as your own. Lead me to conquer. *Unknown.* APN-2 *Fr.* Minnetare Songs.

Make new friends, but keep the old. New Friends and Old Friends. Joseph Parry. ITBLP

Make no demands of those you are about to sacrifice to the winds. Wrong Room, The. Anna Mendelssohn. VaPo

Make no mistake; there will be no forgiveness. Easter Hymn. Alec Derwent Hope. ChIV-2; GI

Make one place ev'rywhere. (LL) Temper (1), The. George Herbert. NoP-4; NoP-5

(Make one place everywhere.) (LL) NoP-4; NoP-5

Make over the alleys and gardens to birdsong. Before. Sean O'Brien. EmeKit

Make pleasing music, and not wild uproar. (LL) 'How Many Bards Gild the Lapses of Time!'. John Keats. CenSon; OxAEP-2

Make quiet, so quiet, your awesome bearing. *Unknown.* ColAnChi *Fr.* Classic of Odes.

Make Someone Happy. Betty Comden and Adolph Green. ReLy

Make the Bed. Stephen Cushman. AWTN

Make the Bedlamp Tipsy with Oil. Philodemus. WoPoe, *tr. by* James Laughlin

Make the bedlamp tipsy with oil. Make the Bedlamp Tipsy with Oil. Philodemus. WoPoe, *tr. by* James Laughlin

Make the greate God thy Fort, and dwell. Psalme 91. Bible, *O.T.* NPeEn, *tr. by* Thomas Carew

Make the Man Love Me. Dorothy Fields. ReLy

Make the poem like the hood. Three Legged Chairs. Lamont B. Steptoe. OxAAAP

Make the unseen visible. It Speaks. Kang Ŭn'gyo. EcSo, *tr. by* Ann Y. Choi

Make there my tomb, beneath the lime-tree's shade. By the Same. Charlotte Smith. CenSon; RWP

Make thyself known, Sibyl, or let despair. Leonardo's "Mona Lisa." Edward Dowden. GSo

Make way, make way. Stream's Song, The. Lascelles Abercrombie. OBMV

Make way, make way, give leave to rove. Little Good Fellows, The. Herman Melville. NCAP

Make with the Feet. Harold Adamson. ReLy

Make you scream your own name they carry razors between their teeth. Enemies. Tish Benson. BRtP

Make you wonder. Bible Buckle, The. Rozell Caldwell. BtF

Make Your Body a Heart. Rosita Copioli. CItWP, *tr. by* Cinzia Sartini Blum and Lara Trubowitz

Make Your Mark. David Barker. TreFP

Make Your Radiant Twining Curls. Mohammed Iqbal. WoPoe, *tr. by* Frances W. Pritchett

Make your radiant twining curls. Make Your Radiant Twining Curls. Mohammed Iqbal. WoPoe, *tr. by* Frances W. Pritchett

Make yourself a beggar and a fool, then come in search of me. *Unknown.* SLW, *tr. by* Marjolijn De Jager, Sayd Bahodin Majrouh and André Velter

Make yourself my father's follower. *Unknown.* SLW, *tr. by* Marjolijn De Jager, Sayd Bahodin Majrouh and André Velter

Makeme. *Unknown.* SonAtl, *tr. by* Lester Browne, Rob Holden and Myrna Teirrel

Make/n My Music. Angela Jackson. SeSe

Maker of Songs. Hazel Hall. FiBr

Maker of worlds and tender father of sparrows, The. For My Son Johnny. Anne Porter. OxBoAm

Maker on High, The. Saint Columba. NePenScot, *tr.* by Edwin Morgan

Makers of perpetuum mobile seem to have become almost extinct, The. Makers of Perpetuum Mobile, The. Harry Edmund Martinson. MotU, *tr.* by Lennart Bruce

Makes him to his own blood strange. (LL) Intellect. Ralph Waldo Emerson. APN-1; NoP-4; NoP-5

Makes lime for Mammon's tower. (LL) Ravaged Villa, The. Herman Melville. APN-2; TCAPo

Makes me wish. After the 200th White Person Locks Her Car Door at Me. Bruce A. Jacobs. BtF

Makes Sense. Ted Greenwald.

"Who / 'd / of / thought / the / morning / 'd / be / so / late." AHA

Makes that small *oh* turning over. (LL) How Many Times. Marie Howe. BeAl; LaCa; P180

Makes the eye happy. Buson. EH, *tr.* by Robert Hass

Makes Them Wild. Susan Bright. TiP2

Makes Time so vicious in his reaping. (LL) For a Dead Lady. Edwin Arlington Robinson. APT-1; HeIP-4; InoFa; MoAmPo; NAMCP V.1; NoAM; OxBoAm; TCAPo; TFi

Makes You Go Oohhh! Kalamu ya Salaam. SpirFl *Fr.* New Orleans Haiku.

Make-Up. Cheryl Clarke. WiU

Make-Up. Maurice Kilwein Guevara. TouFir

Makhno's Philosophers. John Streeter Manifold. NOBAu

Makin' Jump Shots. Michael S. Harper. ISC; MoASP

Makin' Whoopee. Gustave Kahn. OBCoV

Making a Bed. Howard Moss. OxBoAm

Making a Love Poem. Leonard Nathan. IaFF

Making a Statement. Dave Jeddie Smith. RoV

Making America Strong. Fred Voss. StAl

Making Babies. Hilary Llewellyn-Williams. TCAWP

Making Camp ("When their eyes opened, it was more than morning.") David Wagoner. VCAP

Making Camp ("You've found the place in time—no permanent shade.") David Wagoner. PoCoUp

Making Chicago. Dennis Schmitz. IllVoic

Making Contact. Virginia Satir. TWF

Making Conversation. Maggie Hannan. MFPA

Making Ends Meet. Thomas Sayers Ellis. InTrad

Making Fire. J. P. Dancing Bear. RWB

Making for Planet Alice. Deryn Rees-Jones. MFPA; StAl

Making Friends with Ties. Hugo Williams. PML

Making Hay. Philip Hodgins. NOBAu

Making It. Magdalena Gomez. PueRic

Making It Stick. Lawson Fusao Inada. BAP-97

Making Jam in July. Inna Kabysh. CRWP, *tr.* by Alex Marshall and Fay Marshall

Making Lists [*with music*]. Gladys Cardiff. HATNAP

Making love and omelettes. Pfarr-Schmerz (Village-Anguish). Veronica Forrest-Thomson. HarvBoo

Making Love at the Frost Place. Michael Waters. VisFro

Making love down through the centuries. Here Today. Andrew Elliott. PNI

Making love for ten thousand years on a rockledge. David Campbell. BMAP *Fr.* Ku-ring-gai Rock Carvings.

Making Love in the Meat Locker. Robert Masterson. ICANM

Making love in the Painted Desert. Things I Miss, The. Paula Yup. WhBo

Making Love, Killing Time. Anne Ridler. SacPr

Making love with you. Kenneth Rexroth. NAMCP V.1; PoCho *Fr.* Love Poems of Marichiko, The.

Making Money. Carol Ann Duffy. RSaN

Making Money: Drought Year in Minkler, California. Gary Soto. NoAM

Making of Color, The. Hugh Seidman. YaYoPo

Making of Eve, The. Julia Copus. NeBl

Making of the Cross, The. William Everson. CalPo

Making of the Drum, The. Edward Kamau Brathwaite. EmeKit

Making Our Clowns Martyrs. Jack A. Mapanje. HBAPE; NAfrP

Making our pillows either down, or dust. (LL) Death: "Death, thou wast once an uncouth hideous thing." George Herbert. FSCP; NAEL-6v1; NAEL-7v1; NoP-4; NoP-5; PtR

Making Poems; on the road in Minneapolis. Sekou Sundiata. SpirFl

Making Poetry [*with music*]. Anne Stevenson. MoWP

Making Poison. Margaret Atwood. MotU

Making the batter understand too late. (LL) Pitcher, The. Robert Francis. MoASP; RaBo; WeW-3

Making the flags hang wet. (LL) Rain and the Tyrants. Jules Supervielle. GPTC; WoPoe, *tr.* by David Gascoyne

Making the Jam without You. Maxine W. Kumin. NALW

Making / the Master of Early Dawn. Kakei. EMJL *Fr.* Mad Verse.

Making the Middle Be. Brent MacLaine. Coast

Making the Move. Paul Muldoon. NoAM

Making the Rate (factory journals). Sarah Klassen. ACAMVP

Making the shadows that cross each other's smiles. (LL) Steps. Naomi Shihab Nye. CAP-8; ExTi

Making Tortillas. Alicia Gaspar de Alba. IPoFL

Making tracks. Aleksandr Aleksandrovich Blok. WoPoe *Fr.* Twelve, The.

Makings of Happiness, The. Ronald Wallace. PBCAP

Makpelah. Anna Hajnal. IQMS, *tr.* by Kenneth McRobbie

Malaguena. Federico García Lorca. WED, *tr.* by Robert Bly

Malagueña. Federico García Lorca. RaW *Fr.* Tres Ciudades.

Malaria. Paolo Ruffilli. NeIt, *tr.* by Felix Stefanile

Malay Figures. *Unknown.* EaWin, *tr.* by W. S. Merwin

Malcolm. Lucille Clifton. InoFa; WaAnP

Malcolm Is 'Bout More Than Wearing a Cap. Michael Warr. UnSA

Malcolm Lowry. Epitaph. Malcolm Lowry. OBCoV

Malcolm Mooney's Land. William Sydney Graham. NePenScot; NPeEn

Malcolm Spoke / Who Listened? Haki R. Madhubuti. ESEAA

Malcolm X. Gwendolyn Brooks. IllVoic; OxAAAP

Maldive Shark, The. Herman Melville. APN-2; BrAP; ColAP; NAAL-3; NAAPv.1; NCAP; NoP-4; NoP-5; OxBoAm; TCAPo; WaAnP

Maldonne. Michel Leiris. YaTCFP

Maldoror. Comte de Lautréamont.

"I am filthy. Lice gnaw me. Swine, when they look at me, vomit. The scabs." PFTM-1

Male. Howard Phelps Putnam. *See* Romeo and Juliet.

Male, The. Carla Harryman. PmAP

Male Grownups. Hoda Hussein. PoArWo, *tr.* by Cornelia Al-Khaled

Male in the Women's Locker Room, A. Natasha Saje. MAAN

Male is not less the soul nor more, he too is in his place, The. Walt Whitman. ErotSp *Fr.* I Sing the Body Electric.

Male Nipples. Brenda Hillman. ExTi

Male poets run, lifting their feet like pros, The. On Watching a Young Man Play Tennis. Kelly Cherry. LPSFW

Male Rage Poem. Pier Giorgio Di Cicco. PML

Malecón, El. Harryette Mullen. RD

Malediction. Barry Spacks. RaF

Malediction. *Unknown.* WoPoe, *tr.* by Arthur Waley

Malediction, A. Peter Didsbury. BeAl

Malediction upon Myself. Elinor Wylie. ColAP

Malefic Return, The. Ramón López Velarde. OBVE, *tr.* by Samuel Beckett

Malenki Robot. Ken Smith. BeAl

Malepractice and maleabsence issue is loneliness & limiting to-. Men and Birth: the Unexplainable. Haki R. Madhubuti. RaBo

Malest Cornifici Tuo Catullo. Allen Ginsberg. BB

Malfeasance, The. Alan Bold. OBSP

Malice. Fawzi Karim. IrPoTo, *tr.* by Saadi A. Simawe

Malice of Innocence, The. Denise Levertov. BodElec

Malicious Envy rode. Edmund Spenser. RaF *Fr.* Faerie Queene, The.

Malicious insect, little vengeful bee. To an Angry Bee. John Clare. CenSon

Malignant gnomes who write reviews in Rhodes, The. Prologue to the Aetia. Callimachus. WoPoe, *tr.* by Stanley Lombardo and Diane Rayor

Malines. James Kenneth Stephen. OBCoV

Malines. Paul Verlaine. SxFrPo, *tr.* by Martin Sorrell

Mall, The. William Jon Watkins. IaFF

Mallard nests among the reeds, The. Mallard Nests, The. *Hungarian Oral Tradition.* IQMS, *tr.* by Watson Kirkconnell

Mallard Nests, The. *Hungarian Oral Tradition.* IQMS, *tr.* by Watson Kirkconnell

Mallards, The. *Unknown.* CCL1 *Fr.* Guan-ju.

M'alléger / me dépouiller. Avare. Michel Leiris. YaTCFP

Malleus Maleficarum 4. Maureen Seaton. ExTi

Mal'Occhio. Jennifer Martelli. OPRER

Malta. John Forbes. NOBAu

Maltese Dog, A. Tymnes. Spl; WoPoe, *tr.* by Edmund Charles Blunden

Malvern at a Distance. John Keble. OxBSo

Malvern Hill. Herman Melville. APN-2; CBCWP; ColAP; PCW

Malvern Hills. Joseph Cottle.

Ratiocinative. STuOW

Malvolio in San Francisco. Jack Gilbert. YaYoPo

Mama. Claire Kageyama. UnSA

Mama. Timothy Liu. WiU

Mama. Rohan B. Preston. AmPoNex

Mama, Come Back. Nellie Wong. UnSA

Mama, come back. Mama, Come Back. Nellie Wong. UnSA

Mama danced. Josephine Baker Museum, The. Elizabeth Alexander. FuFl

Mama Dot. Frederick D'Aguiar. Oth

Mama Dot Warns Against an Easter Rising. Frederick D'Aguiar. Oth

Mama Elsie's ninety now. Little Man around the House. Yusef Komunyakaa. OxAAAP

Mama had hips the shape of Iowa. Indian Locks. Jessica Smucker Falcón. ACAMVP

Mama I Remember. Marilyn Nelson Waniek. OxAAAP

Mama is mending / my underwear. Night before Good-Bye, The. Mitsuye Yamada. CFP

Mama Loves Janis Joplin. Richard Speakes. SwNoth

Mama pulls the prayer-cloth. Sweet Hour. Diane Gilliam Fisher. SweBea

Mama said I was a girl. Mama Said. Andrea Shipley. BeDoSh

Mamá. Go see for yourself. Tomás. Luis Lopez. GeoH

Mama's God. Carolyn M. Rodgers. OxAAAP

Mama's Magic. Glenis Redmond. BRtP

Mame. Jerry Herman. ReLy

MAME was singing. Queen of the Blues. Gwendolyn Brooks. NALW; SeSe

Mami is part of that silent tribe that didn't bother to learn English. SpaNglisH. Lissette Norman. BRtP

Mamie. Carl Sandburg. APT-1

Mamie beat her head against the bars of a little Indiana town and. Mamie. Carl Sandburg. APT-1

Mamie's Blues. "Jelly Roll." Morton. NAAPv.2

Mamma Goes Where Papa Goes. Jack Yellen. ReLy

Mamma! mamma! two eaglets cried. Taking Time to Grow. Mary Mapes Dodge. SWaP

Mammals. Lesley Dauer. NAPBL

Mammals cling so! It must come. Vigil. Blair Gibb. Prnts

Mammon Marriage. George Macdonald. SacPr

Mammoth morning moved grey flanks and groaned, A. Walking Wounded. Vernon Scannell. OBWP

Mammy mine / Your little rollin' stone that rolled away. Rock-a-Bye Your Baby with a Dixie Melody. Sam M. Lewis and Joe Young. ReLy

Mams, pig-sick of oilstains in the wash, The. Breaking the Chain. Tony Harrison. UV

Mam'selle. Mack Gordon. ReLy

Man. Sir John Davies. Fr. Nosce Teipsum.

Man. Oscar Hahn. TCLAP, tr. by Sandy McKinney

Man. George Herbert. BASC; FSCP; NAEL-6v1; NAEL-7v1; NoP-4; NoP-5

Man. Christopher Southgate. NewEx

Man. Henry Vaughan. OBEV

Man. Humbert Wolfe. MoBrPo

Man: "Consider: if we measured the Four Oceans." Chuang Tzu. SonAtl, tr. by Peter Aldman, Alek Stamnitz and P. L. Win

Man, A. / I think it is a man. My Dream About the Poet. Lucille Clifton. TRP

Man, A / Who sleeps by the window was. Tale of Bananas, A. Víctor Hernández Cruz. PueRic

Man, A. Binyo Ivanov. CSCBP, tr. by Georgi Belev and Lisa Sapinkopf

Man, A. Nicanor Parra. VCWP, tr. by W. S. Merwin

Man, The. Man and Woman Go Through the Cancer Ward. Gottfried Benn. PFTM-1

Man, The. Kenneth Koch. BAP-04

Man, The. The Woman. Hans Arp. PFTM-1

Man, The / was / less man. Finished Poem. Michelle Calhoun Green. BtF

Man, a man, a kingdom for a man!, A. John Marston. NoSic Fr. Satires.

Man, a Woman, A. Vincent Buckley. BMAP

Man, a woman, an old man. They are in a hut. The man holds a news-, A. Hair Tonic. Gisèle Prassinos. PFTM-1

Man, a woman there, A. (LL) Andraitx—Pomegranate Flowers. D. H. Lawrence. NAMCP V.1; NoP-4; NoP-5

Man across the street is imitating, The. Window Seat at the Paradise. Lee Upton. AmAlph

Man adrift on a slim spar, A. Stephen Crane. APN-2; NAAPv.1; NoP-4; NoP-5

Man against the Sky, The. Edwin Arlington Robinson. TCAPo

Man Alone. Louise Bogan. NoP-4; NoP-5

Man alone at the third-floor window, The. West Strand Visions. James Simmons. ModIr; PBCIP

Man alone gets up while the sea's still dark, The. Morning Star. Cesare Pavese. GPTC, tr. by William Arrowsmith

Man and a Woman, A. Roberto Fernández Retamar. PML, tr. by Mark Weiss

Man and a Woman, A. Juan Gelman. BLPSL, tr. by Rene de Costa, Rigas Kappatos and Eleni Paidoussi

Man and a Woman Absolutely White, A. André Breton. ConPit, tr. by Clayton Eshleman

Man and a woman are sitting at a table, A. Seen through a Window. David Ferry. ItP

Man and a woman recite their dreams, A. Tracing of an Evening. David Shapiro. PmAP

Man and a Woman Standing in the Rain in Front of a Candy Store, A. Jennifer Bartlett. ICANM

Man and Beast. Léopold Sédar Senghor. PFTM-1

Man and Boy. John N. Morris. PoA 2002

Man and His Image, The. Jean de La Fontaine. OBVE, tr. by Elizur Wright

Man and Machine. Robert Morgan. LPSFW

Man and the Echo. William Butler Yeats. NAMCP V.1

Man and the Tree, The. Philip Mead. NOBAu

Man and Wife. Robert Lowell. ColAP; VCAP

Man and Wife. Anne Sexton. CAP-8

Man and Woman Absolutely White, A. André Breton. PFTM-1

Man and Woman Go Through the Cancer Ward. Gottfried Benn. PFTM-1

Man and woman lie on a white bed, A. Happiness. Louise Glück. HarvBoo; WaAnP

Man and woman walking, A. Feather, The. Lilian Bowes-Lyon. LW

Man at leisure. Cassia flowers fall. Bird-Singing Stream. Wang Wei. ChinPo, tr. by Ye Weilian [or Yeh Wei-lien or Wai-lim Yip]

Man at the table across from mine, The. Man Eating. Jane Kenyon. OxBoAm

Man awakes every morning, A. Daily Grind. BJ Ward. IaFF

Man Be Merie as Bryd on Berie. Unknown. SacPr

Man beats his wife on the mountainside, A. Mines in Sepia Tint, The. Steve Griffiths. TCAWP

Man begins to think about a wolf, A. Fable of the Hunter. Jorge Esquinca. PML, tr. by Robert Jones

Man behind you spoke to the tracery, The. Walkways, The. John Ashbery. BodElec

Man bent over his guitar, The. Man with the Blue Guitar, The. Wallace Stevens.

Man blew away, A. Blizzard, The. Roger McDonald. NOBAu

Man Born to Farming, The. Wendell Berry. InGu; IPoFL

Man came, unfortunate bridge, A. Tiresias. Karen Press. TSAP Fr. Tiresias in the City of Heroes.

Man Can Complain, Can't He?, A [with music]. Ogden Nash. NBLV

Man Carrying Bale. Harold Monro. MoBrPo

Man comes last: he's got to. Gregorio Scalise. ItPo, tr. by Gayle Ridinger

Man comes to the door (a million times), A. Million times, A. Jessemyn Meyerhoff. WhBo

Man Condemned to Death, The. Jean Genet. CAGL, tr. by David Fisher and Guy Wernham

Man could love a girl like you; in fact, A. Albery Allson Whitman. NAAPv.1 Fr. Octoroon, The.

Man, could you in yourself the vermin all behold. "Angelus Silesius." GePo Fr. Cherubical Wanderer, The.

Man crosses a river, spends time on the other side, crosses again that evening, A. Heraclitus. Leslie Rondin. MotU

Man crosses the street in rain, A. Shoulders. Naomi Shihab Nye. AtGh; TWF

Man cuts brush, A. Verge. James Schuyler. AHA

Man dear, did you never hear of buxom Molly Bloom at all. Post Ulixem Scriptum. James Joyce. OBCoV

Man differs more from Man, than Man from / Beast. (LL) Satire [or Satyre or Satyr] against [Reason and] Mankind, A. John Wilmot, 2d Earl of Rochester. BASC; NOSC; OBSV

Man Doesn't Exist. Vicente Aleixandre. RaW, tr. by Lewis Hyde

Man, dreame no more of curious mysteries. Fulke, 1st Baron Brooke Greville. NOSC; NoSic Fr. Caelica.

Man earns greatness, A. Sam Bass. Gene Shuford. TiP2

Man Eating. Jane Kenyon. OxBoAm

Man eats a chicken every day for lunch, A. Spiritual Chickens. Stephen Dobyns. StAl

Man enters a florist's, A. At the Florist's. Jacques Prévert. BeAl, tr. by Lawrence Ferlinghetti

Man Escaped, A. Lewis Warsh. BodElec

Man Falls at Work, A. Ber Grin. Prolet, tr. by Amelia Glaser

Man feared that he might find an assassin, A. Stephen Crane. APN-2; NAAPv.1; NoP-4; NoP-5

Man feels humiliated, A. Instinct, The. Jack Myers. BodElec

Man filled grain, A. Tattered Sack, The. Devara Dasimayya. WoPoe, tr. by A. K. Ramanujan

Man filled with the gladness of living, A. Table. Richard Tillinghast. MAAN

Man Flammonde, from God knows where, The. Flammonde. Edwin Arlington Robinson. NoAM

Man flees suffocation. René Char. AF

Man flees suffocation. Man flees suffocation. René Char. AF

Man flying over bridge with orange sunset on shirt. Ten Still Lives. Juan Felipe Herrera. LiTh

Man! Foolish Man! On Exodus 3: 14: "I am that I am." Matthew Prior. ChIV-1

Man Frail, and God Eternal. Isaac Watts. InvLi; NPeEn; OBVE; OxBEV; SacPr

(Our God, Our Help.) NoP-4; NoP-5; WaAnP

Man freed his body of itself, The. Evening Before, The. José Ángel Valente. RaW, *tr. by* Hardie St. Martin

Man from Changi, The. Graeme Hetherington. NOBAu

Man from my country spoke to the world, A. I Was One of Them. Gurram Jashuva. HotL, *tr. by* V. Narayana Rao

1. The Man from Nod. Don McKay. NLPA *Fr.* Matériel.

Man from Strathbogie, The. Olive Mary Finnin. NOBAu

Man from the Death Institute. Novica Tadic. VCWP, *tr. by* Charles Simic

Man from Washington, The. James Welch. HATNAP; NoAM; PoPoPo; RaBo; WaAnP

Man Gets Off Work Early, A. Thomas Lux. PoDa

Man getting on a bus carrying a huge sack of crushed cans, A. Leslie Scalapino. WhBo

Man git his feet set in a sticky mudbank, A. Riverbank Blues. Sterling Allen Brown. MakPoe

Man gnaws his eyes, his blood and his bowels. Journey to the End of Night. Bernard Bador. ConPit, *tr. by* Clayton Eshleman

Man goes down the street, A. Song of the Alpine Hunter. Paul Van Ostaijen. TuT, *tr. by* Theo Dorgan

Man got stuck in the door, A. For the Sake of Two Screws. Yi Yônju. EcSo, *tr. by* Yung-Hee Kim

Man grows old and indolent, A. (LL) But I Am Growing Old and Indolent. Robinson Jeffers. APT-1; ColAP

Man had just married an automobile, A. Automobile, The. Russell Edson. RaBo; SUP

Man half Alan and half Uncle Arnold, A. Impetus. Mary Leader. NAPBL

Man has been in the VAH Library all day long, A. Simon J. Ortiz. NAAL-5 *Fr.* Poems from the Veterans Hospital.

Man has been standing, A. Tunnel, The. Mark Strand. HeIP-4

Man has finally hanged himself and rejoiced, The. Window, The. Marianne Boruch. AmAlph

Man has forgot his Origin; in vain. Jones Very. APN-1 *Fr.* Origin of Man, The.

Man has forgot his Origin; in vain. Origin of Man, The. Jones Very.

Man has found no comfort in the grave, The. (LL) Man Who Dreamed of Faeryland, The. William Butler Yeats. NAEL-6v2; NAEL-7v2; NoAM

Man has nought so much his own. Bonds of Friendship, The. Simon Dach. GePo, *tr. by* Ingrid Waløe-Engel

Man hath a weary pilgrimage. Remembrance. Robert Southey. TreFP

Man hauling coal in the street is stilled forever, A. Negative, The. Arthur Sze. AmAlph

Man He Killed, The. Thomas Hardy. ChAP; FaBoWar; HarvBoo; HeIP-4; ItP; MoBrPo; NIP-4; OBWP; TFi; WeW-3

Man held his hands to his heart as he danced, The. Of the Ever-Changing Agitation in the Air. Jorie Graham. ExTi

Man. His Bowl. His Raspberries, The. Claudia Rankine. GT

Man I could have been works for a vital institution, *is* a vital institution, The. Man I Could Have Been, The. Roddy Lumsden. NeBrP

Man I had a love for, The. Old Woman's Lamentations, An. François Villon. MoBrPo; OBMV, *tr. by* John Millington Synge

Man I Love and I Have a Typical Evening the Night Richard M. Nixon Dies, The. Jim Elledge. ReTh

Man I Love and I Shop at Jewel, The. Jim Elledge. IllVoic; ReTh

Man I Love, The. Ira Gershwin. ReLy

Man I married twice, The. Reject Jell-O. Lucille Day. CalPo; MPUn

Man I was when I was part of it, The. (LL) Beware of Ruins. Alec Derwent Hope. NAMCP V.1; NoAM

Man, if I said once, "I know." Islands, The. Randall Jarrell. ItP

Man, if you God as balm, as light, and sweetness take. "Angelus Silesius." GePo *Fr.* Cherubical Wanderer, The.

Man, if your heart is gold, and if your soul is pure. "Angelus Silesius." GePo *Fr.* Cherubical Wanderer, The.

Man, if you're dead, why are you leading. Sonny's Purple Heart. Adrian C. Louis. ReTh

Man Impregnated. Moniza Alvi. NeBl

Man in a lawn chair, A. Last Day of August, The. Naomi Shihab Nye. CAP-8

Man in a restaurant shook hands with someone, A. Considering How Exaggerated Music Is. Leslie Scalapino. FTOS

Man in a Semi-Detached House. John Thorpe. AHA

Man in a Shell, The. Angela Ball. ExTi

Man in Blue, A. James Schuyler. FTOS; PmAP; WaAnP

Man in California says he understands me, A. Long Distance. Aleda Shirley. ExTi

Man in His Life, A. Yehuda Amichai. VCWP, *tr. by* Benjamin Harshav

Man in his life has no time to have, A. Man in His Life, A. Yehuda Amichai. VCWP, *tr. by* Benjamin Harshav

Man in Love, A. Lady Mary Wortley Montagu. LW

Man in love with a tree goes to live with him awhile before getting married, A. Tree. Juan Carlos Galeano. PML, *tr. by* Delia Poey

Man in Miami, The. Kevin Prufer. LiTh

Man in Moonlight. Robert Penn Warren. *Fr.* Promises.

Man in My Bed Like Cracker Crumbs, A. Sandra Cisneros. SweBea

Man in Petersham. John A. Scott. PML

Man in repose: the cassia flowers falling. Birdsong Torrent. Wang Wei. CCL1, *tr. by* Jerome P. Seaton

Man in righteousness arrayed [*or* array'd], The. To Sally. John Quincy Adams. APN-1

Man in solitary passes by, A. In solitary. Wopko Jensma. TSAP

Man, in some lan. Oliver Pitcher. EGAG *Fr.* Harlem: Sidewalk Icons.

Man in Space. Billy Collins. BeAl; CAP-8

Man in terror of impotence, A. Ninth Symphony of Beethoven Understood at Last as a Sexual Message, The. Adrienne Rich. PFTM-2

Man in the black suit delivers a eulogy, The. Eulogy, The. Carol Muske-Dukes. InoFa; PBCAP

Man in the Blue Smock, The. Günter Eich. GTCP; PML, *tr. by* Reinhold Grimm

Man in the clot of colors—which are people, A. La Guardia, the Story. Jane Mead. BodElec

Man in the Dead Machine, The. Donald Hall. OtW

Man in the Honeysuckle, The. David Campbell. BMAP

Man in the Middle of the Street. Petronius Arbiter. WoPoe, *tr. by* Tim Reynolds

Man in the Moon. Linda Hogan. HATNAP

Man in the Moon Stayed up To Late, The. John Ronald Reuel Tolkien. OBSP

Man in the Moon, The. Alvin Greenberg. OPRER

Man in the next office, The. Hubris. Mary Karr. NIL-7

Man in the VA Hospital, The. Betsy Colquitt. TiP2

Man in the Valley of Women, A. Chris Greenhalgh. NeBl

Man in the white room next door wrote this, I think: wrote this thinking I wanted to read it, The. For the Reader (Blank Book). Laura Mullen. ExTi

Man in the White Suit, The. Nick Drake. NeBl

Man In the Wilderness Asked [of] Me [*or* said to me], The [*or* A]. Mother Goose. Spl

Man in the World Lodging. *Unknown.* CCL1,

Man into Whose Yard You Should Not Hit Your Ball, The. Thomas Lux. P180

Man is approaching, A. Man Went to See the Doltons, A. Giovanna Pollarolo. TANSG, *tr. by* Marjorie Agosin

Man is bending his wife, A. Conjugal. Russell Edson. PmAP

Man is blest which can indure, The. Verses Written by a Gentlewoman upon the Jaylors Conversion. Anne Dowriche. EMWP

Man Is Born in Tao. Chuang Tzu. BLT, *tr. by* Thomas Merton

Man Is Dead, A. Claire Gebeyli. PoArWo, *tr. by* Mona Takyeddine Amyuni

Man is Dumb, A. Franz Werfel. GTCP, *tr. by* Irmgard Hunt

Man is following me, A. Jennifer Rankin. BMAP

Man is haunted by his father's ghost, A. Shakespearean Sonnet. R. S. Gwynn. IaFF

Man is leaning on a cold iron rail, A. Man Who Loved Islands, The. Derek Walcott. BodElec; NoAM

Man is lonely: the moon shines all the brighter. Chiu Tsz-yung. ColAnChi *Fr.* Cantonese Love-Songs.

Man is most anxious not to stir. That Corner. Blanaid Salkeld. IrLP

Man is no microcosm, and they detract. Habitation, The. Ralph Knevet. NOSC

Man is permitted much. Elements, The. John Henry, Cardinal Newman. SacPr

Man is seated before me, and there, The. Autograph. Francisco Hernandez. PML, *tr. by* John Oliver Simon

Man is shut in. Man-today. Andrée Chedid. HAWP, *tr. by* Mirène Ghossein and Samuel Hazo

Man is squeezing oranges in my kitchen, A. Aubade. Paula Cunningham. NIrP

Man is still alive, The. Amnesty. Ivan Venediktovich Elagin. TCRusP, *tr. by* Bertram D. Wolfe

Man Is The Highest Thing. "Angelus Silesius." GePo *Fr.* Cherubical Wanderer, The.

Man Is What He Wills to Be [*with music*]. Mrs. Henry Linden. CBWP-4

Man knocked three times, A. Madam and the Wrong Visitor. Langston Hughes. SAmP

Man knows not love—such love as woman feels. Woman's Love. *Unknown.* TreFP

Man lays his heavy, square paw on her dress, The. Apple, The. Radu Andriescu. PML, *tr. by* the author and Adam J. Sorkin *and* Irina Grigorescu Pan

Man letters the sign for his grocery in Arabic and English, A. Steps. Naomi Shihab Nye. CAP-8; ExTi

Man, like others, formed by God, A. Saxons of Flint, The. *Unknown.* OBWVE, *tr. by* Mary C. Llewelyn

Man Listening to Disc. Billy Collins. OxBoAm

Man looking into the sea. Grave, A. Marianne Moore. APT-1; HeIP-4; NAAPv.2; NAMCP V.1; NoAM; NoP-4; NoP-5; TFi; TRP; WeW-3

Man looks back on the land as it, A. Nostalgia. Xue Di. PML, *tr. by* Wang Ping and Keith Waldrop

Man Lost by a River, A. Michael C. Blumenthal. RaBo

Man Lying in a Hallway. Huw Jones. TCAWP

Man Lying on a Wall. Michael Longley. ModIr; NPeEn; PNI

Man May Change, A. Marvin Bell. PoDa

Man may longe lyves wene. *Unknown.* OHMEL

Man may make a Remark, A. Emily Dickinson. SAmP

Man May Tear a Jewel, A. Bhartrihari. WoPoe, *tr. by* Barbara Stoler Miller

Man may tear a jewel, A. Man May Tear a Jewel, A. Bhartrihari. WoPoe, *tr. by* Barbara Stoler Miller

Man Meets a Woman in the Street, A. Randall Jarrell. NoP-4; NoP-5

Man, mek me tell yu, dat was a fete. Dance Hall. Geoffrey Philp. WaCA

Man Named Troy, A. Reginald Shepherd. IllVoic

Man needs nothing so much as a strip of sea, A. About to Fall. Blas de Otero. RaW, *tr. by* Hardie St. Martin

Man needs something animal, A. Mr. Bloomer's Birds. William D. Barney. TiP2

Man of 1794, A. Donald Justice. PoDa

Man of action dials the telephon, A. (LL) Bachelor. William Meredith. NoAM; PoA 2002

Man of God is drunken without wine, The. Jelaluddin Rumi. TAL *Fr.* Dīvāni Shamsi Tabrīz.

Man of Green Hill. Song of the Man of Green Hill, The. Kao Ch'i. ColAnChi, *tr. by* Jonathan Chaves

Man of his age, he believed in the things. What My Father Believed. Robert Wrigley. RoV

Man of Law's Epilogue, The. Geoffrey Chaucer. NAEL-7v1 *Fr.* Canterbury Tales, The.

Man of Life Upright, The. Thomas Campion. NoSic

Man of No Attachments. Soyo Taeneung. BecRai, *tr. by* Kim Daljin, Kim Won-Chung and Christopher Merrill

Man of numbers, The. Numerology. Jerome Rothenberg. FTOS

Man, of precarious science vain. William Somervile. DiBP

Man of the House. Bob Hicok. SUP

Man of the House, The [*with music*]. David Wagoner. NAMCP V.2; NoAM

Man on a Fire Escape. Edward Hirsch. OxBoAm; UrbNat

Man on the Bed, The. Debora Greger. PoSol

Man on the Dump, The. Wallace Stevens. APT-1; NAMCP V.1; NAWM-7v2; NoAM; OxBoAm

Man on the Edge. Heberto Padilla. VCWP

Man on the Horizon, The. Gerallt Lloyd Owen. BBMWP, *tr. by* Joseph P. Clancy

Man on the Hotel Room Bed, The. Galway Kinnell. VCAP

Man on the Tower, The. Charles Rafferty. AmPoNex

Man plays a violin on the roof, A. Rooftop Violin. No Hyangnim. EcSo, *tr. by* Aimee N. Kwon

Man plowing starts at the side of a field, A. Woodcut on the Cover of Robert Frost's *Complete Poems*, The. Hayden Carruth. VisFro

Man Proposes, God Disposes. Bachner, Miroslav Košek and Hanuš Löwy. INSAB

Man pulling radishes, The. Issa. EH; IPoFL; PtR, *tr. by* Robert Hass

Man pulling the boat, A. Yasui. EMJL *Fr.* Mad Verse.

Man Rapes 25 in fight. Up, Up, Home & Away. John Forbes. NOBAu

Man Reading Homer, A. Nishiwaki Junzaburo. CAoMJL1, *tr. by* Hosea Hirata

Man risked his life to write the words, A. I Love You Sweatheart. Thomas Lux. SUP

Man Root, The. Kazuko Shiraishi. PFTM-2, *tr. by* Ikuko Atsumi and Kenneth Rexroth

Man Running. Richard Wilbur. OxBoAm

Man said to the universe, A. Stephen Crane. APN-2; BRP; NAAPv.1; OBSV; TCAPo; WeW-3

Man said unto his Angel, A. Kings, The. Louise Imogen Guiney. SacPr

Man sat in the felon's tank, alone, A. In the Tank. Thom Gunn. NoAM

Man sat staring at a doll's house, A. Doll's House, A. Kit Wright. EmeKit

Man Saves Own Life. Aaron Anstett. AmPoNex

Man saw a ball of gold in the sky, A. Stephen Crane. OxBoAm

Man says lilacs against white houses, two sparrows, one streaked, in a thinning birch, A. Spring Drawing 2. Robert Hass. CAP-8

Man Seeking Experience Enquires His Way of a Drop of Water, The. Ted Hughes. OxAEP-2

Man sees a tiny couple in the distance, and thinks they might be his mother and father, A. Optical Prodigal, The. Russell Edson. PmAP

Man sells post-cards, A. (LL) Bad times: / The cars pass. George Oppen. APT-2; PFTM-1

Man She Called Honey, and Married, The. Alberto A. Ríos. ReTh

Man should clear a space for himself, A. Clearing a Space. Brendan Kennelly. BeAl

Man should have no thought for property, A. Property. Robert Garioch. FaBoWar

Man should seek great glory, and not broad, A. (LL) To John Donne ("Who shall doubt, Donne, where [*or* whe'er] I a poet be[e].") Ben Jonson. NoP-4; NoP-5

Man sits in a timelessness, The. Rescue, The. Robert Creeley. VCAP

Man Splitting Wood in the Daybreak, The [*with music*]. Galway Kinnell. OxBoAm; VCAP

Man standing at the bus stop, A. Tuesday 9:00 AM. Denver Butson. P180

Man staring at a small lake sees, A. Fishing in Winter. Ralph Burns. MoASP

Man still light of foot, but ageing, took, A. Thinking of Mr D. Thomas Kinsella. NoAM

Man Struck Twenty Times by Lightning, The. Maxine Chernoff. PmAP

Man talking to his ex-wife on the phone, A. Sonnet. Robert Hass. NAMCP V.2

Man tears a chunk of bread off the brown loaf, A. Where We Are. Stephen Dobyns. StAl

Man That Got Away, The. Ira Gershwin. ReLy

Man that had six mortal wounds, a man, A. Cuchulain Comforted. William Butler Yeats. PoCho

Man that hath a handsome wife, The. Things Forbidden. *Unknown.* NoSic

Man that hath great griefs I pity not, The. Pain. Thomas Edward Brown. SacPr

Man, That Is Born of a Woman. Rosanna Warren. ExTi; PfSP

Man, that is borne of a woman is of a few dayes, and full of trouble. Bible, *O.T.* OBVE *Fr.* Job.

Man that mates wi' Poverty, The. Comfort in Puirtith. Helen B. Cruickshank. EdScPo

Man that sees by chance his picture made, A. Robert Bridges. NoAM *Fr.* Growth of Love, The.

Man the hare has met, The. Names of the Hare, The. *Unknown.* WoPoe, *tr. by* Seamus Heaney

Man Then Suddenly Stops Moving, A [*with music*]. Alberto A. Ríos. NAMCP V.2; NoAM

Man throws ten thousand shovels of grael at a window screen, A. El periférico, or Sleep. Joshua Clover. NeAmPo

Man traveled in Europe among Fauves, A. Night Shadows. William Carpenter. PoSol

Man Undergoes Pain Sitting at a Piana, A. Michael Palmer. OxBoAm

Man United. *Unknown.* FaBoVe

Man up early. Muskmelon, horsebean. In the Bitter Country. Mary Ruefle. AmAlph

Man walks a dusty road, A. Olmos. Dennis Nurkse. OPRER

Man walks beside them, A. White Oxen. Louis Simpson. NAMCP V.2; NoAM

Man Walks By with a Loaf of Bread on His Shoulder, A. César Vallejo. PoetW; TCLAP, *tr. by* Clayton Eshleman

Man walks by with a loaf of bread on his shoulder, A. Man Walks By with a Loaf of Bread on His Shoulder, A. César Vallejo. PoetW; TCLAP, *tr. by* Clayton Eshleman

(Man walks by with a baguette on his shoulder, A.) PoCho

Man walks into a bar and says, A. Boot Theory. Richard Siken. LegDan

Man walks on the bridge and gives away the change in his, A. Sri Sri. HotL *Fr.* Some People Laugh, Some People Cry.

Man Walks through His Life, A. Jane Hirshfield. MAAN

Man walks towards town, A. Late Hour, The. Mark Strand. AWTN

Man wanted to see the world, A. Promised Land, The. Jorge Fernández Granados. RMCMP, *tr. by* John Oliver Simon

Man wants an aeroplane to like him, A. He doesn't like it, but he. Categories, The. Russell Edson. SUP

Man wants but little here below. Wants of Man, The. John Quincy Adams. APN-1

Man wants to make love to the crippled man's sister, The. Words of a Toast, The. Denis Johnson. LaCa

Man was made of social earth. Ralph Waldo Emerson. APN-1 *Fr.* Initial, Dæmonic, and Celestial Love.

Man Was Made to Mourn, a Dirge. Robert Burns. TreFP

Man was thinking about his mother, The. Runner, The. Allen Grossman. PoCho

Man was walking through the nursery, The. Bear of the Human Family, A. Kazuko Shiraishi. WoBe, *tr. by* Samuel Grolmes and Yumiko Tsumura

Man watches a woman disrobe in a window, A. Voyeur. David Moolten. BloBone

Man Watching, The. Rainer Maria Rilke. RaBo; WED, *tr. by* Robert Bly

Man waxy, The--he jogs along the fields. Arthur Rimbaud. OBWP *Fr.* Eighteen-Seventy.

Man Wearing Bird. Denise Levertov. UpMys

Man went forth one day at eve, A. Tragedy. George Russell. MoBrPo

Man Went to See the Doltons, A. Giovanna Pollarolo. TANSG, *tr. by* Marjorie Agosin

Man, what is hope? . . . a horrifying whore. On Hope. Sándor Petőfi. IQMS, *tr. by* Peter Zollman

Man White, Brown Girl and All That Jazz / Upon the Occasion of His Marriage. Gloria C. Oden. GT

Man Who Beat Hemingway, The. Martín Espada. MoASP

Man Who Beat Up Homosexuals Reported to Have AIDS Virus. Richard Howard. NAMCP V.2

Man Who Became Old, The. Alberto A. Ríos. NoAM

Man who buries his house in the sand, The. Houses. Agha Shahid Ali. NIP-4

Man Who Came to the Last Floor, The. Víctor Hernández Cruz. PueRic

Man Who Closed Shop, The. Stephen Dunn. NIP-4

Man Who Couldn't Believe, The. David Citino. UpMys

Man Who Devoured Himself, The. Nasri Hajjaj. Eno, *tr. by* Ibrahim Muhawi

Man Who Didn't Know What Was His, The. Robert Bly. PML

Man Who Didn't Sign, The. Radoi Ralin. CSCBP, *tr. by* Georgi Belev and Lisa Sapinkopf

Man who doesn't love boys and single-foot horses and dogs, his heart will never know pleasure, The. Theognis. CAGL *Fr.* Second Book of Theognis, The.

Man Who Dreamed of Faeryland, The. William Butler Yeats. NAEL-6v2; NAEL-7v2; NoAM

Man who dropped death on Hiroshima, The. Hiroshima. Marie Luise Kaschnitz. GTCP, *tr. by* Lisel Mueller

Man who feels the dear disease, The. Man in Love, A. Lady Mary Wortley Montagu. LW

Man Who Feigns Deafness, The. Nguyễn Khuyến. WoPoe, *tr. by* Nguyen Ngoc Bich

Man who fiercest charged in fight, The. Stonewall Jackson. Herman Melville. NCAP

Man who fixed his eyes, A. Sentences After *Defence of Poetry*. Paul Goodman. BodElec

Man who had fallen among thieves, A. E. E. Cummings. ChIV-2; NoAM

Man, who had no rivals in the love, A. Man and His Image, The. Jean de La Fontaine. OBVE, *tr. by* Elizur Wright

Man Who Hanged Himself, The. Martin Birnbaum. Prolet, *tr. by* Amelia Glaser

Man Who Hated the Spring, The. Winifred Holtby. RSaN

Man who hated the spring was cold and narrow, cold as water and narrow as a steel blade, The. Man Who Hated the Spring, The. Winifred Holtby. RSaN

Man who, having collapsed, rises, takes steps, is insane. Forced March. Miklós Radnóti. AF

Man Who Invented Pain, The. Craig Raine. EmeKit

Man who ironed, The. Jelly Bean Policy, The. Jose Angel Figueroa. RWB

Man who is free and read, The. Various Songs of Leisure. Jungkwan Haean. BecRai, *tr. by* Kim Daljin, Kim Won-Chung and Christopher Merrill

Man who is very angry, A. 9th Untitled Poem. Pedro Juan Pietri. PueRic

Man Who Killed Himself to Avoid August, The. Maureen Seaton. ExTi

Man Who Knew the Words to "Louie, Louie", The. David Keller. SwNoth

Man who lives for only making money, The. Nice Work If You Can Get It. Ira Gershwin. ReLy

Man who lost both legs, A. Monologue at the Chinook Bar and Grill. Tess Gallagher. BodElec

Man Who Loved Islands, The. Derek Walcott. BodElec; NoAM

Man Who Loved White Chocolate, The. Robert Kelly. PFTM-2

Man who loves me, A. Troubadour Love. Olga Nolla. TANSG, *tr. by* Paula Vega

Man who loves *rancheras* holds out his hand, The. Turns at the Dance. Diana García. TouFir

Man Who Makes Brooms, The. Naomi Shihab Nye. LoL

Man Who Married Magdalene, The. Anthony Hecht. ChIV-2

Man Who Married Magdalene, The [*with music*]. Louis Simpson. NoAM

Man who melts a plastic garbage bag, The. Donald Morrill. LiTh

Man who needs space in his mind for important things, The. Eraser. Juan Carlos Galeano. PML, *tr. by* Delia Poey

Man Who Offers Me His Chest, The. Hala Mohammad. PoArWo, *tr. by* Cornelia Al-Khaled

Man who raped her, The. December 12th. Zachary Scott Robbins. BtF

Man Who Reads Homer, A. Nishiwaki Junzaburo. WoPoe, *tr. by* Masaya Saito

Man who seemed, A. Regulation equipment. Joyce Mansour. MFP, *tr. by* Martin Sorrell

Man who sold his lawn to standard oil, The. War against the Trees, The. Stanley Kunitz. NAMCP V.1

Man who spreads the cow-muck, The. Gardening. Tudur Dylan Jones. BBMWP, *tr. by* Elin ap Hywel

Man who stands above the bird, his knife, The. Thanksgiving. Mac Hammond. P180

Man who stood beside me, The. Sweet Will. Philip Levine. PoA 2002; VCAP

Man who tells you which is the whiter wash, The. Love and How It Becomes Important in Our Day to Day Lives. Miller Williams. PoA 2002

Man who thinks God is too kind, The. God Correctly Understood. J. Gordon Coogler. VerBaPo

Man Who Thinks He Can, The. Walter D. Wintle. ITBLP

Man Who Tried to Rape You, The. Erin Belieu. AmPoNex

Man who walks in the black wind; the dry reeds rustle quietly, A. On the Marshy Pastures. Georg Trakl. WED, *tr. by* Robert Bly

Man Who wants no children, The. Five Smooth Stones. Deborah Digges. ExTi

Man Who Wishes to Feed on Mahogany, The. Annie Dillard. UpMys

Man Who Wrote Yeats, the Man Who Wrote Mozart, The. Michael Hartnett. ModIr

Man whose height his fear improved he, The. Medgar Evers. Gwendolyn Brooks. ESEAA; NoP-4; NoP-5

Man Whose Name Rhymes with Peace, A. Nathaniel Tarn. WANABP

Man Whose Pharynx Was Bad, The. Wallace Stevens. OxBoAm

Man whose vacant mind prepares him to the sport, The. Michael Drayton. DiBP *Fr.* Polyolbion [*or* Poly-Oobion].

Man will keep a horse for prestige, A. Gateposts. Medbh McGuckian. MakPoe; ModIr; PBCIP

Man will put a large-headed nail, The. Of Green Steps and Laundry. Ralph Gustafson. NoP-4

Man with a Hat, A. Sunday Ayewanu. NeNiPo

Man with a heart, A. Man with a Hat, A. Sunday Ayewanu. NeNiPo

Man with a Hole in His Face, The. Jack Coulehan. BloBone

Man with a scythe: the torrent of his swing. Gardens No Emblems. Donald Davie. OBGa

Man with His Kids on a Table, The. Larry Kearney. Eno

Man with incomplete words on his roof, The. Karen Press. TSAP

Man with laughing eyes stopped smiling, The. Arabic. Naomi Shihab Nye. CAP-8; PoArWo

Man with Long Legs, The. Dacia Maraini. CItWP, *tr. by* Cinzia Sartini Blum and Lara Trubowitz

Man With Night Sweats, The. Thom Gunn. CABP; CalPo; HarvBoo; PoPoPo

Man with the big mouth, The. And Again. Alison Fell. LW

Man with the Blue Guitar, The. Wallace Stevens.
   "I cannot bring a world quite round." RaBo
   "Poetry is the subject of the poem." NAMCP V.1

Man with the glass eye, The. Leonard Neufeldt. ACAMVP

Man with the goats has seen this light before, The. Landscape with a Calm. T. J. Clark. BAP-04

Man with the gold lighter lights five, The. Watching the Men Walk. Nance Van Winckel. PoDa

Man with the green cigarette strolls down the path. Jungle Night. "K." FaBoWar

Man with the Hoe, The. Edwin Markham. APN-2; BRP; CalPo; GS; MoAmPo; NAAPv.1; OxBoAm; TCAPo; TFi

Man with the Hoe, The. Les A. Murray. UpMys

Man with the red hat, The. Glazunoviana. John Ashbery. VCAP

Man with the Saxophone, The. Ai. CFP; SeSe

Man with the Wooden Leg, The [*with music*]. Katherine Mansfield. FaBoWar

Man with Three Friends, The. Dora Greenwell. SacPr

Man with wrinkly lips, The. Amiti´ Amoureuse. Gregorio Scalise. ItPo, tr. by Gayle Ridinger

Man without a Middle, The. Angela Sorby. AmPoNex

Man, you funny thing. I Wanna Be Loved. Edward Heyman and Billy Rose. ReLy

Man you know, assured and kind, The. Almost Human. Cecil Day Lewis. NAMCP V.1; NoAM

Man, you too, aren't you, one of these rough followers of the criminal? In the Servants' Quarters. Thomas Hardy. FaBoVe; MoBrPo

Management is pleased to announce, The. Jazz at the Intergalactic Nightclub. Michael McClure. SeSe

Manager lady of this, The. Incognito Lounge, The. Denis Johnson. ReTh

Managing the Common Herd: Two Approaches for Senior Management. Julie O'Callaghan. BeAl

Managing the house is a big problem. Rāmprasād Sen. SinGod, tr. by Rachel Fell McDermott

Mañana desnuda, el diamante, La. Mañana, La. José Ángel Valente. RaW

Mañana (Is Soon Enough for Me). Dave Barbour and Peggy Lee. ReLy

Mañana, La. José Ángel Valente. RaW

Manatee tries a diet of only sea grass, but still stays fat, The. Why, on a Bad Day, I Can Relate to the Manatee. Denise Duhamel. SUP

Man-brained and man-handed ground-ape, physically, The. Original Sin. Robinson Jeffers. MoAmPo

Manchester by Night. Mathilde Blind. ViWPN

Manda decir que no estén en Su lugar. Eduardo Milán. RMCMP

Mandala. Yamamura Bochō. CAoMJL1, tr. by Leith Morton

Mandalay. Rudyard Kipling. BRP; HarvBoo; MoBrPo; NPeEn; OxAEP-2

Mandan Chief, The. Fanny Crosby. SWaP

Mandap. Elsa Cross. RMCMP

Mandap. Elsa Cross. RMCMP, tr. by Margaret Sayers Peden

Mandarin Who Couldn't Do Anything, The. Vietnamese Oral Tradition. CaDao, tr. by John Balaban

Mandarins Got Their Raise, The. Tu Mo. WoPoe, tr. by Nguyen Ngoc Bich

Mandoline. Paul Verlaine. OBMV, tr. by Arthur Symons

Mandorla. Paul Celan. PoSu, tr. by Michael Hamburger

Manes P. Aground Off Fort Dufferin, The. Robert J. Gibbs. Coast

Manet's Olympia. Margaret Atwood. NAMCP V.2

Man-Fate, The [with music]. William Everson. NoAM

Manfred. Lord Byron. NAEL-6v2; NAEL-7v2; NOBRP
 "Stars are forth, the moon above the tops, The." AmFaPo; TreFP
 "We are the fools of time and terror: Days." AmFaPo

Mangel-Bury, The. Ivor Gurney. HarvBoo

Mango. Unknown. SonAtl, tr. by Martha Belton, Kurt Ganzl, F. Silai and Jim Yarris

Mango, A. Joyce Mansour. SurWo, tr. by Mary Beach

Mango on the Mango Tree, The. Robert Penn Warren. NoAM Fr. Mexico is a Foreign Country: Five Studies in Naturalism.

Mango Poem. Regie Cabico. WiU

Mangoes. Richard Tipping. NOBAu

Mangoes are not cigarettes. Mangoes. Richard Tipping. NOBAu

Mango's Core, The. Patricia Blanco. AFaM

Mangosteens. Daniel Hall. NoP-4

Mangrove. John Blight. NOBAu

Manhattan. Lorenz Hart. ReLy

Manhattan, a small hotel. Thursday. Miklós Radnóti. IQMS, tr. by John Wain

Manhattan dance Latin. Side 12. Víctor Hernández Cruz. PueRic

Manhattan faces and eyes forever for me. (LL) Give Me the Splendid Silent Sun. Walt Whitman. CBCWP; MoAmPo

Manhattan / I'm up a tree. Down in the Depths. Cole Porter. ReLy

Manhattan is really as grand as it's painted. Moon About Town. E. Y. Harburg. ReLy

Manhattan Lullaby. Norma Farber. SSCS; TLR

Manhattan Lullaby. Rachel Lyman Field. HHAm; TLR

Manhattan Madness. Irving Berlin. ReLy

Manhattan, Manhattan. Manhattan Madness. Irving Berlin. ReLy

Manhattan May Day Midnight. Allen Ginsberg. WhBo

Manhattan Pastures. Sandra Hochman. YaYoPo

Manhattan Valley. Lynn Melnick. IIR

Manhole Covers. Karl Shapiro. NAMCP V.2; NoAM

Maniac, The. Agnes Strickland. CenSon

Maniac, The (2). Mary Bryan. CenSon

Maníacos y locos. Heriberto Yépez. RMCMP

Maniacs and crazies. Heriberto Yépez. RMCMP, tr. by Mark Weiss

Maniac's Song, The. Ann Taylor. NOBRP

Manic: A Conversation with Jimi Hendrix. Tim Seibles. OPRER

Manic-depressive Lincoln, national hero! Lincoln. Delmore Schwartz. APT-2

Manichean Geography I. Tom Paulin. PNI

Manicheans did no Idols make, The. Fulke, 1st Baron Brooke Greville. SacPr Fr. Caelica.

Manifest Destiny. Suheir Hammad. PoArWo

Manifest, The. Olga Nolla. TANSG, tr. by Paula Vega

Manifesto. Peter E. Murphy. UrbNat

Manifesto, A. José Santos Chocano. TCLAP, tr. by Andrew Rosing

Manifesto of Futurism, The. Filippo Tommaso Marinetti.
 "We had stayed up all night, my friends and I, under hanging mosque lamps." PFTM-1

Manifesto of Surrealism (1924). André Breton.
 Three Excerpts. PFTM-1

Manifesto on Ars Poetica. Frank Mkalawile Chipasula. HBAPE; NAfrP; PML

Manifesto: The Mad Farmer Liberation Front. Wendell Berry. GoPo; IPoFL

Manifesto: The Mad Farmer Liberation Front. Wendell Berry.
 "So, friends, every day so something." UpMys

Manila Bay. Eugene Fitch Ware. OBCoV

Manila is full of the black ruins of my life. Lament Beginning w/a Line after Cavafy. Eric Gamalinda. ReBoTo

Manila Paper. Cyn Zarco. ReBoTo

Mani-Mani Gatha. Jackson Mac Low. PFTM-1

Mankend I cale, wich lyith in frale. Unknown. SacPr

Mankind on a little globe. Twenty Billion Light Years of Loneliness. Shuntaro Tanikawa. PoetW, tr. by Harold Wright

Mankind owns four things. Antonio Machado Ruiz. WED Fr. Moral Proverbs and Folk Songs.

Mankind should hope. Mary Savage. LW Fr. Letter to Miss E.B. on Marriage.

Manly Ferry. John Philip. NOBAu

Manly Love. Donald Malloch. CAGL

Manly Sports. Marion Bernstein. NePenScot

Man-maker, make white! (LL) White Things. Anne Spencer. InGu; NAAPv.2

Man-Moth, The. Elizabeth Bishop. APT-2; MoAmPo; NALW; NAMCP V.2; NoAM

Man-Myth: Puberty. Jean-Baptiste Tati-Loutard. SonAtl, tr. by Gregory Beaven and Kurt Ganzl

Manna. Joseph Stroud. CalPo; GeoHom

Manna. James Tate. GM

Mannequins. Daniel Mark Epstein. ReTh

Manner in which we are present at this time and to and fro appears, we come to point of view before us, The. Lyn Hejinian. AWPTFC Fr. Happily.

Manner of Her Will and What She Left to London and to All Those in It, at Her Departing, The. Isabella Whitney. NoSic
 "I whole in body, and in mind." NoP-5

Mannerly Margery Milk and Ale. John Skelton. NAEL-6v1; NAEL-7v1; NoP-4; NoP-5

Manners. Pamela Alexander. ExTi

Manners. Elizabeth Bishop. EMP; GoPo; NOxBChV

Manners [with music]. Howard Nemerov. NBLV

Manners may prevail. (LL) Abraham to kill him. Emily Dickinson. ChIV-1; SoSe-8

Manning the controls, faith. At the Controls. Robert Vas Dias. OtW

Mannyelanong. Huw Jones. BBMWP, tr. by the author

Manodharma with Mr. Y. Takehisa Kosugi. WhBo

Man-of-War Hawk, The. Herman Melville. APN-2; OWoS

Manon Reassures Her Lover. Martha Elizabeth. PasH

Manong Chito Tells Manong Ben about His Dream over Breakfast at the Manilatown Cafe. Vince Gotera. ReBoTo

Manong with a Thousand Tribal Visions, The. Al Robles. ReBoTo

Manor Garden, The. Sylvia Plath. HarvBoo

Manora. Pimone Triplett. NAPBL

Man—pitiful insect. Qiyuge. Unknown. CCL1, tr. by Burton Watson

Man's a carnation. Green and Gold. Ani Ilkov. CSCBP, tr. by Georgi Belev and Lisa Sapinkopf

Man's [a] Sliding Mood, A. Mary Elizabeth Fullerton. NOBAu

Man's ambition is to conquer the world, A. Unknown. NAAPv.2

Man's and woman's bodies lay without souls. Childish Prank, A. Ted Hughes. CABP; NPeEn

Man's body at auction, A. Walt Whitman. SAmP Fr. I Sing the Body Electric.

Man's Civil[l] War[re]. Robert Southwell. NoSic

Man's Country. Daryl Hine. IllVoic

Man's Days. Eden Phillpotts. OBEV

Man's dead, The. Edward Hopper Retrospective, The. Tony Quagliano.
PoSol

Mans disposition is for to requite. Revenge. Robert Herrick. RaF

Man's got a heart, A. Reviewing the Situation. Lionel Bart. ReLy

Man's Heart, A. Charles MacKay.
Earl and the Girl, The. STuOW

Mans Knowledge, Ignorance in the Misteries of God. William Drummond of
Hawthornden. SacPr

Man's Life. Inscription in Osmington Church, Dorset. *Unknown*. NPeEn

Man's life, A? Empty water bubbles. Deathbed Song. Pou Kuksa. BecRai,
tr. by Christopher Merrill

Man's Life a Sojourning. *Unknown*. CCL1,

Man's life is laid in the loom of time. Loom of Time, The. *Unknown*.
ITBLP

Man's life is like a Sparrow, mighty King! William Wordsworth. OWoS *Fr.*
Ecclesiastical Sonnets.

Man's life is warm, glad, sad, 'twixt loves and graves. Leigh Hunt. NPeEn
Fr. Fish, the Man, and the Spirit, The.

Man's life is well compared to a feast. Comparison of the Life of Man, A.
Richard Barnfield. NoSic

Man's life's a tragedy: his mother's womb. De Morte. Sir Henry Wotton.
BASC; NOSC

Man's mother is very sick, A. Man, A. Nicanor Parra. VCWP, *tr. by* W. S.
Merwin

Man's Natural Infirmity. John Day. InvLi

Man's Requirements, A. Elizabeth Barrett Browning. RACG; ViWPN

Mans Youth it is a field of large desires. Fulke, 1st Baron Brooke Greville.
WaAnP *Fr.* Caelica.

Manse, The. Alastair Reid. EdScPo

Mansion. A. R. Ammons. AmFaPo; OxBoAm

Mansion Beach. Elizabeth Spires. PoDa

Mansion is full of spiders, The. Pick up. Soon. Pamela Alexander. ExTi

Mansize. Maura Dooley. NeBl

Mantanza to Welcome Spring. Jimmy Santiago Baca. PmAP

Man-thunder, woman-lightning. Opus 17. Witter Bynner. APT-1, *tr. by*
Emanuel Morgan

Mantilla. Medbh McGuckian. NAMCP V.2

"Mantis." Louis Zukofsky. NAAPv.2

Mantis! praying mantis! since your wings' leaves. "Mantis." Louis Zukofsky.
NAAPv.2

Mantle [*with music*]. William Heyen. MoASP; ReTh

Mantle ran so hard, they said. Mantle. William Heyen. MoASP; ReTh

Mantles. Kit Wright. NoP-5

Man-today. Andrée Chedid. HAWP, *tr. by* Mirène Ghossein and Samuel Hazo

Man-Torpedo-Boat. Tessa Rumsey. LegDan

Mantra for a Classless Society, or Mr. Roget's Neighborhood. Harryette
Mullen. WANABP

Mantreya Upanishad, The. *Unknown. Fr.* Upanishads, The.

Manual System. Carl Sandburg. APT-1

Manuel. Rafael Campo. WiU *Fr.* Ten Patients, and Another.

Manuel de Río, natural. Requiem. José Hierro. RaW

Manuel del Río, born. Requiem. José Hierro. RaW

Manufacturing. Rae Armantrout. AWPTFC

Manuscript. Angelina Muñiz Huberman. MirDau, *tr. by* Aurora Camacho

Manuscript Found in a Book of Joseph Conrad. Jorge Luis Borges. PoetW, *tr.
by* Alastair Reid

Manuscript in a Bottle. Pablo Antonio Cuadra. BLPSL, *tr. by* Rene de Costa,
Rigas Kappatos and Eleni Paidoussi

Manuscript in a Bottle. Pablo Antonio Cuadra. TCLAP, *tr. by* Ann McCarthy
de Zavala and Grace Schulman

Manuscript with Illumination. Robert Fitzgerald. APT-2

Manx. Mary Russell Mitford. DiBP

Many a lip is gaping for drink. Eliza Cook. STuOW; VerBaPo *Fr.* Song of the
Seaweed.

Many a long, long year ago. Alarmed Skipper, The. James Thomas Fields.
NBLV

Many a man gets bewitched by the elves. Heinrich von Morungen. GePo

Many a man joined the club. Julia A. Moore. STuOW *Fr.* Temperance
Reform Clubs.

Many a New Day. Oscar Hammerstein, II. ReLy

Many a poet in his lay. May. Dafydd ap Gwilym. CABP

Many a soldier's kiss dwells on these bearded lips. (LL) Wound-Dresser, The.
Walt Whitman. AmWaPo; APN-1; CBCWP; ColAP; NAAL-3; NAAL-5;
NAAPv.1; OBWP; PCW; TCAPo

Many a swan-white breast. (LL) Dead at Clonmacnois [*or* Clonmacnoise], The.
Angus O'Gillan. OBEV; OBMV, *tr. by* Thomas William Hazen Rolleston

Many a year has fled away. My Old Palette. Christopher Pearse Cranch.
APN-1

Many American flags, The. Grand Entry, The. Gary Snyder. NoAM

Many and many a time. (LL) Coronal, A. William Carlos Williams.
OxBoAm; TCAPo

Many and More. Maya Angelou. LW

Many Are Called. Rick Barot. LegDan

Many Are Called. Edwin Arlington Robinson. GI

Many are from the Maldives. Where Babies Come From. James Tate.
NAMCP V.2

Many are making love. Privilege of Being. Robert Hass. NIP-4
(Many are making love. Up above, the angels.) CAP-8; ItP; NAMCP V.2

Many are the hills. Written After Climbing Kaguyama to Survey the Land.
Emperor Jomei. WoPoe, *tr. by* Helen Craig McCullough

Many are thy tones, O Ocean. Sea Cadences. Henrietta Cordelia Ray.
CBWP-3

Many builders there have been. Love Nest, The. Otto Harbach. ReLy

Many children are fathered, fondled by parents. Fates of Men. Peter Reading.
PML

Many creatures don't have one. Penelope Shuttle. NewEx

Many entrances. Open. Everywhere. But reaching nowhere. Wandering. Poetry.
Kim Chôngnan. EcSo, *tr. by* Peter H. Lee

Many fair hours have been buried here. Millinery District. Charles Reznikoff.
APT-2

Many films begin with a funeral. Mara Malanova. CRWP, *tr. by* Nika
Skandiaka

Many find Quintia stunning. I find her attractive. Catullus. NAWM-7v1 *Fr.*
Carmina [Charles Martin Translation].

Many folks are in a snit. Freud's Butcher. Charles Bernstein. BodElec

Many girls I've met. Maybe This Is Love. Lew Brown, B. G. DeSylva and
Ray Henderson. ReLy

Many good angels helped me on my journey. Heart, The. Patrick Warner.
Coast

Many Happy Returns. Ted Berrigan. AHA

Many in aftertimes will say of you. Christina Georgina Rossetti. CABP;
MakPoe; OxBSo *Fr.* Monna Innominata.

Many ingeni[o]us lovely things are gone. Nineteen Hundred and Nineteen.
William Butler Yeats. NAMCP V.1

Many long years ago, I loved a youth. Blight of Love, The. Mary E. Tucker.
CBWP-1

Many, many things. Basho. TAL

Many mellow Cydonian suckets. Miss Lee [*or* Rosalie Lee]. Thomas Holley
Chivers. STuOW

Many men with lofty aims. Folks Who Live on the Hill, The. Oscar
Hammerstein, II. ReLy

Many, monstrous, tumbled, dun-gray boulders, The. You Were Broken.
Giuseppe Ungaretti. STV, *tr. by* John Frederick Nims

Many nights on the road. Basho. EH, *tr. by* Robert Hass

Many of the stories circulating about my escapades are not true. Explanation.
Christine Hume. LegDan

Many. / One. (LL) Alone. Tomas Transtrómer. StAl; WoPoe, *tr. by* Robin
Fulton

Many people have drifted away. My Phone Rings Endlessly. Ch'oe Sûngja.
EcSo, *tr. by* Mickey Hong

Many people have gathered together. Foot Race Song. *Unknown*. OBVE, *tr.
by* Frank Russell

Many policemen wear upon their shoulders. Sergeant Brown's Parrot. Kit
Wright. OPOU

Many prophets have failed, their voices silent. Ode to Failure. Allen
Ginsberg. CAP-8

Many red devils ran from my heart. Stephen Crane. NAAPv.1

Many Said. Kakkai Patiniyar Naccellaiyar. WoPoe, *tr. by* George L. Hart III

Many said. Many Said. Kakkai Patiniyar Naccellaiyar. WoPoe, *tr. by*
George L. Hart III

Many say Japan has neither a poetics nor a language in which poetry can be
written. Fujii Sadakazu. PFTM-2 *Fr.* Where is Japanese Poetry?

Many sewing days ago. Listening Macaws, The. Hazel Hall. APT-1;
NAAPv.2

Many shapes of wings. Environs. Larry Eigner. FTOS

Many ships that left our country, The. Exiles, The. Iain Crichton Smith.
HarvBoo; NePenScot

Many slandered him. *Various authors*. CATKP *Fr.* Songs of Flying Dragons.

Many Soldiers. Edgar Lee Masters. TCAPo

Many strange mountains in Shu and Han. Imitating the Old Poems. Pao
Chao. CCL1, *tr. by* Burton Watson

Many things to absorb I teach to help you become eleve of mine. To a Western
Boy. Walt Whitman. APN-1

Many thoughts converge and finally disappear. Lonely Hermitage. Master
Naong. BecRai, *tr. by* Kim Daljin, Kim Won-Chung and Christopher
Merrill

Many Thousand Go. *Unknown*. SSUS

Many thousand gone. (LL)   No More Auction Block.   *Unknown.*   ISC; RaBo

Many times I wait there for my father.   Buffalo.   Molly Peacock.   OxBoAm

Many times the mountains have turned from green to yellow.   Muso Soseki. ZenPo, *tr. by* Takashi Ikemoto and Lucien Stryk

Many will love you; you were made for love.   Many Will Love You.   Mathilde Blind.   ViWPN

Many winters ago our wise ancestors predicted that a great.   Dancing Speech of O-No'-Sa, The.   *Iroquois Oral Tradition.*   NAAPv.1

Many winters have gone by.   Dora Markus and Her Actors.   Gregorio Scalise. ItPo, *tr. by* Gayle Ridinger

Many Worlds Are Walked Once.   Kojo Laing.   HBAPE

Many years, and one of them a little harder.   Eugenio Montale.   WoPoe *Fr.* Motets [Mottetti].

Many years from now.   Glass of Ancient Wine, A.   Gzar Hantoosh.   IrPoTo, *tr. by* Saadi A. Simawe and Ellen Doré Watson

Many years from now, when I am a little heap of silenced dust, play.   To the Children.   Gabriela Mistral.   SpanPo, *tr. by* Kate Flores

Many years have passed, mica.   Accomplices.   Bei Dao.   AF, *tr. by* Bonnie S. McDougall

Many years have slipped by since.   Yi Hwang.   CATKP *Fr.* Twelve Songs of Tosan.

Many-colored sandal, A.   Sappho.   SaLy, *tr. by* Diane Rayor

Many-headed Hydra, or the people, The.   Common People, The.   Rowland Watkyns.   AngWePo; BASC

Manyo Shu, Part 3 of 4.   *Various authors. tr. by* Lafcadio Hearn

  "O pine-tree standing."   TAL, *tr. by* Arthur Waley

  "Plum-blossom, The."   TAL

Manyo Shu, Part 2 of 4.   *Various authors.*

  "May the men who are born."   TAL

  "Men of valor, The."   TAL

Mao & Matisse.   Ed Friedman.   PrTe

Map.   Gerardo Deniz.   RMCMP, *tr. by* Mónica de la Torre

Map.   Michele Glazer.   IAoNAP

Map.   Linda Hogan.   ExTi

Map.   Raymond Radiguet.   CuPo

Map.   Martin Sorescu.   VCWP, *tr. by* Russell-Gebbett

Map, The.   Elizabeth Bishop.   APT-2; ColAP; NAMCP V.2

Map, The [*with music*].   Gary Soto.   NoAM; WaAnP

Map Burnt Through.   Joanna Rawson.   AmPoNex

Map of Europe, A.   Derek Walcott.   BrAP

Map of Montana in Italy, A.   Richard Hugo.   CAP-8

Map of My Country.   John Holmes.   CA

Map of my native country is all edges, A.   Map of My Country.   John Holmes. CA

Map of places passes, The.   Map of Places, The.   Laura Riding Jackson. APT-2; NAMCP V.1

Map of Simplicities, A.   James Applewhite.   LPSFW

Map of the City, A.   Thom Gunn.   NAEL-6v2; NAEL-7v2; NoP-4; NoP-5

Map of the Kingdom, A.   David Wright.   ACAMVP

Map of the Winter Sky, The.   Margherita Guidacci.   CItWP, *tr. by* Cinzia Sartini Blum and Lara Trubowitz

Map of the world is felt from the inside. Rough around the, The.   Map of the World, The.   Anna Couani.   BMAP

Map of the World, The.   Anna Couani.   BMAP

Map of Verona, A.   Henry Reed.   HarvBoo

Map Reading.   Raymond Garlick.   AngWePo

Map Room, The.   Joshua Clover.   BAP-97; NeAmPo

Map shows me where it is you are, The.   Private Letter to Brazil, A.   Gloria C. Oden.   ESEAA

  (Map shows me where it is you are. I, The.)   GT

Map the dominie had tacked up, The.   St Kilda.   Neil Curry.   NLP

Mapa.   Gerardo Deniz.   RMCMP

Mapas.   Alberto Blanco.   RMCMP

Mapas, Los / se hacen los domingos.   Fabio Morabito.   RMCMP

Maple.   Bill Griffiths.   Oth *Fr.* Building: The New London Hospital.

Maple and the Pine, The.   Robert Garioch.   NPeEn

Maple Bridge Night Mooring.   Chang Chi.   ColAnChi; NDACCP, *tr. by* Gary Snyder

Maple Leaf.   "Shu Ting."   VCWP

Maple Syrup.   Donald Hall.   CAP-8

Maple Syrup Sonnet ("For over ten years now.")   Bernadette Mayer.   NYP2

Maple Syrup Sonnet ("Syrup's up again.")   Bernadette Mayer.   NYP2

Maple Tree, The.   John Clare.   OxBSo

Maple with its tassel[l] flowers of green, The.   Maple Tree, The.   John Clare. OxBSo

Mapmaker's Song, The.   Gwyneth Lewis.   BBMWP, *tr. by* the author and Richard Poole

Mapooram.   *Aborigine Oral Tradition.*   NOBAu, *tr. by* Fred Biggs

Mappa Mundi.   Philip Gross.   BeAl

Maps.   Alberto Blanco.   RMCMP, *tr. by* Michael Wiegers

Maps.   Bruce Guernsey.   IllVoic

Maps are drawn / on Sundays.   Fabio Morabito.   RMCMP, *tr. by* Geoff Hargreaves

Maps, his father said, are history.   Winners.   Katherine Frost.   Prnts

Maqabane.   Tatamkulu Afrika.   TSAP

Maquinarias.   David Huerta.   RMCMP

Mar 7 SIGNAL.   Hannah Weiner.   PFTM-2 *Fr.* Clairvoyant Journal.

Mar Egeo.   Manuel Ulacia.   RMCMP

Mar sin marinos, ni buques fantasmas.   Yramín y el Mar.   Manuel Vázquez Montalbán.   RaW

Mara sighs over the silks laid out on the rosewood windowsill.   Silk Light of Advent, The.   Gillian Allnutt.   NeBrP

Marated Bastilled age, A.   Boris Nartsissov.   TCRusP, *tr. by* John Glad

Marathon.   Cyrus Cassells.   WiU

Marathon.   Louise Glück.

  Song of Obstacles.   LW

Marathon.   John Powell Ward.   TCAWP

Marble.   Zulaykha Abu-Risha.   PoArWo, *tr. by* Clarissa C. Burt

Marble Beads.   Delmira Agustini.   TANSG, *tr. by* Mark McCaffrey

"Marble I thought thee, and brickwork I find thee!" the Tourist may answer. (LL)   Arthur Hugh Clough.   FaBoVe; NoP-5; OxAEP-2 *Fr.* Amours de Voyage.

Marble on the milk of this night.   Marble.   Zulaykha Abu-Risha.   PoArWo, *tr. by* Clarissa C. Burt

Marble one so warmed would speak, A. (LL)   To a Fair Lady Playing with a Snake.   Edmund Waller.   CABP; NOSC

Marble Prophecy, The.   Josiah Gilbert Holland.

  "Laocöon! thou great embodiment."   APN-1

Marble surfaces.   Joanne Burns.   BMAP

Marbled Chuckle in the Savannahs.   Kenward Elmslie.   FTOS

Marblehead's a rocky place.   Royall Tyler.   NAAL-3 *Fr.* Contrast, The.

Marble-Top.   Elwyn Brooks White.   AmWit

Marcelina.   Natalia Toledo.   RMCMP

Marcelina.   Natalia Toledo.   RMCMP, *tr. by* Alberto A. Ríos

March.   Elizabeth Jane Coatsworth.   Spl

March.   Elizabeth Jane Coatsworth.   Spl

March: "I'm going to your fair."   Ekaterina Iosifova.   CSCBP, *tr. by* Georgi Belev and Lisa Sapinkopf

March [*with music*].   Henrietta Cordelia Ray.   CBWP-3

March.   Rosemerry Wahtola Trommer.   GeoH

March.   Marina Ivanovna Tsvetaeva.

  "They took quickly, they took hugely."   AF

March . . . Someone has walked across the snow.   Vacancy in the Park. Wallace Stevens.   SAmP

March 1, The.   Robert Lowell.   AmWaPo; PoetW; PoPoPo

March 2, The.   Robert Lowell.   AmWaPo

3-4-00.   Jack Collom.   BAP-04

March 12, 1999.   Alex Rawls.   AnSo *Fr.* What's Your Sign?

March 9 1976.   Brian Meeks.   WaCA

March Again.   Philip Booth.   PfSP

March Blizzard.   John Tagliabue.   GoPo

March comes, / and Eastern bluebird shows himself.   This Year's Drive to Appomattox.   Eleanor Ross Taylor.   CBCWP

March Crescent Moon Song.   Andrew Schelling.   WANABP

March Day in London, A.   Amy Levy.   VWP

March Elegy.   Arkadii Dragomoschenko.   ItGoST, *tr. by* Elena Balashova and Lyn Hejinian

March Evening.   Harry Edmund Martinson.   WED, *tr. by* Robert Bly

March Evening.   Leonard Alfred George Strong.   MoBrPo

March Hares.   Andrew Young.   SAmP

March has come to the bridge head.   Poem by the Bridge at Ten-shin.   Li Po. InoFa; NDACCP; OBVE, *tr. by* Ezra Pound

March in the Ranks Hard-Prest, and the Road Unknown, A.   Walt Whitman. AmWaPo; CBCWP; NAAL-3; PCW

March in Transylvania.   Lajos Áprily.   IQMS, *tr. by* Adam Makkai

March into Virginia, Ending in the First Manassas, The.   Herman Melville. *See* March into Virginia, The.

March into Virginia, The.   Herman Melville.   NCAP

  (March into Virginia, Ending in the First Manassas, The.)   AmWaPo

March Lambs.   Bobi Jones.   ATSWP, *tr. by* Robert Minhinnick

March, now, and almost the season.   Small Girl Brings an Injured Bird into the Surgery, A.   Michael O'Reilly.   BloBone

March of Dawn, The.   Yi Hyangji.   EcSo, *tr. by* Catherine J. Kim

March of the Cordilleras, The.   Raúl Zurita.   TCLAP, *tr. by* Jack Schmitt

March of the Rebel Angels.   John Milton.   TreFP *Fr.* Paradise Lost.

March strikes the ice of the sky.   Peter Huchel.   *See* March with its sharp pick.

March strongly forth, my Muse, whilst yet the temperate air.   Michael Drayton.   NOSC *Fr.* Polyolbion [*or* Poly-Oobion].

March, The.   Mary Ruefle.   AmAlph

March toward the Front, The.   Odysseus Elytis.   AF, *tr. by* Edmund Keeley and George Savidis

March went out like a lion.   June Is Bustin' Out All Over.   Oscar Hammerstein, II.   ReLy

March, when the ground softened.   Burial, The.   Ellen Bryant Voigt.   InoFa

March wind blows the garden gate.   Riding the Lion, Riding the Lamb.   Karen Chamberlain.   GeoH

March with its sharp pick.   Landscape Beyond Warsaw.   Peter Huchel.   PoSu
(March strikes the ice of the sky.)   AF

Marche à l'amour, La.   Gaston Miron.
"Tu as les yeux pers des champs de rosées."   YaTCFP

Marché aux Oiseaux.   Richard Wilbur.   OWoS

Marche Funèbre.   Gunnar Ekelof.   PFTM-2 *Fr.* Mölna Elegy.

Märchen, The.   Randall Jarrell.   HarvBoo

Marching armies of the past, The.   Confederate Memorial Day.   *Unknown.*   CBCWP

Marching Song.   George Dillon.   PoA 2002

Marching Still.   Minna Irving.   CBCWP

Marching through Georgia.   Henry Clay Work.   APN-2; CBCWP

Marcia and I went over the curve.   Millions of Strawberries.   Genevieve Taggard.   NOxBChV

Marco Bozzaris.   Fitz-Greene Halleck.
"At midnight, in his guarded tent."   APN-1

Marco Polo.   Marvin Bell.   BodElec

Marconi, of course, and the whisper.   Signal Hill.   Randall Maggs.   Coast

Marconi's Cottage.   Medbh McGuckian.   ModIr

Marcus Aurelius.   Dezső Kosztolányi.   IQMS, *tr. by* Earl M. Herrick

Marcus Curtius.   Oliver St. John Gogarty.   OBMV

Mardi Gras.   Paul Laraque.   OGAHCP, *tr. by* Boadiba and Jack Hirschman

Mardi Gras Premortem.   Ann Townsend.   NeAmPo

Mardohai Simhon claimed the silk scarf he wore around his neck was a mirror.   Mirror and Scarf.   Edmond Jabès.   YaTCFP, *tr. by* Rosmarie Waldrop

Mardohai Simhon prétendait que le mouchoir de soie qu'il portait.   Miroir et le mouchoir, Le.   Edmond Jabès.   YaTCFP

Mare lies down in the grass where the nest of the skylark is hidden, The.   Mare, The.   Vernon Watkins.   OBWVE

Mare, The [*with music*].   Vernon Watkins.   OBWVE

Marea roja.   José Luis Rivas.   RMCMP

Mares.   Juan Ramón Jiménez.   RaW

Marfa Lights, The.   W. S. Merwin.   BodElec

Margaret, are you grieving.   Spring and Fall [To a Young Child].   Gerard Manley Hopkins.   BrAP; CABP; ClHu; CtM; HeIP-4; InoFa; NAEL-6v2; NAEL-7v2; NAMCP V.1; NIL-7; NIP-4; NoAM; NoP-4; NoP-5; OPOU; PoPoPo; PtR; TFi; TRP; WaAnP

Margaret Fuller Slack.   Edgar Lee Masters.   APT-1; RACG

Margaret Fuller Slack.   Edgar Lee Masters.   APT-1; IllVoic; RACG *Fr.* Spoon River Anthology.

Margaret/Haskell Indian School.   Carolyn Marie Dunn.   ReEnLa

Margaret Morse.   From the Green Book of Yfan.   Rolfe Humphries.   APT-2

Margarita, A. (LL)   Of Time and the Line.   Charles Bernstein.   FTOS; NIL-7; NoP-5; PFTM-2; PmAP; ReTh; WaAnP

Margarita first possest [*or* possessed].   Chronicle, The; a Ballad.   Abraham Cowley.   OxAEP-1

Margarita the sea is gleaming.   Story for Margarita.   Rubén Darío.   PtR, *tr. by* Maggie Dietz

Margaritae Sororis.   W. E. Henley.   MoBrPo; OBEV *Fr.* Echoes.

Marged.   Gillian Clarke.   MoWP

Margery kempe twisted olfactory phoneme.   Solstice / Surgery.   A. Di Michele.   AnSo

Margin Prayer from an Ancient Psalter.   Ian Duhig.   EmeKit; NeBl

Marginal Field, The.   Stephen Spender.   PoA 2002

Marginal Way.   Renée Gregorio.   ICANM

Marginalia.   Stephanie Brown.   AmPoNex

Marginalia.   Billy Collins.   PoA 2002

Marginalia.   Richard Wilbur.   PoA 2002

Marginalization of Poetry, The.   Mitch Highfill.   HeMarv

Marginalization of Poetry, The.   Bob Perelman.   FTOS

Margins of season.   Hunger.   Jeffrey Renard Allen.   RD

Marguerite.   Rubén Darío.   SpanPo, *tr. by* Anita Volland

Maria 1.   Asaf Halet Çelebi.   NaPG, *tr. by* Talat Sait Halman

Maria 2.   Asaf Halet Çelebi.   NaPG, *tr. by* Talat Sait Halman

Maria, she said. No city river.   Scuba Diver Recovers the Body of a Drowned Child, The.   Gerald William Barrax.   GT; OxAAAP

Maria to Henric.   *Unknown.*   EMWP

Maria Wentworth.   Thomas Carew.   NPeEn
(Inscription on the Tomb of the Lady Mary Wentworth, The.)   CavPo

Mariachi beckon, their guitars, The.   On Plaza Garibaldi.   Nellie Wong.   OpBo

Marian Hymn.   Christiania Whitehead.   NeBl

Marian Sector.   David Craig.
"In the morning, when the sun."   UpMys

Mariana.   R. F. Langley.   HarvBoo

Mariana.   Alfred Tennyson.   NAEL-6v2; NAEL-7v2; NOBRP; OBEV; OxAEP-2; TFi

Mariana II.   Maria Arrillaga.   TANSG

Mariana Trench.   Joanna Klink.   LegDan

Marianne Faithfull's Cigarette.   Gerry Gomez Pearlberg.   WiU

Marías, Old Indian Mothers.   Rigoberto González.   GeoHom

Maridunum.   Douglas Phillips.   AngWePo

Marie antoinette / slice, The.   After / the Moratorium Reading.   Nigel Roberts.   NOBAu

Marie Farrar, born in April.   Concerning the Infanticide, Marie Farrar.   Bertolt Brecht.   WoPoe, *tr. by* Hoffman Reynolds Hays

Marie Hamilton's to the kirk gane.   Queen's Marie, The [Version from Scott's Minstresy].   *Unknown.*   OBEV

Marie Lucille.   Gwendolyn Brooks.   TLR

Marie moder, wel thee be!   *Unknown.*   OHMEL

Marie [*or* Mary] Magdalens Complaint at Christs Death.   Robert Southwell.   ChIV-2

Marigold nowhere turns from the sun, The.   To Henry Darnley, King of Scots.   George Buchanan.   NePenScot, *tr. by* Robert Crawford

Marigold, The.   George Wither.   NOSC; SacPr *Fr.* Collection of Emblemes, Ancient and Moderne, A.

Marijuana.   Chase Twichell.   WANABP

Marijuana joints make circles.   Round Irving High School.   Cheryl Boyce Taylor.   WiU

Marikudo in Kalibo, 1979.   Dominador I. Ilio.   ReBoTo

Marilyn.   Ōoka Mokoto.   PFTM-2, *tr. by* Thomas Fitzimmons

Marilyn Climbs Out of the Pool.   Tracey Herd.   NeBl

Marilyn Monroe Indian.   Leo Romero.   ReTh

Marina.   T. S. Eliot.   APT-1; CABP; HeIP-4; NAEL-6v2; NAEL-7v2; NPeEn; OxBEV

Marina.   Eugenio Montejo.   BLPSL, *tr. by* Rene de Costa, Rigas Kappatos and Eleni Paidoussi

Marin-An.   Gary Snyder.   CalPo

Marina's Daughters, 1964.   Rebecca Spears.   TiP2

Marine Snow at Mid-Depths and Down.   Thomas Lux.   AmAlph

Marine Surface, Low Overcast.   Amy Clampitt.   GPTC; OxBoAm

Marine Vignette.   Robert Montgomery.   STuOW *Fr.* Omnipresence of the Deity, The.

Mariners call them devil fish.   Octopus.   Caitríona O'Reilly.   NIrP; StAl

Mariner's Hymn.   Caroline Anne Bowles Southey.   TreFP

Mariner's Ideal Epitaph.   Juan Ramón Jiménez.   SpanPo, *tr. by* Kate Flores

Marines look vernal, The.   Sound Bite.   Frederick D'Aguiar.   NeBrPo; Oth

Marionetas son metáforas perfectas, Las.   Eduardo Milán.   RMCMP

Marionette.   Maher Sabry.   AnVo, *tr. by* Mohamed Enani

Mariposa.   Rigoberto González.   BeDoSh

Mariposa Lily, The.   Ina Coolbrith.   NAAPv.1

Marisel.   Juan Gonzalo Rose.   BLPSL, *tr. by* Rene de Costa, Rigas Kappatos and Eleni Paidoussi

Maritae Suae.   William Philpot.   OBEV

Marital quarrels are not poetic.   Temptation.   Salwa Al-Neimi.   PoArWo, *tr. by* Subhi Hadidi and Nathalie Handal

Maritime.   Reginald Shepherd.   AmPoNex

Maritime Ode.   Fernando Pessoa. *tr. by* Susan M. Brown and Edwin Honig
"Ah, pirates, pirates, pirates!"   PFTM-1

Maritime Pastoral.   Ted Benttinen.   PoCoUp

Mark [*with music*].   John Tranter.   NoAM

Mark 14:26–42; And when they had sung.   Boris Leonidovich Pasternak.   GI *Fr.* St. Mark.

Mark 16:19–20; So then the Lord Jesus, after.   A. E. Housman.   GI

Mark 5:21–43; And when Jesus had crossed.   Czeslaw Milosz.   GI *Fr.* St. Mark.

Mark a circle and start digging here.   Zero.   Susan Stewart.   AmAlph

Mark Antony's Valentine.   Steven Marx.   IaFF

Mark but this flea, and mark in this.   Flea, The.   John Donne.   AmFaPo; BASC; BrAP; FSCP; NAEL-6v1; NAEL-7v1; NBLV; NIL-7; NIP-4; NoP-4; NoP-5; NoSic; OxAEP-1; TFi; WaAnP

Mark finished it himself, choosing midnight.   Mark.   John Tranter.   NoAM

Mark how this polished [*or* polish'd] Eastern sheet.   Fancy, A.   Thomas Carew.   NOSC
(Marke how this polisht Easterne sheet.)   PBRV

Mark is a fag scratched in blue ink. Geometry Class. Mark Bibbins. AmPoNex; WiU

Mark mar ha forest 1 a boundary manic a land a. Secret History of the Dividing Line. Susan Howe.

Mark of Resistance, A. Adrienne Rich. PoA 2002

Mark Stern. Frederick Feirstein. RA

Mark Stern Wakes Up. Frederick Feirstein. RA

Mark, The. Robert Patrick Dana. OPRER

Mark Twain said he wouldn't want to be a boy again. Origins, Divergences. Cynthia Ozick. TaR

Mark where the pressing wind shoots javelin-like. George Meredith. NAEL-6v2; OBEV *Fr.* Modern Love.

Mark yon round parson, fat and sleek. Robert Lloyd. OBSV *Fr.* Familiar Epistle to J. B. Esq, A.

Mark you how the peacock's eye. Peacock's Eye, The. Gerard Manley Hopkins. OWoS

Mark you the floor[e]? that square and speckled stone. Church-Floor[e], The. George Herbert. NOSC

Marked by no fence. Jackson Mac Low. APSN *Fr.* Presidents of the United States of America, The.

Marked Ones, The. Gyula Illyés. IQMS, *tr.* by John Brander and John Wilkinson

Marked with D. Tony Harrison. InoFa; NAEL-6v2; NAEL-7v2; NAMCP V.2 *Fr.* School of Eloquence, The.

Marked you, by yon thatched farm that skirts the down—. Village Maid, The. Mary F. Johnson. CenSon

Marker at Auschwitz, The. Rational Man. Muriel Rukeyser. AF

Marker reads: "Western Cattle Trail", The. Thinking About Cows at Ten O'Clock in the Morning, Abilene. Naomi Shihab Nye. TiP2

Marker slants, flowerless, day's almost done, The. John Berryman. BrAP; CAP-8; InoFa; NAMCP V.2; PoPoPo; VCAP *Fr.* Dream Songs.

Market day. Mwatabu Okantah. BtF

Marketplace. Günter Eich. MotU, *tr.* by David Walker

Market's Closing. Shin Kyŏngnim. CAMKP, *tr.* by David R. McCann

Marketwoman of Luanda. Maria Eugénia Lima. HAWP, *tr.* by Julia Kirst

Marking of Folders. Anne Anderton. UV

Marking Time. Peter Steele. NOBAu

Marks [*with music*]. Linda Pastan. NIL-7; NIP-4

Marks the English Left on the Map. Peter Finch. Oth

Marksman's Work, The. Nathaniel Southgate Shaler. PCW

Marlene Dietrich is singing a lament. Blue Angel, The. Allen Ginsberg. BB

Marlo Thomas in Seven Parts and Epilogue. Jeffery Conway. WiU

Marmalade. Elizabeth Delmore. NLP

Marmion. Sir Walter Scott. TreFP

Marmion. Sir Walter Scott.
    "Along the bridge Lord Marmion rode." FaBoWar
    "Heap on more wood!—the wind is chill." ChrPo; OBCP
    Jealous Twain, The. DiBP
    Lochinvar. ChAP; NAEL-6v2; NAEL-7v2; NePenScot; NPBRoP; OxAEP-2; TFi
    (Marmion.) TreFP
    Nelson, Pitt, Fox. OBEV
    Poor Yarrow. DiBP
    (Song.) NOBRP
    (Young Lochinvar.) OBNV

Maroon Woman, feisty and sensual with Oshun beauty. Palenque Queen by Habana's Shores. Askia Muhammad Touré. BRtP

Marooned in it, stealthy as fishes, we may even be dead. (LL) Mess Deck. Alan Ross. FaBoWar; PoWW

Marpessa's Choice [*with music*]. Yannis Ritsos. VCWP, *tr.* by Edmund Keeley

Marquis de Sade has gone back inside the erupting volcano, The. Marquis de Sade, The. André Breton. WoPoe, *tr.* by Jack Rogow and Bill Zavatsky

Marquis de Sade, The. André Breton. WoPoe, *tr.* by Jack Rogow and Bill Zavatsky

Marquisite, false diamond. Salamander. Ingrid de Kok. TSAP

Marriage. Wendell Berry. WaAnP

Marriage. Stephanie Brown. BodElec

Marriage. Mary Elizabeth Coleridge. LW; NALW; PEW; PoBW; ViWPN; VWP

Marriage. Gregory Corso. NoP-4; NoP-5; PmAP; TRP

Marriage. Mary Weston Fordham. CBWP-2

Marriage. Amy Gerstler. PmAP

Marriage. Marianne Moore. APT-1; ColAP; MoWP; NAAPv.2; NALW; OxBoAm

Marriage. Friederike Roth. GTCP, *tr.* by Irmgard Hunt

Marriage. Carol Rumens. MoWP

Marriage. Walter James Turner. NOBAu

Marriage. William Carlos Williams. PoA 2002

Marriage: "First, it was the common magic." Richard Frost. PoDa

Marriage: "Marriage marriage is like you say everything everything in stereo stereo fall fall on the bed bed at dawn dawn because you work work all night." Anne Waldman. PoDa

Marriage, A. Michael C. Blumenthal. PoPoPo

Marriage, A. Robert Creeley. RaBo

Marriage, A. Anne Stevenson. MoWP

Marriage, A. Ronald Stuart Thomas. BeAl; TCAWP

Marriage, The. Mary Dalton. Coast

Marriage, The. Anne Stevenson. NALW

Marriage, The [*with music*]. Mark Strand. NoAM

Marriage, The [*with music*]. Anna Wickham. ItWoWo

Marriage, The. Yvor Winters. NAAPv.2

Marriage à la Mode. John Dryden.
    "Whil'st Alexis lay prest [*or* press'd]." NPeEn
    "Why should a foolish marriage vow." NAEL-6v1; NAEL-7v1; NIL-7; NIP-4

Marriage and Love. Caroline Elizabeth Norton.
    "Laura was lightsome, gay, and free from guile." VWP

Marriage and Midsummer's Night [*with music*]. Linda Gregg. OxBoAm

Marriage and Money. Sir Charles Sedley. OBSV *Fr.* Happy Pair, The.

Marriage has gone the way of God! (LL) Ballad of Religion and Marriage, A. Amy Levy. NPeEn; ViWPN; VWP

Marriage in Eden, The. William Williams. OBWVE *Fr.* View of Christ's Kingdom, A.

Marriage in the Nineties, A. Alfred Corn. WiU

Marriage in the Sixties, A. Adrienne Rich. OxBoAm

Marriage is a going forth. Marriage Song for Many Voices. Jennifer Weinblatt. MPUn

Marriage is not / a house or even a tent. Habitation. Margaret Atwood. WeW-3

Marriage Market, The. Martin Farquhar Tupper. STuOW

Marriage marriage is like you say everything everything in stereo stereo fall fall on the bed bed at dawn dawn because you work work all night. Marriage. Anne Waldman. PoDa

Marriage of a Virgin, The. Dylan Thomas. ChIV-2

Marriage of Death, The. László Szabédi. IQMS, *tr.* by J. G. Nichols

Marriage of Heaven and Hell by William Blake, The. Alex Rawls. AnSo

Marriage of Heaven and Hell in Española. Joan Logghe. ICANM

Marriage of Heaven and Hell, The. William Blake. WaAnP

Marriage of Heaven and Hell, The. William Blake. NAEL-6v2; NAEL-7v2; NOBRP
    "Once I saw a Devil in a flame of fire." NAEL-6v2
    Proverbs of Hell.
    Pride of the Peacock, The. RaBo
    Song of Liberty, A. NAEL-6v2; NAEL-7v2

Marriage of Hector and Andromache, The. Sappho. OBVE, *tr.* by Guy Davenport

Marriage of St Katharine, by the same, A; in the Hospital of St John at Bruges. Dante Gabriel Rossetti. CenSon

Marriage of Sorts, A. Pamela Alexander. YaYoPo

Marriage Patois. Megan Sexton. PoDa

Marriage Proposal. Sarah Messer. LegDan

Marriage Ring, The. George Crabbe. OBEV; OxBEV

Marriage Song for Many Voices. Jennifer Weinblatt. MPUn

Marriage Vow [*with music*]. Mrs. Henry Linden. CBWP-4

Marriage Vow, The. Letitia Elizabeth Landon. VWP

Married Love. Kuan Tao Shēng. PasH; WoPoe, *tr.* by Chung Ling and Kenneth Rexroth

Married Love [*with music*]. Liz Rosenberg. NIL-7

Married Lover, The. Coventry Patmore. OBEV; OxAEP-2; SacPr *Fr.* Angel in the House, The.

Married State, A. Katherine Philips. BASC; NAEL-7v1
    (Marryd state affords but little Ease, A.) BrAP

Married state affords but little ease, A. Married State, A. Katherine Philips. BASC; NAEL-7v1

Marrow of time; eternity in brief. Church Festivals. Christopher Harvey. NOSC

Marry. Linda Smukler. WiU

Marrying. Charles Harper Webb. SUP

Marrying Again [*with music*]. Mei Yao Ch'en. ColAnChi, *tr.* by Burton Watson

Marrying maiden, The / Undertakings bring misfortune. *Unknown.* PFTM-1 *Fr.* I Ching [*or* The Book of Changes *or* The Classic of Changes].

Mars and Venus. Rachel Hadas. GS

Mars, brilliant lord of the sky's fifth sphere. To Mars, a Prayer for Peace. Janus Pannonius. IQMS, *tr.* by Anthony Barrett

Mars is braw in crammasy. Bonnie Broukit Bairn, The. Hugh MacDiarmid. EdScPo; FaBoVe; HarvBoo; NePenScot

Mars Needs Terrorists. K. Silem Mohammad. BAP-04

Marsh Song—At Sunset. Sidney Lanier. TCAPo *Fr.* Hymns of the Marshes.

Marshes of Glynn, The. Sidney Lanier. NAAPv.1; NoP-5 *Fr.* Hymns of the Marshes.

Marshland merges with a tarry sea. Candle at Canterbury, A. Tessa Rose Chester. MFPA

Marshlands. Emily Pauline Johnson. SWaP

Marshmallow Man, The. Jean Follain. MotU, *tr. by* Louise Imogen Guiney

Marsh's Plants Bewilder, The. *Unknown.* WoPoe, *tr. by* Barbara Hughes Fowler

Marsh's plants bewilder, The. Marsh's Plants Bewilder, The. *Unknown.* WoPoe, *tr. by* Barbara Hughes Fowler

Marshy retainer, A. (LL) He lived—childhood summers. Lorine Niedecker. APT-2; ItP; NAAPv.2

Marsilion sees his people's martyrdom. *Unknown.* NAWM-5v1; NAWM-7v1 *Fr.* Song of Roland, The.

Marsyas. Sir Charles G. D. Roberts. NoP-4

Marta we found the little box. Protect Me, My Talisman. Milo De Angelis. NeIt, *tr. by* Lawrence Venuti

Martha. Walter De la Mare. MoBrPo

Martha and Mary. Gabriela Mistral. GI, *tr. by* Doris Dana

Martha Blake. Austin Clarke. ModIr; OxBEV

Martha Blake at Fifty-one. Austin Clarke. ModIr; NPeEn

Martha, like most eagle mothers. Endangered Species. William Cook. FTtHH

Martha's Wall. Paul Durcan. IrLP

Martial. Thom Gunn. OBGa, *tr. by* Peter Porter

Martial. Epigram XLVII, Book X [*see also* "Things that make a life to please, The" *by* Sir Richard Fanshawe]. Ben Jonson. OBVE

Martial [*or* Marshall *or* My Friend], the thing[e]s that do [*or* for to] attain [*or* attayne]. Happy Life, The. Martial. NoSic; OBVE, *tr. by* Henry Howard, Earl of Surrey

Martial, the things that do attain. Martial. See Happy Life, The.

Martial Variations. Amelia Rosselli. *tr. by* Lawrence R. Smith
"In the lethargy which follows the machinations of the." PFTM-2, *tr. by* Lawrence R. Smith

Martian Landscape. Abbie Huston Evans. APT-1

Martian Sends a Postcard Home, A. Craig Raine. NAEL-6v2; NAEL-7v2; NAMCP V.2; NoAM; NoP-4; NoP-5; NPeEn; WaAnP

Martin. Pamela Stewart. ExTi

Martin and My Father. David Hernandez. UnSA

Martin Buber in the Pub. Max Harris. NOBAu

Martin Luther King. Aileen Fisher. HHAm

Martin was too peaceful for me. Martin and My Father. David Hernandez. UnSA

Martinet aux ailes trop larges. Martinet, Le. René Char. YaTCFP

Martins. Mike Jenkins. AngWePo

Martin's Blues. Michael S. Harper. NAAL-5

Marty was the first holy man I knew. Tishah B'Ov / 1952. David Meltzer. TaR

Martyr, The. Scott Cairns. UpMys

Martyr, The. Herman Melville. CBCWP; ColAP; NCAP; TCAPo

Martyr is like lightning that glitters and is then snuffed out, A. *Unknown.* SLW, *tr. by* Marjolijn De Jager, Sayd Bahodin Majrouh and André Velter

Martyr of Antioch, The. Henry Hart Milman.
"For thou didst die for me, O Son of God!" SacPr

Martyr Poets—did not tell, The. Emily Dickinson. APN-2

Martyr wears a crown, The. Be He Ezra Pound, Kennedy, or King. Belle Randall. GifTon

Martyrdom. Yolanda Bedregal. TANSG, *tr. by* Carolyne Wright

Martyrdom and Triumph of Sergei Korolev. Andrew Duncan. VaPo

Martyrdom like radiance of a clear night sky. Artist and Medium. Sarah Klassen. ACAMVP

Martyrdom of Saint Sebastian, The. Eugenio Florit. TCLAP, *tr. by* Peter Fortunato

Martyred Tamarind, The. Alberto Ferreira Gomes. NAfrP, *tr. by* Gerald M. Moser

Martyrology 7, The. B. P. Nichol.
Hill Songs of Saint Orm, The. PFTM-2
Monotones. PFTM-2
Scraptures: 17th Sequence. PFTM-2

Marty's Mother. Stephen Kessler. GeoHom

Maru Mori brought me. Ode to My Socks. Pablo Neruda. AmFaPo, *tr. by* Stephen Mitchell

Maru Mori brought me. Ode to My Socks. Pablo Neruda. RaBo; TCLAP; TRP; WED, *tr. by* Robert Bly

Marvel Mystery Oil. Elliot Fried. SUP

Marvellous Grass. Nuala Ni Dhomhnaill. PBCIP, *tr. by* Michael Hartnett

Marvellous how the house builds itself. Rise. Pat Winslow. PoCu

Marvell's garden, that place of solitude. Marvell's Garden. Phyllis Webb. BrAP

Marvelous and escape, The. (LL) Roses. Barbara Guest. NoP-4; NoP-5

Marvelous Beast. Patti Tana. PasH

Marvelous Father. Dana Levin. PoChi

Marvelous four-cylindered beast. Mechanical Cow, The. Robley, Jr. Wilson. PBCAP

Marvelous is this wall-stone—but the fates broke. Ruin, The. *Unknown.* NAWM-7v1, *tr. by* Lee Patterson

Marvelous Land of Indefinitions, The. Lorenzo Thomas. PmAP

Marvelous thing I have mused in my mind, A. Mirabile Misterium. *Unknown.* SacPr

Marx the Sign Painter. Edgar Lee Masters. NoAM *Fr.* New Spoon River, The.

Marxist to Liberals, A. David Lindley. NLP

Mary. Philip Appleman. GI

Mary. Bertolt Brecht. GI

Mary. Lucille Clifton. BBASP

Mary. Sterling Plumpp.
"Daybreak wakes." FuFl
"I wonder." FuFl

Mary and Gabriel. Rupert Brooke. ChIV-2

Mary and *mare*, anagrammatized. Epigram, A Supposed Construction. John Taylor. NOSC

Mary and the Bramble. Lascelles Abercrombie. OBMV

Mary at Peace with the Risen Lord. Rainer Maria Rilke. GI

Mary at the Feet of Christ. Felicia Dorothea Hemans. CenSon

Mary Celeste. Judith Nicholls. OBSP

Mary Desti's Ass. Frank O'Hara. FTOS

Mary, don't You Weep. Honorée Fanonne Jeffers. BtF

Mary, fate lent me a moment of pleasure. Ballad. John Clare. NPBRoP

Mary, full of the mercy only. Sister Mary Appassionata Lectures the Folklore Class: Doctrines of the Strawberry. David Citino. UpMys

Mary had a little lamb. Mary's Lamb [*or* Mary and Her Lamb]. Sarah Josepha Buell Hale. BRP; SWaP

Mary had a little lamb. Little Lamb, A. *Unknown.* OBCoV

Mary Hamilton. *Unknown.* NePenScot; NoP-4; NoP-5

Mary has a thingamajig clamped on her ears. Manual System. Carl Sandburg. APT-1

Mary hath born allone. James Ryman. OHMEL

Mary Hogan's Quatrains. James Gleashure.
"I care little for people's suspicions." IrLP

Mary Hogan's Quatrains. Máire Mhac an tSaoi. ModIr, *tr. by* Patrick Crotty

Mary Hynes. Anthony Raftery. IrLP

Mary! I want a lyre with other strings. To Mary Unwin. William Cowper. CenSon; OBEV

Mary Kröger. Louise Erdrich. UpMys

Mary laid her Child among. Carol. Norman Nicholson. OBCP

Mary leave thy lowly cot. Song. John Clare. NPBRoP

Mary Magdalene. Saunders Lewis. BBMWP, *tr. by* Joseph P. Clancy

Mary Magdalene. Louise Erdrich. CAP-8

Mary Magdalene. Saunders Lewis. OBWVE, *tr. by* Gwyn Morgan

Mary Magdalene (I). Boris Leonidovich Pasternak. AF, *tr. by* Lydia Pasternak Slater

Mary Magdalene, that easy woman. Lent. William Robert Rodgers. ModIr; PNI

Mary Magdalene's Left Foot. Andrew Hudgins. UpMys

Mary Martin, leader of the Lost Boys. Peter Pan in North America. Robin Becker. ReTh

Mary Mihalik. Ed Ochester. LiTh

Mary, more than quite contrary, bars the door. Visit, The. Lesley Duncan. EdScPo

Mary Morelle Show, The. Denise Nico Leto. UnSA

Mary Morison. Robert Burns. NePenScot; OBEV

"Mary mother, dost thou sleep?" Mary's Dream. *Unknown.* OBWVE, *tr. by* C. C. Bell

Mary [*or* Marie] Hamilton [Version from Motherwell's Manuscript]. *Unknown.* NoP-4

Mary [*or* Marie] Magdalene. George Herbert. SacPr

Mary Pickford, doll divine. To Mary Pickford—Moving Picture Actress. Vachel Lindsay. IllVoic

2. Mary Presented at the Temple. Rainer Maria Rilke. WED *Fr.* Life of the Virgin Mary, The.

Mary prevents the day; she rose to weep. Gardener, The. Rowland Watkyns. NOSC

Mary Rockwell, 1950. Juliana Baggott. RWB

Mary rose up, as one in sleep might rise. Jesus Wept. William Michael Rossetti. CenSon

Mary sat musing on the lamp-flame at the table. Death of the Hired Man, The. Robert Frost. APT-1; HeIP-4; MoAmPo; NAAL-5; NAAPv.2; NoP-4; OxBoAm; SAmP; TCAPo

Mary Smith had a college education. Personality. Johnny Burke. ReLy

Mary Stuart. Edwin Muir. EdScPo

Mary the Cook-Maid's Letter to Dr. Sheridan. Jonathan Swift. NPeEn

Mary, the Scots are sots in any case. Joseph Brodsky. TCRusP *Fr.* Sonnets on the Statue of Mary, Queen of Scots, in the Luxembourg Gardens, Paris.

Mary Trevellyn to Miss Roper. Arthur Hugh Clough. FaBoVe *Fr.* Amours de Voyage.

Mary Warren's Sampler. Nicole Cooley. NeAmPo

Mary, your great. Jesus Suckles. Anne Sexton. PFTM-2

Maryette Myers. Julia A. Moore.
    Hic Finis Rapto 5. STuOW

Maryland. James Ryder Randall. *See* My Maryland.

Maryland, my Maryland! (LL) My Maryland. James Ryder Randall. CBCWP; PCW

Mary's a Grand Old Name. George M. Cohan. NAAPv.2; ReLy

Mary's Dream. Van K. Brock. AllShUp; SwNoth

Mary's Dream. Lucille Clifton. NALW

Mary's Dream [*with music*]. *Unknown.* OBWVE, *tr. by* C. C. Bell

Mary's Ghost. Thomas Hood. NPBRoP

Mary's Lamb [*or* Mary and Her Lamb]. Sarah Josepha Buell Hale. BRP; SWaP

Mary's poem vision. Gold on Oak Leaves Said Young. George Oppen. BodElec

Mary's Song. Marion Angus. EdScPo; LW

Mary's Song. Charles Causley. OBCP

Mary's Song. Sylvia Plath. AFaM; ChIV-2

4. Mary's Visit with Elizabeth. Rainer Maria Rilke. WED *Fr.* Life of the Virgin Mary, The.

Mary's Visitation. Rainer Maria Rilke. GI

Mas-Soñer / Restaurat—Any. House, The. Robert Creeley. FTOS

Masaccio's *Expulsion from Paradise.* Julia Copus. MFPA

Masculinity. Robert Crawford. PML

Mashed potatoes cannot hurt you, darling. Giving Potatoes. Adrian Mitchell. NBLV

Mask. Sapardi Djoko Damono. WoPoe, *tr. by* John H. McGlynn

Mask. Stephen Spender. MoBrPo

Mask, A. John Milton. OxAEP-1 *Fr.* Comus; a Masque Presented at Ludlow Castle.

Mask, The. Elizabeth Barrett Browning. VWP

Mask, The. Laura Riding Jackson. HarvBoo

Mask [*or* Masque] of Anarchy, The. Percy Bysshe Shelley. NPBRoP; OBSV; OxAEP-2
    "As I lay asleep in Italy." NPeEn; WoPoe

Mask of Anger, A. Lyn Hejinian. FTOS

Mask of Evil, The [*with music*]. Bertolt Brecht. PoSu; WoPoe, *tr. by* Hoffman Reynolds Hays

Mask of Gaiety, The. Letitia Elizabeth Landon. VWP

Masks. Kim Ch'unsu [*or* Chun-soo]. CAMKP, *tr. by* Anthony, Brother of Taizé

Masks! O Masks. Prayer to the Masks. Léopold Sédar Senghor. YaTCFP, *tr. by* Hoyt Rogers

Mason, The. Aloysius Bertrand. BLT, *tr. by* E. D. Hartley

Mason, The. Aloysius Bertrand. MotU, *tr. by* Michael Benedikt

Mason Abraham Knupfer is singing, trowel in hand, scaffolded, The. Mason, The. Aloysius Bertrand. BLT, *tr. by* E. D. Hartley

Mason Abraham Knupfer is singing, trowel in hand, The. Mason, The. Aloysius Bertrand. MotU, *tr. by* Michael Benedikt

Masons, cart drivers and occasional fishermen. Havana Harbor. Nancy Morejón. TANSG, *tr. by* Joy Renjilian-Burgy

Mason's finger, The. Buson. EH, *tr. by* Robert Hass

Masons, when they start upon a building. Scaffolding. Seamus Heaney. ChAP

Masque of Blackness, The. Geoffrey Hill. NoAM *Fr.* Lachrimae; or Seven Tears Figured in Seven Passionate Pavans.

Masque of Christmas, The. Ben Jonson. ChrPo

Masque of May, The. John Millington Synge. IrLP

Masque of Queens, The. Ben Jonson.
    "Help, help all tongues to celebrate this wonder." NOSC

Masque of the Inner Temple and Gray's Inne, The. Francis Beaumont.
    Fourth Song, The. NOSC

Masquerading. May Probyn. NPeEn; VWP

Masques! O Masques! Prière aux Masques. Léopold Sédar Senghor. YaTCFP

Mass. Mairi MacInnes. MoWP

Mass. César Vallejo. TCLAP *Fr.* Spain, Take [Away] This Cup from Me [España, Aparta de Mí Este Cáliz].

Mass. César Vallejo. StAl *Fr.* Spain, Take Away This Cup from Me [España, Aparta de Mí Este Cáliz].

Mass at Dawn. Roy Campbell. OxAEP-2

Mass Graves. Charles Reznikoff.

Mass hysteria, wave after breaking wave. Willowware Cup. James Merrill. VCAP

Mass is Over, The. Sara Berkeley. PBCIP

Mass is over, they have gone in peace, The. Mass is Over, The. Sara Berkeley. PBCIP

Mass of ledged rock, A. Winter Nocturne: The Hospital. Alter Brody. APT-2

Massachusetts to Virginia. John Greenleaf Whittier. NAAPv.1

Massacre, October '66. Wole Soyinka. AF; NAMCP V.2

Massacre of the Boys. Tadeusz Rózewicz. AF; GI; HP

Massacre of the Innocents. Alec Derwent Hope. GI

Massacre of the Innocents, The. Giovanni Giambattista.
    "Yet on the other side, faine would he start." OBVE

Massacre of the Innocents, The (after Brueghel). Holger Teschke. GTCP, *tr. by* Reinhold Grimm

Massacres. Charles Reznikoff. APSN

Massed peaks pierce. Overnight at a Buddhist Mountain Temple. Mike O'Connor. CSKM

Massenet. Antony Butts. OBCoV

Masses. César Vallejo. PoCho; WED *Fr.* España, Aparta de me Este Caliz.

Masses of mountain peaks. T'ung Pass. Chang Yang-hao. WoPoe, *tr. by* Sam Hamill

Masses, The. Cornelius Mathews. APN-1 *Fr.* Poems on Man in His Various Aspects under the American Republic.

Masseuse, The. Olga Broumas. WiU

Massimo del Panino, Il. Del Ray Cross. FreRad

Massive rock head but the guy's eyes dart. O Pioneers! Jane Miller. GifTon

Massive Stoner. Michael Savitz. FreRad

Mast / Inaudibly soars; bole-like, tapering, The. George Oppen. APT-2; PFTM-1

Mastectomy Poems, The. Alicia Ostriker.
    Bridge, The. ExTi
    Healing. ExTi
    Wintering. ExTi

Master—. Her Habit. Lucie Brock-Broido. ExTi

Master, The. Bryn Griffiths. TCAWP

Master, The. Edwin Arlington Robinson. CBCWP; MoAmPo

Master and Guest. Mary Elizabeth Coleridge. ViWPN; VWP

Master and Man. Sterling Allen Brown. OxBoAm

Master and the Dog, The. Ignacy Krasicki. WoPoe, *tr. by* Jerzy Peterkiewicz and Burns Singer

Master and the slave go hand in hand, The. Sonnet. Edwin Arlington Robinson. APN-2

Master Chia. Li Shang-yin. ColAnChi, *tr. by* James J. Y. Liu

Master craftsman sits like Rodin's, The. Devil's Workshop, The. Yusef Komunyakaa. PoA 2002

Master Hunt, anon, foot-hot, The. Geoffrey Chaucer. DiBP *Fr.* Book of the Duchesse, The.

Master Jen has long been famous. Thanking Doctor Jen. Li K'ai-hsien. ColAnChi, *tr. by* Jonathan Chaves

Master Joshu and the dog. Soen. ZenPo, *tr. by* Takashi Ikemoto and Lucien Stryk

Master Mind, The. Carla Harryman. MotU

Master of an Expanse. Fabio Morabito. PML, *tr. by* E. Bell

Master of Auschwitz, angel of death. For the Bones of Josef Mengele, Disinterred June 1985. Robert Bringhurst. NIP-4

Master of beauty, craftsman of the snowflake. John Berryman. InvLi; PLBUT *Fr.* Eleven Addresses to the Lord.

Master of the Golden Glow, The. James Schuyler. FTOS

Master only left old Mistus. Frances Ellen Watkins Harper. SWaP *Fr.* Aunt Chloe.

Master send me. Gone. Calvin Forbes. BtF

Master Shih's medical fame, because of Master Ch'en. Sent to the Master Physician, "Almond Orchard" Shih. Li K'ai-hsien. ColAnChi, *tr. by* Jonathan Chaves

Master Speed, The. Robert Frost. GoPo

Master stood upon the mount, and taught, The. Progress. Matthew Arnold. ChIV-2

Master, they say that when I seem. Prayer. Clive Staples Lewis. SacPr

Master Tung's Western Chamber Romance. Tung Chieh-yüan. Chapter 2. ColAnChi, *tr. by* Li-li Ch'en

Master Weldon, will you answer. (LL) Leaving San Francisco. Marilyn Chin. CalPo; GeoHom

Master Zhang has an inborn craving for wine. To Zhang Xu. Li Qi. CCL1, *tr. by* Stephen Owen

Masters. Selima Hill. MoWP *Fr.* Accumulation of Small Acts of Kindness, The.

Masters, The. Gillian Conoley. BodElec

Masters, The. Francis Saltus Saltus. "Come! show your jolly tricks, and be possessed." VerBaPo

Master's cabin's overrun by mice, The. For Christine at the Frost Farm. Daniel Tobin. VisFro

Masters go abrod to vew the towne, The. Ludovico Ariosto. OxBEV *Fr.* Orlando Furioso.

Masters, in this Hall. French Noel. William Morris. ChrPo

Master's Sermon, The. Han Yong'un [*or* Yongwun]. CAMKP, *tr. by* Sammy Solberg

Masters, the mock orange is blooming in Syracuse without scent, having been bred. Of Distress Being Humiliated by the Classical Chinese Poets. Hayden Carruth. WoPoe

Master-songs are ended, and the man, The. Walt Whitman. Edwin Arlington Robinson. APN-2; NCAP; TCAPo; ViWalt

Masterworks of Ming. Kay Ryan. GoPo

Master—you were having your veins cleaned out of Me—. Prescient. Lucie Brock-Broido. ExTi

Mastiff, of true English blood, A. John Gay. DiBP *Fr.* Fables: First Series.

Mastiffs, as austere. Homer. DiBP *Fr.* Odyssey.

Mastiff-Worrying Fly, The. Ludovico Ariosto. DiBP *Fr.* Orlando Furioso.

Mastodon Teeth. Sybil Pittman Estess. TiP2

Masts at Dawn. Robert Penn Warren. NoP-4; NoP-5; VCAP *Fr.* Island of Summer.

Masts—loose paddles—hulls. Sea. *Unknown.* SonAtl, *tr. by* Lester Browne, P. Ensor and Edward Kandy

Mata Hari Blues or Why I Will Never Be a Spy. Jewell M. Handy. BRtP

Matachines, The. Charles Tomlinson. ICANM

Match beaten by frail wind lights the cave, A. Radical Neck. Bob Hicok. AmAlph

Match Me Such Marvel. William Basil Tickell Jones. UV

Match me such marvel save in college port. Match Me Such Marvel. William Basil Tickell Jones. UV

Match me such marvel save in Eastern clime. John William Burgon. UV *Fr.* Petra.

Match that Darkened the Sun, The. *Unknown.* SonAtl, *tr. by* Richard Blecker and Etienne Karekezi

Match with the Moon, A. Dante Gabriel Rossetti. NPeEn; OxBEV

Match-bark of the younger dog sets fire to, The. Table-Birds. Kenneth Mackenzie. BMAP; NOBAu

Matches. Im Yŏngjo. CAMKP, *tr. by* Edward W. Poitras

Matches among other things that were not allowed. Burnt Child, The. W. S. Merwin. NoAM

Matching Flowers. Kate Foley. Prnts

Matchmaker. Sheldon Harnick. ReLy

Matchmaker, matchmaker, make me a match. Matchmaker. Sheldon Harnick. ReLy

Mater Dolorosa. William Barnes. OBEV

Mater Dolorosa. Eugene Jolas. APT-2

Materialism. Lőrinc Szabó. IQMS, *tr. by* Laurence James

Material's Daughter. Aaron Shurin. FTOS

Matériel. Don McKay. NLPA

    3. The Base. NLPA

    2. Fates Worse Than Death. NLPA

    1. The Man from Nod. NLPA

    4. Stretto. NLPA

Maternal Earth stirs redly from beneath. Roy Campbell. MoBrPo *Fr.* Flaming Terrapin, The.

Maternal Love. *Unknown.* CATKP, *tr. by* Peter H. Lee

Maternity [*with music*]. Alice Thompson Meynell. InoFa; PEW; VWP

Maternity. Anna Swirszczynska [*or* Swir]. PoChi, *tr. by* Czeslaw Milosz and Leonard Nathan

Matey. Patrick MacGill. PoWW

Math is as old as Medusa's left tit, The. Boy. Negro Survival 101 or Poem for Tiger Woods and Other Multiethnic *Other's.* Crystal Williams. RD

Mathemaku for Beethoven. Bob Grumman. AnSo

Mathemaku No. 16. Bob Grumman. AnSo

Mathemaku No. 17. Bob Grumman. AnSo

Mathematician's Dream, The. Reuel Denney. YaYoPo

Mathematicians take a huge area like a whole world. To Myself. Abba Kovner. AF, *tr. by* Shirley Kaufman

Mathenge. Marjorie Oludhe Macgoye. HBAPE

Mathilde in Normandy. Adrienne Rich. YaYoPo

Mathios Paskalis among the Roses. George Seferis. PFTM-1; PoetW, *tr. by* Edmund Keeley and Philip Sherrard

Matière de Bretagne. Paul Celan. WoPoe, *tr. by* Margaret Guillemin and Katherine Washburn

Matière de Bretagne. Paul Celan. VCWP, *tr. by* Michael Hamburger

Matilde, sleeping / that feverish sleep, a day or a year. Final. Pablo Neruda. WoPoe, *tr. by* Ben Belitt

Matin Hymn. Josephine D. Henderson Heard. CBWP-4

Matin Song. Thomas Heywood. OBEV

Matinee. Susan Clements. UnSA

Matinée Idylls. Molly Bendall. AmPoNex

Mating. Yang Wei-chen. ColAnChi, *tr. by* John Timothy Wixted

Matins. Molly Peacock. ExTi

Matins and Lauds. Marie Ponsot. CLPP

Matins. Denise Levertov. BrAP; NoAM

Matins: James Brown and His Famous Flames Tour the South, 1958. David Wojahn. PBCAP *Fr.* Mystery Train: A Sequence.

Matins [*or* Mattens], or Morning Prayer. Robert Herrick. BASC

Matins: "Sun shines; by the mailbox, leaves, The." Louise Glück. MoWP

Matins: "Unreachable father, when we were first." Louise Glück. InvLi; MoWP

Matisse: Blue Nude, 1952. Dionisio D. Martinez. TouFir

Matisse, Cut Outs. Trasi Johnson. BtF

Matisse: "The Red Studio." W. D. Snodgrass. GS

Matisse was no hedonist. He articulated ideas with pleasure. Mao & Matisse. Ed Friedman. PrTe

Matmiya. Mary Tallmountain. HATNAP; IPoFL; LoL

Matriatism. Charlotte Perkins Stetson Gilman. CalPo

Matrix. Dorothy, Duchess of Wellington Wellesley. "Spiritual, the carnal, are one, The." OBMV

Matrix alive in limb, pseudopod, tenthrill, voice. Economics of Metonymy: sic transit. Skip Fox. AnSo

Matsushima. Sora. EMJL, *tr. by* Haruo Shirane

Matt the Gooseherd. Mihály Fazekas. *tr. by* Thomas Kabdebo "'"But good Sir, look here"—said he." IQMS, *tr. by* Thomas Kabdebo

Matter. Nedelcho Ganev. CSCBP, *tr. by* Georgi Belev and Lisa Sapinkopf

Matter. Alexander Gerov. CSCBP, *tr. by* Georgi Belev and Lisa Sapinkopf

Matter. Michele Glazer. IAoNAP

Matter. Carla Harryman. FTOS

Matter. Joan Houlihan. IAoNAP

Matter is palsy: the land heaving, water. From Heraclitus. Alan Dugan. PoA 2002

Matter? More than anything else. For Gil and Other Incurables. Renée Weiss and Theodore Weiss. BodElec

Matter of Control, A. Diana García. TouFir

Matter of Division, A. Frankie Paino. AmPoNex

Matter / of fact. Catherine Walsh. Oth *Fr.* Pitch.

Matters of Policy. Charles Bernstein. FTOS

Matthew 8, 28 ff. Richard Wilbur. UpMys

Matthew 10:1. Philip Larkin. GI *Fr.* St. Matthew.

Matthew 1:18–25: Now the birth of Jesus Christ took place. Philip Appleman. GI *Fr.* St. Matthew.

Matthew 13:1–9; That same day Jesus. Stephen Mitchell. GI *Fr.* St. Matthew.

Matthew 19:16–24; And behold, one came up to him. Anna Kamienska. GI *Fr.* St. Matthew.

Matthew 21:1–11. Boris Leonidovich Pasternak. GI *Fr.* St. Matthew.

Matthew 2:1–12; Now when Jesus was born. T. S. Eliot. GI *Fr.* St. Matthew.

Matthew 21:18–22; In the morning. Donald Hall. GI *Fr.* St. Matthew.

Matthew 2:16–18; Then Herod, when he saw. Julia Hartwig. GI *Fr.* St. Matthew.

Matthew 22:1–14; And again Jesus spoke to them. Edwin Arlington Robinson. GI *Fr.* St. Matthew.

Matthew 22:15–22; Then the Pharisees went and. Desanka Maksimovic. GI *Fr.* St. Matthew.

Matthew 24:15–31. William Butler Yeats. GI *Fr.* St. Matthew.

Matthew 25:14–30; "For it will be as when a man." Jorge Luis Borges. GI *Fr.* St. Matthew.

Matthew 26:17–29. Rainer Maria Rilke. GI *Fr.* St. Matthew.

Matthew 26:47–56; While he was still speaking, Judas came. Boris Leonidovich Pasternak. GI *Fr.* St. Matthew.

Matthew 27:11–24; Now Jesus stood before. René Daumal. GI *Fr.* St. Matthew.

Matthew 27:3–10; When Judas, his betrayer, saw. Zbigniew Herbert. GI *Fr.* St. Matthew.

May be refin'd [or refined], and join th' [or the] angelic train. (LL)   On Being Brought from Africa to America.   Phillis Wheatley.   ColAP; FaBoA; ISC; NAAL-3; NAAL-5; NAAPv.1; NALW; NoP-4; NoP-5; OxBEV; OxBoAm; RWP; SacPr

May! be thou never graced with birds that sing.   [Epitaph] In Obitum M.S., X° Maij [or Maii], 1614.   William Browne.   OBEV

May begin, and in doing so be undone. (LL)   And "Ut Pictura Poesis" Is Her Name.   John Ashbery.   EMP; VCAP

May breath for a dead moment cease as jerking your.   Curse.   Frank Bidart.   OxBoAm

May cast a leafy shadow.   Unica Zurn's Loam Bowl.   A. Di Michele.   AnSo

May come up with bird-din.   Nuts in May.   Louis MacNeice.   MoBrPo

May crown Thy Feet, that could not crown Thy Head. (LL)   Coronet, The.   Andrew Marvell.   BASC; BrAP; FSCP; NAEL-6v1; NAEL-7v1; NoP-4; NoP-5; NOSC; PBRV; SacPr

May Day.   Jinkag Haesim.   BecRai, *tr.* by Kim Daljin, Kim Won-Chung and Christopher Merrill

May Day.   Dinah Livingstone.   RSaN

May Day, 1917.   W. N. Ewer.   RSaN

May every reference cease.   Pagan.   R. Williams Parry.   BBMWP, *tr.* by Martin Davis

May find you planting lentils on my grave. (LL)   Prodigal Son, The.   Edwin Arlington Robinson.   GI; MoAmPo

May God above.   Curse on Mine-Owners, A.   *Unknown.*   RaF

May God be praised for woman.   On Woman.   William Butler Yeats.   ChIV-1

May God bless your home.   Marriage Vow.   Mrs. Henry Linden.   CBWP-4

May God Go with You, Son.   C. Wright.   FaBoWar

May God, in whose hand is the lot of each land.   Our Dear Native Island.   Edward Lysaght.   IrV

May God let him be invited to our home!   *Unknown.*   SLW, *tr.* by Marjolijn De Jager, Sayd Bahodin Majrouh and André Velter

May God prohibit you from any pleasure as you travel.   *Unknown.*   SLW, *tr.* by Marjolijn De Jager, Sayd Bahodin Majrouh and André Velter

May [God's] mercy and power be bestowed plentifully upon this kingship, and may safety and piety be granted to both the religious and the secular [branches].   Ahmad ibn Muhammad Ibn Darrāj al-Qasṭallī.   HiArP, *tr.* by James T. Monroe

May have killed the cat; more likely.   Curiosity.   Alastair Reid.   SoSe-8; WaAnP

May he have new life like the fall.   John Coltrane: An Impartial Review.   Alfred B. Spellman.   EGAG

May he lose his way on the cold sea.   Archilochus.   OBVE; WoPoe, *tr.* by Guy Davenport

May he that bade me trust him, but did not come.   Malediction.   *Unknown.*   WoPoe, *tr.* by Arthur Waley

May he who brings / Flowers tonight.   Kikaku.   ZenPo, *tr.* by Takashi Ikemoto and Lucien Stryk

May I ask you a question?.   Narrows, The.   Anne Rouse.   MFPA

May I be born without hands for 500 lifetimes, for a.   Old Monks Drinking.   Seido Ray Ronci.   AmZen

May i feel said he.   E. E. Cummings.   HeIP-4; NAMCP V.1; NBLV; NoP-5; OBCoV; OxBoAm; PoPoPo

May I for my own self song's truth reckon.   *Unknown.*   APT-1; HeIP-4; NoP-4; NoP-5; OxBoAm; TCAPo; WaAnP; WoPoe *Fr.* Ripostes of Ezra Pound.

May I, goldencrowned Aphrodite.   Sappho.   SaLy, *tr.* by Diane Rayor

May I learn the shape of that hurt.   For the D.   Anthony McNeill.   WaCA

May I say, "It is Nestus Gurley." (LL)   Nestus Gurley.   Randall Jarrell.   HeIP-4; InGu

May I with Mary choose the better part.   Mary English.   EMWP

May in My Lai.   Menna Elfyn.   ATSWP, *tr.* by Robert Minhinnick

May in the Green-Wood.   *Unknown.*   OBEV

May is a pious fraud of the almanac.   James Russell Lowell.   APN-1; TCAPo *Fr.* Under the Willows.

May Isis heal me.   *Unknown.*   HW

May Isis heal me as she healed her son Horus.   May Isis heal me.   *Unknown.*   HW

May-June, 1940.   Robinson Jeffers.   MoAmPo

May Levine.   Susan Fromberg Schaeffer.   TaR

May Morning.   George Buchanan.   PBRV

May morning, A.   Blossom, The.   Eavan Boland.   ItP

May morning at Minsmere, A.   May Day.   Dinah Livingstone.   RSaN

May Mowing Clover.   Lisa Lewis.   SweBea

May my Irish grandfather from Tyrells Pass.   Buzz Plane, The.   Robert Francis.   OtW

May my little boy.   Let Him Not Grow Up.   Gabriela Mistral.   BeAl, *tr.* by Ursula K. Le Guin

May my love become an alder tree.   Yi Chŏngbo.   CATKP, *tr.* by Wen Hsia-min

May not have been in vain. (LL)   David Gascoyne.   ChIV-2; NoP-4; NoP-5; OBWP *Fr.* Miserere.

May one sorrow every day.   Wish, A.   John Millington Synge.   IrLP

May one who fought in honor for the South.   Lincoln's Grave.   Maurice Thompson.   CBCWP

May Ours Not Be.   Funso Aiyejina.   NAfrP

May ours not be like the story.   May Ours Not Be.   Funso Aiyejina.   NAfrP

May! queen of blossoms.   May.   Edward, 2d Baron Thurlow Hovell-Thurlow.   OBEV

May Queen, The.   Alfred Tennyson.   TreFP

May rains.   Buson.   EH, *tr.* by Robert Hass

May reach—tho' lost on earth—the ear of Heaven! (LL)   To Night.   Charlotte Smith.   NAEL-6v2; NAEL-7v2

May say Alas but cannot help or pardon. (LL)   Spain [1937].   W. H. Auden.   AF; NAEL-6v2; NAEL-7v2; NAMCP V.1; NoP-4; NoP-5; OBWP

May say their lords have built, but thy lord dwells. (LL)   To Penshurst.   Ben Jonson.   BASC; CABP; NAEL-6v1; NAEL-7v1; NoP-4; NoP-5; NOSC; OxBEV; PBRV; TFi; WaAnP

May Song.   Johann Wolfgang von Goethe.   STV, *tr.* by John Frederick Nims

May Song.   Félix Lope de Vega Carpio.   SpanPo, *tr.* by Kate Flores

May sun—whom, The.   Tulip Bed, The.   William Carlos Williams.   OBGa

May the Lord bless you and keep you.   Blessing Attributed to Saint Clare, The.   Clare of Assisi.   BBASP, *tr.* by Regis J. Armstrong

May the maiden.   Song for "The Jacquerie."   Sidney Lanier.   NCAP

May the man who has cruelly murdered his sire.   Horace.   NBLV *Fr.* Epodes.

May the men who are born.   Kakinomoto no Hitomaro.   TAL *Fr.* Manyo Shu, Part 2 of 4.

May the rain cloud be bountiful to you when the rain cloud pours, O time of love union in al-Andalus!   Ibn al-Khaṭīb.   HiArP, *tr.* by James T. Monroe

May the Saddest Memory.   Birthday Wishes to a Husband.   Lizelia Augusta Jenkins Moorer.   CBWP-3

May the smell of thyme and lavender accompany us on our journey.   On Pilgrimage.   Czeslaw Milosz.   AmFaPo; BeAl, *tr.* by the author and Robert Hass

May the tide / that is entering even now.   Blessing the boats.   Lucille Clifton.   CFP

May the wind blow sweetness.   *Unknown.*   WoPoe *Fr.* Rig Veda.

May the wind blows sweetness.   *Unknown.*   WoPoe *Fr.* Vedic Hymns.

May the youths love me by my words and songs.   Fragment 17.   Anacreon.   CAGL, *tr.* by Eugene O'Connor

May there be an afterlife.   Prayer for the Man Who Mugged My Father, 72.   Charles Harper Webb.   MAAN

May they stumble [or wander], stage by stage.   Travel[l]er's Curse after Misdirection[, The].   Robert Graves.   MoBrPo; NBLV; OBCoV

May toss[e] him to my breast. (LL)   Pulley, The.   George Herbert.   BASC; BBASP; BrAP; ChIV-1; FSCP; HeIP-4; InvLi; NAEL-6v1; NAEL-7v1; NoP-4; NoP-5; NOSC; OBEV; OxAEP-1; TFi; WaAnP

May Tree, The.   Jean Earle.   TCAWP

May very well cost you your life. (LL)   Poem About My Rights.   June Jordan.   ISC; NoAM; WaAnP

May was murder, a hooligan spring.   Old Photograph, An.   Iwan Llwyd.   BBMWP, *tr.* by Richard Poole

May winds and sorrows.   Sappho.   SaLy, *tr.* by Diane Rayor

May you be found cut to pieces by a trenchant sword.   *Unknown.*   SLW, *tr.* by Marjolijn De Jager, Sayd Bahodin Majrouh and André Velter

May you live forever. In that eternity.   Curse on Herod, A.   Amy Witting.   ChIV-2; NOBAu

May you perish on the field of honor, my beloved!   *Unknown.*   SLW, *tr.* by Marjolijn De Jager, Sayd Bahodin Majrouh and André Velter

May you rejoice, Paeon lord, who rule.   Women at the Temple.   Herodas.   HePo, *tr.* by Barbara Hughes Fowler

May / You rest in peace.   Monologue with Commentary.   Andrey Andreievich Voznesensky.   RusPo, *tr.* by Robert Arthur Douglas Ford

May you sleep on the breast of a tender companion.   Sappho.   SaLy, *tr.* by Diane Rayor

May your journey, Uaithne, be in the name of the Holy Spirit.   Fionnghuala Inghean Uí Domhnaill Bhriain.   EMWP

May—1941.   Valentine Penrose.   SurPaPo, *tr.* by Mary Ann Caws

Maya to Herself and Then to Her Gardener.   Reetika Vazirani.   NAPBL

Mayakovsky in Paris.   Andrey Andreievich Voznesensky.   TCRusP, *tr.* by Daniel Weissbort

Mayan Astronomer in Hell's Kitchen, A.   Martín Espada.   PoDa

Mayan Glyphs Unread, The.   William Bronk.   APSN

Mayan Princess fronts the Gulf, The.   Elegy at Mustang Island.   Isabel Nathaniel.   TiP2

Maybe Alone on My Bike.   William Stafford.   ArBi

Maybe because I was married and felt secure and dead.   Visiting My Gravesite: Talbott Churchyard, West Virginia.   Irene McKinney.   PBCAP

Maybe Desdemona.   Dan Johnson.   IaFF

Maybe He looked indeed.   Salvator Mundi: Via Crucis.   Denise Levertov.
UpMys

Maybe human, bereft. (LL)   Skeins o Geese.   Kathleen Jamie.   GPPA;
MoWP; NeBrP

Maybe I knew it wouldn't last long that night, that the joys of us.   Different
Strokes Bar, San Francisco, The.   Forrest Hamer.   GeoHom

Maybe I Should Change My Ways.   John Latouche.   ReLy

Maybe I should go back to the white leather.   Desnos Reading the Palms of
Men on Their Way to the Gas Chambers.   Stephen Berg.   TaR

Maybe I should have saved those leftover dreams.   Here's That Rainy Day.
Johnny Burke.   ReLy

Maybe, if she didn't have adobe walls between her.   Riding the Eye.   Frances
Payne Adler.   FiBr

Maybe if you saw Hiroshima.   Maybe Then.   Idea Vilariño.   CFP; TANSG, tr.
by Louise B. Popkin

Maybe I'm a king. (LL)   Story That Could Be True, A.   William Stafford.
NTCP; RaBo

Maybe I'm Amazed.   Jim Carroll.   PmAP

Maybe I'm old-fashioned.   When I Fall in Love.   Edward Heyman.   ReLy

Maybe I'm seven in the open field.   Sudden Journey.   Tess Gallagher.   NIL-7;
NIP-4

Maybe I'm sick, I've been shivering.   Chill, A.   Bella Akhatovna
Akhmadulina.   TCRusP, tr. by Kathy Lewis and Bob Perelman

Maybe it happens this way.   How Little We Know.   Johnny Mercer.   ReLy

Maybe it is the shyness of the pride.   Surge, The.   Molly Peacock.   PasH

Maybe it isn't choirs of cherbubim with perfect pitch.   O Paradise.   William
Trowbridge.   ReLy

Maybe it was.   Why I Left the Church.   Richard Garcia.   SUP

Maybe it was the Bichot.   Poetry Makes Rhythm in Philosophy.   Ishmael
Reed.   EGAG

Maybe it was the music.   This Heart of Mine.   Arthur Freed.   ReLy

Maybe it's not the city you thought.   Like This.   Carol Muske-Dukes.   ExTi

Maybe it's the time I spend in high school classrooms.   Why I Forgive My
Younger Self Her Transgressions.   Ruth L. Schwartz.   NeAmPo

Maybe morning lightens up.   For My Grandmother, Bridget Halpin.   Michael
Hartnett.   ModIr; PBCIP

Maybe on his way to Gadsden.   Walt Whitman in Alabama.   Jake Adam York.
ViWalt

Maybe one day we will have.   After a Reading at a Black College.   Toi
Derricotte.   FuFl

Maybe our failed hopes rise like tulips.   Tulips.   Mark Halperin.   PoDa

Maybe she does her homework.   In Praise of Zigzags.   Jane O. Wayne.
InvLad

Maybe that day I met Clarissa Dalloway.   Woman in the Moon, The.   Nadya
Aisenberg.   PfS

Maybe that is what he was after.   Sweet Ruin.   Tony Hoagland.   FaoP

Maybe that "quest thing."   For LeRoi Jones.   Steve Jonas.   EGAG

Maybe that's why I don't like.   Jackie Kay.   MoWP Fr. Adoption Papers, The.

Maybe / the burning bush.   Miracle.   Kathe Davis.   AmZen

Maybe the street is tired of being a street.   New Year.   Naomi Shihab Nye.
LoL

Maybe the sun gave me the pow'r.   Almost Like Being in Love.   Alan Jay
Lerner.   ReLy

Maybe the winds die down tomorrow.   Balitaw.   Bataan Faigao.   ReBoTo

Maybe Then.   Idea Vilariño.   CFP; TANSG, tr. by Louise B. Popkin

Maybe there is an evening meant.   Runt of a Dream, A.   Arthur Rimbaud.
WoPoe, tr. by Denis Goacher

Maybe This Is Love.   Lew Brown, B. G. DeSylva and Ray Henderson.   ReLy

Maybe we are the same darkness the same words.   Gloria Gervitz.   MirDau Fr.
Yiskor.

Maybe what Thomas means when he says grace.   Reading Aquinas.   Michael
Heffernan.   WeW-3

Maybe when her eye first gave her trouble, but when I did not yet know.
Contemporary American Poetry.   Alan Feldman.   BAP-01

Maybe you escaped from the marsh.   Bullfrog.   Brendan Galvin.   PoCoUp

Maybe you need to write a poem about grace.   Faint Music.   Robert Hass.
CAP-8

Maybe you thought it was a bird.   Hand, The: "Brightness Falls from the Air."
Gregory Orr.   PoChi

Maybe you've got a little time.   Neckst.   Yosl Cutler.   Prolet, tr. by Amelia
Glaser

Maybe Zizi is right.   Venice Beach: Brief Song.   Dorothy Barresi.   SeSe;
SwNoth

May-day! delightful day!   In Praise of May.   Unknown.   IrV, tr. by Thomas
William Hazen Rolleston

Mayden in the moor lay—.   Unknown.   OHMEL

Mayest find thy Darling in an Urne. (LL)   Thomas Carew.   See Mayst find thy
darling in an urn.

Mayflies.   Richard Wilbur.   CAP-8

Mayfly.   Louis MacNeice.   ModIr

Mayo Monologues.   Michael Longley.
Self-Heal.   ModIr

Mayo Tao, The.   Derek Mahon.   BeAl

Mayombe-bombe-mayombé!   Sensemayá.   Nicolás Guillén.   PFTM-1

Mayor.   Yehuda Amichai.   PoSu, tr. by Assia Gutmann

Mayor couldn't be here, but he sends his grand whereases, The.   State Poetry
Day.   Ronald Wallace.   PBCAP

Mayor Harold Washington has been dead.   Chicago on the Day Brother
Increases His Chances of Reaching Age 21.   Taiyon J. Coleman.   BRtP

Mayor of Scuttleton, The.   Mary Mapes Dodge.   SWaP

May-Pole, The.   Robert Herrick.   CavPo

May's Invocation after a Tardy Spring [with music].   Henrietta Cordelia Ray.
CBWP-3

Maytime, loveliest season.   Sadness in Spring.   Unknown.   OBWVE, tr. by
Gwyn Jones

Mazatlan: Sea.   Robert Creeley.   APSN

Maze is round and blue and green, The.   Marriage of Sorts, A.   Pamela
Alexander.   YaYoPo

Maze, The.   Joanne Kyger.   BB

Maze Without a Minotaur.   Dana Gioia.   RA

Mazeppa.   Lord Byron.
Bring forth the horse! The horse was brought.   TreFP

Mazing around my mind like moths at a shaded candle.   Ghosts.   Robert
Bridges.   OxBEV

Mbaye Dyôb! I want to say your name and your honor.   Taga for Mbaye Dyôb.
Léopold Sédar Senghor.   PFTM-1

McDermott's War Song.   G. W. Hunt.
"Dogs of war are loose and the rugged russian bear, The."   FaBoWar

McDonald's, Scottsboro, April, 1997.   Anthony Walton.   RD

McTaggart.   Kenneth White.   EdScPo

Me.   Chairil Anwar.   PoetW, tr. by Burton Raffel

Me?   Nirasana Kavulu.   HotL, tr. by V. Narayana Rao

Me.   Lady Ukon.   WoPoe, tr. by Howard S. Levy

Me, a fellow who powders his face.   Performer, Male.   No Ch'ŏnmyŏng.
CAMKP, tr. by David R. McCann

Me a poet! My daughter with maimed limb.   Tony Harrison.   NAMCP V.2 Fr.
School of Eloquence, The.

Me against the world.   Charles Bukowski.   OxBoAm

Me and Baby.   Ana Castillo.   IllVoic

Me and Marlene sit tight in her truck.   Our Lady of the Laundromat.   Belle
Waring.   PBCAP

Me and My Bike.   Dylan Thomas.
"How stern you appear."   ArBi

Me and my brother would jump off the porch.   Pushing.   Christopher Gilbert.
LTA; SoSe-8

Me and My Girl.   Douglas Furber and Noel Gay.   ReLy

Me and my new bike.   We.   Ryn Gargulinski.   ArBi

Me and Russia.   Velemir Khlebnikov.   TCRusP, tr. by Kathy Lewis and Bob
Perelman

Me and the Devil Blues.   Robert Johnson.   APT-2; OxBoAm

Me as an Archaeologist.   John MacKenzie.   Coast

Me at the Bottom of the Sea.   Alfonsina Storni.   TCLAP, tr. by Andrew Rosing

Me back to my mountain and far, far, west. (LL)   August on Sourdough, a Visit
from Dick Brewer.   Gary Snyder.   LoL; NAAL-5

Me clairvoyant.   G. K. Chesterton.   UV Fr. Variations on an Air Composed on
Having to Appear in a Pageant as Old King Cole.

Me colmó el sol del poniente.   Canción.   Juan Ramón Jiménez.   RaW

Me da terror irme con toda la sangre metida entre la carne y el corazón.
Hacho.   Pedro Serrano.   RMCMP

Me dejo guiar porque he dejado ir.   Eduardo Milán.   RMCMP

Me, for example.   Say Girls in Shoe Ads: "I Go for a Man Who's Tall!"
Robley, Jr. Wilson.   PBCAP

Me from Myself—to banish.   Emily Dickinson.   NALW; TCAPo; TRP

Me glad fi see yuh come back, bwoy.   No Lickle Twang.   Louise Bennett.
NAMCP V.2

Me go to Morant Bay.   Morant Bay.   Unknown.   FaBoVe

Me good friend Beverley.   Beverley's Saga.   Grace Nichols.   WaCA

Me gusta oler las almohadas, me dices.   Almohadas.   Antonio Deltoro.
RMCMP

Me! he says, hand on his chest.   Myself I Sing.   George Oppen.   FTOS

Me / I am / Royal blue.   Poem for a Doll Bought in a Russian Bazaar.
Marguerite Yourcenar.   YaTCFP, tr. by Martin Sorrell

Me, I like to putz in the kitchen and regard.   Breeze in Translation.   Belle
Waring.   PBCAP

Me I will throw away.   Self-slaved, The.   Patrick Kavanagh.   MoBrPo

Me imperturbe, standing, imperturbable, surveying the big country in rough-hewn, limping language, seeking the barbaric yawp.   Whitman Stock-Taking, Cataloguing.   James Schevill.   ViWalt

Me in Paradise.   Brenda Shaughnessy.   IIR

Me interpreting her reply all the way home. (LL)   Strange Case, The.   Michael Ondaatje.   EmeKit; StAl

Me, Lord? Canst Thou misspend.   Phineas Fletcher.   SacPr

Me lover gone a Colon Bay.   Colon Bay.   *Unknown.*   FaBoVe

"Me loving subjects," sez she.   Queen's After-Dinner Speech, The.   William Percy French.   OBCoV

Me lusteth [*or* list] no longer [*or* lenger] rotten bough[e]s to climb [*or* clymbe].   (LL)   Farewell, love, and all thy law[e]s forever [*or* for ever].   Sir Thomas Wyatt.   GSo; NAEL-6v1; NAEL-7v1; NoSic; OxBSo

Me not no Oxford don.   Listen Mr Oxford Don.   John Agard.   NPeEn; Oth

Me on the Wall.   Ajanta.   HotL, *tr. by* V. Narayana Rao

Me one, way out in the crowd.   Valley Prince.   Mervyn Morris.   WaCA

Me refiero a ti como a dos fieras porque.   Eduardo Milán.   RMCMP

Me reweth, Marie, thi sone and the. (LL)   *Unknown.*   NoP-4; NoP-5

Me she hated.   Stepmother.   Dinah Livingstone.   Prnts

Me show you. Love the only way I know how. (LL)   You Bring Out the Mexican in Me.   Sandra Cisneros.   IllVoic; WaAnP

Me siento solo como un dedo al que le faltara mano.   Domingo.   Antonio Deltoro.   RMCMP

Me so oft my fancy drew.   Choice, The.   George Wither.   OBEV

Me Sobra el Corazón.   Miguel Hernández.   RaW

Me the youngest of the Lumière brothers.   How Old Is the Old Mole?   Marie-Dominique Massoni.   SurWo, *tr. by* Myrna Bell Rochester

Me thinkes tis pretie sport to heare a childe.   Thomas Bastard.   OxBEV

Me thinks I heare some Cavillers object.   John Taylor.   PBRV *Fr.* Comparison betwixt a Whore and a Booke, A.

Me thinks I see our mighty monarch stand.   *Unknown.*   OBSV *Fr.* Royal Angler, The.

Methinks I see, with what a busy haste.   On Zacheus [*or* Zacchaeus].   Francis Quarles.   NOSC

Me thought I passed through th' Idalian groves.   Author's Dream to the Lady Mary, the Countess Dowager of Pembroke, The.   Emilia Lanier and Aemilia Bassano Lanyer.   BASC

Me up at does.   Me Up at Does.   E. E. Cummings.   WeW-3

Me Voy Porque la Espiga y la Aurora No Son Mías.   León Felipe.   RaW

Me when she ironed clothes. (LL)   Deep-Sea Bathing (Inna Reggae Dancehall).   Rohan B. Preston.   AmPoNex; WaCA

Mea Shearim.   Tamara Kamenszain.   MirDau, *tr. by* Roberta Gordenstein

Meadow.   John Engels.   PfSP

Meadow, The.   Peter Fallon.   IPoFL; PBCIP

Meadow, The.   Kate Knapp Johnson.   P180

Meadow, The.   Susan Stewart.   AmAlph

Meadow and Might.   Friederike Roth.
   "Just only alive."   GTCP, *tr. by* Irmgard Hunt

Meadow and the mountain with desire, The.   Attraction.   Ella Wheeler Wilcox.   LW

Meadow brown; across the yonder edge, A.   Joe.   Emily Pauline Johnson.   SWaP

Meadow Bug.   Rossana Ombres.   NeIt

Meadow grass hemming, The.   Loom: Burnt Woods Cemetery, Western Bay, Newfoundland.   Michael Crummey.   Coast

Meadow in Spring.   Gregory Orr.   PfSP

Meadow is venomous but pleasant in autumn, The.   Meadow Saffron.   Guillaume Apollinaire.   WoPoe, *tr. by* Robert Mezey

Meadow, / Meadow.   Golden Meadow, The.   Kim Sowŏl.   CAMKP, *tr. by* David R. McCann

Meadow Mouse, The.   Theodore Roethke.   ChAP; HeIP-4; TRP

Meadow Saffron.   Guillaume Apollinaire.   WoPoe, *tr. by* Robert Mezey

Meadows again!, The. (LL)   Old Song.   Edward Fitzgerald.   OBEV; OxAEP-2

Meadow's mad beneath them, The. They fly like.   March Lambs.   Bobi Jones.   ATSWP, *tr. by* Robert Minhinnick

Meadowsweet.   Rolf Jacobsen.   WoPoe, *tr. by* Roger Greenwald

Meadowsweet.   Kathleen Jamie.   MoWP; PoCu

Meadowsweet, those dizzying flowers.   Meadowsweet.   Rolf Jacobsen.   WoPoe, *tr. by* Roger Greenwald

Meager food and a shabby house: the marks of a scholar.   Higher Living Away from the World.   Hamhur Kiwha.   BecRai, *tr. by* Kim Daljin, Kim Won-Chung and Christopher Merrill

Meal for the Monks, A.   Wang Wei.   CrYelRi, *tr. by* Sam Hamill

Meal of words made by a moth, A.   *Unknown.*   WoPoe *Fr.* Riddles (Exeter Book).

Meal, The.   T. Gwynn Jones.   BBMWP, *tr. by* Anthony Conran

Meal Time [*with music*].   Maggie Pogue Johnson.   CBWP-4

Mean Drunk Poem.   Sharon Thesen.   BrAP

Mean mean mean to be free. (LL)   Runagate Runagate.   Robert Earl Hayden.   APT-2; ESEAA; GM; ISC; OxAAAP; SSLK

Mean to Me.   Roy Turk.   ReLy

Mean wind wanders through the backcourt trash, A.   Glasgow Sonnets.   Edwin Morgan.   RSaN

Meaner Than a Junkyard Dog; or, Turner's Evil Twin.   Turner Cassity.   PoA 2002

Meaning a context or vision to confer with this which could be a book.   Approximately.   Diane Ward.   FTOS

Meaning of a Word, The.   Vincent Woods.   NIrP

Meaning of Life, The.   Patricia Goedicke.   TAPaP

Meaning of Simplicity, The.   Yannis Ritsos.   PFTM-2, *tr. by* Kimon Friar

Meaning of Soup, The.   Gabriel Celaya.   RaW, *tr. by* Robert Mezey and Hardie St. Martin

Meaning of the Look, The.   Elizabeth Barrett Browning.   SacPr

Meaning: this world holds every sort of weather. (LL)   Pelicans.   Judith Wright.   BMAP; OWoS

Meaningful Love.   John Ashbery.   VaPo

Means.   Dennis Phillips.
   "Hounds are either the work of wind, The."   FTOS

Means to Attain the Happy Life, The.   Martial. *See* Happy Life, The.

Meantime from an adjoining chamber came.   Philip Freneau.   NAAL-3 *Fr.* House of Night, The.

Meanwhile a great deal of time has passed.   Dust of Poems, The.   Nathan Yonathan.   NRoS, *tr. by* Esther Raizen

Meanwhile / a young man.   Ana Belén López Pulido.   SPV, *tr. by* Jen Hofer

Meanwhile in Massachusetts Jack Kennedy dreamed.   Meanwhile in Massachusetts.   Jacqueline Kennedy Onassis.   BLPJKO

Meanwhile, in Rwanda.   Patricia Smith.   SpirFl

Meanwhile [*or* Mean while] the Adversary of God and Man.   John Milton.   OBNV *Fr.* Paradise Lost.

Meanwhile, somewhere in the state of Colorado, armed to the teeth.   Simon Armitage.   NoP-5 *Fr.* Killing Time.

Meanwhile the cars continued in a persistent flow down.   C. D. Wright.   AmAlph; ExTi *Fr.* Deepstep Come Shining.

Meanwhile the Troops beneath Patroclus' Care.   Homer.   OBVE *Fr.* Iliad, The.

Meanwhile the Turtle.   Ann Lauterbach.   ExTi

Meanwhile the two men pressed on where the pathway led.   Virgil.   NAWM-5v1; NAWM-7v1 *Fr.* Aeneid [*or* Eneados *or* Aeneis], The.

Meanwhile with Vine there, Clarel stood.   Herman Melville.   APN-2 *Fr.* Clarel: A Poem and Pilgrimage in the Holy Land.

Measure.   Robert Hass.   YaYoPo

Measure, The.   Peter Levitt.   WhBo

Measure for Measure.   Sipho Sepamla.   AF

Measure for Measure.   William Shakespeare.
   "Ay[e], but to die, and go we know not where."   WaAnP
   Take, O Take Those Lips Away.   NoSic; OBEV; TFi
   "What saies my brother?"   OxBEV

Measure me for a burial.   Dimensions.   Laura Riding Jackson.   FuPo

Measured blood beats out the year's delay, The.   Simple Autumnal.   Louise Bogan.   MoAmPo

Measurements.   Louisa Sarah Bevington.   VWP

Measures.   Adam Drinan.   EdScPo

Measure's inherent.   Parade.   Robert Creeley.   BodElec

Measures Taken, The.   Erich Fried.   WoPoe, *tr. by* Michael Hamburger

Measuring Apollo.   Luke Icarus Simon.   PML, *tr. by the author*

Measuring the Tyger.   Jack Gilbert.   BeAl

Meat ants, meat-coloured, greet each other.   Anguish of Ants, The.   David Campbell.   BMAP

Meat Epitaph, The.   Michael Benedikt.   MotU

Meat Michelangelo.   Charles Harper Webb.   LiTh

Meatloaf, you remembered, is the third vegetable. (LL)   Wolf Ridge.   John Ashbery.   BAP-04; VaPo

Mechanical Cow, The.   Robley, Jr. Wilson.   PBCAP

Mechanical Heart.   Josué Ramírez.   RMCMP, *tr. by* Mónica de la Torre

Mechanical-landscape-poem.   Ion Minulescu.   SonAtl, *tr. by* Chris Constantinescu, Dio Marescu, Phoebe Ravenhall and Helen Wilson

Mechanics.   T. R. Hummer.   LPSFW

Mechanics.   Sally Keith.   LegDan

Me—come! My dazzled face.   Emily Dickinson.   APN-2

Meda Songs.   *Unknown.*   APN-2, *tr. by* Henry Rowe Schoolcraft

Medallion.   Sylvia Plath.   HeIP-4

Medallion.   Ezra Pound.   NoP-5; TCAPo *Fr.* Hugh Selwyn Mauberley (Life and Contacts).

Medallion, The.   Herman Melville.   APN-2 *Fr.* Clarel: A Poem and Pilgrimage in the Holy Land.

Meddling Mastiff, The.   John Gay.   DiBP *Fr.* Fables: First Series.

Medea. Euripides.
 Chorus. OBEV, *tr. by* John Byrne Leicester Warren, 3d Baron De Tabley
Medea. Seneca. *tr. by* John Studley
 Deaths of Orphues and Hercules, The. OBVE, *tr. by* John Studley
 Medea's Frenzy. OBVE, *tr. by* John Studley
Medea in Athens. Augusta Davies Webster.
 "Dead is he? Yes, our stranger guest said dead." ViWPN
Medea Speaks. Z Budapest.
 "Medea speaks: / This is God, children, listen up well. The." HW
Medea speaks: / This is God, children, listen up well. The. Z Budapest. HW
 Fr. Medea Speaks.
Medea, you beautiful woman, don't turn around. Letter to Medea. Helga
 Novak. GTCP, *tr. by* Susan L Cocalis
Medea's Frenzy. Seneca. OBVE *Fr.* Medea.
Medea's Incantation. Ovid. OBVE *Fr.* Metamorphoses.
Medgar Evers. Gwendolyn Brooks. ESEAA; NoP-4; NoP-5
Media España ocupaba España entera. De los Años Cuarenta. Jaime Gil de
 Biedma. RaW
Media on War: or, the Square Root of Vietnam. Clarence Major. EGAG
Medical Science. Robin Becker. PBCAP
Medical Student Learns Love and Death, A. Rafael Campo. WiU *Fr.* Song for
 My Lover.
Medicine: "Black hair of my Chinese doctor, The." Tony Hoagland. PoCu
Medicine. Wang Shih-chieng. ColAnChi, *tr. by* Richard John Lynn
Medicine Bearer. Gail Tremblay. HATNAP
Medicine Man. Calvin C. Hernton. EGAG
Medicine Song of an Indian Lover. *Unknown.* APN-2, *tr. by* Charles Fenno
 Hoffman
Medicine Songs. *Unknown.* APN-2, *tr. by* Francis La Flesche
Medieval. Ernst Jandl. OnScMo, *tr. by* Gale Nelson
Medieval town, with frieze, The. What Is Poetry. John Ashbery. HarvBoo
Mediocrity in Love Rejected. Thomas Carew. NoP-4; NoP-5; WaAnP
Meditar. Gerardo Deniz. RMCMP
Meditate. Gerardo Deniz. RMCMP, *tr. by* Mónica de la Torre
Meditate, O mind, on the mystery of Kali. My blissful Mother exists fully
 through every creature! Lex Hixon. HW
Meditate on jagged things. Miscellaneous Bouquet. No Hyegyông. EcSo, *tr.
 by* Ann Y. Choi
Meditate on Kali! Why be anxious? Rämprasäd Sen. SinGod, *tr. by* Rachel
 Fell McDermott
Meditating at midnight. Zhou Xuanjing. WPoS
Meditating on Star Light While Traveling Highway. Anita Endrezze.
 HATNAP
Meditating on the Start of a New Era. Yo Inlô. WoPoe, *tr. by* Jean S. Grigsby
Meditatio. Ezra Pound. ItP
Meditatio Lectoris. Rodrigo Toscano. BAP-04
Meditatio Septima. Francis Quarles. ChIV-1
Meditatio Tertia Decima. Francis Quarles. ChIV-1 *Fr.* Job Militant.
Meditation 3 Can. 1.3. Thy Good Ointment. Edward Taylor. OxBoAm *Fr.*
 Preparatory Meditations: Part 1.
Meditation 6 (Canticles 2:1 I am. . .the lily of the valleys). Edward Taylor. *See*
 Another Meditation at the same Time.
Meditation 8 (First Series). Edward Taylor. ChIV-2; ColAP; NAAL-3;
 NAAL-5; NAAPv.1; NoP-4; NoP-5; TCAPo *Fr.* Preparatory Meditations
 Before My Approach to the Lord's Supper.
Meditation 26. Edward Taylor. NAAL-3 *Fr.* Preparatory Meditations Before
 My Approach to the Lord's Supper.
Meditation 38. Edward Taylor. NAAL-3 *Fr.* Preparatory Meditations Before
 My Approach to the Lord's Supper.
Meditation 42 (First Series). Edward Taylor. NAAL-3; NAAL-5; NAAPv.1
 Fr. Preparatory Meditations Before My Approach to the Lord's Supper.
Meditation 150 (Second Series). Edward Taylor. ColAP; NAAPv.1 *Fr.*
 Preparatory Meditations Before My Approach to the Lord's Supper.
Meditation 16 (First Series). Edward Taylor. NAAL-3; NAAL-5; NAAPv.1
 Fr. Preparatory Meditations Before My Approach to the Lord's Supper.
Meditation 22 (First Series). Edward Taylor. NAAL-3; NAAL-5; NAAPv.1;
 TCAPo *Fr.* Preparatory Meditations Before My Approach to the Lord's
 Supper.
Meditation 39 (First Series). Edward Taylor. NAAPv.1; TCAPo *Fr.*
 Preparatory Meditations Before My Approach to the Lord's Supper.
Meditation, A. Herman Melville. PCW
Meditation: "Animals full of light." William Stafford. WaAnP
Meditation: "I could sit in this hot bath for hours." Roberta Spear. PoCho
Meditation: "Quiet now, sorrow; relax. Calm down, fear." David St. John.
 AmAlph
Meditation: "Sorrow is to be discarded." Mary Sue Koeppel. AmZen
Meditation, The. John Norris. NOSC
Meditation at Kew. Anna Wickham. MoBrPo; NALW

Meditation at Lagunitas. Robert Hass. AmFaPo; CalPo; CAP-8; ColAP;
 FaoP; GeoHom; MakPoe; NAMCP V.2; NoP-4; NoP-5; OxBoAm; StAl;
 VCAP; WaAnP
Meditation at Oyster River. Theodore Roethke. MoAmPo
Meditation at Oyster River. Theodore Roethke. MoAmPo *Fr.* North American
 Sequence.
Meditation Brought About by George Bogin's Translation of Jules Supervielle's
 Poem "The Sea." Michael Burkard. BodElec
Meditation by the Xerox Machine. Doris Safie. PoArWo
Meditation. Can. 1.3. Thy Good Ointment. Edward Taylor. TCAPo *Fr.*
 Preparatory Meditations Before My Approach to the Lord's Supper.
Meditation. Cant.6.11. Edward Taylor. OxBEV
Meditation Celestial & Terrestrial. Wallace Stevens. APT-1
Meditation. Col. 1.18. He is the Head of the Body. Edward Taylor. *Fr.*
 Preparatory Meditations Before My Approach to the Lord's Supper.
Méditation du 8/5/85. Jacques Roubaud. YaTCFP
Meditation 8. Philip Pain. NOSC
Meditation for Christmas, A. Selwyn Image. OBEV
Meditation for His Mistress[e], A. Robert Herrick. NOSC; OBEV
Meditation for this Day. Antonio Machado Ruiz. CLPP, *tr. by* Kenneth
 Rexroth
Meditation hall. Stanford M. Forrester. AmZen
Meditation. Heb. 13.10. We[e] have an Altar. Edward Taylor. ChIV-2; NOSC;
 TCAPo; WaAnP *Fr.* Preparatory Meditations Before My Approach to the
 Lord's Supper.
Meditation in Loudoun County. Thomas Bolt. YaYoPo
Meditation in Seven Days, A. Alicia Ostriker. PBCAP
Meditation in Seven Days, A. Alicia Ostriker. PBCAP; TaR
 "If your mother is a Jew, you are a Jew." TaR
Meditation in the Spring Rain. Wendell Berry. UpMys
Meditation. Joh. 15.5. Without me yee can do nothing. Edward Taylor.
 TCAPo *Fr.* Preparatory Meditations Before My Approach to the Lord's
 Supper.
Meditation. Mal. 4.2. With Healing in His Wings. Edward Taylor. *Fr.*
 Preparatory Meditations Before My Approach to the Lord's Supper.
Meditation. Numb. 28.4.9. One Lamb shalt thou offer in the Morning, and the
 other at Even. And on the Sabbath day two Lambs etc. Edward Taylor.
 ChIV-1; TCAPo *Fr.* Preparatory Meditations Before My Approach to the
 Lord's Supper.
Meditation 8/5/85. Jacques Roubaud. YaTCFP, *tr. by* Rosmarie Waldrop
Meditation on a Bone. Alec Derwent Hope. BrAP; NoAM; WoPoe
Meditation on Gal. 3.16. And to thy Seed Which is Christ. Edward Taylor. *Fr.*
 Preparatory Meditations Before My Approach to the Lord's Supper.
Meditation on Politics at the Quabbin Reservoir. Michael C. Blumenthal.
 PfSP
Meditation on *The Consolation of Philosophy*. Josh Bell. LegDan
Meditation on the Feminine Nature of Shekinah, A. Ann Gottlieb. HW
Meditation on the Great Blue Heron. Kay Murphy. RWB
Meditation on the Past at White Emperor City. Chen Zi'ang. CCL1, *tr. by*
 Stephen Owen
Meditation on the Threshold. Rosario Castellanos. CFP; TANSG, *tr. by*
 Magda Bogin
Meditation on the *Wen-Fu*. Eleanor Wilner. GifTon
Meditation on Yellow. Olive Senior. WaCA
Meditation. Phil. 3 Ult. Our Vile Bodie. Edward Taylor. *Fr.* Preparatory
 Meditations Before My Approach to the Lord's Supper.
Meditation. Rom. 9.5. God blessed forever. Edward Taylor. TCAPo *Fr.*
 Preparatory Meditations Before My Approach to the Lord's Supper.
Meditation. Zech. 9.11. The Pit wherein is no water. Edward Taylor. *Fr.*
 Preparatory Meditations Before My Approach to the Lord's Supper.
Meditations. Margaret Fuller. NAAPv.1; SWaP
Meditations 1: "For the beginning and the end." Duriel Harris. BtF
Meditations and Maxims. Margherita Guidacci. *tr. by* Cinzia Sartini Blum and
 Lara Trubowitz
 "First to feast is love, The. On the scraps of love the fever feasts." CItWP, *tr.
 by* Cinzia Sartini Blum and Lara Trubowitz
 "Tiny dew reinvigorates the tiny grass, The." CItWP, *tr. by* Cinzia Sartini
 Blum and Lara Trubowitz
Meditations in an Emergency. Frank O'Hara. PmAP; VCAP
Meditations in Time of Civil War. William Butler Yeats.
 Ancestral Houses. OBGa
 Road at My Door, The. NPeEn
Meditations of Man's Mortalitie; or, A Way to True Blessedness. Alice
 Sutcliffe.
 Of our losse by Adam, and our gayne by Christ.
 "God by his Wisdome, and all seeing Pow'r." EMWP
Meditations of Mr. Cogito on Redemption. Zbigniew Herbert. GI, *tr. by* John
 Carpenter

Meditations on a World of Stones.   Mahmoud al-Braikan.   IrPoTo, *tr.* by Ralph Saverese and Saadi A. Simawe

Meditations on Persecution.   Mary Mollineux.   EMWP

Meditations on Stevie.   Gordon Chambers.   InTrad

Meditations on the Moon.   Paula Gunn Allen.   HATNAP

Meditations on the Sepulchre in the Garden.   Philip Doddridge.   OBGa

Meditations on the Six Days of the Creation.   Thomas Traherne.   Third Day.   ChIV-1

Meditations, The.   *Unknown.*   "In the casket of the Hours."   TAL

Meditatio[u]n in Wyntir [*or* Winter].   William Dunbar.   CABP

Mediterranean Cooking for Two.   Janet Holmes.   PoDa

Mediterranean, The.   Allen Tate.   APT-2; FuPo; InGu; MoAmPo; NAAPv.2; OxBoAm; WoPoe

Medlars and Sorb-Apples.   D. H. Lawrence.   FaBoVe; NAMCP V.1; NoAM; NPeEn

Medoro's Inscription Book XXIII.   Ludovico Ariosto.   NOBRP *Fr.* Orlando Furioso.

Medrano Academy.   Blaise Cendrars.   CuPo

Medusa.   Louise Bogan.   APT-2; MoAmPo; NAAPv.2; NALW; NAMCP V.1; NoAM; NoP-4; NoP-5; PtR

Medusa.   Amy Clampitt.   VCAP

Medusa.   Carol Ann Duffy.   NAMCP V.2

Medusa.   Sylvia Plath.   NALW

Medusa.   Mariahadessa Ekere Tallie.   BRtP

Medusa: "Ageing woman combs her hair, The."   Ann Turner.   EdScPo

Medusa and Perseus III: Lilith.   Pat Parnell.   HW

Méduse l'auditoire mets sac à côté nord.   Isidore Ducasse Comte de Lautréamont.   Michelle Grangaud.   YaTCFP

Meek Friend! I have been traversing the steep.   Written at the Hotwells, near Bristol.   Charles Lloyd.   CenSon

Meek house with no style, framed.   Babble.   César Vallejo.   IJHIL, *tr.* by John Knoepfle

Meek Shall Disinherit the Earth,The.   Horace Gregory.   APT-2 *Fr.* Chorus for Survival.

Meek twilight! soften the declining day.   Helen Maria Williams.   CenSon *Fr.* Poems.

Meet me at the St Francis.   Iwan Llwyd.   ATSWP, *tr.* by Robert Minhinnick

Meet Me in St. Louis, Louis.   Andrew B. Sterling.   NAAPv.2

Meet, O Lord, on de milk-white horse,/ An' de nineteen wile in his han'.   Meet, O Lord!   *Unknown.*   SSUS

Meet the Beat of My Heart.   Mack Gordon.   ReLy

Meet the Supremes.   David Trinidad.   SwNoth

Meetin the Conjure Woman.   Gary Lilley.   BtF

Meeting.   George Crabbe.   OBEV

Meeting.   Max Jacob.   YaTCFP, *tr.* by Mary Ann Caws

Meeting.   László Kálnoky.   IQMS, *tr.* by Kenneth McRobbie and Zita McRobbie

Meeting, The: "She'll meet me with the gate thrown wide."   Francis Ledwidge.   IrLP

Meeting, The: "When my friend is away from me, I am depressed."   Kabir.   WED, *tr.* by Robert Bly

Meeting, The.   Louise Bogan.   NoAM

Meeting, The.   José Hierro.   RaW, *tr.* by Rachel Benson

Meeting, The.   Isabel Ecclestone MacKay.   PoBW

Meeting, The.   Katherine Mansfield.   LW

Meeting, The.   Harriet Monroe.   IllVoic

Meeting, The.   Muriel Rukeyser.   MoAmPo

Meeting a Bear.   David Wagoner.   WeW-3

Meeting and Passing.   Robert Frost.   OxBoAm; OxBSo

Meeting at Night.   Robert Browning.   BRP; CABP; FaBoVe; HeIP-4; ITBLP; NAEL-6v2; NAEL-7v2; OBEV; OPOU; OxBEV; SoSe-8; TFi

Meeting Bandits.   Yŏngjae, Monk.   CATKP, *tr.* by Peter H. Lee

Meeting by chance and speaking.   Judas Touch, The.   David Malouf.   BMAP

Meeting Ezra Pound.   Miroslav Holub.   MotU, *tr.* by Stuart Friebert and Dana Hábová

Meeting Gaylen's 5th Grade Class.   Miguel Algarín.   PueRic

Meeting his mouth made it so I had house again.   House, Garden, Madness.   Cate Marvin.   PoDa

Meeting in a Lift.   Vladimir Holan.   PML; StAl, *tr.* by Ian Milner and Jarmila Milner

Meeting is hard. Harder, separation.   Without Title (2).   Li Shang-yin.   ChinPo, *tr.* by Ye Weilian [*or* Yeh Wei-lien *or* Wai-lim Yip]

Meeting Mescalito at Oak Hill Cemetery.   Lorna Dee Cervantes.   PBCAP

Meeting My Former Self.   Norman Cameron.   NePenScot

Meeting my former self in a nostalgia.   Meeting My Former Self.   Norman Cameron.   NePenScot

Meeting of Friends, A.   Phillis Levin.   RA

Meeting of the Bards, The.   Written for an Eisteddford, or Meeting of Welsh Bards, Held in London, 22 May 1822.   Felicia Dorothea Hemans.   RWP *Fr.* Siege of Valencia, The.

Meeting of the Waters, The.   Thomas Moore.   ItP

Meeting Place.   Pauline Hawkesworth.   Prnts

Meeting Point.   Louis MacNeice.   ModIr; NPeEn; PNI

Meeting the Angel.   Susan Aizenberg.   ExTi

Meeting the Animal in Washington Square Park.   Luis J. Rodriguez.   FaoP

Meeting the British.   Paul Muldoon.   EmeKit; NAMCP V.2; NoAM; NoP-4; NoP-5; PNI

Meeting, the Departure, The.   Johann Wolfgang von Goethe.   STV, *tr.* by John Frederick Nims

Meeting the Gulf, hosannas silently below. (LL)   Hart Crane.   GM; MoAmPo; NAAL-5; OxBoAm *Fr.* Bridge, The.

Meeting the Master.   Thomas Gannon.   ViWalt

Meeting the Mountains.   Gary Snyder.   NoAM

Meeting Up with the Picaro.   Patricia Smith.   ICANM

Meeting Walter Benjamin.   Karen Solie.   OpeFie

Meeting when all the world was in the bud.   Loves of the Puppets.   Richard Wilbur.   UpMys

Meeting with Time, slack thing, said I.   Time.   George Herbert.   NAEL-6v1; NAEL-7v1

Meeting-House Hill.   Amy Lowell.   APT-1; ColAP; MoAmPo; TCAPo

Meetings.   Paul Éluard.   AF, *tr.* by Lloyd Alexander

Meets our bouquet of death and turns sharp right.. (LL)   Unseen Fire.   Ralph Nixon Currey.   OBWP; PoWW

Meg Merrilies [*or* Merrilees].   John Keats.   NOxBChV
   (Old Meg.)   ITBLP
   (Old Meg She Was a Gipsy.)   NPBRoP

Megaceph, chosen to serve the State.   Ambrose Bierce.   APN-2 *Fr.* Devil's Dictionary, The.

Mehinaku Girl in Seclusion, A.   Cathy Song.   OpBo

Mehitabel S Extensive Past.   Don Marquis.   TriCat

Mehitabel the cat claims that.   Mehitabel S Extensive Past.   Don Marquis.   TriCat

Mehitabel's Extensive Past.   Don Marquis.   "I had some romantic."   AmWit

Mehitabel's Song.   Don Marquis.   GoPo

Mein Kind, wir waren Kinder.   Heinrich Heine.   OBVE, *tr.* by Elizabeth Barrett Browning

Mek me tell you wha me Mudder do.   Wha Me Mudder Do.   Grace Nichols.   NOxBChV

Mekhmekh flowers.   Brightlines.   *Unknown.*   SonAtl, *tr.* by H. Younde

Melampus' Epitaph.   William Drummond of Hawthornden.   DiBP

Melancholiacs, The.   Mary Ruefle.   AmAlph

Melancholic.   Li Ho.   CrYelRi; ErotSp, *tr.* by Sam Hamill

Melancholic dandy, you weep and cut.   Penserosa, La.   Gig Ryan.   VaPo

Melancholy.   Rubén Darío.   SpanPo, *tr.* by Anita Volland

Melancholy.   John Fletcher.   OBEV *Fr.* Nice Valor, The.

Melancholy.   Hwang Jiwoo.   CAMKP, *tr.* by Young-Jun Lee and Scott Swaner
   Mirror 1.   CAMKP, *tr.* by Young-Jun Lee and Scott Swaner
   Mirror 2.   CAMKP, *tr.* by Young-Jun Lee and Scott Swaner
   Mirror 3.   CAMKP, *tr.* by Young-Jun Lee and Scott Swaner

Melancholy.   David Keller.   UrbNat

Melancholy.   Thomas Middleton.   NOSC

Melancholy day in the second month of autumn, A.   Autumn Day, An.   Sun Ch'o.   CCL1, *tr.* by John Frodsham

Melancholy days are come, the saddest of the year, The.   Death of the Flowers, The.   William Cullen Bryant.   TreFP

Melancholy in the Families.   Pablo Neruda.   ConPit, *tr.* by Clayton Eshleman

Melancholy in the Women's Apartments.   Jiang Zong.   CCL1, *tr.* by John Frodsham

Melancholy inside Families.   Pablo Neruda.   RaBo; WED, *tr.* by Robert Bly and James Wright

Melancholy Lay, A.   Marjory Fleming.   NBLV

Melancholy remembrances and vesperal. (LL)   Church of a Dream, The.   Lionel Pigot Johnson.   CABP; OBMV

Melancholy year is dead with rain, The.   Trumbull Stickney.   APN-2

Melanie.   Nathaniel Parker Willis.   "Calm and lovely paradise, A."   APN-1

Melanin.   J. H. Prynne.   PFTM-2

Melba Street.   Deena November.   IJHIL

Melbourne or the Bush.   Philip Mead.   BMAP

Melbourne, Perth, Darwin, Townsville.   Ode to the Air Traffic Controller.   Joshua Beckman.   LegDan

Melchizedek.   John Henry, Cardinal Newman.   SacPr

Meleager.   Ovid.   NOBRP *Fr.* Metamorphoses.

Melinna herself is re-created: notice the face. Nossis. SaLy, *tr.* by Diane Rayor

Melissa Quits School. Lucile Burt. TWF

Melissias denies her love, but her body screams. Rufinus. HePo, *tr.* by Barbara Hughes Fowler

Mellow as the glory roses. (LL) Gloire de Dijon. D. H. Lawrence. NAMCP V.1; NoAM; WaAnP

Mellow moon hangs golden in the sky, The. October. Henrietta Cordelia Ray. CBWP-3

Mellow on Morphine. Dana Shuster. FaBoWar

Mellow on morphine, he smiles and floats. Mellow on Morphine. Dana Shuster. FaBoWar

Mellow the moonlight to shine is beginning. Spinning-Wheel, The. John Francis Waller. IrV

Mellow year is hasting to its close, The. Hartley Coleridge. CenSon *Fr.* Sonnets to the Seasons.

Melodic Trains. John Ashbery. FaoP; GM; NoP-4

Melodies bring memories. Georgia on My Mind. Stuart Gorrell. ReLy

Melody of Wei City. Wang Wei. CCL1, *tr.* by William Dolby

Melon / How well. Ransetsu. ZenPo, *tr.* by Takashi Ikemoto and Lucien Stryk

Melon / In morning dew. Basho. ZenPo, *tr.* by Takashi Ikemoto and Lucien Stryk

Melon Girl. Mei Yao Ch'en. NDACCP, *tr.* by Kenneth Rexroth

Melon Grower, The. Alice Oswald. MFPA; MoWP

Melrose Abbey. Sir Walter Scott. NPBRoP; OxAEP-2 *Fr.* Lay of the Last Minstrel, The.

Melt me. Amanda Nazario. HeMarv

Melt Twa. James Logie Robertson. EdScPo

Melting her candy on the radiator. Cooking. Ayin Adams. BRtP

Melting icicle, a leaking tap, A. During an Illness. Vladimir Holan. WoPoe, *tr.* by Ian Milner and Jarmila Milner

Melting in the hand, sign of the Big Dipper. Swans. Yoshida Issui. CAoMJL1, *tr.* by Leith Morton

Melting into pure water the snow buddha. Stanford M. Forrester. AmZen

Melting melodious words to lutes of amber. (LL) Upon Julia's Voice. Robert Herrick. NPeEn; SoSe-8

Melting Milk. Bill Berkson. PmAP

Melting snow. Issa. EMJL, *tr.* by Haruo Shirane

Melvin, / the large collie. Happiness. Michael Van Walleghen. VisFro

Members of the Orchestra, The. Kevin Hart. NOBAu

Même si la montagne se consume, même si les suivants s'entretuent. Même si la montagne. Jacques Dupin. YaTCFP

Memento. Stephen Spender. HP

Memento Mori. Billy Collins. EmeKit

Memento of the Hours. Linda Bierds. RoV

Memento on the Departure of a Friend, from Yeh, Last Day of the Second Moon. Chia Tao. CSKM, *tr.* by Mike O'Connor

Mementos, 1. W. D. Snodgrass. MoAmPo; NoP-4; NoP-5; OxBoAm; VCAP

Memling. Roland Mathias. AngWePo

Memo. Leslie Ullman. YaYoPo

Memo About the Green Oranges, A. Carol Rumens. MoWP

Memo: For the Race Orators. Sterling Allen Brown. InGu

Memo on Composition. Hwang Jiwoo. CAMKP, *tr.* by Young-Jun Lee and Scott Swaner

Memo to Auden. Anne Rouse. MFPA; NeBrP

Memo to Us (story). Lionel Fogarty. VaPo

Memo, Who Loved Motorcycles. Luis Miguel Aguilar. PML, *tr.* by Robert Jones

Memo: you have only 16 lifetimes. More than 9 Lives. Bruce Beaver. BMAP

Memoir of the Cosmopolite Who Stayed Home. Ron McFarland. RWB

Memoirs. Aleksandr Semionovich Kushner. ItGoST, *tr.* by Paul Graves and Carol Ueland

Memoirs of a Turcoman Diplomat. Denis Devlin. ModIr

Oteli Asia Palas, Inc. ModIr

Memoirs of a Velvet Urinal. Michael Dransfield. BMAP

Memorabilia. Robert Browning. NAEL-6v2; NAEL-7v2; NoP-4; NoP-5; NPeEn; OxBEV; PoPoPo

Memorabilia. Lexie Dean Robertson. TiP2

Memoranda. William Dickey. YaYoPo

Memoranda for Rosario. Maria Elena Caballero-Robb. ReBoTo

Memorandum. Yunna Petrovna Moritz. TCRusP, *tr.* by Daniel Weissbort

Memorandum. Nanao Sakaki. AtGh

Memorandum of Martha Moulsworth Widdowe, The. Martha Dorsett Prynne. EMWP

Memorandum of Martha Moulsworth, Widow, The. Martha Moulsworth. NAEL-7v1

Memoria echa sus cartas, La. Espectros. Jorge Fernández Granados. RMCMP

Memoriae Matris Sacrum. George Herbert.
"Ah Mater, quo te deplorem fonte? Dolores." PBRV

Memoriae Positum R. G. Shaw. James Russell Lowell. CBCWP

Memorial. Marjorie Agosin. TANSG, *tr.* by Celeste Kostopulos-Cooperman

Memorial. Mihály Babits. IQMS, *tr.* by Peter Zollman

Memorial 1: "If you come as softly." Audre Lorde. WaAnP

Memorial: "Burnt sugar skeletons." Charmaine A. Gill. BtF

Memorial: "He who knew to serve as one of the oridnary soldiers." Uri Zvi Greenberg. NRoS, *tr.* by Esther Raizen

Memorial: "If we do not lift quickly the dead bodies from the beaches." William Bronk. PWW2

Memorial Candle. Yelena Shwarts. CRWP, *tr.* by Stephanie Sandler

Memorial Day. Michael Anania. NoAM

Memorial Day. Clara Ann Thompson. CBWP-2

Memorial Day, 1969. T. Carmi. NRoS, *tr.* by Esther Raizen

Memorial Day 1950. Frank O'Hara. OxBoAm

Memorial Drive. Willie Abraham Howard Jr. BtF

Memorial for the City. W. H. Auden.
"Alone in a room Pope Gregory whispered his name." SacPr

Memorial for Trane. Sam Greenlee. SeSe

Memorial Fountain, The. Roy Fisher. NPeEn

Memorial of Mary, The. Felicia Dorothea Hemans. CenSon

Memorial on the Slain at Chickamauga. Herman Melville. CBCWP

Memorial Pillar, The. Felicia Dorothea Hemans. RWP

Memorial Rain. Archibald MacLeish. AmWaPo; MoAmPo; OBWP

Memorial Service. Ayin Tur-Malka. NRoS, *tr.* by Esther Raizen

Memorial Service for the Invasion Beach Where the Vacation in the Flesh Is Over. Alan Dugan. AF; PWW2

Memorial Tablet. Siegfried Sassoon. PoWW

Memorial: "There had to be a way of making a building talk." Yvonne Cullen. NIrP

Memorial to D. C.. Edna St. Vincent Millay.
Elegy. APT-1; InoFa; MoAmPo

Memorial to Triangle Fire Victims. Morris Jacob Rosenfeld. NAAPv.2, *tr.* by Leon Stein

Memorial Verses. Matthew Arnold. CABP; NAEL-6v2; NAEL-7v2

Memorial Wreath. Dudley Randall. CBCWP

Memorials of a Tour in Italy, 1837. William Wordsworth.
(Worm's Life Not Everything, A.) STuOW

Memorials of a Tour of the Continent; 1820. William Wordsworth.
Column Intended by Buonaparte for a Triumphal Edifice in Milan, Now Lying by the Way-Side in the Simplon Pass, The. OxBSo
Hymn for the Boatmen, as They Approach the Rapids under the Castle of Heidelberg. SacPr

Memorials: "Walt Whitman I lay on the grass today." Suzanne Gardinier. ViWalt

Memories. Charles Bernstein. BodElec

Memories: "My name is Lila." Sishtla Uma-Maheswara Rao. HotL, *tr.* by V. Narayana Rao

Memories of a Lost War. Louis Simpson. AmWaPo; OBWP; PWW2

Memories of a Summer Night. Endre Ady. IQMS, *tr.* by Peter Zollman

Memories of Chinatown. Roy McFadden.
Bigamy. PNI

Memories of Horses. Rolf Jacobsen. WED, *tr.* by Robert Bly

Memories of Italy (Broken Sestina). John Ash. NeBrP

Memories of Marriage. Enrique Lihn. TCLAP, *tr.* by John Felstiner

Memories of Mudland-Meadow. István Sinka. IQMS, *tr.* by Adam Makkai

Memories of My Father. Galway Kinnell.
"When I come back to my father's house,.." RaBo

Memories of past struggles were expelled by fear. Catius As Conius Silius Italicus. RomPo *Fr.* Punica, The.

Memories of President Lincoln. Walt Whitman.
Hush'd be the Camps To-Day. SAmP
"O Captain! my Captain! our fearful trip is done." AmWaPo; APN-1; BRP; CBCWP; ChAP; HHAm; MakPoe; MoAmPo; PCW; SAmP; TCAPo; TFi
When Lilacs Last in the Dooryard Bloom'd. APN-1; CBCWP; ColAP; InoFa; MoAmPo; NAAL-3; NAAL-5; NAAPv.1; NAMCP V.1; NCAP; NIL-7; NoP-4; NoP-5; OxBoAm; PCW; PoPoPo; SAmP; TCAPo; TFi; WaAnP
"And I saw askant the armies." FaBoWar

Memories of St. George's Caye. John Rozel Cuthbert. OWABP

Memories of the Day I Gave Birth to a Daughter. Kim Hyesun. EcSo, *tr.* by Youngju Ryu

Memories of West Street and Lepke. Robert Lowell. AF; AmWaPo; CAP-8; EmeKit; ItP; NAAL-5; NAMCP V.2; NoAM; OxBoAm; PWW2; VCAP

Memories of You. Andy Razaf. ReLy

Memories, The. Storing Memories. Belinda Zubicueta Carmona. TANSG, *tr.* by Celeste Kostopulos-Cooperman

Memorised: the curl of your back, your face, an open book. (LL) Tonight of Yesterday. Vona Groarke. NIrP; StAl

Memorium. Ed Robeson. Eno

Memorization. Adisa Vera Beatty. FuFl

Memorizing your face. Ray McNiece. AmZen

Memory. Thomas Bailey Aldrich. TCAPo

Memory. Margaret Walker Alexander. GT

Memory. William Browne. OBEV *Fr.* Britannia's Pastorals.

Memory. Robert Burns. MoASP

Memory. Hayden Carruth. GoPo

Memory. Roque Dalton. BLPSL, *tr.* by Rene de Costa, Rigas Kappatos and Eleni Paidoussi

Memory. Babette Deutsch. PoA 2002

Memory. Ralph Waldo Emerson. APN-1; TCAPo *Fr.* Quatrains.

Memory. Federico García Lorca. PFTM-1 *Fr.* Night (Suite for Piano and Poet's Voice).

Memory. Marin Georgiev.
    2. CSCBP, *tr.* by Georgi Belev and Lisa Sapinkopf
    5. CSCBP, *tr.* by Georgi Belev and Lisa Sapinkopf
    6. CSCBP, *tr.* by Georgi Belev and Lisa Sapinkopf
    7. CSCBP, *tr.* by Georgi Belev and Lisa Sapinkopf

Memory. Oliver Goldsmith. OBEV

Memory: "I hated the Road Runner." Bob Hicok. SUP

Memory. Walter Savage Landor. NPeEn

Memory. Edward Prosser Rhys. *tr.* by Martin Davis
    "Our tight knot! Gentle boy with golden hair." BBMWP, *tr.* by Martin Davis

Memory 1. George Seferis. PoetW, *tr.* by Edmund Keeley and Philip Sherrard

Memory, A. Marceline Desbordes-Valmore. WoPoe, *tr.* by Louis Simpson

Memory, A. Heinrich Heine. WoPoe, *tr.* by Francis C. Golffing

Memory, A. Adah Isaacs Menken. CBWP-1; NAAPv.1; ViWPN

Memory, A. Yi Chŏngbo. CATKP; WoPoe, *tr.* by Kevin O'Rourke

Memory, The. Jane Mead. LaCa

Memory At Last. Wisława Szymborska. PoSu, *tr.* by Magnus F. Krynski

Memory at last has what it sought. Memory At Last. Wisława Szymborska. PoSu, *tr.* by Magnus F. Krynski

Memory cannot make your song everlasting. Ars Poetica. Sándor Weöres. IQMS, *tr.* by Edwin Morgan

Memory, flowering prison. Prison, The. Maria Luisa Spaziani. CItWP, *tr.* by Cinzia Sartini Blum and Lara Trubowitz

Memory from Childhood. Antonio Machado Ruiz. RaW; WED, *tr.* by Robert Bly

Memory Gardens. Robert Creeley. FTOS

Memory hasn't a chord of what the family lost. Stones Speak of an Earthless Sky. Duane Niatum. PoCoUp

Memory, hither come. Song. William Blake. NAEL-6v2

Memory in sea-green with sea-weed grain. Oracle of the Drowned, The. Douglas Oliver. Oth

Memory is as narrow. Angel's Flight. Maxine Scates. PBCAP

Memory is the land standing still. Photograph from Berlin. Silvia Curbelo. CFP

Memory is what has died. Past Perfect. Linda Gregg. BodElec

Memory Lapse. Judith Strasser. CFP

Memory lifts her smoky mirror: 1943. Adrienne Rich. NoP-4; NoP-5 *Fr.* Eastern War Time.

Memory, like a piece of beautiful and imprecise canvas. Memorial. Marjorie Agosin. TANSG, *tr.* by Celeste Kostopulos-Cooperman

Memory of a Dream From the Year 1963. Tadeusz Rózewicz. PoSu

Memory of a Victory. Keith Wilson. AmWaPo

Memory of Bathurst Street. Raymond Souster. BrAP

Memory of Brother Michael. Patrick Kavanagh. HarvBoo

Memory of childhood, of stooping, The. For the Dead. Kevin Prufer. AmPoNex

Memory of Elena, The. Carolyn Forché. LoL; NAMCP V.2; NoAM

Memory of Holland. Hendrik Marsman. TuT, *tr.* by Michael Longley

Memory of love's refrain, The. (LL) Star Dust. Mitchell Parish. NAAPv.2; ReLy

Memory of my dead, black hole through everything / gaping on the Sea of Vertigos. Persephone That Is to Say Double Issue. René Daumal. PFTM-1

Memory of my father is wrapped up in, The. My Father. Yehuda Amichai. BeAl; PtR, *tr.* by Azila Talit Reisenberger

Memory of My Private Childhood. Eunice Odio. TCLAP, *tr.* by Suzanne Jill Levine

Memory of New England, The. Donald Revell. RWB

Memory of Quiet. Rosalie Moore. APT-2

Memory of Sunday. Mairtin O Direain. ModIr, *tr.* by Patrick Crotty

Memory of the Graves. Ko Ŭn. CAMKP, *tr.* by David R. McCann

Memory of the past grows paler with each day. A. Velichansky. TCRusP, *tr.* by Daniel Weissbort

Memory of the War, A. Howard Nemerov. PWW2

Memory of Underdevelopment. No Hyegyông. EcSo, *tr.* by Ann Y. Choi

Memory of Wilmington. Galway Kinnell. OPRER

Memory of Wings. Jabari Asim. BtF

Memory plays its cards. Specters. Jorge Fernández Granados. RMCMP, *tr.* by John Oliver Simon

Memory says: Want to do right? Don't count on me. Adrienne Rich. TaR *Fr.* Eastern War Time.

Memory Sire, The. Barney Bush. HATNAP

Memory Span of a Goldfish Is Three Seconds, The. Traci Paris. ICANM

Memory Table 1, The. Christopher Dewdney. OpeFie

Memory, the cat. Elective Affinities. Jonathan Cott. AHA

Memory 2. George Seferis. PoetW, *tr.* by Edmund Keeley and Philip Sherrard

Memory Waves. Quo Vadis Gex-Breaux. FuFl

Memory's branch quivers. Postcard from Trakl. John Yau. OpBo

Memory's Usefulness. Maria Luisa Spaziani. CItWP, *tr.* by Cinzia Sartini Blum and Lara Trubowitz

Memory's Wedge. Ray DiPalma. PmAP

Memphian mummy, that from age to age, The. Robert Pollok. STuOW *Fr.* Course of Time, The.

Memphis Blues. Sterling Allen Brown. APT-2; InGu; NAMCP V.1

Memres of Alfred Stoker. Christopher Reid.
    "Firs / born Xmas day." FaBoVe

Mem'ries light the corners of my mind. Way We Were, The. Alan Bergman and Marilyn Bergman. ReLy

Men. Dorothy Parker. APT-1

Men. William Stafford. PWW2

Men. Dora Teitelboim. Prolet, *tr.* by Amelia Glaser

Men, The. E. Ethelbert Miller. UnSA

Men, a word of wisdom. Give. Bernard [*or* Bernart] de Ventadour *or* Ventadorn. STV

Men and beasts of the zodiac, The. Winter Dawn. Tu Fu [*or* Du Fu]. BLT, *tr.* by Kenneth Rexroth

Men and Birth: the Unexplainable. Haki R. Madhubuti. RaBo

Men and their mournful romanticisms. Romantic. Margaret Atwood. SweBea

Men and Women. Frederick Seidel. BeAl

Men and Women Have Meaning Only as Man and Woman. Joan Murray. OxBoAm; YaYoPo

Men are drawn to my ass by. Being Aware. Dennis Cooper. PmAP

Men are running across a field. Letter. Mark Strand. NoAM

Men are what they are, and what they do. Intimate Parnassus. Patrick Kavanagh. MoBrPo

Men are willing to observe. Watching "Dark Circle." Denise Levertov. AtGh; UpMys

Men ask the way to Cold Mountain. Way to Cold Mountain, The. Han-shan (Cold Mountain). CCL1; NDACCP, *tr.* by Gary Snyder

Men at Forty. Donald Justice. CAP-8; EMP; InGu; ItP; NAMCP V.2; NoAM; NoP-4; NoP-5; OxBoAm; VCAP

Men at My Father's Funeral. William Matthews. CAP-8

Men at Work. Richard Tipping. NOBAu

Men call you fair [*or* fayre], and you do[e] credit it. Edmund Spenser. NoP-4; NoP-5 *Fr.* Amoretti.

Men choose a crystal goblet filled with wine. God's Ways, Not Our Ways. Henrietta Cordelia Ray. CBWP-3

Men claim the easiest spots. Fishing the White Water. Audre Lorde. GT

Men clothe him with their praise. (LL) West Country, The. Alice Cary. APN-2; SWaP

Men duly understand the river of life. Poem of Unrest, A. John Ashbery. OxBoAm; PoA 2002

Men Fade Like Rocks. Walter James Turner. OBMV

Men flirt in the silvered mirror, eyelids, shadow-. Other Side, The. Minnie Bruce Pratt. WiU

Men Folks ob Today, De. Maggie Pogue Johnson. CBWP-4

Men From the Boys. Kate Clanchy. EdScPo

Men gathered and came up with domination. It Will Be a New World. Ko Chŏnghûi. EcSo, *tr.* by Catherine J. Kim

Men gave it different names: there were many words. Letter to the Survivors. Charles E. Butler. YaYoPo

Men go to women mutely for their peace. Everyday Alchemy. Genevieve Taggard. APT-2; NAAPv.2

Men grew sae cauld, maids sae unkind. Blind Boy's Pranks, The. William Thom. OBEV

Men grow with all that grows. Pablo Neruda. GifTon, *tr.* by William O'Daly

Men have made them gods of love. Pain. George Russell. MoBrPo

Men heard this roar of parleying starlings, saw. February Afternoon. Edward Thomas. NAMCP V.1; NoAM; PoWW

Men Improve with the Years. William Butler Yeats. OxAEP-2

Men in overalls the same color as earth rise from a ditch. Outskirts. Tomas Tranströmer. BLT, *tr. by* Robert Bly

Men in the Hoboken Bar, the. Jonathan Holden. MAAN

Men in the market pride themselves on their knowledge and craft, The. Ch'en Tzu-ang. ColAnChi *Fr.* Poems of Reflection on the Vicissitudes of Life.

Men keep searching the room, The. Fire in Early Morning. Christiane Jacox Kyle. YaYoPo

Men lean toward the wood. Lynching and Burning. Primus St. John. ISC; PoChi

Men leave the car, The. Lorine Niedecker. APT-2

Men led me to him, blindfold and alone. (LL) Rudyard Kipling. HarvBoo; InoFa; NPeEn; WoPoe *Fr.* Epitaphs of the War [1914–1918].

Men Loved Wholly Beyond Wisdom. Louise Bogan. APT-2; ColAP; OxBoAm

Men Made out of Words. Wallace Stevens. APT-1

Men May Talk of Country-Christmasses. Philip Massinger. OBCP

Men must love your lips. Prelude to a Kiss. Tracie Morris. BtF

Men / occupying bedrooms and unemployment lines, on corners, in bars, The. Empty Warriors. Haki R. Madhubuti. RaBo

Men of Dawn, The. Efraín Huerta. TCLAP, *tr. by* Todd Dampier

Men of England, wherefore plough. Song to the Men of England. Percy Bysshe Shelley. CABP; NAEL-6v2; NAEL-7v2; RSaN

Men of old never saw me, The. Yi Hwang. CATKP *Fr.* Twelve Songs of Tosan.

Men of Old, The. Richard Monckton, 1st Baron Houghton Milnes. OBEV; TreFP

Men of science are a brilliant clan, The. Too Close for Comfort. Jerry Bock, Larry Holofcener and George David Weiss. ReLy

Men of Terry Street. Douglas Dunn. WaAnP

Men of the marketplace boast their cunning. Chen Zi'ang. CCL1,

Men of thought! be up, and stirring. Clear the Way. Charles MacKay. TreFP

Men of valor, The. Yamabe no Akahito. TAL *Fr.* Manyo Shu, Part 2 of 4.

Men of wealthy Sestos, every year, The. Christopher Marlowe. AEP *Fr.* Hero and Leander.

Men on Fire. Kriapur (Kristianto Agus Purnomo). PML, *tr. by* Harry Aveling

Men on the Rocks, The. Adam Drinan. EdScPo

Men Only Pretend. *Unknown.* WaAnP

Men prefer an island. Other. Dorothy Livesay. NIL-7

Men rigged my chamfered oak. William Scammell. NewEx

Men Roofing. Eamon Grennan. PBCIP

Men saw the blush and called it Dawn. (LL) Dawn: "Angel, robed in spotless white, An." Paul Laurence Dunbar. NAAPv.1; OxBoAm

Men say they know many things. Henry David Thoreau. NAAL-3

Men seldom make passes. News Item. Dorothy Parker. AmWit; APT-1; NALW; OxBoAm

Men sleep. The cassia blossoms fall. Bird and Waterfall Music. Wang Wei. NDACCP, *tr. by* Kenneth Rexroth

Men sleep / with loose hands that by day are fists. Prayer for Men and Children. Linda Hogan. AtGh

Men, some to bus'ness, some to pleasure take. Alexander Pope. NPeEn; OBSV; OxBEV *Fr.* Epistle [II,] to a Lady[: Of the Characters of Women].

Men speak lightly of frustration. Cormorant. Lucien Stryk. IllVoic

Men stare at me more than at women. William Oxley. NewEx

Men start digging in the ground. Missing in Action. Yusef Komunyakaa. InGu

Men still make steel in the hellish mill. Why We Are Forgiven. Bruce Weigl. BodElec

Men swell the current,—many of them wear. Mary E. Tucker. SWaP

Men Talk. Stephen P. Dunn. NIP-4

Men talking, The. Eclogue. George Oppen. APT-2; FTOS

Men that are safe, and sure, in all they do[e]. Epistle Answering to One That Asked to Be Sealed of the Tribe of Ben, An. Ben Jonson. BASC

Men That Once Were, The. Owen Gruffydd.

"Old, old/ To live on, wretched to behold." OBWVE

Men that worked for England, The. Elegy in a Country Churchyard. G. K. Chesterton. FaBoWar; MoBrPo; OBWP

Men There Were Then, The. Howard White. PML

Men Together. Richard Murray Vaughan. Coast

Men truck I-45 up and down Oklahoma. White Roses. David Biespiel. AmPoNex

Men turn to rocks. Answer to Herrick, An. Harry Gilonis. Oth

Men! / u shouldn't listen 2 your selfish heart. Why Must U Be Unfaithful (4 Women). Tupac Shakur. FTtHH

Men went to Catraeth, keen their war-band. Aneirin. OBWVE *Fr.* Gododdin, The.

Men went to Catraeth. The luxury liner. Elegy for the Welsh Dead, in the Falkland Islands, 1982. Anthony Conran. TCAWP

Men went to Gododdin, laughter-loving. Aneirin. OBWP *Fr.* Gododdin, The.

Men were my buttresses, my castellated towers. Grands Seigneurs, Les. Dorothy Molloy. BeAl

Men / who cannot eat dried oats, who. Two Princes, The. Michael Stillman. IaFF

Men Who Come Behind, The. Henry Lawson. NOBAu

Men Who Killed My Brother, The. Edward Bartók-Baratta. LiTh

Men Who March Away. Thomas Hardy. OBWP; PoWW

Men Who Ride for Fun, The. Walter G. Kendall. ArBi

Men with much toil, and time, and pain. Female Wits, The: A Song by a Lady of Quality. *Unknown.* NOSC

Men with picked voices chant the names. Overture to a Dance of Locomotives. William Carlos Williams. GM

Men with Small Heads. Thomas Lux. SUP

Men with the heads of eagles. Margaret Atwood. NAMCP V.2; NoAM *Fr.* Circe / Mud Poems.

Men without rank, excrement spatulas. Guchu. ZenPo, *tr. by* Takashi Ikemoto and Lucien Stryk

Men wore human skins, The. Skin. Linda Hogan. ReEnLa

Men working on the building going up here have got these great, The. Sanctity, The. C. K. Williams. BodElec

Men would often go hunting rabbits, The. Hunting Rabbits. Peter Skrzynecki. BMAP

Menace of the Flower, The. Alfonso Reyes. TCLAP, *tr. by* Samuel Beckett

Ménage à Trois. Gwyneth Lewis. MoWP

Ménage à Trois. Howard Moss. VCAP

Menage, The. Carl Rakosi. FTOS

Menaka says, Hey listen, Mountain King. Śāradā Bhāndārī. SinGod, *tr. by* Rachel Fell McDermott

Menaphon. Robert Greene.

(Samela.) OBEV

(Sephestia's Lullaby.) OBEV

Sephestia's Song to Her Child[e]. NoSic; OxAEP-1

Mend itself. (LL) At Luca Signorelli's Resurrection of the Body. Jorie Graham. NAMCP V.2; NoP-5

Mend your fishing line and rod. Yun Sŏndo. CATKP *Fr.* Angler's Calendar, The.

Mendacity. Alfred Edgar Coppard. OBMV

Mendigo, El. Francisco Brines. RaW

Mending. Ingrid de Kok. TSAP

Mending. Joe Denham. OpeFie

Mending Sump. Kenneth Koch. NAMCP V.2; NoAM; VisFro

Mending Wall. Robert Frost. APT-1; BrAP; BRP; ChAP; ClHu; CtM; EMP; HarvBoo; HelP-4; ITBLP; MoAmPo; NAAL-5; NAAPv.2; NAMCP V.1; NoAM; NoP-4; NoP-5; OxBoAm; PoPoPo; RaF; SAmP; SoSe-8; TCAPo; TFi; WeW-3

Mendocino Memory. June Jordan. ASA

Mendocino Rose. Garrett Kaoru Hongo. WeW-3

Mene Tekel. Frigyes Karinthy. IQMS, *tr. by* Aaron Kramer

Menelaus. Derek Walcott. BrAP

Meng Jiangnü at the Long Wall. *Unknown.* CCL1, *tr. by* Arthur Waley

Meng Jung, Gainfully Unemployed. Chia Tao. CSKM, *tr. by* Mike O'Connor

Meng: To a Man. *Unknown.* CCL1, *tr. by* H. A. Giles

Mengele Shitting. Jason Sommer. NAPBL

Menial twilight sweeps the storefronts along Lexington. Claudette Colvin Goes to Work. Rita Dove. FuFl; NAMCP V.2

Mennonite Farm Wife. Janet Kauffman. ACAMVP

Mennonite Funeral in the Shenandoah Valley. Jane Rohrer. ACAMVP

Mennonites. Julia Kasdorf. ACAMVP; NeAmPo; PBCAP

Men's fascination with Nintendo is. Nintendo. Treasure Williams. BRtP

Men's Harbour, The. John Burnside. PML

Men's hearts love gold and jade;. Lodging with the Old Man of the Stream. Po Chü-i. BLT, *tr. by* Arthur Waley

Men's hearts, with mirth in view. (LL) *Unknown.* NAEL-6v1; NAEL-7v1; NAWM-7v1 *Fr.* Sir Gawain and the Green Knight [Marie Borroff Translation].

Men's Room in the College Chapel, The. W. D. Snodgrass. MoAmPo

Men's Talk. Len Roberts. PML

Men's Vices. Joyce Mansour. NAWM-7v2, *tr. by* Serge Gavronsky

Men's vices. Men's Vices. Joyce Mansour. NAWM-7v2, *tr. by* Serge Gavronsky

Menses. Edna St. Vincent Millay. APT-1; BrAP; RACG

Menstrual Irregularities. Pak Sŏwŏn. EcSo, *tr. by* Julie C. Park

Mental Cases. Wilfred Owen. NAMCP V.1; NoAM

Mental Hospital Sitting-Room, A. Elizabeth Jennings. MoWP

Mental Terrorism. Kevin Powell. InTrad

Mental Traveller, The. William Blake. ChIV-2; NAEL-6v2; WoPoe

Mental Traveller's Landfall, The. Chris Wallace-Crabbe. BMAP

Mentem Mortalia Tangunt. John Close. STuOW *Fr.* In Respectful Memory of Mr. Yarker.

Mentioning of Souls. Gerald Stern. PLBUT

Mentor. Timothy Murphy. PoDa

Mentors. Gwendolyn Brooks. ESEAA

Ments of a rift in a crusted so as Fairy. Clark Coolidge. AHA

Menus. Blaise Cendrars. GPTC, *tr. by* Ron Padgett

Me—of Me? (LL) Me from Myself—to banish. Emily Dickinson. NALW; TCAPo; TRP

Meop. Albert Goldbarth. IllVoic

Merce of Egypt. Charles Olson. APT-2; NoP-4; NoP-5

Mercenary Soldier, The. *Unknown.*
  "No money yet, why then let's terrify with swords." FaBoWar

Merchant of Death. Ramabai Espinet. WaCA

Merchant of Venice, The. William Shakespeare.
  Casket Song, A. NoSic; TFi
  "Go, draw aside the curtain, and discover." OxAEP-1
  "How sweet the moonlight sleeps upon this bank!" TreFP
  "In sooth, I know not why I am so sad." OxAEP-1
  (Love.) OBEV
  Moonlight. OxAEP-1
  (Tell Me Where Is Fancy Bred.) NAEL-6v1
  "Then must the Jew be mercifull." OxBEV

Merchant, to secure his treasure, The. Ode, An. Matthew Prior. NoP-4; NoP-5; NPeEn

Merchant's Daughter. Thomas Meyer. AnSo

Merchants from Cathay. William Rose Benét. MoAmPo

Merchant's Joy, The. Chang Yü. ColAnChi, *tr. by* Jonathan Chaves

Merchant's Joy, The [*with music*]. Lu Yu. ColAnChi, *tr. by* Burton Watson

Merci Bien, Monsieur. Carlota Caulfield. TANSG, *tr. by* Chris Allen

Mercian Hymns. Geoffrey Hill.
  "And it seemed, while we waited, he began to walk to- / wards us." NAEL-7v2; NAMCP V.2; NoAM; NoP-4
  "Brooding on the eightieth letter of *Fors Clavigera*." NAMCP V.2
  "Clash of salutation. As keels thrust into shingle." NAMCP V.2; NoAM; NoP-4
  "Cohorts of charabancs fanfared Offa's province and his concern, negotiating the by-ways from Teme to Trent. Their windshields dripped butterflies. Stranded on hilltops they signalled with plumes of steam. Twilight menaced the land." OxBEV
  "Coins handsome as Nero's; of good substance and." NAMCP V.2; NoAM
  "Gasholders, russet among fields. Milldams, marpools." NAEL-7v2; NAMCP V.2; NoAM; NoP-4; NoP-5; NPeEn
  "He adored the desk, its brown-oak inlaid with ebony." NAMCP V.2; NoAM; NoP-4
  "I was invested in mother-earth, the crypt of roots." NAMCP V.2; NoAM
  "King of the perennial holly-groves, the riven sandstone." NAMCP V.2; NoAM; NPeEn; WoPoe
  "Mad are predators, The. Too often lately they harbour." NoP-4; NoP-5
  "Not strangeness, but strange likeness. Obstinate." NAMCP V.2; NoAM; WoPoe
  "'Now when King Offa was alive and dead', they were." NPeEn
  "Pet-name, a common name, A. Best-selling brand, curt." NAMCP V.2; NoAM; WoPoe
  "Princes of Mercia were badger and raven, The. Thrall." NAEL-6v2; NAEL-7v2; NAMCP V.2; NoAM; NoP-4; NoP-5; NPeEn; WoPoe
  "Processes of generation; deeds of settlement." NAEL-7v2; NoP-4
  "So much for the elves' wergild, the true governance." NAMCP V.2; NoAM; WoPoe
  "Strange church smelled a bit 'high,' of censers, The." EmeKit
  "Their spades grafted through the variably-resistant soil." EmeKit

Merciful God, / Choose another people. Merciful God. Kadya Molodovsky. PoCho, *tr. by* Kathryn Hellerstein

Merciful Shore, The. Maria Luisa Spaziani. NeIt, *tr. by* Beverly Allen

Merciless Beauty. Geoffrey Chaucer. NAEL-6v1 *Fr.* Merciles[s] Beaute [*or* Beautée *or* Beauty].

Mercury's Song [to Phaedra]. John Dryden. NOSC

Mercury-vapor yard light on a pole, The. Wilson County Farmer, A. James Applewhite. LPSFW

Mercy. David Baker. Vesp

Mercy. Andrew Lansdown. NOBAu

Mercy. Roddy Lumsden. NeBl

Mercy. *Unknown.* SacPr

Mercy Flight. Anselm Berrigan. HeMarv

Mercy is hendest where sinne is mest. Mercy. *Unknown.* SacPr

Mercy is whiter than laundry. Angels in Winter. Nancy Willard. ColAP

Mercy o' Gode. Pittendrigh Macgillivray. EdScPo

Mercy on me spirit. David Brendon Hopes. UpMys *Fr.* Song of Mercies, A.

Mercy Replies to Justice. Giles, the Younger Fletcher. SacPr *Fr.* Christ's Victory and Triumph.

Mercy Tempering Justice. Francis Quarles. SacPr

Mercy's Reward. Sir Edwin Arnold. DiBP

Mere chance that the patterned lute has fifty strings. Patterned Lute, The. Li Shang-yin. CCL1, *tr. by* A. C. Graham

Mere child dog-eared, A. Old Snapshot. Dimitris Tsaloumas. PML

Mere Pleasure of Flying, The. Jane Duran. MFPA

Merely the landscape of a vanished whim. Versailles. Adrienne Rich. OBGa

Merely to know. On the Spirit of the Heart as Moon-Disk. Kojijū. WoPoe; WPoS, *tr. by* Edwin A. Cranston

Merengue. Mary Ruefle. FaoP

'Mergency Man, The. John Millington Synge. NPeEn

'Mericn Fst Fd. Thom Tammaro. ReTh

Meridian. Amy Clampitt. NAMCP V.2; NIL-7

Meridian. Diana Hartog. NLPA *Fr.* Oasis.

Meridian Hill Terrace. Wendy S. Walters. BtF

Merioneth [*with music*]. John Machreth Rees. OBWVE, *tr. by* Kenneth Hurlstone Jackson

Merits of Writers. Ferenc Kazinczy. IQMS, *tr. by* Watson Kirkconnell

Merk. Eileen Myles. WiU

Merl. Jean Toomer. GT

Merle; Uncle Seagram. Gwendolyn Brooks. ESEAA *Fr.* Children Going Home.

Merlin. Thomas Caldecot Chubb. YaYoPo

Merlín. Gerardo Deniz. RMCMP

Merlin. Gerardo Deniz. RMCMP, *tr. by* Mónica de la Torre

Merlin. Ralph Waldo Emerson. APN-1; NAAL-3
  Merlin I. NAAPv.1; NCAP
  Merlin II. NAAPv.1

Merlin. Geoffrey Hill. TRP

Merlin [*with music*]. Edwin Muir. EdScPo; NePenScot

Merlin I. Ralph Waldo Emerson. NAAPv.1; NCAP *Fr.* Merlin.

Merlin II. Ralph Waldo Emerson. NAAPv.1 *Fr.* Merlin.

Merlin and the Snake's Egg. Leslie Norris. OBSP

Merlin, they say, an English Prophet borne. Fulke, 1st Baron Brooke Greville. WoPoe *Fr.* Caelica.

Merlins Prophecy. William Blake. WoPoe

Mermaid, The. Aliyah Abdul-Salaam. AnVo, *tr. by* Mohamed Enani

Mermaid, The. Ogden Nash. Spl

Mermaid dives deep, A. Mermaid Knows, A. Irene Young. HW

Mermaid Knows, A. Irene Young. HW

Mermaid of Palmares. Harryette Mullen. RD

Mermaid Tank, The. Stephen Knight. NeBl; StAl

Mermaidens' Vesper-Hymn, The. George Darley. NAEL-6v2; NPeEn *Fr.* Syren Songs.

Mermaids Explained. Christopher Reid. NeBrP

Mermaid's / privacy, The. (LL) Necromance. Rae Armantrout. FTOS; PmAP

Mermaid's Song. James C. McCullagh. PoCoUp

Merman, The. Alfred Tennyson. UV

Merops. Ralph Waldo Emerson. APN-1

Merrily the ospreys cry. *Unknown.* CCL1 *Fr.* Guan-ju.

Merrow Down. Rudyard Kipling. NOxBChV *Fr.* Just-So Stories.

MERRY CHR / YSANTHEMUM. (LL) Computer's First Christmas Card, The. Edwin Morgan. NOxBChV; OxBEV

Merry Country Lad, The. Nicholas Breton. NoSic *Fr.* Passionate Shepherd, The.

Merry Cuckoo, The. Edmund Spenser. OWoS

Merry Cuckow, messenger of Spring, The. Merry Cuckoo, The. Edmund Spenser. OWoS

Merry mate amongst the rest, of cloisterers thus told, A. William Warner. NoSic *Fr.* Albion's England.

Merry, merry bells of Yule, The. (LL) Alfred Tennyson. NAEL-6v2; NAEL-7v2; NAWM-7v2; RSR; SoSe-8 *Fr.* In Memoriam A. H. H.

Merry month of May, sunny skies of blue. I've Got the World on a String. Ted Koehler. ReLy

Merry [*or* Merrie] world did on a day, The. Quip, The. George Herbert. BASC; NOSC; OxAEP-1; OxBEV

Merry [*or* Mirry] Margaret. John Skelton. NAEL-6v1; NBLV; NoP-4; NoP-5; NoSic; OBEV; OxBEV; TFi; WaAnP *Fr.* Garland [*or* Garlande *or* Garlands] of Laurel[l], The.

Merry Truce, The. Nathaniel Southgate Shaler. PCW

Merry-Go-Round. Langston Hughes. AmFaPo; BLPJKO; SAmP

Merry-go-round, The. Rainer Maria Rilke. WeW-3, *tr. by* C. F. MacIntyre

Merthe of alle this londe, The. *Unknown.* NPeEn

Merthyr. Glyn Jones. AngWePo

Mertill though my heart should break. To Mertill Who Desired Her to Speak to Clorinda of His Love. Elizabeth Taylor. EMWP

Meru. William Butler Yeats. GSo; NAMCP V.1; NoAM; OxBSo; PoPoPo

Mervell nothyng, Joseph, that Mary be with chyld. *Unknown.* SacPr

Mervyn Clyde Witherup. William Witherup. AtGh

Mes belles lectrices. Corset Mystère, Le. André Breton. YaTCFP

Mes bêtes de la nuit qui venaient boire à la surface. Création de soi, La. André Frénaud. YaTCFP

Mes dents ont arraché des cubes de rire, des sorties d'école de rire. Des fêtes. Annie Le Brun. YaTCFP

Mes statues. Henri Michaux. YaTCFP

Mesa Blanca. Víctor Hernández Cruz. PFTM-2

Mésalliance, A. May Probyn. NPeEn

Mescaline. Allen Ginsberg. PFTM-2

Meseemeth I heard cry and groan. Complaint of the Fair Armoress [*or* Armouress], The. François Villon. OBVE, *tr. by* Algernon Charles Swinburne

Meshes. Elizabeth Robinson. AmPoNex

Mesmeric hunter of the unseen. General Strike. Nancy Joyce Peters. SurWo

Mesopotamia. Rudyard Kipling. HarvBoo; PoWW

(Mesopotamia 1917.) FaBoWar

Mesopotamia 1917. Rudyard Kipling. *See* Mesopotamia.

Mesquite. Robert A. Fink. TiP2

Mess Boy, The. Sydney Wilmer. CAGL

Mess Deck. Alan Ross. FaBoWar; PoWW

Mess With It. Linda France. MFPA

Message. Rosario Ferré. TANSG

Message. Lola Haskins. PfS

Message, The. Mathilde Blind. ViWPN

Message, The. Michael Heffernan. RACG

Message, The. Jeffrey Hillard. AtGh

Message, The. Jacques Prévert. WeW-3, *tr. by* John Frederick Nims

Message About the Times. Remco Campert. TuT, *tr. by* Theo Dorgan

Message: Bottle #32. J. Allyn Rosser. P180

Message Clear. Edwin Morgan. NePenScot

Message from a Cross. Max Harris. NOBAu

Message from Inland. Maura Eichner. UpMys

Message from Ohanapecosh Glacier. W. M. Ransom. GifTon

Message from Outside. Gary Snyder. BodElec

Message from the Photo-Mat. Lawrence Goeckel. ICANM

Message from the Wanderer, A. William Stafford. BrAP

Message from your distant lover is the smell of gunpowder, The. *Unknown.* SLW, *tr. by* Marjolijn De Jager, Sayd Bahodin Majrouh and André Velter

Message in the Bottle,The. Frigyes Karinthy. IQMS, *tr. by* Paul Tabori

Message No. 57. Holley Blackwell. AnSo

Message No. 44. Holley Blackwell. AnSo

Message No. 69. Holley Blackwell. AnSo

Message No. 32. Holley Blackwell. AnSo

Message of King Sakis and the Legend of the Twelve Dreams He Had in One Night, The. *Unknown.* WoPoe, *tr. by* Charles Simic

Message of the Rain, The. Norman H. Russell. ChAP

Message on Cape Cod, The. Afaa Michael Weaver. GT; PBCAP

Message on the Machine. Ken Smith. BeAl

Message that St. Francis preached to the birds, The. St. Francis and the Nun. Carl Dennis. KGB

Message to a Loved One Dead, A. Josephine D. Henderson Heard. CBWP-4

Message to Mary Ferrari in Jo'Burg. Donna Brook. PrTe

Message to the Living. *Unknown.* PoCho, *tr. by* Burton Raffel

Message, we conclude, is inevitable, The. Bachelors, The. Edward Cortez Garrett. ReBoTo

Messages. Nanna Banyiwa Horne. NAfrP

Messages. Jack A. Mapanje. HBAPE

Messalonghi. January 22, 1824. On This Day I Complete My Thirty-sixth Year. Lord Byron. *See* On This Day I Complete My Thirty-sixth Year.

Messe of Nonsense, A. *Unknown.* NOSC

Messenger, The. Thom Gunn. PoA 2002

Messenger, The. Thomas Kinsella.

"It is an August evening, in Wicklow." ModIr

Messenger, The. Jean Valentine. CAP-8

Messenger came in the night, The. "Rachel." FIT, *tr. by* Robert Friend

Messenger, hear what I say. Reinmar der Alte. GePo

Messengers. Louise Glück. ColAP; VCAP; WaAnP

Messengers, The. Steve Chimombo. HBAPE

Messengers, The. Robert Creeley. NAAL-5

Messengers, The [*with music*]. Henrietta Cordelia Ray. CBWP-3

Messiah [a Sacred Eclogue, in Imitation of Virgil's Pollio]. Alexander Pope. ChIV-1

"Rise, crowned with light, imperial Salem, rise!" SacPr

Messiah has sold his blood to the imbecile king, The. Nine Ruba'iyat. Abdul Wahab Al-Bayati. IrPoTo, *tr. by* Carolina Hotchandani and Najat Rahman

Messiah, no rain at all, A. Letter S. Anne Waldman. AHA

Messina, 1908. Alice Thompson Meynell. SacPr

Met, hesitated, left double footsteps, then walked on. (LL) Return to Cardiff. Dannie Abse. AngWePo; TCAWP

Met in the milder shades of Purgatory. (LL) To Mr. H. Lawes On His Airs. John Milton. NoP-4; NoP-5

Met Noel at Cheshire Street. Bill Griffiths. Oth *Fr.* Building: The New London Hospital.

Meta-A and the A of Absolutes. Jay Wright. ESEAA; TRP *Fr.* Logbook of Judgments.

Metacom. John Greenleaf Whittier. AmWaPo

Metacomet. Body of Liberties, The. Peter Gurnis. OnScMo

Metagnomy. Norman Henry Pritchard II. EGAG

Metal and the Flower, The. Patricia K. Page. GPPA

Metal blue sky, the sun, The. Things You Can't Do in Albuquerque or Santa Fe, #11. Bobby Byrd. TiP2

Metal Coughdrops. Tristan Tzara. PFTM-1

Metal Denser Than, and Liquid, A. John Peck. BAP-01

Metal I, the soul the hearth, the blaze that warms, The. "Angelus Silesius." GePo *Fr.* Cherubical Wanderer, The.

Metal smokestack, The. Exercise No. 2. William Carlos Williams. SAmP

Metal-gray, sturdy. Tricycles. Francisco Aragon. InoFa

Metallic mammal. Nocturnal, A. Moon. Nicolás Guillén. PFTM-1

Metal-work. David Morley. NLP

Metamorfosis de la silla. Alberto Blanco. RMCMP

Metamorphoses. Geoffrey Hill.

Re-birth of Venus, The. UpMys

"Through scant pride to be so put out!" UpMys

Metamorphoses. Nikolai Alekseievich Zabolotsky. TCRusP, *tr. by* John Glad

Metamorphoses [Hughes Translation]. Ovid. *tr. by* Ted Hughes

Actaeon. WaAnP, *tr. by* Ted Hughes

Metamorphoses of M. John Peale Bishop. APT-1

Metamorphoses. Ovid. *tr. by* Charles Boer, Ciaran Carson, John Dryden, Arthur Golding, Thom Gunn, Rolfe Humphries, Mary M. Innes, Allen Mandelbaum, John Herman Merivale, Matthew Prior and William Shakespeare

Acteon.

Actaeon and His Hounds. DiBP, *tr. by* Joseph Addison

"And from the Citie Tegea there came the Paragone." OBVE

"And now my work is done: no wrath of Jove." WaAnP, *tr. by* Allen Mandelbaum

Apollo and Daphne. NAWM-7v1, *tr. by* Allen Mandelbaum

Apollo and Hyacinthus. CAGL, *tr. by* Rolfe Humphries

Arethusa Saved. WoPoe, *tr. by* Thom Gunn

Baucis and Philemon. NOSC

Ceres and Proserpina. NAWM-7v1, *tr. by* Allen Mandelbaum

Ceyx and Alcyone. NoSic

Conclusion. OBVE

Cyclops. OBVE

Daedalus. OBVE

Daphne and Apollo. OBVE, *tr. by* Arthur Golding

(Daphne and Apollo.) NPeEn, *tr. by* Arthur Golding

Death of Orpheus, The. WoPoe, *tr. by* Charles Boer

Deucalion and Pyrrha, sole survivors of the Flood, renew Creation by casting stones behind them. NPeEn, *tr. by* John Dryden

Europa and Jove. NAWM-7v1, *tr. by* Allen Mandelbaum

"Floods, by nature enemies to land, The." OBVE

Golden Age, The. NAEL-6v1; NAEL-7v1, *tr. by* Arthur Golding

Io and Jove. NAWM-7v1, *tr. by* Allen Mandelbaum

Iphis and Ianthe. NAWM-7v1, *tr. by* Allen Mandelbaum

Magic.

"Before the Moone should cirlcewise close both hir hornes in one." NPeEn, *tr. by* Arthur Golding

Medea's Incantation. OBVE

Meleager. NOBRP

"Moysting Ayre was whist: no leafe ye could have moving sene, The." OxBEV, *tr. by* Arthur Golding

"My intention is to tell of bodies changed." NAWM-5v1

Myrrha and Cinyras. NAWM-7v1, *tr. by* Allen Mandelbaum

"Near the Cymmerians, in his dark abode." OBVE

"Neare Enna walles there standes a Lake Pergusa is the name." OBVE

"Northern breath, that freezes floods, he binds, The." OBVE

"Not Pallas, not ev'n Spleen it self could blame." OBVE

"Now whyle Hippomenes/ Debates theis things." OBVE

Of the Pythagorean Philosophy. OBVE

"This let me further add, that nature knows." OBVE

"Time was, when we were sow'd, and just began." NPeEn, *tr. by* John Dryden

"Persephone ate seven pomegranate seeds. So What? I'll tell you what." ModIr, *tr. by* Ciaran Carson

Philemon and Baucis.

Baucis and Philemon. OBVE, *tr. by* John Dryden

Procris' Immortal Lelaps: Cephalus' Story. DiBP, *tr. by* Nahum Tate

Prologue. NAWM-7v1, *tr. by* Allen Mandelbaum

Proserpine and Dis. NPeEn, *tr. by* Arthur Golding

Pygmalion. NAWM-7v1, *tr. by* Allen Mandelbaum

"Seeing as the father saw the rosy morn." OBVE

"So, when she saw Narcissus wandering through the lonely countryside, Echo fell in love with him, and followed secretly in his steps." EroLit, *tr. by* Mary M. Innes

"Stones (a miracle to mortal view), The." OBVE

"There was a man here, Samian born, but he." NAWM-5v1

"To thee obeyeth all the East as far as Ganges goes." OBVE

Venus and Adonis. NAWM-7v1, *tr. by* Allen Mandelbaum

Zeus and Ganymede. CAGL, *tr. by* Rolfe Humphries

Metamorphosis. Richard Lemm. Coast

Metamorphosis. Sylvia Plath. PoA 2002

Metamorphosis. Caroline Sprague Smith. StAl

Metamorphosis of a Chair. Alberto Blanco. RMCMP, *tr. by* Joan Lindgren

Metamorphosis of Pigmalions Image, The. John Marston.

"*Pigmalion,* whose hie love-hating minde." PBRV

M'étant penché en cette nuit à la fenêtre. Sur les pas de la lune. Philippe Jaccottet. YaTCFP

Metaphor Crosses the Road, A. Martha McFerren. P180

Metaphor here is the pool, regular, The. Freestyle, on the First of Tishri. Enid Shomer. TaR

Metaphor of Grass in California. Charles Martin. RA

Metaphor, The. Henry Rago.

4. Terror and Love as Fugitives. PoA 2002

Metaphors. Sylvia Plath. HeIP-4; NAMCP V.2; SoSe-8

Metaphors of a Magnifico. Wallace Stevens. TCAPo

Metaphysic of Snow. Donald Finkel. PoA 2002

Metaphysical. Robert Fitzgerald. PoA 2002

Metaphysical Sonnet. Charles Lloyd. CenSon

Metaphysically Niggerish. Wanda Coleman. RD

Metempsicosis del perro. Alfonso D'Aquino. RMCMP

Metempsychosis. Kenneth Slessor. NOBAu

Metempsychosis of the Dog. Alfonso D'Aquino. RMCMP, *tr. by* Rebecca Seiferle

Meteor. Ivan Davidkov. CSCBP, *tr. by* Georgi Belev and Lisa Sapinkopf

Meteor. C. M. Mayo. RWB

Meteor. Larissa Szporluk. BAP-01; LegDan

Meteor of the war, The. (LL) Portent, The. Herman Melville. APN-2; CBCWP; ColAP; InoFa; NAAL-3; NAAPv.1; NCAP; NoP-4; NoP-5; OBWP; OxBoAm; PCW; TCAPo; WaAnP

Meteor Showers—Yosemite. Dixie Salazar. GeoHom

Meteorology. Linda France. MFPA

Meter todas las manos en el agua. Dolores Dorantes. SPV

Methinks (cold fear) bids me bide. Woful Words of the Hart, The. George Turberville. DiBP

Methinks it is good to be here. Lines Written in the Church Yard of Richmond, Yorkshire. Herbert Knowles. SacPr

Methinks, 'tis strange you can't afford. Forsaken Wife, The. Elizabeth Thomas. GoPo; LW

Methinks 'twere no unprecedented feat. William Wordsworth. CenSon *Fr.* River Duddon [A Series of Sonnets], The.

Metho Drinker. Judith Wright. BMAP

Method, The [*with music*]. J. D. McClatchy. MakPoe

Methodical dust shades the combs and pomade. Cuttings. Nick Laird. NIrP

Methodist, The. Evan Lloyd.

"Sons of War sometimes are known, The." OBSV

Methodology. Bruce Andrews. FTOS

Methought a sweet sound from the street uprose. Street Music. Elizabeth Akers Allen. SWaP

Methought I lived in the icy times forlorn. Great Britain Through the Ice: Or, Premature Patriotism. Charles Tennyson Turner. OxBSo

Methought I Saw. John Milton. *See* On His Deceased Wife.

Methought I saw (as I did dream[e] in bed). Vision, The. Robert Herrick. NOSC

Methought I Saw My Late Espousèd Saint. John Milton. *See* On His Deceased Wife.

Methought I saw the footsteps of a throne. William Wordsworth. CenSon

Methought I saw the grave where Laura lay. Sir Walter Ralegh. NoSic *Fr.* Commendatory Verses to Edmund Spenser's Fairy Queen.

Methought I Saw the Grave Where Laura Lay. Sir Walter Ralegh. *See* Vision upon This Concei[p]t of the Faerie [*or* Faery] Queen[e], A.

Methought, one night, I saw, in trance sublime. Vision of Sunday in Heaven, A. Victor James Daley. ChIV-2

Methought [*or* Mee thought] I saw my late espoused saint. On His Deceased Wife. John Milton. NPeEn; OBEV; OxBSo; SacPr; TFi

(Methought I saw my late espousèd Saint.) CABP; GSo; InoFa; NoP-4; PBRV

Meticulous, past midnight in clear rime. Hart Crane. ColAP; NAAL-5 *Fr.* Voyages.

Métier of Blossoming, The. Denise Levertov. MoWP

Metonymy as an Approach to a Real World. William Bronk. APSN

Metre Colombian, The. *Unknown.* UV

Metric Blues. Francis Reginald Scott. IFF

Metric Figure ("There is a bird in the poplars.") William Carlos Williams. MoAmPo

Metrical Feet. Samuel Taylor Coleridge. NIL-7; NIP-4

Metrical Translation of the Song of Macgregor Na Ruara. Anne Grant. RWP

Metrics. Rhina P. Espaillat. FFC

Metro Taxqueña. Carla Faesler Bremer. SPV, *tr. by* Jen Hofer

Metro Taxqueña. Carla Faesler Bremer. SPV

Metropolitan Metaphysics. James Flint. BRtP

Metropolitan / Museum of / Art, The. Miss Pimberton Of. Siv Cedering Fox. PBCAP

Metropolitan Nightmare. Stephen Vincent Benét. APT-2

Metropolitan Railway, The. Sir John Betjeman. OxAEP-2

Metrum Parhemiacum Tragicum. Eugenius Vulgarius. FaBoWar, *tr. by* Helen Waddell

Mewl. Zulaykha Abu-Risha. PoArWo, *tr. by* Clarissa C. Burt

Mexican egg and the clock that will not make me know how to leave you. (LL) Les Luths. Frank O'Hara. NAMCP V.2; NoAM

Mexican Fire Breather, A. Juan Delgado. TouFir

Mexican Loneliness. Jack Kerouac. CLPP

Mexican World Mural / 5 x 25. Juan Felipe Herrera. TouFir

Mexicans Begin Jogging. Gary Soto. CAP-8; LTA; PML; RWB

Mexico City Blues. Jack Kerouac.

One Hundred and Forty-Ninth Chorus. PmAP

113th Chorus. PmAP

127th Chorus. PmAP

211th Chorus. PFTM-2; PmAP

Two Hundred and Twenty-Eighth Chorus. PmAP

Mexico is a Foreign Country: Five Studies in Naturalism. Robert Penn Warren. Mango on the Mango Tree, The. NoAM

Mexico needs mahogany. El Paso Monologue. Ishmael Reed. SpirFl

Mexico Will Be Free. Merced J. de Gonz´les. NAAPv.1, *tr. by Unknown*

Mezuzah. Alan Shapiro. TaR

Mezzo Cammin. Henry Wadsworth Longfellow. APN-1; ColAP; GSo; NAAL-3; NAAPv.1; NCAP; TCAPo

Mezzo Forte. William Carlos Williams. SAmP

M'fingal. John Trumbull.

Canto First : or The Town Meeting A.M.

Town-Meeting, A.M., The. TCAPo

Mi Abuelo. Alberto A. Ríos. NAMCP V.2; NIL-7; PoPoPo; WaAnP

¿Mi Amor? . .¿Recuerdas, dime. Antonio Machado Ruiz. RaW *Fr.* Del Camino.

Mi Estomago / My Belly. Marjorie Agosin. FiBr, *tr. by* Cola Franzen

Mi Mamá, the Playgirl. Richard Garcia. InoFa; SUP

Mi Negrito. Anasuya Isaacs. BRtP

M-I-N-O-R-I-T-Y. Last Visit to Chestnut Middle School. Jaime Shaggy Flores. BRtP

Mi revalueshanary fren is nat di same agen. Mi Revalueshanary Fren. Linton Kwesi Johnson. Oth

Mi Tía Sofía. Carmen Tafolla. TiP2

Mi Tío Baca el Poeta de Socorro. Jimmy Santiago Baca. PmAP

Mi voz fiel como la sombra. Tedi López Mills. RMCMP

Mi voz se fue amoldando a sus tejidos. Dramatis personae. Pura López Colomé. RMCMP

Mia Carlotta. Thomas Augustin Daly. NBLV

Miami Beach. Howard Moss. BodElec

Miami lights beckon. Journalist's Convention 1987. Esther Iverem. InTrad

Miami sunlight, as in a painting. Variations on a Theme by Justice. Paul Mariani. PfSP

Mian: The House of Zhou. *Unknown.* CCL1, *tr. by* James Legge

Mica Country. Robert Morgan. LPSFW

Mica flask moves layout hasty. Tab, The. Clark Coolidge. FTOS

Mica, if you peel carefully. Earth Angel. Jeffrey Skinner. PBCAP

Mica shines on the beach. Extract. Paul Bowles. PoA 2002

Micah. Bible, *O.T. tr. by* King James Version

"But in the last days it shall come to pass." FaBoWar, *tr. by* King James Version

(Mice). Rose Fyleman. NTCP

Mice. Alexander Gerov. CSCBP, *tr. by* Georgi Belev and Lisa Sapinkopf

Mice. Kim Hyesun. EcSo, *tr. by* Youngju Ryu

Mice come first, The. In our bedroom. Virus². Jackie Kay. MFPA

Mice have established themselves in the house and run about in all directions. Mouse, The. Alexei Remizov. MotU, *tr. by* Nancy Condee

Mice in the eaves, and breathe well my dear. Chess Piece Cornered. John Kinsella. BMAP

Mice in the Hay. Leslie Norris. NOxBChV; OBCP

Mice wizards baskets bells. Beautiful House, The. Laura Moriarty. ASA

Michael. Sandra McPherson. MotU

Michael [A Pastoral Poem]. William Wordsworth. NAEL-6v2; NAEL-7v2; NOBRP; OxAEP-2; WaAnP

"While this good household thus were living on." NPBRoP

Michael Angelo: A Fragment. Henry Wadsworth Longfellow.

In the Coliseum. TCAPo

Monologue: The Last Judgment.

"In happy hours, when the imagination." TCAPo

Michael Applebaum became. Only Applebaum Can Make a Tree. Joanne Hart. MiVo

Michael didn't want to go. After the Prom. Lisa D. Chavez. AmPoNex

Michael Is Afraid of the Storm. Gwendolyn Brooks. NOxBChV

Michael Masse. Sam Witt. NeAmPo

Michael Robartes Bids His Beloved Be at Peace. William Butler Yeats. NoAM

(He Bids His Beloved Be at Peace.) IJHIL

Michael Row the Boat Ashore. *Unknown.* APN-2; NAAPv.1; SSUS

Michael sets before Adam in vision what shall happ'n till the Flood. John Milton. NPeEn

Michael writes to tell me his dream. Mark Doty. WiU *Fr.* Atlantis.

"Michaelangelo" the Elder. Bob Kaufman. OxAAAP

Michaelmas. Veronica Forrest-Thomson. HarvBoo

Michaelmas. Norman Nicholson. MoBrPo

Michael's Dream. Mark Doty. WiU *Fr.* Atlantis.

Michal her modest flames sought to conceal. Abraham Cowley. ChIV-1 *Fr.* Davideis.

Micheál Mac Liammóir. Paul Durcan. PBCIP

Michelangelo didn't lose any fingers. Hawthorne Metal, Detroit, 1939. Marcus Cafagña. MAAN

Michele. Afaa Michael Weaver. BtF

Michele has become another dead little girl. An easy poem. Poet Goes about Her Business, The. Linda Gregg. PtR

Michelle Granguad Creating Anagrams. Paul Lloyd and Rosemary Lloyd. YaTCFP

Michié Préval li donnin gran bal. Calinda. *Unknown.* SSUS

Michigan Boulevard. Jun Fujita. NAAPv.2

Mick whore, Grandma Maloney, The. Grandmothers in Green and Orange. Frank R. Maloney. GifTon

Mickey Mouse. Christopher Murray. BeDoSh

Mickey says hey / you guys, go throw. Third Shift. Anthony Walton. NAPBL

Micmac woman's body has been disinterred and her, The. Report on Her Remains. Daniel David Moses. HATNAP

Micro 1. Takehisa Kosugi. WhBo

Microbiblion. Simon Wastell.

Micrographic Manuscript, Miniature (1). Esther Ettinger. DTA, *tr. by* Mariana Barr

Micrographic Manuscript, Miniature (2). Esther Ettinger. DTA, *tr. by* Mariana Barr

Microscope [*with music*]. Gwyn Thomas. BBMWP; OBWVE, *tr. by* Joseph P. Clancy

Microscope in Winter, The. Sandra McPherson. VCAP

Microscope revealed a world of miracles, The. Genealogy of Crosses, The. Andrey Andreievich Voznesensky. PFTM-2, *tr. by* Richard McKane

Mid-Friday morn, 10 o'clock, I go to India. Ted Berrigan. AHA *Fr.* Anti-Memoirs.

'Mid / 'mid. Medieval. Ernst Jandl. OnScMo, *tr. by* Gale Nelson

'Mid pleasures and palaces though we may roam. John Howard Payne. APN-1; BRP; TCAPo *Fr.* Clari, the Maid of Milan.

Mid the bind-grass on the plain. Ye-you man-cao: Mid the Bind-Grass. *Unknown.* CCL1, *tr. by* Ezra Pound

Mid the blue waves, by circling seas embraced. Mary Tighe. NOBRP *Fr.* Psyche.

Mid western mountains far away. Patterdale. Isabella Lickbarrow. RWP

Mid-1990s, Scotland, dead of winter. Older Woman, An. Roddy Lumsden. NeBrP

Murder Will Out. *Unknown.* DiBP

Midafternoon in Norfolk. At the Swings. Henry Taylor. MPUn

Midas. John Lyly.

Daphne. NoSic

"'Las, how long shall I." NoSic

(Pan's Song.) OxAEP-1

Pan's Syrinx. NoSic; NPeEn

Song of Apollo. NoSic

Midas, they say, possessed the art of old. Epigram. "Peter Pindar." NIL-7; NIP-4

Midas watched the golden crust. Ungrateful Garden, The. Carolyn Kizer. BrAP

Mid-August at Sourdough Mountain Lookout. Gary Snyder. ColAP; FaoP; LoL; NoP-4; OxBoAm; VCAP; WaAnP

Mid-Autumn Moon. Su Tung-p'o. GifTon, *tr. by* Burton Watson

Midcentury Love Letter. Phyllis McGinley. LW

Mid-Channel. Gwen Harwood. BMAP

Mid-Country Blow. Theodore Roethke. HarvBoo

Mid-day. "H. D." APT-1; NAAL-5; NAAPv.2; NAMCP V.1

Midday. Irmgard Hunt. GTCP, *tr. by* Sam McLean

Midday. Cees Nooteboom. PML, *tr. by* Leonard Nathan and Herlinde Spahr

Midday. Sŏ Chŏngju. CAMKP, *tr. by* David R. McCann

Midday I go to the park alone. One White Dream. Hô Sugyông. EcSo, *tr. by* Youngju Ryu

Mid-day moon lights up the rocky sky, The. Pastoral in Posters, A. Carolyn Wells. SWaP

Mid-Day Moon, The. John Banister Tabb. APN-2

Midday sleep, the veil of sleepy maya. Nina Gabrielian. CRWP *Fr.* Erebuni.

Midday, the sun's rays. Small Park, A. Yi Yuksa. CAMKP, *tr. by* Kyung-Ja Chun

Midden-Battle between Lady Scotstarvit and the Mistress of Newbarns, The. William Drummond of Hawthornden. NePenScot, *tr. by* Allan H. MacLaine

Middle. Jimmie Durham. HATNAP

Middle Age [*with music*]. Patricia Beer. HarvBoo

Middle Age. Arlene L. Mandell. PasH

Middle Age. Luis Omar Salinas. GeoHom

Middle Age, The: "Between TV and computer screens." Roger Fanning. NevBe

Middle aged / couple playing. 40— Love. Roger McGough. OBCoV

Middle- and small-sized needles. *Unknown.* CATKP, *tr. by* Peter H. Lee

Middle Class Blues. Hans Magnus Enzensberger. VCWP, *tr. by the author*, Hans Magnus Enzensberger and Michael Hamburger

Middle Daughter, The. Barbara Kingsolver. FiBr

Middle East, The. Nadia Hazboun Reimer. PoArWo

Middle Manager in Paradise, The. Michael Foley. PNI

Middle of a War, The. Roy Fuller. OBWP; PoWW

Middle of life's journey; I, The. Dante Alighieri. STV *Fr.* Divina Commedia (Selections from Anthologies, in English).

Middle of May, when the iris blows. Iris. Muriel Rukeyser. APSN; ColAP

Middle of the night, she's wide awake, carefully lying as far away as she can from him, The. Question, The. C. K. Williams. NoP-4; NoP-5

Middle of the Way. Galway Kinnell.

"Coals go out, The." RaBo

Middle of the World. D. H. Lawrence. NoAM; WoPoe

Middle Passage. Sonya Brooks. InTrad

Middle Passage. Robert Earl Hayden. APT-2; CAP-8; ColAP; NAAL-5; NAMCP V.2; NoAM; OxAAAP; OxBoAm; TRP; VCAP; WaAnP

Middle Path. Galway Kinnell. PoA 2002

Middle Years, The. Walter McDonald. GoPo

Middle-aged Irish Mothers. Rita Ann Higgins. MoWP

Middleaged Man, The. Louis Simpson. BodElec

Middle-Aged, The. Adrienne Rich. OxBoAm; PoPoPo

Middle-aged white man in a beat-up blue Pinto, The. Lucky One, The. Reginald Shepherd. GT

Middle-aged woman, quite plain, to be polite about it, and somewhat stout, to be more courteous still, A. Dance, The. C. K. Williams. GoPo

Mid-February in America. Cold everywhere but Florida. Patricia Jones. ReTh *Fr.* Billie Holiday Chronicles, The.

Midfield. Basho. EH, *tr. by* Robert Hass

Midges. Edward Robert Bulwer-Lytton.

"She is talking aesthetics, the dear clever creature." VerBaPo

Midland. Mark Van Doren. APT-2

Midlife. Robin Becker. BodElec

Midlife. Joseph Millar. OPRER

Mid-March. Lizette Woodworth Reese. SWaP

Mid-morning paraffin film over the. Cycle of Community. Margaret Avison. GPPA

Mid-morning, walking ocean shoreline. Blackbird Spring. William Heyen. CAP-8

Midnight. Louisa Sarah Bevington. PEW

Midnight. No Break. N. Revathi Devi. HotL, *tr. by* V. Narayana Rao

Midnight. Louise Glück. CAP-8

Midnight. Andreas Gryphius. GePo, *tr. by* George C. Schoolfield

Midnight: "You call." Terrance Hayes. BtF

Midnight. Vicente Huidobro. CuPo

Midnight. Alison Kolodinsky. PasH

Midnight. Michael Roberts. OBMV

Midnight. Thomas, 1st Earl of Dorset Sackville. AEP *Fr.* Mirror for Magistrates.

Midnight. Tu Fu [*or* Du Fu]. CCL1, *tr. by* A. C. Graham

Midnight. Henry Vaughan. ChIV-2

Midnight already and you are still not here. *Unknown.* SLW, *tr. by* Marjolijn De Jager, Sayd Bahodin Majrouh and André Velter

Midnight at Baiae. John Addington Symonds. CAGL *Fr.* Three Visions of Imperial Rome.

Midnight Caller, The. Pak Sôwôn. EcSo, *tr. by* Julie C. Park

Midnight cities cower underfoot, The. Demons of the Cities, The. Georg Heym. WoPoe, *tr. by* Peter Viereck

Midnight Court, The. Brian Merriman. *tr. by* Brendan Behan, David Marcus, Frank O'Connor and Arland Ussher

   Husband's Lament, The. OBVE, *tr. by* Frank O'Connor

   Lament of the Unmarried Girl, The. OBVE, *tr. by* Frank O'Connor

   Unmarried Clergy, The. IrLP, *tr. by* Frank O'Connor

Midnight Diner by Edward Hopper, A. David Ray. PoSol

Midnight Flowers. Eavan Boland. ModIr

Midnight frost. Basho. EH, *tr. by* Robert Hass

Midnight Gladness. Denise Levertov. UpMys

Midnight Harvest, A. Rosamund Marriott Watson. ViWPN

Midnight has come, and the great Christ Church Bell. William Butler Yeats. OxAEP-2 *Fr.* Vision, A.

Midnight in Mississippi. M. Eliza Hamilton. BtF

Midnight in the Assyrian camp! No sound. Rebekah Gumpert Hyneman. SWaP *Fr.* Female Scriptural Characters.

Midnight. June, 1923. Not a stir except for the brough and brouhaha. Third Epistle to Timothy. Paul Muldoon. NoP-5

Midnight Lamentation. Harold Monro.

   "When you and I go down." OBMV

Midnight on the Great Western. Thomas Hardy. OxAEP-2; WoPoe

Midnight or after, and the little lights. Train. Donald Justice. GM

Midnight percussion. Gary Warner. WhBo

Midnight Reports. Lynda Hull. SwNoth

Midnight Rocker, Tiananmen Square, May 27, 1989. Edith Rylander. MiVo

Midnight Run. Jonathan Johnson. AmPoNex

Midnight Saving Time. Adrien Stoutenburg. AWTN

Midnight Skaters, The. Edmund Charles Blunden. MoBrPo; NPeEn; WoPoe

Midnight sleepless heart. Quartets of Inner Whispering. Shakir Samawi. IrPoTo, *tr. by* Chuck Miller and Saadi A. Simawe

Midnight Snack, The. James Merrill. OxBSo *Fr.* Five Old Favorites.

Midnight Song. Pinkie Gordon Lane. GT

Midnight Songs. *Unknown. tr. by* Jeanne Larsen

   "Morning's sun." ColAnChi, *tr. by* Jeanne Larsen

   "My perfume?" ColAnChi, *tr. by* Jeanne Larsen

   "Night after night, I do not." ColAnChi, *tr. by* Jeanne Larsen

   "Night so." ColAnChi, *tr. by* Jeanne Larsen

   "Night so." ColAnChi, *tr. by* Jeanne Larsen

   "Seize the moment!—." ColAnChi, *tr. by* Jeanne Larsen

   "So soon. Today, love, we." ColAnChi, *tr. by* Jeanne Larsen

   "Sun sinks low, The. I." ColAnChi, *tr. by* Jeanne Larsen

   "Through the front gate." ColAnChi, *tr. by* Jeanne Larsen

   "When I started wanting." ColAnChi, *tr. by* Jeanne Larsen

Midnight sound / Leap up. Masaoka Shiki. ZenPo, *tr. by* Takashi Ikemoto and Lucien Stryk

Midnight Special. *Unknown.* APT-1

Midnight storm. Trees walking off across the fields in fury. Light. Michael Ondaatje. NIP-4

Midnight Sun. Johnny Mercer. APT-2; ReLy

Midnight sun was larger than the bridge, its reds, almost flame like blood, The. Hare, The. Silvia Eugenia Castillero. SPV, *tr. by* Jen Hofer

Midnight sun with phantom glare, The. Russian Student's Tale, The. Mathilde Blind. VWP

Midnight Supper. Ruth L. Schwartz. NeAmPo

Midnight Tennis Match, The [*with music*]. Thomas Lux. MoASP

Midnight. The flowing water of Hu T'o River. Midnight. Jěn Jui. CFP; WoPoe, *tr. by* Chung Ling and Kenneth Rexroth

Midnight. The wind yawing nor-east. Haddock Fishermen. George Mackay Brown. NoP-4; NoP-5

Midnight the years last day the last. New Year's Eve, 1938. John Frederick Nims. ChrPo

Midnight Thought, A. On the Death of Mrs. E. H. and Her Little Daughter. Elizabeth Thomas. NOSC

Midnight Vapor Light Breakdown. Betsy Sholl. LTA

Midnight Velada, The. María Sabina. PFTM-1 *Fr.* Midnight Velada, The.

Midnight Velada, The. María Sabina. *tr. by* Henry Munn

   "Ah, Jesu Kri." PFTM-2, *tr. by* Henry Munn

   Midnight Velada, The. PFTM-1

Midnight Vigil. Fran Haraway. HHAm

Midnight wakes into noon. Dream Cloud. Lindiwe Mabuza. HAWP

Midnight was come, when every vital thing. Thomas, 1st Earl of Dorset Sackville. AEP *Fr.* Mirror for Magistrates.

Midnight Woman to the Bobby, A. Claude McKay. NAMCP V.1

Midnight / You heavy laden, it's midnight. Street of Dreams. Sam M. Lewis. ReLy

Midnights of consciousness, still, and even. Endsight. Michael Dransfield. BMAP

Mid-noon is past;—upon the sultry mead. William Wordsworth. CenSon *Fr.* River Duddon [A Series of Sonnets], The.

Mid-Ocean. Emily Jane Pfeiffer. ViWPN

Midrashim: Proverbs 6:6. David Curzon. *See* Proverbs 6:6.

Midst all the dark and knotty snares,. Neither Durst Any Man From That Day Ask Him Any More Questions. Richard Crashaw. ChIV-2

'Midst dreary labyrinths of mental night? (LL) Invokes Reason. Mary Robinson. CenSon; RWP

Midston House. David Schubert. OxBoAm

Midstream they met. Challenger and champion. Swans, The. Clifford Dyment. TCAWP

Midsummer. William Cullen Bryant. GSo

Midsummer. Nicholas Christopher. UrbNat

Midsummer: "Two yearling deer." Sam Hamill. WANABP

Midsummer. Alexander L. Posey. APN-2

Midsummer. Sherod Santos. GeoHom

Midsummer. Derek Walcott.

   "Camps hold [*or* held] their distance—[of] brown chestnuts and grey smoke, The." PoetW

   "Certain things here are quietly American." NAEL-6v2; NAEL-7v2; NoP-4; NoP-5

   "Chicago's avenues, as white as Poland." UrbNat

   Gauguin. NoAM

   "Oak inns creak in their joints as light declines, The." NoAM

Midsummer Farewell. Jerry Craven. TiP2

Midsummer Night's Dream, A. William Shakespeare.

   Fairies' Lullaby, The. NoSic

   (Fairy Land, 1.) OBEV

   (Fairy Land, 2.) OBEV

   Helena's Humble Petition. DiBP

   Lunatic, the Lover, and the Poet, The. IJHIL; WaAnP

   Music of the Hound, The. DiBP

   "Ousel cock, so black of hue, The." NoSic

   "Tis strange my Theseus, that these lovers speake of." OxBEV

Midsummer stretches before me with a cat's yawn. Port of Spain. Derek Walcott. NoAM

Midsummer, Tobago. Derek Walcott. MakPoe; OPOU; VCWP

Midsummer's Eve. Deborah Leiter. IaFF

Mid-Term Break. Seamus Heaney. AmFaPo; BeAl; NIL-7; PoPoPo; WaAnP

Midway [*with music*]. Robert Desnos. PFTM-1

Mid-way. Robert Desnos. GPTC, *tr. by* Carole Frankel and William Kulik

Midway between cage and "cachot" (prison) the French language has "cageot" (crate). Crate, The. Francis Ponge. MotU, *tr. by* Cid Corman

Midway in life, attuned to Buddhism. Villa at the Foot of Mount Chungnan. Wang Wei. ChinPo, *tr. by* Ye Weilian [*or* Yeh Wei-lien *or* Wai-lim Yip]

Midway in our life's journey, I went astray. Dante Alighieri. NAWM-5v1 *Fr.* Divina Commedia (Selections from Anthologies, in English).

Midway the hill of science, after steep. To Mr. S. T. Coleridge. Anna Laetitia Barbauld. CABP; NoP-4; WoRP

Mid-West, The. *Unknown.* OBCoV

Midwest, Midcentury. Sharyn Jeanne Skeeter. ISC

Midwest Town. Ruth Delong Peterson. CA

Midwife. Judith Kazantzis. Prnts

Midwife puts a rag in the dead woman's hand, The. Obedience of the Corpse. C. D. Wright. InGu

Midwife's Invocation, A. *Unknown*. WPoS, *tr.* by Michael Coe and Whittaker Gordon

Midwinter and this beech wood's mind. Woods. Gwyneth Lewis. NeBrP

Midwinter. Snow. Olav H. Hauge. WED, *tr.* by Robert Bly

Midwinter spring is its own season. T. S. Eliot. CABP; NAAPv.2; NAEL-6v2; NAEL-7v2; NAMCP V.1; NAWM-7v2; NoAM; NoP-5; OxAEP-2; OxBoAm; TFi *Fr.* Four Quartets.

Midwives, The. Celia Gilbert. ChIV-1

Midwives all were scarecrows, The. Almanac, 1939, An. Kevin Young. AmPoNex

Mid-Year Report: For Haruko. June Jordan. ReTh

Mientras / un hombre joven. Ana Belén López Pulido. SPV

Might and Right [*with music*]. Clarence Day. NBLV

Might have been. This Place Rumored to Have Been Sodom. Robert Duncan. CAGL; CalPo

Might live invisible and dim! (LL) Night, The. Henry Vaughan. BASC; ChIV-1; FSCP; NAEL-6v1; NAEL-7v1; NoP-4; NoP-5; NPeEn; OBEV; OBWVE; OxAEP-1; OxBEV; TFi

Might quicken me all into verb, pure verb. (LL) Oysters. Seamus Heaney. StAl; UV

Might rise from where they slept and go away. (LL) Sheaves, The. Edwin Arlington Robinson. APT-1; ItP; MoAmPo; NAMCP V.1; NoAM; OxBoAm; SoSe-8

Might there have been an echo of self. Music's Wife. Joel Long. AmPoNex

Mightier than the Pen. Kingsley Amis. OBCoV

Mightier than the sword thou art. Pen, The. Mary Weston Fordham. CBWP-2

Mighty Blood, The. A. Anthony Vessup. BtF

Mighty creature is the germ, A. Germ, The. Ogden Nash. APT-2

Mighty empty alien stones of the waterless desert. In the Desert. Dmitry Aleksandrovich Prigov. ItGoST, *tr.* by Robert Reid

Mighty Fortress Is Our God, A. Frederic Henry Hedge and Martin Luther. GePo; SacPr

Mighty growth! The county side, A. Old Oak Tree at Hatfield Broadoak, The. Frederick Locker-Lampson. OxAEP-2

Mighty junction of star with star, A. Ode on Slate, The. Osip Emilevich Mandelstam. WoPoe, *tr.* by Bernard Meares

Mighty Lord Is Money, A. Francisco de Quevedo y Villegas. SpanPo, *tr.* by William M. Davis

Mighty love's consuming fire. Shy Request. Mihály Csokonai Vitéz. IQMS, *tr.* by Adam Makkai and Ena Roberts

Mighty Mother, and her son who brings, The. Alexander Pope. OxAEP-1 *Fr.* Dunciad, The.

Mighty One, The. Ssu-ma Hsiang-ju. CCL1, *tr.* by Burton Watson

Mighty Orion conquered. Korinna [*or* Corinna]. SaLy, *tr.* by Diane Rayor

Mighty Runner, A. Nicarchus of Alexandria. AmWit *Fr.* Variations of Greek Themes.

Mighty Tropicale Orchestra, The. Sean Harvey. SeSe

Mighty wave rush'd o'er him as he spoke, A. Homer. OBVE *Fr.* Odyssey.

Mignon. Johann Wolfgang von Goethe. WoPoe, *tr.* by Anthony Hecht

Mignon [*with music*]. Henrietta Cordelia Ray. CBWP-3

Mignon Aspiring to Heaven. Johann Wolfgang von Goethe. TreFP

Migraciones. Gloria Gervitz.
   "Agua en su silencio de raíz, El." RMCMP

Migraine. Gillian Clarke. Prnts *Fr.* Glass.

Migrant tribe of spiders, A. Encampment at Morning, An. W. S. Merwin. GifTon

Migrants by Night. W. S. Merwin. BodElec

Migration. Jane Griffiths. BeAl; NeBl

Migration. Tony Hoagland. BeAl; PoCho

Migration. David Johnson. ICANM

Migration of Drummond's Organs (After Death), The. Norman Weinstein. WaCA

Migrations. Gloria Gervitz. *tr.* by Mark Schafer
   "Water in its silence of roots." RMCMP, *tr.* by Mark Schafer

Migratory. Mark Doty. AmAlph; BeAl

Migratory bird flew with mirth. Lost Bird. Chenjerai Hove. HBAPE

Miguel, for instance: how, when the man with the bicycle. On Being the Least Feminist Woman You've Ever Met. Paula Cunningham. NIrP

Mih Feel It. Ahdri Zhina Mandiela. WaCA

Mika / But I will not allow you. Sappho. SaLy, *tr.* by Diane Rayor

Mikado, The. William Schwenck Gilbert.
   (Titwillow.) NoP-4; NoP-5

Mike Howe's head with frozen frown. Hobart Town, Van Diemen's Land (11th June, 1837). Hal Porter. NOBAu

Mike moved to the city. Ecology. Tony Hoagland. FaoP

Mike's. Agnes Walsh. Coast

Milagros Mourns the Queen of Scat. Marisa De Los Santos. NAPBL

Milagrosa, La. Víctor Hernández Cruz. TouFir

Milan, August 1943. Salvatore Quasimodo. WoPoe, *tr.* by Peter Russell

Mild and slow and young. Girl Help. Janet Lewis. APT-2; CalPo; HeIP-4

Mild but an endless winter, A. (LL) Buried Graves, The. Brad Leithauser. NoP-4; NoP-5; WaAnP

Mild Citizen. Glyn Maxwell. HarvBoo

Mild Splendor of the various-vested Night! Samuel Taylor Coleridge. CenSon *Fr.* Effusions.

Mild Was the Air. Rosalía de Castro. NAWM-7v2, *tr.* by S. Griswold Morley

Mild was the air. Mild Was the Air. Rosalía de Castro. NAWM-7v2, *tr.* by S. Griswold Morley

Mild-eyed white-haired wedding guest, The. At revolution's end. Lionel Abrahams. TSAP

Mildly hostile point, A. Instinct. Bill Berkson. NYP2

Mildred, if you take the trouble to send me what I want. Katherine Killigrew. EMWP

Mildred's Doves. Henrietta Cordelia Ray. CBWP-3

Mile an' a Bittock, A. Robert Louis Stevenson. OxBEV

Mile at sea, Cake Rock, against the blue, A. Iron Man of the Hoh. Nelson Bentley. GifTon

Mile behind is Gloucester town, A. Gloucester Moors. William Vaughn Moody. APN-2; TCAPo

Mile 49: Ladies and gentlemen. Travel North: The Rules. Jane Epton Seale. TiP2

Mile from Poetry, A. Kris Hemensley.
   "Look! she said you can see." BMAP
   "My poem's in the oven where it." BMAP
   "Place was famed for, The." BMAP
   "Poem by John Thorpe, A." BMAP

Mile, gallon and pound. Metric Blues. Francis Reginald Scott. IFF

Mile or two from Arras town, A. Alastair Buchan (1917). John, 1st Baron Tweedsmuir Buchan. EdScPo

Mile out in the marshes, under a sky, A. Town Dump, The. Howard Nemerov. NIL-7; WaAnP

Milena Jesenká. Edward Hirsch. BodElec

"Miles", and "John Alden" were Synonym. (LL) God is a distant—stately Lover. Emily Dickinson. APN-2; NCAP

Miles are more like time that anything, The. Driving Towards Houston. Paul Christensen. TiP2

Miles blew "so what" on *kind of blue*. So What. Quincy Troupe. PrTe

Miles of frost / On the lake. Buson. ZenPo, *tr.* by Takashi Ikemoto and Lucien Stryk

Miles of pram in the wind and Pam in the gorse track. Potpourri from a Surrey Garden. Sir John Betjeman. NPeEn

Milestone: The Birth of an Ancestor. Eugene B. Redmond. SpirFl

Militance of a Photograph in the Passbook of a Bantu under Detention, The. Michael S. Harper. VCAP

Militaris Cantio. *Unknown*. IQMS, *tr.* by Matthew Mead *and* Ruth Mead

Military Ball, A. Frank O'Hara. BodElec

Military Call-up. Meir Wieseltier. NRoS, *tr.* by Esther Raizen

Military Creed, The. Ernest Crosby. FaBoWar

Military Funeral in the Heat of Day. T. Carmi. NRoS, *tr.* by Esther Raizen

Military Harpist, The. Ruth Pitter. NALW

Military Life, The. Harold Rome. ReLy

Military / in a hurry. Somalia. Nancy Mercado. BRtP

Military-Industrial Complex, The. Robley, Jr. Wilson. PBCAP

Militia, The. John Dryden. OBSV *Fr.* Cymon and Iphigenia.

Milk. Eileen Myles. KGB

Milk. Maurice Riordan. ModIr; NIrP

Milk. Gertrude Stein. MotU *Fr.* Tender Buttons.

Milk for the Cat [*with music*]. Harold Monro. MoBrPo; OBMV

Milk Lorry, The. Les A. Murray. NAMCP V.2

Milk white Hind, immortal and unchang'd, A. John Dryden. UV *Fr.* Hind and the Panther, The.

Milk[e] all the way. (LL) To the Infant Martyrs. Richard Crashaw. ChIV-2; NAEL-6v1; NAEL-7v1; NoP-4; NoP-5

Milkers lace their boots up at the farms, The. (LL) Cock-Crow. Edward Thomas. MoBrPo; NPeEn

Milkfish. Eugene Gloria. OpBo

Milkflowers. Robert Wrigley. PasH

Milkman, The. Isabella Gardner. AFaM

Milkman, Keep Those Bottles Quiet! Don Raye. ReLy

Milkman, keep those bottles quiet! Milkman, Keep Those Bottles Quiet! Don Raye. ReLy

Milkstone. Shin Yu Pai. AmZen

Milkweed. James Wright. ColAP; RaBo

Milkweed and Monarch. Paul Muldoon. NAEL-7v2; NoP-4; NoP-5; PoetW; WaAnP

Milk-white hair-lace wound up all her hairs, A. Woman drest by Age, A. Margaret Lucas Cavendish, Duchess of Newcastle. BrAP; PEW

Milk-Wort and Bog Cotton. Hugh MacDiarmid. EdScPo

Milky rain on the green hills. Chŏng Ch'ŏl. CATKP, tr. by Peter H. Lee

Milky Way. Wei Ying-wu. CCL1, tr. by Marsha Wagner

Milky Way. Milky Way. Wei Ying-wu. CCL1, tr. by Marsha Wagner

Milky Way, The. Sinan Anton. IrPoTo, tr. by the author

Milky Way, The. At the Nachi Kannon Hall. Muso Soseki. EaWin, tr. by W. S. Merwin

Milky Way above, The. Fire Island. May Swenson. PoA 2002

Milkymoonstruck, a cool disposition of storks. Moonstruck Storks. Ahmet Hasim. SonAtl, tr. by Fatih, Nevin Ipek, Nazim and Tamer Yazircioglu

Mill, The. Edwin Arlington Robinson. APT-1; NAAPv.1; NAMCP V.1; NoAM; NoP-4; NoP-5; WeW-3

Mill, the Stone, and the Water, The. Jelaluddin Rumi. WED, tr. by Robert Bly

Milla. Unknown. NOSC

Milla lived eons ago. Milla. Nancy Mercado. FTtHH

Milla, the glory of whose beauteous rays. Milla. Unknown. NOSC

Millares 1965. Rafael Alberti. RaW

Millares 1965. Rafael Alberti. RaW, tr. by Hardie St. Martin

Mille e tre. Paul Verlaine. CAGL, tr. by Alan Stone

Millefiori. Lavinia Greenlaw. MFPA

Millenary. Richard Kenney. PfSP

Millennial Polka. Alicia Ostriker. ExTi

Millennium. Patricia Beer. HarvBoo

Millennium. E. A. Mares. ICANM

Millennium ago, a. Various authors. CATKP Fr. Songs of Flying Dragons.

Millennium Cities. Lawrence Ferlinghetti. WhBo

Miller's daughter, The. Spinning Song. Dame Edith Sitwell. MoBrPo

Miller's Daughter, The. Alfred Tennyson. OBEV

Miller's Prologue, The. Geoffrey Chaucer. NAEL-6v1; NAEL-7v1 Fr. Canterbury Tales, The.

Miller's [or Milleres] Tale, The. Geoffrey Chaucer. NAEL-6v1; NAEL-7v1 Fr. Canterbury Tales, The.

Miller's wife had waited long, The. Mill, The. Edwin Arlington Robinson. APT-1; NAAPv.1; NAMCP V.1; NoAM; NoP-4; NoP-5; WeW-3

Millet Field in My Mind. Ch'ŏn Yanghûi. EcSo, tr. by Aimee N. Kwon

Millet field passes through my mind again as I go to the backyard to gather a few butteburr leaves, A. Millet Field in My Mind. Ch'ŏn Yanghûi. EcSo, tr. by Aimee N. Kwon

Millets in full rows. Unknown. ChinPo, tr. by Ye Weilian [or Yeh Wei-lien or Wai-lim Yip]

Millet's The Gleaners. Matt Simpson. RSaN

Millie's Date. Dannie Abse. BloBone

Millimeters of your life are nine, The. Shooter Rules. Michael Bugeja. LiTh

Millinery District ("Clouds, piled in rows like merchandise, The.") Charles Reznikoff. APT-2

Millinery District ("Many fair hours have been buried here.") Charles Reznikoff. APT-2

Milling of spilled workers. Day Labor. Heather Fuller. Eno

Million billion trillion stars, A. (LL) Man who had fallen among thieves, A. E. E. Cummings. ChIV-2; NoAM

Million Futures of Late, A. Christine Hume. IAoNAP

Million million spermatozoa, A. Fifth Philosopher's Song. Aldous Leonard Huxley. OBCoV

Million times, A. Jessemyn Meyerhoff. WhBo

Millions of stars playing tag in the skies. It Shouldn't Happen to a Dream. Don George. ReLy

Millions of Strawberries. Genevieve Taggard. NOxBChV

Millstones rest their weathered bulk. Lorne, Nova Scotia. Geoffrey Cook. Coast

Milltown Union Bar, The. Richard Hugo. NoAM

Milord I thanke you hartely. Thursday Before New Yeares Day (Being on the Satterdy) the Maide, by Councell of On, She Trustid Well, Excussid Herself on This Wise to Milord, The. Marie Collyn. EMWP

Milor's good food all fits the season. (LL) Yu-li: Fine Fish to Net. Unknown. CCL1; OBVE, tr. by Ezra Pound

Milo's from home; and, Milo being gone. Epigram. Martial. OBVE, tr. by Elijah Fenton

Milton. Henry Wadsworth Longfellow. GSo; NAAPv.1

Milton. Edwin Muir. OxBSo

Milton. Henrietta Cordelia Ray. CBWP-3

Milton. John Banister Tabb. APN-2

Milton by Firelight. Gary Snyder. BB; NAMCP V.2

Milton, his face set fair for Paradise. Milton. Edwin Muir. OxBSo

Milton. William Blake.

"And every Space that a Man views around his dwelling-place." BLT

"But the Wine-press of Los is eastward of Golgonooza, before the Seat." NOBRP

"But turning toward Ololon in terrible majesty Milton." OxAEP-2

"I come in self-annihilation and the grandeur of inspiration." NPBRoP

"Into this pleasant Shadow all the weak & weary." NOBRP

(Jerusalem.) OBEV; OxAEP-2; UV

Preface. BrAP; CABP; ChIV-1; ClHu; CtM; HeIP-4; NAEL-7v2; NAWM-7v2; NOBRP; NoP-4; NPeEn; OxBEV; TFi; WoPoe

"There is a place where Contrarities are equally True." NOBRP

Milton, the airport driver, retired now. Becoming Milton. Coleman Barks. RaBo; RaF

Milton! thou shouldst be living at this hour. London 1802. William Wordsworth. BrAP; CenSon; HeIP-4; InoFa; NAEL-6v2; NAEL-7v2; NIL-7; NIP-4; NOBRP; NoP-4; NoP-5; OxAEP-2; TFi; UV

Milton was not my father's favourite poet. John Milton and My Father. Patricia Beer. HarvBoo

Milwaukee, 1966. Mrs. Post's 6th-Hour English Class. Susan Firer. VisFro

Mimesis. Elizabeth Garrett. MFPA

Mimetic. Ann Lauterbach. PmAP

Mimi. Paul Muldoon and Gerald Stern. GPPA

Mimic Muse, The. Samuel Hoffenstein.

"With rue my heart is laden." NBLV

Mimikòs. Luigi Fontanella. NeIt, tr. by Michael Palma

Mimnermus in Church. William Johnson Cory. OBEV

Mimshi Maiden, The. Hugh Raymond McCrae. NOBAu

Mina Bell's Cows. Wesley McNair. TRP

Mind. Jorie Graham. WaAnP

Mind. Richard Wilbur. OxBoAm; SoSe-8; VCAP

Mind, and some thin longing that ensnared it, The. Skull. Edward Weismiller. YaYoPo

Mind as though in the void, The. Sikong Tu. CCL1 Fr. Twenty-Four Modes of Poetry.

Mind becomes a field of snow, The. Invention of Heaven, The. Dean Young. P180

Mind Debarred, A. William Wordsworth. NPBRoP Fr. Prelude, The; Growth of a Poet's Mind [1805 version].

Mind, don't be duped by others' sneers. Rāmprasād Sen. SinGod, tr. by Rachel Fell McDermott

Mind has shown itself at times, The. For the Marriage of Faustus and Helen. Hart Crane. APT-2; NoAM; OxBoAm

Mind, how do you think you'll find Her? Rāmprasād Sen. SinGod, tr. by Rachel Fell McDermott

Mind, I'm talking to you. Rāmkumār Nandī Majumdār. SinGod, tr. by Rachel Fell McDermott

Mind in its [or the] purest play is like some bat. Mind. Richard Wilbur. OxBoAm; SoSe-8; VCAP

(Mind in its purest play is like some bat.) ColAP

Mind invents its own inadequacies, The. Dangerous Doubts. Lorenzo Thomas. AnSo; FuFl

Mind is a city like London, The. Mind Is an Ancient and Famous Capital, The. Delmore Schwartz. APT-2; NAMCP V.2; NoAM

Mind Is an Enchanting Thing, The. Marianne Moore. APT-1; HeIP-4; MoAmPo; NAAL-5; NAAPv.2; NoP-4; NoP-5

Mind led body. Vertigo. Anne Stevenson. PoDa

Mind, let's go to an estate that's decent. Rāmdulāl Nandī. SinGod, tr. by Rachel Fell McDermott

Mind of a child who knows he is dying opens with the radiance, The. David McFadden. NLPA

Mind of man is this world's true dimension, The. Fulke, 1st Baron Brooke Greville. NOSC Fr. Treaty of Human Learning, A.

Mind of Squash, The. Naomi Shihab Nye. IPoFL

Mind of the people is like mud, The. Talking with Soldiers. Walter James Turner. MoBrPo

Mind Over Matter. Gloria Frym.

"Only two know the meaning of us." ASA

Mind Reborn in Streatham Common, A. Richard Percival Lister. OBCoV

Mind returns to it always, The. Paul Blackburn. APSN Fr. Selection of Heaven, The.

Mind set free in the Dharma-realm. Ryushu Shutaku. ZenPo, tr. by Takashi Ikemoto and Lucien Stryk

Mind the Gap. Maura Dooley. BeAl

Mind Wanting More. Holly Hughes. AmZen

Mind, why this separation from the Mother's feet? Rāmprasād Sen. SinGod, tr. by Rachel Fell McDermott

Mind, with its own eyes and ears, The. Mind's Liberty, The. W. H. Davies. MoBrPo

Mind, you're still not rid of your illusions. Rāmprasād Sen. SinGod, *tr. by* Rachel Fell McDermott.

Mind-Body Problem. Katha Pollitt. KGB; OxBoAm

Minde through thee divines on endlesse things, The. Thomas Lodge. PBRV *Fr.* Scillaes Metamorphosis.

Mindful of the shambles of the day. Nightwalker. Thomas Kinsella.

Minding Ruth. Aidan Carl Mathews. PBCIP

Minding You. Catherine Byron. Prnts

Mind-Reader, The. Richard Wilbur. NoAM

Minds awake in bodies that were asleep. Pandora and the Moon. Merrill Moore. MoAmPo

Mind's circle increases death, The. Still without Life. Rosalie Moore. CalPo; YaYoPo

Mind's disguise is permanence, The. Mind's Disguise, The. Rosalie Moore. APT-2; YaYoPo

Mind's Disguise, The. Rosalie Moore. APT-2; YaYoPo

Mind's immortal, but the man is dead, The. (LL) Time and the Garden. Yvor Winters. APT-2; HarvBoo; MoAmPo; NoAM

Mind's Liberty, The. W. H. Davies. MoBrPo

Mine. Mary E. Tucker. CBWP-1

Mine and the sea-wind's. (LL) Rose, The. Theodore Roethke. APT-2; TRP

Mine angry and defrauded young? (LL) Rudyard Kipling. FaBoWar; NBLV; OPOU; PoWW; WoPoe *Fr.* Epitaphs of the War [1914–1918].

Mine are the night and morning. Song of Nature. Ralph Waldo Emerson. APN-1

Mine arms embrace my God, yet I. Ralph Erskine. SacPr *Fr.* Believer's Riddle, The.

Mine be a cot beside the [*or* a] hill. Wish, A. Samuel Rogers. OBEV; OxAEP-2

Mine be the strength of spirit fierce and free. Alfred Tennyson. CenSon

Mine be thy love, and thy love's use their treasure. (LL) William Shakespeare. CAGL; HeIP-4; NAEL-6v1; NAEL-7v1; NoP-4; NoP-5; NoSic; OxAEP-1; PBRV; WaAnP *Fr.* Sonnets.

Mine Enemy is growing old. Emily Dickinson. RaBo; RaF

Mine eye and heart are at a mortal war. William Shakespeare. HeIP-4 *Fr.* Sonnets.

Mine eyes did ne'er. William Wordsworth. NPBRoP *Fr.* Home at Grasmere [1800 version].

Mine eyes have seen the glory of the coming of the Lord. Battle Hymn [*or* Battle-Hymn] of the Republic, The. Julia Ward Howe. AmWaPo; APN-1; BRP; CBCWP; HHAm; NAAPv.1; NoP-5; OBWP; OxBoAm; SWaP; TCAPo; TFi

Mine eyes, like clouds, were drizzling rain. Rainbow; or Curious Covenant, The. Robert Herrick. ChIV-1

Mine high estate, power and auctority. Sir Thomas More. NoSic

Mine is a body that should die at sea! Burial. Edna St. Vincent Millay. InoFa

Mine is a labyrinth, not the heroics or high noon. Migration. David Johnson. ICANM

Mine is the ungloved. John Mole. NewEx

Mine, O thou lord of life, send my roots rain. (LL) Thou Art Indeed Just, Lord. Gerard Manley Hopkins. BrAP; InvLi; MoBrPo; NAEL-6v2; NAEL-7v2; NAMCP V.1; NoAM; NoP-4; NoP-5; SacPr; TFi; WaAnP

Mine [*or* Myne *or* Myn] own[e] John Poyntz, since [*or* sins] ye delight to know. Sir Thomas Wyatt. NoSic; NPeEn; OBSV; OBVE *Fr.* Satires.

Mine Own John Poins. Sir Thomas Wyatt. *See* Of the Courtier's Life.

Mine, says the cat, putting out his paw of darkness. Cat's song, The. Marge Piercy. BrAP

Mine was a trading family. Inscribed on the Doors of My Bookshelves. Yang Hsün-chi. ColAnChi, *tr. by* John Timothy Wixted

Mine with inner, weather. (LL) Tree at My Window. Robert Frost. APT-1; MoAmPo; NAMCP V.1; NoAM

Mine—by the Right of the White Election! Emily Dickinson. APN-2; NAAL-3; NALW; NoP-4; NoP-5; WPoS

Mined Country. Richard Wilbur. PWW2

Minefield, The. Diane Thiel. AmWaPo; RaF

Mine—long as Ages steal! (LL) Mine—by the Right of the White Election! Emily Dickinson. APN-2; NAAL-3; NALW; NoP-4; NoP-5; WPoS

Mineral Kingdom. Jacques Dupin. VCWP, *tr. by* Paul Auster

Miners. Branko Miljkovic. WoPoe, *tr. by* Charles Simic

Miners. Wilfred Owen. MoBrPo; OBWVE; OxAEP-2

Miner's Ballad, The. Lewis Morris. AngWePo

Miner's Family, The. Yosl Grinshpan. Prolet, *tr. by* Amelia Glaser

Miners hunted down the corn by the mounted division. 1984 Tour of Britain, The. Ken Smith. RSaN

Minerva Jones. Edgar Lee Masters. APT-1; IllVoic *Fr.* Spoon River Anthology.

Mines. Bruce Weigl. PoAgWa

Mines in Sepia Tint, The. Steve Griffiths. TCAWP

Ming, Ming. Masterworks of Ming. Kay Ryan. GoPo

Ming will be over to make way for the Ch'ing, The. Barbarian Suite. Marilyn Chin. OpBo

Mingled the moonlight with daylight—the last in the narrowing west. Thomas Hardy. Walter De la Mare. NoAM

Mingling with the holiday crowd. Fish 2. Fidelito Cortes. ReBoTo

Mingus at The Showplace. William Matthews. OxBoAm; PoA 2002; SeSe

Mingus Speaks: Found Poems. George Barlow. ISC

Miniature. Yannis Ritsos. GPTC; VCWP, *tr. by* Edmund Keeley

Miniature Dialogue. Edmund Wilson. OBCoV

Miniature in brass-rimmed frame, A. Cromwell: The Last Portrait. David Lindley. NLP

Miniaturist, The. Maurice Kilwein Guevara. AmPoNex; TouFir

Minimal, The. Theodore Roethke. NAMCP V.1; NoAM; OxBoAm

Minimal Ulysses. Jorge Fernández Granados. RMCMP, *tr. by* John Oliver Simon

Mínimos Ulises. Jorge Fernández Granados. RMCMP

Minister. Anne Stevenson. InoFa

Minister, The. Fenton Johnson. APT-1

Minister has all his notes in place, The. Richard Heller. FaBoWar

Minister said it wad [*or* wald] dee, The. Last Lauch. Douglas Young. EdScPo; NBLV

Ministers are rehabilitated. Nothing-Never. János Székely. IQMS, *tr. by* Geroge Gömöri

Minister's enunciations cut like knives, The. Prophecy, The. Robert Wrigley. SwNoth

Miniver Cheevy, child of scorn. Miniver Cheevy. Edwin Arlington Robinson. AmWit; APT-1; ChAP; ClHu; ColAP; EMP; HeIP-4; MoAmPo; NAAL-5; NAAPv.1; NAMCP V.1; NBLV; NoAM; NoP-4; NoP-5; OBSV; OxBoAm; RaBo; SoSe-8; TCAPo; TFi; WaAnP

Miniver Cheevy, Jr [*parody*]. David Fisher Parry. NBLV

Minks, The. Toi Derricotte. FuFl; UrbNat

Minneapolis Poem, The. James Wright. CAP-8; NAMCP V.2; NoAM

Minneapolis. / We talk of here and there. Dokusan: Visit to Katagiri Roshi. Diane Di Prima. AmZen

Minnelied. W. H. Auden. CAGL *Fr.* Three Posthumous Poems.

Minnesota Farmers Blame Bad Crop on Jews. Robert Hershon. PrTe

Minnesota Fats Describes His Youth. Elizabeth Alexander. AmPoNex

Minnetare Songs. *Unknown.*

New Moon Ceremonies.

"Buffalo are coming. We will feed and feast. We wish to be fortunate and we expect it, The." APN-2

"I want the robes, the skins of the game animals, the meat of the game animals. Bring them to me. Let us enjoy ourselves." APN-2

"If the clouds come good, our tobacco will grow. We will be happy." APN-2

"Spring from the earth, food for our children. Give us good health. Let us grow up, and become ripe." APN-2

Song of the Bald Eagle. APN-2

Song of the Bear. APN-2

Song of the Elk. APN-2

Song of the Gun. APN-2

Song of the Pheasant. APN-2

Song of the Weasel. APN-2

Song of the White Man. APN-2

Minnie had a house. Housing Poem, The. Dian Million. ReEnLa

Minnie Henderson. Colleen Beeson. TiP2

Minnie, I canna caa my minnie. Douglas Young. OBVE

Minnie May House she had to go. Julia A. Moore. STuOW *Fr.* William House and Family.

Minnie, the Moocher. Cab Calloway, Clarence Gaskill and Irving Mills. ReLy

Minnows and Flowers. Wintu Oral Tradition. NAAPv.1 *Fr.* Six Dream Songs.

Minoan Distance, The. Alan Williamson. FaoP

Minoen récent 1 (Aiguières d'Hagia Triada). Lorand Gaspar. YaTCFP

Minor Bird, A. Robert Frost. APT-1; OWoS; SAmP

Minor Figure. Mary Ruefle. ExTi

Minor God, A. Gu Cheng. WoBe *Fr.* Liquid Mercury.

Minor Miracle. Marilyn Nelson. CAP-8

Minor Poet, A. Amy Levy. VWP

Minor Poets, The. Damon Krukowski. OnScMo

Minor Van Gogh (He Speaks), A. Alicia Ostriker. RACG

Minority. Imtiaz Dharker. NeBl

Minotaur. Carl Phillips. AmAlph

Minotaur at Supper, The: Spare the Noritake and the Spode. D. A. Powell. IAoNAP; WiU

Minotaur lived, The. Death in Venice. Gareth Alban Davies. BBMWP, *tr. by* the author

Minotaur Next Door, The. Greg Pape. PBCAP

Minott, Lee, Willard, Hosmer, Meriam, Flint. Hamatreya. Ralph Waldo Emerson. APN-1; NAAL-3; NCAP

Minstrel. Michael Dransfield. BMAP

Minstrel, The. Sir Walter Scott. OxAEP-2 *Fr.* Lay of the Last Minstrel, The.

Minstrel austere, I honour you with gloom. Berzsenyi. Árpád Tóth. IQMS, *tr. by* Watson Kirkconnell

Minstrel Boy to the war is gone, The. Minstrel Boy, The. Thomas Moore. ChAP; FaBoWar; OxAEP-2

Minstrel Man. Langston Hughes. AmFaPo; ItP

Minstrel's Song. Ted Hughes. OBCP

Minted flesh of leaves, The. Town Garden, A. Tony Lucas. OBGa

Minute ago I came from the well, A. Woman, The. Kristina Rungano. HAWP

Minute Amphibian. Silvia Eugenia Castillero. SPV, *tr. by* Jen Hofer

Minute before Meeting, The. Thomas Hardy. OxBSo

Minute flowers harden. Depend. Lilies of the Valley. Jon Silkin. NoAM

Minute I heard my first love story, The. Jelaluddin Rumi. LoL, *tr. by* Coleman Barks

Minute I was born, The. Three Point Five Nine. Patricia Young. BrAP

Minute of Consciousness, The. Imamu Amiri Baraka. APSN

Minute the sun comes out, The. Isabel Fraire. CFP, *tr. by* Thomas Hoeksema

Minutes grow tedious, Time too slowly moves. Maria to Henric. *Unknown.* EMWP

Minutes of Hasiba, The. Holger Teschke. FaBoWar, *tr. by* Margitt Lehbert

Minutes ooze into a honeycomb gold, The. Spring Smoke. Arthur Sze. MAAN

Minutiae 3. P. F. Widdows. FaBoWar

Mips and ma the mooly moo. Theodore Roethke. NBLV *Fr.* Praise to the End!

Mira dances, how can her ankle bells not dance? Ankle Bells. Mirabai. WED, *tr. by* Robert Bly

Mira says: Without the energy that lifts mountains, how am I to live? (LL) All I Was Doing Was Breathing. Mirabai. WED; WoPoe; WPoS, *tr. by* Robert Bly

Mirándose. Francisco Brines. RaW

Mirabai says, The heat of midnight tears will bring you to God. (LL) Heat of Midnight Tears, The. Mirabai. WED; WPoS, *tr. by* Robert Bly

Mirabeau B. / (Buonaparte) Lamar. Mirabeau B. Lamar. A. L. Crouch. TiP2

Mirabeau B. Lamar. A. L. Crouch. TiP2

Mirabeau Bridge. Guillaume Apollinaire. WoPoe, *tr. by* Richard Wilbur

Mirabeau Bridge, The. Guillaume Apollinaire. OBVE

Mirabell: Books of Number. James Merrill.

    "It starts in the small hours. An interlude." NoAM

Mirabile Misterium. *Unknown.* SacPr

Miracle. Kathe Davis. AmZen

Miracle. Nikolai Kanchev. CSCBP, *tr. by* Georgi Belev and Lisa Sapinkopf

Miracle. Wen Yi-tuo [*or* Wen I-to]. PFTM-1

Miracle, The. Boris Leonidovich Pasternak. GI, *tr. by* Nina Kossman

Miracle, The. George Young. BloBone

Miracle Country. Dana Gelinas. SPV, *tr. by* Jen Hofer

Miracle for Breakfast, A. Elizabeth Bishop. OxBoAm; PoA 2002

Miracle Glass Co. Charles Simic. MakPoe

Miracle Indeed, A. Swami Purohit. OBMV

Miracle Mart. Wisława Szymborska. PoSu, *tr. by* Adam Czerniawski

Miracle mongers. Bedwetters. Hair-shirted wonder workers. Shirkers of the soggy soggy earth. Saints. Amy Gerstler. ExTi

Miracle of F6/18, The. Leontia Flynn. NIrP

Miracle of the children the brilliant. Exodus. George Oppen. ChIV-1

Miracle seekers bring offerings of money, candy, and teddy bears. Earthly Light. Marcia Southwick. PuP-23

Miracles. Conrad Potter Aiken. MoAmPo; TCAPo

Miracles. Carol Muske-Dukes. AmAlph; ExTi

Miracles. Walt Whitman. SAmP

Miracles of St. Sebastian, The. G. C. Waldrep. LegDan

Miracles secret and open flow from the teacher. Two Kinds of Miracles. Jelaluddin Rumi. WED, *tr. by* Robert Bly

Miraculous Dawn. R. Williams Parry. OBWVE, *tr. by* Joseph P. Clancy

Miraculous Grass. Nuala Ni Dhomhnaill. ModIr, *tr. by* Seamus Heaney

Miraculous Image. Miranda Field. LegDan

MIRACULOUS love's wounding! *Unknown.* NoSic

Miraculous Mandarin, The. Deborah Tall. PoDa

Miraculous Marriage of Zarife Dominquez. Patricia Dubrava. MPUn

Miraculous Panoptic Precipitations. Christine Hume. IAoNAP

Miraculous Ship, The. Delmira Agustini. TCLAP, *tr. by* Karl Kirchwey

Miraculous Weapons, The. Aimé Césaire. PFTM-1

Mirage. R. P. Blackmur. APT-2

Mirage. Hashim Shafiq. IrPoTo, *tr. by* Ralph Saverese and Saadi A. Simawe

Mirages. Kapka Kassabova. StAl

Miranda. W. H. Auden. NoAM; NPeEn *Fr.* Sea and the Mirror, The.

Miranda. Kathleen Kirk. IaFF

Mira's Will. Mary Leapor. CABP; NoP-4; NPeEn; OxBEV; PEW

Miriam. Marjorie Agosin. MirDau, *tr. by* Monica Bruno Galmozzi

Miriam's Song. Eleanor Wilner. FiBr; TaR

Miro la espuma, su delicadeza. Espuma. Claudio Rodríguez. RaW

Miro la música de Schumann. De cómo Robert Schumann fue vencido por los demonios. Francisco Hernandez. RMCMP

Miroir. Guillaume Apollinaire. YaTCFP

Miroir et le mouchoir, Le. Edmond Jabès. YaTCFP

Mirror. Guillaume Apollinaire. YaTCFP *Fr.* Heart, Crown, and Mirror.

Mirror. James Merrill. BeAl; PoA 2002

Mirror. Sylvia Plath. MoWP; NIL-7; NIP-4; OxBoAm; StAl

Mirror. Mieko Shiomi. WhBo

Mirror. Yi Sang. CAMKP, *tr. by* Walter Lew

Mirror 1. Hwang Jiwoo. CAMKP *Fr.* Melancholy.

Mirror 2. Hwang Jiwoo. CAMKP *Fr.* Melancholy.

Mirror 3. Hwang Jiwoo. CAMKP *Fr.* Melancholy.

Mirror, A. Jean Follain. BLT

Mirror, The. Dafydd ap Gwilym. WoPoe, *tr. by* Daniel Huws

Mirror, The. Michael Davitt. BeAl; PBCIP, *tr. by* Paul Muldoon

Mirror, The. Louise Glück. CAP-8; OxBoAm

Mirror, The. Robert Graves. NOxBChV

Mirror, The. Boris Leonidovich Pasternak. TCRusP, *tr. by* Bogdan Boychuk and Mark Rudman

Mirror, The. Wanted. Mercedes Roffé. TANSG, *tr. by* Kathryn Kopple

Mirror, The. Isaac Rosenberg. NAMCP V.1; NoAM

Mirror, The. "Shu Ting." PFTM-2, *tr. by* Dennis Ding, Fang Dai and Edward Morin

Mirror and Scarf. Edmond Jabès. YaTCFP, *tr. by* Rosmarie Waldrop

Mirror for Magistrates.

    Complaint of Henry Duke of Buckingham, The.

      Midnight. AEP

    Induction, The.

      Induction, The. NoSic

Mirror for the Twentieth Century, A. Adonis. AF, *tr. by* Abdullah Al-Udhari

Mirror Image. Louise Glück. StAl

Mirror in February. Thomas Kinsella. MakPoe; NAMCP V.2; NoAM

Mirror in the Deserted Hall, The. Felicia Dorothea Hemans. NOBRP

Mirror is not your body hanging from the wall, The. Me on the Wall. Ajanta. HotL, *tr. by* V. Narayana Rao

Mirror Lake, The. Summer Song. Li Po. NDACCP, *tr. by* William Carlos Williams

Mirror Lake's waters are moon-clear. Li Po. CrYelRi; ErotSp *Fr.* Women of Yueh.

Mirror, let us through the glass. W. H. Auden. *Fr.* For the Time Being; a Christmas Oratorio.

Mirror of a Day Chiming Marigold, The. Diane Wakoski. NALW

Mirror of a Moment, The. Paul Éluard. NAWM-7v2, *tr. by* Lloyd Alexander

Mirror of emptiness. Lake, The. Gertrude Pape. SurWo, *tr. by* Her de Vries

Mirror of Matsuyama, The. Sharon Hashimoto. CFP; OpBo

Mirror of poets, mirror of our age. Upon Ben Johnson [*or* Jonson]. Edmund Waller. NOSC

Mirror of the Battle. Ayin Tur-Malka. NRoS, *tr. by* Esther Raizen

Mirror. Roll away. Underneath (7). Jorie Graham. BodElec

Mirrored. Giancarlo Majorino. ItPo, *tr. by* Gayle Ridinger

Mirrored by stream / Swallow darts—. Saimaro. ZenPo, *tr. by* Takashi Ikemoto and Lucien Stryk

Mirrors. Sarah Arvio. KGB *Fr.* Visits from the Seventh.

Mirrors. Marta Kornblith. MirDau, *tr. by* Roberta Gordenstein

Mirrors. Ibrahim Nasrallah.

    "Outside my image in the frame." Eno

Mirrors at 4 A.M. Charles Simic. AWTN

Mirrors in the Room. Rodney M. McNeil. InTrad

Mirrors, The! The. Amelia Rosselli. CItWP, *tr. by* Cinzia Sartini Blum and Lara Trubowitz

Mirth, Spring, to linger in a garden fair. Khwaja Shams-ad-din Muhammad Hafiz. TAL *Fr.* Odes.

Mirth, with thee I mean to live. (LL) L'Allegro. John Milton. BASC; NAEL-6v1; NAEL-7v1; NoP-4; NoP-5; NOSC; OBEV; PBRV; PoPoPo; TFi

Mirza, scribe me a circle beneath. Amanuensis. Mimi Khalvati. MoWP

Mis Mai. Dafydd ap Gwilym.

    "Duw gwyddiad mai da y gweddai." CABP

Mis Pies ¡Qué Hondos en la Tierra! Juan Ramón Jiménez. RaW

Misanthropos. Thom Gunn.
Elegy on the Dust. NoAM
Last Man, The. OxAEP-2
Misanthropos. William Shakespeare. DiBP *Fr.* Timon of Athens.
Miscarriage. Joseph P. Clancy. AngWePo
Miscarriage. Jane Duran. PoCu; StAl
Miscarriage, Midwinter. Kate Clanchy. MoWP
Miscarried, mishandled—a lifetime's affairs. On the West Tower in Guozhou. Ts'en Shen. CCL1, *tr. by* Stephen Owen
Miscegenation. Natasha Trethewey. LegDan
Miscellaneous Bouquet. No Hyegyông. EcSo, *tr. by* Ann Y. Choi
Miscellaneous Feelings in the Sui Garden. Yüan Mei. ColAnChi, *tr. by* Jonathan Chaves
Miscellaneous Poem. T'ao Ch'ien. CCL1, *tr. by* Gladys Yang and Yang Xianyi, Gladys Yang *and* Hu Shiguang
Miscellaneous Poem on Rural Life. Liu Yin. ColAnChi, *tr. by* John Timothy Wixted
Misconceptions. Robert Browning. OBEV
Misconstrued, The. Bruce Berger. GeoH
Misdeal. Michel Leiris. YaTCFP, *tr. by* Keith Waldrop
Misdemeanor. Sharon Zetter. BeDoSh
Mise au monde, La. Jean-Michel Maulpoix. YaTCFP
Mise Eire. Eavan Boland. NAMCP V.2
Miser. Elizabeth Garrett. NeBl
Miserable ant. Yamaguchi Seishi. CAoMJL1, *tr. by* Alfred H. Marks and Takashi Kodaira
Miserable Estate of the World Before the Incarnation of God. William Drummond of Hawthornden. SacPr
Miserable I lie in desire. Archilochus. SaLy, *tr. by* Diane Rayor
Misere. Ifigenija Simonovic. PoCu, *tr. by* Anthony Rudolf
Miserere. David Gascoyne.
Ecce Homo. ChIV-2; NoP-4; NoP-5; OBWP
Misericord. The Misery Cord. Misery Cord (In Memory of F. S. Murray), The. Les A. Murray. UpMys
Misericordia! James Lipton. NBLV
"Miseries of Courtiers" by Æneas Sylvius Ricolomini, The. Alexander Barclay. *Fr.* Eclogues.
Miserimus. Adah Isaacs Menken. CBWP-1
Miserly. Michel Leiris. YaTCFP, *tr. by* Cole Swensen
"Miserrimus!" and neither name nor date. Gravestone upon the Floor in the Cloisters of Worcester Cathedral, A. William Wordsworth. SacPr
Miser's Only Friend, The. George Crabbe. DiBP *Fr.* Dealer and the Clerk, The.
Misery. Andreas Gryphius. WoPoe, *tr. by* Christopher Benfey
Misery. Rumen Leonidov. CSCBP, *tr. by* Georgi Belev and Lisa Sapinkopf
Misery. Edward Robert Bulwer-Lytton.
8.
Sordid Scene. STuOW
Misery and Splendor. Robert Hass. BeAl; OxBoAm; PtR; VCAP
Misery Cord (In Memory of F. S. Murray), The. Les A. Murray. UpMys
Misfits, The. Paul Muldoon. GPPA
Misfortune sometimes is a prize. Wooden Leg. James McIntyre. VerBaPo
Misfortunes of Elphin, The. Thomas Love Peacock.
War Song of Dinas Vawr, The. CABP; FaBoWar; NAEL-6v2; NOBRP; NPeEn; OxAEP-2
Misgivings. William Matthews. BeAl; PoDa
Misgivings. Herman Melville. APN-2; NAAL-3; NCAP; OxBoAm; TCAPo
Misguided Angels. Gale Renée Walden. ReTh
Misremembered Lyric, A. Denise Riley. NPeEn; Oth
Misremembered lyric: a soft catch of its song, A. Misremembered Lyric, A. Denise Riley. NPeEn; Oth
Miss Adair. Thomas Holley Chivers. STuOW
Miss Bitter. N. M. Bodecker. NTCP
Miss Blues's Child. Langston Hughes. ChAP; SAmP
Miss Buss and Miss Beale. *Unknown.* OBCoV
Miss Chang is Missing. Adrienne Su. PoDa
Miss Cho Composes in the Cafeteria. James Tate. WeW-3
Miss Clement's Second Grade. Maryfrances Cusumano Wagner. UnSA
Miss Congeniality. Maxine Chernoff. SUP
Miss Edith's Modest Request. Bret Harte. NOxBChV
Miss Florence Jackson. David Huddle. PBCAP
Miss Foggerty's Cake. *Unknown.* NBLV
Miss Gee. W. H. Auden. UV; WaAnP
Miss Gee Meets W. H. Auden in Heaven. Vanessa Haley. PfS
Miss Havisham. Olga Orozco. TCLAP, *tr. by* Stephen Tapscott
Miss Havisham's Letter. Julia Copus. MFPA

Miss Helen Slingsby was my maiden aunt. Aunt Helen. T. S. Eliot. FTtHH; NPeEn
Miss Ivy, tell me supmn. Wha Fe Call I'. Valerie Bloom. FaBoVe
Miss J. Hunter Dunn, Miss J. Hunter Dunn. Subaltern's Love-Song, A. Sir John Betjeman. BrAP; NoAM; OxAEP-2
Miss Jane jus hear from Merica. Pass fi White. Louise Bennett. NAMCP V.2
Miss July Grows Older. Margaret Atwood. NAMCP V.2
Miss Kilmansegg and Her Precious Leg. Thomas Hood.
Miss Kilmansegg's Birth. OBCoV
Miss Kilmansegg's Birth. Thomas Hood. OBCoV *Fr.* Miss Kilmansegg and Her Precious Leg.
Miss Lee [*or* Rosalie Lee]. Thomas Holley Chivers. STuOW
Miss Marnell. Austin Clarke. OxBEV
Miss Mary Mack. Lisa Buscani. AmPoNex
Miss Millay Says Something Too. Samuel Hoffenstein. NBLV
Miss Nettie was mystery to me at nine. Mistletoe Kills. Charlotte Renk. TiP2
Miss Nostalgia lurks in fishnet, in bustier. Americana. Paisley Rekdal. RWB
Miss October. Rachel Loden. RWB
Miss Otis Regrets. Cole Porter. ReLy
Miss Otis regrets she's unable to lunch today. Miss Otis Regrets. Cole Porter. ReLy
Miss Pimberton Of. Siv Cedering Fox. PBCAP
Miss R. looks at the mantel-piece, which must mean something. (LL) Evening in the Sanitarium. Louise Bogan. GPTC; NALW; NIL-7; OxBoAm
Miss Rafferty wore taffeta. Private Dining Room, The. Ogden Nash. AmWit; OBCoV
Miss Riley stands above me, fading fast. Bailey Gatzert: The First Grade, 1945. Lonny Kaneko. LTA
Miss Rosie. Lucille Clifton. ESEAA
Miss Rosie Mae. Miss Rosie Mae Watches Elvis Presley on The Ed Sullivan Show. Herbert Martin. AllShUp
Miss Rosie Mae Watches Elvis Presley on The Ed Sullivan Show. Herbert Martin. AllShUp
Miss Scarlet, Mr. Rhett and other Latter-Day Saints. Maya Angelou. OxAAAP
Miss ship. Clark Coolidge. AHA
Miss T. Walter De la Mare. NTCP
Miss third-person-singular-about-to-be-devoured, she's. Casus Belli. Caroline Finkelstein. PfS
Miss Tourist. Lord Kitchener. PML
Miss Universe, for Thy Name's Sake, Amen. (LL) Boom! Howard Nemerov. NBLV; NIL-7; NIP-4
Miss Wilson's eyes, opaque. Public School No. 18: Paterson, New Jersey. Maria Gillan. UnSA
Miss you, miss you, miss you. Miss You. David Cory. ITBLP
Miss you. / Should I say it. Road Away, The. Kim Sowŏl. CAMKP, *tr. by* David R. McCann
Missa joe. Seitlhamo Motsapi. TSAP
Mrs. Post's 6th-Hour English Class. Susan Firer. VisFro
Missing. Moniza Alvi. NeBl
Missing. Tracey Herd. MFPA
Missing. John McAuliffe. NIrP
Missing. Gardner McFall. OtW
Missing. Joseph Stroud. CalPo
Missing, The. Thom Gunn. CAGL; EMP; NAMCP V.2; NoP-4; NoP-5; WaAnP
Missing, The. Yannis Ritsos. AF, *tr. by* Edmund Keeley
Missing a kick. Jack Kerouac. WhBo
Missing All—prevented Me, The. Emily Dickinson. APN-2
Missing and spurious it might be i think, A. do you think so? Ode to Toge. Mark Prejsnar. AnSo
Missing — Believed Drowned. Michael Greening. FaBoWar
Missing consonant, silent vowel in everyone. Small Lower-Middle-Class White Southern Male. Rodney Jones. OxBoAm
Missing Dates. William Empson. HarvBoo; MakPoe; MoBrPo; NAMCP V.1; NoAM; NoP-5; NPeEn; OxBEV; StAl
Missing France. Jules Supervielle. MFP, *tr. by* Martin Sorrell
Missing God. Dennis O'Driscoll. BeAl
Missing head tells yet of the sacred day, The. Victory of Samothrace, The. Rubén Darío. GS, *tr. by Unknown*
Missing in Action. Yusef Komunyakaa. InGu
Missing Jew, The. Rodger Kamenetz. TaR
Missing Out. Eli Alon. NRoS, *tr. by* Esther Raizen
Missing Patriarch, The. Afaa Michael Weaver. PBCAP
Missing so much and so much? (LL) To a Fat Lady Seen from the Train. Frances Darwin Cornford. MoBrPo; OBMV; OxBEV; UV; WeW-3

Missing Supper. Tim Suermondt. PA9/11

Missing the noise of the sea at night. Nocturnal. John Haines. GifTon

Missing the Sea. Derek Walcott. OxBEV

Missing You. "Shu Ting." VCWP, tr. by Carolyn Kizer and Y. H. Zhao

Mission. Bei Dao. WoBe, tr. by Iona Man-Cheong and Eliot Weinberger

Mission Dolores. Hoa Nguyen. WANABP

Mission Impossible. Elizabeth Smither. BeAl

Mission Poem. Tarin Towers. AmPoNex; PuP-23

Mission San José. Carmen Tafolla. TiP2

Mission Street Song. Jon Paul Fiorentino. PoPra

Mission Thief. Forrest Gander. WoBe

Mission to the Frontier. Wang Wei. CCL1, tr. by Jerome P. Seaton

Mission Work-Boat. Unknown. NOBAu, tr. by Mungayana Nundhirribala

Missionary, The. Mrs. Henry Linden. CBWP-4

Mississippi. Rita Dove. AmAlph; StAl

Mississippi. Milán Füst. IQMS, tr. by István Tótfalusi

Mississippi. E. Ethelbert Miller. GT

Mississippi: Bell Zone 1. Jerry W., Jr. Ward. BtF

Mississippi Blues. Lamont B. Steptoe. SpirFl

Mississippi China woman, / why do you wear blue jeans in the city? Lost Name Woman. Shirley Lim. UnSA

Mississippi Girls, Plaited. Chelle Miko. RWB

Mississippi on the Doorstep. Sam Cornish. BtF

Mississippi river empties into the gulf. Lucille Clifton. NAMCP V.2

Mississippi steamed in July. Civil Rights. Ira Sadoff. LTA

Missoula Softball Tournament. Richard Hugo. MoASP

Missouri, she's a mighty river. Unknown. APN-2

Mist. Eugen Gomringer. PFTM-2, tr. by Jerome Rothenberg

Mist. Henry David Thoreau. NAAPv.1

Mist drizzles down on your tangled brown hair. Twenty Years Later, to a Friend. Andrea Potos. FiBr

Mist hangs of late, A. Different. Marga Kool. TuT, tr. by Joan McBreen

Mist in the Meadows. John Clare. NPeEn

Mist is thick, The. On the wide river, the water-plants float smoothly. Lonely Wife, The. Li Po. NAAPv.2; NIL-7, tr. by Florence Ayscough and Amy Lowell

Mist Maiden, The. Henrietta Cordelia Ray. CBWP-3

Mist rises, The. George Stanley. NLPA Fr. Mountains and Air.

Mist where Genesis begins, The. (LL) To the Man after the Harrow. Patrick Kavanagh. ModIr; WaAnP

Mistake, A. Czeslaw Milosz. BeAl, tr. by Renata Gorczynski and Robert Hass

Mistake, The. James Fenton. BeAl

Mistake, The. Theodore Roethke. OBCoV Fr. Three Epigrams.

Mistaken. Mary Elizabeth Coleridge. PoBW

Mistaken for the place of angels. (LL) Angels of Juárez, Mexico, The. Ray Gonzalez. TiP2; TouFir

Mistaken Identity. Lewis Warsh. BodElec

Mistakes. Judith Taylor. SUP

Mister Death. (LL) Buffalo Bill's Lament. E. E. Cummings. HeIP-4; InoFa; NAMCP V.1; NIP-4; OxBoAm; StAl; WaAnP

Mister Five by Five. Don Raye. ReLy

Mister Shylock was stingy. I've Got Five Dollars. Lorenz Hart. ReLy

Mister Snow. Oscar Hammerstein II. ReLy

Mister Williams / lets youn me move. Uncle Iv Surveys His Domain from His Rocker. Jonathan Williams. NBLV

Mister Winkler Winkler oh. Devil and the Princess. Unknown. FaBoVe

Misterios del tacto, Los. Coral Bracho. RMCMP

Mistletoe. Mary E. Tucker. CBWP-1

Mistletoe Kills. Charlotte Renk. TiP2

Mistress Agnes. János Arany. IQMS, tr. by William N. Loew

Mistress Agnes in the streamlet. Mistress Agnes. János Arany. IQMS, tr. by William N. Loew

Mistress Mary is dead and gone! (LL) Telling the Bees. John Greenleaf Whittier. APN-1; ColAP; NAAPv.1; NoP-4; NoP-5; OxBoAm; TCAPo

Mistress of all my senses can invite. To Caelia. Richard Duke. NOSC

Mistress of My Own Being. Ifi Amadiume. HAWP

Mistress, The. Abraham Cowley.
  Against Fruition. NOSC
  Against Hope. NOSC
  (On Hope.) CABP
  (Platonic Love.) NoP-4
  Platonic[k] Love. NoP-5
  Spring, The. OxAEP-1
  Wish, The. BASC; NoP-4; NoP-5; NOSC; OBEV; OxAEP-1; PBRV
  Written in Juice of Lem[m]on. CABP

Mistress, The. Pamela Gillilan. Prnts

Mistress, The. C. K. Williams. StAl

Mistress, The: A Song. John Wilmot, 2d Earl of Rochester. NOSC; NPeEn (Mistress, The.) OxAEP-1

Mistress to the Spirit of Her Lover, The. Charlotte Dacre. RWP

Mists, and the winds that warn, Stranger, O stranger! (LL) Snow on a Mountain. Dom Moraes. NoP-4; NoP-5

Mists are brooding on the fields, The. Autumn Song. József Bajza. IQMS, tr. by Watson Kirkconnell

Mists disappear, the water, The. Morning. Judith Herzberg. TuT, tr. by Joan McBreen

Mists Over the River. William Carlos Williams. ColAP

Misty. Johnny Burke. ReLy

Misty brown of my mourning flees, The. Adam, Where Art Thou? Endre Ady. IQMS, tr. by Anton N. Nyerges

Misty grasses. Buson. EH, tr. by Robert Hass

Misty moon. Tenth Wedding Anniversary (July 3, 1994): Tsuki Oboro Totsugishi Yoru No Sora Datta. Violet Kazue De Cristoforo. CalPo

Misty rain. Basho. EH, tr. by Robert Hass

Misty trees hide in crinkled hills' blue green. Returning Clouds. Ching An. CSKM, tr. by Jerome P. Seaton

Misty waves in the distance. Springtime South of the Yangtze. K'o Chun. CrYelRi, tr. by Sam Hamill

Misunderstanding, A. Maggie Nelson. PoDa

Misunderstood. Lizelia Augusta Jenkins Moorer. CBWP-3

Mitayo, The. Manuel González Prada. SpanPo, tr. by Kate Flores

Mitchells, The. Les A. Murray. PML

Mithras, God of the morning, our trumpets waken the Wall! Rudyard Kipling. NoAM Fr. Puck of Pook's Hill.

Mithridates. Ralph Waldo Emerson. APN-1; NCAP

Mithridates, he died old. (LL) A. E. Housman. BrAP; CABP; HeIP-4; NAEL-6v2; NAEL-7v2; NAMCP V.1; NoAM; NoP-4; NoP-5; TFi Fr. Shropshire Lad, A.

Mitigation. Kate Clanchy. EdScPo

Mitten Song, The. Marie Louise Allen. NTCP

Mix a Pancake. Christina Georgina Rossetti. NTCP

Mix a Pancake. Christina Georgina Rossetti. NTCP Fr. Sing-Song.

Mixed. Tess Gallagher. AmZen

Mixed Feelings. John Ashbery. WeW-3

Mixed Marriage. Diana Der Hovanessian. TWW

Mixed Marriage. Joan Logghe. MPUn

Mixed Marriage, The. Paul Muldoon. PNI

Mixed Weather. Sydney Tremayne. EdScPo

Mixed with morning dew? (LL) Isatou Died. Lenrie Peters. HBAPE; PoetW

Mixed with quartz grains, rose and amethyst. (LL) Sandpiper. Elizabeth Bishop. APT-2; HeIP-4; NoP-5; OWoS

Mixture of smells, The. Bower of Roses, A. Louis Simpson. PWW2

Mixtures of this garden, The. In the Garden: Villa Cleobolus. Lawrence Durrell. OBGa

Miyoko San. Mary Fenollosa. NAAPv.1

Miz Rosa Rides the Bus. Angela Jackson. IllVoic

Mizzle. Jay Parini. PfSP

Mm / I'm a little bit in love. Little Bit in Love, A. Betty Comden and Adolph Green. ReLy

Mmenson. Edward Kamau Brathwaite. OPOU

Mnemonic. Li-Young Lee. UnSA

Mnemosyne. Madison Cawein. APN-2

Mnemosyne. Trumbull Stickney. APN-2; CtM; NAAPv.2; TCAPo

Mo déjà roulé tout la côte / Pancor ouar pareil belle Layotte. Belle Layotte. Unknown. SSUS

Mo parlé Rémon, Rémon. Rémon. Unknown. SSUS

Moan in the dark, A. (LL) Black Slip. Terry Wolverton. SUP; WiU

Mob of dressing-tables is grazing, A. Duchesses. David Campbell. NOBAu

Mob, The. Calvin C. Hernton. OxAAAP

Mobile, The. Sean Dunne. ModIr Fr. Sydney Place.

Mobile City. Machine Wilkins. ArBi

Mobile, immaculate and austere. Pastoral, A. Geoffrey Hill. NPeEn

Möbius Strip. Anne Simpson. IFF

Möbius Strip-Tease. Alec Derwent Hope. OBCoV

Moby Dick. Herman Melville.
  "Call me Ishmael." GoPo
  "Ribs and terrors in the whale, The." APN-2; ChIV-1

Moby grape jam on the stereo. Some Sixties. Ray Gonzalez. MiVo

Mock class, A. My mother and I. Orientation: Wittenberg University, 1983. A. Van Jordan. NevBe

Mock On, Mock On, Voltaire, Rousseau. William Blake. ChIV-1; NAEL-6v2; NAEL-7v2; NAWM-7v2; NoP-4; NoP-5; NPeEn; TFi

Mock Orange. Louise Glück. CAP-8; MakPoe; NAMCP V.2; NoAM; OxBoAm; PoPoPo; VCAP

Mock Song, The. John Wilmot, 2d Earl of Rochester. NoP-5

Mocking Bird, The. Sidney Lanier. APN-2; TCAPo

Mocking Fairy, The. Walter De la Mare. MoBrPo

Mocking taunt, See then whether you shall be master!, The. (LL) Walt Whitman. ColAP; NAWM-7v2; NoP-4; NoP-5; SAmP; WaAnP *Fr.* Song of Myself.

Mocking-bird, A. Boyce House. TiP2

Mockingbird, The. Charles Bukowski. PmAP; WaAnP

Mocking-Bird, The. Joseph Rodman Drake. APN-1

Mocking-Bird, The. Richard Hovey. APN-2

Mockingbird, The. Randall Jarrell. OWoS

Mockingbird, knowing he owned the tree, The. Bluejay and the Mockingbird, The. Howard Nemerov. BodElec

Mockingbird leans, A. Letter to a Poet. Robert Hass. YaYoPo

Mockingbird Month. Mona Van Duyn. OWoS

Mocking-Bird's Song, The. *Unknown.* APN-2, *tr. by* Alice C. Fletcher

Moðöe word fræt. Me þæt þuhte. *Unknown.* NoP-5

Mode of France, The. *Unknown.* PBRV

Model, The. May Probyn. VWP

Model Children of the Regime, The. Nguyễn Chí Thiện. VCWP, *tr. by* Huynh Sanh Thông

Model children of the regime, The. Model Children of the Regime, The. Nguyễn Chí Thiện. VCWP, *tr. by* Huynh Sanh Thông

Model of the Universe, A. Norman Fischer. WhBo

Model yachts contend in seas sheltered, The. Conservatory Pond, Central Park, New York, New York. Joel Brouwer. AmPoNex

Models. Howard Nemerov. AF

Moder Phoebe. *Unknown.* FaBoVe

Moderation Is Not a Negation of Intensity, But Helps Avoid Monotony. John Tagliabue. GoPo

Moderation Kills (Excusez-Moi, je Suis Sick as a Dog). David Kirby. P180

Moderato. Susan Wicks. MFPA

Modern biographers worry, The. Romantics: Johannes Brahms and Clara Schumann. Lisel Mueller. GoPo

Modern circus, The. Pierre McOrlan. MFP, *tr. by* Martin Sorrell

Modern Craft. Hart Crane. CAGL

Modern Day Sisphus. Jeffrey McDaniel. LaCa

Modern delinquents. Vices of the Modern World. Nicanor Parra. CLPP, *tr. by* Jorge Elliott

Modern English. Jeffery Conway. WiU

Modern Female Fashions. Mary Robinson. NOBRP

Modern Fine Gentleman, The. Soame Jenyns.
"Just broke from school, pert, impudent, and raw." OBSV

Modern Fine Lady, The. Soame Jenyns.
"For love no time has she, or inclination." OBSV

Modern Hiawatha, The. George A. Strong. OBCoV; UV *Fr.* Song of Milkanwatha, The.

Modern Horn of Plenty, a magic coffer, A. Deep-Freeze. Nuala Ni Dhomhnaill. MoWP

Modern Love. Douglas Dunn. NPeEn

Modern Love. George Meredith.

Sonnet 1. CABP; GSo; NAEL-6v2; NAEL-7v2; NoP-4; NoP-5; NPeEn; WaAnP

Sonnet 2. NAEL-6v2; NAEL-7v2

Sonnet 3. NAEL-6v2

Sonnet 6. WaAnP

Sonnet 15. NAEL-6v2

Sonnet 16. NAEL-6v2

Sonnet 17. NAEL-6v2; NAEL-7v2; NoP-5; NPeEn; WaAnP

Sonnet 23. NAEL-6v2; WaAnP

Sonnet 30. CABP; NoP-4; NoP-5

Sonnet 34. NPeEn; OxBEV

Sonnet 35. NAEL-6v2

Sonnet 42. NAEL-6v2

Sonnet 43. NAEL-6v2; OBEV

Sonnet 47. OxBEV; WaAnP

Sonnet 48. NAEL-6v2; NoP-4; NoP-5

Sonnet 49. NAEL-6v2; NAEL-7v2; NoP-4; NoP-5

Sonnet 50. GSo; NAEL-6v2; NAEL-7v2; NoP-4; NoP-5; NPeEn; OxAEP-2; OxBEV; TFi

Modern Love. Anne Ridler. SacPr

Modern Love. Gerald Stern. BodElec

Modern Love. Ann Townsend. LegDan; LiTh

Modern Love: "Early evening, five minutes before." Jan Beatty. SweBea

Modern Love Poem, A. Candice Nicole Love. BRtP

Modern Major-General, The. William Schwenck Gilbert. *See* I Am the Very Model [*or* Pattern] of a Modern Major-General.

Modern malady of love is nerves, The. Nerves. Arthur Symons. CABP

Modern Male Fashions. Mary Robinson. NOBRP

Modern Man I sing, The. (LL) One's-Self I Sing. Walt Whitman. ColAP; NAAPv.1; NAMCP V.1; TCAPo; WaAnP

Modern Mother, The. Alice Thompson Meynell. VWP

Modern on the Surface. Nia Francisco. HATNAP

Modern Poet, A. Howard Nemerov. ViWalt

Modern Science has destroyed his reputation. Hyena, The. Cees Buddingh'. TuT, *tr. by* John Hughes

Modern Secrets. Shirley Lim. OPOU; StAl; UnSA

Modern Sorcery. Charles Simic. StAl

Modern Times. Fergus Allen. NIrP

Modern Times. Nicanor Parra. AF, *tr. by* Miller Williams

Modern Traveller, The. Joseph Hilaire Pierre Belloc.
Maxim Gun, The. FaBoWar

Modern Western History. Britton Wilkie. AHA

Modest chair people painted grey. People. Hans Arp. PFTM-1

Modest Muse a veil with pity throws, The. John Duncombe. STuOW *Fr.* Feminead, or Female Genius, The.

Modest Proposal, A. Ted Hughes. CABP

Modest rose puts forth a thorn, The. William Blake. NOBRP *Fr.* Songs of Experience.

Modest sinner stood behind, The. Navigation. Ralph Knevet. NOSC

Modo and Alciphron. Sylvia Townsend Warner. MoBrPo

Modotti. Adrienne Rich. NoP-5

Modris. Peter Thabit Jones. AngWePo

Modris sits on the warm doorstep. Modris. Peter Thabit Jones. AngWePo

Modulation. Robert Clinton. PoDa

Modulation is that footfalling, A. Footfalling. Laura Riding Jackson. NAMCP V.1

Moe Belle Jackson's husband. Battle, The. Gwendolyn Brooks. FTtHH

Moggy's Wedding. Charles Robert Thatcher. NOBAu

Moguer ("Anochecido, grandes nubes ahogan el pueblo.") Juan Ramón Jiménez. RaW

Moguer ("Dusk. Enormous clouds press down on the town.") Juan Ramón Jiménez. RaW, *tr. by* Hardie St. Martin

Mohács. Károly Kisfaludy. *tr. by* Watson Kirkconnell
"Sighing, O greet you and mourn you, O meadow of burial, Mohács." IQMS, *tr. by* Watson Kirkconnell

Mohawk lover who told her he stripped all his clothes, The. Deer Cloud. Susan Clements. UnSA

Mohini Chatterjee. William Butler Yeats. NoAM

Moi / Je suis. Poème pour une poupée achetée dans un bazar russe. Marguerite Yourcenar. YaTCFP

Moi l'Empereur ordonne ma sépulture: cette montagne hospitalière. Édit Funéraire. Victor Segalen. YaTCFP

Moi-Même. Carmen Bruna. SurWo, *tr. by* Natalie Kenvin

Moindre fêlure, La. Félicité. Jean Follain. YaTCFP

Moishele, Moishele / Moses Maimonides. Double Dactyls. Eric Salzman. OBCoV

Moist Moon People. Carl Sandburg. MoAmPo

Moist the jade dew that borders the flowers. Thinking of My Family on an Autumn Day. Yang Wen-li. WoPoe, *tr. by* Nancy Hodes and Tung Yuan-fang

Mokuboji Temple. Issa. ZenPo, *tr. by* Takashi Ikemoto and Lucien Stryk

Moldering Hulk, The. Antonio Machado Ruiz. SpanPo, *tr. by* Kate Flores

Moldering hulk, The. Moldering Hulk, The. Antonio Machado Ruiz. SpanPo, *tr. by* Kate Flores

Mole, The. Al-Muntafil. RaBo, *tr. by* Robert Bly

Mole, The. Nathan Alterman. FIT, *tr. by* Robert Friend

Mole, The. Christine D'Haen. TuT, *tr. by* Dennis O'Driscoll

Molecatcher. Albert D. Mackie. EdScPo

Mole Catcher. Edmund Charles Blunden. OBMV

Moles, The. Mark Cox. MAAN

Moles in Spring. Dave Jeddie Smith. PfSP

Molino. Maggie Nelson. HeMarv

Moll doll his chin. Yet. Mary Dalton. OpeFie

Mollusc. Les A. Murray. NAMCP V.2; UpMys

Molly Means. Margaret Abigail Walker. NALW

Molly Mog [or The Fair Maid of the Inn]. John Gay. OBCoV

Molly Pitcher. Laura Elizabeth Richards. HHAm

Mölna Elegy. Gunnar Ekelof. *tr. by* Muriel Rukeyser and Leif Sjöberg
Leavetaking. PFTM-2, *tr. by* Muriel Rukeyser and Leif Sjöberg
Marche Funèbre. PFTM-2, *tr. by* Muriel Rukeyser and Leif Sjöberg

Moly. Thom Gunn. CABP; NAMCP V.2; NoAM; NPeEn

Mom and Dad Getting Older. Sarah Rosenblatt. AmPoNex

Mom and Dad have abandoned the family home and retired to Palm. Empress of Sighs. Beth Lisick. AmPoNex

Mom and Dad must have believed they had found a safe place. Paysage Moralisé. Stephen Burt. LegDan

Mom Did Marilyn, Dad Did Fred. Jack Myers. ReTh

Mom is smart. Fēng Mèng-lung. ColAnChi; WoPoe *Fr.* Mountain Songs.

Mom says getting to the new home is a snap. Empress of Sighs. Beth Lisick. BAP-97

Mom told me how she "worked on" hers. Faith. Charles Harper Webb. Vesp

Mom Used to Listen to Erroll Garner. Everett Goodwin. BtF

Mom you'll know this as a wordgame, strategy to get truth's attention. Fred Wah. NLPA *Fr.* This Dendrite Map: Father / Mother Haibun.

Moment: "I saw a young deer standing." Hildegarde Flanner. APT-2; ASA

Moment. C. G. Hanzlicek. GeoHom

Moment. Angela Jackson. BtF

Moment-/ airly air / borne. Roy Kiyooka. NLPA *Fr.* Pear Tree Pomes.

Moment ("Clear moments are so short.") Adam Zagajewski. StAl, *tr. by* Renata Gorczynski

Moment, A. Mary Elizabeth Coleridge. LW; PEW

Moment, A. John Todhunter. IrLP

Moment, The. Margaret Atwood. OpeFie

Moment, The. Kathleen Jessie Raine. MoWP

Moment, The. Lőrinc Szabó. IQMS *Fr.* Cricket Music.

Moment before the comber turns into, A. Comber, The. Michael Longley. NAMCP V.2

Moment comes to me, A. This Bridge Across. Christopher Gilbert. ESEAA; GT

Moment I am told, The. Physical Geography. Mahe Jabeen. HotL, *tr. by* V. Narayana Rao

Moment of desire! the moment of desire! the virgin, The. William Blake. ErotSp; OxBEV *Fr.* Visions of the Daughters of Albion.

Moment of Love, A. Awwad Nasir. IrPoTo, *tr. by* Ralph Saverese and Saadi A. Simawe

Moment of Mourning, A. Donia El-Amal Ismail. PoArWo

Moment of My Father's Death, The. Sharon Olds. NIP-4

Moment of the First Day, The. Kalamu ya Salaam. AnSo

Moment of Waking, The. John Tranter. BMAP

Moment of War, A. Laurie Lee. OBWP

Moment Please, A. Samuel Allen. FuFl; SSLK

Moment she died, my mother's dancedresses, The. Sorting Through. Liz Lochhead. StAl

Moment the Two Worlds Meet, The. Sharon Olds. NAMCP V.2

Moment when, after many years, The. Moment, The. Margaret Atwood. OpeFie

Moment yellow, just as four years later when, A. Lyn Hejinian. PmAP *Fr.* My Life.

Moment yellow, just as four years later, when my father returned home from the war, A. Lyn Hejinian. NAMCP V.2 *Fr.* My Life.

Momentos Felices. Gabriel Celaya. RaW

Moments after death, I found my voice. Result, The. Robert Crawford. NeBrP

Moment's memory to that laurelled head, A. (LL) Coole Park, 1929. William Butler Yeats. CABP; OBMV

Moments of great calm. Kneeling. Ronald Stuart Thomas. WaAnP

Moments of Summer. Rachel Hadas. RA

Moments pass, The. Moment. C. G. Hanzlicek. GeoHom

Moments pass unchanged. Predicted. Secreting. White Trace Close. Christine Monhollen. Eno

Moments that hands without a vine...laughter. Ivano Fermini. ItPo, *tr. by* Gayle Ridinger

Momentum and wash of the undefined. Platonic Subject. Ann Lauterbach. PmAP

Momma a carrot grows underground. Potlicker Blues. Calvin Forbes. GT

Momma cat died in the weeds. Practicing Eulogies. Gary Soto. NAMCP V.2

Momma had words for us. Momma Sayings. Harryette Mullen. ISC; ItWoWo; TiP2

Momma in Red. Karen Williams. BRtP

Momma is a big-boned, Nordic looking. For the White Lady Holding Me. Crystal Williams. AmPoNex

Momma Sayings. Harryette Mullen. ISC; ItWoWo; TiP2

Momma told me to write to you today. Letter to Daddy, A. *Unknown, fr. Terezin Concentration Camp.* INSAB

Mommie, she says, "I've never met you and daddy." Learning to See Crooked. Gerald Locklin. SUP

Mommy mommy come and see. Ballad from Childhood. Audre Lorde. WaAnP

Mommy, Mommy! / Please be holy. Between Saint and Witch. Kim Sǔnghǔi. EcSo, *tr. by* K. Kim Richards and Steffen Richards

"Mommy, take me home. I'm a changed boy!" Ontogeny. Jarold Ramsey. NIP-4

Mom's in the kitchen telling stories. Vesta's Father. Julia Kasdorf. PBCAP

Mon avion en flammes mon château inondé de vin du Rhin. Allo. Benjamin Péret. YaTCFP

Mon cheval arrêté sous l'arbre plein de tourterelles. Chanson. "St.-John Perse." YaTCFP

Mon Pouchkine. Nathalie Quintane. YaTCFP

Mona Lisa. Ray Evans and Jay Livingston. ReLy

Mona Lisa. Walter Pater. OBMV

Mona Lisa. Edith Wharton. GS

Mona Lisa, A. Angelina Weld Grimké. APT-1; NAAPv.2

Mona lisa mona lisa mona lisa Mona Lisa mona lisa The. Message No. 44. Holley Blackwell. AnSo

Mona Lisa Tea Towel, The. Nigel Roberts. BMAP

Monadnoc. Ralph Waldo Emerson.
   "Every morn I lift my head." APN-1

Monangamba Estate. Antonio Jacinto. SonAtl, *tr. by* Michael Cruz, Mary Jay and Lisa Martin

Monarch of Gods and Dæmons, and all Spirits. Prometheus Unbound. Percy Bysshe Shelley. NAEL-6v2; NAEL-7v2; NOBRP

Monarch of Han, he doted on beauty, yearned for a bewitching temptress. Song of Lasting Regret, The. Po Chü-i. ColAnChi, *tr. by* Paul W. Kroll

Monarch saw the gambols flag, The. Sir Walter Scott. DiBP *Fr.* Lady of the Lake, The.

Monarche, The. Sir David Lyndsay.
   After the Flood. ChIV-1

Monarchs. Sharon Olds. CAP-8

Monarchs of Parque Tranquilidad. Robin Becker. UrbNat

Monarchs Steering. Shirley Lim. GeoHom

Monasteries Lift Gold Domes, The. Yocheved Bat-Miriam. FIT, *tr. by* Robert Friend

Monastery. Ivan Davidkov. CSCBP, *tr. by* Georgi Belev and Lisa Sapinkopf

Monastery. Yevgeny Borisovich Rein. TCRusP, *tr. by* Daniel Weissbort

Monastery, The. Pure Sound Pavilion of the Riverside Temple, The. Muso Soseki. EaWin, *tr. by* W. S. Merwin

Monastery, The. Sir Walter Scott.
   (Book of Books, The.) ChIV-1

Monastery gate. Mitsu Suzuki. WhBo

Monastery Orchard in Early Spring, The. Kathleen Norris. UpMys

Monastic Poems: Four Glosses. *Unknown.* WoPoe.

Monastîr. Cynan. BBMWP, *tr. by* Sally Roberts Jones

Monday. Romelia Alarcón de Folgar. TANSG, *tr. by* Alison Ridley

Monday. Week in the Life of the Ethnically Indeterminate, A. Elena Georgiou. WiU

Monday. Nikki Giovanni. InGu

Monday, 3 December. Norman Fischer. WANABP *Fr.* Success.

Monday a boy who cannot lift. Space. Maura Stanton. OPRER

Monday evening, E. 22nd. Lilacs in NYC. Mark Doty. WiU

Monday has the long face. Monday. Romelia Alarcón de Folgar. TANSG, *tr. by* Alison Ridley

Monday I expect a letter from you. Weekly Agenda of Love. M. Sami Aşar. NaPG, *tr. by* Talat Sait Halman

Monday, Monday. David Trinidad. SwNoth

Monday Morning. Audrey Shafer. BloBone

Monday morning broke. Rub a Dub Style inna Regent Park. Lillian Allen. WaCA

Monday Night at Pedro's. Sandra M. Castillo. TouFir

Monday night i went to the san francisco art institute to see nathaniel dorsky's silent film trilogy. Trilogy. Del Ray Cross. FreRad

Monday night was for doing the brasses. Portrait in a Brass Gong. Mick North. NLP

Monday rue Christine. Guillaume Apollinaire. CuPo

Mondays are meshed with Tuesdays. Too Many Names. Pablo Neruda. VCWP, *tr. by* Alastair Reid

Monday's child is fair of face. Birthdays. Mother Goose. NBLV

Mondays, he trails burr-like fragments. Marriage. Carol Rumens. MoWP

Mondays my aunt awoke with the first cockrow, in the orange dawn. Those Rainy Mornings. Frank Mkalawile Chipasula. HBAPE

Mondo. Sojun Mel Weitsman and Zen Center Sangha. WhBo

Mondo Henbane. Charles Wright. PfSP

Mondrian's Forest. Wendy Battin. AmWaPo

Monet never knew. Monet's Lilies Shuddering. Lawrence Ferlinghetti. PmAP

Monet Refuses the Operation. Lisel Mueller. IllVoic

Monet tires of painting lilies. From Where I Stand. Elena Georgiou. WiU

Monet's Lilies Shuddering. Lawrence Ferlinghetti. PmAP

Monet's "Waterlilies" [(*for Bill and Sonja*)]. Robert Earl Hayden. AmFaPo; GT

Money. Richard Armour. NBLV

Money. W. H. Davies. OBEV; OBMV

Money. Beckian Fritz Goldberg. AmAlph

Money. Philip Larkin. NPeEn

Money. Howard Nemerov. VCAP; WeW-3

Money. Bob Perelman. FTOS

Money. C. K. Williams. OxBoAm

Money As Water. Kurt Brown. SUP

Money burns the pocket, pocket hurts. Seventh Street. Jean Toomer. APT-2; NAAPv.2

Money ghost lives in the hands of many men, The. Parody. Chungji. BecRai, *tr. by* Kim Daljin, Kim Won-Chung and Christopher Merrill

Money, Money. *Unknown.* CABP

Money, money, now hay goode day! Money, Money. *Unknown.* CABP

Money Song, The. Harold Rome. ReLy

Mongoloid Child Handling Shells on the Beach, A. Richard Snyder. NIL-7

Mongo's open hands. Shaking Hands with Mongo. Martín Espada. SeSe

Monique. Cynthia Hogue. LiTh

Monitors. Geoffrey Holloway. NLP

Monk. Gaston Neal. BtF

Monk. John Taggart. FTOS; PFTM-2

Monk, A. Geoffrey Chaucer. OBCoV *Fr.* Canterbury Tales, The.

Monk, The. Thomas Kinsella. BBASP

Monk at the Five Spot. Crepuscule with Nellie. Charles Simic. SeSe

Monk Chun of Shu with a Green Brocade Lute. Listening to the Lute Played by Monk Chun from Shu. Li Po. ChinPo, *tr. by* Ye Weilian [*or* Yeh Wei-lien *or* Wai-lim Yip]

Monk coveted the moon in the well, The. Moon in the Well, The. Yi Kyubo. CATKP, *tr. by* Kevin O'Rourke

Monk from Shu with his green lute-case walked, The. Listening to a Monk from Shu Playing the Lute. Li Po. WoPoe, *tr. by* Vikram Seth

Monk in the Kitchen, The. Anna Hempstead Branch. APT-1; MoAmPo

Monk neighbors on three sides, a wall on the fourth. Written on a Summer Day in the City. Ch'i-chi. CSKM, *tr. by* Burton Watson

Monk sips morning tea, A. Basho. EH, *tr. by* Robert Hass

Monk Stood Beside a Wheelbarrow, The. Jane Hirshfield. AmZen

Monk stood beside a wheelbarrow, weeping, The. Monk Stood Beside a Wheelbarrow, The. Jane Hirshfield. AmZen

Monk that slept here must, after all, have been a man, The. *Unknown.* CATKP, *tr. by* Kevin O'Rourke

Monk ther was, a fair for the maistrye [*or* maistrie], A. Geoffrey Chaucer. OBCoV *Fr.* Canterbury Tales, The.

Monk was preaching: strong his earnest word, The. Legend, A. Adelaide Anne Procter. SacPr

Monkey. Vladislav Felitsianovich Khodasevich. TCRusP, *tr. by* Daniel Weissbort

Monkey. Bruce Weigl. AmAlph

Monkey Blues. Michael Brownstein. AHA

Monkey cries accompany the dawn. Crossing the Mountain, I Follow the Chin-chu River. Hsieh Ling-yün. CrYelRi, *tr. by* Sam Hamill

Monkey Hill. Stan Rice. PoCho

Monkey House. Betsy Sholl. SUP

Monkey knows, The. *Unknown.* SonAtl, *tr. by* Pila Cahanna and Owen Forrest

Monkey-eaters. Takahashi Mutsuo. PFTM-2, *tr. by* Hiroaki Sato

Monkeyland. Sándor Weöres. IQMS; WoPoe, *tr. by* Edwin Morgan

Monkeys at the laboratory. Do Not Put Dead Monkeys in the Freezer. Martín Espada. TouFir

Monkeys cry: dawn, they know. From Chin-Chu Creek, Past the Ridge, Along the Stream. Hsieh Ling-yün. ChinPo, *tr. by* Ye Weilian [*or* Yeh Wei-lien *or* Wai-lim Yip]

Monkey's Journey, The. Mahmoud al-Braikan. IrPoTo, *tr. by* Ralph Saverese and Saadi A. Simawe

Monkey's Pride. John Forbes. BMAP

Monkeys, The. Marianne Moore. APT-1

Monkeys' world the world we face, The. (LL) Monkeyland. Sándor Weöres. IQMS; WoPoe, *tr. by* Edwin Morgan

Monk's bowl. Stanford M. Forrester. AmZen

Monk's bowl, The. Tom Montag. AmZen *Fr.* Ben Zen Poems.

Monk's dissonant hat. Bandstand. Michael S. Harper. SeSe

Monk's Dream. Dave Etter. SeSe

Monk's Misterioso. Sydney March. BtF

Monks recite the sutras in honor of the Founder. Face to Face with My Lover on Daito's Anniversary. Ikkyu Sojun. ErotSp, *tr. by* Sam Hamill

Monk's World. Imamu Amiri Baraka. NAMCP V.2

Mon'motapa's coast. John Dyer. STuOW *Fr.* Fleece, The.

Monmouth. John Dryden. NPeEn

Monna Innominata. Christina Georgina Rossetti.
  "Come back to me, who wait and watch for you." OxBSo
  "I dream of you to wake: would that I might." OxBSo
  ""I, if I perish, perish"—Esther spake." OxBSo
  "I loved you first: but afterwards your love." OxBSo
  "I wish I could remember the [*or* that] first day." LW; OxBSo
  "If there be any one can take my place." OxBSo
  ""Love me, for I love you"—and answer me." OxBSo
  "Many in aftertimes will say of you." CABP; MakPoe; OxBSo
  "O my heart's heart, and you who are to me." OxBSo
  "Thinking of you, and all that was, and all." OxBSo
  "Time flies, hope flags, life plies a wearied wing." OxBSo
  "Trust me, I have not earned your dear rebuke." OxBSo
  "Youth gone, and beauty gone if ever there." GSo; OxBSo

Monodrama. Bill Knott. BodElec

Monody on Doctor Olmsted. Edgar Allan Poe. TCAPo

Monody: "To have known him, to have loved him." Herman Melville. APN-2; NAAL-3; NAAPv.1; NoP-4; NoP-5; PoPoPo; TCAPo

Monody to the Sound of Zithers. Kay Boyle. PoA 2002

Monologue. Gottfried Benn. AF, *tr. by* Christopher Middleton

Monologue, A. Mihai Ursachi. PML, *tr. by* the author and Adam J. Sorkin

Monologue at the Chinook Bar and Grill. Tess Gallagher. BodElec

Monologue for an Onion. Suji Kwock Kim. LegDan

Monologue for Cassandra. Wisława Szymborska. PoSu, *tr. by* Grazyna Drabik

Monologue for Selah Bringing Spring to Whylah Falls. George Elliott Clarke. OpeFie

Monologue of the Falconer's Wife. Colette Inez. PuP-23

Monologue of the Magdalene. John Peck. HarvBoo

Monologue with Commentary. Andrey Andreievich Voznesensky. RusPo, *tr. by* Robert Arthur Douglas Ford

Monologue with Its Wife. Gunnar Ekelof. WED, *tr. by* Robert Bly

Monomaniacal Possessor of the Firmament. Hans Arp. MotU, *tr. by* Bethany Schneider

Monoon Season. Yusef Komunyakaa. AmAlph

Monosyllable, The. Josephine Jacobsen. OxBoAm

Monotomy. Gabriella Sica. CItWP, *tr. by* Cinzia Sartini Blum and Lara Trubowitz

Monotones. B. P. Nichol. FTOS

Monotones. B. P. Nichol. PFTM-2 *Fr.* Martyrology 7, The.

Monotonies of my retinas. Processions, The. Mário de Andrade. TCLAP, *tr. by* Jack E. Tomlins

Monotony Song, The. Theodore Roethke. ChAP

Monsieur Étienne de Silhouette. Some Frenchmen. John Updike. NBLV

Monsieur Ezra Pound croit que. Another Canto. John Bingham Morton. UV

Monsieur, your ribcage. Man without a Middle, The. Angela Sorby. AmPoNex

Monsoon. Elsa Cross. RMCMP, *tr. by* Margaret Sayers Peden

Monsoon Day Fable, A. Jayanta Mahapatra. VCWP

Monsoon Girl. Harry Clifton. PBCIP

Monsoon Season Opens Children's Eyes. Chông Hwajin. EcSo, *tr. by* Julie C. Park

Monsoon Song. James Cordeiro. PoDa

Monster and the sacrifice are one, The. Head and Torso of the Minotaur. John Reibetanz. IFF

Monster owl, A. Lorine Niedecker. NAAPv.2

Monster seized the shrieking girl, The. Samuel Carter. STuOW *Fr.* Avenger, The.

Monster, The. Karen L. Mitchell. GT

Monster's Dream, The. William Reichard. AmPoNex

Monstrance. János Pilinszky. PoSu, *tr. by* Peter Jay

Monstrous Pictures of Whales. Dennis Schmitz. GeoHom

Mont Blanc. Percy Bysshe Shelley. BrAP; NAEL-6v2; NAEL-7v2; NIP-4; NOBRP; NoP-4; NoP-5; NPBRoP

Mont Ventoux. Jan Kal. ArBi, *tr. by* John Irons

Montana Pastoral. James Vincent Cunningham. APT-2; MoAmPo; OxBoAm

Montana's Biggest Weekend. Whitney Ward. FTtHH

Monterey. David Schubert. APT-2

Monterrey Sun. Alfonso Reyes. TCLAP, *tr. by* Samuel Beckett

Montes, los olivos, Los. Arabian Knight. Manuel Ulacia. RMCMP

Montesano Unvisited. Richard Hugo. OxBoAm

Montezuma. Diane Di Prima. BB

Month gone and the day coming up like a bad cold, The. Saturday 6 a.m. Charles Wright. GeoHom

Month of plants and of honey. Alexander MacDonald. NePenScot *Fr.* Song of Summer.

Month of rain ends—. Tanka. Lenard D. Moore. SpirFl

Month of roses. And my rhymes. Spring. Rubén Darío. SpanPo, *tr.* by Anita Volland

Month of roses. My poems. Springtime. Rubén Darío. TCLAP, *tr.* by Lysander Kemp

Month she died, the. Ein Leben. Dan Pagis. FIT, *tr.* by Robert Friend

Months after the Muse. Illustration, The [—a Footnote]. Denise Levertov. PoA 2002

Months and years have flown. Passing Through Ch'ien-hsi, Third Month, 405. T'ao Ch'ien. CrYelRi, *tr.* by Sam Hamill

Montreal. Abraham Moses Klein. BrAP

Monument, A. Vladislav Felitsianovich Khodasevich. TCRusP, *tr.* by John Glad

Monument, The. Elizabeth Bishop. NAMCP V.2; NoAM; TRP

Monument to Birds (Max Ernst). Luiza Neto Jorge. SurWo, *tr.* by Jean R. Longland

Monumental Memorial of Marine Mercy, A. Richard Steere. TCAPo

Monumental, millennial decrepitude. Dream Avenue. Charles Simic. StAl

Monuments for a Friendly Girl at a Tenth Grade Party. William Stafford. NoAM

Monuments, The. John Ash. EmeKit

Monutments of political yearning occur in the shopkeepers' vaults, The. Allegory of Good Government. Rod Mengham. VaPo

Monzón. Elsa Cross. RMCMP

Moochie likes to keep on playing. Moochie. Eloise Greenfield. NTCP

Moochkap. Boris Leonidovich Pasternak. TCRusP, *tr.* by Bogdan Boychuk and Mark Rudman

Mood Indigo. William Matthews. WeW-3

Mood of Depression, The. Georg Trakl. WED, *tr.* by Robert Bly

Moods. Sara Teasdale. APT-1

Moods 1. Della Cruscans. STuOW

Moods 2. Della Cruscans. STuOW

Moods 3. William Parsons. STuOW

Moody child and wildly wise, A. Motto to "The Poet." Ralph Waldo Emerson. NCAP

Mool oio clish brodge. Junt. Norman Henry Pritchard II. EGAG

Moon. Nathan Alterman. FIT, *tr.* by Robert Friend

Moon. Katie Donovan. NIrP

Moon. Nicolás Guillén. PFTM-1

Moon. Giovanni Raboni. ItPo, *tr.* by Gayle Ridinger

Moon. Henry Rowe. OBEV

Moon. Takahashi Shinkichi. ZenPo, *tr.* by Takashi Ikemoto and Lucien Stryk

Moon, The. Witter Bynner. APT-1

Moon, The. (LL) Niagara. Adelaide Crapsey. APT-1; NAAPv.2

Moon, The. W. H. Davies. MoBrPo

Moon, The. Robert Duncan. APSN *Fr.* Passages.

Moon, The. Gunnar Ekelof. AWTN, *tr.* by Robert Bly

Moon, The. Juan Ramón Jiménez. MotU, *tr.* by Hoffman Reynolds Hays

Moon, The. Percy Bysshe Shelley. OBEV

Moon, The. Martha Silano. AmPoNex

Moon, The. Robert Louis Stevenson. TLR

Moon, The. *Unknown.* FaBoVe

Moon, a ring of crimson snapped in two, The. Long-Barrow Princess 2. Elizaveta Kuzmina-Karavayeva. ARWW, *tr.* by Catriona Kelly

Moon, a sweeping scimitar, dipped in the stormy straits, The. Winged Man. Stephen Vincent Benét. MoAmPo

Moon About Town. E. Y. Harburg. ReLy

Moon above the milky field, The. Night-Piece. Léonie Adams. MoAmPo

Moon and Apple. Rolf Jacobsen. WED, *tr.* by Robert Bly

Moon and Farmstead. Sándor Weöres. IQMS, *tr.* by Edwin Morgan

Moon and Firestone, The. Diana Hartog. NLPA *Fr.* Oasis.

Moon and Hare. Takahashi Shinkichi. ZenPo, *tr.* by Takashi Ikemoto and Lucien Stryk

Moon and Spectator, The. Léonie Adams. APT-2

Moon and the flowers, The. Issa. EH; NIL-7, *tr.* by Robert Hass

Moon and the Night and the Men, The. John Berryman. GPTC; PWW2; VCAP

Moon and the Pleiades have set, The. Sappho. SaLy, *tr.* by Diane Rayor

Moon and the Yew Tree, The. Sylvia Plath. BBASP

Moon / Another hour has come through the opening. Sentry. Dennis Saleh. GeoHom

Moon, as though something dead. West, The (Fourth Version). Georg Trakl. GTCP, *tr.* by Robert Firmage

Moon at Sea. Nikolai Stepanovich Gumilyov. TCRusP, *tr.* by Mary Jane White

Moon be thanked for what, The. Your Absence. Arthur Nortje. TSAP

Moon became mired on our bed, The. Ana Istarú. TANSG, *tr.* by Mary Jane Treacy

Moon behind High Tranquil Leaves, The. Robert Malise Bowyer Nichols. OBMV

Moon broken, she said. (LL) Broken Moon. Carole Satyamurti. BeAl; MoWP

Moon Came Late, The. Mary Mapes Dodge. SWaP

Moon came late to a lonesome bog, The. Moon Came Late, The. Mary Mapes Dodge. SWaP

Moon clouds over, the alley-cats start to fight, The. David Wheatley. NIrP *Fr.* Sonnets to James Clarence Mangan.

Moon comes out, both full and bright, The. Ah. *Unknown.* CCL1 *Fr.* Yue-chu [Translations].

Moon comes up, a white cow, The. Leonard Refuses to Atone. Louise Erdrich. UpMys

Moon Compasses. Robert Frost. ITBLP

Moon Dance (Listen Sylvia). Tony Nduka Otiono. NeNiPo

Moon Daughters. Artress Bethany White. BtF

Moon did not become the sun, The. Stationery. Agha Shahid Ali. BeAl

Moon dips low and the stars grow dim. Moon Dips Low, The. Wei Chuang. CCL1, *tr.* by Lois Fusek

Moon Dips Low, The. Wei Chuang. CCL1, *tr.* by Lois Fusek

Moon does shine as bright as day. (LL) Namby-Pamby. A Panegyric on the New Versification, Address'd to A———— P————, Esq. ("All ye poets of the age.") Henry Carey. NPeEn; OBSV; UV

Moon drops one or two feathers into the field, The. Beginning. James Wright. ColAP; VCAP

Moon Eclipse Exorcism. *Unknown.* WoPoe, *tr.* by Armand Schwerner

Moon falls in shape of little metal plates against my face. Remembrance of the Founts of Night. Theo Van Doesburg. PFTM-1

Moon Festival. Bei Dao. WoBe, *tr.* by Iona Man-Cheong and Eliot Weinberger

Moon Festival. Tu Fu [*or* Du Fu]. NDACCP, *tr.* by Kenneth Rexroth

Moon Fishing. Greta Knutson. YaTCFP, *tr.* by Mary Ann Caws

Moon flashes in Her blessed face, The. Mahārāja Rāmkrsna Rāy. SinGod, *tr.* by Rachel Fell McDermott

Moon Folly. Fannie Stearns Gifford. RACG *Fr.* Songs of Conn the Fool, The.

Moon god's light, The. Kitahara Hakushū. CAoMJL1, *tr.* by Janine Beichman

2: The Moon Ground. James Dickey. OtW *Fr.* Apollo.

Moon had, The. Jack Kerouac. WhBo

Moon hangs in the air, A. David Campbell. BMAP

Moon hangs on a clouded sky, The. Clouded Sky. Miklós Radnóti. GifTon; HP, *tr.* by Stephen Berg, F. J. Marks, S. J. Marks and Steven Polgar

Moon hangs on a nettle tree, The. Crescent Moon. Ch'ôn Yanghûi. EcSo, *tr.* by Aimee N. Kwon

Moon has a face like the clock in the hall, The. Moon, The. Robert Louis Stevenson. TLR

Moon has a halo, there will be wind, The. I Remember the Blue River. Mei Yao Ch'en. NDACCP, *tr.* by Kenneth Rexroth

Moon has already left the cliffs, The. Moon at Sea. Nikolai Stepanovich Gumilyov. TCRusP, *tr.* by Mary Jane White

Moon has fallen on her back, The. Night-Piece. Frances Horovitz. LW

Moon has gone to her rest, The. Nocturne. Wilfrid Scawen Blunt. OBMV

Moon Has Set, The. Sappho. WoPoe, *tr.* by Kenneth Rexroth

Moon has set, The. Moon Has Set, The. Sappho. WoPoe, *tr.* by Kenneth Rexroth

Moon has set, The. Sappho. WoPoe, *tr.* by Jim Powell

Moon Haze. Amy Lowell. NAAPv.2

Moon, he didn't come back. He Didn't Come Back. Nanduri Subbarao. HotL, *tr.* by V. Narayana Rao

Moon hung low 'mid clouds enshrined, The. Fading Skiff, The. Henrietta Cordelia Ray. CBWP-3

Moon in a blue sky, morning loneliness, the need to have children. Blue Sky in Morning. Rob MacKenzie. Oth

Moon in a Mason Jar. Robert Wrigley. RoV

Moon in China Bazaar. Pathabhi. HotL, *tr.* by V. Narayana Rao

Moon in her new era, the. CXLII. Pita Amor. TANSG, *tr.* by Shaun Griffin and Emma Sepúlveda-Pulvirenti

Moon in Llŷn is pregnant, The. Moons of Llŷn, The. Alan Llwyd. BBMWP, *tr.* by Joseph P. Clancy

Moon in midsky, high. Buson. SoOfWa, *tr.* by Sam Hamill

Moon in the bureau mirror, The. Insomnia. Elizabeth Bishop. AWTN

Moon in the dewdrop is the real moon, The. Allen Ginsberg. WhBo

Moon in the Mirror. Brenda Brooks. ArBi

Moon in the pond, The. Missing France. Jules Supervielle. MFP, *tr.* by Martin Sorrell

Moon in the sky, floating overhead. On My Pneumonia. Mihály Csokonai Vitéz. IQMS, *tr.* by Joseph Leftwich

Moon in the streets, The. Patrick Friesen. ACAMVP

Moon in the Well, The. Yi Kyubo. CATKP, *tr.* by Kevin O'Rourke

Moon in Your Hands, The. "H. D." APT-1; OxBoAm *Fr.* Sigil.

Moon inducts the lovers in the ferns, The. (LL) Sydney Cove, 1788. Peter Porter. BrAP; NoAM

Moon Is a Diamond, The. Arthur Sze. TAPaP

Moon is a poor woman, The. Sidney Keyes. NoP-4; NoP-5; OBWP *Fr.* Foreign Gate, The.

Moon is a sow, The. Song for Ishtar. Denise Levertov. MoWP; NALW; NAMCP V.2; NoAM

Moon is a white sliver, The. I Am Singing Now. Luci Tapahonso. UnSA

Moon is able to command the valley tonight, The. Moist Moon People. Carl Sandburg. MoAmPo

Moon is always female and so, The. Moon Is Always Female, The. Marge Piercy. NoAM; WaAnP

Moon is an exile, The. Niyi Osundare. HBAPE *Fr.* Moonsongs.

Moon is bright in the far sky, the night deep on the empty mountain, The. Cuckoo. Woljo Toan. BecRai, *tr. by* Kim Daljin, Kim Won-Chung and Christopher Merrill

Moon is cold over the sand-dunes, The. Shore Grass. Amy Lowell. APT-1; NAMCP V.1

Moon is distant from the Sea, The. Emily Dickinson. TCAPo

Moon is full, The. Bob Marley's Dead. Rachel Manley. WaCA

Moon is one, The. Teaching Numbers. Gary Soto. NOxBChV

Moon is out this morning, The. P. M. T. Dorothy Porter. BMAP

Moon is put up, The. Moon in China Bazaar. Pathabhi. HotL, *tr. by* V. Narayana Rao

Moon Is Rising, The. *Unknown.* TAL

Moon is sick, The. Panic of Birds, The. Olena Kalytiak Davis. AmPoNex

Moon is singing eloquently, The. Sea Song. Luis Omar Salinas. GeoHom

Moon is so full, and the weather, The. Bubbles. Celia de Fréine. NIrP, *tr. by* the author

Moon is sunk, and heaven's resplendent stars, The. Anne Batten Cristall. RWP *Fr.* Thelmon and Carmel; An Irregular Poem.

Moon is the mother of pathos and pity, The. Lunar Paraphrase. Wallace Stevens. SAmP

Moon Is the Number 18, The. Charles Olson. APT-2; HarvBoo; PFTM-2

Moon is thin with fear, The. Jaham Sings of the Fear of the Moon. Eric Ormsby. IFF

Moon is tied to a few strings, The. Cardplayers, The. Jack Spicer. APSN

Moon is waning, September sublime, The. After the Deluge. Pierre Jean Jouve. YaTCFP, *tr. by* Lee Fahnestock

Moon is white on pear blossoms, The. Yi Chonyŏn. CATKP, *tr. by* Peter H. Lee

Moon Landing. W. H. Auden. EmeKit; OxAEP-2

Moon Landing, 1969. Mary Jane Nealon. ArBi

Moon light is on the floor luminous, The. Calm Night Thought. Li Po. NDACCP, *tr. by* Ezra Pound

Moon/light quarter/back sack. Samuel F. Reynolds. SpirFl

Moon like a bloody animal eye over the inlet, A. June 15, 1992: Widow's Walk, Harpswell, Maine. Sandra M. Gilbert. InoFca

Moon lives in all the alone places, The. Meditations on the Moon. Paula Gunn Allen. HATNAP

Moon makes a sign, The. Another wave comes in. Beach, Later. Dennis Saleh. GeoHom

Moon Mountain. Muso Soseki. EaWin, *tr. by* W. S. Merwin

Moon moves up the outback ridge and they turn chewing. Flying Kangaroos. Coral Hull. PoCoUp

Moon nails a long horn, The. Second Anniversary. Federico García Lorca. SpanPo, *tr. by* Rachel Benson and Robert O'Brien

Moon never lets me down, The. Notes on a Moonwatcher. Kenneth Gangemi. PoCoUp

Moon now from old Avon's stream, The. Rural Lyre, The. Ann Yearsley. RWP

Moon on Friday Night, The. Susan Goyette. Coast; OpeFie

Moon on the Cold Flood Festival. Tu Fu [*or* Du Fu]. CrYelRi, *tr. by* Sam Hamill

Moon on the one hand, the dawn on the other, The. Early Morning, The. Joseph Hilaire Pierre Belloc. Spl; TLR

Moon on the porch thumps his tail when I climb. Moon on the Porch. Eloise Klein Healy. CalPo

Moon over Prague. Vitězslau Nezval. AF, *tr. by* Ewald Osers

Moon over the Mountain Pass, The. Li Po. TAL

Moon passes her hands softly over my eyes. Moon, The. Gunnar Ekelof. AWTN, *tr. by* Robert Bly

Moon penny bright as silver. Moon, The. *Unknown.* FaBoVe

Moon plays horn, leaning on the shoulder of the dark universe, The. Bird. Joy Harjo. SeSe

Moon, plum blossoms. Issa. EH, *tr. by* Robert Hass

Moon Poem. Max Jacob. AF, *tr. by* Michael Brownstein

Moon, Rain, Riverbank. Tu Fu [*or* Du Fu]. CrYelRi, *tr. by* Sam Hamill

Moon rattles like a fragment of angry candy. (LL) Cambridge ladies who live in furnished souls, The. E. E. Cummings. BrAP; HeIP-4; MakPoe; NAAPv.2; NAMCP V.1; NoAM; NoP-4; NoP-5; TCAPo; WaAnP

Moon reaches out, The. Cycles. Nzadi Z. Keita. BtF

Moon rises as Shizu rises from her couch, The. Earth Quake. Ruth Stone. ExTi

Moon rises over White Heron Island, The. Farewell to Yin Shu. Li Po. CrYelRi, *tr. by* Sam Hamill

Moon Rising, A. *Unknown.* CCL1 *Fr.* Yue-chu [Translations].

Moon rising white, A. *Unknown.* CCL1 *Fr.* Yue-chu [Translations].

Moon River. Johnny Mercer. ReLy

Moon River. Joe Wenderoth. NAPBL

Moon River / Wider than a mile. Moon River. Johnny Mercer. ReLy

Moon rolls over the roof and falls behind, The. Continuum. Allen Curnow. HarvBoo

Moon, round moon, moon that shines. *Unknown.* CATKP, *tr. by* Kevin O'Rourke

Moon rows burning, The. Nocturn. Herman van den Bergh. TuT

Moon Sails Out, The. Federico García Lorca. AmFaPo, *tr. by* Robert Bly

Moon set, a crow caws. Maple Bridge Night Mooring. Chang Chi. ColAnChi; NDACCP, *tr. by* Gary Snyder

Moon sets, The. A crow caws. Night at Anchor by Maple Bridge. Chang Chi. NDACCP, *tr. by* Kenneth Rexroth

Moon shadows on internment camp. Shonan Suzuki. NAAPv.2

Moon Shatters on Alabama Avenue, The. Martín Espada. PueRic

Moon shines on valley. *Unknown.* WoPoe *Fr.* Three Gypsy Songs.

Moon shines while billions. Moon. Takahashi Shinkichi. ZenPo, *tr. by* Takashi Ikemoto and Lucien Stryk

Moon, somnolent, white. Sadakichi. NAAPv.1 *Fr.* Tanka.

Moon, Sun, Sleep, Birds, Live. Kenneth Patchen. WeW-3

Moon swims to the fore in the pale heavens, The. Gethsemane. Irina Ermakova. CRWP, *tr. by* Daniel Weissbort

Moon that pushes her way, The. Ode to Knight Kip'a. Ch'ungdam, Master. CATKP, *tr. by* Peter H. Lee

Moon the color of an empty movie screen, A. Enough. Cindy Day Roberts. LaCa

Moon, the dried weeds, The. William Carlos Williams. APT-1

Moon: the lighted hall of a bell. Personal Atlas. Rosalie Moore. YaYoPo

Moon, The / nicotine of a kiss. Absence. Luljeta Lleshanaku. WoBe, *tr. by* Henry Israeli

Moon, the year is over. Remembering Leopardi's Moon. Giacomo Leopardi. WoPoe, *tr. by* Stephen Berg

Moon; then turns about, and earthward, too, is clear, The. (LL) On the Ineffable Inspiration of the Holy Spirit. Catharina Regina von Greiffenberg. WoPoe; WPoS, *tr. by* Michael Hamburger

Moon this evening, The. Saiokuken Socho. SoOfWa, *tr. by* Sam Hamill

Moon through total darkness hurrying, The. Demons. Alexander Sergeyevich Pushkin. WoPoe, *tr. by* D. M. Thomas

Moon to the north of Aldebarán lights up in the estuary, The. Red Tide. José Luis Rivas. RMCMP, *tr. by* Alastair Reid

Moon tonight, The. Issa. EH, *tr. by* Robert Hass

Moon Tree Cliff. Muso Soseki. EaWin, *tr. by* W. S. Merwin

Moon trees keep growing and growing, The. Moon Tree Cliff. Muso Soseki. EaWin, *tr. by* W. S. Merwin

Moon turns in the sky, The. Thamar and Amnon. Federico García Lorca. WED, *tr. by* Robert Bly

Moon upon her fluent Route, The. Emily Dickinson. APN-2

Moon was a thick slab of yellow cheese between thin slices of toasted clouds, The. Sam Jackson. Frank Marshall Davis. APT-2

Moon Was Gliding the River, The. Juan Ramón Jiménez. SpanPo, *tr. by* Eloise Roach

Moon was gliding the river, The. Moon Was Gliding the River, The. Juan Ramón Jiménez. SpanPo, *tr. by* Eloise Roach

Moon was in eclipse last night: the stars, The. Eclipse of the Moon. Mary Susannah Robbins. PfS

Moon was like a full cup tonight, The. Cows at Night, The. Hayden Carruth. GifTon; PoA 2002

Moon was round!, The. Whisperer, The. James Stephens. IrV

Moon Winx Motel. Emily Hiestand. ReTh

Moon Winx with its neon eyes and sly smile, The. Moon Winx Motel. Emily Hiestand. ReTh

Moon, worn thin to the width of a quill. Moon's Ending. Sara Teasdale. APT-1

Moon you could hang a coat on, A. Sean Dunne. ModIr *Fr.* Sydney Place.

Moonburn. Laura H. Kennedy. PasH

Moonburn. Marge Piercy. NAMCP V.2

Moondown: crows caw. Frost, a skyful. Night-Mooring at Maple Bridge. Chang Chi. ChinPo, *tr. by* Ye Weilian [*or* Yeh Wei-lien *or* Wai-lim Yip]

Moon-Hops. Ted Hughes. CABP

Mooni. Henry Clarence Kendall. OBEV

Moonless darkness stands between. Gerard Manley Hopkins. OBCP

Moonless Night. Louise Glück. AWTN

Moonlight. Aloysius Bertrand. MotU, *tr. by* James Weeks

Moonlight. Kim Caldwell. ReEnLa

Moonlight. Berta Hart Nance. TiP2

Moonlight. Michael Ryan. BodElec

Moonlight. William Shakespeare. OxAEP-1 *Fr.* Merchant of Venice, The.

Moonlight. Paul Verlaine. NAWM-7v2, *tr. by* Carlyle Ferren MacIntyre

Moonlight Alert. Yvor Winters. PWW2

Moonlight and Gas. Constance Naden. ViWPN; VWP

Moonlight and the sound of pines are things we all know. Han-shan Te-ch'ing. CSKM, *tr. by* Red Pine

Moonlight Becomes You. Johnny Burke. ReLy

Moonlight Cocktail. Kim Gannon. ReLy

Moonlight falls by my bed, The. Night Thoughts. Li Po. WaAnP, *tr. by* Arthur Sze

Moonlight in front of my bed. Still Night Thoughts. Li Po. ColAnChi; ItP, *tr. by* Burton Watson

Moonlight in the kitchen is a sign of God. Anne Carson. BodElec; OxBoAm; WoBe *Fr.* Truth About God, The.

Moonlight in Vermont. John Blackburn and Karl Suessdorf. ReLy

Moonlight lingers down the air. Robert Penn Warren. GPTC *Fr.* Promises.

Moonlight now on Malibu. Air and Angels. Kenneth Rexroth.

Moonlight on stubbleshining. Nocturne. Yvor Winters. APT-2

Moonlight / On Swanee's muddy shore. Rockin' Chair. Hoagy Carmichael. ReLy

Moonlight on the Lake. Kunle Adebajo. NeNiPo

Moonlight pearls on my breast like solder. She Speaks to Her Husband, Asleep. Robert Schultz. AWTN

Moonlight Ride, A. Harriet Hamilton King. VWP

Moonlight shines cold on white bones, The. (LL) Travelling Northward. Tu Fu [*or* Du Fu]. BLT; CCL1; NDACCP, *tr. by* Kenneth Rexroth

Moonlight shines on the lotus pond. Kim Sujang. CATKP; WoPoe, *tr. by* Kevin O'Rourke

Moonlight slanting. Basho. EH, *tr. by* Robert Hass

Moonlight through my gauze curtains. Skein, The. Emperor Wu of Han. CAP-8, *tr. by* Carolyn Kizer

Moonlit Apples. John Drinkwater. OBMV

Moonlit Night. Kim Namjo. CAMKP, *tr. by* David R. McCann and Hyunjae Yee Sallee

Moonlit night / By melon flowers. Kaya Shirao. ZenPo, *tr. by* Takashi Ikemoto and Lucien Stryk

Moonlit Night ("In Fuzhou, far away, my wife is watching.") Tu Fu [*or* Du Fu]. WoPoe, *tr. by* Vikram Seth

Moonlit Night Thinking of My Brothers. Tu Fu [*or* Du Fu]. NDACCP, *tr. by* David Hinton

Moonlit Night ("This same moon hangs over Fu-chou.") Tu Fu [*or* Du Fu]. CrYelRi, *tr. by* Sam Hamill

Moonlit Night ("Tonight, moon over Fu-chou.") Tu Fu [*or* Du Fu]. ChinPo, *tr. by* Ye Weilian [*or* Yeh Wei-lien *or* Wai-lim Yip]

Moonrise. "H. D." PoA 2002

Moonrise. Gerard Manley Hopkins. MoBrPo

Moonrise. *Unknown.* CCL1 *Fr.* Yue-chu [Translations].

Moonrise as Abstraction. Paul Mariani. PfSP

Moonrise in the Rockies. Ella Higginson. SWaP

Moonrise Over Battlefield. Edgell Rickword. PoWW

Moons . . . Tides. Andrew J. Baldwin. BtF

Moon's a devil jester, The. Traveler, The. Vachel Lindsay. MoAmPo

Moon's a path, The. Hansel, Gretel and Ruby Redlips. Anita Endrezze. HATNAP

Moon's Bed, the Bride's Bed, The. W. S. Rendra. WoPoe, *tr. by* Burton Raffel

Moon's bed, the bride's bed, The. Moon's Bed, the Bride's Bed, The. W. S. Rendra. WoPoe, *tr. by* Burton Raffel

Moon's brightness turns a freezing blue, The. Hayim Lenski. FIT, *tr. by* Robert Friend

Moon's Cadaver, The. Clara Silva. TANSG, *tr. by* Celeste Kostopulos-Cooperman

Moon's driving, waxing light may suit, The. For My Mother Magnetic Poetry Series. Gideon Ferebee. BtF

Moon's dropped child!, The. (LL) Fame. Charlotte Mew. HarvBoo; NPeEn; VWP

Moon's Ending. Sara Teasdale. APT-1

Moons of Llŷn, The. Alan Llwyd. BBMWP, *tr. by* Joseph P. Clancy

Moon's the same old moon, The. Bunan. ZenPo, *tr. by* Takashi Ikemoto and Lucien Stryk

Moon-Shadows. Adelaide Crapsey. APT-1

Moonshine. Walter De la Mare. OBCoV

Moonshine. Richard Murphy. IrLP

Moonshine. David Wheatley. NIrP

Moonshine Sonata. John Tranter. KGB

Moonshot, A. Giant Rocket. Wes Magee. NOxBChV

Moonsnow '77. Michael Hartnett. ModIr

Moonsongs. Niyi Osundare.
"Frantic as a prentice poet." HBAPE
"Ikoyi / The moon here." NAfrP
"Madding moon, A." HBAPE
"Moon is an exile, The." HBAPE
"We called the statue." HBAPE

Moonstones. David Trinidad. WiU

Moonstruck. Hugh MacDiarmid. NAEL-6v2

Moonstruck Storks. Ahmet Hasim. SonAtl, *tr. by* Fatih, Nevin Ipek, Nazim and Tamer Yazircioglu

Moon-talk. Edgell Rickword. OxBSo

Moor / Point my horse. Basho. ZenPo, *tr. by* Takashi Ikemoto and Lucien Stryk

Moor, The. Ralph Hodgson. MoBrPo

Moor, The. Ronald Stuart Thomas. OBWVE; WaAnP

Moor Girl's Well, The. Rosamund Marriott Watson. ViWPN

Moored at Maple Bridge. Ching An. CSKM, *tr. by* Jerome P. Seaton

Moored boat, A. Buson. EH, *tr. by* Robert Hass

Moored for the Night at the Lan-chi Riverside Courier Station. Yang Wan-li. GifTon, *tr. by* Paul Hansen

Moorer Denies Holyfield in Twelve. Olena Kalytiak Davis. AmPoNex; MoASP

Moore's Paradox. John Koethe. OxBoAm

Mooring at River Ch'in-Huai. Tu Mu. ChinPo, *tr. by* Ye Weilian [*or* Yeh Wei-lien *or* Wai-lim Yip]

Mooring at Twilight in Yuyi District. Wei Ying-wu. CCL1, *tr. by* Witter Bynner

Mooring by Jiangzhen in the Evening. Lo Pin-wang. CCL1, *tr. by* Stephen Owen

Mooring on Chien-Te River. Meng Hao Jan. NDACCP, *tr. by* Gary Snyder

Moorland. Ronald Stuart Thomas. StAl

Moorland blazing and a bomber's moon, The. Dornier, The. Gladys Mary Coles. TCAWP

Moose, The. Elizabeth Bishop. NAAL-5; NALW; NoP-4; NoP-5; StAl; WaAnP

Moose has fallen smoothly, without sound, The. Ritual for the Dead, Lake Sakami, Quebec, 1980. Linda Bierds. RoV

Moose has lost his way, A. Duluth, Minnesota. Connie Wanek. UrbNat

Moose in the Morning, Northern Maine. Mona Van Duyn. ColAP

Moose that once presided over games, The. Adirondack Moosehead. Jeffrey Harrison. PoA 2002

Moose's heart, The. Fire Barns. Jordan Davis. HeMarv

Morada oscura del sentido. Palabras. Elsa Cross. RMCMP

Moraine Lake. Brian Henry. PoCoUp

Moral. Dominique Fourcade. OnScMo

Moral, The. W. E. Henley. OxAEP-2

Moral Alphabet, A. Joseph Hilaire Pierre Belloc.
"A stands for Archibald who told no lies." NoAM
"B stands for Bear. When bears are seen." NoAM
"E stands for egg." NoAM
"K for the Klondyke, a country of gold." NoAM
"R the reviewer, reviewing my book." NoAM

Moral climbs whose name should be a wreath, A. (LL) Mr. Pope. Allen Tate. APT-2; ColAP; FuPo; NAMCP V.1; NoAM

Moral Poem, A. James Vincent Cunningham. APT-2

Moral Proverbs and Folk Songs. Antonio Machado Ruiz. *tr. by* Robert Bly
"All things die and all things live forever." WED, *tr. by* Robert Bly
"Between living and dreaming." WED, *tr. by* Robert Bly
"Beyond living and dreaming." WED, *tr. by* Robert Bly
"But art? / It is pure and intense play." WED, *tr. by* Robert Bly
"But look in your mirror for the other one." RaBo; WED, *tr. by* Robert Bly
"don't trace out your profile." RaBo, *tr. by* Robert Bly
"Eye you see is not, The." WED, *tr. by* Robert Bly
"Form your letters slowly and well." WED, *tr. by* Robert Bly
"I love Jesus, who said to us." WED, *tr. by* Robert Bly
"If it's good to live." WED, *tr. by* Robert Bly
"In my solitude." WED, *tr. by* Robert Bly
"It is good knowing that glasses." WED, *tr. by* Robert Bly
"Look for your other half." RaBo, *tr. by* Robert Bly
"Mankind owns four things." WED, *tr. by* Robert Bly
"Narcissism / is an ugly fault." RaBo; WED, *tr. by* Robert Bly

"Pay attention now." WED, *tr. by* Robert Bly

"To die. . .To fall like a drop." WED, *tr. by* Robert Bly

"To talk with someone." WED, *tr. by* Robert Bly

"What the poet is searching for." WED, *tr. by* Robert Bly

"When I am alone." WED, *tr. by* Robert Bly

"You say nothing is created new?" WED, *tr. by* Robert Bly

Moral Tale, A. Roger Woddis. UV

Moralist of Bananas, The. Michael Benedikt. MotU

Morality Play, A: Preface. George Oppen. APSN *Fr.* Some San Francisco Poems.

Morality, thou deadly bane. Robert Burns. OBSV *Fr.* Dedication to G**** H******* Esq, A.

Morall Fabillis of Esope the Phrygian, The. Robert Henryson. (Cock and the Fox, The.) NAEL-7v1

  Taill of the Uponlandis Mous, and the Burges Mous. NePenScot

  (Tale of the Upland Mouse and the Burgess Mouse, The.) OBNV

  (Two Mice, The.) NePenScot

Morant Bay. *Unknown.* FaBoVe

Morbid. Nancy Eimers. ExTi

Morcels: Between the Lines. Theresa Hak Kyung Cha. ASA

More. Ai. GT

More. Gertrude Stein. TCAPo *Fr.* Tender Buttons.

More a Man Has the More a Man Wants, The. Paul Muldoon. ModIr

More Abandoned, The More Divine, The. "Angelus Silesius." GePo *Fr.* Cherubical Wanderer, The.

More about God (But with Some Reservations). Victor Hugo. SxFrPo, *tr. by* A. M. and E. H. Blackmore

More amorous than Solomon. (LL) Worm Fed on the Heart of Corinth, A. Isaac Rosenberg. NPeEn; PoWW

More and More. Margaret Atwood. LW

More and more lately, as, not even minding the slippages yet, the aches and sad softenings. Repression. C. K. Williams. GoPo; NoP-4; NoP-5

More and more to yesterdays. (LL) Ding-Donging. Laura Riding Jackson. NAMCP V.1; NoP-4; NoP-5

More and More Woman. Pierre Jean Jouve. YaTCFP, *tr. by* Mary Ann Caws

More Bagpipe Music. E. O. Parrott. UV

More beautiful and soft than any moth. Landscape near an Aerodrome, The. Stephen Spender. MoBrPo; NAMCP V.1; NoAM

More beautiful than the notable moon and its ennobled light. Paean to the Sun, A. Ingeborg Bachmann. GTCP, *tr. by* Reinhold Grimm

More beautiful than the remarkable moon and its noble light. To the Sun. Ingeborg Bachmann. GPTC, *tr. by* Peter Filkins

More Beautiful Than Your Eyes. Sa'id 'Aql. ErotSp, *tr. by* Naomi Shihab Nye and Matthew Sorenson

More bitter is our weeping. Magyar Messiahs, The. Endre Ady. IQMS, *tr. by* Anton N. Nyerges

More brave than me:more blond than you. (LL) I sing of Olaf glad and big. E. E. Cummings. AF; AmFaPo; AmWaPo; BrAP; ColAP; FaBoWar; HeIP-4; NAAL-5; NAAPv.2; NAMCP V.1; NoAM; NoP-4; OBSV; OBWP; PoWW; WaAnP

More Care for the Neck Than for the Intellect. J. Gordon Coogler. VerBaPo

More Chagall than Chagall. Luisa Futuransky. MirDau, *tr. by* Celeste Kostopulos-Cooperman

More dear, both for themselves and for thy sake! (LL) Lines Composed a Few Miles above Tintern Abbey on Revisiting the Banks of the Wye During a Tour, July 13, 1798. William Wordsworth. AmFaPo; BrAP; CABP; HeIP-4; NAEL-6v2; NAEL-7v2; NAWM-7v2; NIL-7; NoP-4; NoP-5; NPeEn; OxAEP-2; OxBEV; PoPoPo; TFi

More delicate than the historians' are the map-makers' colors. (LL) Map, The. Elizabeth Bishop. APT-2; ColAP; NAMCP V.2

More domestic than elegant, leaves and pigeons. Urban Pastoral. Babette Deutsch. MakPoe

More durable than bronze, higher than Pharaoh's. Horace. WaAnP *Fr.* Odes.

More Earnest Prayer of Christ, The. Scott Cairns. UpMys

More fertile than they think, or know. Offspring, The. Liz Rosenberg. PoA 2002

More fleeting than my shadow is. Hans Faverey. WoBe *Fr.* Eighteen Poems.

More for asparagus than asparagus does. Angry with China. Douglas Messerli. FTOS

More Foreign Cities. Charles Tomlinson. HarvBoo

More Fun In The New World. Karen Solie. OpeFie; PoPra

More geese than swans now live, more fools than wise.. (LL) Silver Swan, The. Orlando Gibbons. HeIP-4; NAEL-6v1; NoP-4; NoP-5; OPOU; OWoS; WaAnP

More grotesque than a row of laundromats. Novelty Shop, The. Duane Niatum. ReTh

More haughty than the rest, the wolfish race. John Dryden. NOSC *Fr.* Hind and the Panther, The.

More I read the papers, The. Love Is Here to Stay. Ira Gershwin. ReLy

More I Remember More. Joe Brainard.

  "I remember biting on a little piece of flesh inside my mouth until a very sweet sort of pain came." AHA

More I wonder, The. Observation, An. Kay Sage. SurWo

More I'm with you, the more I can see, The. Everything I Have Is Yours. Harold Adamson. ReLy

More Important Than the Design of Cities Will Be the Design of Their Decay. Tessa Rumsey. LegDan

More in number, five. Works and Days. David Baker. PoDa

More It Snows, The. Alan Alexander Milne. NTCP

More I've viewed this world, the more I've found, The. Fancy. Thomas Moore. CenSon

More Joy in Heaven. Howard Nemerov. NoAM

More Light! More Light! [*for Heinrich Blücher and Hannah Arendt*]. Anthony Hecht. AF; EmeKit; EMP; GPTC; HP; NoAM; NoP-4; OBWP; PWW2; TaR; VCAP

More like a stock than like a vine. (LL) Vine, The. Robert Herrick. CavPo; EroLit; NAEL-6v1; NAEL-7v1; NoP-4; NoP-5

More love or more disdain I crave. Against Indifference. Charles Webbe. OBEV

More Lovely than Antiquity. Witter Bynner. NoP-4; NoP-5

More Loving One, The. W. H. Auden. ItP; OxBoAm

More luck to honest poverty. For A' That and A' That. Shirley Brooks. UV

More man / Than myth, more myth. Tambourine Tommy. Thomas Sayers Ellis. NAPBL

More memories than if I'd lived a thousand years! Spleen LXXVI. Charles Baudelaire. SxFrPo, *tr. by* James McGowan

More of a Corpse Than a Woman. Muriel Rukeyser. NALW

More of double. Gertrude Stein. NAMCP V.1 *Fr.* Tender Buttons.

More often than not he stops at the headrig to light. Cauliflowers. Paul Muldoon. ModIr; NAMCP V.2

More painful, love is, The. Kim Namjo. CAMKP *Fr.* Love's Cursive.

More Poem. Dennis Scott. WaCA

More powerful than the government. Giles Goodland. NewEx

More Rain. David Baker. LiTh

More Rain. Ben Scammell. NLP

More Reformation. Daniel Defoe.

  "To sin's a vice in nature, and we find." OBSV

More song. birds follow the sun. Lady's Days. Larry Neal. SeSe

More surprising than a moving statue. Apparition, The. Bernard O'Donoghue. NoP-4

More than a brother to me, Jonathan. Peter Abelard. EroLit, *tr. by* John Boswell

More than a King's my Word dos rule to day. Elizabeth Tipper. EMWP; NOSC *Fr.* Pilgrim's Viaticum; or, The Destitute, But Not Forlorn.

More Than Anything. Doreen Baingana. BtF

More than anything else. I Cherish That Love. Kabir. WoPoe, *tr. by* Pritish Nandy

More than anything, I wanted Charlie. David Trinidad. WiU *Fr.* Eighteen to Twenty-One.

More than eager to rid himself of a father. Studies in Desire. Pimone Triplett. AmPoNex

More than ever I want to see. Basho. EH, *tr. by* Robert Hass

More than love. *Unknown.* SonAtl, *tr. by* Mohammed Attiyah and Lubna Khader

More than most fair [*or* fayre], full of the living fire [*or* fyre]. Edmund Spenser. NoP-5; OxBSo *Fr.* Amoretti.

More than my brothers are to me. (LL) Alfred Tennyson. CAGL; NAEL-6v2; NAEL-7v2 *Fr.* In Memoriam A. H. H.

More than my sixteen rented houses and their eighty or so rooms. Broom. Deborah Digges. SweBea

More than 9 Lives. Bruce Beaver. BMAP

More Than Once in Caves. Mark McMorris. IAoNAP

More than polished stone. I Am Root. Claribel Alegría. PoetW; VCWP, *tr. by* Carolyn Forché

More than Suspect. André Breton. AF, *tr. by* Mary Ann Caws

More than the beetles turned russet. Colophon. Dean Young. PoDa

More than the color. *Unknown.* ArkPo, *tr. by* Helen Craig McCullough

More than the Grave is closed to me. Emily Dickinson. APN-2

More than They that Watch for the Morning. May Probyn. VWP

More than this I scarce can die. (LL) Fare Thee Well. Lord Byron. NOBRP; NPBRoP

More than thyself to love thy neighbor. (LL) Latest Decalogue, The. Arthur Hugh Clough. BrAP; CABP; ChIV-1; NAEL-6v2; NAEL-7v2; NoP-4; NoP-5; NPeEn; OBSV; OxBEV; SacPr; TFi; WeW-3; WoPoe

More Than We Dream. Hayan Charara. PrTe

More Than You Know. Edward Eliscu and Billy Rose. ReLy

More then most faire, full of the living fire. Edmund Spenser. *See* More than most fair [*or* fayre], full of the living fire [*or* fyre].

More Trouble with the Obvious. Michael Van Walleghen. IllVoic

More whyght thou art than primrose leaf my Lady Galatee. Ovid. OBVE *Fr.* Metamorphoses.

More ye desire her, the sooner ye miss, The. How to Obtain Her. *Unknown.* NoSic

More years pass and the book does not leave the drawer. Next to Last Draft, The. C. D. Wright. GPPA

Morenz. Tim Bowling. IFF

Moreover the Lord answered Job, and said. Bible, *O.T.* OBVE *Fr.* Job.

Moreover, there with them appear. Michael Wigglesworth. *See* Thus everyone before the throne.

Morgana La Fay. John Wieners. AHA

Morgan's curls are matted. Henry Morgan's March on Panama. A. G. Prys-Jones. AngWePo

Morgan's father will be mailed to her. Complete with Starry Night and Bourbon Shots. Albert Goldbarth. BAP-97

Morisseau-Leroy. Max Manigat. OGAHCP, *tr. by* Boadiba and Jack Hirschman

Morn. Josephine D. Henderson Heard. CBWP-4

Morn hath risen clear and bright, The. Expulsion of Hagar, The. Eloise Bibb. CBWP-4

Morn on her rosy couch awoke. Poetry. Lydia Huntley Sigourney. SWaP

Morning. Fadhil Assultani. IrPoTo, *tr. by* Raghid Nahhas

Morning. Joanna Baillie. *Fr.* Winter Day, A.

Morning: "Where was I last night? In whose arms?" Miryana Basheva. CSCBP, *tr. by* Georgi Belev and Lisa Sapinkopf

Morning. Louisa Sarah Bevington. PEW

Morning. William Blake. WoPoe

Morning. Louise Bogan. APT-2

Morning. William Browne. NOSC *Fr.* Britannia's Pastorals.

Morning: "Why do we bother with the rest of the day." Billy Collins. WaAnP

Morning. Jeni Couzyn. HAWP

Morning. Duo Duo. PoetW, *tr. by* Maghiel van Crevel

Morning. Judith Herzberg. TuT, *tr. by* Joan McBreen

Morning. Vincente Huidobro. CuPo

Morning. Glyn Jones. AngWePo

Morning. Pauline Kaldas. PoArWo

Morning. Alfred Lichtenstein. GTCP, *tr. by* Michael Hamburger

Morning: "Main thing is not to oversleep, so as later not to have to run for dear life, The." Mara Malanova. CRWP, *tr. by* Nika Skandiaka

Morning. Gabriela Mistral. TANSG, *tr. by* Maria Giachetti [*or* Jacketti]

Morning. Mary Oliver. NIL-7

Morning. Ron Padgett. NYP2

Morning. Arthur Rimbaud. SxFrPo, *tr. by* Martin Sorrell

Morning. Yannis Ritsos. StAl, *tr. by* Nikos Stangos

Morning. Giuseppe Ungaretti. PFTM-1

Morning: "Naked morning, the day's transparent." José Ángel Valente. RaW, *tr. by* Hardie St. Martin

Morning. Wang Wei. TAL

Morning. Franz Wright. AmAlph

Morning, A. Douglas Livingstone. TSAP

Morning, A. Mark Strand. CAP-8

Morning After. Langston Hughes. NAMCP V.1; NBLV; NoAM; OBCoV

Morning After My Death, The. Larry Levis. OPRER

Morning After, The. Dory Langdon Previn. ReLy

Morning After, The. Johari M. Rashad. PasH

Morning After, The. Dorothy, Duchess of Wellington Wellesley. OBMV

Morning after the night, The. Raymond of the Rooftops. Paul Durcan. EmeKit

Morning after the storm, townsmen found, The. After the Storm. Henri Faust. YaYoPo

Morning after Woe, The. Emily Dickinson. TCAPo

Morning among the Hills. James Gates Percival. TreFP

Morning and evening. Goblin Market. Christina Georgina Rossetti. BrAP; NAEL-6v2; NAEL-7v2; NALW; NOxBChV; OBNV; OxAEP-2; OxBEV; ViWPN; VWP; WaAnP

Morning and Evening Calm. James Keir Baxter. HarvBoo

Morning and evening calm: the Lord has spoken. Morning and Evening Calm. James Keir Baxter. HarvBoo

Morning and night I bring. Cottage Song. John Drinkwater. UV

Morning and night I found. Same Cottage—But Another Song, of Another Season. Max Beerbohm. UV

Morning arose, and its beauties were beaming, The. Cornelius Whur. STuOW *Fr.* Rose-Covered Grave, The.

Morning at the Window. T. S. Eliot. OxBEV; PoA 2002; TCAPo

Morning Athletes. Marge Piercy. MoASP

Morning Baking, The. Carolyn Forché. LoL

Morning Becomes Electric. Bruce Dawe. BMAP

Morning Bird Songs. Tomas Tranströmer. WED, *tr. by* Robert Bly

Morning breaks like a pomegranate, The. Wedding Morn. D. H. Lawrence. MoBrPo

Morning breeze. Buson. EH, *tr. by* Robert Hass

Morning broke like an egg. Eggs. Susan Wood. SoSe-8

Morning / broods. Strawberrying. Maurice Kenny. HATNAP

Morning brought strong rain. Harlem Haiku: A Scrapbook. Jabari Asim. InTrad

Morning Buddhism. E. Ethelbert Miller. BtF

Morning Call. Richard Murphy. ModIr

Morning came with not a cloud in view, The. Albery Allson Whitman. NAAPv.1 *Fr.* Octoroon, The.

Morning Chamber Orchestra Near Piney Crick, Wyoming, 7 A.M., The. William Borden. MiVo

Morning Coffee. György Petri. VCWP, *tr. by* Geroge Gömöri and Clive Wilmer

Morning coffee, The. I'm not sure why I drink it. Prose Poem. Ron Padgett. NYP2

Morning comes, and thickening clouds prevail, The. Clouded Morning, The. Jones Very. GSo

Morning comes, not slow with reddening gold, The. Frederick Goddard Tuckerman. APN-2 *Fr.* Sonnets: First Series, 1854–1860.

Morning comes, the night decays, the watchmen leave their stations, The. William Blake. NAEL-7v2 *Fr.* America: A Prophecy.

Morning dawned full darkly, The. William Edmonstoune Aytoun. NePenScot *Fr.* Execution of Montrose, The.

Morning dew was on your lip, The. Red Poppy, The. I. D. Hooson. BBMWP, *tr. by* Gillian Clarke

Morning Exercises. Nina Cassian. CFP; PoSu, *tr. by* Andrea Deletant and Brenda Walker

Morning flushes its gray light across where I collect a face, rimmed. Great Stories of the Chair. Ted Berrigan. AHA

Morning frost cocoons my car. Gurney Tears. Audrey Shafer. BloBone

Morning frost / Mount Fuji. Tantan. ZenPo, *tr. by* Takashi Ikemoto and Lucien Stryk

Morning glories pleasure for a day. Violins tickling. Stephanie Koufman. PfS

Morning glories, The. Basho. SoOfWa, *tr. by* Sam Hamill

Morning glories, yes. Issa. WED, *tr. by* Robert Bly

Morning glory. Issa. IllVoic *Fr.* Issa: A Suite of Haiku.

Morning glory also, The. Basho. EH, *tr. by* Robert Hass

Morning Glory Pool. Sandra McPherson. MotU

Morning glory / So pure. Kakei. ZenPo, *tr. by* Takashi Ikemoto and Lucien Stryk

Morning glory!, The. Chiyojo. WPoS

Morning has its flat first light, its blaze, The. New. Jennifer Maiden. BMAP

Morning hour of mutual separation has replaced that of mutual proximity and the moment of our mutual separation from the sweetness of our proximity has come, The. Ahmad ibn 'Abd Allāh Ibn Zaydūn. HiArP, *tr. by* James T. Monroe

Morning Hours. Rossana Ombres. NeIt *Fr.* Excursion to Ravenna of A Young Girl with Her Parents.

Morning Hymn. Joseph Beaumont. SacPr

Morning Hymn. Thomas Ken. NOSC; SacPr

Morning Hymn. Charles Wesley. NPeEn

Morning I asked you to marry me, The. Marry. Linda Smukler. WiU

Morning, if this late withered light can claim. Zonnebeke Road, The. Edmund Charles Blunden. OBWP

Morning in America. John Koethe. OxBoAm

Morning in Norfolk. George Barker. HarvBoo

Morning in the Burned House. Margaret Atwood. NAMCP V.2

Morning in the Hospital Solarium. Sylvia Plath. BodElec

Morning in the Islands. John Hollander. ColAP

Morning is so gray that the grass is gray and the side of the white horse grazing, The. On Learning of a Friend's Illness. C. K. Williams. WaAnP

Morning Jitters. John Ashbery. FTOS; PoA 2002

Morning Letter, A. Robert Duncan. PoA 2002

Morning light. Stanford M. Forrester. AmZen

Morning Light at Wanship, Utah. Dave Jeddie Smith. BodElec

Morning light creaks down again!, The. (LL) Aubade: "Jane, Jane, / Tall as a crane." Dame Edith Sitwell. MoBrPo; NALW; NAMCP V.1; NoAM

Morning Love Song. Marge Piercy. PasH

Morning. / Me and my things. Morning Window, A. Alaa Khalid. AnVo, *tr. by* Mohamed Enani

Morning *Minyan*. Marcia Falk. ASA

Morning muezzin in orange and a mosquito. Clark Coolidge. FTOS *Fr.* At Egypt.

Morning, Noon and Night. Mark Strand. BAP-97

Morning of buttered toast. Not-Yet. Jane Hirshfield. BeAl; ExTi

Morning of Drunkenness. Arthur Rimbaud. SxFrPo, tr. by Martin Sorrell

Morning of Every Sin, The. Maysoun Saqr Al-Qasimi. tr. by Subhi Hadidi
  "I'm not sleeping now." PoArWo, tr. by Subhi Hadidi
  "Salty like my seashores." PoArWo, tr. by Subhi Hadidi
  "Voice is never enough, The." PoArWo, tr. by Subhi Hadidi

Morning of swift grey skies, A. Signals. Kerry Hardie. NIrP

Morning of the Last Farewell, The. Miyazawa Kenji. CAoMJL1, tr. by Hiroaki Sato

Morning on the Lièvre. Archibald Lampman. BrAP

Morning Paper, Society Page. Naomi Shihab Nye. CAP-8

Morning Person. Vassar Miller. GoPo

Morning Poem. Mary Oliver. EMP

Morning Quatrains, The. Charles Cotton. NOSC

Morning Radio. Derek Mahon. RWPCtW

Morning Radio. Deirdre Shanahan. RWPCtW

Morning rain of Wei city. Melody of Wei City. Wang Wei. CCL1, tr. by William Dolby

Morning rain of Wei city wets the white dust, The. Song for Wei City, A. Wang Wei. TAL

Morning reflections over the miso soup. Alan Chong Lau. WhBo

Morning Ride. Lola Ridge. NAAPv.2

Morning Ride. Unknown. ArBi

Morning Roar of the City, The. Slavko Mihalic. PoSu, tr. by Charles Simic

Morning. Rosamonde. Anne Batten Cristall. RWP

Morning seems to have no light to spare. Edward Hopper's Seven A.M. John Hollander. PoSol

Morning Set. Joe Denham. OpeFie

Morning shone in cloudless beauty bright, The. George Crabbe. Fr. Tales of the Hall.

Morning sleep / it's sweeter than your palms. Stella Morotskaya. CRWP, tr. by Vitaly Chernetsky

Morning Snowfield. Reg Saner. PoCoUp

Morning Song. Conrad Potter Aiken. NoAM; NoP-5 Fr. Senlin; a Biography.

Morning Song and Evening Walk. Sonia Sanchez. InGu

Morning Song in the Jungle. Rudyard Kipling. NoAM Fr. Second Jungle Book, The.

Morning Song: "Love set you going like a fat gold watch." Sylvia Plath. BeAl; ColAP; HarvBoo; HeIP-4; ItWoWo; NAAL-5; NAMCP V.2; NIL-7; NIP-4; NoP-4; NoP-5; PoPoPo; VCAP; WaAnP

Morning Song of Senlin. Conrad Potter Aiken. See Morning Song.

Morning Songs. Robert E. Penn. WiU

Morning space. Louise Herlin. MFP, tr. by Martin Sorrell

Morning space expands the building's. Morning space. Louise Herlin. MFP, tr. by Martin Sorrell

Morning spent itself, The. Street Fair: The Quartet. Marvin Bell. BodElec

Morning Splendour of the Tisza, The. György Bessenyei. IQMS, tr. by Gavin Ewart

Morning Star. Cesare Pavese. GPTC, tr. by William Arrowsmith

Morning Star. C. D. Wright. TAPaP

Morning Star, The. Paul S. Piper. AmZen

Morning star goes under cover, The. Der von Kürenberg. GePo

Morning star has set, The. A lark. Yi Myŏnghan. CATKP, tr. by Peter H. Lee

Morning Stroll, A. Yi Sanghûi. EcSo, tr. by Jennifer M. Lee

Morning Sun. Hsiao Yen [or Emperor Wu of Liang]. CCL1, tr. by Anne Birrell

Morning Sun. Louis MacNeice. MoBrPo

Morning sun cradles a bowl of apples. Part of a Larger Country. Jeanne Bryner. SweBea

Morning sun emblazons. Roy Kiyooka. NLPA Fr. Pear Tree Pomes.

Morning sun outside D'Agostino's, a young man bends. Beatrix Gates. WiU Fr. Triptych.

Morning sun shines in the lonely window, The. On the Mountain. Chunbong Manwoo. BecRai, tr. by Kim Daljin, Kim Won-Chung and Christopher Merrill

Morning sun shines on silk coin windows. Morning Sun. Hsiao Yen [or Emperor Wu of Liang]. CCL1, tr. by Anne Birrell

Morning sweet with bird song and the low grasses, A. Ancient Themes: The Night. Jeff Gundy. ACAMVP

Morning Swim. Maxine W. Kumin. CAP-8

Morning swoops down on her with words, chews. Learning Window. James Longenbach. NAPBL

Morning that I first loved you, The. New Clouds, The. William Carlos Williams. HarvBoo

Morning Thesis. Christiania Whitehead. NeBl

Morning they set out from home, The. I Was Not There. Karen Gershon. HP

Morning They Shot Tony Lopez, Barber and Pusher Who Went Too Far, 1958, The. Gary Soto. PBCAP

Morning to Remember, A; or, E Pluribus Unum. Edward Dorn. NoAM

Morning traffic murmurs like an ocean. West Willow. Reginald Shepherd. AmPoNex; IllVoic

Morning Travel. Chia Tao. CSKM, tr. by Mike O'Connor

Morning uptown, quiet on the street. Song Form. Imamu Amiri Baraka. ChAP

Morning wakes; the Huntsman sounds, The. John Gay. DiBP Fr. Fables: First Series.

Morning Walk in Autumn to South Valley Passing an Abandoned Village. Liu Tsung-yüan. ChinPo, tr. by Ye Weilian [or Yeh Wei-lien or Wai-lim Yip]

Morning Watch, The. Jones Very. APN-1

Morning when the things again come back, The. Thanks to the Things. Rutger Kopland. VCWP, tr. by James Brockway

Morning Window, A. Alaa Khalid. AnVo, tr. by Mohamed Enani

Morning with a baby crying with all its might. Ogiwara Seisensui. CAoMJL1, tr. by Donald Keene

Morning Work. D. H. Lawrence. MoBrPo

Morning-Glory, The. Sarah Helen Whitman. ColAP

Morning—only the seed of Noon. (LL) I shall keep singing! Emily Dickinson. APN-2; GoPo

Mornings. Sarah Kirsch. PFTM-2 Fr. Kite-Flying.

Mornings are his, The. Waterwings. Cathy Song. NoAM

Morning's at seven. Pippa Passes, But I Can't Get Around This Truck. Margaret Blaker. NBLV

Mornings / before the sun's liquid. Lagoons, Hanlan's Point. Raymond Souster. BrAP

Morning's early rime, The. Shadows of Trees on the Lawn, January. Einir Jones. BBMWP, tr. by Joseph P. Clancy

Mornings he hobbles around. Man in the VA Hospital, The. Betsy Colquitt. TiP2

Mornings I carve washers from bars of sheet metal at the large press. Making the Rate (factory journals). Sarah Klassen. ACAMVP

Morning's News, The. Wendell Berry. UpMys

Mornings run their course, clear and deserted, The. Grappa in September. Cesare Pavese. RaBo, tr. by William Arrowsmith

Morning's sun. Unknown. ColAnChi Fr. Midnight Songs.

Mornings we hold on for noon. Green Cadillac. Eric Tretheway. Coast

Mornings we walked on air, moments. Carnation. Lily, Lily, Rose. Susan Wood. TiP2

Morningside Park. Stephen Burt. LegDan

Morning-Watch, The. Henry Vaughan. AngWePo; BASC; NOSC

Morns are meeker than they were, The. Emily Dickinson. ChAP; SAmP

Morns are meeker than they were, The. Morns are meeker than they were, The. Emily Dickinson. ChAP; SAmP

Morn's Recompense. Clement Andrews. CAGL

Moroccans with the carpets, The. Patrizia Cavalli. NeIt; VCWP, tr. by Kenneth Koch

Moroni is a foreigner. Moroni on the Mormon Temple / Angel on the Wall. Eloise Klein Healy. GeoHom

Moroni on the Mormon Temple / Angel on the Wall. Eloise Klein Healy. GeoHom

Morphemes in section. Morphemics. Jack Spicer. PmAP

Morphemics. Jack Spicer. PmAP

Morpheus, the humble god, that dwells. Song, A. Sir John Denham. NOSC

Morphine, Or The Cutting Stone. Erin Mouré. OpeFie

Morris Winchevsky. Ber Grin. Prolet, tr. by Amelia Glaser

Morrow every listen. Colloam. P. Inman. FTOS

Mors et Vita. James Edwin Campbell. TCAPo

Morse. Les A. Murray. NoP-4; NoP-5

Morse Lesson. Joy Corfield. FaBoWar

Morsels of my lifework: the story of a professional party hostess. Sonnet. D. A. Powell. NeAmPo

Mort de Guillaume Apollinaire, La. Tristan Tzara. YaTCFP

Mort, j'en parle, La. Claire Lejeune. YaTCFP

Mort, Le. Howard Buck. YaYoPo

Mortal Combat. Mary Elizabeth Coleridge. VWP

Mortal flesh is full of grief. Vanity of the World, The. Siôn Cent. OBWVE, tr. by Joseph P. Clancy

Mortal Lease, The: V. Edith Wharton. LW

Mortal Limit. Robert Penn Warren. InGu

Mortal my mate, bearing my rock-a-heart. To His Watch. Gerard Manley Hopkins. MoBrPo

Mortal Partner, The. René Char. YaTCFP, tr. by Nancy Kline

Mortal Practice. Gabriel Zaid. TCLAP, tr. by Mónica Hernández-Cancio

Mortal Remains. Kimiko Hahn. PA9/11

Mortal Roundness. Clarence Major. EGAG

Mortality. R. Williams Parry. BBMWP, tr. by Martin Davis

Mortality [*or* Mortalitie], behold and fear[e]!   Francis Beaumont.   OBEV *Fr.* On the Tombs in Westminster Abbey.

Mortality shrinks back—because.   May.   T. Arfon Williams.   BBMWP, *tr. by* Emyr Lewis

Morte d'Arthur.   Alfred Tennyson.   NIP-4; OBNV; OxAEP-2 *Fr.* Morte d'Arthur.

Morte d'Arthur.   Alfred Tennyson.
   Epic, The [Morte d'Arthur].   NAEL-6v2; NAEL-7v2
   Morte d'Arthur.   NIP-4; OBNV; OxAEP-2

Mortel Partenaire, Le.   René Char.   YaTCFP

Mortician's Twelve-year-old Son, The.   Ai.   CAP-8

Mortification.   George Herbert.   FSCP; NOSC

Morts vont vite, the dead go fast, the next day absent!, *Les.*   Proverb.   Kenneth Koch.   OxBoAm

Morwenna, Julie, don't forget me, Kate. (LL)   New Diary, A.   Dannie Abse.   AngWePo; NoAM

Mosca se detiene sobre el vidrio, La.   En la ventana.   Carla Faesler Bremer.   SPV

Moscow is yelling down the line.   On the Air.   Julian May.   RWPCtW

Moscow / like a Christmas-tree.   Capitals.   Raymond Garlick.   AngWePo

"Moscow" Pool.   Pyotr Vegin.   TCRusP, *tr. by* Daniel Weissbort

Moscow Station, The.   Yevgeny Borisovich Rein.   ItGoST, *tr. by* Judith Hemschemeyer

Mosel, The.   Caroline Clive.   PoBW

Moses: A Story of the Nile.   Frances Ellen Watkins Harper.
   Death of Moses, The.
    "Oh never on that mountain."   TCAPo

Moses and the Princess.   Peter Dickinson.   NOxBChV

Moses, from whose loins I sprung.   Jew, The.   Isaac Rosenberg.   ChIV-1; MoBrPo

Moses His Birth and Miracles.   Michael Drayton.
   "In time the Princess playing with the child."   ChIV-1

Moses in Infancy.   Jones Very.   ChIV-1

"Moses" of Michael Angelo, The.   Robert Browning.   GS

Moses, who spake with God as with his friend.   Death of Moses, The.
   "George Eliot."   ChIV-1

Mosqueda doesn't believe it for one minute.   Jacob Mosqueda Wrestles with the Angels.   Rolando Hinojosa.   AmWaPo

Mosques into snow-palaces; banks, bagnios.   City Under Snow.   Gwyn Williams.   AngWePo

Mosquito.   Master Naong.   BecRai, *tr. by* Kim Daljin, Kim Won-Chung and Christopher Merrill

Mosquito, A.   Brad Leithauser.   StAl

Mosquito and tick.   Sunday Dinner, A.   David Bottoms.   PoDa

Mosquito at my ear.   Issa.   ChAP; EH, *tr. by* Robert Hass

Mosquito Kingdom.   Ernesto Cardenal.   VCWP, *tr. by* Donald D. Walsh

Mosquito Knows, The.   D. H. Lawrence.   NPeEn

Mosquito lives, The.   Mosquito, The.   Dan Pagis.   FIT, *tr. by* Robert Friend

Mosquito, may you fly, a swift courier for me.   Meleager.   HePo

Mosquito, may you fly, a swift courier for me.   HePo, *tr. by* Barbara Hughes Fowler

Mosquito, The.   D. H. Lawrence.   NPeEn

Mosquito, The.   Dan Pagis.   FIT, *tr. by* Robert Friend

Mosquitoes, shameless and shrill of voice, sucking the blood.   Meleager.   HePo

Mosquitoes, shameless and shrill of voice, sucking the blood.   Meleager.   HePo, *tr. by* Barbara Hughes Fowler

Moss Burning.   Marianne Boruch.   AmAlph

Moss covered paths between scarlet peonies.   Visit to the Hermit Ts'ui.   Ch'ien Ch'i.   NDACCP, *tr. by* Kenneth Rexroth

Moss covers his stone bed fresh.   Weeping for the Zen Master Boyan.   Chia Tao.   CCL1, *tr. by* Stephen Owen

Moss in the gratings / of a sewer vent.   January 1965, Looking on.   Kenneth Irby.   FTOS

Moss of His Skin, The.   Anne Sexton.   NALW

Mossbawn.   Seamus Heaney.   HarvBoo; PNI
   Seed Cutters, The.   IPoFL; PNI
   Sunlight.   BeAl; ModIr; WaAnP

Moss-covered bucket that hangs in the well, The. (LL)   Old Oaken Bucket, The.   Samuel Woodworth.   BRP; TCAPo

Moss-covered stone lane, an old empty temple, A.   Sleeping in Pulil Hermitage.   Jaewol Kyunghun.   BecRai, *tr. by* Kim Daljin, Kim Won-Chung and Christopher Merrill

Moss-Gathering.   Theodore Roethke.   BLT

Most Americans like kids.   On What the Army Does with Heads.   Michael Casey.   YaYoPo

Most Ancient Names of Fire, The.   Roberto Sosa.   ErotSp, *tr. by* Jo Anne Engelbert

Most beautiful girl in the college, The.   Courtney, Mentioned in Passing, Years After.   Robyn Sarah.   NoP-5

Most Beautiful Girl in the World, The.   Lorenz Hart.   ReLy

Most beautiful girl in the world used the pad of her finger to, The.   Testifying to Beauty.   Ronny Someck.   IrPoTo, *tr. by* Vivian Eden

Most beautiful order is still, The.   Cucina.   Martine Bellen.   TAPaP

Most beautiful! the red-flowering eucalyptus.   Torso, The / Passages 18.   Robert Duncan.   CAGL; HarvBoo; OxBoAm; PmAP

Most beautiful! the red-flowering eucalyptus.   Robert Duncan.   CAGL *Fr.* Passages.

Most Beds are Beds.   Sylvia Plath.   ChAP *Fr.* Bed Book, The.

Most beloved body, The.   Paper River, The.   Chase Twichell.   WANABP

Most brightly of all burned the hair of my evening loved one.   Night Ray.   Paul Celan.   AF, *tr. by* Michael Hamburger

Most charming sir, most learned young master.   Letter to Carlos Pellicer.   Eunice Odio.   TCLAP, *tr. by* Martha Collins

Most days back then I would walk by the shrike tree.   Shrike Tree.   Lucia Maria Perillo.   RoV

Most days Group V. practiced on seeing through.   One Filament against the Firmament.   Matthea Harvey.   IAoNAP; PoDa

Most days, this wild weather.   Blondie.   Jean Earle.   TCAWP

Most difficult thing about looking at a bird is convincing yourself that you are looking at anything, The.   In Referring to What Does Not Exist.   Skip Fox.   AnSo

Most Excellent Song Which Was Solomon's, The.   Michael Drayton.
   "By night within my bed, I roamed here and there."   ChIV-1

Most explicit— / the sense of trap.   Age.   Robert Creeley.   FTOS; PmAP

Most fear to be. (LL)   Childhood's Retreat.   Robert Duncan.   NAMCP V.2; NoAM

Most glorious Lord of Life that on this day.   Edmund Spenser.   ChIV-2; NoSic; SacPr; WaAnP *Fr.* Amoretti.

Most glorious Lord of life, that on this day.   Edmund Spenser. *See* Sonnet 68:
   "Most glorious Lord of Life that on this day."

Most gunmen.   Cowboy Sayings.   *Unknown.*   CA

Most happy letters fram'd by skilfull trade.   Edmund Spenser.   NAEL-7v1

Most high, all powerful, good Lord.   Canticle of the Creatures.   Saint Francis of Assisi.   WoPoe, *tr. by* James Schuyler

Most High, all-powerful, good Lord.   Canticle of the Brother Sun, The.   Saint Francis of Assisi.   BBASP, *tr. by* Regis J. Armstrong and Ignatius C. Brady

Most Holy Night, that still dost keep.   Night, The.   Joseph Hilaire Pierre Belloc.   OBEV

Most holy Satyr.   Holy Satyr.   "H. D."   MoAmPo

Most is your name the name of this dark stone.   Rainy Mountain Cemetery.   N. Scott Momaday.   HATNAP; ICANM

Most learned Father Grimold.   With His Book, Of Gardening.   Walafrid Strabo.   WoPoe, *tr. by* Tim Reynolds

Most lights are made to see by.   Lighthouse.   Jane Hirshfield.   WANABP

Most likely whatever glimpse we caught.   Letter to Russel Barron.   Robert Gibb.   SwNoth

Most modern nature lovers have a personal scale of values that tells them.   William Wordsworth (1770-1850).   Gavin Ewart.   NoAM

Most mornings I get away, slip out.   Run before Dawn.   William Stafford.   MoASP

Most mornings I wake up slowly. That's just.   Another Song.   Scott Cairns.   UpMys

Most mornings we go running side by side.   Morning Athletes.   Marge Piercy.   MoASP

Most near, most dear, most loved and most far.   Sonnet to My Mother.   George Barker.   OxBSo; RaBo

Most noble empress, you have heard of me?   William Shakespeare.   OxAEP-1 *Fr.* Antony and Cleopatra.

Most Notoriously Absent North American Bird in Her Face, The.   Skip Fox.   AnSo

Most, O maid's child, thy choice and worthy the winning. (LL)   Spring:
   "Nothing is so beautiful as Spring."   Gerard Manley Hopkins.   BrAP; GoPo; GSo; MoBrPo; NAEL-6v2; NAEL-7v2; NAMCP V.1; NoAM; OBMV; TFi

Most of eternity hides.   Life of Eternity, The.   Gene Frumkin.   ICANM

Most of It, The.   Robert Frost.   APT-1; BLT; NAMCP V.1; NoP-4; NoP-5; OxBoAm; TRP; WaAnP; WeW-3

Most of our bodies will melt.   Lucy's Bones.   Christine Evans.   TCAWP

Most of the mass of the universe.   Vast Problem Still Obscure.   Siri von Reis.   PoDa

Most of these minor samurai draw a stipend of three koku.   Kyoto Minor Retainer.   Dōyaku Sensei, Master Artery.   EMJL, *tr. by* Haruo Shirane

Most of us have an agenda, The.   Burning Multitude, The.   Menna Elfyn.   ATSWP, *tr. by* Robert Minhinnick

Most people believe you're blind.   Stevie Wonder.   Lyn'elle Patrice Chapman.   BtF

Most people don't know. Woman Who Raised Dogs, The. Lisa D. Chavez. AmPoNex

Most people, I suppose, would rather not wash one. Washing the Cow's Skull. David C. Yates. TiP2

Most poets to a muse that is stone-deaf cry. On the Oxford Book of Victorian Verse. Hugh MacDiarmid. MoBrPo

Most popular "act" in, The. Black Boys Play the Classics. Toi Derricotte. ExTi; SpirFl

Most prolific seem to be imports, The. Water: City Wildlife and Greenery. Alfred Corn. UrbNat

Most sacred fire, that burnest mightily. Edmund Spenser. NAEL-6v1; NAEL-7v1 *Fr.* Faerie Queene, The.

Most Saturday afternoons. Weepies, The. Paul Muldoon. NoAM; PNI

Most simple things repel. Mac Wellman. HeMarv *Fr.* Rat Minaret: Miniaturist-Divan, The.

Most Sweet It Is with Unuplifted Eyes. William Wordsworth. CenSon *Fr.* Poems Composed or Suggested During a Tour, in the Summer of 1833.

Most terrible was our hero in battle blows. From the Irish. James Simmons. ModIr; PBCIP; PNI

Most, The. Revolutionary. Willie Perdomo. InTrad

Most things are colorful things—the sky, earth, and sea. White Things. Anne Spencer. InGu; NAAPv.2

Most times the lines are invisible as threats. Signals and Demarcations. Quincy Troupe. PrTe

Most truly hono[u]red, and as truly dear. To Her Father, with Some Verses. Anne Bradstreet. NAAL-3; NAAL-5; NAAPv.1; NALW

Most Unbelievable Part, The. Marjorie Agosin. TANSG, *tr. by* Cola Franzen

Most unbelievable part, The. Most Unbelievable Part, The. Marjorie Agosin. TANSG, *tr. by* Cola Franzen

Most unexpectedly it happens, just. Victor Record Catalog. David Schubert. APT-2

Most unusual thing I ever stole, The? A snowman. Stealing. Carol Ann Duffy. EmeKit

Most Vital Thing in Life, The. Grenville Kleiser. SoSe-8

Most Welshmen are worthless. Case History. Dannie Abse. TCAWP

Most what I know of war is what I learned. Memory of the War, A. Howard Nemerov. PWW2

Most who die, the more we live, The. (LL) What If a Much of a Which of a Wind. E. E. Cummings. HarvBoo; MoAmPo; NAAL-5; PoA 2002

Mostly it happens in the first year. Non-Accidental Injury Slides. Geoffrey Holloway. NLP

Mostly Mick Jagger. Catie Rosemurgy. BAP-97

Mostly Mozart at Planting Fields Arboretum. David Zeiger. MiVo

Mostly my nightmares are dull. On autumn nights. Mostly My Nightmares Are Dull. Andrew Hudgins. UpMys

Mostly, the men. Western Trail Cook, 1880. Sharyn Jeanne Skeeter. ISC

Mostly we occupy ocular zones, clinging. How the Rainbow Works. Al Young. ESEAA

Mostly, we try to keep it from happening. Guardian Life. Michael Klein. WiU

Mot et la mouche, Le. René Daumal. YaTCFP

Mote it is to trouble the mind's eye, A. William Shakespeare. OxAEP-1 *Fr.* Hamlet.

Motel pool wasn't flat as safety, The. Tides, The. Michael Klein. WiU

Motel Story. Maggie Nelson. AmPoNex

Motets [Mottetti]. Eugenio Montale. *tr. by* Dana Gioia
  "Black and white, The." WoPoe, *tr. by* Dana Gioia
  "Far away, still I was with you." WoPoe, *tr. by* Dana Gioia
  "Frost on the windowpanes; the sick." WoPoe, *tr. by* Dana Gioia
  "Here is the sign: it trembles." WoPoe, *tr. by* Dana Gioia
  "I had almost lost." WoPoe, *tr. by* Dana Gioia
  "If the green lizard darts." WoPoe, *tr. by* Dana Gioia
  "Long goodbyes, the whistles in the dark, The." WoPoe, *tr. by* Dana Gioia
  "Many years, and one of them a little harder." WoPoe, *tr. by* Dana Gioia
  "You know this: I must lose you again and cannot." WoPoe, *tr. by* Dana Gioia

Moth ate words; a marvellous event, A. *Unknown.* NoP-4

Moth belated,—sun and zephyr-kist, A. To a Moth that Drinketh of the Ripe October. Emily Jane Pfeiffer. ViWPN

Moth house is taking over, Sir Footfall. Mac Wellman. HeMarv *Fr.* Rat Minaret: Miniaturist-Divan, The.

Moth, I thought, munching a word, A. Cynewulf. OPOU *Fr.* Riddles (Exeter Book).

Moth under the eaves, The. Prelude to Winter. William Carlos Williams. SAmP

Mothball Fleet: Benicia, California. John Haines. PWW2

Mother. Willem Elsschot. TuT, *tr. by* Peter van de Kamp

Mother. Josephine D. Henderson Heard. CBWP-4

Mother. Vladimir Holan. PoSu, *tr. by* Ian Milner and Jarmila Milner

Mother. Attila József. IQMS, *tr. by* Vernon Watkins

Mother. Ussin Kerim. PML, *tr. by* William Matthews

Mother. Karl Lubomirski. PML, *tr. by* Renate Latimer

Mother. Nancy Morejón. TCLAP, *tr. by* Kathleen Weaver

Mother. Nancy Morejón. TANSG, *tr. by* Joy Renjilian-Burgy

Mother. Daphne Rock. Prnts

Mother: "Funniest of all was birth." Vera Pavlova. CRWP *Fr.* Signs of Life.

Mother. Kristina Rungano. HAWP

Mother. River. Shuntaro Tanikawa. VCWP, *tr. by* Harold Wright

Mother. A. Isobel Thrilling. Prnts

Mother, A: "Mother in the green sweater walks and walks along the street, The." Kadya Molodovsky. CFP, *tr. by* Kathryn Hellerstein

Mother, The. Gwendolyn Brooks. CAP-8; ESEAA; IllVoic; ISC; MoWP; NAAL-5; NALW; OxAAAP; OxBoAm; PoPoPo *Fr.* Street in Bronzeville, A.

Mother, The. Caroline Clive. VWP

Mother, The. Marie Howe. LaCa

Mother, The. Sharon Olds. PBCAP

Mother, The. Dora Sigerson Shorter. VWP

Mother, The. Dame Edith Sitwell. MoWP

Mother, The. Anne Stevenson. BeAl

Mother, The: "On Monday she stood at the wooden wash-tub." George Mackay Brown. EdScPo

Mother, The: "She stands in the dead center like a star." W. D. Snodgrass. BrAP

Mother, a mother was born, A. (LL) Maternity. Alice Thompson Meynell. InoFa; PEW; VWP

Mother, a Young Wife Leans to Sew. Geraldine Connolly. SweBea

Mother, among the dustbins and the manure. Mother, among the Dustbins. Stevie Smith. BrAP

Mother and Child. Ronald Stuart Thomas. RSR

Mother and child! whose blending tears. Memorial Pillar, The. Felicia Dorothea Hemans. RWP

Mother and Daughter. Augusta Davies Webster.
  "Her father lessons me I at times am hard." ViWPN
  "Little child she, half defiant came, A." VWP
  Love's Mourner. ViWPN; VWP
  "She will not have it that my day wanes low." OxBSo; ViWPN
  "Since first my little one lay on my breast." ViWPN; VWP
  "Sometimes, as young things will, she vexes me." ViWPN
  "That she is beautiful is not delight." ViWPN
  "That some day death who has us all for jest." VWP
  "There's one I miss. A little questioning maid." ViWPN; VWP

Mother and father are in heaven— / Amen. Chronica. Else Lasker-Schüler. PFTM-1

Mother, and Given Girl. *Unknown.* SonAtl, *tr. by* Alec Sett, A. Valderin and Tamer Yazircioglu

Mother and her son tug, A. Pietà. Christopher Davis. Vesp

Mother and I. Takahashi Shinkichi. ZenPo, *tr. by* Takashi Ikemoto and Lucien Stryk

Mother and Poet. Elizabeth Barrett Browning. InoFa; NAEL-6v2; NALW; ViWPN; VWP

Mother and Son. Alden Nowlan. RaBo

Mother and Son. Karen Swenson. PoChi

Mother and Son. Allen Tate. MoAmPo

Mother, any distance greater than a single span. Simon Armitage. BeAl *Fr.* Book of Matches.

Mother blackbird I've been feeding, The. Flight. Sarah Wardle. BeAl; PoCu

Mother, blood irises unfold. Santorini Daughter. Julie Fay. NAPBL

Mother called to her own son, The. Boy Changed into a Stag Clamours at the Gate of Secrets, The. Ferenc Juhász. IQMS, *tr. by* David Wevill

Mother, come home; mother, come home. *Sioux Oral Tradition.* NAAPv.1 *Fr.* Ghost-Dance Songs.

Mother Corn Assumes Leadership. *Unknown. Fr.* Hako, The.

Mother Dawning. Janine Canan. HW

Mother dear, may I go downtown. Ballad of Birmingham. Dudley Randall. HeIP-4; ISC; NIL-7; NIP-4; NoAM; NoP-4; NoP-5; SoSe-8; WaAnP

Mother, Dear Mother. Elma Mitchell. Prnts

Mother Dies. Saitō Mokichi. *tr. by* Hiroaki Sato and Burton Watson
  "From far off I have brought medicines, she watches me because I am her son." WoPoe, *tr. by* Hiroaki Sato and Burton Watson

Mother disappeared below the rim. Cleaning the Cistern. Anna Ruth Ediger Baehr. ACAMVP

Mother does knitting, The. Familial. Jacques Prévert. CLPP; FaBoWar; PoAgWa, *tr. by* Lawrence Ferlinghetti

Mother Doesn't Want a Dog. Judith Viorst. NBLV

Mother Doorstep. Victor James Daley. NOBAu

Mother: Dorcas Good, The. Nicole Cooley. NeAmPo

Mother eats seaweed and plum pickles.   Pearls.   Lee Ann Roripaugh.   AmPoNex

Mother Egret.   *Vietnamese Oral Tradition.*   CaDao, *tr.* by John Balaban

Mother fetched the fruit from the mango grove.   Mango Poem.   Regie Cabico.   WiU

Mother, for months a mist has been before me.   Light in Darkness.   Mary E. Tucker.   CBWP-1

Mother Goblin's Lullaby.   Jack Prelutsky.   NOxBChV

Mother Goose Up-to-Date.   Louis Untermeyer.

   Archibald MacLeish Suspends the Five Little Pigs.   MoAmPo

   (Edgar A. Guest Syndicates the Old Woman Who Lived in a Shoe.)   MoAmPo

   Edna St. Vincent Millay Exhorts Little Boy Blue.   MoAmPo

   John Masefield Relates the Story of Tom, Tom, the Piper's Son.   MoAmPo

   Walter de la Mare Tells the Listener about Jack and Jill.   MoAmPo

Mother has brought me a lavender tree. (LL)   Love from a Foreign City.   Lavinia Greenlaw.   EmeKit; MFPA; MoWP

Mother has lupus.   Dear World.   Paula Gunn Allen.   FiBr; HATNAP

   (Mother has lupus. She says that it's a disease.)   FiBr

Mother Hubbard's Tale.   Edmund Spenser.

   Fox and the Ape Go to Court, The.   NoSic

Mother, I am eighteen this year.   Cherished Daughter, The.   *Unknown.*   WoPoe, *tr.* by Nguyen Ngoc Bich

Mother, I am mothering you now.   I'm My Own Mother, Now.   Stella P. Chipasula.   HAWP

Mother, I am older than your picture.   Calling Out the Names.   Carol Gordon.   FiBr

Mother, I bow to gold.   Mighty Lord Is Money, A.   Francisco de Quevedo y Villegas.   SpanPo, *tr.* by William M. Davis

Mother, I Cannot Mind My Wheel.   Walter Savage Landor.   NAEL-6v2; NAEL-7v2; OBEV; OBVE

Mother, I didn't mean to slight you but.   Reluctant Light.   Naomi Long Madgett.   FuFl

Mother / I have an iron gun.   Poem of a Militant.   Jorge Rebelo.   PML

Mother, I leave thee—thou hast been.   Slave Girl's Farewell, The.   "Ada."   NAAPv.1

Mother, I listen hard to hear you speak.   Praisesong: From Son to Mother.   Lenard D. Moore.   BtF

Mother, I love you so.   Human Affection.   Stevie Smith.   NALW

Mother I never knew.   Issa.   EH, *tr.* by Robert Hass

Mother, I weep.   Issa.   SoOfWa, *tr.* by Sam Hamill

Mother, I'll / tell you. Let me tell you it's.   Persephone, to Demeter.   Marilyn Krysl.   HW

Mother, I'm trying.   Another Poem for Mothers.   Erin Belieu.   PoChi

Mother in the green sweater walks and walks along the street, The.   Mother, A.   Kadya Molodovsky.   CFP, *tr.* by Kathryn Hellerstein

Mother Ireland.   Eavan Boland.   PoA 2002

Mother, it pains me that I must confide.   Winter Offerings.   Frank Ormsby.   PNI

Mother Kali, the destroyer, is the giver.   Lamps Are Brought In, The.   George Kalamaras.   Vesp

Mother Lakshmi's Poem.   Cassia Berman.   HW

Mother lies in travail bed, The.   Newly Dead and Newly Born.   Eliza Ogilvy.   VWP

Mother Love.   Rita Dove.   AFaM

Mother Love.   Elaine Feinstein.   HarvBoo

Mother Love.   Stevie Smith.   Spl

Mother love is a mighty benefaction.   Mother Love.   Stevie Smith.   Spl

Mother loves me loves me not.   Veno Taufer *and* Michael Scammell.   WoPoe   *Fr.* Prayers and Games of the Water People, The.

Mother, make *me* Your treasurer.   Rāmprasād Sen.   SinGod, *tr.* by Rachel Fell McDermott

Mother, Mother, Are You All There?   Felicia Lamport.   NBLV

Mother, Mother, my Dear Mother.   Katie Kádár.   *Hungarian Oral Tradition.*   IQMS, *tr.* by Adam Makkai

Mother, mother, what illbred aunt.   Disquieting Muses, The.   Sylvia Plath.   NALW; NAMCP V.2

Mother moves through the World.   Persephone.   Cynthia Cruz.   IAoNAP

Mother Nature.   Amy Fusselman.   HeMarv

Mother Nature, how fair has your invention's grace.   Lake of Zurich, The.   Friedrich Gottlieb Klopstock.   GePo, *tr.* by George C. Schoolfield

Mother of Andromeda, The.   Julie Fay.   NAPBL

Mother of Darkness, Our Lady.   Winter-Worship.   Charles Wright.   PfSP

Mother of fictions.   Prayer to Eve, A.   Kathleen Norris.   HW; UpMys

Mother of God, everyone is invited.   Congress of the Insomniacs, The.   Charles Simic.   EmeKit

Mother of God! no lady thou.   Our Lady.   Mary Elizabeth Coleridge.   OBEV; OBMV; ViWPN

Mother of God that's Lady of the Heavens.   Prayer of the Old Woman.   François Villon.   MoBrPo, *tr.* by John Millington Synge

Mother of God, The.   William Butler Yeats.   BBASP; ChIV-2; ChrPo

Mother of God, whose burly love.   On the Eve of the Feast of the Immaculate Conception: 1942.   Robert Lowell.   PWW2

Mother of God, you tired Mary.   Géza Páskándi.   IQMS   *Fr.* Language Memory.

Mother of heaven, regina of the clouds.   Le Monocle de Mon Oncle.   Wallace Stevens.   TCAPo

Mother of Hermes! and still youthful Maia!   Fragment of an Ode to Maia Written on May Day, 1818.   John Keats.   OBEV

Mother of Judas, The.   Yevgeny Mikhailovich Vinokurov.   GI, *tr.* by Anthony Rudolf

Mother of King Matthias, The.   János Arany.   IQMS, *tr.* by Neville Masterman

Mother of Men and Bearded like a male.   Sonnets to Some Sexual Organs.   Howard Phelps Putnam.   OxBoAm

Mother of my birth, for how long were we together.   Kaddish.   David Ignatow.   GoPo; RaBo; TaR

Mother of our own dear mother, good old grandam, wake and smile!   Grandmother, The.   Victor Hugo.   TreFP

Mother of salt and slate.   Salmon, The.   Duane Niatum.   PoCoUp

Mother of Sorrow.   Litany.   David Craig.   UpMys

Mother of the concierge and the concierge will let everything, The.   Monday rue Christine.   Guillaume Apollinaire.   CuPo

Mother of the long silences.   Mother of Us All.   Cathy Song.   PoDa

Mother of the muses, we are taught, The.   Memory.   Walter Savage Landor.   NPeEn

Mother of the road. (LL)   Prayer to Eve, A.   Kathleen Norris.   HW; UpMys

Mother of the Universe.   Yoko Ono.   HW

Mother of Us All.   Cathy Song.   PoDa

Mother of Us All, The.   Gertrude Stein.

   Concluding Aria.   PFTM-2

Mother of us all, The.   *Unknown.*   HW   *Fr.* Homeric Hymns.

"Mother, oh mother! where shall we hide us?"   Others.   James Reeves.   Spl

Mother: / Only hours after your death.   Another Poem to My Mother.   Clementina Suárez.   TANSG, *tr.* by Janet N. Gold

Mother, / perhaps you cannot stay asleep any longer.   Prague Spring 6.   Ko Chŏnghûi.   EcSo, *tr.* by Catherine J. Kim

Mother plasma. Father fire.   Glacier's Daughters, The.   David Brendon Hopes.   UpMys

Mother rinsed her menstrual rags.   Point of No Return.   Jane Glazer.   FiBr

Mother Ruin.   Linda Gregerson.   ExTi

Mother Sabbath.   Nikolai Alekseievich Klyuyev.   TCRusP, *tr.* by John Glad

Mother said thirty years ago.   Miss Florence Jackson.   David Huddle.   PBCAP

Mother said to call her if the H bomb exploded.   Belief.   Josephine Miles.   NoAM

Mother sat / with hunger on her hands.   Child's Parliment.   Chenjerai Hove.   HBAPE

Mother shake the cherry-tree.   Let's Be Merry.   Christina Georgina Rossetti.   TLR

Mother shake the cherry-tree.   Christina Georgina Rossetti.   TLR   *Fr.* Sing-Song.

Mother she looks like stands at the counter snapping beans, The. (LL)   Tahoe in August.   Robert Hass.   CalPo; NoP-4; NoP-5

Mother shook her head and sadly smiled, The.   Albery Allson Whitman.   NAAPv.1   *Fr.* Octoroon, The.

Mother . . . Sister . . . Daughter.   Jean Binta Breeze.   RSaN

Mother somewhere you flying over me with love and close careless caress.   Fred Wah.   NLPA; OpeFie   *Fr.* This Dendrite Map: Father / Mother Haibun.

Mother, squatting hurts.   Kseniya Marennikova.   CRWP, *tr.* by Daniel Weissbort

Mother the Wardrobe Is Full of Infantrymen.   Roger McGough.   RSaN

Mother then must suck the Son, The. (LL)   Bible, *N.T.*   ChIV-2; NOSC   *Fr.* St. Luke.

Mother throws her voice in loops, The.   Two Couples.   Debra Bruce.   FFC

Mother to Her Waking Infant, A.   Joanna Baillie.   CABP; NoP-4; NoP-5; WaAnP; WoRP

Mother to Son.   Jenny Factor.   PoChi

Mother to Son.   Langston Hughes.   AmFaPo; BLPJKO; ChAP; ISC; NAAL-5; NTCP; SAmP; TWF; WaAnP; WoPoe

Mother tongue.   Celia de Fréine.   NIrP, *tr.* by the author

Mother Tongue.   Rebecca Seiferle.   ExTi

Mother Tongue.   Jon Stallworthy.   NoAM

Mother, two days ago he left.   Susan Hahn.   Vesp   *Fr.* Holiday.

Mother, unroll the bolts and name.   Naming the Fabrics.   Julia Alvarez.   FFC

Mother used to tell us about a white forest in Russia.   Suspicion.   Alejandra Pizarnik.   TANSG, *tr.* by Susan Bassnett

Mother wanted the dowry of rice.   Arranged Marriage, The.   *Vietnamese Oral Tradition.*   CaDao, *tr.* by John Balaban

Mother was a crack of light.   Three Floors.   Stanley Kunitz.   LoL

Mother, we were a heavy burden for you.   Mother, We Were a Heavy Burden.   Stein Mehren.   PML, *tr.* by Olav Grinde

Mother, what trick of light.   Mirror of Matsuyama, The.   Sharon Hashimoto.   CFP; OpBo

Mother, who read and thought and poured herself into me.   Arioso Dolente.   Anne Stevenson.   NoP-5; Prnts

Mother with Child.   Lenore Keeshig-Tobias.   FFC

Mother with the life-giving power now comes.   *Unknown.*   APN-2 *Fr.* Hako, The.

Mother wrote to say: "Stay / in Europe. Soak up as much beauty as you."   John Cage.   APSN *Fr.* Diary: How to Improve the World (You Will Only Make Matters Worse).

Mother, / You did not leave me an inheritance of.   Mother's Inheritance.   Fawziyya Abu Khalid.   CFP, *tr.* by Kamal Boullata

Mother, you know there is a place somewhere called Paris.   Right Meaning, The.   César Vallejo.   MotU; PoDa; RaBo; WED, *tr.* by Robert Bly

Mother, you never said it wasn't true.   Lines in the Sand.   Richard Sanger.   IFF

Mother, you were born.   Peter Levitt.   WhBo

Mother / You're always finding ways to amuse Yourself.   Kamalākānta Bhattācārya.   SinGod, *tr.* by Rachel Fell McDermott

Motherfucker I just found out my boyfriend's a prostitute.   Cruising for Prostitutes.   Jennifer L. Knox.   FreRad

Motherhood.   Mathilde Blind.   ViWPN *Fr.* Ascent of Man, The.

Motherhood.   Georgia Douglas Johnson.   NAAPv.2; OxAAAP

Motherhood.   May Swenson.   NoP-4; NoP-5

Motherhood is so final, Nita.   Mariana II.   Maria Arrillaga.   TANSG

Mothering.   Carla Harryman.   FTOS

Mother-in-law.   U. A. Fanthorpe.   MoWP *Fr.* Only Here for the Bier.

Mother-in-law, do not stamp.   *Unknown.*   CATKP, *tr.* by Wen Hsia-min

Mother-in-Law of the Marquis de Sade, The.   Jennifer Maiden.   NOBAu

Motherland.   Rose Ausländer.   PoCho, *tr.* by Eavan Boland

Motherland.   Jo Shapcott.   NeBrP

Mother-May-I.   Kathleen Jamie.   BeAl

Mothers: "In the still of night."   Kay Boyle.   PoChi

Mothers.   Nikki Giovanni.   OxAAAP

Mothers.   Haki R. Madhubuti.   FuFl

Mothers.   Francis Saltus Saltus.   VerBaPo

Mothers and Daughters.   David Campbell.   BMAP

Mothers are hardest to forgive.   Adversary, The.   Phyllis McGinley.   SoSe-8

Mother's Charge, The.   Charlotte Perkins Stetson Gilman.   SWaP

Mother's dance blossomed in beauty at last.   My Mother Dances a Ballad.   István Sinka.   IQMS, *tr.* by Adam Makkai

Mothers, Daughters.   Shirley Kaufman.   PoChi

Mother's Day.   Daisy Zamora.   LoL, *tr.* by Margaret Randall

Mother's Day at McDonald's.   Patricia Elam.   BtF

Mother's dream, A.   Nocturne.   Alaide Foppa.   TANSG, *tr.* by Celeste Kostopulos-Cooperman

Mother's face looked tired and worn, The.   Skeptic, The.   Clara Ann Thompson.   CBWP-2

Mother's father.   Big Zeb Johnson.   Everett Hoagland.   GT; OxAAAP

Mother's Feet.   Kim Sŭnghŭi.   EcSo, *tr.* by K. Kim Richards and Steffen Richards

Mother's Heart, The.   Caroline Elizabeth Norton.   NPBRoP

Mother's Inheritance.   Fawziyya Abu Khalid.   CFP, *tr.* by Kamal Boullata

Mother's Lace.   Shonto Begay.   NOxBChV

Mother's Lament, The.   Helen Selina Blackwood, Countess of Dufferin and Clandeboye.   VWP

Mother's Lament, The.   Mary E. Tucker.   CBWP-1

Mother's letter, torn open, A.   1948: Jews.   Adrienne Rich.   OxBoAm

Mother's Love, A.   Josephine D. Henderson Heard.   CBWP-4

Mother's Love, A.   Ellen Johnston.   VWP

Mother's Mark.   Jana Beranová.   TuT, *tr.* by Aidan Sharkey

Mother's Nerves.   X. J. Kennedy.   ChAP

Mothers of America / let your kids go to the movies!   Ave Maria.   Frank O'Hara.   CLPP; HarvBoo; MakPoe; NoP-4; NoP-5; PmAP; PoPoPo; VCAP

Mother's Past.   Reed Whittemore.   BodElec

Mother's past is full of old cars with very large fenders.   Mother's Past.   Reed Whittemore.   BodElec

Mother's Pearls.   Bao-Long Chu.   AmWaPo

Mother's Quest, A.   William Wordsworth.   STuOW *Fr.* Sailor's Mother, The.

Mother's Recall.   Mary Weston Fordham.   CBWP-2

Mother's Room.   Nicky Rice.   Prnts

Mother's Song.   *Unknown.*   WoPoe, *tr.* by Stephen Berg

Mother's Song, The.   *Unknown.*   OBCP, *tr.* by Peter Freuchen

Mother's Tale, The.   Ai.   CAP-8

Mother's Voice.   Robert Creeley.   NAMCP V.2

Mother's Winter Guests.   Tammy Armstrong.   Coast

Motherseed.   Sandra Maria Esteves.   BRtP

Mother-to-Be's Book of melt down anticipation and scientific renderings, A.   Encyclopedia Botanica.   Lee Ann Brown.   VaPo

Moth-force a small town always has.   Strength of Fields, The.   James Dickey.   VCAP

Motho Ke Motho Ka Batho Babang (A Person Is a Person Because of Other People).   Jeremy Cronin.   AF

Moths.   Adam Zagajewski.   BLT, *tr.* by Renata Gorczynski, Benjamin Ivry and C. K. Williams

Moth's kiss, first, The!   Robert Browning.   OBEV *Fr.* In a Gondola.

Moths, The.   W. S. Merwin.   HeIP-4

Moths watched us through.   Moths.   Adam Zagajewski.   BLT, *tr.* by Renata Gorczynski, Benjamin Ivry and C. K. Williams

Motion.   Sikong Tu.   CCL1 *Fr.* Twenty-Four Modes of Poetry.

Motion.   Yi Sang.   CAMKP, *tr.* by Edward Mack

Motion guided a lotion, A.   Lack of Balance but not Fatal, A.   Jackson Mac Low.   FTOS

Motion of gathering loops of water, The.   Glass Bubbles, The.   Samuel Greenberg.   APT-1; OxBoAm

Motion of the Cypher.   Ray DiPalma.   FTOS

Motion Pictures: 15.   Barbara Guest.   BodElec

Motion Pictures: 4.   Barbara Guest.   BodElec

Motionless Faces.   Carlos Drummond de Andrade.   PFTM-1

Motionless—His sons.   Death Bed.   Thomas Kinsella.   PBCIP

Motions and means, on land and sea anew.   Steamboats, Viaducts, and Railways.   William Wordsworth.   CenSon; NAEL-6v2; NAEL-7v2

Motion's Holdings.   A. R. Ammons.   NAMCP V.2; NoAM

Motive.   Catherine Imbriglio.   IAoNAP

Motive.   Muriel Rukeyser.   PoA 2002

Motive.   Reginald Shepherd.   NeAmPo

Motive for Mayhem, A.   Abigail Child.   FTOS

Motive for Metaphor, The.   Wallace Stevens.   APT-1; BrAP; MoAmPo; NAMCP V.1; OxBoAm

Motley.   Peter Davison.   NBLV

Motley.   Walter De la Mare.   PoWW

Motley's the Only Wear.   William Shakespeare.   OBCoV *Fr.* As You Like It.

Moto Perpetuo.   Dionisio D. Martinez.   NAMCP V.2

Motor mouth overflow has tapered off. I head home. Dish with CQ how Wayne's a wife-beater.   Diddly Squat From Cyberspace.   Kenward Elmslie.   NYP2

Motor Oil Queen.   Cheryl Burke.   WiU

Motor stops, the boat thuds mud—the river's bed, The.   After the Flood.   John Foulcher.   NOBAu

Motorboat's charge, The.   Sexual Love.   Eva Salzman.   MoWP

Motorcycle roaring in the distance—, A.   Aunt Toni's Heart.   Rafael Campo.   RA

Motorcycle Ward.   David Moolten.   BloBone

Motorcyclists, The.   James Tate.   NAMCP V.2; NoAM; ReTh

Mots d'Heures: Gousses, Rames.   Luis d'Antin Van Rooten.

"Jacques s'apprête."   OBCoV

"Lit-elle messe, moffette."   OBCoV

"Polis poutre catalane."   OBCoV

"Pousse y gâte, pousse y gâte."   OBCoV

Mottled hands cupped deep.   Hands in the Motion of Prayer.   Sojourner Kincaid Rolle.   GeoHom

Motto.   Langston Hughes.   ItP; NAMCP V.1

Motto.   Yüan Mei.   WoPoe, *tr.* by Jerome P. Seaton

Motto for a Sun Dial.   James Vincent Cunningham.   APT-2 *Fr.* Epigrams: A Journal.

Motto Tell me, thou skilful shepherd's swain.   Michael Drayton.   AEP

Motto, The.   Abraham Cowley.   NOSC

Motto, The.   In this day and age.   Bruce George.   BRtP

Motto to "Illusions."   Ralph Waldo Emerson.   *See* Illusions.

Motto to "The Poet."   Ralph Waldo Emerson.   NCAP

Mouche et l'Océan, La.   Jean Tardieu.   YaTCFP

Mouche se balançait, Une.   Mouche et l'Océan, La.   Jean Tardieu.   YaTCFP

Mouettes, Les.   *Unknown.*   CCL1 *Fr.* Guan-ju.

Moules à la Marinière.   Elizabeth Garrett.   MFPA

Moulton Transformations.   Dixie Salazar.   GeoHom

Mound of dung. (LL)   Muliebrity.   Sujata Bhatt.   HarvBoo; MoWP; NeBrP

Mounds of Human Heads.   Osip Emilevich Mandelstam.   WoPoe, *tr.* by Mark Rudman

Mounds of Human Heads Are Wandering into the Distance.   Osip Emilevich Mandelstam.   AF

Mounds of human heads recede in mist. Mounds of Human Heads. Osip Emilevich Mandelstam. WoPoe, *tr. by* Mark Rudman

Mount Ararat. Louise Glück. ColAP

Mount Auburn! loveliest city of the dead. Richard Henry Wilde. APN-1 *Fr.* Hesperia.

Mt. Auburn Owl. Pamela Alexander. AmAlph

Mount Bromley Hymn. John Peck. PoCoUp

Mount Chung-Nan. Wang Wei. ChinPo, *tr. by* Ye Weilian [*or* Yeh Wei-lien *or* Wai-lim Yip]

Mount Fuji. Kaneko Mitsuharu. WoPoe, *tr. by* James Kirkup and Akiko Takemoto

Mount Fuji [Selections, 1943]. Kusano Shimpei. CAoMJL1, *tr. by* Leith Morton

Mount Kearsarge. Donald Hall. LoL

Mount Kearsarge shines with ice; from hemlock branches. Mount Kearsarge Shines. Donald Hall. PfSP

Mount Ko's nine-bend pool. Nine Songs of Mount Ko. Yi I. CATKP, *tr. by* Peter H. Lee

Mount Ko's nine-bend pool. Yi I. CATKP *Fr.* Nine Songs of Mount Ko.

Mount. Leave your living to the wise. Where the Sun Ends. Peter Davison. ChIV-1

Mt. Lykaion. Trumbull Stickney. NAAPv.2 *Fr.* Sonnets from Greece.

Mount Melleray. Sean O Riordain. ModIr, *tr. by* Patrick Crotty

Mount of Olives, The. Shirley Kaufman. DTA

Mount Palomar's parabola. Contracting Universe, The. William J. Tait. EdScPo

Mount rides into the seething alcove. (LL) Women of Rubens, The. Wisława Szymborska. PoSu; VCWP

Mount Shasta: "Behold the dread Mt. Shasta, where it stands." John Rollin Ridge. APN-2; CalPo

Mount Sumeru—my fist! Kiko. ZenPo, *tr. by* Takashi Ikemoto and Lucien Stryk

Mount T'ai is one tall mountain rising. Song of Mount T'ai. Lu Chi. CrYelRi, *tr. by* Sam Hamill

Mt. Tamalpais. Kenneth Rexroth. CalPo *Fr.* Andrée Rexroth.

Mount, The. Léonie Adams. MoAmPo

Mount Zhongnan. Wang Wei. CCL1, *tr. by* Jerome P. Seaton

Mountain, The. Louise Glück. NoAM

Mountain, The. Hashim Shafiq. IrPoTo, *tr. by* Ralph Saverese and Saadi A. Simawe

Mountain, The. Jones Very. NCAP

Mountain air Living air. Place of Fire, A. "Zelda." NRoS, *tr. by* Esther Raizen

Mountain and lake. I Ching. Diane Di Prima. SeSe

Mountain and the squirrel, The. Fable. Ralph Waldo Emerson. APN-1; NBLV; OxBoAm; TFi

Mountain Ash without Cedar Waxwings. Robert Pack. PfSP

Mountain bird comes, A. Tobong Mountain. Pak Tujin. CAMKP, *tr. by* Edward W. Poitras

Mountain Building. Víctor Hernández Cruz. PueRic

Mountain Chant, The. *Unknown. tr. by* Washington Matthews
  First Daylight Song. APN-2
  First Song of the Exploding Stick. APN-2
  First Song of the Thunder. APN-2; TCAPo
  Invocation To Dsilyi N'Eyani. APN-2; TCAPo
  Last Daybreak Song. APN-2
  Last Song of the Exploding Stick. APN-2; NAAPv.1
  Last Words of the Prophet. APN-2
  One of the Awl Songs. APN-2; NAAPv.1
  Sixth Song of the Holy Young Men. APN-2
  (Song of Sequence.) TCAPo
  Song of the Prophet. APN-2
  Song of the Rising Sun Dance. APN-2
  Twelfth Song of the Holy Young Men. APN-2
  Twelfth Song of the Thunder. APN-2

Mountain cuckoo, The. Buson. EH, *tr. by* Robert Hass

Mountain cuckoo, The. Issa. EH, *tr. by* Robert Hass

Mountain Dialogue. Li Po. NDACCP, *tr. by* David Hinton

Mountain doesn't call me, The. Mountain Life. Chimi Sucho. BecRai, *tr. by* Kim Daljin, Kim Won-Chung and Christopher Merrill

Mountain Drinking Song. Li Po. CrYelRi, *tr. by* Sam Hamill

Mountain Excursion. Jinkag Haesim. BecRai, *tr. by* Kim Daljin, Kim Won-Chung and Christopher Merrill

Mountain Fern, The. Arthur G. Geoghegan. IrV

Mountain Flowers. Kim Sowŏl. CAMKP, *tr. by* David R. McCann

Mountain Folk. Kim Ch'anghyŏp. CATKP, *tr. by* Peter H. Lee

Mountain gone. In a Glazed-Over World. Carl Mayfield. ICANM

Mountain Greenery. Lorenz Hart. ReLy

Mountain is only a moorland, The. Language Is Only Words, A. Myrddin ap Dafydd. BBMWP, *tr. by* Anthony Conran

Mountain is silent, The. Sŏng Hon. CATKP, *tr. by* Peter H. Lee

Mountain Life. Baekoon Kyunghan. BecRai, *tr. by* Kim Daljin, Kim Won-Chung and Christopher Merrill

Mountain Life. Chimi Sucho. BecRai, *tr. by* Kim Daljin, Kim Won-Chung and Christopher Merrill

Mountain Life. Chungji. BecRai, *tr. by* Kim Daljin, Kim Won-Chung and Christopher Merrill

Mountain Life. Hueng Guobin. BecRai, *tr. by* Kim Daljin, Kim Won-Chung and Christopher Merrill

Mountain Life. Pyungyang Ungee. BecRai, *tr. by* Kim Daljin, Kim Won-Chung and Christopher Merrill

Mountain Lion. Barry Goldensohn. MAAN

Mountain Lion. D. H. Lawrence. FaBoVe

Mountain Living. Han-shan Te-ch'ing. *tr. by* James M. Cryer
  "Through a few splinters of." WoPoe, *tr. by* James M. Cryer

Mountain mist / Torches dropped. Kaya Shirao. ZenPo, *tr. by* Takashi Ikemoto and Lucien Stryk

Mountain Mountainous in Parturition, A. Voltaire. WoPoe, *tr. by* Robert Fitzgerald

Mountain mountainous in parturition, A. Mountain Mountainous in Parturition, A. Voltaire. WoPoe, *tr. by* Robert Fitzgerald

Mountain of books half-finished, A. Surf. Kiyoko Nagase. ItWoWo, *tr. by* Kijima Hajime

Mountain of Dreams. Aziz Samawi. IrPoTo, *tr. by* Alex Bellem

Mountain of interbeing. Deer Park. Wang Wei. WhBo

Mountain over Aberdare, The. Alun Lewis. AngWePo; TCAWP

Mountain Peak Grave. Miriam Sagan. WANABP

Mountain Pule. James King Annand. EdScPo

Mountain Rain. Paek Sŏk. CAMKP, *tr. by* Kyunghwan Choi

Mountain range, The. Temple of Eternal Light. Muso Soseki. EaWin, *tr. by* W. S. Merwin

Mountain receives, The. Pei Di and Wang Wei. CCL1 *Fr.* Wheel River.

Mountain road ends here, The. Lyell's Hypothesis Again. Kenneth Rexroth. APSN; APT-2; NAAPv.2

Mountain road is steep, the stone steps are dangerous, The. Spring Thoughts Sent to Tzu-an. Yü Hsüan-chi. WoPoe, *tr. by* Geoffrey Waters

Mountain Sanctuaries. Felicia Dorothea Hemans. CenSon *Fr.* Sonnets, Devotional and Memorial.

Mountain sheep are sweeter, The. Thomas Love Peacock. CABP; FaBoWar; NAEL-6v2; NOBRP; NPeEn; OxAEP-2 *Fr.* Misfortunes of Elphin, The.

Mountain sinks into the sea, The. Seung Sahn. WhBo

Mountain snow. Seasons in Santa Fe. Gerald Vizenor. HATNAP

Mountain Songs. Fĕng Mĕng-lung. *tr. by* Richard W. Bodman
  Feeling the Itch. ColAnChi; WoPoe, *tr. by* Richard W. Bodman
  Fooling Mom. ColAnChi, *tr. by* Richard W. Bodman
  My Old Man's Small. ColAnChi; WoPoe, *tr. by* Richard W. Bodman
  No Old Lady. ColAnChi, *tr. by* Richard W. Bodman
  Smart. ColAnChi; WoPoe, *tr. by* Richard W. Bodman

Mountain sounds carry a chill wisdom. 106. Shih Shu. CSKM, *tr. by* James H. Sanford

Mountain Spring, A. Ch'u Ch'uang I. CCL1; NDACCP; WaAnP, *tr. by* Kenneth Rexroth

Mountain stream in wild bamboo, A. On Chung Mountain. Wang An-shih. CrYelRi, *tr. by* Sam Hamill

Mountain Stream, The. John Ceiriog Hughes. OBWVE, *tr. by* Kenneth Hurlstone Jackson

Mountain Streams. Rhydwen Williams. *tr. by* Meic Stephens
  "Listen. / The rejoicing of waters fills my ears this evening." BBMWP, *tr. by* Meic Stephens

Mountain Stroll. Ch'ôn Yanghûi. EcSo, *tr. by* Aimee N. Kwon

Mountain Talk. A. R. Ammons. LPSFW; OxBoAm

Mountain Temple. Yi Tal. CATKP, *tr. by* Peter H. Lee

Mountain Tops. Lizelia Augusta Jenkins Moorer. CBWP-3

Mountain View with Figures. Paul Mariani. PfSP

Mountain Walk, A. Tu Mu. CCL1, *tr. by* R. F. Burton

Mountain / Whose woman have you brought home to our mountain city? Rasikcandra Rāy. SinGod, *tr. by* Rachel Fell McDermott

Mountain—Buddha's body, The. Sotoba, Layman. ZenPo, *tr. by* Takashi Ikemoto and Lucien Stryk

Mountain-light suddenly fails in the west, The. In Summer at the South Pavilion Thinking of Xing. Meng Hao Jan. CCL1, *tr. by* Witter Bynner

Mountains. Gaylord Brewer. AmPoNex

Mountains. Alice Oswald. MFPA; StAl

Mountain's a palace, A. Written in the Mountains. Kuan Hsiu. WoPoe, *tr. by* Jerome P. Seaton

Mountains and Air. George Stanley. NLPA
  "Big fish on the line." NLPA

Munition Wages. Madeline Ida Bedford. FaBoWar

Mur est massif, de pierre pleine, dur, fini, Le. Mur, Le. Michel Deguy. YaTCFP

Mur, Le. Michel Deguy. YaTCFP

Mural. Dominique Fourcade. OnScMo

Mural, Ch'ien-ming Temple. Lu Yu. CrYelRi, *tr.* by Sam Hamill

Murder. Yury Timofeievich Galanskov. TCRusP, *tr.* by Olive Dehn

Murder. Lucy Grealy. KGB

Murder, He Says. Frank Loesser. ReLy

Murder Machine 43. Kurt Schwitters. PFTM-1

Murder One. Allen Fisher. Oth *Fr.* Emergent Manner.

Murdered himself, to show some manful deed. (LL) Sardanapalus. Henry Howard, Earl of Surrey. NAEL-6v1; NAEL-7v1; NoSic

Murdered Luggage. Jose Angel Figueroa. PueRic

Murderer, The. Christopher Davis. OPRER

Murderer and Sarapis, The. Palladas. WoPoe, *tr.* by Tony Harrison

Murderer has been injecting her remorselessly, The. Dune Road, Southampton. Frederick Seidel. BeAl

Murderer is a Cow, The. Gerard Woodward. BeAl

Murderer spread his palliasse, A. Murderer and Sarapis, The. Palladas. WoPoe, *tr.* by Tony Harrison

Murderer's little daughter, The. Sympathetic Portrait of a Child. William Carlos Williams. APT-1; NAMCP V.1

Murderers, The. Paul Van Ostaijen. PFTM-1

Murderous little world once our objects had gazes. Our lives. Epitaph: Zion. Anne Carson. NAMCP V.2

Murder's not my forte. Eugenio Montale. ItPo, *tr.* by Gayle Ridinger

Murdoch, whet thy knife, that we may shave our crowns to the Great King. Shaving of Murdoch, The. Murdoch O'Daly. IrV, *tr.* by Standish O'Grady

Mûres, Les. Francis Ponge. YaTCFP

Murge with your white stones and green olives. Second Image Sequence. Umberto Piersanti. NeIt, *tr.* by Stephen Sartarelli

Murillo's Magdalen. William Ellery Channing. APN-1

Murk was the night: nor star, nor moon. Young Man Naughty's Adventure. Charlotte Brontë. VWP

Murky water of the North-Sea. North-Sea, The. Albert Verwey. TuT, *tr.* by Tony Curtis and Tony Curtis

Murmur. Esther Iverem. GT

Murmur. Adelia Prado. TANSG, *tr.* by Ellen Doré Watson

Murmur of a Bee, The. Emily Dickinson. MoAmPo

Murmur of the city sounded on, The. Day-dream, A. Mary Elizabeth Coleridge. VWP

Murmur of the mourning ghost, The. Sydney Thompson Dobell. OBEV *Fr.* Nuptial Eve, A.

Murmur, The. Arthur Sze. PoChi

Murmuring. Kofi Anyidoho. NAfrP

Murmuring of Bees, has ceased, The. Emily Dickinson. APN-2

Murmurings in a Field Hospital. Carl Sandburg. IllVoic

Murocercados / circodesnudos. Dolores Dorantes. SPV

Murphy's Law. Alan Jenkins. OxBSo

Murry, on finding *le Bon Dieu.* On Reading "God." G. K. Chesterton. OBCoV

Musa. Gerardo Deniz. RMCMP

Muscat Pruning. William Everson. APT-2

Muscular, maddened, and wrecking cornstalks. Lear Of Whylah Falls. George Elliott Clarke. OpeFie

Muscular sky of Minnesota is more than I can fathom, The. Autumn Song. Spencer Reece. LegDan

Muse. Sophia De Mello Breyner. VCWP, *tr.* by Ruth Fainlight

Muse. Gerardo Deniz. RMCMP, *tr.* by Mónica de la Torre

Muse. Linda Pastan. Vesp

Muse. Rebecca Seiferle. PoChi

Muse. Jo Shapcott. NeBrP; StAl

Muse, The. Anna Andreyevna Akhmatova. WoPoe, *tr.* by Stanley Burnshaw

Muse, The. Anna Andreyevna Akhmatova. PoetW, *tr.* by Max Hayward and Stanley Kunitz

Muse, The. Abraham Cowley. CABP; PBRV *Fr.* Pindarique Odes.

Muse, The. Alfred de Musset. WoPoe *Fr.* Night in May, A.

Muse, The. Ovid. NAWM-7v1 *Fr.* Metamorphoses.

Muse, The. Eleanor Wilner. GifTon

Muse and Drudge. Harryette Mullen.
   "Ain't your fancy." FaoP

Muse and Poet. Robert Bridges. OBMV

Muse as Medusa, The. May Sarton. HW; NALW

Muse, disgusted at an age and clime, The. On the Prospect of Planting Arts and Learning in America. George Berkeley. OxBEV
   (In happy climes, the seat of innocence.) ASA

Muse in Late November. Jonathan Henderson Brooks. ChIV-1

Muse in the New World, The. Walt Whitman. MoAmPo *Fr.* Song of the Exposition.

Muse Is Always the Other Woman, The. Constance Urdang. PBCAP

Muse Is Gone, The. Robert Long. MAAN

Muse of Fire, A. William Shakespeare. OxAEP-1 *Fr.* King Henry V.

Muse of Poetry came down one day, The. In Memoriam Paul Laurence Dunbar. Henrietta Cordelia Ray. CBWP-3

Muse of Satire, The. Mary Kinzie. PoA 2002

Muse of the many-twinkling feet! whose charms. Waltz, The. Lord Byron.

Muse of Water, A. Carolyn Kizer. FFC; VCAP

Muse teach me the song. Muse. Sophia De Mello Breyner. VCWP, *tr.* by Ruth Fainlight

Musée des Beaux Arts. W. H. Auden. BeAl; BrAP; CABP; ClHu; EMP; GS; HeIP-4; NAEL-6v2; NAEL-7v2; NAMCP V.1; NIL-7; NoAM; NoP-4; NoP-5; NPeEn; OxAEP-2; OxBEV; OxBoAm; PoPoPo; RaBo; RSaN; SoSe-8; TFi; TRP; WaAnP

Muses. Ani Ilkov. CSCBP, *tr.* by Georgi Belev and Lisa Sapinkopf

Muses are turned gossips; they have lost, The. Washing-Day. Anna Laetitia Barbauld. BrAP; NAEL-7v2; PEW; WoRP

Muses' Elysium [*or* Elizium]. Michael Drayton.
   Description of Elizium, The. PBRV

Muses' Elysium X, The. Michael Drayton.
   "*Satyr* O never ask how I came to this place." AEP

Muses' evening, as their morning-star, The. (LL) To Lucy, Countess of Bedford, with Mr. Donne's Satires. Ben Jonson. NAEL-6v1; NAEL-7v1

Muse's Favor, The. Priscilla Jane Thompson. CBWP-2

Muses' friend, The (grey-eyed Aurora), yet. William Browne. NOSC *Fr.* Britannia's Pastorals.

Muses, help me; sorrow swarmeth. Shepherd's Sorrow, Being Disdained in Love, The. Thomas Lodge. NoSic

Muses that fame's loose feathers beautify. George Chapman. OxBSo *Fr.* Coronet for His Mistress Philosophy, A.

Museum. Josep-Enric Dallerès. SonAtl, *tr.* by Eleanor Davidson, Richard Hacken, Alberto José Miyara and Anna Platt

Museum. Catherine Imbriglio. IAoNAP

Museum. Joe Wenderoth. BodElec

Museum, The. Wisława Szymborska. PoSu, *tr.* by Magnus F. Krynski

Museum Attendant, The. Archibald MacLeish. GM

Museum Cashier, The. Yona Harvey. BtF

Museum man!, The. Lorine Niedecker. NAAPv.2

Museum of pigs cries in my ears, A. Thanks to the pigs, I finished college. Ringing in My Ears. Yi Hyangji. EcSo, *tr.* by Catherine J. Kim

Museum Piece. Iorwerth Cyfeilog Peate. BBMWP, *tr.* by Joseph P. Clancy

Museum Piece. Richard Wilbur. NIL-7; NIP-4; TRP

Museum Piece (ca. Now). Teresa Palma Acosta. TiP2

Museum Vase. Robert Francis. APT-2

Museums. Louis MacNeice. MoBrPo

Museums offer us, running from among the buses. Museums. Louis MacNeice. MoBrPo

Mushroom. Takahashi Shinkichi. ZenPo, *tr.* by Takashi Ikemoto and Lucien Stryk

Mushroom Clouds. John Engman. AtGh

Mushroom Gatherers, The. Adam Mickiewicz. OxBEV, *tr.* by Donald Davie

Mushrooms. Moira Clark. Prnts

Mushrooms. Sylvia Plath. StAl

Music. Eugenio de Andrade. VCWP, *tr.* by Alexis Levitin

Music. Madison Cawein. APN-2

Music. William Congreve. OxAEP-1 *Fr.* Mourning Bride, The.

Music. Abraham Cowley. OxAEP-1

Music. Christopher Pearse Cranch. APN-1

Music. George Du Maurier. OBEV

Music. John Fletcher *and* William Shakespeare. NOSC *Fr.* King Henry VIII.

Music. Josephine D. Henderson Heard. CBWP-4

Music. David Huddle. MiVo

Music. Natasha Josefowitz. PasH

Music. Vladislav Felitsianovich Khodasevich. TCRusP, *tr.* by Daniel Weissbort

Music. Amy Lowell. ColAP

Music. Wilfred Owen. CAGL

Music. Rohan B. Preston. WaCA

Music. Henry David Thoreau. APN-1

Music— / a naked woman. Music. Juan Ramón Jiménez. WED, *tr.* by Robert Bly

Music, The. Mirabai. WED, *tr.* by Robert Bly

Music and Poetry of the Indians. *Unknown.* APN-2, *tr.* by John Tanner

Music Appreciation. Floyd Skloot. MiVo

Music At The Heart Of Thinking 22. Fred Wah. OpeFie

Music At The Heart Of Thinking 42. Fred Wah. OpeFie

Music at the Heart of Thinking 52. Fred Wah. OpeFie

Music At The Heart Of Thinking 54. Fred Wah. OpeFie

Music divides the evening. Tu Do Street. Yusef Komunyakaa. AmAlph; AmWaPo; CAP-8; LTA; NAMCP V.2; OxBoAm; SwNoth

Music for Brass. Günter Grass. AF, *tr. by* Christopher Middleton

Music for Homemade Instruments. Harryette Mullen. AWPTFC; BAP-01

Music for Martyrs. Gwendolyn Brooks. OxAAAP

Music for the Cows. Jim Johnson. MiVo

Music For Two Players 2. Mieko Shiomi. WhBo

Music has charms to soothe a savage breast. William Congreve. OxAEP-1 *Fr.* Mourning Bride, The.

Music historian explains the monkeybread tree to us, A. Salt. Günter Eich. MotU, *tr. by* David Walker

Music I heard with you was more than music. Conrad Potter Aiken. ItP; OxBoAm *Fr.* Discordants.

Music in Camp. John Reuben Thompson. CBCWP

Music in the Age of Iron. Alberto Blanco. CLPP, *tr. by* Julian Palley

Music in the granite hill. (LL) Men Loved Wholly Beyond Wisdom. Louise Bogan. APT-2; ColAP; OxBoAm

Music in the Meadow. Alice Wirth Gray. MiVo

Music is / more than model. SOUND is ProFound Sense. Kalamu ya Salaam. AnSo

Music is played. Play, The. Celebration. Joseph Ceravolo. FTOS

Music is your mistress. For duke ellington. Reuben Jackson. ESEAA

Music it was I heard, and music too. Lines Suggested by Hearing Music on the Boston Common at Night. Thomas Cole. APN-1

Music, *jazz*, comes in, The. (LL) Reuben, Reuben. Michael S. Harper. CAP-8; LoL; NAMCP V.2

Music Like Water, The. Jane Hirshfield. PasH

Music, Maestro, Please! Herb Magidson. ReLy

Music Master. Jelaluddin Rumi. ErotSp, *tr. by* Coleman Barks

Music met Leviathan returning, A. Peter Quennell. MoBrPo *Fr.* Leviathan.

Music Mother. Naomi Feigelson Chase. MiVo

Music my rampart, and my only one. (LL) On Hearing a Symphony of Beethoven. Edna St. Vincent Millay. ItP; MoAmPo

Music no one has ever heard, The. (LL) I Am a Cameraman. Douglas Dunn. EmeKit; StAl

Music of a Tree, The. Walter James Turner. MoBrPo

Music of Colours: The Blossom Scattered. Vernon Watkins. AngWePo

Music of Colours—White Blossom. Vernon Watkins. AngWePo; TCAWP

Music of Forefended Spheres, The. Coventry Patmore. NPeEn *Fr.* Victories of Love, The.

Music of Indifference. Samuel Beckett. YaTCFP, *tr. by* Mary Ann Caws and Jean-Pierre Cauvin

Music of Spheres. Jean Follain. BLT

Music of the Altai Mountains. Kelvin Corcoran. Oth

Music of the Hound, The. William Shakespeare. DiBP *Fr.* Midsummer Night's Dream, A.

Music of the Spheres. Anthony Barnett. Oth

Music of the Spheres. Robert Morgan. PoA 2002

Music of Words, The. Lu Chi. WoPoe *Fr.* Art of Writing, The.

Music, on fat bellied instruments, The. In Britain. Peter Didsbury. StAl

Music One Looks Back On, The. Stephen Dobyns. GoPo

Music rang out in the garden, The. In the Evening. Anna Andreyevna Akhmatova. FiBr, *tr. by* Judith Hemschemeyer

Music seemed to be so reminiscent, The. My Old Flame. Sam Coslow. ReLy

Music: Sexual misery is wearing you out. Ceriserie. Joshua Clover. BAP-01

Music stole in; and all the idle chatter. Music Stole In. Wilfrid Wilson Gibson. RWPCtW

Music Swims Back to Me. Anne Sexton. ColAP; MiVo; VCAP

Music That Makes Me Dance. Bob Merrill. ReLy

3. The Music. Madeline DeFrees. FiBr *Fr.* Figures for a Carrousel.

Music: the breathing of statues. Perhaps. On Music. Rainer Maria Rilke. WED, *tr. by* Robert Bly

Music to sleep in. (LL) Orfeo. Jack Spicer. APSN; CalPo

Music We Dance To, The. Rebecca Seiferle. PoDa

Music, when soft voices die. To —. Percy Bysshe Shelley. HeIP-4; NAEL-6v2; NAEL-7v2; OBEV; OxAEP-2; OxBEV; TFi

Music without Strings, The. Kabir. WED, *tr. by* Robert Bly

Musica. Philip Dacey. MiVo

Musical Instrument, A. Elizabeth Barrett Browning. BrAP; CABP; NAEL-6v2; NoP-4; NoP-5; NPeEn; OBEV; PEW; PoPoPo; ViWPN; VWP

Musical monkey is dressed like a flunkey, The. John Mole. OBCoV *Fr.* Penny Toys.

Musical Monkey, The. John Mole. OBCoV *Fr.* Penny Toys.

Musical Pumpkin-Hut. Heinrich Albert. GePo, *tr. by* George C. Schoolfield

Musical Saw. David Kresh. MiVo

Musicall Consort, A. Thomas Churchyard.

  "That humor now, declines for age drawes on." PBRV

Musician. Louise Bogan. APT-2

Musician, The. Philip Dacey. MiVo

Musician, The. Martinus Nijhoff. TuT, *tr. by* Desmond Egan

Musician, The. David Wright. NLP

Musician Talks about "Process," The. Rita Dove. ESEAA; PoDa

Musicians gone. Amateur Drummer. Roberta Gould. MiVo

Musician's Widow. Anne Stevenson. BeAl

Musicians wrestle everywhere. Emily Dickinson. APN-2

Music[k]'s Duel[l] [*ad. fr. the Latin of* Strada]. Richard Crashaw. NAEL-7v1; NPeEn

Music's Wife. Joel Long. AmPoNex

Musidora's Vision. Henrietta Cordelia Ray. CBWP-3

Musieu Bainjo. *Unknown.* SSUS

Musique de l'indifférence. Samuel Beckett. YaTCFP

Musketaquid. Ralph Waldo Emerson. APN-1

Muskoxen. Jeanette Lynes. Coast

Muskrats rose from the marsh. After the Storm. Edmond Yi-teh Chang. OpBo

Muslims in London are screaming, The. News, The. Harvey Shapiro. PrTe

Musophilus; or, Defence of All Learning. Samuel Daniel.

  "Behold how every man, drawn with delight." NoSic

  (Imperial Eloquence.) NAEL-7v1

  Poet and Critic. NoSic; PBRV

  Poetry in England. NoSic

  "Sacred Religion, mother of form and fear." NoSic

  Stonehenge. NPeEn

Muspilli. *Unknown.* GePo, *tr. by* Carroll Hightower

Mussel Rock/Lowtide—Santa Cruz, California 1959. Jeff Tagami. OpBo

Must Be Freed. Lizelia Augusta Jenkins Moorer. CBWP-3

Must be open to choices. Woman's Portrait, The. Wisława Szymborska. FiBr, *tr. by* Grazyna Drabik and Sharon Olds

Must be there's a neighbor upstairs whom we'll never meet. Superior. Gerardo Deniz. RMCMP, *tr. by* Mónica de la Torre

Must both remain as strangers still to you. (LL) Yourself. Jones Very. APN-1; OxBoAm

Must come upon you unmotivated as a poem. Hour of the Siesta, The. Judith Ortiz Cofer. PueRic

Must fall. (LL) Power of Taste, The. Zbigniew Herbert. PoetW; PoSu, *tr. by* Bogdana Carpenter and John Carpenter

Must I *always* be stuck in the audience at these poetry-readings, never. Juvenal. RomPo *Fr.* Satires.

Must I live here, with Scripture on my walls. Bed-Sitting Room, The. W. H. Davies. TCAWP

Must I shoot the. Watts. Conrad Kent Rivers. OxAAAP

Must I then see, alas! eternal night. Elegy over a Tomb. Edward Herbert, 1st Baron Herbert of Cherbury. OBEV; OBWVE

Must it be so? Should foreignness begin. Oskar Loerke. GTCP *Fr.* At the Edge of the Great City.

Must learn in life to die [*or* dy] like thee. (LL) Hymn to the Name and Hono[u]r of the Admirable Saint[e] Teresa, A. Richard Crashaw. BASC; FSCP; NoP-4; OBEV

Must not be uprooted! (LL) Okot P'Bitek. NAMCP V.2; PoetW *Fr.* Song of Lawino.

Must now be postponed for fifteen years! (LL) Golden Bells. Po Chü-i. BLT; CCL1, *tr. by* Arthur Waley

Must quiet a heart accused by its own fear. (LL) At Cooloolah. Judith Wright. BMAP; HarvBoo

Must raise you high among the run of men. (LL) If in the years to come you should recall. Edna St. Vincent Millay. HeIP-4; NAAPv.2

Must soon partake his grave. (LL) Epitaph on a Hare. William Cowper. NoP-4; NoP-5; PoPoPo

Must then my crimes become thy scandal too? To Antenor. Katherine Philips. EMWP

Must thou from Afric reinforce thy gang? James Grainger. STuOW *Fr.* Sugar Cane, The.

Must we part, Von Hügel, though much alike. William Butler Yeats. OBMV *Fr.* Vacillation.

Must you dance ev'ry dance. Change Partners. Irving Berlin. ReLy

Must you have a part in everything? (LL) Smell. William Carlos Williams. MoAmPo; OxBoAm; RaBo

Must you leave, John Holmes, with the prayers and psalms. Somewhere in Africa. Anne Sexton. InoFa; NALW

Must you with hot irons burn out both mine eyes? William Shakespeare. OxAEP-1 *Fr.* King John.

Mustache, The. Sabrina Orah Mark. LegDan

Mustaches on the last Russian Czar. (LL)   Grandparents.   Robert Lowell. ColAP; NAMCP V.2; WaAnP

Mustapha.   Fulke, 1st Baron Brooke Greville.

(Chorus of Priests.)   NoSic; OxAEP-1

Chorus Primus of Bashaws or Cadis.   NOSC

Chorus Sacerdotum.   NAEL-6v1; NAEL-7v1; OxBEV

(From Mustapha.)   NoP-4

Mutability.   Rachel Hadas.   ExTi

Mutability.   William Wordsworth.   CenSon; HeIP-4; NAEL-6v2; NAEL-7v2; NoP-4; NoP-5; OBEV Fr. Ecclesiastical Sonnets.

Mutability Checkers.   Randolph Healy.   Oth

Mutability Claims to Rule the World.   Edmund Spenser.   NoSic Fr. Faerie Queene, The.

Mutability ("Flower that smiles today, The.")   Percy Bysshe Shelley.   NAEL-6v2; NoP-4; NoP-5

Mutability ("We are as clouds that veil the midnight moon.")   Percy Bysshe Shelley.   NAEL-6v2; NAEL-7v2

Mutable Earth.   Louise Glück.   BodElec

Mutation.   William Cullen Bryant.   NCAP

Mutations.   Robert Fitzgerald.   APT-2

Mutations ("Face with red cavernous gashes a things possibly living in them, A.")   Carla Harryman.   BAP-04 Fr. Baby.

Mutations ("In the air cuddling with the wildest regions. Reproducing one trauma after another.")   Carla Harryman.   BAP-04 Fr. Baby.

Mute as it is, the river.   River Song.   Ben Howard.   PoCoUp

Mute is thy wild harp, now, O Bard sublime!   To the Shade of Burns. Charlotte Smith.   NoP-4; NoP-5; WaAnP

Mute Poem.   Laura Solórzano.   SPV, tr. by Jen Hofer

Mute Prophets.   Nicholas Samaras.   OPRER

Mute Swan, The.   Constance Merritt.   AmPoNex

Mute Swans.   Neil Curry.   NLP

Mute Trout.   Terrance Hayes.   RD

Mute was the marble. / Mutely glimmered the glass.   Yevgeny Aleksandrovich Yevtushenko.   VCWP,

Muted, The.   John Smith.   Coast

Muted Music.   Robert Penn Warren.   APT-2; NAMCP V.1

Muted pluck, pluck of the embroiderer's needle, The.   Muted, The.   John Smith.   Coast

Muted Tones.   Paul Verlaine.   SxFrPo, tr. by Martin Sorrell

Mutes, The.   Denise Levertov.   BeAl; CAP-8; ErotSp; NALW; OxBoAm

Mutineer's Ballad, The.   Peter Kocan.   NOBAu

Mutton.   Gertrude Stein.   NAMCP V.1 Fr. Tender Buttons.

Mutton Bird Man.   Rhyll McMaster.   NOBAu

Mutual Congratulations of the Poets Anna Seward and Hayley, The.   Richard Porson.   OBSV

Mutual forgiveness of each vice.   Gates of Paradise, The.   William Blake.

Mutual Problem.   William Cole.   OBCoV

"Muvver was barfin' 'er biby one night," A.   Unknown.   NOxBChV,

Muy Lejos.   Blas de Otero.   RaW

Muybridge.   Linda Bierds.   AmAlph

Muzzle and jowl and beastly brow.   Fearful Symmetry.   Basil Bunting.   PoA 2002

My age fallen away like white swaddling.   Age.   Philip Larkin.   OxBEV

My age is three hundred and seventy-two.   Sleepy Giant, The.   Charles Edward Carryl.   NOxBChV,

My airplane is flames my castle flooded with Rhenish wine.   Hello.   Benjamin Péret.   YaTCFP, tr. by Mary Ann Caws

My Alba.   Allen Ginsberg.   CLPP

My Ambition.   James Laughlin.   GifTon; PoA 2002

My ancestor was called on to go out.   Wind at Your Door, The.   Robert David Fitzgerald.   NOBAu

My ancestors arose from graves.   What the Dead Do.   Jackie Graves.   BRtP

My ancestors weren't hippies, cotton.   Botanical Fanaticism.   Thylias Moss.   TRP

My Androgynous Years.   James Harms.   NeAmPo

My angel!   Holiday Present.   Ilya Abu Madi.   NAAPv.2, tr. by George Dimitri Selim

My Angel Sister, though thy lovely form.   On a Lock of Miss Sarah Seward's Hair Who Died in her Twentieth Year.   Anna Seward.   CenSon

My Angeline.   Harry Bache Smith.   NBLV

My anointed knuckles, a hierophant inhabits fingertips at midnight, a greenglow sacrifice.   Shy Breathing of the Radiator, The.   Night Sighs.   Jill Hartman.   PoPra

My apparition rose from the fall of lead.   Civilian and Soldier.   Wole Soyinka.   AF; PoetW

My apple-tree, my willow.   Yunna Petrovna Moritz.   ItGoST, tr. by Daniel Weissbort

My Arab Steed.   Caroline Elizabeth Norton.   NPBRoP

My ardours for emprize nigh lost.   On an Invitation to the United States. Thomas Hardy.   FaBoA

My Arima mountains closer.   Forever Arima.   Cheryl Boyce Taylor.   WiU

My arm for a pillow.   Buson.   EH, tr. by Robert Hass

My arms are given.   Absolution.   Diane Ward.   FTOS

My arms are round you, and I lean.   To the Oaks of Glencree.   John Millington Synge.   InoFa; MoBrPo

My Army Cross Over.   Unknown.   SSUS

My aspens dear, whose airy cages quelled.   Binsey Poplars (Felled 1879). Gerard Manley Hopkins.   NAEL-6v2; NAEL-7v2; NAMCP V.1; NoAM; PtR

My atheist lover.   Grand Canyon.   Ken Pobo.   RWB

My attention is a wild / animal: it will if idle.   Pet Panther.   A. R. Ammons. NoP-4; NoP-5

My Atthis, although our dear Anaktoria.   Sappho.   PtR, tr. by Willis Barnstone

My Auld Hector.   James Hoggard.   DiBP

My Aunt and the Sun.   Michael Burkard.   BodElec

My Aunt Jane.   Unknown.   FaBoVe

My Aunt Jane she took me in.   My Aunt Jane.   Unknown.   FaBoVe

My Aunt Maria.   Mary Morelle Show, The.   Denise Nico Leto.   UnSA

My aunt was an herb doctor, one-eyed with crooked yellow teeth.   To-ta Ti-om. Peter Blue Cloud.   HATNAP

My aunts washed dishes while the uncles.   Paper Matches.   Paulette Jiles. NIL-7; NIP-4

My Autobiography.   Ted Berrigan.   OxBoAm

My ax sinks in.   Buson.   EMJL, tr. by Haruo Shirane

My baby contemplates the toy catalog.   20 July 1994.   Virginia Cerenio. ReBoTo

My baby is sleeping overhead.   Dream Maiden, A.   Harriet Hamilton King. VWP

My Baby Just Cares for Me.   Gustave Kahn.   ReLy

My baby sister used to get.   Michele.   Afaa Michael Weaver.   BtF

My baby's gone.   Blues: My Baby's Gone.   Alfred B. Spellman.   EGAG

My bakelite mantel set pulled him in.   Whatever Happened to Conway Twitty? Tim Thorne.   BMAP

My bands of silk and miniver.   Full Moon.   Elinor Wylie.   NALW; NoP-4; NoP-5; StAl

My Baptismal Birthday [or Birth-Day].   Samuel Taylor Coleridge.   ChIV-2

My bar is somewhat further down the street.. (LL)   Third Avenue in Sunlight. Anthony Hecht.   OxBoAm; VCAP

My Bas-Sheva.   Moishe Nadir.   Prolet, tr. by Amelia Glaser

My Bawty is a cur I dearly like.   Allan Ramsay.   DiBP Fr. Gentle Shepherd, The.

My beautiful bird in the eternal the downspouts call you but don't think about. Pale Blue Line in a Forced Episode, I Cut a Hole in the Flag of the Republic.   Simone Yoyotte.   SurWo, tr. by Myrna Bell Rochester

My beautiful boy you have killed me. (LL)   Ballygrand Widow.   Deborah Randall.   BeAl; NeBl

My beautiful lover, one day you will be killed.   Unknown.   SLW, tr. by Marjolijn De Jager, Sayd Bahodin Majrouh and André Velter

My beautiful, my beautiful! thou standest meekly by.   Scorcher's Farewell to His Steed, The.   Charles Dryden.   ArBi

My beautiful picture of pirates and treasure.   Jigsaw Puzzle.   Russell Hoban. NTCP

My beautiful trembler! how wildly she shrinks!   Ellen Learning to Walk. Frances Sargent Osgood.   ColAP

My bed is unmade: sheets on the floor.   Death Is Sitting at the Foot of My Bed. Oscar Hahn.   TCLAP, tr. by Sandy McKinney

My bed was soft, the early night was bliss.   Petronius Arbiter.   RomPo, tr. by J. P. Sullivan

My bedroom window can be seen from the viewing deck.   Panopticon. Brenda Shaughnessy.   LegDan

My beloved.   Love I Gave You Once, The.   Faiz Ahmad Faiz.   PtR, tr. by Mahbub-ul-Haq

My Beloved.   Charles Simic.   OxBoAm

My beloved, come and sit a moment close to me.   Unknown.   SLW, tr. by Marjolijn De Jager, Sayd Bahodin Majrouh and André Velter

My Belovèd Compares Herself to a Pint of Stout.   Paul Durcan.   EmeKit; StAl

My beloved has visited me and my moments have become sweet. My beloved listened to me.   Alī ibn Abd Allāh Shushtarī.   HiArP, tr. by James T. Monroe

My beloved hath a vineyard.   Vineyard of My Beloved, The.   Priscilla Jane Thompson.   CBWP-2

My beloved, I have nothing to offer you.   Unknown.   SLW, tr. by Marjolijn De Jager, Sayd Bahodin Majrouh and André Velter

My beloved! If you turn your back upon the enemy, do not come home again! Unknown.   SLW, tr. by Marjolijn De Jager, Sayd Bahodin Majrouh and André Velter

My beloved is / Dead in Diên Biên Phu. My Beloved Is Dead in Vietnam. Thuong Vuong-Riddick. IFF

My Beloved Is Dead in Vietnam. Thuong Vuong-Riddick. IFF

My beloved little billiard balls. Poem to Some of my Recent Poems. James Tate. NoAM

My beloved, my sun, rise above the horizon and obliterate my nights of exile. *Unknown*. SLW, *tr. by* Marjolijn De Jager, Sayd Bahodin Majrouh and André Velter

My beloved spake, and said unto me. Bible, *O.T.* OPOU *Fr.* Song of Solomon, The [*or* The Song of Songs].

My beloved, the breath of the universe. Butterfly frozen in stone, A. Shakir Li'aibi. IrPoTo, *tr. by* Ralph Saverese and Saadi A. Simawe

My Ben [See also "An Ode for Him"]. Robert Herrick. BASC

My best friend Bruce. Fireflies in a Jar. DJ Renegade. FuFl

My Bethel is a house of God between slagheap and factory. Bafflement. J. Eirian Davies. BBMWP, *tr. by* Sion Eirian

My Bicycle Bell. Dobashi Jiji. ArBi, *tr. by* Edward Lueders and Koriyama Naoshi

My Big German Bra. Jennifer L. Knox. FreRad

My birthplace is the brown heather-land. Steen Steensen Blicher. SonAtl, *tr. by* Peter Hansen, Maria Palmer and Asa Winter

My black brothers. Grand Central by Night. Yosl Grinshpan. Prolet, *tr. by* Amelia Glaser

My black cat doesn't know. Savoir Faire. Claribel Alegría. VCWP

My black face fades. Facing It. Yusef Komunyakaa. AmAlph; AmFaPo; AmWaPo; EMP; ESEAA; FTtHH; InoFa; ItP; NAMCP V.2; NoP-5; OxBoAm; PLBUT; PoAgWa; PoPoPo; StAl; TRP

My black hair tangled. Lady Izumi. ErotSp, *tr. by* Sam Hamill

My black hills have never seen the sun rising. Shancoduff. Patrick Kavanagh. HarvBoo; WoPoe

My black mother birthed me. Afro-American. Henry Dumas. OxAAAP

My black mulberries, my swarthy woman, my gypsy. Black Mulberries. Bedri Rahmi EyuboĞlu. NaPG, *tr. by* Talat Sait Halman

My Blackness Is the Beauty of This Land. Lance Jeffers. ISC; OxAAAP

My Blessed Lord, how doth thy Beautious Spouse. Edward Taylor. ColAP; NAAPv.1 *Fr.* Preparatory Meditations Before My Approach to the Lord's Supper.

My Blessed Lord, that Golden Linck that joyns. Edward Taylor. TCAPo *Fr.* Preparatory Meditations Before My Approach to the Lord's Supper.

My blissful Mother exists fully through every creature! Lex Hixon. HW

My Blood Brother. Frank Mkalawile Chipasula. HBAPE; PML

My blood came late. No-one celebrated. Blood. Judith Barrington. FiBr

My blood sits upright in a chair. Blood. Franz Wright. AmAlph

My blood so red. Call, The. *Unknown*. OBEV

My Bloodhound. Barry Cornwall. DiBP

My blue boy sleeps under the stack's huge shadow. (LL) Primer, The. Josephine Jacobsen. NoP-4; NoP-5

My Blue Heaven. George Whiting. ReLy

My Blue Piano. Else Lasker-Schüler. GTCP, *tr. by* Irmgard Hunt

My Blue Piano. Else Lasker-Schüler. PoCho, *tr. by* Eavan Boland

My blueveined child. (LL) Flower Given to My Daughter, A. James Joyce. OBMV; PtR; RaBo

My boat slowed on the still water. Return, The. William Heyen. CAP-8

My Body. Joan Larkin. WiU

My body being dead, my limbs [*or* lims] unknown. Preparative, The. Thomas Traherne. BASC

My body breaking. (LL) Lucille Clifton. *See* Always for your never named sake.

My body in the walls captived. Sir Walter Ralegh. CABP

My body is a mystery. Instinct. Edith Södergran. PFTM-1

My body is a torn mattress. Would You Wear My Eyes? Bob Kaufman. GT

My body is a white thing in the sun, now. Morning After My Death, The. Larry Levis. OPRER

My body is a wide house. House of Changes. Jeni Couzyn. BrAP

My body is like an illusory flower: no way to touch it. Illusory Hermitage. Master Naong. BecRai, *tr. by* Kim Daljin, Kim Won-Chung and Christopher Merrill

My body is like deadwood my thoughts are like ashes. Han-shan Te-ch'ing. CSKM, *tr. by* Red Pine

My body is weary to death of my mischievous brain. Nebuchadnezzar. Elinor Wylie. ChIV-1; MoAmPo

My body leaves you drop by drop. Absence. Gabriela Mistral. SpanPo, *tr. by* Kate Flores

My body opens over San Francisco like the day. Splittings. Adrienne Rich. HarvBoo

My body remembers. Making Tortillas. Alicia Gaspar de Alba. IPofL

My Body Rock 'Long Fever. *Unknown*. SSUS

My body, you are an animal. I Talk to My Body. Anna Swirszczynska [*or* Swir]. BLT

My body's idle, doing perfectly nothing. Autumn Pool. Po Chü-i. NDACCP, *tr. by* David Hinton

My Bohemia (Fantasy). Arthur Rimbaud. SxFrPo, *tr. by* Martin Sorrell

My Bomb. Beckian Fritz Goldberg. ExTi

My bones burned down. Meetin the Conjure Woman. Gary Lilley. BtF

My Bones Predict. Anne Wilkinson. *See* Tigers Know from Birth.

My bones predict the striking hour of thunder. Tigers Know from Birth. Anne Wilkinson. IFF

My boots stayed damp with suppuration. Road Home, The. Andrew Hudgins. AmWaPo

My borders rise like the neat pile of white hankies. Borders. Margaret Randall. ICANM

My Boy Willie. *Unknown*. MakPoe

My boyfriend, the Infidel, is dying of old age. My Boyfriend, the Infidel. Jeni Olin. FreRad

My brain burns with hate of you. Paradox. Anna Wickham. LW

My brain is like the ravaged shores—the sand. At Night. Frances Darwin Cornford. MoBrPo

My breath is a red bird. Yellow Blight. Cemal Süreya. NaPG, *tr. by* Talat Sait Halman

My brethren all attend. Zealous Puritan, The. *Unknown*. NOSC

My brethren, you see with your own eyes what we are. Funeral Oration. *Unknown*. IQMS, *tr. by* Alan Jenkins

"My bride is not coming, alas!" says the groom. Thomas Hardy. MoBrPo *Fr.* Satires of Circumstance in Fifteen Glimpses.

My bright and beauteous Bride. (LL) Love: "All thoughts, all passions, all delights." Samuel Taylor Coleridge. NPBRoP; OBEV

My Broad Back. Paul Laraque. OGAHCP, *tr. by* Boadiba and Jack Hirschman

My Broken Heart. Fanny Howe. ExTi

My Brother. Chavali Bangaramma. HotL, *tr. by* V. Narayana Rao

My Brother. Hendrik de Vries. TuT, *tr. by* Peter van de Kamp

My Brother. Mikhail Naimy. NAAPv.2, *tr. by* Sharif Elmusa and Gregory Orfalea

My brother and I. Miriam. Marjorie Agosin. MirDau, *tr. by* Monica Bruno Galmozzi

My brother and I planned to meet. Black Hole, The. Robert Pack. OtW

My Brother and the Brazier. Im Hwa. CAMKP, *tr. by* Jiwon Shin

My brother being the eldest had / for his bike the most elaborate. Our Bicycles. James Laughlin. ArBi

My brother came from the field. And My Brother Was Silent. Amir Gilboa. NRoS, *tr. by* Esther Raizen

My brother Charles. Ooly Pop a Cow. David Huddle. GoPo

My brother comes home from work. You Can Have It. Philip Levine. AmFaPo; CAP-8; EMP; NAMCP V.2; NoP-4; NoP-5; OxBoAm; VCAP

My brother flies. Those Who Wrestle with the Angel for Us. Brigit Pegeen Kelly. OtW

My brother, good morning: my sister, good night. (LL) Early Morning, The. Joseph Hilaire Pierre Belloc. Spl; TLR

My brother is deep in his library book. Which is causing my stepfather great agitation. Sunday Afternoon. Franz Wright. AmAlph

My brother is skull and skeleton now. Epitaph. William Montgomerie. EdScPo

My brother Jack was nine in May. Baby's Debut, The. James Smith. NPBRoP

My brother Jamie lost me all. Mary Stuart. Edwin Muir. EdScPo

My brother kept. Wheels. Jim Daniels. P180

My Brother Lives Too Far Away. Mark Van Doren. OxBoAm

My Brother, my brother. Jane Johnston Schoolcraft. NAAPv.1 *Fr.* Forsaken Brother, a Chippewa Tale, The.

My brother sent me ribs for my birthday. 1-800-HOT-RIBS. Catherine Bowman. P180

My brother, / staggering amidst the shiny glass mountains of the North Pole. Hymn of Love, The. György Sárközi. IQMS, *tr. by* Adam Makkai

My brother thinks it's best to distract my sister. Return, 2, The. Catherine Barnett. PoCho

My brother thought they were freaks. Everly Brothers, The. Floyd Skloot. SwNoth

My brother was afraid, even as a boy, of going blind—so deeply. How Some of It Happened. Marie Howe. ExTi

My brother works at the telegraph office in the station. Canto Three. Tonino Guerra. PML, *tr. by* Adria Bernardi

My brother, you suffered. My Brother. Hendrik de Vries. TuT, *tr. by* Peter van de Kamp

My Brothers. Haki R. Madhubuti. ISC

My Brother's Anger. Patricia Goedicke. LiTh

My brother's done for, by all human law. János Arany. IQMS *Fr.* Toldi.

My brothers i will not tell you. My Brothers. Haki R. Madhubuti. ISC

My Brothers Make a Lantern. David Scott Ward. AmPoNex

My brudder build a house in Paradise. Build a House in Paradise. *Unknown.* SSUS

My brudder sittin' on de tree of life. Roll, Jordan, Roll. *Unknown.* NAAPv.1

My brudder, tik keer Satan, / My army cross ober. My Army Cross Over. *Unknown.* SSUS

My brudder, want to get religion? Lonesome Valley, The. *Unknown.* SSUS

My Buddy. Richard Hugo. SeSe

My bumpy road to sexual maturity was paved with the death of communist dictators. Dictators. Péter Zilahy. PML, *tr. by* Judith Sonnabend

My butterfly breaths. Haiku # 135. Kalamu ya Salaam. BtF

My Canary. Josephine D. Henderson Heard. CBWP-4

My candle burned alone in an immense valley. Valley Candle. Wallace Stevens. SAmP

My candle burns a flame of jade. Meditating on the Start of a New Era. Yo Inlŏ. WoPoe, *tr. by* Jean S. Grigsby

My candle burns at both ends. First Fig. Edna St. Vincent Millay. AmWit; APT-1; BLPJKO; BRP; ChAP; NAAPv.2; NALW; NAMCP V.1; NIL-7; NoAM; NoP-4; NoP-5; OxBoAm; PoA 2002

My candle burns up lank and fair. Resurrection. Margiad Evans. OBWVE

My carefree Namesake, this the art. Martial. RomPo, *tr. by* Peter Whigham

My Careful Life. Frank Ormsby. PBCIP

My careful life says: "No surrender." My Careful Life. Frank Ormsby. PBCIP

My cares comen evere anewe—. *Unknown.* OHMEL

My case is this. Sir John Davies. NoSic *Fr.* Gulling[e] Sonnets, The.

My cat. Issa. EH, *tr. by* Robert Hass

My Cat Jeoffry. Christopher Smart. BrAP; CABP; HeIP-4; NAEL-6v1; NAEL-7v1; NoP-4; NoP-5; NPeEn; OBWVE; OxAEP-1; PoPoPo; TriCat; TRP; WaAnP; WeW-3 *Fr.* Jubilate Agno.

My Chakabuku Mama: A Comic Tale. Jewelle Gomez. BAP-01

My cheeks still feel their breath: how can it be. On the Transitory. Hugo von Hofmannsthal. WoPoe, *tr. by* Naomi Replansky

My child and I hold hands on the way to school. September, the First Day of School. Howard Nemerov. GoPo

My Child Blossoms Sadly. Yehuda Amichai. PLBUT, *tr. by* Ruth Nevo

My child, I do this for you. I give this to you. *Unknown.* APN-2 *Fr.* Minnetare Songs.

My child is lying on my knees. Father's Hymn for the Mother to Sing. George Macdonald. SacPr

My child, my child, thou leav'st me! I shall hear. Madeline, A Domestic Tale. Felicia Dorothea Hemans. RWP

My child, my sister. Invitation au Voyage, L'. Charles Baudelaire. ItP; WoPoe, *tr. by* Richard Wilbur

My child never played the piano. Moderato. Susan Wicks. MFPA

My child perished like the sky when it broke. Kŭ' siut Song. *Unknown.* APN-2, *tr. by* Franz Boas

My Child Smells of Peace. Yehuda Amichai. NRoS, *tr. by* Esther Raizen

My child, we were two children. Mein Kind, wir waren Kinder. Heinrich Heine. OBVE, *tr. by* Elizabeth Barrett Browning

My childhood all a myth. Myth, The. Edwin Muir. HarvBoo

My childhood are rememberances of a court in Seville. Portrait. Antonio Machado Ruiz. SpanPo, *tr. by* Dorren Bell

My Childhood in Another Part of the World. Rafael Campo. NeAmPo

My childhood is a sphere. Childhood. Thomas Traherne. SacPr

My childhood is all memories of a patio in Sevilla. Portrait. Antonio Machado Ruiz. STV, *tr. by* Robert Bly and John Frederick Nims

My childhood is memories of a patio in Seville. Portrait. Antonio Machado Ruiz. ItP; RaBo; WED; WoPoe, *tr. by* Robert Bly

My Childhood Trees. Edith Södergran. WoPoe, *tr. by* Stina Katchadourian

My childhood trees stand tall in the grass. My Childhood Trees. Edith Södergran. WoPoe, *tr. by* Stina Katchadourian

My Childhood-Home I See Again. Abraham Lincoln. APN-1; NAAPv.1; PtR

My childhood's trees stand rejoicing around me: O human! Homecoming. Edith Södergran. WPoS

My Children. Lance Jeffers. OxAAAP

My Children Visit the Zendo. Tom Greening. WhBo

My children, when at first I liked the whites. *Arapaho Oral Tradition.* APN-2 *Fr.* Ghost-Dance Songs.

My Chinese uncle, gouty, deaf, half-blinded. Grotesques. Robert Graves. OBCoV

My Christ, by Thee. (LL) Thanksgiving to God for His House, A. Robert Herrick. BASC; CavPo; NOSC

My Christmas; Mum's Christmas. Sarah Forsyth. OBCP

My City. James Weldon Johnson. NAAPv.1

My Class Draws a Blank on Robbie Burns. Richard Lemm. Coast

My clear windowpane moon. (LL) Love Song: "I love you, I love you, is my song." Pablo Neruda. ErotSp; GifTon, *tr. by* William O'Daly

My clock is fast. I don't know how fast. I wanted. Term, The. Oni Buchanan. LegDan

My closest and dearest! Dirge on the Death of Art O'Leary. Eileen O'Connell. IrV, *tr. by* Eleanor Hull

My Cloth of Gold. Ina Coolbrith. SWaP

My clothes are standing up without me. When You Wish Upon a Star That Turns into a Plane. James Harms. SwNoth

My clothes somersault in the dryer. At thirty. Laundromat, The. Dorianne Laux. SUP

My clumsiest dear, whose hands shipwreck vases. Love Poem. John Frederick Nims. IllVoic; PoA 2002

My Cockroach Lover. Martín Espada. UrbNat

My cock's great size results in one delight. *Unknown.* PriapPo *Fr.* Priapus Poems, The.

My Cocoon tightens—Colors tease. Emily Dickinson. APN-2; NAAL-3

My cold sandwich sits on books. Bookshop in Winter. Margo Lockwood. PfS

My colleague knows by heart the morbid verse. Lunch and Afterwards. Dannie Abse. BloBone

My colored child / hood wuz mostly music. Make/n My Music. Angela Jackson. SeSe

My Coloring Book. Fred Ebb. ReLy

My comforts drop and melt away like snow. Answer, The. George Herbert. FaBoVe; NPeEn

My company. (LL) Hellhound on My Trail. Robert Johnson. APT-2; PFTM-2

My Company. Sir Herbert Read. PoWW

My Compleinte. Thomas Hoccleve. Hoccleve Remembers His Madness. NPeEn

My comrades / Inasmuch as they are comrades do not need to study the map. Abba Kovner. NRoS, *tr. by* Esther Raizen

My Confessional Sestina. Dana Gioia. PoA 2002; RA

My contemplation dazzles in the End. Anticipation, The. Thomas Traherne. BASC

My contemporary. He died, not I. To a Poet. Ágnes Nemes Nagy. PoSu, *tr. by* Bruce Berlind

My copy of his *Introductory Lectures*. First Time Reading Freud. Douglas Goetsch. NevBe

My Corpses. Benjamin Paloff. NevBe

My cottage door opens on the water. At Home. Wang An-shih. CrYelRi, *tr. by* Sam Hamill

My cotton shirts float on the line. Women, The. Cyrus Cassells. UnSA

My Country. Tony Hoagland. SUP

My Country. D. Natsagdorzh. SonAtl, *tr. by* Bat-Erdene Baabar, Susie Drost, Clare Eaton and S. Erdenebat

My Country. Jaime Torres Bodet. TCLAP, *tr. by* Sonja Karsen

My Country Audit. Mildmay Fane, 2d Earl of Westmorland. NOSC

My country does not belong to me. Poet's Fate, A. Awwad Nasir. IrPoTo, *tr. by* Saadi A. Simawe and Daniel Weissbort

My Country in Darkness. Eavan Boland. PoCho

My country is an asylum where madmen. Dead Erect, The. Malika O'Lahsen. HAWP

My country is at the break of Spring. Anne Pauker. Nokhem Vaysman. Prolet, *tr. by* Amelia Glaser

My country need not change her gown. Union. Emily Dickinson. FaBoA

My country now is like a barge. Richard II Forty. Louis Aragon. WoPoe, *tr. by* Peter Dale

My country, O my land, my friends. Purgatorio. Hart Crane. PoA 2002

My country, that nobly could dare. For the Fourth of July. Eliza Lee Cabot Follen. SWaP

My country, 'tis of thee. Rational Anthem, A. Ambrose Bierce. CalPo

My Country 'Tis of Thee. William Edward Burghardt DuBois. NAAPv.1

My country, 'tis of thee. America. Samuel Francis Smith. TCAPo

My country wasn't sold, it was stolen. *Unknown.* WhBo

My Country Weeps. Andreas Gryphius. WoPoe, *tr. by* John Peck

My country, what road do you take? Lusitanian Song. János Vajda. IQMS, *tr. by* Jean Overton Fuller

My courage fails me when I grasp my water jar. *Unknown.* SLW, *tr. by* Marjolijn De Jager, Sayd Bahodin Majrouh and André Velter

My Cousin Abe, Paul Antschel and Paul Celan. Jacqueline Osherow. TaR

My Cousin Agueda [or Agatha]. Ramón López Velarde. OBVE; TCLAP, *tr. by* Samuel Beckett

My cousin at the dye factory, who stutters. How Much Is This One? Pak Nohae. CAMKP, *tr. by* Scott Swaner

My cousin Gene (he's really only a second cousin) has a shoe he picked up at Dachau. Dachau Shoe, The. W. S. Merwin. AmWaPo; MotU

My Creed. Alice Cary. TreFP

My Cutey's Due at Two-to-Two Today. Leo Robin. ReLy

My cuticles are a mess. Oh honey, by the way. Motorcyclists, The. James Tate. NAMCP V.2; NoAM; ReTh

My Dad. Laura Whipple. CA

My dad cracks a joke and two men laugh. Show Biz Parties. Elizabeth Claman. OPRER

My dad is a cook. My Family. Nyere-Gibran Miller. BtF

My Dad Versus Ginsberg. Sion Eirian. BBMWP, tr. by Robert Minhinnick

My dad worked there, part-time, knew about. Powerhouse, The. Keith Wilson. ICANM

My dad works late in a coffee shop. My Dad. Laura Whipple. CA

My Dada. Judith Kazantzis. Prnts

My daddy has paid the rent. Good Times. Lucille Clifton. FTtHH; HHAm; SoSe-8; TRP

My daddy rides me piggy-back. Piggy-back. Langston Hughes. TLR

My daddy said, 'My son, my son'. Bad Report—Good Manners. Spike Milligan. NOxBChV

My Daddy, Whenever He Went Some Place. David Huddle. PBCAP

My Dad's Wallet. Raymond Carver. GoPo

My Damon was the first to wake. Meeting. George Crabbe. OBEV

My Dance. Blaise Cendrars. CuPo

My Dance. Blaise Cendrars. YaTCFP, tr. by Ron Padgett

My Dancing Day. Unknown.
    "To-morrow shall be my dancing day." ChrPo

My Daphne's hair is twisted gold. John Lyly. NoSic Fr. Midas.

My Dark Fathers. Brendan Kennelly. PBCIP; StAl

My Dark Night Has Come Round Again. Unknown. WoPoe Fr. Sweeney Astray.

My dark night has come round again. Unknown. WoPoe Fr. Sweeney Astray.

My Dark Rosaleen! (LL) Dark Rosaleen. Owen Roe MacWard. IrV; OBEV; OxAEP-2, tr. by James Clarence Mangan

My darling, all around us people clamor. Love Is the Thing. Ned Washington. ReLy

My darling, / Best of all. Aprin Çor Tigin. NaPG, tr. by Talat Sait Halman

My Darling Clementine. Percy Montrose. ASA

My darling dear, my daisy flower. John Skelton. NoSic Fr. Garland [or Garlande or Garlands] of Laurel[1], The.

My darling lady readers. Mystery Corset, The. André Breton. PFTM-1

My darling / life is a woman who belongs to everyone. Like a Stranger. Melisa Gürpınar. NaPG, tr. by Talat Sait Halman

My darling little Lou how I love you. Guillaume Apollinaire. PFTM-1 Fr. Poems for Lou.

My darling makes me mother to their youth. (LL) Augusta Davies Webster. ViWPN; VWP Fr. Mother and Daughter.

My Darling, My Darling. Frank Loesser. ReLy

My darling, my love. In the Greenwood. Desmond O'Grady. IrLP

My darling, thou wilt never know. On the Death of Emily Jane Brontë. Charlotte Brontë. VWP

My darling with the rosy face—at one glance. Şeyh Galib. NaPG, tr. by Talat Sait Halman

My darling, you know how much I like to see the light on a. Black Hairs, The. Heinz Pasman. RaBo, tr. by Robert Bly

My darlings, do you hear me? Trim the fires! (LL) My Lighthouses. Helen Hunt Jackson. APN-2; ColAP

My darling's features, painted by the light. George Henry Boker. APN-2 Fr. Sonnets: A Sequence on Profane Love.

My Darlings' Shoes. Unknown. TreFP

My daugher's eyes are blue as Georgian Bay. Ferry to South Baymouth, The. Bruce Meyer. IFF

My daughter. (LL) Marina. T. S. Eliot. APT-1; CABP; HeIP-4; NAEL-6v2; NAEL-7v2; NPeEn; OxBEV

My daughter. Dime after Dime. Mary Weems. SpirFl

My daughter, at eleven. Little Girl, My String Bean, My Lovely Woman. Anne Sexton. AFaM; NAAL-5

My daughter came home from school one day. Battle, Over and Over Again, The. Safiya Henderson-Holmes. UnSA

My daughter has a birthmark hidden under her left arm. Hunger and Imagination. Teresa Whitman. MiVo

My daughter has turned against eggs. Age six. Eggs. Sharon Olds. AFaM

My daughter of the Mabinogion name. Rhiannon. T. Harri Jones. AngWePo

My daughter plays on the floor. Spelling. Margaret Atwood. NALW; NoAM

My daughter sings under a brick arch. Falling Bricks. Jim Daniels. PML

My daughter spreads her legs. After Reading Mickey in the Night Kitchen for the Third Time Before Bed. Rita Dove. CAP-8; LoL; NAMCP V.2; OxAAAP; ReTh

My daughter tells me. Astrology? Jean Valerie. BtF

My daughter works each night. Destinies. Hashim Shafiq. IrPoTo, tr. by Saadi A. Simawee and Ellen Doré Watson

My daughter, writer, sits and floats. (LL) Well, spring overflows the land. Lorine Niedecker. NAAPv.2; NAMCP V.1

My day in the hills. Sound of Music, The. Oscar Hammerstein, II. ReLy

My daydreams lie buried in autumn leaves. September in the Rain. Al Dubin. ReLy

My days pass with the beads of the rosary. Shakir Li'aibi. IrPoTo, tr. by Ralph Saverese and Saadi A. Simawe

My days, these days, begin on a road called Rugby. Rugby Road. George Garrett. LPSFW

My days were a thing for me to live. For One Who Gayly Sowed His Oats. Countee Cullen. APT-2; NAAPv.2

My Dead. "Rachel." FIT, tr. by Robert Friend

My dead Love came to me, and said. Apparition, The. Stephen Phillips. OBEV

My dead piled up, thick, fragrant, on the fire escape. Marilyn Chin. See Dead piled up, thick, fragrant, on the fire escape, The.

My dead self in. Year I Found, The. Dieter Weslowski. IJHIL

My Dear and Only Love. James Graham, Marquess of Montrose. OxBEV

My dear and only Love, I pray. My Dear and Only Love. James Graham, Marquess of Montrose. OxBEV

My dear Brother, with courage bear the crosse. Sonnet sent to Blackness to Mr. John Welsch, by the Lady Culross, A. Elizabeth Melville, Lady Culross. EMWP

My dear child, my darling daughter. Dear Child, My Darling Daughter. Hungarian Oral Tradition. IQMS, tr. by Anthony Edkins

My dear children, do you remember the morning. Driving West in 1970. Robert Bly. PoA 2002

My Dear Editor Manchette. Quote Me Wrong Again and I'll Slit the Throat of Your Pet Iguana. David St. John. RACG

My dear, I wonder if before the end. To D———, Dead by Her Own Hand. Howard Nemerov. PoA 2002

My Dear Little Fellow. László Mécs. IQMS, tr. by Watson Kirkconnell

My dear Maria, my long absent friend. Epistle, An. Elizabeth Hands. PoBW

My dear Odysseus. Letter to an Exile. Claribel Alegría. TANSG, tr. by Louise B. Popkin

My dear old village. Issa. SoOfWa, tr. by Sam Hamill

My Dear One is mine as mirrors are lonely. W. H. Auden. NoAM; NPeEn Fr. Sea and the Mirror, The.

My dear son I am well thanks be to God. Home News. Ahmed Tidjani-Cissé. NAfrP; PML, tr. by Gerald Moore

My dear Telemachus, / The Trojan War. Odysseus to Telemachus. Joseph Brodsky. BLT, tr. by George L. Kline

My dear, / Today a letter from Berlin. Letter from Berlin, A. Jon Stallworthy. OBWP

My dear, you would not believe the weather here. Belvedere Marittimo. Greg Williamson. AmPoNex; NeAmPo

My dearly loved friend how oft have we. Michael Drayton. PBRV

My dearest consort, my more loved heart. Dying Husband's Farewell, The. Phineas Fletcher. SacPr

My dearest dust, could not thy hasty day. Lady Catherine Dyer. InoFa Fr. Sir William Dyer, Knight.

My Dearest Dust: Epitaph on the Monument of Sir William Dyer at Colmworth, 1641. Lady Catherine Dyer. InoFa Fr. Sir William Dyer, Knight.

My dearest friend is struck, and I must stern beware. He Loves. David Schirmer. GePo, tr. by George C. Schoolfield

My dearest rival, lest our love. Sir John Suckling. CavPo

My dearest, To let you or the world know. Forfeiture, The. Henry King, Bishop of Chichester. NOSC

My dearest, you may pray now it is Lent. To My Daughter Catherine on Ashwednesday 1645, Finding Her Weeping at Prayers, Because I Would Not Consent to Her Fasting. Katherine Thimelby Aston. EMWP

My death grazes just out of sight. Sister Death. Penny Harter. TWW

My death was arranged by special plans in Heaven. New England Bachelor, A. Richard Eberhart. MoAmPo; NoAM

My debt to you, Belovèd. Debts. Jessie Belle Rittenhouse. TCAPo

My deere doghter Venus, quod Saturne. Geoffrey Chaucer. NPeEn Fr. Canterbury Tales, The.

My Delight and Thy Delight. Robert Bridges. OBEV

My departure made the leaves gather more quickly. Not a Balancing Act. Claire Needell. OnScMo

My desire is. Clarity. 'Enayat Jaber. PoArWo, tr. by Wen Chin Ouyang

My Destiny. Mirza Asadullah Khan Ghalib. WED, tr. by Robert Bly and Sunil Dutta

My destiny did not include reunion with my Friend. My Destiny. Mirza Asadullah Khan Ghalib. WED, tr. by Robert Bly and Sunil Dutta

My disaffected gaze falls on the city. Côte de Liesse. Daryl Hine. NoP-4

My disordered perfumed clouds are still damp. Cloud Hairdress. Chao Luanluan. CCL1, tr. by Chung Ling and Kenneth Rexroth

My doctor's given me a massive can. Tamoxifen. Alison Mosquera. PoCu

My Dog. John Kendrick Bangs. ITBLP

My Dog. Marchette Chute. WHSW

My dog came through the pinewoods dragging a dead fox. Wings. Mary Oliver. PoCoUp

My dog lay dead five days without a grave. Pardon, The. Richard Wilbur. BrAP; InoFa; NIL-7; NoAM

My dog (the trustiest of his kind). John Gay. DiBP *Fr.* Fables: First Series.

My dog's assumed my alter ego. Strange Case, The. Michael Ondaatje. EmeKit; StAl

My Dolphin, you only guide me by surprise. Dolphin. Robert Lowell. NAMCP V.2; NoAM; OxBoAm; VCAP; WaAnP

My dove, my beautiful one. James Joyce. ChIV-1

My Dream. Christina Georgina Rossetti. ViWPN; VWP

My dream a drink with Lonnie Johnson we discuss the code. Ted Berrigan. NoAM *Fr.* Sonnets, The.

My Dream About the Cows. Lucille Clifton. TRP

My Dream About the Poet. Lucille Clifton. TRP

My dream confirms it. After the Funeral. Paulette Roeske. Vesp

My dream is the dream of a pond. Gifts. "Shu Ting." VCWP

My dream mentor sits in his room overlooking the city. My Dream Mentor. Leontia Flynn. NIrP

My dream of America. Chinese Hot Pot. Wing Tek Lum. UnSA

My dream won't last long. Words. Gu Cheng. WoBe, *tr. by* Joseph R. Allen

My Dreams. Charlotte Brontë. *See* Again I find myself alone.

My dreams, my works must wait till after hell. Gwendolyn Brooks. NoP-4; NoP-5; WaAnP

My Dreams, My Works, Must Wait Till After Hell. Gwendolyn Brooks. IllVoic *Fr.* Gay Chaps at the Bar.

My dreams of scaling. Artifice of War, The. Brandon D. Johnson. BtF

My dress is silent when I tread the ground. *Unknown.* NoP-4

My driver's license is lapsing and so I appear. Vision Test, The. Mona Van Duyn. FFC

My dugout flibbles. *Unknown.* SonAtl, *tr. by* Mrs. G. Ben, Daniel A. Reboussin and M. Sello

My Dusty Kinsfolk. John Ormond. TCAWP

My dusty kinsfolk in the hill. My Dusty Kinsfolk. John Ormond. TCAWP

My duties took me to a spot by the sea. Bald Mountain. Wang An-shih. ColAnChi, *tr. by* Victor H. Mair

My eager waiting heart can bear no more. He Comes Not To-night. Josephine D. Henderson Heard. CBWP-4

My ear perceives no paltry difference. Blood and Gold. Endre Ady. IQMS, *tr. by* Watson Kirkconnell

My earlobe in your mouth, my lips and tongue on your breasts, my palms pressed. Helas! Hung Hung. PML, *tr. by* Steve Bradbury

My early Mistress, now my ancient Muse. Preface to *The Progress of Learning.* Sir John Denham. NOSC

My ears (shaped just like his). World, The. Alice Jones. ASA

My Easter Dove. Henrietta Cordelia Ray. CBWP-3

My Een are Nae on Calvary. Sorley MacLean. EdScPo, *tr. by* Douglas Young

My eggs will never be dry. Diner. RoByn Baron. BRtP

My eldest sister arrived home that morning. Cuba. Paul Muldoon. ModIr; PNI; StAl

My emblem is an arrow. John Fairfax. NewEx

My empire of flamboyans. Areyto. Víctor Hernández Cruz. PmAP

My empty face. Issa. IllVoic *Fr.* Issa: A Suite of Haiku.

My Enemies. Sophie Hannah. HarvBoo

My enemies, polished inside their caskets. My Enemies. Sophie Hannah. HarvBoo

My enemy came nigh. Hate. James Stephens. MoBrPo

My English Teacher. Chava Pinchas-Cohen. DTA, *tr. by* Miriyam Glazer

My English teacher is a journalist. My English Teacher. Chava Pinchas-Cohen. DTA, *tr. by* Miriyam Glazer

My entire life / has been spent / in refugee camps. Wired In. Lamont B. Steptoe. UnSA

My epithalamion. Lee Ann Brown. VaPo

My Erotic Double. John Ashbery. EMP; VCAP

My errors my loves my unlucky star. Sonnet: My Errors My Loves My Unlucky Star. Luis de Camões [*or* Camãoes *or* Camoëns]. WoPoe, *tr. by* David Wevill

My Estate. John Norris. NOSC

My Exorcist Mother. Patricia Adelman. Prnts

My eye descending from the Hill, surveys. Sir John Denham. OxAEP-1; OxBEV *Fr.* Cooper's Hill.

My eye is not on Calvary. Calvary. Sorley MacLean. EdScPo; NePenScot

My eyes already touch the sunny hill. Walk, A. Rainer Maria Rilke. RaBo; WED, *tr. by* Robert Bly

My Eyes are. Courage! John G. de la Parra, Jr. BeDoSh

My eyes are. Dina Gatina. CRWP, *tr. by* Chris Jones

My eyes are full of rivers and trees tonight. After a Train Journey. May Sarton. GM

My eyes are the enemy's eyes. Enemy's Eyes, The. Emma Lee Warrior. HATNAP

My eyes can be closed by the last shadow. Love Beyond Death. Francisco de Quevedo y Villegas. BLPSL, *tr. by* Rene de Costa, Rigas Kappatos and Eleni Paidoussi

My eyes eavesdrop on their lashes! Eichu. ZenPo, *tr. by* Takashi Ikemoto and Lucien Stryk

My eyes fixed on the mountains and my ears on the zither. At My Study. Yun Sŏndo. CATKP, *tr. by* Chi-gyu Kim [*or* Kim Chonggil]

My Eyes Have Seen and Chosen. Meinloh von Sevelingen. GePo, *tr. by* J. W. Thomas

My eyes have seen and chosen for me a handsome youth. My Eyes Have Seen and Chosen. Meinloh von Sevelingen. GePo, *tr. by* J. W. Thomas

My eyes have seen what my hand did. (LL) Dolphin. Robert Lowell. NAMCP V.2; NoAM; OxBoAm; VCAP; WaAnP

My eyes, peasant woman milking the light. True Man, A. Attila József. IQMS, *tr. by* Edwin Morgan

My eyes transfixed on the road, I strained in their light to see. Tryst. Yahya Kemal [Beyatlı]. NaPG, *tr. by* Talat Sait Halman

My eyes wax and wane. 13 June 1994. Virginia Cerenio. ReBoTo

My face is grass. Legacy. Maurice Kenny. HATNAP

My face. Whenever I take a breath I hear cracking. (LL) Mark Strand. CAP-8; NAMCP V.2 *Fr.* Dark Harbor.

My faint spirit was sitting in the light. From the Arabic: An Imitation. Percy Bysshe Shelley. OBEV

My faith / is a great weight. Small Wire. Anne Sexton. InvLi

My Faith Looks Up to Thee. Ray Palmer. SacPr

My Faithful Mother Tongue. Czeslaw Milosz. VCWP, *tr. by* the author, Robert Hass and Robert Pinsky

My Family. Nyere-Gibran Miller. BtF

My family expected I would be born on Armistice Day. Four November 9ths. Anne-Marie Levine. PA9/11

My family married me off. Lament. Liu Chi-hsün. WoPoe, *tr. by* Tony Barnstone and Chou Ping

My family married me to a lost horizon. Lost Horizon. Hsi-chün. ColAnChi, *tr. by* Anne Birrell

My family tree is mist and darkness. Family History. Irving Feldman. VCAP

My family's all so squalid. Dressing Up. Jackie Kay. MoWP

My fan is preaching abstinence but I want a miracle. Lullaby. Debra Gregerman. AmPoNex

My fantasies were always. Dried Flowers. Carmen Celia Beltrán. NAAPv.2

My Fate. Anne Wharton. EMWP

My fater / was a graduate. Texas Boomer. John Collin Murphey. TiP2

My Father. Yehuda Amichai. BeAl; PtR, *tr. by* Azila Talit Reisenberger

My Father. Manuela Fingueret. MirDau, *tr. by* Roberta Gordenstein

My father. Two Poems for the Good Given. Robert Sund. WhBo

My father always wanted me to draw roses. Bo Tree. Patricia Pogson. Prnts

My father and I have no place to go. Thoreau. Timothy Liu. AmPoNex; GifTon; OPRER

My father and I play checkers. Photograph, 1958. Patricia Young. BrAP

My Father and Me Making Dresses: Together. D. A. Powell. WiU

My father and me making dresses: together. My Father and Me Making Dresses: Together. D. A. Powell. WiU

My father and mother, my brother and sister. Sightseers, The. Paul Muldoon. StAl

My father and mother, two tiny figures. Clouds above the Sea. Philip Levine. PML

My father and my mother never quarrelled. Because. James Philip McAuley. BMAP; NOBAu; StAl

My Father and the Fig Tree. Naomi Shihab Nye. IPoFL

(My Father and the Figtree.) UnSA

My father arranges the window like a stage. Diane Arbus, New York. Nicole Cooley. AmPoNex

My Father at 85. Robert Bly. OxBoAm

My father at the dictionary-stand. Supernatural Love. Gjertrud Schnackenberg. MakPoe; NoAM; NoP-4; NoP-5; StAl; VCAP

My father at the front window. Upturn. Anne-Marie Fyfe. Prnts

My Father at the North Street Boarding House. James Kimbrell. AmPoNex

My father bequeathed me no wide estates. Heirloom. Abraham Moses Klein. NIL-7

My Father Breaks the Neighbor's Nose. Hayan Charara. AmPoNex

My father burned us all. ash. Cigarettes. Lucille Clifton. PoChi

My father buying me the bicycle that time. New Cycle, A. Edward Field. ArBi

My father calls me up. Public Garden with a Weeping Tree. Mary Ruefle. AmAlph

My father came home with a new glove. Catch. George Bilgere. RaF

My father came today: an awaited visit. Ithaca-Liverpool. Gladys Mary Coles. Prnts

My father carries me across a field. George Szirtes. BeAl

My father casts brass. My Father the Foundryman. Alexander Pomerantz. Prolet, *tr. by* Amelia Glaser

My father cinched the rope. In the Well. Andrew Hudgins. P180

My father could not say the words. My Father's Tongue. Juanita Brunk. ACAMVP

My Father, Counting Sheep. Kate Foley. Prnts

My father detested the drivers who slowed down. Slowing Down for Death. Hal Sirowitz. PA9/11

My father died at the age of eighty. Honey. James Wright. MotU

My father died Christmas Eve in. Death of My Father, The. Robert J. Gibbs. Coast

My father died near evening, having spent. Truth, The. Frankie Paino. AmPoNex; FaoP

My father died of a heart attack / during an afternoon nap. Upkeep. Miriam Goodman. UnSA

My father dies and is buried in his Brooks Brothers suit. Halfway Through the Book I'm Writing. Lynn Emanuel. ExTi

My father fought their war four years or so. Yehuda Amichai. FIT, *tr. by* Robert Friend

My father got on his horse and went to the field. Infancy. Carlos Drummond de Andrade. BeAl; TCLAP, *tr. by* Elizabeth Bishop

My father had a lot of friendly enemies. Father-Sequence. Luigi Fontanella. NeIt, *tr. by* Michael Palma

My father hated moonlight. Moonlight. Berta Hart Nance. TiP2

My father, he was a mountaineer. Ballad of William Sycamore, The. Stephen Vincent Benét. MoAmPo

My Father, his mouth full of nails. Nails. Gary Gildner. PBCAP

My Father, How Long! *Unknown.* SSUS

My father, in a 1956 gray suit. Dance of the Letters. Vince Gotera. FTtHH; OpBo

My Father in New Zealand. George Bowering. BrAP

My Father in the Night Commanding No. Louis Simpson. HeIP-4; NAMCP V.2; NoAM; OxBoAm

My father in the snowy window, face incandescent. Riding the Empire Builder, 1948. David Wojahn. GM

My father is a hand-. William J. Harris. ISC; UnSA

My father is breathing through. During the Eclipse. Pascale Petit. PoCu

My father is deceas'd. Come, Gaveston. Christopher Marlowe. CAGL *Fr.* Edward the Second.

My father is looking at the end of his life. Journey. Cathy Song. ExTi

My Father Is Shrinking. Susan Wicks. BeAl

My father is sleeping. His noble face. Distant Footsteps, The. César Vallejo. RaBo, *tr. by* James Wright and John Knoepfle

My father is standing on a railroad platform. Departure. Louise Glück. GM

My father is telling me the story of Samuel. Calling, A. W. S. Merwin. BodElec

My Father, it is surely a blue place. Gwendolyn Brooks. ChAP *Fr.* Street in Bronzeville, A.

My father just passed me. Almost Communication. Rita Ann Higgins. ArBi

My father kept a stove. Smoke. Jacob Polley. BeAl

My father knew the weight of words. In Season. Lisa Suhair Majaj. PoArWo

My father laughing over the morning paper. Reading Before We Read, Horoscope and Weather. Wyatt Prunty. RA

My father, let no similes eclipse. In Memoriam. Michael Longley. ModIr; PNI

My father lifts the crippled airman's body. Colonel. Andrew Hudgins. UpMys

My father limps on the leg that healed short. Hook. Floyd Skloot. MoASP

My father, listening. Exiles. Diana Der Hovanessian. OPRER

My father, looking for trouble, would find it. Man of the House, The. David Wagoner. NAMCP V.2; NoAM

My father loved more than anything to. Working in the Rain. Robert Morgan. GoPo

My father loves with the knuckles. Aphelion. Joseph Sherman. Coast

My Father Makes a Lightbox for Vivienne Westwood. Nicolette Golding. Prnts

My father moved through dooms of love. E. E. Cummings. ColAP; NAAL-5; NAMCP V.1; NoAM; NoP-4; OxBoAm; WaAnP; WoPoe

My father never sweat. Tendered. Sandy Feinstein. IaFF

My father once broke a man's hand. Winter Stars. Larry Levis. GeoHom

My father once told me that as a boy. Site of My Grandfather's House, The. Dominador I. Ilio. ReBoTo

My father paces the upstairs hall. Spree. Maxine W. Kumin. NoAM

My father passed with his penny letters. Hamnavoe. George Mackay Brown. EdScPo

My Father Plaits His Granddaughter's Hair. Joseph Sherman. Coast

My father read the World Telegram & Sun. War Stories. Harvey Shapiro. PWW2

My father recommended safety. Belonging to a New Family. Mohammad Bennis. NAfrP, *tr. by* Charles Doria and Sharif Elmusa

My Father Recounts a Story from His Youth. Kevin Prufer. AmPoNex

My father rode a horse. I Remember. Fay M. Yauger. TiP2

My father said I could not do it. Leaving, The. Brigit Pegeen Kelly. IllVoic; YaYoPo

My father sang for himself. His Father, Singing. Leslie Norris. TCAWP

My father sat in his chair recovering. Out. Ted Hughes. FaBoWar; NAMCP V.2

My father saw it back in 1910. Halley's Comet. Norman Nicholson. NoP-4; NoP-5

My father says, 'They've found water'. Water on the Moon. Stephanie Norgate. PoCu

My father sits at the kitchen table. Snow. Regina DeCormier-Shekejian. TWW

My father sits in his chair and snores. Sleeping Father. David Chin. InvLad

My father sits quietly in his brown Naugahyde chair watching / TV with the remote control. Portrait of Assimilation. Chrystos. UnSA

My father speaks in riddles. Song for My Father, A. Dimitris Tsaloumas. PML

My Father Speaks to Me from the Dead. Sharon Olds. NAMCP V.2

My father stands in the warm evening. Starlight. Philip Levine. BeAl

My father stands next to my mother. Cuban-American Gothic. Virgil Suárez. AmPoNex

My Father: "Staunin noo aside his braw bress-haunled coffin." Duncan Glen. EdScPo

My father taught me to measure. Numbers. Allison Joseph. NeAmPo

My father tells me of the time. Echo of the Ax, The. Al Pittman. PML

My Father the Foundryman. Alexander Pomerantz. Prolet, *tr. by* Amelia Glaser

My father the hawk. Latvian Songs. Johannes Bobrowski. AF

My father, the juggler at the circus. Balls and Hoops. Martin Sorescu. PML, *tr. by* Adam J. Sorkin and Lidia Vianu

My father, the least happy. John Montague. PNI *Fr.* Rough Field, The.

My Father Travels. Dilip Chitre. WoPoe

My father travels on the late evening train. My Father Travels. Dilip Chitre. WoPoe

My father used to say. Silence. Marianne Moore. APT-1; HarvBoo; NAAPv.2; NALW; OxBoAm; PtR; TRP; WoPoe

My father was a city schoolmaster. John Hewitt. *Fr.* Freehold.

My father was a Cornish customs officer. Naturalised. Cyril Hodges. AngWePo

My father was a dictator. Revolution. Brian G. Gilmore. SpirFl

My father was a servant-boy. Mixed Marriage, The. Paul Muldoon. PNI

My father was a Toltec. Toltec, The. Ana Castillo. IllVoic

My father was an enormous man. Sticks. Thomas Sayers Ellis. LegDan; NAPBL

My father was on the tractor up ahead. First Time I Heard Elvis, The. Steven Huff. NevBe

My father was six-fingered. Across the canvas, stretched tight, Bruni taught him to guide the soft brush. Dactyls. Vladislav Felitsianovich Khodasevich. TCRusP, *tr. by* Mary Jane White

My Father Went to Funerals. Howard Nelson. RaBo

My father wept aloud in the night. My Mother. Every Man His Own Cross. Dick Barnes. CalPo

My father! when I saw thee last. To Father. Mary E. Tucker. CBWP-1

My father, who works with stone. Story of How a Wall Stands, A. Simon J. Ortiz. HATNAP

My Father with Cigarette Twelve Years Before the Nazis Could Break His Heart. Philip Levine. TaR

My father with great sadness used to say. Plowman of Rákos Under the Turks. Károly Kisfaludy. IQMS, *tr. by* Watson Kirkconnell

My father worked with a horse-plough. Follower. Seamus Heaney. CABP; IPoFL; PNI; PtR

My father would have cherished an heir. Inheritance. Michael Donaghy. PML

My father would not show us. Ingrid de Kok. TSAP

My father yelled, "Turn that damn thing down!" Jungle Music. Warren Woessner. MiVo; SwNoth

My father, you say. Reply. Reiner Kunze. PoSu, *tr. by* Ewald Osers

My Fatherland is dead. Motherland. Rose Ausländer. PoCho, *tr. by* Eavan Boland

My Father's Angels. Ger Killeen. AmPoNex

My father's angels. My Father's Angels. Ger Killeen. AmPoNex

My Father's Back. Edward Hirsch. VCAP

My father's back. Secret Love. Milton Kessler. UnSA

My father's body is the narrow grave. Host. Bruce Bond. Vesp

My father's body was a globe of fear. Letters & Other Worlds. Michael Ondaatje. BrAP; NAMCP V.2; NoAM; NoP-4; NoP-5

My Father's Caul. Susan Wicks. MoWP

My Father's Clothes. Pascale Petit. Prnts

My Father's Country. Joyce Lee. NOBAu

My Father's Death. Constance Urdang. PBCAP

My Father's Dreams. Cynthia Fuller. Prnts

My father's eyes were blue. To Human Skin. Cheryl Savageau. TWW

My father's face. My father would not show us. Ingrid de Kok. TSAP

My father's father came. Legend. Louise Glück. TaR

My Father's Fights. Stuart Dybek. TaR

My Father's First Baseball Game. Afaa Michael Weaver. PBCAP

My Father's First Fight. Deborah DeNicola. NevBe

My Father's Funeral. Karl Shapiro. TaR

My Father's Garden. David Wagoner. NIL-7; NIP-4

My Father's Geography. Afaa Michael Weaver. GT; OxAAAP; PBCAP

My Father's Girlfriend. E. Ethelbert Miller. SpirFl

My Father's Hats. Mark Irwin. P180

My father's head has become a mystery to him. Sudden Movements. Bob Hicok. AmAlph

My father's heart is on television. Medical Science. Robin Becker. PBCAP

My Father's Heroes ("He gloried in the feats.") Allison Joseph. SeSe

My Father's Heroes ("Not JFK, not MLK.") Allison Joseph. NeAmPo

My father's hobby was collecting sneezes. No stamps or coins for him. "The stuff of life," he said, "of life." My Father's Hobby. Morton Marcus. PoDa

My father's Holsteins. Those Mornings. Robert Kinsley. IPoFL

My Father's House. Sam Cornish. AllShUp

My Father's House. Calvin Forbes. ESEAA

My Father's House. Narlan Matos-Teixera. PML, tr. by the author and Al Zolynas

My Father's Hurricane. Fred Chappell. InGu

My father's in my fingers, but my mother's in my palms. Genetics. Sinéad Morrissey. BeAl; MoWP; NIrP

My Father's Irish Setters. James Merrill. StAl

My Father's Love Letters [or Loveletters]. Yusef Komunyakaa. InGu; NAMCP V.2; OxAAAP

(My Father's Loveletters.) ISC; PoPoPo

My Father's Memorial Day. Yehuda Amichai. PoCho, tr. by the author and Ted Hughes

My father's, mother's, brother's deaths I pardon. John Dryden. STuOW Fr. Don Sebastian.

My Father's Neck. Robert Bly. BodElec

My father's parents sold fish. Erdywurble. Carole Satyamurti. Prnts

My Father's Pornography. David Wojahn. ReTh

My Father's Retirement. A. Van Jordan. SpirFl

My Father's Shadow. Dorothy Nimmo. Prnts

My Father's Singing. Marc J. Sheehan. MiVo

My Father's Song. Simon J. Ortiz. HATNAP; NIL-7

My Father's Story. Priscilla Jane Thompson. CBWP-2

My Father's Tongue. Juanita Brunk. ACAMVP

My Father's Trapdoors. Peter Redgrove. PML

My Father's Wedding. Robert Bly. NAMCP V.2; NoAM; RaBo

My Father's Whistle. Len Roberts. MiVo

My father's white uncle became. Todd. Stewart Conn. EdScPo; NePenScot

My father's womb. Wardrobes. Nicolette Golding. Prnts

My Father's Words. Lucy Hamilton. Prnts

My Father's Workshop. Anna Swirszczynska [or Swir]. GifTon, tr. by Czeslaw Milosz and Leonard Nathan

My father—that kind smiling hero—went. After the Battle. Victor Hugo. SxFrPo, tr. by A. M. and E. H. Blackmore

My Favorite Monk Is. Connie Deanovich. AmPoNex

My Favorite Things. Oscar Hammerstein, II. ReLy

My favourite phlebotomist speaks with. Celia de Fréine. NIrP Fr. Price on My Head, A.

My favourite view of people. Fish Shop Windows. Geoffrey Dutton. NOBAu

My fear is a filly. Neighing of the Fingers. Aziz Samawi. IrPoTo, tr. by Alex Bellem

My feet are elms, roots in the earth. They Tell Me I Am Lost. Maurice Kenny. HATNAP

My feet mark the passage of time. Waiting. Donald Woods. CAGL

My feet shall tread no more thy mossy side. To the Wissahiccon. Frances Anne Kemble. APN-1

My Feet, So Deep in the Earth. Juan Ramón Jiménez. RaW, tr. by Ralph Nelson and Rita García Nelson

My feet they are sore, and my limbs they are weary. Orphan Child, The. Charlotte Brontë. VWP

My feet were nourished on her breasts all night. (LL) George Meredith. NAEL-6v2; WaAnP Fr. Modern Love.

My fever's over 98 point 6, and still. Belated Lament. Attila József. IQMS, tr. by John P. Sadler

My Field Guide. Erin Belieu. NAPBL

My fifteen year old. Some Tentative Definitions 7. Kwame Dawes. WaCA

My fiftieth year had come and gone. William Butler Yeats. RaBo Fr. Vacillation.

My Fifty-Plus Years Celebrate Spring. Luis Omar Salinas. GeoHom

My Final Agonies. Benjamin Péret. PFTM-1

My fine web sparkles. Christmas Spider, The. Michael Richards. Spl

My fingers. Message in the Bottle,The. Frigyes Karinthy. IQMS, tr. by Paul Tabori

My first and last two corpses felt perhaps the mildest pain in passing. My Corpses. Benjamin Paloff. NevBe

My first, as thy name is Joseph, labour so in knowledge to increase. Sarah Goodhue. EMWP

My first big love was cosmically correct. My Chakabuku Mama: A Comic Tale. Jewelle Gomez. BAP-01

My first bridge was a log—a slippery one across a muddy creek. Bridges. Carlos Reyes. NevBe

My first is in life (not contained within heart). Riddle-Me-Ree. Liz Lochhead. OPOU

My First Marriage. Kabir. WED, tr. by Robert Bly

My First Name, Wystan. W. H. Auden. AmWit Fr. Academic Graffiti.

My First Riot: Bronx, NYC. Safiya Henderson-Holmes. UnSA

My first sense of politics—of something waiting for me, outside—came from falling bombs in wartime newsreels. Man with His Kids on a Table, The. Larry Kearney. Eno

My first thought was, he lied in every word. Childe Roland to the Dark Tower Came. Robert Browning. NAEL-6v2; NAEL-7v2; NAWM-7v2; NoP-4; NoP-5; OBNV; PoPoPo; WaAnP

My first vivid memory of you / mamacita. Alma Villanueva. UnSA

My first week in Cambridge a car full of white boys. Boston Year. Elizabeth Alexander. GT; OPRER

My First Weeks. Sharon Olds. BeAl

My fishing boat sails the river. I love spring in the mountains. Song of Peach Tree Spring. Wang Wei. WoPoe, tr. by Tony Barnstone, Willis Barnstone and Xu Haixin

My flag is blue and sprouts a fish rampant, locked in and let loose by two bracelets. Flag, The. Pablo Neruda. PoetW, tr. by Nathaniel Tarn

My Flesh in its Sweat. Giancarlo Majorino. ItPo, tr. by Gayle Ridinger

My flesh is at a distance from me. Virgin, The. Laura Riding Jackson. ChIL-2

My flesh is consumed with love. (LL) Kenneth Rexroth. APSN; NAAPv.2 Fr. Love Poems of Marichiko, The.

My Flower at Paoa-ka-lani. Queen Lili'u-o-ka-lani. See Ku'u Pua I Paoakalani.

My flowery and green age was passing away. Petrarch. OBMV; OxBEV; WoPoe Fr. Sonnets to Laura.

My Flu. Michael Donaghy. StAl

My Fly. C. K. Williams. AmFaPo

My foe outstretched [or outstretch'd] beneath the tree. (LL) William Blake. NAEL-6v2; NAEL-7v2; NoP-4; NoP-5; NPBRoP; NPeEn; OxAEP-2; OxBEV; SoSe-8; TFi; WaAnP; WeW-3 Fr. Songs of Experience.

My folder of poems. Weather. Hettie Jones. PrTe

My Folk, What Have I Done Thee? William Herebert. SacPr

My Folly of Being. Gherasim Luca. YaTCFP, tr. by Michael Tweed

My food was pallid till I heard it ring. King Midas. Howard Moss. OxBoAm

My fool asks: Do the years spell a path to later. Little Round. Li-Young Lee. Vesp

My Foolish Heart. Ned Washington. ReLy

My footsteps in this street. Here. Octavio Paz. STV, tr. by John Frederick Nims

My foundling, my fondling, my frolic first-footer. Blason, A. Alec Derwent Hope. NOBAu

My four foot-eleven mother was world wise yet unburdened. Sharing is Hereditary. Kalamu ya Salaam. FuFl

My fourthe housbonde was a revelour. Geoffrey Chaucer. NPeEn Fr. Canterbury Tales, The.

My frame hath often trembled with delight. William Wordsworth. CenSon Fr. River Duddon [A Series of Sonnets], The.

My Friend. Christina Georgina Rossetti. InoFa

My Friend. David St. John. BodElec

My friend, a man I love as wholly. My Friend. David St. John. BodElec

My friend Bill Hupp leaves this week. Hungry Ghost Surrenders His Tackle Box, A. Maj Ragain. AmZen

My friend conceived the soul hereafter dwells. Aspiration. Edward William Thomson. SacPr

My friend Deane took me into the Yuba Goldfields. No Shadow. Gary Snyder. WANABP

My friend from Asia has powers and magic, he plucks a blue leaf from the young blue-gum. Credo. Robinson Jeffers. MoAmPo; OxBoAm

My friend go gently, for Time is as you know it to be, since there is no avoiding an easy life in spite of the present trace of hardship. King of Granada Yūsuf III. HiArP, tr. by James T. Monroe

My friend, he looked, and our eyes met; an arrow came in. Faithfulness. Mirabai. WED, tr. by Robert Bly

My friend Henry signs his note by accident. Poems of Delight. Liz Rosenberg. IJHIL

My friend, hold back your heart from enemies. Khwaja Shams-ad-din Muhammad Hafiz. WoPoe Fr. Three Poems on Friendship.

My friend, I went to the market and bought the Dark One. It's True I Went to the Market. Mirabai. WED; WPoS, tr. by Robert Bly

My friend: / In what language shall we begin our conversation? Brief Letter to Donald Walsh (in memoriam). Angel Cuadra. AF, tr. by Katherine Rodriguez Nieto

My friend is dwelling in the eastern mountain. To Tan Ch'iu. Li Po. TAL

My Friend Is Making Himself. Philip Schultz. MAAN

My friend, judge not me. Epitaph. Unknown. NOSC

My friend, limb-loosening. Archilochus. SaLy, tr. by Diane Rayor

My friend Priapus with myself shall rise? (LL) Quaerè. George Farewell. NPeEn; OBCoV

My friend said, Let's go down to the river. Bright Light of Responsibility, The. Jennifer L. Knox. BAP-97

My friend says I was not a good son. Yesterday. W. S. Merwin. GoPo; OxBoAm; PML; PoChi; RaBo

My friend the blue paisley shirt is always assured. Blue Paisley Shirt, The. Thomas William Shapcott. BMAP

My Friend the Cuckold. Morris Gilbert Bishop. OBCoV

My friend, the football coach in San Antonio. Mocking-bird, A. Boyce House. TiP2

My friend, the stain of the Great Dancer has penetrated my body. Music, The. Mirabai. WED, tr. by Robert Bly

My Friend, the Things That Do Attain. Martial. See Happy Life, The.

My friend / they don't care. There It Is. Jayne Cortez. BRtP

My friend, thou sorrowest for thy golden prime. Return of Youth, The. William Cullen Bryant. TreFP

My friend tree. Lorine Niedecker. APT-2; NAAPv.2

My friend wakes up into the. My Friend Is Making Himself. Philip Schultz. MAAN

My friend wears boots to sleep. Following Her to Sleep. Jeffrey McDaniel. NeAmPo

My Friendly People. Frank Mkalawile Chipasula. HBAPE

My Friends. Boris Abramovich Slutsky. TCRusP, tr. by Daniel Weissbort

My friends appreciate my way of life. Two Poems Written While Drunk. T'ao Ch'ien. CCL1, tr. by Gladys Yang and Yang Xianyi

My friends are borne to one another. Martin Buber in the Pub. Max Harris. NOBAu

My friends are real, though very few.. (LL) Money. W. H. Davies. OBEV; OBMV

My Friend's Dog. Meret Oppenheim. SurPaPo, tr. by Catherine Schelbert

My friends hunted in packs, had themselves photographed. Ancient Evenings. Michael Hofmann. EmeKit; NeBrP

My friends, I love your fame; I joy to raise. Joel Barlow. See Too much of Europe, here transplanted o'er.

My friends in tanks were burnt. My Friends. Boris Abramovich Slutsky. TCRusP, tr. by Daniel Weissbort

My friend's sweet love came into town. Song to Hymen: 1942. Anthony Richardson. PoWW

My friends, which of these two to choose? Unknown. SLW, tr. by Marjolijn De Jager, Sayd Bahodin Majrouh and André Velter

My friends who knew me. Wait Till You See Her. Lorenz Hart. ReLy

My frowning students carve. E. S. L. Charles Martin. RA

My Funny Valentine. Chris Greenhalgh. NeBl

My Funny Valentine. Lorenz Hart. ReLy

My Future Just Passed. George Marion, Jr. ReLy

My Galley. Petrarch. See Galley, The.

My galley charged with forgetfulness. Sonnet: "My Galley Charged." Sir Thomas Wyatt. AEP; GSo

My Galley [Charged with Forgetfulness]. Sir Thomas Wyatt. See also Sonnet: "My Galley Charged."

My galley [or galy] charged with forgetfulness. Petrarch. OBVE; OxBEV; WeW-3 Fr. Sonnets to Laura.

My Garden. Thomas Edward Brown. OBEV; OBGa; UV

My Garden. P. R. Hines. UV

My Garden, My Daylight. Jorie Graham. AFaM

My garment may no man put by. (LL) Swan, The. Jay Macpherson. NoP-4; NoP-5; WaAnP

My Gauri / You've come home! Kamalākānta Bhattācārya. SinGod, tr. by Rachel Fell McDermott

My Generation. Kabura Zakama. NeNiPo

My generation is dying, after long lives. Judith Wright. HarvBoo Fr. Shadow of Fire: Ghazals, The.

My generous muse, assistance lend. Favourite Swain, The. Elizabeth Hands. WoRP

My gentle friend! I hold no creed so false. Retirement. Henry Timrod. APN-2

My gentle son is performing tricks for me on his bicycle. Visitation Rites. Jack Myers. ArBi

My Ghost may feel that thine is near. (LL) Alfred Tennyson. NAEL-6v2; NAEL-7v2 Fr. In Memoriam A. H. H.

My girl says she'll take no one else as a lover. Catullus. STV

My girl, thou gazest much. Lover to His Lady, The. Plato. NoSic, tr. by George Turberville

My Girlfriends. Erich Fried. AF, tr. by Georg Rapp

My girlfriend's eyes are nothing like the Sun. I Never Saw a Goddess Go. Austin Hummell. AmPoNex

My glad feet shod with the glittering steel. Skater, The. Sir Charles G. D. Roberts. BrAP; IFF

My glittering sky, high, clear, profound. Lovers, The. Marya Alexandrovna Zaturenska. MoAmPo

My Gloriana. Bessie. Alvin Aubert. SeSe

My God, a verse is not a crown. Quidditie [or Quiddity], The. George Herbert. NOSC

My God and King! to thee. Anguish. Henry Vaughan. OxAEP-1

My God, how wonderful Thou art. Frederick William Faber. SacPr

My God, I heard this day. Man. George Herbert. BASC; FSCP; NAEL-6v1; NAEL-7v1; NoP-4; NoP-5

My God! I know, I feel thee mine. Charles Wesley. NoP-5 Fr. Hymns.

My God, I thank Thee who hast made. Thankfulness. Adelaide Anne Procter. SacPr

My God, I'm wounded by my sin. To God: an Anthem, Sung in the Chapel at White-Hall, Before the King. Robert Herrick. ChIV-1

My God most glad to look, most prone to hear [or heere]. Bible, O.T. OBVE

My God, my God, what queer corner am I in? In the Deep Museum. Anne Sexton. BrAP; MoAmPo; WaAnP

My God, sometimes I cannot pray. Unuttered Prayer. Josephine D. Henderson Heard. CBWP-4

My God, than they? (LL) Ice Storm. Robert Earl Hayden. APT-2; ESEAA

My God, the poore expressions of my Love. George Herbert. PBRV

My God! till I receiv'd thy stroke. William Cowper. ChIV-1 Fr. Olney Hymns.

My God to thee I dedicate. Short Oblation of This Smal Work by the Writer Gatherer Thereof to Our Most Sweet and Merciful God, A. Dame Gertrude More. EMWP

My God, what a dream I had. Us Two. Nina Cassian. PoSu, tr. by Nina Cassian

My God, when I walk [or walke] in those groves. Religion. Henry Vaughan. OxAEP-1

My God, where is that ancient heat towards Thee. Sonnet. George Herbert. NOSC

My God, Why Are You Crying? Molly Peacock. PasH

My godmother invited my cousin. My Cousin Agueda [or Agatha]. Ramón López Velarde. OBVE; TCLAP, tr. by Samuel Beckett

My Gospel Is. Chris Forhan. PoDa

My gostly fader, I me confesse. Charles, Duc d' Orléans. OHMEL

My Government. Matthew Rohrer. LegDan

My Grace Is Sufficient. Josephine D. Henderson Heard. CBWP-4

My grampaw was a smooth black, way back then. Little Girl Talk. Delores S. Williams. OxAAAP

My Grandfather Always Promised Us. Liam Rector. UrbNat

My Grandfather and His Apple-Tree. John Ormond. AngWePo; TCAWP

My grandfather, dead long before I was born. Charles Reznikoff. APT-2

My grandfather died one morning in dampness. Him, His Place. Liam Rector. BodElec

My grandfather Ezra painted a gigantic face. Iconoclast. Ann Elizabeth Hostetler. ACAMVP

My grandfather is chugging along the back roads. Chronicle. David Wheatley. NIrP

My grandfather placed wood. Mythology. Earle Thompson. HATNAP

My grandfather said to me. Manners. Elizabeth Bishop. EMP; GoPo; NOxBChV

My Grandfather Walks in the Woods. Marilyn Nelson Waniek. ESEAA

My grandfather wore white. Boiling, The. Kevin Young. OxAAAP

My grandfather's clock was too large for the shelf. Grandfather's Clock. Henry Clay Work. ITBLP

My Grandfather's Hammer. Charles Behlen. TiP2

My Grandfather's Hat. Judith Ortiz Cofer. TouFir

My grandfather's old house. Rooftops. Lyubomir Levchev. CSCBP, tr. by Georgi Belev and Lisa Sapinkopf

My grandfather's painted grandfather. Cracked Portraits. Agha Shahid Ali. OpBo

My Grandfather's Poems. Edward Hirsch. TaR

My grandma on my mother's side had a little clock which never. Tonton Macoutes Steal Dreams. Bobby Medard. OGAHCP, tr. by Boadiba and Jack Hirschman

My Grandmother. Elizabeth Jennings. HarvBoo; NoP-4; NoP-5

My grandmother. This Is the Poem I Never Meant to Write. Colleen J. McElroy. FTtHH

My Grandmother. Karl Shapiro. TaR

My Grandmother Died in the Early Hours of the Morning. T. Harri Jones. AngWePo; TCAWP

My grandmother doesn't hear me call; a white mist licks. Conch. Eva Salzman. MoWP

My grandmother Eliza. Grandmother Eliza. Nora Dauenhauer. FTtHH

My grandmother goes to visit a friend. My Grandmother's Birthday. Susan Thomas. LiTh

My grandmother had a house. My father bought it. Family Tree, The. Catalina Cariaga. ReBoTo

My grandmother had a small shelf of books. Footbinding. Patricia Beer. NoP-4

My grandmother is waiting for me to come home. Gwendolyn Brooks. ESEAA Fr. Children Going Home.

15. My Grandmother Learns to Drive. David McFadden. NLPA

My grandmother Lola, with her beautiful sagging face and her fine. 1930. Aurora Levins Morales. PueRic

My grandmother moves to my mind in context of sorrow. My Grandmother. Karl Shapiro. TaR

My grandmother / rakes up chicken shit / mixed with mud / to feed her roses. Upside Down Basket, The. Alan Chong Lau. UnSA

My grandmother taught me the delicate trick. Blowing Eggs. Anne Caston. NAPBL

My grandmother's. Door. Valerie Worth. CA

My Grandmother's Birthday. Susan Thomas. LiTh

My Grandmother's Burial Ground. Elizabeth Cook-Lynn. HATNAP

My Grandmother's Funeral. Thomas Lux. WeW-3

My Grandmother's Love Letters. Hart Crane. BeAL; GPTC; NAAPv.2; NoAM; NoP-4; NoP-5; OxBoAm; PtR; WaAnP

My grandmothers were strong. Lineage. Margaret Abigail Walker. ItP; ItWoWo; NALW; OxWW

My granny used to say that if a shadow. August the First: The Shadow. Patel Speaks. Marjorie Oludhe Macgoye. HBAPE

My grass hut. Yasui. EMJL Fr. Mad Verse.

My Grave. Ella Wheeler Wilcox. SWaP

My great God, You been a tenderness to me. Black Mother Praying. Owen Dodson. ISC

My great-grandfather fell in top hat and tails. Self-Portrait. Michael Longley. PML

My Greatgreatuncle the Archbishop. Ruth Whitman. TaR

"My green leaves are more beautiful." Leaves. Frank Asch. NTCP

My Greenhouse. Edwin Morgan. OBGa

My grief and my pain! a mortal disease is love. Love Is a Mortal Disease. Unknown. IrV, tr. by Eleanor Hull

My grief, like dense clouds, cannot be dispersed. Unknown. NAAPv.2

My grief, my grief, maid without sin. Body's Speech, The. Unknown. IrLP, tr. by Frank O'Connor

My grief on the men of the stories. Era's End. Mairtin O Direain. ModIr, tr. by Patrick Crotty

My Grief on the Sea. Biddy Cussrooee. IrLP; OBEV, tr. by Douglas Hyde

My grief, quoth I, is called Ignorance. Rachel Speght. NAEL-7v1 Fr. Dream[e], The [or A].

My groom, I fear, has grown. We Are Easily Reduced. HeidiLynn Nilsson. NeAmPo

My Ground. Marie Luise Kaschnitz. PFTM-2, tr. by Lisel Mueller

My Gun Has So Many Places to Hide. David Lazar. LiTh

My gun shines in the misty air. Picket before Bull Run, The. John Day. TreFP

My hair barely covered my forehead. Song of Ch'ang-Kan (Yueh-Fu), The. Li Po. ChinPo, tr. by Ye Weilian [or Yeh Wei-lien or Wai-lim Yip]

My hair coming down in the middle of a conversation. (LL) Slips. Medbh McGuckian. MoWP; NAMCP V.2

My hair is a palm tree. Forbidden. Unoma Nguemo Azuah. NeNiPo

My hair is grey, but not with years. Prisoner of Chillon, The. Lord Byron. BrAP; NPBRoP

My hair is springy like the forest grasses. Black Woman. Naomi Long Madgett. GT; ISC

My hair, scalp. (LL) Her ankles are watches. George Oppen. APT-2; PFTM-1

My hair went on a diet of its own accord. Bald Truth, The. Bob Hicok. MAAN

My hair's tightly plaited. I've Got an Apple Ready. John Walsh. NOxBChV

My half-brother had dark sad eyes, wheaten hair. Green One over There, The. Katia Kapovich. P180

My half-sister comes to me to be painted. Sitting, The. Medbh McGuckian. CABP; ModIr; PNI

My hand. Comparison of Hands One Day Late Summer El Sobrante. Wendy Rose. HATNAP

My Hand is Extended for the Peace of the Galilee. Ramy Ditzanny. NRoS, tr. by Esther Raizen

My Hand is Lady Mori's Hand. Ikkyu Sojun. ErotSp, tr. by Sam Hamill

My hand is Lady Mori's hand. My Hand is Lady Mori's Hand. Ikkyu Sojun. ErotSp, tr. by Sam Hamill

My hand is lonely for your clasping, dear. You and I. Henry Alford. ITBLP

My hand is up. It goes up to my father's dark coat. Atavistic: Traces after the Rain. Juan Felipe Herrera. TouFir

My hand is weak and delicate. Your Hand in Mine. Alaide Foppa. TANSG, tr. by Celeste Kostopulos-Cooperman

My hand moved furiously. Short Poem. Kenneth Carroll. SpirFl

My hand within you. Arms and the Woman. Dorothy Livesay. PoBW

My hands are murder-red. Many a plump head. Strawberrying. May Swenson. NAMCP V.2; VCAP

My hands are smooth, the grooves. Workaholic. Nadia Hazboun Reimer. PoArWo

My hands are wrinkled from the cold. Pale Ant. Ellease Southerland. GT

My hands bones were life-sized, my feet bones. Lecture #1. Brenda Coultas. HeMarv

My hand's crabbed up with scribbling. Copier. Unknown. SonAtl, tr. by Colin Thewley

My hands creep forward on the hot sand. Sand. Nina Cassian. PoSu, tr. by Nina Cassian and Naomi Lazard

My hands did numb to beauty. I Held a Shelley Manuscript. Gregory Corso. BB; PmAP

My hands here, gentle, where her breasts begin. No Continuing City. Michael Longley. PNI

My hands ooze over you. Portraits of a Moment. Keith Gilyard. SpirFl

My hands released at last, the cliff soars. Kanemitsu-Kogun. ZenPo, tr. by Takashi Ikemoto and Lucien Stryk

My hands that guide a needle. Instruction. Hazel Hall. NAAPv.2

My hands turn to claws, tear. Bedouin Eyes. Dima Hilal. PoArWo

My Handy Man. Andy Razaf. ReLy

My Handy Man Ain't Handy No More. Andy Razaf. ReLy

My happiness swelled. Tomas Transtromer. WoBe Fr. Haiku.

My harbouring arms. (LL) Midsummer, Tobago. Derek Walcott. MakPoe; OPOU; VCWP

My hasty pen, about to write unkind. Another Letter to a Friend. Mary Mollineux. PoBW

My hat vanished. Charles Stein. WhBo

My Head and My Knees. Mirza Asadullah Khan Ghalib. WED, tr. by Robert Bly and Sunil Dutta

My head and shoulders, and my book. Signature of All Things, The. Kenneth Rexroth. APSN; APT-2; OxBoAm; TRP

My head battered against the culvert wall, nose. My Manhood. Rodney Jones. OxBoAm

My head felt stabbed. I Would Not Recommend Love. Harold Norse. CLPP

My head filled with TV images. Looking for Indians. Cheryl Savageau. TWW

My head is bald, my breath is bad. Late-Flowering Lust. Sir John Betjeman. BrAP

My head is spinning to the right. Kseniya Marennikova. CRWP, tr. by Daniel Weissbort

My head is unhappy. Poem in Time of Winter. Ray Mathew. NOBAu; OBCoV

My head, my heart, mine Eyes, my life, nay more. Letter to Her Husband, Absent upon Public[k] Employment, A. Anne Bradstreet. BrAP; HeIP-4; NAAL-3; NAAL-5; NAAPv.1; NALW; NoP-4; NoP-5; PEW; PoPoPo; WaAnP

My head so big. Narrative: Ali. Elizabeth Alexander. ESEAA; MoASP

My headlights raise them up: a dash. Census of Animal Bodies: Driving Home. Madeline DeFrees. UrbNat

My head's too full of memories for my own good. Spoon Maker's Daughter, The. Susan Utting. Prnts

My Heart. Abd al-Rahim Salih al-Rahim. IrPoTo, *tr.* by Saadi A. Simawe and Daniel Weissbort

My Heart. Myriad Stars, Part 132. Bingxin. CFP, *tr.* by Michelle Yeh

My Heart. Laura Kasischke. AmPoNex

My Heart. Moishe Nadir. Prolet, *tr.* by Amelia Glaser

My Heart. Frank O'Hara. OxBoAm

My heart aches and a drowsy numbness pains. Ode to a Nightingale. John Keats. AmFaPo; BrAP; BRP; CABP; ClHu; HeIP-4; NAEL-6v2; NAEL-7v2; NAWM-7v2; NIL-7; NOBRP; NoP-4; NoP-5; NPBRoP; NPeEn; OBEV; OWoS; OxBEV; PoPoPo; SoSe-8; TFi; WaAnP

My Heart and I. Elizabeth Barrett Browning. VWP

My heart and my body want to separate. Friedrich von Hausen. GePo

My heart beat speeds up. Letter to My Mother. Mary McGinnis. ICANM

My heart beats in the first spring. Nguyen Quang Thieu. PML *Fr.* Eleven Parts of Feeling.

My heart, being hungry, feeds on food. My Heart, Being Hungry. Edna St. Vincent Millay. AFaM

My Heart Belongs to Daddy. Cole Porter. ReLy

My heart broke loose on the wind. (LL) Poetry. Pablo Neruda. PoetW; VCWP, *tr.* by Alastair Reid

My heart burns in flames of sorrow. Mihri Hatun. OLP, *tr.* by Walter Andrews, Najaat Black and Mehmet Kalpakli

My heart can't go on any longer. Miguel Hernández. PoCho, *tr.* by Timothy Baland

My heart did heave, and there came forth, O God! Affliction (3). George Herbert. NOSC

My heart doesn't ache; sometimes though it rages. (LL) One Life. Adrienne Rich. CAP-8; OxBoAm

My Heart, Faithful. Ramón López Velarde. BLPSL, *tr.* by Rene de Costa, Rigas Kappatos and Eleni Paidoussi

My heart, faithful, has earned itself the shadow. My Heart, Faithful. Ramón López Velarde. BLPSL, *tr.* by Rene de Costa, Rigas Kappatos and Eleni Paidoussi

My heart fell dead before. (LL) All in green went my love riding. E. E. Cummings. HeIP-4; NAAPv.2; NoAM; NoP-4; NoP-5; OxBoAm; WaAnP

My heart gives you love. (LL) Dirge for Two Veterans. Walt Whitman. APN-1; BLT; CBCWP; ItP; MoAmPo

My heart grows sick when home I come. My Only Friends. Ebenezer Elliott. DiBP

My heart has grown rich with the passing of years. Solitary, The. Sara Teasdale. MoAmPo

My Heart has Known its Winter. Arna Bontemps. GT

My heart has made its mind up. Valentine. Wendy Cope. NoP-4; NoP-5

My heart has mighty love. My Heart. Moishe Nadir. Prolet, *tr.* by Amelia Glaser

My heart has thanked [*or* thank'd] thee, Bowles! for those soft strains. Samuel Taylor Coleridge. CenSon *Fr.* Effusions.

My heart is. Black Heart as Ever Green, The. Carolyn M. Rodgers. IllVoic

My Heart Is a Hobo. Johnny Burke. ReLy

My heart is broken (oh my God). Contrition. Ralph Knevet. ChIV-2

My heart is crusty. Love Ghost. Mimi Goese. HeMarv

My heart is heavy in my breast—my eyes are full of tears. Woods of Kylinoe, The: Song of the Irish Emigrant in North America. Ellen Fitz-Simon. IrV

My Heart Is High Above. Alexander Scott. OBEV

My Heart Is in Merioneth. *Unknown.* OBWVE, *tr.* by Richard Llwyd

My heart is in woe. Downfall of the Gael, The. Fearflatha O'Gnive. IrV, *tr.* by Sir Samuel Ferguson

My heart is just as heavy. Grief. *Unknown.* OBWVE, *tr.* by Aneirin Talfan Davies

My heart is like a singing bird. Birthday, A. Christina Georgina Rossetti. CABP; LW; NAEL-6v2; NAEL-7v2; NALW; OBEV; PEW; TFi; UV; ViWPN; VWP

My heart is like one asked to dine. Unexpected Pleasure, An. *Unknown.* UV

My heart is like the failing hearth. Letitia Elizabeth Landon. NOBRP; NPBRoP *Fr.* Golden Violet, The.

My heart is lost. What can I now expect? Mary Sidney Wroth, Countess of Montgomery. OxBSo

My heart is not of wax; nor may it one compare. She Boasts Her Constancy. Johann Rist. GePo, *tr.* by George C. Schoolfield

My heart is very faint and low. Dying Child, The. Mary Howitt. VWP

My heart leaps up when I behold. Song to Be Sung by the Father of Infant Female Children. Ogden Nash. MoAmPo

My heart leaps up when I behold. My Heart Leaps Up [When I Behold]. William Wordsworth. ChAP; ITBLP; NAEL-6v2; NAEL-7v2; NOBRP; NoP-4; NoP-5; PoPoPo; SacPr; TFi; WaAnP

My heart leaps up with streams of joy. Word, The. Stevie Smith. MoWP

My heart, like a bird ahover joyously. Voyage to Cythera, A. Charles Baudelaire. WoPoe, *tr.* by Frederick Morgan

My heart, my dove, my snail, my sail, my. Song. Cynthia Zarin. NIL-7; NoP-4; NoP-5

My heart, O God, is void of love. Malice. Fawzi Karim. IrPoTo, *tr.* by Saadi A. Simawe

My heart overflows with love, so what is this wine for? Imprisoned God, The. Murad Mikha'il. IrPoTo, *tr.* by Christina Coyle and Sadok Masliyah

My heart perceives nothing. Stockade prisoners on hunger strike: Nani Mo Mite Inai Kokoro No Hi Ga Tsuzuki Kogen Natsu Takenawa. Violet Kazue De Cristoforo. CalPo

My heart said this to me: "I have no role to play." *Unknown.* SLW, *tr.* by Marjolijn De Jager, Sayd Bahodin Majrouh and André Velter

My heart sits back and wonders. Lest We Forget. Patricia A. Holt Abner. BRtP

My heart still feels the weight of that remember'd chain. (LL) Sonnet 7: "Like an enfranchised bird, who wildly springs." Caroline Elizabeth Norton. CenSon; VWP

My heart still loves, will break. (LL) Words for Love. Ted Berrigan. NYP2; PmAP

My Heart Stood Still. Lorenz Hart. ReLy

My heart tells me. Mexico Will Be Free. Merced J. de Gonz´les. NAAPv.1, *tr.* by Unknown

My heart tells me. Zaragoza Clubs. SWaP *Fr.* Héroes del Cinco de Mayo.

My Heart Thinks as the Sun Comes Up. Solomon ibn Gabirol. WoPoe, *tr.* by Peter Cole

My heart thinks as the sun comes up. My Heart Thinks as the Sun Comes Up. Solomon ibn Gabirol. WoPoe, *tr.* by Peter Cole

My heart trembles at the raw sound of a woman's voice as if drawing together tightly thin, colored silk. Living Voice. Kawai Suimei. CAoMJL1, *tr.* by Leith Morton

My heart was heavy, for its trust had been. Forgiveness. John Greenleaf Whittier. GSo

My heart was like a bird that fluttered joyously. Voyage to Cythera, A. Charles Baudelaire. SxFrPo, *tr.* by James McGowan

My heart was petrified. Mermaid, The. Aliyah Abdul-Salaam. AnVo, *tr.* by Mohamed Enani

My heart, you might pierce it and take it. RaF, *tr.* by Abraham Halpern

My heart Your heart. London Air. Ted Berrigan. AHA

My heart's cloth I shall spread before the Savior's feet. Yelena Shwarts. TCRusP, *tr.* by Anna Barker and Daniel Weissbort

My heart's delight, I must for love forget you. Felo de Se. Elinor Wylie. NAAPv.2

My heart's in the Highlands, my heart is not here. My Heart's in the Highlands. Robert Burns. ITBLP

(Farewell to the Highlands, farewell to the North.) ChAP

My heart's in the kitchen, my heart is not here. Maria Jane Jewsbury. VWP

My heart's in the kitchen, my heart is not here. My heart's in the kitchen, my heart is not here. Maria Jane Jewsbury. VWP

My heart's on my fist. Tomb of the Kings, The. Anne Hébert. WoPoe, *tr.* by A. Poulin, Jr.

My heart's true bride has slept two thousand years. Tomb of Hegeso, The. Mihály Babits. IQMS, *tr.* by Watson Kirkconnell

My heid did yak yester nicht. Magryme, The. William Dunbar. FaBoVe

My height: just av'rage. It Amazes Me! Carolyn Leigh. ReLy

My Heritage! It is to live within. My Heritage. Adah Isaacs Menken. CBWP-1

My high hand makes fine patterns. Reason. Philippe Jaccottet. MFP, *tr.* by Martin Sorrell

My highway is unfeatured air. Hymn of the Earth. William Ellery Channing. APN-1

My hips are a desk. Secretary Chant, The. Marge Piercy. BrAP

My Hobby on the Mountain. Hamhur Kiwha. BecRai, *tr.* by Kim Daljin, Kim Won-Chung and Christopher Merrill

My home(did you know?)—my home. Mariella Bettarini. CItWP *Fr.* Poet's Home, The.

My home over there, my home over there. That Mountain Far Away. *Unknown.* CA, *tr.* by Herbert Joseph Spinden

My home was at Cold Mountain from the start. Han-shan (Cold Mountain). BB, *tr.* by Gary Snyder

My homeland is in your eyes, my duty on your lips. Circe. Gabriel Zaid. TCLAP, *tr.* by Andrew Rosing

My homeland is infinitely far. Staying in Luoxiang County for the Evening. Chen Zi'ang. CCL1, *tr.* by Stephen Owen

My homestead lies beside a clear stream. Homestead. Tu Fu [*or* Du Fu]. CrYelRi, *tr.* by Sam Hamill

My honeybunch's peeper are nothing like neon. Dim Lady. Harryette Mullen. IaFF

My hope and treasure lies above. (LL) [Here Follows Some] Verses upon the Burning of Our House [July 10th, 1666. Copied Out of a Loose Paper]. Anne Bradstreet. BASC; ColAP; EMWP; MakPoe; NAAL-3; NAAL-5; NAAPv.1; NALW; NoP-4; NoP-5; NOSC; PEW; SacPr; TCAPo

My Hope Is in God. *Unknown.* SacPr

My hope is on what is to come. Anthem for Doomed Youth. Raymond Garlick. AngWePo

My horse has wings. Ride, The. Lucinda Roy. GT

My horse is halting! Halt thine own as well, comrade, I am afraid! Translated from the German or the Bosnian. Max Jacob. GPTC, *tr. by* John Ashbery

My horse / thickens. *Unknown.* SonAtl, *tr. by* Greg Gao and Lee Sombur

My hotel room's small. 63rd and broadway. Reuben Jackson. ESEAA

My House. Robert Adamson. BMAP

My house gutted. Hokushi. ZenPo, *tr. by* Takashi Ikemoto and Lucien Stryk

My house, I say. But hark to the sunny doves. Robert Louis Stevenson. NPeEn; OxBEV

My house is empty but for a pair of boots. Flooded Valley, The. Roland Mathias. AngWePo

My house is poor; those that I love have left me. Winter Night. Po Chü-i. CCL1, *tr. by* Arthur Waley

My house is so small. School Street. Matthew Zapruder. LegDan

My house is the red earth; it could be the center of the world. My House Is the Red Earth. Joy Harjo. ICANM

My house is torn down. Done With. Ann Stanford. CalPo

My house lies west of Thousand Mile Bridge. Madman, The. Tu Fu [*or* Du Fu]. CrYelRi, *tr. by* Sam Hamill

My House Not Made with Hands. Helen Hunt Jackson. SWaP

My house was a house of winds. Wind. Dana Levin. AmPoNex

My house with criss-cross beams is remote from the world. I Sit in My Lofty Study. Hsieh T'iao. CCL1, *tr. by* John Frodsham

My hovering[e] thought[e]s would fly to heaven. Man's Civil[l] War[re]. Robert Southwell. NoSic

My husband. My Husband, Before Leaving. *Unknown.* EaWin; WoPoe, *tr. by* J. Moussaieff Masson and W. S. Merwin

My husband, / and don't put the blame. Dear Mr. Whitman. Mark Kraushaar. ViWalt

My Husband, Before Leaving. *Unknown.* EaWin; WoPoe, *tr. by* J. Moussaieff Masson and W. S. Merwin

My Husband Discovers Poetry. Diane Lockward. PoDa

My husband gives me an A. Marks. Linda Pastan. NIL-7; NIP-4

My husband had a knack of knowing things. Message, The. Michael Heffernan. RACG

My husband has a crush on Myrna Loy. Video Blues. Mary Jo Salter. P180; WaAnP

My husband made me juice. Two Men, Two Grapefruits. Donna Masini. KGB

My husband with no band. Mixed Marriage. Joan Logghe. MPUn

My Husband's Birthday. Josephine D. Henderson Heard. CBWP-4

My Husband's Bride. Beckian Fritz Goldberg. PfS

My Husband's Tongue Is Bitter. Okot P'Bitek. NAMCP V.2 *Fr.* Song of Lawino.

My hut / Thatched. Issa. ZenPo, *tr. by* Takashi Ikemoto and Lucien Stryk

My ice skates on a wall. Cold Lost Marbles. William S. Burroughs. BB

My Ideal. Leo Robin. ReLy

My Idlest Dreams. Li Yu [*or* Li Hou-Chu]. CCL1, *tr. by* Sam Houston Brock

My idlest dreams go farthest. My Idlest Dreams. Li Yu [*or* Li Hou-Chu]. CCL1, *tr. by* Sam Houston Brock

My Imperialism. Tamura Ryuichi. AF; PFTM-2; VCWP, *tr. by* Christopher Drake

My Indian Grandmother Speaks to Animals. John E. Smelcer. PoCoUp

My Indigo. Li-Young Lee. CAP-8

My Infelice's face, her brow, her eye. Portrait, A. Thomas Dekker. OxAEP-1

My insatiable memory is like. Olga Fiodorovna Berggolts. TCRusP, *tr. by* Daniel Weissbort

My intention is to tell of bodies changed. Ovid. NAWM-5v1 *Fr.* Metamorphoses.

My intimate companion. Who can keep a blazing fire tied in a cotton cloth? Lex Hixon. HW

My inventory is small, a singular dance. Annihilation's Trio: Three Irrational Sonnets Begging the Question of Being and Act. Jay Wright. ICANM

My island spirit. *Unknown.* NAAPv.2

My jacket old, with narrow seam. My Jacket Old. Herman Melville. TCAPo

My jade body, like my gold hairpins. Spring Night. Chu Shu-chen. NDACCP, *tr. by* Kenneth Rexroth

My Japanese mother-in-law. Coffee, Markets, Blossoms. Gary Snyder. WANABP

My job is to watch leaves fall. Out of Time. Laura Fargas. CFP

My Journal. Adelaide Anne Procter. VWP

My Joy, My Jockey, My Gabriel. George Barker. MoBrPo *Fr.* First Cycle of Love Poems.

My joys are those of the spare autumn birds. Epilogue. Dimitris Tsaloumas. PML

My king summoned this sick and aged body. Lament on the Water. Pak Illo. CATKP, *tr. by* Peter H. Lee

My kingdom for a horse! Kingdom. Leopold Staff. PoSu, *tr. by* Adam Czerniawski

My kingdom is of this world. Audrey Poetker-Thiessen. ACAMVP

My kite is three feet broad, and six feet long. Kite, The. Adelaide O'Keeffe. NOxBChV

My Knicks Are Going to Beat Your Spurs—NBA Souvenir Bracelet 1999 for My Long Distance Love. Catherine Bowman. MoASP

My Lady Carries Stones. Nick Piombino. FTOS

My Lady Greensleeves. *Unknown.* OxAEP-1

My lady, how comes it about—what all can see. Michelangelo Buonarroti. PoDa, *tr. by* John Frederick Nims

My lady love. Tea Making. Antoinette Scudder. PoBW

My Lady, the Amazement of the Land, the Lone Star. Lady Who Ascends into the Heavens, The. *Unknown.* HW, *tr. by* Samuel Noah Kramer and Diane Wolkstein

My lady walks her morning round. Henchman, The. John Greenleaf Whittier. OBEV

My Lady's Eyes Are Hazel. Nazim Hikmet. NaPG, *tr. by* Talat Sait Halman

My Lady's Grave. Emily Jane Brontë. *See* Song: "Linnet in the rocky dells, The."

My lady's presence makes the roses red. Henry Constable. NIL-7; NIP-4; OBGa *Fr.* Diana.

My Lady's Tears. *Unknown. See* I Saw My Lady Weep.

My lamp and life, both shall in Thee abide. (LL) Morning-Watch, The. Henry Vaughan. AngWePo; BASC; NOSC

My land is bare of chattering folk. Sanctuary. Dorothy Parker. NBLV

My land, my love, sleep well. (LL) Nightsong: City. Dennis Brutus. HBAPE; PoetW; WoPoe

My landlord called at 11:00 P.M. Intrusion, The. Biljana Dragoslav Obradović. LiTh

My large magnetic card flag proudly displays Old Glory. Land of the Discount Price, Home of the Brand Name. Harryette Mullen. Eno

My Last Afternoon with Uncle Devereux Winslow. Robert Lowell. GPTC; NoP-4; NoP-5

My Last Dance. Julia Ward Howe. APN-1

My Last Duchess. Robert Browning. AmFaPo; BrAP; CABP; ClHu; CtM; HeIP-4; ITBLP; MakPoe; NAEL-7v2; NAWM-7v2; NIL-7; NIP-4; NoP-4; NoP-5; NPeEn; OxBEV; PoPoPo; SoSe-8; TFi; TRP; WaAnP

My Last Hustler. Richard Howard. NAMCP V.2

My last modernist poem, #2 (or, mugshot). Evie Shockley. RD

My Last Name. Nicolás Guillén. TCLAP, *tr. by* Robert Marquez and David Arthur McMurray

My Last Night in Bahia. Carolyne Wright. RoV

My last night in California. California. David St. John. SwNoth

My Last Tooth. *Unknown.* VerBaPo

My latest thought brick for an abundant supply for home and clothes. Bill Griffiths. Oth *Fr.* Building: The New London Hospital.

My laugh was an ancient, a very ancient laugh. Soaring. Kim Sŭnghŭi. EcSo, *tr. by* K. Kim Richards and Steffen Richards

My Least Skirtable Deficiency. HeidiLynn Nilsson. NeAmPo

My leg stiffens. The crutch that holds me has become my aromatic rosary. Weaning of Furniture-Nutrition. Juan Felipe Herrera. BodElec

My legs are long. To Trace from Hebrew. Ece Ayhan. PFTM-2, *tr. by* Murat Nemet-Nejat

My legs fell asleep in an attempt. Drinking Beer with Sir. Cindy Goff. LaCa

My Legs Señor. William S. Burroughs. BB

My legs shimmer like fish. Bathroom. Elaine Feinstein. HarvBoo

My lemon-colored. Bringing My Son to the Police Station to Be Fingerprinted. Shoshauna Shy. P180; PoDa

My Lesbia let us love and live. Catullus. *See* Lesbia / live with me.

My letters! all dead paper, mute and white! Elizabeth Barrett Browning. CenSon; OxAEP-2 *Fr.* Sonnets from the Portuguese.

My Lief Is Faren in Londe. *Unknown.* NAEL-6v1; NAEL-7v1

My liege, I did deny no prisoners. William Shakespeare. FaBoWar *Fr.* King Henry IV, Pt. I.

My Life. Lyn Hejinian.
   "Moment yellow, just as four years later when, A." PmAP
   "Moment yellow, just as four years later, when my father returned home from the war, A." NAMCP V.2
   "Tree rows in orchards are capable of patterns. What, The." FTOS
   What is the Meaning Hung from that Depend. OxBoAm

My life. Happy Marriage. Taslima Nasrin. P180

My Life. Mark Strand. NoAM

My life as a bat. Life. Jo Shapcott. StAl

My Life Asleep. Jo Shapcott. BeAl; NeBrP

My life becomes too hard, so I go away. Asylum. Herman Fong. BAP-97

My Life Before I Knew It. Lawrence Raab. GoPo

My Life by Somebody Else. Mark Strand. CAP-8

My Life by Water. Lorine Niedecker. APT-2; NAAPv.2; NAMCP V.1; OxBoAm

My life closed twice before its close. Emily Dickinson. APN-2; ColAP; HeIP-4; LW; MoAmPo; NAAL-3; NAAL-5; NAAPv.1; NAMCP V.1; NIL-7; NIP-4; NoAM; NoP-5; OxBoAm; SacPr; SAmP; TCAPo; TFi

My life had taken the form of a small square. Small Square, The. Sophia De Mello Breyner. VCWP, tr. by Ruth Fainlight

My life has been tedious. Release. Peter Schjeldahl. AHA

My life has been the poem I would have writ. Henry David Thoreau. APN-1; NAAPv.1; NCAP; TCAPo

My Life in Yonago. Sharon Mesmer. HeMarv

My Life Is a————. Frederick Locker-Lampson. OBCoV

My life is bitter with thy love; thine eyes. Anactoria. Algernon Charles Swinburne. RACG

My life is hung up. Lorine Niedecker. APT-2

My life is like the summer rose. Lament of the Captive, The. Richard Henry Wilde. APN-1; ColAP; TCAPo

My life is my own bible. Wife of Bath Speaks in Brixton Market. Jean Binta Breeze. MoWP

My life is spent in dissipation and wantonness! Abu Bakr ibn Abd al-Malik Ibn Quzman. HiArP, tr. by James T. Monroe

My life is what it chose for me. Black Drag Queen. A. Van Jordan. BtF

My Life, my Strength, my Joy, my All. (LL) Hymn to My God in a Night of My Late Sickness[e], A. Sir Henry Wotton. NOSC; SacPr

My life seems dull and flat. Epitaph on a Pet Cat. Joachim Du Bellay. TriCat, tr. by Ralph Nixon Currey

My Life: "Somehow it got into my room." Joe Wenderoth. BodElec; NAPBL; P180

My Life with Horses. Polly Clark. NeBl; StAl

My life's a maze of seeming traps. Ralph Erskine. SacPr Fr. Believer's Riddle, The.

My life's a pleasure and a pain. Ralph Erskine. SacPr Fr. Believer's Riddle, The.

My life's blossom might have bloomed on all sides. Edgar Lee Masters. APT-1 Fr. Spoon River Anthology.

My Lighthouses. Helen Hunt Jackson. APN-2; ColAP

My lips are sweet, inspired with Stella's kiss. (LL) Sir Philip Sidney. NAEL-6v1; NAEL-7v1; NoSic Fr. Astrophil and Stella.

My lips are zippered shut. White Paintings I. Laura Mullen. RoV

My lips came with a caravan of slaves. History of My Face. Khaled Mattawa. AmPoNex

My Listener. Chase Twichell. WANABP

My little book, as o'er thy page so white. Written in a Blank-Paper Book Given to the Author by a Friend. Mary Russell Mitford. PoBW

My little box. Little Box from Olinalá, The. Gabriela Mistral. TANSG, tr. by Maria Giachetti [or Jacketti]

My little crazy beloved was serving me dinner, and through the dining room's open window. Soup and the Clouds, The. Charles Baudelaire. MotU, tr. by Edward K. Kaplan

My Little Girl Went to the Sea. Federico García Lorca. SpanPo, tr. by Rachel Benson and Robert O'Brien

My little girl went to the sea. My Little Girl Went to the Sea. Federico García Lorca. SpanPo, tr. by Rachel Benson and Robert O'Brien

My little girl's face was white as snow. Grieving for My Little Girl. Yi Kyubo. CATKP, tr. by Kevin O'Rourke

My little ship, three-masted. Unknown. WoPoe Fr. Mourning Songs of Greece.

'My Little Sister'. Abba Kovner. tr. by Shirley Kaufman
    Far, Far a City Lies. HP

My little sister likes to try my shoes. Poem for My Sister. Liz Lochhead. EdScPo; ItWoWo

My little son comes running with open arms! Poem. Thomas McGrath. PoChi

My little son enters. Transformations. Tadeusz Różewicz. ChAP, tr. by Czeslaw Milosz

My little son, laughing, singing... Poem. Thomas McGrath. GifTon

My little son, when you could command marvels. Geoffrey Hill. NAMCP V.2; NoAM; UpMys Fr. Funeral Music.

My little son, who looked from thoughtful eyes. Coventry Patmore. OBEV; OxAEP-2; SoSe-8 Fr. Unknown Eros, The.

My little towns are scared of the dark. Nightstart. Malick Fall. SonAtl, tr. by Gregory Beaven, Nene Ndiaye Diop, Kurt Ganzl, Saul Goode, Eileen Julien, Lilyan Kesteloot, Aliko Songolo, Jean-Marie Volet and Kenneth Wilburn

My Little Woman. Asaf Halet Çelebi. NaPG, tr. by Talat Sait Halman

My lizard, my lively writher. Wish for a Young Wife. Theodore Roethke. NAAL-5; NAMCP V.1; NoAM; NoP-4; NoP-5; WaAnP

My Loneliness. Thérèse 'Awwad. PoArWo, tr. by Kamal Boullata

My long scythe whispered and left the hay to make. (LL) Mowing. Robert Frost. APT-1; ColAP; HarvBoo; ITBLP; NAAL-5; TRP; WaAnP

My long two-pointed ladder's sticking through a tree. After Apple-Picking. Robert Frost. APT-1; BrAP; IPoFL; ItP; MoAmPo; NAAL-5; NAAPv.2; NAMCP V.1; NoAM; NoP-5; OxBoAm; SAmP; SoSe-8; TCAPo; TFi; TRP; WaAnP

My long white hair is framed by green mountains. Han-shan Te-ch'ing. CSKM, tr. by Red Pine

My lord and my God, I have hoped in Thee. Mary Stuart, Queen of Scots. NePenScot, tr. by Agnes Strickland

My lord, as I was sewing in my closet. William Shakespeare. OxAEP-1 Fr. Hamlet.

My Lord granted me such a heart. Yunus Emre. NaPG, tr. by Talat Sait Halman

My lord, hearing lately of your opulence in promises and your house. Epistle to a Patron, An. Frank Templeton Prince. HarvBoo; OxBEV

My lord / i know my presence irritates you. Confidentially Yours. Wopko Jensma. TSAP

My Lord, I take the liberty of submitting a case. Rhyfel y Sais Bach. John Stuart Williams. TCAWP

My Lord, I'm coming from the war. Prayer After War. Endre Ady. IQMS, tr. by Anton N. Nyerges

My Lord Is Full of Delight. Unknown. TAL

My Lord, my Lord, what shall I do? Heaven Bell A-Ring. Unknown. SSUS

My Lord recalls Ferrara? How walls. Nikolaus Mardruz to his Master Ferdinand, Count of Tyrol, 1565. Richard Howard. NoP-4; NoP-5

My Lord, what a mornin'. Unknown. NoP-4

My Lord, What a Mornin'. Unknown. NoP-4

My lords, here's something marvelous. Butcher of Abbeville, The. Unknown. NAWM-7v1, tr. by Ned Dubin

My lords, if you have time to spare. Three Hunchbacks, The. Unknown. NAWM-7v1, tr. by Ned Dubin

My Lost Brother. Ben Scammell. NLP

My Lost Youth. Henry Wadsworth Longfellow. APN-1; BrAP; ITBLP; NAAL-3; NAAPv.1; OBEV; OxBoAm; TCAPo; TFi

My Lot to Spin the Purple: that the Tabernacle Should Be Made. D. A. Powell. IAoNAP

My lov'd [or loved], my honor'd [or honored], much respected friend. Cotter's Saturday Night [nscribed to Robert Aiken [or R. A****], Esq.], The. Robert Burns. NOBRP; TreFP

My love / there are no accidents. Sol/o. Seitlhamo Motsapi. TSAP

My Love. Nanduri Subbarao. HotL, tr. by V. Narayana Rao

My love, / When you were here there was. Letter, A. Li Po. NDACCP, tr. by William Carlos Williams

My Love about his Business in the Barn. Paula Meehan. MoWP

My Love? alas! I must not call you Mine. To J.G. on the News of His Marriage. "Ephelia." LW

My love and I asked little of the world. Right to Love, The. Gene Lees. ReLy

My love came up from Barnegat. Puritan's Ballad, The. Elinor Wylie. OxBoAm

My love, capture me, embrace me! Unknown. SLW, tr. by Marjolijn De Jager, Sayd Bahodin Majrouh and André Velter

My love, come quickly and appease him. Unknown. SLW, tr. by Marjolijn De Jager, Sayd Bahodin Majrouh and André Velter

My love, come quickly to subdue it. Unknown. SLW, tr. by Marjolijn De Jager, Sayd Bahodin Majrouh and André Velter

My love don't let me, going to sleep. Quicksand. Michael Hartnett. IrLP

My love dwelt in a northern land. Romance. Andrew Lang. NePenScot

My Love For You. Unknown. Spl

My love, / for you the thousand oaths. To My Beloved. R. G. Ka. Prolet, tr. by Amelia Glaser

My Love Has Departed. Chippewa Oral Tradition. NAAL-5; OBVE, tr. by Frances Densmore
    (Woman's Song.) NAAPv.1

My Love Has Departed. Frances Densmore. APT-1 Fr. Chippewa Music.

My love hot on your scent on the cusp of winter. (LL) Adrienne Rich. LW; NIL-7 Fr. Contradictions: Tracking Poems.

My Love, I Speak to You of a Love. Leila Ferraz. SurWo, tr. by Jean R. Longland

My love, I speak to you of a love. My Love, I Speak to You of a Love. Leila Ferraz. SurWo, tr. by Jean R. Longland

My love, if I die and you don't. Pablo Neruda. TCLAP, tr. by Stephen Tapscott

My love, if I write a song for you. Sonnet. Veronica Forrest-Thomson. EdScPo; HarvBoo; MoWP

My Love in her attire doth show her wit. Madrigal. Unknown. HeIP-4; NAEL-6v1; NIP-4; OBEV; TFi

My love is as a fe[a]ver, longing still.   William Shakespeare.   AEP; NAEL-6v1; NAEL-7v1; OxAEP-1 *Fr.* Sonnets.

My love is coming! I take dinner early.   *Unknown.*   CATKP, *tr. by* Kevin O'Rourke

My Love is Like a Lily.   Kim Ly Bui-Burton.   PasH

My love is like a river or a fist with forty fingers.   Enia.   Seitlhamo Motsapi.   TSAP

My love is like Mies van der Rohe's.   Dea ex Machina.   John Updike.   UV

My love / Is like the grasses.   Ono no Yoshiki.   TAL *Fr.* Kokin Shu.

My Love is of a birth as rare.   Definition of Love, The.   Andrew Marvell.   BASC; BrAP; FSCP; ITBLP; NAEL-6v1; NAEL-7v1; NoP-4; NoP-5; NOSC; NPeEn; OBEV; OxBEV; PBRV; PtR; TFi; WaAnP

My Love is Past.   Thomas Watson.   NoSic

My love is sick—she has begun to turn.   My Love Is Sick.   Craig Arnold.   NAPBL

My love is strengthened, though more weak in seeming.   William Shakespeare.   OBEV *Fr.* Sonnets.

My love is strung with the ancient.   John MacKenzie.   Coast

My love, jump into bed with me and do not fear.   *Unknown.*   SLW, *tr. by* Marjolijn De Jager, Sayd Bahodin Majrouh and André Velter

My love late walking in the rain's white aisles.   My Love Late Walking.   James Keir Baxter.   BrAP

My love lies underground.   Hymn to Priapus.   D. H. Lawrence.   OBMV

My love, like my hair, is pure.   Song of White Hair, A.   Chuo Wen-chün.   CCL1, *tr. by* Chung Ling and Kenneth Rexroth

My love lives down by the butchery.   All but Lost.   Mark Bibbins.   LegDan

My love looks like a girl to-night.   Bride, The.   D. H. Lawrence.   InoFa; NAMCP V.1; NoAM

My love must be a kind of blind love.   I Only Have Eyes for You.   Al Dubin.   ReLy

My love, my lord.   Verses Expressing the Feelings of a Lover.   Sor Juana Inés de la Cruz.   SpanPo, *tr. by* Samuel Beckett

My Love, my Love, it was a day in June.   Sinfonia Eroica.   Amy Levy.   ViWPN

My love, my love, my love, why have you left me alone? (LL)   I hear an army charging upon the land.   James Joyce.   CtM; IrLP

My love of you was life and not a breath. (LL)   Christina Georgina Rossetti.   CABP; MakPoe; OxBSo *Fr.* Monna Innominata.

My love, open my tomb and see.   *Unknown.*   SLW, *tr. by* Marjolijn De Jager, Sayd Bahodin Majrouh and André Velter

My love shall in my verse ever live young. (LL)   William Shakespeare.   HeIP-4; NAEL-6v1; NAEL-7v1; NoSic; OxAEP-1; PBRV *Fr.* Sonnets.

My love, swear that you will come to me.   *Unknown.*   SLW, *tr. by* Marjolijn De Jager, Sayd Bahodin Majrouh and André Velter

My love, the tragic night was crying with sobs.   Intruder, The.   Delmira Agustini.   BLPSL, *tr. by* Rene de Costa, Rigas Kappatos and Eleni Paidoussi

My love, this is the bitterest, that thou.   Any Wife to Any Husband.   Robert Browning.   RACG

My love was light the old wives said.   Tennessee Williams.   PoA 2002 *Fr.* Shuttle, The.

My love was walking in the sun.   Shallow-Water Warning.   Helen Adam.   APT-2

My love whose hair is woodfire.   Free Union.   André Breton.   YaTCFP, *tr. by* Mary Ann Caws

My love, you are timely come, let me lie by your heart.   Door and the Window, The.   Henry Reed.   HarvBoo

My loved one is far away.   *Unknown.*   NAAPv.2

My loved ones drift into nothingness.   Fuselage Installation.   Juan Felipe Herrera.   BodElec

My lovely readers.   Mystery Corset, The.   André Breton.   YaTCFP, *tr. by* Mary Ann Caws

My lovely, sweet Ipsithilla.   Catullus.   ErotSp, *tr. by* Sam Hamill

My Lover.   Wendy Cope.   MoWP

My lover cannot take a joke.   *Unknown.*   SLW, *tr. by* Marjolijn De Jager, Sayd Bahodin Majrouh and André Velter

My lover is a lotus blossom.   *Unknown, fr. Egyptian hieroglyphics.*   ErotSp, *tr. by* Sam Hamill

My lover is asleep.   Peaceful Sunday.   Charlotte Gardelle.   CuPo

My lover is Hindu and I am a Muslim.   *Unknown.*   SLW, *tr. by* Marjolijn De Jager, Sayd Bahodin Majrouh and André Velter

My lover is the ornament around my neck.   *Unknown.*   SLW, *tr. by* Marjolijn De Jager, Sayd Bahodin Majrouh and André Velter

My lover once informed me that miles davis was a real man 'cause he didn't take no shit.   On the Other Side.   Benin Williams.   BRtP

My lover prefers sky-colored eyes.   *Unknown.*   SLW, *tr. by* Marjolijn De Jager, Sayd Bahodin Majrouh and André Velter

My lover prefers well mannered garden flowers.   *Unknown.*   SLW, *tr. by* Marjolijn De Jager, Sayd Bahodin Majrouh and André Velter

My lover rests near where the flowers are.   *Unknown.*   SLW, *tr. by* Marjolijn De Jager, Sayd Bahodin Majrouh and André Velter

My lover wants me to kiss him in the foliage of the blackberry bush.   *Unknown.*   SLW, *tr. by* Marjolijn De Jager, Sayd Bahodin Majrouh and André Velter

My lover wants to keep my tongue inside his mouth.   *Unknown.*   SLW, *tr. by* Marjolijn De Jager, Sayd Bahodin Majrouh and André Velter

My lover was a wonderer.   Sylvia.   Meic Stevens.   BBMWP, *tr. by* the author

My lover was dozing on armfuls of flowers.   *Unknown.*   SLW, *tr. by* Marjolijn De Jager, Sayd Bahodin Majrouh and André Velter

My lover wears only boxer shorts.   Symbols of Fertility.   Audrey Poetker-Thiessen.   ACAMVP

My lovers aren't members of the gentry.   Mille e tre.   Paul Verlaine.   CAGL, *tr. by* Alan Stone

My Loves.   Julián de Casal.   BLPSL, *tr. by* Rene de Costa, Rigas Kappatos and Eleni Paidoussi

My Love's Dark Place Is Fragrant Like Narcissus.   Ikkyu Sojun.   ErotSp, *tr. by* Sam Hamill

My Luve's [*or* love's *or* love is *or* luve is] like a red, red rose.   Robert Burns.   *See* Oh my Love is like a red, red rose.

My loving frende, amorous Bune.   Lettre Sende by on Yonge Woman to A-noder, Whiche Aforetyme Were Felowes To-geder, A.   *Unknown.*   EMWP

My lute, awake! Perform the last.   My Lute, Awake!   Sir Thomas Wyatt.   NAEL-6v1; NAEL-7v1; NoP-4; NoP-5; NoSic; OBEV; TFi; WaAnP; WoPoe

(My lute, awake! perfourme the last.)   NPeEn; OxBEV; PBRV

My lute, be as thou wast [*or* wert] when thou didst grow.   To His Lute.   William Drummond of Hawthornden.   NOSC

(My lute, be as thou wert when thou didst grow.)   GSo

"My lute, be as thou wert when thou didst grow."   William Drummond of Hawthornden. *See* To His Lute.

My lute be still for I have done. (LL)   My Lute, Awake!   Sir Thomas Wyatt.   NAEL-6v1; NAEL-7v1; NoP-4; NoP-5; NoSic; OBEV; TFi; WaAnP; WoPoe

My LYRE! oh, let thy soothing power.   To My Lyre.   Eliza Cook.   VWP

My Magic Wheel.   N. P. Tyler.   ArBi

My mama done tol' me.   Blues in the Night.   Johnny Mercer.   APT-2; ReLy

My Mama is Magic!   Mama's Magic.   Glenis Redmond.   BRtP

My Mama Moved among the Days.   Lucille Clifton.   ItWoWo

My Mamma is a mean old sing.   Insulted.   Priscilla Jane Thompson.   CBWP-2

My Mammogram.   J. D. McClatchy.   WiU

My Man Caliban!   James Richardson.   RD

My man loved me so much.   So Long.   Jayne Cortez.   LW; OxAAAP

My Man o' War.   Andy Razaf.   ReLy

My Man Pa Replies.   Li Ho.   ColAnChi, *tr. by* Burton Watson

My man said *Howl*.   Ginsburg.   Thomas C. Howell IV.   BRtP

My man, Willard Franklin 'The Bunny' Goodjarrah.   Story of Frankie . . . My Man, The.   Archie Weller.   BMAP

My Manhood.   Rodney Jones.   OxBoAm

My Mary.   John Clare.   NOBRP; NPBRoP

My Mary.   William Cowper. *See* To Mary.

My Maryland.   James Ryder Randall.   CBCWP; PCW

(Maryland.)   APN-2

My Masters.   Sandor Csoori.   VCWP, *tr. by* Len Roberts

My Meat and Drink.   Jones Very.   InvLi

My meditation turns to thinking.   Sonnet.   Giorgio Baffo.   EroLit, *tr. by* Wayland Young

My Melancholy Baby.   George Norton.   ReLy

My memory disrobes at night.   My Memory.   Monica Mansour [*or* Mansur].   MirDau, *tr. by* Maria Xirinachs

My memory is.   Charles Olson.   PFTM-2

My memory is short, and braine is dry.   Anne Bradstreet.   TCAPo *Fr.* Four Ages of Man, The.

My Message.   Cecil Rajendra.   PoetW

My Metaphors are but dull Tacklings tag'd.   Edward Taylor.   TCAPo *Fr.* Preparatory Meditations Before My Approach to the Lord's Supper.

My Mind.   Rāmprasād Sen.   SinGod, *tr. by* Rachel Fell McDermott

My mind is dazzled.   Shrine Priestess of Ise.   ArkPo, *tr. by* Robert H. Brower and Earl Miner

My mind is foolish.   Sŏ Kyŏngdŏk.   CATKP, *tr. by* Peter H. Lee

My mind is intact, but the shapes.   Robert Penn Warren.   NoAM *Fr.* Island of Summer.

My mind is sad and weary thinking how.   Odell.   James Stephens.   MoBrPo

My mind is worn out, my features grown sharp and gaunt.   Sitting at Night with My Nephew Who Has Just Come from Afar.   Su Tung-p'o.   TAL

My mind lets go a thousand things.   Memory.   Thomas Bailey Aldrich.   TCAPo

My Mind, my helmsman. Rāmprasād Sen. SinGod, *tr.* by Rachel Fell McDermott

My mind [*or* minde *or* mynde] to me a kingdom [*or* kyngdome] is. My Mind to Me a Kingdom Is. Sir Edward Dyer. WaAnP

My Mind to Me a Kingdom Is. Sir Edward Dyer. WaAnP
    (In Praise of a Contented Mind.) NAEL-6v1; NoSic
    (Sweet and pleasant Sonnet, entitled: My mind to me a kingdom is, A.) BASC

My mind to me mangles iron. An error is mirror to the truth. Stephen Rodefer. PmAP *Fr.* Plane Debris.

My mind was once the true survey. Mower's Song, The. Andrew Marvell. BASC; CtM; NAEL-6v1; NAEL-7v1; NOSC

My Mind's Got a Mind of Its Own. Butch Hancock. WhBo

My mission was to sell pottery from booth 109. Tradition and Change. Nora Naranjo-Morse. ReTh

My Mistress. *Unknown.* NOSC; OBCoV

My mistress' eyes are nothing like the sun. William Shakespeare. AEP; CABP; HeIP-4; NAEL-6v1; NAEL-7v1; NIL-7; NIP-4; NoP-5; NoSic; OxAEP-1; OxBEV; PoPoPo; SoSe-8; TFi; WaAnP; WeW-3 *Fr.* Sonnets.

My mistress in a hive of bees. *Unknown.* EroLit

My mistress loves no woodcocks. My Mistress. *Unknown.* NOSC; OBCoV

My Mistresse sayes she'll marry none but me. Catullus. OBVE

My moccasins are black obsidian. Song of the Black Bear, The. *Unknown.* RaBo

My Mocking Bird. Josephine D. Henderson Heard. CBWP-4

My mojito in La Bodeguita. My daiguiri in El Floridita. Drinking Mojitos in Cuba Libre. Harryette Mullen. RD

My monument is done, my task is ended. Epilogue. Miklós Zrínyi. IQMS, *tr.* by Michael Hatwell

My Moral Life. Mark Halliday. SUP

My mortar shell I remember well. My Hand is Extended for the Peace of the Galilee. Ramy Ditzanny. NRoS, *tr.* by Esther Raizen

My most respected / comrades of posterity! Vladimir Vladimirovich Mayakovsky. AF *Fr.* At the Top of My Voice.

My mother. That Jewish Crusader. Diana Anhalt. MirDau

My mother. My Mother's Friend. Lily Brett. HP

My Mother. Virginia Cerenio. ReBoTo

My Mother. Claude McKay. GT

My Mother. Claude McKay. OxAAAP

My Mother. Robert Mezey. GoPo; TaR

My Mother. William Bell Scott. GSo

My Mother. Jane Taylor. ITBLP

My Mother. John Wieners. BB

My Mother. John Wieners. PmAP

My mother and I debate. Black Walnut Tree, The. Mary Oliver. MakPoe

My Mother and I Had a Discussion One Day. Denise Sweet. ReEnLa

My Mother and My Sisters. Simon J. Ortiz. ICANM

My mother asks if I read about the sculptor. Caged Stone. Martha Vertreace. IllVoic

My mother at thirty was as luminous as a Puerto Rican dawn over the cream sand beaches. Old. Rosario Morales. PfS

My mother, blind from the swamp-gas. Some women marry houses. Sarah Messer. SweBea

My mother bore me in the southern wild. William Blake. AmFaPo; CABP; ChAP; HeIP-4; NAEL-6v2; NAEL-7v2; NAWM-7v2; NOBRP; NoP-4; NoP-5; OBEV; PoPoPo; TFi *Fr.* Songs of Innocence.

My mother can't recall the exact. You don't Know What Love Is. Ken Harris. AnSo

My Mother Cunning, Yet Innocent. Gloria Vando. TouFir

My Mother Dances a Ballad. István Sinka. IQMS, *tr.* by Adam Makkai

My Mother Dear. *Hawaiian Oral Tradition.* NAAPv.1

My mother did not have a garden. Mother. Nancy Morejón. TANSG, *tr.* by Joy Renjilian-Burgy

My Mother Didn't Learn. Leo Romero. ICANM

My mother died when I was already old. Moviola. Elena Clementelli. CItWP, *tr.* by Cinzia Sartini Blum and Lara Trubowitz

My mother disappeared in a shoddy. Cold River. Joan Larkin. WiU

My Mother Dressed for the Wedding. Stevie Krayer. Prnts

My mother dressed for the wedding. My Mother Dressed for the Wedding. Stevie Krayer. Prnts

My mother drives the goat. Pictures. Sarah Kirsch. AF, *tr.* by Wayne Kvam

My mother even hated. 1956, The Year My Sister, Using Her Ill Health Once Again, Blackmailed My Parents into an Accordion. Susan Firer. MiVo

My mother / feigned living. I Watched. Kimmika L. H. Williams. BtF

My mother forbad us to walk backwards. Short Talk on Walking Backwards. Anne Carson. OpeFie

My mother found herself one late summer. Diana Brandt. ACAMVP

My mother / gathers gladiolas: the little tubes. Arguments of Everlasting. Brigit Pegeen Kelly. PoDa

My mother gave me the prayer to Saint Theresa. What Every Woman Should Carry. Maura Dooley. NeBl; StAl

My mother groaned! [*or* groan'd! *or* groand!] my father wept. William Blake. IJHIL; NAEL-6v2; NAEL-7v2; NPBRoP; OxAEP-2; OxBEV; PoPoPo *Fr.* Songs of Experience.

My mother had no patio garden. Mother. Nancy Morejón. TCLAP, *tr.* by Kathleen Weaver

My mother had two faces and a frying pot. From the House of Yemanjá. Audre Lorde. NALW; NAMCP V.2; NoAM; NoP-4; NoP-5

My mother hands me the still form of a worker bee. Worker Bee, The. Allan Cooper. Coast

My Mother Has Forgotten My Name. Neeltje Maria Min. TuT, *tr.* by Peter van de Kamp

My mother has forgotten my name. My Mother Has Forgotten My Name. Neeltje Maria Min. TuT, *tr.* by Peter van de Kamp

My mother has gone and bought herself a piglet. Family. Vona Groarke. BeAl

My mother hated gesturing. My speech. Handnotes. Lyn Moir. Prnts

My mother hates her life. World in My Mother's Hair, The. Lisa Glatt. SUP

My mother hates the sea. Sea Chanty. Gregory Corso. BB

My mother held me by my hand. Dead Child Speaks, A. Nelly Sachs. HP; PoSu

My mother held us to her. My mother's house hold. Ingrid de Kok. TSAP

My mother, I cannot endure. Mother. Willem Elsschot. TuT, *tr.* by Peter van de Kamp

My Mother, If She Had Won Free Dance Lessons. Cornelius Eady. ISC

My mother in her Old World pose. In the New World. Florence Elon. ASA

My mother / In her youth it was a great. Sappho. SaLy, *tr.* by Diane Rayor

My Mother, in memoriam. Fadhil Assultani. IrPoTo, *tr.* by Melissa Brown and Saadi A. Simawe

My Mother in Old Age. Eric Ormsby. NIP-4

My Mother in Three Acts. Jane Cooper. ExTi

My mother is a. Natural High. Jean Binta Breeze. Prnts

My Mother is a God Fearing Woman. Cornelius Eady. ISC

My Mother is a whore without a dagger. Already Night, Already Day. Hedva Harechavi. DTA, *tr.* by Miriyam Glazer

My Mother is Alabama. My Mother. Melvin E. Lewis. BtF

My mother is casual when I ask. Cooking Lesson. Zarina Mullan Plath. SweBea

My mother is concerned that I haven't met a nice boy to settle down with. Ex-Boyfriends Named Michael. Justin Chin. WiU

My mother is here. Charles Simic. AF

My mother is sometimes a summer hotel with cheerful blue and. Vow. Nina Nyhart. PfS

My mother killed cats. Act of Mercy. Sarah Klassen. ACAMVP

My mother lay on her side to birth me. Coyotismo. Janice Gould. ReEnLa

My mother lies spread-eagle upon the bed. In My Mother's Room. Colleen J. McElroy. GT

My Mother, Life. John Godfrey. FTOS

My Mother, Listening to Flowers. Naomi Feigelson Chase. PfS

My mother lives here, I am told. Searching. Cathy Grindrod. Prnts

My mother lives in a house. My House. Robert Adamson. BMAP

My mother made Big Macs and beds. Making Ends Meet. Thomas Sayers Ellis. InTrad

My mother, Nettie, and her sister, Lelia. Sober Ghost. Michael Burkard. LaCa

My mother never forgave my father. Portrait, The. Stanley Kunitz. CAP-8; GoPo; InvLad; NAAPv.2; NAMCP V.1; PoCho; RaBo

My mother never gave me pomegranates. Persephone's Daughter. Anne MacLeod. EdScPo

My mother never heard of Freud. Nomenclature. Alan Dugan. BodElec

My mother never taught me sweeping. How I Learned to Sweep. Julia Alvarez. FFC; RA; SweBea

My Mother Once Told Me. Yehuda Amichai. WoPoe, *tr.* by Barbara Harshav and Benjamin Harshav

My mother once watched. San Francisco Sunrise. Diane Ackerman. UrbNat

My mother opened her eyes wide. Lesson of the Sugarcane, The. Judith Ortiz Cofer. TouFir

My mother peers. 1973. Reuben Jackson. GT

My mother phoning from far off. Breathing Exercises. Leonard Nathan. PBCAP

My mother recognized. Hiroshima Maiden. Lee Ann Roripaugh. AmWaPo

My mother, red-haired. At the Powwow. Cheryl Savageau. TWW

My mother said, "If just once more." Mother's Nerves. X. J. Kennedy. ChAP

My mother said later that, to the shovel operators, we must have looked like. Visiting the Site of One of the First Churches My Grandfather Pastored. T. Crunk. YaYoPo

My mother said, "Of course." Donald Hall. GoPo

My mother said what she thought. Discipline of Marriage, The. Chana Bloch. FaoP

My mother says I must not pass. Witch in the Glass, The. Sarah Morgan Bryan Piatt. NAAPv.1

My mother sent me into the swirling. Fool's Errand. Zachariah Wells. IFF

My mother sent us to the school. Shoemaker, The. *Unknown.* FaBoVe

My mother sings me a song. Russian Fables. Sarah Klassen. ACAMVP

My mother sold life insurance. Job. Erika Meitner. NevBe

My mother teaches me the fading skills. Things That Are Lost. Kerry Hardie. MoWP

My mother tells me she dreamed. Soloing. Philip Levine. OPRER

My mother, the sage of Aliceville, Alabama. Annie Pearl Smith Discovers Moonlight. Patricia Smith. GT; OtW; OxAAAP

My mother told me that after he left us. Father (Part 1). Harryette Mullen. OxAAAP; TiP2

My mother told me the story, and I believed it. Drowning, The. David Lehman. MAAN

My Mother Tongue. Gary Daniel. OGAHCP, *tr. by* Boadiba and Jack Hirschman

My mother took me because she couldn't. Madre Sofía. Alberto A. Ríos. NAAL-5; NAMCP V.2; NoAM

My mother tried to teach me how. Dinner. Laura Kasischke. SweBea

My mother used to say "Bury me with a band." Bury Me with a Band. Ofelia Zepeda. ReEnLa

My mother wants to know. Brown Circle. Louise Glück. CFP

My mother was a braid of black smoke. My Mother was a Braid. Charles Simic. MotU

My mother was a doe in another time. My Nightingale. Rose Ausländer. PoCho, *tr. by* Eavan Boland

My mother was a Florentine. Elizabeth Barrett Browning. NALW *Fr.* Aurora Leigh.

My mother was a romantic girl. Papa Love Baby. Stevie Smith. NALW

My mother was my midwife. Midwife. Judith Kazantzis. Prnts

My mother was not impressed with her beauty. Christmas Eve: My Mother Dressing. Toi Derricotte. BtF

My mother was one of the great mothers. Second Elegy. Aida Cartagena de Portalatin. TANSG, *tr. by* Emma Jane Robinett

My mother was sewing: pajamas for us, always. Sewing. Marianne Boruch. SweBea

My mother was telling me. Picture of My Mother. Meg Bateman. MoWP

My mother was very small. My Mother. Gabriela Mistral. TANSG, *tr. by* Maria Giachetti [*or* Jacketti]

My mother watches videos. Video Mama. Jack Ridl. SwNoth

My mother went to work each day. Nurse, The. Dorianne Laux. PoDa

My mother went with no more warning. Lost Woman, The. Patricia Beer. MoWP

My mother, when young, scrubbed laundry in a tub. In an Iridescent Time. Ruth Stone. MoAmPo; NALW; OxWW

My mother with her long, dangling earrings. Blazon. Dinah Berland. SUP

My Mother! With the angels now. Mrs. Louise B. Weston. Mary Weston Fordham. CBWP-2

My mother wore a cat-fur collar which she stroked until its sparks lit up the cellar. (LL) We Were So Poor. Charles Simic. MotU; StAl; VCAP

My Mother Would Be a Falconress. Robert Duncan. FTOS; OxBoAm; RaBo; WoPoe

My mother would drift away. (LL) Great Blue Heron, The. Carolyn Kizer. InoFa; InvLad; WaAnP

My mother writes from Trenton. My Mother. Robert Mezey. GoPo; TaR

My mother—preferring the strange to the tame. Intruder, The. Carolyn Kizer. CAP-8

My mother's an expert at one thing. Lullaby. Louise Glück. MoWP

My Mother's Body. Enid Shomer. NevBe

My Mother's Burial. Sean O Riordain. ModIr, *tr. by* Patrick Crotty

My Mother's Clothes. Pascale Petit. Prnts

My Mother's Friend. Lily Brett. HP

My Mother's Hands. Ellen M. Huntington Gates. ITBLP

My Mother's Hard Row to Hoe. Fred Chappell. InGu

My mother's house hold. Ingrid de Kok. TSAP

My mother's insomnia over at last. Chain, The. Maxine W. Kumin. TaR

My mother's kitchen was asleep. Entropy. Faith Shearin. SweBea

My Mother's Lips. C. K. Williams. EmeKit

My mother's maids [*or* maydes] when they did sew [*or* sowe] and spin [*or* spynne]. Sir Thomas Wyatt. NoSic *Fr.* Satires.

My mother's mother died. From My Mother's Home. Leah Goldberg. FIT, *tr. by* Robert Friend

My mother's mother, widowed very young. Find Work. Rhina P. Espaillat. PoA 2002

My mother's name was Mary. Mary's a Grand Old Name. George M. Cohan. NAAPv.2; ReLy

My mother's old leather handbag. Handbag. Ruth Fainlight. OPOU; StAl

My mother's phantom hovers here. Behind Bars, Sel. Fadwa Tuqan. AF, *tr. by* Hatem Hussaini

My Mother's Sabbath Days. Irena Klepfisz. TaR

My Mother's Skin. Pascale Petit. PoCu

My mother's uncle was physician to the Persian Shah. Eternal Present, The. Gabriel Preil. FIT, *tr. by* Robert Friend

My Mother's Voice. Mary E. Tucker. CBWP-1

My mother's voice scrapes the ocean floor. Dream of Birth, The. Judith Ortiz Cofer. PueRic

My Mother's Wedding. Boris Hristov. CSCBP, *tr. by* Georgi Belev and Lisa Sapinkopf

My Mother's Young Sister. Roy McFadden. PNI

My mountains, God has company in heaven. In High Places. Harriet Monroe. PoA 2002

My mouth doth water, and my breast doth swell. Sir Philip Sidney. NAEL-6v1; NAEL-7v1 *Fr.* Astrophil and Stella.

My mouth hovers across your breasts. Adrienne Rich. LW; NIL-7 *Fr.* Contradictions: Tracking Poems.

My mouth is on fire. Let it burn. (LL) Billie in Silk. Angela Jackson. ReTh; SeSe

My mouth is yours, devour it and be not afraid. *Unknown.* SLW, *tr. by* Marjolijn De Jager, Sayd Bahodin Majrouh and André Velter

My movable empire between Athens and Megara. Damastes (Also Known As Procrustes) Speaks. Zbigniew Herbert. PoSu, *tr. by* John Carpenter

My mudder, you follow Jesus. I Wish I Been Dere. *Unknown.* SSUS

My murderer is no thief. Ivan Venediktovich Elagin. TCRusP, *tr. by* John Glad

My Muse. Eugenio Montale. ItPo, *tr. by* Gayle Ridinger

My muse bad, *Bedford* write, and that was she. (LL) On Lucy, Countess of Bedford. Ben Jonson. BASC; NAEL-7v1; NOSC

My muse came up from the creek. Virginian Arcady. Anne Rouse. NeBl

My Muse had slept, and none had known[e] my mind[e]. (LL) Samuel Daniel. GSo; NoP-5; OBEV *Fr.* Sonnets to Delia.

My muse is distant: one could say. My Muse. Eugenio Montale. ItPo, *tr. by* Gayle Ridinger

My muse is in the sulks to-day. Knitting. Mary E. Tucker. CBWP-1

My muse now hap[p]y, lay thy self to rest. Mary Sidney Wroth, Countess of Montgomery. BASC; NAEL-7v1 *Fr.* Pamphilia to Amphilanthus.

My Muse, the Whore. Linda France. NeBl

My muse was imprisoned once. I Can No Longer Care for the Dying. Brenda J. Moossy. PoArWo

My Muse what ails this ardour. Sir Philip Sidney. *Fr.* Countesse of Pembroke's Arcadia, The.

My Mysterious Body. Rane Arroyo. BeDoSh

My Name. Daniel Berrigan. AF

My Name and I. Robert Graves. NoAM

My name is Antigone: I was buried alive. Opprobium. Rosario Ferré. TANSG

My Name Is Dimitri. John Ashbery. BodElec

My name is Fermin. Tobera. Jeff Tagami. OpBo

My name is George Nathaniel Curzon. *Various authors.* OBCoV *Fr.* Balliol Rhymes.

My name is Henri. Listen. It's morning. Work Song. Mark Levine. AmPoNex

My name is Isaac Woodard, my tale I'll tell you. Blinding of Isaac Woodard, The. Woody Guthrie. PWW2

My name is James A. Wright, and I was born. At the Executed Murderer's Grave. James Wright. VCAP

My name is Johnson. Madam's Past History. Langston Hughes. HHAm; NAMCP V.1; NoAM; SAmP

My name is Lila. Memories. Sishtla Uma-Maheswara Rao. HotL, *tr. by* V. Narayana Rao

My name is Lisa Jarnot and I am a terrorist. I can tell you how it happened to me. Girl Who Couldn't Be Loved, The. Lisa Jarnot. LegDan

My name is Michel. Anti-Foucault Poem, The. Sandra Nelson. SUP

My name is O'Kelly, I've heard the Revelly. Shillin' a Day. Rudyard Kipling. NAMCP V.1; NoAM

My name is Parrot, a bird [*or* byrd] of paradise. John Skelton. NoSic *Fr.* Speak [*or* Speke], Parrot.

My name is Shlomit. I was born in Afula, in Galilee. My Name is Shlomit. Shlomit Baytelman. MirDau, *tr. by* Elizabeth Horan

My name is Solomon Levi. Old Cracked Tune, An. Stanley Kunitz. LoL; TaR

My name is Stanford Barnes, I come from Nobleville town. State of Arkansas, The. *Unknown.* APN-2

My name isn't Lucius; I never grew up. Poem of the Praises, The. Albert Goldbarth. ViWalt

My name it is Nell, quite [*or* right] candid I tell. Nell Flaherty's Drake. *Unknown.* IrV

My name, my speech, my self I had forgot. Rudyard Kipling. InoFa *Fr.* Epitaphs of the War [1914–1918].

My name skimmed by the. Name, The. Mariella Bettarini. CItWP, *tr. by* Cinzia Sartini Blum and Lara Trubowitz

My name? Where am I coming from? Where am I going? A fusillade of question marks. (LL) Belfast Confetti. Ciaran Carson. NPeEn; PNI

My name's James, enlightenment's my game. Hi. William Kulik. BodElec

My Name's Not Rodriguez. Luis J. Rodriguez. BRtP

My name's Philip Marlowe, the chivalrous shamus. Raymond Chandler: The Big Sleep. Basil Ransome-Davies. OBCoV

My Native Costume. Martín Espada. TouFir

My native land is up there. At Gold Hill Monastery. Su Tung-p'o. NDACCP, *tr. by* Kenneth Rexroth

My nature singing in me is your nature singing. Singing & Doubling Together. A. R. Ammons. NoAM

My neck a toothsome feeding ground. vespered swarms had drunk of me before this new batman. D. A. Powell. FaoP

My Neighbor. Roque Dalton. AF, *tr. by* Richard Schaaf

My neighbor, a scientist and art-collector, telephones me in a. Burning of Paper instead of Children, The. Adrienne Rich. HarvBoo; VCAP

My neighbor brings me bottom fish. My Garden, My Daylight. Jorie Graham. AFaM

My neighbor cruises with a lug wrench on his lap. Going Postal. Paul Christensen. LiTh

My neighbor, drunk, stood on his lawn and yelled. Heat Lightning in a Time of Drought. Andrew Hudgins. CAP-8

My neighbor to the East has. Rain in the Aspens. Su Tung-p'o. NDACCP, *tr. by* Kenneth Rexroth

My neighbor used to come to our hut. Rwanda. Ai. CFP

My Neighborhood. Stuart Dybek. PBCAP

My neighborhood at dusk: boys swooping circles. Gentrification. Erika Meitner. RWB

My neighbor's almost ex-husband, an auto salesman with a different car. Late Summer Litany. Julie Moulds. AmPoNex

My neighbor's boy has lifted his father's shotgun and stolen. Snowy Egret. Bruce Weigl. UrbNat

My neighbors on the right. Next Door. Mei Yao Ch'en. NDACCP, *tr. by* Kenneth Rexroth

My neighbour, Mrs Fanshaw, is portly-plump and gay. Stately as a Galleon. Joyce Grenfell. OBCoV

My nerves my nerves I'm going mad. Girl Machine. Kenward Elmslie. AHA; NYP2

My New Angels. Sinéad Morrissey. MFPA

My new grad-school roommates and I are attending. Dear Derrida. David Kirby. BAP-01

My new house. Pei Di and Wang Wei. CCL1 *Fr.* Wheel River.

My new neighbors keep asking, are you. Settled In. Michael David Madonick. IllVoic

My new Province is a land of bamboo-groves. Eating Bamboo-Shoots. Po Chü-i. CCL1; OBVE, *tr. by* Arthur Waley

My New York Street Sings. Esther Shumyatsher. Prolet, *tr. by* Amelia Glaser

My newly rented home commands a view of the temple hall. Solitary Falcon above the Buddha Hall of the Monastery of Universal Purity, A. Mei Yao Ch'en. WoPoe, *tr. by* Jonathan Chaves

My next bite is my last. On the Venom Farm. Ruth Padel. EmeKit

My night awake. Muriel Rukeyser and Leif Sjoberg. AWTN *Fr.* Speed of Darkness, The.

My Night with Frederico García Lorca (As Told by Edouard Roditi). Jaime Manrique. WiU

My Nightingale. Rose Ausländer. PoCho, *tr. by* Eavan Boland

My nipples tick. Small Hotel, A. Selima Hill. NeBrP

My noble, lovely, little Peggy. Letter to the Honourable Lady Margaret Cavendish Holles-Harley, A. Matthew Prior. NoAM

My Noiseless Entourage. Charles Simic. CAP-8

My noontime nap. Issa. SoOfWa, *tr. by* Sam Hamill

My normal dwelling is the lungs of swine. Autobiography of a Lungworm. Roy Fuller. NoAM

My northern pines are good enough for me. Boston. Edwin Arlington Robinson. APN-2

My nose cuts the air. Life-Saving Medal. Philippe Soupault. PFTM-1

My nosegays are for Captives. Emily Dickinson. NCAP

My November Guest. Robert Frost. StAl

My Number. Sandra Alcosser. ExTi

My number is small. A hundred pounds of water. My Number. Sandra Alcosser. ExTi

My obsession. (LL) Documentary. Claribel Alegría. LoL; VCWP

My October Song. Yuri Suhl. Prolet, *tr. by* Amelia Glaser

My office has grown cold today. Poem to a Taoist Hermit on Quanjiao Mountain, A. Wei Ying-wu. CCL1, *tr. by* Witter Bynner

My old acquaintances the mice. Mice. Alexander Gerov. CSCBP, *tr. by* Georgi Belev and Lisa Sapinkopf

My old druid, winter. Heart. Dieter Weslowski. InvLad

My Old Flame. Sam Coslow. ReLy

My old flame, my wife! Old Flame, The. Robert Lowell. ItP; NoAM

My Old Friend Hospital. Julia Darling. PoCu

My old friend takes off from the Yellow Crane Tower. To See Meng Hao-Jan Off to Yang-Chou. Li Po. ChinPo, *tr. by* Ye Weilian [*or* Yeh Wei-lien *or* Wai-lim Yip]

My old home. Issa. EMJL, *tr. by* Haruo Shirane

My Old Kentucky Home. Stephen Collins Foster. APN-2

(My Old Kentucky Home.) FaBoA

My Old Letters. Horatius Bonar.

"Evening brings all home. For that we wait, The." SacPr

My old man. Charles Bukowski. CalPo; OxBoAm; PmAP

My old man used to take the dog. Beer. Milk. The Dog. My Old Man. Kim Addonizio. RoV

My old man's a white old man. Cross. Langston Hughes. ColAP; GT; HarvBoo; NAMCP V.1; NoP-4; NoP-5; SAmP; SoSe-8

My old man's ears. Buson. EH, *tr. by* Robert Hass

My Old Man's Small. Fĕng Mĕng-lung. ColAnChi; WoPoe *Fr.* Mountain Songs.

My old man's small, shriveled and shrunk. Fĕng Mĕng-lung. ColAnChi; WoPoe *Fr.* Mountain Songs.

My old men are dying. Boris Abramovich Slutsky. TCRusP, *tr. by* Daniel Weissbort

My Old Palette. Christopher Pearse Cranch. APN-1

My old thighs / How thin. Shiseki. ZenPo, *tr. by* Takashi Ikemoto and Lucien Stryk

My old time daddy. Lover's Return. Langston Hughes. SAmP

My old village lies. Issa. SoOfWa, *tr. by* Sam Hamill

My old Welsh neighbor over the way. Robin, The. John Greenleaf Whittier. OWoS

My oldest sister wears thick glasses. My Mother and My Sisters. Simon J. Ortiz. ICANM

My ole man took me to the fulton fish market. Knees of a Natural Man. Henry Dumas. GT; OxAAAP

My once dear love; hapless that I no more. Surrender, The. Henry King, Bishop of Chichester. NOSC

My One. Heather McHugh. BAP-01

My one blood-uncle laughs. Three Men in a Tent. Marilyn Nelson Waniek. ESEAA

My One Brother. Mary Dalton. OpeFie

My one puny hut leads right off to the slopes. Distant View from a Grass Hill. Gensei. WoPoe, *tr. by* Burton Watson

My Only Friends. Ebenezer Elliott. DiBP

My only love was dead. (LL) In the Mile End Road. Amy Levy. PEW; RACG; ViWPN

My Opinion. Charles, 6th Earl of Dorset Sackville. BASC

My Orcha'd in Lindèn Lea. William Barnes. FaBoVe; NPeEn; OxBEV

My orchid-me had need to keep in thrall. Botany. Dan Beachy-Quick. IAoNAP

My Other Life. Peter Serchuk. PoDa

My other self is floating above a crowd. Body Doubled. Lynne Cohen. PfS

My outspread hands. Rin Ishigaki. WoPoe, *tr. by* Naoshi Koriyama and Edward Lueders

My own Belovèd, who hast lifted me. Elizabeth Barrett Browning. CenSon *Fr.* Sonnets from the Portuguese.

My own darling. Eibhlin Dubh O'Connell. WoPoe *Fr.* Death of Art O'Leary, The.

My own dim life should teach me this. Alfred Tennyson. NAEL-6v2; NAEL-7v2 *Fr.* In Memoriam A. H. H.

My Own Epitaph. John Gay. InoFa; NIL-7; NIP-4; NPeEn; OxBEV

My Own Fate. Lionel Pigot Johnson. SacPr

My own flesh and blood—dear sister, dear Ismene. Antigone [Fagles Translation]. Sophocles. NAWM-5v1, *tr. by* Robert Fagles

My own heart let me have. More pity on. Nell Altizer. FFC *Fr.* ("Love Letters to Her Who Lives [Alas!] Away").

My Own Heart Let Me More Have Pity On. Gerard Manley Hopkins. MoBrPo; NoP-4; NoP-5

My Own Little Piece of Hollywood. James Harms. AmPoNex

My own Maria!—Ah my own—my own! Maniac, The (2). Mary Bryan. CenSon

My own mind is very hard to me. Carrying My Mind Around. *Tlingit Oral Tradition.* TCAPo

My Ox Duke. John Dyer. NPeEn

My ox is called. Ox. *Unknown.* SonAtl, *tr. by* F. Josephs and Silke Werner

My Pain. Yu Wang. CFP, *tr.* by Tang Chao

My pain is not a generation's pain. Pain, The. Sion Eirian. BBMWP, *tr.* by Robert Minhinnick

My pain[e], still smothered [*or* smother'd] in my grieved bre[a]st. Mary Sidney Wroth, Countess of Montgomery. NAEL-6v1; NAEL-7v1; NOSC; PEW *Fr.* Pamphilia to Amphilanthus.

My pal the struggling sculptor, poor as dirt. Conjurer's Honor. Joel Brouwer. RWB

My pale muse, night creature, maybe a vampire, my pale Medusa. Marketplace. Günter Eich. MotU, *tr.* by David Walker

My pants, the hue of fire, are slipping down my thighs. *Unknown.* SLW, *tr.* by Marjolijn De Jager, Sayd Bahodin Majrouh and André Velter

My Papa knows you, and he says you're a man who makes reading for / books. Miss Edith's Modest Request. Bret Harte. NOxBChV

My Papa's Waltz. Theodore Roethke. AmFaPo; APT-2; BeAl; BrAP; CAP-8; ClHu; ColAP; EMP; HeIP-4; NAAL-5; NAMCP V.1; NBLV; NIL-7; NIP-4; NoAM; NoP-4; NoP-5; NOxBChV; OxBoAm; PoPoPo; RaBo; TFi; TRP; WaAnP

My Parents. Stephen Spender. HarvBoo

My parents are old; my family is poor. *Unknown.* NAAPv.2

My parents felt those rumblings. Hongo Store 29 Miles Volcano Hilo, Hawaii, The. Garrett Kaoru Hongo. PoPoPo

My parents had teased that if I ever. James McMichael. GeoHom *Fr.* Each in a Place Apart.

My Parents, Know It Well. Carlos German Belli. TCLAP, *tr.* by Maureen Ahern and David Tipton

My parents, know it well. My Parents, Know It Well. Carlos German Belli. TCLAP, *tr.* by Maureen Ahern and David Tipton

My parents' papers lie round me. Protected Species. Susan Wicks. MFPA

My parents were fish. Digging in the Streets of Gold. Barry Seiler. UnSA

My parents were married the year. 1945. Leslie Ullman. ExTi

My parents were virgins. Vera Pavlova. CRWP *Fr.* Signs of Life.

My passion is full of seeds issuing secretly from heraclitus and nietzsche. Adonis. PFTM-2 *Fr.* Desire Moving Through the Maps of the Material.

My patent pardouns ye may see. Sir David Lyndsay. OBSV *Fr.* Ane Satire [*or* Satyre] of the Three [*or* Thrie] Estaitis.

My patron has truly opened up my eyes. What Really Goes on in the College of Cardinals. *Unknown.* CAGL, *tr.* by James J. Wilhelm

My Peggy is a young thing. Allan Ramsay. *Fr.* Gentle Shepherd, The.

My Pen. Tom Pickard. Oth

My pensive Public, wherefore look you sad? Playhouse Musings. James Smith. OxAEP-2

My pensive Sara! thy soft cheek reclined [*or* reclin'd]. Samuel Taylor Coleridge. NAEL-6v2; NAEL-7v2; NOBRP; NoP-4; NoP-5; NPBRoP; NPeEn *Fr.* Effusions.

My People. Langston Hughes. APT-2; NOxBChV; OxAAAP; TWF

My People. Else Lasker-Schüler. GTCP, *tr.* by Michael Hamburger

My People are destroyed for lack of Knowledge.—Hosea 4:6. Jones Very. ChIV-1

My people / pass through gardens untouched by the toxic pollen of lilies. My People. Kona Macphee. StAl

My perennial nest. (LL) Her breast is fit for pearls. Emily Dickinson. HeIP-4; PoBW

My perfume? *Unknown.* ColAnChi *Fr.* Midnight Songs.

My period had come for Prayer. Emily Dickinson. APN-2; BBASP

My personal revenge will be your children's. Revenge. Luis Enrique Mejía Godoy. BeAl, *tr.* by Dinah Livingstone

My Philosophy. Dan Nielsen. SUP

My Philosophy of Life. John Ashbery. BodElec; OxBoAm

My Phone Rings Endlessly. Ch'oe Sûngja. EcSo, *tr.* by Mickey Hong

My photograph already looks historic. Middle of a War, The. Roy Fuller. OBWP; PoWW

My Picture Left in Scotland. Ben Jonson. NAEL-6v1; NAEL-7v1; NPeEn; PtR

My Picture-Gallery. Walt Whitman. NAAL-3

My pictures blacken in their frames. Death of the Day. Walter Savage Landor. NoP-4

My Pietà. Thomas Heise. LegDan

My pilgrimage fail. (LL) For Life I Had Never Cared Greatly. Thomas Hardy. NAMCP V.1; NoAM

My place is on Cold Mountain. Han-shan (Cold Mountain). GifTon, *tr.* by Red Pine

My 'place of clear water'. Anahorish. Seamus Heaney. HarvBoo; PBCIP

My Plan. Marchette Chute. WHSW

My Playmate. John Greenleaf Whittier. APN-1

My pleasant home! where erst when sad and faint. Charles Lloyd. CenSon

My poem would eat nothing. Poem You Asked For, The. Larry Levis. CalPo; PBCAP

My poems are all jagged at the edges. Judgement. Meiling Jin. CFP

My poem's epic, and is meant to be. Lord Byron. BrAP *Fr.* Don Juan.

My poem's in the oven where it. Kris Hemensley. BMAP *Fr.* Mile from Poetry, A.

My poet, thou canst touch on all the notes. Elizabeth Barrett Browning. CenSon *Fr.* Sonnets from the Portuguese.

My Poetess' Eyes. Katherine Cottle. IaFF

My poetess is not blond, like the rest of the world. My Poetess' Eyes. Katherine Cottle. IaFF

My Poetry. Lajos Kassák. IQMS, *tr.* by Adam Makkai

My poetry is exacting a confession. Manifesto on Ars Poetica. Frank Mkalawile Chipasula. HBAPE; NAfrP; PML

My poetry will not be. Sandro Penna. CAGL, *tr.* by John McRae

My poor expecting Heart beats for thy Breast. To My Heavenly Charmer. Martha Sansom. LW

My poor old Chloe! gentle playfellow. On Trust. Caroline Anne Bowles Southey. DiBP

My Portion. Dániel Berzsenyi. IQMS, *tr.* by Peter Zollman

My Portion is Defeat—today. Emily Dickinson. APN-2; FaBoWar; OBWP; PCW

My Portuguese-bred aunt. Conversation Piece. Eunice De Souza. NAMCP V.2

My prayers have been answered, if they were prayers. I live. At Seventy-Five: Rereading an Old Book. Hayden Carruth. TAPaP

My precious heart, my handsome soldier son. To My Soldier Son. Zseni Várnai. IQMS, *tr.* by Peter Zollman

My Pretty Rose-Tree. William Blake. NAEL-6v2; NAEL-7v2; NOBRP; NPBRoP *Fr.* Songs of Experience.

My primary teachers o the Thirties. Primary Teachers. Alastair MacKie. EdScPo

My prime of youth is but a frost of cares. Tichborne's Elegy. Chidiock Tichborne. AmFaPo; HeIP-4; InoFa; NIL-7; NoP-4; NoP-5; NoSic; PoPoPo; TFi; WeW-3

(My prime of youth is but a froste of cares.) NPeEn; OxBEV; PBRV

My Psychic. James Kimbrell. LegDan

My pulse beats fire—my pericranium glows. William Tennant. NePenScot *Fr.* Anster Fair.

My pulses rushed, and, quick, to saddle! Meeting, the Departure, The. Johann Wolfgang von Goethe. STV, *tr.* by John Frederick Nims

My purpose here is to advance into. Residence at C———. Lisa Robertson. OpeFie

My Pushkin. Nathalie Quintane. YaTCFP, *tr.* by Mary Ann Caws

My Queen her sceptre did lay down. Regina. Mary Elizabeth Coleridge. NALW; PoBW

My Queen, the air has burst in flame. Hackney Coach, The. Endre Ady. IQMS, *tr.* by Anton N. Nyerges

My question eagerly did I renew. William Wordsworth. STuOW *Fr.* Resolution and Independence.

My quiet kin, must I affront you. Preliminary to Classroom Lecture. Josephine Miles. NoAM

My quietness has a man in it, he is transparent. In Memory of My Feelings. Frank O'Hara. APSN; ColAP; HarvBoo

My quirt dangles freely. Departing in Early Morning. Tu Mu. CrYelRi, *tr.* by Sam Hamill

My radios came at all hours, on different days. My Radios. Todd Swift. RWPCtW

My ragged cloak is streaked with mountain shadows. After Shih-te. Shih Shu. CSKM, *tr.* by James H. Sanford

My raincoat cleaned. And she will. (LL) Selecting a Reader. Ted Kooser. P180; PBCAP

My Ravine. Dan Chiasson. LegDan

My Real Dwelling. Ikkyu Sojun. ItP, *tr.* by John Stevens

My real name got lost in the letter. Subtraction Song. Sally Keith. LegDan

My reason for raising a cat was not to catch you. Mad Rout of the Rat, The. Yi Kyubo. CATKP, *tr.* by Kevin O'Rourke

My reckless race is run, green youth and pride be past,. Gloze Upon This Text, *Dominus iis opus habet*, A. George Gascoigne. ChIV-2

My religion makes no sense. Anne Carson. BodElec; OxBoAm; WoBe *Fr.* Truth About God, The.

My Required Tool. Justin Cain. MAAN

My resurrective verses shed people. Mantilla. Medbh McGuckian. NAMCP V.2

My Revolution. Rosario Morales. PueRic

My revolution is not starched and ironed. My Revolution. Rosario Morales. PueRic

My Rich Uncle, Whom I Only Met Three Times. Marge Piercy. UnSA

My Riches I Have Squandered. Spread with Honey. D. A. Powell. IAoNAP

My rifle cocked, in savage calm. Hunter's Song at Nightfall, The. Johann Wolfgang von Goethe. STV, *tr.* by John Frederick Nims

My Right Hand Don't Leave Me No More. Carter Revard. HATNAP

My Rights. Susan Coolidge. SWaP

My Ringless Fingers on the Steering Wheel Tell the Story. Laura Boss. UnSA

My Rival's House. Liz Lochhead. CFP; EdScPo; EmeKit

My robe hangs in the garden. Peter Levitt. WhBo

My rod is made of fine bamboo. Angling. *Unknown*. WoPoe, tr. by Nguyen Ngoc Bich

My Rodeo. Jack Grapes. SUP

My Romance. Lorenz Hart. ReLy

My Room. Marceline Desbordes-Valmore. WoPoe, tr. by Edmund Charles Blunden

My Room at Aunt Eura's, 1937. Wilma Elizabeth McDaniel. GeoHom

My room has two doors. Window, The. Kay Sage. SurWo

My room is at the far end of a courtyard and behind some shops. Visitation. Max Jacob. YaTCFP, tr. by Moishe Black and Maria Green

My room is blue, the carpet's blue. Blue Room, The. Richard Edwards. Spl

My room's a square and candle-lighted boat. Country Bedroom, The. Frances Darwin Cornford. MoBrPo

My roots are buried deep in Texas ground. Old Oak Speaks, The. Margaret Bell Houston. TiP2

My Rubaiyat. Sadakichi.
   12. NAAPv.1
   37. NAAPv.1
   42. NAAPv.1
   44. NAAPv.1
   46. NAAPv.1
   48. NAAPv.1
   52. NAAPv.1
   58. NAAPv.1

My Sad Captains. Thom Gunn. NAEL-6v2; NAEL-7v2; NAMCP V.2; NoAM; NoP-4; NoP-5; NPeEn; PoPoPo; WaAnP

My sad heart is burnt black in the fire. Figani Ramazan Çelebi. OLP, tr. by Walter Andrews, Najaat Black and Mehmet Kalpakli

My sad moon. Two Poems for My Son, Ali. Abdul Wahab Al-Bayati. IrPoTo, tr. by Carolina Hotchandani and Najat Rahman

My Sad Self. Allen Ginsberg. BrAP; VCAP

My sails by tempest riven. Kenless Strand, The. Sydney Goodsir Smith. WoPoe

My sanguine and adventurous dear. Samuel Hoffenstein. AmWit Fr. Love-songs, at Once Tender and Informative.

My saul and life stand up and see. Martin Luther. SacPr

My Savior, let me hear Thy voice tonight. I'll Follow Thee. Clara Ann Thompson. CBWP-2

My school work will twist a ribbon of the trans-canada into a gordian knot. Escapology. Ian Samuels. PoPra

My sculptor husband, when he *was* mine, possessed. Bride of Quietness, The. Kelly Cherry. FFC

My Sea Has One Island. Hong Yunsuk. CAMKP, tr. by Genell Y. Poitras

My Second Marriage to My First Husband. Alice Fulton. EmeKit

My secrets cry aloud. Open House. Theodore Roethke. NoAM

My senses are stirred. Kitahara Hakushū. CAoMJL1, tr. by Donald Keene

My seventh summer the Rosenbergs burned Sing Sing Prison. Out in the Cold. Ellen A. Rosen. PfS

My Shadow. W. Hodgson Burnett. UV

My Shadow. Robert Louis Stevenson. ChAP; ITBLP; ItP; UV

My shadow in waves. Ray McNiece. AmZen

My shadow spoke to me saying. What the Shadow Said in the Presence of the Poem. Abd al-Karim Kassid. IrPoTo, tr. by Chuck Miller and Saadi A. Simawe

My Shadow's Stature. John James Piatt. APN-2

My shared bedroom's window. Elegies for Paradise Valley. Robert Earl Hayden. NAMCP V.2

My Shattered Sister. Naomi Quinonez. FTtHH

My shattered phancy stole away from mee. Edward Taylor. NOSC Fr. Preparatory Meditations Before My Approach to the Lord's Supper.

My Sheep Are Thoughts. Sir Philip Sidney. NoSic Fr. Countess of Pembroke's Arcadia, The.

My sheep are thoughts, which I both guide and serve. Sir Philip Sidney. NoSic Fr. Countess of Pembroke's Arcadia, The.

My Shining Archipelago. Ansel Talvikki. NeAmPo

My Shining Hour. Johnny Mercer. ReLy

My Ship. Ira Gershwin. ReLy

My Ship Does Not Need a Helmsman. Alan Chong Lau. OpBo

My ship has sails that are made of silk. My Ship. Ira Gershwin. ReLy

My ship is sinking. Sunken Ship, The. Salma Khadra Jayyusi. PoArWo, tr. by Suneet Chopra

My ship laden with forgetfulness passes through a harsh sea, at. Petrarch. NAWM-7v1 Fr. Sonnets to Laura.

My shirt got torn to rags. Géza Páskándi. IQMS Fr. Language Memory.

My shirt is a token and symbol. Shirt. Carl Sandburg. CA

My shoelaces come untied. Pak Mogwŏl [or Mokwŏl]. CAMKP Fr. Nature of Gravel, The.

My Shoes. Charles Simic. EmeKit; OxBoAm; VCAP

My shoes are mulberry with dew. Prayers. Sadi. SonAtl, tr. by Roya Colandier and K. Young

My Shtetl on the Dnestr. Ber Grin. Prolet, tr. by Amelia Glaser

My sight's sharp as a sunflower. Alberto Caeiro. OpeFie Fr. Sheep's Vigil for a Fervent Person.

My silks and fine array. Song. William Blake. RACG

My sin! my sin, my God, these cursed dregs. Edward Taylor. NAAPv.1; TCAPo Fr. Preparatory Meditations Before My Approach to the Lord's Supper.

My sister. Sisters. Wendy Cope. ItWoWo

My sister and I. O That Summer. Ginger Andrews. SUP

My sister and I used to play this game called Red Hot. Red Hot. Laurie Anderson. OxWW

My sister and I've come out of the blizzard. Out of the Blizzard. Lesley-Anne Bourne. Coast

My sister, between us lie. To Rose. Roberta Hill. ReEnLa

My sister comes, quietly. Blanco. Gary Soto. GeoHom

My sister doesn't write poems. In Praise of My Sister. Wisława Szymborska. PoSu

(My sister does not write poems.) BLT

My sister got me the script. I couldn't. Sanctuary. Norman Dubie. BodElec

My sister in her well-tailored silk blouse hands me. Photos, The. Diane Wakoski. NIP-4

My Sister Laura. Spike Milligan. NTCP

My sister Laura's bigger than me. My Sister Laura. Spike Milligan. NTCP

My sister loved milkweed, flower and plant. Weed, The. Genevieve Taggard. APT-2

My sister, my child. Invitation to the Voyage. Charles Baudelaire. SxFrPo, tr. by James McGowan

My sister! my sweet sister! if a name. Epistle to Augusta. Lord Byron. NPBRoP

My sister picks up her daughters at the bus stop. Four Hours. Denise Duhamel. LiTh

My sister rises from our bed hours before dawn. Listen Carefully. Philip Levine. EmeKit

My sister rubs the doll's face in mud. Kid, The. Ai. GT; NoAM

My sister singing the Kyrie. Near Burning. Kathleen Peirce. PBCAP

My Sister, the Empress. Ileana Malancioui. ItWoWo, tr. by Dan Dutescu

My Sister's Jeans. Selima Hill. NeBrP

My Sisters, O My Sisters. May Sarton. NALW

My Sister's Sleep [rev. vers.]. Dante Gabriel Rossetti. NAEL-6v2; NAEL-7v2

My sisters, tie your veils around like waistbands. *Unknown*. SLW, tr. by Marjolijn De Jager, Sayd Bahodin Majrouh and André Velter

My Sixth Grade Sex Life: Milne Elementary, New Orleans. Brad Richard. BeDoSh

My sixty-year-old 'forty-year-old' sister. My Sister's Jeans. Selima Hill. NeBrP

My skin is pumiced to a fault. Fado Singer. Wole Soyinka. HBAPE

My skin is white, but my name is foreign, a dark inflection. Jewish. Harvey M. Plotnick. OPRER

My skin shimmers with all the colours. Charles Hadfield. NewEx

My sleek, smooth machine's lying in a drift. After Snow-Mobiling. Alec Bond. VisFro

My Sleeping Husband. Nzadi Z. Keita. BtF

My small, my beautiful land, all of a summer. All of a Summer. Jakov Steinberg. FIT, tr. by Robert Friend

My smalltown bell. Fernando Pessoa. SonAtl, tr. by Becca, Lester Browne, Audrey Cooper, Celia Martin and Patti Oliver

My smile mocked your speed. Lame Boy Returns, The. Juan Delgado. TouFir

My snout chews the field like a prow. Riddle. *Unknown*. SonAtl

My Sodger Laddie. *Unknown*. FaBoWar

My Son. Yehuda Amichai. WoPoe, tr. by Barbara Harshav and Benjamin Harshav

My son always asks this question. Birth Postponed, A. Mailabattula Satish Chandar. HotL, tr. by V. Narayana Rao

My son, come pierce my soul with a sword. Ballad of the Scarecrow Christ. Elder Olson. ChIV-2

My son had a hard time learning the concept of shadow. At first, to him. Shadow. Josip Novakovich. BAP-97

My son has birds in his head. Daedalus. Alastair Reid. WaAnP

My son his hands unsteady. New Blade. Anzai Hitoshi. PML, tr. by Leith Morton

My son, / I guess there lives a god. To My Son. Mun Chônghui. EcSo, tr. by Catherine J. Kim

My Son, Let Me Grasp Your Hand. *Arapaho Oral Tradition.* NAAPv.2

My Son, My Executioner. Donald Hall. LoL; TRP

My son / she saids. Homemade Smiles. Jose Angel Figueroa. PueRic

My Son Shows Me a Photograph of Michael Jordan Performing a Slam Dunk. Louis Phillips. ReTh

My son Siôen of Anglesey, I am without flattery. To Siôn Lloyd: the Mother's Advice to Her Heir. Catherin Owen Llwyd. EMWP

My son smells of peace when I lean over him. Two Songs of Peace. Yehuda Amichai. AF, *tr. by* Assia Gutmann

My son squats in the snow in his blue snowsuit. Illuminations. Louise Glück. HarvBoo; NALW

My son swings from black railings. Sean Dunne. ModIr *Fr.* Sydney Place.

My son tells his aunt. San Diego Poem, A: January-February 1973. Simon J. Ortiz. OtW

My son, trenches dug deep by my hands. When You Grow Up. Anadad Eldan. NRoS, *tr. by* Esther Raizen

My son was killed while laughing at some jest. I would I knew. Rudyard Kipling. NPeEn; PoAgWa *Fr.* Epitaphs of the War [1914–1918].

My son, you are a sweet bitter shadow. On Your Twenty-First Birthday. Joan Austin Geier. FFC

My son, you loved telling the story of Prince Nata. T'ang Hsien-tsu. ColAnChi *Fr.* Twenty-two Quatrains on Receiving the Obituary Notice for my Son Shih-Chü.

My Song is for All Men. Peter Blackman.
  "Sometimes all night I kept vigil with men stripped of their flesh." RSaN

My song will rest while I rest. I struggle along. I'll get back to the corn and the open fields. Evening Song. Sherwood Anderson. PoA 2002

My Son's Wedding, My Daughter's. Barbara Hurd. NevBe

My sorrow, deep sorrow, incessant returning. Metrical Translation of the Song of Macgregor Na Ruara. Anne Grant. RWP

My sorrow, when she's here with me. My November Guest. Robert Frost. StAl

My soul doth magnify the Lord,. Song of the Virgin Mary, The. Miles Coverdale. ChIV-2

My soul doth pant towards thee. Prayer, A. Jeremy Taylor. SacPr

My soul from the nethermost Hell! (LL) Wilderspin. Mary Elizabeth Coleridge. ViWPN; VWP

My soul grieved seven times: the first time when it tried to attain. Seven Stages, The. Kahlil Gibran. BBASP, *tr. by* Michael Beard and Adnan Haydar

My soul has grown deep like the rivers. (LL) Negro Speaks of Rivers, The. Langston Hughes. APT-2; BLPJKO; ColAP; CtM; HarvBoo; HeIP-4; ISC; NAAL-5; NAAPv.2; NAMCP V.1; NIL-7; NIP-4; NoAM; NoP-4; NoP-5; OxAAAP; RaBo; SSLK; TCAPo; TFi; WaAnP; WeW-3

My soul is a castle, ancient, known to be haunted. Lady of the White Castle, The. Endre Ady. IQMS, *tr. by* Dermot Spence and Paul Tabori

My soul is a dark ploughed field. Broken Field, The. Sara Teasdale. APT-1

My soul is all things. Ladies of Dimbaza, The. Carole Boston Weatherford. FiBr

My soul is awakened, my spirit is soaring. Anne Brontë. VWP

My soul is clanging like a cimbalom gone mad. Reply to Petőfi. János Arany. IQMS, *tr. by* Madeline Mason

My soul is hard as stone. I slept with the wind. Crust on Fresh Snow. Rolf Jacobsen. WoPoe, *tr. by* Olav Grinde

My soul is like a kite. Kite, The. Olga Sulchinskaya. CRWP, *tr. by* Richard McKane

My Soul is like to a little painful Bee. Spiritual Meditation upon a Bee, A. Amey Hayward. EMWP

My soul is not at rest. There comes a strange. Nathan Brown. SacPr

My soul looked down from a vague height, with Death. Show, The. Wilfred Owen. MoBrPo; OBWVE; OxBEV

My soul looks over the courtyard. Early in the morning. Jules Supervielle. MFP, *tr. by* Martin Sorrell

My soul parted from me last night. Elegy on Mael Mhedha, his Wife. Muireadhach Albanach Ó Dálaigh. NePenScot, *tr. by* Thomas Owen Clancy

My Soul Sinks. Hayyim Nahman Bialik. FIT, *tr. by* Robert Friend

My Soul, Sit Thou a Patient Looker-on. Francis Quarles. NIP-4

My Soul, there is a country [*or* countrie]. Peace. Henry Vaughan. FSCP; OBEV; OxAEP-1; OxBEV; RSR; TFi; WeW-3

My soul was created from matter. Matter. Nedelcho Ganev. CSCBP, *tr. by* Georgi Belev and Lisa Sapinkopf

My soul was mantled with dark shadows, born. Despondency and Aspiration. Felicia Dorothea Hemans. RWP

My soul would sing of metamorphoses. Ovid. NAWM-7v1 *Fr.* Metamorphoses.

My soul yearns for you. *Unknown.* NaPG, *tr. by* Talat Sait Halman

My soul[e] I'll [*or* Ile] pour[e] into thee. (LL) Night-Piece, to Julia, The. Robert Herrick. NAEL-6v1; NAEL-7v1; NoP-4; NoP-5; NOSC; OBEV; TFi

My soul's an atom in the world of mind. Metaphysical Sonnet. Charles Lloyd. CenSon

My Soul's Wardrobe. Sharon Dolin. PoCoUp

My spading fork turning the earth turns. Earthworm. Robert Francis. APT-2

My Spanish isn't enough. Elena. Pat Mora. NIL-7; UnSA

My Special Friend (Is Back in Town). Andy Razaf. ReLy

My Special Madness. Rikki Ducornet. SurWo

My special madness. My Special Madness. Rikki Ducornet. SurWo

My spirit and flesh, parting now. At the End. Richard Ryan. PBCIP

My spirit is too weak—mortality. On Seeing the Elgin Marbles. John Keats. CenSon; GSo; NAEL-6v2; NAEL-7v2; NIL-7; NIP-4

My Spirit Longeth for Thee. John Byrom. SacPr (Desiderium.) OxAEP-1

My spirit longeth for Thee. My Spirit Longeth for Thee. John Byrom. SacPr

My spirit to yours dear brother. To Him That Was Crucified. Walt Whitman. ChIV-2

My Spirit Will Not Haunt the Mound. Thomas Hardy. FaBoVe; MoBrPo

My Spirit's Complement. Henrietta Cordelia Ray. CBWP-3

My Spiritual State. Mirza Asadullah Khan Ghalib. WED, *tr. by* Robert Bly and Sunil Dutta

My spotless[e] love ho[o]vers, with purest wings. Samuel Daniel. OBEV *Fr.* Sonnets to Delia.

My spring is just this. Issa. SoOfWa, *tr. by* Sam Hamill

My Stars. Abraham ibn Ezra. WoPoe, *tr. by* Robert Mezey

My Statues. Henri Michaux. YaTCFP, *tr. by* Mary Ann Caws and Patricia Terry

My stepdaughter and I circle round and round. Loud Music. Stephen Dobyns. P180

My steps along this street. Here. Octavio Paz. TCLAP, *tr. by* Charles Tomlinson

My steps lead me to a junction of three roads. Juan Chi. ColAnChi *Fr.* Songs of My Soul.

My steps led me here, and so I circle the pond. Playing at Jeoksun Pond on a Moonlit Night. Master Naong. BecRai, *tr. by* Kim Daljin, Kim Won-Chung and Christopher Merrill

My stick fingers click with a snicker. Player Piano. John Updike. WeW-3

My stock has gone down and my tailor has sent. Companion's Progress, A. Paul Laurence Dunbar. GT

My stock lies dead, and no increase. Grace. George Herbert. ChIV-1

My Story. Carla Harryman. PmAP

My story is much too sad to be told. Cole Porter. *See* Until the day.

My Strawberry. Helen Hunt Jackson. SWaP

My streetlamp is so glacially alone in the night. Light Pole. Rolf Jacobsen. WED, *tr. by* Robert Bly

My strength plucked up the hills. Hegemon's Lament, The. Hsiang Chi. CCL1, *tr. by* Burton Watson

My student says he wrote a poem. Office Hour. Carol Lem. GeoHom

My Students. Ron Koertge. IaFF

My Students against the Cemetery Pines. Keith Ratzlaff. ACAMVP

My students look at me expectantly. Mountain, The. Louise Glück. NoAM

My Study. Edward Palmer Thompson. RSaN

My suite is just, just lord to my suite hark. Bible, *O.T.* OBVE

My summer robes. Basho. EH, *tr. by* Robert Hass

My sun has gone down in drum suite penumbra. Umbra. Lloyd Addison. EGAG

My supermarket is bigger than your supermarket. That's. Supermarket. Peter Meinke. PBCAP

My Susanna. Anne Portugal. SCFWP *Fr.* Bath, The.

My sweet, beloved companion. Litany. Margit Kaffka. IQMS, *tr. by* Paul Tabori

My sweet old etcetera. E. E. Cummings. HeIP-4; NAMCP V.1; OBWP; PoAgWa

My sweetest Dorothy, said John. Dorothy's Dower. Phoebe Cary. NAAPv.1

My sweetest Lesbia let us live and love. My Sweetest Lesbia. Catullus. BrAP; NoP-5; WaAnP, *tr. by* Thomas Campion

My sweetest Lesbia, let us live and love. Catullus. *See* Lesbia / live with me.

My Sweetest Lesbia [Let Us Live and Love]. Catullus. *See* Carmen 5.

My sweet-faced, tattle-tale brother was born blind. Twins, The. Mona Van Duyn. VCAP

My swirling wants. Your frozen lips. Valediction Forbidding Mourning, A. Adrienne Rich. BrAP; NAAL-5; NAMCP V.2; NoAM; NoP-4; NoP-5; OxBoAm; WaAnP

My sword at my waist, I climb a high tower. Li Po. ColAnChi *Fr.* Poems in an Old Style.

My symptoms have become bizarre. As the silver liquid is drained from my. Dear, I Love. Todd Colby. HeMarv

My : T. Ernst Jandl. OnScMo, *tr. by* Craig Watson

My tailor is against parting. Against Parting. Natan Zach. HP; PoSu

My tamed predator, so old now.   This Is for Megan.   Polly Brown.   PfS

My Taste for Trash.   Chase Twichell.   ExTi

My taste in women, Flaccus? Give me one.   Martial.   RomPo, tr. by Peter Whigham

My Tattoo.   Mark Doty.   WiU

My tea is nearly ready and the sun has left the sky.   Lamplighter, The.   Robert Louis Stevenson.   ITBLP; NePenScot

My teachers are dead men. I was too young.   Autopsy.   Arthur Nortje.   HBAPE

My tears became desire that illuminates.   Na'ili [or Yeni-Zada Mustafa Efendi].   OLP, tr. by Walter Andrews, Najaat Black and Mehmet Kalpakli

My teeth have ripped out cubes of laughter.   Festivals.   Annie Le Brun.   YaTCFP, tr. by Mary Ann Caws

My temples covered all in white, I'm.   Scolding My Sons.   T'ao Ch'ien.   PoChi, tr. by David Hinton

My temples throb, my pulses boil.   To Minerva.   Thomas Hood.   NBLV

My Tenth Birthday.   Robert Adamson.   BMAP

My Terrorist Notebook.   Lisa Jarnot.   Eno

My Test Market.   Rachel Loden.   CalPo; PoDa; VisFro

My thatched hut.   Muso Soseki.   EaWin, tr. by W. S. Merwin

My thatched hut's plenty.   Reclusive.   Wang Fan-chih.   CrYelRi, tr. by Sam Hamill

My Thatched Roof Is Ruined by the Autumn Wind.   Tu Fu [or Du Fu].   CCL1, tr. by Stephen Owen

My thinning hair.   Issa.   IllVoic Fr. Issa: A Suite of Haiku.

My thoughts are perfumed when toward you they turn.   Autumn Verses.   Rubén Darío.   SpanPo, tr. by Kate Flores

My thoughts are with a boat.   Kakinomoto no Hitomaro.   TAL

My thoughts go back to a heavenly dance.   Song Is Ended (But the Melody Lingers On), The.   Irving Berlin.   ReLy

My thoughts hold mortal[l] strife.   Madrigal.   William Drummond of Hawthornden.   NOSC

My thoughts, like sailors becalmed in Cape Town harbor.   Sailor's Harbor.   Henry Reed.   MoBrPo

My thoughts, my grief! are without strength.   Poem Written in Time of Trouble by an Irish Priest Who Had Taken Orders in France, A.   Unknown.   OBMV, tr. by Augusta, Lady Gregory

My thoughts of you always involve something trivial.   Happy Letter, A.   Hwang Tonggyu.   CAMKP, tr. by Anthony, Brother of Taizé

My thoughts the guests, which would thereon have fed. (LL)   Edmund Spenser.   NIP-4; OxBSo Fr. Amoretti.

My thoughts turn faithfully to my cigarette.   Cigarette.   Kim Sowŏl.   CAMKP, tr. by David R. McCann

My thoughts turn south.   White City, A.   James Schuyler.   OxBoAm

My three sisters are sitting.   Women.   Adrienne Rich.   TRP

My throats / a hungry saxophone.   Ohnedaruth.   Angela Jackson.   SeSe

My Tibetanness.   PML

My time he said was not my own.   Private But Sulphurous.   Tom Matthews.   PNI

My Times Are in Thy Hand.   Anna L. Waring.   SacPr

My Toilette, Patches, all the World, Adieu! (LL)   Lady Mary Wortley Montagu.   BrAP; NoP-5 Fr. Six Town Eclogues.

My tongue is a pink fire.   Word is an Egg, The.   Niyi Osundare.   NAfrP

My Tongue Paints a Path.   Eugene B. Redmond.   ISC

My tongue paints a path of fire.   My Tongue Paints a Path.   Eugene B. Redmond.   ISC

"My towers at last!"   Herman Melville.   Conrad Potter Aiken.   NoAM

My Train.   Barbara Ras.   NAPBL

My Treasure.   John Oxenham.   SacPr

My tree stands somewhere in the world.   Mail.   Sarah Kirsch.   MotU, tr. by Peter Spycher

My trewest tresowre sa trayturly was taken.   Song of the Passion, A.   Richard Rolle of Hampole.   SacPr

My trip begins.   My Trip.   Adam David Miller.   FuFl

My Trip in a Dream to the Lady of Heaven Mountain A Farewell to Several Gentlemen of Eastern Lu.   Li Po.   CCL1, tr. by Elling O. Eide

My Triumph.   John Greenleaf Whittier.   APN-1

My Triumph lasted till the Drums.   Emily Dickinson.   APN-2; BrAP; OBWP; PoAgWa

My Trouble.   Diane Wakoski.   NALW

My trouble is.   Packrat.   Naomi Long Madgett.   FuFl

My trouble / is that I have the spirit of Gertrude Stein.   My Trouble.   Diane Wakoski.   NALW

My True Love Hath My Heart.   Naomi Mitchison.   LW

My true love hath my heart and I have hers.   Strugnell's Bargain.   Wendy Cope.   UV

My true love hath my heart [or hart], and I have his.   Sir Philip Sidney.   NoSic; NPeEn; OxBEV; PtR; TFi; UV Fr. Countesse of Pembroke's Arcadia, The.

My True Love Hath My Heart and I Have His.   Patricia Stockbridge.   UV

My Turn.   Glyn Maxwell.   NeBrP

My TV Came down with a Chill.   Willard R. Espy.   TLR

My Twentieth Century.   Claudia Keelan.   RoV

My twentieth summer I got a job in Door Locks.   Assembler.   Debra Allbery.   PBCAP

My twin brother swears that at age thirteen.   Old Testament, The.   Philip Levine.   TaR

My twin, the nameless one, wild in the woods.   John Berryman.   HarvBoo Fr. Dream Songs.

My two friends, the love of one's two sons is not heresy, so surely you will both establish my innocence concerning the matter.   'Alī ibn 'Aṭiyya Abū l-Hasan al-Bulughghīnī al-Mursī Ibn az-Zaqqāq.   HiArP, tr. by James T. Monroe

My Two Lives.   Ernest Sandeen.   PoA 2002

My two-score years and ten are over.   On the Voyage to Jerusalem.   Judah Ha-Levi. tr. by Emma Lazarus

My Uma has come!   Kamalākānta Bhattācārya.   SinGod, tr. by Rachel Fell McDermott

My uncle always insisted.   Always Throw the First Punch.   Miguel Algarin.   PueRic

My uncle is buried at Sheik Bad'r.   Luxury.   Yehuda Amichai.   PoSu, tr. by Assia Gutmann

My Uncle Is My Honor and a Guest in My House.   Etheridge Knight.   BodElec

My uncle likes me too much.   Gwendolyn Brooks.   ESEAA Fr. Children Going Home.

My uncle made chairs, tables, balanced doors on, dug out.   Ogun.   Edward Kamau Brathwaite.   NAMCP V.2

My uncle said, "This is Elijah's wine."   On the Eve of the Warsaw Uprising.   Robin Becker.   TaR

My Uncle the Levitator.   Rafael Pérez Estrada.   PML, tr. by Steven J. Stewart

My uncle was a ranger.   Frontier Mystery.   Berta Hart Nance.   TiP2

My uncle was going overseas.   Lawson Fusao Inada.   AmWaPo Fr. Legends from Camp.

My Uncruel April, My Totally Equal Unfortold April Unfolded.   Lee Ann Brown.   VaPo

My Version.   Kit Wright.   NoP-5

My very own queen, my everything.   Muhibbi.   NaPG, tr. by Talat Sait Halman

My victory, my triumph, my memory, my fabulous.   King with His Queen, The.   Monica Ferrell.   IIR

My village / Dragonflies.   Buson.   ZenPo, tr. by Takashi Ikemoto and Lucien Stryk

My violin is out of shape. The tunes don't come forth well.   For Gwendolyn Brooks: As I Civilize a Space.   Dolores Kendrick.   FuFl

My virgin womb ha'e met. (LL)   O Wha's the Bride?   Hugh MacDiarmid.   NAMCP V.1; OxBEV; RaBo

My Voice.   Rafael Campo.   AmPoNex

My voice drifts to the ceiling, like a stream of incense, filling.   I'll Never Know No Sunday in This Weekday Room.   Sabah As-Sabah.   InTrad

My Voice Faithful as a Shadow.   Tedi López Mills.   RMCMP, tr. by Esther Allen

My voice is sweeter than the lute.   Siren, The.   Violet Fane.   VWP

My Voice Not Being Proud.   Louise Bogan.   APT-2

My voice rings down through thousands of years.   Sappho's Reply.   Rita Mae Brown.   OxWW

My voice to thee it self extreamly strayning.   Bible, O.T.   PBRV Fr. Psalms.

My voice went on, its tones varying.   Dramatis Personae.   Pura López Colomé.   RMCMP, tr. by Forrest Gander

My waist her swallows it's a key that's bent my.   Glorious.   Marla Jernigan.   AnSo

My Wales?   Gerwyn Williams.   BBMWP, tr. by the author and Richard Poole

My walls outside must have some flowers.   Truly Great.   W. H. Davies.   OBMV

My war pits sleep's enthrallments.   Quality of Striving, The.   Chase Twichell.   WANABP

My wardrobe door will not stay closed these days.   Presence, The.   Medbh McGuckian.   PNI

My watch tells me the time in Calcutta.   Modern Times.   Fergus Allen.   NIrP

My Way.   Kim Koengp'il.   CATKP, tr. by Chi-gyu Kim [or Kim Chonggil]

My Way.   Liz Lochhead.   BeAl

My way is from woe to wonder.   Near-Johannesburg Boy, The.   Gwendolyn Brooks.   ESEAA; FuFl; IllVoic

My way is in the sand flowing [Author's own English vers. of his "Je suis ce cours de sable qui glisse"].   Samuel Beckett.   ModIr; YaTCFP, tr. by the author

My weary bosom fill. (LL)   Maids, not to you my mind doth change.   Michael Field.   NAEL-7v2; ViWPN; VWP

My weary eyes shall close like folding flowers in sleep. (LL)   Columbine, The.   Jones Very.   ColAP; GSo; WaAnP

My wedding-ring lies in a basket.   Wedding-Ring.   Denise Levertov.   CAP-8; NIL-7

My Welsh Home.   John Morgan.   AngWePo

My Wheel and I.   Alberto A. Bennett.   ArBi

My whining lover, what needs all.   Against Absence.   Sir John Suckling.   CavPo

My white canoe, like the silvery air.   Camp of Souls, The.   Isabella Valancy Crawford.   BrAP

My white coat waits in the corner.   Talking to the Family.   John A. Stone.   BloBone

My white mare on the Punjabi plains, the stamp of her hooves.   Ghazal 5.   Kuldip Gill.   IFF

My whole eye was sunset red.   Eye and Tooth.   Robert Lowell.   CAP-8

My whole family has died.   All That Really Happens.   Joe Wenderoth.   BodElec

My whole life has led me here.   Woolworth's.   Donald Hall.   ItP; OBCoV

My whole life long? (LL)   Night Song at Amalfi.   Sara Teasdale.   APT-1; MakPoe; MoAmPo

My whole mouth, all of it, is yours.   Unknown.   SLW, tr. by Marjolijn De Jager, Sayd Bahodin Majrouh and André Velter

My Wicked Wicked Ways.   Sandra Cisneros.   ItWoWo; WaAnP

My / wide eyes watch.   Unknown.   SonAtl, tr. by Ed Allison, Wilson Berra and M. Veya

My wife, a psychiatrist, sleeps.   Why Do Poets Write?   TAPaP

My Wife and Children.   Jaan Kaplinski.   BLT

My wife and children were waiting for ice cream.   My Wife and Children.   Jaan Kaplinski.   BLT

My wife and I lived all alone.   Ballad of the Despairing Husband.   Robert Creeley.   RaBo

My wife asks.   Father's Day.   E. Ethelbert Miller.   OxAAAP

My wife has left me. the child.   Specimen.   Christopher Pilling.   NLP

My wife I sing from the other shore.   My Wife I Sing.   André Velter.   YaTCFP, tr. by Rosemary Lloyd

My wife is always knitting, knitting.   Stitches.   Takahashi Shinkichi.   ZenPo, tr. by Takashi Ikemoto and Lucien Stryk

My wife is ill!   Thomas Jefferson.   Lorine Niedecker.   HarvBoo; NAMCP V.1

My wife is left-handed.   For Hettie.   Imamu Amiri Baraka.   GT

My wife left me, taking the two kids.   Hungry.   Luis J. Rodriguez.   FTtHH

My wife pokes fun at the way I say pencil and Pennsylvania.   Ohio River Region.   Terrance Hayes.   RD

My wife said something.   Something Nice.   Jack Forbes.   FTtHH

My wife stays home and stares at the amaryllis.   Deep Ecology.   Michael C. Blumenthal.   PfSP

My wife, who has perfect recall, won't sleep with me.   Perfect Recall.   Jack Myers.   SUP

My wife whose hair is a brush fire.   Free Union.   André Breton.   PFTM-1

My wife's therapist is explaining how counterproductive anger is.   My Wife's Therapist.   Angelo Verga.   PoDa

My will.   Erin Mouré.   NLPA Fr. Wittgenstein Letters to Mel Gibson's Braveheart, The.

My window, barely attached by its butterfly hinge.   Matinée Idylls.   Molly Bendall.   AmPoNex

My window, framed in pear-tree bloom.   Villeggiature.   Edith Nesbit.   LW; PEW

My window shook all night in Camden Town.   Responsibilities.   Anthony Cronin.   PBCIP

My window, window.   Window, The.   Enrique Gonzáles Martínez.   TCLAP, tr. by Elizabeth Gordon

My windows are sprayed by the tide.   Beach House.   Stanley Noyes.   ICANM

My windows now are giant drops of dew.   Bright Day, A.   W. H. Davies.   OBWVE

My windows open to the autumn night.   Cadgwith.   Lionel Pigot Johnson.   SacPr

My wine you drink, my bread you snap. (LL)   This Bread I Break.   Dylan Thomas.   ChIV-2; GI; TRP

My Wish for My Land.   Randolph Stow.   NOBAu

My wish for my land is that ladies be beautiful.   My Wish for My Land.   Randolph Stow.   NOBAu

My woman says she'd rather have me.   Catullus.   ErotSp, tr. by Sam Hamill

My woman says there is no one whom she'd rather marry.   Catullus.   NAWM-7v1 Fr. Carmina [Charles Martin Translation].

My woman used to tell me.   Texas Corrido.   Unknown.   NAAPv.2

My Woman's Transparence.   Amina Saïd.   HAWP; NAfrP, tr. by Eric Sellin

My woman's transparence.   My Woman's Transparence.   Amina Saïd.   HAWP; NAfrP, tr. by Eric Sellin

My womb was sealed.   Nanny.   Lorna Goodison.   NAMCP V.2

My wont is not to write in verse.   Imprisoned Recusant Writes to His Wife, An.   Francis Tregian.   NoSic

My words are the poor footmen of your pride.   Full Orchestra.   Kenneth Slessor.   OxBSo

My work done, I lean on the window-sill.   Charles Reznikoff.   APT-2; NAAPv.2

My work is done.   Angel.   John Henry, Cardinal Newman.   SacPr

My world has been laid low, and the wind blows.   Quatrain without Sparrows, Helpful Bells or Hope.   Thomas McCarthy.   PBCIP

My Worst Fear.   Cyn Zarco.   ReBoTo

My Worst Nightmare.   Kate Light.   AmPoNex

My worst nightmare was to be the couple.   My Worst Nightmare.   Kate Light.   AmPoNex

My worthy [or woorthy] Lord, I pray you wonder not.   Gascoigne's Woodmanship.   George Gascoigne.   NoSic
   (My worthy Lord, I pray you wonder not.)   CABP; PBRV

My Wrist Split Open.   Steve Healey.   LegDan

My years on earth were short, but long for me.   On a Shipmate, Pero Moniz, Dying at Sea.   Luis de Camões [or Camõens or Camoëns].   OxBEV; WoPoe, tr. by Roy Campbell

My yellow mou'd mistress, I bid you adieu.   My Sodger Laddie.   Unknown.   FaBoWar

My Yellow Straw Hat.   Lessie Jones Little.   TLR

My yesterday was dream, tomorrow earth.   He Points Out the Brevity of Life, Unthinking and Suffering, Surprised by Death.   Francisco de Quevedo y Villegas.   WoPoe, tr. by Willis Barnstone

My young love said to me, 'My brothers won't mind'.   She Moved through the Fair.   Padraic Colum.   IrLP

My young son claimed total recall from the sperm last bathnight, which stopped me like a clock.   First Second, The.   Ian Duhig.   NeBl

My youth? I hear it mostly in the long, volleying.   Poet at Seventeen, The.   Larry Levis.   GeoHom

My zenith was luckily happier than my night.   Heinrich Heine.   WoPoe Fr. Dying in Paris.

Mykonos.   Edwin Denby.   NYP2

Myn owne John poyntz sins ye delight to know.   Sir Thomas Wyatt.   See Of the Courtier's Life.

Mynstrelles Songe.   Thomas Chatterton.   CABP

Mynstrelle's Songe ("O! synge untoe mie roundelaie").   Thomas Chatterton.   OxAEP-1

Myomectomy Cycle, The.   Tracie Morris.
   4.   RD

Myopia.   Biancamaria Frabotta.   CItWP, tr. by Cinzia Sartini Blum and Lara Trubowitz

Myopic Child, A.   Yannis Ritsos.   P180, tr. by Gwendolyn MacEwen and Nikos Tsingos

Myriad carven statues, A.   At the Summit.   Robert Phillips.   Vesp

Myriad differences resolved by sitting, all doors opened, The.   Reizan.   ZenPo, tr. by Takashi Ikemoto and Lucien Stryk

Myriad insects.   Konchu Kazu Aru Yube Ako Iyo-Iyo Seicho Shitari.   Violet Kazue De Cristoforo.   CalPo

Myriad Stars, Part 132.   Bingxin.   CFP, tr. by Michelle Yeh

Myriad times, Ptolemy, your father, myriad times.   Antipater of Sidon.   HePo, tr. by Barbara Hughes Fowler

Myriad unfolds from a progression of strokes, The.   Before Sunrise.   Arthur Sze.   WANABP

Myrie a tyme I telle in May.   Unknown.   OHMEL

Myrie it is whil somer ylast.   Unknown.   OHMEL

Myrie songen the monkes binne Ely.   Unknown.   OHMEL

Myrres vous y. (LL)   John Skelton.   See Trinity, The. Amen.

Myrrha and Cinyras.   Ovid.   NAWM-7v1 Fr. Metamorphoses.

Myrtle.   John Ashbery.   NAAL-5

Myrtle.   Ted Kooser.   InvLad

Myrtle bush grew shady, The.   Jealousy.   Mary Elizabeth Coleridge.   LW

Myself.   Adah Isaacs Menken.   CBWP-1; NAAPv.1; ViWPN

Myself borne safely through it. (LL)   Recent Past, The.   C. S. Giscombe.   GT; OxAAAP

Myself I Sing.   George Oppen.   FTOS

Myself in the Disguise of an Ancient Queen.   Takahashi Mutsuo.   PFTM-2 Fr. Self-Portraits.

Myself outside at night.   Moonsnow '77.   Michael Hartnett.   ModIr

Myself, Rousseau, a Few Others.   William Meredith.   YaYoPo

Myself unholy, from myself unholy.   Gerard Manley Hopkins.   SacPr

Myself unto myself will give.   Holy Office, The.   James Joyce.   NoAM

Myself When I Am Real.   Al Young.   OxAAAP

Myself when young did eagerly frequent.   Omar Khayyám.   CABP; TRP Fr. Rubáiyát of Omar Khayyám [of Naishápúr], The.

Myself with a Glory Hole.   Takahashi Mutsuo.   PFTM-2 Fr. Self-Portraits.

Myselves / The grievers.   Ceremony after a Fire Raid.   Dylan Thomas.   AF

Mysteries. Terence Winch. OxBoAm

Mysteries, The. "H. D." APT-1

Mysteries, The. Brenda Hillman. ExTi

Mysteries of Caesar, The. Anthony Hecht. NoP-4

Mysteries of Life. Mary E. Tucker. CBWP-1

Mysteries of Small Houses. Alice Notley. ExTi

Mysteries of The Incarnation: "She Said Yeah." Kathleen Norris. UpMys

Mysteries of Touch, The. Coral Bracho. RMCMP, tr. by Mónica de la Torre

Mysteries of Udolpho, The. Ann Radcliffe.
  Butterfly to His Love, The. RWP

Mysterious. Sadiq al-Saygh. IrPoTo, tr. by Ralph Saverese and Saadi A. Simawe

Mysterious, Ancient World of Mine. Sergey Aleksandrovich Yesenin. TCRusP, tr. by Nigel Stott

Mysterious Night! when our first parent knew. To Night. Joseph Blanco White. GSo; OBEV; OxAEP-2
  (Mysterious night, when the first man but knew.) CenSon

Mysterious Nothing! how shall I define. Sonnet to Nothing. Thomas Beck. NOBRP

Mysterious shapes, with wands of joy and pain. Dreams. Helen Hunt Jackson. APN-2

Mysterious things within you, The. Ahmad al-Mushari Al-'Udwani. BBASP Fr. Signs.

Mysterious valley fountain, The. Gem Creek. Muso Soseki. EaWin, tr. by W. S. Merwin

Mystery. Langston Hughes. APT-2

Mystery. Octavio Paz. TCLAP, tr. by Muriel Rukeyser

Mystery. Lizette Woodworth Reese. SWaP

Mystery, The. Jeni Couzyn. HAWP

Mystery, The. Paul Laurence Dunbar. APN-2; NAAPv.1

Mystery, The. Ralph Hodgson. InvLi; MoBrPo

Mystery, The. Sara Teasdale. PasH

Mystery Boy Looks for Kin in Nashville. Robert Earl Hayden. NoAM; NoP-4; NoP-5

Mystery Corset, The. André Breton. PFTM-1

Mystery Corset, The. André Breton. YaTCFP, tr. by Mary Ann Caws

Mystery: God, Man's Life, born into man. Virgin and Child, by Hans Memmeling, A; in the Academy of Bruges. Dante Gabriel Rossetti. CenSon

Mystery: Katharine, the bride of Christ. Marriage of St Katharine, by the same, A; in the Hospital of St John at Bruges. Dante Gabriel Rossetti. CenSon

Mystery of Emily Dickinson, The. Marvin Bell. CAP-8; InvLad

Mystery of Profession great, The. Anne Docwra. EMWP

Mystery of the Charity of Charles Péguy, The. Geoffrey Hill.
  "Crack of a starting pistol. Jean Jaurès." NAMCP V.2
  "Violent contrariety of men and days; calm." FaBoWar

Mystery of the Missing Century, The. Tracey Herd.
  "I stopped the car and stepped out onto gravel." NeBl
  "We are sailing on a charming bay." NeBl

Mystery of the Three Horns, The. Jules Laforgue. WoPoe, tr. by William Jay Smith

Mystery Story. Howard Nemerov. NBLV

Mystery Train: A Sequence. David Wojahn.
  Assassination of John Lennon as Depicted by the Madame Tussaud Wax Museum, Niagara Falls, Ontario, 1987, The. P180; PBCAP
  At Graceland with a Six Year Old, 1985. AllShUp; PBCAP
  Buddy Holly Watching *Rebel Without a Cause*, Lubbock, Texas, 1956. PBCAP
  Colorizing: Turner Broadcasting Enterprises, Computer Graphics Division, Burbank, California, 1987. PBCAP
  Custom Job: Hank Williams, Jr., and the Death Car, 1958. PBCAP
  Fab Four Tour Deutschland: Hamburg, 1961. PBCAP
  Homage: Light from the Hall. PBCAP
  Matins: James Brown and His Famous Flames Tour the South, 1958. PBCAP
  "Mystery Train" Janis Joplin Leaves Port Arthur for Points West, 1964. GM; PBCAP
  Tattoo, Corazon: Ritchie Valens, 1959. PBCAP
  Trashmen Shaking Hands with Hubert Humphrey at the Opening of Apache Plaza Shopping Center, Suburban Minneapolis, August 1963, The. PBCAP
  Woody Guthrie Visited by Bob Dylan: Brooklyn State Hospital, New York, 1961. PBCAP; SwNoth

"Mystery Train" Janis Joplin Leaves Port Arthur for Points West, 1964. David Wojahn. GM; PBCAP Fr. Mystery Train: A Sequence.

Mystic. D. H. Lawrence. BLT

Mystic and Cavalier. Lionel Pigot Johnson. MoBrPo

Mystic in the morning, half asleep, A. Bachelor. William Meredith. NoAM; PoA 2002

Mystic Magi, The. Robert Stephen Hawker. OBCP

Mystic shadow, bending near me. Stephen Crane. IJHIL

Mystical Chorus. Johann Wolfgang von Goethe. WoPoe Fr. Faust.

Myth. Muriel Rukeyser. APT-2; NAAL-5; NALW; NIL-7; OxBoAm

Myth, The. Edwin Muir. HarvBoo

Myth of Myself. Sri Sri. HotL, tr. by V. Narayana Rao and A. K. Ramanujan

Myth of Tea Boy, The. Leontia Flynn. NIrP

Myth of the Blaze. George Oppen. PFTM-2

Mythic Fragment. Louise Glück. NoAM

Mythical Founding of Buenos Aires, The. Jorge Luis Borges. TCLAP, tr. by Alastair Reid

Mythical Journey, The. Edwin Muir. NoAM

Mythistorima. George Seferis. tr. by Edmund Keeley and Philip Sherrard
  Bottle in the Sea. WoPoe, tr. by Edmund Keeley and Philip Sherrard

Mythology. Marilyn Hacker. NoAM; ReTh

Mythology. Andrew Motion. NeBrP

Mythology. Earle Thompson. HATNAP

Mythology of Cures, The. Susan Goyette. OpeFie

Mythology of Heavenly Messengers, The. Rebecca Seiferle. ICANM

Mythology of Snow, A. Violette Newton. TiP2

Myths. Nazik al-Mala'ika. IrPoTo, tr. by Ferial J. Ghazoul

Myths and Texts. Gary Snyder.
  Hunting.
    First Shaman Song. PFTM-2
    This Poem Is for Bear. PFTM-2
    This Poem Is for Deer. GeoHom

Myths of separation from the Earth, The. Friedrich Hölderlin. WoPoe Fr. Seasons, The.

Myths of the Disappearance. Monica Ferrell. LegDan

Myxomatosis. Philip Larkin. NoAM

N

N. William Heyen. AtGh

N. Kiini Ibura Salaam. BRtP

N i'm waitin for the light to turn green. Green Boots n Lil Honeys. Ruth Forman. SpirFl

N. N. Miryana Basheva. CSCBP, tr. by Georgi Belev and Lisa Sapinkopf

N. N. Tries to Remember the Words of a Prayer. Stanislaw Baranczak. GI, tr. by Kevin Windle

N T. Charles Wesley. ChIV-2

N.V., my girlfriend then, who laughed nonstop. Memoirs. Aleksandr Semionovich Kushner. ItGoST, tr. by Paul Graves and Carol Ueland

"N" Word, The. Mona Lisa Saloy. FuFl

Na Agrícola. Natalia Toledo. RMCMP

Na Aurea. Natalia Toledo. RMCMP, tr. by Alberto A. Ríos

Na Aurea. Natalia Toledo. RMCMP

Na hermila limón. Natalia Toledo. RMCMP

Na Hermila Limón. Natalia Toledo. RMCMP, tr. by Alberto A. Ríos

Na Hyesôk's Complex. Kim Sǔnghǔi. EcSo, tr. by K. Kim Richards and Steffen Richards

Na tacha. Natalia Toledo. RMCMP

Na Tacha. Natalia Toledo. RMCMP

Na Victórica litru. Natalia Toledo. RMCMP

Na Victórica Litru. Natalia Toledo. RMCMP, tr. by Alberto A. Ríos

Naaman's Song. Rudyard Kipling. ChIV-1

Naäy, noä mander o' use to be callin' 'im Roä. Old Roä. Alfred Tennyson. DiBP

Naayawva Taawi. Wendy Rose. UnSA

Nabara, The. Cecil Day Lewis. OBNV

Naches River. Just below the falls. Woman Bathing. Raymond Carver. PasH

Nací rompiendo las telas del alba. Cielo Min. Natalia Toledo. RMCMP

Nacogdoches Speaks. Karle Wilson Baker. TiP2

Nacreous land had no dust, The. Kuan Hsiu. CCL1, tr. by Edward H. Schafer

Nada es tan necesario al hombre como un trozo de mar. A Punto de Caer. Blas de Otero. RaW

Nadar. Richard Howard. GS

Nadine held my hand when we were kids. Miss Mary Mack. Lisa Buscani. AmPoNex

Nadine, Resting on Her Neighbor's Stoop. Judy Grahn. NALW Fr. Common Woman, The.

Nae hat. Hitch-Haiku. Alan Jackson. EdScPo

Nae muckle love in that dour look. Photograph. Raymond Vettese. EdScPo

Nae sign o' thow yet. Ay, that's me, John Watt o' Dockenhill.   Dockens afore his Peers.   Charles Murray.   NePenScot

Nae wi the gallus captains.   Sodgers, The.   Alexander Scott.   EdScPo

Nagasaki.   Mort Dixon.   ReLy

Nagasaki Style.   Kinoshita Mokutarō.   CAoMJL1, *tr. by* Leith Morton

Nagging reminders: the black ghost-melancholy vision.   Ovid.   RomPo *Fr.* Tristia.

Naglfar.   Monica Youn.   LegDan

Nahum 2.10.   Francis Quarles.   ChIV-1

Naiad changes / Quick as these.. (LL)   Gardener Janus Catches a Naiad.   Dame Edith Sitwell.   MoBrPo; OBGa

Nail, The.   Vasco [*or* Vasko] Popa.   PoSu *Fr.* Games.

Nail in the Grass, The.   Christopher Smart.   STuOW *Fr.* Hop-Garden, The.

Nail it, but he can't do that, Tom. (LL)   Becoming Milton.   Coleman Barks.   RaBo; RaF

Nail scratching at the glass, The.   Crossroads, The.   Maria Luisa Spaziani.   CItWP, *tr. by* Cinzia Sartini Blum and Lara Trubowitz

Nail the shutters closed.   Protecting the Children from Hurricanes.   Jean Nordhaus.   PfSP

Nàile from Iona, Nàile from above.   Lullaby of Donald Gorm, by his Nurse.   *Unknown.*   EMWP

Nailed eagles beryl alter vasish.   Hill Figures.   Maggie O'Sullivan.   Oth

Nailed like illegible bronze on the futureless future. (LL)   Fishnet.   Robert Lowell.   PoetW; VCAP

Nails.   Gary Gildner.   PBCAP

Nails dropped off a roof onto flagstone.   Ice Floe.   Arthur Sze.   WhBo

Nails out and took it with me, The. (LL)   Surprise in the Peninsula, A.   Fleur Adcock.   EmeKit; MoWP

Naima.   Edward Kamau Brathwaite.   WoPoe

Naked.   Issa.   EH, *tr. by* Robert Hass

Naked among the Trees.   Norman Cameron.   OxBEV

Naked and as if in silence.   *Mi Estomago* / My Belly.   Marjorie Agosin.   FiBr, *tr. by* Cola Franzen

Naked and the Nude, The.   Robert Graves.   SoSe-8

Naked, astride an elephant.   Yannis Ritsos.   PFTM-2 *Fr.* Second Series.

Naked blond head.   Peace.   Jonetta Barras.   ISC

Naked body maybe, A.   Nudity.   Gabriella Sica.   CItWP, *tr. by* Cinzia Sartini Blum and Lara Trubowitz

Naked child is running, A.   War Photograph.   Kate Daniels.   CFP

Naked clarity.   Tennis.   Pierre Drieu la Rochelle.   CuPo

Naked earth is warm with Spring, The.   Into Battle.   Julian Grenfell.   FaBoWar; OBEV; OBMV; OBWP

Naked Face.   Yannis Ritsos.   PFTM-2, *tr. by* Kimon Friar and Kostas Myrsiades

Naked Face, The.   Andrée Chedid.   HAWP, *tr. by* Mirène Ghossein and Samuel Hazo

Naked Girl and Mirror.   Judith Wright.   NALW

Naked, he climbed to the wolf's lair.   Holy Thursday.   Geoffrey Hill.   UpMys

Naked, he lies in the blinded room.   Soledad.   Robert Earl Hayden.   APT-2

Naked I came, naked I leave the scene.   James Vincent Cunningham.   APT-2; TRP; WoPoe *Fr.* Five Epigrams.

Naked / I float among the wreckage with steel mustaches.   Joyce Mansour.   SurPaPo *Fr.* Pericoloso Sporgersi.

Naked I Saw You.   Padraic Pearse.   WoPoe, *tr. by* Desmond O'Grady

Naked I saw you.   Naked I Saw You.   Padraic Pearse.   WoPoe, *tr. by* Desmond O'Grady

Naked in eastern mournin sun.   Funeral.   Gary Lilley.   BtF

Naked is the earth.   Poem.   Antonio Machado Ruiz.   WoPoe, *tr. by* John Dos Passos

Naked Jaina monk, A.   Pleasure.   A. K. Ramanujan.   PoetW; VCWP

Naked Man, The.   Michael Crummey.   IFF

Naked morning, the day's transparent.   Morning.   José Ángel Valente.   RaW, *tr. by* Hardie St. Martin

Naked she lay, clasped in my longing arms.   Imperfect Enjoyment, The.   John Wilmot, 2d Earl of Rochester.   BASC; NAEL-7v1; NoP-5

Naked Truth, The.   Marianne van Hirtum.   SurWo, *tr. by* Myrna Bell Rochester

Naked truth: that's not her, The.   Naked Truth, The.   Marianne van Hirtum.   SurWo, *tr. by* Myrna Bell Rochester

Naked Vision.   Gwen Harwood.   EmeKit; StAl

Naked without either cover or dress.   Pen, The.   Solomon ibn Gabirol.   WoPoe, *tr. by* Peter Cole

Naked woman and a dead dwarf, A.   Stephen Crane.   APN-2

Naked woman at the window, The.   Untitled (February 2000).   Michael Palmer.   BAP-01

Namby-Pamby. A Panegyric on the New Versification, Address'd to A————P————, Esq. ("All ye poets of the age.")   Henry Carey.   NPeEn; OBSV; UV

Namby-Pamby; or, A Panegyric on the New Versification ("Naughty Paughty Jack-a-Dandy.")   Henry Carey.   OBSV

Name.   Alan Davies.
"Personality syndrome, The."   FTOS

Name, A.   Linda Pastan.   TaR

Name, The.   Mariella Bettarini.   CItWP, *tr. by* Cinzia Sartini Blum and Lara Trubowitz

Name, The.   Shrine.   Octavio Paz.   EroLit

Name Alissa, The.   In Which Names.   Ilse Aichinger.   AF, *tr. by* Allen H. Chappel

Name and the spirit are inseparable, The.   Onomastics and the Falling Snow.   Steve Orlen.   PoDa

The name *Caliban* derives from cannibal.   At *The Tempest* with a Pregnant Wife.   Charles Harper Webb.   IaFF

Name confronts you, The.   Shap.   Mick North.   NLP

Name Drawn from the Names, The.   Juan Ramón Jiménez.   RaW, *tr. by* Robert Bly

Name in a footnote. Faceless name.   Crispus Attucks.   Robert Earl Hayden.   ESEAA

Name, Many Names, A.   Anne Simpson.   Coast

Name not to be worn out with the years, A. (LL)   Ezra Pound.   APT-1; OBVE; OxBoAm; WoPoe *Fr.* Homage to Sextus Propertius.

Name of god, The.   Imtiaz Dharker.   NeBl

Name of Jesus, The.   John Newton.   SacPr

Name of my heroine, simply "Rose."   Tale of a Pony, The.   Bret Harte.   OBNV

Name of my mother's bowling team, The.   Wade's Hoggers.   Debbra Palmer.   FiBr

Name of the author is the first to go, The.   Forgetfulness.   Billy Collins.   EMP; FaoP; PoA 2002; StAl

Name of the living God, The. (LL)   Naming the Living God.   Kathleen Norris.   InvLi; UpMys

Name of the product I tested is *Life*, The.   Consumer's Report, A.   Peter Porter.   EmeKit; NoP-4; NoP-5

Name only once.   America.   Kofi Awoonor.   HBAPE

Name stained in colored glass.   Joshua Clark.   Maurice Kenny.   FTtHH

Name the Oldest Member of Your Family.   Kalamu ya Salaam.   OPRER

Named *Albion*. (LL)   Geoffrey Hill.   NAEL-7v2; NAMCP V.2; NoAM; NoP-4; NoP-5; NPeEn *Fr.* Mercian Hymns.

Named and unnamed and renamed.   Leaving Eden.   Ralph Dickey.   ESEAA

Named for a color, I slept in your pocket.   Having Cut the Sparrow's Heart.   Malinda Markham.   IAoNAP

Nameless Love, The.   John Henry Mackay.   CAGL, *tr. by* Hubert Kennedy

Nameless One, A.   Margaret Avison.   BrAP; HeIP-4

Nameless One, The.   James Clarence Mangan.   OBEV

Nameless Pain.   Elizabeth Stoddard.   SWaP

Nameless Spirit.   Gustavo Adolfo Bécquer.   NAWM-7v2, *tr. by* Bruce Phenix

Nameless spirit.   Nameless Spirit.   Gustavo Adolfo Bécquer.   NAWM-7v2, *tr. by* Bruce Phenix

Nameless Thing.   Robert Penn Warren.   BodElec

Nameless / Weed quickening.   Chiun.   ZenPo, *tr. by* Takashi Ikemoto and Lucien Stryk

Nameless Woman.   No Ch'ŏnmyŏng.   CAMKP, *tr. by* David R. McCann

Nameless Woman, A.   No Ch'ŏnmyŏng.   WoPoe, *tr. by* Ko Won

Name—of it—is "Autumn," The.   Emily Dickinson.   NCAP

Name—of it—is "Autumn," The.   Name—of it—is "Autumn," The.   Emily Dickinson.   NCAP

Names.   Medora C. Addison.   YaYoPo

Names: "She was Eliza for a few weeks."   Wendy Cope.   BeAl; PoCu

Names.   Gerald Dawe.   PNI

Names.   Robert Earl Hayden.   GT

Names.   William Matthews.   PfSP; PoCoUp

Names.   Jelaluddin Rumi.   RaBo

Names, The.   Robert Browning.   OxBSo

Names, The.   Billy Collins.   FTtHH

Names and sorrows.   D. Rubin Green.   CAGL

Names creeping out everywhere, The. (LL)   Lying Awake.   Thomas Hardy.   FaBoVe; NPeEn

Names flow from her mouth as so many hearty allies.   Rival, A.   Rachel Wetzsteon.   NeAmPo

Names for everything I touch.   Hollow Thesaurus, The.   Roger McDonald.   BMAP

Names for the moon.   As a Blow, from the West.   Carl Phillips.   FaoP

Names in the Bark.   Rod Mengham.   VaPo

Names of Horses.   Donald Hall.   AmFaPo; BeAl; GoPo; IPoFL; SoSe-8; TRP; TWF

Names of Summer, The: A War Memory.   Harold L. Johnson.   BtF

Names of the dead, The.   Remembrance Day.   Ida G. M. Gerhardt.   TuT, *tr. by* Robert Greacen

Names of the fallen, The. Remembrance Day. Ida G. M. Gerhardt. TuT, *tr.* by Michael Longley

Names of the Hare, The. *Unknown.* WoPoe, *tr.* by Seamus Heaney

Names of Waitie and Boudinot, The. Ode to Sequoyah. Alexander L. Posey. NAAPv.2

Names. / She and my uncles looked for names. Number Our Days. Norbert Hirschhorn. BloBone

Names will change. Election Time. Lamont B. Steptoe. UnSA

Namesake. Imtiaz Dharker. NeBl

Naming Day, A. Odia Ofeimun. HBAPE

Naming It. Leontia Flynn. NIrP

Naming of Cats is a difficult matter, The. Naming of Cats, The. T. S. Eliot. AmWit; NBLV

Naming of Cats, The. T. S. Eliot. AmWit; NBLV

Naming of Flowers, The. Jennie Osborne. Prnts

Naming of Parts. Henry Reed. AmFaPo; BrAP; FaBoWar; MoBrPo; NAEL-6v2; NAEL-7v2; NoP-4; NoP-5; OxBEV; PoPoPo; RaBo; SoSe-8; TFi; UV; WaAnP *Fr.* Lessons of the War.

Naming Power. Wendy Rose. OxWW

Naming the Animals. Anthony Hecht. ChIV-1

Naming the Animals. Lisel Mueller. IllVoic

Naming the Fabrics. Julia Alvarez. FFC

Naming the Living God. Kathleen Norris. InvLi; UpMys

Naming's over. Day is done. (LL) Adam's Task. John Hollander. NAMCP V.2; NIL-7; NIP-4; NoP-4; NoP-5; OxBoAm; WoPoe

Nan robh sinn an Talasgar air an tràigh. Tràighean. Sorley MacLean. EdScPo

Nanas de la Cebolla. Miguel Hernández. RaW

Nancy Hanks. Rosemary Benét. NTCP

Nani. Alberto A. Ríos. MakPoe; SoSe-8; UnSA; WaAnP

Nani Worries about Her Father's Happiness in the Afterlife. Ana Castillo. FTtHH

Nanny. Lorna Goodison. NAMCP V.2

Nanny Tanya. Yevgeny Borisovich Rein. ItGoST, *tr.* by Judith Hemschemeyer

Nansen. Gary Snyder. BB

Nant yr Eira. Will Ifan. BBMWP, *tr.* by Joseph P. Clancy

Nantucket. William Carlos Williams. HarvBoo; OxBoAm; TRP; WeW-3

Naola Beauty Academy, New Orleans, Louisiana, 1943. Natasha Trethewey. NeAmPo; SpirFl; SUP

Napkin that is shredded into a cupful of snow. (LL) Soup, The. Gary Soto. NoP-4; NoP-5

Napoleon. Walter De la Mare. NPeEn; OxBEV; Spl; WoPoe

Napoleon. Miroslav Holub. ChAP; PoSu, *tr.* by Kaca Plakova

Napoleon. William Makepeace Thackeray. FaBoWar

Napoleon after Sedan. Arthur Rimbaud. OBWP *Fr.* Eighteen-Seventy.

Napoleon was a little guy. Napoleon. P. G. Wodehouse. ReLy

Napoleon's Farewell. Lord Byron. NPBRoP

Napoli Again. Richard Hugo. AF

Napolo has spoken: Death. Messengers, The. Steve Chimombo. HBAPE

Napped half the day. Issa. EH, *tr.* by Robert Hass

Napping at midday. Issa. EH, *tr.* by Robert Hass

Naranja de luz abierta, La. Alfonso D'Aquino. RMCMP

Narcissa. Gwendolyn Brooks. NTCP

Narcissism / is an ugly fault. Antonio Machado Ruiz. RaBo; WED *Fr.* Moral Proverbs and Folk Songs.

Narcissus. Gerda Mayer. LW

Narcissus and Echo. Fred Chappell. PoA 2002

Narcissus Learning the Words to This Song. Reginald Shepherd. WiU

Narcissus to Echo. Edgar Bogardus. YaYoPo

Narration. George Seferis. PoetW, *tr.* by Edmund Keeley and Philip Sherrard

Narrative. Russell Atkins. EGAG; GT

Narrative: Ali. Elizabeth Alexander. ESEAA; MoASP

Narrative Charm for Ibbotroyd. Maggie O'Sullivan. Oth; PFTM-2

Narrative of the Life and Times of John Coltrane: Played by Himself, A. Michael S. Harper. SeSe

Narrative of the Life of Frederick Douglass, an American Slave. Frederick Douglass.
  Parody, A. NAAL-3; NAWM-7v2

Narrative of the Men and Women Who Became Stars. Nathaniel Tarn. ICANM

Narrative Poem. Joe Wenderoth. LegDan

Narrator, The. Milo De Angelis. NeIt, *tr.* by Lawrence Venuti

NARRATOR: Suddenly someone wakes me. Still half-asleep, I see standing in front. Douglas Messerli. FTOS *Fr.* Along Without: A Fiction in Film for Poetry.

Narrator was shot by the sniper he was describing, The. Democratic Vistas. David Berman. LegDan

Narrow black veins on the map, The. Highway Poems. Lisel Mueller. IllVoic

Narrow Fellow in the Grass, A. Snake, The. Emily Dickinson. ClHu; HeIP-4; NAAL-3; NALW; NAMCP V.1; NIP-4; NoAM; NoP-4; NoP-5; SAmP; SoSe-8; TFi; TRP; WaAnP; WeW-3; WoPoe

Narrow Fellow in the Grass, A. Emily Dickinson. *See* Snake, The.

Narrow for love that must be fitted in. Sophie Hannah. NewEx

Narrow Path, The. Norman Henry, II Pritchard. GT

Narrow Road to the Deep North, The. Paul Muldoon. HarvBoo

Narrow streets cut into the wide highway at Choan, The. Old Idea of Choan by Rosoriu. Lu Chao-lin. NDACCP, *tr.* by Ezra Pound

Narrows, The. Anne Rouse. MFPA

Nasal whine of power whips a new universe. Hart Crane. MoAmPo *Fr.* Bridge, The.

Naseby, now no longer England's shame, The. John Dryden. STuOW *Fr.* Astraea Redux.

Nasica raped the doctor's pretty lad. Martial. CAGL *Fr.* Epigrams.

Naskeag. Alfred Corn. VCAP

Nasser is dead. Arthur Nortje. TSAP

Nasturtium petals alight. *ZZZZZ.* Carl Rakosi. NAAPv.2

Nasturtium Scanned. Judith Rodriguez. BMAP

Nasty surprise in a sandwich, A. God, A Poem. James Fenton. NAMCP V.2; NoAM; NoP-4; NoP-5; OBCoV

Nat Love: Black Cowboy. Lee Bennett Hopkins. HHAm

Nat Turner in the Clearing. Alvin Aubert. FuFl

Natal Address to My Child, March 19th 1844, A. Eliza Ogilvy. VWP

Natalia. Natalia Toledo. RMCMP

Natalia. Natalia Toledo. RMCMP, *tr.* by Alberto A. Ríos

Natalie gets discovered in her pit by an old, drunken transient. Connie Deanovich. ReTh *Fr.* Ephemera Today on "All My Children."

Natasha, the White Donkey, and I. Paek Sŏk. CAMKP, *tr.* by Kyunghwan Choi

Nathaniel, born Hathorne, you who set. Secret, The. Suzanne Noguere. FFC

Nathaniel to Ruth. Emily Jane Pfeiffer. ViWPN

Nation, indivisible, with liberty and justice for all. (LL) Topography. Sharon Olds. GoPo; OxBoAm; WaAnP

Nation is broken, but hills and rivers remain, The. Spring View. Tu Fu [*or* Du Fu]. WaAnP, *tr.* by Arthur Sze

Nation is coming, a nation is coming, A. *Sioux Oral Tradition.* NAAPv.1 *Fr.* Ghost-Dance Songs.

Nation Is Like Ouselves, The. Imamu Amiri Baraka. PmAP

Nation is ruined, but mountains and rivers remain, The. Spring View. Tu Fu [*or* Du Fu]. ColAnChi; NDACCP, *tr.* by Gary Snyder

Nation of hayricks spotting the green solace, A. Airman Who Flew over Shakespeare's England, The. Hyam Plutzik. APT-2; PWW2

Nation of trees, drab green and desolate gray [*or* grey], A. Australia. Alec Derwent Hope. BMAP; BrAP; NAMCP V.1; NoAM; NoP-4; NoP-5

Nation true to honor's cause, The. On the Great Western Canal of the State of New York. Philip Freneau. APN-1

National Anthem. Ferenc Kölcsey. IQMS, *tr.* by Earl M. Herrick, Watson Kirkconnell and Adam Makkai

National anthem at sunrise, The. Two Songs for Hendrix. James McManus. RWB

National Cemetery, Beaufort, South Carolina, The. Josephine D. Henderson Heard. CBWP-4

National Cold Storage Company contains, The. National Cold Storage Company. Harvey Shapiro. WoPoe

National Depression Awareness Week. Mary Ruefle. IJHIL

National Federation is a grand and glorious band, The. All We Ask Is Justice. Mrs. Henry Linden. CBWP-4

National Hero, The. Gojko Djogo. AF, *tr.* by Michael March

National Museum Hallway. Kim Hyesun. EcSo, *tr.* by Youngju Ryu

National Painting, The. Joseph Rodman Drake. GS

National Painting [*or* Paintings], The. Fitz-Greene Halleck. APN-1 *Fr.* Croaker Papers, The.

National Police Headquarters. Nicolás Guillén. PFTM-1 *Fr.* Daily Daily, The.

National Song. Sándor Petőfi. IQMS, *tr.* by Adam Makkai

National Thoughts. Yehuda Amichai. PFTM-2, *tr.* by Stephen Mitchell

National Trust. Tony Harrison. HarvBoo; NAEL-6v2; NAEL-7v2; RSaN *Fr.* School of Eloquence, The.

Nations die. *Japanese Figures 1. Unknown.* EaWin, *tr.* by W. S. Merwin

Nation's lost diplomacy. Scroll No. 2. Cecil Taylor. EGAG

Native. Rae Armantrout. PFTM-2

Native American Birds, The. Annie Finch. RWB

Native Guard. Natasha Trethewey. LegDan

Native moments—when you come upon me—ah you are here now. Native Moments. Walt Whitman. NAAPv.1

Native peoples. Shaking Hands with Murder. Sir Osbert Sitwell. RSaN

Native Soil. Marin Georgiev. CSCBP, *tr.* by Georgi Belev and Lisa Sapinkopf

Native Stone.   Octavio Paz.   TCLAP, *tr. by* Muriel Rukeyser

Natives, The.   David Mura.   WeW-3

Natives are all inside the houses.   Ceylon.   Nishiwaki Junzaburo.   CAoMJL1, *tr. by* Hosea Hirata

Natives are restless tonight, The.   Drummer, The.   Philip Dacey.   MiVo

Natives camped on the hatches, who sang through the, The.   Calenture, The.   Randolph Stow.   BMAP

Native's letter.   Arthur Nortje.   BrAP; HBAPE; TSAP

Natives of America, The.   Ann Plato.   TCAPo

Nativities.   U. A. Fanthorpe.   NoP-4

Nativity.   Li-Young Lee.   Vesp

Nativity.   Craig Powell.   NOBAu

Nativity.   Aidan Rooney-Céspedes.   NIrP

Nativity, A.   Rudyard Kipling.   ChrPo; GI

Nativity, The.   William Drummond of Hawthornden.   RSR

Nativity, The.   Mary Weston Fordham.   CBWP-2

Nativity, The.   Clive Staples Lewis.   ChIV-2

Nativity, The.   Henry Vaughan.   ChrPo

Nativity of Christ[e], The.   Robert Southwell.   OxBEV

Nativity of Our Lord and Saviour Jesus Christ, The.   Christopher Smart.   ChrPo; NPeEn; OxBEV; SacPr *Fr.* Hymns and Spiritual Songs for the Fasts and Festivals of the Church of England.

Nativity of St. John the Baptist, The.   Christopher Smart.   ChIV-2 *Fr.* Hymns and Spiritual Songs for the Fasts and Festivals of the Church of England.

Nativity [*or* Nativitie].   John Donne.   ChrPo *Fr.* Holy Sonnets.

Nativity Play, The.   Gwyn Thomas.   BBMWP, *tr. by the* author

Nativity Poem.   Louise Glück.   GI; HarvBoo

Natural.   Ellen Doré Watson.   PoDa

Natural, The.   Sikong Tu.   CCL1 *Fr.* Twenty-Four Modes of Poetry.

Natural Child, The.   Helen Leigh.   WoRP

Natural demeanor warm and soft.   Tune: "Rapt with Wine, Loudly Singing; Joy in Spring's Coming."   Kuan Yün-shih.   ColAnChi, *tr. by* Richard John Lynn

Natural Disaster.   David Swanger.   GeoHom

Natural Functions.   Jonathan Cott.   AHA

Natural High.   Jean Binta Breeze.   Prnts

Natural History.   Chana Bloch.   ASA

Natural History.   Harold Monro.
   "Vixen woman, The."   OBMV

Natural History.   Giampiero Neri.   ItPo, *tr. by* Gayle Ridinger

Natural History.   Elwyn Brooks White.   PtR

Natural History: "Late afternoon, autumn equinox."   Sam Hamill.   PoChi

Natural image is a moving image, The.   Moving Image, The.   Elizabeth Brewster.   Coast

Natural Selection.   Constance Naden.   VWP *Fr.* Evolutional Erotics.

Natural Selection.   Alan Shapiro.   PoA 2002

Natural Son.   Richard Murphy.   BeAl; ModIr *Fr.* Price of Stone, The.

Natural thirst that never can be quenched.   Dante Alighieri.   NAWM-7v1 *Fr.* Divine Comedy, The (Mandelbaum Translation).

Natural Woman.   Judith Taylor.   SUP

Natural world is a spiritual house, where the pillars, that are alive, The.   Intimate Associations.   Charles Baudelaire.   WoPoe, *tr. by* Robert Bly

Naturaleza Viva.   Jorge Guillén.   RaW

Naturalised.   Cyril Hodges.   AngWePo

Naturalist, A.   William O'Daly.   PoChi

Naturalization.   Erich Fried.   GTCP, *tr. by* Reinhold Grimm

Naturalization Papers.   Myriam Moscona.   CFP, *tr. by* Cynthia Steele

Naturally.   Audre Lorde.   ISC

Naturally it is night.   Air.   W. S. Merwin.   CAP-8

Nature: "Hand that tries to shake a hand, A."   Marvin Bell.   PfSP

Nature.   Henry Wadsworth Longfellow.   ITBLP; NAAPv.1

Nature.   Edmund Spenser.   AEP

Nature [1836].   Ralph Waldo Emerson.   APN-1
   (Motto to "Nature.")   NCAP

Nature [1844].   Ralph Waldo Emerson.   APN-1

Nature: "In a corn field."   No Hyangnim.   EcSo, *tr. by* Aimee N. Kwon

Nature ("Bubbling brook doth leap when I come by, The.")   Jones Very.   ColAP

Nature Alive.   Jorge Guillén.   RaW, *tr. by* James Wright

Nature and Art.   Johann Wolfgang von Goethe.   STV, *tr. by* John Frederick Nims

Nature and Nature's Laws lay hid in Night.   Intended for Sir Isaac Newton.   Alexander Pope.   WeW-3

Nature Be Damned.   Anne Wilkinson.   BrAP

Nature, Beside Herself.   James Galvin.   WaAnP

Nature causes brass to oxidize.   X-Ray.   Else Von Freytag-Loringhoven.   SurPaPo

Nature centres into balls.   Circles.   Ralph Waldo Emerson.   APN-1; TCAPo

Nature drives me crazy, how it repeats.   Echo to Narcissus.   Michele Glazer.   IAoNAP

Nature herself doth Scotchmen beasts confess.   John Cleveland.   OBSV *Fr.* Rebel Scot, The.

Nature is a temple, where the living.   Correspondences.   Charles Baudelaire.   SxFrPo, *tr. by* James McGowan

Nature is a temple whose living colonnades.   Correspondences.   Charles Baudelaire.   NAWM-7v2, *tr. by* Richard Wilbur

Nature is only for the smug or the empty.   Dapper Street.   J. C. Bloem.   TuT, *tr. by* Desmond Egan

Nature is so near: the rooks in the college garden.   Oxford.   W. H. Auden.   OxAEP-2

Nature is there, outside. One takes a walk.   Leslie Kaplan.   SCFWP *Fr.* Règne.

Nature makes clear the windy air.   Kwŏn Homun.   CATKP, *tr. by* Peter H. Lee

Nature Morte.   Louis MacNeice.   NAMCP V.1; NoAM

Nature Note: The California Poison Oak.   Helen Pinkerton.   CalPo

Nature of a river is to run, The.   Rivers.   Homero Aridjis.   PoCoUp, *tr. by* George McWhirter

Nature of Braille, The.   Anthony Butts.   AmPoNex

Nature of Gravel, The.   Pak Mogwŏl [*or* Mokwŏl].   CAMKP, *tr. by* Edward W. Poitras
   Eternity of Pure Color.   CAMKP, *tr. by* Edward W. Poitras
   Today.   CAMKP, *tr. by* Edward W. Poitras

6. The Nature of Love.   David Citino.   UpMys *Fr.* Sister Mary Appassionata Lectures the Pre-Med Class.

Nature of Suffering, The.   Amy Gerstler.   ExTi

Nature of the Siren, The.   Cynewulf.   WoPoe, *tr. by* Richard Wilbur

Nature of Things, The.   Kathleen Ossip.   BAP-01

Nature Poem.   Cornelius Eady.   PfSP

Nature Poem.   Adrian Mitchell.   Spl

Nature Poetry.   Meg Kearney.   UrbNat

Nature Queries [*or* Epistle to Mr. Fox, from Hampton Court].   Lord John Hervey.   STuOW

Nature requires five; custom gives seven.   Hours of Sleep.   *Unknown.*   NBLV

Nature selects the longest way.   Northern Suburb, A.   John Davidson.   NePenScot; NPeEn

Nature Study.   Craig Raine.   NoAM

Nature Study.   Trevor Winkfield.   KGB

Nature that taught my silly dog, God wat.   Dumb Advocate, A.   *Unknown.*   DiBP

Nature, That Washed Her Hands in Milk.   Sir Walter Ralegh.   NoP-4

Nature, That Washed [*or* Washt] Her Hands in Milk[e].   Sir Walter Ralegh.   NAEL-6v1; NAEL-7v1; NoP-4; NoP-5

Nature Was Caught in the Nets of Your Life.   Paul Éluard.   NAWM-7v2, *tr. by* Lloyd Alexander

Nature was caught in the nets of your life.   Nature Was Caught in the Nets of Your Life.   Paul Éluard.   NAWM-7v2, *tr. by* Lloyd Alexander

Nature, which is the vast creation's soul.   To Mr. Henry Lawes.   Katherine Philips.   NoP-4; NoP-5

Nature withheld Cassandra in the skies.   Fragment of a Sonnet.   Pierre de Ronsard.   OBVE, *tr. by* Keats

Nature's decorations glisten.   Christopher Smart.   OBCP *Fr.* Hymns and Spiritual Songs for the Fasts and Festivals of the Church of England.

Nature's first green is gold.   Nothing Gold Can Stay.   Robert Frost.   APT-1; ColAP; MoAmPo; NAAL-5; OxBoAm; PtR; SoSe-8; TWF; WaAnP

Nature's lay idiot [*or* ideot], I taught thee to love.   John Donne.   BASC; NoP-4; NoP-5; OxAEP-2 *Fr.* Elegies.

Nature's Minor Chords.   Henrietta Cordelia Ray.   CBWP-3

Nature's Questioning.   Thomas Hardy.   BrAP

Nature's Reply to Mutability.   Edmund Spenser.   MakPoe *Fr.* Faerie Queene, The.

Nature's Sympathy with the Poet.   Sir Walter Scott.   OxAEP-2

Nature's Uplifting.   Henrietta Cordelia Ray.   CBWP-3

Nature—sometimes sears a Sapling.   Emily Dickinson.   NAAL-3

Natus de Muliere, Brevi Vivens.   Emilio Villa.   ItPo, *tr. by* Gayle Ridinger

Natzweiler.   Rutger Kopland.   VCWP, *tr. by* James Brockway

Naughty Boy.   Robert Creeley.   HeIP-4; NAMCP V.2; NoAM

Naughty Paughty Jack-a-Dandy.   Namby-Pamby; or, A Panegyric on the New Versification.   Henry Carey.   OBSV

Naughty Preposition, The.   Morris Gilbert Bishop.   NBLV

Nautical Ballad, A.   Charles Edward Carryl.   *See* Walloping Window-Blind, The.

Nautilus Island's hermit.   Skunk Hour.   Robert Lowell.   BrAP; CAP-8; ColAP; EmeKit; HarvBoo; HeIP-4; IJHIL; MoAmPo; NAAL-5; NAMCP V.2; NIL-7; NIP-4; NoAM; NoP-4; NoP-5; OxBoAm; PoetW; PoPoPo; TFi; TRP; VCAP; WaAnP

Navajo medicine woman gets up early, The.   Dawn of the Navajo Woman, The.   Terry Blackhawk.   PoDa

Naval Base (Part III), The.   Jeremy Cronin.   AF

Naval Trainees Learn How to Jump Overboard, The.   David Wagoner.   VCAP

Navidad, St. Nicholas Ave.   Alfred Corn.   NoP-4; NoP-5

Navidades.   Gerardo Deniz.   RMCMP

Navigable sorrow. (LL)   Our Lady of the Snows.   Robert Hass.   CAP-8; GoPo

Navigation.   Philip Booth.   PfSP

Navigation.   Ralph Knevet.   NOSC

Navigation.   Ronald Stuart Thomas.   HarvBoo

Navigation's gone haywire. Who's to blame?   Shipwreck Poem.   Karen Volkman.   NeAmPo

Navigator: "This lazy prince of tennis balls and lutes."   May Sarton.   PWW2

Navigators, The.   Walter James Turner.   OBMV

Navy Field.   William Meredith.   PWW2

Navy near-black cut in with lemon, fruity bright lime green.   Lure, 1963.   Denise Riley.   Oth

Nay, be content—our door that opens wide.   Fall.   George Cabot Lodge.   APN-2

Nay, but I fancy somehow, year by year.   Robert Louis Stevenson.   OxBSo

Nay, *Clytus*, you that cou'd advise—.   Nathaniel Lee.   FaBoWar *Fr.* Rival Queens; or, Alexander the Great, The.

Nay, Death, thou art a shadow! Even as light.   Lux Est Umbra Dei.   John Addington Symonds.   GSo

Nay, do not dream, designer dark.   Death's Valley.   Walt Whitman.   GS

Nay, Doll, quoth Roger, now you're caught.   Dol and Roger.   Laetitia Pilkington.   PEW

Nay fie, Platonics, still adoring.   Epithalamy.   Alexander Brome.   NOSC

Nay, he could sail a yacht both nigh and large.   Cabin-Boy, The.   George, 2d Duke of Buckingham Villiers.   NOSC

Nay, if there's room for poets in this world.   Fifth Book.   Elizabeth Barrett Browning.   PEW

Nay, if you threaten, all is over.   Sydney, Lady Morgan Owenson.   RWP *Fr.* Lay of an Irish Harp, or Metrical Fragments, The.

Nay, lady, sit; if I but wave this wand.   John Milton.   OxAEP-1 *Fr.* Comus; a Masque Presented at Ludlow Castle.

Nay, let me own it is but vain regret.   Continuity of Life.   William Bell Scott.   OxBSo

Nay, Margaret, thou trickster.   Tricky Margaret.   Mary Macleod.   EMWP

Nazareth.   Rosario Castellanos.   GI, *tr. by* Magda Bogin

Nazi Song.   Paul Éluard.   AF, *tr. by* Lloyd Alexander

Nazi within me thinks it's time to take charge, The.   Confession.   Stephen Dobyns.   GoPo; SUP

Nazis.   Ira Sadoff.   LTA; OPRER

Ndaani' batanaya'.   Víctor Terán.   RMCMP

Ne hath my soule but fyr and yse.   *Unknown.*   OHMEL

N-e-m-e-s-i-s Blues.   A. Van Jordan.   PoCho

Ne Me Tangito.   Charlotte Mew.   VWP

Ne Plus Ultra.   Samuel Taylor Coleridge.   WaAnP

Neaera when I'm there is adamant.   George Buchanan.   OBVE, *tr. by* James Vincent Cunningham

Neanderthal Funeral.   Martin Mooney.   NIrP

Neanderthal, with Help from Cave and Bear, Invents the Flute.   David Citino.   PoDa

Near.   William Stafford.   CAP-8

Near a shrine in Japan he'd swept the path.   Tour.   Carol Snow.   P180

Near a window.   Will-o'-Wisp.   Nancy Morejón.   TANSG, *tr. by* Joy Renjilian-Burgy

Near an Old Prison.   Frances Darwin Cornford.   OBMV

Near, and more near, without sight or sound.   Anniversaries.   May Probyn.   VWP

Near are we, Lord.   Tenebrae.   Paul Celan.   PoetW, *tr. by* John Felstiner

Near Avon's bank, on Arden's flowery plain.   He Repeats the Song of Colin, a Discerning Shepherd [*or* Elegy 18].   William Shenstone.

Near blackened alcoves.   Railway Allotments.   M. R. Peacocke.   OBGa

Near Burning.   Kathleen Peirce.   PBCAP

Near Cartego, up river from Puerto Limon.   After Barranquillo, before Belize.   Matthew Kearney.   MAAN

Near Damascus.   W. S. Di Piero.   ChIV-2

Near Dawn.   Eric Tretheway.   PfSP

Near dawn our old live oak sagged over.   Hurricane.   John Balaban.   UrbNat

Near evening, in Fairhaven, Massachusetts.   Migratory.   Mark Doty.   AmAlph; BeAl

Near evening, the first days.   Walk After Rain.   Douglas Burnet Smith.   Coast

Near Frost's Grave.   David Smith.   VisFro

Near high tide.   Nightfishing.   Charles McDonald.   NLP

Near House, The.   Mark Van Doren.   APT-2

Near, in the aorta's arch.   Paul Celan.   GTCP, *tr. by* John Felstiner

Near Kitami Station on the Odakyū Line.   Itō Hiromi.   PFTM-2, *tr. by* Leith Morton

Near Lanivet, 1872.   Thomas Hardy.   NoAM

Near Martinpuich that night of hell.   Leveller, The.   Robert Graves.   FaBoWar

Near Nunnerie, where Daer and Potrail meet.   First Light.   Stewart Conn.   EdScPo

Near Perigord.   Ezra Pound.   APT-1

Near Rhydcymerau.   Rhydcymerau.   David Gwenallt Jones.   BBMWP; OBWVE, *tr. by* Anthony Conran

Near Roscoe and Coldwater.   Amy Uyematsu.   OpBo

Near Rose's Chop Suey and Jinosuke's grocery.   Argument: On 1942, An.   David Mura.   PoPoPo

Near San Ardo the grasses tremble.   Our Life in California.   Gary Young.   GeoHom

Near Sheridan.   Robin Becker.   PoCoUp

Near Shinobazu Pond.   Takahashi Shinkichi.   ZenPo, *tr. by* Takashi Ikemoto and Lucien Stryk

Near Speech, The.   Mark McMorris.   AmPoNex

Near the campus, every night.   Cockroaches of Liberation.   Martín Espada.   TouFir

Near the celebrated Lido where the breeze is fresh and free.   Longfellow's Visit to Venice.   Sir John Betjeman.   OBCoV

Near the City of Petersburg.   V. N. and C. I, The.   Maggie Pogue Johnson.   CBWP-4

Near the curving harbor where pine trees father.   Heart's Ease.   Paul Hoover.   PmAP

Near the Cymmerians, in his dark abode.   Ovid.   OBVE *Fr.* Metamorphoses.

Near the Desert Test Sites.   Sherod Santos.   GeoHom

Near the dry river's water-mark we found.   Note Left in Jimmy Leonard's Shack, A.   James Wright.   NoP-4; NoP-5; StAl

Near the end of an extremely important discourse.   Discourse on Peace, The.   Jacques Prévert.   CLPP, *tr. by* Lawrence Ferlinghetti

Near the Front.   Nathaniel Southgate Shaler.   PCW

Near the Lizhou Ferry.   Wen T'ing-yün.   CCL1, *tr. by* Witter Bynner

Near the Mill.   Hayim Lenski.   FIT, *tr. by* Robert Friend

Near the Mississippi.   Steve Gehrke.   AmPoNex

Near the mountain's summit, when the bells.   Fox, The.   R. Williams Parry.   OBWVE, *tr. by* Gwyn Williams

Near the Place Maubert, at the spot where each morning early I wait for the bus.   Three Shops, The.   Francis Ponge.   WED, *tr. by* Robert Bly

Near the red blade of a furred poinsettia.   Pasteur on the Rue Vauquelin.   Linda Bierds.   AmAlph

Near the Rio Grand.   Del Marie Rogers.   TiP2

Near the shrine, humped back.   Clay Image.   Takahashi Shinkichi.   ZenPo, *tr. by* Takashi Ikemoto and Lucien Stryk

Near the Vipsanian columns where the aqueduct.   Martial.   OBVE; OxBEV, *tr. by* Peter Porter

Near the wall of a house painted.   Near the Wall of a House.   Yehuda Amichai.   BBASP; PFTM-2, *tr. by* Chana Bloch

Near to me as my flesh, my flesh and blood.   Allen Tate.   PoA 2002

Near Twelve Mile Point.   Lance Henson.   HATNAP

Near us, a retarded woman was vomiting. (LL)   Visit, A.   Anna Swirszczynska [*or* Swir].   CFP; PoSu, *tr. by* Czeslaw Milosz and Leonard Nathan

Near where I lived there was a fenced schoolyard.   Where Blind Sorrow Is Taught to See.   Suzanne Gardinier.   AmPoNex

Near yonder copse, where once the garden smiled.   Oliver Goldsmith.   TreFP *Fr.* Deserted Village, The.

Near your eyes.   George Oppen.   APT-2; PFTM-1

Nearby creatures of the air.   Antonio Porta.   ItPo *Fr.* Essences.

Neare Enna walles there standes a Lake Pergusa is the name.   Ovid.   OBVE *Fr.* Metamorphoses.

Nearer her they get, The. (LL)   What mystery pervades a well!   Emily Dickinson.   NAAL-3; NAAPv.1; NCAP

Nearer Home.   Phoebe Cary.   SacPr

Nearer, My God, to Thee.   Sarah Flower Adams.   InvLi; SacPr; TCAPo

Nearer to Thee! (LL)   Nearer, My God, to Thee.   Sarah Flower Adams.   InvLi; SacPr; TCAPo

Nearest Dream recedes—unrealized, The.   Emily Dickinson.   APN-2

Nearing Again the Legendary Isle.   Cecil Day Lewis.   MoBrPo *Fr.* Magnetic Mountain, The.

Nearing Long Moons.   J. L. Jacobs.   AmPoNex

Nearing the end.   Mervyn Clyde Witherup.   William Witherup.   AtGh

Nearing the Snow-Line.   Oliver Wendell Holmes.   APN-1

Near-Johannesburg Boy, The.   Gwendolyn Brooks.   ESEAA; FuFl; IllVoic

Nearly a hundred when she died.   Grandmother, a Caribbean Indian, Described by My Father.   Yvonne Sapia.   NIL-7; UnSA

Nearly a Sky Half Clear, Not Yet Half Light.   Yüan Chěn.   CCL1, *tr. by* John A. Scott

Nearly a sky half clear, not yet half light.   Nearly a Sky Half Clear, Not Yet Half Light.   Yüan Chěn.   CCL1, *tr. by* John A. Scott

Nearly a Valediction.   Marilyn Hacker.   PoDa

Nearly Circle. Heather Ramsdell. AmPoNex

Nearly everyone had left that bar in the middle of winter except the. Deer Dancer. Joy Harjo. NAMCP V.2

Nearly midnight. Windows open. Summertime. Through Time's Segments. István Vas. IQMS, *tr. by* Daniel Gerard Hoffman

Nearly Nowhere. Catherine Walsh. Oth

Nearly right, The. To the Tune of The Coventry Carol. Stevie Smith. WoPoe

Nearly ripe for worms. (LL) Face. Jean Toomer. NoP-4; NoP-5

Nearly Three Million Years Ago. Mohamed Lasheen. AnVo, *tr. by* Mohamed Enani

Nearness. David Lindley. NLP

Nearness of You, The. Ned Washington. ReLy

Nearness to Tremendousness, A. Emily Dickinson. TCAPo

Nearsighted child has taken off her glasses, The. Country Stars. William Meredith. VCAP

Near-Sightedness. Edmond Yi-teh Chang. OpBo

Neat greens of Monument Hill, The. Plumburst. John Kinsella. NeBl

Neatened flat, storing heat and white. (LL) Women, The. Eavan Boland. MoWP; NAMCP V.2

Neblina veraniega. David Huerta. RMCMP

Nebraska. Barbara Guest. FTOS

Nebuchadnezzar. Elinor Wylie. ChIV-1; MoAmPo

Nebuchadnezzar's Kingdom-Come. David Rowbotham. ChIV-1; NOBAu

Necessarie Praier in Meeter Against Vices, A. Frances Manners Nevill, Lady Abergavenny. EMWP

Necessary Dirge, A. Ogden Nash. AmWit; APT-2

Necessitie and Benefit of Affliction, The. Anne Lok. EMWP

Necessities. Mei Yao Ch'en. CrYelRi, *tr. by* Sam Hamill

Necessity. E. Y. Harburg. ReLy

Necessity. Langston Hughes. APSN; RaBo

Necessity. Keith Ratzlaff. ACAMVP

Necessity of Fate, The. Jane Barker. EMWP

Neck lodged under a stick, The. Hen, The. Ellen Bryant Voigt. CAP-8

Neck tucked in. Heron. Peter Sanger. Coast

Necking. Sharon Olds. FaoP

Necklace of flame, little dropped hearts. Tattoos. Charles Wright. BodElec

Necklace of human bones. Regalia in Immediate Demand! Philip Whalen. BB

Necklace: Rich Pink Corona Round a Flashing Yellow Heart. Kathleen Crown. FiBr

Neckst. Yosl Cutler. Prolet, *tr. by* Amelia Glaser

Neckties. Liz Lochhead. NePenScot; OBCoV

Necrological. John Crowe Ransom. FuPo; NAAPv.2

Necromance. Rae Armantrout. FTOS; PmAP

Necromancy. Rikki Ducornet. SurWo

Necromancy: The Last Days of Brian Jones, 1968. David Wojahn. SwNoth

Necropolis of Pantàlica. Insomnia. Salvatore Quasimodo. AWTN, *tr. by* Allen Mandelbaum

Nectar of Ápan, The. Enrique Gonzáles Martínez. TCLAP, *tr. by* Elizabeth Gordon

Need. Dionisio D. Martinez. FaoP

Need, The. Sewing a Dress. Lorine Niedecker. APT-2

Need for Armor, A. Eileen Stratidakis. PasH

Need for Attention, The. William Wadsworth. KGB

Need for Censorship, The. Reiner Kunze. PoSu, *tr. by* Michael Hamburger

Need for Shoes, The. Molly Bendall. InvLad

Need I that you exist and show yourself any more than in these songs. (LL) Not Heaving from My Ribb'd Breast Only. Walt Whitman. APN-1; CAGL

Need Increasing Itself by Rounds. Kathleen Peirce. PBCAP

Need not trouble him at all. (LL) Chancelor's Gravel-Drive, The. Po Chü-i. CCL1; WoPoe, *tr. by* Arthur Waley

Need of Being Versed in Country Things, The. Robert Frost. APT-1; NAMCP V.1; NoAM; SAmP; TCAPo; TRP

Need the warld ken? (LL) Comin[g] thro' [*or* through] the Rye. Robert Burns. FaBoVe; GoPo; OxAEP-2

Need to Die, The. César Vallejo. ConPit, *tr. by* Clayton Eshleman and Jorge Guzman

Need to Win, The. Chuang Tzu. BLT, *tr. by* Thomas Merton

Needing someone. Discover Me. Opal Palmer Adisa. GT

Needle and Thread. Pan Chao. WoPoe, *tr. by* Richard Mather and Rob Swigart

Needle and Thread. Pan Zhao. WPoS, *tr. by* Richard Mather

Needle and Thread, The. Pan Chao. ColAnChi

Needle growing in ancient basalt. Mac Wellman. HeMarv *Fr.* Rat Minaret: Miniaturist-Divan, The.

Needle running in white crêpe de chine, A. Made of Crêpe de Chine. Hazel Hall. FiBr

Needled by death for change, for simple change. Vegetable Garden, The. Wyatt Prunty. OBGa

Needled red tea roses were distorted, The. Her Purse, at the Winter Solstice. Susan Hahn. PoDa

Needles. Lucia Maria Perillo. IllVoic

Needlework. Mimi Khalvati. MFPA

Needlework. Elaine Terranova. PoDa

Needling / threading nighttime sewing machine. What Were You Patching? Ruth Lisa Schechter. UnSA

Needs. A. R. Ammons. NIL-7; NIP-4

Needy knife-grinder! whither are you going? Friend of Humanity and the Knife Grinder, The. George Canning *and* John Hookham Frere. OBCoV; UV

Neep-Fields by the Sea, The. Violet Jacob. EdScPo

Ne'er fash your *thumb* what *gods* decree. Horace. NPeEn, *tr. by* Robert Fergusson

Ne'er to be found again[e]. (LL) To Daffodils [*or* Daffadills]. Robert Herrick. BASC; NoP-4; NOSC; OBEV; OxAEP-1; TFi; TreFP

Negative. Kevin Young. LegDan

Negative, The. Arthur Sze. AmAlph

Negative Garden. Sylvia Legris.
  Earth, Critical Earth.
    12. PoPra
    13. PoPra
    14. PoPra
    15. PoPra
    16. PoPra
    17. PoPra
  Tongue Graft Variations.
    1. PoPra
    2. PoPra
    3. PoPra
    4. PoPra
    5. PoPra

Negatives. Charles Wright. PoA 2002

Neglect it. How to kill a living thing. Eibhlín Nic Eochaidh. StAl

Neglected Muse! of this our western clime. James Kirke Paulding. APN-1 *Fr.* Backwoodsman, The.

Neglected Wife, The. Yi Talch'ung. WoPoe, *tr. by* Jean S. Grigsby

Neglectful Edward. Robert Graves. MoBrPo

Negotiation. Leroy McLucas. EGAG

Negotium Perambulans. Peter Redgrove. OBGa

Negro. Langston Hughes. NAAPv.2

Negro, The / With the trumpet at his lips. Trumpet Player. Langston Hughes. BrAP

Negro Ballot, The. Lizelia Augusta Jenkins Moorer. CBWP-3

Negro blood flowing on his brown. Amelia Rosselli. ItPo, *tr. by* Gayle Ridinger

Negro Boy, The. David Samwell. AngWePo

Negro Boy's Tale, The. Amelia Alderson Opie. RWP

Negro Dies, A. Berysh Vaynshteyn. Prolet, *tr. by* Amelia Glaser

Negro Girl, The. Mary Robinson. RWP

Negro girls. Pictures. Clarence Major. EGAG

Negro Has a Chance, The. Maggie Pogue Johnson. CBWP-4

Negro Hero. Gwendolyn Brooks. AmWaPo; ColAP; OxBoAm; PWW2; RACG; WaAnP

Negro Heroines. Lizelia Augusta Jenkins Moorer. CBWP-3

Negro holds firmly the reins of his four horses, the block swags underneath on its tied-over chain, The. Walt Whitman. NoP-5 *Fr.* Song of Myself.

Negro, in the middle of the field, bleeds beneath a bright blade, A. Negro Dies, A. Berysh Vaynshteyn. Prolet, *tr. by* Amelia Glaser

Negro Love Song, A. Paul Laurence Dunbar. APN-2; ColAP; SSLK

Negro on the Subway. Malka Lee. Prolet, *tr. by* Amelia Glaser

Negro Schools, The. Lizelia Augusta Jenkins Moorer. CBWP-3

Negro Sermon—Simon Legree, A. Vachel Lindsay. MoAmPo

Negro Song. Sarah Barkan. Prolet, *tr. by* Amelia Glaser

Negro Speaks of Rivers, The. Langston Hughes. APT-2; BLPJKO; ColAP; CtM; HarvBoo; HeIP-4; ISC; NAAL-5; NAAPv.2; NAMCP V.1; NIL-7; NIP-4; NoAM; NoP-5; OxAAAP; RaBo; SSLK; TCAPo; TFi; WaAnP; WeW-3

Negro Spiritual. Claude McKay. APT-1

Negro Survival 101 or Poem for Tiger Woods and Other Multiethnic *Other's*. Crystal Williams. RD

Negro Woman, A. William Carlos Williams. SAmP

Negroes. Matthew Watley. BtF

Negroes don bow ties. Negroes. Matthew Watley. BtF

Negromania, Negrophilia, Negrophobia.   C. S. Giscombe.   RD

Negro's Complaint, The.   William Cowper.   CABP; ItP

Negrosaurus wrecks. (LL)   Theory on Extinction or what happened to the dinosaurs?   Kenneth Carroll.   AmPoNex; SpirFl

NEHI Strawberry Down-and-Away.   Luis Lopez.   GeoH

Neige, La.   Yves Bonnefoy.   YaTCFP

Neighbor.   Langston Hughes.   APSN; OxBoAm; PFTM-1

Neighbor.   Richard Hugo.   GifTon

Neighbor.   Bahiyyih Maroon.   SpirFl

Neighborhood / of tiny shaded yards.   Ortamezar—The Jewish Quarter.   Ivan Teofilov.   CSCBP, tr. by Georgi Belev and Lisa Sapinkopf

Neighborhood animals are circling the yard, The.   Giving the House Away.   Julie King.   SweBea

Neighborhood dog is climbing up the side of a house, A.   Neighborhood Dog, The.   Russell Edson.   OxBoAm

Neighborhood of Make-Believe, The.   Thomas Lux.   LaCa

Neighborhood of my youth.   Trip Through the Mind Jail, A.   Raul Salinas.   FaBoA

Neighboring Storms.   Greg Williamson.   AmPoNex

Neighbors.   Antonio Deltoro.   RMCMP, tr. by Christian Viveros-Fauné

Neighbors.   Yi Cha.   PML, tr. by Wang Ping and Richard Sieburth

Neighbors' dog will not stop barking, The.   Another Reason Why I don't Keep a Gun in the House.   Billy Collins.   OxBoAm; SUP

Neighbor's Elm, The.   Robert Ayres.   UrbNat

Neighbor sits in his window and plays the flute, The.   Music.   Amy Lowell.   ColAP

Neighbours.   Gillian Clarke.   TCAWP

Neighbour's Pear Tree.   Tony Curtis.   AngWePo

Neighing of the Fingers.   Aziz Samawi.   IrPoTo, tr. by Alex Bellem

Neil Diamond.   Poet Sings His Painting, The.   Lloyd Richardson.   WaCA

Neil Young.   Tom Clark.
"In a strange game I saw myself."   AHA

Neither a jade carriage nor a golden palanquin is precious.   My Hobby on the Mountain.   Hamhur Kiwha.   BecRai, tr. by Kim Daljin, Kim Won-Chung and Christopher Merrill

Neither a lender nor a borrower be.   Postmodern: A Definition.   Joseph Like.   ReTh

Neither battle nor fiendish pogrom.   Memorial to Triangle Fire Victims.   Morris Jacob Rosenfeld.   NAAPv.2, tr. by Leon Stein

Neither Blood Nor Bowed.   Dorothy Parker.   AmWit

Neither can you crack a nut. (LL)   Fable: "Mountain and the squirrel, The."   Ralph Waldo Emerson.   APN-1; NBLV; OxBoAm; TFi

Neither childhood / nor future.   Confession.   George Oppen.   HarvBoo

Neither cloud nor rain casts.   Logging Trestle.   Mary Barnard.   APT-2

Neither does the world answer but.   Sic transit.   Skip Fox.   AnSo

Neither Durst Any Man From That Day Ask Him Any More Questions.   Richard Crashaw.   ChIV-2

Neither father nor lover. (LL)   Elegy for Jane.   Theodore Roethke.   APT-2; BrAP; ColAP; InoFa; MoAmPo; NAMCP V.1; NoP-4; NoP-5; PoPoPo; PtR; TFi; TRP; WaAnP; WeW-3

Neither for stars nor moon.   Evening Primrose.   Kim Namjo.   CAMKP, tr. by David R. McCann and Hyunjae Yee Sallee

Neither had said they were going to climb to it.   Source, The.   David Wagoner.   VCAP

Neither Here nor There.   William Robert Rodgers.   MoBrPo

Neither Innocence or Experience.   Dambudzo Marechera.   NAfrP

Neither is simple.   Thomas Kinsella.   HarvBoo Fr. Notes.

Neither leaving, nor wishing that they were staying.   Key, The.   Peter Scupham.   HarvBoo

Neither of them.   Thing.   Elin ap Hywel.   BBMWP, tr. by the author

Neither of them was better than the other.   From Plane to Plane.   Robert Frost.   MoAmPo

Neither of them were thinking of me then.   Long Walk Home, The.   Robert Fleming.   BtF

Neither on horseback nor seated.   Walt Whitman at Bear Mountain.   Louis Simpson.   TRP; ViWalt

Neither our vices nor our virtues.   Poetry, a Natural Thing.   Robert Duncan.   CalPo; NAMCP V.2; NoAM; OxBoAm; PmAP; TRP

Neither Out Far Nor In Deep.   Robert Frost.   APT-1; BrAP; NAMCP V.1; NoAM; NoP-4; NoP-5; OxBoAm; TRP; WeW-3; WoPoe

Neither sheep nor cows crisscross our lives as much.   Afterlife of Trees, The.   Brian Bartlett.   Coast

Neither the interminable patches of land.   Like This.   Lajos Kassák.   IQMS, tr. by Edwin Morgan

Neither the mailboxes nor the windows would tell me.   Morbid.   Nancy Eimers.   ExTi

Neither the sorrows of afternoon, waiting in the silent house.   Pentecost.   Dana Gioia.   PoDa; Vesp

Neither the wild tulip, poignant.   Palm Sunday.   Amy Clampitt.   OxBoAm

Neither will I put myself forward as others may do.   Eternal Masculine.   William Rose Benét.   MoAmPo

Neither wish death, nor fear his might. (LL)   Happy Life, The.   Martial.   NoSic; OBVE, tr. by Henry Howard, Earl of Surrey

Neither yes nor no: she is entire.   Mavena.   Radovan Ivsic.   YaTCFP, tr. by Mary Ann Caws

Neither yielding to rain.   November 3rd.   Miyazawa Kenji.   CAoMJL1, tr. by Hiroaki Sato

Neither your hard crystal silence of solid rock.   Nocturnal Sea.   Xavier Villaurrutia.   CAGL, tr. by Fanny Arango-Ramos and William Keeth

Nel mezzo del camin I found myself / in the middle class.   Circle Jerk.   Andrei Codrescu.   PmAP

Nell.   Rodney Jones.   IllVoic

Nell Flaherty's Drake.   Unknown.   IrV

Nellie Gives into Blanche.   Leslie Simon.   FFC

Nellie named her Blanche for white and French. two.   Nellie Gives into Blanche.   Leslie Simon.   FFC

Nelly Trim.   Sylvia Townsend Warner.   MoBrPo

Nelly's Lament for the Pirnhouse Cat.   Ellen Johnston.   VWP

Nelson, Pitt, Fox.   Sir Walter Scott.   OBEV Fr. Marmion.

Nemo Canem Impune Lacessit.   Robert Garioch.   EdScPo

Nemoroso.   Baldomero Garcilaso de la Vega.   BLPSL, tr. by Rene de Costa, Rigas Kappatos and Eleni Paidoussi

Neo-Classic.   James Merrill.   AmWit

Neon Signs.   Langston Hughes.   APSN; PFTM-1

Neon stripes tighten my wall.   Zebra Goes Wild Where the Sidewalk Ends, The.   Henry Dumas.   GT

Neonatology.   Elizabeth Alexander.
"Giving birth is like jazz, something from silence."   FaoP

Neonbright orange.   Robben Island Sequence.   Dennis Brutus.   HBAPE

Nepenthe.   George Darley.
(Hundred-sunned Phenix.)   OWoS
"Hurry me Nymphs! O, hurry me."   NPeEn
"O blest unfabled incense tree."   OBEV

Nepenthe.   Charlotte Smith.   NoP-4; NoP-5

Nephew, I must to Scotland. Thou stay'st here.   Christopher Marlowe.   CAGL Fr. Edward the Second.

Neptune Goes to the Greeks.   Homer.   NOSC Fr. Iliad, The.

Nero.   Shuntaro Tanikawa.   PoetW, tr. by Harold Wright

Nero / Another summer is coming soon.   Nero.   Shuntaro Tanikawa.   PoetW, tr. by Harold Wright

Nero commanded; but withdrew his eyes.   Cruelties.   Robert Herrick.   CavPo

Nerve, The.   Glyn Maxwell.   BeAl

Nerve Meter, The.   Antonin Artaud.   YaTCFP, tr. by Mary Ann Caws and Patricia Terry

Nerve pivots and that space, A.   Finite Intuition.   Milo De Angelis.   NeIt, tr. by Lawrence Venuti

Nerves.   Arthur Symons.   CABP

Nerves.   Anne Waldman.   BodElec

Nerves are France, and Italy, and Spain, The.   Body, The: A Fancy.   Margaret Lucas Cavendish, Duchess of Newcastle.   STuOW

Nerves, blind attraction to.   Nerves.   Anne Waldman.   BodElec

Nervous Prostration.   Anna Wickham.   MoWP

Nervous Systems.   Greg Williamson.   LegDan

Nervy with neons, the main drag.   At Barstow.   Charles Tomlinson.   NoAM

Nes From Nowhere.   John Lucas.   RSaN

Nescit Vox Missa Reverti.   James Vincent Cunningham.   APT-2

Ness.   Lawson Fusao Inada.   WhBo

Nessa.   Paul Durcan.   IrLP

Nest.   Amanda Dalton.   NeBl Fr. Room of Leaves.

Nest, The.   Carol Moldaw.   UrbNat

Nest, The.   Andrew Young.   Spl

Nest for Everyone, A.   Roberta Spear.   GeoHom

Nest of Hats, A.   Annie Foster.   NLP

Nest on the high Burren of Inishma'an.   Synge's Chair.   Maryhelen Snyder.   ICANM

Nest yon winged artist builds, The.   Unknown.   CCL1 Fr. Que-chao [Translations].

Nesting of Layer Protocols.   Kit Robinson.   FTOS

Nestle-down Cottage.   Mary Weston Fordham.   CBWP-2

Nests in Elms.   Michael Field.   NAEL-7v2; VWP

Nests of golden porridge shattered in the silky-oak trees.   Equanimity.   Les A. Murray.   NOBAu

Nestus Gurley.   Randall Jarrell.   HeIP-4; InGu

Net, The.   George Mackay Brown.   WaAnP

Net, The.   William Robert Rodgers.   IrLP; ModIr; PNI

Net, The.   Edith Södergran.   WoPoe, tr. by David McDuff

Net Breaker, The.   Brewster Ghiselin.   APT-2

Net of Place, The. Paul Blackburn. PFTM-2; PmAP

Nettle. *Unknown.* WoPoe *Fr.* Two Swedish Riddles.

Nettlebed Road. Naomi Mitchison. EdScPo

Nettles in May. Euros Bowen. BBMWP; OBWVE, *tr.* by the author and Joseph P. Clancy

Nettles in May. Euros Bowen. BBMWP, *tr.* by Joseph P. Clancy

Network, The. Arthur Sze. OpBo

Network of the Imaginary Mother, The. Robin Morgan. "As it was in the beginning." HW

Neural, feral fix on the beautiful movie face, A. Song of the Ransom of the Dark. Bruce Smith. BAP-04

Neurasthenia [*with music*]. Agnes Mary Frances Robinson. NPeEn

Neuroanatomy Summer. Marc J. Straus. BloBone

Neurosis. Elizabeth Bartlett. MoWP

Neutral Tones. Thomas Hardy. CABP; HeIP-4; MoBrPo; NAEL-6v2; NAEL-7v2; NAMCP V.1; NoAM; NoP-4; NoP-5; NPeEn; TFi; WaAnP

Neutrality. Sidney Keyes. MoBrPo

Neutrality. Eman Mersaal. AnVo, *tr.* by Mohamed Enani

Neutrality Loathsome. Robert Herrick. ChIV-1; NoP-4; NoP-5

Neutrino (means little one). Jason Christie. PoPra

Nevada es silenciosa, La. Miguel de Unamuno. RaW

Nevada Red Blues. Adrian C. Louis. AtGh

Never a day, never a day passes. Europe's Prisoners. Sidney Keyes. PoWW

Never able to enter. Farmers. Kathleen Peirce. PBCAP

Never afraid of those huge creatures. Horseback. Carolyn Kizer. MoASP

Never Again. Noël Coward. ReLy

Never Again. Jaroslav Seifert. AF *Fr.* Bombing of the Town of Kralupy, The.

Never again another garden like. Never Again Another Garden. Sándor Weöres. IQMS, *tr.* by Bruce Berlind and Mária Kőrösy

Never again, Orpheus. Antipater of Sidon. WoPoe, *tr.* by Kenneth Rexroth

Never Again the Same. James Tate. BodElec

Never Again Would Birds' Song Be The Same. Robert Frost. APT-1; NAMCP V.1; NIP-4; NoAM; NoP-4; NoP-5; OWoS; OxBoAm; SoSe-8

Never anyone but you in spite of stars and solitudes. Never Anyone but You. Robert Desnos. YaTCFP, *tr.* by Mary Ann Caws

"Never Apologize; Never Explain." Philip Whalen. BB

Never argue with your heart. Why Shouldn't It Happen to Us? Mann Holiner. ReLy

Never ask me whose. (LL) A. E. Housman. BrAP; MoBrPo; NAMCP V.1; NoAM; NoP-4; NoP-5; OBEV *Fr.* Shropshire Lad, A.

Never Before. Philip Levine. NevBe

Never before without a ring. My Ringless Fingers on the Steering Wheel Tell the Story. Laura Boss. UnSA

Never, believe me, / Appear the Immortals. Visit of the Gods, The. Samuel Taylor Coleridge. OBVE

Never better, mad as a hatter. Sweater Weather: A Love Song to Language. Sharon Bryan. GoPo

Never between the branches has the sky. Brilliant Sky. Jean Joubert. GifTon, *tr.* by Denise Levertov

Never can worldly tumults violate. Return. T. H. Parry-Williams. BBMWP, *tr.* by Joseph P. Clancy

Never closer the whole rest of our lives. (LL) Seamus Heaney. BeAl; BLT; InoFa; ItP; NoP-5; PML; PNI *Fr.* Clearances.

Never comes now the through-and-through clear. Not-Returning, The. Ivor Gurney. HarvBoo

Never could bring myself. Jesus' Song. Esther Louise. BtF

Never could carry a tune. Zing! Went the Strings of My Heart. James F. Hanley. ReLy

Never did I learn to share. Expanding. To My Twin Sister Who Died at Birth. Kathleene West. GifTon

Never Did I See Such Loves Nor Such Separations. İlhan Berk. NaPG, *tr.* by Talat Sait Halman

Never / did I speak with her. Silk of a Soul. Zbigniew Herbert. BeAl, *tr.* by Peter Dale Scott

Never do I let any word of this leak out. (LL) Yi Sang. CAMKP; PFTM-1 *Fr.* Crow's-Eye View.

Never does it. One is whole. One is not. Kathleen Fraser. PfS

Never Eat Oranges! John Nelson. GeoH

Never for us those dreams aforetime shown. Of the Earth, Earthy. Rosamund Marriott Watson. ViWPN

Never forget. Ishikawa Takuboku. CAoMJL1, *tr.* by Carl Sesar

Never forget / We walk on hell. Issa. ZenPo, *tr.* by Takashi Ikemoto and Lucien Stryk

Never forgot to put in my pocket. (LL) Once I got a postcard from the Fiji Islands. Jaan Kaplinski. StAl; TAPaP; WhBo, *tr.* by the author, Sam Hamill and Riina Tamm

Never Give a Bum an Even Break [*with music*]. James Welch. NoAM

Never giving thought to fame. On Entering His Coffin. Baiho. ZenPo, *tr.* by Takashi Ikemoto and Lucien Stryk

Never Gonna Dance. Dorothy Fields. ReLy

Never got, and never thought, and yet. Sonnet. Karen Volkman. IAoNAP

Never had the old man made such a journey. Father, The. Maura Eichner. UpMys

Never has such turmoil. Turmoil, The. Sorley MacLean. HarvBoo

Never in all my life have I seen. Rat, O Rat. Christopher Logue. EmeKit

Never in its path before, she sat, legs crossed, facing east. She. Hurakán: A Two Way Poem. Linda M. Rodriguez Guglielmoni. FTtHH

Never, in the way of the Great Poets. Poem on the First Day of Spring. Peter Cooley. PoDa

Never Land. Yusef Komunyakaa. ReTh

Never Let Me Go. Ray Evans and Jay Livingston. ReLy

Never let me go. Never Let Me Go. Ray Evans and Jay Livingston. ReLy

Never love with all your heart. Song in Spite of Myself. Countee Cullen. ISC; ItP

Never mind how or why—. White. Grace Nichols. Oth

Never mind the fantasy about the tweezers and the tongue. Skin. Brian Henry. AmPoNex; LegDan

Never more, when the day is o'er. Fountain's Abbey. Letitia Elizabeth Landon. NPBRoP

Never Mororcco. Tessa Rumsey. LegDan

Never, never may the fruit be plucked from the bough. Never May the Fruit Be Plucked. Edna St. Vincent Millay. AFaM; APT-1

Never on this side of the grave again. Life's Parallels, A. Christina Georgina Rossetti. NAEL-6v2; NAEL-7v2

Never Pain to Tell Thy Love. William Blake. *See* Love's Secret.

Never Pharaoh's Night. In the Desert. Herman Melville. NCAP

Never reaching the promised land in Canada. Tribute to Chief Joseph, A. Duane Niatum. AmWaPo

Never recorded either. (LL) Buzz in the Window. Ted Hughes. NAMCP V.2; NoAM

Never saw you look. Easter Parade. Irving Berlin. ReLy

Never seek to tell thy love [*see also* "I told my love I told my love"]. Love's Secret. William Blake. ITBLP; NPeEn; OxBEV

Never shall a young man. For Anne Gregory. William Butler Yeats. NAEL-6v2; NAEL-7v2; OxAEP-2

Never Shall I Forget. Elie Wiesel. HP

Never shall I forget that night. Never Shall I Forget. Elie Wiesel. HP

Never shall I take an old man as a lover. *Unknown.* SLW, *tr.* by Marjolijn De Jager, Sayd Bahodin Majrouh and André Velter

Never since a child. You're Lucky to Me. Andy Razaf. ReLy

Never so much as. An oblique angle. Primitive oath, blood horizon. Macula of Light, A. Forrest Gander. OnScMo

Never such innocence again. (LL) MCMXIV. Philip Larkin. FaBoWar; HarvBoo; NAEL-6v2; NAEL-7v2; NAMCP V.2; NoAM; NoP-4; NoP-5; OBWP; OxAEP-2; PoAgWa

Never Swat a Fly. Lew Brown, B. G. DeSylva and Ray Henderson. ReLy

Never take her away. Song. Vinícius de Moraes. WoPoe, *tr.* by Richard Wilbur

Never talk ahead. Joanne Kyger. WhBo

Never talk down to a glowworm. Glowworm. David McCord. NTCP

Never Tell [*with music*]. *Unknown.* OBWVE, *tr.* by Anthony Conran

Never tell me that not one star of all. Star in a Stoneboat, A. Robert Frost. APT-1

Never than, the look. Anyway. Ted Greenwald. BAP-04

Never the loaves and fishes multiplied. Christ Seen by Flemish Painters. Elizabeth Jennings. HarvBoo

Never think she loves him wholly. Appraisal. Sara Teasdale. MoAmPo

Never to be lonely like that. Face to Face. Adrienne Rich. NAMCP V.2; NoAM

Never Too Late. Robert Greene. Palmer's Ode, The. NoSic

Never Too Late. John Taggart. FTOS

Never too many fish in a swift creek,. Jelaluddin Rumi. RaBo *Fr.* Three Quatrains.

Never touched a drop last night. That Face. Ralph Blane and Hugh Martin. ReLy

Never treat others with scorn. Love Thy Neighbor. Mack Gordon. ReLy

Never turns him to the bride. (LL) A. E. Housman. HarvBoo; MoBrPo; NoP-4; NoP-5; NPeEn *Fr.* Shropshire Lad, A.

Never until the mankind making. Refusal to Mourn the Death, by Fire, of a Child in London, A. Dylan Thomas. AF; BrAP; FaBoWar; HarvBoo; HeIP-4; MoBrPo; NAMCP V.2; NoAM; NoP-4; NoP-5; OBWVE; OxAEP-2; PoAgWa; PoWW; TFi; WaAnP

Never wake up in a million years. (LL) First Night, A. Peter Kane Dufault. NoP-4; NoP-5

Never weather-beaten sail[e] more willing bent to shore. O Come Quickly! Thomas Campion. NPeEn; OBEV; OxAEP-1

Never—yes, never—before these months just passed. Acquaintance with Time in Early Autumn. Robert Penn Warren. NAAL-5

Never yet could I endure. The Archpoet. EroLit *Fr.* Confession, The.

Never-Dead, The. Anna Couani. BMAP

Nevertheless. Marianne Moore. HarvBoo; NAAPv.2; NoP-4; NoP-5; SoSe-8

Nevertheless (I'm in Love with You). Bert Kalmar and Harry Ruby. ReLy

Nevertheless the Moon. Muriel Rukeyser. AWTN

Nevrazumitelny. Wendy Mulford. Oth

New. Gillian Conoley. RoV

New. Jennifer Maiden. BMAP

New Age, The. Stevie Smith. NAEL-6v2; NAEL-7v2

New/Aguas Buenas/Jersey. Víctor Hernández Cruz. TouFir

New air has come around us. Dakota: October, 1822, Hunkpapa Warrior. Rod Taylor. WeW-3

New Apartment. Linda Hogan. HATNAP; UnSA

New Approach Needed [*with music*]. Kingsley Amis. NoAM

New Ark Space. Imamu Amiri Baraka. EGAG *Fr.* Poem of Destiny, A.

New Arrival. Kenneth Mackenzie. BMAP

New Baby, The. Fred Emerson Brooks. VerBaPo

New Birth, The. Jones Very. APN-1; NCAP; OxBoAm; SacPr

New Blade. Anzai Hitoshi. PML, *tr. by* Leith Morton

New Blue Bike, A. C. J. Stevens. ArBi

New Boogaloo. Willie Perdomo. BRtP

New books of poetry will be written. Coronal, A. William Carlos Williams. OxBoAm; TCAPo

New book—the making and breaking of me—ringing out from the Tower of the Supreme Hour!, A. Supreme Hour, The. Viktor Aleksandrovich Sosnora. ItGoST, *tr. by* F. D. Reeve

New Bottom. Dylan Iorwerth. BBMWP *Fr.* Sand.

New Boy, The. Peter E. Murphy. OPRER

New Bride, The. Catherine Smith. BeAl

New Brooms, The. Odia Ofeimun. NAfrP

New Clouds, The. William Carlos Williams. HarvBoo

New Colossus, The. Emma Lazarus. AmFaPo; APN-2; CA; CtM; FaBoA; GS; GSo; HHAm; NAAPv.1; NIL-7; NoP-4; NoP-5; OxBoAm; SWaP; TCAPo

New Comers. Melinda Goodman. WiU

New Constructions. John Ashbery. KGB

New Corrido of Laredo. *Unknown.* NAAPv.2

New Courtly Sonet, [*or* Sonnet] of the Lady Greensleeves, A. *Unknown.* NoSic; NPeEn; PBRV

New Crops for a Free Man. Ai. BodElec

New Cycle, A. Edward Field. ArBi

New day cancels dread, The. Psalm: The New Day. Mark Jarman. AWTN

New Days for Old, Old Days for New. Philip Levine. TaR

New decade, the teacher cried, *A.* My Mother's Young Sister. Roy McFadden. PNI

New Diary, A [*with music*]. Dannie Abse. AngWePo; NoAM

New discovery may lie. The deer in that beautiful place lay down their bones: I must wear mine. (LL) Deer Lay Down Their Bones, The. Robinson Jeffers. APT-1; GPTC; NoAM

New Dog. Mark Doty. InoFa; WiU *Fr.* Atlantis.

New doth the sun appear. Change Should Breed Change. William Drummond of Hawthornden. OBEV

New Dream, A (Wuski A-Baw-Tan). Jennifer Pierce Eyen. ReEnLa

New Dub, A. "Mbala." WaCA

New England. Edwin Arlington Robinson. HeIP-4; MoAmPo; PoPoPo

New England Bachelor, A. Richard Eberhart. MoAmPo; NoAM

New England first a wilderness was found. America. Phillis Wheatley. TCAPo

New England Pilgrimage. Phyllis McGinley. AmWit

New England, Springtime. Norman Dubie. AmAlph

New England Wind. Eileen Myles. PmAP

New falconer. Invocation. Sana'i. BBASP, *tr. by* Nasrollah Pourjavady and Peter Lamborn Wilson

New flaws. Food rotting within a safe context. First the food. Heather Ramsdell. IAoNAP *Fr.* Vague Swimmers.

New flood came, transcending Ipoly's banks. Lőrinc Szabó. IQMS *Fr.* Cricket Music.

New foal, The. Issa. EH, *tr. by* Robert Hass

New Friends and Old Friends. Joseph Parry. ITBLP

New from Ethiopia and the Sudan, The. John Pepper Clark Bekedermo. HBAPE

New Ghost, The. Fredegond Maitland Shove. SacPr

New ghosts weep over lost battles. Facing the Snow. Tu Fu [*or* Du Fu]. CrYelRi, *tr. by* Sam Hamill

New grass, the new lambs, The. Pastorale for Spring. Al Zolynas. SUP

New Gravity. Robin Robertson. StAl

New Guard forms, is present and correct, The. Guard-Room. Peter Scupham. WaAnP

New Guide, A. Kenneth Koch. BodElec

New Hampshire. T. S. Eliot. NoAM; WeW-3 *Fr.* Landscapes.

New Hampshire. Howard Moss. GoPo

New Heart, The. Semyon Isaakovich Kirsanov. CLPP, *tr. by* Anselm Hollo

New Heaven, New War[re]. Robert Southwell. ChIV-2

(New Heaven, New War.) NoP-4

New Heavens for Old. Amy Lowell. APT-1; NAMCP V.1

New House. Geraldine Connolly. SweBea

New House, The. Edward Thomas. MoBrPo; OBEV; OBWVE

New houses grasp our hillside. Andante. Gwen Harwood. HarvBoo

New hunt / the morning bent, A. Clark Coolidge. APSN *Fr.* At Egypt.

New Illiterate Lay-Teachers, The. Rowland Watkyns. BASC

New Incidents in the Life of Shelley. Robert Johnstone. "Not from our dreams, not from our daft cadres." PNI

New Indian Medicine [*with music*]. Emma Lee Warrior. HATNAP

New Inn, The. Ben Jonson. "It was a beauty that I saw." ItP

(Vision of Beauty, A.) BASC; NOSC

New Intelligence, The. Timothy Donnelly. LegDan

New Jersey Boys. Robert Coles. BloBone

New Jersey Turnpike [*with music*]. Richard Cumbie. NBLV

New Jerusalem, The. Allan M. Laing. UV

New Jerusalem, The. *Unknown. See* Hierusalem.

New Joke, The. Deborah Bacharach. FiBr

New Knighthood, The. Rudyard Kipling. UV

New knowledge of reality, A. (LL) Not Ideas about the Thing but the Thing Itself. Wallace Stevens. APT-1; OxBoAm; PFTM-2; SAmP; StAl

New Language, The. Elizabeth Robinson. OnScMo

New laugh, The. Woman Dragged by Welsh Corgis. Joan Retallack. FTOS

New life, new birth, or a Nation's tomb? (LL) Crime of the Ages, The. Augusta Cooper Bristol. APN-2; PCW

New Life, The. Louise Glück. BodElec

New Life, The. Lisa Jarnot. LegDan

New light gives new directions, Fortunes new. George Chapman. NoSic; PBRV *Fr.* Hero and Leander.

New light on an old bike. Moon in the Mirror. Brenda Brooks. ArBi

New little boy moved in next door, A. New Little Boy, The. Harry Behn. TLR

New Little Boy, The. Harry Behn. TLR

New Love and the Gentle Heart. Dante Alighieri. RaBo

New love and the gentle heart are the same thing. New Love and the Gentle Heart. Dante Alighieri. RaBo

New Man, The. Jones Very. APN-1; TCAPo

New Mennonite Replies to Julia Kasdorf, A. David Wright. ACAMVP

New Mex Hip. Anne MacNaughton. ICANM

New Mexican Mountain. Robinson Jeffers. NoAM

New Mexico. Douglas Kent Hall. ICANM

New Mexico Time. Mary McGinnis. ICANM

New Mistress, The. A. E. Housman. MoBrPo *Fr.* Shropshire Lad, A.

New Miz Praise de Lawd, The. Nicole Breedlove. InTrad

New Monthly Magazine, 44 286–8. Letitia Elizabeth Landon. Stanzas on the Death of Mrs Hemans. VWP

New Moon. Tu Fu [*or* Du Fu]. ChinPo, *tr. by* Ye Weilian [*or* Yeh Wei-lien *or* Wai-lim Yip]

New Moon Ceremonies. *Unknown. Fr.* Minnetare Songs.

New moon hangs like an ivory bugle, The. Penny Whistle, The. Edward Thomas. MoBrPo

New moon! New king! Marriage of Death, The. László Szabédi. IQMS, *tr. by* J. G. Nichols

New moon stirs pangs of love, The. First Love. Vidyapati. ErotSp, *tr. by* Sam Hamill

New moon, The. Yannis Ritsos. PFTM-2 *Fr.* Second Series.

New Moon, The. William Gilmore Simms. APN-1

New Moon, The. *Unknown.* WoPoe *Fr.* Two Swedish Riddles.

New Mother. Sharon Olds. PasH

New Mr Barnsley Something, The. Geoff Hattersley. NeBl

New Music, A. Haniel Long. APT-1

New Nephilim, A. Afaa Michael Weaver. OxAAAP

New Netherland, 1654. Grace Schulman. OPRER

New Noah, The [*with music*]. Adonis. AF, *tr. by* Abdullah Al-Udhari

New Organ, The [*with music*]. Josephine D. Henderson Heard. CBWP-4

New Orleans. Ralph Adamo. AnSo

New Orleans. Joy Harjo. HATNAP

New Orleans Engagement. Dave Jeddie Smith. LPSFW

New Orleans Haiku. Kalamu ya Salaam.

All Nite Long. SpirFl

Everywhere You Eat. SpirFl

French Quarter Intimacies. SpirFl

Funeraled Fare Well. SpirFl

Height, Breadth, Depth. SpirFl

Makes You Go Oohhh! SpirFl

New Orleans Rainbow. SpirFl

Our Natures Rise. SpirFl

Quarter Moon Rise. SpirFl

Round Midnight, Place de Congo. SpirFl

Secondline Send Off. SpirFl

Spice of Life, The. SpirFl

Spiritual Geography. SpirFl

St. Louis Cemetery Crypt. SpirFl

Sunrise on the River. SpirFl

Til Death Do Us Part. SpirFl

New Orleans Rainbow. Kalamu ya Salaam. SpirFl *Fr.* New Orleans Haiku.

New Orpheus, The. Christopher Howell. RoV

New Our Father, The. Priscilla Baird Hinckley. HW

New peace hangs like moss, A. New Sestina, The. Kevin Simmonds. BtF

New Periods—of Pain. (LL) Pain Has an Element of Blank. Emily Dickinson. APN-2; ColAP; HeIP-4; MoAmPo; NAAL-3; NAAPv.1; OxBoAm; SWaP; TCAPo

New Person, A. John Ridland. CalPo

New Philosophy of Composition, or, How to Ignore the Non-Reasoning Creature Capable of *Speeech* Perched Outside Your Bathroom Window, A. Olena Kalytiak Davis. NAPBL

New Picnic Time. Peter Gizzi. OnScMo

New pier is concrete, the streets are paved, The. Love Song. Samuel Maio. CalPo

New Poem. Holley Blackwell. AnSo

New Poem (for Jack Spicer), A. Robert Duncan. FTOS

New Point of View, A. Martial. DiBP *Fr.* Epigrams.

New Presbyter is but old Priest writ[t] large. (LL) On the New Forcers of Conscience Under the Long Parliament. John Milton. BASC; NAEL-6v1; NOSC; PBRV

New Prince, New Pomp[e]. Robert Southwell. ChrPo; NoSic; SacPr; WaAnP

New Race, The. Aubrey Thomas De Vere. IrV

New Realism. Joseph Ceravolo. PmAP

New Reality Is Better Than a New Movie!, A. Imamu Amiri Baraka. NAMCP V.2; NoAM; WaAnP

New Release, A. Alice Fulton. AllShUp

New ridge spreads underneath. Volcanoes, offten, A. Wandering Curves. Keith Waldrop. PmAP

New Rock n Roll, The. Brendan Cleary. NeBl

New Rule. Anne Carson. NoP-5

New Rule, The. Jelaluddin Rumi. RaBo, *tr. by* Coleman Barks and Robert Bly

New salem in patches of snow. Late Winter in Menard County. John Knoepfle. IllVoic

New schemes, not even dream'd of once before. Thomas Baker. STuOW *Fr.* Steam Engine; or, The Power of the Flame, The.

New sensation, A. "H. D." APT-1 *Fr.* Tribute to the Angels.

"New Sensibility" or not, The. Wordsworths: William and Dorothy, The. Thomas Lux. BodElec

New Sentience, The. Alan Davies. FTOS

New Sermons and Preachings of the Christ of Elqui (1979). Nicanor Parra. "Who are my friends / the sick / the weak / the poor in spirit." GI

New Sestina, The. Kevin Simmonds. BtF

New shoes, new shoes. Choosing Shoes. Ffrida Wolfe. ChAP

New snow. Garry Gay. CalPo

New snow covers everything, The. Possibility. Charles Coe. UrbNat

New Song. Vincente Huidobro. CuPo

New Song, A. Seamus Heaney. CABP

New Song of Solomon. Cyrus Cassells. WiU

New Southern Exposure. Hettie Jones. PrTe

New Spirit, The. Glenn Godfrey. OWABP

New Spirit, The. Hank Lazer.
8 / (in transit). AnSo
Teshuva: heading south. AnSo

New Spoon River, The. Edgar Lee Masters.
Marx the Sign Painter. NoAM
Unknown Soldiers. InoFa; NoAM

New Stanzas for *Amazing Grace.* Allen Ginsberg. WhBo

New Stanzas to Augusta. Joseph Brodsky. *tr. by* George L. Kline
"September came on Tuesday." WoPoe, *tr. by* George L. Kline

New Stars, The. Martinus Nijhoff. WoPoe, *tr. by* Raphael Rudnik

New stirrings converge in the mist. Anti-mnemonic self-vaccination. Joyce Mansour. MFP, *tr. by* Martin Sorrell

New Storefront. Russell Atkins. GT

New styles of architecture, a change of heart. (LL) Petition. W. H. Auden. NAEL-6v2; NAEL-7v2

New Suit, The. Nidia Sanabria de Romero. ChAP, *tr. by* Arnaldo D. Larrosa and Naomi Shihab Nye

New Sweater. Kees Ouwens. TuT, *tr. by* Peter van de Kamp

New Tarantella. Paul Griffin. UV

New Tenants, The. Edwin Arlington Robinson. NoAM

New Testament, The. Nike Adesuyi. NeNiPo

New Testament, The. Who Will Throw the First Stone? Clara Silva. TANSG, *tr. by* Celeste Kostopulos-Cooperman

New, the feel of sand after sea. Viola Recalls. Chris Terrio. IaFF

New Time. Leslie Scalapino.
"There's still on the rim of night (having been in it) which is (in night)." ExTi

New Toy, The. Thomas Hardy. ChAP

New Verses for June 7, 1951. Jan Hanlo. TuT, *tr. by* Eamon Grennan

New Version of the Psalms of David, Fitted to the Tunes Used in Churches, A. Bible, *O.T.*
[Psalm 104]. STuOW
[Psalm 104]. STuOW

New View of Sunday Cycling, A. *Unknown.* ArBi

New volcano has erupted, A. Crusoe in England. Elizabeth Bishop. APT-2; EmeKit; FaBoVe; NAMCP V.2; OxBoAm; PoPoPo; RACG

New Vows. Louise Erdrich. CAP-8

New Wife, The. Wang Chien. BLT

New Windows [*The stewardess gave me—I had just / turned six—a white eyelet sweater. / It was late November, 1968. "This is America," / she told me, "cold, not like the West Indies. / One needs a jacket of some kind here."*]. Claudia Rankine. GT

New World. Sally Roberts Jones. AngWePo

New World A-Comin'. Edward Kamau Brathwaite. NoP-4; NoP-5 *Fr.* Arrivants: A New World Trilogy, The.

"New World" Interview. Bruce Sweet. MiVo

New World Symphony, A. Kit Wright. NBLV

New World, The. Imamu Amiri Baraka. NoAM; NoP-4; PmAP

New World, The. Valerie Martínez. TouFir

New World, The. Jones Very. APN-1; OxBoAm

New Year. Aimé Césaire. YaTCFP, *tr. by* Clayton Eshleman and Annette Smith

New Year. Philip Larkin. ChrPo

New Year. Naomi Shihab Nye. LoL

New Year: "Let me dive to the bottom of the hotel pool." Jason Shinder. NevBe

New Year. Christopher Smart. ChrPo *Fr.* Hymns and Spiritual Songs for the Fasts and Festivals of the Church of England.

New Year, The. Mark Strand. NAMCP V.2 *Fr.* Elegy for My Father.

New Year, The. *Unknown.* OBCP

New Year, The. Nathaniel Parker Willis. TreFP

New year arrived, The. Issa. SoOfWa, *tr. by* Sam Hamill

New Year Behind the Asylum. David Constantine. BeAl

New year, forth looking out of Janus' gate. Edmund Spenser. NoSic *Fr.* Amoretti.

New Year Greeting, A. W. H. Auden. HarvBoo; NAMCP V.1

New year has dawned and we meet it with gladness, The. New Year's Morning; or, the First Day of the Year. Mrs. Henry Linden. CBWP-4

New Year Letter. W. H. Auden.

New Year Letter [*for mexican*]. Edward Kamau Brathwaite. GT

New Year's. Charles Reznikoff. TaR

New Year's: A Short Pantoum. Greg Williamson. NoP-5

New Year's Card, A. Hwang Insuk. EcSo, *tr. by* Peter H. Lee

New Year's Day. Issa. EH, *tr. by* Robert Hass

New Year's Day. Issa. IllVoic *Fr.* Issa: A Suite of Haiku.

New Year's Day. Robert Lowell. ChrPo; TRP

New Year's Day came quietly and left silently. Karl Yoneda. NAAPv.2

New Year's Day on Angel Island. Karl Yoneda. NAAPv.2

New Year's Eve. John Davidson.
Imagination. MoBrPo

New Year's Eve. Lavinia Greenlaw. MFPA

New Year's Eve. Thomas Hardy. MoBrPo; NAMCP V.1; NoAM

New Year's Eve. Yang Wen-li. WoPoe, *tr. by* Nancy Hodes and Tung Yuan-fang

New Year's Eve, 1938. John Frederick Nims. ChrPo

New Year's Eve at the Home of Tu Wei. Tu Fu [*or* Du Fu]. CrYelRi, *tr. by* Sam Hamill

New Year's Eve in Bismarck, North Dakota. Kathleen Norris. UpMys

New Year's Eve, in Hospital. Philip Levine. MAAN

New Year's Eve Poem 1965. Peter Levi. OxAEP-2

New Year's first poem. Buson. SoOfWa, *tr. by* Sam Hamill

New Year's Gift, A. William Cartwright. OxAEP-1

New Year's holiday. Spring Wind on the Riverbank at Kema. Buson. EH, *tr. by* Robert Hass

New Year's Letter in Warsaw, A. Andrey Andreievich Voznesensky. TCRusP, *tr. by* Daniel Weissbort

New Year's Morning. Elmaz Abinader. PoArWo

New Year's morning. Issa. EH, *tr. by* Robert Hass

New Year's Morning; or, the First Day of the Year. Mrs. Henry Linden. CBWP-4

New Year's Ode, 1731. Colley Cibber.

   "Ye grateful Britons, bless the year." STuOW

New Year's [*or* Year] Song. Ted Hughes. OBCP

New Year's Poem. Margaret Avison. BrAP

New Year's Prayer: 1976. Sŏ Chŏngju. CAMKP, *tr. by* David R. McCann

New Year's Season and Its Poetasters, The. Trần Tế Xu'o'ng. WoPoe, *tr. by* Nguyen Ngoc Bich

New Year's white morning of hard new ice, A. New Rule. Anne Carson. NoP-5

New Yeir Gift to the Quene Mary, quhen scho come first Hame, 1562, Ane. Alexander Scott.

   "Welcum, illustrat Ladye, and oure Quene!" NePenScot

New York. Steven Blevins. PoCoUp

New York. Larry Fagin. AHA *Fr.* Parade of the Caterpillars, The.

New York. Federico García Lorca. RaBo; RaW; WED, *tr. by* Robert Bly

New York: "I read over my lines." Hugh Seidman. PA9/11

New York, 1927. Anne Marie Macari. NevBe

New York! At first I was bewildered by your beauty. To New York. Léopold Sédar Senghor. PoetW; WoPoe, *tr. by* Melvin Dixon

New York City. Michael Castro. UrbNat

New York City fails to be spectacular from my teacher's car. Short History of Autumn, A. Anselm Berrigan. HeMarv

New York Face, A. Edwin Denby. APT-2

New York Five A.M. Man with the Saxophone, The. Ai. CFP; SeSe

New York has had it, newsmen all proclaim. New York Sonnet. Judith Rodriguez. NOBAu

New York is a wonderful town. Who Knows? Harold Rome. ReLy

New York is the Old Country to me. Old Countries. Aurora Levins Morales. PueRic

New York Knicks are making front-page news, The. This Old Man. Jackie Sheeler. BRtP

New York!/ Mad mermaid. New York. Alexander Pomerantz. Prolet, *tr. by* Amelia Glaser

New York Minute. Joe Osterhaus. AmPoNex

New York, New York. Betty Comden and Adolph Green. ReLy

New York Newsday: Truth, Justice and Vomit. Paul Beatty. InTrad

New York Notebooks, The. Howard Moss. BodElec

New York Poem, The. Sam Hamill. WANABP

New York Seizures. Eugene B. Redmond. BRtP; FuFl

New York, smog-dim under August. Edwin Denby. AHA *Fr.* Snoring in New York.

New York Sonnet. Judith Rodriguez. NOBAu

New York Spring. Linda France. MFPA

New York Tory, to His Friend in Philadelphia, A. Philip Freneau. AmWaPo

New Yorkers. Edward Field. GoPo

New York's lovely weather / hurts my forehead. Bean Spasms. Ted Berrigan. AHA; PmAP

New York's lovely weather hurts my forehead. For You. Ted Berrigan. AHA

New Zealand. James Keir Baxter. NoP-4; NoP-5

Newark. Evan Braunstein. FTtHH

Newark is a glass jaw, listless in the center of the ring. Newark. Evan Braunstein. FTtHH

New-Born Baby's Song, The. Frances Darwin Cornford. MoWP; NIL-7

Newborn, diaper-clad, same as a child. Star Child. Thomas Sayers Ellis. NeAmPo

Newborn Found Alive in Shallow Grave. David Citino. LiTh

Newborn Lover. Vivian Lamarque. CItWP, *tr. by* Cinzia Sartini Blum and Lara Trubowitz

Newcombe at the Croydon Gallery. Arthur Nortje. HBAPE

New-Comer, A. Herman Melville. *Fr.* Clarel: A Poem and Pilgrimage in the Holy Land.

Newcomers on the hill have cut the trees. Broken View, A. Robert Francis. APT-2

New-Courtier, The. Alexander Brome. BASC

New-England Boy's Song about Thanksgiving Day, The. Lydia Maria Child. *See* Thanksgiving Day.

Newer headstones tense against the cold, The. Churchyard under Snow. David Scott. NLP

Newfoundland is, or was, full of interesting people. Interesting People of Newfoundland. John Ashbery. VaPo

Newly Born Twins. Helen Farish. BeAl

Newly Dead and Newly Born. Eliza Ogilvy. VWP

Newly Discovered "Homeric" Hymn, A. Charles Olson. NoAM

Newly wed girl, pregnant already, The. *Unknown.* WoPoe *Fr.* Gathasaptasati, The.

Newly Wed Girl, The. *Unknown.* WoPoe *Fr.* Gathasaptasati, The.

Newlyweds, The. John Updike. OBCoV

News. William Kloefkorn. LiTh

News, The. Maxine Chernoff. LiTh

News, The. John Godfrey Saxe. NBLV

News, The. Harvey Shapiro. PrTe

News, The. *Unknown.* RWPCtW

News bulletin from Keith Lampe. Joanne Kyger. BB

News continued release. Ed Roberson. EGAG

News for the Delphic Oracle. William Butler Yeats. NoAM

News from a foreign [*or* forein *or* forrein] country came. Thomas Traherne. OBEV *Fr.* Third Century, The.

News, Indeed!—pray do you call it news, The. News, The. John Godfrey Saxe. NBLV

News Item. Dorothy Parker. AmWit; APT-1; NALW; OxBoAm

News of a Baby. Elizabeth Riddell. ItWoWo

News of battle!—news of battle! Edinburgh after Flodden. William Edmonstoune Aytoun.

News of the Changes. Bryan Aspden. AngWePo

News of the Cranes. Rodney Jones. InGu

News of the Occluded Cyclone. Alice Fulton. WeW-3

News of the Phoenix. Arthur James Marshall Smith. BrAP; IFF

News of the World. Meena Alexander. BRtP

News of us spreads like a storm. Pounding Rain. Jackie Kay. MFPA; PoBW

News of Your Death. Callimachus. WoPoe, *tr. by* Stanley Lombardo and Diane Rayor

News of your death. News of Your Death. Callimachus. WoPoe, *tr. by* Stanley Lombardo and Diane Rayor

NEWS peels off my arms and legs in a wind that doesn't quite hurt. The, The. What Say. John Godfrey. FTOS

News So Seldom Comes. Wen T'ing-yün. CCL1, *tr. by* Glen Baxter

News Story. Clarence Major. EGAG

News Update. John Balaban. AF

News which might well reach you, The / before this letter? / Your *Ellen.* (LL) Ellen West. Frank Bidart. NAMCP V.2; RACG

New-sawed. Lorine Niedecker. NAMCP V.1

Newsboy. Albert D. Mackie. EdScPo

Newscast. Jared Angira. NAfrP

Newscast, The. Ian Hamilton. FaBoWar; NPeEn; PoAgWa

Newspaper. Blaise Cendrars. YaTCFP, *tr. by* Ron Padgett

Newspaper, The. Penina Moise *and* Edward N. Calisch. SWaP

Newspaper, glanced at by chance, A. It has something to do with final words. Gladys Cardiff. ReEnLa

Newspaper is a collection of half-injustices, A. Stephen Crane. APN-2

Newspaper on the table, The. Self-Portrait as Still Life. Donald Justice. OxBoAm

Newspaper says the boy killed by someone. Detroit, Tomorrow. Philip Levine. PoA 2002

Newspapers on the Plateau. Irina Mashinskaya. CRWP, *tr. by the author*

Newsreel. Cecil Day Lewis. MoBrPo

Newton's Descent. Irene Plazewska. SurWo

New-year bells are wrangling with the snow, The. (LL) Year's End. Richard Wilbur. GoPo; HeIP-4; MoW

Nexhedxí ne nayani xpiaani. Marcelina. Natalia Toledo. RMCMP

Next. Carla Harryman. BAP-04 *Fr.* Baby.

Next Afternoon. Molly Peacock. OxBoAm

Next and Last. Chase Twichell. AmZen

Next Bend in the Road, The. Michael Fried. PoCho

Next, bidding all draw near on bended knees. Alexander Pope. OBSV *Fr.* Dunciad, The.

Next Day. Randall Jarrell. AmFaPo; HarvBoo; NAMCP V.2; NoAM; NoP-4; NoP-5; VCAP; WeW-3

Next day, I am almost afraid, The. Last Night. Sharon Olds. StAl

Next Door. Laini Mataka. ISC

Next Door. Mei Yao Ch'en. NDACCP, *tr. by* Kenneth Rexroth

Next door a woman is hanging. Clean Sheets. Lisa D. Chavez. AmPoNex

Next Heaven [*or* Heav'n] my vows to thee (O sacred Muse!). Upon the Saying That My Verses Were Made by Another. Anne Killigrew. BASC; CABP; EMWP; NALW; PEW

Next it was Austria we. Glenn on Monk's Mountain. Nathaniel Mackey. OxAAAP

Next Malcolm Poem, The. Peter Harris. BtF

Next millennium you'll have to search quite hard. V. Tony Harrison. NAMCP V.2

Next Morning. *Unknown*. WoPoe, *tr. by* Andrew Schelling

Next morning. Next Morning. *Unknown*. WoPoe, *tr. by* Andrew Schelling

Next, Please. Philip Larkin. CABP; GPTC; HarvBoo; MoBrPo

Next Poem, The. Dana Gioia. NoP-4; NoP-5

Next summer she'll be too old for naps. Balance. James Harris. PasH

Next they invented alphabets. Cabalistic Rabbis, The. Rosita Kalina. MirDau, *tr. by* Roberta Gordenstein

Next thing, I wake up in a swaying bunk. Journey: the North Coast. Robert Gray. BMAP

Next time my mother comes to visit, The. Libation. Palorine Williams. Prnts

Next time she came when the moon was windblown. Night Visit. Adriann Roland Holst. TuT, *tr. by* Paula Meehan

Next time you are doing something absolutely ordinary, or even better, The. Small Sentence to Drive Yourself Sane. Lew Welch. WhBo

Next time you walk by my place. Look Here. Pamela Alexander. ExTi

Next to even. Kyoriku. EMJL, *tr. by* Haruo Shirane

Next to Last Draft, The. C. D. Wright. GPPA

Next to Last Prayer. Pimone Triplett. LegDan

Next to my office where I edit poems ("Can poems be edited?") there is the Chicago Models Club. Editing *Poetry*. Karl Shapiro. IllVoic

Next to my own skin, her pearls. My mistress. Warming Her Pearls. Carol Ann Duffy. BeAl; EdScPo; MakPoe; MoWP; NAMCP V.2; NeBrP; NePenScot; NoP-4; NoP-5; PoBW

Next to of course god america i. E. E. Cummings. FaBoA; NAAL-5; NAMCP V.1; NBLV; NoP-4; NoP-5; OBWP; OxBoAm; PoAgWa; PoWW; RaBo; StAl; TFi; WaAnP

Next to the *Café Chaos*. Olga Broumas. BodElec

Next to the fair ascent our steps we traced. Samuel Boyse. OBGa *Fr.* Triumphs of Nature, The.

Next to the fourteen excellent reasons. Dream of the Just, The. Dana Gelinas. SPV, *tr. by* Jen Hofer

Next to the fresh grave of my beloved grandmother. Ireland 1972. Paul Durcan. PBCIP; PoAgWa

Next to the gate. Generations. Siva Reddy. HotL, *tr. by* V. Narayana Rao

Next to the white window. Jan Freeman. OxWW *Fr.* Autumn Sequence.

Next to the wine. Claustrophobia. Sean O Riordain. ModIr, *tr. by* Patrick Crotty

Next to Tut. Jon Veinberg. GeoHom

Next Two Tablets, The. Armand Schwerner. BodElec

Next unto God, to whom I owe. To Retiredness. Mildmay Fane, 2d Earl of Westmorland. NOSC

Next War, The. Sir Osbert Sitwell. PoWW

Next Year, in Jerusalem. Shirley Kaufman. UnSA

Next year the grave grass will cover us. Street Corner College. Kenneth Patchen. APT-2; CLPP; MoAmPo

Next year we are to bring the soldiers home. Homage to a Government. Philip Larkin. NAMCP V.2; NoAM; OxBEV

Nexus. Rita Dove. OxAAAP

Ngoh m' sick gong tong hwa. Going Home. Wing Tek Lum. UnSA

Ngungalari. Archie Weller. RACG

Ni guicaa ta Juan míchi. Guibá xti min. Natalia Toledo. RMCMP

Ni oui, ni non: elle est entière. Mavena. Radovan Ivsic. YaTCFP

Nia, Imani, Kuchajaculia. Shout Out. Sekou Sundiata. FaoP

Niagara. Adelaide Crapsey. APT-1; NAAPv.2

Niagara. Joseph Rodman Drake. APN-1

Niagara. Vachel Lindsay. AmWit *Fr.* Niagara.

Niagara. Vachel Lindsay.

    Niagara. AmWit

    "What marching men of Buffalo." AmWit

Niagara Falls. Alan Dugan. PoA 2002

Niagara or Vesuvius is deferred. (LL) George Meredith. NPeEn; OxBEV *Fr.* Modern Love.

4: The Niagara River Speaks Three Languages. Alicia Gaspar de Alba. FTtHH *Fr.* Elemental Journey: Anniversary Gift.

Nialls' cottage had one, The. Hearth Song. John Montague. PNI

Nicaragua Water Fire. Gioconda Belli. TANSG, *tr. by* Steven F. White

Nicaraguan Triptych. Rubén Darío. TCLAP, *tr. by* Lysander Kemp

Nice old temple against a green mountain, A. At Hongbub Temple. Daegak Euchon. BecRai, *tr. by* Kim Daljin, Kim Won-Chung and Christopher Merrill

Nice Place, A. Lawson Fusao Inada. WhBo

Nice Sister-Scholars Need Loving, Too. David Earl Jackson. BtF

Nice Thing About Counting Stars, The. Dwight Okita. UnSA

Nice Valor, The. John Fletcher.

    Melancholy. OBEV

Nice Work If You Can Get It. Ira Gershwin. ReLy

Nicest child I ever knew, The. Charles Augustus Fortescue. Joseph Hilaire Pierre Belloc. NoAM

Nicholas by the River. Nance Van Winckel. RoV

Nicholas Ned. Laura Elizabeth Richards. NTCP

Nicholas the ridiculous: you will always be 27 and impossible. No more expectations. D. A. Powell. NeAmPo

Nick and the Candlestick. Sylvia Plath. ItP; NALW

Nickel, what is nickel, it is originally rid of a cover. Gertrude Stein. NAAPv.2 *Fr.* Tender Buttons.

Nickel Wine and Deep Kisses. Patricia Smith. BRtP

Nickleplate moon, The. Kansas City West Bottoms. Edward Dahlberg. PoA 2002

Nicodemus. Howard Nemerov. GI; TaR

Nicola. William Scammell. NLP

Nicolas Guillen brought me your letter, written. Letter to Miguel Otero Silva, in Caracas. Pablo Neruda. AF, *tr. by* Robert Bly

Nicotine. Art Beck. CalPo

Nietzsche is pietsche. Graffiti. Alice Archer Sewall James. NBLV

Nieve, La. Jorge Guillén. RaW

Nigeria in the Year 1999. Catherine Obianuju Acholonu. HBAPE

Nigeria of the Seventies. Molara Ogundipe-Leslie. HAWP

Nigger and Some Poofters, A. Nigel Roberts. BMAP

Nigger in a Photograph, The. Ece Ayhan. PFTM-2, *tr. by* Murat Nemet-Nejat

Nigger Song: An Odyssey. Rita Dove. OxAAAP

Nigger Sweat. Edward Baugh. EmeKit; WaCA

Niggerlips was the high school name / for me. Martín Espada. UnSA

Nigger-Lover is a song, spat out. Song. Cornelius Eady. ESEAA

Nigger-Lover is a song, spat out. Song. Cornelius Eady. GT

Nigger-Reecan Blues. Willie Perdomo. InTrad

Nigger's Leap, New England. Judith Wright. NOBAu

Nighingale, The. János Arany. IQMS, *tr. by* Peter Zollman

Night. Marjorie Agosin. ExTi

Night. Frances Bellerby. MoWP

Night. William Rose Benét. MoAmPo

Night. William Blake. ITBLP; OBEV *Fr.* Songs of Innocence.

Night. Augusta Cooper Bristol. APN-2

Night. Anne Brontë. VWP

Night. Longing, a Documentary. Anne Carson. BAP-01

Night. Justin Chin. AmPoNex

Night. Hartley Coleridge. OxBSo

Night. Mary Dorcey. PoBW

Night. Paul Laurence Dunbar. InvLi

Night. Duo Duo. PoetW, *tr. by* Donald Finkel and Li Guohua

Night. Josephine D. Henderson Heard. CBWP-4

Night. Robinson Jeffers. ColAP; MoAmPo

Night. Etheridge Knight. GT

Night. Henry Wadsworth Longfellow. APN-1

Night. Gabriela Mistral. TANSG, *tr. by* Maria Giachetti [*or* Jacketti]

Night. Gabriela Mistral. WoPoe, *tr. by* Alice Jane McVan

Night. Percy Bysshe Shelley. *See* To Night.

Night. Maurya Simon. InvLad

Night. Cherie Forman Spencer. TiP2 *Fr.* Desert Symphony.

Night. Gerald Stern. BodElec

Night. Sara Teasdale. NOxBChV

Night. Tony Towle. AHA

Night: "From this night on God let me eat." Jean Valentine. AFaM

Night: "Your hand is heavy, Night, upon my brow." Wole Soyinka. WaAnP; WoPoe *Fr.* Idanre and Other Poems (1967).

Night. Jones Very. InvLi

Night, The. Joseph Hilaire Pierre Belloc. OBEV

Night, The. Myra Cohn Livingston. TLR

Night, The. Henry Vaughan. BASC; ChIV-2; FSCP; NAEL-6v1; NAEL-7v1; NoP-4; NoP-5; NPeEn; OBEV; OBWVE; OxAEP-1; OxBEV; TFi

Night 1. Salim Hatubou. SonAtl, *tr. by* Carole Beckett, Kurt Ganzl, Eva Mallenby, Eric Milan, Christophe Mirambeau, Martin Ottenheimer and Simon Young

Night 9. Salim Hatubou. SonAtl, *tr. by* Carole Beckett, Kurt Ganzl, Eva Mallenby, Eric Milan, Christophe Mirambeau, Martin Ottenheimer and Simon Young

Night: a street, a streetlight; drugstore. Aleksandr Aleksandrovich Blok. TCRusP *Fr.* Dances of Death.

Night above the Town. Thomas Lux. SeSe

Night Abraham Called to the Stars, The. Robert Bly. OxBoAm; PoCho

Night After Bushfire. Judith Wright. BMAP

Night After Night. Shen Yüeh. CCL1, *tr.* by Anne Birrell

Night after night from my small bed. Hooters. Meic Stephens. AngWePo; TCAWP

Night after night from our camp on Sugar Loaf Hill. Influence of Natural Objects, The. James Simmons. PNI

Night after night, I do not. *Unknown.* ColAnChi *Fr.* Midnight Songs.

Night after night I turn off the light. Prayer, The. Leanne O'Sullivan. NIrP

Night after night, it was very nearly enough. Whippoorwill in the Woods, A. Amy Clampitt. OWoS

Night again. Again the grim sky closes. Night over Birkenau. Tadeusz Borowski. HP, *tr.* by Tadeuszt Pióro

Night Alone, The. Meleager. AWTN, *tr.* by Dudley Fitts

Night; an Epistle to Robert Lloyd. Charles Churchill.
"Spectators only on this bustling stage." OBSV

Night and a Distant Church. Russell Atkins. EGAG

Night and a starless sky. Shipwreck. Mary Weston Fordham. CBWP-2

Night, and beneath star-blazoned summer skies. South, The. Emma Lazarus. APN-2; ColAP; NAAPv.1

Night and Dawn. Khwaja Shams-ad-din Muhammad Hafiz. WED, *tr.* by Robert Bly and Leonard Lewisohn

Night and Day. Cole Porter. ReLy

Night and day arrive, and day after day goes by. For My Son Noah, Ten Years Old. Robert Bly. GoPo; LoL; RaBo

Night and Death. Joseph Blanco White. *See* To Night.

Night and evening, morning, every day. Recommendation. Andrey Andreievich Voznesensky. RusPo, *tr.* by Robert Arthur Douglas Ford

Night. And I am drinking smoky black tea from China. Gabriel Preil. FIT, *tr.* by Robert Friend

Night and Morning. *Unknown.* OBWVE

Night, and part of the world locked in silence. Killer Dog. Gwyn Thomas. BBMWP, *tr.* by Joseph P. Clancy

Night and Sleep. Jelaluddin Rumi. WoPoe, *tr.* by Robert Bly

Night, and the coffers are empty. Jewel, The. Mary Ruefle. AmAlph

Night and the distant rumbling; for the train. Last Evening, The. Rainer Maria Rilke. FaBoWar, *tr.* by C. F. MacIntyre and Carlyle Ferren MacIntyre

Night and the House. Sophia De Mello Breyner. StAl, *tr.* by Richard Zenith

Night and we heard heavy and cadenced hoofbeats. Return, The. John Peale Bishop. APT-1

Night arches England, and the winds are still. Walter De la Mare. MoBrPo

Night as dark as the inside. Roy Campanella: January, 1958. E. Ethelbert Miller. FuFl

Night at Anchor by Maple Bridge. Chang Chi. NDACCP, *tr.* by Kenneth Rexroth

Night at Dunkirk. Louis Aragon. FaBoWar, *tr.* by Malcolm Cowley and Rolfe Humphries

Night at times revives a curious plant. Candle, The. Francis Ponge. WED, *tr.* by Robert Bly

Night at Tongbak Temple. Pak Chaesam. CAMKP, *tr.* by David R. McCann and Jiwon Shin

Night Attack, A. Siegfried Sassoon. BrAP

Night attendant, a B.U. sophomore, The. Waking in the Blue. Robert Lowell. AmFaPo; MoAmPo; NAMCP V.2

Night Beach. Vic Coccimiglio. InvLad

Night before Good-Bye, The. Mitsuye Yamada. CFP

Night before Larry Was Stretched, The. *Unknown.* IrV

Night Before the First Day of School, The. E. Ethelbert Miller. SpirFl

Night before the first, The. Night Before the First Day of School, The. E. Ethelbert Miller. SpirFl

Night before the last day of January, The. Kona Macphee. BeAl

Night before they came, The. Tuscaloosa: Riversong. Honorée Fanonne Jeffers. RD

Night before they meant to pluck his eyes, The. Among Philistines. R. S. Gwynn. RA

Night before we flew your body home air freight, The. O Mother My Giant Redwood. Judith Hemschemeyer. FiBr

Night Bird, The. Larry Kramer. GeoHom

Night Blindness. Jocelyn Emerson. IAoNAP

Night Blooming Jasmine. Diane Wakoski. GeoHom

Night bulb that reveals ash on my sleeve, The. (LL) Waiting: "Isolation of exile is a gutted, The." Arthur Nortje. HBAPE; TSAP

2. Night Bus to Montreal. David McFadden. NLPA

Night Café. Gottfried Benn. PFTM-1

Night Call. Annie Finch. VisFro

Night Call. George Young. BloBone

Night called me, The. Foxfire. Andy Young. AnSo

Night Came in the Drowsy Living Room, The. Delmira Agustini. BLPSL, *tr.* by Rene de Costa, Rigas Kappatos and Eleni Paidoussi

Night came in the drowsy living room, The. Night Came in the Drowsy Living Room, The. Delmira Agustini. BLPSL, *tr.* by Rene de Costa, Rigas Kappatos and Eleni Paidoussi

Night Chant, The. *Navajo Oral Tradition.* NAAL-5 *Fr.* Night Chant, The.

Night Chant, The. Arthur Rimbaud.
"In Tsegihi." PFTM-1

Night Chant, The. *Unknown.* APN-2, *tr.* by Washington Matthews
(Last Song in the Rock.) NAAPv.1
Night Chant, The. NAAL-5
Prayer of First Dancers. NAAPv.1
(Song in the Rock.) NAAPv.1

Night Clouds. Amy Lowell. MoAmPo

Night clouds scumble overhead, some. Night in San Francisco. Carolyn Miller. UrbNat

Night Coach. Phillis Levin. RA

Night: "Cold remote islands, The." Louise Bogan. APT-2; NAMCP V.1; NoP-4; NoP-5; WaAnP

Night comes and extinguishes the numbers and the year. Jaan Kaplinski. ErotSp

Night comes so people can sleep like fish. Jelaluddin Rumi. WoPoe, *tr.* by Coleman Barks and John Moyne

Night covers the pond with its wing. Pond, The. Louise Glück. ColAP; WaAnP

Night creeps in, The. Twilight. Ch'en Yün. WoPoe, *tr.* by Henry Hart

Night / creeps in, The. Night, The. Myra Cohn Livingston. TLR

Night Crossing in Ice. Randall Maggs. Coast

Night Crow. Theodore Roethke. NAAL-5

Night Dances, The. Sylvia Plath. AmFaPo; MoWP

Night darkens the middle of the road. Asphalt. Chimalum Nwankwo. NAfrP

Night, Death, Mississippi. Robert Earl Hayden. CAP-8; ColAP; NAMCP V.2; NoP-4; NoP-5; OxAAAP; PoPoPo; VCAP

Night deepens. Buson. EH, *tr.* by Robert Hass

Night departs, a black bull, The. Vigil. Juan Ramón Jiménez. SpanPo, *tr.* by Willis Barnstone

Night descends while. Round About Midnight, Opus #6. Percy Johnston. EGAG

Night designs a darkness of horseweed. Slowly, Slowly, Horses. Julianne Buchsbaum. LegDan

Night disembowels itself on the rocks. Evil Port. Bernard Bador. ConPit, *tr.* by Clayton Eshleman

Night draws near in a mountain village. Ch'ŏn Kŭm. CATKP, *tr.* by Peter H. Lee

Night Driving. Jane Draycott. MoWP

Night Duty in the Palace, Dreaming of a Hsien-yu Temple. Po Chü-i. CrYelRi, *tr.* by Sam Hamill

Night Falling Fast. Mary Jo Bang. PoDa

Night falls on single vision zombies everywhere. Ken Edwards. Oth *Fr.* Five Nocturnes, after Derek Jarman.

Night feast at the Tsos. Tu Fu [*or* Du Fu]. ChinPo, *tr.* by Ye Weilian [*or* Yeh Wei-lien *or* Wai-lim Yip]

Night Feast, Zuo Family Village. Tu Fu [*or* Du Fu]. CCL1, *tr.* by David Lattimore

Night Feed. Eavan Boland. NAMCP V.2 *Fr.* Domestic Interior.

Night Feeding. Muriel Rukeyser. NAMCP V.2; NoP-4; NoP-5

Night ferry. Arthur Nortje. TSAP

Night Ferry to Naxos 1. Monica Youn. LegDan

Night Ferry to Naxos 2. Monica Youn. LegDan

Night Fishing. Caroline Price. Prnts

Night Flight. Marion Alexopoulos. NOBAu

Night Flight: New York. Muriel Rukeyser and Leif Sjoberg.
"Believe that we bloom upon this stalk of time." YaYoPo

Night Flower. Geoffrey Lehmann. NOBAu

Night Flute, The. Beryle Williams. MiVo

Night for menace with weary eyes. (LL) Trenches, The. Frederic Manning. NOBAu; PoWW

Night forked stigmata. Different Horizon. Aimé Césaire. VCWP

Night from a railroad car window. Window. Carl Sandburg. APT-1

Night frost / Pulsing wings. Iio Sogi. ZenPo, *tr.* by Takashi Ikemoto and Lucien Stryk

Night full of talking that hurts, A. Jelaluddin Rumi. RaBo; WoPoe *Fr.* Three Quatrains.

Night Fun. Judith Viorst. TLR

Night Funeral in Harlem. Langston Hughes. APT-2

Night Game, The. Robert Pinsky. TaR

Night Gives Old Woman the Word. Gail Tremblay. HATNAP; ItWoWo

Night had passed away among the hills, A. Morning among the Hills. James Gates Percival. TreFP

Night Hair. Raquel Chalfi. DTA, *tr. by* Karen Alkalay-Gut

Night Harvest. Lam Thi My Da. PoCho, *tr. by* Martha Collins and Thuy Dinh

Night Has a Thousand Eyes, The. Francis William Bourdillon. BRP; OBEV

Night has engulfed both firelit hall and sparrow. (LL) Jarrow. Carol Rumens. RSaN; StAl

Night Haul. Joe Denham. OpeFie

Night he died, earth's images all came, The. Poet. Peter Viereck. MoAmPo

Night Herons. Gary Snyder. GeoHom

Night herons nest in the cypress. Night Herons. Gary Snyder. GeoHom

Night hides our thefts; all faults then pardon'd be. Robert Herrick. CavPo

Night, Hornby Island. Danielle Janess. IFF

Night hung o'er Virginia's forest wild, The. Capt. Smith and Pocahontas. Eloise Bibb. CBWP-4

Night I fell in love with you I lost my watch, The. Perfect Timing. Sarah Maguire. LW

Night, I Know All About You. Yolanda Bedregal. TANSG, *tr. by* Carolyne Wright

Night I lost you, The. Five Stages of Grief, The. Linda Pastan. WaAnP

Night I made love to you, The. Illegitimate Poem. Vivian Lamarque. CItWP, *tr. by* Cinzia Sartini Blum and Lara Trubowitz

Night I met Marilyn it was raining, The. Night I Met Marilyn, The. Chris Greenhalgh. NeBl

Night I Met Marilyn, The. Chris Greenhalgh. NeBl

Night I returned home, The. Yet Another Home. Yun Tongju. CAMKP, *tr. by* Kay Richards and Steffen Richards

Night I woke to find the sheets wet from you, The. Bruise of This, The. Mark Wunderlich. NeAmPo; P180

Night I Won the Crown in the National Eisteddfod of My Dreams, The. Elinor Wyn Reynolds. BBMWP, *tr. by* the author

Night in a Room by the River. Tu Fu [*or* Du Fu]. AWTN; CrYelRi, *tr. by* Sam Hamill

Night in a World, A. Heather McHugh. InvLad

Night in Al-Hamra. Sa'di Yusuf. BeAl; PoAgWa, *tr. by* Khaled Mattawa

Night in Elphin goes slow, The. Author of this is Ossian, The. *Unknown.* NePenScot, *tr. by* Derick Thomson

Night in Gracie's Face. Jayne Anne Phillips. MotU

Night in Hell. Arthur Rimbaud. SxFrPo, *tr. by* Martin Sorrell

Night in June, A. Duncan Campbell Scott. IFF

Night in Kolozsvár. Lajos Áprily. IQMS, *tr. by* Watson Kirkconnell

Night in May, A. Alfred de Musset. *tr. by* Claire Nicholas White

Muse, The. WoPoe, *tr. by* Claire Nicholas White

Poet, The. WoPoe, *tr. by* Claire Nicholas White

Poet, The. WoPoe, *tr. by* Claire Nicholas White

Night in Nigeria. Ellease Southerland. GT

Night in San Francisco. Carolyn Miller. UrbNat

Night in the Ashes. Agnes Walsh. Coast

Night in the basement of a concrete structure now in ruins. Let Us Be Midwives! Kurihara Sadako. ItWoWo, *tr. by* Richard H. Minear

Night in the Ghetto. *Unknown, fr. Terezin Concentration Camp.* INSAB

"Night" in the Medici Chapel. Michelangelo Buonarroti. WoPoe, *tr. by* William Jay Smith

Night in the Palace with Ch'ien Hui. Po Chü-i. NDACCP, *tr. by* David Hinton

Night in the Shape of a Bison. Joyce Mansour. SurWo, *tr. by* Mary Beach

Night in the sky. Paris Is Paris Again. Alan Jay Lerner. ReLy

"Night in the Tropics" (1858-59?). Michael Waters. MiVo

Night in the Villa by the River. Tu Fu [*or* Du Fu]. TAL

Night is a cup of evil, The. A watchman's stinging. Black Cup, The. César Vallejo. WoPoe, *tr. by* Tony Barnstone and Willis Barnstone

Night is a furrow, a queasy, insistent wound, The. Heavy the flies hang, slow wheel the lingering birds. Nightletter. Charles Wright. PoA 2002

Night is a ship of mother-of-pearl and gold. Nocturne of Hope. Yolanda Bedregal. TANSG, *tr. by* Carolyne Wright

Night is already falling, enfolding the mountain. Sappers, The. Hayim Hefer. NRoS, *tr. by* Esther Raizen

Night is bait, The. Tercios del Muerte. Gerry Gordon. MiVo

Night is beautiful, The. My People. Langston Hughes. APT-2; NOxBChV; OxAAAP; TWF

Night is bitter, The. Man That Got Away, The. Ira Gershwin. ReLy

Night is caught on the web of her wings, The. Sonnet for an SR-71. P. L. Delano. OtW

Night is cold and frosty, The. Winter Night, A. Priscilla Jane Thompson. CBWP-2

Night is come, like to the day, The. Sir Thomas Browne. SacPr *Fr.* Religio Medici.

Night is covered with signs. The body and face of man, The. Akiba. Muriel Rukeyser. TaR

Night is darkening round me, The. Emily Jane Brontë. *See* Spellbound.

Night is darkening round me, The. Spellbound. Emily Jane Brontë. NPeEn

Night is dewy as a maiden's mouth, The. Summer's Night, A. Paul Laurence Dunbar. APN-2; NAAPv.1; NoP-4; NoP-5

Night is everywhere. Cuba. Sandra M. Castillo. TouFir

Night is falling. Sound 8. Kang Ŭn'gyo. CAMKP, *tr. by* Tae Yang Kwak

Night Is Freezing Fast, The. A. E. Housman. BrAP

Night Is My Nudity. Georges Bataille. YaTCFP, *tr. by* Rosemary Lloyd

Night is my sister, and how deep in love. Edna St. Vincent Millay. OxBSo

Night Is Near [*or* Neir] Gone, The. Alexander Montgomerie. OBEV

Night is on the downland, on the lonely moorland. Night on the Downland. John Masefield. MoBrPo

Night Is out of Sight, The. Pedro Juan Pietri. PueRic

Night is quiet. All creatures are resting. Spring Night at Bamboo Pavillion, Presenting a Poem to Subprefect Qian about His Staying for Good in Blue Field Mountains. Wang Wei. WoPoe, *tr. by* Tony Barnstone, Willis Barnstone and Xu Haixin

Night is so long, The. Issa. WED, *tr. by* Robert Bly

Night is still, The. The unfailing surf. James Vincent Cunningham. APT-2

Night is too long to the sleepless, The. Kenneth Rexroth. APT-2 *Fr.* Love Poems of Marichiko, The.

Night Is Young and You're So Beautiful, The. Irving Kahal and Billy Rose. ReLy

Night It Rained Life, The. Devarakonda Balagangadhara Tilak. HotL, *tr. by* V. Narayana Rao

Night Journal. Charles Wright. CAP-8; InGu

Night Journey. Alfred Noyes. SacPr

Night Journey. Theodore Roethke. AmFaPo; BeAl; GM; GoPo

Night Journey of a River, The. William Cullen Bryant. APN-1

Night Lake. Jean Valentine. LaCa

Night Letter. Stanley Kunitz. AF

Night licks the backyard with its reptile tongue. Clockface. Rhyll McMaster. BMAP

Night Light. Kate Barnes. GoPo

Night Light. Anne Winters. PtR

Night Light. Anne Winters. BeAl *Fr.* Elizabeth Near and Far.

Night, lighter than day! Night, more than brilliant night. On the Birth of Jesus. Andreas Gryphius. GePo, *tr. by* George C. Schoolfield

Night Litany. Ezra Pound. TCAPo

Night long, knocking on barn boards, the scuffling mare moves. Postcard from the Coast. Katrina Roberts. NAPBL

Night long on the jade staircase, white. Jade-Staircase Grievance. Li Po. NDACCP, *tr. by* David Hinton

Night lowers its drapes, residues of light harbored between the wrinkles on my forehead. Jeopard, The. Silvia Eugenia Castillero. SPV, *tr. by* Jen Hofer

Night lowers upon the city, upon the deserted streets. At Nightfall, 1/27/91. Pinhas Sadeh. NRoS, *tr. by* Esther Raizen

Night Meeting. Thomas McGrath. BodElec

Night Mirror. Li-Young Lee. WaAnP

Night Mirror, The. John Hollander. VCAP

Night mist leaves us yearning for a new location, The. Floating Houses. David Wojahn. WaAnP

Night Mooring on the Jiande River, A. Meng Hao Jan. CCL1, *tr. by* Witter Bynner

Night Morring at Cow's Creek: I Think of the Old Man. Li Po. CCL1, *tr. by* C. H. Kwock and Vincent McHugh

Night Music. Linda Gregg. BLT

Night my brother was stabbed, The. Jojo's. Christopher Davis. LiTh

Night never falls here. No Man's Land. Iwan Llwyd. BBMWP, *tr. by* the author

Night ("Now Ev'ning fades! her pensive step retires.") Ann Radcliffe. NOBRP

Night ("O'er the dim breast of ocean's wave.") Ann Radcliffe. CenSon

Night of Battle. Yvor Winters. PoA 2002; PWW2

Night of Fathers. Valerie Martínez. TouFir

Night of Hell. Arthur Rimbaud. *tr. by* Louise Varese

"Decidedly we are out of the world. No longer any sound." AWTN, *tr. by* Louise Varese

Night of love, A. Second Madrigal, The. Anna Swirszczynska [*or* Swir]. BLT

Night of March 20, 1994, The. Declaration of Love to Kurt Cobain. Hector Avellán. PML, *tr. by* Marco Morelli

Night of My Blood (1971). Kofi Awoonor.

At the Gates. VCWP

Night of my cousin's wedding, The. Anne Sexton. NAAL-5; NAMCP V.2 *Fr.* Death of the Fathers, The.

Night of my first cell meeting it was pouring rain, The.   Looking for Trouble. Roque Dalton.   TCLAP, *tr. by* Richard Schaaf

Night of nations. On a death-dense bassoon.   Prayer for the Great Lunatic. László Mécs.   IQMS, *tr. by* Paul Tabori

Night of Sleepless Love.   Federico García Lorca.   CAGL *Fr.* Sonetos del Amor Oscuro [Sonnets of Dark Love].

Night of Terror.   Giuseppe Gioacchino Belli.   PoCho, *tr. by* Miller Williams

Night of the day, The.   Lunar Frost.   Mary Kinzie.   IllVoic

Night of the Fourth: A Recollection, The.   Victor Hugo.   SxFrPo, *tr. by* A. M. and E. H. Blackmore

Night of the Hunter.   Paul Hoover.   LiTh

Night of the Living, Night of the Dead.   Kim Addonizio.   RoV

Night of the Scorpion.   Nissim Ezekiel.   BrAP

Night of the Shirts, The.   W. S. Merwin.   VCAP

Night of the wedding she got into bed.   No Balls at All.   *Unknown.*   FaBoWar

Night of Trafalgar, The.   Thomas Hardy.   MoBrPo; OBMV *Fr.* Dynasts, The.

Night on high the two of us in full moon, I began to cry and you were laughing, The.   Federico García Lorca.   CAGL *Fr.* Sonetos del Amor Oscuro [Sonnets of Dark Love].

Night on the Boulevard.   Lőrinc Szabó.   IQMS, *tr. by* Laurence James

Night on the Downland.   John Masefield.   MoBrPo

Night on the Great River.   Meng Hao Jan.   NDACCP, *tr. by* Kenneth Rexroth

Night Operations, Coastal Command RAF.   Howard Nemerov.   AF; PWW2

Night Ottawa brought down the budget, The.   Spleen.   August Kleinzahler. PmAP

Night, our [*or* the] black summer, simplifies her smells.   Nights in the Gardens of Port of Spain.   Derek Walcott.   NAEL-6v2; NAEL-7v2; NoP-4; NoP-5; PoetW

Night Out, A.   Douglas Houston.   TCAWP

Night over Birkenau.   Tadeusz Borowski.   HP, *tr. by* Tadeusz Pióro

Night over Georgia; mist across the heights.   Ode on the Hills of Georgia. Alexander Sergeyevich Pushkin.   WoPoe, *tr. by* Peter Viereck

Night Owl.   Ch'oe Sûngja.   EcSo, *tr. by* Mickey Hong

Night Owl.   M. Wyrebek.   PoCho

Night owl peered at me, A.   Night Owl.   Ch'oe Sûngja.   EcSo, *tr. by* Mickey Hong

Night passes on, and the bright day appears.   *Unknown.*   NAWM-7v1 *Fr.* Song of Roland, The.

Night Patrol, The.   Arthur Graeme West.   FaBoWar

Night Person, The.   Richard Frost.   AWTN

Night Picnic.   Charles Simic.   BAP-01

Night Piece.   "Ern Malley."   BMAP

Night Piece.   Juan Ramón Jiménez.   WED, *tr. by* Robert Bly

Night Piece.   John Streeter Manifold.   MoBrPo

Night Piece.   Robin Skelton.   IFF

Night Piece on Death.   Thomas Parnell.
    "How deep yon azure dyes the sky!"   OxAEP-1

Night Piece, The: "Fog drifts slowly down the hill, The."   Thom Gunn.   ASA

Night Piece: the Trojans outside Troy.   Homer.   OBVE *Fr.* Iliad, The.

Night Raid.   Desmond Hawkins.   PoWW

Night Rain.   Countee Cullen.   GT

Night Rain.   Karen L. Mitchell.   GT

Night Rain: A Wall Collapses—Sent To My Neighbors.   Yang Shih-ch'i. ColAnChi, *tr. by* Jonathan Chaves

Night Rain at Luster Gap.   Yang Wan-li.   NDACCP, *tr. by* David Hinton

Night Rain on the Rivers Hsiao and Hsiang.   Yi Illo.   CATKP, *tr. by* Peter H. Lee

Night rain whispers outside the window, The.   Poem That Came Easily, A. Yun Tongju.   CAMKP, *tr. by* Kay Richards and Steffen Richards

Night Rains: A Letter to Go North.   Li Shang-yin.   ChinPo, *tr. by* Ye Weilian [*or* Yeh Wei-lien *or* Wai-lim Yip]

Night rattles with nightmares, The.   From the Night-Window.   Douglas Dunn. EdScPo

Night Ray.   Paul Celan.   AF, *tr. by* Michael Hamburger

Night: reading Meng Chiao's poems.   Reading the Poetry of Meng Chiao: Two Poems.   Su Tung-p'o.   ColAnChi; WoPoe, *tr. by* Burton Watson

Night rests like a ball of fur on my tongue. (LL)   Adolescence—2.   Rita Dove. AmAlph; AWTN; ISC; NAAL-5; NAMCP V.2; NoAM; PoPoPo; VCAP

Night reunites the house and its silence.   Night and the House.   Sophia De Mello Breyner.   StAl, *tr. by* Richard Zenith

Night Ride On 21.   Mustafa Ziyalan.   PML, *tr. by* the author

Night Robert Frost Died, The.   Lyn Lifshin.   VisFro

Night Roof.   *Unknown.*   SonAtl, *tr. by* G. Basuti, Evan Palle and M. Seane

Night roof is a right-round city, The.   Night Roof.   *Unknown.*   SonAtl, *tr. by* G. Basuti, Evan Palle and M. Seane

Night rose up from the earth.   Valley of Zapata, The.   Veronica Volkow. RMCMP, *tr. by* Margaret Sayers Peden

Night Seasons.   Stephen Kuusisto.   TAPaP

Night Sentence.   Christine Hume.   IAoNAP

Night: Setting out from Shih-Kuan Pavilion.   Hsieh Ling-yün.   ChinPo, *tr. by* Ye Weilian [*or* Yeh Wei-lien *or* Wai-lim Yip]

Night Shadows.   William Carpenter.   PoSol

Night Shift, after Drinking Dinner, Container Corporation of America, 1972. Kevin Stein.   IllVoic

Night Shift at the Fruit Cannery.   Ilze Mueller.   CFP

Night sighs, The.   Surrogate Mothers.   Andrea M. Wren.   InTrad

Night Sitting.   Ching An.   CSKM, *tr. by* Jerome P. Seaton

Night Sky.   Bei Dao.   WoBe, *tr. by* Iona Man-Cheong and Eliot Weinberger

Night Sky.   Louise Erdrich.   HATNAP

Night Sky, The.   Sean Dunne.   ModIr *Fr.* Sydney Place.

Night Sky, The.   Charles G. D. Roberts.   GSo

Night—sky bird's world.   Myth of the Blaze.   George Oppen.   PFTM-2

Night Sky Hiss.   Jonathan Griffin.   Oth

Night sky is only a sort of carbon paper, The.   Insomniac.   Sylvia Plath. AWTN

Night, sleep, death and the stars. (LL)   Clear Midnight, A.   Walt Whitman. AWTN; SAmP; Spl

Night slips, trailing behind it.   Tryst.   Lavinia Greenlaw.   BeAl

Night snow / Neighbor's cock.   Kagami Shiko.   ZenPo, *tr. by* Takashi Ikemoto and Lucien Stryk

Night so.   *Unknown.*   ColAnChi *Fr.* Midnight Songs.

Night so.   *Unknown.*   ColAnChi *Fr.* Midnight Songs.

Night sometimes revives a singular plant whose light decomposes furnished. Candle, The.   Francis Ponge.   MotU, *tr. by* Cid Corman

Night Song.   Lajos Áprily.   IQMS, *tr. by* Watson Kirkconnell

Night Song at Amalfi.   Sara Teasdale.   APT-1; MakPoe; MoAmPo

Night Song for a Child.   Charles Williams.   OBEV

Night Song of the Los Angeles Basin.   Gary Snyder.   PfSP; UrbNat

Night Song of the Personal Shadow.   György Petri.   VCWP, *tr. by* Geroge Gömöri and Clive Wilmer

Night splintered into stars, The.   Ashes.   Alejandra Pizarnik.   TCLAP, *tr. by* Frank Graziano and María Rosa Fort

Night Strategies.   David Bottoms.   PoChi

Night, street, a lamp, a chemist's window.   Aleksandr Aleksandrovich Blok. OBVE *Fr.* Dances of Death.

Night street an onyx eye unblinking, empty.   Black on Black.   Bruce A. Jacobs.   BtF

Night (Suite for Piano and Poet's Voice).   Federico García Lorca. *tr. by* Jerome Rothenberg
    At the Poorhouse.   PFTM-1, *tr. by* Jerome Rothenberg
    Below.   PFTM-1, *tr. by* Jerome Rothenberg
    Comet.   PFTM-1, *tr. by* Jerome Rothenberg
    Great Sadness, The.   PFTM-1, *tr. by* Jerome Rothenberg
    In a Corner of the Sky.   PFTM-1, *tr. by* Jerome Rothenberg
    Memory.   PFTM-1, *tr. by* Jerome Rothenberg
    One.   PFTM-1, *tr. by* Jerome Rothenberg
    Prelude.   PFTM-1, *tr. by* Jerome Rothenberg
    Sketches.   PFTM-1, *tr. by* Jerome Rothenberg
    Star, A.   PFTM-1, *tr. by* Jerome Rothenberg
    Swath.   PFTM-1, *tr. by* Jerome Rothenberg
    Ursa Major.   PFTM-1, *tr. by* Jerome Rothenberg
    Venus.   PFTM-1, *tr. by* Jerome Rothenberg
    Whole Works, The.   PFTM-1, *tr. by* Jerome Rothenberg

Night. Summer Meteors. A Comet.   James Thomson.   NPeEn *Fr.* Seasons, The.

Night Sweat.   Robert Lowell.   HarvBoo; OxBoAm

Night sweet are you.   Litany, A.   Frank O'Hara.   BodElec

Night takes feelings to the window.   Birds Leaving.   Johanna Kruit.   TuT, *tr. by* Medbh McGuckian

Night takes on its own elegance.   Approaching August.   Sandra Alcosser. PfSP

Night Talk in a Dream Chamber.   Ikkyu Sojun.   ErotSp, *tr. by* Sam Hamill

Night Taxi.   Thom Gunn.   BeAl

Night that cuts between you and you, A.   People at Night.   Denise Levertov. CLPP

Night that has no star lit up by God, The.   New World, The.   Jones Very. APN-1; OxBoAm

Night that orders everyone to sleep, The.   Live Walls.   Mahe Jabeen.   HotL, *tr. by* V. Narayana Rao

Night the Fifth.   Edward Young.   *Fr.* Night Thoughts.

Night the Eighth: Camerados.   Bayard Taylor.   APN-2 *Fr.* Echo Club, The.

Night, The Porch, The.   Mark Strand.   CAP-8; KGB

Night the Second: All or Nothing.   Bayard Taylor.   APN-2 *Fr.* Echo Club, The.

Night the Sixth: Hadramaut.   Bayard Taylor.   APN-2 *Fr.* Echo Club, The.

Night, the wet, the onyx-faced.   Elementary.   Muriel Spark.   MoWP

Night Things.   Greg Kuzma.   InvLad

Night Thoughts.   David Gascoyne.

Nightwatchers, The.   RWPCtW

Night Thoughts.   Heinrich Heine.   WoPoe, *tr. by* Mark Rudman

Night Thoughts.   Li Po.   WaAnP, *tr. by* Arthur Sze

Night Thoughts.   Lu Yu.   WoPoe, *tr. by* Kenneth Rexroth

Night Thoughts.   Lu Yu.   NDACCP; WoPoe, *tr. by* Kenneth Rexroth

Night Thoughts.   Edward Young.   OxAEP-1 *Fr.* Night Thoughts.

Night Thoughts Concerning a Dream.   Daniel Casper von Lohenstein.   GePo, *tr. by* George C. Schoolfield

Night Thoughts.   Edward Young.

Night the Fifth.

Pudeur Française, La.   STuOW

Night Thoughts.   OxAEP-1

"What am I? and from whence?—I nothing know."   SacPr

Night Thoughts While Traveling.   Tu Fu [*or* Du Fu].   CrYelRi, *tr. by* Sam Hamill

Night Thoughts While Travelling ("Light breeze rustles the reeds, A.")   Tu Fu [*or* Du Fu].   NDACCP, *tr. by* Kenneth Rexroth

Night Thoughts: "Your kind of night, David, your kind of night."   Henri Coulette.   CalPo

Night Toad.   Susan Wicks.   MoWP; StAl

Night Traffic Near Winchester, Virginia.   Dave Jeddie Smith.   LPSFW

Night Train.   Robert Francis.   GM

Night Tree, The.   Jane Draycott.   MoWP

Night trembles long on the water before you sleep, The.   Stone of the Arabian woman, The.   Shakir Li'aibi.   IrPoTo, *tr. by* Ralph Saverese and Saadi A. Simawe

Night tumbles into town, bruised.   Night Tumbles into Town by Rail.   Kim Roberts.   AmPoNex

Night Tumbles into Town by Rail.   Kim Roberts.   AmPoNex

Night, two o'clock: moonlight. The train has stopped.   Tomas Tranströmer. *See* 2 a.m.: moonlight. The train has stopped.

Night universe scallop-edged with his faces—, A.   Some Metaphysics of Junior Wells.   Sandra McPherson.   SeSe

Night unwraps the true stuff of the world.   Olga Martynova.   CRWP, *tr. by* Elaine Feinstein

Night Up in the Tower.   Tu Fu [*or* Du Fu].   ChinPo, *tr. by* Ye Weilian [*or* Yeh Wei-lien *or* Wai-lim Yip]

Night usually computes itself in stars.   News of the Occluded Cyclone.   Alice Fulton.   WeW-3

Night / Virgins.   Sappho.   SaLy, *tr. by* Diane Rayor

Night Vision.   Lucille Clifton.   BodElec; GifTon; UnSA

Night Vision of the Gulf War.   Dale Jacobson.   AmWaPo

Night Visit.   Adriann Roland Holst.   TuT, *tr. by* Paula Meehan

Night Visit, The (22).   Khwaja Shams-ad-din Muhammad Hafiz.   WED, *tr. by* Robert Bly and Leonard Lewisohn

Night Visitor, A.   Robert Greene.   NoSic

Night Waitress.   Lynda Hull.   SwNoth

Night Walking.   Robert Penn Warren.   BodElec

Night warmed by an african moon.   To Tania.   Alda do Espirito Santo.   SonAtl, *tr. by* Simon Lewis and Krystyna Ziemba

Night was clean as the bone of a rabbit blown hollow, The.   New Vows.   Louise Erdrich.   CAP-8

Night Was Growing Cold, The.   *Unknown.*   WHSW

Night was growing old, The.   In the Night.   *Unknown.*   NBLV

Night was mighty dark so you could hardly see, The.   Shine On, Harvest Moon.   Jack Norworth.   NAAPv.2

Night was stormy and dark, The town was shut up in sleep:, The.   Speculators, The.   William Makepeace Thackeray.   OBCoV; OBSV

Night wasn't over / when the moon stood beside my bed.   Prison Daybreak, A.   Faiz Ahmad Faiz.   AF, *tr. by* Agha Shahid Ali

Night Watch.   Wang An-shih.   CrYelRi, *tr. by* Sam Hamill

Night Watch in the Laboratory.   Ann Townsend.   NAPBL

Night Watchman of Pont-au-Change, The.   Robert Desnos.   AF, *tr. by* Carolyn Forché

Night We Called It a Day, The.   Tom Adair.   ReLy

Night we stayed at Summit Temple, The.   Inscribed at Summit Temple.   Li Po.   CCL1; WoPoe, *tr. by* Elling O. Eide

Night We Stole a Full-Lenght Mirror, The.   Greta Stoddart.   MoWP

Night wears a garment.   Street Lamps in Early Spring.   Gwendolyn B. Bennett.   NAAPv.2

Night, welcome art thou to my mind destrest [*or* distressed].   Mary Sidney Wroth, Countess of Montgomery.   NoP-4; NoP-5 *Fr.* Pamphilia to Amphilanthus.

Night when she first gave birth, The.   Mary.   Bertolt Brecht.   GI

Night will be all dried moths on the windows, The.   Sprites.   Richard Jackson.   VisFro

Night Will Never Stay, The.   Eleanor Farjeon.   NTCP

Night will stay as it is: an old maid, grey to the tip of her braid, The.   Honey of a Wild Bee.   Abraham Sutskever.   MotU, *tr. by* Ruth R. Wisse

Night Wind, The.   Emily Jane Brontë.   NAEL-6v2; NAEL-7v2; NALW; NIL-7 (In summer's mellow midnight.)   VWP

Night Winds.   Adelaide Crapsey.   APT-1; NAAPv.2; TCAPo

Night with a Friend, A.   Li Po.   CCL1, *tr. by* Burton Watson

Night with Hamlet, A.   Vladimir Holan.   ConPit, *tr. by* Clayton Eshleman, Frantisek Galan and Michael Heim

"When passing from nature to being."   PFTM-2, *tr. by* Clayton Eshleman, Frantisek Galan and Michael Heim

Night with Lions, A.   Randall Jarrell.   StAl *Fr.* Lost World, The.

Night with the Vampire, The.   Fadil Azzawi.   IrPoTo, *tr. by* Ralph Saverese and Saadi A. Simawe

Night without end. I cannot sleep.   Night Without End.   *Unknown.*   NDACCP, *tr. by* Kenneth Rexroth

Night without end. Loneliness.   Kenneth Rexroth.   APSN; APT-2 *Fr.* Love Poems of Marichiko, The.

Night Without Stars, A.   Nancy Eimers.   ExTi

Night Words.   Isabel Meyrelles.   SurWo, *tr. by* Jean R. Longland

Night Work.   Sharan Strange.   FuFl

Night, Work.   Yi Sanghûi.   EcSo, *tr. by* Jennifer M. Lee

Night wounded, The.   Roça.   Maria Manuela Margarido.   HAWP, *tr. by* Julia Kirst

Night you called to tell me, The.   Electricity.   Lavinia Greenlaw.   MoWP; NeBrP

Night you died I heard your cello shift, The.   For Peter, My Cousin.   Barbara Nickel.   IFF

Night you left I hooked my heart to that silver, The.   Letters to a Vanishing Fiancée.   James Kimbrell.   LegDan

Night-bird sight.   Summer.   Luciana Frezza.   CItWP, *tr. by* Cinzia Sartini Blum and Lara Trubowitz

Night-Blooming Cereus, The.   Robert Earl Hayden.   APT-2; ESEAA; ItP

Night-Blooming Flowers.   Felicia Dorothea Hemans.   NOBRP

Night-Blooming Jasmine, The.   Audre Lorde.   ColAP

Nightbook.   Dan Beachy-Quick.   IAoNAP

Nightclass.   Diana Hartog.   NLPA *Fr.* Oasis.

Nightclub.   Billy Collins.   FaoP; GoPo; SUP

Nightclub, A: on the Jacksboro Highway.   Robert Trammell.   TiP2

Night-dreams trace on Memory's wall.   Ralph Waldo Emerson.   APN-1; TCAPo *Fr.* Quatrains.

Nightfall.   Walter Davies.   OBWVE; WoPoe, *tr. by* Anthony Conran

Nightfall.   Michael Field.   VWP

Nightfall.   Gwen Harwood.   BMAP

Nightfall.   C. Robert Lloyd.   ICANM

Nightfall.   Alexander L. Posey.   APN-2

Nightfall . . . grass on the back.   Landscape.   Maria Manuela Margarido.   HAWP, *tr. by* Julia Kirst

Nightfall. Clouds scatter and vanish.   Turning Year, The.   Su Tung-p'o.   NDACCP, *tr. by* Kenneth Rexroth

Nightfall of nations brilliant after war. (LL)   Troop Train.   Karl Shapiro.   AmWaPo; APT-2; OxBoAm; PWW2; WaAnP

Nightfall: "Shadows dart, the wind has risen."   Ekaterina Iosifova.   CSCBP, *tr. by* Georgi Belev and Lisa Sapinkopf

Nightfall. The Coolness of My Watered Garden.   Juan Ramón Jiménez.   SpanPo, *tr. by* Eloise Roach

Nightfall. The coolness of my watered garden.   Nightfall. The Coolness of My Watered Garden.   Juan Ramón Jiménez.   SpanPo, *tr. by* Eloise Roach

Nightfall: the town's chromatic nocturne wakes.   Game of Chess, A.   Gwen Harwood.   MakPoe

Nightfire.   Brad Daugherty.   BeDoSh

Nightfishing.   Charles McDonald.   NLP

Nightfishing.   Gjertrud Schnackenberg.   WeW-3

Nighthawks.   Samuel Yellen.   PoSol

Night-hours. The edge of a fuller moon.   Captain Lavender.   Medbh McGuckian.   NAMCP V.2

Nightingale, The.   Mark Akenside.   OBEV

Nightingale, The.   Euros Bowen.   BBMWP, *tr. by* R. Gerallt Jones

Nightingale, The.   Sir Philip Sidney.   PBRV (Philomela.)   OxAEP-1

Nightingale, The.   William Strode.   OBVE

Nightingale as soone as Aprill bringeth, The.   Nightingale, The.   Sir Philip Sidney.   PBRV (Nightingale, as soon as April bringeth, The.)   NAEL-6v1; NAEL-7v1; NoP-4; NoP-5

Nightingale has a lyre of gold, The.   W. E. Henley.   MoBrPo *Fr.* Echoes.

Nightingale / My clogs.   Boncho.   ZenPo, *tr. by* Takashi Ikemoto and Lucien Stryk

Nightingale near the House, The.   Harold Monro.   MoBrPo

Nightingale of Uncle Yair, The.   Devorah Amir.   DTA, *tr. by* Linda Zisquit

Nightingale / Rarely seen.   Takai Kito.   ZenPo, *tr. by* Takashi Ikemoto and Lucien Stryk

Nightingale Sang in Berkeley Square, A.   Eric Maschwitz.   ReLy

Nightingale, whose happy noble hart, The.   Steele Glas, The.   George Gascoigne.

Nightingales.   Robert Bridges.   MoBrPo; OBEV; OBMV; TFi

Nightingales, The.   Harri Webb.   AngWePo; TCAWP

Nightingale's Nest, The.   John Clare.   NAEL-7v2; NPeEn

Nightingale's song / this morning.   Issa.   ZenPo, *tr. by* Takashi Ikemoto and Lucien Stryk

Nightingales' tongues, your majesty?   Figgie Hobbin.   Charles Causley.   NOxBChV

Nightingales warbled without.   In the Garden at Swainston.   Alfred Tennyson.   OBEV

Nightjar.   John McAuliffe.   NIrP

Nightletter.   Charles Wright.   PoA 2002

Night-life. Letters, journals, bourbon.   Origins and History of Consciousness.   Adrienne Rich.   NIP-4

Nightline: An Interview with the General.   Ronald Wallace.   PBCAP

Nightlong I Wander.   Li Yu [*or* Li Hou-Chu].   CCL1, *tr. by* Sam Houston Brock

Nightlong I wander aimlessly about the palace lawn.   Nightlong I Wander.   Li Yu [*or* Li Hou-Chu].   CCL1, *tr. by* Sam Houston Brock

Nightlong waiting and listening, being schooled.   Owl.   Robert Mezey.   AWTN

Nightly News, The.   Daniel Anderson.   AmPoNex

Nightmare.   Matilde Salganicoff.   MirDau, *tr. by* Celeste Kostopulos-Cooperman

Nightmare 1.   Abdul Maqsoud Abdul Karim.   NAfrP, *tr. by* Clarissa C. Burt

Nightmare 3.   Abdul Maqsoud Abdul Karim.   NAfrP, *tr. by* Clarissa C. Burt

Nightmare, A.   Christina Georgina Rossetti.   EroLit

Nightmare, [A *or* The].   William Schwenck Gilbert.   OBCoV *Fr.* Iolanthe.

Nightmare, The.   Abdul Wahab Al-Bayati.   IrPoTo, *tr. by* Farouk Abdel Wahab

Nightmare, The.   Wang Yen-Shou.   CCL1, *tr. by* Arthur Waley

Nightmare Abbey.   Thomas Love Peacock.

   (Three Men of Gotham.)   OBEV; OxAEP-2

Nightmare begins responsibility. (LL)   Nightmare Begins Responsibility.   Michael S. Harper.   ESEAA; GT; LoL; NAMCP V.2; OxAAAP; PoPoPo; VCAP

Nightmare Begins Responsibility.   Michael S. Harper.   ESEAA; GT; LoL; NAMCP V.2; OxAAAP; PoPoPo; VCAP

Nightmare Boogie.   Langston Hughes.   APSN; APT-2; NAMCP V.1; OxBoAm

Nightmare flickers.   Cyclone.   Remi Raji Oyelade.   NeNiPo

Nightmare leaves fatigue.   Louis MacNeice.   ModIr; PNI *Fr.* Autumn Journal.

Nightmare Number Three.   Stephen Vincent Benét.   MoAmPo

Nightmare of beasthood, snorting, how to wake.   Moly.   Thom Gunn.   CABP; NAMCP V.2; NoAM; NPeEn

Nightmares.   Marie Étienne.   YaTCFP, *tr. by* Marilyn Hacker

Nightmares Fit to Arouse Misgivings.   Mohamed Lasheen.   AnVo, *tr. by* Mohamed Enani

Nightmarkets, The.   Alan Wearne.

   Division of O'Dowd, The.   BMAP

   Elise.   BMAP

   Terri.   BMAP

Night-Mooring at Maple Bridge.   Chang Chi.   ChinPo, *tr. by* Ye Weilian [*or* Yeh Wei-lien *or* Wai-lim Yip]

Night-Mooring near Maple Bridge, A.   Chang Chi.   CCL1, *tr. by* Witter Bynner

Night-Mullins River.   Colville N. Young.   OWABP

Night-Music.   Muriel Rukeyser.

   "When those who can never again forgive themselves."   PoA 2002

Night-Piece.   Léonie Adams.   MoAmPo

Night-Piece.   Joy Davidman.   YaYoPo

Night-piece.   "Ern Malley."   BMAP

Night-Piece.   Frances Horovitz.   LW

Nightpiece.   Judith Johnson Sherwin.   YaYoPo

Night-Piece, The.   Virgil.   MakPoe *Fr.* Aeneid [*or* Eneados *or* Aeneis], The.

Night-Piece, to Julia, The.   Robert Herrick.   NAEL-6v1; NAEL-7v1; NoP-4; NoP-5; NOSC; OBEV; TFi

Nightrider.   Tatamkulu Afrika.   TSAP

Nights.   Lyn Hejinian.   BAP-01

Nights.   Alda Lara.   HAWP, *tr. by* Julia Kirst

Nights: "Drunk and weeping. It's another."   Harvey Shapiro.   PA9/11

Nights After Rain When the Moon.   Kwŏn Homun.   WoPoe, *tr. by* Kevin O'Rourke

Nights after rain when the moon.   Nights After Rain When the Moon.   Kwŏn Homun.   WoPoe, *tr. by* Kevin O'Rourke

Nights as they'll be in his rough arms. (LL)   Grenoble Café.   Jean Garrigue.   APT-2; OxBoAm

Night's best of all. Night brings delight.   Propertius.   EroLit *Fr.* Elegies.

Nights come, The.   My days pass with the beads of the rosary.   Shakir Li'aibi.   IrPoTo, *tr. by* Ralph Saverese and Saadi A. Simawe

Night's Delights.   Kaspar Stieler.   GePo, *tr. by* Ingrid Waløe-Engel

Night's drifts, The.   Winter Daybreak above Vence, A.   James Wright.   VCAP

Night's Fall.   William Sydney Graham.   WoPoe

Night's glass towers, Rapunzel'd by the sun.   Skyscrapers.   Star Black.   PA9/11

Nights in Fresno.   Luis Omar Salinas.   GeoHom

Nights in Siuna.   Rebecca Gordon.   FiBr

Nights in the castle we dream of hounds.   Stories from the Tower.   Monica Ferrell.   LegDan

Nights in the Constellation of the Tree Stepping from its Robe.   Beckian Fritz Goldberg.   AmAlph

Nights in the Gardens of Port of Spain.   Derek Walcott.   NAEL-6v2; NAEL-7v2; NoP-4; NoP-5; PoetW

Nights like this: on the cold apple-bough.   Adrienne Rich.   HarvBoo *Fr.* Not Somewhere Else, But Here.

Nights like this you could forget.   Tilts, Point Lance, The.   Agnes Walsh.   Coast

Night's moonlight lake was neither water nor air. (LL)   Reality Is an Activity of the Most August Imagination.   Wallace Stevens.   APT-1; NAMCP V.1; NoAM; OxBoAm

Nights of 1964–66: The Old Reliable.   Marilyn Hacker.   OxBoAm; VCAP

Nights of 1964–1966: The Old Reliable.   Marilyn Hacker.   RA

Nights she counted coins from my father's vending machines.   Stories.   Philip Schultz.   PoDa

Nights we lie beside her, our mouths.   Workers (attendants).   Nick Flynn.   IIR

Nights when I lie.   To The Barbarian.   Else Lasker-Schüler.   PFTM-1

Nights with the Star-Ladle Over the House.   Beckian Fritz Goldberg.   AmAlph

Nights Without Hope (Rebetiko Song).   Yannis Papaionnou.   WoPoe, *tr. by* Gail Holst-Warhaft

Nightsong.   Frank Mkalawile Chipasula.

   Dusk.   HBAPE

Nightsong.   Thamnaret.   WoPoe, *tr. by* Ronald Perry

Nightsong: City.   Dennis Brutus.   HBAPE; PoetW; WoPoe

Nightspell.   Jon Furberg.   IFF

Nightstart.   Malick Fall.   SonAtl, *tr. by* Gregory Beaven, Nene Ndiaye Diop, Kurt Ganzl, Saul Goode, Eileen Julien, Lilyan Kesteloot, Aliko Songolo, Jean-Marie Volet and Kenneth Wilburn

Nightsweats.   Richard Tayson.   AmPoNex; WiU

Nighttime.   René Crevel.   CAGL, *tr. by* Michael Taylor

Night-time.   Ricardo Jaimes Freyre.   SonAtl, *tr. by* Lisa Martin and Eva Asensio Vicente

Night-time.   Mongane Wally Serote.   TSAP

Nighttime am a fallin'.   Put Your Arms Around Me, Honey.   Junie McCree.   ReLy

Night-Time: Starting to Write.   Bernard Spencer.   AWTN

Nighttrains.   Jayne Cortez.   PFTM-2

Nightwalker.   Thomas Kinsella.

   "Foot of the tower. An angle where the darkness, The."   PBCIP

Nightwatcher:/ Fast falls the night unfurling its vile veil.   Frank Mkalawile Chipasula.   HBAPE *Fr.* Nightsong.

Nightwatchers, The.   David Gascoyne.   RWPCtW *Fr.* Night Thoughts.

Nightwatchman.   Deborah Randall.   NeBl

Night-watchmen think of dawn and things auroral.   Blindman's Buff.   Peter Viereck.   MoAmPo

Night-wind shook the tapestry round an ancient palace-room, The.   Juana.   Felicia Dorothea Hemans.   RWP

Nihilist as Hero, The.   Robert Lowell.   VCAP

Nijinsky's Dog.   Susan Hahn.   IllVoic

Nijinski.   George Seferis.   MotU, *tr. by* Edmund Keeley and Philip Sherrard

Nijinsky.   Parker Tyler.   PoA 2002

Nijmi en Nima.   Juan Gregorio Regino.   RMCMP

Nijun uchan yibua nga kjín.   Nijmi en Nima.   Juan Gregorio Regino.   RMCMP

Nike.   Ernest Bryll.   FaBoWar, *tr. by* Czeslaw Milosz

Nike.   Nengi Ilagha.   NeNiPo

Nike of Samothrace.   Wingless Victory, The.   Hervey Allen.   YaYoPo

Nikki-Rosa.   Nikki Giovanni.   FaBoA; FuFl; GT; HeIP-4; InGu; ISC; OxAAAP; SSLK; UnSA

Nikolaus Mardruz to his Master Ferdinand, Count of Tyrol, 1565.   Richard Howard.   NoP-4; NoP-5

Nile, The.   Leigh Hunt.   CenSon; GSo

Nimbus rhomboid on gamboled happenstance.   Plate Pieces.   Jerry McGuire.   AnSo

Nimis Compos Mentis. Leslie Monsour. CalPo

Nimium Fortunatus. Robert Bridges. MoBrPo

Nimmers, The. John Byrom. OxAEP-1

Nimrod gazed across the plain. Tower of Babel, The. Laurance Wieder. ChIV-1

Nina. Noël Coward. ReLy

Nina got out. Bruce and Nina. Clarence Major. BodElec

Niña, La / con los ojos dichosos. Dolor, El. Francisco Brines. RaW

Nina Simone. Lance Jeffers. SeSe

Nine adulteries, 12 liaisons, 64 fornications and something approaching a rape. Temperaments, The. Ezra Pound. NAMCP V.1; NoAM; OBCoV

Nine delightful birthmarks. Mikhail Alekseievich Kuzmin. CAGL, tr. by Simon Karlinsky

Nine dragons—how fluent their undulations! Apotheosis. Wu Yun. ColAnChi, tr. by Edward H. Schafer

Nine Flower Mountain. Finn Wilcox. CSKM

Nine humors split and woven, The. Hsüeh T'ao [or Xue Tao]. WoPoe Fr. Trying on New-Made Clothes: Three Poems.

Nine hundred thousand prisoners of war. To Her of Whom They Dream. Paul Éluard. AF, tr. by Lloyd Alexander

Nine Little Goblins, The. James Whitcomb Riley. NOxBChV

Nine miles from here. Miklós Radnóti. See I fell next to him. His body rolled over.

Nine months I waited in the dark beneath. Pro Sua Vita. Robert Penn Warren. MoAmPo

Nine months in the belly. Ernst Mirville. OGAHCP, tr. by Boadiba and Jack Hirschman

Nine of Clubs, Cleveland, Ohio. Dorothy Barresi. SwNoth

911. Jim Daniels. LiTh

9 PM Summer. Mary Sue Koeppel. AmZen

Nine Ruba'iyat. Abdul Wahab Al-Bayati. IrPoTo, tr. by Carolina Hotchandani and Najat Rahman

Nine Sentiments, The. Michael Ondaatje. NLPA; OpeFie

Nine Songs of Mount Ko. Yi I. CATKP, tr. by Peter H. Lee

"Mount Ko's nine-bend pool." CATKP, tr. by Peter H. Lee

"Where is the eighth bend?" CATKP, tr. by Peter H. Lee

"Where is the fifth bend?" CATKP, tr. by Peter H. Lee

"Where is the first bend?" CATKP, tr. by Peter H. Lee

"Where is the fourth bend?" CATKP, tr. by Peter H. Lee

"Where is the ninth bend?" CATKP, tr. by Peter H. Lee

"Where is the second bend?" CATKP, tr. by Peter H. Lee

"Where is the seventh bend?" CATKP, tr. by Peter H. Lee

"Where is the sixth bend?" CATKP, tr. by Peter H. Lee

"Where is the third bend?" CATKP, tr. by Peter H. Lee

Nine Songs, The. Ch'u Yüan. CCL1, tr. by David Hawkes

Nine souls more went in her: the long-boat still. Lord Byron. OxBEV Fr. Don Juan.

Nine swallows sat on a telephone wire. Swallows, The. Elizabeth Jane Coatsworth. TLR

9000 Jackals Swimming to Boston. "Lucebert." PFTM-2, tr. by Peter Nijmeijer

Nine Times a Night. Unknown. EroLit

Nine times out of ten. Airs and Graces. Peter Fallon. PBCIP

9–10. Inger Christensen. PFTM-2 Fr. Alphabet.

Nine white chickens come. Black November Turkey, A. Richard Wilbur. OWoS

Nine years and three days later I drop to the earth. Blind-Sided. Rick Mulkey. AmPoNex

Nineteen. Elizabeth Alexander. GT; InTrad; PoPoPo

1980. C. S. Giscombe. GT

1980. Wayne Koestenbaum. WiU Fr. Erotic Collectibles.

1980. Abraham Sutskever. HP Fr. Poems from a Diary.

1980 VI. Wendell Berry. UpMys Fr. Sabbaths.

1985 I. Wendell Berry. UpMys Fr. Sabbaths.

1985 III. Wendell Berry. UpMys Fr. Sabbaths.

1984 Tour of Britain, The. Ken Smith. RSaN

1980, I was returned to the city exposed. Zombies. Lavinia Greenlaw. BeAl; NeBrP

1981 and. Adupe. Jayne Cortez. ESEAA

1980–1990: A Poet's Personal Review. Asha Bandele. InTrad

1915. Anna Andreyevna Akhmatova. WoPoe, tr. by Stephen Berg

1915. Roger McDonald. NOBAu

1915: A Pre-Raphaelite Ending, London. Richard Howard. RACG

1915 Interior. Clarence Major. OxAAAP

1956. Thomas Kinsella. ModIr Fr. Anniversaries.

1956. Maxine Scates. PBCAP

1956, The Year My Sister, Using Her Ill Health Once Again, Blackmailed My Parents into an Accordion. Susan Firer. MiVo

1953 Re-entry. Time Presses Me. Lee Ranaldo. HeMarv

1940. Bertolt Brecht. HP, tr. by John Willet

1948: Jews. Adrienne Rich. OxBoAm

1945. Ed Leeflang. TuT, tr. by Peter van de Kamp

1945. Leslie Ullman. ExTi

1941. Robert Garioch. FaBoWar

1946, 1957. J. D. McClatchy. WiU Fr. First Steps.

1914. Max Jacob. PFTM-1

MCMXIV. Philip Larkin. FaBoWar; HarvBoo; NAEL-6v2; NAEL-7v2; NAMCP V.2; NoAM; NoP-4; NoP-5; OBWP; OxAEP-2; PoAgWa

1914 Box, The. Marcel Duchamp. PFTM-1

1914–1918 The Young to the Old. W. J. Gruffydd. BBMWP, tr. by Robert Minhinnick

1905. David Ignatow. TaR

Nineteen Hundred and Nineteen. William Butler Yeats. NAMCP V.1

Nineteen hundred and ninety-nine. Conor O'Callaghan. NIrP Fr. Loose Change.

1904. Frederick Morgan. WeW-3

1919. Donald Revell. BodElec

1990. Bob Holman. FTtHH

1994. Lucille Clifton. FuFl

1994 Inventory. Toi Derricotte. SpirFl

1992. Wayne Koestenbaum. WiU Fr. Erotic Collectibles.

Nineteen Old Poems, The. Unknown. tr. by Anne Birrell

"Green, green riverside grass." ColAnChi, tr. by Anne Birrell

1907: A man digs a deepwell on a hilltop, harnessing. Condensed History of Beauty, A. Maurice Manning. LegDan

1978, Remembering 1962. C. S. Giscombe. GT

1974. Abraham Sutskever. BBASP Fr. Poems from a Diary.

1974: My Story in a Late Style of Fire. Larry Levis. BodElec

1971. J. D. McClatchy. WiU Fr. First Steps.

1979 II. Wendell Berry. UpMys Fr. Sabbaths.

1977. Wayne Koestenbaum. WiU Fr. Erotic Collectibles.

1977. Jeffrey McDaniel. LaCa

1973. Reuben Jackson. GT

1916 Seen from 1921. Edmund Charles Blunden. NoP-4; NoP-5

1965. Frankie Paino. AmPoNex

1967, Detroit. My grandfather watches. Time, Temperature. Jim Daniels. LTA

1966. David Rivard. PBCAP

1963 in / became poem. Clark Coolidge. AHA Fr. Ing.

1962 At the Edge of Town. C. S. Giscombe. GT

Nineteen Sonnets. Elinor Wylie.

"In our content, before the autumn came." NALW

1910. Federico García Lorca. PtR, tr. by Greg Simon and Steven F. White

1930. Aurora Levins Morales. PueRic

1935. Stephen Vincent Benét. MoAmPo

1936–1986. Eitan Kalinski. NRoS, tr. by Esther Raizen

1933. Kenneth Fearing. APT-2; FTtHH

1928 film star's breasts, The. Caught. Carole Bernstein. AmPoNex

1925. Edwin Honig. NoAM Fr. To Restore a Dead Child.

1929. W. H. Auden. OxAEP-2

1926. Weldon Kees. OxBoAm

19 January 1944. Salvatore Quasimodo. AF, tr. by Jack Bevan

99.9 FM Radio Nostalgia. Keith Bennett. RWPCtW

90 North. Randall Jarrell. HarvBoo; NAMCP V.2; NoAM; NoP-5; PtR; StAl; VCAP

96 Vandam. Gerald Stern. P180

Ninety-Mile, The. Laurie Duggan. BMAP Fr. Ash Range, The.

Ninety-Nine. Elizabeth Godley. NOxBChV

Nineveh, Tyre. Memphis Blues. Sterling Allen Brown. APT-2; InGu; NAMCP V.1

Ninguna. Frontera. Francisco X. Alarcón. CalPo

Ninguna / No. Frontera / Border. Francisco X. Alarcón. GeoHom

Ninny's Tomb. Patricia Beer. HarvBoo

Niño buscaba su voz, El. Niño Mudo, El. Federico García Lorca. RaW

Niño de la Jaula Vacía, El. José Hierro. RaW

Niño Mudo, El. Federico García Lorca. RaW

Niño Tras un Cristal. Luis Cernuda. RaW

Nintendo. Treasure Williams. BRtP

Ninth Canticle, The. George Wither. ChIV-1

Ninth Elegy. Rainer Maria Rilke. Fr. Duino Elegies, The [David Young Translation].

Ninth Elegy: Fort Capuzzo. Hamish Henderson. FaBoWar Fr. Elegies for the Dead in Cyrenaica.

Ninth Evening Voluntary. William Wordsworth. SacPr

Ninth Month. Victoria Redel. BeAl

9.1.59: II. Pablo Picasso. CLPP, *tr. by* Paul Blackburn
9.1.59: VI. Pablo Picasso. CLPP, *tr. by* Paul Blackburn
Ninth Symmetrical Poem. Michael Palmer. HarvBoo
Ninth Symphony. Michael Brownstein. MotU
Ninth Symphony of Beethoven Understood at Last as a Sexual Message, The.
    Adrienne Rich. PFTM-2
9th Untitled Poem. Pedro Juan Pietri. PueRic
Ninth Vertical Poetry. Roberto Juarroz.
    "To die, but far away." VCWP
Niobe. Henrietta Cordelia Ray. CBWP-3
Niobe is very old now. Bus Ride. Kate Daniels. PBCAP
Niobe lives in the desert, too. Ethiopia. Kate Daniels. PBCAP
Nip in the blossom[e] all our hopes and thee. (LL) Picture of Little T. C. in a
    Prospect of Flowers, The. Andrew Marvell. BASC; FSCP; NAEL-6v1;
    NAEL-7v1; NoP-4; NoP-5; OBEV; OxAEP-1; TFi; WaAnP
Nirvâna. Sidney Lanier. NCAP
Nirvana. James Tate. BodElec
Nirvana. Rosamund Marriott Watson. VWP
Nirvana. John Hall Wheelock. MoAmPo
Nirvana: "After you left me, I was so lonely and sad, I became but an
    apparition, a ghost of who I had been." Nin Andrews. AmZen
Nisei Picnic: From an Album, A. David Mura. LoL
Nisei: Second Generation Japanese-American. James Masao Mitsui. GifTon;
    OpBo
Niversity of *Gottingen*. (LL) George Canning and John Hookham Frere.
    NPBRoP; OBCoV *Fr.* Rovers, The; or, The Double Arrangement.
Nixon Names Elvis Honorary Federal Narcotics Agent at Oval Office Ceremony,
    1973. David Wojahn. AllShUp
Nizam the pederast, whose delight in boys. Surprise, Surprise. *Unknown.*
    EroLit, *tr. by* Derek Parker
No. Mark Doty. EmeKit
No. Joy Harjo. PrTe
No! Thomas Hood. OBCoV
No. Patti Tana. PasH
No. Treasure, The. U Tam'si Tchicaya. PFTM-2, *tr. by* Pierre Joris
No. Idea Vilariño. TANSG, *tr. by* Louise B. Popkin
No. 5, Judith. Rebekah Gumpert Hyneman. SWaP *Fr.* Female Scriptural
    Characters.
No acabamos nunca de entender. No acabamos nunca. Francisco Segovia.
    RMCMP
No airy stretch of sky to rest my eyes on. Non Te Rapiet Quisquam de Manua
    Mea. Sydney E. Jerrold. SacPr
No Altarpiece. J. Kates. GI
No altarpiece includes the painter. No Altarpiece. J. Kates. GI
No ancestral bones of ours. Visit to the Village, A. Michael Smith. PBCIP
No angel has descended here. Visitation, The. Jan Owen. NOBAu
No angel speaks to me. Muse. Linda Pastan. Vesp
No answers. Only questions. (LL) In the Absence of Bliss. Maxine W.
    Kumin. NAMCP V.2; NoAM; TaR
No Argument Tonight. Tijan M. Sallah. NAfrP
No Baby Must Weep. Mongane Wally Serote.
    1. TSAP
    2. TSAP
    3. TSAP
No Balls at All. *Unknown.* FaBoWar
No barometer but yellow. One, The. James Dickey. BodElec
No bells rang in her house. The silver plate. Miss Marnell. Austin Clarke.
    OxBEV
No belly, / no cry. (LL) Starry Night, The. Anne Sexton. ColAP; NAAL-5;
    NAMCP V.2; NoAM; VCAP
No better lost than any other woman. Canzone. Marilyn Hacker. NoAM
No better lost than any other woman. Marilyn Hacker. NAMCP V.2 *Fr.*
    Taking Notice.
No Bharatpur Bird Sanctuary in India, or Pantanal. Faithful Daughter Dreams
    of Spring Break While Installing a Bird Feeder for Her Mother by a
    Window in the Courtyard of Safe Harbour, The. Vivian Shipley. ExTi
No birds in the window, just snow grains. Sitting, Wedding Morning. Tony
    Trigilio. AmZen
No bird-song floated down the hill. River Path, The. John Greenleaf Whittier.
    TreFP
No bitterness: our ancestors did it. Ave Caesar. Robinson Jeffers. NAMCP
    V.1; NoAM; OxBoAm
No Bloody Matter 43 42. Michael Haslam. Oth *Fr.* Continual Song.
No Bobolink—reverse His Singing. Emily Dickinson. SWaP
No / Border. Border. Francisco X. Alarcón. CalPo
No Boundaries. Liz Rosenberg. InvLad
No Break. N. Revathi Devi. HotL, *tr. by* V. Narayana Rao
No breath of air to break the wave. Giaour, The. Lord Byron. NOBRP

No bridge. Buson. EH, *tr. by* Robert Hass
No Brigadier throughout the Year. Emily Dickinson. OWoS
No burning leaf; prithee, let no bird call. (LL) God's World. Edna St. Vincent
    Millay. APT-1; ITBLP; MoAmPo
No butler, no second maid, no blood upon the stair. Crime Club. Weldon
    Kees. OxBoAm
No call upon anyone but the timber drifting in the waves. Lament for the
    Makers. Jack Spicer. FTOS
No canta el agua en la rueda. Movimiento Perpetuo. Gerardo Diego. RaW
No Categories! Stevie Smith. NoP-4; NoP-5
No Child. Padraic Colum. OBMV
No Choice. Norman Alexander MacCaig. EdScPo
No Classes! Ella Wheeler Wilcox. APN-2; SWaP
No cloud, no relic of the sunken day. Samuel Taylor Coleridge. NPBRoP
No cloud or rain all night long. Wang Ping. KGB *Fr.* Rain, Clouds, Eight
    Thousand Miles of Roads.
No clouds overhead. Mother and Child. Ronald Stuart Thomas. RSR
No clue. In a Dublin Museum. Sheila Wingfield. MoWP
No cold philosophy nor cynic sneer. Louis. Maurice Frederick Fitzhardinge
    Berkeley, 1st Baron Fitzhardinge. DiBP
No collier comes from the belly of earth. After the Exam. Gwyn Williams.
    BBMWP, *tr. by* Christopher Meredith
No combat did he unleash, as panting. Portrait of José Cemí. José Lezama
    Lima. TCLAP, *tr. by* Gregory Rabassa
No Coming to God without Christ. Robert Herrick. SacPr
No congregation. pasts to shake. Alley Blues. Wayde Compton. IFF
No connection. The train would be six hours. Maundy Thursday. Jenő Dsida.
    IQMS, *tr. by* Geroge Gömöri and Clive Wilmer
No conozco los pantanos bálticos. Y nunca quise. Tedi López Mills.
    RMCMP
No Consolation. Norman Alexander MacCaig. HarvBoo
No Continuing City. Michael Longley. PNI
No cotton picking that day. California Entertainment, 1936. Wilma Elizabeth
    McDaniel. GeoHom
No counterman expects stumps. Hiroshima Day at the Riviera Coffeeshop.
    Andrea Collins. AtGh
No! cover not the fault. The wise revere. Frederick Goddard Tuckerman.
    TCAPo *Fr.* Sonnets: Second Series, 1854–1860.
No Coward Soul is Mine. Emily Jane Brontë. CABP; InvLi; NAEL-6v2;
    NAEL-7v2; NALW; NoP-4; NoP-5; OxAEP-2; PEW; PoPoPo; TRP; VWP;
    WPoS
(No Coward Soul.) BrAP
No crosswords ever. No Words Empty. Beau Sia. HeMarv
No curtain. Anne Portugal. SCFWP *Fr.* Bath, The.
No, Daisy! lift not up thy ear. To a Spaniel. Walter Savage Landor. DiBP
No danger that worms will attack; thrill them to death. Sounds. John Cage.
    PFTM-2 *Fr.* Song Books.
No days that dawn can match for her. Rachel. Lizette Woodworth Reese.
    TCAPo
No Deal. Lee Ranaldo. HeMarv
No Decía Palabras. Luis Cernuda. RaW
No Delicacies. Ingeborg Bachmann. PoSu, *tr. by* Mark Anderson
No Deposit. Earle Thompson. HATNAP
No Deposit Returns. Carlos Cumpian. ReTh
No Derry slubberdegullion with college airs. Ian Duhig. NeBl
No desire to die. Taneda Santoka. CAoMJL1, *tr. by* Burton Watson
No detail here, nothing but you. Unbroken gaze. Glance in White Space.
    Clark Coolidge. FTOS
No Dice. Annie Foster. NLP
No diff' no how. (LL) Dead in There. Langston Hughes. APSN; NAMCP
    V.1
No disrespect, mi boss. Nigger Sweat. Edward Baugh. EmeKit; WaCA
No Doubt. Margaret Lucas Cavendish, Duchess of Newcastle. STuOW
No doubt about it. Issa. EH, *tr. by* Robert Hass
No doubt I need a year of hallucinating. Confessions. Iman Mirsal. NAfrP,
    tr. by Clarissa C. Burt
No doubt: the sun. Monterrey Sun. Alfonso Reyes. TCLAP, *tr. by* Samuel
    Beckett
No doubts defend? (LL) Time Passing, Beloved. Donald Davie. HarvBoo;
    NoP-4; NoP-5
No Dream. Maria Mikhailovna Shkapskaya. ARWW, *tr. by* Catriona Kelly
No dreams. Wopko Jensma. TSAP
No duerme nadie por el cielo. Nadie, nadie. Ciudad sin Sueño. Nocturno del
    Brooklyn Bridge. Federico García Lorca. RaW
No dust speck anywhere. Shofu. ZenPo, *tr. by* Takashi Ikemoto and Lucien
    Stryk
No eagle stays a wind in cosmic motion. Walk On. Sheena Blackhall.
    EdScPo

No earthbound morning is this. Cemetery at Petit Saconnex, The. Deema K. Shehabi. PoArWo

No easy thing to bear, the weight of sweetness. Weight of Sweetness, The. Li-Young Lee. RaBo

No emblem, this; not a ducal banner. Bonfire in April. Norman Kreitman. EdScPo

No empty bed blues. 29 Songs. Louis Zukofsky.

No en Palacios de Mármol. Pedro Salinas. RaW

No End Point. Muso Soseki. EaWin, tr. by W. S. Merwin

No end to this separation, no limit to this cruel pain. Muhibbi. NaPG, tr. by Talat Sait Halman

No es la suavidad. Francisco Segovia. RMCMP

No es necesario que muera alguien. Claudia Hernández de Valle-Arizpe. RMCMP Fr. Hemicránea.

No es verdad que el cielo y su compás de espera. Al Zarpar. Gerardo Diego. RaW

No esteem for the stately caps and carriages of consequence. Long Lines Sent to Ling Hu-Ch'u before He Comes to Visit My Tumbledown Home. Po Chü-i. NDACCP, tr. by David Hinton

No Existe el Hombre. Vicente Aleixandre. RaW

No eye that sees could fail to remark you. Luna Moth. Carl Phillips. CAP-8; PoDa

No faculty not ill at ease. After a Long Illness. Robert Duncan. PFTM-2

No fairy story. Kona Macphee. BeAl

No fear of losing my sanity. Jolanda Insana. CItWP Fr. Colic Passion, The.

No ferns, but. Solitude of Glass, The. Yvor Winters. APT-2

No fiction was it of the antique age. William Wordsworth. CenSon; OxBSo Fr. River Duddon [A Series of Sonnets], The.

No finer gift could come to man. Tiruvalluvar. WoPoe Fr. Kural, The.

No flowers now to wear at. Waning of the Harvest Moon, The. John Wieners. PmAP

No Fool, the God of Salt. Alan Michael Parker. NeAmPo

No fool, the God of Salt, beloved by all. No Fool, the God of Salt. Alan Michael Parker. NeAmPo

No foot of man, commend thyself to God! (LL) Sonnet—Silence. Edgar Allan Poe. ColAP; TCAPo

No, for I'll save it! Seven years since. Apparent Failure. Robert Browning. NAEL-6v2

No foreign sky protected me. Requiem. Anna Andreyevna Akhmatova. AF; PoetW; WoPoe, tr. by Max Hayward and Stanley Kunitz

No form at all—it's impossible to imagine its being. Lyn Hejinian. FTOS Fr. Oxota: A Short Russian Novel.

No fortune base shall ever alter me. (LL) Sir Walter Ralegh. See No fortune base, nor frail, shall alter me.

No Foundation. John Hollander. OBCoV

No fragrance yet the fold. Harry Guest. NewEx

No funeral gloom, my dears, when I am gone. William Allingham. OxBEV

No future hope no fear for evermore. (LL) Cobwebs. Christina Georgina Rossetti. CABP; NAEL-6v2; NAEL-7v2; NALW; VWP

No Gain. Muso Soseki. EaWin, tr. by W. S. Merwin

No glow of promises this time. Light Leaving a Small Harbour. Chairil Anwar. SonAtl, tr. by Peter Lennon and Tracey Yuan

No, go back into your exile, go back quick. After Wiriyamu Village Massacre by Portuguese. Jack A. Mapanje. AF

No, Go On. Maura Dooley. LW

No Goalies. Phil Iton. ArBi

No God. Dennis Cooper. PmAP

No God but me thou shalt adore. Fourfold Exercise for the Believer in His Lodging on Earth, A. Ralph Erskine. SacPr

No God's rain petals. Woe. Ethan Paquin. IIR

No going back. Hour of Fear. J. Dyfnallt Owen. BBMWP, tr. by Gillian Clarke

No good hangin' onto a full cup. Bop for Laotzu. Hester G. Storm. WhBo

No Goodbyes. Paul Monette. InoFa

No gorgeous coat has he. My Mocking Bird. Josephine D. Henderson Heard. CBWP-4

No greater curse. Company I Keep, The. Nissim Ezekiel. BrAP

No Grudge. Lionel Fogarty. BMAP

No Guarantee. Craig Crist-Evans. MAAN

No Hands. Gillian Clarke. TCAWP

No Hands. Helena Nelson. ArBi

No Hast But Good. George Gascoigne. NoSic Fr. Gascoigne's Memories.

No Hatchet Job. Luz Maria Umpierre. PueRic

No hay centros pero el círculo existe. Carla Faesler Bremer. SPV

No hay porqué, hay órdenes de canto. Eduardo Milán. RMCMP

No he amado bastante. Fabio Morabito. RMCMP, tr. by Geoff Hargreaves

"No!" He Said. Wole Soyinka. HBAPE

No he venido a cantar, podéis llevaros la guitarra. No He Venido a Cantar. León Felipe. RaW

No Heaven. David St. John. FaoP

No Help. Sarah Morgan Bryan Piatt. NCAP

No / Historical figure. In the Fields or on the Hill. Pierre Reverdy. YaTCFP, tr. by Patricia Terry

No hoof, no foot, no wheel. To a Coal Miner in Madrid, New Mexico. Luis Lopez. GeoH

No house of stone. Elements, The. W. H. Davies. MoBrPo

No human face is. Brown Curtain, The. Alberto Giacometti. SurPaPo, tr. by Mary Ann Caws

No, I am not death wishes of sacred rapists, singing on candy. Bob Kaufman. GT

"No, I have tempered haste." Mount, The. Léonie Adams. MoAmPo

No, I'll not, carrion, comfort you. Comfort. Sonnet 5. Nell Altizer. FFC

No, I'm not going to. De Souza Prabhu. Eunice De Souza. FaBoVe; NAMCP V.2

No: I'm unmoved: nor can thy charming muse. Reply to Mr.———, The. Elizabeth Singer Rowe. BASC

No Images. Waring Cuney. APT-2; NIP-4; SSLK

No Immunity. Dolores de Iruretagoyena de Humphrey. ReBoTo

No importa el año. Leyendo a Virgilio. Tedi López Mills. RMCMP

No, in the New World, happiness is enforced. 'In the New World Happiness is Allowed'. Peter Porter. BMAP

No inheritance. Old Man To-The-Point. Muso Soseki. EaWin, tr. by W. S. Merwin

No interval of manner. George Oppen. APT-2; HarvBoo; PFTM-1

No introspective chaos . . . I accept. Lettres d'un Soldat. Wallace Stevens.

No, it does not happen. Snakes. A. K. Ramanujan. NoP-4; NoP-5; WaAnP

No, it is not only the date clusters. Middle East, The. Nadia Hazboun Reimer. PoArWo

No, it is not too soon. Forest Trees of the Sea. Unknown. WoPoe, tr. by Alfons L. Korn and Mary Kawena Pukui

No, it is not wise. (LL) Is It Wise? Stevie Smith. NAEL-6v2; NAEL-7v2

No it was no dream of coming death. Louis Zukofsky. OxBoAm

No, it was not under a strange sky. Anna Andreyevna Akhmatova. PFTM-1

No, it was only a touch of dysentery, he said. He was doing fine. Taking of the Koppie, The. Uys Krige. FaBoWar

No it wasn't. Nothingmas Day. Adrian Mitchell. NOxBChV

No Jive. Raymond R. Patterson. BRtP

No kings be crowned [or crown'd], but they some covenants make. (LL) Sir Philip Sidney. NAEL-6v1; NAEL-7v1; OxAEP-1 Fr. Astrophil and Stella.

No knowing what to do. Wailer. Kim Sŭnghŭi. EcSo, tr. by K. Kim Richards and Steffen Richards

No Labor-Saving Machine. Walt Whitman. APN-1

No lake is so still but that it has its wave. Unknown. Spl

No language is neutral. I use to haunt the beach at. No Language Is Neutral. Dionne Brand. NLPA

No leaf-shaking blast of winds. Simonides. SaLy, tr. by Diane Rayor

No, let it stay. It speaks but truth. First Grey Hair, The. Mary E. Tucker. CBWP-1

No Letter. Mary E. Tucker. CBWP-1

No, Liberty! People, he must not die! Set Him Apart! Victor Hugo. SxFrPo, tr. by A. M. and E. H. Blackmore

No Lickle Twang. Louise Bennett. NAMCP V.2

No life but this one. Peter Levitt. WhBo

No light to guide but the moon's pallid ray. Henry More. NOSC Fr. Psychozoia, or, the Life of the Soul.

No like place. Kim Hunter. RD

No limbo this week. Or next. Now it turns out. Limbo Dancer, The. Josephine Jacobsen. FFC

No lo puedes decir, pero io vives. Raíz, La. Luis Rosales. RaW

No longer are the forests green. Storms. Steel Usurps the Forests; Silence Dethrones Dialogue. Bible, Apocrypha. HBAPE

No longer, as before, plying with whirring wings. Anyte. SaLy, tr. by Diane Rayor

No longer, as before, will you wake at dawn and flap. Anyte. HePo Fr. Epigrams.

No longer can I tar[r]y. (LL) Aucthour Maketh Her Wyll and Testament, The. Isabella Whitney. EMWP; NoP-4

No longer dreaming plowing on through thick mud? (LL) Lateral Disregard. Harry Mathews. BAP-04; NYP2

No longer eating meat or dairy products or refined sugar. Acupuncture and Cleansing at 48. Len Roberts. BodElec

No longer for me is there anything late. All is late. Tomorrow the Past Comes. Ion Caraion. AF, tr. by Marguerite Dorian

No longer mourn for me when I am dead. William Shakespeare. HeIP-4; InoFa; NAEL-6v1; NAEL-7v1; NoP-5; NoSic; OxAEP-1; TFi; WaAnP Fr. Sonnets.

No longer, O honeytongued, holyvoiced maidens.   Alcman.   SaLy, *tr. by* Diane Rayor

No longer shall I exult in the floating seas and arch.   Anyte.   HePo *Fr.* Epigrams.

No longer slings back rot-guts G&Ts before 2 a.m.   Haymarket, The.   John Keene.   FuFl

No longer throne of a goddess to whom we pray.   Full Moon.   Robert Earl Hayden.   GT

No longer torn by what she knows.   Poor Relation, The.   Edwin Arlington Robinson.   APT-1

No longer truth, though shown in verse, disdain.   George Crabbe.   OxAEP-1 *Fr.* Village, The.

No longer will I draw water from the spring at dusk.   *Unknown.*   SLW, *tr. by* Marjolijn De Jager, Sayd Bahodin Majrouh and André Velter

No longer will I fling up my neck, exulting.   Anyte.   SaLy, *tr. by* Diane Rayor

No longer with us, you are that man I once feared.   Absence.   Jaime Jacinto.   ReBoTo

No look back.   George Stanley.   NLPA *Fr.* Mountains and Air.

No love deserves the death it has.   Phonemics.   Jack Spicer.   PmAP

No, Love Is Not Dead.   Robert Desnos.   WoPoe, *tr. by* Bill Zavatsky

No, love is not dead in this heart and these eyes and this mouth which announced the beginning of this burial.   No, Love Is Not Dead.   Robert Desnos.   SurPaPo, *tr. by* Mary Ann Caws

No Love, No Nothin'.   Leo Robin.   ReLy

No lovelier city than all of this.   Toast.   Thomas McCarthy.   PBCIP

No lover saith, I love, nor any other.   Paradox, The.   John Donne.   NOSC

'No' Madonnas, The.   Gwyneth Lewis.   TCAWP

No Man Can Hinder Me.   *Unknown.*   SSUS

No man can print a kiss[e]: lines may deceive. (LL)   Fulke, 1st Baron Brooke Greville.   NoSic; OBEV; OxBEV; PBRV *Fr.* Caelica.

No man can serve two masters.   Bible, *N.T.*   OBVE *Fr.* St. Matthew.

No man knows.   When A Woman Gets Blue.   Norman Jordan.   ISC

No man outlives the grief of war.   Permanence of the Young Men, The.   William Soutar.   EdScPo

No man takes the farm.   John Masefield.   UV

No manner of address will do.   Metamorphoses.   Geoffrey Hill.

No Man's Land.   Tom French.   NIrP

No Man's Land.   Iwan Llwyd.   BBMWP, *tr. by* the author

No Man's Land.   José Ángel Valente.   RaW, *tr. by* Hardie St. Martin

No man's trust let woman claim.   Roman Earl, The.   *Unknown.*   OBVE, *tr. by* Douglas Hyde

No Man's Wood.   W. H. Davies.   OBGa

No Map.   Stephen Dobyns.   GoPo

No Master, High or Low!   William Morris.   RSaN

No matter by what hand or trick. (LL)   Sonnet: "Of thee, kind boy, I ask no red and white."   Sir John Suckling.   BASC; CavPo; NoP-4; NoP-5; NOSC

No matter how he scrubbed, every day.   Meat Michelangelo.   Charles Harper Webb.   LiTh

No matter how I concealed them, even the.   Osip Emilevich Mandelstam.   PFTM-1 *Fr.* Tristia.

No matter how long.   Not Masterpieces, Planting Astonishments.   John Tritica.   ICANM

No matter how many times I try I can't stop my father.   How Many Times.   Marie Howe.   BeAl; LaCa; P180

No matter how often you knock.   Hotel Lullaby.   Srikanth Reddy.   IIR

No matter how small.   Smalltown Memorials.   Geoff Page.   BMAP

No matter how thunderous the chorus.   True Descenders.   James Kimbrell.   AmPoNex; NAPBL

No Matter What, After All, and That Beautiful Word So.   Hayden Carruth.   BeAl

No matter what I say.   Eel-Grass.   Edna St. Vincent Millay.   APT-1

No matter what life you lead.   Snow White and the Seven Dwarfs.   Anne Sexton.   PoPoPo

No Matter What Sign You Are.   Jeni Olin.   FreRad

No matter what we are and who.   Routine.   Arthur Guiterman.   GoPo

No matter what you did to her, she said.   Yeah Yeah Yeah.   Roddy Lumsden.   EdScPo; NeBl

No Matter Where We Go.   Henrik Nordbrandt.   VCWP, *tr. by* Henrik Norbrandt and Alexander Taylor

No matter where we go, we always arrive too late.   No Matter Where We Go.   Henrik Nordbrandt.   VCWP, *tr. by* Henrik Norbrandt and Alexander Taylor

No meat, no mind, no consciousness.   Unchanged.   Michael McClure.   WANABP

No mind, no Buddha.   Shozan.   ZenPo, *tr. by* Takashi Ikemoto and Lucien Stryk

No mind, no Buddha, no being.   Tekkan.   ZenPo, *tr. by* Takashi Ikemoto and Lucien Stryk

No mind, no Buddhas, no live beings.   Chifu.   ZenPo, *tr. by* Takashi Ikemoto and Lucien Stryk

No mistakes made here.   Broken and Beirut.   Suheir Hammad.   PoArWo

No Moment Past This One.   Stephen Dobyns.   IJHIL

No money for lunch so I rode an elevator to the top of the ONB.   Vision (2).   Sherman Alexie.   UnSA

No money to bury him.   Ballad of the Man Who's Gone.   Langston Hughes.   SAmP

No money yet, why then let's terrify with swords.   *Unknown.*   FaBoWar *Fr.* Mercenary Soldier, The.

No monument. Let me be ash.   Codicil: Including the cost of a monument and inscription.   M. Travis Lane.   Coast

No monument stands over Babii Yar.   Babii Yar.   Yevgeny Aleksandrovich Yevtushenko.   HP; VCWP, *tr. by* George Reavey

No monuments or landmarks guide the stranger.   Country without a Mythology, A.   Douglas Le Pan.   BrAP

No Moon.   Nancy Eimers.   ExTi

No Moon at All.   Redd Evans and David Mann.   ReLy

No moon at all.   No Moon at All.   Redd Evans and David Mann.   ReLy

No More.   Idea Vilariño.   BLPSL, *tr. by* Rene de Costa, Rigas Kappatos and Eleni Paidoussi

No more alone sleeping, no more alone waking.   Marriage.   Mary Elizabeth Coleridge.   LW; NALW; PEW; PoBW; ViWPN; VWP

No More Auction Block.   *Unknown.*   ISC; RaBo
  (Many Thousand Gone.)   APN-2; NAAPv.1; TCAPo

No more be[e] grieved [*or* greev'd] at that which thou hast done.   William Shakespeare.   HeIP-4; NAEL-6v1; NAEL-7v1; NoP-5; NoSic; OxAEP-1; PBRV; RaF *Fr.* Sonnets.

No More Boomerang.   Oodgeroo of the tribe Noonuccal.   BMAP

No more by cold philosophy confined.   Sir Samuel Egerton Brydges.   CenSon

No more diving into the wreck. From this point on.   Up from the Wreck Conjuring Montana Sonnet.   Steven Davenport.   RWB

No more dying. (LL)   Ode to Joy.   Frank O'Hara.   PmAP; WaAnP

No more exercises of style for him.   Younger Poet, A.   Peter Schjeldahl.   PoA 2002

No more for sin's dark stain the debt of death to pay. (LL)   Garden, The.   Jones Very.   APN-1; OxBoAm

No more he comes, who this way came and went. (LL)   London Poets.   Amy Levy.   PEW; ViWPN

No more head shaving.   Chitsu.   ZenPo, *tr. by* Takashi Ikemoto and Lucien Stryk

No More Hiroshimas.   James Kirkup.   RSaN

No more I seek, the prize is found.   Harbor, The.   William Ellery Channing.   APN-1

No more in any house can I be at peace.   Dream, A.   Charles Williams.   OBEV

No more in supermarkets will her good taste choose.   Dining.   Douglas Dunn.   InoFa

No more jazz.   No More Jazz at Alcatraz.   Bob Kaufman.   CalPo

No More Jazz at Alcatraz.   Bob Kaufman.   CalPo

No more let Greece her bolder fables tell.   On the Famous Voyage.   Ben Jonson.

No more my visionary soul shall dwell.   Pantisocracy.   Samuel Taylor Coleridge.   CenSon

No more, no more.   Riddle, The.   Alexander Brome.   NOSC

No more, no more Jewish townships in Poland.   Elegy.   Antoni Slonimski.   HP, *tr. by* Isaac Komen

No more, no more—oh, never more returning.   Felicia Hemans.   Letitia Elizabeth Landon.   NPBRoP

No more of talk where God or Angel Guest.   John Milton.   OxBEV *Fr.* Paradise Lost.

No more poem! he raged, eye red.   More Poem.   Dennis Scott.   WaCA

No More Rain Fall for Wet You.   *Unknown.*   SSUS

No more shall walls, no more shall walls confine.   Hosanna.   Thomas Traherne.   ChIV-2

No more soaring, said the hawk with a gunshot wound.   Red Tail Sonnet.   Ira Sadoff.   PfSP

No more [of] talk where God or Angel Guest.   John Milton.   NAEL-6v1; NAWM-5v1; NAWM-7v1; NoP-4; NoP-5 *Fr.* Paradise Lost.

No More Than One Allowed.   Duo Duo.   PoetW, *tr. by* Maghiel van Crevel

No more than one memory allowed.   No More Than One Allowed.   Duo Duo.   PoetW, *tr. by* Maghiel van Crevel

No more the black walnut's delineated.   Seneca Street.   Michael Collier.   PfSP

No more the English girls may go.   High Germany.   Edward Richard Burton Shanks.   OBMV

No more the scarlet maples flash and burn.   December.   Christopher Pearse Cranch.   APN-1; TCAPo

No more walks in the wood.   Old-Fashioned Song, An.   John Hollander.   NoP-4; NoP-5; OxBoAm

No more we search our hearts of hearts.   On With the Dance! Let Freud Be Unconfined!   William J. Tait.   EdScPo

No more with overflowing light. For a Dead Lady. Edwin Arlington Robinson. APT-1; HeIP-4; InoFa; MoAmPo; NAMCP V.1; NoAM; OxBoAm; TCAPo; TFi

No more you weave, Persephone. To Persephone. Harold Vinal. YaYoPo

No mountains or ocean, but we had orchards. Produce. Debra Allbery. PBCAP

No Music. Richard Chess. TaR

No, my body is neither a pelican nor a water lily. Adonis. PFTM-2 Fr. Desire Moving Through the Maps of the Material.

No namable danger to the season. Notes: From the Wait. Rachel Tzvia Back. DTA

No Name for It. Harry Edmund Martinson. WED, tr. by Robert Bly

No need to cling. Naito Joso. ZenPo, tr. by Takashi Ikemoto and Lucien Stryk

No Need to Discourage Dreams. Ihab Khalifa. AnVo, tr. by Mohamed Enani

No need to go. Jefferson Company, The. Clarence Major. BodElec

No never again without sense. Now Melanctha Had neither Home, nor Regular Occupation. Life Was Just Beginning for Her. Piera Oppezzo. CItWP, tr. by Cinzia Sartini Blum and Lara Trubowitz

No new poems his brush will trace. On Hearing Someone Sing a Poem by Yuan Zhen. Po Chü-i. CCL1, tr. by Arthur Waley

No news of him. Tanka. Toki Zenmaro. CAoMJL1, tr. by Makoto Ueda

No Newspapers. Mary Elizabeth Coleridge. NPeEn

No nightfall in June. Love Poem. John Purser. EdScPo

No, no, fair heretic, it needs must be. Sir John Suckling. CavPo

No, no; for my virginity. True Maid, A. Matthew Prior. NAEL-6v1; NAEL-7v1; NIP-4; NPeEn; WaAnP

No, no! Go from me. I have left her lately. Ezra Pound. ColAP; MoAmPo; NAAPv.2; NIL-7; NIP-4; TCAPo Fr. Ripostes of Ezra Pound.

No, no, go not to Lethe, neither twist. Ode on Melancholy. John Keats. BrAP; CABP; NAEL-6v2; NAEL-7v2; NAWM-7v2; NIL-7; NoP-4; NoP-5; NPBRoP; NPeEn; OBEV; OxAEP-2; OxBEV; TFi; WaAnP

No, No, Nanette. K. Schippers. TuT, tr. by Dennis O'Driscoll

No, no, no, I know I was not important as I moved. Come Dance with Kitty Stobling. Patrick Kavanagh. HarvBoo; NAMCP V.1; NoAM; NPeEn

No, no, no, no, my dear, let be. (LL) Sir Philip Sidney. NAEL-6v1; NAEL-7v1; NoP-4; NoP-5; NoSic Fr. Astrophil and Stella.

—No, no, no, she tells me. Why bring it back? Argument: on 1942, An. David Mura. LoL

No, No, Nora. Gustave Kahn. ReLy

No, No Nostalgia! Stephanie Brown. BodElec

No, no shakespeare not your gloomy melancholy. To be or not to be is a kink you've cleverly cast. Changes—Five. Norman J. Loftis. EGAG

No no the dead have no brothers. Hydra, The. W. S. Merwin. NAMCP V.2

No no: they definitely were. Testimony. Dan Pagis. PoSu, tr. by Stephen Mitchell

No. No. They were certainly. Evidence. Dan Pagis. FIT, tr. by Robert Friend

No noise, except the vellum pages getting bruised by the fingers of Master Huylten. Tulip Merchant, The. Aloysius Bertrand. MotU, tr. by James Weeks

No noise subtracts it. It won't leave, or scatter jokes or fathoms, no tiny failing. Karen Volkman. IAoNAP

No, not much, the old song. Kitchen Terrarium. Linda McCarriston. PfS

No, not the sort of boy for whom on does. For R. J. C. (Summer, 1936). Margot Heinemann. RSaN

No, not under the vault of alien skies. Requiem. Anna Andreyevna Akhmatova. NAWM-7v2, tr. by Judith Hemschemeyer

No, not under the vault of another sky. Requiem 1935-1940. Anna Andreyevna Akhmatova. tr. by Richard McKane

No, not writers for Heaven's sake. That bunch of slobbers. Brothers and Sisters. Michael Foley. PNI

No oasis anymore; and beauty. Beach. Tiziano Rossi. ItPo, tr. by Gayle Ridinger

No Obligation. Victoria Mary Sackville-West. PoBW

No occasion to. (LL) British Journalist, The. Humbert Wolfe. OBCoV; OxBEV

No Offense. Kevin Young. LTA

No Old Lady. Fĕng Mĕng-lung. ColAnChi Fr. Mountain Songs.

No olvida. No se aleja. Gorrión. Claudio Rodríguez. RaW

No one. Poem Arrested at Daybreak. Julia de Burgos. TANSG, tr. by Heather Rosario Sievert

No One. Kim Chiha. CAMKP, tr. by David R. McCann

No One. Lilian Moore. TLR

No one asks. Martín Espada. LTA

No one believes in the calm. Belief. Philip Levine. ColAP

No one belongs to the path. Strangers. Huda Ablan. PoArWo, tr. by Nathalie Handal and Ibrahim Muhawi

No one calls me that here. No one. Tísica. Diana García. TouFir

No one calls you beautiful. Adolescence. Allison Joseph. AmPoNex

No one can hurt me. They've tried to kill me. Alone. Anna Andreyevna Akhmatova. GifTon, tr. by Stephen Berg

No one can know about women. There are those. Mary Magdalen. Saunders Lewis. BBMWP, tr. by Joseph P. Clancy

No one comes to this garden. The dawn. Garden Temple, The. Patrick Lane. IFF

No one disputes that it is our duty to provide for the rehabilitation of. Concerning the Rehabilitation of the Disabled from the Wars of Israel. Arye Sivan. NRoS, tr. by Esther Raizen

No one feels half of what we know. (LL) Song of the Bowmen of Shu [1954]. Bunno [Wen Wang or King Wen]. NDACCP; OBVE, tr. by Ezra Pound

No one forgives you for what. Dear Ez. Christopher Pilling. NLP

No one has named the colors. At Fort Clark. Carol Coffee Reposa. TiP2

No one has seen your face, and yet a thousand. Cries We Make, The (64). Khwaja Shams-ad-din Muhammad Hafiz. WED, tr. by Robert Bly and Leonard Lewisohn

No one has yet looked at. (LL) Beach Glass. Amy Clampitt. MoWP; NAMCP V.2; NoAM; NoP-4; NoP-5; VCAP

No One Heard Him Call. Dorothy Aldis. TLR

No one hears her. Whippoorwill Calls, The. Beverly McLoughland. HHAm

No one in the Arrowhead Pub believed. Man on the Tower, The. Charles Rafferty. AmPoNex

No One in the Wide Wilderness of the Wood. Fernando Pessoa. WoPoe, tr. by Katherine Washburn

No one in the wide wilderness of the wood. No One in the Wide Wilderness of the Wood. Fernando Pessoa. WoPoe, tr. by Katherine Washburn

No one is awake in the campgrounds. First Sober Morning, The. Cindy Goff. LaCa

No one is safe. The streets are unsafe. Social Security. Terence Winch. P180

No one kneads us again out of earth and clay. Psalm. Paul Celan. GTCP; PoetW; PoSu, tr. by John Felstiner

No one kneads us anew from earth and clay. Psalm. Paul Celan. WoPoe, tr. by Margaret Guillemin and Katherine Washburn

No one knew the secret of my flutes. Something Whispered in the Shakuhachi. Garrett Kaoru Hongo. WhBo

No one knows. Matches. Im Yŏngjo. CAMKP, tr. by Edward W. Poitras

No one knows. (LL) Kenneth Rexroth. APSN; NAAPv.2 Fr. Love Poems of Marichiko, The.

No one knows if he opened his eyes. Inhumation. Kathleen Jamie. GPPA

No one knows what's in it, not even. Marvel Mystery Oil. Elliot Fried. SUP

No one knows where the undertaker lives. Owl In Daytime, The. Thylias Moss. GT

No one knows why he came, or why he turned away, and did not climb the hill. (LL) Snowbanks North of the House. Robert Bly. BodElec; CAP-8; RaBo

No one likes to mention the gate of eternity. Ancient New Parents. Robin Behn. AmAlph

No one lives in Cape George lighthouse. Fern Kidnappings, The. Jeanette Lynes. Coast

No one moulds us again out of earth and clay. Psalm. Paul Celan. BBASP; HP; OBVE, tr. by Michael Hamburger

No one needs to ask. Reinmar der Alte. GePo

No one, not even Cambridge, was to blame. A. E. Housman. W. H. Auden. OxAEP-2

No one notices what I am doing by the border fence. Jaffa, July 1948. Hamutal Bar Yosef. DTA, tr. by Shirley Kaufman

No one offered you a courtyard. Gu Cheng. WoBe Fr. Liquid Mercury.

No one publishes my poems. Wonderful in Poetry, or a Victim of Goldfish, The. Konstantin Pavlov. CSCBP, tr. by Georgi Belev and Lisa Sapinkopf

No one really dies in the myths. Singers Change, the Music Goes On, The. Linda Gregg. BAP-01; OxBoAm

No one. Red notes sounding in a grey trolley town. (LL) Boston Year. Elizabeth Alexander. GT; OPRER

No one remembers ever having seen. No One Remembers. Léon Damas. SurPaPo, tr. by Mary Ann Caws

No one sees me. Fathoms up. Angel. Ruth Padel. MFPA; NeBrP

No one shall leave this place. Caption for "The Child from Vallecas" by Velázquez. León Felipe. RaW, tr. by Julio de la Torre

No one should ask the other. After Making Love. Stephen Dunn. EMP; PoA 2002

No One So Much As You. Edward Thomas. TCAWP

No one speaks a word. (LL) Off from Swing Shift. Garrett Kaoru Hongo. GeoHom; ReTh

No one to busy. Masaoka Shiki. CAoMJL1, tr. by Burton Watson

No one understood the perfume. Gacela of Unforeseen Love. Federico García Lorca. RaW, tr. by W. S. Merwin

No one walks when the guardian drum sounds. Thinking of My Brothers on a Moonlit Night. Tu Fu [or Du Fu]. TAL

No one wanted to dance with us. Junior High Dance. Allison Joseph. UnSA

No one wants to look at my disaster. Nodding Cranes. Vicki Hudspith. PA9/11

No one was at the door. Chained. Rayaprolu Subbarao. HotL, *tr. by* V. Narayana Rao

No one wears yellow like you excessive and radiant storehouse of sun. Daphne Marlatt. NLPA *Fr.* Touch to My Tongue.

No one will believe this story I'm telling, so it must be true. Sonnet: Tattoo Tears. Sherman Alexie. PrTe; WaAnP

No One Will Put the Cid up. Only a Small Girl Addresses Him and That to Tell Him to Go Away. The Cid Finds He Has to Make Camp Outside of Town, on the Sand of the Riverbank. *Unknown.* WoPoe *Fr.* Excerpts from *The Poem of the Cid.*

No one's dancing here tonight. Dance, The. Daniel Halpern. ChAP

No one's fated or doomed to love anyone. Adrienne Rich. PoBW *Fr.* Twenty-one Love Poems.

No one's here I'm alone with the violin of silence. Silence. Carlos Edmundo de Ory. PML, *tr. by* Steven J. Stewart

No ornaments but the double bed and open. Outer Banks, The. Emily Grosholz. RA

No other man has come down that way with his foot so big. Hallelujah Terrible. Matthew Lippman. BAP-97

No other man, unless it was Doc Hill. Edgar Lee Masters. APT-1; IllVoic *Fr.* Spoon River Anthology.

No other seagull, no ocean—the true / Music. (LL) Improvisations on a Sentence by Poe. Jack Spicer. APSN; CalPo; OxBoAm

No other woman can truthfully say she was cherished. Catullus. NAWM-7v1 *Fr.* Carmina [Charles Martin Translation].

No other word will do. For that's what it was. Gravy. Gravy. Raymond Carver. BeAl; LaCa

No palm me up, you dutty brute. Midnight Woman to the Bobby, A. Claude McKay. NAMCP V.1

No Pardon. Friedrich Hölderlin. WoPoe, *tr. by* Vyt Bakaitis

No part of her will fade. African Queen. Willem M. Roggeman. TuT, *tr. by* Gabriel Rosenstock

No part of the hand was hungry. Julie Kalendek. PfS

No Pasarán. Aaron Kurtz. Prolet, *tr. by* Amelia Glaser

No Passenger was known to flee. Emily Dickinson. SAmP

No peacocks will strut in my yard. Estate. Agi Mishol. DTA, *tr. by* Tsipi Keller

No pets in the projects. Owl and the Lightning, The. Martín Espada. TouFir; UrbNat

No place I love to visit more. Thoughts. Amanda Ros. VerBaPo

No place is extreme. Nanni Cagnone. ItPo, *tr. by* Gayle Ridinger

No Place Is Here or There. Oscar Hahn. BLPSL, *tr. by* Rene de Costa, Rigas Kappatos and Eleni Paidoussi

No place is here or there. No Place Is Here or There. Oscar Hahn. BLPSL, *tr. by* Rene de Costa, Rigas Kappatos and Eleni Paidoussi

No Place Like Home. Llawdden. OBWVE, *tr. by* Gwyn Jones

No planet revolves around the Sun. Law. Tiziano Rossi. ItPo, *tr. by* Gayle Ridinger

No Platonic [*or* Platonique] Love. William Cartwright. NOSC; NPeEn

No pleasant fruit or blossom gaily smiled. Philip Freneau. NAAL-3 *Fr.* House of Night, The.

No, please don't. On Thinking of Photographing My Fantasies. Nellie Wong. OpBo

No poem has yet been written. On the Growth of Hair in Middle Age. Kjell Hjern. PML, *tr. by* Leif Sjöberg and William Jay Smith

No poem you send. Buson. TAL

No poetry before ours. Filippo Tommaso Marinetti. PFTM-1 *Fr.* Zang Tumb Tuuum.

No point in crying justice. Prescription. Donald Woods. CAGL

No point in leaving you a long list. What I Leave to My Son. Du Tử' Lĕ. WoPoe, *tr. by* Nguyen Ngoc Bich

No point mortgages wilt in daynights. Mac Wellman. HeMarv *Fr.* Rat Minaret: Miniaturist-Divan, The.

No poisoned image yours against the sky. Hemlock at Sunset, A. Alec Brock Stevenson. FuPo

No population, roofs that move. Unusual View of the Town. J. P. Ward. AngWePo

No praying allowed, no sneezing. Warnings. Nicanor Parra. AF, *tr. by* Miller Williams

No Precedent. Muso Soseki. EaWin, *tr. by* W. S. Merwin

No priests. No tiring-women. If you please. Jezebel to the Eunuchs. Eleanor Brown. MFPA

No Problem, But Not Easy. Michael Harlow. BeAl

No! put the work down! No, not another stitch! Unfinished Sewing, The. Evdokiya Rostopchina. ARWW, *tr. by* Catriona Kelly

No, Quetzalcoatl, don't come back. Pentti Saarikoski. VCWP *Fr.* Invitation to the Dance.

No quiero, pese a todo. Fabio Morabito. RMCMP

No Rack can torture me. Emily Dickinson. NALW; TCAPo

No radio after eight. Easter for Joe. Kenward Elmslie. AHA

No reason for worry. Groom of the Animal-Bride. Paulann Petersen. FiBr

No reason given. Allan Graham. ICANM

No record tells of lance opposed to lance. William Wordsworth. CenSon *Fr.* River Duddon [A Series of Sonnets], The.

No red ammo spells a tin sign screwed. Steve's Commando Paintball, San Adriano, California. Joel Brouwer. AmPoNex

No rest! No rest on this bleak earth for me;. Crazed. Mary E. Tucker. CBWP-1; RACG

No Return. Hô Sugyông. EcSo, *tr. by* Youngju Ryu

No Return. William Matthews. P180

No Rewriting. Eileen Myles. BAP-04

No rice—In that hour. Basho. TAL

No riches from his scanty store. Song, A. Helen Maria Williams. WoRP

No ring, no Wedding. *Unknown.* BASC

No Road. Philip Larkin. MoBrPo; OxAEP-2

No Road Back. *Unknown.* CCL1,

No room at the crowded inn for you. And why? To the Virgin Mary. Andreas Gryphius. WoPoe, *tr. by* Christopher Benfey

No room in the inn, of course. What the Donkey Saw. U. A. Fanthorpe. OBCP

No round-shouldered pitchers here. Seamus Heaney. GI

No runner clears the final fence. Unfinished Race, The. Norman Cameron. OxBSo

No se sabe. Ana Belén López Pulido. SPV

No Second Deirdre. Máire Mhac an tSaoi. IrLP

No Second Troy. William Butler Yeats. HarvBoo; NAEL-6v2; NAEL-7v2; NAMCP V.1; NoAM; NoP-5; OxAEP-2; TFi; WaAnP; WeW-3

No, señora rodriguez. Ancestral Messengers / Composition 13. Ntozake Shange. AFaM; GT; IPoFL

No Shadow. Gary Snyder. WANABP

No sharp edges to this poet, who strolls. Contemporary Poet, A. Steve Wilson. AmPoNex

No, she's brushing a boy's hair. (LL) Facing It. Yusef Komunyakaa. AmAlph; AmFaPo; AmWaPo; EMP; ESEAA; FTtHH; InoFa; ItP; NAMCP V.2; NoP-5; OxBoAm; PLBUT; PoAgWa; PoPoPo; StAl; TRP

No ship of all that under sail or steam. Immigrants. Robert Frost. AmFaPo

No Shoes No Shirt No Service. Gary Snyder. BB

No sign is made while empires pass. Continuity. George Russell. MoBrPo

No Sign of Blood. Faiz Ahmad Faiz. AF, *tr. by* Naomi Lazard

No Sign of Life. Jorge Teillier. TCLAP, *tr. by* Carolyne Wright

No sign of men on the empty mountain. Deer Park. Wang Wei. CrYelRi, *tr. by* Sam Hamill

No Simple Explanations [(*to the Memory of Larry Neal*)]. Jayne Cortez. GT

"No, sir," said General Sherman. Edmund Clerihew Bentley. OBCoV *Fr.* Clerihews.

No situation presents itself. Every Time We Say Goodbye. James Cushing. SeSe

No sky and no earth at all. Hashin. NIL-7, *tr. by* Daniel C. Buchanan

No sleep. The sultriness pervades the air. House-Top, The. Herman Melville. APN-2; BrAP; CBCWP; NAAL-3; NAAPv.1; NCAP; OxBoAm; TCAPo

No sleeping wind will bear my head. Hourglass Lying Down. Alice Rahon. SurWo, *tr. by* Nancy Deffebach and Vanina Deler

No soldiers in the scenery. Clear Day and No Memories, A. Wallace Stevens. OxBoAm

No son. No moon. Veil. János Pilinszky. IQMS, *tr. by* Peter Jay

No sooner come [*or* came] but gone, and fallen [*or* fall'n] asleep. On My Dear Grandchild Simon Bradstreet, [Who Died on 16TH November, 1669, Being But A Month And One Day Old]. Anne Bradstreet. NAAL-3

(No sooner came, but gone, and fall'n asleep.) ColAP

No sooner downstairs after the night's rest. I See You Dancing, Father. Brendan Kennelly. BeAl

No sooner had they carried their martinis. Drinks in the Town Square. Rachel Wetzsteon. AmPoNex; NeAmPo

No Sorry. Catherine Bowman. BAP-97; RaF; SUP

No sound. Devil's Destroying Angel Exploded, The. Tom Pickard. Oth

No sound from the stone. This Is a Blessing, This Is a Curse. Chard DeNiord. PfSP

No sound is dissonant which tells of Life. (LL) This Lime-Tree Bower My Prison. Samuel Taylor Coleridge. HeIP-4; NAEL-6v2; NAEL-7v2; NoP-5; NPBRoP; OBGa; OxAEP-2

No sound of any storm that shakes. Hillcrest. Edwin Arlington Robinson. APT-1

No specious splendour of this stone. Cornelian, The. Lord Byron. CAGL; TreFP

No speed of wind or water rushing by. Master Speed, The. Robert Frost. GoPo

No spinsterlollypop for me—yes—we have. Dozen Cocktails—Please, A. Else Von Freytag-Loringhoven. APT-1

No spring, nor summer beauty hath such grace. John Donne. BASC; FSCP; NOSC *Fr.* Elegies.

No square poet's job. (LL) Haiku: "Eastern guard tower." Etheridge Knight. ESEAA; InGu

No stab thy [*or* the] soul[e] can kill. (LL) Lie, The. Sir Walter Ralegh. NAEL-6v1; NAEL-7v1; NoP-4; NoP-5; NoSic; NPeEn; OxBEV; PBRV; PoPoPo; TFi; WaAnP

No star gleam. Up Tchoupitoulas Nom de Guerre. Jessica Freeman. AnSo

No stir in the air, no stir in the sea. Inchcape Rock, The. Robert Southey. NPBRoP; OBNV; OBSP; OxAEP-2

No Story So Divine. Samuel Crossman. SacPr

No such antagonism. Dint. Tony Lopez. VaPo

No such thing as a prose poem. Nicole Markotić. PoPra

No sudden thing of glory and fear. Advent Meditation. Alice Thompson Meynell. RSR

No sun—no moon! No! Thomas Hood. OBCoV

No, Superman Was Not the Only One. Katharyn Howd Machan. ReTh

No Surprises. Rochelle Mass. Eno

No Swan So Fine. Marianne Moore. BrAP; NALW; NoP-4; NoP-5; OxBoAm

No talent. Issa. EH, *tr. by* Robert Hass

No Te Veo, Bien Sé. Pedro Salinas. RaW

No tears and no fears. Wes "Scoop." Nisker. WhBo

No telling where: down the hill. Where Souls Go. August Kleinzahler. StAl

No, Thank You, John. Christina Georgina Rossetti. NAEL-6v2; NAEL-7v2; PtR

No Thanks, No. 70. E. E. Cummings. PFTM-1

No, That Can't Be. Erica Pedretti. MotU, *tr. by* Stuart Friebert

No, the serpent did not. Theology. Ted Hughes. NAEL-6v2; NAEL-7v2; NoAM; NoP-4; NoP-5

No theory will stand up to a chicken's guts. No Theory. David Ignatow. RaBo

No; they have heads to think, and hearts to feel. Hannah More. NPBRoP *Fr.* Slavery.

No thing existed, nor did nothing exist. *Unknown.* WoPoe *Fr.* Rig Veda.

No thing existed, nor did nothing exist. *Unknown.* WoPoe *Fr.* Vedic Hymns.

No thing is great on this side of the grave. Heaviness May Endure for a Night, But Joy Cometh in the Morning. Christina Georgina Rossetti. SacPr

No, this is my body. (LL) Beauty and the Beast. Gillian Conoley. BodElec; RoV

No; thou'rt a fool, I'll swear, if e'er thou grant. Abraham Cowley. NOSC *Fr.* Mistress, The.

No, throwing yourself under a train like Tolstoy's Anna. Meditation on the Threshold. Rosario Castellanos. CFP; TANSG, *tr. by* Magda Bogin

No thunder blasts Jove's plant, nor can. Occasioned by Seeing a Walk of Bay Trees. Mildmay Fane, 2d Earl of Westmorland. NOSC

No thyng is to man so dere. Praise of Women. Robert Mannyng. OBEV

No ticket could touch. (LL) Soul Music. Baron Wormser. LTA; SwNoth

No Time. Billy Collins. OxBoAm

No time, no room, no thought, or writing can. Mary Sidney Wroth, Countess of Montgomery. PEW

No! Time, thou shalt not boast that I do change. William Shakespeare. OxAEP-1 *Fr.* Sonnets.

No, 'tis in vain to seek for bliss. Felicity. Isaac Watts. SacPr

No Title. Sam Gardiner. NIrP

No Title. David Schubert. APT-2

No tongue but bumbles, has. Mac Wellman. HeMarv *Fr.* Rat Minaret: Miniaturist-Divan, The.

No Tool or Rope or Pail. Bob Arnold. GoPo; IPoFL; OPRER

No touch, but forever and ever this. (LL) At Baia. "H. D." APT-1; ColAP; PoBW

No towers tremble now at the blast of my sighs. De Profundis. László Kálnoky. IQMS, *tr. by* Edwin Morgan

No townsman, Perikles, will blame us for groaning. Archilochus. SaLy, *tr. by* Diane Rayor

No trace anywhere of life, you say, pah, no difficulty there. Imagination Dead Imagine. Samuel Beckett. PFTM-2

No trace is left upon the vulgar mind. Charles Tennyson Turner. CenSon

No Transport. Tony Lopez. Oth

No trellisses, no vines. Thom Gunn. FaBoA

No Trespassing (Private Beach). Katayoon Zandvakili. AmPoNex

No truck. Camille Martin.

    Mawkish me. AnSo

    Pseudo slammer. AnSo

    Repo winter. AnSo

No use getting hysterical. Little Miracle. Molly Peacock. IFF

No use in my going. Blue Monday. Langston Hughes. SAmP

No use to aim that sextant now. Song. Reuel Denney. YaYoPo

No use waiting for it to stop. Apples. Shirley Kaufman. AFaM

No village dames and maidens now are seen. Samuel Jackson Pratt. OBGa *Fr.* Cottage Pictures.

No walk today;—November's breathings toss. Thomas Doubleday. CenSon

No walls confine! Can nothing hold my mind? Insatiableness. Thomas Traherne. BBASP; NOSC

No wandering poets. To TS Eliot. Abdul Wahab Al-Bayati. IrPoTo, *tr. by* Carolina Hotchandani and Najat Rahman

No water so still as the / dead fountains of Versailles. No swan. No Swan So Fine. Marianne Moore. BrAP; NALW; NoP-4; NoP-5; OxBoAm

No waters breed or break. (LL) Next, Please. Philip Larkin. CABP; GPTC; HarvBoo; MoBrPo

No Way Back to the Past. Allen Ginsberg. BodElec

No weather is ill. *Unknown.* FaBoVe

No, we'll be wits, and then men must be fools. (LL) Emulation, The. Sarah Fyge Egerton. CABP; PEW

No West Indians that I could see at my grandfather's funeral. 1962 At the Edge of Town. C. S. Giscombe. GT

No whimsy of the purse is here. Inscription for the Moss-Hut at Dove Cottage. William Wordsworth. OBGa

No. Who can bear it. Only someone. Demeter, Waiting. Rita Dove. BodElec

No winter shall abate the spring's increase [*or* springs encrease]. (LL) Love's Growth. John Donne. NoP-4; NoP-5; NOSC; NPeEn; PBRV

No woman yet has understood. It's a Hard, Hard World for a Man. P. G. Wodehouse. ReLy

No, Women don't Cry. Opal Palmer Adisa. WaCA

No wonder I'm a poet. Manila Paper. Cyn Zarco. ReBoTo

No Wonder Our Fathers Died. Ogden Nash. AmWit

No words are left. Saitō Mokichi. CAoMJL1, *tr. by* Amy Vladek Heinrich

No Words Empty. Beau Sia. HeMarv

No words for the Way. Yosano Akiko. CAoMJL1, *tr. by* Janine Beichman

No, worldling, no, 'tis not thy gold. Second Rapture, The. Thomas Carew. BASC

No worldly dust in Chongmyung Temple. At Chonymyung Temple. Daegak Euchon. BecRai, *tr. by* Kim Daljin, Kim Won-Chung and Christopher Merrill

No Worst, There Is None. Pitched Past Pitch of Grief. Gerard Manley Hopkins. GSo; HeIP-4; MoBrPo; NAEL-6v2; NAEL-7v2; NAMCP V.1; NoAM; NoP-4; NoP-5; OxAEP-2; PoPoPo; TFi; WoPoe

(No worst, there is none.) BrAP

No' yirdit thaim. (LL) Eemis-Stane, The. Hugh MacDiarmid. EdScPo; NAEL-6v2; NePenScot; NPeEn

No, you never will bind him. God (3). Marina Ivanovna Tsvetayeva. WPoS, *tr. by* Paul Graves

Noah. Roy Daniells. GoPo

Noah. Ricardo Pau-Llosa. Vesp

Noah. Margit Szécsi. IQMS, *tr. by* Agnes Arany-Makkai

Noah, looking out of the safe Ark. Flood, The. Patricia Beer. HarvBoo

Noah's Ark. Roger McGough. OBSP

Noah's Flood. *Unknown.*

    "Noye, to me thou arte full able." InvLi

Noah's Flood. Michael Drayton.

    "By this the sun had sucked up the vast deep." NOSC

    "Hundred years the Ark in the building was, A." ChIV-1

Noah's Raven. W. S. Merwin. ChIV-1

Nobel prize, The. Noble Funerals Arranged. Piet Hein. WoPoe, *tr. by* Martin Allwood

Nobilnes and grit magnificens, The. Orpheus and Eurydice. Robert Henryson.

Noble Balm, The. Ben Jonson. OBEV

Noble, enduring, ever-renewed peace do I attribute exclusively to his highness, the best of Caliphs, A. *Unknown.* HiArP, *tr. by* James T. Monroe

Noble Funerals Arranged. Piet Hein. WoPoe, *tr. by* Martin Allwood

Noble gods at the board. Herman Melville. TCAPo *Fr.* Clarel: A Poem and Pilgrimage in the Holy Land.

Noble hart, that harbours vertuous [*or* virtuous] thought, The. Edmund Spenser. NoSic *Fr.* Faerie Queene, The.

Noble horse with courage in his eye, The. Aristocrats. Keith Douglas. FaBoWar; NAEL-6v2; NAEL-7v2; NAMCP V.1; NoAM; NoP-4; NoP-5; OBWP

Noble King of Brentford, The. King of Brentford's Testament *abr, The.* William Makepeace Thackeray. OBNV

Noble lady from the province: sitting together. In the Dying Afternoon. Ramón López Velarde. BLPSL, *tr. by* Rene de Costa, Rigas Kappatos and Eleni Paidoussi

Noble Nature, The. Ben Jonson. *See* It Is Not Growing Like a Tree.

Noble range it was, of many a rood, A. Leigh Hunt. OBGa *Fr.* Story of Rimini, The.

Noble Ritter Hugo, Der.   Ballad by Hans Breitmann.   Charles Godfrey Leland.   APN-2; TCAPo

Noble Sisters.   Christina Georgina Rossetti.   VWP

Noble Six Hundred! (LL)   Charge of the Light Brigade, The.   Alfred Tennyson.   BRP; CABP; ChAP; FaBoWar; NAEL-6v2; NAEL-7v2; NoP-4; NoP-5; OBWP; OxAEP-2; OxBEV; TFi; UV

Noble Structure, A.   Julia A. Moore.   STuOW *Fr.* Centennial Celebration, The.

Noblest bodies are but gilded clay.   Samuel Harding.   NOSC

Noblest of men, woo't die?   William Shakespeare.   OxAEP-1 *Fr.* Antony and Cleopatra.

Nobly, nobly Cape Saint Vincent to the North-west died away.   Home-Thoughts, from the Sea.   Robert Browning.   NAEL-6v2; NAEL-7v2

Nobly, the great priest.   Buson.   SoOfWa, *tr. by* Sam Hamill

Nobody.   Robert Graves.   HarvBoo

Nobody.   Novica Tadic.   VCWP, *tr. by* Charles Simic

Nobody, ancient mischief, nobody.   Nobody.   Robert Graves.   HarvBoo

Nobody but Lester let Lester leap.   Lester Leaps In.   Al Young.   ESEAA; SeSe

Nobody but you.   Charles Bukowski.   IJHIL

Nobody can please her except God.   Mrs. Biswas Breaks Her Connection with Another Relative.   Reetika Vazirani.   AmPoNex

Nobody can save you but.   Nobody but you.   Charles Bukowski.   IJHIL

Nobody Comes.   Thomas Hardy.   NAMCP V.1

Nobody comes up from the sea as late as this.   You Will Know When You Get There.   Allen Curnow.   EmeKit; NoP-4

Nobody does any waiting.   Jackson Mac Low.   FTOS *Fr.* Pronouns, The—A Collection of 40 Dances—For the Dancers.

Nobody has ever offered.   Personal Footnote, A.   Gavin Ewart.   FaBoWar

Nobody heard him, the dead man.   Not Waving but Drowning.   Stevie Smith.   AmFaPo; BrAP; CABP; CtM; EmeKit; EMP; HarvBoo; HeIP-4; IJHIL; InoFa; MakPoe; MoWP; NAEL-6v2; NAEL-7v2; NALW; NAMCP V.1; NoAM; NoP-4; NoP-5; NPeEn; OxAEP-2; OxBEV; PoPoPo; StAl; TFi; UV; WaAnP; WeW-3

Nobody Here But Us.   Richard Garcia.   OPRER; TouFir

Nobody. I, myself.   Lemon and Rosemary.   Veronica Forrest-Thomson.   Oth

Nobody in the lane, and nothing, nothing but blackberries.   Blackberrying.   Sylvia Plath.   BeAl; NAAL-5; NAMCP V.2; NoAM; PoPoPo

Nobody in the widow's household.   Passing Through.   Stanley Kunitz.   BodElec; LoL

Nobody is ever missing. (LL)   John Berryman.   BrAP; CAP-8; HarvBoo; NAAL-5; NAMCP V.2; NoP-4; NoP-5; OxBoAm; VCAP *Fr.* Dream Songs.

Nobody knew, not even you.   Secret Love.   Paul Francis Webster.   ReLy

Nobody knew when it would start again.   Schizophrenic.   Patricia K. Page.   HeIP-4

Nobody knocks at my door. Nobody comes to hit me.   Invocation.   Maria Elena Cruz Varela.   VCWP, *tr. by* Mairym Cruz-Bernal

Nobody Knows of Trouble I've Had.   Unknown.   TCAPo

Nobody knows nor shall know. (LL)   don't Kill Yourself.   Carlos Drummond de Andrade.   PoCho; TCLAP, *tr. by* Elizabeth Bishop

Nobody knows the other side.   Jack Kerouac.   PmAP *Fr.* Mexico City Blues.

Nobody Knows the Trouble I've Had.   Unknown.   APN-2; NAAPv.1; SSUS

Nobody knows what I feel about Freddy.   Freddy.   Stevie Smith.   LW

Nobody Knows You When You're Down and Out.   Jimmie Cox.   GoPo

Nobody lies in this earth.   Cemetery in Pernambuco: Our Lady of Light.   João Cabral de Melo Neto.   TCLAP, *tr. by* Jane Cooper

Nobody loses all the time.   E. E. Cummings.   NBLV

Nobody Makes a Pass at Me.   Harold Rome.   ReLy

Nobody mentioned war.   Malcolm.   Lucille Clifton.   InoFa; WaAnP

Nobody noogers the shaff of a sloo.   On a Flimmering Floom You Shall Ride.   Carl Sandburg.   APT-1

Nobody,not even the rain,has such small hands. (LL)   Somewhere i have never travelled,gladly beyond.   E. E. Cummings.   BLPJKO; BrAP; MoAmPo; NAAL-5; NoP-4; NoP-5; PtR

Nobody nowhere they've all gone home.   Sleep.   Ajanta.   HotL, *tr. by* V. Narayana Rao

Nobody on earth has a book of matches.   Race of the Kingfishers.   Ray A. Young Bear.   HATNAP

Nobody read him, the poor sod.   Not Wavell but Browning.   Gavin Ewart.   UV

Nobody reads me.   Poet's Tango, The.   Jack Foley.   CalPo

Nobody Riding the Roads Today.   June Jordan.   NoAM

Nobody says: Ah, that is the place.   Places.   Thomas Hardy.   HarvBoo

Nobody Sleeps.   Stanley Plumly.   BodElec

Nobody told me when I was born.   Mirage.   Hashim Shafiq.   IrPoTo, *tr. by* Ralph Saverese and Saadi A. Simawe

Nobody told the flowers to come up nobody.   Ikkyu Sojun.   WoPoe *Fr.* Four Poems.

Nobody understands so let the Rabbi.   Prayer.   Stephen Berg.   TaR

Nobody waits at the foot of the stairs any more.   Anatoly Steiger.   TCRusP, *tr. by* Paul Schmidt

Nobody wants it to rain at a wedding.   Vows.   Shirley Kaufman.   TaR

Nobody's going to come in.   No Rewriting.   Eileen Myles.   BAP-04

Nobody's Heart.   Lorenz Hart.   ReLy

Nobody's heart belongs to me.   Nobody's Heart.   Lorenz Hart.   ReLy

Nobody's Hell.   Douglas Goetsch.   AmPoNex

Nobody's serious when they're seventeen.   Romance.   Arthur Rimbaud.   AmFaPo, *tr. by* Paul Schmidt

No-caring louder brothers. (LL)   Illusion.   Colleen J. McElroy.   ISC; OxAAAP

Noche baja su cortinaje, residuos de luz se resguardan entre las arrugas de mi, La.   Jeopardo, El.   Silvia Eugenia Castillero.   SPV

Noche blanca en que el agua cristalina.   Miguel de Unamuno.   RaW *Fr.* En Casa Ya.

Noche subió desde la tierra, La.   En el Valle de Zapata.   Veronica Volkow.   RMCMP

Noche Triste de Octubre, 1959.   Jaime Gil de Biedma.   RaW

Noche, Una.   Michael Palmer.   WoBe

Nocturn: "Moon rows burning, The."   Herman van den Bergh.   TuT

Nocturnal.   Romelia Alarcón de Folgar.   TANSG, *tr. by* Alison Ridley

Nocturnal.   John Haines.   GifTon

Nocturnal Garden.   Nikolai Alekseievich Zabolotsky.   TCRusP, *tr. by* Kathy Lewis and Bob Perelman

Nocturnal honey that glides down from the flanks, The.   White on White.   Maria Luisa Spaziani.   NeIt, *tr. by* Beverly Allen

Nocturnal Reverie, A.   Anne Finch, Countess of Winchilsea.   BrAP; NAEL-6v1; NAEL-7v1; NALW; NoP-4; NoP-5; OxAEP-1; OxBEV

Nocturnal Sea.   Xavier Villaurrutia.   CAGL, *tr. by* Fanny Arango-Ramos and William Keeth

Nocturnal Visits.   Claribel Alegría.   CFP; TANSG; VCWP, *tr. by* Darwin Flakoll

Nocturnal, you sword-fight.   Luis Cernuda.   CAGL, *tr. by* Rick Lipinski

Nocturnal[l] upon Saint Lucy's [*or* S. Lucy's *or* S. Lucies] Day, Being the Shortest Day, A.   John Donne.   BASC; CABP; NAEL-6v1; NAEL-7v1; NoP-4; NoP-5; NOSC; OxAEP-1; TFi

Nocturne.   Mário de Andrade.   TCLAP, *tr. by* Jack E. Tomlins

Nocturne.   David Barber.   AmPoNex

Nocturne: "Moon has gone to her rest, The."   Wilfrid Scawen Blunt.   OBMV

Nocturne: "Moonlight on stubbleshining."   Yvor Winters.   APT-2

Nocturne.   Rubén Darío.   SpanPo, *tr. by* Kate Flores

Nocturne.   Rubén Darío.   TCLAP, *tr. by* Lysander Kemp

Nocturne.   Angie Estes.   GeoHom

Nocturne.   Alaide Foppa.   TANSG, *tr. by* Celeste Kostopulos-Cooperman

Nocturne.   James McAuley.   BMAP

Nocturne.   John Crowe Ransom.   APT-1

Nocturne: "Now! they are ripe, these fruits of a jealous fate."   "St.-John Perse."   YaTCFP, *tr. by* Richard Howard

Nocturne: "One night / One night full of perfumes, music of wings and murmurs."   José Asunción Silva.   BLPSL, *tr. by* Rene de Costa, Rigas Kappatos and Eleni Paidoussi

Nocturne.   Xavier Villaurrutia.   TCLAP, *tr. by* Xavier Leroux

Nocturne.   Ellen Bryant Voigt.   UrbNat

Nocturne: "I can see the whole city, lights edging the harbor like yellow pins in uneven."   Katie Ford.   LegDan

Nocturne: "Long day was bright, The."   Frances Wynne.   IrLP

Nocturne: "Street is pure black and there are no seasonal traces, The."   Pierre Reverdy.   MotU, *tr. by* Michael Benedikt

Nocturne: "To the interior, limbs folded."   Valerie Martínez.   TouFir

Nocturne: "Topple the house down, wind."   Lizette Woodworth Reese.   PoBW

Nocturne: "Voici mûrs, ces fruits d'un ombrageux destin, Les."   "St.-John Perse."   YaTCFP

Nocturne and Elegy.   Emilio Ballagas.   CAGL, *tr. by* Fanny Arango-Ramos and William Keeth

Nocturne at Bethesda.   Arna Bontemps.   ChIV-2; NAAPv.2; OxAAAP

Nocturne at Danieli's, A.   Sir Owen Seaman.   UV

Nocturne, Aubade, and Vesper: "To call it a wet dream would be too barren."   James Wright.   BodElec

Nocturne by Ben Shahn.   Ronald Stuart Thomas.   OxAEP-2

Nocturne (I Accompanied You).   Léopold Sédar Senghor.   WoPoe, *tr. by* Melvin Dixon

Nocturne in a Deserted Brickyard.   Carl Sandburg.   APT-1; MoAmPo

Nocturne Militaire.   Thomas McGrath.   AF

Nocturne, Morningside Heights.   Karl Kirchwey.   PA9/11

Nocturne: My Sister Life.   Erin Belieu.   NeAmPo

Nocturne of Hope.   Yolanda Bedregal.   TANSG, *tr. by* Carolyne Wright

Nocturne of the Statue.   Xavier Villaurrutia.   TCLAP, *tr. by* Dana Stangel

Nocturne of the Wharves.   Arna Bontemps.   ColAP; GT

Nocturne (She Flies She Flies). Léopold Sédar Senghor. WoPoe, tr. by John Reed and Olive Wake

Nocturne: The Eternal. Xavier Villaurrutia. GifTon, tr. by Eliot Weinberger

Nocturnes: "He closed the deal on the night. A real." Dionisio D. Martinez. TouFir

Nocturno de Washington. Pablo Medina. BodElec

Nod. Christopher Davis. AmPoNex

Nod. Walter De la Mare. MoBrPo

Nod their cloned heads. (LL) In the Pea Patch. Maxine W. Kumin. AFaM; CAP-8

Nodding Cranes. Vicki Hudspith. PA9/11

Nodding, its great head rattling like a gourd. Original Sin [: A Short Story]. Robert Penn Warren. FuPo

Node. Imamu Amiri Baraka. EGAG

Nodes of light on the table. Florilegium. Eric Tretheway. PfSP

No[e] marvel [or mervaile] that I grieve, who like want see. (LL) Mary Sidney Wroth, Countess of Montgomery. BASC; EMWP; NOSC Fr. Pamphilia to Amphilanthus.

Noël. Joseph Hilaire Pierre Belloc. UV

Noel; Christmas Eve, 1913. Robert Bridges. ChrPo; OBCP; SacPr

Noel, noel, noel, / Noel, noel, noel! Unknown. NoP-4

No-Good Blues. Yusef Komunyakaa. OxBoAm

NOIRE, telle âme en exil s'achemine lentement vers. Secrète au Grand Jour. Habib Tengour. YaTCFP

Noise. Ferreira Gullar. TCLAP, tr. by Renato Rezende

Noise absorbed. Larry Eigner. ASA

Noise began in my belly, The. For Carlos Charles Bucillio. Alice Sadongei. HATNAP

Noise goes nowhere down the corridor, The. Sunday Morning Services. Michael S. Smith. ArBi

Noise in thousands of fissures my sight. Angélica Tornero. SPV, tr. by Jen Hofer

Noise of hammers once I heard. Hammers, The. Ralph Hodgson. MoBrPo

Noise of the Village, The. Unknown. OBVE, tr. by Frances Densmore

Noise outside. Spring. Pinkie Gordon Lane. GT

Noise suffocates the song, The. Ultrasound. Maria Luisa Spaziani. CItWP, tr. by Cinzia Sartini Blum and Lara Trubowitz

Noise That Time Makes, The. Merrill Moore. MoAmPo

Noise the pillow makes wakes me, The. Permit. Syto Cavé. OGAHCP, tr. by Boadiba and Jack Hirschman

Noise throws down, The. Immortal Pilots, The. Chase Twichell. PfSP

Noise Time makes in passing by, The. Merrill Moore. See Noise That Time Makes, The.

Noise Will Start Tomorrow, The. Jeanne Megnen. SurWo, tr. by Guy Ducornet

Noiseless at first, a spray. Rainbow Over the Seine, A. Mary Jo Salter. ExTi

Noiseless Patient Spider, A. Walt Whitman. APN-1; BLT; BrAP; ColAP; CtM; HeIP-4; ITBLP; MoAmPo; NAAL-3; NAAL-5; NAAPv.1; NCAP; NIL-7; NoP-4; NoP-5; OxBoAm; PoPoPo; SAmP; TCAPo; TFi; WaAnP; WoPoe

Noiseless Wheel, The. James Benjamin Kenyon. ArBi

Noises from underground made gibber some. John Berryman. CAP-8 Fr. Dream Songs.

Noises in the Dark. Liz Lochhead. EdScPo

Noisy banging and tuning of growth, The. (LL) Sticks. Thomas Sayers Ellis. LegDan; NAPBL

Nok Lady in Terracotta. Ifi Amadiume. HAWP

Nokh Aushvits (After Auschwitz). Jerome Rothenberg. TaR

No—Leave My Heart to Rest. Thomas Moore. CenSon

No—leave my heart to rest, if rest it may. No—Leave My Heart to Rest. Thomas Moore. CenSon

Noli Me Tangere. Jan Polkowski. AF, tr. by Michael March

Nomad, A. Jean Daive. MFP, tr. by Martin Sorrell

Nomad, A. Nomad, A. Jean Daive. MFP, tr. by Martin Sorrell

Nomad Exquisite. Wallace Stevens. APT-1; ColAP; WaAnP

Nomad House. Malva Flores. tr. by Jen Hofer
    "Body of morning glorious." RMCMP, tr. by Jen Hofer

Nomad of the Sky, The. Anna Cascella. CItWP, tr. by Cinzia Sartini Blum and Lara Trubowitz

Nombre Conseguido de los Nombres, El. Juan Ramón Jiménez. RaW

Nomenclature. Alan Dugan. BodElec

Nomenclaturik. Harry Hearson. OBCoV

Nominalist and Realist. Ralph Waldo Emerson. APN-1

Nominalist in me invents, The. Chanson Philosophique. Timothy Steele. PoA 2002

Nomine Domini / Theotocopoulos. High Renaissance. George Starbuck. AmWit; NBLV

Nommo. Zizwe Ngafua. BRtP

Nommo: how we come to speak. Devorah Major. BRtP

No-More-Daughters's. Ko Ŭn. CAMKP, tr. by Kevin O'Rourke

Non Dimenticar. Bill Berkson. AHA

Non Dolet. Oliver St. John Gogarty. OBMV

Non, l'amour n'est pas mort en ce coeur et ces yeux et cette bouche qui proclaimait ses funérailles commencées. Non l'amour n'est pas mort. Robert Desnos. YaTCFP

Non / Le personnage historique. Dans les champs ou sur la colline. Pierre Reverdy. YaTCFP

Non Linear. Phyllis Webb. NLPA Fr. Naked Poems.

Non Nobis. Henry Cust. OBEV

Non Omnis Moriar. Manuel Gutiérrez Nájera. BLPSL, tr. by Rene de Costa, Rigas Kappatos and Eleni Paidoussi

Non Omnis Moriar. Allen Tate. FuPo

Non Pax—Expectatio. Francis Thompson. OxBSo

Non Piu Leggevano. Árpád Tóth. IQMS, tr. by Jess Perlman

Non Sequitur. Margot Schilpp. AmPoNex

Non Sum Qualis Eram Bonae sub Regno Cynarae. Ernest Dowson. CABP; ClHu; HeIP-4; MoBrPo; NoP-4; NoP-5; OBEV; OBMV; TFi (Cynara.) NAEL-6v2; NAEL-7v2

Non Te Rapiet Quisquam de Manua Mea. Sydney E. Jerrold. SacPr

Non Ti Fidar. Louis Zukofsky. WaAnP

Non-Accidental Injury Slides. Geoffrey Holloway. NLP

Non-cognitive aspects of the City. Joseph Jarman. EGAG

Non-Combatant, The. Sir Henry John Newbolt. FaBoWar

Nondescript express in from the South, A. Gare du Midi. W. H. Auden. StAl

Nondescript, The. Peter Scupham. HarvBoo

None. Duo Duo. PoetW, tr. by Maghiel van Crevel

None are like you, Shulamite. (LL) Hebrew of your poets, Zion, The. Charles Reznikoff. APT-2; ChIV-1

None but a Muse in love, can tell. On Fruition. Sir Charles Sedley. NOSC

None but my Lely [or Lilly] ever drew a mind[e]. (LL) To My Worthy Friend Mr. Peter Lely [or Lilly]. Richard Lovelace. BASC; CavPo; GS; NOSC

None can experience stint. Emily Dickinson. NCAP

None could ever say that she. Catullus. OBVE

None is like Jeshuron's God. Charles Wesley. NoP-4

None is, slight things do lightly please. (LL) His Grange, or Private Wealth. Robert Herrick. BASC; CavPo

None of the computers can say. Airport. W. S. Merwin. OtW

None of the songs myself and can't pronounce them, these are my greatest hits. (LL) Map Room, The. Joshua Clover. BAP-97; NeAmPo

None of them come! (LL) Dame Edith Sitwell. MoBrPo; MoWP; NALW; OBCoV Fr. Façade.

None of this makes any sense. Ghost-Who-Walks, The. Colleen J. McElroy. GT

None of this world do I care for. When He Met Julia, He Greeterd Her Thus. Bálint Balassi. IQMS, tr. by Adam Makkai

None of us are the Waltons, Ricki Lake said that. Tricks for the Barmaid. Roddy Lumsden. NeBl

None of us remembers these, the days. Summer 1983. Mary Jo Salter. RA

None of your business. (LL) Jesus Dies. Anne Sexton. PFTM-2; RACG

None with swift feet. (LL) Dance Figure. Ezra Pound. HeIP-4; MoAmPo

None'll come, and then a lot'll. (LL) On Tomato Ketchup. Unknown. NBLV; Spl

Non-Emigrant, The. Lotte Kramer. Prnts

Non-Military Statements. Dunya Mikhail. WoBe, tr. by Liz Winslow

Non-native plantings stuck into lawns. Cougar. Brendan Galvin. UrbNat

Nonplussed. Ken Bolton. BMAP

Nonresistance, or love Mennonite style. Diana Brandt. ACAMVP

Non-sense. Unknown. NPeEn

Nonsense [or Nonsence]. Richard Corbet. FaBoVe

Nonsense Rhyme, A. James Whitcomb Riley. NOxBChV

Nonsense: these Buddha teachings. 73. Shih Shu. CSKM, tr. by James H. Sanford

Nonsense Verses. Charles Lamb. OBCoV

Non-Stop. James Tate. BodElec

Nonti Nzimande died long, long ago. Children of Nonti, The. Mafika Pascal Gwala. TSAP

Noodling. Narda Bush. MAAN

Nook. George Barlow. GT

Noon. John Clare. OxAEP-2

Noon. Thomas Hornsby Ferril. APT-2

Noon. Issa. EH, tr. by Robert Hass

Noon. Robinson Jeffers. MoAmPo

Noon. 12:45 already. Maya Bejerano. DTA Fr. Hymns of Job.

Noon—A Certain. Yi Sang. CAMKP, tr. by Edward Mack

Noon. A stale Saturday. The hills. What Could Happen. Dorianne Laux. BodElec; GeoHom; RoV

Noon heat in the yard, The. Hen Woman. Thomas Kinsella. ModIr; NPeEn; PBCIP

Noon in the intermountain plain. Headwaters. N. Scott Momaday. ICANM; NoP-4; NoP-5; WaAnP

Noon is half the passion of light. Noon. Thomas Hornsby Ferril. APT-2

Noon. Lysander. Anne Batten Cristall. RWP

Noon Office. James Schuyler. BodElec

Noon on Alameda Street. Hildegarde Flanner. CalPo

Noon on the mountain! Walt Whitman. Emanuel Carnevali. PoA 2002

Noon Point. Clark Coolidge. PmAP

Noon sun beats down the leaf; the noon. Grapes Making. Léonie Adams. APT-2

Noon Talk at Georgia's Coffee Shop. Allison Joseph. BtF

Noon Walk on the Asylum Lawn. Anne Sexton. OBGa

Noonday Axeman. Les A. Murray. NAEL-7v2; NoP-4; NoP-5

Noonday Rest. Mathilde Blind. ViWPN

Noonday square, The. Plane leaves, dust. Max Jacob at Saint Benoît. Rosanna Warren. OPRER

Noonday Vision, A. Frances Anne Kemble. PoBW

No-one has ever seen me. And the seasons. Memorial. Mihály Babits. IQMS, tr. by Peter Zollman

Nooo!/ me nah call him. Wasting Time. Opal Palmer. FaBoVe

Nor all earth's flowers, how fair. (LL) Slim Cunning Hands. Walter De la Mare. NIL-7; NIP-4; WeW-3

Nor all that glisters, gold! (LL) Ode on the Death of a Favo[u]rite Cat, Drowned in a Tub [or Bowl] of Gold Fishes. Thomas Gray. BrAP; ClHu; CtM; ItP; NAEL-6v1; NAEL-7v1; NBLV; NoP-5; OBCoV; OxBEV; TFi; WaAnP

Nor all your Tears wash out a Word of it. (LL) Omar Khayyám. CABP; CtM; TRP Fr. Rubáiyát of Omar Khayyám [of Naishápúr], The.

Nor am I a mother. I am not an Amazon—a warrior. Bronislava Volková. Vesp

Nor antlers through the thickness of his curls. (LL) Arms and the Boy. Wilfred Owen. BrAP; MoBrPo; OxBEV; WeW-3

Nor blame my weakness, till like me ye love! (LL) Tyranny of Love, The. Mary Robinson. CenSon; RWP

Nor can who has passed a month in the death cells. Ezra Pound. PWW2 Fr. Cantos.

Nor delayed the wingèd saint. John Milton. NOSC Fr. Paradise Lost.

Nor did the peach complain. (LL) Blue-Fly, The. Robert Graves. NAEL-6v2; NAEL-7v2; NAMCP V.1; NoAM

Nor dread nor hope attend. Death. William Butler Yeats. OxAEP-2

Nor ever chast[e], except you ravish me[e]. (LL) John Donne. BASC; BrAP; CABP; ClHu; FSCP; GSo; HeIP-4; InvLi; NAEL-6v1; NAEL-7v1; NIL-7; NIP-4; NoP-4; NoP-5; NOSC; NPeEn; OxAEP-1; OxBSo; PBRV; PoPoPo; SacPr; SoSe-8; TFi; WaAnP Fr. Holy Sonnets.

Nor ever did a wise one. (LL) Impromptu on Charles II. John Wilmot, 2d Earl of Rochester. BASC; NBLV; OBSV; OxAEP-1

Nor fear the God whom priests and kings have made. (LL) To the Poor. Anna Laetitia Barbauld. NoP-4; NoP-5

Nor happiness, nor majesty, nor fame. Sonnet: Political Greatness. Percy Bysshe Shelley. CenSon

Nor has my father nor his father. I Have Not Signed a Treaty with the United States Government. Chrystos. UnSA

Nor heed my craft or art. (LL) In My Craft or Sullen Art. Dylan Thomas. AmFaPo; BrAP; HeIP-4; NAMCP V.2; NIL-7; NIP-4; NoAM; NoP-4; NoP-5; OPOU; PoPoPo; RaBo; TCAWP; WaAnP; WeW-3; WoPoe

Nor heed the rumble of a distant Drum! (LL) Omar Khayyám. CABP; TRP Fr. Rubáiyát of Omar Khayyám [of Naishápúr], The.

Nor home, but Thee. (LL) None other Lamb, none other Name. Christina Georgina Rossetti. InvLi; SacPr

Nor human. (LL) My Imperialism. Tamura Ryuichi. AF; PFTM-2; VCWP, tr. by Christopher Drake

Nor in the integrated suburbs, / after ballet class. (LL) Soft Targets. Essex Hemphill. GT; OxAAAP

Nor knows he makes the shadow, he pursues! (LL) Constancy to an Ideal Object. Samuel Taylor Coleridge. NAEL-6v2; NOBRP

Nor last, forget thy faithful dogs; but feed. Virgil. DiBP Fr. Georgics.

Nor let thy wisdom make me wise. (LL) Alfred Tennyson. NAEL-6v2; NAEL-7v2 Fr. In Memoriam A. H. H.

Nor lingered Paris in the lofty house. Homer. OBVE Fr. Iliad, The.

Nor long the Trench or lofty Walls oppose. Homer. OBVE Fr. Iliad, The.

Nor look'd I back, till to a far off wood. Philip Freneau. TCAPo Fr. House of Night, The.

Nor moon. Fragment. Adelaide Crapsey. APT-1

Nor my prudence, love, can heal your wounded stare. (LL) Dream of Jealousy, A. Seamus Heaney. NoP-4; NoP-5

Nor pause in fearful dread before the opening grave! (LL) Ode to Death. Charlotte Smith. NoP-4; NoP-5

Nor Pirate, though a Prince he be. (LL) Upon Kind[e] and True Love. Aurelian Townshend. NOSC; WaAnP

Nor poverty the mind appal[l]. (LL) William Blake. BrAP; NAEL-6v2; NAEL-7v2; NOBRP; NoP-4; NoP-5; NPBRoP Fr. Songs of Experience.

Nor riches to the virtues of my love. George Chapman. OxBSo Fr. Coronet for His Mistress Philosophy, A.

Nor seek[e] him so[e] given [or giv'n] to flying. (LL) Mary Sidney Wroth, Countess of Montgomery. BASC; LW; NAEL-6v1; NAEL-7v1; NoP-4; NoP-5; NOSC; OxBEV Fr. Pamphilia to Amphilanthus.

Nor should this, perchance. William Wordsworth. OxAEP-2 Fr. Prelude, The; Growth of a Poet's Mind [1805 version].

Nor skin nor hide nor fleece. Lethe. "H. D." APT-1; MoAmPo; TCAPo

Nor strange it is, to us who walk in bonds. Frederick Goddard Tuckerman. APN-2; TCAPo Fr. Sonnets.

Nor success make proud. (LL) Rock and Hawk. Robinson Jeffers. APT-1; CalPo; ColAP; NAMCP V.1; NoAM; OxBoAm

Nor taste that bliss, which Phaon did not share. (LL) Foresees her Death. Mary Robinson. CenSon; RWP

Nor the full moon more quick to chill. (LL) Voices from the Other World. James Merrill. CAP-8; VCAP

Nor thirteen pence a day. (LL) Grenadier. A. E. Housman. OBMV; OBWP

Nor truth nor good did they know. Gloss. Padraic Fiacc. PNI

Nor used this complaint, nor have thought the day to be so long. (LL) Constant Penelope sends to thee, careless Ulysses. Unknown. NoSic; NPeEn, tr. by Ovid

Nor vaunt the balm, to heal a lover's wound. (LL) Contemns Philosophy. Mary Robinson. CenSon; RWP

Nor what he is, nor whither he's to go. (LL) Seneca. BASC; OBVE Fr. Thyestes.

Nor with the muse's laurel unbestowed. (LL) Sonnet: To the River Lodon. Thomas, the Younger Warton. CenSon; OxBSo

Nora. Nengi Ilagha. NeNiPo

Nora. Jean Toomer. MotU

Norbert Dentressangle Van, The. Sophie Hannah. HarvBoo

Noreen. Peter Meinke. IaFF

Norfolk sprang [or sprung] thee, Lambeth holds thee dead. Epitaph for [or on] Thomas Clere. Henry Howard, Earl of Surrey. NoSic; OxBSo

(Norfolk sprang thee, Lambeth holds thee dead.) PBRV

(Norfolk sprung thee, Lambeth holds thee dead.) NoP-4

Norfolk Sprung Thee, Lambeth Holds Thee Dead. Henry Howard, Earl of Surrey. See Epitaph for [or on] Thomas Clere.

Norgberto Hernandez—Photographed Falling September Eleventh. David Reibetanz. IFF

Noria, La. Pedro Serrano. RMCMP

Norma. Sonia Sanchez. UnSA

Normal Behavior of the Famas. Julio Cortázar. TCLAP, tr. by Paul Blackburn

Normal Madness. George Santayana.
    "When I discover that the substance of the beautiful is a certain rhythm." TCAPo

North. Lance Henson. HATNAP

North. Roger Mitchell. PoCoUp

North. Tony Towle. PmAP

North. Rosanna Warren.
    1. Over Prairie. OtW

North America. Nanao Sakaki. WhBo

North American Sequence. Theodore Roethke.
    Far Field, The. ColAP; NAMCP V.1; NoAM
    Meditation at Oyster River. MoAmPo
    Rose, The. TRP

North American Time. Adrienne Rich.
    "Suppose you want to write." LoL

North and South. Linda France. NeBl

North and south of my cottage, spring waters everywhere. Guest Arrives, A. Tu Fu [or Du Fu]. ColAnChi, tr. by Victor H. Mair

North Brunswick Street Lullaby. John McAuliffe. NIrP

North Corridor. Michael Collier. GM

North Country Village, A. Susanna Blamire. RWP

North Dakota, North Light. N. Scott Momaday. HATNAP

North Fork. Amy Clampitt. PfSP

North Haven. Elizabeth Bishop. InoFa; NAMCP V.2

North Infinity Street. Conrad Potter Aiken. InGu

North of Amsterdam. Larry Rubin. ArBi

North of Berwick. Sydney Tremayne. EdScPo

North of Dark. Medicine Man. Calvin C. Hernton. EGAG

North of Diamond Lake, the Cascades, crossmarks. Urban Renewal 12. Major L. Jackson. IIR

North of my grandfathers house. North. Lance Henson. HATNAP

North of my lodge, south of my lodge, spring rivers all. Guest Arrives, A. Tu Fu [or Du Fu]. CCL1, tr. by Burton Watson

North of our science, east of the hashish dream. Inglorious Milton, The. Francis Letters. NOBAu

North Philadelphia, Trenton, and New York. Richmond Lattimore. APT-2

North Point North. John Koethe. PoDa

North Sea. Jeffery Day. PoWW

North Sea. Duo Duo. PFTM-2, tr. by Tony Barnstone and Newton Liu

North Shore Park. Brent MacLaine. Coast

North Star. L. S. Asekoff. BodElec

North Star, The [with music]. John Morris-Jones. OBWVE, tr. by Anthony Conran

North: the watered-down sun. Ideal, The. T. R. Hummer. LTA

North Tower of Golden Fort, The. Kao Shih. CCL1, tr. by Stephen Owen

North Wales girl was once my passion, A. Two-Faced Too. Unknown. OBWVE, tr. by Glyn Jones

North we climb the Taihang Mountains. Song on Enduring the Cold. Ts'ao Ts'ao. CCL1; ColAnChi, tr. by Burton Watson

North wind blows the flying rain, The. Looking at the Morning Rain. Hsieh T'iao. CCL1, tr. by John Frodsham

North wind heard is heard always, A. Reverberation. Maurice Kenny. HATNAP

North Wind, The. Frederick van Eeden. TuT, tr. by Michael Longley

North-born horses do not think of Yueh in the south. Ku Feng (After the Style of Ancient Poems). Li Po. ChinPo, tr. by Ye Weilian [or Yeh Wei-lien or Wai-lim Yip]

North-East. Unknown. WoPoe, tr. by Seamus Heaney

Northeast Suite. Pamela Alexander. AmAlph

North-east wind did briskly blow, The. Bryan and Pereene. James Grainger. STuOW

Northeast wind was the wind off the lake, The. Cook County. Archibald MacLeish. IllVoic

Northern Boulevard. Edwin Denby. NYP2

Northern breath, that freezes floods, he binds, The. Ovid. OBVE Fr. Metamorphoses.

Northern Elegies. Anna Andreyevna Akhmatova. GPTC, tr. by Judith Hemschemeyer

Northern Exposure. Charles Simic. NAMCP V.2

Northern Farmer: New Style. Alfred Tennyson. NAEL-6v2; OBCoV; OxAEP-2

Northern har, A. Unknown. FaBoVe

Northern landscape. (LL) John Montague. ModIr; PBCIP; PNI Fr. Dead Kingdom, The.

Northern Morning, A. Alistair Elliot. StAl

Northern Pike. James Wright. PLBUT

Northern snows invade the city. Facing the Snow. Tu Fu [or Du Fu]. CrYelRi, tr. by Sam Hamill

Northern Spring, A. Frank Ormsby.
Apples, Normandy, 1944. PNI
Soldier Bathing. PNI

Northern Suburb, A [with music]. John Davidson. NePenScot; NPeEn

Northern Sun, The. Sherwin Bitsui. LegDan

Northern Vigil, A. Bliss Carman. BrAP; OBEV

Northern woods are fat, The. Ripe. Todd Davis. ACAMVP

North-Sea, The. Albert Verwey. TuT, tr. by Tony Curtis and Tony Curtis

Northward beyond the Lapps to the world's end, the frozen. Juvenal. CAGL Fr. Satires.

Northward I came, and knocked in the coated wall. Rodez. Donald Davie. HarvBoo

Northwest Passages. Daryl Hine. BrAP

Norway. Linda Gregerson. AmAlph

Nos asusta ver que el bosque. Claridad del silencio. Francisco Segovia. RMCMP

Nosce Teipsum. Sir John Davies. NoSic
Affliction. WoPoe
Man.
"I know my soul hath power to know all things." OBEV
Reasons drawn from Divinity. SacPr

Nose. Ambrose Bierce. APN-2 Fr. Devil's Dictionary, The.

Nose, The [with music]. Iain Crichton Smith. OBSP

Nose, The. Ruth Stone. InvLad

Nose cone of a rocket, The. Reverse Engineering. Robert Johnson. TiP2

Nose of the pick-up lifted, The. Scattering Ashes. David Scott. NLP

Nose only above water. Sandra: At the Beaver Trap. Michael S. Harper. NoAM

Nose went away by itself, The. Nose, The. Iain Crichton Smith. OBSP

Nosebleed, Gold Digger, KGB, Henry James, Handshake. David Kirby. SUP

Nosebleed, The / Of the cottonwood. Land of God. Texas. Caley O'Dwyer. TiP2

Nosegay, A. John Reynolds. OBEV

Nosing about for worms. Robin (The bird that was devoured by the cat in the garden of the house). Fawzi Karim. IrPoTo, tr. by Chuck Miller and Saadi A. Simawe

Nostalgia. Lajos Áprily. IQMS, tr. by Watson Kirkconnell

Nostalgia. Stephen Berg. OPRER

Nostalgia. Christopher Buckley. SeSe

Nostalgia: "Way. . .way back. . .nine hills away." Musa Ćatim Ćatić. SonAtl, tr. by Merica Delic and Ziva Pecavar

Nostalgia. Billy Collins. BeAl

Nostalgia. Darryl Holmes. InTrad

Nostalgia: "O, fruitful district Corozal!" Dolores B. Lin. OWABP

Nostalgia. Louis MacNeice. OxAEP-2

Nostalgia. No Ch'ŏnmyŏng. CAMKP, tr. by Mickey Hong

Nostalgia. Charles Rossiter. PasH

Nostalgia. Robert Ivanovich Rozhdestvensky. TCRusP, tr. by Daniel Weissbort

Nostalgia. Aharon Shabtai. WoBe, tr. by Peter Cole

Nostalgia. Xue Di. PML, tr. by Wang Ping and Keith Waldrop

Nostalgia and Complaint of the Grandparents. Donald Justice. NAMCP V.2; NoAM

Nostalgia, Cheryl, Is the Best Heroin. Arielle Greenberg. LegDan

Nostalgia comes with the smell of rain, you know. (LL) Nostalgia of the Lakefronts. Donald Justice. InGu; NoP-5

Nostalgia del sol en los terrados, La. Arte Poética. Jaime Gil de Biedma. RaW

Nostalgia is the elixir drained. Lyn Hejinian. CalPo Fr. Redo.

Nostalgia of the Infinite. Barbara Guest. BAP-04

Nostalgia of the Lakefronts. Donald Justice. InGu; NoP-5

Nostalgia, or a Painful Return to Memories. Stefan Tsanev. CSCBP, tr. by Georgi Belev and Lisa Sapinkopf

Nostalgic Song for My Beloved. Adolf Wolfli. PFTM-1

Nostalgic song for my beloved. Nostalgic Song for My Beloved. Adolf Wolfli. PFTM-1

Noster was a ship of swank, The. Noster, The. E. E. Cummings. OBCoV

Nostoi. Rodolfo Di Biasio. NeIt, tr. by Stephen Sartarelli

Nostos. Louise Glück. CAP-8

Nostradamus Predicts the Destruction of Chicago. Maureen Seaton. IllVoic

Nostrum. Christopher Pilling. PoCu

Not. Mona Lisa Tea Towel, The. Nigel Roberts. BMAP

Not a Balancing Act. Claire Needell. OnScMo

Not a Cage. Joan Retallack. FTOS

Not a Care in the World. John Latouche. ReLy

Not a Christian, not a Buddhist, not a Confucian either. Natsume Soseki. CAoMJL1, tr. by Burton Watson

Not a drum was heard, not a funeral note. Burial of Sir John Moore, The. Charles Wolfe. FaBoWar; GoPo; IrV; NOBRP; OBEV; OBWP; OxAEP-2; OxBEV; TFi; TreFP; UV

Not a head stands out. Post. Pierre Reverdy. CuPo

Not a Herod's oath that cannot change. (LL) Mind Is an Enchanting Thing, The. Marianne Moore. APT-1; HeIP-4; MoAmPo; NAAL-5; NAAPv.2; NoP-4; NoP-5

Not a hill to highlight the landscape. No Goalies. Phil Iton. ArBi

Not a homeland. Upside Down Picture, An. Mahdi Muhammad Ali. IrPoTo, tr. by Salaam Yousif

Not a leaf stirring. Buson. EH, tr. by Robert Hass

Not a Letter. Yvonne Cullen. NIrP

Not a line of her writing have I. Thoughts of Phena. Thomas Hardy. HarvBoo; NoP-4; NPeEn

Not a mote in the light above. Tsugen Jakurei. ZenPo, tr. by Takashi Ikemoto and Lucien Stryk

Not a one out of place. (LL) Naola Beauty Academy, New Orleans, Louisiana, 1943. Natasha Trethewey. NeAmPo; SpirFl; SUP

Not a Paris Review Interview. Frank Templeton Prince.
"Surely he undertakes." PoCho

Not a poem on your absence. Speaking Your Name. Alejandra Pizarnik. TANSG, tr. by Susan Bassnett

Not a pretty tree. Shagbark. Faye George. PoCoUp

Not a prophet, he says of himself. Witness, The. Rose Drachler. TaR

Not a red rose or a satin heart. Valentine. Carol Ann Duffy. BeAl; EdScPo

Not a shank of the long lane upwards. Brechfa Chapel. Roland Mathias. AngWePo

Not a Sous Had He Got. Thomas Ingoldsby. UV

Not a sous had he got,—not a guinea or note. Not a Sous Had He Got. Thomas Ingoldsby. UV

Not a Sparrow. Tess Gallagher. AmZen

Not a star but a planet not. Morning Star, The. Paul S. Piper. AmZen

Not a thing could I see. Frustrated. May Probyn. VWP

Not A Ton Notation. Jerry McGuire. AnSo

Not a twig or a leaf on the old tree. Withered Tree, A. Han Yü. CCL1, *tr. by* A. C. Graham

Not a word! Not a word! Allen Ginsberg. WhBo

Not a word, or to the knowing. Ecstatic Longing. Johann Wolfgang von Goethe. STV, *tr. by* John Frederick Nims

Not About Death. Bulat Shalvovich Okudzhava. RusPo, *tr. by* Robert Arthur Douglas Ford

Not About Poems. Carolyn M. Rodgers. OxAAAP

Not / above / a juggler's. John Frederick Nims. PoA 2002 *Fr.* Six-Cornered Snowflake, The.

Not Adlestrop [*with music*]. Dannie Abse. NoAM

Not Adlestrop, no—besides, the name. Dannie Abse. *See* Not Adlestrop.

Not again in this flesh will I see. Wendell Berry. UpMys *Fr.* Sabbaths.

Not all insects but certain insects. Reckless Sonnet. Kimiko Hahn. CAP-8

Not All, Only a Few, Return As the Rose or the Tulip. Mirza Asadullah Khan Ghalib. WoPoe, *tr. by* Adrienne Rich

Not all, only a few, return as the rose or the tulip. Not All, Only a Few, Return As the Rose or the Tulip. Mirza Asadullah Khan Ghalib. WoPoe, *tr. by* Adrienne Rich

Not all that tempts one's wand'ring eyes. Fred. Ian Duhig. NeBl

Not all these legends, I suppose. Popular Mythologies. Vernon Scannell. OBCoV

Not alwayes give a melting kiss. Johannes Secundus. OBVE *Fr.* Basia.

Not always should the tear's ambrosial dew. Samuel Taylor Coleridge. CenSon *Fr.* Effusions.

Not an acquiescence of surrender. War Is Over, The. Ben Doyle. LegDan

Not an editorial-writer, bereaved with bartlett. Portrait of the Poet as Landscape. Abraham Moses Klein. NoAM

Not an epilogue, but everything coming to an end. Anatoly Steiger. TCRusP, *tr. by* Paul Schmidt

Not and tries less once tries tries AH, GOD. (LL) Falling. James Dickey. InGu; NoAM

Not any higher stands the Grave. Emily Dickinson. SAmP

Not apocalypse. (LL) Note on the Iliad. Raymond Garlick. AngWePo; TCAWP

Not as a bird with twelve black wings and en eye. Meeting the Angel. Susan Aizenberg. ExTi

Not, as it used to be, round. Poison, The. Hans Magnus Enzensberger. VCWP, *tr. by* the author Michael Hamburger

Not as she is, but as she fills his dream. (LL) In An Artist's Studio. Christina Georgina Rossetti. NAEL-6v2; NAEL-7v2; NALW; NoP-4; NoP-5; PEW; ViWPN; VWP

Not as they promised us it would be in the Rapture. Prayer for the End of the World. Raylene Hinz-Penner. ACAMVP

Not as though storks were sorry that they'd brought the child. Page Torn from a Notebook. Ruth Herschberger. OxBoAm

Not as we are but as we must appear. Geoffrey Hill. NAMCP V.2; NoAM *Fr.* Funeral Music.

Not at first sight, nor with a dribbled shot. Sir Philip Sidney. *See* Not at [the] first sight, nor with a dribbled shot.

Not at Home. Robert Graves. CABP

Not at Home. Elizabeth Jennings. BeAl

Not at Home to Callers. Tree in Winter. Emily Dickinson. NOxBChV

Not at [the] first sight, nor with a dribbled shot. Sir Philip Sidney. NAEL-6v1; NAEL-7v1 *Fr.* Astrophil and Stella.

Not Bad, Dad, Not Bad. Jan Heller Levi. P180

Not because of his eyes. Turtle, The. William Carlos Williams. EmeKit; PtR; RaBo; SAmP

Not because of victories. Te Deum. Charles Reznikoff. ChIV-1; NAAPv.2; NAMCP V.1; OxBoAm

Not Being Oedipus. John Heath-Stubbs. EmeKit

Not bird not badger not beaver not bee. Lament for the Makers. Frank Bidart. PtR

Not blinking or resting, as if never to alight. (LL) From the Childhood of Jesus. Robert Pinsky. EmeKit; HarvBoo; OxBoAm; WaAnP

Not Body. Jennifer Grotz. LegDan

Not British; certainly. Expatriates. Ronald Stuart Thomas. AngWePo

Not / But near another you have a timid. Anacreon. SaLy, *tr. by* Diane Rayor

Not but they die, the teasers and the dreams. Teasers, The. William Empson. HarvBoo

Not by growth / But the. Drawing. George Oppen. APT-2; PFTM-1

Not by the railing tongues of angry men. Slavery. Jones Very. NCAP

Not Caesar's deeds, nor all his honours won. To Clement Edmonds, on His *Caesar's Commentaries* Observed, and Translated. Ben Jonson. NOSC

Not caring to observe the Wind. Of Loving at First Sight. Edmund Waller. NOSC

Not, Celia, that I juster am. Song to Celia. Sir Charles Sedley. OxBEV

Not cherry blossoms. Buson. SoOfWa, *tr. by* Sam Hamill

Not comin' back tonight, matey. Matey. Patrick MacGill. PoWW

Not Courageous. Marie Luise Kaschnitz. GTCP, *tr. by* Reinhold Grimm

Not days, not years. Lilies. Erica Funkhouser. PfS

Not Dead, but Sleeping [*with music*]. Clara Ann Thompson. CBWP-2

Not Dead Yet. Allen Ginsberg. BodElec

Not easy to state the change you made. Love Letter. Sylvia Plath. LW; PtR

Not enough. Field Trip. Kevin Young. GT

Not envying shades which haply yet may throw. William Wordsworth. CenSon

Not even. Albert Speer. W. D. Snodgrass. NoAM

Not even among them in question form. (LL) Veil. Marjorie Welish. OnScMo; PmAP

Not even death could make these men alike. Cemetery in Punta Arenas. Enrique Lihn. TCLAP; VCWP, *tr. by* David Unger

Not even Hercules saw in the yard of the Hesperides' land. About a Transdanurban Almond Tree. Janus Pannonius. IQMS, *tr. by* Adam Makkai

Not even if it is you. (LL) Ringless. Diane Wakoski. FTtHH; NALW

Not even I—would undo me so! (LL) Going, The. Thomas Hardy. HarvBoo; InoFa; NAMCP V.1; OxAEP-2

Not Even Mythology. Yannis Ritsos. AF, *tr. by* Edmund Keeley

(Not even the lame grass can answer this *what is this*). Meanwhile the Turtle. Ann Lauterbach. ExTi

Not even you, Gerry Adams, deserve to be murdered. Bloomsday Murders, 16 June 1997, The. Paul Durcan. StAl

Not ever knowing what she does in the shower. Fixture, A. Bill Berkson. NYP2

Not every man has gentians in his house. Bavarian Gentians. D. H. Lawrence. BrAP; CABP; HarvBoo; NAEL-6v2; NAEL-7v2; NAMCP V.1; NoAM; NoP-4; NoP-5; NPeEn; OxBEV; PoPoPo; TFi; TRP; WaAnP

Not every man knows what he shall sing at the end. End, The. Mark Strand. TRP

Not everyone is so skilled. Anorexia. Alice Jones. AFaM; BloBone

Not evident at "The Sailor's Rest." (LL) Three wide / Funnels raked aft, and the masts slanted, The. George Oppen. APT-2; PFTM-1

Not, exactly, green. Green Crab's Shell, A. Mark Doty. NAMCP V.2

Not expunged. Nocturne, Morningside Heights. Karl Kirchwey. PA9/11

Not Falling. Lynne McMahon. ExTi

Not falling, not ignoring. Nan-o-myo. ZenPo, *tr. by* Takashi Ikemoto and Lucien Stryk

Not far from the railroad tracks, near the fickle post office. Rustle of History's Wings, as They Used to Say Then, The. Yehuda Amichai. BeAl, *tr. by* Chana Bloch and Stephen Mitchell

Not far west of here. September: Nederland, Colorado. Jonathan Holden. PfSP

Not foam at all. Certainly. Quickly and Fully. Linda Bierds. AmAlph

Not for a long time now has anyone waited for me. Leah Goldberg. FIT, *tr. by* Robert Friend

Not for a moment shall I allow. Cyclus. Toeti Herarty. WoPoe, *tr. by* Harry Aveling

Not for Burning. Joyce Sutphen. PoDa

Not for me the general renowned nor the well-groomed lady. Ideal General, The. Archilochus. FaBoWar, *tr. by* A. Watson Bain

Not for me today the *vox angelica*. Sunday Shopping. George Scarbrough. PoDa

Not for nothing did we read the theologians. Mikhail Alekseievich Kuzmin. CAGL, *tr. by* Michael Green

Not for that city of the level sun. Not for That City. Charlotte Mew. ChIV-2; HarvBoo; MoBrPo; VWP

Not for the Imperial City am I bound. Tune: "Partridge Sky" At Po-shan Monastery. Hsin Ch'i-chi. ColAnChi, *tr. by* Jiaosheng Wang

Not for these lovely blooms that prank your chambers did I come. Indeed. Rendezvous. Edna St. Vincent Millay. APT-1; NALW; OxBoAm

Not for thy gothic trumpet's martial rage. To Boccaccio. Thomas Russell. OxBSo

Not for us alone did the god, Nicias. Theocritus. HePo *Fr.* Idylls.

Not for you would the winds. Kerensky. Lola Ridge. APT-1

Not forgetting Ko-jen, that. More Foreign Cities. Charles Tomlinson. HarvBoo

Not frail, while's man, all frailty. Man on the Horizon, The. Gerallt Lloyd Owen. BBMWP, *tr. by* Joseph P. Clancy

Not free from faults, nor yet too vain to mend. (LL) Essay on Criticism, An. Alexander Pope. NAEL-6v1; NAEL-7v1; TFi

Not from our dreams, not from our daft cadres. Robert Johnstone. PNI *Fr.* New Incidents in the Life of Shelley.

Not from this anger, anticlimax after. Not from This Anger. Dylan Thomas. PoA 2002

Not full of fish—that's imprecise—but full. Fish Pond, The [1993]. Sydney Lea. PfSP

Not glad, like those that have new hopes, or suits. To the Same [Robert, Earl of Salisbury] [Upon the Accension of the Treasurership to Him]. Ben Jonson. NOSC

Not Gone Yet. John Swanwick Drennan. IrLP

Not good any more, not beautiful. Face, The. Randall Jarrell. InGu

Not great truths do I ask you. Words to My Mother. Alfonsina Storni. TANSG, tr. by Mark McCaffrey

Not having is not the end of greed. Not Having. Dianne Edenfield Edwards. ICANM

Not he who in spring goes out to the field. Who Will Be My Friend Always. Claudio Rodríguez. RaW, tr. by W. S. Merwin

Not heart, not soul, and not their joined intent. Communiqués from Yalta, The. R. P. Blackmur. APT-2

Not Heat Flames Up and Consumes. Walt Whitman. APN-1

Not Heaving from My Ribb'd Breast Only. Walt Whitman. APN-1; CAGL

Not hell but a street, not. 209 Canal. Richard Howard. OxBoAm

Not here and now but now and here. James Harrison. WhBo

Not *Here* Orinda lies, but *Here* she lives. (LL) Wiston Vault. Katherine Philips. BASC; NOSC

Not hiding behind a ski mask, the man. Homing In. Lilace Mellin Guignard. LiTh

Not honey, / not the plunder of the bee. Fragment 113. "H. D." APT-1; NAAPv.2

Not hopeless, round this calm sepulchral spot. Spark Divine, A. Sir Francis Hastings Doyle. DiBP

Not hurled precipitous from steep to steep. William Wordsworth. CenSon *Fr.* River Duddon [A Series of Sonnets], The.

Not I, not I, but the wind that blows through me! Song of a Man Who Has Come Through. D. H. Lawrence. HarvBoo; RaBo; TRP

Not I, not I, but the wind that blows through me! D. H. Lawrence. RaBo; TRP *Fr.* Song of a Man Who Has Come Through.

Not I, you idiot, not self, but we, we—waves. Scilla. Louise Glück. WaAnP

Not Ideas about the Thing but the Thing Itself. Wallace Stevens. APT-1; OxBoAm; PFTM-2; SAmP; StAl

Not if you crawled from there to here, you hear? Sonnet. Eleanor Brown. BeAl

Not, I'll not, carrion comfort, Despair, not feast on thee. Carrion Comfort. Gerard Manley Hopkins. BBASP; BrAP; CABP; GSo; HeIP-4; ItP; MakPoe; NAEL-6v2; NAEL-7v2; NAMCP V.1; NoAM; NoP-4; NoP-5; TFi; WaAnP

Not in a silver casket cool with pearls. Sonnet 11. Edna St. Vincent Millay. WaAnP

Not in but past. Rosanna Warren. OtW *Fr.* North.

Not in envy, ire, or grief. Farewell to the Muse, A. Maria Jane Jewsbury. VWP

Not in Marble Palaces. Pedro Salinas. RaW, tr. by W. S. Merwin

Not in rich furniture, or fine array. Holy [or H.] Communion, The. George Herbert. ChIV-1

Not in sunk Spain's prolonged death agony. To the Hungarian Nation. Matthew Arnold. OxBSo

Not in the chimney, but in the gas-pipes. Mikhail Aizenberg. ItGoST, tr. by J. Kates

Not in the days of Adam and Eve, but when Adam. In the Days of Prismatic Color. Marianne Moore. NAMCP V.1

Not in the poet is the poem or. George Barker. OxAEP-2

Not in the sky. Lost Pleiad, The. William Gilmore Simms. APN-1

Not in the solitude. Hymn of the City. William Cullen Bryant. NAAPv.1

Not in the street and not in the square. Sequel to 'A Reminiscence," The. Amy Levy. VWP

Not in the world of light alone. Oliver Wendell Holmes. APN-1 *Fr.* Autocrat of the Breakfast Table, The.

Not in this way, I said, dragging the little pink blanket along the bottom. Sentimental Suffering of the Oyster of Smoke. Rossana Ombres. CItWP, tr. by Cinzia Sartini Blum and Lara Trubowitz

Not in time's inches or blood's whispering. Time's Muteness. Gareth Alban Davies. BBMWP, tr. by Joseph P. Clancy

Not in vain I vow to be faithful. Mole, The. Nathan Alterman. FIT, tr. by Robert Friend

Not JFK, not MLK. My Father's Heroes. Allison Joseph. NeAmPo

Not just I, the whole world. Longing, A. Abburi Ramakrishna Rao. HotL, tr. by V. Narayana Rao and David Shulman

Not just the body—be it. Abundance. Carl Phillips. PuP-23

Not knowing. Issa. EH, tr. by Robert Hass

Not Knowing. Gary Soto. NoP-4; NoP-5

Not Knowing He's Dead. Kim Hyesun. EcSo, tr. by Youngju Ryu

Not knowing its strength. Mosquito. Master Naong. BecRai, tr. by Kim Daljin, Kim Won-Chung and Christopher Merrill

Not Knowing Nijinsky or Diaghilev. Rachel Zucker. LegDan

Not leaving your. For Gen the New Head Priest of Erin-ji. Muso Soseki. EaWin, tr. by W. S. Merwin

Not less because in purple I descended. Tea at the Palaz of Hoon. Wallace Stevens. AmFaPo; APT-1; NAMCP V.1; OxBoAm; PoA 2002; WoPoe

Not less nor more, but even that word alone. (LL) Dante Gabriel Rossetti. BrAP; GSo; NAEL-6v2; NAEL-7v2 *Fr.* House of Life, The.

Not less nor more than five and forty years ago. In Heytesbury Wood. Siegfried Sassoon. OBGa

Not lichen, not yet here when this began. Beggar Outside Cape Town Station, A. Sarah Ruden. AmPoNex

Not like a sock. The one. Mary Maher. NewEx

Not like flowers in the city. Free Verse. Charles Reznikoff. APT-2; NAAPv.2

Not Like That. Adrienne Rich. EmeKit

Not like the brazen giant of Greek fame. New Colossus, The. Emma Lazarus. AmFaPo; APN-2; CA; CtM; FaBoA; GS; GSo; HHAm; NAAPv.1; NIL-7; NoP-4; NoP-5; OxBoAm; SWaP; TCAPo

Not like the cypress. Yehuda Amichai. FIT, tr. by Robert Friend

Not like the white filmstars, all rib. Indian Movie, New Jersey. Chitra Divakaruni. NIL-7; UnSA

Not listening, not listening. (LL) Tenebrae. Denise Levertov. EMP; NoP-4; NoP-5

Not long ago a whole sun. Miryana Basheva. CSCBP, tr. by Georgi Belev and Lisa Sapinkopf

Not long ago I sat here with my mother. Berkeley Marina at Dusk, The. Dan Clurman. WhBo

Not long ago, I studied medicine. What the Body Told. Rafael Campo. AmPoNex; BloBone; NeAmPo; WiU

Not loved enough, nor yet quite lost. Suniti Namjoshi. NewEx

Not magnitude, not lavishness. Greek Architecture. Herman Melville. NoP-4

Not many moonlit nights. Reading Seferis. Sam Hamill. GifTon

Not many trees survive our satellite. Nervous Systems. Greg Williamson. LegDan

Not marble hard and enduring. From My Notebook. Pablo Neruda. TAPaP, tr. by Willis Barnstone

Not marble, nor the g[u]ilded monuments. William Shakespeare. AEP; CABP; CtM; GSo; HeIP-4; NAEL-6v1; NAEL-7v1; NIL-7; NIP-4; NoP-4; NoP-5; NoSic; NPeEn; OxAEP-1; OxBSo; PBRV; WaAnP *Fr.* Sonnets.

Not marching [now] in the fields of T[h]rasimene. Doctor Faustus. Christopher Marlowe. NAEL-7v1

Not Martha nor Diana—only a woman. On Vermeer's *Young Woman with a Water Jug* (1658) in the Metropolitan Museum. Helen Pinkerton. FFC

Not Masterpieces, Planting Astonishments. John Tritica. ICANM

Not Me. Shel Silverstein. *See* Slithergadee, The.

Not met and married with the year's whole turn of grief. James Agee. APT-2 *Fr.* Lyrics.

Not Mine. Betty Comden and Adolph Green. ReLy

Not mine own[e] fear[e]s, nor the prophetic[k] soul[e]. William Shakespeare. NAEL-6v1; NAEL-7v1; NoP-5; NoSic; OxAEP-1 *Fr.* Sonnets.

Not Mine the Years Time Took Away. Andreas Gryphius. WoPoe, tr. by John Peck

Not mine the years time took away. Not Mine the Years Time Took Away. Andreas Gryphius. WoPoe, tr. by John Peck

Not much more than being. Louis Zukofsky. APT-2 *Fr.* 29 Poems.

Not Much Singing. Charles Bukowski. BodElec

Not my best side, I'm afraid. Not My Best Side. U. A. Fanthorpe. EmeKit; MoWP

Not my final face, a map of how to get there. Who's Joking with the Photographer? Anne Stevenson. BeAl; MoWP

Not my hands but green across you now. Lady in Kicking Horse Reservoir, The. Richard Hugo. CAP-8; NAMCP V.2; NoAM; NoP-4; NoP-5; VCAP

Not My Knees. Stazja McFayden. ArBi

Not nails but the hammer. Ventriloquy. Andrew Zawacki. IAoNAP

Not no socialism/communism classical, but some power to the people jazz. Daniel Gray-Kontar. SpirFl

Not noisily, but solemnly and pale. John Gould Fletcher. PoA 2002 *Fr.* Irradiations.

Not noisy. No singing, no dancing, no carrying on. (LL) Confession. Stephen Dobyns. GoPo; SUP

Not, not yet, this ever revolving speculum of abeyances and ardor. Ascension Provisos. Andrew Zawacki. IAoNAP

Not of father nor of mother. Song of Blodeuwedd, The. *Unknown.* NoP-4; WoPoe, tr. by Robert Graves

Not of itself [or it selfe] but thee. (LL) Song. To Celia ("Drink to me only with thine eyes.") Ben Jonson. AmFaPo; ClHu; NAEL-6v1; NAEL-7v1; NoP-4; NoP-5; NOSC; OxAEP-1; OxBEV; SoSe-8; TFi; UV; WaAnP

Not of steep mountain trails or perilous ascents. Spring Passion. Yu Xuanji. CCL1, tr. by Genevieve Wimsatt

Not of the princes and prelates with periwigged charioteers. Consecration, A. John Masefield. MoBrPo

Not of the spirituality of the mind. Sikong Tu. CCL1 *Fr.* Twenty-Four Modes of Poetry.

Not of the wealthy, Coral Gables class. House Sparrows. Anthony Hecht. OWoS

Not of This World. Sheri Hostetler. ACAMVP

Not only can I not remember anecdotes that are racy. What's in a Name? Some Letter I Always Forget. Ogden Nash. AmWit

Not only her stone face, laid back staring in the ferns. Pygmalion's Image. Eiléan Ní Chuilleanáin. MakPoe

Not only how far away, but the way that you say it. Henry Reed. BrAP; NAEL-6v2; NAEL-7v2; NIL-7; NIP-4; NoP-4; NoP-5; NPeEn; OxBEV; PoWW *Fr.* Lessons of the War.

Not only marble, but the plastic toys. Wendy Cope. NIL-7

Not Only the Eskimos. Lisel Mueller. GoPo

Not only the rape. Objection Overruled. Jackie Hardy. NeBl

Not Ophelia. Allison Joseph. IaFF

Not oriental Indus' crystal streams. Lady Cicely Wemyss. James I, King of England. NOSC

Not over-kind nor over-quick in study. Edna St. Vincent Millay. NALW *Fr.* Sonnets from an Ungrafted Tree.

Not Palaces. Stephen Spender. MoBrPo; NoAM

Not Pallas, not ev'n Spleen it self could blame. Ovid. OBVE *Fr.* Metamorphoses.

Not past conceiving but past care. (LL) Distant Fury of Battle, The. Geoffrey Hill. FaBoWar; NoP-4; NoP-5; WaAnP

Not Pastoral Enough. Veronica Forrest-Thomson. EdScPo

Not probable—The barest Chance. Emily Dickinson. TCAPo

Not Quiet. Ibrahim al-Osta Omar. SonAtl, *tr.* by Abdul Kalam Azad and Ibrahim Ighneiwa

Not quite dark yet. Buson. EH, *tr.* by Robert Hass

Not quite midnight. My candle stutters. Another Vigil at San Quentin. Alison Luterman. RaF

Not quite yet. First, / around the corner for a visit. Dining Out with Doug and Frank. James Schuyler. OxBoAm

Not recognize a sister? (LL) Eel, The. Eugenio Montale. STV; WeW-3

Not reigns of kings now vanished. Picture, A. Aleksandr Semionovich Kushner. TCRusP, *tr.* by Daniel Weissbort

Not Responsible. Caroline Finkelstein. PoA 2002

Not say, "Alas! I did not know him at all." (LL) U.S. Sailor with the Japanese Skull, The. Winfield Townley Scott. APT-2; ICANM; OxBoAm

Not Sense. Gail Tremblay. WeW-3

Not serious about drugs. Angel. John Forbes. NOBAu

Not shaking the grass. (LL) And the Days Are Not Full Enough. Ezra Pound. SpI; StAl

Not, Silence, for thine idleness I raise. To Silence. Alice Thompson Meynell. VWP

Not Singing. Kate Daniels. PBCAP

Not Sleeping. Ch'i-chi. CSKM, *tr.* by Burton Watson

Not slowly wrought, nor treasured for their form. Snowflakes. Howard Nemerov. NAMCP V.2

NOT SNOW. Michael McClure. WANABP *Fr.* Haiku Rows.

Not so dear was Lyde to the Clarian poet, not so truly. Ovid. RomPo *Fr.* Tristia.

Not So Good Night in the San Pedro of the World, A. Charles Bukowski. PoA 2002

Not so long ago, the world was complete. Georgy Vladimirovich Ivanov. TCRusP, *tr.* by Daniel Weissbort

Not so that Pair whose youthful spirits dance. William Wordsworth. CenSon *Fr.* River Duddon [A Series of Sonnets], The.

Not so with me as with the little page. Ausiàs March. STV

Not some writhing in a tortuous canine province. Will Alexander. BAP-04 *Fr.* Solea of the Simooms.

Not sometimes, but to him that heeds the whole. Frederick Goddard Tuckerman. TCAPo *Fr.* Sonnets: First Series, 1854–1860.

Not Somewhere Else, But Here. Adrienne Rich.
   Amends. HarvBoo
   To the Days. AmFaPo; BeAl; LoL
   What Kind of Times Are These. ExTi; LoL; WaAnP

Not Spring's. Arbutus. Adelaide Crapsey. APT-1

Not starting from the top. Turvy-Topsy. Paul Groves. TCAWP

Not stitched to air or water but to both. Definition of a Waterfall. John Ormond. AngWePo

Not strangeness, but strange likeness. Obstinate. Geoffrey Hill. NAMCP V.2; NoAM; WoPoe *Fr.* Mercian Hymns.

Not such a sad story: the woman wakes to an observation. Residue. Paula McLain. AmPoNex

Not summer. Oak Tree. Gwyn Williams. BBMWP, *tr.* by Christopher Meredith

Not Surfing Some Days. Rick Noguchi. AmPoNex

Not Surprising. Gertrude Stein. OxBoAm *Fr.* Book Concluding with As A Wife Has a Cow a Love Story, A.

Not Swans. Susan Bartels Ludvigson. P180

Not taking the scarf from her head. Death. Peter France. TCRusP, *tr.* by Gennady Aygi

Not that his writing isn't moving when. For a Cowper Paperweight. Charles North. NYP2

Not that I am losing my grip: I am just tired of summer. Joseph Brodsky. StAl *Fr.* Part of Speech, A.

Not that I cared about the other women. Colder. Erica Jong. LW

Not that I'm a Punchinello. I Hear Music. Frank Loesser. ReLy

NOT that in colour it was like thy hair. Bracelet, The. John Donne. NoSic

Not that of a truce. Wildling Peace. Yehuda Amichai. NRoS, *tr.* by Esther Raizen

Not that the earth is changing, O my God! On Refusal of Aid between Nations. Dante Gabriel Rossetti. OxAEP-2

Not that the Pines were darker there. Long Voyage, The. Malcolm Cowley. SoSe-8

Not that they die but that they die like sheep. (LL) Leaden-eyed, The. Vachel Lindsay. StAl; TCAPo

Not that thy fair hand. Cloris' Charms Dissolved by Eudora. Anne Killigrew. BASC

Not that we are not all. To a Man Dying on His Feet. William Carlos Williams. APT-1

Not the attendance of stones. Black Maps. Mark Strand. PoA 2002

Not the austere. Dikes on Fundy Bay. Liliane Welch. Coast

Not the beautiful youth with features of bloom & brightness. Beauty. Walt Whitman. WeW-3

Not the city lights. We want. View. Rae Armantrout. AWPTFC

Not the dumb earth, wherein they set their graves. (LL) Cassandra. Louise Bogan. APT-2; MoAmPo; NALW; NAMCP V.1

Not the epithet. Lovely. Erin Belieu. ExTi

Not the Fear of Shivering. Gülten Akın Cankoçak. NaPG

Not the five feet of water to your chin. Epitaph. Charles Reznikoff. APT-2; OxBoAm

Not the Furniture Game. Simon Armitage. BeAl

Not the glittering shudder in the ear, the high whine of the wasp. Applause. Carol Muske-Dukes. AmAlph

Not the heat flames up and consumes. Live Oak, with Moss. Walt Whitman. NAAL-5

Not the man who wishes to feed on mahogany. Man Who Wishes to Feed on Mahogany, The. Annie Dillard. UpMys

Not the night poem. Instead of Reading Marcus Aurelius. Claudia Keelan. RWB

Not / the nude but. Josée Lapeyrère. SCFWP *Fr.* Skirt, The.

Not the profound *dark.* Oblique Prayer. Denise Levertov. SacPr

Not the recipe grandmother slipped the girl. Date Nut Bread. Ann Townsend. SweBea

Not the sharp torture of the critic's pen. To an Author who Loved Truth More than Fame. Bessie Rayner Parkes. VWP

Not the shouted poetry. Monkey's Pride. John Forbes. BMAP

Not the songs that nobly tell. Stanzas on the Psalms. Thomas Warton, the Elder. ChIV-1

Not the thunk of pumpkins, thicklidded. First Harvest. Monica Raymond. PfS

Not the walls of the furled city. Wolf of Gubbio, The. William Matthews. P180

Not the wooden spoon. Zapato, El. Richard Garcia. TouFir

Not their own words. The art of the performer. (LL) For the Twentieth Century. Frank Bidart. KGB; OxBoAm

Not them, O no, but you in them I love. (LL) Sir Philip Sidney. NAEL-6v1; NAEL-7v1 *Fr.* Astrophil and Stella.

Not There. Tess Gallagher. NIP-4

Not these cut heads posed in a breathless room. Flower Poem. Alec Derwent Hope. BMAP

Not these tall towers of no song. Hart Crane. Paul Engle. YaYoPo

Not thirsting for battle. Return. Yoseph Sarig. NRoS, *tr.* by Esther Raizen

Not this. Ron Silliman. *See* Not this. / What then?

Not this human sadness. Basho. EH, *tr.* by Robert Hass

Not this room. Denials. Eric Gamalinda. ReBoTo

Not this. / What then? Ron Silliman. PmAP *Fr.* Tjanting.

Not this with Cataracts and Creeks. (LL) Waterfall [*or* Water-Fall], The. Henry Vaughan. AngWePo; NAEL-6v1; NAEL-7v1; NoP-4; NoP-5; NOSC; OBWVE; OxAEP-1; SacPr; WaAnP

Not this world, but a dream. Winter Night. Stanislav Kostka Neumann. SonAtl, *tr.* by Dorli Meek, Ziva Pecavar and Josef Pettersen

Not This—This Here! Clarence Major. EGAG

Not thither, Caesar, yet. Katherine Philips. NOSC *Fr.* Corneille's Pompey.

Not three years since—and now he asks my name! Model, The. May Probyn. VWP

Not to ask, not to be answered. Unthronged Oracle, The. Laura Riding Jackson. OxBoAm

Not to be believed, this blunt savage wind. Papermill. Joseph Kalar. APT-2

Not to be just a "skinny sado-masochist." Homage To Charlotte Rampling. Todd Swift. OpeFie

Not to be spattered by his blood—this, even then. Not to Be Spattered by His Blood. Edna St. Vincent Millay. PtR

Not to believe the phoebes wept. (LL) Need of Being Versed in Country Things, The. Robert Frost. APT-1; NAMCP V.1; NoAM; SAmP; TCAPo; TRP

Not to die, as in cold-hands dead. Drink and Agriculture. Dave Etter. IllVoic

Not to Keep. Robert Frost. AmWaPo

Not to let ourselves know. Even Now You Are Leaving. Tess Gallagher. LaCa

Not to mention the crystal goblet and—somehow—the wine. (LL) Litany: "You are the bread and the knife." Billy Collins. BeAl; CAP-8; NoP-5; OxBoAm; SUP

Not to the swift, the race. Reliance. Henry Van Dyke. ITBLP

Not to touch, she said to me, anything sticky. Nightpiece. Judith Johnson Sherwin. YaYoPo

Not to you / Unborn generations. Sentiments for a Dedication. Archibald MacLeish. APT-1

(Not too far past) may to their wits be brought. (LL) Michael Drayton. NOSC; NoSic *Fr.* Idea.

Not Translation, Not Poetry. Daryl Ngee Chinn. LTA

Not twenty miles from where I work. Getting to Sleep in New Jersey. John A. Stone. BloBone

Not twice a twelvemonth [*or* twelve-month] you appear in Print. Epilogue to the Satires, in Two Dialogues. Alexander Pope.

Not Tyrants. Reed Bye. AHA

Not unlike themselves. (LL) Wishes for Sons. Lucille Clifton. CAP-8; SUP

Not until. Paul Celan. AmFaPo *Fr.* Zeitgehoft.

Not until my father had led her into the paddock. Nell. Rodney Jones. IllVoic

Not unto thee—oh! not to thee! (LL) Woman and Fame. Felicia Dorothea Hemans. ViWPN; VWP

Not unto us, O Lord. Non Nobis. Henry Cust. OBEV

Not utter, not. Male Nipples. Brenda Hillman. ExTi

Not very anxious. Issa. EH, *tr.* by Robert Hass

Not very long ago. Orange Poem, The. George MacBeth. OBCoV

Not Virgil, not Beatrice. Detroit Addendum. Murray Jackson. OxAAAP

Not Wavell but Browning. Gavin Ewart. UV

Not Waving but Drowning. Stevie Smith. AmFaPo; BrAP; CABP; CtM; EmeKit; EMP; HarvBoo; HeIP-4; IJHIL; InoFa; MakPoe; MoWP; NAEL-6v2; NAEL-7v2; NALW; NAMCP V.1; NoAM; NoP-4; NoP-5; NPeEn; OxAEP-2; OxBEV; PoPoPo; StAl; TFi; UV; WaAnP; WeW-3

Not Weary Yet. *Unknown.* SSUS

Not what my hands have done. Horatius Bonar. SacPr

Not when at Falkirk in the English camp. Royalty. James Logie Robertson. EdScPo

Not when leaves are brown and sere. When I Would Die. Josephine D. Henderson Heard. CBWP-4

NOT, where the stairway turns in the dark. Jennie McGrew. Edgar Lee Masters. RACG

Not wide but a wing. Table, The. Ray DiPalma. FTOS

Not *Winds* to *Voyagers* at Sea. Abraham Cowley. ChIV-2 *Fr.* Pindarique Odes.

Not with a bang but a whimper. (LL) Hollow Men, The. T. S. Eliot. APT-1; BrAP; HarvBoo; NAAL-5; NAEL-7v2; NoP-5; OBMV; OxBoAm; WaAnP

Not with more glories, in th'ethereal plain. Alexander Pope. OxAEP-1 *Fr.* Rape of the Lock, The: An Heroi-Comical Poem in Five Cantos.

Not with public words can his greatness. Elegy for Jim Larkin. Patrick Kavanagh. ModIr

Not with your tribe's spears I write. Tattoo Writing. Fawziyya Abu Khalid. CFP, *tr.* by Kamal Boullata

Not without glory fought. (LL) Henry Reed. BrAP; NAEL-6v2 *Fr.* Lessons of the War.

Not Without Hope Pulsing My Breast. San Juan de la Cruz. SpanPo, *tr.* by James Edward Tobin

Not without hope pulsing my breast. Not Without Hope Pulsing My Breast. San Juan de la Cruz. SpanPo, *tr.* by James Edward Tobin

Not without hope we suffer and we mourn. (LL) Elegiac Stanzas: Suggested by a Picture of Peele Castle, in a Storm, Painted by Sir George Beaumont. William Wordsworth. NAEL-6v2; NAEL-7v2; NOBRP; NoP-4; NPBRoP; NPeEn; WaAnP

Not Wordsworth's genius, Pestalozzi's love. Sonnet 14. Amos Bronson Alcott. APN-1

Not Writing Poems about Children. Carolyn Kizer. PoChi

Not Yet. William Cullen Bryant. NCAP

Not Yet. Mary Elizabeth Coleridge. PoBW

Not yet become a Buddha. Issa. EH, *tr.* by Robert Hass

Not yet dead, not yet alone. Osip Emilevich Mandelstam. OBVE

Not yet does parting summer gentle the Sun's steeds. Titus Calpurnius Siculus. RomPo *Fr.* Eclogues.

Not Yet 40, My Beard is Already White. Lew Welch. CalPo

Not yet will those measureless fields be green again. Cenotaph, The. Charlotte Mew. OxAEP-2

Not you, lean quarterlies and swarthy periodicals. To the Film Industry in Crisis. Frank O'Hara. GPTC; OxBoAm

Not young and not renewable, but man. (LL) Mirror in February. Thomas Kinsella. MakPoe; NAMCP V.2; NoAM

Not your winged lust but his must now change suit. William Empson. UV *Fr.* Death of the King's Canary, The.

Not-a. Yosl Cutler. Prolet, *tr.* by Amelia Glaser

Nota: man is the intelligence of his soil. Comedian as the Letter C, The. Wallace Stevens. TCAPo

Notable Dinner, A [*with music*]. Lizelia Augusta Jenkins Moorer. CBWP-3

Notations of Ten Summer Minutes. Norman Alexander MacCaig. EmeKit; NPeEn

Note. Joan Brossa. StAl, *tr.* by Arthur Terry

Note. Mary Abigail Dodge (Gail Hamilton). SWaP

Note. Carla Harryman. BAP-04 *Fr.* Baby.

Note. Dimitris Tsaloumas. BMAP

Note, A. Clark Coolidge. AHA

Note, The. To Raise the Blind on Purpose. Stephanie Sallaska. SUP

Note, The. Melvin B. Tolson. GT

Note Delivered by Female Impersonator. Heather McHugh. RACG

Note Folded Thirteen Ways. Richard Garcia. TouFir

Note for Robert Henryson, A. Robin Fulton. EdScPo

Note from a Loving Wife. Mariahadessa Ekere Tallie. RaF

Note from Capri to Richard Ryan on the Adriatic Floor. Richard Hugo. PWW2

Note how the bear. Hispaniola. Amy Clampitt. NAMCP V.2

Note Left in Jimmy Leonard's Shack, A. James Wright. NoP-4; NoP-5; StAl

Note of a trumpet was eating the heart of a thunderbolt, The. Sons d'un Cornet, Li. *Unknown.* WoPoe, *tr.* by Willard Trask

Note of Thanks, A. Wyatt Prunty. RA

Note old chestnut tie in foreground. Tie, The. William Heyen. GM

Note on Commercial Theatre. Langston Hughes. NAAL-5

(Notes on the Broadway Theatre.) SSLK

Note on Local Flora. William Empson. OxAEP-2; OxBEV

Note on my Son's Face, A. Toi Derricotte. ISC

Note on the Iliad. Raymond Garlick. AngWePo; TCAWP

Note on the L and N. Richmond Lattimore. GM

Note on the Lessons of Antipoetry. Nicanor Parra. WoBe, *tr.* by Liz Werner

Note on Wyatt, A. Kingsley Amis. WeW-3

Note, Passed to Superman. Lucille Clifton. ReTh

Note the stump, a peach tree. We had to cut it down. Places and Ways to Live. Richard Hugo. NIP-4

Note to My Liberal Feminist Sister, A. Nanna Banyiwa Horne. NAfrP

Note to Olga (1966), A. Denise Levertov. NALW

Note to Skip on Max and Maxine, A. Bill Lavender. AnSo

Note to the Ophthalmologist. Dolores Kendrick. FFC

Note to the reader: this is not a poem. Helen Ivory. StAl

Note to Tony Towle (After WS), A. Charles North. FTOS; PmAP

Notebook, Two. Edmond Jabès. AF, *tr.* by Rosmarie Waldrop

Notebook of a Return to the Native Land. Aimé Césaire.

"Islands scars of the water." PFTM-1

Notebook of a Schnook, The. Samuel Hoffenstein.

1. AmWit

2. AmWit

Notes. Thomas Kinsella.

Brotherhood. HarvBoo

Talent and Friendship. HarvBoo

Notes. Friend, A. Paul Klee. PFTM-1

Notes. Friedrich Wilhelm Nietzsche. WoPoe *Fr.* Zarathustra.

Notes About My Face. Michael Burkard. BAP-01

Notes at Edge. Judith Wright.

Brevity. HarvBoo

Notes for a History of Poetry. David Daiches. PoA 2002

Notes for a Poem from the Middle Passage of Years. Lamont B. Steptoe. SpirFl

Notes for a Poem on Being Asian American. Dwight Okita. NIL-7; UnSA

Notes for a Revised Sonnet. Edward Pygge. OBCoV

Notes for a Sermon on the Mount. Nin Andrews. BAP-01

Notes for a Sonnet. Edward Pygge. OBCoV

Notes for a Southern Road Map. Phyllis McGinley. NBLV

Notes for Echo Lake 3. Michael Palmer. PmAP; WaAnP

Notes for My Son. Alex Comfort. MoBrPo; RSaN *Fr.* Song of Lazarus, The.

Notes for the Legend of Salad Woman [*with music*]. Michael Ondaatje. NoAM

Notes for the Park Keeper. Peter Bland. OBGa

Notes From a Chinese Love Manual. Sarah Gorham. White Tiger Leaps, The. FFC

Notes from a Nonexistent Himalayan Expedition. Wisława Szymborska. AmFaPo; ItP, *tr. by* Stanislaw Barańczak and Clare Cavanagh

Notes from the Childhood and the Girlhood. Gwendolyn Brooks.
  (Ballad of Late Annie, The.) ColAP
  Do Not Be Afraid of No. ColAP; PtR
  Old Relative. ColAP
  Parents: People Like Our Marriage Maxie and Andrew, The. ColAP
  "Pygmies Are Pygmies Still, Though Percht on Alps." ColAP
  Sunday Chicken. ColAP
  Throwing Out the Flowers. ColAP

Notes from the Defense of Colin Ferguson. Sekou Sundiata. ESEAA

Notes: From the Wait. Rachel Tzvia Back. DTA

Notes from Underground: W. H. Auden on the Lexington Avenue IRT. Grace Schulman. ExTi

Notes in Jerusalem. Nicholas Samaras. TWW

Notes of a Cold War Veteran. Natalya Gorbanevskaya. CRWP, *tr. by* Daniel Weissbort

Notes on a Blizzard. Maxine W. Kumin. MoW

Notes on a Departure. Wanda Coleman. RD

Notes on a Moonwatcher. Kenneth Gangemi. PoCoUp

Notes on a Visit to Le Tuc d'Audoubert. Clayton Eshleman. PmAP

Notes on living inside the lightbulb. Gillian Allnutt. NeBrP

Notes on My Contemporaries. Michael Hartnett.
  Person as Dreamer: We Talk about the Future, The. PBCIP

Notes on the Art of Memory. Diane Di Prima. SeSe

Notes on the Broadway Theatre. Langston Hughes. *See* Note on Commercial Theatre.

Notes on the Peanut. June Jordan. NAMCP V.2; NoAM

Notes on the tuned frame of strings. Sub Contra. Louise Bogan. APT-2; WaAnP

Notes to my Daughters. Shirley Kaufman. PoChi

Notes Toward a Poem of Revolution. Diane Di Prima. Eno

Notes toward a Supreme Fiction. Wallace Stevens. APT-1
  It Must Be Abstract.
    "First idea was not our own, The. Adam." ColAP
    "It feels good as it is without the giant." ColAP
    "Major abstraction is the idea of man, The." ColAP
    "Lasting visage in a lasting bush, A." NAMCP V.1
    "On a blue island in a sky-wide water." NAMCP V.1
    "Soldier, there is a war between the mind." AmWaPo; ColAP; NoAM; WaAnP

Not-France. Carla Harryman. PFTM-2

Nothin' be as terrible. Jenny in Sleep. Dolores Kendrick. ESEAA

Nothing. Basil Bunting. BrAP

Nothing. Cheryl Clarke. PoBW

Nothing. Terrance Hayes. RD

Nothing. Linda Hogan. ExTi

Nothing: "Now, this beginning." Douglas Lochhead. Coast

Nothing. Pak Chaesam. CAMKP, *tr. by* David R. McCann and Jiwon Shin

Nothing about that life. Little Dance Outside the Ruins of Unreason. Carl Phillips. NAPBL

Nothing about the first abandonment. Belongings. Catherine Davis. FFC

Nothing ades to Loves fond fire. Song. Elizabeth Wilmot, Countess of Rochester. EMWP; LW

Nothing, and is nowhere, and is endless. (LL) High Windows. Philip Larkin. HarvBoo; NAEL-6v2; NAEL-7v2; NAMCP V.2; NoAM; PoetW; PoPoPo

Nothing anymore Nothing. Venice Lost. Günter Kunert. GTCP, *tr. by* Reinhold Grimm

Nothing as miserable has happened before. Long Island Night, The. Howard Moss. OxBoAm

Nothing at Newbegins. Clark Coolidge. AHA *Fr.* Ing.

Nothing behind the door, behind the curtain. To Open. Antonio Porta. PFTM-2, *tr. by* Paul Vangelisti

Nothing but a hovel now. Ruin, The. Dafydd ap Gwilym. OBWVE, *tr. by* Rolfe Humphries

Nothing but a plain black boy. (LL) Gwendolyn Brooks. ESEAA; InoFa; NAMCP V.2; NoAM *Fr.* Street in Bronzeville, A.

Nothing but a resonance. Voice, The. May Muzaffar. PoArWo, *tr. by* Tahia Abdel Nasser

Nothing but Bad News. Jennifer Richter. MoASP

Nothing but Curves. Menna Elfyn. BBMWP, *tr. by* Elin ap Hywel

Nothing but Death. Pablo Neruda. WED, *tr. by* Robert Bly

Nothing but grey seen through the arch. Arc de Triomphe. Bert Meyers. CalPo

Nothing but miracles. (LL) Miracles. Carol Muske-Dukes. AmAlph; ExTi

Nothing / but reason. Tanka. Toki Zenmaro. CAoMJL1, *tr. by* Makoto Ueda

Nothing can be done about the rain in your meal. Same Corpse, The. Kojo Laing. HBAPE

Nothing can satisfy. (LL) Hamlen Brook. Richard Wilbur. HarvBoo; VCAP; WeW-3

Nothing can soak. Ode to Brother Joe. Anthony McNeill. WaCA

Nothing comforts me, not Gloria Swanson. Ikon. Timothy Liu. ReTh

Nothing Could Take Away the Bear-King's Image. Ray A. Young Bear. HATNAP

Nothing derivative here. Litrajure of Everyday Life, The. Michael C. Blumenthal. NoAM

Nothing else has ever been. (LL) One minute of sitting, one inch of Buddha. Manzan. WhBo; ZenPo, *tr. by* Takashi Ikemoto and Lucien Stryk

Nothing endures, / Not even love. Nothing Endures. Countee Cullen. NAAPv.2

Nothing escapes. Turbulence and Tongue. Anthony Barnett. Oth

Nothing Ever Changes My Love for You. Jack Segal. ReLy

Nothing ever delivers but the opacity of words. Aimé Césaire. ConPit *Fr.* Configurations.

Nothing first-hand. I'm not your Saul. No burst. Knowledge of God. John Frederick Nims. InvLi

Nothing for a dirty man. All That Is Lovely in Men. Robert Creeley. RaBo

Nothing Gold Can Stay. Robert Frost. APT-1; ColAP; MoAmPo; NAAL-5; OxBoAm; PtR; SoSe-8; TWF; WaAnP

Nothing had been said. (LL) Morning Exercises. Nina Cassian. CFP; PoSu, *tr. by* Andrea Deletant and Brenda Walker

Nothing Happened. Smile. HotL, *tr. by* V. Narayana Rao

Nothing Happened. Belle Waring. PBCAP

Nothing happens, nothing happens, then suddenly, quick as a wink, and slick as a mink's prick, Time thrusts through the time of no-Time. (LL) There's a Grandfather's Clock in the Hall. Robert Penn Warren. NAMCP V.1; NoAM; NoP-4; NoP-5

Nothing has happened. Poem on Death. Inger Christensen. GPTC, *tr. by* Susanna Nied

Nothing has to be ugly. Luck of the dumb. To We Who Were Saved by the Stars. Lorna Dee Cervantes. TouFir

Nothing he had done before. Architect. Adrienne Rich. BAP-01

Nothing hurts but the foot is insistent. Democracy. Suzanne Gardinier. NeAmPo

Nothing I wouldn't do for the woman I sleep with. Nothing. Cheryl Clarke. PoBW

Nothing in Art. J. Kates. IaFF

Nothing in my body escapes me. Song of a Prisoner. Jack Spicer. APSN

Nothing in That Drawer. Ron Padgett. PmAP; PoDa

Nothing in the air to call me here. What You Find in the Woods. James Longenbach. NAPBL

Nothing in the cry. Basho. SoOfWa, *tr. by* Sam Hamill

Nothing is at one with nature. Nature, Beside Herself. James Galvin. WaAnP

Nothing is better, I well think. Leper, The. Algernon Charles Swinburne. OxBEV

Nothing is changed: against the dining-room windows. Guest, The. Anna Andreyevna Akhmatova. ErotSp, *tr. by* Max Hayward and Stanley Kunitz

Nothing is deeper. Short Song. T. Carmi. WoPoe, *tr. by* Grace Schulman

Nothing Is Enough. Laurence Binyon. MoBrPo

Nothing is happening. And the Grass Did Grow. Ralph Angel. PoA 2002

Nothing is left to dig, little to make. Jarrow. Carol Rumens. RSaN; StAl

Nothing is plumb, level or square. Love Song: I and Thou. Alan Dugan. AmFaPo; NAMCP V.2; NoAM

Nothing is quite alien or quite recognizable at this speed. Barbie's Ferrari. Lynne McMahon. P180; RWB

Nothing is sacred now but Villany. (LL) Alexander Pope. NPeEn; OBSV *Fr.* Epilogue to the Satires, in Two Dialogues.

Nothing is so beautiful as Spring. Spring. Gerard Manley Hopkins. BrAP; GoPo; GSo; MoBrPo; NAEL-6v2; NAEL-7v2; NAMCP V.1; NoAM; OBMV; TFi

Nothing is sweeter than love, all other riches. Nossis. SaLy, *tr. by* Diane Rayor

Nothing is thought. Hyphen's Hyphen. Susan Gevirtz. OnScMo

Nothing is unexpected or sworn impossible. Archilochus. SaLy, *tr.* by Diane Rayor

Nothing left of the house. Taneda Santoka. CAoMJL1, *tr.* by Burton Watson

Nothing. Let me pass please. I am an Englishwoman. (LL) Phrase Book. Jo Shapcott. MoWP; NeBrP; PoAgWa; StAl

Nothing like her ever came his way before. Semi-Skilled Lover. Maureen Duffy. LW

Nothing like the others, even as a child. Home Again among Gardens and Fields. T'ao Ch'ien. NDACCP, *tr.* by David Hinton

Nothing longed for. Yoketsu. ZenPo, *tr.* by Takashi Ikemoto and Lucien Stryk

Nothing matters. Beyond Recall. Sharon Bryan. P180

Nothing more hesitant. Garden Note II, March. Janet Lewis. APT-2

Nothing more strong. Adamantine Perfection of Desire, The. Jane Hirshfield. WhBo

Nothing move thee. Poem. Saint, of Avila Theresa. WoPoe, *tr.* by Yvor Winters

Nothing much just. Nothing Much. Allison Harris. WhBo

Nothing nastier than a white person! Great Palaces of Versailles, The. Rita Dove. ESEAA; NAMCP V.2; NoAM

Nothing New. Ella Wheeler Wilcox. APN-2

Nothing New Beneath the Sun. George M. Cohan. ReLy

Nothing, not even fear of punishment. Young Girls. Patricia K. Page. BrAP; StAl

Nothing, not even the chokingly sentimental, is as predictable as the self-confidence of the unwittingly trivial gesture. Foolish Treasures. Lorenzo Thomas. AnSo

Nothing, nothing at all. Shell. Takahashi Shinkichi. ZenPo, *tr.* by Takashi Ikemoto and Lucien Stryk

Nothing of All That. Jan G. Elburg. TuT, *tr.* by Pat Boran

Nothing [*or* Nothin'] very bad happen to me lately. John Berryman. EMP; NAMCP V.2; NoAM; VCAP *Fr.* Dream Songs.

Nothing pleases me anymore. No Delicacies. Ingeborg Bachmann. PoSu, *tr.* by Mark Anderson

Nothing recognizable exists here. Farasa. Nicholas Samaras. TWW

Nothing remains but memory— and the suffuring of thos who would walk into the soft hands of a killer for a crumb of bread. (LL) Boy at the Paterson Falls. Toi Derricotte. BtF; PBCAP

Nothing resting in its own completeness. Incompleteness. Adelaide Anne Procter. TreFP

Nothing sings in our bodies. Nothing. Linda Hogan. ExTi

Nothing so far but moonlight. Nothing So Far. Laura Riding Jackson. APT-2; ColAP

Nothing so foreign but th' athletic hind. John Armstrong. STuOW *Fr.* Art of Preserving Health, The.

Nothing so true as what you once let fall. Epistle [II,] to a Lady[: Of the Characters of Women]. Alexander Pope. NAEL-6v1; NAEL-7v1

Nothing so true as what you once let fall. Epistle [II,] to a Lady[: Of the Characters of Women]. Alexander Pope. CABP; WaAnP

Nothing takes me back. Autumn's End. Christopher Buckley. PfSP

Nothing that is not there and the nothing that is. (LL) Snow Man, The. Wallace Stevens. AmFaPo; APT-1; ColAP; GoPo; HarvBoo; HeIP-4; IJHIL; MoW; NAAL-5; NAAPv.2; NAMCP V.1; NoAM; NoP-4; NoP-5; OxBoAm; PoA 2002; PoPoPo; SoSe-8; StAl; TCAPo; TRP; WaAnP; WeW-3

Nothing that is shall perish utterly. Dedication. Henry Wadsworth Longfellow. TCAPo

Nothing That Is, The. Ralph Angel. BodElec

Nothing that you say, The. (LL) Félix Lope de Vega Carpio. OxBEV; WoPoe *Fr.* Pentecost Castle, The.

Nothing: the nothing for which there's no reward. (LL) Thinking of the Lost World. Randall Jarrell. NAAL-5; NAMCP V.2; NoAM; StAl

Nothing, this foam, this virgin verse. Toast. Stéphane Mallarmé. SxFrPo, *tr.* by A. M. and E. H. Blackmore

Nothing! thou elder brother ev'n [*or even*] to shade. Upon Nothing. John Wilmot, 2d Earl of Rochester. NOSC; OBSV; OxAEP-1; OxBEV

Nothing to be said about it, and everything. Dying. Robert Pinsky. PoA 2002; VCAP

Nothing to do but work. Pessimist, The. Ben King. NBLV

Nothing was as we'd thought, the sea. Effort at Speech. Ellen Bryant Voigt. WaAnP

Nothing was broken, and we made surprisingly little noise. (LL) Ancient Evenings. Michael Hofmann. EmeKit; NeBrP

Nothing was ever what it claimed to be. Sonnet. Karen Volkman. IAoNAP

Nothing was foreseen. Prologue to a Time That Is Not Itself. Eunice Odio. TCLAP, *tr.* by Martha Collins

Nothing was left of me. Dream of Burial, A. James Wright. InoFa

Nothing Whatsoever. Fujiwara no Yasusue. WoPoe, *tr.* by Donald Keene

Nothing whatsoever. Nothing Whatsoever. Fujiwara no Yasusue. WoPoe, *tr.* by Donald Keene

Nothing. When we realized you weren't here. Did I Miss Anything? Tom Wayman. P180

Nothing will ease the pain to come. Annuciation, The. Elizabeth Jennings. ChrPo

Nothing will keep. Personal Letter No. 3. Sonia Sanchez. ESEAA; SSLK

Nothing would sleep in that cellar, dank as a ditch. Root Cellar. Theodore Roethke. CAP-8; ColAP; HarvBoo; HeIP-4; NoP-4; NoP-5; OxBoAm; VCAP

Nothing you tell me nothing. Gloria Gervitz. MirDau *Fr.* Yiskor.

Nothingmas Day. Adrian Mitchell. NOxBChV

Nothingness. T'aego, National Preceptor. CATKP, *tr.* by Peter H. Lee

Nothingness, for the, The. Paul Celan. PoSu

Nothing-Never. János Székely. IQMS, *tr.* by Geroge Gömöri

Nothing's going to become of anyone. Play. A. R. Ammons. PoA 2002

Nothing's sadder than my sister's grave. Mount Ararat. Louise Glück. ColAP

Nothing's undoing among the self-stung unfolding of things. (LL) In Praise of Han Shan. Charles Wright. BAP-04; OxBoAm

Notice. Steve Kowit. BLT

Notice [*with music*]. Robert Lowell. NoAM

Notice to Tourists. Della Cruscans. STuOW

Notice with what careful nonchalance. Portrait. Hyam Plutzik. TaR

Notice yourself ever. As in life you don't. (LL) Misremembered Lyric, A. Denise Riley. NPeEn; Oth

Noticing a man unable. Gerry McGrath. BeAl

Notion of Grace, A. Brenda J. Moossy. PoArWo

Not-loving. Sylvia Kantaris. LW

Notre Dame. Osip Emilevich Mandelstam. TCRusP, *tr.* by John Glad

Notre Dame. Osip Emilevich Mandelstam. OBVE, *tr.* by James Greene

Notre Dame, Sainte Chapelle, Sacré Coeur by foot—. Debora Greger. NoP-4 *Fr.* Lives of the Saints.

Notre Paire. Robert Desnos. YaTCFP

Notre paire quiète, ô yeux! Notre Paire. Robert Desnos. YaTCFP

Not-Returning, The. Ivor Gurney. HarvBoo

Not[t] ceasing offrings [*or* off'rings] to love while I Live. (LL) Mary Sidney Wroth, Countess of Montgomery. BASC; EMWP; NoP-5; NOSC *Fr.* Pamphilia to Amphilanthus.

Not-too-near slip softly by, The. Convalescence. David McCord. AmWit

Not-Yet. Jane Hirshfield. BeAl; ExTi

Nou goth sonne under wode. *Unknown.* NoP-4; NoP-5

Nought can anoy them. (LL) Bible, *O.T.* BASC; PBRV *Fr.* Psalms.

Nought may endure but Mutability. (LL) Mutability ("We are as clouds that veil the midnight moon.") Percy Bysshe Shelley. NAEL-6v2; NAEL-7v2

Nought to me! So I choose to say. Michael Field. PoBW

Nought to me! So I choose to say. Nought to me! So I choose to say. Michael Field. PoBW

Nought vnder heauen so strongly doth allure. Edmund Spenser. NoSic *Fr.* Faerie Queene, The.

Noun's a thing, A. A verb's the thing it does. Grammar Lesson, The. Steve Kowit. P180

Nouns of Assemblage. Stephen Dobyns. BodElec

Nouns, verbs couple like years, Water comes, listens. (LL) Fiddlers. Dave Jeddie Smith. CAP-8; NAMCP V.2

Nourishment of Little Birds, The. Raymond Queneau. YaTCFP, *tr.* by Teo Savory

Nous ne savons rien. Mort de Guillaume Apollinaire, La. Tristan Tzara. YaTCFP

Nous vieillissions, lui le feuillage et moi la source. Voix, Une. Yves Bonnefoy. YaTCFP

Nov 22, 1988. Ishmael Reed. ESEAA

Nova, pure periphery, glassed into the immobile black, a few light. Shooting Star. Joanna Klink. IAoNAP

Nova Scotia Fish Hut. Charles Bruce. Coast

Novel. Fred Moramarco. SUP

Novel, The. Richard Jones. GifTon

Novel, The. Denise Levertov. BrAP

Novel, The. Adrienne Rich. CAP-8

Novel of High Life, A. Thomas Haynes Bayly. OxAEP-2

Novelist Speaks, The. Ann Lauterbach. KGB

Novelle; My Grandmother Is Waiting For Me To Come Home. Gwendolyn Brooks. ESEAA *Fr.* Children Going Home.

Novels from a Fragment in Progress. Bob Kaufman. EGAG

Novelty Shop, The. Duane Niatum. ReTh

Novelty today, tomorrow a ruin from the past, buried and, A. I Speak of the City. Octavio Paz. VCWP, *tr.* by Eliot Weinberger

November. William Cullen Bryant. APN-1; GSo; TreFP

November. Hartley Coleridge. CenSon *Fr.* Sonnets to the Seasons.

November: "Shimmering spreads of golden fire." James Hoggard. TiP2

November: "When the hangman's bored he turns dangerous." Tomas Tranströmer. WoBe, *tr. by* Robin Fulton

November. William Dean Howells. APN-2

November. John Keble. OBEV *Fr.* Forest Leaves in Autumn.

November. Lucy Larcom.
  "This is the month sunrise skies." TCAPo

November [*with music*]. Henrietta Cordelia Ray. CBWP-3

November 1st. Jessica Freeman. AnSo

November 19. David Lehman. PoDa

November 20, 1999. Alex Rawls. AnSo *Fr.* What's Your Sign?

November 25, 1963. Thomas Whitbread. TiP2

November 26, 1992: Thanksgiving at the Sea Ranch, Contemplating Metempsychosis. Sandra M. Gilbert. InoFa; PoDa

November 11, 1919. In Centralia, Washington, the air. Everest. Kimiko Hahn. PrTe

November 1936. Paul Éluard. AF, *tr. by* Gilbert Bowen

November, a godless month, full of. American Dream, An. Mary Ruefle. AmAlph

November and a snarling gale. Doctor, The. Mary Dalton. OpeFie

November and Aunt Jemima. Thylias Moss. TRP

November, and the Sunday twilight fallen. Lines, The. Andrew Motion. NeBrP

November Blue. Alice Thompson Meynell. MoBrPo

November Cotton Flower. Jean Toomer. ColAP; NAAPv.2; NAMCP V.1; NoAM; OxBoAm

November, 1806. William Wordsworth. OBWP

November Harvest. Anita Endrezze. HATNAP

November Landscape, A. Sarah Helen Whitman. ColAP

November light drains fast; the shadowed street. Guys. Sheenagh Pugh. TCAWP

November Night. Adelaide Crapsey. APT-1; NAAPv.2; Spl; TCAPo

November! November! Smoke outrunning branches, reefs. Breath. Bill Berkson. NYP2

November on Heaven Mountain, the wind like a knife. Song for General Zhao. Ts'en Shen. CCL1, *tr. by* Stephen Owen

November rips gold foil from the oak ridges. Damon's Lament for His Clorenda, Yorkshire, 1654. Lupercio Leonardo de Argensola. WoPoe, *tr. by* Geoffrey Hill

November '63: eight months in London. Immigrant. Fleur Adcock. OPOU

November sun, The. Tomas Tranströmer. WoBe *Fr.* Haiku.

November Surf. Robinson Jeffers. CalPo

November the 1st. Gold leaves. Autumn. Charles Wright. GeoHom

November 3rd. Miyazawa Kenji. CAoMJL1, *tr. by* Hiroaki Sato

November through a Giant Copper Beech [*with music*]. Edwin Honig. NoAM

November 22, 1983. Sherman Alexie. ReTh

November Woods. S. J. Marks. BodElec

November's chill blast on the rough beach is howling. Female Exile, The. Charlotte Smith. NPBRoP

Novgorod: Coming of the Saints. Johannes Bobrowski. WoPoe, *tr. by* John Peck

Novice was sitting on a cornice, A. Illustration. John Ashbery. NAAL-5

Novitiates sing Ave. Miss Scarlet, Mr. Rhett and other Latter-Day Saints. Maya Angelou. OxAAAP

Now. Robert Browning. OxBSo

Now. Christopher Gilbert. GT; OxAAAP

Now. Thomas Ken. SacPr

Now. Margaret Abigail Walker. OxAAAP

Now a monastery on southern river-banks. Written on a Wall at Hsiu-Ching Monastery in Wu-Ch'ang. Li Po. NDACCP, *tr. by* David Hinton

Now a year after your death, fish-mother, skate. Skate. Jean Valentine. CAP-8

Now absence is a habit it is time. Poem. Burns Singer. EdScPo

Now after absurd recollections and all sorts of things. All Over Again. Ataol BehramoĞlu. NaPG, *tr. by* Talat Sait Halman

Now after the sabbath. Czeslaw Milosz. GI *Fr.* St. Matthew.

Now again the world is shaken. Foundation. Henry Van Dyke. SacPr

Now, alas, it is too late. Samuel Hoffenstein. OBCoV *Fr.* Songs of Fairly Utter Despair.

Now all day long the man who is not dead. Mother and Son. Allen Tate. MoAmPo

Now all day long until the sun went down. Homer. BLPJKO *Fr.* Odyssey, The.

Now all our guests have come and gone away. Sonnet 16. Ronald David Laing. EdScPo

Now all that scintillation is a chore. Untrimming the Tree. John N. Morris. ChrPo

Now all that sound of laughter, sound of singing. Rosalía de Castro. STV

Now all the dogs with folded paws. Suburban Song. Elizabeth Riddell. NOBAu

Now all the truth is out. To a Friend Whose Work Has Come to Nothing. William Butler Yeats. MoBrPo; OBMV; OxAEP-2; WoPoe

Now all the world she knew is dead. Sir John Betjeman. OxAEP-2 *Fr.* House of Rest.

Now and Again: An Autobiography of Basket. Angie Estes. ExTi

Now and Then. Alice B. Fogel. CFP

Now and Then. Robert Peterson. GeoHom

Now and then a lost sea gull flutters into. Sea We Read About, The. Philip Levine. GeoHom

Now and then I find myself. Now and Then. Robert Peterson. GeoHom

Now and then there will arise. Song. *Unknown.* OBVE, *tr. by* Frances Densmore

Now another's land—Will spring return again to stolen fields? Will Spring Return to Stolen Fields? Yi Sanghwa. CAMKP, *tr. by* David R. McCann

Now as at all times I can see in the mind's eye. Magi, The. William Butler Yeats. ChIV-2; GI; HarvBoo; NAMCP V.1; NoAM; NPeEn; OxAEP-2; PoA 2002; TRP

Now / As day breaks, light. Novgorod: Coming of the Saints. Johannes Bobrowski. WoPoe, *tr. by* John Peck

Now as I was young and easy under the apple boughs. Fern Hill. Dylan Thomas. AmFaPo; AngWePo; BrAP; CABP; ChAP; ClHu; EMP; GPTC; HarvBoo; HeIP-4; IPoFL; MoBrPo; NAEL-6v2; NAEL-7v2; NAMCP V.2; NIL-7; NIP-4; NoAM; NoP-4; NoP-5; OBWVE; PoPoPo; SoSe-8; TCAWP; TFi; TRP; WaAnP

Now as I watch the progress of the plague. Missing, The. Thom Gunn. CAGL; EMP; NAMCP V.2; NoP-4; NoP-5; WaAnP

Now, as my hand rolls up the blind to reach its hook of jade. Sorrow for Spring. Li Ching. CCL1, *tr. by* Alan Ayling and Duncan Mackintosh

Now as the golden. Sunday Morning in Old San Juan. Julio Marzán. PueRic

Now, as the stars unfleece themselves. Night. Maurya Simon. InvLad

Now as the train bears west. Night Journey. Theodore Roethke. AmFaPo; BeAl; GM; GoPo

Now as they went on their way. Anna Kamienska. GI *Fr.* St. Luke.

Now as to the names (how much less than the natures. Leigh Hunt. *Fr.* Blue-Stocking Revels; or, The Feast of the Violets.

Now, at a particular spot on the radio dial, "—in this corner, wearing purple trunks." Reception Good. Kenneth Fearing. APT-2

Now, at last, even Nikifor's a suitor. Vladimir Uflyand. TCRusP, *tr. by* Daniel Weissbort

Now at night preserves itself as a black bird. Mei-Mei Berssenbrugge. AWPTFC *Fr.* Kali.

Now at the turn of the year this coil of clay. Mad Potter, The. John Hollander. ColAP; VCAP

Now autumn beats like music at my breast. Texas Autumn. Grace Noll Crowell. TiP2

Now banished art, but yet alas how shall? (LL) Sir Philip Sidney. NAEL-6v1; NAEL-7v1; NoP-5 *Fr.* Astrophil and Stella.

Now, be cruel. Vinegar of Cruelty. Kim Suyŏng. CAMKP, *tr. by* Young-Jun Lee

Now, because of you, symmetry and asymmetry interest me *equally*. Outsider: Minnie Evans. Sandra McPherson. ExTi

Now Bekotsidi, that am I. For them I make. Song of Bekotsidi, The. *Unknown.* OBVE, *tr. by* Washington Matthews

Now bithenk thee, gentilman. *Unknown.* OHMEL

Now, brighter than the host that all night long. Daybreak. Richard Henry Dana. APN-1

Now burst above the city's cold twilight. Six O'Clock. Trumbull Stickney. APN-2; OxBoAm

Now bygynneth Glotoun for to go to shryfte. William Langland. NPeEn

Now can you see the monument? It is of wood. Monument, The. Elizabeth Bishop. NAMCP V.2; NoAM; TRP

Now comes the Course-of-things, shaped like an Ox. Sidney Lanier. TCAPo *Fr.* Clover.

Now comes the evening of the mind. Evening of the Mind, The. Donald Justice. VCAP

Now comes the good rain farmers pray for(and). E. E. Cummings. NoAM

Now cometh alle ye that been y-brought. God, the Port of Peace. John Walton. SacPr

Now cometh alle ye that ben ibroght. Boethius. OBMV *Fr.* Consolation of Philosophy, The ("De Consolacione Philosophie").

Now Crockett said, "You gentlemen are free." Michael Lind. TiP2 *Fr.* Alamo, The: An Epic.

Now crowds on crowds around the goddess press. Alexander Pope. NAEL-6v1; NAEL-7v1 *Fr.* Dunciad, The.

Now cumis aige quhair yewth hes bene. William Dunbar. SacPr

Now Daphne—daughter of the river-god. Ovid. NAWM-7v1 *Fr.* Metamorphoses.

Now, darling. It's time you strapped me back on that wheel.   Second Circle. Srikanth Reddy.   LegDan

Now day and night sit balanced.   Peter Blue Cloud.   ChAP *Fr.* Within the Seasons.

Now did you mark a falcon.   Noble Sisters.   Christina Georgina Rossetti. VWP

Now didn't Suzdal and Moscow.   Holy Russia.   Maksimilian Aleksandrovich Voloshin.   TCRusP, *tr. by* Bob Perelman

Now, do you doubt that your Bird was true? (LL)   Split the Lark—and you'll find the Music.   Emily Dickinson.   APN-2; ChIV-2; NoP-4; NoP-5; TCAPo

Now down among red lotus plunged.   Dike of the Cormorants.   Wang Wei. CCL1, *tr. by* Jerome P. Seaton

Now dusk is on Houston: flat and breastless.   Sunset on the Bayou.   Sybil Pittman Estess.   TiP2

Now each creature joys the other.   Ode.   Samuel Daniel.   NoSic

Now Energy's bound to diminish.   Ether Insatiable.   May Kendall.   CABP

Now entertain conjecture of a time.   William Shakespeare.   FaBoWar; OxAEP-1 *Fr.* King Henry V.

Now, Epicure.   Alchemist, The.   Ben Jonson.

Now, ere sweet Summer bids its long adieu.   Robert Bloomfield.   NPBRoP *Fr.* Farmer's Boy, The.

Now even my chest is parched like a mummy. I lack even the strength to drink sorrow.   Driving During a Shower.   Kim Hyesun.   EcSo, *tr. by* Youngju Ryu

Now every day the bracken browner grows.   September.   Mary Elizabeth Coleridge.   ViWPN

Now every man at my request.   *Unknown.*   OBCP

Now every thing that shadowy thought.   In Festubert.   Edmund Charles Blunden.   OBMV

Now Ev'ning fades! her pensive step retires.   Night.   Ann Radcliffe.   NOBRP

Now fades the last long streak of snow.   Alfred Tennyson.   NAEL-6v2; NAEL-7v2; NPeEn; WaAnP *Fr.* In Memoriam A. H. H.

Now faintly the falling sun.   Chengtu.   Tu Fu [*or* Du Fu].   TAL

Now farewel World, in which is not my treasure.   Farewel to the World, A.   Michael Wigglesworth.   SacPr

Now fetch me out the Turkish concubines.   Christopher Marlowe.   FaBoWar *Fr.* Tamburlaine the Great, Part 2.

Now *Fight Cancer* is there. (LL)   Sunny Prestatyn.   Philip Larkin.   NAMCP V.2; NoAM; OBCoV

Now first, as I shut the door.   New House, The.   Edward Thomas.   MoBrPo; OBEV; OBWVE

Now first of all he means the night.   Song for the Middle of the Night, A.   James Wright.   WeW-3

Now for a little I have fed on loneliness.   Fruit of Loneliness.   May Sarton.   PoA 2002

Now for my story. For many years.   Delirium.   Norman J. Loftis.   SpirFl

Now for that slawnders sake.   *Unknown.*   PBRV *Fr.* Jack of the North.

Now for the first time on the night of your death.   Thomas Merton.   BLT

Now for the long years when I could not love you.   In Recompense.   Eda Lou Walton.   LW

Now for the opening of the Truth, which is our strength and stay.   Some More Scruples Clear'd.   Elizabeth Hincks.   EMWP

Now from the marshlands under the mist-mountains.   *Unknown.*   OPOU *Fr.* Beowulf.

Now Front to Front the hostile Armies stand.   Homer.   OBVE *Fr.* Iliad, The.

Now gently winding up the fair ascent.   Homer.   OBVE *Fr.* Odyssey.

Now, George the third rules not alone.   On the Conflagrations at Washington.   Philip Freneau.   AmWaPo; APN-1

Now gie me back my milkin' stool.   Sonsy Milkmaid, The.   Emily Jane Pfeiffer.   ViWPN

Now ginnes this goodly frame of temperaunce.   Edmund Spenser.   *Fr.* Faerie Queene, The.

Now Glutton begins to go to shrift.   William Langland.   NAEL-6v1; NAEL-7v1 *Fr.* Vision of Piers Plowman, The.

Now, God be thanked Who has matched us with His hour.   Rupert Brooke.   NPeEn; OBWP; PoA 2002

Now God is truly naught, and if He aught may be.   "Angelus Silesius."   GePo *Fr.* Cherubical Wanderer, The.

Now God preserve, as you well do deserve.   Masque of Christmas, The.   Ben Jonson.   ChrPo

Now Good-night.   Good Night.   Eleanor Farjeon.   NOxBChV

Now goth sonne under wode.   *Unknown.*   OHMEL

Now goth sonne under wode,—.   *Unknown.*   OHMEL

Now Go'th Sun Under Wood.   *Unknown.*   NoP-4; NoP-5

Now gowans sprout, an' lavrocks sing.   Ode to Mr. F— [*or* Mr. Forbes].   Allan Ramsay.   OBVE

Now graceful truce suspends the burning war.   Joel Barlow.   APN-1 *Fr.* Columbiad, The.

Now grapes are plush upon the vines.   Contrary Theses (I).   Wallace Stevens.   SAmP

Now Great and Awesome in My Heart.   Francisco de Quevedo y Villegas.   SpanPo, *tr. by* William M. Davis

Now great and awesome in my heart.   Now Great and Awesome in My Heart.   Francisco de Quevedo y Villegas.   SpanPo, *tr. by* William M. Davis

Now green the larch; the hedges green.   Spring Comes to the Suburbs.   Phyllis McGinley.   APT-2

Now grimy April comes again.   For City Spring.   Stephen Vincent Benét.   NBLV

Now had th' Almighty Father from above.   John Milton.   NIL-7; NIP-4 *Fr.* Paradise Lost.

Now hardly here and there a hackney-coach.   Description of the Morning, A.   Jonathan Swift.   BrAP; HeIP-4; NIL-7; NoP-4; NoP-5; OxAEP-1; OxBEV; PoPoPo; SoSe-8; TFi

Now has the wind a sound.   Wind.   Lizette Woodworth Reese.   APT-1

Now have I brought a woork to end which neither Joves fierce [*or* feerce] wrath.   Ovid.   OBVE *Fr.* Metamorphoses.

Now Have I Fed and Eaten Up the Rose.   Gottfried Keller.   WoPoe, *tr. by* James Joyce

Now have I fed and eaten up the rose.   Now Have I Fed and Eaten Up the Rose.   Gottfried Keller.   WoPoe, *tr. by* James Joyce

Now he comes! will he come? alas, no, no! (LL)   Seafarer, The.   Henry Howard, Earl of Surrey.   NoSic; NPeEn

Now he has seen the girl Hsiang-Hsiang.   Chinese Ballad.   Mao Tse-tung.   OxBEV, *tr. by* William Empson

Now He Knows All There Is to Know: Now He Is Acquainted with the Day and Night.   Delmore Schwartz.   VisFro

Now, he recalls the lamentable wail.   John Pierpont.   APN-1 *Fr.* Airs of Palestine.

Now he will forget you. (LL)   Spell for Jealousy.   Jeni Couzyn.   BrAP; HAWP

Now hear this, lovers, my friends.   Yunus Emre.   NaPG, *tr. by* Talat Sait Halman

Now heaven be thanked. I am out of love again!   Freedom.   Jan Struther.   LW

Now Heaven conduct thee with a parent's love! (LL)   To Mr. S. T. Coleridge.   Anna Laetitia Barbauld.   CABP; NoP-4; WoRP

Now Henry Jones and William Brown.   Smithville Tandem Bike, The.   W. T. Goodge.   ArBi

Now Here of the Golden Throne, looking out from where she stood on the summit of Olympus, was quick to observe two things.   Homer.   EroLit *Fr.* Iliad, The.

Now here's a story 'bout Minnie, the Moocher.   Minnie, the Moocher.   Cab Calloway, Clarence Gaskill and Irving Mills.   ReLy

Now his nose's bridge is broken, one eye.   On Hurricane Jackson.   Alan Dugan.   TRP

Now holde [*or* hoold] your[e] pees, my tale I wol beginne [*or* biginne *or* bigynne]. (LL)   Geoffrey Chaucer.   NAEL-6v1; NAEL-7v1; WaAnP *Fr.* Canterbury Tales, The.

Now homing tradesmen scatter through the streets.   Place Pigalle.   Richard Wilbur.   HeIP-4; PWW2

Now I am a fan of silence.   Marina Boroditskaya.   CRWP, *tr. by* Ruth Fainlight

Now I am a lute filled with this wandering description. (LL)   Chinese Villanelle.   John Yau.   PmAP; WaAnP

Now! I am as beautiful as the very blossoms themselves.   Formula to Secure Love.   *Cherokee Oral Tradition.*   NAAPv.1

Now I am dry bones and my face a stony skull staring in yellow surprise at the / sun sun. . . . . (LL)   Between the World and Me.   Richard Wright.   FTtHH; ISC; SSLK

Now I am glad to be one whom people ignore.   At a Reception.   Karen Gershon.   LW

Now I Am Going.   León Felipe.   RaW, *tr. by* W. S. Merwin

Now I am like a seaweed.   Reborn.   Edison Mpina.   NAfrP

Now I am slow and placid, fond of sun.   With Child.   Genevieve Taggard.   MoAmPo; NAAP.v.2

Now, I am stirring like a seed in China. (LL)   Pruned Tree, The.   Howard Moss.   BeAl; VCAP

Now I become myself. It's taken.   Now I Become Myself.   May Sarton.   TWF

Now I begin again to refuse to say the things.   Mechanics.   T. R. Hummer.   LPSFW

Now I can tell you. Hearing the shrill leaves.   Thrasher in the Willow by the Lake, The.   Robert Pack.   ColAP

Now I don't have to leave this place not for anybody.   Free Abandonment Blues, The.   Jean Valentine.   BodElec

Now I feel safe.   Red Bird.   Gerald Stern.   UrbNat

Now I find myself dried.   Psalm 2.   Mahmoud Darwish.   AF, *tr. by* Denys Johnson-Davies

Now I find peace in everything around me.   Williams Was Wrong.   Greg Delanty.   WaAnP

Now, I gain the Mountain's Brow. John Dyer. NPeEn *Fr.* Grongar Hill.

Now I go down here and bring up a moon. Auctioneer. Carl Sandburg. NOxBChV

Now I have a gas stove. Life of a Cucapá Woman, The. Heriberto Yépez. RMCMP, *tr. by* Harry Polkinhorn

Now I have found thee I will evermore. Upon the Crucifix. William Alabaster. NoSic

Now I have nothing. Even the joy of loss. Stella Benson. LW

Now i have read your book of everything. Ballad of the Rainmaker. Maik Nwosu. NeNiPo

Now I have Vallejo with me on the desk, his troubled words, and. End of Communism, The. Rodney Jones. IllVoic

Now I invest the world. What is Beautiful. Jay Wright. GT

Now I know enough. Not a Letter. Yvonne Cullen. NIrP

Now I know there are bored, beautiful people everywhere. Nine of Clubs, Cleveland, Ohio. Dorothy Barresi. SwNoth

Now I know they're all the same. A standing cock. Linda France. MFPA *Fr.* On the Game.

Now I know you'll be born. (LL) Heartsong. Jeni Couzyn. BeAl; HAWP

Now: "I long for my voice that found you." Cengiz Bektaş. NaPG, *tr. by* Talat Sait Halman

Now I love you. In the Midst of Possibility. Gabriel Fitzmaurice. IrLP

Now I may wither into the truth. (LL) Coming of Wisdom with Time, The. William Butler Yeats. HarvBoo; SoSe-8

Now I Prize Yellow Strawberries. José Garcia Villa. WoPoe

Now i prize yellow strawberries. Now I Prize Yellow Strawberries. José Garcia Villa. WoPoe

Now I promise the shriek that the pressure of days, the pressure of days will be weapon. Karen Volkman. LegDan

Now I realize that I love you. Italy 1942. Franco Fortini. ItPo, *tr. by* Gayle Ridinger

Now I say in structuring the simple slips a seems. Essay on Concrete, An. Douglas Messerli. FTOS

Now I see her face. Basho. SoOfWa, *tr. by* Sam Hamill

Now I see its whiteness. Dead Butterfly, The. Denise Levertov. NoP-4

Now I see moon rise like primitive memory. Because of Duties, Zimmer Had Forgotten the Forest. Paul Zimmer. AtGh

Now I see them sitting me before a mirror. Sonnet. Michael Palmer. HarvBoo; MakPoe

Now I see you. Grandfather. Joseph Stroud. GeoHom

Now I sing again. Roses for the folks we know, A. Seitlhamo Motsapi. TSAP

Now I sit my child on the jut. Stance. Kate Clanchy. BeAl

Now I think I hear the laments. François Villon. NAWM-7v1 *Fr.* Testament, The.

Now I Want All My Letters White Again. Cristina Campo. CItWP, *tr. by* Cinzia Sartini Blum and Lara Trubowitz

Now I was thinking of those bacteria. Analogy. János Székely. IQMS, *tr. by* Geroge Gömöri

Now I will ask for one true word beyond. Grandfather and Grandmother in Love. David Mura. TRP

Now I will do nothing but listen. Walt Whitman. SAmP *Fr.* Song of Myself.

Now I will do to you what you came here for me to do. (LL) Prayer to the Sockeye Salmon. *Unknown.* WoPoe; WPoS, *tr. by* Jane Hirshfield

Now I will enter the house of affliction. Love's Dozen. Jay Wright.

Now if the dull and thankless heart declare. Malediction upon Myself. Elinor Wylie. ColAP

Now if thou hast one dram of Grace. Catullus. OBVE,

Now I'll see whether Siva. Raghunāth Dās. SinGod, *tr. by* Rachel Fell McDermott

Now in a thought, now in a shadowed word. L'Envoi. Edwin Arlington Robinson. ITBLP

Now in an hour you have me, tight, and loose me. Fool, The. Kenneth Mackenzie. BMAP

Now, in another part of the country. Spending the Night. Scott Hightower. BeDoSh

Now in more subtle wreaths I will entwine. Thomas Carew. EroLit *Fr.* Rapture, A.

Now in my middle years I glean. Serene Words. Gabriela Mistral. SpanPo, *tr. by* Muriel Kittel

Now in the dawn before it dies, the eagle swings. Story of a Well-made Shield, The. N. Scott Momaday. HATNAP

Now in the Golden Stag's mossy courtyard, where. Death of Shakespeare, The. Gyula Juhász. IQMS, *tr. by* J. G. Nichols

Now in the helicopters the casual will. George Oppen. AmWaPo; NAMCP V.1 *Fr.* Of Being Numerous.

Now in the jasmine arbour. Happiness. Mihály Csokonai Vitéz. IQMS, *tr. by* Paul Tabori

Now in the palace gardens warm with age. Trumbull Stickney. APN-2 *Fr.* Eride.

Now in the patron's mansion see the wight. Richard Savage. OBSV *Fr.* Progress of a Divine, The.

Now in the suburbs and the falling light. Father and Son. Stanley Kunitz. AF; TaR, *tr. by* Jack Bevan

Now in the tight trench you go. Jim Powell. CalPo *Fr.* Time and Light.

Now in this fest, this holy fest. Nunc Puer Nobis Natus Est. James Ryman. SacPr

Now in this while gan Daedalus a wearinesse to take. Ovid. OBVE *Fr.* Metamorphoses.

Now in thy dazzling half-oped eye. Mother to Her Waking Infant, A. Joanna Baillie. CABP; NoP-4; NoP-5; WaAnP; WoRP

Now incense fills the air. After Yeats. Allen Ginsberg. FTOS

Now, innocent, within the deep. M., Singing. Louise Bogan. ColAP; NoAM; WaAnP

Now is a ship / which captain am. E. E. Cummings. EmeKit; Spl

Now is it? You'll remember Mercury. (LL) First Men on Mercury, The. Edwin Morgan. EdScPo; NePenScot

Now is Jonas the Jwe jugged to drowne. *Unknown.* NPeEn *Fr.* Patience.

Now is the globe shrunk tight. Snowdrop. Ted Hughes. HarvBoo

Now Is the Month of Maying. *Unknown.* NoSic

Now is the month of maying. Now Is the Month of Maying. *Unknown.* NoSic

Now is the time for mirth. To Live Merrily, and To Trust to Good Verses. Robert Herrick. BASC; CavPo; NOSC

Now is the time for the burning of the leaves. Laurence Binyon. NPeEn *Fr.* Burning of the Leaves, The.

Now is the time of year when bees are wild. Equinox. Elizabeth Alexander. ExTi

Now is the time when the great urban heart. City Christmas. Phyllis McGinley. ChrPo; OBCoV

Now is the winter of our discontent. William Shakespeare. OxBEV *Fr.* King Richard III.

Now isn't it time. Birthday Cake. Paul Goodman. BodElec

Now Israel. Bible, *O.T.* NPeEn

Now it begins. The sun plunges down. Season of Locking-In, The. Christiane Jacox Kyle. YaYoPo

Now it belongs not to my care. Richard Baxter. NOSC

Now it grows dark. Hymn to Night. Melville Cane. MoAmPo

Now it hangs on the back of the kitchen chair. Father's Old Blue Cardigan. Anne Carson. StAl

Now it is almost night, from the bronzey soft sky. Storm in the Black Forest. D. H. Lawrence. FaBoVe

Now it is autumn and the falling fruit. Ship of Death, The. D. H. Lawrence. BrAP; GPTC; MoBrPo; NAEL-6v2; NAEL-7v2; NAMCP V.1; NoAM; NoP-4; NoP-5; OxAEP-2; OxBEV

Now it is evening, the light rushes to fall. Vespers. Peter Cooley. Vesp

Now it is late winter. Two Spring Charms. *Unknown.* WoPoe, *tr. by* James Wright

Now it is midsummer and the long sun shines. For Hokey and Henrietta. Norman Nicholson. NoP-4

Now it is nearly time when, quivering on its stem. Harmony of Evening, The. Charles Baudelaire. SxFrPo, *tr. by* James McGowan

Now it is over, the midnight funeral that parts. On the New Year. Christopher Okigbo. PoetW

Now / it is shame that becomes the grains. Kiss Me, Then Give Birth to Me. Cemal Süreya. NaPG, *tr. by* Talat Sait Halman

Now it only feels good when it bleeds. (LL) Logic in the House of Sawed-Off Telescopes. Jeffrey McDaniel. AmPoNex; LegDan; NeAmPo

Now it so happened she came. That Black Girl Fulô. Jorge de Lima. TCLAP, *tr. by* Elizabeth Gordon

Now it's a way of remembering, dark by dark, the rows. No Moon. Nancy Eimers. ExTi

Now it's in all the novels, what's pornography to do? Peter Porter. OBCoV *Fr.* Sanitized Sonnets, The.

Now it's time for me to go to my society. Zuni Dancers. Eric Mottram. Oth

Now, it's true that Happiness was a little cockeyed and her dress was a particular yellow. Happiness. Crystal Williams. RD

Now Jesus had not yet come to the village. Rainer Maria Rilke. GI *Fr.* St. John.

Now Jesus stood before the governor. René Daumal. GI *Fr.* St. Matthew.

Now Johnson would go up to join the [great] simulacra of men. Robert Duncan. APSN; NAMCP V.2 *Fr.* Passages.

Now, Joy is born of parents poor. Joy and Pleasure. W. H. Davies. OBMV

Now kept it flat and raked the walls and shrubs. (LL) Frederick Goddard Tuckerman. APN-2; NoP-4; TCAPo *Fr.* Sonnets: Second Series, 1854–1860.

Now late. Scholar Recruit, The. Pao Chao. FaBoWar, *tr. by* Arthur Waley

Now leave the check-reins slack. To the Man after the Harrow. Patrick Kavanagh. ModIr; WaAnP

Now let me come unto that stately tree.   Emilia Lanier and Aemilia Bassano Lanyer.   MakPoe *Fr.* Description of Cooke-ham [*or* Cookham], The.

Now let my habitude be where the vine.   Donald Davidson.   FuPo *Fr.* Hermitage.

Now let my pen been choakt with gall.   Epitaph, uppon Cassandra Mac Willms Wife to Sr Thomas Ridgway Earle of London Derry by ye Lady A. S., An. Lady Anne Harris Southwell.   EMWP

Now let no charitable hope.   Let No Charitable Hope.   Elinor Wylie.   APT-1; ColAP; IJHIL; MoAmPo; NAAPv.2; NALW; NAMCP V.1; OxBoAm

Now let the cycle sweep us here and there.   "H. D."   APT-1 *Fr.* Sigil.

Now let the legless boy show the great lady.   In the Children's Hospital.   Hugh MacDiarmid.   BrAP; NAEL-6v2; NAEL-7v2

Now let us unto some fair Medow goe.   Margaret Maule, Countess of Panmure.   EMWP

Now let[t] your constancy your hono[u]r prove. (LL)   Mary Sidney Wroth, Countess of Montgomery.   BASC; NAEL-7v1 *Fr.* Pamphilia to Amphilanthus.

Now Liddesdale [*or* Liddisdale] has ridden a raid.   Jock o' the Side [*Version from Poetical Museum; Albyn's Anthology 2*].   *Unknown.*   IBB

Now Liddisdale [*or* Liddesdale] has lain long [*or* layen lang] in.   Dick o' the Cow.   *Unknown.*   IBB

Now life in the houses of flesh help us.   Hymn for Seedtime and a Safe Harvest (Arval Hymn).   *Unknown.*   WoPoe, *tr.* by Janet Lembke.

Now light congeals. Soon the late summer air.   Now Light Congeals.   Thomas Blackburn.   StAl

Now light the candles; one; two; there's a moth.   Repression of War Experience.   Siegfried Sassoon.   AF; NAMCP V.1; NoAM

Now lighted windows climb the dark.   Manhattan Lullaby.   Rachel Lyman Field.   HHAm; TLR

Now like the Lady of Shalott.   Before the Mirror.   Elizabeth Stoddard.   SWaP

Now listen, honey, 'bout a new dance craze.   Walkin' the Dog.   Shelton Brooks.   ReLy

Now, listen. / I want you new girls, every morning.   To the Virgins, to Make the Most of Time.   Gavin Ewart.   OBCoV

Now listen, you watermelons.   Issa.   WED, *tr.* by Robert Bly

Now, little Edward, say why so.   William Wordsworth.   STuOW *Fr.* Anecdote for Fathers [*Showing how the Art of Lying may be Taught*].

Now, luck yet send us, and a little wit.   Ben Jonson.   NAEL-7v1 *Fr.* Volpone.

Now manhood and garbroyls I chaunt, and martial horror.   Virgil.   OBVE *Fr.* Aeneid [*or* Eneados *or* Aeneis], The.

Now may we turn aside and dry our tears.   Inis Fal.   Egan O'Rahilly.   OBMV, *tr.* by James Stephens

Now maybe you can tell me what a hundred grand looks like. (LL)   Soybeans.   Thomas Alan Orr.   GoPo; IPoFL

Now Melanctha Had neither Home, nor Regular Occupation. Life Was Just Beginning for Her.   Piera Oppezzo.   CItWP, *tr.* by Cinzia Sartini Blum and Lara Trubowitz

Now mirk December's dowie face.   Daft Days, The.   Robert Fergusson.   CABP; NPeEn; OxAEP-1; OxBEV

Now Miss Sarah, if you please.   I'll See You Again.   Noël Coward.   ReLy

Now Morn her rosie steps in th' Eastern Clime.   John Milton. *Fr.* Paradise Lost.

Now morn her rosy steps in th' eastern clime.   John Milton.   NAEL-6v1

Now mountains are separating us.   *Unknown.*   SLW, *tr.* by Marjolijn De Jager, Sayd Bahodin Majrouh and André Velter

Now must I grieve and fret my little way.   Solace.   Margaret Abigail Walker.   OxAAAP

Now must I these three praise.   Friends.   William Butler Yeats.   NoAM

Now my father always has to come to terms.   Autobiographical Moment, An.   Ya'ir Hurvits.   PML, *tr.* by Lois Bar-yaacov

Now My Life Has Gained Some Meaning.   Walther von der Vogelweide.   GePo, *tr.* by J. W. Thomas

Now my mind's been brought to such a state—and it's your fault.   Catullus.   STV

Now my right hand.   "H. D."   APT-1; NAAL-5 *Fr.* Walls Do Not Fall, The.

Now, My Usefullness Over [*with music*].   Edwin Honig.   NoAM

Now near the end of the middle stretch of road.   Jersey Rain.   Robert Pinsky.   BAP-01

Now, not a tear begun.   Woman Mourned by Daughters, A.   Adrienne Rich.   InoFa

Now o'er the one half-world.   William Shakespeare.   OxAEP-1 *Fr.* Macbeth.

Now, o'er the tesselated pavement strew.   Mary Robinson.   NPBRoP *Fr.* Sappho and Phaon.

Now, o'er the tessellated pavement strew.   Previous to her Interview with Phaon.   Mary Robinson.   CenSon; RWP

Now of that vision I, bereaven.   Francis Thompson.   MoBrPo *Fr.* Grace of the Way.

Now of wemen this I say, for me.   In Prais[e] of Women [*or* Wemen].   William Dunbar.   CABP; NoP-4; WaAnP

Now old, my heart is at peace.   In Reply to Wei Dan.   Lingche.   CCL1, *tr.* by Stephen Owen

Now on the battlefield.   Warrior's Lament, A.   Nnamdi Olebara.   PoAgWa, *tr.* by Chinweizu

Now, on the fifteenth day of the seventh month, the heavens open their doors.   Transformation Text on Mahāmaudgalyāyana Rescuing His Mother from the Underworld.   *Chinese Oral Tradition.*   ColAnChi, *tr.* by Victor H. Mair

Now on the first day of Unleavened Bread the disciples came to Jesus.   Rainer Maria Rilke.   GI *Fr.* St. Matthew.

Now on their coasts our conquering navy rides.   John Dryden.   OxAEP-1 *Fr.* Annus Mirabilis.

Now on you is the hungry equinox.   Kentucky Mountain Farm.   Robert Penn Warren.

Now once more gray mottled buckeye branches.   Andrée Rexroth.   Kenneth Rexroth.   APT-2; ASA; NAMCP V.1

Now only praise makes me cry.   Paul Goodman.   BodElec *Fr.* Sentences for Matthew Ready, Series 2.

Now only the dying and as the sky closes its shutter I say.   End of the City, The.   Kevin Prufer.   LegDan

"Now," or never or can't be. . ."this question," now that "was easy."   Short sorry.   Kari Edwards.   BAP-04

Now ore the sea from her old Love comes she.   Christopher Marlowe.   PBRV *Fr.* Ovids Elegies Book 1.

Now our boys have such toys.   Toys.   Gemino H. Abad.   ReBoTo

Now, Parrot, my sweet bird, speak our yet once again.   John Skelton.   NoSic *Fr.* Speak [*or* Speke], Parrot.

Now place your hand on her back. Now struggle and shove him off.   Heather Ramsdell.   IAoNAP *Fr.* Vague Swimmers.

Now polish the crucible.   "H. D."   NALW *Fr.* Tribute to the Angels.

Now ponder well, you parents dear.   Babes in the Wood, The.   *Unknown.*   OBNV; OxAEP-1

Now Pontius Pilate is to judge the cause.   Emilia Lanier.   EMWP; NAEL-6v1; NALW; NOSC *Fr.* Salve Deus Rex Judaeorum.

"Now pray, where are you going, child?"   *Unknown.*   OBSP

Now precedent songs, farewell—by every name farewell.   Now Precedent Songs, Farewell.   Walt Whitman.   NAAL-3

Now preye I to hem alle that herkne this litel tretis or rede.   Geoffrey Chaucer.   NAEL-6v1; NAEL-7v1 *Fr.* Canterbury Tales, The.

Now remember, old pal, when you get back home. (LL)   Give My Regards to Broadway.   George M. Cohan.   NAAPv.2; ReLy; TCAPo

Now rides this renk thurgh the ryalme of Logres.   *Unknown.*   NPeEn *Fr.* Sir Gawain and the Green Knight [*Middle English Text Selections*].

Now rises this poet's soul.   Jimmy Santiago Baca.   ICANM *Fr.* Healing Earthquakes.

Now Roland feels that he is at death's door.   *Unknown.*   FaBoWar *Fr.* Song of Roland, The.

Now, round my favored grot let roses rise.   Phaon Awakes.   Mary Robinson.   CenSon; RWP

Now round my favoured grot let roses rise.   Mary Robinson.   NPBRoP *Fr.* Sappho and Phaon.

Now, said the cook, I will teach you.   How to Stuff a Pepper.   Nancy Willard.   AFaM

Now scarce is heard the zephyr's sigh.   *Unknown.*   CCL1 *Fr.* Gu-feng [*Translations*].

Now seals the fair creation from my sight. (LL)   To S. M., a Young African Painter.   Phillis Wheatley.   ColAP; MakPoe; NAAL-3; NAAL-5; NAAPv.1; NoP-4; NoP-5

Now seems sweeter than flowers. (LL)   Hibakusha's Letter (1955), The.   David Mura.   AtGh; OpBo

Now, Serena, be not coy.   To His Love When He Had Obtained Her.   Sir Walter Ralegh.   NoSic

Now shall I walk.   Best Friend, The.   W. H. Davies.   OBMV

Now shall the long homesickness have an end.   Nineteen Sonnets.   Elinor Wylie.

Now shall the praises of the Lord be sung.   First Song of Moses, The.   George Wither.   ChIV-1

Now she guards her chalice in a temple of fear.   Ted Berrigan.   BodElec

Now She Is like the White Tree-Rose.   Cecil Day Lewis.   MoBrPo *Fr.* From Feathers to Iron.

Now She Is Unadorned.   Milo De Angelis.   NeIt, *tr.* by Lawrence Venuti

Now she was ready, in an aura of moth-balls.   Clearing Out.   Val Warner.   EdScPo

Now she's ninety I walk through the local park.   Winter Visit, A.   Dannie Abse.   NoAM

Now shine, now rain, and rain becomes shine.   Now Shine, Now Rain.   Kim Sisŭp.   CATKP, *tr.* by Chi-gyu Kim [*or* Kim Chonggil]

Now shout into my dream. These trumpets snored.   Farewell in a Dream.   Stephen Spender.   MoBrPo

Now shrynketh rose and lilye-flour.   *Unknown.*   OHMEL

Now side by side, with like unweary'd care.   Homer.   OBVE *Fr.* Iliad, The.

Now since the members of the World we view. Lucretius. OBVE *Fr.* De Rerum Natura (On the Nature of Things).

Now Sleeps the Crimson Petal. Alfred Tennyson. NIL-7 *Fr.* Princess, The.

Now sleeps the crimson petal, now the white. Alfred Tennyson. NAEL-6v2; NAEL-7v2; NoP-4; NoP-5; NPeEn; OxAEP-2; TFi; WoPoe *Fr.* Princess, The.

Now sleeps the crimson petal, now the white. Alfred Tennyson. NIL-7 *Fr.* Princess, The.

Now slowly winding from the mountain's head. John Jones. AngWePo *Fr.* Holywell.

Now smoke rivals smoke in its idiots' race. Engine Driver. Bobi Jones. ATSWP, *tr. by* Robert Minhinnick

Now, sometimes in my sorrow shut. Alfred Tennyson. CAGL; NAEL-6v2; NAEL-7v2; NAWM-7v2 *Fr.* In Memoriam A. H. H.

Now spring has come. Primavera. Antonio Machado Ruiz. WoPoe, *tr. by* Samuel Menashe

Now Spring returning beckons the little boats. Priapos of the Harbor. Antipater of Sidon. WoPoe, *tr. by* Dudley Fitts

Now stands our love on that still verge of day. James Agee. APT-2 *Fr.* Sonnets.

Now stood Eliza on the wood-crown'd height. Erasmus Darwin. STuOW *Fr.* Botanic Garden, The.

Now sulkies come haunting softwheeled down the. Ghost at Anlaby, The. Randolph Stow. NOBAu

Now take my word for jewel in the open light. (LL) Coal. Audre Lorde. ESEAA; NAAL-5; NALW; NAMCP V.2; NoAM; NoP-4; NoP-5; VCAP

Now tell me, my merry woodman. Estray, The. Forceythe Willson. APN-2

Now tell me where my easy rider gone. Easy Rider Blues. Blind Lemon Jefferson. GM

Now Thank We All Our God. Martin Rinckhart. GePo; SacPr, *tr. by* Catherine Winkworth

Now that all your distance surrounds me. Distance. Andrea Zanzotto. VCWP

Now that black ground and bushes. [Winter Sketches I]. Charles Reznikoff. PoA 2002

Now that death has fled these quiet corridors. (LL) Another Poem for Me (after Recovering from an O.D.). Etheridge Knight. LaCa; OxAAAP

Now that Fate is dead and gone. Song. Dame Edith Sitwell. MoBrPo

Now that father's leaves are falling. Acorn Speaks, The. Theo Sontrop. TuT, *tr. by* Theo Dorgan

Now that few people need. Not a *Paris Review* Interview. Frank Templeton Prince.

Now that he has a child. Karai Senryū. EMJL, *tr. by* Makoto Ueda

Now that he's free, relatively, often he shuffles. Holiday, The. Hans Magnus Enzensberger. VCWP, *tr. by* the author and Michael Hamburger

Now that his name has turned to elegy. Photo of My Father in a Snowbound Train. David Wojahn. GM

Now that I am all but blind. Tribute to Neruda the Poet Collector of Seashells. William Carlos Williams. NAAPv.2

Now that I am fifty-six. Rondel. Muriel Rukeyser. NoP-4; NoP-5

Now That I Am Forever with Child. Audre Lorde. NALW; NAMCP V.2; OxAAAP

Now that I am old I get up very early. Growing Old (1). Yüan Mei. WoPoe, *tr. by* Arthur Waley

Now That I Have Grown Up, Mother. Clementina Suárez. TANSG, *tr. by* Janet N. Gold

Now that I have seen Tor House. Tor House. William Everson. APT-2

Now that I have your face by heart, I look. Song for the Last Act. Louise Bogan. NoP-4; NoP-5

Now that I have your heart by heart, I see. (LL) Song for the Last Act. Louise Bogan. NoP-4; NoP-5

Now that I know. Knowledge. Louise Bogan. APT-2; NAMCP V.1; PoA 2002

Now that I know so much, I know better. Lion of Judah, The. Jan Emmens. WoPoe, *tr. by* Adrienne Rich

Now that I know where circus children. Temporary Losses. Dionisio D. Martínez. NAMCP V.2

Now that I, tying thy glass mask tightly. Laboratory, The (Ancien Régime). Robert Browning. NAEL-6v2; NAEL-7v2; OBEV

Now that is the absolute scream of anguish! (LL) Looking Out from Death. Duo Duo. AF; PML, *tr. by* Gregory Lee and Fred Moramarco

Now that I've been married for almost four weeks, Mama. Anne Stevenson. MoWP *Fr.* Correspondences.

Now that I've kicked in thirty-two. For My Birthday. Attila József. IQMS, *tr. by* Adam Makkai

Now that I've nearly done my days. Things That Matter, The. Edith Nesbit. VWP

Now that I've wasted. My Alba. Allen Ginsberg. CLPP

Now that my body grows woman-like I look at men. Flowering, A. Michael Longley. PML

Now that my ears are connected to a random answer machine. Present Tense. Harryette Mullen. PrTe

Now that of absence the most irksome night. Sir Philip Sidney. NAEL-6v1; NAEL-7v1 *Fr.* Astrophil and Stella.

"Now that poor, wayward Jane is big with child." Repentance. Louis Untermeyer. NBLV

Now that sea's over that island. Basil Bunting. HarvBoo

Now that spring's returned, I like to get up early. Early Rising. Tu Fu [*or* Du Fu]. CrYelRi, *tr. by* Sam Hamill

Now that the April of your Youth. Edward Herbert, 1st Baron Herbert of Cherbury. OxAEP-1

Now that the city with its masonries. At Villequier. Victor Hugo. SxFrPo, *tr. by* A. M. and E. H. Blackmore

Now that the fragrance. *Unknown.* ArkPo, *tr. by* Robert H. Brower and Earl Miner

Now that the men have gone off to the choleric wars. Stay Behind, The. Andrew Elliott. PNI

Now that the midday heate doth scorch my shame. William Alabaster. OxBEV

Now that the owl-light—in the time between. Owl. John Hollander. OWoS

Now that the rain is spent. Again with Music. Kay Smith. Coast

Now that the smog. Millennium. E. A. Mares. ICANM

Now that the sun has set beyond the western range. At the Mountain-Lodge of the Buddhist Priest Ye Waiting in Vain for My Friend Ding. Meng Hao Jan. CCL1, *tr. by* Witter Bynner

Now that the Sunset of Hope. Rosalía de Castro. SpanPo, *tr. by* Kate Flores

Now that the sunset of hope for my life. Now that the Sunset of Hope. Rosalía de Castro. SpanPo, *tr. by* Kate Flores

Now that the time has come wherein. Advice from Poor Robin's Almanack. *Unknown.* OBCP

Now that the time seems all mine. Patrizia Cavalli. NeIt; VCWP, *tr. by* Judith Baumel

Now that the triumphant march has entered the last street [corners]. Come Thunder. Christopher Okigbo. HBAPE; NAMCP V.2; VCWP; WaAnP

Now that the Winter's gone, the earth hath lost. Spring, The. Thomas Carew. CavPo; NoP-4; NoP-5; PBRV

Now that the worst is over, they predict. Blizzard, The. Phillis Levin. P180

Now that the young buds are tipped with a falling sun. Early Spring. Sidney Keyes. MoBrPo

Now that there's no self, let's proceed to the general self. Eduardo Milán. RMCMP *Fr.* Five.

Now that war is in the air, e'en the parson in his lair. W. T. Stead. FaBoWar *Fr.* War against War in South Africa.

Now that we are close. From This Moment On. Cole Porter. ReLy

Now that we / We have arrived at. Light & Love. Cathal McCabe. NIrP

Now that we have had our day, you. Love in Age. George Bruce. EdScPo

Now that we have had the rice and flowers. Shuffle Off to Buffalo. Al Dubin. ReLy

Now that we move and we breathe apart. You Have to Strike Back. Kate Lilley. BMAP

Now that we're almost settled in our house. In Memory of Major Robert Gregory. William Butler Yeats. IrV; NAEL-6v2; NAEL-7v2; NAMCP V.1; WaAnP

Now that we're alone we can talk prince man to man. Elegy of Fortinbras. Zbigniew Herbert. PoSu; VCWP; WoPoe, *tr. by* Czeslaw Milosz

Now that we're nothing, for example. Eduardo Milán. RMCMP, *tr. by* Roberto Tejada

Now that we're okay, I guess we should finish. As Always. James Harms. NAPBL

Now that we've come to the end. Avenue, The. Paul Muldoon. PBCIP

Now that we've done our best and worst, and parted. Busy Heart, The. Rupert Brooke. MoBrPo

Now that we've finally arrived here. Breaking the Rock Down. Ralph Angel. BodElec

Now that ye be assemblld heer. Lady Margaret Howard. EMWP

Now that you lie. Before Sleep. Anne Ridler. SacPr

Now That Your Eyes Are Shut. Elinor Wylie. APT-1

Now that your nebula, O noble Count, sheds. Luis de Góngora y Argote. SpanPo *Fr.* Fable of Polyphemus and Galatea.

Now that your surgery's. Plunder. Debra Bruce. IllVoic

Now that's the kind of thing. Andy Weaver. PoPra *Fr.* Were the Bees.

Now the air is visible again, floating. In a Motel Room at Dawn. Malena Mörling. AmPoNex

Now the archbishop comes to Lawrence. Toque de queda: Curfew in Lawrence. Martín Espada. PueRic

Now the bat circles on the breeze of eve. Sonnet. Ann Radcliffe. CenSon

Now the BBC once wrote to me and said 'Dear Norman Long'. Norman Long. RWPCtW *Fr.* We Can't Let You Broadcast That.

Now the birds begin to crow. It is time for them to crow. Blues for the Lonely. Jeremy Robson. SeSe

Now the birth of Jesus Christ took place in this way. Philip Appleman. GI *Fr.* St. Matthew.

Now the bitter pangs of hope deferred. Mail Has Come, The. Mary E. Tucker. CBWP-1

Now the body is the body's flower. Pastoral, The. Charles North. NYP2

Now the bright morning Star, Dayes harbinger. John Milton. PBRV

Now the children of the future tried to come to terms. Children of the Future. Jalauddin Mansur Nuriddin. SpirFl

Now the City Has Fallen. Andrew Waterhouse. BeAl

Now the day is over. Hymn. Sabine Baring-Gould. SacPr; WHSW

Now the declining sun 'gan downwards bend. Nightingale, The. William Strode. OBVE

Now the eleven disciples went to Galilee. William Butler Yeats. GI *Fr.* St. Matthew.

Now the equivocal lightning flashes. Summer Thunder, The. Howard Moss. OxBoAm

Now the fireflies of our youth. Kenneth Rexroth. APSN *Fr.* Love Poems of Marichiko, The.

Now the golden looks are spent. Rounds and Garlands Done, The. Léonie Adams. APT-2

Now the honey flow is over. Autumn Bees on Broccoli Blossoms Gone-by. Gary Margolis. PfSP

Now the ice lays its smooth claws on the sill. Scotland's Winter. Edwin Muir. EdScPo; NePenScot

Now the last day of many days. To Jane: The Recollection. Percy Bysshe Shelley. NPBRoP

Now the lovely autumn morning breathes its freshness in earth's face. Run to Death. Amy Levy. ViWPN

Now the milk lorry is a polished submarine. Milk Lorry, The. Les A. Murray. NAMCP V.2

Now the moon is rising. Song. Antonio Machado Ruiz. SpanPo, *tr. by* Kate Flores

Now the New Year draws near, and the night passes. *Unknown.* NAEL-6v1; NAEL-7v1; NAWM-7v1 *Fr.* Sir Gawain and the Green Knight [Marie Borroff Translation].

Now the old ways that have brought us. At a Country Funeral. Wendell Berry. UpMys

Now the parade is coming! Triumphal March. Rubén Darío. SpanPo, *tr. by* Charles Guenther

Now the person you loved. Ashes. Malena Morling. InoFa

Now the potato plants are flowering. They've lit up their streets. Gaslight. Rolf Jacobsen. WoPoe, *tr. by* Roger Greenwald

Now the rain is falling, freshly, in the intervals between sunlight. Spring Rain. Robert Hass. BodElec

Now the rich cherry, whose sleek wood. Country Summer. Léonie Adams. MoAmPo

Now the sea moves up the lawn for him as those nearby view his life passing before their eyes. Mark Bibbins. BAP-04 *Fr.* Blasted Fields of Clover Bring Harrowing and Regretful Sighs.

Now the seasons are closing their files. Year's End. Ted Kooser. PBCAP

Now the shadows flee and vanish. Hymn. William Williams. AngWePo

Now the shiades o' the elems da stratch muore an muore. William Barnes. OBEV

Now the sky begins to turn upon its hub. Heart and Clock. Charles Reznikoff. NAMCP V.1

Now the splendor of the Patriarch's Garden. For Myo's Departure for Anzen-ji. Muso Soseki. EaWin, *tr. by* W. S. Merwin

Now the stars flush with joy. Song to the Mother of the World. Suzanne Ironbiter. HW

Now the summer air exerts its syrupy drag on the half-dark. Archive of Confessions, a Genealogy of Confessions, An. Joshua Clover. NeAmPo

Now the sun is an applegreen blindness through the swells, a white blas on the sea face, flaking and shoaling. Les A. Murray. NAMCP V.2 *Fr.* Buladelah-Taree Holiday Song Cycle, The.

Now the sun's gane out o' sight. Up in the Air. Allan Ramsay. OxBEV

Now the table is set, a covenant to endure. Elf Shots. Peter Riley. Oth

Now the thing the Negro has GOT to do—. View from the Corner. Samuel Allen. SSLK

Now the twin-light of my eyes. Bible, *O.T. See* I will lift up mine eyes unto the hills, from whence cometh my help.

Now the Two Are One. Frederick D'Aguiar. WaCA *Fr.* GDR.

Now the white violet blooms and narcissus that loves. Meleager. HePo

Now the white violet blooms and narcissus that loves. Meleager. HePo, *tr. by* Barbara Hughes Fowler

Now the wings of our thoughts belong to one angel. Angel on the Beach, An. Hamutal Bar Yosef. DTA, *tr. by* Shirley Kaufman

Now Thebes stood in good estate, now Cadmus might thou say. Ovid. *Fr.* Metamorphoses.

Now then. *Yana Oral Tradition.* ASA, *tr. by* Edward Sapir

Now there are gold reflections on the water. In Time of Gold. "H. D." PoA 2002

Now there comes / The Christmas rose. New Year's [*or* Year] Song. Ted Hughes. OBCP

Now there is a slit in the blue fabric of air. Fragments. Stephen Dobyns. CAP-8

Now there is none of the living who can remember. Epitaph for a Concord Boy. Stanley Young. ChAP

Now there is nothing more to strip away. Winter Tree. Im Yŏngjo. CAMKP, *tr. by* Edward W. Poitras

Now there was a man of the Pharisees, named Nicode'mus. Howard Nemerov. GI *Fr.* St. John.

Now there you are sitting in traffic waiting for a gap so you can scoot on. Monday. Nikki Giovanni. InGu

Now there'll be a new mantra, Mother. Najrul Islām. SinGod, *tr. by* Rachel Fell McDermott

Now there's a pause in the journey. Texas Eclogues. Frederick Turner. TiP2

Now they are condemned. Old Gods, The. John Burnside. NeBrP

Now they are old, on dull mornings. May Tree, The. Jean Earle. TCAWP

Now they are resting. Fine Work with Pitch and Copper. William Carlos Williams. OxBoAm

Now! they are ripe, these fruits of a jealous fate. Nocturne. "St.-John Perse." YaTCFP, *tr. by* Richard Howard

Now they have gone. St Brides: Sea-Mail. Don Paterson. NeBrP

Now they tell me I'm like those August children digging. Now They Tell Me. Franck Venaille. YaTCFP, *tr. by* Mary Ann Caws

Now thin mists temper the slow-ripening beams. Garden in September, The. Robert Bridges. OBGa

Now, thirty years on, I shift. Headmaster. John Tripp. AngWePo

Now, this beginning. Nothing. Douglas Lochhead. Coast

Now this happened on one of the nights of utter exhaustion. On a Stone Pillow. Haim Guri. NRoS, *tr. by* Esther Raizen

Now, this is it, the toilsome journey's end. Imre Madách. IQMS *Fr.* Tragedy of Man.

Now this particular girl. Spinster. Sylvia Plath. LW; SoSe-8

Now thise foweles syngen and maken her blisse. *Unknown.* OHMEL

Now thou art dead, no eye shall ever see. Upon His Spaniel[l] Tracie [*or* Tracy]. Robert Herrick. DiBP

Now thou hast lov'd me one whole day. Woman's Constancy. John Donne. NBLV; NOSC

(Now thou hast loved me one whole day.) NoP-4; NoP-5

Now thou hast seen my heart. Was it too near? Confessional, The. Frederick William Faber. CenSon

Now through the ocean in great haste they flunder. Luis de Camões [*or* Camões *or* Camoëns]. OBVE *Fr.* Lusiads, The.

Now tidy your house. Chicago Zen. A. K. Ramanujan. NAMCP V.2

Now Time's Andromeda on this rock rude. Andromeda. Gerard Manley Hopkins. OxAEP-2

Now to a softer theme descends my muse. Stephen Duck. OBGa *Fr.* On Richmond Park.

Now to Aurora, borne by dappled steeds. Walter Savage Landor. NOBRP *Fr.* Gebir.

Now to be clean he must abandon himself. Swan Bathing, The. Ruth Pitter. MoBrPo

Now to depart from all this complication. Departure of the Prodigal Son, The. Rainer Maria Rilke. GI

Now to dispose the dead, the care remains. Homer. OBVE *Fr.* Odyssey.

Now, to tense stillness as the door is slammed. Their Thoughts Cling to Everything They See on the Way. Allen Afterman. NOBAu

Now to the author of *Toldi* my spirit flies through space. To János Arany. Sándor Petőfi. IQMS, *tr. by* Madeline Mason

Now, today, and, my oh my! don't these greens taste good. (LL) First Green of Spring, The. David Budbill. BeAl; GoPo; IPoFL

Now toils the Heroe; trees on trees o'erthrown. Homer. OBVE *Fr.* Odyssey.

Now touch the air softly. Pavane for the Nursery, A. William Jay Smith. MoAmPo

Now trouble comes between the forest's selves. Russian New Year. Bill Berkson. NYP2; PmAP

Now up in Kalu's Temple. Robert Kelly. WhBo *Fr.* Flowers of Unceasing Coincidence, The.

Now useless drapings of a funeral. Albery Allson Whitman. NAAPv.1 *Fr.* Octoroon, The.

Now van to van the foremost squadrons meet. John Dryden. OBWP *Fr.* Annus Mirabilis.

Now war and vengeance claim. Firdowsi. TAL *Fr.* Shahnamah, The.

Now was there made fast by the touris wall. James I, King of Scotland. OBGa

Now we are back to normal, now the mind is. Louis MacNeice. OxAEP-2 *Fr.* Autumn Journal.

Now we are leaving. Issa. SoOfWa, *tr. by* Sam Hamill

Now we are like that flat cone of sand. Yes. Tess Gallagher. StAl

Now we are on the chapter of pleats. House of Dior. Robyn Schiff. LegDan

Now we are silent. Evil Time. Hermann Hesse. IJHIL, tr. by James Wright

Now we enter a strange world, where the Hessian Christmas. After the Industrial Revolution, All Things Happen at Once. Robert Bly. OxBoAm

Now we have heard stories of high valor. Unknown. CABP Fr. Beowulf.

Now we hear the tamarack fall. Coming Out on Solid Ground After the Ice Age. Gary Paul Nabhan. PoCoUp

Now we know what it costs. Summer and Smoke. Manuel Vázquez Montalbán. RaW, tr. by Robert Mezey

Now we must come to the net. Coming to the net (for Arthur Ashe). Brian G. Gilmore. BtF; SpirFl

Now we must praise heaven-kingdom's Guardian. Caedmon's Hymn. Caedmon. NoP-5, tr. by John Pope

Now we must praise the Protector of the heavenly kingdom. Caedmon's Hymn. Caedmon. PoCho, tr. by Unknown

Now we will count to twelve. Keeping Quiet. Pablo Neruda. TWF, tr. by Alastair Reid

Now westward Sol had spent the richest beam[e]s. Music[k]'s Duel[l]. Richard Crashaw. NAEL-7v1; NPeEn

Now what have I to live for. (LL) Long Time Back, A. Unknown. EaWin; WoPoe, tr. by J. Moussaieff Masson and W. S. Merwin

Now what my mother told me one day as we sat at dinner together. Walt Whitman. BLT Fr. Sleepers, The.

Now, when he and I meet, after all these years. Bitch. Carolyn Kizer. GifTon; OxBoAm; PoA 2002; StAl

Now when I walk around at lunchtime. Personal Poem. Frank O'Hara. CAP-8; CLPP; OxBoAm; PmAP

'Now when King Offa was alive and dead', they were. Geoffrey Hill. NPeEn Fr. Mercian Hymns.

Now, when the rustic wears the social smile. Henry Kirke White. STuOW Fr. Clifton Grove.

Now when the solemn Rites of Pray'r were past. Homer. OBVE Fr. Iliad, The.

Now when we had gone down again to the sea and our vessel. Homer. WaAnP Fr. Odyssey.

Now, whether it were by peculiar grace. William Wordsworth. UV Fr. Resolution and Independence.

Now why must I disturb a dream of bliss. Leigh Hunt. Fr. Story of Rimini, The.

Now whyle Hippomenes/ Debates theis things. Ovid. OBVE Fr. Metamorphoses.

Now will I open unto thee—whose heart. Unknown. TAL Fr. Bhagavad-Gita, The.

Now will we plunge into the frigid dark. Autumn Song. Charles Baudelaire. SxFrPo, tr. by James McGowan

Now wilt me take for Jesus' sake. Prayer, A. Katharine Tynan Hinkson. SacPr

Now wind torments the field. February: Thinking of Flowers. Jane Kenyon. LoL

Now winter downs the dying of the year. Year's End. Richard Wilbur. GoPo; HeIP-4; MoW

Now Winter Nights. Robert Hass. BodElec

Now Winter Nights Enlarge. Thomas Campion. NAEL-7v1; NoP-4; NoP-5; NPeEn; OxAEP-1; OxBEV; PBRV; PtR

(Winter Nights.) NOSC

Now winter's standing at the door. Winter. Yuri Suhl. Prolet, tr. by Amelia Glaser

Now, with your palms on the blades of my shoulders. Dead Still. Andrey Andreievich Voznesensky. PasH, tr. by Richard Wilbur

Now wither all earth's gallantries! Autumn. Mihály Tompa. IQMS, tr. by Watson Kirkconnell

Now wolde I fayn som myrthes make. A. Godwin. OHMEL

Now won't you listen, honey, while I say. After You've Gone. Henry Creamer. ReLy

Now / you are / a mirror. Bloom-Girl. Unknown. SonAtl, tr. by Alan Brierly and B. Ouane

Now you are a priest. Priest. "H. D."

Now you are going, what can I do but wish you. Poet's Farewell to His Teeth, The. William Dickey. PoA 2002

Now you aren't here I find. Mansize. Maura Dooley. NeBl

Now you have burned your books, you'll go with nothing. Ghazal 37. John Thompson. Coast

Now you have come. Foot-Washing, The. A. R. Ammons. ChIV-2

Now you have freely given me leave to love. To a Lady That Desired I Would Love Her. Thomas Carew. BASC; CavPo

Now you hear what the house has to say. Insomnia. Dana Gioia. AWTN

Now you lean across the table, fingers. Malleus Maleficarum 4. Maureen Seaton. ExTi

Now you look down. The waters of childhood are there. (LL) Where Are the Waters of Childhood? Mark Strand. EmeKit; EMP; VCAP; WeW-3

Now you may rest forever. To Himself. Giacomo Leopardi. NAWM-7v2, tr. by Ottavio M. Casale

Now you nerve. Flurred, avid as the raw. Sonnet. Karen Volkman. IAoNAP

Now you see it: the autumn of me. Lear Expands His Last Words to Cordelia. Sheryl Cornett. IaFF

Now you take ol Rufus. He beat drums. For Freckle-Faced Gerald. Etheridge Knight. ESEAA

Now you think that is right, sah? Talk the truth. Carpenter's Complaint, The. Edward Baugh. OBCoV

Now your grave is sinking. Rainbow-Colored Whale, The. Ferenc Juhász. WoPoe, tr. by David Wevill

Now you've made. Jo Shapcott. MoWP Fr. Roses, The.

Nowadays. Fred Ebb. ReLy

Nowadays. Tushar Roy. WoPoe, tr. by Ron D. K. Banerjee

Nowadays it's rather nobby. I've a Shooting Box in Scotland. Cole Porter. NAAPv.2

Nowe, Parott, my swete byrde, speke owte yet ons agayn. John Skelton. See Now, Parrot, my sweet bird, speak our yet once again.

Nowel, el, el, el, el! Unknown. OHMEL

Nowell Sing We. Unknown. ChrPo

Nowell sing we, both all and some. Nowell Sing We. Unknown. ChrPo

Nowhere else but on the mouth. How He Should Like to Be Kissed. Paul Fleming. GePo, tr. by Harold B. Segel

Nowhere in this world have I a home. Basho 3. Cees Nooteboom. TuT, tr. by Michael O'Loughlin

Nowhere, nowhere is there any trace of blood. No Sign of Blood. Faiz Ahmad Faiz. AF, tr. by Naomi Lazard

Nowhere on this earth. Each Step. Jane Hirshfield. WhBo

Now—I cannot get warm: slowing. This August's Phloxes. Gennady Aygi. WoBe, tr. by Peter France

Nowness and nowness sings the crow. Michael Palmer. APSN

No-Word Hut. Muso Soseki. EaWin, tr. by W. S. Merwin

Now's the Time for Love. Sait Faik. NaPG, tr. by Talat Sait Halman

Now—wagon full of thunder. Wagon Full of Thunder. Louis Oliver. HATNAP

Nox Nocti Indicat Scientiam. William Habington. BASC; NPeEn; OBEV; OxBEV Fr. Castara.

Nox was lit by lux of Luna, The. Carmen Possum. Unknown. NBLV

Noye, to me thou arte full able. Unknown. InvLi Fr. Noah's Flood.

Ntozake Shange's Broadway opening. Broadway Opening. Miguel Algarin. PueRic

Nu. Melvin B. Tolson. NAMCP V.1 Fr. Harlem Gallery.

Nu sculon herigean heofonrices weard. Cædmon's Hymn, West Saxon Version. Caedmon. NoP-5

Nuair a bha mi òg. Oideadhadh Ceart. Aonghas MacNeacail. EdScPo

Nuair a ràinig sinn an t-eilean. An dàrna eilean. Derick Thomson. EdScPo

Nuance. Amy Lowell. NAAPv.2

Nub. Chris Wallace-Crabbe. BMAP

Nubarrones, runas echadas. Cachorros, Los. Pura López Colomé. RMCMP

Nubbed leaves, The. Artichoke. Robin Robertson. NeBrP

Nuchal, a Fragment. Thomas Kinsella. PBCIP

Nuchika torichibi, in Orok, small dream. The newspaper clipping where. Fujii Sadakazu. PFTM-2 Fr. Where is Japanese Poetry?

Nuclear ecstasy on the picket line. Cheap Replicas of the Eiffel Tower. Elton Glaser. PBCAP

Nuclear Peril. Pinkie Gordon Lane. BtF

Nuclear Umbrella. Heberto Padilla. AF, tr. by Alastair Reid

Nuclear Winter. Thomas McGrath. AtGh; GifTon

Nuclear Winter. Edward Nobles. P180

Nuclear Winter. Nicholas Samaras. AtGh

Nude by Edward Hopper, A. Lisel Mueller. PoSol

Nude Descending a Staircase. X. J. Kennedy. NIP-4; PoA 2002

Nude on a Horsehair Sofa by the Sea. Matthea Harvey. IAoNAP

Nude Womon Spotted in Cappuccino Cup as Advertising Dollar co-opts another life. Bahiyyih Maroon. SpirFl

Nudes. Rodney Jones. MAAN

Nudes—stark and glistening. Louse Hunting. Isaac Rosenberg. FaBoWar; NAEL-6v2; NAEL-7v2; NAMCP V.1; NoAM; NoP-4; NoP-5; OxAEP-2; OxBEV

Nudity. Gabriella Sica. CItWP, tr. by Cinzia Sartini Blum and Lara Trubowitz

Nudo de Claridad. Miguel Algarin. PmAP

Nuestro Marine. Elaine Romero. RWB

Nueva York. Oficina y Denuncia. Federico García Lorca. RaW

Nuit Blanche, La. Rudyard Kipling. MoBrPo; UV

Nuit Blanche, Une. Emily Warn. FiBr

Nuit est ma nudité, La. Georges Bataille. YaTCFP

Nuits partagées.   Paul Éluard.
 "Je m'obstine à mêler des fictions aux redoutables réalités."   YaTCFP
Nul seigneur je n'appelle, et pas de clarté dans la nuit.   Amen.   Jacques Réda.
 YaTCFP
Nullarbor.   William Hart-Smith.   BMAP
Nullo.   Jean Toomer.   APT-2
Numb to Number.   Tina Darragh and P. Inman.   Eno
Number 1 bus jerks to a stop at Mass. Ave., The.   Untitled.   Eli Goodwin.
 BtF
No. 6.   Charles Bukowski.   P180
#6 Sepulveda.   Harryette Mullen.   RD
Number in the boxhouse registry, A.   Beyond fences.   Mafika Pascal Gwala.
 TSAP
Number of positions to take with respect to the present, A.   Form of Chiasmus;
 The Chiasmus of Forms, The.   Michael Davidson.   PmAP
Number Our Days.   Norbert Hirschhorn.   BloBone
Number, Weight, and Measure.   Abraham Cowley.   NOSC
Numberless are the world's wonders, but none.   Sophocles.   BLPJKO Fr.
 Antigone.
Numbers.   Bible, O.T. tr. by William Tyndale
 Balaam's Blessing.   OBVE
Numbers: "I like the generosity of numbers."   Mary.   P180; PoDa
Numbers: "My father taught me to measure."   Allison Joseph.   NeAmPo
Numbers from one to ten, however, are called.   God.   Annie Dillard.   UpMys
Numbers, Letters.   Imamu Amiri Baraka.   PFTM-2
Numbing current of the Demerol, The.   Tom Sleigh.   InoFa Fr. Work, The.
Numeri XIII.   John Hall.   ChIV-1
Numerology.   Jerome Rothenberg.   FTOS
Numerology.   David Wheatley.   NIrP
Numerous host of dreaming saints succeed, A.   John Dryden.   OBSV Fr.
 Absalom and Achitophel.
Numinous, golden as Cappadocian bishops.   Sunflowers at Prime.   Tim
 Lilburn.   OpeFie
Nun Takes the Veil, A.   Bernard O'Donoghue.   ModIr
Nun went past, and her girdle swung, A.   From a Travel Diary.   T. H. Parry-
 Williams.   BBMWP, tr. by Anthony Conran
Nunc Puer Nobis Natus Est.   James Ryman.   SacPr
Nunc Viridant Segetes.   Sedulius Scottus.   NAWM-5v1, tr. by Helen Waddell
Nungesser und Coli Sind Verreckt.   Benjamin Péret.   AF, tr. by Keith
 Hollaman
Nun's Dance, The.   Cho Chihun.   CAMKP, tr. by Kevin O'Rourke
Nuns fret not at their convent's narrow room.   Sonnet.   William Wordsworth.
 BrAP; CenSon; GSo; NIL-7; NIP-4; NoP-4; OBEV
Nuns Go Walking.   Aldo Palazzeschi.   PFTM-1
Nuns of Childhood, The: Two Views.   Maxine W. Kumin.   FFC; WaAnP
Nun's Priest's [or Nonne Preestes] Tale, The.   Geoffrey Chaucer.   NAEL-6v1;
 NAEL-7v1 Fr. Canterbury Tales, The.
Nu-plastik Fanfare Red.   Judith Rodriguez.   BMAP
Nuptial Dialogues.   Edward Ward.
 Dialogue between a Squeamish Cotting Mechanic and His Sluttish Wife, in
 the Kitchen.   WaAnP
Nuptial Eve, A.   Sydney Thompson Dobell.
 Ballad of Keith of Ravelston, The.   OBEV
Nuptial Material.   Pablo Neruda.   ConPit, tr. by Clayton Eshleman
6a: Nuptial Sleep.   Dante Gabriel Rossetti.   NAEL-6v2; NAEL-7v2 Fr. House
 of Life, The.
Nuremberg.   Kenneth Slessor.   BMAP
Nurse, The.   Dorianne Laux.   PoDa
Nurse, The.   R. Gerallt Jones.   BBMWP, tr. by Robert Minhinnick
Nurse a terror theory back.   Principles, When I Felt Them.   Prageeta Sharma.
 HeMarv
Nurse grits her teeth, stubs out the cigarette, The. (LL)   David Wojahn.
 PBCAP; SwNoth Fr. Mystery Train: A Sequence.
Nurse speaks of christmas, The.   Jerry Kilbride.   WhBo
Nurse was in a hospital, A.   Syllabling.   Sean O Riordain.   ModIr, tr. by
 Patrick Crotty
Nurse Whitman.   Sharon Olds.   ViWalt
Nursed on the blood of your inheritance. (LL)   America, I Do Not Call Your
 Name Without Hope.   Pablo Neruda.   AF; TCLAP, tr. by Robert Bly
Nurse-life Wheat within his greene huske growing, The.   Fulke, 1st Baron
 Brooke Greville.   NoP-4; NoP-5 Fr. Caelica.
Nursery.   No Hyangnim.   EcSo, tr. by Aimee N. Kwon
Nursery Rhyme.   Gavin Ewart.   UV
Nursery Rhyme.   Kit Robinson.   FTOS
Nursery Rhyme.   May Sarton.   NOxBChV
Nursery Rhyme in Eight Strophes.   Rossana Ombres.   CItWP, tr. by Cinzia
 Sartini Blum and Lara Trubowitz
Nursery Rhyme of Innocence and Experience.   Charles Causley.   NOxBChV

Nursery Song.   Anna Wickham.   NOxBChV
Nursery Vignette.   Edmund Wilson.   OBCoV Fr. Easy Exercises in the Use of
 Difficult Words.
Nurses.   Julia Darling.   PoCu
Nurses, The.   Rudyard Kipling.   NoAM Fr. Land and Sea Tales.
Nurse's Dole in the Medea, The.   Lord Byron.   OBVE
Nurse's Song ("When the voices of children are heard on the green.")   William
 Blake.   NAEL-6v2; NAEL-7v2; NPBRoP; RACG Fr. Songs of Innocence.
Nurse's Song ("When the voices of children are heard on the green / And
 whisperings [or whisprings] are in the dale.")   William Blake.   NPBRoP;
 PtR Fr. Songs of Experience.
Nursing her child.   Issa.   EH, tr. by Robert Hass
Nursing her I felt alive.   Ardor.   Donald Hall.   CAP-8
Nursing Home, 3rd Shift.   David Craig.   UpMys
Nursing the Sunburn.   Judith Vollmer.   SwNoth
Nursling.   Kathleen Ossip.   BeAl; PoCho
Nurture.   Maxine W. Kumin.   CAP-8; PoA 2002
Nushu.   Margaret Randall.   ICANM
Nut, The / Ripens on the tree.   Mandala.   Yamamura Bochō.   CAoMJL1, tr.
 by Leith Morton
Nut Castle.   John Ashbery.   VaPo
Nut-brown maid of Grasmere plays, The.   Eclogue: Clerk of the Weather.
 William Scammell.   NLP
Nut-brown Maid, The.   Unknown.   NoSic; OBEV
Nuthatch.   David Wagoner.   OWoS
Nuts in May.   Louis MacNeice.   MoBrPo
Nutting.   John Clare.   CenSon
Nutting.   William Wordsworth.   NAEL-6v2; NAEL-7v2; NOBRP; WaAnP
Nuu dxi rirayá gueela nua sicarú.   Natalia.   Natalia Toledo.   RMCMP
Nü-yue ji-ming: The Cock Is Crawin' (scoticè).   Unknown.   CCL1, tr. by
 James Legge
Nwinnng buht nawuNNN baheegwinnng. (LL)   12th Horse Song of Frank
 Mitchell (Blue), The.   Frank Mitchell.   APSN; FTOS, tr. by Jerome
 Rothenberg
N-word, The.   Evie Shockley.   BRtP
Nymph and shepherd raise electric tridents.   Chances "R."   Allen Ginsberg.
 CAGL
Nymph and swain, Sheelah and Dermot hight, A.   Pastoral Dialogue, A.
 Jonathan Swift.   IrLP
Nymph Complaining for the Death of Her Faun [or Fawn], The.   Andrew
 Marvell.   BASC; HeIP-4; NAEL-6v1; NAEL-7v1; RACG
Nymph Fanarett, supposed to be.   Penance, A.   Francis Daniel Pastorius.
 NOSC
Nymph of the Fountain to Charlotte, The.   Anne Grant.   PoBW
Nymph turnd home, The. He fell to felling downe.   Homer.   OBVE Fr.
 Odyssey.
Nymphidia.   Michael Drayton.
 (Queen Mab's Chariot.)   NPeEn
Nymphs and Shepherds dance no more.   John Milton.   OxBEV Fr. Arcades.
Nymph's [or Nimphs] Reply to the [Passionate] Shepherd [or Sheepheard], The.
 Sir Walter Ralegh.   AEP; AmFaPo; BrAP; CABP; ClHu; HeIP-4; NAEL-
 6v1; NAEL-7v1; NBLV; NIL-7; NIP-4; NoP-4; NoP-5; NoSic; NPeEn;
 PoPoPo; RACG; TFi; TRP; UV; WaAnP; WeW-3
 (Her Reply.)   BLPJKO; OBEV
Nymph's Secret, A.   Ben Jonson.   OBEV
Nymph's Song to Hylas, The.   William Morris.   OBEV
Nyogen Senzaki, the erstwhile Zen teacher.   Picking Up Stones.   Lawson
 Fusao Inada.   WANABP
Nyooz. belt up. (LL)   Tom Leonard.   NePenScot; NPeEn Fr. Unrelated
 Incidents.
NyQuil.   Raymond Carver.   LaCa
Nyx.   Catherine Pozzi.   YaTCFP, tr. by Mary Ann Caws
Nyx.   Catherine Pozzi.   YaTCFP

O

Ö.   Rita Dove.   StAl; WeW-3
O a gallant set were they.   Huguenot, A.   Mary Elizabeth Coleridge.   SacPr
O Adam, where are you?   What a Trying Time.   Unknown.   SSUS
O Africa, where I baked my bread.   Lance Jeffers.   OxAAAP
O! Africans! Here I sing you.   When Africa Speaks.   Jude Chudi Okpala.   BtF
O All Down within the Pretty Meadow.   Kenneth Patchen.   WeW-3
O all the problems other people face.   Alcoholic.   John Berryman.   BodElec
O all ye nations of the Lord.   Thomas Norton.   SacPr
O all you lands, the treasures of your joy.   Bible, O.T.   CABP Fr. Psalms.
O! And I forsooth in love!   William Shakespeare.   OBCoV Fr. Love's
 Labour's Lost.

O another deluge of wind and rain.   Cathedral in the Thrashing Rain. Takamura Kotaro.   CAoMJL1, *tr.* by Hiroaki Sato

O Antioch, my Antioch, my city!   Henry Wadsworth Longfellow.   AWPTFC *Fr.* Judas Maccabaeus.

O antique city on St. Lawrence shore.   Quebec.   Henrietta Cordelia Ray. CBWP-3

O anti-verdurous phallic were'n not for your pouring height.   Ode to Coit Tower.   Gregory Corso.   CLPP

O Aridon, bring back my wealth.   Fate of Vultures, The.   Tanure Ojaide. NAfrP

O Art, high gift of Heaven! how oft defamed.   Art.   Washington Allston. APN-1

O Artemis of Delos and lovely Ortygia.   Nossis.   SaLy, *tr.* by Diane Rayor

O Autumn! how I love thy pensive air.   Written in Autumn.   Mary Tighe. CenSon; OxBSo

O Autumn, laden with fruit, and stained.   To Autumn.   William Blake. NAEL-6v2; NAEL-7v2

O autumn winds.   Issa.   SoOfWa, *tr.* by Sam Hamill

O autumn winds.   Prince Shiki.   SoOfWa, *tr.* by Sam Hamill

O Baba! Look at this Cadak tree.   Dīnrām.   SinGod, *tr.* by Rachel Fell McDermott

O barbarous Corsica, locked in by crags.   Seneca.   RomPo, *tr.* by J. P. Sullivan

O bards! weak heritors of passion and of pain!   Miserimus.   Adah Isaacs Menken.   CBWP-1

O be swift.   Helmsman, The.   "H. D."   GPTC; OxBoAm

O! bear me witness, night.   William Shakespeare.   OxAEP-1 *Fr.* Antony and Cleopatra.

O beato solitudo! where have I flown to?   High.   Philip Lamantia.   CalPo

O beauteous God! uncircumscribed treasure.   Prayer, A.   Jeremy Taylor. SacPr

O beautiful adolescent, O young man.   Lanza 51.   Filippo Scarlatti.   CAGL, *tr.* by James J. Wilhelm

O beautiful for spacious skies.   America the Beautiful.   Katharine Lee Bates. APN-2; BLPJKO; FaBoA; HHAm; OxBoAm

O beech, unbind your yellow leaf, for deep.   Ghostly Tree.   Léonie Adams. APT-2; MoAmPo

O beloved of my twenty-seven senses, I.   Anna Blume.   Kurt Schwitters. NAWM-7v2, *tr.* by David Britt

O Best of All Nights, Return and Return Again.   James Laughlin.   GifTon

O Bid Me Not to Wander.   Susanna Blamire.   NPBRoP

O bird crying on the acacia tree, alike are our sorrows.   Andalusian Exile, An. Ahmad Shauqi.   BBASP, *tr.* by M. Mustafa Badawi and John Heath-Stubbs

O Black and unknown bards of long ago.   O Black and Unknown Bards. James Weldon Johnson.   APT-1; ColAP; HeIP-4; NAAPv.1; NAMCP V.1; OxBoAm; TCAPo; WaAnP

O Blanca Virgen.   *Peralta Family Oral Tradition.*   ASA

O blessed breeding sun! draw from the earth.   William Shakespeare.   OxAEP-1 *Fr.* Timon of Athens.

O blessed Solitude. (LL)   Woman Alone, A.   Denise Levertov.   BodElec; MoWP

O blest unfabled incense tree.   George Darley.   OBEV *Fr.* Nepenthe.

O blest with Taste, with Genius blest.   Moods 3.   William Parsons.   STuOW

O blithe New-comer! I have heard.   To the Cuckoo.   William Wordsworth. NOBRP; NPBRoP; UV

O blonde thing! (LL)   Sylvia's Death.   Anne Sexton.   InoFa; NAAL-5; NALW

O Bonnie Man, Lovely Man.   Meg Bateman.   EdScPo

O born in days when wits were fresh and clear.   Matthew Arnold.   OxBEV *Fr.* Scholar Gypsy, The.

O boss of ashes boss of dust.   Maurice Manning.   LegDan

O breake my hart quoth he, O breake and dye.   Michael Drayton.   CAGL *Fr.* Piers Gaveston [1619].

O Britain, infamous for suicide!   Edward Young.   STuOW *Fr.* Night Thoughts.

O Brothers, don't Get Weary.   *Unknown.*   SSUS

O brothers mine, take care! Take care!   White Witch, The.   James Weldon Johnson.   APT-1

O brothers mine, today we stand.   Fifty Years.   James Weldon Johnson.   InGu

O, but how white is white, white from shadows come.   Music of Colours: The Blossom Scattered.   Vernon Watkins.   AngWePo

O but the wind is keen.   My Cloth of Gold.   Ina Coolbrith.   SWaP

O but we talked at large before.   Sixteen Dead Men.   William Butler Yeats. OBWP

O Caledonia! stern and wild.   Sir Walter Scott.   NePenScot *Fr.* Lay of the Last Minstrel, The.

O Calendar of the Century.   Melvin B. Tolson.   APT-2 *Fr.* Libretto for the Republic of Liberia.

O Canada!   G. C. Waldrep.   LegDan

O Captain! my Captain! our fearful trip is done.   Walt Whitman.   AmWaPo; APN-1; BRP; CBCWP; ChAP; HHAm; MakPoe; MoAmPo; PCW; SAmP; TCAPo; TFi *Fr.* Memories of President Lincoln.

O Carib Isle!   Hart Crane.   APT-2; NoAM; OxBoAm; PFTM-1

O Carmelita, know ye not.   Carmelita.   Mirabeau Buonaparte Lamar.   TiP2

O casket of sweet sounds, wherein there lieth.   To a Piano.   Mary Elizabeth Coleridge.   OxBSo

O caterpillar, daughter of the butterfly.   Svetlana Ivanova.   CRWP, *tr.* by Jenefer Coates

O Chatterton, how very sad thy fate!   To Chatterton.   John Keats.   CenSon

O chief director of the growing race.   Ad Quintilianum.   Martial.   RomPo, *tr. by* Robert Louis Stevenson

O Child, Do Not Fear the Dark and Sleep's Dark Possession.   Delmore Schwartz.   NOxBChV

O child, when you go down to sleep and sleep's secession.   O Child, Do Not Fear the Dark and Sleep's Dark Possession.   Delmore Schwartz. NOxBChV

O Christ of God! whose life and death.   Vesta.   John Greenleaf Whittier. SacPr

O Christ, our hope, our heart's desire, Redeption's only spring!   *Unknown.* SacPr, *tr. by* John Chandler

O Christ, who in Gethsemane.   Prayer.   Henrietta Cordelia Ray.   CBWP-3

O city ladies.   George Oppen.   APT-2; PFTM-1

O city metropole, isle riverain!   Montreal.   Abraham Moses Klein.   BrAP

O Come, All Ye Faithful.   *Unknown.*   SacPr, *tr. by* Frederick Oakeley

O come my brethren and sisters too.   On to Glory.   *Unknown.*   SSUS

O come, O come, Emmanuel.   *Unknown.*   SacPr, *tr. by* John Mason Neale

O Come Quickly!   Thomas Campion.   NPeEn; OBEV; OxAEP-1

O! come quickly, glorious Lord, and raise my spright to thee. (LL)   O Come Quickly!   Thomas Campion.   NPeEn; OBEV; OxAEP-1

O come, soft rest of cares, come Night.   George Chapman.   OBEV *Fr.* Hero and Leander.

O come, thou Wisdom from on high.   *Unknown.*   RSR

O come to me in my dreams love!   Lines to———.   Mary Weston Fordham. CBWP-2

O Come to My Heart, Lord Jesus.   Emily E. S. Elliott.   SacPr

O Constellations of the early night.   Constellations, The.   William Cullen Bryant.   APN-1

O cord of life!   Princess Shokushi.   ArkPo, *tr. by* Robert H. Brower and Earl Miner

O could I flow like thee, and make thy stream.   Sir John Denham.   NPeEn *Fr.* Cooper's Hill.

O could I sing as you have fought.   Edward Young.   STuOW *Fr.* Foreign Address, The.

O coupon life.   Psychic Killed by Train.   Ron Overton.   PrTe

O courteous Christkind guest, most gracious host.   To a Crucifix.   Anna Wickham.   MoBrPo

O Courtesy, O Harborage Most Sweet.   Luís De León.   SpanPo, *tr. by* Brenda M. Sackett

O courtesy, O harborage most sweet.   O Courtesy, O Harborage Most Sweet. Luís De León.   SpanPo, *tr. by* Brenda M. Sackett

O crownless soul of Ishmael!   Hemlock in the Furrows.   Adah Isaacs Menken. CBWP-1

O cruel Death, give three things back.   Three Things.   William Butler Yeats. OBMV

O cruel Love! on thee I lay.   John Lyly.   NoSic *Fr.* Sapho and Phao.

O Cuckoo! shall I call thee Bird.   To the Cuckoo.   F. H. Townsend.   UV

O Cuckoo! shall I call thee Bird.   Examination Question.   *Unknown.*   OBCoV

O cuckoo that sang to us and art fled.   Lament for the Cuckoo.   Alcuin. NAWM-5v1

O cupbearer, our complaints are addressed to you; we have called upon you even though you do not listen!   Muhammad ibn Abd al-Malik Ibn Zuhr. HiArP, *tr. by* James T. Monroe

O Daniel.   *Unknown.*   SSUS

O darkness, mine! I shall always be a Finn. (LL)   James Tate.   EmeKit; OxBoAm *Fr.* I Am A Finn.

O David, highest in the list.   Christopher Smart.   NPeEn; OxBEV *Fr.* Song to David, A.

O David, if I had.   That Harp You Play So Well.   Marianne Moore.   MoAmPo

O Day! he cannot die.   Death Scene, A.   Emily Jane Brontë.   OxAEP-2

O Day of Rest and Gladness.   Christopher Wordsworth.   SacPr

O de Lamb done been down here an' died.   Sinner Won't Die No More. *Unknown.*   SSUS

O de vinter, O de vinter, O de vinter 'll soon be ober, chilen.   Winter, The. *Unknown.*   SSUS

O dea certe! (LL)   Edmund Spenser.   NAEL-6v1; NoP-5; OBEV *Fr.* Shepherd's Calender, The.

O dear! How disgusting is life!   Edward Lear.   NOxBChV

O Death in Life, the days that are no more! (LL) Alfred Tennyson. CABP; CtM; NAEL-6v2; NAEL-7v2; NIL-7; NIP-4; NoP-4; NoP-5; OxAEP-2; OxBEV; PoPoPo; TFi; TreFP Fr. Princess, The.

O Death! thou dauntless vanquisher of earth. Robert Montgomery. STuOW Fr. Omnipresence of the Deity, The.

O Death! where is thy Sting? (LL) Ode: The Dying Christian to His Soul. Alexander Pope. ChIV-2; SacPr

O Death! Why dost thou steal the great. In Memoriam Frederick Douglass. Eloise Bibb. CBWP-4

O deep, creating Light. Gordon Bottomley. MoBrPo Fr. Suilven and the Eagle.

O Deep of Heaven, 'tis thou alone art boundless. Night Sky, The. GSo

O Dieu, Purifiez nos coeurs! Night Litany. Ezra Pound. TCAPo

O, dim, forsaken mirror! Mirror in the Deserted Hall, The. Felicia Dorothea Hemans. NOBRP

O distant, distant; deep unapproachable; receive always. Distant, The. Yannis Ritsos. VCWP, tr. by Edmund Keeley

O Divine Mother. Prayer to the Divine Mother, A. Andrew Harvey. HW

O do, Lord, remember me! Lord, Remember Me! Unknown. APN-2

O do not disturb the Archbishop. Archbishop, The. Dana Gioia. OxBoAm

O do you see the waters of the Yellow River pouring. Fragmented Address to the FBI. Diane Di Prima. BB

O Donald! Ye Are Just the Man. Susanna Blamire. LW

O Donal[l] Oge, if you go across the sea. Donal[l] Oge [or Og]: Grief of a Girl's Heart. Augusta, Lady Gregory. IrLP, tr. by Augusta, Lady Gregory and Lady Gregory

O Donall Oge, if you will go across the sea. O Donall Oge : The Grief of a Girl's Heart. Irish Oral Tradition. IrV, tr. by Eleanor Hull

O Donall Oge : The Grief of a Girl's Heart. Irish Oral Tradition. IrV, tr. by Eleanor Hull

O don't you see the waters of the Yellow River pouring. Bring On the Wine. Li Po. CCL1, tr. by Elling O. Eide

O doves of the arāk and the bān trees; take pity; to not redouble my sorrows with [your] mourning. Ibn al-Arabi. HiArP, tr. by James T. Monroe

O! Drimin donn dílis! the landlord has come. Drimin Donn Dílis. John Walsh. IrV

O Duty / Why hast thou not the visage of a sweetie or a cutie? Kind of an Ode to Duty. Ogden Nash. AmWit

O early one morning I walked out like Agag. Streets of Laredo, The. Louis MacNeice. FaBoWar; OBWP

O Earth, adore creative power. Creation. Mary Weston Fordham. CBWP-2

O earth, if it is earth, O earth all-in-daylight where we came. For Mycea. Édouard Glissant. YaTCFP, tr. by Brent Hayes Edwards

O Earth, lie heavily upon her eyes. Rest. Christina Georgina Rossetti. GSo; OBEV

O Earth, unhappy planet born to die. Edna St. Vincent Millay. HeIP-4 Fr. Epitaph for the Race of Man.

O / Elevator for America. Noon—A Certain. Yi Sang. CAMKP, tr. by Edward Mack

O English mother, in the ruddy glow. In Snow. William Allingham. OxBSo

O Eros of the mountains, of the earth. Eros. Michael Field. NAEL-7v2; VWP

O Eros, silently smiling one, hear me. Hymn to Eros. Denise Levertov. LW

O Eve. Rosemary C. Hildebrandt. PuP-23

O Eve. That rubricose ball is no apple. Plump fist rubbing rub. O Eve. Rosemary C. Hildebrandt. PuP-23

O, ever dear! thy precious, vital powers. Sonnet 31. Anna Seward. PoBW

O evil Angel, set me free! (LL) Clever Woman, A. Mary Elizabeth Coleridge. ViWPN; VWP

O faithful eyes, day after day as I see and know you—unswerving faithful and beautiful—going about your ordinary work unnoticed. Edward Carpenter. CAGL Fr. Towards Democracy.

O faithless world, and thy more faithless part. Poem Written by Sir Henry Wotton, in His Youth, A. Sir Henry Wotton. NoSic

O false and treacherous probability. Fulke, 1st Baron Brooke Greville. SacPr Fr. Caelica.

O famished Prodigal, in vain. Echo. John Banister Tabb. APN-2

O fan of white silk. Pan Chieh-yû. See Fan of white silk, A.

O fare you well, my brudder, fare you well by de grace of God. Fare Ye Well. Unknown. SSUS

O! farewell, my country—my kindred—my lover. Exile of Erin, The. Unknown. NOBAu

O far-off rose of long ago. Far-Off Rose, A. Josephine Preston Peabody. TCAPo

O farther, farther, farther sail! (LL) Passage to India. Walt Whitman. APN-1; NAAPv.1; NCAP

O Father, I acknowledge, Job replied. Bible, O.T. ChIV-1 Fr. Paraphrase Upon Job, A.

O fickle muse, feather ball tossed between men, you come when you want to. Matthea Harvey. IAoNAP Fr. Thermae.

O finicky cat. Richard Wright. APT-2

O flea! whatever you do. Issa. EH, tr. by Robert Hass

O fleece, billowing even down the neck! Head of Hair. Charles Baudelaire. SxFrPo, tr. by James McGowan

O fleece, that down the neck waves to the nape! Her Hair. Charles Baudelaire. NAWM-7v2, tr. by Dorren Bell

O Florida, Venereal Soil. Wallace Stevens. NAAPv.2; TCAPo

O flowers, strewn today. Song of Tuṣita Heaven. Wŏlmyŏng, Master. CATKP, tr. by Peter H. Lee

O Flowery Mountain slopes. On the Slope of Hua Mountain. Unknown. WoPoe, tr. by Chung Ling and Kenneth Rexroth

O foolish tears, go back! In Vain. Adah Isaacs Menken. CBWP-1

O foolish wisdom sought in books! Longing. Ina Coolbrith. SWaP

O foot, O leg, O thighs for which I rightly died. Philodemus. HePo Fr. Epigrams.

O! [or Oh] for a bowl of fat canary. John Lyly. NoSic Fr. Alexander and Campaspe.

O for a Muse of fire, that would ascend. William Shakespeare. OxAEP-1 Fr. King Henry V.

O, for my sake do you with Fortune chide. William Shakespeare. OxAEP-1 Fr. Sonnets.

O for ten years, that I may overwhelm. John Keats. NAEL-6v2; NAEL-7v2; NPBRoP Fr. Sleep and Poetry.

O for that warning voice which he who saw. John Milton. NAEL-6v1; NAWM-7v1; NoP-5; OxAEP-1 Fr. Paradise Lost.

O Friend! I know not which way I must look. Written in London, September, 1802. William Wordsworth. SacPr

O friend, understand: the body. Mirabai. WPoS

O friends, I am mad. Mirabai. WPoS

O friends on this Path. Mirabai. WPoS

O, from what power hast thou this powerful might. William Shakespeare. OxAEP-1 Fr. Sonnets.

O, fruitful district Corozal! Nostalgia. Dolores B. Lin. OWABP

O furrowed plaintive face. Hurrier, The. Harold Monro. MoBrPo

O gay thrush! (LL) Thrush in the syringa sings, A. Basil Bunting. HarvBoo; WoPoe

O generation of the thoroughly smug. Salutation. Ezra Pound. HeIP-4; MoAmPo; NAAPv.2; OxBoAm

O gentle Sleep, come, wave thine opiate wing. On Dreams, October 15, 1782. Sir Samuel Egerton Brydges. CenSon

O girl picking cotton in a long dense field. Transplanting Song. Korean Oral Tradition. CATKP, tr. by Peter H. Lee

O give me a home where the buffalo roam. Unknown. See Oh give me a home where the buffalo roam.

O glorious dump, how shall I sing your praise! Dump, The. Yelena Shwarts. ItGoST, tr. by Catriona Kelly and Michael Molnar

O God. Else Lasker-Schüler. BBASP, tr. by Robert P. Newton

O God, / I have bound myself to you to the exclusion of all else. Kwaja Abdullah Ansari. BBASP Fr. Intimate Conversations with God.

O God, in the dream the terrible horse began. Dream, The. Louise Bogan. MoAmPo; NALW; NoAM

O God, my dream! I dreamed that you were dead. On the Threshold. Amy Levy. LW

O God! O Montreal! Samuel Butler. OBSV

O God, O Venus, O Mercury, patron of thieves. Lake Isle, The. Ezra Pound. OBCoV; OxBoAm; PoA 2002

O God of Hosts, thine Ear incline. Hymn. Unknown. NOBRP

O god of spring forgive me. Pete Winslow. CLPP

O God, where do they tend—these struggling aims? Robert Browning. SacPr Fr. Pauline [or Pauline; A Fragment of a Confession].

O God, why hast thou thus. Bible, O.T. BASC Fr. Psalms.

O Goddess! hear these tuneless numbers, wrung. Ode to Psyche. John Keats. NAEL-6v2; NAEL-7v2; NOBRP; NoP-4; NoP-5; NPBRoP; OBEV; OxAEP-2; TFi

O Gods, it is terrible to be buried this way. Shades of the Newly Buried Complain to the Gods, The. Unknown. WoPoe, tr. by John S. Major

O golden child the world will kill and eat. (LL) Mary's Song. Sylvia Plath. AFaM; ChIV-2

O Golden Fleece she is where she lies tonight. George Barker. MoBrPo Fr. Secular Elegies.

O golden-tongued Romance with serene lute! On Sitting Down to Read King Lear Once Again. John Keats. CABP; GSo; NAEL-6v2; NAEL-7v2; NoP-4; NoP-5; NPBRoP; PoPoPo

O! good my lord, tax not so bad a voice. William Shakespeare. OxAEP-1 Fr. Much Ado about Nothing.

O grammar rules, O now your virtues show. Sir Philip Sidney. NoP-5 Fr. Astrophil and Stella.

O Grandfather Dust. Glenn Kletke. IFF

O grant me darkness! Let no gleam. But in That Sleep of Death What Dreams May Come? Mary Elizabeth Coleridge. VWP

O grant that like to Peter I.   John Keats.   ChIV-2 *Fr.* Three Undated Fragments.

O grasses wet with dew, yellow fallen leaves.   Glimpse, A.   Frances Darwin Cornford.   OBMV

O Grave, keep shut lest I be shamed. (LL)   C. L. M.   John Masefield.   InoFa; MoBrPo

O graveyard, O graveyard.   Lay This Body Down.   *Unknown.*   SSUS

O Great Apposition of the World.   Michel Deguy.   YaTCFP, *tr. by* Clayton Eshleman

O Great Buddha.   Kikaku.   SoOfWa, *tr. by* Sam Hamill

O Great Mary.   Litany to Our Lady.   Eugene O'Curry and *Unknown.*   HW

O great mountain Bodhidharma.   To Bodhidharma.   Tenshin Reb Anderson.   WhBo

O great tone-master! low thy massive head.   Beethoven.   Henrietta Cordelia Ray.   CBWP-3

O guide my judgment and my taste.   Christopher Smart.   ChIV-1 *Fr.* Hymns for the Amusement of Children.

O.H.M.S.   Ian Hamilton Finlay.   EdScPo

O Hada Cibernetica.   Carlos German Belli. *tr. by* Maureen Ahern and David Tipton

Why Have They Moved Me.   TCLAP, *tr. by* Maureen Ahern and David Tipton

O Hand of Fire / gatherest. (LL)   Hart Crane.   MoAmPo; NAAL-5; OxBoAm *Fr.* Bridge, The.

O Happy Dames, That May Embrace.   Henry Howard, Earl of Surrey. *See* Seafarer, The.

O happy Earth! reality of Heaven!   Percy Bysshe Shelley.   NAEL-7v2 *Fr.* Queen Mab.

O happy [*or* happie] dames, that may embrace.   Seafarer, The.   Henry Howard, Earl of Surrey.   NoSic; NPeEn

O Happy people, where good princes reign.   Guillaume de Salluste Du Bartas.   NoSic *Fr.* Divine Weeks and Works, The.

O happy Thames, that didst my Stella bear.   Sir Philip Sidney.   OxAEP-1 *Fr.* Astrophil and Stella.

O happy Tithon! if thou know'st thy harp.   Sir William Alexander, Earl of Stirling.   OBEV *Fr.* Aurora.

O harbor for the rich and poor.   Ville de Nice, La.   Kenneth Koch.   AmWit

O, Harry! thou hast robb'd me of my youth.   William Shakespeare.   OxAEP-1 *Fr.* King Henry IV, Pt. I.

O hateful hellish snake, what furie furst.   Edmund Spenser.   NAEL-6v1; NAEL-7v1 *Fr.* Faerie Queene, The.

O have ye na heard o' the fause Sakelde?   Kinmont Willie.   *Unknown.*   IBB

O he is a rest that requires.   Anna Trapnell.   PBRV *Fr.* Cry of a Stone, A [*or* The].

O heart green acre sown with salt.   Upward Look, An.   James Merrill.   CAP-8; NAMCP V.2; PoPoPo

O heart, small urn.   "H. D."   APT-1 *Fr.* Walls Do Not Fall, The.

O heavenly color, London town.   November Blue.   Alice Thompson Meynell.   MoBrPo

O Heavens!   *Unknown.*   ChinPo, *tr. by* Ye Weilian [*or* Yeh Wei-lien *or* Wai-lim Yip]

O Heavens! O Earth! heer I must pause a space.   Sir William Mure.   PBRV *Fr.* Cry of Blood, and of a Broken Covenant, The.

O Hector, thou wert rooted in my heart.   Homer.   OBVE *Fr.* Iliad, The.

O height dispersed and head.   Happiness in the Trees.   Joseph Ceravolo.   OxBoAm

O Hell-born Tyranny! how blest the land.   To Tyranny.   John Thelwall.   CenSon

O help us, Lord! Each hour of need.   Henry Hart Milman.   SacPr

O helpless few in my country.   Ezra Pound.   MoAmPo; NAMCP V.1; NoAM; PoA 2002 *Fr.* Lustra.

O here it is! And there it is!   Mervyn Laurence Peake.   NOxBChV

O Hero Akimbo on the Mountains of To-morrow.   George Barker.   RSaN

"O Hero, Hero!" thus he cried full oft.   Christopher Marlowe.   EroLit *Fr.* Hero and Leander.

O hideous little bat, the size of snot.   Fly, The.   Karl Shapiro.   NAMCP V.2; NoAM; SoSe-8

O Hitler's a non-smoker.   Ballad of the Taxi Driver's Cap.   Hamish Henderson.   RSaN

O holy, blessed, glorious Trinity.   Ben Jonson.   SacPr

O holy Justice! Hiding your puissance.   Invocation.   Benedek Virág.   IQMS, *tr. by* Watson Kirkconnell

O holy talk show host.   Wish Foundation, The.   Carol Muske-Dukes.   PBCAP

O holy virgin! clad in purest white.   To Morning.   William Blake.   OxAEP-2

O Holy Water.   Margot Ruddock.   OBMV

O Honored Hera, who often descending from heaven.   Nossis.   SaLy, *tr. by* Diane Rayor

O Hope! thou soother sweet of human woes!   To Hope.   Charlotte Smith.   RWP

O house, o sloping field, o poplar trees whose tall arms salute.   Elaine Randell.   Oth *Fr.* Snoad Hill Poems, The.

O! How can Love exulting Reason quell!   Contemns its Power.   Mary Robinson.   CenSon

O! How disorder'd our machine.   Edward Young.   STuOW *Fr.* Resignation.

O, how I faint when I of you do write.   William Shakespeare.   CAGL; OxAEP-1 *Fr.* Sonnets.

O how I know all the answers.   Out of illness.   Lionel Abrahams.   TSAP

O how much I would like—.   Osip Emilevich Mandelstam.   PFTM-1

O[h] how much more doth beauty beauteous seem.   William Shakespeare.   AEP; OBEV *Fr.* Sonnets.

O how my mind.   Confusion.   Christopher Hervey.   UV

O, how sick and weary I.   In a Myrtle [*or* Mirtle] Shade.   William Blake.   ChIV-1

O how that glittering taketh me! (LL)   Upon Julia's Clothes.   Robert Herrick.   BASC; BrAP; CABP; CavPo; ClHu; HeIP-4; NAEL-6v1; NAEL-7v1; NBLV; NIL-7; NIP-4; NoP-4; NoP-5; NOSC; OBEV; OxAEP-1; OxBEV; PoPoPo; TFi; TRP; UV; WaAnP; WeW-3; WoPoe

O hundred-towered Prague.   City With Towers.   Vitězslav Nezval.   PFTM-1

O, hungry heart.   Heart-Hungry.   Josephine D. Henderson Heard.   CBWP-4

O! I Could Laugh to Hear the Midnight Wind.   Charles Lamb.   CenSon

O! I do love thee, meek Simplicity!   Samuel Taylor Coleridge.   CenSon *Fr.* Sonnets Attempted in the Manner of Contemporary Writers.

O I forbid you, maidens a' [*or* all].   Tam Lin.   *Unknown.*   OBEV; OBNV

O I had a future.   I Had a Future.   Patrick Kavanagh.   NoAM

O, I hae come from far away.   Witch's Ballad, The.   William Bell Scott.   OBEV; RACG

O I ha'e Silence left. (LL)   Hugh MacDiarmid.   NAEL-6v2; NAEL-7v2 *Fr.* Drunk Man Looks at the Thistle, A.

O I hae tint my rosy cheek.   *Unknown.*   FaBoVe

O, I have been wounded.   Battle of Inverlochy, The.   *Unknown.*   EMWP

O I repented, wore my pious cloak.   Sadi.   WoPoe, *tr. by* Dick Davis

O I say you Joe.   William Blake.   *Fr.* Island in the Moon, An.

O Ihu, lett me neuer forgett thy byttur passion.   For Thy Sake Let the World Call Me Fool.   *Unknown.*   SacPr

O I'm a jolly old cowboy.   *Unknown.*   CA

O I'm a professional.   Sung in a Graveyard.   Anna Wickham.   ItWoWo

O, I'm not myself at all, Molly dear, Molly dear.   I'm Not Myself at All!   Samuel Lover.   IrV

O I'm off to Hullaboola where the climate's never cooler.   Folk Song.   Bruce Beaver.   OBCoV

O, insatiable monster! Could'st thou not.   Requiem.   Mary Weston Fordham.   CBWP-2

O is it Love or is it Fame.   Oh, Is It Love?   Amy Levy.   ViWPN

O islets green, Nature's immortal gems.   Hymn to the Thousand Islands.   Henrietta Cordelia Ray.   CBWP-3

O! it is pleasant, with a heart at ease.   Fancy in Nubibus.   Samuel Taylor Coleridge.   CenSon

O Jean, my Jean, when the bell ca's the congregation.   Tam i' the Kirk.   Violet Jacob.   EdScPo; NePenScot

O Jesu Parvule.   Hugh MacDiarmid.   EdScPo

O Jesus, drink of me. (LL)   Better Resurrection, A.   Christina Georgina Rossetti.   ViWPN; VWP

O Jolly brick, with kindly wrinkled face.   Holland Brick, A.   Wallace Bruce.   VerBaPo

O, Jordan bank was a great old bank!   One More River.   *Unknown.*   APN-2

O joy of creation.   What the Bullet Sang.   Bret Harte.   APN-2; CalPo; OBEV

O joy, too high for my low style to show.   Sir Philip Sidney.   NAEL-6v1; NAEL-7v1; OxAEP-1 *Fr.* Astrophil and Stella.

O Karma, Dharma, pudding and pie.   Philip Appleman.   GoPo

O Kate! thou dear Partner, through joy and through strife!   Domestic Poems.   Thomas Hood.

O Keeper of the Sacred Key.   In State, Part 1.   Forceythe Willson.   APN-2

O King of Terrors, whose unbounded sway.   To Death.   Anne Finch, Countess of Winchilsea.   NoP-4; NoP-5

O king, whose greatness none can comprehend.   William Drummond of Hawthornden.   SacPr *Fr.* Hymn to the Fairest Fair, A.

O kiss, which dost those ruddy gems impart.   Sir Philip Sidney.   NAEL-6v1; NAEL-7v1; OxBSo *Fr.* Astrophil and Stella.

O la grande apposition du monde.   Michel Deguy.   YaTCFP

O Lady amorous, / Merciless lady.   Canzonetta: A Bitter Song to His Lady.   Pier Moronelli da Fiorenza.   OBVE, *tr. by* Dante Gabriel Rossetti

O ladyis fair of Troy and Grece, attend.   Robert Henryson.   NPeEn *Fr.* Testament of Cresseid, The.

O land of elegance, where every grace.   Farewell to France.   Sarah Hamilton.   CenSon

O Language you.   Robert Kelly.   WhBo *Fr.* Flowers of Unceasing Coincidence, The.

O leave me easy, leave me alone. (LL)   Libertine, The.   Louis MacNeice.
ModIr; NAMCP V.1; NoAM

O Leerie, see a little child and nod to him to-night! (LL)   Lamplighter, The.
Robert Louis Stevenson.   ITBLP; NePenScot

O, lest the world should task you to recite.   William Shakespeare.   OxAEP-1
Fr. Sonnets.

O let him whose sorrow.   H. S. Oswald.   SacPr, tr. by F.E. Cox

O let me be in loving nice.   Punctilio.   Mary Elizabeth Coleridge.   OBEV;
PoBW

O let me, Lady, silence calumny.   Protestation.   Bertrans de Born.   WoPoe, tr.
by John Peale Bishop

O let me soar on steadfast wing.   Prayer.   Dennis Brutus.   AF

O let the solid ground.   Alfred Tennyson.   NAEL-6v2 Fr. Maud [A
Monodrama].

O lett it be for ever told.   Jane Hawkins.   EMWP

O Liberty, God-gifted.   To the Bartholdi Statue.   Ambrose Bierce.   APN-2

O life! what letts thee from a quicke decease?   I Dye Alive.   Robert Southwell.
SacPr

O Life, who art thou that with scarcely scanned.   Life Plastic.   Michael Field.
VWP

O Life! without thy chequered scene.   William Wordsworth.   SacPr

O Light Invisible, we praise Thee!   T. S. Eliot.   SacPr Fr. Rock, The.

O Light, 'tis I, who from death's other shores.   Helen.   Paul Valéry.   OBVE

O lips full of lust and of laughter.   Algernon Charles Swinburne.   UV Fr.
Dolores.

O / little / bird.   Roy Kiyooka.   NLPA Fr. Pear Tree Pomes.

O little broken doll, dropped in the well.   Broken Doll, The.   Nuala Ni
Dhomhnaill.   ModIr, tr. by John Montague

O Little Brother.   Tree.   Zulaykha Abu-Risha.   PoArWo, tr. by Clarissa C.
Burt

O little friend, your nose is ready; you sniff.   Dog.   Harold Monro.   MoBrPo

O little one, this longing is the pits.   Marilyn Hacker.   EmeKit

O Little Town of Bethlehem.   Phillips Brooks.   APN-2; ChrPo; SacPr; TCAPo

O Living Flame of Love.   San Juan de la Cruz.   SpanPo, tr. by Stephen
Stepanchev

O living flame of love.   O Living Flame of Love.   San Juan de la Cruz.
SpanPo, tr. by Stephen Stepanchev

O living will that shalt endure.   Alfred Tennyson.   NAEL-6v2; NAEL-7v2 Fr.
In Memoriam A. H. H.

O lonely workman, standing there.   Thomas Hardy.   NAMCP V.1; NoAM Fr.
Satires of Circumstance in Fifteen Glimpses.

O Lord All-Merciful, be merciful to me. (LL)   Before the Beginning.
Christina Georgina Rossetti.   InvLi; SacPr

O Lord, Help Me to Live Through This Night.   Osip Emilevich Mandelstam.
WoPoe, tr. by Clarence Brown and W. S. Merwin

O Lord, help me to live through this night.   O Lord, Help Me to Live Through
This Night.   Osip Emilevich Mandelstam.   WoPoe, tr. by Clarence Brown
and W. S. Merwin

O lord, I dred, and that I did not dred.   Bible, O.T.   OBVE

O Lord I shall be whole in deed.   Jeremie .17.   Bible, Apocrypha.   ChIV-1

O Lord, in me there lieth nought.   Bible, O.T.   NAEL-7v1; NoSic; OBVE

O Lord in me there lieth nought.   Bible, O.T.   PEW Fr. Psalms.

O Lord, in your courtesy.   Praise of Diseases.   Jacopone da Todi.   WoPoe, tr.
by L. R. Lind

O Lord my God, make thou my hart repentant for to be.   Necessarie Praier in
Meeter Against Vices, A.   Frances Manners Nevill, Lady Abergavenny.
EMWP

O Lord! my heart is sick.   Eternity of God, The.   Frederick William Faber.
SacPr

O Lord of Light! A Mystic Sage Returns to Realms of Eternity!   Askia
Muhammad Touré.   FuFl; SeSe; SpirFl

O Lord our Lord, how excellent is thy name in all the earth!   Bible, O.T.
NAWM-5v1 Fr. Psalms.

O Lord, our Sovereign.   Bible, O.T.   InvLi Fr. Psalms.

O Lord, praise be.   Giotto.   Rafael Alberti.   WoPoe, tr. by Carolyn Tipton

O Lord, sir, let me live, or let me see my death!   William Shakespeare.
OxAEP-1 Fr. All's Well That Ends Well.

O Lord, that rul'st the human heart.   Bible, O.T. See O Lord our Lord, how
excellent is thy name in all the earth!

O Lord, the hard-won miles.   Prayer, A.   Paul Laurence Dunbar.   SacPr

O Lord thou seest my wrongs abound.   Ode XV.   Thomas Stanley.   ChIV-1

O Lord, turn not away thy face.   Lamentation, The.   John Marckant.   SacPr

O Lord two things I thee require.   Proverb, XXX.   John Hall.   ChIV-1

O Lord, with whom subduer Love.   Anacreon.   SaLy, tr. by Diane Rayor

O Lorde oure gouvernoure, howe excellent is thy name.   Bible, O.T. See O
Lord our Lord, how excellent is thy name in all the earth!

O lost moon sisters / crescent in hair.   Diane Di Prima.   BB

O love, be fed with apples while you may.   Sick Love.   Robert Graves.
HarvBoo; NPeEn; OxAEP-2

O Love of God, How Strong and True.   Horatius Bonar.   SacPr

O love, round as the watermelon.   Unknown.   CATKP, tr. by Peter H. Lee

O Love! that stronger art than wine.   Aphra Behn.   LW

O Love That Wilt Not Let Me Go.   George Matheson.   SacPr

O loveliest daughter of Hsieh.   Elegy.   Yüan Chĕn.   CrYelRi; ErotSp, tr. by
Sam Hamill

O lovely age of gold!   Torquato Tasso.   OBVE Fr. Aminta.

O lovely Galatea, sweeter than.   Luis de Góngora y Argote.   SpanPo Fr. Fable
of Polyphemus and Galatea.

O lovely thing.   Bible, O.T.   PEW Fr. Psalms.

O ludicrous and pensive trinity.   Romeo and Juliet.   Howard Phelps Putnam.
OxBoAm

O luely, luely cam she in.   Tryst [or Trysting Place], The.   William Soutar.
EdScPo; NePenScot; NPeEn

O Lusty May, with Flora queen!   Lusty May.   Unknown.   OBEV

O Luxury.   Guy W. Longchamps.   GoPo

O Magdalen!   Oskar Pastior.   OnScMo, tr. by Christopher Middleton

O magic wheel.   My Magic Wheel.   N. P. Tyler.   ArBi

O, Magyar.   Unknown.   IQMS, tr. by Watson Kirkconnell

O, Magyar, think no German true.   O, Magyar.   Unknown.   IQMS, tr. by
Watson Kirkconnell

O make me a mask and a wall to shut from your spies.   O Make Me a Mask.
Dylan Thomas.   PoA 2002

O Man, forgive thy mortal foe.   Forgiving.   Alfred Tennyson.   SacPr

O Man unkynde.   Unknown.   OHMEL

O Man! what Inspiration was thy Guide.   Glass.   Anne Finch, Countess of
Winchilsea.   OxBEV

O! Mankinde.   See! Here, My Heart.   Unknown.   NoP-4; NoP-5

O, Mare Atlanticum.   Sleep of my lions, The.   Douglas Livingstone.   TSAP

O Margie, Marge, Dear Margaret.   Oswald von Wolkenstein.   GePo, tr. by J.
W. Thomas

O marvel, fruit of fruits, I pause.   My Strawberry.   Helen Hunt Jackson.
SWaP

O [or Oh] Mary, at the window be.   Mary Morison.   Robert Burns.
NePenScot; OBEV

O Mary, go and call the cattle home.   Forgotten Song.   John Ashbery.
HarvBoo

O Mary, go and call the cattle home.   Sands of Dee, The.   Charles Kingsley.
OxAEP-2

O Mary / The girls in the convent.   O Mary.   Freda Downie.   MoWP

O massa take dat new bran coat / And hang it on de wall.   Away Down in
Sunbury.   Unknown.   SSUS

O me no weary yet.   Not Weary Yet.   Unknown.   SSUS

O 'Melia, my dear, this does everything crown!   Ruined Maid, The.   Thomas
Hardy.   FaBoVe; HeIP-4; NAEL-6v2; NAEL-7v2; NBLV; NIL-7; NoP-5;
TFi; TRP

    (O'Melia, my dear, this does everything crown!)   NoP-4; PoPoPo

O melody, what children strange are these.   Lines.   Ina Coolbrith.   SWaP

O member, will you linger?   Children Do Linger.   Unknown.   SSUS

O memory! that which I gave thee.   Flight.   Charles Stuart Calverley.
OBCoV

O merchants! oh turn to the Lord!   Having Prayed for, and Made Much
Mention of the Merchants, She Sings the Following Hymn to Them.   Anna
Trapnell.   EMWP

O Merlin in your crystal cave.   Merlin.   Edwin Muir.   EdScPo; NePenScot

O michti ladi, owr leding/tw haf.   Ieuan ap Hywel Swrdwal.   AngWePo

O mickle yeuks the keckle doup.   Justice to Scotland.   Unknown.   NBLV

O might those sigh[e]s and tear[e]s return[e] again[e].   John Donne.   SacPr Fr.
Holy Sonnets.

O mighty Cæsar! dost thou lie so low?   William Shakespeare.   OxAEP-1 Fr.
Julius Caesar.

O Mighty Nothing! unto thee.   And He Answered Them Nothing.   Richard
Crashaw.   ChIV-2; SacPr

O mightye Muse.   George Puttenham.   PBRV Fr. Partheniades.

O miraculous blown country.   Mental Traveller's Landfall, The.   Chris
Wallace-Crabbe.   BMAP

O miss, I'll give you a paper of pins.   Unknown.   TLR

O mistress mine, where are you roaming?   William Shakespeare. See O[h]
Mistress Mine.

O Mistris mine where are you roming?   William Shakespeare. See O[h]
mistress mine, where are you roaming?

O months of blossoming, months of transfigurations.   Lilacs and the Roses,
The.   Louis Aragon.   OBWP, tr. by Louis MacNeice

O moon, / Go to the West, and.   Prayer to Amitāyus.   Kwangdŏk.   CATKP, tr.
by Peter H. Lee

O moon, rise high.   Song of Ch'ŏngŭp.   Unknown.   CATKP, tr. by Peter H.
Lee

O Mors! Quam Amara Est Memoria Tua Homini Pacem Habenti In Substantiis
Suis.   Ernest Dowson.   OBMV

O mortal boy we cannot stop. To the Powers of Desolation. Genevieve Taggard. APT-2

O mortal folk you may behold and see. Stephen Hawes. NoSic; OBEV *Fr.* Pastime of Pleasure, The.

O mortal virtue and immortal sin. Pride. Mary Elizabeth Coleridge. ViWPN

O Most High, you willed to create me a poet and now it is time for me to present a report. Report. Czeslaw Milosz. BodElec, *tr. by the author and Robert Hass*

O mother I believe. . .O mother I believe. Heaven Bells, The. *Unknown.* SSUS

O Mother My Giant Redwood. Judith Hemschemeyer. FiBr

O mother, open the window wide. At Last. Elizabeth Siddal. VWP

O mother / what have I left out. Allen Ginsberg. BB; CLPP *Fr.* Kaddish.

O Mother-heart! when fast the arrows flew. Niobe. Henrietta Cordelia Ray. CBWP-3

O mountain Stream! the Shepherd and his Cot. William Wordsworth. CenSon *Fr.* River Duddon [A Series of Sonnets], The.

O Muse! relate (for you can tell alone). Alexander Pope. OxBEV *Fr.* Dunciad, The.

O Muses! I beseech you, fire my heart with song. Ekaterina Urusova. ARWW *Fr.* Heroides: Dedicated to the Muses.

O my aged uncle Arly! Incidents in the Life of My Uncle Arly. Edward Lear. OBCoV

  (O my agèd Uncle Arly!) NOxBChV

O my coy darling, still. Ode to a Dressmaker's Dummy. Donald Justice. NoAM

O [*or* Oh] my dark Rosaleen. Dark Rosaleen. Owen Roe MacWard. IrV; OBEV; OxAEP-2, *tr. by James Clarence Mangan*

O my daughters. Behold This and Always Love It. Meridel Le Sueur. HW

O my Dear Animals. Salvatore Quasimodo. SonAtl, *tr. by Gregory Beaven and Favorita '68*

O my dear father! Restoration, hang. William Shakespeare. OxAEP-1 *Fr.* King Lear.

O my deir hert, young Jesus sweit. Balulalow. John James. OBEV

O my eyes where are you, you that found a face so wonderful? Old Age. Milán Füst. IQMS, *tr. by Edwin Morgan*

O my fair warrior! William Shakespeare. OxAEP-1 *Fr.* Othello.

O My God Do Not Part Me from Thee. Esrefoğlu. WoPoe, *tr. by Taner Baybars*

O my God do not part me from thee. O My God Do Not Part Me from Thee. Esrefoğlu. WoPoe, *tr. by Taner Baybars*

O my heart is the unlucky heir of the ages. Personal History; for My Son. Ruthven Todd. EdScPo

'O, My Heart Is Woe'. *Unknown.* ChIV-2

O my heart's heart, and you who are to me. Christina Georgina Rossetti. OxBSo *Fr.* Monna Innominata.

O my insatiable muse. Alfred de Musset. WoPoe *Fr.* Night in May, A.

O my King Emanuel, my Emanuel above. King Emanuel. *Unknown.* SSUS

O my Lord. Rabi'a al-Adawiyya. WPoS

O my Lord. Rabi'a al-Adawiyya. WPoS

O my lost husband! let me ever mourn. Homer. OBVE *Fr.* Iliad, The.

O my love, my wife! William Shakespeare. OxAEP-1 *Fr.* Romeo and Juliet.

O my love, what gift of mine. Gift. Rabindranath Tagore. AmFaPo, *tr. by William Radice*

O my lover, blind me. Tired Woman, The. Anna Wickham. MoBrPo

Oh my Love is like a red, red rose. Red, Red Rose, A. Robert Burns. BrAP; ChAP; CtM; GoPo; HeIP-4; ITBLP; NAEL-6v2; NAEL-7v2; NePenScot; NIL-7; NIP-4; NOBRP; NoP-4; NoP-5; NPBRoP; NPeEn; OxAEP-2; OxBEV; PoPoPo; TFi; UV; WaAnP

  (My Luve's [*or* love's *or* love is *or* luve is] like a red, red rose.) OxBEV; UV

O my merciful Lord God, you, who are one in three. Jane Vaughan. EMWP

O my mother Nut. Hymn to Nut. *Unknown.* HW

O my much praised but-not-altogether-satisfactory lady. (LL) Bathtub [*or* Bath Tub], The. Ezra Pound. NIP-4; TRP; WeW-3

O My Name It Is Sam Hall. Randall Jarrell. PWW2

O! my offense is rank, it smells to heaven. William Shakespeare. OxAEP-1 *Fr.* Hamlet.

O my seven-stringed board. Drawer. Zbigniew Herbert. VCWP, *tr. by Czeslaw Miosz and Peter Dale Scott*

O my son, farewell! Song for a Fallen Warrior. *Unknown.* AmWaPo; APN-2, *tr. by John Mason Browne*

O, my strong-minded sisters, aspiring to vote. Advice Gratis to Certain Women. Phoebe Cary. APN-2

O my tiny child. Magic Words to Cure a Sick Child. *Eskimo Oral Tradition.* PoChi

O Myland Woman. Dus Mapun. SonAtl, *tr. by Edward Etepa, Nancy Gallas, Daniel Perissa, Kate Webster and Albert Wendt*

O narrow is the house where we are born. Valley-Folk. Fred Cogswell. Coast

O Nature! thou didst rear me for thine own. Felicia Dorothea Hemans. NPBRoP *Fr.* Thoughts during Sickness.

O Nature, thou to me was cruel. Address to Nature on its Cruelty, An. Ellen Johnston. VWP

O Nature! thou whom I have thought to love. Emily Jane Pfeiffer. ViWPN *Fr.* To Nature.

O, never say that I was false of heart. William Shakespeare. OBEV; OxAEP-1 *Fr.* Sonnets.

O night betrayed by darkness not its own. (LL) Night, Death, Mississippi. Robert Earl Hayden. CAP-8; ColAP; NAMCP V.2; NoP-4; NoP-5; OxAAAP; PoPoPo; VCAP

O Night, O sleepless tossing, longing. Night Alone, The. Meleager. AWTN, *tr. by Dudley Fitts*

O Noble and Most High in Beauty, Thou. Luis de Góngora y Argote. SpanPo, *Fr.* River Duddon

O noble and most high in beauty, thou. O Noble and Most High in Beauty, Thou. Luis de Góngora y Argote. SpanPo, *tr. by Ian Fletcher*

O nocturnal garden, secret organ. Nocturnal Garden. Nikolai Alekseievich Zabolotsky. TCRusP, *tr. by Kathy Lewis and Bob Perelman*

O none but gods have power their love to hide. George Chapman. OxAEP-1 *Fr.* Hero and Leander.

O North! as thy romantick vales I leave. At a Village in Scotland. William Lisle Bowles. NPBRoP

O! nothing earthly save the ray. Al Aaraaf. Edgar Allan Poe. APN-1

O nothing in this corporal earth of man. Francis Thompson. MoBrPo; OBMV *Fr.* Heart, The.

'O Now the Drenched Land Wakes'. Kenneth Patchen. CLPP

O now the drenched land wakes. 'O Now the Drenched Land Wakes'. Kenneth Patchen. CLPP

O, one I need to love me. Friends—With a Difference. Mary Elizabeth Coleridge. VWP

O orange were her underclothes. Epithalamium in Olive Drab. William Jay Smith. PWW2

O Osbert father Osbert. To Osbert Sitwell. Cyril Connolly. OBCoV

O our Mother the Earth, O our Father the Sky. Song of the Sky Loom. *Tewa Oral Tradition.* WoPoe, *tr. by Herbert J. Spinden*

O owl! Issa. EH, *tr. by Robert Hass*

O Paddy dear, and did you hear the news that's going round? Wearing of the Green, The. Dion Boucicault. IrV

O Painter of the fruits and flowers. Garden. John Greenleaf Whittier. OBGa

O Paleys [*or* palace], whylom [*or* whilom] croune [*or* crown] of houses all[e]. Geoffrey Chaucer. OBEV *Fr.* Troilus and Criseyde [*or* Criseide].

O Paradise. William Trowbridge. SUP

O, pardon me, thou bleeding piece of earth. William Shakespeare. OxAEP-1 *Fr.* Julius Caesar.

O Paris. Blaise Cendrars. YaTCFP *Fr.* Prose du Transsibérien et de la Petite Jeanne de France.

O patient shore, that canst not go to meet. Tides. Helen Hunt Jackson. LW

O Peace, O Dove, O shape of the Holy Ghost. To Peace. Richard Watson Dixon. OxAEP-2

O Pearl and Breasted World. George Barker. PoA 2002 *Fr.* Cycle of Six Lyrics.

O peerless marble marvel! what of grace. Venus of Milo, The. Henrietta Cordelia Ray. CBWP-3

O pensive Passenger! do not deny. Moods 2. Della Cruscans. STuOW

O perfite light, quhilk schaid away. Alexander Hume. NPeEn *Fr.* Of the Day Estivall.

O perfite light, quhilk schaid away. Of the Day Estivall. Alexander Hume. NePenScot

O pine-tree standing. Hakutsu. TAL *Fr.* Manyo Shu, Part 3 of 4.

O Pioneers! Jane Miller. GifTon

O place us, dear Saviour! in some small retreat. Eliza Robertson. PoBW *Fr.* Poetical Epistle to an Absent Friend, A.

O pleasant exercise of hope and joy! William Wordsworth. NAEL-6v2; NAEL-7v2 *Fr.* Prelude, The; Growth of a Poet's Mind [1850 version].

O, po' sinner, O, now is yo' time. What Yo' Gwine to [*or* t'] Do When Yo' [*or* de] Lamp Burn Down? *Unknown.* APN-2

O poet gifted with the sight divine! Milton. Henrietta Cordelia Ray. CBWP-3

O poet rare and old! Astræa. John Greenleaf Whittier. APN-1

O poor Catullus, stupid long enough! Catullus. STV,

O poor me! / Who am going out to fight the enemy. Song of the Lenape Warriors Going against the Enemy, The. *Unknown.* APN-2, *tr. by John Heckwelder*

O pr / gress verily thou art m. E. E. Cummings. UV

O pray! Example take too, and have care. (LL) After the Pleasure Party [Lines Traced under an Image of Amor Threatening]. Herman Melville. APN-2; NAAL-3; OxBoAm

O precious codex [or code], volume, tome. To a Thesaurus. Franklin Pierce Adams. AmWit; NBLV

O Quadriga. Charles Olson. BodElec

O queen o sludge, maist royal mousse. To a Mousse. W. N. Herbert. NeBl

O quick quick quick, quick hear the song sparrow. T. S. Eliot. NAEL-6v2; NoAM Fr. Landscapes.

O radiant luminary of light interminable. Prayer to the Father of [or in] Heaven, A. John Skelton. SacPr

O raging seas, and mighty Neptune's reign! Coming Homeward out of Spain. Barnabe Googe. NoSic
   (O ragyng Seas.) NPeEn

O rare Narcissus! sunny-haired! Echo's Complaint. Henrietta Cordelia Ray. CBWP-3

O! Reason! vaunted Sovereign of the mind! Rejects the Influence of Reason. Mary Robinson. CenSon; RWP

O, remember me in your garden. Letter, A. Viktor Aleksandrovich Sosnora. ItGoST, tr. by Maia Tekses

O Restless Heart, Be Still! Henrietta Cordelia Ray. CBWP-3

O Robertson of Inverawe. Song of Sorrow, A. Mary Cameron. EMWP

O roc, don't ridicule the small black birds. Yi T'aek. CATKP, tr. by Peter H. Lee

O rock o' jubilee, poor fallen soul. Rock o' Jubilee. Unknown. SSUS

O rocking boat, rocking boat poised on the wave. Boat Song. Henrietta Cordelia Ray. CBWP-3

O Roger, Mackerel, Riley, Ned, Nellie, Chester, Lady Ghost. (LL) Names of Horses. Donald Hall. AmFaPo; BeAl; GoPo; IPoFL; SoSe-8; TRP; TWF

O rosary that recalled my tear. Aithbhreac Inghean Corcadail. NePenScot, tr. by Derick Thomson

O[h] Rose, thou art sick. William Blake. BrAP; CABP; ClHu; HeIP-4; NAEL-6v2; NAEL-7v2; NAWM-7v2; NIL-7; NIP-4; NOBRP; NoP-4; NoP-5; NPBRoP; NPeEn; OPOU; OxAEP-2; OxBEV; PoPoPo; SoSe-8; TFi; TRP; WaAnP; WeW-3 Fr. Songs of Experience.

O Rourk's noble fare. Description of an Irish Feast, The. Hugh MacGowran. OBCoV, tr. by Jonathan Swift

O ruddier than the cherry! John Gay. NAEL-6v1 Fr. Acis and Galatea: An English Pastoral Opera.

O run, Mary, run, Hallelu, hallelu! Resurrection Morn, The. Unknown. SSUS

O Sacred Head Now Wounded. Paul Gerhardt. SacPr, tr. by James Waddell Alexander

O sacred head, now wounded. Paul Gerhardt. GePo

O sacred Head, now wounded, With grief and shame weighed down. O Sacred Head Now Wounded. Paul Gerhardt. SacPr, tr. by James Waddell Alexander

O sacred Providence, who from end to end. Providence. George Herbert. BASC

O sacred Providence, who from end to end. George Herbert. AngWePo Fr. Providence.

O sad Ulysses in decline, seer. Ulysses. Umberto Saba. WoPoe, tr. by Stephen Sartarelli

O Sadducees and Pharisees. Ballad of the Grapes. George Sterling. CalPo

O sailing stars! Star Song. Henrietta Cordelia Ray. CBWP-3

O St. James Road. Federico García Lorca. PFTM-1 Fr. Night (Suite for Piano and Poet's Voice).

O Saisons, O Châteaux. Arthur Rimbaud. WoPoe, tr. by Padraic Fallon

O save thy children blue Ontario! John Neal. APN-1 Fr. Battle of Niagara, The.

O saw ye bonny Lesley. Bonnie Lesley. Robert Burns. OBEV

O saw ye not fair Ines? Fair Ines. Thomas Hood. OBEV

O say, have you seen at the Willows so green. Ballad of the Emeu, The. Bret Harte. NBLV

O say not thou art left of God. Desolation. John Henry, Cardinal Newman. SacPr

O say to all of the inhāja, the full moons of the time, and the lions of the thicket. Abu Ishaq al-Ilbin. HiArP, tr. by James T. Monroe

O sea-gulls that are crying. Unknown. TAL

O seasons, O châteaux. O Saisons, O Châteaux. Arthur Rimbaud. WoPoe, tr. by Padraic Fallon

O seasons, o châteaux. Arthur Rimbaud. SxFrPo, tr. by Martin Sorrell

O! seize again thy golden quill. To Della Crusca. The Pen. Hannah Cowley. NOBRP

O Shadow, in thy fleeting form I see. Shadow, The. John Banister Tabb. APN-2

O, she doth teach the torches to burn bright! William Shakespeare. WaAnP Fr. Romeo and Juliet.

O she took the babe still sick slick from the waterbag. Four Black Bogmen, The. Elder Olson. APT-2

O shield me from his rage, celestial Powers! Esther Johnson. LW

O shining, sapphire seat. Sailed. Ina Coolbrith. NAAPv.1

O short shrift's the best shrift to give to this Festschrift! Unlikely Obbligato of Andersonstown. Kit Wright. OBCoV

O Shout Away. Unknown. SSUS

O shout, O shout, O shout away. O Shout Away. Unknown. SSUS

O Silent God, Thou whose voice afar in mist and mystery hath left our ears an-hungered in these fearful days. Litany of [or at] Atlanta, A. William Edward Burghardt DuBois. APT-1; NAAPv.1; OxAAAP; TCAPo

O silver splendor, marvelous! Vision of Moonlight, A. Henrietta Cordelia Ray. CBWP-3

O [or Oh] silver-throated swan. Dying Swan, The. Thomas Sturge Moore. OBMV

O, silver tree! Langston Hughes. See Oh, silver tree!

O Simplicitas. Madeleine L'Engle. OBCP Fr. Three Songs of Mary.

O! sing ye a dirge for the loved and the lost. Tribute to a Lost Steamer. Mary Weston Fordham. CBWP-2

O Singer of Persephone! Theocritus: A Villanelle. Oscar Wilde. WaAnP

O, Sire, is this the path? "H. D." NAAL-5 Fr. Walls Do Not Fall, The.

O Sister. Nelly Sachs. AF, tr. by Matthew Mead

O sister of wealth. Andal. WPoS Fr. Tiruppavai, The.

O sister, / where do you pitch your tent? O Sister. Nelly Sachs. AF, tr. by Matthew Mead

O sky & earth! How ye are linked together. Lago Maggiore. Thomas Cole. APN-1

O sleepy city of reeling wheelchairs. Wheelchair Butterfly, The. James Tate. NAMCP V.2; NoAM

O small and squat. Songs of the Fruits and Sweets of Childhood. Lorna Goodison. VCWP

O smooth flatterers, go over sea. Reflection and Advice. Ezra Pound. OBSV

O snowflake clouds, O feath'ry clouds. Cloud Song. Henrietta Cordelia Ray. CBWP-3

O so white, O so soft, O so sweet is she! (LL) Ben Jonson. BASC; NAEL-7v1; NoP-4; NoP-5; NOSC; NPeEn Fr. Celebration of Charis in Ten Lyric[k] Pieces [or Peeces], A.

O soft embalmer of the still midnight! To Sleep. John Keats. ItP; NIP-4; OBEV; OxBSo

O soldiers, soldiers, get ye back, I pray! Saved. Adah Isaacs Menken. CBWP-1

O solitary wand'rer! whither stray. Laura to Petrarch. Mary Robinson. CenSon

O Solitude, I said, sweet Solitude! Solitude. Helen Hunt Jackson. SWaP

O Solitude! If I Must With Thee Dwell. John Keats. AmFaPo; CenSon; IJHIL

O Solitude! to thy sequester'd vale. By the Same. To Solitude. Charlotte Smith. CenSon; RWP

O! Solomon! let us try again. (LL) Solomon and the Witch. William Butler Yeats. ChIV-1; NoAM; WoPoe

O some tell me that a nigger won't steal. Run, Nigger, Run! Unknown. SSUS

O son of man, by lying tongues adored. On the Russian Persecution of the Jews. Algernon Charles Swinburne. OxBSo

O Sorrow! John Keats. OBEV Fr. Endymion: A Poetic Romance.

O Sorrow, cruel fellowship. Alfred Tennyson. NAEL-6v2; NAEL-7v2; NAWM-7v2 Fr. In Memoriam A. H. H.

O Sorrow, wilt thou live with me. Alfred Tennyson. NAEL-6v2; NAEL-7v2 Fr. In Memoriam A. H. H.

O sorrowful and ancient days. Metrum Parhemiacum Tragicum. Eugenius Vulgarius. FaBoWar, tr. by Helen Waddell

O soul, canst thou not understand. Aridity. Michael Field. OBMV

O soul, 'tis thine in season meet. Ode on Theoxenos. Pindar. CAGL, tr. by John Addington Symonds

O soul, why shouldst thou downcast be? Hope Thou in God. Josephine D. Henderson Heard. CBWP-4

O Southland! James Weldon Johnson. InGu

O Southland! O Southland! James Weldon Johnson. InGu

O spare a tear for poor Tom Hood. Elegy on Thomas Hood. Martin Fagg. UV

O splendour of God's glory bright. Saint Ambrose. SacPr, tr. by Robert Bridges

O stagnant east-wind, palsied mare. Room on a Garden, A. Wallace Stevens. NoP-4; NoP-5; OBGa

O stamping-ground of the shod Word! So hard. Geoffrey Hill. UpMys Fr. Locust Songs.

O Star (the fairest one in sight). Choose Something like a Star. Robert Frost. APT-1; BLPJKO; MoAmPo

O! start a revolution, somebody! O! Start a Revolution. D. H. Lawrence. RSaN

O stay, sweet warbling woodlark stay. Address to the Woodlark. Robert Burns. OWoS

O stiffly shapen houses that change not. Suburbs on a Hazy Day. D. H. Lawrence. OBMV

O stony grey soil of Monaghan. Stony Grey Soil. Patrick Kavanagh. HarvBoo; ModIr

O stormy, stormy world. Happiness Makes Up in Height for What It Lacks in Length. Robert Frost. MoAmPo; SoSe-8

O strategic map of disasters, hungry America. On Walt Whitman's Birthday. Anne Waldman. ViWalt

Ô[h] strive not[t] still to heap[e] disdain[e] on me[e]. Mary Sidney Wroth, Countess of Montgomery. NOSC Fr. Pamphilia to Amphilanthus.

O study Nature! and with thought profound. Unknown. OBGa Fr. Rise and Progress of the Present Taste in Planning Parks, Pleasure Grounds, Gardens, etc, The.

O subtile secret of the air. Distance. Helen Hunt Jackson. SWaP

O subtle, musky, slumbrous clime! To the South. Maurice Thompson. CBCWP

O suitably-attired-in-leather-boots. Fragment of a Greek Tragedy. A. E. Housman. WoPoe

O summer snail. Issa. SoOfWa, tr. by Sam Hamill

O sun, and moonlight shining in the woods. Carmen Saeculare. Charles Hubert Sisson. OBVE, tr. by Christopher Smart

O sun, be his protection. Branwen's Starling. R. Williams Parry. OBWVE, tr. by Gwyn Jones

O suns [or sun] and skies and clouds of June. October's Bright Blue Weather. Helen Hunt Jackson. ITBLP

O sway, and swing, and sway. First Extra, The. Amy Levy. ViWPN

O SWEET and bitter monuments of pain. Upon the Ensigns of Christ's Crucifying. William Alabaster. NoSic

O sweet dead artist and seer, O tender prophetic priest. Ernest Francisco Fenollosa. APN-2 Fr. East and West.

O sweet incendiary! shew here thy art. Richard Crashaw. NPeEn Fr. Flaming Heart, The.

O sweet, sad, singing river. Song. Henrietta Cordelia Ray. CBWP-3

O sweet spontaneous. E. E. Cummings. IPoFL; NAAL-5; NAAPv.2; NAMCP V.1; NoAM; RaBo; TCAPo

O sweet woods, the delight of solitariness! Sir Philip Sidney. NoSic Fr. Countesse of Pembroke's Arcadia, The.

O Sweetie, O Hon, in this weather—split sea pea. Crossed-Over, Fiend-Snitched, X-ed Out. Mary Jo Bang. BAP-01

O swiftly, re-light the flame. "H. D." NALW Fr. Tribute to the Angels.

O sylvan priest of nature! rightly thou. Thought at Walden, A. Henrietta Cordelia Ray. CBWP-3

O Sylvia, Sylvia. Sylvia's Death. Anne Sexton. InoFa; NAAL-5; NALW

O sympathy, of birth divine. Well-Aimed Tear, The [or To Della Crusca]. Hannah Cowley. STuOW

O! synge untoe mie roundelaie. Thomas Chatterton. CABP

O Tan-Faced Prairie-Boy. Walt Whitman. CAGL

O Taste and See. Denise Levertov. AFaM; BeAl; ChIV-1; IPoFL; NoP-4; NoP-5; PoPoPo

O tell me the truth about love. (LL) W. H. Auden. NoP-5; StAl Fr. Twelve Songs.

O tell me where, in lands or seas. Ballade of the Ladies of Time Past. François Villon. WoPoe, tr. by Richard Wilbur

O tender time that love thinks long to see. Vision of Spring in Winter, A. Algernon Charles Swinburne. NPeEn

O Tender under Her Right Breast. George Barker. MoBrPo Fr. Second Cycle of Love Poems.

O tender-heartedness right bitter grown. Fragmenti. Ezra Pound. PoA 2002

Ô terre, si c'est terre, ô toute-en-jour où nous sommes venus. Pour Mycéa. Édouard Glissant. YaTCFP

O, that I knew which side I fought for! (LL) Hesitating Veteran, The. Ambrose Bierce. CBCWP; PCW

O that my prayers could raiment you in splendour. Fair Raiment. John Oxenham. SacPr

O That Summer. Ginger Andrews. SUP

O, that the Holy Angels would indite. Quarto Centennial, The. Josephine D. Henderson Heard. CBWP-4

O that the lilies and roses were mine. J. Gordon Coogler. VerBaPo

O, that the years had language! time would / tell. Judith. Eloise Bibb. CBWP-4

O, that there were, indeed, some hidden charm—. To Ancestry. John Thelwall. CenSon

O! that this too too solid flesh would melt. William Shakespeare. OxAEP-1; WaAnP Fr. Hamlet.

O [or Oh] that 'twere possible. Alfred Tennyson. NAEL-6v2; OBEV Fr. Maud [A Monodrama].

O! that we now had here. William Shakespeare. FaBoWar; OxAEP-1 Fr. King Henry V.

O the beautiful garment. "H. D." HarvBoo Fr. Flowering of the Rod, The.

O the beautiful garment. Flowering of the Rod, The. "H. D."

O the blessedness of life! It's lucky, no doubt. Life. T. H. Parry-Williams. BBMWP, tr. by Richard Poole

O the Chimneys [And though after my skin worms destroy this body, yet in my flesh shall I see God. JOB 19:26]. Nelly Sachs. AF; HP; PoetW, tr. by Michael Roloff

O! / The constellation glitters. Stars abound. Passages 37. Robert Duncan. FTOS

O the days gone by! O the days gone by! Days Gone By, The. James Whitcomb Riley. APN-2

O the deep, deep love of Jesus! Samuel Trevor Francis. SacPr

O the engineer's joys! to go with a locomotive! Walt Whitman. HHAm Fr. Song of Joys, A.

O the Harbour of Fowey. Harbour of Fowey, The. Sir Arthur Thomas Quiller-Couch. OBCoV

O, the Month of May. Thomas Dekker and others. NoSic Fr. Shoemaker's Holiday, The.

O the month of May, the merry month of May. Thomas Dekker and others. NoSic Fr. Shoemaker's Holiday, The.

O the mountaineer to the summit clear. Her Majesty. Arthur Waugh. ArBi

O the night of the weeping children! Nelly Sachs. HP

O the Night of the Weeping Children! Nelly Sachs. HP

O the opal and the sapphire of that wandering western sea. Beeny Cliff. Thomas Hardy. CABP; OxAEP-2

O the Raggedy Man! He works fer Pa. Raggedy Man, The. James Whitcomb Riley. ITBLP

O, the rain, the weary, dreary rain. Twenty Golden Years Ago. James Clarence Mangan. OxBEV

O the sad day! Sad Day, The. Thomas Flatman. OBEV

O the sweeping past of the ruined sky! (LL) Bracelet of Grass, The. William Vaughn Moody. APN-2; NAAPv.1; TCAPo

O, the Temeraire no more! (LL) Temeraire, The. Herman Melville. APN-2; FaBoWar

O the ten-, twelve-, twenty-story clouds. Altitude. Stanley Plumly. OtW

O there is blessing in this gentle breeze. William Wordsworth. NAEL-6v2; NAEL-7v2 Fr. Prelude, The; Growth of a Poet's Mind [1850 version].

O there is blessing in this gentle breeze. William Wordsworth. Fr. Prelude, The; Growth of a Poet's Mind [1805 version].

O these wakeful[l] wounds of thine! On the Wounds of Our Crucified Lord. Richard Crashaw. NAEL-6v1; NAEL-7v1

O, / these wild trees. Hymn for Lanie Poo. Imamu Amiri Baraka. BB

O they took my blessed Lawd. He Never Said a Mumblin' Word. Unknown. APN-2

O this weather! this weather! Hot Day In Sydney, A. Unknown. NOBAu

O, thou art far away from me—dear boy! To My Brother. Mary Bryan. CenSon

O Thou, beloved of my twenty seven senses. Anna Blossom Has Wheels. Kurt Schwitters. PFTM-1

O thou, by Nature taught. Ode to Simplicity. William Collins. OBEV; OxAEP-1

O thou great Wrong, that, through the slow-paced years. Death of Slavery, The. William Cullen Bryant. CBCWP; PCW

O thou little tree which I planted a few years ago. Homeland. Mahdi Muhammad Ali. IrPoTo, tr. by Salaam Yousif

O thou! meek Orb! that stealing o'er the dale. Her Address to the Moon. Mary Robinson. CenSon; RWP

O thou most terrible, most dreaded power. To Death. Mary Tighe. CenSon; NPBRoP

O thou, my lovely boy, who in thy power. William Shakespeare. HeIP-4; NAEL-6v1; NAEL-7v1; NoP-5 Fr. Sonnets.

O thou new comer [or newcomer] who seek'st Rome in Rome. Rome. Joachim Du Bellay. FaBoWar, tr. by Ezra Pound

O Thou of Little Faith! George Macdonald. SacPr

O thou slight word, most like to breath, and made. Death. Mary Elizabeth Coleridge. ViWPN

O thou, that art my Light, my Life, my Way. (LL) Francis Quarles. BASC; NOSC; OxAEP-1; SacPr Fr. Emblems (Fragments).

O Thou that in the heavens does dwell! Holy Willie's Prayer. Robert Burns. BrAP; CABP; NAEL-6v2; NAEL-7v2; NOBRP; NoP-5; NPBRoP; OBCoV; OBSV; TFi

(O Thou, wha in the heavens dost dwell.) NePenScot; NoP-4

O Thou, that sit'st upon a throne. Song to David, A. Christopher Smart. NAEL-6v1; NAEL-7v1; OBWVE

O Thou That Sleep'st like Pig in Straw. Sir William Davenant. NOSC

O Thou, the first, the greatest friend. First Six Verses of the Ninetieth Psalm, The. Robert Burns. ChIV-1

O thou, the wonder of all day[e]s! Dirge of Jephthah's Daughter, The. Robert Herrick. ChIV-1

O Thou, to Whom in Ancient Time. John Pierpont. TCAPo

O Thou, to whom, in ancient time. O Thou, to Whom in Ancient Time. John Pierpont. TCAPo

O thou undaunted daughter of desires! Richard Crashaw. OBEV; WoPoe Fr. Flaming Heart, The.

O Thou unknown, Almighty Cause. Prayer, in the Prospect of Death, A. Robert Burns. TreFP

O thou unknown disturber of my rest. To———. Mary Bryan. CenSon

O thou vast Ocean! ever-sounding Sea! Address to the Ocean. Barry Cornwall and Adelaide Anne Procter. TreFP

O thou! whatever title suit thee. Address to the Deil. Robert Burns. NePenScot

O Thou, who all things hast of nothing made. Bible, O.T. SacPr

O thou! / Who from "*a wilderness of Suns.*" Ode to Della Crusca. Hannah Cowley. NOBRP

O thou who never harbored fear. Sonnet. Eloise Bibb. CBWP-4

O thou who standest 'mid the bards of old. On Kean's Hamlet. Washington Allston. APN-1

O thou who sweetly bend'st my stubborn will. In Desolation. John Beaumont. SacPr

O Thou Whose Face Hath Felt the Winter's Wind. John Keats. CenSon

O thou! whose fancies from afar are brought. To H. C., Six Years Old. William Wordsworth. NPBRoP

O Thou! whose name too often is profaned. To Friendship. Charlotte Smith. RWP

O thou whose pow'r o'er moving worlds presides. Boethius. OBVE *Fr.* Consolation of Philosophy, The ("De Consolacione Philosophie").

O thou, with dewy locks, who lookest down. To Spring. William Blake. NAEL-6v2; NAEL-7v2; OBEV

O Thought, now you'll have to think the same thing forever! (LL) Fourth Floor, Dawn, Up All Night Writing Letters. Allen Ginsberg. HarvBoo; InvLad

O thow Minstral that cannest so note and pipe. John Lydgate. OxBEV *Fr.* Daunce of Death, The.

O three-toned green little place with trees. Waxwings. Milton Kessler. InvLad

O! thy bright eyes must answer now. Emily Jane Brontë. PEW; VWP

O Tim, my own Tim I must call 'ee—I will! Thomas Hardy. FaBoVe *Fr.* Bride-Night Fire, The.

O Time the fatal wrack of mortal things. Anne Bradstreet. ColAP *Fr.* Contemplations.

"O Time! who know'st a lenient hand to lay." William Lisle Bowles. *See* Time and Grief.

O timeless guest!—so soon returned art thou. To———. Mary Bryan. CenSon

O Times most bad. Upon the Troublesome Times. Robert Herrick. CavPo

O To Be A Dragon. Marianne Moore. APT-1; ChIV-1; NAAL-5; NALW

O to be blind! Blind Man at the Fair, The. Joseph Campbell. IrV

O[h], to be in England. Home-Thoughts, from Abroad. Robert Browning. CABP; ClHu; HeIP-4; NAEL-6v2; NAEL-7v2; NoP-4; NoP-5; OBEV; TFi; UV

O to be in the news again—now as fashion runs. Robert Adamson. BMAP *Fr.* Sonnets to be Written from Prison.

O to Be Up and Doing. Robert Louis Stevenson. ITBLP

O to break loose, like the chinook. Waking Early Sunday Morning. Robert Lowell. HarvBoo; NAMCP V.2; OxBoAm; VCAP

O [*or* Oh], to have a little house! Old Woman of the Roads, The. Padraic Colum. IrV; MoBrPo; OBEV

O to make the most jubilant song! Song of Joys, A. Walt Whitman.

O To Scuttle From the Battle. Justin Richardson. UV

O to scuttle from the battle and to settle on an atoll far from brutal mortal neath a wattle portal! O To Scuttle From the Battle. Justin Richardson. UV

O, to see you again. Covered in spring. (LL) In the Clear Long After. Olena Kalytiak Davis. NAPBL; PoDa

O tongue / licking. To an Old Jaundiced Woman. William Carlos Williams. APT-1

O, Traveller to Najran, convey to my two companions, when the day breaks. Writing on Aisha's Tomb. Abdul Wahab Al-Bayati. IrPoTo, *tr. by* Farouk Abdel Wahab

O treacherous scent, O thorny sight. Another for the Briar Rose. William Morris. OxBEV

O [*or* Oh] turn away those cruel eyes. Relapse, The. Thomas Stanley. NOSC; OBEV

O two-horned moon, you love the parties that last all night. Philodemus. HePo *Fr.* Epigrams.

O Tyrant / Tell me, how did you manage to build all these dungeons in your heart? Picture of a Tyrant. Hashim Shafiq. IrPoTo, *tr. by* Melissa Brown and Saadi A. Simawe

O urge me not to wander. O Bid Me Not to Wander. Susanna Blamire. NPBRoP

O vale and lake, within your mountain-urn. Felicia Dorothea Hemans. CenSon *Fr.* Records of the Spring of 1834.

O Virtuous Light. Elinor Wylie. MoAmPo

O Visionary who adjust your lens. Higher Empiricism, The. Francis C. Golffing. PoA 2002

O Vocables of Love. Laura Riding Jackson. APT-2

Ô vous mes nuits, ô noires attendues. Nyx. Catherine Pozzi. YaTCFP

O wad this braw hie-heapit toun. Prows O' Reekie, The. Lewis Spence. NePenScot

O Wakonda, you see me a poor man. Prayer of a Warrior (Assiniboine). *Unknown.* AmWaPo, *tr. by* Edwin Thompson Denig

O walk Jordan long road. Religion So Sweet. *Unknown.* SSUS

O, Was my Heart but form'd for Woe. One Thing Needful Generally Neglected, The. Samuel Davies. SacPr

O wastfull riot, never well content. Lucan. OBVE *Fr.* Civil War [Bellum Civile] *or* Pharsalia.

O wat ye what my Minnie did. Wat ye what my Minnie did. Robert Burns. EroLit

O waters running pure and crystal clear. Baldomero Garcilaso de la Vega. SpanPo *Fr.* Eclogue 1.

O Wave God who broke through me today. Burning Island. Gary Snyder. APSN; VCAP

O wearisome condition of humanity! Fulke, 1st Baron Brooke Greville. *See* O[h] wearisome condition of humanity.

O weary Champion of the Cross, lie still. Cardinal Newman. Christina Georgina Rossetti. NAEL-6v2; NAEL-7v2

O weary pilgrims, chanting of your woe. Robert Bridges. MoBrPo *Fr.* Growth of Love, The.

O Wendy, Arthur. Maurice Kenny. HATNAP

O were it but a venial sin, and I asleep. Virgin, The. Ruth Herschberger. OxBoAm

O Were My Love Yon Lilac[k] Fair. Robert Burns. OBEV

O wha my babie-clouts will buy? Rantin' Dog, the Daddie o't, The. Robert Burns. FaBoVe

O wha' the bride that cairries the bunch. Hugh MacDiarmid. NPeEn *Fr.* Drunk Man Looks at the Thistle, A.

O Wha's Been Here Afore Me, Lass? Hugh MacDiarmid. *See* O Wha's the Bride?

O wha's the bride that carries the bunch. O Wha's the Bride? Hugh MacDiarmid. NAMCP V.1; OxBEV; RaBo

(O wha's the bride that cairries the bunch.) EdScPo; WoPoe

O what a loud and fearful shriek was there. Samuel Taylor Coleridge. OxBSo *Fr.* Effusions.

O what a luxury it be. O Luxury. Guy W. Longchamps. GoPo

O what a magic comfort are boys to men! Fragment 652. Euripides. CAGL, *tr. by* John Addington Symonds

O what a physical effect it has on me. In Love with You. Kenneth Koch. PoDa

O what a strange parcel of creatures are we. On an Unsociable Family. Elizabeth Hands. NPeEn; WoRP

O what a tangled web we weave. Word of Encouragement, A. J. R. Pope. NBLV

O! what a thing is Love? who can define. Edward Taylor. SacPr

O what a weary while it is to stand. Eternity. James Whitcomb Riley. GSo

O, what can ail thee, knight at arms. Answer to a Kind Enquiry. Mary Holtby. UV

O what can ail thee, knight-at-arms [*or* wretched wight]. Belle Dame sans Merci, La [A Ballad]. John Keats. BrAP; BRP; CABP; ClHu; CtM; HeIP-4; NAEL-6v2; NAEL-7v2; NAWM-7v2; NOBRP; NoP-4; NoP-5; NPBRoP; NPeEn; OBEV; OBSP; OxAEP-2; OxBEV; PoPoPo; SoSe-8; TFi; TRP; UV; WaAnP; WoPoe

O what can you give me? Idris Davies. AngWePo *Fr.* Gwalia Deserta.

O what could be more nice. Light Listened. Theodore Roethke. MoAmPo

O What Is That Sound [Which So Thrills the Ear]. W. H. Auden. FaBoWar; PoAgWa

(Ballad.) MoBrPo

(Quarry, The.) WaAnP

O what will a' the lads do. When Maggy Gangs Away. James Hogg. CABP; NPBRoP

O [*or* Oh] when our clergy at the dreadful day. On Those That Deserve It. Francis Quarles. NOSC

O [*or* Oh] when the saints go marchin' [*or* marching] in. When the Saints Go Marchin' [*or* Marching] In. *Unknown.* TCAPo

O when you come in summer time. Blue Tail Fly or Jimmy Cracked Corn, The. Daniel Decatur Emmett. TCAPo

O when you were little, you were really big. Duet. Theodore Roethke. OBCoV

O where are Mina Bell's cows who gave no milk. Mina Bell's Cows. Wesley McNair. TRP

O where are they now, your harridan nuns. Nuns of Childhood, The: Two Views. Maxine W. Kumin. FFC; WaAnP

O [*or* Oh] where are you going? says [*or* said] Milder to Malder. Cutty Wren, The. *Unknown.* UV

O where does the dancer dance. Song. Judith Wright. BrAP

O where have you been, Lord Randal my son?   Lord Randal[l].   *Unknown*. CtM; HeIP-4; InoFa; NAEL-6v1; NAEL-7v1; NIL-7; NoP-4; NoP-5; NPeEn; OxBEV; PoPoPo; TFi; TRP; WaAnP; WeW-3

"O where [*or* whare] have you [*or* hae ye] been, my dear, dear [*or* dearest dear *or* long, long] love."   Demon Lover, The.   *Unknown*.   TFi; WeW-3

O, Where Were We Before Time Was.   Max Dunn.   NOBAu

O where will you go when the blinding flash.   Terminal Colloquy.   Charles Martin.   AtGh

O whirly-water.   Lawn Sprinkler, The.   Queen Lili'u-o-ka-lani.   WoPoe, *tr.* by Alfons L. Korn and Mary Kawena Pukui

O whistle, and I'll come to you [*or* ye], my lad.   Whistle, and I'll Come to You, My Lad.   Robert Burns.   OxAEP-2

O whitewashed chapel.   Greece.   Gunnar Ekelof.   BLT

O whither dost thou flye? Cannot my vow.   William Habington.   OxBSo *Fr.* Castara.

O Whither will you lead the Fair.   Countess of Anglesey lead Captive by the Rebels, at the Disforresting of Pewsam, The.   Sir William Davenant.   PBRV

O who can ever gaze his fill.   Death's Echo.   W. H. Auden.   IJHIL

O who rides by night thro' the woodland so wild?   Erl-King, The.   Johann Wolfgang von Goethe.   OBVE; STV

   (Who is it that rides through the forest so fast?)   NOBRP

O[h], who shall from this dungeon raise.   Dialogue between the Soul and [the] Body, A.   Andrew Marvell.   BASC; BrAP; FSCP; NAEL-6v1; NAEL-7v1; NoP-4; NoP-5; OxAEP-1; OxBEV; SoSe-8; TFi

O who will show me those delights on high?   Heaven.   George Herbert.   WoPoe

O who would not sleep with the brave? (LL)   Lancer.   A. E. Housman.   MoBrPo; OBWP

O why do you walk through the fields in gloves.   To a Fat Lady Seen from the Train.   Frances Darwin Cornford.   MoBrPo; OBMV; OxBEV; UV; WeW-3

O, why should Nature niggardly restraine!   Michael Drayton.   PBRV *Fr.* Idea.

O wife, wife, wife! As if the sacred name.   Last Giustiniani, The.   Edith Wharton.   APN-2

O[h] wild West Wind, thou breath of Autumn's being.   Ode to the West Wind.   Percy Bysshe Shelley.   BrAP; CenSon; ClHu; HeIP-4; MakPoe; NAEL-6v2; NAEL-7v2; NAWM-7v2; NIL-7; NIP-4; NOBRP; NoP-4; NoP-5; NPeEn; OBEV; OxAEP-2; OxBEV; OxBSo; PoPoPo; TFi; TRP; WaAnP; WeW-3

O wind, rend open the heat.   "H. D."   HeIP-4; MoAmPo; TCAPo; TRP *Fr.* Garden, The.

O Wind, thou hast thy kingdom in the trees.   Michael Field.   VWP

O Winter Aphrodite! O acute.   To the Winter Aphrodite.   Michael Field.   VWP

O wistful eyes that haunt the gloom of sleep.   Unborn.   John Le Gay Brereton.   NOBAu

O Woman of Three Cows, agra [*or* agragh] [don't let your tongue thus rattle!].   Woman of Three Cows, The.   *Unknown*.   OBCoV, *tr.* by James Clarence Mangan

O wondrous age! a wondrous age we live in.   Beelah Viaduct, The.   John Close.   STuOW

O, wondrous depth to which my soul is stirr'd.   Music.   Josephine D. Henderson Heard.   CBWP-4

O wondrous thing it is.   Excitation.   Lorenzo Thomas.   FTOS

O words are lightly spoken.   Rose Tree, The.   William Butler Yeats.   OBMV

O world, I cannot hold thee close enough!   God's World.   Edna St. Vincent Millay.   APT-1; ITBLP; MoAmPo

O world invisible, we view thee.   Kingdom of God, The.   Francis Thompson.   SacPr

O World, O Life, O Time.   Percy Bysshe Shelley.   NAEL-6v2; NAEL-7v2

O world, thou choosest not the better part!   George Santayana.   APN-2; TCAPo *Fr.* Sonnets.

O worship the King all glorious above.   Sir Robert Grant.   SacPr

O would I were where I would be!   Suspiria.   *Unknown*.   OBEV

O wreche [*or* wretch], be war [*or* beware], this warld [*or* world] will wend the[e] fro.   William Dunbar.   SacPr

O ye, all ye that walk in Willowwood.   Dante Gabriel Rossetti.   NAEL-6v2; OxBSo *Fr.* House of Life, The.

O ye dead Poets, who are living still.   Poets, The.   Henry Wadsworth Longfellow.   GSo

O ye gentle breeze which wafts to me.   Ku'u Pua I Paoakalani.   Queen Lili'u-o-ka-lani.   SWaP

O ye numberless.   Samuel Taylor Coleridge.   NAEL-7v2 *Fr.* Religious Musings.

O Ye Tongues.   Anne Sexton.   NALW

   Third Psalm.   NALW

O [*or* A *or* Oh] ye wha are sae guid yoursel.   Address to the Unco Guid, or the Rigidly Righteous.   Robert Burns.   ChIV-1; OxBEV

O ye who have vanquished the land and retain it.   New Race, The.   Aubrey Thomas De Vere.   IrV

O ye who ride upon the wandering gale.   To the Clouds.   Susan Evance.   CenSon

O ye wretched Scots.   John Skelton.   OBSV *Fr.* How the Doughty Duke of Albany like a Coward Knight Ran Away Shamefully.

O Years! and Age! Farewell.   Robert Herrick.   CavPo

O yee, whome lorde of lande and waters wyde.   Seneca.   OBVE *Fr.* Thyestes.

O, Yellow Pond.   *Unknown*.   CCL1 *Fr.* Travels of Mu, Son of Heaven, The.

O' Yes.   Lamont B. Steptoe.   ISC

O' yes.   O' Yes.   Lamont B. Steptoe.   ISC

O Yes? Do they come on horses.   So Mexicans Are Taking Jobs from Americans.   Jimmy Santiago Baca.   LTA; UnSA

O yes I told her.   For the Angry White Student Who Wanted to Know.   Wendy Rose.   FTtHH

O yes. I've had to give up somewhat here.   Dry Eleven Months.   John Berryman.   BodElec

O yes, the Chinese Garden! Do you remember.   Chinese Garden, The.   Horace Gregory.   OBGa

O yesterday the cutting edge drank thirstily and deep.   To-morrow.   John Masefield.   MoBrPo

O yes—you understand, I say.   "H. D."   NAAPv.2; NALW; NAMCP V.1 *Fr.* Tribute to the Angels.

O Yonge fresshe folks, he or she.   Love Unfeigned, The.   Geoffrey Chaucer.   OBEV

O you in that little bark.   Michael Palmer.   CAP-8

O you lovers that are so gentle, step occasionally.   Rainer Maria Rilke.   RaBo *Fr.* Sonnets to Orpheus.

O you so long dead.   To My Brother: Killed: Hammont Wood: October, 1918.   Louise Bogan.   AmWaPo

O you, / Who came upon me once.   Carrefour.   Amy Lowell.   LW

O you who eat with someone else's teeth.   Toothpuller Who Wanted to Turn a Mouth into a Grinding Machine, The.   Francisco de Quevedo y Villegas.   WoPoe, *tr.* by Willis Barnstone

O you who guard over.   Andal.   WPoS *Fr.* Tiruppavai, The.

O you who have aimed / At my heart with the dart / Of a piercing glance.   King of Granada Yūsuf III.   HiArP, *tr.* by James T. Monroe

O you whom I often and silently come where you are that I may be with you.   O You Whom I Often and Silently Come.   Walt Whitman.   APN-1

O you would clothe me in silken frocks.   Wild Goat, The.   Claude McKay.   RACG

O young man who composes the poem.   Brigid Fitzgerald.   EMWP

O younge [*or* yonge] fres[s]he folkes, he or she.   Geoffrey Chaucer.   OBEV *Fr.* Troilus and Criseyde [*or* Criseide].

O zummer clote! when the brook's a-glidèn [*or* a-sliden].   Clote, The.   William Barnes.   FaBoVe; NPeEn

Oafs emit the fundament.   Stewed and Fraught with Birds.   Stephen Rodefer.   VaPo

Oak coffin covered with vines, An.   Furtherness.   Mary Ruefle.   BAP-01

Oak inns creak in their joints as light declines, The.   Derek Walcott.   NoAM *Fr.* Midsummer.

Oak oak! like like / it then.   Drunken Winter.   Joseph Ceravolo.   NYP2; OxBoAm

Oak sky. (LL)   Drunken Winter.   Joseph Ceravolo.   NYP2; OxBoAm

Oak, The.   Aleksandr Semionovich Kushner.   TCRusP, *tr.* by Daniel Weissbort

Oak, The.   George Pope Morris.   *See* Woodman, Spare That Tree.

Oak Tree.   Gwyn Williams.   BBMWP, *tr.* by Christopher Meredith

Oak tree, The.   Basho.   EH, *tr.* by Robert Hass

Oak tree in my front yard dies, The.   For a Bitter Season.   George Garrett.   LPSFW

Oakland.   Robert Grenier.

   "Open the door Oakland."   FTOS

Oakland Blues.   Ishmael Reed.   CalPo

Oaks and Squirrels.   Anne Porter.   ChIV-1

Oaks are stricken by a serious illness, The.   More than Suspect.   André Breton.   AF, *tr.* by Mary Ann Caws

Oaks, how subtle and marine, The.   Bearded Oaks.   Robert Penn Warren.   APT-2; ColAP; EMP; FuPo; InGu; MoAmPo; NAAL-5; NAMCP V.1; NoAM; NoP-4; NoP-5; PoA 2002

Oaktown CA.   Reginald Lockett.   FTtHH

Oars, heavy with seaweed, at rest in humid mists, The.   Oars Heavy with Seaweed, The.   Karel Van de Woestijne.   TuT, *tr.* by Michael Longley

Oars Heavy with Seaweed, The.   Karel Van de Woestijne.   TuT, *tr.* by Michael Longley

Oarsman, The.   Paul Valéry.   YaTCFP, *tr.* by Mary Ann Caws and Patricia Terry

Oasis. Diana Hartog. NLPA

  Chimney Ranch. NLPA

  Creation, 3:30 p.m., the Fifth Day. NLPA

  Entry. NLPA

  Glass. NLPA

  Infra-Red. NLPA

  Link Between Reader and Writer, The. NLPA

  Meridian. NLPA

  Moon and Firestone, The. NLPA

  Nightclass. NLPA

  Seventh Day, The. NLPA

  "Sound of each other, rustling, The." NLPA

  Thirst for Knowledge, A. NLPA

Oasis, An. Agnes Mary Frances Robinson. VWP

Oasis, light incarnate. (LL) World Without Objects Is a Sensible Emptiness, A. Richard Wilbur. MoAmPo; NoAM; PoA 2002; UpMys

Oath, The. Allen Tate. InGu

Oaths. Thomas Brown. OBCoV

Oatmeal. Galway Kinnell. EmeKit; FaoP; StAl

Ob all de subjects I kin read. Men Folks ob Today, De. Maggie Pogue Johnson. CBWP-4

Obbligato from a Public Gallery. Jared Angira. NAfrP

Obeah Mama Dot. Frederick D'Aguiar. Oth

Obedience / Intention to Hunt. Malinda Markham. IAoNAP

Obedience of the Corpse. C. D. Wright. InGu

Obedient Girl, The. Marjorie Agosin. ExTi

Obedient girl, The. Obedient Girl, The. Marjorie Agosin. ExTi

Obelisk Inscriptions. Queen Hatshepsut.

  "I have done this with a loving heart for my father Amun." HAWP

Ober de mountains, slick as an eel. Boatman's Dance. Daniel Decatur Emmett. APN-1

Oberon's Feast. Robert Herrick. NOSC

Obessions Are Important. Primus St. John. BtF

Obey Your Parents. William Bingham Tappan. VerBaPo

Obeying orders, I journeyed to the distant capital. Recalling Old Times. Xiang Xiu. CCL1, tr. by Burton Watson

Obit. Robert Lowell. PoetW; VCAP

Obit on Parnassus. F. Scott Fitzgerald. AmWit; NBLV

Obiter Dicta. Joseph Hilaire Pierre Belloc. OBCoV

Obituary. Steve Chimombo. HBAPE

Obituary. Kenneth Fearing. IllVoic

Object among dreams, you sit here with your shoes off, An. Girl in a Library, A. Randall Jarrell. InGu; NoAM

Object of Burial Is Intent, The. Rebecca Reynolds. AmPoNex

Objection Overruled. Jackie Hardy. NeBl

Objection to Being Stepped On, The. Robert Frost. NBLV; OBCoV

Objectivist Lamp. Carl Rakosi. NAAPv.2

Objectivists are metaphysical. Edward Hopper. Anthony Rudolf. PoSol

Objects. Yevgeny Mikhailovich Vinokurov. TCRusP Fr. History.

Objects. Richard Wilbur.

  "There's classic and there's quaint." UpMys

Objects clutter the shiny air and flash. In Communication with a UFO. Helen Chasin. YaYoPo

Objects in Mirror Are Closer Than They Appear. Reginald Shepherd. RD

Objects in Mirror are Closer Than They Appear. Jeffrey Skinner. PBCAP

Objects in the mirror are mirrors. Charm of the Highway Strip, The. Jim Behrle. FreRad

Objects of Desire. Monifa Atungaye Love. BtF

Obligation to Be Happy, The. Linda Pastan. PoA 2002

Obligations of Civil to Religious Liberty. William Wordsworth. SacPr Fr. Ecclesiastical Sonnets.

Obliged by frequent visits of this man. Flecknoe, an English Priest at Rome. Andrew Marvell. BASC

Oblique cloud of purple smoke, An. Woman Walking. William Carlos Williams. ColAP

Oblique light on the trite, on brick and tile. Courtyards in Delft. Derek Mahon. ModIr; NPeEn; PBCIP; PNI

Oblique Prayer. Denise Levertov. SacPr

Oblique Rain. Fernando Pessoa.

  "Inside, the church lights up today's rain." PFTM-1, tr. by Susan M. Brown and Edwin Honig

Obliterate / mythology as you unwind. Cavern, The. Charles Tomlinson. ICANM

Obliterating face and hands. Hamish Henderson. EdScPo Fr. Elegies for the Dead in Cyrenaica.

Oblivion. Fanny Carrión de Fierro. TANSG, tr. by Sally Cheney Bell

"Oblivion, that's all. I never dream" he said. Dreaming. Fleur Adcock. OxBSo

Oblivion: "Twilight hours are always gruff and gory." Ahmet Muhip Dıranas. NaPG, tr. by Talat Sait Halman

Oboe. Laurence McKinney. NBLV

O-Bon: Dance for the Dead. Garrett Kaoru Hongo. LoL

Obscur et froncé. Arthur Rimbaud. EroLit, tr. by Kenneth McLeish

Obscure, The. Norman Dubie. NoAM

Obscure and little seen my way. Charlotte Brontë. VWP

Obscure Night of the Soul, The. San Juan de la Cruz. See Dark Night, The.

Obscure Night of the Soul, The. San Juan de la Cruz. OBMV, tr. by Arthur Symons

Obscurely yet most surely called to praise. Praise in Summer. Richard Wilbur. NoP-4; UpMys

Obscurest night involved [or involv'd] the sky. Castaway, The. William Cowper. BrAP; NAEL-6v1; NAEL-7v1; NOBRP; NoP-4; NoP-5; NPeEn; OxBEV; PoPoPo; TRP

Obscurity of Woman's Worth. Caroline Elizabeth Norton. VWP

Obsequies of Stuart. John Randolph Thompson. CBCWP

Obsequious squeaker. Golden-Mantled Ground Squirrel. Sandra Alcosser. PfSP

Observance. Barbara Unger. TWW

Observant of the way she told. Tact. Edwin Arlington Robinson. NoAM

Observation. Tim Griffin. FreRad

Observation. Dorothy Parker. APT-1; NAMCP V.1; OxBoAm

Observation, An. Kay Sage. SurWo

Observation Car. Alec Derwent Hope. NAMCP V.1; NoAM

Observation Generall from Their Eating, Etc., The. Roger Williams. SacPr (Of Eating and Entertainment.) TCAPo

Observation ("Virgin-Mother stood at distance (there), The.") Robert Herrick. ChIV-2

Observations. Luvuyo Mkangelwa. NAfrP

Observations and Experiments. Annie Dillard. UpMys

Observations in the Art of English Poesie. Thomas Campion.

  (Laura). OBEV

  (Rose-Cheek'd Laura, Come.) CABP

  "Rose-cheeked Laura, come." NAEL-6v1; NAEL-7v1; NoP-4; NoP-5; NOSC; TFi; TRP; WaAnP

Observations of Egyptian Artifacts. Britton Wilkie. AHA

Observe how he negotiates his way. Swimmer. Robert Francis. APT-2; WeW-3

Observe the weary birds ere night be done. Orinda to Lucasia. Katherine Philips. BASC; NOSC

Observed Observer, The. Alan Gould. BMAP

Obsessed, bewildered / By the shipwreck. George Oppen. NAMCP V.1 Fr. Of Being Numerous.

Obsessed by betrayal. Palm Leaf of Mary Magdalene. Cheryl Clarke. WiU

Obsession. Robert Desnos. SurPaPo, tr. by Mary Ann Caws

Obsession. Angelina Muñiz Huberman. MirDau, tr. by Aurora Camacho

Obsession: "Knife on the fruit dish, The." Pak Sôwôn. EcSo, tr. by Julie C. Park

Obsidian sculpted lips slip. Doll Museum, The. Carlyle Reedy. Oth

Obsolescence of Thou, The. Rodney Jones. PoA 2002

Obvious is the rottenness through your head. (LL) Penis, The. Dafydd ap Gwilym. EroLit; WoPoe, tr. by Dafydd Johnston

Obvious, The. Anna Couani. BMAP

Obvious, The. Jeffrey McDaniel. AmPoNex

Obvious Tradition, The. Bill Berkson. NYP2

Occam's Razor. Thomas Rain Crowe. AmZen

Occasion and expediency determines the form, The. (LL) Past Is the Present, The. Marianne Moore. APT-1; OxBoAm

Occasional Man, An. Ralph Blane and Hugh Martin. ReLy

Occasional mornings when an early fog. Housewife. Josephine Miles. APT-2

Occasional Poem. Larry Fagin. AHA Fr. Parade of the Caterpillars, The.

Occasional Poem 7.1.72. Roy Fisher. HarvBoo

Occasioned by Reading Mrs. M. Robinson's Poems. Martha Hanson. CenSon

Occasioned by Seeing a Walk of Bay Trees. Mildmay Fane, 2d Earl of Westmorland. NOSC

Occasions. Michael Murphy. NIrP

Occassional Loquats. Gus Blaisdell. ICANM

Occupant of the Hose. Larissa Szporluk. NeAmPo

Occupation. Suji Kwock Kim. LegDan

Occupations of Hell. John Milton. NOSC Fr. Paradise Lost.

Occupies a wide mind, a wide consciousness. Wide Mind. Joanne Kyger. WANABP

Occupy the poem. They stake. Abandoing All Pretense, the Vandals. Alan Michael Parker. NAPBL

Occurrences and all that failed to occur.   Didactic Poem on the Nature of History, A.D. 1954.   Helmut Heissenbüttel.   PFTM-2, *tr. by* Jerome Rothenberg

Occurrences, The ("Simplest / Words say the grass blade, The.")   George Oppen.   APT-2

Ocean.   Peter Balakian.   PfSP

Ocean / in the bed of a.   Answers, The.   Ed Robeson.   Eno

Ocean, The.   Lord Byron.   *See* Apostrophe to the Ocean.

Ocean, The.   Lord Byron.   *Fr.* Childe Harold's Pilgrimage.

Ocean, The.   Nathaniel Hawthorne.   APN-1

Ocean, The.   Moschus.   OBVE, *tr. by* Percy Bysshe Shelley

Ocean, The.   Charles Olson.   APT-2 *Fr.* Maximus Poems, The.

Ocean, an Ode.   Edward Young.
   "Who sings the source."   STuOW

Ocean begat ground.   February Ground.   Edward Dahlberg.   APT-2

Ocean has its silent caves, The.   Ocean, The.   Nathaniel Hawthorne.   APN-1

Ocean has not been so quiet for a long while, The.   Evening Ebb.   Robinson Jeffers.   NoAM
   (Ocean has not been so quiet for a long while; five night- / herons, The.)   v(BLT

Ocean Liner.   Ko Changsu.   WoPoe, *tr. by* the author

Ocean Liner.   Peter Schjeldahl.   AHA

Ocean Musing, An.   Henrietta Cordelia Ray.   CBWP-3; SWaP

Ocean of Light.   Phineas Fletcher.   NOSC
   (Vast Ocean of light, whose rayes surround.)   PBRV

Ocean of the Streams of Story.   Primus St. John.   GT

Ocean Spirit.   Song for Smooth Waters.   Haida.   CA

Ocean State.   Stephen Burt.   LegDan

Ocean strives with forth the boat to kiss, The. (LL)   Sonnet: "Slide soft, fair forth, and make a crystal plain."   William Drummond of Hawthornden.   NOSC; OxBSo

Ocean takes so long, The.   Year in Hawaii.   Marianne Boruch.   AmAlph

Ocean to Cynthia, The.   Sir Walter Ralegh.   NoSic

Ocean too has Winter-Views serene, The.   George Crabbe.   WoPoe *Fr.* Borough, The.

Ocean with its large mouth swallowed him, The.   Kenji Takezo Becomes Water.   Rick Noguchi.   NeAmPo

Oceanoceanoceanoceanocean.   Concrete Seascape.   William Harmon.   PoDa

Oceans.   Juan Ramón Jiménez.   RaW; WED, *tr. by* Robert Bly

Ocean's Love to Cynthia, The.   Sir Walter Ralegh.
   "Butt stay my thoughts, make end, geve fortune way."   NPeEn
   (Ocean to Cynthia, The.)   NoSic
   (21th: and last booke of the Ocean to Scinthia, The.)   PBRV

Ocean's Tribute, The.   Robinson Jeffers.   NAAPv.2

Ocean-Spoil Alive, O!   Alfred Tennyson.   STuOW *Fr.* Enoch Arden.

Och, Johnny, I hardly knew ye! (LL)   Johnny, I Hardly Knew Ye.   *Unknown.*   FaBoWar; IrV; NPeEn; PoAgWa

Ochre Iron.   Peter Blue Cloud.   HATNAP

O'Clock.   Fanny Howe.
   "Edge of the dome is slipping, The."   FTOS
   "You float inside your water."   FTOS

Ocol rejects the old type.   Okot P'Bitek.   NAMCP V.2; PoetW *Fr.* Song of Lawino.

Octans the Octant.   Alan Robert Wilson.   Coast

Octaves.   Edwin Arlington Robinson.

Octavia.   Italo Calvino.   MotU *Fr.* Invisible Cities.

Octet Before Winter.   Claire Malroux.   VCWP, *tr. by* Marilyn Hacker

October.   William Cullen Bryant.   APN-1

October.   Paul Claudel.   YaTCFP, *tr. by* James Lawler

October.   Mary Weston Fordham.   CBWP-2

October.   Robert Earl Hayden.   ESEAA

October.   Paul Hamilton Hayne.   APN-2

October.   Helen Hunt Jackson.   APN-2

October: "It's nuthatch on the box elder outside the window."   David Brendon Hopes.   UpMys

October.   Denise Levertov.   TRP

October.   Henrietta Cordelia Ray.   CBWP-3

October.   Edmund Spenser.   NAEL-6v1; NAEL-7v1 *Fr.* Shepherd's Calender, The.

October.   Edward Thomas.   CABP; HarvBoo; NoAM

October.   Yvor Winters.   APT-2

October 1.   Karl Shapiro.   MoAmPo

October 1, 1999.   Alex Rawls.   AnSo *Fr.* What's Your Sign?

X: October 1 (*morning*).   Susan Hahn.   Vesp *Fr.* Holiday.

October 7, 1994.   Ruth Lepson.   PfS

October 31, 1981.   Albert Huffstickler.   TiP2

October 23, 1983.   June Jordan.   SeSe

October 27th.   Vera Gheraducci.   CItWP, *tr. by* Cinzia Sartini Blum and Lara Trubowitz

October 31st 1994 7:30 am, on a street in Syracuse New York I'm a black female.   "C" ing in Colors: Blue.   Safiya Henderson-Holmes.   SpirFl

October, A Copper-Crawed Cock.   Nikolai Alekseievich Klyuyev.   TCRusP, *tr. by* John Glad

October, a copper-crawed cock.   October, A Copper-Crawed Cock.   Nikolai Alekseievich Klyuyev.   TCRusP, *tr. by* John Glad

October air was warm and musky, blowing, The.   Soybeans.   Thomas Alan Orr.   GoPo; IPoFL

October & winter had begun.   My Indian Grandmother Speaks to Animals.   John E. Smelcer.   PoCoUp

October Death.   Kiamsha Madelyn Leeke.   BtF

October, 1803 ("When, looking on the present face of things.")   William Wordsworth.   CenSon

October Falls in Black and White.   Joe Lothamer.   GeoH

October, flower of my peril—.   Indian Summer.   Cristina Campo.   CItWP, *tr. by* Cinzia Sartini Blum and Lara Trubowitz

October, Gothic October: no lovers loiter, lounge.   George Elliott Clarke.   Coast *Fr.* Blue Elegies.

October has come—already now the wood.   Autumn (A Fragment).   Alexander Sergeyevich Pushkin.   WoPoe, *tr. by* Edwin Morgan

October Is Here.   Mrs. Henry Linden.   CBWP-4

October, Isle of Skye.   Carter Revard.   NoP-4

October its brilliance.   In October.   Claire Malroux.   VCWP, *tr. by* Marilyn Hacker

October: "It's odd to have a separate month. It."   Bill Berkson.   NYP2

October Journey.   Margaret Walker Alexander.   GT

October Maples, Portland.   Richard Wilbur.   UpMys

October Marriage.   Dennis Nurkse.   PA9/11

October night nesting on the stadium.   Halftime.   Adam Lefevre.   MoASP

October: no frost.   Taproots.   Dorothy Marie Rice.   FuFl

October Nocturne, An.   Yvor Winters.   OtW

October Observed, Hudson Falls, New York in Bill's Back Yard.   Richard Elman.   PoCoUp

October Opera for Kate.   Angus Calder.   EdScPo

October Poem.   Tamura Ryuichi.   AF, *tr. by* Christopher Drake

October Redbreast, The.   Alice Thompson Meynell.   MoBrPo

October Robin, An.   Ted Hughes.   NOxBChV

October robin kept, An.   October Robin, An.   Ted Hughes.   NOxBChV

October Salmon[, An].   Ted Hughes.   EmeKit

October 7th.   Zachary Scott Robbins.   BtF

October. They decide it is time to move.   Sestina for the House.   Ronald Wallace.   PBCAP

October Tune.   Joseph Brodsky.   VCWP, *tr. by* the author and Joseph Brodsky

October, Yellowstone Park.   Maxine W. Kumin.   ExTi; PfSP

October's Bright Blue Weather.   Helen Hunt Jackson.   ITBLP

October's gold is dim—the forests rot.   Sonnet.   David Gray.   OxAEP-2

Octobre.   Paul Claudel.   YaTCFP

Octopus.   Arthur Clement Hilton.   UV

Octopus.   Caitríona O'Reilly.   NIrP; StAl

Octopus, An.   Marianne Moore.   NAMCP V.1; OxBoAm

Octopus, The.   James Merrill.   CAP-8

Octopus in hot sauce.   Just the Two of Us.   Kate Jennings.   BMAP

Octopus in one hand, cookbook in the other, he nearly.   Mediterranean Cooking for Two.   Janet Holmes.   PoDa

Octopus traps.   Basho.   EMJL, *tr. by* Haruo Shirane

Octopuses caught in floating pots.   Basho.   WED, *tr. by* Robert Bly

Octoroon, The.   *Sels.*   Albery Allson Whitman.   NAAP V.1

Oda a la Cebolla.   Pablo Neruda.   IPoFL

Oda a la Manzana.   Pablo Neruda.   IPoFL

Oda para Leticia.   Oscar Bermeo.   IJHIL

Odakyu line is always crowded I go on standing, The.   Near Kitami Station on the Odakyū Line.   Itō Hiromi.   PFTM-2, *tr. by* Leith Morton

Odd Case of Mr. Gill.   William Wordsworth.   STuOW *Fr.* Goody Blake and Harry Gill.

Odd day, An. For the first time in years.   View from a Cab, The.   Henry Taylor.   NBLV

Odd gift, certainly, An.   One.   Spirit Level.   Anthony Conran.   TCAWP

Odd music, / cutting through horn blasts and squawks of traffic, asserts.   Organist's Black Carnation, The.   Laurence Lieberman.   BodElec

Odd to close my eyes during the day and open them at night.   Robert Glück.   WiU *Fr.* Visit, The.

Odd Years, The.   Jeffery Conway.   BeDoSh

Odd, *You* should fear the touch.   Ne Me Tangito.   Charlotte Mew.   VWP

Odds were a hundred to one against me, The.   They All Laughed.   Ira Gershwin.   APT-2; ReLy

Ode.   Elizabeth Alexander.   GT; PoPoPo

Ode: "Bards of passion and of mirth." John Keats. OBEV; OxAEP-2

Ode: "Do ye quail but to hear, Carolinians." William Gilmore Simms. PCW

Ode: "Here I'm perched on a sheer cliff." Attila József. IQMS, *tr.* by Susanne K. Walther

Ode: "I hate that drum's discordant sound." John Scott of Amwell. NIP-4; OxAEP-1

   (Drum, The.) FaBoWar; PoAgWa

Ode: "Lend me your great sound, your fine smooth speed." Valery Larbaud. YaTCFP, *tr.* by Mary Ann Caws *and* Jean-Pierre Cauvin and Patricia Terry

Ode: "Now each creature joys the other." Samuel Daniel. NoSic

Ode: "Prête-moi ton grand bruit, ta grande allure si douce." Valery Larbaud. YaTCFP

Ode: "Raven croaks before me, A." Theophile De Viau. WoPoe, *tr.* by Phillip Holland

Ode: "Sleep sweetly in your humble graves." Henry Timrod. CBCWP; ColAP; MakPoe; NAAPv.1

   (Lines.) APN-2

   (Lines.) PCW

   (Ode Sung at Magnolia Cemetery.) TCAPo

Ode: "Spacious firmament on high, The." Joseph Addison. ChIV-1; NPeEn; OxBEV

   (Spacious Firmament on High, The.) CtM

Ode: "Urals post-master, this is your." Barry MacSweeney. Oth

Ode: "Vengeance will sit above our faults; but till." John Donne. SacPr

Ode: "We are the music-makers." Arthur William Edgar O'Shaughnessy. OBEV

   (We Are the Music Makers.) CABP

Ode: "Weep, ah weep love's losing, love's with its dwelling-place." Imr el Kais. TAL *Fr.* Mu'allaqat, The.

Ode: "Where have you gone blue middle of a decade? the gates creak. a sigh is so vastly different." D. A. Powell. NAPBL

Ode. Thomas Gray. *See* Ode on the Death of a Favo[u]rite Cat, Drowned in a Tub [*or* Bowl] of Gold Fishes.

Ode. Richard Lovelace. CavPo

Ode. Hugh Maxton. PBCIP

Ode 1.9 / To Thaliarchus. Horace. PtR *Fr.* Odes.

Ode 3.29: To Maecenas. Horace. NPeEn; OBVE *Fr.* Odes.

Ode 5: "Of thee the Northman by his beachèd galley." George Santayana. APN-2

Ode 6: "Lachon has brought home the bacon." Bacchylides. PoCho, *tr.* by David R. Slavitt

Ode 1.2: To Leuconoë. Horace. WoPoe *Fr.* Odes.

Ode 1.5: Quis Multa Gracilis. Horace. WoPoe *Fr.* Odes.

Ode 1.8: "Lydia, in Heavens Name." Horace. OBVE *Fr.* Odes.

Ode 1.9: To Thaliarchus: "Thou seest the Hills candied with Snow." Horace. OBVE *Fr.* Odes.

Ode 1.9: "You see how, white with snows to the north of us." Horace. STV *Fr.* Odes.

Ode 1.21: To Apollo and Diana ("Dianam tenerae dicite virgines"). Horace. OBVE *Fr.* Odes.

Ode 1.22: "Virtue, dear friends, needs no 'defense'." Horace. OBVE *Fr.* Odes.

Ode 1.23: To Chloë. Horace. OBVE *Fr.* Odes.

Ode 1.25: Ribald Romeos Less and Less Berattle ("Parcius iunctas quatiunt fenestras"). Horace. STV *Fr.* Odes.

Ode 2.8: "If for all the promises you regard so lightly." Horace. STV *Fr.* Odes.

Ode 2.18: "Gold or iv'ry's not intended." Horace. OBVE *Fr.* Odes.

Ode 3.7: "Dear Moly, why so oft in tears?" Horace. OBVE *Fr.* Odes.

Ode 3.9: Dialogue between Horace and Lydia, A ("Donec gratus eram"). Horace. OBVE *Fr.* Odes.

Ode 3.30: This Monument Will Outlast (Exegi monumentum aere perennius). Horace. WoPoe *Fr.* Odes.

Ode 3: "Of late, what time the Bear turned round." Anacreon. NoSic *Fr.* Odes.

Ode 4.7: "Snow dissolv'd no more is seen, The." Horace. NAEL-6v1; NAEL-7v1 *Fr.* Odes.

Ode 4.7: "Snows dissolving, grass returns to meadow." Horace. WoPoe *Fr.* Odes.

Ode 4.7 To L. Manlius Torquatus. Horace. NPeEn *Fr.* Odes.

Ode 3. 30. Horace. PoCho *Fr.* Odes.

Ode, An: "Almighty Power! who rul'st this world of storms!" Anne Batten Cristall. RWP

Ode, An: "Merchant, to secure his treasure, The." Matthew Prior. NoP-4; NoP-5; NPeEn

   (Song.) OBEV

Ode against Despair. Joseph Warton.

   Spleen, Le. STuOW

Ode for Him [*or* Ben Jonson], An. Robert Herrick. BASC; NoP-5; NOSC; WaAnP

Ode for Orville and Wilbur Wright. David Moolten. OtW

Ode for the American Dead in Asia. Thomas McGrath. *See* Ode for the American Dead in Korea.

Ode for the American Dead in Korea. Thomas McGrath. AmWaPo; StAl

   (Ode for the American Dead in Asia.) RaBo

Ode for Walt Whitman. Federico García Lorca. PFTM-1

Ode: Hastening His Friend into the Country. Eldred Revett. NOSC

Ode: In a Few Hours. Hans Lodeizen. TuT, *tr.* by Eamon Grennan

Ode in May. Sir William Watson. OBEV

Ode in Praise of the Coalminer, An. Gwilym R. Tilsley. *tr.* by Joseph P. Clancy

   "Boy strides boldly from his June of youth, The." BBMWP, *tr.* by Joseph P. Clancy

Ode in Praise of the Farmer. Geraint Bowen. *tr.* by Gillian Clarke

   Poet's Prelude, The. BBMWP, *tr.* by Gillian Clarke

Ode in the Time of Hesitation. William Vaughn Moody.

   9. AmWaPo

Ode in Time of Hesitation, An. William Vaughn Moody. APN-2; CBCWP; NAAPv.1

Ode Inscribed to the Infant Son of S.T. Coleridge, Esq. Mary Robinson. RWP

   "Sweet baby boy, accept a stranger's song." NPBRoP

Ode, Inscribed to W. H. Channing. Ralph Waldo Emerson. AmWaPo; APN-1; ColAP; NAAL-3; NAAPv.1; NCAP; NoP-4; NoP-5; OxBoAm; TCAPo; WaAnP

Ode: Intimations of Immortality from Recollections of Early Childhood. William Wordsworth. BrAP; HeIP-4; NAEL-6v2; NAEL-7v2; NAWM-7v2; NOBRP; NoP-4; NoP-5; NPeEn; OBEV; OxBEV; PoPoPo; TFi; TRP; WaAnP

   "Our birth is but a sleep and a forgetting." ITBLP

   "Thought of our past years in me doth breed, The." SacPr

Ode Long Kesh. Barry MacSweeney. Oth

Ode of Imr El-Qais, The. Imr el Kais. WoPoe, *tr.* by Robert Bringhurst

Ode of Signs. Muhammad 'Abd al-Hayy. NAfrP, *tr.* by Alistair Elliot and Matthew Sorenson

Ode: Of Wit. Abraham Cowley. NAEL-6v1; NAEL-7v1; NOSC

   (Ode to Wit.) OxAEP-1

Ode on a Bicycle on Halsted Street in a Sudden Summer Thunderstorm. Paul Carroll. IllVoic

Ode on a Distant Prospect of Eton College. Thomas Gray. NAEL-6v1; NAEL-7v1; NoP-4; NoP-5; OxAEP-1

Ode on a Grecian Urn. John Keats. BLPJKO; BrAP; ClHu; HeIP-4; MakPoe; NAEL-6v2; NAEL-7v2; NAWM-7v2; NIP-4; NOBRP; NoP-5; NPBRoP; OBEV; OxBEV; TFi; WaAnP

Ode on a Grecian Urn Summarized. Desmond Skirrow. NIL-7; NIP-4

Ode on Arrival. Carl Rakosi. BodElec

Ode on Indolence. John Keats. NAEL-6v2; NAEL-7v2; NPBRoP

Ode on Melancholy. John Keats. BrAP; CABP; NAEL-6v2; NAEL-7v2; NAWM-7v2; NIL-7; NoP-4; NoP-5; NPBRoP; NPeEn; OBEV; OxAEP-2; OxBEV; TFi; WaAnP

Ode on Reincarnation. Ernest Francisco Fenollosa.

   "Here let me sit, in this empty, cool, terraced hall." APN-2

   "I remember an ancient Chinese picture kept over there in Daitokuji." APN-2

Ode on Slate, The. Osip Emilevich Mandelstam. WoPoe, *tr.* by Bernard Meares

Ode on Solitude. Alexander Pope. HeIP-4; NAEL-6v1; NIL-7; NOSC; SacPr; WaAnP

Ode on the Birth of Our Saviour, An. Robert Herrick. ChrPo

Ode on the Death of a Favo[u]rite Cat, Drowned in a Tub [*or* Bowl] of Gold Fishes. Thomas Gray. BrAP; ClHu; CtM; ItP; NAEL-6v1; NAEL-7v1; NBLV; NoP-5; OBCoV; OxBEV; TFi; WaAnP

   (Ode.) NoP-4

   (On a Favorite Cat Drowned in a Tub of Gold Fishes.) OxAEP-1

Ode on the Death of Haig's Horse. Douglas Garman.

   "Bury the Great Horse." UV

Ode on the Death of Mr. Henry Purcell. John, Duke of Buckingham and Normandy Sheffield.

   Blue Pencil, The. STuOW

Ode on the Death of [Mr.] Thomson. William Collins. NAEL-6v1; NAEL-7v1

Ode on the Death of the Duke of Wellington. Alfred Tennyson.

Ode on the Hills of Georgia. Alexander Sergeyevich Pushkin. WoPoe, *tr.* by Peter Viereck

Ode on the Mammoth Cheese. James McIntyre. VerBaPo

Ode on the Passion. Thomas Warton, the Elder. ChIV-2

Ode on the Poetical Character. William Collins. NAEL-6v1; NAEL-7v1; NoP-4; NoP-5; WaAnP

Ode on the Popular Superstitions of the Highlands of Scotland, An. William Collins. OxAEP-1

Ode on the Twentieth Century. Henrietta Cordelia Ray. CBWP-3

Ode on the Visit of the Shah of Persia. Joseph Gwyer.
 "Intoxicating draughts he never does drink." VerBaPo

Ode on the Whole Duty Of Parents. Frances Darwin Cornford. MoWP

Ode on Theoxenos. Pindar. CAGL, tr. by John Addington Symonds

Ode on Truth: Addressed to George Dyer. Anne Batten Cristall. RWP

Ode Recited at the Harvard Commemoration (July 21, 1865). James Russell Lowell. APN-1; CBCWP; OBWP; PCW

Ode: Rule, Brittania! David Mallet and James Thomson. See Rule, Britannia!

Ode: Salute to the French Negro Poets. Frank O'Hara. PFTM-2

Ode (scoticè). Unknown. CCL1 Fr. Jun-zi yu-yi [Translations].

Ode Sung at Magnolia Cemetery. Henry Timrod. See Ode: "Sleep sweetly in your humble graves."

Ode Sung at the Opening of the International Exhibition. Alfred Tennyson. STuOW

Ode: The Capris. Mark Halliday. P180

Ode: The Dying Christian to His Soul. Alexander Pope. ChIV-2; SacPr
 (Dying Christian to His Soul, The.) OBEV

Ode to a Beautiful Nude. Pablo Neruda. WaAnP, tr. by Nathaniel Tarn

Ode to a Ditch. Unknown. VerBaPo

Ode to a Dressmaker's Dummy. Donald Justice. NoAM

Ode to a Jacobin. Unknown. UV

Ode to a Long Sorrow. Ricardo Molinari. TCLAP, tr. by Inés Probert

Ode to a Maintenance Man and His Family. Kay Boyle. GifTon

Ode to a Nightingale. John Keats. AmFaPo; BrAP; BRP; CABP; ClHu; HeIP-4; NAEL-6v2; NAEL-7v2; NAWM-7v2; NIL-7; NOBRP; NoP-4; NoP-5; NPBRoP; NPeEn; OBEV; OWoS; OxBEV; PoPoPo; SoSe-8; TFi; WaAnP

Ode to Bicycles. Pablo Neruda. ArBi, tr. by Margaret Sayers Peden

Ode to Bill. John Ashbery. NoP-5

Ode to Bohemians. Ron Padgett. NYP2

Ode to Borrowdale in Cumberland. Amelia Alderson Opie. RWP

Ode to Brother Joe. Anthony McNeill. WaCA

Ode to César Vallejo. Pablo Neruda. TCLAP, tr. by Stephen Tapscott

Ode to Chaplin. Zoltán Jékely. IQMS, tr. by Joseph Leftwich

Ode to Charles Fourier. André Breton. tr. by Kenneth White
 "Fourier what have they done with your keyboard." PFTM-2, tr. by Kenneth White

Ode to Coit Tower. Gregory Corso. CLPP

Ode to Death. Charlotte Smith. NoP-4; NoP-5

Ode to Della Crusca. Hannah Cowley. NOBRP

Ode to DJ. Trebor Healey. BeDoSh

Ode to Duty. William Wordsworth. NAEL-6v2; NAEL-7v2; NOBRP; OBEV

Ode to Election Day. Anselm Berrigan. HeMarv

Ode to Evening. William Collins. CABP; NAEL-6v1; NAEL-7v1; NoP-4; NoP-5; OBEV; OxAEP-1; TFi

Ode to Evening. Joseph Warton. OxAEP-1

Ode to Failure. Allen Ginsberg. CAP-8

Ode to Fanny. John Keats. NPBRoP

Ode to Federico García Lorca. Pablo Neruda. ConPit, tr. by Clayton Eshleman

Ode to Francisco Salinas. Luís De León. SpanPo, tr. by Edwin Morgan

Ode to Governor Capper, An. J. P. Dunn. VerBaPo

Ode to H. Bodkin, Esq., Secretary to the Society for the Suppression of Mendicity. Thomas Hood. NPBRoP

Ode to Himself, An ("Where dost [or; do'st] thou careless[e] lie."). Ben Jonson. BASC; CABP; NoP-4; NoP-5; NOSC; NPeEn; OxAEP-1; PBRV; WaAnP

Ode to Jackson Pollock. Michael McClure. PmAP

Ode to Joy. Frank O'Hara. PmAP; WaAnP

Ode to Knight Chukchi. Tŭgo [or Tŭgogok]. CATKP, tr. by Peter H. Lee

Ode to Knight Kip'a. Ch'ungdam, Master. CATKP, tr. by Peter H. Lee

Ode to Language. Robert Kelly. PFTM-2; SeSe

Ode to Laziness. Pablo Neruda. TCLAP, tr. by William Carlos Williams

Ode to Lovers. Sir John Suckling. UV

Ode to Master [or Mr.] Anthony Stafford to Hasten Him into the Country, An. Thomas Randolph. BASC; NOSC; OBEV

Ode to Meaning. Robert Pinsky. MakPoe; OxBoAm

Ode to Miss Hoyland. Thomas Chatterton. STuOW

Ode: To Miss Margaret Pulteney [Daughter of Daniel Pulteney, Esq., in the Nursery]. Ambrose Philips. OxAEP-1; STuOW; UV

Ode to Mozart. Maura Stanton. MiVo

Ode to Mr. F— [or Mr. Forbes]. Allan Ramsay. OBVE

Ode to My Car. Gig Ryan. BMAP

Ode to My Flint and Boom Bolivia. Michael Costello. BAP-04

Ode: To My Pupils. W. H. Auden. MoBrPo

Ode to My Socks. Pablo Neruda. AmFaPo, tr. by Stephen Mitchell

Ode to My Socks. Pablo Neruda. RaBo; TCLAP; TRP; WED, tr. by Robert Bly

Ode to Nea. Thomas Moore. IrLP

Ode to Our Young Pro-consuls of the Air. Allen Tate. PWW2

Ode to Peace. Mary Weston Fordham. CBWP-2

Ode to Pornography. Jack Anderson. PoA 2002

Ode to Psyche. John Keats. NAEL-6v2; NAEL-7v2; NOBRP; NoP-4; NoP-5; NPBRoP; OBEV; OxAEP-2; TFi

Ode to Rhys ap Maredudd of Tywyn. Dafydd Nanmor. OBWVE, tr. by H. Idris Bell

Ode to Salt. Pablo Neruda. TCLAP, tr. by Margaret Sayers Peden

Ode to Salt. Pablo Neruda. WED, tr. by Robert Bly

Ode to Sappho. Elizabeth Oakes-Smith. ColAP

Ode to Sequoyah. Alexander L. Posey. NAAPv.2

Ode to Simplicity. William Collins. OBEV; OxAEP-1

Ode to Singer. Paul Van Ostaijen. TuT, tr. by Peter van de Kamp

Ode to Spring. Anna Laetitia Barbauld. OxAEP-1

Ode to St Crispin's Day. R.H. Ellis.
 "Walk up, walk up, my bonny boys." FaBoWar

Ode to Stephen Dowling Bots, Dec'd. Mark Twain. See Emmeline Grangerford's Ode to Stephen Dowling Bots, Dec'd.

Ode to Suburbia. Eavan Boland. PBCIP

Ode to Swansea. Vernon Watkins. OBWVE

Ode to the Air Traffic Controller. Joshua Beckman. LegDan

Ode to the Angels Who Move Perpetually toward the Dayspring of Their Youth. Paul Carroll. IllVoic

Ode to the Apple. Pablo Neruda. IPoFL, tr. by Ken Krabbenhoft

Ode to the Bicycle. Cees Buddingh'. ArBi, tr. by John Irons

Ode to the Bourgeois Gentleman. Mário de Andrade. GPTC, tr. by Jack E. Tomlins

Ode to the Cat. Pablo Neruda. VCWP, tr. by John Hollander

Ode to the Computer. Inna L'vovna Lisnyanskaya. CRWP, tr. by Ruth Fainlight

Ode to the Confederate Dead. Allen Tate. AmWaPo; APT-2; CBCWP; ColAP; FuPo; HeIP-4; InGu; MoAmPo; NAAPv.2; NAMCP V.1; NoAM; NoP-4; NoP-5; OBWP; OxBoAm; TFi; WaAnP

Ode to the Diencephalon. W. H. Auden. OxAEP-2

Ode to the End of Summer. Phyllis McGinley. NBLV

Ode to the King. Edward Young.
 "Old Ocean's praise." STuOW

Ode to the Lemon. Pablo Neruda. PoetW, tr. by Margaret Sayers Peden

Ode to the Maggot. Yusef Komunyakaa. CAP-8

Ode to the Medieval Poets. W. H. Auden. GoPo

Ode to the Northeast Wind. Charles Kingsley. OxAEP-2

Ode to the Onion. Pablo Neruda. BeAl, tr. by Stephen Mitchell

Ode to the Onion. Pablo Neruda. IPoFL, tr. by Ken Krabbenhoft

Ode to the Pious Memory of the Accomplished Young Lady, Mrs. Anne Killigrew. John Dryden. See To the Pious Memory of the Accomplished [or Accomplisht] Young Lady, Mrs. Anne Killigrew, [Excellent in the Two Sister-Arts of Poesie and Painting. An Ode].

Ode to the Seagull. Pablo Neruda. GPTC, tr. by Margaret Sayers Peden

Ode to the Seasons. Unknown. CATKP, tr. by Peter H. Lee

Ode to the Setting Sun. Francis Thompson.
 Sun, The. MoBrPo

Ode to the Severn Bridge. Harri Webb. TCAWP

Ode to the Sun. Eloise Bibb. CBWP-4

Ode to the Urge. Ricardo Castillo. PML, tr. by Robert Jones

Ode. To The Virginian Voyage. Michael Drayton. See To the Virginian Voyage.

Ode to the West Wind. Percy Bysshe Shelley. BrAP; CenSon; ClHu; HeIP-4; MakPoe; NAEL-6v2; NAEL-7v2; NAWM-7v2; NIL-7; NIP-4; NOBRP; NoP-4; NoP-5; NPeEn; OBEV; OxAEP-2; OxBEV; OxBSo; PoPoPo; TFi; TRP; WaAnP; WeW-3

Ode to the Yard Sale. Gary Soto. WaAnP

Ode to Toge. Mark Prejsnar. AnSo

Ode to Walt Whitman. Pablo Neruda. ViWalt, tr. by Willis Barnstone

Ode to Walt Whitman ("Along the East River and the Bronx."). Federico García Lorca. ViWalt, tr. by Betty Jean Craige

Ode to Wit. Abraham Cowley. See Ode: Of Wit.

Ode to Yangji. Unknown. CATKP, tr. by Peter H. Lee

Ode to Your Back. Gloria Vando. TouFir

Ode, upon a Question Moved, Whether Love Should Continue Forever?, An. Edward Herbert, 1st Baron Herbert of Cherbury. BASC; OxAEP-1; OxBEV

Ode upon Doctor Harvey. Abraham Cowley. NPeEn

Ode upon the New Year. Nahum Tate. STuOW

Ode with a Lament. Pablo Neruda. ConPit, *tr.* by Clayton Eshleman

Ode Written in the Beginning of the Year 1746. William Collins. *See* How Sleep the Brave.

Ode Written in the Peak[e], An. Michael Drayton. NOSC

Ode XV. Thomas Stanley. ChIV-1

Odell. James Stephens. MoBrPo

Odes. Anacreon. *tr.* by Anomos

Ode 3. NoSic

Odes. Khwaja Shams-ad-din Muhammad Hafiz.

"Flower-tinted cheek, the flowery close, A." TAL

"From Canaan Joseph shall return, whose face." TAL

"I cease not from desire till my desire." TAL, *tr.* by Gertrude Lowthian Bell

"Mirth, Spring, to linger in a garden fair." TAL

"Rose has flushed red, the bud has burst, The." TAL

"What is wrought in the forge of the living and life." TAL

"Where is my ruined life, and where the fame." TAL, *tr.* by Gertrude Lowthian Bell

"Wind from the east, oh Lapwing of the day." TAL, *tr.* by Gertrude Lowthian Bell

Odes and Days. Bruce Beaver.

Day 20. BMAP

Odes to Nea. Thomas Moore.

(Ode to Nea.) IrLP

Odes. Horace.

Exegi Monumentum. WaAnP, *tr.* by James Michie

Ode 1.2. WaAnP, *tr.* by James Michie

Ode 2.7. WaAnP, *tr.* by James Michie

(Diffugere Nives.) OBVE, *tr.* by Samuel Johnson

(Fifth Ode of Horace. Lib. I, The.) NPeEn; OxBEV; PBRV, *tr.* by John Milton

(IV, 1. To Venus.) OBVE, *tr.* by Samuel Johnson

Ode 1.9 / To Thaliarchus. PtT, *tr.* by David Ferry

Ode 3.29: To Maecenas. NPeEn; OBVE, *tr.* by John Dryden

Ode 1.2: To Leuconoë. WoPoe, *tr.* by David Ferry

Ode 1.5: Quis Multa Gracilis. WoPoe, *tr.* by Stephen Sandy

Ode 1.8. OBVE

Ode 1.9: To Thaliarchus. OBVE, *tr.* by Sir Richard Fanshawe

Ode 1.9. STV, *tr.* by John Frederick Nims

Ode 1.21: To Apollo and Diana ("Dianam tenerae dicite virgines"). OBVE

Ode 1.22. OBVE

Ode 1.23: To Chloë. OBVE, *tr.* by Branwell Brontë

Ode 1.25: Ribald Romeos Less and Less Berattle ("Parcius iunctas quatiunt fenestras"). STV

Ode 2.8. STV

Ode 2.18. OBVE, *tr.* by Christopher Smart

Ode 3.7. OBVE

Ode 3.9: Dialogue between Horace and Lydia, A ("Donec gratus eram"). OBVE, *tr.* by Robert Herrick

Ode 3.30: This Monument Will Outlast (Exegi monumentum aere perennius). WoPoe, *tr.* by Ezra Pound

Ode 4.7. NAEL-6v1; NAEL-7v1, *tr.* by Samuel Johnson

Ode 4.7. WoPoe, *tr.* by Michael O'Brien

Ode 4.7 To L. Manlius Torquatus. NPeEn, *tr.* by Sir Richard Fanshawe

Ode 3. 30. PoCho, *tr.* by David Ferry

(Reconciliation: A Modern Version, The.) NBLV, *tr.* by Robert Herrick

(To Aristius Fuscus.) OBVE, *tr.* by Samuel Johnson

(To Lydia.) OBVE

(To Venus.) OBVE, *tr.* by Samuel Johnson

Odeur nocturne, indéfinissable et qui m'apporte un doute obscur, Une. Léon-Paul Fargue. YaTCFP

Odi et Amo. Catullus. WoPoe, *tr.* by Frank Bidart

Odor has remained among the sugarcane, An. Dictators, The. Pablo Neruda. AF, *tr.* by Robert Bly

Odor like an acid sword made, An. Youth. Pablo Neruda. WED, *tr.* by Robert Bly

Odor of a Metal Is Not Strong, The. Merrill Moore. OxBSo

Odor of algaroba, lure of release. Fructus. Genevieve Taggard. APT-2

Odor of Irish Spring, the stench of Ivory, The. (LL) Soap. Gerald Stern. CAP-8; TaR

Odor of pines hangs heavy this morning, The. Last night. Remains. Dorothy Marie Rice. FuFl

Odour I bequeath, The. (LL) Unprofitablenes. Henry Vaughan. NAEL-7v1; NOSC

Odour of sanctity, The. Candles. Little Cloth, The. Hilary Llewellyn-Williams. TCAWP

Odour. 2. Cor. 2, The. George Herbert. ChIV-2

Odours of spring, my sense ye charm. On Receiving a Branch of Mezereon Which Flowered at Woodstock, December 1809. Mary Tighe. RWP

O'Driscoll drove with a song. Host of the Air, The. William Butler Yeats. IrV

Odysseus. W. S. Merwin. NoP-4; NoP-5

Odysseus and Argus. Homer. DiBP *Fr.* Odyssey.

Odysseus and the Swineherd. Homer. DiBP *Fr.* Odyssey.

Odysseus has come home, to the gully farm. Homecoming, The. James Keir Baxter. BrAP

Odysseus heard the sirens; they were singing. Sirens, The. John Streeter Manifold. MoBrPo

Odysseus rested on his oar, and saw. Second Voyage, The. Eiléan Ní Chuilleanáin. EmeKit; ModIr; NPeEn

Odysseus to Telemachus. Joseph Brodsky. BLT, *tr.* by George L. Kline

Odysseus's Secret. Stephen Dunn. PML

Odyssey. Bernard Bador. ConPit, *tr.* by Clayton Eshleman

Odyssey, The. Andrew Lang. OBEV

Odyssey, The. Sipho Sepamla. AF

Odyssey, The. Homer. NAWM-5v1; NAWM-7v1, *tr.* by Robert Fitzgerald

"Now all day long until the sun went down." BLPJKO, *tr.* by Robert Fitzgerald

"We bore down on the ship at sea's edge." WoPoe, *tr.* by Robert Fitzgerald

Odyssey. Homer.

"And now the Queene of women had intent." OBVE

"And then went down to the ship." ColAP; MoAmPo; NAAL-5; NoAM; OBVE; PFTM-1, *tr.* by Ezra Pound

Argos. ModIr, *tr.* by Michael Longley

Butchers, The. ModIr; NPeEn

(Canto 1.) BrAP, *tr.* by Ezra Pound

"Cave we found, but vacant all within, The." OBVE

End of the Suitors, The. OBVE

Execution of the faithless maids. OBVE, *tr.* by Alexander Pope

From Book 11. WaAnP, *tr.* by Richmond Lattimore

Gardens of Alcinous, The. OBGa; OBVE, *tr.* by Alexander Pope

Gardens of Alcinous, The. OBVE

"God who mounts the winged winds, The." OBVE

"He ended, nor the Argicide refus'd." OBVE

"Just then, forgetful of the strict command." OBVE

Laertes. ModIr, *tr.* by Michael Longley

"Mighty wave rush'd o'er him as he spoke, A." OBVE

"Now gently winding up the fair ascent." OBVE

"Now toils the Heroe; trees on trees o'erthrown." OBVE

"Nymph turnd home, The. He fell to felling downe." OBVE

Odysseus and Argus. DiBP, *tr.* by William Maginn

Odysseus and the Swineherd. DiBP, *tr.* by George Chapman

Phemios and Medon. ModIr

"She thus; when I had great desire to prove." OBVE

Suitors watch Ulysses string the bow, The. OBVE, *tr.* by Alexander Pope

"There grew two olives, closest of the grove." OBVE

"This spoke, a huge wave tooke him by the head." OBVE

"Thus charg'd he; nor Argicides denied." OBVE

"Trembling the spectres glide, and plaintive vent." OBVE

Ulysses Describes His Visit to the Underworld. WaAnP, *tr.* by George Chapman

Ulysses Insults over the Cyclops. NOSC

Ulysses Invokes the Dead. NOSC

Ulysses Reunited with Penelope. NOSC; OBVE, *tr.* by George Chapman

"While thus he thought, a monst'rous wave up-bore." OBVE

"With many a weary step, and many a groan." UV

"Youth there was, Elpenor was he nam'd, A." OBVE

Odyssey of Big Boy. Sterling Allen Brown. NAMCP V.1

Odyssey or "On Absence," The. Chimako Tada. VCWP, *tr.* by Naoshi Koriyama

Oedipus. John Dryden.

"When Athens all the Graecian state did guide." NOSC

Oedipus. Josephine Miles. SoSe-8

Oedipus and the Riddle. Jorge Luis Borges. WoPoe, *tr.* by John Hollander

Oedipus at Colonus. Sophocles.

Colonus' Praise. OBVE, *tr.* by William Butler Yeats

"Endure what life God gives and ask no longer span." OBMV, *tr.* by William Butler Yeats

Oedipus the King. Sophocles. NAWM-5v1, *tr.* by Robert Fagles

Oedipus to the Third Power. Gerardo Deniz. RMCMP, *tr.* by Mónica de la Torre

O'er a dark field I held my dubious way. Philip Freneau. TCAPo *Fr.* House of Night, The.

O'er Esthwaite's lake, serene and still.   On Esthwaite Water.   Isabella Lickbarrow.   NPBRoP; RWP; WaAnP

O'er me, alas! thou dost to much prevail.   Anne Finch, Countess of Winchilsea.   NPeEn Fr. Spleen, The: A Pindaric Poem.

O'er paths and fields.   William Wordsworth.   NPBRoP Fr. Prelude, The; Growth of a Poet's Mind [1805 version].

O'er the Crossing.   Unknown.   SSUS

O'er the dim breast of ocean's wave.   Night.   Ann Radcliffe.   CenSon

O'er the glad waters of the dark blue sea.   Corsair, The.   Lord Byron.

O'er the glad waters of the dark blue sea.   Lord Byron.   Fr. Corsair, The.

O'er the Hills.   Francis Hopkinson.   TCAPo

O'er the hills far away, at the birth of the morn.   O'er the Hills.   Francis Hopkinson.   TCAPo

O'er the land of the free, and the home of the brave. (LL)   Star-Spangled Banner, The.   Francis Scott Key.   AmWaPo; HHAm; NoP-4; UV

O'er the Muir Amang the Heather.   Jean Glover.   RACG

O'er the round throat her little head.   Harebell and Pansy.   Laurence Binyon.   CABP

O'er the tall cliff that bounds the billowy main.   Bids Farewell to Lesbos.   Mary Robinson.   CenSon; RWP

O'er this huge town, rife with intestine wars.   Manchester by Night.   Mathilde Blind.   ViWPN

O'er twilight fields the autumnal gossamer? (LL)   William Wordsworth.   CenSon; OxBSo Fr. River Duddon [A Series of Sonnets], The.

O'erladen with sad musings, till the tear.   Charles Tennyson Turner.   CenSon Fr. Supposed to Be Written By One On Whom the Death of an Excellent Woman Has Forced the Conviction of a Future State.

Oeuf, Un.   Max Jacob.   YaTCFP

Oeuvre.   Lucien Stryk.   IllVoic

Of a coat's satin pocket. (LL)   Fare, The.   Molly Peacock.   ExTi; InoFa

Of a cold day. (LL)   Early in the Morning.   Louis Simpson.   TRP; WaAnP

Of a copy of nothing.   Burning Interior, A.   David Shapiro.   BAP-04

Of a Country Life.   James Thomson.
    "How sweet and innocent are country sports."   UV

Of a day I had rued. (LL)   Dust of Snow.   Robert Frost.   APT-1; ChAP; NAAPv.2; NAMCP V.1; OxBoAm; PtR; SAmP; SoSe-8; WaAnP; WeW-3

Of a demon in my view. (LL)   Alone.   Edgar Allan Poe.   APN-1; ItP; NAAL-3; NAAPv.1

Of a full feast; and the out-courts of glory. (LL)   Son-Days [dayes].   Henry Vaughan.   AngWePo; NOSC

Of a Good Prince and an Evil.   Timothy Kendall.   NoSic

Of a good universe next door; let's go. (LL)   Pity This Busy Monster,Manunkind.   E. E. Cummings.   HarvBoo; NAMCP V.1

Of a Husbandman.   Joshua Sylvester.   NOSC

Of a lady fair to see.   Lines to Mrs. M. C. Turner.   Eloise Bibb.   CBWP-4

Of a love or a season? (LL)   Reluctance.   Robert Frost.   ITBLP; MoAmPo

Of a messmate's opened vein. (LL)   Eliza Cook.   STuOW; VerBaPo Fr. Song of the Seaweed.

Of a newborn child. (LL)   John Berryman.   PoPoPo; VCAP Fr. Dream Songs.

Of a Rose, a Lovely Rose.   Unknown.   OBEV

Of a rose, a lovely rose.   Unknown.   OHMEL

Of a rosy ear. (LL)   Rosy Ear.   Zbigniew Herbert.   BeAl; PML, tr. by Czeslaw Milosz

Of A' the Airts [the Wind Can Blaw].   Robert Burns.   NoP-4; NoP-5
    (I Love My Jean.)   NPBRoP; OxBEV
    (Jean.)   OBEV

Of a' the waters that can hobble.   Robert Fergusson.   NePenScot

Of a vast expanding pearl. (LL)   Kenneth Rexroth.   APSN; APT-2; NAAPv.2; NAMCP V.1 Fr. Love Poems of Marichiko, The.

Of about one year and a half. (LL)   Henry Reed.   BrAP; NAEL-6v2; NAEL-7v2; NIL-7; NIP-4; NoP-4; NoP-5; NPeEn; OxBEV; PoWW Fr. Lessons of the War.

Of Adam's first wife, Lilith, it is told.   Dante Gabriel Rossetti.   NAEL-7v2 Fr. House of Life, The.

Of aid from them—She was the Universe. (LL)   Darkness.   Lord Byron.   CABP; NAEL-6v2; NAEL-7v2; NPBRoP; TreFP

Of all are living, or have been. (LL)   Queens.   John Millington Synge.   MoBrPo; OBMV

Of All Despondencies.   Enrique Lihn.   VCWP, tr. by Alastair Reid

Of all despondencies, death-despair must be the worst.   Of All Despondencies.   Enrique Lihn.   VCWP, tr. by Alastair Reid

Of All Distances the Best Possible One.   Patrizia Cavalli.   CItWP, tr. by Cinzia Sartini Blum and Lara Trubowitz

Of all God's mercies, is my posy [or posie] still. (LL)   Posy [or Posie], The.   George Herbert.   ChIV-1; NOSC

Of all great Nature's tones that sweep.   Implicit Faith.   Aubrey Thomas De Vere.   SacPr

Of all implements, the pitchfork was the one.   Pitchfork, The.   Seamus Heaney.   OxBEV

Of all instants the most.   Instants 1.   Jacqueline Risset.   SCFWP, tr. by Serge Gavronsky

Of all its pow'r disarms! (LL)   Farewell[l] to America, A. To Mrs. S. W. Phillis Wheatley.   NoP-4; NoP-5

Of all that God has shown me.   Mechthild von Magdeburg.   WPoS

Of all that Orient lands can vaunt.   Haschish, The.   John Greenleaf Whittier.   APN-1; NCAP

Of all that shines below. (LL)   Sun-Flower, The.   Dora Greenwell.   EroLit; VWP

Of all the Bible stories that they tell.   Revenge 1.   Giuseppe Gioacchino Belli.   WoPoe, tr. by Anthony Burgess

Of all the birds I know, few can.   Toucan, The.   Pyke, Jr. Johnson.   NTCP

Of all the birds that rove and sing.   Jenny Wren.   Walter De la Mare.   OWoS

Of all the buttons I ever opened, you were the one.   Belly Button Song.   Menna Elfyn.   ATSWP, tr. by Robert Minhinnick

Of all the causes which conspire to blind.   Alexander Pope.   MakPoe; NoP-4; NoP-5; OxAEP-1; WaAnP Fr. Essay on Criticism, An.

Of all the cities far and wide.   Sandblast Girl and the Acid Man, The.   May Kendall.   ViWPN

Of all the cities in Romanian lands.   John Dryden.   NOSC Fr. Theodore and Honoria.

Of all the creatures, in the world, that be.   John Oldham.   OBVE Fr. Satires.

Of all the dogs around me, spotted, black, and hairy.   Kim Sujang.   CATKP, tr. by Kevin O'Rourke

Of all the flowers rising now.   Maritae Suae.   William Philpot.   OBEV

Of all the girls that are so smart.   Sally in Our Alley.   Henry Carey.   OBEV; OxAEP-1

Of all the huntresses.   Patrizia Cavalli.   NeIt

Of all the kings that ever here did reign.   Sir Philip Sidney.   NoSic Fr. Astrophil and Stella.

Of all the lives I cannot live.   Dickinson.   Anne Finch.   FFC

Of all the mighty nations of the sun. (LL)   Africa.   Claude McKay.   APT-1; FTtHH; NAAL-5

Of all the people in the mornings at the mall.   Old Liberators, The.   Robert Hedin.   GoPo; P180

Of all the people who went into the snowy mountains.   Gu Cheng.   PFTM-2; VCWP Fr. Bulin File, The.

Of all the rides since the birth of time.   Skipper Ireson's Ride.   John Greenleaf Whittier.   APN-1; NAAPv.1; NCAP

Of all the self destructive stories.   To the Coming of the Decade.   Simone Waight.   OWABP

Of all the ships upon the blue.   Captain Reece.   William Schwenck Gilbert.   OBCoV

Of all the Souls that stand create—.   Choice.   Emily Dickinson.   NAAL-3

Of all the Sounds despatched abroad.   Wind, The.   Emily Dickinson.   APN-2

Of all the thoughts of God that are.   Sleep, The.   Elizabeth Barrett Browning.   ChIV-1; OxAEP-2

Of all the times when not to speak is best.   Three Silences.   Rachel Hadas.   RA

Of all the torments, all the cares.   Rivals.   William Walsh.   OBEV

Of all the world's enjoyments.   Fisherman's Song, The.   Thomas D'Urfey.   NOSC

Of All There Is.   C. Mikal Oness.   GeoHom

Of all things living.   Sweet Potato.   Takahashi Shinkichi.   ZenPo, tr. by Takashi Ikemoto and Lucien Stryk

Of all those streets that blur into the sunset [or wander to the west].   Limits.   Jorge Luis Borges.   PoetW, tr. by Alastair Reid

Of all those who reach earth by falling. (LL)   Sudden Journey.   Tess Gallagher.   NIL-7; NIP-4

Of all women that ever were born.   Unknown.   NAWM-7v1

Of all your poems.   So Gallantly Streaming: To the Poet.   Carter Ratcliff.   PA9/11

Of alle the enemies that I can fynde.   Unknown.   OHMEL

Of an incongruous century. (LL)   Dissonance.   Amy Lowell.   APT-1; NAAPv.2

Of an Orchard.   Katharine Tynan Hinkson.   SacPr

Of Anantanarayanan— / M. Anantanarayanan. (LL)   I Missed His Book, but I Read His Name.   John Updike.   NoP-4; NoP-5

Of Another Fashion.   Emilio Ballagas.   CAGL, tr. by Fanny Arango-Ramos and William Keeth

Of any beast none is more faithful found.   Faithfullest Beast, The.   Philipp Camerarius and Vera Moller.   DiBP, tr. by John Molle

Of Art & Memory.   Norman Dubie.   AmAlph

Of asphodel, that greeny flower.   Asphodel, That Greeny Flower.   William Carlos Williams.

Of asphodel, that greeny flower, the least.   William Carlos Williams.   HarvBoo; PoA 2002 Fr. Paterson.

Of banks and stones and every blooming thing. (LL)   Inniskeen Road: July Evening.   Patrick Kavanagh.   NAMCP V.1; NoAM; NPeEn; OxBSo; StAl

Of Being Numerous.   George Oppen.
  "Amor fati / The love of fate."   NAMCP V.1
  "Emotions are engaged, The."   NAMCP V.1
  "For the people of that flow."   NAMCP V.1
  "Great stone, The / Above the river."   NAMCP V.1
  "I cannot even now."   PWW2
  "It is the air of atrocity."   AmWaPo; NAMCP V.1
  "Now in the helicopters the casual will."   AmWaPo; NAMCP V.1
  "Obsessed, bewildered / By the shipwreck."   NAMCP V.1
  "So spoke of the existence of things."   NAMCP V.1
  "They await / War, and the news."   AmWaPo
  "We are pressed, pressed on each other."   NAMCP V.1
  "Whether, as the intensity of seeing increases, one's distance from Them, the
    people , does not also increase."   NAMCP V.1
Of Birds.   Tom Mandel.   OnScMo
Of births and deaths and bridal nights. (LL)   In the Room.   James Thomson.
  NePenScot; OxBEV
Of black flesh after flame. (LL)   Portrait in Georgia.   Jean Toomer.   APT-2;
  InGu; NAAPv.2; NAMCP V.1; NoP-4; NoP-5
Of blackberry eating in late September. (LL)   Blackberry Eating.   Galway
  Kinnell.   BeAl; CAP-8; InvLad; NIL-7; NIP-4; SoSe-8; WaAnP
Of boats, of boats.   Passage.   Peter Rafferty.   NLP
Of breakage, and the sweat runs off them. (LL)   Rain Dance.   Susan Wicks.
  MFPA; MoWP
Of Breakfast, then of walking to the pond.   Good Appetite.   Mark Van Doren.
  Spl
Of Brennbaum "The Impeccable." (LL)   Ezra Pound.   MoAmPo; NAAPv.2 Fr.
  Hugh Selwyn Mauberley (Life and Contacts).
Of British beasts the Buck is king.   Upon the Duke of Buckingham.
  Unknown.   BASC
Of Bronze—and Blaze.   Aurora.   Emily Dickinson.   APN-2; NCAP; PCW
Of C# minor and the calms of C. (LL)   Pupil, The.   Donald Justice.   GoPo;
  PoCho
Of carrying a stick? (LL)   Critics and Connoisseurs.   Marianne Moore.   APT-
  1; BrAP; NAAPv.2; NAMCP V.1; NoAM; OxBoAm
Of cat-gut lace. (LL)   Boogie: 1 a.m.   Langston Hughes.   APSN; APT-2;
  NAMCP V.1
Of cat-gut lace. (LL)   Nightmare Boogie.   Langston Hughes.   APSN; APT-2;
  NAMCP V.1; OxBoAm
Of Children on Wood.   Malinda Markham.   IAoNAP
Of Clovers, and of Noon! (LL)   His Feet are shod with Gauze.   Emily
  Dickinson.   IPoFL; SAmP
Of Cold Winds.   Margaret Lucas Cavendish, Duchess of Newcastle.   EMWP
Of colour, wilting a little in the unseasonable heat. (LL)   Pink Rose Rings, The.
  Tracey Herd.   MFPA; NeBl
Of Commerce and Society: Variations on a Theme.   Geoffrey Hill.
  "Statesmen have known visions. And, not alone."   UpMys
Of composts shall the Muse disdain to sing?   James Grainger.   VerBaPo Fr.
  Sugar Cane, The.
Of course I burned what I wrote.   Salamander.   Robert Thomas.   FaoP
Of course, I don't know very much.   Frances Ellen Watkins Harper.
  NAAPv.1; NALW Fr. Aunt Chloe.
Of course I gave in.   What a Boy Does Not Say.   Christopher Bursk.   MAAN
Of course I know it ends.   Mark Doty.   AmAlph Fr. Fog Argument.
Of course, I left it, the tuning hammer.   Piano Tuning.   Marianne Boruch.
  AmAlph
Of course I love them, they are my children.   Mother, The.   Anne Stevenson.
  BeAl
Of course I tried to tell him.   Poets Hitchhiking on the Highway.   Gregory
  Corso.   BB
Of course it had been madness even to bring it up.   E Pur Si Muove.   George
  Bradley.   YaYoPo
Of course it is made of would, and want.   Regarding the Monument.   Scott
  Cairns.   UpMys
Of course it's all over the morning news.   Through These Halls.   Judy Jordan.
  AmPoNex
Of course no one sets out to discover.   Discovery.   Brian Henry.   AmPoNex
Of course only days after I meet you I am imagining.   Only Days.   Melanie
  Hope.   WiU
Of course, something is missing.   Moving and St Rage.   Kathy Fagan.   ExTi
Of course the dead outnumber us.   Death's Door.   Thom Gunn.   InoFa
Of course, the entire effort is to put my [or one] self.   Thoughts During an Air
  Raid.   Stephen Spender.   MoBrPo
Of course, the familiar rustling of programs.   Peripeteia.   Anthony Hecht.
  VCAP
Of course there's always a last everything.   Sonnet: The Last Things.   Gavin
  Ewart.   OxBSo
Of course they had servants, dressed for dinner.   Andrew Taylor.   BMAP Fr.
  Travelling to Gleis-Binario.

Of course, we have Guide Dogs For The Blind.   Who Likes the Idea of Guide
  Cats?   Gavin Ewart.   NOxBChV
Of course, we must die.   Charles Reznikoff.   APT-2
Of Course, We Would Wish.   Irving Feldman.   VCAP Fr. All of Us Here.
Of course, we would wish them angelic lookouts.   Irving Feldman.   VCAP Fr.
  All of Us Here.
Of course what called you was lovely. A girl gone.   Beauty, That Lying Bitch.
  Paula McLain.   AmPoNex
Of course Zimmer was late for the gig.   Duke Ellington Dream, The.   Paul
  Zimmer.   PBCAP
Of Course—I prayed.   Emily Dickinson.   APN-2; MoAmPo; TCAPo
Of Courtesy.   Arthur Guiterman.   Spl
Of crow, time's surge begins again. (LL)   Resurrection at West Lake.   Eric
  Tretheway.   Coast; PfSP
Of darkness and tears. (LL)   Winter Nightfall.   Robert Bridges.   MoBrPo;
  OBEV
Of De Witt Williams on His Way to Lincoln Cemetery.   Gwendolyn Brooks.
  ESEAA; InoFa; NAMCP V.2; NoAM Fr. Street in Bronzeville, A.
Of death / the barber.   Death the Barber.   William Carlos Williams.   OxBoAm
Of Deaths, Days, Futures, Nations ("Do i need to (need to).")   Jen Hofer.   Eno
Of Deaths, Days, Futures, Nations ("On the corner of plato and national army a
  man early.")   Jen Hofer.   Eno
Of Deaths, Days, Futures, Nations ("Question, the action, the speech, the taxi,
  the proof, the reference, forgotten, The.")   Jen Hofer.   Eno
Of devils, you and I would live in peace. (LL)   Ready for Flight.   Eavan
  Boland.   IrLP; OxBSo
Of dirt, and spit, and poetry. (LL)   Meadowsweet.   Kathleen Jamie.   MoWP;
  PoCu
Of Distress Being Humiliated by the Classical Chinese Poets.   Hayden Carruth.
  WoPoe
Of Dogs and Ostriches.   Eve Merriam.   TaR
Of dust the primal Adam came.   Kosmos.   Julia Ward Howe.   ColAP
Of dying. (LL)   I Give You Back.   Joy Harjo.   AmWaPo; HATNAP; LoL
Of eager and extravagant anger. (LL)   Lovers, The.   William Robert Rodgers.
  IrLP; PNI
Of earthly civilization, what shall we say?   Tidings.   Czeslaw Milosz.
  BodElec, tr. by Lillian Vallee
Of Earthly Love.   Susanna Valentine Mitchell.   LW
Of Eating and Entertainment.   Roger Williams.   See Observation Generall from
  Their Eating, Etc., The.
Of elephop and telephong! (LL)   Eletelephony.   Laura Elizabeth Richards.
  NBLV; NOxBChV; NTCP
Of emptiness soon forgotten. (LL)   Robert Creeley.   NAMCP V.2; WoBe Fr.
  Life and Death.
Of English Verse.   Edmund Waller.   CABP; NOSC
Of every command. (LL)   Every Day.   Ingeborg Bachmann.   CFP; PoSu, tr.
  by Daniel Huws
Of everything, a little stayed.   Residue.   Carlos Drummond de Andrade.
  TCLAP, tr. by Virginia de Araújo
Of fading pleasures in successive night. (LL)   Sonnet 6. To the Torrid Zone.
  Helen Maria Williams.   CenSon; NOBRP
2. Of Faith.   Timothy Steele.   PoA 2002 Fr. Three Notes Toward Definitions.
Of famine fed upon all entrails—.   Abdiel.   Lord Byron.   DiBP
Of fantasye is all oure fare.   John Gower.   SacPr Fr. This World fares as a
  Fantasy.
Of feathered fouls, that fan the buxom air.   Fashioned After the Manner of
  Master Geoffrey Chaucer in His Assembly of Fowls.   Thomas Warton, the
  Elder.   ChIV-1
Of February, 1918. (LL)   In the Waiting Room.   Elizabeth Bishop.   APT-2;
  BrAP; CAP-8; FTtHH; GPTC; HeIP-4; NAAL-5; NALW; NAMCP V.2;
  NoAM; NoP-4; NoP-5; OxBoAm; PoetW; VCAP
Of feeling no pain? (LL)   Painkillers.   Thom Gunn.   AllShUp; SwNoth
Of feet both human and holy. (LL)   Annie Pearl Smith Discovers Moonlight.
  Patricia Smith.   GT; OtW; OxAAAP
Of Fiction and Things.   Josué Ramírez.   RMCMP, tr. by Margaret Sayers
  Peden
Of fields, of forts, and floods, unknown to fame.   Colley Cibber.   STuOW Fr.
  Another [Birthday Ode], 1743.
Of finite hearts that yearn. (LL)   Two in the Campagna.   Robert Browning.
  ItP; NAEL-6v2; NAEL-7v2; NoP-4; NoP-5; NPeEn; OxAEP-2; OxBEV;
  TFi
Of Fire.   Agha Shahid Ali.   AmAlph
Of first and last, and midst, and without end. (LL)   William Wordsworth.
  NAEL-6v2; NAEL-7v2 Fr. Prelude, The; Growth of a Poet's Mind [1850
  version].
Of fleiss and bon and full of lif. (LL)   John Gower.   NPeEn; OxBEV Fr.
  Confessio Amantis.
Of flesh. O star of men! (LL)   Camp in the Prussian Forest, A.   Randall Jarrell.
  FaBoWar; HP; MoAmPo; OBWP; PoWW; PWW2

Of flying birds and beasts that craw. *Unknown.* CATKP, *tr. by* Kevin O'Rourke

Of folly studious, even of vices vain. William Shenstone. STuOW *Fr.* Describing the Sorrow of an Ingenuous Mind on the Melancholy Event of a Licentious Amour [*or* Elegy 26].

Of Forced Sightes and Trusty Ferefulness. Jorie Graham. PoPoPo

Of Gardens. Rene Rapin. OBGa *Fr.* Of Gardens.

Of Gardens. Rene Rapin. *tr. by* John, the Younger Evelyn Of Gardens. OBGa

Of George and Caroline! (LL) Lilliputian Ode on Their Majesties' Accession, A. Henry Carey. FaBoVe; NPeEn; OBCoV

Of George, and Property. Thomas, the Younger Warton. STuOW *Fr.* On the Marriage of the King.

Of grass, the myriad dewdrops twinkle round. (LL) James Thomson. NAEL-6v1; NAEL-7v1 *Fr.* Seasons, The.

Of Gravity and Angels. Jane Hirshfield. PasH

Of Green Steps and Laundry. Ralph Gustafson. NoP-4

Of hacked, beheaded coconuts towards home. (LL) Nights in the Gardens of Port of Spain. Derek Walcott. NAEL-6v2; NAEL-7v2; NoP-4; NoP-5; PoetW

Of Haloes & Saintly Aspects. Sherod Santos. PfSP

Of happiness, haply hysterics. Is. (LL) Gwendolyn Brooks. InoFa; NAMCP V.2; NoP-4; NoP-5; OxAAAP; WeW-3 *Fr.* Womanhood, The.

Of Heaven, and hope to have it after all. (LL) Argument of His Book, The. Robert Herrick. BASC; CavPo; NAEL-6v1; NAEL-7v1; NoP-4; NoP-5; NOSC; NPeEn; OxAEP-1; PoPoPo; SacPr; TFi; WaAnP; WoPoe

Of Heaven Considered as a Tomb. Wallace Stevens. PoA 2002

Of Heaven or Hell I have no power to sing. William Morris. NAEL-6v2 *Fr.* Earthly Paradise, The.

Of Helen's brothers, one was born to die. George Santayana. APN-2 *Fr.* Sonnets.

Of her, her only, of herself alone! (LL) Petrarch. NAWM-5v1; NAWM-7v1 *Fr.* Sonnets to Laura.

Of her Jacks, Latin. Jane. Philip Hammial. BMAP

Of her removed and soul-infused regard. George Chapman. OxBSo *Fr.* Coronet for His Mistress Philosophy, A.

Of him, even third or fourth hand. (LL) Has Anyone Seen the Boy? Jelaluddin Rumi. RaBo; WoPoe, *tr. by* Coleman Barks and John Moyne

Of himself to think this: she does not. Lady and Gentleman. Richard Weber. IrLP

Of hireling wolves whose Gospel[l] is their maw. (LL) To the Lord General Cromwell. John Milton. NAEL-6v1; NoP-5; NOSC; WaAnP

(Of hireling wolves, whose Gospel is their maw.) (LL) GSo; NoP-4; PoPoPo

Of His Conversion. William Alabaster. NPeEn

Of His Dear Son, Gervase. Sir John Beaumont. OBEV *Fr.* Of My Dear Son, Gervase Beaumont.

Of his glory. *So farewell.* (LL) Upon Ben Jo[h]nson. Robert Herrick. NoP-4; NoP-5

Of his hands and fingers, we know nothing. (LL) Incident. Imamu Amiri Baraka. AF; NoAM

Of His Life. Wayne Dodd. BLT

Of his long marvellous letters but kept none. (LL) Who's Who. W. H. Auden. GoPo; MoBrPo; NAMCP V.1; NoAM

Of his Mistress, upon Occasion of her Walking in a Garden. Henry Constable. NIL-7; NIP-4; OBGa *Fr.* Diana.

Of History and Hope. Miller Williams. InGu; RWB

Of History, really beginning. (LL) Sea Is History, The. Derek Walcott. BrAP; NAMCP V.2

Of honest Theft. To my good friend Master Samuel Daniel. Sir John Harington. PBRV

Of hope, and smiles on you with cheer sublime. (LL) Steamboats, Viaducts, and Railways. William Wordsworth. CenSon; NAEL-6v2; NAEL-7v2

Of horrors that happen so? (LL) Apparition, The—A Retrospect. Herman Melville. APN-2; NAAPv.1; NCAP; TCAPo

Of Human Knowledge. Sir John Davies. "Why did my parents send me to the schools." ChIV-1

Of ice. Deceptively reserved and flat. Octopus, An. Marianne Moore. NAMCP V.1; OxBoAm

Of intellectual, of emotional quiet, the merest hint, would have meant inconceivable capitulation. (LL) Repression. C. K. Williams. GoPo; NoP-4; NoP-5

Of interest to John Calvin and Thomas Aquinas. Why God Permits Evil: For Answers to This Question of Interest to Many Write Bible Answers, Dept. E-7. Miller Williams. InGu

Of it all. (LL) Personal Letter No. 3. Sonia Sanchez. ESEAA; SSLK

Of Jacopo del Sellaio. Ezra Pound. APT-1 *Fr.* Ripostes of Ezra Pound.

Of John Davidson. Hugh MacDiarmid. HarvBoo; NePenScot; OxBEV

Of Joy Illimited: Polyphonic Soundings: Shore to Ship. Anna Rabinowitz. KGB

Of Lalage and Barbara. (LL) Private Dining Room, The. Ogden Nash. AmWit; OBCoV

Of Late. George Starbuck. AmWaPo

Of late it has dawned on me that it's futile. Tune: "Rouged Lips." Wang Kuo-wei. ColAnChi, *tr. by* Jiaosheng Wang

Of late / Since I parted from Liadin. Liadan and Curithir. Kuno Meyer. IrLP

Of late, what time the Bear turned round. Anacreon. NoSic *Fr.* Odes.

Of lead and emerald. Note to Olga (1966), A. Denise Levertov. NALW

Of Life and Death. Ben Jonson. TreFP

Of lilies rusted, rotting, wet / With rain. (LL) Room on a Garden, A. Wallace Stevens. NoP-4; NoP-5; OBGa

Of longing, Termia, the sharp specifics know. End of July. John Peck. HarvBoo

Of lost connections. (LL) Memories of West Street and Lepke. Robert Lowell. AF; AmWaPo; CAP-8; EmeKit; ItP; NAAL-5; NAMCP V.2; NoAM; OxBoAm; PWW2; VCAP

Of love. Sappho. SaLy, *tr. by* Diane Rayor

Of love and death in the Garrison State I sing. Karl Shapiro. BodElec *Fr.* Bourgeois Poet, The.

Of Love, Death and the Sea-Squirt. Chris Greenhalgh. NeBl

Of love he sang, full hearted one. Forced Music, A. Robert Graves. MoBrPo

Of love's austere and lonely offices? (LL) Those Winter Sundays. Robert Earl Hayden. AmFaPo; APT-2; CAP-8; ChAP; ColAP; CtM; ESEAA; GoPo; ISC; MakPoe; NAAL-5; NAMCP V.2; NIL-7; NIP-4; NoAM; NoP-4; NoP-5; OxAAAP; OxBoAm; PoPoPo; RaBo; SoSe-8; SSLK; StAl; TFi; WaAnP; WeW-3

Of Loving at First Sight. Edmund Waller. NOSC

Of LSD, Peyote, Psilocybin, Amanita, Benzedrine, Valium / and aspirin. (LL) Destruction. Joanne Kyger. BLT; GoPo

Of madness cured me. (LL) For My Contemporaries. James Vincent Cunningham. APT-2; OxBoAm; VCAP; WaAnP

Of making many books there is no end. Of Modern Books. Carolyn Wells. SWaP

Of mankind. (LL) Thread suns. Paul Celan. BBASP; OBVE; VCWP, *tr. by* Michael Hamburger

Of man's delight and man's desire. Ballad of Passive Paederasty, A. Aleister Crowley. CAGL

Of Man's [*or* Mans] First Disobedience, and the Fruit. John Milton. NAEL-6v1; OxAEP-1 *Fr.* Paradise Lost.

Of Many Worlds in This World. Margaret Lucas Cavendish, Duchess of Newcastle. NOSC; NPeEn

Of Marilyn, and Marijuana. Kenneth Rosen. NevBe

Of memory there was also a song of. Under My Breath. Anne Waldman. BodElec

Of men and girls. (LL) Charles Olson. APT-2; PmAP *Fr.* Maximus Poems, The.

Of Mere Being. Wallace Stevens. APT-1; BLPJKO; NAAPv.2; NAMCP V.1; NoP-4; NoP-5; OxBoAm; PtR; WoPoe

Of Mere Plastic. David Trinidad. KGB

Of mighty love the wings for this me give. (LL) In Spayn. Sir Thomas Wyatt. NoSic; OPOU

Of Miles Davis. William Ford. SeSe

Of Modern Books. Carolyn Wells. SWaP

Of Modern Poetry. Wallace Stevens. ColAP; NAAL-5; NAAPv.2; NAMCP V.1; NoAM; OxBoAm; WaAnP

Of Money. Barnabe Googe. NBLV; NoSic; SoSe-8

Of Mortain. Herman Melville. APN-2 *Fr.* Clarel: A Poem and Pilgrimage in the Holy Land.

Of Moulds and Mushrooms. Ruthven Todd. NePenScot

Of Movement towards a Natural Place. J. H. Prynne. PFTM-2

Of my bosom I have made a bed. *Unknown.* SLW, *tr. by* Marjolijn De Jager, Sayd Bahodin Majrouh and André Velter

Of my crust. I Undressed Myself. Thérèse 'Awwad. PoArWo, *tr. by* Kamal Boullata

Of My Dear Son, Gervase Beaumont. Sir John Beaumont. Of His Dear Son, Gervase. OBEV

Of my drowsy mouth. (LL) Breasts. Charles Simic. RaBo; WaAnP

Of My Nipple Ring Halos. Edwin Torres. HeMarv

Of myself, a survivor. Self-Portrait at Thirteen Years of Age. Homero Aridjis. WoBe, *tr. by* George McWhirter

Of Myself [*or* My Self]. Abraham Cowley. BASC

Of Nelson and the North. Battle of the Baltic. Thomas Campbell. OBEV

Of Neptune's empire [*or* Empyre] let us sing. Hymn in Praise of Neptune, A. Thomas Campion. OBEV

Of Night. Molly Peacock. IFF

Of no removes! (LL) Fine Knacks for Ladies. John Dowland. NoP-4; NoP-5; NoSic; NPeEn; PBRV

Of Nobility. Fulke, 1st Baron Brooke Greville. *Fr.* Treatise of Monarchy, A.

Of nothing, nothing, nothing—nothing at all. (LL)　End of the World, The. Archibald MacLeish.　BrAP; GSo; MoAmPo; NAMCP V.1; NoAM; OxBSo; TFi

Of now done darkness I wretch lay wrestling with (my God!) my God. (LL)　Carrion Comfort.　Gerard Manley Hopkins.　BBASP; BrAP; CABP; GSo; HeIP-4; ItP; MakPoe; NAEL-6v2; NAEL-7v2; NAMCP V.1; NoAM; NoP-4; NoP-5; TFi; WaAnP

Of obedience, faith, adhesiveness.　Thought.　Walt Whitman.　HHAm

Of of Titmouse.　Michael Portnoy.　HeMarv

Of Ohio and Michigan. (LL)　Double Elegy.　Michael S. Harper.　ESEAA; NAMCP V.2; NoAM; WaAnP

Of old, under Emperor Gui.　Sea, The.　Mu Hua.　CCL1, tr. by David Knechtges

Of old when folk lay sick and sorely tried.　On Hygiene.　Joseph Hilaire Pierre Belloc.　MoBrPo

Of old when Nature, in her verve defiant.　Giantess, The.　Charles Baudelaire.　OBVE, tr. by Roy Campbell

Of One and Two, of All.　Paul Eluard and Andre Breton.　YaTCFP, tr. by Mary Ann Caws

Of one that is so far and bright.　Hymn to the Virgin.　Unknown.　RSR

Of one whose occupation was to die. (LL)　Souvenir.　Edwin Arlington Robinson.　APT-1; NoAM

Of oon that is so faire and bright.　Unknown.　OHMEL

Of our amusements ask you?—We amuse.　George Crabbe.　Fr. Borough, The.

Of our chosen place.　Map Burnt Through.　Joanna Rawson.　AmPoNex

Of our dear West. (LL)　David Jones.　HarvBoo; NAMCP V.1; NoAM Fr. Anathemata, The.

Of our desires the farther [or farder] down[e] to slide. (LL)　Mary Sidney Wroth, Countess of Montgomery.　BASC; NAEL-6v1; NAEL-7v1; PEW Fr. Pamphilia to Amphilanthus.

Of our fierce doings! (LL)　Samuel Taylor Coleridge.　FaBoWar; PoAgWa Fr. Fears in Solitude [Written in April, 1798, during the Alarm of an Invasion].

Of our jasmine-white Lord. (LL)　Vein of sapphires, A.　Mahadevi.　WoPoe; WPoS, tr. by Jane Hirshfield

Of our like minds. (LL)　Fan Letter, A.　Amy Gerstler.　BAP-97; BodElec

Of our losse by Adam, and our gayne by Christ.　Alice Sutcliffe.　Fr. Meditations of Man's Mortalitie; or, A Way to True Blessedness.

Of our trials & our last bride. (LL)　John Berryman.　EMP; MakPoe; NoP-4; NoP-5; WaAnP Fr. Dream Songs.

Of our white-on-white. (LL)　Snow Light, The.　May Sarton.　APT-2; NBLV

Of ourselves, the talking engines of our day. (LL)　Late Echo.　John Ashbery.　PoA 2002; WaAnP

Of Oxfordshire and Gloucestershire. (LL)　Adlestrop.　Edward Thomas.　CtM; HarvBoo; NAEL-6v2; NAEL-7v2; NAMCP V.1; NoP-4; NoP-5; OBEV; UV; WaAnP

Of pain, and knowing the meaning. (LL)　Brinkwomanship.　Leontia Flynn.　NIrP; StAl

Of pale cold light that was alive. (LL)　Signature of All Things, The.　Kenneth Rexroth.　APSN; APT-2; OxBoAm; TRP

Of past misadventure? (LL)　"H. D."　HarvBoo; NAAL-5 Fr. Walls Do Not Fall, The.

Of Paul and Silas it is said.　Emily Dickinson.　ChIV-2; SacPr

Of Peace.　Fulke, 1st Baron Brooke Greville.　Fr. Treatise of Monarchy, A.

Of perhaps meaning otherwise? (LL)　Wind, the Clock, the We, The.　Laura Riding Jackson.　APT-2; FaBoVe

Of person rare, strong limbs, and manly shape.　Sonnet Written upon My Lord Admiral Seymour, A.　John Harington.　NoSic

Of pinyon / pine. (LL)　Gary Snyder.　APSN; PFTM-2 Fr. Mountains and Rivers without End: The Market.

Of pleasure. (LL)　Word Plum, The.　Helen Chasin.　NIL-7; NIP-4

Of Politics, & Art.　Norman Dubie.　AmAlph; P180

Of Poor B.B.　Bertolt Brecht.　GTCP; WoPoe, tr. by Michael Hamburger

Of Power, Money, Cheese, Real Estate, Conboberation, Hoohah.　Mac Wellman.　FTOS Fr. Terminal Hip.

Of Promises and Prophecy.　Steve Chimombo.　HBAPE

Of quality and fabric more divine. (LL)　William Wordsworth.　NAEL-6v2; NAEL-7v2 Fr. Prelude, The; Growth of a Poet's Mind [1850 version].

Of Rain and Air.　Wayne Dodd.　BLT

Of raindrops across the windowpanes. (LL)　Memory from Childhood.　Antonio Machado Ruiz.　RaW; WED, tr. by Robert Bly

Of ralsis. (LL)　Ing.　Walter Conrad Arensberg.　APT-1; NAAPv.2

Of rapid floods and cruel winds.　Rapid Floods.　Kata Szidónia Petröczy.　IQMS, tr. by Marie B. Jaffe

Of red berries. Will he wake? (LL)　Scenes from the Life of the Peppertrees.　Denise Levertov.　NoP-4; NoP-5

Of remembrance, whispers out of time. (LL)　Self-Portrait in a Convex Mirror.　John Ashbery.　CAP-8; NAMCP V.2; OxBoAm

Of Riches.　Stephanie Williams.　AnSo

Of rising up. (LL)　Post-colonial Tale, A.　Joy Harjo.　BodElec; PrTe

Of Robert Frost.　Gwendolyn Brooks.　NoAM; VisFro

Of Saint Theresa in her wild lament. (LL)　Groundhog, The.　Richard Eberhart.　APT-2; BrAP; InoFa; MoAmPo; NAAPv.2; NAMCP V.1; NoAM; RaBo; TFi; TRP; WaAnP

Of satin close down on her. (LL)　Viewing the Body.　W. D. Snodgrass.　CAP-8; InoFa

Of seeing myself without fruit. (LL)　Song of the Barren Orange Tree.　Federico García Lorca.　AmFaPo; RaW, tr. by W. S. Merwin

Of Simple Intent.　Pamela Uschuk.　AtGh

Of simple tastes and mind content! (LL)　Oliver Wendell Holmes.　APN-1; OxBoAm Fr. Autocrat of the Breakfast Table, The.

Of Sir Frauncis Walsingham Sir Phillipp Sydney, and Sir Christopher Hatton, Lord Chancelor.　Unknown.　PBRV

Of Sleep.　Martha, Lady Giffard.　EMWP

Of Solitude.　Abraham Cowley.　BASC

Of some muted horn muted with sea sound.　Tone, The.　Judson Crews.　ICANM

Of some Pharaoh's daughter. (LL)　Language Issue, The.　Nuala Ni Dhomhnaill.　ModIr; NPeEn, tr. by Paul Muldoon

Of someone greater than I can understand? (LL)　Empty Church, The.　Ronald Stuart Thomas.　AngWePo; EmeKit

Of St Stephen.　Francis Quarles.　NOSC

Of Stars.　Margaret Lucas Cavendish, Duchess of Newcastle.　NOSC

Of Stone.　Ani Ilkov.　CSCBP Fr. Orbis Tertius.

Of such a wit the world should have no more. (LL)　Ode for Him [or Ben Jonson], An.　Robert Herrick.　BASC; NoP-5; NOSC; WaAnP

Of such an intense azure.　Blue City, The.　Alfred Wellington Purdy.　NoP-4

Of Suicide.　John Berryman.　NoAM

Of summer, around the empty field. (LL)　Boy Juggling a Soccer Ball, A.　Christopher Merrill.　MoASP; PML

Of Sweet Rest.　Joyce Mansour.　HAWP, tr. by Mary Beach

Of th' eternal silence. (LL)　Noel; Christmas Eve, 1913.　Robert Bridges.　ChrPo; OBCP; SacPr

Of that late death took all my heart for speech. (LL)　In Memory of Major Robert Gregory.　William Butler Yeats.　IrV; NAEL-6v2; NAEL-7v2; NAMCP V.1; WaAnP

Of that medusa strange.　Statue of Medusa, The.　GS

Of that mysterious race. (LL)　Poem: "At night Chinamen jump."　Frank O'Hara.　NAMCP V.2; NoAM; PmAP

Of that passion that light within.　To the Poets: To Make Much of the World.　George Oppen.　BodElec

Of that table in the café.　Cafe.　Czeslaw Milosz.　PoSu, tr. by Jan Darowski

Of that which once was great, is [or has] passed [or pass'd] away. (LL)　On the Extinction of the Venetian Republic.　William Wordsworth.　NPBRoP; OBEV

Of the abandoned world. (LL)　Wake.　Tess Gallagher.　InoFa; StAl

Of the Animal Spirits.　Margaret Lucas Cavendish, Duchess of Newcastle.　PEW

Of the beauty of kindness I speak.　Kindness.　Thomas Sturge Moore.　OBMV

Of the Birth and Bringing Up of Desire.　Edward, 17th Earl of Oxford De Vere.　NoSic

Of the Blessed Sacrament of the Altar ("Angels' eyes, whom veils cannot deceive, The.")　Robert Southwell.　OBEV

Of the Blessed Sacrament of the Altar [or Aulter] ("In paschall feast, the end of a[u]ncient rite.")　Robert Southwell.　OBEV

Of the body: most.　Loose Hinge.　Carl Phillips.　FaoP

Of the bog curlew or the sea-going eider. (LL)　Avatar, The.　Kerry Hardie.　NIrP; StAl

Of the box's top, both wearing pretty nightcaps. (LL)　Porcelain Couple, The.　Donald Hall.　BAP-97; CAP-8

Of the broad road that stretches and the roadside fire. (LL)　Song of a Traveller, The.　Robert Louis Stevenson.　MoBrPo; OBEV

Of the broken pieces of our lives. (LL)　Liberation.　Abena Busia.　HAWP; PoetW

Of the cave must tell you, "Yes, you can go back." (LL)　Return, The.　Molly Peacock.　PasH; RA

Of the Changes of Life.　William Dunbar.　WoPoe

Of the Cosmic Light! (LL)　O Lord of Light! A Mystic Sage Returns to Realms of Eternity!　Askia Muhammad Touré.　FuFl; SeSe; SpirFl

Of the country of my pleasure. (LL)　History of Sexual Preference, A.　Robin Becker.　BodElec; ExTi

Of the Courtier's Life.　Sir Thomas Wyatt.　NoSic; NPeEn; OBSV; OBVE Fr. Satires.

Of the Creator. And he waits for the world to begin. (LL)　Leviathan.　W. S. Merwin.　ChIV-1; NoAM

Of the dark past.　Ecce Puer.　James Joyce.　AmFaPo; ChIV-2; NoAM

Of the Day Estivall.　Alexander Hume.　NePenScot

"O perfite light, quhilk schaid away."　NPeEn

Of the dog in ancient story.　Mary Howitt.　DiBP Fr. Sketches of Natural History.

Of the Earth, Earthy. Rosamund Marriott Watson. ViWPN

Of the Epiphany. John Beaumont. SacPr

Of the Ever-Changing Agitation in the Air. Jorie Graham. ExTi

Of the eyes of my Annie. (LL) For Annie. Edgar Allan Poe. APN-1; ColAP; OBEV; TCAPo

Of the far Waterfall like Doom. (LL) Tarantella. Joseph Hilaire Pierre Belloc. BLPJKO; MoBrPo; OBMV; UV

Of the Father's love begotten Ere the worlds began to be. Prudentius. SacPr, tr. by John Mason Neale

Of the fathoms of set eyes. (LL) Fire at Alexandria, The. Theodore Weiss. NoAM; PoA 2002; SAmP

Of the Finished World. Lucie Brock-Broido. MakPoe; WaAnP

Of the first league out from land? (LL) Exultation is the going. Emily Dickinson. APN-2; TCAPo

Of the first morning of the world. (LL) Kenneth Rexroth. APSN; NAMCP V.1 Fr. Love Poems of Marichiko, The.

Of the first Paradice there's nothing found. On St. James's Park, as Lately Improved by His Majesty. Edmund Waller. BASC; NOSC; OBGa

Of the fish the bone remained. Afterwards. Günter Grass. GTCP, tr. by Irmgard Hunt

Of the four fuschia plants that hung. Robin's Nest, A. Mary Jo Salter. OWoS

Of the four louts who threw him off the dock. Finished Man, A. Richard Wilbur. NAMCP V.2

Of the general, the skin of her arms slowly going red. (LL) Skin: "Never mind the fantasy about the tweezers and the tongue." Brian Henry. AmPoNex; LegDan

Of the great moon. (LL) Letter, The. Amy Lowell. NAAPv.2; NALW; PoBW

Of the Great Worm in the Sky? (LL) Hornworm: Autumn Lamentation. Stanley Kunitz. AmFaPo; BodElec; ItP

Of the hundreds of deaths that inhabit me. Death in the Afternoon. Angel González. RaW, tr. by David Ignatow

Of the ills we daily see. Social Life, The. Lizelia Augusta Jenkins Moorer. CBWP-3

Of the Indigo Combo. (LL) Melvin B. Tolson. APT-2; NAMCP V.1; OxBoAm; PFTM-1 Fr. Harlem Gallery.

Of the Last Verses in the Book. Edmund Waller. BASC; NoP-4; NoP-5; NOSC; NPeEn; OxBEV; PoPoPo; SacPr

"Seas are quiet when the winds give o'er, The." OBEV

Of the Light. John Ashbery. NAMCP V.2

Of the long sepulcher that hid death and hides me? (LL) How Much Longer Will I Be Able to Inhabit the Divine Sepulcher. John Ashbery. FTOS; HarvBoo; OxBoAm; PmAP

Of the look of a room on returning thence. (LL) Walk, The. Thomas Hardy. NAEL-6v2; NAEL-7v2; NPeEn; OxBEV

Of the many known and proven. Curing Homosexuality. Jim Everhard. CAGL

Of the many men whom I am, whom we are. We Are Many. Pablo Neruda. VCWP, tr. by Alastair Reid

Of the Marriage of the Dwarfs. Edmund Waller. NPeEn

Of the moon. They can't see / Not yet. (LL) Small Frogs Killed on the Highway. James Wright. NAMCP V.2; NoAM

Of the nearest / Ear. (LL) Watch Repair. Charles Simic. NAMCP V.2; NoP-4; NoP-5

Of the no need. "H. D." NALW; NAMCP V.1 Fr. Tribute to the Angels.

Of the not born, yet buried, here's the tomb. (LL) To Fine Lady Would-Be. Ben Jonson. NoP-4; NOSC

Of the old house, only a few, crumbled. House That Was, The. Laurence Binyon. MoBrPo

Of the other he's more of an Emerson. (LL) James Russell Lowell. APN-1; NAAPv.1; OxBoAm; TCAPo Fr. Fable for Critics, A.

Of the pains this indifferent Union. Notes on a Departure. Wanda Coleman. RD

Of the planet of which they were part. (LL) Planet on the Table, The. Wallace Stevens. APT-1; NAMCP V.1; OxBoAm; PoPoPo; SAmP

Of the primeval Priests assum'd [or assumed] power. Book of Urizen [or First Book of Urizen], The. William Blake. NOBRP

Of the Progress of the Soul: The Second Anniversary. John Donne.

Second Anniversary [or Anniversarie], The.

"We now lament not, but congratulate." NOSC

"We see in authors, too stiff to recant." NOSC

Of the Pythagorean Philosophy. Ovid. OBVE Fr. Metamorphoses.

Of the realm of the nebulae! (LL) Star-Struck Utopias of 2000. "Antler." PoCoUp; RWB

Of the Reed That the Jews Set in Our Saviour's Hand. William Alabaster. NoSic; NPeEn

Of the Remembered. David St. John.

"I will tell you. Maybe." GeoHom

"Twin memory, we all seek it." GeoHom

Of the Resurrection. Miles Coverdale. ChIV-2

Of the right way. As to How Much. Louis Zukofsky. APT-2

Of the salted bream. (LL) Fish shop. Basho. WoPoe; ZenPo, tr. by Takashi Ikemoto and Lucien Stryk

Of the shocked boy's twenty-year-old jacket. (LL) Weakness, The. Bernard O'Donoghue. ModIr; NoP-4

Of the sixty-two. Poetry of America, The. Juan Felipe Herrera. TouFir

Of the sleeves, I remember their weight, like wet wool. Uniform, The. Marvin Bell. MAAN

Of the species *Pipistrellus pipistrellus*. Lecture Upon the Bat, A. Caitríona O'Reilly. MoWP; NIrP

Of the stars? (LL) Road Home, The. Gillian Allnutt. NeBrP; StAl

Of the stars, that fact, Johnny Dominguez. (LL) Photograph: Migrant Worker, Parlier, California, 1967. Larry Levis. CalPo; GeoHom

Of the Tallahatchie. (LL) Bones of My Father, The. Etheridge Knight. BodElec; OxAAAP

Of the teeth of rats. (LL) On winter mornings. Richard Wright. APT-2; NoP-5

Of the Terrible Doubt of Appearances. Walt Whitman. APN-1; CAGL

Of the Theam of Love. Margaret Lucas Cavendish, Duchess of Newcastle. PEW

Of the three, one blackheart man lives. Black Heart. Kwame Dawes. WaCA

Of the thumbprint searing her immutable brow. (LL) Sonnet in Primary Colors. Rita Dove. InoFa; PfS

Of the toy's purchase with the length of life. (LL) Blight. Ralph Waldo Emerson. APN-1; BrAP; NCAP; OxBoAm; TCAPo

Of the unnamed poor. (LL) Minneapolis Poem, The. James Wright. CAP-8; NAMCP V.2; NoAM

Of the very world he made. (LL) Christopher Smart. ChrPo; NPeEn; OxBEV; SacPr Fr. Hymns and Spiritual Songs for the Fasts and Festivals of the Church of England.

Of the Wars in Ireland. John Harington. NoSic

Of the war's obscenity. (LL) Fabrication of Ancestors. Alan Dugan. AmWaPo; CBCWP; NAMCP V.2; NoAM

Of the ways things happen to fall. (LL) Table Talk. Wallace Stevens. NoP-4; NoP-5

Of the Weather. John Gay. NPeEn

Of the world's business. (LL) Mrs. Small. Gwendolyn Brooks. GT; ItWoWo

Of thee and thy house, which doth in eating heal. (LL) John Donne. BASC; ChIV-1; NAEL-6v1; NAEL-7v1; NIP-4; NoP-4; NoP-5; OxBSo Fr. Holy Sonnets.

Of Thee I Sing. Ira Gershwin. ReLy

Of thee, kind boy, I ask no red and white. Sonnet. Sir John Suckling. BASC; CavPo; NoP-4; NoP-5; NOSC

Of thee the Northman by his beachèd galley. Ode 5. George Santayana. APN-2

Of their iniquity. (LL) Ballad Which Anne Askew[e] Made and Sang When She Was in Newgate, The. Anne Askew. CABP; EMWP; NoP-4; NoP-5; NoSic; SacPr; WaAnP

Of their "ole Massa," who had made the sale. Albery Allson Whitman. NAAPv.1 Fr. Octoroon, The.

Of their passage. On Third Avenue. Mina Loy. APT-1; HarvBoo

Of their unthinking Drums. (LL) I dreaded that first Robin, so. Emily Dickinson. APN-2; MoAmPo; NAAL-3; NAAL-5

Of them and rolled her head away. (LL) Last Words of My English Grandmother, The. William Carlos Williams. APT-1; InoFa; NAMCP V.1; PtR; RaBo; SAmP

Of these men and their music. (LL) Here Where Coltrane Is. Michael S. Harper. CAP-8; ESEAA

Of these the false Achitophel was first. John Dryden. OxBEV Fr. Absalom and Achitophel.

Of things beyond our reason or control. (LL) Sound of the Sea, The. Henry Wadsworth Longfellow. ITBLP; TCAPo

Of things exactly as they are. (LL) Wallace Stevens. NAMCP V.1; NoAM; RaBo Fr. Man with the Blue Guitar, The.

Of things moving back to where they came from. (LL) Procession at Candlemas, A. Amy Clampitt. NAMCP V.2; PoPoPo

Of this bad world the loveliest and the best. On a Dead Hostess. Joseph Hilaire Pierre Belloc. MoBrPo

Of This Cloth Doll Which. Michael Palmer. NoP-4; NoP-5

Of this day's glorious feast and revel. Unknown. CCL1,

Of this fair[e] volume which we World do[e] name. Book, The. William Drummond of Hawthornden. ChIV-3

(Of this faire Volumne which wee World doe name.) SacPr

Of this handful of cyclamen. (LL) Cyclamens. Michael Field. ViWPN; VWP

Of this ruined house. (LL) Although the wind. Lady Izumi. WoPoe; WPoS, tr. by Mariko Aratani and Jane Hirshfield

Of this turning age. (LL) Oh Beloved, Since the Origin We Have Been. Bâkî. OLP; WoPoe, tr. by Walter Andrews, Najaat Black and Mehmet Kalpakli

Of this world's Theatre in which we stay. Edmund Spenser. CABP; NAEL-7v1; NoP-4; NoP-5 Fr. Amoretti.

Of those base things called men. (LL) To Celinda. Elizabeth Singer Rowe. BASC; PEW

Of three eyes, I would still give two for one. Third Eye, The. Jay Macpherson. IFF

Of thy life [or lyfe], Thomas, this compass[e] well mark. Golden Mean, The. Henry Howard, Earl of Surrey. OBVE

Of thy lyfe [or life], Thomas, this compass well mark. Horace. OBVE, PEW

Of Time and the Line. Charles Bernstein. FTOS; NIL-7; NoP-5; PFTM-2; PmAP; ReTh; WaAnP

Of time as horizontal paths. Choir. Cecil Taylor. EGAG

Of too much was our talk, of. Zürich, the Stork Inn. Paul Celan. BBASP; HP, tr. by Michael Hamburger

Of touch they are, and poor I am their straw. (LL) Sir Philip Sidney. NAEL-6v1; NAEL-7v1 Fr. Astrophil and Stella.

Of Treason [epigram]. Sir John Harington. NoSic; NPeEn; OBCoV; OxBEV; SoSe-8

   (Epigram IV.v: Of Treason.) NOSC

Of unapplauding hands and broken song. (LL) My Dark Fathers. Brendan Kennelly. PBCIP; StAl

Of underground streams, what I see is a limestone landscape. (LL) In Praise of Limestone. W. H. Auden. HarvBoo; NAEL-6v2; NAEL-7v2; NAMCP V.1; NoAM; NoP-4; NoP-5; OxBoAm; WaAnP

Of unremembered seas. (LL) So I Said I Am Ezra. A. R. Ammons. ColAP; NAAL-5; NAMCP V.2; NoAM; OxBoAm; WaAnP

Of unsaciable purchasers. Robert Crowley. PBRV

Of vacant darkness and to cease. (LL) Alfred Tennyson. NAEL-6v2; NAEL-7v2 Fr. In Memoriam A. H. H.

Of vast import to the nation. (LL) Pastoral: "When I was younger." William Carlos Williams. APT-1; SAmP

Of veins, purple as violets? (LL) Hippolytus Temporizes. "H. D." APT-1; HarvBoo; RACG

Of victory what remains for us is just. To El Mingo (with Whom I Share Eva Victoria and Anahi Paz). Alicia Partnoy. CFP, tr. by Gail Wronsky

Of Violence. G. Travis Regier. LiTh

Of Walter White's Father in the Rain. Houston A., Jr. Baker. SeSe

Of wars o western. Disasters. George Oppen. BodElec

Of water, water, water. (LL) Lifeguard, The. James Dickey. NoP-4; NoP-5; SoSe-8

Of what avail are palaces in hell. Mátyás Nyéki Vörös. IQMS Fr. Hell.

Of what is past, or passing, or to come. (LL) Sailing to Byzantium. William Butler Yeats. AmFaPo; BLPJKO; BrAP; CABP; ClHu; EMP; HarvBoo; HeIP-4; MoBrPo; NAEL-6v2; NAEL-7v2; NAMCP V.1; NAWM-7v2; NIL-7; NIP-4; NoAM; NoP-4; NoP-5; NPeEn; OBMV; OWoS; OxBEV; PoPoPo; RaBo; SoSe-8; TFi; WaAnP; WeW-3; WoPoe

Of what the others never set eyes on. (LL) Desert Flowers. Keith Douglas. HarvBoo; NPeEn

Of what the tree might do. (LL) Robert Frost. RaBo; TCAPo Fr. Hill Wife, The.

Of what we are, together, here. (LL) What we, when face to face we see. Arthur Hugh Clough. ChIV-2; SacPr

Of which the first is love. the sad, unrepeatable fact. And Forgive Us Our Traspasses. Sinéad Morrissey. MoWP; NIrP

Of which there is nothing left. (LL) Barbara. Jacques Prévert. AF; GPTC, tr. by Harriet Zinnes

Of which there's left / Nothing. (LL) Barbara. Jacques Prévert. MFP; YaTCFP, tr. by Martin Sorrell

Of wild geese. (LL) Above the boat. Kikaku. BLT; ZenPo, tr. by Takashi Ikemoto and Lucien Stryk

Of wilding in his hand. (LL) Two April Mornings, The. William Wordsworth. NAEL-6v2; NAEL-7v2; NPBRoP

Of Wilmington winces with the dawn, he has just. Long Man, The. Mark Ford. NeBrP

Of Woman Torn. Suheir Hammad. PoArWo

Of world without integument. Red Clay. Candice Favilla. ExTi

Of writing many books there is no end. Aurora Leigh. Elizabeth Barrett Browning. VWP

Of you. Little Mother. Guido Gezelle. TuT, tr. by Mary E. O'Donnell

Of You. Norman Alexander MacCaig. PoCu

Of you I have no memory, keep no promise. Living Together. Edgar Bowers. PoDa

Of young men and boys. (LL) Thousand Killed, A. Bernard Spencer. FaBoWar; OBWP

Of your daughters: Zeus, Father. Korinna [or Corinna]. SaLy, tr. by Diane Rayor

Of Your Father's Indiscretions and the Train to California. Lynn Emanuel. OxBoAm

Of your path. (LL) Garden. "H. D." APT-1; NAMCP V.1; NoAM

Of your path. (LL) "H. D." HeIP-4; MoAmPo; TCAPo; TRP Fr. Garden, The.

Of your reaches. (LL) Peaches. Donald Hall. BeAl; NoP-4; NoP-5

Of your torn and distraught life. (LL) Delia Rexroth ("California rolls into.") Kenneth Rexroth. CalPo; PoCho

Of your trouble, Ben, to ease me. Ben Jonson. NAEL-7v1 Fr. Celebration of Charis in Ten Lyric[k] Pieces [or Peeces], A.

Of your unforgettable perfection. (LL) Letting Go. Daryl Hine. NoP-4; NoP-5

Of Youth He Singeth. Robert Wever. See In Youth Is Pleasure.

Ofay-watcher looks back. Mongane Wally Serote. NAfrP; TSAP

Ofertas. Gerardo Deniz. RMCMP

Off . . . / over / that way. Philip Whalen. WhBo

Off Brighton Pier. Alan Ross. OBWP

Off Duty [or To Della Crusca]. Hannah Cowley. STuOW

Off Februar the fyiftene nycht. William Dunbar. NePenScot

Off Februar the fyiftene nycht. William Dunbar.

Off Ferry Road, the toilet of a garage where. Brigitte Bardot in Grangetown. Tony Curtis. TCAWP

Off from Swing Shift. Garrett Kaoru Hongo. GeoHom; ReTh

Off go the crows from the roof. Crows in a Strong Wind. Cornelius Eady. ESEAA; InvLad

Off Havana the ocean is green this morning. Havana Birth. Susan Mitchell. OxBoAm

Off Highway 106. Cherrylog Road. James Dickey. ColAP; NIL-7; NIP-4; WaAnP; WeW-3

Off Hurricane Creek where. Remembering Wind Mountain at Sunset. Fred Chappell. LPSFW

Off in the forest. Found. Johann Wolfgang von Goethe. STV, tr. by John Frederick Nims

Off Interstate 20. Widow Zebach. Charles Behlen. TiP2

Of[f] Lentren in the first mornyng [or morning]. William Dunbar. SacPr

Off Scollay Square, back from the subway, stands. Epitaph for the Old Howard. Byron Vazakas. APT-2

Off that landspit of stony mouth-plugs. Medusa. Sylvia Plath. NALW

Off the Back of a Lorry. Tom Paulin. ModIr; PBCIP

Off the Beaten Track. Peter Rafferty. NLP

Off the Dutchesse. Elizabeth Taylor. EMWP

Off the Korean Coast, beyond Wonsan. Memory of a Victory. Keith Wilson. AmWaPo

Off the wall those prickles. Qiang-you-ci: Off the Wall. Unknown. CCL1, tr. by V. W. X.

Off to Pasárgada. Manuel Bandeira. TCLAP, tr. by Candace Slater

Off to Philadelphia in the Morning. Dennis Brutus. GT

Off to Philadelphia in the morning. Off to Philadelphia in the Morning. Dennis Brutus. GT

Off to work. Karai Senryū. EMJL, tr. by Burton Watson

Off-color eyes that shine through lobes. Studs. Michael S. Harper. CAP-8; ESEAA

Offensive, The. Keith Douglas. PoWW

Offer it up plank it down. Ooftish. Samuel Beckett. NoAM

Offered in Thanks for a Present of Wine and a Goose. Yu Hsin. CCL1, tr. by John Frodsham

Offering. Debra Allbery. PBCAP

Offering. Thomas McGrath. RaBo

Offering. Sharan Strange. FuFl; GT

Offering, An [with music]. Eloise Bibb. CBWP-4

Offering Congratulations to the Enlightened Reign [with music]. Ou-yang Chiung. ColAnChi, tr. by Lois Fusek

Offering for the Cat, An [with music]. Mei Yao Ch'en. ColAnChi, tr. by Burton Watson

Offers the boon of Death. (LL) Compensation. Paul Laurence Dunbar. APN-2; NAAPv.1

Offers you security, and free rides to cops. (LL) Subway, The. Edwin Denby. APT-2; NYP2

Office Depot Parking Lot. Del Ray Cross. FreRad

Office Feng Shui. Shin Yu Pai. WANABP

Office Geraniums. Laura Newburn. UrbNat

Office Hour. Carol Lem. GeoHom

Office Party. Phyllis McGinley. ChrPo; OBSV

Office Window. Llewelyn Wyn Griffith. AngWePo

Office work: a wearisome jumble. Poem without a Category. Liu Cheng. ColAnChi, tr. by Burton Watson

Officer Adolphus Jay. Briefly Eavesdropping on Walt Whitman, Virginia, 1863. Tim Suermondt. ViWalt

Officers and Gentlemen Down Under. John Brookes. FaBoWar

Officers' Mess. Gavin Ewart. FaBoWar

Official acropolis outdoes the most colossal conceptions of modern barbarity, The. Cities. Arthur Rimbaud. MotU, *tr.* by Louise Varese

Official history that, The. For Maximino Palomo. Teresa Palma Acosta. TiP2

Official Love Story. Linda Gregg. BodElec

Official Piety. John Greenleaf Whittier. NCAP

Official Versions. Mark Pawlak. PrTe

Officials are quick to disembark. Singing Girls (Written in Jest). Tu Fu [*or* Du Fu]. CrYelRi, *tr.* by Sam Hamill

Officials checked to make certain we'd. John Cage. APSN *Fr.* Diary: How to Improve the World (You Will Only Make Matters Worse).

Official's little son, The. Karai Senryū. EMJL, *tr.* by Makoto Ueda

Offpsring, The. Liz Rosenberg. PoA 2002

Off'rings of the Eastern[e] kings of old, The. Royal[l] Presents. Nathaniel Wanley. SacPr

Offset, The. Wyatt Prunty. PfSP

Off-shore, by islands hidden in the blood. Charles Olson. NAMCP V.2; NoAM; PmAP *Fr.* Maximus Poems, The.

Offspring. Naomi Long Madgett. GT; OxAAAP; SoSe-8

Oft had I heard of Lucy Gray. William Wordsworth. NPBRoP *Fr.* Lucy.

Oft haive I hard, bot ofter fund it treu. Christen Lyndesay to Ro. Hudsone. Christian Lindsay. EMWP

Oft have I brooded on defeat and pain. Success. Emma Lazarus. SWaP

Oft have I heard thee mourn the wretched lot. Charles Churchill. OBSV *Fr.* Prophecy of Famine, The.

Oft have I lain in those dear days of old. Memories of St. George's Caye. John Rozel Cuthbert. OWABP

Oft have I said, the praise of doing well. Matthew Prior. ChIV-1 *Fr.* Pleasure: The Second Book of Solomon on the Vanity of the World.

Oft have I seen a hot o'erweening cur. William Shakespeare. DiBP *Fr.* King Henry VI, Pt. II.

Oft have I seen at some cathedral door. Divina Commedia. Henry Wadsworth Longfellow. APN-1; BrAP; TCAPo

Oft have I strove t'asscend that lofty ground. To Dame—Augustin nun on her curious gum-work. Jane Barker. EMWP

Oft have you hinted to your brother peer. Alexander Pope. OBGa *Fr.* Epistle to Lord Burlington.

Oft I had heard of Lucy Gray. Lucy Gray; or, Solitude. William Wordsworth. NAEL-6v2; NAEL-7v2; NOBRP; OxAEP-2; WaAnP

Oft in my thought full busily have I sought. Oft in My Thought. Charles D'Orleans. NoP-4; NoP-5

Oft in the hall I have heard my people. *Unknown.* HeIP-4 *Fr.* Beowulf.

Oft in the lone church-yard at night I've seen. Robert Blair. OxAEP-1 *Fr.* Grave, The.

Oft In the Stilly Night. Thomas Moore. WaAnP
   (Light of Other Days, The.) OBEV

Oft I've implored the gods in vain. Prayer for Indifference, A. Fanny [*or* Frances] Macartney Greville. OxBEV

Oft let me wander, at the break of day. Sun-Rise: Sonnet, A. Ann Radcliffe. CenSon

Oft mighty elephants by little Moors are led. Powerful Servants. Friedrich von Logau. GePo, *tr.* by George C. Schoolfield

Oft o'er my brain does that strange fancy roll. Sonnet Composed on a Journey Homeward; the Author Having Received Intelligence of the Birth of a Son, 20 September 1796. Samuel Taylor Coleridge. OxBSo

Oft to the Wanderer, weary of exile. Wanderer, The. *Unknown.* NAWM-5v1, *tr.* by Charles W. Kennedy

Oft when I've seen some lonely mansion stand. Richard Payne Knight. OBGa *Fr.* Landscape, The.

Oft, when my lips I open to rehearse. To Shakspeare. Frances Anne Kemble. SWaP

Oft with true sighs, oft with uncalled tears. Sir Philip Sidney. NAEL-6v1; NAEL-7v1 *Fr.* Astrophil and Stella.

Often. Jane Kenyon. LoL *Fr.* Having It Out with Melancholy.

Often a friend will greet me thus. Hartmann von Aue. GePo

Often after we make love. Old Man, The. Penelope Shuttle. LW

Often beneath the wave, wide from this ledge. At Melville's Tomb. Hart Crane. APT-2; HarvBoo; InoFa; MoAmPo; NAAL-5; NAMCP V.1; NoAM; NoP-4; NoP-5; OxBoAm; PoA 2002; WaAnP

Often, for pastime, mariners will ensnare. Albatross, The. Charles Baudelaire. OWoS, *tr.* by Richard Wilbur

Often I Am Permitted to Return to a Meadow. Robert Duncan. ColAP; HarvBoo; NAMCP V.2; OxBoAm; PFTM-2; PmAP; WaAnP

Often I go to bed as soon after dinner. Jane Kenyon. LoL *Fr.* Having It Out with Melancholy.

Often I have seen things that others have also seen. Conflict Between the Eyes and the Gaze, The. César Vallejo. ConPit, *tr.* by Clayton Eshleman

Often I inhabit my body. Stepping Aside. Andrée Chedid. HAWP, *tr.* by Harriet Zinnes

Often I mistake the opening in my soul for a knife. Halo Factory, The. Dave Brinks. AnSo

Often I return to that room—abject. Denied, The. Lisa Sewell. AmPoNex

Often I sit in the sun and brooding over the city, always. Dennis Lee. BrAP *Fr.* Civil Elegies.

Often I think of my Jewish friends. Pripet Marshes, The. Irving Feldman. TaR

Often I think of the beautiful town. My Lost Youth. Henry Wadsworth Longfellow. APN-1; BrAP; ITBLP; NAAL-3; NAAPv.1; OBEV; OxBoAm; TCAPo; TFi

Often I turn on people / in rather strange and / inexplicable ways. Maxfield Parrish. Eileen Myles. WiU

Often, I wonder, who is this stranger. Keys. Barbara J. Garshman. PasH

Often I'm lonely—some Crusoe. Lonely. Vasyl Symonenko. SonAtl, *tr.* by Dmytro Romanyk, Iryna Romanyk and Tamara Romanyk

Often in summer, on a tarred bridge plank standing. Wild Bees. James Keir Baxter. NoP-4; NoP-5

Often I've seen friends brake when I drive the car. Bicycle Slow Race, The. Claire Bateman. ArBi

Often keening on her daughter's tomb, Kleina. Anyte. SaLy, *tr.* by Diane Rayor

Often of late. Images of San Luis. Luis Lopez. GeoH

Often on this her daughter's tomb did Cleina grieve. Anyte. HePo *Fr.* Epigrams.

Often one wonders what the snake does all day in its pit. Old Trembling, An. Marvin Bell. PfSP

Often rebuked, yet always back returning. Stanzas. Emily Jane Brontë. BrAP; CtM; NALW; OBEV; OxBEV; PEW; VWP

Often the start went wrong. Start. Martin Sorescu. VCWP, *tr.* by Michael Hamburger

Often times / parents. Wishbone. Frank X. Walker. SpirFl

Often up the back steps he came. Landscape with Dog. Paul Mariani. PfSP

Often, when bored, the sailors of the crew. Albatross, The. Charles Baudelaire. SxFrPo, *tr.* by James McGowan

Often, when I leave home. On Shutting the Door. Lotte Kramer. Prnts

Often When Warring. Thomas Hardy. GSo

Often you come with your bird on your wrist. Often You Come. Franck André Jamme. YaTCFP, *tr.* by Mary Ann Caws

Oft-Repeated Dream, The. Robert Frost. TCAPo *Fr.* Hill Wife, The.

Oggy! Oggy! Oggy! Land of Song. Nigel Jenkins. AngWePo

Ogot, you invertebrate charlatan! Entelechy on the Libidinal Fringe. E. San Juan, Jr. ReBoTo

Ogres and Pygmies. Robert Graves. NAMCP V.1; NoAM

Ogun. Edward Kamau Brathwaite. NAMCP V.2

Ogun's Friend. Jayne Cortez. FTtHH

Oh. René Ricard. AHA

Oh. . .how the sky is in flame! Man Who Is Out of Work Talks to His Son about the Sunset, The. L. Miller. Prolet, *tr.* by Amelia Glaser

Oh, a hidden power is in my breast. Song of the Moon. Priscilla Jane Thompson. CBWP-2

Oh! a private buffoon is a light-hearted loon. William Schwenck Gilbert. NBLV *Fr.* Yeoman of the Guard.

Oh, America / The sun sets in you. Evening Land, The. D. H. Lawrence. FaBoA

Oh amiable rain. Rain. Charlotte Gardelle. CuPo

Oh, and yet I see that I will return to you anyway, and throw myself at your feet and cry a lot over my sins, until my crime will be pardoned. Marino Ceccoli. CAGL, *tr.* by Jill Claretta Robbins

Oh angels! will ye never sweep the drifts from my door? Drifts That Bar My Door. Adah Isaacs Menken. CBWP-1

Oh, answer me! (LL) Answer Me. Adah Isaacs Menken. CBWP-1; PoBW; ViWPN

Oh, Astonishing Love. Javier Sologuren. BLPSL, *tr.* by Rene de Costa, Rigas Kappatos and Eleni Paidoussi

Oh, Athelstane, the faithful! Athelstane. Priscilla Jane Thompson. CBWP-2

Oh, Atonement. Bruce Weigl. MAAN

Oh, baby, baby, baby dear. Song. Edith Nesbit. PEW

Oh, be but still, you half-part of my breast! Departure Aria. Johann Christian Günther. GePo, *tr.* by George C. Schoolfield

Oh, beautiful bicycle, noiselessly gliding. Bicycler's Song, A. *Unknown.* ArBi

Oh beloved, since the origin we have been / the slaves of the shah of love. Oh Beloved, Since the Origin We Have Been. Bâkî. OLP; WoPoe, *tr.* by Walter Andrews, Najaat Black and Mehmet Kalpakli

Oh, Bill / Why can't you behave. Always True to You in My Fashion. Cole Porter. ReLy

Oh, black Persian cat! Mujer. William Carlos Williams. SAmP

Oh! blame not the bard, if he fly to the bowers. Thomas Moore. NPeEn

Oh, blessed ease! no more of heaven I ask. Written in the Workhouse. Thomas Hood. CenSon

Oh! blest beyond all daughters of the earth! Mary at the Feet of Christ. Felicia Dorothea Hemans. CenSon

Oh Boney was a warrior. Boney. *Unknown.* FaBoVe

Oh bright-glancing Silver, who marriage has made. Stroll-Joy. Johann Klaj. GePo, *tr. by* George C. Schoolfield

Oh, broken-hearted lover. Decline of Love, The. William E. H. Lecky. IrLP

Oh, brown skinny girl with eyes like chips of mica. Tita's Poem. Aurora Levins Morales. PueRic

Oh, but it is dirty! Filling Station. Elizabeth Bishop. NoP-4; NoP-5; PoetW; PtR; VCAP; WeW-3

Oh, but to fade, and live we know not where. Shakespearian Readings. Phoebe Cary. SWaP

Oh, can we love and live? Pray, let us die. Love's Sun. William Cavendish, Duke of Newcastle. NOSC

Oh! can'st thou bear to see this faded frame. Her Last Appeal to Phaon. Mary Robinson. CenSon; RWP

Oh! canst thou bear to see this faded frame. Mary Robinson. NPBRoP *Fr.* Sappho and Phaon.

Oh child let yourself. Prayer of Mothers Who Unintentionally Failed Their Children. Vivian Lamarque. CItWP, *tr. by* Cinzia Sartini Blum and Lara Trubowitz

Oh chimes set high on the sunny tower. Over the Roofs. Sara Teasdale. ColAP

Oh Cibernetic Fairy. Down with the Money-Exchange. Carlos German Belli. TCLAP, *tr. by* Maureen Ahern and David Tipton

Oh, climb to my lips. Sadakichi. NAAPv.1 *Fr.* Tanka.

Oh come, my beloved! from thy winter abode. California Madrigal. Bret Harte. APN-2

Oh, come to me in dreams, my love! Stanzas. Mary Wollstonecraft Shelley. LW

Oh come with me by moonlight, love. Cherokee Love Song, A. John Rollin Ridge. APN-2

Oh, come with old Khayyam and leave the Wise. Omar Khayyám. UV *Fr.* Rubáiyát of Omar Khayyám [of Naishápúr], The.

Oh, could I but sing as the minstrels of old! Lines to Emma. Priscilla Jane Thompson. CBWP-2

Oh Could I Raise the Darken'd Veil. Nathaniel Hawthorne. APN-1

Oh! could I see as thou hast seen. On Hearing a Description of a Prairie. Fanny Crosby. SWaP

Oh country, marvel of the earth! Not Yet. William Cullen Bryant. NCAP

Oh! craven, craven! while my brothers fall. George Henry Boker. APN-2; PCW

Oh Cruel Was the Press-Gang. *Unknown.* FaBoWar

Oh cry, what are you doing, disturbing. Sheyhülislâm Bahâyî. OLP, *tr. by* Walter Andrews, Najaat Black and Mehmet Kalpakli

Oh damned rooster, I would like to strangle you! *Unknown.* SLW, *tr. by* Marjolijn De Jager, Sayd Bahodin Majrouh and André Velter

Oh, Damon, if thou ever wers't. To Damon. To Inquire of Him if He Cou'd Tell Me by the Style, Who Writ Me a Copy of Verses that Came to Me in an Unknown Hand. Aphra Behn. EMWP

Oh, daybreak streets. Blood of Daybreak, The. Chŏng Hyŏnjong. CAMKP, *tr. by* John M. Frankl

Oh dead punk lady with the knack. Victim, The. Thom Gunn. SwNoth

Oh, dear! Oh, me! Oh, my! Song. Gregory Corso. BB

Oh, dear! / The Christian virtues will disappear! Christian Virtues. Charlotte Perkins Stetson Gilman. SWaP

Oh dear what can the matter be? Saturday Night. Victoria Wood. OBCoV

Oh, dearest loss, sweet illusion. Sonnet 32. Fernando de Herrera. BLPSL, *tr. by* Rene de Costa, Rigas Kappatos and Eleni Paidoussi

Oh Deat' he is a little man. Lord, Remember Me. *Unknown.* SSUS

Oh! Death will find me, long before I tire. Sonnet. Rupert Brooke. NoP-4; NoP-5

Oh, Dem Golden Slippers! James A. Bland. APN-2

Oh Dick! You may talk of your writing and reading. Thomas Moore. OBCoV *Fr.* Fudge Family in Paris, The.

Oh didn't it "" "" "." Spyrytual. Russell Atkins. EGAG

Oh, ditch of all ditches. Ode to a Ditch. *Unknown.* VerBaPo

Oh, don't you remember Sweet Betsey from Pike. *Unknown.* APN-2; TCAPo

Oh Earth! The dues that you exact weigh far too much. *Unknown.* SLW, *tr. by* Marjolijn De Jager, Sayd Bahodin Majrouh and André Velter

Oh, East is East, and West is West, and never the twain shall meet. Ballad of East and West, The. Rudyard Kipling. OBNV

Oh east wind, come, what news from that garden. Sünbülzâde Vehbî. OLP, *tr. by* Walter Andrews, Najaat Black and Mehmet Kalpakli

Oh Eliza look at your Uncle Jim! Soldiers' Chorus from Faust. *Unknown.* NOBAu

Oh! Erin my country, my ancestor's home! Song to Erin. Mary Weston Fordham. CBWP-2

Oh, ever skilled [*or* skill'd] to wear the form we love! To Hope. Helen Maria Williams. CenSon; OxBSo

Oh! ever thus from childhood's hour. Thomas Moore. UV *Fr.* Lalla Rookh.

Oh fate, take pity on my suffering country. Zrínyi's Second Song. Ferenc Kölcsey. IQMS, *tr. by* Adam Makkai

Oh, For a Bowl of Fat Canary. John Lyly. *See* Serving Men's Song, A.

Oh, for a drink, to-night. Charmion's Lament. Eloise Bibb. CBWP-4

Oh for a lodge in some vast wilderness. William Cowper. *Fr.* Task, The.

Oh for a poet—for a beacon bright. Sonnet. Edwin Arlington Robinson. APN-2; NCAP

Oh for far-off monkeyland. Monkeyland. Sándor Weöres. IQMS; WoPoe, *tr. by* Edwin Morgan

Oh! for imperial Polydamna's art. Nepenthe. Charlotte Smith. NoP-4; NoP-5

O[h]! for some honest lover's ghost. Sonnet. Sir John Suckling. BASC; CavPo; OxBEV

Oh for that rose of Bolshevism which holds. Anathema. Maranatha! John Wheelwright. APT-2

Oh, for the holiness which is a needle. Apprentice Is Amazed, The. David Craig. UpMys

Oh for the love of God, sleep, don't let it come to this! *Unknown.* SLW, *tr. by* Marjolijn De Jager, Sayd Bahodin Majrouh and André Velter

Oh for the wings of a dove. Song. Agnes Mary Frances Robinson. VWP

Oh for words with which. In the Potting Shed. Sir Osbert Sitwell. OBGa

Oh force of your insistent pellicule. Erin Mouré. NLPA *Fr.* Wittgenstein Letters to Mel Gibson's Braveheart, The.

Oh Fortune, thy wresting wavering state. Queen of England Elizabeth I. CABP; PEW

Oh, foully slighted Ethiope maid! Song, The. Priscilla Jane Thompson. CBWP-2

Oh Friend, few happier moments have been mine. William Wordsworth. NPBRoP *Fr.* Prelude, The; Growth of a Poet's Mind [1805 version].

Oh friend, I love you, think this over. Why Arrange the Pillows. Kabir. WED, *tr. by* Robert Bly

Oh friend, we arrived too late. Friedrich Hölderlin. RaBo *Fr.* Bread and Wine.

Oh! Fucking Halkirk. *Unknown.* FaBoWar

Oh, gallant was the first love, and glittering and fine. Pictures in the Smoke. Dorothy Parker. NBLV

Oh, Galuppi, Baldassaro, this is very sad to find! Toccata of Galuppi's, A. Robert Browning. FaBoVe; NAEL-6v2; NAEL-7v2; NoP-5; UV

(Oh Galuppi, Baldassare, this is very sad to find!) NoP-4

Oh, genius of Stratford, return! To Shakespeare. Nina Nikolaevna Berberova. TCRusP, *tr. by* John Glad

Oh gentle Venus, ease a tarse. John Wilmot, 2d Earl of Rochester. EroLit *Fr.* Sodom; or The Quintessence of Debauchery.

Oh girl among roses, oh pressure of doves. Ode with a Lament. Pablo Neruda. ConPit, *tr. by* Clayton Eshleman

Oh give it Motion—deck it sweet. Emily Dickinson. NCAP

Oh give me a home where the buffalo roam. Home on the Range, A. *Unknown.* APN-2

(O give me a home where the buffalo roam.) TCAPo

Oh give me that you prize the most. Her Gift. Annie Hindle. PoBW

Oh, give my youth, my faith, my sword. Louise Imogen Guiney. TCAPo *Fr.* Knight Errant, The.

Oh! give to me of the bright green leaves. I Am Fashion's Toy. Mary E. Tucker. CBWP-1

Oh, give us of your oil, our lamps go out. For Richer, For Poorer. Emily Hickey. PoBW

Oh, give us pleasure in the flowers today. Prayer in Spring, A. Robert Frost. BLPJKO

Oh, God, beyond the wit of the genius. Prayer. Dániel Berzsenyi. IQMS, *tr. by* Peter Zollman

Oh God, don't let anyone be like me. Fuzuli. OLP, *tr. by* Walter Andrews, Najaat Black and Mehmet Kalpakli

Oh God, Fuck Me. Ruth L. Schwartz. BeAl

Oh, God, God!—Calm down. Which One Is the Grown-up? Haiku. Liz Rosenberg. InvLad

Oh God! my heart is thine. In the Valley. Priscilla Jane Thompson. CBWP-2

Oh God of mercy, oh wild God. (LL) Dancing, The. Gerald Stern. CAP-8; LoL; UnSA

Oh God, that I were dead! (LL) Mariana. Alfred Tennyson. NAEL-6v2; NAEL-7v2; NOBRP; OBEV; OxAEP-2; TFi

Oh, God, the full-faced moon is smiling at me. Coming Home. Elizabeth Tibbetts. SweBea

Oh God! what a lovely war. Cavalier's Farewell, The. Guillaume Apollinaire. WoPoe, *tr. by* Anne Greet

Oh golden life, waken! Fortunate night! Johann Klaj. GePo

Oh green green willow wonderfully red flower. Ikkyu Sojun. WoPoe *Fr.* Four Poems.

Oh happy hero come, oh enter, worthy groom. To Be Read above the Castle-Gate, When His Princely Highness Rode in to His Marriage Bed. Simon Dach. GePo, *tr. by* George C. Schoolfield

Oh happy shades—to me unblest! Shrubbery, The. William Cowper. OBGa

Oh, hark the dogs are barking, love. Banks of the Condamine, The. *Unknown.* NOBAu

Oh he is worn with toil! the big drops run. Robert Southey. CenSon

Oh, he was a handsome trotter, and he couldn't be completer. How We Drove the Trotter. W. T. Goodge. NOBAu

Oh, hear a pensive captive's prayer. Anna Laetitia Barbauld. NPBRoP

Oh, Heaven! it was a frightful and pitiful sight to see. Calamity in London; Family of Ten Burned to Death. William McGonagall. VerBaPo

Oh heavens how these crying people spoil the beautiful geological scene. (LL) New Age, The. Stevie Smith. NAEL-6v2; NAEL-7v2

Oh heavens, why do you cry? Is your beloved seen. Zati. OLP, *tr. by* Walter Andrews, Najaat Black and Mehmet Kalpakli

Oh hell, what do mine eyes. Milton by Firelight. Gary Snyder. BB; NAMCP V.2

Oh hey, All-Destroyer. Najrul Islām. SinGod, *tr. by* Rachel Fell McDermott

Oh hold me, for I am afraid. (LL) Woman to Man. Judith Wright. BMAP; BrAP; NoP-4; NoP-5; StAl

Oh, how can I live in a torture so wild. Disappointment. Mary E. Tucker. CBWP-1

Oh how can love exulting reason quell? Mary Robinson. NPBRoP *Fr.* Sappho and Phaon.

Oh, how cool. Buson. CalPo, *tr. by* Yonejiro (Yone) Noguchi

Oh, how cool. Yonejiro (Yone) Noguchi. NAAPv.2 *Fr.* Japanese Hokkus.

Oh, how fastidious you once were. Georgy Vladimirovich Ivanov. TCRusP, *tr. by* Daniel Weissbort

Oh! How his pointed language, like a dart. Cant. 5.6 & c. Elizabeth Singer. ChIV-1

Oh! How I Hate to Get Up in the Morning. Irving Berlin. NAAPv.2; ReLy; TCAPo

Oh, how I love Humanity. World State, The. G. K. Chesterton. SacPr

OH HOW I WANT THEE FAME! Mad Sonnet: Fame. Michael McClure. BB

Oh how I wanted to be a dancer. Soul Train. Allison Joseph. AmPoNex; ExTi; SUP

Oh how I wish that an embargo. Nurse's Dole in the Medea, The. Lord Byron. OBVE

Oh, how slowly he goes. Chalk and Soot. Wassily Kandinsky. PFTM-1

Oh, How the Hand the Lover Ought to Prize. Aphra Behn. LW

Oh, how the lilacs are this May! Bulging-large bunches fell. Sergey Gandlevsky. ItGoST, *tr. by* Philip Metres

Oh, how the world has altered since some fifty years ago! Song of the Modern Time. Eliza Cook. VWP

Oh humming all and. Detach, Invading. Ron Padgett. FTOS

Oh hush thee, my baby. Carol, A. Cecil Day Lewis. ChrPo

Oh! I admit his talent,—there's no lack. Contemporary Criticism, A. William Wetmore Story.

Oh I am a Yankee sailor boy. Sailor Boy's Song. *Unknown.* CA

Oh / I am thinking. Frances Densmore. APT-1 *Fr.* Chippewa Music.

Oh, I am wild—wild! Sale of Souls. Adah Isaacs Menken. CBWP-1

Oh, I can cook, too, on top of the rest. I Can Cook, Too. Betty Comden and Adolph Green. ReLy

Oh, I can smile for you, and tilt my head. Certain Lady, A. Dorothy Parker. NIL-7; NIP-4

Oh! I could toil for thee o'er burning plains. To Phaon. Mary Robinson. CenSon; RWP

Oh / I got a message from below. Pack Up Your Sins and Go to the Devil. Irving Berlin. ReLy

Oh, I got plenty o' nuthin'. I Got Plenty o' Nuthin'. Ira Gershwin. ReLy

Oh, I have no illusions as to what. Penelope. James Harrison. NIP-4

Oh! I have slipped the surly bonds of Earth. High Flight. John Gillespie, Jr. Magee. ITBLP; OtW; PoWW

Oh, I have told thee every secret care. Charles Lloyd. CenSon

Oh I suppose I should. Le Médecin Malgré Lui. William Carlos Williams. PoA 2002

Oh, I went down South for to see my Sal. Polly Wolly Doodle. *Unknown.* TCAPo

Oh, I would have these tongues oracular. At a Symphony. Louise Imogen Guiney. APN-2

Oh, if my power might equal my desire. Lady Charlotte Guest. Goronva Camlan. AngWePo

Oh If the Gods Would Make Me Rich. Martial. WoPoe, *tr. by* William Matthews

Oh if the gods would make me rich, you said. Oh If the Gods Would Make Me Rich. Martial. WoPoe, *tr. by* William Matthews

Oh! if thou lov'st me, love me not so well! Jane Cross Simpson. CenSon

Oh! if you love her. Advice to a Lover. S. Charles Jellicoe. IrLP

Oh I'll die I'll die I'll die. Stark Electric Jesus. Malay Roy Choudhury. PFTM-2

Oh, ill-starred Ethiopia. Address to Ethiopia. Priscilla Jane Thompson. CBWP-2

Oh, I'm 10 Months Pregnant. Ntozake Shange. GT

Oh, I'm a good old Rebel. Rebel, The. Innes Randolph. AmWaPo; NBLV

Oh, I'm sailin' away my own true love. Boots of Spanish Leather. Bob Dylan. NoP-5

(Oh, I'm sailing away my own true love.) NoP-4

Oh in eighteen hundred and forty-one. Poor Paddy Works on the Railway. *Unknown.* GM

Oh, in the merry month of May. Bonny Barbara Allan. *Unknown.* HeIP-4

Oh, in the pen, oh, in the pen. Penological Study: Southern Exposure. Robert Penn Warren.

Oh Indian watching from the doorway. Who Knows? José Santos Chocano. TCLAP, *tr. by* Andrew Rosing

Oh, it is done, my love, my death, my life, my prize. To the Superhuman Adelmund, When She Would Undo the Kiss Already Done. Philipp von Zesen. GePo, *tr. by* George C. Schoolfield

Oh, It's You Again. Carl Mayfield. ICANM

O[h] joy[e]s! Infinite sweetness! with what flowers [*or* flowres]. Morning-Watch, The. Henry Vaughan. AngWePo; BASC; NOSC

Oh Kali. Janine Canan. HW

Oh Kali Full of Brahman! Rāmprasād Sen. SinGod, *tr. by* Rachel Fell McDermott

Oh Keep the Poet Hence. Thomas Carper. PoA 2002

Oh king, whose head alone can rule Earth's company. Concerning the King of Sweden. Georg Rudolph Weckherlin. GePo, *tr. by* George C. Schoolfield

Oh! la bonne petite pluie qui sait si bien. Pluie de Printemps, La. Tu Fu [*or* Du Fu]. CCL1, *tr. by* Marie-Jean-Léon, Marquis d'Hervey de Saint-Denys

Oh, Lady, Be Good! Ira Gershwin. ReLy

Oh Lana Turner we love you get up. (LL) Poem: "Lana Turner has collapsed!" Frank O'Hara. CAP-8; CLPP; FTOS; ItP; OxBoAm; PmAP

Oh! lay me by yon peaceful stream. *Unknown.* RWP *Fr.* Aged Bard's Wish, The.

Oh, lead me to a quiet cell. Portrait of the Artist. Dorothy Parker. AmWit

Oh! leave the Past to bury its own dead. To One Who Would Make a Confession. Wilfrid Scawen Blunt. GSo

Oh, let me not serve so, as those men serve. John Donne. BASC *Fr.* Elegies.

Oh, let me run and hide. Spring Ecstasy. Lizette Woodworth Reese. MoAmPo

Oh! let that day from time be blotted quite. On the Fatal Day January 30, 1648. Thomas Fairfax, Baron Fairfax of Cameron. NOSC

Oh, let us fly without delay. Bungalow in Quogue. P. G. Wodehouse. ReLy

Oh! Liberty! transcendent and sublime! To Liberty. Mary Robinson. OxBSo

Oh Life. Yi Kyŏngnim. EcSo, *tr. by* Peter H. Lee

Oh, life is a glorious cycle of song. Comment. Dorothy Parker. AmWit; LW; NBLV; NIL-7; NIP-4; OBCoV

Oh life, long as an epic. Tatiana Bek. ItGoST, *tr. by* Richard McKane

Oh limpid spring! that dost surpass. To Mother Luddwels Cave and Spring. Martha, Lady Giffard. EMWP

Oh List to My Song! [*with music*]. Clara Ann Thompson. CBWP-2

Oh, listen, sister. Can't Help Lovin' Dat Man. Oscar Hammerstein, II. ReLy

Oh Living Lord, I still will laud thy name. Other Song of the Faithful, for the Mercies of God, An. Michael Drayton. ChIV-1

Oh London I once more to thee do speak. Mary Adams. EMWP

Oh, long, long / The snow has possessed the mountains. Grass on the Mountain, The. *Unknown.* APT-1, *tr. by* Mary Austin

Oh look, / a flock of kayakers. Observation. Tim Griffin. FreRad

Oh, Lord! I lift my heart. Prayer, A. Priscilla Jane Thompson. CBWP-2

Oh Lord, I want some valiant soldier. Some Valiant Solider. *Unknown.* SSUS

Oh Lord! Once again your long and dismal night is here. *Unknown.* SLW, *tr. by* Marjolijn De Jager, Sayd Bahodin Majrouh and André Velter

Oh, lost and unforgotten friend. Desiderato. William Johnson Cory. CAGL

Oh, lovely Mary Donnelly, my joy, my pride [*or* it's you I love best]. Lovely Mary Donnelly. William Allingham. IrV

Oh lustrous! the king's army. Great War Dance, The. *Unknown.* WoPoe, *tr. by* Constance A. Cook

Oh lute that I would like to see demolished! *Unknown.* SLW, *tr. by* Marjolijn De Jager, Sayd Bahodin Majrouh and André Velter

Oh, ma honey. Alexander's Ragtime Band. Irving Berlin. NAAPv.2; ReLy; TCAPo

Oh Ma Kali, for a long time now. Mahendranāth Bhattācārya. SinGod, *tr. by* Rachel Fell McDermott

Oh, Magyar, keep immovably. Appeal. Mihály Vörösmarty. IQMS, *tr. by* Watson Kirkconnell

Oh man, be born of God: for at His Godhead's throne. "Angelus Silesius." GePo *Fr.* Cherubical Wanderer, The.

Oh Man is the highest type of animal existing. Joanne Kyger. WhBo

Oh, man's capacity / For spiritual sorrow. Crucifixion, The. Alice Thompson Meynell. SacPr

Oh, Mary, this London's a wonderful sight. Mountains of Mourne, The. William Percy French. OBCoV

Oh Mary, this Tatton's a wonderful sight. Tatton Parachute Training School. *Unknown.* FaBoWar

O[h] me[e], the time is [*or* has] come to part. Mary Sidney Wroth, Countess of Montgomery. NOSC *Fr.* Pamphilia to Amphilanthus.

Oh memory of my beloved, you are my one true lover! *Unknown.* SLW, *tr. by* Marjolijn De Jager, Sayd Bahodin Majrouh and André Velter

Oh Menelaus. On Hearing the First Cuckoo. Richard Church. OBMV

Oh Mercy. Tony Hoagland. SUP

Oh! Mercy Mercy Me! A Family Gathers to Marvin Gaye. Laura Soul Brown. FTtHH

Oh, might it die or rest at last! (LL) Percy Bysshe Shelley. HeIP-4; NoP-4; NoP-5 *Fr.* Hellas.

Oh Mind, you don't know how to farm. Rāmprasād Sen. SinGod, *tr. by* Rachel Fell McDermott

Oh, Missouri, she's a mighty river. *Unknown.* FaBoA

O[h] mistress mine, where are you roaming? William Shakespeare. AEP; ClHu; NAEL-6v1; NBLV; NoP-4; NoP-5; NoSic; TFi; WoPoe *Fr.* Twelfth Night.

Oh, moon, you and I have something to share. Oh, Moon. Běkes. IrPoTo, *tr. by* Salah Ahmed Baban

Oh, Mother, Mother, oh what a cipher. Carl Michael Bellman. WoPoe *Fr.* Fredman's Epistlar, 1790.

Oh mother my mouth is full of stars. Song of the Dying Gunner A.A.1. Charles Causley. FaBoWar; PoWW

Oh Mother, so many times. Mother with Child. Lenore Keeshig-Tobias. FFC

Oh Mother, the brightness of the birch tree's bark in this November. Fred Wah. NLPA *Fr.* This Dendrite Map: Father / Mother Haibun.

Oh, murmuring reef. To a Tropic Reef. Hugh Fuller. OWABP

Oh Muse! I crave a favor. Muse's Favor, The. Priscilla Jane Thompson. CBWP-2

Oh! must that task, that mournful task, be thine? (LL) Laments her Early Misfortunes. Mary Robinson. CenSon; RWP

Oh, my belovèd, have you thought of this. Edna St. Vincent Millay. HeIP-4; LW

Oh my black[e] soul[e]! now thou art summoned. John Donne. OxAEP-1 *Fr.* Holy Sonnets.

Oh my bride, my bride. (LL) I Remember. Stevie Smith. NIL-7; PoAgWa

Oh my children, the new blood of ancient Thebes. Oedipus the King. Sophocles. NAWM-5v1, *tr. by* Robert Fagles

Oh, my fine, my honey-colored Duke of Marmalade! Elegy for the Duke of Marmalade. Luis Palés Matos. TCLAP, *tr. by* Ellen G. Matilla and Diego de la Texera

Oh, my God is in the whirlwind. Song of the Whirlwind. Fenton Johnson. OxAAAP

Oh my God! Once again you send me the dark night. *Unknown.* SLW, *tr. by* Marjolijn De Jager, Sayd Bahodin Majrouh and André Velter

*Oh my god—*you. Robert Creeley. WoBe *Fr.* Life and Death.

Oh, my golden slippers am [*or* are] laid away. Oh, Dem Golden Slippers! James A. Bland. APN-2

Oh *my* Good, *my* Beauty! Atrocious fanfare in which I do not waver! Morning of Drunkenness. Arthur Rimbaud. SxFrPo, *tr. by* Martin Sorrell

Oh, my hatred, my majestic hatred. Sacred Hatred. João da Cruz e Sousa. TCLAP, *tr. by* Flavia Vidal

Oh, my heart is beating wildly. When I'm Not Near the Girl I Love. E. Y. Harburg. ReLy

Oh my heart, you must remain alone. Solo for the Lone Intuition, A. Shakir Samawi. IrPoTo, *tr. by* Chuck Miller and Saadi A. Simawe

Oh! my heart's in a whirl. Peg O' My Heart. Alfred Bryan. NAAPv.2

Oh, my, here comes a crazy wench. Prague Spring 8. Ko Chônghûi. EcSo, *tr. by* Catherine J. Kim

Oh my idol of the temple, in the dark of night. Nesimi. OLP, *tr. by* Walter Andrews, Najaat Black and Mehmet Kalpakli

Oh my love beyond the mountains, gaze at the moon. *Unknown.* SLW, *tr. by* Marjolijn De Jager, Sayd Bahodin Majrouh and André Velter

Oh my love! If in my arms you tremble so. *Unknown.* SLW, *tr. by* Marjolijn De Jager, Sayd Bahodin Majrouh and André Velter

Oh, my loved Harp! companion dear! Address to My Harp. Mary Tighe. NPBRoP

Oh my mimics, my gangly girls. Daffodils. Karen Volkman. NeAmPo

Oh my Mind, worship Kali. Rāmprasād Sen. SinGod, *tr. by* Rachel Fell McDermott

Oh my Mind! You're just spinning. Rāmprasād Sen. SinGod, *tr. by* Rachel Fell McDermott

Oh, my mother was frightened by a shotgun they say. You Can't Get a Man with a Gun. Irving Berlin. ReLy

Oh, my rash hand! what has thou idly done? Written at Rossana. November 18, 1799. Mary Tighe. CenSon

Oh! my sleigh and my fast horse! Sleigh, The. Sergey Aleksandrovich Yesenin. RusPo, *tr. by* Robert Arthur Douglas Ford

Oh, my truelove, is part of it. Old Love in Song, An. Elizabeth Madox Roberts. APT-1

Oh, neighbours! what had I a-do for to marry! Hooly and Fairly. Joanna Baillie. RACG; WoRP

Oh! never did the dark-soul'd Atheist stand. Robert Montgomery. STuOW *Fr.* Omnipresence of the Deity, The.

Oh never on my youthful ear. My Mother's Voice. Mary E. Tucker. CBWP-1

Oh never on that mountain. Frances Ellen Watkins Harper. TCAPo *Fr.* Moses: A Story of the Nile.

Oh never try to knock on rotten wood. Admonitions. Sylvia Plath. WaAnP

Oh never weep for love that's dead. Dead Love. Elizabeth Siddal. LW

Oh No. Robert Creeley. HeIP-4

Oh no. Oh Yes. Joseph Stroud. GeoHom

Oh no categories I pray. (LL) No Categories! Stevie Smith. NoP-4; NoP-5

Oh, no! we never mention her, her name is never heard. Oh, No! We Never Mention Her. Thomas Haynes Bayly. STuOW

Oh, Noa, Noa! William Cole. NBLV

Oh, Nobody knows the trouble I've seen. *Unknown.* SacPr

Oh nobody's a long time. Lonesome Boy Blues. Kenneth Patchen. APT-2

Oh, not more subtly silence strays. To the Beloved. Alice Thompson Meynell. VWP

Oh, now I feel as though another sense. On the Group of the Three Angels Before the Tent of Abraham, by Raffaelle, in the Vatican. Washington Allston. APN-1

Oh, now, now the white fury of the spring. White Fury of the Spring, The. Lizette Woodworth Reese. APT-1

Oh, Oh, you will be sorry for that word! Edna St. Vincent Millay. HeIP-4; NALW

Oh one day as anoder, / Hallelu, hallelu! Hallelu, Hallelu. *Unknown.* SSUS

Oh [*or* O] Fairest of the Rural Maids. William Cullen Bryant. APN-1

Oh [*or* O] how comely it is and how reviving. John Milton. OBEV; OxAEP-1 *Fr.* Samson Agonistes.

Oh [*or* O] many a day have I made good ale in the glen. Outlaw of Loch Lene, The. Jeremiah Joseph Callanan. IrLP; OBEV, *tr. by* Jeremiah Joseph Callanan

Oh [*or* O], no more, no more, too late. John Ford. NOSC *Fr.* Broken Heart, The.

Oh [*or* O] say, [*or* O! say] can you see, by the dawn's early light. Star-Spangled Banner, The. Francis Scott Key. AmWaPo; HHAm; NoP-4; UV

Oh [*or* O], slow to smite and swift to spare. Death of Lincoln, The. William Cullen Bryant. NAAPv.1

(Oh, slow to smite and swift to spare.) NCAP

Oh [*or* O] that those lips had language! Life has passed [*or* pass'd]. On the Receipt of My Mother's Picture out of Norfolk [the Gift of My Cousin Ann Bodham]. William Cowper. OxAEP-1

Oh [*or* O] thou great Power, in whom I move. Hymn to My God in a Night of My Late Sickness[e], A. Sir Henry Wotton. NOSC; SacPr

Oh [*or* O!] what a plague is Love! Phillida Flouts Me [*or* The Disdainful Shepherdess]. *Unknown.* OBEV

Oh [*or* O], young Lochinvar is come out of the west. Sir Walter Scott. ChAP; NAEL-6v2; NAEL-7v2; NePenScot; NPBRoP; OxAEP-2; TFi *Fr.* Marmion.

Oh pale, white forms, clear forms. Antiphony. João da Cruz e Sousa. TCLAP, *tr. by* Nancy Vieira Couto

Oh Pangs of Love! Robert Desnos. SurPaPo, *tr. by* Mary Ann Caws

Oh, pedestals of ivory, breathing structure. To a Pair of Legs. Francisco de Terrazas. BLPSL, *tr. by* Rene de Costa, Rigas Kappatos and Eleni Paidoussi

Oh pile of white shirts who is coming. Night of the Shirts, The. W. S. Merwin. VCAP

Oh! place me where the burning noon. Petrarch. RWP *Fr.* Sonnets to Laura.

Oh, Poet of our Race. Poet of Our Race. Maggie Pogue Johnson. CBWP-4

Oh praise Him, praise Him, praise without an end or aim. Zealous Admonition to Praise. Catharina Regina von Greiffenberg. GePo, *tr. by* George C. Schoolfield

Oh praise the lowly stalk. Grass. Vera Pavlova. CRWP, *tr. by* Maura Dooley and Terence Dooley

Oh, Priest Pangeivi, you let go. Funeral Eva. Koroneu. RaBo

Oh princess of your land, whom Holstein cousin names. To the Great City of Moscow, as He Was Leaving June 25, 1636. Paul Fleming. GePo, tr. by George C. Schoolfield

Oh, pure and sportive little child. To a Little Colored Boy. Priscilla Jane Thompson. CBWP-2

Oh, pure virgin, come to your window. O Blanca Virgen. Peralta Family Oral Tradition. ASA

Oh raw, raw. Transporter. Oni Buchanan. LegDan

Oh Reason, vaunted sovereign of the mind. Mary Robinson. NPBRoP Fr. Sappho and Phaon.

Oh Rilke, I want to sit down calm like you. Michael Ondaatje. BrAP Fr. Tin Roof.

Oh River, gentle River! gliding on. Night Journey of a River, The. William Cullen Bryant. APN-1

Oh, rock-a-by, baby mouse, rock-a-by, so! Mouse's Lullaby, The. Palmer Cox. NOxBChV; TLR

Oh rooster, wait a little with your song! Unknown. SLW, tr. by Marjolijn De Jager, Sayd Bahodin Majrouh and André Velter

Oh ruined tomb, oh scattered bricks, my beloved is no more than dust. Unknown. SLW, tr. by Marjolijn De Jager, Sayd Bahodin Majrouh and André Velter

Oh sacred Time! how soon thou'rt gone! Midnight Thought, A. On the Death of Mrs. E. H. and Her Little Daughter. Elizabeth Thomas. NOSC

Oh, said a piece of tree bark in the wind, and the night froze. Sound of the Resurrected Dead Man's Footsteps (#2). Marvin Bell. TAPaP

Oh say not that my heart is cold. Song. Charles Wolfe. OxAEP-2

Oh, say you can hear / On the Watergate tapes. Final Curtain. Roger Woddis. UV

Oh! scorn me not as a fameless thing. Song of the Rushlight. Eliza Cook. VWP

Oh see how thick the goldcup flowers. A. E. Housman. MoBrPo Fr. Shropshire Lad, A.

Oh send to me an apple that hasn't any kernel. Unknown. WoPoe, tr. by Gwyn Williams

Oh Sensibility! Thou busy nurse. Addressed to Sensibility. Ann Yearsley. RWP

Oh sensibility, thou dangerous gift. On Sensibility: A Fragment. Isabella Lickbarrow. RWP

Oh! she is very old. I lay. Africa. Joaquin Miller. APN-2

Oh, she may be weary. Try a Little Tenderness. Jimmy Campbell, Reginald Connelly and Harry Woods. ReLy

Oh, she said. For Elaine de Kooning. Hilda Morley. PmAP

Oh, she / the well remembered. Cytherea. Carlos Montemayor. BLPSL, tr. by Rene de Costa, Rigas Kappatos and Eleni Paidoussi

Oh she thinks in song. She Thinks in Song. Femi Osofisan. NAfrP

O[h], she walked unaware of her own increasing beauty. She Walked Unaware. Patrick MacDonogh. IrLP

Oh! she was a lovely girl. Only One Eye. Lillian E. Curtis. VerBaPo

Oh, she was almost speechless! nor could hold. Charles Lloyd. CenSon

Oh, she was beautiful in every part! To Elinor Wylie. Edna St. Vincent Millay. NAAPv.2

Oh, she was sad, oh, she was sad. She Didn't Mean to Do It. Daisy Fried. P180; PoDa

Oh! Shepherd John is good and kind. Shepherd John. Mary Mapes Dodge. SWaP

Oh, show us the way to the next whisky-bar. Alabama Song. Bertolt Brecht. PFTM-1

Oh, Sí; Romper la Copa. Juan Ramón Jiménez. RaW

Oh, sick I am to see you, will you never let me be? A. E. Housman. MoBrPo Fr. Shropshire Lad, A.

Oh sigh, thou stealest (the herald of the breast). Mary Robinson. NPBRoP Fr. Sappho and Phaon.

Oh Sigh! thou steal'st, the herald of the breast. To a Sigh. Mary Robinson. CenSon; RWP

Oh, silver tree! Jazzonia. Langston Hughes. ColAP; NAAPv.2

(O, silver tree!) OxAAAP

Oh sister, he is so swift and tall. Apprehension. Hannah Flagg Gould. SWaP

Oh, skies of those days, skis of luminous signals and meteors. Constellation: Prose Poem. Bruno Schulz. ArBi, tr. by Celina Wieniewska

Oh, slow to smite and swift to spare. William Cullen Bryant. See Oh [or O], slow to smite and swift to spare.

Oh some are fond of red wine, and some are fond of white. Captain Stratton's Fancy. John Masefield. MoBrPo; OBEV

Oh! Southey! Southey! cease thy varied song! Lord Byron. WaAnP Fr. English Bards and Scotch Reviewers [1812 version].

Oh spare me, spare me. Maya Bejerano. DTA Fr. Hymns of Job.

Oh spare the busy morning fly! Humanity. Han Yü. CCL1, tr. by H. A. Giles

Oh springtime of unquenched desires. Unknown. SLW, tr. by Marjolijn De Jager, Sayd Bahodin Majrouh and André Velter

Oh springtime! The pomegranate trees are blooming. Unknown. SLW, tr. by Marjolijn De Jager, Sayd Bahodin Majrouh and André Velter

Oh! Stalin is my darling, my darling, my darling. Stalin Moy Golubchik. "Sagittarius." OBCoV

Oh stay at home, my lad, and plough. A. E. Housman. FaBoWar

Oh strong-ridged and deeply hollowed. Smell. William Carlos Williams. MoAmPo; OxBoAm; RaBo

Oh Sumptuous moment. Emily Dickinson. NAAL-3

Oh! surely for thee were the gates ajar. Rev. Samuel Weston. Mary Weston Fordham. CBWP-2

Oh! surely 'tis a theme sublime. Dedicated to the Right Rev'd D. A. Payne. Mary Weston Fordham. CBWP-2

Oh! Susanna. Stephen Collins Foster. TCAPo

(Susanna.) APN-2

Oh, sweet gifts brought forth for my misfortune. Sonnet 10. Baldomero Garcilaso de la Vega. BLPSL, tr. by Rene de Costa, Rigas Kappatos and Eleni Paidoussi

Oh, talk not to me of a name great in story. Stanzas Written on the Road between Florence and Pisa. Lord Byron. BrAP; NAEL-6v2; NAEL-7v2

Oh, tell me why you make the school. Retrospection. Dunstan Shaw. NOBAu

Oh that girl with the Binh Tien hairdo. Girl with the Binh Tien Hairdo, The. Vietnamese Oral Tradition. CaDao, tr. by John Balaban

Oh that I was my Sylvia's stays! Poem Left in a Lady's Toilet. James Eyre Weeks. IrLP

Oh that I were all soul, that I might prove. Upon Platonic Love: To Mistress Cicely Crofts, Maid of Honour. Sir Robert Aytoun. NOSC

Oh That My Heart Could Hit Upon a Strain. Nicholas Breton. WaAnP

Oh! That my young life were a lasting dream! Dreams. Edgar Allan Poe. NCAP; OxBoAm

Oh! that the desert [or desart] were my dwelling-place. Lord Byron. Fr. Childe Harold's Pilgrimage.

Oh, that they had pity, the men we serve so truly! Cry of the Animals, The. Mary Howitt. VWP

Oh [or O] that those lips had language! Life has passed [or pass'd]. On the Receipt of My Mother's Picture out of Norfolk, the Gift of My Cousin Ann Bodham. William Cowper. OxAEP-1

Oh the anguish of these secret meetings. Kenneth Rexroth. APSN; APT-2; NAAPv.2 Fr. Love Poems of Marichiko, The.

Oh, the comfort—the inexpressible comfort of feeling safe with a person. Friendship. Dinah Maria Mulock Craik. ITBLP

Oh, the days when I was young. Richard Brinsley Sheridan. OxAEP-1 Fr. Duenna, The.

Oh, the Fern! the Fern!—the Irish hill Fern! Mountain Fern, The. Arthur G. Geoghegan. IrV

Oh, the Gingkos. Edward Field. BodElec

Oh! the Golden Age. William Browne. NOSC Fr. Britannia's Pastorals.

Oh, the gorgeous leaves of autumn! Autumn Leaves. Clara Ann Thompson. CBWP-2

Oh, the hireling sun in a slipshod way. Field of the Cloth of Gold, The. Patrick Joseph Hartigan. NOBAu

Oh the long and dreary Winter! Henry Wadsworth Longfellow. TreFP Fr. Song of Hiawatha, The.

Oh the maggots marched down Pitt Street. Maggot Song. Unknown. NOBAu

Oh the magnificence of hell! Hell. Edith Södergran. PFTM-1

Oh the nighttime beating of the soul's wings. Song of the Western Countries. Georg Trakl. WED, tr. by Robert Bly

Oh the north countree is a hard countree. Ballad of Yukon Jake, The. Edward E., Jr. Paramore. TCAPo

Oh! the old swimmin'-hole! whare the crick so still and deep. Old Swimmin'-Hole, The. James Whitcomb Riley. APN-2; BRP

Oh, the pleasing, pleasing anguish. Joseph Addison. STuOW Fr. Rosamond.

Oh the rose of keenest thorn! Iniquity of the Fathers upon the Children, The. Christina Georgina Rossetti. FaBoVe

Oh, the sea is deep. Song for a Suicide. Langston Hughes. OxAAAP

Oh the sound of her silk sleeves. Emperor Wu of Han. EaWin, tr. by W. S. Merwin

Oh, the sweet contentment. Coridon's Song. John Chalkhill. NOSC

Oh, the wild joys of living! the leaping from rock up to rock. Robert Browning. ITBLP Fr. Saul.

Oh! the world gives little of love or light. Song of the Ugly Maiden. Eliza Cook. VWP

Oh there hasn't been much change. Grange, The. Stevie Smith. OBCoV

Oh, there once was a Puffin. There Once Was a Puffin. Florence Page Jaques. NTCP

Oh there once was a woman. How to Continue. John Ashbery. OxBoAm

Oh they came, their eyes blank. Voice for the Sirens, A. Maura Stanton.

YaYoPo

Oh! / They say some people long ago. Birth of the Blues, The. Lew Brown, B. G. DeSylva and Ray Henderson. ReLy

Oh, think not I am faithful to a vow! Edna St. Vincent Millay. NAAPv.2

Oh this man. Magnificat. Michele Roberts. PoBW

Oh Those Smokestacks. Nelly Sachs. GTCP, tr. by Reinhold Grimm

Oh! thou dead / And everlasting witness! whose unsinking. Lord Byron. ChIV-1 Fr. Cain: A Mystery.

Oh, thou eternal Homer! I have now. Lord Byron. FaBoWar Fr. Don Juan.

Oh, thou immortal bard! Byron. J. Gordon Coogler. VerBaPo

Oh, thou! in Hellas deemed of heavenly birth. Lord Byron. NAEL-6v2; NAEL-7v2 Fr. Childe Harold's Pilgrimage.

Oh thou, meek orb, that stealing o'er the dale. Mary Robinson. NPBRoP Fr. Sappho and Phaon.

Oh Thou, that sit's upon a throne. Christopher Smart. See O Thou, that sit'st upon a throne.

O[h] that swingest [or swing'st] upon the waving hair[e] [or ear or eare]. Grasshopper, The [To My Noble Friend Mr Charles Cotton: Ode]. Richard Lovelace. BASC; CavPo; NAEL-6v1; NAEL-7v1; NoP-4; NoP-5; NOSC; OBEV; TFi; WaAnP

Oh! thou who dry'st the mourner's tear. Comforter, The. Thomas Moore. SacPr

Oh, thou! whose tender smile most partially. Sonnet Addressed to My Mother. Mary Tighe. NoP-4

¡Oh Tiempo, Dame Tu Secreto. Juan Ramón Jiménez. RaW

Oh, 'tis little Mary Cassidy's the cause of all my misery. Little Mary Cassidy. Francis A. Fahy. IrV

Oh to be a bride. Bride, The. Bella Akhatovna Akhmadulina. MPUn

Oh, to be in England. Home Truths from Abroad. Unknown. UV

Oh, to be more than you can be. Recruiting Poster. Hillel Schwartz. BAP-97

Oh to be one of them, the wine whispered to me. (LL) Old World, The. Charles Simic. CAP-8; StAl

Oh, to be ready for it, unfucked, ever-fucked. Me in Paradise. Brenda Shaughnessy. IIR

Oh, to be somebody's moon! Looking at the Moon. Vivian Lamarque. CItWP, tr. by Cinzia Sartini Blum and Lara Trubowitz

Oh, to close my desk, lay by my pen. Sigh of the Old Cattleman, The. Jas. D. Thorn. TiP2

Oh, to my sobs, Galatea, you are harder than a stone. Baldomero Garcilaso de la Vega. BLPSL Fr. First Eclogue.

Oh, to vex me, contraries [or contraryes] meet in one. John Donne. BASC; ChIV-2; NAEL-7v1; NOSC; WaAnP Fr. Holy Sonnets.

Oh town of the hundred doors. Jerusalem. Manuela Fingueret. MirDau, tr. by Roberta Gordenstein

Oh transient sorrows, light as morning dews. To My Brother. Mary Bryan. NPBRoP

Oh Trial. Unknown. FaBoVe

Oh! wake the chace where I may hear. Unknown. RWP Fr. Aged Bard's Wish, The.

O[h] waly, waly, up the [or yon] bank. Waly, Waly [Love Be Bonny]. Unknown. NOSC; OBEV; TFi

Oh, wash-woman, / Arms elbow-deep in white suds. Song to a Negro Wash-woman, A. Langston Hughes. NAAPv.2

Oh! waves in the sunlight gleaming. Sonnet to My First Born. Mary Weston Fordham. CBWP-2

Oh we know. (LL) Song for Those Who Know. Hans Magnus Enzensberger. PoSu; VCWP, tr. by the author and Michael Hamburger

O[h] wearisome condition of humanity. Fulke, 1st Baron Brooke Greville. NAEL-6v1; NAEL-7v1; OxBEV Fr. Mustapha.

Oh, weep for Mr. and Mrs. Bryan! Lion, The. Ogden Nash. TLR; WHSW

Oh! Weep for Those. Lord Byron. ChIV-1

Oh, Wellington! (or "Villainton") for fame. Lord Byron. Fr. Don Juan.

Oh, were the white waves. Sadakichi. NAAPv.1 Fr. Tanka.

O[h] Wert Thou in the Cauld Blast. Robert Burns. FaBoVe; NePenScot; NoP-4; NoP-5; NPeEn; OxAEP-2; PoPoPo

Oh, What a Beautiful Mornin'! Oscar Hammerstein, II. ReLy

Oh, what a bevy of beauties. They Couldn't Compare to You. Cole Porter. ReLy

Oh, what a kiss. Modern Mother, The. Alice Thompson Meynell. VWP

Oh! what a pain is here! All through the night. What Cannot Be. John Addington Symonds. CAGL

Oh what a pity, Oh! don't you agree. Innocent England. D. H. Lawrence. NPeEn; OBCoV

Oh! what a thing is man? Lord, who am I? Edward Taylor. NAAL-3 Fr. Preparatory Meditations Before My Approach to the Lord's Supper.

Oh, what a waste of feeling and of thought. Gifts Misused. Letitia Elizabeth Landon. VWP

Oh, what am I but an engine, shod. Nothing New. Ella Wheeler Wilcox. APN-2

Oh, what could the ladye's beauty match. Proud Ladye, The. Letitia Elizabeth Landon. NAEL-7v2

Oh, what delight to be given the right. Cocktails for Two. Sam Coslow. ReLy

Oh, what do we geese wear for clothes? What Do We Geese Wear For Clothes? Unknown. OWoS, tr. by W. D. Snodgrass

Oh / What has happened to me? Head Over Heels in Love. Mack Gordon. ReLy

Oh, what hath death with souls like thine to do? (LL) To Elizabeth Barrett Browning, in 1861. Dora Greenwell. PoBW; VWP

Oh what is Man, great Maker of mankind. Acclamation, An. John Davies. SacPr

Oh what it must have cost the angels. Rainer Maria Rilke. WED Fr. Life of the Virgin Mary, The.

Oh! What It Seemed to Be. Bennie Benjamin, Frankie Carle and George David Weiss. ReLy

Oh, what sound of gold going. Sunset. Juan Ramón Jiménez. SpanPo, tr. by Kate Flores

Oh what's the matter? What's the matter? Goody Blake and Harry Gill. William Wordsworth.

Oh, when I come to die. Give Me Jesus. Unknown. SacPr

Oh, when I flung my heart away. Healed. Dorothy Parker. AmWit

Oh, when I was in love with you. A. E. Housman. MoBrPo Fr. Shropshire Lad, A.

Oh when the early morning at the seaside. East Anglian Bathe. Sir John Betjeman. NoP-4; NoP-5

Oh, when the sky is choked with smoke. Getting Away: Verses and Choruses for Various Voices. Wendell Berry. PoCoUp

Oh, Whence Comes the Gladness? [with music]. Priscilla Jane Thompson. CBWP-2

Oh where are you going with your lovelocks [or love-locks] flowing. Amor Mundi. Christina Georgina Rossetti. NoP-4; NoP-5; PEW; RACG

Oh! where shall I bury my poor dog Tray. Cynotaph, The. Richard Harris Barham. DiBP

Oh! wherefore come ye forth, in triumph from the North. Battle of Naseby, The. Thomas Babington Macaulay, 1st Baron Macaulay. FaBoWar; OxAEP-2

Oh whistle I'll come to ye. Ultrasound. Kathleen Jamie. StAl

Oh, who has not heard of the Wooyeo Ball. Wooyeo Ball, The. Unknown. NOBAu

Oh who is that young sinner with the handcuffs on his wrists? A. E. Housman. CAGL; NPeEn; SoSe-8

Oh who that ever lived and loved. Egg, The. Clarence Day. NBLV

Oh why are not all those close ties which enfold. Fragment 3. Sydney, Lady Morgan Owenson. PoBW

Oh, why don't I work like the other men do? Unknown. GM

Oh! why hath not the mind. William Wordsworth. NAEL-6v2; NAEL-7v2 Fr. Prelude, The; Growth of a Poet's Mind [1850 version].

Oh, why left I my hame? Exile's Song, The. Robert Gilfillan. TreFP

Oh, why so late, when tired leaves are falling. Oh, Why So Late. József Kiss. IQMS, tr. by Peter Zollman

Oh! Wilberforce, our star of hope. Golden Jubilee of Wilberforce. Mrs. Henry Linden. CBWP-4

Oh, Wilderness were Paradise enow! (LL) Omar Khayyám. CABP; OBEV; TRP; WoPoe Fr. Rubáiyát of Omar Khayyám [of Naishápúr], The.

Oh! will you never let me be? These Foolish Things (Remind Me of You). Eric Maschwitz. ReLy

Oh woe is me! Oh misery! (LL) Thorn, The. William Wordsworth. NAEL-7v2; NPBRoP

Oh, Woe Ith Me! Bruce Lansky. ArBi

Oh Woman, Blessed Woman! [with music]. Mrs. Henry Linden. CBWP-4

Oh, woman, woman, in thy brightest hour. Appeal to Women, An. "Ada." SWaP

Oh World, Why Do You Thus Pursue Me? Sor Juana Inés de la Cruz. SpanPo, tr. by Muriel Kittel

Oh world, why do you thus pursue me? Oh World, Why Do You Thus Pursue Me? Sor Juana Inés de la Cruz. SpanPo, tr. by Muriel Kittel

Oh would to God he would but pitty mee. Richard Barnfield. CAGL Fr. Affectionate Shepherd [or Shephearde], The.

Oh would you know why Henry sleeps. Inhuman Henry. A. E. Housman. NBLV

Oh! ye bright Stars! that on the ebon fields. Sappho's Address to the Stars. Mary Robinson. CenSon; RWP

Oh, ye who in those Houses hold. Lines. Frances Sargent Osgood. NAAPv.1

Oh ye! who teach the ingenuous youth of nations. Lord Byron. Fr. Don Juan.

Oh Yes. Joseph Stroud. GeoHom

Oh yes the page is blank. Oh. René Ricard. AHA

Oh, yes! they love through all this world of ours! Elizabeth Barrett Browning. CenSon Fr. Sonnets from the Portuguese.

O[h], yet we trust that somehow good. Alfred Tennyson. BrAP; CABP; ItP; NAEL-6v2; NAEL-7v2; NoP-5; WaAnP Fr. In Memoriam A. H. H.

Oh, you crazy girls from Laredo.   Viejas Locas.   Harryette Mullen.   TiP2

Oh! you great big brute.   You Can't Stop Me from Lovin' You.   Mann Holiner.   ReLy

'Oh you kid!' / Shouted Id.   Adventures of Id, The.   Morris Gilbert Bishop.   OBCoV

Oh you my nights, oh dark awaited.   Nyx.   Catherine Pozzi.   YaTCFP, tr. by Mary Ann Caws

Oh you, once mighty Hungary, gone to seed.   To the Hungarians.   Dániel Berzsenyi.   IQMS, tr. by Adam Makkai

Oh your face is there a mirror days.   First Love.   Robert Creeley.   ICANM

Ohio River Region.   Terrance Hayes.   RD

Ohlone walk among us, setting fire to the stipa, The.   California Coast.   Jean V. Gier.   ReBoTo

Ohnedaruth.   Angela Jackson.   SeSe

O'Hussey's Ode to the Maguire.   James Clarence Mangan.   CABP

Oí en el muro la grieta.   Grieta, La.   Carla Faesler Bremer.   SPV

Oí pisadas presurosas.   Navidades.   Gerardo Deniz.   RMCMP

Oideachadh Ceart.   Aonghas MacNeacail.   EdScPo

Oil.   Hansjörg Mayer.   WeW-3

Oil brown smog over Denver.   Who Runs America?   Allen Ginsberg.   FaBoA

Oil Field Road off Clyte Escarpment.   James Hoggard.   TiP2

Oil for extreme unction must be blessed, The.   Rule, The.   Richard Wilbur.   UpMys

Oil on Troubled Waters.   Amryl Johnson.   Oth Fr. Rainbow Dragon Trilogy.

Oil Slick.   Judith Thurman.   SSCS

Oil Well Fire.   Grace Ross.   TiP2

Oiled Sweater.   John Wilkinson.   VaPo

Oileus by his brother's side stood close and would not thence.   Homer.   OBVE Fr. Iliad, The.

Oil-slick, slack shocks, ancient engine.   Apples on Champlain.   Richard Kenney.   NoP-4; NoP-5

Oily rag at her feet in the warehouse of scents, An.   Studio, The (Homeage to Alice Neel).   Alicia Ostriker.   ExTi

Oily ring shimmering, scintillating round the stern.   Daphne Marlatt.   BrAP Fr. Steveston.

Oink as Taunt.   Roger Fanning.   NAPBL

Ojichan was a fisherman/farmer.   Fisherman, The.   Janice Mirikitani.   OpBo

Ojo en el centro del triángulo.   Templo.   Natalia Toledo.   RMCMP

Ojos de nubes bicolores.   Na tacha.   Natalia Toledo.   RMCMP

OK Corral East: Brothers in the Nam.   Horace Coleman.   AmWaPo

OK Neal / aethereal Spirit.   Elegy for Neal Cassady.   Allen Ginsberg.   CLPP

Ok ok ok ok.   Chickadee Encounter.   Don McKay.   OpeFie

Ok, right here's the first dry pavement geyser.   Concrete Delivery Delayed by Goose and Gosling Crossing, Late March, Mallett's Bay.   Richard Kenney.   PfSP

OK. So she got back the baby.   Onesided Dialog.   June Jordan.   NoAM

Ok Sunday, An.   Sheer Strips.   Bill Berkson.   AHA

Oka-san keeps stuffing rags under.   Lee Ann Roripaugh.   AmWaPo Fr. Heart Mountain, 1943.

Okato-Otaia.   Sándor Petőfi.   IQMS, tr. by Anton N. Nyerges

Okay, I remember the book pretty well.   Farmer's Evidence, The.   Gwyneth Lewis.   ATSWP, tr. by Robert Minhinnick

Okay let's go swimming.   Trout Quintet, The.   Frank O'Hara.   BodElec

Okay, my starsick beauty.   Unknown Shores.   Théophile Gautier.   WoPoe, tr. by D. M. Thomas

Okay son—I'm going.   Forced Labour.   Manuel González Prada.   SonAtl, tr. by Dave French, Lisa Martin and Lisandro Pena

Okay, Toots.   Gustave Kahn.   ReLy

Okay. We're stuck with one lives and those.   Heartbreak Hotel Piano-Bar.   Richard Speakes.   SwNoth

Okeydoekey Tribe, The.   Chrystos.   WiU

Okies wrapped their, The.   First Spring in California, 1936.   Wilma Elizabeth McDaniel.   CalPo; GeoHom

Oklahoma lies on top of us like a sod quilt.   We Go Away at Home.   Jack Myers.   TiP2

Okra to Greens /.   Ntozake Shange.

Different Love Poem / We Need a Change, A.   UnSA

Ol Abshire.   Houseboat Ferry.   Jessica Freeman.   AnSo

Ol' Hannah.   Doc Reese.   PFTM-1

Ol' Man River.   Oscar Hammerstein, II.   APT-2; ReLy

Ol' plantation wither.   For Consciousness.   Mervyn Morris.   WaCA

Ola en la mano es la balanza, Una.   Arcano 8: La Justicia.   Veronica Volkow.   RMCMP

Olayimika.   Toyin Adewale.   NeNiPo

Old.   Rosario Morales.   PfS

Old, The / Old winds that blew.   Night Winds.   Adelaide Crapsey.   APT-1; NAAPv.2; TCAPo

Old Adam, the Carrion Crow.   Thomas Lovell Beddoes.   TFi Fr. Death's Jest Book.

Old Age.   Maxwell Bodenheim.   TaR

Old Age.   Anne Bradstreet.   TCAPo Fr. Four Ages of Man, The.

Old Age.   Caroline Clive.   VWP

Old Age.   Milán Füst.   IQMS, tr. by Edwin Morgan

Old Age.   Rolf Jacobsen.   WED, tr. by Robert Bly

Old Age [with music].   John Morris-Jones.   OBWVE, tr. by Anthony Conran

Old Age.   Ou-yang Hsiu.   NDACCP, tr. by Kenneth Rexroth

Old Age: "Another winter."   Buland Al-Haidari.   PML, tr. by Hamid Algar and Mounah Abdallah Khouri

Old Age: "Such a wizened creature." [with music].   Eliza Keary.   WaAnP

Old Age Gets Up [with music].   Ted Hughes.   NoAM

Old age has come and I am glad.   Tune: "Nien-nu Is Charming."   Chu Tun-ju.   ColAnChi, tr. by James Robert Hightower

Old age hastens on, as each fleet hour passes.   Farewell to Spring.   Wang Wei.   CCL1, tr. by John Francis Davis

Old age in the towns.   War.   Miguel Hernández.   AF; RaBo

Old age is.   To Waken an Old Lady.   William Carlos Williams.   OxBoAm; SoSe-8; WeW-3

Old age, lookit, it's stupid, a big fart.   Edwin Denby.   NYP2

"Old age never comes alone"—it brings sighs.   Old Age.   John Morris-Jones.   OBWVE, tr. by Anthony Conran

Old age (the name that others give it).   In Praise of Darkness.   Jorge Luis Borges.   GPTC, tr. by Hoyt Rogers

Old age, wise curber of the blood's ebullience.   Plea to Old Age.   Lajos Áprily.   IQMS, tr. by Dorren Bell

Old, and a Fever.   Po Chü-i.   NDACCP, tr. by David Hinton

Old and abandoned by each venal friend.   On Lord Holland's Seat near Margate, Kent.   Thomas Gray.   NPeEn

Old, and abandoned by each venal friend.   Thomas Gray.   OBGa

Old and bearded sun, good soldier sun.   To the Sun of the War.   Rafael Alberti.   RaW, tr. by Rachel Benson

74: Old and New Art (St Luke the Painter).   Dante Gabriel Rossetti.   SacPr Fr. House of Life, The.

Old and New Year Ditties.   Christina Georgina Rossetti.

Passing Away, Saith the World, Passing Away.   NoP-4; NoP-5; ViWPN

Old and the New, The.   Clara Ann Thompson.   CBWP-2

Old and Traveling.   Yuan Mei.   GifTon, tr. by Jerome P. Seaton

Old anorak green.   Oth Fr. Wait, A.

Old Apple Trees.   W. D. Snodgrass.   CAP-8

Old April wanes, and her last dewy morn.   Last of April, The.   John Clare.   CenSon

Old Arm-Chair, The.   Eliza Cook.   VWP

Old as I am, for ladies' love unfit.   Cymon and Iphigenia.   John Dryden.   OBNV

Old Australian Ways.   Andrew Barton Paterson.   NOBAu

Old Bachelor Brother.   Brad Leithauser.   NoP-4; NoP-5; RA

Old Barbarossa.   Sleeping Heroes.   Edward Richard Burton Shanks.   OBMV

Old Barbed Wire, The.   Unknown.   FaBoWar

Old Belle, An.   Lizette Woodworth Reese.   SWaP

Old Bike, The.   Unknown.   ArBi

Old Black ladies.   Weeksville Women.   Elouise Loftin.   ISC

Old Black Ladies Standing on Bus Stop Corners #2.   Quincy Troupe.   OxAAAP

Old black man was stood on the block, The.   Legend.   Sterling Allen Brown.   OxBoAm

Old Boards.   Robert Bly.   GoPo

Old Boatman of Death's River, The.   R. Williams Parry.   OBWVE, tr. by Joseph P. Clancy

Old Boatman, The.   R. Williams Parry.   BBMWP, tr. by Anthony Conran

Old Bob-white and Chipbird, The.   Few of the Bird-Family, A.   James Whitcomb Riley.   NOxBChV

Old Bud Romick weighed three hundred pounds if he weighed an ounce.   Old Bud.   James Wright.   MotU

Old Buildings, The.   Pedro Juan Pietri.   UnSA

Old calendar, The.   Buson.   EH, tr. by Robert Hass

Old Cat Care.   Richard Hughes.   OBMV

Old Cat's Confessions, An.   Christopher Pearse Cranch.   APN-1

Old Cat's Dying Soliloquy, An.   Anna Seward.   OxBEV

Old Champagne Glass.   Eddy Van Vliet.   VCWP

Old Chapel, The.   Alun Cilie.   BBMWP, tr. by Joseph P. Clancy

Old, Childless, Husbandless.   Ruth Pitter.   PoBW

Old, childless, husbandless, bereaved, alone.   Old, Childless, Husbandless.   Ruth Pitter.   PoBW

Old Christmas Morning.   Roy Helton.   MoAmPo

Old Circles.   Jennifer Rankin.   BMAP

Old City, The.   Ivan Teofilov.   CSCBP, tr. by Georgi Belev and Lisa Sapinkopf

Old Clock on the Stairs, The. Henry Wadsworth Longfellow. TreFP

Old cob swan his cygnets thus addressed, An. Edmund Wilson. OBCoV *Fr.* Easy Exercises in the Use of Difficult Words.

Old Complex, The. John Ashbery. FTOS

Old cormorant keeper, The. Buson. EH, *tr. by* Robert Hass

Old Corruption. William Blake. NPBRoP

Old Countries. Aurora Levins Morales. PueRic

Old Country, The. Carl Rakosi. BodElec

Old Couple. Charles Simic. PoPoPo

Old Coyote. . . [/] "If he hadn't looked back." Telling About Coyote. Simon J. Ortiz. ICANM

    (Old Coyote . . . / "If he hadn't looked back.") PFTM-1

Old Cracked Tune, An. Stanley Kunitz. LoL; TaR

Old Creek. Muso Soseki. EaWin, *tr. by* W. S. Merwin

Old Crib, The. Mary E. Tucker. CBWP-1

Old crow of Shang Mountain, you are cruel! Song of the Crow Pecking at My Scarred Donkey. Wang Yü-ch'eng. WoPoe, *tr. by* Jonathan Chaves

Old Currawong. Jennifer Rankin. BMAP

Old Dan'l. Leonard Alfred George Strong. MoBrPo

Old daughter, small traveler. Making the Jam without You. Maxine W. Kumin. NALW

Old Days, The. Raymond Carver. LaCa

Old Dedication. Luciana Frezza. CItWP, *tr. by* Cinzia Sartini Blum and Lara Trubowitz

Old desolate place tonight. Old Chapel, The. Alun Cilie. BBMWP, *tr. by* Joseph P. Clancy

Old Devil Moon. E. Y. Harburg. ReLy

Old dissembler who lived out his lie, An. James Vincent Cunningham. APT-2; OxBoAm *Fr.* Epigrams.

Old dissembler who lived out his lie, An. Epigrams. James Vincent Cunningham.

Old docker with gutted cheeks, An. Charlottetown Harbour. Milton Acorn. Coast

Old Dog. Michael L. Johnson. UrbNat

Old dog barks backward without getting up, The. Robert Frost. SoSe-8 *Fr.* Ten Mills.

Old dog bends his head listening, The. Issa. WED, *tr. by* Robert Bly

Old dog listens, The. Issa. SoOfWa, *tr. by* Sam Hamill

Old dog, The. Issa. EH, *tr. by* Robert Hass

Old dog used to herd me through the street, The. Turnabout. Linda Pastan. NIP-4

Old Dreams. Ivor Gurney. HarvBoo

Old Dust. Li Po. CrYelRi, *tr. by* Sam Hamill

Old Eagle. Fred Emerson Brooks.
    "From thine eyrie, the crag." VerBaPo

Old Eben Flood, climbing alone one night. Mr Flood's Party. Edwin Arlington Robinson. AmFaPo; APT-1; ClHu; ColAP; HeIP-4; MoAmPo; NAAL-5; NAAPv.1; NAMCP V.1; NIL-7; NIP-4; NoAM; NoP-4; NoP-5; OxBoAm; SoSe-8; TCAPo; TFi; TRP; WaAnP; WeW-3

Old Eddie's face, wrinkled with river lights. Glory Trumpeter, The. Derek Walcott. GT; NAEL-6v2; NAEL-7v2; NoP-4; NoP-5; SeSe

Old elm that murmured in our chimney top. Fallen Elm, The. John Clare. RSaN

Old England! thy name shall yet warrant thy fame. Entry of the Marines [*or* The Red Cross of England]. Eliza Cook. STuOW

Old English Riddle. Cynewulf. OPOU *Fr.* Riddles (Exeter Book).

Old escapes into the new, The. (LL) Purification, A. Wendell Berry. TWF; UpMys

Old Familiar Faces, The. Charles Lamb. OBEV; OxAEP-2; OxBEV

Old fang in the boot trick. Five chambered. Heart. Catherine Bowman. ExTi

Old farmer, nearing death, asked, The. Field Day. William Robert Rodgers. PNI

Old Farmer, The. Ch'i-chi. CSKM, *tr. by* Burton Watson

Old Farmer Wall, of Manor Hall. Legend of Manor Hall, The. Thomas Love Peacock. NPBRoP

Old fat fish of everlasting life. Lines on a Carp. Gary Snyder. WaAnP

Old fear of the dark has not returned, The. Edge, The. Fred Cogswell. IFF

Old feeble Winter to gay Spring resigns. On an Early Spring. Mary Julia Young. CenSon

Old fellow, old one. Poem For My Father. Graham Allen. AngWePo

Old Fisherman. Ou-yang Hsiu. BLT

Old fisherman spends his night beneath the western cliffs. Old Fisherman. Ou-yang Hsiu. BLT

Old fisherman spent the night here, under the western cliff, An. Old Fisherman, The. Liu Tsung-yüan. CCL1, *tr. by* Witter Bynner

Old Fisherman, The. Emily Grosholz. RA

Old Fisherman, The. George Campbell Hay. EdScPo

Old Fisherman, The. Liu Tsung-yüan. CCL1, *tr. by* Witter Bynner

Old Fitz, who from your suburb grange. To E. Fitzgerald. Alfred Tennyson. NPeEn

Old Flame, The. Robert Lowell. ItP; NoAM

Old Florist. Theodore Roethke. APT-2

Old folk used to say, The. Cows and Alabama Folklore. Kathryn Takara. FTtHH

Old Folks at Home. Stephen Collins Foster. APN-2

Old Folks' Room, The. *Unknown.* TreFP

Old Folsom Prison. William Matthews. OPRER

Old Fools, The. Philip Larkin. EmeKit; HarvBoo

Old forms are like birdhouses that, The. Poetry. Greg Kuzma. PoA 2002

Old fort brims with yellow leaves, The. To a Friend Bound East. Wen T'ing-yün. CCL1, *tr. by* Witter Bynner

Old Fort Griffin. Berta Hart Nance. TiP2

Old Fort Phantom Hill. Larry Chittendon. TiP2

Old Fortunatus. Thomas Dekker *and others.*
    Fortune and Virtue. NoSic
    Priest's Song, A. NoSic

Old Freedman, The. Priscilla Jane Thompson. CBWP-2

Old Friend. Dimitris Tsaloumas. BMAP

Old friend from schooldays, An. Letter from Brazil, A. Louis Simpson. BodElec

Old friend has prepared chicken and millet dumpling, An. In Passing an Old Friend's Farm. Meng Hao Jan. CCL1, *tr. by* Soame Jenyns

Old friend, kind friend! lightly down. To My Old Schoolmaster. John Greenleaf Whittier. ColAP

Old friend, you. Back from the Word-Processing Course, I Say to My Old Typewriter. Michael C. Blumenthal. NoAM

Old Friends. "Peter Pindar." DiBP

Old friends, nearing senility. On Coming to Nothing. Richard Moore. PoA 2002

Old Fritz, on this rotating bed. Flat One, A. W. D. Snodgrass. NAMCP V.2

Old General Artichoke lay bloated on his bed. Old Land Dog, The. Sir John Betjeman. OBCoV

Old Gentleman, An. Alain Bosquet. PML, *tr. by* William Jay Smith

Old gilt vane and spire receive, The. Late, Last Rook, The. Ralph Hodgson. MoBrPo

Old Gladys, in lime polyester slacks. At Rose's Range. R. S. Gywnn. TiP2

Old Gods, The. John Burnside. NeBrP

Old green witch, An. *Unknown.* WoPoe *Fr.* Two Swedish Riddles.

Old grey goat of a mountain, An. Grey. Einir Jones. BBMWP, *tr. by* Joseph P. Clancy

Old Guidebook to Prague, An. Frank Kuppner.
    "Architecture is when the sun shines on a facade daily." NePenScot
    "It being my almost invariable habit." EdScPo

Old guy put down his beer, The. Do the Dead Know What Time It Is? Kenneth Patchen. MoAmPo

Old Henri is dying. Death of Old Men, The. *Unknown.* SonAtl, *tr. by* Charles Dendi and S. Marne

Old Hokum Buncombe, The. Robert E. Sherwood. NBLV

Old Home, The. Amanda Ros. VerBaPo

Old Homestead, The. Mattie J. Peterson.
    "I sometimes alligators heard." VerBaPo

Old horse, I've pushed you hard. Sick Horse. Tu Fu [*or* Du Fu]. CrYelRi, *tr. by* Sam Hamill

Old Hotel, The. Kim Hyesun. CAMKP, *tr. by* Jiwon Shin

Old House Blues. William Kulik. BodElec

Old house leans upon a tree, The. Deserted. Madison Cawein. TCAPo

Old House, The. Franta Bass. INSAB

Old House, The. Amy Levy. PEW; ViWPN; VWP

Old Houses. Melvin B. Tolson. GT

Old Houses on the Quays. Augusta Peaux. TuT, *tr. by* Tony Curtis

Old houses were scaffolding once. Image. Thomas Ernest Hulme. NPeEn

Old Huntsman, The. William Wordsworth. STuOW *Fr.* Simon Lee [Original Version].

Old Husband Suspects Adultery, An. Gavin Ewart. NoAM

Old Hut. Muso Soseki. EaWin, *tr. by* W. S. Merwin

Old Idea of Choan by Rosoriu. Lu Chao-lin. NDACCP, *tr. by* Ezra Pound

Old Ila, to show his fine delicate taste. On Lord Ila's Improvements, near Hounslow Heath. Philip Dormer Stanhope, 4th Earl of Chesterfield. OBGa

Old in Overijssel. René van Riessen. TuT, *tr. by* Robert Greacen

Old Indian Granny, The. Chrystos. ReEnLa

Old inventive Poets, had they seen, The. William Wordsworth. CenSon *Fr.* River Duddon [A Series of Sonnets], The.

Old Ironsides. Oliver Wendell Holmes. AmWaPo; APN-1; BRP; NAAL-3; NAAPv.1; NCAP; OxBoAm; TCAPo; TFi

Old Italians Dying, The. Lawrence Ferlinghetti.

Old Japan. Tanka. Toki Zenmaro. CAoMJL1, *tr.* by Makoto Ueda

Old Jockey, The. Frederick Robert Higgins. OBMV

Old Joe Clark. *Unknown.* APN-2

Old Joe is gone, who saw hot Percy goad. James Russell Lowell. TCAPo *Fr.* Biglow Papers, The.

Old Joe Jones. Laura Elizabeth Richards. TLR

Old Joe Jones and his old dog Bones. Old Joe Jones. Laura Elizabeth Richards. TLR

Old Joe the stray dog. Ray McNiece. AmZen

Old Joke. Alan Shapiro. PtR

Old joy returns in holy presence, An. (LL) Come into Animal Presence. Denise Levertov. AmFaPo; HeIP-4

Old King Cole ("Me clairvoyant"). G. K. Chesterton. UV *Fr.* Variations on an Air Composed on Having to Appear in a Pageant as Old King Cole.

Old King Cotton. Sterling Allen Brown. InGu

Old Ladies. Will Allen Dromgoole. WeW-3

Old ladies and tulips, model boats. Kensington Gardens. Muriel Spark. OBGa

Old lady Shih, braving acerbity, pokes in her three-foot beak. To Go with Shih K'o's Painting of an Old Man Tasting Vinegar. Huang T'ing-chien. ColAnChi, *tr.* by Burton Watson

Old lady writes me in a spidery style, An. Letter from Brooklyn, A. Derek Walcott. BrAP

Old Land Dog, The. Sir John Betjeman. OBCoV

Old Leaves from the Chinese Earth. Sadanand Rege. WoPoe, *tr.* by Dilip Chitre

Old Lem. Sterling Allen Brown. APT-2; NAMCP V.1

Old Letters. Edward Dowden. IrLP

Old Liberators, The. Robert Hedin. GoPo; P180

Old light smoulders in her eye, An. Pity. Trumbull Stickney. ColAP

Old Light, The. Moses Glyn Jones. BBMWP, *tr.* by Mike Jenkins

Old Lobsterman, The. John Townsend Trowbridge. APN-2

Old Love. Tu Mu. CCL1, *tr.* by H. A. Giles

Old Love in Song, An. Elizabeth Madox Roberts. APT-1

Old love, wake up, it's time. Plaisir. Lucile Adler. ICANM

Old love would seem as though not love today. Old Love. Tu Mu. CCL1, *tr.* by H. A. Giles

Old Lovers. Carl Rakosi. NAAPv.2

Old Lutheran Bells at Home, The. Wallace Stevens. NoAM

Old Mackenzie Trail, The. William Lawrence Chittenden. TiP2

Old, mad, blind, despised, and dying king, An. England in 1819. Percy Bysshe Shelley. CenSon; NAEL-6v2; NAEL-7v2; NAWM-7v2; NoP-4; NoP-5; NPBRoP; OxAEP-2; OxBEV; OxBSo; PoPoPo; TFi

Old Maid's Reverie, An. *Unknown.*

Old Maid's Soliloquy. Maggie Pogue Johnson. CBWP-4

Old Malediction, An. Horace. NoAM; OBCoV; WoPoe, *tr.* by Anthony Hecht

Old Man: "On his tired memory a splendid." Petar Alipiev. CSCBP, *tr.* by Georgi Belev and Lisa Sapinkopf

Old Man. Geoffrey Holloway. NLP

Old Man. Edward Thomas. HarvBoo; NPeEn; OxBEV; StAl; TCAWP

Old man. Chinese Figures 2. *Unknown.* EaWin, *tr.* by W. S. Merwin

Old man, The. Birdfoot's Grampa. Joseph Bruchac. UnSA

Old man, The. Buson. EH, *tr.* by Robert Hass

Old Man, The. Charles Reznikoff. OxBoAm

Old Man, The. Penelope Shuttle. LW

Old Man, The. He Was Lucky. Anna Swirszczynska [or Swir]. CFP; HP; PoSu, *tr.* by Magnus J. Krynski and Robert A. Maguire

Old Man Advancing. Muso Soseki. EaWin, *tr.* by W. S. Merwin

Old man among the reeds mistrust of the poet. Basho. Cees Nooteboom. LWR, *tr.* by John M. Coetzee

Old Man and the Sun, The. Vicente Aleixandre. RaW, *tr.* by W. S. Merwin

Old Man at Leisure. Muso Soseki. EaWin, *tr.* by W. S. Merwin

Old Man at the Crossing, The. Leonard Alfred George Strong. OBMV

Old man babbles on! Ye gods, I swear, The. Idler Listening to Socrates Discussing Philosophy with His Boy-Friends, An. Edward Cracroft Lefroy. CAGL

Old man bending I come among new faces, An. Wound-Dresser, The. Walt Whitman. AmWaPo; APN-1; CBCWP; ColAP; NAAL-3; NAAL-5; NAAPv.1; OBWP; PCW; TCAPo

Old Man by the Brook, The. William Wordsworth. TreFP

Old Man Climbs a Tree, The. Wendell Berry. PoCoUp

Old man fishing in the cold river-snow, An. (LL) River-Snow. Liu Tsung-yüan. CCL1; ItP, *tr.* by Witter Bynner

Old Man from Darjeeling. *Unknown.* NTCP

Old Man from Peru, An. *Unknown. See* Limerick: "There was an old man of [or from] Peru / Who dreamt [or dreamed] he was eating his shoe."

Old man going a lone highway, An. Building the Bridge. Will Allen Dromgoole. WeW-3

Old man grinned and bowed low with a groan, The. Albery Allson Whitman. NAAPv.1 *Fr.* Octoroon, The.

Old Man Ho. To Kengai Osho of Engaku-ji. Muso Soseki. EaWin, *tr.* by W. S. Merwin

Old man in a lodge within a park, An. Chaucer. Henry Wadsworth Longfellow. APN-1; HeIP-4; OBEV; TCAPo; TFi; WoPoe

Old Man in a Moon Loft [*with music*]. T. Glynne Davies. OBWVE, *tr.* by the author

Old Man in Meditation. Henrik Nordbrandt. PML, *tr.* by Anne Born

Old Man in Retirement. Muso Soseki. EaWin, *tr.* by W. S. Merwin

Old man in the rushes the poet's suspicion. Basho 1. Cees Nooteboom. TuT, *tr.* by Michael O'Loughlin

Old Man Inside Me, The. Dambudzo Marechera. NAfrP

Old man inside me, The. Old Man Inside Me, The. Dambudzo Marechera. NAfrP

Old Man Is Like Moses, The. Vicente Aleixandre. GifTon, *tr.* by Lewis Hyde

Old Man Leaves Party. Mark Strand. PoDa

Old man mumbling in his dotage, or crying child, unborn? (LL) For Malcolm X. Margaret Abigail Walker. FTtHH; OxAAAP

Old Man Ocean. Russell Hoban. TLR

Old Man Ocean, how do you pound. Old Man Ocean. Russell Hoban. TLR

Old Man of Few Words. Muso Soseki. EaWin, *tr.* by W. S. Merwin

Old Man of Verona, The. Claudian. OBVE, *tr.* by Abraham Cowley

Old Man on a Bike. Peter Sizer. ArBi

Old Man on the River Bank, An. George Seferis. AmFaPo

Old Man, or Lad's-Love,—in the name there's nothing. Old Man. Edward Thomas. HarvBoo; NPeEn; OxBEV; StAl; TCAWP

Old Man Pondered. John Crowe Ransom. MoAmPo

Old Man Potchikoo. Louise Erdrich. HATNAP

Old man pushing seventy. Written in a Carefree Mood. Lu Yu. ColAnChi, *tr.* by Burton Watson

Old man sat by the chimney side, The. Old Folks' Room, The. *Unknown.* TreFP

Old man, seated, his boiled turnip eyes, The. Miracle, The. George Young. BloBone

Old man sent for Papa, The. Family. Ai. TiP2

Old man shuffles to the fish market, The. Georgy Vladimirovich Ivanov. TCRusP, *tr.* by Daniel Weissbort

Old man sitting on the roof, The. Above Vitebsk. Shirley Kaufman. TaR

Old Man Sunshine—listen, you! But Not for Me. Ira Gershwin. ReLy

Old Man To-The-Point. Muso Soseki. EaWin, *tr.* by W. S. Merwin

Old Man Travelling. William Wordsworth. *See* Animal Tranquillity and Decay.

Old Man Travelling [Animal Tranquillity and Decay, a Sketch]. William Wordsworth. NPeEn; OBWP

Old Man, we always called him, The. Katakalos. Rosemary Catacalos. TiP2

Old man, we do not speak of crosses. (LL) Father and Daughter. Sonia Sanchez. FFC; GT

Old Man with a Beard. Edward Lear. *See* There Was an Old Man With a Beard.

Old Man's Comforts and How He Gained Them, The. Robert Southey. UV (Old Man's Comforts, The.) TreFP

Old man's eagle mind, An. (LL) Acre of Grass, An. William Butler Yeats. HarvBoo; NAMCP V.1; NoAM

Old man's lazy, The. Peter Blue Cloud. HATNAP; LTA

Old Man's Monologue with Death, The. Enrique Lihn. GPTC, *tr.* by David Unger

Old Man's Sigh, The. A Sonnet. Samuel Taylor Coleridge. CenSon

Old man's son was killed far away in the Staked Plains, An. Colors of Night, The. N. Scott Momaday. MotU

Old man's tale, a tale for men gray-hair'd, An. Willie Baird. Robert Williams Buchanan.

Old Man's Thought of School, An. Walt Whitman. AmFaPo

Old Man's Winter Night, An. Robert Frost. APT-1; GPTC; ItP; MoAmPo; NAMCP V.1; NoAM; OxBoAm

Old Man's Wish, The. Walter Pope. NOSC

Old Mansion. John Crowe Ransom. FuPo; HeIP-4

Old Mare, The. Elizabeth Jane Coatsworth. MoAmPo

Old mare whose eyes. Weakness. Alden Nowlan. StAl

Old master held up fluff, The. Kaigen. ZenPo, *tr.* by Takashi Ikemoto and Lucien Stryk

Old master of deep communion, beyond boundaries, An. Man of No Attachments. Soyo Taeneung. BecRai, *tr.* by Kim Daljin, Kim Won-Chung and Christopher Merrill

Old masters posed themselves at a window, The. Stilts and Other Vehicles. Richard Sale. TiP2

Old mayor climbed the belfry tower, The. High Tide on the Coast of Lincolnshire, 1571, The. Jean Ingelow. OxAEP-2

Old Meg. John Keats. *See* Meg Merrilies [or Merrilees].

Old Meg she was a gipsy [*or* gypsy]. Meg Merrilies [*or* Merrilees]. John Keats. NOxBChV

Old Men, The. Walter De la Mare. MoBrPo

Old Men, The. Rudyard Kipling. OBSV

Old Men and Old Women Going Home on the Street Car. Merrill Moore. MoAmPo

Old men and women, The. July. Sonia Sanchez. GT

Old men, as time goes on, grow softer, sweeter. Silence of Women, The. Liz Rosenberg. NIL-7

Old Men at Pevensey. Rudyard Kipling. NoAM *Fr.* Puck of Pook's Hill.

Old men in the hills, The. Perlas. Víctor Hernández Cruz. TouFir

Old Men in the Leaf Smoke, The. Archibald MacLeish. IllVoic

Old Men of Athens, The. Gail Holst-Warhaft. GI

Old Men Playing Basketball. B. H. Fairchild. MoASP; P180; PoCho

Old men rake the yards for winter, The. Old Men in the Leaf Smoke, The. Archibald MacLeish. IllVoic

Old men say, The. Bering Bridge, The. Roald Hoffmann. PfSP

Old men teach me animal spirits. Animal Spirits. John E. Smelcer. PoCoUp

Old Menalcas on a day. Robert Greene. NoSic *Fr.* Never Too Late.

Old men's wives, The. Old Men of Athens, The. Gail Holst-Warhaft. GI

Old Micon, once, and Canthus, Micon's foster-child. Titus Calpurnius Siculus. RomPo *Fr.* Eclogues.

Old moder Phoebe how happy you be. Moder Phoebe. *Unknown.* FaBoVe

Old Molly Means was a hag and a witch. Molly Means. Margaret Abigail Walker. NALW

Old monastery north of the city, The. Leaving Ch'in-chou. Tu Fu [*or* Du Fu]. CrYelRi, *tr. by* Sam Hamill

Old Mongoose, The—*for Mac.* Murray Jackson. OxAAAP

Old Monks Drinking. Seido Ray Ronci. AmZen

Old Monterey. Charles Warren Stoddard. CalPo

Old moon fades, the flies tune their voices, The. New Days for Old, Old Days for New. Philip Levine. TaR

Old moon is tarnished, The. Sea Lullaby. Elinor Wylie. OxBoAm

Old moon, old moon / what do I tell you? Crater. Lisa Williams. AmPoNex

Old Moon With Her Youth In Her Arms. Gale Swiontkowski. PasH

Old Mortality. Sir Walter Scott.
    (Call, The.) OBEV
    Sound, Sound the Clarion. OxAEP-2

Old Mother Hubbard. *Unknown.* DiBP

Old Mother Twitchett had [*or* has] but one eye. Mother Goose. NTCP

Old Mountain. Muso Soseki. EaWin, *tr. by* W. S. Merwin

Old Movies. Robley, Jr. Wilson. PoA 2002

Old Mr. Christopher sailed an egg. Columbus Circle Swing. William Jay Smith. PWW2

Old Mythologies. John Montague. NoP-4; NoP-5

Old Neighborhood, The. Andrea Carter Brown. PA9/11

Old Neighborhood, The. Gerald Costanzo. OPRER

Old Nelly's Birthday. Ruth Pitter. NALW

Old newspaper!, An. Ishikawa Takuboku. PoCho, *tr. by* Sanford Goldstein and Seishi Shinoda

Old newspapers nobody's ever got to read again. (LL) Twenty-Year Marriage. Ai. CAP-8; GT; NAMCP V.2; NoAM; WaAnP

Old Noah he had an ostrich farm and fowls on the largest scale. Wine and Water. G. K. Chesterton. ChIV-1; MoBrPo

Old Nobility, The [*epigram*]. Friedrich von Logau. GePo, *tr. by* George C. Schoolfield

Old now, / your eyes nearly blank. Benjamin Banneker Sends His *Almanac* to Thomas Jefferson. Jay Wright. VCAP

Old Oak Speaks, The. Margaret Bell Houston. TiP2

Old Oak Tree at Hatfield Broadoak, The. Frederick Locker-Lampson. OxAEP-2

Old Oaken Bucket, The. Samuel Woodworth. BRP; TCAPo
    (Bucket, The.) APN-1

Old Ocean's praise. Edward Young. STuOW *Fr.* Ode to the King.

Old, old house by the side of the sea, An. Katrina on the Porch. Alice Cary. APN-2

Old, old/ To live on, wretched to behold. Owen Gruffydd. OBWVE *Fr.* Men That Once Were, The.

Old [*or* Ould] Orange Flute, The. *Unknown.* OBCoV

Old orchard, full of smoking air, The. Wild Grapes. Kenneth Slessor. BrAP

Old Oscar, how feebly thou crawl'st to the door. Dying Oscar. David Macbeth Moir. DiBP

Old People. Michael Davitt. PBCIP, *tr. by* Michael Hartnett

Old people are like birds. City Pigeons. Helen Chasin. WeW-3

Old People Speak of Death, The. Quincy Troupe. OxAAAP

Old Peter Grimes made fishing his employ. George Crabbe. NPBRoP; OBNV *Fr.* Borough, The.

Old Pettigrew. Melvin B. Tolson. GT

Old Photograph Album. Linda Pastan. TaR

Old Photograph, An. Iwan Llwyd. BBMWP, *tr. by* Richard Poole

Old photographs would have her bookish, sitting. Ma. Paul Muldoon. PNI

Old piece of string!, An. (LL) Wheelchair Butterfly, The. James Tate. NAMCP V.2; NoAM

Old Pilot, The. Donald Hall. OtW

Old Pirate in These Waters, An. Ali Püsküllüoğlu. WoPoe, *tr. by* Murat Nemet-Nejat

Old Platthis often thrust away her morning's sleep. Leonidas of Tarentum. HePo, *tr. by* Barbara Hughes Fowler

Old Poem [*with music*]. *Unknown.* WoPoe, *tr. by* Burton Watson

Old Poems. David Shapiro. KGB

Old poet loves peacock feathers, The. Han-Shan Fashions a Myth. George Scarbrough. PoA 2002

Old Poet, Poetry's final subject glimmers months ahead. don't Grow Old. Allen Ginsberg.

Old Poetess Makes a Child, The. Ken Harris. AnSo

Old poets foster'd under friendlier skies. Alfred Tennyson. GSo

Old pond:/ frog-jump-in. Basho. TAL

Old pond / Leap-splash. Basho. ZenPo, *tr. by* Takashi Ikemoto and Lucien Stryk

Old Pond, An. Basho. EMJL, *tr. by* Haruo Shirane

Old pond, The. Basho. NIL-7, *tr. by* R. H. Blyth

Old pond, The. Basho. EH, *tr. by* Robert Hass

Old pond—a frog jumps in, kerplunk!, The. Basho. NIL-7, *tr. by* Allen Ginsberg

Old pond full of flags and fenced around, The. John Clare. NPeEn

Old pond—frogs jumped in—sound of water. Basho. NIL-7, *tr. by* Lafcadio Hearn

Old post town, two or three houses. Buson. EMJL *Fr.* Spring Breeze on the Kema Embankment.

Old Postcards. Günter Eich. AF, *tr. by* Stuart Friebert

Old Priest, The. Vladimir Holan. PoSu, *tr. by* George Theiner

Old priest Peter Gilligan, The. Ballad of Father Gilligan, The. William Butler Yeats. IrV; MoBrPo

Old Prison, The. Judith Wright. BMAP

Old Professor, The. John Holmes. APT-2

Old Pump-house, Llanwrtyd Wells. Ruth Bidgood. TCAWP

Old radio, its dial showing all the names of the cities, glows again in the dark, The. Sominex. Dan Pagis. MotU, *tr. by* Stephen Mitchell

Old Rattler, we have know each other long. To the Rattlesnake. Vaida Stewart Montgomery. TiP2

Old recluse lives under the cliff, The. Taoist Song. Wang Yang-ming. CrYelRi, *tr. by* Sam Hamill

Old Relative. Gwendolyn Brooks. ColAP *Fr.* Notes from the Childhood and the Girlhood.

Old Revolution. Hans Magnus Enzensberger. GTCP, *tr. by* Reinhold Grimm

Old Rhythm, old Metre. Judith Wright. HarvBoo *Fr.* Notes at Edge.

Old Roä. Alfred Tennyson. DiBP

Old road curves off the highway, The. Old Road, The. Aimée Grunberger. PoCoUp

Old Road Map, The. Arthur Waugh. ArBi

Old Road, The. Aimée Grunberger. PoCoUp

Old Rocket. Knight Horsfield. DiBP

Old Roscoff [*after* Corbière]. Tristan Corbière. WoPoe, *tr. by* Derek Mahon

Old Rugged Cross, The [*with music*]. George Bennard. NAAPv.2; TCAPo

Old Russian spits up a plum, The. Man Then Suddenly Stops Moving, A. Alberto A. Ríos. NAMCP V.2; NoAM

Old sailor in old times, An. Flying Down to Rio. Edward Eliscu and Gustave Kahn. ReLy

Old Saint's Prayer, The [*with music*]. Priscilla Jane Thompson. CBWP-2

Old Salt Kossabone. Walt Whitman. WaAnP

Old Salt Woman. Luci Tapahonso. ICANM

Old Sam. Stanley Holloway. OBCoV

Old Satan told me to my face. I Know When I'm Going Home. *Unknown.* SSUS

Old School, The. Sean Dunne. ModIr *Fr.* Sydney Place.

Old Scotia's jocund Highland reel. Sydney, Lady Morgan Owenson. RWP *Fr.* Lay of an Irish Harp, or Metrical Fragments, The.

Old shepherd's dog, like his master, was grey, The. Old Friends. "Peter Pindar." DiBP

Old Shepherd's Prayer. Charlotte Mew. MoBrPo

Old Ship of Zion, The [Maryland version]. *Unknown.* SSUS

Old Ship of Zion, The [North Carolina version]. *Unknown.* SSUS

Old Ships, The. James Elroy Flecker. MoBrPo; OBMV

Old ships are preserved. George Oppen. FTOS *Fr.* Some San Francisco Poems.

Old silent pond, An. Basho. BLPJKO, *tr. by* Harry Behn

Old singer, a young stag, I am Deor, An. Deor. *Unknown.* WoPoe, *tr. by* Peter Russell

Old Sister Death bit you off. On the Death of Muriel Rukeyser. Billy Marshall-Stoneking. BMAP

Old Skinflint. Wilfrid Wilson Gibson. OBMV

Old Slavemarket: St. Augustine, Fla. George Garrett. LPSFW

Old Snaps, The. Derek Mahon. IrLP

Old Snapshot. Dimitris Tsaloumas. PML

Old Soldier. Padraic Colum. OBMV

Old Soldier. Louis Simpson. PWW2

Old Song. Edward Fitzgerald. OBEV; OxAEP-2

Old Song. *Unknown.* ChinPo, *tr. by* Ye Weilian [*or* Yeh Wei-lien *or* Wai-lim Yip]

Old Song. *Unknown.* RaBo

Old Song. Andrey Andreievich Voznesensky. VCWP, *tr. by* Vera Dunham and William Jay Smith

Old Song Ended, An. J. D. McClatchy. ChrPo

Old Song of the Musk Ox People. Brian Swann. PoCoUp

Old Song Resung, An. William Butler Yeats. *See* Down by the Salley Gardens.

Old song with new words, An. Song. Yen Shu. CrYelRi, *tr. by* Sam Hamill

Old, sore heart, the battered, foundered, faithful heart, snorting again, stamping in its stall, The. (LL) Love: Beginnnings. C. K. Williams. OxBoAm; StAl

Old South Boston Aquarium stands, The. For the Union Dead. Robert Lowell. AmWaPo; BrAP; CAP-8; CBCWP; ColAP; EMP; FaBoA; HarvBoo; HeIP-4; NAAL-5; NAMCP V.2; NoAM; NoP-4; NoP-5; OBWP; OxBoAm; PoetW; PoPoPo; PtR; TFi; TRP; VCAP; WaAnP; WeW-3

Old Squire, The. Wilfrid Scawen Blunt. OBEV

Old / star / shuts her bleary eyes, The. Federico García Lorca. PFTM-1 *Fr.* Night (Suite for Piano and Poet's Voice).

Old Stoic, The. Emily Jane Brontë. BrAP; NALW; OBEV; OxAEP-2
  (Riches I hold in light esteem.) VWP

Old Stone Age. Frances Angela. Prnts

Old Stories. Rita Joe. Coast

Old Story. Kenneth Fearing. AmWit

Old Story, An. Edwin Arlington Robinson. MoAmPo; OxBoAm

Old Style Poem. Li Po. CrYelRi, *tr. by* Sam Hamill

Old Susan. Walter De la Mare. MoBrPo

Old Sussex Road, The. Ian Serraillier. NTCP

Old sweetheart of mine!—Is this her presence here with me, An. Old Sweetheart of Mine, An. James Whitcomb Riley. BRP

Old Swimmin'-Hole, The. James Whitcomb Riley. APN-2; BRP

Old Tai's Wine Shop. Li Po. CCL1; WoPoe, *tr. by* Elling O. Eide

Old Testament, The. Philip Levine. TaR

Old Thanksgiving game, The. Female Cousins at Thanksgiving. Paul Ruffin. TiP2

Old, the mad, the blind have fairest daughters, The. Beauty of Job's Daughters, The. Jay Macpherson. ChIV-1; IFF

Old, the young—they sit, The. Sitting on Farm Lawn on Sunday Afternoon. Robert Penn Warren. LPSFW

Old, their big shoulders humped, The. Stations. Philip Booth. GM

Old time, old shifting trade—time there is for the luffing sheets. Pindar. WoPoe *Fr.* Olympian Odes, The.

Old Timers. Carl Sandburg. NoAM

Old Tips. Jean Earle. TCAWP

Old Tongue. Jackie Kay. EdScPo

Old Tongue, The. Herbert Williams. AngWePo; TCAWP

Old Trees with Hands Sawing the Air. Margit Szécsi. IQMS, *tr. by* Agnes Arany-Makkai

Old Trembling, An. Marvin Bell. PfSP

Old Trojan Chiefs See Helen, The. Homer. OBVE *Fr.* Iliad, The.

Old Veteran and Napoleon, The. János Garay. IQMS, *tr. by* Watson Kirkconnell

Old Vicarage, Grantchester, The. Rupert Brooke. MoBrPo; NoP-4; NoP-5

Old violence is not too old to beget new values. (LL) Bloody Sire, The. Robinson Jeffers. PoA 2002; PWW2

Old Walt went seeking / And finding. (LL) Old Walt. Langston Hughes. HarvBoo; HeIP-4; ViWalt

Old Walt Whitman / Went finding and seeking. Old Walt. Langston Hughes. HarvBoo; HeIP-4; ViWalt

Old warder of these buried bones. Alfred Tennyson. NAEL-6v2; NAEL-7v2 *Fr.* In Memoriam A. H. H.

Old waste tip has gone, The. Waste. Grahame Davies. BBMWP, *tr. by the* author

Old watch: their, The. Vapor Trail Reflected in the Frog Pond. Galway Kinnell. AF; OBWP; VCAP

Old Water. Jeff Gundy. ACAMVP

Old well. Buson. EH, *tr. by* Robert Hass

Old Wharf Canto. Jared Angira. NAfrP

Old white beard of God is blowing, The. EVA Psalm. Raymond Roseliep. OtW

Old White Russian, An. Ch'en Meng-chia. WoPoe, *tr. by* Harold Acton and Ch'en Shih-hsiang

Old wife, An. Things One Would Like to Send Away. *Unknown.* EMJL, *tr. by* Edward Putzar

Old wine gone. Tune: "Four Pieces of Jade." Kuan Han-ch'ing. ChinPo, *tr. by* Ye Weilian [*or* Yeh Wei-lien *or* Wai-lim Yip]

Old wines for those who will. Chanson Delice. Beatrice E. Harmon. YaYoPo

Old Witherington [*with music*]. Dudley Randall. NoAM

Old Wives' [*or* Wife's] Tale, The. George Peele.
  Song. FaBoVe; NoSic; NPeEn; OxBEV; TFi
  Spread, Table, Spread. NoSic
  (Summer Song, A.) OBEV
  "Three merry men, and three merry men." NoSic
  (Voice from the Well [of Life Speaks to the Maiden], The.) NoSic
  (When As the Rye Reach to the Chin.) NoP-4

Old Wives' Tale. Olga Broumas. FiBr

Old Wives' Tales. Constance Urdang. PBCAP

Old wolf, I said. Case, The. Karen Volkman. LegDan

Old Woman. Iain Crichton Smith. EdScPo; HarvBoo; NePenScot; OxBEV

Old Woman, An. David Gwenallt Jones. OBWVE, *tr. by* H. Idris Bell

Old Woman, The. Joseph Campbell. IrV; MoBrPo

Old Woman, The. Moishe Nadir. Prolet, *tr. by* Amelia Glaser

Old Woman, The [*with music*]. Beatrix Potter. NTCP

Old Woman, The. Iain Crichton Smith. WoPoe

Old woman across the way, The. Whipping, The. Robert Earl Hayden. PoCho; SoSe-8; SSLK

Old Woman and the Sandwiches, The. Libby Houston. OBSP

Old woman at the teahouse, The. Buson. EMJL *Fr.* Spring Breeze on the Kema Embankment.

Old woman leans against the pine tree, The. Stefan Tsanev. CSCBP, *tr. by* Georgi Belev and Lisa Sapinkopf

Old woman likes to melt her husband. She puts him in a, An. Feeding the Dog. Russell Edson. RaBo

Old Woman Nature. Gary Snyder. BB; NoAM; RaBo

Old Woman of Beare Regrets Lost Youth, The. *Unknown.* OBMV, *tr. by* Frank O'Connor

Old Woman of Beare, The. *Unknown.* WoPoe, *tr. by* Brendan Kenneally

Old Woman of Berkeley, The. Robert Southey. NPBRoP

Old Woman of the Roads, The. Padraic Colum. IrV; MoBrPo; OBEV

Old Woman, Outside the Abbey Theater, An. Leonard Alfred George Strong. MoBrPo

Old Woman Reclining. Claudia Buckholts. PfS

Old Woman Remembers, An. Sterling Allen Brown. ISC

Old woman sits on a bench before the door and quarrels, The. Fawn's Foster-Mother. Robinson Jeffers. NAMCP V.1; NoAM

Old woman sits on a broken pillar, The. Old Woman, The. Moishe Nadir. Prolet, *tr. by* Amelia Glaser

Old woman standing, An. Saviour. Zindzi Mandela. HAWP

Old woman, time and your own. To Grandmother on Her Going. Gail Tremblay. HATNAP

Old Woman's Lamentations, An. François Villon. MoBrPo; OBMV, *tr. by* John Millington Synge

Old Women. Judith Ortiz Cofer. PueRic

Old Women, The. George Mackay Brown. EdScPo; NoP-4; NoP-5; WaAnP

Old Women, The. Rolf Jacobsen. WED, *tr. by* Robert Bly

Old Women, The. Naomi Long Madgett. OxAAAP

Old Women and Love. Kay Smith. Coast

Old women are moving. Old Women's Summer. Katie Donovan. NIrP

Old Women Fishing from Bridges. Darrell Bourque. Vesp

Old Women of Toronto. Miriam Waddington. IFF

Old Women's Summer. Katie Donovan. NIrP

Old wood stands uncut, of long years' space, an. Ovid. CABP *Fr.* Elegies.

Old wooden steps to the front door, The. Time Past, A. Denise Levertov. NAMCP V.2; NoAM

Old World, The. Charles Simic. CAP-8; StAl

Old World Monkeys. Sam Truitt. AmPoNex *Fr.* Anamorphosis Eisenhower.

Old wound in my ass, The. Fabrication of Ancestors. Alan Dugan. AmWaPo; CBCWP; NAMCP V.2; NoAM

Old WPA Swimming Pool in Martins Ferry, Ohio, The. James Wright. CAP-8

Old Year, The [*with music*]. John Clare. OBCP

Old Year, The. Priscilla Jane Thompson. CBWP-2

Old Year's gone away, The. Old Year, The. John Clare. OBCP

Old Yellow Shop, The. Abbie Huston Evans. APT-1

Old yew, which graspest at the stones. Alfred Tennyson. NAEL-6v2; NAEL-7v2; NAWM-7v2; NoP-5; NPeEn; WaAnP *Fr.* In Memoriam A. H. H.

Olden Days, The. Joseph Hall. OBSV *Fr.* Virgidemiarum.

Olden Love-making. Nicholas Breton. NoSic

Older, but no wiser than the defect of love. (LL) New World, The. Imamu Amiri Baraka. NoAM; NoP-4; PmAP

Older Child, The. Kimiko Hahn. CAP-8

Older children pedal past, The. Learning the Bicycle. Wyatt Prunty. ArBi

Older, more generous. Gift, The. N. Scott Momaday. NoP-4; NoP-5

Older than any hope I ever knew. (LL) Because. James Philip McAuley. BMAP; NOBAu; StAl

Older Woman, An. Roddy Lumsden. NeBrP

Older women wise and tell Anna, The. Birth Stone. Lorna Goodison. VCWP

Oldest human fossil, The. Fire. Mark O'Connor. NOBAu

Oldest Living Thing in L.A., The. Larry Levis. P180; UrbNat

Oldest man in the world wears shoes, The. Passage. Billy Marshall-Stoneking. BMAP; NOBAu

Oldest Place, The. Thomas Kinsella. PBCIP *Fr.* One.

Old-Fashioned Garden. Cole Porter. OBGa

Old-Fashioned Song, An. John Hollander. NoP-4; NoP-5; OxBoAm

Old-fashioned uncouth measurer of the day. To an Hour-Glass. John Clare. CenSon

Oldies But Goodies. Grace Bauer. MiVo

Old-Saxon Fragment. *Unknown.* OBCoV

Old-Testament Gospel. William Cowper. ChIV-2 *Fr.* Olney Hymns.

Old-time pond, from off whose shadowed depth, An. Basho. NIL-7, *tr. by* Clara A. Walsh

Old-time Priapuses could take their pick. *Unknown.* PriapPo *Fr.* Priapus Poems, The.

Old-Time Religion. *Unknown.* APN-2

Old-world machinery of beework, The. Bees Stumble. Molly McQuade. PoDa

Old-World Thicket, An. Christina Georgina Rossetti. VWP

Ole King Cotton. Old King Cotton. Sterling Allen Brown. InGu

Ole Satan is busy old man. Come Go With Me. *Unknown.* SSUS

Oleander: coral. Garden, The. Rae Armantrout. FTOS

O'Leary was a poet—for a while. Shadrach O'Leary. Edwin Arlington Robinson. APT-1

Olfactory paradise. Love Poem. E. K. Caldwell. PasH

Olga Orozco. Olga Orozco. TCLAP, *tr. by* Stephen Tapscott

Olga Poems. Denise Levertov. NAMCP V.2
   "By the gas-fire, kneeling." InoFa

Olga's House. Natalia Toledo. RMCMP, *tr. by* Alberto A. Ríos

Olía la cabaña. Vida que Uno Lleva, La. Gabriel Celaya. RaW

Olive garden for the nightingales, The. (LL) Painted Head. John Crowe Ransom. APT-1; FuPo; NAMCP V.1; NoAM

Olive Garden, The. Rainer Maria Rilke. GI

Olive, The. A. E. Housman. NoAM

Olive Tree, The. Felicia Dorothea Hemans. CenSon *Fr.* Sonnets, Devotional and Memorial.

Olive Trees. Bernard Spencer. NoAM

Olive trees grow silently in patches on the shoulders, The. Los Olivos. Michael Lieberman. BloBone

Oliver Twist can't do this. Marlene Philip. NOxBChV

Oliver's climbed upon a hilly crest. *Unknown.* FaBoWar *Fr.* Song of Roland, The.

Olives. Catharine Savage Brosman. PoDa

Olla, La. David Huerta. RMCMP

Olmos. Dennis Nurkse. OPRER

Olney Hymns. William Cowper.
   Contentment. ChIV-2
   (Contrite Heart, The.) NPeEn
   Ephraim Repenting. ChIV-1
   (Fountain, The.) ChIV-1
   Future Peace and Glory of the Church, The. InvLi
   House of Prayer, The. ChIV-2
   Hymn. SacPr
   (Hymn 10.) ChIV-1
   Light Shining out of Darkness. CABP; NoP-4; NoP-5; NPeEn; OxBEV; SacPr; TFi
   Lovest Thou Me? ChIV-2
   Old-Testament Gospel. ChIV-2
   Retirement. SacPr
   Sardis. ChIV-1
   Sower, The. ChIV-2
   "There is a fountain filled with blood." SacPr
   Wisdom. ChIV-1

Olsanski Cemetery, The. Yury Iofe. TCRusP, *tr. by* John Glad

Olympia 12. Pindar. WaAnP *Fr.* Olympian Odes, The.

Olympia 11—For Agesidamus of the Westwind Locrians: Winner in the Boys' Boxing Match. Pindar. WoPoe *Fr.* Olympian Odes, The.

Olympian 1. Pindar. *Fr.* Olympian Odes, The.

Olympian Eleven. Pindar. *Fr.* Olympian Odes, The.

Olympian [Muses], round my mind. Alcman. SaLy, *tr. by* Diane Rayor

Olympian Odes, The. Pindar. *tr. by* Robert Fagles
   Olympia 12. WaAnP, *tr. by* Richmond Lattimore
   Olympian 1. *tr. by* Ambrose Philips
    "Water is preeminent and gold, like a fire." PoCho, *tr. by* Frank J. Nisetich
   Olympian Eleven.
    Olympia 11—For Agesidamus of the Westwind Locrians: Winner in the Boys' Boxing Match. WoPoe, *tr. by* Robert Fagles

Olympus, no medal like the light in each other's eye. (LL) To Hermes. Alfred Corn. CAGL; WiU

Omagh Post Office Rhyme. *Unknown.* FaBoVe

Oman. Gu Cheng. WoBe, *tr. by* Joseph R. Allen

Omar pointed to a pink man. Growing Up with a Sears Catalog in Benghazi, Libya. Khaled Mattawa. LegDan

Ombre qui est dans la lumière, L'. Sérénité. Philippe Jaccottet. YaTCFP

Ombres 1. Habib Tengour. YaTCFP *Fr.* Au pays des morts.

Ombres 2. Habib Tengour. YaTCFP *Fr.* Au pays des morts.

Ombres 3. Habib Tengour. YaTCFP *Fr.* Au pays des morts.

Ombres 10. Habib Tengour. YaTCFP *Fr.* Au pays des morts.

O-mei Mountain Moon. Li Po. CrYelRi, *tr. by* Sam Hamill

O'Melia, my dear, this does everything crown! Thomas Hardy. *See* O 'Melia, my dear, this does everything crown!

Omens. Cyd Adams. TiP2

Omens. Marianne Boruch. AmAlph

Omens. *Unknown.* WoPoe, *tr. by* Alexander Carmichael

Omens are for example hearing someone say victory as they pass you in the street. Anne Carson. MoWP *Fr.* Beauty of the Husband, The.

Omens on the Road to Burgos. *Unknown.* WoPoe *Fr.* Excerpts from *The Poem of the Cid.*

Omera. Marjorie Oludhe Macgoye. HBAPE

Omeros. Derek Walcott.
   Book 1.
    1. NAMCP V.2; WaAnP
    1. WaAnP
    2. WaAnP
    2. WaAnP
    3. WaAnP
    Chapter 3. NAMCP V.2
    Chapter 9. NAMCP V.2
    Chapter 13. NAMCP V.2
   Book 3. NAMCP V.2
    Chapter 25. NAMCP V.2
   Book 6. NAMCP V.2
    Chapter 49. NAMCP V.2
   Book 7.
    Chapter 64. NAMCP V.2
   Chapter 38, Part 3. NoP-5
   "He yawned and watched the lilac horns of his island." NAEL-7v2; NoP-4

Ominous anger of masses of men, The. On the Eastern Front. Georg Trakl. WED, *tr. by* Robert Bly

"Omit needless words!" Preface Shrink Lit: Elements of Style. Maurice Sagoff. NBLV

Omnibus across the bridge, An. Symphony in Yellow. Oscar Wilde. MoBrPo; NoAM; OPOU

Omnibus, The. Vera Bulich. ARWW, *tr. by* Catriona Kelly

Omnipotent and steadfast God. Stephen Vincent Benét. CBCWP *Fr.* John Brown's Body.

Omnipotent Olympus' king meanwhile. Virgil. NAWM-5v1; NAWM-7v1 *Fr.* Aeneid [*or* Eneados *or* Aeneis], The.

Omnipresence of the Deity, The. Robert Montgomery.
   Fore and Aft. STuOW
   Marine Vignette. STuOW
   On the Revolution. STuOW
   Request, A. STuOW

Omnivore. Harryette Mullen. OxAAAP

Omoide no Tsukimi. Gus Blaisdell. ICANM

Omoro Sōshi, The. *Unknown. tr. by* Christopher Drake
   "Before light became time." WoPoe, *tr. by* Christopher Drake

Omphalos. Michele Leggott. VaPo

On. Paul Muldoon. GPPA

On a Bank [*or* Banck] as I Sat[e] [a-]Fishing; a Description of the Spring. Sir Henry Wotton. AmFaPo; BASC; NOSC

On a Bashful Shepherd. "Ephelia." PEW

On a Bas-relief of Pelops and Hippodameia. Mary Elizabeth Coleridge. ViWPN

On a battu le cheval, au mois de Mai and they ate him. Overloaded Horse, The. Ted Joans. EGAG

On a Beautiful Woman. Mary Russell Mitford. CenSon

On a Bed of Guernsey Lilies. Christopher Smart. BBASP

On a Bench in a Park. Anne Wilkinson. BrAP

On a Bicycle. Yevgeny Aleksandrovich Yevtushenko. ArBi, *tr. by* Peter Levi and Robin Milner-Gulland

On a Bird Singing in its Sleep. Robert Frost. APT-1

On a Birthday. John Millington Synge. OBMV

On a blasted heath in Maryland. Bargain at Half the Price, A. Henry Taylor. LPSFW

On a blue island in a sky-wide water. Wallace Stevens. NAMCP V.1 *Fr.* Notes toward a Supreme Fiction.

On a bone-white dish. (LL) Song: "Afternoon cooking in the fall sun." Robert Hass. ASA; LoL; NAMCP V.2

On a Bougainvillaea Vine at the Summer Palace [*or* in Haiti]. Barbara Howes. MoAmPo

On a broad plain in a universe of. Matters of Policy. Charles Bernstein. FTOS

On a brown isle of Lough Corrib. Celibacy. Austin Clarke. ModIr

On a Canaanite Stone in the Dead Sea. Mahmoud Darwish. PML, *tr. by* Muna Asali van Engen

On a Carrier Who Died of Drunkenness. Lord Byron. NBLV

On a Cat Aging. Sir Alexander Gray. TriCat

(On a Cat, Ageing.) EdScPo

On a cat's fur soft as pollen. Spring is a Cat, The. Yi Jang'hi. WoPoe, *tr. by* Ko Changsu

On a Certain Engagement South of Seoul. Hayden Carruth. AmWaPo; PWW2; WaAnP

On a Certain Field in Auvers. John Haines. OPRER

On a Certain Lady at Court. Alexander Pope. OBEV

On a Chaplain's Nose. Francisco de Quevedo y Villegas. WoPoe, *tr. by* Roy Campbell

On a chilly, clear night. Peepers. Howard Nelson. MiVo

On a Clear Day You Can See Forever. Alan Jay Lerner. ReLy

On a clear night in Live Oak you can see. Walking Down the Road. Adrienne Rich. NIL-7; NIP-4

On a clear spring windless sky. Feathered Robe, The. Gary Snyder. BodElec

On a clear winter's evening. Winter Twilight. Anne Porter. APT-2

On a Clergyman's Horse Biting Him. *Unknown.* NBLV

(Steed Bit His Master, The.) ChIV-1

On a Cock at Rochester [*with music*]. Sir Charles Sedley. NOSC; NPeEn; OBCoV

On a Cold Autumn Day. Bonnie Nims. TLR

On a cold frosty morning in the month of September. Wreck of the Old 97. David Graves George. GM

On a cold night. Solitary. Lance Henson. HATNAP

On a cold night I came through the cold rain. James Vincent Cunningham. TRP; VCAP

On a Columnar Self. Emily Dickinson. APN-2; NoP-4; NoP-5

On a convoy from Bong Son to Hue we stop at a Vietnamese graveyard. Convoy. Bruce Weigl. MotU

On a cool September day, the soup commences. Cooking Catalogue. Jill Breckenridge. SweBea

On a Cuckoo's Song. Pyungyang Ungee. BecRai, *tr. by* Kim Daljin, Kim Won-Chung and Christopher Merrill

On a Curate's Complaint of Hard Duty. Jonathan Swift. OBCoV

On a Dark Night. John F. Deane. StAl

On a dark night in a stinking slum. Adam. Honor Arundel. RSaN

On a day like any other day. Disappearances, The. Vijay Seshadri. BeAl; StAl

On a day when sunlight fell through rifts of wind, he came to me limping and said, "Try and draw my face." Poem's Visit, A. Kang Ŭn'gyo. CAMKP, *tr. by* Tae Yang Kwak

On a day when sunlight pours like barium, a woman is hanging laundry. Woman Hanging Laundry. Kang Ŭn'gyo. EcSo, *tr. by* Ann Y. Choi

On a day—alack the day! William Shakespeare. OBEV *Fr.* Love's Labour's Lost.

'On a day—alack the day!'. William Shakespeare. *See* Blossom, The.

On a Dead Child [*with music*]. Robert Bridges. NoAM; OBMV; OxAEP-2

On a Dead Hostess. Joseph Hilaire Pierre Belloc. MoBrPo

On a Deathbed. T'aego, National Preceptor. CATKP, *tr. by* Peter H. Lee

On a dime. (LL) Fact. Langston Hughes. APSN; OxBoAm; PFTM-1

On a dirt road lies a dead beetle. Seen from Above. Wisława Szymborska. BLT

On a Discovery Made Too Late. Samuel Taylor Coleridge. CenSon; GSo *Fr.* Effusions.

On a dish on the table, nothing but your head. Meal, The. T. Gwynn Jones. BBMWP, *tr. by* Anthony Conran

On a dish recline the peaches. Brilliant yellow, burnt vermillion. In Cézanne's studio, we're dappled with joy. Liliane Welch. Coast

On a Drawing by Flavio. Philip Levine. BodElec

On a Drop of Dew. Andrew Marvell. BASC; FSCP; NIL-7; NOSC

On a Dying Planet. Fadil Azzawi. IrPoTo, *tr. by* Ralph Saverese and Saadi A. Simawe

On a Fair Lady, Looking in the Glass. Richard Leigh. NOSC

On a Falling Group in the Last Judgement of Michael Angelo, in the Cappella Sistina. Washington Allston. APN-1

On a Favorite Cat Drowned in a Tub of Gold Fishes. Thomas Gray. *See* Ode on the Death of a Favo[u]rite Cat, Drowned in a Tub [*or* Bowl] of Gold Fishes.

On a Feast. Francis Quarles. ChIV-2

On a Field Trip at Fredericksburg. Dave Jeddie Smith. LPSFW; PoPoPo

On a Fine Crop of Peas Being Spoiled by a Storm. Henry Jones. OBGa

On a flat road runs the well-train'd runner. Runner, The. Walt Whitman. BLT; ItP; SAmP

On a Flimmering Floom You Shall Ride. Carl Sandburg. APT-1

On a Fly Drinking out of [*or* from] His Cup. William Oldys. OBEV; OxAEP-1; OxBEV

On a Forsaken Lark's Nest. Mathilde Blind. ViWPN; VWP

On a Fortification at Boston Begun by Women [American edition]. Benjamin Tompson. NOSC

On a Friend's Taking a Journey. Elizabeth Teft. PoBW

On a Frightful Dream. John Codrington Bampfylde. CenSon

On a fully broken-in animal's back. Definition of Your Attraction. János Pilinszky. StAl, *tr. by* Peter Jay

On a General Election. Joseph Hilaire Pierre Belloc. NPeEn; OBSV; OxBEV

On a Gentlewoman that Sung and Played upon a Lute. William Strode. NOSC

On a Gentlewoman Walking in the Snow. William Strode. *See* On Chloris Walking in the Snow.

On a Girdle. Edmund Waller. BASC; NoP-4; NOSC; OBEV; TFi

On a Girl Who Took Action for Breach of Promise. Amanda Ros. VerBaPo

On a glacial stone. (LL) Come Not the Seasons Here. Edwin John Pratt. NoP-4; NoP-5

On a gnarled and naked tree. (LL) Song for a Dark Girl. Langston Hughes. InoFa; NAAL-5; NAAPv.2; NAMCP V.1; NoP-4; NoP-5; SAmP

On a golden pane. In the Rearview Mirror. Karl Krolow. GTCP, *tr. by* Reinhold Grimm

On a Good Leg and Foot. William Strode. NOSC

105: On a Happy Love. Asclepiades. GPTC,

On a highway over the marshland. Flames and Dangling Wire. Robert Gray. BMAP; NOBAu

On a Hill Above Your House. Julia Alvarez. PfSP

On a hill far away stood an old rugged cross. Old Rugged Cross, The. George Bennard. NAAPv.2; TCAPo

On a hill near Petersburg. James Hugo Johnston. Maggie Pogue Johnson. CBWP-4

On a hillside somewhere in Sorrento Valley. Sorrento Valley. John Koethe. OxBoAm

On a holy day when sails were blowing southward. Straying Student, The. Austin Clarke. ModIr; NPeEn

On a hook he hangs. Yamaguchi Seishi. CAoMJL1, *tr. by* Alfred H. Marks and Takashi Kodaira

On a Hopeful Youth. Owen Felltham [*or* Feltham]. NOSC

On a hot summer night, heavy with stars. By Starlight on Narin Strand. Jean Bleakney. NIrP

On a Juniper-Tree, Cut Down to Make Busks. Aphra Behn. BASC

On a Kazoo. Dennis Lee. IFF

On a Lady Indifferent to Poetry. Sappho. STV, *tr. by* John Frederick Nims

On a Lady's Writing. Anna Laetitia Barbauld. PEW

On a Leander Gem which Miss Reynolds, My Kind Friend, Gave Me. John Keats. ItP

On a Line from Valéry. Carolyn Kizer. FFC; GifTon

On a Lock of Milton's Hair. Leigh Hunt. NPBRoP

On a Lock of Miss Sarah Seward's Hair Who Died in her Twentieth Year. Anna Seward. CenSon

On a long misty. Ryokan. EMJL, *tr. by* Haruo Shirane

On a lucky day with an auspicious name. Nine Songs, The. Ch'u Yüan. CCL1, *tr. by* David Hawkes

On a Maid of Honour Seen by a Scholar in Somerset Garden. Thomas Randolph. OBGa

On a map it is precise and rectilinear as a chessboard. Prose Poem, The. Campbell McGrath. PoDa

On a Midsummer Eve. Thomas Hardy. FaBoVe

On a midsummer night, on a night that was eerie with stars. August Night. Sara Teasdale. MoAmPo

On a moonlight evening, in the month of May. Julia A. Moore. VerBaPo *Fr.* Croquet by Moonlight.

On a morning ramble I visit a great mountain. Seeking out Master Chan on Incense Mountain. Meng Hao Jan. ColAnChi, *tr. by* Daniel Bryant

On a needful day. Comfort-Maker. Jerry W., Jr. Ward. ISC

On a night as clear and warm as tonight. Coventry. Conor O'Callaghan. NIrP

On a Night of Snow. Elizabeth Jane Coatsworth. MoAmPo

On a Night of the Full Moon [*with music*]. Audre Lorde. NALW

On a Nook Called Fairyland. Henrietta Cordelia Ray. CBWP-3

On a [p < suddenly . . . on a > was shot thro with a dyed. Scattering as Behavior Toward Risk. Susan Howe. PFTM-2

On a Painted Woman [*with music*]. Percy Bysshe Shelley. NBLV

On a Painting. Ching An. CSKM, *tr. by* Jerome P. Seaton

On a Painting by a Member of the Northwest Visionary School. Averill Curdy. RWB

On a Painting by Patient B of the Independence State Hospital for the Insane. Donald Justice. NoAM

On a Painting by Wang the Clerk of Yen Ling. Su Tung-p'o. BLT, *tr. by* Kenneth Rexroth

On a Painting of Fish Being Caught, A Song. Li Tung-yang. ColAnChi, *tr. by* John Timothy Wixted

On a Painting of Kenshin Attacking Shingen. Rai San'yo. EMJL, *tr. by* Haruo Shirane

On a Peacock. Thomas Heyrick. OWoS

On a Phrase from Southern Ohio. James Wright. LTA

On a Picture Painted by Herself [*or Her self*], Representing Two Nymphs [*or Nimphs*] of Diana's, One in a Posture to Hunt, the other Bath[e]ing. Anne Killigrew. BASC; NOSC

On a Piece of Tapestry. George Santayana. APN-2

On a piece of toilet paper. Bladder Song. Leonard Nathan. BLT

On a Pig's Head. Charles Tomlinson. NoAM

On a Political Prisoner. William Butler Yeats. OBMV

On a Portrait of a Falcon. Tu Fu [*or* Du Fu]. CrYelRi, *tr. by* Sam Hamill

On a Portrait of the Poet. Po Chü-i. CrYelRi, *tr. by* Sam Hamill

On a Portrait of Two Beauties. Hồ Xuân Huong. PoDa, *tr. by* John Balaban

On a Portrait of Wordsworth by B. R. Haydon. Elizabeth Barrett Browning. HeIP-4

On a Procession with the Prince of Wales. Joseph Gwyer. "At evening too the dazzled light." VerBaPo

On a purple, sun-shot evening. On a Sunny Evening. *Unknown, fr. Terezin Concentration Camp.* INSAB

On a Raft. Lőrinc Szabó. IQMS *Fr.* Cricket Music.

On a Rainy Autumn Night. Ch'oe Ch'iwŏn. CATKP, *tr. by* Peter H. Lee

On a Raised Beach. Hugh MacDiarmid. NePenScot "All is lithogenesis – or lochia." NPeEn

On a ranch down near the Texas-Mexico border. Chalk Draw Ranch. Sherry Craven. TiP2

On a Replica of the Parthenon. Donald Davidson. FuPo

On a Return from Egypt. Keith Douglas. NoP-4; NoP-5

On a Rhine Steamer. James Kenneth Stephen. FaBoA; OBCoV *Fr.* England and America.

On a rocky ledge. Tomas Tranströmer. WoBe *Fr.* Haiku.

On A Romantic Lady. Mary Monck. RACG

On a roof in the Old City. Jerusalem. Yehuda Amichai. BeAl, *tr. by* Chana Bloch and Stephen Mitchell

On a Ruined House in a Romantic Country. Samuel Taylor Coleridge. CenSon *Fr.* Sonnets Attempted in the Manner of Contemporary Writers.

On a Sabbath eve, at dusk on a summer day. Song of Lies on Sabbath Eve, A. Yehuda Amichai. PoSu, *tr. by* Chana Bloch

On a Sabbath late. Mountains. Gaylord Brewer. AmPoNex

On a saddle without a horse. Journey Through Hell. Nicanor Parra. WoPoe, *tr. by* Miller Williams

On a Santiago street. Hero, The. Pablo Neruda. GifTon, *tr. by* William O'Daly

On a Saturday afternoon in summer. Under House Arrest. Dennis Brutus. AF

On a sheet of paper. Arithmetical Progression of the Verb "To Be." Walter Conrad Arensberg. APT-1

On a Shipmate, Pero Moniz, Dying at Sea. Luis de Camões [*or Camões or Camoëns*]. OxBEV; WoPoe, *tr. by* Roy Campbell

On a shore washed by desolate waves, *he* stood. Alexander Sergeyevich Pushkin. WoPoe *Fr.* Bronze Horseman, The.

On a sideboard where the sun falls. (LL) Man in Blue, A. James Schuyler. FTOS; PmAP; WaAnP

On a snug evening I shall watch her fingers. Piano after War. Gwendolyn Brooks. ESEAA

On a Soldier Fallen in the Philippines [*with music*]. William Vaughn Moody. AmWaPo

On a Soldier Killed in the Great War. R. Williams Parry. OBWVE, *tr. by* H. Idris Bell

On a spring hillside. Ki no Tsurayuki. WoPoe, *tr. by* Steven D. Carter

On a spring morning of young wood, green wood. Burning the Dreams. Muriel Rukeyser. AF

On a squeaking cart, they push the usual stuff. Removal from Terry Street, A. Douglas Dunn. FaBoVe; NoP-4; NoP-5; NPeEn; StAl

On a Squirrel Crossing the Road in Autumn, in New England. Richard Eberhart. APT-2; HeIP-4

On a Stanza by Rilke. Thomas Swiss. PoDa

On a starless night and still. On Being Asked to Write a School Hymn. Charles Causley. OxAEP-2

On a starred [*or* starr'd] night Prince Lucifer uprose. Lucifer in Starlight. George Meredith. CABP; ChIV-1; CtM; GSo; NAEL-6v2; NAEL-7v2; NoP-4; NoP-5; OBEV; OxBEV; OxBSo; TFi

On a starry, wintry night. Christ Child, The. Mary Weston Fordham. CBWP-3

On a stone disk palette from ancient America. Transparencies. Bruce Bond. Vesp

On a Stone Pillow. Haim Guri. NRoS, *tr. by* Esther Raizen

On a Stone Thrown at a Very Great Man, But Which Missed Him. "Peter Pindar." NBLV

On a street clogged with chatter, young men and women. Spontaneous Monument. Meredith Walters. IIR

On a summer day in the month of May. Big Rock Candy Mountains, The. *Unknown.* FaBoA

On a Summer Night. Elmaz Abinader. CFP

On a summer Sunday I saw the sun. Summer Sunday. *Unknown.* WoPoe, *tr. by* John Gardner

On a Sunbeam. Thomas Heyrick. NOSC

On a sunny brae alone I lay. Day Dream, A. Emily Jane Brontë. NALW

On a Sunny Evening. *Unknown, fr. Terezin Concentration Camp.* INSAB

On a Theme by Frost. Robert Francis. VisFro

On a Theme from Julian's Chapter 20. Denise Levertov. UpMys

On a Theme from Nicolas of Cusa. Clive Staples Lewis. SacPr

On a 3 1/2 Oz. Lesser Yellowlegs, Departed Boston August 28, Shot Martinique September 3. Eamon Grennan. P180

On a train in Texas German prisoners eat. Defeat. Witter Bynner. APT-1; PWW2

On a Tree Fallen Across the Road (To Hear Us Talk). Robert Frost. GoPo

On a tributary of the Amazon. Lass of Aughrim, The. Paul Muldoon. NoAM; PBCIP

On a Trip. Hagiwara Sakutaro. CAoMJL1, *tr. by* Hiroaki Sato

On a Vase of Gold-Fish [*with music*]. Charles Tennyson Turner. NPeEn

On a veranda. Mukai Kyorai. EMJL, *tr. by* Haruo Shirane

On a verdant summer islet. Burial of a Fairy Queen. Mary E. Tucker. CBWP-1

On a View of Pasadena from the Hills. Yvor Winters. HarvBoo

On a Violet in Her Breast. Thomas Stanley. NOSC

On a Virtuous Young Gentlewoman That Died Suddenly. William Cartwright. OBEV

On a Visit. Alun Llywelyn-Williams. BBMWP, *tr. by* Joseph P. Clancy

On a Visit to Ch'ung Chen Taoist Temple. Yü Hsüan-chi. ColAnChi, *tr. by* Chung Ling and Kenneth Rexroth

On a Weekend in September. Vassar Miller. TiP2

On a Wet Summer. John Codrington Bampfylde. OxBSo

On a white corner these voices are heard. Good-for-nothings on a White Corner. Ernesto Lumbreras. RMCMP, *tr. by* Rebecca Seiferle

On a Winter Night. May Sarton. ItWoWo

On a Winter's Night. Shin Kyŏngnim. CAMKP, *tr. by* Anthony, Brother of Taizé

On a winter's night long time ago. Noël. Joseph Hilaire Pierre Belloc. UV

On a withered branch. Basho. TAL

On a Woman. Robert Williams. OBWVE, *tr. by* H. Idris Bell

On African Writing. Jack A. Mapanje. HBAPE

On Air. Gillian Clarke. RWPCtW

On Alabama Ave., Paterson, NJ, 1954. Rachel De Vries. UnSA

On Alderman W———: The History of His Life. John Cunningham. OBCoV

On All Fours. Benjamin Péret. PFTM-1

On all that strand. Roundelay. Samuel Beckett. ModIr; OxBEV

On an Æolian Harp. George Cabot Lodge. APN-2

On an afternoon when you're sitting. With Your Mother in a Café. Shaun Levin. PML

On an Amorous Old Man.   David Mallet.   NePenScot

On an Ancient Tomb East of the Village.   Po Chü-i.   TAL

On an Anniversary [with music].   John Millington Synge.   OBMV

On an apple-ripe September morning.   Tarry Flynn.   Patrick Kavanagh.   IPoFL; ModIr

On an Autumn Evening Listening to Reverend Yeh Play the Ch'in.   Ch'i-chi.   CSKM, tr. by Burton Watson

On an Early Spring.   Mary Julia Young.   CenSon

On an East Wind from the Wars.   Alan Dugan.   AF; GPTC

On an Engraving by Casserius.   Alec Derwent Hope.   HarvBoo

On an evening in June, alone with anxious mediations, ready by mobbed light, I come again, taste to taste, with my own self-inoculations.   Sign Under Test.   Charles Bernstein.   BAP-04

On an Indian Tomineois, the Least of Birds.   Thomas Heyrick.   NOSC

On an Infant Dying as Soon as Born.   Charles Lamb.   OBEV

On an Infant Which Died before Baptism.   Samuel Taylor Coleridge.   SacPr

On an Invitation to the United States.   Thomas Hardy.   FaBoA

On an Irish Retriever.   Frances Anne Kemble.   DiBP

On an Island.   John Millington Synge.   FaBoVe; MoBrPo; NPeEn; OxBEV

On an old grand piano.   Ekaterina Vlasova.   CRWP, tr. by Peter France

On an Unfinished Statue.   George Santayana.   APN-2

On an Unsociable Family.   Elizabeth Hands.   NPeEn; WoRP

On and on, always on and on.   Unknown.   CCL1,

On and On: An Ancient Song (Yueh-Fu).   Li Ho.   ChinPo, tr. by Ye Weilian [or Yeh Wei-lien or Wai-lim Yip]

On and on in the white clouds.   Sent to the Taoist of Dragon Mountain, Hsu Fa-leng.   Liu Ch'ang-ch'ing and William H. Nienhauser.   ColAnChi

On Angels.   Czeslaw Milosz.   AF; BBASP; WaAnP, tr. by the author

On Anna Laetitia Aikin.   Mary Scott.   RWP
  (On Anna Laetitia Barbauld (née Aikin).)   NPBRoP

On Another's Sorrow.   William Blake.   InvLi; OxAEP-2 Fr. Songs of Innocence.

On any sheet the least display of mind. (LL)   Considerable Speck, A.   Robert Frost.   MoAmPo; SAmP

On Apologies.   Jean Valerie.   SpirFl

On Arno's bosom, as he calmly flows.   John Pierpont.   APN-1 Fr. Airs of Palestine.

On Arriving at Oeo Temple.   Jinkag Haesim.   BecRai, tr. by Kim Daljin, Kim Won-Chung and Christopher Merrill

On Artistic Freedom in the Nationalist Era.   Salman Masalha.   PML, tr. by Vivian Eden

On attendait que l'homme étendu en travers du chemin se réveillât.   Plus Lourd.   Pierre Reverdy.   YaTCFP

On august 12, 1982, the first Trident-class submarine, the USS.   Black Beauty, A Praise.   David Romtvedt.   AtGh

On August 1st in Texas everybody sweats.   August 1, 1966.   Pat Stodghill.   TiP2

On Autumn.   Chungji.   BecRai, tr. by Kim Daljin, Kim Won-Chung and Christopher Merrill

On autumn nights.   David Vogel.   FIT, tr. by Robert Friend

On autumn nights the rapid weaver sings.   Autumn Night, An.   Hsieh T'iao.   CCL1, tr. by John Frodsham

On Balaam's Ass.   Francis Quarles.   ChIV-1

On Bald Mountain.   A. Kadir.   NaPG, tr. by Talat Sait Halman

On Ballycastle Beach.   Medbh McGuckian.   PBCIP

On Basho's "Frog."   Sengai Gibon.   ZenPo, tr. by Takashi Ikemoto and Lucien Stryk

On Bathing.   Thomas, the Younger Warton.   OxBSo

On Beauty [or Beauety].   James Thomson.
  "This happy place with all delights abounds."   UV

On Becoming a Mermaid.   Lorna Goodison.   NAMCP V.2

On Becoming a Tiger.   Lorna Goodison.   GT

On Being a Householder.   Alan Dugan.   NAMCP V.2; NoAM

On Being a Poet in Sierra Leone.   Syl Cheney-Coker.   HBAPE

On Being a Woman [with music].   Dorothy Parker.   BrAP

On Being Asked for a War Poem.   William Butler Yeats.   FaBoWar; NIP-4; OBWP; OxAEP-2; PoAgWa; PoWW

On Being Asked My Opinion About an Autopsy.   Robin Behn.   AmAlph

On Being Asked to Write a Poem Against the War in Vietnam.   Hayden Carruth.   AmWaPo; PoAgWa

On Being Asked to Write a Poem for 1979.   Jack A. Mapanje.   AF; NAfrP

On Being Asked to Write a School Hymn.   Charles Causley.   OxAEP-2

On Being Brought from Africa to America.   Phillis Wheatley.   ColAP; FaBoA; ISC; NAAL-3; NAAL-5; NAAPv.1; NALW; NoP-4; NoP-5; OxBEV; OxBoAm; RWP; SacPr

On Being Cautioned against Walking on an Headland Overlooking the Sea, Because It Was Frequented by a Lunatic.   Charlotte Smith.   CenSon; NAEL-7v2; NPeEn; WoRP

On Being Disabled by Light at Dawn in the Wilderness.   G. E. Murray.   IllVoic

On Being Forced to Part with his Library for the Benefit of his Creditors.   William Stanley Roscoe.   CenSon

On Being Head of the English Department.   Pinkie Gordon Lane.   GT

On Being in the Midwest.   Diana Chang.   FiBr

On Being Kicked Out of the Harold Washington Library Center for Napping on the Floor.   Thom Ward.   OPRER

On being reproaced by saintly mediators for bad budgeting.   Anna Mendelssohn.   VaPo

On Being the Least Feminist Woman You've Ever Met.   Paula Cunningham.   NIrP

On Being Told I don't Speak Like a Black Person.   Allison Joseph.   OPRER

On Bellosguardo, when the year was young.   To Vernon Lee.   Amy Levy.   VWP

On Belmont, low riders.   Hotel Fresno.   Dixie Salazar.   GeoHom

On Ben Dorain.   Duncan Ban MacIntyre.   Fr. Last Farewell to the Hills.

On black St. Stephen's steeple. (LL)   Backyard.   Diane Di Prima.   PmAP; WaAnP

On board the Victory Line Bus.   Assimilation.   Eugene Gloria.   ReBoTo

On Boiled Rice Mountain.   For Du Fu.   Li Po.   CCL1, tr. by David Young

On Bond the Usurer.   Unknown.   NOSC

On Boston Common a red star.   Winter's Tale, A.   Sylvia Plath.   FaBoA

On Bourbon Street. I changed it at a bank.   After Finding a One Hundred Dollar Bill.   David Chapman Berry.   PoA 2002

On boys and girls the middle parts get mated.   Unknown.   PriapPo Fr. Priapus Poems, The.

On broad hills, the broken backs of mountains.   Pissaro's Tomb.   Patrick Lane.   BrAP

On Brooklyn Bridge I saw a man drop dead.   Charles Reznikoff.   APT-2; NAAPv.2; NAMCP V.1

On Brutus, an Ode.   John, Duke of Buckingham and Normandy Sheffield.   Heavy Going.   STuOW

On Buddha's birthday.   Basho.   SoOfWa, tr. by Sam Hamill

On Buddha's birthday.   Kikaku.   SoOfWa, tr. by Sam Hamill

On Buddha's deathday.   Basho.   SoOfWa, tr. by Sam Hamill

On Building a Nest: St. Peter's, Saskatchewan.   Susan Goyette.   Coast

On Butler who can think without rage.   John Oldham.   OBSV Fr. Satire, A.

On Buying a Dog.   Edgar Klauber.   NTCP

On Buying a Horse [with music].   Unknown.   NBLV

On came the whirlwind—like the last.   Charge at Waterloo.   Sir Walter Scott.   FaBoWar

On can never tell what November will be in Texas.   Visit, The.   Gene Shuford.   TiP2

On Cantey Street a visitor came by.   Mr. Watts and the Whirlwind.   William D. Barney.   TiP2

On Catullus.   Walter Savage Landor.   OBEV

On certain days a sweat folds in over her, covering her as weather covers a little city.   Bathroom.   Fanny Howe.   ExTi

On charts they fall like lace.   Delos.   Lawrence Durrell.   OxAEP-2

On Chloris Walking in the Snow.   William Strode.   NPeEn
  (Chloris in the Snow.)   OBEV
  (On a Gentlewoman Walking in the Snow.)   NOSC

On Christians, Mercy Will Fall [with music].   Unknown.   OBWVE, tr. by D. Myrddin Lloyd

On Christmas.   John Codrington Bampfylde.   CenSon

On Christmas Day I weep.   Christmas Mourning.   Vassar Miller.   ChIV-2; MoAmPo

On Christmas Day to My Heart.   Clement Paman.   ChrPo; NOSC; RSR

On Chung Mountain.   Wang An-shih.   CrYelRi, tr. by Sam Hamill

On Cimbing Mount Green Crag in Yongjia.   Hsieh Ling-yün.   CCL1, tr. by John Frodsham

On city breezes borne. (LL)   London Plane-Tree, A.   Amy Levy.   PEW; ViWPN

On Clarastella walking in Her Garden.   Robert Heath.   NOSC

On Class and Desire.   Chuck Wachtel.   PrTe

On clear days.   Ap'ae Island 1—Diving Women.   No Hyangnim.   EcSo, tr. by Aimee N. Kwon

On Climbing Stone Drum Mountain, Near Shangshu.   Hsieh Ling-yün.   CCL1, tr. by John Frodsham

On Climbing the Heights on the Ninth Day of the Ninth Moon.   Tu Fu [or Du Fu].   TAL

On Climbing the Highest Peak of Stone Gate.   Hsieh Ling-yün.   CCL1, tr. by John Frodsham

On Climbing the Highest Peak of Stone Gate Mountain.   Hsieh Ling-yün.   ColAnChi, tr. by Richard W. Bodman

On Climbing the Mountain Where Buddha Trained.   Mokusen.   ZenPo, tr. by Takashi Ikemoto and Lucien Stryk

On Climbing the Phoenix Tower at Chinling.   Li Po.   TAL

On Coahuila Street. Heriberto Yépez. RMCMP, *tr.* by Mark Weiss

On cold and dusty mornings, the fog. Retired Postman Recalls the Old Route, A. C. J. Sage. RWB

On Coming to Nothing. Richard Moore. PoA 2002

On Commonwealth Avenue and Brattle Street. Diana Der Hovanessian. UrbNat

On Commonwealth, on Marlborough. Technologies. George Starbuck. YaYoPo

On Communists. Ebenezer Elliott. NBLV

On Consulting "Contemporary Poets of the English Language." Anthony Thwaite. OxBEV

On Contact Opens Its Indigo Pit. Coral Bracho. PFTM-2, *tr.* by Forrest Gander

On Covering the Bones of Chang Chin, the Hired Man. Liu Tsung-yüan. WoPoe, *tr.* by Jan W. Walls

On Crossing the Rhine Bridge at Cologne by Night. Ernst Stadler. GTCP, *tr.* by Michael Hamburger

On Cupid's bow how are my heart-strings bent. Sir Philip Sidney. NoSic *Fr.* Astrophil and Stella.

On Damons Loveing of Clora. Damaris, Lady Masham. EMWP

On dark nights, when thoughts fly like nightbirds. It Is Important. Gail Tremblay. WeW-3

On Death. Anne Killigrew. ChIV-1

On Death. Maurice Manning. LegDan

On Death. Sándor Weöres. IQMS, *tr.* by Alan Dixon

On death and beauty—till a bullet stopped his song. (LL) All Day It Has Rained. Alun Lewis. AngWePo; NAEL-6v2; NoP-4; NoP-5; OBWP; OBWVE; RSaN; TCAWP; WaAnP

On December 22, 1882, an old newspaper. Broken Glass. Victoria Edwards Tester. ICANM

On deck. And love's the burning boy. (LL) Casabianca. Elizabeth Bishop. NIL-7; NoP-5; WoPoe

On Derry's Walls. Kerry Hardie. NIrP

On Desire. A Pindarick. Aphra Behn. EMWP

On Digital Extremities [*limerick*]. Frank Gelett Burgess. CalPo

On Dinah. Francis Quarles. ChIV-1

On Display. Thomas Sayers Ellis. InTrad

On Don Surly. Ben Jonson. NAEL-6v1; NAEL-7v1

On Donne's Poetry. Samuel Taylor Coleridge. NAEL-6v2; NAEL-7v2; UV

On Dorothea Lange's Photograph "Migrant Mother" (1936). Helen Pinkerton. FFC

On Dover Cliffs. July 20, 1787. William Lisle Bowles. CenSon

On DOVE's green brink the fair TREMELLA stood. Erasmus Darwin. NOBRP *Fr.* Botanic Garden, The.

On Dragon Hill. Li Po. CrYelRi, *tr.* by Sam Hamill

On Dreams, October 15, 1782 [*with music*]. Sir Samuel Egerton Brydges. CenSon

On Dry Land. Pedro Salinas. RaW, *tr.* by Donald Hall

On Dutch's Death. Robert Coles. BloBone

On each receding bush. Second Song. Charles Tomlinson. WoBe

On ear and ear two noises too old to end. Sea and the Skylark, The. Gerard Manley Hopkins. OBMV

On Earth. Olga Broumas. BodElec

On earth. (LL) Plague Victims Catapulted Over Walls Into Besieged City. Thomas Lux. AmAlph; KGB

(Just as she did on earth.) (LL) BeAl; P180

On earth as it is in heaven. (LL) Talk Show, The. Albert Goldbarth. CAP-8; IllVoic; ReTh

On Education, December 1789. Elizabeth Bentley. WoRP

On either side of a rock-paved lane. St Kilda's Parliament: 1879–1979. Douglas Dunn. NePenScot

On either side of the white line. James Vincent Cunningham. APT-2

On either side the *Jervis Bay* the convoy was dipping. Michael Thwaites. FaBoWar *Fr.* Jervis Bay, The.

On either side the river lie. Lady of Shalott, The. Alfred Tennyson. BrAP; NAEL-6v2; NAEL-7v2; NOBRP; NoP-4; NoP-5; OBEV; OBNV; OBSP; OxAEP-2; TFi; WaAnP

On El Camino Del Mar. Variations for the Piano. Siv Cedering. MiVo

On Eleanor Freeman, Who Died 1650, Aged 21. *Unknown.* OBEV

On Elijah's Chariot. Endre Ady. IQMS, *tr.* by Anton N. Nyerges

On Elizabeth Montagu. Mary Scott. RWP

On Encountering Trouble. Ch'u Yüan. CCL1, *tr.* by David Hawkes

On English Monsieur. Ben Jonson. AEP; NBLV; NoP-4; NoP-5

On Entering His Coffin. Baiho. ZenPo, *tr.* by Takashi Ikemoto and Lucien Stryk

On Entries Emptiness. Dennis Phillips. FTOS

On Esthwaite Water. Isabella Lickbarrow. NPBRoP; RWP; WaAnP

On every slave a pigeon loft to kick in the light of his decline. 9000 Jackals Swimming to Boston. "Lucebert." PFTM-2, *tr.* by Peter Nijmeijer

On every street. Going Up. Sam Liptsin. Prolet, *tr.* by Amelia Glaser

On every thought I have the countless shadows fall. Light and Shadow. Hugh MacDiarmid. HarvBoo

On Exodus 3: 14: "I am that I am." Matthew Prior. ChIV-1

On Exploration. James Galvin. TAPaP

On extending the olive branch to my own self. Harriet Jacobs. SpirFl

On Failing the Examination. Meng Chiao. ColAnChi, *tr.* by Burton Watson

On Failing to Translate. Hugh Maxton. IrLP

On Fairford Windows. William Strode. NOSC

On Falling Asleep by Firelight. William Meredith. ChIV-1; NoAM

On Fame. John Keats. CenSon *Fr.* Two Sonnets on Fame.

On Feather Beds. John Armstrong. STuOW *Fr.* Art of Preserving Health, The.

On feeling, blue blaze of noon. Bow and Arrow. Derec Llwyd Morgan. BBMWP, *tr.* by Joseph P. Clancy

On fields oer which the reaper's hand has passed. Henry David Thoreau. APN-1

On filling a car with gasoline. Gathas. *Unknown.* WhBo

On Finding a Swastika Carved on a Tree in the Hills above Heidelberg. Kevin Prufer. AmPoNex; LegDan

On Finding an Old Photograph. Wendy Cope. HarvBoo

On Fire. Andrew Feld. LegDan

On Fire. David Morley. NLP

On First Looking into Chapman's Hesiod. Peter Porter. NOBAu

On First Looking into Chapman's Homer. John Keats. BrAP; BRP; CABP; CenSon; ClHu; CtM; GSo; HeIP-4; NAEL-6v2; NAEL-7v2; NAWM-7v2; NIL-7; NIP-4; NOBRP; NoP-4; NoP-5; NPBRoP; NPeEn; OBEV; OPOU; OxAEP-2; OxBEV; OxBSo; PoPoPo; SoSe-8; TFi; TRP; UV; WaAnP; WoPoe

On First Looking into Krafft-Ebing's *Psychopathosexualis* [*or Psychopathia Sexualis*]. Oliver St. John Gogarty. UV

On First Reading *Romeo and Juliet.* Diane Lockward. IaFF

On Flower Wreath Hill. Kenneth Rexroth. APT-2; BodElec

On foot. On Foot I Had to Walk Through the Solar Systems. Edith Södergran. WPoS

On Foot I Had to Walk Through the Solar Systems. Edith Södergran. WPoS

On Forgetting Your Father's Face. Crystal Williams. RD

On forgotten tracks, in unnamed places. On Forgotten Tracks. Abdelwahab Meddeb. YaTCFP, *tr.* by Charlotte Mandell

On Fourteen Maple Street. Barbara Winder. MiVo

On Fourteenth street the bugles blow. Ballad of the Salvation Army. Kenneth Fearing. AmWit

On Francis Drake. *Unknown.* NOSC; NPeEn; PBRV

On Fridays he'd open a can of Jax. My Father's Love Letters [*or Loveletters*]. Yusef Komunyakaa. InGu; NAMCP V.2; OxAAAP

On Fridays we would gather at Lucy's. Last at Lucy's, The. John Tripp. TCAWP

On Fruition. Sir Charles Sedley. NOSC

On Gallia's land I saw thy faded form. To Freedom. Joseph Hucks. CenSon

On Galveston Beach. Barbara Howes. MoAmPo

On Gask's deserted ancient hall. Ghost of Fadon, The. Joanna Baillie. NOBRP

On Gay Wallpaper. William Carlos Williams. APT-1; MoAmPo

On Genessarett. Josephine D. Henderson Heard. CBWP-4

On Geoffrey Grigson. Cyril Connolly. OBCoV

On George Herbert's "The Temple" Sent to a Gentlewoman. Richard Crashaw. OxAEP-1

On Giles and Joan. Ben Jonson. NAEL-6v1; NAEL-7v1

On Giving My Father a Book About Roses. Robin Behn. AmAlph

On God. Maurice Manning. LegDan

On God's Law. Francis Quarles. ChIV-1

On Going Deaf. Anne Stevenson. PoCu

On Going Without Saying. Jean Bleakney. NIrP

On Groin. Ben Jonson. NOSC

On Growing Old. John Masefield. MoBrPo

On Growing Up the Darker Berry. Harriet Jacobs. ISC

On Guard. Marge Piercy. PoDa

On Gut. Ben Jonson. NoP-4; NoP-5; NPeEn; PoPoPo

On Happiness. Pacifico Massimi. CAGL *Fr.* Hecateleguim.

On Having Been an Experimental Sacred Cow for Four Years, and a Token African on Faculty. Kofi Awoonor. HBAPE

On Hearing a Description of a Prairie. Fanny Crosby. SWaP

On Hearing a Flute at Night from the Wall of Shouxiang. Li Yi. CCL1, *tr.* by Witter Bynner

On Hearing a New Escalation. Richard Hugo. AmWaPo; PoA 2002

On Hearing a Pipe. Buhyu Sunsoo. BecRai, *tr.* by Kim Daljin, Kim Won-Chung and Christopher Merrill

On Hearing a Symphony of Beethoven. Edna St. Vincent Millay. ItP; MoAmPo

On Hearing of the Intention of a Gentleman to Purchase the Poet's Freedom. George Moses Horton. APN-1

On Hearing Someone Sing a Poem by Yuan Zhen. Po Chü-i. CCL1, *tr. by* Arthur Waley

On hearing that a small herd of buffalo. Buffalo Poem #1. Geary Hobson. UrbNat

On Hearing That the Students of Our New University Have Joined the Agitation against Immoral Literature. William Butler Yeats. NoAM

On hearing / that twelve. News, The. Maxine Chernoff. LiTh

On Hearing the Airlines Will Use a Psychological Profile to Catch Potential Skyjackers. Stephen Dunn. OtW; SUP

On Hearing the First Cuckoo. Richard Church. OBMV

On Hearing the Song of the Geese. Haewŏn. BecRai, *tr. by* Kim Daljin, Kim Won-Chung and Christopher Merrill

On Hearing the Sound of a Komunko While Passing a Mansion. Chunghur Hyujung. BecRai, *tr. by* Kim Daljin, Kim Won-Chung and Christopher Merrill

On Hellespont, guilty of true love's blood. Hero and Leander. Christopher Marlowe. NAEL-6v1; NAEL-7v1; NoP-5; NoSic

On her chest. (LL) Motherhood. May Swenson. NoP-4; NoP-5

On her dark breast with indifferent hand. (LL) Cleopatra. Anna Andreyevna Akhmatova. FaBoWar; PoetW, *tr. by* Max Hayward and Stanley Kunitz

On Her Decision to Stop Wearing Clothes. Mahadevi. ErotSp; WPoS, *tr. by* Jane Hirshfield

On her evening off. For the Woman Who Dressed Up to Listen to Gigli on the Radio. Jane Duran. MFPA

On Her Loving Two Equally. Aphra Behn. NALW; NIL-7; NIP-4

(Song.) EMWP; OxAEP-1

On her ninetieth birthday, we found her. Brick. Kristin Kovacic. SweBea

On her own, beware, she will. (LL) I am accused of tending to the past. Lucille Clifton. ISC; NAMCP V.2

On Her Portrait. Sor Juana Inés de la Cruz. WoPoe, *tr. by* Robert Mezey

On Her Portrait. Sor Juana Inés de la Cruz. SpanPo, *tr. by* Kate Flores

On her 36th birthday, Thomas had shown her. Wingfoot Lake. Rita Dove. CAP-8; NAMCP V.2; PoPoPo

(On her 36th birthday.) UnSA

On Her Vanity. Wilfrid Scawen Blunt. GSo

On Her Way. Gertrude Stein. PFTM-1

On her way down. Birth and Death of Bette Davis, The. Jackie Kay. MoWP

On her way to the beach. Young Girl. Carl Rakosi. APT-2

On high may dwell with thee. (LL) Church's One Foundation, The. Samuel John Stone. SacPr; UV

On High Street. Andrea Hollander Budy. UrbNat

On highway edges the sparrows. Winter Landscape. Luciana Notari. CItWP, *tr. by* Cinzia Sartini Blum and Lara Trubowitz

On him. (LL) Sir Nose D'VoidofFunk. Thomas Sayers Ellis. FuFl; NeAmPo

On him the unpetitioned heavens descend. Counsel of Moderation, A. Francis Thompson. MoBrPo

On Himself. Cyril Connolly. OBCoV

On Himself. David Wright. OPOU

On Himself, upon Hearing What Was His Sentence. James Graham, Marquess of Montrose. NePenScot; NOSC; NPeEn

(His Metrical Prayer.) ChIV-2

On Himself[e] ("Here down my wearied [*or* wearyed] limbs I'll [*or* Ile] lay.") Robert Herrick. BASC

On Himself[e] ("I fear[e] no Earthly Powers.") Robert Herrick. CavPo

On Himself[e] ("I will no longer kiss.") Robert Herrick. CavPo

On Himself[e] ("Lost to the world; lost to my selfe [*or* myself]; alone.") Robert Herrick. NPeEn

On Himselfe ("Weepe for the dead, for they have lost this light.") Robert Herrick. NOSC

On hire is al my lyf ylong. *Unknown.* OHMEL

On his airy perch among the branches. Fox and the Crow, The. Jean de La Fontaine. OBVE, *tr. by* Marianne Moore

On his Baldness. Po Chü-i. CCL1, *tr. by* Arthur Waley

On His Birthday. Greg Williamson. NAPBL

On His Blindness. John Milton. BLPJKO; CABP; ChIV-2; CtM; GSo; HeIP-4; ITBLP; ItP; NAEL-6v1; NIL-7; NoP-4; NOSC; NPeEn; OBEV; OxBSo; PoPoPo; SacPr; SoSe-8; TFi; TRP; WaAnP; WeW-3

(Sonnet 19.) BASC

(When I Consider How My Light Is Spent.) BrAP; NoP-5

On His Books [*epigram*]. Joseph Hilaire Pierre Belloc. MoBrPo; NBLV; WeW-3

On His Deceased Wife. John Milton. NPeEn; OBEV; OxBSo; SacPr; TFi

(On His Dead Wife.) WaAnP; WeW-3

(Methought I Saw.) NoP-4; NoP-5

(Methought I Saw My Late Espousèd Saint.) BrAP; CABP; NAEL-6v1; PBRV

(Sonnet.) NOSC

(Sonnet 23.) MakPoe

On his first visit to Puerto Rico. Coca-Cola and Coco Frío. Martín Espada. ReTh; UnSA

On his free weekends he took. Military-Industrial Complex, The. Robley, Jr. Wilson. PBCAP

On His Late Majesty's Gracious Gift to the Universities. Joseph Trapp. OxBEV

On His Mistress Drown'd [*or* Drowned]. Thomas Spratt. STuOW

On His Mistress Going from Home [Song]. *Unknown.* NOSC

On His Mistress [*or* Mistris]. John Donne. CABP; FSCP; NAEL-6v1; NAEL-7v1; NoSic; NPeEn; OxAEP-1 *Fr.* Elegies.

On His Mistress [*or* Mistris], the Queen of Bohemia. Sir Henry Wotton. BASC; NOSC; NPeEn; OxBEV; TFi

(Elizabeth of Bohemia.) OBEV

On his return, he finds from the man rhyming peace. Man Whose Name Rhymes with Peace, A. Nathaniel Tarn. WANABP

On His Royal Blindness Paramount Chief Kwangala. Jack A. Mapanje. AF

On His Royal Highness His Expedition Against the Dutch. Elizabeth Polwhele. EMWP

On His Seventy-Fifth Birthday. Walter Savage Landor. *See* I Strove With None.

On his tired memory a splendid. Old Man. Petar Alipiev. CSCBP, *tr. by* Georgi Belev and Lisa Sapinkopf

On his way to the open hearth where white-hot steel. My Father's Garden. David Wagoner. NIL-7; NIP-4

On his wedding night. Sons of War. Samih Al-Qasim. FaBoWar, *tr. by* Abdullah Al-Udhari

On Hope. *See* Against Hope.

On Hope. Sándor Petőfi. IQMS, *tr. by* Peter Zollman

On hot nights now, in the smell of trees and water. Lazarus' Sister. Elaine Feinstein. HarvBoo

On hot summer mornings my aunt set glasses. Water. Leslie Norris. AngWePo; OBWVE

On How Robert Schumann Was Defeated by Demons. Francisco Hernandez. RMCMP, *tr. by* Christian Viveros-Fauné

On Hsin-P'ing Tower. Li Po. NDACCP, *tr. by* David Hinton

On humming rubber along this white concrete. Driving in Oklahoma. Carter Revard. HATNAP

On hurling insults, the other gone mad. (LL) At the Mosque. Chairil Anwar. PML; PoetW, *tr. by* Burton Raffel

On Hurricane Jackson. Alan Dugan. TRP

On Hygiene. Joseph Hilaire Pierre Belloc. MoBrPo

On Imagination. Phillis Wheatley. NAAPv.1; NoP-5; OxWW; RWP

On Impermanence. Jamie Meyerhoff. WhBo

On Induction of the Hand. Clark Coolidge. NYP2; PmAP

On Inhabiting an Orange. Josephine Miles. NoAM; PoA 2002; WaAnP

On Inheriting Departure. HeidiLynn Nilsson. NeAmPo

On Iona the last Gaelic speaker has died. Long Silence, The. Kenneth Steven. EdScPo

On its highest leaves. Ibycus. SaLy, *tr. by* Diane Rayor

On Its Way. May Swenson. SoSe-8

On its way I see. Kathleen Jessie Raine. NALW

On Jacob Tonson, His Publisher. John Dryden. OBSV

On Jacob's Purchase. Francis Quarles. ChIV-1

On Jam. Joseph Hilaire Pierre Belloc. NBLV

On Jealousy. Esther Johnson. LW

On Jordan's Bank. Lord Byron. ChIV-1

On Joshu's Nothingness. Saisho. ZenPo, *tr. by* Takashi Ikemoto and Lucien Stryk

On July 14, 1954 Frida Kahlo, who had swallowed the world. Rising Bodies. Mary Ruefle. AmAlph

On Justifying Cuckoo La Goose. Marianne Vitale.

"*Who trusteth in hilarity.*" HeMarv

On Karma at 9.11.85. Bobby Byrd. TiP2

On Kean's Hamlet. Washington Allston. APN-1

On Killing a Tax Collector. Murragh O'Daly. WoPoe, *tr. by* Richard O'Connell

On Killing Myself. Hwang Hyŏn. CATKP, *tr. by* Chi-gyu Kim [*or* Kim Chonggil]

On Labor Day the last barbecue smoke. Fiber Optics. Joseph Millar. PoDa

On Lady A———. Nicolas Bentley. OBCoV

On Lady Anne Hamilton. Richard Brinsley Sheridan. NPeEn; OBCoV

On Lady Poltagrue, A Public Peril. Joseph Hilaire Pierre Belloc. MoBrPo; OBCoV

On land and sea I strove with anxious care. Rudyard Kipling. InoFa; WoPoe *Fr.* Epitaphs of the War [1914–1918].

On Late-acquired Wealth *or* Riches. *Unknown.* OBVE, *tr. by* William Cowper

On late-night television, two U.S. scientists talk about why the U.S. Simon J. Ortiz. OPRER

On Lazarus Raised From Death. Henry Colman. ChIV-2

On Learning of a Friend's Illness. C. K. Williams. WaAnP

On leave, I sat on marsh grass, watched. Soldier on the Marsh, A. Andrew Hudgins. CBCWP

On Leaving Prison. Luís De León. SpanPo, *tr. by* Brenda M. Sackett

On Leaving Some Friends at an Early Hour. John Keats. CenSon

On Leaving the Artists' Colony. Bruce Bawer. RA

On leaving the city. Seven Beginnings. Olesya Nikolayeva. ItGoST, *tr. by* Richard Graves and Carol Ueland

On Lending a Punch-Bowl. Oliver Wendell Holmes. TreFP

On Liberty and Slavery. George Moses Horton. APN-1; NAAPv.1

On Lieutenant Shift. Ben Jonson. OBSV

On light's reflected word. (LL) Heron, The. Vernon Watkins. AngWePo; TCAWP

On Linden, when the sun was low. Hohenlinden. Thomas Campbell. CABP; NOBRP; NPBRoP; OBWP; TFi

On Lisi's Golden Hair. Francisco de Quevedo y Villegas. WoPoe, *tr. by* Roy Campbell

(When You Shake Loose Your Hair.) SpanPo

On little rented chairs with gilded backs. (LL) Evening Musicale. Phyllis McGinley. AmWit; OBCoV

On Living. Nazim Hikmet. PoetW, *tr. by* Randy Blasing and Mutlu Konuk

On Living with a Fat Woman in Heaven. Sidney Burris. SwNoth

On London fell a clearer light. Summer in England, 1914. Alice Thompson Meynell. SoSe-8

On lonely. Mother. Karl Lubomirski. PML, *tr. by* Renate Latimer

On Long Island, they moved my clapboard house. Whitman. Larry Levis. ReTh; ViWalt

On longer evenings. Coming. Philip Larkin. MoBrPo

On Looking into Henry Moore. Dorothy Livesay. BrAP

On Lookout: Guadalupe River Ranch. William Virgil Davis. TiP2

On Lord Cobham's Garden. Nathaniel Cotton. OBGa

On Lord Holland's Seat near Margate, Kent. Thomas Gray. NPeEn

On Lord Holland's Seat near Margate, Kent. Thomas Gray. OBGa

On Lord Ila's Improvements, near Hounslow Heath. Philip Dormer Stanhope, 4th Earl of Chesterfield. OBGa

On lottery blotting paper, 8-spot (click, click). (LL) Fred Wah. NLPA; OpeFie *Fr.* This Dendrite Map: Father / Mother Haibun.

On Love. Diophanes of Myrina. WoPoe, *tr. by* Dudley Fitts

On Love. Hsü Tsai-ssu. CrYelRi; ErotSp, *tr. by* Sam Hamill

On Loving Once and Loving Often. Elizabeth Tollet. LW

On Lucy, Countess of Bedford. Ben Jonson. BASC; NAEL-7v1; NOSC

On Maguire's Winter Campaign. Eochaidh Ó Heóghusa. PBRV

On makeshift. On Makeshift Bedding. Vidya. WoPoe, *tr. by* Andrew Schelling

On Makeshift Bedding. Vidya. WoPoe, *tr. by* Andrew Schelling

On Man, on Nature, and on Human Life. William Wordsworth. NAEL-6v2; NAEL-7v2 *Fr.* Recluse, The.

On Mankind. Attila József. IQMS, *tr. by* Adam Makkai

On Mankind. Mihály Vörösmarty. IQMS, *tr. by* Valerie Becker Makkai and Neville Masterman

On Mr. Dryden, Renegade. Aphra Behn. FaBoVe

On May-day, when the lark began to rise. *Unknown.* NoSic *Fr.* Court of Love, The.

On me dit que là-bas les plages sont noires. On me dit que là-bas. André Breton. YaTCFP

On Me, the Imported Skies. Willy Clay. PoA 2002

On Melancholy. *Unknown.* NOSC

On Michael Angelo. Washington Allston. APN-1

On ministers, on actors. Public Beach No. 2. Andrey Andreievich Voznesensky. RusPo, *tr. by* Robert Arthur Douglas Ford

On Mr Milton's "Paradise Lost." Andrew Marvell. BASC; CABP; FSCP; NOSC

On Monday she stood at the wooden wash-tub. Mother, The. George Mackay Brown. EdScPo

On Monsieur's Departure. Queen of England Elizabeth I. CABP; NAEL-6v1; NAEL-7v1; NALW; WaAnP

On Mortality. Henry Colman. ChIV-1

On most nights now. Papa. Barbara Marsh. Prnts

On Mother's Day. Aileen Fisher. NTCP

On Mount Chorae he struck two roebucks. *Various authors.* CATKP *Fr.* Songs of Flying Dragons.

On Mr. Edward Howard, upon His British Princes. Charles, 6th Earl of Dorset Sackville. OBSV

On Mr. G. Herberts booke intituled the Temple of Sacred Poems, sent to a Gentlewoman. Richard Crashaw. FSCP

On Mr. George Herbert's Book, The Temple. Richard Crashaw. CABP

On Mr. Paine's Rights of Man. Philip Freneau. NAAL-3; NAAL-5; NAAPv.1

On Mr. Rice the Manciple of Christ Church in Oxford. Richard Corbet. NOSC

On Mrs. Montagu. Ann Yearsley. RWP

On Mundane Acquaintances. Joseph Hilaire Pierre Belloc. OBCoV

On Muranowska Street. Myra Sklarew. TaR

On Music. Rainer Maria Rilke. WED, *tr. by* Robert Bly

On my altar. Peter Levitt. WhBo

On My Birthday, July 21. Matthew Prior. OBEV

On My Boy Henry. Elizabeth Egerton, Lady Brackley. EMWP

On My Child's Death. Joseph, Freiherr von Eichendorff. WoPoe, *tr. by* W. D. Snodgrass

On My Dear Grandchild Simon Bradstreet, [Who Died on 16TH November, 1669, Being But A Month And One Day Old]. Anne Bradstreet. NAAL-3

(On My Dear Grandchild Simon Bradstreet Who Died on 16 November, 1669, Being But a Month, and One Day Old.) ColAP

On my desk, a set of labels. City Gent. Craig Raine. NoAM

On my desk is a small bottle. Jasmine. E. Ethelbert Miller. GT; OxAAAP

On my desk is a stone with "Amen" carved on it, one survivor fragment. Jewish Time Bomb, The. Yehuda Amichai. RaF, *tr. by* Chana Bloch and Chana Kronfeld

On my disdain for the world. Through the Half-Opened Window. Léon Damas. YaTCFP, *tr. by* Mary Ann Caws

On my far-off journey all round the Four Seas. Far-Off Journey. Ts'ao Chih. CCL1, *tr. by* John Frodsham

On my father's feet are the shoes of dead comrades. Shoes of Dead Comrades, The. Jackie Kay. NeBrP; RSaN

On my father's memorial day. My Father's Memorial Day. Yehuda Amichai. PoCho, *tr. by* the author and Ted Hughes

On My First Daughter. Ben Jonson. BASC; NAEL-6v1; NAEL-7v1; NoP-4; NoP-5; NOSC; WaAnP

On My First Son. Ben Jonson. AmFaPo; BASC; BrAP; CABP; ClHu; InoFa; MakPoe; NAEL-6v1; NAEL-7v1; NIL-7; NIP-4; NoP-4; NoP-5; NOSC; NPeEn; OxBEV; PBRV; PoPoPo; RaBo; SUP; TFi; TRP; WaAnP; WeW-3; WoPoe

On My Fortieth Birthday. John Tripp. AngWePo

On my fourteenth birthday. Curtis Fuller. Rick Madigan. SeSe

On My Fourteenth Wedding Anniversary I Ride on Trains. Cornelia Veenendaal. GM

On my honorable Grandmother, Elizabeth Countess of Shrewbury. Lady Jane Cavendish. EMWP

On My Joyful Departure from the Same City. Samuel Taylor Coleridge. NBLV

On my knees to cry, *Who the hell are you, kid?.* (LL) Roundhouse Voices, The. Dave Jeddie Smith. ColAP; GM; NoAM; VCAP; WaAnP

On my livingroom wall hangs a Navajo rug. Storm Pattern. Greg Pape. PBCAP

On my Northwest coast in the midst of the night a fisherman's group stands watching. Torch, The. Walt Whitman. SAmP

On my old battledress tonight, my sweet. (LL) Goodbye. Alun Lewis. AngWePo; NAEL-6v2; NoP-4; NoP-5; OBWP; PoWW; TCAWP

On my one visit to your bijou apartment. Effects. John McAuliffe. NIrP

On My Own. Philip Levine. PtR

On my parents' honeymoon, my mother stood not. Sole of Dover. William Loran Smith. LaCa

On my pillow bit by bit waking. Start of Autumn: Hearing a Cicada While Sick in Bed. Ch'i-chi. CSKM, *tr. by* Burton Watson

On My Pneumonia. Mihály Csokonai Vitéz. IQMS, *tr. by* Joseph Leftwich

On my sea. My Sea Has One Island. Hong Yunsuk. CAMKP, *tr. by* Genell Y. Poitras

On my thigh, and mockery was still the unforgivable sin. (LL) Blasphemy, A. Rodney Jones. IllVoic; WeW-3

On my third day in Paris. From Paris on a Postcard. Yosano Akiko. CAoMJL1, *tr. by* Janine Beichman

On my Visitt to WS Which I Dreamt of That Night. Lucy Hutchinson. EMWP

On my wall hangs a Japanese carving. Mask of Evil, The. Bertolt Brecht. PoSu; WoPoe, *tr. by* Hoffman Reynolds Hays

On my walls there are three. Photographs of My Father. Judith Ortiz Cofer. ExTi

On My Way Back to Kojokdae. Jungkwan Ilson. BecRai, *tr. by* Kim Daljin, Kim Won-Chung and Christopher Merrill

On My Way from South Mountain to North Mountain, I Glance at the Scenery from the Lake. Hsieh Ling-yün. ColAnChi, *tr. by* Kang-i Sun Chang

On my way home from school. Testing-Tree, The. Stanley Kunitz. APT-2

On my way to bringing you the leotard. Dream of the Unified Field, The. Jorie Graham. NAMCP V.2

On My Wedding Day. Sarah Fyge Egerton. EMWP

On my winter walk. Hugo Majer. Spl

On Myself. Anne Finch, Countess of Winchilsea. NoP-4; NoP-5

On ne se baigne pas deux fois dans le même fleuve. Rue Ravignan, La. Max Jacob. YaTCFP

On Neal's Ashes. Allen Ginsberg. BB; PmAP

On New Waters. Endre Ady. IQMS, *tr. by* Anton N. Nyerges

On New Year's Day. Basho. SoOfWa, *tr. by* Sam Hamill

On New Year's Day. Nantembo. ZenPo, *tr. by* Takashi Ikemoto and Lucien Stryk

On New Year's Day. Marge Piercy. MoW

On News. Thomas Traherne. OBEV *Fr.* Third Century, The.

On nights like this, when bayou and lagoon. Orgie. Madison Cawein. APN-2

On nights when hail / falls noisily. Lady Izumi. WoPoe, *tr. by* Willis Barnstone

On Non-Violence & Observation. Jim Cohn. WhBo

On Not Being Milton. Tony Harrison. CABP; HarvBoo; NAMCP V.2; NoP-4; NoP-5 *Fr.* School of Eloquence, The.

On Not Being Your Lover. Medbh McGuckian. IrLP; PBCIP; PNI

On Not Finding Frost's Grave in the Dark. Bruce Weigl. VisFro

On Not Flying to Hawaii. Alison Luterman. P180

On Not Shoplifting Louise Bogan's *The Blue Estuaries*. Julia Alvarez. WaAnP

On Nursing. Jenny Factor. PoChi

On Observing a Large Red-Streak Apple. Philip Freneau. NAAL-3

On ocean's long reach, on parables of God? (LL) Spider, The. Richard Eberhart. NoAM; PoA 2002

On, Off, Over. Richard Price. EdScPo

On old Cold Crendon's windy tops. John Masefield. *Fr.* Reynard the Fox.

On Old River Mountain. Fall River Song. Li Po. CrYelRi, *tr. by* Sam Hamill

On Old Zhang's Pine Tree. Sung Chih-Wen. CCL1, *tr. by* Stephen Owen

On Oliver Goldsmith. David Garrick. OxBEV

On, on to the darkest continent. Dedicated to Dr. W. H. Sheppard. Maggie Pogue Johnson. CBWP-4

On one fix'd point all nature moves. On the Uniformity and Perfection of Nature. Philip Freneau. TCAPo

On one of my afternoon walks I was struck—as if hated—from behind. As Like As Not. Fanny Howe. AFaM

On one side the hedge, on the other the brook:. Common Path, The. Glyn Jones. AngWePo

On one summer's day, sun was shining fine. Bill Bailey, Won't You Please Come Home. Hughie Cannon. NAAPv.2

On One Who Died Discovering Her Kindness. John, Duke of Buckingham and Normandy Sheffield. OBEV

On open downland we're as open as he—. Long-Man. Grace Nichols. Oth

On Opening. Mark Wunderlich. NAPBL

On Originality. Bill Manhire. HarvBoo

On other fields and other scenes the morn. Burnt Lands. GSo

On Our Crucified Lord, Naked and Bloody. Richard Crashaw. *See* Upon the Body of Our Blessed Lord, Naked and Bloody.

On our heads. Vertical. Michel Leiris. YaTCFP, *tr. by* Cole Swensen

On Our Last Evening on This Land. Mahmoud Darwish. PoetW *Fr.* Eleven Stars over Andalusia.

On our last evening on this land we chop our days. Mahmoud Darwish. PoetW *Fr.* Eleven Stars over Andalusia.

On our lone pathway bloomed no earthly hopes. Sarah Helen Whitman. NAAPv.1 *Fr.* Sonnets from the Series Relating to Edgar Allan Poe.

On our meat and on us all. (LL) Grace for a Child. Robert Herrick. NAEL-6v1; TFi

On our native soil, the martyr's drops of blood. *Unknown.* SLW, *tr. by* Marjolijn De Jager, Sayd Bahodin Majrouh and André Velter

On our way home from the factory. Teenagers. Ivan Teofilov. CSCBP, *tr. by* Georgi Belev and Lisa Sapinkopf

On our way home, leaving absolutely nothing behind us. (LL) Sunday in Great Tew. Peter McDonald. ModIr; PNI

On our way to school, in the ditch. In Memory of Sir Hiram Maxim (1840–1916). Hans Magnus Enzensberger. GTCP, *tr. by* Reinhold Grimm

On our wedding day we climbed the top. Manhattan Pastures. Sandra Hochman. YaYoPo

On Oxford. A Parody. John Keats. OxAEP-2

On pale afternoons. Autumnal. Rubén Darío. SpanPo, *tr. by* Anita Volland

On parent knees, a naked new-born child. Epigram. Sir William Jones. OBEV

On parquet. Simon Cutts. PoSol *Fr.* Pianostool Footnotes.

On Parting. Edward Coote Pinkney. APN-1; TCAPo

On Parting with a Friend. Mary Weston Fordham. CBWP-2

On Parting with the Buddhist Pilgrim Ling-Ch'ě. Liu Ch'ang-ch'ing. CCL1; WoPoe, *tr. by* Witter Bynner

On Passing the New Menin Gate. Siegfried Sassoon. NAEL-6v2; NAEL-7v2; NAMCP V.1; NoAM; NoP-4; NoP-5; OBMV; PoWW

On Peter Robinson. Francis, Lord Jeffrey Jeffery. NBLV

On Phoenix Tower in Chin-Ling. Li Po. NDACCP, *tr. by* David Hinton

On Pilgrimage. Czeslaw Milosz. AmFaPo; BeAl, *tr. by* the author and Robert Hass

On Playwright ("Playwright convict of public wrongs to men."). Ben Jonson. NoP-4; NoP-5

On Plaza Garibaldi. Nellie Wong. OpBo

On Poems. Rudolph Smith. OWABP

On Poetry. Franco Buffoni. ItPo, *tr. by* Gayle Ridinger

On Poetry. Yi Kyubo. CATKP, *tr. by* Kevin O'Rourke

On Poetry: a Rhapsody. Jonathan Swift. OBSV

On Ponkawtasset, since, we took our way. Henry David Thoreau. NCAP

On Portents. Robert Graves. HarvBoo

On prancing steed with nodding plume, I join their hunting sports. (LL) Tennyson's Poems. Josephine D. Henderson Heard. CBWP-4; SWaP

On Professor Coué. Charles Cuthbert Inge. OBCoV

On Pym. William Drummond of Hawthornden. NOSC

On quarry walls the spleenwort spreads. Rockferns. Norman Nicholson. MoBrPo

On Queen Caroline's Deathbed. Alexander Pope. NPeEn

On Rachmaninoff's Birthday #158. Frank O'Hara. AHA

On Raglan Road on an autumn day I met her first and knew. On Raglan Road. Patrick Kavanagh. BeAl

On Rainy Days. *Unknown.* ArBi

On rainy leaves / Glow. Ōshima Ryōta. ZenPo, *tr. by* Takashi Ikemoto and Lucien Stryk

On rainy Monday nights of an eternal November. (LL) Classic Ballroom Dances. Charles Simic. CAP-8; NAMCP V.2; WaAnP; WeW-3

On Reading a Recent Greek Poet. Bertolt Brecht. WoPoe, *tr. by* John Peck

On Reading Aloud My Early Poems. John Williams. WeW-3

On Reading an Archeological Article. Molara Ogundipe-Leslie. HBAPE

On Reading "God." G. K. Chesterton. OBCoV

On Reading Jules Renard's Diary. Miguel de Unamuno. RaW, *tr. by* Robert Bly and Hardie St. Martin

On Reading Namwha Sutra. Jungkwan Haean. BecRai, *tr. by* Kim Daljin, Kim Won-Chung and Christopher Merrill

On Reading Poems to a Senior Class at South High. David Chapman Berry. SoSe-8

On Reading Rumi. Mimi Khalvati. MFPA

On Reading *The Book of Odes*. Cao Bá Quát. AWTN, *tr. by* Huỳnh Sanh Thông

On Reading the Life of Haroun Er Reshid. Madison Cawein. APN-2

On reading the new physics—Creation and Cosmology. Cosi Fabian. HW

On Reading the Seas and Mountains Classic. Ch'ien T'ao and James Robert Hightower. ColAnChi

On Reading Virgil. Tedi López Mills. RMCMP, *tr. by* C. M. Mayo

On Receiving a Branch of Mezereon Which Flowered at Woodstock, December 1809. Mary Tighe. RWP

On Receiving My Letter of Termination. Yüan Hung-tao. ColAnChi, *tr. by* Jonathan Chaves

On Receiving News of the War. Isaac Rosenberg. HarvBoo; MoBrPo; OBWP; OxAEP-2; PoWW

On Re-entering the Lavender City. Conor O'Callaghan. NIrP

On Refusal of Aid between Nations. Dante Gabriel Rossetti. OxAEP-2

On Rembrant; Occasioned by His Picture of Jacob's Dream. Washington Allston. APN-1

On Removing Spiderweb. Les A. Murray. NAMCP V.2

On Reporting the Murder of a Young Prostitute. Judith Vollmer. LiTh

On Re-recording Mozart. Susan Wicks. OxBSo

On Richmond Park. Stephen Duck. OBGa *Fr.* On Richmond Park.

On Richmond Park. Stephen Duck.

   On Richmond Park. OBGa

On Roads. Ber Grin. Prolet, *tr. by* Amelia Glaser

On roadsides, / in fall fields. Goldenrod. Mary Oliver. NIL-7

On Rodin's "L'Illusion, Sœur d'Icare." Trumbull Stickney. APN-2

On Roofs of Terry Street. Douglas Dunn. NPeEn

On Rosh Hashanah, I didn't bow. Remembering Our Fathers. Chava Pinchas-Cohen. DTA, *tr. by* Miriyam Glazer

On Russian Poetry (1996-2000). Yana Tokareva. *tr. by* Daniel Weissbort

   2. CRWP, *tr. by* Daniel Weissbort

On S. John the Baptist. Thomas Stanley. ChIV-2

On Sabbath days, on circuit days. Gaelic Long Tunes, The. Les A. Murray. UpMys

On St. Honore Street. Tenebrae. Suze Baron. OGAHCP, *tr. by* Boadiba and Jack Hirschman

On Sale. Léon Damas. YaTCFP, *tr. by* Mary Ann Caws

On sale at every English station. Variation on a Theme of Baudelaire. David Ricks. PoA 2002

On Sanazar's being honoured with six hundred Duckets by the Clarissimi of Venice, for composing an Elegiack Hexastick of The City. A Satyre. Richard Lovelace. PBRV

On Sandro's Flora. Trumbull Stickney. APN-2

On Sarah Street on the South Side. Pittsburgh Poem. Jan Beatty. SweBea

On Saturday sailed from Bremen. Gerard Manley Hopkins. *Fr.* Wreck of the Deutschland, The.

On Saul and David. Francis Quarles. ChIV-1

On Scott's Poem "The Field of Waterloo." Thomas Erskine, 1st Baron Erskine. NBLV

On scuffed chaise-longues in Europe's drawing-rooms. Sobieski-Stuarts. Robert Crawford. EdScPo

On Seeing a Bird-Catcher. Eliza Cook. VWP

On Seeing a Dead Lamb. Dic Jones. BBMWP, *tr. by* Gillian Clarke

On Seeing a '57 Chevy Cruising 16th and O. Grace Bauer. RWB

On Seeing a Hair of Lucretia Borgia. Walter Savage Landor. NPeEn; PtR; WeW-3

On Seeing a Piece of Our Artillery Brought into Action. Wilfred Owen. GSo

On Seeing an Old Poet in the Café Royal. Sir John Betjeman. OxBEV; UV

On Seeing Man with a Guitar at the Moma. James Stewart. ICANM

On Seeing the Elgin Marbles. John Keats. CenSon; GSo; NAEL-6v2; NAEL-7v2; NIL-7; NIP-4

On Seeing the Picture of Æolus by Pelegrino Tibalbi, in the Institute at Bologna. Washington Allston. APN-1

On Seeing the Reformation Memorial in Geneva. Gyula Illyés. IQMS, *tr. by* John Wilkinson

On Seeing Wang Leave for the South. Liu Ch'ang-ch'ing. CCL1, *tr. by* Witter Bynner

On Sensibility: A Fragment. Isabella Lickbarrow. RWP

On Shakespear[e]. John Milton. BrAP; CABP; NAEL-6v1; NAEL-7v1; NoP-4; NoP-5; NOSC; PoPoPo

  (On Shakespeare.) CABP; NoP-4; PoPoPo

On shining heights where Thought with stately tread. Emerson. Henrietta Cordelia Ray. CBWP-3

On Shutting the Door. Lotte Kramer. Prnts

On Sidewalks, on Streetcorners, as Girls. Allison Joseph. IllVoic

On Silver Wings. Naomi Shemer. NRoS, *tr. by* Esther Raizen

On Sir G. B. his defeat. Alexander Brome. PBRV

On Sir Henry Ferrett, M.P. John Bingham Morton. OBCoV

On Sir J—— S—— Saying in a Sarcastic Manner, My Books Would Make Me Mad. Elizabeth Thomas. CABP

On Sir John Hill, M. D., Playwright. David Garrick. NBLV

On Sir John Vanbrugh [Architect]. Abel Evans. NPeEn

On Sir Robert Cotton the Antiquary. Thomas Randolph. NOSC

On Sir Walter Rawleigh at His Execution. *Unknown.* NOSC

On Sitting Down to Read *King Lear* Once Again. John Keats. CABP; GSo; NAEL-6v2; NAEL-7v2; NoP-4; NoP-5; NPBRoP; PoPoPo

On Sitting Down to Write, I Decide Instead to Go to Fred Herko's Concert. Diane Di Prima. PmAP

On Slavery. Maria Frances Cecelia Cowper. BrAP *Fr.* Task, The.

On Slow Learning. Scott Cairns. UpMys

On Solitude. Abraham Cowley. *See* Of Solitude.

On some bright morning filled with lovingkindness. (LL) Cups. Gwen Harwood. EmeKit; HarvBoo

On Some Elegies on a Lap-Dog. *Unknown.* DiBP

On some red day in a burst of fists on a new horizon! (LL) I Have Seen Black Hands. Richard Wright. APT-2; GPTC

On some rude fragment of the rocky shore. Written on the Sea Shore.— October, 1784. Charlotte Smith. CenSon; RWP

On Some Shells Found Inland. Trumbull Stickney. APN-2

On Some South African Novelists. Roy Campbell. MoBrPo; OBCoV; OxAEP-2; OxBEV

On Some Violets Planted in My Garden by a Friend. Elizabeth Cobbold. CenSon

On Something, that Walks Somewhere. Ben Jonson. BASC; NAEL-6v1; NAEL-7v1

On South Africa. Kim C. Lee. InTrad

On South Street, above a burning trashcan, a rasta. Reel Around the Shadow. James Harms. NAPBL

On Sparrows. Suji Kwock Kim. LegDan

On Speed, or How We Murdered Nostalgia. James Stewart. ICANM

On Spending Some Time at the Bai'an Pavilion. Hsieh Ling-yün. CCL1, *tr. by* John Frodsham

On Spies. Ben Jonson. FaBoVe; NoP-4; NoP-5; NPeEn; WoPoe

On Spring. Li Ch'ing-chao. NDACCP, *tr. by* Kenneth Rexroth

On Springfield Mountain there did dwell. Springfield Mountain. *Unknown.* TCAPo

On St. James's Park, as Lately Improved by His Majesty. Edmund Waller. BASC; NOSC; OBGa

On starry heights. Conflict of Convictions, The. Herman Melville. APN-2; CBCWP

On Stella's Birthday, 1718/1719. Jonathan Swift. NIP-4

On sticky summer Sunday afternoons. Elwood Collins: Summer of 1932. Dave Etter. IllVoic

On Stony Pierian Spurs. Osip Emilevich Mandelstam. TCRusP, *tr. by* John Glad

On Stopping Late in the Afternoon for Steamed Dumplings. Toi Derricotte. AFaM

On Striking His Wife's Dog. Sir John Harington. *See* To His Wife, for Striking Her Dog.

On such a day as this. Soundings. Paula Gunn Allen. HATNAP

On such a ground, musick 'twill be to die. (LL) On Christmas Day to My Heart. Clement Paman. ChRPo; NOSC; RSR

On such a morning as this. In Memory of Basil, Marquess of Dufferin and Ava. Sir John Betjeman. OBWP

On Such a Night As This. Marshall Barer. ReLy

On such a night, or such a night. Emily Dickinson. TCAPo

On such occasions. Letter to My Assailant. Suzanne Lummis. SUP

On summer afternoons I sit. La Vie C'est la Vie. Jessie Redmond Fauset. NAAPv.2

On summer nights I sleep naked. Letter of Recommendation. Yehuda Amichai. PoCho, *tr. by* the author and Ted Hughes

On summer nights the world. Late Hours. Lisel Mueller. GoPo

On Sunday in mid-winter, when wild iris. Foghorn, A. Brenda Hillman. FaoP

On Sunday mornin' I seek my Lord. Jine 'Em. *Unknown.* SSUS

On Sunday morning he'd be there. Disappeared, The. Iwan Llwyd. BBMWP, *tr. by* Grahame Davies

On Sunday the hawk fell on Bigging. Hawk, The. George Mackay Brown. BeAl; NoP-4; WaAnP

On Sundays, from upstairs, a grown man's voice. Light's Reading, The. Alan Williamson. PoSol

On Sundays I watch the hermits coming out of their holes. Studying the Language. Eiléan Ní Chuilleanáin. EmeKit; NPeEn

On Sundays in summer when I was a child. On Sundays in Summer. Kay Smith. Coast

On Sundays the children would go to check. Petrograd Side, The. Lev Vladimir Loseff. TCRusP, *tr. by* Henry Pickford

On Sundays when the weather's good, traditionally. Provincial Sundays. Ramón López Velarde. TCLAP, *tr. by* Julián Manríquez

On sunnier days a new coat of arms made the ocean high. Boats. Bernadette Mayer. FTOS

On sunny summer Sunday afternoons in Harlem. Passing. Langston Hughes. APSN; APT-2; OxBoAm; SAmP

On Sweet Coffee. Ábrahám Barcsay. IQMS, *tr. by* Thomas Kabdebo

On Sweet Coffee. Ábrahám Barcsay. IQMS, *tr. by* Peter Zollman

On Sweet Killen Hill. Tom MacIntyre. IrLP

  (Sweet Killen Hill.) PBCIP

On Swimming. Adam Zagajewski. P180, *tr. by* Clare Cavanagh

On Talladega Mountain in the likker raids. (LL) Kissie Lee. Margaret Abigail Walker. NALW; RaF

On tape and late at night. Late Night Radio. Geoff Page. BMAP

On Teaching the Young. Yvor Winters. APT-2; MakPoe; NoAM

On that day in autumn, when winter. Engraving, An. Aleksandr Petrovich Tkachenko. ItGoST, *tr. by* Maia Tekses

On that day she will hold love / in her hands. (LL) Jasmine. E. Ethelbert Miller. GT; OxAAAP

On that, even. Then your soul's the ship. (LL) Drew trips over his shadow by the pool. Gwyneth Lewis. NeBl; StAl

On that first day in history. First Day, The. Geriant Løvgreen. BBMWP, *tr. by* the author

On that great, that awful day,. Dies IrÆ. Thomas Babington Macaulay, 1st Baron Macaulay. ChIV-2

On that last night before we went. Alfred Tennyson. NAEL-6v2; NAEL-7v2 *Fr.* In Memoriam A. H. H.

On That Mountain. Rachel Hadas. ExTi

On that unfashionable gyre again. (LL) Gyres, The. William Butler Yeats. NAMCP V.1; NoAM

On the 3 of September, 1651. Katherine Philips. BASC; EMWP; PBRV; WaAnP

On the 5th of December 1791 Wolfgang Amadeus. Mozart in Heaven. Manuel Bandeira. TCLAP, *tr. by* Dudley Poore

On the 85th night of 19__ there were 280 days left in the year. My Broken Heart. Fanny Howe. ExTi

On the abandoned tennis court in the coconut grove. Trópico. Nicholas Christopher. PoCho

On the Adequacy of Landscape. Wallace Stevens. SAmP

On the advice of Praxilla. Aristophanes of Byzantium. WoPoe, *tr. by* Sam Hamill

On the Air. Julian May. RWPCtW

On the Amtrak from Boston to New York City. Sherman Alexie. NAMCP V.2; PoPoPo

On the Anniversary of Her Grace. Bruce Weigl. StAl

On the Anniversary of My Father's Death. Michael Lieberman. BloBone

On the Anniversary Of Your Death. Karen L. Mitchell. GT

On the Antiquity of Microbes. Strickland W. Gillilan. NBLV

On the Antiquity of Warfare. George Starbuck. AmWit

On the Aphorism "L'Amitié est l'Amour sans Ailes." Charlotte Smith. CABP; PEW

On the Approach of Autumn. Amelia Alderson Opie. CenSon

On the Armada That Battled Against England. Luis de Góngora y Argote. SpanPo, *tr. by* Ian Fletcher and Brian Soper

On the Asylum Road. Charlotte Mew. MoBrPo; VWP

On the Atchison, Topeka and the Santa Fe. Johnny Mercer. ReLy

On the avenue the faces change each day. Hope. F. D. Reeve. PoA 2002

On the Babel-Builders. Francis Quarles. ChIV-1

On the Back of a Photograph. János Pilinszky. PoSu; StAl, *tr. by* Peter Jay

On the back trails, in sun glasses. Kenyatta Listening to Mozart. Imamu Amiri Baraka. PmAP

On the balcony. Tomas Tranströmer. WoBe *Fr.* Haiku.

On the balcony of the tower. Exile in Japan. Su Man-shu. BLT, *tr. by* Kenneth Rexroth

On the bald street breaks the blank day. (LL) Alfred Tennyson. BrAP; HeIP-4; InoFa; NAEL-6v2; NAEL-7v2; NAWM-7v2; NoP-5; NPeEn; OxBEV; SoSe-8; WaAnP *Fr.* In Memoriam A. H. H.

On the Bank of a Stream by Taedun Temple. Choeui Eusoon. BecRai, *tr. by* Kim Daljin, Kim Won-Chung and Christopher Merrill

On the banks of her butterfly pond. Fishing Among the Learned. Nikky Finney. SpirF

On the Banks of the Duero. Antonio Machado Ruiz. STV, *tr. by* John Frederick Nims

On the banks of Tywi river there's a rainbow of one shade. Great Glasshouse at the National Botanic Garden of Wales. Tudur Dylan Jones. BBMWP, *tr. by* Elin ap Hywel

On the Baptized Ethiopian. Richard Crashaw. ChIV-2; NoP-4; NoP-5, *tr. by* Richard Crashaw

   (Acts 8; On the Baptized Æthiopian.) SacPr

On the Bare Roadway. Antonio Machado Ruiz. RaW, *tr. by* Charles Guenther

On the bare slope, wind in my hair. Invasion. Anna Enquist. TuT, *tr. by* Peter van de Kamp

On the bare veld where nothing ever grows. Veld Eclogue: The Pioneers, A. Roy Campbell. OBSV

On the Bath of Pallas. Callimachus. HePo *Fr.* Hymns.

On the Bay. Richard Watson Gilder. APN-2

On the Beach. Tom Clark. BodElec

On The Beach. John Corben. Spl

On the Beach. Jane Hirshfield. ExTi

On the Beach. Manuel Ulacia. RMCMP, *tr. by* Indran Amirthanayagam

On the Beach at Fontana. James Joyce. MoBrPo; OBMV; RaBo

On the Beach at Night. Walt Whitman. APN-1; MoAmPo; NoP-4; PtR; SAmP; TCAPo

On the Beach at Night Alone. Walt Whitman. APN-1

On the Beach One Day. Fraser Sutherland. Coast

On the beach there's a seafood place, simple, just a shack thrown up by survivors of the shipwreck. At Funchal. Tomas Tranströmer. MotU; WED, *tr. by* Robert Bly

On the Bearing of Waitresses. Rodney Jones. ReTh

On the bedscreen's folding panels, gold glimmers and fades. Gold Glimmers and Fades. Wen T'ing-yün. CCL1, *tr. by* Glen Baxter

On the Bell Frieze of a Roman Church. René Char. WoPoe, *tr. by* Mark Rudman

On the beryl-rimmed rebecs of Ruby. Lily Adair. Thomas Holley Chivers. APN-1

On the Bible. Thomas Traherne. ChIV-1

On the Bible. *Unknown.* NOSC

On the Bird Which Still Flew, Though Its Head Was Severed. Janus Pannonius. IQMS, *tr. by* Anthony Barrett

On the Birth of Good and Evil During the Long Winter of '28. Philip Levine. CAP-8

On the Birth of His Son. Su Tung-p'o. OBVE; WoPoe, *tr. by* Arthur Waley

On the Birth of Jesus. Andreas Gryphius. GePo, *tr. by* George C. Schoolfield

On the birthday of our most Pure Savior. Conversational Melody, A Good Verse, A. Nikolai Alekseievich Klyuyev. TCRusP, *tr. by* John Glad

On the Birth-Day of Queen Katherine. Anne Killigrew. EMWP

On the blackened ridge of Psara. Destruction of Psara, The. Dionysios Solomos. WoPoe, *tr. by* Edmund Keeley and Philip Sherrard

On the blank stones of the landing. (LL) Colossus, The. Sylvia Plath. BrAP; MoWP; NALW; NAMCP V.2; NoAM; NoP-4; NoP-5; VCAP; WoPoe

On the blue waves. Muso Soseki. EaWin, *tr. by* W. S. Merwin

On the bottom of the sky. Burning Shewolf. Vasco [*or* Vasko] Popa. PFTM-2; VCWP, *tr. by* Charles Simic

On the boundary of snow and melting. Georgy Vladimirovich Ivanov. TCRusP, *tr. by* Daniel Weissbort

On the breast of our deepest dreams, is that the mad pomegranate tree? (LL) Mad Pomegranate Tree, The. Odysseus Elytis. GPTC; WoPoe, *tr. by* Edmund Keeley and Philip Sherrard

On the bridges. Kenneth Rexroth. APSN *Fr.* Love Poems of Marichiko, The.

On the bridges, on the bridges; swooping and rising, whirling and circling. Song of the Soul of Chicago. Sherwood Anderson. MotU

On the bright road to Rome, beyond Mantua. Italian Eclogues. Derek Walcott. BAP-97

On the Buses with Dostoyevsky. Geoff Hattersley. NeBl

On the business of moving mica. Gu Cheng. WoBe *Fr.* Liquid Mercury.

On the butcher block table. Silver. Jill Bialosky. PoDa

On the cabin-roof I lie. Strenuous Life, The. Henry Sidgwick. OBCoV

On the Calligraphy of Black Chant. Ed Roberson. EGAG

On the Card[e]s, and Dice. Sir Walter Ralegh. ChIV-2

On the Carpet, Staring at Myself. Slavko Mihalic. PoSu, *tr. by* Peter Kastmiler

On the ceiling of the dim pavilion. End of the Affair, The. E. San Juan, Jr. ReBoTo

On the chalk cliff edge struggles the final field. Marginal Field, The. Stephen Spender. PoA 2002

On the Changes in France. János Batsányi. IQMS, *tr. by* Matthew Mead

On the Christmaswhite plains of the floured and flowering kitchen table. Bread of this World; Praises III, The. Thomas McGrath. RaBo

On the Cicada: In Prison. Lo Pin-wang. ColAnChi, *tr. by* Stephen Owen

On the city limits where I live. City Limits, The. Attila József. IQMS, *tr. by* Anton N. Nyerges

On the civic amenity landfill site. Mr and Mrs Scotland Are Dead. Kathleen Jamie. EmeKit; MoWP

On the Civilization of the Western Aboriginal Country. Philip Freneau. APN-1

On the Closing of Millom Ironworks. Norman Nicholson. RSaN

On the Coast near Sausalito. Robert Hass. OxBoAm

On the Coast of Coromandel. Sir Osbert Sitwell. MoBrPo

On the Cold Food Festival, Entertaining at the Southern Estate—the Guests Were Li Chiu-ho, Ma Nan-yeh, Wei Tung-kao, Li Hu-ch'uan, Huang K'ung-ts'un, Li Lung-t'ang, and Hu Hu-shan. Li K'ai-hsien. ColAnChi, *tr. by* Jonathan Chaves

On the Collar of Tiger. Jonathan Swift. DiBP

On the Concert. Trumbull Stickney. APN-2

On the Concord River. Henrietta Cordelia Ray. CBWP-3

On the Conditions of Place. Michael Anania. IllVoic

On the Conflagrations at Washington. Philip Freneau. AmWaPo; APN-1

On the Congo. Harry Edmund Martinson. WED, *tr. by* Robert Bly

On the Cork Packet, 1837. Thomas Baker. STuOW *Fr.* Steam Engine; or, The Power of the Flame, The.

On the Corner. Kit Robinson. FTOS

On the corner of plato and national army a man early. Of Deaths, Days, Futures, Nations. Jen Hofer. Eno

On the corner—116th and Lenox. Harlem Freeze Frame. Lebert Bethune. GT

On the Countess Dowager of Pembroke. William Browne. BASC; TFi

   (Epitaph on the Countess[e] Dowager of Pembroke.) OBEV

   (On the Death of Marie, Countess[e] of Pembroke.) NOSC

On the Countess of Dorchester. Charles, 6th Earl of Dorset Sackville. OBEV

   (Song: "Dorinda's sparkling wit, and eyes.") NOSC

On the cow shed. Basho. EH, *tr. by* Robert Hass

On the crest of the hills. Hezutsu Tosaku. EMJL, *tr. by* Burton Watson

On the Cross. Anna Kamienska. GI, *tr. by* David Curzon and Grażyna Drabik

On the crowded street I want to stop. Natasha Trethewey. RD *Fr.* Storyville Diary.

On the crowded subway. Bicentennial Anti-Poem for Italian-American Women. Daniela Gioseffi. FTtHH; UnSA

On the Dakota prairie an Indian girl was given many gifts. Calling Up the Spirit of the Lost Child. Maggie Penn. TWW

On the damp margin of the sea-beat shore. Anna Seward. CenSon

On the dark earth. (LL) Holy Longing, The. Johann Wolfgang von Goethe. ItP; RaBo; WoPoe, *tr. by* Robert Bly

On the darkening Green. (LL) William Blake. AmFaPo; NAEL-6v2; NAEL-7v2; NPBRoP; OxAEP-2 *Fr.* Songs of Innocence.

On the day a fourteen year old disappeared in Ojai, California. Use of Poetry, The. Michael Ryan. BodElec

On the day after her death. She Came to Say Farewell. Anna Swirszczynska [*or* Swir]. PoChi, *tr. by* Czeslaw Milosz and Leonard Nathan

On the day I was born. My Stars. Abraham ibn Ezra. WoPoe, *tr. by* Robert Mezey

On the day of a funeral. Mirrors. Marta Kornblith. MirDau, *tr. by* Roberta Gordenstein

On the day of his birth. Benjamín. Benjamin Alire Sáenz. TiP2

On the day of the explosion. Explosion, The. Philip Larkin. BrAP; EmeKit; InoFa; ItP; MakPoe; NAEL-6v2; NAEL-7v2; NAMCP V.2; NoAM; NoP-4; NoP-5; NPeEn; OxAEP-2; WeW-3

On the Day of Washing the Buddha in the Year Ting-wei (1607), I Dreamed That My Late Son Shih-ch'ü Was Holding a Book, and Appeared To Be Quite Happy. He Said That He Had Earned His Chin-shih Degree in the Underworld. After We Sighed and La. T'ang Hsien-tsu. ColAnChi, *tr. by* Jonathan Chaves

On the day of your scan, I make a soup. Soup, The. Peggy Penn. SweBea

On the day the poppies. Woodpecker. Sandra Alcosser. PfSP

On the day the sienna-skinned man. Killing Floor. Ai. NAMCP V.2; NoAM; WaAnP

On the day the war ended. Day the War Ended, The. Randall Swingler. RSaN

On the day the world ends. Czeslaw Milosz. FaoP; WoPoe *Fr.* Voices of Poor People.

On The Day They Buried My Mother. Miguel Piñero. PueRic

On the day when the Savoy. Projection. Langston Hughes. PFTM-1

On the day you were born the joyworkers warmed. Poem for a daughter who is already born. Ronny Someck. IrPoTo, *tr. by* Vivian Eden

On the dead oak tree bough. (LL) Gallows, The. Edward Thomas. MoBrPo; NAMCP V.1; NoAM

On the Death of a Colleague. Stephen Dunn. InoFa; P180

On the Death of a German Philosopher. Stevie Smith. OBCoV

On the Death of a New Born Child. Mei Yao Ch'en. WoPoe, *tr. by* Kenneth Rexroth

On the Death of a Nightingale. Thomas Randolph. BASC

On the Death of a Particular Friend. James Thomson. OBEV *Fr.* On the Death of Mr. William Aikman the Painter.

On the Death of a Young Gentleman. Phillis Wheatley. SacPr

On the Death of an Infant of Five Days Old, being a Beautiful but Abortive Birth. Elizabeth Boyd. CABP

On The Death of an Oxford Proctor. Thomas Vaughan. "When he did read how did we flock to hear." AngWePo

On the Death of Anne Brontë. Charlotte Brontë. VWP

On the Death of Dr [*or* Mr] Robert Levet [a Practiser in Physic]. Samuel Johnson. ChIV-2; NAEL-6v1; NAEL-7v1; NoP-4; NoP-5; NPeEn; OBEV; OxAEP-1; OxBEV; TFi; WaAnP

On the Death of Emily Jane Brontë. Charlotte Brontë. VWP

On the Death of Friends in Childhood. Donald Justice. ColAP; NAMCP V.2; OxBoAm

On the Death of His Son. Lewis Glyn Cothi. WoPoe, *tr. by* Gwyn Williams

On the Death of Joseph Rodman Drake. Fitz-Greene Halleck. APN-1

On The Death of King Matthias. *Unknown.* IQMS, *tr. by* Joseph Leftwich

On the Death of Ludwig Erhard. Hal Colebatch. NOBAu

On the Death of Marie, Countess[e] of Pembroke. William Browne. *See* On the Countess Dowager of Pembroke.

On the Death of Mistress Mary Prideaux. William Strode. NOSC

On the Death of Mr. Crashaw. Abraham Cowley. BASC

On the Death of Mr. Persall's Little Daughter, in the Beginning of the Spring, at Amsterdam. *Unknown.* NOSC

On the Death of Mr. Pope. *Unknown.* NPeEn

On the Death of Mr. Richard West. Thomas Gray. *See* Sonnet [on the Death of Mr. Richard West].

On the Death of Mr. William Aikman the Painter. James Thomson. On the Death of a Particular Friend. OBEV

On the Death of Mr. William Hervey [*or* Harvey]. Abraham Cowley. OBEV "It was a dismal and a fearful night." OxAEP-1

On the Death of Mrs. Bowes. Lady Mary Wortley Montagu. LW

On the Death of Mrs. Throckmorton's Bulfinch. William Cowper. BrAP

On the Death of Muriel Rukeyser. Billy Marshall-Stoneking. BMAP

On the Death of My Dear Friend and Play-Fellow Mrs. E. D. Having Dream'd the Night Before I Heard Thereof that I Had Lost a Pearl. Jane Barker. EMWP; PoBW

On the Death of My First and Dearest Child, Hector Philips. Katherine Philips. InoFa; NAEL-6v1; NAEL-7v1

On the Death of My Tomcat Murr. Vladislav Felitsianovich Khodasevich. TCRusP, *tr. by* Mary Jane White

On the Death of Nizar Qabbani. Mohja Kahf. PoArWo

On the death of philip whalen. Mark S. Kuhar. AmZen

On the Death of Priscilla Farmer. Charles Lloyd. NPBRoP

On the Death of Ronald Ryan. Bruce Dawe. BMAP

On the Death of Sir Philip Sidney. Henry Constable. OBEV (To Sir Philip Sidney's Soul.) NoSic

On the Death of the Duke of Clarence. Joseph Gwyer. "Albert Victor loved his mother." VerBaPo

On the Death of the Ferryman, Glaucus. Antiphilus. WoPoe, *tr. by* W. S. Merwin

On the Death of the Late Earl of Rochester. Aphra Behn. BASC; EMWP; NoP-4; NoP-5; WaAnP

On the Death of the Most Reverend Priest. Jinkag Haesim. BecRai, *tr. by* Kim Daljin, Kim Won-Chung and Christopher Merrill

On the Death of the Noble and Gentle Woman, Lady Joanna Kelley. Elizabeth Jane Leon. EMWP

On the Death of the Poet's Daughter Sato. Issa. WoPoe, *tr. by* Conrad Totman

On the Death of the Rev. Mr. George Whitefield [1770]. Phillis Wheatley. ColAP; NAAL-3; NAAL-5; NAAPv.1; SacPr; WaAnP

On the Death of William Linley, esq. William Lisle Bowles. OxBSo

On the Debt My Mother Owed to Sears Roebuck. Edward Dorn. TRP

On the Decipherment of "Linear B." Alfred Wellington Purdy. BrAP

On the deck of Patrick Lynch's boat I sat in woeful plight. County of Mayo, The. Thomas Flavell. OBEV, *tr. by* George Fox

On the Declaration of Joy. Fathi Abdullah. AnVo, *tr. by* Mohamed Enani

On the Departure of the Nightingale. Charlotte Smith. RWP; WoRP

On the desert, between pale mountains, our cries. Two Songs of Advent. Yvor Winters. APT-2; NAAPv.2

On the Desire to Be Precise. Natan Zach. NRoS, *tr. by* Esther Raizen

On the Detraction Which Followed upon My Writing Certain Treatises ("Book was writ[t] of late called [*or* call'd] *Tetrachordon*, A.") John Milton. OxBSo

On the Detraction Which Followed upon My Writing Certain Treatises ("I did but prompt the age to quit their [*or* thir] clogs.") John Milton. NoP-4 (I Did but Prompt the Age.) NoP-5 (Sonnet 12: On the Detraction Which Followed upon My Writing Certain Treatises.) BASC

On the Doctors' Telling Him that till He Left off Making Verses He Was Not Fit to be Discharged. James Carkesse. NOSC

On the dream sidewalk. Denise Levertov. UpMys *Fr.* Embracing the Multipede.

On the Dress of the Hungarians. József Gvadányi. IQMS *Fr.* Village Notary's Journey to Buda, A.

On the Duke of Buckingham, Slain by Felton, the 23rd August, 1628. Owen Felltham [*or* Feltham]. NOSC

On the Dunes. Sara Teasdale. TCAPo

On the Eastern Front. Georg Trakl. WED, *tr. by* Robert Bly

On the eastern seacoast lives a sick man. Inscribed on a Painting by Myself. Ni Tsan. ColAnChi, *tr. by* Jonathan Chaves

On the Eastern Way at the city of Lo-yang. Song. Sung Tzu-hou. WoPoe, *tr. by* Arthur Waley

On the edge. (LL) Paean to Place. Lorine Niedecker. APSN; APT-2; FTOS

On the edge of the road. (LL) Old Cracked Tune, An. Stanley Kunitz. LoL; TaR

On the Edition of Mr. Pope's Works with a Commentary and Notes. Thomas Edwards. OxBSo

On the eerily StarWars campus. Anthelmintic. Chris O. Cook. FreRad

On the electrified ocean. Evening Scene, An. Zhao Zhenkai. VCWP, *tr. by* Chen Maiping and Bonnie S. McDougall

On the Elk, Unwitnessed. Alan Dugan. YaYoPo

On the Elvis Mailing List. Neal Bowers. AllShUp; SwNoth

On the Emigration to America [and Peopling the Western Country]. Philip Freneau. ColAP; NAAL-3; NAAL-5; NAAPv.1; OxBoAm

On The Empress's Mind. John Ashbery. RACG

On the empty mountain, seeing no one. Deer Enclosure. Wang Wei. ColAnChi, *tr. by* Richard W. Bodman and Victor H. Mair

On the Entrance of the Castle Bridge. Simon Dach. GePo, *tr. by* George C. Schoolfield

On the Euthanasia of a Pet Dog. Elizabeth Smither. BeAl

On the Eve of Aphrodite. Tracy Philpot. IAoNAP

On the Eve of His Execution. Prince Otsu. WoPoe,

On the Eve of His Execution. Chidiock Tichborne. *See* Tichborne's Elegy.

On the Eve of Our Mutually Assured Destruction. C. D. Wright. AtGh

On the Eve of the Feast of the Immaculate Conception: 1942. Robert Lowell. PWW2

On the eve of the Festival of The Potato Harvest. Dionysus. Genrik Veniaminovich Sapgir. ItGoST, *tr. by* J. Kates

On the Eve of the Warsaw Uprising. Robin Becker. TaR

On the eve of your tranfusion. Anemia. Rosamond Zimmerman. PfS

On the Evening of a Wedding. Graham Foust. IIR

On the everlasting / snow. (LL) Notes from a Nonexistent Himalayan Expedition. Wisława Szymborska. AmFaPo; ItP, *tr. by* Stanislaw Barańczak and Clare Cavanagh

On the Expected General Rising of the French Nation in 1792. Anna Laetitia Barbauld. CABP; NPBRoP

On the Extinction of the Venetian Republic. William Wordsworth. NPBRoP; OBEV

On the Facets: The Flashing. Coral Bracho. PFTM-2, *tr. by* Thomas Hoeksema

On the fake snowbank. Penguins. Stefan Tsanev. CSCBP, *tr. by* Georgi Belev and Lisa Sapinkopf

On the Famous Voyage. Ben Jonson.
 "By this time had they reached the Stygian pool." NOSC

On the Far Edge of Kilmer. Gerald Stern. LoL

On the Farm. Ronald Stuart Thomas. NoP-4; NoP-5; NPeEn; OxBEV; TCAWP

On the Farther Wall, Marc Chagall. Phyllis McGinley. OBSV *Fr.* Spectator's Guide to Contemporary Art.

On the Fatal Day January 30, 1648. Thomas Fairfax, Baron Fairfax of Cameron. NOSC

On the Feast of Saint John the Evangelist. David Brendon Hopes. UpMys

On the Ferris Wheel rising to the full moon. No Way Back to the Past. Allen Ginsberg. BodElec

On the Ferry, Toward Patras. Emily Grosholz. RA

On the 15th day of November in the year of the motorcar. Ted Berrigan. NYP2 *Fr.* Sonnets, The.

On the fifth of September. Candle's Fly, The. Moses Glyn Jones. BBMWP, *tr. by* Mike Jenkins

On the first cool day in half a year. Sky. Richard Katrovas. LTA

On the first day. Pledge of Allegiance. Carl Hancock Rux. SpirFl

On the first day, eighth moon. Journey North, The. Tu Fu [*or* Du Fu]. CrYelRi, *tr. by* Sam Hamill

On the first day, gazing idly about him. Adam. Yevgeny Mikhailovich Vinokurov. TCRusP, *tr. by* Daniel Weissbort

On the first day of Autumn. Autumn. Michael Schein. ArBi

On the first day when light came through the curtain. Widow. William Stafford. CAP-8

On the first good day of yard work. Alchemy. Alan Michael Parker. AmPoNex

On the first of January. Clare Pollard. NeBl *Fr.* Friday Night at the End of a Millennium, A.

On the first of May. Mountain Greenery. Lorenz Hart. ReLy

On the first of the Feast of Feasts. Epilogue. Robert Browning. ChIV-2

On the first page of my dreambook. Empire of Dreams. Charles Simic. BLT; VCAP

On the five thousandth evening of our love. Iwan Goll. GTCP, *tr. by* Reinhold Grimm

On the flat road a man at last appears. Light Snow-Fall after Frost, A. Thomas Hardy. WaAnP

On the fleet streams, the Sun, that late arose. Anna Seward. WoRP *Fr.* Sonnets.

On the Flightiness of Thought. *Unknown.* IrV, *tr. by* Kuno Meyer

On the Flooding of Prague, which Arose from Continuous Rain in the Year 1596. Elizabeth Jane Leon. EMWP

On the Fly-Leaf of Pound's Cantos. Basil Bunting. HarvBoo; NAMCP V.1; NoAM

On the forest path. Asagumori. Kenneth Rexroth. GifTon

On the fourteenth day of April. Dust Storm Disaster. Woody Guthrie. APT-2

On the fourth day of his fasting. Henry Wadsworth Longfellow. TCAPo *Fr.* Song of Hiawatha, The.

On the fourth day the phone wires talked. I-5 Incident. Juan Delgado. AmPoNex; GeoHom

On the fourth of July. Nightfire. Brad Daugherty. BeDoSh

On the Fourth of July in Sitka, 1982. Ishmael Reed. FaoP

On the Fragile Labyrinth. José Emilio Pacheco. STV, *tr. by* John Frederick Nims

On the Fringe. Amina Saïd. HAWP, *tr. by* Eric Sellin

On the fringe of nothingness. On the Fringe. Amina Saïd. HAWP, *tr. by* Eric Sellin

On the front page of the Chronicle. New Mr Barnsley Something, The. Geoff Hattersley. NeBl

On the Frozen Lake. William Wordsworth. WoPoe *Fr.* Prelude, The; Growth of a Poet's Mind [1805 version].

On the Fruit-Providing Autumn Season. Catharina Regina von Greiffenberg. WPoS, *tr. by* Michael Hamburger

On the Funeral of Dr. Livingston. Joseph Gwyer.
 "Heap on more grass was his request." VerBaPo

On the galloping cusp of the new now. Mark S. Kuhar. AmZen

On the Game. Linda France.
 What I Know Now. MFPA

On the Glittering Beaches. Tracey Herd. MFPA

On the Good Ship Lollipop. Sidney Clare. ReLy

On The Gospel. Francis Quarles. ChIV-2

On the Grass. Paul Verlaine. SxFrPo, *tr. by* Martin Sorrell

On the grass airfield, a wife. Private Airplane. Chase Twichell. ExTi

On the Grasshopper and [the] Cricket. John Keats. CenSon; NIL-7; NIP-4; OxAEP-2

On the grave-posts of the village. (LL) Henry Wadsworth Longfellow. APN-1; NAAPv.1 *Fr.* Song of Hiawatha, The.

On the Great Frost (1634). William Cartwright. NOSC

On the Great Plains in March. Stark Weather. William Trowbridge. LiTh

On the Great Wall. Rudyard Kipling. *Fr.* Puck of Pook's Hill.

On the Great Western Canal of the State of New York. Philip Freneau. APN-1

On the green / with lignum vitae balls and ivory markers. Bowls. Marianne Moore. APT-1

On the ground, ruining the harvest. (LL) Sudden Appearance of a Monster at a Window. Lawrence Raab. BLT; SUP

On the Group of the Three Angels Before the Tent of Abraham, by Raffaelle, in the Vatican. Washington Allston. APN-1

 (On the Group of the Three Angels Before the Tent of Abraham, by Rafaelle, in the Vatican.) GS

On the Growth of Hair in Middle Age. Kjell Hjern. PML, *tr. by* Leif Sjöberg and William Jay Smith

On the Guincho. Emyr Humphreys. BBMWP, *tr. by* Elin ap Hywel

On the half-finished bridge. (LL) First snow. Basho. EH; NIL-7, *tr. by* Robert Hass

On the Hall of Precious Virtue. Yang Shih-ch'i. ColAnChi, *tr. by* Jonathan Chaves

On the harbor freeway. Dog Suicide. Wanda Coleman. GeoHom

On the hard road of life and death. Requiem for the Dead Sister. Wŏlmyŏng, Master. CATKP; WoPoe, *tr. by* Peter H. Lee

On the Head of a Pin. Thomas McGrath. GifTon

On the Headland. Bayard Taylor. CAGL

On the Heart's Beginning to Cloud the Mind. Robert Frost. GM

On the hill he had climbed all winter. Hunger of the Lemur, The. Matthew Rohrer. NeAmPo

On the hillside. Bilberries. Gerda Mayer. Spl

On the hillside, and after a while I nodded back to him. (LL) Crucifixion. Hayden Carruth. BodElec; PLBUT

On the Holy Scriptures. Francis Quarles. ChIV-2

On the Home Front—1942. Edwin Denby. OxBoAm

On the Hon. George Nathaniel Curzon, Commoner of Balliol. *Various authors.* OBCoV *Fr.* Balliol Rhymes.

On the horizon where the sun descends. Yew of Llanddeiniolen, The. W. J. Gruffydd. BBMWP, *tr. by* Joseph P. Clancy

On the Hudson. Nokhem Vaysman. Prolet
 "Sail me." Prolet, *tr. by* Amelia Glaser

On the Ice. Gordon Rodgers. Coast

On the idle hill of summer. A. E. Housman. FaBoWar; MoBrPo; OBWP *Fr.* Shropshire Lad, A.

On the Imprint of the First English Edition of "The Works of Max Beerbohm." Max Beerbohm. OBCoV

On the Inclusion of Miniature Dinosaurs in Breakfast Cereal Boxes. John Updike. OBCoV

On the Ineffable Inspiration of the Holy Spirit. Catharina Regina von Greiffenberg. WoPoe; WPoS, *tr. by* Michael Hamburger

On the Inhumanity of the Slave Trade. Ann Yearsley.
 Death of Luco. NPBRoP

On the inner walls. (LL) Stone. Charles Simic. CAP-8; ChAP

On the Inscription Over the Head of Christ on the Cross. Henry Colman. ChIV-2

On the iris / Kite's. Buson. ZenPo, *tr. by* Takashi Ikemoto and Lucien Stryk

On the Irish Club. Jonathan Swift. OBSV

On the Island. Dennis Brutus. AF

On the Island. David Helwig.
 "Sudden risk of birds, A." Coast

On the Island. Gerald Stern. WaAnP

On the Island of the Spirits of the Dead. Two Sisters, The. *Aborigine Oral Tradition.* NOBAu, *tr. by* Manoowa

On the Islands of All Winds. Aimé Césaire. VCWP

On the Job. Ira Sadoff. PfSP

On the kitchen wall a flash. World Outside, The. Denise Levertov. TRP

On the Lady Arabella.　Richard Corbet.　NOSC

On the Lake.　Victoria Mary Sackville-West.　OBMV

On the land we made.　Work to Be Done.　Sam Cornish.　BtF

On the Landing of William III [or A Hymn of Praise for Three Great Salvations].　Isaac Watts.　STuOW

On the large highway of the awful air that flows.　Fish-Hawk, The.　John Hall Wheelock.　APT-1

On the last day.　Secret of Fire.　Abdul Wahab Al-Bayati.　PML, tr. by Bassam Kahlil Frangieh

On the Last Day of the World.　Sherod Santos.　GeoHom

On the last day of the year we have so much to be thankful for.　Last Day of the Year; or, New Year's Eve, The.　Mrs. Henry Linden.　CBWP-4

On the last words of Trumpeldor.　From the Songs of the Land of Zion and Jerusalem.　Yehuda Amichai.　NRoS, tr. by Esther Raizen

On the Late Improvements at Nuneham, the Seat of the Earl of Harcourt.　William Whitehead.　OBGa

On the Late Massacre [or Massacher] in Piedmont [or Piemont].　John Milton.　BrAP; CABP; GSo; HeIP-4; NAEL-6v1; NIL-7; NoP-4; NoP-5; NPeEn; OBWP; OxBEV; OxBSo; PoPoPo; TFi; TRP; WaAnP; WeW-3

(Sonnet 18 [On the Late Massacre in Piedmont].)　BASC

On the late shift, front desk.　Transient Hotel Sky at the Hour of Sleep.　Martín Espada.　ReTh

On the Lawn at the Drug Rehab Center.　Jane Mead.　LaCa

On the Ledge.　Louis Simpson.　PWW2

On the ledge today, the circus.　Clinic Day.　Diana Fitzgerald Bryden.　OpeFie

On the length and breadth of the marvellous marshes of Glynn.　(LL)　Sidney Lanier.　NAAPv.1; NoP-5 Fr. Hymns of the Marshes.

On the Life of Man.　Francis Quarles.　ChIV-2

On the Life of Man.　Sir Walter Ralegh. See What Is Our Life?

On the Line.　Emmy Bridgwater.　SurWo

On the Line.　Ruth Padel.　MFPA; NeBrP

On the lonely mountain.　Pei Di and Wang Wei.　CCL1 Fr. Wheel River.

On the long shore, lit by the moon.　Goose Fish, The.　Howard Nemerov.　HeIP-4; NAMCP V.2; NIL-7; NIP-4; NoAM; NoP-4; NoP-5

On the look of Death.　(LL)　There's a certain Slant of light.　Emily Dickinson.　APN-2; BrAP; ColAP; HeIP-4; MoAmPo; NAAL-3; NAAL-5; NAAPv.1; NALW; NAMCP V.1; NAWM-7v2; NCAP; NoAM; NoP-4; NoP-5; OxBoAm; PoPoPo; SAmP; SoSe-8; TCAPo; TFi

On the Lord Gen[eral] Fairfax at the Siege of Colchester.　John Milton.　NOSC

(Sonnet 15 [On the Lord General Fairfax at the Siege of Colchester].)　BASC

On the Loss of Friends.　James F. Montgomery.　SacPr

On the Love of Two Boys.　Angelo Poliziano.　CAGL Fr. Greek Epigrams.

On the low margin of a murmuring stream.　Visions Appear to her in a Dream.　Mary Robinson.　CenSon; RWP

On the low margin of a murmuring stream.　Mary Robinson.　NPBRoP Fr. Sappho and Phaon.

On the Luxembourg Gallery.　Washington Allston.　APN-1

On [or Of] the Manner of Addressing Clouds.　Wallace Stevens.　PoA 2002

On the maple wood we placed our elbows.　Wrist-wrestling father.　Orval Lund.　GoPo

On the Marriage at Cana.　Rainer Maria Rilke.　GI

On the Marriage of the King.　Thomas, the Younger Warton.

Of George, and Property.　STuOW

On the Marshy Pastures.　Georg Trakl.　WED, tr. by Robert Bly

On the Medusa of Leonardo da Vinci in the Florentine Gallery.　Percy Bysshe Shelley.　GS

On the Memorial building's.　Under Cancer.　John Hollander.　NAMCP V.2

On the Metamorphoses Brought About By Emotion: The Rebellion of the Eyes.　Andrey Andreievich Voznesensky.　PFTM-2, tr. by Anselm Hollo

On the metro the man across.　Here's Looking at You Francis Bacon.　Joan Retallack.　FTOS

On the Mississippi.　James Applewhite.　IaFF

On the Mississippi.　Hamlin Garland.　APN-2

On the moon's round cay.　Lullaby.　Unknown.　SonAtl, tr. by S. L. Lee, Wendy North and Colin Wilberts

On the Morning of Christ's Nativity.　John Milton.　BASC; ChrPo; NAEL-6v1; NAEL-7v1; NoP-4; NoP-5; PBRV; WaAnP

Hymn on the Morning of Christ's Nativity.　OBEV

"It was the winter wild[e]."　NPeEn; OxBEV

On the morning of my would be wedding.　My epithalamion.　Lee Ann Brown.　VaPo

On the morning of the funeral.　Winston Churchill.　David Scott.　NLP

On the Motor Bus.　Alfred Denis Godley.　NBLV

On the Mountain.　Chunbong Manwoo.　BecRai, tr. by Kim Daljin, Kim Won-Chung and Christopher Merrill

On the mountain.　Kenneth Rexroth.　NAAPv.2 Fr. Love Poems of Marichiko, The.

On the Mountain.　Wang Wei.　CCL1, tr. by Jerome P. Seaton

On the mountain, Epicydes the hunter seeks.　Callimachus.　HePo, tr. by Barbara Hughes Fowler

On the mountain, in the old oak's domain.　Isolation.　Alphonse Marie Louis de Lamartine.　SxFrPo, tr. by A. M. and E. H. Blackmore

On the Mountain of Boiled Rice I met Tu Fu.　To Tu Fu.　Li Po.　TAL

On the Move.　Thom Gunn.　CalPo; NoP-4; NoP-5; OxAEP-2; TRP; WaAnP

On the Murder of an Ice Cream Man.　Hayan Charara.　AmPoNex

On the Murder of Lieutenant José del Castillo by the Falangist Bravo Martinez, July 12, 1936.　Philip Levine.　AmWaPo; WaAnP

On the narrow path.　Pei Di and Wang Wei.　CCL1 Fr. Wheel River.

On the Nature of Desire.　David Lehman.　PfSP

On the Nature of the Iconic.　Gustaf Sobin.　WoBe

On the New Forcers of Conscience Under the Long Parliament.　John Milton.　BASC; NAEL-6v1; NOSC; PBRV

On The New Inn: Ode. To Himself.　Ben Jonson.　BASC

On the New Year.　Christopher Okigbo.　PoetW

On the night beach, quiet beside the blue.　Morning.　Glyn Jones.　AngWePo

On the night of the Belgian surrender the moon rose.　Moon and the Night and the Men, The.　John Berryman.　GPTC; PWW2; VCAP

On the Night of the Day the Worlds Ends.　Lucile Adler.　ICANM

On the night of the execution.　Execution, The.　Alden Nowlan.　BrAP; StAl

On the night road from El Rama the cows.　Second Poem from Nicaragua Libre: War Zone.　June Jordan.　NoAM

On the ninth, we entered the country on iron horse rails.　Spirit of '76, The.　Friederike Mayröcker.　PFTM-2, tr. by Anselm Hollo

On the Numerous Access of the English to Wait upon the King in Flanders.　Katherine Philips.　BASC; NOSC

On the Occasion of One Dr. Fell's Challenge to Translate an Epigram of Matrial's.　Martial. See Doctor Fell.

On the Occurrence of a Spell of Arctic Weather in May, 1858.　Paul Hamilton Hayne.　APN-2

On the offering mound, a dead roe.　Unknown.　ColAnChi Fr. Classic of Odes.

On the old plum tree.　Ransetsu.　SoOfWa, tr. by Sam Hamill

On the one side—a leg thin and short.　Complicated and Innovative Orthopedic Surgery.　Ramy Ditzanny.　NRoS, tr. by Esther Raizen

On the one: the same.　Hold it Steady.　Honorée Fanonne Jeffers.　BRtP

On the Oregon Coast.　Robert Bly.　BodElec

On the Oregon Coast.　Galway Kinnell.　NAMCP V.2; NoAM

On the Origin of Evil.　John Byrom.　NPeEn

On the Origin of the Contrary.　Miroslav Holub.　VCWP, tr. by Stuart Friebert

On the other hand in other words.　Robert Kelly.　WhBo Fr. Flowers of Unceasing Coincidence, The.

On the Other Side.　Czeslaw Milosz.　PoSu, tr. by Jan Darowski

On the Other Side.　Benin Williams.　BRtP

On the other side of a mirror there's an inverse world, where the insane go sane.　Antimatter.　Russell Edson.　OxBoAm

On the other side of the border.　Kith.　Marion Lomax.　NeBl

On the Other Side of the Door.　Jeff Moss.　TWF

On the other side of the moon.　Land Where the Good Songs Go, The.　P. G. Wodehouse.　ReLy

On the other side of the sliding glass door.　On the Other Side.　Joanne Kyger.　WANABP

On the Otis Redding Bridge.　Judson Mitcham.　SwNoth

On the Oxford Book of Victorian Verse.　Hugh MacDiarmid.　MoBrPo

On the Pains of Translating Miklós Radnóti.　Frederick Turner.　RA

On the Painting of the Sistine Chapel.　Michelangelo Buonarroti.　WoPoe,

On the palm of her hand the others drew.　Cage.　Salman Masalha.　PML, tr. by Vivian Eden

On the phoenix terrace, phoenix at play.　Ascend the Phoenix Terrace.　Li Po.　ChinPo, tr. by Ye Weilian [or Yeh Wei-lien or Wai-lim Yip]

On the phonograph, the voice.　Reunion.　Carolyn Forché.　NAMCP V.2; NoAM

On the Picture of a Child.　Henrietta Cordelia Ray.　CBWP-3

On the Pier.　Brenda Hillman.　PoA 2002

On the Plain of Kulikovo.　Aleksandr Aleksandrovich Blok.　TCRusP, tr. by Denis Johnson and Kathy Lewis

On the Ploughman [or Plough-Man].　Francis Quarles.　NOSC; SacPr

On the Poet, Arthur O'Shaughnessy—.　Dante Gabriel Rossetti.　OBCoV

On the Poet Coming of Age.　Lorna Dee Cervantes.　TouFir

On the poop-deck my sad heart drips.　Cheated Heart.　Arthur Rimbaud.　SxFrPo, tr. by Martin Sorrell

On the Porch at the Frost Place, Franconia, NH.　William Matthews.　VisFro

On the Porch—Denton, Texas.　Martha Elizabeth.　TiP2

On the power of a great, silly grin.　(LL)　Mexicans Begin Jogging.　Gary Soto.　CAP-8; LTA; PML; RWB

On the Prince's Death, to the King.　Sir Robert Aytoun.　NOSC

On the Projected Kendal and Windermere Railway.　William Wordsworth.　CenSon

On the Prospect of Planting Arts and Learning in America.   George Berkeley.   OxBEV

(Verses on the Prospect of Planting Arts and Learning in America.)   ASA; FaBoA

On the quays of Papeete, the dawlding white-ducked colonists.   Derek Walcott.   NoAM *Fr.* Midsummer.

On the Queen's Return from the Low Countries.   William Cartwright.   OBEV

On the Rails.   Reed Bye.   AHA

On the Railway Platform.   Randall Jarrell.   GM

On the raked sand, besides a no-smoking sign.   Kyoto 1—Kinkaku-ji.   William Kistler.   WhBo

On the Rapid Extension of the Suburbs.   John Thelwall.   CenSon

On the rapids of the St. Lawrence.   Henrietta Cordelia Ray.   CBWP-3

On the Readiness for Sacrifice.   Reuven ben Yoseph.   NRoS, *tr. by* Esther Raizen

On the Receipt of My Mother's Picture out of Norfolk, the Gift of My Cousin Ann Bodham.   William Cowper.   OxAEP-1

On The Reedy Lake.   János Vajda.   IQMS, *tr. by* Jean Overton Fuller

On the reef of Norman's Woe! (LL)   Wreck of the Hesperus, The.   Henry Wadsworth Longfellow.   APN-1; BRP; NAAPv.1; OBNV; TCAPo; TreFP

On the Relative Merit of Friend and Foe, Being Dead.   Donald Thompson.   FaBoWar

On the Religion of Nature.   Philip Freneau.   NAAL-3; NAAL-5

On the Removal of the Fascist American Right from Power.   Etheridge Knight.   BodElec

On the restaurant terrace, we're face to face.   Ordinary Song, An.   Chairil Anwar.   PoetW, *tr. by* Burton Raffel

On [*or Of*] the Resurrection of Christ.   William Dunbar.   ChIV-2

On the Returne of King Charles 2nd.   Ann Lee.   EMWP

On the Revolution.   Robert Montgomery.   STuOW *Fr.* Omnipresence of the Deity, The.

On the River.   Tu Fu [*or Du Fu*].   CCL1, *tr. by* Burton Watson

On the river, every day these heavy rains.   On the River.   Tu Fu [*or Du Fu*].   CCL1, *tr. by* Burton Watson

On the River on a Spring Day.   Yi Illo.   CATKP, *tr. by* Peter H. Lee

On the riverbanks farmers threw.   Josée Lapeyrère.   SCFWP *Fr.* Apples.

On the Road.   Clark Coolidge.   NYP2

On the Road.   Prodigal Son, The.   Leah Goldberg.   GI, *tr. by* Robert Friend

On the Road.   Ninon Neckar.   ArBi

On the Road: A Spring Day at Ling-Feng.   Ching An.   CSKM, *tr. by* Jerome P. Seaton

On the road between Spanish-Town.   West Indian Primer.   Elizabeth Alexander.   NIL-7

On the Road Home.   C. G. Hanzlicek.   GeoHom

On the road, the mountains.   My Fifty-Plus Years Celebrate Spring.   Luis Omar Salinas.   GeoHom

On the road through. (LL)   Celebration: "How wonderful, Tomasito!"   Thomas McGrath.   GifTon; PoChi

On the Road to Damascus, Maryland.   Enid Dame.   UnSA

On the road to Damascus, Maryland.   On the Road to Damascus, Maryland.   Enid Dame.   UnSA

On the Road to Denver in a Coat and Tie, I Think of My Old Friend Master Red Pine and the Example He Inspires.   Mike O'Connor.   WANABP

On the Road to Erewhon.   Allen Curnow.   HarvBoo

On the road to Hallucination.   On a Certain Field in Auvers.   John Haines.   OPRER

On the Road to Homer Noble Farm.   Kim Waller.   VisFro

On the Road to San Romano.   André Breton.   PFTM-1

On the road to the bay was a lake of rushes.   Bay, The.   James Keir Baxter.   BrAP; HarvBoo; StAl

On the Road to the Sea.   Charlotte Mew.   PoBW

On the Road to T'ien-t'ai.   Yuan Mei.   GifTon, *tr. by* Jerome P. Seaton

On the Road to Woodlawn.   Theodore Roethke.   InoFa

On the road we met a blackman.   Twenty-Six Ways of Looking at a Blackman.   Raymond R. Patterson.   ESEAA

On the roadside.   Tanka.   Ishikawa Takuboku.   CAoMJL1, *tr. by* Makoto Ueda

On the rock / Waves can't reach.   Tantan.   ZenPo, *tr. by* Takashi Ikemoto and Lucien Stryk

On the rocks of my mind's country. (LL)   Back?   T. Harri Jones.   AngWePo; TCAWP

On the rocky slope, blossoming.   Hoin.   ZenPo, *tr. by* Takashi Ikemoto and Lucien Stryk

On the ruins of Synagogue Cheva Bikur, built in 1887.   Monarchs of Parque Tranquilidad.   Robin Becker.   UrbNat

On the runway at the Roxy, the drag queen.   Take Good Care of Yourself.   Mark Wunderlich.   NeAmPo; ReTh; WiU

On the Russian Persecution of the Jews.   Algernon Charles Swinburne.   OxBSo

On the salt plaza.   Skull of the Horse.   Thomas McGrath.   BodElec

On the Same.   Roy Campbell.   OBCoV

On the Same [Death of My Dear Brother, Mr. H.S., Drowned]: The Boat.   William Hammond.   NOSC

On the Same Picture.   Walt Whitman.   GS

On the Sand Dune.   Kawamura Yoichi.   GifTon, *tr. by* Naoshi Koriyama and Edward Lueders

On the school platform, draping the folding seats.   Political Meeting.   Abraham Moses Klein.   BrAP

On the Sea.   Judah Ha-Levi. *tr. by* Gabriel Levin
"Greetings ladies, kith and kin."   WoPoe, *tr. by* Gabriel Levin

On the Sea.   John Keats.   NoP-4

On the Sea.   Gabriella Sica.   CItWP, *tr. by* Cinzia Sartini Blum and Lara Trubowitz

On the Sea.   Bayard Taylor.   TreFP

On the sea fringe.   To Eugene P. Loveman.   Alexander Bergman.   AmWaPo

On the sea-floor a stone bell, tolling.   August Sleepwalker, The.   Zhao Zhenkai.   VCWP

On the sea-shore, smell of iodine.   Regina Derieva.   CRWP, *tr. by* Kevin Carey

On the second floor of the Worcester Center Mall, 7:15 P.M., March 3.   Lines Started Outside Filene's Basement.   James R. Scrimgeour.   OPRER

On the Second Tristia of Ovid.   Elizabeth Jane Leon.   EMWP

On the secret map the assassins.   Rivers and Mountains.   John Ashbery.   NoAM; TRP

On the Setting Up of Mr. Butler's Monument in Westminster Abbey.   Samuel Wesley.   NBLV

On the Seven Bishops.   Anne Fychan.   EMWP

On the seventh day.   Love Affair 36.   Jennifer Rankin.   BMAP

On the shallot the dew.   Dew on the Shallot.   *Unknown.*   CCL1, *tr. by* Anne Birrell

On the shore fish toss in the stretched nets of Simon, James, and John.   Abundant Catch (Luke 5:4–10).   Czeslaw Milosz.   GI

On the shores of my animal there was a zoo.   Letter to Einstein Beginning Dear Albert.   Paul Hoover.   IllVoic

On the shores of Parrot Island, waves beat on the sand.   Parrot Island.   Liu Yu Hsi.   CCL1, *tr. by* Marsha Wagner

On the Shores of Szántód.   Ferenc Jankovich.   IQMS, *tr. by* Madeline Mason

On the Sicilian strand a hare well wrought.   Ausonius.   OBVE

On the side of freedom stand? (LL)   Slave Mother, The: A Tale of the Ohio.   Frances Ellen Watkins Harper.   ColAP; NAAPv.1

On the side of the vaulted library of Augustus.   Santa Maria Antiqua.   István Vas.   IQMS, *tr. by* Geroge Gömöri and Clive Wilmer

On the Situation of Highbury.   Katherine Austen.   EMWP

On the sixth day, as I rode.   Geoffrey Hill.   UpMys *Fr.* Genesis.

On the Sixth Day of the War.   Mac Lojowski.   AmZen

On the Sixth Day the Word Is Taken from Me.   Lisa Beskin.   PoDa

On the sixth day we came. (LL)   Animals, The.   Edwin Muir.   ChIV-1; CtM; HeIP-4; MoBrPo

On the sixty-fifth floor where you wrote.   Peregrine Falcon, New York City.   Robert Cording.   UrbNat

On the Slave-Trade.   Isabella Lickbarrow.   RWP

On the Slope of Hua Mountain.   *Unknown.*   WoPoe, *tr. by* Chung Ling and Kenneth Rexroth

On the Slope of the Desolate River.   Rabindranath Tagore.   OBMV *Fr.* Gitanjali.

On the Soft and Gentle Motions of Eudora.   Anne Killigrew.   PoBW

On the Sonnet.   John Keats. *See* If by Dull Rhymes Our English Must Be Chained.

On the South Downs.   Sara Teasdale.   MoAmPo

On the Spartan Dead at Thermopylae.   Simonides.   WeW-3, *tr. by* Peter Jay

On the Spirit Adulterated by the Flesh.   Thomas Warton, the Elder.   ChIV-1

On the Spirit of the Heart as Moon-Disk.   Kojijū.   WoPoe; WPoS, *tr. by* Edwin A. Cranston

On the Spot Where Shih-chia Tzu Sits in Meditation.   Ching An.   CSKM, *tr. by* Jerome P. Seaton

On the spot you think the dream is. (LL)   My Life Asleep.   Jo Shapcott.   BeAl; NeBrP

On the spread the boy unbuckles like an old leather belt.   Detail from "Set for a Southern Gothic."   Brian Teare.   LegDan

On the Spur of the Moment.   Tu Fu [*or Du Fu*].   CCL1, *tr. by* Burton Watson

On the stage I stumbled.   Indian Blood.   Mary Tallmountain.   FiBr; UnSA

On the stage, mirrored many times.   Stripper, The.   Anita Endrezze.   ReTh

On the state-sanctioned murder of shaka sankofa.   Suheir Hammad.   BRtP

On the Statue of a Player at Svaika.   Alexander Sergeyevich Pushkin.   CAGL, *tr. by* Michael Green

On the Statue of an Angel, by Bienaimé, in the Possession of J.S. Copley Greene, Esq.   Washington Allston.   APN-1

On the steps of the Pentagon I tucked my skull.   Revised Notes for a Sonnet.   Edward Pygge.   OBCoV

On the stiff twig up there.   Black Rook in Rainy Weather.   Sylvia Plath.   BrAP; NIL-7; NoP-4

On the stillest day.   Windmill.   Gillian Clarke.   TCAWP

On the Strange Apparitions at Christ's Death.   Henry Colman.   ChIV-2

On the Street Corner.   L. Mattes.   Prolet, tr. by Amelia Glaser

On the street I see three guys.   Orizaba Blues: 64th Chorus.   Jack Kerouac.   WhBo

On the street today, I sold.   Sanctions.   Sadiq al-Saygh.   IrPoTo, tr. by Emily Howard and Salaam Yousif

On the Street Where You Live.   Alan Jay Lerner.   ReLy

On the Strength of All Conviction and the Stamina of Love.   Jennifer Michael Hecht.   GoPo

On the Subject of Poetry.   W. S. Merwin.   TAPaP

On The Subway.   Sharon Olds.   LTA

On the Sunny Side of the Street.   Dorothy Fields.   ReLy

On the surface, foam and roar.   Under the Surface.   Frances Ridley Havergal.   SacPr

On the Swag.   Ronald Allison Kells Mason.   SacPr

On the Sweet Comfort Brought by Grace.   Catharina Regina von Greiffenberg.   "I look."   WPoS

On the table.   Few Things, A.   Gerhard Rühm.   PFTM-2, tr. by Rosmarie Waldrop

On the table, a book of glass.   Book of Glass, A.   David Shapiro.   PmAP

On the table, in a blaze, the knife awakened. (LL)   Angel of Dread, The.   Miklós Radnóti.   ConPit; PFTM-1, tr. by Clayton Eshleman and Gyula Kodolanyi

On the table, these last mouthfuls. (LL)   Glass, The.   Sharon Olds.   NIL-7; NIP-4

On the tallest day in time, the dead came back.   V-J Day.   John Ciardi.   OtW; PWW2

On the Tattered Edges.   Amina Saïd.   HAWP; NAfrP, tr. by Eric Sellin

On the tattered edges of my unravelling memory.   On the Tattered Edges.   Amina Saïd.   HAWP; NAfrP, tr. by Eric Sellin

On the ten-below-zero day, it was on.   Space Heater, The.   Sharon Olds.   P180

On the Tennis Court at Night.   Galway Kinnell.   MoASP

On the Third Day.   János Pilinszky.   IQMS, tr. by Adam Makkai

On the Third Day I Wait on the Emperor at a Banquet and Describe the Reflection of the Candles in the Serpentine.   Yu Chien-wu.   CCL1, tr. by John Frodsham

On the third day of my marriage.   Wretched Married Life (Folk Song from Koch'ang).   Korean Oral Tradition.   CATKP, tr. by Peter H. Lee

On the third day she went down to the kitchen.   Wang Chien.   BLT

On the third finger of my left hand.   Ceremony.   William Stafford.   CAP-8

On the Thirteenth Day of Christmas.   Charles Causley.   OBCP

On the 30th of June to God.   Lady Jane Cavendish.   EMWP

On the 31st day of August in the year 1914.
Guillaume Apollinaire.   AF

(31st day of August 1914, The.)   Guillaume Apollinaire.   PFTM-1

On the thousand mile road through Yang Pass.   Bidding Farewell to Secretary Chou.   Yu Hsin.   CrYelRi, tr. by Sam Hamill

On the Three Children in the Fiery Furnace.   Henry Colman.   ChIV-1

On the Threshold.   Amy Levy.   LW

On the Threshold.   Pierre Reverdy.   CuPo

On the threshold no one.   Road.   Pierre Reverdy.   CuPo

On the threshold of heaven, the figures in the street.   To an Old Philosopher in Rome.   Wallace Stevens.   APT-1; ColAP; NAMCP V.1; NoAM

On the threshold of the black cave.   Ecce Homo.   Meirion Pennar.   BBMWP, tr. by Martin Davis

On the throne of many hues, Immortal Aphrodite.   Sappho.   SaLy, tr. by Diane Rayor

On the tidal mud, just before sunset.   Daybreak.   Galway Kinnell.   BLT; ChAP

On the Tisza.   Endre Ady.   IQMS, tr. by Anton N. Nyerges

On the Tomb of the Unknown Soldier.   László Mécs.   IQMS, tr. by Watson Kirkconnell

On the Tombs in Westminster Abbey.   Francis Beaumont.

Lines on the Tombs in Westminster.   OBEV

(On the Tombs in Westminster Abbey.)   OxAEP-1

On the tombs of granite.   Jewish Cemetery at Berlin-Weissensee, The.   Günter Kunert.   GTCP, tr. by Reinhold Grimm

On the Tower of Gathering Remoteness.   Su Tung-p'o.   TAL

On the Town's Honest Man.   Ben Jonson.   NOSC

On the Train.   Lynn Davies.   Coast

On the train / old ladies playing football.   Going Uptown to Visit Miriam.   Víctor Hernández Cruz.   PueRic

(On the train.)   LoL

On the Transitory.   Hugo von Hofmannsthal.   WoPoe, tr. by Naomi Replansky

On the Triumph of Judith.   Félix Lope de Vega Carpio. See Judith.

On the trunk of a haunted tree. (LL)   Haunted Oak, The.   Paul Laurence Dunbar.   ColAP; NAAPv.1

On the tube, the old parade.   Thanksgiving.   Ed Ochester.   SUP

On the Turning Up of Unidentified Black Female Corpses.   Toi Derricotte.   CFP; OxAAAP

On the twentieth, at a certain moment.   Christmas 1956.   György Petri.   VCWP, tr. by Geroge Gömöri and Clive Wilmer

On the twenty-fifth of October.   T. Glynne Davies.   BBMWP Fr. Ruins.

On the 21st March 1960.   I Remember Sharpeville.   Sipho Sepamla.   AF

On the Two Great Floods.   Francis Quarles.   ChIV-1

On the typographical bushes that the poem forms along a road.   Blackberries.   Francis Ponge.   WED, tr. by Robert Bly

On the Uncountable Nature of Things.   Ellen Hinsey.   StAl

On the Uniformity and Perfection of Nature.   Philip Freneau.   TCAPo

On the University Carrier Who Sick'n'd [or Sickened] in the Time of His Vacancy [, Being Forbid to go to London, by Reason of the Plague].   John Milton.   NOSC; OxAEP-1

On the Unusual Cold and Rainy [or Rainie] Weather in the Summer, 1648.   Robert Heath.   NOSC

On the "Unusual" Lifestyle of the Cucapá Indians as Recorded by R. W. Hardy, British Lieutenant, While Exploring the Gulf of California.   Heriberto Yépez.   RMCMP, tr. by Harry Polkinhorn

On the uptown lexington avenue express: Martin Luther King Day 1995.   Duriel Harris.   SpirFl

On the Vanity of Earthly Greatness.   Arthur Guiterman.   AmWit; APT-1; HeIP-4

On the Venom Farm.   Ruth Padel.   EmeKit

On the Verge of the Path.   Barbara Guest.   OxBoAm

On the Viking Raids.   Unknown.   WoPoe

On the village square.   Fingerprints.   Iwan Llwyd.   BBMWP, tr. by Geriant Løvgreen

On the Voyage to Jerusalem.   Judah Ha-Levi. tr. by Emma Lazarus

2.   SWaP, tr. by Emma Lazarus

On the Wall of a KZ-Lager.   János Pilinszky.   AF; HP; PoSu

On the Wall of Cloud-Friend Hut.   Muso Soseki.   EaWin, tr. by W. S. Merwin

On the Wall of My Age.   Lajos Áprily.   IQMS, tr. by Paul Tabori

On the war day, mainly the soldiers got going.   Dec. 7, 1941.   Josephine Miles.   OxBoAm

On the warm July river.   Inner Tube.   Michael Ondaatje.   NAMCP V.2; NoAM

On the wasteland that stretches.   Job Hunting.   Brian Patten.   RSaN

On the water, solid.   George Oppen.   APT-2; PFTM-1

On the Waterfront.   Michael Foley.   PNI

On the way down through clouds.   Landing.   James P. Lenfestey.   OtW

On the way home after seeing you.   Letter Written With the Left Hand, A.   Ko Chônghûi.   EcSo, tr. by Catherine J. Kim

On the way home from school, a child is struck.   Acorn, The.   Gail Mazur.   ExTi

On the way to bed a) Take the staircase.   In Case of Monsters.   Stephen Knight.   NeBl

On the Way to Ch'ôngju.   Ko Chônghûi.   EcSo, tr. by Catherine J. Kim

On the Way to Durham, N.C.   Kofi Awoonor.   BrAP

On the way to God the difficulties.   Lal Ded.   WoPoe; WPoS, tr. by Coleman Barks

On the Way to Kew.   W. E. Henley.   MoBrPo Fr. Echoes.

On the way to lower Broadway.   Poem of Chalk, The.   Philip Levine.   P180

On the Way to Mind.   Milo De Angelis.   NeIt, tr. by Lawrence Venuti

On the Way to Pa-ling.   Yüan Mei.   ColAnChi, tr. by Jonathan Chaves

On the Way to the Garden (77).   Khwaja Shams-ad-din Muhammad Hafiz.   WED, tr. by Robert Bly and Leonard Lewisohn

On the way to the grove you'll pass the Fates.   Edgar Lee Masters.   TCAPo Fr. Spoon River Anthology.

On the Way to the Mission.   Duncan Campbell Scott.   BrAP

On the way to the outhouse.   Basho.   EH, tr. by Robert Hass

On the Way to the Sitter's.   Gary Margolis.   PfSP

On the Way to the Zendō.   Philip Whalen.   WANABP

On the way to you.   Vera Pavlova.   CRWP, tr. by Steven Seymour

On the way up from Sheet I met some children.   To Edward Thomas.   Alun Lewis.   PoWW

On the weekends.   Snag.   Rosanna Deerchild.   PoPra

On the Welch.   Unknown.   AngWePo

On the Welsh Language.   Katherine Philips.   EMWP; NoP-5; NOSC

(On the Welch Language.)   NoP-4

On the west side people are singing as though drunk.   Tohono O'odham.   NAAPv.1 Fr. Songs for Treating Sickness, Sung durring the Four Parts of the Night.

On the west side they are singing, the women hear it. Tohono O'odham. NAAPv.1 *Fr.* Songs for Treating Sickness, Sung durring the Four Parts of the Night.

On the west, thornveld, teeth on trees. Ecotone. Ingrid de Kok. TSAP

On the West Tower in Guozhou. Ts'en Shen. CCL1, *tr. by* Stephen Owen

On the White Wall. Paek Sŏk. CAMKP, *tr. by* Kyunghwan Choi

On the whole, we conclude the Romans won't do it, and I sha'n't. (LL) Arthur Hugh Clough. FaBoWar; OxAEP-2; PoAgWa; WaAnP *Fr.* Amours de Voyage.

On the wide level of a mountain's head. Time, Real and Imaginary. Samuel Taylor Coleridge. OBEV

On the Willow Bank. Yen Chen. WoPoe, *tr. by* Arthur Sze

On the wind, a drifting echo. Christmas Night. Lawrence Sail. OBCP

On the windows, the dirty film. Finder, The. Robin Blaser. FTOS

On the Wing. Christina Georgina Rossetti. VWP

On the wings of the buck and wing. (LL) Buckdancer's Choice. James Dickey. HeIP-4; NAMCP V.2; NoAM; NoP-4; NoP-5

On the Wounds of Our Crucified Lord. Richard Crashaw. NAEL-6v1; NAEL-7v1

On the wrist a watch. Last Things, The. Gwyn Thomas. BBMWP, *tr. by the author*

On the Yard. Etheridge Knight. RaBo

On their ankles and arms girls wore. Second Language. Shari Miller Wagner. ACAMVP

On their daily trips. Going to Work. Nancy Mercado. PA9/11

On their way to school. Colour. Tony Marinho. NeNiPo

On These Conditions. Gerardo Diego. RaW, *tr. by* Ralph Nelson

On these sandy dikes I shake the world's dust from my clothes. On Spending Some Time at the Bai'an Pavilion. Hsieh Ling-yün. CCL1, *tr. by* John Frodsham

On these southern roads. Buson. SoOfWa, *tr. by* Sam Hamill

On Thinking of Photographing My Fantasies. Nellie Wong. OpBo

On Third Avenue. Mina Loy. APT-1; HarvBoo

On this April afternoon as Texas heat revs up. Duet. Betsy Colquitt. TiP2

On this bald hill the new year hones its edge. Parliament Hill Fields. Sylvia Plath. NALW

On this blest [*or* blessed] day may no dark cloud, or shower. To the Countess of A—. Written on the Anniversary of Her Marriage. Charlotte Smith. RWP

On this coast where they once arrived destined. In Memoriam. Samuel Maio. CalPo

On This Day. M. B. Goffstein. NTCP

On this day, give or take a week or two over. Ash Wednesday, 2002. Andrea Carter Brown. PA9/11

On This Day I Complete My Fortieth Year. Peter Porter. BMAP

On This Day I Complete My Thirty-sixth Year. Lord Byron. BrAP; CAGL; NAEL-6v2; NAEL-7v2; NoP-4; NoP-5; NPBRoP; NPeEn; OBWP

(Messalonghi. January 22, 1824. On This Day I Complete My Thirty-sixth Year.) NOBRP

On this day my city was struck by a dust storm—while I was. Dust Storm, The. Yusuf Rakha. AnVo, *tr. by* Mohamed Enani

On this day, the sun. Hiroshima. "Agyeya." WoPoe, *tr. by* Agyeya and Leonard Nathan

On this day tradition allots. New Year Greeting, A. W. H. Auden. HarvBoo; NAMCP V.1

On this day when you have needed to sleep forever. Healing Animal. Joy Harjo. SeSe

On This Earth. Juanita Brunk. ACAMVP

On this earth, in this life, as I read your story, you're lonely. Adrienne Rich. NAAL-5 *Fr.* Atlas of the Difficult World, An.

On this feast day, oh, cursèd day and hour! Christopher Marlowe. WaAnP *Fr.* Hero and Leander.

On this fourth day in a row of rain. Yellow Slicker, The. Stuart Dischell. GoPo

On this high hill in a year's turning. (LL) Poem in October. Dylan Thomas. AngWePo; NAEL-6v2; NAEL-7v2; NAMCP V.2; NoAM; NPeEn; OxAEP-2; PoA 2002; SoSe-8; TCAWP; UV

On This Island. W. H. Auden. HarvBoo; NAEL-6v2; NAEL-7v2; NAMCP V.1; OxBEV

(Look, Stranger.) MoBrPo

On this island where I was born. I Never Saw Great Lakes. Nancy Morejón. TANSG, *tr. by* Joy Renjilian-Burgy

On this lone Isle, whose rugged rocks affright. Sonnet: Suppos'd to Be Written at Lemnos. Thomas Russell. NOBRP

On this long farm facing Rila Mountain. Summer. Binyo Ivanov. CSCBP, *tr. by* Georgi Belev and Lisa Sapinkopf

On this map white. A state thick as a fist. Map of Montana in Italy, A. Richard Hugo. CAP-8

On this night. Seder Night with My Ancestors. Joanne Limburg. BeAl; NeBl

On this road, this road. Nettlebed Road. Naomi Mitchison. EdScPo

On this side, and on that, men see their friends. Robert Blair. OxAEP-1 *Fr.* Grave, The.

On This Side of the River. Stephen Berg. GifTon; TAPaP

On this side the engine room, on that side the boiler. Submarine. Brian Henry. LegDan

On this summer night. Chikako. WoPoe; WPoS, *tr. by* Edwin A. Cranston

On this tower as I leave our homeland. On Hsin-P'ing Tower. Li Po. NDACCP, *tr. by* David Hinton

On Those That Deserve It. Francis Quarles. NOSC

On Those Two Unparalleld Friends, Sr: G: Lisle and Sr: C: Lucas, Who Were Shott to Death at Colechester. Hester Lee Pulter. EMWP

On three crosses of a tree. Charm Rhyme, A. *Unknown.* FaBoVe

On thy grey bark, in witness of my flame. Pietro Metastasio. RWP, *tr. by* Charlotte Smith

On thy stars below in Frederick town! (LL) Barbara Frietchie. John Greenleaf Whittier. AmWaPo; APN-1; CBCWP; ColAP; HHAm; ITBLP; NCAP; OxBoAm; PCW; TFi

On thy stupendous summit, rock sublime! Beachy Head. Charlotte Smith. RWP

On thy wild banks, by frequent torrents worn. To the River Arun. Charlotte Smith. CenSon; RWP

On Time. Richard Hughes. MoBrPo

On Time. John Milton. OBEV; SacPr

On Time, Death, and Eternity. Robert Peter. VerBaPo

On time for every meal. Sister Mary Appassionata Lectures the Home Ec Class: The Feast. David Citino. UpMys

On to Glory. *Unknown.* SSUS

On Tobacco. Charles Cotton. OBSV

On Tomato Ketchup. *Unknown.* NBLV; Spl

(Tomato Ketchup.) Spl

On Top of It All. Keith Gilyard. SpirFl

On top of two buildings. Gum. Jean Toomer. APT-2; NAMCP V.1

On t'other side there stood destruction bare. Geoffrey Chaucer. FaBoWar *Fr.* Canterbury Tales, The.

On Track. Kathleene West. FFC

On Translating "Eugene Onegin." Vladimir Vladimirovich Nabokov. APT-2

(Eugene Onegin Stanza, The.) WoPoe

On Transportation. Benjamin Paloff. UrbNat

On Trees. Alan Dugan. NoAM

On Trust. Caroline Anne Bowles Southey. DiBP

On Trying to Imagine the Kiwi Pregnant. Clarence Major. GT

On Tuesday morn at half-past six o'clock. James Rigg. James Hogg. NPBRoP

On Tuesdays Rafaela's husband comes home late because that's the nighe he plays dominoes. Rafaela Who Drinks Coconut & Papaya Juice on Tuesdays. Sandra Cisneros. AFaM

On Turning Ten. Billy Collins. TWF

On TV. Lyle Glazier. OPRER

On two occasions in the past twelve months. Lawrence. Tony Hoagland. SUP

On Two Souldiers Killing One Another for a Groat. Samuel Wesley. "Full doelful Tales have oft been told." VerBaPo

On typographical bushes constituted by the poem along a road which leads neither beyond things nor to the spirit. Blackberries. Francis Ponge. YaTCFP, *tr. by* Serge Gavronsky

On utter foreignness, before he fills and sails down. (LL) Sled Burial, Dream Ceremony. James Dickey. NoP-4; NoP-5

On vague hills the prophet bird. Carol. W. S. Merwin. YaYoPo

On Vermeer's *Young Woman with a Water Jug* (1658) in the Metropolitan Museum. Helen Pinkerton. FFC

On Veronica. Rita Dove. AmAlph

On Viewing Two Different Date Rape Movies. Allison Joseph. LiTh

On village green, whose smooth and well-worn sod. Disappointment, A. Joanna Baillie. WoRP

On vinegar and sour fish sauce Rome's legions stemmed avalanches. Drugs of War, The. Les A. Murray. BMAP

On Visiting a Taoist Master in the Daitian Mountains and Not Finding Him. Li Po. CCL1, *tr. by* Arthur Cooper

On Visiting Shorin Temple, Where Bodhidharma Once Lived. Soen. ZenPo, *tr. by* Takashi Ikemoto and Lucien Stryk

On Visiting Sokei, Where the Sixth Patriarch Lived. Tesshu. ZenPo, *tr. by* Takashi Ikemoto and Lucien Stryk

On Visiting Taoist Recluse of Tai-Tien-Shan and Not Finding Him. Li Po. ChinPo, *tr. by* Ye Weilian [*or* Yeh Wei-lien *or* Wai-lim Yip]

On Visiting Westminster Abbey. Amanda Ros. VerBaPo

On Vulture Peak. Peak of the Held-Up Flower, The. Muso Soseki. EaWin, *tr. by* W. S. Merwin

On Waitakere Dam. Sinéad Morrissey. NIrP

On waking up, I remembered Peter Doyle. It must have been. Walt Whitman and the Birds. Eugenio de Andrade. ViWalt, *tr.* by Alexis Levitin

On Walking Backwards. Anne Carson. *See* Short Talk on Walking Backwards.

On Wallace's Track. Henry the Minstrel (Blind Harry). DiBP *Fr.* Sir William Wallace.

On Walt Whitman's Birthday. Anne Waldman. ViWalt

On warm days in September the high school band. High School Band, The. Reed Whittemore. P180

On washday in the good old bad old days. Washday Battles. Geoffrey Summerfield. NOxBChV

On Washing. John Armstrong. STuOW *Fr.* Art of Preserving Health, The.

On Washington's Birthday Yancey the haberdasher. Americana 3. Carl Rakosi. APT-2

On Watching a Young Man Play Tennis. Kelly Cherry. LPSFW

On Waterloo's ensanguined plain. On Scott's Poem "The Field of Waterloo." Thomas Erskine, 1st Baron Erskine. NBLV

On Wednesday last, in the vicinity. Lost and Found. Jane Griffiths. NeBl

On Wednesday night. Wednesday Night Prayer Meeting. Jay Wright. ISC

On weekends, my husband pays the bills, files away our life. On Weekends. Carli Carrara. PfS

On weekends we climbed the bus out of Paris. To Valenton: Impressions circa 1947. Liliane Richman. TWW

On Wellington. Lord Byron. FaBoWar; OBSV; OxAEP-2 *Fr.* Don Juan.

On Wenlock Edge the wood's in trouble. A. E. Housman. BrAP; HarvBoo; MoBrPo; NAEL-6v2; NAEL-7v2; NAMCP V.1; NoP-4; NoP-5; OxAEP-2; TFi *Fr.* Shropshire Lad, A.

On went She, and due north her journey took. (LL) With Ships the sea was sprinkled far and nigh. William Wordsworth. CenSon; WoPoe

On Westwall Downes [*or* On Westwell Downs]. William Strode. NOSC; NPeEn

On wet sidewalks at the close of fall. Witch-Hazel Wood, The. Emily Hiestand. UrbNat

On what foundation stands the warrior's pride. Juvenal. FaBoWar; OBWP; OxBEV *Fr.* Vanity of Human Wishes, The; The Tenth Satire of Juvenal [Imitated].

On What the Army Does with Heads. Michael Casey. YaYoPo

On what they hunger to become. (LL) Boat People. Yusef Komunyakaa. AF; PoPoPo

On which God moves, and treads beneath his feet the All! (LL) Sonnet: "And so, as this great sphere (now turning slow)." Frederick Goddard Tuckerman. ColAP; WaAnP

On which God moves, and treads beneath his feet the All! (LL) Sonnets: "Starry flower, the flower-like stars that fade, The." Frederick Goddard Tuckerman. APN-2; NAAPv.1

On which the heavenly spheres revolve. (LL) Coventry Patmore. NAEL-6v2; NAEL-7v2 *Fr.* Angel in the House, The.

On Whitsunday morning. Dunt Dunt Dunt Pittie Pattie. *Unknown.* FaBoVe

On ["Who Wrote Icon Basilike" by Dr.] Christopher Wordsworth, Master of Trinity. Benjamin Hall Kennedy. OBCoV

On Wilshire I lunched with a woman dead. Brilliant Windows. Larry Kramer. GeoHom

On windy, woodchopping afternoons. (LL) All I Want. Luci Tapahonso. ItWoWo; UnSA

On Winter. Mary Leapor. PEW

On winter afternoons. Portrait of My Father, Militant Communist. Jorge Teillier. TCLAP, *tr.* by Carolyne Wright

On winter days, about the gloamin hour. Auld Sanct-Aundirans—Brand the Builder. Tom Scott. EdScPo

On winter mornings. Richard Wright. APT-2; NoP-5

On Winter Nights. Nijole Miliauskaite. VCWP, *tr.* by Jonas Zdanys

On winter nights, the dead. What the Dead Fear. Kim Addonizio. SUP

On winter nights, when my grandmother. On Winter Nights. Nijole Miliauskaite. VCWP, *tr.* by Jonas Zdanys

On Wishes. Mahmoud Darwish. VCWP, *tr.* by Denys Johnson-Davies

On With the Dance! Let Freud Be Unconfined! William J. Tait. EdScPo

On with the jalapeño Christmas lights! It's only the end. Sabotage. Anselm Berrigan. HeMarv

On Woman. William Butler Yeats. ChIV-1

On Worldly Prelates. Charles Wesley. ChIV-2

On yeir begines ane other endis. Godlie Instructione for Old and Young, Ane. *Unknown.* EMWP

On Yellow-Crane Tower, Farewell to Meng Hao-Jan Who's Leaving for Yang-Chou. Li Po. NDACCP, *tr.* by David Hinton

On yet, sad Verse: though those bright starres, from whence. Samuel Daniel. *Fr.* Civil Wars, The.

On yonder oak, upon its lordliest height. Mistletoe. Mary E. Tucker. CBWP-1

On your bare rocks, O barren moors. Barren Moors, The. William Ellery Channing. APN-1

On Your Own. Tess Gallagher. LaCa

On your own premises. (LL) I Am in Danger—Sir. Adrienne Rich. HarvBoo; NAAL-5; NALW

On your piano a plaster Beethoven stands. Picture Postcard from Our Youth. Dan Pagis. VCWP, *tr.* by Stephen Mitchell

On your slender body. For the Courtesan Ch'ing Lin. Wu Tsao. WoPoe, *tr.* by Chung Ling and Kenneth Rexroth

On your throne, a marvel of art, immortal. Sappho. STV

On Your Twenty-First Birthday. Joan Austin Geier. FFC

On Zacheus [*or* Zacchaeus]. Francis Quarles. NOSC

Once. Sharon Olds. NAMCP V.2

Once. Siv Widerberg. NTCP, *tr.* by Verne Moberg

Once a day the rocks, with little warning. Naskeag. Alfred Corn. VCAP

Once a dream did weave a shade. William Blake. NOBRP *Fr.* Songs of Innocence.

Once a flock of stately peacocks. Patrician Peacocks and the Overweening Jay, The. Guy Wetmore Carryl. TCAPo

Once a girl, all April-fresh. Fazil Abdulovich Iskander. ItGoST, *tr.* by Avril Pyman

Once a Green Sky. Bob Hicok. AmAlph

Once a little boy, Jack, was, oh! ever so good. Sad Story of a Little boy That Cried, The. *Unknown.* OBSP

Once a little boy was dreaming. Parables, I. Antonio Machado Ruiz. STV, *tr.* by John Frederick Nims

Once a man jumped out of a streetcar, but so clumsily that he fell under an automobile. Event on the Street, An. Daniil Kharms. AF

Once a man makes a decision. To the Reverend Bagam. Muyong Sooyon. BecRai, *tr.* by Kim Daljin, Kim Won-Chung and Christopher Merrill

Once a Meiji Voice. *Unknown.* NAAPv.2

Once, a pre-med white boy laced his fingers into mine. Warning to Young Bright Sisters / White AM. Culture 101A. Michelle T. Clinton. InTrad

Once a Shoot of Heaven. Beckian Fritz Goldberg. PuP-23

Once a time is how the baby asks for a story. Height of the Season, The. Maxine W. Kumin. FFC

Once a two day holiday, the most sacred stretches. At the New Moon: Rosh Hodesh. Marge Piercy. TaR

Once a woman fell from the sky. This woman who fell from the sky was. Woman Who Fell from the Sky, The. Joy Harjo. BodElec

Once a woman who had nine sons. Dead Brother, The. *Hungarian Oral Tradition.* IQMS, *tr.* by Adam Makkai

Once a year. Dylan Iorwerth. BBMWP *Fr.* Sand.

Once a year up the long road from Jericho. Hot summer. Mothballs. Visiting the West Bank. S. V. Atalla. PoArWo

Once again. Isabel Meyrelles. SurWo, *tr.* by Jean R. Longland

Once Again, Anne Frank. Elina Wechsler. MirDau, *tr.* by Darrell Lockhart

Once Again Another Century Ahead. Joanne Kyger. WANABP

Once again I hear. Kenneth Rexroth. NAAPv.2 *Fr.* Love Poems of Marichiko, The.

Once again / I wipe the bedspread. Day's End. Ann Townsend. SweBea

Once again Love [Eros], the loosener of limbs, shakes me. Sappho. EroLit, *tr.* by Josephine Balmer

Once again love has hold. That Which Is Enough for Love. Luis Cernuda. CAGL, *tr.* by Rick Lipinski

Once again on Easter Day before the rain washed away the lamb's blood. Easter Feast. Stratis Haviaras. MotU

Once again, someone took me. Line Up. Forrest Hamer. OPRER

Once again that loosener of limbs, Love. Sappho. SaLy, *tr.* by Diane Rayor

Once Again the Mind. Faiz Ahmad Faiz. AF, *tr.* by Naomi Lazard

Once again the pine-tree sung. Ralph Waldo Emerson. APN-1 *Fr.* Woodnotes II ("As sunbeams stream through liberal space").

Once again the threshold worn down from so much waiting, the night unhung nearer. Innard. Silvia Eugenia Castillero. SPV, *tr.* by Jen Hofer

Once Alien Here. John Hewitt. CABP; PNI

Once Allen Ginsberg stopped to pee at a bookstore in New Jersey. Allen Ginsberg. Toi Derricotte. PBCAP

Once, among the transports, was one with children—two freight. Children. Charles Reznikoff. FTOS

Once an artist went overseas. Looking Thru Those Eyeholes. Russell Soaba. PML

Once, and but once found in thy company. John Donne. FSCP; NoSic *Fr.* Elegies.

Once and for all. (LL) Dark Room, The. Enrique Lihn. TCLAP; VCWP, *tr.* by David Unger

Once and for all I will lie down here like a dead man. Faces I Love, The. Gerald Stern. LoL

Once as abroad I stray'd. Transfiguration. Ralph Chubb. CAGL

Once as I in my study sat and saw. Hourglass, The. Joseph Beaumont. NOSC

Once, as in the darkness I lay asleep by night. Nightmare, The. Wang Yen-Shou. CCL1, *tr.* by Arthur Waley

Once As Thoth Beside The Sea. Cort Day. IIR

Once at a merry wedding feast. St. George Tucker. NBLV Fr. Cynic, The.

Once at Cold Mountain, troubles cease. Like a Drifting Boat. Han-shan (Cold Mountain). CCL1, tr. by Gary Snyder

Once, but is the eternity that awaits you. (LL) Bright Field, The. Ronald Stuart Thomas. AngWePo; TCAWP

Once by the Pacific. Robert Frost. APT-1; GSo; HeIP-4; MoAmPo; NIL-7; PtR; TRP; WeW-3

Once careless of her children. Sioux Woman Defends Her Children, The. Chippewa Oral Tradition. NAAL-5

Once circle round our Sun—and o'er. Edward Edwin Foot. STuOW Fr. Christening the Prince.

Once corpses left the city behind them, dead. Earthquake. Unknown. PoCho, tr. by Burton Raffel

Once Cypris sent to Europa a sweet dream. Europa. Moschus. HePo, tr. by Barbara Hughes Fowler

Once Death has spoken, the words are final. To My Daughter. Margit Mikes. IQMS, tr. by Susanne K. Walther

Once der was a meetin' in de wilderness. Brer Rabbit, You's de Cutes' of 'Em All. James Weldon Johnson. APT-1

Once did She hold the gorgeous east in fee. On the Extinction of the Venetian Republic. William Wordsworth. NPBRoP; OBEV

Once, driving the dirt road. Homesteading. Eric Trethewey. Coast

Once evening's fallen you prepare for a voyage. Once Evening's Fallen. Claude Esteban. YaTCFP, tr. by Rosemary Lloyd

Once, far over the breakers. Yosano Akiko. CFP, tr. by Kenneth Rexroth

Once, fast along the ridge, we stopped where bush opened. More Than Once in Caves. Mark McMorris. IAoNAP

Once Father raised. Transits. Sharan Strange. InTrad

Once, for a dare. After the Deluge. Wole Soyinka. HBAPE

Once for that time we met. I Have Folded This Letter in Ten Places. Tim Griffin. FreRad

Once, happier people lived here. Theresienstadt's Hospital. Unknown, fr. Terezin Concentration Camp. INSAB

Once haunted. Love Letter. Katayoon Zandvakili. AmPoNex

Once he comes to live on the outside of her, he will not sleep. What No One Could Have Told Them. C. D. Wright. GPPA; PoChi

Once home, you'll throw yourself on an unmade bed. Like Thousands of Others. Aleksandr Petrovich Tkachenko. ItGoST, tr. by Maia Tekses

Once hooked ever after lives in lack, The. Nescit Vox Missa Reverti. James Vincent Cunningham. APT-2

Once I am sure there's nothing going on. Church Going. Philip Larkin. BrAP; CABP; EMP; HarvBoo; HeIP-4; MoBrPo; NAEL-6v2; NAEL-7v2; NAMCP V.2; NIL-7; NIP-4; NoAM; NoP-4; NoP-5; SoSe-8; TFi; WaAnP

Once I came to paradise. It was empty. An abandoned village in a remote forest of deciduous trees. Once I Came to Paradise. Harry Edmund Martinson. MotU, tr. by Thomas H. Vance and Vera Vance

Once I did, I escaped. Being Free. Leanne O'Sullivan. PoCu

Once I entered. Like Ana. Nina Cassian. PoSu, tr. by Nina Cassian

Once I fell in the ocean when. This Time. Michael Palmer. NAMCP V.2

Once I fished a wren. Wren. Beckian Fritz Goldberg. AmAlph

Once I found a cowboy who thought he could. Mae West Chats It Up with Bessie Smith. Colleen J. McElroy. BAP-01

Once I gave birth to living metaphors. Not Writing Poems about Children. Carolyn Kizer. PoChi

Once I goosestepped across the square. Résumé. Bei Dao. AF, tr. by Bonnie S. McDougall

Once I gorged myself in a peach grove. To an Ancient Tune. Unknown. CrYelRi, tr. by Sam Hamill

Once I got a postcard from the Fiji Islands. Jaan Kaplinski. StAl; TAPaP; WhBo, tr. by the author, Sam Hamill and Riina Tamm

Once, I grew long hair. Very True Confessions. Sidney Burris. SwNoth

Once I had a taste. Remembrance of Strange Hospitality. Yelena Shwarts. ItGoST; StAl; VCWP, tr. by Michael Molnar

Once I had dreamed of return to a sunlit land. Old Dreams. Ivor Gurney. HarvBoo

Once, / I heard him. Paul Celan. GTCP, tr. by John Felstiner

Once, I knew a fine song. Stephen Crane. APN-2; IJHIL

Once I left the room. Field, The. Tom Sleigh. PoDa

Once I liked pablum. Once. Siv Widerberg. NTCP, tr. by Verne Moberg

Once I lived in capitals. Italic. Roger McGough. OBCoV

Once i lived on pillars in a green house. Under a Soprano Sky. Sonia Sanchez. FuFl

Once I lived the life of a millionaire. Nobody Knows You When You're Down and Out. Jimmie Cox. GoPo

Once I looked inside / the darkness. Hermit Crab, The. Mary Oliver. WaAnP

Once I loved a man. Baby, Baby All the Time. Bobby Troup. ReLy

Once I met a poet who spent his life. Poet, The. Fadil Azzawi. IrPoTo, tr. by Ralph Saverese and Saadi A. Simawe

Once I pass'd through a populous city imprinting my brain for future use with its shows, architecture, customs, traditions. Once I Pass'd through a Populous City. Walt Whitman. NAAL-3; NAAL-5; NAAPv.1; RaBo; SAmP

Once I read a story. Story, The. Dan Pagis. PoSu, tr. by Stephen Mitchell

Once I saw a Devil in a flame of fire. William Blake. NAEL-6v2 Fr. Marriage of Heaven and Hell, The.

Once I seen a human ruin. Ambrose Bierce. APN-2 Fr. Devil's Dictionary, The.

Once I shone afar like a. Kenneth Rexroth. APSN Fr. Love Poems of Marichiko, The.

Once I used to brag about my handy man. My Handy Man Ain't Handy No More. Andy Razaf. ReLy

Once I used to study languages dead for millenia. Olesya Nikolayeva. CRWP, tr. by Catriona Kelly

Once I was a boy. Group Portrait with Ukuleles. Keith Ratzlaff. ACAMVP

Once I was a poor man's son. Natsume Soseki. CAoMJL1, tr. by Burton Watson

Once I was a sentimental thing. Spring Can Really Hang You Up the Most. Fran Landesman. ReLy

Once I was in love with a woman. Temporary Situation, A. David St. John. BodElec

Once, I was martyred. Wake Up, Yousif. Yousif al-Sa'igh. IrPoTo, tr. by Ralph Saverese and Saadi A. Simawe

Once I was sitting on the right hand side of god in Paradise. Hwang Jiwoo. CAMKP Fr. Melancholy.

Once I was wood from a worthless old fig tree. Horace. PriapPo Fr. Satires.

Once I was yellow-haired, and ringlets fell. Youth and Age. Unknown. IrV, tr. by Eleanor Hull

Once I was young / Yesterday, perhaps. I Didn't Know What Time It Was. Lorenz Hart. ReLy

Once I wished I might rehearse. Freedom. Ralph Waldo Emerson. APN-1

Once idly in his hall King Olave sat. King's Sabbath, The. Archibald Lampman. IFF

Once in a bar in Transylvania. Night with the Vampire, The. Fadil Azzawi. IrPoTo, tr. by Ralph Saverese and Saadi A. Simawe

Once in a dream (for once I dreamed of you). On the Wing. Christina Georgina Rossetti. VWP

Once, in [a] finesse of fiddles found I ecstasy. Embankment, The (The fantasia of a fallen gentleman on a cold, bitter night). Thomas Ernest Hulme. OPOU

Once, in a foreign country, I was suddenly ill. Widening Spell of the Leaves, The. Larry Levis. PBCAP

Once, in a house I will inherit in a land I can't explain. Comings and Goings. Ann Townsend. NAPBL

Once in a Lifetime, Snow. Les A. Murray. NoP-4; NoP-5

Once in a room in Blackpool we had to make do. Blindfold, The. Greta Stoddart. BeAl; MoWP

Once in a seaside town with time to kill. John Hewitt. ModIr Fr. Freehold.

Once in a thousand years. Fragrance of the Udumbara, The. Muso Soseki. EaWin, tr. by W. S. Merwin

Once in a while. Ishikawa Takuboku. PoCho, tr. by Sanford Goldstein and Seishi Shinoda

Once in a while, it I lie still and am quiet. Training Horses. Jack Myers. MAAN

Once in a while somebody fights for breath. Vanishing Lung Syndrome. Miroslav Holub. VCWP

Once in a while / we'd find a patch. Children, The. William Carlos Williams. SAmP

Once in Africa I heard voices waling, then turned a bend. Deer on a Beach. Anne Simpson. Coast

Once in Canandaigua, hitchhiking from Ann Arbor. Faces. John Ciardi. WeW-3

Once, in dream. To Rilke. Denise Levertov. UpMys

Once in late summer I walked into. Meadow. John Engels. PfSP

Once in Love with Amy. Frank Loesser. ReLy

Once in Mexico an old man was. Visions. William Stafford. NoAM

Once, in my early thirties, I saw. Jane Kenyon. LoL Fr. Having It Out with Melancholy.

Once in our customed walk a wounded bird. To My Brother. Mary Bryan. CenSon

Once, in Santa Fe. Raylene Hinz-Penner. ACAMVP

Once, in summer. Picking Blueberries, Austerlitz, New York, 1957. Mary Oliver. NAAL-5

Once, in the city of Kalamazoo. Kalamazoo. Vachel Lindsay. AmWit

Once, in the Colosseum—that. Lizard, The. Alphonse Marie Louis de Lamartine. SxFrPo, tr. by A. M. and E. H. Blackmore

Once in the dark of night. Dark Night, The. San Juan de la Cruz. BBASP; STV; WeW-3, *tr. by* Kieran Kavanaugh and Otilio Rodriguez

Once in the 40s. William Stafford. GoPo

Once, in the Giant's Ring, I closed my eyes. Home. Frank Ormsby. ModIr; PBCIP; PNI

Once in the Jurassic, about 150 million years ago. Smokey the Bear Sutra. Gary Snyder. WhBo

Once in the Phoenix tower the phoenix made her nest. On Climbing the Phoenix Tower at Chinling. Li Po. TAL

Once in the winter. Forsaken, The. Duncan Campbell Scott. BrAP

Once it belonged to my teacher. Fan. Jinkag Haesim. BecRai, *tr. by* Kim Daljin, Kim Won-Chung and Christopher Merrill

Once it had gorged itself. On a Pig's Head. Charles Tomlinson. NoAM

Once it smiled a silent dell. Valley of Unrest, The. Edgar Allan Poe. APN-1; NAAL-3

Once it was enough simply. Reaching the Horizon. Robert Mezey. GeoHom

Once late at night staying in Menton. Laughing All the Way. Liz Cashdan. Prnts

Once long ago a wolf strolled down. Wolf and the Sow, The. Marie de France. NAEL-7v1, *tr. by* Harriet Spiegel

Once long ago when at the desert's edge. Three Holy Kings, The. Rainer Maria Rilke. ChrPo, *tr. by* Edward Snow

Once looked Gudrun. *Unknown.* OBVE *Fr.* Elder Edda, The.

Once loving is a gen'ral Fashion. On Loving Once and Loving Often. Elizabeth Tollet. LW

Once more a winter sky surrounds my sight. Winter Sky. John Cope. GeoH

Once more by the roadside fallen, Lord. Until New Spring or Death. Árpád Tóth. IQMS, *tr. by* Madeline Mason

Once more, dear friends, you meet beneath. Anniversary Poem. John Greenleaf Whittier. PCW

Once more drifting clouds gather in the western sky. Dusk. Shuntaro Tanikawa. PoetW, *tr. by* Harold Wright

Once more following the blue grief of the evening. In Hellbrunn. Georg Trakl. WED, *tr. by* Robert Bly

Once more he sees his companions' faces. Survivor, The. Primo Levi. HP, *tr. by* Ruth Feldman

Once more I come to the white page of art. Cost of Seriousness, The. Peter Porter. NoAM

Once more it is April with the first light sifting. Before a Departure in Spring. W. S. Merwin. PoDa

Once more, listening to the wind and rain. Return, The. Arna Bontemps. GT

Once More, Once More. Velemir Khlebnikov. TCRusP, *tr. by* Kathy Lewis and Bob Perelman

Once More, Our God, Vouchsafe to Shine! [*with music*]. Samuel Sewall. SacPr

Once more the changed year's turning wheel returns. Dante Gabriel Rossetti. NoP-4 *Fr.* House of Life, The.

Once more the country calls. Ode to Our Young Pro-consuls of the Air. Allen Tate. PWW2

Once more the leaves. Seattle, Autumn, 1933. Alfred Encarnacion. OpBo

Once more the perfect pattern falls asleep. Replica, The. Vernon Watkins. AngWePo

Once more the poem woke me up. Little Furnace. Brenda Hillman. BodElec

Once more the storm is howling, and half hid. Prayer for My Daughter, A. William Butler Yeats. BrAP; ItP; NAEL-6v2; NAEL-7v2; NAMCP V.1; NoAM; NoP-4; NoP-5; RaBo; TFi; WaAnP

Once More to Lilla. Mihály Csokonai Vitéz. IQMS, *tr. by* Adam Makkai

Once more unto the breach, dear friends, once more. William Shakespeare. OxAEP-1; WaAnP *Fr.* King Henry V.

Once more you pass her house, deep in thought. Song Inscribed on an Earthenware Vessel. *Unknown.* WoPoe, *tr. by* John L. Foster

Once mother said: My little pet. Animal Crackers in My Soup. Irving Caesar and Ted Koehler. ReLy

Once, my braids swung heavy as ropes. Butcher's Wife, The. Louise Erdrich. HATNAP; NoP-4; NoP-5

Once my clothes were shabby. All I Need Is the Girl. Stephen Sondheim. ReLy

Once my husband's father, army-new. At Ease. Elinor Benedict. MAAN

Once naked, once even intangible. (LL) Pleasure. A. K. Ramanujan. PoetW; VCWP

Once near San Ysidro. Earth and Rain, the Plants & Sun. Simon J. Ortiz. NAAL-5

Once near the Border. David Mura. MAAN

Once noble custom was: by blood on battleground. Old Nobility, The. Friedrich von Logau. GePo, *tr. by* George C. Schoolfield

Once on a charger there was laid. Salome. Charles Lamb and Mary Lamb. ChIV-2

Once, on a lone sorry night, your ruins, Fort Huszt, did I enter. Huszt. Ferenc Kölcsey. IQMS, *tr. by* Watson Kirkconnell

Once on a Night in the Delta: A Report From Hell. Etheridge Knight. BodElec

Once on a night of sparkling sin. Vengeance. Shmuel Kreyter. Prolet, *tr. by* Amelia Glaser

Once on a summer night. Fanny Howe. FaoP *Fr.* Passion, The.

Once on a time, a monarch, tired with whooping. Apple Dumplings and a King, The. "Peter Pindar." OBSV

Once on a train from Baden-Baden. Rizal's Ghost. Eugene Gloria. ReBoTo

Once, on that highway where a traveler works hard. Pornography, Nebraska. Sandra McPherson. ReTh

Once on the brow of yonder Hill I stopped. Home at Grasmere [1800 version]. William Wordsworth.

Once on the mountain's balmy lap reclined. James F. Montgomery. NOBRP *Fr.* Brahmin, The.

Once...once upon a time. Martha. Walter De la Mare. MoBrPo

Once one year, and I don't know when. Wanderer's Bouquet. Sŏ Chŏngju. CAMKP; WoPoe, *tr. by* David R. McCann

Once / only. Winemaking. Gwyn Williams. BBMWP, *tr. by* Christopher Meredith

Once Orlov ate too many ground peas and died. Incidents. Daniil Kharms. MotU, *tr. by* George Gibian

Once our healing nurse, now you're. Venus de Milo. Gottfried Keller. WoPoe, *tr. by* John Peck

Once over, the fierce battle. At Toriwpn. Cho Chihun. CAMKP, *tr. by* David R. McCann

Once past the icefalls and the teeth of. On the Road to Erewhon. Allen Curnow. HarvBoo

Once past the sixth block. Country Bus Station. Shin Kyŏngnim. CAMKP, *tr. by* David R. McCann

Once piece, two pieces, three pieces. Laundry Song, The. Wen Yi-tuo [*or* Wen I-to]. NAAPv.2

Once, playing cricket, beneath a toast-dry hill. Curriculum Vitae. Robert Gray. NOBAu

Once public treasurer, a farmer now. *Unknown.* PriapPo *Fr.* Priapus Poems, The.

Once riding in Old Baltimore. Incident. Countee Cullen. APT-2; ChAP; NAAL-5; NAAPv.2; NAMCP V.1; NoAM; NoP-4; NoP-5; NOxBChV; NTCP; PoPoPo; PtR; SSLK

Once she dressed in silks and lace. She's Funny That Way (I Got a Woman, Crazy for Me). Richard A. Whiting. ReLy

Once she was a beauty. Miner's Family, The. Yosl Grinshpan. Prolet, *tr. by* Amelia Glaser

Once some people were visiting Chekhov. Chocolates. Louis Simpson. OBCoV

Once someone loved this piece of junk. Garage Sale as a Spiritual Exercise, The. Thomas M. Disch. GI

Once, taking a train into Chicago. Freight Cars. Stephen Dobyns. GM

Once the Dream Begins. Yusef Komunyakaa. RoV

Once the goal's reached. Kishu. ZenPo, *tr. by* Takashi Ikemoto and Lucien Stryk

Once, the mighty waves of ocean. Precious Pearl, The. Priscilla Jane Thompson. CBWP-2

Once the nation's chief was honored by the company of one. Notable Dinner, A. Lizelia Augusta Jenkins Moorer. CBWP-3

Once the web was perfect. Spider. Iwan Llwyd. ATSWP

Once the world was waiting for a song. History of Poetry, The. Peter Cooley. P180

Once their fruit is picked. Zea. Richard Wilbur. NoP-5

Once there came a man. Stephen Crane. OxBoAm

Once there occurred a miracle. Sheep School. Sándor Weöres. IQMS, *tr. by* Adam Makkai and Donald E. Morse

Once there was. From an ass to an analyst and back. Joyce Mansour. MFP, *tr. by* Martin Sorrell

Once there was a chain; strong as a destiny. Break, The. Delmira Agustini. TANSG, *tr. by* Mark McCaffrey

Once there was a father. Sons Changed Into Stags, The. József Erdélyi. IQMS, *tr. by* Watson Kirkconnell

Once there was a fence here. Former Barn Lot. Mark Van Doren. MoAmPo

Once there was a future when we were very young. Architecture. Jocelyn Emerson. IAoNAP

Once there was a little boy. Switch on the Night. Ray Bradbury. OBSP

Once there was a little girl. Little Girl of the Black Forest. Lise Deharme. SurWo, *tr. by* Franklin Rosemont

Once there was a man. Story of the Man Whose Tastes Were Too Refined. Charles Rafferty. AmPoNex

Once there was a man named Mr. Artesian and his activity was tremendous. Mr. Artesian's Conscientiousness. Ogden Nash. NBLV

Once there was a man who filmed his vacation. Vacation, The. Wendell Berry. GoPo

Once there was a shock. After a Death. Tomas Tranströmer. VCWP, *tr. by* Robert Bly

Once there was a soldier boy. Bulat Shalvovich Okudzhava. TCRusP, *tr. by* Daniel Weissbort

Once there was a thing called Spring. Spring Is Here. Lorenz Hart. ReLy

Once there was a woman went out to pick beans. Hairy Toe, The. *Unknown.* OBSP

Once there was an elephant. Eletelephony. Laura Elizabeth Richards. NBLV; NOxBChV; NTCP

Once there was an Indian-speaking priest. Plawej ans L'nui'site'w (Partridge and Indian-Speaking Priest). Rita Joe. Coast

Once There Was Light. Jane Kenyon. LoL *Fr.* Having It Out with Melancholy.

Once there were 50 Marías. Other Marías. Diana García. TouFir

Once there were none and the dark air was dumb. Nightingales, The. Harri Webb. AngWePo; TCAWP

Once they stood tiptoe, dewy, poised. Dream Lover. Mark DeFoe. SwNoth

Once they were sticks and stones. Names. Robert Earl Hayden. GT

Once to the verge of yon steep barrier came. Recluse, The. William Wordsworth.

Once upon. Fairy Tale, A. Bogdan Boychuk. WoPoe, *tr. by* David Ignatow

Once upon a midnight dreary, while I pondered [*or* ponder'd], weak and weary. Raven, The. Edgar Allan Poe. APN-1; BRP; ChAP; ColAP; HeIP-4; ITBLP; NAAL-3; NAAL-5; NAAPv.1; NCAP; NIL-7; NIP-4; NoP-4; NoP-5; OBNV; OWoS; OxBoAm; TCAPo; TFi; TreFP; UV; WaAnP

Once upon a Seesaw with Charlie Chan. Cyn Zarco. ReBoTo

Once Upon a Time. Lee Adams. ReLy

Once upon a time. After. Wendy Wilder Larsen. NevBe

Once upon a time. Troy. Maher Sabry. AnVo, *tr. by* Mohamed Enani

Once upon a time. Chernobyl. Mary Jo Salter. AtGh; FFC

Once Upon a Time: "Every morning you used to play hooky." Cahit Külebi. NaPG, *tr. by* Talat Sait Halman

Once upon a time a girl with moonlight in her eyes. Once Upon a Time. Lee Adams. ReLy

Once upon a time, a young man. Volunteer's Fairy Tale, A. Fred Moramarco. PML

Once upon a time an ancient man had fine. Splendid Stags, The. József Erdélyi. IQMS, *tr. by* Thomas Land

Once upon a time, Ap'ae Island. Ap'ae Island 45—Once Upon a Time. No Hyangnim. EcSo, *tr. by* Aimee N. Kwon

Once upon a time / Before I took up smiling. Blue Moon. Lorenz Hart. ReLy

Once upon a time, children. Storytime. Judith Nicholls. OBSP

Once upon a time, I practiced moves in a mirror. Resurrection of Elvis Presley, The. Ai. AllShUp

Once upon a time / in a nameless country. History. Elin ap Hywel. ATSWP, *tr. by* Robert Minhinnick

Once upon a time, the goddesses settled down. First Merseburg Spell. *Unknown.* GePo, *tr. by* Carroll Hightower

Once upon a time there was a girl called Annabell. Annabell and the Witches. Mick Gowar. OBSP

Once upon a time / there was a lonely wolf. Fable. János Pilinszky. OBVE; PoSu

Once upon a time there was a roof covered with tin. Owl and the Mouse, The. Viktor Aleksandrovich Sosnora. TCRusP, *tr. by* Denis Johnson and Kathy Lewis

Once upon a time there was a story. Story of a story, The. Vasco [*or* Vasko] Popa. StAl, *tr. by* Anne Pennington

Once upon a time there was a triangle. Vasco [*or* Vasko] Popa. PoSu *Fr.* Yawn of Yawns, The.

Once upon a time there was a yawn. Vasco [*or* Vasko] Popa. PoSu *Fr.* Yawn of Yawns, The.

Once upon a time there was an infinity of echoes. Vasco [*or* Vasko] Popa. PoSu *Fr.* Yawn of Yawns, The.

Once upon a time there was an Italian. Columbus. Ogden Nash. EMP; FaBoA; NAAPv.2; NoP-4; NoP-5

Once upon a time there were three. Variations. Maurice Scully. Oth

Once upon a time there were two brothers. History of My Life, The. John Ashbery. OxBoAm

Once upon a time there would be the bluest bitch of the pack. Three. Jen Hofer and Ofelia Perez Sepúlveda. SPV

Once upon the Iceland's solitary strand. Broken Oar, The. Henry Wadsworth Longfellow. OxBSo

Once upon time, a horse and its rider came to a place where squares of light shone. Yellow House Writes a Story for the Boy, The. Robin Behn. AmAlph

Once, walking home, I passed beneath a tree. Music of a Tree, The. Walter James Turner. MoBrPo

Once was a boy, age fifteen year. Hiram Helsel. Julia A. Moore. VerBaPo

Once we had a knocker. Lazy. Lu Yu. NDACCP, *tr. by* Kenneth Rexroth

Once we knew the world well. Wisława Szymborska. AF, *tr. by* Grazyna Drabik

Once we knew the world well. Once we knew the world well. Wisława Szymborska. AF, *tr. by* Grazyna Drabik

Once, we loved our sister satellite. Firmament on High. Laurence Goldstein. OtW

Once we painted our house and went into it. How the Real Bible Is Written. William Stafford. CAP-8

Once we played at love together. Once We Played. Mathilde Blind. LW

Once we presumed to found ourselves for good. Disappearing Island, The. Seamus Heaney. BodElec

Once we saw the nest. Nest, The. Carol Moldaw. UrbNat

Once We Were Farmers. Elsa Rediva E'der. ReBoTo

Once we were farmers. Once We Were Farmers. Elsa Rediva E'der. ReBoTo

Once we were wayfarers, then seafarers, then airfarers. Post Early for Space. Peter J. Henniker-Heaton. HHAm

Once we've laboriously. After "Mindwalk." Denise Levertov. UpMys

Once, when Heracles was ten months old, Alcmena. Theocritus. HePo *Fr.* Idylls.

Once, / When I lived. Nature Poem. Cornelius Eady. PfSP

Once when I looked up at the sky. Setting Sun, The. Kodama Kagai. CAoMJL1, *tr. by* Leith Morton

Once when I read the funnies. Looking. Robert Kelly. FTOS

Once, when I ventured on your deeps, Piranha. (LL) Old Malediction, An. Horace. NoAM; OBCoV; WoPoe, *tr. by* Anthony Hecht

Once when I walked into a room. Between Ourselves. Audre Lorde. ISC

Once when I was eight we came home in the dark. Stories I Tell My Daughter. Deborah A. Miranda. FiBr

Once When I Was in the Eighth Grade. Maurice Kilwein Guevara. AmPoNex

Once when I was teaching "Dover Beach." Sea of Faith. John Brehm. RaF

Once when I was Thoth. Once As Thoth Beside The Sea. Cort Day. IIR

Once when I was tree. Root Song. Henry Dumas. ISC

Once when I was very scared. Riddle, A. Charlotte Zolotow. NTCP

Once when I was young, Juanito. Mother's Tale, The. Ai. CAP-8

Once, when I wasn't very big. Cat and the Pig, The. Gerard Benson. NOxBChV

Once when our blacktop city. Ants on the Melon. Virginia Hamilton Adair. AFaM; StAl

Once when our eyes were clean as noon, our rooms. Cana. Thomas Merton. ChIV-2

(Once when our eyes were clean as noon.) GI

Once when the moon was out about three quarters. White Clover. Marvin Bell. CAP-8; InvLad; VCAP

Once when the snow of the year was beginning to fall. Runaway, The. Robert Frost. MoAmPo; SAmP

Once when young I lay and listened. To the Tune "The Fair Maid of Yu." Chiang Chieh. NDACCP, *tr. by* Kenneth Rexroth

Once, while a famous town lay torn and burning. Braveries. Robert Pinsky. HarvBoo

Once while hunting in the shady lurking wood he [Dionysus] was delighted by the rosy form of a young comrade. Nonnus. CAGL *Fr.* Dionysiaca.

Once, with a certain pride, we kept attempts. Spot the Ball. Frank Ormsby. PBCIP; PNI

Once with all the gusto of a twin-jet airplane. Collaboration: Storming the Beaches. Anthony Caleshu. NIrP

Once within a little grove a shepherdess I spied. Encounter, An. Guido Cavalcanti. NAWM-7v1, *tr. by* James J. Wilhelm

Once, years after your death, I dreamt. Dream, The. Irving Feldman. TaR; VCAP

Once you called at midnight. Anne Michaels. StAl *Fr.* Sublimation.

Once you leave home, you should be free. Upon Entering the Priesthood: A Warning. Jinkag Haesim. BecRai, *tr. by* Kim Daljin, Kim Won-Chung and Christopher Merrill

Once you said. What She Said to Her Girl-Friend. Maturaikkataiayattar Makan Vennakan. WoPoe, *tr. by* A. K. Ramanujan

Once you said joking slyly, *If I'm killed.* Faithful, The. Jane Cooper. AmWaPo

Once you showed me a poem. Wild Birds. E. A. Mares. ICANM

Once you told me my father never wept. Ancestral Burden. Alfonsina Storni. TCLAP, *tr. by* Andrew Rosing

Once you were immortal in the flame. Spark, The. Brenda Hillman. FaoP

Once you've bought into the suspension of disbelief. Purchase, The. Clarence Major. TAPaP

Once you've had one boy you can imagine all the rest. You can stand with other girls like you. Talking About Boys. Lisa Glatt. SUP

Once-in-a-Lifetime, Never-to-Be-Repeated, A. Emyr Lewis. BBMWP, *tr. by* the author

Once-in-Passing, The. Louis MacNeice. ModIr *Fr.* Hand of Snapshots, A.

Once-Over, The. Robert Pollok. STuOW *Fr.* Course of Time, The.

One. James Berry. NOxBChV

One. Federico García Lorca. PFTM-1 *Fr.* Night (Suite for Piano and Poet's Voice).

One. John Heath-Stubbs. OBCoV

One. Thomas Kinsella.
 Finistère. PBCIP
 Oldest Place, The. PBCIP
 38 Phoenix Street. ModIr

One. Edward Kleban. ReLy

One. John Roberts. ASA

One. Ntozake Shange. FaoP *Fr.* For Colored Girls Who Have Considered Suicide When the Rainbow Is Enuf.

One. Constance Fenimore Woolson. SWaP *Fr.* Two Women.

One, The. James Dickey. BodElec

One, The. Patrick Kavanagh. MoBrPo

(1) A man and woman looking for lilies. Lily Events. *Unknown.* PFTM-1

One a part of his famous society. (LL) Abraham. Delmore Schwartz. ChIV-1; TaR

One admires the American form of these sightings. Apparition, The. Carol J. Pierman. ReTh

One afternoon in her loft. Need for Shoes, The. Molly Bendall. InvLad

One afternoon in my room. True Story, A. Marvin Bell. BodElec

One afternoon in winter. (LL) Beauty and Sadness. Cathy Song. NAMCP V.2; NoAM

One afternoon the last week in April. Axe Handles. Gary Snyder. CAP-8; ColAP; LoL; NAMCP V.2; NoAM; PmAP; PoPoPo; TWF; VCAP

One among the Roses. Edmund Charles Blunden. OBGa

1 An old story. Gongula. Jerry McGuire. AnSo

One anchorage of sand appears as another dissolves away. Po Chü-i. NDACCP *Fr.* Waves Sifting Sand.

21th: and last booke of the Ocean to Scinthia, The. Sir Walter Ralegh. PBRV

One ant and another. Gathered Ants. Tachibana Akemi. EMJL, *tr. by* Haruo Shirane

One arm hooked around the frayed strap. Yellow Light. Garrett Kaoru Hongo. GeoHom; OpBo; WaAnP

One Art. Elizabeth Bishop. AmFaPo; APT-2; BLPJKO; BrAP; CAP-8; EMP; HarvBoo; IJHIL; MakPoe; NAAL-5; NALW; NAMCP V.2; NoAM; NoP-4; NoP-5; OxBoAm; PoetW; PoPoPo; SoSe-8; StAl; VCAP; WaAnP

One at one table. Automat. David Ray. PoSol

One at Rest, The. Hô Sugyông. EcSo, *tr. by* Youngju Ryu

One autumn afternoon when I was nine. Jeni Couzyn. CFP *Fr.* Christmas in Africa.

One autumn eve, when, sharp and chill. Buying a Cycle. Walter Parke. ArBi

One Autumn night, in Sudbury town. Henry Wadsworth Longfellow. APN-1 *Fr.* Tales of a Wayside Inn.

One bath / After another. Issa. ZenPo, *tr. by* Takashi Ikemoto and Lucien Stryk

One be the nail another the pincers. Vasco [*or* Vasko] Popa. PoSu *Fr.* Games.

One beautiful morning in the month of May all was serene and / quiet. May. Mrs. Henry Linden. CBWP-4

One being led? I don't know, The. Scaffold in Winter. János Pilinszky. PoSu, *tr. by* Peter Jay

One Blessing had I than the rest. Emily Dickinson. SWaP

One Body. Margaret Gibson. AmZen

One Book, The. Velemir Khlebnikov. TCRusP, *tr. by* Kathy Lewis and Bob Perelman

One bough in the land of eternal banishment. Yi Sang. CAMKP; PFTM-1 *Fr.* Crow's-Eye View.

One boy, Saint Dwyn, my bauble. Lament for Siôn y Glyn. Lewis Glyn Cothi. OBWVE, *tr. by* Joseph P. Clancy

One Breath. Antler. WhBo

One breath began the world, one can take it back again. Flesh. Katie Ford. LegDan

One Budding-Talent Wang. Han-shan (Cold Mountain). ColAnChi, *tr. by* Red Pine

1. Burned Christ to a crisp. 2. On the Betty Crocker burner. 50 Years in the Career of an Aspiring Thug. Suzanne Wise. AmPoNex; LegDan

One by one, as harvesters, all heavy laden. Sacheverell Sitwell. MoBrPo *Fr.* Agamemnon's Tomb.

One by one, I crushed the letters. Fire and Embers. Leonor Scliar-Cabral. MirDau, *tr. by* Regina Igel

One by one I've gathered up my feelings of love. *Unknown.* CATKP, *tr. by* Kevin O'Rourke

One by one many leaves. It. Muso Soseki. EaWin, *tr. by* W. S. Merwin

One by one, the ancient. Next Year, in Jerusalem. Shirley Kaufman. UnSA

One by one / the small refusals. Text of necessity. Ingrid de Kok. TSAP

One by one they appear in. My Sad Captains. Thom Gunn. NAEL-6v2; NAEL-7v2; NAMCP V.2; NoAM; NoP-4; NoP-5; NPeEn; PoPoPo; WaAnP

One cadaver said to the other. Basic Science. Fanny Howe. ExTi

One can care for boulders. Playfully Inscribed on a Large Boulder. Wang Wei. CCL1, *tr. by* David Lattimore

One can glimpse Apollo in the door of each thing. Deeds Done and Suffered by Light. Clayton Eshleman. APSN

One can rest in a war. One Can Rest. Binyo Ivanov. CSCBP, *tr. by* Georgi Belev and Lisa Sapinkopf

One can sigh, but a lifetime is needed to finish it. When the Day Comes. Mirza Asadullah Khan Ghalib. WED, *tr. by* Robert Bly and Sunil Dutta

One candle. Robert Kelly. WhBo *Fr.* Flowers of Unceasing Coincidence, The.

One cannot live in the same room twice. (LL) Variation on Heraclitus. Louis MacNeice. NAMCP V.1; NoAM

One can't / have it. Coming Right Up. A. R. Ammons. OBCoV

1. cause when he laughs at my jokes or tells me he likes my clothes it can't be anything but the truth. 10 Reasons Why I Fall in Love with Inaccessible Straight Boys Every Damn Time. Richard Murray Vaughan. Coast

One childhood day. Integration. Angela Shannon. BtF

One Christmas Night in Pontgibaud. After Hilaire Belloc. Max Beerbohm. UV

One Coat of Paint. John Ashbery. OxBoAm

One cold and dismal night. Unidentified Flying Object on an Errand of Love. Mihangel Morgan. BBMWP, *tr. by* Martin Davis

One cold freezing morning I lay dis body down. Every Hour in the Day. *Unknown.* SSUS

One collector of the psalms. Gloss. Brooks Haxton. PoCho

One constant in a world of variables. Homo Suburbiensis. Bruce Dawe. BMAP

One could do worse than be a swinger of birches. (LL) Birches. Robert Frost. AmFaPo; APT-1; BrAP; FaBoVe; HarvBoo; HeIP-4; ITBLP; MoAmPo; NAAL-5; NAAPv.2; NAMCP V.1; NoAM; NoP-4; NoP-5; OxBoAm; PoPoPo; SAmP; SoSe-8; TCAPo; TFi; TRP; WaAnP

One crown that no one seeks. Emily Dickinson. ChIV-2

One Crucifixion is recorded—only. Emily Dickinson. APN-2

One cunning bosom-sin blows quite away. (LL) Sin (1). George Herbert. NoP-4; NoP-5; OxAEP-1; WaAnP

One current flows, the other does not. Stone Stream. Pou Kuksa. BecRai, *tr. by* Kim Daljin, Kim Won-Chung and Christopher Merrill

One Day! J. Wilbur Chapman. SacPr

One Day. J. ch'ôn Yanghûi. EcSo, *tr. by* Aimee N. Kwon

One day. Room of One's Own, A. Hoda Hussein. PoArWo, *tr. by* Cornelia Al-Khaled

One day. Imogene Elizabeth Kennedy. PFTM-2, *tr. by* Edward Kamau Brathwaite

One day. One day. Imogene Elizabeth Kennedy. PFTM-2, *tr. by* Edward Kamau Brathwaite

One Day. Ray Mathew. NOBAu

One Day. Bobbi Sykes. BMAP

One Day. Boris Vian. YaTCFP, *tr. by* Rosemary Lloyd

One day, a simple one. Kh'hob dikh lib. Yuri Suhl. Prolet, *tr. by* Amelia Glaser

One day as he did raunge the fields abroad. Edmund Spenser. NoSic *Fr.* Faerie Queene, The.

One day at noon I crossed. Sandy Yard, The. Edith Jay Scovell. HarvBoo

One day, feeling hungry, I swallowed the moon. One day, feeling hungry. Gwyneth Lewis. NeBrP

One day he perched on a tree with dew. Migratory Bird. Chenjerai Hove. HBAPE

One day he realized. Orpheus. Stephen Perry. MiVo

One day he woke up tired, bone-tired. Passing of the Old Man, The. Albert Huffstickler. TiP2

One day I asked the donkey where are. From the Precious Tears of the Donkey. Kazuko Shiraishi. WoBe, *tr. by* Samuel Grolmes and Yumiko Tsumura

One day, I decided to postpone believing the tale until the school bell rings. Voices. Sumaiya El-Sousy. PoArWo, *tr. by* Atef Abu-Seif and Nathalie Handal

One day I dreamt myself. To the Child That Never Was. Emma Sepúlveda-Pulvirenti. TANSG, *tr. by* Shaun Griffin

One day I forgot Jerusalem and my right arm is withered. Warning, A. Grace Paley. TaR

One Day I Know the Page. Amina Saïd. PoArWo, *tr. by* Lucy McNair

One day I saw a ship pass close by. Pelican, The. Adelia Prado. TCLAP, *tr. by* Marcia Kirinus

One day I saw Chicago river move. Chicago. Margaret Walker Alexander. GT

One day I suddenly notice this object within my sight for ten years. One Day I Suddenly Notice. Jean Follain. MotU, *tr. by* Mary Feeney and William Matthews

One day I went and bought a fake fur coat. How I Had to Act. Molly Peacock. FFC

One day I went to London. Maurice Carpenter. RSaN *Fr.* Ballad of John Nameless, The.

One day I went walking and. Man in a Shell, The. Angela Ball. ExTi

One day I wrote her name upon the strand. Edmund Spenser. BrAP; CABP; HeIP-4; NAEL-6v1; NAEL-7v1; NoP-4; NoP-5; NoSic; OxBSo; PoPoPo; TFi; WaAnP; WeW-3 *Fr.* Amoretti.

One Day I Wrote Her Name Upon the Strand. Edmund Spenser. *See* Sonnet 75: "One day I wrote her name upon the strand."

One day I'll lift the telephone. Elegy for My Father, Who Is Not Dead. Andrew Hudgins. RA

One day in a popular quarter of Kharkov. Images. Valery Larbaud. BLT, *tr. by* William Jay Smith

One day in the bluest of summer weather. Bird Language. Christopher Pearse Cranch. APN-1

One day in the forest there was somebody. Stranger, The. W. S. Merwin. OxBoAm

One day love. On the Evening of a Wedding. Graham Foust. IIR

One day, my father chopped down. Too Young to Know. Cornelius Eady. PfSP; WaAnP

One day my husband came home with a jar of generic peanut butter. Marriage. Stephanie Brown. BodElec

One day, not here, you will find a hand. Again. Charlotte Mew. MoBrPo

One day of kindergarten had scared. Second-Grade Incident from Robert Frost's Childhood, A. Joe Aimone. VisFro

One day of my life I had a girlfriend, The. Last Ditch. Jason Schneiderman. BeDoSh

One day one young Creole candio. Criole Candjo. George Washington Cable. APN-2

One day, perhaps when you are. How the Earth Loves You. David Waltner-Toews. ACAMVP

One day / she fell. Monosyllable, The. Josephine Jacobsen. OxBoAm

One day soon he'll tell her it's time to start packing. Drifters. Bruce Dawe. BMAP; NoAM

One day swallows another day. Lemon for Me, A. No Ch'ŏnmyŏng. CAMKP, *tr. by* Mickey Hong

One day the Amorous Lysander. Disappointment, The. Aphra Behn. BASC; BrAP; CABP; EMWP; EroLit; NAEL-7v1; NALW; NoP-4; NoP-5; NOSC; PEW; WaAnP

One day, / the apolitical. Apolitical Intellectuals. Otto René Castillo. AF, *tr. by* Margaret Randall

One day the Chinese Bird of Royalty, Fum. Fum and Hum, the Two Birds of Royalty. Thomas Moore. OBSV

One day the gift arrives—outside your door. Gift, The. Kevin Hart. RSR

One day the Nouns were clustered in the street. Permanently. Kenneth Koch. NoP-4; NoP-5; OxBoAm; PmAP; PoA 2002

One day the time had come. Visit, The. Toon Tellegen. TuT, *tr. by* Peter van de Kamp

One day they said. Purdah, 1. Imtiaz Dharker. NeBl

One day,—'twas on a summer afternoon. Leigh Hunt. NOBRP *Fr.* Story of Rimini, The.

One day we notice that the sun. Feeding the Sun. Bill Knott. PBCAP

One day we will make our perfect journey. Trans-Siberian Express, The. Don Paterson. EdScPo

One Day We'll Be Able to Talk to the Dead. Jackie Wills. PoCu

One day when heaven was filled with his praises. One Day! J. Wilbur Chapman. SacPo

One day when the sun shone on the water and Golden. Introduction to a Prayer. Fritzi Harmsen van Beek. WoPoe, *tr. by* Claire Nicholas White

One day you finally knew. Journey, The. Mary Oliver. StAl; TWF

One day you got tired. Portrait of the artist. Wopko Jensma. TSAP

One day you wake up. From Here to Eternity. Mary Ruefle. AmAlph

One day you will see clearly. Door, The: anticipation of wisdom. Kapka Kassabova. StAl

One day you will slip into an airport. Regret. Michael Lieberman. BloBone

One decade into the 20th century. Imagist at Coney Island. Maura Eichner. UpMys

One December Night. Denise Levertov. BodElec

(1) Did the people of Viet Nam use lanterns of stone? Denise Levertov. *See* Did the people of Viet Nam.

One didn't know the name of Tarzan's monkey. Shibboleth. Michael Donaghy. NeBrP

One died, and the soul was wrenched out. Street Musicians. John Ashbery. PoPoPo

One Dismal Night. San Juan de la Cruz. SpanPo, *tr. by* Kate Flores

One dismal night. One Dismal Night. San Juan de la Cruz. SpanPo, *tr. by* Kate Flores

One does not bathe twice in the same stream, said the philosopher Heraclitus. Rue Ravignan, The. Max Jacob. YaTCFP, *tr. by* John Ashbery

1. Don't see him. Don't phone or write a letter. Two Cures for Love. Wendy Cope. OBCoV

One door alone is shut, one chamber still. (LL) Gone. Mary Elizabeth Coleridge. OBEV; PoBW; VWP

One dot / Grainily shifting we at roadside and. Bee, The. James Dickey. AmFaPo

One doth not stroke me, nor the other strike. (LL) To Fool or Knave. Ben Jonson. NoP-4; NoP-5

One dread knocked out another. Elegy 11: Ford. Eric Mottram. Oth

One Dream. Li Yu [*or* Li Hou-Chu]. CCL1, *tr. by* Sam Houston Brock

One dream of passion and of beauty more! Properzia Rossi. Felicia Dorothea Hemans. NPBRoP; RWP; ViWPN; VWP

One dream that scarce outlasts the burning of a candle or a petal's fall. One Dream. Li Yu [*or* Li Hou-Chu]. CCL1, *tr. by* Sam Houston Brock

One drop of dharma water. Ancient Origin. Muso Soseki. EaWin, *tr. by* W. S. Merwin

One drop of wine wherewith wild rain has mixed. (LL) And in the Hanging Gardens. Conrad Potter Aiken. APT-1; MoAmPo

One duck stood on my toes. Feeding Ducks. Norman Alexander MacCaig. HarvBoo

One Duke and twenty [*or* twentie] places. (LL) Epitaph on the Duke of Buckingham. *Unknown.* BASC; NPeEn; PBRV

One eagle after another. Gone Are Those We Love. Fadwa Tuqan. CFP, *tr. by* Kamal Boullata

1-800-HOT-RIBS. Catherine Bowman. P180

01 84. Michael Haslam. Oth *Fr.* Continual Song.

One either believes in God. In California. Kathy Fagan. GeoHom

One end is moo, the other, milk. (LL) Cow, The. Ogden Nash. NBLV; NoP-4; NoP-5

One evening an exceptionally abstract communication came over the airwaves. Henri Michaux. PFTM-2 *Fr.* Saisir.

One evening, breaking a jeep journey at Capuzzo. Hamish Henderson. FaBoWar *Fr.* Elegies for the Dead in Cyrenaica.

One evening in August, the light already failing. Elegy for the Unknown Soldier. Michael O'Loughlin. PBCIP

One evening in February I came near to dying here. Alone. Tomas Tranströmer. StAl; WoPoe, *tr. by* Robin Fulton

One evening, oh Senghor. Dialogue of the Colours. Buland Al-Haidari. IrPoTo, *tr. by* Hussein Kadhim and Christopher Merrill

One evening, walking in the public way. Statue Horse. William Wordsworth. NPBRoP

One evening, we entered our room with. Flight from the Marriage Bed. Lisa M. Carbone. PasH

One evening when a genial air. Nightfall. Gwen Harwood. BMAP

One evening, when gorse was burning. Early Days. John Stuart Williams. TCAWP

One ever hangs where shelled roads part. At a Calvary near the Ancre. Wilfred Owen. ChIV-2; GI

One ewe. Shepherd's Night Count. Jane Yolen. TLR

One Explanation of Beauty. Mark Wunderlich. AmPoNex

One eye crystal, one eye flame, it arrives. Mimi Khalvati. NewEx

One eye without a head to wear it. Phyllis McGinley. OBSV *Fr.* Spectator's Guide to Contemporary Art.

One face looks out from all his canvas[s]es. In An Artist's Studio. Christina Georgina Rossetti. NAEL-6v2; NAEL-7v2; NALW; NoP-4; NoP-5; PEW; ViWPN; VWP

One failure on. Their Sex Life. A. R. Ammons. OBCoV; OxBoAm

One Faith and No Faith [*epigram*]. Friedrich von Logau. GePo, *tr. by* George C. Schoolfield

One fall after another. The snow. Mother Ruin. Linda Gregerson. ExTi

One fantee wave. Dame Edith Sitwell. OBMV *Fr.* Gold Coast Customs.

One fat poppy dawdles. Garden of Eden, The. Ágnes Nemes Nagy. IQMS, *tr. by* Hugh Maxton

One fatal mistake that is made today is gossip. Gossip. Mrs. Henry Linden. CBWP-4

One feels like an animal. Sinking Feeling, A. Amy Gerstler. BodElec

One Filament against the Firmament. Matthea Harvey. IAoNAP; PoDa

One Fine Day. János Pilinszky. PoSu, *tr. by* Peter Jay

One fine day. Traumerei. David Shapiro. BodElec

One fine morning, in a land of very gentle people, a superb man. Royalty. Arthur Rimbaud. MotU, *tr. by* Louise Varese

One fine morning they move in for the pinch. Lurid Confessions. Steve Kowit. SUP

One Flesh. Julia Casterton. Prnts

One Flesh. Elizabeth Jennings. LW; NoP-4; NoP-5; OxAEP-2; Prnts

One Flower and Another Flower. Hwang Tonggyu. CAMKP, *tr. by* Anthony, Brother of Taizé

One flower at a time, please. Bouquets. Robert Francis. ChAP

One flower lying behind the bars.   One Flower and Another Flower.   Hwang Tonggyu.   CAMKP, *tr.* by Anthony, Brother of Taizé

One Fond Embrace.   Thomas Kinsella.
"Enough."   ModIr

One foot in Eden still, I stand.   One Foot in Eden.   Edwin Muir.   EdScPo; NoAM

One foot on the floor, one knee in bed.   Evening Wind.   Robert Mezey.   PoSol

One For a Keepsake Album.   Ferenc Kölcsey.   IQMS, *tr.* by Adam Makkai

One for All Newborns.   Thylias Moss.   OxAAAP

One For Balassi.   Ferenc Kölcsey.   IQMS, *tr.* by George Sutherland Fraser

One for Charlie Mingus.   Quincy Troupe.   SpirFl

One For Miss Pardo's Travel Diary.   Mihály Vörösmarty.   IQMS, *tr.* by Adam Makkai

One for My Baby (And One More for the Road).   Harold Arlen and Johnny Mercer.   ReLy

One For Pope Paul.   Janus Pannonius.   IQMS, *tr.* by George Burrough and Adam Makkai

One for the "Ancient Gypsy."   Gyula Juhász.   IQMS, *tr.* by Adam Makkai

One for the Anthologies.   Gavin Ewart.   OBCoV

147. 67.   Peter Riley.   VaPo *Fr.* Excavations.

One fourth second after the earth had rolled.   Celebration.   Gene Shuford.   TiP2

One from another, nor needs no other. (LL)   Kiwi Bird in the Kiwi Tree, The.   Charles Bernstein.   FTOS; NAMCP V.2

One from One Leaves Two.   Ogden Nash.
"I pray the Lord my soul to take."   NBLV

One: "From Sappho to myself, consider the fate of women."   Carolyn Kizer.   CAP-8; VCAP *Fr.* Pro Femina.

One garland.   Divorcing.   Denise Levertov.   NALW

One generation passeth away, and another generation cometh: but the earth abideth for ever. Ecclesiastes 1:4.   Jones Very.   ChIV-1

One Girl at the Boys Party, The.   Sharon Olds.   OxBoAm

One Girl's Dance.   Leah Aini.   DTA, *tr.* by Miriyam Glazer

One girl's dance.   One Girl's Dance.   Leah Aini.   DTA, *tr.* by Miriyam Glazer

One glance was enough.   In the Ritz at Meknes.   Manuel Ulacia.   RMCMP, *tr.* by Indran Amirthanayagam

I go to Zoo.   Bill Griffiths.   Oth *Fr.* Building: The New London Hospital.

One Golgotha.   Douglas Livingstone.   TSAP

One good mistress deserves another.   Paul Eluard and Benjamin Péret.   SurPaPo *Fr.* 152 Proverbs Mis au Goût du Jour.

One got peace of heart at last, the dark march over.   After War.   Ivor Gurney.   HarvBoo

One grandchild runs with a net.   Butterfly Net, The.   John Bensko.   YaYoPo

One grandma.   Two Grandmas.   Stanley H. Barkan.   UnSA

One granite ridge.   Piute Creek.   Gary Snyder.   OxBoAm

One grey and foaming day.   R. P. Blackmur.   APT-2

One half of me was up and dressed.   Gentle Check, The.   Joseph Beaumont.   NOSC

One hand on her hip, one hand.   Nathaniel Mackey.   OxAAAP *Fr.* Song of the Andoumboulou.

One hand's arthritic and chained to the pendulum.   Hands of the Old Métis, The.   Maurice Kilwein Guevara.   NAPBL

One hard cold after another came.   Winter 1967.   Lenard D. Moore.   ISC

One Hard Look.   Robert Graves.   MoBrPo

One has learned to allow a tiny space in the head for contingency.   What Was My Choice?   Fawzi Karim.   IrPoTo, *tr.* by Chuck Miller and Saadi A. Simawe

One Heart's Enough for Me.   Auguste Mignon.   TreFP

One heaven and earth.   Cave of the Thousand Pines.   Muso Soseki.   EaWin, *tr.* by W. S. Merwin

101: The One Hope.   Dante Gabriel Rossetti.   BrAP; GSo; NAEL-6v2; NAEL-7v2 *Fr.* House of Life, The.

One horse you gave me, The.   Appaloosa, The.   Afaa Michael Weaver.   GT

One hound alone has crossed the dreary height.   Deep-Toned Jowler, The.   James Hogg.   DiBP

One hound alone has crossed the dreary height.   James Hogg.   DiBP *Fr.* Mador of the Moor.

1. How comely glisten the rounded cheeks and the swelling thighs!   Fatness.   Alan Ansen.   GPTC

One hugs me.   Vasco [*or* Vasko] Popa.   PoSu *Fr.* Raw Flesh.

One human being.   Issa.   EH, *tr.* by Robert Hass

152 Proverbs Mis au Goût du Jour.   Paul Eluard and Benjamin Péret. *tr.* by Julien Levy
"One good mistress deserves another."   SurPaPo, *tr.* by Julien Levy

One Hundred and Fifty Years.   Jack Davis.   BMAP

One Hundred and Forty-Ninth Chorus.   Jack Kerouac.   PmAP *Fr.* Mexico City Blues.

110 Degrees in Dallas.   Frederick Turner.   TiP2

113th Chorus.   Jack Kerouac.   PmAP *Fr.* Mexico City Blues.

125th Street.   Langston Hughes.   APT-2; NAMCP V.1

127th Chorus.   Jack Kerouac.   PmAP *Fr.* Mexico City Blues.

100 Differences Between Poetry and Prose.   Tom Leonard.   Oth

One Hundred Eighty.   Giusi Busceti.   ItPo, *tr.* by Gayle Ridinger

151st Psalm, The.   Karl Shapiro.   TaR

152 Into 5,*El Centro Palabra de Fe.*   M. L. Williams.   GeoHom

One Hundred Lines for the Coast.   Kojo Laing.   HBAPE

100 Love Sonnets.   Pablo Neruda.
17.   BeAl, *tr.* by Stephen Tapscott
89.   BeAl, *tr.* by Stephen Tapscott

One hundred million Africans slaughtered.   100 Million.   Matthew Watley.   BtF

119. 3.   Peter Riley.   VaPo *Fr.* Excavations.

175. 123.   Peter Riley.   VaPo *Fr.* Excavations.

171. 115.   Peter Riley.   VaPo *Fr.* Excavations.

100 Times.   Arnold J. Kemp.   BtF

125th Street and Abomey.   Audre Lorde.   OxAAAP

One hundred watts blinded me.   Notes on living inside the lightbulb.   Gillian Allnutt.   NeBrP

One Hut.   Muso Soseki.   EaWin, *tr.* by W. S. Merwin

One I didn't go on, The.   Bike Ride with Older Boys.   Laura Kasischke.   ArBi

1. I know that none of this goes anywhere.   Arrythmia (1–10).   Dallas Angguish.   BeDoSh

One I loathed, my one malignant foe, The.   Posthumous Revenge.   Francis Saltus Saltus.   VerBaPo

One I Love (Belongs to Someone Else), The.   Gustave Kahn.   ReLy

One I Love, The.   *Unknown.*   CCL1, *tr.* by Anne Birrell

One I love, The.   One I Love, The.   *Unknown.*   CCL1, *tr.* by Anne Birrell

One. / I smelt the weird Atlantic.   Thomas Kinsella.   PBCIP *Fr.* One.

1 I'd like to roll my cigarette through life.   Attitudes.   Sotère Torregian.   AHA

One in All, The.   Margaret Fuller.   SWaP

One in the boat cried out.   Door, The.   Leonard Alfred George Strong.   MoBrPo

One Inch of Love Is an Inch of Ashes.   Anne Waldman.   AmZen

One instant I was asleep in bed; the next.   You Missed the Earthquake, Bill.   Charles Harper Webb.   GeoHom

One is always nearer by not keeping still. (LL)   On the Move.   Thom Gunn.   CalPo; NoP-4; NoP-5; OxAEP-2; TRP; WaAnP

One is dying of desire to see me if only for a moment.   *Unknown.*   SLW, *tr.* by Marjolijn De Jager, Sayd Bahodin Majrouh and André Velter

One is Genius Itself—the other Beauty.   FigTree.   Stephanie Strickland.   ExTi

One is One.   Marie Ponsot.   ExTi

One is so seldom struck by lightning.   For the Poet Who Said Poets Are Struck by Lightning Only Two or Three Times.   Peter Klappert.   NBLV

One is whole. One is not.   Kathleen Fraser.   PfS

1. It's a long way from China to Bremen. How late is it?   Tea Merchant, The.   H. C. Artmann.   MotU, *tr.* by Stuart Friebert

One I've not seen. (LL)   As I saw.   George Oppen.   APT-2; PFTM-1

One Kind of Freedom Speaks.   Erich Fried.   AF, *tr.* by Georg Rapp

One kind of logic is a road cut into the side of a steep, wooded hill.   Glimpse of Terrain.   Thomas Bolt.   YaYoPo

One kind of rain gets to be.   Eight Elegies.   Rick Barot.   LegDan

One kisses Ramén goodnight on Bank Street in the Village.   Kissing Ramén.   Michael Lassell.   WiU

One Knows Not What One Is.   "Angelus Silesius."   GePo *Fr.* Cherubical Wanderer, The.

One knows nothing of their life. The sea.   Minor Poets, The.   Damon Krukowski.   OnScMo

One lady poet was a nymphomaniac and wrote for Vanity Fair.   Lady Poets With Foot Notes, The.   Ernest Hemingway.   IllVoic

One leaves his leaves at home.   Great Mullen.   William Carlos Williams.   OxBoAm

One less.   Lost Body.   Terry Ehret.   GifTon

One Life.   Andrew Motion.   HarvBoo

One Life.   Adrienne Rich.   CAP-8; OxBoAm

One Life to Live.   Ira Gershwin.   ReLy

One lifetime in office.   Chinese Figures 1.   *Unknown.*   EaWin, *tr.* by W. S. Merwin

One lily scented all the dark. It grew.   One Night.   Lizette Woodworth Reese.   APN-2

One Little Boy.   *Unknown.*   NOxBChV

One little hour in jeopardy. (LL)   To a Calvinist in Bali.   Edna St. Vincent Millay.   NAMCP V.1; NoAM

One little kiss.   Remember.   Irving Berlin.   ReLy

One little mess of whelks, so he may 'scape! (LL)   Caliban upon Setebos; or, Natural Theology in the Island.   Robert Browning.   NAEL-6v2; NAEL-7v2; OxAEP-2

One lone tree.   Larger Loneliness, A.   Eli Bosnick.   IJHIL

One long and humid afternoon.   Love Song.   Rofel G. Brion.   PML; ReBoTo

One long-dead.   Another Revenant.   Denise Levertov.   UpMys

One look at you and I knew.   No Hands.   Helena Nelson.   ArBi

One looks around and sees.   Perspectives.   Chiqui Vicioso.   TANSG, tr. by Emma Jane Robinett

One looks from the train.   Orient Express, The.   Randall Jarrell.   BeAl

One Lost, The.   Isaac Rosenberg.   MoBrPo

One lost track of the story.   Among Strangers.   Silvia Curbelo.   OPRER

One lovely summer afternoon when balmy breezes blew.   To Clements' Ferry.   Josephine D. Henderson Heard.   CBWP-4; SWaP

One Man.   William Scammell.   NLP

One man except, the only son of light.   John Milton.   NOSC Fr. Paradise Lost.

One man made a ladder.   Return: Buffalo.   Linda Hogan.   BodElec

One man shall smile one day and say goodbye.   Cambodia.   James Fenton.   AF; PoAgWa; StAl

One man won't say anything.   Star-Spangled.   Michele Glazer.   OPRER

One man's dick had the quaint.   Wayne Koestenbaum.   WiU Fr. Erotic Collectibles.

One Man's Family.   Rosemary Catacalos.   FTtHH

One Meat Ball.   Thomas Lux.   ReTh

One midnight, after a day when lilies.   Digging.   Donald Hall.   CAP-8

One Million Men Marching 2.   Bernard Keller.   BtF

One minute of sitting, one inch of Buddha.   Manzan.   WhBo; ZenPo, tr. by Takashi Ikemoto and Lucien Stryk

One moment, and that realm is ours! On, on, dark rolling stream! (LL)   Indian Woman's Death-Song, The.   Felicia Dorothea Hemans.   NoP-4; NoP-5; NPBRoP; PEW; RWP

One Moment My Hope Rises Up On Wings.   Baldomero Garcilaso de la Vega.   SpanPo, tr. by Edwin Morgan

One moment my hope rises up on wings.   One Moment My Hope Rises Up On Wings.   Baldomero Garcilaso de la Vega.   SpanPo, tr. by Edwin Morgan

One moment past our bodies cast.   Rudyard Kipling.   NoAM Fr. Second Jungle Book, The.

One moon of joy I knew.   Neglected Wife, The.   Yi Talch'ung.   WoPoe, tr. by Jean S. Grigsby

One moon seen, in all the waters, The.   Xuanjue.   CCL1 Fr. Canticle of the Way.

One Moon Seen, The.   Xuanjue.   CCL1 Fr. Canticle of the Way.

One More Brevity.   Robert Frost.   APT-1

One More Bruised Heart!   Louisa Sarah Bevington.   VWP

One more bruised heart laid bare! one victim more!   One More Bruised Heart!   Louisa Sarah Bevington.   VWP

One more day gone, / done, found in / the form of days.   Again.   Robert Creeley.   NAMCP V.2; VCAP

One more little spirit to Heaven has flown.   Little Libbie.   Julia A. Moore.   SWaP

One More New Botched Beginning.   Stephen Spender.   NoAM

One more night my blood.   O Wendy, Arthur.   Maurice Kenny.   HATNAP

One more of those perfections.   You Get What You Pay For.   Allen Curnow.   HarvBoo

One More Once.   Reuben Jackson.   BtF

One More River.   Unknown.   APN-2

One More River to Cross.   John Beecher.   InGu

One More Sign.   Roberta Hill Whiteman.   HATNAP

One more unfortunate.   Bridge of Sighs, The.   Thomas Hood.   BRP; OBEV; OxAEP-2; TreFP

One morn before me were three figures seen.   Ode on Indolence.   John Keats.   NAEL-6v2; NAEL-7v2; NPBRoP

One Morn I Left Him in His Bed.   Elizabeth Stoddard.   SWaP

One morn I left him in his bed.   One Morn I Left Him in His Bed.   Elizabeth Stoddard.   SWaP

One morning a peasant.   Wall of Genesis, The.   Ahmed Taha.   AnVo, tr. by Mohamed Enani

One Morning Beside a Pond.   Rofel G. Brion.   ReBoTo

One morning early I met armoured cars.   Toome Road, The.   Seamus Heaney.   StAl

One morning I shall find.   Maisie.   James Merrill.   HeIP-4

One morning I was a-walking down.   Unknown.   TCAPo

One morning I'll come home.   Love in the Time of Cholera.   Gzar Hantoosh.   IrPoTo, tr. by Saadi A. Simawe and Ellen Doré Watson

One morning in April, a short time ago.   Julia A. Moore.   VerBaPo Fr. Little Libbie.

One morning in June above Yosemite Valley, John Muir learned.   Sierra Bear.   David Bottoms.   GifTon

One morning in spring.   Fife Tune.   John Streeter Manifold.   FaBoWar; NBLV; NOBAu

One morning just like that they arrive.   Mercedès F. Guignard.   OGAHCP Fr. They're Leaving with a Bridle Round the Neck.

One Morning: "Looking for distinctive stones, I found the dead otter."   Eamon Grennan.   P180

One morning of August.   Lament for MacGregor of Glenstrae.   Mrs. MacGregor of Glanstrae.   NePenScot, tr. by Iain Crichton Smith

One mummy walks on snow.   Mummies.   Nicanor Parra.   TCLAP, tr. by Thomas Merton

One musician is sure.   Harp, The.   Ralph Waldo Emerson.   APN-1

One must completely destroy all logic in Variety Theater performances.   Filippo Tommaso Marinetti.   PFTM-1 Fr. Variety Theater Manifesto, The.

One must have a mind of winter.   Snow Man, The.   Wallace Stevens.   AmFaPo; APT-1; ColAP; GoPo; HarvBoo; HeIP-4; IJHIL; MoW; NAAL-5; NAAPv.2; NAMCP V.1; NoAM; NoP-4; NoP-5; OxBoAm; PoA 2002; PoPoPo; SoSe-8; StAl; TCAPo; TRP; WaAnP; WeW-3

One must have breakfasted often on automobile primer.   Note to Tony Towle (After WS), A.   Charles North.   FTOS; PmAP

One must, to find your tomb.   Mariner's Ideal Epitaph.   Juan Ramón Jiménez.   SpanPo, tr. by Kate Flores

One name for it is knowledge. (LL)   Robert Penn Warren.   NAAL-5; NAAPv.2 Fr. Audubon: A Vision.

One name, Ianthe, shall not die. (LL)   Walter Savage Landor.   NOBRP; NPeEn; OxBEV; TFi; WeW-3 Fr. Ianthe.

One need not be a Chamber—to be Haunted.   Emily Dickinson.   APN-2; ItP; NAAPv.1; NALW

One needs sand from the sea, we have known.   Rossana Ombres.   NeIt Fr. Excursion to Ravenna of A Young Girl with Her Parents.

One net made of the sweetest tears.   Fisher King.   Imani Tolliver.   BtF

Bobbi was as surprised as she could be by the.   Bunch of Pictures Back from the Drugstore, A: The Four Good Ones.   Robert Masterson.   ICANM

One Night.   Constantine P. Cavafy.   CAGL; EroLit, tr. by Edmund Keeley and Philip Sherrard

One Night.   Lizette Woodworth Reese.   APN-2

"One night," a doctor said, "last fall."   Ambrose Bierce.   APN-2 Fr. Devil's Dictionary, The.

One night, after a storm, the sort of storm.   Peace of Lodi, The.   Norman Dubie.   BodElec

One night all tired with the weary day.   Gnat, The.   Joseph Beaumont.   NOSC

One Night America: A Boy and His Blowtorch.   M. Loncar.   NAPBL

One night as I lay on my bed.   Death.   Unknown.   OBWVE, tr. by Aneirin Talfan Davies

One night as I lay on the green hill.   My Father's Whistle.   Len Roberts.   MiVo

One night, as I was pondering of late.   John Oldham.   NOSC Fr. Satyr, A.

One Night at Victoria Beach.   Gabriel Okara.   PoetW

One night / deep in middle age.   Situation No. 7: The Poison Lover.   David Citino.   UpMys

One Night I Count the Stars.   Yun Tongju.   CAMKP, tr. by Kay Richards and Steffen Richards

One night I dreamt that in a gleaming hall.   Digby Mackworth Dolben.   OxBSo

One night I heard my parents calling.   Cold Wood.   Alan Shapiro.   WaAnP

One night I was home alone.   Eileen's Vision.   Eileen Myles.   BodElec

One night in late October.   Judged by the Company One Keeps.   Unknown.   NBLV

One night of tempest I arose and went.   Night and Morning.   Unknown.   OBWVE

One night on Monterey Bay the death-freeze of the century.   Adrienne Rich.   GeoHom; WaAnP Fr. Atlas of the Difficult World, An.

One night / One night full of perfumes, music of wings and murmurs.   Nocturne.   José Asunción Silva.   BLPSL, tr. by Rene de Costa, Rigas Kappatos and Eleni Paidoussi

One night our block leader set a competition.   Soup.   Tony Curtis.   TCAWP

One Night Stand.   Kenward Elmslie.   FTOS

One night the cows broke through the fence and got into the alfalfa field.   Bloating and Its Remedies.   Jim Heynen.   MotU

One night the tide went out.   Sea, The.   Esther Morgan.   BeAl

One night two hunters, drunk, came in the tent.   At the Piano.   Andrew Hudgins.   UpMys

One night, when I couldn't sleep.   Trick, The.   John Mole.   NOxBChV

One night when I was traveling home.   Negro on the Subway.   Malka Lee.   Prolet, tr. by Amelia Glaser

One Night When We Paused Half-way.   Kate Clanchy.   MFPA

One Night With a Stranger at 30.   Lisa Glatt.   AmPoNex

One no bigger than the head of a pencil, The.   Spiders I Have Known.   W. S. Merwin.   MotU

One noonday, at my window in the town.   Ball's Bluff.   Herman Melville.   AmWaPo; CBCWP; FaBoWar; OBWP; OxBoAm

One. now another. one.   W. D. Snodgrass.   InvLad Fr. Snow Songs.

One observes them, one expects them. Turkeys Observed. Seamus Heaney. OWoS

One o'Clock. Philippe Soupault. AF, tr. by Eden Paul

One o'Clock at Night. Mina Loy. OxBoAm

One o'clock in the letter-box. Meeting, The. Muriel Rukeyser. MoAmPo

One of Essence's Entrances. Clark Coolidge. NYP2

One of her hands holds a pomegranates. Pallas. Cyrus Atabay. GTCP, tr. by Reinhold Grimm

One of King Henry's favourites began. Groom of the Chamber's Religion in King Henry the Eighth's Time, A. John Harington. NoSic; PBRV

One of me stuttered and one. Andrew Zawacki. LegDan Fr. Viatica.

One of my wings beat faster. Growing Up. William Stafford. CAP-8

One of our race's great lights has gone out to the world. Paul Laurence Dunbar. Mrs. Henry Linden. CBWP-4

One of our race's greatest needs in this country today. Y. M. C. A, The. Mrs. Henry Linden. CBWP-4

One of the Awl Songs. Unknown. APN-2; NAAPv.1 Fr. Mountain Chant, The.

One of the Boys. James Simmons. ModIr; PNI

One of the Citizens. Rodney Jones. InGu

One of the cool things about Jeff Derksen is that it's hard to tell. Darren Wershler-Henry. PoPra Fr. Ten Out of Ten, or, Why Poetry Criticism Sucks in 2003.

One of the criminals who were hanged railed at him. Jorge Luis Borges. GI Fr. St. Luke.

One of the few pleasures of writing. Publication Date. Franz Wright. AmAlph

One of the first things we learn in school is. Raising My Hand. "Antler." IJHIL

One of the guests arrives with irises, all. Hostess. Laura Kasischke. PoDa

One of the Lives. W. S. Merwin. OxBoAm

One of the Lords of Life. David J. Rothman. GeoH

One of the most formidable artistic panoramas of all time. Darren Wershler-Henry. PoPra Fr. Ten Out of Ten, or, Why Poetry Criticism Sucks in 2003.

One of the mysteries of the body is why the heart does not. Why the Heart Never Develops Cancer. Bill Mohr. SUP

One of the ones that Midas touched. Emily Dickinson. APN-2

One of the oxen said. Christmas Poem, A. Dick Davis. ChrPo

One of the Strangest. May Swenson. APT-2; OWoS

One of them was a Turk. Ravine. Luke Icarus Simon. PML, tr. by the author

One of these days she will lie there and be dead. Grimalkin. Thomas Lynch. EmeKit

One of those back roads, the day you wanted to go to the diner. Capstone. Ethan Paquin. LegDan

One of those days. I Remember Dexedrine. 1970. Pamela Brown. BMAP

One of those great, garishly emerald flies that always look freshly generated from fresh excrement. My Fly. C. K. Williams. AmFaPo

One of those times I knew even then. Pleasure. Dean Young. IllVoic

One of Us. Kathleen Jamie. GPPA

One of us said, how odd. "H. D." NALW; NAMCP V.1 Fr. Tribute to the Angels.

One of you is lying. (LL) Unfortunate Coincidence. Dorothy Parker. AmWit; LW; NoP-4; NoP-5; OxBoAm

One of your breaths contains. One Breath. Antler. WhBo

One / O-N-E. Sophie, Climbing the Stairs. Dolores Kendrick. ESEAA

One. One. Laurie Duggan. BMAP Fr. Ash Range, The.

One or More Together. John Godfrey. FTOS

One or mostly. And I am lonely and small in all this, goodnight. Dana Lisa Lustig. AnSo

One or two lines to thee I'll here commend. To the Reader, in Vindication of This Book. Elizabeth Bradford. EMWP

One ought to learn. The Winter Trees. Winter Trees. Ágnes Nemes Nagy. IQMS, tr. by Ila Egon

One Page in The American Heritage Dictionary. Carole Oles. PoA 2002

One pair ridiculous gorilla slippers; 3 pairs of cheap shit sunglasses. Kenneth Goldsmith. HeMarv Fr. Punk.

One pale morning in June at four o'clock. Rolf Jacobsen. See Pale morning in June 4 A.M., A.

One parks the bike. The yard is full of rounded. Leslie Kaplan. SCFWP Fr. L'Excès-L'usine.

One Perfect Rose. Dorothy Parker. AmWit; APT-1; NAAPv.2; NALW; NAMCP V.1; NBLV; NIL-7; NIP-4; NoP-4; NoP-5; OBCoV

One person believes in nothing and another dislikes poetry. Lyn Hejinian. NAMCP V.2 Fr. Oxota: A Short Russian Novel.

One Petition Lofted into the Ginkgos. Gabriel Gudding. PoDa

One plans extraordinary things, masked balls. Leslie Kaplan. SCFWP Fr. Règne.

1.5. George Elliott Clarke. Coast Fr. Blue Elegies.

One Polar Bear, The. Peter Sears. OPRER

One pucker lipping Lion's whelp (in flesh). Lion. John Wheelwright. AmWit

One Quick Quiz. Paula Sergi. SweBea

One quick scratch. Lighting a Fire. X. J. Kennedy. NOxBChV

One Ran Before. Yvor Winters. CalPo

One Reality, The. Frances Ridley Havergal. SacPr

One reason. Why Your Grandfather Stopped Playing the Viola. Alice Wirth Gray. MiVo

One Red-haired Summer, The. Andrea Potos. FiBr

One remains, the many change and pass, The. Percy Bysshe Shelley. NPeEn Fr. Adonais; An Elegy on the Death of John Keats.

One remembers hysterical laughter. Land of Cotton. Gilbert Sorrentino. FTOS

One rooster does not weave a morning. Weaving the Morning. João Cabral de Melo Neto. IPoFL; TCLAP, tr. by Galway Kinnell

One Saturday morning he went to the river to play. From the Childhood of Jesus. Robert Pinsky. EmeKit; HarvBoo; OxBoAm; WaAnP

One scene as I bow to pour her coffee. Vacation. William Stafford. BLT

One seated on the bench leaning forward isn't you, The. Moon Fishing. Greta Knutson. YaTCFP, tr. by Mary Ann Caws and Jean-Pierre Cauvin

One Seated on the Stones of Cheops, The. Marcelle Ferry. SurWo, tr. by Myrna Bell Rochester

One, seated on the stones of Cheops, The. One Seated on the Stones of Cheops, The. Marcelle Ferry. SurWo, tr. by Myrna Bell Rochester

One Second. Innokenty Fiodorovich Annensky. WoPoe, tr. by Stephen Berg

One Secret That Has Carried, The. Jason Shinder. OPRER

One sees pictures of Dante. Carl Phillips. OxAAAP

One sees the leaves let go, and sees the leaves falling. Further Pulsations. Marvin Bell. PfSP

One sees the trees ahead and the shadows underneath them. Pulsations. Marvin Bell. PfSP

1. Select a clean surface, avoiding dirt and litter. Field Guide to Western Intimacy. Tenaya Darlington. IIR

One Self. Laura Riding Jackson. HarvBoo

One Sentence on Tyranny. Gyula Illyés. IQMS, tr. by Adam Makkai, Károly Nagy and Vernon Watkins

One shares the century. (LL) Knowledge not of sorrow, you were, The. George Oppen. APT-2; PFTM-1

One ship drives east and another drives west. Winds of Fate, The. Ella Wheeler Wilcox. BRP

One ship, one only. Few Days in the South in February, A. Eleanor Ross Taylor. CBCWP; InGu

One Should Not Talk to a Skilled Hunter about What Is Forbidden by the Buddha [Hsiang-yen]. Gary Snyder. CAP-8

One showing the eggs unbroken. (LL) Explosion, The. Philip Larkin. BrAP; EmeKit; InoFa; ItP; MakPoe; NAEL-6v2; NAEL-7v2; NAMCP V.2; NoAM; NoP-4; NoP-5; NPeEn; OxAEP-2; WeW-3

One side black sheen three side purple. Cold in the North (After Yueh-Fu). Li Ho. ChinPo, tr. by Ye Weilian [or Yeh Wei-lien or Wai-lim Yip]

One side of his world is always missing. Riding a One-eyed Horse. Henry Taylor. HeIP-4

One side of the potato-pits was white frost. Christmas Childhood, A. Patrick Kavanagh. ModIr

One silent night of late. Cheat of Cupid; or, The Ungentle Guest, The. Robert Herrick. OBVE

One single word of heartfelt kindness. Kindness. Mary E. Tucker. CBWP-1

One singular sensation. One. Edward Kleban. ReLy

One sips of self-understanding. Passing Clouds. Chase Twichell. WaAnP

One Size Fits All: A Critical Essay. David Lehman. OBCoV

One Skit, Then Another. Yannis Ritsos. MotU, tr. by Martin McKinsey

One small boy longs for summer. Mafika Pascal Gwala. TSAP

One Snapshot I Couldn't Take in France, The. Al Young. SpirFl

One sneeze / Skylark's. Yayu. ZenPo, tr. by Takashi Ikemoto and Lucien Stryk

One sock that isn't anywhere you look. (LL) Numbers: "I like the generosity of numbers." Mary. P180; PoDa

One son of God, The. Unknown. WoPoe Fr. Turo, Rescuer of the Sun and Moon.

One son was a jewel to me. On the Death of His Son. Lewis Glyn Cothi. WoPoe, tr. by Gwyn Williams

One Song. Geoffrey Philp. WaCA

One, sorrow. Magpies. Unknown. OWoS

One sound. Then the hiss and whir. Garden, The. Louise Glück. VCAP

One spring day, to catch the moon. To Catch the Moon. Chu Yohan. CAMKP, tr. by Chong Bum Kim

One star. Apostacy, The. Thomas Traherne. OxBEV; SacPr

One star already out, the world's the cosmos now. Crossing Rice Fields at Nightfall. Ko Ŭn. CAMKP, tr. by Anthony, Brother of Taizé

One star fell and another as we walked. Conrad Potter Aiken. MoAmPo *Fr.* Preludes for Memnon; or, Preludes to Attitude.

One step. Climbing the Ridge. Rosemerry Wahtola Trommer. GeoH

One Step at a Time. Joseph Morris. ITBLP

One step at a time to return. Wisconsin Horse, The. Simon J. Ortiz. PFTM-2

One Stick Song. Sherman Alexie. PrTe

One stone. Inventory. Jacques Prévert. STV, *tr. by* John Frederick Nims

One stone at Domazan is enough. Bogomil in Languedoc. John Mathias. AmWaPo

One Strategy for Loving the World. Mona Van Duyn. ExTi

One! strikes the clock in the belfry tower. Frederick B. Needham. VerBaPo *Fr.* Round of the Clock, The.

One stroke at a time, now and then in spare moments. Inscription Etched by Water. Pak Tujin. CAMKP, *tr. by* Edward W. Poitras

One Struggle More, and I Am Free. Lord Byron. CAGL

One student (white). Images. Naomi Long Madgett. LTA

One summer afternoon old Jean Lafitte. Portrait of a Pirate. Stanley E. Babb. TiP2

One summer day. Ant Farm. Thylias Moss. PoDa

One summer day I chanced to stray. Old-fashioned Garden. Cole Porter. OBGa

One summer he stole the jade buttons. Of Your Father's Indiscretions and the Train to California. Lynn Emanuel. OxBoAm

One summer I saw the old wing. Rebirth. Beckian Fritz Goldberg. ExTi

One summer, in a letter, you wrote me. High and Dry. Justin Quinn. NIrP

One surely tires eventually of the frequent references—the gossip. Reading the Unpublished Manuscripts of Louis MacNeice at Kinsale Harbour. Desmond O'Grady. PBCIP

One sweetly solemn thought. Nearer Home. Phoebe Cary. SacPr

One syllable from Pedasos, Erato. *Unknown.* PriapPo *Fr.* Priapus Poems, The.

One that is ever kind said yesterday. Folly of Being Comforted, The. William Butler Yeats. HeIP-4; IJHIL; IrLP; NAEL-6v2; NAEL-7v2

One that resembles or emulates a swan. Definition of Swan, The. Geoffrey Nutter. IAoNAP

One that works Hollyhock Alley, The. Saxophone Julie. Susan Firer. MiVo

1. The Master holds the glowing iron with tongs over the anvil. Blacksmith's Shop, The. H. C. Artmann. MotU, *tr. by* Stuart Friebert

One the Morening the King was Taken Ill my Dreame of Him. Frances Feilding. EMWP

1, the rust-red one, hide-gleaming. Cattle-count. *Unknown.* SonAtl, *tr. by* Kurt Ganzl and Saul Gaoude

One theory is that acid wastes in the blood. Nobody Sleeps. Stanley Plumly. BodElec

One, they're spooking, two, they're opening letters. Un-American Women, The. John Tranter. BMAP

One thing does not exist: Oblivion. Everness. Jorge Luis Borges. TCLAP, *tr. by* Richard Wilbur

One thing has a shelving bank. Drumlin Woodchuck, A. Robert Frost. APT-1; NoAM

One thing in all things have I seen. Secret, The. George Russell. MoBrPo

One thing is sure. Pulse, The. Mark Van Doren. MoAmPo

One Thing Needful Generally Neglected, The. Samuel Davies. SacPr

One Thing That Can Save America, The. John Ashbery. FaBoA; NoAM; OxBoAm; PmAP

One thing that literature would be greatly the better for. Very Like a Whale. Ogden Nash. APT-2; GPTC

One thinks of *one* as a pronoun employed principally. One. John Heath-Stubbs. OBCoV

One third of my life has been spent in this practice and you. Sojun Mel Weitsman and Zen Center Sangha. WhBo

One: This is the way it must be. Erotic Suite. Olga Nolla. TANSG, *tr. by* Paula Vega

One thought the recurring "image" in the poet's song. Handbook of Versification. Gilbert Sorrentino. PoA 2002

One Thousand Days, The. Lucie Brock-Broido. AWPTFC

1134. 39. Peter Riley. VaPo *Fr.* Excavations.

One thousand saxophones infiltrate the city. Battle Report. Bob Kaufman. ISC

One threw a dirt clod and it ran, and when it paused. One Threw a Dirt Clod and It Ran. Andrew Hudgins. CAP-8

One Time. Douglas Livingstone. NoP-4

One time / Columbus said this island and the seas. Time of Turtles. Grace Perry. NOBAu

One time at Springfield. (LL) Edgar Lee Masters. ColAP; IllVoic; NAMCP V.1; NoAM; OxBoAm *Fr.* Spoon River Anthology.

One time in the middle of "Goin' Down Slow." Stereo Time with Booker Little. Rick Madigan. SeSe

One time of the year. It is as if infancy were the whole of incarnation. Luci Shaw. SacPr

One time only, just one time hold my bosom against yours. *Unknown.* SLW, *tr. by* Marjolijn De Jager, Sayd Bahodin Majrouh and André Velter

One time the moon was full and—our blind selves! Sweetness. Michael Savitz. FreRad

One time, to a coast of light. (LL) Flames and Dangling Wire. Robert Gray. BMAP; NOBAu

One time Vincent snapped Melinda's arm. Vincent. Peter Meinke. LiTh

One time when the wind blows it is years. Glimpses. William Stafford. BodElec

One to destroy, is murder by the law. Edward Young. FaBoWar

One Too Many Mornings. David Rivard. PBCAP

One Tourist's Cologne. Hal Colebatch. NOBAu

One Train May Hide Another. Kenneth Koch. GPTC; NAMCP V.2; OxBoAm

One truth is clear, WHATEVER IS, IS RIGHT. (LL) Alexander Pope. NAEL-6v1; NAWM-7v2 *Fr.* Essay on Man, An.

One Tuesday in Summer. James McAuley. NOBAu

One Twenty Pub, The. Wisława Szymborska. StAl, *tr. by* Dennis O'Driscoll

One two. Ballad: Of Motion. Billy Mills. Oth

One, two, and three. Leaves. Countee Cullen. GT

One, two—no, five doves. Ta Ta Cha Cha. Rita Dove. AmAlph

One Two or Three. Philippe Soupault. SurPaPo, *tr. by* Mary Ann Caws *and* Jean-Pierre Cauvin and Patricia Terry

One, two, three. Toward the Corner. Laura Riding Jackson. NOxBChV

One, two, three. Washington Square Park and a Game of Chess. Christopher Stanard. SpirFl

1, 2, 3, 4. Buster Keaton Looks in the Woods for His Love Who is a Real Cow. Rafael Alberti. GPTC, *tr. by* Mark Strand

One two three four five six seven eight nine and ten. Kneeling. Gertrude Stein. PFTM-1

One, Two, Three—Gough! Eve Merriam. NTCP

One! two! three! . .testing! One! two! three! . .testing! One! Rehearsal for a Parade. Stefan Tsanev. CSCBP, *tr. by* Georgi Belev and Lisa Sapinkopf

1-2-3 was the number he played but today the number came 3-2-1. Dirge. Kenneth Fearing. AmWit; APT-2; NAAPv.2; NIL-7; NIP-4; OxBoAm

1/Vacant. Nadir Lasana Bomani. BtF

One vague track. Wind Burial 3. Hwang Tonggyu. CAMKP, *tr. by* Anthony, Brother of Taizé

One wading a Fall meadow finds on all sides. Beautiful Changes, The. Richard Wilbur. NAAL-5; NIL-7; OxBoAm

One wants so many things. Intended, The. Mary Ruefle. AmAlph

One was a bay cowhorse from Piedra & the other was a washed-out palomino. Elegy with a Bridle in Its Hand. Larry Levis. AmAlph

One was a stammerer, the other dumb. (LL) Tony Harrison. HarvBoo; NAEL-6v2; NAEL-7v2; NAMCP V.2 *Fr.* School of Eloquence, The.

One was always going when the other was coming back. Ponds, in Love. C. D. Wright. GPPA

One was more wise than the other. (LL) Man feared that he might find an assassin, A. Stephen Crane. APN-2; NAAPv.1; NoP-4; NoP-5

One watch had passed, and still sweet slumber shed. Firdowsi. TAL *Fr.* Shahnamah, The.

One way there was of muting in the mind. Edna St. Vincent Millay. NALW *Fr.* Sonnets from an Ungrafted Tree.

One We Knew. Thomas Hardy. NAEL-6v2; NAEL-7v2

One went off to be. Headlands. Jack Hirschman. CLPP

One wept whose only child was dead. Maternity. Alice Thompson Meynell. InoFa; PEW; VWP

One West Coast. Al Young. GeoHom

One whistle, a short husky breath. Not There. Tess Gallagher. NIP-4

One whit the wiser when he ate those words. (LL) Riddles. *Unknown.* NoP-4; NoP-5, *tr. by* Richard Hamer

One White Dream. Hô Sugyông. EcSo, *tr. by* Youngju Ryu

One White Face in the Place, The. Sydney Lea. SwNoth

One white foot, try him. On Buying a Horse. *Unknown.* NBLV

One white star. (LL) Incantation: "White well, A." Elinor Wylie. APT-1; NAMCP V.1

One who comes with a broom, The. Five A.M. Na Hûidôk. EcSo, *tr. by* Peter H. Lee

One who could repeat the Summer day, The. Emily Dickinson. NCAP

One who first gave birth to our people, The. *Unknown.* ColAnChi *tr. by* Jeffrey Riegel *Fr.* Classic of Odes.

One who has pulled his oar in a start of storm, The. Simile. Ágnes Nemes Nagy. PoSu, *tr. by* Frederic Will

One Who Is at Home, The. Franciso Albanez. RaBo, *tr. by* Robert Bly

One who is not, we see: but one, whom we see not, is. Algernon Charles Swinburne. CABP *Fr.* Heptalogia, The.

One who lifted his arms with joy, first time across the. Inventory. Joan Larkin. WiU

One who lights the wood stove, The. February. Charles Simic. CAP-8

One who played tunes, nights under the limetrees. Musician, The. Martinus Nijhoff. TuT, *tr. by* Desmond Egan

One who rows a storm at the inception. Comparison, A. Ágnes Nemes Nagy. IQMS, *tr. by* Alan Dixon

One who says: I was almost alive or nearly dead, The. Angel Atrapado 7. John Yau. BodElec

One who should drown him too. (LL) I Looked Up from My Writing. Thomas Hardy. NAMCP V.1; NoAM; WaAnP

One who speaks does not know; one who knows does not speak. After Reading Lao Tzu. Po Chü-i. CrYelRi, *tr. by* Sam Hamill

One who will remain standing when I die, The. (LL) I Am Not I. Juan Ramón Jiménez. RaBo; WED, *tr. by* Robert Bly

One who works. One Who Works and Buys Himself Books. Shmuel HaNagid. WoPoe, *tr. by* Peter Cole

One Who Works and Buys Himself Books. Shmuel HaNagid. WoPoe, *tr. by* Peter Cole

One who writes us is now doing four plays a year, The. Paavo Haavikko. VCWP *Fr.* Short Year, The.

One who'd seen it all turned her face away, The. She was proud, made prouder. Madonna. Blanca Varela. MotU, *tr. by* Martha Moody

One whom I knew, a student and a poet. Epitaph. Alex Comfort. MoBrPo

One whom some were certainly following was one who was completely charming. Picasso. Gertrude Stein. NAAPv.2; NAMCP V.1

One Who's in Love with Love, The. Hagiwara Sakutaro. CAoMJL1; PFTM-1, *tr. by* Hiroaki Sato

One whose love will never end. Accompanying a Gift. Lizelia Augusta Jenkins Moorer. CBWP-3

One whose majestic presence ever here. In Memoriam Frederick Douglass. Henrietta Cordelia Ray. CBWP-3

One Wife for One Man. Frank Aig-Imoukhuede. PML

One windy days. Spring. Judith Ortiz Cofer. PueRic

One winter he was the best. In Memory of My Friend the Bassoonist John Lenox. Donald Justice. BodElec

One Winter Night in August. X. J. Kennedy. OBSP

One Wintry Day. Pyong-hwa Cho. PoetW, *tr. by* Peter H. Lee

One with the Essence of the boundless world. (LL) Pantheist's Song of Immortality, The. Constance Naden. ViWPN; VWP

'One with this world'. *Unknown.* FaBoA, *tr. by* A. L. Kroeber

One Woman. Sandra Maria Esteves. PueRic

One woman has nothing out of place. Criminal. Stephen Dunn. MoASP

One woman seeks more. One Woman. Sandra Maria Esteves. PueRic

One Word. Gabriela Mistral. TCLAP, *tr. by* Doris Dana

One word is too often profaned. To—. Percy Bysshe Shelley. OBEV; OxAEP-2; TFi

One word less. Whatever. Wes "Scoop." Nisker. WhBo

One word presents itself before others: simplify. You have. Intellectual Life, The. Damon Krukowski. OnScMo

One word two vowels one active situation at a time. Never Too Late. John Taggart. FTOS

One work of art without content, The. (LL) Piano Tuner's Wife, The. Karl Shapiro. NAMCP V.2; NoAM

One world at a time, remarked Thoreau. Point of View, A. Constance Carrier. APT-2

One would never suspect there were so many vices. Destruction of Sodom, The. Daryl Hine. ChIV-1

One would remember still. Laventie. Ivor Gurney. NAMCP V.1

One writes, that "Other friends remain." Alfred Tennyson. NAEL-6v2; NAEL-7v2 *Fr.* In Memoriam A. H. H.

One Writing against His Prick. *Unknown.* NOSC

1 x 2. Hedva Harechavi. DTA, *tr. by* Miriyam Glazer

One xxxvii. Laurie Duggan. BMAP *Fr.* Epigrams of Martial, The.

One Year. N. M. Bodecker. TLR

One Year Ago. Adah Isaacs Menken. CBWP-1

One year ago—a ringing voice. Only a Year. Harriet Beecher Stowe. TreFP

One year, as I was sleeping. Good Angel, The. Rafael Alberti. RaW, *tr. by* John Haines

One year I lived in high romance. Deteriora. William Johnson Cory. CAGL

One Year Later. Robyn Zappala. PfS

One year the town Republicans. Alderman. Marilyn Nelson Waniek. LTA

1. You are not going anywhere. How to Look at Mexican Highways. Mónica de la Torre. LegDan

One you shake your head over, The. Prom. Francine Witte. PfS

One You Wanted to Be Is the One You Are, The. Jean Valentine. BodElec; ExTi

One-armed explorer, The. Gardens of Zuñi, The. W. S. Merwin. GifTon

One-Armed Man in the Undergrowth, The. Bertolt Brecht. PoSu, *tr. by* Derek Bowman

One-coach Penn Central is bound, The. On My Fourteenth Wedding Anniversary I Ride on Trains. Cornelia Veenendaal. GM

One-day Snow. T. Arfon Williams. BBMWP, *tr. by* Emyr Lewis

One-eyed prison-warder, A. Ayíasma. Gunnar Ekelof. WoPoe, *tr. by* W. H. Auden and Leif Sjöberg

One-line poem? Why not one-word poem? Kazuaki Tanahashi. WhBo

Onely in thy wig, Sister, does the sky clear. Americana. Sam Witt. NeAmPo

One-Page Novel. David Gewanter. NAPBL

One's alone in this: making masks. Eduardo Milán. RMCMP, *tr. by* Roberto Tejada

One's at God's finding; t'other at his owne, T'. (LL) On the Ploughman [*or* Plough-Man]. Francis Quarles. NOSC; SacPr

One's Correspondence. Connie Bensley. OBCoV

One's Country. Jonathan Griffin. Oth

Ones Forgotten, The. Haim Guri. NRoS, *tr. by* Esther Raizen

One's grand flights, one's Sunday baths. Sense of the Sleight-of-Hand Man, The. Wallace Stevens. MoAmPo; NoAM; OxBoAm; PoA 2002; WeW-3

Ones his age who shook my hand, The. Men at My Father's Funeral. William Matthews. CAP-8

Ones I could see, ones I could not. (LL) View of the Library of Congress from Paul Laurence Dunbar High School. Thomas Sayers Ellis. FuFl; GT

Ones Living by Their Virtue Say, The. Uri Zvi Greenberg. NRoS, *tr. by* Esther Raizen

One's own body from its instant and heat. (LL) Six Young Men. Ted Hughes. OBWP; PoAgWa; PoWW

Ones you fear most of all: ask where you were, The. (LL) For the Record. Adrienne Rich. NIL-7; NIP-4; VCAP

Onesided Dialog. June Jordan. NoAM

Onesided, stripped of its ghosts. Eccles Street, Bloomsday, 1982. Harry Clifton. PBCIP

One's-Self I sing, a simple separate person. One's-Self I Sing. Walt Whitman. ColAP; NAAPv.1; NAMCP V.1; TCAPo; WaAnP

One-Star, The. Jamie McKendrick. NeBrP

One-story is disheartening, A. Pyromaniac, The. Wyatt Prunty. LiTh

OneThousand Bullfrogs Rejoice. Larissa Szporluk. LegDan

One-two! One-two! Footsteps of an Owl and Ants Lament, The. Viktor Aleksandrovich Sosnora. TCRusP, *tr. by* Kathy Lewis

One-Upmanship. Miriam Chaikin. NTCP

Ongoing. Naomi Shihab Nye. PoArWo

Onion. Katha Pollitt. RaBo

Onion. Wisława Szymborska. PoSu, *tr. by* Grazyna Drabik *and* Sharon Olds

Onion. *Unknown.* WoPoe *Fr.* Riddles (Exeter Book).

Onion Bucket. Lorenzo Thomas. GT

Onion Days. Carl Sandburg. IllVoic

Onion Fields. Robert Francis. APT-2

Onion is frost, An. Lullaby of the Onion. Miguel Hernández. AF; WED, *tr. by* Robert Bly

Onion is frost, The. Lullabies of the Onion. Miguel Hernández. RaW, *tr. by* Philip Levine

Onion loves the onion, The. Onions. Lorna Crozier. OpeFie

Onion, / luminous flask. Ode to the Onion. Pablo Neruda. BeAl, *tr. by* Stephen Mitchell

Onion, Memory, The. Craig Raine. NAEL-6v2; NAEL-7v2; NAMCP V.2; NoAM; NoP-4; NoP-5

Onion / shining flask. Ode to the Onion. Pablo Neruda. IPoFL, *tr. by* Ken Krabbenhoft

Onion, The. John Thompson. Coast

Onions. Lorna Crozier. OpeFie

Onions. William Matthews. CAP-8; EmeKit

Onlookers. Luci Shaw. SacPr

Only a beige slat of sun. Mind Wanting More. Holly Hughes. AmZen

Only a bell, a bird, the stillness break. Immense Hour. Juan Ramón Jiménez. SpanPo, *tr. by* Edward F. Gahan

Only a Blush. Mary E. Tucker. CBWP-1

Only a Boche. Robert W. Service. BrAP

Only a brief sleep everywhere. O God. Else Lasker-Schüler. BBASP, *tr. by* Robert P. Newton

Only a chimney. (LL) Song of Smoke. Kevin Young. LegDan; P180

Only a cottage border. Changes. May Probyn. VWP

Only a Curl. Elizabeth Barrett Browning. TreFP

Only a few hours ago the water with its hooves. Mud-Flat. Willem Jan Otten. TuT, *tr. by* Peter van de Kamp

Only a few weeks ago, the sonogram of Jean's womb. Sonogram, The. Paul Muldoon. BeAl; NAMCP V.2; P180

Only a little shall we speak of thee. Mary Elizabeth Coleridge. PoBW; VWP

Only a man harrowing clods. In Time of "The Breaking of Nations." Thomas Hardy. BrAP; ChIV-1; HarvBoo; MoBrPo; NAEL-6v2; NAEL-7v2; NAMCP V.1; NoAM; NoP-4; NoP-5; OBEV; OBWP; OPOU; OxAEP-2; PoWW; TFi; WeW-3

Only a mother could manufacture such a story. Diary (Underworld). Rachel Zucker. LegDan

Only a part of me shall triumph in this. Boult to Marina. "Ern Malley." BMAP

Only a picture from a blue tin box. Cape Enrage. Lynn Davies. Coast

Only a single ray, but suddenly. Hayyim Nahman Bialik. FIT, tr. by Robert Friend

Only a Thought. Charles MacKay. STuOW

Only a Year. Harriet Beecher Stowe. TreFP

Only after all this time. This. Yvonne Cullen. NIrP

Only after radiant adulterous sex could I see the world. Time 5. Yi Kyôngnim. EcSo, tr. by Peter H. Lee

Only Alice. Josephine Jacobsen. FFC

Only an avenue, dark, nameless, without end. (LL) Old Man. Edward Thomas. HarvBoo; NPeEn; OxBEV; StAl; TCAWP

Only an Englishman. Dylan Iorwerth. BBMWP Fr. Sand.

Only animal that commits suicide, The. Only Animal, The. Franz Wright. AmAlph

Only Applebaum Can Make a Tree. Joanne Hart. MiVo

Only barbarians forget about their fallen. Veterans. Aleksey Shelvakh. PML, tr. by J. Kates

Only Birmingham, who took a double back flip. Fish I Remember. Suzanne Lummis. SUP

Only by balancing move. (LL) Machines. Michael Donaghy. NeBrP; StAl

Only calm here is the trees, waiting, The. Girl Named Spring, A. Betsy Sholl. PBCAP

Only calmness will reassure. Honey. Robert Morgan. BLT

Only casually invited, and that several months ago. (LL) Poem: "Eager note on my door said "Call me", The." Frank O'Hara. NAMCP V.2; NoAM; OxBoAm; PmAP

Only Cherries? Kenneth Patchen. RaF

Only child, he draws a child. On Giving My Father a Book About Roses. Robin Behn. AmAlph

Only Choice, The. Jawad Yaqoob. IrPoTo, tr. by Chuck Miller and Saadi A. Simawe

Only consonants and vowels. (LL) Survey of Literature. John Crowe Ransom. AmWit; NBLV

Only Daughter, The. Laura Riding Jackson. FuPo

Only Days. Melanie Hope. WiU

Only Death. Mary Doughtery Bartlett. ICANM

Only Death. Pablo Neruda. ConPit; PFTM-1, tr. by Clayton Eshleman

Only Democracy (in the Middle East), The. Rami Saari. PML, tr. by Lisa Katz

Only deposed kings can know. (LL) Deposition from Love, A. Thomas Carew. BASC; CavPo

Only Dream, The. Semezdin Mehmedinović. PML, tr. by Antonela Glavinic and Kathleen Jamie

Only emperor is the emperor of ice-cream, The. (LL) Emperor of Ice-Cream, The. Wallace Stevens. APT-1; BeAl; BrAP; EMP; HeIP-4; InoFa; NAAL-5; NAAPv.2; NAMCP V.1; NAWM-7v2; NIL-7; NIP-4; NoAM; NoP-4; NoP-5; OxBoAm; PoPoPo; PtR; TCAPo; TFi; TRP; WaAnP; WeW-3

Only evidence remaining from his existence was his coat, The. Underneath Oblivion. Yannis Ritsos. AF, tr. by Minas Savas

Only for one another. (LL) Naked Vision. Gwen Harwood. EmeKit; StAl

Only for You. Else Lasker-Schüler. BBASP, tr. by Robert P. Newton

Only for you my tea roses. Yury Pavlovich Odarchenko. TCRusP, tr. by Theodore Weiss

Only Fortunate Thing, The. Joe Wenderoth. BodElec

Only genuine awakening results in that. Nensho. ZenPo, tr. by Takashi Ikemoto and Lucien Stryk

Only ghost I've ever seen, The. Foundling, The. Rebecca Seiferle. ICANM

Only head in the sky, The. Giraffe. Stanley Plumly. ChAP

Only Here for the Bier. U. A. Fanthorpe.
Mother-in-law. MoWP

Only here that I roll my dope. Nursing the Sunburn. Judith Vollmer. SwNoth

Only His Son Is With God. "Angelus Silesius." GePo Fr. Cherubical Wanderer, The.

Only if Love Should Pierce You. Salvatore Quasimodo. StAl, tr. by Jack Bevan

Only in air. Anguish & Metaphor. Gustaf Sobin. WoBe

Only in Creve Coeur. In Creve Coeur, Missouri. Rosanna Warren. PoPoPo

Only in Poetry. Ajip Rosidi. WoPoe, tr. by Harry Aveling

Only in-between of her I've ever seen, The. Madonna del Parto: Our Lady of Birth-Giving. Jennifer Richter. FiBr

Only Indirectly. Giulia Niccolai. CItWP, tr. by Cinzia Sartini Blum and Lara Trubowitz

Only job I didn't like, quit, The. What I Wouldn't Do. Dorianne Laux. ExTi

Only joy, now here you are. Sir Philip Sidney. NAEL-6v1; NAEL-7v1; NoP-4; NoP-5; NoSic Fr. Astrophil and Stella.

Only language of loss left in the world is Arabic, The. Ghazal. Agha Shahid Ali. AmAlph; PML

Only last month I was drunk with him. Trilobytes. Kent Johnson. AtGh

Only last week, walking the hushed fields. Father and Son. Frederick Robert Higgins. OBMV

Only legend I have ever loved is, The. Pomegranate, The. Eavan Boland. CABP; NAMCP V.2; NoP-4; NoP-5

Only life you could save, The. (LL) Journey, The. Mary Oliver. StAl; TWF

Only Love. Wizlaw von Rügen. OnScMo, tr. by W. D. Snodgrass

Only Love and Love's longing fills my singing. Only Love. Wizlaw von Rügen. OnScMo, tr. by W. D. Snodgrass

Only miracle I ever wanted as a kid, The. Blonde Ambition. Maureen Seaton. ReTh

Only Mount Fuji. Buson. EMJL, tr. by Haruo Shirane

Only News I know, The. Emily Dickinson. APN-2

Only night heals again. (LL) "H. D." APT-1; MoAmPo Fr. Songs from Cyprus.

Only Now I Realize. Luis Lopez. GeoH

Only, of course, they can't sustain the part.. (LL) Fireflies in the Garden. Robert Frost. BLPJKO; SAmP

Only official method, of course, The. Transport of the Dead. Gaylord Brewer. Vesp

Only once more and not again—the larches. In Ampezzo. Trumbull Stickney. APN-2

Only One Eye. Lillian E. Curtis. VerBaPo

Only one fleeting. Ato Tobira. ArkPo, tr. by Edwin A. Cranston

Only one flower. Stanford M. Forrester. AmZen

Only One Life. Unknown. TreFP

Only one of me. One. James Berry. NOxBChV

Only One of My Deaths. Dean Young. P180

Only one old woman. Fugue. Stephen Perry. MiVo

Only one person lives. Being (Human). John Fitzgerald. BBMWP, tr. by Joseph P. Clancy

Only [or Onely] a little more. His Poetry His Pillar. Robert Herrick. NOSC

Only parts of the pain of living. Detroit 1958. Al Young. ESEAA

Only passages of a poetry, no more. No matter how many times the cards are handled. Structure of Rime XXIII. Robert Duncan. FTOS

Only people who should really sin, The. Inter-Office Memorandum. Ogden Nash. APT-2

Only person I've seen all morning, The. Mythology of Cures, The. Susan Goyette. OpeFie

Only poem to write I now have in mind, The. Only Poem, The. Robert Penn Warren. BodElec

Only possible utilisation of electricity "in the arts," The. Electricity Breadthwise. Marcel Duchamp. PFTM-1

Only relics left are those long, The. Monuments for a Friendly Girl at a Tenth Grade Party. William Stafford. NoAM

Only seconds behind. (LL) Minefield, The. Diane Thiel. AmWaPo; RaF

Only shadows follow your footsteps now. Biding Farewell to My Cousin, Haeil, on His Return Home. Buhyu Sunsoo. BecRai, tr. by Kim Daljin, Kim Won-Chung and Christopher Merrill

Only sharpen a knifeblade along its mate's hip. Ballad of Alcohol Valley, The. Ronny Someck. IrPoTo, tr. by Vivian Eden

Only Silly Faggots Know. Perry Brass. CAGL

Only Silly Faggots Know only faggots know. Only Silly Faggots Know. Perry Brass. CAGL

Only teaching on Tuesdays, book-worming. Memories of West Street and Lepke. Robert Lowell. AF; AmWaPo; CAP-8; EmeKit; ItP; NAAL-5; NAMCP V.2; NoAM; OxBoAm; PWW2; VCAP

Only temple he delights to fill, The. (LL) Enoch. Jones Very. ChIV-1; TCAPo

Only the Beards Are Different. Bruce Dawe. RSR

Only the chemist can tell, and not always the chemist. Edgar Lee Masters. APT-1; IllVoic Fr. Spoon River Anthology.

Only the clouds were new. Beast with Two Backs, The. Andrew Taylor. NOBAu

Only the compass, keeping hope alive. Logbook of a Lost Caravan. Gyula Illyés. PFTM-1

Only the crudest. Death by Fruit. Kay Ryan. PoDa

Only the ear of the labyrinth. Story of the Labyrinth, The. Veronica Volkow. RMCMP, tr. by Margaret Sayers Peden

Only the feathers floating around the hat. Icarus. Edward Field. OtW

Only the Hand That Stirs Knows What's in the Pot. Luz Maria Umpierre. PueRic

Only the light industry of snow. Man in the White Suit, The. Nick Drake. NeBl

Only the lion and the cock. After Galen. Oliver St. John Gogarty. OBMV

Only the millionth person. Oh Mercy. Tony Hoagland. SUP

Only the moon. Tagami Kikusha [*or* Kikusha-Ni]. SoOfWa, *tr. by* Sam Hamill

Only the moon suspects the truth. Man Doesn't Exist. Vicente Aleixandre. RaW, *tr. by* Lewis Hyde

Only the most obvious questions. Hearing Loss. Christian Wiman. AmPoNex; PoDa

Only the new dust falling through the air. (LL) My Grandmother. Elizabeth Jennings. HarvBoo; NoP-4; NoP-5

Only the plants remain sinless and pure. Carbon Dioxide. Ágnes Nemes Nagy. IQMS, *tr. by* Adam Makkai

Only the shoots. Buson. SoOfWa, *tr. by* Sam Hamill

Only the stones at first. Heavenly Feast, The. Gjertrud Schnackenberg. AFaM

Only the Sun. István Sinka. IQMS, *tr. by* William Price Turner

Only the truly bourgeois. Qantas Bags. Laurie Duggan. BMAP

Only the van's half inch of steel. Kluane, the Yukon. Nathaniel Tarn. WANABP

Only the very worst despair is as cold. December Offensive. Anna Enquist. TuT, *tr. by* Peter van de Kamp

Only the voice, the skin, the polished. Love. Rosario Castellanos. FiBr, *tr. by* Carolyne Wright

Only the wanderer. Song. Ivor Gurney. HarvBoo

Only the wind sings. Mary Celeste. Judith Nicholls. OBSP

Only the Zen-man knows tranquillity. Fugai. ZenPo, *tr. by* Takashi Ikemoto and Lucien Stryk

Only then and not before. S.O.S. Léon Damas. PFTM-1

Only these black translucent wings. Murmur. Esther Iverem. GT

Only they are left me, they are faithful still. My Dead. "Rachel." FIT, *tr. by* Robert Friend

Only thing I have of Jane MacNaughton, The. Leap, The. James Dickey. NIL-7; NIP-4

Only thing I remember from high school math is that the, The. First Proof. Traci Paris. ICANM

Only thing that can be relied on, The. Snow on Saddle Mountain, The. Miyazawa Kenji. ColAP; NoAM; OxBoAm; WaAnP, *tr. by* Gary Snyder

Only thing that would grieve with me, The. (LL) When I Am Asked. Lisel Mueller. GoPo; PoA 2002

Only think, dearest Louisa, what fearful scenes we have witnessed! Arthur Hugh Clough. NPEeN *Fr.* Amours de Voyage.

Only this table by the draughty window. Autumn Supper. Dimitris Tsaloumas. BMAP

Only three things on earth seem useful or soothing to me. Dear Boy George. Amy Gerstler. SUP

"Only through Me!"..The clear, high call comes pealing. Dies Ire-Dies Pacis. John Oxenham. SacPr

Only those deficient in idealism object. Premature Burial Gazette. Angela Ball. RWB

Only time I ever watched *Dallas*, The. Soap. Jane Coleman. ReTh

Only time I forget is down the pit, The. Close Shave. Jackie Kay. MoWP

Only to fail again! (LL) I never hear the word "escape." Emily Dickinson. NCAP; SAmP

Only to live. River of Bees, The. W. S. Merwin. HeIP-4; VCAP

Only travelers of the Middle Passage / own. (LL) Poem: "Poems are not places." Sterling Plumpp. GT; OxAAAP

Only true likeness of myself, The. (LL) My Shoes. Charles Simic. EmeKit; OxBoAm; VCAP

Only truth you know now is your hunger, The. Disorder, The. Marilyn Chin. LoL

Only 20 Years Old. Gideon Rosenthal. NRoS, *tr. by* Esther Raizen

Only twenty-four graves in the churchyard at Golden. Golden, New Mexico. Mark Ivey. ICANM

Only two know the meaning of us. Gloria Frym. ASA *Fr.* Mind Over Matter.

Only two of us. Day Surgery Pre-Op. Helena Minton. PfS

Only two patient eyes to stare. Faded Pictures. William Vaughn Moody. TCAPo

Only until this cigarette is ended. Edna St. Vincent Millay. HeIP-4; NAAPv.2

Only unto God. (LL) Haiku for My Brothers. Ira B. Jones. BtF; FTtHH

Only war that matters is the war against the imagination, The. Diane Di Prima. PFTM-2 *Fr.* Rant.

Only Way, The. W. N. Ewer. FaBoWar

Only way to be quiet, The. Poetry. Frank O'Hara. AHA

Only, we die in earnest— that's no jest. (LL) What Is Our Life? Sir Walter Ralegh. NAEL-7v1; NoSic; SoSe-8

Only what returns love. (LL) Matins: "Unreachable father, when we were first." Louise Glück. InvLi; MoWP

Only When My Heart Freezes. Alden Nowlan. RaBo

Only with Radiance. Margit Szécsi. IQMS, *tr. by* Kenneth McRobbie

Only Woman Awake, The. Kabir. WED, *tr. by* Robert Bly

Only women went down. Canning Cellar, Early Sixties. Judith Vollmer. SweBea

Only Yak in Batesville, Virginia, The. Oni Buchanan. IIR; LegDan

Only You. Fanny Carrión de Fierro. TANSG, *tr. by* Sally Cheney Bell

Only your plastic night light dusts its pink. Night Light. Anne Winters. PtR

Only your plastic night light dusts its pink. Anne Winters. BeAl *Fr.* Elizabeth Near and Far.

Onomastics and the Falling Snow. Steve Orlen. PoDa

Onondaga Madonna, The. Duncan Campbell Scott. BrAP

Onoto-face. Hammock. Blaise Cendrars. CuPo

Ons in your grace I knowe I was. What Once I Was. Sir Thomas Wyatt. WaAnP

Onset tense: no tone to set. So'net 3. Paul Dutton. IFF

Onset, The. Robert Frost. APT-1; MoAmPo

Onto a charcoal kiln. Natsume Soseki. CAoMJL1, *tr. by* Makoto Ueda

Onto the hallowit steid bryng in, thai cry. Virgil. OBVE *Fr.* Aeneid [*or* Eneados *or* Aeneis], The.

Onto the twin and contrasting altars I pour my libations. Libations. Ferenc Kölcsey. IQMS, *tr. by* Adam Makkai

Ontogeny. Jarold Ramsey. NIP-4

Ontology. Rutger Kopland. TuT, *tr. by* Seamus Deane

Onward, Christian Soldiers. Sabine Baring-Gould. SacPr

Onward led the road again. Hell Gate. A. E. Housman. NoAM

Onward! though ever in our march. William Bingham Tappan. VerBaPo *Fr.* Song of the Three Hundred Thousand Drunkards in the United States.

Onycha. Michael Field. ViWPN

Ooftish. Samuel Beckett. NoAM

Ooh My Soul. Charles Harper Webb. NevBe

Ooly Pop a Cow. David Huddle. GoPo

Oompah Oompah Oompah, fattening. Pumpkins. Tim Lilburn. OpeFie

Oonu see mi dyin trail! Jesus Is Condemned to Death. Pamela Mordecai. WaCA

Ooo-la-la! remarked Reynaldo. "Tonight." Reynaldo in Paris. Leon Stokesbury. IaFF

Ooooh, oooooh, ooooh, says the voice of a girl. Nights. Lyn Hejinian. BAP-01

Oor Hamlet. Adam McNaughtan. EdScPo

Oor Location. Janet Hamilton. NePenScot

Oorlog winnen en gedood worden, De. Zelfrepeterend gedicht. Sybren Polet. LWR

Opal. Amy Lowell. NALW

Opal heart of afternoon, The. Bracelet of Grass, The. William Vaughn Moody. APN-2; NAAPv.1; TCAPo

Opal Sea, The. Ella Higginson. SWaP

Opal Trees, The. David St. John. RoV

Opaque Copper. Roberto Guillermo Monzón. SonAtl, *tr. by* Eleanor Davidson

Open a crack in the wall and kiss me on the mouth. *Unknown*. SLW, *tr. by* Marjolijn De Jager, Sayd Bahodin Majrouh and André Velter

Open Air Where. Larry Eigner. PmAP

Open area outdoors, preferably the courtyard of a church or other religious structure, An. Realtheater Piece Two. Jerome Rothenberg. FTOS

The. Open. Box. Carla Harryman. BAP-04 *Fr.* Baby.

Open city / uncluttered as a map. Night Taxi. Thom Gunn. BeAl

Open Door, The. Elizabeth Jane Coatsworth. TLR

Open door and oh no, The. Any moment (12/4/69 4:30 A.M. chicago). Ed Roberson. EGAG

Open door: white water. Song of the Little Miss by the Green Rill. *Unknown*. ChinPo, *tr. by* Ye Weilian [*or* Yeh Wei-lien *or* Wai-lim Yip]

Open eye, An. (LL) You Fit into Me. Margaret Atwood. IFF; NALW; NAMCP V.2; NoAM

Open Heart. Sekou Sundiata. SpirFl

Open here. Paul Reps. WhBo

Open House. Theodore Roethke. NoAM

Open it. First Book, The. Rita Dove. LoL

Open Kitchen, The. Kimiko Hahn. PrTe

Open Letter. Owen Dodson. OxAAAP

Open Letter from a Constant Reader. Mona Van Duyn. OxBoAm

Open Letter to All Black Poets, An. Samuel F. Reynolds. SpirFl

Open Letter to the Entertainment Industry, An. Beau Sia. BRtP

Open Letter to Voyager II, An. John Updike. OtW

Open lips for sucking and pouting were all stopped up with a plug that wouldn't come out. Carla Harryman. BAP-04 *Fr.* Baby.

Open mouth open through. Ted Greenwald. FTOS *Fr.* Word of Mouth.

Open one's hand. Curriculum vitae. Marie-Claire Bancquart. MFP, *tr. by* Martin Sorrell

Open? Open. Shut? Shut. (LL) Cardinal Ideograms. May Swenson. NoP-4; NoP-5

Open Poem. Melinda Goodman. WiU

Open Prospect. William Wordsworth. CenSon *Fr.* River Duddon [A Series of Sonnets], The.

Open Secrets. Gwendolyn MacEwen. LW

Open Sesame. Edward Field. SUP

Open sesame / by day. Federico García Lorca. PFTM-1 *Fr.* Night (Suite for Piano and Poet's Voice).

Open shop on the strip: Vietnamese barber. Haircut. David Huddle. AmWaPo

Open the book of tales you knew by heart. Living Memory. Adrienne Rich. OxBoAm; TRP

Open the cupboard, cherries rounded up in the darkness. Swallower. Beckian Fritz Goldberg. ExTi

Open the Door. Miriam Sagan. ICANM

Open the door Oakland. Robert Grenier. FTOS *Fr.* Oakland.

Open the door where I knock weeping. Traveller, The. Guillaume Apollinaire. WoPoe, *tr.* by Rachel Blau

Open the door! you order. Eighth Symphony Interruptus. Brian Levison. RWPCtW

Open the final book: November spills. Of the Finished World. Lucie Brock-Broido. MakPoe; WaAnP

Open the windows. Youth of the Language, The. Euros Bowen. BBMWP, *tr.* by Joseph P. Clancy

Open the windows. Spring Forward. Martin Steingesser. PoCoUp

Open thy gates. To Heaven. Robert Herrick. ChIV-2

Open, Time. Louise Imogen Guiney. APN-2

Open up this door where I knock weeping. Voyager, The. Guillaume Apollinaire. CuPo

Open Windows. Victor Hugo. SxFrPo, *tr.* by A. M. and E. H. Blackmore

Open Windows. Sara Teasdale. ColAP

Open-Air Museum. Michael Thorpe. Coast

Opened my veins—unhaltable. Marina Ivanovna Tsvetayeva. PoCho, *tr.* by Angela Livingstone

Opened Orange of Light, The. Alfonso D'Aquino. RMCMP, *tr.* by Rebecca Seiferle

Opened tissues feel. Ian Patterson. VaPo *Fr.* Hardihood.

Opener. Chris Wallace-Crabbe. BMAP *Fr.* Bits and Pieces, The.

Open-Eyed Blind Man, An. Yi Yônju. EcSo, *tr.* by Yung-Hee Kim

Opening a vein he called my radial. 40 Days and 40 Nights. Henri Cole. PoPoPo

Opening Act. Jayne Cortez. EGAG

Opening Day. David McKain. AtGh

Opening in Santa Fe, The. Raylene Hinz-Penner. ACAMVP

Opening like a marigold. I Will Not Be Your Sickness. Marge Piercy. BrAP

Opening of a Door, The. (LL) Suspense. Emily Dickinson. MoAmPo; TCAPo

Opening of an Offensive. Hamish Henderson. FaBoWar

Opening of Eyes. Laura Riding Jackson. OxBoAm

Opening scene, The. The yellow, coal-fed fog. Poem with Refrains. Robert Pinsky. TaR

Opening Service, An. Clara Ann Thompson. CBWP-2

Opening the Cage. Edwin Morgan. NIL-7

Opening the dry white papers is kissing a bone. (LL) History. Maura Dooley. NeBl; StAl

Opening the screen door, you find a fat spider. Earthstar. Arthur Sze. AmAlph

Openly send word to Algol and Procyon.. (LL) For Heather, Entering Kindergarten. Roberta Hill Whiteman. HATNAP; NoAM

Openly, yes / with the naturalness. Black Earth. Marianne Moore. APT-1; NAMCP V.1

Open-mouthed quail, The. Something or Other. Ron Padgett. FTOS

Opens blue and cool on a hot morning. (LL) Pleasures. Denise Levertov. NAMCP V.2; NoAM

Opens his arms like a trough for me to dive into. (LL) Please Can I Have a Man. Selima Hill. BeAl; NeBrP

Operation Redwing in the Pacific, 1956. Seventeen. N. William Heyen. AtGh

Operations: Desert Shield, Desert Storm. Eleanor Wilner. FiBr

Operators Are Standing By. John Ashbery. BodElec

Ophelia. Alice Friman. IaFF

Ophelia. Richard Hedderman. IaFF

Ophelia. Christopher Pilling. NLP

Ophelia. Michael Stillman. IaFF

Ophelia. Susan Terris. IaFF

Ophelia. Vernon Watkins. TCAWP

Ophelia: "Always the daughter." Elizabeth Burns. EdScPo

Ophelia had gathering hands and yet he was lost to her. As Birds in Rain. Kirsten Kaschock. IaFF

Ophelia hangs still tangible. Delacroix's Version. Kirsten Dierking. IaFF

Ophelia in Utah. Kathleen Lynch. IaFF

Ophelia, in Winter. Judith H. Montgomery. IaFF

Ophelia on a Graveled Garden Walk in Purgatory. Ryan Van Cleave. IaFF

Ophelia: Ope not thy ponderous and marble. On the Mississippi. James Applewhite. IaFF

Ophelia Speaks. Tracy Youngblom. IaFF

Ophelia Writes Home. William Greenway. IaFF

Ophelia's Confession. Tracey Herd. BeAl; StAl

Ophelia's Death. William Shakespeare. OxAEP-1 *Fr.* Hamlet.

Ophelia's Rant before She's Heavy with Drink. Leilani R. Hall. IaFF

Ophelia's Song. William Shakespeare. NoSic *Fr.* Hamlet.

Ophelia's Songs, 2 ("And will he not come again"). William Shakespeare. NoSic *Fr.* Hamlet.

Opinion is a flitting thing. Emily Dickinson. SAmP

Opinion of Hagar, The. Alicia Ostriker. TaR

Opium Fantasy, An. Maria White Lowell. APN-2; NAAPv.1

Opium, horse, nothing. Sappers. Yusef Komunyakaa. AmAlph

Opium-Eater, The. Mary E. Tucker. CBWP-1

Oppa. Jim Linebarger. TiP2

Oppenheimer. Antonia Quintana Pigno. AtGh

Oppenheim's Cup and Saucer. Carol Ann Duffy. LW

Opportunity. Harry Graham. OBCoV

Opportunity. Helen Hunt Jackson. SWaP

Opportunity. Edward Rowland Sill. APN-2

Opposite of Green, The. Alvin Aubert. ISC

Opposite of Nostalgia, The. Eric Gamalinda. PoDa

Opposite of Ornate and Rhetorical Poetry, The. José Martí. TCLAP

Opposite to Melancholy. William Strode. NOSC

Opposites Attack. Jeffrey McDaniel. LegDan

Opposites attract. Wake Up (Call). Bill Berkson. AHA

Oppositions. Judith Wright. HarvBoo *Fr.* Shadow of Fire: Ghazals, The.

Oppress'd with grief, oppress'd with care. Despondency, an Ode. Robert Burns. NPBRoP

Oppression. Jimmy Santiago Baca. AF

Opprobium. Rosario Ferré. TANSG

Oprah Out of Control. R. S. Gwynn. PoDa

Optical Illusion, An. Daniil Kharms. MotU, *tr.* by George Gibian

Optical Prodigal, The. Russell Edson. PmAP

Optician has a Glass Heart, An. H. C. Artmann. PFTM-2, *tr.* by Harriett Watts

Optician has a glass heart with plexiglass hinges, An. Optician has a Glass Heart, An. H. C. Artmann. PFTM-2, *tr.* by Harriett Watts

Optimism, / trust, / fearless. Scum & Slime. John Giorno. PmAP

Opting for Early Retirement. Tom Leonard. Oth

Opulence. Jorie Graham. NoP-4

Opus 118. Arthur Davison Ficke. APT-1, *tr.* by Anne Knish

Opus 131. Arthur Davison Ficke. APT-1, *tr.* by Anne Knish

Opus 17. Witter Bynner. APT-1, *tr.* by Emanuel Morgan

Opus 2. Witter Bynner. APT-1, *tr.* by Emanuel Morgan

Opus from Space. Pattiann Rogers. PoCoUp

89. Op. Posth. No. 12. John Berryman. CAP-8 *Fr.* Dream Songs.

91. Op. Posth. No. 14. John Berryman. CAP-8 *Fr.* Dream Songs.

Opusculum paedagogum. Study of Two Pears. Wallace Stevens. APT-1; BLT; NAMCP V.1; NoAM; OxBoAm

Or a great song. (LL) Rainer Maria Rilke. RaBo; WED,

Or a Play. Leslie Scalapino. FTOS

Or an old man upon a winter's night. (LL) On Being Asked for a War Poem. William Butler Yeats. FaBoWar; NIP-4; OBWP; OxAEP-2; PoAgWa; PoWW

Or animate an hour of vacant ease. (LL) William Wordsworth. NAEL-6v2; NAEL-7v2 *Fr.* Prelude, The; Growth of a Poet's Mind [1850 version].

Or Anything Resembling It. Michael Palmer. BodElec; CAP-8; WoBe

Or anywhere. H. D. NAAL-5 *Fr.* Walls Do Not Fall, The.

Or as in jewelry shops, do gems. (LL) Edward Taylor. NAAL-3; NAAL-5; NAAPv.1; TCAPo *Fr.* Preparatory Meditations Before My Approach to the Lord's Supper.

Or as the bridal bed. (LL) Swimmer, The. Brendan Kennelly. PBCIP; PML

Or better, be with me— / Yours, Fly. (LL) Letter to Bee. Emily Dickinson. OxBoAm; SAmP; TLR

Or buried lie in purple beds of thyme. (LL) Cover me with your everlasting arms. Frances Anne Kemble. CenSon; SWaP

Or certain ones. There are Bed and Breakfast flags. Primer about the Flag, A. Marvin Bell. GifTon

Or come again. My Ben. Robert Herrick. BASC

Or, conversely, hungers. Beethoven, Opus 111. Amy Clampitt. NAMCP V.2; NIP-4; NoP-4; NoP-5

Or curtained close such scene from ev'ry [or every] future view. (LL)   Ode on the Poetical Character.   William Collins.   NAEL-6v1; NAEL-7v1; NoP-4; NoP-5; WaAnP

Or dead in the Mississippi mud. (LL)   Poem for Myself (Or Blues for a Mississippi Black Boy), A.   Etheridge Knight.   InGu; PoPoPo

Or die and so forget what love ere meant. (LL)   On Monsieur's Departure. Queen of England Elizabeth I.   CABP; NAEL-6v1; NAEL-7v1; NALW; WaAnP

   (Or die and so forget what love e'er meant.) (LL)   LW; PEW

Or does it explode? (LL)   Langston Hughes.   APSN; APT-2; BrAP; GT; HeIP-4; NAMCP V.1; NIL-7; NIP-4; NoP-4; NoP-5; OxBoAm; RaBo; SAmP; SSLK; WaAnP *Fr.* Lenox Avenue Mural.

Or dying, there at least may die. (LL)   Alfred Tennyson.   InoFa; NAEL-6v2; NAEL-7v2 *Fr.* In Memoriam A. H. H.

Or Else.   Heather McHugh.   InoFa

Or else orange red spiraling.   Josée Lapeyrère.   SCFWP *Fr.* Apples.

Or else this very moment dies— / *Strephon.* (LL)   Strephon to Celia. A modern Love-Letter.   Mary Leapor.   BrAP; RACG

Or every man be blind. (LL)   Tell all the Truth but tell it slant.   Emily Dickinson.   APN-2; ColAP; GoPo; HeIP-4; NAAL-3; NAAL-5; NAAPv.1; NALW; NAMCP V.1; NAWM-7v2; NoAM; NoP-4; NoP-5; OxBoAm; TCAPo; WaAnP; WeW-3

Or for some other reason. (LL)   Gulls.   Jorie Graham.   AWPTFC; BAP-01

Or gathers seaward, ebbing out of mind. (LL)   Slow Pacific Swell, The.   Yvor Winters.   APT-2; CalPo; ColAP; HarvBoo; NAMCP V.1

Or glittering starlight without thee is sweet. (LL)   John Milton.   UV; WoPoe *Fr.* Paradise Lost.

Or hawk[e] of the tower [or towre]. (LL)   John Skelton.   NAEL-6v1; NBLV; NoP-4; NoP-5; NoSic; OBEV; OxBEV; TFi; WaAnP *Fr.* Garland [or Garlande or Garlands] of Laurel[l], The.

Or hear the old Triton blow his wreathèd horn. (LL)   World Is Too Much with Us, The.   William Wordsworth.   BRP; CABP; CenSon; ClHu; GSo; HeIP-4; IJHIL; ItP; NAWM-7v2; NOBRP; NoP-4; NoP-5; NPBRoP; OBEV; PoPoPo; RaBo; SacPr; SoSe-8; TFi; TRP; WeW-3

Or hear the clanging of doors. (LL)   I Have Gone into My Prison Cell. Shakuntala Hawoldar.   CFP; HAWP

Or help to half-a-crown. (LL)   Man He Killed, The.   Thomas Hardy.   ChAP; FaBoWar; HarvBoo; HeIP-4; ItP; MoBrPo; NIP-4; OBWP; TFi; WeW-3 *Fr.*

Or her kisses where a serpent hides. (LL)   Returning, We Hear the Larks. Isaac Rosenberg.   HarvBoo; NAEL-6v2; NAEL-7v2; NAMCP V.1; NoAM; OBWP; PoWW; StAl

Or hope relief.. (LL)   Elegy over a Tomb.   Edward Herbert, 1st Baron Herbert of Cherbury.   OBEV; OBWVE

Or I shall live your epitaph to make.   William Shakespeare.   OxAEP-1 *Fr.* Sonnets.

Or if I die. (LL)   William Blake.   NAEL-6v2; NAEL-7v2; NBLV *Fr.* Songs of Experience.

Or if thou dar'st to climb the highest trees.   Richard Barnfield. *See* If thou wilt come and dwell with me at home.

Or, in eternal slumbers bid them rest. (LL)   Sappho's Conjectures.   Mary Robinson.   CenSon; RWP

Or is it a great tide that covers the rock-pool.   "H. D."   WPoS *Fr.* Sagesse.

Or is it a shadow? (LL)   Tenebris.   Angelina Weld Grimké.   APT-1; NAAPv.2; OxAAAP; OxBoAm

Or its advantage—Blue. (LL)   I watched the Moon around the House.   Emily Dickinson.   APN-2; NCAP

Or just some human sleep. (LL)   After Apple-Picking.   Robert Frost.   APT-1; BrAP; IPoFL; ItP; MoAmPo; NAAL-5; NAAPv.2; NAMCP V.1; NoAM; NoP-5; OxBoAm; SAmP; SoSe-8; TCAPo; TFi; TRP; WaAnP

Or known what death could do. (LL)   Carentan O Carentan.   Louis Simpson. AmWaPo; OBWP; PWW2; WoPoe

Or love, either. (LL)   Spinster.   Sylvia Plath.   LW; SoSe-8

Or love me [or mee] less [or lesse], or love me [or mee] more.   Song: "Or love me less, or love me more."   Sidney Godolphin.   NOSC

Or man sui generis. (LL)   Lying in Bed on a Summer Morning.   Carl Rakosi. APT-2; NAAPv.2

Or, maybe you could just.   Unbeginning, The.   Brenda Hillman.   RoV

Or More. (LL)   One need not be a Chamber—to be Haunted.   Emily Dickinson.   APN-2; ItP; NAAPv.1; NALW

Or music [or musique] be[e] but[t] in sweet [or deere] thoughts of love? (LL) Mary Sidney Wroth, Countess of Montgomery.   BASC; PBRV *Fr.* Pamphilia to Amphilanthus.

Or music when the sound is spent. (LL)   Thine Own.   Josephine D. Henderson Heard.   CBWP-4; SWaP

Or not, as the case may be. (LL)   Any Lover to Any Beloved.   Faiz Ahmad Faiz.   RaF; WoPoe, *tr. by* Naomi Lazard

Or not untrue and not unkind. (LL)   Talking in Bed.   Philip Larkin.   NAEL-6v2; NAEL-7v2; NAMCP V.2; NoP-4; NoP-5; PoetW; PoPoPo

Or nothing. (LL)   Ourselves or Nothing.   Carolyn Forché.   BodElec; GifTon

Or other names. (LL)   Leaving the Motel.   W. D. Snodgrass.   NIL-7; NIP-4

Or overcoat. Still faces already lunar. (LL)   Semaphoring chorus.   George Oppen.   APT-2; PFTM-1

Or pleasures, seldom reached, again pursued. (LL)   Nocturnal Reverie, A. Anne Finch, Countess of Winchilsea.   BrAP; NAEL-6v1; NAEL-7v1; NALW; NoP-4; NoP-5; OxAEP-1; OxBEV

   (Or pleasures, seldom reach'd, pursu'd.) (LL)   CABP; NPeEn

Or rather the sacred fish with the golden faces.   Callimachus.   HePo *Fr.* Galatea.

Or scorn, or pity on me take.   Dream, The.   Ben Jonson.   NOSC

Or shake his trust in God! (LL)   Last Man, The.   Thomas Campbell. NOBRP; NPBRoP

Or skin's the *inevitable* appearance, the only castle, location only.   Light, Bright, Etc.   C. S. Giscombe.   RD

Or so men think who walk a different tree. (LL)   Aspens.   Edward Thomas. FaBoVe; NPeEn; OxBEV

Or so the story is told. (LL)   Dream On.   James Tate.   BodElec; OxBoAm; PtR

Or something very like Him. (LL)   Arthur Hugh Clough.   BrAP; CABP; NoP-4; NPeEn; OxBEV; SacPr; WaAnP *Fr.* Dipsychus [and the Spirit].

Or stain a point with blood. (LL)   Ghostly Tree.   Léonie Adams.   APT-2; MoAmPo

Or take a day or two, my days are numbered. (LL)   Unborn Child, An.   Derek Mahon.   BeAl; CABP; PNI; WoPoe

Or teach himself to pray. (LL)   Lives.   Derek Mahon.   BeAl; EmeKit; ModIr; PBCIP

Or, tell you what, let's save it for THE END. (LL)   Man Who Loved Islands, The.   Derek Walcott.   BodElec; NoAM

Or that favorite kid who gives the moon its glow. (LL)   Ego.   Denise Duhamel. NeAmPo; SUP

Or that of my Alexis, I am lost. (LL)   On Her Loving Two Equally.   Aphra Behn.   NALW; NIL-7; NIP-4

Or the ball can guess where it's going next. (LL)   Do you think I know what I'm doing?   Jelaluddin Rumi.   IJHIL; LoL, *tr. by* Coleman Barks

Or the canvas Malevich never painted.   Vertigo.   Michael Murphy.   NIrP

Or the Chinese chest of drawers taken.   Orchestrion.   Edward Kleinschmidt. MiVo

Or the day's vanity, the night's remorse. (LL)   Choice, The: "Intellect of man is forced to choose, The."   William Butler Yeats.   NoAM; WaAnP

Or the dazzling crystal. (LL)   What I Expected.   Stephen Spender.   MoBrPo; NAMCP V.1; NoAM; OxAEP-2

Or the dog / may / bark. (LL)   Ye-you si-jun: Lies a Dead Deer.   *Unknown.* APSN; CCL1; NDACCP, *tr. by* Ezra Pound

Or the Earl—an Earl? (LL)   Did the Harebell loose her girdle.   Emily Dickinson.   FaBoVe; NCAP

Or the father of your child. (LL)   Love Song: "One long and humid afternoon." Rofel G. Brion.   PML; ReBoTo

Or the first murther. (LL)   Doomsday.   Elinor Wylie.   NoP-4; NoP-5; SacPr

Or the old grasshopper molasses-mouthed. (LL)   Frederick Goddard Tuckerman.   APN-2; NoP-5 *Fr.* Sonnets.

Or the prophetic sibillance of song. (LL)   Mad Potter, The.   John Hollander. ColAP; VCAP

Or the radiant sisters the Pleiades. (LL)   On the Beach at Night.   Walt Whitman.   APN-1; MoAmPo; NoP-4; PtR; SAmP; TCAPo

Or the "sculpture" of rhyme. (LL)   Ezra Pound.   HarvBoo; MoAmPo; NPeEn *Fr.* Hugh Selwyn Mauberley (Life and Contacts).

Or the spike.   Like a Bulrush.   Marianne Moore.   APT-1

Or the strict contract between love and grief? (LL)   Linda Pastan.   InvLi; SoSe-8 *Fr.* Imperfect Paradise, The.

Or the unimaginable touch of Time. (LL)   William Wordsworth.   CenSon; HeIP-4; NAEL-6v2; NAEL-7v2; NoP-4; NoP-5; OBEV *Fr.* Ecclesiastical Sonnets.

Or to the play goes but some purse to nip. (LL)   Sir Revel.   Samuel Rowlands. NoSic; OBCoV

Or too little. (LL)   Destruction.   Shakuntala Hawoldar.   CFP; HAWP

Or view the Lord of the unerring bow.   Lord Byron.   GS *Fr.* Childe Harold's Pilgrimage.

Or was myself—too small? (LL)   I took my Power in my Hand.   Emily Dickinson.   ChIV-1; SAmP

Or we be lost among the stars. (LL)   Calverly's.   Edwin Arlington Robinson. APT-1; NAAPv.1; NAMCP V.1; NoAM

Or what is closer to the truth.   When I Buy Pictures.   Marianne Moore.   APT-1; ColAP

Or where is man so[e] uncontrolled [or uncontrou'd] a lord? (LL)   Verses Written by Mrs. Hutchinson.   Lucy Hutchinson.   BASC; NOSC

Or whether we shall be victorious, or utterly quell'd and defeated. (LL)   As I Lay with My Head in Your Lap Camerado.   Walt Whitman.   CAGL; CBCWP; NAAL-3; NCAP

Or whistling, I am not a little boy. (LL)   Ball Poem, The.   John Berryman. ChAP; MoAmPo; NoAM

Or why could you not be stopping? (LL)   Stars Stand Up, The.   *Unknown.* IrLP; IrV, *tr. by* Eleanor Hull

Or women reading, a glow on resting hands. (LL)   In the shop, she, her mother, and grandmother.   Charles Reznikoff.   APT-2; NAAPv.2

Or you may guess. (LL)   Winter: My Secret.   Christina Georgina Rossetti.   NAEL-6v2; NAEL-7v2; NPeEn; VWP

Oración de la noche para la persona imborrable. Palabras.   Oración del 21 de agosto.   David Huerta.   RMCMP

Oración del 21 de agosto.   David Huerta.   RMCMP

Oración: "Que estás en la tierra, Padre nuestro."   Gloria Fuertes.   RaW

Oracle.   Fanny Carrión de Fierro.   TANSG, *tr. by* Sally Cheney Bell

Oracle.   Gale Renée Walden.   RWB

Oracle Night.   Michael Brownstein.
"Oracle night / the porch is frozen."   FTOS

Oracle night / the porch is frozen.   Michael Brownstein.   FTOS *Fr.* Oracle Night.

Oracle of the Drowned, The.   Douglas Oliver.   Oth

Oracle of the market! thence you drew.   Camelus Saltat: Continued.   George Meredith.   OxBSo

Oracles for Youth.   Caroline Gilman.
What Will Be Your Destiny?   SWaP

Oracular Degeneration.   Karl Kirchwey.   KGB

Orage tire une marge argentée, L'.   Joyce Mansour.   YaTCFP

Oral Messages.   Lawrence Ferlinghetti.
"I am waiting for my case to come up."   PmAP

Oral Tradition, The.   Eavan Boland.   PBCIP

Orange, The.   Wendy Cope.   GoPo

Orange Birch Bolete (Leccinum versipelle).   Harry Gilonis.   Oth *Fr.* Forty Fungi.

Orange Buds by Mail from Florida.   Walt Whitman.   NAAL-3

Orange butterflies and aqua sequins.   Ntozake Shange.   FaoP *Fr.* For Colored Girls Who Have Considered Suicide When the Rainbow Is Enuf.

Orange Coral, tan sea-cork, fishnets.   Mastodon Teeth.   Sybil Pittman Estess.   TiP2

Orange gleams athwart a crimson soul.   You! Inez!   Alice Moore Dunbar-Nelson.   NAAPv.2

Orange in.   Gertrude Stein.   NAAPv.2 *Fr.* Tender Buttons.

Orange leaf on every finger bowl,: dozen tongues, a, An.   Imperfect Is Our Paradise, The.   Joy Katz.   NeAmPo

Orange on its way.   On Its Way.   May Swenson.   SoSe-8

Orange Poem, The.   George MacBeth.   OBCoV

Orange stripes on his head shoot forward into the future, The.   Turtle, A.   Robert Bly.   MotU

Orange, the brilliant slug.   Redwood Haiku.   Lew Welch.   WhBo

Orange Tree Glistens, The.   Malinda Markham.   IAoNAP

Orange Tree, The.   Ben Belitt.   APT-2

Oranges.   Fruit.   Kenward Elmslie.   FTOS

Oranges.   Frank O'Hara.   AHA

Oranges.   Gary Soto.   CAP-8; NAMCP V.2; NoAM; WeW-3

Oranges and lemons, say the bells of St. Clement's.   *Unknown.*   OxBEV

Oranges Returned, The.   Gilbert Sorrentino.   FTOS

Oration, The.   Carolyn Kizer.   PoDa

Oration on Death, An.   Manoah Bodman.
"What rich profusion here."   APN-1

Orator Prigg.   William Blake.   OBSV

Oratorio for a Concentration Camp.   János Pilinszky.   IQMS, *tr. by* Adam Makkai

Orator's Epitaph, The.   Henry Peter Brougham, 1st Baron Brougham and Vaux.   NBLV

Orbis Tertius.   Ani Ilkov.
Of Stone.   CSCBP, *tr. by* Georgi Belev and Lisa Sapinkopf

Orbit.   Gig Ryan.   BMAP

Orbit.   Mark Van Doren.   OxBoAm

Orbit I describe in my environment, The.   Orbits.   Nina Cassian.   PoSu, *tr. by* Naomi Lazard

Orbits.   'Aisha Arnaout.   PoArWo, *tr. by* Mona Fayad

Orbits.   Nina Cassian.   PoSu, *tr. by* Naomi Lazard

Orchard.   "H. D."   APT-1; MoAmPo

Orchard, The.   Brigit Pegeen Kelly.   FaoP

Orchard dying, The.   Mary Kinzie.   FFC

Orchard in the Spring.   Jane Rohrer.   BodElec

Orchard in the Woods.   Charles Bruce.   Coast

Orchard of Figs in the Fall, An.   Diana García.   TouFir

Orchard Pavilion.   Wang Pin-chih.   ChinPo, *tr. by* Ye Weilian [*or* Yeh Wei-lien *or* Wai-lim Yip]

Orchard-Pit, The.   Dante Gabriel Rossetti.   NAEL-6v2

Orchards in July.   Zbigniew Machej.   BLT

Orchestra; or, A Poem[e] of Da[u]ncing.   Sir John Davies.   NoSic (Dancing Justified.)   NAEL-6v1
Speach of Love persuading men to learn Dancing, The.   NPeEn
"Where lives the man that never yet did heare."   OxBEV

Orchestration.   Jane Mayes.   PasH

Orchestrion.   Edward Kleinschmidt.   MiVo

Orchid.   Cassiano Ricardo.   SonAtl, *tr. by* Audrey Cooper, Sue Lawley and Celia Martin

Orchid and Rock.   Stephen Mitchell.   WhBo

Orchid Door, The.   *Unknown.*   WoPoe, *tr. by* Jean S. Grigsby

Orchid Flower, The.   Sam Hamill.   AmZen; WANABP

Orchid House, The.   Medbh McGuckian.   CABP

Orchid Pavilion.   Sun Ch'o.   ChinPo, *tr. by* Ye Weilian [*or* Yeh Wei-lien *or* Wai-lim Yip]

Orchid Pavilion.   Wang Hsi-chih.   ChinPo, *tr. by* Ye Weilian [*or* Yeh Wei-lien *or* Wai-lim Yip]

Orchid seems like, The.   Orchid.   Cassiano Ricardo.   SonAtl, *tr. by* Audrey Cooper, Sue Lawley and Celia Martin

Orchid-lipped, loose-jointed, purplish, indolent flowers.   Himalayan Balsam.   Anne Stevenson.   OxAEP-2

Orchids.   Theodore Roethke.   ColAP; HarvBoo; TRP; WaAnP

Orchids in the valley, The.   Yi Hwang.   CATKP *Fr.* Twelve Songs of Tosan.

Ordeal of Love, The.   Joan Raymund.   IaFF

Order and the Days, The.   Alicia Galaz Vivar.   TANSG, *tr. by* Oliver Welden

Order is a lovely thing.   Monk in the Kitchen, The.   Anna Hempstead Branch.   APT-1; MoAmPo

Order of the Dead, The.   John Pepper Clark Bekederemo.   HBAPE

Ordered verbal syntactic space, An.   Syntactic and Verbal.   Giulia Niccolai.   CItWP, *tr. by* Cinzia Sartini Blum and Lara Trubowitz

Orderly traffic, a normal day.   From Los Angeles Looking South.   Eloise Klein Healy.   WiU

Ordinance, The.   Luis Cabalquinto.   ReBoTo

Ordinance on Arrival.   Naomi Lazard.   BLT; P180

Ordinarily / when the Messenger, otherwise known.   Vocational Guidance, with Special Reference to the Annunciation of Simone Martini.   Richard Howard.   BodElec

Ordinary, The.   Ray McNiece.   AmZen

Ordinary, as Love.   Susan Griffin.   GifTon

Ordinary Country Girl, An.   Dean Phelps.   RWB

Ordinary Evening, An.   Noelle Kocot.   LegDan

Ordinary Evening in New Haven, An.   Wallace Stevens.
"Last leaf that is going to fall has fallen."   NAMCP V.1

Ordinary God.   Donald Davie.   InvLi

Ordinary men. (LL)   Sorrow Song.   Lucille Clifton.   BodElec; CFP

Ordinary Song, An.   Chairil Anwar.   PoetW, *tr. by* Burton Raffel

Ordinary Women, The.   Wallace Stevens.   NAAPv.2

Ordnance Survey in the Northern Counties.   Mick North.   NLP

Ordonnance.   Thomas McGrath.   GifTon

Ordovician Fossil Algae.   Lindley Williams Hubbell.   APT-2

O're [*or* O'er] the smooth enamel'd [*or* enameled *or* enamelled] green.   John Milton.   OBEV *Fr.* Arcades.

Oread.   "H. D."   APT-1; BrAP; ColAP; HeIP-4; MoAmPo; MoWP; NAAL-5; NAAPv.2; NALW; NAMCP V.1; NoAM; NPeEn; OxBoAm; PoPoPo; TCAPo

Oregon.   Bob Kaufman.   EGAG; GT

Oregon Inlet.   Mary Beath.   ICANM

Oregon Landscape with Lost Lover.   Olga Broumas.   GifTon

Orf.   Ted Hughes.   NAMCP V.2; NoAM

Orfeo.   Jack Spicer.   APSN; CalPo

Organic Music.   Takehisa Kosugi.   WhBo

Organist Confesses to His Mirror, The.   John Purser.   EdScPo

Organist's Black Carnation, The.   Laurence Lieberman.   BodElec

Organizing a Drawer.   Yi Sanghûi.   EcSo, *tr. by* Jennifer M. Lee

Orgasm 0.   Steve Jonas.   EGAG

Orgie.   Madison Cawein.   APN-2

Orient Express, The.   Randall Jarrell.   BeAl

Oriental histories relate, The.   John 1:14 (1964).   Jorge Luis Borges.   GI

Oriental ink drawing, An.   Counting.   Judith Ortiz Cofer.   PueRic

Oriental, you give and give. No Christian ever gave like you.   Karl Shapiro.   BodElec *Fr.* Bourgeois Poet, The.

Orientation from Afar.   Silvana Colonna.   ItPo, *tr. by* Gayle Ridinger

Orientation: Wittenberg University, 1983.   A. Van Jordan.   NevBe

Oriflamme.   Jessie Redmond Fauset.   NAAPv.2

Origami.   Jay Griswold.   AtGh

Origami.   Greg Williamson.   NAPBL

Origin.   Robin Behn.   AmAlph

Origin.   Rosario Castellanos.   TANSG, *tr. by* Magda Bogin

Origin Charm Against Uncertain Injuries. Ansel Talvikki. NeAmPo

Origin of Baseball, The. Kenneth Patchen. APT-2; CLPP

Origin of Fear, The. Robert McDowell. CalPo

Origin of Landscape or the End of Mercy, The. Odysseus Elytis. VCWP

Origin of Man, The. Jones Very.
"Man has forgot his Origin; in vain." APN-1

Origin of Music, The. Dannie Abse. BloBone

Origin of Order, The. Pattiann Rogers. PoA 2002

Origin of the Holy One is Heavenly God Mountain, The. Song of Entertaining the Holy One. *Korean Oral Tradition.* CATKP, *tr. by* Peter H. Lee

Origin of the Snake, The. *Unknown.* NOxBChV

Original Face. Henri Cole. BeAl

Original. / Ragged-round. Malcolm X. Gwendolyn Brooks. IllVoic; OxAAAP

Original Sequence. Philip Booth. ChIV-1

Original Sin. Robinson Jeffers. MoAmPo

Original Sin [: A Short Story]. Robert Penn Warren. FuPo

Original Summer Girl, The. Carolyn Wells. SWaP

Originally it does not need. Laughing Mountain. Muso Soseki. EaWin, *tr. by* W. S. Merwin

Originally you could pass by. Gu Cheng. WoBe *Fr.* Liquid Mercury.

Origins. Vincent Buckley. BMAP

Origins. Forrest Hamer. GeoHom

Origins. Joan Larkin. WiU

Origins. Leonard Nolens. TuT, *tr. by* Michael O'Loughlin

Origins. Eric Ormsby. NoP-4; NoP-5

Origins. Carl Rakosi. FTOS

Origins and History of Consciousness. Adrienne Rich. NIP-4

Origins, Divergences. Cynthia Ozick. TaR

Origins of Naval Artillery. Thomas Dibdin. FaBoWar

Origins—they are dim in time, colossally. Night Ferry. Arthur Nortje. TSAP

Orilla de la Noche. José Luis Hidalgo. RaW

ORINDA and ROSANIA. (LL) To Mrs M. A. at Parting. Katherine Philips. NAEL-6v1; NAEL-7v1

Orinda, and the Fair Astrea gone. To the Author of Agnes de Castro. Delariviere Manley. EMWP

Orinda to Lucasia. Katherine Philips. BASC; NOSC

Orinda to Lucasia Parting, October, 1661, at London. Katherine Philips. BASC

Oriole. Yüan Chěn. CrYelRi, *tr. by* Sam Hamill

Oriole chattering shattering cruel dreams. Vanishing Spring Moves to Regret. Yu Xuanji. CCL1, *tr. by* Genevieve Wimsatt

Oriole eats yellow berries, The. Husband and Wife. *Vietnamese Oral Tradition.* CaDao, *tr. by* John Balaban

Oriole sings in the greening grove, The. Summer in the South. Paul Laurence Dunbar. GT

Oriole Song. Hsueh Chao-yun. CrYelRi, *tr. by* Sam Hamill

Orioles and orioles. Love Song. Ch'iao Chi. CrYelRi, *tr. by* Sam Hamill

Orioles sang in a thousand hamlets. Spring South of the River. Tu Mu. CCL1, *tr. by* R. F. Burton

Oriole's swinging nest! (LL) Fall 1961. Robert Lowell. OBWP; OxBoAm; PoAgWa

Orion. Adrienne Rich. BrAP; NAMCP V.2; NIP-4; NoAM; NoP-4; NoP-5

Orion. Charles Tennyson Turner. GSo

Orizaba Blues: 64th Chorus. Jack Kerouac. WhBo

Orkeny / This Life. Andrew Greig. StAl

Orlanda Blues: 24th Chorus. Jack Kerouac. WhBo

Orlando Furioso. Ludovico Ariosto. *tr. by* John Harington and William Parsons
"Alcyna met them at the outer gate." OBVE

Astolfo flies by Chariot to the Moon, where he collects Orlando's lost wits. NPeEn

"Blessed angell not a word replies, The." OBVE

"Go soule, go sweetest soule for ever blest." OBVE

Greyhound in Slip. DiBP, *tr. by* Sir John Harington

"Masters go abrod to vew the towne, The." OxBEV, *tr. by* John Harington

Mastiff-Worrying Fly, The. DiBP, *tr. by* Sir John Harington

Medoro's Inscription Book XXIII. NOBRP

"Soon after, he a crystal stream espying." NoSic

"Thus much he prayed, and thence away he went." NoSic

Trial of Endurance, A. DiBP, *tr. by* Sir John Harington

Tumbler, The. DiBP, *tr. by* Sir John Harington

Ormsby Slatter. Mr. Slatter. N. M. Bodecker. TLR

Ornate iron gates, The. Ornate Iron Gates. Das Lanzilloti. IJHIL

Ornate with Smoke. Sterling Plumpp. FuFl

Ornithology. Lynda Hull. SeSe

Ornithology. Laini Mataka. ISC

Ornithomorphous monsters. Usurers, The. Nicolás Guillén. PFTM-1

Orokashisa Tada Ni Natsu No Hi O Kurashi Mukou Castle Rock. Violet Kazue De Cristoforo. CalPo

Orotava Road, The. Basil Bunting. NoAM

Orphan, An. Malhas Thurayya. PoArWo, *tr. by* Nasser Farghaly

Orphan, The. Glover Davis. GeoHom

Orphan Child, The. Charlotte Brontë. VWP

Orphan Girl, An. Mrs. Henry Linden. CBWP-4

Orphan Miranda walks over my writing book. Tiger Lady. Miguel Algarin. PueRic

Orphanhood. Hayyim Nahman Bialik. FIT, *tr. by* Robert Friend

Orphean Song. Sally Keith. LegDan

Orpheus. John Fletcher *and* William Shakespeare. *See* Music.

Orpheus. John Kinsella. BMAP

Orpheus. Linda Pastan. MiVo

Orpheus. Stephen Perry. MiVo

Orpheus. Elizabeth Madox Roberts. MoAmPo

Orpheus Alone. Mark Strand. OxBoAm

Orpheus, An! an Orpheus! yes, Faith may grow bold. William Wordsworth. STuOW *Fr.* Power of Music, The.

Orpheus and Eurydice. Jorie Graham. OxBoAm; VCAP

Orpheus and Eurydice. Robert Henryson.
"Syne nethir-mare he went quhare Pluto was." NePenScot

Orpheus and Eurydice. Geoffrey Hill. TRP

Orpheus. Eurydice. Hermes. Joanna Klink. IAoNAP; LegDan

Orpheus, Eurydice, Hermes. Rainer Maria Rilke. WoPoe, *tr. by* Franz Wright

Orpheus liked the glad personal quality. Syringa. John Ashbery. APSN; GPTC; NoAM; VCAP

Orpheus Meets Eurydice in the Underworld. Sue Sinclair. Coast

Orpheus with his lute made trees. John Fletcher *and* William Shakespeare. NOSC *Fr.* King Henry VIII.

Orphic Night. James Longenbach. NevBe

Orpingalik's My Breath: Eskimo Song. Stephen Berg. GifTon

Ortamezar—The Jewish Quarter. Ivan Teofilov. CSCBP, *tr. by* Georgi Belev and Lisa Sapinkopf

Orthography. Ambrose Bierce. APN-2; CalPo *Fr.* Devil's Dictionary, The.

Orthone. Philip Pendleton Cooke. APN-1

Os acordáis: Europa estaba en ruinas. Elegía y Recuerdo de la Canción Francesa. Jaime Gil de Biedma. RaW

Os miro. Ceniza en Oxford. Francisco Brines. RaW

Oscar Hummel. Edgar Lee Masters. APT-1 *Fr.* Spoon River Anthology.

Oscar Wilde. W. H. Auden. AmWit *Fr.* Academic Graffiti.

Oscar Wilde. Ulick O'Connor. IrLP

Oscar Wilde. Dorothy Parker. NALW; NAMCP V.1 *Fr.* Pig's-Eye View of Literature, A.

Osceola. Walt Whitman. NAAL-3

Oscuros cristales, Los. Dolores Dorantes. SPV

Oshi. James L. White. ReTh

Oshi has a very large Buddha in him, one that can change. Oshi. James L. White. ReTh

Oshun the River Goddess. *Unknown.* WoPoe, *tr. by* Ulli Beier

Osip Mandelstam. Seamus Deane. PBCIP

Osiris. Jane Hirshfield. BodElec

Ospreys, The. *Unknown.* CCL1 *Fr.* Guan-ju.

Ospreys Woo, The. *Unknown.* CCL1 *Fr.* Guan-ju.

Osso Buco. Billy Collins. CAP-8

Ostella forth of Town: To My Heart. John Tatham. NOSC

Ostia Will Receive You. Friederike Mayröcker. PFTM-2, *tr. by* Beth Bjorklund

Ostia Will Receive You. Friederike Mayröcker. GTCP, *tr. by* Reinhold Grimm

Ostracized as we are with God. Apology of Genius. Mina Loy. APT-1

Ostriches & Grandmothers! Imamu Amiri Baraka. BrAP

Oswald Dead. Ferreira Gullar. TCLAP, *tr. by* Renato Rezende

Otagamiad. Jane Johnston Schoolcraft. SWaP

O-ta-pa! / I am creeping on your track. *Unknown.* APN-2 *Fr.* War Dance.

O-ta-pa! / Why run you from us when you. *Unknown.* APN-2 *Fr.* War Dance.

Oteli Asia Palas, Inc. Denis Devlin. ModIr *Fr.* Memoirs of a Turcoman Diplomat.

Othello. William Shakespeare.
Death of Othello. OxAEP-1
"Her father lov'd me; oft invited me." FaBoWar; OxAEP-1; WaAnP
"I will in Cassio's lodging lose this napkin." OxAEP-1
"It is the cause, it is the cause, my soul [*or* (my soule)]." OxBEV
"O my fair warrior!" OxAEP-1

Other. Robert Creeley. OxBoAm

Other. Dorothy Livesay. NIL-7

Other. Ronald Stuart Thomas. AngWePo

Other, The. Rosario Castellanos. TCLAP, *tr. by* Maureen Ahern

Other, The. Ted Hughes. EmeKit

Other, The. Constance Fenimore Woolson. SWaP *Fr.* Two Women.

Other Alamo, The. Martín Espada. AmWaPo

Other Contexts. Ted Berrigan. AHA

Other country, is it anticipated or half-remembered? The. In Your Mind. Carol Ann Duffy. EmeKit; StAl

Other day, The. Columbus. Walter Helmut Fritz. GTCP, *tr. by* Reinhold Grimm

Other Day, The. Richard Jackson. PfSP

Other day, The. Old Country, The. Carl Rakosi. BodElec

Other day I chanced to meet a soldier friend of mine, The. Oh! How I Hate to Get Up in the Morning. Irving Berlin. NAAPv.2; ReLy; TCAPo

Other day i looked out of the window and saw a, The. Endangered Nouns. David Antin. PFTM-2

Other day it fell, The. William Browne. DiBP *Fr.* Shepherd's Pipe, The.

Other day, when I opened my eyes, a wasp was knocking against the windowpane, The. Account of the Marvels Whispered in a Mannequin's Ear. Jorge Fernández Granados. RMCMP, *tr. by* John Oliver Simon

Other Days, The. Hayim Hefer. NRoS, *tr. by* Esther Raizen

Other familiar monsters surface along with my white republican uncle. Turkey People. Brynn Noelle Saito. FTtHH

Other Forms of Slaughter. Catherine Obianuju Acholonu. HAWP; HBAPE

Other girls are starting with new loves, The. *Unknown.* SLW, *tr. by* Marjolijn De Jager, Sayd Bahodin Majrouh and André Velter

Other Half of Me, The. Jack Lawrence. ReLy

Other Heritage, The. Aurora Levins Morales. PueRic

Other kids romped around the playground; their voices, The. Myopic Child, A. Yannis Ritsos. P180, *tr. by* Gwendolyn MacEwen and Nikos Tsingos

Other Life, The. Nina Cassian. PoSu, *tr. by* Cristian Andrei and Daniel Weissbort

Other Lives of the Romantics. Jane Flanders. PBCAP

Other Lovers. Jackie Kay.

"What was it you said again there by the river." NeBrP

Other Marías. Diana García. TouFir

Other night from Court returning late, The. Upon Mr Thomas Murrays Fall. Sir Robert Aytoun. NePenScot

Other One, One. André Velter. YaTCFP, *tr. by* Mary Ann Caws *and* Jean-Pierre Cauvin

Other one, the one called Borges, is the one things happen to, The. Borges and I. Jorge Luis Borges. MotU, *tr. by* James E. Irby

Other one who walks by your side, The. (LL) Antonio Machado Ruiz. RaBo; WED *Fr.* Moral Proverbs and Folk Songs.

Other option's to become a bird, The. Way Out, A. Fleur Adcock. MoWP

Other patients are ill otherwise, and do. Robert Pinsky. NoAM *Fr.* Essay on Psychiatrists.

Other people ride. Bumping on an Ass. Wang the Zealot. CCL1, *tr. by* C. H. Kwock *and* Vincent McHugh and Vincent McHugh

Other people too have friends that they love. Yuan Zhen to Bo Juyi. Yüan Chên. CCL1, *tr. by* Arthur Waley

Other People's Glasshouses. Ruth Pitter. OBGa

Other People's Pain. Mary Gomez Parham. OWABP

Other Places, The. Charles E. Butler. YaYoPo

Other props are gone, The. Je t'adore. Thomas Kinsella. NAMCP V.2; NoAM

Other secretes a sexual differentiation. Baroque Excess of Pig Latin and. Jill Hartman. PoPra

Other Side, The. Seamus Heaney. PNI

Other Side, The. Minnie Bruce Pratt. WiU

Other Side of a Mirror, The. Mary Elizabeth Coleridge. NAEL-7v2; NALW; ViWPN; VWP

Other Side of the House, The. Rita Dove. AmAlph

Other Side of the Mountain, The. Kit Wright. StAl

Other Side of the River, The. Charles Wright. InGu; OxBoAm; VCAP

Other Simulation, The. Patrizia Valduga. CItWP, *tr. by* Cinzia Sartini Blum and Lara Trubowitz

Other Song of the Faithful, for the Mercies of God, An. Michael Drayton. ChIV-1

Other states were carved or born. Cattle. Berta Hart Nance. TiP2

Other stones the era tell. William Cowper. OBGa

Other Syllabus, The. Chenjerai Hove. HBAPE

Other than a chickadee which I had bought from. Animal Liberation. Genny Lim. FTtHH

Other than Your two red feet, Syama. Kamalākānta Bhattācārya. SinGod, *tr. by* Rachel Fell McDermott

Other Tiger, The. Jorge Luis Borges. PoetW, *tr. by* Alastair Reid

Other Tiger, The. Jorge Luis Borges. TCLAP, *tr. by* Norman Thomas Di Giovanni

Other Tongue, The. Dasu Sriramulu. HotL, *tr. by* V. Narayana Rao

Other Tongues. Lynne Weiss. PfS

Other Tradition, The. John Ashbery. FTOS; PmAP

Other Voice, The. Tom Paulin. PNI

Other voice in a silence of blood, 'neath the noise of the ash, The. (LL) Discord in Childhood. D. H. Lawrence. HarvBoo; IJHIL

Other way Satan went down, Th'. John Milton. NAEL-6v1 *Fr.* Paradise Lost.

Other weddings are so shrewd on the sofa, short. Epithalament. Brenda Shaughnessy. LegDan

Other wings flew into the stone. (LL) Red Lilies. Barbara Guest. FTOS; PmAP

Other Woman, The. Eavan Boland. IrLP

Other Woman, The. Marion Lomax. LW

Other World, The. Dmitry Vasil'evich Bobyshev. ItGoST, *tr. by* Michael Van Walleghen

Other World, The: "So here is the old buck." Robert Wrigley. P180

Other-Directed. Turner Cassity. PoA 2002

Others. James Reeves. Spl

Others abide our question. Thou art free. Shakespeare. Matthew Arnold. BrAP; GSo; HeIP-4; NoP-4; NoP-5; OBEV; OxAEP-2; OxBSo; PoPoPo

Others always skip over the word. In Praise of Bic Pens. David Hilton. P180

Others are all from here, The. Address. Leonard Nolens. TuT, *tr. by* Michael O'Loughlin

Others argue, and not a few. Michael Wigglesworth. NAAL-3 *Fr.* Day of Doom, The [First Section].

Others divided closets full of mother's things. Final Disposition. Jane Glazer. FiBr

Others dress up in their new clothes for the feast, The. *Unknown.* SLW, *tr. by* Marjolijn De Jager, Sayd Bahodin Majrouh and André Velter

Others endure Man's rule: he therefore deems. Unconquered Air, The. Florence Earle Coates. OtW

Others have described. Earthly Beauty, An. Jane Hirshfield. PLBUT

Others have not been lucky as we. Half Century. Maeve Kelly. IrLP

Others, I am not the first. A. E. Housman. MoBrPo *Fr.* Shropshire Lad, A.

Others know how to forge metals. 94. Shih Shu. CSKM, *tr. by* James H. Sanford

Others made the decisions, others spoke on their behalf. They. Missing, The. Yannis Ritsos. AF, *tr. by* Edmund Keeley

Others may pity me but you shall not be ashamed. To My Children. Karen Gershon. ItWoWo

Others plant for profit, The. Clear Skies, Still Sea. *Vietnamese Oral Tradition.* CaDao, *tr. by* John Balaban

Others see a rush, a carnival, a million. Some People. A. K. Ramanujan. VCWP

Others taunt me with having knelt at well-curbs. For Once, Then, Something. Robert Frost. APT-1; NAMCP V.1; NoAM; OxBoAm

Others were more economical than I. But I. Persuasion. Joyelle McSweeney. LegDan

Others will gain what I lose. Memory's Usefulness. Maria Luisa Spaziani. CItWP, *tr. by* Cinzia Sartini Blum and Lara Trubowitz

Otherwise: "I got out of bed." Jane Kenyon. AmFaPo; BeAl; GoPo; LoL; OxBoAm; P180; PLBUT; PoCu; StAl

Otherwise kill me. (LL) Prayer Before Birth. Louis MacNeice. BeAl; FaBoVe; HarvBoo; PNI

Otherwise not a leaf stirs. (LL) Floating Trees. C. D. Wright. AmAlph; InGu

Otherwise, what was I doing in his arms. (LL) Sex with a Famous Poet. Denise Duhamel. KGB; NeAmPo

Otra vez el umbral gastado por tantas esperas, la noche descolgada más cerca. Entraña. Silvia Eugenia Castillero. SPV

Otranto. Barbara Guest. FTOS

Ottava Rima: Lear. Cecilia Woloch. IaFF

Otter, An. Ted Hughes. NAMCP V.2; NoAM

Otter, The. Seamus Heaney. IrLP; NoAM; PNI

Otter is known, The. Lutra, the Fisher. James McMichael. CalPo

Otto. Theodore Roethke. HarvBoo

Où donc. Claire Lejeune. YaTCFP

Où donc sera le texte coronaire? Où donc. Claire Lejeune. YaTCFP

Où est la lettre? Portrait. Bernard Noël. YaTCFP

Où Es-Tu. Benjamin Péret. YaTCFP

O-U-G-H. Charles Battell Loomis. NBLV

Où sont les neiges des neiges? Ted Berrigan. BodElec

Oude man tussen het riet achterdocht van de dichter. Basho. Cees Nooteboom. LWR

Ought to be told to come and take him in. (LL) Runaway, The. Robert Frost. MoAmPo; SAmP

Oui ça se fait aussi bien. Bibliothèque. Pierre Alféri. YaTCFP

Oui féminine et grasse et vermeille. De plus en plus femme. Pierre Jean Jouve. YaTCFP

Ounce code orange. Clark Coolidge. NYP2; WhBo

Our 17th Street Years. Bruce Weigl. BodElec

Our affair had just begun. Hester Prynne Recalls a Sunday in June. Kathleen Norris. UpMys

Our age bereft of nobility. Poem for Painters, A. John Weiners. BB

Our androgynous Lover! (LL) But God is Silent / Psalm 114. Bible, O.T. InvLi; UpMys

Our arms have grown. At the Black Edge. Ger Killeen. AmPoNex

Our Ashes. Horst Bienek. AF

Our Assholes Are Different. Arthur Rimbaud. CAGL, tr. by Paul Schmidt

Our assholes are different from theirs. I used to watch. Our Assholes Are Different. Arthur Rimbaud. CAGL, tr. by Paul Schmidt

Our Baby is a Living Prayer. Ko Chônghûi. EcSo, tr. by Catherine J. Kim

Our beauty is to us that which to men. Sir Richard Fanshawe. OBVE Fr. Il Pastor Fido.

Our Bicycles. James Laughlin. ArBi

Our birth is but a sleep and a forgetting. William Wordsworth. ITBLP Fr. Ode: Intimations of Immortality from Recollections of Early Childhood.

Our Birth-Cord. Kofi Anyidoho. NAfrP

Our blind fingers. Speaking Hands. Elizabeth Woody. FiBr

Our blue boat drifts. Birdwatching at Fan Lake. Anita Endrezze. HATNAP

Our boat going upstream barely moves by the inch. Sailing Through the Gorges. Yang Wan-li. WoPoe, tr. by Kuangchi C. Chang

Our boat touches the bank. Thomas A. Clark. Oth Fr. Sixteen Sonnets.

Our bodies, still young under. Our Bodies. Denise Levertov. CAP-8; ErotSp

Our brains ache, in the merciless iced east winds that knive us. Exposure. Wilfred Owen. NAMCP V.1; NoAM; OBWP; PoWW; TCAWP

Our bugles sang truce, for the night-cloud had lowered [or lower'd]. Soldier's Dream, The. Thomas Campbell. OxAEP-2

Our Burden Bearer. Phillips Brooks. SacPr

Our candles, lit, re-lit, have gone down now. Twelfth Night. Peter Scupham. OBCP

Our canoe idles in the idling current. Floating. Kenneth Rexroth. BodElec

Our Canterburye's great Cathedrall Bell. Upon Arch-bishop Laud, Prisoner in the Tower. 1641. Unknown. PBRV

Our cars were always used and named after singers. Lips. Lance Larsen. AmPoNex

Our children my love. Little Phantoms. Oscar Hahn. PML, tr. by James Hoggard

Our children / stand and stare. Circa. Tom Mitchelson. BRtP

Our Christian savages expect. He Shook off the Beast. Charles Wesley. ChIV-2

Our Christmas Tree. Wendell Berry. ChrPo

Our Christmas tree is. Our Christmas Tree. Wendell Berry. ChrPo

Our churches are burning. Bad Times. Lenard D. Moore. BRtP

Our city declines, the world is still bleak. Beginnings. Peter Sirr. PBCIP

Our city has scrubbed the sleep. Smile. Reuben Jackson. BtF

Our clear-eyed guide said it is the slick. Cold Quilt. Michael McFee. PoA 2002

Our Club Work. Mrs. Henry Linden. CBWP-4

Our country, in fenced areas, in cool shady streets. (LL) One Thing That Can Save America, The. John Ashbery. FaBoA; NoAM; OxBoAm; PmAP

Our Country of Origin. Rafael Campo. WiU Fr. Song for My Lover.

Our cup of joy was overfilled. Dialogue, A. Lizelia Augusta Jenkins Moorer. CBWP-3

Our Daily Bread. César Vallejo. TCLAP, tr. by James Wright

Our dancing and mortal wine. (LL) Horses in Flowers. Sappho. OBVE; WoPoe, tr. by Guy Davenport

Our darkness which can make us think it dark. (LL) Sonnet of Black Beauty. Edward Herbert, 1st Baron Herbert of Cherbury. NoP-5; NOSC

Our darling's now completely frappé! (LL) L'Enfant Glacé. Harry Graham. NBLV; OBCoV

Our days were a joy, and our paths through flowers. (LL) After a Journey. Thomas Hardy. HarvBoo; NPeEn; OxAEP-2; OxBEV

Our Dean of Something thought it would be good. Classroom at the Mall, The. R. S. Gwynn. RA

Our Dear Friend Charles. Collaboration: Letter to Charlie Chaplin. Peter Orlovsky. CLPP

Our Dear Native Island. Edward Lysaght. IrV

Our Destiny. Denizé Lauture. OGAHCP, tr. by Boadiba and Jack Hirschman

Our destiny is not. Our Destiny. Denizé Lauture. OGAHCP, tr. by Boadiba and Jack Hirschman

Our Dog Chasing Swifts. U. A. Fanthorpe. Spl

Our Dog Jock. James Payn. DiBP

Our dream of safety has to disappear. (LL) Leap Before You Look. W. H. Auden. NoAM; PLBUT

Our dreams create the babes we bear. Mother, The. Dame Edith Sitwell. MoWP

Our drift-wood fire burns drowsily. Florida Beach, The. Constance Fenimore Woolson. APN-2

Our dropping Autumn morning clears apace. Robert Browning. OBGa Fr. Sordello.

Our earth in 1969. Doggerel by a Senior Citizen. W. H. Auden. NBLV

Our earth, the whole of it, is alive, they say. Gaea. William Stafford. PfSP

Our Earth Will Not Die. Niyi Osundare. HBAPE

Our eldest son is like Ishmael, Jacob is like you. Charles Reznikoff. ChIV-1 Fr. Israel.

Our end is Life. Put out to sea. (LL) Thalassa. Louis MacNeice. BrAP; WoPoe

Our enemies are nothing to look at. Ha . . . No Shadows. Kim Suyŏng. CAMKP, tr. by Anthony, Brother of Taizé

Our England is a garden that is full of stately views. Glory of the Garden, The. Rudyard Kipling. OBGa

Our England's victor dead: who can express. Acrostick Eligie on the Death of the No Less Prudent than Victorious Prince Oliver Lord Protector, An. Elianour Havey. EMWP

Our epic violence in bleak bars, in bed, in art. (LL) Some Girls. Susanne Doyle. CalPo; FFC

Our eyes have viewed the burnished vineyards where. Letter to a Friend. Robert Penn Warren. MoAmPo

Our faces are the. Poem No. 1. Carolyn M. Rodgers. ISC

Our fancies are but joys all unexprest. Fragment, A. Henrietta Cordelia Ray. CBWP-3

Our Father. Eliza Cook. VWP

Our Father. David Craig. UpMys

Our Father. James Schuyler. ChIV-2

Our father death speaks through the child our father. Blank Misgivings. Andrew Crozier. VaPo

Our Father which art in heaven. Lord's Prayer. Nicanor Parra. GI, tr. by Miller Williams

Our Father who art in heaven. Jacques Prévert. CLPP

Our Father who art in heaven, I am drunk. Praying Drunk. Andrew Hudgins. RA; UpMys

Our Father, who art speechless. N. N. Tries to Remember the Words of a Prayer. Stanislaw Baranczak. GI, tr. by Kevin Windle

Our father works in us. Father of Women, A [Ad Sororem E. B.]. Alice Thompson Meynell. NALW

Our Fathers. Bible, Apocrypha. OBVE Fr. Ecclesiasticus.

Our Fathers. Ta'Lease Niche Cleveland. BRtP

Our fathers of the atomic industry. Liturgy for Trinity, A. Barbara La Morticella. AtGh

Our fathers took oaths as of old they took wives. Oaths. Thomas Brown. OBCoV

Our Fear. Zbigniew Herbert. VCWP

Our first love that glows in the quiet blue. To an Immortal Solitude Where We Now Pitch Our Stately Tent. Tahsin Saraç. NaPG, tr. by Talat Sait Halman

Our first night on the long Huai river. Watching the New Moon, I Compose These Verses to Show to My Fellow-Travelers, Stranded with Me. Ho Hsun. CCL1, tr. by John Frodsham

Our Flag. Unknown. CA

Our fleet divides, and straight the Dutch appear. John Dryden. BASC; FaBoWar Fr. Annus Mirabilis.

Our flesh that was a battle-ground. Litany of the Dark People, The. Countee Cullen. ChIV-2

Our folk's first origin. Hou Ji (Lord Millet), Progenitor of Zhou. Unknown. CCL1, tr. by William Jennings

Our fontanelle, the trout's dimpled feet. (LL) Flower Master, The. Medbh McGuckian. ModIr; PNI

Our footprints. (LL) Day We Die, The. Southern Bushmen Oral Tradition. BLT; WoPoe, tr. by Arthur Markowitz

Our fossilized bones. Srategies for Survival. Beryle Williams. AtGh

Our fourth night of being, her children. Mary Stewart Hammond. InoFa Fr. Blessings.

Our friend there—he's a little queer. Herman Melville. APN-2 Fr. Clarel: A Poem and Pilgrimage in the Holy Land.

Our friends came buoyant dances came. Hobbyhorse, The. Sezai Karakoç. NaPG, tr. by Talat Sait Halman

Our friends go with us as we go. Non Dolet. Oliver St. John Gogarty. OBMV

Our friendship, Robert, firm through twenty years. Letter to Robert Frost, A. Robert Silliman Hillyer. MoAmPo

Our front yard bursts with clover and dandelions. Hair of the Field. Tony Barnstone, Willis Barnstone and Haixin Xu. ViWalt

Our future plunges with the whale. Whales. Morton Marcus. GeoHom

Our future will be marvelously exciting. Make a Miracle. Frank Loesser. ReLy

Our gang dug down two feet. With two feet left. Signalmen, The. Philip Stephens. AmPoNex

Our Gardener here, James Phillips see. Philip Yorke. OBGa

Our generation had no Spain. For Eric Blair. Siùsaidh NicNèill. EdScPo

Our genes have junk in them. Not all the messages. Meaner Than a Junkyard Dog; or, Turner's Evil Twin. Turner Cassity. PoA 2002

Our geodesic dome-shaped lodge. Personification of a Name, The. Ray A. Young Bear. HATNAP

Our God, Our Help. Isaac Watts. *See* Man Frail, and God Eternal.

Our God, our help in ages past. Man Frail, and God Eternal. Isaac Watts. InvLi; NPeEn; OBVE; OxBEV; SacPr

Our Godless Days. Alan Llwyd. BBMWP, *tr. by* Joseph P. Clancy

Our Grandmothers. Maya Angelou. BrAP

Our grandmother's apartment had been reduced some years before the end of her life. Last Simplicity, The. Francis Ponge. MotU, *tr. by* Cid Corman

Our Grandsons Will Be Astonished. Ilya Grigoryevich Ehrenburg. TCRusP, *tr. by* Denis Johnson

Our Ground Time Here Will Be Brief. Maxine W. Kumin. NAMCP V.2; OtW

Our Growing Day. Jean Toomer. NAAPv.2

Our guide is Turk-proud. From Ruin. Julie Suk. PoA 2002

Our hairdresser friend. Dmitry Kuzmin. PML, *tr. by* Vitaly Chernetsky

Our hands crushed. Elaine Randell. Oth *Fr.* Snoad Hill Poems, The.

Our hands grope in vain. Going Home. Catherine Obianuju Acholonu. HAWP

Our heads on fire. (LL) Paper Matches. Paulette Jiles. NIL-7; NIP-4

Our hearths are gone out, and our hearts are broken. Raven Days, The. Sidney Lanier. APN-2; TCAPo

Our hearts are filled with pride to-day. Welcome to Hon. Frederick Douglass. Josephine D. Henderson Heard. CBWP-4

Our héarts' charity's héarth's fíre, our thóughts' chivalry's thróng's Lórd. (LL) Wreck of the Deutschland, The. Gerard Manley Hopkins. NAMCP V.1; NoAM; OxAEP-2; OxBEV; WaAnP

Our hearts still listen for the landward bells. (LL) Irishman in Coventry, An. John Hewitt. ModIr; PNI

Our hips. About Our Hips. Harriet Jacobs. SpirFl

Our home is all too fragile, rather like. Creative Poverty. László Szabédi. IQMS, *tr. by* J. G. Nichols

Our honest neighbor's rolled. Keith Abbott. WhBo

"Our hope is for knowledge," said Reb Mendel. But not all his disciples were of this opinion. Edmond Jabès. PFTM-2 *Fr.* Book of Questions, The.

Our horses neigh to each other [/] As we are departing. (LL) Taking Leave of a Friend ("Blue mountains to the north of the walls.") Li Po. NDACCP; PoCho; WaAnP, *tr. by* Ezra Pound

Oure Ho[o]ste gan to swere as he were wood. Geoffrey Chaucer. NAEL-6v1; NAEL-7v1; WaAnP *Fr.* Canterbury Tales, The.

Our house is an old farmhouse, whose properties. Farmhouse, The. Reed Whittemore. GoPo

Our Hunting Fathers. W. H. Auden. HarvBoo; NoAM

Our hut puffs streaks of hope. Country Life. Chenjerai Hove. HBAPE

Our intestines puke out images. TV Dinner. Michael Warr. BRtP

Our Island Home. Charles Timothy Brooks. APN-1

Our Islet out of Helgoland, dismissed. Islet the Dachs. George Meredith. DiBP

Our Jatti, palace wrestler of Mysore. At Forty. A. K. Ramanujan. VCWP

Our journey had advanced. Emily Dickinson. APN-2; SoSe-8

Our joy, a rampart to the mind. (LL) Passing Strange, The. John Masefield. MoBrPo; OBEV

Our karma led. Reply to a Friend's Poem. Muso Soseki. EaWin, *tr. by* W. S. Merwin

Our Kind. William Stafford. WaAnP

Our kisses are mountain mallow. Khobayza. Zulaykha Abu-Risha. PoArWo, *tr. by* Clarissa C. Burt and Nathalie Handal

Our Kitty. Carol Muske-Dukes. BAP-01

Our knowledge is historical, flowing, and flown. (LL) At the Fishhouses. Elizabeth Bishop. AmFaPo; APT-2; BeAl; CAP-8; Coast; ItP; NAAL-5; NALW; NAMCP V.2; OxBoAm; PoetW; PoPoPo; VCAP

Our Lady. Mary Elizabeth Coleridge. OBEV; OBMV; ViWPN

Our Lady. John Godfrey. PmAP

Our Lady. Carl Phillips. CAP-8

Our Lady Moon still hidden. Federico García Lorca. PFTM-1 *Fr.* Night (Suite for Piano and Poet's Voice).

Our Lady of Ardboe. Paul Muldoon. PBCIP

Our Lady of the Caves. Our Lady of the Three-Pronged Devil. Clayton Eshleman. PFTM-2

Our Lady of the Laundromat. Belle Waring. PBCAP

Our Lady of the Snow. (LL) "H. D." NAAPv.2; NAMCP V.1 *Fr.* Tribute to the Angels.

Our Lady of the Snows. Robert Hass. CAP-8; GoPo

Our Lady of the Three-Pronged Devil. Clayton Eshleman. PFTM-2

Our Lady's Lullaby. Richard Verstegan. *See* Lullaby: "Upon my lap my sovereign sits."

Our Lady's Song. *Unknown*. OBEV

Our Land. Yannis Ritsos. AmFaPo, *tr. by* Edmund Keeley

Our Land. Aharon Shabtai. WoBe, *tr. by* Peter Cole

Our last free summer we mooned about at odd hours. Chrysalides. Thomas Kinsella. ModIr

Our last resort. Lovers wading back to shore. Wellfleet. Timothy Liu. AmPoNex

Our lawn in stripes, the cat's pyjamas. Whole School of Bourgeois Primitives, A. Christopher Reid. NeBrP

Our Life in California. Gary Young. GeoHom

Our life in the world is only a great dream. Awakening from Drunkenness on a Spring Day. Li Po. TAL

Our Life in This World. Sami Mansei. WoPoe, *tr. by* Steven D. Carter

Our life in this world. Our Life in This World. Sami Mansei. WoPoe, *tr. by* Steven D. Carter

Our life is changed; their coming our beginning. (LL) Horses, The. Edwin Muir. BeAl; CABP; EmeKit; HeIP-4; MoBrPo; NAMCP V.1; NePenScot; NoAM; NPeEn; PoAgWa; TRP; WaAnP; WeW-3

Our life—impossible to ignore. (LL) Indian Singing in 20th Century America. Gail Tremblay. HATNAP; LTA; ReEnLa

Our life-sick hearts and turn them into dust. (LL) Last Word, A. Ernest Dowson. GSo; MoBrPo

Our Limitations. Oliver Wendell Holmes. NCAP

Our little Death from which we daily. Sleep is a Deep and Many Voiced Flood. Robert Duncan. CLPP

Our Little Sister is Worried. *Unknown*. NDACCP; WoPoe, *tr. by* Kenneth Rexroth

Our little tantrum, flushed and misery-hollow. Rebeca in a Mirror. Judith Rodriguez. BrAP

Our lives are Swiss. Emily Dickinson. APN-2

Our lives avoided tragedy. Pantoum of the Great Depression. Donald Justice. InGu; MakPoe; NoP-5

Our lives no longer feel ground under them. Stalin Epigram, The. Osip Emilevich Mandelstam. AF; WoPoe, *tr. by* Clarence Brown and W. S. Merwin

Our lives unfold between the sickle and the sword. Between Sickle and Sword. Yekhi'el Mar. NRoS, *tr. by* Esther Raizen

Our lives—the one leisurely, the other busy. To My Old Friend Lee. Chunghur Hyujung. BecRai, *tr. by* Kim Daljin, Kim Won-Chung and Christopher Merrill

Our Lord. Nezahualcoyotl. WoPoe, *tr. by* Thelma D. Sullivan

Our Lord, Immanuel [*or* Our Lord Emmanuel!]. (LL) O Little Town of Bethlehem. Phillips Brooks. APN-2; ChrPo; SacPr; TCAPo

Our Lost Angels. Scott Cairns. UpMys

Our lost virginities will never be regained. Labane. Annette M'Baye d'Erneville. HAWP, *tr. by* Brian Baer

Our Love. Xavier Villaurrutia. TCLAP, *tr. by* Michael Surman

Our Love Is Like Byzantium. Henrik Nordbrandt. VCWP, *tr. by* Henrik Norbrandt *and* Alexander Taylor

Our love is like Byzantium. Our Love Is Like Byzantium. Henrik Nordbrandt. VCWP, *tr. by* Henrik Norbrandt and Alexander Taylor

Our love is not found in our respective. Poem. Carlos German Belli. BLPSL, *tr. by* Rene de Costa, Rigas Kappatos and Eleni Paidoussi

Our love is the autumn languish. Our Love. Jo Nelson. PasH

Our love rhymes with: cub scout, clod-hopper, trouble-shooter, sore. Marriage Proposal. Sarah Messer. LegDan

Our love shall live, and later life renew. (LL) Edmund Spenser. BrAP; CABP; HeIP-4; NAEL-6v1; NAEL-7v1; NoP-4; NoP-5; NoSic; OxBSo; PoPoPo; TFi; WaAnP; WeW-3 *Fr.* Amoretti.

Our love which had a thousand leaves. (LL) Winter. Sheila Wingfield. LW; MoWP

Our love will not come back on fortune's wheel. Obit. Robert Lowell. PoetW; VCAP

Our Man. Ben Doyle. LegDan

Our masks are gauze and screen our faces for those unlike us only. Come Over and Help Us; a Rhapsody. John Wheelwright. APT-2

Our mind is full of sorrow, who will know of our grief? (LL) Song of the Bowmen of Shu [1915]. Bunno [Wen Wang or King Wen]. FaBoWar; NDACCP; OBVE, *tr. by* Ezra Pound

Our ministers were a heroic faction. War Cabinet, The. Myrddin ap Dafydd. BBMWP, *tr. by* Richard Poole

Our mither tongue wis dung doun. Widdershins. Ellie McDonald. EdScPo

Our morning hymn this is, and song at evening. (LL) Sir Philip Sidney. NAEL-6v1; NoSic *Fr.* Countesse of Pembroke's Arcadia, The.

Our mother. Incidence. Rae Armantrout. FTOS

Our Mother. Susan Griffin. HW

Our mother and fathers. Sister Mary Appassionata Proves to the Entomology Class That Woman and Man Descended from the Cricket. David Citino. UpMys

Our mother cautions us. Our Mother Talks about Metaphor. Susan Griffin. TAPaP

Our Mother *Eve,* who tasted of the Tree. Emilia Lanier and Aemilia Bassano Lanyer. PBRV *Fr.* Salve Deus Rex Judaeorum.

Our mother knew our worth. Our Kind. William Stafford. WaAnP

Our Mother Talks about Metaphor. Susan Griffin. TAPaP

Our mother was the pussy-cat, our father was the owl. Children of the Owl and the Pussy-Cat, The. Edward Lear. OBCoV

Our mother who art of the universe. Mother of the Universe. Yoko Ono. HW

Our Mother who art in Earth and Heaven. New Our Father, The. Priscilla Baird Hinckley. HW

Our mothers and fathers. Fighters For Life. Michael Rosen. RSaN

Our mothers tremble vibrate. Shekhinah as mute, The. Alicia Ostriker. SweBea

Our mothers / when asked. Feminism. Carolyn M. Rodgers. OxAAAP

Our mothers will always be. Our Mothers. Melanie Hope. BtF

Our mothers wrung hell and hardtack from row. American Sonnet (10). Wanda Coleman. WaAnP

Our names do not appear. (LL) Diving into the Wreck. Adrienne Rich. CAP-8; ColAP; EmeKit; HarvBoo; HeIP-4; MakPoe; MoWP; NAAL-5; NALW; NAMCP V.2; NIL-7; NIP-4; NoAM; NoP-4; NoP-5; OxBoAm; OxWW; PoPoPo; StAl; TWF; WaAnP

Our nation's future is coming into view. Live at Club Mozambique. Charles Simic. BodElec

Our Natures Rise. Kalamu ya Salaam. SpirFl *Fr.* New Orleans Haiku.

Our Naughty Time [*epigram*]. Friedrich von Logau. GePo, *tr. by* George C. Schoolfield

Our new / service orientation. Charles Bernstein. NAMCP V.2 *Fr.* Lives of the Toll Takers, The.

Our Noble Booker T. Washington. Mrs. Henry Linden. CBWP-4

Our old cat has kittens three—. Choosing Their Names. Thomas Hood. NOxBChV

Our Old Home. Yi Yŏnju. EcSo, *tr. by* Yung-Hee Kim

Our old neighbor. Lost Wood, The. Renée Weiss and Theodore Weiss. PoCoUp

Our olives safe from mildew. Florence: Sleeping in Fog. Adam Drinan. EdScPo

Our oneness is the wrestlers', fierce and close. Wrestling. Louisa Sarah Bevington. LW; PEW

Our orchestra / is the cat's nuts. Shoot It Jimmy! William Carlos Williams. APT-1

Our Other Sister. Jeffrey Harrison. PoDa

Our own calm journey on for human sake. (LL) Nile, The. Leigh Hunt. CenSon; GSo

Our Own Land. Anna Andreyevna Akhmatova. StAl, *tr. by* Richard McKane

Our Own—Progression F. James Russell Lowell.
"This hand-to-mouth, pert, rapid, nineteenth century." TCAPo

Our Paris part of Belfast has. Intimate Letter 1973. Padraic Fiacc. PNI

Our park empty. Three O'Clock Love Song. Michael S. Harper. GT

Our Parodies are Ended. Horace Twiss. UV

Our parodies are ended. These our authors. Our Parodies are Ended. Horace Twiss. UV

Our party scattered at yellow dusk and I came home to bed. After Getting Drunk, Becoming Sober in the Night. Po Chü-i. BLT, *tr. by* Arthur Waley

Our passions are most like to floods and stream[e]s. Sir Walter Ralegh to the Queen. Sir Walter Ralegh. NoSic

Our pastures are bitten and bare. Men on the Rocks, The. Adam Drinan. EdScPo

Our people spread the news each day. Spartan Mother, The. Benedek Virág. IQMS, *tr. by* Joseph Leftwich

Our Photograph[s]. Frederick Locker-Lampson. NBLV

Our pleasure now. Hurricane Doris. Lorenzo Thomas. FTtHH

Our private green honey. (LL) Gentle Communion. Pat Mora. NIL-7; NIP-4

Our provincial city's narrow streets send me a. Lost Behind the Back of God. Gyula Juhász. IQMS, *tr. by* Adam Makkai

Our Red Wheelbarrow. Larry Goodell. ICANM

Our revels now are ended. These our actors. William Shakespeare. ASA; UV *Fr.* Tempest, The.

Our Richard Allen in his early youth. Rt. Rev. Richard Allen. Josephine D. Henderson Heard. CBWP-4

Our romance won't end on a sorrowful note. They Can't Take That Away from Me. Ira Gershwin. ReLy

Our ruins run back to memory. Cavafy in Redondo. Mark Jarman. GeoHom

Our sacred Muse, of Israel's Singer sings. Michael Drayton. ChIV-1 *Fr.* David and Goliath.

Our sad farewell at the red tower. To the Tune: Beautiful Barbarian. Wei Chuang. CrYelRi, *tr. by* Sam Hamill

Our safe inventory of pain. And I was wrong. (LL) Fond Memory. Eavan Boland. ModIr; NAMCP V.2

Our sardine fishermen work at night in the dark of the moon; daylight or moonlight. Purse-Seine, The. Robinson Jeffers. AmFaPo; NAAPv.2; NAMCP V.1; NoAM; NoP-4; NoP-5; WeW-3

Our Savior Christ tracing the bordering hills. Thomas Deloney. ChIV-2 *Fr.* Destruction of Jerusalem, The.

Our Saviour's Passion. Mary Sidney Herbert, Countess of Pembroke.
"He placed all rest, and had no resting place." SacPr

Our Scholar travels yet the loved hill-side [*or* hillside]. (LL) Thyrsis. Matthew Arnold. NAEL-6v2; NAEL-7v2; NoP-4; NoP-5; OBEV; WaAnP

Our Second Night. Viki Radden. BtF

Our senses, without reason, are naught worth. Robert Hayman. NOSC *Fr.* Owen's Epigrams.

Our Sharpeville. Ingrid de Kok. HAWP

Our shells clacked on the plates. Oysters. Seamus Heaney. StAl; UV

Our ship, the Sea Smithy, swerved out of the tradewinds. On the Congo. Harry Edmund Martinson. WED, *tr. by* Robert Bly

Our single purpose was to walk through snow. Polar Exploration. Stephen Spender. NoAM

Our sires who once in freedom's cause. Slave, The. "Ada." NAAPv.1

Our sister dear, what joy for us! Conversation between Me and the Women. Anna Petrovna Bunina. ARWW, *tr. by* Sibelan Forrester

Our Sister's dance! Dance of Sister Rain. Eugène Marais. SonAtl, *tr. by* Joost Daalder, Peter Daskler and Alistair Turner

Our Skin Is Paper. Hilary Booth. SurWo

Our skin loosely lies. Long Division; a Tribal History. Wendy Rose. OPRER

Our skin, strenuously tutored to appreciate the vernacular. Skin. Marjorie Welish. PmAP

Our skins ache of emergence / dark o' the moon. (LL) Loba Addresses the Goddess, The / or The Poet as Priestess Addresses the Loba-Goddess. Diane Di Prima. HW; PmAP

Our Son's Profession. Ha Thi Thao. WoPoe, *tr. by* Nguyen Ngoc Bich

Our Speaker This Morning. Chris Willerton. TiP2

Our speech slurs now. Nook. George Barlow. GT

Our Spring Needs Shoveling. Haniel Long. APT-1

Our Square of Lawn. Matthea Harvey. LegDan

Our storm[e] is past, and that storm[e]'s tyrannous rage. Calm[e], The. John Donne. NoSic; PBRV

Our story didn't make the six o'clock news. The other story did. The one. Sand. Dominique Parker. SpirFl

Our story isn't a file of photographs. For an Album. Adrienne Rich. VCAP

Our suffering would be unbearable if we couldn't regard it as a. Letter to Youki. Robert Desnos. AF, *tr. by* Carolyn Forché

Our Sun. George Seferis. AF

Our Sunday Rest. Don Aminado. TCRusP, *tr. by* John Glad

Our talk was of Too Much, of. Zurich, at the Stork. Paul Celan. PoetW, *tr. by* John Felstiner

Our Task. Henrietta Cordelia Ray. CBWP-3

Our teachers prepared us years ahead. Dancing the Tarantella at the County Farm. Sandra Alcosser. ExTi

Our texas economy. Charles S. Taylor. TiP2

Our thatch house perched where land ends. Thatch House. Tu Fu [*or* Du Fu]. NDACCP, *tr. by* David Hinton

Our thin, tough bodies were identical. Pole Vaulting. Maura Stanton. PoA 2002

Our thoughts and prayers rise to the jet. From Ground Zero. Everett Hoagland. FuFl

Our tight knot! Gentle boy with golden hair. Edward Prosser Rhys. BBMWP *Fr.* Memory.

Our Tongue. Ferenc Kazinczy. IQMS, *tr. by* Watson Kirkconnell

Our Town. Thornton Wilder.
"First Act was called the Daily Life, The." ASA

Our trees are aspens, but people. Another Version. Lisel Mueller. IllVoic

Our tree's shadow is green at night. At Night. Boris Hristov. CSCBP, *tr. by* Georgi Belev and Lisa Sapinkopf

Our true form is the blurb. Ron Silliman. BAP-04 *Fr.* VOG.

Our twentieth century was going to improve on the others. Century's Decline, The. Wisława Szymborska. CFP, *tr. by* Stanisław Barańczak *and* Clara Cavanagh and Clare Cavanagh

Our two soules therefore, which are one. John Donne. UV *Fr.* Valediction: Forbidding Mourning, A.

Our veins are open to shadow, and our fingertips. Eel in the Cave, The. Robert Bly. GoPo

Our Village, that's to say not Miss Mitford's. Our Village—by a Villager. Thomas Hood. FaBoVe; OBSV

Our Village—by a Villager. Thomas Hood. FaBoVe; OBSV

Our vision is our voice. Anthem, An. Sonia Sanchez. UnSA

Our Voice. Noémia da Sousa. HAWP, *tr. by* Jacques-Noël Gouat

Our voice has risen, conscious and barbarous. Our Voice. Noémia da Sousa. HAWP, *tr.* by Jacques-Noël Gouat

Our voices follow each other. For Letters. Yvonne Cullen. NIrP

Our voices waved upwards into a tide / that wrapped itself around the island. Island within Island. Henry Dumas. GT

Our waking hours write bitter things. Reconciliation. Dora Greenwell. PoBW

Our way of life. Lionel Abrahams. TSAP

Our way of life. It's a Woman's World. Eavan Boland. ItWoWo

Our whole body frantic for the leap and the sweet light that follows. (LL) Tagging. Maureen Seaton. ExTi; IllVoic

Our words do not lie apart. Holy Order. Gemino H. Abad. ReBoTo

Our World Is Less Full Now That Mr. Fuller Is Gone. Kalamu ya Salaam. ISC

Our world is very little in the sky. Measurements. Louisa Sarah Bevington. VWP

Our years are driven wild. Yeti. John Haines. PoCoUp

Our youth was gay but rough. One of the Boys. James Simmons. ModIr; PNI

Our youth was happy: why repine. Tears of the Dying. Walter Savage Landor. NPeEn

Oure [*or* Owre] Ho[o]st upon his stiropes stood ano[o]n. Geoffrey Chaucer. NAEL-7v1 *Fr.* Canterbury Tales, The.

Oure kinge went forth to Normandy. *Unknown.* NoP-4; NoP-5; WaAnP

Oure kyng went forth to Normandy. *Unknown.* OHMEL

Ours is group solitude. Eugenio Montale. ItPo, *tr.* by Gayle Ridinger

Ours is the ancient story. For Daughters of Magdalen. Countee Cullen. ChIV-2

Ourselves become our own best sacrifice! (LL) In the Holy Nativity of Our Lord God. Richard Crashaw. NAEL-6v1; NAEL-7v1

Ourselves or Nothing. Carolyn Forché. BodElec; GifTon

Ourselves we do inter with sweet derision. Emily Dickinson. APN-2

Ourstory. Carole Satyamurti. BeAl; MoWP

Ousel cock, so black of hue, The. William Shakespeare. NoSic *Fr.* Midsummer Night's Dream, A.

Out. Eleanor Brown. MFPA

Out. Ted Hughes. FaBoWar; NAMCP V.2

Out and across the Atlantic ocean. Thoughts from a 747. Dana Gilkes. BtF

Out back, Lotte's feeding pillow cases. Typing the Letters. John A. Scott. BMAP

Out beyond ideas of wrongdoing and rightdoing. Jelaluddin Rumi. BLT, *tr.* by Coleman Barks

Out for a walk, after a week in bed. Urban Convalescence, An. James Merrill. ColAP; NAAL-5

Out from the tight railway seams along Highway 101. Elkhorn Slough. Abigail Albrecht. GeoHom

Out Here. Roger Mitchell. PoCoUp

Out here in the exact middle of the day. Edward Hopper and the House by the Railroad. Edward Hirsch. PoSol

Out here on Cottage Grove it matters. The galloping. Pyrography. John Ashbery. HarvBoo; VCAP

Out here there. Robert Creeley. WoBe *Fr.* Life and Death.

Out here, where any rambling bed—of sea-. Reach, The. Carl Phillips. GT

Out here where the crows turn around. Country Wisdoms. Maggie Anderson. PBCAP

Out in Arizona where the bad men are. Rag Time Cowboy Joe. Grant Clarke. ReLy

Out in the Cold. Ellen A. Rosen. PfS

Out in the Dark. Edward Thomas. MoBrPo; OBWVE; OxBEV

Out in the dark over the snow. Out in the Dark. Edward Thomas. MoBrPo; OBWVE; OxBEV

Out in the Desert. Josephine D. Henderson Heard. CBWP-4

Out in the elegy country, summer evenings. Blue Suburban. Howard Nemerov. ColAP

Out in the Fields [with God]. Elizabeth Barrett Browning. ITBLP

Out in the high waves. Saigyō. WoPoe, *tr.* by Steven D. Carter

Out in the late amber afternoon. In Shadow. Hart Crane. NAAPv.2

Out in the marsh reeds. Ki no Tsurayuki. WoPoe, *tr.* by Kenneth Rexroth

Out in the night. Lazy Man's Haiku, The. John Ridland. CalPo

Out in the Open. Tomas Tranströmer. WED, *tr.* by Robert Bly

Out in the silent Rockies. Outcast, The. P. G. Wodehouse. UV

Out in the sky the great dark clouds are massing. Ships That Pass in the Night. Paul Laurence Dunbar. ColAP

Out in the streets, the phantoms of utopia. Phantoms of Utopia. Julianne Buchsbaum. LegDan

Out in the sun the goldfinch flits. Hollow Wood, The. Edward Thomas. OWoS

Out in this desert we are testing bombs. Trying to Talk with a Man. Adrienne Rich. AtGh

Out, John. Thomas Haynes Bayly. OBCoV

Out my window, the loop canal. Loop Canal, The. Nikolai Alekseievich Zabolotsky. TCRusP, *tr.* by Denis Johnson and Kathy Lewis

Out of a blue heaven, a shower of strontium-90. Daily Papers. Marguerite Yourcenar. YaTCFP, *tr.* by Martin Sorrell

Out of a clear blue sky. All I Do Is Dream of You. Arthur Freed. ReLy

Out of a fired ship, which, by no way. Burnt Ship, A. John Donne. FaBoWar; OBWP

Out of a hat. Out of Our Hands. Cathy Song. PoA 2002; UnSA

Out of a high school writing contest. Poetry and Post, Texas. Betsy Colquitt. TiP2

Out of a Hundred. Mary Ruefle. AmAlph

Out of a hundred people. Contribution to Statistics, A. Wisława Szymborska. PtR; TWF, *tr.* by Stanisław Barańczak *and* Clara Cavanagh and Clare Cavanagh

Out of a love poem that you used to know by heart. (LL) Forgetfulness. Billy Collins. EMP; FaoP; PoA 2002; StAl

Out of a pure blue sky, on East River dusk. Holding Mode, A. John Ashbery. VaPo

Out of a ripple in the sea grass. Of Haloes & Saintly Aspects. Sherod Santos. PfSP

Out of a Sudden. Tom Raworth. Oth

Out of Africa arises a silence. Art of Hurricanes, The. Víctor Hernández Cruz. TouFir

Out of Africa of the suckling. Out of Africa. Grace Nichols. MoWP

Out of an Epigram of Martial. Martial. OBVE, *tr.* by Sir John Denham

Out of Blake's Bakery they sauntered, shopping bag full of warm bread. Frank's Song. Reed Bye. AHA

Out of Boredom. Luljeta Lleshanaku. WoBe, *tr.* by Henry Israeli

Out of Bounds. Priscilla Borthwick. Prnts

Out of Bounds. Harry Mathews. OnScMo

Out of Bronx subway June forest. Edwin Denby. AHA; NYP2

Out of burlap sacks, out of bearing butter. They Feed They Lion. Philip Levine. CalPo; CAP-8; ItP; NAMCP V.2; NoAM; NoP-4; NoP-5; OxBoAm; StAl; VCAP

Out of Cana. Maura Eichner. "Eat bread. Drink wine. Try to sing the song." UpMys

Out of chaos. Yün-k'an Tzu. ColAnChi, *tr.* by Jerome P. Seaton

Out of churned aureoles. Marine Surface, Low Overcast. Amy Clampitt. GPTC; OxBoAm

Out of East Gate. East Gate, The. *Unknown.* ChinPo, *tr.* by Ye Weilian [*or* Yeh Wei-lien *or* Wai-lim Yip]

Out of enraged, iron-colored flags. Anxiously Autumn Arrives. Miklós Radnóti. ConPt, *tr.* by Clayton Eshleman and Gyula Kodolanyi

Out of Exile. John Burnside. EdScPo

Out of her salt hips. Ocean. Peter Balakian. PfSP

Out of here / or me. (LL) Inner Tube. Michael Ondaatje. NAMCP V.2; NoAM

Out of Hiding. Li-Young Lee. NoP-5; PoDa

Out of his cottage to the sun. Old Dan'l. Leonard Alfred George Strong. MoBrPo

Out of Horace. James Wright. NOSC

Out of Illness. Lionel Abrahams. TSAP

Out of it all but this remains. Dead Cities. Madison Cawein. APN-2

Out of kindness comes redness and out of rudeness comes comes rapid same question. Gertrude Stein. NAAPv.2 *Fr.* Tender Buttons.

Out of love for You. Dīnrām. SinGod, *tr.* by Rachel Fell McDermott

Out of marsh out of the bronchial. Let Me Remind You You Are Still under Oath. Nance Van Winckel. RWB

Out of me unworthy and unknown. Edgar Lee Masters. CBCWP; MoAmPo; NAMCP V.1; NoAM; OxBoAm; TFi *Fr.* Spoon River Anthology.

Out of midsummer's blazing most not night. E. E. Cummings. NoAM

Out of Mobile I saw a rusty [*or* '60] Ford. Plain. Miller Williams. RWB

Out of my flesh that hungers. On a Night of the Full Moon. Audre Lorde. NALW

Out of my mother's womb. Job. I. John Hall. ChIV-1

Out of My Own Pocket. Martha Collins. ExTi

Out of Our Hands. Cathy Song. PoA 2002; UnSA

Out of range of the classical station, I enter. Road Down Home. James Applewhite. LPSFW

Out of respect for the elders of the village where he finds himself sober for the first time in years. Prodigal Son Considers a Diplomatic Career, The. Dionisio D. Martinez. PoDa

Out of respect for what cannot be said. Out of Respect. Victor Segalen. YaTCFP, *tr.* by Mary Ann Caws *and* Jean-Pierre Cauvin and Patricia Terry

Out of sight, out of mind. Sand in My Shoes. Frank Loesser. ReLy

Out of Sleep. Allen Curnow. BrAP

Out of that pain. Rasta Reggae. Mervyn Morris. WaCA

Out of the American provinces. Cheerleaders. Lisa Coffman. AmPoNex

Out of the Blizzard. Lesley-Anne Bourne. Coast

Out of the blueness. Back Yard, The. Peter Balakian. PfSP

Out of the bosom of the Air. Snow-Flakes. Henry Wadsworth Longfellow. APN-1; BrAP; CtM; ITBLP; MoW; NCAP; NoP-4; NoP-5; TCAPo

Out of the church she followed [or follow'd] them. Maude Clare. Christina Georgina Rossetti. ViWPN

Out of the clover and blue-eyed grass. Driving Home the Cows. Kate Putnam Osgood. CBCWP

Out of the cocoon. (LL) "H. D." NAAPv.2; NALW; NAMCP V.1 Fr. Tribute to the Angels.

Out of the complicated house, come I. Hills, The. Frances Darwin Cornford. MoBrPo

Out of the Cradle Endlessly Rocking. Walt Whitman. APN-1; ColAP; HeIP-4; MoAmPo; NAAL-3; NAAL-5; NAAPv.1; NAWM-7v2; NCAP; NoP-4; NoP-5; OWoS; OxBoAm; SAmP; TRP

Out of the crowd, I have seen you travelling south of Pardoo. Witch Doctor's Magic Flight, The. Smiler Narautjarri. NOBAu, tr. by George von Brandenstein

Out of the dark. Open Door, The. Elizabeth Jane Coatsworth. TLR

Out of the dark cup. From the Telephone. Florence Ripley Mastin. LW

Out of the Darkness. Voltairine de Cleyre. SWaP

Out of the darks and deeps of space. Tryst, The. Harriet Prescott Spofford. SWaP

Out of the Deep. Clara Ann Thompson. CBWP-2

Out of the Depths. Moishe Nadir. Prolet, tr. by Amelia Glaser

Out of the depths of a heart of love. Valentine, A. Priscilla Jane Thompson. CBWP-2

Out of the dusk a shadow. Evolution. John Banister Tabb. APN-2

Out of the earth. I Sing for the Animals. Teton Sioux Oral Tradition. TCAPo

Out of the earth, out of the air, out of the water. Richard Murphy. PBCIP Fr. Battle of Aughrim, The.

Out of the earth to rest or range. Passing Strange, The. John Masefield. MoBrPo; OBEV

Out of the East in purple robes. Ancient "Kayán", The. Endre Ady. IQMS, tr. by Watson Kirkconnell

Out of the east window a storm. Wednesday of Holy Week, 1940. Kenneth Rexroth. ChIV-1

Out of the factory chimney tall. Smoke Animals. Rowena Bastin Bennett. CA

Out of the farmhouse. Revelation on a Summer Walk. John O'Brien. PoCoUp

Out of the flowers. (LL) Temple bell stops, The. Basho. WED; WoPoe, tr. by Robert Bly

Out of the focal and foremost fire. Little Giffen. Francis Orrery Ticknor. CBCWP; PCW

Out of the forest I come with my flowers, singing, all alone. (LL) Little Red-Cap. Carol Ann Duffy. MoWP; NeBrP; NoP-5

Out of the ghetto streets where a Jewboy. Autobiographical. Abraham Moses Klein. BrAP; NoAM

Out of the gray steel of imagination. Spring & Asura. Miyazawa Kenji. CAoMJL1, tr. by Hiroaki Sato

Out of the green of spring. Old Mountain. Muso Soseki. EaWin, tr. by W. S. Merwin

Out of the grey air grew snow and more snow. Snow. William Robert Rodgers. ModIr

Out of the habit, I remembered nothing. I Object, said the Object. Mairi MacInnes. MoWP

Out of the hills of Habersham. Song of the Chattahoochee. Sidney Lanier. APN-2; ColAP; TCAPo

Out of the hills the trees bulge. Charles Reznikoff. APT-2

Out of the house or be the wife I want. Martial. RomPo, tr. by Peter Whigham

Out of the Identical. Gustaf Sobin. PmAP

Out of the inside insane outside ratside batside ouchside cry. Sarcophagus. Larry Goodell. ICANM

Out of the Italian [madrigal]. Giovanni Giambattista. OBVE, tr. by Richard Crashaw

Out of the lamplight. Mice in the Hay. Leslie Norris. NOxBChV; OBCP

Out of the least shift in the wind, out of. Shirt Collar, The. Ann Townsend. NAPBL

Out of the life lived, out of the love spent. (LL) Urban Convalescence, An. James Merrill. ColAP; NAAL-5

Out of the marvellous as he had known it. (LL) Seamus Heaney. EmeKit; ModIr; NoP-5; NPeEn; StAl Fr. Squarings.

Out of the maternal watery blue lines. Ted Hughes. OWoS Fr. Curlews [Lift].

Out of the mud two strangers came. Two Tramps in Mud Time. Robert Frost. APT-1; MoAmPo; NAMCP V.1; NoAM; OxBoAm; SAmP

Out of the Night. Emily Jane Pfeiffer.

"So the river—yes, the river; I have come to that at last." VWP

Out of the night and the north. Train Dogs, The. Emily Pauline Johnson. IFF

Out of the Past there has come a Face. Face from the Past, A. Menella Bute Smedley. VWP

Out of the shadow, I am come in to you whole a black holy man. Study Peace. Imamu Amiri Baraka. APSN

Out of the shadows of your being, so sick and still a shade under it. Daphne Marlatt. NLPA Fr. Touch to My Tongue.

Out of the soil and rock. Gary Snyder. BodElec

Out of the stirrings of the Yellow Sea. Circle, The. Keith Wilson. AmWaPo

Out of the tomb, we bring Badroulbadour. Worms at Heaven's Gate, The. Wallace Stevens. NAMCP V.1; NoAM

Out of the tree of life. Best Is Yet to Come, The. Carolyn Leigh. ReLy

Out of the tuft of hair between his eye. Lotus Sutra. Norman Fischer. WANABP

Out of the Wailing. Stephen Caldwell Wright. ISC

Out of the waste you can spin. Gavin Selerie. Oth Fr. Roxy.

Out of the water call. Logbook of Judgments. Jay Wright.

Out of the window. Ana Belén López Pulido. SPV, tr. by Jen Hofer

Out of the window a sea of green trees. Open Windows. Sara Teasdale. ColAP

Out of the wind's and the rain's way. (LL) Old Woman of the Roads, The. Padraic Colum. IrV; MoBrPo; OBEV

Out of the winds' and the waves' riot. Ebb Tide. Marjorie Lowry Christie Pickthall. IFF

Out of the wine-pot cry'd the fly. Fly, The. Philip Ayres. OBVE

Out of the Winter-Tree Into the Spring-Tree. Hwang Jiwoo. CAMKP, tr. by Young-Jun Lee and Scott Swaner

Out of the wood of thoughts that grows by night. Cock-Crow. Edward Thomas. MoBrPo; NPeEn

Out of their heart's poverty, for worn men. (LL) Everyday Alchemy. Genevieve Taggard. APT-2; NAAPv.2

Out of their loneliness for each other. Spirit of Place: Great Blue Heron. William Stafford. PfSP

Out of their slumber Europeans spun. Snow in Europe. David Gascoyne. NPeEn

Out of their torments men carved a flower. New Year. Aimé Césaire. YaTCFP, tr. by Clayton Eshleman and Annette Smith

Out of these depths. De Profundis. David Gascoyne. PoWW

Out of this close horizon there are animals. New Picnic Time. Peter Gizzi. OnScMo

Out of This World. Johnny Mercer. ReLy

Out of those wild, in- / visible circuits, a. Irises. Gustaf Sobin. APSN

Out of Time. Laura Fargas. CFP

Out of touch, we say. Staying in Touch. Bill Pearlman. ICANM

Out of tube and tune. South Bound: Facing North. Geraldine Monk. Oth

Out of Tune. W. E. Henley. MoBrPo

Out of tune with the crowd since young. Home to Farm. Unknown. ChinPo, tr. by Ye Weilian [or Yeh Wei-lien or Wai-lim Yip]

Out of waters warm. Man. Oscar Hahn. TCLAP, tr. by Sandy McKinney

Out of what secret English summer evening. To the Nightingale. Jorge Luis Borges. PoCho, tr. by Alastair Reid

Out of which all miracles leap. (LL) At Darien Bridge. James Dickey. InGu; LPSFW

Out of Work, Out of Touch, Out of Sorts. Catherine Davis. FFC

Out of your head the sky is taken. Monotones. B. P. Nichol. FTOS

Out of your sleep arise and wake. Unknown. NoP-5

Out of your whole life give but a moment! Now. Robert Browning. OxBSo

Out on Killiney Hill that night, you said. Spring Night. Richard Kell. IrLP

Out on the bare grey roads, I pass. Touch It. Robert Mezey. CalPo; GeoHom

Out on the high "bird islands," Ciboux and Hertford. Cape Breton. Elizabeth Bishop. Coast

Out on the lawn I lie in bed. Summer Night, A. W. H. Auden. NPeEn

Out on the prairie the small owls call. Funeral. Vaida Stewart Montgomery. TiP2

Out on the windy hill. Shepherd's Dog, The. Leslie Norris. OBCP

Out, Out—. Robert Frost. AmFaPo; APT-1; ColAP; HarvBoo; HeIP-4; InoFa; ItP; NAAL-5; NAMCP V.1; OxBoAm; SoSe-8; TCAPo; TRP; WaAnP

Out past the airfield there's a house. For Brigid. M. Travis Lane. Coast

Out scouting for sound counsels? How to prosper? Ausiàs March. STV

Out strolling on a spring day. Tune: "Thinking of the Imperial Capital." Wei Chuang. ColAnChi, tr. by John Timothy Wixted

Out the window, a kid-robin on a branch. Volunteers. Hilda Raz. ExTi

Out the window, Colombia, out the window. Sharon Doubiago. PBCAP Fr. South America Mi Hija.

Out There. Bill Berkson. NYP2

Out There. Breyten Breytenbach. VCWP

Out there, beyond the boundary fence, beyond. Singing Bones, The. Randolph Stow. BMAP

Out there in the sun—in the rain. (LL) Rooms. Charlotte Mew. HarvBoo; MoWP; PoBW; PoCho

Out, thou silly moon-struck elf. Idiot-Born, The. Eliza Cook. VWP

Out through the fields and the woods. Reluctance. Robert Frost. ITBLP; MoAmPo

Out through the neighborhood with nothing more. Downtown Bus, The. Wyatt Prunty. PoDa

Out upon It! Sir John Suckling. See Constant Lover, A [or The].

Out upon it! I have loved [or lov'd]. Sir John Suckling. BASC; CavPo; NAEL-6v1; NAEL-7v1; NBLV; NoP-4; NOSC; NPeEn; OxAEP-1; OxBEV; PBRV Fr. Poem with the Answer, A.

Out, upon the deep old ocean. On Genessarett. Josephine D. Henderson Heard. CBWP-4

Out walking in July. Released on Parole. James McAuley. BMAP

Out walking in the frozen swamp one gray [or grey] day. Wood-Pile, The. Robert Frost. APT-1; ColAP; MoW; NAAL-5; NAAPv.2; NAMCP V.1; NoAM; NoP-4; NoP-5; OxBoAm; SAmP

Out walking in the swamp picking cowslip, marsh marigold. First Green of Spring, The. David Budbill. BeAl; GoPo; IPoFL

Out West. Bill Manhire. EmeKit

Out west there is apparently such a dearth of. Light and Dark, East and West. Robert Hershon. PrTe

Out where silver-blue distance is calling. Over Texas Hills. Maude E. Cole. TiP2

Out where the hand-clasp's a little stronger. Out Where the West Begins. Arthur Chapman. BRP

Out Where the West Begins. Arthur Chapman. BRP

Out where the West begins. Pathogenesis. Philip Whalen. WANABP

Out where yr going. (LL) I Know a Man. Robert Creeley. AmFaPo; CAP-8; ICANM; NAMCP V.2; NIP-4; NoP-4; NoP-5; OxBoAm; StAl; VCAP

Out Whistling. Dave Jeddie Smith. PfSP

Out with my dog at dawn—we couldn't sleep—. Two Ember Days in Alabama. Andrew Hudgins. RA

Outbound. Greg Williamson. NoP-5

Outbound, your bark awaits you. Were I one. Godspeed. John Greenleaf Whittier. GSo

Outcast. Claude McKay. APT-1; NAAPv.2; NAMCP V.1; OxAAAP

Outcast, The. Josephine D. Henderson Heard. CBWP-4

Outcast, The. James Stephens. MoBrPo

Outcast, The. P. G. Wodehouse. UV

Outcries. Hélène d'Oettingen. CuPo

Outdoor Chums in the Forest. Ann Townsend. ExTi

Outer Banks, The. Emily Grosholz. RA

Outer Banks, The. Muriel Rukeyser. APT-2

Outer Layers of Nervousness, The. Alan Davies. FTOS

Outer provinces are never secure, The. Peace with Honor. Philip Appleman. AmWaPo

Outer—from the Inner, The. Emily Dickinson. APN-2

Outlaw, The. Seamus Heaney. NIL-7

Outlaw of Loch Lene, The. Jeremiah Joseph Callanan. IrLP; OBEV, tr. by Jeremiah Joseph Callanan

Outlaw we sometimes love to chase and embrace. (LL) I'm Dealing with My Pain. Denise Duhamel. NeAmPo; SUP

Outlaws. Whitney Montgomery. TiP2

Outlaw's Song, The. Joanna Baillie. OBEV

Outlaws stripped everyone down to the bone, The. Unknown. SLW, tr. by Marjolijn De Jager, Sayd Bahodin Majrouh and André Velter

Outliving / Them all, all. Issa. ZenPo, tr. by Takashi Ikemoto and Lucien Stryk

Outlook. Crystal Bacon. UrbNat

Outlook wasn't brilliant for the Mudville nine that day, The. Ernest Lawrence Thayer. See It looked extremely rocky for the Mudville nine that day.

Out-of-Body Experience. Jim Crenner. PoDa

Outpacing bargain, vocable and prayer. (LL) For the Marriage of Faustus and Helen. Hart Crane. APT-2; NoAM; OxBoAm

Out-Patients. Carole Satyamurti. PoCu; StAl

Outpost Soldier, The. Vietnamese Oral Tradition. CaDao, tr. by John Balaban

Outposts. F. W. D. Bendall. FaBoWar

Outrigger. Charles Bernstein. PFTM-2

Outside. Audre Lorde. BrAP

Outside / a moon starting up. Sharing. Alan Yount. PasH

Outside a rain steady and hard as nails. Dwelling. Emily Warn. GifTon

Outside Amarillo, you thing you will never get anywhere. Way of Words, The. Martha Elizabeth. TiP2

Outside another storm is howling; more. Prayer for My Daughters, A. Thomas O'Grady. Coast

Outside Bristol Rovers Football Ground. Ballad of Billy Rose, The. Leslie Norris. AngWePo

Outside everything visible and invisible a blazing maple. Testimony of Light,The. Carolyn Forché. AFaM; ExTi

Outside, in fact, there wasn't any change. Patrizia Cavalli. NeIt

Outside in floral, vegetating thought. Fall Under. To Succumb to; Come under an Influence or Power. Amy Newman. IAoNAP

Outside in the Open. Adriann Roland Holst. TuT, tr. by Desmond Egan

Outside, in the rain, on the edge of evening. Dick and Colin at the Salmon Nets. Naomi Mitchison. MoWP

Outside / it is suddenly dark. Entries for a Possible Poem. Sargon Boulus. Eno

Outside.(it was New York and beautifully,snowing. (LL) I was sitting in mcsoreley's. outside it was New York and beauti- / fully snowing. E. E. Cummings. NAMCP V.1; NoAM

Outside memory worship never dies. Sappho's Gymnasium. T. Begley and Olga Broumas. GifTon

Outside my door. To the Tune "The Drunken Young Lord." Unknown. WoPoe, tr. by C. H. Kwock and Vincent McHugh and Vincent McHugh

Outside my door four roses. Four Roses. Susan Wood. TiP2

Outside my image in the frame. Ibrahim Nasrallah. Eno Fr. Mirrors.

Outside my window a cow is giving birth. Calf. Katrina Porteous. BeAl; NeBl

Outside my window a lorry misses gear. Weekend at Home. John Pook. AngWePo

Outside my window an English spring was. Game, The. Eavan Boland. PtR

Outside my window the wasps. Flight. B. H. Fairchild. PoA 2002

Outside New York, a high place where with one glance you take in the houses where eight million human beings live. Schubertiana. Tomas Tranströmer. WED, tr. by Robert Bly

Outside nothing's really changed. Patrizia Cavalli. ItPo, tr. by Gayle Ridinger

Outside of Havana. Jewish Cemetery in Guanabacoa, The. Ruth Behar. MirDau

Outside of This, That Is. Barbara Guest. NYP2

Outside our bedroom window. Descant. Jane Mayes. PasH

Outside/ outside myself/ there is a world. William Carlos Williams. NoAM Fr. Paterson.

Outside Pisa. Chitra Divakaruni. OpBo

Outside Room Six. Lynn Emanuel. ReTh

Outside somewhere, beneath an atmosphere. Allegory. Rafael Campo. RA

Outside space and time, the deer wander, at once swift and languid. Deer. Juan José Arreola. MotU, tr. by W. S. Merwin

Outside the Bureau all the trams and trains. Laid Off. Francis Webb. BMAP

Outside the City. Tu Fu [or Du Fu]. NDACCP, tr. by David Hinton

Outside the curtain rain trickles on. Tune: "Sand Washed by Waves." Li Yü. ColAnChi, tr. by Jiaosheng Wang

Outside the Depot. Betsy Sholl. LTA

Outside the Door. Marie Luise Kaschnitz. GTCP, tr. by Reinhold Grimm

Outside the great clanging cathedrals of rust and smoke. Poem Written under an Archway in a Discontinued Railroad Station, Fargo, North Dakota, A. James Wright. GM

Outside the Hospital. Joe Wenderoth. BodElec

Outside the hospital the sun lighted the leaves. Triptych. Christopher Pilling. NLP

Outside the hotel window, unenlightened pigeons. Jain Bird Hospital in Delhi, The. William Meredith. VCAP

Outside the house an ash-tree hung its terrible whips. Discord in Childhood. D. H. Lawrence. HarvBoo; IJHIL

Outside the house: lilacs, white and lilac. Yojimbo. Miriam Sagan. WANABP

Outside, the last kids holler. Leaving the Motel. W. D. Snodgrass. NIL-7; NIP-4

Outside the night was cold, the snow was deep. Charles Reznikoff. NAAPv.2; OxBoAm Fr. Testimony.

Outside the Party. Julia Ward Howe. SWaP Fr. Lyrics of the Street.

Outside the porthole life, or what is. Flight. George Oppen. OtW

Outside the rest home. Nice Place, A. Lawson Fusao Inada. WhBo

Outside the second grade room. Girl Who Loved the Sky, The. Anita Endrezze. HATNAP

Outside the tent on the Little Fork. Horace Kephart. Robert Morgan. LPSFW

Outside the theater I felt. Emetic. Lawrence L. White. IAoNAP

Outside the vineyard is a caravan. Graffiti from the Gare Saint-Manqué. Marilyn Hacker. FaoP

Outside the window, stanchion-barred. In Prison. Paul Verlaine. EdScPo, tr. by Neil Munro

Outside the window the McGill smelter. Lynn Emanuel. AtGh

Outside the world was full, plural. Christmas Tree, The. Patricia Beer. OBCP

Outside their door, a tiny narcissus. April, New Hampshire. Sharon Olds. BodElec

Outside, time and famous dates passed. Women in the Cold War. Alison Fell. RSaN

Outside where the storm goes cracked. Caption for a Miniature. Joanne Kyger. BB

Outside You Cannot Breathe. Jasper Bernes. IAoNAP

Outside your temple wall. To the Unnamed Buddhist Nun Who Burned Herself to Death on the Night of June 3, 1966. Diane Di Prima. BB

Outsider, The. Syl Cheney-Coker. HBAPE

Outsider: Minnie Evans. Sandra McPherson. ExTi

Outskirts. Tomas Transtrӧmer. BLT, tr. by Robert Bly

Outstretched on this bed. Confession for Forgiveness, A. Unknown. IrV, tr. by Alfred Perceval Graves

Outward. Louis Simpson. EmeKit

Outweighing all, heavy out of the souvenir bundle. Three American Women and a German Bayonet. Winfield Townley Scott. PWW2

Outwit me, Lord, if ever hence. Security. Charles Leo O'Donnell. SacPr

Outwitted. Edwin Markham. CalPo; MoAmPo; NAAPv.1

Outwitting barren ground! (LL) In Topaz. Toyo Suyemoto. ASA; NAAPv.2

Outworn year has altered his apparel, The. Elegy. Miklós Zrínyi. IQMS, tr. by Watson Kirkconnell

Ouvertes / aux rouge-gorges. Tahar Bekri. YaTCFP Fr. Retour en Tunisie.

Ovation. Carol Muske-Dukes. AmAlph

Oven. Laura Kasischke. NAPBL

Oven Bird, The. Robert Frost. APT-1; GSo; HeIP-4; ItP; NAAL-5; NAAPv.2; NAMCP V.1; NoAM; NoP-4; NoP-5; OWoS; OxBoAm; TCAPo; WaAnP

Over a dark and quiet empire. Two Poems. Andrey Andreievich Voznesensky. VCWP, tr. by Patricia Blake and William Jay Smith

Over a dock railing, I watch the minnows, thousands, swirl. Prayer. Jorie Graham. AWPTFC; PtR

Over a Drink. Mererid Puw Davies. BBMWP, tr. by the author

Over a purple covered mountain. Distorted Sun. Akira Togawa. NAAPv.2

Over a sea with death acquainted, yet forever chaste. (LL) Ragged Island. Edna St. Vincent Millay. ColAP; NoP-4; NoP-5; WaAnP

Over against each other lie the lines. Merry Truce, The. Nathaniel Southgate Shaler. PCW

Over all the hills now. Song of the Traveler at Evening. Johann Wolfgang von Goethe. STV, tr. by John Frederick Nims

Over all their property. (LL) White Clover. Marvin Bell. CAP-8; InvLad; VCAP

Over an ash-fawn beach fronting a sea which keeps. Fiascherino. Charles Tomlinson. NoAM

Over an oil drum the workmen warm. Break. Ben Howard. UrbNat

Over and back. At Ithaca. "H. D." ColAP

Over and over / again. (LL) Love Poem: "Speak earth and bless me with what is richest." Audre Lorde. NAMCP V.2; NoAM; PoBW

Over and over, like a Tune. Emily Dickinson. TCAPo

Over and Over Stitch. Jorie Graham. VCAP

Over back where they speak of life as staying. Investment, The. Robert Frost. APT-1; GoPo

Over by the horses. Belle Isle Men, The. Anthony Butts. AmPoNex

Over Coffee. Bob Hicok. AmPoNex

Over every elm, the. You Too Lie down. Dennis Lee. TLR

Over Fayetteville, Arkansas. Arkansas Testament, The. Derek Walcott. CBCWP

Over Govino Bay, looking up from the water's edge, the landscape resembles nothing so much as the hills above Genova. Aubade. Charles Wright. MotU

Over his keys the musing organist. James Russell Lowell. APN-1 Fr. Vision of Sir Launfal, The.

Over in the fields the wind provokes. Malines. Paul Verlaine. SxFrPo, tr. by Martin Sorrell

Over King Yu Mountain with a Friend. Ching An. CSKM, tr. by Jerome P. Seaton

Over Manhattan Bridge. Brooklyn. Afaa Michael Weaver. SpirFl

Over Manhattan island when gales subside. City Without Smoke. Edwin Denby. NYP2

Over meadows of Brittany, the lark. Death of Time. Robert Penn Warren. BodElec

Over misted blue hills and distant water. To Judge Han Chuo at Yangzhou. Tu Mu. CCL1, tr. by A. C. Graham

Over Mount Kemenes howls Boreas in rage. Horace. Dániel Berzsenyi. IQMS, tr. by Peter Zollman

Over my desk Georgia O'Keeffe says. Calling, A. Maxine W. Kumin. PoA 2002

Over my head. Roots in the Air. Shirley Kaufman. TaR

Over my head, I see the bronze butterfly. Lying in a Hammock at William Duffy's Farm in Pine Island, Minnesota. James Wright. CAP-8; ColAP; ItP; MakPoe; NAMCP V.2; OxBoAm; StAl; TRP; VCAP; WaAnP

Over my shoulder. Jimmy Santiago Baca. ICANM Fr. Healing Earthquakes.

Over My Shoulder. Harry Woods. ReLy

Over my shoulder in Danbury, Connecticut, as I drove. Wonder, The. Thylias Moss. ChAP

Over northeast mountains. Voyeur's Dream. Barney Bush. HATNAP

Over now / The dream is over now. Never Again. Noël Coward. ReLy

Over, O over / the thorn. (LL) Psalm: "No one kneads us again out of earth and clay." Paul Celan. GTCP; PoetW; PoSu, tr. by John Felstiner

Over, o over / the thorn. (LL) Psalm: "No one moulds us again out of earth and clay." Paul Celan. BBASP; HP; OBVE, tr. by Michael Hamburger

Over oceans sped he, Attis, in the speediest of ships. Catullus. STV

Over Ohio. Michael C. Blumenthal. OtW

Over our naked guilt. (LL) Net, The. William Robert Rodgers. IrLP; ModIr; PNI

Over, Over. Thomas Love Peacock. OxAEP-2 Fr. Maid Marian.

Over paddies / At its foot. Issa. ZenPo, tr. by Takashi Ikemoto and Lucien Stryk

1. Over Prairie. Rosanna Warren. OtW Fr. North.

Over Puerto Rican agony lawyers' screams in slums. (LL) Vow, A. Allen Ginsberg. CLPP; OBWP

Over rips and tears and / thin places. (LL) Nameless One, A. Margaret Avison. BrAP; HeIP-4

Over Sir John's Hill. Dylan Thomas. AngWePo; NPeEn; TCAWP

Over strip-raked iron rooves. Snow. Atanas Dalchev. SonAtl, tr. by Tamara Romanyk and Frederick Spencer

Over Texas Hills. Maude E. Cole. TiP2

Over the Arafura sea, the China sea. For John Chappell. Gary Snyder. InoFa

Over the ball of it. Pisgah-Sights. I. Robert Browning. ChIV-1

Over the bed's cliff my legs dangle. Miser. Elizabeth Garrett. NeBl

Over the clay-laden estuary a. Bye Bye Blackbird. John James. Oth

Over the Coast Range, silver horns of cloud. House of Breath. Ken Gerner. GifTon

Over the crying comes the sugar, the cooing. Part One: The Orders Begin. Carmen Naranjo. TANSG, tr. by Shaun Griffin and Emma Sepúlveda-Pulvirenti

Over the downs there were birds flying. On the South Downs. Sara Teasdale. MoAmPo

Over the dragon rock the moon appears. Lament for Prince Chagoo. Unknown. WoPoe, tr. by Jean S. Grigsby

Over the earth I come. Soldier's Song. Unknown. APN-2, tr. by Stephen Return Riggs

Over the earth they come. Pilgrims, The. Ella Krylova. CRWP, tr. by Yury Drobyshev and Carol Rumens

Over the empty fields a black kite hovers. Kite, The. Aleksandr Aleksandrovich Blok. FaBoWar, tr. by Frances Cornford and Esther Polinowsky Salaman

Over the fence. Emily Dickinson. FaBoVe

Over the fields. They come in Spring. (LL) In the Fields. Charlotte Mew. MoBrPo; OxAEP-2

Over the Garden Wall. Eleanor Farjeon. ChAP

Over the great windy waters, and over the clear crested summits. Arthur Hugh Clough. NoP-5 Fr. Amours de Voyage.

Over the heather the wet wind blows. W. H. Auden. FaBoWar Fr. Twelve Songs.

Over the hills. Witches' Ride, The. Karla Kuskin. NOxBChV; TLR

Over the Hills and far away. (LL) John Gay. NAEL-6v1; NPeEn; OxBEV Fr. Beggar's Opera, The.

Over the hills and far away, and a crescent moon. (LL) Gypsy, The. Edward Thomas. NAMCP V.1; NoAM; NoP-4

Over the Hills and Far Away, or, The Recruiting Officer. Unknown. FaBoWar

Over the housetops. Captured Goddess, The. Amy Lowell. NAAL-5; NAAPv.2

Over the land freckled with snow half-thawed. Thaw. Edward Thomas. MoBrPo; OxAEP-2; OxBEV; Spl

Over the long road. Kikaku. SoOfWa, tr. by Sam Hamill

Over the low, barnacled, elephant-colored rocks. Meditation at Oyster River. Theodore Roethke. MoAmPo

Over the low, barnacled, elephant-colored rocks. Theodore Roethke. MoAmPo Fr. North American Sequence.

Over the monstrous shambling sea. Sidney Lanier. TCAPo Fr. Hymns of the Marshes.

Over the month of June the rain is falling. Rain is Falling, The. Homero Aridjis. STV; TCLAP, tr. by John Frederick Nims

Over the mountains a plane bumbles in. Night-Time: Starting to Write. Bernard Spencer. AWTN

Over the mountains / And over the waves. Love Will Find Out the Way. *Unknown*. OBEV

Over the peak spreading clouds. Hakuyo. ZenPo, *tr. by* Takashi Ikemoto and Lucien Stryk

Over the Pillow. *Unknown*. CCL1, *tr. by* Marsha Wagner

Over the pillow I made a thousand kinds of vows. Over the Pillow. *Unknown*. CCL1, *tr. by* Marsha Wagner

Over the plum snow, the train's blond smoke. Carolyn Forché. GM

Over the Rainbow. E. Y. Harburg. NAAPv.2; ReLy

Over the rim of the glass. Ghost in the Martini, The. Anthony Hecht. NoP-4; NoP-5

Over the river and through the wood. Thanksgiving Day. Lydia Maria Child. NTCP; WHSW

Over the Roofs. Sara Teasdale. ColAP

Over the roof-tops race the shadows of clouds. John Gould Fletcher. PoA 2002 *Fr.* Irradiations.

Over the salt and table at a friendly meal. (LL) May he lose his way on the cold sea. Archilochus. OBVE; WoPoe, *tr. by* Guy Davenport

Over the sea our galleys went. Robert Browning. OBEV *Fr.* Paracelsus.

Over the sheer stone cliff-face, over springs and star clusters. By a Waterfall. David Wagoner. NAMCP V.2

Over the soughing of the sombre wind. Summer Poem, A. Jayanta Mahapatra. VCWP

Over the tender, bow'd locks of the corn. (LL) Summer Dawn. William Morris. GSo; OBEV; OxAEP-2; OxBEV

Over the testicles of bulls, over the seven pigeon-stained saints. Boudica. Paol Keineg. OnScMo, *tr. by* Keith Waldrop

Over the top! The wire's thin here, unbarbed. Night Patrol, The. Arthur Graeme West. FaBoWar

Over the up-turned boat, at night. Boat on the Shore. Andrey Andreievich Voznesensky. RusPo, *tr. by* Robert Arthur Douglas Ford

Over the utmost hill at length I sped. Percy Bysshe Shelley. OBWP *Fr.* Revolt of Islam, The.

Over the wall. (LL) Two Trees. Ellen Bryant Voigt. CAP-8; InGu

Over the wharves at Provincetown. At Provincetown. Daniel Gerard Hoffman. YaYoPo

Over the white fishpond. Descent and Defeat. Georg Trakl. WED, *tr. by* Robert Bly

Over the white steppes. Sad Voices, The. Ricardo Jaimes Freyre. TCLAP, *tr. by* Iver Lofving

Over the wide cold leaves of time you arrive, stained. Little Ode to Melancholy. Ricardo Molinari. TCLAP, *tr. by* Inés Probert

Over the years, a tip would take on time's finish. Old Tips. Jean Earle. TCAWP

Over the years, horses have changed to Land-Rovers. Judith Wright. BMAP *Fr.* For a Pastoral Family.

Over their edge of earth. Little Clan, The. Frederick Robert Higgins. OBMV

Over their small bones. (LL) Blessing. Imtiaz Dharker. BeAl; MoWP

Over There. George M. Cohan. FaBoA; ReLy

Over there, a fly buzzed—bad. Nursling. Kathleen Ossip. BeAl; PoCho

Over there are faith, life, virtue in the sun. (LL) Report on Experience. Edmund Charles Blunden. NPeEn; OBMV; OBWP; OxBEV; PoAgWa

Over there in the other country. Malenki Robot. Ken Smith. BeAl

Over there, people. Veronique Tadjo. NAfrP, *tr. by* Faustine Boateng Gyima

Over these blunted, these tormented hills. Kanheri Caves. Dom Moraes. NoP-4; NoP-5

Over / they all left. Empty. Vegunta Mohana Prasad. HotL, *tr. by* V. Narayana Rao

Over this city of transparent buildings, the zodiac staggers, bombed. Plate Glass. T. R. Hummer. LPSFW

Over this the foresayd lay. John Skelton. PBRV *Fr.* Colin Clout.

Over thresholds of welcome dream with wet and moonlit skin. (LL) Elegy for Drowned Children. Bruce Dawe. BMAP; NOBAu

Over to your place. (LL) Poem You Asked For, The. Larry Levis. CalPo; PBCAP

Over 2000 Illustrations and a Complete Concordance. Elizabeth Bishop. APT-2; HarvBoo; NAMCP V.2; NoAM; OxBoAm; PoetW; VCAP

Over us stands the broad electric face. Terminal. Karl Shapiro. GM

Over *Voice of America*. Dennis Finnell. SwNoth

Over water / Sharp sickles. Buson. ZenPo, *tr. by* Takashi Ikemoto and Lucien Stryk

Over you, Hermes fights. Korinna [*or* Corinna]. SaLy, *tr. by* Diane Rayor

Over-all picture is winter, The. William Carlos Williams. GS; OxBoAm *Fr.* Pictures from Brueghel.

Overburdened with sorrow now. Another Song. William Ross. NePenScot, *tr. by* Derick Thomson

Overcoat, The. Alda Merini. CItWP, *tr. by* Cinzia Sartini Blum and Lara Trubowitz

Overcome by fatigue, there Boaz lay. Boaz Asleep. Victor Hugo. SxFrPo

Overfire: Andante. Phillip Foss. ICANM

Overflow. Nada El-Hage. PoArWo, *tr. by* Nathalie El-Hani

Overflow advances across strawberry. Natural Disaster. David Swanger. GeoHom

Overflow between her breasts. I shall call her Peace. (LL) Peace. Tibullus. PBCIP; PNI, *tr. by* Michael Longley

Overflowed with good deeds. (LL) My Father. Yehuda Amichai. BeAl; PtR, *tr. by* Azila Talit Reisenberger

Overflowing compost scum bucket. Rich Ink, Still Slightly Moist. J. B. Bryan. ICANM

Overflowing Willow. Ernesto Lumbreras. RMCMP, *tr. by* Rebecca Seiferle

Overgrown roads around here refract water-and-mirror mirages, The. Island Celebration. Kenward Elmslie. FTOS

Overhead, as the day breaks, a child is crying. (LL) Juan Ramón Jiménez. SpanPo; WoPoe *Fr.* Ten Short Poems.

Overhead at night, above the planet. Alice Notley. PFTM-2 *Fr.* Désamère.

Overhead, the match burns out. Disregard. Ai. NoAM

Overheard in County Sligo. Gillian Clarke. HarvBoo; StAl; TCAWP

Overheard in the Love Hotel. Robert Polito. KGB

Overheard, / late, this morning: *don't blame*. Singing. Carl Phillips. CAP-8

Over-Heart, The. John Greenleaf Whittier. ChIV-2

Overland to the Islands. Denise Levertov. PmAP

Overlander, The. *Unknown*. NOBAu

Overloaded Horse, The. Ted Joans. EGAG

Overmastering of the mud, The. 4 Variations On. Gerrit Kouwenaar. PFTM-2, *tr. by* Peter Nijmeijer

Overnight / a playful pony. Pony in Kukutis's Ear, A. Marcelijus Martinaitis. TWW, *tr. by* Laima Sruoginis

Overnight, and quietly. Beneath the scratchy leaf we thicken and expand so fast you can't believe. Mind of Squash, The. Naomi Shihab Nye. IPoFL

Overnight at a Buddhist Mountain Temple. Mike O'Connor. CSKM

Overnight at Headquarters. Tu Fu [*or* Du Fu]. NDACCP, *tr. by* David Hinton

Overnight, very. Mushrooms. Sylvia Plath. StAl

Overnight Winder: Texas. William Virgil Davis. TiP2

Overruled. John Greenleaf Whittier. NCAP

Overshot. Wythop Mill. Annie Foster. NLP

Overspread with Salty Soil. Tayankannanar. WoPoe, *tr. by* George L. Hart III

Overture. A. V. Christie. NAPBL

Overture. Christopher Okigbo. NAMCP V.2 *Fr.* Heavensgate.

Overture. Linda Pastan. MiVo

Overture to a Dance of Locomotives. William Carlos Williams. GM

Overture: Watermelon City. Elizabeth Alexander. NAPBL

Overworked. Lucy Partlow. BRtP

Ovid in Love. Ovid. WoPoe *Fr.* Amores.

Ovid in the Third Reich. Geoffrey Hill. CABP; HarvBoo; HP; NAMCP V.2; NoAM; NPeEn; OxBEV

Ovid is the surest guide. Written in an Ovid. Matthew Prior. OBCoV

Ovid Twice Exiled. Jerzy Ficowski. PoSu, *tr. by* Frank J. Corliss, Jr. and Grazyna Sandel

Ovid would never have guessed how far. Brueghel in Naples. Dannie Abse. NIP-4

Ovid's Banquet of Sense. George Chapman.
    Corinna Bathes. OxAEP-1
    Ear's Delight, The. NoSic

Ovids Elegies Book 1. Christopher Marlowe.
    "Now ore the sea from her old Love comes she." PBRV

Ovid's Metamorphoses Book 6. Arthur Golding.
    " . . . This Damsell was not famous for the place." PBRV

Owdham Footbo'. Ammon Wrigley. FaBoVe

Owed to Eminem. June Jordan. BRtP

Owed to New York. Byron Rufus Newton. NBLV

Owen Tudor. Hugh Holland. AngWePo

Owen Tudor to Queen Katherine. Michael Drayton. NoSic *Fr.* England's Heroical Epistles.

Owens. Biographia Literaria. Joan Retallack. FTOS

Owen's Bracelet. Robert Hayman. NOSC *Fr.* Owen's Epigrams.

Owen's Epigrams. Robert Hayman.
    Owen's Bracelet. NOSC
    Saturn's Three Sons. NOSC

Ower t'ills o Bingley. Blake Morrison. FaBoVe *Fr.* Ballad of the Yorkshire Ripper, The.

Owl. John Hollander. OWoS

Owl. George MacBeth. EmeKit

Owl. Robert Mezey. AWTN

Owl. Sylvia Plath. OWoS

Owl. Sŏ Chŏngju. WoPoe, *tr. by* Kevin O'Rourke

Owl. Ted Walker. NOxBChV

Owl, The. Chia Yi. ColAnChi, *tr.* by James Robert Hightower

Owl, The. Chia Yi. CCL1, *tr.* by Burton Watson

Owl, The. Walter De la Mare. OWoS

Owl, The. Edward Thomas. AF; ChAP; NAEL-6v2; NAEL-7v2; NAMCP V.1; NIP-4; NoAM; NoP-4; NoP-5; OBWVE; OWoS; OxAEP-2; PoCho; TCAWP; TFi; TRP

Owl, The. Robert Penn Warren. MoAmPo

Owl,— / Au / The owl, The. Song of the Owl. *Unknown.* APN-2, *tr.* by Henry Wadsworth Longfellow

Owl and the Lightning, The. Martín Espada. TouFir; UrbNat

Owl and the Moon, The. Kabir. WED, *tr.* by Robert Bly

Owl and the Mouse, The. Viktor Aleksandrovich Sosnora. TCRusP, *tr.* by Denis Johnson and Kathy Lewis

Owl and the Pussy-Cat [*or* Pussycat] went to sea, The. Owl and the Pussy-Cat [*or* Pussycat], The. Edward Lear. BLPJKO; BRP; CABP; ChAP; CtM; NBLV; NoP-4; NoP-5; NOxBChV; NPeEn; NTCP; OBCoV; OBSP; OWoS; TFi; TLR; TriCat; WaAnP; WoPoe

Owl / calls. Night Song of the Los Angeles Basin. Gary Snyder. PfSP; UrbNat

Owl drifts slowly through the canyon where three flickers worry a pitted oak for grubs, An. Gary Young. GeoHom *Fr.* If He Had.

Owl feather is rolling in this direction and beginning to sing, The. Tohono O'odham. NAAPv.1 *Fr.* Songs for Treating Sickness, Sung durring the Four Parts of the Night.

Owl hid his eyes, The. Candle. Penelope Rosemont. SurWo

Owl In Daytime, The. Thylias Moss. GT

Owl-light in a tree house [1", 2", 3", or 4" of silence]. 3rd Light Poem: For Spencer, Beate, & Sebastian Holst—12 June 1962. Jackson Mac Low. PFTM-2

Owl of Minerva Takes Flight in the Evening, The. E. San Juan, Jr. ReBoTo

Owl of the wildwood I. Owl, The. Walter De la Mare. OWoS

Owl shriek'd at thy birth, an evil sign, The. William Shakespeare. OxAEP-1 *Fr.* King Henry VI, Pt. III.

Owl sings, The. Premonition. Lucha Corpi. ASA, *tr.* by Catherine Rodriguez-Nieto

Owl Village. Alice Oswald. MoWP

Owl Wives. Nigel Wells. AngWePo

Owl Writes a Detective Story, The. Gavin Ewart. OBCoV

Owls. Charles Baudelaire. OWoS, *tr.* by Richard Howard

Owls. Louise Erdrich. TRP

Owls are calling / "Come, come." Issa. ZenPo, *tr.* by Takashi Ikemoto and Lucien Stryk

Owls at the Shakespeare Festival. William Stafford. IaFF

Owl's Landscape, An. Jon Veinberg. GeoHom

Owls mimic human speech. Meng Chiao. CCL1 *Fr.* Laments of the Gorges.

Owned by a heat:—*There is something in my heart like a burning Fire—shut up in my bones*-hear me, hear me. Of Joy Illimited: Polyphonic Soundings: Shore to Ship. Anna Rabinowitz. KGB

Owner of the drink of life. Water Woman. Catherine Obianuju Acholonu. HAWP

Owner of the field, The. Buson. EH, *tr.* by Robert Hass

Ownership. Ina Coolbrith. SWaP

Ownership. Lizette Woodworth Reese. MoAmPo

Ox. *Unknown.* SonAtl, *tr.* by F. Josephs and Silke Werner

Ox, The. Russell Edson. RaBo

Ox bridle tossed, vows taken. Reito. ZenPo, *tr.* by Takashi Ikemoto and Lucien Stryk

Ox Cart Man. Donald Hall. GoPo; IPoFL; LoL

Ox Looks at Man, An. Carlos Drummond de Andrade. IPoFL; PoetW; PtR; TCLAP, *tr.* by Mark Strand

Ox of my childhood, steaming. Far Away and Long Ago. Rubén Darío. PFTM-1; SpanPo, *tr.* by Denise Levertov

Ox Turned Loose. Muso Soseki. EaWin, *tr.* by W. S. Merwin

Oxaitoq's Song. *Inuit Oral Tradition.* ErotSp, *tr.* by Sam Hamill

Oxaitoq's Song. *Unknown.* APN-2, *tr.* by Franz Boas

Oxcarts Are Now on Their Way, The. Juan Ramón Jiménez. SpanPo, *tr.* by Alice Sternberg

Oxen, The. Thomas Hardy. CABP; ChAP; ChrPo; CtM; HarvBoo; MoBrPo; NAMCP V.1; NoAM; OBCP; OxAEP-2; PoCho; SoSe-8; TFi; TRP; WeW-3

Oxen's muzzles drip with bloody slaver, The. Razglednica (3). Miklós Radnóti. IQMS, *tr.* by Peter Zollman

Oxford. W. H. Auden. OxAEP-2

Oxford Booklicker. Gwyneth Lewis. MoWP; NeBl *Fr.* Parables & Faxes.

Oxford Cheese Ode. James McIntyre.

"Ancient poets ne'er did dream, The." VerBaPo

Oxford Gardens. Charles McDonald. NLP

Oxford, since late I left thy peaceful shore. To Oxford. Thomas Russell. CenSon

Oxford Street? William Wordsworth. STuOW *Fr.* Power of Music, The.

Oxford-Act, The. Alicia D'Anvers.

True Relation of their Practice at Oxford Town when there an Act is, A. EMWP

Ox-head dot, wasp waist, mouse tail. Ox-Head Dot. Arthur Sze. ICANM

Oxhead McIntosh, out of White Plains. San Diego Goodbye—*1944, Jacksaw Arena.* Murray Jackson. OxAAAP

Oxhead Temple. Ssu-k'ung Shu. ColAnChi, *tr.* by Hellmut Wilhelm

Oxota: A Short Russian Novel. Lyn Hejinian.
Chapter 188. FaoP

Oxota: A Short Russian Novel. Lyn Hejinian.
Book 2. PFTM-2
Chapter Seven. NAMCP V.2
Chapter 203. NAMCP V.2
"No form at all—it's impossible to imagine its being." FTOS

Ox-sized cauldron, Kleubotos gave, An. Anyte. SaLy, *tr.* by Diane Rayor

Ox-team and the automobile, The. Meeting, The. Harriet Monroe. IllVoic

Oya Now. Ifi Amadiume. NAfrP

Oye Mundo/Sometimes. Jesús Papoleto Meléndez. UnSA

Oyente. Gerardo Deniz. RMCMP

Oyster, the fragrance, greenleaf, An. Outside of This, That Is. Barbara Guest. NYP2

Oyster, the size of an average pebble, is of more rugged appearance, The. Oyster, The. Francis Ponge. PFTM-1

Oyster, the size of an average pebble, looks tougher, its color is less uniform, The. Oyster, The. Francis Ponge. YaTCFP, *tr.* by Serge Gavronsky

Oyster-Eaters, The. John Blight. NOBAu

Oystering. Richard Howard. NoAM

Oysters. Seamus Heaney. StAl; UV

Oysters. Jonathan Swift. ErotSp

Oysters and Zarzuelas. Maria Ercilla. FiBr

Oysters we ate. Death of the Fathers, The. Anne Sexton.

Ozymandias. Tom Raworth. Eno

Ozymandias. Percy Bysshe Shelley. BLPJKO; BrAP; BRP; CABP; CenSon; ChAP; ClHu; CtM; GSo; HeIP-4; MakPoe; NAEL-6v2; NAEL-7v2; NIL-7; NIP-4; NoP-4; NoP-5; NPBRoP; NPeEn; OPOU; OxBEV; OxBSo; PoPoPo; PtR; SoSe-8; TFi; UV; WaAnP

Ozymandias. Horace Smith. CenSon
(In Egypt's Sandy Silence.) NPBRoP

Ozymandias Revisited. Morris Gilbert Bishop. NBLV; UV

P

P.C. Plod versus the Dale St. Dog Strangler. Roger McGough. OBSP

P. M. T. Dorothy Porter. BMAP

P.O.E. Lincoln Kirstein. APT-2; PoWW; PWW2

P.S. I Love You. Johnny Mercer. ReLy

P.W.T. Tom Weatherly. EGAG

P Word Poem, The. Leticia R. Benson. InTrad

Pa dropped the baby. Pa poem 1: firstborn. Patrick Friesen. ACAMVP

Pa poem 1: firstborn. Patrick Friesen. ACAMVP

Pa poem 4: naked and nailed. Patrick Friesen. ACAMVP

Pájaro de papel en el pecho, Un. Vida. Vicente Aleixandre. RaW

Pájaros anidan en mis brazos, Los. Pájaros Anidan, Los. Gloria Fuertes. RaW

Pájaros Anidan, Los. Gloria Fuertes. RaW

Pabellón. Elsa Cross. RMCMP

Pablo. Dieter Weslowski. InvLad

Pablo, come here and look at this. On Seeing Man with a Guitar at the Moma. James Stewart. ICANM

Pablo Neruda. Jose Angel Figueroa. PueRic

Pachycephalosaurus. Richard Armour. ChAP

Pacific. Robert Fitzgerald. PWW2

Pacific 1945-1995. Allen Curnow. HarvBoo

Pacific Crossing. Vince Gotera. ReBoTo

Pacific is nothing like its name, The. Elegy as Evening, as Exodus. James Harms. GeoHom

Pacific Lament. Charles Olson. NAMCP V.2

Pacifist, The. Joseph Hilaire Pierre Belloc. FaBoWar; OBCoV; PoAgWa

Pack of wild colts went smoking by, The. In Fields of Sleepdreaming. Delmira Agustini. TANSG, *tr.* by Mark McCaffrey

Pack, The. Frank Prewett. HATNAP

Pack train, stage coach, pony express, climb over the mountain passes. James Henry Daugherty. HHAm *Fr.* Trail Breakers.

Pack Up Your Sins and Go to the Devil. Irving Berlin. ReLy

Package for Another World. Jemal Sharah. NOBAu

Packing for the Future: Instructions. Lorna Crozier. OpeFie

Packing Herring. Helga Novak. MotU, *tr.* by Ann Maria Celona

Packrat. Naomi Long Madgett. FuFl

Packs of wolves howl on sidewalks. Wolves. Y. A. Rontsh. Prolet, *tr.* by Amelia Glaser

Pact, A. Robert Hass. BodElec

Pact, A. Ezra Pound. APT-1; ColAP; NAAL-5; NAAPv.2; NAMCP V.1; NoAM; NoP-5; RaF; ViWalt; WaAnP

Pact that we made was the ordinary pact, The. From a Survivor. Adrienne Rich. LoL; NALW

Pad, Pad. Stevie Smith. NPeEn; OxBEV

Padded Steps/Sister Song (a litany). Quo Vadis Gex-Breaux. FuFl

Padding down the street, the. No Shoes No Shirt No Service. Gary Snyder. BB

Paddle-song. *Unknown.* SonAtl, *tr.* by Mo Alexander, Edward Astley and Karun Badel

Paddlin' Madelin' Home. Harry Woods. ReLy

Paddling. Sue Sinclair. Coast

Paddy fields at Chang'gu, in the fifth month. Chang'gu: A Poem Written on the Twenty-Seventh Day of the Fifth Month. Li Ho. CCL1, *tr.* by John Frodsham

Padmapani. Breyten Breytenbach. PoetW, *tr.* by André Brink

Padraic O'Conaire—Gaelic Storyteller. Frederick Robert Higgins. OBMV

Padre ministers to stumps of men, The. Remembrance. M. R. Peacocke. NLP

Pads or pull-ons—*that.* Diapers for My Father. Alice Friman. IaFF

Padua 1717. Charles Reznikoff. *See* Luzzato.

Paean. Samuel Carter. STuOW *Fr.* London.

Paean to Place. Lorine Niedecker. APSN; APT-2; FTOS

Paean to the Dawn, A. Bayard Taylor. CAGL

Paean to the Sun, A. Ingeborg Bachmann. GTCP, *tr.* by Reinhold Grimm

Paengnokdam: White Deer Lake. Chŏng Chiyong. CAMKP, *tr.* by Anthony, Brother of Taizé

Pagan. R. Williams Parry. BBMWP, *tr.* by Martin Davis

Paganly. Trinidad Tarrosa Subido. InvLi

Pagan's myths through marble lips are spoken, The. Worship. John Greenleaf Whittier. ChIV-2

Page dramatically estranged, nor lacking, A. Casting Sequences. Marjorie Welish. FTOS

Page from a Diary. Desmond O'Grady. NoAM

Page is being beaten, A. Let's Say. Bob Perelman. PmAP

Page is printed, The. (LL) Thought-Fox, The. Ted Hughes. BrAP; HeIP-4; MakPoe; NAMCP V.2; NoAM; NoP-5; NPeEn; StAl; WaAnP

Page of Short Poems, A. Eugene McCarthy.
  "Ending." HHAm

Page 1, line 8, for incorrigible read unredeemable. Errata. Jane Griffiths. NeBl

Page opens to snow on a field: boot-holed month, black hour, The. Elegy. Carolyn Forché. ExTi; LoL

Page to Commemorate Colonel Suárez, Victor at Junín, A. Jorge Luis Borges. PoetW, *tr.* by Alastair Reid

Page Torn from a Notebook. Ruth Herschberger. OxBoAm

Pageant of the Seasons and the Months, The. Edmund Spenser. OxAEP-1

Pages of history open, The. The dead enter. Elegy. Sandra M. Gilbert. PoA 2002; WaAnP

Pages of the album, The. Sonatina in Yellow. Donald Justice. ColAP

Pagliacci Pizza wants me. Sweet Red Peppers, Sun-Drieds, the Hearts of Artichokes. Martha Silano. AmPoNex

Pāhkahkos. Louise Bernice Halfe. ReEnLa

Paid on Both Sides. W. H. Auden.
  (Chorus: "To throw away the key and walk away.") MoBrPo

Pain. Thomas Edward Brown. SacPr

Pain. Alan Davies.
  "This evening / Is the only evening." Eno

Pain [*with music*]. Enrique Gonzáles Martínez. TCLAP, *tr.* by Samuel Beckett

Pain. Dionisio D. Martinez. OPRER

Pain. Lupenga Mphande. NAfrP

Pain. George Russell. MoBrPo

Pain. Charles Simic. BodElec

Pain, The. Jeni Couzyn. HAWP

Pain, The. Sion Eirian. BBMWP, *tr.* by Robert Minhinnick

Pain, The. John Graham-Pole. BloBone

Pain and labor of oppression gave the Western world its birth. Pharaohs of Today, The. Lizelia Augusta Jenkins Moorer. CBWP-3

Pain ebbs. Languor After Pain. Adelaide Crapsey. NAAPv.2

Pain Has an Element of Blank. Emily Dickinson. APN-2; ColAP; HeIP-4; MoAmPo; NAAL-3; NAAPv.1; OxBoAm; SWaP; TCAPo

Pain of deception, The. EMJL *Fr.* Mad Verse.

Pain of loving you, The. Young Wife, A. D. H. Lawrence. MoBrPo

Pain or Joy. Christina Georgina Rossetti. OWoS

Pain Strikes Sparks on Me, the Pain of Terezin. *Unknown, fr. Terezin Concentration Camp.* INSAB

Pain was pulled down over his eyes like a fool's hat. God, A. Ted Hughes. GI

Pain—expands the Time. Emily Dickinson. APN-2

Painful husbandman with sweaty brows, The. George Wither. NOSC *Fr.* Collection of Emblems, Ancient and Moderne, A.

Painful to look up. Underneath (1). Jorie Graham. BodElec

Pain—I'm pro it. First Chance Twice. Fanny Howe. FTOS

Painkiller. Jane Mayhall. PoCho

Painkillers. Thom Gunn. AllShUp; SwNoth

Pains and Gains. Edward, 17th Earl of Oxford De Vere. NoSic

Pains flip me around, The. Conception. Joseph Ceravolo. FTOS

Pains of Sleep, The. Samuel Taylor Coleridge. AWTN; NAEL-6v2; NAEL-7v2; NPBRoP

Paint Castlemaine in colours that will hold. Andrew Marvell. OBSV *Fr.* Last Instructions to a Painter, The.

Paint last the King, and a dead shade of night. Andrew Marvell. OBSV *Fr.* Last Instructions to a Painter, The.

Paint my crib a. Poem for Ernie Henry. Gloria Tropp. EGAG

Paint outdoors? Impressionist. Paul Foreman. TiP2

Painted Cup, The. William Cullen Bryant. APN-1

Painted Cup, The. Michael Palmer. FTOS

Painted Head. John Crowe Ransom. APT-1; FuPo; NAMCP V.1; NoAM (Painting: A Head.) MoAmPo

Painted Ladies, The. Del Ray Cross. FreRad

Painted on a monumental scale. Cotton and Gladiolas. Joy Lahey. AnSo

Painted, perfect, patient, I couch myself. Pornography. Angela Shaw. PuP-23

Painted Windows. Gloria Fuertes. RaW, *tr.* by Philip Levine

Painted with fancies of malignant power! (LL) Philip Freneau. NAAL-3; TCAPo *Fr.* House of Night, The.

Painter. Zbigniew Herbert. AF, *tr.* by John Carpenter *and* Bogdana Carpenter

Painter, A. Thomas Cole. APN-1

Painter, The. John Ashbery. EmeKit; NoP-4; NoP-5; PoPoPo; YaYoPo

Painter Asks, The. John Yau. BodElec

Painter descends into the world, The. In the Labyrinth of Elements. Duane Niatum. PoCoUp

Painter Dreaming in the Scholar's House, The. Howard Nemerov. StAl

Painter of Dante's awful ferry-ride, The. Poem, The. Babette Deutsch. PoA 2002

Painter of Destinies, A. Molly Bendall. NAPBL

Painters. Muriel Rukeyser. NAAL-5

Painter's eye follows relation out, The. Painter Dreaming in the Scholar's House, The. Howard Nemerov. StAl

Painter's Son, The. Frank O'Hara. BodElec

Painting. Jane Hirshfield. ExTi

Painting. André Salmon. CuPo

Painting, The. Jack Hirschman. BodElec

Painting, The. Maryhelen Snyder. ICANM

Painting, The. *Vietnamese Oral Tradition.* CaDao, *tr.* by John Balaban

Painting: A Head. John Crowe Ransom. *See* Painted Head.

Painting: A Head. John Crowe Ransom. MoAmPo

Painting Drunken Twilight. George Barlow. GT

Painting / (Frida Kahlo). Elizabeth Alexander. GT

Painting It In. Anne Stevenson. PfSP

Painting of an endless field where grass waits, A. Picture on the Purple Wall, the. Steve Wilson. AmPoNex

Painting on a T'ang Dynasty Water Vessel. Bruce Weigl. AmAlph

Painting the Angel. Martin Mooney. NIrP

Painting the Eaves. Tony Towle. PmAP

Painting the Gate. May Swenson. TLR; WeW-3

Painting the Islands. Michael Crummey. Coast

Painting the Nude. Eric Dyer. BloBone

Painting to be Constructed in Your Head. Yoko Ono. WhBo

Painting To Hammer a Nail. Yoko Ono. WhBo

Painting with My Daughter. Ann Elizabeth Hostetler. ACAMVP

Painting would have been the best way to get things over, A. In Memoriam. Martin Johnston. BMAP; NOBAu

Paints one himself in oil. (LL) Two Artists, The. Constance Naden. ViWPN; VWP

Pair, The / Of cranes suddenly. Lost Cranes. Shi Zhiyuan. CSKM

Pair of blackbirds, A. In Modern Dress. Craig Raine. NoAM

Pair of clouded yellows, A. Exits. Patricia Pogson. NLP

Pair of feet, born so nimble, A. Street Angel, The. K'o Chia Tsang. WoPoe, *tr. by* Kai-yu Hsu

Pair of heavy scissors lay across the sky, A. Sevens (Version 3): In the Closed Iris of Creation. Marvin Bell. CAP-8

Pair of Shoes, A [*with music*]. Theodore Weiss. NoAM

Pair of soft, black eyes, A. Home Greeting, A. Priscilla Jane Thompson. CBWP-2

Pair of strange new birds in the maple tree, A. "Never Apologize; Never Explain." Philip Whalen. BB

Paired Things. Kay Ryan. CalPo

País de la calle. Laura Solórzano. SPV

País de los milagros, El. Dana Gelinas. SPV

Paisleys squirm with spermatozoa. Neckties. Liz Lochhead. NePenScot; OBCoV

Pajaro the men thigh deep in mud. Song of Pajaro. Jeff Tagami. OpBo

Pal Mal Comic, Or. Leslie Scalapino. Eno

Pal was her friend, her lover, and, dismissed. Love's Progress. James Vincent Cunningham. APT-2

Palabrarmás. Cecilia Vicuña. *tr. by* Suzanne Jill Levine

"I saw a word in the air." TANSG, *tr. by* Suzanne Jill Levine

Palabras. Elsa Cross. RMCMP

Palabras un millón de veces repetidas. Corazón mecánico. Josué Ramírez. RMCMP

Palace clocks are stiff as coats of mail, The. Howard Moss. PoA 2002 *Fr.* King Midas.

Palace Cook's Tale. Joan Aiken. NOxBChV

Palace great is builded rich and round. Torquato Tasso. NoSic *Fr.* Godfrey of Bulloigne; or, The Recoverie of Jerusalem [Gerusalemme Liberata].

Palace halls loomed high, encaged in purple vapor. Kuan Hsiu. CCL1, *tr. by* Edward H. Schafer

Palace in smoky light. Ezra Pound. APT-1 *Fr.* Cantos.

Palace of Art, The. Alfred Tennyson. NOBRP

Palace of Fine Arts in San Francisco, The. Fidelito Cortes. ReBoTo

Palace of Mourners, A. Patrick Sylvain. BRtP

Palace of the Gnomes. Maria Gowen Brooks. APN-1 *Fr.* Zophiël or, the Bride of Seven.

Palace Poem. Ts'ao Ching-chao. WoPoe, *tr. by* Nancy Hodes and Tung Yuan-fang

Palace Song. Po Chü-i. NDACCP, *tr. by* Gary Snyder

Palace-Burner, The. Sarah Morgan Bryan Piatt. NAAPv.1; NCAP; SWaP

Palaces and hovels, the leaden eye of the authorities. Trotsky in Mexico. Dmitry Vasil'evich Bobyshev. ItGoST, *tr. by* Michael Van Walleghen

Palaestra (athletics room). Matthea Harvey. IAoNAP *Fr.* Thermae.

Palaestral Study, A. Edward Cracroft Lefroy. CAGL

Palais des Arts. Louise Glück. VCAP

Palanquin, The. Devulapalli Krishna Sastri. HotL, *tr. by* V. Narayana Rao

Palaver is finished, The. (LL) T. S. Eliot. NAEL-6v2; NoAM *Fr.* Landscapes.

Pale. Jane Routh. PoCu

Pale Ant. Ellease Southerland. GT

Pale as the morning star. White Stallion, The. Abu-l-Salt Umayyah. WoPoe, *tr. by* Cola Franzen

Pale blossoms, each balanced on a single jointed stem. Carnations. Theodore Roethke. BLT

Pale Blue Casket, The. Oliver Pitcher. EGAG

Pale Blue Line in a Forced Episode, I Cut a Hole in the Flag of the Republic. Simone Yoyotte. SurWo, *tr. by* Myrna Bell Rochester

Pale brows, still hands and dim hair. Lover Mourns for the Loss of Love, The. William Butler Yeats. IrLP; WeW-3

Pale Cynthia! lovely goddess of the night. Thoughts in Midnight Hours. Fanny Crosby. SWaP

Pale Ebenezer thought it wrong to fight. Pacifist, The. Joseph Hilaire Pierre Belloc. FaBoWar; OBCoV; PoAgWa

Pale moon disappears, The. In the Shadows of the Wu-t'ung Tree. *Unknown.* CrYelRi, *tr. by* Sam Hamill

Pale morning in June 4 A.M., A. Country Roads. Rolf Jacobsen. WED, *tr. by* Robert Bly

(One pale morning in June at four o'clock.) BLT

Pale morning light, dying in shadows, loving the earth in midday rays. Picasso's Balcony. Bob Kaufman. EGAG

Pale mornings, and. Magpie's Shadow, The. Yvor Winters. APT-2

Pale nuns of St. Joseph are here, The. Island of the Three Marias. Alberto A. Ríos. NoAM

Pale ocean rock! that, like a phantom shape. Rockall. Epes Sargent. APN-1

Pale orchid sunrise snaking through fog. Ghost Frost. Roger Weingarten. VisFro

Pale ravener of horrible meat. (LL) Maldive Shark, The. Herman Melville. APN-2; BrAP; ColAP; NAAL-3; NAAPv.1; NCAP; NoP-4; NoP-5; OxBoAm; TCAPo; WaAnP

Pale, struggling blossoms of mankind. Our Father. Eliza Cook. VWP

Pale water flowers. Coralie. Frederick Goddard Tuckerman. NCAP

Paleness of hunger, The. Mutineer's Ballad, The. Peter Kocan. NOBAu

Palenque Queen by Habana's Shores. Askia Muhammad Touré. BRtP

Palest shadow on the middle rock. Hungry Knight, The. Barbara Guest. NYP2

Palest wash of stone-rubbed ink. Recalling a Sung Dynasty Landscape. Jane Hirshfield. WANABP

Palestine. Marvin X. BRtP

Palimpsest, A. Michael Field. ViWPN; VWP

Palindrome. Lisel Mueller. WeW-3

Palindromic. Ken Babstock. OpeFie

Palinode. "Ern Malley." BMAP

Palinode. Oliver St. John Gogarty. OBMV

Palinode, A. Edmund Bolton. NoSic

Pall. Laura Kasischke. AmPoNex

Pall Hanging over Manila. Mila D. Aguilar. ReBoTo

Pallas. Cyrus Atabay. GTCP, *tr. by* Reinhold Grimm

Pallid and moonlike in the smog. Man Can Complain, Can't He?, A. Ogden Nash. NBLV

Pallid cuckoo, The. Late Winter. James McAuley. BMAP

Pallid domed eulogy nested effort. Bill Lavender. AnSo *Fr.* Pentacl.

Pallid Harrier. Colin Simms. Oth

Pallor. Agnes Mary Frances Robinson. VWP

Palm. Rainer Maria Rilke. WED,

Palm, The. Roy Campbell. MoBrPo

Palm at the end of the mind, The. Of Mere Being. Wallace Stevens. APT-1; BLPJKO; NAAPv.2; NAMCP V.1; NoP-4; NoP-5; OxBoAm; PtR; WoPoe

Palm at the Entrance to the Arm, A. Marla Jernigan. AnSo

Palm Leaf of Mary Magdalene [*with music*]. Cheryl Clarke. WiU

Palm of the hand, The / Is not aware of dying as. Fumi Saito. WoPoe, *tr. by* Edith Marcombe Shiffert and Yuki Sawa

Palm Reader. Dabney Stuart. PfSP

Palm Reader, The. Nicholas Christopher. NoP-4; NoP-5

Palm Sunday. Amy Clampitt. OxBoAm

Palm Sunday Maple Syrup Poem. Bernadette Mayer. NYP2

Palm—the Vine—the Cedar—each hath power, The. Felicia Dorothea Hemans. CenSon *Fr.* Sonnets, Devotional and Memorial.

Palm Tree, A. Rosario Castellanos. TCLAP, *tr. by* Myralyn F. Allgood

Palm Tree, The. Felicia Dorothea Hemans. ViWPN

Palm Tree King. John Agard. EmeKit; Oth

Palmer, The. Robert Greene. NoSic

Palmer's Ode, The. Robert Greene. NoSic *Fr.* Never Too Late.

Palms. June Sylvester. PasH

Palm-Tree, The. John Greenleaf Whittier. NCAP

Palm-trees do have. Cloud Rains. Oumarou Watta. NAfrP

Palo Alto: the Marshes. Robert Hass. GeoHom

Paloma blanca en mi ventana, Una. Miro su ojo, el misterio del mundo gira en su ojo seco. Visitación. Mónica Nepote. SPV, *tr. by* Jen Hofer

Palomino, horse of shadows. Revenant. Rita Dove. AmAlph

Palpable / ours. (LL) Snapshots of a Daughter-in-Law. Adrienne Rich. MoWP; NAAL-5; NALW; NAMCP V.2; NIL-7; NIP-5; NoAM; NoP-4; NoP-5; PoPoPo; WaAnP

Palpable, principal, unearthly, is alive. Marianas, a stillness gathering. Mariana Trench. Joanna Klink. LegDan

Palpitar / que nos fuiste. Dolores Dorantes. SPV

Palpitate / that you left us. Dolores Dorantes. SPV, *tr. by* Jen Hofer

Palpo la noche dormida en tu fronda. Su alquimia de morir junto a una piedra blanca. Regresión del sauce. Ernesto Lumbreras. RMCMP

Paltry Nude Starts on a Spring Voyage, The. Wallace Stevens. PoA 2002

Pamphilia to Amphilanthus. Mary Sidney Wroth, Countess of Montgomery.

　　Crown[e] of Sonnets [*or* Sonetts] Dedicated to Love, A.

　　　Sonnet 1. BASC; CABP; EMWP; MakPoe; NAEL-6v1; NAEL-7v1; NoP-4; NoP-5; NPeEn; PBRV

　　　Sonnet 2. BASC; EMWP; NoP-5; NPeEn; OxBSo; PBRV

　　　Sonnet 3. BASC; NoP-5; OxBSo

　　　Sonnet 5. BASC

　　　Sonnet 13. BASC; EMWP

　　　(Cupid Lost.) LW

　　　(Faulce hope which feeds butt to destroy, and spill.) BrAP

　　　(Love a child is ever criing.) BrAP

　　Song 2. NOSC

　　Song 4. NAEL-6v1; NAEL-7v1

　　Song. EMWP

Song. BASC; LW; NAEL-6v1; NAEL-7v1; NoP-4; NoP-5; NOSC; OxBEV
Song. NOSC
Sonnet 6. NAEL-6v1; NAEL-7v1; NOSC; PEW
Sonnet 6. NOSC
Sonnet 7. BASC
Sonnet 8. PEW
Sonnet 9. BASC; NAEL-7v1; NOSC
Sonnet 11. BASC; NoP-5
Sonnet 14. BASC; CABP; EMWP; NAEL-6v1; NAEL-7v1; NOSC
Sonnet 19. BASC; EMWP; NOSC
Sonnet 21. PEW
Sonnet 22. BASC; EMWP; NoP-5; NOSC
Sonnet 23. BASC; PBRV
Sonnet 25. NoP-5
Sonnet 27. NOSC
Sonnet 32. NOSC
Sonnet 34. BASC; NAEL-7v1; PEW
Sonnet 35. BASC; NAEL-6v1; NAEL-7v1; PEW
Sonnet 37. NoP-4; NoP-5
Sonnet 38. EMWP
Sonnet 39. NoP-5
Sonnet 42. BASC
Sonnet 48. NOSC
(When Nights Black Mantle Could Most Darknes Prove.) BrAP
Pan as the Son of Penelope. Joanne Kyger. BB
Pan Cogito on Virtue. Zbigniew Herbert. PoSu, *tr.* by Adam Czerniawski
Pan, Echo, and the Satyr. Moschus. OBVE, *tr.* by Percy Bysshe Shelley
Pan loved his neighbour Echo—but that child. Pan, Echo, and the Satyr. Moschus. OBVE, *tr.* by Percy Bysshe Shelley
Panama. Patrick Sylvain. InTrad
Pancake with its burnt side down, A. Cakes Continue to Rise. Rick Agran. AmPoNex
Pancakes? You really say peace, joy and *pancakes?*. Daumenbreite. John Redmond. NIrP
Pandora and the Moon. Merrill Moore. MoAmPo
Pandora's Box. Sarah Kirsch. PFTM-2, *tr.* by Wayne Kvam
Pandora's Songs. Trumbull Stickney. APN-2 *Fr.* Prometheus Pyrphoros.
Pandosto: The Triumph of Time. Robert Greene.
(Fawnia.) OBEV
Pane of glass and fifty yards away, A. (LL) West Strand Visions. James Simmons. ModIr; PBCIP
Pane of glass separated Altamirano hill, A. Self-Portrait at Six Years of Age. Homero Aridjis. WoBe, *tr.* by George McWhirter
Panel board of the table, The. Nature Alive. Jorge Guillén. RaW, *tr.* by James Wright
Pang of the long century of rains, The. Lament of Edward Blastock, The. Dame Edith Sitwell. OBMV
Pang, The / Of famine fed upon all entrails—men. Lord Byron. DiBP *Fr.* Darkness.
Pangloss's Song: A Comic-Opera Lyric. Richard Wilbur. NBLV; NoAM
Pangolin, The. Marianne Moore. APT-1; NAAPv.2; NAMCP V.1; NoAM; WaAnP
Pangur Bán. *Unknown.* TriCat, *tr.* by Robin Ernest William Flower
(Student and His Cat, The.) IrV
Panic. Austin Hummell. LiTh
Panic. Archibald MacLeish. MoAmPo
Panic Bird, The. Robert Phillips. BeAl; P180; PoCu
Panic Grass. Charles Upton.
"When I was very young." CLPP
Panic of Birds, The. Olena Kalytiak Davis. AmPoNex
Panope. Dame Edith Sitwell. MoBrPo
Panopticon. Steve McCaffery.
"Homines qouque si taceant, vocem invenient libri." FTOS
Panopticon. Brenda Shaughnessy. LegDan
Panorama. Romelia Alarcón de Folgar. TANSG, *tr.* by Alison Ridley
Panorama 2. Romelia Alarcón de Folgar. TANSG, *tr.* by Alison Ridley
Pan's Song. John Lyly. *See* Pan's Syrinx.
Pan's Syrinx. John Lyly. NoSic; NPeEn *Fr.* Midas.
Pan's Syrinx was a girl[e] indeed. John Lyly. NoSic; NPeEn *Fr.* Midas.
Pansie, Thistle, all with prickles set, The. William Browne. NPeEn *Fr.* Britannia's Pastorals.
Pantheist's Song of Immortality, The. Constance Naden. ViWPN; VWP
Panther. Ogden Nash. AmWit
Panther, The. Rainer Maria Rilke. WoPoe, *tr.* by W. D. Snodgrass
Panther, The. Rainer Maria Rilke. ASA; NAWM-7v2, *tr.* by Stephen Mitchell
Panther, The. Rainer Maria Rilke. GTCP, *tr.* by Walter Arndt
Panther, The. Rainer Maria Rilke. PoCho, *tr.* by Robin Robertson

Pantisocracy. Samuel Taylor Coleridge. CenSon
Pantoum. John Ashbery. MakPoe
Pantoum: In a Texas Farm-House Kitchen. Edyth Renshaw. TiP2
Pantoum of the Great Depression. Donald Justice. InGu; MakPoe; NoP-5
Pantoum of the Working Classes. Sean Thomas Dougherty. LiTh
Pantoumstone for a Dying Breed. Beth Lisick. AmPoNex
Pantoun for Chinese Women. Shirley Lim. FiBr
Panty Raid. Terri Ford. PoDa
Pao-you ku-ye: Bitter Blade. *Unknown.* CCL1, *tr.* by Arthur Cooper
Papa. Barbara Marsh. Prnts
Papa called her Pearl when he came home. Taking in Wash. Rita Dove. OxAAAP
Papa drank and ate. Ironing. Nellie Wong. FFC
Papa Love Baby. Stevie Smith. NALW
Papá smelled of the fine *tabaco* and the dried blood. El Malibú. Richard Blanco. AmPoNex
Papalote Creek. Stephen Harrigan. TiP2
Paparazzi, The. Ai. ExTi
Papa's Letter. *Unknown.* WeW-3
Papasan. Doug Anderson. AmWaPo
Papaya: Lancaster County. Juanita Brunk. ACAMVP
Paper 8. Dominique Batraville. OGAHCP, *tr.* by Boadiba and Jack Hirschman
Paper 18. Dominique Batraville. OGAHCP, *tr.* by Boadiba and Jack Hirschman
Paper 33. Dominique Batraville. OGAHCP, *tr.* by Boadiba and Jack Hirschman
Paper 43. Dominique Batraville. OGAHCP, *tr.* by Boadiba and Jack Hirschman
Paper Anniversary. Muriel Rukeyser. NoAM
Paper arks drift on a concrete lake. Park, A. Theo Sontrop. TuT, *tr.* by Ruth Hooley
Paper bags fall to the ground, The. Seed, The. Franco Fortini. PML, *tr.* by Paul Lawton
Paper before him, The. Election pincers. Mafika Pascal Gwala. TSAP
Paper bird I have in my chest, A. Life. Vicente Aleixandre. RaW, *tr.* by Robert Bly
Paper Boat—Sent to Mother. Bingxin. CFP, *tr.* by Michelle Yeh
Paper clip of light falls, A. In Bed with James Tate. Regie Cabico. BRtP
Paper Doll. Johnny S. Black. ReLy
Paper gardens are perhaps richer in memories than, The. Accessories Shop, The. Pierre McOrlan. MFP, *tr.* by Martin Sorrell
Paper kite, A. Buson. EMJL, *tr.* by Haruo Shirane
Paper Matches [*with music*]. Paulette Jiles. NIL-7; NIP-4
Paper Memorial Stone. Yi Sang. CAMKP; PFTM-1, *tr.* by Walter Lew
Paper Nautilus, The. Marianne Moore. HarvBoo; MakPoe; NAAL-5; NAAPv.2; NALW; NAMCP V.1
Paper on Humor. Andrei Codrescu. PmAP
Paper quilt grows cold, the temple light dim, The. After the Snow in the Mountains. Yi Chehyŏn. CATKP, *tr.* by Chi-gyu Kim [*or* Kim Chonggil]
Paper River, The. Chase Twichell. WANABP
Paper table cloth was tastefully bleak, The. Nimis Compos Mentis. Leslie Monsour. CalPo
Paper was pale, The. Etching. Samuel Greenberg. APT-1
Papermill. Joseph Kalar. APT-2
Paper's merciless in reminding us, The. Killers. Cordelia Candelaria. FTtHH
Papers on my desk out of hand, The. Example, The. Paul Zimmer. OPRER
Papers say the heat is here to stay, The. Nocturne. David Barber. AmPoNex
Paperweight, The. Gjertrud Schnackenberg. MoW; VCAP
Papi worked the factory. Workers. David Hernandez. IllVoic
Papi Working. Julia Alvarez. WaAnP
Papier d'argent. Joyce Mansour. YaTCFP
Papilio. Carol Frost. PfSP
Papistry Storm'd. William Tennant.
Sang First. NePenScot
Papua-woman / Buka-woman. O Myland Woman. Dus Mapun. SonAtl, *tr.* by Edward Etepa, Nancy Gallas, Daniel Perissa, Kate Webster and Albert Wendt
Papyrus. Ezra Pound. APT-1; PFTM-1
Par avion. Aerogrammes. Russell Leong. OpBo
Par la fenêtre ouverte à demi. Léon Damas. YaTCFP
Par respect de l'indicible, nul ne devra plus divulguer le mot GLOIRE ni commettre le caractère BONHEUR. Par Respect. Victor Segalen. YaTCFP
Para-Olympic Legacy, The. Jeni Olin. FreRad
Para qué sirve todo eso te digo tu fiebre tu sollozo. Maquinarias. David Huerta. RMCMP
Para ti, niña Aitana. Remontando los Ríos. Rafael Alberti. RaW
Parable. Richard Wilbur. HarvBoo

"To whom the Tempter impudent replied." ChIV-2

Paradise Saved. Alec Derwent Hope. OxBSo

Paradiso. Cornelius Eady. OxAAAP

Paradoja de nuestro pensamiento, La. Teoría de la luz. Alberto Blanco. RMCMP

Paradox. Anna Wickham. LW

Paradox in our thinking, The. Theory of Light. Alberto Blanco. RMCMP, *tr. by* Gustavo V. Segade

Paradox, The. John Donne. NOSC

Paradox, The. Paul Laurence Dunbar. TCAPo

Paradoxes and Oxymorons. John Ashbery. FTOS; HeIP-4; NAMCP V.2; NoAM; NoP-5; PmAP; PoPoPo

Paragon of Animals, The. Alexander Pope. NAEL-6v1; NAEL-7v1; SacPr; TFi *Fr.* Essay on Man, An.

Paragon, The. Coventry Patmore. NAEL-6v2; NAEL-7v2 *Fr.* Angel in the House, The.

Paragraph 36. Hayden Carruth. BodElec

Paragraph from English Speaking World. Clarence Major. EGAG

Paragraphs. Hayden Carruth.

"Day very solid February 12th, 1944, A." StAl

"Exact beat from, The." StAl

"High above themselves. Above everything, flux, ooze." StAl

"In filthy Puerto Rico lives a bird with no." BodElec

Paragraphs from a Day-Book. Marilyn Hacker.

"Thought thrusts up, homely as a hyacinth." PoA 2002

Paraguay. Carl Rakosi. FTOS

Parakeets fly through my head when I see you in profile. Wink. Benjamin Péret. YaTCFP, *tr. by* Mary Ann Caws *and* Jean-Pierre Cauvin

Parallax. Arthur Sze. GifTon

Parallel tracks of silver. Cascades of Death. Angelina Muñiz Huberman. MirDau, *tr. by* Aurora Camacho

Paralyzed. Willie Abraham Howard Jr. BtF

Paranoia. Salwa Al-Neimi. PoArWo, *tr. by* Subhi Hadidi and Nathalie Handal

Paranoia. Leonard Nolens. TuT, *tr. by* Michael O'Loughlin

Paranoid Egotist, A. Dan Nielsen. SUP

Paraphrase [*ad. fr.* the Bible, Proverbs, 6, 6]. Samuel Johnson. ChIV-1

Paraphrase of Part of the Book of Ecclesiates, A. Henry Howard, Earl of Surrey.

"I, Solomon, David's son, King of Jerusalem." ChIV-1

"When I bethought me well, under the restless sun." ChIV-1

"When that repentant tears hath cleansed clear from ill." ChIV-1

Paraphrase of the Latter part of the Sixth Chapter of St. Matthew, A. James Thomson. ChIV-2

Paraphrase on Oenone to Paris, A. Aphra Behn. EMWP

Paraphrase on the Book of Job, A. Bible, *O.T.*

"All Nature felt a reverential shock." STuOW

Chase of the Metaphor, The. STuOW

"I cannot stifle this gigantick woe." STuOW

"With teats distended with their milky store." STuOW

Paraphrase on the Canticles, A. Elizabeth Singer Rowe.

Chapter II. PEW

Paraphrase Upon Job, A. Bible, *O.T.*

Chapter 2.

Chapter 2 (Fragment). NOSC

Chapter 42. ChIV-1

Paraphrase Upon Part of the CXXXIX Psalm, A. Thomas Stanley. ChIV-1

Parasites. John Gwyn Griffiths. BBMWP, *tr. by* Richard Poole

Paratroopers are Weeping, The. Hayim Hefer. NRoS, *tr. by* Esther Raizen

Parchment and paper left clean. Making of Color, The. Hugh Seidman. YaYoPo

Pardon. Jane Kenyon. LoL *Fr.* Having It Out with Melancholy.

Pardon / the lag / in writing you. Francisco X. Alarcón. LTA

Pardon, The. Richard Wilbur. BrAP; InoFa; NIL-7; NoAM

Pardon, Lord, the lips that dare. John Greenleaf Whittier. SacPr *Fr.* Andrew Rykman's Prayer.

Pardon me, boy. Chattanooga Choo-Choo. Mack Gordon. ReLy

Pardon me buddy, I didn't mean to bug you. Homeless Compleynt. Allen Ginsberg. BodElec

Pardon me father if I am a disappointment to what you. Pardon Me. Ismael Hurreh. PML

Pardon me, if when I want. Pablo Neruda. GifTon, *tr. by* William O'Daly

Pardon me, Miss. Real Live Girl. Carolyn Leigh. ReLy

Pardon my boldness, madam; here's the clout. (LL) To a Lady with Child that Asked [*or* Ask'd] an Old Shirt. Richard Lovelace. BASC; NOSC

Pardon, oh, pardon, that my soul should make. Elizabeth Barrett Browning. CenSon *Fr.* Sonnets from the Portuguese.

Pardon sweete flower of matchless Poetrie. Choise of valentines, The. Thomas Nashe. PBRV

Pardon us for uttering a handful. New Netherland, 1654. Grace Schulman. OPRER

Pardon, ye glowing ears; need will it out. Joseph Hall. NoSic *Fr.* Virgidemiarum.

Pardoned in heaven, the first by the throne! (LL) Lost Leader, The. Robert Browning. NAEL-6v2; NAEL-7v2

Pardoner's Introduction, The. Geoffrey Chaucer. NAEL-6v1; NAEL-7v1; WaAnP *Fr.* Canterbury Tales, The.

Pardoner's Prologue, The. Geoffrey Chaucer. NAEL-6v1; NAEL-7v1; WaAnP *Fr.* Canterbury Tales, The.

Pardoner's Tale, The. Geoffrey Chaucer. NAEL-6v1; NAEL-7v1; WaAnP *Fr.* Canterbury Tales, The.

Parece como si el mundo caminase de espaldas. Hijos de la Tierra. Blas de Otero. RaW

Paredón. Ricardo Pau-Llosa. OPRER

Paregoric Babies. Jim Carroll. PmAP

Parent. Josephine Miles. NALW

Parent, The. Ogden Nash. Spl

Parent to Children. Robert Graves. OxAEP-2

Parentage. Alice Thompson Meynell. InoFa; NALW; NPeEn; VWP

Parental Critic, The [*with music*]. Keith Preston. NBLV

Parental Ode to My Son, A. Thomas Hood. OBCoV *Fr.* Domestic Poems.

Parental Recollections. Mary Lamb. OxBEV

(Child, A.) OBEV

Parents. Marta Kornblith. MirDau, *tr. by* Roberta Gordenstein

Parents. William Meredith. NAMCP V.2

Parents. Hilda Morley. PmAP

Parents cluster across the street. Hostage. Dixie Partridge. LiTh

Parents' Pantoum. Carolyn Kizer. MakPoe

Parents: People Like Our Marriage Maxie and Andrew, The. Gwendolyn Brooks. ColAP *Fr.* Notes from the Childhood and the Girlhood.

Parents take their children into the deepest Oregon forests. Robert Bly. LoL *Fr.* Anger Against Children.

Parents They Would Be, The. Joe-Anne McLaughlin-Carruth. PoA 2002

Parfois nous rêvons de jeunes femmes brunes un peu folles. Éloge de Robert Desnos. Franck Venaille. YaTCFP

Parfum Exotique. Padraic Fallon. IrLP

Paring the Apple. Charles Tomlinson. TRP

Paris. Ingeborg Bachmann. VCWP, *tr. by* Mark Anderson

Paris. Miklós Radnóti. IQMS, *tr. by* Zsuzsanna Ozsváth and Frederick Turner

Paris, 7 A.M. Elizabeth Bishop. PoA 2002

Paris and Menelaus. Homer. OBVE *Fr.* Iliad, The.

Paris—Christmas 1938. Edwin Rolfe. APT-2

Paris Cinquième. Antonio Cisneros. TCLAP *Fr.* Loneliness.

Paris Honeymoon, A. Frank Ormsby.

L'Orangerie. ModIr

Paris Is Not the Same. Eric Maschwitz. ReLy

Paris Is Paris Again. Alan Jay Lerner. ReLy

Paris is six feet higher than Mexico. Rousseau Le Douanier. "Lucebert." PFTM-2, *tr. by* Peter Nijmeijer

Paris Latin Quarter. Femi Osofisan. NAfrP

Paris Visitation. Michael Brownstein. FTOS

Parish. Norman Dubie. AmAlph

Parish Register, The. George Crabbe.

Park, A. Theo Sontrop. TuT, *tr. by* Ruth Hooley

Park Elms. Charles Ghigna. UrbNat

Park is filled with night and fog, The. Spring Night. Sara Teasdale. MoAmPo

Park mole. Merilene M. Murphy. BtF

Park of the Dead. Gerrit Komrij. TuT, *tr. by* Peter van de Kamp

Park Poem. Paul Blackburn. PmAP

Parked in the fields. Forms of Love, The. George Oppen. ItP

Parked in the office john, going. Value Added in Smashing a German Roach on the Bathroom Door, The. Luis Cabalquinto. ReBoTo

Parking Lot. Leslie Monsour. CalPo

Parking lots of K-Mart are not safe, The. There are video cameras on school buses. Times. Lola Haskins. LiTh

Parkinson's Disease. Galway Kinnell. FaoP

Parle. Pierre Albert Jourdan. YaTCFP

Parlement of Foules, The. Geoffrey Chaucer.

Catalogue of the Birds. NPeEn

Rondel. OWoS

(Roundel.) NPeEn; OPOU

"With that mine hand in his he took anon." OBGa

Parley of Beasts.　Hugh MacDiarmid.　ChIV-1; MoBrPo; NAMCP V.1; NoAM; OBMV

Parliament Hill Fields.　Sylvia Plath.　NALW

Parliament of grasshoppers is in the field, A.　Questions.　Federico García Lorca.　WED, *tr. by* Robert Bly

Parmenides Machine, A.　Charles Stein.　PFTM-2

Parnassus Rising.　James Richardson.　RD

Parody.　Chungji.　BecRai, *tr. by* Kim Daljin, Kim Won-Chung and Christopher Merrill

Parody, A.　Frederick Douglass.　NAAL-3; NAWM-7v2 *Fr.* Narrative of the Life of Frederick Douglass, an American Slave.

Parody of Bishop Percy.　Samuel Johnson.　OBCoV

Parody of the Other Woman.　Shen Manyuan.　CCL1, *tr. by* Anne Birrell

Paroles du poème, Les.　André Frénaud.　YaTCFP

Parousia.　John Burnside.　NeBrP

PARRA LAUGHS like he's condemned to hell.　Something Like That. Nicanor Parra.　WoBe, *tr. by* Liz Werner

Parrot at Sea, A.　Yelena Shwarts.　ItGoST, *tr. by* Catriona Kelly

Parrot Island.　Liu Yu Hsi.　CCL1, *tr. by* Marsha Wagner

Parrot Parted from Her Cage.　Hsüeh T'ao [*or* Xue Tao].　CCL1, *tr. by* Jeanne Larsen

Parrot, The.　Wilfrid Wilson Gibson.　OBMV

Parrots.　Selima Hill.　MoWP

Parrot's Complaint.　John Skelton.　NPeEn

Parrot's Soliloquy.　John Skelton.　NoSic *Fr.* Speak [*or* Speke], Parrot.

Parrot's voice snaps out, The.　"Psittachus Eois Imitatrix Ales ab Indis." Sacheverell Sitwell.　MoBrPo

Parry, of all my friends the best.　Invitation, The.　Goronwy Owen.　OBWVE, *tr. by* George Burrow

Parsifal.　Paul Verlaine.　SxFrPo, *tr. by* Martin Sorrell

Parsifal has conquered the Maidens, their sweet.　Parsifal.　Paul Verlaine. SxFrPo, *tr. by* Martin Sorrell

Parsley.　Rita Dove.　AmAlph; CAP-8; EMP; ESEAA; LoL; NAAL-5; NAMCP V.2; NIL-7; NoAM; NoP-4; NoP-5; PoPoPo; VCAP; WaAnP

Parsnip, The.　Ogden Nash.　ChAP

Parson and the Plowman Described, The.　Geoffrey Chaucer.　SacPr *Fr.* Canterbury Tales, The.

Parson, these things in thy possessing.　Happy Life of a Country Parson, The. Alexander Pope.　UV

Parson's Case, The.　Jonathan Swift.
　"Thy curate's place, thy fruitful wife."　UV

Parson's Introduction, The.　Geoffrey Chaucer.　NAEL-6v1; NAEL-7v1 *Fr.* Canterbury Tales, The.

Parśvanatha.　Robert Bringhurst.　GifTon

Part 4: Cri Madonna.　Lynnette Roberts.　MoWP *Fr.* Gods with Stainless Ears.

Part Evil.　Jessica Freeman.　AnSo

Part eye, part tear, unwilling to recognize us. (LL)　Stone Canyon Nocturne. Charles Wright.　ColAP; GeoHom; NAMCP V.2; VCAP

Part for the Whole.　Robert Francis.　PoA 2002

Part Four: Rebirth.　Sonia Sanchez.　PfS

Part of a Bird.　Nina Cassian.　PoSu, *tr. by* Andrea Deletant and Brenda Walker *and* Andrea Deletant

Part of a Larger Country.　Jeanne Bryner.　SweBea

Part of a Letter to the Codignola Boy.　Pier Paolo Pasolini.　VCWP, *tr. by* David Stivender *and* J. D. McClatchy

Part of a Novel, Part of a Poem, Part of a Play.　Marianne Moore.
　Hero, The.　PoA 2002
　Steeple-Jack, The.　APT-1; ColAP; FTtHH; HarvBoo; NAAPv.2; NAMCP V.1; NoAM; NoP-4; NoP-5; OxBoAm; PoA 2002; PoPoPo

Part of an Irregular Fragment Found in a Dark Passage of the Tower.　Helen Maria Williams.　RWP
　"Rise, winds of night! Relentless tempests rise!"　NPBRoP

Part of an Ode, A.　Ben Jonson. *See* It Is Not Growing Like a Tree.

Part of Eve's Discussion.　Marie Howe.　P180

Part of me flies upward.　Dead Cartesian, The.　Chris Wallace-Crabbe.　PoA 2002

Part of my charm.　Look for You Yesterday, Here You Come Today.　Imamu Amiri Baraka.　SSLK

Part of our nation of our fanatic sun. (LL)　Soul and Body of John Brown, The. Muriel Rukeyser.　CBCWP; MoAmPo

Part of something at last. (LL)　Death of Janis Joplin, The.　Robert Phillips. SwNoth; TiP2

Part of Speech, A.　Joseph Brodsky. *tr. by* the author and Daniel Weissbort
　"And when "the future" is uttered, swarms of mice."　StAl, *tr. by* the author and Daniel Weissbort
　"As for the stars, they are always on."　StAl, *tr. by* Daniel Weissbort
　"If anything's to be praised, it's most likely how."　StAl, *tr. by* Daniel Weissbort

"In the little town out of which death sprawled over the classroom map." StAl, *tr. by* Daniel Weissbort
　"Not that I am losing my grip: I am just tired of summer."　StAl, *tr. by* the author and Daniel Weissbort
　"You've forgotten that village lost in the rows and rows."　StAl, *tr. by* the author and Daniel Weissbort

Part of the Bee's Body Embedded in the Flesh, The.　Carol Frost.　CAP-8

Part of the Bridge.　Peter Didsbury.　NeBrP

Part of the crowd that day.　Ken Smith.　BeAl

Part of the darkness lived. Furred or scaled.　First Relations.　Pamela Alexander.　PfSP

Part of the difference between floating and going down. (LL)　Yellow Glove. Naomi Shihab Nye.　LoL; PoArWo

Part of the Effect of the Public Scene Is to Importune the Passing Viewer.　Erin Belieu.　AmPoNex

Part of the field, A. Trumpets sound and two men enter.　Joseph Brodsky. TCRusP *Fr.* Sonnets on the Statue of Mary, Queen of Scots, in the Luxembourg Gardens, Paris.

Part of the Lay of Sigrdrifa.　*Unknown.*　OBVE

Part of the soul that doubts, again and again, The.　Cures.　David Rivard. AllShUp; SwNoth

Part of What I Mean.　Frank Gaspar.　UrbNat

Part One: The Orders Begin.　Carmen Naranjo.　TANSG, *tr. by* Shaun Griffin and Emma Sepúlveda-Pulvirenti

Part otter, part snake, part bird the bird Anhinga.　Waterbird.　May Swenson. NoP-4; NoP-5; OxBoAm

Partake as doth the Bee.　Emily Dickinson.　TCAPo

Partaker in my happiest mood.　Companion, The.　*Unknown.*　ArBi

Parted [*with music*].　Clara Ann Thompson.　CBWP-2

Parted by death, we'd strangle on our tears.　Dreaming of Li Po.　Tu Fu [*or* Du Fu].　CrYelRi, *tr. by* Sam Hamill

Parthenea, an Elegy.　Elizabeth Singer Rowe.　PoBW

Partheniades.　George Puttenham.
　"O mightye Muse."　PBRV

Parthenon at Nashville, The.　Joe Bolton.　AmPoNex

Parthenon, The.　Herman Melville.　NCAP

Parthenophil and Parthenophe.　Barnabe Barnes.
　"Jove, for Europa[e]s love took[e] shape of bull."　OxBSo
　"Lovely Maya, Hermes' mother."　NoSic
　Sestina.　NoSic; NPeEn; WaAnP
　Sestine 4.　MakPoe
　"Why do I draw this coole releeving ayer."　PBRV

Parthian Powers.　John Milton.　NOSC

Parti Pris.　Louis Aragon.　YaTCFP

Partial.　Louis Aragon.　YaTCFP, *tr. by* Mary Ann Caws *and* Jean-Pierre Cauvin

Partial Explanation, The.　Charles Simic.　P180

Partial Muse, has from my earliest hours, The.　Charlotte Smith.　CenSon; RWP

Particle Limericks.　Alan Robert Wilson.　IFF

Particularly Effortless He Lay.　Walter Höllerer.　GTCP, *tr. by* Irmgard Hunt

Parting [*with music*].　A. R. Ammons.　NoAM

Parting.　Chŏng Chisang.　CATKP, *tr. by* Peter H. Lee

Parting.　William Johnson Cory.　CAGL

Parting.　Frances Anne Kemble.　PoBW

Parting.　Li Po.　CrYelRi, *tr. by* Sam Hamill

Parting.　Wang Wei.　CCL1, *tr. by* Stephen Owen

Parting, The.　Sara Berkeley.　PBCIP

Parting, The.　Michael Drayton.　OBEV

Parting, The.　Josephine D. Henderson Heard.　CBWP-4

Parting as Descent.　John Berryman.　MoAmPo

Parting at Morning.　Robert Browning.　CABP; HeIP-4; NAEL-6v2; NAEL-7v2; OBEV; SoSe-8; TFi

Parting by Moonlight in a River Pavilion.　Wang Po.　CCL1, *tr. by* Stephen Owen

Parting Gift.　Elinor Wylie.　APT-1

Parting in Wartime.　Frances Darwin Cornford.　NIP-4

Parting Kiss, The [*with music*].　Josephine D. Henderson Heard.　CBWP-4

Parting Lovers, The.　Mrs. Henry Linden.　CBWP-4

Parting makes simple sense.　Katia Kapovich.　CRWP, *tr. by* Richard McKane

Parting Roundel.　Jemal Sharah.　NOBAu

Parting Song, A.　Felicia Dorothea Hemans.　NPBRoP; VWP

Parting the curtains on the other world.　Yunna Petrovna Moritz.　ItGoST, *tr. by* Daniel Weissbort

Parting turns to fire.　*Unknown.*　CATKP, *tr. by* Kevin O'Rourke

Parting with Hsin Chien at Hibiscus Tavern.　Wang Ch'ang-ling.　NDACCP, *tr. by* Gary Snyder

Parting, without a Sequel. John Crowe Ransom. MoAmPo; NoP-4; NoP-5; SoSe-8

Partitions. Franco Buffoni. ItPo, *tr.* by Gayle Ridinger

Partout les. Jacques Roubaud. YaTCFP

Partout / sous les objets la. Partout les. Jacques Roubaud. YaTCFP

Parts of a Mystery. Charlotte Osgood Carter. AHA

Parts of a Thornbush, The. *Unknown.* SonAtl, *tr.* by Alan Brierly, Saul Goode and S. Wendo

Party. Eddy Van Vliet. VCWP, *tr.* by John Van Tiel

Party, The. Margaret Avison. PoA 2002

Party, The. Donald Finkel. OPRER

Party, The. Antigone Kefala. BMAP

Party, The. William Robert Rodgers. PNI

Party, The. Ben Scammell. NLP

Party at Hydra. Irving Layton. HeIP-4

Party balloons rub against each other. Balloons. Dan Pagis. FIT, *tr.* by Robert Friend

Party Crash. René Ricard. AHA

Party Favour [*with music*]. Daniel David Moses. HATNAP

Party for your Right to Fight. Public Enemy. ISC

Party holds you down and you lie still, The. Nguyễn Chí Thiện. VCWP *Fr.* Sundry Notes.

Party on Shipboard. George Oppen. APT-2; PFTM-1

Party on Women's Day, A. Olesya Nikolayeva. ItGoST, *tr.* by Paul Graves and Carol Ueland

Party She Outdid Herself, The. Craig Arnold. NAPBL

Party suddenly condensed, The. Thirteen Ways of Looking at a Hoover. Anthony Conran. TCAWP

Party was no good again, The. Europa. Rolfe Humphries. APT-2

Party's Over, The. Abu Nuwas. SonAtl, *tr.* by Latifa, Malika and Yusuf

Party's Over, The. Betty Comden and Adolph Green. ReLy

Party's over, The. The bursting zanies and their night. Party's Over, The. Abu Nuwas. SonAtl, *tr.* by Latifa, Malika and Yusuf

Parvati. Sujata Bhatt. MoWP

Parvenant. Arthur Hugh Clough. OBCoV *Fr.* Spectator ab Extra.

Pascual the Shepherd. Dorothy Molloy. NIrP

Pasha will see you tonight, The. Effendi. Reed Bye. AHA

Paso del Norte. Ray Gonzales. TiP2

Paso Robles, San Luis Obispo, San Luis Obispo. David Oliveira. CalPo; GeoHom

Pasolini. Robert Glück. WiU

Pass by a tree. Passing Music for a Tree. Mieko Shiomi. WhBo

Pass, Crow. (LL) Examination at the Womb-Door. Ted Hughes. NAEL-6v2; NAEL-7v2; NoP-4; NoP-5

Pass fi White. Louise Bennett. NAMCP V.2

Pass it along to Stand-to. (LL) David Jones. NAMCP V.1; NoAM *Fr.* In Parenthesis.

Pass it on. (LL) Listen Children. Lucille Clifton. ISC; NOxBChV

Pass not, but wonder, and amazed stand. Upon the Much Lamented Death of the Right Honourable, the Lady Elizabeth Langham. Bathsua Pell Makin. EMWP

Pass of Death, The. George Darley. NOBRP

Pass round the glass for the breeze has arisen and the stars have slackened the reins of night travel. Abu Bakr Ibn 'Ammār. HiArP, *tr.* by James T. Monroe

Pass the tambourine, let me bash out praises. Way We Live, The. Kathleen Jamie. NeBrP; StAl

Pass to thy Rendezvous of Light. Emily Dickinson. NAWM-7v2

Pass where the winds pause before they cross. *Unknown.* CATKP, *tr.* by Peter H. Lee

Passacaglia. Don Hymans. BAP-97

Passage. Elizabeth Alexander. FuFl; ISC

Passage. Billy Marshall-Stoneking. BMAP; NOBAu

Passage. Peter Rafferty. NLP

Passage. Penelope Rosemont. SurWo

Passage. *Unknown. tr.* by Billy Marshall-Stoneking

   "See there, that tree is a digging stick." WoPoe, *tr.* by Billy Marshall-Stoneking

Passage, The. Adonis. VCWP, *tr.* by Samuel Hazo

Passage, The. Rita Dove. ESEAA

Passage from a Letter to William Charles Jarvis, September 28, 1820. Thomas Jefferson. TWF

Passage of the Mountain of St. Gothard, The. Georgiana Cavendish, Duchess of Devonshire. RWP

Passage of the Patowmac through the Blue Ridge, The. One More River to Cross. John Beecher. InGu

Passage over Water. Robert Duncan. NAMCP V.2; NoAM

Passage to India. Walt Whitman. APN-1; NAAPv.1; NCAP

Passages. Robert Duncan.

Feast, The. APSN

Fire, The. APSN

In Blood's Domaine. PFTM-2

Moon, The. APSN

Torso, The. CAGL

Transgressing the Real. APSN

Tribal Memories. APSN

Up Rising. APSN; NAMCP V.2

Passages 37. Robert Duncan. FTOS

Passamaquoddy Song of the Stars. Rita Joe. Coast

Passchendaele. Angus Martin. EdScPo

Passé, Le. Jacques Roubaud. YaTCFP

Pass[e] rascal deer [*or* Rascall Deare], strike me the largest doe. (LL) La Bella Bona-Roba. Richard Lovelace. NOSC; OxBEV

Passed guard tower. Kyotaro Komuro. NAAPv.2

Passed On. Bernard Spencer. FaBoWar

Passenger feels the sparks penetrate his halo, The. Real Moment, The. Eduardo Anguita. BLPSL, *tr.* by Rene de Costa, Rigas Kappatos and Eleni Paidoussi

Passenger Opposite, The. Elma Mitchell. NePenScot

Passenger Shanty. W. H. Auden. OBCoV

Passengers. Billy Collins. GoPo; OtW; PLBUT

Passengers afloat on many thousand feet. Night Flight. Marion Alexopoulos. NOBAu

Passer Mortuus Est. Edna St. Vincent Millay. MoAmPo

Passer-by, A. Robert Bridges. MoBrPo; OBEV

Passer-by, these are words. But instead of reading. Passer-by, These are Words. Yves Bonnefoy. P180

Passes gently over us. (LL) Happiness. Louise Glück. HarvBoo; WaAnP

Passes slowly. (LL) Tug against the river. George Oppen. APT-2; PFTM-1

Passing. Cheryl Clarke. WiU

Passing. Toi Derricotte. OPRER

Passing. Langston Hughes. APSN; APT-2; OxBoAm; SAmP

Passing. Carl Phillips. BtF; PoPoPo

Passing a Ruined Palace. Wen T'ing-yün. CCL1, *tr.* by Kenneth Rexroth

Passing Away. Augusta Davies Webster. ViWPN

Passing away from you, love. Passing Away. Augusta Davies Webster. ViWPN

Passing Away, Saith the World, Passing Away. Christina Georgina Rossetti. NoP-4; NoP-5; ViWPN *Fr.* Old and New Year Ditties.

Passing by a Mountain Village at Dusk. Chia Tao. CSKM, *tr.* by Mike O'Connor

Passing by the swamp of cafés. Mountain Stroll. Ch'ôn Yanghûi. EcSo, *tr.* by Aimee N. Kwon

Passing by Where Hsu, "The Wine-Flushed Immortal," Used to Live. Ching An. CSKM, *tr.* by Jerome P. Seaton

Passing Clouds. Chase Twichell. WaAnP

Passing clouds roll grimly on, The. Shower. Jacob Winkler Prins. TuT, *tr.* by Tony Curtis and Tony Curtis

Passing Hidden Fragrance Temple. Wang Wei. CCL1, *tr.* by Jerome P. Seaton

Passing House, The. Beckian Fritz Goldberg. AmAlph

Passing Mr. Sung's Old House. Tu Fu [*or* Du Fu]. CrYelRi, *tr.* by Sam Hamill

Passing Music for a Tree. Mieko Shiomi. WhBo

Passing my floor. Elevator. Sanford Fraser. NevBe

Passing of Arthur, The. Samuel Carter. STuOW *Fr.* Arthur Mervyn; A Tale of Social Grievances.

Passing of Arthur, The. Alfred Tennyson. NAEL-6v2; NAEL-7v2 *Fr.* Idylls of the King.

Passing of the Old Man, The. Albert Huffstickler. TiP2

Passing of the Old Year. Mary Weston Fordham. CBWP-2

Passing On. Menna Elfyn. ATSWP, *tr.* by Robert Minhinnick

Passing Piedras Blancas. Abigail Albrecht. GeoHom

Passing Seven-League Rapids. Meng Hao Jan. ColAnChi, *tr.* by Daniel Bryant

Passing Show, The. Ambrose Bierce. APN-2

Passing spring, The. Buson. EMJL, *tr.* by Haruo Shirane

Passing Strange, The. John Masefield. MoBrPo; OBEV

Passing stranger! you do not know how longingly I look upon you. To a Stranger. Walt Whitman. APN-1; OxBoAm; SAmP

Passing the American graveyard, for my birthday. Poem for My Twentieth Birthday. Kenneth Koch. PoA 2002

Passing the bread shop with hungry eyes. Making It. Magdalena Gomez. PueRic

Passing the Crematorium. Frank Ormsby. ModIr

Passing the man on the rack and the man with the knife in his back. Dyne. René Char. MotU, *tr.* by Franz Wright

Passing the Night. Tu Fu [*or* Du Fu]. CrYelRi, *tr. by* Sam Hamill

Passing the Temple of Teeming Fragrance. Wang Wei. ChinPo, *tr. by* Ye Weilian [*or* Yeh Wei-lien *or* Wai-lim Yip]

Passing Through. Constantine P. Cavafy. CAGL, *tr. by* Edmund Keeley and Philip Sherrard

Passing Through. Stanley Kunitz. BodElec; LoL

Passing Through. Patrick Williams. PNI

Passing Through Ch'ien-hsi, Third Month, 405. T'ao Ch'ien. CrYelRi, *tr. by* Sam Hamill

Passing Through Experiences. Robert Adamson. BMAP

Passing through huddled and ugly walls. Harbor, The. Carl Sandburg. APT-1; ColAP; NAMCP V.1

Passing through passing. Sake Gold. William Heyen. AmZen

Passing Through This House. Brother Yao. BtF

Passing Tianmen Street in Chang'an and Seeing a Distant View of Zhongnan Mountains. Po Chü-i. CCL1, *tr. by* Arthur Waley

Passion. Michael Ryan. BodElec

Passion. Penelope Shuttle.

  Passion. LW

Passion and Love. Paul Laurence Dunbar. ErotSp

Passion at Forty. Jane Barnes. PfS

Passion circles round our body, A. Gregorio Scalise. ItPo, *tr. by* Gayle Ridinger

Passion killings, plane crashes, overdoses. Encyclopedia of Rhythm and Blues, The. Anthony Walton. RD

Passion makes the boredom. Illusion Collector, Age 37, The. Keith Abbott. WhBo

Passion of Jesus Considered as an Uphill Race, The. Alfred Jarry. PFTM-1

Passion of M'Phail, The. Horace Gregory.

  This Is the Place to Wait. MoAmPo

Passion of Our Lord painted by an anonymous hand from the Circle of Rhenish Masters, The. Zbigniew Herbert. GI, *tr. by* Adam Czerniawski

Passion of Ravensbrück. János Pilinszky. AF; GI; HP; PoSu, *tr. by* Ted Hughes

Passion of Ravensbrück, The. János Pilinszky. IQMS, *tr. by* Ted Hughes

Passion of the Queen, The. Virgil. NAWM-5v1; NAWM-7v1 *Fr.* Aeneid [*or* Eneados *or* Aeneis], The.

Passion, The. Fanny Howe.

  "His legs were long and thin, his knees bent and feet crossed." FaoP

  "In the old way the old wood." FaoP

  "Knees trembled but she touched the veins, The." FaoP

  "Once on a summer night." FaoP

  "She put her hand." FaoP

  "Then I'll bear the torch and the needle." FaoP

  "This angel clung to boats." FaoP

Passion Week. William Everson. SacPr

Passionate beyond the will. (LL) Alchemist, The. Louise Bogan. APT-2; MoAmPo; NAAPv.2; NAMCP V.1

Passionate Man[']s Pilgrimage, The. Sir Walter Ralegh. ChIV-2; NoP-5; NoSic; NPeEn; OxBEV; TFi

  (His Pilgrimage.) BLPJKO; OBEV

  (Passionate Man's Pilgrimage, The.) NoP-4

  (Verses made by Sir Walter Raleigh the Night before he was Beheaded.) OxAEP-1

Passionate Pilgrim, The. *Various authors.*

  Philomel. OBEV

  (Crabbed Age and Youth.) NoSic; OBEV

Passionate Professor, The [*with music*]. Bert Leston Taylor. NBLV

Passionate Profiteer to His Love, The [*par. of* Passionate Shepherd to His Love, The *by* Christopher Marlowe]. "Sagittarius." OBCoV

Passionate Sheepheard to his Love, The. Christopher Marlowe. *See* Passionate Shepherd to His Love, The.

Passionate Shepherd, The. Nicholas Breton.

  Merry Country Lad, The. NoSic

Passionate Shepherd to His Love, The. Christopher Marlowe. BLPJKO; ClHu; HeIP-4; ITBLP; MakPoe; NAEL-6v1; NAEL-7v1; NBLV; NIL-7; NIP-4; NoP-5; NoSic; OBEV; OxAEP-1; OxBEV; TFi; TRP; WaAnP; WeW-3; WoPoe

  (Come Live With Me and Be My Love.) UV

  (Passionate Sheepheard to his Love, The.) BrAP; NPeEn; PBRV

Passionate Summer's dead! the sky's a-glow, The. October. Paul Hamilton Hayne. APN-2

Passionate World, The. Anne Michaels. BeAl; PoDa

Passive sea of white foam, A. Poetic Reflections Enroute To, and During, The Funeral and Burial of Henry Dumas, Poet. Eugene B. Redmond. ISC

Passover. Linda Pastan. TaR

Passover: the Injections. William Heyen. HP

Passport photo booth flashes, The. Sean Dunne. ModIr *Fr.* Sydney Place.

Password of the twentieth century: Communications (as if we had to invent them), The. Funeral of Poetry, The. Karl Shapiro. APT-2; OxBoAm

Past. Pablo Neruda. VCWP, *tr. by* Alastair Reid

Past, The. Ralph Waldo Emerson. WoPoe

Past, The [*with music*]. Mary Weston Fordham. CBWP-2

Past, The. Ha Jin. NIL-7

Past, The. Li Yu [*or* Li Hou-Chu]. CCL1, *tr. by* Sam Houston Brock

Past, The. William Oandasan.

  8. FTtHH

  Words of Tayko-mol. HATNAP

Past, The. Jacques Roubaud. YaTCFP, *tr. by* Françoise Gramet and Richard Sieburth

Past, The. Betsy Sholl. ExTi

Past, The. Fyodor Ivanovich Tyutchev. WoPoe, *tr. by* Charles Tomlinson

Past, The. Sarah Helen Whitman. TCAPo

Past, a glacier, gripped the mountain wall, the. Full Moon at Tierz: Before the Storming of Huesca. John Cornford. OBWP; RSaN

Past All Understanding. Heather McHugh. ExTi

Past and Present. John Peale Bishop. InGu

Past and present wilt—I have filled them, emptied them, The. Walt Whitman. CAGL; ColAP; NAWM-7v2 *Fr.* Song of Myself.

Past Andreevsky market. Portrait of the Blockade through Genre Painting, Still Life, and Landscape, A. Yelena Shwarts. CRWP, *tr. by* James McGavran

Past begins to move at night, The. My Husband's Bride. Beckian Fritz Goldberg. PfS

Past bush paths tarred by tireless treading. Excursion. Niyi Osundare. HBAPE

Past can be no more, The. Now. Thomas Ken. SacPr

Past castle, brewery, over a sandstone bridge. Cockermouth. David Wright. NLP

Past eddies dangerous and rock-reefs wild. Boat, The. Ferenc Kazinczy. IQMS, *tr. by* Watson Kirkconnell

Past empty rooms full of men, the. Robert Sheppard. Oth *Fr.* Empty Diaries/ Twentieth Century Blues 24.

Past hurts, George, but sing and be merry, The. Old Song. Andrey Andreievich Voznesensky. VCWP, *tr. by* Vera Dunham *and* H. W. Tjalsma and William Jay Smith

Past is only fit to be regretted, The. Past, The. Li Yu [*or* Li Hou-Chu]. CCL1, *tr. by* Sam Houston Brock

Past Is, The. Margaret Randall. ICANM

Past is the antithesis of burglary, The. Imagine. Empire of Lights, The. John Glenday. NeBrP

Past Is the Present, The. Marianne Moore. APT-1; OxBoAm

Past its southeasterly mouth many times, yes, but I hadn't drifted into the Huerfano until June. Commentary. Andrew Schelling. AmZen

Past Madonna dell'Orto, then under the galleries which run through the center of town. Visit to Fadin. Eugenio Montale. MotU, *tr. by* Charles Wright

Past Midnight. Edmund Wilson. PoA 2002

Past Midnight, My Daughter Awakened by Miles Davis' *Kind of Blue*. Kevin Stein. IllVoic

Past mishaps might be attributed to an incomplete understanding. Flight. Louis Jenkins. GoPo

Past. No matter how poised the shape. Poet Dives, The. Willem Jan Otten. TuT, *tr. by* Micheal O'Siadhail

Past One o'Clock . . . . Vladimir Vladimirovich Mayakovsky. AF, *tr. by* George Reavey

Past parentage or gender. Silence, A. Amy Clampitt. MoWP

Past Perfect. Linda Gregg. BodElec

Past Perm and Glitz. Charlotte Renk. TiP2

Past, present, future: unattainable. Hakuin. ZenPo, *tr. by* Takashi Ikemoto and Lucien Stryk

Past Qualm of Hours. Marla Jernigan. AnSo

Past Ruined Ilion Helen Lives. Walter Savage Landor. *See* Ianthe.

Past ruined [*or* ruin'd] Ilion Helen lives. Walter Savage Landor. NOBRP; NPeEn; OxBEV; TFi; WeW-3 *Fr.* Ianthe.

Past scenic laybys and stag warning signs. Tony Harrison. NAMCP V.2 *Fr.* School of Eloquence, The.

Past second cock-crow yacht masts in the harbor go slowly white. Robert Penn Warren. NoP-4; NoP-5; VCAP *Fr.* Island of Summer.

Past, subject to Judgement, A. (LL) New Year Greeting, A. W. H. Auden. HarvBoo; NAMCP V.1

Past the angular maguey fields, a ride on the optic nerve. Into Mexico. Mona Van Duyn. VCAP

Past the bananas and mangoes. Crossing the River to Juárez. Pat LittleDog. TiP2

Past the fierce Guardians. Poem in November. Shirley Kaufman. GifTon

Past the fourth cloverleaf, by dwindling roads. Buckroe, after the Season, 1942. Virginia Hamilton Adair. APT-2

Past the pedestrians, beyond exhausts. Early Evening. Edward Byrne. ViWalt

Past the platforms of the beloved leader. Documentary Film. Holger Teschke. GTCP, *tr. by* Reinhold Grimm

Past the salt flats, the grave of the sea, the sky. Erosion. Christopher Merrill. OPRER

Past Thinking of Solomon. Francis Thompson. ChIV-1

Past three again! Honest to God, what are you doing? Coffee Imp, The. Bella Akhatovna Akhmadulina. ItGoST, *tr. by* F. D. Reeve

Past Time. Edith Jay Scovell. HarvBoo

Past Yü-ku Tower glides the river Ch'ing. Tune: "The Bodhisattva's Golden Headdress." Hsin Ch'i-chi. ColAnChi, *tr. by* Jiaosheng Wang

Pasteur on the Rue Vauquelin. Linda Bierds. AmAlph

Pastheen Finn. *Irish Oral Tradition*. IrV,

Pastiche. Elinor Wylie. NALW

Pastime. Henry VIII, King of England. NoSic

Pastime Café. W. M. Ransom. GifTon

Pastime of Pleasure, The. Stephen Hawes. OBGa
    Epitaph of Graunde [*or* La Graunde] Amoure, The. NoSic; OBEV
    True Knight [*or* True Knighthood], The. OBEV

Pastime of the Queen of Fairies, The. Margaret Lucas Cavendish, Duchess of Newcastle. BASC; NAEL-6v1

Pastime with good company. Pastime. Henry VIII, King of England. NoSic

Past-Lives Therapy. Charles Simic. StAl

Pastor Praises the Creator, The. UpMys

Pastora. Mario Florián. BLPSL, *tr. by* Rene de Costa, Rigas Kappatos and Eleni Paidoussi

Pastoral ("In cold stiff soils the bleaters oft complain.") John Dyer. STuOW *Fr.* Fleece, The.

Pastoral ("Wild rove the flocks, no burdening fleece they bear.") John Dyer. STuOW *Fr.* Fleece, The.

Pastoral: "Ghosts of summer learn, The." George Garrett. InGu

Pastoral: "So soft in the hemlock wood." Robert Silliman Hillyer. MoAmPo

Pastoral: ""Lumpish trollop, the !"" Dominic Bevan Wyndham Lewis. UV

Pastoral: "Slopes of the sun and vine, and thou dark stream." George Cabot Lodge. APN-2

Pastoral: "Huge upon the hazy plain." Archibald MacLeish. GM

Pastoral: "We're passing the whole summer, all of us." Geoffrey Nutter. IAoNAP

Pastoral: "Dove walks with sticky feet, The." Kenneth Patchen. CLPP

Pastoral: "Annette came through the meadows." Henrietta Cordelia Ray. CBWP-3

Pastoral: "This is a place of ease." Marion Strobel. PoA 2002

Pastoral: "You see that forest on the height?" John Stuart Williams. TCAWP

Pastoral: "Little sparrows, The." William Carlos Williams. SAmP

Pastoral: "When I was younger." William Carlos Williams. APT-1; SAmP

Pastoral, A: "Mobile, immaculate and austere." Geoffrey Hill. NPeEn

Pastoral, A: "Sun looks o'er the mountain fair, The." F. V. N. (Franklin Verzelius Newton) Painter. ArBi

Pastoral, The: "Now the body is the body's flower." Charles North. NYP2

Pastoral Ballad by John Bull, A. Thomas Moore. OBSV

Pastoral Courtship, A. Thomas Randolph. BASC

Pastoral Dialogue. Anne Killigrew. LW

Pastoral Dialogue, A. Jonathan Swift. IrLP

Pastoral Eclogue upon the Death of Sir Philip Sidney Knight, A. Lodowick Bryskett. NoSic

Pastoral in Posters, A. Carolyn Wells. SWaP

Pastoral on the King's Death, The; [Written in 1648]. Alexander Brome. NOSC

Pastoral Poesy. John Clare. NAEL-7v2

Pastoral with Internet Porn. Jennifer L. Knox. FreRad

Pastorale. Michael Hofmann. HarvBoo

Pastorale for Spring. Al Zolynas. SUP

Pastries were awfully dry, The. What I Disliked About the Pleistocene Era. Patty Seyburn. LegDan

Pasture is best, freshly, A. How to Play Night Baseball. Jonathan Holden. MoASP

Pasture, The. Robert Frost. APT-1; BLPJKO; ItP; MoAmPo; NAAL-5; NAAPv.2; SAmP; TLR; TRP; WHSW

Pastures spewing infinite tiny bells. You pimp. (LL) Labor Day. Louise Glück. NIL-7; NoAM

Pat on the head, A. To an Angel in the House. John Sparrow. OBCoV

Pat Taffe and Arkle. Tracey Herd. MFPA

Pat your foot. Leadbelly Gives an Autograph. Imamu Amiri Baraka. PmAP

Patch of Old Snow, A. Robert Frost. WeW-3

Patch-Shaneen. John Millington Synge. FaBoVe

Patchwork-paneled the mitered heart remade. Quilt. Valerie Wohlfeld. SweBea

Pater Filio. Robert Bridges. OBEV

Paternity. Sydney Lea. PfSP

Paterson. William Carlos Williams.
    Delineaments of the Giants, The. NoAM
    "Edward/ Paterson has grown older." NoAM
    Episode 17. APT-1
    "It is dangerous to leave written that which is badly written." PFTM-2
    Paterson, Book V: The River of Heaven. HarvBoo; PoA 2002
    Preface. NoAM
    Preface. NAMCP V.1; NoAM
    Sunday in the Park. NoAM
    "Thought clambers up." NAMCP V.1

Paterson, Book V: The River of Heaven. William Carlos Williams. HarvBoo; PoA 2002 *Fr.* Paterson.

Paterson lies in the valley under the Passaic Falls. William Carlos Williams. NoAM *Fr.* Paterson.

Paterson: The Falls. William Carlos Williams. APT-1; ColAP

Paterson—the Strike. William Carlos Williams. TCAPo *Fr.* Wanderer, The: A Rococo Study.

Path, The. Konstantin Iakovlevich Vanshenkin. TCRusP, *tr. by* Daniel Weissbort

Path, The / down the slope. Trail, The. Myra Stillborn. ArBi

Path by which we twain did go, The. Alfred Tennyson. CAGL; NAEL-6v2; NAEL-7v2; NAWM-7v2 *Fr.* In Memoriam A. H. H.

Path formatted, A. A chapter. Textile 12. Marjorie Welish. VaPo

Path goes on and on, The. Brussels: Simple Frescos 2. Paul Verlaine. SxFrPo, *tr. by* Martin Sorrell

Path I'm following, The. Yury Pavlovich Odarchenko. TCRusP, *tr. by* Theodore Weiss

Path leads up to your house, and stops, The. Makpelah. Anna Hajnal. IQMS, *tr. by* Kenneth McRobbie

Path lies through Gethsemane, The. (LL) From Stone to Steel. Edwin John Pratt. BrAP; NoP-4; NoP-5

Path Marked with Breadcrumbs, A. Tony Lopez. Oth

Path, now paved, winds around the sea's edge, The. Marginal Way. Renée Gregorio. ICANM

Path of Affection, The. Laila 'Allush. PoArWo, *tr. by* Abdelwahab M. Elmessiri

Path of Independence, The. *Unknown*. TreFP

Path of the Ashtrees, The. Pei Di and Wang Wei. CCL1 *Fr.* Wheel River.

Path of the Just, The. John Henry, Cardinal Newman. SacPr

Path strewn with a sprinkling of red, A. Tune: "Treading on Fragrant Grass." Yen Shu. ColAnChi, *tr. by* Jiaosheng Wang

Path that Leads to Nowhere, The. Corinne Roosevelt Robinson. ITBLP

Path the stream scribbles, The. Sensualist Speaks on Faith, A. Dina Ben-Lev. AmPoNex

Path through a field of red flowers, A. Midday. Sŏ Chŏngju. CAMKP, *tr. by* David R. McCann

Path to Han-shan's place is laughable, The. Body Asking Shadow. Han-shan (Cold Mountain). BB; CCL1; NDACCP, *tr. by* Gary Snyder

Path to the Milky Way Leads Through Los Angeles, The. Joy Harjo. NAMCP V.2; StAl

Path to the simples, deep in red moss. Dedicated to the Hermit Cui. Ch'ien Ch'i. CCL1, *tr. by* Jerome P. Seaton

Path to the White Moon, The. John Ashbery. PtR

Path winds through secret peaks and valleys, The. At the Hermitage of Master Fu. Wang Wei. CrYelRi, *tr. by* Sam Hamill

Pathetic Lament, A. Eliza Cook. VerBaPo

Pathetic tale of the sea I will unfold, A. Tale of the Sea, A. William McGonagall.

Pathetic were their words, and well they aimed. Philip Freneau. NAAL-3 *Fr.* House of Night, The.

Pathogenesis. Philip Whalen. WANABP

Pathological Beings. David Huerta. RMCMP, *tr. by* Mark Schafer

Pathologist. Ellen Dudley. OPRER

Pathology literally speaking is a flower garden. William Carlos Williams. TCAPo *Fr.* Kora in Hell.

Pathology of Colours. Dannie Abse. BloBone; NIP-4; NoAM; TCAWP

Pathology of Proximity, The. Mark Bibbins. AmPoNex

Paths of Light. Amina Saïd. YaTCFP, *tr. by* Mary Ann Caws *and* Jean-Pierre Cauvin

Paths of the Mirror. Alejandra Pizarnik. PFTM-2, *tr. by* Jason Weiss

Pathway of light! o'er thy empurpled zone. Sonnet 6. To the Torrid Zone. Helen Maria Williams. CenSon; NOBRP

Pathway of the sinking moon, The. On the Sea. Bayard Taylor. TreFP

Patience. Elaine Feinstein. MoWP

Patience. William Schwenck Gilbert.
Bunthorne's Song. CABP
If You're Anxious for to Shine in the High Aesthetic Line. NAEL-6v2; NAEL-7v2; NBLV
Patience. Kay Ryan. EMP
Patience. *Unknown.*
Jonah and the Whale. NPeEn
Patience: "Patience is the wideness of the night." Phyllis Webb. BrAP
Patience des anges endormis entre les caissons bleus du ciel. Mise au monde, La. Jean-Michel Maulpoix. YaTCFP
Patience is the wideness of the night. Patience. Phyllis Webb. BrAP
Patience is / wider than one. Patience. Kay Ryan. EMP
Patience of angels sleeping amid the sky's blue casings. Giving Birth, The. Jean-Michel Maulpoix. YaTCFP, *tr. by* Mark Polizzoti
Patience of the lambs was exhausted, The. Sacred Wrath. Vahan Tekeyan. GI
Patience, Though I Have Not. Sir Thomas Wyatt. NoP-4; NoP-5
Patience to love like boards, The. (LL) Still without Life. Rosalie Moore. CalPo; YaYoPo
Patient is a twelve-year-old white female, The. Rafael Campo. WiU *Fr.* Ten Patients, and Another.
Patient Joe; or, The Newcastle Collier. Hannah More. WoRP
Patient Pan, The. Ralph Waldo Emerson. APN-1
Patient, The. Mary Karr. PoA 2002
Patio. Jorge Luis Borges. TCLAP, *tr. by* Robert Fitzgerald
Patio. Manuel A. Viray. ReBoTo
Patmos. Friedrich Hölderlin. OBVE; WoPoe, *tr. by* David Gascoyne
Patois. Marianne Vitale. HeMarv
Patriarch, The. Robert Burns. ChIV-1
Patriarch Peaks. Muso Soseki. EaWin, *tr. by* W. S. Merwin
Patriarch wrestled with the angel long, The. Jacob Wrestling with the Angel. Jones Very. ChIV-1
Patrician Peacocks and the Overweening Jay, The. Guy Wetmore Carryl. TCAPo
Patriot, A: Blois, Early Summer 1792. William Wordsworth. NPBRoP *Fr.* Prelude, The; Growth of a Poet's Mind [1805 version].
Patriot, The. Nissim Ezekiel. EmeKit; FaBoVe
Patriotic Songs. Yehuda Amichai.
"Even my loves are measured by wars." PoSu
"I have nothing to say about the war." PoSu
"Let the memorial hill remember, instead of me." PoSu
"Town I was born in was destroyed by shells, The." PoSu
"War broke out in autumn at the empty border, The." PoSu
Patriotic turns to face, The. Question of Covenants, A. Gerald Dawe. PNI
Patriotics. David Baker. LiTh
Patriotism. Sir Walter Scott. OxAEP-2
Patriots' Day. Richard Wilbur. ItP
Patriot's Progress, The. Horace Twiss. UV
Patroclus Fights and Dies. Homer. NAWM-7v1 *Fr.* Iliad, The.
Patroclus Spears Thestor. Homer. OBVE *Fr.* Iliad, The.
Patrolling Barnegat. Walt Whitman. APN-1
Patron of all those who do good by stealth. December: Prayer to St. Nicholas. John Heath-Stubbs. OBCP
Patron of verse, O *Halifax*, attend. To the Right Honourable Charles Lord Halifax [one of the Lords Justices appointed by his Majesty]. Ambrose Philips.
Patsy Cline. Richard Speakes. SwNoth
Patterdale. Isabella Lickbarrow. RWP
Pattern, The. Michael Longley. BeAl
Pattern, The. Paula Meehan. ModIr
Pattern is only ever of animal success, The. Museum. Joe Wenderoth. BodElec
Pattern[e] of your love, A. (LL) Canonization, The. John Donne. BASC; BrAP; CABP; FaBoVe; FSCP; NAEL-6v1; NAEL-7v1; NAWM-5v1; NIL-7; NIP-4; NoP-4; NoP-5; NOSC; NPeEn; PBRV; PoPoPo; SoSe-8; TFi; TRP; WaAnP; WoPoe
Patterned cloud of feathers stands attentive, A. Meditation on the Great Blue Heron. Kay Murphy. RWB
Patterned Lute, The. Li Shang-yin. CCL1, *tr. by* A. C. Graham
Patterns. Amy Lowell. AmFaPo; AmWaPo; APT-1; MoAmPo; NoP-4; NoP-5; WHSW
Patterns. Roberta Hill Whiteman. HATNAP
Patterns. Judith Wright. HarvBoo *Fr.* Shadow of Fire: Ghazals, The.
Patting goodbye, doubtless they told the lad. S.I.W. Wilfred Owen. NAMCP V.1
Patton. Lincoln Kirstein. PWW2
Patty cake, patty cake / bake me a man. Cornbread Blues. Vincent Woodward. BtF

Patty: Hi, Mom! I'm home! / Cathy: From the beginning, I. Double Trouble. David Trinidad. PmAP; SUP
Patty-cake, patty-cake. It Never Rains. Anthony Hecht. AmWit
Patty-cake, patty-cake / Marcus Antonius. Tact. Paul Pascal. WeW-3
Paul Butterfield, Dead at 44. Robert Gibb. SwNoth
Paul Celan: A Grave and Mysterious Sentence. Edward Hirsch. TaR
Paul Claudel. Nakano Shigeharu. CAoMJL1, *tr. by* Miriam Silverberg
Paul Claudel was a poet. Paul Claudel. Nakano Shigeharu. CAoMJL1, *tr. by* Miriam Silverberg
Paul comes from Toronto on Sunday. I Am Not a Conspiracy Everything Is Not Paranoid the Drug Enforcement Administration Is Not Everywhere. Susan Musgrave. NIL-7; NoAM
Paul Dempster had a handsome tackle box. Curse on a Thief, A. X. J. Kennedy. RaF
Paul Eluard. Anne Waldman. AHA
Paul Faber, Surgeon. George Macdonald.
That Holy Thing. OBEV
That Holy Thing. SacPr
Paul Laurence Dunbar [*for Herbert Martin*]. Robert Earl Hayden. ESEAA; GT; InoFa; NoP-4; NoP-5
Paul Laurence Dunbar. Mrs. Henry Linden. CBWP-4
Paul Laurence Dunbar in The Tenderloin. Ishmael Reed. EGAG; ESEAA
Paul Revere Speaks. Myra Cohn Livingston. HHAm
Paul Revere's Ride [The Landlord's Tale]. Henry Wadsworth Longfellow. AmWaPo; BLPJKO; BRP; ChAP; ColAP; HHAm; ITBLP; NAAPv.1; NOxBChV; OBNV; OxBoAm; TCAPo; TFi; WaAnP *Fr.* Tales of a Wayside Inn.
Paul set the bags down, told how they had split. Venison. Karen Chase. NIL-7
Paul Verlaine at the Grave of Lucien Létinois. Bin Ramke. OPRER
Paul / when the leaves. Lorine Niedecker. APT-2
Paula Becker to Clara Westhoff. Adrienne Rich. VCAP
Paula of the trembling brown cheeks and silent tears. For Paula Cooper. Jackie Warren-Moore. SpirFl
Pauline. Felicia Dorothea Hemans. RWP
Pauline, mine own, bend o'er me—thy soft breast. Pauline [*or* Pauline; A Fragment of a Confession]. Robert Browning.
Pauline [*or* Pauline; A Fragment of a Confession]. Robert Browning.
"O God, where do they tend—these struggling aims?" SacPr
Paulo and Francesca. Leigh Hunt. NPBRoP *Fr.* Story of Rimini, The.
Paulownia leaf that gently falls, rippling the windless air—whose footprint is it?, The. I Cannot Know. Han Yong'un [*or* Yongwun]. CAMKP, *tr. by* Sammy Solberg
Pause. Eamon Grennan. NIL-7
Pause. Octavio Paz. STV, *tr. by* John Frederick Nims
Pause, A. Christina Georgina Rossetti. VWP
Pause of Joe, The. Imamu Amiri Baraka. FTOS
Pause of sorrow hangs upon the world, A. Reflections on the Death of Louis XVI. Ann Yearsley. RWP
Pause, Pause. Kevin Prufer. PoDa
Pause stranger at the porch: nothing beyond. Gateway to the Sea—St. Andrews. George Bruce. EdScPo
Pauses to sing. (LL) Such a moon. Buson. WoPoe; ZenPo, *tr. by* Takashi Ikemoto and Lucien Stryk
Pausing at the edge of the wood. Cassandra and Friend. Norman Henry, II Pritchard. GT
Pauve piti Lolotte a mouin. Lolotte. *Unknown.* SSUS
Pavane. Ronald Stuart Thomas. HarvBoo
Pavane for the Nursery, A. William Jay Smith. MoAmPo
Pavane on Mr Wray's Locations, A. Tony Baker. Oth
Pavement here was feverish today, The. Eviction Fight. N. D. Korman. Prolet, *tr. by* Amelia Glaser
Pavement slippery, people sneezing. January, 1795. Mary Robinson. NAEL-7v2; NPBRoP; OxBEV; WoRP
Pavese Said Death Will Come Bearing Your Eyes. Erica Bernheim. LegDan
Pavilion. Elsa Cross. RMCMP, *tr. by* Margaret Sayers Peden
Pavilion for Listening to Fragrance, The. Chang Yü. WoPoe, *tr. by* Jonathan Chaves
Pavilion on the Pier, The. Byron Vazakas. APT-2
Pavlovsk. Anna Andreyevna Akhmatova. RusPo, *tr. by* Robert Arthur Douglas Ford
Pawiak 1943. Jerzy Ficowski. PoSu, *tr. by* Frank J. Corliss, Jr. and Grazyna Sandel
Pawing us who dealt them war and madness. (LL) Mental Cases. Wilfred Owen. NAMCP V.1; NoAM
Pawkie Duke, The. David Rorie. EdScPo
Pawnee War-Song. *Unknown.* APN-2, *tr. by* Daniel Garrison Brinton
Pawnshop, The. Chu Hsiang. WoPoe, *tr. by* Kai-yu Hsu

Pax. D. H. Lawrence. PLBUT

Pay attention now. Antonio Machado Ruiz. WED *Fr.* Moral Proverbs and Folk Songs.

Pay Cash Only. James Sherry. FTOS

Pay close attention: the world that appears now. Lesson in Observation, A. Dan Pagis. AF, *tr. by* Stephen Mitchell

Pay Up or Else. Luci Tapahonso. ReTh

Pay Your Debts. Mrs. Henry Linden. CBWP-4

3. Paying Respects. Mary Stewart Hammond. InoFa *Fr.* Blessings.

Payre: a metrical tag. Throwing Out at / of (Com)pare (Dis)pair, A. Tina Darragh. ChAP

Pays où les écriteaux ont des ongles, Un. Soleilland. Edmond Jabès. YaTCFP

Pays reçu au plus creux du sommeil. Terre originelle. Anne Hébert. YaTCFP

Paysage Moralisé. W. H. Auden. HarvBoo; MoBrPo

Paysage Moralisé. Stephen Burt. LegDan

Paysagesque. Norman Henry, II Pritchard. GT

P.C., X, 36. Max Beerbohm. UV

Peace. Jonetta Barras. ISC

Peace. Ella Bat-Tzion. PoCho, *tr. by* Moshe Dor and Barbara Goldberg

Peace. Rupert Brooke. NPeEn; OBWP; PoA 2002

Peace. John Gower. SacPr *Fr.* Address to the King, An.

Peace. George Herbert. NOSC; TreFP

Peace. Samuel Speed. SacPr

Peace. Tibullus. PBCIP; PNI, *tr. by* Michael Longley

Peace. Henry Vaughan. FSCP; OBEV; OxAEP-1; OxBEV; RSR; TFi; WeW-3

Peace #3. Alma Villanueva. FFC

Peace and Mercy and Jonathan. First Thanksgiving of All. Nancy Byrd Turner. ChAP

Peace, and this cot, and thee, heart-hono[u]red [*or* heart-honour'd] Maid! (LL) Samuel Taylor Coleridge. NAEL-6v2; NAEL-7v2; NOBRP; NoP-4; NoP-5; NPBRoP; NPeEn *Fr.* Effusions.

Peace? and to all the world? sure, one. Nativity, The. Henry Vaughan. ChrPo

Peace and War. Rowland Watkyns. AngWePo

Peace Be Still. Esther Iverem. BtF

Peace be with you! Savage mountain roads don't seem to retard you. Eighth Eclogue. Miklós Radnóti. IQMS, *tr. by* Peter Zollman

Peace; come away: the song of woe. Alfred Tennyson. NAEL-6v2; NAEL-7v2 *Fr.* In Memoriam A. H. H.

Peace Corps Volunteer Comes Home, The. Carolyne Wright. RoV

Peace Discovers the Poet. George Chapman. NOSC *Fr.* Tears of Peace, The or Euthymia Raptus.

Peace has surely come by now to heal it completely. On a Visit. Alun Llywelyn-Williams. BBMWP, *tr. by* Joseph P. Clancy

Peace, Horror. Miklós Radnóti. AF, *tr. by* Emery E. George

Peace in thy hands / Peace in thine eyes. Ghost, The. Walter De la Mare. MoBrPo

Peace is a sea. Peace. Ella Bat-Tzion. PoCho, *tr. by* Moshe Dor and Barbara Goldberg

Peace is declared, an' I return. Return, The. Rudyard Kipling. MoBrPo

Peace is like salt which seasons all our meat. Peace and War. Rowland Watkyns. AngWePo

Peace is the next in order, first in end. Fulke, 1st Baron Brooke Greville. NOSC *Fr.* Treatise of Monarchy, A.

Peace. Let men, who cannot be brothers. Wendell Berry. UpMys *Fr.* Window Poems.

Peace, my heart's blab! Be ever dumb:. Silence: A Sonnet. Henry King, Bishop of Chichester. NOSC

Peace of Death, The. George Chapman. NOSC *Fr.* Tears of Peace, The or Euthymia Raptus.

Peace of great doors be for you, The. For You. Carl Sandburg. MoAmPo

Peace of Lodi, The. Norman Dubie. BodElec

Peace of Wild Things, The. Wendell Berry. BeAl; GoPo; InGu; IPoFL; PLBUT

Peace on Earth. No Hyegyông. EcSo, *tr. by* Ann Y. Choi

Peace! Peace! God of our fathers grant us Peace! Prayer for Peace, A. Severn Teackle Wallis. CBCWP

Peace, peace, my hony [*or* honey], do not cry. Edward Taylor. NAAL-3 *Fr.* God's Determinations [touching his Elect].

Peace Plan: Meditation on the 9 Stages of "Peacemaking" as Tribute to Senator Claiborne Pell: 1997. Michael S. Harper. PuP-23

Peace, Rain, Plenty. *Unknown.* SonAtl, *tr. by* Alan Brierly

Peace, Shepherd, peace! What boots it singing on? Genius Loci. Margaret Louisa Woods. OBEV

Peace, So That. Greg Kuzma. AmWaPo

Peace Studies. Lynne McMahon. ExTi

Peace that hallows rudest ways. (LL) Forerunners. Ralph Waldo Emerson. APN-1; OBEV

Peace the End of the Good Man. Robert Blair. OxAEP-1 *Fr.* Grave, The.

Peace to all living things. One of the Lords of Life. David J. Rothman. GeoH

Peace to all such! but were there one whose fires. Alexander Pope. OxBEV; TRP *Fr.* Epistle to Dr. Arbuthnot.

Peace to all such! but were there one whose fires. Alexander Pope. NPeEn *Fr.* Epistle to Dr. Arbuthnot.

Peace to each swain, who rural rapture owns. George, the Younger Colman. OBGa *Fr.* London Rurality.

Peace to Lord Hamlet, I have never heard. Grave Doubts. Patricia Beer. NoP-4

Peace to the odalisque, the facile slave. Emily Jane Pfeiffer. VWP
   "Peace to the odalisque, whose morning glory." ViWPN

Peace to these little broken leaves. Leaves. W. H. Davies. MoBrPo

Peace to this awful dome!—when straight I heard. Philip Freneau. NAAL-3 *Fr.* House of Night, The.

"Peace upon earth!" was said. We sing it. Christmas: 1924. Thomas Hardy. OBCP

Peace with Honor. Philip Appleman. AmWaPo

Peace, you ungracious clamours! peace, rude sounds! William Shakespeare. OxAEP-1 *Fr.* Troilus and Cressida.

Peaceable Kingdom. Barbara Leslie Jordan. ExTi

Peaceful eyes my only wealth. Paul Verlaine. SxFrPo, *tr. by* Martin Sorrell

Peaceful Life. Dainin Katagiri. WhBo

Peaceful Our Valley, Fair and Green. Dorothy Wordsworth. NALW
   (Cottage in Grasmere Vale, A.) NPBRoP
   (Grasmere—a Fragment.) NAEL-7v2; PEW

Peaceful Sentiment. Judy Kronenfeld. RWB

Peaceful Shepherd, The. Robert Frost. MoAmPo

Peaceful Sunday. Charlotte Gardelle. CuPo

Peacefull, and young, Herculean silence bore. George Chapman. NOSC *Fr.* Tears of Peace, The or Euthymia Raptus.

Peacefully upon its plantlike stem. (LL) Flowers by the Sea ("When over the flowery, sharp pasture's.") William Carlos Williams. APT-1; MoAmPo; NAMCP V.1; NoAM

Peacetime. Peter McDonald. ModIr

Peacetime. Tom Paulin. FaBoWar

Peach. Lance Larsen. AmPoNex

Peach. Shen Yüeh. CCL1, *tr. by* Anne Birrell

Peach and plum I planted were my own, The. Tu Fu [*or* Du Fu]. CrYelRi *Fr.* Random Pleasures.

Peach Blossom and Pigeon (painting by Kiso). Takahashi Shinkichi. ZenPo, *tr. by* Takashi Ikemoto and Lucien Stryk

Peach Blossom Spring, The ("Ying clan disrupted Heaven's ordinance, The.") T'ao Ch'ien. CCL1, *tr. by* James Robert Hightower

Peach Blossom Stream. Chou Pang-yen. CrYelRi, *tr. by* Sam Hamill

Peach Blossoms. Yüan Chên. CrYelRi, *tr. by* Sam Hamill

Peach blossoms are red, willow catkins white. Spring Day. Yu Chien-wu. ColAnChi, *tr. by* Victor H. Mair and Tsu-Lin Mei

Peach flowers turn the dew crimson. Dawn on the Mountain. Wang Wei. NDACCP, *tr. by* Ezra Pound

Peach, The. Takahashi Shinkichi. ZenPo, *tr. by* Takashi Ikemoto and Lucien Stryk

Peachblossom is redded because rain fell overnight, The. Morning. Wang Wei. TAL

Peach-Blossom Spring ("Ch'in's First Emperor ravaged the sense.") T'ao Ch'ien. NDACCP, *tr. by* David Hinton

Peaches. Siv Cedering Fox. PBCAP

Peaches. Donald Hall. BeAl; NoP-4; NoP-5

Peaches. Paul Muldoon and Gerald Stern. GPPA

Peaches and Cream. Mudrooroo Narogin. BMAP

Peaches: "In the only moment of ecstasy I have." Anne-Marie Oomen. NevBe

Peachstone. Dannie Abse. AngWePo; WeW-3

Peachtree, The. Denise Levertov. TaR

Peacock Display. David Wagoner. OWoS

Peacock of Motherhood, The. Anna Jackson. BeAl

Peacock Southeast Flew, A. *Unknown.* ColAnChi, *tr. by* Anne Birrell

Peacock southeast flew, A. Peacock Southeast Flew, A. *Unknown.* ColAnChi, *tr. by* Anne Birrell

Peacock takes its perch upon the county hall, A. Peacock Takes Its Perch, A. Endre Ady. IQMS, *tr. by* Sir Maurice Bowra

Peacock, The. James Merrill. OWoS

1 The Peacock. Conor O'Callaghan. NIrP *Fr.* Loose Change.

Peacock's Eye, The. Gerard Manley Hopkins. OWoS

Peacocks' radiance, The. Unicorn, The. Gertrud Kolmar. GTCP, *tr. by* Henry A. Smith

Peak, and not yet the baseline of the human.. (LL) Easter 1984. Les A. Murray. ChIV-2; UpMys

Peak of the Held-Up Flower, The. Muso Soseki. EaWin, *tr. by* W. S. Merwin

Peaks gather. Tune: "Sheep on the Mountain Slope." Chang Yang-hao. ChinPo, *tr. by* Ye Weilian [*or* Yeh Wei-lien *or* Wai-lim Yip]

Pealing, The. Olga Broumas. BodElec

Peanut Sat on a Railroad Track, A. *Unknown.* TLR

Pear. Susan Stewart. AmAlph

Pear Leaves Redden, Cicada's Song is Done, The. Ou-yang Hsiu. GifTon, *tr. by* Jerome P. Seaton

Pear Tree. "H. D." ColAP; MoAmPo; PtR; TCAPo

Pear Tree, The. Edna St. Vincent Millay. MoAmPo

Pear tree a siamese cat named cooper and me, The. Roy Kiyooka. NLPA *Fr.* Pear Tree Pomes.

Pear Tree Pomes. Roy Kiyooka. NLPA

Pear tree that last year, The. Shimmer. James Schuyler. NoP-5; VCAP

Pear tree's white blossoms tincture the night air, The. Roy Kiyooka. NLPA *Fr.* Pear Tree Pomes.

Pearl. Irène Hamoir. SurWo, *tr. by* Myrna Bell Rochester

Pearl. Barry MacSweeney.
    Pearl Alone. Oth
    Pearl Says. Oth
    Shells Her Auburn Hair Did Show, The. Oth

Pearl Alone. Barry MacSweeney. Oth *Fr.* Pearl.

Pearl Avenue runs past the high-school lot. Ex-Basketball Player. John Updike. TRP

Pearl blooms ring kingfisher plumes. Her Tiara Flowers. Shen Manyuan. CCL1, *tr. by* Anne Birrell

Pearl Harbor. Robinson Jeffers. PWW2

Pearl of the White Breast. *Irish Oral Tradition.* IrV, *tr. by* George Petrie

Pearl or Perle. *Unknown.*
    "Pearl, the precious prize of a king." NoP-4; NoP-5, *tr. by* Sara DeFord
    "Perle, plesaunte to prynces paye." NoP-4; NoP-5

Pearl Says. Barry MacSweeney. Oth *Fr.* Pearl.

Pearl, The. Matth. 13:45. George Herbert. BASC; ChIV-2; FSCP; NOSC; OxBEV

Pearl, the precious prize of a king. *Unknown.* NoP-4; NoP-5 *Fr.* Pearl or Perle.

Pearle's Poem. Primus St. John. GT

Pearlmother dawn. It is fairly true. Abhorring a Vacuum. Chris Wallace-Crabbe. BMAP

Pearls. Janet Fisher. MFPA

Pearls. Alan Gould. NOBAu

Pearls. Lee Ann Roripaugh. AmPoNex

Pearls. Léopold Sédar Senghor. VCWP, *tr. by* Melvin Dixon

Pearl-teardrops roll and gather. Huang E. ColAnChi, *tr. by* Jonathan Chaves

Pears are green as new jade, The. Servant Boy Delivers, The. Tu Fu [*or* Du Fu]. CrYelRi, *tr. by* Sam Hamill

Pear's Complaint. Greg Youmans. FTtHH

Peas. *Unknown.* NTCP

Peasant, A. Ronald Stuart Thomas. AngWePo; OBWVE; OxBEV

Peasant, The. Vladimir Uflyand. TCRusP, *tr. by* Daniel Weissbort

Peasant Girl of the Rhone, The. Felicia Dorothea Hemans. RWP

Peasant Poet, The. John Clare. WaAnP

Peasant Who Saw God, The. Abraham Sutskever. MotU, *tr. by* Ruth R. Wisse

Peasants. Syl Cheney-Coker. NAfrP

Peasants, The. Alun Lewis. OxBEV; PoWW; TCAWP

Peasant's child, The. Basho. EH, *tr. by* Robert Hass

Peasants Waiting for Rain. G. S. Sharat Chandra. PoA 2002

Peasants watch them die, The. (LL) Peasants, The. Alun Lewis. OxBEV; PoWW; TCAWP

Peau de Chagrin of State Street, The. Oliver Wendell Holmes. TCAPo

Pebble, The. Zbigniew Herbert. AmFaPo; PoetW, *tr. by* Czeslaw Milosz and Peter Dale Scott

Pebble, The. Elinor Wylie. ChIV-1; MoAmPo

Pebble ripples the lake, A. By Water Divined. Kathleen West. GifTon

Pebble swells to a boulder at low speed, A. Electronic Sound. May Swenson. APT-2

Pebbles. Herman Melville. NCAP

Pecan, The Toucan, The. Robert Williams Wood. NBLV

Pecans. Paul Foreman. TiP2

Peces de piel fugaz. Coral Bracho. RMCMP

Pêche Lunaire. Greta Knutson. YaTCFP

Pecking by ones or twos the rainbowed gutter. (LL) First Early Mornings Together. Robert Pinsky. ColAP; WaAnP

Pecos Bill in Decline. Stephen Harrigan. TiP2

Pedagogy. Lin Max. MiVo

Pedaling Paranoia. Jane Mayes. ArBi

Pedalling Man, The. Russell Hoban. NOxBChV

Pedestrian. George Oppen. NAMCP V.1

Pediatrics. Carol Muske-Dukes. PBCAP

Pedigree of Honey, The [vers. 2]. Emily Dickinson. SAmP

Pedlar. *Unknown.* OBVE *Fr.* Wei Wind.

Pedlar, The. Charlotte Mew. NOxBChV

Pedlar's Song, The. William Shakespeare. *See* When Daffodils Begin to Peer.

Pedro's mother greets us on the street. Monday Night at Pedro's. Sandra M. Castillo. TouFir

Peeking in through. Praxilla. ErotSp, *tr. by* Sam Hamill

Peeking into the cauldron of phenomena. Cauldron, The. David Huerta. RMCMP, *tr. by* Mark Schafer

Peeking over the horizon of day. Pretty White Girls. James E. Cherry. BtF

Peel back the squirming tentacles. Gutting. Joe Denham. OpeFie

Peel Me a Grape. Dave Frishberg. ReLy

Peel me a grape, crush me some ice. Peel Me a Grape. Dave Frishberg. ReLy

Peeled pencil, choke. Gertrude Stein. NAMCP V.1 *Fr.* Tender Buttons.

Peeling an apple somewhere far away. (LL) Primer of the Daily Round, A. Howard Nemerov. GoPo; NoP-4; NoP-5; WeW-3

Peeling Pippins. Mary Tallmountain. HATNAP

Peeling the Orange. Mary Ruefle. AmAlph

Peepers. Howard Nelson. MiVo

Peeping Tom Tom Girl. Marisela Norte. GeoHom

Peerage. Stephanie Williams. AnSo

Peering and peering, but I can't even see the sky. (LL) In the Mountains. Han-shan (Cold Mountain). CCL1; NDACCP, *tr. by* Gary Snyder

Peering coyly, i said. Centennial Year for the Spirits. Sister Elizabeth Hope Goodwin. FTtHH

Peering, in depth. Backgrounds Observed. Jean Earle. TCAWP

Peerless handcuffs. Protective and Defensive Devices. Mark Pawlak. PrTe

Peerless Lady, The. Wang Wei. NDACCP, *tr. by* William Carlos Williams

Peewits quiffed like Elvis reel from rocks. Incomplete History of Rock Music in the Hebrides, An. Donald S. Murray. EdScPo

Peg O' My Heart. Alfred Bryan. NAAPv.2

Pegasus Lost. Elinor Wylie. MoAmPo

Pegasus the Winged Horse. Alan Robert Wilson. Coast

Peggy. Allan Ramsay. OBEV

Peggy Browne. Turlough Carolan. OxBEV, *tr. by* Austin Clarke

Peggy Everett, my first girlfriend, explains. Single Urge, The. Baron Wormser. NevBe

Pelican, The. Adelia Prado. TCLAP, *tr. by* Marcia Kirinus

Pelican Chorus, The. Edward Lear. OBSP

Pelicans. Robinson Jeffers. MoAmPo

Pelicans. Judith Wright. BMAP; OWoS

Pelleas and Ettarre. Alfred Tennyson. NAEL-6v2 *Fr.* Idylls of the King.

Pelleas and Melisande. Newman Levy. AmWit

Peloria the dog's upper lip kept curling. Charles Olson. PFTM-2

Pembrokeshire Buzzards. Tony Curtis. TCAWP

Pen, The. Muhammad Al-Ghuzzi. NAfrP, *tr. by* John Heath-Stubbs and May Jayyusi

Pen, The. Mary Weston Fordham. CBWP-2

Pen, The. Galway Kinnell. BodElec

Pen, The. Solomon ibn Gabirol. WoPoe, *tr. by* Peter Cole

Pen, The. Jean Valentine. BodElec

Pen filled with ink dark. Blood. Lucien Stryk. BodElec

Pen is an index finger, The. Castration of the Pen. Erica Jong. NALW

Pen slides, The. Valerio Magrelli. NeIt

Pen Vine and Scroll. John Taggart. FTOS

Penal Law. Austin Clarke. ModIr; OxBEV

Penalty for Bigamy Is Two Wives, The. William Matthews. SwNoth

Penalty of Love, The. Sidney Royce Lysaght. IrV

Penance. Sherman Alexie. MoASP

Penance, A. Francis Daniel Pastorius. NOSC

Penance and the Work Week. Gaylord Brewer. Vesp

Penché contre un grand fleuve, infiniment mes rames. Rameur, Le. Paul Valéry. YaTCFP

Pencil's Sleep, The. Tymoteusz Karpowicz. PoSu

Péndulos de hilo. Casa de Olga, La. Natalia Toledo. RMCMP

Pendulum, The. Norman Dubie. AmAlph

Pendulum, The. Árpád Tóth. IQMS, *tr. by* Watson Kirkconnell

Penelope. James Harrison. NIP-4

Penelope. Dorothy Parker. FaBoWar; PoAgWa

Penelope as a *garçon manqué*. Mythology. Marilyn Hacker. NoAM; ReTh

Penelope for her *Ulisses* sake. Edmund Spenser. NoP-4; PBRV

Penelope, for her Ulisses sake. Edmund Spenser. NoP-5 *Fr.* Amoretti.

Penelope pulls home. Kiltartan Legend. Padraic Fallon. ModIr

Penelope, the screaming is all over. Irina Ratushinskaya. CRWP, *tr.* by Alan Myers

Penelope, who really cried. (LL) Ancient Gesture, An. Edna St. Vincent Millay. NALW; NIL-7

Penelope's Song. Louise Glück. NAMCP V.2

Penetrates space. (LL) Rose, The ("Rose is obsolete, The.") William Carlos Williams. APT-1; NAAPv.2; OxBoAm

Penetration. Michael Field. VWP

P'eng-li commands three rivers. Sailing into the South Lake. Chan Fang-sheng. ChinPo, *tr.* by Ye Weilian [*or* Yeh Wei-lien *or* Wai-lim Yip]

Penguin Jane Austen, The. Debora Greger. OWoS

Pen-guin. The Sword-fish, The. Robert Williams Wood. NBLV

Penguins. Artur Miedzyrzecki. PoSu, *tr.* by John Batki and Artur Miedzyrzecki

Penguins. Stefan Tsanev. CSCBP, *tr.* by Georgi Belev and Lisa Sapinkopf

P'eng-ya Road. Tu Fu [*or* Du Fu]. CrYelRi, *tr.* by Sam Hamill

P'eng-Ya Song. Tu Fu [*or* Du Fu]. NDACCP, *tr.* by David Hinton

Peninsula. Jenny Mueller. IAoNAP

Peninsula church, A. October's last Sunday. Within. Philip Booth. PoCoUp

Peninsula, The. Seamus Heaney. HarvBoo

Penis is the ultimate attachment: body's gimmick, A. All Suffering Comes from Attachment. Ron Koertge. SUP

Penis, The. Dafydd ap Gwilym. EroLit; WoPoe, *tr.* by Dafydd Johnston

Penitence. John Burnside. StAl

Penitent Considers Another Coming of Mary, A. Gwendolyn Brooks. NoAM

Penitent, The. Anne Brontë. SacPr

Penitential Cries of Jupiter Hammond, The. Gary Smith. GT

Penitential Psalms. Sir Thomas Wyatt.
　Prologue. ChIV-1

Penn Central Station at Beacon, N.Y, The. Ed Ochester. GM

Pennies from Heaven. Johnny Burke. ReLy

Pennies in a stream. Moonlight in Vermont. John Blackburn and Karl Suessdorf. ReLy

Penniless Lovers. Eugenio de Andrade. VCWP, *tr.* by Alexis Levitin

Pennsylvania Deutsch. Christopher Darlington Morley. NBLV

Pennsylvania Station in New York, The. Pennsylvania Station. Langston Hughes. GM

Pennsylvania to the coast of Ecuador, my mother calling her aunt. Long Distance. Maurice Kilwein Guevara. TouFir

Penny. *Unknown.* FaBoVe

Penny Ballad of Elvious Ricks. R. G. Vliet. TiP2

Penny Men. Rigoberto González. GeoHom

Penny Toys. John Mole.
　Musical Monkey, The. OBCoV
　Song of the Hat-Raising Doll. OBCoV

Penny Whistle, The. Edward Thomas. MoBrPo

Pennycandystore beyond the El, The. Lawrence Ferlinghetti. HeIP-4

Penobscot. George Oppen. HarvBoo

Penological Study: Southern Exposure. Robert Penn Warren.
　Wet Hair: If Now His Mother Should Come. NoAM

Pense au beateau qui s'éloigne du quai, qui se sépare lentement de la terre. Valérie-Catherine Richez. YaTCFP *Fr.* Petite âme.

Pensées sous les nuages. Philippe Jaccottet. YaTCFP

Penserosa, La. Gig Ryan. VaPo

Pensive at eve on the hard world I mus'd [*or* mused]. Samuel Taylor Coleridge. CenSon *Fr.* Sonnets Attempted in the Manner of Contemporary Writers.

Pensive gnu, the staid aardvark, The. For an Amorous Lady. Theodore Roethke. NBLV

Pensive, how parochial. Essence. Judson Crews. ICANM

Pentacl. Bill Lavender.
　22. AnSo
　25. AnSo

Pentecost. Gerrit Achterberg. TuT, *tr.* by Dennis O'Driscoll

Pentecost. Martha Collins. Vesp

Pentecost. David Craig. UpMys

Pentecost. Gwyneth Lewis. MFPA; NeBrP

Pentecost Castle, The. Félix Lope de Vega Carpio. HarvBoo, *tr.* by Geoffrey Hill
　"And you my spent heart's treasure." OxBEV; WoPoe, *tr.* by Geoffrey Hill
　"Down in the orchard." WoPoe, *tr.* by Geoffrey Hill
　"Splendidly-shining darkness." WoPoe, *tr.* by Geoffrey Hill
　"They slew by night." WoPoe, *tr.* by Geoffrey Hill

Pentecost: "Neither the sorrows of afternoon, waiting in the silent house." Dana Gioia. PoDa; Vesp

Pentecostal flames. Parnassus Rising. James Richardson. RD

Pentelogia. Francis Quarles.
　"What is the *World?* A great *Exchange* of ware." PBRV

Penumbra es el camino, El. Arca del día, El. Dana Gelinas. SPV

Penumbra is the way, The. Ark of Day, The. Dana Gelinas. SPV, *tr.* by Jen Hofer

Penyberth. Gwynn Ap Gwilym. BBMWP, *tr.* by Joseph P. Clancy

Poem Written under an Archway in a Discontinued Railroad Station, Fargo, North Dakota, A. James Wright. GM

Peona! ever have I long'd to slake. John Keats. NAEL-6v2; NAEL-7v2 *Fr.* Endymion: A Poetic Romance.

Peonage System, The. Lizelia Augusta Jenkins Moorer. CBWP-3

Peonies. Harry Edmund Martinson. WoPoe, *tr.* by Leif Sjöberg and William Jay Smith

Peonies. Mark Wunderlich. PoDa

Peonies are heavy with dew, The. To the Tune: Beautiful Barbarian. *Unknown.* CrYelRi, *tr.* by Sam Hamill

Peonies at Dusk. Jane Kenyon. LoL

Peonies hold so much rain, they've collapsed, The. Peonies, The. Susan Goyette. Coast

Peonies scattering. Buson. EH, *tr.* by Robert Hass

Peonies, The. Susan Goyette. Coast

Peonies / The strange pink colour of Chinese porcelains. Afterglow. Amy Lowell. NAAPv.2

Peonies: "Young girls walk by looking like wedding, The." Susan Firer. SweBea

Peony Afternoon. Sŏ Chŏngju. VCWP, *tr.* by David R. McCann

Peony and a Lion, A. Ani Ilkov. CSCBP, *tr.* by Georgi Belev and Lisa Sapinkopf

Peony in my hair. Dancing Girl, The. Yosano Akiko. CAoMJL1, *tr.* by Janine Beichman

Peony Lover. Lee Ann Roripaugh. AmPoNex

Peony petals scatter, The. Buson. EMJL, *tr.* by Haruo Shirane

People. Hans Arp. PFTM-1

People. Bob Merrill. ReLy

People. Jean Toomer. GT

People, The. Donald Evans. BBMWP, *tr.* by Gillian Clarke

People, The. Elizabeth Madox Roberts. NOxBChV

People along the sand, The. Neither Out Far Nor In Deep. Robert Frost. APT-1; BrAP; NAMCP V.1; NoAM; NoP-4; NoP-5; OxBoAm; TRP; WeW-3; WoPoe

People always say to me. Question, The. Karla Kuskin. NTCP

People Are a Temple, The. Gennady Aygi. WoBe, *tr.* by Peter France

People Are Dropping Out of Our Lives. Albert Goldbarth. SwNoth

People are eating dinner in that country north of Legge's Lake, The. Les A. Murray. BMAP *Fr.* Bulahdelah—Taree Holiday Song Cycle, The.

People are made of places. They carry with them. Where I Come From. Elizabeth Brewster. Coast

People are making a camp of branches in that country at Arnhem Bay, The. Song Cycle of the Moon-Bone. *Unknown.* NOBAu, *tr.* by Ronald M. Berndt

People are putting up storm windows now. Storm Windows. Howard Nemerov. VCAP

People are queer / They're always crowing. Life Is Just a Bowl of Cherries. Lew Brown. ReLy

People are saying that I am your enemy, The. To Julia de Burgos. Julia de Burgos. TCLAP, *tr.* by Grace Schulman

People are very small and shrink, The. At the Other End of the Telescope. George Bradley. P180

People are watching my eyes. Memorial Drive. Willie Abraham Howard Jr. BtF

People ask about Cold Mountain Way. Han-shan (Cold Mountain). WoPoe, *tr.* by E. Bruce Brooks

People ask the way to Cold Mountain. Han-shan (Cold Mountain). ColAnChi, *tr.* by Red Pine

People at Night [(*Derived from Rilke*)]. Denise Levertov. CLPP

People at the Pay Telephone, The. Victoria McCabe. OPRER

People brag / People boast. Is It True What They Say About Dixie? Irving Caesar and Sammy Lerner. ReLy

People came to listen, The. Chartist Meeting. Mike Jenkins. AngWePo

People come from all over to consult me, bringing their limbs. Margaret Atwood. NALW *Fr.* Circe / Mud Poems.

People don't swallow bullshit wholesale like they used to. What Becomes Us. Sharon Mesmer. HeMarv

People from the Valley, The. Keith Wilson. ICANM

People get married all the time. but not in congo square. eight o'clock in the morning. Moment of the First Day, The. Kalamu ya Salaam. AnSo

People Getting Divorced. Lawrence Ferlinghetti. NoAM

People go naked men and women, The. Admirals (Columbus). Suzanne Gardinier. NeAmPo

People have praised my way of life. Yun Sŏndo. CATKP *Fr.* Angler's Calendar, The.

People have the oddest kinks. Martial. EroLit, *tr. by* James Michie

People hold, The. Coming Down. Rick London. Eno

People I love the best, The. To Be of Use. Marge Piercy. GoPo; IPoFL; TWF

People in his homeland thought him mad. In Memory of Ho Chi-chen. Li Po. CrYelRi, *tr. by* Sam Hamill

People in My Family. Grace Paley. TaR

People in the houses behind Searsport are dancing, The. Dancing in Vacationland. Stephen Dobyns. EmeKit

People, kind people, please buy my powder and rouge. *Unknown.* CATKP, *tr. by* Kevin O'Rourke

People know what the land knows, The. Carl Sandburg. APT-1 *Fr.* People, Yes, The.

People laugh at me for having no old lady. Fĕng Mĕng-lung. ColAnChi *Fr.* Mountain Songs.

People lived there. Now we live there. (LL) Lynching and Burning. Primus St. John. ISC; PoChi

People mistake you; you mistake yourself. (LL) Somebody Else. Jackie Kay. BeAl; NeBl

People, more people. Tayo-jo. SoOfWa, *tr. by* Sam Hamill

People need poetry, The. Osip Mandelstam. Seamus Deane. PBCIP

People, No, The. Vicki Raymond. NOBAu

People of color untie-dyed. Got nothing to lose. Souvenir from Anywhere. Harryette Mullen. WANABP

People of Figs. Nidaa Khoury. DTA, *tr. by* Karen Alkalay-Gut

People of Fire. Nidaa Khoury. DTA, *tr. by* Karen Alkalay-Gut

People of Fire. Nidaa Khoury. PoArWo, *tr. by* Linda Zisquit

People of Grapes. Nidaa Khoury. PoArWo, *tr. by* Linda Zisquit

People of my country, of my village, The. Towards a New Resolve. Pak Inhwan. CAMKP, *tr. by* Scott Swaner

People of my time are passing away: my, The. In View of the Fact. A. R. Ammons. OxBoAm

People of Olives. Nidaa Khoury. DTA, *tr. by* Karen Alkalay-Gut

People of Pomegranates. Nidaa Khoury. DTA, *tr. by* Karen Alkalay-Gut

People of the Earth 8. Ko Chŏnghŭi. EcSo, *tr. by* Catherine J. Kim

People of the Future. Ted Berrigan. PFTM-2

People of the Other Village, The. Thomas Lux. PoCho; StAl; SUP

People of Unrest. Margaret Walker Alexander. GT

People on Sunday. Edwin Denby. NYP2

People on the next block over from yours, you know?, The. Ashbery Explains. Clark Coolidge. NYP2

People on the streets draw up and stare, The. Umbra Vitae. Georg Heym. GTCP, *tr. by* Christopher Middleton

People one, and one supplies the King, The. (LL) Homer. OBGa; OBVE *Fr.* Odyssey.

People open up like doors. Gossip. Angela Sorby. AmPoNex

People, pay attention. Corrido of the Uprooted Ones. *Unknown.* NAAPv.2

People / People who need people. People. Bob Merrill. ReLy

People Possess Four Things. Antonio Machado Ruiz. WoPoe, *tr. by* Robert Bly

People round off this planet, The. Roots. Bill Berkson. AHA; NYP2

People sat up from skin-baking or shade-seeking. Diver-Bird. Mike Jenkins. TCAWP

People say, "The one you love is unfaithful." Twelve Lies, The. Jelaluddin Rumi. WED, *tr. by* Robert Bly

People see gardens and houses. Mikhail Alekseievich Kuzmin. CAGL, *tr. by* Michael Green

People sit numbly at the counter. I Sing the Body Electric. Philip Levine. ViWalt

People tell me not. People tell me. *Unknown.* SonAtl, *tr. by* Lou Arthurs and Andrew Wegley

People that build their houses inland. Inland. Edna St. Vincent Millay. HarvBoo

People that I sing to. (I'm So) Weary of It All. Noël Coward. ReLy

People, then, knew what they wanted and how to get it, The. (LL) Hotel Lautréamont. John Ashbery. FTOS; HarvBoo

People visiting all day. Buson. EH, *tr. by* Robert Hass

People vs. the People, The. Kenneth Fearing. MoAmPo

People were passive, The. Lawson Fusao Inada. AmWaPo *Fr.* Legends from Camp.

People who buy flowers in Ch'ang-an. Song of Selling Flowers. Tsung Ch'en. ColAnChi, *tr. by* Jonathan Chaves

People who come out of nowhere to try to put into words any part of what. All Writing Is Garbage. Antonin Artaud. PFTM-1

People who hate us crowd into our dreams, people who want us. David McFadden. NLPA

People who have no children can be hard. Gwendolyn Brooks. PoA 2002 *Fr.* Womanhood, The.

People who have what they want are very fond of telling people. Terrible People, The. Ogden Nash. APT-2

People who live here, The. How the Heart Aches. N. V. M. Gonzalez. ReBoTo

People who live outside of people. That Place Isn't Far. Na Hûidôk. EcSo, *tr. by* Peter H. Lee

People who want to live beside the ocean are fundamentalists. Lakes. David Donnell. NoAM

People who watch me hang my coat, The. Leaving the Old Gods. Janet McAdams. OPRER

People will live on, The. Carl Sandburg. MoAmPo; NoAM *Fr.* People, Yes, The.

People Will Say We're in Love. Oscar Hammerstein, II. ReLy

People Will Talk. Orban Veli Kanik. NaPG, *tr. by* Talat Sait Halman

People working fields. Issa. SoOfWa, *tr. by* Sam Hamill

People, Yes, The. Carl Sandburg.

    "Little girl saw her first troop parade and asked, "What are those?", The." HHAm

    "People know what the land knows, The." APT-1

    People, Yes, The. MoAmPo; NoAM

    "People, yes, the people, The." APT-1

    "They have yarns / Of a skyscraper so tall they had to put hinges." MoAmPo

    "You can go now yes go now. Go east or west, go north or." HHAm

People—people of my kind, my own, The. To the Lacedemonians. Allen Tate. NoAM

People's abuse. Muso Soseki. EaWin, *tr. by* W. S. Merwin

People's Literary, De. Maggie Pogue Johnson. CBWP-4

Peoples of the Americas. Let Them Call It Jazz. Stewart Brown. WaCA

People's Republic, The. John A. Vanek. RWB

Peoria. M. Loncar. NAPBL

Pepper. Joe Osterhaus. NAPBL

Peppertrees, the peppertrees!, The. Scenes from the Life of the Peppertrees. Denise Levertov. NoP-4; NoP-5

Per Iter Tenebricosum. Oliver St. John Gogarty. OBMV

Peradventure of old, some bard in Ionian Islands. Henry Wadsworth Longfellow. APN-1 *Fr.* Elegiac Verse.

Perambulator Poems, I-VII. David McCord.

    When I Was Christened. OBCoV

Perception of an object costs. Emily Dickinson. APN-2

Perch, The. Galway Kinnell. PML; PoDa

Perchance, Iago, I will ne'er go home. My bones. Epilogue for Emilia. Rachel Beck. IaFF

Perchance, the friend who cheered thy early years. Judge Not. Josephine D. Henderson Heard. CBWP-4

Perchance to Dream. Mary Low. SurWo

Perched, a stained skull. Grey Kirk in the Mearns. Gillian Ferguson. EdScPo

Perched on a steep slate roof: the first. Four Crows at Dusk. Betsy Sholl. SUP

Perched on his balcony of pleasure. Dialogue, The. Funso Aiyejina. NAfrP

Perched on the chimney on one leg. Who Cares for the Blind Stork. Blaga Dimitrova. CSCBP, *tr. by* Georgi Belev and Lisa Sapinkopf

Perched on the edge of. Nine Flower Mountain. Finn Wilcox. CSKM

Percussion, salt and honey. Sappho. WoPoe,

Perdam Sapientiam Sapientum. William Habington. ChIV-2 *Fr.* Castara.

Perdita. Louis MacNeice. PoA 2002

Perdita's Song. Annie Finch. IaFF

Peregrin, Wandering Hunter of Faces. José María Eguren. TCLAP, *tr. by* Iver Lofving

Peregrine. Barton Sutter. UrbNat

Peregrine Falcon, New York City. Robert Cording. UrbNat

Peregrinus A. Two Strangers, The. Manuel A. Viray. ReBoTo

Perennial. Susan Hahn. IllVoic

Perennial Garden. Marianne Boruch. AmAlph

Perennial snow on the mountain. Imagination of Flowers, The. Lee Upton. AmAlph

Perennial tears descend in gems. (LL) Valley of Unrest, The. Edgar Allan Poe. APN-1; NAAL-3

Perfect. Hugh MacDiarmid. NePenScot; NoP-4; OxBEV; WoPoe

Perfect Child, The. Adrian Porter. NBLV

Perfect Circle. Richard Lemm. Coast

Perfect City Code. Richard Blanco. LegDan

Perfect Couple, The.   Good Marriage, A.   Giovanna Pollarolo.   TANSG, *tr. by* Marjorie Agosin

Perfect Example of a Paralysed Larynx, A.   Stephanie Norgate.   PoCu

Perfect god puts forth no dogma, cant, The.   Perfect God, The.   Thomas Lux.   WaAnP

Perfect half-moon glistens, A.   True Illumination Is Habitude.   Sam Hamill.   AmZen

Perfect Heart, The.   Shara McCallum.   AmPoNex; P180

Perfect is the silence of this golden day.   Elis.   Georg Trakl.   WoPoe, *tr. by* Robert Firmage

Perfect Life, The.   Jorge Carrera Andrade.   TCLAP, *tr. by* Dudley Fitts

Perfect little body, without fault or stain on thee.   On a Dead Child.   Robert Bridges.   NoAM; OBMV; OxAEP-2

Perfect Orchestra, The.   Henrietta Cordelia Ray.   CBWP-3

Perfect Peace.   Frances Ridley Havergal.   SacPr

Perfect Reactionary, The.   Hughes Mearns.   NTCP

Perfect Reader.   Mary Ruefle.   AmAlph

Perfect Recall.   Jack Myers.   SUP

Perfect Timing.   Sarah Maguire.   LW

Perfect Work.   Bill Berkson.   AHA

Perfection.   Oliver St. John Gogarty.   IrLP

Perfection, of a kind, was what he was after.   Epitaph on a Tyrant.   W. H. Auden.   AF; HeIP-4; NoAM; OxBEV; WaAnP

Perfection of Wisdom Suite, A: Hymns for the Perfection of Wisdom in Paradise.   Andrew Schelling.   WANABP

Perfection Wasted.   John Updike.   GoPo

Perfectly balanced, he bends in the shallow water.   Great Blue Heron.   Del Marie Rogers.   TiP2

Perfectly beautiful, perfectly ignorant of it. (LL)   Piazza di Spagna, Early Morning.   Richard Wilbur.   NoP-4; NoP-5

Perfectly tired.   Imperfect Poetry and Meaningless Poetry.   Iijima Koichi.   TAPaP, *tr. by* Naoshi Koriyama *and* Edward Lueders *and* Edward Lueders

Perfecto Flores.   Jimmy Santiago Baca.   TRP

Perfil / Filoso perfil.   Dolores Dorantes.   SPV

Performance.   Paul McRay.   SwNoth

Performance.   Les A. Murray.   PML

Performance, The.   James Dickey.   FaBoWar; InGu

Performance Angel.   Yi Sang.   CAMKP, *tr. by* Edward Mack

Performance at Hog Theater, A.   Russell Edson.   PmAP; PoCho

Performance Poem.   Bob Holman.   KGB

Performance Sequence.   Rick London.   Eno

Performance Test.   Prageeta Sharma.   HeMarv

Performances, assortments, résumés.   Hart Crane.   MoAmPo; NAAL-5; OxBoAm *Fr.* Bridge, The.

Performer, Male.   No Ch'ŏnmyŏng.   CAMKP, *tr. by* David R. McCann

Perfume / of flowers! A haw, The.   Charles Olson.   RaBo

Perfume, The.   John Donne.   FSCP; NoSic *Fr.* Elegies.

Perfume of the ginger-flowers, The.   Ginger-flowers.   Kenneth Mackenzie.   BMAP

Perfumed springs ripple over skeletal outcrops.   After Shih-te.   Shih Shu.   CSKM, *tr. by* James H. Sanford

Perfumist, The.   Jorge Fernández Granados.   RMCMP, *tr. by* John Oliver Simon

Perfumista, La.   Jorge Fernández Granados.   RMCMP

Perhaps.   John Brandi.   ICANM

Perhaps.   Perhaps One Day There Will Be Ways.   Armanda Guiducci.   CItWP

Perhaps.   "Shu Ting."   BLT, *tr. by* Carolyn Kizer and Y. H. Zhao

Perhaps all that's lacking.   Hampstead Heath.   Manuel Ulacia.   RMCMP, *tr. by* Indran Amirthanayagam

Perhaps he left the newspaper stand that morning.   Jack Johnson Does the Eagle Rock.   Cornelius Eady.   ESEAA; MoASP

Perhaps he will fall. (LL)   Wilderness Gothic.   Alfred Wellington Purdy.   BrAP; HeIP-4; NoP-4

Perhaps he will press his warm lips.   Lebanon.   Frank O'Hara.   CAGL

Perhaps I am one of them. (LL)   Midnight.   Jĕn Jui.   CFP; WoPoe, *tr. by* Chung Ling and Kenneth Rexroth

Perhaps I asked too large.   Emily Dickinson.   TCAPo

Perhaps I may allow, the Dean.   Jonathan Swift.   OxBEV *Fr.* Verses on the Death of Dr. Swift, D.S.P.D, Occasioned by Reading a Maxim in Rochefoucauld.

Perhaps if she stood for an hour like that.   Woman at Lit Window.   Eamon Grennan.   BLT

Perhaps if we are lucky.   *Zuni Oral Tradition*.   NAWM-7v2 *Fr.* Prayer at the Winter Solstice, A.

Perhaps in hell time has.   Lover Digresses, The.   Luis Cernuda.   CAGL, *tr. by* Rick Lipinski

Perhaps it is not so important that the dead man lives.   Book of the Dead Man #33, The.   Marvin Bell.   PoA 2002

Perhaps it was the fishing boat.   My Father's Words.   Lucy Hamilton.   Prnts

Perhaps it's a question of what.   Black Poppy (At the Temple).   David St. John.   BodElec

Perhaps It's as You Say.   Peter Everwine.   GeoHom

Perhaps it's the bomb craters.   Perhaps.   John Brandi.   ICANM

Perhaps it's the smell of printing ink.   Compositor, The.   Greg Delanty.   WaAnP

Perhaps I've got to write better longer thinking of it [as].   On Induction of the Hand.   Clark Coolidge.   NYP2; PmAP

Perhaps, like everything, it has its flow and ebb.   My Cousin Abe, Paul Antschel and Paul Celan.   Jacqueline Osherow.   TaR

Perhaps No Poem at All But All I Can Say and I Cannot Be Silent.   Denise Levertov.   SacPr

Perhaps on a sunday.   Day Song.   Lance Henson.   HATNAP

Perhaps One Day There Will Be Ways.   Armanda Guiducci.   CItWP

Perhaps one morning the sky will be.   Imani in Sunburst Summer: A Chant.   Askia Muhammad Touré.   SpirFl

Perhaps she loves best. (LL)   In Minako Wada's House.   Brad Leithauser.   NoP-4; NoP-5

Perhaps the ankle of a horse is holy.   There Are Two Worlds.   Larry Levis.   BodElec

Perhaps the rain on the roof is some hyper-phrenetic code from Shadowland.   Skip Fox.   AnSo

Perhaps the smile and tender tone.   Alfred Tennyson.   NAEL-6v2 *Fr.* Maud [A Monodrama].

Perhaps the street I've gone into and come out of.   For Many Years.   Kemal Ozer.   NaPG, *tr. by* Talat Sait Halman

Perhaps the Time of Blood.   Franco Fortini.   ItPo, *tr. by* Gayle Ridinger

Perhaps the time of blood is on the return.   Perhaps the Time of Blood.   Franco Fortini.   ItPo, *tr. by* Gayle Ridinger

Perhaps the World Ends Here.   Joy Harjo.   IPoFL; MakPoe; ReEnLa; SweBea

Perhaps the world will end at the kitchen table, while we are laughing and crying, eating of the last sweet bite. (LL)   Perhaps the World Ends Here.   Joy Harjo.   IPoFL; MakPoe; ReEnLa; SweBea

Perhaps there has never before been such an open sea.   Invisible Hand.   L. S. Asekoff.   BodElec

Perhaps there is no point in seeking.   Twelve Stones. Chapter 1: Prologue.   Yuasa Hangetsu.   CAoMJL1, *tr. by* Leith Morton

Perhaps there will always be yellow buses.   About Benwell.   Gillian Allnutt.   RSaN

Perhaps these thoughts of ours.   Perhaps.   "Shu Ting."   BLT, *tr. by* Carolyn Kizer and Y. H. Zhao

Perhaps they heard we don't understand them.   What the Japanese Perhaps Heard.   Rachel Rose.   BAP-01

Perhaps we ought to be ashamed and aren't.   Ottava Rima: Lear.   Cecilia Woloch.   IaFF

Perhaps you have seen The Dinner Party, tables set with linens and.   Dinner, The.   Rosario Morales.   PueRic

Perhaps you have sworn.   Jane Duran.   Prnts *Fr.* Silences from the Spanish Civil War.

Perhaps you may of Priam's Fate enquire.   Virgil.   NPeEn *Fr.* Aeneid [*or* Eneados *or* Aeneis], The.

Perhaps you'll tire of me, muses.   Misgivings.   William Matthews.   BeAl; PoDa

Perhaps you're sitting up in bed, and have tilted.   Diana Hartog.   NLPA *Fr.* Oasis.

Perhaps you've read the papers.   Julia A. Moore.   STuOW *Fr.* To My Friends and Critics.

Pericles and Aspasia.   Walter Savage Landor.
   Corinna, from Athens, to Tanagra.   OBEV
   Dirce.   NAEL-6v2; NoP-4; NoP-5; NPeEn; OBEV; OxAEP-2; OxBEV; TFi; WeW-3; WoPoe

Pericles, Prince of Tyre: A Commentary.   Reginald Shepherd.   IaFF

Pericles.   William Shakespeare.
   "Terrible child-bed hast thou had, my dear, A."   OxAEP-1

Pericoloso Sporgersi.   Joyce Mansour.   *tr. by* Mary Ann Caws *and* Jean-Pierre Cauvin
   "Naked / I float among the wreckage with steel mustaches."   SurPaPo, *tr. by* Mary Ann Caws *and* Jean-Pierre Cauvin

Peridot.   Rebecca Reynolds.   AmPoNex

Perimedes [*or* Perimedes, the Blacksmith].   Robert Greene.
   (Phillis and Coridon).   NoSic

Period.   Ronald Stuart Thomas.   HarvBoo

Period / a tollbooth a jammed F sharp.   Lost Rules of Usage.   Susan Stewart.   AmAlph

Periodic Table of Ethereal Elements.   Lucie Brock-Broido.   AWPTFC

Periodista / su padre.   Gauguin.   Manuel Vázquez Montalbán.   RaW

Peripeteia.   Anthony Hecht.   VCAP

Periphery.   Ruth Stone.   NALW

Periwig, A.   Rowland Watkyns.   NOSC

Perl Poem.   Leontia Flynn.   NIrP

Perla at the Mexican Border Assembly Line of Dolls.   Rigoberto González.   AmPoNex

Perlas.   Víctor Hernández Cruz.   TouFir

Perle, plesaunte to prynces paye.   *Unknown*.   NoP-4; NoP-5 *Fr.* Pearl or Perle.

Permanence in Change.   Johann Wolfgang von Goethe.   STV, *tr. by* John Frederick Nims

Permanence of the just-yesterday, The.   Mathemaku No. 16.   Bob Grumman.   AnSo

Permanence of the Young Men, The.   William Soutar.   EdScPo

Permanent Tourists, The.   Patricia K. Page.   BrAP

Permanently.   Kenneth Koch.   NoP-4; NoP-5; OxBoAm; PmAP; PoA 2002

Permit.   Syto Cavé.   OGAHCP, *tr. by* Boadiba and Jack Hirschman

Permit Marissa in an artless Lay.   To Almystrea.   Mary Lee, Lady Chudleigh.   EMWP

Permit me, Madam, to invade.   To the Wife of a Non-interventionist Statesman (March 1938).   Edgell Rickword.   RSaN

Permit me to warn you.   Charles Reznikoff.   NAAPv.2

Permit Me Voyage.   James Agee.   MoAmPo; YaYoPo

Permit me voyage, love, into your hands. (LL)   Hart Crane.   AmFaPo; ColAP *Fr.* Voyages.

Pero cómo decírtelo si eres.   Pero Cómo Decírtelo.   Carlos Bousoño.   RaW

Pero es más triste todavía, mucho más triste.   Cuerpo y el Alma, El.   Vicente Aleixandre.   RaW

Pero luego, en el trayecto imaginario de un automóvil blanco.   Cuatro.   Ofelia Perez Sepúlveda.   SPV

Peroration, Concerning Genius.   Robert Pinsky.   NoAM *Fr.* Essay on Psychiatrists.

Perpetua.   Olga Broumas.   ErotSp

Perpetual Infirmity of Hope.   Sor Juana Inés de la Cruz.   SpanPo, *tr. by* Muriel Kittel

Perpetual *Look* Physics: 17/5.   Bernard Collin.   YaTCFP, *tr. by* Mary Ann Caws *and* Jean-Pierre Cauvin

Perpetual Motion.   Gerardo Diego.   RaW, *tr. by* Ralph Nelson

Perpetually Attempting to Soar.   Mary Ruefle.   AmAlph

Perpétuel *voyez* physique, 17/5.   Bernard Collin.   YaTCFP

Perpetuum Mobile.   Philip Whalen.   WANABP *Fr.* Epigrams & Imitations.

Perpetuum Mobile: The City.   William Carlos Williams.   APT-1

Perplex'd and troubl'd at his bad success.   John Milton.   *Fr.* Paradise Regained [*or* Regain'd].

Perplexing forest.   Tomas Tranströmer.   WoBe *Fr.* Haiku.

Perplexity: A Poem.   Elizabeth Hands.   WoRP

Perro Negro Duerme Sobre la Luz, Un.   León Felipe.
   "Yo no soy nadie: un hombre."   RaW

Persecutions Purifie.   Robert Herrick.   SacPr

Persephone.   Cynthia Cruz.   IAoNAP

Persephone.   Ziporah Hildebrandt.   HW

Persephone.   Michael Longley.   NPeEn; PBCIP

Persephone.   Kathleen Norris.   HW

Persephone.   Susan Wicks.   MoWP

Persephone 2.   Cynthia Cruz.   IAoNAP

Persephone, 1978.   Thomas McCarthy.   ModIr

Persephone ate seven pomegranate seeds. So What? I'll tell you what.   Ovid.   ModIr *Fr.* Metamorphoses.

Persephone in America.   Alison Townsend.   FiBr

Persephone That Is to Say Double Issue.   René Daumal.   PFTM-1

Persephone, to Demeter.   Marilyn Krysl.   HW

Persephone Underground.   Rita Dove.   FFC

Persephone (Unplugged).   Stephen Burt.   LegDan

Persephone's Daughter.   Anne MacLeod.   EdScPo

Persephone's Journey.   Patricia Monaghan.   HW

Persephone's Notes.   Caroline Finkelstein.   PfS

Perseus.   Robert Earl Hayden.   NoAM

Perseverance.   Jas. Mardis.   TiP2

Perseverance.   Martin Sorescu.   VCWP, *tr. by* D. J Enright and Joana Russell-Gebbett

Persian Miniature, A.   Mimi Khalvati.   MoWP

Persian miniature for gerry and marlene, A.   Roy Kiyooka.   NLPA *Fr.* Pear Tree Pomes.

Persian Parables.   Aleksander Wat.   *tr. by* Czeslaw Milosz
   "By a great, swift water."   AF; WoPoe, *tr. by* Czeslaw Milosz

Persian Version, The.   Robert Graves.   EMP; NAMCP V.1; NoAM; NoP-4; NoP-5; OBWP; StAl; WeW-3

Persimmons.   Li-Young Lee.   CAP-8; NAAL-5; NAMCP V.2; NIL-7; NIP-4; NoP-4; NoP-5; OPRER

Persistence of Memory, the Failure of Poetry, The.   Robert Phillips.   LiTh

Persistence of Nature in Our Lives, The.   Andrew Hudgins.   WeW-3

Persistence of Song, The.   Howard Moss.   GoPo; NoP-4; NoP-5

Person, The.   Charles Hubert Sisson.   HarvBoo

Person as Dreamer: We Talk about the Future, The.   Michael Hartnett.   PBCIP *Fr.* Notes on My Contemporaries.

Person, for you, is a book, A.   Writer.   Joe Wenderoth.   BodElec

Person has to try on many lives, A.   Fitting Room, The.   Angela Jackson.   BtF

Person is reflected by the whirlpool, not the face, A.   Ekaterina Boyarskikh.   CRWP, *tr. by* Richard McKane

Person is very self-conscious about his head, A.   Thoughts on One's Head.   William Meredith.   VCAP

Person of superior integrity, The.   Lao Tzu.   ColAnChi *Fr.* Tao Te Ching.

Person of water, eye-shine, thigh.   Person of.   Pamela Alexander.   AmAlph

Person of whom you speak is dead, The.   Imperfect Sonnet, The.   Philip Whalen.   WANABP

Person place thing tree.   Diana Helen Melhem.   PoArWo *Fr.* Country.

Person sleeping under the chair, The.   Chair.   Hagiwara Sakutaro.   PFTM-1

Person, The.   Lyn Hejinian.
   "Solitude flared out, The."   FTOS

Person we love, The.   Shadow.   Fazil Hüsnü Daglarca.   NaPG, *tr. by* Talat Sait Halman

Person who feeds me.   Kim Namjo.   CAMKP *Fr.* Love's Cursive.

Person who made a song, The.   Sin Hŭm.   CATKP, *tr. by* Peter H. Lee

Person who's whole possesses four legs, A.   Gwyneth Lewis.   BBMWP *Fr.* Wholeness.

Personae Separatae.   Eugenio Montale.   AF, *tr. by* William Arrowsmith

Personal.   Peter Rafferty.   NLP

Personal Ad.   Joanna Fuhrman.   AmPoNex

Personal Atlas.   Rosalie Moore.   YaYoPo

Personal Column.   Basil Bunting.   BrAP

Personal Column.   Tom Paulin.   PNI

Personal Footnote, A.   Gavin Ewart.   FaBoWar

Personal Helicon.   Seamus Heaney.   BrAP; NPeEn; WaAnP

Personal Histories, The.   Michael Burkard.   BodElec

Personal History; for My Son.   Ruthven Todd.   EdScPo

Personal History of Hands, A.   Lori Jakiela.   ReTh

Personal Letter No. 3.   Sonia Sanchez.   ESEAA; SSLK

Personal Poem.   Frank O'Hara.   CAP-8; CLPP; OxBoAm; PmAP

Personal Poem # 7.   Ted Berrigan.   NYP2

Personal Poem # 8.   Ted Berrigan.   NYP2

Personal Portrait, A.   Guiguis Shoukry.   AnVo, *tr. by* Mohamed Enani

Personality.   Johnny Burke.   ReLy

Personality.   Agnes Mary Frances Robinson.   VWP

Personality syndrome, The.   Alan Davies.   FTOS *Fr.* Name.

Personals.   Star Black.   KGB

Personals.   C. D. Wright.   AmAlph; PtR

Personals Ad.   Allen Ginsberg.   NAMCP V.2

Personification of a Name, The.   Ray A. Young Bear.   HATNAP

Person's Tale, The.   U. A. Fanthorpe.   NoP-4

Perspective.   David Huddle.   PfSP

Perspective.   Lisa Pegram.   BtF

Perspective He Would Mutter Going to Bed.   Jack Gilbert.   YaYoPo

Perspective Lovesong.   "Ern Malley."   BMAP

Perspective of lines or, The.   Arroyo, The.   Brenda Hillman.   ExTi

Perspective seen as trickling light oblit- error impact.   Solfège parasite.   Camille Martin.   AnSo

Perspectives.   Chiqui Vicioso.   TANSG, *tr. by* Emma Jane Robinett

Perspectives on the Second World War.   Irena Klepfisz.   TaR

Persuasion.   Joyelle McSweeney.   LegDan

Persuasion.   Patty Seyburn.   AmPoNex

Persuasion.   William Wordsworth.   OWoS *Fr.* Ecclesiastical Sonnets.

Persuasions to Joy; a Song.   Thomas Carew.   OBEV

Peru Eye, the Heart of the Lamp.   Clark Coolidge.   APSN

Perugia.   Art Lange.   PmAP

Pervasive and.   Theoretical People.   Paul Hoover.   IllVoic

Perversion, A.   Christopher Reid.   OBCoV

Pèse-nerfs, Le.   Antonin Artaud.
   "Acteur on le voit comme à travers des cristaux, Un."   YaTCFP

Peso muerto de la tierra, El.   Tedi López Mills.   RMCMP

Pessimist, The.   Ben King.   NBLV

Pessimist's Vision, The.   Constance Naden.   ViWPN; VWP

Pest.   Major L. Jackson.   LegDan

Pet Panther.   A. R. Ammons.   NoP-4; NoP-5

Pet Shop.   Philip Whalen.   WhBo

Petal shower, A.   Basho.   EH, *tr. by* Robert Hass

Petals fall in the fountain, The.   Ts'ai Chi'h.   Ezra Pound.   NoP-4; NoP-5

Petals fall, The.   Buson.   EH, *tr. by* Robert Hass
Petals of the water-lilies tremble, The.   Intoxication of Love.   Li Po.   CCL1, *tr. by* Judith Gautier and James Whitall [*or*Whittal]
Petals on a wet, black bough. (LL)   In a Station of the Metro.   Ezra Pound.   APT-1; BrAP; ChAP; ColAP; HeIP-4; MoAmPo; NAAL-5; NAAPv.2; NAMCP V.1; NIL-7; NIP-4; NoAM; NoP-5; NPeEn; OxBoAm; PoA 2002; PoPoPo; TCAPo; TFi; WaAnP; WeW-3
Pete at the Zoo.   Gwendolyn Brooks.   TLR
Pete Rose hit number.   On Karma at 9.11.85.   Bobby Byrd.   TiP2
Petelia Tablet, The.   *Unknown.*   WoPoe, *tr. by* Robert Bringhurst
Peter.   Marianne Moore.   APT-1; NoP-4
Peter and John.   Elinor Wylie.   MakPoe; MoAmPo
Peter and Mother.   David Schubert.   OxBoAm
Peter and the Dyke.   Paul Farley.   NeBrP
Peter Bell.   William Wordsworth.
　"Is it some party, in a parlour."   NPBRoP
　"There's something in a flying horse."   NPBRoP
Peter Bell the Third.   Percy Bysshe Shelley.
　"Devil now knew his proper cue, The."   OBSV
　"Hell is a city much like London."   OBSV
　Sin.   NPBRoP
Peter broke the ragged branch to push his nostrils closer.   West Paddocks.   Arthur Davies.   NOBAu
Peter died in a paper tiara cut.   Tiara.   Mark Doty.   MakPoe; WaAnP
Peter Grimes.   George Crabbe.   NPBRoP; OBNV *Fr.* Borough, The.
Peter Maurin (1877–1949).   David Craig.
　"Peter pumped Dorothy's hand."   UpMys
Peter Pan in North America.   Robin Becker.   ReTh
Peter pumped Dorothy's hand.   David Craig.   UpMys *Fr.* Peter Maurin (1877–1949).
Peter Quince at the Clavier.   Wallace Stevens.   APT-1; HeIP-4; MoAmPo; NAAL-5; NAMCP V.1; NAWM-7v2; NoAM; NoP-4; NoP-5; OxBoAm; SAmP; TCAPo; TFi
Peter, Tom, David, Jim and Howard are gone.   Condemned Site.   Mona Van Duyn.   MakPoe
Peter's not friendly. He gives me sideways looks.   John Berryman.   ChIV-2 *Fr.* Dream Songs.
Pete's Poem.   Cyd Adams.   TiP2
Petit Guignol.   Philip Hammial.   BMAP
Petit Mal.   Richard Foerster.   Vesp
Petit Testament.   "Ern Malley."   BMAP
Petit, the Poet.   Edgar Lee Masters.   ColAP; MoAmPo; NAMCP V.1; NoAM; TCAPo *Fr.* Spoon River Anthology.
Petite âme.   Valérie-Catherine Richez.
　"Pense au beateau qui s'éloigne du quai, qui se sépare lentement de la terre."   YaTCFP
Petite Auto, La.   Guillaume Apollinaire.   YaTCFP
Petition.   W. H. Auden.   NAEL-6v2; NAEL-7v2
Petition.   Brigit Pegeen Kelly.   ExTi
Petition.   Malinda Markham.   IAoNAP
Petition, A.   Frances Anne Kemble.   LW
Petition for an Absolute Retreat, The.   Anne Finch, Countess of Winchilsea.
　"Give me, O indulgent fate!"   NOSC
Petition for Langston Hughes, A.   Clarence Major.   EGAG
Petition for Reconciliation.   Cynddelw Brydydd Mawr.   OBWVE, *tr. by* Joseph P. Clancy
Petition for Replenishment.   C. D. Wright.   AmAlph
Petition from the Chain Gang at Newcastle to Captain Furlong the Superintendent, A.   Francis MacNamara.   NOBAu
Petition Hecate at the seal.   Jill Hartman.   PoPra
Petition, The.   Thomas Beedome.   NOSC
Petition to Father and Son and Holy Ghost, A.   *Unknown.*   SacPr
Petitioners are full of prayers.   Lament of Swordy Well, The.   John Clare.   FaBoVe
Pet-name, a common name, A. Best-selling brand, curt.   Geoffrey Hill.   NAMCP V.2; NoAM; WoPoe *Fr.* Mercian Hymns.
Petra.   John William Burgon.
　"Match me such marvel save in Eastern clime."   UV
Petrarch watched a plague: it took.   Prognosis.   George Starbuck.   YaYoPo
Petrified Echoes.   Vasco [*or* Vasko] Popa.   PoSu *Fr.* Yawn of Yawns, The.
Petrograd Side, The.   Lev Vladimir Loseff.   TCRusP, *tr. by* Henry Pickford
Petrushka's valentine pivots on its pin. (LL)   Wine Menagerie, The.   Hart Crane.   APT-2; NoAM
Pettiness, A. (LL)   Snake.   D. H. Lawrence.   AmFaPo; BrAP; CABP; ChAP; HarvBoo; HeIP-4; NAEL-6v2; NAEL-7v2; NAMCP V.1; NoAM; NoP-4; NoP-5; OxBEV; TFi; UV; WaAnP
Petty Bourgeoisie, The.   Roque Dalton.   TCLAP, *tr. by* Richard Schaaf
Petty Time.   Claudio Rodríguez.   RaW, *tr. by* Robert Mezey

Peupliers agités par le vent froid.   Encore le froid.   Paul De Roux.   YaTCFP
Pewits Nest.   John Clare.   FaBoVe
Pewter.   Jack Gilbert.   BodElec
Pewter loons, ceramic bunnies, and faux bamboo.   Mail Order Catalogs.   William Matthews.   ReTh
Peyote Poem.   Michael McClure.
　"Clear—the senses bright—sitting in the black chair—Rocker."   BB
Pez.   José Luis Hidalgo.   RaW
Pez Dorado.   Ann Spanel.   PfS
Pfarr-Schmerz (Village-Anguish).   Veronica Forrest-Thomson.   HarvBoo
Phaedra.   Osip Emilevich Mandelstam.   OBVE, *tr. by* James Greene
Phaedria's Island: The Faerie Queene II.vi. 12–17.   Edmund Spenser. *See* Legend of the Knight of the Red Crosse, or of Holinesse, The.
Phaenomena.   Aratus. *tr. by* Barbara Hughes Fowler
　"Beneath both the feet of Boötes you may see."   HePo
　Proem.   HePo
　Weather Signs.   HePo
Phallometer, a device invented and placed in use, A.   Doggerel for the Great Czech Phallometer.   Richard Katrovas.   MAAN
Phantasia for Elvira Shatayev.   Adrienne Rich.   ItP; NALW
Phantasies (After Robert Schumann).   Emma Lazarus.
　Evening.   APN-2
Phantasmagoria.   Sinan Anton.   IrPoTo, *tr. by* the author
Phantasus.   Arno Holz.
　"In the Thiergarten, on a bench, I'm sitting and smoking."   GTCP, *tr. by* Reinhold Grimm
Phantom.   Samuel Taylor Coleridge.   NAEL-6v2
Phantom Anthems.   Robert Grenier.
　Easter Roses.   FTOS
Phantom Haiku/Silent Film.   Jacqueline Osherow.   ExTi
Phantom Light of All Our Day, The [*You will live more than millions of years, an era of millions, / But in the end I will destroy everything that I have created, / The earth will become again part of the Primeval Ocean . . .*].   Nathaniel Mackey.   GT
Phantom of Clouds, A.   Guillaume Apollinaire.   PFTM-1
Phantom Pain.   Linda Bierds.   AmAlph
Phantoms of Utopia.   Julianne Buchsbaum.   LegDan
Phantom-Wooer, The.   Thomas Lovell Beddoes.   NAEL-6v2; WaAnP
Phaon Awakes.   Mary Robinson.   CenSon; RWP
15. Phaon Awakes.   Mary Robinson.   NPBRoP *Fr.* Sappho and Phaon.
Phaon Forsakes Her.   Mary Robinson.   CenSon; RWP
Pharaoh.   Jane Kenyon.   LoL
Pharaohs of Today, The.   Lizelia Augusta Jenkins Moorer.   CBWP-3
Pharaoh's Palace.   David Wojahn.   AllShUp
Pharao's Daughter.   Michael Moran.   ChIV-1
Pharmacy.   Aaron Anstett.   AmPoNex
Pharoah's Army Got Drowned.   Lynn Domina.   OPRER
Pharonnida.   William Chamberlayne.
　Bad Landlord, The.   NOSC
Phase Four.   John Berryman.   BodElec
Phases.   Wallace Stevens.
　"This was the salty taste of glory."   FaBoWar
　"What shall we say to the lovers of freedom."   FaBoWar
Pheasant and chicken, chicken is a peculiar bird.   Gertrude Stein.   NAAPv.2; NAMCP V.1 *Fr.* Tender Buttons.
Pheasant cries, The.   Issa.   EH, *tr. by* Robert Hass
Pheasant on His Morning Flight, A.   Hsiao Kang.   ColAnChi, *tr. by* Victor H. Mair and Tsu-Lin Mei
Pheasant Plucker's Son, The.   Mick North.   NLP
Phemios and Medon.   Michael Longley.   ModIr *Fr.* Odyssey.
Phenomenology of Anger, The.   Adrienne Rich.   PFTM-2; WaAnP
Phenomenology of Stones, The.   Thomas McCarthy.   PBCIP
Phenomenon, A.   Job Degenaar.   TuT, *tr. by* Aidan Sharkey
Pheobus, arise! / And paint the sable skies.   Invocation.   William Drummond of Hawthornden.   OBEV
Philadelphia.   Arthur Guiterman.   AmWit *Fr.* Lyric Baedeker, The.
Philadelphia / a disguised southern city.   Elegy (for MOVE and Philadelphia).   Sonia Sanchez.   ESEAA
Philadelphia is burning and water.   Overture: Watermelon City.   Elizabeth Alexander.   NAPBL
Philadelphia: Spring, 1985.   Sonia Sanchez.   ESEAA; FuFl
Philaenion is small and swart, but her hair curls more.   Philodemus.   HePo *Fr.* Epigrams.
Philanthropist and the Jelly-fish, The.   May Kendall.   ViWPN; VWP
Philip and Mildred.   Adelaide Anne Procter.   VWP
Philip has stolen a tie.   Philip the Store Policeman.   Lesley Dauer.   AmPoNex
Philip Sparrow.   John Skelton.   OBCoV

Philip the Store Policeman.   Lesley Dauer.   AmPoNex

Philip van Artevelde.   Sir Henry Taylor.
   Elena's Song.   OBEV; RACG

Philip Whalen's Hat.   Joanne Kyger.   BB

Philippians 1.23.   Francis Quarles.   ChIV-2

Philippine Figures.   *Unknown*.   EaWin, *tr.* by W. S. Merwin

Phillida and Coridon.   Nicholas Breton.   NoSic; OBEV *Fr.* Honourable
   Entertainment Given to the Queen's Majesty in Progress at Elvetham, 1591,
   The.

Phillida Flouts Me [*or* The Disdainful Shepherdess].   *Unknown*.   OBEV

Phillis and Coridon.   Robert Greene.   NoSic

Phillis, let's shun the common fate.   Song.   Sir Charles Sedley.   NPeEn

Phillis 2.   Thomas Lodge.   *See* Love Guards [*or* Guides] the Roses of Thy Lips.

Philly in the Light.   Honorée Fanonne Jeffers.   RD

Philo the gentleman, the fortune teller.   Sir John Davies.   NoSic *Fr.* Epigrams.

Philoctetes.   Henry Reed.   HarvBoo

Philodendron Named Joan, A.   Joan Jobe Smith.   SUP

Philodes, if Desire, sweet Blandishment.   To Diodorus, Dorotheus, Callicrates et
   al.   Meleager.   CAGL, *tr.* by Daryl Hine

Philomel.   Richard Barnfield.   OBEV *Fr.* Passionate Pilgrim, The.

Philomel.   Sydney Goodsir Smith.   EdScPo

Philomela.   Matthew Arnold.   OBEV; OWoS

Philomela.   John Crowe Ransom.   APT-1; FuPo; NoAM; OBSV

Philomela.   Sir Philip Sidney.   *See* Nightingale, The.

Philosopher and the Lover; To a Mistress Dying, The.   Sir William Davenant.
   See Lover and Philosopher.

Philosopher's Conquest, The.   Mark Strand.   OxBoAm

Philosophers have measured [*or* measur'd] mountains.   Agony [*or* Agonie],
   The.   George Herbert.   CABP; FSCP

Philosophers, The: Lao-Tzu.   Po Chü-i.   BLT, *tr.* by Arthur Waley

Philosopher's Stone.   Jorie Graham.   AWPTFC

Philosopher's Stone, The.   Konrad Bayer. *tr.* by Walter Billeter
   Electrical Hierarchy, The.   PFTM-2, *tr.* by Walter Billeter

Philosophic Taed, The.   William Soutar.   EdScPo; NePenScot

Philosophical Emancipation, The.   Rafael Zepeda.   SUP

Philosophical Inquiry into the Nature of the Human Cock, A.   Nin Andrews.
   AmZen

Philosophical Songs.   Charles North.   KGB

Philosophy.   Rubén Darío.   SpanPo, *tr.* by Muna Lee

Philosophy.   Elsa Gidlow.   PoBW

Philosophy.   Amy Levy.   ViWPN

Philosophy, A.   Jean R. Désiré.   OGAHCP, *tr.* by Boadiba and Jack Hirschman

Philosophy of Life.   Dániel Berzsenyi.   IQMS, *tr.* by Watson Kirkconnell

Philosophy of white blood cells, The.   Immanuel Kant.   Miroslav Holub.
   VCWP

Philosophy the great and only Heir.   Abraham Cowley.   BASC *Fr.* Pindarique
   Odes.

Philothea (Lydia Child).   James Russell Lowell.   TCAPo *Fr.* Fable for
   Critics, A.

Phlebas the Phoenician, a fortnight dead.   T. S. Eliot.   NPeEn; OBVE; OxBEV
   Fr. Waste Land, The.

Phlegmatic winter on a bed of snow.   Born in Winter.   Francis Quarles.
   NOSC

Phlox is having fun, the purple phlox, The.   Next Afternoon.   Molly Peacock.
   OxBoAm

Phnom Penh Morning.   Yin Luoth.   SonAtl, *tr.* by Carole Gibson, Zaniah
   Marshallsay and Anne Swann

Phoebe in a Rosebush.   Clyde Watson.   NTCP

Phoebe on a Bicycle.   D. W. Faulkner.   ArBi

Phoebus.   James Russell Lowell.   TCAPo *Fr.* Fable for Critics, A.

Phoebus and Boreas.   Jean de La Fontaine.   WoPoe, *tr.* by Marianne Moore

Phœbus Apollo, from Olympus driven.   Christopher Pearse Cranch.   APN-1 *Fr.*
   Seven Wonders of the World.

Phoebus, make haste, the day's too long, be gone.   Another.   Anne Bradstreet.
   BASC

Phoebus, sitting one day in a laurel tree's shade.   James Russell Lowell.
   TCAPo *Fr.* Fable for Critics, A.

Phoebus with Admetus.   George Meredith.   OBEV

Phoenician Statuette, A.   Nina Gabrielian.   CRWP, *tr.* by Peter France

Phoenix.   Elizabeth Kay.   Prnts

Phoenix and the Turtle, The.   William Shakespeare.   NoP-5; NoSic; OBEV;
   OxAEP-1; OxBEV
   (Phoenix and Turtle, The.)   CABP; NPeEn; PBRV

Phoenix are at play on their terrace, The.   City of Choan, The.   Li Po.
   NDACCP, *tr.* by Ezra Pound

Phoenix is rising, The.   Transformation.   Adria Klinger.   PasH

Phoenix tail on scented silk, flimsy layer on layer.   Li Shang-yin.   WoPoe, *tr.*
   by A. C. Graham

Phoenix, The.   Arthur Christopher Benson.   OBEV

Phoenix, The.   Cynewulf. *tr.* by Frank Kuenstler
   "When stars are hid in the western wave, dimmed at dawn."   WoPoe, *tr.* by
   Frank Kuenstler

Phoenix, The.   Yi Hyangji.   EcSo, *tr.* by Catherine J. Kim

Phoenixes and Sparrows.   *Vietnamese Oral Tradition*.   CaDao, *tr.* by John
   Balaban

Phoenixes compete, so do sparrows.   Phoenixes and Sparrows.   *Vietnamese
   Oral Tradition*.   CaDao, *tr.* by John Balaban

Phol and Wotan rode through the forest.   Second Merseburg Spell.   *Unknown*.
   GePo, *tr.* by Carroll Hightower

Phone Booth at the Corner, The.   Juan Delgado.   TouFir

Phone Call From Immortality—From Agnes to Mr. Kundera, A.   Kim
   Chŏngnan.   EcSo, *tr.* by Peter H. Lee

Phone Call to Rutherford.   Paul Blackburn.   PFTM-2

Phone for the fish-knives, Norman.   How to Get On in Society.   Sir John
   Betjeman.   OBSV; UV

Phone rings. Night. Queer loneliness. Such nights exist even at the end of the
   twentieth century.   Phone Call From Immortality—From Agnes to Mr.
   Kundera, A.   Kim Chŏngnan.   EcSo, *tr.* by Peter H. Lee

Phone Sex.   Richard Tayson.   WiU

Phonemics.   Jack Spicer.   PmAP

Phooie!   Robert Garioch.   FaBoWar

Phosphor Reading by His Own Light.   Wallace Stevens.   APT-1

Phosphoric / site that freezes.   Dolores Dorantes.   SPV, *tr.* by Jen Hofer

Photo Genic.   Olga Broumas.   ExTi

Photo of a Rotary Crew, Sour Lake Oilfield, 1904.   Roger Jones.   TiP2

Photo of My Father in a Snowbound Ranch.   David Wojahn.   GM

Photo of Ron Carter, Playing His Bass.   Cornelius Eady.   BtF

Photo of the Author with a Favorite Pig.   William Matthews.   WaAnP

Photo: on a hill a yellow house, white portico, A.   From an Album.   Genrik
   Veniaminovich Sapgir.   ItGoST, *tr.* by J. Kates

Photo Safari.   Bruce Berger.   PoCoUp

Photo Taken in Winter, 1944.   Barbara Unger.   TWW

Photograph.   Lucille Clifton.   OxAAAP

Photograph.   Raymond Vettese.   EdScPo

Photograph, The.   Christopher Pearse Cranch.   APN-1 *Fr.* Seven Wonders of
   the World.

Photograph, The.   Myra Schneider.   Prnts

Photograph, 1958.   Patricia Young.   BrAP

Photograph and White Tulips.   Dannie Abse.   TCAWP

Photograph from Berlin.   Silvia Curbelo.   CFP

Photograph is crowded with the dim figures of dimly remembered people, The.
   Wedding, The.   Franz Wright.   MotU

Photograph is handsome of the young man, The.   Mei-Mei Berssenbrugge.
   Eno *Fr.* Safety.

Photograph: Migrant Worker, Parlier, California, 1967.   Larry Levis.   CalPo;
   GeoHom

Photograph of a Bawd Drinking Raleigh Rye.   Natasha Trethewey.   NeAmPo

Photograph of a Boy.   Carlos Sahagún.   RaW, *tr.* by David Ignatow

Photograph of a Child, Japanese-American Evacuation, Bainbridge Island,
   Washington, March 30, 1942.   James Masao Mitsui.   OpBo

Photograph of My Parents.   Silvia Curbelo.   TouFir

Photograph of the Courthouse Square, 1950s.   Betty Adcock.   TiP2

Photograph of the Girl.   Sharon Olds.   NAMCP V.2

Photographed / face by face.   Saitō Sanki.   CAoMJL1, *tr.* by Masaya Saito

Photographed— / prisoners of war shout commands.   Saitō Sanki.   CAoMJL1,
   tr. by Masaya Saito

Photographs.   Alec Wilder.   ReLy

Photographs, fading already, recall my discomfort.   Getting It Wrong, Again.
   Steve Griffiths.   AngWePo

Photographs from a Book: Six Poems.   David Ferry.
   Photographs from a Book: Six Poems.   FaBoA

Photographs of My Father.   Judith Ortiz Cofer.   ExTi

Photographs of Old New York.   Alfred Corn.   PoA 2002

Photographs of Pioneer Women.   Ruth Dallas.   BeAl

Photographs were yellow where death is a bidden slow form splitting cells
   through the day.   Masters, The.   Gillian Conoley.   BodElec

Photoheliograph (For Lady A.).   Harry Crosby.   APT-2

Photos.   Hugh Seidman.   BodElec

Photos, The.   Diane Wakoski.   NIP-4

Photos and clippings fade.   Archives.   Michael S. Harper.   MoASP

Photos of a Salt Mine.   Patricia K. Page.   NAMCP V.2; NIP-4; NoAM

Photovoltaic.   T. Begley and Olga Broumas.   TAPaP

Photrum.   Anna Mendelssohn.   VaPo

Phrase Book.   Jo Shapcott.   MoWP; NeBrP; PoAgWa; StAl

Phrase-Book.   Veronica Forrest-Thomson.   HarvBoo

Phraseology.   Jayne Cortez.   EGAG

Phyllis. Jacqueline Johnson. BRtP

Phyllis. Thomas Lodge.
   Love Guards [*or* Guides] the Roses of Thy Lips. NoSic
   ('Love guards the roses'.) AEP
   (Phillis 2.) OBEV
   (Phillis 1.) OBEV

Phyllis. Lola Ridge. NAAPv.2

Phyllis' face is a weathered sign. Phyllis. Lola Ridge. NAAPv.2

Phyllis, loving Demophoon. Cometas. ErotSp, *tr. by* Sam Hamill

Phyllis [*or* Phillis] [*or* Progress of Love, The]. Jonathan Swift. OBCoV; OBSV

Phyllyp Sparowe [*or* Philip Sparrow *or* Phillip Sparrow]. John Skelton.
   (Cat of Carlyshe Kynde, A.) TriCat
   "Pla ce bo." NoP-4; NoP-5
   "*Pla ce bo!* Who is there, who?" NoSic

Physical Comparison With Professors and Others. Robert Pinsky. NoP-4; NoP-5 *Fr.* Essay on Psychiatrists.

Physical Geography. Mahe Jabeen. HotL, *tr. by* V. Narayana Rao

Physical Universe. Louis Simpson. CAP-8

Physical-education slides. Hullo, Inside. Max Fatchen. NOxBChV

Physician of eminence, some years ago, A. Lady and the Doctor, The. Helen Leigh. WoRP

Physicians' Fortune, The [*epigram*]. Friedrich von Logau. GePo, *tr. by* George C. Schoolfield

Physics. Eva Salzman. MoWP

Physics of Ochun, The. Víctor Hernández Cruz. PueRic

Physics of Sudden Light, A. Alberto A. Ríos. TAPaP

Physics says: go to sleep. Of course. Sciences Sing a Lullabye, The. Albert Goldbarth. SUP

π. Wisława Szymborska. PoSu, *tr. by* Adam Czerniawski

π deserves our full admiration. π. Wisława Szymborska. PoSu, *tr. by* Adam Czerniawski

Pia who is Pia. Pia. Feriha Aktan. NaPG

Pianist Joe Sullivan, The. Thing About Joe Sullivan, The. Roy Fisher. HarvBoo

Pianist looks like an airline pilot who's afraid to land, The. Greta Goetz. FreRad *Fr.* Construction Papers.

Pianist's funeral passes, The. Sean Dunne. ModIr *Fr.* Sydney Place.

Piano. D. H. Lawrence. BrAP; CABP; GoPo; HarvBoo; HeIP-4; MoBrPo; NAEL-6v2; NAEL-7v2; NAMCP V.1; NIL-7; NoAM; NoP-4; NoP-5; OPOU; TFi; TRP; WeW-3

Piano, The. D. H. Lawrence. PtR; WeW-3

Piano, The: "I try to imagine the lid closing but it won't." Sarah Manguso. IIR

Piano after War. Gwendolyn Brooks. ESEAA

Piano and Drums. Gabriel Okara. NIP-4

Piano has crawled into the quarry, The. Hauled. War Ballad. Andrey Andreievich Voznesensky. WoPoe, *tr. by* Stanley Moss

Piano is correctly tuned slightly out of tune, The. Equal Temperament. Lin Max. MiVo

Piano keys sit stiff and stark, sterile, The. Echoes. Naomi Long Madgett. SeSe

Piano kissed by a slender hand, The. Paul Verlaine. SxFrPo, *tr. by* Martin Sorrell

Piano Man. Joyce Jenkins. ASA

Piano Solo. Nicanor Parra. PoetW; TCLAP, *tr. by* William Carlos Williams

Piano Tuner's Wife, The. Karl Shapiro. NAMCP V.2; NoAM

Piano Tuning. Marianne Boruch. AmAlph

Piano's bone-white oars are pressed, The. Au Café Noir. Mark McMorris. IAoNAP

Pianostool Footnotes. Simon Cutts.
   "On parquet." PoSol

Piao-you-mei: Like Fallie Fruit. *Unknown.* CCL1, *tr. by* V. W. X.

Piazza di Spagna, Early Morning. Richard Wilbur. NoP-4; NoP-5

Piazza Gimma. Fabio Morabito. RMCMP, *tr. by* Geoff Hargreaves

Piazza Gimma. Fabio Morabito. RMCMP

Piazza Piece. John Crowe Ransom. APT-1; ColAP; CtM; FuPo; HarvBoo; HeIP-4; InGu; MoAmPo; NAMCP V.1; NoAM; NoP-4; NoP-5; OxBoAm; TFi

Piazza San Marco. Jean-Pierre Rosnay. PML, *tr. by* J. Kates

Piazza Tragedy, A. Eugene Field. NBLV

Pibroch. J. D. McClatchy. OxBoAm

Pibroch of Donald Dhu. Sir Walter Scott. FaBoWar

Pibroch's note, discountenanced or mute, The. Decadence; or, The Umbrella. William Wordsworth. STuOW

Picadilly or Paradise. John Yau. BodElec

Picasso. Gertrude Stein. NAAPv.2; NAMCP V.1

Picasso and Anarchism. Leslie Scalapino. FTOS

Picasso flies into a rage at Braque. Picasso Visits Braque. Harold Norse. CLPP

Picasso made me tough and quick, and the world. Memorial Day 1950. Frank O'Hara. OxBoAm

Picasso Shag. M. Loncar. AmPoNex

Picasso Visits Braque. Harold Norse. CLPP

Picasso / you give us Things. E. E. Cummings. TCAPo

Picasso's Balcony. Bob Kaufman. EGAG

Piccadilly. Letitia Elizabeth Landon. RWP *Fr.* Scenes in London.

Pick a card, any card. Tyranny of Choice. Elizabeth Garrett. NeBl; StAl

Pick a fern, pick a fern, ferns are high. Song of the Bowmen of Shu [1954]. Bunno [Wen Wang *or* King Wen]. NDACCP; OBVE, *tr. by* Ezra Pound

Pick a pomegranate. *Unknown.* SonAtl, *tr. by* Nezahat Iplici and Emile Tremont

Pick ferns, pick ferns. *Unknown.* ChinPo, *tr. by* Ye Weilian [*or* Yeh Wei-lien *or* Wai-lim Yip]

Pick the flowers by the handful. *Unknown.* SLW, *tr. by* Marjolijn De Jager, Sayd Bahodin Majrouh and André Velter

Pick Yourself Up. Dorothy Fields. ReLy

Picked offhand by the angels to demonstrate. Saint Ursula of Llangwyryfon. Gwyn Williams. AngWePo

Pickerel have infinite, small bones, and skins. In Answer to Amy's Question What's a Pickerel. Stanley Plumly. PfSP

Picket before Bull Run, The. John Day. TreFP

Picketing Supermarkets. Tom Wayman. NIP-4

Pickety Fence, The. David McCord. NTCP

Pickin Em Up and Layin Em Down. Maya Angelou. NBLV

Picking Blueberries, Austerlitz, New York, 1957. Mary Oliver. NAAL-5

Picking Cotton. Mary Loving Blanchard. TiP2

Picking grapes alone in the late autumn sun. Picking Grapes in an Abandoned Vineyard. Larry Levis. GeoHom

Picking grapes from a paper bag, sucking the misted skin. Produce of Cyprus. Alison Brackenbury. RSaN

Picking Up Stones. Lawson Fusao Inada. WANABP

Picking up toward evening. Mission Thief. Forrest Gander. WoBe

Picking violets. Ryokan. WoPoe, *tr. by* Burton Watson

Pickle dogs come down. Rose is a Rose is a Rose is a Rose. Emmett Williams. PFTM-2

Pickpocket leaves. Autumn. Robert Peterson. GeoHom

Picks broke the green-mossed clod. Basin Pond. Tu Mu. CCL1, *tr. by* R. F. Burton

Picks up a water snake. Cobweb. Haniel Long. APT-1

Pickup. Paul Allen. ReTh

Picnic. Kenward Elmslie. FTOS

Picnic. Jane Hirshfield. FiBr

Picnic. Nellie Wong. OpBo

Picnic, The: "It is the picnic with Ruth in the spring." John Logan. NevBe; TRP

Picnic, an Homage to Civil Rights, The. Afaa Michael Weaver. ISC; LTA; PoPoPo

Picnic by the Xie River, A. T'ao Ch'ien. CCL1, *tr. by* William Acker

Picnic on the Bay Bridge. Morton Marcus. GeoHom

Picnic to the Earth. Shuntaro Tanikawa. PoetW, *tr. by* Harold Wright

Picnic-goers beautified themselves, The. Embarkation for Cythera, The. David Ferry. GS

Pict Song, A. Rudyard Kipling. NAMCP V.1; NoAM *Fr.* Puck of Pook's Hill.

Pictis houndis were nocht of sic speed, The. Hector Boece [*or* Boethius]. DiBP *Fr.* Buik of the Cronicles of Scotland.

Picture. Bekes Jr. IrPoTo, *tr. by* Muhamad Tawfiq Ali

Picture, A. Michael Field. VWP

Picture, A. Aleksandr Semionovich Kushner. TCRusP, *tr. by* Daniel Weissbort

Picture, A. Henrietta Cordelia Ray. CBWP-3

Picture, A. B. P. Shillaber. TreFP

Picture, The. Einir Jones. BBMWP, *tr. by* Joseph P. Clancy

Picture and book remain. Acre of Grass, An. William Butler Yeats. HarvBoo; NAMCP V.1; NoAM

Picture has no grammar, A. It has neither evil nor good. Shall Gaelic Die? Iain Crichton Smith. NPeEn

Picture me. Postcard from Cuernavaca. Michael Hofmann. HarvBoo

Picture me, the shy pupil at the door. Pupil, The. Donald Justice. GoPo; PoCho

Picture of a Japanese Farmer, Woodland, California, May 20, 1942. James Masao Mitsui. OpBo

Picture of a Man. Calvin Forbes. ISC

Picture of a Nativity. Geoffrey Hill. NoAM; UpMys

Picture of a Tyrant. Hashim Shafiq. IrPoTo, *tr. by* Melissa Brown and Saadi A. Simawe

Picture of Eakins and a couple of other people, A. David Ferry. FaBoA

Picture of Elvis late at night at the piano, The. Elvis Sings Gospel. Fleda Brown Jackson. AllShUp

Picture of J. T. in a Prospect of Stone, The. Charles Tomlinson. NoP-4; NoP-5; NPeEn; WaAnP

Picture of Little J. A. in a Prospect of Flowers, The ['He was spoilt from childhood by the future, which he mastered rather early and apparently without great difficulty']. John Ashbery. PmAP; WaAnP

Picture of Little T. C. in a Prospect of Flowers, The. Andrew Marvell. BASC; FSCP; NAEL-6v1; NAEL-7v1; NoP-4; NoP-5; OBEV; OxAEP-1; TFi; WaAnP

Picture of My Mother. Meg Bateman. MoWP

Picture of my Mother's Family, A. Wing Tek Lum. OpBo

Picture of Sappho, The. Caroline Elizabeth Norton. VWP

Picture of the Body, The. Ben Jonson. NOSC Fr. Eupheme.

Picture on the front, The. Picture Postcard. Billy Marshall-Stoneking. BMAP

Picture on the Purple Wall, The. Steve Wilson. AmPoNex

Picture Postcard. Billy Marshall-Stoneking. BMAP

Picture Postcard from Our Youth. Dan Pagis. VCWP, tr. by Stephen Mitchell

Picture Postcards. Miklós Radnóti. AF

Picture Shakespeare just like the domed. My Students. Ron Koertge. IaFF

Picture the lost world in. Critique. Anthony Barnett. Oth

Picture wants to be upside down, head, The. Norgberto Hernandez—Photographed Falling September Eleventh. David Reibetanz. IFF

Picture yourself drinking with your father. Painting the Angel. Martin Mooney. NIrP

Picture-Palaces. Philip Heseltine. OBCoV

Pictures. Sarah Kirsch. AF, tr. by Wayne Kvam

Pictures. Clarence Major. EGAG

Pictures are falling from my walls, The. Note to the Reader: This is Not a Poem. Helen Ivory. StAl

Pictures come striding into the room, The. Evening. Mark McMorris. AmPoNex

"Pictures from Brueghel." William Carlos Williams. See Parable of the Blind, The.

Pictures from Brueghel. William Carlos Williams.
    Haymaking. NAMCP V.1; NoAM
    Hunters in the Snow, The. GS; OxBoAm
    Landscape with the Fall of Icarus. BrAP; NAAL-5; NAAPv.2; NAMCP V.1; NoAM; NoP-5; OtW; OxBoAm; PoPoPo
    Parable of the Blind, The. SAmP
    ("Pictures from Brueghel.") GI

Pictures hold up the walls, The. Shadow That Draws the Light, The. Natalia Toledo. RMCMP, tr. by Alberto A. Ríos

Pictures in the Smoke. Dorothy Parker. NBLV

Pictures of Maurice Among Funeral Flowers. Amittai F. Aviram. WaAnP

Pictures of the Floating World. Miyazawa Kenji. PFTM-1

Picturesque, The. George Oppen. APSN Fr. Some San Francisco Poems.

Picture-Writing. Henry Wadsworth Longfellow. APN-1; NAAPv.1 Fr. Song of Hiawatha, The.

Piddling ant has its bibble of gall, The. Unknown. SonAtl, tr. by Helen Bell and Patti Oliver

Pidgin Pinch. William Jay Smith. PWW2

Pie in the Sky: Part 2. Tina Darragh. OnScMo

Pie Para el Niño de Vallecas de Velázquez. León Felipe. RaW

Pièce à grand spectacle. Louis Aragon. YaTCFP

Piece of Coffee, A. Gertrude Stein. NAMCP V.1 Fr. Tender Buttons.

Piece of Advice, A. Gyula Illyés. IQMS, tr. by Adam Makkai

Piece of Bone, The. Katerina Pinosová. SurWo

Piece of burned meat, A. Jane Kenyon. LoL Fr. Having It Out with Melancholy.

Piece of forest, A. Still Life. Raymond Garlick. AngWePo

Piece of meat lost in cabbage stew, A. Our Birth-Cord. Kofi Anyidoho. NAfrP

Piece of the Loot, A. Wang the Zealot. CCL1, tr. by C. H. Kwock and Vincent McHugh and Vincent McHugh

Piece of the Storm, A. Mark Strand. BeAl; CAP-8; WaAnP

Piececitos. Gabriela Mistral. ItP, tr. by Doris Dana

Piecemeal the summer dies. Exeunt. Richard Wilbur. HeIP-4

Pieces. Paul Lake. PoDa

Pieces. Duane Niatum. HATNAP

Pieces from a Mortal Duet. Mario Luzi. tr. by Gayle Ridinger
    Postscriptum. ItPo, tr. by Gayle Ridinger

Pieces of a green / bottle. (LL) Between Walls. William Carlos Williams. APT-1; NAAPv.2

Pieces of Coal. Huw Menai. AngWePo Fr. Back in the Return.

Pieces of coal, hewn from the deeps of earth. Huw Menai. AngWePo Fr. Back in the Return.

Pieces of Henry. Taylor Graham. CalPo

Pieces of the One and a Half Legged Man. Peter Klappert. Court of Divine Justice, The. YaYoPo

Pieces o'Six—XVIII. Jackson Mac Low. FTOS

Pieces o'Six—XXIV. Jackson Mac Low. FTOS

Pied Beauty. Gerard Manley Hopkins. AmFaPo; BrAP; CABP; ChAP; ClHu; CtM; HeIP-4; InvLi; ITBLP; MoBrPo; NAEL-6v2; NAEL-7v2; NAMCP V.1; NIL-7; NoAM; NoP-4; NoP-5; NPeEn; OBEV; OBMV; OxAEP-2; OxBEV; PoCho; PoPoPo; RaBo; SacPr; SoSe-8; TFi; UV; WaAnP; WeW-3

Pied Beauty. Stanley J. Sharpless. UV

Pied / pear. Roy Kiyooka. NLPA Fr. Pear Tree Pomes.

Pied Piper of Hamelin, The. Robert Browning. NOxBChV; OBNV; OBSP "Into the street the Piper stept." OxAEP-2

Pied Piper, The. John Ashbery. YaYoPo

Piedra en el agua de la cordura, Una. Coral Bracho. RMCMP

Piedra en la arena. Coral Bracho. RMCMP

Piedra es una frente donde los sueños gimen, La. Federico García Lorca. RaW Fr. Llanto por Ignacio Sánchez Mejías.

Piensa en esa estatua abierta en el corazón de la ciudad. Mónica Nepote. SPV

Pienso en dificultad, en geometría. Cena de un 10 de Abríl. Carla Faesler Bremer. SPV

Pier, a great concrete semicircle, The. Pacific Crossing. Vince Gotera. ReBoTo

Pier of Yokohama under the Umbrella, The. Im Hwa. CAMKP, tr. by Jiwon Shin

Pier, The. Garrett Kaoru Hongo. OpBo

Pier: Under Pisces, The. James Merrill. NoAM

Pierced tongue. Do-it-yourself lisp. Kate Light. PoDa Fr. Five Urban Love Songs.

Piercing chill. Buson. EMJL, tr. by Haruo Shirane

Piercing shrieks race in. Strike of the Coal Miners. Ber Grin. Prolet, tr. by Amelia Glaser

Piercing winter frost, and winds, and darkened air, The. (LL) November. William Cullen Bryant. APN-1; GSo; TreFP

Pier-Glass, The. Robert Graves. NoAM

Pierre ou eau. André Du Bouchet. YaTCFP

Pierre put the gold in the morning into the ring-machine, and prayed. Ring, The. Harry Mathews. NYP2

Pierrot Says. Jules Laforgue. SonAtl, tr. by Gregory Beaven and Kurt Ganzl

Piers are pummelled by the waves, The. Fall of Rome, The. W. H. Auden. NPeEn; OxBEV

Piers Gaveston [1619]. Michael Drayton.
    "And thus like slaves we sell our soules to sinne." CAGL
    "O breake my hart quoth he, O breake and dye." CAGL
    "This Edward in the Aprill of his age." CAGL
    "Why doe I quake my down-fall to reporte?" CAGL

Piers Plowman Shows the Way to Saint Truth. William Langland. NAEL-6v1; NAEL-7v1 Fr. Vision of Piers Plowman, The.

Pietà. Allen Afterman. NOBAu

Pietà. Christopher Davis. Vesp

Pietà. Alastair MacKie. EdScPo

Pietà. Rainer Maria Rilke. GI

Pietà. Wisława Szymborska. VCWP

Pietà. Ronald Stuart Thomas. NPeEn

Pietà: "What she holds is the unimaginable." Mariève Rugo. PfS

Pietá. Martyn Crucefix. PML

Pietá. James McAuley. BMAP

Pietà's Over, The. Paul Durcan. PBCIP

Pietà's Over—and, now, my dear, droll, husband, The. Pietà's Over, The. Paul Durcan. PBCIP

"Pietrofesso," I'd repeat to Mr. Wright, the science teacher in / Junior High. Having the Wrong Name for Mr. Wright. Helen Barolini. UnSA

Pig, The. Unknown. OBCoV

Pig, Goat, Sheep. Jean de La Fontaine. WoPoe, tr. by Bruce Boone and Robert Glück

Pig Killing Day. Donald Evans. BBMWP, tr. by Gillian Clarke

Pig lay on a barrow dead, The. View of a Pig. Ted Hughes. OxAEP-2; OxBEV

Pig Melons. John Kinsella. NeBl

Pig on the page is crying, The. First Empathy. J. Allyn Rosser. NevBe

Pig Pino oink ochet. Psalm for the Damnation of Pig Pino Oink Ochet, Who Unlike His Victims Will Neither Die nor Disappear, Because He Was Never Human. Jack Agüeros. PrTe

Pigeon Makes His Request, The. Issa. WED, tr. by Robert Bly

Pigeon purrs in the wood; the wood has gone, The. Geoffrey Hill. NoAM Fr. Apology for the Revival of Christian Architecture in England, An.

Pigeon, The / The pigeon. Song of the Pigeon. Unknown. CATKP, tr. by Peter H. Lee

Pigeon-house of letters, The. Letter. Miguel Hernández. WED, *tr. by* Robert Bly

Pigeons. David Hernandez. UnSA

Pigeons. Lilian Moore. SSCS

Pigeons. Conor O'Callaghan. NIrP

Pigeons. Vikram Seth. OWoS

Pigeons. Daniel Tobin. UrbNat

Pigeons. Baron Wormser. UrbNat

Pigeons, The. William Heyen. CAP-8

Pigeons are cityfolk. Pigeons. Lilian Moore. SSCS

Pigeons are the spiks of Birdland. Pigeons. David Hernandez. UnSA

Pigeons / Are tossing. Pigeons. Alison Fell. EdScPo

Pigeons do when they're knitting. (LL) Wild Oats. Norman Alexander MacCaig. NePenScot; NPeEn

Pigeons have survived, The. Closure Opening Its Trap. Suzanne Wise. AmPoNex

Pigeons on the grass alas. Gertrude Stein. NAAPv.2; OWoS *Fr.* Four Saints in Three Acts.

Pigeons: "Pigeons / Are tossing." Alison Fell. EdScPo

Pigeons shake their wings on the copper church roof. Fourth Floor, Dawn, Up All Night Writing Letters. Allen Ginsberg. HarvBoo; InvLad

Pigeons swing across the square, The. Pigeons. Vikram Seth. OWoS

Pigeons that peck at the grass in Trinity Churchyard, The. Trinity Place. Phyllis McGinley. AmWit; MoAmPo; SoSe-8

Piggy-back. Ramy Ditzanny. NRoS, *tr. by* Esther Raizen

Piggy-back. Langston Hughes. TLR

Piglets go by, smart as you please, The. Samch'ŏnp'o. Paek Sŏk. CAMKP, *tr. by* Kyunghwan Choi

Pigmalion, whose hie love-hating minde. John Marston. PBRV *Fr.* Metamorphosis of Pigmalions Image, The.

Pigmy headhunters and killer apes play basketball at the Y. Pygmy Headhunters and Killer Apes, My Lover and Me. Laurel Ann Bogen. CalPo; SUP

Pigs. Les A. Murray. StAl

Pig's-Eye View of Literature, A. Dorothy Parker. APT-1; BrAP

  Alfred Lord Tennyson. NALW

  D. G. Rossetti. NALW

  George Sand. NALW; NAMCP V.1

  Harriet Beecher Stowe. NALW

  Lives and Times of John Keats, Percy Bysshe Shelley, and George Gordon Noel, Lord Byron, The. NALW

  Oscar Wilde. NALW; NAMCP V.1

  Thomas Carlyle. NALW

  Walter Savage Landor. NALW

Pigtail. Tadeusz Rózewicz. BeAl; HP; PoSu, *tr. by* Adam Czerniawski

Pike. Ted Hughes. BrAP; HeIP-4; NAEL-6v2; NAEL-7v2; NAMCP V.2; NoP-4; NoP-5; NPeEn; OxBEV; WaAnP

Pike, The. Amy Lowell. APT-1; NAMCP V.1

Pike, The. Theodore Roethke. MoASP

Pike, three inches long, perfect. Pike. Ted Hughes. BrAP; HeIP-4; NAEL-6v2; NAEL-7v2; NAMCP V.2; NoP-4; NoP-5; NPeEn; OxBEV; WaAnP

Pilate. Donald Davie. GI

Pilate Remembers. William E. Brooks. ChIV-2

Pilate's Wife. Nina Kossman. GI

Pilate's Wife's Dream. Charlotte Brontë. VWP

Pilchard-Curing Song, The. Alice Oswald. MFPA

Pile high the hickory and the light. Winter Night. Edna St. Vincent Millay. APT-1

Pile of discards on the sidewalk, A. Sunday Morning. David Ray. AllShUp

Pile of Feathers. Gerald Stern. LoL

Pile of hides. Strips & scraps of flannel. Peeling the Orange. Mary Ruefle. AmAlph

Pile the bodies high at Austerlitz and Waterloo. Grass. Carl Sandburg. AmWaPo; ColAP; FaBoWar; InoFa; MoAmPo; NAAL-5; NAAPv.2; NAMCP V.1; NoAM; NoP-4; NoP-5; OBWP; OxBoAm; PoAgWa; PoPoPo; StAl; TCAPo; TFi; WaAnP

Piled deep below the screening apple-branch. Orchard-Pit, The. Dante Gabriel Rossetti. NAEL-6v2

Piled for burning/ Brushwood. Boncho. ZenPo, *tr. by* Takashi Ikemoto and Lucien Stryk

Pilgrim, The. Nicanor Parra. VCWP

Pilgrim Song, The. John Bunyan. OxBEV *Fr.* Pilgrim's Progress, The.

Pilgrimage. Yoshioka Minoru. PFTM-2, *tr. by* Eric Selland

Pilgrimage, The. George Herbert. BASC; NAEL-6v1; NAEL-7v1; NOSC

Pilgrimage, The. Henry Vaughan. ChIV-2

Pilgrimage along the migratory roads, a voyage to ancestral / sources. Song of the Initiate. Léopold Sédar Senghor. VCWP, *tr. by* Melvin Dixon

Pilgrims, The. Ella Krylova. CRWP, *tr. by* Yury Drobyshev and Carol Rumens

Pilgrims, The. Adelaide Anne Procter. SacPr

Pilgrims in Mexico. *Unknown.* OBCP

Pilgrim's Progress, The. John Bunyan.

  Christian Loses His Burden. SacPr

  Pilgrim Song, The. OxBEV

  Shepherd Boy Sings [in the Valley of Humiliation], The. OBEV; SacPr

  (Valiant-for-Truth's Song.) NPeEn

  (Valiant's Song.) NOSC

Pilgrim's Viaticum; or, The Destitute, But Not Forlorn. Elizabeth Tipper.

  To a Young Lady That Desired a Verse of My Being Servant One Day and Mistress Another. EMWP; NOSC

Pillar of cloud by day. Exodus. Jarret Keene. Vesp

Pillar of Fame, The. Robert Herrick. NIP-4

Pillar of the Cloud, The. John Henry, Cardinal Newman. ChIV-1; InvLi; NPeEn; SacPr

Pillar [*or* Piller] perished [*or* pearisht] is whe[a]rto I le[a]nt, The. Sir Thomas Wyatt. NoSic; OBVE; OxBEV; PBRV

Pillow. Li-Young Lee. NAMCP V.2

Pillow, The. Herman Melville. APN-2 *Fr.* Clarel: A Poem and Pilgrimage in the Holy Land.

Pillowed on your thighs in a dream garden. Song of the Dream Garden. Ikkyu Sojun. ErotSp, *tr. by* Sam Hamill

Pillows. Antonio Deltoro. RMCMP, *tr. by* Christian Viveros-Fauné

Pillows know, they say. Lady Ise. ArkPo, *tr. by* Helen Craig McCullough

Pilot from the Carrier, A. Randall Jarrell. PoWW

Pilots, Man Your Planes. Randall Jarrell. MoAmPo

Pilot's Psalm, The. *Unknown.* PoWW

Pimpled, pubescent, teeny-bop. Rite of Passage. Gearóid Mac Lochlainn. NIrP, *tr. by* the author

Pin has a head, but has no hair, A. Christina Georgina Rossetti. VWP

Pin your little tail on glittering star, come. Sarah Kirsch. PFTM-2 *Fr.* Kite-Flying.

Pinch him, pinch him black and blue. John Lyly. NoSic *Fr.* Endimion.

Pinch of Salt, A. Robert Graves. MoBrPo

Pindar is imitable by none. Pindarique Odes. Abraham Cowley.

Pindaric on the Death of our Late Sovereign: with an Ancient Prophecy on His Present Majority, A. Aphra Behn. BASC

Pindaric Poem, A. Anne Finch, Countess of Winchilsea.

  Hymn, The. ChIV-1

Pindaric, to the Athenian Society, A. Elizabeth Singer Rowe. BASC

Pindarick To Mrs. Behn on her Poem on the Coronation, A. *Unknown.* EMWP

Pindaricque on the Grunting of a Hog, A. Samuel Wesley.

  "Freeborn Pindaric never does refuse." VerBaPo

Pindarique Odes. Abraham Cowley.

  Hymn to Light. OxAEP-1

  Muse, The. CABP; PBRV

  Resurrection, The. ChIV-2

  To Mr. Hobs. BASC

  To the Royal Society. BASC

Pinder. Mick North. NLP

Pine. Kimiko Hahn. PoDa

Pine. Chase Twichell. WaAnP

Pine, The. Saunders Lewis. OBWVE, *tr. by* Gwyn Morgan

Pine Bark Bread. Hamhur Kiwha. BecRai, *tr. by* Kim Daljin, Kim Won-Chung and Christopher Merrill

Pine boat a-shift [fr. *the Chinese of the* Confucian Odes]. *Unknown.* APSN; APT-1; NDACCP; OBVE, *tr. by* Ezra Pound

Pine cones. Forest Family. Lawson Fusao Inada. WhBo

Pine Cones. Dave Jeddie Smith. CAP-8

"Pine flower's blooming," says. Sŏ Chŏngju. VCWP, *tr. by* David R. McCann

Pine Is Standing Lonely, A. Heinrich Heine. NAWM-7v2, *tr. by* Hal Draper

Pine Island. Reginald Gibbons. RWB

Pine mushroom. Basho. EH, *tr. by* Robert Hass

Pine needles. Masaoka Shiki. CAoMJL1, *tr. by* Burton Watson

Pine needling. Paul Reps. WhBo

Pine or two, A. On a Painting. Ching An. CSKM, *tr. by* Jerome P. Seaton

Pine pierces the hills' whiteness, The. Epiphany. Andrea Zanzotto. VCWP

Pine Planters, The. Thomas Hardy. FaBoVe

Pine seedling somewhere springs, A. Remember It, My Soul. Eduard Friedrich Mörike. WoPoe, *tr. by* W. D. Snodgrass

Pine Shade. Muso Soseki. EaWin, *tr. by* W. S. Merwin

Pine shadow falls on the tent wall, The. Diane Di Prima. WhBo

Pine tree, A. Turtle Head Stupa. Muso Soseki. EaWin, *tr. by* W. S. Merwin

Pine tree shivers like a match flame, The. End of Winter. Liz Rosenberg. IJHIL

Pine tree sways in the smoke, The. Wood in Sound, A. Takahashi Shinkichi. ZenPo, *tr. by* Takashi Ikemoto and Lucien Stryk

Pine trees murmur in the wind. Sitting and Teaching at Night. Jinkag Haesim. BecRai, *tr. by* Kim Daljin, Kim Won-Chung and Christopher Merrill

Pine trees will not converse with foreigners. Their aim. Zipangu. Charles Tomlinson. WoBe

Pine Whisk, The. Yu Chao. CSKM, *tr. by* Paul Hansen

Pineneedles cast a quivering shadow on. Journey of a Doe. Chava Pinchas-Cohen. DTA, *tr. by* Miriyam Glazer

Pines and the Sea, The. Christopher Pearse Cranch. ColAP

Pines at Hakone, The. Charles Tomlinson. WoBe *Fr.* Zipangu.

Pines charred, temple wrecked, all from the fighting. After the Rebellion, Visiting West Mountain Temple. Ch'i-chi. CSKM, *tr. by* Burton Watson

Pines moan when the wind passes, The. Beach. Sophia De Mello Breyner. VCWP, *tr. by* Ruth Fainlight

Pines were dark on Ramoth hill, The. My Playmate. John Greenleaf Whittier. APN-1

Pines Without Peer, The. Kelly Cherry. FFC

Pinetree. Ágnes Nemes Nagy. PoSu, *tr. by* Bruce Berlind

Pinetree thicket dances, The. Chickcharnies. *Unknown.* SonAtl, *tr. by* Edward Kamau Brathwaite, Lester Browne, Eden Marshall and Myrna Teirrel

Pingpong bagmen & a ho & anuther. Ewe's Candy Canes Red Sea Outerbank. Jessica Freeman. AnSo

Pining. Zhang Shuai. CCL1, *tr. by* Anne Birrell

Pink. Gertrude Stein. MotU *Fr.* Book Concluding with As A Wife Has a Cow a Love Story, A.

Pink and a bit soft-bodied, with a somewhat jazzy. Robert Pinsky. NoP-4; NoP-5 *Fr.* Essay on Psychiatrists.

Pink blossoms, The. Blooming Death. . .Blossoms. Andre O. Hoilette. BRtP

Pink car is in my head, The. Pink Car, The. Mark Halliday. P180

Pink Car, The. Mark Halliday. P180

Pink confused with white. Pot of Flowers, The. William Carlos Williams. APT-1

Pink Diapers. Donna Brook. PrTe

Pink Dog. Elizabeth Bishop. NALW

Pink gondola floats, A. How Many More Minutes Until We Can Devour Our Breached Contract? Joanna Fuhrman. PrTe

Pink Locust, The. William Carlos Williams. SAmP

Pink looks as pink, pink looks as pink, as pink as pink supposes, suppose. Gertrude Stein. MotU *Fr.* Book Concluding with As A Wife Has a Cow a Love Story, A.

Pink magnolias, the punishment. Lee Varon. PfS

Pink Maniac, A. Ray DiPalma. PmAP

Pink neon lit window full of plaster of parts and resin, The. Real Indian Leans Against, The. Chrystos. UnSA

Pink petals of peach blossom. Peach Blossom and Pigeon (painting by Kiso). Takahashi Shinkichi. ZenPo, *tr. by* Takashi Ikemoto and Lucien Stryk

Pink Poem. Jackie Warren-Moore. SpirFl

Pink Rose Rings, The. Tracey Herd. MFPA; NeBl

Pink Slip at Tool & Dye. Dave Jeddie Smith. NoAM

Pink Triangles. Larry Wayne Johns. LiTh

Pinned on our picnic blankets. Listening to Mozart at Meadow Brook. Patricia Hooper. MiVo

Piñon Nuts. Dixie Salazar. UnSA

Pins. Menna Elfyn. ATSWP, *tr. by* Robert Minhinnick

Pin's Fee, or Painting with Star, A. David Shapiro. BodElec

Pin-swin or spine-swine, The. His Shield. Marianne Moore. NALW

Pints. Celia de Fréine. NIrP *Fr.* Price on My Head, A.

Pinup of Rita Hayworth was taped, A. Post-Modernism. James Galvin. GifTon

Pinwheel, A. Ōkuma Kotomichi. EMJL, *tr. by* Peter Flueckiger

Pioneer artists had a canvas as wide, The. Cattle Brands. Vaida Stewart Montgomery. TiP2

Pioneer Lane. Michael Dransfield. NOBAu

Pioneer: The Vignette of an Oil-Field. Lexie Dean Robertson. TiP2

Pioneers. Aileen Fisher *and* Olive Rabe. CA

Pioneers. Lillian M. Fisher. HHAm

Pious magistrate! sound his praise throughout, A. Official Piety. John Greenleaf Whittier. NCAP

Pious men. We Must Be Assured That a Fine Poet Will Be Born, Even after Fifteen Years. Ali Mansour. AnVo, *tr. by* Mohamed Enani

Pious One, The. Gabriela Mistral. BBASP, *tr. by* Doris Dana

Pious Selinda goes to prayers [*or* pray'rs]. Pious Selinda [*or* Celinda]. William Congreve. NPeEn

Pious sire of Arla reared her youth, The. Enthusiast, The. Arla. Anne Batten Cristall. RWP

Pious wish to whiteness gone over—, A / or nothing. (LL) Queen Anne's Lace. William Carlos Williams. APT-1; BrAP; MoAmPo; NAAL-5; NAAPv.2; NAMCP V.1; NoAM; NoP-4; NoP-5; OxBoAm

Pipe, The. Stéphane Mallarmé. MotU, *tr. by* Michael Benedikt

Pipe, The. Takahashi Shinkichi. ZenPo, *tr. by* Takashi Ikemoto and Lucien Stryk

Pipe and Can II. Thomas Bonham. OBEV

Pipe of Tobacco, A. Isaac Hawkins Browne.
"Blest leaf! whose aromatic gales dispense." UV

Piper coming from far away is you, The. Keeping Going. Seamus Heaney. ModIr

Pipes at Lucknow, The. John Greenleaf Whittier. FaBoWar

Pipes in the streets were playing bravely, The. Cha Till Maccruimein (Departure of the 4th Camerons). Ewart Alan Mackintosh. FaBoWar

Pipes of the misty moorlands. Pipes at Lucknow, The. John Greenleaf Whittier. FaBoWar

Pipe is dozie, the pipie is fey, The. 51st Highland Division's Farewell to Sicily, The. Hamish Henderson. EdScPo

Piping Down the Valleys Wild. William Blake. ChAP; ClHu; HeIP-4; NoP-4; NOxBChV; SoSe-8; TFi *Fr.* Songs of Innocence.

Piping of our slender, peaceful reeds, The. Prologue. Oliver Wendell Holmes. NCAP

Piping of plenty. (LL) To Waken an Old Lady. William Carlos Williams. OxBoAm; SoSe-8; WeW-3

Pipistrelles. Kathleen Jamie. NeBrP

Pipits sit up, sprinkle, dont give it motion, stay. Pallid Harrier. Colin Simms. Oth

Pipling. Theodore Roethke. OBCoV *Fr.* Three Epigrams.

Pippa Passes. Robert Browning.
Pippa's Song. BRP; ITBLP; NTCP; OBEV
(Song.) TFi

Pippa Passes, But I Can't Get Around This Truck. Margaret Blaker. NBLV

Pippa's Song. Robert Browning. BRP; ITBLP; NTCP; OBEV *Fr.* Pippa Passes.

Pip's sister, Mrs Joe Gargery. Hit Men, The. Philippa Lawrence. Prnts

Piquant. Roddy Lumsden. NeBrP

Pique at Parting, A. Sarah Morgan Bryan Piatt. NCAP

Pirate Ditty. Robert Louis Stevenson. NPeEn *Fr.* Treasure Island.

Pirate Don Durk of Dowdee, The. Mildred Plew Meigs. ChAP

Pirate Story. Robert Louis Stevenson. NOxBChV

Pirates of Penzance, The. William Schwenck Gilbert.
I Am the Very Model [*or* Pattern] of a Modern Major-General. NoP-5
"I am the very pattern of a modern major-gineral." UV
(Modern Major-General, The.) NBLV

Pisan Cantos and the first books of *Paterson*, The. Andy Weaver. PoPra *Fr.* Were the Bees.

Pisces. Ronald Stuart Thomas. CABP

Pisgah-Sights. I. Robert Browning. ChIV-1

Pisgah-Sights. II. Robert Browning. ChIV-1

Pismo, 1959. Robert Vasquez. GeoHom

Pissaro's Tomb. Patrick Lane. BrAP

Pissing in the snow. Issa. EH, *tr. by* Robert Hass

Pissing off the Back of the Boat into the Nivernais Canal. William Matthews. CAP-8

Pistachio Ice Cream. Annemarie Jacir. PoArWo

Pistyll Rhaeadr and Wrexham steeple. Seven Wonders of North Wales, The. *Unknown.* OBWVE

Pit, The. David Ignatow. BodElec

Pit, The. Lucien Stryk. AmWaPo

Pit indeed of Sin: No water's here:, A. Edward Taylor. TCAPo *Fr.* Preparatory Meditations Before My Approach to the Lord's Supper.

Pit of some fruit might be what I'm about, The. Riffing. Rick Barot. NeAmPo

Pit Ponies, The. Leslie Norris. ChAP

Pit Viper. N. Scott Momaday. HATNAP

Pit—but Heaven over it, A. Emily Dickinson. APN-2; NCAP

Pitch. Catherine Walsh.
"Matter / of fact." Oth

Pitch black night gave me two deep black eyes, The. Generation, A. Gu Cheng. PFTM-2; VCWP, *tr. by* Sam Hamill

Pitcher shot her husband, The. Softball at Julia Tutwiler Prison. R. T. Smith. MoASP

Pitcher, The. Robert Francis. MoASP; RaBo; WeW-3

Pitcher, The. Yüan Chĕn. CCL1, *tr. by* Arthur Waley

Pitchfork, The. Seamus Heaney. OxBEV

Pitching and darting across the roadway. Phoebe on a Bicycle. D. W. Faulkner. ArBi

Pitching Coups. Ron Wellburn. MoASP

Pitiful dupes of old illusion, lost. Sparrows in a Hillside Drift. James Wright. ColAP

Pitiful Prioress, The. Geoffrey Chaucer. DiBP *Fr.* Canterbury Tales, The.

Pitiless war of love I fought, A. Sandro Penna. CAGL, *tr. by* John McRae

Pitman's Common Sense Arithmetic, 1917. Alan Brownjohn. Common Sense. NoP-5; NOxBChV

Pitman's Lovesong, A. *Unknown.* FaBoVe

Pitt. Samuel Taylor Coleridge. CenSon *Fr.* Effusions.

Pittancer, The. Brian Catling. VaPo

Pittsburgh. Hayden Carruth. PoChi

Pittsburgh, 1948, The Music Teacher. Gerald William Barrax. PoDa

Pittsburgh Poem. Jan Beatty. SweBea

Pity. Trumbull Stickney. ColAP

Pity, A. We Were Such a Good Invention. Yehuda Amichai. FIT, *tr. by* Robert Friend

Pity, Lord, pity on my poor town. Pueblo. Luis Palés Matos. TCLAP, *tr. by* Barry Luby

Pity Me! Fu Hsüan. ColAnChi, *tr. by* Anne Birrell and Burton Watson

Pity me! my body is female. Pity Me! Fu Hsüan. ColAnChi, *tr. by* Anne Birrell and Burton Watson

Pity me not because the light of day. Edna St. Vincent Millay. MoAmPo; OxBoAm

Pity not! The Army gave. Rudyard Kipling. HarvBoo *Fr.* Epitaphs of the War [1914–1918].

Pity of the Leaves, The. Edwin Arlington Robinson. APN-2; MoAmPo

Pity poor lovers who may not do what they please. Envy of Poor Lovers, The. Austin Clarke. IrLP

Pity the Bastards. Tom French. BeAl; NIrP

Pity the Bathtub Its Forced Embrace of the Human Form. Matthea Harvey. LegDan

Pity the bathtub that belongs to the queen its feet. Pity the Bathtub Its Forced Embrace of the Human Form. Matthea Harvey. LegDan

Pity the drunks in this late April snow. Pity the Drunks. David Constantine. StAl

Pity the heart, my lovely doe. Poem in Parts. Judah Ha-Levi. WoPoe, *tr. by* Ammiel Alcalay

Pity the Man Who English Lacks [*after the Irish of* David O'Bruaidar]. Michael Hartnett. PBCIP

Pity the man who stands alone. Thoughts While Broadcasting. Ronald Frankau. RWPCtW

Pity the poor weightlifter. Baldanders. Christopher Reid. NPeEn

Pity the Slain that Laid Away Their Lives. Iris Tree. RSaN

Pity the tune bereft of singers. Song for the Music in the Warsaw Ghetto. Jacqueline Osherow. TaR

Pity This Busy Monster,Manunkind. E. E. Cummings. HarvBoo; NAMCP V.1

Pity would be no more. William Blake. NAEL-6v2; NAEL-7v2; NOBRP; NPBRoP; OxAEP-2 *Fr.* Songs of Experience.

Pitying the Farmer. Li Shen. ColAnChi, *tr. by* Burton Watson

Pitzeem and the Mare. Robert Bly. CAP-8

Piute Creek. Gary Snyder. OxBoAm

Piyis ĕkwa ĕ-tipiskâk ĕkwa. His Flute, My Ears. Gregory Scofield. IFF

Pizza and Pretense. Nerissa S. Balce. ReBoTo

Pizza's a populous island. Mariya Kildibekova. CRWP, *tr. by* Roy Fisher

Pla ce bo. John Skelton. NoP-4; NoP-5 *Fr.* Phyllyp Sparowe [*or* Philip Sparrow *or* Phillip Sparow].

Placable Caps, The. Hannibal Vito Acconci. AHA

Place, The. Mónica Nepote. SPV, *tr. by* Jen Hofer

Place, The ("Afternoon it changes.") Robert Creeley. BodElec

Place and Date. Leonard Nolens. TuT, *tr. by* Michael O'Loughlin

Place and the formula recede with the echo to win back the fallow lands, The. Rituals. Annie Le Brun. YaTCFP, *tr. by* Mary Ann Caws *and* Jean-Pierre Cauvin

Place devoted to death, A. At noon, when I came out, the sun. Dossers at the Imperial War Museum. Joyce Herbert. TCAWP

Place for Everything, A. Louis Jenkins. GoPo; IJHIL

Place for Four-Letter Words. Peter Sears. ArBi

Place for No Story, The. Robinson Jeffers. APT-1

Place from which no one has ever come back. (LL) Ecstasy. Sharon Olds. EmeKit; MoWP; StAl

Place has its undertone. Not all. Past, The. Fyodor Ivanovich Tyutchev. WoPoe, *tr. by* Charles Tomlinson

Place in thy memory, dearest, A. Song. Gerald Griffin. IrLP

Place is the corner of Empty and Bleak, The. Nighthawks. Samuel Yellen. PoSol

Place is the focus. What is the language. In Defence of Metaphysics. Charles Tomlinson. MoBrPo

Place Names. Thomas Merton. ChIV-1 *Fr.* Geography of Lograire, The.

Place of Fire. Johannes Bobrowski. PoSu

Place of Fire, A. "Zelda." NRoS, *tr. by* Esther Raizen

Place of suffering, a golgotha, A. Black Flower. Walter Pavlich. TWW

Place of the Damned [*or* Damn'd], The. Jonathan Swift. ChIV-2; OBSV

Place park. By the Light of the Silvery Moon. Edward Madden. NAAPv.2; ReLy

Place Pigalle. Richard Wilbur. HeIP-4; PWW2

Place, Places. Melvin Dixon. ISC

Place Setting. Johari M. Rashad. PasH

Place there is, where proudly raised there stands, A. Samuel Daniel. NoSic *Fr.* Civil Wars, The.

Place was famed for, The. Kris Hemensley. BMAP *Fr.* Mile from Poetry, A.

Place Where He Arose, The. George Barlow. GT

Place where I was born, The. Idea of Islands, The. Judith Ortiz Cofer. PueRic

Place Where the Rainbow Ends, The. Paul Laurence Dunbar. SacPr

Place Without Shame, A. David Baraza. FTtHH

Place you never thought to, A. Mad Wolf in Lunar Web, Mad Crow on the Beach. Mac Wellman. FTOS

Placed on this isthmus of a middle state. Alexander Pope. WeW-3 *Fr.* Essay on Man, An.

Placed these worlds in us. (LL) Lost Pilot, The. James Tate. AmWaPo; EmeKit; InoFa; NAMCP V.2; NoAM; OBWP; OtW; OxBoAm; PWW2; WaAnP

Placements I. Clayton Eshleman. PFTM-1

Place-Names of China. Alan Bennett. UV

Places. PfS

Places. Luciana Frezza. CItWP, *tr. by* Cinzia Sartini Blum and Lara Trubowitz

Places. Thomas Hardy. HarvBoo

Places and Ways to Live. Richard Hugo. NIP-4

Places we love exist only through us. Places We Love. Ivan V. Lalic. StAl, *tr. by* Francis R. Jones

Placid Man's Epitaph, A. Thomas Hardy. MoBrPo

Plagiarism. Ben Marcus. HeMarv

Plagiarist, The. Bruce Berger. GeoH

Plague and sores beyond relief. Les Congés du Lépreux. Jean Bodel. WoPoe, *tr. by* Frank Templeton Prince

Plague of Dead Sharks. Alan Dugan. NoAM; PtR

Plague of God, the Rod of God, The. Sister Ann Zita Shows Us the Foolishness of the Forbidden Books. Len Roberts. BodElec

Plague of Starlings, A. Robert Earl Hayden. ESEAA; NoAM; WaAnP

Plague take all your pendants, say I! Robert Browning. OBGa

Plague Victims Catapulted Over Walls Into Besieged City. Thomas Lux. AmAlph; KGB

Plaid is formed of yellow block and black, A. It Says, I Did So. Mary Jo Bang. KGB

Plain. Miller Williams. RWB

Plain, The. Sándor Weöres. BLT

Plain and purl across the ribs of the world. (LL) Poem Ended by a Death. Fleur Adcock. NAEL-6v2; NAEL-7v2; NoP-4; NoP-5

Plain be the phrase, yet apt the verse. Utilitarian View of the Monitor's Fight, A. Herman Melville. AmWaPo; APN-2; ColAP; NAAL-3; NAAPv.1; NCAP

Plain Cap. *Unknown.* CCL1 *Fr.* Su-guan.

Plain chair or two back. Susan Howe. AWPTFC *Fr.* Chair.

Plain Dealing. Alexander Brome. NOSC

Plain Dealing's Downfall. *Unknown.* OBSV

Plain Fools. Alexander Pope. OBSV *Fr.* Essay on Criticism, An.

Plain heart seeing into plain heart. (LL) Late Indian summer's. Sun Bu-er. WoPoe; WPoS, *tr. by* Jane Hirshfield

Plain Language from Truthful James. Bret Harte. APN-2; CalPo; OBCoV; UV

Plain of Donnerdale, The. William Wordsworth. CenSon *Fr.* River Duddon [A Series of Sonnets], The.

Plain old dope isn't always an artist, A. My Pushkin. Nathalie Quintane. YaTCFP, *tr. by* Mary Ann Caws *and* Jean-Pierre Cauvin

Plain Ole Brother Blues. Jarvis Q. DeBerry. BRtP

Plain Poems: A Fairwater Daybook. Tom Montag.

    April 30, 2001 (1). AmZen

    July 6, 2001 (2). AmZen

    May 9, 2001 (4). AmZen

    May 25, 2001 (1). AmZen

Plain Sense of Things, The. Wallace Stevens. APT-1; EmeKit; NAAL-5; NAMCP V.1; NoAM; OxBoAm

Plain Song for Comadre, A. Richard Wilbur. NoP-5

Plain Talk. William Jay Smith. MoAmPo

Plain was grassy, wild and bare, The.   Dying Swan, The.   Alfred Tennyson.   OWoS

Plain wood table, the obligatory, A.   Art of Interpretation, The.   Julia Copus.   NeBl

Plain Words to the Spaniel.   John Gay.   DiBP *Fr.* Fables: First Series.

Plain-clothes inspectors are operating in this store.   Time for Blushing, A.   Fergus Allen.   IrLP

Plainest Narrative, The.   William Bronk.   APSN

Plainsong.   Carol Ann Duffy.   MoWP

Plaint.   Chu Shu-chen.   NDACCP, *tr. by* Kenneth Rexroth

Plaint.   Ebenezer Elliott.   OBEV; SacPr

Plaisir.   Lucile Adler.   ICANM

Plaisirs de la Porte, Les.   Francis Ponge.   YaTCFP

Plait of Hair, The.   Alice V. Stuart.   PoBW

Plaiting a dark red love-knot into her long black hair. (LL)   Highwayman, The.   Alfred Noyes.   BRP; ChAP; ITBLP; NOxBChV; OBNV; OBSP

Plan, The.   Rae Armantrout.   AWPTFC; BAP-01

Plan, The.   Jack Turner.   BAP-97

Plan for a Curriculum of the Soul, A.   Charles Olson.   PFTM-2

Plan is the body, The.   Snow; a fear of dying.   Matt Robinson.   Coast

Plan of the City of O. The great square.   Michael Palmer.   HarvBoo *Fr.* Series.

Plan of the Klan.   Michelle T. Clinton.   InTrad

Plane Debris.   Stephen Rodefer.
   "My mind to me mangles iron. An error is mirror to the truth."   PmAP

Plane Four.   Velemir Khlebnikov.   PFTM-1 *Fr.* Zangezi.

Plane song.   Dana Lisa Lustig.   AnSo

Plane tilts in to Nashville, The.   Homecoming Singer, The.   Jay Wright.   OxBoAm; VCAP

Planes flew low over the house, The.   These Are Not Brushstrokes.   Cyrus Cassells.   GT

Planes Landing.   Jamie Grant.   NOBAu

"Planet doesn't explode of itself, A," said drily.   Earth.   John Hall Wheelock.   SoSe-8

Planet Earth.   Patricia K. Page.   BeAl; IFF

Planet Earth Speaks, The.   Alma Villanueva.   HW

Planet Jupiter, The.   Epes Sargent.   APN-1

Planet on the Table, The.   Wallace Stevens.   APT-1; NAMCP V.1; OxBoAm; PoPoPo; SAmP

Planetarium.   Adrienne Rich.   BrAP; CAP-8; EMP; NALW; NAMCP V.2; NIL-7; NIP-4; NoAM; VCAP

Planh for the Young English King.   Bertrans de Born.   APT-1, *tr. by* Ezra Pound

Planisféria, Map of the World, Lisbon, 1554.   Ellen Hinsey.   AmPoNex

Planks.   C. D. Wright.   CAP-8

Planning the Perfect Evening.   Rita Dove.   GT *Fr.* Suite for Augustus, A.

Plans.   Maxine W. Kumin.   TLR

Plans Gone Up In Smoke.   Sándor Petőfi.   IQMS, *tr. by* Leslie A. Kery

Plant a corkscrew willow.   Mountain Peak Grave.   Miriam Sagan.   WANABP

Plant kernels quickly, three or four together.   Promise, A.   Teresa D. Cader.   PfSP

Plant saw the beauty of water, The.   Hibiscus on the Lake.   Chavali Bangaramma.   HotL, *tr. by* V. Narayana Rao

Plant them with shadows in mind, under a dying.   Day Lilies: Instructions and an Elegy.   Christopher Merrill.   PfSP

Plant trees. Exactly against this tree.   Paavo Haavikko.   WoPoe *Fr.* Fifteen Epigrams in Praise of the Tyrant.

Plantain.   Pak Sŏwŏn.   EcSo, *tr. by* Julie C. Park

Plantain.   *Unknown.*   SonAtl, *tr. by* Lester Browne, Joseph Harden, Myrna Teirrel and M. Wyatt

Plantain est une espèce de, Le.   Pour nourrir les petits oiseaux.   Raymond Queneau.   YaTCFP

Plantain is, The.   Nourishment of Little Birds, The.   Raymond Queneau.   YaTCFP, *tr. by* Teo Savory

Plantain suckers dib the dirt.   Plantain.   *Unknown.*   SonAtl, *tr. by* Lester Browne, Joseph Harden, Myrna Teirrel and M. Wyatt

Plantains.   Tu Mu.   CCL1, *tr. by* R. F. Burton

Planter's Charm.   Fay M. Yauger.   TiP2

Planter's Daughter, The.   Austin Clarke.   IrLP; ModIr; NAMCP V.1; NPeEn; OxBEV

Planting.   George Wither.   NOSC *Fr.* Collection of Emblemes, Ancient and Moderne, A.

Planting a Sequoia.   Dana Gioia.   CalPo; GeoHom

Planting Bamboos.   Po Chü-i.   CCL1, *tr. by* Arthur Waley

Planting Flowers on the Eastern Embankment.   Po Chü-i.   OBGa, *tr. by* Arthur Waley

Planting Initiation Song.   *Unknown.*   WoPoe; WPoS, *tr. by* Francis La Flesche

Planting Onions.   Jane Flanders.   IPoFL

Planting Potatoes during Chernobyl.   Tom Bryan.   EdScPo

Planting rice seedlings.   Basho.   EMJL, *tr. by* Haruo Shirane

Planting Roses.   Phillis Levin.   FFC

Planting the Poplar.   Louise Imogen Guiney.   NAAPv.1

Plantings.   Catalina Cariaga.   AFaM

Plants against the light, The.   Dec. 28, 1974.   James Schuyler.   OxBoAm

Plants she loved, all growing things.   Musician's Widow.   Anne Stevenson.   BeAl

Plants succulent, distinct, each in its own atmosphere, The.   At the Stanley Spencer Exhibition.   John Riley.   Oth

Planxty Irwin.   David Brendon Hopes.   UpMys

Plashes the Fountain.   Paul Celan.   OBVE, *tr. by* Michael Hamburger

Plasnewydd Square.   Christopher Meredith.   TCAWP

Plastic blue eyes.   Cobra Pilot.   Don Receveur.   OtW

Plastic Cup, The.   Kim Roberts.   AmPoNex

Plastic freezer bag filled with cocaine, worn, A.   Dancing to the Track Singers at the Nightclub.   Judith Berke.   SwNoth

Plastic Sense (1947 version).   Malcolm de Chazal.   YaTCFP, *tr. by* Mary Ann Caws *and* Jean-Pierre Cauvin

Plastic Sense (1948 version).   Malcolm de Chazal.   YaTCFP, *tr. by* Mary Ann Caws *and* Jean-Pierre Cauvin

Plastic surgery lacerated the woman's eye, making it into an absurdly aged trick-elephant's eye, The.   Performance Angel.   Yi Sang.   CAMKP, *tr. by* Edward Mack

Plastic transistor from Japan, A.   First Radio.   Michael McFee.   SwNoth

Plastic Virgin.   Gloria Fuertes.   RaW, *tr. by* Philip Levine

Plate 134. By Eakins. 'A cowboy in the West'.   David Ferry.   FaBoA

Plate Glass.   T. R. Hummer.   LPSFW

Plate Pieces.   Jerry McGuire.   AnSo

Plate tectonics: like blackened pieces.   Whole Earth Catalogue, The.   Albert Goldbarth.   CAP-8

Plateaus / The trunks of enormous.   Savage, Our Fathers, The.   B. H. Boston.   GeoHom

Plates and bowls.   Basho.   EH, *tr. by* Robert Hass

Platform One.   Ted Hughes.   NoP-5

Platinum fur and brass revolver shine.   Song.   Michael McClure.   BB

Plato does not grant city rights to the poet.   My Dance.   Blaise Cendrars.   YaTCFP, *tr. by* Ron Padgett

Plato excludes the poet from the city.   My Dance.   Blaise Cendrars.   CuPo

Plato of the clear, dreaming eye and brave.   Maidenhair.   Michael Field.   OxBSo

Plato Told Him.   E. E. Cummings.   NoAM; OxBoAm

Plato told / him:he couldn't.   Plato told.   E. E. Cummings.   OxBoAm

Plato was a fascist.   Until He Comes.   Trasi Johnson.   InTrad

Platon n'accorde pas droit de cité au poète.   Ma Danse.   Blaise Cendrars.   YaTCFP

Platonic.   Dudley, 3d Baron North North.   NOSC

Platonic Blow, The.   W. H. Auden.
   "Mad to be had, to be felt and smelled. My lips."   EroLit

Platonic is a pretty name.   Platonic.   Dudley, 3d Baron North North.   NOSC

Platonic Lady, The.   John Wilmot, 2d Earl of Rochester.   NOSC

Platonic Love.   Curt Anderson.   PoA 2002

Platonic Love.   Edward Herbert, 1st Baron Herbert of Cherbury.   NOSC

Platonic Love.   Elizabeth Singer Rowe.   BASC

Platonic Subject.   Ann Lauterbach.   PmAP

Platonic[k] Love.   Abraham Cowley.   NoP-5 *Fr.* Mistress, The.

Plato's Dog.   John A. Scott.   BMAP

Platypus, The.   *Aborigine Oral Tradition.*   NOBAu

Plawej ans L'nui'site'w (Partridge and Indian-Speaking Priest).   Rita Joe.   Coast

Play.   A. R. Ammons.   PoA 2002

Play.   Frank Asch.   NTCP

Play 1.   Identity A Poem.   Gertrude Stein.   PFTM-1

Play is one paragraph, The.   Realistic Bar and Grill, A.   David Shapiro.   PmAP

Play it across the table.   Cahoots.   Carl Sandburg.   APT-1

Play It Again, Salmonella.   Jeffrey McDaniel.   AmPoNex; SUP

Play it once.   Saturday Night.   Langston Hughes.   MoAmPo

Play No Ball.   Gerard Benson.   NOxBChV

Play that thing, / Jazz band!   Jazz Band in a Parisian Cabaret.   Langston Hughes.   MoAmPo

Play that thing, you jazz mad fools!   Jazz Band.   Frank Marshall Davis.   SeSe

Play the devil with one's emotions. (LL)   Seven-Sided Poem.   Carlos Drummond de Andrade.   PoetW; TCLAP; VCWP, *tr. by* Elizabeth Bishop

Play the tune again: but this time.   Lesson in Music, A.   Alastair Reid.   WaAnP

"Play up! play up! and play the game!" (LL)   Vitaï Lampada.   Sir Henry John Newbolt.   FaBoWar; OBWP; UV

Play us one we've never heard before.   Repertoire, A.   Michael Donaghy.
    NeBrP

Playboy.   Richard Wilbur.   CAP-8; NAMCP V.2; NoAM

Playboy of the Demi-World[: 1938], The.   William Plomer.   UV

Played backwards on his grandson's eyes. (LL)   Grandfather.   Michael S.
    Harper.   ESEAA; VCAP; WaAnP

Player Piano.   John Updike.   WeW-3

Player Piano, The.   Randall Jarrell.   OxBoAm

Players.   E. Ethelbert Miller.   SpirFl

Players dance on the field, The. The ball, as white.   Between Worlds.
    Benjamin Alire Sáenz.   TiP2

Playful Poem.   Chiao-jan.   CCL1, tr. by Stephen Owen

Playfully Inscribed on a Large Boulder.   Wang Wei.   CCL1, tr. by David
    Lattimore

Playground, The.   Gregory Harrison.   NOxBChV

Playhouse Musings.   James Smith.   OxAEP-2

Playing at Jeoksun Pond on a Moonlit Night.   Master Naong.   BecRai, tr. by
    Kim Daljin, Kim Won-Chung and Christopher Merrill

Playing ball—so it's like paradise, not because it's in the past, we're on a.
    Leslie Scalapino.   BodElec Fr. That they were at the beach—aeolotropic
    series.

Playing Basketball with the Viet Cong.   Kevin Bowen.   MoASP

Playing Fields.   Michelle M. Maihiot.   PfS

Playing for England.   David Scott.   NLP

Playing for Love.   Amanda R. Evans.   BeDoSh

Playing for Time.   Christopher Buckley.   SeSe

Playing Solitaire [for Jessica].   Thulani Davis.   GT

Playing the Flute for the TMR Class.   Jane Epton Seale.   MiVo

Playing the Goldberg Variations on Sunday Morning.   Bill Holm.   MiVo

Playing the Machine.   Howard Nemerov.   BodElec

Playing the Messiah.   Jean Binta Breeze.   MoWP

Playing the Part.   Nina Nyhart.   PfS

Playland.   Richard Foerster.   SwNoth

Plays.   Walter Savage Landor.   NBLV

Playwright convict of public wrongs to men.   On Playwright.   Ben Jonson.
    NoP-4; NoP-5

Plaza and the Flaming Orange Trees, The.   Antonio Machado Ruiz.   SpanPo,
    tr. by Kate Flores

Plaza de Mayo.   Dacia Maraini.   CFP, tr. by Gail Wronsky

Plaza Has a Tower, The.   Antonio Machado Ruiz.   SpanPo, tr. by Angel Flores

Plea for a Captive.   W. S. Merwin.   NoAM

Plea for Mercy, A.   Kwesi Brew.   WoPoe

Plea for My Heart's Sake.   Naomi Long Madgett.   SeSe

Plea for Peace.   Frank Prewett.   HATNAP

Plea of Texas, The.   Mary Austin Holley.   TiP2

Plea, The.   Calvin Forbes.   BtF

Plea to Boys and Girls, A.   Robert Graves.   NAEL-6v2

Plea to Old Age.   Lajos Áprily.   IQMS, tr. by Dorren Bell

Plea to Those Who Matter.   James Welch.   WaAnP

Pleading eyebrows, intoxicating eyes!   Song.   Ch'in Kuan.   CrYelRi, tr. by
    Sam Hamill

Pleasant Comedy of Patient Grissell [or Grissel or Grissill], The.   Thomas
    Dekker and others.

    Golden Slumbers.   NoSic; OxAEP-1; OxBEV

    Happy Heart, The.   NoSic

    (Sweet Content.)   OBEV

Pleasant journey, little book.   To the Lady with a Book.   Unknown.   IrLP, tr.
    by Frank O'Connor

Pleasant Joys of Brotherhood, The.   James Simmons.   OBCoV; PBCIP; PML

Pleasant land of counterpane, The. (LL)   Land of Counterpane, The.   Robert
    Louis Stevenson.   BLPJKO; ChAP; NBLV; NTCP; PtR; TLR; WHSW

Pleasant place I was at today, A.   Woodland Mass, The.   Dafydd ap Gwilym.
    OBWVE, tr. by Gwyn Williams

Pleasant sight it was when, having clomb.   William Wordsworth. Fr. Prelude,
    The; Growth of a Poet's Mind [1805 version].

Pleasant smell of frying sausages, A.   Mixed Feelings.   John Ashbery.
    WeW-3

Pleasant Songs of the Sweetheart Who Meets You in the Fields.   Unknown.
    WoPoe Fr. Conversations in Courtship.

Pleasant to wander.   Friedrich Hölderlin.   WoPoe Fr. Tinian.

Pleasd with thy Place.   Epictetus.   NPeEn, tr. by George Chapman

Please.   To One Afflicted with Adolescence.   Anna Cascella.   CItWP, tr. by
    Cinzia Sartini Blum and Lara Trubowitz

Please.   Laura Kasischke.   NAPBL

Please.   Yusef Komunyakaa.   OxAAAP

Please be silent, now my country, while I fill the speaker's place.   Negro
    Schools, The.   Lizelia Augusta Jenkins Moorer.   CBWP-3

Please bring.   Can't Oh.   Del Ray Cross.   FreRad

Please Call Me by My True Names.   Thich Nhat Hanh.   WhBo

Please can I have a man who wears corduroy.   Please Can I Have a Man.
    Selima Hill.   BeAl; NeBrP

Please come forth.   Midwife's Invocation, A.   Unknown.   WPoS, tr. by
    Michael Coe and Whittaker Gordon

Please don't ask me, America.   America.   Dunya Mikhail.   IrPoTo; WoBe, tr.
    by Liz Winslow

Please don't be offended if I preach to you a while.   Look for the Silver Lining.
    B. G. DeSylva.   ReLy; TCAPo

Please draw the fear bigger.   Dracula.   Yi Sanghûi.   EcSo, tr. by Jennifer M.
    Lee

Please, father, dear father, come home[!]. (LL)   Come Home, Father[!].   Henry
    Clay Work.   APN-2; NAAPv.1

Please forgive this platitude.   Fine and Dandy.   Paul James.   ReLy

Please give me a potted may meadow.   At the Delicatessen Shop.   Ernst Jandl.
    GTCP, tr. by Michael Hamburger

Please God, forsake your water and dry bread.   To a Nun.   John Ormond.
    NoP-4

Please hang a moon up and tune up the cellos.   Here Come the Dreamers.
    Marshall Barer.   ReLy

Please help us keep your memory alive.   Under the Roof of Memory.   Peter
    Davison.   InoFa

Please Master.   Allen Ginsberg.   CAGL

Please master can I touch your cheek.   Please Master.   Allen Ginsberg.
    CAGL

Please open it and look again.   Textbook.   Im Yŏngjo.   CAMKP, tr. by
    Edward W. Poitras

Pease Pass the Biscuit.   Ogden Nash.   AmWit

"Please, Please, Please" on the charts permits.   David Wojahn.   PBCAP Fr.
    Mystery Train: A Sequence.

Please refrain from frankly ogling your neighbor's.   Locker Room Etiquette.
    Craig Arnold.   MoASP

Please remove that tendril from my armrest.   3D Matchmove Artist, The.   Kit
    Robinson.   BAP-04

Please, Sir Second-born.   Unknown.   ColAnChi Fr. Classic of Odes.

Please teacher / Teach me something.   Pick Yourself Up.   Dorothy Fields.
    ReLy

Please the Carrots.   Dave Brinks.   AnSo

Please, to wait. It is a week since I have been.   What Bottom Said When He
    Came Home.   Eva Hooker.   IaFF

Please, when you ask me in this dream.   Threnody for Sunrise.   Richard Cecil.
    BodElec

Pleased in his loneliness, he often lies.   Shepherd Boy, The.   John Clare.
    CABP

Pleased to the last, she likes the luscious food.   John Wilkes.   EroLit Fr. Essay
    on Woman.

Pleasure.   David Constantine.   BeAl

Pleasure.   Allison Joseph.   PasH

Pleasure.   Carl Phillips.   BAP-04

Pleasure.   A. K. Ramanujan.   PoetW; VCWP

Pleasure.   Delmore Schwartz.   OxBoAm

Pleasure.   Dean Young.   IllVoic

Pleasure a writer knows is the pleasure all sages enjoy, The.   Lu Chi.   WoPoe
    Fr. Art of Writing, The.

Pleasure Boat, The [or Pleasure-Boat, The].   Richard Henry Dana.   APN-1

PLEASURE FEARS ME, FOOT ROSE, FOOT BREATH.   Michael McClure.
    BB Fr. Ghost Tantras.

Pleasure is / when you rarely cook.   Tachibana Akemi.   EMJL, tr. by Haruo
    Shirane

Pleasure is / when you understand.   Tachibana Akemi.   EMJL, tr. by Haruo
    Shirane

Pleasure It Is.   William Cornish.   NPeEn

Pleasure must slip.   Condom Tree, The.   Chase Twichell.   EmeKit

Pleasure of Feeling Inside Your Body, The.   Rochelle Lynn Holt.   PasH

Pleasure of Princes, The.   Alec Derwent Hope.   BrAP

Pleasure of Ruins, The.   J. D. McClatchy.   PoA 2002

Pleasure Reconciled to Virtue.   Ben Jonson.   NAEL-6v1

    (Comus's Song.)   OBCoV

    (Hymn to Comus.)   NOSC

Pleasure: The Second Book of Solomon on the Vanity of the World.   Matthew
    Prior.

    "Oft have I said, the praise of doing well."   ChIV-1

Pleasures.   Radmila Lazić.   PoCho, tr. by Charles Simic

Pleasures.   Denise Levertov.   NAMCP V.2; NoAM

Pleasures I took from life, The.   Ghost of a Ghost, The.   Brad Leithauser.   RA

Pleasures of a Door.   Francis Ponge.   YaTCFP, tr. by Lee Fahnestock

Pleasures of Heaven, The.   Ben Jonson.   TreFP

Pleasures of Hope, The. Thomas Campbell.
  Part One.
    "'Tis summer eve, when heaven's ethereal bow." TreFP
Pleasures of Melancholy, The. Thomas, the Younger Warton.
  "Beneath yon ruin'd abbey's moss-grown piles." OxAEP-1
Pleasures of Merely Circulating, The. Wallace Stevens. PtR
Pleasures of Retirement, The. Edward Benlowes. NOSC *Fr.* Theophia.
Pleasures of the Door, The. Francis Ponge. WoPoe, *tr. by* Raymond Federman
Pleasures of the Door, The. Francis Ponge. MotU, *tr. by* Lane Dunlop
Pleasures of the Flesh. Anne Barrows. AFaM
Pleasures of the Imagination. Peter McDonald. PNI
Pleated lampshade, slightly askew, The. Midnight Gladness. Denise Levertov. UpMys
Pleated strata of air, The. Marina Kudimova. CRWP, *tr. by* Catriona Kelly
Pleaure Given by Suspicion with the Rhetoric of Crying, The. Sor Juana Inés de la Cruz. BLPSL, *tr. by* Rene de Costa, Rigas Kappatos and Eleni Paidoussi
Pledge. Lawson Fusao Inada. WhBo
Pledge. Gerwyn Williams. BBMWP, *tr. by* the author and Richard Poole
Pledge. Great Master Wonhyo. BecRai, *tr. by* Kim Daljin, Kim Won-Chung and Christopher Merrill
Pledge, The. Adelaide Crapsey. NAAPv.2
Pledge of Allegiance. Carl Hancock Rux. SpirFl
Pledge of Allegiance to the Family of Earth, A. Mim Kelber. HW
Pleiades, The. Mary Barnard. APT-2
Pleiades disappear, The. Sappho. WoPoe, *tr. by* Sam Hamill
Plenteous place is Ireland for hospitable cheer, A. Fair Hills of Ireland, The. *Unknown.* OBEV, *tr. by* Sir Samuel Ferguson
Plenteous ransom [*or* rannzome] shall come with him [*or* com with hym], I say, / And shall redeem [*or* redeme] all our iniquity [*or* iniquitie]. (LL) Bible, *O.T.* NoSic; OBVE
Plentiful light. Electricity of Blossoms. Lorenzo Thomas. FTOS
Plenty. Naomi Feigelson Chase. PfS
Plenty. Allison Joseph. SweBea
Plenty Time Pass Fast, Fas Dey So. Cheryl Boyce Taylor. WiU
Plot, The. William Dickey. YaYoPo
Plot Against the Giant, The. Wallace Stevens. SAmP
Plot shrinks, The. 67 Words with One Vowel and One Consonant. Christophe Tarkos. YaTCFP, *tr. by* Stacy Doris
Plough, The. Richard Henry Horne. OBEV
Plough and a Spade, A. Nguyễn Trãi. WoPoe, *tr. by* Nguyen Ngoc Bich
Plough and a spade, that's all, A. Plough and a Spade, A. Nguyễn Trãi. WoPoe, *tr. by* Nguyen Ngoc Bich
Plough, sow and reap. Charles Reznikoff. FTOS *Fr.* Jews in Babylonia.
Ploughing the land. Basho. EH, *tr. by* Robert Hass
Ploughing the seas like the pirate child. On the Sea. Gabriella Sica. CItWP, *tr. by* Cinzia Sartini Blum and Lara Trubowitz
Ploughman. John Tripp. TCAWP
Ploughman: In Welsh Uplands, The. A. G. Prys-Jones. AngWePo
Ploughman, The. Oliver Wendell Holmes. CA
Ploughman, whose gnarly hand yet kindly wheeled. Waving of the Corn, The. Sidney Lanier. APN-2
Plowboy was something his something as I nibbled the lobe, The. Winter Wheat. Paul Muldoon. GPPA
Plowdens, Finns. Beginnings. Robert Earl Hayden. NAAL-5
Plower, The. Padraic Colum. MoBrPo
Plowing: A Memory. Hamlin Garland. ChAP
Plowing of Piers's Half-acre, The. William Langland. NAEL-6v1; NAEL-7v1 *Fr.* Vision of Piers Plowman, The.
Plowman of Rákos Under the Turks. Károly Kisfaludy. IQMS, *tr. by* Watson Kirkconnell
Plows keep striking, large stones, their. Harrowing. Douglas Messerli. FTOS
Pluck from their dark and rocky bed. Moods 1. Della Cruscans. STuOW
Pluck, pluck, pluck, the thick plantain. *Unknown.* NDACCP, *tr. by* Ezra Pound
Pluck the Fruit and Taste the Pleasure. Thomas Lodge. OxAEP-1 *Fr.* Robert, Second Duke of Normandy.
Pluck the quince. Cai-fan: Pluck the Quince. *Unknown.* CCL1, *tr. by* Ezra Pound
Plucking The Rushes. *Unknown.* OBVE, *tr. by* Arthur Waley
Plucking the vine leaves, hear my song. *Unknown.* CCL1 *Fr.* Cai-ge [Translations].
Pluie de Printemps, La. Tu Fu [*or* Du Fu]. CCL1, *tr. by* Marie-Jean-Léon, Marquis d'Hervey de Saint-Denys
Pluie retrouvant ce qui est perdu, La. Pluie retrouvant, La. Valentine Penrose. YaTCFP

Plum and the snow both claim the spring, The. Snow and the Plum, The—1. Lu Mei-Po. TAPaP, *tr. by* Red Pine
Plum blossom breeze. Stanford M. Forrester. AmZen
Plum Blossom Poem, The. Gary Snyder. ASA
Plum Blossom Scent. Basho and Yaba. EMJL, *tr. by* Haruo Shirane
Plum Blossoms. Li Ch'ing-chao. ErotSp, *tr. by* Sam Hamill
  (To the Tune: Plum Blossoms.) CrYelRi
Plum blossoms float by on the spring water. Song of the Yodo River. Buson. EH, *tr. by* Robert Hass
Plum blossoms here and there. Buson. EH, *tr. by* Robert Hass
Plum blossoms in bloom. Buson. SoOfWa, *tr. by* Sam Hamill
Plum blossoms / One's nose. Onitsura. ZenPo, *tr. by* Takashi Ikemoto and Lucien Stryk
Plum blossoms scent. Buson. WoPoe, *tr. by* Tony Barnstone, Willis Barnstone and Haixin Xu
Plum Crazy. Kate Sontag. SweBea
Plum in bloom. Issa. IllVoic *Fr.* Issa: A Suite of Haiku.
2. Plum Island. Pamela Alexander. AmAlph *Fr.* Foxlight.
Plum scent / Haloing. Buson. ZenPo, *tr. by* Takashi Ikemoto and Lucien Stryk
Plum Stones. Michael McClure.
  Fifteen. WANABP
  Fourteen. WANABP
  Seven. WANABP
Plum tree breaks out in bees, The. April. Charles Wright. GeoHom
Plum Tree by the House, The. Oliver St. John Gogarty. OBEV
Plum Window. Muso Soseki. EaWin, *tr. by* W. S. Merwin
Plum without the snow isn't very special, The. Snow and the Plum, The—2. Lu Mei-Po. TAPaP, *tr. by* Red Pine
Plumbers. Susan Miles. NOxBChV
Plum-blossom, The. Yamabe no Akahito. TAL *Fr.* Manyo Shu, Part 3 of 4.
Plumburst. John Kinsella. NeBl
Plume. Richard Kenney. NoP-4
Plumes of pampas grass. Issa. EH, *tr. by* Robert Hass
Plume-shaped and pampered, the flames. Hunter. Linda Bierds. AmAlph
Plummet, The. Edward Dowden. IrLP
Plumpuppets, The. Christopher Darlington Morley. ChAP
Plums in blossom. Buson. EH, *tr. by* Robert Hass
Plums on the ground. Conservancies. Josephine Miles. AFaM
Plums used to be black. Fruitbowl 1. Imani E. Wilson. BtF
Plum-viewing. Buson. ZenPo, *tr. by* Takashi Ikemoto and Lucien Stryk
Plunder. Debra Bruce. IllVoic
Plunge beneath the still green waters of the Grand Canal. (LL) Lost Fugue for Chet. Lynda Hull. LaCa; SeSe
Plunge deep. Ascent. Anne Morrow Lindbergh. OtW
Plunge the green wave, and bid thy griefs subside. (LL) Visions Appear to her in a Dream. Mary Robinson. CenSon; RWP
Plunges into the heart and is gone. (LL) Panther, The. Rainer Maria Rilke. ASA; NAWM-7v2, *tr. by* Stephen Mitchell
Plunging limbers over the shattered track, The. Dead Man's Dump. Isaac Rosenberg. NAEL-6v2; NAEL-7v2; NAMCP V.1; NoAM; NoP-5; OBWP; PoWW; WaAnP
Plus Lourd. Pierre Reverdy. YaTCFP
Plus the lust pardonable, these days anon. Past Qualm of Hours. Marla Jernigan. AnSo
Plush hills, the raw materials, fall away. Sudden Rain in the Green Mountains, A. Stephen Burt. IIR
Plutonian Ode. Allen Ginsberg. AtGh
  "What new element before us unborn in nature? Is there a new thing under the sun?" CLPP
Pluvia. Donald Hall. PfSP
Pluvius, this whole city on his nerves. Spleen LXXV. Charles Baudelaire. SxFrPo, *tr. by* James McGowan
Pneumoconiosis. Duncan Bush. AngWePo; TCAWP
Po' Boy Blues. Langston Hughes. ColAP; NAMCP V.1
Po' los' boy, bebby, / Evahmo'. (LL) Southern Road. Sterling Allen Brown. APT-2; InGu; NAMCP V.1; OxAAAP
Po, the unrivalled poet. To Li Po on a Spring Day. Tu Fu [*or* Du Fu]. TAL
Pocahontas. Ed Ochester. SUP
Pocket, it is Poems by Pierre Reverdy. (LL) Step Away from Them, A. Frank O'Hara. NAMCP V.2; OxBoAm; PtR; VCAP; WoPoe
Pockets. Ernst Jandl. GTCP, *tr. by* Michael Hamburger
Pockets of Haze. Lewis MacAdams. AHA
Pockets of our greatcoats full of barley, The. Requiem for the Croppies. Seamus Heaney. NAMCP V.2; OBWP
Pockets puffed with bottles. Here. Lawrence Joseph. UrbNat
Poe. Mina Loy. APT-1
Poe: An Assay (1). Jane Hirshfield. BAP-04

Poe and Longfellow. James Russell Lowell. APN-1; OxBoAm; TCAPo *Fr.* Fable for Critics, A.

Poe In Dust. Allen Ginsberg. CLPP

Poe Story, A. Anthony Butts. AmPoNex

Poem. John Cornford. RSaN

Poem. Paul Dermée. CuPo

Poem. Pablo Neruda. CLPP, *tr. by* Kenneth Rexroth

Poem: "And I went up to that chandeliered place." Calvin C. Hernton. GT

Poem: "And if it snowed and snow covered the drive." Simon Armitage. HarvBoo; NeBrP; StAl

Poem: "And tomorrow morning at 8 o'clock in Springfield, Massachusetts." Frank O'Hara. ItP

Poem: "Angel kissed my alphabet, The." James Tate. NAMCP V.2

Poem: "Anyway the time has come to explain." Jack Kerouac. CLPP

Poem: "Are you Alive, Dead or DeadAlive?" Mohammed Iqbal. SonAtl, *tr. by* V. Allison, Harjeet Singh Gill and Nasreen Shaikh

Poem: "As the cat." William Carlos Williams. ChAP; HarvBoo; NoP-4; NoP-5; OxBoAm; PoPoPo; SoSe-8

Poem: "As the full moon rises." Kenneth Rexroth. GifTon

Poem: "At night Chinamen jump." Frank O'Hara. NAMCP V.2; NoAM; PmAP

Poem: "Blue snow is turning black, The." Aleksandr Trifonovich Tvardovsky. RusPo, *tr. by* Robert Arthur Douglas Ford

Poem: "By the road to the contagious hospital." William Carlos Williams. *See* Spring and All.

Poem: "Eager note on my door said "Call me", The." Frank O'Hara. NAMCP V.2; NoAM; OxBoAm; PmAP

Poem: "Every morning I forget how it is." Charles Simic. CAP-8

Poem: "Figures in the fields against the sky!" Antonio Machado Ruiz. WoPoe, *tr. by* John Dos Passos

Poem: "Frail sound of a tunic trailing, A." Antonio Machado Ruiz. WoPoe, *tr. by* John Dos Passos

Poem: "From us, like appendicitis." Andrey Andreievich Voznesensky. RusPo, *tr. by* Robert Arthur Douglas Ford

Poem: "Greater cities are, The." Víctor Hernández Cruz. PueRic

Poem: "Green things are flowers too." Frank O'Hara. PoA 2002

Poem: "Here. Forget." Charles Bernstein. FTOS

Poem: "Horizon line." Raymond Radiguet. CuPo

Poem: "I am beginning to alter." Bernadette Mayer. NYP2

Poem: "I could become a great grinning host." Jack Kerouac. CLPP

Poem: "I demand that the human race." Jack Kerouac. CLPP

Poem: "I don't know as I get what D.H. Lawrence is driving at." Frank O'Hara. CAP-8

Poem: "I lived in the first century of world wars." Muriel Rukeyser. FTtHH; NAMCP V.2; RaF; WaAnP

Poem: "I play tennis with the shells." Paul Dermée. CuPo

Poem: "I stand in full armor." Paul Klee. PFTM-1

Poem: "I think I came close to being insane a few months ago." C. K. Williams. BodElec

Poem: "I'm like all lovers, wanting love to be." Lesbia Harford. NOBAu

Poem: "In danger of which." Ray DiPalma. FTOS

Poem: "In sand." Chimalum Nwankwo. NAfrP

Poem: "In the early evening, as now, a man is bending." Louise Glück. MoWP

Poem: "Is it a plane in the sky." Paul Dermée. CuPo

Poem: "Lana Turner has collapsed!" Frank O'Hara. CAP-8; CLPP; FTOS; ItP; OxBoAm; PmAP

Poem: "Late butterflies gliding through the air." Timothy Liu. NeAmPo; TAPaP

Poem: "Lead drains from your heart on the left side, The." Tony Towle. AHA

Poem: "Life, A / of collecting pollen." Shin Yu Pai. AmZen

Poem: "Light clarity avocado salad in the morning." Frank O'Hara. OxBoAm

Poem: "Like a bird." Philip Whalen. AHA

Poem: "Little bones of." Michael O'Brien. KGB

Poem: "Mule kicked out in the trees, A. An Early." Norman Dubie. BodElec

Poem: "My little son comes running with open arms!" Thomas McGrath. PoChi

Poem: "My little son, laughing, singing..." Thomas McGrath. GifTon

Poem: "Naked is the earth." Antonio Machado Ruiz. WoPoe, *tr. by* John Dos Passos

Poem: "Nothing move thee." Saint, of Avila Theresa. WoPoe, *tr. by* Yvor Winters

Poem: "Now absence is a habit it is time." Burns Singer. EdScPo

Poem: "Our love is not found in our respective." Carlos German Belli. BLPSL, *tr. by* Rene de Costa, Rigas Kappatos and Eleni Paidoussi

Poem: "Red eiderdown at the window, A." Raymond Radiguet. CuPo

Poem: "Rose fades, The." William Carlos Williams. NIL-7

Poem: "Slash my back with a sickle." Hô Sugyông. EcSo, *tr. by* Youngju Ryu

Poem: "Sometimes I wish that I were Helen-fair." Lesbia Harford. NOBAu

Poem: "There was something I can't bring myself." Denis Johnson. OPRER

Poem: "Think with your body." Víctor Hernández Cruz. PueRic

Poem: "Twenty-first, The. Night. Monday." Anna Andreyevna Akhmatova. RusPo, *tr. by* Robert Arthur Douglas Ford

Poem: "War and greed stop food." Hugh Seidman. BodElec

Poem: "We think to create festivals." Antonio Machado Ruiz. WoPoe, *tr. by* John Dos Passos

Poem: "Were I a king, I could command content." Edward, 17th Earl of Oxford De Vere. NoSic

(Weare I a Kinge I coulde commande content.) PBRV

Poem: "When I carry my little son in the cold." Thomas McGrath. GifTon

Poem: "When I look at the falling leaves." Marina Ivanovna Tsvetayeva. RusPo, *tr. by* Robert Arthur Douglas Ford

Poem: "When I was still a child." Lesbia Harford. NOBAu

Poem: "When the rich pass proudly by." Wang Fan-chih. CrYelRi, *tr. by* Sam Hamill

Poem: "Yellow, Loveliest, enters my city." İlhan Berk. NaPG, *tr. by* Talat Sait Halman

Poem: "You hear that heroic big land music?" Alice Notley. PmAP

Poem: "You, my photographer, you, most aware." Delmore Schwartz. PoA 2002

Poem: "You who come from my village." Wang Wei. NDACCP, *tr. by* Gary Snyder

Poem: "Your head it waves outside." Víctor Hernández Cruz. PueRic

Poem 2 (for Duckie Simpson of Black Uhuru). Audrey Ingram-Roberts. WaCA

Poem [2]: "I loved my friend." Langston Hughes. NAAPv.2; NTCP

Poem # 3: "Today, I'm wearing new love." Sybil J. Roberts. BtF

Poem 12. Mary Oliver. PoCoUp *Fr.* West Wind.

Poem 15. Pablo Neruda. BLPSL, *tr. by* Rene de Costa, Rigas Kappatos and Eleni Paidoussi

Poem 20. Pablo Neruda. BLPSL, *tr. by* Rene de Costa, Rigas Kappatos and Eleni Paidoussi

Poem 143. Charles Olson. APSN; ColAP *Fr.* Maximus Poems, The.

Poem, A. Luis Rogelio Nogueras. PML, *tr. by* Mark Weiss

Poem, A: "Poem made of words, A." Marie Luise Kaschnitz. GTCP, *tr. by* Reinhold Grimm

Poem, A: "What is there that we can do or say." Ezekiel Mphahlele. AF

Poem, The. Homero Aridjis. TCLAP, *tr. by* Eliot Weinberger

Poem, The: "Coming late, as always." W. S. Merwin. CAP-8

Poem, The: "If you start to write a poem." Clementina Suárez. TANSG, *tr. by* Janet N. Gold

Poem, The: "It discovers by night." Donald Hall. BeAl

Poem, The: "Painter of Dante's awful ferry-ride, The." Babette Deutsch. PoA 2002

Poem, The: "Rise Oedipus, and if thou canst unfold." Thomas Morton. NAAL-3

Poem about Breath [*with music*]. David Wagoner. NoAM

Poem About Death, A. Burns Singer. EdScPo

Poem about heartbreak that go on and on. June Jordan. StAl

Poem about Morning. William Meredith. GoPo

Poem About My Rights. June Jordan. ISC; NoAM; WaAnP

Poem About My Study at the Back of the House. Chan Fang-sheng. CCL1, *tr. by* John Frodsham

Poem About Myself. George P. Elliott. ASA

Poem about People. Robert Pinsky. VCAP

Poem about Poems about Vietnam, A. Jon Stallworthy. NoAM

Poem about Rain. Nikolai Alekseievich Zabolotsky. TCRusP, *tr. by* Daniel Weissbort

Poem about the Blue Horse. Sergey Morozov. TCRusP, *tr. by* Daniel Weissbort

Poem about the Future. Hans Magnus Enzensberger. PoSu, *tr. by* Michael Hamburger

Poem: "About the size of an old-style dollar bill." Elizabeth Bishop. Coast; NAMCP V.2; NoAM; PoetW; PoPoPo; VCAP

Poem, after A. E. Housman. Hugh Kingsmill. UV

(What, Still Alive.) NBLV

Poem again, of several parts, each having to do, A. David Ferry. FaBoA *Fr.* Photographs from a Book: Six Poems.

Poem against Catholics. James Fenton and John Fuller. OBSV

Poem Against the First Grade. George Venn. TWF

Poem Against the Horizon, The. David Young. MotU

Poem Against the State (Of Things): 1975. June Jordan. ISC

Poem Americans Are Going to Have to Memorize Soon, A. Clarence Major. EGAG

Poem Arrested at Daybreak. Julia de Burgos. TANSG, *tr. by* Heather Rosario Sievert

Poem as Mask, The. Muriel Rukeyser. APT-2; NAAL-5; NALW; NAMCP V.2

Poem ascends, The. (LL) Jacob's Ladder, The. Denise Levertov. APSN; BrAP; ChIV-1; NAAL-5; PFTM-2

Poem Beginning "The." Louis Zukofsky. APT-2

[Dedication]. NAMCP V.1

Fifth Movement: Autobiography. NAMCP V.1; PFTM-1; TaR

First Movement: "And out of olde bokes, in good feith." NAMCP V.1

Poem Beginning with a Line by Cavafy [with music]. Derek Mahon. PNI

Poem Beginning with a Line by Frank Lima. Lisa Jarnot. LegDan; VaPo

Poem Beginning with a Line by Pindar, A. Robert Duncan. PmAP; VCAP

Poem Beginning with a Line from Frost. Dan Chiasson. VisFro

Poem Beginning With a Line of Wittgenstein. Donald Hall. PoA 2002

Poem: "Big animals: despondent / at table: unsated, The." Paul Klee. PFTM-1

Poem by David McCord from the Boston Transcript, A. Poem by David McCord, A. John Wheelwright. OxBoAm

Poem by John Thorpe, A. Kris Hemensley. BMAP *Fr.* Mile from Poetry, A.

Poem by the Bridge at Ten-shin. Li Po. InoFa; NDACCP; OBVE, *tr. by* Ezra Pound

Poem comes to the man who is ready for her, The. Sandra Kohler. FiBr *Fr.* Ars Poetica Feminae.

Poem Composed at the Command of the Emperor. Li Po. ChinPo, *tr. by* Ye Weilian [*or* Yeh Wei-lien *or* Wai-lim Yip]

Poem Composed During a Brownout. Fidelito Cortes. ReBoTo

Poem Ended by a Death [*with music*]. Fleur Adcock. NAEL-6v2; NAEL-7v2; NoP-4; NoP-5

Poem Entitled the Day and the War, A. James Madison Bell. Though Tennyson the Poet King. CBCWP

Poem Fifty. Nancy Morejón. TANSG, *tr. by* Joy Renjilian-Burgy

Poem Films Itself, The. J. S. Harry. BMAP

Poem for a Daughter. Anne Stevenson. StAl

Poem for a daughter who is already born. Ronny Someck. IrPoTo, *tr. by* Vivian Eden

Poem for a "Divorced" Daughter. Horace Coleman. ISC

Poem for a Doll Bought in a Russian Bazaar. Marguerite Yourcenar. YaTCFP, *tr. by* Martin Sorrell

Poem for a New Girlfriend. Joseph Millar. NevBe

Poem for a New Year. Rachel Wetzsteon. NeAmPo

Poem for a Younger Son. William Scammell. NLP

Poem for Adlai Stevenson and Yellow Jackets. David Young. P180

Poem for an Anniversary. Cecil Day Lewis. CABP

Poem for Artemis (3.22). Horace. WED, *tr. by* Robert Bly

Poem for Black Hearts, A. Imamu Amiri Baraka. NAMCP V.2; SSLK; WaAnP

Poem for Black Relocation Centers, A. Etheridge Knight. ESEAA *Fr.* Two Poems for Black Relocation Centers.

Poem for Central America. Hilary Booth. SurWo

Poem for Claude. Ray DiPalma. FTOS

Poem for Cocksuckers, A. John Wieners. CAGL

Poem for Deep Thinkers, A. Imamu Amiri Baraka. APSN

Poem for Dizzy. Betty Adcock. InoFa

Poem for Easter. Robert Kelly. ErotSp

Poem for Ed "Whitey" Ford, A. Jonathan Holden. MoASP

Poem for El Lissitzky. Ron Padgett. NYP2

Poem for Elliot Carter on His 90th Birthday. Alan Dugan. BodElec

Poem for Emily, A. Miller Williams. InGu; WeW-3

Poem for Ernie Henry. Gloria Tropp. EGAG

Poem for George Helm: Aloha Week 1980. Eric Chock. OpBo

Poem for George Miles. Dennis Cooper. WiU

Poem for Gonzales, California, The. Morton Marcus. GeoHom

Poem for Halfwhite College Students. Imamu Amiri Baraka. OxAAAP

Poem for Harry Houdini. Leroy V. Quintana. ICANM

Poem for July 4, 1994. Sonia Sanchez. SpirFl

Poem for (for Langston Hughes), A. Nikki Giovanni. SSLK

Poem for "Magic", A. Quincy Troupe. FTtHH; ISC

(Poem For "Magic," A.) LoL

Poem for Mankind and Its Hope. Clementina Suárez. TANSG, *tr. by* Janet N. Gold

Poem for Maurice O'Shea, A. Geoffrey Lehmann. NOBAu

Poem for Max Nordau, A. Edwin Arlington Robinson. APN-2

Poem for Mr. Li in Early Spring. Tu Fu [*or* Du Fu]. CrYelRi, *tr. by* Sam Hamill

Poem for Museum Goers, A. John Wieners. BB

Poem for My Brother Returning to My Farm. Tu Fu [*or* Du Fu]. CrYelRi, *tr. by* Sam Hamill

Poem for My Father. Graham Allen. AngWePo

Poem for My Father. Toi Derricotte. LiTh

Poem for My Father. Alejandra Pizarnik. TANSG, *tr. by* Susan Bassnett

Poem for My Father, A. Sonia Sanchez. OxAAAP

Poem for My Father; for Quincy Trouppe, Sr. Quincy Troupe. MoASP

(Poem for My Father.) AF; LTA

Poem For My Nephew. Nikki Giovanni. NOxBChV

Poem for My Sister. Liz Lochhead. EdScPo; ItWoWo

Poem for My Sons. Minnie Bruce Pratt. WiU

Poem for My Twentieth Birthday. Kenneth Koch. PoA 2002

Poem for Myself (Or Blues for a Mississippi Black Boy), A. Etheridge Knight. InGu; PoPoPo

(Poem for Myself, A.) AF

Poem for Natalia Ginzburg. Anita Helle. OPRER

Poem for Old Walt. Lawrence Ferlinghetti. ViWalt

Poem for Painters, A. John Wieners. BB

Poem for Pancho Gonzales. Leroy V. Quintana. ICANM

Poem for Players, A. Al Young. LTA; OxAAAP

Poem for R. Kim Ly Bui-Burton. PasH

Poem for Salt. Leroy V. Quintana. P180

Poem for Sigmund. Lorna Crozier. LW

Poem for Speculative Hipsters, A. Imamu Amiri Baraka. NAMCP V.2; NoAM

Poem for Teacup Mantlepiece Poets Palpitating Poot Booty Plagiarists Imprisoned in Ivy League White Supremacist Mental Biological Warfare Labs. Tony Medina. InTrad

Poem for Têt. Ted Sexauer. WhBo

Poem for the Children. Carolyn Beard Whitlow. FFC

Poem for the End. Honor Moore. WiU

Poem for the Father. Alejandra Pizarnik. TCLAP, *tr. by* Frank Graziano and María Rosa Fort

Poem for the Insane, A. John Wieners. PmAP

(Poem for the insance, A.) BB

Poem for the Land. Mahmoud Darwish.

"I am the witness of the massacre." PoAgWa, *tr. by* Sabri Hafiz and Sarah Maguire

Poem for the Man Who Said Shit. David Clewell. OPRER

Poem for the Purchase of a First Bra. Allison Joseph. BtF

Poem for the Sefirot as a Wheel of Light, A. Naftali Bacharach. PFTM-1

Poem for the Shechina. Cassia Berman. HW

Poem for the Womb. Jennifer O'Grady. AmPoNex

Poem for the Young White Man Who Asked Me How I, an Intelligent, Well-Read Person Could Believe in the War Between Races. Lorna Dee Cervantes. FTtHH; PBCAP; PoPoPo

Poem for Those of You Who Are Sometimes Troubled by Barking Dogs and Low Flying Jets, A. Steve Sanfield. WhBo

Poem for Trapped Things, A. John Wieners. BB; PmAP

Poem for Trish, A. Gavin Moses. InTrad

Poem for vipers, A. John Wieners. BB

Poem for Willie Best, A. Imamu Amiri Baraka. NAAL-5

Poem for Writers, A. Lee Harwood. Oth

Poem for You, A. Paul Laraque. BRtP

Poem for Yuan Zhen. Po Chü-i. CCL1, *tr. by* Arthur Waley

Poem from a Three Year Old. Brendan Kennelly. StAl

Poem from Llanybri. Lynnette Roberts. AngWePo; TCAWP

Poem from Sierra Madre. Mila D. Aguilar. ReBoTo

Poem. Timothy Liu. AmPoNex

Poem in November. Shirley Kaufman. GifTon

Poem in October. Dylan Thomas. AngWePo; NAEL-6v2; NAEL-7v2; NAMCP V.2; NoAM; NPeEn; OxAEP-2; PoA 2002; SoSe-8; TCAWP; UV

Poem in Parts. Judah Ha-Levi. WoPoe, *tr. by* Ammiel Alcalay

Poem in Praise of My Husband (Taos). Diane Di Prima. BB

Poem In Progress. Ken Harris. AnSo

Poem in Thanks. Thomas Lux. GoPo

Poem in the Shape of a Saxophone. T. R. Hummer. SeSe

Poem in Three Parts. S. J. Marks. BodElec

Poem in Time of Winter. Ray Mathew. NOBAu; OBCoV

Poem in Which I Refuse Contemplation. Rita Dove. NAAL-5

Poem is a holy glass— put, A. Art. José Asunción Silva. SonAtl, *tr. by* Eleanor Davidson, Carole Gibson and Lisa Martin

Poem is like a palm, A. Palm Sunday Maple Syrup Poem. Bernadette Mayer. NYP2

Poem is not the place where beauty is cherished, A. Speaking of the Poem. Christoph Meckel. GTCP, *tr. by* Reinhold Grimm

Poem is the cry of its occasion, The. Another Duffer. Sam Hamill. BodElec

Poem is ugly and they make it uglier, The. Nokh Aushvits (After Auschwitz). Jerome Rothenberg. TaR

Poem is what has neither name, nor rest, nor place, nor home, The.   Excess of Poetry.   Jacques Garelli.   YaTCFP, *tr.* by Mary Ann Caws *and* Jean-Pierre Cauvin

Poem Left in a Lady's Toilet.   James Eyre Weeks.   IrLP

Poem, like the clitoris, is there, A.   Pleasure.   David Constantine.   BeAl

Poem Looking for a Reader, A.   Haki R. Madhubuti.   ISC

Poem Looking in a Mirror, A.   Awwad Nasir.   IrPoTo, *tr.* by Ralph Saverese and Saadi A. Simawe

Poem made of words, A.   Poem, A.   Marie Luise Kaschnitz.   GTCP, *tr.* by Reinhold Grimm

Poem must complete the cycle of full release, A.   Talking.   Miguel Algarin.   PueRic

Poem No. 1.   Carolyn M. Rodgers.   ISC

Poem No. 1.   Yi Sang.   CAMKP *Fr.* Crow's-Eye View.

Poem No. 2.   Yi Sang.   CAMKP; PFTM-1 *Fr.* Crow's-Eye View.

Poem No. 3.   Yi Sang.   CAMKP; PFTM-1 *Fr.* Crow's-Eye View.

Poem No. 5.   Yi Sang.   CAMKP; PFTM-1 *Fr.* Crow's-Eye View.

Poem No. 7.   Yi Sang.   CAMKP; PFTM-1 *Fr.* Crow's-Eye View.

Poem No. 9.   Yi Sang.   CAMKP *Fr.* Crow's-Eye View.

Poem No. 10: Butterfly.   Yi Sang.   CAMKP; PFTM-1 *Fr.* Crow's-Eye View.

Poem No. 13.   Yi Sang.   CAMKP *Fr.* Crow's-Eye View.

Poem No. 15.   Yi Sang.   CAMKP; PFTM-1 *Fr.* Crow's-Eye View.

Poem of a Distant Childhood.   Noémia da Sousa.   HAWP, *tr.* by Allan Francovich and Kathleen Weaver

Poem of a Militant.   Jorge Rebelo.   PML

Poem of Adulthood, A.   Stephen Harrigan.   TiP2

Poem of any Virgin.   Jorge de Lima.   PFTM-1

Poem of Attrition, A.   Etheridge Knight.   GT; OxAAAP

Poem of Blessing.   Uri Zvi Greenberg.   NRoS, *tr.* by Esther Raizen

Poem of Chalk, The.   Philip Levine.   P180

Poem of Death, A.   George MacBeth.   HP *Fr.* Rumanian of Maria Banus, The.

Poem of Destiny, A.   Imamu Amiri Baraka.

"New Ark Space."   EGAG

Poem of Flight, The.   Philip Levine.   OtW

Poem of Jacobus Sadoletus on the Statue of Laocoon, The.   Jacopo Sadoleto.   GS, *tr.* by H. S. Wilkinson

Poem of Lewis.   Iain Crichton Smith.   EdScPo

Poem of Medicine Puns.   *Unknown.*   ColAnChi; WoPoe, *tr.* by Victor H. Mair

Poem of My Sleeping Sorrow.   Julia de Burgos.   TANSG, *tr.* by Heather Rosario Sievert

Poem of Return.   Jofre Rocha.   NAfrP, *tr.* by Don Burness

Poem of Seven Sorrows.   Wang Ts'an.   CCL1, *tr.* by John Frodsham

Poem of Sorrow.   Ts'ai Yen.   CCL1, *tr.* by John Frodsham

Poem of the Dawn and the Night.   Rodolfo Di Biasio.   NeIt, *tr.* by Stephen Sartarelli

Poem of the End.   Marina Ivanovna Tsvetayeva.   *tr.* by Elaine Feinstein and David McDuff

"I didn't want this, not."   OBVE

"Last bridge I won't."   EroLit, *tr.* by Elaine Feinstein

"Like a thick horse's mane."   WoPoe, *tr.* by David McDuff

Poem of the Frost and Snow.   Lewis Morris.   OBWVE, *tr.* by Anthony Conran

Poem of the Gifts.   Jorge Luis Borges.   TCLAP, *tr.* by Ben Belitt

Poem of the Girl from Velázquez.   Ricardo Molinari.   TCLAP, *tr.* by Inés Probert

Poem of the mind in the act of finding, The.   Of Modern Poetry.   Wallace Stevens.   ColAP; NAAL-5; NAAPv.2; NAMCP V.1; NoAM; OxBoAm; WaAnP

Poem of the Praises, The.   Albert Goldbarth.   ViWalt

Poem of the Sea and of Her.   Carlos Oquendo de Amat.   BLPSL, *tr.* by Rene de Costa, Rigas Kappatos and Eleni Paidoussi

Poem of Unrest, A.   John Ashbery.   OxBoAm; PoA 2002

Poem on Bread.   Vernon Scannell.   NOxBChV

Poem on Death.   Inger Christensen.   GPTC, *tr.* by Susanna Nied

Poem on Divine Providence.   Orientius.   *tr.* by John Peck

"Bulk of these years is already gone out of mind, The."   WoPoe, *tr.* by John Peck

Poem on Dry Mountain (A Zen Garden).   Muso Soseki.   EaWin, *tr.* by W. S. Merwin

Poem on His Death-Bed.   Cynddelw Brydydd Mawr.   OBWVE, *tr.* by Joseph P. Clancy

Poem on His Death-Bed.   Meilyr Brydydd.   OBWVE, *tr.* by Joseph P. Clancy

Poem on Losing One's Teeth.   Han Yü.   GifTon, *tr.* by Kenneth O. Hanson

Poem on My Birthday.   Peter Cooley.   NevBe

Poem on My Son's Birthday.   Jim Carroll.   AHA

Poem on Returning to Dwell in the Country.   T'ao Ch'ien.   WoPoe, *tr.* by William Acker

Poem on Stone House Mountain, A.   Hsieh Ling-yün.   CCL1, *tr.* by John Frodsham

Poem on the attitude adopted.   Erol Güney's Cat.   Orhan Veli Kanik.   WoPoe, *tr.* by Talat Sait Halman

Poem on the Bill Lately Passed for Regulating the Slave-Trade, A.   Helen Maria Williams.   RWP

Poem on the First Day of School.   Peter Cooley.   NevBe; PoA 2002

Poem on the First Day of Spring.   Peter Cooley.   PoDa

Poem on the Fugitive Slave Law, A.   Elymas Payson Rogers.

In 'Fifty Congress Passed a Bill.   CBCWP

Poem on the Limits for My Writing Group: Atlantic Center for the Arts, New Smyrna Beach, Florida.   Diane Di Prima.   AmZen

Poem, on the Supposition of an Advertisement Appearing in a Morning Paper, of the Publication of a Volume of Poems, by a Serving-Maid, A.   Elizabeth Hands.   WoRP

Poem on the Supposition of the Book Having Been Published and Read, A.   Elizabeth Hands.   WoRP

Poem on the Wandering Immortal.   Kuo P'o.   ColAnChi, *tr.* by Burton Watson

Poem, or Beauty Hurts Mr. Vinal.   E. E. Cummings.   FaBoA; HarvBoo; MoAmPo; NAAL-5; NAAPv.2; PFTM-1; TRP

Poem out of Childhood.   Muriel Rukeyser.

"In adolescence I knew travellers."   AmWaPo

Poem: "Poems are not places."   Sterling Plumpp.   GT; OxAAAP

Poem Recalls the Poet, The.   Glyn Maxwell.   NeBrP

Poem Seen in a Motel Fan.   Alberto Blanco.   CLPP, *tr.* by John Oliver Simon

Poem Sent to a Traveler.   Pao Ling-hui.   CCL1, *tr.* by Anne Birrell

Poem should be palpable and mute, A.   Ars Poetica.   Archibald MacLeish.   APT-1; BrAP; ColAP; HeIP-4; IllVoic; ItP; MoAmPo; NAAPv.2; NAMCP V.1; NIL-7; NIP-4; NoP-4; NoP-5; OxBoAm; PoA 2002; PoPoPo; StAl; TFi; WaAnP; WeW-3

Poem should not mean, A / But be. (LL)   Ars Poetica: "Poem should be palpable and mute, A."   Archibald MacLeish.   APT-1; BrAP; ColAP; HeIP-4; IllVoic; ItP; MoAmPo; NAAPv.2; NAMCP V.1; NIL-7; NIP-4; NoP-4; NoP-5; OxBoAm; PoA 2002; PoPoPo; StAl; TFi; WaAnP; WeW-3

Poem Some People Will Have to Understand, A.   Imamu Amiri Baraka.   GT; RaBo

Poem spins over the head of a man, The.   Poem, The.   Homero Aridjis.   TCLAP, *tr.* by Eliot Weinberger

Poem Stalin, The.   Adriano Spatola.   PFTM-2, *tr.* by Paul Vangelisti

Poem That Came Easily, A.   Yun Tongju.   CAMKP, *tr.* by Kay Richards and Steffen Richards

Poem That Took the Place of a Mountain, The.   Wallace Stevens.   NAMCP V.1; TWF

Poem That Was Once Called "Desperate" But Is Now Striving to Become the Perfect Love Poem.   Richard Jackson.   BAP-97

Poem to a Taoist Hermit on Quanjiao Mountain, A.   Wei Ying-wu.   CCL1, *tr.* by Witter Bynner

Poem to Answer the Question: How Old Are Fleas?   *Unknown.*   Spl

Poem to Be Read and Sung ("I know there is a person.")   César Vallejo.   TCLAP, *tr.* by Clayton Eshleman

Poem to Be Read and Sung ("I know there is someone.")   César Vallejo.   WED, *tr.* by Robert Bly and James Wright

Poem To Be Read at 3 a.m.   Donald Justice.   GoPo; StAl *Fr.* American Sketches (for William Carlos Williams).

Poem to Galway Kinnell, A.   Etheridge Knight.   BodElec

Poem to Gentiles.   Maxwell Bodenheim.   TaR

Poem to Her Daughter.   Mwana Kupona Msham.

"Daughter, take this amulet."   HAWP

Poem to His Grace the Duke of Marlborough, A.   Joseph Addison.   OBWP *Fr.* Campaign, The.

Poem to Line My Casket with, Ramona.   Josh Bell.   IIR; LegDan

Poem to Ma Ferguson.   Charles S. Taylor.   TiP2

Poem to Mr Thomas and Mr Frost.   Glyn Maxwell.   NoP-5 *Fr.* Letters to Edward Thomas.

Poem to My Death.   Julia de Burgos.   TCLAP, *tr.* by Grace Schulman

Poem to my uterus.   Lucille Clifton.   BeAl; CAP-8; NAMCP V.2; PoCu

Poem to Ophelia.   Kate Horsley.   ICANM

Poem to Shout in the Ruins.   Louis Aragon.   PFTM-1

Poem to Show the Trouble That Befell Him When He Was at Sea, A.   Thomas Prys.   OBWVE, *tr.* by Gwyn Williams

Poem to Some of my Recent Poems.   James Tate.   NoAM

Poem Unwritten, The.   Denise Levertov.   CAP-8

Poem Upon the Forcible Entry by Cat into a Poem Originally Upon Trilliums.   M. Travis Lane.   Coast

Poem Upon the Lisbon Disaster; or, An Inquiry into the Adage, "All Is for the Best."   Voltaire. *tr.* by Anthony Hecht

"Woeful mankind, born to a woeful earth!"   WoPoe, *tr.* by Anthony Hecht

Poem upon the page is as massive as, The.   Ted Berrigan.   PFTM-2 *Fr.* Sonnets, The.

Poem With a Limp.   Roger McGough.   OBCoV

Poem with Incense Paper.   Liliane Giraudon.   SCFWP, *tr.* by Serge Gavronsky

Poem with Light on Its Shoulder. Mary Ann Samyn. AmPoNex

Poem with Referees. James Sanders. AnSo

Poem with Refrains. Robert Pinsky. TaR

Poem with Skin. Octavio Armand. TCLAP, *tr. by* Carol Maier

Poem with the Answer, A. Sir John Suckling.

 Constant Lover, A [*or* The]. BASC; CavPo; NAEL-6v1; NAEL-7v1; NBLV; NoP-4; NOSC; NPeEn; OxAEP-1; OxBEV; PBRV

 (Out upon It!) NoP-5

Poem with Two Seasons Right Now. S. J. Marks. BodElec

Poem without a Category. Liu Cheng. ColAnChi, *tr. by* Burton Watson

Poem without a Freight Train or a Pocket Watch. Thom Ward. NevBe

Poem without a Hero. Anna Andreyevna Akhmatova. *tr. by* Lenore Mayhew *and* William McNaughton and William McNaughton

 Epilogue. PFTM-2, *tr. by* Lenore Mayhew *and* William McNaughton and William McNaughton

Poem without a Single Bird in It, A. Jack Spicer. BodElec

Poem without a Title. Charles Simic. CAP-8

Poem without Beginning or End. Patrick Warner. Coast

Poem without Music. José Hierro. TAPaP, *tr. by* Stephen Berg

Poem Wrapped Around Quotation from Samantha Power. Donna Brook. PrTe

Poem wrestles you, The. George Stanley. NLPA *Fr.* Mountains and Air.

Poem Written by Sir Henry Wotton, in His Youth, A. Sir Henry Wotton. NoSic

Poem Written for the Celebration of the Fourth Anniversary of President Lincoln's Emancipation Proclamation, A. James M. Whitfield.

 From Year to Year the Contest Grew. CBCWP

Poem Written in a Copy of *Beowulf*. Jorge Luis Borges. PoetW, *tr. by* Alastair Reid

Poem Written in Answer to His Majesty's Question: "What Is There in the Mountains?" T'ao Hung Ching. ColAnChi, *tr. by* Stephen Owen

Poem Written in Time of Trouble by an Irish Priest Who Had Taken Orders in France, A. *Unknown.* OBMV, *tr. by* Augusta, Lady Gregory and Lady Gregory

Poem You Asked For, The. Larry Levis. CalPo; PBCAP

Poema de casa. Laura Solórzano. SPV

Poema del habla. Laura Solórzano. SPV

Poema incesante. Laura Solórzano. SPV

Poema mudo. Laura Solórzano. SPV

Poema para los Californios Muertos. Lorna Dee Cervantes. NAMCP V.2; PoPoPo

Poema temprano. Laura Solórzano. SPV

Poème Amoureux. Gisèle Prassinos. YaTCFP

Poème est ce qui n'a ni nom, ni repos, ni lieu, ni demeure, Le. Démesure de la poésie. Jacques Garelli. YaTCFP

Poème pour une poupée achetée dans un bazar russe. Marguerite Yourcenar. YaTCFP

Poemectomy. John Dickson. IllVoic

Poemes Negres. Tristan Tzara.

 Dance of the Greased Women, The. PFTM-1

Poem-Object. André Breton. PFTM-1

Poems. Helen Maria Williams.

 Sonnet to Twilight. CenSon

Poems: "I think that I shall never read." Thomas M. Disch. PoA 2002; UV

Poems: "When you come back to me." Ruth Stone. BeAl; PoCho; StAl; TAPaP

Poems after Beirut. Mahmoud Darwish. *tr. by* Abdullah Al-Udhari, Lena Jayyusi *and* W. S. Merwin and Christopher Middleton

 We Travel Like Other People. AF

Poems After Drinking Wine. Ch'ien T'ao. ColAnChi, *tr. by* James Robert Hightower

Poems are bullshit unless they are. Black Art. Imamu Amiri Baraka. ESEAA

Poems are not places. Poem. Sterling Plumpp. GT; OxAAAP

Poems at the Porthole. Lorine Niedecker. FTOS

Poems Come to Me in the Night. Alice Sadongei. HATNAP

Poems Composed or Suggested During a Tour, in the Summer of 1833. William Wordsworth.

 Most Sweet It Is with Unuplifted Eyes. CenSon

Poems Concerning the Slave Trade. Robert Southey.

 (Poems on the Slave Trade.) NPBRoP

 Sonnet 6. CenSon

Poems for a Little Boy. Gabriella Sica. *tr. by* Cinzia Sartini Blum and Lara Trubowitz

 "I wish I were spring water." CItWP, *tr. by* Cinzia Sartini Blum and Lara Trubowitz

Poems for Lou. Guillaume Apollinaire.

 "My darling little Lou how I love you." PFTM-1

Poems for My Cousin. Josephine Jacobsen. APT-2

Poems for My Daughter. Horace Gregory. MoAmPo

Poems for Rasmia. Gzar Hantoosh. IrPoTo, *tr. by* Saadi A. Simawe and Ellen Doré Watson

Poems from a Country House. Miriam Goodman. PfS

Poems from a Diary. Abraham Sutskever. *tr. by* Cynthia Ozick

 1980. HP, *tr. by* Cynthia Ozick

 1974. BBASP, *tr. by* Cynthia Ozick

Poems from Prison. Nazim Hikmet. NaPG, *tr. by* Talat Sait Halman

Poems from Saint Pelagia Prison. Philippe Soupault. AF, *tr. by* Eden Paul

Poems from Subway to Work. Peter Orlovsky. CLPP

Poems from the Erotic Left. Ana María Rodas. TANSG, *tr. by* Zoë Anglesey

Poems from the Margins of Thom Gunn's Moly. Robert Duncan.

 Preface to the Suite. FTOS

Poems from the Veterans Hospital. Simon J. Ortiz.

 8:50 AM Ft. Lyons VAH. NAAL-5

 Travelling. NAAL-5

Poems in an Old Style. Li Po. *tr. by* Victor H. Mair

 "Ages have passed since the stately Odes flourished." ColAnChi, *tr. by* Victor H. Mair

 "My sword at my waist, I climb a high tower." ColAnChi, *tr. by* Victor H. Mair

 "There was a sojourner in Ying who intoned "White Snows."" ColAnChi, *tr. by* Victor H. Mair

Poems in Praise of Practically Nothing. Samuel Hoffenstein.

 "You buy some flowers for your table." OBCoV

 "You buy yourself a new suit of clothes." OBCoV

 "You go to high school, even college." AmWit

 "You hire a cook, but she can't cook yet." OBCoV

 "You leap out of bed; you start to get ready." AmWit

 "You're a good girl; you're gray with virtue." AmWit

Poems in the Greek Anthology Mode. Nissim Ezekiel.

 "When the female railway clerk." OBCoV

Poems of Delight. Liz Rosenberg. IJHIL

Poems of Love, The. Padraic Fallon. IrLP

Poems of Memory. Anne Cluysenaar.

 "Knife reduces a polished oval, The." Prnts

Poems of Nine to Ten P.M. Nazim Hikmet. NaPG, *tr. by* Talat Sait Halman

Poems of Our Climate, The. Wallace Stevens. APT-1; NAMCP V.1; NoP-4; NoP-5; OxBoAm; SoSe-8

Poems of Reflection on the Vicissitudes of Life. Ch'en Tzu-ang. *tr. by* Victor H. Mair

 "I close my door and trace the transformations of nature." ColAnChi, *tr. by* Victor H. Mair

 "I dwell in seclusion and observe the creative process." ColAnChi, *tr. by* Victor H. Mair

 "I dwell in the forest nursing a long illness." ColAnChi, *tr. by* Victor H. Mair

 "Men in the market pride themselves on their knowledge and craft, The." ColAnChi, *tr. by* Victor H. Mair

Poems of the Atomic Bomb. Tōge Sankichi. *tr. by* Richard H. Minear

 Dying. PFTM-2, *tr. by* Richard H. Minear

Poems of the Mediterranean. Fazil Hüsnü Daglarca. *tr. by* Talat Sait Halman

 "You say / Stars." NaPG, *tr. by* Talat Sait Halman

Poems of the Pope, The. Nicanor Parra. VCWP, *tr. by* Edith Grossman

Poems on Man in His Various Aspects under the American Republic. Cornelius Mathews.

 Journalist, The. APN-1

 Masses, The. APN-1

 Sculptor, The. APN-1

Poems on Poetry. Yüan Hao-wen.

 "I know my foolishness, a mere ant trying to shake a tree." ColAnChi, *tr. by* John Timothy Wixted

Poems on the Slave Trade. Robert Southey. *See* Sonnet 6: "High in the air exposed the slave is hung."

Poems seeking the image of the sense storm. Don Quixote and the Flour Mills. Safaa Fathy. AnVo, *tr. by* Mohamed Enani

Poems to Blok. Marina Ivanovna Tsvetayeva. *tr. by* Bob Perelman, Aleksandar Petrov and Shirley Rihner

 "Cupolas flame, in Moscow where I live." TCRusP, *tr. by* Bob Perelman, Aleksandar Petrov and Shirley Rihner

 "Den—for the beast, A." TCRusP, *tr. by* Bob Perelman, Aleksandar Petrov and Shirley Rihner

 "Gentle ghost." TCRusP, *tr. by* Bob Perelman, Aleksandar Petrov and Shirley Rihner

 "They thought: Human!" TCRusP, *tr. by* Bob Perelman, Aleksandar Petrov and Shirley Rihner

 "Your name—a bird on my hand." TCRusP, *tr. by* Bob Perelman, Aleksandar Petrov and Shirley Rihner

"You're going by, west of the sun." TCRusP, *tr.* by Bob Perelman, Aleksandar Petrov and Shirley Rihner

Poems to My Father. Mick North. NLP

Poem's Visit, A. Kang Ŭn'gyo. CAMKP, *tr.* by Tae Yang Kwak

Poems We Can Understand. Paul Hoover. PmAP; WaAnP

Poe's House. Juan Ramón Jiménez. MotU, *tr.* by Sandra Hoben

Poesía asesinó un cadáver, La. Con Palabras Distintas. José Ángel Valente. RaW

Poesía Es un Arma Cargada de Futuro, La. Gabriel Celaya. RaW

Poésie se fait dans un lit comme l'amour, La. Sur la Route de San Romano. André Breton. YaTCFP

Poesy. Oliver Wendell Holmes. TreFP

Poet. Karl Shapiro. MoAmPo; NoAM

Poet. Peter Viereck. MoAmPo

Poet, A. Thomas Hardy. NAMCP V.1; NoAM

Poet, A. Jules Supervielle. YaTCFP, *tr.* by Patricia Terry

Poet, The. Matthew Arnold. NPEen *Fr.* Resignation.

Poet, The. Fadil Azzawi. IrPoTo, *tr.* by Ralph Saverese and Saadi A. Simawe

Poet, The. William Cullen Bryant. NAAL-3; NCAP

Poet, The. Dale R. Carver. FaBoWar

Poet, The. Paul Laurence Dunbar. NAAPv.1; TCAPo

Poet, The. Gerrit Komrij. TuT

Poet, The. Alfred de Musset. WoPoe *Fr.* Night in May, A.

Poet, The. Alfred de Musset. WoPoe *Fr.* Night in May, A.

Poet, The. Sir Walter Scott. TreFP

Poet, The. Achsa W. Sprague.
    Scene 3.
      "'Tis near the time. I'm glad 'tis getting late." SWaP

Poet, The. Walt Whitman. MoAmPo *Fr.* By Blue Ontario's Shore.

Poet, The: "Voice of the drum slowly unravels, The." Clotaire Saint-Natus. OGAHCP, *tr.* by Boadiba and Jack Hirschman

Poet: A Lying Word. Laura Riding Jackson. HarvBoo

Poet alone in my country, A. On Being a Poet in Sierra Leone. Syl Cheney-Coker. HBAPE

Poet Among Those Who Are Also Poets. Syl Cheney-Coker. NAfrP

Poet and Botanist. Constance Naden. ViWPN; VWP

Poet and Critic. Samuel Daniel. NoSic; PBRV *Fr.* Musophilus; or, Defence of All Learning.

Poet and His Book, The. Edna St. Vincent Millay. MoAmPo

Poet and Person. Denise Levertov. GifTon

Poet and Saint! to thee alone are given. On the Death of Mr. Crashaw. Abraham Cowley. BASC

Poet as a penguin, A. The. Birds. Frieda Hughes. NeBl; StAl

Poet Asks His Love About the Enchanted City of Cuenca, The. Federico García Lorca. CAGL *Fr.* Sonetos del Amor Oscuro [Sonnets of Dark Love].

Poet Asks His Love to Write to Him, The. Federico García Lorca. CAGL *Fr.* Sonetos del Amor Oscuro [Sonnets of Dark Love].

Poet at Eighteen, The. Dick Allen. PoA 2002

Poet at Night-Fall, The. Glenway Wescott. PoA 2002

Poet at Seven, The. Donald Justice. WeW-3

Poet at Seventeen, The. Larry Levis. GeoHom

Poet at Work. Richard Tipping. BMAP

Poet, be seated at the piano. Mozart, 1935. Wallace Stevens. MiVo

Poet by the fireside cries, A. Sean Dunne. ModIr *Fr.* Sydney Place.

Poet, conserver of the infinite faces of the living, The. René Char. PFTM-1 *Fr.* Leaves of Hypnos.

Poet digs deep for the poem, The. Buried Poem, The. Ismail. HotL, *tr.* by V. Narayana Rao

Poet Dives, The. Willem Jan Otten. TuT, *tr.* by Micheal O'Siadhail

Poet, do not fear tautologies. Repetition. Zoya Ezrokhi. CRWP, *tr.* by Daniel Weissbort

Poet Dreamt of Heaven, The. *Unknown.* TreFP

Poet felt the rain, The. Rain. Margiad Evans. OBWVE

Poet Fishing, The. Gwyneth Lewis. ATSWP, *tr.* by Robert Minhinnick

Poet Gets Drowsy on the Road, The. Frederick Turner. TiP2

Poet Goes about Her Business, The. Linda Gregg. PtR

Poet Grows Old, The. Oliver Wendell Holmes. TCAPo

Poet Grows Older, The. Charles Wright. MotU

Poet has by now travelled a distance, spanning mental universe, The. Iovis XIX: Why That's a Blade Can Float. Anne Waldman. PFTM-2

Poet has passed away, The. Or rather, snuffed. Polina Barskova. CRWP, *tr.* by Peter France

Poet has worked all night in the basement on lofty things, The. Prose Poem, The. Roy Scheele. MotU

Poet Haunted, The. Wendy Rose. ReEnLa

Poet Hipponax lies here, The. Epitaph: Justice. Theocritus. WoPoe, *tr.* by Fred Chappell

Poet hung himself today, A. Mirrors in the Room. Rodney M. McNeil. InTrad

Poet in New York. Federico García Lorca.
    "While the Chinaman was crying on the roof." WED, *tr.* by Robert Bly

Poet in the Desert, The. Charles Erskine Scott Wood.
    1. APT-1

Poet in the House, A. Cathy Song. SweBea

Poet in the Kitchen. Margit Mikes. IQMS, *tr.* by Susanne K. Walther

Poet in theory worships the moon, The. Moonlight and Gas. Constance Naden. ViWPN; VWP

Poet is a fake, The. Autopsychography. Fernando Pessoa. WoPoe, *tr.* by Keith Bosley

Poet is a little God, The. (LL) Ars Poetica. Vincente Huidobro. PFTM-1; TCLAP, *tr.* by David Guss

Poet is a long animal, The. Another Genealogy. Luiza Neto Jorge. SurWo, *tr.* by Jean R. Longland

Poet is a pumping-station turning the landscape into words, The. Basho 4. Cees Nooteboom. TuT, *tr.* by Michael O'Loughlin

Poet is about to write a poem, The. Poem on Bread. Vernon Scannell. NOxBChV

Poet Is Dead, The. William Everson. NoAM

Poet is like a church, an abandoned one, The. Poet Is Like a Church, The. David Starkey. Vesp

Poet is not a jukebox, so don't tell me what to write, A. Poet Is Not a Jukebox, A. Dudley Randall. BRtP; NoAM

Poet is one who writes verses, A. Who Is a Poet. Tadeusz Rózewicz. VCWP

Poet is Piqued, The [*or* Anna Matilda]. Robert Merry. STuOW

Poet is Scornful, The. Julia A. Moore. STuOW *Fr.* To My Friends and Critics.

Poet Is Served Her Papers, The. Lorna Dee Cervantes. TouFir

Poet is working upstairs, The. Sean Dunne. ModIr *Fr.* Sydney Place.

Poet Laments the Coming of Old Age, The. Dame Edith Sitwell. BrAP; NAEL-6v2; NAMCP V.1; NoAM

Poet, let passion sleep. Art, II. Alfred Noyes. OBEV

Poet Lied, The. Odia Ofeimun. HBAPE

Poet, Lover, Birdwatcher. Nissim Ezekiel. BrAP

Poet man walks between dreams. Prologomena to a Poetics. Jerome Rothenberg. PFTM-2

Poet must work with brush and paper, The. Written on a Cold Evening. Yang Wan-li. ColAnChi, *tr.* by Jonathan Chaves

Poet nailed on, The. I am a Camera. Bob Kaufman. PFTM-2

Poet of Nature, thou hast wept to know. To Wordsworth. Percy Bysshe Shelley. CenSon; NAEL-6v2; NAEL-7v2; NoP-4; NoP-5; NPBRoP; NPeEn

Poet of Our Climate, A. Katha Pollitt. PoA 2004

Poet of Our Race. Maggie Pogue Johnson. CBWP-4

Poet of the dead leaves driven like ghosts. Shelley. Charles Simic. TRP

Poet of the Hortobágy, The. Endre Ady. IQMS, *tr.* by Anton N. Nyerges

Poet of the serene and thoughtful lay! Wordsworth. Charlotte L. Forten Grimke. TCAPo

Poet on 'Poets on Poets', A: And Other Poems. Mererid Puw Davies. BBMWP, *tr.* by the author

Poet Pedro Pietri. Jose Angel Figueroa. PueRic

Poet professor in autumn years. Personals Ad. Allen Ginsberg. NAMCP V.2

Poet put Old Prussian, A. Who Would Have Thought It. Marie Luise Kaschnitz. PFTM-2, *tr.* by Lisel Mueller

Poet Questions the Ant, The. Cornelius Whur. STuOW *Fr.* Village Musings.

Poet Recognizing the Echo of the Voice, A. Diane Wakoski. NIP-4

Poet recounts his life first to men, The. Biography, Poetry, Destiny. León Felipe. RaW, *tr.* by W. S. Merwin

Poet Reflects On Her Solitary Fate, The. Sandra Cisneros. FFC

Poet Reveals All, The. William Wordsworth. STuOW *Fr.* Thorn, The.

Poet Ridiculed by Hysterical Academics, The. W. D. Snodgrass. BrAP

Poet should learn with his eyes, A. Kshemendra. EaWin; WoPoe *Fr.* Kavikanthabharana.

Poet Sings His Painting, The. Lloyd Richardson. WaCA

Poet Speaks the Truth, The. Federico García Lorca. CAGL *Fr.* Sonetos del Amor Oscuro [Sonnets of Dark Love].

Poet Speaks with Love by Telephone, The. Federico García Lorca. CAGL *Fr.* Sonetos del Amor Oscuro [Sonnets of Dark Love].

Poet stopped on the edge of night, The. Robert Frost: The Road Taken. William Jay Smith. VisFro

Poet to a Poet. Salman al-Tajir. SonAtl, *tr.* by Abdul Kalam Azad

Poet to Tiger. May Swenson. PoBW

Poet tosses stones into the lake, The. Seven Voluntary Labors and One Seditious Act. Nicanor Parra. WoBe, *tr.* by Liz Werner

Poet, Trying to Surprise God, The. Peter Meinke. PBCAP

Poet Turned Lawyer, The. John Donne. OBSV *Fr.* Satires.

Poet Upstairs, The.   Sean Dunne.   ModIr *Fr.* Sydney Place.

Poet Visits Egypt and Israel, The.   Maxine W. Kumin.   TaR

Poet wandering on, through Araby, The.   Percy Bysshe Shelley.   NPBRoP *Fr.* Alastor; or, The Spirit of Solitude.

Poet wears a hat, The.   Siesta.   Adelia Prado.   TCLAP, *tr. by* Marcia Kirinus

Poet: What Ever Happened to Luther?   Haki R. Madhubuti.   SpirFl; UnSA

Poet: "Wind dying, I find a city deserted, except for crowds of, The."   Keith Waldrop.   OnScMo

Poet, write! / Not of a purpose dark and dire.   Crime of the Ages, The.   Augusta Cooper Bristol.   APN-2; PCW

Poeta Fit, Non Nascitur.   Lewis Carroll.   OBSV

Poeta Fui.   Julia Budenz.   FFC

Poeta le cuenta su vida primero a los hombres, El.   Biografía, Poesía y Destino.   León Felipe.   RaW

Poète, Un.   Jules Supervielle.   YaTCFP

Poetic License.   Leonard Nolens.   TuT, *tr. by* Michael O'Loughlin

Poetic License.   Ron Padgett.   OxBoAm

Poetic Reflections Enroute To, and During, The Funeral and Burial of Henry Dumas, Poet.   Eugene B. Redmond.   ISC

Poetic State, A.   Czeslaw Milosz.   MotU, *tr. by* the author and Robert Hass

Poetic Voice.   Rebecca Seiferle.   TAPaP

Poetical Epistle tae Cullybackey Auld Nummer.   Thomas Given.   FaBoVe

Poetical Epistle to an Absent Friend, A.   Eliza Robertson.
  "O place us, dear Saviour! in some small retreat."   PoBW

Poetical Happiness.   Frederick Tennyson.   CenSon

Poetical Question Concerning the Jacobites, Sent to the Athenians, A.   Elizabeth Singer Rowe.   BASC

Poetics.   Manuel Bandeira.   TCLAP, *tr. by* Candace Slater

Poetics.   August Kleinzahler.   PmAP; WaAnP

Poetics.   Yusef Komunyakaa.   WaAnP

Poetics.   Cesare Pavese.   TAPaP, *tr. by* Geoffrey Brock

Poetresses Petition, The.   Margaret Lucas Cavendish, Duchess of Newcastle.   BrAP
  (Poetress's Petition, The.)   CABP

Poet[r]ess's Hasty Resolution, The.   Margaret Lucas Cavendish, Duchess of Newcastle.   BASC; NAEL-7v1

Poetry.   Madison Cawein.   APN-2

Poetry.   Mary Elizabeth Fullerton.   GI; NOBAu

Poetry: "It's a bit like looking through the big window."   Nick Laird.   NIrP

Poetry: "Many entrances. Open. Everywhere. But reaching nowhere. Wandering."   Kim Chôngnan.   EcSo, *tr. by* Peter H. Lee

Poetry: "Old forms are like birdhouses that, The."   Greg Kuzma.   PoA 2002

Poetry: "Poetry is motion graceful."   Nikki Giovanni.   WaAnP

Poetry: "Who broke these mirrors."   Sa'di Yusuf.   IrPoTo, *tr. by* Khaled Mattawa

Poetry.   Pablo Neruda.   PoetW; VCWP, *tr. by* Alastair Reid

Poetry.   Frank O'Hara.   AHA

Poetry: "Beautiful woman, A."   Ismail.   HotL, *tr. by* V. Narayana Rao

Poetry: "In the same way that the mindless diamond keeps."   Don Paterson.   P180

Poetry: "Invited onto the grounds of the god."   Jane Miller.   GifTon; TAPaP

Poetry / Is something refined.   Sugar Poem.   Aurora Levins Morales.   PueRic

Poetry.   Lydia Huntley Sigourney.   SWaP

Poetry.   Xavier Villaurrutia.   TCLAP, *tr. by* Dana Stangel

Poetry [1921 version]: "I, too, dislike it: there are things that are important beyond all this fiddle."   Marianne Moore.   AmFaPo; APT-1; ColAP; HeIP-4; MoAmPo; NAAL-5; NAAPv.2; NALW; NAMCP V.1; NIP-4; NoAM; NoP-4; NoP-5; OxBoAm; PoPoPo; TCAPo; TFi; WaAnP

Poetry [1925 Version].   Marianne Moore.   NIL-7

Poetry [1967 Version].   Marianne Moore.   BrAP; HarvBoo; NIL-7; OxBoAm

Poetry: A Chronic Disease.   Yi Kyubo.   CATKP, *tr. by* Kevin O'Rourke

Poetry, a Natural Thing.   Robert Duncan.   CalPo; NAMCP V.2; NoAM; OxBoAm; PmAP; TRP

Poetry, almost blind like a camera.   Jack Spicer.   PmAP *Fr.* Imaginary Elegies.

Poetry and Post, Texas.   Betsy Colquitt.   TiP2

Poetry and Religion.   Les A. Murray.   UpMys; WaAnP

Poetry and Science.   Hugh MacDiarmid.   HarvBoo

Poetry and Thought.   René Daumal.   MotU; YaTCFP, *tr. by* Michael Wood

Poetry Became.   Margaret Randall.   ICANM

Poetry begins here. Brand new summer.   Thank You for Being You.   Matthew Zapruder.   NevBe

Poetry Bug, The.   Barry Spacks.   PoA 2002

Poetry Calendar, A.   Chimako Tada.   VCWP, *tr. by* Naoshi Koriyama *and* Edward Lueders

Poetry Despises Your Attempts at Domesticity.   Juliana Baggott.   SweBea

Poetry Detective.   Edwin Torres.   HeMarv

Poetry ends like a rope. (LL)   Book of Music, A.   Jack Spicer.   APSN; CalPo; OxBoAm

Poetry for the Goddess.   William T. Crawley III.   InTrad

Poetry fro Dummies.   Joel Dailey.   AnSo

Poetry holds the written veil across its face, shyly.   Yahya Beg.   OLP, *tr. by* Walter Andrews, Najaat Black and Mehmet Kalpakli

Poetry in America.   Julia Kasdorf.   ACAMVP

Poetry in England.   Samuel Daniel.   NoSic *Fr.* Musophilus; or, Defence of All Learning.

Poetry Is a Destructive Force.   Wallace Stevens.   APT-1; RaBo

Poetry Is a Heavenly Crime.   Vincente Huidobro.   TCLAP, *tr. by* W. S. Merwin

Poetry Is a Kind of Money.   Kay Ryan.   OxBoAm

Poetry is a loose term and only.   Some Poetry.   Freda Downie.   MoWP

Poetry Is a Weapon Loaded with the Future.   Gabriel Celaya.   RaW, *tr. by* Robert Mezey

Poetry is always seeking something special. To men with.   From Hear to Air.   Douglas Messerli.   FTOS

Poetry is like a swoon, with this difference.   Klupzy Girl, The.   Charles Bernstein.   PmAP

Poetry is made in a bed like love.   On the Road to San Romano.   André Breton.   YaTCFP, *tr. by* Mary Ann Caws *and* Jean-Pierre Cauvin

Poetry is made in bed like love.   On the Road to San Romano.   André Breton.   PFTM-1

Poetry is motion graceful.   Poetry.   Nikki Giovanni.   WaAnP

Poetry is not an answer.   Call of the Wild, The.   Kalamu ya Salaam.   FuFl

Poetry Is Not You.   Rosario Castellanos.   TANSG, *tr. by* Magda Bogin

Poetry is the Art of Not Succeeding.   Joe Salerno.   PoDa

Poetry is the subject of the poem.   Wallace Stevens.   NAMCP V.1 *Fr.* Man with the Blue Guitar, The.

Poetry is the supreme fiction, madame.   High-Toned Old Christian Woman, A.   Wallace Stevens.   NAAL-5; NAAPv.2; NoAM; OxBoAm

Poetry is verdant—in spring.   Poetry is Verdant.   Jaan Kaplinski.   TAPaP, *tr. by* the author, Sam Hamill and Riina Tamm

Poetry? It's a hobby.   What the Chairman Told Tom.   Basil Bunting.   BrAP; EmeKit; NAMCP V.1; NoP-4

Poetry Jump-Up.   John Agard.   NOxBChV

Poetry Makes Rhythm in Philosophy.   Ishmael Reed.   EGAG

Poetry murdered a corpse.   With Plain Words.   José Ángel Valente.   RaW, *tr. by* Robert Mezey and Hardie St. Martin

Poetry of America, The.   Juan Felipe Herrera.   TouFir

Poetry of Departures.   Philip Larkin.   BeAl; BrAP; HeIP-4

Poetry of earth can never die, The.   Grasshopper and the Cricket, The.   Olga Sedakova.   ItGoST, *tr. by* Catriona Kelly

Poetry of earth is never dead, The.   On the Grasshopper and [the] Cricket.   John Keats.   CenSon; NIL-7; NIP-4; OxAEP-2

Poetry of Motion, The.   Raymond Garlick.   AngWePo

Poetry of Roses, The.   Franco Fortini.   ItPo, *tr. by* Gayle Ridinger

Poetry Reading.   Anna Swirszczynska [or Swir].   BLT; TAPaP, *tr. by* Czeslaw Milosz and Leonard Nathan

Poetry Reading at the Varna Ruins.   John Balaban.   TAPaP

Poetry Reading at West Point, A.   William Matthews.   P180

Poetry readings have to be some of the saddest.   Poetry readings.   Charles Bukowski.   GoPo

Poetry sickness makes the old-age sickness even worse.   Speaking My Mind.   Ch'i-chi.   CSKM, *tr. by* Burton Watson

Poetry stops before the end of the margin.   100 Differences Between Poetry and Prose.   Tom Leonard.   Oth

Poetry That Is Life.   Almad Shamlu.   PML, *tr. by Unknown*

Poetry's a Way Not a Subject.   Norman Fischer.   WANABP

Poetry's Beginning.   Gail Hosking Gilberg.   VisFro

Poets.   Kay Boyle.   TAPaP

Poets.   X. J. Kennedy.   OPRER

Poets.   James Laughlin.   TAPaP

Poets, The.   Henry Wadsworth Longfellow.   GSo

Poets, The.   Afaa Michael Weaver.   FuFl

Poets and storytellers.   American Literature.   Lisel Mueller.   PoSol

Poet's Arbour in the Birchwood, The.   Edward Williams.   OBWVE, *tr. by* Kenneth Hurlstone Jackson

Poets are dying because they are told to die, The.   Occasional Poem 7.1.72.   Roy Fisher.   HarvBoo

Poets are going home now, The.   Ingathering.   Carolyn Kizer.   ExTi

Poets are usually pure, rugged.   Lament for Lu Yin.   Meng Chiao.   CCL1, *tr. by* Stephen Owen

Poets arrive and shake hands, The.   World Poetry Circuit.   Alfred A. Yuson.   ReBoTo

Poet's Biography.   Belkis Cuza Malé.   TANSG, *tr. by* Pamela Carmell

Poet's Calendar, The.   Henry Wadsworth Longfellow.   APN-1

Poet's Confession, A.   Gwyneth Lewis.   BeAl

Poet's Corner, The.   Laura Riding Jackson.   FuPo

Poet's daily chore, The.   Lens.   Anne Wilkinson.   BrAP

Poet's Death, A. Cheryl Clarke. WiU

Poet's death and sex thoughts rode me, A. Poet's Death, A. Cheryl Clarke. WiU

Poet's Delay, The. Henry David Thoreau. TCAPo

Poet's Destiny, The. Lady Jane Francesca Wilde. VWP

Poets, do not sneer at everything. Lake, The. Tom Clark. AHA

Poet's Farewell to His Teeth, The. William Dickey. PoA 2002

Poet's Fate, A. Awwad Nasir. IrPoTo, *tr. by* Saadi A. Simawe and Daniel Weissbort

Poet's Garret, The. Mary Robinson. RWP

Poets Have Their Ear to the Ground. Peter De Vries. UV

Poet's Heart, The. Richard Jones. GifTon

Poets Hitchhiking on the Highway. Gregory Corso. BB

Poet's Home, The. Mariella Bettarini. *tr. by* Cinzia Sartini Blum and Lara Trubowitz

"My home(did you know?)—my home." CItWP, *tr. by* Cinzia Sartini Blum and Lara Trubowitz

Poet's home is a chair, The. Metamorphosis of a Chair. Alberto Blanco. RMCMP, *tr. by* Joan Lindgren

Poets, I want to follow them all. On Originality. Bill Manhire. HarvBoo

Poet's Ideal, The. Henrietta Cordelia Ray. CBWP-3

Poets / in a company. Dancing Concerning a Form of Women, A. Robert Duncan. FTOS

Poets in Late Winter. Mona Van Duyn. ExTi; PfSP

Poet's Insurance Risk, The. Myrddin ap Dafydd. BBMWP, *tr. by* Gillian Clarke

Poets light but Lamps, The. Emily Dickinson. APN-2; HeIP-4; TCAPo

Poets loiter all their leisure. Hour Glass, The. Edward Quillinan. NOBRP

Poet's Lot, The. Letitia Elizabeth Landon. NPBRoP; RWP

Poet's lovely faith creates, The. Poet's Lot, The. Letitia Elizabeth Landon. NPBRoP; RWP

Poet's Loves, The. Hywel ab Owain Gwynedd. OBWVE, *tr. by* Gwyn Williams

Poets may boast, as safely vain. Of English Verse. Edmund Waller. CABP; NOSC

Poet's Ministrants, The. Henrietta Cordelia Ray. CBWP-3

Poets, minor or major, should arrange to remain slender. Poets. Kay Boyle. TAPaP

Poet's Obligation. Pablo Neruda. PoetW; VCWP, *tr. by* Alastair Reid

Poet's Obligation, The. Pablo Neruda. TWF, *tr. by* William Ward Ayer

Poets of Missouri stare at astonishing winter, The. Poets in Late Winter. Mona Van Duyn. ExTi; PfSP

Poets of the south. Chrysanthemums. Ko Ŭn. CAMKP, *tr. by* Kevin O'Rourke

Poets often use many words to say a simple thing. Fly Me to the Moon (In Other Words). Bart Howard. ReLy

Poets on Poets. Nin Andrews. KGB

Poets on[e]ly that can tell, The. (LL) On a Picture Painted by Herself [*or Her self*], Representing Two Nymphs [*or Nimphs*] of Diana's, One in a Posture to Hunt, the other Bath[e]ing. Anne Killigrew. BASC; NOSC

Poet's or Playwright's Function, The. Giovanni Jacopo meditates. Douglas Livingstone. TSAP

Poet's Poem, The. Kama Kamanda. SonAtl, *tr. by* Gregory Beaven and Christophe Mirambeau

Poet's Prayer, The. *Unknown.* OBSV

Poet's Prelude, The. Geraint Bowen. BBMWP *Fr.* Ode in Praise of the Farmer.

Poet's Resurrection, The. Jenő Dsida. IQMS, *tr. by* Peter Zollman

Poets say that all who love are blind, The. I Got It Bad and That Ain't Good. Paul Francis Webster. ReLy

Poet's Shuffle, The. Calvin Forbes. GT; LTA

Poets sing of a love forlorn. Ballade of Poetic Material. Helen Smith Bevington. AmWit

Poet's Tango, The. Jack Foley. CalPo

Poets, the sages, the seers of the land!, The. (LL) Woman's Future. May Kendall. ViWPN; VWP

Poet's Wife, A. Cho Wen-chun. NAAPv.2, *tr. by* Amy Lowell

Poet's Wish, The; an Ode. Allan Ramsay. OBVE

Poet's Work. Lorine Niedecker. APT-2; HarvBoo; NAAPv.2; NAMCP V.1; OxBoAm; PoCho

Pogrom. Ed. Hoornik. TuT, *tr. by* Mary E. O'Donnell

Point, The. David Bromige. FTOS

Point, The. Robert Earl Hayden. ESEAA

Point, The. Evan Jones. NOBAu

Point, The. John Montague. PNI *Fr.* Great Cloak, The.

Point and Counter-Point in All Things. Jane Mead. NAPBL

Point at Issue, The. William Wordsworth. SacPr *Fr.* Ecclesiastical Sonnets.

Point Grey. Daryl Hine. BrAP

Point, I imagine, is, The. Point, The. Evan Jones. NOBAu

Point is not that Troy, The. On Living with a Fat Woman in Heaven. Sidney Burris. SwNoth

Point is not the point—, The. Point, The. David Bromige. FTOS

Point of hill. Stairway to Heaven. Robert Creeley. FTOS

Point of moonlight, A. Inside: George Gaines at Graterford Prison, 1981. David Keplinger. AmPoNex

Point of No Return. Jane Glazer. FiBr

Point of View, A. Constance Carrier. APT-2

Point Shirley. Sylvia Plath. NIL-7; NIP-4

Pointed Out Like the Stars. Alice Rahon. SurWo, *tr. by* Myrna Bell Rochester

Pointed reproach of the enemy, The. Fuzuli. OLP, *tr. by* Walter Andrews, Najaat Black and Mehmet Kalpakli

Pointless homesickness. Pointless shudderings. Willow in Spring Wind: A Showing. Jorie Graham. ExTi

Pointless Journey. Yolanda Bedregal. TANSG, *tr. by* Carolyne Wright

Pointless objects riddle, The. Wopko Jensma. TSAP

Pointless Pride of Man, The. *Unknown.* FaBoVe

Points at me. (LL) Day They Cleaned Up the Border, The: El Salvador, February, 1981. Wendy Rose. AmWaPo; HATNAP

Poise of my hands reminded me of yours. (LL) Villanelle: "It is the pain, it is the pain, endures." William Empson. HarvBoo; NAMCP V.1; NoAM; TRP; UV; WaAnP

Poised between going on and back, pulled. Base Stealer, The. Robert Francis. NTCP; PML

Poised on this limestone bridge, grey now. Sunken Gardens (Huntington, IN), The. Shari Miller Wagner. ACAMVP

Poised smiling on your charger. Heavens Cherubim High Horsed or The Meeting of the Two Sevens (May 1977). Velma Pollard. WaCA

Poison. William Heyen. RaF

Poison, The. Hans Magnus Enzensberger. VCWP, *tr. by* the author, Hans Magnus Enzensberger and Michael Hamburger

Poison, 1959. David Wojahn. PoDa

Poison flower that in my garden grew, The. Poison Flower, The. Mary Elizabeth Coleridge. PEW

Poison Tree, A. William Blake. NAEL-6v2; NAEL-7v2; NoP-4; NoP-5; NPBRoP; NPeEn; OxAEP-2; OxBEV; SoSe-8; TFi; WaAnP; WeW-3 *Fr.* Songs of Experience.

Poisoned Man, The. James Dickey. CAP-8

Poisoned wheat let. Garvey's Head as Value. Norman Weinstein. WaCA

Poisonfield. Glyn Maxwell. HarvBoo

Poisonous Illusions. Abd al-Rahim Salih al-Rahim. IrPoTo, *tr. by* Saadi A. Simawe and Daniel Weissbort

Poking up from the ground barely above my knees. Little Pines. Ch'i-chi. CSKM, *tr. by* Burton Watson

Poland/1931. Jerome Rothenberg. FTOS

Poland works nicely. Story So Far, The. John Clarke. UV

Polar. Jacqueline Senard. SurWo, *tr. by* Myrna Bell Rochester

Polar Bear. William Jay Smith. TLR

Polar Bear never makes his bed, The. Polar Bear. William Jay Smith. TLR

Polar Cub. Judith Nicholls. NOxBChV

Polar DEW has just warned that, The. Your Attention Please. Peter Porter. OBWP

Polar Exploration. Stephen Spender. NoAM

Polar Explorer, A. Joseph Brodsky. WaAnP, *tr. by* the author

Polar she-bear, dirty ivory, The. Arctic Spring. Denise Levertov. PfS

Polderland. Hendrik Marsman. TuT, *tr. by* Seamus Deane

Polderland. Hendrik Marsman. TuT, *tr. by* Michael Longley

Pole at the Village Pagoda, The. *Vietnamese Oral Tradition.* CaDao, *tr. by* John Balaban

Pole Boat at Honey Island. Sandra Alcosser. PoDa

Pole Star, The. Coslett Coslett. OBWVE, *tr. by* Kenneth Hurlstone Jackson

Pole Vaulter. David Allan Evans. MoASP

Pole Vaulting. Maura Stanton. PoA 2002

Pole your three winged galleons. Han-shan (Cold Mountain). ColAnChi, *tr. by* Red Pine

Poles / are within us, The. Paul Celan. PoetW, *tr. by* John Felstiner

Poles rode out from Warsaw against the German, The. Abnormal Is Not Courage, The. Jack Gilbert. YaYoPo

Polestar. K. Psaila. SonAtl, *tr. by* Xenia Broughton, Dorli Meek, Steven Ostermann, Emma Priest and Tamara Romanyk

Polestar. Christopher Stahl. BeDoSh

Police / being poisoned, The. List of the Delusions of the Insane / What They Are Afraid Of, A. David Antin. APSN

Police came once when I was doing my death dance, The. Mad Cow Tries to Write the Good Poem, The. Jo Shapcott. MoWP

Police killed her brother. Rant, Rave and Ricochet. Luis J. Rodriguez. IllVoic

Police Report. Devarakonda Balagangadhara Tilak. HotL, *tr. by* V. Narayana Rao

Police State. M-1 and Sticman. FTtHH

Policeman does not blow his whistle, The. A. Velichansky. TCRusP, *tr. by* Daniel Weissbort

Pólis, place defended. Nanni Cagnone. ItPo *Fr.* Vaticinio.

Polis poutre catalane. Luis d'Antin Van Rooten. OBCoV *Fr.* Mots d'Heures: Gousses, Rames.

Polish Colours. Maria Pawlikowska-Jasnorzewska. SonAtl, *tr. by* Sue Eley and Katarzyna Pollonska

Polish Girl Standing on a Chair, A. J. B. Charles. TuT, *tr. by* Gregory O'Donoghue

Polish Knot, The. Tomasz Jastrun. AF, *tr. by* Michael March *and* Jaroslaw Anders

Polish Rider, The. Derek Walcott. WoPoe

Polished and polished. Basho. SoOfWA, *tr. by* Sam Hamill

Polished linoleum shone there. Brass taps shone. Seamus Heaney. InoFa *Fr.* Clearances.

Polished now. Need for Armor, A. Eileen Stratidakis. PasH

Polite Debate, A. Princess Nukada. SonAtl, *tr. by* Mitsuko Ishino, Hiroko Ohara, Phoebe Ravenhall and Wakiko Tsujimoto

Politeness fades. After Long Silence. Jane Hirshfield. WANABP

Politer and politer and politer. (LL) City Christmas. Phyllis McGinley. ChrPo; OBCoV

Political. Rita Dove. FFC

Political art, let it be, A. Short Speech to My Friends. Imamu Amiri Baraka. ESEAA

Political House that Jack Built, The. William Hone. NOBRP
  "This is THE MAN—all shaven and shorn." OBCoV

Political Life of Palm Trees, The. Sandra Del Valle. RWB

Political Meeting. Abraham Moses Klein. BrAP

Political Parties. Fereydun Rafiq Hilmi. IrPoTo, *tr. by* Muhammad Ali

Political Poem. Imamu Amiri Baraka. AF; NoAM; PmAP

Political Prisoner. Fadil Azzawi. IrPoTo, *tr. by* Melissa Brown and Salaam Yousif

Politician is an arse upon, A. Politician, A. E. E. Cummings. NBLV

Politicians came into my room last night. How It Happened. Mark Smith-Soto. RWB

Politicians, heart and soul. Poll Star. Felicia Lamport. NBLV

Politicians, The. Miyazawa Kenji. WhBo

Politicisation of the North Wind, The. David Morley. NLP

Politics. William Butler Yeats. AmFaPo; GoPo; HeIP-4; ItP; NAMCP V.1; PLBUT

Politics of Memory, The. Kevin Hearle. CalPo

Politics of Narrative, The: Why I Am a Poet. Lynn Emanuel. SUP

Polka. Diane Jarvenpa. MiVo

Polka Dots and Moonbeams. Johnny Burke. ReLy

Poll. Ed Roberson. EGAG

Poll Star. Felicia Lamport. NBLV

Pollen. Wyn Cooper. UrbNat

Polly Perkins. *Unknown.* OBCoV

Polly perks and Walter Gabriel, old Dan Archer late at plough. Friends Beyond. Stella Davis. RWPCtW

Polly Wolly Doodle. *Unknown.* TCAPo

Polly's Tree. Sylvia Plath. AmFaPo

Polonius. Miroslav Holub. WoPoe, *tr. by* Ian Milner

Polonius is still alive. To Be or Not To Be. Brian G. Gilmore. SpirFl

Polwart on the Green. Allan Ramsay. NPeEn; OxBEV

Polyaenus' daughter, Scyllis, came to the wide gates. Diotimus. HePo *Fr.* Epigrams.

Polychromatic beauty. Nectar of Ápan, The. Enrique Gonzáles Martínez. TCLAP, *tr. by* Elizabeth Gordon

Polydamas, your depth in augry. Homer. NOSC *Fr.* Iliad, The.

Polydeukes. Alcman. SaLy, *tr. by* Diane Rayor

Polyglot in Paradise, A [*or* On the Death of an Aged and Honoured Relative]. Isaac Watts. STuOW

Polyhedral kernels of wisdom. Mikhail Yeryomin. ItGoST, *tr. by* J. Kates

Polyhymnia. George Peele.
  (Farewell to Arms, A.) OBEV; OBWP; OxAEP-1
  (Farewell to the Court.) NoSic
  "His golden locks time hath to silver turned [*or* turn'd]." NIP-4; NoP-4; NoP-5; NPeEn; OxBEV; TFi

Polyolbion [*or* Poly-Oobion]. Michael Drayton.
  "By thine own named town made famous in thy fall." NOSC
  Coursing, the. DiBP
  "March strongly forth, my Muse, whilst yet the temperate air." NOSC
  Poly-Olbion Song 6.
    "What spirit can lift you up, to that immortall praise." PBRV

"Then Frome (a nobler flood) the Muses doth implore." NOSC
"Where she, of all the plains of Britain that doth bear." NOSC
"With solitude what sorts, that there's not wondrous rife?" NOSC

Polyphemus. Virgil. NoSic *Fr.* Aeneid [*or* Eneados *or* Aeneis], The.

Polyphemus, Galatea with apples pelts your flocks. Theocritus. HePo *Fr.* Idylls.

Polyphemus' Love Song. Luis de Góngora y Argote. SpanPo *Fr.* Fable of Polyphemus and Galatea.

Polystylistics. Nina Iskrenko. PFTM-2, *tr. by* John High

Polystylistics is when a knight from the Middle Ages. Polystylistics. Nina Iskrenko. PFTM-2, *tr. by* John High

Pomade. Aleksei Eliseievich Kruchyonykh.
  "3 poems." PFTM-1

Pomegranate. Jean Janzen. GeoHom

Pomegranate, The. Eavan Boland. CABP; NAMCP V.2; NoP-4; NoP-5

Pomegranate, calais lily, sprig of rosemary, meanwhile we do not, A. Portrait of Unknown. Rachel Zucker. IAoNAP

Pomegranates. Jane Hirshfield. AFaM

Pomelo, The. *Unknown.* WoPoe, *tr. by* Anne Birrell

Pomme arac. Derek Walcott. FaBoVe *Fr.* Sainte Lucie.

Pomme Rouge, La. Jean Follain. YaTCFP

Pomona. William Morris. NPeEn; OxBEV; WoPoe

Pompeii: Plaster Casts. Peter Scupham. HarvBoo

Pompeius, chief of all my friends, with whom. Horace. OBWP

Pompeius, shief of all my friends, with whom. Horace. WaAnP *Fr.* Odes.

Pomposo (insolent and loud). Charles Churchill. OBSV *Fr.* Ghost, The.

Pond. Martin Sorescu. BeAl, *tr. by* David Constantine and Ioana Russell-Gebbett

Pond, The. Louise Glück. ColAP; WaAnP

Pond, The. Mervyn Morris. PML

Pond and Peace. Geoffrey Nutter. IAoNAP

Pond in the Woods, A. Thomas Rain Crowe. AmZen

Pond was a deep pond once, The. Pond. Martin Sorescu. BeAl, *tr. by* David Constantine and Ioana Russell-Gebbett

Pond will deepen toward the center like a plate, A. Blue Willow. Jody Gladding. P180

Ponder, darling, these busted statues. E. E. Cummings. NIL-7; NIP-4

Ponder my words, if so that any be. Request to the Graces, An. Robert Herrick. NOSC

Ponds, in Love. C. D. Wright. GPPA

Pondy Woods. Robert Penn Warren. MoAmPo

Pone Venus esta tarde nuevamente. Lucero de la Tarde. Francisco Segovia. RMCMP

Ponies, Twynyrodyn. Meic Stephens. AngWePo

Ponme como un sello sobre tu corazón, como una marca sobre tu brazo. Tiempo de bailar los árboles. Pedro Pérez Conde. RMCMP

Ponnage Pool, The. Helen B. Cruickshank. NePenScot

Pont y Caniedydd. Alun Llywelyn-Williams. OBWVE, *tr. by* Joseph R. Clancy

Pontiac, The. Meditation in Loudoun County. Thomas Bolt. YaYoPo

Pontiac, dressed in his French officer's uniform. Starved Rock. James Ballowe. IllVoic

Pontius Pilate, remembered as a Roman. And Pilate Said. Joy Davidman. YaYoPo

Pontoon. Kit Robinson. FTOS

Pontoosuce. Herman Melville. APN-2; NCAP; TCAPo

Pontypool. Richard Hall. AngWePo

Pontypool! thou dirtiest of dirty places. Pontypool. Richard Hall. AngWePo

Pony boy though it's spring we're still apart. Thinking of My Little Boy. Tu Fu [*or* Du Fu]. ColAnChi; WoPoe, *tr. by* David Lattimore

Pony Express. Stephen Dobyns. SUP

Pony in Kukutis's Ear, A. Marcelijus Martinaitis. TWW, *tr. by* Laima Sruoginis

Pooh! Walter De la Mare. OBCoV

Pool. Pedro Serrano. RMCMP, *tr. by* Geoff Hargreaves

Pool, The. "H. D." APT-1; HarvBoo; NAMCP V.1

Pool is a Godless spout. James Haug. MoASP

Pool is Full of Autumn Sky, Rippled by Gentle Breezes, The. Ou-yang Hsiu. ErotSp, *tr. by* Jerome P. Seaton

Pool of lagoon moving. Leslie Scalapino. PfS *Fr.* Sight.

Pool of moonlight on my bed this late hour, A. Quiet Night Thoughts. Li Po. CrYelRi, *tr. by* Sam Hamill

Poor, The. X in My Name, The. Francisco X. Alarcón. CalPo

Poor, The. Letitia Elizabeth Landon. VWP

Poor, The. Jones Very. SacPr

Poor, The ("It's the anarchy of poverty.") William Carlos Williams. MoAmPo

Poor Adam and Eve were from Eden turned out. *Unknown.* Spl

Poor Angels. Edward Hirsch. PoA 2002

Poor beggars!—they'll never see 'ome! (LL)   Widow at Windsor, The. Rudyard Kipling.   NAEL-6v2; NAEL-7v2; NoAM

Poor Bess Turpin, I pytty thy case as farr as I can.   Isobel Beaumont and John Coleman.   EMWP

Poor box, A.   Issa.   EH, *tr. by* Robert K. Haas

Poor boy. Poor boy.   I'm Glad I'm Not Young Any More.   Alan Jay Lerner. ReLy

Poor Boy: Portrait of a Painting.   John Ash.   HarvBoo

Poor bugger drank all the time, The.   Legend.   Shin Kyŏngnim.   CAMKP, *tr. by* Kevin O'Rourke

Poor But Honest.   *Unknown.*   NBLV

Poor child of sorrow! who did'st boldly spring.   To a Rejected Sonnet. William Ewart Gladstone.   CenSon

Poor Christian Looks at the Ghetto, A.   Czeslaw Milosz.   HP; PoSu; VCWP *Fr.* Voices of Poor People.

Poor composer.   Marina Boroditskaya.   CRWP, *tr. by* Ruth Fainlight

Poor Crow!   Mary Mapes Dodge.   SWaP

Poor Cyrene was minding her own mountain.   Road Trip as Clues, A.   Tracy Philpot.   IAoNAP

Poor devil that I am, being so attacked.   Palladas.   OBVE, *tr. by* Tony Harrison

Poor Dog Tray.   Thomas Campbell.   DiBP

Poor dog, whom rival poets strive.   On Some Elegies on a Lap-Dog. *Unknown.*   DiBP

Poor dwelling near valley mouth.   Wang Wei.   NDACCP, *tr. by* Ezra Pound

Poor Erin's daughter cross'd the main.   Erin's Daughter.   Lydia Huntley Sigourney.   SWaP

Poor Ezekiel, what.   Ezekiel Saw de Wheel.   Honorée Fanonne Jeffers.   AnSo

Poor faithful Trouncer! thou canst lead no more.   Robert Bloomfield.   DiBP *Fr.* Farmer's Boy, The.

Poor fellow, what is it to you.   Verses.   Sir Charles Hanbury Williams. OBWVE

Poor, fond deluded heart! wilt thou again.   Mary Tighe.   CenSon

Poor Girl's Meditation, The.   *Unknown.*   OBMV, *tr. by* Padraic Colum

Poor Hal caught his death standing out a spout.   Fatal Love.   Matthew Prior. NBLV

Poor heart, unsatisfied!   Shadow and Sunrise.   Henrietta Cordelia Ray. CBWP-3

Poor hill farmer astray in the grass.   Lonely Farmer, The.   Ronald Stuart Thomas.   NoP-4

Poor Houses, The.   Ed Roberson.   GT

Poor, impious Soul! that fixes its high hopes.   Aspiration.   Adah Isaacs Menken.   CBWP-1; ViWPN

Poor in my youth, and in life's later scenes.   On Late-acquired Wealth *or* Riches.   *Unknown.*   OBVE, *tr. by* William Cowper

Poor Irus' faithful wolf-dog, here I lie.   Vincent Bourne.   DiBP,

Poor Julia's heart was in an awkward state.   Lord Byron.   NOBRP *Fr.* Don Juan.

Poor lad once and a lad so trim, A.   Jean Richepin's Song.   Herbert Trench. OBMV

Poor Linley! I shall miss thee sadly, now.   On the Death of William Linley, esq. William Lisle Bowles.   OxBSo

Poor little Ada Queetie has departed this life.   Nancy Luce.   VerBaPo *Fr.* Poor Little Hearts.

Poor little diary, with its simple thoughts.   Augusta Davies Webster.   NPeEn; ViWPN *Fr.* Castaway, A.

Poor little Foal of an oppressed Race!   Samuel Taylor Coleridge.   OxAEP-2 *Fr.* Effusions.

Poor Little Hearts.   Nancy Luce.
   "Poor little Ada Queetie has departed this life."   VerBaPo

Poor little, pretty, fluttering [*or* flutt'ring] thing.   Adriani Morientis ad Animam Suam.   Emperor Hadrian.   OBVE, *tr. by* Matthew Prior

Poor Little Rich Girl.   `Noël Coward.   ReLy

Poor man has misplaced the silk, The.   Stray Dogs, Foaming.   Thom Ward. AmPoNex

Poor man's clothes are ragged, quick to soil, A.   Lice, The.   Mei Yao Ch'en. CrYelRi, *tr. by* Sam Hamill

Poor man's clothes—ragged and easy to get dirty, A.   Shih-hou Pointed Out to Me That from Ancient Times There Had Never Been a Poem on the Subject of Lice.   Mei Yao Ch'en.   ColAnChi, *tr. by* Burton Watson

Poor man's heart through half the year, The. (LL)   Sir Walter Scott.   ChrPo; OBCP *Fr.* Marmion.

Poor Man's Life, The.   Claude Innocent.   OGAHCP, *tr. by* Boadiba and Jack Hirschman

Poor Man's Pig, The.   Edmund Charles Blunden.   MoBrPo

Poor man's sins are glaring, The.   Rich and Poor; or, Saint and Sinner. Thomas Love Peacock.   OBSV; OxBEV

Poor melancholy bird—that all night long.   To a Nightingale.   Charlotte Smith. CenSon; OxBSo; RWP

Poor Merry-Andrew, in the neuk.   Robert Burns.   OBCoV

Poor Merry-andrew, in the [*or* a] neuk.   Robert Burns.   OBCoV

Poor Mick was trotting on to the town.   River, The.   Charlotte Grace O'Brien. IrV

Poor moth, I can't help you.   I Can't Help You.   Ryszard Krynicki.   BLT

Poor mother, my martyr.   Mother.   Ussin Kerim.   PML, *tr. by* William Matthews

Poor Naomi.   *Unknown.*   APN-2

Poor Negro Sadi, The.   Charlotte Dacre.   RWP

Poor Nietzsche in Turin, eating sausage his mother.   Supple Wreath of Myrtle, A.   Robert Hass.   RoV

Poor North.   Mark Strand.   NAMCP V.2

Poor old bait got sick & died, The.   Jackson Mac Low.   APSN *Fr.* Presidents of the United States of America, The.

Poor Old Lady.   *Unknown.*   NOxBChV

Poor old lady, she swallowed a fly.   *Unknown.*   NOxBChV

Poor old man, The. (LL)   Note Left in Jimmy Leonard's Shack, A.   James Wright.   NoP-4; NoP-5; StAl

Poor old sister, you have cared for this man and you want to see him again. Tohono O'odham.   NAAPv.1 *Fr.* Songs for Treating Sickness, Sung durring the Four Parts of the Night.

Poor [*or* Poore] bird! I do not envy thee.   Robin, The.   George Daniel. NPeEn

Poor Paddy Maguire, a fourteen-hour day.   Patrick Kavanagh.   ModIr; NPeEn *Fr.* Great Hunger, The.

Poor Paddy Works on the Railway [*with music*].   *Unknown.*   GM

Poor people fish mostly with snare nets.   On a Painting of Fish Being Caught, A Song.   Li Tung-yang.   ColAnChi, *tr. by* John Timothy Wixted

Poor people who do not have the price of a fence ask son Jim to be a fence. Good Son Jim.   Russell Edson.   SUP

Poor Pierrot.   Otto Harbach.   ReLy

Poor Ploughman to a Gentleman for Whom He Had Taken a Little Pains, A. George Turberville.   NoSic

Poor Professor Higgins!   Rain in Spain, The.   Alan Jay Lerner.   ReLy

Poor quarter, A.   Issa.   ZenPo, *tr. by* Takashi Ikemoto and Lucien Stryk

Poor Relation, The.   Edwin Arlington Robinson.   APT-1

Poor Relation, The; or, Pious Hope Frustrated.   Martin Farquhar Tupper. STuOW

Poor restless Dove, I pity thee.   Captive Dove, The.   Anne Brontë.   VWP

Poor Rosy.   *Unknown.*   SSUS

Poor Rosy, poor gal; / Poor Rosy, poor gal.   Poor Rosy.   *Unknown.*   SSUS

Poor Ruth.   Liudmila Petrushevskaya.   CRWP, *tr. by* Daniel Weissbort

Poor savage, doubting that a river flows.   Watching the Dance.   James Merrill. NIL-7; NIP-4

Poor Singing Dame, The.   Mary Robinson.   NAEL-7v2

Poor song.   Tape, The.   Myra Cohn Livingston.   NTCP

Poor[e] soul[e], the centre [*or* center] of my sinful[l] earth.   William Shakespeare.   BrAP; HeIP-4; NAEL-6v1; NAEL-7v1; NoP-4; NoP-5; OBEV; OxAEP-1; SacPr; TFi; WaAnP *Fr.* Sonnets.

Poor thing. She never hurt a soul. What beasts they are. (LL)   Power.   Audre Lorde.   NoAM; WaAnP

Poor thing stands their vainly, The.   Birdsong 2.   *Unknown, fr.* Terezin Concentration Camp.   INSAB

Poor tired Tim! It's sad for him.   Tired Tim.   Walter De la Mare.   NTCP

"Poor wanderer," said the leaden sky.   Subalterns, The.   Thomas Hardy. MoBrPo; NoAM

Poor wayfaring man of grief, A.   Stranger and His Friend, The.   James F. Montgomery.   SacPr

Poor Wayfaring Stranger.   *Unknown.*   SacPr

Poor wearied pilgrim—in this toiling scene! (LL)   To the Moon.   Charlotte Smith.   CenSon; RWP

Poor Woman.   Hŏ Nansŏrhŏn.   CATKP, *tr. by* Peter H. Lee

Poor woman at a shuttle, tears on her cheeks, A.   Poor Woman, A.   Yu Mongin.   CATKP, *tr. by* Peter H. Lee

Poor Women in a City Church.   Seamus Heaney.   BrAP

Poor Yarrow.   Sir Walter Scott.   DiBP *Fr.* Marmion.

Poor Zelda.   Cindy Day Roberts.   LaCa

Poore desolate Gardin, smile no more on me.   To the Gardin att O: [Owthorpe] 7:th.   Lucy Hutchinson.   EMWP

Poor[e] eyes be[e] blind, the light behold no[e] more.   Mary Sidney Wroth, Countess of Montgomery.   NoP-5 *Fr.* Pamphilia to Amphilanthus.

Poore [*or* Povre] widwe [*or* wyde *or* widow] somde[e]l stape in age, A. Geoffrey Chaucer.   NAEL-6v1; NAEL-7v1 *Fr.* Canterbury Tales, The.

Poorly Matched.   Prageeta Sharma.   HeMarv

Poorly matched the world and she.   Poorly Matched.   Prageeta Sharma. HeMarv

Pop.   Vona Groarke.   NIrP

Popcorn-can cover.   Lorine Niedecker.   NAAPv.2; NAMCP V.1

Pope.   Manuel González Prada.   SpanPo, *tr. by* William M. Davis

Pope Alexander VI.   Geoffrey Lehmann.   NOBAu

Pope at 7:00 P.M., The. Eloise Klein Healy. SUP

Pope from penance purgatorial, The. George Buchanan. OBVE, *tr. by* James Vincent Cunningham

Pope of cosmology addresses a convention, The. Anthropic Principle, The. Harryette Mullen. AWPTFC

Pope, The. A. E. Housman. NPeEn; OBCoV

Pope's Carnations Knew Him. Thom Gunn. OBGa

Pope's Penis, The. Sharon Olds. CAP-8; NAMCP V.2; OxBoAm

Popeye in the 19th Century. Tom Ahern. OnScMo

Popeye writes only for the ledger. Popeye wasn't mad. Popeye in the 19th Century. Tom Ahern. OnScMo

Popeye's Last Words. Tom Ahern. OnScMo

Popish Plot, The. John Dryden. BrAP *Fr.* Absalom and Achitophel.

Poplar. Silver Poplar at Sunrise. Constance Egemo. PoCoUp

Poplar Field, The. William Cowper. BrAP; OxBEV

Poplar Leaf, The. George Seferis. PFTM-1

Poplars. Music. Eugenio de Andrade. VCWP, *tr. by* Alexis Levitin

Poplars are felled [*or* fell'd], farewell to the shade, The. Poplar Field, The. William Cowper. BrAP; OxBEV

Poplars are standing there still as death. Southern Mansion. Arna Bontemps. APT-2; GT

Poplars have grown their winter cotton, The. Boleros #36. Jay Wright. MoW

Poplars shaken in the cold wind. Cold Again, The. Paul De Roux. YaTCFP, *tr. by* Stephen Romer

Pop-out eyes belong to Baldwin, The. Of Miles Davis. William Ford. SeSe

Poppa Greer happened. Slim Lands a Job? Sterling Allen Brown. NAAPv.2

Poppies. Yolanda Bedregal. TANSG, *tr. by* Carolyne Wright

Poppies. Nesta Wyn Jones. BBMWP, *tr. by* Anthony Conran

Poppies in October. Sylvia Plath. NAMCP V.2; NoAM; OxBoAm; StAl

Poppies of This Year. Gennady Aygi. TCRusP, *tr. by* Peter France

Poppies on the Wheat. Helen Hunt Jackson. APN-2; ColAP

Poppies, that scattered o'er this arid plain. Thomas Doubleday. CenSon

Poppy, The. Sarah Hamilton. CenSon

Poppy, The. Francis Thompson. MoBrPo

Poppy Heads. Neil Curry. NLP

Poppy seeds from a North Bennington garden. Thermos, The. Arthur Sze. PoChi

Poppy thane. Pendle dust. Boldo sachet gaudles. Lesson from the Cockerel. Maggie O'Sullivan. Oth

Poppy there, companion to repose, The. Philip Freneau. NAAL-3 *Fr.* House of Night, The.

Poppy under a young. Necromance. Rae Armantrout. FTOS; PmAP

Popryshchin. Nikolai Alekseievich Zabolotsky. TCRusP, *tr. by* Daniel Weissbort

Popul Vuh, The. *Unknown. tr. by* Dennis Tedlock

"Truly now." WoPoe, *tr. by* Dennis Tedlock

"Wait!" WoPoe, *tr. by* Dennis Tedlock

Popular Heart is a Cannon first, The. Emily Dickinson. TCAPo

Popular Mechanics. Charles Simic. EmeKit

Popular Mythologies. Vernon Scannell. OBCoV

Populated by dolls and clowns. Waltz for Debby. Gene Lees. ReLy

Population. Mark Halliday. ItP

Population. George Oppen. PoA 2002

Por el sur y por el norte. Esta Es Mi Tierra. Edison Coleman. OWABP

Por entre manos húmedas que agitas blandamente. Pez. José Luis Hidalgo. RaW

Por levante, vientos blanquecinos sobre mis lindes distribuidos. Angélica Tornero. SPV

Por los campos luchados se extienden los heridos. Herido, El. Miguel Hernández. RaW

¿Por qué vacilamos ese día frente al bosque. Premonición. Francisco Segovia. RMCMP

Porcelain Bells. Medbh McGuckian.
    Speaking Into the Candles. ModIr

Porcelain Childhood. Katherine Sánchez. LiTh

Porcelain Couple, The. Donald Hall. BAP-97; CAP-8

"Porcelain is personal," he smiles. For His Ring and Watch on the Night Stand. Gladys Cardiff. HATNAP

Porcelain Pavilion, The. Nikolai Stepanovich Gumilyov. TCRusP, *tr. by* Mary Jane White

Porch in Snow. Joanna Klink. LegDan

Porch sitting hairbraiding. Initiation. Monifa Atungaye Love. ISC

Porchlight coming on again, The. 1926. Weldon Kees. OxBoAm

Porcupine, The. Galway Kinnell. NAAL-5

Poring on Caesar's death with earnest eye. Julius Caesar and the Honey-Bee. Charles Tennyson Turner. OxBSo

Porno-Bach. Shuntaro Tanikawa. PoetW, *tr. by* Harold Wright

Pornographer, The. Robert Hass. YaYoPo

Pornographic Poem. John Giorno. CAGL

Pornography. Angela Shaw. PuP-23

Pornography, Nebraska. Sandra McPherson. ReTh

Porobability and Birds. Russell Atkins. EGAG

Porphyria's Lover. Robert Browning. BrAP; NAEL-6v2; NAEL-7v2; NoP-5; OBEV

Porphyry of Elements, A. Garrett Kaoru Hongo. GeoHom *Fr.* Cruising 99.

Port of Call. Hwang Tonggyu. CAMKP, *tr. by* Kevin O'Rourke

Port of Holy Peter. John Masefield. OBMV

Port of Many Ships. John Masefield. OBMV

Port of Spain. Derek Walcott. NoAM

Port Phillip Night. Francis Webb. BMAP

Port Talbot. John Davies. AngWePo

Port, The. Bernadette Mayer. FTOS

Port Townsend Poems. Pinkie Gordon Lane. BtF

Port, walls. Djinns, The. Victor Hugo. SxFrPo, *tr. by* A. M. and E. H. Blackmore

Portait le ciel en tête. Terre, La. Amina Saïd. YaTCFP

Porte Dorée. Léopold Sédar Senghor. PoetW, *tr. by* Melvin Dixon

Portent, The. Herman Melville. APN-2; CBCWP; ColAP; InoFa; NAAL-3; NAAPv.1; NCAP; NoP-4; NoP-5; OBWP; OxBoAm; PCW; TCAPo; WaAnP

Porter. Marilyn Nelson Waniek. ESEAA

Porter and keepers, when they're civil. His Rule of Behaviour: If You Are Civil, I Am Sober. James Carkesse. NOSC

Porter on the Trail, A. Larry Rottman. ViWalt

Porter to th' infernal[l] gate is Sin, The. Phineas Fletcher. NOSC *Fr.* Locusts, or Appolyonists, The.

Porter's Love Song to a Chambermaid, A. Andy Razaf. ReLy

Porth Cwyfan. Roland Mathias. AngWePo; TCAWP

Portia. Kathleen Kirk. IaFF

Portinaio. Julie Agoos. YaYoPo

Portion of this yew. Transformations. Thomas Hardy. BrAP; TRP

Portishead Suite. Rick Barot. NeAmPo

Portly prince, and goodly to the sight, A. John Dryden. OBSV *Fr.* Hind and the Panther, The.

Portobello. M. Travis Lane. Coast

Portofino. Spencer Reece. LegDan

Portrait. Manuel Bandeira. TCLAP, *tr. by* Candace Slater

Portrait. Kenneth Fearing. APT-2; MoAmPo

Portrait. Mary Leader. NAPBL

Portrait. Antonio Machado Ruiz. SpanPo, *tr. by* Dorren Bell

Portrait. Antonio Machado Ruiz. STV, *tr. by* Robert Bly and John Frederick Nims

Portrait. Cecília Meireles. TCLAP, *tr. by* Luiz Fernández García

Portrait. Bernard Noël. YaTCFP

Portrait. Bernard Noël. YaTCFP, *tr. by* Michael Tweed

Portrait. Hyam Plutzik. TaR

Portrait. Miklós Radnóti. IQMS, *tr. by* Thomas Land

Portrait. Leopold Staff. PoSu, *tr. by* Adam Czerniawski

Portrait. Constance Urdang. OPRER

Portrait. Judith Wright. SoSe-8

Portrait, A. Walter De la Mare. NoAM

Portrait, A. Thomas Dekker *and others*. OxAEP-1

Portrait, A. Michael Field. VWP

Portrait, A. Eman Mersaal. AnVo, *tr. by* Mohamed Enani

Portrait, The. Stanley Kunitz. CAP-8; GoPo; InvLad; NAAPv.2; NAMCP V.1; PoCho; RaBo

Portrait by a Neighbor. Edna St. Vincent Millay. BLPJKO; ItWoWo

Portrait du Père, Le. Abdellatif Laâbî. YaTCFP

Portrait d'une Femme. Ezra Pound. APT-1; BrAP; MoAmPo; NAAL-5; NAMCP V.1; NoAM; NoP-4; NoP-5; OxBoAm; TCAPo *Fr.* Ripostes of Ezra Pound.

Portrait from the Infantry. Alan Dugan. AF; AmWaPo; PWW2

Portrait in a Brass Gong. Mick North. NLP

Portrait in Black Paint, with a Very Sparing Use of Whitewash. Elinor Wylie. NALW

Portrait in Georgia. Jean Toomer. APT-2; InGu; NAAPv.2; NAMCP V.1; NoP-4; NoP-5

Portrait in Rhythm and Blues. Dick Lourie. PrTe

Portrait ("My childhood is memories of a patio in Seville.") Antonio Machado Ruiz. ItP; RaBo; WED; WoPoe, *tr. by* Robert Bly

Portrait of a Bishop. Evan Lloyd. AngWePo

Portrait of a Child. Corey Marks. LegDan

Portrait of a Family. Carlos Drummond de Andrade. TCLAP, *tr. by* Virginia de Araújo

Portrait of a Girl.   Conrad Potter Aiken.   MoAmPo

Portrait of a Girl with Comic Book.   Phyllis McGinley.   APT-2

Portrait of a House Detective.   Hans Magnus Enzensberger.   HP; PoSu, *tr. by* Michael Hamburger

Portrait of a Lady.   T. S. Eliot.   APT-1; OxBoAm

Portrait of a Lady.   Alan Jenkins.   NeBrP

Portrait of a Lady.   William Carlos Williams.   HarvBoo; NAAL-5; NAAPv.2; NAMCP V.1; NoAM; NoP-5; OxBoAm; WaAnP

Portrait of a Lady Walking.   Djuna Barnes.   APT-1

Portrait of a Machine.   Louis Untermeyer.   MoAmPo

Portrait of a Married Couple.   Margaret Scott.   NOBAu

Portrait of a Motorcar.   Carl Sandburg.   APT-1

Portrait of a Nun.   Bobi Jones.   OBWVE, *tr. by* Joseph P. Clancy

Portrait of a Pirate.   Stanley E. Babb.   TiP2

Portrait of a Pregnant Woman.   Bobi Jones.   OBWVE, *tr. by* Joseph P. Clancy

Portrait of a Victorian Author.   Martin Farquhar Tupper.   STuOW

Portrait of an Engine Driver.   Bobi Jones.   OBWVE, *tr. by* Joseph P. Clancy

Portrait of an Overpopulated Woman.   Bobi Jones.   BBMWP, *tr. by* Joseph P. Clancy

Portrait of Assimilation.   Chrystos.   UnSA

Portrait of Auntie Blodwen.   Elwyn Davies.   AngWePo

Portrait of Jonah with woman.   Marie-Claire Bancquart.   MFP, *tr. by* Martin Sorrell

Portrait of José Cemí.   José Lezama Lima.   TCLAP, *tr. by* Gregory Rabassa

Portrait of Mary Stuart, Holyrood.   Lewis Spence.   EdScPo

Portrait of My Father and His Grandson.   Richard Jones.   IllVoic

Portrait of My Father as the Boy of Winander.   Jenny Mueller.   IAoNAP

Portrait of My Father, Militant Communist.   Jorge Teillier.   TCLAP, *tr. by* Carolyne Wright

Portrait of Myself with Arshile Gorky and Gertrude Stein.   Jerome Rothenberg.   FTOS

Portrait of Plisetskaya.   Andrey Andreievich Voznesensky.   RusPo, *tr. by* Robert Arthur Douglas Ford

Portrait of Silverio Franconetti.   Federico García Lorca.   SpanPo, *tr. by* Rachel Benson and Robert O'Brien

Portrait of the Artist.   Wopko Jensma.   TSAP

Portrait of the Artist.   Dorothy Parker.   AmWit

Portrait of the Artist, A.   Thomas Kinsella.   HarvBoo

Portrait of the Artist as a Prematurely Old Man.   Ogden Nash.   APT-2

Portrait of the Artist as an Old Man.   Michael Dransfield.   BMAP

Portrait of the Beautiful Unknown Woman.   Juan Sánchez Peláez.   BLPSL, *tr. by* Rene de Costa, Rigas Kappatos and Eleni Paidoussi

Portrait of the Blockade through Genre Painting, Still Life, and Landscape, A.   Yelena Shwarts.   CRWP, *tr. by* James McGavran

Portrait of the Boy as Artist.   Barbara Howes.   MoAmPo

Portrait of the Father, The.   Abdellatif Laâbi.   YaTCFP, *tr. by* Pierre Joris

Portrait of the Marginalized.   Ch'oe Sûngja.   EcSo, *tr. by* Mickey Hong

Portrait of the Painter Hans Theo Richter and His Wife Gisela in Dresden, 1933.   Tony Curtis.   TCAWP

Portrait of the Poet as Landscape.   Abraham Moses Klein.   NoAM

Portrait of the Town Leonard.   Louise Erdrich.   UpMys

Portrait of Unknown.   Rachel Zucker.   IAoNAP

Portrait of Woman in Long Black Dress / Aurelia.   Juan Felipe Herrera.   TouFir

Portrait Piece.   Mieko Shiomi.   WhBo

Portrait: "There is in his daughter's gaze."   David St. John.   PoDa

Portrait with Background.   Oliver St. John Gogarty.   OBMV

Portraits at the Epicenter.   Pimone Triplett.   LegDan

Portraits of a Moment.   Keith Gilyard.   SpirFl

Portraits of the Ladies.   Elizabeth Crowell.   PfS

Portraits of Tudor Statesmen.   U. A. Fanthorpe.   EmeKit; OxBEV

Portraiture.   Anita Scott Coleman.   OxAAAP

Portrush. Walking dead streets in the dark.   Archæologist, The.   James Simmons.   PBCIP

Ports of death are sins; of life, good deeds, The.   Of Life and Death.   Ben Jonson.   TreFP

Portugal Laurel, The.   John Wright.   BloBone

Portuguese in Mergui, The.   George Green.   P180

Portuguese Mistake.   Oswald de Andrade.   TCLAP, *tr. by* Flavia Vidal

Pose in the murderer's shadow. (LL)   King Kong Meets Wallace Stevens.   Michael Ondaatje.   BrAP; NIL-7

Posies.   Agnes Mary Frances Robinson.   VWP

Posited.   James McMichael.   GeoHom

Position is so well-known, the.   Inside Diameter.   Clarence Major.   PmAP

Position is where you.   Window, The.   Robert Creeley.   FTOS; NoAM; PmAP

Position of the Sparrow, The.   Takahashi Shinkichi.   ZenPo, *tr. by* Takashi Ikemoto and Lucien Stryk

Positions of the Body, 8.   Carol Snow.   ASA

Positions remain the same, their, The.   What It Means to be Avant-Garde.   Lee Bartlett.   ICANM

Positively on my own again, heart broken so long ago I hardly notice.   Where the Weather Suits My Clothes.   John Godfrey.   PmAP

Possessed.   Charles Baudelaire.   ErotSp, *tr. by* Richard Howard

Possessed, The.   Mahmoud al-Braikan.   IrPoTo, *tr. by* Ralph Saverese and Saadi A. Simawe

Possessing what the owners can but own. (LL)   Summer Morning, A.   Richard Wilbur.   NBLV; StAl

Possession.   Richard Aldington.   MoBrPo

Possession.   Caitríona O'Reilly.   StAl

Possession of Yesterday.   Jorge Luis Borges.   WoPoe, *tr. by* Nicomedes Suarez Arauz

Possessions.   Ivor Gurney.   NPeEn

Possessive Case, The.   Lisel Mueller.   GoPo

Posset for Nature's Breakfast, A.   Margaret Lucas Cavendish, Duchess of Newcastle.   STuOW

Possibiliites: Remembering Malcolm X.   Haki R. Madhubuti.   SpirFl

Possibilities ("If casual concourse did the world compose.")   Sir Richard Blackmore.   STuOW *Fr.* Creation.

Possibilities ("In the wide womb of possibility.")   Sir Richard Blackmore.   STuOW *Fr.* Creation.

Possibility.   Charles Coe.   UrbNat

Possibility.   Tiziano Rossi.   ItPo, *tr. by* Gayle Ridinger

Possibility, The.   James Fenton.   HarvBoo

Possible.   Ruth L. Schwartz.   WiU

Possible Man, The.   A. V. Christie.   NAPBL

Possibly a child is not damaged immediately.   Lackawanna.   Galway Kinnell.   GM

Possum lay on the tracks fully dead, The.   Lull, The.   Molly Peacock.   OxBoAm

'Possum under the owl's claw, The.   As a Child, Sleepless.   W. D. Snodgrass.   PoA 2002

Possum with four crazed paws, The.   Nest for Everyone, A.   Roberta Spear.   GeoHom

Post.   Pierre Reverdy.   CuPo

Post Card.   Guillaume Apollinaire.   AF; FaBoWar, *tr. by* Oliver Bernard

Post Card (Central Park).   Rachel Zucker.   IAoNAP

Post Early for Space.   Peter J. Henniker-Heaton.   HHAm

Post Heads.   Johanna Kruit.   TuT, *tr. by* Eamon Grennan

Post Mortem.   Robinson Jeffers.   MoAmPo

Post Mortem.   Sinéad Morrissey.   NIrP

Post Mortem.   Wole Soyinka.   PoetW

Post Operative.   Thomas William Shapcott.   BMAP

Post Script.   Bret Lott.   MAAN

Post Scriptum.   Mark Todd.   GeoH

Post Ulixem Scriptum.   James Joyce.   OBCoV

Post-boy drove with fierce career, The.   Alice Fell; or, Poverty.   William Wordsworth.   OBNV

Postcard.   Margaret Atwood.   NoAM

Postcard Element in Winter, The.   Charles North.   NYP2

Postcard (Found on His body after He Was Killed by the Nazis).   Miklós Radnóti.   RaBo, *tr. by* Stephen Berg, S. J. Marks and Steven Polgar   (Postcards.)   HP

Postcard from a Travel Snob.   Sophie Hannah.   MFPA

Postcard from Cuernavaca.   Michael Hofmann.   HarvBoo

Postcard from Greece, A.   A. E. Stallings.   PoA 2002

Postcard from Kashmir.   Agha Shahid Ali.   NAMCP V.2; NIL-7

Postcard from London, A.   Cathal McCabe.   NIrP

Postcard from North Antrim, A.   Seamus Heaney.   PBCIP; PNI

Postcard from Okemah, A.   Terrance Hayes.   LegDan

Postcard from Robert Frost's Grave.   Wyn Cooper.   VisFro

Postcard from the Coast.   Katrina Roberts.   NAPBL

Postcard from the Garden.   Marge Piercy.   NoAM

Postcard from the Volcano, A.   Wallace Stevens.   APT-1; GPTC; NAMCP V.1; NoAM; PoCho; SAmP; WeW-3

Postcard from Trakl.   John Yau.   OpBo

Postcard to Walt Whitman from Siena.   Stanley Moss.   ViWalt

Postcards.   Miklós Radnóti.   *See* Postcard (Found on His body after He Was Killed by the Nazis).

Postcards from God (1).   Imtiaz Dharker.   NeBl

Postcards from the Maginot Line.   W. S. Merwin.   MotU

Post-colonial Tale, A.   Joy Harjo.   BodElec; PrTe

Post-Communion Striptease.   Jill Alexander Essbaum.   NAPBL

Poster.   Ferreira Gullar.   TCLAP, *tr. by* Renato Rezende

Poster Girl's Defence, The.   Carolyn Wells.   SWaP

Poster of Our Dazzling Victory at Saarbrucken, A. Arthur Rimbaud. OBWP *Fr.* Eighteen-Seventy.

Posterity. Dennis Joseph Enright. OBCoV

Posterity hath many fates bemoaned. On Sir Robert Cotton the Antiquary. Thomas Randolph. NOSC

Posterity was always a great reader. Posterity. Dennis Joseph Enright. OBCoV

Poster's stone hand grips, The. Fist, The. Tatamkulu Afrika. TSAP

Postfeminism. Brenda Shaughnessy. AmPoNex; LegDan

Post-historic herbivore, A. On the Inclusion of Miniature Dinosaurs in Breakfast Cereal Boxes. John Updike. OBCoV

Posthuman. Maura Stanton. BodElec

Posthumous. Michael O'Loughlin. PBCIP

Posthumous Rehabilitation. Tadeusz Rózewicz. HP, *tr. by* Adam Czerniawski

Posthumous Revenge. Francis Saltus Saltus. VerBaPo

Postman comes when I am still in bed, The. Sick Child, A. Randall Jarrell. NoP-4; OxBoAm

Postman's Bell Is Answered Everywhere, The. Horace Gregory. MoAmPo

Postman's Knock. Dorothy Molloy. NIrP

Postmaster's Children, The. Betsy Sholl. PfS

Postmen like doctors go from house to house. (LL) Aubade: "I work all day, and get half-drunk at night." Philip Larkin. AWTN; BodElec; BrAP; CABP; EMP; NAEL-6v2; NAEL-7v2; NAMCP V.2; NoP-4; NoP-5; PoetW; SoSe-8; StAl; TRP; WaAnP

Postmodern: A Definition. Joseph Like. ReTh

Postmodern Maturity. Tony Towle. KGB

Post-Modernism. James Galvin. GifTon

Postmortem. Maurice Kilwein Guevara. AmPoNex

Post-Obits and the Poets. Martial. OBVE; RompPo, *tr. by* Lord Byron

Post-obits rarely reach a poet. (LL) Post-Obits and the Poets. Martial. OBVE; RompPo, *tr. by* Lord Byron

Post-operative. Helen Kitson. PoCu

Postponed Nightmare. Sandor Csoori. VCWP, *tr. by* Len Roberts and László Vértes

Postponement of Self. Laura Riding Jackson. OxBoAm

Post-Recessional. G. K. Chesterton. UV

Post-Revolutionary Letter. Carolyne Wright. RoV

Postscript. Seamus Heaney. ASA; GoPo; StAl

Post-Script: for Gweno. Alun Lewis. AngWePo

Postscript: "There are some questions one should know by heart." Henri Coulette. CalPo

Postscript to an Elegy. Gibbons Ruark. PoA 2002

Postscripts 2. Dennis Brutus. HBAPE

Postscriptum. Mario Luzi. ItPo *Fr.* Pieces from a Mortal Duet.

Postwar. Bei Dao. WoBe, *tr. by* Iona Man-Cheong and Eliot Weinberger

Post-War Procession. Anita Lahey. IFF

Posy, A: "Dear love, I am resolved with thee to live." Sir Robert Aytoun. NOSC

Posy [*or* Posie], The. George Herbert. ChIV-1; NOSC

Pot. Tiziano Rossi. ItPo, *tr. by* Gayle Ridinger

Pot Burial. Tom Paulin. ModIr

Pot of Flowers, The. William Carlos Williams. APT-1

Pot of Red Lentils, A. Peter Pereira. IPoFL

Pot of Tea, A. Robert W. Service. PoWW

Pot Roast. Mark Strand. AmFaPo

Potato, A. Robert Bly. MotU

Potato, The. Lillian E. Curtis. VerBaPo

Potato Blight. David Lindley. NLP

Potato Bug. Charles Webb. UrbNat

Potato Bug Exterminators. James McIntyre. "When we do trace out nature's laws." VerBaPo

Potato crops are flowering. Summer of Lost Rachel, The. Seamus Heaney. NIL-7

Potato Harvest, The. Sir Charles G. D. Roberts. BrAP; NIL-7

Potato Manifesto, The. Cynthia Hwang. FTtHH

Potato Pie. Abba Kovner. AF

Potato reminds one of an alert desert stone, The. Potato, A. Robert Bly. MotU

Potato Thief. Pentti Saarikoski. VCWP, *tr. by* Herbert Lomas

Potato-Digger's Song, The. Thomas Caulfield Irwin. IrV

Potatoes. David Donnell. NIP-4

Potatoes. Linda Hogan. AFaM; IPoFL

Potatoes in flower. Zinaida Bykova. CRWP, *tr. by* Robert Reid

Potatoes of the corner store sing, The. At Kino Viejo, Mexico. Alberto A. Ríos. NoAM

Potent dreamings of whose scent are wizard-locked beneath its glows, The. (LL) Mirror, The. Isaac Rosenberg. NAMCP V.1; NoAM

Potentiality collapses into fact, the wave. Unicorn, The. John Smith. Coast

Potflower on the windowsill says to me, The. Power of Suicide, The. Muriel Rukeyser. NALW

Potholes. Linda Hogan. UrbNat

Potlicker Blues. Calvin Forbes. GT

Potpourri from a Surrey Garden. Sir John Betjeman. NPeEn

Potted Swan. Paul Dehn. "Devil damn thee black, thou cream-faced loon—, The." OBCoV

Potted tulips. Sacco and Vanzetti. Ber Grin. Prolet, *tr. by* Amelia Glaser

Potter. Michael O'Reilly. BloBone

Potter's Field. Prageeta Sharma. HeMarv

Potter's House, The. Katie Donovan. NIrP

Potters I rose up with in a hurry. Contemporary. Alejandrino Hufana. ReBoTo

Potters move like shy dancers, The. Potter's House, The. Katie Donovan. NIrP

Potter's Wheel, The [*for Jane*]. Calvin Forbes. GT

Pottery cup, broken handle. Life, Having Become Still. Brenda Brooks. IFF

Poughkeepsie. Emyr Humphreys. BBMWP, *tr. by* Elin ap Hywel

Pound bran all you please. Burmese Figures. *Unknown.* EaWin, *tr. by* W. S. Merwin

Pound stood at center stage of Caio Melisso. Two Worlds. Julia Older. TWW

Pounding and Gism. Antonin Artaud. ConPit, *tr. by* Albert James Arnold and Clayton Eshleman

Pounding Rain. Jackie Kay. MFPA; PoBW

Pound-note was the best kind of passport, A. Emigration Trains, The. Thomas McCarthy. PBCIP

Pounds and Ounces. Michael Brownstein. AHA

Pour and say again and again and yet again. Meleager. HePo, *tr. by* Barbara Hughes Fowler

Pour Commencer. Jon Stallworthy. NoAM

Pour for Heliodora Persuasion and pour for Cypris. Meleager. HePo

Pour for Heliodora Persuasion and pour for Cypris. Meleager. HePo, *tr. by* Barbara Hughes Fowler

Pour Mycéa. Édouard Glissant. YaTCFP

Pour nourrir les petits oiseaux. Raymond Queneau. YaTCFP

Pour O pour that parting soul in song. Song of the Son. Jean Toomer. InGu; ISC; MakPoe; NAAPv.2; NAMCP V.1; NIL-7; NIP-4; OxAAAP

Pour out the dark wine, Miriamne. Romancero. Lex Banning. NOBAu

Pour Prendre Congé. Dorothy Parker. AmWit

Pour secrecy upon the dying page. (LL) I Held a Shelley Manuscript. Gregory Corso. BB; PmAP

Pour the unhappiness out. Another Weeping Woman. Wallace Stevens. PoA 2002

Pouring orange into GRAPE and grape into ORANGE forever. (LL) Ballad of Orange and Grape. Muriel Rukeyser. ChAP; NoAM; NoP-4; NoP-5; WaAnP

Pouring the hot day. Basho. EMJL, *tr. by* Haruo Shirane

Pourquoi je deviens un saint. Oliver Cadiot. YaTCFP

Pourquoi que je vis. Boris Vian. YaTCFP

Pousse y gâte, pousse y gâte. Luis d'Antin Van Rooten. OBCoV *Fr.* Mots d'Heures: Gousses, Rames.

Poverty. Julia Darling. RSaN

Poverty in London. Samuel Johnson. NPeEn; OBSV; OxAEP-1 *Fr.* London: A Poem in Imitation of the Third Satire of Juvenal.

Poverty Knock. *Unknown.* FaBoVe

Poverty makes all things faded. Zilch Movement. Georges Castera. OGAHCP, *tr. by* Boadiba and Jack Hirschman

Poverty moved into my homestead. Abuse Poems: For Kodzo and Others. Komi Ekpe. PFTM-2, *tr. by* Kofi Awoonor

Poverty much maligned but beautiful. Mysteries of Small Houses. Alice Notley. ExTi

Poverty, remorseless spectre. Christmas Eve, South, 1865. Mary E. Tucker. CBWP-1

Powder!, The. Zaps of Zombifying Powder. Denizé Lauture. OGAHCP, *tr. by* Boadiba and Jack Hirschman

Powdered milk, chocolate bars, canned fruit, tea. Food Packages: 1947. Adrienne Rich. TaR

Powell march 1991. Lucille Clifton. *See* Powell (officer charged with the beating of rodney king).

Powell (officer charged with the beating of rodney king). Lucille Clifton. RACG

(Powell march 1991.) ESEAA

Power. Hart Crane. MoAmPo *Fr.* Bridge, The.

Power. Audre Lorde. NoAM; WaAnP

Power. Adrienne Rich. CAP-8; ColAP; NALW; NAMCP V.2; NIL-7

Power. Alma Villanueva. ItWoWo

Power above powers, O heavenly Eloquence. Samuel Daniel. NoSic *Fr.* Musophilus; or, Defence of All Learning.

Power and the Glory, The. Siegfried Sassoon. OBMV

Power Cut. Seamus Deane. PBCIP

Power Equality. Party for your Right to Fight. Public Enemy. ISC

Power failure. Waking, you try the switches. Dream Prison. Barbara Myers. IFF

Power from God claimed [*or* claim'd *or* claym'd], than God himself[e] to trust. (LL) John Donne. BASC; FSCP; NAEL-6v1; NAEL-7v1; NoP-4; NoP-5; OxAEP-1; SacPr *Fr.* Satires.

Power in the People, The. Robert Herrick. BASC

Power is on the earth and in the air, A. Midsummer. William Cullen Bryant. GSo

Power of Love, The. Charlotte Dacre. NOBRP

Power of Music, The. William Wordsworth. Oxford Street? STuOW

Power of One. Walta Borawski. CAGL

Power of Prayer, The. Rita Ann Higgins. MoWP

Power of Song, The. Euros Bowen. BBMWP, *tr.* by the author

Power of Spleen, The. Anne Finch, Countess of Winchilsea. NPeEn *Fr.* Spleen, The: A Pindaric Poem.

Power of Suicide, The. Muriel Rukeyser. NALW

Power of Taste, The. Zbigniew Herbert. PoetW; PoSu, *tr.* by Bogdana Carpenter and John Carpenter *and* Bogdana Carpenter

Power of the awful wind, whose hollow blast. To Winter. Amelia Alderson Opie. CenSon

Power of the Soul. Sheilah Glover. HW

Power of Words, The. Letitia Elizabeth Landon. VWP

Power [*or* pow'r] must it maintain, A. (LL) Horatian Ode upon Cromwell's Return from Ireland, An. Andrew Marvell. BASC; CABP; FSCP; NAEL-7v1; NoP-4; NoP-5; NOSC; NPeEn; OBEV; OBWP; OxAEP-1; OxBEV; PBRV; PoPoPo; TFi; WaAnP

Power Plant, The. Julianne Buchsbaum. LegDan

Power Quest, Sooke Park. Jarold Ramsey. PoCoUp

Power speaks only out of sleep and blackness, The. Below Loughrigg. Fleur Adcock. BrAP

Power that dwelleth in sweet sounds to waken, The. Spirit's Mysteries, The. Felicia Dorothea Hemans. RWP

Power, that gives with liberal hand, The. On the Religion of Nature. Philip Freneau. NAAL-3; NAAL-5

Power, the Enchanted World. George Oppen. FTOS

Powerful sea of lemons, A. Odyssey. Bernard Bador. ConPit, *tr.* by Clayton Eshleman

Powerful Servants [*epigram*]. Friedrich von Logau. GePo, *tr.* by George C. Schoolfield

Powerhouse, The. Keith Wilson. ICANM

Powerless. Rawia Morra. PoArWo *Fr.* Ghurba.

Powerline Incarnation, The. Les A. Murray. NAMCP V.2

Powers of Darkness. Abraham Cowley. NOSC

Powers of the Pen, The. Evan Lloyd. Helen like the Rose. AngWePo; OBWVE

Powers of the Sonnet. Ebenezer Elliott. CenSon

Powers of Thirteen. John Hollander.
"After the midwinter marriages—the bride of snow." VCAP
"At thirteen already single-minded Abraham." OxBoAm
"Is it the plenitude of seasons, then, the number." OxBoAm
"Just the right number of letters—half the alphabet." OxBoAm
"Like some ill-fated butterfly, the literalists." VCAP
"So we came at last to meet, after the lights were out." VCAP
"These two tales I tell of myself and the life I led." VCAP
"What she and I had between us once, America." VCAP
""Yes, go on! This is plain talk of plainer feelings now,."" VCAP

Powers that be in solemn conclave sat, The. A Bas la Gloire! Edward Wyndham Tennant. FaBoWar

Powwow. Carroll Arnett. LTA

Powwow. W. D. Snodgrass. SoSe-8

Powwow at the End of the World, The. Sherman Alexie. WaAnP

Powwow Polaroid. Sherman Alexie. UnSA

Pox fa that pultron Povertie. Francis Sempill. NePenScot *Fr.* Banishment of Poverty by His Royal Highness James Duke of Albany, The.

Pox of the statesman that's witty, A. Cabal at Nickey Nackeys, The. Aphra Behn. NOSC

Poza. Pedro Serrano. RMCMP

Pozo Basket. Glenna Luschei. GeoHom

Practical Concerns. William J. Harris. EGAG

Practice. Peter Bailey. WhBo

Practice. Thomas Sayers Ellis. NeAmPo

Practice. Meg Schoerke. PoDa

Practice: For Derek Walcott. Thomas Sayers Ellis. NAPBL

Practice of Magical Evocation, The. Diane Di Prima. PmAP

Practice resurrection. (LL) Manifesto: The Mad Farmer Liberation Front. Wendell Berry. GoPo; IPoFL

"Practice your scream" I said. Jerome Rothenberg. FTOS; PFTM-2 *Fr.* Khurbn.

Practicing. Marie Howe. FaoP

Practicing Eternity. Susan Elbe. FiBr

Practicing Eulogies. Gary Soto. NAMCP V.2

Practicing Their Diffidence, the Vandals. Alan Michael Parker. LegDan

Pragmatist. Ken Babstock. OpeFie

Prague in the Midday Sun. Vítězslav Nezval. AF, *tr.* by Ewald Osers

Prague: Old Woman in the Street. Daniel Berrigan. UpMys

Prague Spring 6. Ko Chŏnghûi. EcSo, *tr.* by Catherine J. Kim

Prague Spring 8. Ko Chŏnghûi. EcSo, *tr.* by Catherine J. Kim

Prairie. Daphne Marlatt. NLPA *Fr.* Touch to My Tongue.

Prairie, The. Francis Ponge. AF, *tr.* by Beth Archer

Prairie Friend. Maude E. Cole. TiP2

Prairie Houses. Barbara Guest. PmAP

Prairie Long Poem. Jon Paul Fiorentino. PoPra

Prairie Spring. Willa Sibert Cather. NAAPv.2

Prairie Spring. Loren C. Eiseley. PoCho

Prairie Sunset, A. Walt Whitman. TCAPo

Prairie-grass dividing, its special odor breathing, The. Prairie-Grass Dividing, The. Walt Whitman. APN-1

Prairies, The. William Cullen Bryant. APN-1; ColAP; NAAL-3; NAAL-5; NCAP; TCAPo
"These are the gardens of the Desert, these." ITBLP

Prairies are broad, and the woodlands are wide, The. Stolen White Girl, The. John Rollin Ridge. APN-2; NAAPv.1

Praise. Anne K. Smith. PasH

Praise and Prayer. Sir William Davenant. OBEV *Fr.* Gondibert.

Praise be for my children. Trumpet Voluntary in Praise of My Four Children. Alvaro Cardona-Hine. ICANM

Praise be to Him who is not contained in any region nor reached by any vision. Ahmad ibn Muhammad 'Abd Rabbihi. HiArP, *tr.* by James T. Monroe

Praise Father, Son, and Holy Ghost. (LL) Morning Hymn. Thomas Ken. NOSC; SacPr

Praise for an Urn. Hart Crane. MoAmPo; NAAPv.2; NoAM; WeW-3

Praise him. (LL) Pied Beauty. Gerard Manley Hopkins. AmFaPo; BrAP; CABP; ChAP; ClHu; CtM; HeIP-4; InvLi; ITBLP; MoBrPo; NAEL-6v2; NAEL-7v2; NAMCP V.1; NIL-7; NoAM; NoP-4; NoP-5; NPeEn; OBEV; OBMV; OxAEP-2; OxBEV; PoCho; PoPoPo; RaBo; SacPr; SoSe-8; TFi; UV; WaAnP; WeW-3

Praise him for the place he picked. Death in the Aquarium. Richard Hugo. CAP-8

Praise him that ay[e]. Bible, *O.T.* ChIV-1; OxBEV *Fr.* Psalms.

Praise in Summer. Richard Wilbur. NoP-4; UpMys

Praise is devotion fit for mighty minds. Sir William Davenant. OBEV *Fr.* Gondibert.

Praise, member, praise God, I praise my Lord until I die. Praise, Member. *Unknown.* SSUS

Praise monsters if you mean to rise. Doxology. Jim Powell. CalPo

Praise, my soul, the King of heaven. Bible, *O.T.* SacPr

Praise of a Collie. Norman Alexander MacCaig. EdScPo; NePenScot; PoCho

Praise of a Yellow Skin, The, or An Elizabeth in Gold. John Collop. NOSC

Praise of Diseases. Jacopone da Todi. WoPoe, *tr.* by L. R. Lind

Praise of Duke Wu of Wei. *Unknown.* CCL1 *Fr.* Qi-yu [Translations].

Praise of Dust, The. G. K. Chesterton. MoBrPo

Praise of Faith, The. John Hall. ChIV-2

Praise of Godly Love Out of 1 John. 4, The. John Hall. ChIV-2

Praise of His Lady, A. John Heywood. OBEV

Praise of Italian Chip-Shops. W. N. Herbert. NeBl

Praise of Spenser. William Browne. OxAEP-1

Praise of Women. Robert Mannyng. OBEV

Praise Poem to Christ, A. Catrin Ferch Gruffydd ab Ieuan ap Llywelyn Fychan. EMWP

Praise Psalm of the City-Dweller. April Bernard. NIL-7

Praise song. Lucille Clifton. P180

Praise Song for My Mother. Grace Nichols. Prnts

Praise Song for the Oba of Benin. *Unknown.* WoPoe, *tr.* by John Bradbury

Praise the Daughter. Melanie Hope. BtF

Praise the Lord. Hyperbole. David Craig. UpMys

Praise the Tortilla, Praise the Menudo, Praise the Chorizo. Ray Gonzales. UnSA

Praise to boredom: to the summer solstice. Psalm for an Anniversary. Grace Schulman. PoA 2002

Praise to God, immortal praise. Hymn 2. Anna Laetitia Barbauld. SacPr

Praise to my older brother, the seventeen-year-old boy. Attic, The. Marie Howe. ExTi

Praise to the empty schoolroom, when the folders. Pause, Pause. Kevin Prufer. PoDa

Praise to the End! Theodore Roethke.
   "Mips and ma the mooly moo." NBLV

Praise to the Holy Creator, who has placed his throne upon. Invocation to the Conference of the Birds. Farid-uddin Attar. BBASP, tr. by C.S. Nott

Praise to the Lord, the Almighty, the King of creation. Praise to the Lord the Almighty. Joachim Neander. SacPr, tr. by Catherine Winkworth

Praise to the Tattoo Mistress. Mririda n'Ait Attik. WoPoe, tr. by Daniel Halpern and Paula Paley

Praise (2). George Herbert. ChIV-1

Praise Ye the Lord, O Celebrate His Fame [with music]. Peleg Folger. ChIV-1

Praise youth's hot blood if you will, I think that happiness. Age in Prospect. Robinson Jeffers. MoAmPo

Prais[e]d be Diana[']s fair[e] and harmles[s] light. Homage to Diana. Sir Walter Ralegh. NoSic; NPeEn

Praised be God, and Lord Jesus, Lord Jesus. Three Kings of Bethlehem, The. Attila József. IQMS, tr. by Istvan Fekete

Praised be man, he is existing in milk. Jack Kerouac. PmAP Fr. Mexico City Blues.

Praised be the moon of books! that doth above. In the Reading-Room of the Brtish Museum. Louise Imogen Guiney. APN-2

Praised be the poet, who the sonnet's claim. To Mr. Henry Cary, On the Publication of his Sonnets. Anna Seward. CenSon

Praised be the wooden table. Odysseus Elytis. VCWP

Praised beyond all Enids be. In Morfudd's Arms. Dafydd ap Gwilym. OBWVE, tr. by Rolfe Humphries

Praises of a Country Life, The. Horace. BASC Fr. Epodes.

Praises of the Bantu Kings (1–10). Jerome Rothenberg. FTOS

Praises, Tamalpais, / Perfect in Wisdom and Beauty. Lew Welch. BB

Praises to Him for aye! (LL) For Deliverance from a Fever. Anne Bradstreet. NAAL-3; NAAPv.1; NALW

Praisesong: From Son to Mother. Lenard D. Moore. BtF

Praising Thy worth, despite his cruel hand. (LL) William Shakespeare. CABP; NAEL-6v1; NAEL-7v1; NIL-7; NIP-4; NoP-5; NoSic; NPeEn; OxAEP-1; OxBEV; OxBSo; PoPoPo; TFi; TreFP Fr. Sonnets.

Prawns de Jo. Selima Hill. MoWP

Praxinoa at home? Theocritus. HePo Fr. Idylls.

Pray All de Member. Unknown. SSUS

Pray but one prayer for me 'twixt thy closed lips. Summer Dawn. William Morris. GSo; OBEV; OxAEP-2; OxBEV

Pray for my soul. More things are wrought by prayer. Alfred Tennyson. SacPr Fr. Idylls of the King.

Pray for the little acrobat with the yellow. Max Jacob. Guy Goffette. YaTCFP, tr. by Marilyn Hacker

Pray for the Lovers. Jayne Cortez. ISC

Pray how did she look? Was she pale, was she wan? On Lady Anne Hamilton. Richard Brinsley Sheridan. NPeEn; OBCoV

Pray on, pray on; / Pray on dem light us over. Pray On. Unknown. SSUS

Pray tell me, sir, whose dog are you? (LL) Epigram Engraved on the Collar of a Dog Given [or Which I Gave] to His Royal Highness. Alexander Pope. NTCP; OxBEV

Pray thee, take care, that tak'st my book[e] in hand. To the Reader. Ben Jonson. BASC; NoP-4; NoP-5

Pray to what earth does this sweet cold belong. Henry David Thoreau. NCAP

Pray where would lamb and lion be. Saunders Be Damned. Anne Wilkinson. BrAP

Pray why are you so bare, so bare. Haunted Oak, The. Paul Laurence Dunbar. ColAP; NAAPv.1

Pray why should any man complain. On Sir G. B. His Defeat. Alexander Brome. PBRV

Pray you fetch him hither. William Shakespeare. NPeEn Fr. Cymbeline.

Pray you I pray on new. III. Jennifer Scappettone. BAP-04

Prayer. Hartley Coleridge. GSo

Prayer. Elaine Feinstein. HarvBoo

Prayer. Gabriela Mistral.
   "Like those jars that women put out to catch the dew of night." WPoS

Prayer. James F. Montgomery. SacPr

Prayer. Kathleen Jessie Raine. BBASP

Prayer. Rudaki. WoPoe, tr. by Geoffrey Squires

Prayer. Grace Schulman. PuP-23

Prayer. Hugo Williams. EmeKit; NPeEn

Prayer (1): "Prayer the Church's banquet, Angels' age." George Herbert. AngWePo; BASC; GSo; NAEL-6v1; NAEL-7v1; NoP-4; NoP-5; NOSC; OBWVE; OxAEP-1; OxBSo; PoPoPo; TFi

Prayer #3: "I have pondered." Jeff Tweedy. IIR

Prayer 20. Catherine of Siena (Saint Catherine).
   "We were enclosed." WPoS

Prayer: "Sometimes, when we're lying after love." Kim Addonizio. RoV

Prayer: "We praise only you. We cringe with shame like crumbs." Afsar. HotL, tr. by V. Narayana Rao

Prayer: "I want a god." Francisco X. Alarcón. RaF

Prayer: "God bless the chick in Alaska." Ginger Andrews. SUP

Prayer: "Nobody understands so let the Rabbi." Stephen Berg. TaR

Prayer: "I left Cornell / with half a wit; six mismated socks." Daniel Berrigan. AF

Prayer: "Oh, God, beyond the wit of the genius." Dániel Berzsenyi. IQMS, tr. by Peter Zollman

Prayer: "Let my words." Joseph Bruchac. UnSA

Prayer: "O let me soar on steadfast wing." Dennis Brutus. AF

Prayer: "Grant that no Hobgoblins fright me." John Day. Spl

Prayer: "Some days, although we cannot pray, a prayer." Carol Ann Duffy. EdScPo; HarvBoo; MoWP; NeBrP; NePenScot; NoP-4; NoP-5; OxBSo; RWPCtW

Prayer: "God, I need a job because I need money." Alan Dugan. NoAM

Prayer: "With Him who sets the lily on the stem." Hildegarde Flanner. CalPo

Prayer: "You are here on earth, our Father." Gloria Fuertes. GPTC; RaW, tr. by John Haines

Prayer: "Echo of the clocktower, footstep." Dana Gioia. NoP-4; NoP-5

Prayer: "Over a dock railing, I watch the minnows, thousands, swirl." Jorie Graham. AWPTFC; PtR

Prayer: "Let innocence remain." Pierre Albert Jourdan. YaTCFP, tr. by Mary Ann Caws and Jean-Pierre Cauvin

Prayer: "Bones in your foot that were shattered, The." Richard Lambert. PoCu

Prayer: "Every hour I am disappearing." Carole Glasser Langille. Coast

Prayer: "Sweet Jesus, let her save you, let her take." Dorianne Laux. OPRER

Prayer: "Master, they say that when I seem." Clive Staples Lewis. SacPr

Prayer: "Here I work in the hollow of God's hand." Alice Oswald. NeBrP

Prayer: "O Christ, who in Gethsemane." Henrietta Cordelia Ray. CBWP-3

Prayers: "My shoes are mulberry with dew." Sadi. SonAtl, tr. by Roya Colandier and K. Young

Prayer: "Pray for my soul. More things are wrought by prayer." Alfred Tennyson. SacPr Fr. Idylls of the King.

Prayer: "God, though [or although] this life is but a wraith." Louis Untermeyer. MoAmPo

Prayer: "Bless my life—its inks." Carolyne Wright. SweBea

Prayer, A. Sir Thomas More. InvLi

Prayer, A. Katharine Tynan Hinkson. SacPr

Prayer, A: "God / save this country." Devarakonda Balagangadhara Tilak. HotL, tr. by V. Narayana Rao

Prayer, A: "If I popped in at Downing Street." Max Beerbohm. UV

Prayer, A: "My soul doth pant towards thee." Jeremy Taylor. SacPr

Prayer, A: "O beauteous God! uncircumscribed treasure." Jeremy Taylor. SacPr

Prayer, A: "O Lord, the hard-won miles." Paul Laurence Dunbar. SacPr

Prayer, A: "Oh, Lord! I lift my heart." Priscilla Jane Thompson. CBWP-2

Prayer, A: "When I look back upon my life nigh spent." George Macdonald. SacPr

Prayer, The. John Galsworthy. UV

Prayer, The. Leanne O'Sullivan. NIrP

Prayer, The ("Wilt Thou not visit me?") Jones Very. APN-1

Prayer After War. Endre Ady. IQMS, tr. by Anton N. Nyerges

Prayer at the End. Saunders Lewis. BBMWP, tr. by Joseph P. Clancy

Prayer at the Winter Solstice, A. Zuni Oral Tradition. tr. by Ruth L. Bunzel
   "Perhaps if we are lucky." NAWM-7v2, tr. by Ruth L. Bunzel

Prayer at the Winter Thanksgiving. Unknown. CCL1, tr. by James Legge

Prayer Before Birth. Louis MacNeice. BeAl; FaBoVe; HarvBoo; PNI

Prayer: "Bestow a blessing on the young men, because the time has come." Haim Guri. NRoS, tr. by Esther Raizen

Prayer bites Her skin, A. When She Can't Sleep. Judith Sornberger. FiBr

Prayer Flag. Miriam Sagan. WANABP

Prayer for a Future Beyond Ideology and War. Kelly Cherry. AtGh; RWB

Prayer for a Good Death, A. Toni Kan. NeNiPo

Prayer for a Marriage. Steve Scafidi. GoPo

Prayer for August 21. David Huerta. RMCMP, tr. by Mark Schafer

Prayer for Charity, A. Jeremy Taylor. SacPr

Prayer for Continuation. Susan Griffin. AtGh

Prayer for His Wife and Children, Written in Newgate. George Wither. SacPr

Prayer for Indifference, A. Fanny [or Frances] Macartney Greville. OxBEV
   Prayer for Indifference, A. OBEV

Prayer for Marilyn Monroe. Ernesto Cardenal. TCLAP, tr. by Robert Pring-Mill

Prayer for Men and Children. Linda Hogan. AtGh

Prayer for My Children. Kate Daniels. PoCho

Prayer for My Daughter, A. William Butler Yeats. BrAP; ItP; NAEL-6v2; NAEL-7v2; NAMCP V.1; NoAM; NoP-4; NoP-5; RaBo; TFi; WaAnP

Prayer for My Daughters, A. Thomas O'Grady. Coast

Prayer for My Father. Robert Bly. PoA 2002

Prayer for My Son. James Applewhite. BLT

Prayer for My Son, A. William Butler Yeats. OxAEP-2; RaBo

Prayer for Old Age, A. William Butler Yeats. ItP

Prayer for Peace, A. Severn Teackle Wallis. CBCWP

Prayer for Sleep, A. Michael Hartnett. BeAl

Prayer for Texas, A. Grace Noll Crowell. TiP2

Prayer for the End of the Century, A. Heberto Padilla. VCWP

Prayer for the End of the World. Raylene Hinz-Penner. ACAMVP

Prayer for the Everglades. Lola Haskins. RWB

Prayer for the Great Family. Gary Snyder. WeW-3

Prayer for the Great Lunatic. László Mécs. IQMS, tr. by Paul Tabori

Prayer for the Journey. Unknown. SacPr

Prayer for the Living, A. Asha Bandele. InTrad

Prayer for the Man Who Mugged My Father, 72. Charles Harper Webb. MAAN

Prayer for the Speedy End of Three Great Misfortunes. Unknown. OBMV, tr. by Frank O'Connor

Prayer in Darkness, A. G. K. Chesterton. MoBrPo

Prayer in Four Verses. Pak Mogwŏl [or Mokwŏl]. WoPoe, tr. by Chi-gyu Kim [or Kim Chonggil]

Prayer in Spring, A. Robert Frost. BLPJKO

Prayer, in the Prospect of Death, A. Robert Burns. TreFP

Prayer is the little implement. Emily Dickinson. APN-2

Prayer of a Warrior (Assiniboine). Unknown. AmWaPo, tr. by Edwin Thompson Denig

Prayer of a Woman in Charge of Berry Picking in Knights Inlet. Unknown. WPoS

Prayer of an Unbeliever. Lizette Woodworth Reese. SacPr

Prayer of Columbus. Walt Whitman. NCAP

Prayer of Dedication. Cosi Fabian. HW

Prayer of First Dancers. Navajo Oral Tradition. NAAPv.1 Fr. Night Chant, The.

Prayer of Hezekiah, The. George Wither. ChIV-1

Prayer of Jabez, too, should be our prayer, The. Prayer of Jabez, The. Jones Very. ChIV-1

Prayer of Miss Budd, The. Marilyn Nelson. BtF

Prayer of Mothers Who Unintentionally Failed Their Children. Vivian Lamarque. CItWP, tr. by Cinzia Sartini Blum and Lara Trubowitz

Prayer of Nature, The. Lord Byron. TreFP

Prayer of Nehemiah, The. George Wither. ChIV-1

Prayer of Richard De Castre. Richard of Caistre. SacPr

Prayer of St. Francis of Assisi for Peace. Saint Francis of Assisi. BLPJKO

Prayer of the Old Woman. François Villon. MoBrPo, tr. by John Millington Synge

Prayer of the Wanderer. Katie Donovan. NIrP

Prayer on the Threshold of Tomorrow. Vahan Tekeyan. AF, tr. by Diana Der Hovanessian and Marzbed Margossian

Prayer That Will Be Answered, A. Anna Kamienska. BLT

Prayer the Church's banquet, Angels' age. Prayer (1). George Herbert. AngWePo; BASC; GSo; NAEL-6v1; NAEL-7v1; NoP-4; NoP-5; NOSC; OBWVE; OxAEP-1; OxBSo; PoPoPo; TFi

(Prayer the Churches banquet, Angels age.) BrAP; FSCP; NPeEn; OxBEV; PBRV; SacPr

Prayer to Amitāyus. Kwangdŏk. CATKP, tr. by Peter H. Lee

Prayer to Aphrodite. Sappho. WoPoe, tr. by Alfred Corn

Prayer to Be with Mercurial Women. Roddy Lumsden. BeAl; EdScPo; NeBl

Prayer to Eshbu-Elegba. Jeffrey Renard Allen. RD

Prayer to Eve, A. Kathleen Norris. HW; UpMys

Prayer to Go to Paradise with the Donkeys, A. Francis Jammes. GPTC; WoPoe, tr. by Richard Wilbur

Prayer to God. Esther Kello. EMWP

Prayer to Jesus 1. Richard Rolle of Hampole. SacPr

Prayer to my lady of Paphos. Sappho. HW, tr. by Mary Barnard

Prayer to My Mother. Pier Paolo Pasolini. VCWP, tr. by Norman MacAfee and Luciano Martinengo

Prayer to Saint Grobianus. Roger McGough. NOxBChV

Prayer to Shadows on my Wall. Mark McMorris. IAoNAP

Prayer to the Boys of San Antonio. Ray Gonzalez. LiTh

Prayer to the Divine Mother, A. Andrew Harvey. HW

Prayer to the Father of [or in] Heaven, A. John Skelton. SacPr

Prayer to the Gods of the Night. Unknown. WoPoe, tr. by David Ferry

Prayer to the Masks. Léopold Sédar Senghor. YaTCFP, tr. by Hoyt Rogers

Prayer to the Muse of Ordinary Life. Kate Daniels. ExTi; PoDa

Prayer to the New Year, A. Fadwa Tuqan. PoArWo, tr. by Samira Kawar

Prayer to the Pacific. Leslie Marmon Silko. NAMCP V.2; NoP-4; PoPoPo; WeW-3

Prayer to the Sockeye Salmon. Unknown. WoPoe; WPoS, tr. by Jane Hirshfield

Prayer to the Virgin of Chartres. Henry Adams. APT-1

Prayer to the Wind, A. Thomas Carew. CavPo

Prayer upon Cutting down the Sacred Tree. Unknown. APN-2, tr. by John G. Bourke

Prayer yo Hymen. Unknown. NOSC

Prayers. Henry Charles Beeching. OBEV; SacPr

Prayers and Games of the Water People, The. Veno Taufer and Michael Scammell. tr. by Holton Milne

"Mother loves me loves me not." WoPoe, tr. by Holton Milne

Prayers and Sayings of the Mad Farmer. Wendell Berry. UpMys.

Prayers and words and lights. (LL) Kaddish. Charles Reznikoff. NAAPv.2; TaR

Prayers, Dorcas, Fellowship, and Children's Groups! Gwladys Rhys. W. J. Gruffydd. OBWVE, tr. by Myrddin Lloyd

Prayers have deadlines too. October 7th. Zachary Scott Robbins. BtF

Prayers: I. Kadya Molodovsky. WPoS, tr. by Kathryn Hellerstein

Prayers, The. Brian Coffey. Oth

Prayers of Steel. Carl Sandburg. BeAl; MoAmPo; SSCS

Praying and to be married? It was rare. Isaac's Marriage. Henry Vaughan. ChIV-1

Praying Drunk. Andrew Hudgins. RA; UpMys

Praying ("I was kneeling in the willow when.") Cynthia Cruz. IAoNAP

Praying ("In the middle of the night.") Cynthia Cruz. IAoNAP

Praying ("Into the ice ravaged rag-weed and phlox.") Cynthia Cruz. IAoNAP

Praying ("When I was set in that field.") Cynthia Cruz. IAoNAP

Praying-Mantis, A. Annie Charlotte Dalton. IFF

Praysing that Greeke who did these mysteries find. Argument of the Third Booke, The. Lucy Hutchinson. EMWP

Preacher and the Slave, The. Joe Hill. APT-1

Preacher quoted, and the cranks, The. Bad Break!, A. W. T. Goodge. NOBAu

Preacher: Ruminates behind the Sermon, The. Gwendolyn Brooks. InvLi Fr. Street in Bronzeville, A.

Preacher spoke of little things, The. Little Things. Unknown. ArBi

Preacher took from Solomon's Song, The. Rose Window. Herman Melville. APN-2

Preamble = sardanapalus. Tristan Tzara. PFTM-1 Fr. Dada Manifesto on Feeble and Bitter Love.

Preamble to a Tale of Acadie. Henry Wadsworth Longfellow. APN-1; NAAPv.1; NoP-4; TCAPo; UV Fr. Evangeline: A Tale of Acadie.

Pre-Breakfast Rant, A. Andrew Greig. BeAl

Precautions. Martin Sorescu. VCWP, tr. by Joana Russell-Gebbett and Paul Muldoon

Precedence. Horatius Bonar. SacPr

Precept of Silence, The. Lionel Pigot Johnson. MoBrPo; SacPr

Precepts for City Living. Vladimir Burich. TCRusP, tr. by Daniel Weissbort

Precio de la Verdad. Carlos Bousoño. RaW

Preciosa and the Wind. Federico García Lorca. STV, tr. by John Frederick Nims

Preciosilla. Gertrude Stein. NAAPv.2; NAMCP V.1

Precious in the light of the early sun the Housatonic. From a Train Window. Edna St. Vincent Millay. GM

Precious jewel. Big Glen, The. Colette Ni Ghallchóir. NIrP, tr. by the author

Precious Lord, take my hand. Take My Hand, Precious Lord. Thomas A. Dorsey. APT-2; ISC; NAAPv.2

Precious Moments. Carl Sandburg. MoAmPo

Precious Pearl, The. Priscilla Jane Thompson. CBWP-2

Precious Stones. Christina Georgina Rossetti. ChAP

Precious stones that my mother. Yocheved Bat-Miriam. FIT, tr. by Robert Friend

Precious—moldering pleasure—'tis, A. Emily Dickinson. APN-2

Precipice. Yi Sang. CAMKP; PFTM-1 Fr. Critical Condition.

Precipice, The. Judith Wright. BMAP

Precise German documentary reveals the horrors of Auschwitz, The. Shame. Matilde Salganicoff. MirDau, tr. by Celeste Kostopulos-Cooperman

Precisely. Daisy Zamora. LoL, tr. by Margaret Randall

Precisely because I do not have. Precisely. Daisy Zamora. LoL, tr. by Margaret Randall

Precisely because you are alive. Word before the Last about Loss, A. Linda Zisquit. DTA

Precisely the way you divide your small change between two. Paavo Haavikko. WoPoe Fr. Fifteen Epigrams in Praise of the Tyrant.

Precision, A. Winter Voyage. Anne-Marie Albiach. PFTM-2, *tr. by* Joseph Simas

Precision, The. Linda Gregg. PoDa

Precision German Craftsmanship. Matthew Rohrer. NAPBL; NeAmPo

Predator's excuse is always good, The. Lamb and the Wolves, The. Ignacy Krasicki. WoPoe, *tr. by* Jerzy Peterkiewicz and Burns Singer

Predestination. Robert Herrick. SacPr

Predicter of Famine, The. William Carlos Williams. APT-1

Prediction. Michael Lieberman. BloBone

Prediction, The. Mark Strand. CAP-8; NAMCP V.2; NoP-4; NoP-5; VCAP

Predictions about a Black Car. Mark Wunderlich. LegDan

Pre-eminent among scholars. Martial. RomPo, *tr. by* Peter Whigham

Preface. Han Yong'un [*or* Yongwun]. CAMKP, *tr. by* Sammy Solberg

Preface: "And did those feet in ancient time." William Blake. BrAP; CABP; ChIV-1; ClHu; CtM; HeIP-4; NAEL-7v2; NAWM-7v2; NOBRP; NoP-4; NPeEn; OxBEV; TFi; WoPoe *Fr.* Milton.

Preface: "Rigor of beauty is the quest. But how will you find beauty when it is locked." William Carlos Williams. NoAM *Fr.* Paterson.

Preface: "To make a start." William Carlos Williams. NAMCP V.1; NoAM *Fr.* Paterson.

Preface or The Drama of Absence in an Eternal Heart. Roger Gilbert-Lecomte. PFTM-1

Preface Shrink Lit: Elements of Style. Maurice Sagoff. NBLV

Preface to a Twenty Volume Suicide Note. Imamu Amiri Baraka. AmFaPo; BB; ESEAA

Preface [to God's Determinations], The. Edward Taylor. NAAL-3; NAAPv.1; NOSC; OxBEV; OxBoAm; TCAPo; WaAnP *Fr.* God's Determinations [touching his Elect].

Preface to I Am Rain. Hilary Booth. SurWo

Preface to *Leaves of Grass* [1855]. Walt Whitman. TWF

Preface to *The Progress of Learning*. Sir John Denham. NOSC

Preface to the Suite: "Childhood, boyhood, young manhood." Robert Duncan. FTOS *Fr.* Poems from the Margins of Thom Gunn's Moly.

Preference. Langston Hughes. APSN

Preference. Elinor Wylie. APT-1

Pregnancy. Sandra McPherson. LoL

Pregnant, I Come. Joseph Ceravolo. NYP2

Pregnant Lady Playing Tennis, The. Karen Volkman. AmPoNex

Pregnant Poets Swim Lake Tarleton, New Hampshire. Barbara Ras. NAPBL

Pregnant Woman. Bobi Jones. BBMWP, *tr. by* Joseph P. Clancy

Pregnant Woman. Ingrid Jonker. HAWP, *tr. by* Jack Cope and William Plomer

Pregnant woman, A. Three Bodies. Anna Swirszczynska [*or* Swir]. PoChi, *tr. by* Czeslaw Milosz and Leonard Nathan

Prehistoric Burials. Siegfried Sassoon. MoBrPo

Prejudice. Georgia Douglas Johnson. NAAPv.2

Prejudice. Lizelia Augusta Jenkins Moorer. CBWP-3

Preliminary Studies for the Frankfurt Readings 1984. Ernst Jandl. PFTM-2, *tr. by* Jerome Rothenberg

Preliminary to Classroom Lecture. Josephine Miles. NoAM

Prelude. Marilyn Chin. LoL

Prelude I: "Winter for a moment takes the mind; the snow." Conrad Potter Aiken. APT-1; NAAPv.2; OxBoAm *Fr.* Preludes for Memnon; or, Preludes to Attitude.

Prelude II: "Two coffees in the Español, the last." Conrad Potter Aiken. APT-1; NoAM *Fr.* Preludes for Memnon; or, Preludes to Attitude.

Prelude VI: "This is not you? These phrases are not you?" Conrad Potter Aiken. MoAmPo *Fr.* Preludes for Memnon; or, Preludes to Attitude.

Prelude XIX: "Watch long enough, and you will see the leaf." Conrad Potter Aiken. OxBoAm *Fr.* Preludes for Memnon; or, Preludes to Attitude.

Prelude XXXIII: "Then came I to the shoreless shore of silence." Conrad Potter Aiken. OxBoAm *Fr.* Preludes for Memnon; or, Preludes to Attitude.

Prelude LVI: "Rimbaud and Verlaine, precious pair of poets." Conrad Potter Aiken. NoAM *Fr.* Preludes for Memnon; or, Preludes to Attitude.

Prelude LVII: "One star fell and another as we walked." Conrad Potter Aiken. MoAmPo *Fr.* Preludes for Memnon; or, Preludes to Attitude.

Prelude: "Along the roadside, like the flowers of gold." John Greenleaf Whittier. APN-1 *Fr.* Among the Hills.

Prelude: "As one, at midnight wakened by the call." Wilfrid Wilson Gibson. MoBrPo

Prelude: "Bullock / slowly, The." Federico García Lorca. PFTM-1 *Fr.* Night (Suite for Piano and Poet's Voice).

Prelude: "Drum skin whip." Edward Kamau Brathwaite. WaAnP

Prelude: "Is it the long dry grass that is so erotic." Fleur Adcock. MoWP

Prelude: "Shelley's a garden." George Elliott Clarke. OpeFie

Prelude: "Still south I went and west and south again." John Millington Synge. MoBrPo; OBMV

Prelude, The; Growth of a Poet's Mind [1805 version]. William Wordsworth.
"Another maid there was, who also breathed." NPBRoP
"As oftentimes a river, it might seem."
　Among Royalists: Blois, Spring 1792. NPBRoP
　"I quitted and betook myself to France." OxAEP-2
　Patriot, A: Blois, Early Summer 1792. NPBRoP
　Tourist's Unconcern, A: Paris, Dec. 1791. NPBRoP
Books.
　"Thirteen years / Or haply less, I might have seen, when first." OxAEP-2
Cambridge and the Alps.
　Crossing the Alps. NPBRoP
　(Golden Hours: Calais and the Rhone, July 1790.) NPBRoP
　"I, too, have been a Wanderer; but, alas!" OxAEP-2
　Mind Debarred, A. NPBRoP
　Simplon Pass, The. CABP
Conclusion.
　"Child of my parents, sister of my soul." NPBRoP
　(Climbing of Snowdon.) NPBRoP
　"In one of these excursions, travelling then." OxAEP-2
　"It was a Summer's night, a close warm night." MakPoe
Introduction—Childhood and School-Time.
　"Fair seed-time had my soul, and I grew up." OxAEP-2
　Glad Preamble, The. NPBRoP; WaAnP
　On the Frozen Lake. WoPoe
Residence at Cambridge.
Residence in France and French Revolution.
　Eternal Justice: Morecambe Sands, Aug. 1794. NPBRoP
　"It was a beautiful and silent day." OxAEP-2
　Sleep No More: Paris, Oct. 1792. NPBRoP
　War and Alienation: London and Wales, 1793–4. NPBRoP
Residence in London.
　London Beggar, The. NPBRoP; WaAnP
　London Images. WaAnP
　"Those days are now." OxAEP-2
School-Time.
　"Nor should this, perchance." OxAEP-2
Summer Vacation.
　(Dedicated Spirit, A.) NPBRoP
　"While thus I wander'd, step by step led on." OxAEP-1
"Was it for this." NPeEn
"When from our better selves we have too long." AmFaPo

Prelude, The; Growth of a Poet's Mind [1850 version; Selections from Anthologies]. William Wordsworth.
Books.
　"Here must we pause; this only let me add." NAEL-6v2; NAEL-7v2
　"Oh! why hath not the mind." NAEL-6v2; NAEL-7v2
　"There was a boy;—ye knew him well, ye cliffs." NAEL-7v2; NOBRP
Cambridge and the Alps.
　"That very day." NAEL-6v2; NAEL-7v2
　"When the third summer freed us from restraint." NAEL-6v2; NAEL-7v2
Conclusion. NAEL-6v2; NAEL-7v2
"Even as a river,—partly (it might seem)."
　"Even as a river,—partly (it might seem)." NAEL-6v2; NAEL-7v2
France (Concluded).
　"I summoned my best skill, and toiled, intent." NAEL-6v2; NAEL-7v2
　"O pleasant exercise of hope and joy!" NAEL-6v2; NAEL-7v2
Imagination and Taste, How Impaired and Restored. NAEL-6v2; NAEL-7v2
Introduction—Childhood and School-Time. NAEL-6v2; NAEL-7v2
　"Fair seed time had my soul, and I grew up." NoP-5
　Influence of Natural Objects [in Calling Forth and Strengthening the Imagination in Boyhood and Early Youth]. OxBEV
Residence at Cambridge.
　"It was a dreary morning when the wheels." NAEL-6v2; NAEL-7v2
Residence in France and French Revolution.
　"Domestic carnage now filled the whole year." NAEL-6v2; NAEL-7v2
Residence in London.
　"As the black storm upon the mountain top." NAEL-6v2; NAEL-7v2
Retrospect Love of Nature Leading to Love of Mankind.
　"Rambling school-boy, thus, A." NAEL-6v2; NAEL-7v2
Same subject (Continued) [Imagination and Taste, How Impaired and Restored].
　"Here, calling up to mind what then I saw." NAEL-6v2; NAEL-7v2
School-Time. NAEL-6v2; NAEL-7v2
Summer Vacation.
　"Among the favorites whom it pleased me well." NAEL-6v2; NAEL-7v2

"As one who hangs down-bending from the side." NAEL-6v2; NAEL-7v2

Prelude: The Wayside Inn. Henry Wadsworth Longfellow. APN-1 *Fr.* Tales of a Wayside Inn.

Prelude: "This fugitive between the Earth and Sky." Tu Fu [*or* Du Fu]. TAL

Prelude to a Kiss. Irving Gordon and Irving Mills. ReLy

Prelude to a Kiss. Tracie Morris. BtF

Prelude to a Poem. Kim Ch'unsu [*or* Chun-soo]. CAMKP, *tr. by* Kevin O'Rourke

Prelude to a Volume Printed in Raised Letters for the Blind. Oliver Wendell Holmes. APN-1

Prelude to *Among the Hills*. John Greenleaf Whittier. *See* Prelude: "Along the roadside, like the flowers of gold."

Prelude to *An American Anthology*. Edmund Clarence Stedman. APN-2

Prelude to an Evening. John Crowe Ransom. MoAmPo *Fr.* Sixteen Poems in Eight Pairings.

Prelude to 'Blood and Ash'. Justinas Marcinkevičius. SonAtl, *tr. by* Terese Gustiene, Justinas Marcinkevičius, Dorli Meek, Tamara Romanyk and Alfredas Zalys

Prelude to Nothing. Sonia Sanchez. GT

Prelude to Part the First. James Russell Lowell. APN-1 *Fr.* Vision of Sir Launfal, The.

Prelude to the Fall. Kate Schmitt. IJHIL

Prelude to Winter. William Carlos Williams. SAmP

Preludes for Memnon; or, Preludes to Attitude. Conrad Potter Aiken.

(Cloister.) MoAmPo

Prelude I. APT-1; NAAPv.2; OxBoAm

Prelude II. APT-1; NoAM

Prelude LVI. NoAM

Prelude LVII. MoAmPo

Prelude VI. MoAmPo

Prelude XIX. OxBoAm

Prelude XXXIII. OxBoAm

Preludes: "Winter evening settles down, The." T. S. Eliot. APT-1; BrAP; HeIP-4; NAAPv.2; NAMCP V.1; OBMV; OxBoAm; PtR; TCAPo; WeW-3

Prelusive. Herman Melville. *Fr.* Clarel: A Poem and Pilgrimage in the Holy Land.

Premature Burial Gazette. Angela Ball. RWB

Premature Elegy. Buland Al-Haidari. IrPoTo, *tr. by* Hussein Kadhim and Christopher Merrill

Premeditations. Geoff Page. NOBAu

Pre-Memory. Nikolai Stepanovich Gumilyov. TCRusP, *tr. by* Denis Johnson and Kathy Lewis

Première, seconde elle, La. Choriste. Pierre Alféri. YaTCFP

Premièrement. La Maison est restée là-bas. Cauchemars. Marie Étienne. YaTCFP

Premise, a solace—deciduous dress, A. Sonnet. Karen Volkman. IAoNAP

Premonición. Francisco Segovia. RMCMP

Premonition. Lucha Corpi. ASA, *tr. by* Catherine Rodriguez-Nieto

Premonition. Francisco Segovia. RMCMP, *tr. by* Michael Wiegers

Premonition, The. Theodore Roethke. HarvBoo

Preparation. Thomas Edward Brown. OBEV

Preparation. William Johnson Cory. OxBSo

Preparation. Czeslaw Milosz. WoPoe, *tr. by* the author and Robert Hass

Preparation for the Big Emptiness. Kapka Kassabova. StAl

Preparations. Tony Curtis. TCAWP

Preparations. *Unknown*. *See* Guest, The.

Preparations for Seder. Michael S. Glaser. UnSA

Preparative, The. Thomas Traherne. BASC

Preparatory Meditations Before My Approach to the Lord's Supper. Edward Taylor.

"All Dull, my Lord, my Spirits flat, and dead." NOSC; TCAPo

Another Meditation at the same Time. NOSC; TCAPo; WaAnP

"Dull. Dull indeed! What shall it e'er be thus?" ChIV-1

"Like to the marigold, I blushing close." ChIV-2

(Meditation 6 (Canticles 2:1 I am. . .the lily of the valleys).) OxBoAm

Meditation 8 (First Series). ChIV-2; ColAP; NAAL-3; NAAL-5; NAAPv.1; NoP-4; NoP-5; TCAPo

Meditation 26. NAAL-3

Meditation 38. NAAL-3

Meditation 42 (First Series). NAAL-3; NAAL-5; NAAPv.1

Meditation 150 (Second Series). ColAP; NAAPv.1

Meditation 16 (First Series). NAAL-3; NAAL-5; NAAPv.1

Meditation 22 (First Series). NAAL-3; NAAL-5; NAAPv.1; TCAPo

Meditation 39 (First Series). NAAPv.1; TCAPo

Meditation. Can. 1.3. Thy Good Ointment. TCAPo

(Meditation. Cant.6.11.) OxBEV

Meditation. Col. 1.18. He is the Head of the Body.

"My Metaphors are but dull Tacklings tag'd." TCAPo

Meditation. Heb. 13.10. We[e] have an Altar. ChIV-2; NOSC; TCAPo; WaAnP

Meditation. Joh. 15.5. Without me yee can do nothing. TCAPo

Meditation. Mal. 4.2. With Healing in His Wings.

"Fiery Darts of Satan stob my heart, The." TCAPo

Meditation. Numb. 28.4.9. One Lamb shalt thou offer in the Morning, and the other at Even. And on the Sabbath day two Lambs etc. ChIV-1; TCAPo

Meditation on Gal. 3.16. And to thy Seed Which is Christ.

"Lord with thine Altars Fire, mine Inward man." TCAPo

Meditation. Phil. 3 Ult. Our Vile Bodie.

"Here is a Mudwall tent, whose Matters are." TCAPo

Meditation. Rom. 9.5. God blessed forever. TCAPo

Meditation. Zech. 9.11. The Pit wherein is no water.

"Pit indeed of Sin: No water's here:, A." TCAPo

"My shattred phancy stole away from mee." NOSC

Prologue. NAAL-3; NAAL-5; NAAPv.1; TCAPo

Reflexion, The. ChIV-1; TCAPo

Should I with Silver Tooles Delve through the Hill. ChIV-2

"State, a state, oh! dungeon state indeed, A." ChIV-1

"Stupendious love! all saints astonishment." SacPr

"Thy human frame, my glorious Lord, I spy." ChIV-1

"View, all ye eyes above, this sight which flings." NOSC

Was Ever Heart Like Mine? SacPr

"What shall I say, my Lord? With what begin?" ChIV-2

"Why should my bells, which chime thy praise, when thou." ChIV-2

"Ye angells bright, pluck from your wings a quill." ChIV-2

Preparatory Meditations: Part 1 (Complete). Edward Taylor.

Meditation 3 Can. 1.3. Thy Good Ointment. OxBoAm

Prepare your wreaths, Aonian maids divine. To the Muses. Mary Robinson. CenSon; RWP

Prepare your wreaths, Aonian maids divine. Mary Robinson. NPBRoP *Fr.* Sappho and Phaon.

Prepare yourself to hear the worst! That Was Before I Met You. P. G. Wodehouse. ReLy

Preparedness. Edwin Markham. MoAmPo; NAAPv.1

Preparing for Snow. Mark Ivey. ICANM

Preparing schmaltz for matzoh balls. Preparations for Seder. Michael S. Glaser. UnSA

Preparing the Dead. Paulette Roeske. IllVoic

Preparing the Nets at New Stuyahok. John Brandi. AtGh

Preparing to Live Among the Old. Stephen Corey. PoA 2002

Preparing to live for ever. (LL) Lifetime devoted to literature, A. Judith Rodriguez. BrAP; NOBAu

Preposterous is that Government, (and rude). Ill Government. Robert Herrick. CavPo

Pre-Raphaelite Notebook, A. Geoffrey Hill. NoAM

Prerogative of Lieder, The. Ray DiPalma. FTOS

Presage of mirth and hospitality. (LL) Philip Freneau. NAAL-3; TCAPo *Fr.* House of Night, The.

Presbyterian Study. Tom Paulin. PBCIP

Presbyterians, The. John Dryden. NOSC *Fr.* Hind and the Panther, The.

Prescient. Lucie Brock-Broido. ExTi

Prescient, my hands soothing. Walt Whitman in the Civil War Hospitals. David Ignatow. ViWalt

Prescott, press my Ascot waistcoat. Ascot Waistcoat. David McCord. NBLV

Prescott Slur contains, The. Prescott Slur, The. Reed Bye. AHA

Prescription. Donald Woods. CAGL

Prescription of Painful Ends. Robinson Jeffers. APT-1; MoAmPo

Preseli. Waldo Williams. BBMWP, *tr. by* Anthony Conran

Presence, The. Medbh McGuckian. PNI

Presence, The. Elder Olson. IllVoic

Presence, The. Pier Paolo Pasolini. ItPo, *tr. by* Gayle Ridinger

Presence and Process. Michael Thorpe. Coast

Presence of God, The. David Craig. UpMys

Presence of the Dance / The Resolution of the Music, The. Robert Duncan. FTOS

Presence. Opposites. Absence. Forces exercising pressure against. Alicia Kozameh. MirDau *Fr.* Saltos Sobre El Exilio.

Presence that ignites the, The. Blessing. Reed Bye. AHA

Presence was spectrum-blue, The. "H. D." APT-1 *Fr.* Walls Do Not Fall, The.

Presences. Lauris Edmond. PoCu

Presences Perfected. Siegfried Sassoon. MoBrPo

Presences that constitute life do so by entering life, The. Lyn Hejinian. Eno *Fr.* Fatalist, The.

Present, The. Michael Donaghy. BeAl

Present, The. Marie Laurencin. CuPo

Present, The.   Adelaide Anne Procter.   TreFP

Present, The.   Maria Luisa Spaziani.   CItWP, tr. by Cinzia Sartini Blum and Lara Trubowitz

Present Crisis, The.   James Russell Lowell.   TreFP

Present Divinity. (LL)   It feels a shame to be Alive.   Emily Dickinson. AmWaPo; FaBoWar; PCW

Present Evening, The.   Eugenio Florit.   TCLAP, tr. by Hoffman Reynolds Hays

Present From Ted.   Margaret Avison.   GPPA

Present from the Emperor's New Concubine, A.   Pan Chieh-yû.   NDACCP; WoPoe, tr. by Kenneth Rexroth

Present Moments.   David McElroy.   TiP2

Present of a watch?, The.   Watch, The.   Gwyneth Lewis.   ATSWP, tr. by Robert Minhinnick

Present pain never come to an end. (LL)   Ejected Wife, The.   Yüan-ti. OBVE; OxBEV, tr. by Arthur Waley

Present reigned supreme, The.   Home Coming.   Lenrie Peters.   HBAPE

Present Tense.   Harryette Mullen.   PrTe

Present Time Best Pleaseth, The.   Robert Herrick.   CavPo

Presentation of Two Birds to My Son, A.   James Wright.   YaYoPo

Presente.   Inés Hernández-Ávila.   ReEnLa

Presented to the Taoist Paragon Mao.   Cheng Huan.   ColAnChi, tr. by Edward H. Schafer

Presented to Wei Ba, Gentleman in Retirement.   Tu Fu [or Du Fu].   CCL1, tr. by Burton Watson

Presentiment—is that long Shadow—on the lawn.   Emily Dickinson.   APN-2; HeIP-4

Presently.   Seven Stimuli.   Mei Ch'eng.   ColAnChi, tr. by Victor H. Mair

Presently at our touch the teacup stirred.   Voices from the Other World.   James Merrill.   CAP-8; VCAP

Presents from My Aunts in Pakistan.   Moniza Alvi.   MFPA

Preserve for us rebellion, lightning, the illusory agreement, a laugh for. Unbending Prayer.   René Char.   AF

Preserve thy sighs, unthrifty girl[e].   Soldier Going to the Field, The.   Sir William Davenant.   FaBoWar; OBWP

Preserve us, Lucy.   Richard Wilbur.   UpMys Fr. Eye, The.

Preserves its blue heat down my throat. (LL)   Song: "Yellow coverlet, A." Rosanna Warren.   ExTi; MakPoe; PfSP

Preserves us, not for specialists. (LL)   April Inventory.   W. D. Snodgrass. BrAP; ColAP; EMP; GPTC; NAMCP V.2; NoAM; NoP-4; OxBoAm; TRP; VCAP; WaAnP

Preserving, The.   Kevin Young.   GT

President George W. Bush must feel.   Theological.   Dick Lourie.   PrTe

President has thus disclosed, The.   Door of Hope, The.   Lizelia Augusta Jenkins Moorer.   CBWP-3

Presidents.   Michael Heffernan.   EmeKit

Presidents, The [with music].   Lizelia Augusta Jenkins Moorer.   CBWP-3

Presidents of the United States of America, The.   Jackson Mac Low.   APSN

Presocratic, Surfing, Breathing Cosmology Blues, The.   Christopher Buckley. BodElec

Presque Isle, Maine.   Tammy Armstrong.   Coast

Press ahead, beloved children.   Uncle Rube to the Young People.   Clara Ann Thompson.   CBWP-2

Press me to your bread-fruit chest.   Cultural Trip, A.   Opal Palmer Adisa.   GT

Press of the Spoon River Clarion was wrecked, The.   Edgar Lee Masters. OBSV Fr. Spoon River Anthology.

Press On.   Park Benjamin.   TreFP

Press on! surmount the rocky steeps.   Press On.   Park Benjamin.   TreFP

Press Play.   Rebecca Wolff.   LegDan

Press'd by the Moon, mute arbitress of tides.   Charlotte Smith.   See Pressed by the moon, mute arbitress of tides.

Pressed by the Moon, Mute Arbitress of Tides.   Charlotte Smith.   CenSon; NALW

(Sonnet. Written in the Church-Yard at Middleton in Sussex.)   CABP; NPEEn; WaAnP; WoRP

(Written in the Church-yard at Middleton in Sussex.)   NAEL-7v2; NoP-4; NoP-5; PEW

Pressed to the wall, dying, but[—]fighting back! (LL)   If We Must Die. Claude McKay.   APT-1; ColAP; ISC; NAAL-5; NAAPv.2; NAMCP V.1; NoAM; OxAAAP; OxBoAm; SSLK; TFi

Pressgang at Shihao Village, The.   Tu Fu [or Du Fu].   CCL1, tr. by Jerome P. Seaton

Pressgang, The.   Tu Fu [or Du Fu].   CCL1, tr. by H. A. Giles

Pressing my breasts.   Yosano Akiko.   CAoMJL1, tr. by Janine Beichman

Pressing my lips. (LL)   Kenneth Rexroth.   APSN; APT-2; NAAPv.2; NAMCP V.1 Fr. Love Poems of Marichiko, The.

Pressing out the diasporic snow. (LL)   Dream-Language of Fergus, The. Medbh McGuckian.   MoWP; NAMCP V.2

Preston.   Unknown.   FaBoVe

Pre-Teen Trot.   Helen Adam.   ASA

Prête-moi ton grand bruit, ta grande allure si douce.   Ode.   Valery Larbaud. YaTCFP

Pretext.   Stephen Rodefer.   PmAP

Prettiest shadows were impalpable, so I stored them, The.   Izzy.   Ira Sadoff. BodElec

Pretty.   Jayne Anne Phillips.   MotU

Pretty.   Stevie Smith.   NAEL-6v2; NAEL-7v2; NAMCP V.1; NoAM; NoP-4

Pretty Baby.   Gustave Kahn.   ReLy

Pretty Beads.   Dick Gallup.   AHA

Pretty Blue Apron.   James McMichael.   PtR

Pretty fingers as white as snow move rapidly.   On Hearing the Sound of a Komunko While Passing a Mansion.   Chunghur Hyujung.   BecRai, tr. by Kim Daljin, Kim Won-Chung and Christopher Merrill

Pretty Girl Is Like a Melody, A.   Irving Berlin.   ReLy

Pretty little dress, . . .stockings full of holes.   Ernst Mirville.   OGAHCP, tr. by Boadiba and Jack Hirschman

Pretty Maid, The.   Paul Fort.   OBMV

Pretty Piece of Tail.   Harryette Mullen.   OxAAAP

Pretty Redhead, The.   Guillaume Apollinaire.   GPTC, tr. by James Wright

Pretty Soon.   Edith Bruck.   AF, tr. by Ruth Feldman

Pretty soon, the age of the talk show.   Hush Yo Mouf.   Thomas Sayers Ellis. InTrad

Pretty soon / when people hear a quiz show expert.   Pretty Soon.   Edith Bruck. AF, tr. by Ruth Feldman

Pretty sportive happy creature.   To a Young Lady's Dog.   Thomas Blacklock. DiBP

Pretty White Girls.   James E. Cherry.   BtF

Pre-Uplift of the Sierra.   Brenda Hillman.   RoV

Prevailing winds lied in intent, The.   Statuary.   John Ashbery.   NoAM

Previous to her Interview with Phaon.   Mary Robinson.   CenSon; RWP

12. Previous to her Interview with Phaon.   Mary Robinson.   NPBRoP Fr. Sappho and Phaon.

Previsioning death in advance, our doom is delayed.   Foresight.   Lincoln Kirstein.   OBWP; PoWW

Prewar stadium and a prewar game, A.   Dynamo Stadium, 1980.   Aleksandr Petrovich Tkachenko.   ItGoST, tr. by Maia Tekses

Prey.   Michael Dorris.   PoCoUp

Prey.   Ken Gerner.   GifTon

Prey.   Peter Makuck.   UrbNat

Preying mantis.   Dancing in my city.   Tatamkulu Afrika.   TSAP

Priam and Achilles.   Homer.   NOSC Fr. Iliad, The.

Priapean Corpus, The.   Unknown. tr. by Eugene O'Connor

"Bailiff, why your useless plaints about."   RomPo, tr. by Eugene O'Connor

"Having left behind its cutting."   RomPo, tr. by Eugene O'Connor

"I ask you to witness, Priapus."   RomPo, tr. by Eugene O'Connor

"Romans, I appeal to you."   RomPo, tr. by Eugene O'Connor

"To your question: why are my private parts."   RomPo, tr. by Eugene O'Connor

"What business, this? What reason should we give."   RomPo, tr. by Eugene O'Connor

Priapos of the Harbor.   Antipater of Sidon.   WoPoe, tr. by Dudley Fitts

Priapus and the Pool.   Conrad Potter Aiken.

(Portrait of a Girl.)   MoAmPo

"When trout swim down Great Ormond Street."   NoAM

Priapus, may this shady roof forever.   Tibullus.   PriapPo, tr. by Richard W. Hooper

Priapus Poems, The.   Unknown.   PriapPo, tr. by Richard W. Hooper

Priapus, seeing Cimon's rigid rod.   Antipater of Thessalonica.   CAGL, tr. by Daryl Hine

Price of Disrespect, The.   Lizelia Augusta Jenkins Moorer.   CBWP-3

Price of Stone, The.   Richard Murphy.

Convenience.   ModIr

Kylemore Castle.   ModIr

Natural Son.   BeAl; ModIr

Roof-Tree.   ModIr

Price on My Head, A.   Celia de Fréine.

Inside.   NIrP, tr. by the author

Pints.   NIrP, tr. by the author

Testing, testing.   NIrP, tr. by the author

Price seemed reasonable, location, The.   Telephone Conversation.   Wole Soyinka.   NAMCP V.2; NoP-4; NoP-5; PoetW; WaAnP

Priceless is one's incantation.   Hakuin.   ZenPo, tr. by Takashi Ikemoto and Lucien Stryk

Pride.   Mary Elizabeth Coleridge.   ViWPN

Pride.   Jackie Kay.   NeBl

Pride.   Yusef Komunyakaa.   PoA 2002

Pride: "It becomes your soul: that sucking, itch that."   V. B. Price.   ICANM

Pride of the Fourth and Liquid Element. Luis de Góngora y Argote. SpanPo, *tr. by* J.M. Cohen

Pride of the fourth and liquid element. Pride of the Fourth and Liquid Element. Luis de Góngora y Argote. SpanPo, *tr. by* J.M. Cohen

Pride of the Peacock, The. William Blake. RaBo *Fr.* Marriage of Heaven and Hell, The.

Prière. Pierre Albert Jourdan. YaTCFP

Prière aux Masques. Léopold Sédar Senghor. YaTCFP

Priest. "H. D."
   "You come late." GifTon

Priest and the Mulberry-Tree, The. Thomas Love Peacock. OxAEP-2 *Fr.* Crotchet Castle.

Priest gets lost in prayer, The. Mission. Bei Dao. WoBe, *tr. by* Iona Man-Cheong and Eliot Weinberger

Priest in charge, The. Karai Senryū. EMJL, *tr. by* Makoto Ueda

Priest in the Sabbath Dawn Addresses His Somnolent Mistress, A. Peter Didsbury. EmeKit

Priest of Beauty, the Anointed One, The. Poet's Destiny, The. Lady Jane Francesca Wilde. VWP

Priest of Christ, The. Thomas Ken. SacPr

Priest of the spruce of the north, send all your people to work for us. Rain Song of the Shu'-wi Chai' än (Snake Society), A. *Unknown.* APN-2, *tr. by* Matilda Coxe Stevenson

Priest, the Levite, the Samaritan, and the man who fell among thieves meet in heaven to talk over old times, The. Good Samaritan et Al, The. Stephen Mitchell. GI

Priestess of Love. Ann Elizabeth Hostetler. ACAMVP

Priestly poverty—. Buson. SoOfWa, *tr. by* Sam Hamill

Priests have a problem, The. Hakeldama. Zbigniew Herbert. GI, *tr. by* John Carpenter *and* Bogdana Carpenter

Priests make a brothel's flushest clients. To Master Groggy, From Afar. Dōyaku Sensei, Master Artery. EMJL, *tr. by* Haruo Shirane

Priests of Apollo, sacred be the room[e]. Sacrifice to Apollo, The. Michael Drayton. NOSC

Priests, prophets, helpless. She's beside herself. Virgil. EroLit *Fr.* Aeneid [*or* Eneados *or* Aeneis], The.

Priest's Song, A. Thomas Dekker *and others.* NoSic *Fr.* Old Fortunatus.

Priests, the elders, and the scribes, The. Death and Resurrection. Priscilla Jane Thompson. CBWP-2

Priez pour le petit saltimbanque à croix. Max Jacob. Guy Goffette. YaTCFP

Prig offered Pig the first chance at dessert. Manners. Howard Nemerov. NBLV

Prikaz. André Salmon. CuPo

Primaleon of Greece. Anthony Munday.
   Beauty Bathing. OBEV

Primaries, conventions, elections. Dream of Instant Total Representation, The. Anselm Hollo. PmAP

Primary Lessons in Political Economy. Amitava Kumar. IPoFL

Primary Teachers. Alastair MacKie. EdScPo

Primavera. Antonio Machado Ruiz. WoPo, *tr. by* Samuel Menashe

Prime. W. H. Auden. NAMCP V.1 *Fr.* Horae Canonicae.

Prime Time. Barry Silesky. LiTh

Primer, The. Josephine Jacobsen. NoP-4; NoP-5

Primer about the Flag, A. Marvin Bell. GifTon

Primer for Blacks. Gwendolyn Brooks. ISC

Primer for the Small Weird Loves, A. Richard Siken. LegDan

Primer Lesson. Carl Sandburg. MoAmPo

Primer of the Daily Round, A. Howard Nemerov. GoPo; NoP-4; NoP-5; WeW-3

Primitive Place. Mildred Weston. FFC

Primitiveness of a Cup, The. Nishiwaki Junzaburo. CAoMJL1, *tr. by* Hosea Hirata

Primo Levi. Emrys Roberts. BBMWP, *tr. by* Richard Poole

Primos. Sandra M. Castillo. TouFir

Primrose, The. John Clare. CenSon

Primrose, The. Robert Herrick. OBEV

Primrose of the Rock, The. William Wordsworth. TreFP

Primrose there, the violet darkly blue, The. Philip Freneau. NAAL-3 *Fr.* House of Night, The.

Primroses; salutations; the miry skull. Pre-Raphaelite Notebook, A. Geoffrey Hill. NoAM

Primula veris. Randolph Healy. Oth

Prince. Ann Sansom. NeBl

Prince Arthur. Sir Richard Blackmore.
   Crystal Palaces, The. STuOW

Prince Genji was in love with me in the eleventh century. Put his hand. Lover. Catherine Wagner. IIR

Prince Hamlet thought Uncle a traitor. Hamlet. Stanley J. Sharpless. NBLV

Prince New Year, welcome to thy throne. To the New Year. Priscilla Jane Thompson. CBWP-2

Prince of Aquitania, in His Torn-down Tower, The. Jaime Gil de Biedma. RaW, *tr. by* Lewis Hyde

Prince of Huai-nan, The. Ballad in Imitation of "The Prince of Huainan." Pao Chao. CCL1, *tr. by* Burton Watson

Prince of the Dance. Cecil Rajendra. PML

Prince of the Powers of the Air. Debora Greger. PoDa

Prince Rupert's Drop, The. Jane Draycott. OxBSo

Prince Tan of Yen knew how to treat a man—. In Praise of Ching K'o. Ch'ien T'ao. ColAnChi, *tr. by* James Robert Hightower

Prince, The [. . . *si quid mea carmina possunt, nulla dies umquam memori vos eximet aevo, dum domus Aeneae Capitoli immobile saxum accolet . . .*]. Edgar Bowers. InGu

Prince Went Wandering, A. Hsieh T'iao. CCL1, *tr. by* John Frodsham

Prince who said an English Senate can, The. Anne Merryweather. EMWP

Prince, with Wonder, sees the stately Tow'rs, The. Virgil. OBVE *Fr.* Aeneid [*or* Eneados *or* Aeneis], The.

Princes of Mercia were badger and raven, The. Thrall. Geoffrey Hill. NAEL-6v2; NAEL-7v2; NAMCP V.2; NoAM; NoP-4; NoP-5; NPeEn; WoPoe *Fr.* Mercian Hymns.

Prince's Progress, The. Christina Georgina Rossetti.
   Bride Song. OBEV

Princess, A. (LL) Hazel Tells LaVerne. Katharyn Howd Machan. ReTh; SUP

Princess and the Pea, The. Helen Smith Bevington. AmWit

Princess is sad, and in anguish reposes, The. Sonatina. Rubén Darío. SpanPo, *tr. by* John Crow

Princess is sad, The. What ails the Princess? Sonatina. Rubén Darío. TCLAP, *tr. by* Lysander Kemp

Princess of Scotland, The. Rachel Annand Taylor. NePenScot

Princess of the nights, be welcome. Night's Delights. Kaspar Stieler. GePo, *tr. by* Ingrid Waløe-Engel

Princess Parade. Sarah Gorham. FFC

Princess slept uneasily, The. Princess and the Pea, The. Helen Smith Bevington. AmWit

Princess Sŏnhwa, / After a secret affair. Song of Sŏdong. Mu, King of Paekche. CATKP, *tr. by* Peter H. Lee

Princess that your love was not responded. Elegy for Joan the Mad One. Federico García Lorca. BLPSL, *tr. by* Rene de Costa, Rigas Kappatos and Eleni Paidoussi

Princess, The. Alfred Tennyson.
   "Ask me no more: the moon may draw the sea." NAEL-6v2; NAEL-7v2
   (Blow, Bugle, Blow.) OBEV
   "Deep in the night I woke: she, near me, held." EroLit
   "Home they brought her warrior dead." OxAEP-2
   Now Sleeps the Crimson Petal. NIL-7
   "So sang the gallant glorious chronicle." OBGa
   "So was their sanctuary violated."
      "Come down, O maid, from yonder mountain height." NAEL-6v2; NAEL-7v2; NPeEn; OBEV; OxBEV
      "Now sleeps the crimson petal, now the white." NAEL-6v2; NAEL-7v2; NoP-4; NoP-5; NPeEn; OxAEP-2; TFi; WoPoe
      (Song.) OPOU
      (Summer Night.) OBEV
      Woman's Cause Is Man's, The. NAEL-6v2; NAEL-7v2
   Splendour [*or*Splendor] Falls, The. ClHu; CtM; HeIP-4; NAEL-6v1; NAEL-7v1; NoP-4; NoP-5; TFi
   "Sweet and low, sweet and low." ChAP; NAEL-6v2; NAEL-7v2
   "There sinks the nebulous star we call the Sun."
      "Tears, idle tears, I know not what they mean." CABP; CtM; NAEL-6v2; NAEL-7v2; NIL-7; NIP-4; NoP-4; NoP-5; OxAEP-2; OxBEV; PoPoPo; TFi; TreFP

Princess Victoria, The. Letitia Elizabeth Landon. RWP

Príncipe de Aquitania, En Su Torre Abolida. Jaime Gil de Biedma. RaW

Principles of Scarcity, Doctrines of Growth. David Citino. UpMys

Principles, When I Felt Them. Prageeta Sharma. HeMarv

Print documentcheap ink said. Not This—This Here! Clarence Major. EGAG

Printed in "The Times," May 1859. Alfred Tennyson.
   Riflemen Form. STuOW

Printemps, Le / This shadow ecstasy, a palm, a. Coarse rigors. Stephanie Williams. AnSo

Printer's Error. P. G. Wodehouse. OBCoV

Printer's Error, The. Aaron Fogel. OxBoAm; P180

Printing the stones. (LL) Otter, The. Seamus Heaney. IrLP; NoAM; PNI

Printing-Press, The. Christopher Pearse Cranch. APN-1 *Fr.* Seven Wonders of the World.

Prints left by the eyes that read these lines, The. Secondhand Book. Antonio Deltoro. RMCMP, *tr. by* Christian Viveros-Fauné

Prioresse, A. Geoffrey Chaucer. BrAP; NPeEn *Fr.* Canterbury Tales, The.

Priorities at Friday Ranch. William Stafford. BodElec

Pripet Marshes, The. Irving Feldman. TaR

Prism, A: Wet With Wars. Sinan Anton. IrPoTo, *tr. by* the author

Prism crystal sets towards the axis, The. Chromatin. J. H. Prynne. PFTM-2

Prisms. Laura Riding Jackson. APT-2; ColAP

Prison. Mahmoud Darwish. AF, *tr. by* Denys Johnson-Davies

Prison. Mahmoud Darwish. AF, *tr. by* Denys Johnson-Davies

Prison, The. Shmuel HaNagid. WoPoe, *tr. by* T. Carmi

Prison, The. Maria Luisa Spaziani. CItWP, *tr. by* Cinzia Sartini Blum and Lara Trubowitz

Prison Daybreak, A. Faiz Ahmad Faiz. AF, *tr. by* Agha Shahid Ali

Prison Evening, A. Faiz Ahmad Faiz. BeAl; VCWP, *tr. by* Agha Shahid Ali

Prison gets to be a friend, A. Emily Dickinson. APN-2; NCAP

Prison in Windsor Castle. Henry Howard, Earl of Surrey. NoSic (So Cruel Prison.) CABP; NoP-4; NoP-5

Prison, San Elizario, Texas, The. Ray Gonzales. TiP2

Prison Song. Alan Dugan. PoA 2002; YaYoPo

Prison to Prison. Nazim Hikmet. NaPG, *tr. by* Talat Sait Halman

Prison, *zona*, the camps, Taldái-Kustanái, and the low road. Marina Kudimova. CRWP, *tr. by* Catriona Kelly

Prisoned in Windsor, He Recounteth His Pleasure There Passed. Henry Howard, Earl of Surrey. CABP; NAEL-6v1; NAEL-7v1 *Fr.* Windsor Castle.

Prisoner. Muin Pzaki. NAAPv.2

Prisoner, The. Keith Douglas. HarvBoo

Prisoner, The. Dunya Mikhail. IrPoTo, *tr. by* Liz Winslow

Prisoner, The. Charles Tennyson Turner. CenSon

Prisoner, The. A Fragment. Emily Jane Brontë. NAEL-6v2; NAEL-7v2; NALW; NoP-5

"Still let my tyrants know, I am not doomed to wear." IJHIL; NoP-4; OBEV

Prisoner of Chillon, The. Lord Byron. BrAP; NPBRoP

Prisoner Scolds, The. STuOW

Prisoner of Los Angeles (2). Wanda Coleman. CalPo; GeoHom

Prisoner of Love. Clarence Gaskill and Leo Robin. ReLy

Prisoner of Zenda, The. Richard Wilbur. NBLV; OBCoV

Prisoner ran forward, The. First his head. Essay on Death. Hayden Carruth. BodElec

Prisoner Scolds, The. Lord Byron. STuOW *Fr.* Prisoner of Chillon, The.

Prisoners. Randall Jarrell. AmWaPo

Prisoners. Yusef Komunyakaa. AmAlph

Prisoners [*with music*]. Denise Levertov. NoAM; VCAP

Prisoners, The. Alexander Brome.
"Come a *brimmer* (my bullies) drink whole ones or nothing." PBRV

Prisoners, The. Stephen Spender. MoBrPo

Prisoners, committed to death, The. Hunger. Jerome Rothenberg. APSN

Prisoner's Dream, The. Eugenio Montale. PoetW, *tr. by* Jonathan Galassi

Prisoner's Lay, A. George Wither.
"First think, my soul, if I have foes." SacPr

Prisoners of Saint Lawrence, The. Martín Espada. PoCho; TouFir

Prisoners of War. John Jarmain. FaBoWar

Prisoner's Song, A. Sinan Anton. IrPoTo, *tr. by* the author

Prisons. George Crabbe. *Fr.* Borough, The.

Prisons. Lőrinc Szabó. IQMS, *tr. by* Edwin Morgan

Pristine but jagged, maniacal but clear-thinking. Darren Wershler-Henry. PoPra *Fr.* Ten Out of Ten, or, Why Poetry Criticism Sucks in 2003.

Prithee die and set me free. Out of an Epigram of Martial. Martial. OBVE, *tr. by* Sir John Denham

Privacy. Lionel Abrahams. TSAP

Privacy. Olga Broumas. PasH

Privacy. Carla Harryman. MotU

Privacy. C. D. Wright. AmAlph

Private, A. Edward Thomas. TCAWP

Private, The. Robert Adamson. BMAP

Private Airplane. Chase Twichell. ExTi

Private Bottling, A. Don Paterson. EmeKit; NePenScot

Private But Sulphurous. Tom Matthews. PNI

Private Dining Room, The. Ogden Nash. AmWit; OBCoV

Private John Ball Wounded in the Wood. David Jones. TCAWP *Fr.* In Parenthesis.

Private Letter to Brazil, A. Gloria C. Oden. ESEAA

Private madness has prevailed, A. O Virtuous Light. Elinor Wylie. MoAmPo

Private Occasion in a Public Place, A. David Antin. PmAP

Private of the Buffs; or, The British Soldier in China. Sir Francis Hastings Doyle. FaBoWar; OBEV

Private Sadness. Bob Kaufman. ISC

Private Sorrow, A. George Oommen. PML

Private Theatricals. Louise Imogen Guiney. PoBW

Private Thoughts. Clyde A. Wray. BtF

Private Truce. Lőrinc Szabó. IQMS, *tr. by* Peter Zollman

Privets Come into Season at High Tide [*with music*]. Ted Greenwald. FTOS

Privilege of Being. Robert Hass. NIP-4

Privilege to die, The. (LL) Heart asks Pleasure—first, The. Emily Dickinson. APN-2; MoAmPo; NAAL-3; NoP-4; NoP-5; OxBoAm; PoPoPo; PtR; TCAPo

Privileged fill the imperial ranks, The. At Li's Mountain Hermitage. Wang Wei. CrYelRi, *tr. by* Sam Hamill

Privy-Love for My Landlady. George Farewell. OBCoV

Prize Cat, The. Edwin John Pratt. BrAP

Prize for Good Conduct. Kenneth Allott. OBWP

Pro Bono Publico. Alamgir Hashmi. PML

Pro Femina. Carolyn Kizer.
Erotic Philosophers, The. NoP-5; OxBoAm
One. CAP-8; VCAP
Three. BrAP; FTtHH; NALW
Two. FFC; VCAP

Pro Patria. T. Gwynn Jones.
"Thirty soldiers, exhausted and grim-faced." BBMWP, *tr. by* Elin ap Hywel

Pro Patria. Adah Isaacs Menken. CBWP-1

Pro Patria Mori. Thomas Moore. OxAEP-2

Pro patria mori. (LL) Dulce et Decorum Est. Wilfred Owen. AmFaPo; BrAP; CABP; EMP; FaBoWar; HarvBoo; HeIP-4; InoFa; ItP; MoBrPo; NAEL-6v2; NAEL-7v2; NAMCP V.1; NIL-7; NIP-4; NoAM; NoP-4; NoP-5; OBWP; OxBEV; PoAgWa; PoPoPo; PoWW; RaBo; TCAWP; TFi; TRP; WaAnP

Pro Sua Vita. Robert Penn Warren. MoAmPo

Probability in the yard is this, The. Russell Atkins. GT

Probability in the yard, The:. Russell Atkins. EGAG

Probable Cause. Thomas McGrath. GifTon

Probably. Keith Preston. NBLV

Probably I am an ordinary middle-class. Fire. Adam Zagajewski. PoCho, *tr. by* Renata Gorczynski

Probably take you several hundred years / to get / out! (LL) Imamu Amiri Baraka. NAMCP V.2; PFTM-1 *Fr.* Why's / Wise.

Probably the most human thing I do. Eleanor Brown. NeBl

Probably the song of a temple prostitute, priestess of the second caste. Armand Schwerner. PFTM-2 *Fr.* Tablets, The.

Probably to relate to the notes on 4-dim'l perspective. Cast Shadows. Marcel Duchamp. PFTM-1

Probatioun Officeres Tale, The. Gerard Benson. NBLV

Problem, A. Alexander Gerov. CSCBP, *tr. by* Georgi Belev and Lisa Sapinkopf

Problem, A. Carolyn Wells. SWaP

Problem, The. Ralph Waldo Emerson. APN-1; NAAL-3

Problem, The. Thom Gunn. NAMCP V.2

Problem, The. Len Roberts. PML

Problem here is that, The. Sherbet. Cornelius Eady. GT; LTA

Problem is not the letter X, The. Malcolm Is 'Bout More Than Wearing a Cap. Michael Warr. UnSA

Problem of Anxiety, The. John Ashbery. BAP-97

Problem was a different sense of form, The. Problem Was, The. Joyce Sutphen. PoA 2002

Problem with childhood, The. Chapped Lips. Dean Young. SUP

Problems With Hurricanes. Víctor Hernández Cruz. PmAP

Procedure. Ann Lauterbach. BodElec

Procedures for Underground. Margaret Atwood. NALW

Proceeds by chance. Natural Selection. Alan Shapiro. PoA 2002

Process. Charles Leo O'Donnell. SacPr

Process calls for twenty heads to stare, The. David Wojahn. PBCAP *Fr.* Mystery Train: A Sequence.

Processes activities break drop and disappear, The. Allen Fisher. Oth *Fr.* Emergent Manner.

Processes of generation; deeds of settlement. Geoffrey Hill. NAEL-7v2; NoP-4 *Fr.* Mercian Hymns.

Procession, A. Southern wails. A yellow. Southern Birth. Kevin Powell. AmPoNex; InTrad

Procession, The. Sarah Rosenblatt. AmPoNex

Procession at Candlemas, A. Amy Clampitt. NAMCP V.2; PoPoPo

Procession of death. Allegory of the Supermarket. Stephanie Brown. AFaM; SUP

Procession of ghosts shuffles by, The.   Carnival at the River.   Robert Greacen.
PNI
Processional.   James Merrill.   PoDa
Processions, The.   Mário de Andrade.   TCLAP, *tr. by* Jack E. Tomlins
Processions that lack high stilts have nothing that catches the eye.   High Talk.
William Butler Yeats.   FaBoVe; RaBo
Proclaim liberty throughout.   Inscription on the Liberty Bell.   Bible, *O.T.*   CA
Proclamation on North Mountain.   K'ung Chih-kuei.   CCL1, *tr. by* James
Robert Hightower
Proclamation without Pretention.   Tristan Tzara.   NAWM-7v2, *tr. by* Mary Ann
Caws *and* Jean-Pierre Cauvin
Procne.   Peter Quennell.   MoBrPo
Procne, Philomela, and Itylus.   Philomela.   John Crowe Ransom.   APT-1;
FuPo; NoAM; OBSV
Proconsul of Bithynia.   To Petronius Arbiter.   Oliver St. John Gogarty.
OBMV
Procrastination.   George Crabbe.   NOBRP; NPBRoP *Fr.* Tales.
Procrastination.   Martial.   OBVE, *tr. by* Abraham Cowley
Procris' Immortal Lelaps: Cephalus' Story.   Ovid.   DiBP *Fr.* Metamorphoses.
Proctor buys a pupil ices, The.   Edward Gorey.   AmWit
Procuress, The.   Herodas.   HePo, *tr. by* Barbara Hughes Fowler
Proddy Heebie Jeebies, The.   Alan Jackson.   EdScPo
Prodigal, The.   Elizabeth Bishop.   APT-2; ChIV-2
Prodigal Daughter.   Angelina Muñiz Huberman.   MirDau, *tr. by* Aurora
Camacho
Prodigal Daughter, The.   Dorothy Barresi.   SweBea
Prodigal Son, The.   Robert Bly.   ChIV-2
Prodigal Son, The.   Cynan.   *tr. by* Sally Roberts Jones
"It was all go with the jazz-band and all go with the dance."   BBMWP, *tr. by*
Sally Roberts Jones
Prodigal Son, The.   Leah Goldberg.   GI, *tr. by* Robert Friend
Prodigal Son, The.   Rudyard Kipling.   NoAM *Fr.* Kim.
"Prodigal Son," The.   W. S. Merwin.   GI *Fr.* "Prodigal Son," The.
"Prodigal Son," The.   W. S. Merwin.
"Prodigal Son," The.   GI
Prodigal Son, The.   Edwin Arlington Robinson.   GI; MoAmPo
Prodigal Son Considers a Diplomatic Career, The.   Dionisio D. Martinez.
PoDa
Prodigal Son in His Own Words, The: Bees.   Dionisio D. Martinez.   NAMCP
V.2
Prodigal Son is kneeling in the husks, The.   Prodigal Son, The.   Robert Bly.
ChIV-2
Prodigals.   Phoebe Cary.   SacPr
Prodigies flooded the market—the magnetic corset.   History of Photography, A.
Mary Karr.   PoA 2002
Prodigy, The.   Lola Haskins.   MiVo
Prodigy.   Charles Simic.   AF; AmWaPo; EMP; NAMCP V.2; NoP-5; VCAP
Produce.   Debra Allbery.   PBCAP
Produce from the colonies.   Pierre McOrlan.   MFP, *tr. by* Martin Sorrell
Produce of Cyprus.   Alison Brackenbury.   RSaN
Produce, Produce.   Susan Wheeler.   KGB
Produce the urn that Hannibal contains.   Juvenal.   OBVE *Fr.* Satires.
Product.   George Oppen.   HarvBoo
Product of Evolution, I Invest in a Mutual Fund, A.   Amanda Pecor.   BodElec
Product of peoples on two sides of a narrow sea, The.   Lyle Donaghy, Poet,
1902-1949.   George Buchanan.   PNI
Proem: "Bad Verse I sing, and since 'twere best, I deem."   Charles Lee.
STuOW
Proem: "From Zeus let us begin, him we mortals never."   Aratus.   HePo *Fr.*
Phaenomena.
Proem: "I love the old melodious lays."   John Greenleaf Whittier.   APN-1
Proem: To Brooklyn Bridge.   Hart Crane. *See* To Brooklyn Bridge.
Profaning the Dead.   Carole Bernstein.   AmPoNex
Professor Alpha Umphers.   Chitterling King, The.   Melvin B. Tolson.   EGAG
Professor and Ginger are standing in the space in front, The.   Gilligan's Island.
Tim Dlugos.   ReTh
Professor invites me to his "Black Lit" class; they're, A.   Passing.   Toi
Derricotte.   OPRER
Professor Kelleher and the Charles River.   Desmond O'Grady.   PBCIP
Professor Robinson each summer beats.   Don's Holiday.   George Rostrevor
Hamilton.   OBCoV
Professor's Song, A.   John Berryman.   BrAP; HeIP-4; NoAM
Professor's Wife, The.   Flora Garry.   EdScPo
Profile / knife-filed profile.   Dolores Dorantes.   SPV, *tr. by* Jen Hofer
Profile of Rose.   Glyn Jones.   OBWVE
Profit and Loss.   John Oxenham.   SacPr
Profit?—Loss?   Profit and Loss.   John Oxenham.   SacPr

Profit may and will the pain[e]s requite, The. (LL)   Dream[e], The [*or* A].
Rachel Speght.   BASC; EMWP
Profiteers.   Alexander Pope.   OBSV *Fr.* First Epistle of the First Book of
Horace Imitated, The.
Profuse announcement.   Paul Celan.   PoetW, *tr. by* John Felstiner
Prognosis.   Debra Bruce.   IllVoic
Prognosis.   George Starbuck.   YaYoPo
Program Notes.   Ruth Roston.   MiVo
Programmed to beat *guaguanco*. (LL)   Ode.   Elizabeth Alexander.   GT;
PoPoPo
Progress.   Matthew Arnold.   ChIV-2
Progress.   Robert Conquest.   OBCoV
Progress.   Samuel Hoffenstein.   OBCoV
Progress.   Barrett Watten.
"Isolate *and.*"   FTOS
"Relax, / stand at attention, and."   PmAP
Progress: "Jacaranda blindings."   Bernard Bador.   ConPit, *tr. by* Clayton
Eshleman
Progress: "There was a time when peace at evening."   Violet Helen
Friedlaender.   RWPCtW
Progress of a Divine, The.   Richard Savage.
"Now in the patron's mansion see the wight."   OBSV
Progress of Liberty, The.   Mary Robinson.
Book 1.
Conclusion to Book 1.   RWP
Progress of Man, The. A Didactic Poem.   Anti-Jacobins, The and George
Canning *and* William Gifford.
Canto First.   NOBRP
Progress of Poesy, The.   Thomas Gray.   OBEV
"In climes beyond the solar road."   OxAEP-1
Progress of the Colonies. Troubles with the Natives.   Joel Barlow.   AmWaPo
Fr. Columbiad, The.
Progressions of Spacetime: I.   Allen Fisher.   Oth *Fr.* Stepping Out.
Progressive Insanities of a Pioneer.   Margaret Atwood.   BrAP
Progressive Man's Indignation, A.   Dimitris Tsaloumas.   BMAP
Prohibition, The.   John Donne.   NOSC
Project.   Piera Oppezzo.   CItWP, *tr. by* Cinzia Sartini Blum and Lara
Trubowitz
Project: Flag.   Tadeusz Borowski.   AF, *tr. by* Larry Rafferty, Meryl Natchez
and Tadeusz Pioro
Project for Freight Trains, A.   David Young.   GM
Project of Linear Inquiry, The.   Michael Palmer.   PmAP
Projected Scenario of a Performance to Be Given Before the UN.   Lawson
Fusao Inada.   FaBoA
Projection.   Langston Hughes.   PFTM-1
Projector O film still! Capitalist Projections.   Brenda Coultas.   HeMarv
Prokosch in Tehran, 1978.   Dominador I. Ilio.   ReBoTo
Prolegomenon to a Theodicy, A.   Kenneth Rexroth.
"Bell / Too softly and too slowly tolled, The."   PFTM-1
"Grammar of cause, The."   PFTM-1
Proletarian Portrait.   William Carlos Williams.   BLT; OxBoAm; SAmP
"Prolific and the Devourer," The.   W. H. Auden.
From "The Prolific and the Devourer."   GI
Prolog.   Paul Christensen.   TiP2 *Fr.* Houston: An Ode.
Prologomena to a Poetics.   Jerome Rothenberg.   PFTM-2
Prologue.   Miguel Algarin.   PueRic *Fr.* Angelitos Negros: A Salsa Ballet.
Prologue.   Oliver Wendell Holmes.   NCAP
Prologue.   William Langland.   NPeEn; OxBEV
Prologue.   Audre Lorde.   ESEAA
Prologue.   Archibald MacLeish.   MoAmPo
Prologue.   Ovid.   NAWM-7v1 *Fr.* Metamorphoses.
Prologue.   Milestone: The Birth of an Ancestor.   Eugene B. Redmond.   SpirFl
Prologue.   Virgil.   NAWM-5v1; NAWM-7v1 *Fr.* Aeneid [*or* Eneados *or*
Aeneis], The.
Prologue: "And the way goes on in the worn earth."   Archibald MacLeish.
NoAM *Fr.* Conquistador.
Prologue: "Editor, / Here are the lines my mind fathomed."   Dan Beachy-
Quick.   LegDan
Prologue: "Ends of all, who for the scene do write, The."   Ben Jonson.   ASA
Fr. Epicoene; or, The Silent Woman.
Prologue: "Exult each patriot heart!—this night is shewn."   Royall Tyler.
NAAL-3 *Fr.* Contrast, The.
Prologue: "I have come down."   Odia Ofeimun.   HBAPE; NAfrP
Prologue: "I wrote this when the sky was still serene."   Mihály Vörösmarty.
IQMS, *tr. by* Peter Zollman
Prologue: "Lord, can a crumb of dust the earth outweigh."   Edward Taylor.
NAAL-3; NAAL-5; NAAPv.1; TCAPo *Fr.* Preparatory Meditations Before
My Approach to the Lord's Supper.

Prologue: "Love, to give law unto his subject hearts." Sir Thomas Wyatt. ChIV-1 *Fr.* Penitential Psalms.

Prologue: "Obliterating face and hands." Hamish Henderson. EdScPo *Fr.* Elegies for the Dead in Cyrenaica.

Prologue: The rain fell hard on the Jacqueline Kennedy Onassis auction. Weather Report. Brenda Coultas. HeMarv

Prologue: "Under the shadow of the gloomy night." Samuel Rowlands. NOSC

Prologue: "We Who with Songs Beguile Your Pilgrimage." James Elroy Flecker. OBMV; UV *Fr.* Golden Journey to Samarkand, The.

Prologue at Sixty. W. H. Auden. NAMCP V.1

Prologue from Amboyna: "As needy gallants in the scriv'ners' hands." John Dryden. OBSV *Fr.* Amboyna; or, The Cruelties of the Dutch to the English Merchants.

Prologue in Heaven. Johann Wolfgang von Goethe. *Fr.* Faust.

Prologue Spoken by Mr[.] Garrick at the Opening of the Theatre in Drury Lane, 1747. Samuel Johnson. NAEL-6v1; NAEL-7v1; NoP-4; NoP-5; OxAEP-1

Prologue [Spoken by Mr. Horden]: "First Adventurer for her fame I stand, The." Delariviere Manley. EMWP *Fr.* Lost Lover, The.

Prologue, The: "To sing of wars, of captain[e]s, and of kings." Anne Bradstreet. BASC; BrAP; EMWP; NAAL-3; NAAL-5; NAAPv.1; NALW; NoP-4; NoP-5; OxBoAm; PEW; TCAPo

"I am obnoxious to each carping tongue." WoPoe

Prologue to a Comedy. Wisława Szymborska. MotU, *tr. by* Krystyna Piorkowski

Prologue to a Time That Is Not Itself. Eunice Odio. TCLAP, *tr. by* Martha Collins

Prologue to Hugh Kelly's *A Word to the Wise.* Samuel Johnson. NPeEn; OxAEP-1

Prologue to the Aetia. Callimachus. WoPoe, *tr. by* Stanley Lombardo and Diane Rayor

Prologue to The Collected Poems. Dylan Thomas. *See* Author's Prologue.

Prologues are over. It is a question, now, The. Asides on the Oboe. Wallace Stevens. MoAmPo

Prolonged horizontal pleasures. Q.E.D. Mary Low. SurWo

Prolonged Sonnet: When the Troops were Returning from Milan. Niccolò degli Albizzi. FaBoWar; OBVE; PoAgWa, *tr. by* Dante Gabriel Rossetti

Prom. Francine Witte. PfS

Promesa. Francisco Segovia. RMCMP

Prometheus. Lord Byron. OxAEP-2

Prometheus. Robert Horan. YaYoPo

Prometheus. Charles Tomlinson. HarvBoo

Prometheus: "As, when the squire and tinker, Wood." Jonathan Swift. WaAnP

Prometheus fashioned man. Michael Field. ViWPN

Prometheus Pyrphoros. Trumbull Stickney. Pandora's Songs. APN-2

Prometheus Unbound. Percy Bysshe Shelley. NAEL-6v2; NAEL-7v2; NOBRP

"There the voluptuous nightingales." OWoS

PROMETHEUS, when first from heaven high. Sir Edward Dyer. NoSic

Promiscuity. Lisa Fishman. AmPoNex

Promise! Mafika Pascal Gwala. NAfrP

Promise. Francisco Segovia. RMCMP, *tr. by* Michael Wiegers

Promise. Joe Wenderoth. BodElec

Promise, A. Teresa D. Cader. PfSP

Promise, The. Toi Derricotte. GT

Promise, The. Sharon Olds. ExTi

Promise, The. Heberto Padilla. TCLAP, *tr. by* Alexander Coleman and Alastair Reid

Promise, The ("I come the rushing wind that shook the place.") Jones Very. NCAP

Promise, The: "In the dream I had when he came back, not sick." Marie Howe. LaCa

Promise me no promises. Promises like Pie-Crust. Christina Georgina Rossetti. NAEL-6v2; NAEL-7v2; NPeEn

Promise me you will not forget Portofino. Portofino. Spencer Reece. LegDan

Promise of Peace. Robinson Jeffers. MoAmPo

Promise This, When You be Dying. Emily Dickinson. SWaP

Promise to California, A. Walt Whitman. APN-1

Promised Land, The. Jorge Fernández Granados. RMCMP, *tr. by* John Oliver Simon

Promises. Liz Lochhead. RSaN

Promises. Richard Shelton. GifTon

Promises. Robert Penn Warren.
Gold Glade. TRP
Infant Boy at Midcentury.
"When the century dragged, like a great wheel stuck at dead center." MoAmPo
Man in Moonlight.
Lullaby: Moonlight Lingers. GPTC
School Lesson Based on Word of Tragic Death of Entire Gillum Family. FuPo

Promises like Pie-Crust. Christina Georgina Rossetti. NAEL-6v2; NAEL-7v2; NPeEn

Promising Author. Carolyn Kizer. GeoHom

Promontory. Arthur Rimbaud. SxFrPo, *tr. by* Martin Sorrell

Promotion, The. James Tate. OxBoAm

Prompt sadness of Schumann and Tchaikovsky. From Bowling Green. Al Young. ESEAA

Prompting of my shadow, The. Roberto Juarroz. VCWP *Fr.* Seventh Vertical Poetry.

Prone. Edgar Allan Poe. STuOW *Fr.* For Annie.

Prone, I stretch myself upon a mountain where it's grassy. Elegy on a Broom Bush. Árpád Tóth. IQMS, *tr. by* Neville Masterman

Pronghorn's all four legs had caught in the fence & it had worn one side of its face, The. Matter. Michele Glazer. IAoNAP

Pronoun Woven. Derek Beaulieu. PoPra

Pronounced or heard, hid here in the late spring. Ian Patterson. VaPo *Fr.* Hardihood.

Pronouns, The—A Collection of 40 Dances—For the Dancers. Jackson Mac Low.
1st Dance—Making Things New—6 February 1964. FTOS; PFTM-2; PmAP
2nd Dance—Seeing Lines—6 February 1964. PFTM-2
6th Dance—Doing Things With Pencils—17–18 February 1964. PmAP
12th Dance—Getting Leather by Language—21 February 1964. PmAP
27th Dance—Walking—22 March 1964. FTOS

Proof. Brendan Kennelly. PBCIP

Proof, The. Richard Wilbur. InvLi; UpMys

Proof of Immortality. William Carlos Williams. PoA 2002

Proofs. Tadeusz Rózewicz. PoSu; StAl, *tr. by* Adam Czerniawski

Propaganda of the Poet, The. R. Williams Parry. BBMWP, *tr. by* Anthony Conran

Proper New Ballad Entitled [*or* Intituled] The Fairies' [*or* Faeryes] Farewell, or God-a-Mercy Will, A. Richard Corbet. BASC; NOSC; OxBEV; PBRV

Proper of Time, a brief history, a love story, A. (LL) Very Rich Hours, The. Nick Drake. BeAl; NeBl

Proper Schooling, A. Aonghas MacNeacail. EdScPo

Proper Song, Entitled: Fain Would I Have a Pretty Thing to Give unto My Lady, A. *Unknown.* NoSic

Proper way to eat a fig, in society, The. Figs. D. H. Lawrence. EroLit

Properties of a Good Greyhound, The. Dame Juliana Berners. DiBP; WoPoe, *tr. by* Seamus Heaney

Property. Robert Garioch. FaBoWar

Property of Benjamin. In Mr. Turner's Fields. Sam Cornish. OxAAAP

Properzia Rossi. Felicia Dorothea Hemans. NPBRoP; RWP; ViWPN; VWP

Prophecies or Memories or Display-Board Newspapers. Andrea Zanzotto. *tr. by* Gayle Ridinger
"Eva, forma futuri." ItPo, *tr. by* Gayle Ridinger

Prophecy. Donald Hall. NoP-5; OxBoAm

Prophecy. Elinor Wylie. ItWoWo

Prophecy, The. József Bajza. IQMS, *tr. by* Judith Kroll

Prophecy, The. Robert Wrigley. SwNoth

Prophecy from a severed ear. At the romance of sawdust and stuffing. [Basic system code]. Sandy Baldwin. AnSo

Prophecy of a Ten Ton Cheese. James McIntyre. VerBaPo

Prophecy of Famine, The. Charles Churchill.
"Oft have I heard thee mourn the wretched lot." OBSV
"Two boys, whose birth beyond all question springs." OBSV

Prophecy stopped; traffic started. (LL) When the Young Husband. Donald Hall. CAP-8; OxBoAm

Prophet. Tom Clark. OxBoAm

Prophet, The. Rose Drachler. TaR

Prophet Lost in the Hills at Evening, The. Joseph Hilaire Pierre Belloc. SacPr

Prophet stood, The. Psalm of Silk. Malachi. WaCA

Prophet tribe with burning eyes set forth, The. Gypsies on the Move. Charles Baudelaire. GS, *tr. by* Unknown

Prophet works hard at dreaming, The. Prophet, The. Rose Drachler. TaR

Prophetic Powers. *Unknown.* APN-2, *tr. by* Henry Rowe Schoolcraft

Prophetic Soul. Dorothy Parker. LW

Prophetissa. Diane Di Prima. PFTM-2

Prophet's Lantern, The. David Lehman. KGB

Prophets say to Know Thyself: I say it can't be done, The. Karl Shapiro. BodElec *Fr.* Bourgeois Poet, The.

Propinquity. Alastair Reid. EdScPo

Proportions of the Street, The. Ágnes Nemes Nagy. MotU, *tr. by* Bruce Berlind

Proposal. Maggie Nelson. HeMarv

Proposal. Bayard Taylor. TreFP

Proposed Elegy for Hart Crane. Merrill Gilfillan. AHA

Proposition. Robert Pinsky. NoAM *Fr.* Essay on Psychiatrists.

Proposition and Invocation. Homer. NOSC *Fr.* Iliad, The.

Propped against the crowded bar. Naima. Edward Kamau Brathwaite. WoPoe

Propped against the crowded bar. Trane. Edward Kamau Brathwaite. NAMCP V.2

Propped on tough bamboo. Third Time Wandering to Cloud Sluice Peak. Ching An. CSKM, *tr. by* Jerome P. Seaton

Props assist the House, The. Emily Dickinson. APN-2; GoPo; WPoS

Proputty, proputty, proputty—canter an' canter awaäy. (LL) Northern Farmer: New Style. Alfred Tennyson. NAEL-6v2; OBCoV; OxAEP-2

Proscenium Moon. Dave Brinks. AnSo

Prose 22. Michael Palmer. HarvBoo *Fr.* Series.

Prose 31. Michael Palmer. HarvBoo *Fr.* Series.

Prose du Transsibérien et de la Petite Jeanne de France. Blaise Cendrars.

"Autant d'images-associations que je ne peux pas développer dans mes vers." YaTCFP

"Dis, Blaise, sommes-nous bien loin de Montmartre?" YaTCFP

"En ce temps-là j'étais en mon adolescence." YaTCFP

"O Paris." YaTCFP

Prose for Des Esseintes. Donald Davie. OBVE

Prose for Two Voices. Jack Foley. CalPo

Prose of the Trans-Siberian and Little Jean of France. Blaise Cendrars. CuPo

Prose of the Trans-Siberian and of Little Jeanne of France, The. Blaise Cendrars. YaTCFP, *tr. by* Ron Padgett

Prose of the Trans-Siberian and of Little Jeanne of France, The. Blaise Cendrars.

"Back then I was still young." PFTM-1

Prose of the World Order. Jean Day. BAP-04

Prose Poem: "Morning coffee, The. I'm not sure why I drink it." Ron Padgett. NYP2

Prose Poem, The. Campbell McGrath. PoDa

Prose Poem, The. Roy Scheele. MotU

Prose Poems. Liz Rosenberg.

"Edith B——and her mother on a Sunday afternoon." UnSA

Prosecutor. William Baer. LiTh

Proserpine. Caitríona O'Reilly. NIrP

Proserpine and Dis. Ovid. NPeEn *Fr.* Metamorphoses.

Prospect. Ambrose Bierce. APN-2 *Fr.* Devil's Dictionary, The.

Prospect. Sydney Lea. PfSP

Prospect of a Landscape, Beginning with a Grove, The. Jane Barker. BASC

Prospect of Eden, The. John Milton. NAEL-6v1; NAWM-7v1; NoP-5; OxAEP-1 *Fr.* Paradise Lost.

Prospect of Heaven Makes Death Easy, A. Isaac Watts. NoP-4; NoP-5

Prospect of the Future, The. Mrs. Henry Linden. CBWP-4

Prospect of the Interior. Scott Cairns. UpMys

Prospect Park. David Schubert. APT-2

Prospect seen as false: the listening, The. Provisional. Reginald Shepherd. UrbNat

Prospecting. Margaret Avison. GPPA

Prospective Immigrants Please Note. Adrienne Rich. AmFaPo

Prospects. Anthony Hecht. ItP

Prospects. Tony Towle. PA9/11

Prospectus and Specimen of an Intended National Work by William and Robert Whistlecraft...Relating to King Arthur and His Round Table. John Hookham Frere.

"I've often wish'd that I could write a book." NOBRP

Prospectus to *The Recluse*. William Wordsworth. NAEL-6v2; NAEL-7v2 *Fr.* Recluse, The.

Prosper / O / cell. Ronald Johnson. APSN *Fr.* Ark.

Prospero. Michael Stillman. IaFF

Prospero kept the island as his heart. Heart-Shaped Island, A. J. P. Dancing Bear. IaFF

Prospero Listens to the Night. Jack Gilbert. BodElec

Prospice. Robert Browning. InoFa; ITBLP; NAEL-6v2; NAEL-7v2

Prostitutes at Smiller's Bar beside the dusty road, The. Cheerful Girls at Smiller's Bar, 1971, The. Jack A. Mapanje. HBAPE; NAfrP

Prostitute's Notebook, The. Leslie Burgess. PfS

Prostitute's shack, The. Issa. EH, *tr. by* Robert Hass

Prostrate from the heat the earth withdrew. Attraction. Georgi Rupchev. CSCBP, *tr. by* Georgi Belev and Lisa Sapinkopf

Protect Me, My Talisman. Milo De Angelis. NeIt, *tr. by* Lawrence Venuti

Protect the gleaming, battered soul of her. Faith #1. InTrad

Protected. I was bent. I Told Them I Should Be Here. Kate Schmitt. IJHIL

Protected Species. Susan Wicks. MFPA

Protected Venezuela, the rare, The. Lost Plaza Is Everywhere, The. Rafael Campo. AmPoNex

Protecting the Children from Hurricanes. Jean Nordhaus. PfSP

Protective and Defensive Devices. Mark Pawlak. PrTe

Protective instinct among the Emperor penguins, The. Penguins. Artur Miedzyrzecki. PoSu, *tr. by* John Batki and Artur Miedzyrzecki

Protest. Amal Al-Juburi. PoArWo, *tr. by* Salih J. Altoma

Protest. Romelia Alarcón de Folgar. TANSG, *tr. by* Alison Ridley

Protest at Los Alamos, August 2000. Judith Strasser. RWB

Protest Poem. Mendi Lewis Obadike. RD

Protest Poem. Vernon Scannell. OBCoV

Protest Poem, A. David Wright. ACAMVP

Protestant graveyard was a forbidden place, The. Weeping Headstones of the Isaac Becketts, The. Paul Durcan. PBCIP

Protestation. Bertrans de Born. WoPoe, *tr. by* John Peale Bishop

Protesting at the Nuclear Test Site. Denise Levertov. PoCoUp

Prothalamion. David Craig.

"Brother we are like weeds growing." UpMys

Prothalamion. Robert Silliman Hillyer.

"Hills turn hugely in their sleep, The." MoAmPo

Prothalamion. Edmund Spenser. BrAP; NoSic; NPeEn; OBEV; OxAEP-1; OxBEV; TFi; WoPoe

"With that I saw two swans of goodly hue [*or* hew]." OWoS

Prothalamium. Arthur James Marshall Smith. BrAP

Protocols. Randall Jarrell. AmWaPo

Proton Decay. Robert Pack. ColAP

Proud and beautiful city of Moscow, The. History Lessons. Seamus Deane. PBCIP; PNI

Proud Aristagoras, whose vineyard lacks. *Unknown.* PriapPo *Fr.* Priapus Poems, The.

Proud as Apollo on his forked hill. Alexander Pope. OBSV *Fr.* Epistle to Dr. Arbuthnot.

Proud associate told me, A. Fresno Truth, The. Lawson Fusao Inada. GeoHom

Proud Boast, A. Robert Burns. DiBP

Proud Egyptian [*or* Aegyptian] queen, her Roman guest, The. And She Washed His Feet with Her Tear[e]s, and Wiped Them with the Hairs of Her Head. Sir Edward Sherburne. NOSC

Proud fountains, wave your plumes. Fountains. Sir Osbert Sitwell. MoBrPo

Proud Hogen Mogen's, we will make you bow. On His Royal Highness His Expedition Against the Dutch. Elizabeth Polwhele. EMWP

Proud is my Magyar descent, far to eastward my lineage sprouted. Köcsey. Ferenc Kölcsey. IQMS, *tr. by* Watson Kirkconnell

Proud Lady, The. Robin Ernest William Flower. IrLP

Proud Ladye, The. Letitia Elizabeth Landon. NAEL-7v2

Proud Maisie is in the wood. Sir Walter Scott. CABP; NAEL-6v2; NAEL-7v2; NePenScot; NOBRP; OBEV; OxBEV; RACG; TFi *Fr.* Heart of Midlothian, The.

Proud, majestic Southern sun, The. Husband's Return, The. Priscilla Jane Thompson. CBWP-2

Proud Music of the Storm. Walt Whitman. APN-1

Proud *Paulus* late my secrecies revealing. Of honest Theft. To my good friend Master Samuel Daniel. Sir John Harington. PBRV

Proud Preston poor people. Preston. *Unknown.* FaBoVe

Proud Queen of the Earth Gods, Supreme Among the Heaven Gods. *Unknown.* HW *Fr.* Loud Thundering Storm.

Proud Riders. Harold Lenoir Davis. APT-2

Proud Shore For Legends, A. Nicki Jackowska. RSaN

Proud word you never spoke, but you will speak. Walter Savage Landor. OBEV *Fr.* Ianthe.

Proudly and peacefully[!]. (LL) Sword of Robert Lee, The. Abram Joseph Ryan. CBCWP; PCW

Proudly swept the rain by the cliffs. Aloha'oe. Queen Lili'u-o-ka-lani. SWaP

Proust's Madeleine. Kenneth Rexroth. NAMCP V.1; NoAM; TRP

Prove It on Me Blues. Gertrude "Ma." Rainey. NAAPv.2

Provenance. Joseph Stroud. PoChi

Proverb. Kenneth Koch. OxBoAm

Proverb, XXX. John Hall. ChIV-1

Proverbial Advice on Marriage. *Unknown.* NBLV

Proverbial Philosophy. William Blake. DiBP *Fr.* Auguries of Innocence.

Proverbs. Bible, *O.T.*
  Happy he who has found wisdom. HW

Proverbs. Teresa de Jesús. AF, *tr. by* Maria Proser, Arlene Scully *and* James Scully

Proverbs, aphorisms, epigrams. Inverse Proportions. Jack Matthews. PoA 2002

Proverbs from Purgatory. Lloyd Schwartz. PtR

Proverbs of Hell. William Blake. *Fr.* Marriage of Heaven and Hell, The.

Proverbs 6:6. David Curzon. ChIV-1
  (Midrashim: Proverbs 6:6.) WoPoe

Provide, Provide. Robert Frost. APT-1; ChIV-1; HarvBoo; NAMCP V.1; NoAM; NoP-4; NoP-5; OxBoAm; TFi; WeW-3; WoPoe

Providence. George Herbert. BASC
  "O sacred Providence, who from end to end." AngWePo

Providence heavenly passeth living thought. Edmund Spenser. NAEL-6v1; NAEL-7v1 *Fr.* Faerie Queene, The.

Providence Journal V: Israel of Puerto Rico. Afaa Michael Weaver. SpirFl

Province of the Saved, The. Emily Dickinson. TRP

Provinces. C. D. Wright. AmAlph

Provincial Adolescence, A. Michael Foley. PNI

Provincial Sundays. Ramón López Velarde. TCLAP, *tr. by* Julián Manríquez

Proving again that posture is everything. Helicopter Wrecked on a Hill. Christine Hume. BAP-97

Provision a ship for me like a great idea. Miraculous Ship, The. Delmira Agustini. TCLAP, *tr. by* Karl Kirchwey

Provisional. Reginald Shepherd. UrbNat

Provisional Measures. Charles Stein. AHA

Provisionally. Ken Edwards. Oth

Prowling wolf, whose shaggy skin, A. Wolf and the Dog, The. Jean de La Fontaine. OBVE, *tr. by* Elizur Wright

Prows O' Reekie, The. Lewis Spence. NePenScot

Proximities. Robert Pollok. STuOW *Fr.* Course of Time, The.

Proximity. C. Dale Young. LegDan

Prue, my dearest maid, is sick. Upon Prudence Baldwin Her Sickness[e]. Robert Herrick. BASC

Pruned. Misere. Ifigenija Simonovic. PoCu, *tr. by* Anthony Rudolf

Pruned Tree, The. Howard Moss. BeAl; VCAP

Pruner, The. John Oxenham. SacPr

Pruning. Jim Wilson. EdScPo

Prurito. Pedro Serrano. RMCMP

Pruzzian Elegy. Johannes Bobrowski. AF

Prytherch is dead. We have no right. Dai, Live. Jon Dressel. AngWePo

Psalm. Tudor Arghezi. AF, *tr. by* Andrei Bantas *and* Thomas Amherst Perry

Psalm. Lucian Blaga. PFTM-1

Psalm. Paul Celan. WoPoe, *tr. by* Margaret Guillemin and Katherine Washburn

Psalm: "In the small beauty of the forest." George Oppen. APT-2; CalPo; HarvBoo; ItP; NAMCP V.1; OxBoAm; PFTM-2; PoCho; WoPoe

Psalm: "Lord feeds some of His prisoners better than others, The." Reed Whittemore. GoPo

Psalm: "No one kneads us again out of earth and clay." Paul Celan. GTCP; PoetW; PoSu, *tr. by* John Felstiner

Psalm: "No one moulds us again out of earth and clay." Paul Celan. BBASP; HP; OBVE, *tr. by* Michael Hamburger

Psalm: "Psalm on the day, A." Yehuda Amichai. BBASP, *tr. by* Chana Bloch

Psalm: "That from the seed of men." Peter Huchel. AF; AtGh, *tr. by* Daniel S. Simko

Psalm: The New Day. Mark Jarman. AWTN

Psalm: "You've been a long time making up your mind." Charles Simic. StAl

Psalm 1. Genrik Veniaminovich Sapgir. ItGoST, *tr. by* J. Kates

Psalm 2. Mahmoud Darwish. AF, *tr. by* Denys Johnson-Davies

Psalm III: "To God: to illuminate all men. Beginning with Skid Road." Allen Ginsberg. ChIV-1

Psalm 5: "Give ear to my words, O Lord." Ernesto Cardenal. PLBUT; TCLAP, *tr. by* Robert Marquez

Psalm 6: A Psalm of Abraham, Concerning That Which He Beheld Upon The Heavenly Scarp. Abraham Moses Klein. *See* Upon the Heavenly Scarp.

Psalm 8. Bible, *O.T.* InvLi *Fr.* Psalms.

Psalm 23. Bible, *O.T.* InvLi *Fr.* Psalms.

Psalm 23: "Lord to me [*or* mee] a shepherd is, The." *Unknown.* TCAPo *Fr.* Bay Psalm Book, The.

Psalm 50. Bible, *O.T. Fr.* Psalms.

Psalm 52. Quid Gloriaris? Bible, *O.T.* BASC; PBRV *Fr.* Psalms.

Psalm 57. Miserere Mei Deus. Bible, *O.T.* EMWP; PEW *Fr.* Psalms.

Psalm 58: "Do ye, o congregation." Bible, *O.T.* NoP-4; NoP-5, *tr. by Unknown*

Psalm 58: "Judges, who rule the world by laws." Bible, *O.T.* NoP-4; NoP-5, *tr. by* Isaac Watts

Psalm 58. Si Vere Utique. Bible, *O.T.* BASC; NoP-4; NoP-5; NPeEn; PEW *Fr.* Psalms.

Psalm 58: "Ye congregation of the tribes." Bible, *O.T.* NoP-4; NoP-5 *Fr.* Translation of the Psalms of David, A.

Psalm 72. Deus Judicium. Mary Sidney Herbert, Countess of Pembroke. EMWP *Fr.* Psalms.

Psalm 74. Ut Quid, Deus. Bible, *O.T.* BASC *Fr.* Psalms.

Psalm 84. Bible, *O.T.* CABP *Fr.* Psalms.

Psalm 89. Misericordias. Bible, *O.T. Fr.* Psalms.

Psalm 92. Bonum Est Confiteri. Bible, *O.T.* PEW *Fr.* Psalms.

Psalm 100. Bible, *O.T.* CABP *Fr.* Psalms.

Psalm 114. Bible, *O.T.* NoP-5, *tr. by Unknown*

Psalm 114: *In Exitu Israel.* Mary Sidney Herbert, Countess of Pembroke. NoP-5 *Fr.* Psalms.

Psalm 114: "When Israel came from Egypt's coast." Bible, *O.T.* NoP-5 *Fr.* Translation of the Psalms of David, A.

Psalm 114: "When Isr'el, freed from Pharoh's hand." Bible, *O.T.* NoP-5, *tr. by* Isaac Watts

Psalm 117. Laudate Dominum. Bible, *O.T.* ChIV-1; OxBEV *Fr.* Psalms.

Psalm 120. Ad Dominum. Bible, *O.T.* BASC; OxBEV *Fr.* Psalms.

Psalm 121: "I to the hills lift up mine eyes." *Unknown.* GoPo *Fr.* Bay Psalm Book, The.

Psalm 130. De Profundis. Mary Sidney Herbert, Countess of Pembroke. EMWP *Fr.* Psalms.

Psalm 130. De profundis clamavi. Bible, *O.T.* OxBEV *Fr.* Psalms.

Psalm 137. Genrik Veniaminovich Sapgir. ItGoST, *tr. by* J. Kates

Psalm 137. *Unknown.* WoPoe, *tr. by* Miles Coverdale

Psalm 137: "Along the banks where Babel's current flows." [*with music*]. Bible, *O.T.* ChIV-1, *tr. by* Joel Barlow

Psalm 139. Domine, Probasti. Bible, *O.T.* PEW *Fr.* Psalms.

Psalm 142. Voce mea ad Dominum. Bible, *O.T.* PBRV *Fr.* Psalms.

Psalm Against Psalms. Andrew Hudgins.
  "Isaiah ate the blood-red ember." UpMys

Psalm and Lament. Donald Justice. CAP-8; GPTC

Psalm before Sleep. Peter Cooley. Vesp

Psalm: "Each now dropped / Lay your hands upon me, you in the black bent grass, the body in motion." Catherine Imbriglio. IAoNAP

Psalm for Amadou Diallo. Jack Agüeros. PrTe

Psalm for an Anniversary. Grace Schulman. PoA 2002

Psalm for Christmas Day. Thomas Pestel. SacPr

Psalm for Distribution. Jack Agüeros. PrTe

Psalm for the Damnation of Pig Pino Oink Ochet, Who Unlike His Victims Will Neither Die nor Disappear, Because He Was Never Human. Jack Agüeros. PrTe

Psalm for the Next Millennium. Jack Agüeros. PrTe

Psalm of Life, A. Henry Wadsworth Longfellow. AmFaPo; APN-1; BRP; ITBLP; ItP; NAAL-3; NAAL-5; NAAPv.1; TCAPo

"Psalm of Life" for thee is o'er, The. Longfellow. Henrietta Cordelia Ray. CBWP-3

Psalm of Silk. Malachi. WaCA

Psalm on the day, A. Psalm. Yehuda Amichai. BBASP, *tr. by* Chana Bloch

Psalm to the Creatures. Gwilym R. Jones. OBWVE, *tr. by* Joseph P. Clancy

Psalm (Traherne). Dan Beachy-Quick. LegDan

Psalme 91. Bible, *O.T.* NPeEn, *tr. by* Thomas Carew

Psalms. Bible, *O.T. tr. by* Christopher Smart
  Psalm 8. NAWM-5v1
  Psalm 19. NAWM-5v1
  Psalm 23. BLPJKO; NAWM-5v1; NIL-7; NIP-4; TFi; WaAnP
  Psalm 100. WaAnP
  Psalm 104. NAWM-5v1
  Psalm 121. WaAnP
  Psalm 137. NAWM-5v1

Psalms. Bible, *O.T. tr. by* Sir Thomas Wyatt
  Psalm 130. De profundis clamavi. OxBEV, *tr. by* Sir Thomas Wyatt

Psalms. Bible, *O.T. tr. by* New Revised Standard Version
  Psalm 23. InvLi, *tr. by* New Revised Standard Version
  Psalm 50. *tr. by* New Revised Standard Version
    "Hear, O my people, and I will speak." InvLi, *tr. by* New Revised Standard Version
  Psalm 8. InvLi, *tr. by* New Revised Standard Version

Psalms (Chapter 137, Verse 5-6). Manuela Fingueret. MirDau, *tr. by* Roberta Gordenstein

Psalms [David Rosenberg Adaption]. Bible, *O.T.*
  Psalm 6. AHA
  Psalm 36. AHA
  Psalm 58. AHA
  Psalm 90. AHA
  Psalm 139. AHA

Psalms. Bible, *O.T. tr. by* Mary Sidney Herbert, Countess of Pembroke
Psalm 58. Si Vere Utique. BASC; NoP-4; NoP-5; NPeEn; PEW, *tr. by* Mary Sidney Herbert, Countess of Pembroke
Psalm 100. CABP, *tr. by* Mary Sidney Herbert, Countess of Pembroke
Psalm 114: *In Exitu Israel.* NoP-5
Psalm 117. Laudate Dominum. ChIV-1; OxBEV, *tr. by* Mary Sidney Herbert, Countess of Pembroke
Psalm 120. Ad Dominum. BASC; OxBEV, *tr. by* Mary Sidney Herbert, Countess of Pembroke
Psalm 130. De Profundis. EMWP
Psalm 139. Domine, Probasti. PEW, *tr. by* Mary Sidney Herbert, Countess of Pembroke
"Each inmost peece in me is thine." NPeEn, *tr. by* Mary Sidney Herbert, Countess of Pembroke
Psalm 142. Voce mea ad Dominum. PBRV, *tr. by* Mary Sidney Herbert, Countess of Pembroke
Psalm 52. Quid Gloriaris? BASC; PBRV, *tr. by* Mary Sidney Herbert, Countess of Pembroke
Psalm 57. Miserere Mei Deus. EMWP; PEW, *tr. by* Mary Sidney Herbert, Countess of Pembroke
Psalm 72. Deus Judicium. EMWP
Psalm 74. Ut Quid, Deus. BASC, *tr. by* Mary Sidney Herbert, Countess of Pembroke
Psalm 84. CABP, *tr. by* Mary Sidney Herbert, Countess of Pembroke
Psalm 89. Misericordias. *tr. by* Mary Sidney Herbert, Countess of Pembroke
"Gods boundles bownties gods promise ever abyding." PBRV, *tr. by* Mary Sidney Herbert, Countess of Pembroke
Psalm 92. Bonum Est Confiteri. PEW, *tr. by* Mary Sidney Herbert, Countess of Pembroke
Psalter of Avram Haktani, The. Abraham Moses Klein.
(Psalm 6: A Psalm of Abraham, Concerning That Which He Beheld Upon The Heavenly Scarp.) BrAP
Upon the Heavenly Scarp. PoA 2002
Pseudo slammer. Camille Martin. AnSo *Fr.* No truck.
"Psittachus Eois Imitatrix Ales ab Indis." Sacheverell Sitwell. MoBrPo
Psst! / Eh* *bonjour** kids**. Psst! Oliver Cadiot. YaTCFP, *tr. by* the author and Charles Bernstein
Psyche. Mary Tighe.
Canto 1.
Glimpse of Love, A. NOBRP
Canto 2.
Psyche's Return to the Palace of Love. NOBRP
Canto 6.
Dreams of Delight, Farewell. NOBRP
"Let not the rugged brow the rhymes accuse." NoP-4; RWP
Psyche and Eros in Florida. Debora Greger. PoA 2002
Psyche, Before the Tribunal of Venus. Nathaniel Parker Willis. APN-1
Psyche Revised. Rhina P. Espaillat. PoDa
Psyche's Return to the Palace of Love. Mary Tighe. NOBRP *Fr.* Psyche.
Psychiatrist's Song. Louise Bogan. NAAPv.2
Psychic Killed by Train. Ron Overton. PrTe
Psychoalphadiscobetabioaquadoloop, A. Thomas Sayers Ellis. BRtP
Psychologia Christiana. Mihály Babits. IQMS, *tr. by* Peter Zollman
Psychology. Muddle, A. Steve Jonas. EGAG
Psychopathology of Everyday Life, The. William Matthews. NIP-4
Psychotherapy. Nasri Hajjaj. Eno, *tr. by* Ibrahim Muhawi
Psychozoia, or, the Life of the Soul. Henry More.
Contrition. NOSC
Pub empties out, the moon sets. The stars, The. Time Now Please. Adriann Roland Holst. TuT, *tr. by* Paula Meehan
Pub empties, the moon is down, The. Time, Please. Adriann Roland Holst. TuT, *tr. by* Sean Dunne
Pub is the place where good comrades are found, The. Drinking Song. Randall Swingler. RSaN
Public Aid for Niagara Falls. Morris Gilbert Bishop. NBLV
Public Beach (Long Island Sound). Christopher Darlington Morley. NBLV
Public Beach No. 2. Andrey Andreievich Voznesensky. RusPo, *tr. by* Robert Arthur Douglas Ford
Public Broadcast. Philip Booth. PoDa
Public Dinner, A. Thomas Hood. OBCoV
Public Garden, The. Robert Lowell. BrAP; OBGa
Public Garden with a Weeping Tree. Mary Ruefle. AmAlph
Public has no belief, The. Obbligato from a Public Gallery. Jared Angira. NAfrP
Public house screaming. Drunk Man, The. *Unknown.* NOBAu
Public Journal. Phyllis McGinley. NBLV
Public Outcry. Karen Alkalay-Gut. DTA
Public Place (After Olga Broumas), The. Achy Obejas. WiU

Public Prayer. Delmira Agustini. TANSG, *tr. by* Mark McCaffrey
Public Radio Plays Eddie Harris. A. Van Jordan. LegDan
Public School No. 18: Paterson, New Jersey. Maria Gillan. UnSA
Public servant of men's private parts, The. Richard Murphy. ModIr *Fr.* Price of Stone, The.
Public Spirit of the Women, The. *Unknown.* NAAPv.1
Public Stammer, The. Ron Schreiber. PrTe
Publication Date. Franz Wright. AmAlph
Publication—is the Auction. Emily Dickinson. APN-2; GoPo; NAAL-3; NAAPv.1; NALW; NCAP; NoP-4; NoP-5; OxBoAm; TCAPo
Publications Law. Yi Sang. CAMKP, *tr. by* Edward Mack
Publicity. (LL) Mouth, The. Ciaran Carson. ModIr; PNI
Publick Fast on Account of the Afflicted: March 31, 1692. Nicole Cooley. NeAmPo
Public's darling Quintia, first-class, The. *Unknown.* PriapPo *Fr.* Priapus Poems, The.
Puck of Pook's Hill. Rudyard Kipling.
Centurion of the Thirtieth, A.
Cities and Thrones and Powers. BrAP; NOxBChV
Knights of the Joyous Venture, The.
Harp Song of the Dane Women. HarvBoo; NAMCP V.1; RACG
Old Men at Pevensey. NoAM
Runes on Weland's Sword, The. NoAM
On the Great Wall.
Song to Mithras, A. NoAM
Winged Hats, The.
Pict Song, A. NAMCP V.1; NoAM
Puckered breasts like Leiberman's. Grandma in the Shower. Dale M. Kushner. UnSA
Puddle. Ryoko Shindo. CFP, *tr. by* Aoyami Miyuki and Leza Lowitz
Puddock sat by the lochan's brim, A. Puddock, The. John M. Caie. EdScPo
Puddock, The. John M. Caie. EdScPo
Pudeur Française, La. Edward Young. STuOW *Fr.* Night Thoughts.
Pueblo. Luis Palés Matos. TCLAP, *tr. by* Barry Luby
Puente. Americo Casiano. BRtP
Puente de mi soledad. Canción. Emilio Prados. RaW
Pueril. Gerardo Deniz. RMCMP
Puerta, La. Carlos Bousoño. RaW
Puerta Rica. Víctor Hernández Cruz. LoL
Puerto Rican Girls of French Hill, The. Sean Thomas Dougherty. AmPoNex
Puerto Rican girls, The / of French Hill. Puerto Rican Girls of French Hill, The. Sean Thomas Dougherty. AmPoNex
Puerto Rico 1974. This Is Not the Place Where I was Born. Miguel Piñero. PueRic
Puerto Rico Made in Japan. Jose Angel Figueroa. PueRic
Puerto Rico / You lovely island. America. Stephen Sondheim. ReLy
Puertoricanness. Aurora Levins Morales. PueRic
Puff of east wind ruffles, A. Yun Sŏndo. CATKP *Fr.* Angler's Calendar, The.
Puff the magic dragon lived by the sea. Puff the Magic Dragon. Lenny Lipton. ASA
Puffball appears on the hill, The. In Praise of the Puffball. Nancy Willard. PfSP
Puffed up promises. Promises. Liz Lochhead. RSaN
Puffy Jacket. Amy Fusselman. HeMarv
Puir Jamie's killed. A better lad. Fisher Jamie. John, 1st Baron Tweedsmuir Buchan. EdScPo
Puis tel soir de septembre après tous ces jours lumineux. Distance de l'Automne. Jacques Réda. YaTCFP
Pulil Hermitage. Chunghur Hyujung. BecRai, *tr. by* Kim Daljin, Kim Won-Chung and Christopher Merrill
Pulkovo Meridian, The. Vera Inber. *tr. by* Alexander Kaun and Dorothea Prall Radin
"Teeth are bared, the mouth drawn tight, the face, The." FaBoWar, *tr. by* Alexander Kaun and Dorothea Prall Radin
Pull / a / rope. Careful! *Unknown.* SonAtl, *tr. by* Haike Frank and Abioseh Michael Porter
Pull out the tractor and rev her up. Wolf Packet and Rural America. Matthew Wascovich. BeDoSh
Pull over. Your car with its slow. Quivira City Limits. Kevin Young. FuFl; NeAmPo
Pull the car off here. Loving Along Western Rivers. Stephen J. Lyons. PasH
Pulled as I was down phlegmatic Rivers. Drunken Boat, The. Arthur Rimbaud. ConPit, *tr. by* Clayton Eshleman
Pulled from our ruts by the made-to-order gale. Trans Canada. Francis Reginald Scott. BrAP

Pulley, The. George Herbert. BASC; BBASP; BrAP; ChIV-1; FSCP; HeIP-4; InvLi; NAEL-6v1; NAEL-7v1; NoP-4; NoP-5; NOSC; OBEV; OxAEP-1; TFi; WaAnP

 (Gifts of God, The.) TreFP

Pulling a Pig's Tail. Dave Jeddie Smith. PfSP

Pulling in the Nets. C. Mikal Oness. GeoHom

Pulling in the Reins. Yoshimasu Gōzō. PFTM-2, tr. by Richard Arno

Pulling the Chain. Simon Rae. UV

Pulling the Ivy. Julia Copus. MFPA

Pulling up flax after the blue flowers have fallen. Linen Industry, The. Michael Longley. IrLP; ModIr; NoP-4; NoP-5; PBCIP; PNI; StAl

Pulling up / My robes, I draw magic water. Given to Master Ch'ing-lun of Hsia Mountain. Chien Chang. CSKM, tr. by Paul Hansen

Pulls rabbits out of hats. Great Mutando, The. Deryn Rees-Jones. TCAWP

Pulp Fiction. David Baker. MAAN

Pulpit tulips. Easter Pome. B. P. Nichol. OpeFie

Pulsations. Marvin Bell. PfSP

Pulse. Jane Holland. MFPA

Pulse, The. Martha Kapos. Prnts

Pulse, The. Mark Van Doren. MoAmPo

Pulse, The. So. When I take it now the microsystem wild card is almost. Fred Wah. NLPA Fr. This Dendrite Map: Father / Mother Haibun.

Pulse of your revolt stilled, The. My Friendly People. Frank Mkalawile Chipasula. HBAPE

Puma called asking me to remind you. Rosa. Miguel Algarin. PueRic

Pumping Iron. Diane Ackerman. MoASP

Pumpkins. Tim Lilburn. OpeFie

Pumpkins rove the ground, The. In Hecate's Garden. Ziporah Hildebrandt. HW

Punch and Judy. Rose Fyleman. NOxBChV

'Punch,' said Judy. Punch and Judy. Rose Fyleman. NOxBChV

Punch, the Immortal Liar. Conrad Potter Aiken.

 Puppet Dreams, The. MoAmPo

Punctilio. Mary Elizabeth Coleridge. OBEV; PoBW

Punctually at Christmas the soft plush. White Christmas. William Robert Rodgers. MoBrPo

Puncture Near Wittedrif. Gus Ferguson. ArBi

Puncture Wounds: A Baiku. Rowena M. Love. ArBi

Pungent bloom against your shade, A. (LL) O Florida, Venereal Soil. Wallace Stevens. NAAPv.2; TCAPo

Punica, The. Catius As Conius Silius Italicus. tr. by Marcus Wilson

 "At the city's heart stood the shrine to Dido's ghost." RomPo, tr. by Marcus Wilson

 "Death comes in strange forms and contrasting images." RomPo, tr. by Marcus Wilson

 "Furiously along the banks stormed Hannibal." RomPo, tr. by Marcus Wilson

 "Give me Maeonian Homer's resonant tongue." RomPo, tr. by Marcus Wilson

 "Horses which Titan when discharged for the night, The." RomPo, tr. by Marcus Wilson

 "Memories of past struggles were expelled by fear." RomPo, tr. by Marcus Wilson

Punishing God has taken all content. To His Wife. Fyodor Ivanovich Tyutchev. OxBEV, tr. by Henry Gifford and Charles Tomlinson

Punishment. Seamus Heaney. EmeKit; EMP; NAEL-6v2; NAEL-7v2; NAMCP V.2; NoAM; NoP-4; NoP-5; OxAEP-2; PBCIP; PoPoPo; WaAnP

Punishments. Rafael Alberti. AF, tr. by Geoffrey Connell

Punk. Kenneth Goldsmith.

 "One pair ridiculous gorilla slippers; 3 pairs of cheap shit sunglasses." HeMarv

Punk Pantoum. Pamela Stewart. ReTh

Punt gliding under a chain of smiles, A. Tilla Brading. NewEx

3. Punta Blanca. Pamela Alexander. AmAlph Fr. Foxlight.

Punziplaze karmasokist DecoYen Pompieraeian. Purplexicon of Dissynthegrations, A. Abraham Lincoln Gillespie. APT-2

Pupa of pain, I sat and lay one July, A. Mockingbird Month. Mona Van Duyn. OWoS

Pupil, The. Donald Justice. GoPo; PoCho

Puppet diseases are tiny and thread-like, with funereal fur coats and huge ears. Teaching About Disease. Miroslav Holub. MotU, tr. by Dana Hábová and David Young

Puppet Dreams, The. Conrad Potter Aiken. MoAmPo Fr. Punch, the Immortal Liar.

Puppet of the Wolf, The. Margaret Atwood. NoAM

Puppy Called Puberty, A. Adrian Mitchell. StAl

Pups and the Alligator, The. "Peter Pindar." DiBP

Pups and the Fish, The. Jean Ingelow. DiBP Fr. Brothers, and a Sermon.

Purcell in many victories of his. Bounty. Josephine Miles. NoAM

Purchase, The. Clarence Major. TAPaP

Purdah, 1. Imtiaz Dharker. NeBl

Pure air trembles, O pitiless God, The. Noon. Robinson Jeffers. MoAmPo

Pure amnesia of her face, The. August, Los Angeles, Lullaby. Carol Muske-Dukes. PBCAP; PtR

Pure and Applied. Gig Ryan. VaPo

Pure and worthy Mrs. Stowe, The. Dorothy Parker. NALW Fr. Pig's-Eye View of Literature, A.

Pure as a pane of ice. It's a gift. (LL) Love Letter. Sylvia Plath. LW; PtR

Pure blood domestic, guaranteed. Prize Cat, The. Edwin John Pratt. BrAP

Pure breeze billows bed-curtains and blinds, A. Emotion. Zhang Hua. CCL1, tr. by John Frodsham

Pure brush-clover / Basket of flowers. Ōshima Ryōta. ZenPo, tr. by Takashi Ikemoto and Lucien Stryk

Pure contralto sings in the organloft, The. Walt Whitman. FaBoA Fr. Song of Myself.

Pure Dust. Maria Luisa Spaziani. NeIt, tr. by Beverly Allen

Pure Hypothesis, A. May Kendall. VWP

Pure Loneliness, The. Michael Ryan. BodElec

Pure nothing, in the middle of the day. (LL) Daystar. Rita Dove. AmFaPo; BeAl; NIL-7; NIP-4; OxWW

Pure Pop. Allison Joseph. NeAmPo

Pure products of America, The. To Elsie. William Carlos Williams. AmFaPo; APT-1; NAAL-5; NAAPv.2; NAMCP V.1; OxBoAm; PoPoPo; StAl

Pure Sound Pavilion. Wang Shih-chieng. ColAnChi, tr. by Richard John Lynn

Pure Sound Pavilion of the Riverside Temple, The. Muso Soseki. EaWin, tr. by W. S. Merwin

Pure stream, in whose transparent wave. To Leven Water. Tobias Smollett. OBEV

Pure sun dazzled, The. Glazier, The. Stéphane Mallarmé. OBVE, tr. by Keith Bosley

Pure sunlight is strewn all over the lawn. Saturday Afternoon, October. Jonathan Holden. OPRER

Pure Talk. Yi Chinmyŏng. EcSo, tr. by Carolyn U. So

Pure? What does it mean? Fever 103°. Sylvia Plath. NAMCP V.2; NoAM; OxBoAm; PoA 2002; VCAP

Pure white plum blossoms. Buson. SoOfWa, tr. by Sam Hamill

Pure Wife, A. Yan Yanzhi. CCL1, tr. by Anne Birrell

Purest Rage, The. Charles Baxter. SwNoth

Purgatorio. Hart Crane. PoA 2002

Purgatory Chasm. Timothy Donnelly. PoDa

Purification. Doug Anderson. AmWaPo

Purification, A. Wendell Berry. TWF; UpMys

Purist, The. Ogden Nash. MoAmPo; NBLV

Puritan, The. Karl Shapiro. MoAmPo

Puritan against the Wind. Gus Ferguson. ArBi

Puritan Lady, A. Lizette Woodworth Reese. NeAmPo

Puritan Sonnet. Elinor Wylie. MoAmPo Fr. Wild Peaches.

Puritan Way of Death, The. David Baker. Vesp

Puritans. Elaine Equi. PmAP

Puritan's Ballad, The. Elinor Wylie. OxBoAm

Purity of heart is to will one thing. Numerology. David Wheatley. NIrP

PURITY! PURITY! PURITY! Fanny Beznos. SurWo, tr. by Myrna Bell Rochester

Purple. Lullaby "Purple." Eve Merriam. NOxBChV

Purple Blouse. Dan Chiasson. PoCho

Purple & blue Tiffany combo in the. Call for Vertical Integration in the Eye of the Storm, A. Lee Ann Brown. VaPo

Purple Clover. Emily Dickinson. MoAmPo

Purple Cow, The. Frank Gelett Burgess. ASA; BRP; CalPo; NBLV; NTCP; OBCoV; TCAPo; TFi; TLR

Purple Cow, The: Suite. Frank Gelett Burgess. See also Cinq Ans Après.

Purple Cow, The: Suite. Frank Gelett Burgess. CalPo

Purple flowers. Revelation. Natalia Toledo. RMCMP, tr. by Alberto A. Ríos

Purple headland over yonder. Afternoon. Louisa Sarah Bevington. PEW

Purple is the Color of Longing. David Steinberg. PasH

Purple Island, The. Phineas Fletcher.

 (Triumph of the Church, The.) SacPr

 "With her, her sister went, a warlike maid." NOSC

Purple Loosestrife. Ann Townsend. ExTi; NeAmPo

Purple moorstream all down the mountain. Landscape without a Hat. Bobi Jones. ATSWP, tr. by Robert Minhinnick

Purple pill rattles, The. Antidepressant. Adrienne Su. AmPoNex

Purple red brocades. November 1st. Jessica Freeman. AnSo

Purple sleep of the golden wheatfield. Poppies. Yolanda Bedregal. TANSG, tr. by Carolyne Wright

Purple Spot, The. Ramón López Velarde. BLPSL, tr. by Rene de Costa, Rigas Kappatos and Eleni Paidoussi

Purple Thought, The. Houda Al-Na'mani. PoArWo, tr. by Richard McKane

Purple towel on Grove, down comforter on South Davenport. Firsts in No Particular Order. Kimiko Hahn. NevBe

Purple Valleys, The. Madison Cawein. APN-2

Purple William or The Liar's Doom. A. E. Housman. NOxBChV

Purplexicon of Dissynthegrations, A. Abraham Lincoln Gillespie. APT-2

Purpose. Desmond O'Grady. PBCIP

Purpose. Diane Seuss. SweBea

Purpose of Altar Boys, The. Alberto A. Ríos. FTtHH

Purpose of Design Is to Make the Whole Greater Than the Sum of Its Parts, The. Michele Glazer. IAoNAP

Purpose of Nuns, The. Judith Ortiz Cofer. TouFir

Purpose of the blanket, The. Snow. Elizabeth Robinson. IIR

Purpose than that it might be good. (LL) Failing in the Presence of Ants. Gary Soto. CAP-8; PoA 2002

Purposes, to himself, in a broken sleep. (LL) House on a Cliff. Louis MacNeice. HarvBoo; ModIr; NPeEn

Purr, The. Molly Peacock. ExTi; PasH

Purse, A. Gertrude Stein. TCAPo Fr. Tender Buttons.

Purse be full again, or else I must die. This is the wish. That Been to Me My Lives Light and Saviour. Susan Wheeler. ExTi

Purse was not green, it was not straw color, it was hardly seen and, A. Gertrude Stein. TCAPo Fr. Tender Buttons.

Purse-Seine, The. Robinson Jeffers. AmFaPo; NAAPv.2; NAMCP V.1; NoAM; NoP-4; NoP-5; WeW-3

Purse-Seiner Atlantis, The. Agha Shahid Ali. AmAlph

Pursued by one nun or another. Class Bully. Thomas Reiter. SwNoth

Pursuing beauty, men descry. Song. Thomas Southerne. NOSC

Pursuit. Robert Penn Warren. FuPo; MoAmPo

Pursuit[e], The. Henry Vaughan. AngWePo; NOSC; SacPr

Pusey Hughes, a low-grade voter. Unfortunate Occurrence at Cwm-Cadno. A. G. Prys-Jones. AngWePo

Push the boat out, campañeros. At Eighty. Edwin Morgan. PoCu

Push the Feathered Glory. Jennifer Timoner. ICANM

Pushing. Christopher Gilbert. LTA; SoSe-8

Pushing Forty. Alison Fell. EdScPo

Pushing the seed into the ground. Listening to a White Man Play the Blues. Silvia Curbelo. TouFir

Pushing up through smoke. Flames. Tōge Sankichi. FaBoWar, tr. by Richard H. Minear

Push-Pull of This Love, The. Susan Spady. FiBr

Pussies are not gods. They are created beings. Notes for a Sermon on the Mount. Nin Andrews. BAP-01

Puszta in Winter,The. Sándor Petőfi. IQMS, tr. by Watson Kirkconnell

Put a blade of grass between your lips! It too is the Son of God. Blade of Grass, A. Otto Orban. MotU, tr. by George Szirtes

Put a stone in your mouth and keep it. Put a Stone in Your Mouth. Mary Beath. ICANM

Put a sun in Sunday, Sunday. Gertrude Stein. TCAPo Fr. Yet Dish.

Put away your grief [or sadness], it is a mantle of work. (LL) Anne Carson. BodElec; OxBoAm; WoBe Fr. Truth About God, The.

Put dogs on the list. Before You Cut Loose. Simon Armitage. EmeKit

Put 'Em in a Box, Tie 'Em with a Ribbon (And Throw 'Em in the Deep Blue Sea). Sammy Cahn. ReLy

Put Hannibal i' th' scale. Juvenal. OBVE Fr. Satires.

Put Her down—in Italy? (LL) Her—"last Poems." Emily Dickinson. InoFa; NALW

Put his arms around the first man; started to walk. (LL) César Vallejo. PoCho; WED Fr. España, Aparta de me Este Caliz.

Put in mind of his own father and moved to tears. Ceasefire. Michael Longley. NAMCP V.2; StAl

Put in something else like page bonded to a neutrality my brother. Remembered Sequel. Hannah Weiner. FTOS

Put it on record. Identity Card. Mahmoud Darwish. VCWP, tr. by Denys Johnson-Davies

Put me like a seal over your heart, like a mark on your arm. Time for Trees to Dance. Pedro Pérez Conde. RMCMP, tr. by Michael Wiegers

Put off an important decision. 7th Light Poem: For John Cage—17 June 1962. Jackson Mac Low. FTOS

Put off Thy robe of purple, then go on. Good Friday: Rex Tragicus, or, Christ Going to His Cross[e]. Robert Herrick. NOSC

Put on a Happy Face. Lee Adams. ReLy

Put on all the bracelets beads rings. Tuglik's Song. Tuglik. WoPoe, tr. by Stephen Berg

Put on that languor which the world frowns on. Sonnet 120. Marc André Raffalovich. CAGL

Put on your slumming clothes and get your car. Slumming on Park Avenue. Irving Berlin. APT-1

Put out a hand from a window for a long time. Chironomy. Takehisa Kosugi. WhBo

Put out my hand and touched the face of God. (LL) High Flight. John Gillespie, Jr. Magee. ITBLP; OtW; PoWW

Put out the lights and stop the clocks. Madrid [—1937]. Langston Hughes. AF

Put out the lights now! Christmas Tree, The. Cecil Day Lewis. ChrPo

Put out to sea, if wine thou wouldest make. Sent from Egypt with a Fair Robe of Tissue to a Sicilian Vinedresser. Thomas Sturge Moore. OBEV

Put the Blame on Mame. Doris Fisher and Allan Roberts. ReLy

Put the broidery-frame away. Bertha in the Lane. Elizabeth Barrett Browning. ViWPN

Put the palms of your hands together. You There. Judith Barrington. FiBr

Put the sun a thought below his prime. Afternoon in the Garden. Ethel Louisa Mason Anderson. NOBAu

Put to the door—the school's begun. Country School, The. Unknown. TCAPo

Put together how it will. Marla Jernigan. AnSo

Put up a windmill on. Midwest, Midcentury. Sharyn Jeanne Skeeter. ISC

Put up thy gold: go on,—here's gold,—go on. William Shakespeare. OxAEP-1 Fr. Timon of Athens.

Put Your Arms Around Me, Honey. Junie McCree. ReLy

Put your hands into the mire. Wendell Berry. UpMys Fr. Prayers and Sayings of the Mad Farmer.

Put your lips on my mouth. Unknown. SLW, tr. by Marjolijn De Jager, Sayd Bahodin Majrouh and André Velter

Put your mouth on mine. Unknown. SLW, tr. by Marjolijn De Jager, Sayd Bahodin Majrouh and André Velter

Puttin' on the Dog. Everett Hoagland. OxAAAP

Puttin' on the Ritz (Original Version). Irving Berlin. ReLy

Puttin' on the Ritz (Revised Version). Irving Berlin. ReLy

Putting Down the Cat. Billy Collins. BeAl

Putting in the Seed. Robert Frost. APT-1; IPoFL; NAMCP V.1; NoAM; OxBoAm

Putting red reins on you, goat, with a noseband. Anyte. SaLy, tr. by Diane Rayor

Putting the Blame on His Sons. T'ao Ch'ien. CCL1, tr. by William Acker

Putting the reasons for crying aside for the moment, we might concentrate. Instructions on How to Cry. Julio Cortázar. MotU, tr. by Paul Blackburn

Putting the World to Bed. Esther W. Buxton. NOxBChV

Putting up new curtains. Curtains. Ruth Stone. BeAl; InoFa; StAl

Putty globes. Earplugs. Francisco Aragon. BeDoSH

Puzzle assembled, The. Solution. George Oppen. NAMCP V.1

Puzzle faces in the dying elms. Mystery Boy Looks for Kin in Nashville. Robert Earl Hayden. NoAM; NoP-4; NoP-5

Puzzle Pieces. Chana Bloch. ExTi

Puzzled, depressed, uncertain, I decided to shape my. Fortune Cookies. Fred Moramarco. SUP

Puzzling topic, this, A. Should be filed under. Timothy Steele. PoA 2002 Fr. Three Notes Toward Definitions.

Pwllderi. Dewi Emrys James. BBMWP, tr. by Elin ap Hywel

Pygmaleon. John Gower. NPeEn; OxBEV Fr. Confessio Amantis.

Pygmalion. Ovid. NAWM-7v1 Fr. Metamorphoses.

Pygmalion had seen the shameless lives. Ovid. NAWM-7v1 Fr. Metamorphoses.

Pygmalion's Image. Eiléan Ní Chuilleanáin. MakPoe

"Pygmies Are Pygmies Still, Though Percht on Alps." Gwendolyn Brooks. ColAP Fr. Notes from the Childhood and the Girlhood.

Pygmy Headhunters and Killer Apes, My Lover and Me. Laurel Ann Bogen. CalPo; SUP

Pylons, The. Stephen Spender. BrAP; NAMCP V.1; NoAM

P'yŏngyang ajŭlkka / Although P'yŏngyang is my capital. Song of P'yŏngyang. Unknown. CATKP, tr. by Peter H. Lee

Pyramid, The. Brian Henry. LegDan

Pyramids, The. Nick Piombino. FTOS

Pyramus & Thisbe. Devin Johnston. IIR

Pyrenees, The. Jane Duran. Prnts Fr. Silences from the Spanish Civil War.

Pyres, The. Virgil. WoPoe Fr. Aeneid [or Eneados or Aeneis], The.

Pyrography. John Ashbery. HarvBoo; VCAP

Pyromaniac. Wyatt Prunty. LiTh

Pyrrha, what slender well-shap'd beau. Horace. OBVE,

Pythagoras planned it. Why did the people stare? Statues, The. William Butler Yeats. NoAM; WeW-3

Pythagorean, The. Xenophanes. DiBP, tr. by Sir Edwin Arnold

Pythagorean Silence. Susan Howe.
　"Age of earth and us all chattering." PFTM-2
　"He plodded away through drifts of i/ ce." FTOS
Pythagoric Letter, The. Thomas Stanley. NOSC
Pythagoric letter, two ways spread, The. Pythagoric Letter, The. Thomas Stanley. NOSC
Pythian Odes. Pindar. *tr. by* Padraic Fallon and Thomas Meyer
　Pythian Ten.
　　Hyperboreans, The. WoPoe, *tr. by* Padraic Fallon
　Pythian Twelve.
　　For Midas, the Man from Akragas First in the Flute Match. WoPoe, *tr. by* Thomas Meyer
Python-coils of leg and trunk. Oliver Reynolds. TCAWP *Fr.* Tone Poem.
Pythoness, The. Kathleen Jessie Raine. MoBrPo

Q

Q.E.D. Mary Low. SurWo
Qader blew at a cigarette, stuck his head. Road from Biloxi, The. Khaled Mattawa. RWB
Qadesha (Sacred Whore). Cosi Fabian. HW
Qantas Bags. Laurie Duggan. BMAP
Qaus-e Qazah. Shajahana Begum. HotL, *tr. by* V. Narayana Rao
Qiang-you-ci: Off the Wall. *Unknown.* CCL1, *tr. by* V. W. X.
Qianlong the stone-grinder stands to work at his trestle table. Qing Dish, A. Caitríona O'Reilly. NIrP
Qian-shang: Gird Your Loins. *Unknown.* CCL1, *tr. by* Arthur Waley
Qing Dish, A. Caitríona O'Reilly. NIrP
Qing-ying: Buzz Buzz, the Blue Flies. *Unknown.* CCL1, *tr. by* Burton Watson
Qi-yu [Translations]. *Unknown.* CCL1
　Behold That Bay. CCL1, *tr. by* Bishop Thomas Percy
　Chinese Ode, A. CCL1, *tr. by* Sir William Jones
　Praise of Duke Wu of Wei. CCL1, *tr. by* William Jennings
Qiyuge [*with music*]. *Unknown.* CCL1, *tr. by* Burton Watson
Qua Cursum Ventus. Arthur Hugh Clough. OBEV
Quaco Sam. *Unknown.* FaBoVe
Quadroon, The. William Edward Burghardt DuBois. NAAPv.1
Quadroon mermaids, Afro angels, black saints. Ballad of Remembrance, A. Robert Earl Hayden. ESEAA
Quaerè. George Farewell. NPeEn; OBCoV
Quagmire of an overstuffed sofa, The. Infant, The. Oliver Pitcher. EGAG
Quai gris d'où tombe l'appât de neige. Quai gris. Michel Deguy. YaTCFP
Quail in Autumn. William Jay Smith. OWoS
Quails. Takahashi Shinkichi. ZenPo, *tr. by* Takashi Ikemoto and Lucien Stryk
Quaint Mazes. Geoffrey Hill. NoAM *Fr.* Apology for the Revival of Christian Architecture in England, An.
Quake Theory. Sharon Olds. PBCAP
Quaker Graveyard in Nantucket, The. Robert Lowell. ColAP; MakPoe; NAAL-5; NAMCP V.2; NoAM; NoP-5; VCAP; WaAnP
Quaker Oats. Rita Dove. MotU
Quakerdom (The Formal Call). Charles Graham Halpine. IrLP
Qualités d'Apôtre. Gisèle Prassinos. YaTCFP
Quality of Mercy, The. Lee Upton. AmAlph
Quality of Sprawl, The. Les A. Murray. EmeKit; HarvBoo; NoP-4; NoP-5
Quality of Sprawl, The. Les A. Murray.
　"Sprawl is the quality." UpMys
Quality of Striving, The. ("My war pits sleep's enthrallments") Chase Twichell. WANABP
Quality of Striving, The. ("Eye-catching as a dog on a chain.") Chase Twichell. AmZen
Quality of the dirt, the fealty changing under my foot, The. (LL) Derek Walcott. NAEL-6v2; NAEL-7v2; NoP-4; NoP-5 *Fr.* Midsummer.
Quality of Wine. Hayden Carruth. BodElec
Quand il est impossible d'écrire un mot. Quand il est Impossible. Jacques Dupin. YaTCFP
Quand il eut regardé de bien près tous les monstres. Quand il eut Regardé. Eugène Guillevic. YaTCFP
Quand il n'y a plus rien à attendre. Liliane Giraudon.
　"Quand il n'y a plus rien à attendre." YaTCFP
Quand rien n'entraîne rien. Pierre Alféri. YaTCFP
Quant Souvenir Me Ramentoit. Charles, Duc d' Orléans. WoPoe, *tr. by* Fred Chappell
Quanta. Pauline Stainer. MoWP
Quantifiable griefs. The daily kill. Pacific 1945-1995. Allen Curnow. HarvBoo
Quantum Theory. Alberto Blanco. RMCMP, *tr. by* Gustavo V. Segade

Quarrel. Federico García Lorca. RaW, *tr. by* Herbert Baird and William Stafford
Quarrel, The. Conrad Potter Aiken. MoAmPo; StAl
Quarrel, The. Federico García Lorca. AF; WED, *tr. by* Robert Bly
Quarrel, The. Josephine D. Henderson Heard. CBWP-4
Quarrel, The. Stanley Kunitz. APT-2; TaR
Quarrel of the sparrows in the eaves, The. Sorrow of Love, The [1892 Version]. William Butler Yeats. MoBrPo; NAMCP V.1; NoAM; NPeEn; OxBEV
Quarreling person is none other than a person who had not been quarreling, A. Yi Sang. CAMKP; PFTM-1 *Fr.* Crow's-Eye View.
Quarreling with Robert Frost. Michael S. Glaser. VisFro
Quarrels have long been in vogue among sages. Song from the Coptic, A. Johann Wolfgang von Goethe. WoPoe, *tr. by* James Clarence Mangan
Quarry. T. Arfon Williams. BBMWP, *tr. by* Emyr Lewis
Quarry, The. W. H. Auden. *See* O What Is That Sound [Which So Thrills the Ear].
Quarter century ago, A. Wilberforce. Josephine D. Henderson Heard. CBWP-4
Quarter century of exile has passed, A. Georgy Vladimirovich Ivanov. TCRusP, *tr. by* Daniel Weissbort
Quarter Moon Rise. Kalamu ya Salaam. SpirFl *Fr.* New Orleans Haiku.
Quarter of an hour to wait, A. Underground. May Kendall. ViWPN; VWP
Quarter of pleasures where the rich are always waiting. Capital, The. W. H. Auden. NAMCP V.1
Quarter shined on his palm like light entering a hole in the bone, The. Rapist: A Romance. Rigoberto González. LiTh
Quarter-Hour Between God and the Office. Lőrinc Szabó. IQMS, *tr. by* Egon F. Kunz
Quarterly, is it, money reproaches me. Money. Philip Larkin. NPeEn
Quartermaster of the spring, The. First Rondeau: After a French Poet of the Fourteenth Century. Johann Nikolaus Götz. GePo, *tr. by* George C. Schoolfield
Quarter-mile off, A. Frost in Miami. Peter Schmitt. VisFro
Quarter-million, the last great flock of passenger pigeons, A. Derailment. William Heyen. PoCoUp
Quartet. Leonard Nathan. Vesp
Quartet of Daffodils, A. Lorna Goodison. CFP
Quartets of Inner Whispering. Shakir Samawi. IrPoTo, *tr. by* Chuck Miller and Saadi A. Simawe
Quartier Libre. Jacques Prévert. CLPP, *tr. by* Lawrence Ferlinghetti
Quarto Centennial, The. Josephine D. Henderson Heard. CBWP-4
Quartz and Mica. Yolande Villemaire. NLPA, *tr. by* Judith Elaine Cowan
Quartz Pebble, The. Vasco [*or* Vasko] Popa. PoSu *Fr.* Quartz Pebble, The.
Quartz Pebble, The. Vasco [*or* Vasko] Popa. *tr. by* Anne Pennington
　Adventure of the Quartz Pebble, The. PoSu
　Dream of the Quartz Pebble, The. PoSu
　Heart of the Quartz Pebble, The. PoSu
　Love of the Quartz Pebble, The. PoSu
　Quartz Pebble, The. PoSu
　Secret of the Quartz Pebble, The. PoSu
　Two Quartz Pebbles. PoSu
Quasi-crazy tenement fleet, A. Time Bum. Jordan Davis. HeMarv
Quaternary. Gottfried Benn. WoPoe, *tr. by* Teresa Iverson
Quatrain. Sarah Norcliffe Cleghorn. NIP-4
Quatrain. Ayn Al-Qozat Hamadani. BBASP, *tr. by* Nasrollah Pourjavady and Peter Lamborn Wilson
Quatrain: "Before you praise Spring's advent note." Tu Fu [*or* Du Fu]. TAL
Quatrain: Forgive Me Not. Lilla Cabot Perry. RaF
Quatrain: "France's I am; my lookout's glum." François Villon. WoPoe, *tr. by* Richard Wilbur
Quatrain: "We're snug as a bug in a heated house." Adriann Roland Holst. TuT, *tr. by* Sean Dunne
Quatrain without Sparrows, Helpful Bells or Hope. Thomas McCarthy. PBCIP
Quatrains. Ralph Waldo Emerson.
　Climacteric. TCAPo
　"Ever the poet *from* the land." TCAPo
　"Her planted eye to-day controls." APN-1; NoP-4; NoP-5
　Memory. APN-1; TCAPo
　(Self-Reliance.) APN-1
　Shakspeare. TCAPo
　"To clothe the fiery thought." Spl; TCAPo
　"Wilt thou seal up the avenues of ill?" APN-1
Quatrains for Joy. Muhammad Al-Ghuzzi. NAfrP, *tr. by* John Heath-Stubbs and May Jayyusi

Quavering cry, A. Screech-owl? Night, Death, Mississippi. Robert Earl Hayden. CAP-8; ColAP; NAMCP V.2; NoP-4; NoP-5; OxAAAP; PoPoPo; VCAP

Quavering words of those who survived, The. Great Storm, The. Larry D. Thomas. TiP2

Quay recedes, The. Hurrah! Ahead we go! Colonel's Soliloquy, The. Thomas Hardy. FaBoWar; OBWP

¿Qué desavenencia de violín, ahorcado por el alma. Arde el horizonte. Ernesto Lumbreras. RMCMP

¿Qué es tu dueño más que otro dueño. Regala la mentira. Pedro Pérez Conde. RMCMP

Que estás en la tierra, Padre nuestro. Oración. Gloria Fuertes. RaW

Que ferais-je sans ce monde sans visage sans questions [*Author's own French vers. of his* "What would I do without this world faceless incurious"]. Samuel Beckett. YaTCFP

Que l'innocence demeure. Prière. Pierre Albert Jourdan. YaTCFP

¡Qué serena va el agua! Río. Jorge Guillén. RaW

Qué silencio bajo tierra. Miguel de Unamuno. RaW *Fr.* Cancionero *Diario Poético* 1928–1936.

¿Qué te ha hecho cerrar los ojos. Promesa. Francisco Segovia. RMCMP

Que Venga el Poeta. León Felipe. RaW

Quebec. Henrietta Cordelia Ray. CBWP-3

Que-chao. *Unknown.* CCL1
    Dove in the Magpie's Nest, The. CCL1, *tr. by* Clement Allen
    Robber-Bird, The. CCL1, *tr. by* John Francis Davis
    Wedding-Journey of a Princess, The. CCL1, *tr. by* William Jennings

Queen, A. Bella Akhatovna Akhmadulina. TCRusP, *tr. by* Daniel Weissbort

Queen and Huntress. Ben Jonson. *See* Hymn[e] to Cynthia.

Queen and huntress, chaste and fair. Ben Jonson. NOSC *Fr.* Cynthia's Revels.

Queen Anne's Lace. Raymond Souster. BrAP

Queen Anne's Lace. William Carlos Williams. APT-1; BrAP; MoAmPo; NAAL-5; NAAPv.2; NAMCP V.1; NoAM; NoP-4; NoP-5; OxBoAm

Queen asks, The. Kamalākānta Bhattācārya. SinGod, *tr. by* Rachel Fell McDermott

Queen Bee. Dilya Rose. EdScPo

Queen Bess was Harry's daughter. Stand forward partners all! Looking Glass, The. Rudyard Kipling. OBMV

Queen Caroline. *Unknown.* OBCoV

Queen, for her part, all that evening ached, The. Virgil. NAWM-5v1; NAWM-7v1 *Fr.* Aeneid [*or* Eneados *or* Aeneis], The.

Queen Gertrude's Soliloquy. Gail White. IaFF

Queen Hera. Burleigh Muttén. HW

Queen Hera, may your [graceful form]. Sappho. SaLy, *tr. by* Diane Rayor

Queen Herod. Carol Ann Duffy. P180

Queen Ijo's Blues. Carole Boston Weatherford. FuFl

Queen Katherine to Owen Tudor. Michael Drayton. NoSic *Fr.* England's Heroical Epistles.

Queen Mab. Percy Bysshe Shelley.
    "O happy Earth! reality of Heaven!" NAEL-7v2
    "Then in her triumph spoke the Fairy Queen." NAEL-7v2
    To Harriet. NPBRoP

Queen Mab's Chariot. Michael Drayton. NPeEn

Queen Mary, She's My Friend. Stephen Scobie. IFF

Queen Medusa. Burleigh Muttén. HW

Queen Mother of the West peach tree is planted in my yard, A. Late Bloomer at the Front of My Garden. Li Po. ColAnChi, *tr. by* Elling O. Eide

Queen Mother to New Queen. Robert Graves. OBSV

Queen moves with unbounded liberty, The. Pieces. Paul Lake. PoDa

Queen Nefertiti. *Unknown.* TLR

Queen Night, on velvet slippered feet, comes softly down. (LL) James Weldon Johnson. APT-1; NAMCP V.1 *Fr.* Down by the Carib Sea.

Queen of Carthage, The. Louise Glück. AmFaPo

Queen of Corinth, The. John Fletcher.
    Weep No More. OBEV; OxAEP-1

Queen of fragrance, lovely rose. Rose-Bud, The. William Broome. OBEV

Queen of Girlhood, The. Margaret Elizabeth Sangster. ArBi

Queen of Hearts, The. Christina Georgina Rossetti. NPeEn

Queen of herself, the world and me. (LL) Regina. Mary Elizabeth Coleridge. NALW; PoBW

Queen of imagination who wears the sun's hat is the imagined sun's Queen, The. Vin du Masque. Kitasono Katsue. CAoMJL1, *tr. by* John Solt

Queen of martials, the. Homer. NOSC *Fr.* Iliad, The.

Queen of Prussia's Tomb, The. Felicia Dorothea Hemans. RWP

Queen of Sheba, The. Kathleen Jamie. EdScPo; NePenScot; RSaN

Queen of Swords, The. Joanne Limburg. NeBl

Queen of the Blues. Gwendolyn Brooks. NALW; SeSe

Queen of the differentiated sites, administratrix of the. David Jones. AngWePo; TCAWP *Fr.* Tutelar of the Place, The.

Queen of the silver bow!—by thy pale beam. To the Moon. Charlotte Smith. CenSon; RWP

Queen, Queen, Caroline. *Unknown.* TLR

Queen she kept high festival in Windsor's lordly hall, The. Royal Banquet, The. William Edmonstoune Aytoun. OBCoV

Queen she sent to look for me, The. Grenadier. A. E. Housman. OBMV; OBWP

Queen Virtue's court, which some call Stella's face. Sir Philip Sidney. NAEL-6v1; NAEL-7v1 *Fr.* Astrophil and Stella.

Queen was beloved by a jester, A. Cap and Bells, The. William Butler Yeats. MoBrPo; NoAM

Queen wept but thought: It is not appropriate to show such grief, The. *Unknown.* WoPoe *Fr.* Drimeh Kundan.

Queene *Vertues* court, which some call *Stellas* face. Sir Philip Sidney. *See* Queen Virtue's court, which some call Stella's face.

Queenie. Mary Weston Fordham. CBWP-2

Queenie was a blonde, and her age stood still. Joseph Moncure March. OBCoV *Fr.* Wild Party, The.

Queen-Like Closet, The. Hannah Wolley.
    "Ladies, I do here present you." EMWP

Queens. John Millington Synge. MoBrPo; OBMV

Queen's After-Dinner Speech, The. William Percy French. OBCoV

Queen's Answer, The. Queen of England Elizabeth I. EMWP

Queen's Marie, The [Version from Scott's Minstrelsy]. *Unknown.* OBEV

Queens of Hell had lissome necks to crane, The. Tall Girl, The. John Crowe Ransom. OxBSo

Queen's Tears. Tony Curtis. TCAWP

Queen's Wake, The. James Hogg.
    Kilmeny. OBEV; OxAEP-2
    Thirteenth Bard's Song, The. NePenScot

Queer the way. Making Conversation. Maggie Hannan. MFPA

Queer Thing, A. Nancy Keesing. NOBAu

Queer thing about those waters: there are no, A. Across the Bay. Donald Davie. CABP; NAMCP V.2; NoAM

Queerness is an art form. Butterflying. Tatiana De la Tierra. BeDoSh

Quelques raies qui raccourcissent le mur sont des indications pour la police, Les. Ça. Pierre Reverdy. YaTCFP

Quelqu'un m'a dit que tu n'écris plus qu'en anglais. Apollo at Aberdeen. Herménégilde Chiasson. IFF, *tr. by* Fred Cogswell and Jo-Anne Elder

Querido Flaco, / The ride was cool, wasn't it? Us five. Letter to El Flaco on His Birthday. Richard Blanco. NAPBL

Query: "Who left / this wooly caterpillar." Kate Knapp Johnson. NevBe

Quest, The. Denise Levertov. LW

Quest, The. Sharon Olds. P180

Quest of Silence, The. Christopher John Brennan.
    Fire in the Heavens. NOBAu

Quest of the Ideal, The. Henrietta Cordelia Ray. CBWP-3; SWaP

Qu'est-ce qui rôde autour du chauffeur. Chauffeur, Le. Hédi Kaddour. YaTCFP

Qu'est-ce qui vide un nom de sa substance. Emmanuel Hocquard. YaTCFP *Fr.* À Noël.

Question. Edith Södergran. WPoS

Question: "Body my house." May Swenson. APT-2; GPTC; NAMCP V.2; OxBoAm; PtR

Question ("Said the lady, *Can you do*.") Langston Hughes. APSN

Question: "*What up, brother?* the white teen with dreadlocks." A. Van Jordan. BRtP

Question, A. John Millington Synge. MoBrPo; OBMV

Question, A. *Unknown.* NOSC

Question, The. Josephine D. Henderson Heard. CBWP-4

Question, The. Karla Kuskin. NTCP

Question, The: "I dream'd that, as I wander'd by the way." Percy Bysshe Shelley. OBEV; OxBEV

Question, The. Frederick Goddard Tuckerman. APN-2; ColAP

Question, The. C. K. Williams. NoP-4; NoP-5

Question and Answer. Alasdair Maclean. EdScPo

Question and Answer. Kathleen Jessie Raine. MoBrPo

Question and Answer. William Carlos Williams. HarvBoo

Question and Answer, The. Thomas Beedome. NOSC

Question Answered, The [*or* A]. William Blake. ErotSp; NoP-4; NoP-5; OxBEV; WoPoe *Fr.* Several Questions Answered.

Question at Night. Mihály Babits. IQMS, *tr. by* Peter Zollman

Question clear, the answer deep, The. Sodo. ZenPo, *tr. by* Takashi Ikemoto and Lucien Stryk

Question for the Frankfurt School, A. Heberto Padilla. TCLAP, *tr. by* Andrew Hurley and Alastair Reid

Question I am left with is the question of her loneliness, The. Anne Carson. NLPA *Fr.* Glass Essay, The.

Question includes its own, The.   Queen Mary, She's My Friend.   Stephen Scobie.   IFF

Question is: how does one hold an apple, The.   Five Poems about Poetry.   George Oppen.

Question me again. (LL)   Casualty.   Seamus Heaney.   ModIr; NAEL-6v2; NAEL-7v2; NAMCP V.2; PBCIP

Question, Monsieur Gracq advised, had best, The.   Job Interview, The.   Richard Howard.   OxBoAm

Question of Climate, A.   Audre Lorde.   NAMCP V.2; NoAM

Question of Covenants, A.   Gerald Dawe.   PNI

Question of Identity, The.   Kristin Lattany.   OxAAAP

Question of Time, The.   William Peskett.   PNI

Question of Vitamins, A.   Ron Charach.   BloBone

Question, the action, the speech, the taxi, the proof, the reference, forgotten, The.   Of Deaths, Days, Futures, Nations.   Jen Hofer.   Eno

Question the horizon adorned by the bright stars, for I have entrusted a description of my condition to it.   Muhammad ibn Yūsuf Ibn Zumruk.   HiArP, tr. by James T. Monroe

Question Time.   Jack Lindsay.   NOBAu

Question to Life.   Patrick Kavanagh.   MoBrPo

Question, to Lisetta, The.   Matthew Prior.   OBEV

Question was an academic one, The.   Tomorrows.   James Merrill.   AmWit

Questioner Who Sits So Sly, The.   W. H. Auden.   OxAEP-2

Questioning.   Henrietta Cordelia Ray.   CBWP-3

Questioning Faces.   Robert Frost.   APT-1

Questioning Mr Bonnet.   Selima Hill.   MoWP

Questioning Spirit, The.   Arthur Hugh Clough.   SacPr

Questionnaire.   Gunnar Ekelof.   WED, tr. by Robert Bly

Questions.   Marjorie Agosin.   FiBr

Questions: "Since nothing actually exists except You."   Mirza Asadullah Khan Ghalib.   WED, tr. by Robert Bly

Questions.   Oliver Wendell Holmes.   DiBP Fr. Wind-Clouds and Star-Drifts.

Questions: "If I shriek."   Marc Kaminsky.   AtGh

Questions: "Parliament of grasshoppers is in the field, A."   Federico García Lorca.   WED, tr. by Robert Bly

Questions: "Where are you now, little wandering."   William Hurrell Mallock.   DiBP

Questions, The.   Taking a Watermelon as a Paradigm.   Yi Yônju.   EcSo, tr. by Yung-Hee Kim

Questions, The: "What about the people who came to my father's office."   Robert Pinsky.   ColAP; NAMCP V.2; NoAM

Questions about Poetry since Auschwitz.   Tadeusz Rózewicz.   AF, tr. by Robert A. Maguire

Questions about the Sphinx.   Celia Gilbert.   PfS

Questions and Answers.   Diana O'Hehir.   AFaM

Questions Answered.   Li Po.   CrYelRi, tr. by Sam Hamill

Questions of Travel.   Elizabeth Bishop.   ColAP; HarvBoo; OxBoAm

Questmale.   Mark Halliday.   MAAN

Queue.   Tatamkulu Afrika.   TSAP

Queue.   Rashidah Ismaili.   HAWP

Queynt.   Anne Rouse.   NeBl

Quhen Flora Had O'erfret the Firth.   Unknown.   OBEV

Quhen [or When] Noy[e] had maid his Sacrifyce [or sacrifice].   Sir David Lyndsay.   ChIV-1 Fr. Monarche, The.

Quhen Tayis bank wes blumyt brycht.   Tayis Bank.   Unknown.   FaBoVe

Quhen thou art careit to that cuntree.   Virgil.   OBVE Fr. Aeneid [or Eneados or Aeneis], The.

Qui quoi.   Michel Deguy.   YaTCFP

Quia Amore Langueo.   Unknown.   OBEV, tr. by Helen Gardner

Quick and Bitter.   Yehuda Amichai.   VCWP

Quick and the Dead, The.   Galway Kinnell.   BAP-01

Quick, at the feeder, pausing.   Nuthatch.   David Wagoner.   OWoS

Quick embrace.   Staircase.   Marina Ivanovna Tsvetayeva.   ARWW, tr. by Catriona Kelly

Quick hands on spinning ropes.   Dead Horse Bay.   Robert Adamson.   NOBAu

Quick in spite I said unkind.   Brazen Tongue.   William Rose Benét.   MoAmPo

Quick in the April hedge.   House.   Robert Hass.   LoL

Quick Night / easy warmth.   World Is Full of Remarkable Things, The.   Imamu Amiri Baraka.   SSLK

Quick on my feet in those Novembers of my loneliness.   Mad Fight Song for William S. Carpenter, 1966, A.   James Wright.   NoAM

Quick Poem, A.   Adam Zagajewski.   PoCho, tr. by Clare Cavanagh

Quick Sell the Pig.   Matthew Rohrer.   AmPoNex

Quick sparks on the gorse bushes are leaping, The.   Wild Common, The.   D. H. Lawrence.   NAMCP V.1; NoAM

Quick! / We're due at the square.   Adaptation.   Konstantin Pavlov.   CSCBP, tr. by Georgi Belev and Lisa Sapinkopf

Quick, woman, in your net.   Net, The.   William Robert Rodgers.   IrLP; ModIr; PNI

Quickened with touches of transporting fear. (LL)   Fish, the Man, and the Spirit, The.   Leigh Hunt.   OBEV; OxBSo

Quickening.   Lee Miriam Whitman-Raymond.   PfS

Quicker, vivid, she starts up.   Soundtrack.   Lawrence L. White.   IAoNAP

Quickly and Fully.   Linda Bierds.   AmAlph

Quickly, love, be lyrical & let.   La, La, La!   Thomas M. Disch.   NBLV

Quickly, my love, I want to offer you my mouth!   Unknown.   SLW, tr. by Marjolijn De Jager, Sayd Bahodin Majrouh and André Velter

Quickly take a pen.   Of Sweet Rest.   Joyce Mansour.   HAWP, tr. by Mary Beach

Quickness.   Henry Vaughan.   BBASP; NOSC

Quickness which my God hath kissed, A. (LL)   Quickness.   Henry Vaughan.   BBASP; NOSC

Quicksand.   Michael Hartnett.   IrLP

Quicksilver song, The.   Insomnia at the Solstice.   Jane Kenyon.   AWTN

Quidditie [or Quiddity], The.   George Herbert.   NOSC

Quiddity i cannot penetrate or name. (LL)   [American Journal].   Robert Earl Hayden.   ESEAA; ISC

¡Quién pudiera seducir los potentes brazos del sauce!   Herbario.   Laura Solórzano.   SPV

¿Quieres curar las caras de los dioses? Haz máscaras.   Eduardo Milán.   RMCMP

Quiero Dormir.   Jorge Guillén.   RaW

Quiet.   Marjorie Lowry Christie Pickthall.   SacPr

Quiet, The.   Mariiane Mays.   PoPra Fr. (HERO)neck: attempts at a portrait.

Quiet after the rain of morning.   Trumbull Stickney.   ColAP

Quiet among the leaves, a wren.   Wren, A.   Denise Levertov.   PoCoUp

Quiet by the window of the train.   Hunter Home from the Hill, The.   Kerry Hardie.   BeAl; NIrP

Quiet days and quiet evenings.   Inna L'vovna Lisnyanskaya.   CRWP, tr. by Daniel Weissbort

Quiet deepens, The. You will not persuade.   Farewell to Van Gogh.   Charles Tomlinson.   NoP-4; NoP-5

Quiet Desperation.   Louis Simpson.   CAP-8

Quiet Earth, The.   Heid E. Erdrich.   AmPoNex

Quiet Evening.   Louise Glück.   NAMCP V.2

Quiet Evening, Home Away.   Joann Balingit.   ReBoTo

Quiet gathering of a few old friends, A.   Widow in Red Shoes.   Tess Gallagher.   PoCu

Quiet here as the arsonist's noon—everyone in.   After the Argument.   Joyce Peseroff.   PfS

Quiet House, The.   Charlotte Mew.   HarvBoo; NALW; NPeEn

Quiet left by a departing soul, The. (LL)   Rafael Campo.   AmPoNex; WiU Fr. Ten Patients, and Another.

Quiet Life, The.   William Byrd.   NoSic

12. The Quiet Mary Knew with the Risen Christ.   Rainer Maria Rilke.   WED Fr. Life of the Virgin Mary, The.

Quiet Mind, The.   Unknown.   NoSic

Quiet Neighbour, A.   John Heywood.   NoSic

Quiet Night Thought.   Li Po.   CCL1, tr. by Elling O. Eide

Quiet Night Thoughts.   Li Po.   EaWin, tr. by W. S. Merwin

Quiet Night Thoughts.   Li Po.   CrYelRi, tr. by Sam Hamill

Quiet Nights.   Raymond Carver.   EmeKit

Quiet Nights of Quiet Stars (Corcovado).   Antonio Carlos Jobim.   ReLy, tr. by Gene Lees

Quiet Normal Life, A.   Wallace Stevens.   NAAL-5; NoAM

Quiet now, sorrow; relax. Calm down, fear.   Meditation.   David St. John.   AmAlph

Quiet of a silver afternoon, The.   Hello Goodbye.   Sharon Thesen.   BrAP

Quiet Revery, A.   Unknown.   ArBi

Quiet Soul, A.   John Oldham.   OBEV

Quiet Spaces.   Vicente Huidobro.   TCLAP, tr. by Stephen Fredman

Quiet Thing, A.   Fred Ebb.   ReLy

Quiet Town, The.   Richard Dehmel.   GTCP, tr. by Reinhold Grimm

Quiet Until the Thaw.   Jacob Nibenegenesabe.   AmFaPo, tr. by Howard Norman

Quiet upon the terraces.   Chairs in Snow.   Elwyn Brooks White.   ChAP

Quiet Valley, The.   Gwilym R. Jones.   BBMWP Fr. Atomic Factory, The.

Quiet World, The.   Jeffrey McDaniel.   SUP

Quietly.   Kenneth Rexroth.   ErotSp; GoPo

Quietly Discussing My Thoughts with the Collator of Texts Ts'ui.   Ch'i-chi.   CSKM, tr. by Burton Watson

Quietly shining to the quiet Moon. (LL)   Frost at Midnight [1829 version].   Samuel Taylor Coleridge.   BrAP; CABP; NAEL-6v2; NAEL-7v2; NOBRP; NoP-4; NoP-5; NPeEn; PtR; TFi

Quietly step onto a land.   Kayenta Times Yet Dreaming On.   Nia Francisco. HATNAP

Quietly the world lay sleeping.   Birth of Jesus, The.   Josephine D. Henderson Heard.   CBWP-4

Quietly, they take on the color and shape.   Danger, Men in Trees.   Doris Safie. PoArWo

Quietness.   Jelaluddin Rumi.   PtR, *tr.* by Coleman Barks

Quietness of his eyes, The. (LL)   Dog of Art, The.   Denise Levertov. NAMCP V.2; NoAM; WaAnP

Quietness with a Happening.   Gennady Aygi.   WoBe, *tr.* by Peter France

Quill Holler Waller.   Joan Self.   FTtHH

Quilt.   George Elliott Clarke.   OpeFie

Quilt.   Valerie Wohlfeld.   SweBea

Quilt, The.   Chitra Divakaruni.   FiBr

Quilt Complex.   Ricardo Pau-Llosa.   RWB

Quilt of Rights.   Sandra McPherson.   LoL

Quilting.   Lucille Clifton.   SweBea

Quilts.   Kathleen Peirce.   PBCAP

Quimera.   Silvia Eugenia Castillero.   SPV

Quincaillerie.   Jean Follain.   YaTCFP

Quince, The.   Michael Donhauser.   SonAtl, *tr.* by Colin Brown, Kurt Ganzl, Ursula Hobday and Barbara Vogt

Quinn the Eskimo.   Bob Dylan.   RaBo

Quinnapoxet.   Stanley Kunitz.   LoL

Quinquereme of Nineveh from distant Ophir.   Paul Muldoon.   NAMCP V.2 *Fr.* 7, Middagh Street.

Quinquireme of Nineveh from distant Ophir.   Cargoes.   John Masefield. BLPJKO; BRP; CABP; MoBrPo; OBEV; OBMV; TFi

Quintana lay in the shallow grave of coral.   Karl Shapiro.   BodElec *Fr.* Bourgeois Poet, The.

Quip, The.   George Herbert.   BASC; NOSC; OxAEP-1; OxBEV

Quis Optimus Reipublicae Status.   Sir Thomas More.   PBRV

Quise hallarte dentro de mí.   Muerte del beso, La.   Pura López Colomé. RMCMP

Quisiera cantar: ser flor.   Canción.   Rafael Alberti.   RaW

Quite a number of People.   Why I Do It.   Luke E. Ramirez.   OWABP

Quite a posh old house was this.   Recollections of an Old Spook.   Richard Edwards.   NOxBChV

Quite Apart from the Holy Ghost.   Adrian Mitchell.   OBSV

Quite can drown a faint conviction that we may be born in Sin. (LL)   Huxley Hall.   Sir John Betjeman.   CABP; OBSV

Quite for no reason.   I've Been to a Marvelous Party.   Noël Coward.   NBLV; ReLy

Quite is high.   Styro.   Clark Coolidge.   PmAP

Quite Mercenary He Stalked Her.   Ward Abbott.   ICANM

Quite ordinary funeral: the corpse, A.   Cortège of Daughters, A.   Elizabeth Smither.   BeAl

Quite spent with thoughts I left my cell, and lay.   Vanity of Spirit.   Henry Vaughan.   NOSC

Quite unexpectedly as Vasserot.   End of the World, The.   Archibald MacLeish. BrAP; GSo; MoAmPo; NAMCP V.1; NoAM; OxBSo; TFi

Quitting my horse, a cup with you I drank.   So Farewell. And If for Ever, Still for Ever Fare Ye Well.   Wang Wei.   CCL1, *tr.* by W. J. B. Fletcher

Quiver of Questions, A.   Titiola Shoneyin.   NeNiPo

Quivering together /Ears of barley.   Kana-jo, Lady.   ZenPo, *tr.* by Takashi Ikemoto and Lucien Stryk

Quivira City Limits.   Kevin Young.   FuFl; NeAmPo

Qui-yue: In the Seventh Month.   *Unknown.*   CCL1, *tr.* by Arthur Waley

Quo life, the warld is mine.   Flyting o' Life and Daith, The.   Hamish Henderson.   EdScPo

Quondam was I in my lady's grace.   Sir Thomas Wyatt.   NoSic

Quoof.   Paul Muldoon.   FaBoVe; NAMCP V.2; NPeEn; PBCIP; PNI; StAl

Quorum of small black birds, A.   Morning *Minyan.*   Marcia Falk.   ASA

Quotations.   Charles Wright.   NoP-5

Quotations for a Winter Evening.   David Jauss.   PoA 2002

Quote Me Wrong Again and I'll Slit the Throat of Your Pet Iguana.   David St. John.   RACG

Quoth he, My faith as adamantine.   Samuel Butler.   OBSV *Fr.* Hudibras.

Quoth Hudibras.   Samuel Butler.   DiBP *Fr.* Hudibras.

Quoth the Duchess of Cleveland to counselor Knight.   Song.   John Wilmot, 2d Earl of Rochester.   BASC

Quoth tongue of neither maid nor wife.   Sir Henry Taylor.   OBEV; RACG *Fr.* Philip van Artevelde.

Quotidian, The.   Claudia Rankine.   AmPoNex

Qwhen Alexander our kynge was dede.   *Unknown.*   NePenScot

R

R.A.F.   "H. D."   PWW2; WaAnP

R.A.F. (Aged Eighteen).   Rudyard Kipling.   PoWW *Fr.* Epitaphs of the War [1914–1918].

R. Alcona to J. Brenzaida.   Emily Jane Brontë.   *See* Remembrance: "Cold in the earth—and the deep snow piled above thee!"

R.M.S. *Titanic.*   Anthony Cronin.
"Trembling with engines, gulping oil, the river."   PBCIP

R', *n.* **1.** lo.   Lattice at/of (Com)pare (Dis)pair.   Tina Darragh.   FTOS

R the reviewer, reviewing my book.   Joseph Hilaire Pierre Belloc.   NoAM *Fr.* Moral Alphabet, A.

R. W. Emerson.   Rose Terry Cooke.   NAAPv.1

Ra ruzaulú guiiru biaani yagayoo.   Na Agrícola.   Natalia Toledo.   RMCMP

Rabbi and his wife live in the body of Christ, The.   And Cause His Countenance to Shine upon You: *Corpus Christi, Texas.*   Cynthia MacDonald.   AFaM; TiP2

Rabbi Ben Ezra.   Robert Browning.   NAEL-6v2; NAEL-7v2

Rabbi Ben Levi, on the Sabbath, read.   Henry Wadsworth Longfellow.   NCAP; TCAPo *Fr.* Tales of a Wayside Inn.

Rabbi Eleazer opened the palm of his hand.   Circle of the Golem, The. Angelina Muñiz Huberman.   MirDau, *tr.* by Aurora Camacho

Rabbi of condiments.   Garlic, The.   Bert Meyers.   CalPo

Rabbi tells us music on the Sabbath, The.   No Music.   Richard Chess.   TaR

Rabbi, we Gadarenes.   Matthew 8, 28 ff.   Richard Wilbur.   UpMys
(Rabbi, we Gadarenes / Are not ascetics.)   GI

Rabbi's Song, The.   Rudyard Kipling.   ChIV-1

Rabbis wrote, The.   Short History of Judaic Thought in the Twentieth Century, A.   Linda Pastan.   Vesp

Rabbit, The.   Nina Cassian.   PoSu, *tr.* by Christopher Hewitt

Rabbit as King of the Ghosts, A.   Wallace Stevens.   *See* Rabbit Is King of the Ghosts, A.

Rabbit is born, The.   James Harrison and Ted Kooser.   TAPaP *Fr.* Braided Creek.

Rabbit Is King of the Ghosts, A.   Wallace Stevens.   NAMCP V.1; NoAM
(Rabbit as King of the Ghosts, A.)   ItP; NAMCP V.1

Rabbit Shoeshine.   S. K. Kelen.   BMAP

Rabbit: timid brother! My teacher and philosopher!   Perfect Life, The.   Jorge Carrera Andrade.   TCLAP, *tr.* by Dudley Fitts

Rabbiters: A Pastoral, The.   John Kinsella.   NeBl

Rabbit-foot effectiveness, nonentity of.   Eduardo Milán.   RMCMP, *tr.* by Roberto Tejada

Rabble? she groused. (LL)   Said ("Agatha Christie to.")   George Starbuck. AmWit; OBCoV

Rabid or dog-dull. Let me tell you how.   Professor's Song, A.   John Berryman. BrAP; HeIP-4; NoAM

Raccoons are persistent, The.   Animal Zen.   Kathe Davis.   AmZen

Raccoons have invaded the crawl space.   In the Old Neighborhood.   Rita Dove.   SpirFl

Race.   Karen Gershon.   HP

Race, The.   Nuala Ni Dhomhnaill.   PBCIP, *tr.* by Michael Hartnett

Race, The.   Sharon Olds.   InvLad; OxBoAm; RaBo

Race and Battle.   D. H. Lawrence.   ChIV-1

Race is an invention.   I worked on race at the factory.   Kim Hunter.   RD

Race is not to the swift, The.   Samuel Menashe.   D. H. Lawrence.   ChIV-1

Race of the Kingfishers.   Ray A. Young Bear.   HATNAP

Race on Gathering Bites.   Kojo Laing.   HBAPE

Race Question, The.   Naomi Long Madgett.   LTA

Race Relations.   Carolyn Kizer.   LTA

Race round the track of the stadium pupil. (LL)   Stenographers, The.   Patricia K. Page.   BrAP; HeIP-4; NALW; NAMCP V.2; NoAM

Race up into fresh water. (LL)   Salmon Fishing.   Robinson Jeffers.   APT-1; NAAPv.2

Racehorses assemble at the starting barrier, The.   Flemington Racecourse. Kevin Hart.   NOBAu

Racer's Widow, The.   Louise Glück.   MoASP

Rachel.   Lizette Woodworth Reese.   TCAPo

Rachel, 1840, as Phaedra, appears in white-face.   Rachel's Recovery (Fucking with the Angels).   Christy Sheffield Sanford.   AnSo

Rachel: *Crown of Thorns.*   Rebecca Baggett.   FiBr *Fr.* Art of the Amish: A Quilt Exhibition.

Rachel: *Queen Charlotte's Crown.*   Rebecca Baggett.   FiBr *Fr.* Art of the Amish: A Quilt Exhibition.

Rachel (rä'chal), a Ewe.   Linda Pastan.   TaR

Rachel's Recovery (Fucking with the Angels).   Christy Sheffield Sanford. AnSo

Rachelú ladxiduá.   Zenaida.   Natalia Toledo.   RMCMP

Rachmaninoff played, Chaliapin sang. Return. Dmitry Vasil'evich Bobyshev. ItGoST, *tr. by* Michael Van Walleghen

Racine. Frederick Seidel. OxBoAm

Racing each other. Inflight. Gary Gach. WhBo

Racing, reckoning fingers flick. Palladas. OBVE, *tr. by* Tony Harrison

Racists. C. K. Williams. LTA

Racoons shriek. Prayer of the Wanderer. Katie Donovan. NIrP

Radial wheels of the season spiked with knives, The. Charles Tomlinson. NewEx

Radiance. Robert Patrick Dana. Vesp

Radiance in Your Mother's Womb, The. Kabir. WED,

Radiance of that star that leans on me, The. Delay. Elizabeth Jennings. NIL-7; NIP-4; OPOU; StAl

Radiant. James Sherry. FTOS

Radiant child of Leto, farworking Lord Apollo. Old Joke. Alan Shapiro. PtR

Radiant Dog. John Godfrey. FTOS

Radiant Inventory. Christopher Dewdney. OpeFie

Radiant silence in Fiesole. Art of the Fugue, The: A Prayer. James Wright. BBASP

Radiant Silhouette I. John Yau. OpBo

Radiant Silhouette II. John Yau. OpBo

Radiant Silhouette III. John Yau. OpBo

Radiant Silhouette IV. John Yau. OpBo

Radiant Silhouette V. John Yau. OpBo

Radiant soda of the seashore fashions, The. Far Rockaway. Delmore Schwartz. APT-2; OxBoAm

Radiant with vernal grace and summer flowers. Mothers. Francis Saltus Saltus. VerBaPo

Radiated heat—in a campfire. Quantum Theory. Alberto Blanco. RMCMP, *tr. by* Gustavo V. Segade

Radiating Naïveté. Lucie Brock-Broido. OPRER

Radiation. Margaret Gibson. AtGh

Radiation bubbles beneath the skin. Nostradamus Predicts the Destruction of Chicago. Maureen Seaton. IllVoic

Radiation Victim. Colin Thiele. NOBAu

Radiator. Kimiko Hahn. ExTi

Radiator came on and the geraniums died, The. Larry Fagin. AHA *Fr.* Parade of the Caterpillars, The.

Radiator's hissing hot, The. Studio Up Over In Your Ear. Al Young. GT

Radical Departure, A. James Tate. WaAnP

Radical Neck. Bob Hicok. AmAlph

Radical War Song, A. Thomas Babington Macaulay, 1st Baron Macaulay. OBSV

Radio. Antony Dunn. RWPCtW

Radio. Cornelius Eady. ESEAA

Radio. Harriet Monroe. APT-1

Radio. Frank O'Hara. PoA 2002

Radio. Barrett Watten. PmAP

Radio about a foot-and-a-half. Toltecs. Eloise Klein Healy. SUP

Radio Caliban. Peter Porter. RWPCtW

Radio Cricket. Gavin Ewart. RWPCtW

Radio Gibberish. Genrikh Sabgir. TCRusP, *tr. by* Daniel Weissbort

Radio grovels from over the fence, A. Sydney. Robert Harris. NOBAu

Radio is playing downstairs in the kitchen, The. Distances. Eavan Boland. HarvBoo

Radio is teaching my goldfish Jujuitsu, The. Bob Kaufman. CLPP

Radio Nebraska. Erin Belieu. NAPBL

Radio station is filled with goats, The. Now the City Has Fallen. Andrew Waterhouse. BeAl

Radio talk this morning, The. Lorine Niedecker. AtGh

Radio 3. Brian M. Waltham. RWPCtW

Radioactive. Janine Canan. HW

Radioactive Ball, The. Carole Oles. PfSP

Radiophobia. Lyubov Sirota. AtGh, *tr. by* Leonid Levin and Elisavietta Ritchie

Radio's reality when. Monday, Monday. David Trinidad. SwNoth

Radish. N. M. Bodecker. Spl

Radish is / the only dish, The. Radish. N. M. Bodecker. Spl

Radium of the word, A. (LL) Gertrude Stein. Mina Loy. APT-1; MoWP; NAAPv.2; NAMCP V.1; OxBoAm

Radius of the bomb was twelve inches, The. Yehuda Amichai. FaBoWar, *tr. by* Barbara Harshav and Benjamin Harshav *and* Barbara Harshav

Radnoti Quarantine: Razglednicas. John Kinsella. VaPo

Rae Anne Redfield. Glossolalia. Angela Sorby. PoDa

Rafaela Who Drinks Coconut & Papaya Juice on Tuesdays. Sandra Cisneros. AFaM

Raftsmen on their floats. Buson. TAL

Rag of black plastic, shred of a kite. Goodbye, Goldeneye. May Swenson. NoP-4; NoP-5

Rag Time Cowboy Joe. Grant Clarke. ReLy

Rage. Peter Meinke. LiTh

Rage of Achilles, The. Homer. NAWM-7v1 *Fr.* Iliad, The.

Rage of yellow asters, A. Still-Life. Maurice Kenny. UrbNat

Rage, rage against the dying of the light. (LL) Do Not Go Gentle into That Good Night. Dylan Thomas. AmFaPo; BrAP; CABP; ChAP; ClHu; CtM; EMP; HarvBoo; HeIP-4; InoFa; ITBLP; MakPoe; MoBrPo; NAEL-6v2; NAEL-7v2; NAMCP V.2; NIL-7; NIP-4; NoAM; NoP-4; NoP-5; NPeEn; OxAEP-2; PoPoPo; SoSe-8; StAl; TCAWP; TFi; TRP; UV; WaAnP; WeW-3

Rage—goddess, sing the rage of Peleus' son Achilles. Homer. NAWM-7v1 *Fr.* Iliad, The.

Ragged Island. Edna St. Vincent Millay. ColAP; NoP-4; NoP-5; WaAnP

Ragged pilgrim, on the road to nowhere, The. Seven Twilights. Conrad Potter Aiken.

Ragged Sonnet: So Shall I Live. Leonard Nathan. IaFF

Ragged Sonnet: When in a Deep Depression. Leonard Nathan. IaFF

Raggedy Ann. Anne Caldwell. ReLy

Raggedy Man, The. James Whitcomb Riley. ITBLP

Raging cannon-thunder rolls from Bulgaria, A. Razglednica (1). Miklós Radnóti. IQMS, *tr. by* Peter Zollman

Raglan Lane. Brendan Kennelly. BeAl

Ragwort. Anne Stevenson. OPOU

Raid, The. William Everson. NoAM; OtW; PWW2

Raid of the Reidswire, The. *Unknown.* IBB

Raider, The. William Robert Rodgers. MoBrPo

Raiders' Dawn. Alun Lewis. AngWePo; NPeEn; PoAgWa

Railing Rimes Returned upon the Author by Mistress Mary Wrothe. Mary Sidney Wroth, Countess of Montgomery. EMWP

Railings. Sean Dunne. ModIr *Fr.* Sydney Place.

Railroad and a river and a road, A. Low-Level Cross-Country. Howard Nemerov. GM

Railroad Avenue. Langston Hughes. APT-2

Railroad Bill, A Conjure Man. Ishmael Reed. GM

Railroad Blues, The. *Unknown.* GM

Railroad Cars Are Coming, The. *Unknown.* HHAm

Railroad Man for Me, A. *Unknown.* CA

Railroad running west, A. Tohono O'odham. NAAPv.1 *Fr.* Songs for Treating Sickness, Sung durring the Four Parts of the Night.

Railroad Section Leader's Song. *Unknown.* GM

Railroad Station. Takahashi Shinkichi. ZenPo, *tr. by* Takashi Ikemoto and Lucien Stryk

Railroad station, a few, A. Railroad Station. Takahashi Shinkichi. ZenPo, *tr. by* Takashi Ikemoto and Lucien Stryk

Railroad yard in San Jose. In back of the real. Allen Ginsberg. HeIP-4; PtR

Railway Allotments. M. R. Peacocke. OBGa

Railway Boom, 1845, The. Thomas Baker. STuOW *Fr.* Steam Engine; or, The Power of the Flame, The.

Railway Bridge of the Silvery Tay, The. William McGonagall. NePenScot "Beautiful Railway Bridge of the Silvery Tay!" VerBaPo

Railway Children, The. Seamus Heaney. BrAP; OPOU

Railway Signals. Sheenagh Pugh. TCAWP

Railway Station, The. Jejuri Arun Kolatkar. EmeKit

Railway stationery lay upon, The. Railway Stationery, The. Kenneth Koch. OxBoAm

Raiment We Put On, The. Kelly Cherry. FFC

Rain. John Ashbery. FTOS

Rain. Nicaragua Water Fire. Gioconda Belli. TANSG, *tr. by* Steven F. White

Rain. Roo Borson. NoP-4

Rain. Chŏng Chiyong. CAMKP, *tr. by* Kevin O'Rourke

Rain. Margiad Evans. OBWVE

Rain. Charlotte Gardelle. CuPo

Rain. Jeff Gundy. IllVoic

Rain. Vachel Lindsay. RaBo

Rain. Dunya Mikhail. PoArWo, *tr. by* Nathalie Handal and Samira Kawar

Rain. Nishiwaki Junzaburo. CAoMJL1, *tr. by* Hosea Hirata

Rain. Po Chü-i. BLT, *tr. by* Arthur Waley

Rain. Francis Ponge. MotU, *tr. by* Cid Corman

Rain. Danton R. Remoto. ReBoTo

Rain. Takahashi Shinkichi. ZenPo, *tr. by* Takashi Ikemoto and Lucien Stryk

Rain. Gary Soto. NoAM *Fr.* Elements of San Joaquin, The.

Rain. Robert Louis Stevenson. NTCP

Rain. Leslie Ullman. YaYoPo

Rain. Konstantin Iakovlevich Vanshenkin. TCRusP, *tr. by* Daniel Weissbort

Rain. Sándor Weöres. BLT

Rain: "Rain is not surrounded by sleep like a drum." Joseph Ceravolo. OxBoAm

Rain: "From which heaven did you return." Kim Chôngnan. EcSo, *tr.* by Peter H. Lee

Rain: "It's raining, / and still people say there's no God!" Olga Sedakova. CRWP, *tr.* by Catriona Kelly

Rain: "Little ears of corn are parched, The." Ber Grin. Prolet, *tr.* by Amelia Glaser

Rain: "Teacher asked Paul, A." Naomi Shihab Nye. CFP; P180

Rain: "All afternoon it rained, then." Mary Oliver. OxBoAm

Rain: "Rain falling in the courtyard where I watch adopts three manners, each distinct, The." Francis Ponge. WED, *tr.* by Robert Bly

Rain: "Rain, midnight rain, nothing but the wild rain." Edward Thomas. FaBoWar; GPTC; HarvBoo; MakPoe; NAEL-6v2; NAEL-7v2; NAMCP V.1; NoP-4; NoP-5; NPeEn; OBWP; OxBEV; PoAgWa; PoWW; WaAnP

Rain: "As the rain falls." William Carlos Williams. ItP; OxBoAm; WaAnP

Rain, The. Zbigniew Herbert. PoetW, *tr.* by Bogdana Carpenter and John Carpenter *and* Bogdana Carpenter

Rain, The: "All night the sound had." Robert Creeley. AmFaPo; BeAl; BrAP; ColAP; ErotSp; ICANM; InvLad; PmAP; RaBo; TRP; WaAnP

Rain after a Vaudeville Show. Stephen Vincent Benét. MoAmPo

Rain, all night, taps the holly. Robert Penn Warren. LPSFW *Fr.* Some Quiet, Plain Poems.

Rain, and blown sand, and southwest wind. Nova Scotia Fish Hut. Charles Bruce. Coast

Rain and low clouds blown through the valley. On the Anniversary of Her Grace. Bruce Weigl. StAl

Rain: and over the thorned, cliff-eaten. Rainy Easter. William Everson. APT-2

Rain and the thought of rain. Out There. Bill Berkson. NYP2

Rain and the Tyrants. Jules Supervielle. GPTC; WoPoe, *tr.* by David Gascoyne

Rain and thunder beat down and flooded the streets. Cartagena. Gary Snyder.

Rain at Night. Jakov Steinberg. FIT, *tr.* by Robert Friend

Rain at Noon-time. Molara Ogundipe-Leslie. CFP; HAWP

Rain before [*or* Raan afoor] seven. *Unknown.* FaBoVe

Rain brings flowers to this road each spring. From a Dream. Ch'in Kuan. CrYelRi, *tr.* by Sam Hamill

Rain brings me back, The. Patrizia Cavalli. NeIt

Rain by my throw in a. Subtracted Words. P. Inman. FTOS

Rain came. Fog out of the slough and horses. Day after Chasing Porcupines. James Welch. NoAM; WaAnP

Rain came overnight, A. Sin Hūm. CATKP, *tr.* by Peter H. Lee

Rain, Clouds, Eight Thousand Miles of Roads. Wang Ping. "No cloud or rain all night long." KGB

Rain comes down, it comes without our call, The. Winter Rain, The. Jones Very. NCAP

Rain comes down that sparse night rain in october you feel the sad rhythm of fall. Patrick Friesen. ACAMVP *Fr.* Clearing Poems.

Rain comes flapping through the yard, The. Gathering Mushrooms. Paul Muldoon. HarvBoo; ModIr; NAEL-7v2; NoP-4; PBCIP; PNI

Rain comes in through the oculus making a splaashing circle the swimmers. Matthea Harvey. IAoNAP *Fr.* Thermae.

Rain Dance. Susan Wicks. MFPA; MoWP

Rain, dancing, long-haired, The. Reliefs. Octavio Paz. IPoFL, *tr.* by Muriel Rukeyser

Rain Ditch. Pinkie Gordon Lane. ISC

Rain Downriver. Philip Levine. VCAP

Rain drifts forever in this place. Falls of Glomach, The. Andrew Young. EdScPo

Rain drips through. Laurie Duggan. BMAP *Fr.* Dogs.

Rain During Drought. Master Naong. BecRai, *tr.* by Kim Daljin, Kim Won-Chung and Christopher Merrill

Rain During the Cold Food Festival. Su Tung-p'o. CrYelRi, *tr.* by Sam Hamill

Rain Effect. Mary Ruefle. AmAlph

Rain Fall and Wet Becca Lawton. *Unknown.* SSUS

Rain falling in the courtyard where I watch adopts three manners, each distinct, The. Rain. Francis Ponge. WED, *tr.* by Robert Bly

Rain falls on fallen flowers. To the Tune: The Wine Spring. Li Hsun. CrYelRi; ErotSp, *tr.* by Sam Hamill

Rain falls on the faces of my comrades. Rain on the Battlefield. Yehuda Amichai. NRoS, *tr.* by Esther Raizen

Rain falls on the grass. Buson. SoOfWa, *tr.* by Sam Hamill

Rain Falls on Utopia Too. Arnold Rattenbury. RSaN

Rain fell without stopping. Monsoon Season Opens Children's Eyes. Chông Hwajin. EcSo, *tr.* by Julie C. Park

Rain finding once more what is lost, The. Rain Finding Once More, The. Valentine Penrose. YaTCFP, *tr.* by Mary Ann Caws *and* Jean-Pierre Cauvin

Rain Forest. Eric Rolls. NOBAu

Rain had stopped maybe an hour ago, The. On Failing to Translate. Hugh Maxton. IrLP

Rain has beaded the panes. At the Office Early. Ted Kooser. PBCAP

Rain has come, and the earth must be very glad, The. Soaking, The. Ivor Gurney. OxBEV

Rain has stopped, The. The waterfall will roar like that all night. Elizabeth Bishop. MotU *Fr.* Rainy Season; Sub-Tropics.

Rain hisses off the bus and car and taxi tires. Matins. Molly Peacock. ExTi

Rain in April. Kerry Hardie. NIrP

Rain in gray streaks thickens the beard of summer. Near Frost's Grave. David Smith. VisFro

Rain in Ivy. Chase Twichell. AmZen

Rain in May. Jane Hirshfield. GeoHom

Rain in Spain, The. Alan Jay Lerner. ReLy

Rain in Summer. Henry Wadsworth Longfellow. TreFP

Rain in the Aspens. Su Tung-p'o. NDACCP, *tr.* by Kenneth Rexroth

Rain in the bamboo trees under the eaves sounds familiar, The. On Autumn. Chungji. BecRai, *tr.* by Kim Daljin, Kim Won-Chung and Christopher Merrill

Rain, in the courtyard where I watch it fall, comes down at very varied speeds. Rain. Francis Ponge. MotU, *tr.* by Cid Corman

Rain is falling. Sound of Rain, The. Chu Yohan. CAMKP, *tr.* by Chong Bum Kim

Rain is Falling, The. Homero Aridjis. STV; TCLAP, *tr.* by John Frederick Nims

Rain is falling through the roof. After Us. Connie Wanek. P180

Rain is not surrounded by sleep like a drum. Rain. Joseph Ceravolo. OxBoAm

Rain is not the shape of water most like love. Shape of Water Most Like Love, The. David J. Rothman. GeoH

Rain is over and gone!, The. (LL) Written in March [While Resting on the Bridge at the Foot of Brother's Water]. William Wordsworth. ChAP; NAEL-6v2; NTCP

Rain is pissing down, The. Night Song of the Personal Shadow. György Petri. VCWP, *tr.* by Geroge Gömöri and Clive Wilmer

Rain is plashing on my sill, The. Unknown Dead, The. Henry Timrod. AmWaPo; PCW

Rain is raining all around, The. Rain. Robert Louis Stevenson. NTCP

Rain it raineth all around, The. Rain It Raineth, The. Charles Synge Christopher Bowen, Baron Bowen. NBLV; NTCP

Rain it raineth every day, The. Pennsylvania Deutsch. Christopher Darlington Morley. NBLV

Rain It Raineth, The. Charles Synge Christopher Bowen, Baron Bowen. NBLV; NTCP

Rain Journal: London: June '65. Lee Harwood. AHA

Rain keeps falling, The. Rain. Takahashi Shinkichi. ZenPo, *tr.* by Takashi Ikemoto and Lucien Stryk

Rain/Light. Christopher Buckley. PfSP

Rain Lover. Sakinah Carol Muhammad. OWABP

Rain Making. Dana Gilkes. BtF

Rain Man. Drahomira Vandas. SurWo, *tr.* by Guy Ducornet

Rain, midnight rain, nothing but the wild rain. Rain. Edward Thomas. FaBoWar; GPTC; HarvBoo; MakPoe; NAEL-6v2; NAEL-7v2; NAMCP V.1; NoP-4; NoP-5; NPeEn; OBWP; OxBEV; PoAgWa; PoWW; WaAnP

Rain Moving In. John Ashbery. NoP-4

Rain My Wife, The. Tracy Philpot. IAoNAP

Rain Near Heart Lake. Reg Saner. PoCoUp

Rain now stopped on the plain to the west. Composed at the West Wall of Tsou-p'ing Three Days After the Festival of Pure Brightness. Wang Shih-chieng. ColAnChi, *tr.* by Richard John Lynn

Rain of Bicycles, A. Jonathan Harrington. ArBi

Rain of hollow malice, A. Cesare Greppi. ItPo, *tr.* by Gayle Ridinger

Rain of London pimples, The. London Rain. Louis MacNeice. NoP-4; NoP-5

Rain on a Grave. Thomas Hardy. OxAEP-2

Rain on lilac leaves. In the dusk. Taid's Grave. Gillian Clarke. OPOU

Rain on Snow. Leigh Hancock. FiBr

Rain on the Battlefield. Yehuda Amichai. NRoS, *tr.* by Esther Raizen

Rain on the high prairies. Big Swimming. Edwin Ford Piper. APT-1

Rain on the River [1956]. Lu Yu. NDACCP, *tr.* by Kenneth Rexroth

Rain on the River [1970]. Lu Yu. NDACCP, *tr.* by Kenneth Rexroth

Rain on the West Side Highway. Adrienne Rich. WaAnP *Fr.* Twenty-one Love Poems.

Rain or shine each day. Kalamu ya Salaam. SpirFl *Fr.* New Orleans Haiku.

Rain patters on a sea that tilts and sighs. Absences. Philip Larkin. OxBEV

Rain, people, rain! Mocking-Bird's Song, The. *Unknown.* APN-2, *tr. by* Alice C. Fletcher

Rain Please Fall. Shuntaro Tanikawa. PoetW, *tr. by* Harold Wright

Rain Poem. Gabriel Preil. FIT, *tr. by* Robert Friend

Rain Psalm. Leopoldo Lugones. TCLAP, *tr. by* Julie Schumacher

Rain Race, The. Post Wheeler. ArBi

Rain rain go away. Rainsong. Tony Nduka Otiono. NeNiPo

Rain, rain, go to Spain. Mother Goose. FaBoVe

Rain roared through, now. Moon, Rain, Riverbank. Tu Fu [*or* Du Fu]. CrYelRi, *tr. by* Sam Hamill

Rain runs down the glass, The. Wish you were here. (LL) Belvedere Marittimo. Greg Williamson. AmPoNex; NeAmPo

Rain set early in tonight, The. Porphyria's Lover. Robert Browning. BrAP; NAEL-6v2; NAEL-7v2; NoP-5; OBEV

Rain sets more flowers blooming. Tune: "Happiness Approaches." Ch'in Kuan. ColAnChi, *tr. by* Jiaosheng Wang

Rain smothered us, the hail, The. Sign from Heaven, A. Boris Hristov. CSCBP, *tr. by* Georgi Belev and Lisa Sapinkopf

Rain Song. Robert Loveman. ITBLP

Rain Song of the Quer'ränna Chai' än, A. *Unknown.* APN-2, *tr. by* Matilda Coxe Stevenson

Rain Song of the Shu'-wi Chai' än (Snake Society), A. *Unknown.* APN-2, *tr. by* Matilda Coxe Stevenson

Rain sprinkles on the pond. Cho Hön. CATKP, *tr. by* Peter H. Lee

Rain stopped for one afternoon, The. Easter: Wahiawa, 1959. Cathy Song. FTtHH; OpBo

Rain stops falling in this river village, The. In a Village by the River. Li Po. CrYelRi, *tr. by* Sam Hamill

Rain streaming from me. (LL) Trillium. Louise Glück. MoWP; StAl

Rain streams past the gutters, overflowing, The. Modern Love. Ann Townsend. LegDan; LiTh

Rain sweeps in as the gale begins to blow. Wet Day. James McAuley. BMAP

Rain thunders on the roof, The. Different Morning Altogether, A. Dima Hilal. PoArWo

Rain thunderstorms over the Potomac, in Georgetown. Rainscapes, Hydrangeas, Roses, and Singing Birds. Richard Eberhart. MoAmPo

Rain, tobacco juice, spit from the sky. Starvation. Ai. AFaM

Rain Towards Morning. Elizabeth Bishop. OxBoAm *Fr.* Four Poems.

Rain Travel. W. S. Merwin. ColAP; GoPo

Rain tries the one small foot and at length the other. Towards the Land of the Composer. Francis Webb. BMAP

Rain will never stop falling, The. (LL) Shoulders. Naomi Shihab Nye. AtGh; TWF

Rain, with a silver flail. Whale. William Rose Benét. MoAmPo

Rain with its hair gilded by the sun, The. Transfiguration of the Rain. Jorge Carrera Andrade. TCLAP, *tr. by* Michael Surman

Rain with the old sound, with the country sough. Under Cover. Abbie Huston Evans. APT-1

Rainbarrel. Aidan Rooney-Céspedes. NIrP

Rainbearers. Vona Groarke. NIrP

Rain—Birdoswald. Frances Horovitz. StAl

Rainbow. Paul Laraque. OGAHCP, *tr. by* Boadiba and Jack Hirschman

Rainbow, The. Opal Palmer Adisa. GT

Rainbow, The. John Keble. TreFP

Rainbow, The. William Wordsworth. *See* My Heart Leaps Up [When I Behold].

Rainbow at Night. Antonio Machado Ruiz. AF; BLT; WED, *tr. by* Robert Bly

Rainbow Dragon Trilogy. Amryl Johnson.

    Oil on Troubled Waters. Oth

Rainbow for the Christian West, A. René Depestre. *tr. by* Joan Dayan

    Baron-Samedi. PFTM-2, *tr. by* Joan Dayan

    Cap'tain Zombi. PFTM-2, *tr. by* Joan Dayan

    Chango. PFTM-2, *tr. by* Joan Dayan

Rainbow i'th'morning. *Unknown.* FaBoVe

Rainbow; or Curious Covenant, The. Robert Herrick. ChIV-1

Rainbow Over the Seine, A. Mary Jo Salter. ExTi

Rainbow stands and summer passes under, A. (LL) I hear a river thro' the valley wander. Trumbull Stickney. APN-2; NoP-4; NoP-5; OxBoAm

Rainbow-Colored Whale, The. Ferenc Juhász. WoPoe, *tr. by* David Wevill

Rainbows hang in the eddies. City Out of the Boy, The. Jeffrey Skinner. UrbNat

Raindrop Women. Mariahadessa Ekere Tallie. BtF

Raindrops. György Sárközi. IQMS, *tr. by* Roy Fuller

Raindrops are striking a mountain mulberry leaf. Mountain Rain. Paek Sŏk. CAMKP, *tr. by* Kyunghwan Choi

Raindrops fall. To a Man Who is Rob Southland. Nia Francisco. HATNAP

Raindrops on roses and whiskers on kittens. My Favorite Things. Oscar Hammerstein, II. ReLy

Rained milk and blood during the courtship. Miraculous Panoptic Precipitations. Christine Hume. IAoNAP

Rained on. (LL) Shunning an Imperative. Carl Hancock Rux. BRtP; HeMarv

Rainfall Piano. Luis J. Rodriguez. LiTh

Rainforest. Judith Wright. OPOU

Rainmakers, The. Robert Kelly. PmAP

Rains. Nike Adesuyi. NeNiPo

Rains are driven by stiff winds, The. Traveler's Life, A. Sung Fang-hu. CrYelRi, *tr. by* Sam Hamill

Rains brought a new life, The. Monsoon. Elsa Cross. RMCMP, *tr. by* Margaret Sayers Peden

Rain's cold grains are silver-gray, The. Crowded Trolley Car, A. Elinor Wylie. SacPr

Rain's feet, The. Sublimated Mercury. Alice Rahon. SurWo, *tr. by* Myrna Bell Rochester

Rains have come, The. Poem from Sierra Madre. Mila D. Aguilar. ReBoTo

Rains have come, the winds are shrill, The. Rainy Season in California, The. John Rollin Ridge. APN-2

Rain's pounding away, The. Rain. Sándor Weöres. BLT

Rainscapes, Hydrangeas, Roses, and Singing Birds. Richard Eberhart. MoAmPo

Rainsong. Tony Nduka Otiono. NeNiPo

5: Rainstorm: The Gorge. Alicia Gaspar de Alba. FTtHH *Fr.* Elemental Journey: Anniversary Gift.

Rain-sunken roof, grown green and thin. Barn, The. Edmund Charles Blunden. MoBrPo

Rainy Dawn. Joy Harjo. ICANM

Rainy Easter. William Everson. APT-2

Rainy Mountain Cemetery. N. Scott Momaday. HATNAP; ICANM

Rainy Night. Juana de Ibarbourou. TCLAP, *tr. by* Sophie Cabot Black

Rainy Season. Charles Reznikoff. APT-2

Rainy season, The. Buson. EMJL, *tr. by* Haruo Shirane

Rainy Season, The. Linda Hogan. HATNAP; TRP

Rainy Season in California, The. John Rollin Ridge. APN-2

Rainy Season; Sub-Tropics. Elizabeth Bishop.

    Giant Snail. MotU

    Strayed Crab. MotU

Rainy, sore at the whole town. Homage to a Tom-Cat. Thomas Parkinson. ASA

Raise girls but not too many. Han-shan (Cold Mountain). ColAnChi, *tr. by* Red Pine

Raise high the roof. Sappho. SaLy, *tr. by* Diane Rayor

Raise him a tombstone of snow. (LL) Last Rites. Christina Georgina Rossetti. FaBoVe; NPeEn

Raise the Cromlech high! Lament of Maev Leith-Dherg, The. *Unknown.* OBWP, *tr. by* Thomas William Hazen Rolleston

Raise the oars, be carried. Mortal Practice. Gabriel Zaid. TCLAP, *tr. by* Mónica Hernández-Cancio

Raise up your valorous right arm, O Spain. On the Armada That Battled Against England. Luis de Góngora y Argote. SpanPo, *tr. by* Ian Fletcher and Brian Soper

Raised grain of golden oak in sunlight, The. Sudden Tug of the Familiar, The. Faye George. PoDa

Raisin Pumpernickel. Marge Piercy. StAl

Raising a Humid Flag. Thylias Moss. GT

Raising my drooping Head, o'er charg'd with Thought. My Fate. Anne Wharton. EMWP

Raising My Hand. "Antler." IJHIL

Raising my head, I make out my house in the twilight. Buson. EMJL *Fr.* Spring Breeze on the Kema Embankment.

Raising of Icarus, The: Envoi. Guy Goffette. YaTCFP, *tr. by* Marilyn Hacker

Raising that truncheon of an arm. When I Think About America Sometimes (I Think of Ralph Kramden). Dorothy Barresi. ExTi; ReTh

Raising the Dead. Fatima Lim-Wilson. ReBoTo

Raising the Mediating Center and the Field of Evil with the Twenty-Five Thousand Accounts and the Chant of the Ancients. Eduardo Calderón. PFTM-2, *tr. by* F. Kaye Sharon

Raíz, La. Luis Rosales. RaW

Rajah doesn't like Nirvana but he seems. Rajah in Babylon. David Wojahn. IllVoic

Rajah in Babylon. David Wojahn. IllVoic

Rakes of Mallow, The. *Unknown.* OBCoV

Raking leaves / brown as his robe. My Favorite Monk Is. Connie Deanovich. AmPoNex

Ralegh's Prizes. Robert Pinsky. VCAP

Raleigh Was Right. William Carlos Williams. NIL-7; NIP-4; NoAM; PoA 2002; WaAnP; WoPoe

Rales of Easter. . .The sucking. Invitation to a Sabbath. Harry Mathews. NYP2

Rally Song. Mary Weston Fordham. CBWP-2

Ralph Ellison didn't. Forgive and Live. Yusef Komunyakaa. BodElec

Ralph Rhodes. Edgar Lee Masters. APT-1 *Fr.* Spoon River Anthology.

Ram. Gillian Clarke. AngWePo

Ram. Ani Ilkov. CSCBP, *tr. by* Georgi Belev and Lisa Sapinkopf

Ram came last of all. And Abraham, The. Heritage. Haim Guri. HP

Rama says. Two Women Knitting. Mrinal Pande. CFP, *tr. by* Arlene Zide, the author and Mrinal Pande *and* Arlene Zide

Ramallah. Bei Dao. WoBe, *tr. by* Iona Man-Cheong and Eliot Weinberger

Ramallah—January, 2002. Mahmoud Darwish. Eno, *tr. by* Ramsis Amun

Ramat Gan houseware shop, The. Liquidation. Leah Aini. DTA, *tr. by* Miriyam Glazer

Ramayana. Viswanatha Satyanarayana. *tr. by* V. Narayana Rao

Beginning, The. CFP, *tr. by* V. Narayana Rao

Ramble in St. James's Park, A. John Wilmot, 2d Earl of Rochester. BASC

Rambling school-boy, thus, A. William Wordsworth. NAEL-6v2; NAEL-7v2 *Fr.* Prelude, The; Growth of a Poet's Mind [1850 version].

Rameur, Le. Paul Valéry. YaTCFP

Rampaging spectral images. Just Another Gig. Baron James Ashanti. SeSe

Rams. Alasdair Maclean. EdScPo

Ram's Horn, The. John Hewitt. ModIr; PNI

Ramsden. Margaret Avison. GPPA

Rana sent a gold coffer of complicated ivory. Coffer with the Poisonous Snake, The. Mirabai. WED, *tr. by* Robert Bly

Ranch on the Limpia, The. Dorys Crow Grover. TiP2

Rancho. Cecilio Garcia-Camarillo. ICANM

Rançon, La. René[e] Vivien. YaTCFP

Randall, My Son. Donald Davidson. FuPo

Randall, my son, before you came just now. Randall, My Son. Donald Davidson. FuPo

Randolph Field, 1938. R. S. Gwynn. TiP2

Random Pleasures. Tu Fu [*or* Du Fu]. *tr. by* Sam Hamill

"All day, all night, I worry." CrYelRi, *tr. by* Sam Hamill

"Blown by winds, the thistledown." CrYelRi, *tr. by* Sam Hamill

"Dragon sleeps three winter months, A." CrYelRi, *tr. by* Sam Hamill

"Grieved, I idle and doze." CrYelRi, *tr. by* Sam Hamill

"Peach and plum I planted were my own, The." CrYelRi, *tr. by* Sam Hamill

"River swallows know my shack is humble." CrYelRi, *tr. by* Sam Hamill

"T'ao Ch'ien withdrew from all the world." CrYelRi, *tr. by* Sam Hamill

"Unemployed and lazy, I wander around the village." CrYelRi, *tr. by* Sam Hamill

"West of my hut, I grow mulberry." CrYelRi, *tr. by* Sam Hamill

Random (Re-arrangeable) Study for *Views*. Tony Towle. PmAP

Range in the Desert, The. Randall Jarrell. PoWW

Range is French and has a mind of its own, The. Collector's Marginalia, The. Peter Sirr. PBCIP

Range of It, The. Michael Klein. WiU

Range Rovers carry. Three xlvii. Laurie Duggan. BMAP

Range-finding. Robert Frost. NIL-7; NIP-4; NoAM; OBWP

Ranges / of clinker heaps. John Maydew or The Allotment. Charles Tomlinson. OBGa

Ranging Dog the stubble tries, The. John Gay. *Fr.* Fables: First Series.

Rank. Lincoln Kirstein. FaBoA; OBWP; OxBoAm; PWW2

Ranked solid on my shelves. Books. Aneirin Talfan Davies. BBMWP, *tr. by* Catherine Fisher

Rankles in a livid spot. (LL) Fifth-Floor Window, The. Lola Ridge. APT-1; NAAPv.2

Ranks of electroplated cubes, dwindling to glitters. Fixed Ideas. Kenneth Slessor. BMAP

Rannoch, by Glencoe. T. S. Eliot. NAEL-6v2 *Fr.* Landscapes.

Rannoch Moor. Alison Fell. EdScPo

Ransom, The. René[e] Vivien. YaTCFP, *tr. by* Mary Ann Caws *and* Jean-Pierre Cauvin

Rant. Diane Di Prima.

"Only war that matters is the war against the imagination, The." PFTM-2

Rant, Rave and Ricochet. Luis J. Rodriguez. IllVoic

Rantin' Dog, the Daddie o't, The. Robert Burns. FaBoVe

Rap Is. Christopher Stanard. SpirFl

Rap is no mystery. Rap Is. Christopher Stanard. SpirFl

Rape. Jayne Cortez. GT; PmAP

Rape of Chanticleer, the. Geoffrey Chaucer. DiBP *Fr.* Canterbury Tales, The.

Rape of Lucrece, The. Thomas Heywood.

(Matin Song.) OBEV

Rape of Lucrece, The. Ovid. NPeEn *Fr.* Confessio Amantis.

Rape of Lucrece, The. William Shakespeare.

[Before the Rape]. NoSic

Lucrece's Death. NoSic

Rape of the Lock, The: An Heroi-Comical Poem in Five Cantos. Alexander Pope. CABP; NAEL-6v1; NAEL-7v1; NAWM-7v2; NoP-4; NoP-5; OBNV; WaAnP

"Adventurous baron the bright locks admired, The." EroLit

"But anxious cares the pensive nymph oppressed." OxAEP-1

"But when to mischief mortals bend their will." OxAEP-1

"For lo! the board with cups and spoons is crown'd." UV

Hampton Court. OBSV

"'Restore the lock!" she cries; and all around." OxAEP-1

"Sol through white curtains shot a tim'rous ray." NPeEn

"Then grave Clarissa graceful wav'd her fan." NPeEn; OxBEV

Toilet, The. OxAEP-1; OxBEV

Voyage on the Thames, The. OxAEP-1

Raped Poem. Bhairavayya. HotL, *tr. by* V. Narayana Rao

Raphael. Henrietta Cordelia Ray. CBWP-3

Raphael. Priscilla Jane Thompson. CBWP-2

Raphael's Descent. John Milton. NOSC *Fr.* Paradise Lost.

Rapid day is gone; her banner swings the night, The. Evening. Andreas Gryphius. GePo, *tr. by* George C. Schoolfield

Rapid Floods. Kata Szidónia Petröczy. IQMS, *tr. by* Marie B. Jaffe

Rapid Transit. James Agee. MoAmPo

Rapid Transit. Nzadi Z. Keita. BRtP

Rapid Transit. William Carlos Williams. APT-1; OxBoAm

Rapist: A Romance. Rigoberto González. LiTh

Rapist's Villanelle, The [*with music*]. Thomas M. Disch. RA

Rapparees. Richard Murphy. PBCIP *Fr.* Battle of Aughrim, The.

Rappelle-toi. Joyce Mansour. YaTCFP

Rappelle-toi Barbara. Barbara. Jacques Prévert. YaTCFP

Rapt. Irene McKinney. PBCAP

Rapt with the rage of mine own ravisht thogunt. Hymn[e] of Heavenly Beauty [*or* Beautie], An. Edmund Spenser.

Raptor. Ronald Stuart Thomas. EmeKit

Raptor, The. Molly Peacock. PfS

Raptor in the Kitchen. Joyce Peseroff. PoDa

Rapture. Galway Kinnell. FaoP

Rapture, A. Thomas Carew. BASC; CABP; NAEL-6v1; NAEL-7v1; OxAEP-1

"Come, then, and mounted on the wings of Love." EroLit

"I will enjoy thee now my Celia, come." PBRV

"Now in more subtle wreaths I will entwine." EroLit

Rapture, The. Adam Cornford.

"And it came to pass just as they had foretold." CLPP

Rapture, The. Thomas Traherne. NOSC

Rapture of Dry Ice Burning off Skin as the Moment of the Soul's Apotheosis, The. Thylias Moss. NAMCP V.2

Rapunzel. Olga Broumas. ReTh

Rapunzel Rapunzel let down your hair. After-Thought, The. Stevie Smith. MoWP

Rapunzstiltskin. Liz Lochhead. BeAl; MoWP

Rare composition of a poet-knight. Sonnet to a Sonnet. Thomas Hood. CenSon

Rare Is the Wheat-Field in Which There's No Blemish. *Hungarian Oral Tradition*. IQMS, *tr. by* Adam Makkai

Rare medieval Spirit! brooding seer! Dante. Henrietta Cordelia Ray. CBWP-3

Rare perfectbound collection from jwcurry emerges full flannel as the flag, A. Darren Wershler-Henry. PoPra *Fr.* Ten Out of Ten, or, Why Poetry Criticism Sucks in 2003.

Rare sight, a woman lost in the trance. *Unknown*. GifTon, *tr. by* David Ray

Rare smile, The. Portrait. Manuel Bandeira. TCLAP, *tr. by* Candace Slater

Rare, twice-in-a-lifetime form of sport, A. Retort Perfect, The. Justin Richardson. OBCoV

Rare type of gentrie, and true Vertues Starr. Joshua Sylvester. OxBSo *Fr.* Du Bartas: His Divine Weeks and Works.

Rarest commodity here is color, The. Ophelia on a Graveled Garden Walk in Purgatory. Ryan Van Cleave. IaFF

Rarest of the esculents, its distribution. Roger Garfitt. NewEx

Rarity and value of scientific knowledge, The. Poetry and Science. Hugh MacDiarmid. HarvBoo

Raspa. Orlando Ricardo Menes. RWB

Raspberry Sweater, A. Frank O'Hara. AHA

Rasta Reggae. Mervyn Morris. WaCA

Rat, The. W. H. Davies. OBWVE

Rat, The. Karen Kipp. BodElec

Rat, The. *Unknown*. WoPoe, *tr. by* John S. Major

Rat and the Elephant, The. Jean de La Fontaine. OBVE, *tr. by* Marianne Moore

Rat / gnawing the white rabbit deep in sleep. In the Night. Kim Hyesun. CAMKP, *tr. by* Jiwon Shin

Rat Jelly. Michael Ondaatje. EmeKit

Rat makes her way up, The. Explicating the Twilight. Jack Gilbert. WaAnP

Rat Minaret: Miniaturist-Divan, The. Mac Wellman.

  "All the way clear to Aliquippa." HeMarv

  "Blue sky in a human face." HeMarv

  "Endowed fiction of a mouse ear." HeMarv

  "Evil Raven, have paper pity upon those." HeMarv

  "Lost from an airy." HeMarv

  "Most simple things repel." HeMarv

  "Moth house is taking over, Sir Footfall." HeMarv

  "Needle growing in ancient basalt." HeMarv

  "No point mortgages wilt in daynights." HeMarv

  "No tongue but bumbles, has." HeMarv

  "Silvery tells no sphere to go and." HeMarv

  "So perfectly done and yet." HeMarv

  "United bolt and screw." HeMarv

  "Who lowers the unseen hat from on high." HeMarv

Rat, O Rat. Christopher Logue. EmeKit

Rat Song. Margaret Atwood. NIP-4 *Fr.* Songs of the Transformed.

Rat too has a skin (to tan), A. *Unknown*. WoPoe *Fr.* Yung Wind.

Rat! Torturing my *BRAIN!* is the aria. Try-Outs, The. Sharon Olds. PoDa

Rat Trap. Mick Gowar. NOxBChV

Ratatouille. Douglas Dunn. BeAl

Rate of Exchange, The. Nakano Shigeharu. CAoMJL1, *tr. by* Miriam Silverberg

Rather a box of winds. Box. Michele Glazer. IAoNAP

Rather, cars will honk as if to say it's easier. Strictly Speaking. Debra Gregerman. AmPoNex

Rather dead than spotted; and believe it. Then the Ermine. Marianne Moore. PoA 2002

Rather deception than retreat, painted in flesh, in broken arcade, dust and flecks of red remain. Moveable Figures. Heather Ramsdell. IIR

Rather obese Master Shuang, A. Tune: "Po Pu-tuan" Fat Couple. Wang Ho-ch'ing. ColAnChi, *tr. by* James I. Crump

Rather remote, all of it. Vanished Work. Hans Magnus Enzensberger. VCWP, *tr. by* the author, Hans Magnus Enzensberger and Michael Hamburger

Rather than attribute, towards the brush with open sea. (LL) Note to Tony Towle (After WS), A. Charles North. FTOS; PmAP

Rather than break my vow to plum blossoms. 133. Shih Shu. CSKM, *tr. by* James H. Sanford

Rather than deserting someone. Kim Namjo. CAMKP *Fr.* Love's Cursive.

Rather than our bodies the sand. Army Beach with Trumpets. Jack Spicer. APSN

Rather the Bird Flying By and Leaving No Trace. Fernando Pessoa. WoPoe, *tr. by* Edwin Honig

Rathlin. Derek Mahon. ModIr

Ratiocinative. Joseph Cottle. STuOW *Fr.* Malvern Hills.

Ration books voided, there was little to eat. Tía Olivia Serves Wallace Stevens a Cuban Egg. Richard Blanco. NAPBL

Rational. Helen Chalakee Burgess. ReEnLa

Rational Anthem, A. Ambrose Bierce. CalPo

Rational Man. Muriel Rukeyser. AF

Rats, / stone-head rats lay off our grain. Shi-shu: Rats. *Unknown*. CCL1, *tr. by* Ezra Pound

Rats by night such mischief did, The. Fable XXI: The Rat-catcher and Cats. John Gay. OxAEP-1

Rattle [*with music*]. Peter Blue Cloud. HATNAP

Rattle Bag, The. Dafydd ap Gwilym. NBLV; WoPoe, *tr. by* Joseph P. Clancy

Rattler, Alert. Brewster Ghiselin. WeW-3

Rattlesnake Country. Robert Penn Warren. VCAP

Rattlesnake Roundup. Pat Stodghill. TiP2

Rav, The / of Northern White Russia declined. Illustrious Ancestors. Denise Levertov. OxBoAm; PmAP; TaR

Ravaged Villa, The. Herman Melville. APN-2; TCAPo

  (In Shards the Sylvan Vases Lie.) NCAP

Rave. Jasper Bernes. IAoNAP

Ravel: Bolero. Al Young. SpirFl

Ravel of ravishments the raven-black. Rave. Jasper Bernes. IAoNAP

Raven, The. Samuel Taylor Coleridge. NOxBChV

Raven, The. Edgar Allan Poe. APN-1; BRP; ChAP; ColAP; HeIP-4; ITBLP; NAAL-3; NAAL-5; NAAPv.1; NCAP; NIL-7; NIP-4; NoP-4; NoP-5; OBNV; OWoS; OxBoAm; TCAPo; TFi; TreFP; UV; WaAnP

Raven, The. Sarah Helen Whitman. NAAPv.1

Raven croaks before me, A. Ode. Theophile De Viau. WoPoe, *tr. by* Phillip Holland

Raven Days, The. Sidney Lanier. APN-2; TCAPo

Raven eyes blink. Raven is Two-Faced. Robert H. Davis. HATNAP

Raven, from the dim doninions. Raven, The. Sarah Helen Whitman. NAAPv.1

Raven, gather us to that dark breast. Raven Tells Stories. Robert H. Davis. HATNAP

Raven is Two-Faced [*with music*]. Robert H. Davis. HATNAP

Raven Robe Lane. Liu Yu Hsi. CCL1, *tr. by* Stephen Owen

Raven sat upon a tree, A. Sycophantic Fox and the Gullible Raven, The. Guy Wetmore Carryl. NBLV

Raven Tells Stories [*with music*]. Robert H. Davis. HATNAP

Ravenna Bridge. Leslie Norris. AngWePo

Ravens. Georgi Borisov. CSCBP, *tr. by* Georgi Belev and Lisa Sapinkopf

Raven's Beak River at the End. Gary Snyder. PfSP

Raven's Revenge. Tyler Doherty. WANABP

Ravine. Luke Icarus Simon. PML, *tr. by* the author

Ravine on a Cold Evening. Li Ho. ColAnChi, *tr. by* Maureen Robertson

Ravished [*or* Ravisht] in that fair[e] *Via Lactea*. (LL) Upon Julia's Breasts. Robert Herrick. NoP-4; NoP-5; WaAnP

Raw cabbage marinated in vinegar with chilies. Kimchee in Worchester (Mass.). Alfred Corn. WiU

Raw Fish and Vegetables. Takahashi Shinkichi. ZenPo, *tr. by* Takashi Ikemoto and Lucien Stryk

Raw Flesh. Vasco [*or* Vasko] Popa. *tr. by* Anne Pennington

  Be Seeing You. PoSu

  In the Village of My Forefathers. PoSu

  Time Swept Up. PoSu

Rawest, most spontaneous, and most eclectic of post-Langpo texts, The. Darren Wershler-Henry. PoPra *Fr.* Ten Out of Ten, or, Why Poetry Criticism Sucks in 2003.

Rayboy Blk & Bluz. Shirley Bradley LeFlore. SpirFl

Rayflower / About the head. Rayflower. Sándor Weöres. IQMS, *tr. by* Edwin Morgan

Raymond Chandler: The Big Sleep. Basil Ransome-Davies. OBCoV

Raymond of the Rooftops. Paul Durcan. EmeKit

Raynsford, a knight, fit to have served King Arthur. Sir John Raynsford's Confession. John Harington. NoSic

Rayos luminosos penetran el verde ajado del ojo, paracido a un cenote muerto, Los. Quimera. Silvia Eugenia Castillero. SPV

Ray's third new car in half as many years. Family Reunion. Louise Erdrich. HATNAP; NAMCP V.2; NoAM; WaAnP

Razglednica (1). Miklós Radnóti. IQMS, *tr. by* Peter Zollman

Razglednica (2). Miklós Radnóti. IQMS, *tr. by* Peter Zollman

Razglednica (3). Miklós Radnóti. IQMS, *tr. by* Peter Zollman

Razglednica (4). Miklós Radnóti. IQMS, *tr. by* Peter Zollman

Razglednica (4) ("I dropped beside him. Taut as is the cord.") Miklós Radnóti. IQMS, *tr. by* Iain MacLeod

Razglednica (4) ("I fell beside him and his corpse turned over.") Miklós Radnóti. IQMS, *tr. by* Zsuzsanna Ozsváth and Frederick Turner

Razglednica (4) ("I fell beside him. His body—which was taut.") Miklós Radnóti. IQMS, *tr. by* Geroge Gömöri and Clive Wilmer

Razones viudas por las que. Trece intenciones contra el amor trivial. David Huerta. RMCMP

Razor-filching delivery in half-mind. Camille Martin. AnSo *Fr.* No truck.

Razors pain you. Résumé. Dorothy Parker. AmWit; APT-1; EMP; HeIP-4; IJHIL; NALW; NAMCP V.1; NBLV; NoP-4; NoP-5; OxBoAm; PtR; UV

Razzle Dazzle! Whiskers Meets Polly. Michael Stillman. TLR

Razzmatazz. Gilbert Sorrentino. FTOS

Re:composition. Martha Collins. PfS

R-E-M-O-R-S-E. George Ade. NBLV; OBCoV

Re: Robert. Larkin Higgins. VisFro

Re:searches (Fragments, after Anakreon, for Emily Dickinson). Kathleen Fraser. PmAP

Re: The Tobacco Institute. Ron Overton. PrTe

Reach, The. Carl Phillips. GT

Reach and you set this whole harp. Harp/Desire. Katherine Soniat. MiVo

Reach back and bring me the firmness of her hand. (LL) Request to a Year. Judith Wright. BrAP; ItWoWo; NALW; NAMCP V.2; NoAM; NoP-4; NoP-5

Reach my boat. (LL) Maple Bridge Night Mooring. Chang Chi. ColAnChi; NDACCP, *tr. by* Gary Snyder

Reach, with your whiter hands, to me. To the Water Nymphs, Drinking at the Fountain. Robert Herrick. NAEL-6v1

Reaches down like a hood. Although the Sky. Elmaz Abinader. PoArWo

Reaches Sicily. Mary Robinson. CenSon; RWP

Reaching Around. Judith Moffett. ViWalt

Reaching for the cakes of ice. (LL) Charles Reznikoff. ColAP; NAAPv.2 *Fr.* Testimony.

Reaching for the silence. Poem for Those of You Who Are Sometimes Troubled by Barking Dogs and Low Flying Jets, A. Steve Sanfield. WhBo

Reaching out into the sea, passing the waves its exhaust smoking. Mission Work-Boat. *Unknown.* NOBAu, *tr. by* Mungayana Nundhirribala

Reaching the Horizon. Robert Mezey. GeoHom

Reaching to help hurt creatures they usually. Goat, The. Greg Delanty. MAAN

Reaching Yellow River. Roberta Hill Whiteman. HATNAP

Reaction To What You Said. Sonnet L'Abbé. OpeFie

Reactionary Poet, The. Ishmael Reed. ESEAA; GT

Read and committed to the flames, I call. Tony Harrison. CABP; HarvBoo; NAMCP V.2; NoP-4; NoP-5 *Fr.* School of Eloquence, The.

Read here: / This is the story of Evarra-man. Evarra and His Gods. Rudyard Kipling. MoBrPo

Read it not, noble lords. William Shakespeare. OxAEP-1 *Fr.* Coriolanus.

Read me Euripides. Follies of Adam, The. Theodore Roethke. ChIV-1

Read of *Thyestes, Oedipus*, dark suns. Martial. RomPo, *tr. by* Peter Whigham

Read some lines a poet wrote in the exile of his town. Town. Marie-Claire Bancquart. MFP, *tr. by* Martin Sorrell

Read the Bible, it will tell. Bible, The. Lizelia Augusta Jenkins Moorer. CBWP-3

Reader, The. Janet Lewis. APT-2

Reader, The. Wallace Stevens. SAmP

Reader. Epitaph on Sir Philip Sidney Lying in St Paul's without a Monument, to be Fastned upon the Church Door. Edward Herbert, 1st Baron Herbert of Cherbury. NPeEn

Reader / If thou be a Christian and a Freeman. Epitaph for Jonathan Robbins. Philip Freneau. TCAPo

Reader, my story's an old one—and yet. Rebirth. Mereid Hopwood. BBMWP, *tr. by* Elin ap Hywel

Reader of This Page. Maurice Kilwein Guevara. NAPBL

Reader over My Shoulder, The. Robert Graves. NAEL-6v2; NAEL-7v2

Reader unmov'd and Reader unshaken, Reader unsedc'd. Sweet Reader, Flanneled and Tulled. Olena Kalytiak Davis. BAP-01; NAPBL

(Reader unmov'd and Reader unshaken, Reader unseduc'd.) LegDan

Reader, when these dumb stones have told. Another [On the Duke of Buckingham]. Thomas Carew. NOSC

Readers, forgive me. Ten ii. Laurie Duggan. BMAP

Readers. I am ashamed to set myself up as a poet before you. To the Readers. Han Yong'un [*or* Yongwun]. CAMKP, *tr. by* Sammy Solberg

Readers of the *Boston Evening Transcript*, The. *Boston Evening Transcript*, The. T. S. Eliot. APT-1; TCAPo

READIE-SOUNDPIECE (after a suggestion of Hilaire Hiler) (synchro-with Orchestrauto maton). Abraham Lincoln Gillespie. PFTM-2 *Fr.* Readie-Soundpiece (For Bob Brown's Reading Machine).

Readie-Soundpiece (For Bob Brown's Reading Machine). Abraham Lincoln Gillespie.

"READIE-SOUNDPIECE (after a suggestion of Hilaire Hiler) (synchro-with Orchestrauto maton)." PFTM-2

Reading. Joanne Burns. BMAP

Reading. Ruth Stone. ExTi

Reading: "Taste the unnecessary tears." Bei Dao. WoBe, *tr. by* Iona Man-Cheong and Eliot Weinberger

Reading, A. Virginia Hooper. KGB

Reading, The. Gabriel Gbadamosi. HBAPE

Reading, The. Peter Schjeldahl. AHA

Reading a Book on a Winter Night. Kan Chazan. EMJL, *tr. by* Haruo Shirane

Reading a Story to My Child. Primus St. John. PoChi

Reading a used book on evolution I wonder. Active Reader, The. Bob Hicok. AmAlph

Reading Akhmatova in Midwinter. Lavinia Greenlaw. NeBrP

Reading, and reading—little is the gain. Suspiria Noctis. Henry Howard Brownell. APN-2

Reading and singing are good, while speaking is just minutes. Apostle Qualities. Gisèle Prassinos. YaTCFP, *tr. by* Mary Ann Caws *and* Jean-Pierre Cauvin

Reading Aquinas. Michael Heffernan. WeW-3

Reading Before We Read, Horoscope and Weather. Wyatt Prunty. RA

Reading *Bonjour, Tristesse* at the Florence Crittenden Home for Unwed Mothers. Diane Wakoski. GeoHom

Reading Buddhist Classics with Chao at His Temple in the Early Morning. Liu Tsung-yüan. CCL1, *tr. by* Witter Bynner

Reading by Mechanic Light. Thomas McGrath. BodElec; GifTon

Reading Chinese Poetry before Dawn. Jane Hirshfield. WANABP

Reading Chiyo-Ni, 1703-1775, Japanese Woman Haikuist. Miriam Sagan. WANABP

Reading clouds beyond the road. Getting Your Rocks Off. Melvin Dixon. CAGL

Reading Croce. Meirion Pennar. BBMWP, *tr. by* Martin Davis

Reading "Crossing Brooklyn Ferry" on a Summer Morning. Howard Nelson. ViWalt

Reading, Dreaming, Hiding. Kelly Cherry. FFC

Reading Emerson. Cottonmouths are moving mildly. Lake Drummond Dream. Dave Jeddie Smith. VCAP

Reading for Pleasure. Barbara Einzig *and* Jerome Rothenberg. OnScMo

Reading Frank O'Hara in a Mexican Rainstorm. Michael McClure. BB

Reading Hamlet. Anna Andreyevna Akhmatova. PoetW, *tr. by* Max Hayward and Stanley Kunitz

Reading I spilled the wine. Untoward. Ann Lauterbach. BodElec

Reading in Bed. Magi Gibson. EdScPo

Reading in Li Po. After the Last Dynasty. Stanley Kunitz. InvLad

Reading in Place. Mark Strand. OxBoAm

Reading Lao Tzu Again in the New Year. Charles Wright. PfSP; PoA 2002

Reading Lesson, The. Richard Murphy. PBCIP

Reading *Moby-Dick* at 30,000 Feet. Tony Hoagland. OtW

Reading my verses, I liked [*or* like't] them so well. Poet[r]ess's Hasty Resolution, The. Margaret Lucas Cavendish, Duchess of Newcastle. BASC; NAEL-7v1

Reading Myself. Robert Lowell. NAMCP V.2; VCAP; WaAnP

Reading *Othello* and Watching a Girl Skip Rope. Jennifer Hill Kaucher. IaFF

Reading *Paradise Lost* in Protestant Ulster 1984. Seamus Deane. PBCIP

Reading *Pericles* in New London. Alfred Corn. IaFF

Reading Plato. Rick Barot. LegDan

Reading Pornography in Old Age [*with music*]. Howard Nemerov. NAMCP V.2; NoAM

Reading Postures 3. Marcella Durand. IIR

Reading Reverdy. Ron Padgett. OxBoAm

Reading Room. Allison Joseph. NAPBL

Reading Scheme. Wendy Cope. MakPoe; WaAnP

Reading Seferis. Sam Hamill. GifTon

Reading the Bible Backwards. Eleanor Wilner. NoP-4; NoP-5

Reading: The Bus. C. K. Williams. PoCho

Reading the Elephant. Andrew Motion. HarvBoo

Reading the Facts about Frost in *The Norton Anthology*. George Starbuck. PoA 2002

Reading the I Ching. Raquel Chalfi. DTA, *tr. by* Karen Alkalay-Gut

Reading the Japanese Poet Issa (1762–1826). Czeslaw Milosz. WoPoe, *tr. by* the author and Robert K. Haas

Reading the Names. Elizabeth McLagan. FiBr

Reading the Poems of an Absent Friend. Ou-yang Hsiu. NDACCP, *tr. by* Kenneth Rexroth

Reading the Poetry of Meng Chiao: Two Poems. Su Tung-p'o. ColAnChi; WoPoe, *tr. by* Burton Watson

Reading the Signs. Eric Tretheway. PfSP

Reading the Unpublished Manuscripts of Louis MacNeice at Kinsale Harbour. Desmond O'Grady. PBCIP

Reading the Writing. John N. Morris. PoA 2002

Reading this poet makes me wonder who's crazy? Ryokan the Crazy Snow Poet. Al Robles. WhBo

Reading Time : 1 Minute 26 Seconds. Muriel Rukeyser. NIL-7

Reading Tom's poem "To Winter." Larry Fagin. AHA *Fr.* Parade of the Caterpillars, The.

Reading Walt Whitman. Calvin Forbes. ESEAA; ViWalt

Reading Whitman in a Toilet Stall. Timothy Liu. WiU

Reading Whitman's *Democratic Vistas*. Terry Savoie. ViWalt

Reading with the Poets. Stanley Plumly. ViWalt

Reading won't save us from death. Han-shan (Cold Mountain). ColAnChi, *tr. by* Red Pine

Reading Yeats I do not think / of Ireland. Lawrence Ferlinghetti. CLPP

Reading your poems I am aware. Letter to Peter Levi, A. Elizabeth Jennings. OxAEP-2

Reading Yuan Chen on a Boat. Po Chü-i. CrYelRi, *tr. by* Sam Hamill

Readings. Armanda Guiducci. CItWP, *tr. by* Cinzia Sartini Blum and Lara Trubowitz

Readings. Czeslaw Milosz. GI, *tr. by* the author and Lillian Vallee

Readings, Forecasts, Personal Guidance. Kenneth Fearing. MoAmPo

Ready. Dan Pagis. FIT, *tr. by* Robert Friend

Ready for Flight. Eavan Boland. IrLP; OxBSo

Ready she sat with one hand to turn o'er. Leigh Hunt. STuOW *Fr.* Story of Rimini, The.

Ready-Made World. Piera Oppezzo. CItWP, *tr. by* Cinzia Sartini Blum and Lara Trubowitz

Real Comfort. Mary Stanley Bunce Dana. SWaP

Real danger. gambles. and the edge of death. (LL) What You Should Know to Be a Poet. Gary Snyder. APSN; OxBoAm; PFTM-2

Real Devotion of Events, The. Judith Goldman. Eno

Real duel of Apollo, The. Apollo and Marsyas. Zbigniew Herbert. PoSu; WoPoe, *tr. by* Czeslaw Milosz and Peter Dale Scott

Real electric lights light upon the full-sized, The. Fission. Jorie Graham. NAMCP V.2; OxBoAm

Real Estate. David Antin. FTOS

Real Estate. Michael Hannon. GeoHom

Real Estate. Barrett Watten.

4. ASA

Real horse is good, A. Wooden Horse, The. Mary Mapes Dodge. SWaP

Real Indian Leans Against, The. Chrystos. UnSA

Real Life. Frances Driscoll. PfS

Real Live. Ted Berrigan. FTOS *Fr.* Sonnets, The.

Real Live Girl. Carolyn Leigh. ReLy

Real Love Isn't What It Seems. Dahlia Ravikovitch. DTA, *tr. by* Chana Bloch

Real Moment, The. Eduardo Anguita. BLPSL, *tr. by* Rene de Costa, Rigas Kappatos and Eleni Paidoussi

Real rock and rollers have ugly teeth and fucked-up hair. Form a Band, Goddammit. Horehound Stillpoint. BeDoSh

Real Romance, A. Henry Cuyler Bunner. VerBaPo *Fr.* In School House.

Real Thing, The. Eiléan Ní Chuilleanáin. ModIr; MoWP

Real thing is always an imitation, The. Dharmakaya. Philip Whalen. WANABP

Real Toads. Heidi Peppermint. BAP-04

Real unabstract snow, The. (LL) Malcolm Mooney's Land. William Sydney Graham. NePenScot; NPeEn

Realism. Carla Harryman. PmAP

Realism. Tom Mandel. PmAP

Realist of 1939–40, A. Wilma Elizabeth McDaniel. GeoHom

Realistic Bar and Grill, A. David Shapiro. PmAP

Realistic dreams with a whiff of terror. 29-77-02. Artur Miedzyrzecki. PoSu

Réalités cosmiques vanille tabac éveils. Tristan Tzara. YaTCFP

Reality. Sir Aubrey De Vere. SacPr

Reality. Bob Grumman. AnSo

Reality and Desire. Olga Orozco. TCLAP, *tr. by* Stephen Tapscott

Reality being too thorny for my great personality. Bottom. Arthur Rimbaud. MotU, *tr. by* Louise Varese

Reality Demands. Wisława Szymborska. BeAl; VCWP, *tr. by* Stanislaw Barańczak *and* Clara Cavanagh and Clare Cavanagh

Reality happens. Quanta. Pauline Stainer. MoWP

Reality is a question. Terms in Which I Think of Reality, The. Allen Ginsberg. AmFaPo

Reality Is an Activity of the Most August Imagination. Wallace Stevens. APT-1; NAMCP V.1; NoAM; OxBoAm

Reality of Autumn, The. Duane Niatum. HATNAP

Reality Organization. Albert Goldbarth. CAP-8

Reality U.S.A. Mark Halliday. StAl

Reality, yes, reality. Reality and Desire. Olga Orozco. TCLAP, *tr. by* Stephen Tapscott

Reality's Dark Dream. Samuel Taylor Coleridge. IJHIL

Realization, The. Yvor Winters. APT-2; HarvBoo

Realization came from a small thing. Triangle, Comb. No Hyegyông. EcSo, *tr. by* Ann Y. Choi

Realizing the Futility of Life. Po Chü-i. CCL1, *tr. by* Arthur Waley

Real-Life Drama, A. Michael Collier. WaAnP

Really Long Ride, The. Rick Noguchi. NeAmPo

Really the Real. Gary Snyder. WANABP

Really this is one scene and actual in french means now as if the moment were yesteryear. Assuage Bane. Mark Prejsnar. AnSo

Really? / Will all the world find happiness. Really? Sri Sri. HotL, *tr. by* V. Narayana Rao

Realm is here of masquing light, A. Light at Equinox. Léonie Adams. ColAP

Realm of Jabberwocks and Angels' Wings, Widows' Kisses, Corpse Revivers, The. (LL) Cocktails. Ciaran Carson. ModIr; PBCIP

Realtheater Piece Two. Jerome Rothenberg. FTOS

Reanimated, now, and dressed in robes. Robert Pollok. *Fr.* Course of Time, The.

Reapers. Jean Toomer. APT-2; ColAP; GT; InGu; NAAPv.2; NAMCP V.1; NIL-7; NoAM; NoP-4; NoP-5; OxBoAm; PtR; SoSe-8; TRP; WaAnP; WeW-3

Reapers and sowers, gleaners and drovers. Cradle Song. Jim Schley. GoPo

Reaping. Dic Jones. BBMWP, *tr. by* Joseph P. Clancy

Reappearing like bindweed. Candid Camera. Angelo Lumelli. ItPo, *tr. by* Gayle Ridinger

Rear Porches of an Apartment Building, The. Maxwell Bodenheim. APT-1

Rear ruth as the seat, rear her ureaus, cart cheer there. Archeus Terrae. John Peck. HarvBoo

Rear Window. Angela Shaw. NeAmPo

Reared Within the Mountains! *Unknown.* APN-2; TCAPo *Fr.* Mountain Chant, The.

Rear-Guard, The. Siegfried Sassoon. MoBrPo; NAEL-6v2; NAEL-7v2; NAMCP V.1; NoAM; OBWP; PoWW; WaAnP

Rearrange a "Wife's" affection! Emily Dickinson. NALW

Rearview Mirror. Robert Morgan. PoA 2002

Reason. Charlotte Brontë. VWP

Reason. Abraham Cowley. SacPr

Reason. Ralph Hodgson. MoBrPo

Reason. Philippe Jaccottet. MFP, *tr. by* Martin Sorrell

Reason. Clive Staples Lewis. SacPr

Reason. "Said, Pull her up a bit will you, Mac, I want to unload there." [*with music*]. Josephine Miles. ASA; NALW; NoAM; OxBoAm

Reason, The. Eric Pankey. GI

Reason and Faith. Cecil Frances Alexander. SacPr

Reason Fair, A (Liangzhou Song). Wang Han. CCL1, *tr. by* H. A. Giles

Reason for Refusal. Martin Bell. FaBoWar

Reason for Silence, A. Louise Imogen Guiney. SWaP

Reason, I hope I never speak ill of you. To Reason. Carl Dennis. PoA 2002

Reason, in faith thou art well served, that still. Sir Philip Sidney. NAEL-6v1; NAEL-7v1 *Fr.* Astrophil and Stella.

Reason of the saint that he is saintly, The. Reasons of Each, The. Laura Riding Jackson. HarvBoo

Reason, Reason is my middle name. (LL) Reason: "Said, Pull her up a bit will you, Mac, I want to unload there." Josephine Miles. ASA; NALW; NoAM; OxBoAm

Reason we do not learn from history is, The. Ultima Ratio Reagan. Howard Nemerov. AF

Reason why the Park is closed, The. Deceit in the Park. Patrick Hare. OBGa

Reasonable restraints, The. This has been. Joanne. Joanne Kyger. AHA

Reasons. Thomas James. PoCho

Reasons drawn from Divinity. John Davies. SacPr *Fr.* Nosce Teipsum.

Reasons for Attendance. Philip Larkin. NAMCP V.2; PoPoPo

Reasons for Loving the Harmonica. Julie Kane. MiVo

Reasons for the Beginning. Milo De Angelis. ItPo, *tr. by* Gayle Ridinger

Reasons of Each, The. Laura Riding Jackson. HarvBoo

Reasons That Induced Dr. Swift to Write a Poem Called "The Lady's Dressing-Room", The. Lady Mary Wortley Montagu. NAEL-7v1

Reasons to Commute by Bicycle. Frederic William Kirchner. ArBi

Reasons to Meditate. Lisa Cullen. WhBo

Reassurance. Alice Walker. ASA

Reassurance, The. Thom Gunn. NPeEn; StAl

Rebeca in a mirror. Judith Rodriguez. BrAP

Rebecca. E. Ethelbert Miller. ISC

Rebecca Cutlet. Bill Berkson. PmAP

Rebel, A. John Gould Fletcher. MoAmPo

Rebel, The. Innes Randolph. AmWaPo; NBLV

Rebel Scot, The. John Cleveland. BASC

"He that saw hell in his melancholy dream." NOSC

"How? 'Providence', and yet a Scottish crew?" NOSC

"Lord! what a goodly thing is want of shirts." OBSV

"Nature herself doth Scotchmen beasts confess." OBSV

Rebel Tam. Joe Corrie. RSaN

Rebellion against the North Side. Naomi Shihab Nye. WeW-3

Rebellion of the Waters, The. George Darley. NOBRP

Rebellion shook an ancient dust. April Mortality. Léonie Adams. APT-2; CtM; MoAmPo

Rebel's Progress [*with music*]. Tom Earley. OBWVE

Rebirth. Beckian Fritz Goldberg. ExTi

Rebirth. Mereid Hopwood. BBMWP, *tr. by* Elin ap Hywel

Rebirth. Man Giac. EaWin; WoPoe, *tr. by* W. S. Merwin and Nguyen Ngoc Bich

Re-birth of Venus, The. Geoffrey Hill. UpMys *Fr.* Metamorphoses.

Rebirth of Venus, The. Mary Jo Salter. FFC

Rebis. Mitch Highfill. HeMarv

Reborn. Edison Mpina. NAfrP

Re-born Sun, The. (LL) "H. D." APT-1; NAAL-5 *Fr.* Walls Do Not Fall, The.

Rebus Tact. Ray DiPalma. PmAP

Recalcitrant, the empire sleeves of her dress hold back. Diagnosis: My Mother's Breast. Lisa Fishman. AmPoNex

Recall how she lolly-gagged beneath. Forgetting the Sixties. Mark DeFoe. SwNoth

Recalling a Sung Dynasty Landscape. Jane Hirshfield. WANABP

Recalling a Visit from His Majesty. Princess Uchiko. WoPoe,

Recalling Former Travels. Tu Mu.
   "Li Bo put it in a poem, this West-of-the-Waters Abbey." CCL1, *tr. by* A. C. Graham
   "Whirled ten years beyond all bounds." CCL1, *tr. by* A. C. Graham

Recalling Former Travels. Anne Waldman. AmZen

Recalling now the pleasures of the South. Tune: "The Bodhisattva Foreigner." Wei Chuang. ColAnChi, *tr. by* John Timothy Wixted

Recalling Old Times. Xiang Xiu. CCL1, *tr. by* Burton Watson

Recalling our agony, and the way we danced. / The music! (LL) Tree Telling of Orpheus, A. Denise Levertov. APSN; MiVo

Recalling the dead. (LL) Picture of a Nativity. Geoffrey Hill. NoAM; UpMys

Recalling War. Robert Graves. AF; BrAP; HarvBoo; NAMCP V.1; NoAM; OBWP; PoWW

Recapitulations. Karl Shapiro. TaR

Receipt to Cure the Vapours, A. Lady Mary Wortley Montagu. NoP-4; NoP-5; NPeEn; OxBEV; PEW

Received it. (LL) Pike, The. Amy Lowell. APT-1; NAMCP V.1

Recension Day. Duncan Forbes. BeAl

Recent Past, The. C. S. Giscombe. GT; OxAAAP

Recently displayed at the Times Square station, a new Vandyke on the face-cream girl. Art Review. Kenneth Fearing. APT-2; NAAPv.2

Recently I met a friend for the first time in 8 years. Large Little Circle. Lew Welch. WhBo

Reception. Traci Paris. ICANM

Reception, The. June Jordan. NAMCP V.2

Reception Good. Kenneth Fearing. APT-2

Recessional. Robert Kelly. FTOS

Recessional. Rudyard Kipling. BrAP; BRP; CABP; InvLi; MoBrPo; NAEL-6v2; NAEL-7v2; NAMCP V.1; NoAM; NoP-4; NoP-5; NPeEn; OBEV; OxAEP-2; OxBEV; TFi; UV; WaAnP

Recessional. Thomas MacGreevy. ModIr

Recibí de mi madre—igual que otros—la carta que no abrí. Topografía. Josué Ramírez. RMCMP

Recife. Evocation of Recife. Manuel Bandeira. TCLAP, *tr. by* Candace Slater

Recipe. Albert Goldbarth. RWB

Recipe for a Salad. Sydney Goodsir Smith. *See* Salad, A.

Recipe for a Warsaw Novel. Cyprian Norwid. WoPoe, *tr. by* Jerzy Peterkiewicz, Burns Singer and Jon Stallworthy

Reciprocal love, the only love that should concern us here, is the love that. Paul Eluard *and* Andre Breton. PFTM-1 *Fr.* Immaculate Conception, The.

Reciprocity. John Drinkwater. PoA 2002

Reciprocity. Kim Gannon. ReLy

Recitation. Ellease Southerland. GT

Récitation de l'oubli, La. Franck André Jamme. YaTCFP

Recitation of Forgetting, The. Franck André Jamme. YaTCFP, *tr. by* John Ashbery

Recitative: "Farmer's son is good and mad," The. Ronald McCuaig. NOBAu

Recite the dangers chiselled on this face. Lines for a Tomb. Donald Davidson. FuPo

Reckless Sonnet. Kimiko Hahn. CAP-8

Reckoning. Fay Zwicky. NOBAu

Reclaiming our land. Karen Press. TSAP

Recluse, The. Herman Melville. APN-2 *Fr.* Clarel: A Poem and Pilgrimage in the Holy Land.

Recluse, The. William Wordsworth.
   Prospectus to *The Recluse.* NAEL-6v2; NAEL-7v2

Reclusive. Wang Fan-chih. CrYelRi, *tr. by* Sam Hamill

Recogitabo Tibi Omnes Annos Meos. William Habington. ChIV-1

Recognition. Kate Clanchy. MFPA

Recognition. Alejandra Pizarnik. TANSG, *tr. by* Susan Bassnett

Recognition. Eve Wood. BAP-97

Recognition, The. John Berryman. BodElec

Recognition in the body. In Particular. Elena Karina Byrne. PoDa

Recognition of Eve, The. Karl Shapiro. ChIV-1 *Fr.* Adam and Eve.

Recognize his unique and solitary home. (LL) Poem That Took the Place of a Mountain, The. Wallace Stevens. NAMCP V.1; TWF

Recognized Futures. Lisa Suhair Majaj. UnSA

Recollect thou, in thunder. Tallulah. James Matthew Legaré. APN-2

Recollection, A. John Peale Bishop. InGu

Recollection of Gabriela Mistral. Claudia Lars. TCLAP, *tr. by* Nancy Christoph

Recollection of what's been lost. Sunday Afternoon. Rachel Hadas. PA9/11

Recollections. Lita Hunter Krohn. OWABP

Recollections: "Do you remember all the sunny places." Caroline Elizabeth Norton. NPBRoP

Recollections of an Old Spook. Richard Edwards. NOxBChV

Recollections of Being. Nathaniel Tarn. WANABP

Recollections of "Lalla Rookh." John Townsend Trowbridge. APN-2

Recollections of Love. Samuel Taylor Coleridge. NAEL-6v2

Recollections of Siberia. Bella Akhatovna Akhmadulina. RusPo, *tr. by* Robert Arthur Douglas Ford

Recollections of The Arabian Nights. Alfred Tennyson. OBGa

Recommendation. Andrey Andreievich Voznesensky. RusPo, *tr. by* Robert Arthur Douglas Ford

Recommitted. Juan Delgado. TouFir

Recompensed? [*with music*]. Henrietta Cordelia Ray. CBWP-3

Reconciled Flame. Alessandro Ceni. ItPo, *tr. by* Gayle Ridinger

Reconcilement, The. John, Duke of Buckingham and Normandy Sheffield. OBEV

Reconciliation. Cecil Day Lewis. PoWW

Reconciliation. Dora Greenwell. PoBW

Reconciliation. George Russell. OBMV

Reconciliation. Walt Whitman. AmWaPo; APN-1; FaBoWar; MoAmPo; NAAL-3; NAAL-5; NAAPv.1; NoP-4; NoP-5; OBWP; OxBoAm; PCW; WeW-3; WoPoe

Reconciliation: "Do not torment me, woman." Brendan Kenneally. IrLP

Reconciliation, The. Archibald MacLeish. MoAmPo

Reconciliation: A Modern Version, The. Horace. *See* Ode 3.9: Dialogue between Horace and Lydia, A ("Donec gratus eram").

Recondite familiar to your candour, The. (LL) Divestment of Beauty. Laura Riding Jackson. APT-2; HarvBoo

Recondite war on women, The. Douglas Livingstone. TSAP

Reconnaissance. Arna Bontemps. APT-2

Reconnaissance Patrol. August Stramm. GTCP, *tr. by* Reinhold Grimm

Reconsideration of the Blackbird, A. Thylias Moss. ESEAA

Reconstructed Face. Rachel Loden. LiTh

Re-Conversion. Novella Nikolaevna Matveyeva. TCRusP, *tr. by* Nigel Stott

[Record]. Kenneth Irby. BAP-04

Record is nothing, and the hero great. Sonnet. John Byrne Leicester Warren, 3d Baron De Tabley. OxBSo

Record of a Certain Summer. Yi Chinmyông. EcSo, *tr. by* Carolyn U. So

Recorded ambience—this. In the Studio. Charles Tomlinson. RWPCtW

Recorders Ages Hence. Walt Whitman. HeIP-4; MoAmPo; SAmP

Recording the Spirit Voices. David Bottoms. TAPaP

Records of the Spring of 1834. Felicia Dorothea Hemans.
   Remembrance of Grasmere, A. CenSon
   To a Distant Scene. NPBRoP

Recount the years, my song (a mournful round!). Polyglot in Paradise, A [*or* On the Death of an Aged and Honoured Relative]. Isaac Watts. STuOW

Recovered by fisherman who saw. Drowned Radio, The. Charles Bennett. RWPCtW

Recovering Henry levelled and confronted. 4th Weekend. John Berryman. BodElec

Recovery. Marie Howe. LaCa

Recovery. M. Wyrebek. AmPoNex

Recovery, The. Edmund Charles Blunden. MoBrPo

REcreation. Askhari. InTrad

Recreation. Audre Lorde. NIL-7

Recreation. Jane Taylor. OBCoV; PEW; WoRP

Recreational Mathematics. Steve Wilson. AmPoNex

Recruiting Officer, The. George Farquhar.
   Song. IrLP

Recruiting Officer of Shih-hao. Tu Fu [*or* Du Fu]. ColAnChi, *tr. by* Irving Y. Lo

Recruiting Poster. Hillel Schwartz. BAP-97

Recruiting Serjeant, The. Isaac Bickerstaffe.
   "What a charming thing's a battle!" OBCoV; PoAgWa

Recruiting Song. Michael Foster. UV

Recuerdo. Edna St. Vincent Millay. APT-1; ChAP; EMP; ItP; NAAL-5; NAAPv.2; NAMCP V.1; NoAM; PoA 2002

Recuerdo. Emilio Prados. RaW

Recuerdo Infantil. Antonio Machado Ruiz. RaW

Recuerdo Se Va, El. Juan Ramón Jiménez. RaW

Reculver Bay. Vicki Raymond. NOBAu

Recumbent. Carl Phillips. NAPBL

Recumbent against any mirror, any stardom. Mimetic. Ann Lauterbach. PmAP

Recuperation of Sin, A. Scott Cairns. UpMys

Recurrence. Michael White. GifTon

Recurrences. / Coppery light hesitates. Measure. Robert Hass. YaYoPo

Recurring Nightmare, A: My Amputation. Pak Sŏwŏn. EcSo, *tr.* by Julie C. Park

Recursus. Michael Palmer. APSN

Recycling Center. Brenda Hillman. CalPo

Red. Grahame Davies. BBMWP, *tr.* by the author

Red. Eugene Field. CA

Red. Lance Larsen. AmPoNex

" " " " / " " " red ". '. Norman Henry, II Pritchard. EGAG

Red Admiral, The. Charles Hubert Sisson. HarvBoo

Red and the Black, The. Norman Alexander MacCaig. BeAl

Red Apple, The. Jean Follain. YaTCFP, *tr.* by Serge Gavronsky

Red are her eyes, for she was a dove once. She Was a Dove. Gerald Stern. CAP-8

Red as the banner which enshrouds. Metacom. John Greenleaf Whittier. AmWaPo

Red berries wiping rain at the window. Old Circles. Jennifer Rankin. BMAP

Red Bird. Pablo Neruda. *tr.* by Christopher Logue

   "Drunk as drunk on turpentine." PasH; WoPoe, *tr.* by Christopher Logue

Red Bird. Gerald Stern. UrbNat

Red Blossoms. Liu Yu Hsi. CCL1, *tr.* by Burton Watson

Red blossoms of mountain peach crowd the uplands. Red Blossoms. Liu Yu Hsi. CCL1, *tr.* by Burton Watson

Red Book of Hergest, The. *Unknown. tr.* by Ernest Rhys

   Lament for Urien, The. OBMV

Red Brick and Brown Stone. James Schuyler. BodElec

Red canna blooms, A. Canna. Takahashi Shinkichi. ZenPo, *tr.* by Takashi Ikemoto and Lucien Stryk

Red caravan, a greyhound bitch, A. Flame, The. I. D. Hooson. BBMWP, *tr.* by Anthony Conran

Red cassia flowers. If Hot Flowers Come to the Street. R. Meenakshi. WoPoe, *tr.* by Martha Ann Selby

Red Chair (for three voices), The. Emmett Williams.

   "He said it two days ago." PFTM-2

Red Clay. Candice Favilla. ExTi

Red Cliff, The. Su Tung-p'o. NDACCP, *tr.* by Kenneth Rexroth

Red Cliff Rhapsodies. Su Tung-p'o. ColAnChi, *tr.* by Richard Strassberg

Red cliffs and emerald canyons. Yun Sŏndo. CATKP *Fr.* Angler's Calendar, The.

Red Clock. A. Poulin, Jr. OPRER

Red Cloth, The. *Vietnamese Oral Tradition.* CaDao, *tr.* by John Balaban

Red Cloud's Song. *Unknown.* APN-2 *Fr.* Sacred Songs of the Konkau.

Red cockatoo crests caught on coral-trees. Early Arrival: Sydney. Vivian Smith. NOBAu

Red Cow Is Dead, The [*with music*]. Elwyn Brooks White. NBLV

Red Cross Telegram, The. Lotte Kramer. HP

Red Cuckatoo, The. Po Chü-i. CCL1; WoPoe, *tr.* by Arthur Waley

Red D Gypsum. J. H. Prynne.

   "Did you light furtive aggregate late-flow samples." VaPo

Red Desiré. Mick North. NLP

Red dragonfly darts, little, A. Swimming. Carmen Horst. ACAMVP

Red Dress, The. Dorothy Parker. APT-1

Red Dust. Philip Levine. NoAM

Red Dye. Barbara Guest. BodElec

Red eiderdown at the window, A. Poem. Raymond Radiguet. CuPo

Red Embankment. Tu Mu. ColAnChi, *tr.* by John M. Ortinau

Red eye, red foot: the pigeons are finding. Warmer. Martha Collins. UrbNat

Red Flower. Ann Turner. SSCS

Red fool, my laughing comrade. To a Comrade in Arms. Alun Lewis. MoBrPo

Red Geranium and Godly Mignonette. D. H. Lawrence. NoAM

Red gladioli of bleeding feathers. Gladioli by the Sea. Oscar Hahn. TCLAP, *tr.* by Isabel Bize

Red globes of light, the liquor-green, The. William Street. Kenneth Slessor. BMAP

Red Glow in the Sky, A. Aleksandr Aleksandrovich Blok. OBVE

Red granite and black diorite, with the blue. Skeleton of the Future, The. Hugh MacDiarmid. MoBrPo; OBMV

Red Hat, A. Gertrude Stein. MoWP *Fr.* Tender Buttons.

Red Hat, The. Rachel Hadas. OxBoAm; RA; WaAnP

Red High-heeled Shoes. Mihangel Morgan. BBMWP, *tr.* by Martin Davis

Red Hills of Home. Chenjerai Hove. HBAPE; NAfrP

Red horse, A. Louis Zukofsky. PFTM-2 *Fr.* A.

Red horses. It Was War. Miryana Basheva. CSCBP, *tr.* by Georgi Belev and Lisa Sapinkopf

Red Hot. Laurie Anderson. OxWW

Red, Hot and Blue. Cole Porter. ReLy

Red Jacket. Fitz-Greene Halleck. APN-1

Red Judge, The. D. M. Black. EmeKit

Red leaped. Moon, The. Witter Bynner. APT-1

Red Light District Nurse, The. James Fenton and John Fuller. OBCoV

Red light is stuck, A. Why We Are Late. Josephine Miles. NALW

Red Lights of Plenty, The. Tony Harrison. RSaN

Red Lilies. Barbara Guest. PmAP

Red lips are not so red. Greater Love. Wilfred Owen. MoBrPo; NAMCP V.1; NoAM; TFi

Red Lipstick on a Straw. Michael Melo. ReBoTo

Red lotus incense fades on. Sorrow of Departure. Li Ch'ing-chao. NDACCP, *tr.* by Kenneth Rexroth

Red Man's Wife, The. *Unknown.* IrLP, *tr.* by Douglas Hyde

Red men embraced my body's whiteness. Birch Canoe. Carter Revard. NoP-4

Red morning sky. Issa. EH, *tr.* by Robert Hass

Red mouths of lads for love God made. De Puerorum osculis. Giles de Gillies. CAGL

Red mullet, rosy in its sleep. Beaulieu. Clarence Major. FTOS

Red oak leaves rustle in the wind. Leaves of a Dream Are the Leaves of an Onion, The. Arthur Sze. OpBo

Red odd numbers untouched: pleasure beaches, monsoons and sun, The. (LL) Japanese City. Kenward Elmslie. NYP2; PmAP

Red o'er the forest glows the setting sun. John Keble. OBEV *Fr.* Forest Leaves in Autumn.

Red of the dawn! Dawn, The. Alfred Tennyson. NAEL-6v2

Red Onion, Cherries, Boiling Potatoes, Milk. Jane Hirshfield. BeAl

Red Palm, A. Gary Soto. CalPo

Red Pepper. Sue Sinclair. Coast

Red pepper hangs from a nail, The. Mal'Occhio. Jennifer Martelli. OPRER

Red poppy. Ghazal 21. Mirza Asadullah Khan Ghalib. EaWin, *tr.* by Aijaz Ahmad and W. S. Merwin

Red Poppy, The. Louise Glück. MoWP; OxBoAm; PtR

Red Poppy, The. I. D. Hooson. BBMWP, *tr.* by Gillian Clarke

Red Raging Waters, The. Larry D. Thomas. TiP2

Red Rebel Song. Jean Binta Breeze. RSaN

Red, Red Rose, A. Robert Burns. BrAP; ChAP; CtM; GoPo; HeIP-4; ITBLP; NAEL-6v2; NAEL-7v2; NePenScot; NIL-7; NIP-4; NOBRP; NoP-4; NoP-5; NPBRoP; NPeEn; OxAEP-2; OxBEV; PoPoPo; TFi; UV; WaAnP

Red Reed. Bruce Beasley. AmAlph

Red River. Molly Fisk. PasH

Red river, red river. T. S. Eliot. FaBoA *Fr.* Landscapes.

Red rock wilderness, The. Sidney Keyes. OBWP; PoWW *Fr.* Wilderness, The.

Red Rose and a Beggar. "H. D." APSN

Red Rose and a Beggar. "H. D." PFTM-2 *Fr.* Hermetic Definition.

Red Rose, proud Rose, sad Rose of all my days! To the Rose upon the Rood of Time. William Butler Yeats. NAMCP V.1; NoAM

Red rose whispers of passion, The. White Rose, A. John Boyle O'Reilly. OBEV

Red Roses. Anne Sexton. EmeKit

Red roses, in the slender vases burning. Forlorn. William Dean Howells. APN-2

Red Round Sun, The. Louise Herlin. MFP, *tr.* by Martin Sorrell

Red Salamander—Video Store Parking Lot. Mark DeFoe. UrbNat

Red Sandalwood Mouth. Chao Luan-luan. CCL1; NDACCP, *tr.* by Chung Ling and Kenneth Rexroth

Red setter leaping, A. Flames. Pearse Hutchinson. BeAl

Red Shirt, The. Philip Levine. BodElec

Red sky at night, A. *Unknown.* OBCoV

Red slippers in a shop-window, and outside in the street, flaws of grey, windy sleet! Towns in Colour. Amy Lowell.

Red spattered on an orchard path. Thats all. Seed. Charles Buckmaster. BMAP

Red spruce and fir have crossed the broken lines. Orchard in the Woods. Charles Bruce. Coast

Red Squirrel. Bruce Weigl. BodElec

Red Stove Warms the Room, The. *Unknown.* CCL1, *tr.* by Marsha Wagner

Red stove warms the room where a beautiful woman sleeps. Red Stove Warms the Room, The. *Unknown.* CCL1, *tr.* by Marsha Wagner

Red String. Minnie Bruce Pratt. WiU

Red sun comes out of the Eastern corner, The. Li Po. NDACCP, *tr.* by Ezra Pound

Red Sunsets, 1883, The. Mathilde Blind. ViWPN

Red Tail Sonnet. Ira Sadoff. PfSP

Red that iron becomes when held, The. San Joaquin. David Oliveira. GeoHom

Red Tide. José Luis Rivas. RMCMP, *tr.* by Alastair Reid

Red Trousseau. Carol Muske-Dukes. BodElec

Red varnish / Warm flitch. Louis Zukofsky. APT-2 *Fr.* 29 Poems.

Red Velvet Jacket. Lynda Hull. ExTi

Red Water. Dana Levin. AmPoNex

Red Wheat. Gu Cheng. WoBe *Fr.* Liquid Mercury.

Red Wheelbarrow, The. Jack Spicer. OxBoAm

Red Wheelbarrow, The. William Carlos Williams. APT-1; BLPJKO; BLT; BrAP; ChAP; ColAP; EMP; HarvBoo; HeIP-4; MoAmPo; NAAL-5; NAAPv.2; NAMCP V.1; NIL-7; NIP-4; NoAM; NoP-4; NoP-5; OxBoAm; SAmP; SoSe-8; TFi; TRP; TWF; WaAnP; WeW-3

Red Wind from out the East. Red Wind, The. Lionel Pigot Johnson. IrV

Red Wine Stain from Malin to Mizen Head, A. Paula Cunningham. NIrP *Fr.* Dog Called Chance, A.

Red Wool Shirt, The. Alden Nowlan. Coast

Redbreast smoulders in the waste of snow, The. Redbreast, The. Anthony Rye. Spl

Redbreast, The. Anthony Rye. Spl

Redbud. Betsy Sholl. ACAMVP

Red-Dress Girl. Ann Turner. SSCS

Redeem Time Past. William Drummond of Hawthornden. OxAEP-1

Redeemed by what he tried to say. (LL) My Father's Love Letters [*or* Loveletters]. Yusef Komunyakaa. InGu; NAMCP V.2; OxAAAP

Redeemer, The. Cynewulf. *Fr.* Ascension, The.

Redefining "Orthodoxy." Pier Paolo Pasolini. ItPo, *tr. by* Gayle Ridinger

Redemption. George Herbert. BASC; CABP; FSCP; GSo; NAEL-6v1; NAEL-7v1; NoP-4; NoP-5; NOSC; NPeEn; OxBEV; OxBSo; PBRV; PoPoPo; SoSe-8; TFi; WeW-3

Redemption. Pauli Murray. GT

Redemption? because they loved me? or loved me in my words? Audience, The. Richard Silberg. ASA

Redemption hangs upon the nails. (LL) He. Stanley Kunitz. NoP-4; NoP-5

Redemptive definitions fixed in tension my control, or then I. Transom Over Death's Door, A. Jennifer Moxley. VaPo

Redeployment. Howard Nemerov. AmWaPo; OBWP; PoWW

Red-faced and sweating in autumn. Uranium. Robert Morgan. AtGh

Red-Gold Rain, The. Sacheverell Sitwell. MoBrPo

Red-haired hard-of-hearing woman. (LL) Romance. Ann Sansom. MFPA; NeBl

Red-haired horse, A. EMJL *Fr.* Mad Verse.

Red-haired Man's Wife, The. James Stephens. MoBrPo

Red-headed G.I.'s favourite, The. Bombshell. Tracey Herd. NeBl

Red-Headed Intern, Taking Notes. Ramon Guthrie. APT-2

Red-headed laborer streaked with soot, your buzzing fills my ears. Bee. Ivan Tsanev. CSCBP, *tr. by* Georgi Belev and Lisa Sapinkopf

Redivivus. Donald Davidson. FuPo

Red-Man, The. Frank Prewett. HATNAP

Redneck with Hair on His Back. Paul Ruffin. LiTh

Redness: Thinking it Through. Garrett Kaoru Hongo. LTA

Redo. Lyn Hejinian.
"Nostalgia is the elixir drained." CalPo

Redonda suerte. Dolores Dorantes. SPV

Redondo. Ron Koertge. CalPo

Redonnez-leur ce qui n'est plus présent en eux. Redonnez-leur. René Char. YaTCFP

Redress: to receive something, get in exchange. Redness: Thinking it Through. Garrett Kaoru Hongo. LTA

Reds in the Bed. Peter Finch. Oth

Redshanks, The. Julian Bell. OBMV

Red-Tail Hawk and Pyre of Youth. Robert Penn Warren. InGu

Reduced to ash and collected cold from spent flame. Spring and Other Places. David Chaloner. VaPo

Redundant Miners. Mogg Williams. RSaN

Redwing. R. P. Blackmur. APT-2

Redwing Blackbirds. Fred Dings. PoDa

Redwing Sonnets. Julia Alvarez. BodElec

Redwood Haiku. Lew Welch. WhBo

Reed Boat, A. Yusef Komunyakaa. AmAlph

Reed Flowers Turn White. *Unknown.* CCL1, *tr. by* Marsha Wagner

Reeds give, The. Small Song. A. R. Ammons. NAMCP V.2; NoAM

Reeds of Innocence. William Blake. *See* Piping Down the Valleys Wild.

Reel Around the Shadow. James Harms. NAPBL

Re-Emergence of the Trombone, The. Fred Muratori. MiVo

Reencournter with the Goddess. Olga Nolla. TANSG, *tr. by* Paula Vega

Reetika Arranges My Closet. Dorianne Laux. SweBea

Refined Man, The. Rudyard Kipling. NPeEn *Fr.* Epitaphs of the War [1914–1918].

Refinement. Sikong Tu. CCL1 *Fr.* Twenty-Four Modes of Poetry.

Refining Fire [*with music*]. Lizelia Augusta Jenkins Moorer. CBWP-3

Reflected / In the dragonfly's eye—. Issa. ZenPo, *tr. by* Takashi Ikemoto and Lucien Stryk

Reflected in the plate glass, the pies. Night Waitress. Lynda Hull. SwNoth

Reflection. Christina Georgina Rossetti. VWP

Reflection. Mark Turcotte. PoDa

Reflection. Walter James Turner. OBMV

Reflection, The. Elizabeth Singer Rowe. EMWP

Reflection and Advice. Ezra Pound. OBSV

Reflection by a Mailbox. Stanley Kunitz. PWW2

Reflection I desire, The. (LL) Mirror, The. Louise Glück. CAP-8; OxBoAm

Reflection of a wet finger that slipped over the faded oil-cloth, The. Faina Grimberg. CRWP, *tr. by* Richard McKane

Reflection on Babies. Ogden Nash. NBLV

Reflection on El Train Glass. Luis J. Rodriguez. IllVoic

Reflection on the Paintings of Mark Rothko's Chapel, A. Eric Muirhead. TiP2

Reflections. George Crabbe.
Late Wisdom. OBEV

Reflections after a Dry Spell. Charles Martin. PfSP

Reflections After the June 12th March for Disarmament. Sonia Sanchez. ESEAA

Reflections at Dawn [*with music*]. Phyllis McGinley. NBLV

Reflections at Lake Louise. Allen Ginsberg. BBASP; WaAnP

Reflections in a passing mirror. Arthur Nortje. TSAP

Reflections on a Dove. Hamutal Bar Yosef. DTA, *tr. by* Shirley Kaufman

Reflections on a Visit to the Burke Museum, University of Washington, Seattle. Gail Tremblay. HATNAP

Reflections on Growing Older. Quincy Troupe. GT; OxAAAP

Reflections on Hillsborough in Memoriam. T. H. Naisby. NOBAu

Reflections on Ice-breaking. Ogden Nash. APT-2; NAAPv.2; NBLV; NIL-7; NoP-4; NoP-5

Reflections on the Death of Louis XVI. Ann Yearsley. RWP

Reflective. A. R. Ammons. OxBoAm; VCAP

Reflective life separates us from the sources of reflection. Mario Luzi. ItPo *Fr.* In the Dark Body of Metamorphosis.

Reflexion, The. Edward Taylor. ChIV-1; TCAPo *Fr.* Preparatory Meditations Before My Approach to the Lord's Supper.

Reflexions on suicide, & on my father, possess me. Of Suicide. John Berryman. NoAM

Reflexions on the Seizure of the Suez, and on a Proposal to Line the Banks of That Canal with Billboard Advertisements. Howard Nemerov. NBLV

Reforma Agraria. Ian Duhig. ModIr

Reformation of Manners. Daniel Defoe.
"Search all the Christian climes from pole to pole." OBSV
"Yet Ostia boasts of her regeneration." OBSV

Refracted through years, this neon light comes back. Poem in the Shape of a Saxophone. T. R. Hummer. SeSe

Refrain. John Montague. IrLP *Fr.* Great Cloak, The.

Refrain. Reginald Shepherd. RD

Refresh my thoughts of Penelope again. Pan as the Son of Penelope. Joanne Kyger. BB

Refreshing, the wind against the waterfall. Jakushitsu. ZenPo, *tr. by* Takashi Ikemoto and Lucien Stryk

Refrigerator, The. Sue Sinclair. Coast

Refrigerium. Frederick Goddard Tuckerman. TCAPo

Refuge. Randy Blasing. PoA 2002

Refuge. Gyula Illyés. IQMS, *tr. by* Peter Zollman

Refuge at the One Step Down. Belle Waring. PBCAP; SeSe

Refugee. Gideon Ferebee. BtF

Refugee. Laila Halaby. PoArWo

Refugee, A. Lee Ranaldo. HeMarv

Refugee Blues. W. H. Auden. AmFaPo; BeAl; HP; OxAEP-2 *Fr.* Ten Songs.

Refugee Ship. Lorna Dee Cervantes. NAMCP V.2; PoPoPo

Refugee Song, A. *Unknown.* NAAPv.1

Refugees. Donald Davidson. FuPo

Refugees. Chaim Grade. HP, *tr. by* Marc Kaminsky

Refugees. Patrick Sylvain. OGAHCP, *tr. by* Boadiba and Jack Hirschman

Refugees, The. Randall Jarrell. MoAmPo

Refugees, The. Edwin Muir. NoAM

Refusal. Carol Frost. PfSP

Refusal. Colette Ni Ghallchóir. NIrP, *tr. by the author*

Refusal to Inter. Mohammed Khaïr-Eddine. PFTM-2, *tr. by* Pierre Joris

Refusal to Mourn, A. Derek Mahon. ModIr; PNI

Refusal to Mourn the Death, by Fire, of a Child in London, A. Dylan Thomas. AF; BrAP; FaBoWar; HarvBoo; HeIP-4; MoBrPo; NAMCP V.2; NoAM; NoP-4; NoP-5; OBWVE; OxAEP-2; PoAgWa; PoWW; TFi; WaAnP

Refusing food, he scarcely spoke a word. Albery Allson Whitman. NAAPv.1 Fr. Octoroon, The.

Refusing the Call. Enid Shomer. TaR

Refusing worldly worries. Lu-lung Village, Autumn. Hsu Hsuan. CrYelRi, tr. by Sam Hamill

Reg wished me to go with him to the field. My Mother. Claude McKay. GT

Regain'd my freedom with a sigh. (LL) Prisoner of Chillon, The. Lord Byron. BrAP; NPBRoP

Regal is the pleasure, afoot, threading the trees. Spring. Ferenc Faludi. IQMS, tr. by Donald Davie

Regala la mentira. Pedro Pérez Conde. RMCMP

Regalia Figure. Carl Phillips. NAPBL

Regalia in Immediate Demand! Philip Whalen. BB

Regarde-moi et sois couleur. Dompteur de lions se souvient, Le. Tristan Tzara. YaTCFP

Regarder l'enfance. Andrée Chédid. YaTCFP

Regarding Music. Siv Cedering. MiVo

Regarding the Heart. Haewŏn. BecRai, tr. by Kim Daljin, Kim Won-Chung and Christopher Merrill

Regarding the Monument. Scott Cairns. UpMys

Regarding yours, dear Mrs Nightingale. Mrs Nightingale. Martin Fagg. UV

Regarding yours, dear Mrs Worthington. Noël Coward. ReLy; UV Fr. Mrs Worthingtion.

Regardless of the Final Score. Debra Nystrom. LiTh

Regardons autour de nous. Trois leçons de morale. Emmanuel Hocquard. YaTCFP

Regeneration. Henry Vaughan. BASC; ChIV-1; FSCP; NAEL-6v1; NAEL-7v1; NoP-4; NoP-5

Regeneration. Leo Vroman. TuT, tr. by James Liddy

Reggae. Vejay Steede. WaCA

Reggae Cat (for Boston Jack). Kendel Hippolyte. WaCA

Reggae Prophecy. Marion Bethel. WaCA

Reggae Sounds. Linton Kwesi Johnson. WaCA

Reggie the carnation giver, in season. Door Shed, The. Sam Gardiner. NIrP

Régime. Karel Soudijn. TuT, tr. by Ruth Hooley

Regina. Mary Elizabeth Coleridge. NALW; PoBW

Reginald Pugh, The Man Who Came from the Army. Emma Lee Warrior. HATNAP

Region of Unlikeness, The. Jorie Graham. HarvBoo

Register / and escape. In the Room of Never Grieve. Anne Waldman. AmZen

Registering the Little One. Derec Llwyd Morgan. BBMWP, tr. by Catherine Fisher

Registration of 1918. Unknown. NAAPv.2

Règne. Leslie Kaplan. tr. by Serge Gavronsky
  "Before leaving there's always a get-together. The." SCFWP, tr. by Serge Gavronsky
  "Fairs, with fireworks. A mix of people." SCFWP, tr. by Serge Gavronsky
  "Nature is there, outside. One takes a walk." SCFWP, tr. by Serge Gavronsky
  "One plans extraordinary things, masked balls." SCFWP, tr. by Serge Gavronsky
  "Sheets, how to describe them, The? They envelop the." SCFWP, tr. by Serge Gavronsky
  "There are passionate love affairs, often between." SCFWP, tr. by Serge Gavronsky

Regresión del sauce. Ernesto Lumbreras. RMCMP

Regreso a la ciudad. Manuel Ulacia. RMCMP

Regression of the Willow. Ernesto Lumbreras. RMCMP, tr. by Rebecca Seiferle

Regret. Chŏng Sŏ. CATKP, tr. by Peter H. Lee

Regret. Michael Lieberman. BloBone

Regret. Sinch'ung. CATKP, tr. by Peter H. Lee

Regret de la terre, Le. Jules Supervielle. YaTCFP

Regret for a Spider Web. James Wright. MotU

Regret for the Mourning Doves Who Failed to Mate [with music]. Bruce Weigl. UrbNat

Regrets. Joachim Du Bellay. tr. by David Curzon and Denis Devlin
  "Given all my worries over each day's trivia." WoPoe, tr. by David Curzon
  "To walk with sober step, to raise the eyebrow." WoPoe, tr. by Denis Devlin

Regrets untold! Tune: "Memories of the South." Li Yü. ColAnChi, tr. by Jiaosheng Wang

Regretting the Earth. Jules Supervielle. YaTCFP, tr. by Patricia Terry

Regretting the Past. Narihira. WoPoe Fr. Ise Monogatari, The.

Regular Bobbsey Twins. / That story. (LL) Cinderella. Anne Sexton. BrAP; HeIP-4

Regulation equipment. Joyce Mansour. MFP, tr. by Martin Sorrell

Rehab. Richard Katrovas. PoDa

Rehabilitative Report: We Can Still Laugh. Daniel Berrigan. AF

Rehearsal. Baba Lukata. BtF

Rehearsal for a Parade. Stefan Tsanev. CSCBP, tr. by Georgi Belev and Lisa Sapinkopf

Reification won't get you out of the parking lot. Things. Bob Perelman. PmAP

Reign of Chaos, The. Alexander Pope. NoP-4; NoP-5 Fr. Dunciad, The.

Rein up. Ode of Imr El-Qais, The. Imr el Kais. WoPoe, tr. by Robert Bringhurst

Reindeer Report. U. A. Fanthorpe. OBCP

Reinforcements [1]. Raymond Queneau. YaTCFP, tr. by Keith Waldrop

Reinforcements [2]. Raymond Queneau. YaTCFP, tr. by Keith Waldrop

Reisebilder. Edoardo Sanguineti. tr. by Gayle Ridinger
  "I defended Genet on the subject of terror in London." ItPo, tr. by Gayle Ridinger
  "I tell you it was a hard punch to my brain." ItPo, tr. by Gayle Ridinger
  "So it takes very little indeed: a brasserie." ItPo, tr. by Gayle Ridinger
  "To the mini-skirted customs official who with sibyl-dove eyes." ItPo, tr. by Gayle Ridinger

Reizan Osho Visits Me. Muso Soseki. EaWin, tr. by W. S. Merwin

Reject Jell-O. Lucille Day. CalPo; MPUn

Rejected Gift, The. Ida G. M. Gerhardt. TuT, tr. by Ruth Hooley

Rejected Gift, The. Ida G. M. Gerhardt. TuT, tr. by Peter van de Kamp

Rejection, The. Sir Robert Aytoun. NOSC

Rejects the Influence of Reason. Mary Robinson. CenSon; RWP

11. Rejects the Influence of Reason. Mary Robinson. NPBRoP Fr. Sappho and Phaon.

Rejoice. Judson Crews. ICANM

Rejoice in the Abyss. Stephen Spender. AF

Rejoice, join. Bill Griffiths. Oth Fr. Building: The New London Hospital.

Rejoice, O young man, in thy youth (Keep down, down). Peter Bowman. PWW2 Fr. Beach Red.

Rejoice! The Lord is King. Charles Wesley. SacPr

Rejoicing That Attend the Murder of Famous Men, The. Robley, Jr. Wilson. PBCAP

Rejoicing that the Zen Master Pao Has Arrived from Dragon Mountain. Liu Ch'ang-ch'ing. ColAnChi, tr. by Burton Watson

Rejoinder to a Critic. Donald Davie. CABP; NoP-4

Relación de maravillas susurradas al oído de un maniquí. Jorge Fernández Granados. RMCMP

Relapse, The. Thomas Stanley. NOSC; OBEV

Relapse of my stomach problem, A. Holiday Inside an Incubator. Yi Yŏnju. EcSo, tr. by Yung-Hee Kim

Relating / to the care of souls, / it says. Charles Olson. NAMCP V.2 Fr. Maximus Poems, The.

Relations: Old Light / New Sun / Postmistress / Earth / 04421. Philip Booth. GoPo

Relationship. János Pilinszky. IQMS; StAl, tr. by Peter Jay

Relationship between, The. Fiduciary. Randall Mann. PoDa

Relationships. Mahe Jabeen. HotL, tr. by V. Narayana Rao

Relationships. Mona Van Duyn. OxBoAm

Relative Heat Index. Alan Gilbert. FreRad

Relatives are leaning over, staring expectantly, The. "Dreadful Has Already Happened, The." Mark Strand. NoAM; VCAP

Relax for one moment, my Jerry. Let's Not Talk About Love. Cole Porter. ReLy

Relax, / stand at attention, and. Barrett Watten. PmAP Fr. Progress.

Release. Adelaide Crapsey. APT-1; NAAPv.2; OxBoAm

Release. R. S. Gwynn. RA

Release. Femi Osofisan. NAfrP

Release. Peter Schjeldahl. AHA

Release. Lisa Sewell. AmPoNex

Release: "I'm going to slap my anger onto a wet slab." Myra Schneider. PoCu

Release, The. Adah Isaacs Menken. CBWP-1

Released from a wooden box. (LL) Fragging. Yusef Komunyakaa. AmAlph; ESEAA

Released from your cell. For Lolita Lebron. Sandra Maria Esteves. PueRic

Released in his suit of lights, / lifted and laid clear. (LL) Him. Charles Wright. CAP-8; WaAnP

Released on Parole. James McAuley. BMAP

Released [or Releas'd] from the noise of the butcher and baker. Jinny the Just. Matthew Prior. OBEV

Released Seagull. Hakuro Wada. NAAPv.2

Relent at last, you lightnings wrought of steel. To Pál Ányos. Ábrahám Barcsay. IQMS, tr. by Adam Makkai

Relentless, black on white, the cable runs. T-Bar. Patricia K. Page. BrAP; NoAM

Relentlessly Lovelorn, the Non-Sleeper Whispers and Re-Whispers a Magic Charm Against His Wound's Roar. Stephen Margulies. AWTN

Relèvement d'Icare, L': Envoi. Guy Goffette. YaTCFP

Reliance. Henry Van Dyke. ITBLP

Relic. Ted Hughes. EMP; NAEL-6v2; NAEL-7v2; NoP-4

Relic, A. Alaa Khalid. AnVo, *tr.* by Mohamed Enani

Relic, The. John Donne. BASC; FSCP; HeIP-4; NAEL-6v1; NAEL-7v1; NoP-4; NoP-5; NOSC; TFi; WaAnP

Relics. Barbara Baldwin. FiBr

Relics. Robyn Sarah. NoP-5

Relics. Charles Wright. CAP-8

Relics, The. Harry Mathews. NYP2

Relict. Emily Wilson. LegDan

Relief of Myopia, The. U. A. Fanthorpe. Spl

Reliefs. Octavio Paz. IPoFL, *tr.* by Muriel Rukeyser

Relieved, I let the book fall behind a stone. Depressed by a Book of Bad Poetry, I Walk toward an Unused Pasture and Invite the Insects to Join Me. James Wright. EmeKit

Relieves. Octavio Paz. IPoFL

Relieving Guard. Bret Harte. PCW

Religio Laici. John Dryden.
   Conclusion, The. BASC
   "Dim, as the borrow'd beams of moon and stars." BASC; NOSC

Religio Medici. Sir Thomas Browne.
   Colloquy with God, A. SacPr

Religion. Gwendolyn Brooks. OxWW *Fr.* Ulysses.

Religion. Stephen Dunn. Vesp

Religion. Judith W. Steinbergh. PfS

Religion [*with music*]. Henry Vaughan. OxAEP-1

Religion? Huh! Whenever I hear the word. Two Memories. Hugh MacDiarmid. EdScPo

Religion Is That I Love You. Kenneth Patchen. APT-2

Religion So Sweet. *Unknown.* SSUS

Religion stands on tip-toe in our land. George Herbert. PBRV *Fr.* Church Militant, The.

Religion stands, the church blocking the sun. (LL) Landscape near an Aerodrome, The. Stephen Spender. MoBrPo; NAMCP V.1; NoAM

Religions are poems. They concert. Poetry and Religion. Les A. Murray. UpMys; WaAnP

Religious Art. Charlie Smith. PA9/11

Religious cry in their patois of sand and dusk, The. Hotel d'Avignon. G. C. Waldrep. LegDan

Religious man practises reversals, The. B. P. Nichol. PFTM-2 *Fr.* Martyrology 7, The.

Religious Musings. Samuel Taylor Coleridge.
   "O ye numberless." NAEL-7v2

Religious Use of [Taking] Tobacco, A. Robert Wisdome. OBCoV
   (Pipe and Can, I.) OBEV

Religious wars of Europe have been numbered with the past, The. Peonage System, The. Lizelia Augusta Jenkins Moorer. CBWP-3

Relinquishment. Elsa Gidlow. PoBW

Reliquaries, The. Valerie Martínez. TouFir

Reliquaries the size of samovars holding bits of the true cross. Wood. Patricia Y. Ikeda. MotU; WhBo

Reliquary. Hart Crane. PoA 2002

Relish honey. If you please. To a Swallow. Euenus. OBVE, *tr.* by John Peale Bishop

Relishing her moments alone. Callaloo. Chezia Thompson Cager. FTtHH

Reluctance. Robert Frost. ITBLP; MoAmPo

Reluctant, I must take leave from war. Farewell Rhyme. Tu Fu [*or* Du Fu]. CrYelRi, *tr.* by Sam Hamill

Reluctant Light. Naomi Long Madgett. FuFl

Reluctant Prophet. Luci Shaw. SacPr

Remain calm, O Dawn. Soul of a pebble on top of the mountain, The. Shakir Li'aibi. IrPoTo, *tr.* by Ralph Saverese and Saadi A. Simawe

Remains. Tony Harrison. FaBoVe

Remains. Dorothy Marie Rice. FuFl

Remains of an Indian Village. Alfred Wellington Purdy. BrAP

Remaking. Ornate with Smoke. Sterling Plumpp. FuFl

Remark, The. Oliver Pitcher. EGAG

Remarkable that the skin has such resiliency. Monster's Dream, The. William Reichard. AmPoNex

Remark'd [*or* remarked] how ill we all dissembled. (LL) Ode, An: "Merchant, to secure his treasure, The." Matthew Prior. NoP-4; NoP-5; NPeEn

Rembrandt—Self Portrait. Gregory Corso. BB

Remedia Amoris. Elizabeth Thomas. LW

Remedios. Demetria Martinez. ICANM

Remedy for Backache. Judith Taylor. SUP

Remember. Irving Berlin. ReLy

Remember. Ion Caraion. AF, *tr.* by Marguerite Dorian *and* Elliott B. Urdang

Remember. (LL) Remember. Joy Harjo. LoL; OxWW

Remember. Joy Harjo. LoL; OxWW

Remember? Stephen Sondheim. ReLy

Remember? Alice Walker. InvLad

Remember a / monument 'not even entertaining the thought Find. Jennifer Scappettone. Eno *Fr.* Consensus Series.

Remember Barbara. Barbara. Jacques Prévert. AF; GPTC, *tr.* by Harriet Zinnes

Remember Dear Mary. John Clare. WeW-3

Remember Father's Day, the banner says. Gift, The. Jack Myers. TiP2

Remember Gascoigne's lullaby. (LL) George Gascoigne. *See* Remember then this lullaby!

Remember Haiti, Cuba, Vietnam. Andrew Salkey. RSaN

Remember he was poor and country-bred;. Abraham Lincoln. Mildred Plew Meigs. CA

Remember how cold I will be. (LL) Carrowmore. Lucie Brock-Broido. AWPTFC; PoPoPo

Remember how the screen. Skin. Ruth Padel. NeBrP

Remember how we picked the daffodils? Daffodils. Ted Hughes. NAEL-7v2; NoP-5

Remember how we rowed toward the cottage. Crossing the Loch. Kathleen Jamie. EdScPo; MoWP

Remember how we spread our hair on the sea. Lines in Dejection. Jean Valentine. YaYoPo

Remember how you always bore me! (LL) Villeggiature. Edith Nesbit. LW; PEW

Remember how you tried to wash it. Black Water Creek. Walter Holland. BeDoSh

Remember I am a garnet woman. If I Am Too Brown or Too White for You. Wendy Rose. HATNAP

Remember, imbeciles and wits. Basil Bunting. NPeEn; OxBEV *Fr.* Villon.

Remember, Imbeciles and Wits. François Villon. WoPoe, *tr.* by Basil Bunting

Remember in Spanish the island places. (LL) Prisoners of Saint Lawrence, The. Martín Espada. PoCho; TouFir

Remember It, My Soul. Eduard Friedrich Mörike. WoPoe, *tr.* by W. D. Snodgrass

Remember last summer when God turned on the heat. Honeymoon, The. James Simmons. PNI

Remember, Man, Death's grief and sorrow. Remembrance of Death. András Batizi. IQMS, *tr.* by Adam Makkai

Remember Me? Al Dubin. ReLy

Remember [Me]. Christina Georgina Rossetti. ChAP; GSo; InoFa; LW; NoP-4; NoP-5; OBEV; OxAEP-2; PEW; TFi; VWP; WaAnP

Remember me? Remember? Alice Walker. InvLad

"Remember me" implored the Thief! Emily Dickinson. ChIV-2; SacPr

Remember me this summer. New England Wind. Eileen Myles. PmAP

Remember me when I am dead. Simplify Me When I'm Dead. Keith Douglas. EdScPo; FaBoWar; NAMCP V.1; NoAM

Remember me when I am gone away. Remember [Me]. Christina Georgina Rossetti. ChAP; GSo; InoFa; LW; NoP-4; NoP-5; OBEV; OxAEP-2; PEW; TFi; VWP; WaAnP

Remember me when thou comest into thy Kingdom. Discourse of the Good Thief, The. Nicanor Parra. GI, *tr.* by Miller Williams

Remember my little granite pail? Lorine Niedecker. APT-2; NAAPv.2

Remember, my love, the item you saw. Carcass, A. Charles Baudelaire. NAWM-7v2, *tr.* by James McGowan

Remember, my love, the object we saw. Carcass, A. Charles Baudelaire. SxFrPo, *tr.* by James McGowan

Remember Now Thy Creator. Bible, *O.T.* OBVE *Fr.* Ecclesiastes.

Remember now thy Creator in the days of thy youth. Bible, *O.T.* OBVE *Fr.* Ecclesiastes.

Remember our ecstatic parade. Untitled. Robert N. Casper. IIR

Remember? Remember? Remember? Stephen Sondheim. ReLy

Remember Something Like This. Lionel Fogarty. BMAP

Remember Tam o' Shanter's mare! (LL) Tam o' Shanter; A Tale. Robert Burns. CABP; NAEL-6v2; NAEL-7v2; NePenScot; NoP-4; NoP-5; NPBRoP; NPeEn; OBNV; WaAnP

Remember that day we found his books? Robert Frost's Books, Ripton, Vermont, 1980. John Sokol. VisFro

Remember that June before our wedding we spent. First Mango. Vince Gotera. ReBoTo

Remember that leader with the funny mustache? Explaining the Big One. William Stafford. PWW2

Remember the blackness of that flesh. Memento. Stephen Spender. HP

Remember the boy who played with a rope. Emperor of China, The. Shirley Kaufman. BAP-01

Remember the Christmas morning long ago. Happy Time, The. Fred Ebb. ReLy

Remember the goose that. Dario Villa. ItPo, *tr.* by Gayle Ridinger

Remember the Island Where They Build the Fire. Yves Bonnefoy. WoPoe, *tr.* by Galway Kinnell and Richard Pevear

Remember / The jolting flight of my heart. Remember. Joyce Mansour. YaTCFP, *tr.* by Mary Ann Caws *and* Jean-Pierre Cauvin

Remember the Moon Survives. Barbara Kingsolver. FiBr

Remember the old hawker. Ballad of the Cadger. May Kendall. ViWPN

Remember the sky that you were born under. Remember. Joy Harjo. LoL; OxWW

   (Remember the sky you were born under.) IPoFL; NOxBChV

Remember the 1340s? We were doing a dance called the Catapult. Nostalgia. Billy Collins. BeAl

Remember Thee! Remember Thee! Lord Byron. NPeEn

Remember then this lullaby! (LL) Lullaby [*or* Lullabie] of a Lover, The. George Gascoigne. NAEL-6v1; PtR

   (Remember Gascoigne's lullaby.) (LL) NoP-4; NoP-5; WaAnP

Remember this. Fury. Lucille Clifton. LoL

Re-member Us. Judith Anderson. HW

Remember us, remember our names! (LL) Barbershop Ritual. Sharan Strange. InTrad; ISC

Re-member us, / you who are living. Re-member Us. Judith Anderson. HW

Remember when. Sisters. Kimberly Ann Collins. InTrad

Remember when we took those separate flights. At the Terminal. Patricia Hooper. OtW

Remember when you hear them beginning to say Freedom. Alex Comfort. MoBrPo; RSaN *Fr.* Song of Lazarus, The.

Remember when you love, from that same hour. Pastoral Dialogue. Anne Killigrew. LW

Remember, you and I are not supposed. Insight Into Private Affairs . . . Raises Certain Barristers and Magistrates to Such Great Heights. Richard Murray Vaughan. Coast

Remembered [*(for Virginia Louise Ferris)*]. Sterling Plumpp. GT

Remembered Morning. Janet Lewis. MakPoe; SoSe-8

Remembered Music. James Russell Lowell. APN-1

Remembered Sequel. Hannah Weiner. FTOS

Remembered, the perceived, The. (LL) Time: "There was too much, always, then too little." Louise Glück. BAP-01; PtR

Remembering. László Kálnoky. IQMS, *tr.* by Kenneth McRobbie and Zita McRobbie

Remembering. Stephen J. Lyons. PasH

Remembering. Yüan Chěn. CrYelRi; ErotSp, *tr.* by Sam Hamill

Remembering Ancient Days in Yueh. Li Po. CrYelRi, *tr.* by Sam Hamill

Remembering Carrigskeewaun. Michael Longley. PBCIP

Remembering Dennis's Eyes. Geoff Hattersley. NeBl

Remembering Dresden. Van K. Brock. HP

Remembering East Mountain. Li Po. CrYelRi, *tr.* by Sam Hamill

Remembering Emily. Rita Mae Reese. PfS

Remembering Fire. Rodney Jones. InGu

Remembering Frost at Kennedy's Inauguration. Linda Pastan. VisFro

Remembering Golden Bells. Po Chü-i. CCL1, *tr.* by Arthur Waley

Remembering how. Buson. EH, *tr.* by Robert Hass

Remembering Leopardi's Moon. Giacomo Leopardi. WoPoe, *tr.* by Stephen Berg

Remembering Miller. Kay Smith. Coast

Remembering Min Ch'e. Su Tung-p'o. NDACCP, *tr.* by Kenneth Rexroth

Remembering My Father. Zbigniew Herbert. VCWP, *tr.* by John Carpenter *and* Bogdana Carpenter

Remembering My Wife. Su Tung-p'o. ErotSp, *tr.* by Sam Hamill

Remembering Our Excursion in the Past. Li Po. ChinPo, *tr.* by Ye Weilian [*or* Yeh Wei-lien *or* Wai-lim Yip]

Remembering Our Fathers. Chava Pinchas-Cohen. DTA, *tr.* by Miriyam Glazer

Remembering Priest Quang Tri. Doan Van Kham. WoPoe, *tr.* by Nguyen Ngoc Bich

Remembering that island lying in the rain. Remembering That Island. Thomas McGrath. AmWaPo; PWW2

Remembering that war, I'd near believe. Night Operations, Coastal Command RAF. Howard Nemerov. AF; PWW2

Remembering the Ardèche. Emily Grosholz. RA

Remembering the Day I Gave Birth to a Daughter. Kim Hyesun. CAMKP, *tr.* by Jiwon Shin

Remembering the invasion of Grenada by the USA. Bob Dixon. RSaN

Remembering the Night Fountains. I. K. Bonset. TuT, *tr.* by Desmond Egan

Remembering the Pacific. Diane Wakoski. GeoHom

Remembering the Past. Al Robles. ReBoTo

Remembering the shot that seemed to burst with no. Slaughter. Susan Stewart. BodElec

Remembering the 'Thirties. Donald Davie. HarvBoo; NAMCP V.2; NoP-4; NoP-5

Remembering Wind Mountain at Sunset. Fred Chappell. LPSFW

Remembering your face, I see it here. On Dorothea Lange's Photograph "Migrant Mother" (1936). Helen Pinkerton. FFC

Remembers thou in Æsope of a taill. Alexander Montgomerie. PBRV

Remember—the noise of moonlight. In the Lebanese Mountains. Nadia Tuéni. PoArWo, *tr.* by Samuel Hazo

Remembrance. M. R. Peacocke. NLP

Remembrance. Robert Southey. TreFP

Remembrance. Sir Thomas Wyatt. *See* Lover Showeth How He Is Forsaken of Such as He Sometime Enjoyed, The.

Remembrance: "Cold in the earth—and the deep snow piled above thee!" Emily Jane Brontë. BrAP; CABP; MakPoe; NAEL-6v2; NAEL-7v2; NoP-4; NoP-5; NPeEn; OxAEP-2; OxBEV; PEW; PoPoPo; TFi; VWP; WeW-3

   (R. Alcona to J. Brenzaida.) InoFa; NALW

Remembrance Day. Ida G. M. Gerhardt. TuT, *tr.* by Michael Longley

Remembrance Day. Ida G. M. Gerhardt. TuT, *tr.* by Robert Greacen

Remembrance Is Moving, a. Juan Ramón Jiménez. RaW, *tr.* by Robert Bly

Remembrance of Death. András Batizi. IQMS, *tr.* by Adam Makkai

Remembrance of Grasmere, A. Felicia Dorothea Hemans. CenSon *Fr.* Records of the Spring of 1834.

Remembrance of Nature. Felicia Dorothea Hemans. NPBRoP *Fr.* Thoughts during Sickness.

Remembrance of Strange Hospitality. Yelena Shwarts. ItGoST; StAl; VCWP, *tr.* by Michael Molnar

Remembrance of the Founts of Night. Theo Van Doesburg. PFTM-1

Remembrance Sunday. Dennis Joseph Enright. NPeEn

Remigration. Hilde Domin. GTCP, *tr.* by Agnes Stein

Remind Me. Dorothy Fields. ReLy

Remind me who I am. (LL) Touch Me. Stanley Kunitz. APT-2; BeAl; CAP-8; NAMCP V.1; NoP-4; NoP-5; PoDa; StAl

Reminder. Michael Ryan. PoCho

Reminder, The. Thomas Hardy. ChAP; OBCP

Reminder, The. Denise Levertov. PoCoUp

Reminiscence. Vladimir Holan. PoSu, *tr.* by George Theiner

Reminiscence, A. Amy Levy. VWP

Remission. Katherine Frost. Prnts

Remittance Man. Judith Wright. NoAM

Remnants of counterclockwise. If I Blindfold You. Marjorie Welish. FTOS

Rémon. *Unknown.* SSUS

Remontando los Ríos. Rafael Alberti. RaW

Remordimiento en Traje de Noche. Luis Cernuda. RaW

Remorse. Sir John Betjeman. MoBrPo

Remorse. Percy Bysshe Shelley. OBEV

Remorse Dressed Up as Night. Luis Cernuda. RaW, *tr.* by Timothy Baland

Remorse—is Memory—awake. Emily Dickinson. NAAL-3; NoP-4; NoP-5; SAmP

Remote and ineffectual Don. Lines to a Don. Joseph Hilaire Pierre Belloc. MoBrPo; OBSV

Removal from Terry Street, A. Douglas Dunn. FaBoVe; NoP-4; NoP-5; NPeEn; StAl

Remov'd from man, and summer's tuneful groves. Anne Batten Cristall. RWP *Fr.* Thelmon and Carmel; An Irregular Poem.

Remove a stone from an unmarked pile. Yes Yoko Ono. Shin Yu Pai. WANABP

Remove your veil and illuminate the earth. Zeyneb. OLP, *tr.* by Walter Andrews, Najaat Black and Mehmet Kalpakli

Removing the Plate of the Pump on the Hydraulic System of the Backhoe. Gary Snyder. LoL

Renaissance Drunk, A. George Evans. PmAP

Renascence. Edna St. Vincent Millay. BRP; ColAP; MoAmPo

   "All I could see from where I stood." MoAmPo; TCAPo

Renato O. Jones, you maintain my beliefs. Ode to a Maintenance Man and His Family. Kay Boyle. GifTon

Rendered Dog. Sarah Messer. LegDan

Rendezvous. Edna St. Vincent Millay. APT-1; NALW; OxBoAm

Rendezvous. Dom Moraes. NoP-4; NoP-5 *Fr.* Two from Israel.

Rendez-vous derrière l'arbre à songes. Jeune Fille Endormie. Jean Cocteau. YaTCFP

Rendez-vous en juin. Claire Malroux. YaTCFP

Rendezvous of river. Appellants, The. Alice Rahon. SurWo, *tr.* by Myrna Bell Rochester

How did you come to develop the concept of Negritude? Aime Cesaire *and* Rene Depestre. PFTM-1 *Fr.* Discourse on Colonialism.

Renegade. Andrée Chedid. PoArWo, *tr.* by Lucy McNair

Renewal. Michael Field. ViWPN

Renewal, A. James Merrill. CAP-8; VCAP

Renewal by Her Element. Denis Devlin. ModIr

Renewal Notice. Bruce Dawe. BMAP

Renfort [1] ("Je vous dis adieu monsieur mon sergent.") Raymond Queneau. YaTCFP

Renfort [2] ("Je suis vieux et je suis lourd.") Raymond Queneau. YaTCFP

Renoir. Rosanna Warren. GS

Renoir, whose painting I don't much like. Quotations. Charles Wright. NoP-5

Renoir's Bathers. Julie Moulds. AmPoNex

Renoir's people. Swing, The. George Bowering. BrAP

Renouncement. Alice Thompson Meynell. GSo; LW; MoBrPo; OBEV; OBMV; OxBSo; PEW; VWP

Renowned as Black Geordie. Sporting the Plaid. Chris Wallace-Crabbe. NOBAu

Renowned Empress, and Great Britain's Queen. Emilia Lanier and Aemilia Bassano Lanyer. NAEL-7v1 Fr. Salve Deus Rex Judaeorum.

Renowned musician, freeman of the world. To Ferencz Liszt. Mihály Vörösmarty. IQMS, tr. by Alan Dixon

Rent. Jane Cooper. StAl

Rent man knocked, The. Madam and the Rent Man. Langston Hughes. SAmP

Rent overdue. Not a Care in the World. John Latouche. ReLy

Rented House in Maine, The. William Matthews. PfSP

Renting. Charles S. Taylor. TiP2

Renting a Room. Sarah Kirsch. PFTM-2 Fr. Kite-Flying.

Renunciation. Emily Dickinson. APN-2; MoAmPo; NAAL-3

Renunciation. Lizette Woodworth Reese. TCAPo

Renunciation, A. Henry King, Bishop of Chichester. OBEV

Renunciation—is a piercing Virtue. Emily Dickinson. APN-2; NoP-4; NoP-5

Renunciation's agonies. Dīnrām. SinGod, tr. by Rachel Fell McDermott

Rep/resent. Douglas Kearney. BRtP

Repairing the Hubble Telescope. Robert Thomas. FaoP

Repairs are like the fall of Pompeii. Inga Kuznetsova. CRWP, tr. by Max Nemtsov

Repeat after me. Pledge. Lawson Fusao Inada. WhBo

Repeat that, repeat. Cuckoo, The. Gerard Manley Hopkins. MoBrPo

Repeat the capitalism of narrative. Nicole Markotić. PoPra

Repeating fly, blueback, thumbthick—so gross, A. Harriet. Robert Lowell. NoP-4; NoP-5

Repeating three clear tones. (LL) Conrad Potter Aiken. NoAM; NoP-5 Fr. Senlin; a Biography.

Repentance. Andrew Hudgins. UpMys Fr. Liar's Psalm, The.

Repentance. Louis Untermeyer. NBLV

Repenting. Sarah Klassen. ACAMVP

Repertoire, A. Michael Donaghy. NeBrP

Repetition. Zoya Ezrokhi. CRWP, tr. by Daniel Weissbort

Repetition. Eman Mersaal. AnVo, tr. by Mohamed Enani

Repetition and baby. Losing and tiger baby. Water in baby and curling. Carla Harryman. BAP-04 Fr. Baby.

Repetitive Heart, The. Delmore Schwartz.
  "All clowns are masked and all *personae*." OxBoAm
  (For Rhoda.) MoAmPo
  Heavy Bear Who Goes with Me, The. APT-2; ColAP; FTtHH; NAMCP V.2; NoAM; StAl

Replacement Buddhas. Joanne Kyger. WANABP

Replacing rings on her hands. Cat's Cradle. Lynne Wycherley. Prnts

Replica, The. Vernon Watkins. AngWePo

Replication: n. I cannot dream of losing you so I will answer to your gesture. Dear ——. Prageeta Sharma. IIR

Replies. *Vietnamese Oral Tradition*. CaDao, tr. by John Balaban

Reply. Hart Crane. PoA 2002

Reply. Reiner Kunze. PoSu, tr. by Ewald Osers

Reply, A. *Unknown*. NBLV; OxBEV

Reply at an Unknown Place. Yi Hyangji. EcSo, tr. by Catherine J. Kim

Reply (crumped on her desk). Florence H. Williams. WaAnP

Reply From His Coy Mistress, A. Anne Finch. FFC

Reply to a Friend's Poem. Muso Soseki. EaWin, tr. by W. S. Merwin

Reply to a Magistrate. Wang Wei. CrYelRi, tr. by Sam Hamill

Reply to a Poem by Donglim. Pyungyang Ungee. BecRai, tr. by Kim Daljin, Kim Won-Chung and Christopher Merrill

Reply to a Poem by Songgyedang. Buhyu Sunsoo. BecRai, tr. by Kim Daljin, Kim Won-Chung and Christopher Merrill

Reply to Bukko Zenji's Poem at Seiken-ji. Muso Soseki. EaWin, tr. by W. S. Merwin

Reply to Gen'no Osho's Poem. Muso Soseki. EaWin, tr. by W. S. Merwin

Reply to King Sunjo's Poem on Bamboo. Chunghur Hyujung. BecRai, tr. by Kim Daljin, Kim Won-Chung and Christopher Merrill

Reply to Mr.——, The. Elizabeth Singer Rowe. BASC

Reply to Petőfi. János Arany. IQMS, tr. by Madeline Mason

Reply to Prefect Liu. T'ao Ch'ien. CrYelRi, tr. by Sam Hamill

Reply to Reizan Osho. Muso Soseki. EaWin, tr. by W. S. Merwin

Reply to Sir Kukwon's "Sleeping in the Temple in Autumn." Daegak Euchon. BecRai, tr. by Kim Daljin, Kim Won-Chung and Christopher Merrill

Reply to Suzan Osho's Snow Poem. Muso Soseki. EaWin, tr. by W. S. Merwin

Reply to T'ao Ch'ien. Sam Hamill. WANABP

Replycacion, A. John Skelton.
  "Than, if this noble kyng." PBRV

Replying to a Poem from My Cousin Huilian. Hsieh Ling-yün. CCL1, tr. by Burton Watson

Repo winter. Camille Martin. AnSo Fr. No truck.

Report. Johannes Bobrowski. GTCP, tr. by Reinhold Grimm

Report. Czeslaw Milosz. BodElec, tr. by the author and Robert Hass

Report from High School. Terese Svoboda. RWB

Report from the Besieged City [*with music*]. Zbigniew Herbert. AF, tr. by John Carpenter *and* Bogdana Carpenter

Report from the Field. Dorothea Tanning. PoCho

Report from the Skull's Diorama. Yusef Komunyakaa. LTA

Report is in, The. Police Report. Devarakonda Balagangadhara Tilak. HotL, tr. by V. Narayana Rao

Report on Experience. Edmund Charles Blunden. NPeEn; OBMV; OBWP; OxBEV; PoAgWa

Report on Heaven and Hell. Silvina Ocampo. MotU, tr. by Edith Grossman

Report on Her Remains [*with music*]. Daniel David Moses. HATNAP

Report on the Protest in Front of the United States Embassy by the Pino Grande Movement, A. Daisy Zamora. CLPP, tr. by Barbara Paschke

Report Song [in a Dream], A. Nicholas Breton. NoSic

Report to Crazy Horse. William Stafford. NoAM

Report to the Stockholders. John Beecher. InGu

Report to the Stockholders. Reg Saner. PoCoUp

Reported Missing. John Clifford Bayliss. PoWW

Reporting to a future difficult. 'From Escomb, County Durham': July 1990. John Seed. Oth

Reports of a lone lynx in village yards. Fur. William Heyen. PfSP

Repose. Henrietta Cordelia Ray. CBWP-3

Repose of Rivers. Hart Crane. APT-2; ColAP; MoAmPo; NAMCP V.1; OxBoAm

Reprehensibly perfect. (LL) Poetry of Departures. Philip Larkin. BeAl; BrAP; HeIP-4

Repression. C. K. Williams. GoPo; NoP-4; NoP-5

Repression of War Experience. Siegfried Sassoon. AF; NAMCP V.1; NoAM

Repressive desublimation. Lines. David Bromige. FTOS

Reprieve, The. Hans Magnus Enzensberger. PoSu, tr. by Michael Hamburger

Reprieve, The. Elizabeth Garrett. NeBl

Reprieve on the Stoop. Belle Waring. PBCAP

Reprisals. William Butler Yeats. OBWP; PoWW

Reprise. Pamela Alexander. AmAlph

Reproach. Elizabeth Cobbold. CenSon Fr. Sonnets of Laura.

Reproaches Phaon. Mary Robinson. CenSon

Reproachful eyes' / beauty but the. Wrath to Sadness. Robert Grenier. PmAP

Reproduction of Profiles, The. Rosmarie Waldrop.
  Feverish Propositions. FTOS; PFTM-2

Reproof Deserved; or After the Lecture. Sir John Betjeman. OBCoV

Reptilian green the wrinkled throat. Sir Gawaine and the Green Knight. Yvor Winters. NoAM

Republic of the West. James Kenneth Stephen. FaBoA; OBCoV Fr. England and America.

Republicans? We've got a few. In fact. Hayden Carruth. GifTon Fr. Vermont.

Repudiate the Forge. (LL) Dare you see a Soul *at the White Heat?*. Emily Dickinson. APN-2; NALW; OxBoAm; TCAPo; WPoS

Repulse Bay. Marilyn Chin. OpBo

Request. Langston Hughes. APT-2

Request. Shuntaro Tanikawa. VCWP, tr. by Harold Wright

Request, A. Robert Montgomery. STuOW Fr. Omnipresence of the Deity, The.

Request, The. Sharon Olds. BodElec

Request from Tante Tina to the Mennonite Women's Missionary Society to Put Salman Rushdie on the Prayer List, A. David Waltner-Toews. ACAMVP

Request of Alexis, The. Sarah Dixon. LW

Request Radio. Carol Muske-Dukes. AmAlph

Request to a Year [*with music*]. Judith Wright. BrAP; ItWoWo; NALW; NAMCP V.2; NoAM; NoP-4; NoP-5

Request to the Graces, An. Robert Herrick. NOSC

Requiem. Anna Andreyevna Akhmatova. TCRusP, *tr. by* Daniel Weissbort

Requiem: "No foreign sky protected me." Anna Andreyevna Akhmatova. AF; PoetW; WoPoe, *tr. by* Max Hayward and Stanley Kunitz

Requiem: "No, not under the vault of alien skies." Anna Andreyevna Akhmatova. NAWM-7v2, *tr. by* Judith Hemschemeyer

Requiem: "O, insatiable monster! Could'st thou not." Mary Weston Fordham. CBWP-2

Requiem. Annette M'Baye d'Erneville. HAWP, *tr. by* Brian Baer

Requiem: "Houses in country and city." Wang Fan-chih. CrYelRi, *tr. by* Sam Hamill

Requiem: "There was a young belle of old Natchez." Ogden Nash. NoP-4; NoP-5

Requiem: "Under the wide and starry sky." Robert Louis Stevenson. BRP; MoBrPo; NBLV; NePenScot; OBEV; OxBEV; TFi; WaAnP

Requiem for "Bird" Parker, Musician. Gregory Corso. BB

Requiem for James Byrd, Jr. H. Palmer Hall. TiP2

Requiem[:] for Soldiers Lost in Ocean Transports, A: "When, after storms that woodlands rue." Herman Melville. APN-2

Requiem for the Croppies. Seamus Heaney. NAMCP V.2; OBWP

Requiem for the Dead Sister. Wŏlmyŏng, Master. CATKP; WoPoe, *tr. by* Peter H. Lee

Requiem for the Death of a Boy [*tr. fr. the German of* Rilke]. Rainer Maria Rilke. ItP, *tr. by* Randall Jarrell

Requiem for the Left Hand. Nancy Morejón. TANSG, *tr. by* Joy Renjilian-Burgy

Requiem for the Plantagenet Kings. Geoffrey Hill. CABP; NAEL-6v2; NAEL-7v2; NoAM

Requiem for the Spanish Dead. Kenneth Rexroth. CalPo

Requiem in C. Biagio Cepollaro. ItPo, *tr. by* Gayle Ridinger

Requiem ("Manuel de Río, natural.") José Hierro. RaW

Requiem ("Manuel del Río, born.") José Hierro. RaW

Requiem 1935-1940. Anna Andreyevna Akhmatova. *tr. by* Richard McKane

Requiem on I-89. Maxine W. Kumin. CAP-8

Requiem on Poros. Yannis Ritsos. VCWP, *tr. by* Edmund Keeley

Requiescam. Trumbull Stickney. ColAP

Requiescat. Matthew Arnold. OBEV

Requiescat. Leo Ross. TuT, *tr. by* Sean Dunne

Requiescat. Leo Ross. TuT, *tr. by* Eamon Grennan

Requiescat. Oscar Wilde. GoPo; IrV; MoBrPo

Required, as a necessity requires. (LL) Plain Sense of Things, The. Wallace Stevens. APT-1; EmeKit; NAAL-5; NAMCP V.1; NoAM; OxBoAm

Requirements for Suggesting Fats Waller. Connie Deanovich. AmPoNex

Requiring something lovely on his arm. Labor Day. Louise Glück. NIL-7; NoAM

Re-reading Jane. Anne Stevenson. NALW

Re-Rooting. Denise Levertov. UpMys

Rescue. James Tate. YaYoPo

Rescue, The. Robert Creeley. VCAP

Rescue the Dead. David Ignatow. WoPoe

Rescue workers fought today. News continued release. Ed Roberson. EGAG

Rescued Year, The. William Stafford. ColAP

Rescues them at last, as a star absorbs the night. (LL) Other Tradition, The. John Ashbery. FTOS; PmAP

Rescuing gate is wide, The. Like a Mourningless Child. Kenneth Patchen. MoAmPo

Research has shown that ballads were produced by all of society. Hotel Lautréamont. John Ashbery. FTOS; HarvBoo

Research shows that for each discovery. Principles of Scarcity, Doctrines of Growth. David Citino. UpMys

Resemblance Between Your Life and a Dog, The. Robert Bly. CAP-8; OxBoAm

Resentment Near the Jade Steps. Li Po. ErotSp, *tr. by* Sam Hamill (Complaint near the Jade Steps.) CrYelRi

Reservation. Jean Day. ASA

Reservation, The. Susan Clements. UnSA

Reservation Love Song. Sherman Alexie. PoPoPo

Reserve. Lizette Woodworth Reese. SWaP

Reserved Sacrament. James Schuyler. BodElec

Reservoirs. Ronald Stuart Thomas. AngWePo

Residence at C——— ("Give me hackneyed words because.") Lisa Robertson. OpeFie

Residence at C——— ("My purpose here is to advance into.") Lisa Robertson. OpeFie

Residence of truth, The. Dry self-portrait. Lionel Abrahams. TSAP

Resident doctor said, The. Notice. Robert Lowell. NoAM

Residents of the Cocoon, The. Kazuko Shiraishi. WoBe, *tr. by* Samuel Grolmes and Yumiko Tsumura

Residue. Carlos Drummond de Andrade. TCLAP, *tr. by* Virginia de Araújo

Residue. Carlos Drummond de Andrade. GPTC; PoetW; VCWP, *tr. by* Mark Strand

Residue. Paula McLain. AmPoNex

Residues: Thronging the Heart. Gael Turnbull. Oth

Resignation. Matthew Arnold.
Poet, The. NPeEn

Resignation. Paul Laurence Dunbar. SacPr

Resignation. Edward Young.
Runcible Thought, A. STuOW
Seascape. STuOW

Resin. Patricia Pogson. NLP

Resist Confinement. Joette Harland-Watts. InTrad

Resistance. Horst Bienek. AF

Resisting, by embracing, nothingness. (LL) In Santa Maria del Popolo. Thom Gunn. HarvBoo; NPeEn

Resisting Geometry. Ann Elizabeth Hostetler. ACAMVP

Resolute Desire That Enters, The. Arnaut Daniel. STV, *tr. by* John Frederick Nims

Resolution. Charles Leo O'Donnell. SacPr

Resolution, The. Richard Baxter. SacPr

Resolution and Independence. William Wordsworth. NAEL-6v2; NAEL-7v2; NOBRP; NoP-4; NoP-5; OxAEP-2; TFi
Aged, Aged Man, The. STuOW
"Now, whether it were by peculiar grace." UV
"There was a roaring in the wind all night." ITBLP; WoPoe

Resolution in Four Sonnets, of a Poetical Question Put to Me by a Friend, Concerning Four Rural Sisters. Charles Cotton. OxBSo

Resolve. Leslie Ullman. ExTi

Resolve, The. Alexander Brome. NOSC; OBEV

Resolve, The. Mary Lee, Lady Chudleigh. BrAP

Resolve, The. Lady Mary Wortley Montagu. BrAP

Resolves to Take the Leap of Leucata. Mary Robinson. CenSon; RWP

41. Resolves to Take the Leap of Leucata. Mary Robinson. NPBRoP *Fr.* Sappho and Phaon.

Resolving to climb inside the solid mount, to see. (LL) Bright Receding. Heather Ramsdell. AmPoNex; IAoNAP

Resonance. Christopher Gilbert. ESEAA

Resonance. Ruth Stone. BodElec; OxBoAm

Resonance resplendent. Favorable Prospects. Norman Fischer. WANABP

Resort. George Oppen. FTOS

Resound my voice, ye woods that hear me plain. Sir Thomas Wyatt. AEP

Resounding echo of the buddha's words, The. Jessemyn Meyerhoff. WhBo

Resounding Zero, A. Nicanor Parra. WoBe, *tr. by* Liz Werner

Resource and a touch. So ditditdit daah for Bill Tuckett. (LL) Morse. Les A. Murray. NoP-4; NoP-5

Respect for Law and Order, A. John Hughes. PNI

Respect yourself, my brother. Brothers Loving Brothers. Vega. ISC

Respectable Burgher, The. Thomas Hardy. ChIV-2; NoAM

Respectable House. Anne Stevenson. NALW

Respected, Feared, and Somehow Loved. Marjorie Welish. OnScMo; PmAP

Respecting each other's silence. (LL) For Black Women Who Are Afraid. Toi Derricotte. ExTi; FuFl

Respice Finem. Thomas Proctor. NoSic

Respite. Tatamkulu Afrika. TSAP

Resplendent chariot of the sun goes down inside, The. Evening. Mihály Csokonai Vitéz. IQMS, *tr. by* Madeline Mason

Resplendent in the active way. Shelving Fixtures. Gale Nelson. OnScMo

Respond to me: how many. Respond to Me. Lee Ann Brown. VaPo

Respondez! Walt Whitman. NoAM

Respondez! Respondez! / Let every one answer! Let those who sleep be waked! Let none evade—not you, any more than others! Chants Democratic and Native Americans: 5. Walt Whitman. APN-1

Response and Reconciliation. Octavio Paz. WoBe, *tr. by* Eliot Weinberger

Response to Rimbaud's Later Manner. Thomas Sturge Moore. CABP; OBMV

Responsibilities. Anthony Cronin. PBCIP

Responsibility. Lisa Lewis. BodElec

Responsive to the tune of lawns and trees. Dogs in the Morning Light. Bruce Dawe. NoAM

Rest. Christina Georgina Rossetti. GSo; OBEV

Rest ("When round the earth the Father's hands.") George Macdonald. SacPr

Rest ("Who dwelleth in that secret place.") George Macdonald. SacPr

Rest, The. Ezra Pound. MoAmPo; NAMCP V.1; NoAM; PoA 2002 *Fr.* Lustra.

Rest, The. Lawrence Raab. PoA 2002

Rest and look at this goddamned wheelbarrow. Whatever. Red Wheelbarrow, The. Jack Spicer. OxBoAm

Rest, beauty, stillness: not a waif of a cloud. Phantasies (After Robert Schumann). Emma Lazarus.

Rest, beauty, stillness: not a waif of cloud. Emma Lazarus. APN-2 *Fr.* Phantasies (After Robert Schumann).

Rest Due and Taken. Rolando Hinojosa. TiP2

Rest from Loving and Be Living. Cecil Day Lewis. MoBrPo; OBMV

Rest in Love. Diana Helen Melhem.
  "Say french." PoArWo

Rest Is Grace, The. János Pilinszky. IQMS, *tr.* by Adam Makkai

Rest is vanity of vanities, The. (LL) Ecclesiastes. G. K. Chesterton. ChIV-1; MoBrPo

Rest lightly O Earth upon this wretched Nearchos. Epitaph of Nearchos. Ammianus. WeW-3, *tr.* by Dudley Fitts

Rest, little guest. After Annunciation. Anna Wickham. MoBrPo

Rest me with Chinese colours. Song of the Degrees, A. Ezra Pound. APT-1

Rest of It, The. John Wilkinson. VaPo

Rest of Love, The. Carl Phillips. AmAlph

Rest / Of our life must be a palimpsest, The. Palimpsest, A. Michael Field. ViWPN; VWP

Rest of the way will be only going down, The. (LL) Long Hill, The. Sara Teasdale. MoAmPo; TCAPo

Rest thee aged pilgrim, now thy toils are o'er. Death of a Grandparent. Mrs. Jennette Bonneau. Mary Weston Fordham. CBWP-2

Rest! This little Fountain runs. For a Fountain. Barry Cornwall. OBEV

Rest was mismanaged, The. (LL) Gertrude Stein. MotU; TCAPo *Fr.* Tender Buttons.

Rest your heart; let your cares not overcome you. What good will grief and apprehension do you? Mu'tamid, King of Seville. HiArP, *tr.* by James T. Monroe

Restaurant. Maxine Hong Kingston. OpBo

Restaurant is empty, The. On Stopping Late in the Afternoon for Steamed Dumplings. Toi Derricotte. AFaM

Resting [*with music*]. Josephine D. Henderson Heard. CBWP-4

Resting at my open window I gaze out at mountains. Han-shan Te-ch'ing. CSKM, *tr.* by Red Pine

Resting-Place, The. William Wordsworth. CenSon *Fr.* River Duddon [A Series of Sonnets], The.

Restless before the canary, wave of traffic on an inhale, I can just barely see on a dark blue ground black arabesques. Killarney Clary. GeoHom

Restless he rolls about from whore to whore. John Wilmot, 2d Earl of Rochester. OBSV *Fr.* Satire on Charles II, A.

Restless, I walk out in the evening. Lilacs. Karen Solie. OpeFie

Restless Night. Tu Fu [*or Du Fu*]. CCL1, *tr.* by Burton Watson

Restless Night ("As bamboo chill drifts into the bedroom.") Tu Fu [*or Du Fu*]. NDACCP, *tr.* by David Hinton

Restless Night in Camp, A. Tu Fu [*or Du Fu*]. NDACCP, *tr.* by Kenneth Rexroth

Restless, restless, craving rest. Herman Melville. NCAP

Restless that noble day, appeased by soft. Patriots' Day. Richard Wilbur. ItP

Restoration. Jeffrey Skinner. PBCAP

Restoration, A. Brendan Kennelly. IrLP

"Restore the lock!" she cries; and all around. Alexander Pope. OxAEP-1 *Fr.* Rape of the Lock, The: An Heroi-Comical Poem in Five Cantos.

Restore to them what they have no longer. Restore to Them. René Char. YaTCFP, *tr.* by Mary Ann Caws *and* Jean-Pierre Cauvin

Restored Terrace is new and fresh, The. *Unknown.* ColAnChi *Fr.* Classic of Odes.

Restores the else-betrayed, too-human heart. (LL) At a Bach Concert. Adrienne Rich. NIL-7; NIP-4; YaYoPo

Restricting Gate, The. Alan Dent. RSaN

Re-stringing 100 Year Old Wire. John Collin Murphey. TiP2

Restroom. Chitra Divakaruni. UnSA

Result, The. Robert Crawford. NeBrP

Result of an Observation. Lenous Surprice. OGAHCP, *tr.* by Boadiba and Jack Hirschman

Résumé. Bei Dao. AF, *tr.* by Bonnie S. McDougall

Résumé. Dorothy Parker. AmWit; APT-1; EMP; HeIP-4; IJHIL; NALW; NAMCP V.1; NBLV; NoP-4; NoP-5; OxBoAm; PtR; UV

Resurgam [*with music*]. Adah Isaacs Menken. CBWP-1

Resurgam. Marjorie Lowry Christie Pickthall. SacPr

Resurrection. Nicole Cooley. Vesp

Resurrection. George Crabbe. SacPr

Resurrection [*with music*]. Margiad Evans. OBWVE

Resurrection. Joy Harjo. HATNAP

Resurrection. Vladimir Holan. PoSu; StAl, *tr.* by George Theiner

Resurrection. Alfred Noyes. SacPr

Resurrection, The. Abraham Cowley. ChIV-2 *Fr.* Pindarique Odes.

Resurrection, The. Elizabeth Jennings. HarvBoo

Resurrection, The. Nathaniel Wanley. NPeEn

Resurrection, The. William Butler Yeats.
  Two Songs from a Play.
    Everything That Man Esteems. TWF

Resurrection: An Easter Sequence. William Robert Rodgers.
  "It was a lovely night." PNI

Resurrection at West Lake. Eric Tretheway. Coast; PfSP

Resurrection, Imperfect. John Donne. ChIV-2

Resurrection man, father. Sister Mary Appassionata Lectures the Bible Study Class: Homage to Onan. David Citino. UpMys

Resurrection Morn, The. *Unknown.* SSUS

Resurrection of a Mouse. David J. Rothman. GeoH

Resurrection of Elvis Presley, The. Ai. AllShUp

Resurrection of the Body, The. Eric Pankey. PoA 2002

Resurrection of the Flesh, The. Juan Felipe Herrera. TouFir

Resurrections of Layla Al-Attar, The. Jawad Yaqoob. IrPoTo, *tr.* by Chuck Miller and Saadi A. Simawe

Retaliation. Oliver Goldsmith.
  David Garrick. NPeEn; OxBEV
  Edmund Burke. NPeEn; OxBEV
  (Joshua Reynolds.) NPeEn
  Sir Joshua Reynolds. OBCoV; OxBEV

Rethink in the hair department. Time maybe to move on from the fags. (LL) Time Out. Maurice Riordan. BeAl; EmeKit; ModIr

Reticence. May Muzaffar. PoArWo, *tr.* by Tahia Abdel Nasser

Retina fills with skies and expanses of grass, The. Martyrdom. Yolanda Bedregal. TANSG, *tr.* by Carolyne Wright

Retinal burn of warm November light. Dan Guillory. IllVoic *Fr.* Snowpoems.

Retire, my daughter. Fragment of an English Opera. A. E. Housman. OBCoV

Retired Architect, The. Mei-Mei Berssenbrugge.
  3. AWPTFC

Retired Ballerinas, Central Park West. Lawrence Ferlinghetti. NAMCP V.2; NoAM

Retired Friendship, To Ardelia, A. Katherine Philips. BASC

Retired general is talking about restraint, The. Nightline: An Interview with the General. Ronald Wallace. PBCAP

Retired man showed the town, The. His Waves. Rick Noguchi. AmPoNex

Retired [*or* Retyrèd] thought[e]s enjoy their own[e] delight[e]s. Look[e] Home. Robert Southwell. NoSic

Retired Postman Recalls the Old Route, A. C. J. Sage. RWB

Retirement. William Cowper. SacPr *Fr.* Olney Hymns.

Retirement. Henry Timrod. APN-2

Retirement. Henry Vaughan. ChIV-1

Retirement. Yüan Chĕn. CrYelRi, *tr.* by Sam Hamill

Retirement of the Elephant, The. Russell Edson. SUP

Retirement (I). Henry Vaughan. NOSC

Retirement: "Unfamiliar warble 9 times more, An." Joanne Kyger. WANABP

Retiring from court. EMJL *Fr.* Mad Verse.

Retornos a Través de los Colores. Rafael Alberti. RaW

Retornos de un Poeta Asesinado. Rafael Alberti. RaW

Retort Perfect, The. Justin Richardson. OBCoV

Retour d'Ulysse. Marie-Claire Bancquart. YaTCFP

Retour en Tunisie. Tahar Bekri.
  14. YaTCFP
  15. YaTCFP
  16. YaTCFP
  17. YaTCFP
  18. YaTCFP
  19. YaTCFP

Retratos sostienen paredes, Los. Sombra que dibuja la luz, La. Natalia Toledo. RMCMP

Retreat. Árpád Tóth. IQMS, *tr.* by Watson Kirkconnell

Retreat at Haein Temple. Daegak Euchon. BecRai, *tr.* by Kim Daljin, Kim Won-Chung and Christopher Merrill

Retreat from Paradise, The. John Milton. HeIP-4 *Fr.* Paradise Lost.

Retreat of Hsieh Kung, The. Li Po. NAAPv.2, *tr.* by Florence Ayscough *and* Amy Lowell and Amy Lowell

Retreat of Ita Cagney, The. Michael Hartnett. PBCIP

Retreat toward the Spring. Nathaniel Tarn. WANABP

Retreat[e], The. Henry Vaughan. BASC; CABP; ClHu; FSCP; NAEL-6v1; NAEL-7v1; NIP-4; NoP-4; NoP-5; NOSC; NPeEn; OBEV; OBWVE; OxBEV; PBRV; RSR; TFi

Retreating Wind. Louise Glück. CAP-8

Retribution [*with music*]. Lizelia Augusta Jenkins Moorer. CBWP-3

Retribution keeps watch this summer day. Buchenwald. Fedya Filkova. CSCBP, *tr.* by Georgi Belev and Lisa Sapinkopf

Retrieval System, The. Maxine W. Kumin. InvLad; WeW-3

Retrievers in Translation. Mark Doty. AmAlph

Retro Creation. Aidan Rooney-Céspedes. BeAl; NIrP

Retro Lullaby. Beckian Fritz Goldberg. AmAlph

90: Retro me, Sathana! Dante Gabriel Rossetti. ChIV-2 *Fr.* House of Life, The.

Retrospect. Erich Fried. GTCP, *tr.* by Stuart Hood

Retrospect [*with music*]. Josephine D. Henderson Heard. CBWP-4

Retrospect: "Breath of balm—of orange bloom!, A." Ina Coolbrith. CalPo

Retrospect Love of Nature Leading to Love of Mankind. William Wordsworth. *Fr.* Prelude, The; Growth of a Poet's Mind [1850 version].

Retrospection. Charlotte Brontë. "Dream that stole o'er us in the time." PEW

Retrospection [*with music*]. Henrietta Cordelia Ray. CBWP-3

Retrospection. Dunstan Shaw. NOBAu

Retrospective. Ogata Kenzon. WoPoe, *tr.* by Richard L. Wilson

Retrospective. William Scammell. NLP

Retrun of the Muse, The. Sandra M. Gilbert. WaAnP

Returning to Fields and Gardens (1) ("When I was young, I did not fit in.") T'ao Ch'ien. WaAnP, *tr.* by Arthur Sze

Return. Dmitry Vasil'evich Bobyshev. ItGoST, *tr.* by Michael Van Walleghen

Return. Rosario Castellanos. FiBr, *tr.* by Carolyne Wright

Return. Constantine P. Cavafy. PasH, *tr.* by Rae Dalven

Return. Seamus Deane. PBCIP; PNI

Return. Carolyn Forché. BodElec

Return. Robinson Jeffers. HarvBoo

Return. Archibald MacLeish. APT-1

Return. T. H. Parry-Williams. BBMWP, *tr.* by Joseph P. Clancy

Return: "Not thirsting for battle." Yoseph Sarig. NRoS, *tr.* by Esther Raizen

Return. John Wilmot, 2d Earl of Rochester. *See* Song: "Absent from thee, I languish still."

Return. William Wordsworth. CenSon *Fr.* River Duddon, The.

Return, The. John Peale Bishop. APT-1

Return, The. Arna Bontemps. GT

Return, The. Rosario Castellanos. TANSG; TCLAP, *tr.* by Magda Bogin

Return, The. Emily Dickinson. MoAmPo

Return, The. Felicia Dorothea Hemans. RWP

Return, The. Julio Herrera y Reissig. TCLAP, *tr.* by Andrew Rosing

Return, The. Dalia Hertz. FIT, *tr.* by Robert Friend

Return, The. William Heyen. CAP-8

Return, The. Ho Ch'e Ch'ang. CCL1, *tr.* by H. A. Giles

Return, The. Rudyard Kipling. MoBrPo

Return, The. Joanne Limburg. NeBl

Return, The. Thomas McGrath. GifTon

Return, The. Edna St. Vincent Millay. MoAmPo; NAMCP V.1; NoAM

Return, The. Molly Peacock. PasH; RA

Return, The. Ezra Pound. APT-1; MoAmPo; NAAPv.2; NAMCP V.1; NoAM; NPeEn; OxBoAm; TRP; WeW-3 *Fr.* Ripostes of Ezra Pound.

Return, The. Yevgeny Borisovich Rein. ItGoST, *tr.* by Judith Hemschemeyer

Return, The. Theodore Roethke. PoA 2002

Return, The. Tadeusz Rózewicz. HP, *tr.* by Adam Czerniawski

Return, The. T'ao Ch'ien. ColAnChi, *tr.* by James Robert Hightower

Return, The. Evan J. Thomas. AngWePo

Return, The. Tu Fu [*or* Du Fu]. TAL

Return, The: "After washing Paddington loos." Moeen Faruqi. PML

Return, The: "All afternoon my father drove the country roads." Philip Levine. OxBoAm

Return, The: An Elegy. Robert Penn Warren. APT-2

Return, 2, The. Catherine Barnett. PoCho

Return and dwell with me. (LL) Shall Earth no more inspire thee. Emily Jane Brontë. BrAP; VWP

Return, blessed years, when not the jocund spring. Anna Seward. RWP *Fr.* Llangollen Vale.

Return: Buffalo. Linda Hogan. BodElec

Return, Content! for fondly I pursued. William Wordsworth. CenSon *Fr.* River Duddon, The.

Return is not a way of going forward. Roman Poem Number Nine. June Jordan. GT

Return, my joys, and hither bring. Opposite to Melancholy. William Strode. NOSC

Return of an Ikon. Dimitris Tsaloumas. BMAP

Return of Charles II, The. John Dryden. STuOW *Fr.* Astraea Redux.

Return of Persephone, The. Alec Derwent Hope. BMAP; BrAP

Return of Robinson Jeffers, The. Robert Hass. GeoHom

Return of, The. Morgana La Fay. John Wieners. AHA

Return of the Banished. Li Po. CrYelRi, *tr.* by Sam Hamill

Return of the Goddess [Artemis]. Robert Graves. PoA 2002

Return of the Greeks, The. Edwin Muir. NoP-4; NoP-5

Return of the Native. Imamu Amiri Baraka. APSN; OxAAAP

Return of the Native: "This is the true land of fairy tales." Elizabeth Brewster. Coast

Return of the Proconsul, The. Zbigniew Herbert. PoSu

Return of the Prodigals. Kurt Brown. SUP

Return of the Wolves. Anita Endrezze. HATNAP

Return of Ulysses. Marie-Claire Bancquart. YaTCFP, *tr.* by Martin Sorrell

Return of Youth, The. William Cullen Bryant. TreFP

Return often and take me. Return. Constantine P. Cavafy. PasH, *tr.* by Rae Dalven

Return, Sweet Horse, rise. Cortez's Horse. Pat Mora. UnSA

Return Thee, Heart. Alexander Scott. NePenScot

Return thee, heart, hamewart again. Return Thee, Heart. Alexander Scott. NePenScot

Return to Avondale. Eithne Cavanagh. IrLP

Return to Cardiff. Dannie Abse. AngWePo; TCAWP

Return to DeKalb. Lucien Stryk. IllVoic

Return to Frankfurt. Marie Luise Kaschnitz. *tr.* by Beatrice Cameron "Girl thinks if I can only manage, The." ItWoWo, *tr.* by Beatrice Cameron

Return to Harmony 3. Agha Shahid Ali. BAP-97

Return to Hiroshima. Lucien Stryk. AtGh

Return to La Plata, Missouri. Jim Barnes. HATNAP

Return to Normalcy. Joanna Fuhrman. PrTe

Return to Paris. Jules Supervielle. MFP, *tr.* by Martin Sorrell

Return to Scalpay. Norman Alexander MacCaig. NePenScot; NoP-5

Return to Shaoshan. Mao Tse-tung. WoPoe, *tr.* by Willis Barnstone and Ko Ching-po

Return to Temptation. Mary Weems. SpirFl

Return to the City. Manuel Ulacia. RMCMP, *tr.* by Indran Amirthanayagam

Return to the Homeland. Adelina da Silva. NAfrP, *tr.* by Don Burness

Return to the Village. Na'im Araidi. PLBUT, *tr.* by Jay Shir

Return to Tunisia. Tahar Bekri. YaTCFP, *tr.* by Mary Ann Caws *and* Jean-Pierre Cauvin

Return to Wang River. Wang Wei. CrYelRi, *tr.* by Sam Hamill

Return trip seated erect on the singing train in deliberate. Novels from a Fragment in Progress. Bob Kaufman. EGAG

Return 2. Tamara Kamenszain. MirDau, *tr.* by Roberta Gordenstein

Returned from California. Simon J. Ortiz. HATNAP

Returned Soldier, The. John Clare. FaBoWar

Returned to Frisco, 1946. W. D. Snodgrass. PWW2

Returning. Linda Pastan. WeW-3

Returning. Victor Vroomkoning. TuT, *tr.* by Ruth Hooley

Returning a Lawn to the Field It Was. Brendan Galvin. PoCoUp

Returning after I left my home in childhood. Ho Ch'e Ch'ang. NDACCP, *tr.* by William Carlos Williams

Returning at Night to Lumen Mountain. Meng Hao Jan. CCL1, *tr.* by Witter Bynner

Returning / By an unused path—violets. Bakusui. ZenPo, *tr.* by Takashi Ikemoto and Lucien Stryk

Returning by Night to Lu-Men. Meng Hao Jan. NDACCP, *tr.* by Kenneth Rexroth

Returning Clouds. Ching An. CSKM, *tr.* by Jerome P. Seaton

Returning Exile. Iain Crichton Smith. EdScPo

Returning from a funeral. Mukai Kyorai. SoOfWa, *tr.* by Sam Hamill

Returning from Italy. Denise Calvetti Michaels. IPoFL

Returning from its daily quest, my Spirit. To Dante [*or* Sonnet: Guido Cavalcanti to Dante Alighieri]. Guido Cavalcanti. OBVE, *tr.* by Percy Bysshe Shelley

Returning from the Enemy, Part 6. Joy Harjo. CFP

Returning from the Fair. Ivan Davidkov. CSCBP, *tr.* by Georgi Belev and Lisa Sapinkopf

Returning Home to Deer-Gate Mountain at Night. Meng Hao Jan. NDACCP, *tr.* by David Hinton

Returning in Wind and Drizzle to My Home. S. J. Marks. BodElec

Returning Late to Lu-men Shan. Meng Hao Jan. CrYelRi, *tr.* by Sam Hamill

Returning, near morning. Douglas Burnet Smith. Coast *Fr.* Killed, The.

Returning North. Gjertrud Schnackenberg. BeAl

Returning Spring. Pauli Murray. GT

Returning the Water. Angela Shannon. BtF

Returning to Dongrae. Chimi Sucho. BecRai, *tr.* by Kim Daljin, Kim Won-Chung and Christopher Merrill

Returning to Dupawon. Jungkwan Ilson. BecRai, *tr.* by Kim Daljin, Kim Won-Chung and Christopher Merrill

Returning to Fields and Gardens (2) ("I plant beans below the southern hill.") T'ao Ch'ien. WaAnP, *tr.* by Arthur Sze

Returning to Goleufryn. Vernon Watkins. AngWePo; OBWVE

Returning to his vomit. (LL)   William Wordsworth.   NAEL-6v2; NAEL-7v2 *Fr.* Prelude, The; Growth of a Poet's Mind [1850 version].

Returning to My Fields and Gardens.   T'ao Ch'ien.   CrYelRi, *tr. by* Sam Hamill

Returning to My Garden Home: In Respectful Response to the Master of Hua-yang.   Shen Yüeh.   ColAnChi, *tr. by* Richard Mather and Richard B. Mather

Returning to my grandfather's house, after this exile.   Returning to Goleufryn. Vernon Watkins.   AngWePo; OBWVE

Returning to My Hometown.   Chimi Sucho.   BecRai, *tr. by* Kim Daljin, Kim Won-Chung and Christopher Merrill

Returning to Roots of First Feeling.   Robert Duncan.   PoA 2002

Returning to the Port of Authority: A Picaresque.   Constance Urdang.   PBCAP

Returning, we found everything in its place.   History Set, The.   Vincent Woods.   NIrP

Returning, We Hear the Larks.   Isaac Rosenberg.   HarvBoo; NAEL-6v2; NAEL-7v2; NAMCP V.1; NoAM; OBWP; PoWW; StAl

Reuben Bright.   Edwin Arlington Robinson.   APN-2; GSo; MoAmPo; NAMCP V.1; NCAP; NoP-4; NoP-5; OxBoAm

Reuben Pantier.   Edgar Lee Masters.   APT-1 *Fr.* Spoon River Anthology.

Reuben, Reuben.   Michael S. Harper.   CAP-8; LoL; NAMCP V.2

Reuben, Reuben, I've been thinking.   How 'Ya Gonna Keep 'Em Down on the Farm? (After They've Seen Paree).   Sam M. Lewis and Joe Young.   ReLy

Reunion.   Sarah Cortez.   TiP2

Reunion.   T. Crunk.   YaYoPo

Reunion.   Carolyn Forché.   NAMCP V.2; NoAM

Réunion.   Max Jacob.   YaTCFP

Reunion.   Carolyn Kizer.   ExTi

Reunion.   Charles Wright.   CAP-8; OxBoAm

Reunion: A Scenario.   Vern Rutsala.   MotU

Reunión de violonchelos.   Ernesto Lumbreras.   RMCMP

Reunion of Cellos.   Ernesto Lumbreras.   RMCMP, *tr. by* Rebecca Seiferle

Reunited.   Sir Gilbert Parker.   OBEV

Reunited.   Henrietta Cordelia Ray.   CBWP-3

Rev. Andrew Brown, over the Hill to Rest.   Josephine D. Henderson Heard.   CBWP-4

Rev. Samuel Weston.   Mary Weston Fordham.   CBWP-2

Rêve à Barcelone.   Meret Oppenheim.   YaTCFP

Rêve du fleuve, Le.   Éveil.   Robert Melançon.   YaTCFP

Reveal Code: Indra's Net 8.   John Cayley.
    Four Screen Shots.   PFTM-2

Revealing Oneself to a Woman.   Bin Ramke.   YaYoPo

Reveals the deep love sealed in the still face. (LL)   Dom Moraes.   NoP-4; NoP-5 *Fr.* Two from Israel.

Reveille.   A. E. Housman.   CABP; HarvBoo; MoBrPo; NoP-4; NoP-5 *Fr.* Shropshire Lad, A.

Reveille.   Primo Levi.   HP, *tr. by* Ruth Feldman and Brian Swann

Reveille Matin, or Good Morrow to a Friend.   Mildmay Fane, 2d Earl of Westmorland.   NOSC

Revel in the contradictions of love and pain.   Thoreau's Eyes: Two Poems for Kazuaki Tanahashi.   Michael McClure.   WANABP

Revelación.   Natalia Toledo.   RMCMP

Revelation.   Robert Frost.   ChIV-2

Revelation.   Sir Edmund William Gosse.   OBEV

Revelation.   Aaron Pope and Jodi A. Shaw.   IFF

Revelation.   Natalia Toledo.   RMCMP, *tr. by* Alberto A. Ríos

Revelation.   Robert Penn Warren.   NoAM

Révélation, La.   Max Jacob.   YaTCFP

Revelation, The.   Stanley Crouch.   SeSe

Revelation, The.   Max Jacob.   YaTCFP, *tr. by* Moishe Black and Maria Green

Revelation, The.   William Carlos Williams.   SAmP

Revelation: The Movie.   Elton Glaser.   PBCAP

Revelation 5, October 8.   Anne Wentworth.   EMWP

Revelation 8, March 31.   Anne Wentworth.   EMWP

Revelation, A.   Tomas Tranströmer.   WoBe *Fr.* Haiku.

Revelation and Decline.   Georg Trakl.   PFTM-1

Revelation in the Mother Lode.   George Evans.   AF; PmAP

Revelation of St. John the Divine, The.   Bible, *N.T. tr. by* Bathsheba Bowers
    "Spirit saith, come, The."   EMWP, *tr. by* Bathsheba Bowers

Revelation on a Summer Walk.   John O'Brien.   PoCoUp

Revelations.   Harry Thurston.   Coast

Revelations of ice, exactly, The.   Reading Akhmatova in Midwinter.   Lavinia Greenlaw.   NeBrP

Revellers, The.   Felicia Dorothea Hemans.   TreFP

Revelry by Night.   Lord Byron.   NPBRoP *Fr.* Childe Harold's Pilgrimage.

Revelry in Black-and-White.   Ann Lauterbach.   BodElec

Revelry was had, A.   The chair came to pieces.   Fall of Because, The.   David Baratier.   AmPoNex

Revenant.   Rita Dove.   AmAlph

Revenge.   Henry Fielding.   DiBP *Fr.* Tom Thumb the Great.

Revenge—?   Heinrich Heine.   WoPoe, *tr. by* Mark Rudman

Revenge.   Robert Herrick.   RaF

Revenge.   Letitia Elizabeth Landon.   NAEL-7v2; NOBRP; NPeEn

Revenge.   Luis Enrique Mejía Godoy.   BeAl, *tr. by* Dinah Livingstone

Revenge.   Amado Nervo.   TCLAP, *tr. by* Sue Standing

Revenge.   Mary E. Tucker.   CBWP-1

Revenge.   Charles Henry Webb.   RaF

Revenge, The.   Alfred Tennyson.
    "At Flores in the Azores Sir Richard Grenville lay."   OBWP

Revenge—?—as if it were a cure.   Revenge—?   Heinrich Heine.   WoPoe, *tr. by* Mark Rudman

Revenge Fable.   Ted Hughes.   RaF

Revenge: "Hands on the steering wheel."   Sadhu Binning.   PML, *tr. by the* author

Revenge is a naked sword.   Revenge.   Charles Henry Webb.   RaF

Revenge, like habanero peppers, clears.   Revenge, Like Habanero Peppers. Rachel Loden.   LiTh

Revenge of Hamish, The.   Sidney Lanier.   APN-2; NCAP

Revenge 1.   Giuseppe Gioacchino Belli.   WoPoe, *tr. by* Anthony Burgess

Revenge the attitude I need never attend. Not too.   Versailles.   Michael Gizzi. OnScMo

Revenger's Tragedy, The.   Cyril Tourneur.
    "Art thou beguild now? tut, a Lady can."   OxBEV
    "Duke: royall letcher; goe, gray hayrde adultery."   OxBEV

Reverberation.   Maurice Kenny.   HATNAP

Reverence is the nature of my love.   Thich Nhat Hanh *and* Jane Hirshfield. WhBo

Reverend Butler came by.   Madam and the Minister.   Langston Hughes. OxAAAP

Reverend mothers, The.   Foretold Futures.   Giovanna Pollarolo.   TANSG, *tr. by* Marjorie Agosin

Rev Stump is believe it or not for real.   We Will Now Hear the Word of God from Each of Our Beloved Chaplains.   Daniel Berrigan.   UpMys

Reverie.   Henrietta Cordelia Ray.   CBWP-3

Reverie, A.   Joanna Baillie.   WoRP

Reverie, A.   Mary Weston Fordham.   CBWP-2

Reverie of a Mum.   Nancy Keesing.   NOBAu

Reversal of Worlds.   Georgi Rupchev.   CSCBP, *tr. by* Georgi Belev and Lisa Sapinkopf

Re-Verse.   Diane Ward.   FTOS

Reverse Engineering.   Robert Johnson.   TiP2

Reverse Order.   Steve Benson.
    "As sincerely as possible."   FTOS

Reverse the flight of Lucifer.   Task, The.   Ruth Pitter.   BeAl; MoBrPo

Reverse wind blows freeway sounds up-canyon, A.   On the Way to the Zendō. Philip Whalen.   WANABP

Reversible Stitches: my mother and I leaned over a single piece of English. Mary Warren's Sampler.   Nicole Cooley.   NeAmPo

Review from Staten Island.   Gloria C. Oden.   GT

Reviewing Past Lives while Leaf-Burning.   Anita Endrezze.   HATNAP

Reviewing the Situation.   Lionel Bart.   ReLy

Revised Notes for a Sonnet.   Edward Pygge.   OBCoV

Revised Versions, The.   Lawrence Raab.   PoDa

Revisionary Instruments 1.   Kathy Fagan.   ExTi

Revisionism.   Joanne Burns.   BMAP

Revisionism.   Gordon Wardman.   RSaN

Revisionist History: Magic Kingdom.   Robert Wynne.   RWB

Revisionist Poem—Octavio Paz.   Thomas McGrath.   TAPaP

Revisionist work in.   Susan Howe.   VaPo *Fr.* Bed Hangings.

Revisiting Kumkang Pavilion.   Jungkwon Ilson.   BecRai, *tr. by* Kim Daljin, Kim Won-Chung and Christopher Merrill

Revival.   Arthur Hugh Clough.   SacPr

Revival.   Steve Crow.   HATNAP

Revival.   Kevin Young.   OxAAAP

Revival, The.   Henry Vaughan.   InvLi

Revo Lyric.   Kendel Hippolyte.   WaCA

Revocation, A.   Sir Thomas Wyatt.   OBEV

Revolt.   Maura Stanton.   SUP

Revolt Against Poetry.   Antonin Artaud.   ConPit, *tr. by* Clayton Eshleman

Revolt in the Mirror, A.   Wolfgang Bächler.   GTCP; PML, *tr. by* Reinhold Grimm

Revolt of immense estates, The. (LL)   In the Miscroscope.   Miroslav Holub. PoSu; WoPoe, *tr. by* Ian Milner and Jarmila Milner

Revolt of Islam, The.   Percy Bysshe Shelley.
    "Over the utmost hill at length I sped."   OBWP

Revolting against the lips. Dracula. Salwa Al-Neimi. PoArWo, *tr. by* Subhi Hadidi

Revolution. Brian G. Gilmore. SpirFl

Revolution. Emyr Lewis. *tr. by* Robert Minhinnick
"Above us, where the clouds'." ATSWP

Revolution. Enrique Lihn. TCLAP, *tr. by* Jonathan Cohen

Revolution, The. Jack Gilbert. BodElec

Revolution is conceived, The. Cycle. Bobbi Sykes. BMAP

Revolution, said Mr Adams, The. Ezra Pound. PFTM-1 *Fr.* Cantos.

Revolutionary. Willie Perdomo. InTrad

Revolutionary,The. Dezső Kosztolányi. IQMS, *tr. by* Peter Zollman

Revolutionary Letter #1. Diane Di Prima. CLPP

Revolutionary Petunias. Alice Walker. NIL-7

Revolutionary Thoughts. Crystal Williams. BtF

Revolutionary Vision, The. Ira B. Jones. InTrad

Revolving door. Ron Silliman. PFTM-2 *Fr.* Ketjak.

Reward. Kevin Young. SpirFl

Rewarded porters opening their smiles, The. On the Railway Platform. Randall Jarrell. GM

Rewards and Fairies. Roger Woddis. UV

Rewind. Ger Killeen. AmPoNex

Rewind the star back to a burning rind. Stellar Elements. Dan Beachy-Quick. IAoNAP

Rex Mundi. David Gascoyne. NoP-4

Rex regum, for whom praise flows freely. Poem on His Death-Bed. Meilyr Brydydd. OBWVE, *tr. by* Joseph P. Clancy

Rex Whistler—or is it Joe Isuzu?—stretches. Society. Tom Clark. PmAP

Reyerta. Federico García Lorca. RaW

Reynaldo in Paris. Leon Stokesbury. IaFF

Reynard the Fox. John Masefield.
Part 2.
"Fox knew well, that before they tore him, The." OBNV

Rhapsody. William Stanley Braithwaite. TCAPo

Rhapsody. Frank O'Hara. NAMCP V.2; NoAM

Rhapsody, A. Henry Vaughan. NAEL-6v1
"Should we go now a wandering [*or* a-wand'ring], we should meet." BASC

Rhapsody for the Mule. José Lezama Lima. TCLAP, *tr. by* Dudley Fitts, José Rodríguez Feo and Donald D. Walsh

Rhapsody: Keeping Faith. István Vas. IQMS, *tr. by* George Szirtes

Rhapsody on a Windy Night. T. S. Eliot. HeIP-4

Rhapsody on Main Street. Patrick Williams. PNI

Rhapsody on Whistling. Ch'eng-kung Sui. ColAnChi, *tr. by* Douglass A. White

Rheia, submissive in love to Kronos,. Hesiod. RaBo *Fr.* Theogony.

Rhetoric. Francis Ponge. WoPoe, *tr. by* Serge Gavronsky

Rhetors, travellers, neighbours, I've been. Debbie: An Epic. Lisa Robertson. NLPA

Rhiannon. Christine Furnival. TCAWP

Rhiannon. T. Harri Jones. AngWePo

Rhinemaiden. D. L. Crockett-Smith. OxAAAP

Rhinoceros, The. Ogden Nash. MoAmPo

Rhode Island. William Meredith. NoP-4; NoP-5

Rhode Island Is Famous for You. Howard Dietz. ReLy

Rhodoclea, I send you this wreath which I wove with my own hands. Rufinus. HePo, *tr. by* Barbara Hughes Fowler

Rhododaphne. Thomas Love Peacock.
"Magic and mystery, spells Circæan." NOBRP

Rhododendron is happy. Its aloof yet sexual, The. It's a Party (1959). Baron Wormser. SeSe

Rhododendrons. Larry Levis. GeoHom

Rhodora, The [On Being Asked Whence Is the Flower]. Ralph Waldo Emerson. AmFaPo; APN-1; ITBLP; NAAL-3; NAAL-5; NAAPv.1; NoP-4; NoP-5; OxBoAm; TCAPo; TFi

Rhodri. Ronald Stuart Thomas. OxAEP-2

Rhodri Theophilus Owen. Rhodri. Ronald Stuart Thomas. OxAEP-2

Rhonda, Age 15, Emergency Room. Letta Neely. WiU

Rhotruda. Frederick Goddard Tuckerman. NCAP

Rhudine Rhudine. Tony Medina. InTrad

Rhydcymerau. David Gwenallt Jones. BBMWP; OBWVE, *tr. by* Anthony Conran

Rhyfel y Sais Bach. John Stuart Williams. TCAWP

Rhyme. James Laughlin. WeW-3

Rhyme. Sylvia Plath. BodElec

Rhyme for a Child Viewing a Naked Venus in a Painting [of "The Judgement of Paris"]. Robert Browning. NPeEn; OBCoV

Rhyme for Halloween, A. Maurice Kilwein Guevara. TouFir

Rhyme for Night. Joan Aiken. TLR

Rhyme from Lincolnshire, A. *Unknown.* NPeEn

Rhyme is a woman, trying on clothes. Tatyana Voltskaya. CRWP, *tr. by* Daniel Weissbort

Rhyme is after, The. For W. C. W. Robert Creeley. FTOS

Rhyme Is Running Out,The. József Kiss. IQMS, *tr. by* Anthony Edkins

Rhyme nor mars, nor makes, The. His Defence Against the Idle Critic. Michael Drayton. NOSC

Rhyme of Sir Christopher, The. Henry Wadsworth Longfellow. NCAP

Rhyme of the Antique Forest. Henrietta Cordelia Ray. CBWP-3

Rhyme of the Flying Bomb, The. Mervyn Laurence Peake.
"Babe was born in the reign of George, A." FaBoWar

Rhyme of the poet, The. Ralph Waldo Emerson. NAAPv.1 *Fr.* Merlin.

Rhyme, the rack of finest wits. Fit of Rhyme against Rhyme, A. Ben Jonson. NoP-4; NoP-5; PBRV

Rhymeprose on an Owl. Chia Yi. *tr. by* James Robert Hightower
"Year was tan-wo, it was the fourth month, summer's first, The." WoPoe, *tr. by* James Robert Hightower

Rhymeprose on Literature. Lu Chi. ColAnChi, *tr. by* Achilles Fang

Rhymeprose on the Sword Gallery. Li Po. ColAnChi, *tr. by* Elling O. Eide

Rhymes of Learning, The. (LL) Blackstone Rangers, The. Gwendolyn Brooks. ESEAA; NAMCP V.2; NoAM

Rhymes on the Road. Thomas Moore.
Extract 9. Venice. OBSV

Rhymes picked me in a ditch, The. Natalya Gorbanevskaya. CRWP, *tr. by* Daniel Weissbort

Rhythm and Blues. / *Ohh, Ooh, Oh.* Tribute to Duke. Sarah Webster Fabio. FTtHH

Rhythm Is Only a Servant. János Batsányi. IQMS, *tr. by* Joseph Leftwich

Rhythm of the Pestle. Richard Ntiru.
"Listen—listen." EroLit

Rhythm scares them, The. Freestyle (Why They Don't Like Rap). Sonnet L'Abbé. OpeFie

Riachuelo con Lavanderas. Jorge Guillén. RaW

Rib Sandwich. William J. Harris. UnSA

Ribald Romeos less and less berattle. Horace. STV *Fr.* Odes.

Ribbon on Hell's Tree, The. Kristi Garboushian.
10. AmWaPo

Ribbons of iodine. Kelp. Nora Dauenhauer. HATNAP

Ribes rubrum. Elizabeth Garrett. NeBl

Ribh Considers Christian Love Insufficient. William Butler Yeats. BBASP; RaBo

Ribs and terrors in the whale, The. Herman Melville. APN-2; ChIV-1 *Fr.* Moby Dick.

Ribs of leaves lie in the dust, The. Coming of the Cold, The. Theodore Roethke. OBCP

Rice. Mary Oliver. PoCoUp

Rice around the lingam stone will be distributed in the dying sun, The. Karl Shapiro. BodElec *Fr.* Bourgeois Poet, The.

Rice Comes to El Volcán. Virgil Suárez. AmPoNex

Rice fields of cigarette butts of spit on the strange summons, The. Batouque. Aimé Césaire. GPTC, *tr. by* Clayton Eshleman and Annette Smith

Rice is cut and clouds glisten in the fields, The. After the Harvest. Tu Fu [*or* Du Fu]. CrYelRi, *tr. by* Sam Hamill

Rice Papers. Menna Elfyn. BBMWP, *tr. by* Nigel Jenkins

Rice this year ripens so late! Lament of the Farm Wife of Wu. Su Tung-p'o. ColAnChi, *tr. by* Burton Watson

Rich, The. Hans Magnus Enzensberger. GTCP, *tr. by* Reinhold Grimm

Rich and Poor; or, Saint and Sinner. Thomas Love Peacock. OBSV; OxBEV

Rich, black humus, airborne, glimmers gold, The. Descano, California. Chryss Yost. GeoHom

Rich, flashy, puffy-faced. Cabaret. Sterling Allen Brown. APT-2

Rich grass slumbers even in this place of death and the mounded graves seem not at all lonely, The. Song in a Graveyard. Pak Tujin. CAMKP, *tr. by* Edward W. Poitras

Rich Ink, Still Slightly Moist. J. B. Bryan. ICANM

Rich jigsaw'd gone, A. Bill Griffiths. Oth *Fr.* Building: The New London Hospital.

Rich little circle south. Bruce Andrews. FTOS

Rich man has his motorcar, The. Rich Man, The. Franklin Pierce Adams. AmWit; NBLV

Rich Man, The. Franklin Pierce Adams. AmWit; NBLV

Rich night. Will They Always Remember. Tracy Clarke. InTrad

"Rich soil," remarked the Landlord. Dennis Joseph Enright. OBCoV *Fr.* Paradise Illustrated.

Rich Statue, double-faced. To the New Year. Michael Drayton. NOSC

Rich surplus of consciousness rots at the wharves, The. Clouds. Francis Webb. BMAP

Rich worry about getting poor, The. 40. Shih Shu. CSKM, *tr. by* James H. Sanford

Richard and Maurice McDonald. Customer #! Jessica Freeman. AnSo

Richard Brought His Flute. Nancy Morejón. TCLAP, *tr. by* Kathleen Weaver

Richard Cory. Edwin Arlington Robinson. APN-2; ChAP; ColAP; CtM; IJHIL; MoAmPo; NAAL-5; NAAPv.1; NAMCP V.1; NCAP; NoP-4; NoP-5; OxBoAm; PoPoPo; PtR; TCAPo; TFi; WaAnP

Richard II. Veronica Forrest-Thomson. Oth

Richard II Forty. Louis Aragon. WoPoe, *tr. by* Peter Dale

Richard, said he, "though I myself explore." George Crabbe. STuOW *Fr.* Tales of the Hall.

Richard's Blues. Richard Cecil. SeSe

Riches I hold in light esteem. Emily Jane Brontë. *See* Old Stoic, The.

Richmond. John Updike. CBCWP

Richmond Gardens: A Poem. *Unknown.*

  Richmond Gardens: A Poem. OBGa

Richmond Hill. Thomas Maurice.

  Chiswick. OBGa

Richness, quietness, and pleasure. (LL) Invitation au Voyage, L'. Charles Baudelaire. ItP; WoPoe, *tr. by* Richard Wilbur

Rick of Green Wood, The. Edward Dorn. PmAP

Rickety chimney suggests, A. Caravan. Michael Longley. ModIr; PNI

Riddim an' Hardtimes. Lillian Allen. WaCA

Riddle. Gharib Nawaz. BBASP, *tr. by* Nasrollah Pourjavady and Peter Lamborn Wilson

Riddle: "As I went down that yella bank." *Unknown.* FaBoVe

Riddle: "As I went through a guttery gap / I met a wee man with a red cap." *Unknown.* FaBoVe

Riddle: "As I went through yon guttery gap / I met my Uncle Davy." *Unknown.* FaBoVe

Riddle: "Black'm saut'm rough'm glower'm saw." *Unknown.* FaBoVe

Riddle: "Chip chip cherry." *Unknown.* FaBoVe

Riddle: "Cuckoo and the gowk, the." *Unknown.* FaBoVe

Riddle: "From Belsen a crate of gold teeth." William Heyen. HP; SoSe-8

Riddle: "Hickamore hackamore." *Unknown.* FaBoVe

Riddle: "High as the sky it flies." *Unknown.* FaBoVe

Riddle: "Hopper o'ditches, A." *Unknown.* FaBoVe

Riddle: "House full, [a] yard full, [A]." *Unknown.* NTCP

Riddle: "I see them in summer." Tom Dawe. Coast

Riddle: "Invisible, chimerical." Daryl Hine. NoP-4; NoP-5

Riddle: "It has a head like a cat, feet like a cat." *Unknown.* NTCP

Riddle: "Land was white, The." *Unknown.* FaBoVe

Riddle: "Little trotty hetty coat." *Unknown.* FaBoVe

Riddle: "Lives in winter." *Unknown.* NTCP

Riddle: "Long slick black feller." *Unknown.* FaBoVe

Riddle: "My snout chews the field like a prow." *Unknown.* SonAtl

Riddle: On a Kiss, A. William Strode. NOSC

Riddle: "Riddle a riddle as I suppose, A." *Unknown.* FaBoVe

Riddle: "Riddlum riddlum ranty pole." *Unknown.* FaBoVe

Riddle: "Rooted in fresh earth, I am a bush of flies." Henry Hart. WaAnP

Riddle: "Round the house and round the house / and there lies a black glove in the window." *Unknown.* FaBoVe

Riddle: "Round the house and round the house / and there lies a white glove in the window." *Unknown.* FaBoVe

Riddle: "White bird featherless." *Unknown.* FaBoVe; OxBEV

Riddle: "White sheep, white sheep, on a blue hill." *Unknown.* FaBoVe

Riddle: "Wooden belly iron back." *Unknown.* FaBoVe

Riddle: "You are a riddle I would not unravel." Josephine Miles. CalPo

Riddle, A. William Cowper. DiBP

Riddle, A. Daniel Hoffman. PoCho

Riddle, A. *Unknown.* PoCho, *tr. by* John Hollander

Riddle, A: Of the Soul. M. K. Joseph. BeAl

Riddle, A: "Once when I was very scared." Charlotte Zolotow. NTCP

Riddle a riddle as I suppose, A. Riddle. *Unknown.* FaBoVe

Riddle, A: "'Twas in heaven pronounced, and 'twas muttered in hell." Catherine Maria Fanshawe. NOBRP; OxBEV

Riddle, The: "No more, no more." Alexander Brome. NOSC

Riddle cum diddle cum dido. Kindness to Animals. Laura Elizabeth Richards. NTCP

Riddle in the Garden. Robert Penn Warren. NoAM *Fr.* Island of Summer.

Riddle me what marionettes are. Eduardo Milán. RMCMP, *tr. by* Roberto Tejada

Riddle of Noah, The. Maxine W. Kumin. OPRER

Riddle silently sees its image, The. It spins evening. Dusk in the Country. Harry Edmund Martinson. WED, *tr. by* Robert Bly

Riddle we can guess, The. Emily Dickinson. OxBoAm; SAmP

Riddle-Me-Ree. Liz Lochhead. OPOU

Riddles. *Unknown.* NoP-4; NoP-5, *tr. by* Richard Hamer

Riddles (Exeter Book). Cynewulf. *tr. by* Michael Alexander, Gerard Benson, Charles W. Kennedy, Kevin Crossley-Holland, Geoffrey Grigson, Edwin Morgan and Lewis Turco

  Bookworm. WoPoe, *tr. by* Edwin Morgan

  Old English Riddle. OPOU

  Onion. WoPoe, *tr. by* Lewis Turco

  Sun and Moon. WoPoe, *tr. by* Kevin Crossley-Holland

  Swan, The. WoPoe, *tr. by* Geoffrey Grigson

  "This knave came in where he knew she'd be." EroLit, *tr. by* Michael Alexander

Riddles: "He opens her. She can't have him." Kathleen Peirce. PoDa

Riddlum riddlum ranty pole. Riddle. *Unknown.* FaBoVe

Riddym Ravings (The Mad Woman's Poem). Jean Binta Breeze. WaCA

Ride. Josephine Miles. OxBoAm

Ride a cock-horse to Banbury Cross. *Unknown.* OxBEV

Ride, The. Lucinda Roy. GT

Ride, The. Richard Wilbur. CAP-8

Ride Fortune's chariot with care and doubt. Fickle Fortune. Ferenc Faludi. IQMS, *tr. by* Watson Kirkconnell and J. G. Nichols

Ride Me Baby, Ride Me. Felicia L. Morgenstern. BtF

Ride out against the horizon and the orange sun! (LL) Feminine Intuition. Stephanie Brown. AmPoNex; BAP-97

Ride, ride together, for ever ride? (LL) Last Ride Together, The. Robert Browning. EroLit; ITBLP; NAEL-6v2; NAEL-7v2; OBEV

Ride the High Country. Joel Dailey. AnSo

Ride the Turtle's Back. Beth Brant. ItWoWo

Ride-by-Nights, The. Walter De la Mare. ChAP

Rider. Mark Rudman.

  "There was only one problem—the steepness of the hill." ArBi

  "What about that girl in first grade? The one who hopped up on her desk." TaR

Rider, The. Sarah Manguso. BAP-01

Rider, The. Naomi Shihab Nye. ArBi

Rider and horse,—friend, foe,—in one red burial blent! (LL) NAEL-6v2; NAEL-7v2 *Fr.* Childe Harold's Pilgrimage.

Rider in stone, A. To the Gods the Shades Flavinus of the Cavalry Regiment. David Wright. NLP

Ridge, The. John Cowper Powys.

  "Aye! What a thing is the passing of Cronos, the angular-minded." OBWVE

Ridge road takes the ridgespine every way, The. Indirective. James Galvin. VisFro

Ridiculing the Monk Who Builds a Stupa. Jungkwan Haean. BecRai, *tr. by* Kim Daljin, Kim Won-Chung and Christopher Merrill

Ridiculous dreamer. Events Like Palaces. Paz Molina. TANSG, *tr. by* Steven F. White

Ridiculous / How the space between three violins. Cantata. Jack Spicer. APSN

Ridiculous shack of frost is slush, faded, The. March Elegy. Arkadii Dragomoschenko. ItGoST, *tr. by* Elena Balashova and Lyn Hejinian

Ridin' High. Cole Porter. ReLy

Riding. Buson. EH, *tr. by* Robert Hass

Riding a Horse in the Rain. Daegak Euchon. BecRai, *tr. by* Kim Daljin, Kim Won-Chung and Christopher Merrill

Riding a Mule. Kim Ch'unsu [*or* Chun-soo]. CAMKP, *tr. by* Anthony, Brother of Taizé

Riding a One-eyed Horse. Henry Taylor. HeIP-4

Riding Across John Lee's Finger [*for Walter Lowe*]. Stanley Crouch. GT

Riding across the town in a dirty carriage. Riding Over Belmore Park. Robert Harris. BMAP

Riding against the east. To Beachey, 1912. Carl Sandburg. OtW

Riding Backwards on a Train. James Hoch. PoDa

Riding backwards this wooden horse. Kukoku. ZenPo, *tr. by* Takashi Ikemoto and Lucien Stryk

Riding Bike with No Hands. Julia Kasdorf. ArBi

Riding Crop, The. Lu Chi. WoPoe *Fr.* Art of Writing, The.

Riding high. Moons. . .tides. Andrew J. Baldwin. BtF

Riding high into the night. Gas. Gerry Gordon. MiVo

Riding into California. Shirley Lim. GeoHom

Riding Lesson. Robin Becker. NevBe

Riding Lesson. Henry Taylor. GoPo; NBLV

Riding on silver wings are. On Silver Wings. Naomi Shemer. NRoS, *tr. by* Esther Raizen

Riding on the Coast Starlight. Ursula K. Le Guin. PoCoUp

Riding Out at Evening. Linda McCarriston. BBASP; WaAnP

Riding Over Belmore Park. Robert Harris. BMAP

Riding silk, adrift at noon. Basil Bunting. WoPoe *Fr.* Briggflatts [An Autobiography].

Riding the "A." May Swenson. APT-2; GM; OxBoAm

Riding the black express from heaven to hell. Lucifer in the Train. Adrienne Rich. GM

Riding the Currents. Susan Bright. TiP2

Riding the Empire Builder, 1948. David Wojahn. GM

Riding the Eye. Frances Payne Adler. FiBr

Riding the Lion, Riding the Lamb. Karen Chamberlain. GeoH

Riding the North Point Ferry. Wing Tek Lum. OpBo

Riding the Rock Island Through Kansas. Dave Etter. GM

Riding the wide leaf. Kikaku. SoOfWa, tr. by Sam Hamill

Riding Their Bikes. Ellen Kirvin Dudis. ArBi

Riding Westward. John Balaban. GifTon

Rifacimento. Paul Violi. PmAP

Riffing. Rick Barot. NeAmPo

Rifle, The. Tymoteusz Karpowicz. PoSu, tr. by Jan Darowski

Rifle Range: Louisiana. Charles E. Butler. PWW2

Rifled honeycomb, The. John Montague. ModIr Fr. Cave of Night, The.

Riflemen Form. Alfred Tennyson. STuOW Fr. Printed in "The Times," May 1859.

Rifle's beside you like a lover, The. Survivalist. Carolyne Wright. LiTh

Rig Veda. Unknown.

    Creation Hymn. WoPoe, tr. by Frederick Morgan

    Dawn Has Arisen, Our Welfare Is Assured. WoPoe, tr. by Raimundo Panikkar

    Hymn to Night. WoPoe, tr. by Peter Dent and Edwin Gerow

    "May the wind blow sweetness." WoPoe, tr. by Raimundo Panikkar

Rigamarole. William Carlos Williams. APT-1

Rigby. Mark Todd. GeoH

Right among the people coming and going. Lodging House in Town, A. Muso Soseki. EaWin, tr. by W. S. Merwin

Right Arm, The. Paul Muldoon. NoAM

Right at the End of Night. Philippe Jaccottet. VCWP, tr. by Derek Mahon

Right Away. Joel Dailey. AnSo

Right best beloved and most in assurance. Unknown. EMWP

Right Cross, The. Philip Levine. MoASP

Right family connections, The. Andy-the-German Servant of Two Masters. Andrew Duncan. VaPo

Right from the ambiguous start. D-Zug. Julian Croft. NOBAu

Right from the start I have stood on my own feet. I Have Done My Reckoning. Attila József. IQMS, tr. by Michael Hatwell

Right from the start I knew I'd follow you like a grenadier his banner. To a Dead Lady. Antonio Cisneros. TCLAP, tr. by Maureen Ahern and David Tipton

Right Hand, The. Robert Herrick. CavPo

Right hand lead pure. Ali, Bomaye. Hayes Davis. BRtP

Right here I was nearly killed one night in February. Solitude. Tomas Tranströmer. WED, tr. by Robert Bly

Right here the other night something. E. E. Cummings. NoAM

Right here with the others. (LL) Language of the Brag, The. Sharon Olds. FiBr; MakPoe; PBCAP

Right in the Trail. Gary Snyder. PmAP

Right Meaning, The. César Vallejo. MotU; PoDa; RaBo; WED, tr. by Robert Bly

Right now I am the flower girl. Flowers. Margaret Atwood. NoP-4; NoP-5

Right now my love for you is a baby elephant. Baby Elephant, A. Nikolai Stepanovich Gumilyov. TCRusP, tr. by Carl R. Proffer

Right now two black people sit in a jury room. Affirmative Action Blues (1993). Elizabeth Alexander. ExTi; FaoP

Right of Way. Barry Sternlieb. GM

Right of Way, The. William Carlos Williams. APT-1

Right On: White America. Sonia Sanchez. ISC

Right or ruth. Susan Howe. PmAP Fr. Speeches at the Barriers.

Rt. Rev. Richard Allen. Josephine D. Henderson Heard. CBWP-4

Right then. Author's Consent. Mahe Jabeen. HotL, tr. by V. Narayana Rao

Right Thing, The. Pesha Gertler. FiBr

Right Time, The. William Stafford. MotU

Right to Grief, The. Carl Sandburg. IllVoic

Right to Love, The. Gene Lees. ReLy

Right to the end you never got it straight. Mother's Room. Nicky Rice. Prnts

Right under their noses, the green. Dusk of Horses, The. James Dickey. ColAP

Right Use of Prayer, The. Sir Aubrey De Vere. SacPr

Right waves gather, The. (LL) From the Wave. Thom Gunn. NAEL-6v2; NAEL-7v2; NoP-4; NoP-5

Right well I w[r]ote most mighty Soueraine [or soveraine]. Edmund Spenser. NoSic Fr. Faerie Queene, The.

Right words elude me, The. Love. Joan Gordon. Prnts

Righteous Anger. James Stephens. See Glass of Beer, A.

Righteous Man, The. Samuel Butler. OBSV

Rightful One, The. David Ignatow. TaR

Rights. Martha Collins. LiTh

Rights of Way. Thomas Reiter. GM

Rights of Woman, The. Anna Laetitia Barbauld. BrAP; CABP; NAEL-6v2; NAEL-7v2; NoP-4; NoP-5; PEW; WaAnP; WoRP

Rigid Body Sings. James Clerk Maxwell. UV

Rigoletto. Newman Levy. AmWit

Rigor of beauty is the quest. But how will you find beauty when it is locked. William Carlos Williams. NoAM Fr. Paterson.

Rilke's Letter from Rome. Star Black. KGB

Rill of the House of the Luans. Wang Wei. ChinPo, tr. by Ye Weilian [or Yeh Wei-lien or Wai-lim Yip]

Rillons, Rillettes. Richard Wilbur. OBCoV

Rillons, Rillettes, they taste the same. Rillons, Rillettes. Richard Wilbur. OBCoV

Rills of cool water curtained the windows. Crab, The. Dennis O'Donnell. EdScPo

Rilly, / im a brown man. Not no socialism/communism classical, but some power to the people jazz. Daniel Gray-Kontar. SpirFl

Rimbaud and Verlaine, precious pair of poets. Conrad Potter Aiken. NoAM Fr. Preludes for Memnon; or, Preludes to Attitude.

Rimbaud Having a Bath. Robert Adamson. BMAP

Rime of the Ancient Mariner (1817 version). Samuel Taylor Coleridge. NoP-5; WaAnP

Rime of the Ancient Mariner, The (1798 version). Samuel Taylor Coleridge. CABP; HeIP-4; NAEL-6v2; NAEL-7v2; NoP-4; OBEV; OBNV; OxAEP-2; OxBEV; PoPoPo; TFi

    "And now the Storm-blast came, and he." OWoS

    "I fear thee, ancient Mariner!" NPeEn

    "It is an ancient Mariner." AmFaPo

Rime of the Auncient Waggonere, The. William Maginn. ClHu

Rimer. Ambrose Bierce. APN-2 Fr. Devil's Dictionary, The.

Rimer quenches his unheeded fires, The. Ambrose Bierce. APN-2 Fr. Devil's Dictionary, The.

Rims of Distinction: I. Allen Fisher. Oth Fr. Stepping Out.

Rincón. Sandra M. Castillo. TouFir

Rind, inner fruit, and core. (LL) For One Who Gayly Sowed His Oats. Countee Cullen. APT-2; NAAPv.2

Ring, The. Harry Mathews. NYP2

Ring, The. Diane Wakoski. PoA 2002

Ring and the Book, The. Robert Browning.

    "Do you see this square old yellow Book, I toss." FaBoVe

Ring da Till. Wopko Jensma. TSAP

Ring in the Christ that is to be. (LL) Alfred Tennyson. BrAP; ChrPo; CtM; NAEL-6v2; NAEL-7v2; NAWM-7v2; OxAEP-2; RSR; TreFP Fr. In Memoriam A. H. H.

Ring into golden bowls. (LL) Opium Fantasy, An. Maria White Lowell. APN-2; NAAPv.1

Ring is on my hand, The. Bridal Ballad. Edgar Allan Poe. STuOW

Ring, joyous chords!—ring out again! Revellers, The. Felicia Dorothea Hemans. TreFP

Ring of Irony, The. Diane Wakoski. NIL-7

Ring on the Finger. Harold Rome. ReLy

Ring out, wild bells, to the wild sky. Alfred Tennyson. BrAP; ChrPo; CtM; NAEL-6v2; NAEL-7v2; NAWM-7v2; OxAEP-2; RSR; TreFP Fr. In Memoriam A. H. H.

Ring Out Your Bells. Sir Philip Sidney. See Dirge: "Ring out your bells [or belles], let mourning shows [or shewes] be spread."

Ring out your bells [or belles], let mourning shows [or shewes] be spread. Dirge. Sir Philip Sidney. NoSic

    (Ring out your bells, let mourning shows be spread.) NoP-4

Ring peace and freedom in! (LL) Battle Autumn of 1862, The. John Greenleaf Whittier. AmWaPo; CBCWP; PCW

Ring so worn as you behold, The. Marriage Ring, The. George Crabbe. OBEV; OxBEV

Ring Sonnet. Betty Scott Stam. SacPr

Ring That Controlled Erections, The. Unknown. NAWM-7v1, tr. by Ned Dubin

Ring the gong, strike the chimes! Song of the Gong and Chimes. Unknown. CATKP, tr. by Peter H. Lee

Ringed by dark palisades. Resurrection at West Lake. Eric Tretheway. Coast; PfSP

Ringed Plover by a Water's Edge. Norman Alexander MacCaig. NoP-4

Ringing anthemic lies—unpack sizzle thumping hammer sparks as fun stuff & slip it off. Bruce Andrews. BAP-04 Fr. Dang Me.

Ringing Chamber, The. Pauline Stainer. BeAl

Ringing in My Ears. Yi Hyangji. EcSo, tr. by Catherine J. Kim

Ringing out from our blue heavens. Journey. Breyten Breytenbach. AF, *tr. by* Denis Hirson

Ringing phone and a hushed voice, A. Prayer for the Living, A. Asha Bandele. InTrad

Ringing the bell of my bicycle. My Bicycle Bell. Dobashi Jiji. ArBi, *tr. by* Edward Lueders and Koriyama Naoshi

Ringing Words. Mary Kinzie. FFC

Ringless. Diane Wakoski. FTtHH; NALW

Ringlet, The. Jean Sprackland. MoWP

Ringleted Youth of My Love. *Unknown.* IrLP, *tr. by* Douglas Hyde

Ringlety-jing! Nonsense Rhyme, A. James Whitcomb Riley. NOxBChV

Ringmaster's Wife. Fatima Lim-Wilson. ReBoTo

Rings. Joan Michelson. Prnts *Fr.* Departures.

Ringsend. Oliver St. John Gogarty. OBMV

Ringstead Mill. Margot Heinemann. RSaN

Rinsed by the rain, the front garden is clean. Casual Line, A. Chungji. BecRai, *tr. by* Kim Daljin, Kim Won-Chung and Christopher Merrill

Rinsing the choked mud, keeping the colours new. (LL) In Carrowdore Churchyard. Derek Mahon. NoP-4; NoP-5; PBCIP; PNI

Rintrah roars and shakes his fires in the burdened air. Marriage of Heaven and Hell, The. William Blake. WaAnP

Rio. Joel Dailey. AnSo

Río. Jorge Guillén. RaW

Río. Carlos Sahagún. RaW

Río 1. José Luis Rivas. RMCMP

Rio Grande Hills. Berta Hart Nance. TiP2

Riot. Gwendolyn Brooks. NALW; SSLK

Riot, A. Mrs. Henry Linden. CBWP-4

Riot Act, April 29, 1992. Ai. CAP-8; ESEAA; NIL-7

Riot at Winchell's. Bruce Jackson. AmPoNex

Riot in the lute song's propinquity. Propose to be guided by the. Pieces o'Six—XXIV. Jackson Mac Low. FTOS

Riot of forsythia, a six-pack, A. Vandals in the Garden. Alan Michael Parker. NAPBL

Riot; or Half a Loaf is Better than No Bread In a Dialogue between Jack Anvil and Tom Hod, The. Hannah More. PEW

Rioupéroux. James Elroy Flecker. OBEV

Riparto d'Assalto. Ernest Hemingway. AmWaPo

Ripe. Todd Davis. ACAMVP

Ripe Apple. Kim Hyesun. CAMKP, *tr. by* Jiwon Shin

Ripe, Being Plunged into Fire. Friedrich Hölderlin. OBVE, *tr. by* James Blair Leishman

Ripe Plums. *Unknown.* TAL

Ripe plums are dropping. Ripe Plums. *Unknown.* TAL

Ripeness Is All. Peter Viereck. PWW2

Ripeness is all; her in her cooling planet. To an Old Lady. William Empson. NoAM; OxAEP-2; OxBEV

Ripeness Is Rapid. Rosalie Moore. CalPo; YaYoPo

Ripeness is rapid as plum-drop, as invader. Ripeness Is Rapid. Rosalie Moore. CalPo; YaYoPo

Ripening. Wendell Berry. RaBo

Ripostes of Ezra Pound. Ezra Pound.

Δωρια. MoAmPo

Girl, A. MoAmPo; NOxBChV

Immorality, An. AmWit; MoAmPo; TCAPo

Of Jacopo del Sellaio. APT-1

Portrait d'une Femme. APT-1; BrAP; MoAmPo; NAAL-5; NAMCP V.1; NoAM; NoP-4; NoP-5; OxBoAm; TCAPo

Return, The. APT-1; MoAmPo; NAAPv.2; NAMCP V.1; NoAM; NPeEn; OxBoAm; TRP; WeW-3

Seafarer, The. APT-1; HeIP-4; NoP-4; NoP-5; OxBoAm; TCAPo; WaAnP; WoPoe

Silet. MoAmPo

Virginal, A. ColAP; MoAmPo; NAAPv.2; NIL-7; NIP-4; TCAPo

Ripped and rotting in the dark. (LL) 1st Lt. Vernon J. Baker: Hero on the Hill. Jabari Asim. BtF; FuFl

Rippled nut, The. Empty Walnut, The. Gabriela Mistral. TANSG, *tr. by* Maria Giachetti [*or* Jacketti] and Maria Jacketti

Ripples. Ko Un. WhBo

Ripple-topped stream in its best suit, in the ground. (LL) Mi Abuelo. Alberto A. Ríos. NAMCP V.2; NIL-7; PoPoPo; WaAnP

Rippling hospital sheets. Grandmother: Crossing Jordan. Melvin Dixon. ESEAA

Rippling in the ocean of that darkening room. Woman at the Piano. Marya Alexandrovna Zaturenska. MoAmPo

Riprap. Gary Snyder. CalPo; NAAL-5; NAMCP V.2; NoAM; OxBoAm; PmAP; PoCho; PoPoPo; VCAP

Rise. Brenda Shaughnessy. AmPoNex

Rise: "Marvellous how the house builds itself." Pat Winslow. PoCu

Rise and deride this sepulchre of crime. (LL) On Passing the New Menin Gate. Siegfried Sassoon. NAEL-6v2; NAEL-7v2; NAMCP V.1; NoAM; NoP-4; NoP-5; OBMV; PoWW

Rise and Progress of the Present Taste in Planning Parks, Pleasure Grounds, Gardens, etc, The. *Unknown.* OBGa *Fr.* Rise and Progress of the Present Taste in Planning Parks, Pleasure Grounds, Gardens, etc, The.

Rise and shine. Gonna Change My Life. Anne Waldman. AHA

Rise, as my head. (LL) Merce of Egypt. Charles Olson. APT-2; NoP-4; NoP-5

Rise, blossom of the spring. To a Lady on the Rise of Morn. Anne Batten Cristall. RWP

Rise, crowned with light, imperial Salem, rise! Alexander Pope. SacPr *Fr.* Messiah [a Sacred Eclogue, in Imitation of Virgil's Pollio].

Rise from the wrist, o kestrel. Sonnets for the Novachord. "Ern Malley." BMAP

Rise from your virgin sheets, that be. Epithalamium: To Mistress M. A. Martin Lluellyn [*or* Lluelyn]. NOSC

Rise, Grass. Kang Ún'gyo. EcSo, *tr. by* Ann Y. Choi

Rise heart; thy Lord is risen. Sing his praise. Easter. George Herbert. NAEL-6v1; NOSC

Rise odors of ploughed field or flowery mead. (LL) Chaucer. Henry Wadsworth Longfellow. APN-1; HeIP-4; OBEV; TCAPo; TFi; WoPoe

Rise Oedipus, and if thou canst unfold. Poem, The. Thomas Morton. NAAL-3

Rise of Rome, The. Kevin Prufer. LegDan

Rise of the Afternoon is a Wide Glory, The. Jeannette Miller. TANSG, *tr. by* Paula Vega

Rise of the afternoon is a wide glory, The. Rise of the Afternoon is a Wide Glory, The. Jeannette Miller. TANSG, *tr. by* Paula Vega

Rise, shining martyrs. With Meaning. John Weiners. BB

Rise, small bird, to the top of the tree. Celebration. Nuala Ni Dhomhnaill. BeAl

Rise up, brother, be born with me. Pablo Neruda. TCLAP *Fr.* Heights of Macchu Picchu, The.

Rise up, Magyar, the country calls! National Song. Sándor Petőfi. IQMS, *tr. by* Adam Makkai

Rise up, Oh, Tihany's clamorous daughter. To the Echo of Tihany. Mihály Csokonai Vitéz. IQMS, *tr. by* Adam Makkai

Rise up, rise up, / And, as the trumpet blowing. Trumpet, The. Edward Thomas. MoBrPo

Rise up, rise up, now, Lord Douglas, she says. *Unknown.* NoP-4; NoP-5

Rise, winds of night! Relentless tempests rise! Helen Maria Williams. NPBRoP *Fr.* Part of an Irregular Fragment Found in a Dark Passage of the Tower.

Rise, winds of night! Relentless tempests rise! Part of an Irregular Fragment Found in a Dark Passage of the Tower. Helen Maria Williams. RWP

Risen from rented rooms, old ghosts. Winter Ode to the Old Men of Lummus Park, Miami, Florida, A. Donald Justice. WeW-3

Risen from the artificial lake. Porcelain Pavilion, The. Nikolai Stepanovich Gumilyov. TCRusP, *tr. by* Mary Jane White

Risen in a / welter of waters. Birth of Venus, The. Muriel Rukeyser. NALW

Rises toward her day after day, like a terrible fish. (LL) Mirror. Sylvia Plath. MoWP; NIL-7; NIP-4; OxBoAm; StAl

Risest thou thus, dim dawn, again. Alfred Tennyson. NAEL-6v2; NAEL-7v2 *Fr.* In Memoriam A. H. H.

Risible. Stefanie Marlis. AFaM

Risible—used in eliciting laughter, from the Latin *ridere*, to laugh. Risible. Stefanie Marlis. AFaM

Rising. Sam Hamill. AmZen

Rising. Nzadi Z. Keita. BtF

Rising Asleep. Penelope Rosemont. SurWo

Rising Bodies. Mary Ruefle. AmAlph

Rising deluge he descried, The. Vision of Noah, The. May Kendall. VWP

Rising Drunk on a Spring Day. Li Po. CrYelRi, *tr. by* Sam Hamill

Rising early. Morning Travel. Chia Tao. CSKM, *tr. by* Mike O'Connor

Rising hills, the slopes, The. For the Children. Gary Snyder. BeAl

Rising moon revenges herself, The. Lunatics. Bella Akhatovna Akhmadulina. TCRusP, *tr. by* Daniel Weissbort

Rising of the Buffalo Men, The. *Unknown.* NAAPv.2

Rising Spring Waters. Tu Fu [*or* Du Fu]. CrYelRi, *tr. by* Sam Hamill

Rising toward New England along the throughway. Summers of Vietnam. Mary Kinzie. IllVoic

Rising up in time, michael jordan hangs like an icon, suspended in space. Forty-one Seconds on a Sunday in June, in Salt Lake City, Utah. Quincy Troupe. MoASP

Risk. C. K. Williams. PoA 2002

Risk is moral death each time we act, The. Some Girls. Susanne Doyle. CalPo; FFC

Risk of Abstraction, The. Adriano Spatola. PFTM-2, *tr.* by Paul Vangelisti
Risk of Birth, The. Madeleine L'Engle. SacPr
Risks. Joan Larkin. FiBr
Risks. Meng Chiao. CCL1, *tr.* by Graeme Wilson
Risotto at Caffé Proust, The. Painted Ladies, The. Del Ray Cross. FreRad
Rispond Miser, The. Robert MacKay. NePenScot, *tr.* by Derick Thomson
Ristorante San Marco, The. Mary Ferrari. AHA
Rite of Passage. Gearóid Mac Lochlainn. NIrP, *tr.* by the author
Rites. Edward Kamau Brathwaite.
  "Look wha' happen las' week at de Oval!" FaBoVe
Rites and Ceremonies. Anthony Hecht.
  Room, The. PWW2
Rites for Cousin Vit, The. Gwendolyn Brooks. InoFa; NAMCP V.2; NoP-4;
  NoP-5; OxAAAP; WeW-3 *Fr.* Womanhood, The.
Rites of Manhood, The. Alden Nowlan. RaBo
Rites of Participation. Robert Duncan. PFTM-1 *Fr.* Rites of Participation.
Rites of Passage. Robert Duncan.
  "Something is taking place." NAMCP V.2
Rites of spring: roll out. Lighting Up Time. Dennis O'Driscoll. PoDa
Ritual. Anna Ruth Ediger Baehr. ACAMVP
Ritual. Stephen Berg. PfSP
Ritual. Sue Chenette. IFF
Ritual. Rosita Kalina. MirDau, *tr.* by Roberta Gordenstein
Ritual. Gwyneth Lewis. ATSWP, *tr.* by Robert Minhinnick
Ritual. Crystal Williams. RD
Ritual done, sterile as Pilate. Contact. Alison Chisholm. Prnts
Ritual for the Dead, Lake Sakami, Quebec, 1980. Linda Bierds. RoV
Ritual Girl. Frank Mkalawile Chipasula. HBAPE
Ritual of My Legs. Pablo Neruda. ConPit, *tr.* by Clayton Eshleman
Ritual to Read to Each Other, A. William Stafford. GoPo; RaBo; RaF
Rituals. Annie Le Brun. YaTCFP, *tr.* by Mary Ann Caws *and* Jean-Pierre
  Cauvin
Rituals, Yours—and Mine. Kimberly M. Blaeser. ReEnLa
Rival, A. Rachel Wetzsteon. NeAmPo
Rival, The. Sylvia Townsend Warner. MoBrPo
Rival Favourites. William Shakespeare. DiBP *Fr.* Taming of the Shrew, The.
Rival Queens; or, Alexander the Great, The. Nathaniel Lee.
  "Nay, *Clytus*, you that cou'd advise—." FaBoWar
Rivals. William Walsh. OBEV
Rivals. William Walsh *and* Sir George Etherege. OBEV
Rivals, The. James Stephens. OBEV; OBMV
Riven Quarry, The. Gloria C. Oden. GT
River. Jorge Guillén. RaW, *tr.* by Charles Guenther
River. Ted Hughes. NAEL-6v2; NoP-4
River. Shuntaro Tanikawa. VCWP, *tr.* by Harold Wright
River: "River, River." Ivan Metodiev. CSCBP *Fr.* Songs for Orphans Big and
  Small.
River: "They named this stretch of river Postwar." Carlos Sahagún. RaW, *tr.*
  by David Ignatow
River, The. Hart Crane. GM; MoAmPo; NAAL-5; OxBoAm *Fr.* Bridge, The.
River, The. Jacques Prévert. MFP, *tr.* by Martin Sorrell
River, The. Patti Tana. PasH
River, The: "I waded, deepening, into the dark water." Raymond Carver.
  PoDa
River, The: "Poor Mick was trotting on to the town." Charlotte Grace O'Brien.
  IrV
River 1. José Luis Rivas. RMCMP, *tr.* by Alastair Reid
River and Bridge. Meena Alexander. RWB
River and Death, The. Badr Shakir al-Sayyab. PFTM-2, *tr.* by Pierre Joris
River and Fountain. Michael Longley. ModIr
River at Night. Conor O'Callaghan. NIrP
River at Wolf, The. Jean Valentine *and* Anne Frydman. LaCa
River bank is white like silver, The. On the Willow Bank. Yen Chen.
  WoPoe, *tr.* by Arthur Sze
River Bend. Judith Wright. BMAP
River brought down, The. How We Heard the Name. Alan Dugan. NoAM;
  PtR; YaYoPo
River by river, mountain by mountain, sea to sea. (LL) Today's Meditation.
  Antonio Machado Ruiz. AF; WED, *tr.* by Robert Bly
River called the Snake, A. Blueprint for Disaster. Christian Morgenstern.
  WoPoe, *tr.* by David R. Slavitt
River city is as in a picture, The. Climbing Xie Tiao's North Tower at Xuan in
  Autumn. Li Po. CCL1, *tr.* by Elling O. Eide
River crosses the city over a series of falls, The. Charles Tomlinson. WoBe
  Fr. Zipangu.
River Darkens on an Autumn Night, The. Yi Jung. WoPoe, *tr.* by Virginia
  Olsen Baron and Chung Seuk Park

River disappears into haze, The. After Li Ch'ing-Chao. John Brandi.
  ICANM
River Dove: a Lyric Pastoral, The. Samuel Bently. VerBaPo
River Drau flows swiftly here, The. Cycling the Rosental. William Daniel
  Ehrhart. ArBi
River drops from Dragon Gate, The. Descending Through Dragon Gate. Tu
  Fu [*or* Du Fu]. CrYelRi, *tr.* by Sam Hamill
River Duddon [A Series of Sonnets], The. William Wordsworth.
  After-Thought. CenSon; NPBRoP
  American Tradition. CenSon
  Change Me, Some God, Into That Breathing Rose! CenSon
  "Child of the clouds! remote from every taint." CenSon
  Conclusion. CenSon
  Faery Chasm, The. CenSon; OxBSo
  Flowers. CenSon
  "From this deep chasm, where quivering sunbeams play." CenSon
  "How shall I paint thee?—Be this naked stone." CenSon
  Journey Renewed. CenSon
  "KIRK OF ULPHA to the pilgrim's eye, The." CenSon
  "Methinks 'twere no unprecedented feat." CenSon
  "No record tells of lance opposed to lance." CenSon
  "Not hurled precipitous from steep to steep." CenSon
  "O mountain Stream! the Shepherd and his Cot." CenSon
  Open Prospect. CenSon
  Plain of Donnerdale, The. CenSon
  Resting-Place, The. CenSon
  Return. CenSon
  "Return, Content! for fondly I pursued." CenSon
  Same Subject, The. CenSon
  Seathwaite Chapel. CenSon
  "Sole listener, Duddon! to the breeze that played." CenSon
  Stepping-Stones, The. CenSon
  "Take, cradled Nursling of the mountains, take." CenSon
  Tradition. CenSon
  Tributary Stream. CenSon
  (Valedictory Sonnet to the River Duddon.) OBEV
  "What aspect bore the Man who roved or fled." CenSon
  "Whence that low voice?—A whisper from the heart." CenSon
  "Who swerves from innocence, who makes divorce." CenSon
River flows to the East, The. Red Cliff, The. Su Tung-p'o. NDACCP, *tr.* by
  Kenneth Rexroth
River Flute. Po Chü-i. CrYelRi, *tr.* by Sam Hamill
River Girl. Keith Wilson. ICANM
River God, The. Vicki Feaver. MoWP
River God, The. Sacheverell Sitwell. MoBrPo
River God, The. Stevie Smith. BrAP; MoWP
River Guadalquivir, The. Little Ballad of the Three Rivers. Federico García
  Lorca. BLPSL, *tr.* by Rene de Costa, Rigas Kappatos and Eleni Paidoussi
River Han long and wide. Night After Night. Shen Yüeh. CCL1, *tr.* by
  Anne Birrell
River in Dusk. Joanna Klink. IAoNAP
River in its abundance, The. Eros at Temple Stream. Denise Levertov.
  NALW
River in the Meadows, The. Léonie Adams. MoAmPo
River in the street!, A. Streets 2. Paul Verlaine. SxFrPo, *tr.* by Martin Sorrell
River inn spring hangover—half a day's delay. At Ta-an I Got Sick from Wine
  and Had to Lay Over for Half a Day. Governor Wang Invited Me to His
  Place Again. Lu Yu. ColAnChi, *tr.* by Burton Watson
River irises, The. Grass. James Merrill. OxBoAm
River is black jelly, thrilled with reflections, The. Crossing the River. Monica
  Raymond. PfS
River is famous to the fish, The. Famous. Naomi Shihab Nye. LoL
River is largely implicit here, but part, The. Waterborne. Linda Gregerson.
  BAP-01
River is silted with sentiments, Ophelia, The. Snowdrops and Summer
  Snowflakes, Drooping. Reginald Shepherd. IaFF
River Jade-Gray. Tu Fu [*or* Du Fu]. CCL1, *tr.* by Florence Ayscough *and*
  Amy Lowell
River jade-gray; birds gleam white. River Jade-Gray. Tu Fu [*or* Du Fu].
  CCL1, *tr.* by Florence Ayscough *and* Amy Lowell
River Journal. Bruce Weigl. AmAlph
River Meditation. Wendy Johnson. WhBo
River Merchant's Wife, The; A Letter. Li Po. AmFaPo; APT-1; BrAP; ClHu;
  ColAP; EMP; HarvBoo; HeIP-4; MoAmPo; NAAL-5; NAAPv.2; NAMCP
  V.1; NDACCP; NIL-7; NIP-4; NoAM; NoP-4; NoP-5; NPeEn; OBMV;
  OBVE; OxBoAm; PoPoPo; RaBo; RACG; TCAPo; TFi; TRP; WaAnP;
  WeW-3, *tr.* by Ezra Pound

River moon only feet away, storm-lanterns, A.   Brimmed Whole.   Tu Fu [*or* Du Fu].   NDACCP, *tr. by* David Hinton

River Now, The.   Richard Hugo.   VCAP

River of Bees, The.   W. S. Merwin.   HeIP-4; VCAP

River of Bones and Flesh and Blood.   Eugene B. Redmond.   IllVoic

River of diaphanous waters, The.   Blue River.   Muhammad ibn Ghalib al-Rusafi.   WoPoe, *tr. by* Cola Franzen

River of Rivers in Connecticut, The.   Wallace Stevens.   APT-1; FaBoA; NAMCP V.1

River of Seville.   Seguidillas of the Guadalquivir River.   Félix Lope de Vega Carpio.   SpanPo, *tr. by* Denise Levertov

River of sudden, The.   Waterfall.   Gareth Owen.   Spl

River of Time.   River of Bones and Flesh and Blood.   Eugene B. Redmond.   IllVoic

River Otters at Play.   Harry Thurston.   Coast

River Path, The.   John Greenleaf Whittier.   TreFP

River Pavilion.   Tu Fu [*or* Du Fu].   CrYelRi, *tr. by* Sam Hamill

River riven / wandering the length up and down.   B. P. Nichol.   NLPA *Fr.* Inchoate Road.

River, River.   Ivan Metodiev.   CSCBP *Fr.* Songs for Orphans Big and Small.

River Road.   Cyd Adams.   TiP2

River Road.   Stanley Kunitz.   NoAM

River Road Studio.   Barbara Guest.   PmAP

River Rolling Eastward, The.   Li Yu [*or* Li Hou-Chu].   CCL1, *tr. by* Cyril Birch

River Scamander Attacks Achilles.   Homer.   OBVE *Fr.* Iliad, The.

River seemed a broad stream, fenced with folk, The.   János Arany.   IQMS *Fr.* Toldi.

River shaking in the sun, A. (LL)   Windigo.   Louise Erdrich.   NAMCP V.2; NoAM; PoPoPo

River shines in the jungle's, A.   Monoon Season.   Yusef Komunyakaa.   AmAlph

River slopes, already into the midmonth of spring.   On the Spur of the Moment.   Tu Fu [*or* Du Fu].   CCL1, *tr. by* Burton Watson

River slops under the bridge, The.   Flight.   Neal Bowers.   PoDa

River Snow.   Liu Tsung-yüan.   ChinPo, *tr. by* Ye Weilian [*or* Yeh Wei-lien *or* Wai-lim Yip]

River Snow ("These thousand peaks cut off the flight of birds.")   Liu Tsung-yüan.   ColAnChi; NDACCP, *tr. by* Gary Snyder

River Snow ("Thousand peaks: no more birds in flight, A.")   Liu Tsung-yüan.   NDACCP, *tr. by* David Hinton

River Song.   Ben Howard.   PoCoUp

River Song.   Weldon Kees.   OxBoAm

River Song.   Li Po.   ChinPo, *tr. by* Ye Weilian [*or* Yeh Wei-lien *or* Wai-lim Yip]

River Song.   Roberta Spear.   GeoHom

River Song, The.   Wang Yung.   ChinPo, *tr. by* Ye Weilian [*or* Yeh Wei-lien *or* Wai-lim Yip]

River, Stay 'Way from My Door.   Mort Dixon.   ReLy

River Steamer, The.   Edith Jay Scovell.   HarvBoo

River Still To Be Found, A.   Lawrence Ferlinghetti.   BB

River stretches wide, The. It flows on tiredly.   On the Plain of Kulikovo.   Aleksandr Aleksandrovich Blok.   TCRusP, *tr. by* Denis Johnson and Kathy Lewis

River swallows know my shack is humble.   Tu Fu [*or* Du Fu].   CrYelRi *Fr.* Random Pleasures.

River swells onto the flooded banks, The.   Cortes Swamp, The.   Clovis L. Nazareno.   ReBoTo

River takes the land, and leaves nothing, The.   Slip, The.   Wendell Berry.   UpMys

River that flows nowhere, like a sea, The. (LL)   River of Rivers in Connecticut, The.   Wallace Stevens.   APT-1; FaBoA; NAMCP V.1

River through the dirty mill town, The.   First Love, Sixteen Years Old.   Baron Wormser.   NevBe

River Town Packin House Blues.   Quincy Troupe.   LoL

River turns, The.   Pike, The.   Theodore Roethke.   MoASP

River Walk.   John Stuart Williams.   AngWePo

River wandering down.   Robert Creeley.   FTOS

River we are caried by.   Seth Young.
   "*All* says a glass doorknow Parabola ghost."   AnSo

River, while it, The.   Still Life with Minnows.   Sherod Santos.   PfSP

River, why in ceaseless flow.   Maiden and River.   Mary Weston Fordham.   CBWP-2

River winds perfect in the moonlight, The.   Brazos de Dios.   Paul Foreman.   TiP2

River winds through the wilderness, The.   Looking Outside the Cabin Window, I Remember a Line by Li Po.   Charles Wright.   PfSP

Riverbank Blues.   Sterling Allen Brown.   MakPoe

Riverbank, the long rigs.   Broagh.   Seamus Heaney.   FaBoVe; ModIr; NPeEn

Riverbed, The.   Vona Groarke.   MFPA; NIrP

Riverbend.   Marin Georgiev.   CSCBP, *tr. by* Georgi Belev and Lisa Sapinkopf

Rivercraft. Carey neon. Dove-webbing fatigues.   2nd Lesson from the Cockerel.   Maggie O'Sullivan.   Oth

River[-]God's Song, The.   John Fletcher.   NOSC *Fr.* Faithful Shepherdess, The.

River-marsh-drowse.   Lorine Niedecker.   FTOS

River-mirror mirrors the cold sky, The.   Mists Over the River.   William Carlos Williams.   ColAP

Rivers.   Homero Aridjis.   PoCoUp, *tr. by* George McWhirter

Rivers, The.   Giuseppe Ungaretti.   PFTM-1

Rivers and Mountains.   John Ashbery.   NoAM; TRP

River's Answer, The.   Ben Howard.   PoCoUp

Rivers level granite mountains.   Sulpicius Lupercus Servasius.   WoPoe, *tr. by* Kenneth Rexroth

Rivers of this country are sweet, The.   On Swimming.   Adam Zagajewski.   P180, *tr. by* Clare Cavanagh

River's tent is broken; the last fingers of leaf.   T. S. Eliot.   HarvBoo *Fr.* Waste Land, The.

River's up two feet overnight, The.   Rising Spring Waters.   Tu Fu [*or* Du Fu].   CrYelRi, *tr. by* Sam Hamill

Riverside Drive.   Louis Simpson.   CAP-8

Riverside Park.   Rachel Hadas.   OxBoAm

River-Snow.   Liu Tsung-yüan.   CCL1; ItP, *tr. by* Witter Bynner

Riversongs of Arion, The.   Michael Anania.   NoAM

Riviera, The.   Joseph McCarthy, Jr.   ReLy

Riviera, The / On every street a gay casino.   Riviera, The.   Joseph McCarthy, Jr.   ReLy

Rivière du Loup.   Alfred Goldsworthy Bailey.   Coast

Rivulet, The.   William Cullen Bryant.   APN-1

Rivulet-loving wanderer Abraham, The.   Abraham.   Edwin Muir.   ChIV-1

Rizal's Ghost.   Eugene Gloria.   ReBoTo

Rizpah.   Alfred Tennyson.   NPeEn

Road.   No Ch'ŏnmyŏng.   CAMKP, *tr. by* Mickey Hong

Road.   Pierre Reverdy.   CuPo

Road: "They are all asleep, below."   Juan Ramón Jiménez.   WED, *tr. by* Robert Bly

Road, The.   Conrad Potter Aiken.   MoAmPo

Road, The.   Abd al-Rahim Salih al-Rahim.   IrPoTo, *tr. by* Saadi A. Simawe and Daniel Weissbort

Road, The.   Robert Creeley.   BodElec

Road, The.   Kim Sowŏl.   CAMKP, *tr. by* David R. McCann

Road, The.   Shin Kyŏngnim.   CAMKP, *tr. by* Anthony, Brother of Taizé

Road at My Door, The.   William Butler Yeats.   NPeEn *Fr.* Meditations in Time of Civil War.

Road Away, The.   Kim Sowŏl.   CAMKP, *tr. by* David R. McCann

Road Back, The.   Pak Chaesam.   CAMKP, *tr. by* David R. McCann and Jiwon Shin

Road becomes three, The.   Buson.   EMJL *Fr.* Spring Breeze on the Kema Embankment.

Road crew worked all afternoon, The.   Ghost Birches.   Chase Twichell.   PfSP

Road crowds houses almost into the lake, The.   Along Overgrown Paths.   James Schuyler.   BAP-01

Road Down Home.   James Applewhite.   LPSFW

Road from Biloxi, The.   Khaled Mattawa.   RWB

Road from Elmira, The.   Robert Morgan.   LPSFW

Road from Khartoum, The.   Sheree Renée Thomas.   BRtP

Road Home, The.   Gillian Allnutt.   NeBrP; StAl

Road Home, The.   Andrew Hudgins.   AmWaPo

Road I walked home from school, The.   Genus Narcissus.   Natasha Trethewey.   LegDan

Road in Kentucky, A.   Robert Earl Hayden.   ColAP

Road itself was like a stream that men, The.   Edwin John Pratt.   BrAP *Fr.* Towards the Last Spike.

Road Kill.   Netta Gillespie.   AmZen

Road Less Travelled, The.   Alan Jenkins.   WaAnP

Road 1940.   Sylvia Townsend Warner.   RSaN

Road Not Taken, The.   Robert Frost.   APT-1; BLPJKO; BrAP; ChAP; CtM; EMP; HarvBoo; HeIP-4; ITBLP; MoAmPo; NAAL-5; NAAPv.2; NAMCP V.1; NIL-7; NIP-4; NoAM; NoP-4; NoP-5; OxBoAm; PoPoPo; SAmP; SoSe-8; StAl; TCAPo; TFi; TRP; WaAnP

Road of the Dread, The.   Lorna Goodison.   VCWP

Road reaches beyond mountains, The.   Stayover at Pei-Ku-Shan.   Wang Wan.   ChinPo, *tr. by* Ye Weilian [*or* Yeh Wei-lien *or* Wai-lim Yip]

Road running straight ahead.   Taneda Santoka.   CAoMJL1, *tr. by* Burton Watson

Road Show.   Geoff Page.   BMAP

Road through Saluda Gap and down, The. Road from Elmira, The. Robert Morgan. LPSFW

Road to Corruption, The. Pak Nohae. CAMKP, *tr.* by Scott Swaner

Road to Morocco, The. Johnny Burke. ReLy

Road to Patmos, The. John Ennis. PBCIP

Road to Seoul, The. Kim Chiha. CAMKP, *tr.* by David R. McCann

Road to Shu Is Hard, The. Li Po. CCL1; WoPoe, *tr.* by Elling O. Eide

Road to the Presidency. Oneca Hitchman-Britton. BRtP

Road Trip. Alma Stacey Allen. PfS

Road Trip as Clues, A. Tracy Philpot. IAoNAP

Road turned out to be a cul-de-sac, The. Brother and Sisters. Judith Wright. BMAP

Road twisted through tongues of rock, The. Vowels of Another Language, The. Thomas M. Disch. PoA 2002

Road unravels as I go, The. Minstrel. Michael Dransfield. BMAP

Road unwinds like a bandage, The. Clinchfield Station. Charles Wright. LPSFW

Road West, The. Vincent Woods. NIrP

Roadbook: Suite of Hands. Lydia Kwa.

"You must exist. Writing this book depends on it. It has occurred to." OpeFie

Road-Kill. David Johnson. ICANM

Roadkill Coyote. Art Goodtimes. GeoH

Roadmap. Harryette Mullen. ISC

Roads. Peter Huchel. HP; PoSu, *tr.* by Michael Hamburger

Roads. Peter Huchel. AF, *tr.* by Daniel S. Simko

Roads. (LL) I Am Alone. Léopold Sédar Senghor. PoetW; VCWP, *tr.* by Melvin Dixon

Roads. Edward Thomas. HarvBoo

Road's End. Rolf Jacobsen. WED, *tr.* by Robert Bly

Roads have come to their end now, The. Road's End. Rolf Jacobsen. WED, *tr.* by Robert Bly

Roadside flowers are blooming, butterflies on the wing. Su Tung-p'o. WoPoe *Fr.* Roadside Flowers, Three Poems with Introduction.

Roadside Flowers, Three Poems with Introduction. Su Tung-p'o. *tr.* by Burton Watson

"Roadside flowers are blooming, butterflies on the wing." WoPoe, *tr.* by Burton Watson

"Wealth and honor in life were dew on the grass leaf." WoPoe, *tr.* by Burton Watson

"Wild roadside flowers, blooming in boundless numbers." WoPoe, *tr.* by Burton Watson

Roadside Weeds. John Haines. PoCoUp

Roaming life's ocean, if your damaged vessel. Haven of Rest. Mihály Tompa. IQMS, *tr.* by Dorren Bell

Roaming the East Field. Hsieh T'iao. ChinPo, *tr.* by Ye Weilian [*or* Yeh Wei-lien *or* Wai-lim Yip]

Roaming the Via degli Alfani. Late Apostasy, A. V. Penelope Pelizzon. AmPoNex

Roan mare breaking morning ice. Some Reservation Valentines. Patricia Smith. ICANM

Roan Stallion. Robinson Jeffers. NAAPv.2

Roar of the Lion. Xuanjue. CCL1 *Fr.* Canticle of the Way.

Roar of the Lion Voice beyond fear. Xuanjue. CCL1 *Fr.* Canticle of the Way.

Roar of welkome though the welkin, A. Elk, The Whelk, The. Robert Williams Wood. NBLV

Roar, raging torrent! and thou, mighty river. Niagara. Joseph Rodman Drake. APN-1

Roaring alongside he takes for granted, The. Sandpiper. Elizabeth Bishop. APT-2; HeIP-4; NoP-5; OWoS

Roasting alive of rabbis, The. In the Absence of Bliss. Maxine W. Kumin. NAMCP V.2; NoAM; TaR

Robben Island Sequence. Dennis Brutus. HBAPE

Robber, The. Hugh MacDiarmid. OBVE

Robber, The. Walter James Turner. MoBrPo

Robber, The. Louis Untermeyer. STuOW

Robber, with a pike in his hand. (LL) Petrarch. OBMV; OxBEV; WoPoe *Fr.* Sonnets to Laura.

Robber-Bird, The. *Unknown.* CCL1 *Fr.* Que-chao.

Robby, git down wi'tha, wilt tha? Alfred Tennyson. FaBoVe *Fr.* Spinster's Sweet-Arts, The.

Robe, The. Martha Rhodes. ExTi

Robe, The. Jones Very. NCAP

Robe of Golden Thread, The. Autumn Maid Tu (Tu Ch'iu-niang). ColAnChi, *tr.* by Victor H. Mair

Robed Heart, The. Elizabeth Spires. ExTi

Robert. Wendy Rose. HATNAP

Robert Bruce's Address to His Army. Robert Burns. *See* Scots Wha Hae.

Robert Bruce's March to Bannockburn. Robert Burns. *See* Scots Wha Hae.

Robert E. Lee. Julia Ward Howe. CBCWP

Robert Frost. Kim Bridgford. VisFro

Robert Frost. David Keplinger. VisFro

Robert Frost. Robert Lowell. NoAM *Fr.* Writers.

Robert Frost. Robert Lowell. VisFro

Robert Frost. Lex Runciman. VisFro

Robert Frost and I. Ngodup Paljor. WhBo

Robert Frost as Father. Sarah Katherine Mccann. VisFro

Robert Frost at the Net. Daneen Wardrop. VisFro

Robert Frost Discovers Another Road Not Taken. X. J. Kennedy. VisFro

Robert Frost, expatiating. After All. Theodore Weiss. VisFro

Robert Frost in Warsaw. Peter Meinke. VisFro

Robert Frost: The Road Taken. William Jay Smith. VisFro

Robert Frost to Ezra Pound's Daughter from His Deathbed. Gibbons Ruark. VisFro

Robert Frost's Books, Ripton, Vermont, 1980. John Sokol. VisFro

Robert Frost's Chair. Gary Metras. VisFro

Robert Frost's Writing Desk. David Graham. VisFro

Robert G. Shaw. Henrietta Cordelia Ray. CBWP-3

Robert Gould Shaw. Paul Laurence Dunbar. CBCWP; PoPoPo

Robert Graves. Gavin Ewart. NoAM

Robert Graves saw—not the *male-womb* made scary in Euripides. Robin Blaser. NLPA; PFTM-2 *Fr.* Image-Nation.

Robert Herrick. William Cole. AmWit *Fr.* Uncoupled Couplets.

Robert Lowell's Notebook. Edward Pygge. OBCoV

Robert Penn Warren's Book. Anthony Lawrence. BMAP

Robert Sat. Tom Matthews. PNI

Robert, Second Duke of Normandy. Thomas Lodge. Pluck the Fruit and Taste the Pleasure. OxAEP-1

Robert Watches Elizabeth Knitting. Jo Shapcott. MoWP

Robert Wilson. Michael Collier. OPRER

Roberto Meets Cabeza de Vaca in the Desert. Ray Gonzales. TiP2

Robes loosely flowing and aspect as free. Seeing Her Dancing. Robert Heath. NOSC

Robeson at Rutgers. Elizabeth Alexander. OxAAAP

Robin, The. George Daniel. NPeEn

Robin, The. John Greenleaf Whittier. OWoS

Robin Hood. Phyllis McGinley. OBSV *Fr.* Speaking of Television.

Robin Hood and Allen [*or* Allin] -a-Dale. *Unknown.* OxAEP-1

Robin Hood and the Grey Friars. Thomas Love Peacock. OxAEP-2 *Fr.* Maid Marian.

Robin Hood and the Monk. *Unknown.* OBNV

Robin Hood Book, A.

"His acre. His arbour." Oth

"Saracen SAS or Assaseen called Nasir claims on HTV, A." Oth

"32s. 6d. for the chattels of Robert Hod, fugitive, Michaelmas 1230 at York." Oth

"Weakened by loss of blood Robin's last act was to slash his sword." Oth

Robin is nesting at eye level in a blue spruce just outside, A. Birdsong for September 11, 2001. Vivian Shipley. RWB

Robin [*or* Robene] and Makyne. Robert Henryson. OBEV

Robin [*or* Robene] sat on gude green [*or* gud grene] hill. Robin [*or* Robene] and Makyne. Robert Henryson. OBEV

Robin Redbreast. Stanley Kunitz. CAP-8; NoP-4; NoP-5

Robin Redbreast in a cage, A. William Blake. OWoS *Fr.* Auguries of Innocence.

Robin! Robin! call the Springtime. March. Henrietta Cordelia Ray. CBWP-3

Robin (The bird that was devoured by the cat in the garden of the house). Fawzi Karim. IrPoTo, *tr.* by Chuck Miller and Saadi A. Simawe

Robins' green-blue eggs, The. Morning. Louise Bogan. APT-2

Robin's Nest, A. Mary Jo Salter. OWoS

Robinson. Weldon Kees. NoP-5; OxBoAm; StAl

Robinson. Karl Krolow. GTCP, *tr.* by Reinhold Grimm

Robinson at cards at the Algonquin; a thin. Aspects of Robinson. Weldon Kees. OxBoAm

Robinson Crusoe. Franz Kafka. MotU, *tr.* by Edwin Muir and Willa Muir *and* Edwin Muir

Robinson Crusoe breaks a plate on his way out. Revolution, The. Jack Gilbert. BodElec

Robinson Crusoe Daniel Defoe. Maurice Sagoff. NBLV

Robinson's Resignation. Simon Armitage. HarvBoo

Robo. Nick Carbó. NAPBL

Robot Camera. Robert Johnstone. PNI

Roc, The. Mohja Kahf. PoArWo

Roça. Maria Manuela Margarido. HAWP, *tr.* by Julia Kirst

Roches Moutonnees. Ralph Adamo. AnSo

Rochester Extempore. John Wilmot, 2d Earl of Rochester. ChIV-1

Rock, The.   T. S. Eliot.
   "It is hard for those who have never known persecution."   SacPr
   "O Light Invisible, we praise Thee!"   SacPr
Rock, The.   Elizabeth Spires.   ExTi
Rock, The.   Wallace Stevens.   APT-1
   Seventy Years Later.   NAMCP V.1
Rock, The.   Jones Very.   InvLi
Rock and Hawk.   Robinson Jeffers.   APT-1; CalPo; ColAP; NAMCP V.1; NoAM; OxBoAm
Rock and precipice.   Landscape.   Octavio Paz.   OBVE, tr. by Charles Tomlinson
Rock Bottom.   Michael Ondaatje.
   "For you I have slept."   NoP-4
Rock Candy.   A. Wanjiku H. Reynolds.   BRtP
Rock Climbers, The.   Robert Francis.   MoASP
Rock grows brittle, The.   My People.   Else Lasker-Schüler.   GTCP, tr. by Michael Hamburger
Rock in the Garden Allows People In, The.   Malinda Markham.   IAoNAP
Rock is like space, A.   Bath Tub Thought.   Jack Kerouac.   WhBo
Rock is naturalist scripture. The deeper you go the older the story.   Haibun.   Andrew Schelling.   WANABP
Rock it just a tip, and have yourself an ocean that swims from lip to lip.   Rainbarrel.   Aidan Rooney-Céspedes.   NIrP
Rock Me to Sleep[, Mother].   Elizabeth Akers Allen.   APN-2; BRP; ITBLP; SWaP
Rock 'n Roll.   Peter Balakian.   SwNoth
Rock o' Jubilee.   Unknown.   SSUS
Rock o' my soul in de bosom of Abraham.   Rock O' My Soul.   Unknown.   SSUS; TCAPo
Rock of Ages.   Augustus Montague Toplady.   SacPr
Rock of ages, cleft for me.   Rock of Ages.   Augustus Montague Toplady.   SacPr
Rock of Cader Idris, The.   Felicia Dorothea Hemans.   RWP
Rock Pickers.   Cyd Adams.   TiP2
Rock, Rock, Sleep, My Baby.   Clyde Watson.   NTCP
Rock the child, rock the small one.   Unknown.   WoPoe Fr. Kanteletar, The.
Rock there is whose homely front, A.   Primrose of the Rock, The.   William Wordsworth.   TreFP
Rock-a-Bye Your Baby with a Dixie Melody.   Sam M. Lewis and Joe Young.   ReLy
Rockall.   Epes Sargent.   APN-1
Rockall. Malin. Dogger. Finisterre. (LL)   Prayer: "Some days, although we cannot pray, a prayer."   Carol Ann Duffy.   EdScPo; HarvBoo; MoWP; NeBrP; NePenScot; NoP-4; NoP-5; OxBSo; RWPCtW
Rock[e] them, rock[e] them, lullaby [or lullabie].   (LL)   Thomas Dekker and others.   NoSic; OxAEP-1; OxBEV Fr. Pleasant Comedy of Patient Grissell [or Grissel or Grissill], The.
Rockefeller the Center.   Marie Ponsot.   CLPP
Rocket to Russia.   Alison Stone.   SwNoth
Rockferns.   Norman Nicholson.   MoBrPo
Rockhopper, The.   Kimiko Hahn.   PrTe
Rockin' A Man, Stone Blind.   Carolyn Beard Whitlow.   FFC
Rockin' Chair.   Hoagy Carmichael.   ReLy
Rocking.   Gabriela Mistral.   TANSG, tr. by Maria Giachetti [or Jacketti] and Maria Jacketti
Rocking.   Gabriela Mistral.   BBASP; CFP, tr. by Doris Dana
Rocking.   Gabriela Mistral.   SpanPo, tr. by Muriel Kittel
Rocking Chair, The.   Abraham Moses Klein.   HeIP-4
Rocking Horse and the Lady, The.   Pak Inhwan.   CAMKP, tr. by Scott Swaner
Rock-like the souls of men.   Men Fade Like Rocks.   Walter James Turner.   OBMV
Rockpool.   Judith Wright.   HarvBoo Fr. Shadow of Fire: Ghazals, The.
Rocks.   Florence Parry Heide.   NTCP
Rocks.   Takahashi Shinkichi.   ZenPo, tr. by Takashi Ikemoto and Lucien Stryk
Rocks, The. (LL)   Sort of a Song, A.   William Carlos Williams.   APT-1; NAAL-5; NoP-4; NoP-5; WoPoe
Rocks Along the Coast, The.   Jerry Martien.   GeoHom
Rocks are warm, The.   Mission San José.   Carmen Tafolla.   TiP2
Rock's gray place is precise, The.   Translation.   Nicholas Samaras.   YaYoPo
Rocks jagged in morning mist.   John Montague.   PNI Fr. Great Cloak, The.
Rocks rising from the rushing water.   Buson.   EMJL Fr. Spring Breeze on the Kema Embankment.
Rocks, sand, and unrimmed holes. (LL)   Mast / Inaudibly soars; bole-like, tapering, The.   George Oppen.   APT-2; PFTM-1
Rocks spear upward: sky's face split.   Trip on Mount T'ai-P'ing.   K'ung Chih-kuei.   ChinPo, tr. by Ye Weilian [or Yeh Wei-lien or Wai-lim Yip]
Rock-shores of the world and the secret waters. (LL)   Birds.   Robinson Jeffers.   APT-1; NAAPv.2

Rockstar Poet.   Elizabeth Rees.   PfS
Rocky Acres.   Robert Graves.   NoAM
Rod of Jesse, The.   Bible, O.T.   OBVE Fr. Isaiah.
Rode fast convertibles, rose up like the Furies.   Alex, Tiffany, Meg.   Eva Salzman.   MoWP
Rodeo.   David Thomas Roberts.   AnSo
Rodeo Tangent.   Kendra Borgmann.   MoASP
Roderick, The Last of the Goths.   Robert Southey.
   Roderick at Cangas.
      Roderick's Faithful Theron.   DiBP
Roderick's Faithful Theron.   Robert Southey.   DiBP Fr. Roderick, The Last of the Goths.
Rodez.   Donald Davie.   HarvBoo
Rodin's "Gates of Hell."   Jane Greer.   FFC
Rods and Kisses.   Coventry Patmore.   SacPr
Roe-Deer.   Ted Hughes.   NAMCP V.2; NoAM; NOxBChV; OxAEP-2
Rogation Day: Portrush.   James Simmons.   PBCIP
Roger a doleful widower.   Widower's Courtship, The.   Elizabeth Hands.   WoRP
Roger the Dog.   Ted Hughes.   ChAP
Rogero's Song.   George Canning, John Hookham Frere and John Hookham Frere.   NPBRoP; OBCoV Fr. Rovers, The; or, The Double Arrangement.
Rogers in Italy.   Frank O'Hara.   FTOS
Roget, Papier, Schism!   Michael Portnoy.   HeMarv
Rogue and Jar: 4/27/77.   Thulani Davis.   SeSe
Rois ne touchent pas aux portes, Les.   Plaisirs de la Porte, Les.   Francis Ponge.   YaTCFP
Roistering I'll Chaff.   Luis de Góngora y Argote.   SpanPo, tr. by William M. Davis
Rokeby.   Sir Walter Scott.
   (Rover's Adieu [or Farewell], The.)   OBEV
Rokeby Venus, The.   Robert Conquest.   GS
Roland is dead and the ivory broken.   Rockefeller the Center.   Marie Ponsot.   CLPP
Role.   John Redmond.   NIrP
Role of a Lifetime, The.   Floyd Skloot.   IaFF
Role Reversal.   Maria Luisa Spaziani.   CItWP, tr. by Cinzia Sartini Blum and Lara Trubowitz
Rolfe and the Palm.   Herman Melville.   NCAP
Roll Call, The.   Dan Pagis.   HP, tr. by Stephen Mitchell
Roll Call of Bones, The.   César Vallejo.   AF; WED, tr. by Robert Bly
Roll forth, my song, like the rushing river.   Nameless One, The.   James Clarence Mangan.   OBEV
Roll in your skull gone green.   Hoa Nguyen.   WANABP
Roll, Jordan, Roll.   Unknown.   NAAPv.1
Roll on, sad world! Not Mercury or Mars.   Frederick Goddard Tuckerman.   APN-2 Fr. Sonnets.
Roll On, Shining Wheel!   C.T. Mitchell.   ArBi
Roll on, thou ball, roll on!   To the Terrestrial Globe.   William Schwenck Gilbert.   NBLV
Roll on, thou deep and dark blue ocean—roll!   Lord Byron.   UV Fr. Childe Harold's Pilgrimage.
Roll on, thou deep and dark blue ocean—roll!   Lord Byron.   NOBRP Fr. Childe Harold's Pilgrimage.
Roll On, Time, Roll On.   Julia A. Moore.
   "Some people are getting so they think a poor girl."   VerBaPo
Roll the stone from its grave away! (LL)   Maud Muller.   John Greenleaf Whittier.   APN-1; BRP; TreFP
Roll up a long cord.   Anima 1.   Takehisa Kosugi.   WhBo
Roll within themselves.   People of Pomegranates.   Nidaa Khoury.   DTA, tr. by Karen Alkalay-Gut
Roll-Call in the Concentration Camp.   Dan Pagis.   FIT; PoSu, tr. by Robert Friend
Rolled in your fragrances, beautiful turning Earth.   Sphere.   Jules Supervielle.   MFP, tr. by Martin Sorrell
Roller Coaster.   Nicanor Parra.   TCLAP, tr. by Miller Williams
Roller Coaster.   Nicanor Parra.   PoCho, tr. by Miller Williams
Rollercoaster.   Cris Cheek.   Oth
Rollicksome frolicsome rare old cock, A.   Our Dog Jock.   James Payn.   DiBP
Rolling Chinese Wall, The.   Roger Woddis.   UV
Rolling earth stops, The.   Down-hill on a Bicycle.   Louis Untermeyer.   ArBi
Rolling English Road, The.   G. K. Chesterton.   OBEV; OBMV; OxAEP-2; UV
Rolling snow turned peach-color.   Dawn.   Miyazawa Kenji.   WhBo
Rolling the Lawn.   William Empson.   HarvBoo; MoBrPo; OBGa
Rolls and harrows lie at rest beside, The.   Sky Lark, The.   John Clare.   NPeEn
Rolls-Royce Dreams.   Ginger Andrews.   GoPo
   And do they so?   Henry Vaughan.   BASC; SacPr

Roma Higgins. Dave Etter. IllVoic
Roman, The. Sydney Thompson Dobell.
  Timely Hint, A. STuOW
Roman Arbor, The. Ellen Hinsey. YaYoPo
Roman Baths at Nîmes, The. Henri Cole. MakPoe
Roman Earl, The [*with music*]. *Unknown.* OBVE, *tr. by* Douglas Hyde
Roman Elegies. Joseph Brodsky. VCWP, *tr. by* the author and Joseph
  Brodsky
Roman Elegies, The. Johann Wolfgang von Goethe. *tr. by* David Ferry and
  David Luke
  "Here my garden is growing, the flowers of Eros I tend here." EroLit, *tr. by*
    David Luke
  "When you tell me that you were unpopular as a child." WoPoe, *tr. by* David
    Ferry
Roman Evening. Pier Paolo Pasolini. CLPP
Roman Fountain. Louise Bogan. APT-2; NoP-4; NoP-5
Roman Fountain. Rainer Maria Rilke. GS, *tr. by* Edward Snow
Roman had an, A/ artist, a freedman. Jerboa, The. Marianne Moore. NALW
Roman Hunting. William Shakespeare. DiBP *Fr.* Titus Andronicus.
Roman miniature urchin, A. Seeking an Explanation. Richard Emil Braun.
  NoAM
Roman Poem Number Nine. June Jordan. GT
Roman Presents. Martial. OBCP, *tr. by* James Michie
Roman road runs straight and bare, The. Roman Road, The. Thomas Hardy.
  MoBrPo
Roman Study. Louise Glück. BodElec
Roman swallows. Sant'Alessio, Roma. Olga Sedakova. CRWP, *tr. by*
  Catriona Kelly
Roman Thank-You Letter, A. Martial. OBCP, *tr. by* James Michie
Roman threw us a road, a road, The. G. K. Chesterton. OBSV *Fr.* Songs of
  Education.
Roman Tribute, A. Faliscus Grattius. DiBP *Fr.* Cynegeticon Liber.
Roman Tribute, A. John Whitaker. DiBP
Roman Virgil [*or* Vergil], thou that singest. To Virgil [*or* Vergil]. Alfred
  Tennyson. NAEL-6v2
Roman Wall Blues. W. H. Auden. FaBoWar *Fr.* Twelve Songs.
Romance. Andrew Lang. NePenScot
Romance. Edgar Allan Poe. APN-1; NCAP
  (Introduction.) NAAL-3
  (Preface.) NAAL-3
Romance. Charles Reznikoff. NAAPv.2
Romance. Arthur Rimbaud. AmFaPo, *tr. by* Paul Schmidt
Romance. Ann Sansom. MFPA; NeBl
Romance. Walter James Turner. MoBrPo; NOBAu; NOxBChV; OBMV
Romance. Paul Zimmer. ReTh
Romance, A. Ernst Jandl. OnScMo, *tr. by* Brian Schorn
Romance for the Wild Turkey, A. Paul Zimmer. P180
Romance is a world, tiny and curved, reflected in a spoon. Perilous as a.
  Marriage. Amy Gerstler. PmAP
Romance Moderne. William Carlos Williams. APT-1
Romance of Love. *Unknown.* BLPSL, *tr. by* Rene de Costa, Rigas Kappatos
  and Eleni Paidoussi
Romance of the Swan's Nest, The. Elizabeth Barrett Browning. VWP
Romance [*or* Romaunt] of the Rose, The. Guillaume de Lorris.
Romance Somnambulo by Garcia Lorca. Federico García Lorca. AnSo, *tr. by*
  Alex Rawls
Romance to Night, A. Georg Trakl. AF, *tr. by* Daniel Simko
Romance, who loves to nod and sing. Romance. Edgar Allan Poe. APN-1;
  NCAP
Romancero. Lex Banning. NOBAu
Romancero d'une petite lampe. René Depestre. YaTCFP
Romania, Romania. Gerald Stern. MiVo
Romans Angry about the Inner World. Robert Bly. WaAnP
Romans, I appeal to you. *Unknown.* RomPo *Fr.* Priapean Corpus, The.
Romans once indeavoured all they could, The. Upon a Joynted Ring.
  Francellina Stapleton. EMWP
Romantic. Margaret Atwood. SweBea
Romantic Movement, The. Philip Lamantia. CLPP
Romanticism. Claudia Keelan. RoV
Romanticism. Spencer Short. IIR
Romanticism is for flakes. I've Looked Everywhere. J. B. Bryan. ICANM
Romantics: Johannes Brahms and Clara Schumann. Lisel Mueller. GoPo
Romanus Sum. István Vas. IQMS, *tr. by* Geroge Gömöri and Clive Wilmer
Romanus sum—and I held my hand in fire. Romanus Sum. István Vas.
  IQMS, *tr. by* Geroge Gömöri and Clive Wilmer
Romaunt of Cecilia, The. Arthur Waugh. ArBi
Rome. Madison Cawein. APN-2

Rome. Arthur Hugh Clough. OxAEP-2 *Fr.* Amours de Voyage.
Rome. Joachim Du Bellay. FaBoWar, *tr. by* Ezra Pound
Rome. Joachim Du Bellay. WoPoe, *tr. by* Yvor Winters
Rome. Peter Huchel. GTCP, *tr. by* Reinhold Grimm
Rome. "Panormitanus." OBVE, *tr. by* James Vincent Cunningham
Rome disappoints me still; but I shrink and adapt myself to it. Arthur Hugh
  Clough. OxAEP-2 *Fr.* Amours de Voyage.
Rome, do not ask for the Pontiff Paul to be testicle-tested! One For Pope Paul.
  Janus Pannonius. IQMS, *tr. by* George Burrough and Adam Makkai
Rome has a thousand fountains, and in May they sing. Maria Luisa Spaziani.
  NeIt
Rome, I am Scorpus, foremost in the race. Martial. RomPo, *tr. by* Brian Hill
Rome never looks where she treads. Rudyard Kipling. NAMCP V.1; NoAM
  Fr. Puck of Pook's Hill.
Rome still lies gleaming in a yellowish-golden hue. Marcus Aurelius. Dezső
  Kosztolányi. IQMS, *tr. by* Earl M. Herrick
Romeo and Juliet. Howard Phelps Putnam. OxBoAm
  (Male.) OxBoAm
Romeo and Juliet. Sherod Santos. IaFF
Romeo and Juliet. William Shakespeare.
  "Come night! come, Romeo! come, thou day in night!" BLPJKO
  "If I profane with my unworthiest hand." OxAEP-1; SoSe-8
  "O my love, my wife!" OxAEP-1
  "O, she doth teach the torches to burn bright!" WaAnP
Romeo, Grown Old. James Wright. BodElec
Romeo Is Dead. H. Palmer Hall. IaFF
RomeRomeRomeRomeRome. Haiku Monument for Washington, D.C.
  Michael Redhill. IFF
Romira, stay. Call, The. John Hall. NOSC
Romney! expert infallibly to trace. To George Romney, Esq. William
  Cowper. OxBSo
  (Romney! expert infallible to trace.) CenSon
Romp. Dave Etter. WeW-3
Ron. Beatrix Gates. WiU *Fr.* Triptych.
Roncesvalles. Iorwerth Cyfeilog Peate. BBMWP, *tr. by* Nigel Jenkins
Roncevalles. *Unknown.* WoPoe *Fr.* Song of Roland, The.
Rondeau: "Fleas, stink, pigs, mold." Eustache Deschamps. WoPoe, *tr. by*
  David Curzon and Jeffrey Fiskin
Rondeau: "Jenny kissed [*or* kiss'd] me when we met." Leigh Hunt. CABP;
  NBLV; NIL-7; NTCP; OBEV; OxAEP-2; OxBEV
  (Jenny Kiss'd Me.) BRP
  (Jenny Kissed Me.) ITBLP; TFi; UV
Rondeau: "Lord, I'm done for: now Margot." Vincent Voiture. WoPoe, *tr. by*
  William Jay Smith
Rondeau after a Transatlantic Telephone Call [*with music*]. Marilyn Hacker.
  ColAP; NAMCP V.2; NoAM
Rondeau at the Train Stop. Erin Belieu. GifTon; NeAmPo
Rondeau: "They are bodies left unburied." Cheryl Clarke. FFC
Rondeau of the Little Horses. Manuel Bandeira. TCLAP, *tr. by* Candace
  Slater
Rondeau Redoublé. Margaret Avison. IFF
Rondeau Redoublé. Wendy Cope. HarvBoo
Rondeau Tempo. Rossana Ombres. CItWP, *tr. by* Cinzia Sartini Blum and
  Lara Trubowitz
Rondel: "And whan this werk al brought was to an ende." Geoffrey Chaucer.
  OWoS *Fr.* Parlement of Foules, The.
Rondel: "Now that I am fifty-six." Muriel Rukeyser. NoP-4; NoP-5
Rondel of Luve [*or* Love], A. Alexander Scott. OBEV; OxBEV
Rondelet: "Say what you please." May Probyn. VWP
Rondelet: "Which way he went?" May Probyn. VWP
Rondels. Aleister Crowley. CAGL
Rondo: "Did I love thee? I only did desire." George Moore. IrLP
Roof and spire and darkened vane. Autumn Rain, The. Christopher Pearse
  Cranch. TCAPo
Roof beams. Things the Bigger the Better. *Unknown.* EMJL, *tr. by* Edward
  Putzar
Roof broke apart, The. Tomas Tranströmer. WoBe *Fr.* Haiku.
Roof caves in, A. English Sampler, An. Frederick D'Aguiar. Oth
Roof Garden. James Schuyler. OBGa
Roof it again. Batten down. Dig in. Seamus Heaney. PoetW *Fr.* Squarings.
Roof of the old morada, The. Dream 8. Cecilio Garcia-Camarillo. ICANM
Roof over Far Away. Ana Doina. RWB
Roof-poles in those days, The. Tel Aviv 1935. Leah Goldberg. FIT, *tr. by*
  Robert Friend
Roofs over the shops, The. Christmas Eve. Patricia Beer. OBCP
Rooftop. James Kimbrell. AmPoNex
Rooftop Piper. David Hernandez. IllVoic
Rooftop Violin. No Hyangnim. EcSo, *tr. by* Aimee N. Kwon

Rooftops. Lyubomir Levchev. CSCBP, *tr.* by Georgi Belev and Lisa Sapinkopf

Roof-Tree. Richard Murphy. ModIr *Fr.* Price of Stone, The.

Rook. Shari Miller Wagner. ACAMVP

Rook was the first, The. Rook. Shari Miller Wagner. ACAMVP

Rookhope Ryde. *Unknown.* IBB

Rookhope stands in a pleasant place. Rookhope Ryde. *Unknown.* IBB

Rooks. Charles Hamilton Sorley. MoBrPo

Rooks, The. Arthur Rimbaud. FaBoWar, *tr.* by Norman Cameron

Rooks are cawing up and down the trees!, The. Nests in Elms. Michael Field. NAEL-7v2; VWP

Rooks are homing, says. (LL) Our Bodies. Denise Levertov. CAP-8; ErotSp

Rooks: December. Huw Menai. AngWePo

Rooks love excitement. When I walked in under the rookery. Rooks love excitement. Ted Hughes. NOxBChV

Room. Bob Perelman. ASA

Room 5600. Ernesto Cardenal. CLPP, *tr.* by Jonathan Cohen

Room 703. Jane Rohrer. ACAMVP

Room, The. Conrad Potter Aiken. APT-1; InGu; MoAmPo

Room, The. Kevin Hart. StAl

Room, The. Anthony Hecht. PWW2 *Fr.* Rites and Ceremonies.

Room, The. William Soutar. NePenScot

Room, A. Jane Hirshfield. BeAl

Room after room. Love in a Life. Robert Browning. NPEeN; OxBEV

Room contains no sound, The. At 3 A.M. Wendy Cope. LW

Room does not turn its back on grief, A. Room, A. Jane Hirshfield. BeAl

Room fell silent, and all eyes were on him, The. Virgil. NAWM-5v1; NAWM-7v1 *Fr.* Aeneid [*or* Eneados *or* Aeneis], The.

Room 40. Oni Buchanan. LegDan

Room grew dark and at my work desk stood two spirits, The. Visitation. Adriann Roland Holst. TuT, *tr.* by Paula Meehan

Room I entered was a dream of this room, The. This Room. John Ashbery. ItP; OxBoAm

Room in Bloomsbury, A. Sandy Wilson. ReLy

Room in Space [*with music*]. René Char. YaTCFP, *tr.* by W. S. Merwin

Room is dark. . .as you know it, The. From Behind the Closed Door. Buland Al-Haidari. IrPoTo, *tr.* by Hussein Kadhim and Christopher Merrill

Room is full of gold, The. Jason. Anthony Hecht. ColAP

Room is prepared, the incense burned, The. Southern Room Over the River, The. Su Tung-p'o. NDACCP, *tr.* by Kenneth Rexroth

Room is sparsely furnished, The. Thrall. Carolyn Kizer. CAP-8; GifTon; StAl

Room itself, The. The women. The absence of women. Dionisio D. Martinez. NoP-4; NoP-5 *Fr.* What the Men Talk About When the Women Leave the Room.

Room of Leaves. Amanda Dalton.

     Almost Bird. NeBl

     In Love. NeBl

     Nest. NeBl

Room of My Life, The. Anne Sexton. CAP-8; NAMCP V.2; VCAP

Room of One's Own, A. Hoda Hussein. PoArWo, *tr.* by Cornelia Al-Khaled

Room on a Garden, A. Wallace Stevens. NoP-4; NoP-5; OBGa

Room sometimes vacant, sometimes engaged, A. A red-light district, just. Poem for the Womb. Jennifer O'Grady. AmPoNex

Room temperature Sandwich hoods. Right Away. Joel Dailey. AnSo

Room tips, The. Washing Dishes Late at Night. Kathleen Norris. UpMys

Room was cheap and sordid, The. One Night. Constantine P. Cavafy. CAGL; EroLit, *tr.* by Edmund Keeley and Philip Sherrard

Room was suddenly rich and the great bay-window was, The. Snow. Louis MacNeice. HarvBoo; ModIr; NAMCP V.1; NoAM; NPEeN; OPOU; OxAEP-2; OxBEV; PNI; StAl

Room with a View. Robert John Moore. Coast

Room with double beds, side by side, The. What They Left Behind. J. D. McClatchy. OxBoAm

Rooms. Brian Henry. LegDan

Rooms. Kathleen Jamie. MoWP

Rooms. Charlotte Mew. HarvBoo; MoWP; PoBW; PoCho

Rooms. Gertrude Stein.

     "Light in the moon the only light is on Sunday, A." TCAPo

Rooms. Gertrude Stein. *Fr.* Tender Buttons.

Rooms are chosen, then they move on, The. Fall Returns, The. Clark Coolidge. AHA

Rooms Are Never Finished. Agha Shahid Ali. AmAlph

Rooms outlast you. (LL) O city ladies. George Oppen. APT-2; PFTM-1

Rooster. James Tate. WaAnP

Rooster, The. Abu'l Qasim As'ad ibn Billita. WoPoe, *tr.* by Leticia Garza-Falcón and Christopher Middleton

Rooster, The. Aleksandr Semionovich Kushner. ItGoST, *tr.* by Paul Graves and Carol Ueland

Rooster and the Pearl, The. Max Jacob. CuPo

Rooster had hardly crowed when Timofey jumped out of the window onto the roof, The. Beginning of a Beautiful Day (A Symphony), The. Daniil Kharms. AF; MotU, *tr.* by George Gibian

Rooster is already announcing dawn, The. *Unknown.* SLW, *tr.* by Marjolijn De Jager, Sayd Bahodin Majrouh and André Velter

Rooster nights with crests of screams; sleep that's gotten old. Clothes Without the Monk, The. Silvio Giussani. ItPo, *tr.* by Gayle Ridinger

Rooster, you monster with a blood-red crest, a jagged. Rooster, The. Aleksandr Semionovich Kushner. ItGoST, *tr.* by Paul Graves and Carol Ueland

Roosters. Elizabeth Bishop. APT-2; ChIV-2; NALW; NAMCP V.2; OxBoAm

Roosting in a crater with one. Vampire Finch. Robyn Schiff. LegDan

Root. Miklós Radnóti. IQMS, *tr.* by Peter Zollman

Root, The. Luis Rosales. RaW, *tr.* by Ralph Nelson and Rita García Nelson

Root ("Through the root power flashes unseen.") Miklós Radnóti. ConPit, *tr.* by Clayton Eshleman and Gyula Kodolanyi

Root Cellar. Theodore Roethke. CAP-8; ColAP; HarvBoo; HeIP-4; NoP-4; NoP-5; OxBoAm; VCAP

Root of Our Evil, The. D. H. Lawrence. ChIV-2

Root of our present evil is that we buy and sell, The. Root of Our Evil, The. D. H. Lawrence. ChIV-2

Root Song. Henry Dumas. ISC

Root stirs with rushing power, The. Root. Miklós Radnóti. IQMS, *tr.* by Peter Zollman

Rooted, immutable, neighboring / Music. (LL) Conspiracy: "Violin which is following me, A." Jack Spicer. APSN; CalPo

Rooted in fresh earth, I am a bush of flies. Riddle. Henry Hart. WaAnP

Rooted out of my soul? (LL) Edgar Lee Masters. APT-1; OxBoAm *Fr.* Spoon River Anthology.

Rooting, The. Jolanda Insana. CItWP *Fr.* Rooting, The.

Rooting, The. Jolanda Insana. *tr.* by Cinzia Sartini Blum and Lara Trubowitz

Rooting, The. CItWP, *tr.* by Cinzia Sartini Blum and Lara Trubowitz

Rootless tree, A. Sozan-Kyonin. ZenPo, *tr.* by Takashi Ikemoto and Lucien Stryk

Roots. Arthur Ade Amaker. BRtP

Roots. Bill Berkson. AHA; NYP2

Roots. Mawiyah Kai el-Jamah Bomani. BtF

Roots. Seamus Deane. PNI

Roots. Charlotte Watson Sherman. ISC

Roots: "Rudy Weibe, wiping the sweat from his brow." David Waltner-Toews. ACAMVP

Roots 1: big momma speaks to jimmy's wife. Cherryl "Blue." Floyd-Miller. BtF

Roots 2: the conjure woman replies. Cherryl "Blue." Floyd-Miller. BtF

Roots and Branches. Robert Duncan. CalPo; FTOS

Roots and leaves themselves alone are these. Roots and Leaves Themselves Alone. Walt Whitman. APN-1

Roots in the Air. Shirley Kaufman. TaR

Roots of Blue Bells. Nia Francisco. HATNAP

Roots of the camphor tree. Buson. EMJL, *tr.* by Haruo Shirane

Rope is braided in colors of love, The. Wind Turns, The. Nicole Espagnol. SurWo, *tr.* by Myrna Bell Rochester

Rope strung over an abyss. Balancing Act. Elsa Cross. RMCMP, *tr.* by Margaret Sayers Peden

Rope swings in, The. Red-Dress Girl. Ann Turner. SSCS

Ropewalk, The. Henry Wadsworth Longfellow. NCAP

Ropey, lippy, loopy, scribbly. Nasturtium Scanned. Judith Rodriguez. BMAP

Rosa. Miguel Algarin. PueRic

Rosa. Rita Dove. ExTi; FuFl

Rosa dances her feet out. Nudo de Claridad. Miguel Algarin. PmAP

Rosa/Fili. Maria Arrillaga. TANSG

Rosa junonis: milk tears. Syliva Legris. PoPra *Fr.* Negative Garden.

Rosa Luxemburg. Y. A. Rontsh. Prolet, *tr.* by Amelia Glaser

Rosa Mystica. John Gwyn Griffiths. BBMWP, *tr.* by Richard Poole

Rosa Odorata. Jo Shapcott. MoWP *Fr.* Roses, The.

Rosa Rosarum. Agnes Mary Frances Robinson. PoBW

Rosa Sancta. Jo Shapcott. MoWP *Fr.* Roses, The.

Rosabel. Angelina Weld Grimké. PoBW

Rosalind, in a négligée. Early Unfinished Sketch. Austin Clarke. ModIr

Rosalind's [*or* Rosalynde's] Description. Thomas Lodge. *See* Rosaline.

Rosalind's [*or* Rosalynd's] Madrigal[l]. Thomas Lodge. NoSic; OBEV *Fr.* Rosalynde; or Euphues' Golden Legacy.

Rosaline. Thomas Lodge. OBEV *Fr.* Rosalynde; or Euphues' Golden Legacy.

Rosalynde; or Euphues' Golden Legacy.   Thomas Lodge.
   (Rosalind's Madrigal.)   NoP-4; RACG
   (Rosalind's [or Rosalynde's] Description.)   OxAEP-1
   Rosalind's [or Rosalynd's] Madrigal[l].   NoSic; OBEV
   Rosaline.   OBEV
Rosamond.   Joseph Addison.
   King Henry's Song.   STuOW
   Rosamond's Song.   STuOW
Rosamond's Song.   Joseph Addison.   STuOW Fr. Rosamond.
Rosario.   Pedro Serrano.   RMCMP
Rosary.   Pedro Serrano.   RMCMP, tr. by Geoff Hargreaves
Rosary Beads.   Herman Melville.   NCAP
Rosa's Beauty.   Jane Alberdeston Coralin.   BRtP
Rosa's body stopped growing.   Water, White Cotton, and the Rich Man.
   Martín Espada.   PueRic
Rose: "Seated at the core of the rose I weep."   Cemal Süreya.   NaPG, tr. by
   Talat Sait Halman
Rose, The.   "Angelus Silesius."   GePo Fr. Cherubical Wanderer, The.
Rose, The.   Kelly Cherry.   LPSFW
Rose, The.   Gabriela Mistral.   SpanPo, tr. by Kate Flores
Rose, The.   Gabriela Mistral.   WPoS, tr. by Langston Hughes
Rose, The.   Theodore Roethke.   APT-2; TRP
Rose, The.   Theodore Roethke.   TRP Fr. North American Sequence.
Rose, The ("Rose is obsolete, The.")   William Carlos Williams.   APT-1;
   NAAPv.2; OxBoAm
Rose, A.   Sir Richard Fanshawe.   OBEV Fr. Il Pastor Fido.
Rose, A / a / shameless.   Evelina Shats.   CRWP, tr. by Daniel Weissbort
Rose and gold and violet, The.   Afterglow, The.   Henrietta Cordelia Ray.
   CBWP-3
Rose and went a-roving, mother.   Lass A-Laundering.   Unknown.   STV, tr. by
   John Frederick Nims
Rose Aylmer.   Walter Savage Landor.   CABP; NAEL-6v2; NAEL-7v2;
   NOBRP; NoP-4; NoP-5; OBEV; OxAEP-2; TFi; WeW-3
Rose Bay Willow Herb.   Judy Ray.   AtGh
Rose Beetle, The.   W. S. Merwin.   CAP-8
Rose both white and Red, The.   John Skelton.   PBRV Fr. Lawde and Prayse
   Made for Our Sovereigne Lord the Kyng, A.
Rose by the Wayside, The.   D.A. Drown.   TreFP
Rose fades, The.   Poem.   William Carlos Williams.   NIL-7
Rose Family, The.   Robert Frost.   BLPJKO; NIL-7
Rose Farmer, The.   Herman Melville.   APN-2
Rose for a young head, A.   Watcher, The.   James Stephens.   MoBrPo; OBEV
Rose Geranium, The.   Eiléan Ní Chuilleanáin.
   6.   IrLP
Rose, harsh rose.   Sea Rose.   "H. D."   APT-1; HeIP-4; MoWP; NAAPv.2;
   NAMCP V.1; NIL-7; NoAM; NoP-4; NoP-5; OxWW; TRP; WaAnP
Rose has flushed red, the bud has burst, The.   Khwaja Shams-ad-din
   Muhammad Hafiz.   TAL Fr. Odes.
Rose in her hand, a rose in her breast, A.   Kyrielle.   May Probyn.   VWP
Rose is a Rose is a Rose is a Rose.   Emmett Williams.   PFTM-2 Fr.
   Ultimate Poem, The.
Rose is a rose, The.   Rose Family, The.   Robert Frost.   BLPJKO; NIL-7
Rose is a Violin is a Codpiece.   Emmett Williams.   PFTM-2 Fr. Ultimate
   Poem, The.
Rose is obsolete, The.   Rose, The.   William Carlos Williams.   APT-1;
   NAAPv.2; OxBoAm
Rose kissed me today.   Rose-Leaves.   Austin Dobson.
Rose Leaves When the Rose Is Dead.   Marc André Raffalovich.   CAGL
Rose like a fog off a lake at dawn as the bus rolled past, a young man nodding
   sleepily against the glass.   Rise of Rome, The.   Kevin Prufer.   LegDan
Rose might of the winds.   Ronald Johnson.   FTOS Fr. Ark.
Rose Nocturnal.   Xavier Villaurrutia.   GPTC, tr. by Donald Justice
Rose of all the world is not for me, The.   Little White Rose, The.   Hugh
   MacDiarmid.   NePenScot
Rose of Fire.   Antonio Machado Ruiz.   SpanPo, tr. by Kate Flores
Rose of Silence.   Gennady Aygi.   ItGoST, tr. by Peter France
Rose of the Russian nation.   Wild Rose.   Vitalina Tkhorzhevskaya.   CRWP, tr.
   by Daniel Weissbort
Rose of the World, The.   William Butler Yeats.   MoBrPo; NAEL-6v2; NAEL-
   7v2
Rose of Time, The.   Bei Dao.   WoBe, tr. by Iona Man-Cheong and Eliot
   Weinberger
Rose on My Cake, The [with music].   Karla Kuskin.   TLR
Rose Quartz.   Leslie Ullman.   ExTi
Rose, regarded here by your external eyes, The.   "Angelus Silesius."   GePo Fr.
   Cherubical Wanderer, The.
Rose That Bore Jesu, The [with music].   Unknown.   NPeEn

Rose, The / was not searching for the sunrise.   Casida of the Rose.   Federico
   García Lorca.   WED, tr. by Robert Bly
Rose Tree, The.   William Butler Yeats.   OBMV
Rose was sick and smiling died [or di'd], The.   Funeral[l] Rites of the Rose,
   The.   Robert Herrick.   NOSC; OBEV
Rose, were you not extremely sick? (LL)   True Maid, A.   Matthew Prior.
   NAEL-6v1; NAEL-7v1; NIP-4; NPeEn; WaAnP
Rose Window.   Herman Melville.   APN-2
Rose Wreaths, The.   Friedrich Gottlieb Klopstock.   GePo, tr. by J. W. Thomas
Rose-blushing heaven-scented pear ("that pear's a").   On Impermanence.
   Jamie Meyerhoff.   WhBo
Rosebud in the Heather.   Johann Wolfgang von Goethe.   STV, tr. by John
   Frederick Nims
Rose-Bud, The.   William Broome.   OBEV
Rosebush, Less Presumption.   Francisco de Quevedo y Villegas.   SpanPo, tr.
   by William M. Davis
Rosebush, less presumption.   Rosebush, Less Presumption.   Francisco de
   Quevedo y Villegas.   SpanPo, tr. by William M. Davis
Rose-cheeked Laura, come.   Thomas Campion.   NAEL-6v1; NAEL-7v1; NoP-
   4; NoP-5; NOSC; TFi; TRP; WaAnP Fr. Observations in the Art of English
   Poesie.
Rose-Covered Grave, The.   Cornelius Whur.
   "Morning arose, and its beauties were beaming, The."   STuOW
Rose-Leaves.   Austin Dobson.
   Urceus Exit.   OBEV
Rosemary.   John A. Stone.   BloBone
Rosemary for remembrance, Shakespeare wrote.   Wreath for Emmett Till, A.
   Marilyn Nelson.   CAP-8
Rosemary, Rosemary.   Stephen Vincent Benét.   NOxBChV
Roses.   Barbara Guest.   NoP-4; NoP-5
Roses.   Geoffrey Lehmann.   BMAP Fr. Roses.
Roses.   Geoffrey Lehmann.
   Roses.   BMAP
Roses.   Pierre de Ronsard.   WoPoe, tr. by Vernon Watkins
Roses, The.   Jo Shapcott.
   Rosa Odorata.   MoWP
   Rosa Sancta.   MoWP
Roses, The.   Jennifer Snyder.   BodElec
Roses: "There was a rose called Guy de Maupassant."   Gerald Stern.   GPPA
Roses All the Way.   Thomas Baker.   STuOW Fr. Steam Engine; or, The Power
   of the Flame, The.
Roses and Thorns.   Kim Sŭnghŭi.   CAMKP, tr. by Anthony, Brother of Taizé
Roses and tulips Flora gathers here.   David Lloyd.   AngWePo
Roses at first were white.   How Roses Came Red.   Robert Herrick.   NAEL-
   7v1
Roses caged in windows, heighten.   Julia Ward Howe.   SWaP Fr. Lyrics of the
   Street.
Roses curve around the lawn, their pale cheeks.   Appointment in June.   Claire
   Malroux.   YaTCFP, tr. by Marilyn Hacker
Roses for the folks we know, A.   Seitlhamo Motsapi.   TSAP
Roses hence, or Lil[l]ies rather. (LL)   Upon the Infant Martyrs.   Richard
   Crashaw.   NoP-4; NoP-5; NPeEn
Roses in breathing forth their scent.   Celia Singing.   Thomas Stanley.   NOSC
Roses, Late Summer.   Mary Oliver.   NIL-7
Roses, roses of dust, how much hardness.   Poetry of Roses, The.   Franco
   Fortini.   ItPo, tr. by Gayle Ridinger
Roses, roses, roses.   June.   Henrietta Cordelia Ray.   CBWP-3
Roses shed tears on their delicate white petals, The.   Chamber Music.   Li
   Shang-yin.   CCL1, tr. by James J. Y. Liu
Roses, their sharp spines being gone.   John Fletcher and William Shakespeare.
   NOSC; NoSic Fr. Two Noble Kinsmen, The.
Roses were bright red, The.   Spleen.   Paul Verlaine.   SxFrPo, tr. by Martin
   Sorrell
Rosewater and dust the dawn.   Bicycling Away from the Library.   William
   Hedrington.   ArBi
Rosh Chodesh Tisheri.   Vicki Hollander.   HW
Rosh HaShanah.   Aharon Shabtai.   WoBe, tr. by Peter Cole
Rosina Alcona to Julius Brenzaida.   Judith Wright.   InoFa; NALW
Roslyn Malamud the Coup.   Anna Deavere Smith.   OxWW Fr. Fires in the
   Mirror.
Ross's Poems.   Geoffrey Lehmann.
   "What's that bird, Mr Long?"   BMAP
Rostov.   George Sutherland Fraser.   PoWW
Rostov-on-Don.   Flora Garry.   EdScPo
Rosy Ear.   Zbigniew Herbert.   BeAl; PML, tr. by Czeslaw Milosz
Rosy from wine, she rises.   Drinking All Night, Sleeping All Day.   Li Ho.
   CrYelRi, tr. by Sam Hamill
Rot, old crow, a mausoleum.   Unknown.   PriapPo Fr. Priapus Poems, The.

Rot on the vine: in that land were we born. (LL) Mediterranean, The. Allen Tate. APT-2; FuPo; InGu; MoAmPo; NAAPv.2; OxBoAm; WoPoe

Rotary. Christina Pugh. P180

Rotate the husband and expose a hidden side. A letter he wrote from Rio de Janeiro. Anne Carson. NoP-5 *Fr.* Beauty of the Husband, The.

Rotation 1. Kang Ŭn'gyo. EcSo, *tr. by* Ann Y. Choi

Rothko. Del Ray Cross. FreRad

Rothko's Yellow. Dean Young. IllVoic

Rotten Axe-Handle Mountain. Huai Ku. CSKM, *tr. by* Paul Hansen

Rotten fish. Karen Press. TSAP

Rotting Ginsberg, I stared in the mirror naked today. Mescaline. Allen Ginsberg. PFTM-2

Rotting Symbols. Eileen Myles. BodElec

Rottnest Island. Nicholas Hasluck.
  "All day the bicycles come and go." NOBAu
  "Christmas Day. 1696." NOBAu

Rotund, stubby fingered. Tale. Jennifer Rankin. BMAP

Rou-cou spoke the dove. Song of Fixed Accord. Wallace Stevens. SAmP

Rouen. May Wedderburn Cannan. NAEL-6v2; NAEL-7v2; OBWP

Rouen, Place de la Pucelle. Maria White Lowell. APN-2

Rouge. Ann Townsend. ExTi

Rouged hands. Tune: "Hairpin Phoenix." Lu Yu. ChinPo, *tr. by* Ye Weilian [*or* Yeh Wei-lien *or* Wai-lim Yip]

Rough and dark—the Cold Mountain trail. Rough and Dark. Han-shan (Cold Mountain). CCL1; NDACCP, *tr. by* Gary Snyder

Rough are the roads that led me to this place. Rough Are the Roads. Baldomero Garcilaso de la Vega. SpanPo, *tr. by* Edwin Morgan

Rough articles likesiding at others plug making plug. Accessories are. Hints at Distance. Michael Portnoy. HeMarv

Rough Boys. Sam Adams. TCAWP

Rough clouds gather around the valley. Yi Saek. CATKP, *tr. by* Peter H. Lee

Rough Country. Dana Gioia. PfSP

Rough draft, getting rougher, A. Drafts. A. K. Ramanujan. NAMCP V.2

Rough Field, The. John Montague.
  Fault, The.
    Cage, The. PNI
  Home Again.
    Like Dolmens Round My Childhood. ModIr; NoP-4; NoP-5; PBCIP; PNI
  Severed Head, A.
    Grafted Tongue, A. PBCIP
    Lost Tradition, A. PBCIP
  Wild Dog Rose, The. PBCIP

Rough fir, hauled from the hills. And the tree it had been. Making of the Cross, The. William Everson. CalPo

Rough Guide. Grahame Davies. BBMWP, *tr. by* the author

Rough hail rattles thro the trees, The. Eild. Robert Tannahill. NePenScot

Rough man entered the lover's garden, The. Ilahi. Pir Sultan Abdal. WoPoe, *tr. by* Murat Nemet-Nejat

Rough Music. Deborah Digges. ExTi

Rough Road, A. Pao Chao. CCL1, *tr. by* John Frodsham

Rough sleep from the room across the hall. Bronchitis. David Bottoms. PML

Rough weight of it, The. Love the Human. Lucille Clifton. GT

Rough wind, that moanest loud. Dirge, A. Percy Bysshe Shelley. NAEL-7v2

Rough-Cut Head. Keith Ratzlaff. ACAMVP

Roughly figured, this man of moderate habits. Life Cycle of Common Man. Howard Nemerov. NBLV

Round. Robert Pinsky. OxBoAm

Round: "Wondrous life! cried Marvell at Appleton House." Weldon Kees. OxBoAm

Round, The. Stanley Kunitz. BeAl; BodElec; NAMCP V.1

Round About. Ogden Nash. ReLy

Round About Midnight. Bob Kaufman. CalPo

Round About Midnight, Opus #6. Percy Johnston. EGAG

Round and sad-eyed man puffed cigars as if, The. Song of the Round Man. Michael Palmer. NAMCP V.2

Round Fan. Wang Chien. CCL1, *tr. by* Marsha Wagner

Round fortune. Dolores Dorantes. SPV, *tr. by* Jen Hofer

Round gourd dipper could scoop up my cheek, The. Water in a Gourd. Chŏng Hwajin. EcSo, *tr. by* Julie C. Park

Round his left shoulder, as he got up slowly. Lazarus. Ágnes Nemes Nagy. IQMS, *tr. by* Hugh Maxton

Round Irving High School. Cheryl Boyce Taylor. WiU

'Round Killar. Eric Dyer. BloBone

Round Lake. Janet Kauffman. ACAMVP

Round like a circle in a spiral. Windmills of Your Mind, The. Alan Bergman and Marilyn Bergman. ReLy

Round living bulge, more certain today, The. Delivery. Alicia Galaz Vivar. TANSG, *tr. by* Dave Oliphant

'Round Midnight. Bernie Hanighen. ReLy

Round Midnight, Place de Congo. Kalamu ya Salaam. SpirFl *Fr.* New Orleans Haiku.

Round of Life. Richard Outram. IFF

Round of the Clock, The. Frederick B. Needham.
  "One! strikes the clock in the belfry tower." VerBaPo

Round Room, The. Harvena Richter. ICANM

Round, round, more round than the moon. Etsudo Nishikawa. WhBo

Round the cape of a sudden came the sea. Parting at Morning. Robert Browning. CABP; HeIP-4; NAEL-6v2; NAEL-7v2; OBEV; SoSe-8; TFi

'Round the Corn, Sally. Unknown. SSUS

Round the encampments of our saddle-kings. (LL) In the Grounds. Douglas Dunn. NoP-4; NoP-5

Round the house and round the house / and there lies a black glove in the window. Riddle. *Unknown.* FaBoVe

Round the house and round the house / and there lies a white glove in the window. Riddle. *Unknown.* FaBoVe

Round the island of Zipangu. Mimshi Maiden, The. Hugh Raymond McCrae. NOBAu

Round the Palace of Waters gently the wind moves the flowers. Sy-che and the King. Li Po. CCL1, *tr. by* E. Powys Mathers

Round the tall towers blow many mournful winds. Ts'ao Chih. CCL1, *tr. by* John Frodsham

Round the wide earth, from the red field your valour has won. Conquerors, The: The Black Troops in Cuba. Paul Laurence Dunbar. AmWaPo

Round the World with the Rumpus God. Meret Oppenheim. SurPaPo; SurWo, *tr. by* Catherine Schelbert

Round this particular date I have drawn a circle. Sulpicia. Michael Longley. OxBSo; RACG

Round universe, where only spheres can range. Emblem 51. Zbigniew Morsztyn. WoPoe, *tr. by* Jerzy Peterkiewicz and Burns Singer

Roundabout winds wearily down, The. Poem about the Blue Horse. Sergey Morozov. TCRusP, *tr. by* Daniel Weissbort

Roundabouts stolidly turn. Natalya Starodubtseva. CRWP, *tr. by* Daniel Weissbort

Rounded Catalogue Divine Complete, The. Walt Whitman. NAAL-3

Rounded world is fair to see, The. Nature [1844]. Ralph Waldo Emerson. APN-1

Roundel. Geoffrey Chaucer. NPeEn; OPOU

Roundel: "Take, take this cosse, atonys, atonys, my hert!" Charles, Duc d' Orléans. NPeEn

Roundel to My Pipe. Emile Nelligan. IFF, *tr. by* P. F. Widdows

Roundelay: "On all that strand." Samuel Beckett. ModIr; OxBEV

Roundelay, A: "It fell upon a holy eve." Edmund Spenser. NPeEn

Roundelay Between Two Shepherds, A. Michael Drayton. NoP-4; NoP-5

Roundhouse Voices, The. Dave Jeddie Smith. ColAP; GM; NoAM; VCAP; WaAnP

Rounding steeps and jostles were one thing, The. Ferris Wheel, The. Wyatt Prunty. RA

Rounding the Horn. L. S. Asekoff. BAP-97

Rounding the Horn. John Masefield. MoBrPo *Fr.* Dauber.

Roundness. Pierre Drieu la Rochelle. CuPo

Round—oblong—like jam. Contours. Noël Coward. UV

Rounds and Garlands Done, The. Léonie Adams. APT-2

Rounds, The. G. E. Murray. IllVoic

Rouse thee, old Time, thy folded pinions shake. To Time. Mary Julia Young. CenSon

Rousseau Le Douanier. "Lucebert." PFTM-2, *tr. by* Peter Nijmeijer

Rousseau, Voltaire, our Gibbon, and De Staël. Sonnet to Lake Leman. Lord Byron. CenSon; NPBRoP

Route. George Oppen. AF; APSN; APT-2

Route. Philippe Soupault. PFTM-1

Route of Evanescence, A. Hummingbird, A. Emily Dickinson. APN-2; HeIP-4; NAAL-3; NAAL-5; NoP-4; NoP-5; SoSe-8; TCAPo

Route of the Táin, The. Thomas Kinsella. PBCIP

Route Six. Stanley Kunitz. APT-2

Routine. Arthur Guiterman. GoPo

Routine Day Sonnet. A. K. Ramanujan. EmeKit

Routine Things Around the House, The. Stephen Dunn. CAP-8; MAAN

Rover killed the goat. Brave Rover. Max Beerbohm. NBLV

Rover's Adieu [*or* Farewell], The. Sir Walter Scott. OBEV

Rovers, The; or, The Double Arrangement. Anti-Jacobins, The and George Canning, George Ellis *and* John Hookham Frere.
  Rogero's Song. NPBRoP; OBCoV

Roving breezes come and go, the reed-beds sweep and sway, The. Travelling Post Office, The. Andrew Barton Paterson. NOBAu

Roving Lover, The. Frederick Robert Higgins. IrLP

Row after row (this). Stare Decisis. Gale Nelson. OnScMo

Row after row with strict impunity. Ode to the Confederate Dead. Allen Tate. AmWaPo; APT-2; CBCWP; ColAP; FuPo; HeIP-4; InGu; MoAmPo; NAAPv.2; NAMCP V.1; NoAM; NoP-4; NoP-5; OBWP; OxBoAm; TFi; WaAnP

Row gently here, my gondolier; so softly wake the tide. Venetian Air. Thomas Moore. GoPo

Row of black tombs—tall and jagged, A. Michigan Boulevard. Jun Fujita. NAAPv.2

Row, Row, Row. William Jerome. ReLy

Row us out from Desenzano, to your Sirmione row! Frater Ave Atque Vale. Alfred Tennyson. NAEL-6v2; NoP-4; NoP-5

Rowan like a lip-sticked girl, A. Song. Seamus Heaney. TRP

Rowboat was caught in the mudflats, The. A few gulls padded around it. Carla Harryman. ASA

Rowing between Pond and Western Islands. Loon Call, A. Richard Eberhart. ColAP

Rowing in Familiar January. Milo De Angelis. NeIt, tr. by Lawrence Venuti

Rows of cells are unroofed, The. Old Prison, The. Judith Wright. BMAP

Rows of drops like shining buds are hanging. (LL) My work done, I lean on the window-sill. Charles Reznikoff. APT-2; NAAPv.2

Rows of piggy bank fed coins. Scabible. Elouise Loftin. EGAG

Rows of rectangles rise, set into brick. Dearborn North Apartments Chicago, Illinois. Lola Haskins. P180; PoDa

Roxy. Gavin Selerie.
    47. Oth
    52. Oth
    23. Oth

Roy Campanella: January, 1958. E. Ethelbert Miller. FuFl

Royal Angler, The. Unknown.
    "Me thinks I see our mighty monarch stand." OBSV

Royal Avenue Hotel collapses under the breaker's pendulum, The. Clerance. Ciaran Carson. BeAl

Royal Banquet, The. William Edmonstoune Aytoun. OBCoV

Royal Charlie's now awa. Will He No Come Back Again? Unknown. OBEV

Royal Dwellings. Emperor Juntoku. WoPoe, tr. by Howard S. Levy

Royal Education. Winthrop Mackworth Praed. OBSV

Royal feast was done; the King, The. Fool's Prayer, The. Edward Rowland Sill. APN-2; ITBLP

Royal health to the Rising Sun, The. Unknown. BASC

Royal in splendour went down the day. Indian City, The. Felicia Dorothea Hemans. RWP

Royal Manor Road. Gerald Stern. InvLad

Royal Palm. Hart Crane. MoAmPo; NAMCP V.1; NoAM

Royal Portraits, The. William Dean Howells. APN-2

Royal Review, The. William McGonagall.
    "All hail to the Empress of India, Great Britain's Queen." VerBaPo

Royal roads were cow paths, The. Seamus Heaney. PoetW Fr. Sweeney Redivivus.

Royall Palice of the Heichest Hewin, The. Alexander Montgomerie. NePenScot

Royall palice of the heichest hewin, The. Royall Palice of the Heichest Hewin, The. Alexander Montgomerie. NePenScot

Royal[l] Presents. Nathaniel Wanley. SacPr

Royals. James Schuyler. FTOS

Royalty. Arthur Rimbaud. MotU, tr. by Louise Varese

Royalty. James Logie Robertson. EdScPo

Roysters give Roome, for here comes a Lass. Elizabeth Banckes and George James. EMWP

R-p-o-p-h-e-s-s-a-g-r. R-P-O-P-H-E-S-S-A-G-R. E. E. Cummings. NAMCP V.1

RS Thomas. Fadhil Assultani. IrPoTo, tr. by Melissa Brown and Saadi A. Simawe

RSVP. Danielle Pafunda. BAP-04

Rub a Dub Style inna Regent Park. Lillian Allen. WaCA

Rub her choke. Gertrude Stein. NAMCP V.1 Fr. Tender Buttons.

Rubáiyát of Omar Khayyám [of Naishápúr], The. Omar Khayyám. CtM; NAEL-6v2; NAEL-7v2; NoP-4; NoP-5; TRP, tr. by Edward Fitzgerald
    5. OBEV, tr. by Edward Fitzgerald
    7. TRP; UV, tr. by Edward Fitzgerald
    12. CABP; OBEV; TRP; WoPoe, tr. by Edward Fitzgerald
    13. CABP; TRP, tr. by Edward Fitzgerald
    19. CABP; CtM; TRP, tr. by Edward Fitzgerald
    22. TRP, tr. by Edward Fitzgerald
    27. CABP; TRP, tr. by Edward Fitzgerald
    68. CABP, tr. by Edward Fitzgerald
    69. CABP, tr. by Edward Fitzgerald
    70. CABP, tr. by Edward Fitzgerald
    71. CABP; CtM; TRP, tr. by Edward Fitzgerald
    72. CABP, tr. by Edward Fitzgerald
    73. CABP, tr. by Edward Fitzgerald
    74. CABP, tr. by Edward Fitzgerald
    100. TRP, tr. by Edward Fitzgerald
    101. TRP, tr. by Edward Fitzgerald

Rubáiyát of Omar Khayyám [of Naishápúr], The. Omar Khayyám. NPeEn; OxAEP-2; OxBEV; TAL; UV, tr. by Edward Fitzgerald
    "But leave the Wise to wrangle, and with me." OxBEV, tr. by Edward Fitzgerald
    "Here with a Loaf of Bread beneath the Bough." UV, tr. by Edward Fitzgerald
    "'How sweet is mortal Sovranty!' — think some." UV, tr. by Edward Fitzgerald
    "Oh, come with old Khayyam and leave the Wise." UV, tr. by Edward Fitzgerald

Rubai. Nazim Hikmet. WoPoe, tr. by Taner Baybars

Rubaiyat. Mimi Khalvati. MFPA

Rubber. Rolf Jacobsen. See Country Roads.

Rubber Eraser. John Mueller. WhBo

Rubber gloves, for the kitchen—brutish, efficient. Devotion. Dan Pagis. MotU, tr. by Stephen Mitchell

Rubber Knight, The. Tom Ahern. OnScMo

Rubbish Bags. Victor Vroomkoning. TuT, tr. by Dennis O'Driscoll

Rubbish Tip, The. Donald Evans. BBMWP, tr. by Gillian Clarke

Rubens. Washington Allston. APN-1

Rubens. Harriet Monroe. IllVoic

Rubric, The. Virgil. OBVE Fr. Aeneid [or Eneados or Aeneis], The.

Ruby Red's Migrant Camp. Wilma Elizabeth McDaniel. GeoHom

Rubyfruit. Jenny Factor. CalPo

Rückenfigur. Susan Howe. NAMCP V.2

Ruddigore. William Schwenck Gilbert.
    Thought from Ruddigore, A. OBCoV

Ruddy drop of manly blood, A. Friendship. Ralph Waldo Emerson. CAGL

Ruddy fire-glow, like her sister's eyes, The. Lot and His Daughters I. Alec Derwent Hope. ChIV-1

Ruddy-skinned pears. (LL) Late Aubade, A. Richard Wilbur. BrAP; SoSe-8

Rude, from the wide extended Chesapeke. Philip Freneau. TCAPo Fr. House of Night, The.

Rude Mars had th' ordering of their spirits; of Greeks, the learned Maid. Homer. FaBoWar Fr. Iliad, The.

Rude Ranger Rebuked. Caroline Anne Bowles Southey. DiBP

Rudy Weibe, wiping the sweat from his brow. Roots. David Waltner-Toews. ACAMVP

Rue de Rosiers: To My Brother Fred. Liliane Richman. TWW

Rue Ravignan, La. Max Jacob. YaTCFP

Rue Ravignan, The [with music]. Max Jacob. YaTCFP, tr. by John Ashbery

Ru-fen: Along Yew's Banks. Unknown. CCL1, tr. by V. W. X.

Rufino Laughlin / (M.C.). Melvin B. Tolson. NAMCP V.1 Fr. Harlem Gallery.

Rufous Hummingbird. Duane Niatum. PoCoUp

Rufous-Crowned Sparrow Seen Loitering below Possum Kingdom Dam. William D. Barney. TiP2

Rufus Prays. Leonard Alfred George Strong. MoBrPo

Rug of dead butterflies at my feet, A. Ghost. Nina Cassian. PoSu, tr. by Christopher Hewitt

Rugby Road. George Garrett. LPSFW

Rugged billion Miles, A. (LL) Savior must have been, The. Emily Dickinson. ChrPo; SacPr

Ruido en miles de grietas la vista. Angélica Tornero. SPV

Ruin, The. Dafydd ap Gwilym. OBWVE, tr. by Rolfe Humphries

Ruin, The. Richard Hughes. OBMV

Ruin, The. Unknown. WoPoe, tr. by Michael O'Brien

Ruin, The. Unknown. NAWM-7v1, tr. by Lee Patterson

Ruin seize thee, ruthless King! Bard, The [A Pindaric Ode]. Thomas Gray. OxAEP-1

Ruine of this Island, The. Margaret Lucas Cavendish, Duchess of Newcastle. EMWP

Ruined Altar, A. Rosamund Marriott Watson. ViWPN

Ruined and ill—a man of two score. Remembering Golden Bells. Po Chü-i. CCL1, tr. by Arthur Waley

Ruined City, The. Pao Chao. WoPoe, tr. by Michael Bullock and C. J. Chen

Ruined Cottage, The [see also The Wanderer, Book 1 of The Excursion]. William Wordsworth. NAEL-6v2; NAEL-7v2; NoP-4; NoP-5; NPBRoP

Ruined House, The. Jay Parini. VisFro

Ruined Maid, The. Thomas Hardy. FaBoVe; HeIP-4; NAEL-6v2; NAEL-7v2; NBLV; NIL-7; NoP-5; TFi; TRP

Ruined Motel, The. Reginald Gibbons. BodElec

Ruined so many romances. Elena Lazutkina. CRWP, tr. by Robert Reid

Ruined stone temple by the side of a lake, A. Ian Hamilton Finlay. PFTM-2 Fr. Images from the Arcadian Dream Garden.

Ruined Terrace, The. Kao Shih. CCL1, tr. by Stephen Owen

Ruines of Rome: by Bellay. Edmund Spenser.
"Who lists to see, what ever nature, arte." PBRV

Ruines of Time, The. Edmund Spenser. OxAEP-1

Ruins. T. Glynne Davies. tr. by Joseph P. Clancy
1. BBMWP, tr. by Joseph P. Clancy
2. BBMWP, tr. by Joseph P. Clancy
6. BBMWP, tr. by Joseph P. Clancy

Ruins of a Great House. Derek Walcott. BrAP; PoPoPo

Ruins of Drégel have sunk in the clouds, The. Two Pages of Szondi, The. János Arany. IQMS, tr. by Adam Makkai

Ruins of Rome. Joachim Du Bellay. tr. by Edmund Spenser
Antiquitez de Rome. OBVE
"Who list the Romane greatnes forth to figure." OBVE

Ruins of Rome, The. John Dyer. AngWePo

Ruins of Time, The. Luis de Góngora y Argote. WoPoe, tr. by Robert Lowell

Ruins of Walsingham, The. Unknown. NoSic

Ruispiri—A Comic Ballad. Bulat Shalvovich Okudzhava. RusPo, tr. by Robert Arthur Douglas Ford

Rule, The. Richard Wilbur. UpMys

Rule and Its Exception, The. Russell Edson. OxBoAm

Rule, Britannia! David Mallet and James Thomson. OBWP; TreFP; WaAnP Fr. Alfred: A Masque.

RULE: It is important not to wear out the freshness and original taste of a person's. Art of the Nickname, The. Dominique Parker. SpirFl

Rule of law was more often an ideal than a practice. Government and Binding. Mark Prejsnar. AnSo

Rule of Thirds, The. Jack Coulehan. BloBone

Rule of thumb—whatever came out of that mouth. Mouth of Him, The. David Huddle. MAAN

Rule which by obeying grows. Intellect. Ralph Waldo Emerson. APN-1; NoP-4; NoP-5

Ruler, The. Robin Blaser. FTOS

Rules, The. Philip Dacey. SUP

Rules and Ranges for Ian Tyson. Roy Fisher. Oth

Rules break like a thermometer, The. Adrienne Rich. WaAnP Fr. Twenty-one Love Poems.

Rules of Sleep. Howard Moss. VCAP

Rules of the Road, The. Carolyn Leigh. ReLy

Rum Tum Tugger, The. T. S. Eliot. TriCat

Rumanian of Maria Banus, The. George MacBeth.
Poem of Death, A. HP

Rumble, A. Virginia Schonborg. SSCS

Rumble with complacency, a bestiality beyond barking squash proclivity cherry, A. Bruce Andrews. BAP-04 Fr. Dang Me.

Rumination. Dabney Stuart. PfSP

Rummaging a drawer I found the bee glue. Resin. Patricia Pogson. NLP

Rumor. Catherine Imbriglio. IAoNAP

Rumor crecía como un torbellino, El. Jardín de madera. Dana Gelinas. SPV

Rumor had it there had been. Storm Surf. Greg Pape. MoASP

Rumor is Kate is a full blood Tonk, The. Renting. Charles S. Taylor. TiP2

Rumor persisted that the head of Pancho Villa, The. Head of Pancho Villa, The. Ray Gonzales. TiP2

Rumor was growing like a whirlwind, The. Wood Garden. Dana Gelinas. SPV, tr. by Jen Hofer

Rumorosas Pestañas. Miguel Hernández. RaW

Rumors fly and you can't tell where they start. They Say It's Wonderful. Irving Berlin. ReLy

Rumors from an Aeolian Harp. Henry David Thoreau. APN-1

Rumors of it kept my doors sealed. Potato Bug. Charles Webb. UrbNat

Rumor's Rooster. Ray DiPalma. PmAP

Rumoured thief. Sam Smith. NewEx

Rumpelstiltskin Convention. Charles Webb. ReTh

Rumpled, torpid, bored, too tasteful to rhyme. Inspiration. William Matthews. OxBoAm

Rumpelstiltskin. Glyn Maxwell. OBCoV

RUN AWAY from this sub- / scriber for the second time. Reward. Kevin Young. SpirFl

Run before Dawn. William Stafford. MoASP

Run down by fate's spite. Lament for Five Sons Lost in a Plague. Abu Dhu'ayb al-Hudhali. WoPoe, tr. by Omar S. Pound

Run! in the magpie's shadow. Yvor Winters. NAAPv.2 Fr. Magpie's Shadow, The.

Run in warm sun. African Sunrunner. Wanda Winbush-David. BtF

Run like rats from the plague in you. Saint Coleman's Song for Flight/ An Ite Missa Est. Padraic Fiacc. PNI

Run My Hand Under. Andrew Schelling. WhBo

Run, Nigger, Run! Unknown. SSUS

Run out the boat, my broken comrades. Thalassa. Louis MacNeice. BrAP; WoPoe

Run to Death. Amy Levy. ViWPN

Run your tongue down the two tendons both sides. How to Make Love to a Man. Sharon Doubiago. MAAN

Runagate Runagate. Robert Earl Hayden. APT-2; ESEAA; GM; ISC; OxAAAP; SSLK

Runaway. Nancy Mitchell. LaCa

Runaway, The. Robert Frost. MoAmPo; SAmP

Runaway Cow, A. Cathal Ó Searcaigh. ModIr, tr. by Patrick Crotty

Runaway Slave at Pilgrim's Point, The. Elizabeth Barrett Browning. NALW; ViWPN; VWP

Runaway slave came to my house and stopt outside, The. Walt Whitman. HHAm Fr. Song of Myself.

Runaway son, A. Wandering. Muso Soseki. EaWin, tr. by W. S. Merwin

Runaways Café II. Marilyn Hacker. NoAM

Runcible Thought, A. Edward Young. STuOW Fr. Resignation.

Rundown Church (Ballad of the First World War). Federico García Lorca. RaBo; WED, tr. by Robert Bly
(Rundown Church.) AF

Rune. Paul Muldoon. NewEx

Rune of the Finland Woman. Marilyn Hacker. FaoP; RA

Rune Poem, The. Unknown. tr. by James Paul
"We love the daylight." WoPoe, tr. by James Paul

Rune-Maker, The. Frederick Feirstein. RA

Runes on Weland's Sword, The. Rudyard Kipling. NoAM Fr. Puck of Pook's Hill.

Rung from their Marble Caves, repent, repent. (LL) For the Baptiste. William Drummond of Hawthornden. NPeEn; OxBEV; PBRV

Rung from their marble [or flinty] caves "Repent! Repent!" (LL) Saint John Baptist. William Drummond of Hawthornden. OBEV; OxAEP-1

Runnable Stag, A [with music]. John Davidson. OBEV

Runne (Sheepheards) run where Bethleme blest appeares. William Drummond of Hawthornden. NePenScot

Runner, The. Allen Grossman. PoCho

Runner, The. Louis Simpson. AF

Runner, The. Walt Whitman. BLT; ItP; SAmP

Runners creak, The. Dead snow broke like day. Winter Sonnets, The. Vyacheslav Ivanovich Ivanov. TCRusP, tr. by Mary Jane White

Runnin. Jamila Z. Wade. BRtP

Runnin' scared—runnin' scared. Running Scared. Miguel Piñero. PueRic

Running. Brendan Galvin. MoASP

Running [with music]. Leslie Ullman. PBCAP

Running. Richard Wilbur. MoASP

Running and. We are running. Lucille Clifton. PLBUT

Running around here & there. Politicians, The. Miyazawa Kenji. WhBo

Running down the fell, I round a rock. Yew. Elizabeth Delmore. NLP

Running downhill, spilling over, searching and spilling. Flood Water. Unknown. NOBAu, tr. by Mungayana Nundhirribala

Running from death. Death and the Dancer. Muriel Rukeyser. AF

Running from Trouble. Tu Fu [or Du Fu]. CrYelRi, tr. by Sam Hamill

Running Hares. Tessa Rose Chester. MFPA

Running into Snow While Journeying Through the Suburbs. Yu Hsin. CCL1, tr. by John Frodsham

Running Loose around the Castle. Lee McCarthy. IaFF

Running Man. Cornelius Eady. FaoP

Running over the fields. (LL) Days. Philip Larkin. NPeEn; OxAEP-2; OxBEV; PoetW; WaAnP; WoPoe

Running Scared. Miguel Piñero. PueRic

Running water is cold, the river from Eden flows east. Svetlana Kekova. CRWP, tr. by Ruth Fainlight

Running waters, crystal clear and pure. Nemoroso. Baldomero Garcilaso de la Vega. BLPSL, tr. by Rene de Costa, Rigas Kappatos and Eleni Paidoussi

Runoff. William Everson. NoAM

Runs falls rises stumbles on from darkness into darkness. Runagate Runagate. Robert Earl Hayden. APT-2; ESEAA; GM; ISC; OxAAAP; SSLK

Runt of a Dream, A. Arthur Rimbaud. WoPoe, tr. by Denis Goacher

Rupert Winds. George Stanley. NLPA Fr. Mountains and Air.

Rupert winds blowing. George Stanley. NLPA Fr. Mountains and Air.

Ruptured underbelly of a black horse flew overhead, The. Apocrypha of Jacques Derrida, The. Norman Dubie. AmAlph

Rural Gothic. Shan Neilson. IFF

Rural letter box said Toffile Lajway, The. (LL) Robert Frost. APT-1; NoAM; PoA 2002 *Fr.* Two Witches.

Rural Lyre, The. Ann Yearsley. RWP

Rural Scenes. John Clare. CenSon

Rural Sports. John Gay. DiBP

Rush hour. I board the train. Notes from the Defense of Colin Ferguson. Sekou Sundiata. ESEAA

Rush to the Lakes, The [*or* Anna Matilda]. Robert Merry. STuOW

Rushes, The. Kevin Young. LegDan

Rushes float in the stream. Stream with Washerwomen. Jorge Guillén. RaW, *tr.* by Charles Guenther

Rushing at times. Rushing at Times Like Flames. Nelly Sachs. WPoS, *tr.* by Matthew Mead *and* Ruth Mead and Ruth Mead *and* Matthew Mead

Rushing at Times Like Flames. Nelly Sachs. WPoS, *tr.* by Matthew Mead *and* Ruth Mead and Ruth Mead *and* Matthew Mead

Ruskie's Boy. Víctor Hernández Cruz. PueRic

Rusks. Rita Dove. PfSP

Russ Joy Little League. Douglas Carlson. MoASP

Russet leaves of the sycamore, The. Last Days, The. George Sterling. CalPo

Russia. Svetlana Dengina. CRWP, *tr.* by Daniel Weissbort

Russia 1812. Victor Hugo. FaBoWar; OBWP, *tr.* by Robert Lowell

Russia, I give you my divine. Velemir Khlebnikov. PoCho, *tr.* by Paul Schmidt

Russia set thousands and thousands free. Me and Russia. Velemir Khlebnikov. TCRusP, *tr.* by Kathy Lewis and Bob Perelman

Russian, The. Robert Bly. CAP-8

Russian cemetery is too shabby for dawdlers, The. Olsanski Cemetery, The. Yury Iofe. TCRusP, *tr.* by John Glad

Russian Fables. Sarah Klassen. ACAMVP

Russian God, The. Petr Andreevich Vyazemsky. WoPoe, *tr.* by Alan Myers and Alan Meyers

Russian New Year. Bill Berkson. NYP2; PmAP

Russian Soul II, The. John Hollander. NBLV

Russian Student's Tale, The. Mathilde Blind. VWP

Russians Breathing. Philip Hammial. NOBAu

Russians had few doctors on the front line, The. Russian, The. Robert Bly. CAP-8

Russia's Resentment. Lizelia Augusta Jenkins Moorer. CBWP-3

Rust and silence fill the thatch. Wole Soyinka. HBAPE

Rust Eclogues, The: Radnoti, Poetry, and the Strains of Appropriation. John Kinsella. VaPo

Rusted Legacy. Adrienne Rich. PoDa

Rustic inn, our evening resting place, A. (LL) Ruined Cottage, The. William Wordsworth. NAEL-6v2; NAEL-7v2; NoP-4; NoP-5; NPBRoP

Rustic Interior. John Armstrong. STuOW *Fr.* Art of Preserving Health, The.

Rustle from the vale—the Saint has gone out to the fields again, A. Moralist of Bananas, The. Michael Benedikt. MotU

Rustle of a page will haunt us, The. Shma Yisrael (Hear, O Israel). Galina Zelenina. CRWP, *tr.* by Daniel Weissbort

Rustle of Birches. Gennady Aygi. TCRusP, *tr.* by Peter France

Rustle of History's Wings, as They Used to Say Then, The. Yehuda Amichai. BeAI, *tr.* by Chana Bloch and Stephen Mitchell

Rustler. William Stroud. Spl

Rustling dry paper. Richard Wright. APT-2

Rustling of the silk is discontinued, The. Liu Ch'e. Emperor Wu of Han. APT-1; NDACCP; OBVE, *tr.* by Ezra Pound

Rustling the empty, bodiless grains. (LL) Ash. Jayanta Mahapatra. PoA 2002; VCWP

Rusty Man, The. Herman Melville. NCAP

Ruta. Juan Ramón Jiménez. RaW

Ruth. Mary Crockett Hill. AmPoNex

Ruth. Thomas Hood. ChIV-1; NPBRoP; OBEV

Ruth. Elizaveta Kuzmina-Karavayeva. ARWW, *tr.* by Catriona Kelly

Ruth. Norman J. Loftis. SpirFl

Ruth. Colleen J. McElroy. OxAAAP

Ruth Says. Andrew Greig. EdScPo

Ruts. Jonathan Greene. WhBo

Ruts. Arthur Rimbaud. MotU, *tr.* by Louise Varese

Rwanda. Ai. CFP

Rycht potent prince, of hie imperial blude. Dreme, The. Sir David Lyndsay.

Rye Bread. William Stanley Braithwaite. GT

Ryokan the Crazy Snow Poet. Al Robles. WhBo

(Ryokan's scroll). Louis Zukofsky. APT-2

Ryūkyū, land of the sacred *Omoro sōshi.* Final Battle for the Ryūkyū Islands, The. Takamura Kotaro. CAoMJL1, *tr.* by Leith Morton

S

S.F. homebound kearny street. Manong with a Thousand Tribal Visions, The. Al Robles. ReBoTo

S, hiss, primal sound, default letter. Wireless. Michael Symmons Roberts. RWPCtW

S.I.W. Wilfred Owen. NAMCP V.1

S.L.A.M. Giovanna Pollarolo. TANSG, *tr.* by Marjorie Agosin

S sz sz SZ sz SZ sz ZS zs Zs zs zs z. Siesta of a Hungarian Snake. Edwin Morgan. HarvBoo

S. W. Rafael Campo. BloBone

'S Wonderful. Ira Gershwin. ReLy

Saadi. Ralph Waldo Emerson. APN-1

Saba. Henry Dumas. OxAAAP

Sabbath and sweet spices. Susan Howe. PmAP *Fr.* Speeches at the Barriers.

Sabbath Bells. Josephine D. Henderson Heard. CBWP-4

Sabbath Has No End. *Unknown.* SSUS

Sabbath Morning. Marcia Falk. TaR

Sabbath, the pious carry no money. Voice out of the Sabbaths, A. Derek Walcott. WeW-3

Sabbaths. Wendell Berry.

"Another Sunday morning comes."

1979 II. UpMys

1980 VI. UpMys

1985 I. UpMys

1985 III. UpMys

"Where the great trees were felled." PfSP

Sabbaths. Robert Herrick. SacPr

Sabbaths are threefold (as S. Austine sayes:). Sabbaths. Robert Herrick. SacPr

Sable arrested a fine comb. Jack Spicer. FTOS *Fr.* Love Poems.

Sabotage. Anselm Berrigan. HeMarv

Saboteur autumn has riddled the pampered folds. Wild Honey. Francis Webb. NOBAu

Sabrina. John Milton. See Sabrina Fair.

Sabrina Fair. John Milton. OxBEV; WoPoe *Fr.* Comus; a Masque Presented at Ludlow Castle.

Sabrina's Song. John Milton. *See* Song: "By the rushy-fringèd bank."

Sacco and Vanzetti. Ber Grin. Prolet, *tr.* by Amelia Glaser

Sacrament. Countee Cullen. NAAPv.2

Sacrament. Alden Nowlan. StAl

Sacrament of Poverty, The [*for Judy Maines*]. Marilyn Nelson Waniek. ExTi; GT

Sacrament of the Altar, The. *Unknown.* NoP-4; NoP-5

Sacraments, The. Louise Erdrich. UpMys

Sacré Dieu, I said for the very first time. Hinglish. Gerald Stern. BodElec

Sacred and Profane Love, or, There's Nothing New under the Moon Either. Peter De Vries. NBLV; OBCoV

Sacred and secular. Inauguration of Fukusan Dormitory. Muso Soseki. EaWin, *tr.* by W. S. Merwin

Sacred Cow of Hardship, The. Agi Mishol. DTA, *tr.* by Tsipi Keller

Sacred Emily. Gertrude Stein. NAMCP V.1

Sacred Hatred. João da Cruz e Sousa. TCLAP, *tr.* by Flavia Vidal

Sacred marble, clothed in spirit and strength. Venus de Milo. Charles Marie René Leconte de Lisle. GS, *tr.* by *Unknown*

Sacred muse that first[e] made love divine [*or* devine], The. Sir John Davies. NoSic; OxBSo; PBRV *Fr.* Gulling[e] Sonnets, The.

Sacred night / Through masks. Kikaku. ZenPo, *tr.* by Takashi Ikemoto and Lucien Stryk

Sacred or secular. Old Man at Leisure. Muso Soseki. EaWin, *tr.* by W. S. Merwin

Sacred Religion, mother of form and fear. Samuel Daniel. NoSic *Fr.* Musophilus; or, Defence of All Learning.

Sacred Religion! "mother of form and fear." William Wordsworth. CenSon *Fr.* River Duddon [A Series of Sonnets], The.

Sacred Songs of the Konkau. *Unknown. tr.* by Stephen Powers

Acorn Song, The. APN-2

Ki-u-nad'-dis-si's Song. APN-2

Red Cloud's Song. APN-2

Sacred tree midst the fair orchard grew, The. Tree of Knowledge, The. Abraham Cowley. ChIV-1

Sacred Trees. Jayne Cortez. SurWo

Sacred Trinity, The. *Unknown.* IrV, *tr.* by Eleanor Hull

Sacred words?, The. (LL) Ka 'Ba. Imamu Amiri Baraka. ISC; PmAP

Sacred Wrath. Vahan Tekeyan. GI

Sacrifice. Albania and the Death of Enver Hoxha. Will Alexander. PFTM-2

Sacrifice. Melanie Hope. WiU

Sacrifice. Gyula Illyés. IQMS, *tr.* by Marie B. Jaffe

Sacrifice, A. Robert Davenport. NOSC

Sacrifice: An Epistle to Celia, The. Mary Leapor. PEW

Sacrifice of Isaac, The. Rabbi Ephraim ben Jacob. NAWM-7v1, *tr.* by Judah Goldin

Sacrifice, The. Frank Bidart. InoFa; VCAP

Sacrifice, The. Gertrud Kolmar. AF, *tr.* by David Kipp

Sacrifice to Apollo, The. Michael Drayton. NOSC

Sacrifice to Apollo, The. Homer. OBVE *Fr.* Iliad, The.

Sacrificed Author, A. Howard Nemerov. GI *Fr.* Gnomes.

Sacrificial Wolf. Anne Rouse. MFPA; NeBl

Sacrilege. Nina Cassian. StAl, *tr.* by William Jay Smith and Petre Solomon

Sacristy. Rachel Zucker. IAoNAP

Sacude la tristeza y tu ánimo recobra. Miguel de Unamuno. RaW *Fr.* En Casa Ya.

Sad? / (admit it). Picasso Shag. M. Loncar. AmPoNex

Sad and lonely, I sew a bag that holds heaven. From *So Mountain. Vietnamese Oral Tradition.* CaDao, *tr.* by John Balaban

Sad and solemn night, The. Hymn to the North Star. William Cullen Bryant. NCAP

Sad and solemn verse doth please the mind, A. Discourse of Melancholy, A. Margaret Lucas Cavendish, Duchess of Newcastle. NOSC

Sad beauty? Basho. EH, *tr.* by Robert Hass

Sad Birds, The. Harry Mathews. PmAP

Sad Child, A. Margaret Atwood. IJHIL

Sad Children's Song, The. Grace Paley. SoSe-8; TaR

Sad cookies, The. The once and future cookies. Cookie Poem, The. Jeff Gundy. ACAMVP

Sad creature, neck stretched out. Deer. No Ch'ŏnmyŏng. CAMKP, *tr.* by David R. McCann

Sad Day, The. Thomas Flatman. OBEV

Sad Green. Sylvia Townsend Warner. MoBrPo

Sad heart, the gymnast of inertia, does not count. Sad Indian, The. Hart Crane. PoA 2002

Sad Hesper o'er the buried sun. Alfred Tennyson. NAEL-6v2; NAEL-7v2; NoP-5 *Fr.* In Memoriam A. H. H.

Sad, I blame Mister Sky. Tao. *Vietnamese Oral Tradition.* CaDao, *tr.* by John Balaban

Sad, idle, I think of my dead mother. Red Cloth, The. *Vietnamese Oral Tradition.* CaDao, *tr.* by John Balaban

Sad Indian, The. Hart Crane. PoA 2002

Sad is our home. Mumbling. Enrique Banchs. BLPSL, *tr.* by Rene de Costa, Rigas Kappatos and Eleni Paidoussi

Sad is the burying in the sunshine. Rhyme from Lincolnshire, A. *Unknown.* NPeEn

Sad is the man who is asked for a story. Story, A. Li-Young Lee. LoL; RaBo

Sad Night of October 1959. Jaime Gil de Biedma. RaW, *tr.* by Robert Mezey and Hardie St. Martin

Sad nodes. Basho. EH, *tr.* by Robert Hass

Sad, on Broadway next afternoon. Francis Saltus Saltus. VerBaPo *Fr.* In a Book-store.

Sad, purple well! whose bubbling eye. Abel's Blood. Henry Vaughan. OBWVE

Sad refrain I heard, from poet sad, A. Forevermore. Jones Very. NCAP

Sad Remembrance. Mei Yao Ch'en. ColAnChi, *tr.* by Burton Watson

Sad Sestina. Robin Becker. BodElec

Sad Shepherd, The. Ben Jonson.
(Though I Am Young [and Cannot Tell].) NoP-4; NoP-5; WaAnP

Sad Song. Laura Kasischke. PuP-23

Sad Song. *Unknown.* ChinPo, *tr.* by Ye Weilian [*or* Yeh Wei-lien *or* Wai-lim Yip]

Sad Song. *Unknown.* CCL1, *tr.* by Burton Watson

Sad Song, A. Stephen Vincent Benét. NOxBChV

Sad song for weeping. Sad Song. *Unknown.* ChinPo, *tr.* by Ye Weilian [*or* Yeh Wei-lien *or* Wai-lim Yip]

Sad Spring-Song. Sarah Morgan Bryan Piatt. NCAP

Sad Steps. Philip Larkin. BrAP; NAEL-6v2; NAEL-7v2; NAMCP V.2; NoAM; NoP-4; NoP-5; WaAnP

Sad Story of a Little boy That Cried, The. *Unknown.* OBSP

Sad thoughts, avaunt!—the fervor of the year. William Wordsworth. CenSon

Sad, to shut / to shut other. Nearly Circle. Heather Ramsdell. AmPoNex

Sad Voices, The. Ricardo Jaimes Freyre. TCLAP, *tr.* by Iver Lofving

Sad was his countenance, if we can call. Philip Freneau. NAAL-3 *Fr.* House of Night, The.

Sad was the day when my Willie did leave me. Song. John Clare. NPBRoP

Sad was the morn', the sadder week began. Pindaric on the Death of our Late Sovereign: with an Ancient Prophecy on His Present Majority, A. Aphra Behn. BASC

Saddam Hussein the troublesome supplier. Desert Storm. Volker Braun. GTCP, *tr.* by Reinhold Grimm

Saddened by the sun. Leper. Sŏ Chŏngju. CAMKP, *tr.* by David R. McCann

Sadder Man, The. Meelaad Zakaria Youssef. AnVo, *tr.* by Mohamed Enani

Saddest day will have an eve, The. Hope. Clara Ann Thompson. CBWP-2

Saddest noise, the sweetest noise, The. Emily Dickinson. OWoS

Saddhu of Couva, The. Derek Walcott. BodElec

Saddled Ass, The. Jean de La Fontaine. NBLV, *tr.* by Deems Taylor

Sad-hearted, be at peace: the snowdrop lies. O Thou of Little Faith! George Macdonald. SacPr

Sadhu carries a lamp to the Ganges, A. Banaras Is Another Name for the World. George Kalamaras. Vesp

Sadie. Philip Hammial. BMAP

Sadie and Maud. Gwendolyn Brooks. BeAl; ESEAA; NAMCP V.2; NoAM; StAl; WaAnP *Fr.* Street in Bronzeville, A.

Sadie Snuffs a Candle. Dolores Kendrick. ESEAA

Sadie, who was only twelve, wrote each letter down. Ellis Island, September 1907. Andrea Hollander Budy. OPRER

Sadique Judith, La. Claude Cahun. YaTCFP

Sadistic Judith. Claude Cahun. YaTCFP, *tr.* by Mary Ann Caws *and* Jean-Pierre Cauvin

Sadistic Love. Julio Herrera y Reissig. BLPSL, *tr.* by Rene de Costa, Rigas Kappatos and Eleni Paidoussi

Sadly I was treated, sadly I was treated. Tohono O'odham. NAAPv.1 *Fr.* Songs for Treating Sickness, Sung durring the Four Parts of the Night.

Sadly talks the blackbird here. Deserted Home, The. *Unknown.* IrV, *tr.* by Kuno Meyer

Sadly the dead leaves rustle in the whistling wind. Church of a Dream, The. Lionel Pigot Johnson. CABP; OBMV

Sadly, though not. Like a Wind from Lotus Blossoms. Sŏ Chŏngju. CAMKP, *tr.* by David R. McCann

Sadness. Mary Elizabeth Coleridge. ViWPN

Sadness. Stephen Dunn. StAl

Sadness. Shuntaro Tanikawa. VCWP, *tr.* by Harold Wright

Sadness in Spring. *Unknown.* OBWVE, *tr.* by Gwyn Jones

Sadness in the human visage stares, The. At an Exhibition of Historical Paintings, Hobart. Vivian Smith. NOBAu

Sadness of afternoons was unmistakable, The. After the War; When Coltrane Only Wanted to Play Dance Tunes. Matthew Graham. SeSe

Sadness of Couples, The. Barbara Ras. NAPBL

Sadness of Leaving, The. Eileen Myles. PmAP

Sadness of Memory, The. Barbara Ras. NAPBL

Sadness of My Neighbors, The. James Tate. ItP

Sadness of the Sea, The. William Carlos Williams. ColAP

Sadness of their house is hard to defeat, The. There are at least three clocks per room. Clocks. Sinéad Morrissey. MoWP; NIrP

Sadness of Water, The. Paul Claudel. YaTCFP, *tr.* by James Lawler

Sadness of Windows, The. Carole Glasser Langille. Coast

Sadness, stillness in the room. Illness. Franta Bass. INSAB

Sadness, the languor of the human body, The. Paul Verlaine. SxFrPo, *tr.* by Martin Sorrell

Sae lang has Sorrow tenanted. Sae Lang Has Sorrow. Helen B. Cruickshank. EdScPo

Safaddan. Ruth Bidgood. TCAWP

Safe. Linda Bierds. RoV

Safe. Linda Gregerson. AmAlph

Safe. James Walker. OBCP

Safe from the wolf's [*or* wolves] black jaw, and the dull ass's [*or* Asses] hoof[e]. (LL) Ode to Himself, An ("Where dost [*or*; do'st] thou careless[e] lie.") Ben Jonson. BASC; CABP; NoP-4; NoP-5; NOSC; NPeEn; OxAEP-1; PBRV; WaAnP

Safe, here, now. *Unknown.* SonAtl, *tr.* by F. A. Allworth and Albert Mahera

Safe is the man with blunderbuss. Ernest. Malcolm Cowley. APT-2

Safe period. Helen Dunmore. StAl

Safe to say that most men who want. Little Essay on Communication. Stephen Dunn. PoA 2002

Safe upon the solid rock the ugly houses stand. Second Fig. Edna St. Vincent Millay. AmWit; APT-1; BLPJKO; NALW; NoP-4; NoP-5; PoA 2002

Safe, we thought. Safe. Linda Bierds. RoV

Safe-Conduct. Ingeborg Bachmann. PoSu, *tr.* by Daniel Huws

Safe-T-Man. Kate Light. AmPoNex *Fr.* Five Urban Love Songs.

Safety. Mei-Mei Berssenbrugge.
2. Eno

Safety Pins (excerpts). Radoi Ralin. CSCBP, *tr.* by Georgi Belev and Lisa Sapinkopf

Safety-Clutch. Ambrose Bierce. APN-2 *Fr.* Devil's Dictionary, The.

Saffron. David St. John. RoV

Saffron-colored leaves are cresting into their moment, The. It's. Autumnal. Mark Irwin. PuP-23

Saga of Gisli, The. *Unknown.* OBVE, *tr. by* George Johnston

Saga of Jenny, The. Ira Gershwin. ReLy

Sagacity. William Rose Benét. MoAmPo

Sagamore, The. B. P. Shillaber. TreFP

Sage Counsel. Sir Arthur Thomas Quiller-Couch. NBLV

Sage in Unison, The. Harold Stewart. NOBAu

Sage nor saint nor soldier—these were not. At the Monument to Pierre Louÿs. Richard Howard. VCAP

Sagebrush (*Artemisia*) is of the sunflower family, or Compositae. It is. Gary Snyder. APSN *Fr.* Mountains and Rivers without End: The Market.

Sage's Family, The. Francis Ponge. MotU, *tr. by* Cid Corman

Sagesse. "H. D."
   "Or is it a great tide that covers the rock-pool." WPoS

Saginaw Song, The. Theodore Roethke. NBLV

Sah Sin. Tess Gallagher. AmZen

Sahara to America, The. Aleksei Eliseievich Kruchyonykh. Sahara to America, The. PFTM-1

Said. George Starbuck. AmWit

Said a scarecrow swingin' on a pole. If I Only Had a Brain (If I Only Had a Heart) (If I Only Had the Nerve). E. Y. Harburg. ReLy

Said Abner, "At last thou art come! Ere I tell, ere thou speak." Saul. Robert Browning.

Said ("Agatha Christie to.") George Starbuck. AmWit; OBCoV

Said an erudite sinologue: "How." Limerick. R. J. P. Hewison. OBCoV

Said ("Dame Edith Evans to.") George Starbuck. AmWit

Said God, You sisters, ere ye go. Hope and Despair. Lascelles Abercrombie. OBMV

Said I many times. I'm Glad There Is You (In This World of Ordinary People). Paul Madeira. ReLy

Said ("J. Alfred Prufrock to.") George Starbuck. AmWit

Said Jerome K. Jerome to Ford Madox Ford. Mutual Problem. William Cole. OBCoV

Said King Pompey. Dame Edith Sitwell. UV

Said Mario Praz to Mario Pei. Miniature Dialogue. Edmund Wilson. OBCoV

Said Philip Sidney, buttoning his jerkin. Edmund Wilson. OBCoV *Fr.* Easy Exercises in the Use of Difficult Words.

Said, Pull her up a bit will you, Mac, I want to unload there. Reason. Josephine Miles. ASA; NALW; NoAM; OxBoAm

Said the chief of the marriage feast to the groom. Wedding Feast, The. Edgar Lee Masters. ChIV-2

Said the lady, *Can you do*. Question. Langston Hughes. APSN

Said the Lion to the Lioness—'When you are amber dust'. Heart and Mind. Dame Edith Sitwell. LW

Said the speaker. Michael Palmer. APSN

Said the table to the chair. Table and the Chair, The. Edward Lear. ITBLP

Said the Undertaker to the Overtaker. Tweedledee and Tweedledoom. Ogden Nash. OBCoV

Said the Victory of Samothrace. Japanese Beetles [2003]. X. J. Kennedy. AmWit

Said the whitrick to the stoat. Fur Coats. James King Annand. EdScPo

Said the Wind to the Moon, 'I will blow you out;'. Wind and the Moon, The. George Macdonald. NOxBChV

Said to the children, and they fell asleep. (LL) My Father in the Night Commanding No. Louis Simpson. HeIP-4; NAMCP V.2; NoAM; OxBoAm

Said Zwingli to Muntzer. How to Start a War. Phyllis McGinley. OBSV

Saigon River slides past the Old Market, The. Saigon River, The. *Vietnamese Oral Tradition.* CaDao, *tr. by* John Balaban

Sail Away. Noël Coward. ReLy

Sail before the morning breeze. Archipelago, The. Herman Melville. APN-2

Sail is up, Fortune ruleth our helm, The. John Skelton. NoSic *Fr.* Bouge of Court, The.

Sail me. Nokhem Vaysman. Prolet *Fr.* On the Hudson.

Sail, Monarchs, rising and falling. Roots and Branches. Robert Duncan. CalPo; FTOS

Sail, O believer, sail, / Sail over yonder. Sail, O Believer. *Unknown.* SSUS

Sail spread, you're ready. Seeing Off the Mountain Monk Ch'u, Returning to Japan. Chia Tao. CSKM, *tr. by* Mike O'Connor

Sailboats in line. Hokushi. ZenPo, *tr. by* Takashi Ikemoto and Lucien Stryk

Sailed. Ina Coolbrith. NAAPv.1

Sailed. Aaron Shurin. FTOS

Sailing. Richard Kenney. YaYoPo

Sailing. Henrik Nordbrandt. VCWP, *tr. by* Henrik Norbrandt *and* Alexander Taylor and Alexander Taylor

Sailing above our shadow. George Stanley. NLPA *Fr.* Mountains and Air.

Sailing Back to the Capital. Chan Fang-sheng. ChinPo, *tr. by* Ye Weilian [*or* Yeh Wei-lien *or* Wai-lim Yip]

Sailing Down the Han. Wang Wei. CrYelRi, *tr. by* Sam Hamill

Sailing Home from Rapallo. Robert Lowell. InoFa; PoetW; PoPoPo

Sailing into the South Lake. Chan Fang-sheng. ChinPo, *tr. by* Ye Weilian [*or* Yeh Wei-lien *or* Wai-lim Yip]

Sailing on Men River, I heard. Soan. ZenPo, *tr. by* Takashi Ikemoto and Lucien Stryk

Sailing Through the Gorges. Yang Wan-li. WoPoe, *tr. by* Kuangchi C. Chang

Sailing to an Island. Richard Murphy. ModIr; PBCIP

Sailing to Bien Hoa. Bruce Weigl. MotU

Sailing to Byzantium. William Butler Yeats. AmFaPo; BLPJKO; BrAP; CABP; ClHu; EMP; HarvBoo; HeIP-4; MoBrPo; NAEL-6v2; NAEL-7v2; NAMCP V.1; NAWM-7v2; NIL-7; NIP-4; NoAM; NoP-4; NoP-5; NPeEn; OBMV; OWoS; OxBEV; PoPoPo; RaBo; SoSe-8; TFi; WaAnP; WeW-3; WoPoe

Sailor. Langston Hughes. PoA 2002

Sailor. Vicente Huidobro. TCLAP, *tr. by* David Guss

Sailor. Gerry Gomez Pearlberg. WiU

Sailor, A. Ivan Slamnig. PML, *tr. by* Vasa D. Mihailovich and Charles David Wright

Sailor, The. Safaa Fathy. PoArWo, *tr. by* S. V. Atalla

Sailor, The. Geof Hewitt. GoPo

Sailor, The. Sylvia Townsend Warner. OBMV

"Sailorman, I'll give to you." Silver Penny, The. Walter De la Mare. NOxBChV; OBMV

Sailor and the Shark, The. Paul Fort. OBMV, *tr. by* Frederick York Powell

Sailor Boy's Song. *Unknown.* CA

Sailor fishes for herring, The. Aria. Irène Hamoir. SurWo, *tr. by* Myrna Bell Rochester

Sailor leaning on the rail thinks of home, The. One Day. Ray Mathew. NOBAu

Sailor sailor got ashore. Irina Shostakovskaya. CRWP, *tr. by* Daniel Weissbort

Sailor's Carol. Charles Causley. OBCP

Sailor's Harbor. Henry Reed. MoBrPo

Sailor's Mother, The. William Wordsworth.
   Mother's Quest, A. STuOW

Sailors Shielding Their Eyes During Atomic Bomb Test, Bikini, 1947. John Bradley. AtGh

Sailors' Song. Thomas Lovell Beddoes. OxAEP-2

Sailor's Song. Slavko Janevski. WoPoe,

Sailplane, sliver of ice, seen. Flight Instructor. James Applewhite. OtW

Sails out of sleep / Steering for dream. (LL) Now is a ship / which captain am. E. E. Cummings. EmeKit; Spl

Sails shred, the steering goes, and waves roar doom. Storm, The. Adam Mickiewicz. WoPoe, *tr. by* Vyt Bakaitis

Saint. Stéphane Mallarmé. NAWM-7v2, *tr. by* Henry Weinfield

Saint. Stéphane Mallarmé. SxFrPo, *tr. by* A. M. and E. H. Blackmore

St Agnes' Eve—Ah, bitter chill it was! Eve of St. Agnes, The. John Keats. CABP; NAEL-6v2; NAEL-7v2; NOBRP; NoP-4; NoP-5; NPBRoP; NPeEn; OBNV; OxAEP-2; TFi; TRP; WaAnP

St. Agnes' Eve. Alfred Tennyson. OBEV; SacPr

St Andrew's Day, blind November fumbling. St. Andrew's Day. Robert Greacen. PNI

St Andrews town may look right gawsy. To the Principal and Professors of the University of St Andrews, on their Superb Treat to Dr Samuel Johnson. Robert Fergusson. NePenScot

Saint Animal. Chase Twichell. StAl

St. Anzas VI. B. P. Nichol. FTOS

St. Anzas IX. B. P. Nichol. FTOS

St. Aubin d'Aubigne. Paul Dehn. OBWP

Saint Augustine, thy praise was sung by one. Richard Henry Wilde. APN-1 *Fr.* Hesperia.

St. Bees in Winter. William Scammell. NLP

Saint Bernards carry the food bowl, not him. Pasting relics, The. Abel and Abel. Silvio Giussani. ItPo, *tr. by* Gayle Ridinger

St. Bride's. Kathleen Jamie. MoWP; NePenScot

St. Brides: Sea-Mail. Don Paterson. NeBrP

St Brigid's night and we lie in separate beds. Conor O'Callaghan. NIrP *Fr.* Loose Change.

St. Christopher. Austin Clarke. ModIr

Saint Clare. Louise Erdrich. UpMys

St. Clare's Underwear. Barbara Hamby. ReTh

Saint Coleman's Song for Flight/ An Ite Missa Est. Padraic Fiacc. PNI

St. David's Head. Sir Lewis Morris.
   "Salt sprays deluge it, wild waves buffet it, hurricanes rave." AngWePo

St Francias came to me alive last night and tole me. I Dream of St. Francis. Peter Orlovsky. BB

Saint Francis and the Sow. Galway Kinnell. AmFaPo; BeAl; ChAP; NAAL-5; OxBoAm; P180; TWF

St. Francis and the Nun. Carl Dennis. KGB

St. Francis Speaks to Me at a Young Age. Vic Coccimiglio. InvLad

St. Govan [*with music*]. A. G. Prys-Jones. OBWVE

St. Helena Lullaby, A. Rudyard Kipling. FaBoWar; OBMV

Saint in penitence shouts, The. Weddings of Flowers Take Place upon the Stigma, The. María Baranda. RMCMP, *tr. by* Mónica de la Torre

St. Jacob's Church of the Hanging Hand. James Ragan. Vesp

St James's Phenomenon, The. Leigh Hunt.
"Good people all attend now." NPBRoP

St Jerome and His Lion. *Unknown*. TriCat

St Jerome in his study kept a great big cat. St Jerome and His Lion. *Unknown*. TriCat

Saint Jerome lived with a community. Elegy for Wright & Hugo. Norman Dubie. NoAM

St. John. Bible, *N.T. tr. by* Richard Crashaw
"I am the true vine, and my Father is the husbandman." OBVE
"In the beginnin o aa things the Wurd wis there ense." FaBoVe
John 3; But Men Loved Darknesse Rather than Light. ChIV-2

St. John. Jorge Luis Borges.
John 1:14; And the Word became flesh and dwelt among us. GI

St. John. Mary Elizabeth Fullerton.
John 14:1–2. GI

St. John. Gail Holst-Warhaft.
John 1:1 and 14. GI

St. John. Nina Kossman.
John 13:21–30; When Jesus had thus said, he was troubled. GI

St. John. Howard Nemerov.
John 3:1–15; Now there was a man. GI

St. John. Pier Paolo Pasolini.
John 12:24–25; Truly, truly, I say to you. GI

St. John. Rainer Maria Rilke.
John 2:1–12; On the third day there was a marriage. GI

St. John. Rainer Maria Rilke.
John 11:30–44; Now Jesus had not yet come to the village. GI

St. John. Rainer Maria Rilke.
John 20:11–18; But Mary stood weeping outside the tomb. GI

Saint John Baptist. William Drummond of Hawthornden. OBEV; OxAEP-1
(For the Baptist.) ChIV-2; RSR

Saint John divinely counsels us. Praise of Godly Love Out of 1 John. 4, The. John Hall. ChIV-2

St. John, whose love indulg'd my labours past. First Epistle of the First Book of Horace Imitated, The. Alexander Pope.

Saint Judas. James Wright. GI; NAMCP V.2

St Kilda. Neil Curry. NLP

St Kilda's Parliament: 1879–1979. Douglas Dunn. NePenScot

St Kildan Congregation. Derick Thomson. EdScPo

St. Louis. Amy Lowell. NAAL-5

St. Louis Cemetery Crypt. Kalamu ya Salaam. SpirFl *Fr.* New Orleans Haiku.

St. Louis Zoo, The. Carol Frost. CAP-8

St. Luke. W. H. Auden.
Luke 23:26–38; And as they led him away. GI

St. Luke. W. H. Auden.
Luke 23:26–38; And as they led him away. GI

St. Luke. Bible, *N.T. tr. by* Richard Crashaw
"And it came to pass in those days, that there went out a decree from Caesar Augustus." NAWM-5v1
Blessed be the Paps which Thou hast Sucked. ChIV-2; NOSC
"Feare not, litle flocke, for it is your fathers good pleasure to give you the kingdome." OBVE
Luke 7; She Began To Wash His Feet with Teares and Wipe Them with the Haires of Her Head. NOSC; SacPr
"Then drew near unto him all the publicans and sinners." NAWM-5v1

St. Luke. Jorge Luis Borges.
Luke 23:39–43; One of the criminals. GI

St. Luke. Bertolt Brecht.
Luke 2:8–20; And in that region there were shepherds. GI

St. Luke. Ernesto Cardenal.
Luke 16:1–9; He also said to the disciples. GI

St. Luke. T. S. Eliot.
Luke 2:21–40; And at the end of eight days, when he was circumcised. GI

St. Luke. Robert Frost.
Luke 16:19–26; "There was a rich man." GI

St. Luke. Louise Glück.
Luke 2:1–7; In those days a decree went out from Caesar Augustus. GI

St. Luke. Alec Derwent Hope.
Luke 24:36–49; As they were saying this, Jesus. GI

St. Luke. Anna Kamienska.
Luke 1:26–38; In the sixth month the angel Gabriel. GI

St. Luke. Anna Kamienska.
Luke 10:38–42; Now as they went on their way. GI

St. Luke. Czeslaw Milosz.
Luke 5:1–11; While the people pressed upon him. GI

St. Luke. Stephen Mitchell.
Luke 10:25–37; And behold, a lawyer. GI

St. Luke. Eric Pankey.
Luke: 24:13–32; That very day two of them. GI

St. Luke. Rainer Maria Rilke.
Luke 1:39–56: In those days Mary arose. GI

St. Luke. Rainer Maria Rilke.
Luke 15:11–19; And he said, "There was a man." GI

St. Luke. Edwin Arlington Robinson.
Luke 15:20–32; And he arose and came. GI

Saint Margaret of Cortona. Eiléan Ní Chuilleanáin. ModIr

Saint Margaret's Legend. Endre Ady. IQMS, *tr. by* Anton N. Nyerges

St. Mark. Bible, *N.T.*
"Aa this while, Peter wis doun ablò i the yaird." FaBoVe
"And he said, So is the kingdome of God." OBVE
And he said, So soule doth magnifie the Lord. OBVE

St. Mark. Czeslaw Milosz.
Mark 5:21–43; And when Jesus had crossed. GI

St. Mark. Boris Leonidovich Pasternak.
Mark 14:26–42; And when they had sung. GI

Saint Martha. Anna Kamienska. GI, *tr. by* David Curzon and Grażyna Drabik

Saint Mary Magdalene or The Weeper. Richard Crashaw. BASC; ChIV-2 (Weeper, The.) OBEV

St. Matthew. Philip Appleman.
Matthew 1:18–25: Now the birth of Jesus Christ took place. GI

St. Matthew. Bible, *N.T.*
"And seeing the multitudes, he went up." NAWM-5v1
"And seeing the multitudes, he went up into the mountain: and when he was set, his disciples came unto him." BLPJKO
Beatitudes, The. OBVE
"In the end of the sabbath, as it began to dawn toward the first day of the week." NAWM-5v1
"No man can serve two masters." OBVE
"Then one of the twelve, called Judas Iscariot." NAWM-5v1
"When morning has come, all the chief priests and elders of the people." NAWM-5v1

St. Matthew. Jorge Luis Borges.
Matthew 25:14–30; "For it will be as when a man." GI
Matthew 5:1–12; Seeing the crowds, he went up on the mountain. GI

St. Matthew. René Daumal.
Matthew 27:11–24; Now Jesus stood before. GI

St. Matthew. T. S. Eliot.
Matthew 2:1–12; Now when Jesus was born. GI

St. Matthew. Jacob Glatstein.
Matthew 5:38–48; "You have heard that it was said, 'An eye'." GI

St. Matthew. Donald Hall.
Matthew 21:18–22; In the morning. GI

St. Matthew. Julia Hartwig.
Matthew 2:16–18; Then Herod, when he saw. GI

St. Matthew. Zbigniew Herbert.
Matthew 27:3–10; When Judas, his betrayer, saw. GI

St. Matthew. Gail Holst-Warhaft.
Matthew 5:13; You are the salt of the earth. GI

St. Matthew. Ted Hughes.
Matthew 27:45–56; Now from the sixth hour there was darkness. GI

St. Matthew. Anna Kamienska.
Matthew 19:16–24; And behold, one came up to him. GI

St. Matthew. Karl Kirchwey.
Matthew 8:20; And Jesus said to him. GI

St. Matthew. Philip Larkin.
Matthew 10:1. GI

St. Matthew. D. H. Lawrence.
Matthew 6:7–15; "And in praying do not heap up empty." GI

St. Matthew. Desanka Maksimovic.
Matthew 22:15–22; Then the Pharisees went and. GI

St. Matthew. Czeslaw Milosz.
Matthew 4:1–11; Then Jesus was led up by the spirit. GI

St. Matthew. Czeslaw Milosz.
   Matthew 28:1–6; Now after the sabbath. GI
St. Matthew. Stephen Mitchell.
   Matthew 13:1–9; That same day Jesus. GI
St. Matthew. Boris Leonidovich Pasternak.
   Matthew 21:1–11. GI
St. Matthew. Boris Leonidovich Pasternak.
   Matthew 26:47–56; While he was still speaking, Judas came. GI
St. Matthew. Rainer Maria Rilke.
   Matthew 26:17–29. GI
St. Matthew. Rainer Maria Rilke.
   Matthew 27:57–61; When it was evening, there came a rich man. GI
St. Matthew. Edwin Arlington Robinson.
   Matthew 22:1–14; And again Jesus spoke to them. GI
St. Matthew. Theodore Roethke.
   Matthew 7:1–2; "Judge not, that you be not." GI
St. Matthew. Richard Wilbur.
   Matthew 8:28–34; And when he came to the other side. GI
St. Matthew. William Butler Yeats.
   Matthew 24:15–31. GI
   Matthew 28:16–20; Now the eleven disciples went to Galilee. GI
St. Matthew; He also told them a parable. William Carlos Williams.
   Luke 6:39. GI
St. Merri district, The. Robert Desnos. MFP, *tr. by* Martin Sorrell
St. Michael and all Angels. Christina Georgina Rossetti. SacPr
St Patrick's Breastplate. Saint Patrick. SacPr, *tr. by* Frances Alexander
Saint Patrick's Breastplate; or, The Deer's Cry. Saint Patrick. IrV, *tr. by* Kuno Meyer
St. Patrick's Hymn Before Tara. James Clarence Mangan.
   "Christ, as a light." SacPr
St. Paul. Thomas Merton. ChIV-2
St. Peter and the Angel. Denise Levertov. SacPr
St. Peter Claver. Toi Derricotte. LTA; PBCAP
St. Peter once: "Lord, dost Thou wash my feet?" St. Peter. Christina Georgina Rossetti. ChIV-2
Saint Peter sat by the celestial gate. Vision of Judgment, The. Lord Byron. NAEL-6v2
St. Peter's Hospital. Nursery. No Hyangnim. EcSo, *tr. by* Aimee N. Kwon
Saint Ras. Anthony McNeill. WaCA
St. Roach. Muriel Rukeyser. PLBUT
Saint Rose of Lima. Judith Ortiz Cofer. PueRic; TouFir
St Sava's Forge. Vasco [*or* Vasko] Popa. PoSu *Fr.* St Sava's Spring.
St Sava's Journey. Vasco [*or* Vasko] Popa. PoSu; WoPoe *Fr.* St Sava's Spring.
St Sava's Spring. Vasco [*or* Vasko] Popa. *tr. by* Anne Pennington
   Life of St Sava, The. PoSu
   St Sava's Forge. PoSu
   St Sava's Journey. PoSu; WoPoe, *tr. by* Anne Pennington
St. Saviour's, Aberdeen Park, Highbury, London, N. Sir John Betjeman. SacPr
St. Stephen's Day. Patric Dickinson. OBCP
St. Stephen's is a stage. Patriot's Progress, The. Horace Twiss. UV
St. Thomas. Christopher Smart. ChIV-2 *Fr.* Hymns and Spiritual Songs for the Fasts and Festivals of the Church of England.
St. Thomas Aquinas. Charles Simic. OxBoAm
St. Thomas's Day. Gillian Clarke. HarvBoo
Saint Ursula of Llangwyryfon. Gwyn Williams. AngWePo
St. Vincent's. W. S. Merwin. CAP-8; VCAP
Saint Vitus's Dance in October 10. Leonard Nolens. TuT, *tr. by* Michael O'Loughlin
Sainte Lucie. Derek Walcott.
   "Pomme arac." FaBoVe
Sainte-Chapelle. John Taggart. FTOS
Saint-Lô. Samuel Beckett. NPeEn
Saints. Amy Gerstler. ExTi
Saints. Arielle Greenberg. BAP-04; LegDan
Saints. Lana C. Williams. BtF
Saints and Strangers. Andrew Hudgins. *See* At the Piano.
Saints are in such wise from God's own godhead drunk, The. "Angelus Silesius." GePo *Fr.* Cherubical Wanderer, The.
Saints' Encouragement, The. Alexander Brome. BASC
Saint's First Wife Said, The. G. E. Patterson. IIR
Saint's Logic. Linda Gregerson. ExTi; PoDa
Saints of Four Seasons! Feilire of Adamnan, The. *Unknown.* IrV, *tr. by* Patrick Joseph McCall
Saints of Jazz are playing, The. Saints of Jazz. Yevgeny Aleksandrovich Yevtushenko. SeSe

Saisir. Henri Michaux. *tr. by* Pierre Joris
   "One evening an exceptionally abstract communication came over the airwaves." PFTM-2, *tr. by* Pierre Joris
Saith man to man, We've heard and known. No Master, High or Low! William Morris. RSaN
Sakai Harbor. Yosano Akiko. ASA, *tr. by* Janine Beichman
Sake Gold. William Heyen. AmZen
Saki, offer the cup, let them call me a drunkard. Sheyhülislâm Yahya Efendi. OLP, *tr. by* Walter Andrews, Najaat Black and Mehmet Kalpakli
Sakura. Mike O'Connor. WANABP
Sākyamuni Buddha entered nirvana. At My Mother's Funeral. Sabok. BecRai, *tr. by* Kim Daljin, Kim Won-Chung and Christopher Merrill
Salad, A. Sydney Goodsir Smith. NBLV
   (Recipe for a Salad.) OBCoV
Salad Days. Bruce Berger. SwNoth
Salad Days. Susan Musgrave. NoAM
Salad of greens! Salad of greens! Universal Favorite, The. Carolyn Wells. NBLV
Salamander. Ingrid de Kok. TSAP
Salamander. Robert Thomas. FaoP
Salamanders. A. K. Ramanujan. PoetW
Salami. Philip Levine. TRP; WaAnP
Sale. Josephine Miles. APT-2
Sale began—young girls were there, The. Slave Auction, The. Frances Ellen Watkins Harper. APN-2; ColAP; ISC; NAAPv.1; PCW
Sale of a Historian's Library. Yelena Shwarts. ARWW, *tr. by* Catriona Kelly
Sale of Souls [*with music*]. Adah Isaacs Menken. CBWP-1
Salem. T. Rowland Hughes. BBMWP, *tr. by* Sally Roberts Jones
Salem, Indiana, 1983. Richard Newman. LiTh
Sales. Arthur Rimbaud. SxFrPo, *tr. by* Martin Sorrell
Sales Talk for Annie. Morris Gilbert Bishop. NBLV
Salesman, A. E. E. Cummings. NoAM
Salesman is an it that stinks excuse, A. Salesman, A. E. E. Cummings. NoAM
Salgo de ti como tu sombra. Shakti. Elsa Cross. RMCMP
Salisbury Plain. Elizabeth Robinson. AmPoNex
Salisbury Plain. William Wordsworth.
   "Four years each day with daily bread was blest." NPBRoP
Sall God's ain sel' them wile. (LL) Sauchs in the Reuch Heuch Hauch, The. Hugh MacDiarmid. NAMCP V.1; NoAM
Sallie sits beside me as we wait for you and studies the painting of the hot-air ballon. Revisionary Instruments 1. Kathy Fagan. ExTi
Sally [*with music*]. Paul Durcan. IrLP
Sally, I was happy with *you*. Sally. Paul Durcan. IrLP
Sally in Our Alley. Henry Carey. OBEV; OxAEP-1
   (Ballad of Sally in Our Alley, The.) WaAnP
Sally is gone that was so kindly. Ha'nacker Mill. Joseph Hilaire Pierre Belloc. MoBrPo
Sally Simpkin's Lament. Thomas Hood. CABP
Salma in Wonderland. Mona Fayad. PoArWo
Salmon. Jorie Graham. FaoP; StAl
Salmon, The. Duane Niatum. PoCoUp
10 The Salmon. Conor O'Callaghan. NIrP *Fr.* Loose Change.
Salmon Brook. Henry David Thoreau. TCAPo
Salmon Fishing. Robinson Jeffers. APT-1; NAAPv.2
Salmon lying in the depths of Llyn Llifon, The. Ancients of the World, The. Ronald Stuart Thomas. OPOU
Salmon's leap, The. Shannon Estuary Welcomes the Fish, The. Nuala Ni Dhomhnaill. ModIr, *tr. by* Patrick Crotty
Salome. Ai. NoAM
Salomé. Silvia Grénier. SurWo, *tr. by* Natalie Kenvin
Salome. Charles Lamb and Mary Lamb. ChIV-2
Salon de Vers. Orrick Johns. APT-1
Salon, Salon. Louis Cabri. PoPra
Saloon is gone up the creek, The. William Carlos Williams. APT-1 *Fr.* Folded Skyscraper, A.
Saloon with Birds. Christopher Middleton. HarvBoo
Salopian. Peter Reading. NeBrP
Salt. George Barlow. GT
Salt. Günter Eich. MotU, *tr. by* David Walker
Salt. Patricia Y. Ikeda. MotU
Salt. Yusef Komunyakaa. OPRER; UnSA
Salt air flutters them, cradles. Hydrangeas. Joan Houlihan. IAoNAP
Salt comes in with the wind. Turnip Field. John Thompson. Coast
Salt Garden, The. Howard Nemerov. OBGa
Salt grass silent of hooves, the lake stinks. Basil Bunting. PFTM-1

Salt groups itself in a constellation of birds on the cotton tumor.   White Giant Leper of the Countryside.   Tristan Tzara.   YaTCFP, *tr.* by Mary Ann Caws *and* Jean-Pierre Cauvin

Salt Lake, The.   Iwan Goll.   WoPoe, *tr.* by George Hitchcock

"Salt / lick!" deer on waste sing.   Lu-ming: Salt Lick!   *Unknown.*   CCL1, *tr.* by Ezra Pound

Salt Longing.   Austin Hummell.   AmPoNex

Salt on their lips. (LL)   Passionate World, The.   Anne Michaels.   BeAl; PoDa

Salt Pork, The.   Robert Clayton Casto.   HeIP-4

Salt shining behind its glass cylinder.   Morning.   Mary Oliver.   NIL-7

Salt sprays deluge it, wild waves buffet it, hurricanes rave.   Sir Lewis Morris.   AngWePo *Fr.* St. David's Head.

Salt water. and faces dying.   Elegy.   Frank O'Hara.   AHA

Salt Water Story.   Richard Hugo.   NoAM

Saltbox Brothel.   Danielle Pafunda.   BeDoSh

Saltcoats Structuralists, The.   Robert Crawford.   NeBrP

Salter's Gate.   Anne Stevenson.   PfSP

Salting of Snow, A.   Hamish Brown.   EdScPo

Salting the Brae.   Martin Mooney.   NIrP

Saltos Sobre El Exilio.   Alicia Kozameh.   *tr.* by David Davis

   "It's aborbed, perceived, partially picked up. The brighness envelops."   MirDau, *tr.* by David Davis

   "Presence. Opposites. Absence. Forces exercising pressure against."   MirDau, *tr.* by David Davis

   "We will mention it. We will remember and mention."   MirDau, *tr.* by David Davis

Salty like my seashores.   Maysoun Saqr Al-Qasimi.   PoArWo *Fr.* Morning of Every Sin, The.

Salty water, to begin again, The. (LL)   Offering.   Sharan Strange.   FuFl; GT

Salu lú nisadó nexhedxí.   Na hermila limón.   Natalia Toledo.   RMCMP

Saluste du Bartas' Devine Weekes.   Joshua Sylvester.

   "Cunning Painter, that with curious care, The."   PBRV

Salut du jeune soleil, Le.   Léopold Sédar Senghor.   YaTCFP

Salutation.   Robert Herrick.   CavPo; ChIV-2

Salutation.   Ezra Pound.   HeIP-4; MoAmPo; NAAPv.2; OxBoAm

Salutation, A.   Louise Imogen Guiney.   APN-2

Salutation [*or* Salutations], The.   Thomas Traherne.   NoP-4; NoP-5; SacPr   (Salutation, The.)   NoP-4

Salutations to the goddess who dwells in all things as.   Tantric Praise of the Goddess.   *Unknown.*   HW, *tr.* by Jalaja Bonheim

Salute to Property.   Ambrose Philips.   STuOW *Fr.* To the Right Honourable Charles Lord Halifax [one of the Lords Justices appointed by his Majesty].

Salute we must, nor strangers, kin, or friends. (LL)   Salutation.   Robert Herrick.   CavPo; ChIV-2

Salvador.   Paul Muldoon.   NAMCP V.2 *Fr.* 7, Middagh Street.

Salvation.   Scott Cairns.   UpMys

Salvation.   James Kimbrell.   LegDan

Salvation bought, sin sold.   Hermit with Landscape.   Daniel Hall.   YaYoPo

Salvator Mundi: Via Crucis.   Denise Levertov.   UpMys

Salve!   Thomas Edward Brown.   OBEV

Salve Deus Rex Judaeorum.   Emilia Lanier.

   (Eve's Apology in Defense of Women.)   NAEL-7v1

   "Now Pontius Pilate is to judge the cause."   EMWP; NAEL-6v1; NALW; NOSC

Salve Deus Rex Judaeorum.   Emilia Lanier and Aemilia Bassano Lanyer.

   "Our Mother *Eve,* who tasted of the Tree."   PBRV

   "Sith Cynthia is ascended to that rest."   BASC; NoP-4; NoP-5

   To the Queen's Most Excellent Majesty.   NAEL-7v1

Salvos of Mercy.   Ibrahim Nasrallah.

   "In the beginning / The horses said, we need plains."   Eno

Sam.   Lucille Clifton.   UnSA

Sam.   Walter De la Mare.   MoBrPo

Sam Bass.   Gene Shuford.   TiP2

Sam Jackson.   Frank Marshall Davis.   APT-2

Sam, Sam, the butcher man.   *Unknown.*   TLR

Sam was a family embarrassment.   Uncle.   Ellie McDonald.   EdScPo

Samaki.   Seitlhamo Motsapi.   TSAP

Samantha is my.   Samantha Is My Negro Cat.   William J. Harris.   GT

Samantha Is My Negro Cat.   William J. Harris.   GT

Samaritans.   Gerald Stern.   GPPA

Samba.   Robert Pinsky.   BAP-04

Samch'ŏnp'o.   Paek Sŏk.   CAMKP, *tr.* by Kyunghwan Choi

Same Air, The.   Al Zolynas.   SUP

Same as ever to the sight, The. (LL)   Mill, The.   Edwin Arlington Robinson.   APT-1; NAAPv.1; NAMCP V.1; NoAM; NoP-4; NoP-5; WeW-3

Same as, The.   Hotel.   Alfonso D'Aquino.   RMCMP, *tr.* by Rebecca Seiferle

Same Corpse, The.   Kojo Laing.   HBAPE

Same Cottage—But Another Song, of Another Season.   Max Beerbohm.   UV

Same Gesture, The.   John Montague.   ModIr; PNI *Fr.* Great Cloak, The.

Same in Blues.   Langston Hughes.   APSN; APT-2; OxBoAm; SSLK *Fr.* Lenox Avenue Mural.

Same Inside, The [*with music*].   Anna Swirszczynska [*or* Swir].   BLT

Same look which she turn'd [*or* turned] when he rose, The. (LL)   Believe Me, If All Those Endearing Young Charms.   Thomas Moore.   NAEL-6v2; NAEL-7v2

Same low sky, The.   Every Metaphor.   Milo De Angelis.   ItPo, *tr.* by Gayle Ridinger

Same melody of.   Car Music.   Reed Bye.   AHA

Same Month They Bombed Cambodia, The.   Amy Uyematsu.   OpBo

Same rough brown, The. (LL)   Traitor.   Allison Joseph.   IllVoic; SUP

Same Side of the Canoe, The.   Alda do Espirito Santo.   HAWP, *tr.* by Allan Francovich and Kathleen Weaver

Same Subject, The.   William Wordsworth.   CenSon *Fr.* River Duddon, The.

Samela.   Robert Greene.   OBEV

Sammy Davis, Jr.   Jacqueline Jones LaMon.   BRtP

Sammy Lou of Rue.   Revolutionary Petunias.   Alice Walker.   NIL-7

Samocrate, Naso and Nigidius.   Scourge of Folly, The.   John Davies of Hereford.

Sampler City.   Christine Hume.   LegDan

Samson.   Primo Levi.   PML, *tr.* by Ruth Feldman

Samson Agonistes.   John Milton.   BASC; NAEL-6v1

   "All is best, though we oft doubt."   NOSC; OBEV; OxBEV

   "But peace, I must not quarrel with the will."   NoP-5

   "But what is strength without a double share."   ChIV-1

   Deliverer, The.   OBEV; OxAEP-1

   "Just are the ways of God."   InvLi

   Samson before the Prison in Gaza.   OxAEP-1; WoPoe

   Samson's Complaint.   NOSC

Samson Agonistes.   Ogden Nash.   APT-2; OBCoV

Samson before the Prison in Gaza.   John Milton.   OxAEP-1; WoPoe *Fr.* Samson Agonistes.

Samson of Tinnata, the rebel.   Delilah.   Primo Levi.   PML, *tr.* by Ruth Feldman

Samson to His Delilah.   Richard Crashaw.   ChIV-1

Samson's Complaint.   John Milton.   NOSC *Fr.* Samson Agonistes.

Samuel.   Judith Baumel.   TaR

Samuel Brown.   Phoebe Cary.   APN-2; NAAPv.1

Samuel Sewall.   Anthony Hecht.   NBLV

Samuel's Prayer.   John Keble.   ChIV-1

Samurai Song.   Robert Pinsky.   OxBoAm

San Antonio Nights.   Bryce Milligan.   TiP2

San Antonio, / They called you lazy.   San Antonio.   Carmen Tafolla.   TiP2

San Buenaventura.   Maurina Sherman.   GeoHom

San Diego Goodbye—*1944, Jacksaw Arena.*   Murray Jackson.   OxAAAP

San Diego (On a rainy day).   Lamea Abbas Amara.   PoArWo, *tr.* by Nathalie Handal and Mike Maggio

San Diego Poem, A: January-February 1973.   Simon J. Ortiz.   OtW

San Francisco.   Miguel Algarin.   PmAP

2. San Francisco.   Kate Light.   PoDa *Fr.* Five Urban Love Songs.

San Francisco remains in grave personal.   Jeane Dixon's America.   Gerald Costanzo.   ReTh

San Francisco Streets.   Thom Gunn.   CalPo

San Francisco Sunrise.   Diane Ackerman.   UrbNat

San Jacinto.   Mirabeau Buonaparte Lamar.   TiP2

San Jacinto Plaza.   Ray Gonzalez.   UrbNat

San Joaquin.   David Oliveira.   GeoHom

San José: A Poem.   Cynthia Gomez.   FTtHH

San Juan.   June Jordan.   EGAG

San Luis, New Mexico.   Patricia Smith.   ICANM

San Pedro Road.   Robert Hass.   GeoHom

San Quentin 1968.   Robert Peterson.   GeoHom

San Sepolcro.   Jorie Graham.   MoWP; VCAP

Sancho, the Bagman's Dog.   Richard Harris Barham.   DiBP

Sanct Christopher's a muckle sanct and strang.   Sanct Christopher II.   Robert Garioch.   OBVE

Sancta Maria, ora pro nobis.   James Ryman.   OHMEL

Sanctions.   Sadiq al-Saygh.   IrPoTo, *tr.* by Emily Howard and Salaam Yousif

Sanctity.   Patrick Kavanagh.   NoP-4; NoP-5; StAl

Sanctity, The.   C. K. Williams.   BodElec

Sanctofy me, sanctofy me.   Just Now.   *Unknown.*   SSUS

Sanctuary.   Donald Davidson.   APT-1; FuPo

Sanctuary.   Norman Dubie.   BodElec

Sanctuary.   Angelina Muñiz Huberman.   MirDau, *tr.* by Aurora Camacho

Sanctuary.   Dorothy Parker.   NBLV

Sanctuary.   Elinor Wylie.   MoAmPo; NAAPv.2

Sanctuary, The.   Sara Teasdale.   APT-1; NAAPv.2

Sand.   Nina Cassian.   PoSu, *tr.* by Nina Cassian and Naomi Lazard

Sand.   Dylan Iorwerth. *tr. by the author*

  Dafydd.   BBMWP, *tr. by the author*

  Druidstone.   BBMWP, *tr. by the author*

  Garden.   BBMWP, *tr. by the author*

  Horses.   BBMWP, *tr. by the author*

  House of Teletubbies, The.   BBMWP, *tr. by the author*

  New Bottom.   BBMWP, *tr. by the author*

  Sea.   BBMWP, *tr. by the author*

  Surf.   BBMWP, *tr. by the author*

  "That first time."   BBMWP, *tr. by the author*

Sand.   John Jarmain.   FaBoWar

Sand.   Dominique Parker.   SpirFl

Sand.   Hannah Weiner.   PFTM-2

Sand below the border-mountain lies like snow, The.   On Hearing a Flute at Night from the Wall of Shouxiang.   Li Yi.   CCL1, *tr. by* Witter Bynner

Sand, caravans, and teetering sea-edge graves.   Earthen Lot, The.   Tony Harrison.   NPeEn

Sand Dunes.   Robert Frost.   MoAmPo

Sand has the ants, clay ferny weeds for play.   Possessions.   Ivor Gurney.   NPeEn

Sand in Flames.   Nujoum Al-Ghanim.   PoArWo, *tr. by* Clarissa C. Burt

Sand in My Shoes.   Frank Loesser.   ReLy

Sand is a fine grit, The.   Dry Root in a Wash.   Simon J. Ortiz.   HATNAP

Sand is swift, overflowing, The.   Snake.   Dan Pagis.   WoPoe, *tr. by* Stephen Mitchell

Sand Martin, The.   John Clare.   NPeEn

Sand modeller always began by heaping the sand, The.   Entertainer, The.   Bruce Beaver.   NOBAu

Sand Nigger.   Lawrence Joseph.   OPRER

Sand of the Desert in an Hour-Glass.   Henry Wadsworth Longfellow.   NCAP

Sand pyramid, size of a child, each September.   Ant Hill, The.   Cynthia Zarin.   NoP-4; NoP-5

Sand Roads.   Marge Piercy.

  Development, The.   NBLV

Sand, sand. In the university the halls.   Poet Visits Egypt and Israel, The.   Maxine W. Kumin.   TaR

Sand Shark.   Nancy Willard.   PoCoUp

Sand: the crystalline children.   Kneeling Here, I Feel Good.   Marge Piercy.   IPoFL

Sand Wet and Cool, The.   Dennis Brutus.   GT

Sandal and garment of yellow and lotus garlands upon his body of blue.   Jayadeva.   TAL *Fr.* Gita Govinda, The.

Sandal paste dry in the golden bowl.   Waiting.   Rayaprolu Subbarao.   HotL, *tr. by* V. Narayana Rao

Sandalphon.   Henry Wadsworth Longfellow.   TCAPo

Sandalphon.   Ezra Pound.   TCAPo

Sandals on my feet. (LL)   Another year gone.   Basho.   EH; NIL-7, *tr. by* Robert Hass

Sandalwood Comes to My Mind.   Carl Rakosi.   ChIV-1 *Fr.* Exercises in Scriptural Writing (1925–1939).

Sandbags of sugar cannot conceal the gloomy fact.   And the World was Calm.   Chris Wallace-Crabbe.   BMAP

Sandbar at Moore's Creek.   Judy Jordan.   AmPoNex

Sandblast Girl and the Acid Man, The.   May Kendall.   ViWPN

Sandbox. 1952.—*Homage to Joseph Cornell*.   Laura Mullen.   IAoNAP

Sanderlings.   Roland Mathias.   TCAWP

Sandpiper.   Elizabeth Bishop.   APT-2; HeIP-4; NoP-5; OWoS

Sand-Quarry with Moving Figures.   Muriel Rukeyser.   NoP-4

Sandra.   Demetrice A. Worley.   SpirFl

Sandra: At the Beaver Trap.   Michael S. Harper.   NoAM

Sands at my feet, The. (LL)   Venus Transiens.   Amy Lowell.   APT-1; NAAL-5; NAAPv.2; NALW; NAMCP V.1

Sands do not weep on Lafan.   Gwenllian.   Myrddin ap Dafydd.   BBMWP, *tr. by* Anthony Conran

Sands of Dee, The.   Charles Kingsley.   OxAEP-2

Sands of time are sinking, The.   In Emmanuel's Land.   Anne R. Cousin.   SacPr

Sands stretch away like snow, The.   Listening to a Flute at Night near the City Wall.   Li Yi.   CrYelRi, *tr. by* Sam Hamill

Sand-slums are hunble townships, The.   Saturday in the Sand-Slums.   Agostinho Neto.   PoetW, *tr. by* Michael Wolfers

Sand-time Measuring.   Moses Glyn Jones.   BBMWP, *tr. by* Mike Jenkins

Sandwiches.   David Donnell.   NoAM

Sandy cat by the Farmer's chair, The.   Summer Evening.   Walter De la Mare.   MoBrPo

Sandy road, the bright green two-inch lizard, The.   Pen, The.   Jean Valentine.   BodElec

Sandy Yard, The.   Edith Jay Scovell.   HarvBoo

Sang.   Robert MacLellan.   EdScPo

Sang.   Allan Ramsay.   OxBEV

Sang a maiden in a meadow.   Reunited.   Henrietta Cordelia Ray.   CBWP-3

Sang First.   William Tennant.   NePenScot *Fr.* Papistry Storm'd.

Sang of the Outlaw Murray, The.   *Unknown.*   IBB

Sanglant comme la nuit, admirable en effroi, et sensible.   Lamentations au cerf.   Pierre Jean Jouve.   YaTCFP

Sango.   Gabriel Gbadamosi.

  "Sango's son came down to the river."   HBAPE

Sangra la carne expuesta entre las moscas.   Carnicería.   Carla Faesler Bremer.   SPV

Sang-zhong: Hunting the Dodder.   *Unknown.*   CCL1, *tr. by* V. W. X.

Sanitized Sonnets, The.   Peter Porter.

  "It's there, somewhere in the Platonic cold store."   OxBSo

  "Now it's in all the novels, what's pornography to do?"   OBCoV

Sanju Sangendo.   Philip Whalen.   AHA

Sank through easeful.   Diver, The.   Robert Earl Hayden.   MoASP

Sankey Hymns.   Alan Riach.   EdScPo

Sanoe.   Queen Lili'u-o-ka-lani.   SWaP

Sanoe ("Where can you be, Sanoe?")   Queen Lili'u-o-ka-lani.   NAAPv.1

Sans Equity and sans Poise.   *Unknown.*   WoPoe *Fr.* Yung Wind.

Sans teeth, sans eyes, sans taste, sans everything. (LL)   William Shakespeare.   CtM; ITBLP; UV *Fr.* As You Like It.

Sanskrit.   Jayanta Mahapatra.   VCWP

Sant' Angelo d'Ischia.   Edwin Denby.   NYP2

Santa Ana came storming, as a storm might come.   Defense of the Alamo, The.   Joaquin Miller.   AmWaPo

Santa Claus.   Dunya Mikhail.   IrPoTo, *tr. by* Salaam Yousif

Santa Claus.   Dom Moraes.   NoAM

Santa Claus: "Each year when the trees turn white."   Harry Edmund Martinson.   PML, *tr. by* Leif Sjöberg and William Jay Smith

Santa Claus Is Comin' to Town.   Haven Gillespie.   ReLy

Santa Decca.   Oscar Wilde.   OxBSo

Santa en penitencia grita, La.   Bodas de las Flores se Dan Sobre el Estigma, Las. El polen se desprende al comenzar la aurora y en un solo momento la vida se redime y entonces se retira.   María Baranda.   RMCMP

Santa Fe.   Joy Harjo.   ICANM

Santa Fe Railroad, The.   Charles Tomlinson.   ICANM

Santa Fe Sky.   Ann Lauterbach.   OxBoAm

Santa Fe, still the one, The.   American Trains.   Reginald Gibbons.   GM

Santa Fe Trail.   Barbara Guest.   FTOS

Santa Filomena.   Henry Wadsworth Longfellow.   FaBoWar

Santa Maria Antiqua.   István Vas.   IQMS, *tr. by* Geroge Gömöri and Clive Wilmer

Santa Monica.   Charlie Smith.   KGB

Santa Rita Massacre, 1837.   Victoria Edwards Tester.   ICANM

Sant'Alessio, Roma.   Olga Sedakova.   CRWP, *tr. by* Catriona Kelly

Santo Domingo Corn Dance.   Lynn Riggs.   APT-2

Santorin.   James Elroy Flecker.   OBMV

Santorini Daughter.   Julie Fay.   NAPBL

São Paulo! tumult of my life.   Inspiration.   Mário de Andrade.   TCLAP, *tr. by* Jack E. Tomlins

Sap.   Robert Minhinnick.   AngWePo

Sapho and Phao.   John Lyly.

  Sapho's Song.   NoSic

  (Song in Making of the Arrows, The.)   NoSic

Sapho's Kiss.   Efrén Rebolledo.   BLPSL, *tr. by* Rene de Costa, Rigas Kappatos and Eleni Paidoussi

Sapho's Song.   John Lyly.   NoSic *Fr.* Sapho and Phao.

Sapling bent and tied to point the way, A.   Elbow Tree, The.   Wyatt Prunty.   PfSP

Saplings of the green-tipped birch, The.   Never Tell.   *Unknown.*   OBWVE, *tr. by* Anthony Conran

Sappers.   Yusef Komunyakaa.   AmAlph

Sappers, The.   Hayim Hefer.   NRoS, *tr. by* Esther Raizen

Sapphic Fragment [*fr. the Greek of* Sappho].   Sappho.   OBVE, *tr. by* Thomas Hardy

Sapphics.   George Canning *and* John Hookham Frere. *See* Friend of Humanity and the Knife Grinder, The.

Sapphics.   Daryl Hine.   PoA 2002

Sapphics.   Sappho.   NPeEn, *tr. by* Algernon Charles Swinburne

Sapphics Against Anger.   Timothy Steele.   CalPo

Sapphics for Patience.   Anne Finch.   FFC

Sappho.   Christina Georgina Rossetti.   VWP

Sappho. James Wright. NoAM

Sappho and Phaon. *sels.* Mary Robinson. NPBRoP

4. Sappho Discovers her Passion. Mary Robinson. CenSon; NPBRoP; RWP *Fr.* Sappho and Phaon.

Sappho; or, The Resolve. Charlotte Dacre. NOBRP

Sappho Rejects Hope. Mary Robinson. CenSon; RWP

Sappho to Philaenis. John Donne. RACG *Fr.* Elegies.

Sappho was neither woman or man. Greek Metamorphosis. Belkis Cuza Malé. TANSG, *tr. by* Pamela Carmell

Sappho's Address to the Stars. Mary Robinson. CenSon; RWP

23. Sappho's Conjectures. Mary Robinson. CenSon; NPBRoP; RWP *Fr.* Sappho and Phaon.

Sappho's Gymnasium ("For healthy cells please remember.") T. Begley and Olga Broumas. PfS

Sappho's Gymnasium ("Outside memory worship never dies.") T. Begley and Olga Broumas. GifTon

Sappho's Leap. Howard Baker. APT-2

Sappho's Prayer to Venus. Mary Robinson. CenSon; RWP

Sappho's Reply. Rita Mae Brown. OxWW

Sappho's Song. Letitia Elizabeth Landon. NPBRoP; RWP; VWP *Fr.* Improvisatrice, The.

Saraband. Austin Hummell. AmPoNex

Sarabande on Attaining the Age of Seventy-Seven. Anthony Hecht. BAP-01

Saracen SAS or Assasseen called Nasir claims on HTV, A. Alan Halsey. Oth *Fr.* Robin Hood Book, A.

Sarah. Delmore Schwartz. ChIV-1; TaR

Sarah Byng. Joseph Hilaire Pierre Belloc. NoAM

Sarah, my rose, where are you off? Please stop a minute. Lover Under Suspicion. Ádám Pálóczi Horváth. IQMS, *tr. by* J. G. Nichols

Sarah's Choice. Eleanor Wilner. TaR

Sarah's laughter's sudden like a hurdle, like an old lould crow. Sarah's Laughter. Gillian Allnutt. MoWP

Sarah's thinner friend. It's Just As Well About Heather. Chris O. Cook. FreRad

Sarajevo wind, The. Sorrow of Sarajevo, The. Goran Simić. PoAgWa, *tr. by* David Harsent

Sarcophagus. Larry Goodell. ICANM

Sarcophagus. Pauline Stainer. NeBl

Sardanapalus. Henry Howard, Earl of Surrey. NAEL-6v1; NAEL-7v1; NoSic

Sardines. Menna Elfyn. ATSWP, *tr. by* Robert Minhinnick

Sardis. William Cowper. ChIV-2 *Fr.* Olney Hymns.

Sardis. Sappho. SaLy, *tr. by* Diane Rayor

Sari, The. Moniza Alvi. BeAl

Saris go by me from the embassies, The. Woman at the Washington Zoo, The. Randall Jarrell. BrAP; InGu; ItP; OxBoAm; VCAP

Sarpedon's Speech to Glaucus. Homer. NPeEn; OBVE *Fr.* Iliad, The.

Sartor Resartus. Art Goodtimes. GeoH

Sass pumping my gas, The. Copyright Renewal Under the Texaco Star. Jeffrey Dye. PoDa

Sassafras. Barbara Guest. FTOS

Sat a damsel on the hillside. Messengers, The. Henrietta Cordelia Ray. CBWP-3

Sat down near the cigarette stand and surveyed his new scene, just arrived in the Holy City of Benares. (LL) Describe: The Rain on Dasaswamedh Ghat. Allen Ginsberg. BB; FTOS

Sat for three days in a white room. Heroin. Jim Carroll. OBCoV

Sat in a faded teal-blue chair above the sea to watch. Catch, The. Laura Mullen. IAoNAP

Satan Is on Your Tongue. George Barker. MoBrPo *Fr.* Secular Elegies.

Satan Says. Sharon Olds. OxBoAm; PBCAP

Satan with his Angels now fallen into Hell. John Milton. NPeEn

Satan's Camp a-Fire. *Unknown.* SSUS

Satan's Journey. John Milton. NOSC *Fr.* Paradise Lost.

Satan's Summons. John Milton. NOSC

Satasai, The. Bihari. *tr. by* Krishna P. Bahadur

"*What she said to her companion.*" WoPoe, *tr. by* Krishna P. Bahadur

Sated with home, of wife, of children tired. Cui Bono? Horace Smith. NOBRP

Satin Doll. Johnny Mercer. ReLy

Satin Doll. David Wojahn. PBCAP

Satire. Ibn Sharaf. WoPoe, *tr. by* Leticia Garza-Falcón and Christopher Middleton

Satire. *Unknown.* WoPoe, *tr. by* Sir Arthur Grimble

Satire: "This way of writing I observed by some." *Unknown.* BASC

Satire VIII. Joseph Hall. ChIV-2

Satire, A. John Oldham.

"On Butler who can think without rage." OBSV

Satire against Reason and Mankind, A. Grace Buchanan Sherwood. NoP-4

Satire on Charles II, A. John Wilmot, 2d Earl of Rochester. NOSC

"Restless he rolls about from whore to whore." OBSV

Satire on the Rebellion, A. Alexander Brome. BASC

Satire [*or* Satyre *or* Satyr] against [Reason and] Mankind, A. John Wilmot, 2d Earl of Rochester. BASC; NOSC; OBSV

"Were I (who to my cost already am)." CABP; NPeEn; OxBEV

"You see how far Mans wisedom here extends." OxBEV

Satires. John Donne.

Satire 1 [A London Street]. NoSic

Satire 2.

Poet Turned Lawyer, The. OBSV

Satire 3 [Religion]. BASC; FSCP; NAEL-6v1; NAEL-7v1; NoP-4; NoP-5; OxAEP-1; SacPr

Hill of Truth, The. OBSV

Satire 4. OBSV

Satire 5. OBSV

(Satyre 3 [On Religion].) PBRV

Hill of Truth, The. OBSV

(Search for True Religion, The.) NoSic

Hill of Truth, The. OBSV

Satires. Horace. *tr. by* Richard W. Hooper

Satire 1.8. PriapPo, *tr. by* Richard W. Hooper

Satires. Juvenal. *tr. by* John Dryden, William Gifford, Peter Green, Samuel Johnson, Robert Lowell and Henry Vaughan

"But of all the plagues, the greatest is untold." OBSV

"Give store of days, good Jove, give length of years." OBSV

Hannibal ("Produce the urn that Hannibal contains"). OBVE, *tr. by* William Gifford

Hannibal ("Put Hannibal i' th' scale"). OBVE

Hannibal ("Throw Hannibal on the scales, how many pounds"). OBVE

""Life! length of life!" for this, with earnest cries." OBVE

Satire 1. RomPo, *tr. by* Peter Green

Satire 2.

"Northward beyond the Lapps to the world's end, the frozen." CAGL, *tr. by* Peter Green

Satire 6. RomPo, *tr. by* Peter Green

Satire 10. RomPo, *tr. by* Peter Green

Sejanus ("How many men are killed by power, by power"). OBVE

Sejanus ("Some ask for envy'd pow'r; which publick hate"). OBVE

Sejanus ("What crowds by envied power, the wish of all"). OBVE

Sixth Satire. *tr. by* John Dryden

Empress Messalina, The. BASC, *tr. by* John Dryden

Gaudy Gossip, The. BASC, *tr. by* John Dryden

"In Saturn's reign, at Nature's early birth." NPeEn; OBSV; OBVE; OxBEV, *tr. by* John Dryden

Learned Wife, The. BASC, *tr. by* John Dryden

"What care our Drunken Dames to whom they spread?" OxBEV, *tr. by* John Dryden

Tenth Satire. *tr. by* John Dryden

Sejanus. BASC, *tr. by* John Dryden

"When the last Flavius, drunk with fury, tore." OBVE

Satires. John Marston.

Cynic Satire, A. NoSic

Humours. NoSic

Satires. John Oldham.

"Of all the creatures, in the world, that be." OBVE

Satires. Persius. *tr. by* John Dryden

Satire 1. RomPo, *tr. by* Richard Emil Braun

Satire 5. RomPo, *tr. by* Richard Emil Braun

Satire 6. RomPo, *tr. by* Richard Emil Braun

Satires. Sir Thomas Wyatt.

(Mine Own John Poins.) NAEL-6v1; NAEL-7v1; NoP-4; NoP-5; WaAnP

"My mother's maids [*or* maydes] when they did sew [*or* sowe] and spin [*or* spynne]." NoSic

(Myn owne John poyntz sins ye delight to know.) PBRV

Of the Courtier's Life. NoSic; NPeEn; OBSV; OBVE

To Sir Francis Brian. NoSic

Satires of Circumstance in Fifteen Glimpses. Thomas Hardy.

At the Altar-Rail. MoBrPo

At the Draper's. MoBrPo

By Her Aunt's Grave. MoBrPo

In Church. MoBrPo

In the Moonlight. NAMCP V.1; NoAM

In the Restaurant. MoBrPo

Satiric and Censorious Epistle. Francisco de Quevedo y Villegas. *tr.* by Denise Levertov

"I'll not be silent, though you put your finger." SpanPo, *tr.* by Denise Levertov

Satirical Elegy on the Death of a Late Famous General, A. Jonathan Swift. NBLV; NPeEn; OBSV; WaAnP

Satis Passio. Les A. Murray. HarvBoo

Satisfaction, The. Lu Chi. WoPoe *Fr.* Art of Writing, The.

Satisfaction—is the Agent. Emily Dickinson. TCAPo

Satisfied, unsatisfied. "H. D." APT-1 *Fr.* Flowering of the Rod, The.

Satori. Nin Andrews. AmZen

Satori in Fauldhouse. Colin Will. EdScPo

Saturated. Aaron Shurin. FTOS

Saturday. New Comers. Melinda Goodman. WiU

Saturday. Philip Whalen. WhBo

Saturday, 1 December. Norman Fischer. WANABP *Fr.* Success.

Saturday Afternoon. Sue Sinclair. Coast

Saturday Afternoon, October. Jonathan Holden. OPRER

Saturday Afternoon, When Chores Are Done. Harryette Mullen. ISC; OxAAAP

Saturday April 8 Swansea, where Dylan Thomas was born on October 27th, the same day I was born. Maxine Hong Kingston. FaoP

Saturday, April 26, 1973. Poem to Galway Kinnell, A. Etheridge Knight. BodElec

Saturday at the Border. Hayden Carruth. MakPoe; WaAnP

Saturday at the Canal. Gary Soto. P180; TWF

Saturday before Easter, The. Beverlyjean Smith. PfS

Saturday grieves. To the New World. Claudia Keelan. BodElec

Saturday in the '20s, A. Jean Earle. AngWePo

Saturday in the Sand-Slums. Agostinho Neto. PoetW, *tr.* by Michael Wolfers

Saturday, March the first, she rings. Chords. Eamer O'Keefe. Prnts

Saturday Morning. Hugo Williams. GoPo

Saturday Morning, A. Manuel A. Viray. ReBoTo

Saturday morning, Motown. Collection Day. Natasha Trethewey. SpirFl

Saturday Morning Ultimatum. Dan Nielsen. SUP

Saturday morning, Wolverhampton market. Red Desiré. Mick North. NLP

Saturday mornings. Irish-speaking Mynah, The. Gearóid Mac Lochlainn. NIrP, *tr.* by Ciaran Carson

Saturday mornings, before. Bait, The. Eric Chock. OpBo

Saturday mornings in harlem at places. Shop Sonnet. Crystal Williams. RD

Saturday Night. Clark Coolidge. FTOS

Saturday Night. Sir Alan Patrick Herbert. NBLV

Saturday Night. Langston Hughes. MoAmPo

Saturday Night. Victoria Wood. OBCoV

Saturday Night, Arriving in Seoul. Kim Hyesun. CAMKP, *tr.* by Jiwon Shin

Saturday Night Decades. Sterling Plumpp. IllVoic

Saturday night I buy a soda. I Like to Collapse. Joseph Ceravolo. NYP2

Saturday Night in the Village. Giacomo Leopardi. OBVE; WoPoe, *tr.* by Robert Lowell

Saturday night November 1980. Lullabye for a Butch. Melinda Goodman. WiU

Saturday 6 a.m. Charles Wright. GeoHom

Saturday: The Small-Pox. Lady Mary Wortley Montagu. BrAP; NoP-5 *Fr.* Six Town Eclogues.

Saturday Tub, The. Mary Gilmore. NOBAu

Saturday with Dad. Liz Houghton. Prnts

Saturn. Geoffrey Chaucer. NPeEn *Fr.* Canterbury Tales, The.

Saturn. Günter Grass. AF

Saturn. John Keats. NOBRP; OxAEP-2; OxBEV *Fr.* Hyperion.

Saturn. Sharon Olds. RaBo

Saturn Declining. Sándor Weöres. IQMS, *tr.* by Alan Dixon

Saturn's Three Sons. Robert Hayman. NOSC *Fr.* Owen's Epigrams.

Satyr, A. John Oldham.

  London. NOSC

  "One night, as I was pondering of late." NOSC

Satyr Address'd to a Friend That Is About to Leave the University, and Come Abroad in the World, A. John Oldham.

  "If you for orders, and a gown design."

    "If you're so out of love with happiness." OBSV

Satyr, Cunnilinguent: To Herman Melville. Charles Martin. RA

Satyr O never ask how I came to this place. Michael Drayton. AEP *Fr.* Muses' Elysium X, The.

Satyre 3 [On Religion]. John Donne. *See* Satire 3 [Religion].

Satyricon. Petronius Arbiter. *tr.* by J. P. Sullivan

  "However, Eumolpus, our champion in time of trouble and the author of the present harmony." EroLit, *tr.* by J. P. Sullivan

Satyr's Song, The ("Softly Gliding as I Go"). John Fletcher. NOSC *Fr.* Faithful Shepherdess, The.

Satyrus Peregrinans. William Rankins.

  "By this time long-gowned Lumen walked abroad." OBSV

Sauce desbordado. Ernesto Lumbreras. RMCMP

Sauchs in the Reuch Heuch Hauch, The. Hugh MacDiarmid. NAMCP V.1; NoAM

Saudades. Jacqueline Johnson. BtF

Saul. Robert Browning.

  "Oh, the wild joys of living! the leaping from rock up to rock." ITBLP

Sauna 2. Karina Africa-Bolasco. ReBoTo

Sauntering the pavement or riding the country byroad here then are faces. Walt Whitman. APN-1 *Fr.* Leaves of Grass [1855 Version].

Sausage Parade, The. Martha Silano. PoDa

Sausalito, / Little Willow. Sausalito Trash Prayer. Lew Welch. BB

Sausalito Trash Prayer. Lew Welch. BB

Sautéed, baked or fried. Kalamu ya Salaam. SpirFl *Fr.* New Orleans Haiku.

Savage cold of Russian winters, The. Natalya Gorbanevskaya. TCRusP, *tr.* by Daniel Weissbort

Savage Memories. Yehuda Amichai. FIT, *tr.* by Robert Friend

Savage of Aveyron, The. Mary Robinson. RWP

Savage, Our Fathers, The. B. H. Boston. GeoHom

Savage the sea leaped high; on the rocks plunged ponderous breakers. Tempest. Theodore H. Banks, Jr. YaYoPo

Savannah Brass. Verneda Sagay-Lights. BtF

Save As: Salvation. Bill Knott. BodElec

Save breed, to brave him when he takes thee hence.. (LL) William Shakespeare. GSo; HeIP-4; NAEL-6v1; NAEL-7v1; NoP-5; NoSic; WoPoe *Fr.* Sonnets.

Save it all; you do not know. 1915: A Pre-Raphaelite Ending, London. Richard Howard. RACG

Save me from such as me assail. Bible, *O.T.* NoSic

Save that I know Roger Parry and he does not? (LL) Porth Cwyfan. Roland Mathias. AngWePo; TCAWP

Save that the curtains, drawn. New York Minute. Joe Osterhaus. AmPoNex

Save that to die [*or* dye], I leave my love alone. (LL) William Shakespeare. CABP; NoSic; OxAEP-1; PoPoPo; TFi; WeW-3 *Fr.* Sonnets.

Save thou, my rose; in it thou art my all. (LL) William Shakespeare. OBEV; OxAEP-1 *Fr.* Sonnets.

Save to one man, and unto God. (LL) Precept of Silence, The. Lionel Pigot Johnson. MoBrPo; SacPr

Save Us From. Roo Borson. NIL-7

Save us from night. Save Us From. Roo Borson. NIL-7

Save us, the poets, save us, we have but. Bulat Shalvovich Okudzhava. TCRusP, *tr.* by Denis Johnson, Aleksandar Petrov and Shirley Rihner

Saved. Adah Isaacs Menken. CBWP-1

Saving the Appearances. Charles Tomlinson. OxBEV

Savior. Ray Gonzalez. TouFir

Savior, The. Louise Erdrich. UpMys

Savior Is Abducted in Puerto Rico, The. Martín Espada. TRP

Savior must have been, The. Emily Dickinson. ChrPo; SacPr

Saviour. Zindzi Mandela. HAWP

Saviour of mankind, Man, Emmanuel! Hymn Written at the Holy Sepulchre in Jerusalem. George Sandys. SacPr

Sâvitrî; or, Love and Death. *Unknown.* TAL *Fr.* Mahabharata, The.

Savoir Faire. Claribel Alegría. VCWP

Savouring the shade of our teacher's willow. Dog Day Lesson. John Hughes. PNI

Savoy / The home of sweet romance. Stompin' at the Savoy. Andy Razaf. ReLy

Saw a home movie this afternoon. Uncle Charles. Uncle Charles: A Home Movie. J. Bernlef. TuT, *tr.* by Peter van de Kamp

Saw a lamb being born. Lamb. Michael Dennis Browne. RaBo

Saw my shadow on the wall. Shadow Returns, The. Phillis Levin. RA

Saw on the lyric lake the single perfect swan. (LL) First Love. Edwin Rolfe. AmWaPo; APT-2

Saw someone yesterday looked like you did. In the Post Office. Thom Gunn. CAGL

Saw them glittering in the trees. Blake. Lucille Clifton. ExTi

Saw whites clap during a sacred dance. Today Was a Bad Day Like TB. Chrystos. UnSA

Saw ye Jenny Nettles. Jenny Nettles. Allan Ramsay and *Unknown.* NePenScot

Sawdust. Jane Shore. PfSP

Sawing His Wife in Half. Dafydd Rowlands. BBMWP, *tr.* by Meic Stephens

Sawmill. Richard Kenney. NoP-4; NoP-5

Saw-Mill Shack, The. Thomas Rain Crowe. AmZen

Sawmill's whistle for noon would surprise us, The. Map of Simplicities, A. James Applewhite. LPSFW

Saw-toothed blades, the lavish, common flowers, The. (LL) Dandelion Greens. Jane Flanders. AFaM; IPoFL

Sawyers lie outside the shed, The. Boathouse, The. Robert Minhinnick. AngWePo

Sax. Robert Minhinnick. ATSWP

Saxon Legend of Language, The. Mary Weston Fordham. CBWP-2

Saxons of Flint, The. *Unknown.* OBWVE, *tr.* by Mary C. Llewelyn

Saxophone Julie. Susan Firer. MiVo

Saxophonetyx. Cyn Zarco. WaAnP

Sax's and Selves. Mark Halliday. P180

Say. Beckian Fritz Goldberg. PfS

Say a lake decayed: say wind makes a lake of eyes: an eyed lake sees her here. Lies Concerning Speed. Christine Hume. IAoNAP

Say "Cheese!" Fran Landesman. ReLy

Say, crimson rose and dainty daffodil. Nosegay, A. John Reynolds. OBEV

Say, cruel Iris, pretty rake. Gift, The. To Iris, in Bow Street, Covent Garden. Oliver Goldsmith. IrLP

Say *darkness*, say *light*. The eagle. Teresa. R. T. Smith. Vesp

Say, dear Sophia! gentle friend. To Miss Sophia Headle. Dorothea Primrose Campbell. PoBW

Say, Dwarf, for it seems to me. *Unknown.* OBVE *Fr.* Elder Edda, The.

Say for me. / Say forth, say forthwhile, in the name of colors, of real colors, in the name of real colors named. In Nomine. Catherine Imbriglio. IAoNAP

Say french. Diana Helen Melhem. PoArWo *Fr.* Rest in Love.

Say Girls in Shoe Ads: "I Go for a Man Who's Tall!" Robley, Jr. Wilson. PBCAP

Say Good-bye to Big Daddy. Randall Jarrell. MoASP

Say happiness is possible, or more than possible. On Track. Kathleene West. FFC

Say, hast thou track'd a traveller's round. Taormini. John Henry, Cardinal Newman. SacPr

Say! Have you ever met the girl who's the toast of the town. Lady in Red, The. Mort Dixon. ReLy

Say, how shall thoughtless, easy-natured youth. Stanzas Imitated From Psalm 119. Bible, *O.T.* ChIV-1, *tr.* by Thomas Warton, the Elder

Say I were not sixty. Make Believe. Gerda Mayer. Prnts

Say It. Jayne Cortez. SurWo

Say it in sheets of sound. Hoodoo Whisper. Adrian Castro. BRtP

Say it is Tuesday. Tuesday Shaman. Maurice Kilwein Guevara. TouFir

Say it isn't real. Bedtime Stories. Silvia Curbelo. TouFir

Say It Isn't So. Irving Berlin. ReLy

Say it loud, I'm black and I'm proud. Say It Loud—I'm Black and I'm Proud. James Brown *and* Alfred Ellis. ISC

Say It Loud—I'm Black and I'm Proud. James Brown *and* Alfred Ellis. ISC

Say Ja. Tom Mandel. PmAP

Say just one word to me, make one promise. *Unknown.* NaPG, *tr.* by Talat Sait Halman

Say life is the one-way trip, the one-way flight. Watchmaker God. Robert Lowell. InvLi; SoSe-8

Say, little honey / I haven't any money. Great Big Bunch of You, A. Mort Dixon. ReLy

Say me, wight in the brom [*or* broom]. Tell Me, Wight in the Broom. *Unknown.* NAEL-6v1

(Sey me, wight in the broom.) OHMEL

Say milky cocoa we'd say. Funeral. Carol Ann Duffy. InoFa

Say, Montagu, can this unartful verse. On Elizabeth Montagu. Mary Scott. RWP

Say Muses, say; who now in those rich fields. Phineas Fletcher. ChIV-1 *Fr.* Locusts, or Appolyonists, The.

Say my love is easy had. Fighting Words. Dorothy Parker. AmWit

Say not, because no more you see. On the Death of Mr. Persall's Little Daughter, in the Beginning of the Spring, at Amsterdam. *Unknown.* NOSC

Say not of beauty she is good. Beauty. Elinor Wylie. APT-1

Say not the mermaid is a myth. Mermaid, The. Ogden Nash. Spl

Say Not the Struggle Nought Availeth. Arthur Hugh Clough. BrAP; ITBLP; NAEL-6v2; NAEL-7v2; NoP-4; NoP-5; OBEV; OxBEV; SacPr; TFi

Say of them / They knew no Spanish. To the Veterans of the Abraham Lincoln Brigade. Genevieve Taggard. AmWaPo; NAAPv.2

Say over again, and yet once over again. Elizabeth Barrett Browning. CenSon; NAEL-6v2; NAEL-7v2; OxBSo *Fr.* Sonnets from the Portuguese.

Say proudly yet—"'Twas hers who loved me well!" (LL) Properzia Rossi. Felicia Dorothea Hemans. NPBRoP; RWP; ViWPN; VWP

Say--So I'll Say. Giancarlo Majorino. ItPo, *tr.* by Gayle Ridinger

Say Something: A Change Is Gonna Come. Mbali Umoja. BtF

Say, spotless plume, if Damon bade thee go. To My Pen. Mary Julia Young. CenSon

Say, stranger, that this is the tomb of the mare Aethyia. Mnasalces. HePo *Fr.* Epigrams.

Say that a ballad. Speeches at the Barriers. Susan Howe.

Say that thou didst forsake me for some fault. William Shakespeare. OxAEP-1 *Fr.* Sonnets.

Say that we saw Spain die. O splendid bull, how well you fought! Say that We Saw Spain Die. Edna St. Vincent Millay. AmWaPo

Say that you are a poet. Airport. Lenard D. Moore. FuFl

Say that you're lying comfortably under. Journey Out. Rachel Hadas. RA

Say the need's born within the tree. Gum-trees Stripping. Judith Wright. BMAP

Say the words I am. Examining the I. Jean V. Gier. ReBoTo

Say, there's a lamb in the daisies. (LL) For a Lamb. Richard Eberhart. ColAP; SoSe-8

Say this city has ten million souls. W. H. Auden. AmFaPo; BeAl; HP; OxAEP-2 *Fr.* Ten Songs.

Say this to the king: men wrought this shrine. Last Oracle from Delphi. *Unknown.* WoPoe, *tr.* by Katherine Washburn

Say to me: out there are only streets, and cars. Lullaby. Constance Merritt. AmPoNex

Say to them. Speech to the Young Speech to the Progress-Toward (Among Them Nora and Henry III). Gwendolyn Brooks. PLBUT

Say tyrant Custom, why must we obey. Emulation, The. Sarah Fyge Egerton. CABP; PEW

Say what remains when Hope is fled? Boy of Egremond, The. Samuel Rogers. NOBRP

Say what slim youth, with moist perfumes. Horace. OBVE

Say what you please. Rondelet. May Probyn. VWP

Say wherefore is't that Damon flys. On Damons Loveing of Clora. Damaris, Lady Masham. EMWP

Say witty fair one, from what sphere. To the Most Excellently Accomplished Mrs. Katherine Philips. Henry Vaughan. CABP

Say Yes Quickly. Jelaluddin Rumi. RaBo, *tr.* by Coleman Barks

Say yes quickly, before you think too hard. Say Yes Quickly. Sheri Hostetler. ACAMVP

Say you came once as a dragonfly. Dancer, The. Margaret Holley. PoDa

Say you could have come there from Athens, when its empire. Minoan Distance, The. Alan Williamson. FaoP

Say You Love Me. Molly Peacock. CFP; RaF

Say you needed some ideas. Journals, The. Gaylord Brewer. AmPoNex

Say you wake. Loneliness. Franz Wright. AmAlph

Say you wake up one morning without a language. Hypothetical. John K. Samson. PoPra

Say you want to sing right now. Worry. Aaron Anstett. AmPoNex

Sayatasha's Night Chant. *Zuni Oral Tradition.* NAAPv.1 *Fr.* Shalako.

Say-but-the-Word Centurion Attempts a Summary, The. Les A. Murray. UpMys

Saying, The. Ernst Stadler. PoCho

Saying *blackberry, blackberry, blackberry.* (LL) Meditation at Lagunitas. Robert Hass. AmFaPo; CalPo; CAP-8; ColAP; FaoP; GeoHom; MakPoe; NAMCP V.2; NoP-4; NoP-5; OxBoAm; StAl; VCAP; WaAnP

Saying *Dear child*, and all time has disproved. (LL) Faith Healing. Philip Larkin. ChIV-2; GI; NAMCP V.2; NoAM; OxBEV

Saying Farewell at the Monastery After Hearing the Old Master Lecture on "Return to the Source." Gary Snyder. WhBo

Saying Farewell to a Friend. Li Po. TAL

Saying, "Goodbye! Goodbye! Nice to have seen you again." (LL) Bitch. Carolyn Kizer. GifTon; OxBoAm; PoA 2002; StAl

Saying Good-bye in a Ch'in-ling Wineshop. Li Po. CrYelRi, *tr.* by Sam Hamill

Saying Good-bye to a Singing Girl Who Has Decided to Become a Nun. Mo Shih-lung. ColAnChi; WoPoe, *tr.* by Jonathan Chaves

Saying Good-bye to Meng Hao-jan at Yellow Crane Pavilion. Li Po. CrYelRi, *tr.* by Sam Hamill

Saying Goodbye to Very Young Children. John Updike. PoA 2002

Saying nothing I want to understand. (LL) Passing. Carl Phillips. BtF; PoPoPo

Saying the words. Young Woman Stands on the Edge of Her Life, The. Kerry Hardie. NIrP

Saying Your Names. Richard Siken. LegDan

Say-it-again got hold of us, we. Go Left Out of Shantiville. Nathaniel Mackey. OxAAAP

Says a Reverend Priest to a less Rev'rend friend. Epigram. *Unknown.* NOBRP

Says Come here, says. Whistle. Janet Holmes. ExTi

Says I have. Girlfriend. Lori Tsang. BtF

Says Jone to his woife on a whot summer's day.   Jone o' Grinfilt.   Joseph Lees.   NOBRP

Says my Uncle, I pray you discover.   Molly Mog [or The Fair Maid of the Inn].   John Gay.   OBCoV

Says oor gudewife, "The cock is crawin'."   Nü-yue ji-ming: The Cock Is Crawin' (scoticè).   Unknown.   CCL1, tr. by James Legge

Says that it says nothing.   You Can Say That the Bird as the Saying Goes.   Nicholás Maré.   PML, tr. by Gilbert Wesley Purdy

Says Tweed tae Till.   Unknown. See Tweed and Till.

Says Tweed to [tae] Till.   Tweed and Till.   Unknown.   NPeEn

Says yes.   Lao Figures.   Unknown.   EaWin, tr. by W. S. Merwin

Scabible.   Elouise Loftin.   EGAG

Scaffold, The.   Amal Dunqul.   NAfrP, tr. by Sharif Elmusa and Thomas G. Ezzy

Scaffold in Winter.   János Pilinszky.   PoSu, tr. by Peter Jay

Scaffolding.   Seamus Heaney.   ChAP

Scald it and scour it like a doorstep. (LL)   View of a Pig.   Ted Hughes.   OxAEP-2; OxBEV

Scale Force, Cumberland.   Letitia Elizabeth Landon.   NPBRoP; RWP

Scale of Being, The.   Alexander Pope.   WoPoe

Scale of dragon, tooth of wolf.   William Shakespeare.   UV Fr. Macbeth.

Scales, The.   Phyllis Stowell.   AFaM

Scales are a wave in the hand, The.   Arcana 8: Justice.   Veronica Volkow.   RMCMP, tr. by Margaret Sayers Peden

Scalloped synecdoches of satin cloud.   Shells.   Rachel Hadas.   ExTi

Scalp Dance, The.   Zuni Oral Tradition. tr. by Ruth L. Bunzel
    "Indeed, the enemy."   NAWM-7v2, tr. by Ruth L. Bunzel

Scalpel finds the heart, The. The heart is still.   Rafael Campo.   WiU Fr. Song for My Lover.

Scalpel in Hand.   Marjorie Welish.   FTOS

Scampering the pasture, that's how now.   Calf and the Ox, The.   Avianus.   WoPoe, tr. by David R. Slavitt

Scan.   Pat Borthwick.   PoCu

Scan.   Gillian Ferguson.   NeBl

Scan at 8 Weeks.   Helen Dunmore.   BeAl

Scandal, The.   Robert Bly.   GoPo

Scandal of this universe, The.   Door of the Cities.   Munia Samara.   PoArWo, tr. by Amal Amireh

Scandalous man, A.   Mr. Tom Narrow.   James Reeves.   OBSP

Scanning an Afternoon in Winter.   Carole Glasser Langille.   Coast

Scant and straggling her yellow hair, from her lip.   Old Woman, An.   David Gwenallt Jones.   OBWVE, tr. by H. Idris Bell

Scape-Goat, The.   Agnes Mary Frances Robinson.   VWP

Scar.   Lucille Clifton.   CAP-8

Scar, The.   John Hewitt.   PNI

Scarabaeus Sisyphus.   Mathilde Blind.   ViWPN

Scaramouche and Pulcinella.   Weird as Puppets.   Paul Verlaine.   SxFrPo, tr. by Martin Sorrell

Scaramouche waves a threatening hand.   Fantoches.   Paul Verlaine.   OBMV, tr. by Arthur Symons

Scarce American pamphlet.   Memory of New England, The.   Donald Revell.   RWB

Scarce do I pass a day, but that I hear.   Meditation 8.   Philip Pain.   NOSC

Scarce had I slept my wonted round.   Dream, A.   Sir John Suckling.   ChIV-2

Scarce had the morning starre hid from the light.   Richard Barnfield.   CAGL; NoSic Fr. Affectionate Shepherd [or Shephearde], The.

Scarce warms the surface of the deepest pool? (LL)   August.   Elinor Wylie.   APT-1; MoAmPo

Scarcely.   Alfonso Reyes.   TCLAP, tr. by Samuel Beckett

Scarcely a street, too few houses.   Village, The.   Ronald Stuart Thomas.   HarvBoo

Scarcely, I think; yet it indeed may be.   For "An Allegorical Dance of Women" by Andrea Mantegna.   Dante Gabriel Rossetti.   CenSon

Scarcity.   Joanna Klink.   IAoNAP

Scarecrow.   Derick Thomson.   EdScPo

Scarecrow, The.   Walter De la Mare.   MoBrPo

Scarecrow, The.   Charles Simic.   OxBoAm

Scarecrow Eclogue.   Srikanth Reddy.   LegDan

Scarecrows.   James Kirkup.   NOxBChV

Scared Cows.   Douglas Messerli.   FTOS

Scarf, The.   Brendan Kennelly.   IrLP

Scaring Hens.   Peter Finch.   Oth

Scarlet.   Arrow Song.   Chippewa Oral Tradition.   NAAPv.2; TCAPo

Scarlet Crown.   Marc J. Straus.   BloBone

Scarlet Letter, The.   Lee Upton.   AmAlph

Scarlet Skirt.   Víctor Hernández Cruz.   TouFir

Scarred hemlock roots.   Down Stream.   Louise Imogen Guiney.   SWaP

Scars.   William Stafford.   AmFaPo

Scars take us back to places we have been, The.   Memoranda.   William Dickey.   YaYoPo

Scartabello.   Edoardo Sanguineti.   tr. by Gayle Ridinger
    "And now a few questions to end with."   ItPo, tr. by Gayle Ridinger
    "At the offset it was calculated."   ItPo, tr. by Gayle Ridinger
    "Like a disk, a trembling coin spinning on its own diameter."   ItPo, tr. by Gayle Ridinger
    "What you're reading (if you're reading me) are the effects."   ItPo, tr. by Gayle Ridinger
    "Wind shoves my New Year's Day sun in my face, The."   ItPo, tr. by Gayle Ridinger

Scary thing, The.   Dreamsters.   Ani Ilkov.   CSCBP, tr. by Georgi Belev and Lisa Sapinkopf

Scatological History.   Lisa Rye.   MAAN

Scatter of silver dews, A.   Yun Söndo.   CATKP Fr. Angler's Calendar, The.

Scattered, aslant.   Fathers.   Robert Creeley.   FTOS

Scattered brainscape while the fan.   Summertime Late Show.   Edwin Torres.   HeMarv

Scattered Congregation, The.   Tomas Tranströmer.   RaBo; VCWP; WED, tr. by Robert Bly

Scattered Light.   Fanny Howe.   FTOS

Scattered milkweed, valentine.   To My Soul.   Jean Valentine.   YaYoPo

Scattered Moluccas.   Ezra Pound.   TCAPo Fr. Hugh Selwyn Mauberley (Life and Contacts).

Scattered on a lawn. (LL)   Free Verse.   Charles Reznikoff.   APT-2; NAAPv.2

Scattered Psalms.   Jacqueline Osherow.
    9 (Looking through the Window: Psalm 121).   PoDa

Scattering as Behavior Toward Risk.   Susan Howe.   PFTM-2

Scattering Ashes.   David Scott.   NLP

Scattering bloom, The.   Buson.   TAL

Scattering long-haired grief and scored pity. (LL)   For Sidney Bechet.   Philip Larkin.   NoP-4; NoP-5

Scattering of mottled seeds, spots, A.   My Shining Archipelago.   Ansel Talvikki.   NeAmPo

Scatters of eider and shelduck ride.   Exilics: Leaving Lochboisdale, 1919.   Walter Perrie.   EdScPo

Scenario is: I'm six, and an invincible Venusian army of robots, The.   Meop.   Albert Goldbarth.   IllVoic

Scene 1. Front angle, dark sky, or the middle of the universe.   Images.   Kim Chôngnan.   EcSo, tr. by Peter H. Lee

Scene 3.   Achsa W. Sprague. Fr. Poet, The.

Scene 8.   Shin Tongyŏp.   CAMKP Fr. Kŭm River.

Scene 9.   Shin Tongyŏp.   CAMKP Fr. Kŭm River.

Scene, A.   Ani Ilkov.   CSCBP, tr. by Georgi Belev and Lisa Sapinkopf

Scene, The.   Ágnes Nemes Nagy.   PoSu, tr. by Bruce Berlind

Scene: A Bedside in the Witches' Kitchen.   Ramon Guthrie.   APT-2

Scene: A Farm Yard in South Texas.   Seventh Seal, The.   W. E. Bard.   TiP2

Scène de Boudoir.   Edmund Wilson.   OBCoV Fr. Easy Exercises in the Use of Difficult Words.

Scene for the Mornings Preceding the Fire, A.   Ghada El-Shafa'i.   PoArWo, tr. by Atef Abu-Seif and Nathalie Handal

Scene from a Play, Acted at Oxford, Called "Matriculation."   Thomas Moore.   OBSV

Scene from South Hill to North Hill Passing the Lake.   Hsieh Ling-yün.   ChinPo, tr. by Ye Weilian [or Yeh Wei-lien or Wai-lim Yip]

Scene from the Movie Giant.   Tino Villanueva.   ReTh

Scene in a Café.   Saunders Lewis.   BBMWP, tr. by Joseph P. Clancy

Scene is set for dreaming, The.   My Foolish Heart.   Ned Washington.   ReLy

Scene: "Meeting a former friend", The.   Reunion: A Scenario.   Vern Rutsala.   MotU

Scene of Return is Sketched, A.   Mercedes Roffé.   MirDau

Scene of superfluous grace, and wasted bloom.   Anna Seward.   PEW Fr. Colebrook Dale.

Scene on the Banks of the Hudson, A.   William Cullen Bryant.   NAAPv.1

Scene on the Northern Shore of Sicily.   Ann Radcliffe.   RWP

Scene within the paperweight is calm, The.   Paperweight, The.   Gjertrud Schnackenberg.   MoW; VCAP

Scenery bows for you & the skies defer, The.   Torn Ones, The.   John Wilkinson.   VaPo

Scenes for an Elegy.   Michael Klein.   WiU

Scenes from the Door.   Gertrude Stein.   AF

Scenes from the Life of the Peppertrees.   Denise Levertov.   NoP-4; NoP-5

Scenes from the Mesozoic.   Clarence Day.
    "Yesterday explorers found."   OBCoV

Scenes in London.   Letitia Elizabeth Landon.
    Piccadilly.   RWP

Scenes with Harlequins.   Geoffrey Hill.
    "Even now one is amazed."   UpMys

Scene-Script. Giancarlo Majorino. ItPo, *tr. by* Gayle Ridinger

Scent of hyacinths, like a pale mist, lies between me and my book, The. Vernal Equinox. Amy Lowell. APT-1; NAAPv.2

Scent of pencil, a house full, The. How Garnett Mims and the Enchanters Came into Your Life. Bruce Smith. SwNoth

Scent of plum blossoms. Kyoriku. EMJL, *tr. by* Haruo Shirane

Scent of plumeria, and the smell of burning. Warscape, with Lovers. Marilyn Krysl. LiTh

Scent of ripeness from over a wall, A. Unharvested. Robert Frost. APT-1; NAMCP V.1; SAmP

Scent of unseen jasmine on the warm night beach, The. Málaga. Pearse Hutchinson. ModIr; PBCIP

Scented Herbage of My Breast. Walt Whitman. APN-1; NAAL-3; OxBoAm

Scented with days to come. (LL) Girl Help. Janet Lewis. APT-2; CalPo; HeIP-4

Scenting Hounds pursued, The. Hare's Complaint, The. George Turberville. DiBP

Schad paced the length of his studio. Agosta the Winged Man and Rasha the Black Dove. Rita Dove. NAMCP V.2

Schadenfreude. Stephanie Brown. BodElec

Sche broghte him to his chambre tho. Ovid. NPeEn *Fr.* Confessio Amantis.

Schedule of Benefits, A. John N. Morris. PoA 2002

Scheherazade. Gillian Allnutt. NeBrP

Scheherazade. John Ashbery. FaoP

Scheme is tried; and shall it prosper too?, The. Thomas Baker. STuOW *Fr.* Steam Engine; or, The Power of the Flame, The.

Schemhammphorasch. Rose Terry Cooke. NAAPv.1; SWaP

Scherzo. Pamela Alexander. YaYoPo

Scherzo, A. Dora Greenwell. NPeEn

  (Scherzo A Shy Person's Wishes, A.) PEW

Schicksalslied. Friedrich Hölderlin. WoPoe *Fr.* Hyperion.

Schiehallion. Deric Bolton. EdScPo

Schizo de Picasso. Elin Llwyd Morgan. BBMWP, *tr. by* the author

Schizophrenic. Patricia K. Page. HeIP-4

Schizophrenic Africa for us enacts a Spring. Spring Report. Lionel Abrahams. TSAP

Schizophrenic, wrenched by two styles. Codicil. Derek Walcott. NoAM

Schluf mine faygele. Lullaby. Breyten Breytenbach. VCWP, *tr. by* Breyten Breytenbach

Scholar, The. Vijay Seshadri. KGB

Scholar and the Cat, The. *Unknown.* WoPoe, *tr. by* Frank O'Connor

Scholar, compose me a Magyar song. Matthias' Demented Scholar. Endre Ady. IQMS, *tr. by* Anton N. Nyerges

Scholar first my Love implor'd, A. Song. Dorothea Du Bois. LW

Scholar Gypsy, The. Matthew Arnold. NAEL-6v2; NAEL-7v2; NoP-4; NoP-5; OBEV; OxAEP-1; TFi

  "O born in days when wits were fresh and clear." OxBEV

  Scholar Gipsy, The. WaAnP

Scholar Recruit, The. Pao Chao. FaBoWar, *tr. by* Arthur Waley

Scholars. Walter De la Mare. NoAM

Scholars, The. William Butler Yeats. NoP-4; NoP-5

Scholars at the Orchid Pavilion. John Berryman. HarvBoo

Scholar's Cat, The. János Arany. IQMS, *tr. by* Neville Masterman

Scholar's Life, The. Juvenal. NPeEn; OBSV *Fr.* Vanity of Human Wishes, The; The Tenth Satire of Juvenal [Imitated].

School Among the Ruins, The. Adrienne Rich. AmWaPo; CAP-8

School and Nature. Jean Follain. BLT, *tr. by* W. S. Merwin

School and Schoolfellows. Winthrop Mackworth Praed. OxAEP-2

School Children, The. Louise Glück. ColAP; ItP; NAMCP V.2; PoPoPo; WeW-3

School for Scandal, The. Richard Brinsley Sheridan.

  Drinking Song. NPeEn; OxBEV

  (Song: "Here's to the maiden [*or* maid] of bashful fifteen.") IrLP; OxAEP-1

School is gone from Belgrave Place, The. Sean Dunne. ModIr *Fr.* Sydney Place.

School is long closed down, The. A Nos Glorieux Morts. Jan Eijkelboom. TuT, *tr. by* Michael O'Loughlin

School is over. It is too hot. Lonely Street, The. William Carlos Williams. APT-1

School Lesson Based on Word of Tragic Death of Entire Gillum Family. Robert Penn Warren. FuPo *Fr.* Promises.

School lets out for the summer. *Unknown.* NAAPv.2

School of clouds and a bunch, A. Fish. Mariana Romo-Carmona. WiU

School of Denial. Mary Ruefle. ExTi

School of Eloquence, The. Tony Harrison.

  Book Ends. NAEL-6v2; NAEL-7v2; NAMCP V.2

  Classics Society. NoP-4; NoP-5

  Heredity. HarvBoo; NAEL-6v2; NAEL-7v2; NAMCP V.2

  History Classes. NAMCP V.2

  Long Distance. NAEL-6v2; NAEL-7v2

  Marked with D.. InoFa; NAEL-6v2; NAEL-7v2; NAMCP V.2

  National Trust. HarvBoo; NAEL-6v2; NAEL-7v2; RSaN

  On Not Being Milton. CABP; HarvBoo; NAMCP V.2; NoP-4; NoP-5

  Self Justification. NAMCP V.2

  Timer. EmeKit; HarvBoo; NAMCP V.2

  Turns. NAEL-6v2; NAEL-7v2; NAMCP V.2

School of Fish. Eileen Myles. WiU

School Street. Matthew Zapruder. LegDan

School-Boy, The. William Blake. OxAEP-2 *Fr.* Songs of Experience.

Schoolcraft left the Soo—canoes. Lorine Niedecker. FTOS *Fr.* Lake Superior.

Schoolday's stretching time of fear and stress, The. Childhood. Rainer Maria Rilke. GTCP, *tr. by* Felix Pollak

Schoolgirls Hastening. John Shaw Neilson. NOBAu

Schooling, A. Seamus Deane. PNI

Schoolmaster, The. Herodas. HePo, *tr. by* Barbara Hughes Fowler

Schoolmaster once known as, The. History Teacher in the Warsaw Ghetto Rising. Evangeline Paterson. RSaN

Schoolmaster's Story, The. Robert Williams Buchanan. DiBP *Fr.* Willie Baird.

Schoolquine. Alastair MacKie. EdScPo

School's Out. W. H. Davies. OBMV

School-Time. William Wordsworth. NAEL-6v2; NAEL-7v2 *Fr.* Prelude, The; Growth of a Poet's Mind [1850 version].

School-Time. William Wordsworth. *Fr.* Prelude, The; Growth of a Poet's Mind [1805 version].

Schoolyard in April. Kenneth Koch. PoA 2002

Schoolyard tolls as once the graveyard did. Littleton. Michael Bugeja. LiTh

Schooner Flight, The. Derek Walcott. ESEAA; HarvBoo; NAEL-7v2; NAMCP V.2; NoP-4

  Adios, Carenage. NoP-5

Schooners with their pale green lights, The. Dream within a Song, A. Henrietta Cordelia Ray. CBWP-3

Schrimshaw Sailor, The. Gordon Meade. EdScPo

Schssssssss. Martin Steingesser. MoASP

Schubert, or: Notes on the Weather, Vienna. Friederike Mayröcker. OnScMo, *tr. by* Rosmarie Waldrop

Schubertiana. Tomas Tranströmer. WED, *tr. by* Robert Bly

Schute, Bell, Badgery, Lumby. Country Song, A. Douglas Stewart. NOBAu

Schutzstaffeln 45326. Dafydd Rowlands. BBMWP, *tr. by* Meic Stephens

Schwartzkopf's Copters. Sadiq al-Saygh. IrPoTo, *tr. by* Salaam Yousif

Schwinn rests in back seat. American Odalisque. Jane Miller. GifTon

Science. Samuel Davies. SacPr

Science. Michele Glazer. IAoNAP

Science and Human Behavior. John Hollander. YaYoPo

Science and Poetry. James Russell Lowell. NCAP

Science and the Single Girl. Karen Solie. PoPra

Science! bright Beam of Light Divine! Science. Samuel Davies. SacPr

Science Fiction. Kingsley Amis. NAMCP V.2; NoAM

Science! meet daughter of old Time thou art. Edgar Allan Poe. *See* Science! true daughter of Old Time thou art!

Science of Forgetting, The. Brother Yao. BtF

Science of Geology, The. James Milligan.

  "In ages past [animals] lived and died." VerBaPo

Science of the Night, The. Stanley Kunitz. APT-2; ColAP; MoAmPo

Science Revealed. George Eveleigh.

  Divine Mission, A. STuOW

Science, science, science! Venus Hottentot, The. Elizabeth Alexander. ESEAA; InTrad

Science! true daughter of Old Time thou art! Sonnet—To Science. Edgar Allan Poe. NAAPv.1; NCAP; NoP-4; NoP-5; OxBSo; TCAPo

  (Science! meet daughter of old Time thou art.) NAAL-3; NAAL-5; NAAPv.1

Sciences Sing a Lullabye, The. Albert Goldbarth. SUP

Scientific inquiry, seen in a very broad perspective may. Not a Cage. Joan Retallack. FTOS

Scientific Wooing. Constance Naden. VWP *Fr.* Evolutional Erotics.

Scientist has a test tube full of sheep, A. He wonders if he should. Counting Sheep. Russell Edson. SUP

Scientists are in terror, The. Ezra Pound. APSN *Fr.* Cantos.

Scilla. Louise Glück. WaAnP

Scillaes Metamorphosis. Thomas Lodge.
  "Minde through thee divines on endlesse things, The." PBRV
Scion of the high lord Gao Yang. On Encountering Trouble. Ch'u Yüan.
  CCL1, *tr. by* David Hawkes
Scirocco. Jorie Graham. FaoP
Scissors. Fabio Morabito. RMCMP, *tr. by* Geoff Hargreaves
Scissors are ambassadors of cold. They bring us notice of the brilliant cruelties
  that cold is capable of. Scissors. Fabio Morabito. RMCMP, *tr. by* Geoff
  Hargreaves
Scissors Ceremony, The. Michael Longley. EmeKit
Scissors Strokes by the Clock. Laurence Iché. SurWo, *tr. by* Myrna Bell
  Rochester
Scissortails. Teresa Whitman. TWW
Scolded like an impolite child. Saint Martha. Anna Kamienska. GI, *tr. by*
  David Curzon and Grażyna Drabik
Scolding My Sons. T'ao Ch'ien. PoChi, *tr. by* David Hinton
Scold's Mask. Miranda Field. LegDan
Scones. *Unknown.* OBCoV
Scorched with love, the cicada. Kenneth Rexroth. APSN; NAAPv.2 *Fr.* Love
  Poems of Marichiko, The.
Scorcher, The. Edward F. Strange. ArBi
Scorcher's Farewell to His Steed, The. Charles Dryden. ArBi
Scorn. Carol Frost. CAP-8
Scorn not the Sonnet; Critic, you have frowned. Scorn Not the Sonnet [Critic,
  You Have Frowned]. William Wordsworth. CenSon; GSo; HeIP-4; NoP-
  4; NoP-5; NPBRoP; OxBSo; WaAnP
Scorpion. Stevie Smith. NPeEn; OxAEP-2
Scorpion, The. William Plomer. OBMV
Scorpion so wishes to be gone. (LL) Scorpion. Stevie Smith. NPeEn;
  OxAEP-2
Scorpions, The. Alfonso X. NAWM-7v1, *tr. by* Peter Dronke
Scotch. Ruth Padel. MFPA
Scotch and Soda. Jenny Factor. CalPo
Scotch Broth. Robert Crawford. EdScPo
Scotch Drink. Robert Burns. ChIV-1
Scotch God / Kent His. Scotched. Alexander Scott. EdScPo
Scotch God / Kent His / Faither. Alexander Scott. OBCoV; WoPoe *Fr.*
  Scotched.
Scotch mist is a shroud, The. National Depression Awareness Week. Mary
  Ruefle. IJHIL
Scotch Song, A. Joanna Baillie. RWP
Scotch Te Deum. William Kethe. SacPr
Scotched. Alexander Scott. EdScPo
Scotched. Alexander Scott.
  "*Scotch God* / Kent His / Faither." OBCoV; WoPoe
Scotchman Salvage. Joe Denham. OpeFie
Scotland. Sir Alexander Gray. EdScPo
Scotland. Frederick Seidel. BodElec
Scotland: "Green-coated elms stand placidly around." Rayne Mackinnon.
  EdScPo
Scotland: "It was a day peculiar to this piece of the planet." Alastair Reid.
  EdScPo; NePenScot
Scotland 1941. Edwin Muir. CABP; EdScPo; NePenScot
Scotland Small? Hugh MacDiarmid. NePenScot
Scotland the wee, crèche of the soul. Scotland the Wee. Tom Buchan.
  EdScPo
Scotland, when it is given to me. With a Lifting of the Head. Hugh
  MacDiarmid. MoBrPo
Scotland, you have invoked her name. Queen of Sheba, The. Kathleen Jamie.
  EdScPo; NePenScot; RSaN
Scotland's Winter. Edwin Muir. EdScPo; NePenScot
Scots, wha hae wi' Wallace bled. Scots Wha Hae. Robert Burns. NAEL-6v2
Scott and I bent. Heaven. Gary Soto. SwNoth
Scott Joplin. Bill Holm. MiVo
Scot[t]ish Field[e]. *Unknown.*
  Battle of Flodden, The. NoSic
Scottish Mythology. Raymond Vettese. EdScPo
Scottish Names. Raymond Vettese. EdScPo
Scottish Renaissance in Glasgow, The: 1935. Naomi Mitchison. EdScPo
Scott's Dogs at Melrose Abbey. Arthur Henry Hallam. DiBP
Scottsboro. Betsalel Friedman. Prolet, *tr. by* Amelia Glaser
Scottsboro. Y. A. Rontsh. Prolet, *tr. by* Amelia Glaser
Scotty Has His Say. Sterling Allen Brown. APT-2
Scoundrel carries his baseness around like an ID card, The. Answer. Bei Dao.
  PoetW; VCWP, *tr. by* Donald Finkel
Scourge of Folly, The. John Davies of Hereford.
  Author Loving These Homely Meats, The. NPeEn; OBCoV

Scourge of Villainy [*or* Villanie], The. John Marston.
  To Detraction I Present My Poesie. NoSic
  To Everlasting Oblivion. NoSic
Scourge of Villanie, The. John Marston.
  "Fy Satyre fie, shall each mechanick slave." PBRV
Scout. Wendell Ricketts. BRtP
Scrabble. David Starkey. ReTh
Scrambled Eggs and Garlic Pork. Michael Melo. ReBoTo
Scrambled Eggs and Whiskey. Hayden Carruth. GoPo
Scrap. Tomasz Jastrun. AF, *tr. by* Daniel Bourne
Scrape / memory. For Michael Griffith, Murdered Dec. 21, 1986, Howard
  Beach, NY. Jeffrey Renard Allen. BRtP
Scrape the bottom of the hole: gather up the stuff! Digger's Song, The.
  Barcroft Henry Boake. NOBAu
Scraps of moon. Denise Levertov. NAMCP V.2
Scraps of Time. Mrs. Henry Linden. CBWP-4
Scraptures: 17th Sequence. B. P. Nichol. PFTM-2 *Fr.* Martyrology 7, The.
Scraptures: 7th Sequence. B. P. Nichol. FTOS
Scratch a Jew and you'll find a wailing Wall. Wall, The. Eve Merriam. TaR
Scratching. Kikaku. EMJL
Scrawled in Pencil in a Sealed Car. Dan Pagis. PoSu, *tr. by* Robert Friend
Scrawny women of the foundry workers, The. Scrawny Women, The. Gloria
  Fuertes. RaW, *tr. by* Robert Mezey
Scrawny-necked black girls. Dewey Square, 1956. Percy Johnston. EGAG
Scream! Nesta Wyn Jones. BBMWP, *tr. by* Robert Minhinnick
Scream, The. Donald Hall. GS
Scream is a Kind of Coffin, The. Paz Molina. TANSG, *tr. by* Steven F. White
Scream of Abû Nuwàs, The. Jolanda Insana. *tr. by* Cinzia Sartini Blum and
  Lara Trubowitz
  "From wonder to wonder." CItWP, *tr. by* Cinzia Sartini Blum and Lara
  Trubowitz
Scream that climbs a candle, A. Screams in the Dark. Slavko Mihalic.
  PoSu, *tr. by* Charles Simic
Scream that seems to be heard when we step into bright morning, A. Mice.
  Kim Hyesun. EcSo, *tr. by* Youngju Ryu
Scream, The: Edvard Munch (1893). Alan Llwyd. BBMWP, *tr. by* Joseph P.
  Clancy
Screaming and laughing; soaked right through. (LL) Pounding Rain. Jackie
  Kay. MFPA; PoBW
Screaming My Head Off. Vladimir Vladimirovich Mayakovsky. PFTM-1
Screaming through the streets. (LL) Malcolm. Lucille Clifton. InoFa;
  WaAnP
Screams and hair come out. Stella Morotskaya. CRWP, *tr. by* Vitaly
  Chernetsky
Screams in the birth of her fading away. (LL) Lake in Central Park, The. Jay
  Wright. ESEAA; GT
Screams in the Dark. Slavko Mihalic. PoSu, *tr. by* Charles Simic
Screech owls moan in the yellowing. Travelling Northward. Tu Fu [*or* Du
  Fu]. BLT; CCL1; NDACCP, *tr. by* Kenneth Rexroth
Screen of supreme good fortune curved, The. Young Son, The. John Ashbery.
  YaYoPo
Screen Porch. Frederick Marchant. UrbNat
Screening its face amongst lotus stalks. Mahendranâth Bhattâcârya. SinGod,
  tr. by Rachel Fell McDermott
Screens. Barry Silesky. IllVoic
Screes, The. William Scammell. NLP
Screes are speeding down at perfect pitch, The. Screes, The. William
  Scammell. NLP
Screw-Guns. Rudyard Kipling. FaBoWar
Scribble— / the self centred—a latititude. Arrhythmia. Barry McKinnon.
  NLPA
Scribbled at a Cabinet Meeting. Sir Edward Carlson. FaBoVe
Scribblers, The. Walter Savage Landor. OBSV
Scribe, The. Walter De la Mare. OBMV
Scribe, The. *Unknown.* IrV, *tr. by* Kuno Meyer
Scribe, The: "For Weariness My Hand Writes Ill." *Unknown.* IrV, *tr. by*
  Alfred Perceval Graves
Scribes, The. Suzanne Noguere. FFC
Scribes have cast the blame, The. *Unknown.* WoPoe *Fr.* Lamentations.
Scrimmage of appetite everywhere, The. (LL) Delmore Schwartz. APT-2;
  ColAP; FTtHH; NAMCP V.2; NoAM; StAl *Fr.* Repetitive Heart, The.
Script Conference. John Hartley Williams. EmeKit
Scripts I used to write for the young actor, The. Written, Directed by and
  Starring. James Simmons. PBCIP
Scripture of the Golden Eternity, The. Jack Kerouac.
  "Did I create that sky? Yes, for, if it was." CLPP
  "You are the golden eternity because there is." WhBo
Scroll. Lee Upton. AmAlph

Scroll, The.   Kathleen Spivack.   PfS

Scroll 1: "From the Three Emperors and Five Kings down to Hsia, Shang, and Chou."   *Chinese Oral Tradition.*   ColAnChi *Fr.* Expository Tale on King Wu's Expedition Against Chow.

Scroll is open, The.   "Ada."   SWaP

Scroll is open—many a name is written, The.   Scroll is open, The.   "Ada."   SWaP

Scroll No. 1.   Cecil Taylor.   EGAG

Scroll No. 2.   Cecil Taylor.   EGAG

Scroll passes hands in, A.   Fall aster with firefly.   Shin Yu Pai.   AmZen

Scrotal burning, night, all day, night two, A.   Recognition, The.   John Berryman.   BodElec

Scrub.   Edna St. Vincent Millay.   APT-1

Scrub woman for the old bank and jailhouse, The.   Lamentations.   Norman Dubie.   NoAM

Scrubbing the upstairs tub at our first housecleaning job of the day.   Hurricane Sisters Work Regardless, The.   Ginger Andrews.   SweBea

Scuba Diver Recovers the Body of a Drowned Child, The.   Gerald William Barrax.   GT; OxAAAP

Sculler, The.   John Taylor.

"As Gold is better that's in fire tride."   PBRV

Sculptor musing sat one eve, A.   Sculptor's Vision, The.   Henrietta Cordelia Ray.   CBWP-3

Sculptor, The.   Cornelius Mathews.   APN-1 *Fr.* Poems on Man in His Various Aspects under the American Republic.

Sculptor's Vision, The.   Henrietta Cordelia Ray.   CBWP-3

Sculpture.   Joseph Ceravolo.   NYP2

Sculpture Garden.   Austin Hummell.   AmPoNex

Scum & Slime.   John Giorno.   PmAP

Scunner.   Hugh MacDiarmid.   NePenScot

Scyld was still a strong man when his time came.   Ship of Death, A.   Seamus Heaney.   NAEL-6v2; NoP-4

Scyros.   Karl Shapiro.   PWW2

Scythed god whose part is greater than the whole.   *Unknown.*   PriapPo *Fr.* Priapus Poems, The.

Se acabó.   Víctor Terán.   RMCMP

Se Aprovechan.   Irving Feldman.   GS

Sé de tu cuerpo: los arrecifes.   En esta oscura mezquita tibia.   Coral Bracho.   RMCMP

Se dejaba montar como la banca del parque.   Caballo de acero, El.   Dana Gelinas.   SPV

Se déversent.   Tahar Bekri.   YaTCFP *Fr.* Retour en Tunisie.

Se durmió en la cocina como un trapo.   Censoria.   Blas de Otero.   RaW

Se Entró en Mi Frente el Pensamiento Negro.   Juan Ramón Jiménez.   RaW

Se escapan indefectiblemente. Voy.   Arca.   Gerardo Deniz.   RMCMP

Se me aparece blanco en la mañana.   Aparecido, El.   Rafael Alberti.   RaW

¡Se me mueren! Han vivido.   Muerte de Unos Zapatos.   Jorge Guillén.   RaW

Se mete / la humedad.   Ana Belén López Pulido.   SPV

Se murió diez centímetros tan sólo.   Cadáver Ínfimo.   Angel González.   RaW

Se tiene todo a sí mismo el bosque.   Ánimo vegetal.   Francisco Segovia.   RMCMP

Sea.   Marie-Claire Bancquart.   MFP, *tr. by* Martin Sorrell

Sea.   Dylan Iorwerth.   BBMWP *Fr.* Sand.

Sea.   *Unknown.*   SonAtl, *tr. by* Lester Browne, P. Ensor and Edward Kandy

Sea.   Valerie Wohlfeld.   YaYoPo

Sea: "It's he, it's sea. the sea is continuous; a continuous body."   Bernadette Mayer.   NYP2

Sea, The.   Jorge Luis Borges.   TCLAP, *tr. by* John Updike

Sea, The.   E. A. Markham.   EmeKit

Sea, The.   Esther Morgan.   BeAl

Sea, The.   Mu Hua.   CCL1, *tr. by* David Knechtges

Sea, The.   James Reeves.   NOxBChV

Sea, The: "Ladies, why don't you lift a stone."   Yi Hyangji.   EcSo, *tr. by* Catherine J. Kim

Sea and a crescent strip of beach, The.   George Oppen.   APSN *Fr.* Some San Francisco Poems.

Sea and Other Stories, The.   Jennifer Rankin.   NOBAu

Sea and the Canefield, The.   João Cabral de Melo Neto.   TCLAP, *tr. by* Louis Simpson

Sea and the Man, The.   Anna Swirszczynska [*or* Swir].   BLT

Sea and the Mirror, The.   W. H. Auden.

Supporting Cast, Sotto Voce, The.

Miranda.   NoAM; NPeEn

Sea and the Skylark, The.   Gerard Manley Hopkins.   OBMV

Sea and You, The.   Julia de Burgos.   TANSG, *tr. by* Heather Rosario Sievert

Sea Anemones, The.   Gwen Harwood.   BMAP

Sea asks 'How is your life now?', The.   Sea Question, The.   Elizabeth Smither.   BeAl

Sea at evening moves across the sand, The.   Soldiers Bathing.   Frank Templeton Prince.   MoBrPo; OBWP

Sea at Twenty-Four, The.   Kim Chôngnan.   EcSo, *tr. by* Peter H. Lee

Sea awoke at midnight from its sleep, The.   Sound of the Sea, The.   Henry Wadsworth Longfellow.   ITBLP; TCAPo

Sea Bells.   Miriam Waddington.   BrAP

Sea Breeze.   Mitch Highfill.   HeMarv

Sea Breeze.   Stéphane Mallarmé.   WoPoe, *tr. by* Louis Simpson

Sea Breeze.   Stéphane Mallarmé.   SxFrPo, *tr. by* A. M. and E. H. Blackmore

Sea by Dusk.   Joanna Klink.   IAoNAP

Sea Cadences.   Henrietta Cordelia Ray.   CBWP-3

Sea Calm.   Langston Hughes.   APT-2

Sea calm, sky blue, moon just now full.   Year Keng-Wu, Night of the Fifteenth, Facing the Moon, The.   Ch'i-chi.   CSKM, *tr. by* Burton Watson

Sea Canes.   Derek Walcott.   HeIP-4; InoFa

Sea Change.   John Masefield.   OBMV

Sea Chanty.   Gregory Corso.   BB

Sea Chanty.   Suzanne Lummis.   CalPo

Sea crawls from the shore, The.   Old Woman of Beare, The.   *Unknown.*   WoPoe, *tr. by* Brendan Kenneally and Brendan Kennelly

Sea darkening, The.   Basho.   EH, *tr. by* Robert Hass

Sea darkening, The.   Basho.   EMJL, *tr. by* Haruo Shirane

Sea Dreams.   Rosita Copioli.   CItWP, *tr. by* Cinzia Sartini Blum and Lara Trubowitz

Sea Eats the Land at Home, The.   Kofi Awoonor.   EmeKit

Sea, False Philosophy.   Laura Riding Jackson.   APT-2

Sea Fever.   John Masefield.   BLPJKO; BRP; CABP; ChAP; ITBLP; MoBrPo; OxAEP-2; UV; WaAnP

Sea flat out / the light far out, The.   Mazatlan: Sea.   Robert Creeley.   APSN

Sea Grapes: "That sail in cloudless light."   Derek Walcott.   TRP

(Sour Grapes.)   BodElec

Sea Grapes: "That sail which leans on light."   Derek Walcott.   PoetW

Sea, great mercury mirror, The.   Symphony in Gray Major.   Rubén Darío.   SpanPo, *tr. by* Denise Levertov

Sea grows dark, The.   Basho.   WED, *tr. by* Robert Bly

Sea grows rough, The.   Basho.   WED, *tr. by* Robert Bly

Sea Gypsy, The.   Richard Hovey.   BRP; TCAPo

Sea has made a wall for its defence, The.   Shoreline.   Mary Barnard.   APT-2

Sea here used to look, The.   At Darien Bridge.   James Dickey.   InGu; LPSFW

Sea Holly.   Conrad Potter Aiken.   APT-1

Sea howling and moaning by itself, The.   Guillaume Apollinaire.   PFTM-1 *Fr.* Victoire.

Sea Inside the Sea.   Tess Gallagher.   PasH

Sea Iris.   "H. D."   APT-1

Sea is a blue garden of crystal flowers, The.   Sea Surrounded.   Dulce Maria Loynaz.   TANSG, *tr. by* Alan West

Sea is a hungry dog, The.   Sea, The.   James Reeves.   NOxBChV

Sea is a wall, The.   Tomas Tranström.   WoBe *Fr.* Haiku.

'Sea is Awash with Roses, The'.   Kenneth Patchen.   CLPP

Sea is calm tonight [*or* to-night], The.   Dover Beach.   Matthew Arnold.   AmFaPo; BrAP; BRP; CABP; ClHu; CtM; HeIP-4; ITBLP; MakPoe; NAEL-6v2; NAEL-7v2; NIL-7; NIP-4; NoP-4; NoP-5; NPeEn; OxBEV; PoPoPo; TFi; WaAnP; WoPoe

Sea is calm to-night, The.   Dover Beach.   Tom Clark.   OxBoAm

Sea Is Enormous, The.   Juan Ramón Jiménez.   SpanPo, *tr. by* James Wright

Sea is enormous, The.   Sea Is Enormous, The.   Juan Ramón Jiménez.   SpanPo, *tr. by* James Wright

Sea Is History, The.   Derek Walcott.   BrAP; NAMCP V.2

Sea is made of ponds—a cairn of rain, The.   Sea Sonnet.   Alice Oswald.   NeBrP; OxBSo

Sea is moving under our passage, The.   Crossing the Straits.   Richard Greene.   Coast

Sea is the Aegean Sea which goes beyond Alicante.   In Honor of the Sardana and the Tenora.   Max Jacob.   CuPo

Sea Joy.   Jacqueline Kennedy Onassis.   BLPJKO

Sea Love.   Charlotte Mew.   LW; MoBrPo; OxAEP-2; OxBEV

Sea Lullaby.   Elinor Wylie.   OxBoAm

Sea Marke.   John Smith.   TCAPo

Sea Monkeys, The.   Barbara J. Orton.   NeAmPo

Sea of Faith.   John Brehm.   RaF

Sea of feathers billows, A. It billows with happy billows.   Around the Star's Throne.   Hans Arp.   MotU, *tr. by* Bethany Schneider

Sea of Kansas, Ohio Tundra, Time Still Running Out, The.   David Citino.   UpMys

Sea of living silver.   Visions.   Elsa Cross.   TANSG, *tr. by* Patricia Dubrava

Sea of Oblivion.   Takahashi Shinkichi.   ZenPo, *tr. by* Takashi Ikemoto and Lucien Stryk

Sea of Zhang swells to the very sky, The. Written at Jumble-Rock Mountain by the South Sea. Du Shenyan. CCL1, *tr.* by Stephen Owen

Sea opens no door before me, The. On a Canaanite Stone in the Dead Sea. Mahmoud Darwish. PML, *tr.* by Muna Asali van Engen

Sea or Sky? Medbh McGuckian. PBCIP

Sea Owl [*with music*]. Dave Jeddie Smith. RoV

Sea Poppies. "H. D." APT-1; NALW

Sea Question, The. Elizabeth Smither. BeAl

Sea rages to break the silver mountain, The. While Sleeping at the Southern Sea. Chunghur Hyujung. BecRai, *tr.* by Kim Daljin, Kim Won-Chung and Christopher Merrill

Sea Replies to Byron, The. G. K. Chesterton. UV

Sea rocks her thousand of waves, The. Rocking. Gabriela Mistral. BBASP; CFP, *tr.* by Doris Dana

Sea Rose. "H. D." APT-1; HeIP-4; MoWP; NAAPv.2; NAMCP V.1; NIL-7; NoAM; NoP-4; NoP-5; OxWW; TRP; WaAnP

Sea serpent is, The. CXXXIV. Pita Amor. TANSG, *tr.* by Shaun Griffin and Emma Sepúlveda-Pulvirenti

Sea Shells. Lorna Lowe. BtF

Sea shone, The. During War, the Timeless Air. John Seed. Oth

Sea sighs, thieves fly, The. Sigh, The. Nathalie Handal. PoArWo

Sea Similized to Meadows and Pastures, The: the Mariners, to Shepherds: the Mast, to a May-Pole: the Fish, to Beasts. Margaret Lucas Cavendish, Duchess of Newcastle. NoP-4; NoP-5

Sea 6. Chŏng Chiyong. CAMKP, *tr.* by Kevin O'Rourke

Sea slaps the sleeping beach's ear, The. Beyond the Breakers. Joyce Mansour. MFP, *tr.* by Martin Sorrell

Sea Song. Luis Omar Salinas. GeoHom

Sea Song, A. William Shakespeare. NBLV; OBCoV

Sea Sonnet. Alice Oswald. NeBrP; OxBSo

Sea Spray. Marion Margaret Boyd. YaYoPo

Sea Sprite, Hermosa Beach, The. Maurya Simon. GeoHom

Sea stares at my dream, The. Gulf. Dhabya Khamees. PoArWo, *tr.* by Clarissa C. Burt

Sea Stone. Sinéad Morrissey. NIrP

Sea sucks at its own, The. Landcrab II. Margaret Atwood. NIP-4

Sea Surface Full of Clouds. Wallace Stevens. APT-1; MoAmPo

Sea Surrounded. Dulce Maria Loynaz. TANSG, *tr.* by Alan West

Sea, the Memory, and the Woman, The. Seyfettin Başcıllar. NaPG, *tr.* by Talat Sait Halman

Sea to the West. Norman Nicholson. BeAl

Sea took a sailor to its deep.—, The. Supplication. Constantine P. Cavafy. BLT, *tr.* by Rae Dalven

Sea Unicorns and Land Unicorns. Marianne Moore. NALW; PFTM-1

Sea View, The. Charlotte Smith. CenSon; NAEL-7v2

Sea View, Water's Edge, Atlantis. Double Writing. Stephen Knight. NeBl

Sea Violet. "H. D." APT-1; MoWP; NAMCP V.1; NoP-4; NoP-5

Sea was in front of me, The. Dream. No Hyangnim. EcSo, *tr.* by Aimee N. Kwon

Sea Washes Sand Scours Sea. Tom Vander Ven. PoDa

Sea waves are green and wet. Sand Dunes. Robert Frost. MoAmPo

Sea We Read About, The. Philip Levine. GeoHom

Sea whisper'd [*or whispered*] me, The. (LL) Out of the Cradle Endlessly Rocking. Walt Whitman. APN-1; ColAP; HeIP-4; MoAmPo; NAAL-3; NAAL-5; NAAPv.1; NAWM-7v2; NCAP; NoP-4; NoP-5; OWoS; OxBoAm; SAmP; TRP

Sea wind sways on over the endless oceans, The. Sea Wind, The. Harry Edmund Martinson. WED, *tr.* by Robert Bly

Sea Without Poets. Branko Miljkovic. WoPoe, *tr.* by Charles Simic

Sea without sailors, or phantom ships. Yramín and the Sea. Manuel Vázquez Montalbán. RaW, *tr.* by Robert Mezey

Sea woke up, The. Danila Stoyanova. CSCBP, *tr.* by Georgi Belev and Lisa Sapinkopf

Sea World. Eric Berlin. OPRER

Sea yes learns from the canefield, The. Sea and the Canefield, The. João Cabral de Melo Neto. TCLAP, *tr.* by Louis Simpson

Sea yes teaches the canefield, The. Canefield and the Sea, The. João Cabral de Melo Neto. TCLAP, *tr.* by Louis Simpson

Sea-Breeze at Matanzas, The. Epes Sargent. APN-1

Sea-bundle. Jennifer Rankin. BMAP

Sea-Chill. Arthur Guiterman. UV

Seacoast wears you out with damp and heat. White Crane Hill. Su Tung-p'o. ColAnChi; GifTon, *tr.* by Burton Watson

Sea-Cucumber, The. Martin Johnston. BMAP

Sea-Elephant, The. William Carlos Williams. SAmP

Seafarer (c. 10th century), The. *Unknown.*

Seafarer, The. Henry Howard, Earl of Surrey. NoSic; NPeEn (Complaint of the Absence of Her Lover Being upon the Sea.) OBEV (O Happy Dames, That May Embrace.) NAEL-6v1; NAEL-7v1

Seafarer, The. *Unknown.* SacPr, *tr.* by Margaret Williams

Seafarer, The. *Unknown.* OBVE, *tr.* by Michael Alexander

Seafarer, The. *Unknown.* NoP-4

Seafarer, The. *Unknown.* APT-1; HeIP-4; NoP-4; NoP-5; OxBoAm; TCAPo; WaAnP; WoPoe *Fr.* Ripostes of Ezra Pound.

Seafarer, The. *Unknown.*
"Tale I frame shall be found to tally." OBVE

Seafarers. Georg Heym. WoPoe, *tr.* by Christopher Benfey

Seafarers tell of a magic island. My Trip in a Dream to the Lady of Heaven Mountain A Farewell to Several Gentlemen of Eastern Lu. Li Po. CCL1, *tr.* by Elling O. Eide

Sea-foam / And coral! Oh, I'll. Laurel in the Berkshires. Adelaide Crapsey. NAAPv.2

Sea-god, when he walked the beach, shared out, The. Foam. Roland Jones. WoPoe, *tr.* by Anthony Conran

Seagull. Brian McCabe. EdScPo

Seagull, The. Dafydd ap Gwilym. OBWVE; TCAWP, *tr.* by Glyn Jones

Sea-Gull, The. Ogden Nash. OWoS

Seagull, The. Siôn Phylip. OBWVE, *tr.* by Joseph P. Clancy

Sea-Gull and the Ea-Gull, The. Ogden Nash. ReLy

Sea-gull *is* so sorry!, The. Sorrowful Sea-Gull, The. Menella Bute Smedley. VWP

Sea-gull met an ea-gull, A. Sea-Gull and the Ea-Gull, The. Ogden Nash. ReLy

Seagull shrilly in my head, A. Inga Kuznetsova. CRWP, *tr.* by Max Nemtsov

Seagulls. Judith Herzberg. TuT, *tr.* by Greg Delanty

Seagulls. Daria Menicanti. CItWP, *tr.* by Cinzia Sartini Blum and Lara Trubowitz

Seagulls. John Updike. OWoS

Sea-hawks are calling. *Unknown.* CCL1 *Fr.* Guan-ju.

Seal Cave. Brenda Chamberlain. TCAWP

Seal Island. Tom Sexton. PoCoUp

Seal swims like a poodle through the sheet, A. Flaw, The. Robert Lowell. HarvBoo

Seal up the book, all vision's at an end. On the Death of Mr. Pope. *Unknown.* NPeEn

Sealed at their lips like urgent telegrams. (LL) Bicycle. David Malouf. ArBi; BMAP

Sealed in rainlight one. Magic Apple Tree, The. Elaine Feinstein. HarvBoo

Sealed in your pewter coat. Sand Shark. Nancy Willard. PoCoUp

Sea-Limits, The [*rev. vers. of* "From the Cliffs: Noon"]. Dante Gabriel Rossetti. NAEL-6v2

Sealink. Brendan Cleary. NeBl

Seals, The. Pauline Stainer. NeBl

Seals at High Island. Richard Murphy. ModIr; PBCIP

Seals at play off Western Isle, The. Seals, Terns, Time. Richard Eberhart. MoAmPo

Seal's cry has lain against my leg, A. Sheila Nickerson. GifTon

Seals in Penobscot Bay, The. Daniel Gerard Hoffman. YaYoPo

Seals of love, but seal'd in vain, seal'd in vain! (LL) William Shakespeare. NoSic; OBEV; TFi *Fr.* Measure for Measure.

Seals, Terns, Time. Richard Eberhart. MoAmPo

Seal's wide spindrift gaze toward paradise, The. (LL) Hart Crane. ColAP; MoAmPo; OxBoAm; RaBo; TRP; WaAnP; WoPoe *Fr.* Voyages.

Seaman, 1941 [*with music*]. Molly Holden. PoAgWa

Seamen's Mission. Gerald Dawe. PNI

Seamless. Gojusan. ZenPo, *tr.* by Takashi Ikemoto and Lucien Stryk

Seams. Hazel Hall. APT-1

Seamstress stitches on a sewing machine, The. Mikhail Yeryomin. ItGoST, *tr.* by J. Kates

Seamstress, The. Zinaida Nikolayevna Gippius. ARWW, *tr.* by Catriona Kelly

Seamus of the Smart Suit, box player. Harmonies. Thomas Kinsella. ModIr

Sea-palms. *Unknown.* SonAtl, *tr.* by P. Alleyne, Tim Hillier, Terence Madeleine, Jean-Claude Mahoune, Christopher Morau and Alan Starr

Sea-perch over paddocks. Dunes. Salt light everywhere low down. Greenhouse Vanity, The. Les A. Murray. FaBoVe

Sea-Polyp, The. Julia Copus. NeBl

Sea-preserved, heaped with sea-spoils. Picture of a Nativity. Geoffrey Hill. NoAM; UpMys

Sear at the center. Robert Creeley. WoBe *Fr.* Life and Death.

Search. Eleanor Slater. YaYoPo

Search, The. John Hewitt. PNI

Search, The. Inge Hoogerhuis. HW

Search, The. Charles Shaw. NOBAu

Search, The. Maurya Simon. ExTi

Search, The. Henry Vaughan. ChIV-2
   "Leave, leave, thy gadding thoughts." SacPr
Search, The: "Where are the poems I promised." Gabriel Rosenstock. IrLP
Search all the Christian climes from pole to pole. Daniel Defoe. OBSV *Fr.* Reformation of Manners.
Search every land, from Cadiz to the dawn-streaked shores. Juvenal. RomPo *Fr.* Satires.
Search for Apollo, A. Agnes Mary Frances Robinson. VWP
Search for Baby Combover, The. David Kirby. PoDa
Search for My Tongue. Sujata Bhatt.
   "You ask me what I mean." PFTM-2
Search for True Religion, The. John Donne. *See* Satire 3 [Religion].
Search Party. W. S. Merwin. PoA 2002
Search Party. Mary Ruefle. AmAlph
Search the length of your eyes. Joseph speaks to gericault in the studio. Michael Datcher. BRtP
Search to get lost in a great big coat, The. Laura Chester. OnScMo *Fr.* Free Rein.
Searchin'. Jerry Leiber *and* Michael E. Stoller and Michael E. Stoller. FTtHH
Searching. Cathy Grindrod. Prnts
Searching for Gathered Fragrance Temple. Way to the Temple, The. Wang Wei. CrYelRi, *tr. by* Sam Hamill
Searching for *Melinda's Magic Moment.* Allison Joseph. NAPBL
Searching for Mooncakes. Kathe Davis. AmZen
Searching for Pittsburgh. Jack Gilbert. BeAl
Searching Him took. Keppo. ZenPo, *tr. by* Takashi Ikemoto and Lucien Stryk
Searching, seeking. Long Melancholy Tune, A. Li Ch'ing-chao. ColAnChi, *tr. by* Jiaosheng Wang
Searching storehouse eaves. Basho. SoOfWa, *tr. by* Sam Hamill
Searching the darkness for a landing place. (LL) Downstream ("Drifting to meet us on the darkening stage.") Thomas Kinsella. HarvBoo; PBCIP
Searching was easy and memory ripens, The. Blood Donor. Robert Morgan. AngWePo; TCAWP
Searchlights. Kenneth Mackenzie. BMAP
Seared to the Echo. Barry MacSweeney. VaPo
Sgt. Christopher and I are. OK Corral East: Brothers in the Nam. Horace Coleman. AmWaPo
Sears Catalogue, The. Alan Michael Parker. RWB
Sea's Abundant Progeny, The. William Wood. NOSC
Seas are quiet when the winds give o'er, The. Edmund Waller. OBEV *Fr.* Of the Last Verses in the Book.
Seas Incarnadine. R. P. Blackmur. APT-2
Seas of Faith are full again with vain, The. Valentine for Matthew Arnold, A. William Logan. PoA 2002
Seas of Sorrow boil with a rage, Magyar, The. To the Hungarians. Dániel Berzsenyi. IQMS, *tr. by* Adam Makkai
Seas slowly darken. Basho. SoOfWa, *tr. by* Sam Hamill
Sea's Wash in the Hollow of the Heart, The. Denise Levertov. LW
Seascape. Elizabeth Bishop. ColAP; OxBoAm
Seascape. Stanley Noyes. ICANM
Seascape. Arthur Rimbaud. SxFrPo, *tr. by* Martin Sorrell
Seascape. Stephen Spender. NoP-4; NoP-5
Seascape. Edward Young. STuOW *Fr.* Resignation.
Seashell. Rubén Darío. SpanPo, *tr. by* Anita Volland
Sea-Shell, The. Ina Coolbrith. NAAPv.1
Seashell, The. Rubén Darío. TCLAP, *tr. by* Lysander Kemp
Sea-Shore. Ralph Waldo Emerson. APN-1; ColAP
Sea-Sickness. Heinrich Heine. WoPoe, *tr. by* Vernon Watkins
Seaside, The. Lee Harwood. AHA
Seaside, and the fragment of one running. Reliquaries, The. Valerie Martínez. TouFir
Sea-Side Cave, The. Alice Cary. APN-2; ColAP; NAAPv.1
Seaside Cemetery, The. Paul Valéry. YaTCFP, *tr. by* Derek Mahon
Season, The. Anne MacNaughton. ICANM
Season for Hunting, A. Teresa D. Cader. PfSP
Season greeter, The. Yomono Akara. EMJL, *tr. by* Burton Watson
Season late, day late, sun just down, and the sky. Birth of Love. Robert Penn Warren. APT-2; VCAP
Season of Anger. René Depestre. PFTM-2, *tr. by* Pierre Joris
Season of Beginning and End. Zuhur Dixon. CFP, *tr. by* Patricia Alanah Byrne and Salma Khadra Jayyusi
Season of Locking-In, The. Christiane Jacox Kyle. YaYoPo
Season of Loss, A [*with music*]. Jim Barnes. HATNAP
Season of mists and mellow fruitfulness! To Autumn. John Keats. BrAP; CABP; ClHu; CtM; HeIP-4; ITBLP; MakPoe; NAEL-6v2; NAEL-7v2; NAWM-7v2; NIL-7; NIP-4; NOBRP; NoP-4; NoP-5; NPBRoP; NPeEn; OBEV; OxAEP-2; OxBEV; PoPoPo; PtR; RaBo; SoSe-8; TFi; TRP; WaAnP; WeW-3

Season of Paradise, A. José Luis Rivas. RMCMP, *tr. by* Reginald Gibbons
Season of Phantasmal Peace, The. Derek Walcott. EmeKit; GPTC; NAMCP V.2; PoetW; PoPoPo; VCWP
Season of rains: the horizon like an illness. Autumn 1942. Roy Fuller. PoWW
Season of Shadow draws to an end in silence, The. Season of Shadow, The. Yu Hsin. CCL1, *tr. by* John Frodsham
Season Song. Judith Nicholls. Spl
Season Song. *Unknown.* WoPoe, *tr. by* Flann O'Brien and Flann O'Brien
Season turned like the page of a glossy fashion magazine, The. Change, The. Tony Hoagland. BeAl
Season with Angels. Judyth Hill. ICANM
Seasonal. Karen Volkman. AmPoNex
Seasonal, 1991. Roland Flint. PoCho
Seasonal Ramble. Tony Towle. PoDa
Sea-Song, A. Allan Cunningham. OxAEP-2
Seasons. Philip Booth. PfSP
Seasons. Safaa Fathy. PoArWo, *tr. by* S. V. Atalla
Seasons. Giampiero Neri. ItPo, *tr. by* Gayle Ridinger
Seasons, The. Friedrich Hölderlin. *tr. by* David Rattray
   Autumn. WoPoe, *tr. by* David Rattray
   Spring. WoPoe, *tr. by* David Rattray
   Summer. WoPoe, *tr. by* David Rattray
   Winter. WoPoe, *tr. by* David Rattray
Seasons, The. Susan Stewart. PoCho
Seasons, The. James Thomson.
   Autumn.
      Evening and Night. NAEL-6v1; NAEL-7v1
   Hymn on the Seasons, A. CABP
      "These, as they change, Almighty Father! these." InvLi; TreFP
   Spring.
      "Flushed by the spirit of the genial year." OxAEP-1
   Summer.
      Forenoon. Summer Insects Described. NPeEn
      Night. Summer Meteors. A Comet. NPeEn
   Winter.
      "For, see! where Winter comes, himself, confest." NePenScot
      "Keener tempests come: and fuming dun, The." NoP-5
      "'Tis done! Dread Winter spreads his latest glooms." OxAEP-1
Seasons are spirits, you said, each. Grandmother. Regina DeCormier-Shekejian. TWW
Seasons in Santa Fe [*haiku*]. Gerald Vizenor. HATNAP
Seasons of Fire, The. Billy Marshall-Stoneking. NOBAu
Seasons of the Soul. Allen Tate. FuPo
Seasons revolve and the years change, The. Another Spring. Kenneth Rexroth. GoPo
Seasons turn like a great wheel, The. Was It One of the Long Hunters of Kentucky who Discovered Boone at Sunset? Robert Penn Warren. LPSFW
Seat of the Riviera. Child We Won't Have Is Crowding Us in the Front, The. Lyn Lifshin. PfS
Seated at the core of the rose I weep. Rose. Cemal Süreya. NaPG, *tr. by* Talat Sait Halman
Seated at the table. Voyage. Antonio Deltoro. RMCMP, *tr. by* Christian Viveros-Fauné
Seated in a Chinese Painting, He Speaks. Netta Gillespie. AmZen
Seated on her bed legs spread open. Joyce Mansour. HAWP; WoPoe, *tr. by* Willis Barnstone
Seated one day at the organ. Lost Chord, The. Dominic Bevan Wyndham Lewis. UV
Seated one day at the Organ. Lost Chord, A. Adelaide Anne Procter. ITBLP; SacPr; UV; VWP
Seated statue of himself he seems, A. Farm Boy after Summer. Robert Francis. APT-2
Seathwaite Chapel. William Wordsworth. CenSon *Fr.* River Duddon [A Series of Sonnets], The.
Seattle. Arthur Guiterman. AmWit *Fr.* Lyric Baedeker, The.
Seattle, Autumn, 1933. Alfred Encarnacion. OpBo
Sea—turn yr Back on, The. Charles Olson. PFTM-2 *Fr.* Maximus Poems, The.
Sea-View, A. Ann Radcliffe. RWP
Seawall. Julia de Burgos. PoCho, *tr. by* Jack Agüeros
Seaweed. Henry Wadsworth Longfellow. APN-1; ColAP
Seaweed / Between rocks—. Takai Kito. ZenPo, *tr. by* Takashi Ikemoto and Lucien Stryk
Sea-wind and fog hover over the river's waves. Returning in Wind and Drizzle to My Home. S. J. Marks. BodElec
Secluded for a while. Basho. EMJL, *tr. by* Haruo Shirane

Secluded from domestic strife.　Double Transformation, The.　Oliver Goldsmith.　OBCoV; OBNV

Secluded gentleman, The.　Rhapsody on Whistling.　Ch'eng-kung Sui.　ColAnChi, *tr. by* Douglass A. White

Secluded in my chamber.　To the Tune: Lips Painted Red.　Li Ch'ing-chao.　CrYelRi, *tr. by* Sam Hamill

Secluded myself.　I found one word.　Thérèse 'Awwad.　PoArWo, *tr. by* Kamal Boullata

Seclusion.　Sikong Tu.　CCL1 *Fr.* Twenty-Four Modes of Poetry.

Second Advent, The.　Thomas Kelly.　SacPr

2nd afternoon I come, The.　Poem for the Insane, A.　John Wieners.　PmAP

Second Air Force.　Randall Jarrell.　NAAL-5

Second Anniversary.　Federico García Lorca.　SpanPo, *tr. by* Rachel Benson and Robert O'Brien

Second Best.　Rupert Brooke.　MoBrPo

Second Book of Theognis, The.　Theognis. *tr. by* Peter Bing and Rip Cohen
　"Boy and horse, a similar brain: the horse doesn't cry when its rider lies in the dust."　CAGL, *tr. by* Peter Bing and Rip Cohen
　"It's a thrill to love a boy: even Kronos' son, king of immortals, once longed for Ganymede."　CAGL, *tr. by* Peter Bing and Rip Cohen
　"Man who doesn't love boys and single-foot horses and dogs, his heart will never know pleasure, The."　CAGL, *tr. by* Peter Bing and Rip Cohen

Second Circle.　Srikanth Reddy.　LegDan

Second Class Citizen.　Jennifer Lagier.　UnSA

Second Coming, The.　Suzanne Benton.　HW

Second Coming, The.　William Butler Yeats.　BLPJKO; BrAP; CABP; ChIV-2; ClHu; CtM; EMP; GI; HarvBoo; HeIP-4; IrV; MoBrPo; NAAL-3; NAEL-6v2; NAEL-7v2; NAMCP V.1; NIL-7; NIP-4; NoAM; NoP-4; NoP-5; OxAEP-2; OxBEV; PoPoPo; RaBo; RSR; SoSe-8; TFi; TRP; WaAnP; WoPoe

Second Cycle of Love Poems.　George Barker.
　O Tender under Her Right Breast.　MoBrPo

Second dance.　Patrick Friesen.　NLPA *Fr.* Anna.

2nd Dance—Seeing Lines—6 February 1964.　Jackson Mac Low.　PFTM-2 *Fr.* Pronouns, The—A Collection of 40 Dances—For the Dancers.

Second Elegy.　Aida Cartagena de Portalatín.　TANSG, *tr. by* Emma Jane Robinett

Second Epistle to Davie.　Robert Burns.　NePenScot

Second Epode of Horace Translated, The.　Thomas Randolph.　BASC

Second Evening.　Mary F. Johnson.　CenSon

Second Fig.　Edna St. Vincent Millay.　AmWit; APT-1; BLPJKO; NALW; NoP-4; NoP-5; PoA 2002

Second Glance at a Jaguar.　Ted Hughes.　BrAP; NAMCP V.2; NoAM

Second Half of Our Lives, The.　Sarah Rosenblatt.　AmPoNex

Second Hand Rose.　Grant Clarke.　ReLy

Second Hand, The.　Phyllis Webb.　IFF

Second Home.　Julia Copus.　BeAl

Second Hymn to Lenin.　Hugh MacDiarmid.　RSaN

Second Image Sequence.　Umberto Piersanti.　NeIt, *tr. by* Stephen Sartarelli

Second Island, The.　Derick Thomson.　EdScPo

Second Jungle Book, The.　Rudyard Kipling.
　Letting in the Jungle.
　　Morning Song in the Jungle.　NoAM
　　Mowgli's Song Against People.　NOxBChV

Second Language.　Shari Miller Wagner.　ACAMVP

2nd Lesson from the Cockerel.　Maggie O'Sullivan.　Oth

Second Letter to My Nephew Wulang.　Tu Fu [*or* Du Fu].　CCL1, *tr. by* Jerome P. Seaton

Second Life of My Mother.　Jorge Carrera Andrade.　TCLAP, *tr. by* Muna Lee

Second Madrigal, The [*with music*].　Anna Swirszczynska [*or* Swir].　BLT

Second Merseburg Spell.　*Unknown.*　GePo, *tr. by* Carroll Hightower

Second Nature.　Paul Eluard *and* Andre Breton.　SurPaPo, *tr. by* Samuel Beckett

Second Part: "Thus far, my friend, have we retraced the way."　William Wordsworth.　NPBRoP *Fr.* Two-Part Prelude, The.

Second passerby *(he reads):* "The Tables of Destiny! I carve you in letters."　Velemir Khlebnikov.　PFTM-1 *Fr.* Zangezi.

Second Person.　Sam Gardiner.　NIrP

Second Philosopher's Song.　Aldous Leonard Huxley.　OBCoV

Second Poem from Nicaragua Libre: War Zone [*with music*].　June Jordan.　NoAM

Second Poem, The.　Paavo Haavikko.　PFTM-2 *Fr.* Winter Palace, The.

Second Portrait.　Manuela Fingueret.　MirDau, *tr. by* Roberta Gordenstein

Second Psalm: The Signals.　W. S. Merwin.　GifTon

Second Rapture, The.　Thomas Carew.　BASC

Second Review of the Grand Army, A.　Bret Harte.　CBCWP; PCW

Second Rondeau.　Johann Nikolaus Götz.　GePo, *tr. by* George C. Schoolfield

Second Samuel.　Bible, *O.T.*
　David's Lament.　NPeEn; OBVE; OBWP

Second Satire of the Second Book of Horace Imitated, The.　Alexander Pope.
　"With all a woman's virtues but the pox."　OBSV

Second Series.　Yannis Ritsos.
　"Guatemala, Nicaragua, Salvador."　PFTM-2, *tr. by* Kostas Myrsiades
　"In the white egg."　PFTM-2, *tr. by* Kostas Myrsiades
　"Naked, astride an elephant."　PFTM-2, *tr. by* Kostas Myrsiades
　"New moon, The."　PFTM-2, *tr. by* Kostas Myrsiades
　"Seek not, want not, be not."　PFTM-2, *tr. by* Kostas Myrsiades
　"They tagged you an illiterate, those idle bureaucrats."　PFTM-2, *tr. by* Kostas Myrsiades
　"Where is the time to light a cigarette."　PFTM-2, *tr. by* Kostas Myrsiades

Second Sermon on the Warpland, The.　Gwendolyn Brooks.　FuFl

Second Shepherd's Play, The.　*Unknown.*　NAEL-7v1
　(Haylle, Comly and Clene.)　OBEV

Second Sight.　Felicia Dorothea Hemans.　RWP

Second Song.　Charles Tomlinson.　WoBe

Second Song for the Worship of the Goddess at Yu Mountain: "Bidding the Goddess Farewell."　Wang Wei.　ColAnChi, *tr. by* Stephen Owen

Second Story Warehouse.　Edward Hirsch.　NevBe

Second Thoughts.　Michael Field.　LW; ViWPN

Second Time Around, The.　Sammy Cahn.　ReLy

Second time the comet swung by, The.　Gwyneth Lewis.　NeBl; StAl

Second time we met, The.　Hoop Snake.　Rebecca Wee.　P180

Second Tongue.　Gearóid Mac Lochlainn.　NIrP, *tr. by* the author and Séamas Mac Annaidh

Second Voyage, The.　Eiléan Ní Chuilleanáin.　EmeKit; ModIr; NPeEn

Second Warning Sign: the Game Heats Up.　Edoardo Cacciatore.　ItPo *Fr.* Full Powers: Five Warning Signs.

Second Why.　Ron Padgett.　NYP2

Second World War, The.　Elizabeth Jennings.　ItWoWo

Second year of the emperor's reign, in autumn, The.　Journey North.　Tu Fu [*or* Du Fu].　ColAnChi, *tr. by* Hugh M. Stimson

Second-Born Son: Lines for Walt Whitman Composed on Nantucket Island.　Gary Miranda.　ViWalt

Second-Class Citizen.　Slavko Mihalic.　PoSu, *tr. by* Charles Simic

Second-Grade Incident from Robert Frost's Childhood, A.　Joe Aimone.　VisFro

Secondhand Book.　Antonio Deltoro.　RMCMP, *tr. by* Christian Viveros-Fauné

Secondhand Coat.　Ruth Stone.　NALW; NIL-7; NIP-4

Secondline Send Off.　Kalamu ya Salaam.　SpirFl *Fr.* New Orleans Haiku.

Secondly there are the beams or sails.　Night Tree, The.　Jane Draycott.　MoWP

Seconds, The.　Linda Bierds.　RoV

Secrecy.　Samuel Greenberg.　APT-1

Secrecy of Mirrors, The.　Al-Zahra Al-Mansouri.　PoArWo, *tr. by* Nathalie Handal, Richard McKane and Tahia Abdel Nasser

Secret.　Pierre Reverdy.　PFTM-1

Secret, a secret, A.　If This Isn't Love.　E. Y. Harburg.　ReLy

Secret, The.　Charles Bukowski.　RaBo

Secret, The.　Peter Cooley.　PoCoUp

Secret, The.　Fanny Carrión de Fierro.　TANSG, *tr. by* Sally Cheney Bell

Secret, The.　Denise Levertov.　PtR

Secret, The.　Eiléan Ní Chuilleanáin.　MoWP

Secret, The.　Suzanne Noguere.　FFC

Secret, The.　George Russell.　MoBrPo

Secret Agent, A.　Yevgeny Borisovich Rein.　ItGoST, *tr. by* Judith Hemschemeyer

Secret Agent, The.　W. H. Auden.　NAMCP V.1

Secret Brain, The.　Dave Brinks.　AnSo

Secret cistern, forcing its way at last, the. (LL)　Fifth Stanzas. De Arte Poetica.　Olga Sedakova.　ARWW; ItGoST, *tr. by* Catriona Kelly

Secret cone will drop in Rothiemurcus, A.　Forecast for a Quiet Night.　Robin Fulton.　EdScPo

Secret Flowers.　Katherine Mansfield.　LW

Secret Garden, The.　Rita Dove.　NoAM

Secret Garden, The.　Eleanor Wilner.　GifTon

Secret Gratitude, A.　James Wright.　NoAM

Secret History of the Dividing Line.　Susan Howe.
　"In its first dumb form."　FTOS

Secret History of the Mongols, The.　*Unknown. tr. by* Paul Kahn
　Death of Yesugei, The.　WoPoe, *tr. by* Paul Kahn
　Last Battle and Death of Chingis Khan, The.　WoPoe, *tr. by* Paul Kahn
　Temujin Becomes Chingis Khan.　WoPoe, *tr. by* Paul Kahn

Secret in Broad Daylight.　Habib Tengour.　YaTCFP, *tr. by* Mary Ann Caws *and* Jean-Pierre Cauvin

Secret in the Roar, The.   Luis H. Francia.   ReBoTo

Secret Life, A.   Stephen Dunn.   GoPo

Secret Life of Gilbert Bond, The.   Joan Retallack.   FTOS

Secret Life of Musical Instruments, The.   C. D. Wright.   CAP-8

Secret like a lodestar, a ball of pure lead, I thought, A.   Dust Storm.   Gray Jacobik.   BAP-97

Secret Love.   Milton Kessler.   UnSA

Secret Love.   Paul Francis Webster.   ReLy

Secret Love: "It was seven or eight years ago."   Behçet Necatigil.   NaPG, tr. by Talat Sait Halman

Secret Love; or, The Maiden Queen.   John Dryden.
    (Hidden Flame.)   OBEV

Secret many years unseen, A.   Chess Play, The.   Nicholas Breton.   NoSic

Secret Melodies.   Debra Taub.   SurWo

SECRET murder hath been done of late.   Unknown.   NoSic

Secret Notebook.   Eduard Veniaminovich Limonov. tr. by William Tjalsma
    "And it's the summer civil war."   TCRusP, tr. by William Tjalsma
    "Fantastic!"   TCRusP, tr. by William Tjalsma
    For whisper and orchestra.   TCRusP, tr. by William Tjalsma
    "It is good in May, in marvelous wet May, to be the chairman of the All-Russian Extraordinary Committee in the city of Odessa."   TCRusP, tr. by William Tjalsma
    "Japanese restaurant is good in autumn—in dank weather—the hot napkins, the warm sake, The."   TCRusP, tr. by William Tjalsma

Secret of a smile, The.   For the Assignment of the Spirit.   Robert Duncan.   WhBo

Secret of Fire.   Abdul Wahab Al-Bayati.   PML, tr. by Bassam Kahlil Frangieh

Secret of the Quartz Pebble, The.   Vasco [or Vasko] Popa.   PoSu Fr. Quartz Pebble, The.

Secret of these hills was stone, and cottages, The.   Pylons, The.   Stephen Spender.   BrAP; NAMCP V.1; NoAM

Secret pillagers that protect the heart.   Rest of It, The.   John Wilkinson.   VaPo

Secret Rose, The.   William Butler Yeats.   NAEL-6v2; NAEL-7v2

Secret Song of the Heretics.   Kitahara Hakushū.   WoPoe, tr. by Donald Keene

Secret they are, sealed, annealed, and brainless.   Oystering.   Richard Howard.   NoAM

Secret Virginity, The.   "Angelus Silesius."   GePo Fr. Cherubical Wanderer, The.

Secret voyage goes through my mind like distilled ruins, The.   Lime.   Frank Lima.   AHA

Secretary Chant, The.   Marge Piercy.   BrAP

Secretary feels age, The.   Age and the Secretary.   Diana Fitzgerald Bryden.   OpeFie

Secrète au Grand Jour.   Habib Tengour.   YaTCFP

Secreted by long minds, antenna shell—.   Night Sky Hiss.   Jonathan Griffin.   Oth

Secrets.   Letitia Elizabeth Landon.   VWP Fr. Fragments.

Secrets of the Landscape, The.   Jacob Fichman.   FIT, tr. by Robert Friend

Section: America (2): Seen as a Bird.   Nathaniel Tarn.   APSN Fr. Lyrics for the Bride of God.

Section II.   "Mang Ke."   PFTM-2 Fr. Apeherd.

Section V.   Jacques Roubaud.   PFTM-2 Fr. Some Thing Black.

Secular.   Natasha Trethewey.   SpirFl

Secular Elegies.   George Barker.
    "O Golden Fleece she is where she lies tonight."   MoBrPo
    Satan Is on Your Tongue.   MoBrPo

Secular Masque, The.   John Dryden.   BASC; NAEL-6v1; NPeEn; OxAEP-1; OxBEV
    (Song: "All, all of a piece throughout.")   WeW-3

Secular, The.   Chris Wallace-Crabbe.   NOBAu

Secularist, The.   Claudia Keelan.   RoV

Secure in death he keeps the hearts he had.   Death's Guerdon.   Lizette Woodworth Reese.   APN-2

Security.   Shirley Kaufman.   DTA

Security.   Charles Leo O'Donnell.   SacPr

Security-man who stood, arms crossed, outside, The.   Reading Whitman in a Toilet Stall.   Timothy Liu.   WiU

Sed Non Frustra.   Anton Korteweg.   TuT, tr. by Seamus Deane

Sed non satiata.   Charles Baudelaire.   SxFrPo, tr. by James McGowan

Sedans cruised past our bench.   Wayne Koestenbaum.   WiU Fr. Erotic Collectibles.

Seder.   Jeanne Foster.   AFaM

Seder at the Saxons' house, The.   Seder.   Jeanne Foster.   AFaM

Seder Night with My Ancestors.   Joanne Limburg.   BeAl; NeBl

Seder, The.   Enid Dame.   UnSA

Sediment of Lukewarm and Radiant Rain.   Coral Bracho.   TANSG, tr. by Celeste Kostopulos-Cooperman

Seduced and Abandoned.   Radoi Ralin.   CSCBP, tr. by Georgi Belev and Lisa Sapinkopf

Seduced by Analogy.   Bob Perelman.   FTOS

Seducin me.   Asante.   Leticia R. Benson.   InTrad

Seducing the Sparrow.   Sam Hamill.   WANABP

Seduction.   Cornelius Eady.   OxAAAP

Seduction, The.   Archilochus. tr. by Kenneth McLeish
    "I said, "Be mine.""   EroLit, tr. by Kenneth McLeish

See.   LZ Gator Body Collector, The.   Michael Casey.   YaYoPo

See a man who so loves you as your fond S. T. COLERIDGE. (LL)   Metrical Feet.   Samuel Taylor Coleridge.   NIL-7; NIP-4

See a pin and pick it up.   Unknown.   ITBLP

See an old unhappy bull.   Bull, The.   Ralph Hodgson.   MoBrPo; OBMV

See dear Pater with the bills.   Christmas Bills.   Joseph Hatton.   OBCP

See for yourself? (LL)   Telephone Conversation.   Wole Soyinka.   NAMCP V.2; NoP-4; NoP-5; PoetW; WaAnP

See, hear, and am silent. (LL)   I Sit and Look Out.   Walt Whitman.   NAAL-3; NAAPv.1; SAmP

See her come bearing down, a tidy craft!   Note on Wyatt, A.   Kingsley Amis.   WeW-3

See her eager face.   Not Mine.   Betty Comden and Adolph Green.   ReLy

See, here is eternity's shore.   Arrival in Hades.   Edith Södergran.   WoPoe, tr. by David McDuff

See! Here, My Heart.   Unknown.   NoP-4; NoP-5

See, here's the workbox, little wife.   Workbox, The.   Thomas Hardy.   NAEL-6v2; NAEL-7v2

See him recall the day by moral trace, a squint.   Of Movement towards a Natural Place.   J. H. Prynne.   PFTM-2

See how Flora smiles to see.   On Clarastella Walking in Her Garden.   Robert Heath.   NOSC

See how I'm sitting.   Tomas Tranströmer.   WoBe Fr. Haiku.

See how our works endure! (LL)   Rudyard Kipling.   BrAP; NOxBChV Fr. Puck of Pook's Hill.

See how that royal fights.   Christopher Logue.   FaBoWar Fr. War Music.

See how the archèd earth does here.   Upon the Hill and Grove at Bilbrough.   Andrew Marvell.   BASC

See how the brown kelp withers in air.   Landed: A Valentine.   Richard Howard.   PoA 2002

See how the cottonwood bends at the waist.   At the Rio Grande Near the End of the Century.   Ray Gonzalez.   TouFir

See how the flowers, as at parade.   Andrew Marvell.   OBEV Fr. Upon Appleton House [To My Lord Fairfax].

See how the gently falling rain.   Evening Shower in Spring, An.   Tu Fu [or Du Fu].   CCL1, tr. by John Francis Davis

See! How the Nations Rage Together.   Richard Allen.   TCAPo

See how the orient dew.   On a Drop of Dew.   Andrew Marvell.   BASC; FSCP; NIL-7; NOSC

See how the rainbow in the sky.   Justification.   William Strode.   NOSC

See how the sage brush slants before the wind.   Cherie Forman Spencer.   TiP2 Fr. Desert Symphony.

See how the willing earth gave way.   Fall, The.   Edmund Waller.   NOSC

See how they hurry.   At Luca Signorelli's Resurrection of the Body.   Jorie Graham.   NAMCP V.2; NoP-5

See, / how they trace.   Birds in Snow.   "H. D."   APT-1; PoA 2002; WaAnP

See how this being at the neck and bowel.   Fanny Howe.   FaoP Fr. Splinter, The.

See how this violet which before.   On a Violet in Her Breast.   Thomas Stanley.   NOSC

See! Hymen comes; how his torch blazes!   Sir Charles Sedley.   NOSC

See! I am dancing!   Maria Viviana Soto.   ASA, tr. by Alfred Kroeber

See, I was raised on the wild side, border country.   How the Wild South East Was Lost.   Kit Wright.   OBCoV

See in that nook, where bends the K'i.   Unknown.   CCL1 Fr. Qi-yu [Translations].

See It Does Rise.   April Bernard.   KGB

See it does rise, and will not be stalled.   See It Does Rise.   April Bernard.   KGB

See lightning is flashing.   Storm, The.   Sara Coleridge.   NOxBChV

See Lucifer Like Lightning Fall.   John Keble.   ChIV-2

See me, the lord of deep-bosomed earth, who turned Acmonides upside down.   Wings.   Unknown.   HePo, tr. by Barbara Hughes Fowler

See Mount Soracte shining in the snow.   Horace.   PtR Fr. Odes.

See No Indian, Hear No Indian.   Victoria Lena Manyarrows.   TWW

See now, tender anemones are lifting up.   To Spring.   Mihály Fazekas.   IQMS, tr. by Watson Kirkconnell

See, o'er its withering leaves, the musk-rose bend.   Written in a Shrubbery Towards the Decline of Autumn.   Mrs. B. Finch.   CenSon

See, our languishing park's finery fades and falls.   Approaching Winter, The.   Dániel Berzsenyi.   IQMS, tr. by Peter Zollman

See See Rider, see what you done done! See, See Rider. Gertrude "Ma." Rainey. NAAPv.2

See sun, and think shadow. (LL) Anew 21. Louis Zukofsky. APT-2; NAAPv.2

See that day, Lord, did you hear what happened then? Twelve Bar Bessie. Jackie Kay. BeAl; NeBl

See that lady / Dressed so fine? Lady's Boogie. Langston Hughes. APT-2

See that sun in the morning. Side by Side. Harry Woods. ReLy

See the body. It is small and thin. Long Goodbye. Carrie St. George Comer. LegDan

See the chariot at hand here of Love. Ben Jonson. BASC; NAEL-7v1; NoP-4; NoP-5; NOSC; NPeEn Fr. Celebration of Charis in Ten Lyric[k] Pieces [or Peeces], A.

See the Condemned alone within his cell. William Wordsworth. SacPr Fr. Sonnets upon the Punishment of Death.

See the Conqueror mounts in triumph. Christopher Wordsworth. SacPr

See the dreadful tyranny of husbands. Unknown. SLW, tr. by Marjolijn De Jager, Sayd Bahodin Majrouh and André Velter

See the great vultures. Unknown. WoPoe Fr. Three Gypsy Songs.

See the handsome hippopotamus. Hippopotamus. Joanna Cole. NTCP

See the kitten on the wall. William Wordsworth. ChAP Fr. Kitten and [the] Falling Leaves, The.

See the man sit in the corner there naked. Sale of a Historian's Library. Yelena Shwarts. ARWW, tr. by Catriona Kelly

See! the moon is smiling. Eliza in Uncle Tom's Cabin. Eloise Bibb. CBWP-4

See the rat in the jelly. Rat Jelly. Michael Ondaatje. EmeKit

See, the smelle of my sone is as the smell of a feld. Bible, O.T. OBVE Fr. Genesis.

See[!] the smoking bowl before us. Robert Burns. NePenScot; NPeEn

See the world! the tussles. Annunciation, The. Douglas Messerli. FTOS

See them sprawl with earth for bed. Angry Dusk. Jack Lindsay. NOBAu

See there, that tree is a digging stick. Unknown. WoPoe Fr. Passage.

See these slumberers, tight in their shoal. Sardines. Menna Elfyn. ATSWP, tr. by Robert Minhinnick

See, they return; ah, see the tentative. Ezra Pound. APT-1; MoAmPo; NAAPv.2; NAMCP V.1; NoAM; NPeEn; OxBoAm; TRP; WeW-3 Fr. Ripostes of Ezra Pound.

See thon raws o flint arraheids. Arraheids. Kathleen Jamie. EdScPo; GPPA

See those cherries, how they cover. Cherries; a Parable, The. Thomas Moore. OBSV

See those resplendent creatures, as they glide. Fashion. Ada Cambridge. NOBAu

See, through this air, this ocean, and this earth. Alexander Pope. InvLi Fr. Essay on Man, An.

See what a clouded Majesty, and eyes. To My Worthy Friend Mr. Peter Lely [or Lilly]. Richard Lovelace. BASC; CavPo; GS; NOSC

See what a mass of gems the city wears. Impression de Nuit; London. Lord Alfred Bruce Douglas. OBEV

See what the boys in the backroom will have. Boys in the Backroom, The. Frank Loesser. ReLy

See what you miss by being dead? (LL) Curtains. Ruth Stone. BeAl; InoFa; StAl

See, when a fireship in mid ocean blazes. Surrender to Christ. Frederic William Henry Myers. SacPr

See when my English cousin comes. English Cousin Comes to Scotland. Jackie Kay. NOxBChV

See where Capella with her golden kids. Edna St. Vincent Millay. MoAmPo Fr. Epitaph for the Race of Man.

See where she sits upon the grassie [or grassy] green[e]. Edmund Spenser. OBEV Fr. Shepherd's Calender, The.

See where the falling day. Tomorrow. Anna Laetitia Barbauld. PEW

See where the windows are boarded up. Where Are the Waters of Childhood? Mark Strand. EmeKit; EMP; VCAP; WeW-3

See where the wooded slope grows wide. Daphne. Elisabeth Langgässer. GTCP, tr. by Irmgard Hunt

See Willow. James Bertolino. PoCoUp

See with what constant Motion. Gratiana Dancing [or Dauncing] and [or &] Singing. Richard Lovelace. OBEV

See with what simplicity. Picture of Little T. C. in a Prospect of Flowers, The. Andrew Marvell. BASC; FSCP; NAEL-6v1; NAEL-7v1; NoP-4; NoP-5; OBEV; OxAEP-1; TFi; WaAnP

See yonder hallow'd fane, the pious work. Robert Blair. OxAEP-1 Fr. Grave, The.

See you not Heng Mountain towering over Hunan hills. Song of the Vermeil Phoenix. Tu Fu [or Du Fu]. TAL

Seed. Charles Buckmaster. BMAP

Seed. Ruth Stone. PoChi

Seed, The. Franco Fortini. PML, tr. by Paul Lawton

Seed, The. Tomasz Jastrun. AF, tr. by Michael March and Jaroslaw Anders

Seed, The. Vasco [or Vasko] Popa. PoSu Fr. Games.

Seed Cutters, The. Seamus Heaney. IPoFL; PNI Fr. Mossbawn.

Seed Growing Secretly, The. Henry Vaughan. ChIV-2

Seed Leaves. Richard Wilbur. VisFro

Seed, Lord, falls on stony ground, The. Process. Charles Leo O'Donnell. SacPr

Seed went in, The. Planting Potatoes during Chernobyl. Tom Bryan. EdScPo

Seeded in the mud on turtle's back. Sweetgrass. Maurice Kenny. HATNAP

Seeding grit, her body. Fertility Test. Diana Fitzgerald Bryden. OpeFie

Seed-Picture, The. Medbh McGuckian. ModIr; PNI

Seeds. Katie Degentesh. FreRad

Seeds in a dry pod, tick, tick, tick. Edgar Lee Masters. ColAP; MoAmPo; NAMCP V.1; NoAM; TCAPo Fr. Spoon River Anthology.

Seeds of certain grasses that once grew, The. Metaphor of Grass in California. Charles Martin. RA

Seedsman of old Saturn's land. Herman Melville. APN-2 Fr. Clarel: A Poem and Pilgrimage in the Holy Land.

Seedy Henry rose up shy in de world. John Berryman. VCAP Fr. Dream Songs.

Seeing. At the Castle. Jerome Rothenberg. FTOS

Seeing as I was willing to give up my seat for the person who said. Instead of an Animal. Leslie Scalapino. PFTM-2

Seeing as the father saw the rosy morn. Ovid. OBVE Fr. Metamorphoses.

Seeing Auden Off. Philip Booth. PoA 2002

Seeing for a Moment. Denise Levertov. VCAP

Seeing Her Dancing. Robert Heath. NOSC

Seeing Hsia Chan off by River. Po Chü-i. TAL

Seeing is believing. On Sir Henry Ferrett, M.P. John Bingham Morton. OBCoV

Seeing moonlight here at my bed. Thoughts in Night Quiet. Li Po. NDACCP, tr. by David Hinton

Seeing Off a Friend. Stephen Dobyns. EmeKit

Seeing Off a Friend. Li Po. CrYelRi, tr. by Sam Hamill

Seeing Off a Guest at Captain Wang's Headquarters. T'ao Ch'ien. CCL1, tr. by William Acker

Seeing Off the Monk Ts'ung-Ch'ih Returning to the Capital. Chia Tao. CSKM, tr. by Mike O'Connor

Seeing Off the Mountain Monk Ch'u, Returning to Japan. Chia Tao. CSKM, tr. by Mike O'Connor

Seeing people off. Basho. EH, tr. by R. H. Blyth

Seeing Red. Al Young. FTtHH

Seeing Snow. Mun Chônghui. EcSo, tr. by Catherine J. Kim

Seeing Someone Off. Wang Wei. CCL1, tr. by Burton Watson

Seeing St. James's. Ray Mathew. NOBAu

Seeing that there's no other way. After a Death. Roo Borson. NIL-7

Seeing the Beloved in a Dream. Shen Yüeh. ColAnChi, tr. by Richard Mather and Richard B. Mather

Seeing the block of flats, I remember. Where All Were Good to Me, God Knows. Glyn Jones. TCAWP

Seeing the bloodless lips, the ugly knot of salt-coloured hair. Daughter of Zion. Alden Nowlan. Coast

Seeing the bodies lying in heaps. Various authors. CATKP Fr. Songs of Flying Dragons.

Seeing the Bones. Maxine W. Kumin. NoAM

Seeing the drifting sun that gives us our lives. (LL) Vapor Trail Reflected in the Frog Pond. Galway Kinnell. AF; OBWP; VCAP

Seeing the Eclipse in Maine. Robert Bly. InvLad

Seeing the Returning Geese. Lady Ise. WoPoe, tr. by Irma Brandeis and Etsuko Teraski

Seeing the snowman standing all alone. Boy at the Window. Richard Wilbur. GoPo; MoW; NAMCP V.2; OxBoAm; RaBo

Seeing the year end at my brother's home. New Year's Eve at the Home of Tu Wei. Tu Fu [or Du Fu]. CrYelRi, tr. by Sam Hamill

Seeing them like this. Toys. Carl Phillips. CAP-8; ReTh

Seeing these church pews up in the Choir. Where the Grieved Ones Sat. Dolores Kendrick. FuFl

Seeing Things. Seamus Heaney.
  "Claritas. The dry-eyed Latin word." HarvBoo
  "Inishbofin on a Sunday morning." HarvBoo

Seeing thou art fair[e], I bar[re] not thy false playing. Ovid. NPeEn; OBVE Fr. Elegies.

Seeing through the Sun. Linda Hogan. HATNAP

Seeing Wonsunja Off to Kwandong Province. Chunghur Hyujung. BecRai, tr. by Kim Daljin, Kim Won-Chung and Christopher Merrill

Seeing you makes me want to lift up my top. Look at These. Helen Farish. BeAl

SEEing yu. Holley Blackwell. AnSo

SEEing yu last night was an apparition, a beautiful wet child, someone suspended by the ankles in the world. SEEing yu. Holley Blackwell. AnSo

Seek not, my Lesbia, the sequestered dale. Anna Seward. CenSon

Seek not the spirit, if it hide. Sursum Corda. Ralph Waldo Emerson. APN-1

Seek not, want not, be not. Yannis Ritsos. PFTM-2 *Fr.* Second Series.

Seek salvation in the crowd. Song for the New Order. Lionel Abrahams. TSAP

Seek the Lord. Thomas Campion. SacPr

Seek true religion. O where? Mirreus. John Donne. OBSV *Fr.* Satires.

Seek your own Buddha within. To a Fellow Monk. Jaewol Kyunghun. BecRai, *tr.* by Kim Daljin, Kim Won-Chung and Christopher Merrill

Seeking a Hermit on West Mountain and Not Finding Him. Ch'iu Wei. CCL1, *tr.* by John Minford

Seeking an Explanation. Richard Emil Braun. NoAM

Seeking but Not Finding the Recluse. Chia Tao. CSKM, *tr.* by Mike O'Connor

Seeking fresh air. Rattlesnake Roundup. Pat Stodghill. TiP2

Seeking heat men become cold, and look for meaning. David Foster. NOBAu *Fr.* Fleeing Atalanta, The.

Seeking marsh. Wind. Hsüeh T'ao [*or* Xue Tao]. ColAnChi, *tr.* by Jeanne Larsen

Seeking Out His face in a Cup. Fanny Howe. FTOS

Seeking out Master Chan on Incense Mountain. Meng Hao Jan. ColAnChi, *tr.* by Daniel Bryant

Seeking Perfect Total Enlightenment. Difficulty Along the Way. Lew Welch. WhBo

Seeking Spring Beyond the City. Su Tung-p'o. TAL

Seeking the origin, I went to the edge of the pond. Autumn Thought. Choeui Eusoon. BecRai, *tr.* by Kim Daljin, Kim Won-Chung and Christopher Merrill

Seekonk Woods, The. Galway Kinnell. NoAM

Seemed, bringing the small ripped thing to me. (LL) Luna Moth. Carl Phillips. CAP-8; PoDa

Seemingly small her work. Poet in the House, A. Cathy Song. SweBea

Seems I'm always making resolutions. Call Me Irresponsible. Sammy Cahn. ReLy

Seems lak to me de stars don't shine so bright. Sence You Went Away. James Weldon Johnson. ISC

Seems like a long time. Partial Explanation, The. Charles Simic. P180

Seems like every boy I know. Our Texas Economy. Charles S. Taylor. TiP2

Seems she was called Ruth. Poor Ruth. Liudmila Petrushevskaya. CRWP, *tr.* by Daniel Weissbort

Seems that I read, or somebody said. I Thought About You. Johnny Mercer. ReLy

Seems to me I have & am thankful. Ode to My Flint and Boom Bolivia. Michael Costello. BAP-04

Seen. Issa. EH, *tr.* by Robert Hass

Seen from a distance, dappled and picturesque. Cows. Julia Alvarez. PfSP

Seen From Above ("Dead beetle lies on a country road, A.") Wisława Szymborska. PoSu, *tr.* by Grazyna Drabik *and* Sharon Olds

Seen from Above ("On a dirt road lies a dead beetle.") Wisława Szymborska. BLT

Seen from above, the sky. Downward Look, A. James Merrill. CAP-8; StAl

Seen from an Island in Godavari. Ismail. HotL, *tr.* by V. Narayana Rao

Seen from close up, my heart is a lake. (LL) Here I am Once More. Rachida Madani. CFP; HAWP; NAfrP, *tr.* by Eric Sellin

Seen from Over Here ("From the horizon there.") Anne Portugal. YaTCFP, *tr.* by Norma Cole

Seen from Over Here ("Seen from over here.") Anne Portugal. YaTCFP, *tr.* by Norma Cole

Seen from within a heated room. Tough Guy of London, The. Kojo Gyinaye Kyei. EmeKit

Seen in plain daylight. Basho. SoOfWa, *tr.* by Sam Hamill

Seen my lady home las' night. Negro Love Song, A. Paul Laurence Dunbar. APN-2; ColAP; SSLK

Seen on the sea, no sign; no sign, no sign. Dead Wingman, The. Randall Jarrell. PoWW

Seen through a Window. David Ferry. ItP

Seen to be Done. Oumar Ba. SonAtl, *tr.* by Olivier Barlet, Paul Boorde, P. Ellis, Kurt Ganzl and Saul Goode

Seen Words. Hannah Weiner. FTOS *Fr.* Spoke Aug 19.

Seep yourself, clear as water. Exits. Jean Earle. TCAWP

Seer, The. János Batsányi. IQMS, *tr.* by John Fuller

Seer, The. Abd al-Karim Kassid. IrPoTo, *tr.* by Chuck Miller and Saadi A. Simawe

Seersucker Suit. Deborah Digges. PoCho

Sees not my love how time resumes. To a Lady in a Garden. Edmund Waller. NPeEn

Seesaw. Amy Gerstler. MotU

See-saw, Margery Daw. *Unknown.* OxBEV

See'st thou that Cloud as silver cleare. Her Bed. Robert Herrick. PBRV

Seest thou those diamonds which she wears. Robert Herrick. NOSC

Seest thou yonder craggy rock. Complaint of a Lover, The. Anne Killigrew. BASC

Seething hopes all in a trembling hairpin. (LL) Spring View. Tu Fu [*or* Du Fu]. ColAnChi; NDACCP, *tr.* by Gary Snyder

Seething over inwardly. His Confession. The Archpoet. NAWM-7v1, *tr.* by Helen Waddell

Sefarad. Olga Klein Weisz. MirDau, *tr.* by Leslie MacIntosh

Sefarad, it is I who abandons. Sefarad. Olga Klein Weisz. MirDau, *tr.* by Leslie MacIntosh

Segmented line, The. Line of a Poem. Zali Gurevitch. FIT, *tr.* by Robert Friend

Segovia. Ricardo Pau-Llosa. Vesp

Segregated Railway Diner—1946. Robert Winner. LTA

Segregation #1. Carlos German Belli. TCLAP, *tr.* by Isabel Bize

Segue O Teu Destino. Fernando Pessoa. WoPoe, *tr.* by David Wright

Seguidillas of the Guadalquivir River. Félix Lope de Vega Carpio. SpanPo, *tr.* by Denise Levertov

Seh why—bway! Di Brook Di Dry. Jag Chenkó. OWABP

Sehnsucht. Anna Wickham. MoBrPo

Seine de Paris, La. Jean Tardieu. YaTCFP

Seine in Paris, The. Jean Tardieu. YaTCFP, *tr.* by David Kelley

Seine / transcend, be real, The. James Schuyler. FTOS

Seis Cuerdas, Las. Federico García Lorca. RaW *Fr.* Gráfico de la Petenera.

Seis variaciones acerca del amor. Víctor Terán. RMCMP

Seize the moment!—. *Unknown.* ColAnChi *Fr.* Midnight Songs.

SEIZE THIS OPPORTUNITY. 1962 Sonnet. Kept in excellent condition. Classified Ads. Gerardo Deniz. RMCMP, *tr.* by Mónica de la Torre

Seized by a sudden truth I started up at. Short Talk on the Truth to Be Had From Dreams. Anne Carson. OpeFie

Seized with a sudden fancy for fresh meat. *Unknown.* OBVE *Fr.* Homeric Hymns.

Seizing the Day. Judith Ortiz Cofer. PueRic; SwNoth

Seizing the white clouds, crumpling them up, destroying them. (LL) Lonely Wife, The. Li Po. NAAPv.2; NIL-7, *tr.* by Florence Ayscough *and* Amy Lowell and Amy Lowell

Sejanus. Juvenal. BASC *Fr.* Satires.

Sejanus ("How many men are killed by power, by power"). Juvenal. OBVE *Fr.* Satires.

Sejanus ("Some ask for envy'd pow'r; which publick hate"). Juvenal. OBVE *Fr.* Satires.

Sejanus ("What crowds by envied power, the wish of all"). Juvenal. OBVE *Fr.* Satires.

Sel se groupe en constellation d'oiseaux sur la tumeur de ouate, Le. Géant Blanc Lépreux du paysage, Le. Tristan Tzara. YaTCFP

Seldom has a panther's leap. Hans Faverey. WoBe *Fr.* Eighteen Poems.

Selected Poses. Anselm Berrigan. Eno

Selecting a loose vibration from the taut air. Soundwaves. Andrew Sant. NOBAu

Selecting a Reader. Ted Kooser. P180; PBCAP

Selection of Heaven, The. Paul Blackburn.
"Mind returns to it always, The." APSN

Selections from "Quatrains." Kim Yŏngnang. CAMKP, *tr.* by Walter Lew

Selective loggers go where the roots go. (LL) Elegy for a Forest Clear-Cut by the Weyerhaeuser Company. David Wagoner. NAMCP V.2; NoAM

Selective Memory. Robin Becker. PfS

Selective Service. Carolyn Forché. StAl

Self and the Mulberry, The. Marvin Bell. BodElec; CAP-8

Self crowned the day displays its plumage. Hymn Among the Ruins. Octavio Paz. PFTM-2; TCLAP, *tr.* by William Carlos Williams

Self Defense. Ai. ESEAA

Self in Variation, The: Scenes From Meditation. Harvena Richter. ICANM

Self is that small, The. (LL) Hole. Leonard Nathan. CalPo; PBCAP

Self Justification. Tony Harrison. NAMCP V.2 *Fr.* School of Eloquence, The.

Self moving / Moon, mid-air. (LL) Near your eyes. George Oppen. APT-2; PFTM-1

Self must hide from wind and dust, The. On Reading *The Book of Odes*. Cao Bá Quát. AWTN, *tr.* by Huỳnh Sanh Thông

(Self) Portrait. Natasha Trethewey. RD *Fr.* Storyville Diary.

Self Portrait as Nancy Drew, Girl Sleuth. Kristy Nielsen. ReTh

Self Portrait in Froehlichia. Cynthia Cruz. IAoNAP

Self Portrait in Horse Hair Wig. Cynthia Cruz. IIR

Self steps out of the circle, The. What Is Left to Say. Lisel Mueller. PoA 2002

Self Unsatisfied Runs Everywhere, The. Delmore Schwartz. PoA 2002

Self-analysis. Michael Dransfield. BMAP

Self-Analysis. Anna Wickham. MoBrPo

Self-brewing of the amaryllis rising before me, The. Opulence. Jorie Graham. NoP-4

Self-Creation. André Frénaud. YaTCFP, *tr. by* Michael Sheringham

Self-Deceaver, The. Juan Perez de Montalvan. OBVE, *tr. by* Thomas Stanley

Self-Defeating Poem, The. Fadil Azzawi. IrPoTo, *tr. by* the author

Self-Defense. Luljeta Lleshanaku. WoBe, *tr. by* Henry Israeli

Self-Defense of Peaches, The. Nancy Willard. PfSP

Self-Devoted, The. Agnes Strickland. CenSon

Self-Discipline. George Russell. MoBrPo

Self-Evident. James Robinson Planché. OBCoV

Self-Examination. Elaine Terranova. GifTon

Self-Exhortation on Military Themes. Alan Dugan. PWW2

Self-exiled Harold wanders forth again. Lord Byron. NPBRoP *Fr.* Childe Harold's Pilgrimage.

Self-Hatred of Don L. Lee, The. Haki R. Madhubuti. ESEAA

Self-Heal. Michael Longley. ModIr *Fr.* Mayo Monologues.

Self-Love. Joan Larkin. FiBr

Self-Mastery. Henrietta Cordelia Ray. CBWP-3; SWaP

Self-Pity. Philip Hodgins. NOBAu

Self-Pity Is a Kind of Lying, Too. James Schuyler. BodElec

Self-Portrait. Michelangelo Coviello. ItPo *Fr.* Caravaggio.

Self-Portrait. Robert Creeley. NoAM; PmAP

Self-Portrait. Milán Füst. IQMS, *tr. by* Paul Tabori

Self-Portrait. Edward Hirsch. RoV

Self-Portrait. Michael Longley. PML

Self-Portrait. Linda Pastan. ExTi

Self-Portrait. A. K. Ramanujan. NAMCP V.2; NoP-4; NoP-5; PML; PoetW

Self-Portrait. Rainer Maria Rilke. PoCho

Self-Portrait. Gerald Stern. TaR

Self-portrait. Elinor Wylie. APT-1; NAAPv.2

Self-portrait. Yun Tongju. CAMKP, *tr. by* David R. McCann

Self-Portrait [1969]. Frank Bidart. PoCho

Self-Portrait Approaching Promontory, Utah. Michael Pettit. GM

Self-Portrait as a Drowned Man. Jennifer Grotz. NevBe

Self-Portrait as a Warao Violin. Pascale Petit. BeAl

Self-Portrait as Somebody Else. Laura Mullen. ExTi

Self-Portrait as Still Life. Donald Justice. OxBoAm

Self-Portrait as the Letter Y. Tracy K. Smith. LegDan

Self-Portrait at Age Sixteen. Homero Aridjis. WoBe, *tr. by* George McWhirter

Self-Portrait at Age Ten. Homero Aridjis. WoBe, *tr. by* George McWhirter

Self-Portrait at Eleven on a Train. Homero Aridjis. WoBe, *tr. by* George McWhirter

Self-Portrait at Fifty-Four Years Old. Homero Aridjis. WoBe, *tr. by* George McWhirter

Self-Portrait at Fifty-Three. Bruce Weigl. AmAlph

Self-Portrait at Six Years of Age. Homero Aridjis. WoBe, *tr. by* George McWhirter

Self-Portrait at the Health Museum. Lucille Day. Cell, The. ASA

Self-Portrait at Thirteen Years of Age. Homero Aridjis. WoBe, *tr. by* George McWhirter

Self-Portrait at Thirty-Nine. Ted Kooser. PBCAP

Self-Portrait ("Charles on the Trevisan, night bridge.") Charles Wright. OxBoAm

Self-Portrait, Double Exposed. Joanie Mackowski. PoDa

Self-portrait ("Father was a serf.") Sŏ Chŏngju. CAMKP, *tr. by* David R. McCann

Self-portrait ("Father was a serf, seldom came home at night.") Sŏ Chŏngju. WoPoe, *tr. by* Peter H. Lee

Self-Portrait in a Convex Mirror. John Ashbery. CAP-8; NAMCP V.2; OxBoAm

Self-Portrait in the Doorway. Homero Aridjis. WoBe, *tr. by* George McWhirter

Self-Portrait in the New World Order. Reginald Shepherd. RD

Self-Portrait in the Supermarket. Rolf Dieter Brinkmann. GTCP, *tr. by* Reinhold Grimm

Self-Portrait in the Third Person. Biancamaria Frabotta. CItWP, *tr. by* Cinzia Sartini Blum and Lara Trubowitz

Self-Portrait in Tyvek(TM) Windbreaker. James Merrill. NAMCP V.2; OxBoAm

Self-Portrait, Jackson. James Kimbrell. NAPBL

Self-Portrait of the Other. Heberto Padilla. TCLAP; VCWP, *tr. by* Andrew Hurley and Alastair Reid

Self-Portrait on a Summer Evening. Eavan Boland. NPeEn

Self-Portraits. Takahashi Mutsuo. *tr. by* Hiroaki Sato

     Myself in the Disguise of an Ancient Queen. PFTM-2, *tr. by* Hiroaki Sato

     Myself with a Glory Hole. PFTM-2, *tr. by* Hiroaki Sato

Self-portraits by Frida Kahlo. Joanna Rawson. BodElec

Self-Protection. D. H. Lawrence. NoP-4; NoP-5

Self-Reliance. Ralph Waldo Emerson. APN-1

Self-renewing vegetable bliss?, A. (LL) Sonnet Made upon the Groves near Merlou [*or* Merlow] Castle. Edward Herbert, 1st Baron Herbert of Cherbury. NOSC; NPeEn

Self-Repeating Poem. Sybren Polet. LWR, *tr. by* John M. Coetzee

Self-same Power that brought me there brought you, The. (LL) Rhodora, The [On Being Asked Whence Is the Flower]. Ralph Waldo Emerson. AmFaPo; APN-1; ITBLP; NAAL-3; NAAL-5; NAAPv.1; NoP-4; NoP-5; OxBoAm; TCAPo; TFi

Selfsame, the siren, The. Eugenio Montale: The Eel. Paul Muldoon. GPPA

Selfsame toothless voice for death or bridal, The. Bell Speech. Richard Wilbur. MoAmPo

Self-slaved, The. Patrick Kavanagh. MoBrPo

Self-styled reluctant womaniser; less. Tragic Hero. Eleanor Brown. MFPA

Self-Sufficient Blues. Maureen Hynes. IFF

Self-Transformation. Willem Kloos. TuT, *tr. by* Desmond Egan

Self-Unseeing, The. Thomas Hardy. MoBrPo; NAMCP V.1; OxAEP-2; OxBEV; PtR; WeW-3

Selfwriting. Moishe Nadir. Prolet, *tr. by* Amelia Glaser

Sell it, though it sleeps still at its mother's breast! Meleager. HePo, *tr. by* Barbara Hughes Fowler

Selling Wilted Peonies. Yu Xuanji. CCL1, *tr. by* Genevieve Wimsatt

Selva Oscura. Louis MacNeice. HarvBoo

Selves, The. Patricia K. Page. BrAP; GPPA

Semantic Limerick According to Dr. Johnson's Dictionary (Edition of 1765), The. Gavin Ewart. OBCoV

Semantic Limerick According to the Shorter Oxford English Dictionary (1933), The. Gavin Ewart. OBCoV

Semaphoring chorus. George Oppen. APT-2; PFTM-1

Semblance of my elusive love, hold still. Which Contains a Fantasy Satisfied with a Love Befitting It. Sor Juana Inés de la Cruz. ErotSp, *tr. by* Alan S. Trueblood

Semele. Rose Terry Cooke. NAAPv.1

Semele Recycled. Carolyn Kizer. CAP-8; NALW

Semele to Jupiter. William Congreve. OBCoV

Seminar for Backward Pupils. Günter Eich. AF, *tr. by* David Young

Semiotics not of sex but of concealment, the lessons, The. My Father's Pornography. David Wojahn. ReTh

Semi-Revolution, A. Robert Frost. FTtHH

Semi-Skilled Lover. Maureen Duffy. LW

Semyon Semyonovich, having put on his glasses, looks at a pine tree. Optical Illusion, An. Daniil Kharms. MotU, *tr. by* George Gibian

Senate Hearings. Michael McClure. BB

Senators mine our lives for another war. (LL) Remembering That Island. Thomas McGrath. AmWaPo; PWW2

Sence You Went Away. James Weldon Johnson. ISC

Send Him Back Hard By Your Lady's Small Window. *Unknown.* WoPoe, *tr. by* John L. Foster

Send in the Clowns. Stephen Sondheim. ReLy

Send me a shirt and neck-tie. (LL) Home News. Ahmed Tidjani-Cissé. NAfrP; PML, *tr. by* Gerald Moore

Send me jewels from starboard. What It Takes. John Godfrey. FTOS

Send My Spinach. Douglas Florian. NOxBChV

Send New Beasts. Joe Wenderoth. BodElec; LegDan

Send not your wild supplications to the gods dwelling in their lofty abodes. Death of the Man in the Field, The. Haim Guri. NRoS, *tr. by* Esther Raizen

Sending Men Back to the Sea. Mary McGinnis. ICANM

Sending off My Fellow Monk Hae. Baggok Choneung. BecRai, *tr. by* Kim Daljin, Kim Won-Chung and Christopher Merrill

Sending the Mare to Auction. Jana Harris. FiBr

Send-Off, The. Michael Fried. PoCho

Send-Off, The. Wilfred Owen. HarvBoo; MoBrPo; NPeEn; OBWP; OBWVE; OxBEV; PoWW; TCAWP

Seneca Journal 1: "A Poem of Beavers." Jerome Rothenberg. APSN

Seneca Street. Michael Collier. PfSP

Seneca's Troas. Act 2. Chorus. Seneca. *See* After Death Nothing Is.

Senegal Sestina. Odetta D. Norton. BtF

Seneryen! Flame. Cauvin L. Paul. OGAHCP, *tr. by* Boadiba and Jack Hirschman

Senilio Passes, Singing. Martin Bell. OBCoV

Senior Lady Sells Garden Eggs. Kojo Laing. HBAPE

Senlin; a Biography. Conrad Potter Aiken.
  Morning Song. NoAM; NoP-5
  (Morning Song of Senlin.) APT-1; MoAmPo
  "Senlin, walking before us in the sunlight." NAAPv.2

Senlin, walking before us in the sunlight. Conrad Potter Aiken. NAAPv.2 *Fr.* Senlin; a Biography.

Señora, it is true the Greeks are dead. Invocation to the Social Muse. Archibald MacLeish. OxBoAm

Señorita Nina. Nina. Noël Coward. ReLy

Sens Plastique. Malcolm de Chazal. *tr. by* Patricia Terry
  "Bicycle rolls on the road, A." SurPaPo, *tr. by* Patricia Terry

Sens plastique (1947). Malcolm de Chazal.
  "Idiot bêle du regard, L'." YaTCFP

Sens plastique (1948). Malcolm de Chazal.
  "Volupté est la plus puissante sensation que nous ayons de la vitesse, La." YaTCFP

Sensation created by the human voice, The. Great Love Duets. Lorenzo Thomas. AHA

Sensation Type and His Friends, The. Michael Davidson. FTOS

Sensationalism. Larry Levis. AmAlph

Sense. Rae Armantrout. FTOS

Sense of Coolness, A [*for Stanley Crouch*]. Quincy Troupe. GT

Sense of danger must not disappear, The. Leap Before You Look. W. H. Auden. NoAM; PLBUT

Sense of Distance, A. Charles Tomlinson. ICANM

Sense of obligation, A. (LL) Man said to the universe, A. Stephen Crane. APN-2; BRP; NAAPv.1; OBSV; TCAPo; WeW-3

Sense of Proportion, The. Stephen Mitchell. WhBo

Sense of Responsibility, The. Harry Mathews. NYP2

Sense of the Sleight-of-Hand Man, The. Wallace Stevens. MoAmPo; NoAM; OxBoAm; PoA 2002; WeW-3

Sense of the world is short, The. Eros. Ralph Waldo Emerson. APN-1

Sense with keenest edge unused. Pater Filio. Robert Bridges. OBEV

Sensemayá. Nicolás Guillén. PFTM-1

Sensibility: A Poetical Epistle to the Hon. Mrs. Boscawen. Hannah More. RWP

Sensibly shod. (LL) Poem for My Sister. Liz Lochhead. EdScPo; ItWoWo

Sensing the next. Re-Verse. Diane Ward. FTOS

Sensitive male minus labour pains equals poem. Baby Poem Industry Poem, The. W. N. Herbert. NeBl

Sensitive Plant, The. Percy Bysshe Shelley.
  Conclusion. NPeEn

Sensualist Speaks on Faith, A. Dina Ben-Lev. AmPoNex

Sensuality is the most powerful feeling of speed we can have. Plastic Sense (1948 version). Malcolm de Chazal. YaTCFP, *tr. by* Mary Ann Caws *and* Jean-Pierre Cauvin

Sensuous and hilarious wit. Marathon. Cyrus Cassells. WiU

Sent. Hérib Campos Cervera. SonAtl, *tr. by* Eleanor Davidson

Sent as a present from Annam. Red Cuckatoo, The. Po Chü-i. CCL1; WoPoe, *tr. by* Arthur Waley

Sent by another world, I wonder. Another World. Sándor Weöres. IQMS, *tr. by* Adam Makkai and Donald E. Morse

Sent forth the beams which made so fair my race. (LL) Sir Philip Sidney. NAEL-6v1; NAEL-7v1 *Fr.* Astrophil and Stella.

Sent from Egypt with a Fair Robe of Tissue to a Sicilian Vinedresser. Thomas Sturge Moore. OBEV

Sent from the Power. Nag Hammadi Library. WPoS *Fr.* Thunder, The: Perfect Mind.

Sent myself the length. Eleven Rock Poems. Gustaf Sobin. PmAP

Sent out of sight, somewhere becoming rain. (LL) Whitsun Weddings, The. Philip Larkin. BeAl; HeIP-4; NAMCP V.2; NoAM; NoP-4; NoP-5; OxAEP-2

Sent to a Poetry Friend. Ch'i-chi. CSKM, *tr. by* Burton Watson

Sent to Huai Ku. Hsi Chou. CSKM, *tr. by* Paul Hansen

Sent to My Fourth Son, Shao-Wu (to the Tune "Southern Countryside"). Liang Te-sheng. WoPoe, *tr. by* Nancy Hodes and Tung Yuan-fang

Sent to the Magistrate of P'eng-chou. Tu Fu [*or Du Fu*]. CrYelRi, *tr. by* Sam Hamill

Sent to the Master Physician, "Almond Orchard" Shih. Li K'ai-hsien. ColAnChi, *tr. by* Jonathan Chaves

Sent to the Taoist of Dragon Mountain, Hsu Fa-leng. Liu Ch'ang-ch'ing and William H. Nienhauser. ColAnChi

Sent to Yuan Chen at White Cabin Peak. Pao Hsien. CSKM, *tr. by* Paul Hansen

Sent to Zen Master Yun-Shui. Chien Chang. CSKM, *tr. by* Paul Hansen

Sentada ya a la mesa. Viaje. Antonio Deltoro. RMCMP

Sentado en primera fila, diestra en la tablita. Oyente. Gerardo Deniz. RMCMP

Sentados en el tren. Conrail Wax Museum. Manuel Ulacia. RMCMP

Sentence: "Bloated and mesmerized by rasberries." William Matthews. PfSP

Sentence in the evening. Today the boxscores are green. Tonight, A. Ron Silliman. PmAP *Fr.* Paradise.

Sentence, The. Anna Andreyevna Akhmatova. AmFaPo; ItP, *tr. by* Judith Hemschemeyer

Sentence, unapproved, and overruled by Heaven, A. (LL) Prisoner, The. A Fragment. Emily Jane Brontë. NAEL-6v2; NAEL-7v2; NALW; NoP-5

Sentence—Life without a prison—struck, The. Divorcee. C. Webster Wheelock. SoSe-8

Sentences. Nicanor Parra. AF, *tr. by* Miller Williams

Sentences. Thornton Wilder. MotU

Sentences After *Defence of Poetry*. Paul Goodman. BodElec

Sentences do not deliver. Death of Man. "Arudra." HotL, *tr. by* V. Narayana Rao

Sentences for Matthew Ready, Series 2. Paul Goodman.
  "Now only praise makes me cry." BodElec

Sentences we studied are rungs upon the ladder Jacob saw, The. Luzzato. Charles Reznikoff. BBASP

Sentences While Remembering Hiraethog. T. Glynne Davies. OBWVE, *tr. by* R. Gerallt Jones

Sentencing. Natalie Simpson. PoPra

Sentencing goes blithely on its way, The. In a Poem. Robert Frost. AmWit

Sentido de la Sopa, El. Gabriel Celaya. RaW

Sentiers de lumière. Amina Saïd.
  "J'ai dormi trois siècles sur un lit de rochers." YaTCFP

Sentimental Education. Rachel Hadas. RA

Sentimental Elegy, A. Arkadii Dragomoschenko. PFTM-2, *tr. by* Elena Balashova and Lyn Hejinian

Sentimental Journey. Bud Green. ReLy

Sentimental Moment or Why Did the Baguette Cross the Road? Robert Hershon. P180

Sentimental Suffering of the Oyster of Smoke. Rossana Ombres. CItWP, *tr. by* Cinzia Sartini Blum and Lara Trubowitz

Sentiments for a Dedication. Archibald MacLeish. APT-1

Sentimientos pour from your teeth. Tato—Reading at the Nuyorican Poets' Cafe. Miguel Algarin. PmAP

Sentinel of the grave who counts us all! (LL) Ode to the Confederate Dead. Allen Tate. AmWaPo; APT-2; CBCWP; ColAP; FuPo; HeIP-4; InGu; MoAmPo; NAAPv.2; NAMCP V.1; NoAM; NoP-4; NoP-5; OBWP; OxBoAm; TFi; WaAnP

Sentinels, The. Robert Duncan. HarvBoo

S'entre-bâille. Pierre Reverdy. YaTCFP

Sentry. Dennis Saleh. GeoHom

Sentry, sentry, what did you see. Outposts. F. W. D. Bendall. FaBoWar

Sentry, The. Alun Lewis. AngWePo; PoWW; TCAWP

Sentry, The. Wilfred Owen. PoWW
  "We'd found an old Boche dug-out, and he knew." FaBoWar

Separated East, The. Ernest Francisco Fenollosa. APN-2 *Fr.* East and West.

Separately and one. Not Tyrants. Reed Bye. AHA

Separation. Bekes Jr. IrPoTo, *tr. by* Muhamad Tawfiq Ali

Separation. Walter Savage Landor. NPeEn

Separation. W. S. Merwin. NoP-4; NoP-5

Separation by Death. Ibn Hazm al-Andalusi. RaBo, *tr. by* A. R. Nykl

Separation from Clorila, The. José Manuel Martínez de Navarrete. BLPSL, *tr. by* Rene de Costa, Rigas Kappatos and Eleni Paidoussi

Separation on the River Kiang. Li Po. CCL1; NDACCP, *tr. by* Ezra Pound

Separations begin with placement. River Road Studio. Barbara Guest. PmAP

Separations Sequence. Marilyn Hacker.
  15. FaoP

Sephestia's Lullaby. Robert Greene. *See* Sephestia's Song to Her Child[e].

Sephestia's Song to Her Child[e]. Robert Greene. NoSic; OxAEP-1 *Fr.* Menaphon.

Sephirot. Leonor Scliar-Cabral. MirDau, *tr. by* Regina Igel

Sepia strands. So harmless and regal in the hieratic dark. Jill Hartman. PoPra

Sepr. ye 6th 1666 Thursday A Thanks Geving for the Stoping of the Fire in London. Elizabeth, Viscountess Mordaunt. EMWP

September. Mary Elizabeth Coleridge. ViWPN

September. Jennifer Michael Hecht. PLBUT

September. Linda Pastan. InvLad

September. Henrietta Cordelia Ray. CBWP-3

September 1939. Alan Brownjohn. RWPCtW

September, 1918. Amy Lowell. NAAL-5; NAAPv.2

September 1961. Denise Levertov. NAMCP V.2

September 1913. William Butler Yeats. HarvBoo; IrV; NAEL-6v2; NAEL-7v2; NAMCP V.1; NoAM

September 1, 1802. William Wordsworth. OxBSo

September 1, 1939. W. H. Auden. AF; BrAP; HarvBoo; MoBrPo; NAMCP V.1; NoP-5; OxAEP-2; OxBoAm; PoAgWa; PWW2; StAl; WaAnP

September 5. Robert Peterson. GeoHom

September 11. Pat Reed. Eno

9-11-01. Fanny Howe. OxBoAm

September 11, 1973. Emma Sepúlveda-Pulvirenti. CFP; TANSG, *tr. by* Shaun Griffin

9/11/01. Pierre Joris. Eno

9/14/01. David Lehman. PA9/11

9/15/01. David Lehman. PA9/11

September 18. Pat Reed. Eno

September 18, 1958 I took the day off to be born. Human Museum, The. 3 Brenda Coultas. HeMarv

September 22nd. Vera Gheraducci. CItWP, *tr. by* Cinzia Sartini Blum and Lara Trubowitz

September twenty-second, Sir: today. After the Surprising Conversions. Robert Lowell. NAMCP V.2; NoAM; TRP

September 25, 1999. Alex Rawls. AnSo *Fr.* What's Your Sign?

September 30. Sarah Menefee. Eno

September Afternoon at Four O'Clock. Marge Piercy. NIP-4

September came on Tuesday. Joseph Brodsky. WoPoe *Fr.* New Stanzas to Augusta.

September City. Gerald Hausman. UrbNat

September [Days Are Here]. Helen Hunt Jackson. APN-2

September evenings they are here after work. Surfers. Robert Minhinnick. TCAWP

September has come and I wake. Louis MacNeice. NoP-4; NoP-5 *Fr.* Autumn Journal.

September in the Rain. Al Dubin. ReLy

September, let us go. It is time to migrate. I Pastori (The Shepherds). Gabriele D'Annunzio. TWF

September Morning. Colette Inez. PA9/11

September: Nederland, Colorado. Jonathan Holden. PfSP

September Night, A. George Marion McClellan. TCAPo

September rain falls on the house. Sestina. Elizabeth Bishop. APT-2; BrAP; NAAL-5; NAMCP V.2; NIL-7; NoP-4; NoP-5; OxBoAm; PoetW; PoPoPo; PtR; WaAnP

September: six months into the last full. At Thirty. Kyoko Mori. SweBea

September Song. Maxwell Anderson. ReLy

September Song. Geoffrey Hill. EMP; FaBoWar; HarvBoo; HP; NAEL-6v2; NAEL-7v2; NAMCP V.2; NoAM; NoP-4; NoP-5; NPeEn; OBWP; OxBEV; StAl

September, the First Day of School. Howard Nemerov. GoPo

September was when it began. Coming of the Plague, The. Weldon Kees. ChIV-1; StAl

Sepulchres, how thick they stand, The. Meditations on the Sepulchre in the Garden. Philip Doddridge. OBGa

Sepulchrum Domus Mea Est. William Austin. NOSC

Seq. Maggie Hannan. NLP

Sequel of Appomattox. Donald Davidson. CBCWP; FuPo

Sequel to 'A Reminiscence," The. Amy Levy. VWP

Sequence. Kenneth Irby. FTOS

Sequence: "Standing in her basement." Peter E. Murphy. NevBe

Sequence for the First Sunday in Advent. *Unknown.* RSR, *tr. by* L. William Countryman

Ser humano es apenas un desprendimiento, El. Fiel de la balanza, El. Alberto Blanco. RMCMP

Será sacrificado el cautivo. Fiesta de izcalli o décimo octavo mes. Carla Faesler Bremer. SPV

Serbian Postcard 1. Miklós Radnóti. ConPit, *tr. by* Clayton Eshleman and Gyula Kodolanyi

Sere of the sun exploded in the sea. (LL) O Carib Isle! Hart Crane. APT-2; NoAM; OxBoAm; PFTM-1

Serena e iluminada. Marcelina. Natalia Toledo. RMCMP

Serenade. Emanuel Carnevali. APT-2

Serenade. Angie Estes. GeoHom

Serenade. Adelia Prado. TANSG, *tr. by* Ellen Doré Watson

Serenade: "Look out upon the stars, my love." Edward Coote Pinkney. APN-1

Serenade: "Sleep, love sleep." Mary Weston Fordham. CBWP-2; SWaP

Serenade: "Softly, O midnight Hours!" Aubrey Thomas De Vere. OBEV

Serenade: "Who is it sings the gypsies' song to-night." Rosamund Marriott Watson. ViWPN

Serenade, A (Fragment): "Lullaby, O, lullaby!" Thomas Hood. NBLV *Fr.* Domestic Poems.

Serenade: Any Man to Any Woman. Dame Edith Sitwell. NALW

Serenade at Dawn. Árpád Tóth. IQMS, *tr. by* Jess Perlman

Serenade for Ilonka. Jenő Dsida. IQMS, *tr. by* Joseph Leftwich

Serenade for Two Poplars, A. Esther Raab. FIT, *tr. by* Robert Friend and Shimon Sandbank

Serenade in Blue. Mack Gordon. ReLy

Serenades in Virginia. Andrew Hudgins. CBCWP

Serene Words. Gabriela Mistral. SpanPo, *tr. by* Muriel Kittel

Sérénité. Philippe Jaccottet. YaTCFP

Serenity. Philippe Jaccottet. MFP; YaTCFP, *tr. by* Martin Sorrell

Serenity in Stones, The. Simon J. Ortiz. ColAP

Serepta Mason. Edgar Lee Masters. APT-1 *Fr.* Spoon River Anthology.

Seres patológicos. David Huerta. RMCMP

Serf, The. Roy Campbell. MoBrPo; OBMV

Serfs are glad through Lara's wide domain. Lara. Lord Byron.

Sergeant Brown's Parrot. Kit Wright. OPOU

Sergeant-Major Money. Robert Graves. FaBoWar; OBWP

Sergeant's been on a gas course. Gas Drill. Tom Rawling. FaBoWar

Sergeant's Weddin', The. Rudyard Kipling. OBCoV

Sergei Yesenin. Sergey Aleksandrovich Yesenin. Prolet, *tr. by* Amelia Glaser

Serial Toxic Teen. Matthew Wascovich. BeDoSh

Seriamente, en tus ojos era la mar dos niños que me espiaban. Ángel de Arena, El. Rafael Alberti. RaW

Seriema Song. Albert Goldbarth. UrbNat

Series. Michael Palmer.

Prose 22. HarvBoo

Prose 31. HarvBoo

Series of Failures So That I'm Sick of the Word, A. Laura Mullen. IAoNAP

Series of white squares, each, A. Flight. Pamela Alexander. AmAlph; OtW

Series—3, The. Leslie Scalapino. PmAP *Fr.* Crowd and Not Evening Or Light.

Serious Concerns. Wendy Cope. NoP-5; OBCoV

Serious moment for the water is when it boils, A. Boiling Water, The. Kenneth Koch. ItP

Serious of Photographs, A. Iain Sinclair. Oth *Fr.* Ebbing of Kraft, The.

Seriously, these sorts. Gradation. Charles Bernstein. FTOS

Sermon. Emanuel Carnevali. APT-2

Sermon, The. Richard Hughes. OBMV

Sermon on Language. Robert Kelly. WhBo

Serpent, The. Theodore Roethke. NOxBChV

Serpent, The. Jones Very. NCAP

Serpent Finds Eve Alone, The. John Milton. NPeEn *Fr.* Paradise Lost.

Serpent has no feet or hands, The. Samuel Hoffenstein. AmWit *Fr.* Songs about Life and Brighter Things Yet.

Serpent Knowledge. Robert Pinsky. ColAP *Fr.* Explanation of America, An.

Serpent with the eagle in the boughs, The. (LL) Hart Crane. MoAmPo; NAAL-5 *Fr.* Bridge, The.

Serpentine Voices. Diana García. TouFir

Serpiente sangrienta. Tarde de Sol. Mary Gomez Parham. OWABP

Servant, A. Rudyard Kipling. HarvBoo; NPeEn *Fr.* Epitaphs of the War [1914–1918].

Servant Boy Delivers, The. Tu Fu [*or* Du Fu]. CrYelRi, *tr. by* Sam Hamill

Servant of the House. "Sagittarius." UV

Servant of the world's welfare once were you—god bless. Humiliating the Laser-Beam. Ödön Palasovszky. IQMS, *tr. by* Kenneth McRobbie

Servant of thought, a lamp held in one hand. (LL) Distances. Philippe Jaccottet. StAl; VCWP, *tr. by* Derek Mahon

Servant was startled, My. God's Voice. Sunday Ayewanu. NeNiPo

Servant When He Reigneth, A. Rudyard Kipling. ChIV-1

Servant's soul, A. He said I had a servant's soul. Heron, The. Stuart Henson. StAl

Service. Peter Scupham. HarvBoo

Service and strength, God's Angels and Archangels. St. Michael and All Angels. Christina Georgina Rossetti. SacPr

Service is joy, to see or swing. Allow. Tennis. Margaret Avison. IFF

Service Is No Heritage. Nicholas Breton. NoSic

Service Wash. Deryn Rees-Jones. MFPA

Services. Carl Rakosi. ChIV-1

Servile Herd, The. Alexander Pope. OBSV *Fr.* Essay on Criticism, An.

Serving Men's Song, A. John Lyly. NoSic *Fr.* Alexander and Campaspe.

Serving of Water, The. Tino Villanueva. TiP2

Serving the Shogun in the capital. Kodo. ZenPo, *tr. by* Takashi Ikemoto and Lucien Stryk

Serwice [*or* Service] and luve, aboif all vthir [*or* uthir *or* othir] thing. (LL) In Prais[e] of Women [*or* Wemen]. William Dunbar. CABP; NoP-4; WaAnP

Ses Grosses Cuisses. Pablo Picasso. YaTCFP

Sesshin Poem. Norman Fischer. WhBo

Session[s] was held the other day, A.   Wits, The; A Session[s] of the Poets.   Sir John Suckling.   BASC; CABP

Sestina: "Coming to Spain on the first day of the fighting."   Muriel Rukeyser.   AmWaPo *Fr.* Letter to the Front.

Sestina: "Farewell, O Sun."   Sir Philip Sidney.   WaAnP *Fr.* Countesse of Pembroke's Arcadia, The.

Sestina: "He wanted to tell her the weekend idea was "neat.""   James Cummins.   OxBoAm

Sestina: "I have reached, alas, the long shadow." [*tr. of* "Al poco giorno" *by Dante*].   Dante Alighieri.   WoPoe, *tr. by* James Schuyler

Sestina: "I saw my soul at rest upon a day."   Algernon Charles Swinburne.   MakPoe

Sestina: "In fair Provence, the land of lute and rose."   Sir Edmund William Gosse.   MakPoe

Sestina: "September rain falls on the house."   Elizabeth Bishop.   APT-2; BrAP; NAAL-5; NAMCP V.2; NIL-7; NoP-4; NoP-5; OxBoAm; PoetW; PoPoPo; PtR; WaAnP

Sestina: "Then first with locks dishevelled and bare."   Barnabe Barnes.   NoSic; NPeEn; WaAnP *Fr.* Parthenophil and Parthenophe.

Sestina: Altaforte.   Ezra Pound.   APT-1; ColAP; MakPoe; MoAmPo; OxBoAm; TCAPo; WaAnP

Sestina d'Inverno.   Anthony Hecht.   NoAM

Sestina for the House.   Ronald Wallace.   PBCAP

Sestina Halted in a Rain Delay.   Miles Garett Watson.   RWB

Sestina: Here in Katmandu.   Donald Justice. *See* Here in Katmandu.

Sestina in Time of Winter.   Patrick Anderson.   PoA 2002

Sestina of the Geographic Tongue.   Rachel Rose.   IFF

Sestina: Of the Lady Pietra degli Scrovigni.   Dante Alighieri.   MakPoe; NPeEn; OBVE, *tr. by* Dante Gabriel Rossetti

Sestina of the Tramp-Royal.   Rudyard Kipling.   MakPoe; MoBrPo; WaAnP

Sestina on a Train.   Alfred Wellington Purdy. *See* Madwoman on the Train, The.

Sestine 4.   Barnabe Barnes.   MakPoe *Fr.* Parthenophil and Parthenophe.

Sestri Levante / Liguria 2.   Günter Kunert.   GTCP, *tr. by* Reinhold Grimm

Set for a Southern Gothic.   Brian Teare.   LegDan

Set Free.   Sikong Tu.   CCL1 *Fr.* Twenty-Four Modes of Poetry.

Set Her Far from Me, Mirror.   Pedro Salinas.   RaW, *tr. by* W. S. Merwin

Set Him Apart!   Victor Hugo.   SxFrPo, *tr. by* A. M. and E. H. Blackmore

Set in their studious corners, the players.   Chess.   Jorge Luis Borges.   PoetW, *tr. by* Alastair Reid

Set Love in order, thou that lovest Me.   Cantica: Our Lord Christ: Of Order.   Saint Francis of Assisi.   OBVE, *tr. by* Dante Gabriel Rossetti

Set me free, flagpole, why must you deny me the free wind?   Conversation.   Ágnes Nemes Nagy.   IQMS, *tr. by* Adam Makkai

Set me whereas the sun[ne] doth[e] parch [*or* perche] the green [*or* grene].   Petrarch.   NoSic; OxBSo *Fr.* Sonnets to Laura.

Set on rising ground above the village.   Caleb Barnes.   David Wright.   NLP

Set on the soul's acropolis the reason stands.   Reason.   Clive Staples Lewis.   SacPr

Set on this bubble of dead stone and sand.   On an Engraving by Casserius.   Alec Derwent Hope.   HarvBoo

Set Piece.   Houston A., Jr. Baker.   BtF

Set silver cone to tulip flame!   Inscription for a Mirror in a Deserted Dwelling.   William Rose Benét.   MoAmPo

Set Theory.   Alberto Blanco.   RMCMP, *tr. by* Gustavo V. Segade

Set to flame, his eyes.   Martyr, The.   Scott Cairns.   UpMys

Set up the drum.   December.   Maurice Kenny.   HATNAP

Set where the sun strikes free. (LL)   Atlantic City Waiter.   Countee Cullen.   APT-2; NAMCP V.1

Setback.   Susan Wicks.   PoCu

Setback, darling, A.   Death.   Setback.   Susan Wicks.   PoCu

Seth Bingham.   William W. Cook.   SpirFl

Seton Hospital coming down.   Eugene Wukasch, Texas Architect.   Dave Oliphant.   TiP2

Setting.   Joe Denham.   OpeFie

Setting out on my bicycle alone.   Horses.   Henri Cole.   PoDa

Setting out over the sea to the south.   At Kan's Embarkation for Yuan China.   Muso Soseki.   EaWin, *tr. by* W. S. Merwin

Setting Sail.   Gerardo Diego.   RaW, *tr. by* Ralph Nelson

Setting Sun, The.   Kodama Kagai.   CAoMJL1, *tr. by* Leith Morton

Setting sun is splendid, The.   Yun Söndo.   CATKP *Fr.* Angler's Calendar, The.

Setting sun left my heart, The.   Song.   Juan Ramón Jiménez.   RaW, *tr. by* Ralph Nelson and Rita García Nelson

Setting sun—a pool of molten gold, The.   Tune: "Joy of Eternal Union."   Li Ch'ing-chao.   ColAnChi, *tr. by* Jiaosheng Wang

Setting the Table.   Don McKay.   OpeFie

Setting-Up Camp.   Jonathan Gefen.   NRoS, *tr. by* Esther Raizen

Settle Bed, The.   Seamus Heaney.   NoP-5

Settled at Cold Mountain.   Han-shan (Cold Mountain).   CCL1; NDACCP, *tr. by* Gary Snyder

Settled In.   Michael David Madonick.   IllVoic

Settlement.   David Avidan.   NRoS, *tr. by* Esther Raizen

Settlement.   Ingeborg Bachmann.   PoSu, *tr. by* Daniel Huws

Settler, The.   Jones Very.   SacPr

Settlers.   Tom Paulin.   PNI

Settling, white dew.   Nishiyama Soin.   SoOfWa, *tr. by* Sam Hamill

Seva.   Elsa Cross.   RMCMP, *tr. by* Margaret Sayers Peden

Seven.   Michael McClure.   WANABP *Fr.* Plum Stones.

Seven.   Natan Zach.   FIT, *tr. by* Robert Friend

Seven, The.   *Unknown.*   WoPoe, *tr. by* Jerome Rothenberg

Seven ages, first puking and mewling.   "All the World's a Stage."   Victor Gray.   NBLV

Seven Ages of Man.   J. D. Smith.   IaFF

Seven Ages of Man, The.   William Shakespeare.   CtM; ITBLP; UV *Fr.* As You Like It.

Seven Ages, The.   Louise Glück.   PoCho

Seven Beginnings.   Olesya Nikolayeva.   ItGoST, *tr. by* Richard Graves and Carol Ueland

Seven Blind Curves.   Nicole Markotić.   PoPra

Seven Cats Are Happy, The.   Kazuko Shiraishi.   WoBe, *tr. by* Samuel Grolmes and Yumiko Tsumura

Seven Cuban / army officers.   Pornographic Poem.   John Giorno.   CAGL

Seven Days.   Gu Cheng.   WoBe, *tr. by* Joseph R. Allen

Seven Days of Creation, The.   James McAuley.   Seventh Day, The.   BMAP

Seven Days of the Sun, The.   Walter James Turner.   OBMV

Seven days passed and he didn't write. He read until his eyes hurt.   How L'Akhdar Ben Youssef Wrote His Last Poem.   Sa'di Yusuf.   IrPoTo, *tr. by* Khaled Mattawa

Seven Deadly Sins.   Yusef Komunyakaa.   BAP-01

Seven dog-days we let pass.   Queens.   John Millington Synge.   MoBrPo; OBMV

Seven Dwarfs, Each on His Deathbed, Remember Snow White, The.   Ron Koertge.   SUP

Seven Exhortations to Rise, The.   Mei Sheng.   CCL1, *tr. by* John A. Scott

Seven Forbidden Words [*with music*].   Michael Palmer.   HarvBoo

Seven full-paunched eunuchs came to me.   King, The.   Skipwith Cannell.   APT-1

Seven Gifts of the Holy Ghost, The.   John Audelay [*or* Awdelay].   SacPr

Seven hills shudder in silence, The.   Agony . . . A Resurrection, An.   Assumpta Acam-Oturu.   HAWP; NAfrP

Seven Horizons.   Stephen Stepanchev.   PoDa

Seven hours: late afternoon here, lightning.   Divine Will.   Michael Waters.   Vesp

Seven Laments for the War-Dead.   Yehuda Amichai.   PoetW, *tr. by* Chana Bloch

7, Middagh Street.   Paul Muldoon.   Salvador.   NAMCP V.2   Wystan.   NAMCP V.2

Seven o'clock. The seventh day of the seventh month of the year.   Birth, The.   Paul Muldoon.   EmeKit

Seven of Pentacles, The.   Marge Piercy.   IPoFL; TWF *Fr.* Laying Down the Tower.

Seven Old Men, The.   Charles Baudelaire.   OBVE, *tr. by* Roy Campbell

Seven Old Men, The.   Charles Baudelaire.   SxFrPo, *tr. by* James McGowan

7 or 8 Things I Know About Her—A Stolen Biography.   Michael Ondaatje.   MotU

Seven Paintings By Brueghel.   Anne Simpson.   OpeFie

Seven pairs of leopard-skin underpants.   Leopard Skin.   Douglas Stewart.   NOBAu

Seven pinecones.   *Various authors.*   CATKP *Fr.* Songs of Flying Dragons.

Seven Postcards from Dover.   Mary Ruefle.   AmAlph

Seven scythes leaned at the wall.   Taxman.   George Mackay Brown.   NePenScot

Seven Seas rose in the half-dark to make coffee.   Derek Walcott.   WaAnP *Fr.* Omeros.

Seven seas sucked up together, The.   Gesshu Soko.   ZenPo, *tr. by* Takashi Ikemoto and Lucien Stryk

Seven Sides and Seven Syllables.   Edouard J. Maunick.   VCWP, *tr. by* Carolyn Kizer

Seven Sins, The.   *Unknown.*   SacPr

Seven Skins.   Adrienne Rich.   NAMCP V.2

Seven Songs and Song Pictures.   *Unknown.*   PFTM-1

Seven Songs Written During the Qianyuan Era While Staying at Tonggu District. Tu Fu [*or* Du Fu]. *tr. by* Burton Watson

"I have a sister, little sister, living in Zhongli." CCL1, *tr. by* Burton Watson

"I have brothers, younger brothers in a place far away." CCL1, *tr. by* Burton Watson

"Long hoe, long hoe, handle of white wood." CCL1, *tr. by* Burton Watson

"To the south there is a dragon living in a mountain pool." CCL1, *tr. by* Burton Watson

"Traveler, a traveler, Zimei his name, A." CCL1, *tr. by* Burton Watson

Seven Songs Written while Living at T'ung-ku in 759. Tu Fu [*or* Du Fu]. ColAnChi, *tr. by* Geoffrey Waters

Seven Sorrows. Wang Ts'an. ColAnChi

Seven Sorrows, The. Ted Hughes. NAEL-6v2; NAEL-7v2

Seven Spiritual Ages of Mrs. Marmaduke Moore, The. Ogden Nash. MoAmPo

Seven Stages, The. Kahlil Gibran. BBASP, *tr. by* Michael Beard and Adnan Haydar

Seven Stimuli. Mei Ch'eng. ColAnChi, *tr. by* Victor H. Mair

Seven Stones. Marjorie Agosin. TANSG, *tr. by* Cola Franzen

Seven Strangely Exciting Lies. Denise Riley.

Disintegrate Me. Oth

Flip, Flop. Oth

I Take Two of These Tablets Tonight and in the Morning Go on Living. Oth

Seven threads make the shroud. Shroud. George Mackay Brown. NoP-4; NoP-5

Seven Times Six. Giving in Marriage. Jean Ingelow. TreFP *Fr.* Songs of Seven.

Seven Times Three. Love. Jean Ingelow. TreFP *Fr.* Songs of Seven.

Seven Twilights. Conrad Potter Aiken.

"When the tree bares, the music of it changes." MoAmPo

Seven Virgins, The. *Unknown.* OBEV

Seven Voluntary Labors and One Seditious Act. Nicanor Parra. WoBe, *tr. by* Liz Werner

Seven weeks of sea, and twice seven days of storm. Gibraltar. Wilfrid Scawen Blunt. OBEV

Seven wise men, seven fit in their wisdom—seven heroes. On the Seven Bishops. Anne Fychan. EMWP

Seven Wonders of North Wales, The [*with music*]. *Unknown.* OBWVE

Seven Wonders of the World. Christopher Pearse Cranch.

Locomotive, The. APN-1; GM

Photograph, The. APN-1

Printing-Press, The. APN-1

Seven Words, The. Jerzy Ficowski. PoSu, *tr. by* Keith Bosley and Krystyna Wandycz

Seven years ago I went into. Water's Chant, The. Philip Levine. GeoHom

Seven years without milk. Ethiopia. Audre Lorde. AFaM

Seven-hundred tons per inch, I read, is the force in a bomb or shell in. Shrapnel. C. K. Williams. AmWaPo

Sevens (Version 3): In the Closed Iris of Creation. Marvin Bell. CAP-8

Seven-Sided Poem. Carlos Drummond de Andrade. PoetW; TCLAP; VCWP, *tr. by* Elizabeth Bishop

1789. Jackson Mac Low. APSN *Fr.* Presidents of the United States of America, The.

1711. Fugitive Slaves. Gale Jackson. SpirFl

Seventeen feet of canvas. Shoeing the Currach. Mary O'Malley. MakPoe

Seventeen hundred and sixty yards. Enigma No. 6. Augusta Davies Webster. VWP

Seventeen hundred and thirty-nine. Ballad of 'Beau Brocade', The. Austin Dobson. OxAEP-2

1797. Jackson Mac Low. APSN *Fr.* Presidents of the United States of America, The.

Seventeen years ago come March. (LL) Crusoe in England. Elizabeth Bishop. APT-2; EmeKit; FaBoVe; NAMCP V.2; OxBoAm; PoPoPo; RACG

Seventeen years ago you said. À Quoi Bon Dire. Charlotte Mew. MakPoe; NPeEn; OxBEV; VWP

17:II:82. David Meltzer. SeSe

Seventh, The. Attila József. AF; PtR, *tr. by* John Batki

Seventh Avenue. Muriel Rukeyser. NoAM

Seventh Avenue fills at noon with a gray tide of. I Want a Solid Piece of Sunlight and a Yardstick to Measure it With. Tom Postell. EGAG

Seventh Birthday of the First Child. Sharon Olds. PBCAP

Seventh Day, The. Diana Hartog. NLPA *Fr.* Oasis.

Seventh Day, The. James McAuley. BMAP *Fr.* Seven Days of Creation, The.

Seventh Eclogue. Miklós Radnóti. IQMS, *tr. by* Peter Zollman

Seventh Eclogue ("Do you see? Evening falls, fringed with barbed-wire.") Miklós Radnóti. ConPit; PFTM-1, *tr. by* Clayton Eshleman and Gyula Kodolanyi

Seventh Heaven Can Be Seen at First Glance. Nikolai Kanchev. CSCBP, *tr. by* Georgi Belev and Lisa Sapinkopf

7th Light Poem: For John Cage—17 June 1962. Jackson Mac Low. FTOS

Seventh month. Chinese Figures 3. *Unknown.* EaWin, *tr. by* W. S. Merwin

Seventh Month, The. Basho. EMJL, *tr. by* Haruo Shirane

Seventh of July, the suith to say, The. Raid of the Reidswire, The. *Unknown.* IBB

Seventh Seal, The. W. E. Bard. TiP2

Seventh Street [*with music*]. Jean Toomer. APT-2; NAALPv.2

Seventh Symphony,The. Sándor Weöres. IQMS, *tr. by* Bruce Berlind and Mária Kőrösy

7th Untitled Poem. Pedro Juan Pietri. PueRic

Seventh Vertical Poetry. Roberto Juarroz.

"Prompting of my shadow, The." VCWP

Seventy Feet Down. Philip Larkin. NPeEn *Fr.* Livings.

74th Street. Myra Cohn Livingston. SSCS

79 years in a cast-iron box. Box, The. Matthew Sweeney. BeAl

Seventy Six Trombones [*with music*]. Meredith Willson. ReLy

Seventy Years Are Few. Lu Chih. WoPoe, *tr. by* Bruce Carpenter

Seventy Years Later. Wallace Stevens. NAMCP V.1 *Fr.* Rock, The.

Seventy-eight awkward years. Ichigen. ZenPo, *tr. by* Takashi Ikemoto and Lucien Stryk

Seventy-six: done. Fuyo-Dokai. ZenPo, *tr. by* Takashi Ikemoto and Lucien Stryk

Seventy-two years I've hung. Ikuo-Myotan. ZenPo, *tr. by* Takashi Ikemoto and Lucien Stryk

Several months after we lost our way. Natives, The. David Mura. WeW-3

Several of us are quiet in a ring. Manuscript with Illumination. Robert Fitzgerald. APT-2

Several Questions Answered. William Blake.

"He who binds to himself a joy." AmFaPo; NoP-4; NoP-5; SoSe-8; Spl

"Look of love alarms, The." WoPoe

Question Answered, The [*or* A]. ErotSp; NoP-4; NoP-5; OxBEV; WoPoe

Several sentences appear. Konrad Bayer. PFTM-2 *Fr.* Philosopher's Stone, The.

Several Voices Out of a Cloud. Louise Bogan. APT-2; NALW

Severance. Kit Robinson. FTOS

Severed hand flutters, the. Persistence of Memory, the Failure of Poetry, The. Robert Phillips. LiTh

Severer Service of Myself. Emily Dickinson. TRP

Severity of Heaven calls out the angry winds, The. On the Flooding of Prague, which Arose from Continuous Rain in the Year 1596. Elizabeth Jane Leon. EMWP

Severn and Vaga, each old Cambria's pride. Thoughts on Happiness. Francis Homfray. AngWePo

Severn Bore. Catherine Fisher. AngWePo; TCAWP

Sevint Buik, Lines 1029–92, The. Henry the Minstrel (Blind Harry). NePenScot *Fr.* Actis and Deidis of the Illustere and Vailyeand Campioun Schir William Wallace, Knicht of Ellerslie, The.

Sewing. Marianne Boruch. SweBea

Sewing a Dress. Lorine Niedecker. APT-2

Sewing Box, The. Chŏng Hwajin. EcSo, *tr. by* Julie C. Park

Sewing Lesson, The. Kate Lilley. BMAP

Sewing the torn sleeve of my shirt. Sewing the Torn Sleeve. Janet E. Aalfs. FiBr

Sewing Without Mother: A Zuihitsu. Kimiko Hahn. PuP-23

Sex. David Baker. PfSP

Sex. Stefan Brecht.

"Here then is the life-giving activity given to every man: the sexual / act, vivificator." CLPP

Sex. Yona Harvey. BRtP

Sex. Kim Suyŏng. CAMKP, *tr. by* Young-Jun Lee

Sex. Viki Radden. BtF

Sex. David C. Yates. TiP2

Sex: "You can sense, after a slow apprenticeship." Ricardo Feierstein. PML, *tr. by* J. Kates and Stephen A. Sadow

Sex and the Over Forties. Peter Porter. BMAP

Sex, as they harshly call it. Adrienne Rich. NIP-4 *Fr.* Two Songs.

Sex, as they harshly call it. Two Songs. Adrienne Rich. EmeKit; NIL-7

Sex, Consolation for Misery. Pier Paolo Pasolini. CLPP

Sex Everywhere. Srirangam Narayana Babu. HotL, *tr. by* V. Narayana Rao

Sex fingers toes. Dear John, Dear Coltrane. Michael S. Harper. CAP-8; FaoP; FuFl; ISC; LoL; NAAL-5; NAMCP V.2; NIL-7; NIP-4; VCAP

Sex has a way of unclothing limbs. Sex Has a Way. Wendy Lee. PasH

Sex is a power all cherish. Sadakichi. NAAPv.1 *Fr.* My Rubaiyat.

Sex is the curse of life! (LL) Edgar Lee Masters. APT-1; IllVoic; RACG *Fr.* Spoon River Anthology.

Sex violent as an object (whitened quarry of marble). Amelia Rosselli. ItPo, *tr. by* Gayle Ridinger

Sex with a Famous Poet. Denise Duhamel. KGB; NeAmPo

Sex without Love. Sharon Olds. HeIP-4; NIL-7; NIP-4; TRP

Sex—A Five-Minute Briefing. Nina Iskrenko. ItGoST, *tr. by* Patrick Henry, John High and Katya Olmsted

Sexes aren't very nice, The. Samuel Hoffenstein. AmWit *Fr.* Couplets, Rare, Medium, and Well-Done.

Sexes, The. Samuel Hoffenstein. AmWit *Fr.* Couplets, Rare, Medium, and Well-Done.

Sex-life her husband dreamed of, The. Limerick. Laurence Perrine. PoA 2002

Sex-life of Fish, The. William Diaper. OBVE *Fr.* Halieutica.

Sexpot. Charles Bukowski. BeAl

Sexsmith the Dentist. Edgar Lee Masters. GeoHom *Fr.* Spoon River Anthology.

Sext. Jeanne Shannon. ICANM

Sextain: "Sith gone is my delight and only pleasure." William Drummond of Hawthornden. NOSC

Sextain: "With elegies, sad songs, and mourning lays." William Drummond of Hawthornden. NOSC

Sextet. C. Yaphet Brinson. BtF

Sexton is opening up the grave, The. Third Light, The. Michael Longley. PNI

Sexual intercourse began. Annus Mirabilis. Philip Larkin. NBLV; NIP-4

Sexual Jealousy. Carol Frost. CAP-8; PfSP

Sexual Love. Eva Salzman. MoWP

Sexual Water. Pablo Neruda. ConPit; PFTM-1, *tr. by* Clayton Eshleman

Sexy talk show host nods and nods, The. Beside her. Broken Helix. Dina Ben-Lev. AmPoNex

Sexy Things. Anne Waldman. AHA

Sey me, wight in the broom. *Unknown. See* Say me, wight in the brom [*or* broom].

Seyton!—I am sick at heart. William Shakespeare. OxAEP-1 *Fr.* Macbeth.

Shabine sang to you from the depths of the sea. (LL) Schooner Flight, The. Derek Walcott. ESEAA; HarvBoo; NAEL-7v2; NAMCP V.2; NoP-4

Shadblow. Linda Pastan. PoDa

Shade, The. C. K. Williams. BeAl; StAl

Shade o' the vine. Ge-tan: Shade o' the Vine. *Unknown.* CCL1, *tr. by* Ezra Pound

Shade of noble trees spreads in all directions, The. Han-shan Te-ch'ing. CSKM, *tr. by* Red Pine

Shade upon the mind there passes, A. Emily Dickinson. APN-2

Shades. Minnie Bruce Pratt. ExTi

Shades and shadows manifold. Sub Umbra. Leo Bradley. OWABP

Shades of Callimachus, Coan ghosts of Philetas. Ezra Pound. APT-1; OBVE; OxBoAm; WoPoe *Fr.* Homage to Sextus Propertius.

Shades of eve are quickly closing in, The. Night. Josephine D. Henderson Heard. CBWP-4

Shades of night and glimmering dawn are fled, The. Anne Batten Cristall. RWP *Fr.* Thelmon and Carmel; An Irregular Poem.

Shades of Night, The [*par. of* Excelsior *by* Longfellow]. A. E. Housman. NBLV; OBCoV; UV

Shades of night were falling fast, The. Shades of Night, The. A. E. Housman. NBLV; OBCoV; UV

Shades of night were falling fast, The. Excelsior. Henry Wadsworth Longfellow. BRP; GoPo; NAAL-3; OBSP; STuOW; TCAPo; UV

Shades of old Lucretia Borgia! Witchcraft. Carolyn Leigh. ReLy

Shades of the Newly Buried Complain to the Gods, The. *Unknown.* WoPoe, *tr. by* John S. Major

Shadow. Mary Elizabeth Coleridge. VWP

Shadow. Patricia Goedicke. AtGh

Shadow. Josip Novakovich. BAP-97

Shadow. Stephanie Strickland. AtGh

Shadow: "Person we love, The." Fazil Hüsnü Daglarca. NaPG, *tr. by* Talat Sait Halman

Shadow, The. Nathan Alterman. FIT, *tr. by* Robert Friend

Shadow, The. Luis Cernuda. CAGL, *tr. by* Rick Lipinski

Shadow, The. Ben Jonson. OBEV

Shadow, The. John Banister Tabb. APN-2

Shadow, The: "Cheap movie theaters, saloons, fly-by-night markets." Tōge Sankichi. AtGh, *tr. by* Richard H. Minear

Shadow 1. Miyoshi Toyoichiro. GifTon, *tr. by* Naoshi Koriyama *and* Edward Lueders and Edward Lueders

Shadow, A. Abd al-Rahim Salih al-Rahim. IrPoTo, *tr. by* Ralph Saverese and Saadi A. Simawe

Shadow and Sunrise [*with music*]. Henrietta Cordelia Ray. CBWP-3

Shadow Beds. Delmira Agustini. TANSG, *tr. by* Mark McCaffrey

Shadow boxer, fighting. Father of Famine. Richard Ryan. PBCIP

Shadow does not leave my feet, The. David. Charles Reznikoff. ChIV-1

Shadow extends the tree. Thomas A. Clark. Oth

Shadow faces. Chord. Langston Hughes. APSN; OxBoAm

Shadow fruit is falling from the walls. Songs from an Island. Ingeborg Bachmann. VCWP, *tr. by* Mark Anderson

Shadow Grammar. Terence Winch. BAP-97

Shadow his father makes with joined hands, A. Alphabets. Seamus Heaney. NAMCP V.2; NoAM

Shadow in Stone. Janice Mirikitani. OpBo

Shadow int he shiny pilot's jacket, The. Segovia. Ricardo Pau-Llosa. Vesp

Shadow of a Loom, The. Cecilia Vicuña. WANABP

Shadow of Darkness. Gladys May Casely Hayford. HAWP

Shadow of Days to Come. Alejandra Pizarnik. TANSG, *tr. by* Susan Bassnett

Shadow of Fire: Ghazals, The. Judith Wright.
    Dust. HarvBoo
    Oppositions. HarvBoo
    Patterns. HarvBoo
    Rockpool. HarvBoo
    Summer. HarvBoo
    Winter. HarvBoo

Shadow of my silent steed, The. Silent Steed, The. Paul Pastnor. ArBi

Shadow of the night comes on, The. (LL) You, Andrew Marvell. Archibald MacLeish. APT-1; BeAl; BrAP; ColAP; HeIP-4; MoAmPo; NAMCP V.1; NoAM; NoP-4; SoSe-8; TFi; TRP

Shadow of the Rock, The. Frederick William Faber. SacPr

Shadow of the Venetian blind on the painted wall, The. Forties Flick. John Ashbery. FTOS; NoAM

Shadow of War, 1941. Thomas William Shapcott. BMAP

Shadow of wings grew, The. Fight With an Angel. Tadeusz Rózewicz. PoSu, *tr. by* Victor Contoski

Shadow on the shed, The. Subject / Matter. Robin Becker. RWB

Shadow on the wall vanished, The. The sun vanished. Out of a Hundred. Mary Ruefle. AmAlph

Shadow Portrait. Paul Mariani. PfSP

Shadow Returns, The. Phillis Levin. RA

Shadow sits and waits for me, The. (LL) Alfred Tennyson. CAGL; NAEL-6v2; NAEL-7v2; NAWM-7v2 *Fr.* In Memoriam A. H. H.

Shadow, stone, linen, lime, the. Seventh Symphony,The. Sándor Weöres. IQMS, *tr. by* Bruce Berlind and Mária Kőrösy

Shadow That Draws the Light, The. Natalia Toledo. RMCMP, *tr. by* Alberto A. Ríos

Shadow Valley. Robert Morgan. AngWePo

Shadow within the light, The. Serenity. Philippe Jaccottet. MFP; YaTCFP, *tr. by* Martin Sorrell

Shadowboxing [*with music*]. James Tate. MoASP

Shadow-Casting. James Galvin. MoASP

Shadowed by your father. Tracey Herd. StAl *Fr.* Some Mangled Dream Songs for Henry who is twenty-eight years dead and past caring.

Shadowless sun on male bodies. Sandro Penna. CAGL, *tr. by* John McRae

Shadows. John Clare. CenSon

Shadows. Patricia Hubbell. Spl

Shadows. Richard Jackson. SeSe

Shadows. Nesta Wyn Jones. BBMWP, *tr. by* Anthony Conran

Shadows: "Black-blue shadows on red-brown bricks." Avrom Viktor. Prolet, *tr. by* Amelia Glaser

Shadows, The. Jorge Guillén. RaW, *tr. by* Charles Guenther

Shadows: "Shadows can never open their mouths." Jayanta Mahapatra. PML

Shadows become familiar. My Neighborhood. Stuart Dybek. PBCAP

Shadows behind, Before. Ingrid de Kok. TSAP

Shadows can never open their mouths. Shadows. Jayanta Mahapatra. PML

Shadows dart, the wind has risen. Nightfall. Ekaterina Iosifova. CSCBP, *tr. by* Georgi Belev and Lisa Sapinkopf

Shadows / fill the stones. Rain. Chŏng Chiyong. CAMKP, *tr. by* Kevin O'Rourke

Shadows in his eye sockets like shades, The. Richmond. John Updike. CBCWP

Shadows in the Water. Thomas Traherne. NoP-4; NoP-5; WoPoe

Shadows, like Navahoes, wear velvet. Tourist Country. William Stafford. NoAM

Shadows of Chrysanthemums. Edith Jay Scovell. HarvBoo

Shadows of the bicycles are so sharp, The. October 7, 1994. Ruth Lepson. PfS

Shadows of the plane-tree leaves. Sveta Litvak. CRWP, *tr. by* Daniel Weissbort

Shadows of Trees on the Lawn, January. Einir Jones. BBMWP, *tr. by* Joseph P. Clancy

Shadows on azure seawater. (LL) Wild Iris, The. Louise Glück. ColAP; MoWP; NAMCP V.2; StAl

Shadows on the wall. Life Doesn't Frighten Me. Maya Angelou. ChAP

Shadows, shadows, / Hug me round. Escape. Georgia Douglas Johnson. NAAPv.2

Shadows simplify—the beak combing the back is lost. Image Cast by a Body Intercepting Light. Matthea Harvey. IAoNAP

Shadow's Song, The. Yvor Winters. NAAPv.2 *Fr.* Magpie's Shadow, The.

Shadows watched from the three windows, the. House, The. Vincent Woods. NIrP

Shadowy as a blueprint is. Building the Dam. Reuel Denney. YaYoPo

Shadowy daughter of Urthona stood before red Orc, The. America: A Prophecy. William Blake.

Shadrach O'Leary. Edwin Arlington Robinson. APT-1

Shady Grove. *Unknown.* APN-2

Shady grove, my true love. Shady Grove. *Unknown.* APN-2

Shady, shady, flower stamens a tangle. Shady, Shady. Tu Fu [*or* Du Fu]. CCL1, *tr.* by Florence Ayscough *and* Amy Lowell

Shady, shady, the woods before the hall. Harmonizing with a Poem by the Registrar Guo. T'ao Ch'ien. CCL1, *tr.* by William Acker

Shady Soul. Max Jacob. YaTCFP, *tr.* by Mary Ann Caws *and* Jean-Pierre Cauvin

Shaft extracted does not cure the wound!, The. (LL) Petrarch. CenSon; RWP *Fr.* Sonnets to Laura.

Shaft of narrative peers down, The. Soul, The. Ira Sadoff. BodElec

Shaft we raise to them and thee, The. (LL) Concord Hymn. Ralph Waldo Emerson. AmWaPo; BRP; ClHu; ColAP; CtM; FaBoA; HeIP-4; NAAPv.1; NoP-4; NoP-5; OBWP; OxBoAm; PoPoPo; TCAPo; TFi; WaAnP

Shaft[e]sbury. John Dryden. NOSC

Shaftesbury. John Dryden. NPeEn *Fr.* Absalom and Achitophel.

Shagbark. Faye George. PoCoUp

Shagoon 1–4. Andrew Hope III. FTtHH

Shahnamah, The. Firdowsi.
　Birth of Sohráb, The. TAL
　Death of Sohráb, The. TAL

Shake Down the Stars. Eddie DeLange. ReLy

Shake hands, we shall never be friends, all's over. A. E. Housman. CAGL

Shake hole. Marks the English Left on the Map. Peter Finch. Oth

Shake off this sadness, and recover your spirit. Throw Yourself Like Seed. Miguel de Unamuno. PLBUT; RaBo; RaW, *tr.* by Robert Bly

Shake the bed, the blackened child whimpers. Cotton Flannelette. Les A. Murray. PoetW

Shaken. Ellen McGrath Smith.
　2. IaFF
　3. IaFF
　4. IaFF

Shaken, They Cling Again. Li Yu [*or* Li Hou-Chu]. CCL1, *tr.* by John Turner

Shakeout. Diane Ward. FTOS

Shakespeare. Henrietta Cordelia Ray. CBWP-3

Shakespeare: "Others abide our question. Thou art free." Matthew Arnold. BrAP; GSo; HeIP-4; NoP-4; NoP-5; OBEV; OxAEP-2; OxBSo; PoPoPo

Shakespeare as a Waiter. BJ Ward. IaFF

Shakespeare never got to see. Symmetron: You and Brother Will. Jack Rogow. IaFF

Shakespeare No More. Anne MacLeod. EdScPo

Shakespeare!—to such name's sounding, what succeeds. Names, The. Robert Browning. OxBSo

Shakespearean Sonnet. R. S. Gwynn. IaFF

Shakespeare's Eyebrows. Sylvia Adams. IaFF

Shakespeare's Wages. Marvin Bell. IaFF

Shakespearean Readings. Phoebe Cary. SWaP

Shakin All Over. John James. Oth

Shaking Hands with Mongo. Martín Espada. SeSe

Shaking Hands with Murder. Sir Osbert Sitwell. RSaN

Shaking off the red dust. Kim Sŏnggi. CATKP, *tr.* by Peter H. Lee

(Shaking with light—) is born. (LL) Thinking. Jorie Graham. BAP-97; ExTi

Shak-shak. Seitlhamo Motsapi. TSAP

Shakspeare. Ralph Waldo Emerson. TCAPo *Fr.* Quatrains.

Shakti. Elsa Cross. RMCMP

Shakti. Elsa Cross. RMCMP, *tr.* by Margaret Sayers Peden

Shakti. Rae Desmond Jones. BMAP

Shalako. *Zuni Oral Tradition. tr.* by Ruth L. Bunzel
　Dismissal of the Koyemshi. NAWM-7v2
　Sayatasha's Night Chant. NAAPv.1
　House Blessing. NAWM-7v2, *tr.* by Ruth L. Bunzel

Shale. Vona Groarke. MFPA

Shall be a soldier's sepulchre. (LL) Hohenlinden. Thomas Campbell. CABP; NOBRP; NPBRoP; OBWP; TFi

Shall be lifted—nevermore! (LL) Raven, The. Edgar Allan Poe. APN-1; BRP; ChAP; ColAP; HeIP-4; ITBLP; NAAL-3; NAAL-5; NAAPv.1; NCAP; NIL-7; NIP-4; NoP-4; NoP-5; OBNV; OWoS; OxBoAm; TCAPo; TFi; TreFP; UV; WaAnP

Shall become as. Evie Shockley. RD

Shall both rise with me. (LL) Cherry-Tree Carol, The. *Unknown.* ChrPo; HeIP-4; MakPoe; TFi

Shall bring my boats ashore. (LL) Where Go the Boats? Robert Louis Stevenson. NOxBChV; NTCP; TLR; WHSW

Shall brothers [*or* brithers] be for a' that. (LL) For A' That and A' That ["Is there, for honest poverty"]. Robert Burns. BRP; NAEL-6v2; NePenScot; NPBRoP; OxAEP-2; OxBEV; TFi; TreFP; UV

Shall buffet the vexed forests in his rage. (LL) Winter Piece, A. William Cullen Bryant. APN-1; ColAP

Shall do it reverence. (LL) City in the Sea, The. Edgar Allan Poe. APN-1; BrAP; NAAL-3; NAAPv.1; NCAP; NoP-4; NoP-5; OxBoAm; TCAPo; TFi; TRP

Shall Earth no more inspire thee. Emily Jane Brontë. BrAP; VWP

Shall fear to seem untrue. Rejection, The. Sir Robert Aytoun. NOSC

Shall find wings waiting there. (LL) Going Down Hill on a Bicycle. Henry Charles Beeching. ArBi; NOxBChV; OBEV

Shall Gaelic Die? Iain Crichton Smith. NPeEn

Shall hearts that beat no base retreat. Enthusiast, The. Herman Melville. ChIV-1; NAAL-3

Shall I be child of the full moon. Bloody Masculinity. Ifi Amadiume. HAWP

Shall I be one of those obsequious Fools. Liberty, The. Sarah Fyge Egerton. EMWP

Shall I Come, Sweet Love. Thomas Campion. OxAEP-1

Shall I compare her to a summer play? Sonnet on Famous and Familiar Sonnets and Experiences. Delmore Schwartz. TRP

Shall I Compare Thee? T. Alan Broughton. PoDa

Shall I compare thee to a summer's bay. Lateral Disregard. Harry Mathews. BAP-04; NYP2

Shall I compare thee to a summer's day? William Shakespeare. AEP; AmFaPo; BLPJKO; BrAP; CABP; ClHu; CtM; HeIP-4; ITBLP; MakPoe; NAEL-6v1; NAEL-7v1; NIL-7; NoP-5; NoSic; NPeEn; OBEV; OxBEV; OxBSo; PoPoPo; TFi; WaAnP; WeW-3 *Fr.* Sonnets.

Shall I compare thee to a winter's night? Shall I Compare Thee. . .? Anthony Lombardy. IaFF

Shall I Die? *Unknown.* SSUS

Shall I Do This. Swami Purohit. OBMV

Shall I get drunk or cut myself a piece of cake. Cairo Jag. Keith Douglas. HarvBoo; PoWW

Shall I have jealous thoughts to nurse. No Man's Wood. W. H. Davies. OBGa

Shall I love God for causing me to be? Proof, The. Richard Wilbur. InvLi; UpMys

Shall I place a tin wreath upon! (LL) Ezra Pound. ColAP; HarvBoo; MoAmPo *Fr.* Hugh Selwyn Mauberley (Life and Contacts).

Shall I rebuke thee, Ocean, my old love. To the Ocean. Thomas Hood. CenSon

Shall I say how it is in your clothes? How It Is. Maxine W. Kumin. InoFa; NALW; NAMCP V.2; NoAM

Shall I see it again. Shunzei. WoPoe, *tr.* by Valerie Durham

Shall I sonnet-sing you about myself? House. Robert Browning. NAEL-6v2

Shall I strew on thee rose or rue or laurel. Ave atque Vale. Algernon Charles Swinburne. NAEL-6v2; NAEL-7v2; OBEV

Shall I tell you the signs of a New Age coming? New Age, The. Stevie Smith. NAEL-6v2; NAEL-7v2

Shall I tell you what I'm thinking. Old Maid's Reverie, An. *Unknown.* ArBi

Shall I tell you whom I love? William Browne. NOSC *Fr.* Britannia's Pastorals.

Shall I then praise the heavens, the trees, the earth. Anne Bradstreet. NOSC *Fr.* Contemplations.

Shall I, Wasting in Despair. George Wither. OxAEP-1 *Fr.* Fair Virtue, the Mistress of Philarete [Selections from anthologies].

Shall I write pretty poetry. Egoist, The. Anna Wickham. MoWP

Shall last and shine when all of these are gone. (LL) Contemplations. Anne Bradstreet. ColAP; NAAL-3; NAAL-5; NAAPv.1; TCAPo

Shall live my Highland Mary. (LL) Highland Mary. Robert Burns. NPBRoP; OBEV

Shall multi . . . pl . . . p. (LL) Spring's Last Drop, The. Catherine Obianuju Acholonu. HAWP; NAfrP

Shall no more blackened and obscured be. (LL) October. Edward Thomas. CABP; HarvBoo; NoAM

Shall paint this happiest scene with pencil soft. (LL) Written at the Eagle's Nest, Killarney. July 26, 1800. Mary Tighe. CenSon; OxBSo

Shall silence shroud such sin. Declaration of the Death of John Lewes, A. Thomas Gilbart. NoSic

Shall speak to me in their fattening echo, and purr: penetralia. Waterfowl Descending. Sam Witt. NeAmPo

Shall the water not remember *Ember*. Narcissus and Echo. Fred Chappell. PoA 2002

Shall then another do what I have done. Shall Then Another. Kenneth Mackenzie. BrAP; NOBAu

Shall thirst (God's gargoyle!) for these blessings' blows. (LL) Gwyneth Lewis. MoWP; NeBl *Fr.* Parables & Faxes.

Shall we behold "no classes" on God's earth. (LL) No Classes! Ella Wheeler Wilcox. APN-2; SWaP

Shall we call them poets, for having observed. Crew of *Apollo 8*, The. Elaine V. Emans. OtW

Shall We Dance? Oscar Hammerstein, II. ReLy

Shall We Dance. Joe Osterhaus. NAPBL

Shall we dress in skin. Lai with Sounds of Skin. Chryss Yost. CalPo

Shall we forget the shiver. Yury Ivask. TCRusP, *tr. by* John Glad

Shall We Gather at the River? Monifa Atungaye Love. LiTh

Shall we gather at the river. Beautiful River. Robert Lowry. APN-2

Shall we / gentlemen. Hebron. Diane Di Prima. Eno

Shall we go dance the hay? The hay? Report Song [in a Dream], A. Nicholas Breton. NoSic

Shall we hear you again soon, soon? (LL) Nightingales, The. Harri Webb. AngWePo; TCAWP

Shall We Join the Ladies? Marshall Barer. ReLy

Shall we leave it unabated in its place? (LL) Mesopotamia. Rudyard Kipling. HarvBoo; PoWW

Shall yourselves find blessing. (LL) Good King Wenceslas. *Unknown*. ChrPo; SacPr, *tr. by* John Mason Neale

Shallot, A. Richard Wilbur. OxBoAm

Shallow / Bruises blush blue. Ghost of His Hand, The. Nancy Bennett. IFF

Shallows, brighter, The. Pier: Under Pisces, The. James Merrill. NoAM

Shallow-Water Warning. Helen Adam. APT-2

Sham Jew. Matt Morris. MAAN

Shaman and the Red God, The. Nakkiranar. WoPoe,

Shaman Breaks. Gerald Vizenor. HATNAP

Shaman Song. Uvavnuk. WoPoe, *tr. by* Jane Hirshfield

Shaman's Song. *Hungarian Oral Tradition*. IQMS, *tr. by* Adam Makkai

Shame. Ku Sang. CAMKP, *tr. by* Kevin O'Rourke

Shame. Vern Rutsala. OPRER

Shame. Matilde Salganicoff. MirDau, *tr. by* Celeste Kostopulos-Cooperman

Shame. Lőrinc Szabó. IQMS *Fr.* Cricket Music.

Shame. Richard Wilbur. EmeKit; OBCoV; OxBoAm

Shame: "If only I'd known then what I was reaching for." Tom Sleigh. PfSP

Shame, No Statist. Robert Herrick. BASC

Shame of France, The. James Grainger. STuoW *Fr.* Sugar Cane, The.

Shame of Llanfaes, The. Gerallt Lloyd Owen. BBMWP, *tr. by* Ronald Stuart Thomas

Shame of the Writers' Conference. Allison Joseph. BtF

Shame on You. Langston Hughes. APT-2

Shame on you Shakyamuni for setting. Layman's Lament, The. Judyth Collin. WhBo

Shame Place, The. Stephen Dunn. SUP

Shame to my thoughts, how they stray from me! On the Flightiness of Thought. *Unknown*. IrV, *tr. by* Kuno Meyer

Shamed by the Creature. Mildmay Fane, 2d Earl of Westmorland. NOSC

Shameful / Dead grass. Shoha. ZenPo, *tr. by* Takashi Ikemoto and Lucien Stryk

Shameful mask hid his teeth, The. Squares. Pierre Reverdy. PFTM-1

Shameful / These clothes. Sono-Jo, Lady. ZenPo, *tr. by* Takashi Ikemoto and Lucien Stryk

Shamisen is hateful, The. Ecstasy. Yamamura Bochō. CAoMJL1, *tr. by* Leith Morton

Shampoo, The. Elizabeth Bishop. APT-2; HarvBoo; OxBoAm; PtR; StAl; VCAP

Shancoduff. Patrick Kavanagh. HarvBoo; WoPoe

Shandon Bells, The. Francis Sylvester Mahony. *See* Bells of Shandon, The.

Shane O'Neill's Cairn. Robinson Jeffers. NoAM

Shaneen and Maurya Prendergast. Patch-Shaneen. John Millington Synge. FaBoVe

Shang Cup. Louis Zukofsky. APT-2

Shangri-la. Suzanne Lummis. CalPo

Shank-end of day, spit of snow, the call. Robert Penn Warren. NAAPv.2 *Fr.* Audubon: A Vision.

Shannon Estuary 1988. Nuala Ni Dhomhnaill. IrLP

Shannon Estuary Welcomes the Fish, The. Nuala Ni Dhomhnaill. ModIr, *tr. by* Patrick Crotty

12. Shantideva. David McFadden. NLPA

Shantung. Hsi-tseng Tsiang. NAAPv.2

Shantung. Denise Riley. MoWP

Shanty shade figured among the makers, A. Revelry in Black-and-White. Ann Lauterbach. BodElec

Shap. Mick North. NLP

Shapcot, to thee the Fairy [*or* faery] State. Oberon's Feast. Robert Herrick. NOSC

Shape for It, A. Michael Ryan. PoA 2002

Shape of Death, The. May Swenson. APT-2

Shape of talk about sag, The. Ongoing. Naomi Shihab Nye. PoArWo

Shape of the Fire, The. Theodore Roethke. VCAP

Shape of Things, The. Lavinia Greenlaw. MFPA

Shape of Things, The. Phyllis Thompson. ICANM

Shape the lips to an *o*, say *a*. Ö. Rita Dove. StAl; WeW-3

Shape-Changer, The. Chris Wallace-Crabbe. NOBAu

Shaped and vacated. Event, The. Thomas Sturge Moore. OBMV

Shapeless mass of wreck and rubbish lies, A. (LL) Warning, The. Henry Wadsworth Longfellow. APN-1; ChIV-1; NCAP; PCW; TCAPo

Shapeless, the waves rise toward their elements, where the foam of. Orbits. 'Aisha Arnaout. PoArWo, *tr. by* Mona Fayad

Shapelessness, the endlessness, The. Shapelessness, The. Ágnes Nemes Nagy. IQMS, *tr. by* Alan Dixon

Shapes as a series of edges, each edge. Dove. Stanley Plumly. PfSP

Shapes of a Soul. Sarah Morgan Bryan Piatt. NAAPv.1

Shapes of Death, The. Stephen Spender. OBMV

Shapes of Mouths at Parties, The. Naomi Shihab Nye. CAP-8

Shapes of purity—over the wide water. (LL) Goodbye, Goldeneye. May Swenson. NoP-4; NoP-5

Shapeshifter Poems. Lucille Clifton. BodElec; LoL

Shapeshifting. Isabel Gowdie. EMWP

Shaping the red gold of my thoughts. Quartz and Mica. Yolande Villemaire. NLPA, *tr. by* Judith Elaine Cowan

Shards. Enid Shomer. TaR

Shards, The. Michael O'Loughlin.
Bunkers, The. PBCIP

Shards of retribution jut skyward. In Oklahoma. Toni Asante Lightfoot. BtF

Shards of sunlight touch me here. Massacre, October '66. Wole Soyinka. AF; NAMCP V.2

Share fear. Repeat with one lip what. Poem with Skin. Octavio Armand. TCLAP, *tr. by* Carol Maier

Share in perdition. (LL) Lost Soul, A. Jay Macpherson. BrAP; NoP-4; NoP-5

Share my harvest and my home. (LL) Ruth. Thomas Hood. ChIV-1; NPBRoP; OBEV

Share-Croppers. Langston Hughes. SAmP

Shared Custody. Brenda Hillman. RoV

Shared Existence. Ivan Teofilov. CSCBP, *tr. by* Georgi Belev and Lisa Sapinkopf

Shared Life, A. Katherine Soniat. PfSP

Shared Nights. Paul Eluard *and* Andre Breton. YaTCFP, *tr. by* Mary Ann Caws *and* Jean-Pierre Cauvin

Shari Wag El Burka. *Unknown*. FaBoWar

Sharing. Alan Yount. PasH

Sharing bread. Truth. Jean Valentine. BodElec

Sharing Eve's Apple. John Keats. ChIV-1; ErotSp; NBLV

Sharing is Hereditary. Kalamu ya Salaam. FuFl

Sharing Lodging with Hsieh Shih-hou. Mei Yao Ch'en. ColAnChi, *tr. by* Burton Watson

Shark, The. Edwin John Pratt. BrAP

Shark, with your mouth tucked under. Thom Gunn. NOxBChV *Fr.* Three for Children.

Shark Wrangler Goes to Church, The. Jeni Olin. FreRad

Sharks cruising a sky cold as these waters off the coastline. (LL) Gray Day in January in La Jolla. Quincy Troupe. OxAAAP; PrTe

Sharks tooth is perfect for biting, The. The Intent. Canticle. Michael McClure. CalPo

Sharon Resembles a Person. Aharon Shabtai. WoBe, *tr. by* Peter Cole

Sharp as an arrow Orpheus. Orfeo. Jack Spicer. APSN; CalPo

Sharp facets. Jewel Cliff. Muso Soseki. EaWin, *tr. by* W. S. Merwin

Sharp howling winds scattering grit. Desert Crossing. Dambudzo Marechera. NAfrP

Sharping Stone, The. Seamus Heaney. NAEL-7v2

Shatter. Elizabeth Robinson. AmPoNex

Shattered water made a misty din, The. Once by the Pacific. Robert Frost. APT-1; GSo; HeIP-4; MoAmPo; NIL-7; PtR; TRP; WeW-3

Shatterfall. Scutter. Mark, The. Robert Patrick Dana. OPRER

Shaula is radiant to starboard. Liberación. E. A. Mares. ICANM

Shaving. Richard Blanco. AmPoNex; NAPBL

Shaving my head. Sora. EMJL, *tr. by* Haruo Shirane

Shaving of Murdoch, The. Murdoch O'Daly. IrV, *tr.* by Standish O'Grady

She. Mary Dalton. OpeFie

She. Lynn Emanuel. BodElec

She. Christopher Gilbert. OxAAAP

She. Theodore Roethke. NIL-7; StAl

She: "She lives on a moor in the north." Anne Carson. NLPA *Fr.* Glass Essay, The.

She [*with music*]. Richard Wilbur. NIL-7

She adjusts my hip, spine, shoulder. Chest X-Ray. Paula Tatarunis. BloBone

She aims her spears at the cardinal points. Spark of Green. Maria Luisa Spaziani. CItWP, *tr.* by Cinzia Sartini Blum and Lara Trubowitz

She already knows that he had said "*The rest of them.*" Variations. Hédi Kaddour. YaTCFP, *tr.* by Marilyn Hacker

She always said "*tu*" in such a way. Dark Portrait, A. Lawrence Ferlinghetti. PmAP

She answered the phone and heard her answer. Exhaled, The. Katherine Swiggart. IaFF

She answers the bothersome telephone, takes the message, forgets the message, forgets who called. Alzheimer's: The Wife. C. K. Williams. EMP; VCAP

She asked for bread. Mother. Isobel Thrilling. Prnts

She asked me to luncheon in fur. Far from. Oppenheim's Cup and Saucer. Carol Ann Duffy. LW

She asked me why I did such things. Dialogue. Jared Angira. NAfrP

She Asked You. Vladimir Holan. PML, *tr.* by Ian Milner and Jarmila Milner

She Attempts to Tell the Truth About True Romance. Kathy Fagan. ExTi

She awakened me with tears. Sammy Davis, Jr. Jacqueline Jones LaMon. BRtP

She bathed him in the brew of the root. The basin. Derek Walcott. NAMCP V.2 *Fr.* Omeros.

She begins, and my grandmother joins her. I Ask My Mother to Sing. Li-Young Lee. IllVoic; InvLad; LoL; OpBo; PoCho; UnSA

She begins to board the flight. White Bear. Joy Harjo. NAAL-5

She being Brand. E. E. Cummings. EroLit

She believed she was cursed. She believed her guardian angel had. Three Observations on Belief. Tarin Towers. AmPoNex

She blossomed in the country. Country Lassie, The. *Unknown.* TreFP

She blossomed, tall, benevolent, notwithstanding. (LL) Autumn Leaves. Marilyn Chin. ExTi; NAMCP V.2

She Boasts of Her Constancy. Johann Rist. GePo, *tr.* by George C. Schoolfield

She boned three chickens—all except the wings. Bacchanal. Barbara J. Orton. NeAmPo

She bore the goblet in her hand. Two, The. Hugo von Hofmannsthal. GTCP, *tr.* by Walter Kaufmann

She bore three sons. Has two sons. Was twenty-five. Biography of a Woman, The. Ferenc Juhász. ConPit, *tr.* by Clayton Eshleman and Gyula Kodolanyi

She bought the eggplant because her lover. Vegetable Love. Diane Lockward. SweBea

She bows her head. Annunciation, The. Samuel Menashe. GI

She brings that breath, and music too. Visitor, The. W. H. Davies. OBWVE

She brings the Book of Life, obiously. (LL) "H. D." NAAPv.2; NALW; NAMCP V.1; NoAM *Fr.* Tribute to the Angels.

She broke a window in the nearest boat. This Land. Sasha Steensen. Eno

She brought her to her ioyous Paradize. Edmund Spenser. OBGa

She brought home poppies. Karen Press. TSAP

She Called Them Stones. Robert Masterson. ICANM

She calls and calls each vagabond by name. (LL) Vagabond Song, A. Bliss Carman. BRP; IFF; TCAPo

She Calms the Savage Beast with Her Aubade. Grace Bauer. MiVo

She came among us from the South. Enrica, 1865. Christina Georgina Rossetti. NALW

She came as a falling star to the lakes. She the lithesome virgin not to be turned into. My Mother, Life. John Godfrey. FTOS

She came every morning to draw water. Drink of Water, A. Seamus Heaney. TRP

She came, fair Friendship came, with aspect bland. Friendship. Mary Julia Young. CenSon

"She came home, my Lord, and smashed-in the television." Wife Who Smashed Television Gets Jail. Paul Durcan. CABP

She came home smelling of another man. Kiss. Shuntaro Tanikawa. PML, *tr.* by Harold Wright

She came in glowing. Visitor. Aleksandr Aleksandrovich Blok. TCRusP, *tr.* by Geoffrey Thurley

She came on Earth soon after the creation. Fairy Maimounè, The. John Moultrie. NOBRP

She came through the room like an answer in long division. Victorian Idyll, A. David Wagoner. NoAM

She came to my dream. Pak Hyogwan. CATKP, *tr.* by Peter H. Lee

She Came to Say Farewell. Anna Swirszczynska [*or* Swir]. PoChi, *tr.* by Czeslaw Milosz and Leonard Nathan

She came to the village church. Alfred Tennyson. NAEL-6v2 *Fr.* Maud [A Monodrama].

She came to this local bar. Performance. Paul McRay. SwNoth

She came to us walking, at night. Shoemaker's Wife, The. Lotte Kramer. HP

She came up the hill carrying water. Achill Woman, The. Eavan Boland. HarvBoo

She cannot leave it alone. New Toy, The. Thomas Hardy. ChAP

She carried a book, either to imply. "H. D." NAAPv.2; NALW; NAMCP V.1 *Fr.* Tribute to the Angels.

She carried / one daughter. Sistah Flo. Terri L. Jewell. FiBr

She carries it unsteadily, warily. Young Girl with a Pitcher Full of Water, A. David Wagoner. NAMCP V.2; NoAM

She cat, The. Basho. EH, *tr.* by Robert Hass

She channelled love under my skin. Finding. Celia Barry. Prnts

She chooses her clothes in subdued colours. Other Woman, The. Marion Lomax. LW

She cleaned house, and then lay down long. Secret Gratitude, A. James Wright. NoAM

She closes the bathroom door to secure her privacy, slips off her robe. Shower Scene in *Psycho*, The. David Trinidad. ReTh

She closes the gate. Times Like This. Richard Jones. GifTon

She comes each morning. Woman. Kang Ŭn'gyo. CAMKP, *tr.* by Kevin O'Rourke

She comes in late, then settles like a sigh. Introduction to Poetry. Paul Lake. RA

She comes level with him at. Donahue's Sister. Thom Gunn. NoAM

She Comes Not When Noon Is on the Roses. Herbert Trench. IrLP; OBEV

She comes on drenched in a perfume called Self Satisfaction. Mae West. Edward Field. GoPo

She comes to me. (LL) She Comes Not When Noon Is on the Roses. Herbert Trench. IrLP; OBEV

She comes to me squirming in her father's arms. Latching On, Falling Off. Beth Ann Fennelly. NevBe

She comes with fairy footsteps. Little Rose. *Unknown.* TreFP

She concerned him. Melon Grower, The. Alice Oswald. MFPA; MoWP

She could be seen undressing. Gesture and Flight. Ann Lauterbach. BodElec

She could bind the world's winds in a single strand. Rune of the Finland Woman. Marilyn Hacker. FaoP; RA

She could have told him a million times and tried. Last Days. Betsy Struthers. IFF

She could not love him till she saw him clear. Psyche Revised. Rhina P. Espaillat. PoDa

She cross'd, and pass'd him on the other side. (LL) George Crabbe. NOBRP; NPBRoP *Fr.* Tales.

She cursed the circumstance. (LL) Ballad of Sue Ellen Westerfield, The. Robert Earl Hayden. ESEAA; NoAM

She dances Henry away. (LL) John Berryman. CAP-8; EMP; NoP-4; NoP-5 *Fr.* Dream Songs.

She dealt her pretty words like Blades. Emily Dickinson. NIL-7

She delighted to hold a slip of myrtle. Archilochus. SaLy, *tr.* by Diane Rayor

She dens in a garret. Fruit and Flower Painter. Herman Melville. NCAP

She detaches herself from her shadow. She is an old woman and still beautiful. Gloria Gervitz. MirDau *Fr.* Yiskor.

She dialed a number and said. How To Live Through This Night (A Dream). Nina Iskrenko. ItGoST, *tr.* by Patrick Henry, John High and Katya Olmsted

She did not graze on all fours but. Lilith. Ron Koertge. CalPo

She didn't believe the words. Inventing the Hawk. Lorna Crozier. BeAl

She Didn't Mean to Do It. Daisy Fried. P180; PoDa

She Didn't Say "Yes." Otto Harbach. ReLy

She died, as many travellers have died. Found Frozen. Helen Hunt Jackson. NAAPv.1

She died in the upstairs bedroom. Death in Leamington. Sir John Betjeman. MakPoe; NoP-4; NoP-5; OxAEP-2

She does not know. No Images. Waring Cuney. APT-2; NIP-4; SSLK

She does not move. Takes the man's. She Does Not Move. Jean Daive. MFP, *tr.* by Martin Sorrell

She Does Not Remember [*with music*]. Anna Swirszczynska [*or* Swir]. BLT

She does not speak. Jacqueline Goldberg. MirDau *Fr.* Luba.

She doesn't feel the need to erect pergolas. Jolanda Insana. CItWP *Fr.* Rooting, The.

She doesn't get to say much in the official biography.   Anne Carson.   OxBoAm; WoBe *Fr.* Truth About God, The.

She doesn't understand.   Prisoner, The.   Dunya Mikhail.   IrPoTo, *tr. by* Liz Winslow

She doesn't want.   Pumping Iron.   Diane Ackerman.   MoASP

She doesn't wear.   Gwendolyn Brooks.   Haki R. Madhubuti.   ESEAA; FTtHH; OPRER

She done put huh little hands.   Conjured.   Sterling Allen Brown.   NoP-4; NoP-5

She don't look Indian all the time.   Rational.   Helen Chalakee Burgess.   ReEnLa

She dotes on what the wild birds say.   She Dotes.   Edward Thomas.   StAl

She drawled, When Ah itchez, Ah scratchez! (LL)   Requiem: "There was a young belle of old Natchez."   Ogden Nash.   NoP-4; NoP-5

She dreamed along the beaches of this coast.   Palo Alto: the Marshes.   Robert Hass.   GeoHom

She drew an angel down[!]. (LL)   Alexander's Feast; or, The Power of Music [*or* Musique].   John Dryden.   NAEL-6v1; NAEL-7v1; TFi; WaAnP

She drew back; he was calm.   Subverted Flower, The.   Robert Frost.   APT-1; ColAP; NoAM

She Drove a 'Seventies Plymouth.   Robert Minhinnick.   TCAWP

She Dwelt among the Untrodden Ways.   William Wordsworth.   BrAP; HeIP-4; InoFa; NAEL-6v2; NAEL-7v2; NIL-7; NIP-4; NoP-5; NPBRoP; NPeEn; OxAEP-2; UV; WeW-3 *Fr.* Lucy.

She eased the bike onto the park's curved path.   Sonnet at Three-Speed.   J. Lorraine Brown.   ArBi

13. She Endeavours to Fascinate Him.   Mary Robinson.   CenSon; NPBRoP; RWP *Fr.* Sappho and Phaon.

She entered, sore and wan—she could not speak.   Albery Allson Whitman.   NAAPv.1 *Fr.* Octoroon, The.

She even meditates on rites of passage.   Gooseflesh.   Janet Fisher.   MFPA

She even thinks that up in heaven.   Countee Cullen.   APT-2; HeIP-4; NAAPv.2; NAMCP V.1; NIL-7; NIP-4; SSLK; TRP *Fr.* Four Epitaphs.

She exists, but only at midnight, when the wings of the white birds have folded.   She Exists.   Paul Eluard *and* Andre Breton.   YaTCFP, *tr. by* Mary Ann Caws *and* Jean-Pierre Cauvin

She extends the empty cup of her body.   Diminutive.   Nancy Steele.   GifTon

She eyes herself in the mirror.   Salma in Wonderland.   Mona Fayad.   PoArWo

She falls for him, conventional longing well.   Robert Sheppard.   Oth *Fr.* Empty Diaries/Twentieth Century Blues 24.

She fears him, and will always ask.   Eros Turannos.   Edwin Arlington Robinson.   AmFaPo; APT-1; HeIP-4; MoAmPo; NAAPv.1; NAMCP V.1; NoAM; NoP-4; OxBoAm; PoA 2002; PoPoPo; TCAPo; TFi; TRP; WoPoe

She feels her hands, scabrous as fish.   Washerwoman, The.   Veronica Volkow.   VCWP, *tr. by* Forrest Gander

She fell asleep in the kitchen like a dishrag.   Censored.   Blas de Otero.   RaW, *tr. by* Hardie St. Martin

She fell asleep on Christmas Eve: / At length the long-ungranted shade.   My Sister's Sleep.   Dante Gabriel Rossetti.   NAEL-6v2; NAEL-7v2

She fell away in her first ages spring.   Edmund Spenser.   OBEV *Fr.* Daphnaïda.

She fell off the hot tub and broke her wrist.   Wedding Banquet.   Diana O'Hehir.   AFaM

She filled her arms with wood, and set her chin.   Edna St. Vincent Millay.   NALW *Fr.* Sonnets from an Ungrafted Tree.

She flies she flies through the white flat lands, and patiently I take my aim.   Nocturne (She Flies She Flies).   Léopold Sédar Senghor.   WoPoe, *tr. by* John Reed and Olive Wake

She flitted by me on the stair.   Meeting, The.   Isabel Ecclestone MacKay.   PoBW

She folds her wings about her sleeping child. (LL)   Bats.   Randall Jarrell.   ChAP; GoPo; NTCP

She frowned. He was amazed—he could not speak.   Albery Allson Whitman.   NAAPv.1 *Fr.* Octoroon, The.

She gave her body for my meat.   Sacrament.   Countee Cullen.   NAAPv.2

She gave it out as if it were.   Aphrodisiac, The.   Medbh McGuckian.   PBCIP

She gave me childhood's flowers.   Heirloom.   Kathleen Jessie Raine.   NALW

"She gives herself;" there's a poetic thought.   Portrait in Black Paint, with a Very Sparing Use of Whitewash.   Elinor Wylie.   NALW

She gives him his eyes, she found them.   Bride and Groom Lie Hidden for Three Days.   Ted Hughes.   StAl

She gives him paper and a fine-nibbed pen.   Trois Petits Tours et Puis . . .   Marie Ponsot.   ExTi

She gives it to herself.   Gospel According to One Who Always Needs an Audience.   Catherine Imbriglio.   IAoNAP

She glided into.   Youth.   Vernon Rowe.   BloBone

She goes on with her story.   Mother and Son.   Alden Nowlan.   RaBo

She goes upstairs early.   Double Bed.   Carol Rumens.   LW

She Goes with her Brother to the Place of their Forebears.   Kerry Hardie.   NIrP

She got off, according to the diary.   Arrival of My Mother, The.   Keith Wilson.   ICANM

She got pulled down and learned to like it.   Falling.   Joy Katz.   NeAmPo

She graced me with a smile for.   Triangle.   L. Miller.   Prolet, *tr. by* Amelia Glaser

She grew up in bedeviled southern wilderness.   Ballad of Sue Ellen Westerfield, The.   Robert Earl Hayden.   ESEAA; NoAM

She had a horror he would die at night.   Edna St. Vincent Millay.   NALW *Fr.* Sonnets from an Ungrafted Tree.

She had a kind of classy coarseness.   Jazz Rain.   Quo Vadis Gex-Breaux.   FuFl

She had already kissed Antony's dead lips.   Cleopatra.   Anna Andreyevna Akhmatova.   FaBoWar; PoetW, *tr. by* Max Hayward and Stanley Kunitz

She had become, the preacher hollows his voice.   Saint Margaret of Cortona.   Eiléan Ní Chuilleanáin.   ModIr

She had blue eyes and light flaxen hair.   Julia A. Moore.   VerBaPo *Fr.* Hattie House.

She had forgotten how the August night.   Edna St. Vincent Millay.   NALW *Fr.* Sonnets from an Ungrafted Tree.

She had from Monsieur d'Elbœuf. (LL)   Alas! Poor Queen.   Marion Angus.   EdScPo; NePenScot; NPeEn

She had imagined the kiss.   Kiss, The.   Paul Hoover.   SUP

She had in her favor.   Magical Devices.   Clara Silva.   TANSG, *tr. by* Celeste Kostopulos-Cooperman

She Had Known Brothers.   Sherley Anne Williams.   GT

She had life in the blood of her eyes, history in her body. With a.   Felipa, La Filosofa de Rincon que Nació a los 98 Años.   Jose Angel Figueroa.   PueRic

She had never desired him in that way.   Maura.   Thomas Lynch.   EmeKit

She had no saying dark enough.   Robert Frost.   TCAPo *Fr.* Hill Wife, The.

She had nothing.   Girl of Six from the Ghetto Begging in Smolna Street in 1942, A.   Jerzy Ficowski.   HP, *tr. by* Keith Bosley

She had raised the window.   Destination: Tule Lake Relocation Center, May 20, 1942.   James Masao Mitsui.   OpBo

She Had Some Horses.   Joy Harjo.   HATNAP; LoL Drowning Horses.   NAAL-5

She had the stance of a snowdrop.   Elaine Randell.   Oth *Fr.* Snoad Hill Poems, The.

She had thought the studio would keep itself.   Living in Sin.   Adrienne Rich.   NIL-7; NIP-4; NoP-4; OxBoAm; SoSe-8; WaAnP

She had too much so with a smile you took some.   Other, The.   Ted Hughes.   EmeKit

She had travelled through nights and days.   End of the Journey, The.   May Probyn.   VWP

She hadn't found a speck of death. (LL)   How I Learned to Sweep.   Julia Alvarez.   FFC; RA; SweBea

She hangs out his shirts.   Shirts.   Nigel Jenkins.   TCAWP

She has a full beard when I first meet her.   Hand.   Robert E. Penn.   WiU

She has a way of standing as if a belt of weights.   Hope.   Robyn Zappala.   PfS

She has always been clever and poor.   Clever and Poor.   V. Penelope Pelizzon.   AmPoNex; PoDa

She has been burning palaces. "To see."   Palace-Burner, The.   Sarah Morgan Bryan Piatt.   NAAPv.1; NCAP; SWaP

She has been packing all night.   Leaving Yuba City.   Chitra Divakaruni.   GeoHom

She has been shown fear more than once.   Afternoon in Austin.   Betsy Berry.   TiP2

She has done with silkworms and the fieldwork.   Summer.   *Unknown.*   CCL1, *tr. by* John Frodsham

She has finished and sealed the letter.   Parting, without a Sequel.   John Crowe Ransom.   MoAmPo; NoP-4; NoP-5; SoSe-8

She has given all her beauty to the water.   Island Rose.   Hamish Maclaren.   EdScPo

She has gone weeping away. (LL)   Lover Mourns for the Loss of Love, The.   William Butler Yeats.   IrLP; WeW-3

She has had to bear. (LL)   Whipping, The.   Robert Earl Hayden.   PoCho; SoSe-8; SSLK

She has had to learn.   Her Other Language.   Nancy Mattson.   IFF

She has it down. Get dressed. Put the housecoat back on over the suit.   Working Mother.   Kathleen Aguero.   PfS

She has left behind a smooth blank space, fuckable and pure in the Louvre.   Viewing Mona Lisa.   Angela Martin.   FTtHH

She has left me, my pretty.   Song.   Sylvia Townsend Warner.   MoBrPo

She has let herself fall on her bed.   Hans Faverey.   WoBe *Fr.* Eighteen Poems.

She has lighted her lamp, and crowned it with flowers.   Letitia Elizabeth Landon.   NPBRoP *Fr.* Improvisatrice, The.

She has no bosom and no behind. (LL)   This Englishwoman.   Stevie Smith.   NALW; NAMCP V.1

She has one good bumblebee. Head of a White Woman Winking. James Tate. BodElec

She has returned, and she has returned. Morning. Gabriela Mistral. TANSG, *tr. by* Maria Giachetti [*or* Jacketti] and Maria Jacketti

She has squatted down. Woman Resting on a Bundle of Kindling. Margaret Gibson. AmZen

She has to pity him after what happened. Job's Wife. Shirley Kaufman. DTA

She has wounded me. Wound of Love, The. Heinrich von Morungen. NAWM-7v1, *tr. by* Peter Dronke

She hated a *mown lawn*. Mown Lawn, A. Lydia Davis. BAP-01

She hath an art[e] to break[e] them with her eyes. (LL) Thrice Toss[e] These Oaken Ashes in the Air [*or* Ayre]. Thomas Campion. OxBSo; PoCho; TFi; WeW-3

She hath forsaken courtly halls and bowers. Self-Devoted, The. Agnes Strickland. CenSon

She having gainèd both the Wind and Sun. (LL) Fair Singer, The. Andrew Marvell. FSCP; NoP-4; NoP-5

She Hears The Storm. Thomas Hardy. NAEL-6v2; NAEL-7v2

She held me for a night against her bosom. Macon Prairie. Willa Sibert Cather. NAAPv.2

She hers, he his, pursuing. (LL) Dalliance of the Eagles, The. Walt Whitman. HeIP-4; NAAL-3; NAAPv.1; NoP-4; NoP-5; SAmP; TCAPo; TRP; WaAnP

She hoists her thigh over back fences. Bogey-Wife, The. Kathleen Jamie. NeBrP

She holds a candle, advances. Brides of Elvis, The. David Ray. AllShUp

She holds things together, collects bail,. Judy Grahn. NALW *Fr.* Common Woman, The.

She holds to the idea. Visit. Gerald William Barrax. GT

She hugs a white rose to her heart. Kind Valentine. David Schubert. OxBoAm

She hunched in the back seat, and fired. Southern Literature. Andrew Hudgins. LPSFW

She hung her laundry in the morning. Mennonite Farm Wife. Janet Kauffman. ACAMVP

She I love leaves me, and I leave my friends. False Bay. Frank Templeton Prince. HarvBoo

She / impregnates my face. Her hair taken, and in the veins addicted blood. Incantation. Anne-Marie Albiach. OnScMo, *tr. by* Keith Waldrop

She in whose lipservice. Goddess, The. Denise Levertov. NALW

She is a file. Necromancy. Rikki Ducornet. SurWo

She is a mermaid caught in a net. Scherzo. Pamela Alexander. YaYoPo

She is a northern woman, barely more. Winter 40. Patrick Lane. BrAP

She is a reed swaying in blue. Love Song. Earle Thompson. HATNAP

She is about to come. This time. Lovers, The. Dorianne Laux. BodElec; ErotSp

She is all so slight. After Two Years. Richard Aldington. MoBrPo

She Is Always Unwilling to Understand. Paul Éluard. NAWM-7v2, *tr. by* Lloyd Alexander

She is always unwilling to understand, to listen. She Is Always Unwilling to Understand. Paul Éluard. NAWM-7v2, *tr. by* Lloyd Alexander

She is as in a field a silken tent. Silken Tent, The. Robert Frost. APT-1; BrAP; ColAP; NAMCP V.1; NoP-4; NoP-5; OxBSo; TRP; WaAnP; WeW-3

She is crying. Gloria Gervitz. MirDau *Fr.* Yiskor.

She is facetious, of a gentle nature. Epigram VII: Winifred. Hugh Crompton. NOSC

She Is Far from the Land. Thomas Moore. OxAEP-2

She Is Flat on Her Back [*(for K. F.)*]. E. Ethelbert Miller. GT; OxAAAP

She is gathering lotos-seed in the river of Yueh. Girl of Yueh, The. Li Po. TAL

She is gesture. Isn't She Not a Bird. Nina Iskrenko. PFTM-2, *tr. by* Forrest Gander and Mala Kotamraju

She is invigilator; her name is knife. Mother, Dear Mother. Elma Mitchell. Prnts

She is large and matronly. Lui et Elle. D. H. Lawrence. NAMCP V.1; NoAM

She is like a horse grazing. In the Nursing Home. Jane Kenyon. BeAl

She is like this. My Mother. Virginia Cerenio. ReBoTo

She is liquid darkness occult with desire. Christopher Dewdney. FTOS *Fr.* Concordat Proviso Ascendant.

She is lovely. Her eyes are big almonds. Sub Shop Girl. Afaa Michael Weaver. SpirFl

She is madonna in an art. Vachel Lindsay. APT-1 *Fr.* Mae Marsh, Motion Picture Actress.

She is mopping about—she is moping. Beatrix Potter. Lee Upton. AmAlph

She is my right hand woman, my best friend. I know. My Muse, the Whore. Linda France. NeBl

She is neither pink nor pale. Witch-Wife. Edna St. Vincent Millay. APT-1

She is no woman, but a sencelesse stone. (LL) Edmund Spenser. CABP; NAEL-7v1; NoP-4; NoP-5 *Fr.* Amoretti.

She is not dead, but sleepeth. Mrs. Rebecca Weston. Mary Weston Fordham. CBWP-2

She is not fair to outward view. She Is Not Fair to Outward View. Hartley Coleridge. OBEV

She is not happy as the Poets say. On Sandro's Flora. Trumbull Stickney. APN-2

She is of the continent, around her everything is light and I observe her atop the slab in the image of her body. Three. Ofelia Perez Sepúlveda. SPV, *tr. by* Jen Hofer

She is old, and bent, and wrinkled. Marching Still. Minna Irving. CBCWP

She is older than the rocks among which she sits. Mona Lisa. Walter Pater. OBMV

She is one with your joy. (LL) How to Get a Baby. Judith Ortiz Cofer. NIL-7; PueRic

She is pale, her eyes baggy. At Breakfast. Giovanna Pollarolo. TANSG, *tr. by* Marjorie Agosin

She is purposeless as a cyclone; she must move. Cubist Portrait. Marjorie Allen Seiffert. PoA 2002

She is rising. Yes. From the Healing Dark. Alma Villanueva. HW

She is scooped out and bow-like. Stonepicker. Frieda Hughes. StAl

She is Singing to Thee, *Domine!*. Michael Field. VWP

She is sixty. She lives. Greatest Love, The. Anna Swirszczynska [*or* Swir]. PoSu

She is sleeping, so it's quiet. Then it snows in the rooms. Tributary. Leonard Nolens. TuT, *tr. by* Michael O'Loughlin

She is slim again. Baby in the House, A. Patrick Williams. PNI

She is standing on my eyelids. Woman In Love. Paul Éluard. NAWM-7v2, *tr. by* Lloyd Alexander

She is standing on my eyelids. Loving. Paul Eluard *and* Andre Breton. YaTCFP, *tr. by* Mary Ann Caws *and* Jean-Pierre Cauvin

She is standing on my lids. Lady Love. Paul Éluard. OBVE; SurPaPo; WoPoe, *tr. by* Samuel Beckett

She is swinging in a contraption above the heads. Our Kitty. Carol Muske-Dukes. BAP-01

She is talking aesthetics, the dear clever creature. Edward Robert Bulwer-Lytton. VerBaPo *Fr.* Midges.

She Is the Greatest Wealth. Georg Rudolph Weckherlin. GePo, *tr. by* George C. Schoolfield

She is the thing that she despises. (LL) Hue and Cry after Fair Amoret, A. William Congreve. NPeEn; OBEV; OxBEV

She is the touch of pink. Touch, A. Michael Longley. IrLP

She is the woman hanging from the 13th floor. Woman Hanging from the Thirteenth Floor Window, The. Joy Harjo. HATNAP

She is weeping for her lost right arm. Weeping Woman. Denise Levertov. AF; AmWaPo

She is without longinge. (LL) *Unknown. See* Che is with-out longing.

She jes' gits hold of us dataway. (LL) Ma Rainey. Sterling Allen Brown. APT-2; NAAPv.2; NAMCP V.1; OxAAAP

She juliets him from a window in Soho. Short Time. Gavin Ewart. NoAM

She just got here yesterday. Sweet Georgia Brown. Ben Bernie, Kenneth Casey and Maceo Pinkard. ReLy

She just knows that he is guilty as hell. (LL) Knife. Gloria Vando. LiTh; TouFir

She keeps singing a song. Lost Love. Cahit Külebi. NaPG, *tr. by* Talat Sait Halman

She kept an antique shop—or it kept her. My Grandmother. Elizabeth Jennings. HarvBoo; NoP-4; NoP-5

She kept her secret well, oh, yes. My Angeline. Harry Bache Smith. NBLV

She kept her songs, they took so little space. Love Songs in Age. Philip Larkin. OxBEV

She kissed me for good-night. So you'll not tell. (LL) Match with the Moon, A. Dante Gabriel Rossetti. NPeEn; OxBEV

She kneels at the wailing wall. Cherryl "Blue." Floyd-Miller. BtF

She knelt in prayer. A stream of sunset fell. Costanza. Felicia Dorothea Hemans. RWP

She knew him somewhere between five p.m. and the next day. Stains of Stalin. Bill Berkson. NYP2

She knew more about me *than* let us say. Isolate. Clarence Major. PmAP

She knows of doom only what all women know. Laws. Carol Frost. CAP-8

She knows them all. Urchins. Beggars. Left Eye of Odin, The. Regina DeCormier-Shekejian. TWW

She knows where to get cracked eggs, does Nelly. Old Nelly's Birthday. Ruth Pitter. NALW

She languorously swings her tongue. Domesticity of Giraffes, The. Judith Beveridge. BMAP

She lay beside me in the dawn. (LL) Alba. Ezra Pound. TCAPo; WaAnP; WeW-3

She lay, skin down on the moist dirt. Our Grandmothers. Maya Angelou. BrAP

She leaned her head upon her hand. Vashti. Frances Ellen Watkins Harper. NALW

She leaned in a small fist on the cushions, buds in her pajamas. "Make me a story." Blue Shade. Aaron Shurin. FTOS

She leans upon her violent hills at ease. Karle Wilson Baker. TiP2 *Fr.* Some Towns of Texas.

She leaps to her feet. Well-Bred Woman, A. Mervyn Taylor. BRtP

She left me at the silent time. Lines Written in the Bay of Lerici. Percy Bysshe Shelley. NAEL-6v2; NAEL-7v2

She left then, spitting the reek of soil. Shipping the Pictures from Belfast. Catherine Byron. Prnts

She let them leave their jellies at the door. Edna St. Vincent Millay. NALW *Fr.* Sonnets from an Ungrafted Tree.

She licked my salty nose. Old People. Michael Davitt. PBCIP, *tr.* by Michael Hartnett

She lied as much as she could, while she lived. Epitaph: On the Near-Death Experience. Ellis Owen. WoPoe, *tr.* by Anthony Conran

She lies, hip high. George Oppen. APT-2; PFTM-1

She Lies Silent. Christopher Pilling. NLP

She lies silent, her head in The Plague. She Lies Silent. Christopher Pilling. NLP

She lies tonight. Melancholic. Li Ho. CrYelRi; ErotSp, *tr.* by Sam Hamill

She lifts her green umbrellas. Bartok and the Geranium. Dorothy Livesay. BrAP

She liggs ablow my body's lust and luve. Continent o Venus. Alexander Scott. EdScPo

She liked mornings the best—Thomas gone. Weathering Out. Rita Dove. AmAlph; CFP; ESEAA; NAMCP V.2; NoAM

She liked the blue drapes. They made a star. Couple in the Next Room, The. John Ashbery. BodElec

She likes it, the conjugal act. *Unknown.* GifTon, *tr.* by David Ray

She Lived. Lucille Clifton. LoL

She lived beside the Anner. Irish Peasant Girl, The. Charles Joseph Kickham. IrV

She lived in dark times, as we do. Denise Levertov. UpMys *Fr.* Showings, The: Lady Julian of Norwich, 1342-1416.

She lived in the hovel alone, the beautiful child. Scape-Goat, The. Agnes Mary Frances Robinson. VWP

She lives alone now. Poet Reflects On Her Solitary Fate, The. Sandra Cisneros. FFC

She lives in the apartment below me. Singer, The. Chocolate Waters. SUP

She lives in the porter's room; the plush is nicotined. Bitter Sanctuary. Harold Monro. OBMV

She lives on a moor in the north. Anne Carson. NLPA *Fr.* Glass Essay, The.

She Looked At the Sun. Tadeusz Rózewicz. PoSu, *tr.* by Magnus F. Krynski

She looked over his shoulder. Shield of Achilles, The. W. H. Auden. BeAl; NAEL-6v2; NAEL-7v2; NAMCP V.1; NoAM; NoP-4; NoP-5; NPeEn; OxAEP-2; OxBEV; OxBoAm; PoA 2002; WaAnP; WeW-3

She love me, loves me not. Vladimir Vladimirovich Mayakovsky. PFTM-1

She loves especially the Cha Cha Cha. Sweeping the Floor. Martha Rhodes. LaCa

She loves him from a distance. Empty Place, An. Sonia Edwards. BBMWP, *tr.* by Sally Roberts Jones

She Loves Me. Sheldon Harnick. ReLy

She loves—but knows not whom she loves. Thomas Moore. NPBRoP *Fr.* Lalla Rookh.

She lowers her fragrant curtain. Song. Liu Yung. ErotSp, *tr.* by Sam Hamill

She made him an amulet. Wanderer in the Night of the World, A. N. V. M. Gonzalez. ReBoTo

She made the gang sing this song. (LL) Take Me Out to the Ball Game. Jack Norworth. NAAPv.2; TCAPo

She made the trip daily, though. Drapery Factory, Gulfport, Mississippi, 1956. Natasha Trethewey. FuFl; SpirFl

She makes her way through the dark trees. Country Wife, The. Dana Gioia. RA

She may count three little daisies very well. Gertrude Stein. NoP-4; NoP-5 *Fr.* Stanzas in Meditation.

She may not accuse me. Friedrich von Hausen. GePo

She means two things. Stereograph: 1903. Julie Fay. NAPBL

She Mends an Ancient Wireless. Paul Durcan. IrLP; PBCIP

She minds the lilacs. Hopper's Women. Sue Standing. PoSol

She mourned the long-ears. Jugged Hare. Jean Earle. TCAWP

She Moved through the Fair [*with music*]. Padraic Colum. IrLP

She must have been kicked unseen or brushed by a car. Dog's Death. John Updike. GoPo; P180

She must look at her face until she grows to hate it. Harem, The. Maher Sabry. AnVo, *tr.* by Mohamed Enani

She. My people came from Korelitz. Grand Conversation, The. Paul Muldoon. NAMCP V.2

She / never was. Coming Ashore. Lamont B. Steptoe. FuFl

She never will say no. (LL) I Care Not for These Ladies. Thomas Campion. NAEL-7v1; NoP-4; NoP-5; NoSic

She opened the shutters. She hung the sheets over the sill. Morning. Yannis Ritsos. StAl, *tr.* by Nikos Stangos

She orders vegetables over the telephone. Memorial Day, 1969. T. Carmi. NRoS, *tr.* by Esther Raizen

She passed away like morning dew. Early Death. Hartley Coleridge. OBEV

She passed with her mother. What rare beauty! Cowardice. Amado Nervo. BLPSL, *tr.* by Rene de Costa, Rigas Kappatos and Eleni Paidoussi

She peeked out from under. Missing Patriarch, The. Afaa Michael Weaver. PBCAP

She picks me. Women. Zakiyya Malallah. PoArWo, *tr.* by Wen Chin Ouyang

She played me false, but that's not why. Our Photograph[s]. Frederick Locker-Lampson. NBLV

She plays Miles, rolls another joint. Shunning an Imperative. Carl Hancock Rux. BRtP; HeMarv

She points to a star. Fortune Teller, The. Fu'ad Rifqa. BBASP, *tr.* by Sargon Boulus and Samuel Hazo

She presses her dark lips. Girl/Spit. Lisa Coffman. AmPoNex

She pretends to be dead. For Her Children. Martha Rhodes. LaCa

She put away her hats. Mistress, The. Pamela Gillilan. Prnts

She put her hand. Fanny Howe. FaoP *Fr.* Passion, The.

She put him on a snow-white shroud. Little Shroud, The. Letitia Elizabeth Landon. NAEL-7v2

She put the whammy. Three-Headed Womon Song. Wanda Coleman. RD

She raised her head. With hot and glittering eye. Mother's Charge, The. Charlotte Perkins Stetson Gilman. SWaP

She reads, of course, what he's doing, shaking Nixon's hand. Women Who Love Elvis All Their Lives, The. Fleda Brown Jackson. AllShUp

She really misses her boyfriend. Empty Chairs. Maxianne Berger. IFF

She reclines, more or less. Manet's Olympia. Margaret Atwood. NAMCP V.2

She re-enters her life. Returning. Linda Pastan. WeW-3

She remarks how the style of a whole age. Moment of Waking, The. John Tranter. BMAP

She remembered seeing the underpass up ahead. Pink Rose Rings, The. Tracey Herd. MFPA; NeBl

She remembered to the very end. Annunciations. Nuala Ni Dhomhnaill. ModIr, *tr.* by Michael Hartnett

She remembers / an absence of blue. Woman Who Allowed Light to Have Its Way with Her, The. Dannye Romine Powell. PoDa

She rented a little windblown house with two bedrooms and a simple tree. Trial Separation. Marie Harris. PfS

She Replies to Carmel's Letter. Kerry Hardie. BeAl; NIrP

She Replies to the Fat Crimson Bishop. Vincent Woods. NIrP

She retires from life's uncertainties, he plunges. Kundiman. Bataan Faigao. ReBoTo

She rises among boulders. Naked, alone. Bath of Aphrodite. Brewster Ghiselin. APT-2

She rises mostly every day. On a Girl Who Took Action for Breach of Promise. Amanda Ros. VerBaPo

She roamed the meadows long in hope. Recompensed? Henrietta Cordelia Ray. CBWP-3

She rose from the water like a mermaid. Mermaid's Song. James C. McCullagh. PoCoUp

She Rose to His Requirement—Dropt. Emily Dickinson. NAAPv.1; NALW SUP

She said, Creek Daughter. Beneath the Pole of Proud Raven. Jana Harris. SUP

She Said / He Said. Helen Lamb. EdScPo

She said he was a man who cheated. Jack and Jill. James Vincent Cunningham. OxBoAm

She said how come you never. Saturday Morning Ultimatum. Dan Nielsen. SUP

She said, I am wrong to want something more, it's true. Words in the Shadow. Victor Hugo. WoPoe, *tr.* by Louis Simpson

She said, If tomorrow my world were torn in two. Phyllis McGinley. APT-2 *Fr.* I Know a Village.

She said: "I'm god and all." Against a Sickness: To the Female Double Principle God. Alan Dugan. NoAM

She said it was a better way to die. Her Final Show. Rafael Campo. BloBone

She said often around 1929, 1930—especially when I played. Robin Blaser. NLPA *Fr.* Image-Nation.

She said she forgave me. Parted. Clara Ann Thompson. CBWP-2

She said she / woke up with him in. Dreaming Frankenstein. Liz Lochhead. MoWP

She said she'd do. Love Before Dinner. Alfred A. Yuson. ReBoTo

She said that underneath the surface. American Variation on How Rilke Loved a Princess and Got to Stay in Her Castle. Alan Dugan. BodElec

She said they are building the ship. Naglfar. Monica Youn. LegDan

She said, "They gave me of their best." After Aughrim. Emily Lawless. OBEV

She said to him: "It is very nice out." Past, The. Jacques Roubaud. YaTCFP, tr. by Françoise Gramet and Richard Sieburth

She said to me: "How glows." Subalterns. Elizabeth Daryush. OBWP

She said—you want space? She Said / He Said. Helen Lamb. EdScPo

She sang beyond the genius of the sea. Idea of Order at Key West, The. Wallace Stevens. AmFaPo; APT-1; BrAP; ColAP; HarvBoo; HeIP-4; MakPoe; MoAmPo; NAAL-5; NAAPv.2; NAMCP V.1; NAWM-7v2; NIL-7; NIP-4; NoAM; NoP-4; NoP-5; OxBoAm; PoPoPo; SAmP; TFi; WaAnP

She Sat Alone beside Her Hearth. Letitia Elizabeth Landon. NPBRoP

She sat and sang alway. Song. Christina Georgina Rossetti. NAEL-6v2; NAEL-7v2

She sat and wept beside His feet; the weight. "Multum Dilexit." Hartley Coleridge. SacPr

She sat at tea just like the others. First. Going Blind. Rainer Maria Rilke. BLT, tr. by Walter Arndt

She sat by the window opening into the airshaft. Charles Reznikoff. NAAPv.2

She sat like all the others drinking tea. Woman Going Blind. Rainer Maria Rilke. GTCP, tr. by Felix Pollak

She sat on a shelf. Motherhood. May Swenson. NoP-4; NoP-5

She sat on a willow-trunk. Fly, The. Miroslav Holub. NPeEn; PoAgWa; PoetW; PoSu; StAl, tr. by Ian Milner and George Theiner

(She sat on the willow bark.) VCWP

She sat on the Lex line #2. Black Lady, A. Elouise Loftin. EGAG

She sat on the willow bark. Miroslav Holub. See She sat on a willow-trunk.

She sat up on her pillows, receiving guests. Douglas Dunn. InoFa; NoP-4; NoP-5 Fr. Elegies.

She sat upon the pile by her dead lord. Suttee, The. Lydia Huntley Sigourney. NAAPv.1

She sat where the level sands. Africa. Maria White Lowell. NAAPv.1

She sat with fear in her eyes. Fortune Teller, The. Nizar Qabbani. PML, tr. by Issam A. Lakkis, Fred Moramarco and Al Zolynas

She saw on her home street. Survivor, The. Thomas Dorsett. BloBone

She saw the beauty of the sea and could not rival it. Influence of Anxiety at the Seaside with Tea, The. Todd Swift. OpeFie

She saying, You don't have to do anything. One You Wanted to Be Is the One You Are, The. Jean Valentine. BodElec; ExTi

She says. So Now You're Chicana. Carol Lem. GeoHom

She says she is going to kill. Joy Harjo. NAAL-5 Fr. She Had Some Horses.

She says to him, musing, "If you ever leave me." Forty Something. Robert Hass. NAMCP V.2; OxBoAm

She seems to come by wing. Jackson Mac Low. PFTM-2 Fr. Pronouns, The—A Collection of 40 Dances—For the Dancers.

She sees her mouth hit the floor. Gu Cheng. WoBe Fr. Liquid Mercury.

She Sends Him a Postcard of the Sea. Lesley-Anne Bourne. Coast

She Sent Him Away [with music]. Clara Ann Thompson. CBWP-2

She sent him off to war for nothing but a title. (LL) Silent at Her Window. Wang Ch'ang-ling. ColAnChi; CrYelRi, tr. by Sam Hamill

She shakes feathers toward him. Pay Cash Only. James Sherry. FTOS

She, she and she and she. Divestment of Beauty. Laura Riding Jackson. APT-2; HarvBoo

She should have died hereafter. William Shakespeare. SoSe-8 Fr. Macbeth.

She shuffles to the door on faded scuffs. Curandera, La. Diana García. TouFir

She Sighs on Her Jade Lute. Wen T'ing-yün. CCL1, tr. by Witter Bynner

She sights a Bird—she chuckles—. Cat. Emily Dickinson. SAmP

She sings her sorrows no more. Black bottom stomp. Wopko Jensma. TSAP

She sits beside: through four low panes of glass. Nightfall. Michael Field. VWP

She sits in a corner away from the light. Irresistible Light, An. Dorothy Phaire. BtF

She sits in the marketplace. Pearle's Poem. Primus St. John. GT

She sits in the park. Her clothes are out of date. In the Park. Gwen Harwood. BMAP; NIL-7

She sits in the tawny vapour. Wife in London, A. Thomas Hardy. OBWP

She sits naked on a rock. Last Gods. Galway Kinnell. PasH; RaBo

She sits on a smoldering couch. Woman on the Dump, The. Elizabeth Spires. EmeKit

She sits on the mountain that is her home. Night Music. Linda Gregg. BLT

She sits there. Girl at the Window. Pinkie Gordon Lane. FuFl; GT

She sits with. Young Woman at a Window. William Carlos Williams. HHAm

She sits with one hand poised against her head, the. Dialogue. Adrienne Rich. NIL-7; TWF

She skips on to the day's next blue radius. Maggie. Duane Niatum. HATNAP

She sleeps, and I, who used to sleep so sound. Necklace: Rich Pink Corona Round a Flashing Yellow Heart. Kathleen Crown. FiBr

She sleeps, her dreams as clear as diamond edge. Madrigal, a Lullaby for Xan. Marilyn Bowering. IFF

She sleeps in late. House. Selima Hill. BeAl

She sleeps so lightly, that in trembling fear. Hush. Mary Elizabeth Coleridge. PoBW

She slides her finger. In the Season of Suicides. Lisa D. Chavez. LiTh

She smelled like bananas just as sure. Nature of Braille, The. Anthony Butts. AmPoNex

She smiled behind a lawny cloud. Fancy Dress. Dorothea MacKellar. NOBAu

She smokes / slowly, like a bad. Woman with Chrysler. Jeremy Countryman. PoDa

She snorts and stamps upon the eastern hill. Hind of Morning, The. George Campbell Hay. EdScPo

She spans a bridge over a human being. Mei-Mei Berssenbrugge. AWPTFC Fr. Kali.

She Speaks to Her Husband, Asleep. Robert Schultz. AWTN

She speaks with the accent of her wild seas. Stranger, The. Gabriela Mistral. SpanPo, tr. by Kate Flores

She sped the daytime hours. Waiting Wife. Marcella Siegel. TiP2

She spent her money with such perfect style. Rapist's Villanelle, The. Thomas M. Disch. RA

She spent three hundred and sixty four days a year. Grandmother Jackson. David Jackson. OBCP

She spreads her pale legs. In the Purple Bar. Gig Ryan. BMAP

She springs from the ground-clinging thicket, her face. Veneris Venefica Agrestis. Lucio Piccolo. OBVE, tr. by Charles Tomlinson

She spun on the apex of her fragile. Hate Crime. Barry Ballard. LiTh

She stalks me through the yellow flags. Autobiography. Paula Meehan. MoWP

She stamps and shivers. Entering the Mare. Katie Donovan. NeBl

She stands as pale as Parian statues paint. Study (A Soul), A. Christina Georgina Rossetti. NALW; VWP

She stands beside me, stands away. Like Rousseau. Imamu Amiri Baraka. PoA 2002

She stands by the table, poised. Vermeer. Stephen Mitchell. GI

She stands full-throated and with careless pose. Onondaga Madonna, The. Duncan Campbell Scott. BrAP

She stands in the dead center like a star. Mother, The. W. D. Snodgrass. BrAP

She started up from where the lizard lies. On Rodin's "L'Illusion, Sœur d'Icare." Trumbull Stickney. APN-2

She stayed away longer. Gertrude Stein. MotU Fr. Book Concluding with As A Wife Has a Cow a Love Story, A.

She stitched her story on black. Constellation Quilt, The. Mei-Mei Berssenbrugge. OpBo

She stood, a weed tall in the sun. Weed. Paula Gunn Allen. FiBr

She stood breast-high amid the corn. Ruth. Thomas Hood. ChIV-1; NPBRoP; OBEV

She stood nakedly. After Her Man Had Left Her for the Sixth Time That Year (An Uncommon Occurrence). Haki R. Madhubuti. GT

She stopped traffic. Tribal Marks. Saundra Sharp. SpirFl

She stops short at something said to her, holding at arm's length the plate. She Stops Short. Jean Follain. MotU, tr. by Mary Feeney and William Matthews

She struggles with her chopsticks, and I watch her slyly. Chopsticks. Alan Jenkins. PML

She sucked the happiness. Contemporary Jezebel, The. Elin Llwyd Morgan. BBMWP, tr. by the author and Richard Poole

She suffers from excess. Accumulation sits on her like homunculi. Why She Suffers. Anne Valley Fox. ICANM

She takes the plums from him dumbly. (LL) At Les Deux Magots. Maura Dooley. IrLP; LW

She taps, pats, clicks. Black Girl Tap Dancing. Lenard D. Moore. FuFl

She taught me what her uncle once taught her. Seamus Heaney. NoP-5 Fr. Clearances.

She taught me what her uncle taught her. Clearances. Seamus Heaney. EMP; NAMCP V.2; PBCIP; PNI

She taught theater, so we gathered. On the Death of a Colleague. Stephen Dunn. InoFa; P180

She Teaches Him to Reach Out. Martha Elizabeth. PasH

She Tells Her Love While Half Asleep. Robert Graves. WaAnP

She tells me she will find a letter. Woman of Three Minds, The. Thomas Centolella. GifTon

She tells us she felt. Clinic, The. Grace Herman. BloBone

She tests the curb with a chubby boot. For Heather, Entering Kindergarten. Roberta Hill Whiteman. HATNAP; NoAM

She that but little patience knew. On a Political Prisoner. William Butler Yeats. OBMV

She, / the eskimo's woman. Eskimo's Woman, The. Anabel Torres. TANSG, tr. by Celeste Kostopulos-Cooperman

She, the river. Woman. Hira Bansode. CFP; ItWoWo; WoPoe, tr. by Vinay Dharwadker

She thinks if she puts out, her sainthood will be recognized. Robert Mezey. CalPo Fr. Couplets.

She Thinks in Song. Femi Osofisan. NAfrP

She Thinks of Her Beloved. Lu Chi. NDACCP, tr. by Kenneth Rexroth

She thought of no wilder delicacy than the starling eggs she fed him for breakfast. Scorn. Carol Frost. CAP-8

She thus; when I had great desire to prove. Homer. OBVE Fr. Odyssey.

She Ties Her Bandanna. Beth Cuthand. ReEnLa

She told how they used to form for the country dances. One We Knew. Thomas Hardy. NAEL-6v2; NAEL-7v2

She told me she had always fantasized. Black Slip. Terry Wolverton. SUP; WiU

She told the story, and the whole world wept. Harriet Beecher Stowe. Paul Laurence Dunbar. PoPoPo

She told us; take a picture, an art postcard. Persian Miniature, A. Mimi Khalvati. MoWP

She, too, had been taken in, her husband's. Aunt May. Robert A. Fink. TiP2

She took her scarlet knickers off. Gaudy Camp Follower, The. Jack Beeching. RSaN

She took the curious amber charms. La Dame Jaune. Oscar Wilde. IrLP

She took the dappled partridge flecked [or fleckt] with blood. Sonnet. Alfred Tennyson. NAEL-6v2

She transforms scarlet leaves into moths. (LL) Madrigal: "How the tenor warbles in April!" Mary Leader. NAPBL; PoDa

She tried to warn us. Justice of the Peace, The. Alison Luterman. MPUn

She tries to tell him. Audrey Poetker-Thiessen. ACAMVP

She trips across the meadows. April. Henrietta Cordelia Ray. CBWP-3

She trod the edge of land. Forlorn Queen, The. Bryan Guinness. IrLP

She turned in the high pew, until her sight. Church Romance, A. Thomas Hardy. OxAEP-2; OxBSo

She turned to me. Walk Like Freedom. Carolyn M. Rodgers. OxAAAP

She turned to me last night. Other People's Pain. Mary Gomez Parham. OWABP

She turns them over in her slow hands. Mongoloid Child Handling Shells on the Beach, A. Richard Snyder. NIL-7

She twirled the string of golden beads. Illustration of a Picture. Oliver Wendell Holmes. TreFP

[She Unties the Straps of Her Corselette Fire]. Jill Hartman. PoPra

She used to. Emily Dickinson's Defunct. Marilyn Nelson Waniek. ESEAA

She used to flash her fingers through the flame. Heroine. Paul Groves. AngWePo

She used to let her golden hair fly free. Petrarch. NAWM-5v1; NAWM-7v1 Fr. Sonnets to Laura.

She used to say, "There's no rest." Moving My Mother. Karen McKinnon. ICANM

She used to throw her old crockery at the moon. She Used to Throw Her Old Crockery. Venus Khoury-Gata. YaTCFP, tr. by Marilyn Hacker

She uttered what was lodged. Failure of Language, The. Elon G. Eidenier. IaFF

She waited for her century to turn. Blues Spiritual for Mammy Prater. Dionne Brand. WaAnP

She Waits for Me. Unknown. ArBi

She wakes beside a man. Goldilocks. Magi Gibson. EdScPo

She / wakes up each day with the dawn. Crazed Woman, The. Jeannette Miller. TANSG, tr. by Paula Vega

She walked in the garden. Che Sara Sara. Rose Terry Cooke. NAAPv.1; SWaP

She walked nude beside them. Springtime. Norman Henry, II Pritchard. GT

She walked through Grant Park during the red days of summer. Days of 1968. Edward Hirsch. OxBoAm

She Walked Unaware. Patrick MacDonogh. IrLP

She walks down the hall carrying. Han Shan in Santa Rosa. John Tarrant. WhBo

She walks in Beauty like the night. She Walks In Beauty. Lord Byron. AmFaPo; BLPJKO; BrAP; BRP; CABP; HeIP-4; ITBLP; NAEL-6v2; NAEL-7v2; NePenScot; NOBRP; NoP-4; NoP-5; NPBRoP; OBEV; OxAEP-2; OxBEV; PoPoPo; TFi; WaAnP

She walks on ground with feet of clay. Ghanian girl treads the breach. Peerage. Stephanie Williams. AnSo

She walks to a table. Syntax. Wang Ping. PoDa

She walks—the lady of my delight. Shepherdess, The. Alice Thompson Meynell. MoBrPo

She wanted a little room for thinking. Daystar. Rita Dove. AmFaPo; BeAl; NIL-7; NIP-4; OxWW

She wanted her ashes scattered. Marty's Mother. Stephen Kessler. GeoHom

She wanted pretty fine. Aunt Jessie. Wanda Coleman. GT

She wanted to tread the surge of the sea. Beams. Paul Verlaine. SxFrPo, tr. by Martin Sorrell

She Wants. David Baratier. AmPoNex

She wants a man she can just. Roadmap. Harryette Mullen. ISC

She wants me to gather Her fallen robe around me. Woman Who Jumped, The. M. Eliza Hamilton. BtF

She wants me to hear the whole story. Coincidentally. Frederic W. Platt. BloBone

She wants to hear. Sunday Greens. Rita Dove. AmAlph; GT

She was a beautiful animal. Nijinsky's Dog. Susan Hahn. IllVoic

She was a brazen package of smoulder. Party, The. Ben Scammell. NLP

She was a child's purse, full of useless things. (LL) Death of an Irishwoman. Michael Hartnett. EmeKit; PBCIP; StAl

She was a dear little dicky bird. She Was One of the Early Birds. T. W. Connor. OBCoV

She Was a Dove. Gerald Stern. CAP-8

She was a girl. Instrument of Choice. Robert Phillips. GoPo

She Was a Phantom of Delight. William Wordsworth. HeIP-4; NoP-5; NPBRoP; OBEV; TFi

She was a Queen. Hartley Coleridge. OxAEP-2

She was a queen of noble Nature's crowning. She Was a Queen. Hartley Coleridge. OxAEP-2

She was a small dog, neat and fluid. Praise of a Collie. Norman Alexander MacCaig. EdScPo; NePenScot; PoCho

She was a woman obsessed by an old book. Beyond Phigalia. Alec Derwent Hope. BMAP

She was all woman, all women to me. One Flesh. Julia Casterton. Prnts

She was alone that evening—and alone. Lonely Lady, The. Charlotte Brontë. VWP

She was already lean when. Parting. A. R. Ammons. NoAM

She was an evil stepmother. She Does Not Remember. Anna Swirszczynska [or Swir]. BLT

She was at work on a poem about breath. Poem about Breath. David Wagoner. NoAM

She was blushing in the misty green of August. Good Night! Gilbert Sorrentino. FTOS

She was born of wealthy parents, but her only wealth. Agatha. David Citino. UpMys

She was buried on her wedding-day, these words a friend gave. Julia A. Moore. STuOW Fr. Maryette Myers.

She was buying an elixir. Buying. Jean Follain. BLT, tr. by Heather McHugh

She was cleaning—there is always. Black Silk. Tess Gallagher. EmeKit

She was crying in the kitchen. Who Knew. Martha Rhodes. LaCa

She was Eliza for a few weeks. Names. Wendy Cope. BeAl; PoCu

She was Eliza once again. (LL) Names: "She was Eliza for a few weeks." Wendy Cope. BeAl; PoCu

She was four, he was one, it was raining, we had colds. Clasp, The. Sharon Olds. BodElec

She was from Fort Worth, just out of high school. Country Boy, City Girl. Brenda Black White. TiP2

She was given to fits. Crazy Girl, The. Sharan Strange. InTrad

She was in terrible pain the whole day. Wedding, A. James Tate. NoAM

She was interested in prehistory. In the Bath. Jo Shapcott. MoWP

She was just a schoolteacher then. Evening Star. Edward Hirsch. TiP2

She was just risen from her bended knee. Girl at Her Devotions, A. Letitia Elizabeth Landon. VWP

She was little. To My Little Girl. Shakuntala Hawoldar. CFP; HAWP

She was made from scratch in Wisconsin. American Cheese. G. E. Murray. IllVoic

She was most like a rose, when it flushes rarest. Gone Before. Christina Georgina Rossetti. PoBW

She was old. She lived alone in a small house. Knife. Gloria Vando. LiTh; TouFir

She Was One of the Early Birds. T. W. Connor. OBCoV

She was practicing fly fishing. Poet Fishing, The. Gwyneth Lewis. ATSWP, tr. by Robert Minhinnick

She was pure and white, resembling the sun as it rises. Separation by Death. Ibn Hazm al-Andalusi. RaBo, tr. by A. R. Nykl

She was sitting across from me. I Finally Managed to Speak to Her. Hal Sirowitz. P180

She was sitting at her window. Three Ravens. Jamie Meyerhoff. WhBo

She was skilled in music and the dance. Alas! Poor Queen. Marion Angus. EdScPo; NePenScot; NPeEn

She was so small I would scan the crib a half-second. Sharon Olds. *See* She was so small, that sometimes I would walk into.

She was so small, that sometimes I would walk into. Her First Week. Sharon Olds. ExTi

(She was so small I would scan the crib a half-second.) StAl

She was still upset. Bubba Esther, 1888. Ruth Whitman. TaR

She was such a dab hand, my mother. Such a dab hand. They That Wash on Thursday. Paul Muldoon. EMP

She Was Telling It This Way. Laura Tohe. ReEnLa

She was the daughter of a fishmonger, she stood. Theatrical Venus. George Buchanan. PNI

She was the joke of the angels—a girl. Saint Rose of Lima. Judith Ortiz Cofer. PueRic; TouFir

She was the one who lived up country. After Reading "The Country of the Pointed Firs." Jean Garrigue. VCAP

She was the woman who drank us up. Woman Who Drank Us Up, The. Lesley Quayle. Prnts

She was there on the mountain. Flower No More Than Itself, A. Linda Gregg. BBASP; WaAnP

She was thinner, with a mannered gauntness. Bistro Styx, The. Rita Dove. NoP-4; NoP-5

She was too kind, wooed too persistently. Samuel Butler. OxBSo

She was white and flown. Girl Friend Poem # 3. C. D. Wright. CAP-8

She was young! She was pure! She was new! She was nice! Have Some Madeira, M'dear? Michael Flanders. OBCoV

She watched all day that she might see him pass. "George Eliot." LW *Fr.* How Lisa Loved the King.

She watches him reaching for oranges. Art History (Sandro Botticelli). Alena Nádvorníková. SurWo

She waz sullen. Ntozake Shange. ASA *Fr.* For Colored Girls Who Have Considered Suicide When the Rainbow Is Enuf.

She weaves and ends no pattern to day. [Version 1]. *Unknown.* NDACCP, *tr. by* Ezra Pound

(By the river of stars, its brightness.) NDACCP

She weaves away at the bower. To-and-Fro of Saint Theresa. Alfonso Reyes. WoPoe, *tr. by* Samuel Beckett

She weighed / three hundred pounds. Walking the Dog. John Wright. BloBone

She went back to her hometown. Mom and Dad Getting Older. Sarah Rosenblatt. AmPoNex

She went slowly. Bye Bye Barbara. Sally Bellerose. PfS

She went up the hill to pick angelica. Old Poem. *Unknown.* WoPoe, *tr. by* Burton Watson

She wheeled, then sprang, and threw the arm from her. Albery Allson Whitman. NAAPv.1 *Fr.* Octoroon, The.

She whispers to me she says to me she says to me says to me she. Her, Me, and Yochanan. Chava Pinchas-Cohen. DTA, *tr. by* Miriyam Glazer

She who has forgotten. Yr Iaith. Nigel Jenkins. AngWePo

She Who Listens. Elana Klugman. HW

She who to Heaven more Heaven doth annex. On a Virtuous Young Gentlewoman That Died Suddenly. William Cartwright. OBEV

She who worked patiently. Charles Reznikoff. APT-2

She who would take a bath. Anne Portugal. SCFWP *Fr.* Bath, The.

She will be bound with garlands of her own. (LL) If by Dull Rhymes Our English Must Be Chained. John Keats. BrAP; CenSon

She will fly from you. Flight of the Daughter, The. Maisha Baton. ICANM

She will know. (LL) Scuba Diver Recovers the Body of a Drowned Child, The. Gerald William Barrax. GT; OxAAAP

She will not have it that my day wanes low. Augusta Davies Webster. OxBSo; ViWPN *Fr.* Mother and Daughter.

She will take Jesus down. Maid of Need, A. Stephanie Williams. AnSo

She woke to a mockingbird and sensed a lucky day. Ophelia. Susan Terris. IaFF

She woke up under a loose quilt. Evacuee, The. R. Hewett Thomas. ItP

She wonders how people get babies. Facts of Life, The. Ronald Wallace. PBCAP

She worked in the newsagent, redhaired. Graffiti. Julian Croft. NOBAu

She works with the Moors. Showing some skin she lures a. Sadie. Philip Hammial. BMAP

She Would Long. Jean Valentine. PA9/11

She would wake up every morning. Disney's Cinderella. Tennessee Reed. FTtHH

She wouldn't claim her own perfections. Ladders. Deanna Ortiz. ICANM

She wouldn't recognize it. Her Scream Has Been Stolen. Samiya Adelle Bashir. BRtP

She wreaks such havoc in my library. Minding Ruth. Aidan Carl Mathews. PBCIP

She writes to him again. Henri Michaux. GPTC; MotU *Fr.* I Am Writing to You from a Far-Off Country.

She writes to me as if we still shared. Letter from Home in Spanish. Judith Ortiz Cofer. ExTi

Sheaf Mark. Ray DiPalma. FTOS

Sheafe of snakes used heretofore to be, A. To Mr. George Herbert. John Donne. OBVE

Shealtiel, governor of Judah. Haggai. John Chagy. ChIV-1

Shearer man like toast and butter. Indian Bagman's Toast. *Unknown.* FaBoVe

Shearer's Wife, The. Louis Esson. NOBAu

Shearing, The. *Unknown.* OBWVE, *tr. by* Glyn Jones

Sheaves, The. Edwin Arlington Robinson. APT-1; ItP; MoAmPo; NAMCP V.1; NoAM; OxBoAm; SoSe-8

Sheba and Solomon. Ruth Fainlight.

　Invitation, The. MoWP

　Sheba's Tests. MoWP

Sheba worshipped the sun. Ruth Fainlight. MoWP *Fr.* Sheba and Solomon.

Sheba's Tests. Ruth Fainlight. MoWP *Fr.* Sheba and Solomon.

She'd always peeled them. Mushrooms. Moira Clark. Prnts

She'd looks, she'd style. Ovid. EroLit *Fr.* Amores.

Shed the Fear. Anselm Hollo. PmAP

Shed, the wall, and the anonymous cross. (LL) Here is another poem in a picture. Daryl Hine. GS; NoAM

She'd thrust the canyon out of her mind; she never thought of the whispering fall, the ferns, the hawk-haunted. Home. Robinson Jeffers. BodElec

She'd tried to kill herself before. Mary Mihalik. Ed Ochester. LiTh

She'd want, if we were given what we want. (LL) What Do Women Want? Mary Jo Salter. FFC; RA

Shedding our petty pruderies. Mina Loy. NAMCP V.1 *Fr.* Love Songs to Joannes.

Sheep. W. H. Davies. MoBrPo; NPeEn

Sheep. Takahashi Shinkichi. ZenPo, *tr. by* Takashi Ikemoto and Lucien Stryk

Sheep and Lambs. Katharine Tynan Hinkson. OBEV; SacPr

Sheep and the Goat, The. George Macdonald. SacPr

Sheep Child, The. James Dickey. CAP-8; EmeKit; NAMCP V.2; NoAM; VCAP

Sheep Fair Day. Kerry Hardie. BeAl; MoWP; NIrP

Sheep in Fog. Sylvia Plath. NPeEn

Sheep running downhill makes the bell jingle faster with seeming, A. Good Sheep. Heather Ramsdell. IAoNAP

Sheep School. Sándor Weöres. IQMS, *tr. by* Adam Makkai and Donald E. Morse

Sheep was. And a purse dangled from his arm. A sporran jogged between his lies, A. Tune. Robert Kelly. FTOS

Sheep yard of the dead, between poor walls. In a Castilian Graveyard. Miguel de Unamuno. RaW, *tr. by* Donald Hall

Sheepdog Trials in Hyde Park. Cecil Day Lewis. NoAM

Sheepheard, what's Love, I pray thee tell? Sheepheards Description of Love, The. *Unknown.* NPeEn

Sheepheards Description of Love, The. *Unknown.* NPeEn

Sheepheards Sorrow, Being Disdained in Love, The. Thomas Lodge. *See* Shepherd's Sorrow, Being Disdained in Love, The.

Sheep's Vigil for a Fervent Person. Alberto Caeiro.

　"My sight's sharp as a sunflower." OpeFie, *tr. by* Erin Mouré

Sheer, bright-shining spring, spring as it used to be. After Liberation. J. C. Bloem. TuT, *tr. by* Seamus Heaney

Sheer grip and the push of it—growth gets, The. April. Alice Oswald. NeBrP

Sheer naked rock. From the high cliff-cut. Stone Face Falls. William Everson. APT-2

Sheer Strips. Bill Berkson. AHA

Sheet had dried, The. (LL) Duo-Tang. Kenward Elmslie. AHA; FTOS

Sheet of rain, A. Issa. SoOfWa, *tr. by* Sam Hamill

Sheets, how to describe them, The? They envelop the. Leslie Kaplan. SCFWP *Fr.* Règne.

Sheets of water are washed out on the shore as. Shore. Alan Bold. EdScPo

Sheets on the floor, a stick. Distance between Bodies, The. Bill Manhire. HarvBoo

Sheets were frozen hard, and they cut the naked hand, The. Christmas at Sea. Robert Louis Stevenson. ChrPo; NePenScot

Sheffield Ghazal 4: Driving West. Galway Kinnell. NAMCP V.2

She-Ghost of Tiresias. Monica A. Hand. BtF

Sheila and I spent the night talking about French. Scrambled Eggs and Garlic Pork. Michael Melo. ReBoTo

Sheila the Hat. Pat Parnell. HW

Sheila-na-gig, I will make myself a hat. Sheila the Hat. Pat Parnell. HW

Shekhinah as Mute, The. Alicia Ostriker. SweBea

Shekinah is She Who Dwells Within. Meditation on the Feminine Nature of Shekinah, A. Ann Gottlieb. HW

Shelburne Falls. Carrie St. George Comer. LegDan

Shell. Takahashi Shinkichi. ZenPo, tr. by Takashi Ikemoto and Lucien Stryk

Shell / sitting still. Wingaersheek Beach. Marsden Hartley. APT-1

Shell, The. Thomas Holley Chivers. TCAPo

Shell, The. H. M. Sarson. PoWW

Shell, The. James Stephens. IrV; MoBrPo

Shell of objects inwardly consumed, The. My Last Dance. Julia Ward Howe. APN-1

She'll meet me with the gate thrown wide. Meeting, The. Francis Ledwidge. IrLP

She'll not nag if there's no bread for breakfast. To Russian Women. Olga Ivanova. CRWP, tr. by Jenefer Coates

She'll press me. I stay stiff-backed. Poems from a Country House. Miriam Goodman. PfS

Shellbrook. William Barnes. OxBEV

Shell-bursting births, comas, and the mute. Eclogue 4. Andrea Zanzotto. ItPo, tr. by Gayle Ridinger

Shelley. Charles Simic. TRP

Shelley and jazz and lieder and love and hymn-tunes. Louis MacNeice. NPeEn Fr. Autumn Journal.

Shelley's a garden. Prelude. George Elliott Clarke. OpeFie

Shelley's Skylark. Thomas Hardy. CABP

Shelley's Vision. Herman Melville. APN-2

Shells. Rachel Hadas. ExTi

Shells Her Auburn Hair Did Show, The. Barry MacSweeney. Oth Fr. Pearl.

Shelly Beach. Christopher Koch. NOBAu

Sheltered beneath white hawthorn boughs. En un Vergier Soiz Folha D'Albespi. Unknown. WoPoe, tr. by Stanley Burnshaw

Sheltered Garden. "H. D." NAAPv.2

Sheltering Places. Gerald Dawe. PNI

Shelving Fixtures. Gale Nelson. OnScMo

Shemà. Primo Levi. AF; BeAl; FaBoWar; HP; PLBUT; PoAgWa, tr. by Ruth Feldman and Brian Swann

She-Machines, The. Mary O'Donoghue. NIrP

Shen Tao was not afraid. Shen Tao. Will Staple. WhBo

Shenandoah. Delmore Schwartz.
    Let Us Consider Where the Great Men Are. MoAmPo

Shephard loveth thow me vell? Song. Jean Passerat. NPeEn; OBVE, tr. by William Drummond of Hawthornden

Shepheardes boye (no better do him call), A. Edmund Spenser. CAGL

Shepherd's Calender, The. Edmund Spenser.
    Aprill. NAEL-6v1; NoP-5; OBEV
       Ditty, A: In Praise of Eliza, Queen of the Shepherds. OBEV
    August.
       (Roundelay, A: "It fell upon a holy eve.") NPeEn
       "Ye wastefull woodes bear witness of my woe." MakPoe
    May. PBRV
    October. NAEL-6v1; NAEL-7v1
    To His Booke. NAEL-6v1; NAEL-7v1

Shephe[a]rd's Hunting, The. George Wither.
    Sonnet. NOSC

Shepherd. William Stafford. PoA 2002

Shepherd Boy Sings [in the Valley of Humiliation], The. John Bunyan. OBEV; SacPr Fr. Pilgrim's Progress, The.

Shepherd Boy, The. John Clare. CABP

Shepherd Corydon burned with fire for fair Alexis, The. Virgil. CAGL Fr. Eclogues.

Shepherd in Capri. Nishiwaki Junzaburo. CAoMJL1, tr. by Hosea Hirata

Shepherd is blind, the sheep are made of stone, The. To Ovid. Elena Ignatova. ItGoST, tr. by Sibelan Forrester

Shepherd John. Mary Mapes Dodge. SWaP

Shephe[a]rd Paris bore the Spartan bride, The. Theocritus. OBVE Fr. Idylls.

Shepherd Rides on Donkey-Back, The. Sándor Petőfi. IQMS, tr. by Peter Zollman

Shepherd stands at one end of the arena, A. Sheepdog Trials in Hyde Park. Cecil Day Lewis. NoAM

Shepherd, The. William Blake. ChAP; NPBRoP Fr. Songs of Innocence.

Shepherd Thirsis longed to die, The. Giovanni Battista Guarini. EroLit, tr. by Sir Robert Aytoun

Shepherd Who With Your Tender Calls. Félix Lope de Vega Carpio. SpanPo, tr. by Kate Flores

Shepherd, why creep we in this lowly vein. Michael Drayton. NoSic Fr. Shepherd's Garland, The.

Shepherd, Young and Mournful, Grieves Alone, A. San Juan de la Cruz. SpanPo, tr. by James Edward Tobin

Shepherdess, The. Alice Thompson Meynell. MoBrPo
    (Lady of the Lambs, The.) OBEV
    (Shepherdess, The.) CABP; RACG

Shepherds and Flocks. Victor Hugo. SxFrPo, tr. by A. M. and E. H. Blackmore

Shepherds armed with staff and sling. Carol of Patience. Robert Graves. OBCP

Shepherd's Calendar. Bill Griffiths. Oth Fr. Building: The New London Hospital.

Shepherd's Calendar cont'd. Bill Griffiths. Oth Fr. Building: The New London Hospital.

Shepherds' Carol. Norman Nicholson. OBCP

Shepherd's Dale, The. Herman Melville. TCAPo

Shepherd's Dog, The. Leslie Norris. OBCP

Shepherd's Garland, The. Michael Drayton.
    (Daffodil Song, The.) AEP
    "Shepherd, why creep we in this lowly vein." NoSic
    ('Tell me, thou skilful shepherd's swain'.) AEP
    Tenth Eclogue, The.
       Farewell to Whitefoot. DiBP

Shepherds, I sing you, this winter's night. For the Nativity. John Heath-Stubbs. ChrPo

Shepherd's Night Count. Jane Yolen. TLR

Shepherd's [or Shepheards] Calendar, The. John Clare.
    Frolicsome Old Dog, The. DiBP
    Guardian at the Gate, A. DiBP
    July. NPBRoP; WaAnP
    Teased Pet, The. DiBP

Shepherds [or Shepheards], The. Henry Vaughan. ChIV-2

Shepherd's Pipe, The. William Browne.
    Comedy, A. DiBP

Shepherd's Sirena, The. Michael Drayton.
    (Sirena.) OBEV

Shepherd's Song at Christmas. Langston Hughes. ChrPo

Shepherd's Sorrow, Being Disdained in Love, The. Thomas Lodge. NoSic
    (Sheepheards Sorrow, Being Disdained in Love, The.) NPeEn

Shepherd's Tale, The. James Kirkup. OBCP

Shepherd's Tree, The. John Clare. CenSon

Shepherds went their hasty way, The. Christmas Carol, A. Samuel Taylor Coleridge. ChrPo

Shepherd's Wife's Farewell to the Old Pasture, The. István Sinka. IQMS, tr. by Gavin Ewart

Shepherd's Wife's Song, The. Robert Greene. NoSic; RACG Fr. Greene's Mourning Garment.

Sherbet. Cornelius Eady. GT; LTA

Shérdi. Sujata Bhatt. NeBrP

Sheridan at Cedar Creek. Herman Melville. CBCWP

Sheridan's Ride. Thomas Buchanan Read. APN-2; CBCWP; PCW

Sherri told me they had been. Drooling Madness at St. Liz. Charles Bukowski. BodElec

Sherwood. Alfred Noyes. BLPJKO; MoBrPo

She's a big teaser. She took him half the way there. Big Tease. Ania Walwicz. BMAP

She's a copperheaded waitress. Judy Grahn. NALW Fr. Common Woman, The.

She's a Latin from Manhattan. Al Dubin. ReLy

She's a man in the hat she's a bucket of air. Seven blind curves. Nicole Markotić. PoPra

She's all about getting there and being. Feeling Rosemary. Jerry McGuire. AnSo

She's always expecting disaster. Why She Hurries Out, Then Home. Martha Rhodes. OPRER

She's been in too deep and out too far, oh man. Portrait of a Lady. Alan Jenkins. NeBrP

She's calling God, she wants to ask Him. Elena Vasileva. CRWP, tr. by Max Nemtsov

She's combed his neckties out of her hair. Widow, A. Ted Kooser. PBCAP

She's crying. Scene, A. Ani Ilkov. CSCBP, tr. by Georgi Belev and Lisa Sapinkopf

She's daft to refuse the laird o' Cockpen. (LL) Laird o' Cockpen, The. Carolina Oliphant, Baroness Nairne. NOBRP; NPeEn; OxBEV

She's dreaming. Rita Dove. GT

She's empty: hark, she sounds: there's nothing there. Nahum 2.10. Francis Quarles. ChIV-1

She's Funny That Way (I Got a Woman, Crazy for Me). Richard A. Whiting. ReLy

She's heating you some soup. (LL) Old Woman Nature. Gary Snyder. BB; NoAM; RaBo

She's leaving. U-turn. Joy Lahey. AnSo

She's looking for a man physically. Evidently, She Says. Ginger Andrews. SUP

She's looking out of the picture. The bars across her face hold her in the picture and. Motive for Mayhem, A. Abigail Child. FTOS

She's My Love. Augustus Young. IrLP

She's my lover. One or More Together. John Godfrey. FTOS

She's neither ugly nor fearful. Eternity. Alexander Gerov. CSCBP, tr. by Georgi Belev and Lisa Sapinkopf

She's not and never can be mine. (LL) Coventry Patmore. OBEV; OxAEP-2; SacPr Fr. Angel in the House, The.

She's out there again with her five-cent. Another Spring on Olmstead Street. Len Roberts. UrbNat

She's put the child to sleep. Issa. EH, tr. by Robert Hass

She's resting in the bosom of Jesus. (LL) Go Down Death (A Funeral Sermon). James Weldon Johnson. ISC; OxAAAP; SacPr

She's slim and seems distracted, the social worker. Midlife. Joseph Millar. OPRER

She's somewhere in the sunlight strong. Song. Richard Le Gallienne. OBEV

She's there in the way you mark a cross. There. Caroline Natzler. Prnts

Shew, weakenes speaks in prose, but powre in verse. (LL) Samuel Daniel. NoSic; PBRV Fr. Musophilus; or, Defence of All Learning.

She-Who-Watches . . . The Names are Prayer. Elizabeth Woody. OPRER

Shibboleth. Paul Celan. PoetW, tr. by Michael Hamburger

Shibboleth. Michael Donaghy. NeBrP

Shickered As He Could Be. *Unknown.* NOBAu

Shield of Achilles, The. W. H. Auden. BeAl; NAEL-6v2; NAEL-7v2; NAMCP V.1; NoAM; NoP-4; NoP-5; NPeEn; OxAEP-2; OxBEV; OxBoAm; PoA 2002; WaAnP; WeW-3

Shield of Achilles, The. Homer. NOSC Fr. Iliad, The.

Shield of Achilles, The. Homer. NAWM-7v1 Fr. Iliad, The.

Shield of Aeneas, The. Virgil. NAWM-5v1; NAWM-7v1 Fr. Aeneid [or Eneados *or* Aeneis], The.

Shield of Perseus, The. Andrew Duncan. VaPo

Shields Bruttians threw from their doomed shoulders. Nossis. SaLy, tr. by Diane Rayor

Shift. Aaron Anstett. AmPoNex

Shift here, in town, not meanest among squires. On Lieutenant Shift. Ben Jonson. OBSV

Shifting Colors. Robert Lowell. BodElec

Shifting the Sun. Diana Der Hovanessian. GoPo

Shih-hou Pointed Out to Me That from Ancient Times There Had Never Been a Poem on the Subject of Lice. Mei Yao Ch'en. ColAnChi, tr. by Burton Watson

Shikata ga nai. Jodi L. Hottel. RWB

Shillin' a Day. Rudyard Kipling. NAMCP V.1; NoAM

Shilling life will give you all the facts, A. Who's Who. W. H. Auden. GoPo; MoBrPo; NAMCP V.1; NoAM

Shillong. Bernard Gutteridge. PoWW

Shiloh (A Requiem). Herman Melville. AmWaPo; APN-2; CBCWP; ColAP; CtM; NAAPv.1; NoP-4; NoP-5; OBWP; OxBoAm; PCW; PoAgWa; TCAPo

Shiloh Church, 1862: Twenty-Three Thousand. Geoffrey Hill. UpMys Fr. Locust Songs.

Shilpit dog fucks grimly by the close, A. Edwin Morgan. OxBSo

Shimá Shil hoolne'. She Was Telling It This Way. Laura Tohe. ReEnLa

Shimmer. James Schuyler. NoP-5; VCAP

Shimmering in the scrub-brush, A. Little Overture. David Barber. AmPoNex

Shimmering sea is still, The. Dolphins. Bryn Griffiths. TCAWP

Shimmering spreads of golden fire. November. James Hoggard. TiP2

Shinano. Issa. EH, tr. by Robert Hass

Shine On, Harvest Moon. Jack Norworth. NAAPv.2

Shine, Perishing Republic. Robinson Jeffers. APT-1; CalPo; ColAP; HarvBoo; NAAL-5; NAMCP V.1; NoAM; NoP-4; NoP-5; OxBoAm; PoPoPo; TFi; WaAnP

Shine, the square of light on every leaf, The. Paddling. Sue Sinclair. Coast

Shine was up in Harlem damn near drunk. (LL) Dark Prophecy: I Sing of Shine. Etheridge Knight. ESEAA; LTA; PBCAP

Shiner. Maggie Nelson. AmPoNex

Shines / in the mind of heaven God. Ezra Pound. PFTM-1 Fr. Cantos.

Shines farewell on the jewelled saddle, The. (LL) Bite back passion. Spring now sets. Li Shang-yin. CCL1; WoPoe, tr. by A. C. Graham

Shingle Flies. Hugh MacDonald. Coast

Shinier than transparent marble. Sapho's Kiss. Efrén Rebolledo. BLPSL, tr. by Rene de Costa, Rigas Kappatos and Eleni Paidoussi

Shining afternoon was his at last, The. Romaunt of Cecilia, The. Arthur Waugh. ArBi

Shining cup of earthly joy, The. Earthly Joy. Sydney E. Jerrold. SacPr

Shining fauna of that fire, The. (LL) Burning the Christmas Greens. William Carlos Williams. APT-1; ChrPo; NAAL-5; NAMCP V.1; NoAM

Shining indication of yellow consists in there haveing been more of the same color, A. Gertrude Stein. NAMCP V.1 Fr. Tender Buttons.

Shining Posy, The. Anthony Raftery. IrLP, tr. by Eleanor Hull

Shiny Aluminum of God, The. Martín Espada. Vesp

Shiny jewel eye. Lee Ann Brown. VaPo

Shiny record albums scattered over. As You Leave Me. Etheridge Knight. InGu

Shiny roundness of the rim, The. Wheel Building. Kate Taylor. PfS

Ship, The. Bill Griffiths. Oth Fr. Building: The New London Hospital.

Ship, The. J. F. Hendry. EdScPo

Ship, The. Robert Southey. TreFP

Ship at rock, wakes, terns, A. Going to Sea. Douglas Messerli. FTOS

Ship in Yokohama, The. Gary Snyder. MotU

Ship is a She, A. She-Machines, The. Mary O'Donoghue. NIrP

Ship Is Lost, The. William Falconer. OxAEP-1 Fr. Shipwreck, The.

Ship moves, The. 4th of July. William Carlos Williams. PoA 2002

Ship of Death, A. Seamus Heaney. NAEL-6v2; NoP-4

Ship of Death, The ("Now it is autumn and the falling fruit.") D. H. Lawrence. BrAP; GPTC; MoBrPo; NAEL-6v2; NAEL-7v2; NAMCP V.1; NoAM; NoP-4; NoP-5; OxAEP-2; OxBEV

Ship of Redemption. *Vietnamese Oral Tradition.* CaDao, tr. by John Balaban

Ship of State and Grandpa. Howard Phelps Putnam. OxBoAm

Ship of the body, ship of the soul, voyaging, voyaging, voyaging. (LL) Aboard at a Ship's Helm. Walt Whitman. APN-1; PtR

Ship Sets out, The. William Falconer. OxAEP-1 Fr. Shipwreck, The.

Ship, slow and rushing at the same time, can get ahead of the water, The. Night Piece. Juan Ramón Jiménez. WED, tr. by Robert Bly

Ship, Solid and Black, The. Juan Ramón Jiménez. RaW, tr. by Robert Bly

Ship Starting, The. Walt Whitman. TCAPo

Ship That Went Down, The [*with music*]. Adah Isaacs Menken. CBWP-1

Ship Waits in the Harbor, The. Gabriella Leto. CItWP, tr. by Cinzia Sartini Blum and Lara Trubowitz

Ship weighed twenty thousand ton, The. Passenger Shanty. W. H. Auden. OBCoV

Ship Without a Sail, A. Lorenz Hart. ReLy

Ship you've boarded, The. Ark. Gu Cheng. VCWP

Shipboard Song. Yüan Chüeh. ColAnChi, tr. by John Timothy Wixted

Ship-broken Men Whom Stormy Seas Sore Toss. William Fowler. NPeEn

Shipment to Maidanek. Ephim G. Fogel. OBWP; HP

Shipping Forecast, Donegal. Sean Street. RWPCtW

Shipping Out. Fadil Azzawi. IrPoTo, tr. by Ralph Saverese and Saadi A. Simawe

Shipping the Pictures from Belfast. Catherine Byron. Prnts

Shiprecked icily, the windows called away? (LL) Respected, Feared, and Somehow Loved. Marjorie Welish. OnScMo; PmAP

Ships. Douglas Dunn. EdScPo

Ship's master:/ before him, in the waist and before it. David Jones. WoPoe Fr. Anathemata, The.

Ships of state, The. Australorp. Edith Speers. NOBAu

Ships That Pass in the Night. Paul Laurence Dunbar. ColAP

Shipwreck [*with music*]. Mary Weston Fordham. CBWP-2

Shipwreck: "Watching, watching from the shore." Rosalie Moore. CalPo; YaYoPo

Shipwreck. Biancamaria Frabotta. CItWP, tr. by Cinzia Sartini Blum and Lara Trubowitz

Shipwreck in Haven, A. Keith Waldrop.
   "Balancing. Austere. Life." PmAP

Shipwreck Poem. Karen Volkman. NeAmPo

Shipwreck, The. Lord Byron. NPBRoP; NPeEn Fr. Don Juan.

Shipwreck, The. William Falconer.
   Ship Is Lost, The. OxAEP-1
   Ship Sets out, the. OxAEP-1

Shipwrecked Tippoo. William Wyndham. DiBP

Shipyard cranes have come down again. Landscape with One Figure. Douglas Dunn. NePenScot

Shir Asheydim Ansher. Yosl Cutler. Prolet, tr. by Amelia Glaser

Shiraz Moon. Abdul Wahab Al-Bayati. IrPoTo, tr. by Farouk Abdel Wahab

Shirley MacLaine says she believes in reincarnation. Honeybee upon the Tundra. Joan Jobe Smith. SUP

Shirley Temple Surrounded by Lions. Kenward Elmslie. NYP2

Shirt. Robert Pinsky. ColAP; FaoP; HarvBoo; NAAL-5; OxBoAm; StAl

Shirt ("My shirt is a token and symbol.") Carl Sandburg. CA

Shirt blows across the field, A. Storm. Ágnes Nemes Nagy. IQMS, tr. by Hugh Maxton

Shirt Collar, The. Ann Townsend. NAPBL

Shirt I sleep in, The. Dux Bellorum. Max Winter. NeAmPo

Shirt of a Lad, The.   *Unknown*.   OBWVE, *tr. by* Anthony Conran

Shirt Poem, The [*with music*].   Gerald Stern.   ItP

Shirts.   Nigel Jenkins.   TCAWP

Shi-shu: Rats.   *Unknown*.   CCL1, *tr. by* Ezra Pound

Shiva.   Robinson Jeffers.   NoAM

Shiva's Prowess.   Maurya Simon.   ErotSp

Shiver crosses Loch Stenness, A.   Stolen Light.   Stewart Conn.   EdScPo

Shivering.   Emperor, The.   Jonathan Griffin.   Oth

Shivering and hoping no one.   Grandma's Bureau.   Robert Morgan.   WeW-3

Shi-you chang-chu: In the Lowlands.   *Unknown*.   CCL1, *tr. by* Arthur Waley

Shlup, shlup, the dog.   Denise Levertov.   HeIP-4 *Fr.* Six Variations.

Shma Yisrael (Hear, O Israel).   Galina Zelenina.   CRWP, *tr. by* Daniel Weissbort

Shma—listen, receive.   She Who Listens.   Elana Klugman.   HW

Shoal of Silver Angelfish, A.   Edward B. Koster.   TuT, *tr. by* Tony Curtis and Tony Curtis

Shock.   Rudyard Kipling.   InoFa *Fr.* Epitaphs of the War [1914–1918].

Shock.   C. K. Williams.   UrbNat

Shock Along, John, shock along.   Shock Along, John.   *Unknown*.   SSUS

Shock and His Mistress.   John Gay.   DiBP

Shock is that it took, The.   Argument For Small Arms, An.   Karen Solie.   OpeFie

Shock-black bubble-doun-beat bouncing.   Reggae Sounds.   Linton Kwesi Johnson.   WaCA

Shocks of dizziness.   Incantations of the Sea: Moando Coast.   Mukula Kadima-Nzuji.   NAfrP, *tr. by* Gerald Moore

Shoe Shop.   Barton Sutter.   SoSe-8

Shoe the steed with silver.   Sheridan at Cedar Creek.   Herman Melville.   CBCWP

Shoe with legs, A.   Lobster.   Anne Sexton.   ChAP

Shoeing the Currach.   Mary O'Malley.   MakPoe

Shoemaker's Holiday, The.   Thomas Dekker *and others*.
   O, the Month of May.   NoSic

Shoemaker's Wife, The.   Lotte Kramer.   HP

Shoemakker, The.   *Unknown*.   FaBoVe

Shoes, The.   Lola Haskins.   PfS

Shoes, The.   Nina Nyhart.   PfS

Shoes of Dead Comrades, The.   Jackie Kay.   NeBrP; RSaN

Shoes, secret face of my inner life.   My Shoes.   Charles Simic.   EmeKit; OxBoAm; VCAP

Shoeshine Boy.   Maria Eugénia Lima.   HAWP, *tr. by* Julia Kirst

Shoeshine, master?, A.   Shoeshine Boy.   Maria Eugénia Lima.   HAWP, *tr. by* Julia Kirst

Shogun, always on the lookout for ways to increase his glory, The.   Autumn.   Jean Frémon.   YaTCFP, *tr. by* Cole Swensen

Shogun, soucieux d'ajouter à sa gloire, Le.   Automne, L'.   Jean Frémon.   YaTCFP

Shoichi brushed the black.   Awakening.   Lucien Stryk.   BodElec

Sholto Peach Harrison you are no son of mine.   Correspondence between Mr. Harrison in Newcastle and Mr. Sholto Peach Harrison in Hull.   Stevie Smith.   NBLV

Shoni Onions.   Sheenagh Pugh.   AngWePo

Shooshoon.   Félix Morisseau-Leroy.   OGAHCP, *tr. by* Boadiba and Jack Hirschman

Shoot It Jimmy!   William Carlos Williams.   APT-1

Shoot me for.   What Sunni Say.   Elouise Loftin.   EGAG

Shooter Rules.   Michael Bugeja.   LiTh

Shooting a Farmhouse.   Ted Kooser.   PBCAP

Shooting Back.   Thomas Sayers Ellis.   GT

Shooting Crows.   Peter Markus.   AmPoNex

Shooting, Killing, Drug Busts, Cover-Ups, Fuck-Ups, Lighter Sides, Weather, and Sports.   Bruce Jackson.   AmPoNex

Shooting of Dan McGrew, The.   Robert W. Service.   BrAP; BRP; EdScPo; UV

Shooting Script, A [*with music*].   Seamus Heaney.   BodElec

Shooting Star.   Joanna Klink.   IAoNAP

Shooting Star, A.   Edith Matilda Thomas.   ChAP

Shooting the Dogs.   Philip Hodgins.   BMAP

Shooting Whales [*with music*].   Mark Strand.   ColAP

Shootingway Ceremony Prayer.   *Unknown*.   WoPoe; WPoS. *tr. by* Gladys A. Reichard

Shop Sonnet.   Crystal Williams.   RD

Shop windows glow like fish tanks. Even in town.   Beneath Searchlights.   Andrew Hudgins.   UpMys

Shopgirls leave their work, The.   Charles Reznikoff.   APT-2; NAAPv.2; NAMCP V.1

Shoplifter Hands.   Diane Averill.   FiBr

Shoplifters.   Maura Stanton.   ReTh

Shoplifting.   Baron Wormser.   ReTh

Shoppers steer trolleys.   This is Sunday.   Mary O'Donoghue.   NIrP

Shopping.   Agi Mishol.   DTA, *tr. by* Tsipi Keller

Shopping for Midnight.   G. E. Murray.   ReTh

Shops.   Jean Follain.   MotU, *tr. by* Mary Feeney

Shops, the streets are full of old men, The.   Talk.   Roo Borson.   NIP-4

Shore.   Alan Bold.   EdScPo

Shore, The.   W. S. Merwin.   ItP

Shore Bird.   Brewster Ghiselin.   APT-2

Shore Crab.   Gerry Cambridge.   EdScPo

Shore Grass.   Amy Lowell.   APT-1; NAMCP V.1

Shore of Night.   José Luis Hidalgo.   RaW, *tr. by* Hardie St. Martin

Shore people worshipped, we are told, the Mother.   Peter Davison.   YaYoPo *Fr.* Breaking of the Day, The.

Shorebirds in Seasonal Plumage Observed through Binoculars.   Amy Clampitt.   PfSP

Shoreless bath a fabulous boast, A.   Bronislava Volková.   Vesp

Shoreline.   Mary Barnard.   APT-2

Shoreline After Storm.   Eamon Grennan.   PoCoUp

Shoreline, The.   Joe Denham.   IFF

Shorelines.   Howard Moss.   GoPo

Shores.   Sorley MacLean.   EdScPo, *tr. by* Iain Crichton Smith

Shores are crown'd with people, The.   Luis de Camões [*or* Camõens *or* Camoëns].   OBVE *Fr.* Lusiads, The.

Shorn of landmarks, glued to a sere promontory.   "No!" He Said.   Wole Soyinka.   HBAPE

Short afternoon ends, and the year is over, The.   New Year.   Philip Larkin.   ChrPo

Short and Sweet Sonnet Made by One of the Maids of Honour, upon the Death of Queen Elizabeth, which She Sewed upon a Sampler, in Red Silke, A.   *Unknown*.   EMWP

Short Circuit.   Daniel Hall.   OWoS

Short Curse.   John Banks.   STuOW *Fr.* Anna Bullen.

Short Hand.   Lawrence Goeckel.   ICANM

Short History of Autumn, A.   Anselm Berrigan.   HeMarv

Short History of Bill Berkson, A.   Frank O'Hara.   AHA

Short History of Illumination, A.   Matthew Rohrer.   AmPoNex

Short History of Judaic Thought in the Twentieth Century, A.   Linda Pastan.   Vesp

Short History of the Bourgeoisie.   Hans Magnus Enzensberger.   VCWP, *tr. by* the author and Michael Hamburger

Short history of vodka, A.   Ronny Someck.   IrPoTo, *tr. by* Vivian Eden

Short Lexicon of Torture in the Eighties, A.   Edward Hirsch.   VCAP

Short nap / Waking.   Buson.   ZenPo, *tr. by* Takashi Ikemoto and Lucien Stryk

Short Narrative of Breasts and Wombs in Service of Plot Entitled, A.   Claudia Rankine.   BAP-01

Short Narrative of Hand and Face in Service of PLOT, Entitled, A.   Claudia Rankine.   NAPBL

Short night / Scarlet flower.   Issa.   ZenPo, *tr. by* Takashi Ikemoto and Lucien Stryk

Short night, The.   Buson.   EH, *tr. by* Robert Hass

Short Note on the Sparseness of the Language.   Diane Di Prima.   BB

Short Oblation of This Smal Work by the Writer Gatherer Thereof to Our Most Sweet and Merciful God, A.   Dame Gertrude More.   EMWP

Short Poem.   Kenneth Carroll.   SpirFl

Short Poem.   William Carlos Williams.   SAmP

Short Prayer for a Loyalist Hero.   César Vallejo.   TCLAP *Fr.* Spain, Take [Away] This Cup from Me [España, Aparta de Mí Este Cáliz].

Short Revelation Concerning Death and Chaos.   René Daumal.   PFTM-1

Short service, to be sure, A.   Lament for a Leg.   John Ormond.   AngWePo; NoP-4; NoP-5; OBWVE

Short Song.   T. Carmi.   WoPoe, *tr. by* Grace Schulman

Short Song of Congratulation, A [*or* To a Young Heir].   Samuel Johnson.   NAEL-6v1; NPeEn; OBCoV; OBSV; OxAEP-1; OxBEV; TFi; WoPoe

Short Sorry.   Kari Edwards.   BAP-04

Short Speech to My Friends.   Imamu Amiri Baraka.   ESEAA

Short Story.   Ruth Buchman.   PfS

Short Story.   Maura Stanton.   BodElec

Short Story, A.   David Escobar Galindo.   ChAP, *tr. by* Jorge Piche

Short Summary.   Louise Bogan.   APT-2

Short Talk on Gertrude Stein About 9:30.   Anne Carson.   OpeFie

Short Talk on Orchids.   Anne Carson.   OpeFie

Short Talk on Reading.   Anne Carson.   OpeFie

Short Talk on the Sensation of Aeroplane Takeoff.   Anne Carson.   OpeFie

Short Talk on the Truth to Be Had From Dreams.   Anne Carson.   OpeFie

Short Talk on the Youth at Night.   Anne Carson.   OpeFie

Short Talk on Trout.   Anne Carson.   OpeFie

Short Talk on Walking Backwards. Anne Carson. OpeFie
(On Walking Backwards.) StAl

Short Testimony for Anne Whitehead, A. Jane Sowle. EMWP

Short Time [*with music*]. Gavin Ewart. NoAM

Short Wave. Hilary Llewellyn-Williams. RWPCtW; TCAWP

Short Wave. George Szirtes. RWPCtW

Short Year, The. Paavo Haavikko.
"One who writes us is now doing four plays a year, The." VCWP

Shortcut, A. Buson. EH, *tr. by* Robert Hass

Shortened History in Pictures, A. Jamie McKendrick. OxBSo

Shortening the Road. Michael Davitt. PBCIP, *tr. by* Philip Casey

Shorter and shorter now the twilight clips. Autumn. Alice Cary. APN-2

Shorter by two inches, you tell me. Health Check. Penny Feinstein. PoCu

Shorter Life, The. Peter Didsbury. NeBrP

Shortest Day. Arthur Leslie Morton. RSaN

Shortest Day, The. William Dickey. InoFa

Shorthand. Theodore Weiss. BodElec

Shortly after midnight, certain creatures become what they really. Nocturne. Angie Estes. GeoHom

Shortly before it is too late. Hans Faverey. WoBe *Fr.* Eighteen Poems.

Shortly before my death I'm buying. Beating the Drum in Reverse. Miroslav Valek. ArBi, *tr. by* David Short

Shortness of Life. Thomas Fairfax, Baron Fairfax of Cameron. NOSC

Short-Order Cook. Jim Daniels. ReTh

Shot at Random, A. Dominic Bevan Wyndham Lewis. UV

Shot Down at Night. John Frederick Nims. PWW2

Shot down from its enskied formation. Angel in Blythburgh Church, An. Peter Porter. NoP-4; NoP-5

Shot Forth. Paul Celan. WoPoe, *tr. by* Margaret Guillemin and Katherine Washburn

Shot gold, maroon and violet, dazzling silver, emerald, fawn. Prairie Sunset, A. Walt Whitman. TCAPo

Shot of sunlight, A. Albert Memmi. SonAtl, *tr. by* Kurt Ganzl and Saul Goode

Shot of War, A. J. S. Harry. BMAP

Shot? so quick, so clean an ending? A. E. Housman. CAGL *Fr.* Shropshire Lad, A.

Shot through with silver gray light. One Snapshot I Couldn't Take in France, The. Al Young. SpirFl

Shot Who? Jim Lane! Merrill Moore. MoAmPo

Shotgun. Patti Sees. MPUn

Shotgun / blossoming / outward. Maxine Chernoff. PmAP *Fr.* Japan.

Shots at Otters. Colin Simms.
"Lochside silverschistsand disturbed-to-black-below distributed." Oth

Shotts. George MacBeth. EdScPo

Should any to himself for safety fly? To Whom Else Can We Fly? Giles, the Younger Fletcher. SacPr

Should auld acquaintance be forgot. Auld Lang Syne. Robert Burns. NAEL-6v2; NAEL-7v2; NePenScot; NoP-5; NOSC; OBEV; OxAEP-2; OxBEV

Should be clear: the darkness around us is deep. (LL) Ritual to Read to Each Other, A. William Stafford. GoPo; RaBo; RaF

Should be very quiet this morning. Sunday Morning. Robert Grenier. PmAP

Should blaze the path of thunder. (LL) Tableau. Countee Cullen. BLPJKO; NAAPv.2

Should find brief [*or* short] solace there, as I have found. (LL) Sonnet: "Nuns fret not at their convent's narrow room." William Wordsworth. BrAP; CenSon; GSo; NIL-7; NIP-4; NoP-4; OBEV

Should Heaven send me any son. Dorothy Parker. NALW *Fr.* Pig's-Eye View of Literature, A.

Should I Earn My Daily Bread, or Should I Write a Poem? Bishwabimohan Shreshtha. PML, *tr. by* Michael James Hutt

Should I forget your scales. Walking Buddha. Barbara Guest. FTOS

Should I get married? Should I be good? Marriage. Gregory Corso. NoP-4; NoP-5; PmAP; TRP

Should I give in to sleep? This fire's warm. Reading *Paradise Lost* in Protestant Ulster 1984. Seamus Deane. PBCIP

Should I return to consciousness or stay. Conciousness. Ágnes Nemes Nagy. IQMS, *tr. by* Dorren Bell

Should I return to Japan? *Hawaiian Oral Tradition.* NAAPv.2

Should I say the eyes were laced and that the laces were snakes. How Should I Say This? Robert Dow. BAP-97

Should I simplify my life for you? Adrienne Rich. NIL-7 *Fr.* Inscriptions.

Should I Stay or Should I Go? Sarah Rosenblatt. AmPoNex

Should I tell of all the absolute fools. Georgy Vladimirovich Ivanov. TCRusP, *tr. by* Daniel Weissbort

Should I tell what a miracle she was. (LL) Relic, The. John Donne. BASC; FSCP; HeIP-4; NAEL-6v1; NAEL-7v1; NoP-4; NoP-5; NOSC; TFi; WaAnP

Should I wear a shadowed eye. Acceptance. John Wieners. FTOS

Should I with Silver Tooles Delve through the Hill. Edward Taylor. ChIV-2 *Fr.* Preparatory Meditations Before My Approach to the Lord's Supper.

Should Lanterns Shine. Dylan Thomas. OxBEV

Should make her equal to so great a work. (LL) Alexandreis. Anne Killigrew. NoP-4; NoP-5

Should make men atheists, and not women whores. (LL) Rapture, A. Thomas Carew. BASC; CABP; NAEL-6v1; NAEL-7v1; OxAEP-1

Should never be light. That kind of thing feels. Your One Good Dress. Brenda Shaughnessy. AmPoNex

Should she call or not. Donkey Speculates, The. Kazuko Shiraishi. WoBe, *tr. by* Samuel Grolmes and Yumiko Tsumura

Should some ill Painter in a wild design. Horace. OBVE *Fr.* Art of Poetry, The.

Should the bare-ass pavement-pounder. *Unknown.* PriapPo *Fr.* Priapus Poems, The.

Should the building totter, run for an archway! Fallen Tower of Siloam, The. Robert Graves. ChIV-2

Should the lone Wanderer, fainting on his way. Charlotte Smith. RWP

Should the pillar sing, should salt. Lot. David Helwig. NIP-4

Should the schoolboy pull a marble out of his pocket. Should the Schoolboy Pull. Jean Follain. MotU, *tr. by* Mary Feeney and William Matthews

Should the wide world roll away. Stephen Crane. APN-2

Should the years continue to press. Protest Poem. Mendi Lewis Obadike. RD

Should they not have the best of both worlds? Mules. Paul Muldoon. HarvBoo

Should they study me. (LL) Sphinx. Van K. Brock. AllShUp; SwNoth

Should toss with tangle and with shells. (LL) Alfred Tennyson. NAEL-6v2; NAEL-7v2; NAWM-7v2 *Fr.* In Memoriam A. H. H.

Should we go now a wandering [*or* a-wand'ring], we should meet. Henry Vaughan. BASC *Fr.* Rhapsody, A.

Should wear all Time's destruction for a dress. (LL) Poet Laments the Coming of Old Age, The. Dame Edith Sitwell. BrAP; NAEL-6v2; NAMCP V.1; NoAM

Should weep? (LL) Night Winds. Adelaide Crapsey. APT-1; NAAPv.2; TCAPo

Should you ask me, whence these stories? Henry Wadsworth Longfellow. ColAP *Fr.* Song of Hiawatha, The.

Should you come to me. Years from Now. Kim Sowŏl. WoPoe, *tr. by* Kevin O'Rourke

Should you ever forsake me. Soul and Love, The. Albert Verwey. TuT, *tr. by* Tony Curtis and Tony Curtis

Should you revisit us. New Approach Needed. Kingsley Amis. NoAM

Shouldering / a house without a husband. Shouldering. Taro Katay. NAAPv.2

Shouldering its way and shedding the earth crumbs. (LL) Putting in the Seed. Robert Frost. APT-1; IPoFL; NAMCP V.1; NoAM; OxBoAm

Shoulders. Naomi Shihab Nye. AtGh; TWF

Shout, The. Simon Armitage. NoP-5

Shout came from the loquacious ones, A. Welsh Ballad, A. Edmwnd Prys. OBWVE, *tr. by* Gwyn Williams

Shout On, Children. *Unknown.* SSUS

Shout on, chil'en, you never die. Shout On, Children. *Unknown.* SSUS

Shout Out. Sekou Sundiata. FaoP

Shout the Redeemer. (LL) Isaac Watts. *See* Throned, yet adoring!

Shouting, Noel. Rejoice. Judson Crews. ICANM

Shouting Your Name Down the Well. David McFadden. IFF

Shovelful or two of sand has been flung, A. Inside the Iris. Kim Hyesun. EcSo, *tr. by* Youngju Ryu

Shovelin' Coal. Tony Pranses. ArBi

Shoveling Snow with Buddha. Billy Collins. OxBoAm

Shoving another quarter home to make. Honky-Tonk Blues. Walter McDonald. SwNoth

Show, The. Wilfred Owen. MoBrPo; OBWVE; OxBEV

Show an affirming flame. (LL) September 1, 1939. W. H. Auden. AF; BrAP; HarvBoo; MoBrPo; NAMCP V.1; NoP-5; OxAEP-2; OxBoAm; PoAgWa; PWW2; StAl; WaAnP

Show and Tell. Roddy Lumsden. NeBl

Show Biz Parties. Elizabeth Claman. OPRER

Show Me a Rose. John Godfrey. FTOS

Show me a sight. Irish Spinning-Wheel, The. Alfred Perceval Graves. IrV

Show me again the time. Lines to a Movement in Mozart's E-Flat Symphony. Thomas Hardy. NoAM

Show me dear[e] Christ, thy spouse, so bright and clear[e]. John Donne. BASC; FSCP; NAEL-6v1; NAEL-7v1; NoP-4; NoP-5; NOSC; OxBSo; PBRV; WaAnP *Fr.* Holy Sonnets.

Show me himself, himself (bright Sir) O show. Come See the Place Where the Lord Lay. Richard Crashaw. ChIV-2

Show me the flames you brag of, you that be.   On the Great Frost (1634).   William Cartwright.   NOSC

Show me the woman.   Black.   Grace Nichols.   Oth

Show [or Shew] me thy feet; show [or shew] me thy legs, thy thighs.   To Dianeme.   Robert Herrick.   CavPo; NOSC

Show square is filled with all manner of people, The.   Parade.   Amjad Nasir.   IrPoTo, tr. by Ralph Saverese and Saadi A. Simawe

Show them this day you were on Calvary. (LL)   Petrarch.   NAWM-5v1; NAWM-7v1 Fr. Sonnets to Laura.

Show us there's chance at least of winning through. (LL)   To Whistler, American.   Ezra Pound.   FaBoA; PoA 2002

Shower.   Leah Aini.   DTA, tr. by Linda Zisquit

Shower.   Jacob Winkler Prins.   TuT, tr. by Tony Curtis and Tony Curtis

Shower, A.   Amy Lowell.   PoBW

Shower, The.   Kimiko Hahn.   CAP-8

Shower of Secret Things, The.   Nathaniel Mackey.   PmAP

Shower room's peace shattered by boys launched.   Naked Man, The.   Michael Crummey.   IFF

Shower Scene in *Psycho*, The.   David Trinidad.   ReTh

Showing.   Liam Rector.   TRP

Showing a torn sleeve, with stiff and shaking fingers the old man.   Charles Reznikoff.   WoPoe

Showings, The: Lady Julian of Norwich, 1342-1416.   Denise Levertov.
  "God's wounded hand."   UpMys
  "Julian laughing aloud, glad."
    "She lived in dark times, as we do."   UpMys
  "To understand her, you must imagine."   UpMys
  "What she petitioned for was never."   UpMys

Shown in a photo.   Genuflection to Petty Officer First Class Leonette Masters.   Hettie Jones.   PrTe

Shoyn Fergéssin: "I've Forgotten" in Yiddish.   Albert Goldbarth.   TaR

Shrapnel.   C. K. Williams.   AmWaPo

Shrapnel lives in Morton's neck, so his head stays.   Refuge at the One Step Down.   Belle Waring.   PBCAP; SeSe

Shred.   Hoa Nguyen.   WANABP

Shredding at the lower rim of disc of, The.   Leslie Scalapino.   PfS Fr. Sight.

Shrew, The.   Rowland Watkyns.   AngWePo

Shrewd star, who crudes our naming: you should be flame.   Karen Volkman.   IAoNAP; NAPBL; NeAmPo

Shrieking its message the flying death.   Shell, The.   H. M. Sarson.   PoWW

Shrieking man stood in the square, A.   Ballad of the Shrieking Man, The.   James Fenton.   EmeKit

Shrieking plovers / Calling darkness.   Basho.   ZenPo, tr. by Takashi Ikemoto and Lucien Stryk

Shrike Tree.   Lucia Maria Perillo.   RoV

Shrill of one hundred katydids chirring together.   Ripe Apple.   Kim Hyesun.   CAMKP, tr. by Jiwon Shin

Shrill sentence: God is love, The. (LL)   On the Farm.   Ronald Stuart Thomas.   NoP-4; NoP-5; NPeEn; OxBEV; TCAWP

Shrill winds, high sky, monkeys' heart-rending cry.   Climbing on the Double Ninth Day.   Tu Fu [or Du Fu].   ChinPo, tr. by Ye Weilian [or Yeh Wei-lien or Wai-lim Yip]

Shrilling cicada, drunk on drops of dew, you sing.   Meleager.   HePo, tr. by Barbara Hughes Fowler

Shrimp and Her Daughter, The.   Jean de La Fontaine.   WoPoe, tr. by Bruce Boone and Robert Glück

Shrimp Boats, Biloxi.   Campbell McGrath.   AmPoNex

Shrimps.   Nguyễn Văn Lạc.   WoPoe, tr. by Huỳnh Sanh Thông

Shrine.   Octavio Paz.   EroLit

Shrine, The.   "H. D."   ColAP

Shrine, The.   Sara Teasdale.   APT-1

Shrine gate / Through morning mist.   Kikaku.   ZenPo, tr. by Takashi Ikemoto and Lucien Stryk

Shrinking brain, sick of an inner war, The. (LL)   Sidney Keyes.   NoP-4; NoP-5; OBWP Fr. Foreign Gate, The.

Shrinking Lonesome Sestina, The.   Miller Williams.   MakPoe

Shropshire Lad, A.   Sir John Betjeman.   HarvBoo

Shropshire Lad, A.   A. E. Housman.
  "Along the field as we came by."   MoBrPo; WeW-3
  "Be still, my soul, be still; the arms you bear are brittle."   MoBrPo
  Bredon Hill.   MoBrPo; NAEL-6v2; OxAEP-2; SoSe-8; UV
  Carpenter's Son, The.   ChIV-2; MoBrPo; OxAEP-2; UV
  1887.   NIP-4
  (Epilogue: "Terence, this is stupid stuff.")   MoBrPo
  "Far in a western brookland."   NPeEn
  "Farewell to barn and stack and tree."   HarvBoo; MoBrPo
  "From far, from eve and morning."   HeIP-4; MoBrPo; NoP-4; NoP-5
  "I hoed and trenched and weeded."   MoBrPo; WeW-3

  "If it chance your eye offend you."   ChIV-2
  "If truth in hearts that perish."   CAGL
  Immortal Part, The.   MoBrPo; SoSe-8
  "Is my team ploughing."   BrAP; MoBrPo; NAMCP V.1; NoAM; NoP-4; NoP-5; OBEV
  Isle of Portland, The.   MoBrPo
  "It nods and curtseys and recovers."   OxBEV
  "Lads in their hundreds to Ludlow come in for the fair, The."   MoBrPo
  "Look not in my eyes, for fear."   CAGL
  "Loveliest of trees, the cherry now."   BrAP; ChAP; ClHu; MakPoe; MoBrPo; NAEL-6v2; NAEL-7v2; NAMCP V.1; NoAM; NoP-4; NoP-5; PoPoPo; SoSe-8; TFi; WaAnP; WeW-3
  New Mistress, The.   MoBrPo
  "Oh see how thick the goldcup flowers."   MoBrPo
  "Oh, when I was in love with you."   MoBrPo
  "On the idle hill of summer."   FaBoWar; MoBrPo; OBWP
  "On Wenlock Edge the wood's in trouble."   BrAP; HarvBoo; MoBrPo; NAEL-6v2; NAEL-7v2; NAMCP V.1; NoP-4; NoP-5; OxAEP-2; TFi
  "Others, I am not the first."   MoBrPo
  Reveille.   CABP; HarvBoo; MoBrPo; NoP-4; NoP-5
  "Shot? so quick, so clean an ending?"   CAGL
  "Terence, this is stupid stuff."   BrAP; CABP; HeIP-4; NAEL-6v2; NAEL-7v2; NAMCP V.1; NoAM; NoP-4; NoP-5; TFi
  To an Athlete Dying Young.   BrAP; ChAP; CtM; HeIP-4; InoFa; MoBrPo; NAEL-6v2; NAEL-7v2; NAMCP V.1; NIP-4; NoAM; NoP-4; NoP-5; PtR; SoSe-8; TFi; TRP; WaAnP; WeW-3
  "When I was one-and-twenty."   ChAP; HeIP-4; ITBLP; ItP; MoBrPo; NAEL-6v2; NAEL-7v2; NAMCP V.1; NoAM; TFi; WaAnP
  "When I watch the living meet."   HarvBoo; MoBrPo; NoP-4; NoP-5; NPeEn
  "When smoke stood up from Ludlow."   MoBrPo
  "When the lad for longing sighs."   MoBrPo
  "With rue my heart is laden."   HeIP-4; InoFa; MoBrPo; NAEL-6v2; NAEL-7v2; NAMCP V.1; NoAM; NoP-4; NoP-5; PoPoPo; TFi
  Yon Far Country.   HarvBoo; MoBrPo; NoAM; NPeEn; OPOU; OxAEP-2; OxBEV; TFi; WaAnP

Shroud.   George Mackay Brown.   NoP-4; NoP-5

Shrouding of the Duchess of Malfi, The.   John Webster.   OBEV

Shrubbery, The.   William Cowper.   OBGa

Shrunken world, A.   Epistle. To Enrique Caracciolo Trejo.   Donald Davie.   HarvBoo

Shtetl years.   To My Shtetl Years.   Yosl Grinshpan.   Prolet, tr. by Amelia Glaser

Shu is away in the hunting-fields.   *Unknown*.   WoPoe, tr. by Arthur Waley

Shu Swamp, Spring.   May Swenson.   APT-2

Shubble, The.   Walter De la Mare.   OBCoV

Shucks flit the horizon.   Last Warm Day, A.   Katherine Soniat.   PfSP

Shuddered under the feet in waves, then the waves passed. (LL)   Derek Walcott.   NAMCP V.2; WaAnP Fr. Omeros.

Shuffle Off to Buffalo.   Al Dubin.   ReLy

Shuffles.   Brian Bartlett.   IFF

Shuffling papers.   Certificate of Live Birth.   Kimberly M. Blaeser.   UnSA

Shugakuin Garden.   Charles Tomlinson.   WoBe Fr. Zipangu.

Shulamit in Her Dreams.   Marcia Falk.   TaR

Shumeekuli, The.   Andrew Peynetsa.   PFTM-2, tr. by Dennis Tedlock

Shun[ne] delay[e]s, they breed[e] remorse.   Loss[e] in Delay[e].   Robert Southwell.   NoSic

Shunning an Imperative.   Carl Hancock Rux.   BRtP; HeMarv

Shunryu Suzuki.   Jaan Kaplinski.   WhBo

Shush, cicada / Old Whiskers.   Issa.   ZenPo, tr. by Takashi Ikemoto and Lucien Stryk

Shut In.   Robert B. Shaw.   SoSe-8

Shut in from all the world without.   John Greenleaf Whittier.   NoP-5; OBCP Fr. Snow-Bound [or Snow-Bound] [A Winter Idyl].

Shut not me alive away.   Commuted Sentence, The.   Stevie Smith.   OxAEP-2

Shut not so soon; the dull-eyed night.   To Daisies, Not to Shut So Soon[e].   Robert Herrick.   OBEV

Shut Out.   Christina Georgina Rossetti.   NALW

Shut Out That Moon.   Thomas Hardy.   NAMCP V.1; NoAM

Shut, shut the door, good John! (fatigu'd [or fatigued] I said).   Epistle to Dr. Arbuthnot.   Alexander Pope.   NAEL-6v1; NAEL-7v1; NoP-4; NoP-5; OxAEP-1; TFi

Shut the Seven Seas against Us.   George Barker.   MoBrPo Fr. Third Cycle of Love Poems.

Shut up and listen! Sit up.   My Big German Bra.   Jennifer L. Knox.   FreRad

Shut up. Shut up. There's nobody here.   Beast in the Space, The.   William Sydney Graham.   EmeKit; OxAEP-2; PoA 2002; StAl

Shut up they said.   Not Quiet.   Ibrahim al-Osta Omar.   SonAtl, tr. by Abdul Kalam Azad and Ibrahim Ighneiwa

Shut your eyes then. Nursery Rhyme. May Sarton. NOxBChV

Shuts up the story of our days. (LL) Nature, That Washed [*or* Washt] Her Hands in Milk[e]. Sir Walter Ralegh. NAEL-6v1; NAEL-7v1; NoP-4; NoP-5

Shutting my gate, I walk away. All Souls'. Ruth Bidgood. AngWePo

Shuttle, The. Tennessee Williams.
"My love was light the old wives said." PoA 2002

Shuttles of trains going north, going south, drawing threads of blue. Morning Sun. Louis MacNeice. MoBrPo

Shut-winged fish, brown as mushroom. Swifts. Glyn Jones. AngWePo

Shy and timid, Gloom to me. Outcast, The. James Stephens. MoBrPo

Shy breathing of the radiator, The. night sighs. Jill Hartman. PoPra

Shy dawn tenderly. Kalamu ya Salaam. SpirFl *Fr.* New Orleans Haiku.

Shy Geordie. Helen B. Cruickshank. EdScPo

Shy Ones, The. Antonio Deltoro. RMCMP, *tr. by* Christian Viveros-Fauné

Shy Request. Mihály Csokonai Vitéz. IQMS, *tr. by* Adam Makkai and Ena Roberts

Shy speechless sound, The. Osip Emilevich Mandelstam. Spl

Shy, you veil your face on the street. In Peking to a Woman with a Veil. Cho Hwi. CATKP, *tr. by* Peter H. Lee

Shylock. J. B. Mulligan. IaFF

Shyly she knits her brows. Tune: "Drunk in Fairyland." Ou-yang Hsiu. ColAnChi, *tr. by* James Robert Hightower

Shyly the silver-hatted mushrooms make. May. John Shaw Neilson. NOBAu

Shyness and modesty, they said. Disillusionment. Virginia Graham. NBLV

Shyness, the delay to say, The. Sonnet L'Abbé. OpeFie *Fr.* Dumb Animal.

Si canta la cigarra y bajo las pestañas. Biografía Incompleta. Gerardo Diego. RaW

Si cascas como un huevo. Condicional. Gerardo Diego. RaW

Si creciera y las fosas se colmarían de grandes cubos de sales. Mapa. Gerardo Diego. RMCMP

Si el calor dilata, amalgama y fusiona, el frío hace lo opuesto. Tijeras, Las. Fabio Morabito. RMCMP

Si en un plano colocamos un cierto número de pasillos y galerías que se cruzan y se comunican. Esponja, La. Fabio Morabito. RMCMP

Si es difícil trepar por la cucaña. De la Vida en Provincias. Carlos Sahagún. RaW

Si la vie est comme un grand songe. Jour de Pritemps Le Poète Exprime Ses Sentiments au Sortir de l'Ivresse, Un. Li Po. CCL1, *tr. by* Marie-Jean-Léon, Marquis d'Hervey de Saint-Denys

Si l'attendrissant souvenir du verre brisé dans son oeil ne sonne l'heure. Si l'attendrissant souvenir. Dora Maar. YaTCFP

Si le Sage, faisant peu de cas de l'albâtre, vénère le pur Jade onctueux. Éloge du Jade. Victor Segalen. YaTCFP

Si Mi Voz Muriera en Tierra. Rafael Alberti. RaW

Si mince l'infractuosité d'où sortait la voix. Paroles du poème, Les. André Frénaud. YaTCFP

Si Tu Savais. Robert Desnos. YaTCFP

Si votre enfant a une trompe sur le nez, ne soyez pas effrayé par les éléphants. Henri Michaux. YaTCFP *Fr.* Tranches de savoir.

Si yo no cre en mí. Acotamiento. Pedro Serrano. RMCMP

Si yo, por ti, he creado un mundo para ti. Nombre Conseguido de los Nombres, El. Juan Ramón Jiménez. RaW

Siamese Twins in Love. Susan Swartwout. ReTh

Siamese twins: one, maddened by. Twins. Robert Graves. OBCoV

Siân Owen Ty'n-y-Fawnog's the old wife. Salem. T. Rowland Hughes. BBMWP, *tr. by* Sally Roberts Jones

Siberia. James Clarence Mangan. NPeEn

Siberian Wooing. Yevgeny Aleksandrovich Yevtushenko. VCWP, *tr. by* Albert C. Todd *and* James Ragan

Sibling Rivalry. Kenward Elmslie. BAP-04

Sibyl. Robert Adamson. BMAP

Sibyl, The. Agnes Mary Frances Robinson. VWP

Sic counseils ye gave to me, O. (LL) *Unknown. See* Such counsels ye gave to me, O!

Sic transit gloria mundi. Skip Fox. AnSo

Sic transit ("Kingfisher in highest cypress green.") Skip Fox. AnSo

Sic transit ("Neither does the world answer but.") Skip Fox. AnSo

Sic transit ("Thus does the sun.") Skip Fox. AnSo

Sic Transit ("We who were alive, held you in arms, welcomed you to table, to.") Skip Fox. AnSo

Sic Vita. Henry King, Bishop of Chichester. BASC; NOSC

Sic Vita. Henry David Thoreau. *See* I Am a Parcel of Vain Strivings Tied.

Siccine separat amara mors? Knowledge after Death. Henry Charles Beeching. SacPr

Sich a Nice Man Too! Albert Chevalier.
"There's parties ad yer meets about." _ UV

Sicilian Cyclamens. D. H. Lawrence. NAMCP V.1; NoAM

Sicilian Muses, sing we greater things. Virgil. OBVE *Fr.* Eclogues.

Sick. Shel Silverstein. ChAP

Sick. Anne Waldman. AHA

Sick and feverish. Ryunosuke Akutagawa. CAoMJL1, *tr. by* Makoto Ueda

Sick and Old, Same as Ever: A Poem to Figure It All Out. Po Chü-i. NDACCP, *tr. by* David Hinton

Sick and scrawny lies the land, denuded. Appalachian Landscape. John Beecher. InGu

Sick Child, A. Randall Jarrell. NoP-4; OxBoAm

Sick Cicada, A. Chia Tao. NDACCP, *tr. by* David Hinton

Sick Horse. Tu Fu [*or* Du Fu.] CrYelRi, *tr. by* Sam Hamill

Sick Image of My Father Fades, The. John Horder. RaBo

Sick, lost traveler, wandering in the mists of night, A. Sonnet 103. Luis de Góngora y Argote. BLPSL, *tr. by* Rene de Costa, Rigas Kappatos and Eleni Paidoussi

Sick Love. Robert Graves. HarvBoo; NPeEn; OxAEP-2

Sick Man, The. E. du Perron. TuT, *tr. by* Pat Boran

Sick man passing. Buson. EH, *tr. by* Robert Hass

Sick man's lamp guides death, The. Sweater, The. Ivan Radoev. CSCBP, *tr. by* Georgi Belev and Lisa Sapinkopf

Sick Men Sleeping. Kenneth Mackenzie. BMAP

Sick of all his women. Gambit. Tony Curtis. AngWePo

Sick of the mask he slips into every morning. Revolt in the Mirror, A. Wolfgang Bächler. GTCP; PML, *tr. by* Reinhold Grimm

Sick on a journey. Basho. EH, *tr. by* Robert Hass

Sick on a journey. Basho. EMJL, *tr. by* Haruo Shirane

Sick on a journey / Over parched fields. Basho. ZenPo, *tr. by* Takashi Ikemoto and Lucien Stryk

Sick on my journey. Basho. SoOfWa, *tr. by* Sam Hamill

Sick Queen, The. Frances Darwin Cornford. MoWP

Sick Rose, The. William Blake. BrAP; CABP; ClHu; HeIP-4; NAEL-6v2; NAEL-7v2; NAWM-7v2; NIL-7; NIP-4; NOBRP; NoP-4; NoP-5; NPBRoP; NPeEn; OPOU; OxAEP-2; OxBEV; PoPoPo; SoSe-8; TFi; TRP; WaAnP; WeW-3 *Fr.* Songs of Experience.

Sick Woman. John Kinsella. BMAP

Sickens my gut, Yellow Bittern. Yellow Bittern, The. Tom MacIntyre. PBCIP

Sickly. Basho. EH, *tr. by* Robert Hass

Sickly Face at the Bottom of the Ground. Hagiwara Sakutaro. CAoMJL1, *tr. by* Hiroaki Sato

Sickly wolfberry shrub, A. Eve's Monologue. Bella Abramovna Dizhur. ItGoST, *tr. by* Sarah Bliumis

Sickness hangs on a nail. Back Road. Nzadi Z. Keita. BtF

Sickness & the Magnet, The. Christine Hume. IAoNAP

Sick-Room, The. Maria White Lowell. NAAPv.1

Sidanen. Ludovic Lloyd.
"Flee, stately Juno, Samos fro." AngWePo

Side 4. Víctor Hernández Cruz. PueRic

Side 12. Víctor Hernández Cruz. PueRic

Side 18. Víctor Hernández Cruz. PueRic

Side 20. Víctor Hernández Cruz. PueRic

Side 21. Víctor Hernández Cruz. PueRic

Side 22. Víctor Hernández Cruz. PueRic

Side 26. Víctor Hernández Cruz. PueRic

Side 32. Víctor Hernández Cruz. PueRic

Side by side. Larry Eigner. BAP-04

Side by side. September City. Gerald Hausman. UrbNat

Side by Side. Harry Woods. ReLy

Side by side after the meal. Valerio Magrelli. NeIt

Side by side, all morning. Common Ground. Michael Murphy. NIrP

Side by side, their faces blurred. Arundel Tomb, An. Philip Larkin. BeAl; BrAP; ItP; NAMCP V.2; NoP-4; NoP-5; OxAEP-2; WaAnP

Side by side we stood together. Ideological Tango. Radoi Ralin. CSCBP, *tr. by* Georgi Belev and Lisa Sapinkopf

Sidekicks. Ron Koertge. CalPo; P180

Side-room has sweated years and patience, rolls its one eye, The. Hospital Night. Francis Webb. BMAP

Sideshow. John Wilkinson. VaPo

Sidestepping definitions is a normal process which is permission. Rumor. Catherine Imbriglio. IAoNAP

Sidewalk cracks, gumspots, the water, the bits of refuse, The. Silence at Night, The. Edwin Denby. OxBoAm

Sidewalk of days was innocent, The. Trilogy of the Man in Black. Awwad Nasir. IrPoTo, *tr. by* Saadi A. Simawe and Daniel Weissbort

Sidewalk Racer Or, On the Skateboard, The. Lillian Morrison. NTCP

Sidewalks lined with stone cold faces. . .mysterious like the. Land of the Lost. Charles Porter. BtF

Sidewalks of New York, The.   James W. Blake.   TCAPo

Sidewalks ooze but are forgiven, The.   Serial Toxic Teen.   Matthew Wascovich.   BeDoSh

Sidney, Looking for her Mother.   Dolores Kendrick.   ISC

Siècles à venir.   Avenir.   Henri Michaux.   YaTCFP

Siege.   Edna St. Vincent Millay.   APT-1

Siege of Corinth, The.   Lord Byron.
   At the Siege of Corinth.   DiBP

Siege of Valencia, The.   Felicia Dorothea Hemans.
   (Dirge, A ("Calm on the bosom of thy God").)   WoRP
   Dirge.   OBEV
   Meeting of the Bards, The. Written for an Eisteddford, or Meeting of Welsh Bards, Held in London, 22 May 1822.   RWP

¡Siémbrate!   Miguel de Unamuno.   RaW Fr. En Casa Ya.

Siempre Abiertos Tus Ojos.   Gerardo Diego.   RaW

Siempre la frente vendada.   Na Victórica litru.   Natalia Toledo.   RMCMP

Siempre que algo se muere.   Malva Flores.   RMCMP Fr. Turbia dicción.

Siempre será mi amigo no aquel que en primavera.   Siempre Será Mi Amigo.   Claudio Rodríguez.   RaW

Siena.   Lily Thicknesse.   LW

Siena Mi Fe'; Disfecemi Maremma.   Ezra Pound.   MoAmPo; NAAPv.2 Fr. Hugh Selwyn Mauberley (Life and Contacts).

Siento en los brazos cruzados las cortas.   Metro Taxqueña.   Carla Faesler Bremer.   SPV

Siento que el barco mío.   Mares.   Juan Ramón Jiménez.   RaW

Sierra Bear.   David Bottoms.   GifTon

Sierra Cup.   Reg Saner.   PoCoUp

Sierra Kid.   Philip Levine.   GeoHom

Sierra Noon.   C. G. Hanzlicek.   GeoHom

Sierra Walk.   Carolyne Wright.   RoV

Sierras.   Joaquin Miller.   APN-2

Siesta.   Julio Herrera y Reissig.   SonAtl, tr. by Carole Gibson and Lisa Martin

Siesta.   Carmen Horst.   ACAMVP

Siesta.   Antonio Machado Ruiz.   SpanPo, tr. by Kate Flores

Siesta.   Leslie Anne McIlroy.   AmPoNex

Siesta.   Adelia Prado.   TCLAP, tr. by Marcia Kirinus

Siesta in Xbalba.   Allen Ginsberg.
   "So I dream nightly of an embarkation."   CLPP

Siesta of a Hungarian Snake.   Edwin Morgan.   HarvBoo

Sifting fronds of your hair, she talks "style."   Hairdressing.   Patricia Pogson.   NLP

Sigh, A.   Witter Bynner.   APT-1

Sigh, A.   Anne Finch, Countess of Winchilsea.   OxBEV

Sigh, The.   Nathalie Handal.   PoArWo

Sigh, for the petals whirl before the gust!   Selling Wilted Peonies.   Yu Xuanji.   CCL1, tr. by Genevieve Wimsatt

Sigh No More.   William Shakespeare. See Balthasar's Song.

Sigh no more, dealers, sigh no more.   Much Ado about Nothing in the City.   Unknown.   UV

Sigh no more, ladies [sigh no more].   William Shakespeare.   NoSic; UV Fr. Much Ado about Nothing.

Sigh not, Parthenia, that I'me doom'd to dye.   To My Most Honord Cosen, Mrs Somerset on the Unjust Censure Past Upon My Poore Marcelia.   Frances Boothby.   EMWP

Sigh, O thin sigh, through.   Unknown.   CATKP, tr. by Wen Hsia-min

Sigh of the Old Cattleman, The.   Jas. D. Thorn.   TiP2

Sigh with her bosom over me. (LL)   Kingfisher, The.   W. H. Davies.   AngWePo; OBEV; OBWVE

Sighing.   József Bajza.   IQMS, tr. by Watson Kirkconnell

Sighing, and sadly sitting by my Love.   Richard Barnfield.   CAGL; PBRV Fr. Cynthia, with Certain[e] Sonnets.

Sighing I see yon little troop at play.   Charlotte Smith.   RWP

Sighing, O greet you and mourn you, O meadow of burial, Mohács.   Károly Kisfaludy.   IQMS Fr. Mohács.

Sighle of the Lovespot.   Joseph Campbell.   IrLP

Sighs Are Air, and Go to the Air.   Gustavo Adolfo Bécquer.   SpanPo, tr. by Kate Flores

Sighs are my food, drink are my tears.   Sir Thomas Wyatt.   NoSic

Sight.   Pamela Alexander.   AmAlph

Sight.   Wilfrid Wilson Gibson.   MoBrPo

Sight.   Lyn Hejinian and Leslie Scalapino.
   "But I accept a greeting at a place I've never seen, leaning."   PfS
   "Pool of lagoon moving."   PfS
   "Shredding at the lower rim of disc of, The."   PfS
   "Thin silver disc moon shredded at the bottom edge is."   PfS
   "This conscious attempt to see is producing sensations of."   PfS
   "When our movement is due to that of the window."   PfS

Sight in Camp [in the Daybreak Gray and Dim], A.   Walt Whitman.   BLT; CBCWP; InoFa; NAAL-3; NAAL-5; NoAM; SAmP

Sight is my birthright.   Johann Wolfgang von Goethe.   PtR Fr. Faust.

Sight of my father and mother, The.   Wakayama Bokusui.   CAoMJL1, tr. by Donald Keene

Sight of the coffee was good for sore eyes, The.   Upon Receipt of a Pound of Coffee in 1863.   Mary E. Tucker.   CBWP-1

Sight seems colored by the hour.   On Being Disabled by Light at Dawn in the Wilderness.   G. E. Murray.   IllVoic

Sight Unseen.   Kingsley Amis.   NoAM

Sighting the Slave Ship.   Pauline Stainer.   NeBl

Sightseeing.   Rita Dove.   GT

Sightseers, The.   Paul Muldoon.   StAl

Sigil.   "H. D."
   "Are these ashes in my hand."   APT-1
   Moon in Your Hands, The.   APT-1; OxBoAm
   "Now let the cycle sweep us here and there."   APT-1

Sigmund Freud.   Howard Nemerov.   PoA 2002

Sign.   Linda Smukler.   WiU

Sign from Heaven, A.   Boris Hristov.   CSCBP, tr. by Georgi Belev and Lisa Sapinkopf

Sign Illuminated, A.   Roy Fisher.   EmeKit

Sign of the Bite, The.   Ronny Someck.   IrPoTo, tr. by Vivian Eden

Sign of the Times.   Remco Campert.   TuT, tr. by Desmond Egan

Sign of Your Father, The.   Annie Dillard.   UpMys

Sign Under Test.   Charles Bernstein.   BAP-04

Sign Whereby He Knew, The.   Robert Penn Warren.   NAAPv.2 Fr. Audubon: A Vision.

Signal Gun, The.   Mary E. Tucker.   CBWP-1

Signal Hill.   Randall Maggs.   Coast

Signalmen, The.   Philip Stephens.   AmPoNex

Signals.   Yvonne Cullen.   NIrP

Signals.   Kerry Hardie.   NIrP

Signals and Demarcations.   Quincy Troupe.   PrTe

Signature of All Things, The.   Kenneth Rexroth.   APSN; APT-2; OxBoAm; TRP

Signatures.   Tomas Tranströmer.   WoBe, tr. by Robin Fulton

Signed with a flourish, like the dead wife's jeans. (LL)   James Merrill.   BeAl; NIP-4 Fr. Topics.

Signet ring of Heaven, The. (LL)   Death of an Infant.   Lydia Huntley Sigourney.   SWaP; TCAPo

Significance of a Water Animal, The.   Ray A. Young Bear.   HATNAP

Signify the strength of the waves' lash. (LL)   Lear.   William Carlos Williams.   NAAL-5; PoA 2002

Signior Dildo.   John Wilmot, 2d Earl of Rochester.   BASC

Signs.   Ahmad al-Mushari Al-'Udwani.   tr. by Charles Doria and Hilary Kilpatrick
   "Mysterious things within you, The."   BBASP, tr. by Charles Doria and Hilary Kilpatrick
   "You I give no name to / The mysterious things within you / are an untrodden bower."   BBASP, tr. by Charles Doria and Hilary Kilpatrick
   "You I give no name to / The mysterious things within you / are fragrance, light and melody."   BBASP, tr. by Charles Doria and Hilary Kilpatrick

Signs.   Silvia Grénier.   SurWo, tr. by Myrna Bell Rochester

Signs.   Wendy Mnookin.   UrbNat

Signs.   Mariana Romo-Carmona.   WiU

Signs.   Gjertrud Schnackenberg.   PoA 2002; StAl; VCAP

Signs of an Organised Hand.   Paul Grattan.   NIrP

Signs of Life.   Vera Pavlova. tr. by Jason Schneiderman
   Juice.   CRWP, tr. by Jason Schneiderman
   Mother.   CRWP, tr. by Jason Schneiderman

Signs of Spring.   Sir Thomas Browne.   NOSC

Signs of the Times.   Paul Laurence Dunbar.   APN-2

Signs of the Zodiac are fading, The.   Nikolai Alekseievich Zabolotsky.   WoPoe, tr. by Daniel Weissbort

Signs on 42nd Street.   Flash.   Lee Bennett Hopkins.   SSCS

Signs on the Table, The.   Amanda Berenguer.   TANSG, tr. by Louise B. Popkin

Sigurd of yore.   Unknown. Fr. Elder Edda, The.

Sila.   Robert Penn Warren.   NoP-4

Sile Na gCioch.   Pat Parnell.   HW

Silence.   Claribel Alegría.   TANSG, tr. by Darwin Flakoll

Silence.   Eugenio de Andrade.   VCWP, tr. by Alexis Levitin

Silence.   Stefan Brecht.   CLPP

Silence.   Bella Abramovna Dizhur.   ItGoST, tr. by Sarah Bliumis

Silence. Marina Dolia. *tr. by* Daniel Weissbort

2. CRWP, *tr. by* Daniel Weissbort

4. CRWP, *tr. by* Daniel Weissbort

Silence. Miroslav Holub. PoSu, *tr. by* Ian Milner and Jarmila Milner

Silence. Thomas Hood. GSo; OBEV; OxBSo

Silence. Slavko Janevski. WoPoe, *tr. by* Charles Simic

Silence. Tymoteusz Karpowicz. PoSu, *tr. by* Jan Darowski

Silence. Asymmetry 205. Jackson Mac Low. PFTM-2

Silence. Edgar Lee Masters. MoAmPo

Silence. Marianne Moore. APT-1; HarvBoo; NAAPv.2; NALW; OxBoAm; PtR; TRP; WoPoe

Silence. Edgar Allan Poe. *See* Sonnet—Silence.

Silence. James Whitcomb Riley. GSo

Silence. Walter James Turner. MoBrPo

Silence. William Carlos Williams. SAmP

Silence: "In the afternoon hours of autumn heading home." Marin Georgiev. CSCBP, *tr. by* Georgi Belev and Lisa Sapinkopf

Silence: "No one's here I'm alone with the violin of silence." Carlos Edmundo de Ory. PML, *tr. by* Steven J. Stewart

Silence: "This is addressed to you—A century later." Vitalina Tkhorzhevskaya. CRWP, *tr. by* Daniel Weissbort

Silence, 2. Stefan Brecht. CLPP

Silence: 2. Sipho Sepamla. AF

Silence, A. Amy Clampitt. MoWP

Silence, The. Robert Mezey. TaR

Silence, The. Without. Gary Snyder. WhBo

Silence, The. Arthur Sze. WhBo

Silence: A Sonnet. Henry King, Bishop of Chichester. NOSC

Silence Afterwards, The. Rolf Jacobsen. WED, *tr. by* Robert Bly

Silence aimlessly. Silent Time. Hannie Rouweler. TuT, *tr. by* Aidan Sharkey

Silence and Solitude may hint. Uninscribed Monument on One of the Battlefields of the Wilderness, An. Herman Melville. CBCWP

Silence and solitude were vacancy? (LL) Mont Blanc. Percy Bysshe Shelley. BrAP; NAEL-6v2; NAEL-7v2; NIP-4; NOBRP; NoP-4; NoP-5; NPBRoP

Silence, and stealth of day[e]s! 'tis now. Silence and Stealth of Day[e]s! Henry Vaughan. NAEL-6v1; NAEL-7v1; NPeEn

Silence, and whirling worlds afar. Night. Paul Laurence Dunbar. InvLi

Silence Around an Ancient Stone. Rosario Castellanos. TANSG, *tr. by* Magda Bogin

Silence at Night, The. Edwin Denby. OxBoAm

Silence at the End of the World. Amber Coverdale Sumrall. AtGh

Silence between drops of rain, The. (LL) Why Must You Know? John Wheelwright. APT-2; OxBoAm

Silence / between the floorboards. Neighbor. Bahiyyih Maroon. SpirFl

Silence braided her fingers in my hair. Dumb. Hildegarde Flanner. APT-2

Silence brought by the dark night: Eryri's. Nightfall. Walter Davies. OBWVE; WoPoe, *tr. by* Anthony Conran

Silence, cooked like gold, in. Alchemical. Paul Celan. VCWP, *tr. by* Michael Hamburger

Silence I identify with silence. Silences. Alejandra Pizarnik. BLPSL, *tr. by* Rene de Costa, Rigas Kappatos and Eleni Paidoussi

Silence I speak of, the. Silence: 2. Sipho Sepamla. AF

Silence in the middle of traffic. Philip Whalen. Eno *Fr.* Canoeing Up Cabarga Creek.

Silence is a roar. Michael McClure. WANABP *Fr.* Touching the Edge: Dharma Devotions.

Silence is a task that will last all her life. It continues. Gloria Gervitz. MirDau *Fr.* Yiskor.

Silence is sucking the earth dry. Silence. Tymoteusz Karpowicz. PoSu, *tr. by* Jan Darowski

Silence. Noon. The tower of sun, its rapt, circled crowd. Indian Rope Trick. Geoffrey Holloway. NLP

Silence Now, The. May Sarton. FiBr

Silence, now the bells are still. Sunday. J. C. Bloem. TuT, *tr. by* Desmond Egan

Silence of Eyes, A. Fabio Fiallo. SonAtl, *tr. by* Eleanor Davidson

Silence of it takes my breath, The. Orbit. Mark Van Doren. OxBoAm

Silence of knife, The. Morning reflections over the miso soup. Alan Chong Lau. WhBo

Silence of love that cannot sing again. (LL) Christina Georgina Rossetti. GSo; OxBSo *Fr.* Monna Innominata.

Silence of the desert is too strong for the walls of the ranch house, The. Diana Hartog. NLPA *Fr.* Oasis.

Silence of the ether, The. Morning Radio. Derek Mahon. RWPCtW

Silence of the night, a sad, nocturnal. Nocturne. Rubén Darío. TCLAP, *tr. by* Lysander Kemp

Silence of the Stars, The. David Wagoner. PoDa

Silence of the suburb, The. Suburbia. David Ignatow. PoCoUp

Silence of Women, The. Liz Rosenberg. NIL-7

Silence silence silence. [Untitled Concrete Poem]. Eugen Gomringer. GTCP, *tr. by* Reinhold Grimm

Silence slipping around like death, A. Winter Twilight, A. Angelina Weld Grimké. MoW

SILENCE THE EYES! BECALM THE SENSES! Michael McClure. PFTM-2 *Fr.* Ghost Tantras.

Silence / turns the page. Fables of the Beginning and Remains of the Origin. Cecilia Vicuña. WANABP

Silence Wager Stories. Susan Howe. BodElec; FTOS; WoBe

Silence wells up at the mouth, A. Whapmagoostui. Charles Fishman. PoCoUp

Silence whistles in the open spaces. Summer Night. Nathan Alterman. FIT, *tr. by* Robert Friend

Silences. Alejandra Pizarnik. BLPSL, *tr. by* Rene de Costa, Rigas Kappatos and Eleni Paidoussi

Silences from the Spanish Civil War. Jane Duran.

Pyrenees, The. Prnts

Spanish Peasant Boy. Prnts

Silencio, Desnudo, El. Emilio Prados. RaW

Silent, The. Jones Very. NCAP

Silent, about-to-be-parted-from house. Invocation. Denise Levertov. PoA 2002

Silent and Alone. Li Yu [*or* Li Hou-Chu]. CCL1, *tr. by* Florence Ayscough *and* Amy Lowell and Amy Lowell

Silent and alone, I ascend the west tower. To the Tune "Meeting Happiness." Li Yü. WoPoe, *tr. by* Arthur Sze

Silent and alone, I ascended the West Cupola. Silent and Alone. Li Yu [*or* Li Hou-Chu]. CCL1, *tr. by* Florence Ayscough *and* Amy Lowell and Amy Lowell

Silent and alone, I ascended the West Cupola. Together We Know Happiness. *Unknown.* NAAPv.2, *tr. by* Florence Ayscough *and* Amy Lowell and Amy Lowell

Silent and small in your wet sleep. Winter's Tale, A. Wyatt Prunty. RA

Silent Angel, The. James Wright. BodElec

Silent as a nun Aleng Maria prays. Aleng Maria. Eugene Gloria. ReBoTo

Silent as Roses. Gillian Ferguson. NeBl

Silent at Her Window. Wang Ch'ang-ling. ColAnChi; CrYelRi, *tr. by* Sam Hamill

Silent, beyond silence listened for. (LL) Clearances. Seamus Heaney. EMP; NAMCP V.2; PBCIP; PNI

Silent, blue pavilion by the highway, A. Melancholy in the Women's Apartments. Jiang Zong. CCL1, *tr. by* John Frodsham

Silent companions of the lonely hour. To My Books. Caroline Elizabeth Norton. CenSon

Silent conquering army, A. Kirkyard. George Mackay Brown. NePenScot; NPeEn

Silent dinner. Night Sky. Bei Dao. WoBe, *tr. by* Iona Man-Cheong and Eliot Weinberger

Silent, draped in the garments of sacrifice. Adelaida Gertsyk. ARWW, *tr. by* Catriona Kelly

Silent Echo. Robert Burns. DiBP

Silent Generation, The. Louis Simpson. OxBoAm

Silent Globe. Debra Gregerman. AmPoNex

Silent hush, the rusted hinges, The. Who Will Live in Our Houses When We Die? Michael C. Blumenthal. NoAM

Silent in the moonlight, no beginning or end. Two Ramages for Old Masters. Robert Bly. BodElec

Silent is the house: all are laid asleep. Visionary, The. Emily Jane Brontë. NPeEn; OxBEV

Silent lines, The / Are set against each other in the pause. Marksman's Work, The. Nathaniel Southgate Shaler. PCW

Silent Lover, The. Sir Walter Ralegh. OBEV

Silent Night. Joseph Mohr. ChrPo, *tr. by* John Freeman Young

Silent night, holy night. Silent Night. Joseph Mohr. ChrPo, *tr. by* John Freeman Young

Silent Night! Holy Night! Joseph Mohr. SacPr, *tr. by* Jane Campbell

Silent Night, The. Mrs. Henry Linden. CBWP-4

19: Silent Noon. Dante Gabriel Rossetti. BrAP; GSo; NAEL-6v2; NAEL-7v2; NoP-4; NoP-5 *Fr.* House of Life, The.

Silent Nymph, with curious eye. Grongar Hill. John Dyer. CABP; NoP-4; OxAEP-1

Silent old man, The. Old Man of Few Words. Muso Soseki. EaWin, *tr. by* W. S. Merwin

Silent One, The. Ivor Gurney.

Silent One, The. HarvBoo; NAEL-6v2; NAEL-7v2; NAMCP V.1; NoP-4; NoP-5; NPeEn; OBWP; PoWW

Silent Piano, The. Louis Simpson. EmeKit

Silent Promise, A. Jay Emerson Johnson. RSR

Silent Room. Aaron Smith. PA9/11

Silent room—grey with a dusty blight, A. Edith Nesbit. PEW

Silent rounds of mice and roaches begin, The. (LL) Shopgirls leave their work, The. Charles Reznikoff. APT-2; NAAPv.2; NAMCP V.1

Silent Slain, The. Archibald MacLeish. *See* Too-Late Born, The.

Silent, speechless God; the dead, uninterfering God, The. Our Godless Days. Alan Llwyd. BBMWP, *tr. by* Joseph P. Clancy

Silent Steed, The. Paul Pastnor. ArBi

Silent the girl at the spindle. Spinner, The. Nathan Alterman. FIT, *tr. by* Robert Friend

Silent, the Savoy. Harlem Suite. Raymond R. Patterson. FuFl

Silent Time. Hannie Rouweler. TuT, *tr. by* Aidan Sharkey

Silent, upon a peak in Darien. (LL) On First Looking into Chapman's Homer. John Keats. BrAP; BRP; CABP; CenSon; ClHu; CtM; GSo; HeIP-4; NAEL-6v2; NAEL-7v2; NAWM-7v2; NIL-7; NIP-4; NOBRP; NoP-4; NoP-5; NPBRoP; NPeEn; OBEV; OPOU; OxAEP-2; OxBEV; OxBSo; PoPoPo; SoSe-8; TFi; TRP; UV; WaAnP; WoPoe

Silent Woman to the University of Oxford, The. John Dryden. "What Greece, when learning flourished, only knew." NOSC

Silent World Is Our Only Homeland, The. Francis Ponge. AF, *tr. by* Beth Archer

Silentium. Fyodor Ivanovich Tyutchev. WoPoe, *tr. by* Charles Tomlinson

Silentium Amoris. Oscar Wilde. IrLP

Silently and very fast. (LL) Fall of Rome, The. W. H. Auden. NPeEn; OxBEV

Silently, dawn and dusk. Man Reading Homer, A. Nishiwaki Junzaburo. CAoMJL1, *tr. by* Hosea Hirata

Silently I ascend the western pavilion. Li Yü. NDACCP, *tr. by* William Carlos Williams

Silently keeping the secret of your birth. (LL) Planting a Sequoia. Dana Gioia. CalPo; GeoHom

Silently my wife walks on the still wet furze. Berry Picking. Irving Layton. HeIP-4; NIP-4; NoP-4; NoP-5

Silently / she was quieter than breathing now. Juliet's Garden. Charles Tomlinson. OBGa

Silently you stand before me. David Vogel. FIT, *tr. by* Robert Friend

Silesian Weavers, The. Heinrich Heine. NAWM-7v2, *tr. by* Hal Draper

Silet. Ezra Pound. MoAmPo *Fr.* Ripostes of Ezra Pound.

Silhouette. Langston Hughes. NAAL-5; NAMCP V.1 *Fr.* Three Songs about Lynching.

Silhouette, A. Basho. EMJL *Fr.* Mad Verse.

Silk Cotton Tree. *Unknown.* SonAtl, *tr. by* Cheryl Borde and Emma Gonzalez

Silk Light of Advent, The. Gillian Allnutt. NeBrP

Silk of a Soul. Zbigniew Herbert. BeAl, *tr. by* Peter Dale Scott

Silk Robe. Jeffrey Skinner. PBCAP

Silken Snake, The. Robert Herrick. PBRV

Silken Tent, The. Robert Frost. APT-1; BrAP; ColAP; NAMCP V.1; NoP-4; NoP-5; OxBSo; TRP; WaAnP; WeW-3

Silken threads by viewless spinner spun, The. Crossed Threads. Helen Hunt Jackson. APN-2

Silk-spread Blackbird. *Unknown.* SonAtl, *tr. by* Jenny Boarder and Evan Watson

Silk-spread, tawn-beak. Silk-spread Blackbird. *Unknown.* SonAtl, *tr. by* Jenny Boarder and Evan Watson

Silkworm Song of Torchlit Fields. Kao Ch'i. ColAnChi, *tr. by* Jonathan Chaves

Silkworms enter cocoons: harvest time. At the Temple of Kuan Yin in the Rain. Su Tung-p'o. CrYelRi, *tr. by* Sam Hamill

Siller Croun, The. Susanna Blamire. LW; NPBRoP

Silly Boy. *Unknown.* NOSC

Silly boy, wert you but wise. Silly Boy. *Unknown.* NOSC

Silly Fool, The. W. H. Auden. OBMV

Silly Ghost. Natalia Toledo. RMCMP, *tr. by* Alberto A. Ríos

Silly Song, A. Hwansung Jian. BecRai, *tr. by* Kim Daljin, Kim Won-Chung and Christopher Merrill

Silly Spring. Marcelijus Martinaitis. TWW, *tr. by* Laima Sruoginis

Silly widow and her daughters two, The. Geoffrey Chaucer. DiBP *Fr.* Canterbury Tales, The.

Silo Treading. Bruce Beaver. BMAP

Silhouette of a woman appears in my mind as if from a sixteen millimeter film, The. Thoughts about Sari's Jump. Devorah Amir. DTA, *tr. by* Miriyam Glazer

Silva smoak of pine. Wooden Dog. Christopher Middleton. OnScMo

Silver. A. R. Ammons. NoP-4

Silver. Jill Bialosky. PoDa

Silver [*with music*]. Walter De la Mare. MoBrPo

Silver and slick as velvet. Tools. Thomas Rain Crowe. AmZen

Silver answer rang,—"Not Death, but Love", The. (LL) Elizabeth Barrett Browning. CenSon; NoP-4; NoP-5; OBEV; OxAEP-2; PoPoPo *Fr.* Sonnets from the Portuguese.

Silver as / The needle's eye. George Oppen. FTOS *Fr.* Some San Francisco Poems.

Silver bark of beech, and sallow. Counting-out Rhyme. Edna St. Vincent Millay. NOxBChV; SoSe-8

Silver birch is a dainty lady, The. Child's Song in Spring. Edith Nesbit. NOxBChV

Silver chariots, and copper. Seascape. Arthur Rimbaud. SxFrPo, *tr. by* Martin Sorrell

Silver chatter in parks. Silver Talk. Remco Campert. TuT, *tr. by* Theo Dorgan

Silver Clasps. Paul Dermée. CuPo

Silver Creature. Maxwell Boyle. ArBi

Silver dust. Pear Tree. "H. D." ColAP; MoAmPo; PtR; TCAPo

Silver flash from the sinking sun, A. James Weldon Johnson. APT-1; NAMCP V.1 *Fr.* Down by the Carib Sea.

Silver Flask, The ("Sweet, though short, our.") John Montague. PNI *Fr.* Dead Kingdom, The.

Silver half freezing in day. Leslie Scalapino. ASA; WANABP *Fr.* It's Go In / Quiet Illumined Grass / Land.

Silver herring throbbed thick in my seine, The. Kenneth Leslie. IFF; OxBSo *Fr.* By Stubborn Stars.

Silver, into which I force. Paavo Haavikko. PFTM-2 *Fr.* Winter Palace, The.

Silver is the ruby's faded glare. Eye Reflecting the Gold of Fall. Charles North. NYP2

Silver Jubilee. Llewelyn Wyn Griffith. OBWVE

Silver Lucifer, A. Lunar Baedeker. Mina Loy. APT-1; OxBoAm

SILVER OCELOT. Michael McClure. WANABP *Fr.* Haiku Rows.

Silver Penny, The. Walter De la Mare. NOxBChV; OBMV

Silver Platter, The. Nathan Alterman. NRoS, *tr. by* Esther Raizen

Silver Poplar at Sunrise. Constance Egemo. PoCoUp

Silver. Possessed. (LL) I rose from marsh mud. Lorine Niedecker. APT-2; FTOS

Silver rubs rocks and furs the twig. Bounding Line. Genevieve Taggard. APT-2

Silver Sands, The. Richard Blanco. AmPoNex; NAPBL

Silver scales and jade scales. Yun Söndo. CATKP *Fr.* Angler's Calendar, The.

Silver Star. William Stafford. TWF

Silver Swan, The. Orlando Gibbons. HeIP-4; NAEL-6v1; NoP-4; NoP-5; OPOU; OWoS; WaAnP

(Silver Swan[ne], Who Living Had No Note, The.) WoPoe

Silver Swan, The. Kenneth Rexroth. Void Only. WhBo

Silver swan, who living had no note, The. Silver Swan, The. Orlando Gibbons. HeIP-4; NAEL-6v1; NoP-4; NoP-5; OPOU; OWoS; WaAnP

Silver Talk. Remco Campert. TuT, *tr. by* Theo Dorgan

Silver Tassie, The. Robert Burns. OBEV; WoPoe

(Soldier's Farewell, A.) FaBoWar

Silver trumpets rang across the Dome, The. Easter Day. Oscar Wilde. OxAEP-2

Silverfish. Robert Siegel. PfSP

Silver-footed girl was bathing, letting the water, The. Rufinus. HePo, *tr. by* Barbara Hughes Fowler

Silverhaired guard at the museum of fine arts, The. "Moscow" Pool. Pyotr Vegin. TCRusP, *tr. by* Daniel Weissbort

Silver-Paced. Bruce Berger. UrbNat

Silver-scaled Dragon with jaws flaming red, A. Toaster, The. William Jay Smith. NOxBChV

Silver-vested monkey trips, A. Cortège. Paul Verlaine. OBVE, *tr. by* Arthur Symons

Silvery Fountain [*with music*]. Mary E. Tucker. CBWP-1

Silvery red shirt is half covered with dust, The. *Unknown.* NAAPv.2

Silvery tells no sphere to go and. Mac Wellman. HeMarv *Fr.* Rat Minaret: Miniaturist-Divan, The.

Silvia. William Shakespeare. *See* Who Is Silvia [*or* Sylvia]?

Silvio's Complaint: A Song, to a Fine Scotch Tune. Aphra Behn. EMWP; RACG

Simcox. John Heath-Stubbs. OBCoV

Simcox was one of several rather uninteresting. Simcox. John Heath-Stubbs. OBCoV

Similarities try me. Seeing things. Anti-Preening Poem. Anselm Berrigan. Eno

Simile. Ágnes Nemes Nagy. PoSu, *tr. by* Frederic Will

Simile: "As when a heavy bomber in the cloud." William Meredith. PWW2

(Homeric Simile.) OtW

Similes. Charles Reznikoff. APT-2; OxBoAm

Similie. Charlotte Dacre. NOBRP

Simmers on the kitchen stove. Pot of Red Lentils, A. Peter Pereira. IPoFL

Simon Lee [Original Version]. William Wordsworth. Old Huntsman, The. STuOW

Simon Lee, the Old Huntsman; with an incident in which he was concerned. William Wordsworth. NAEL-6v2; NAEL-7v2

Simon the Cyrenian Speaks. Countee Cullen. ChIV-2; MoAmPo; OxAAAP

Simone, laying her life in Perrin's hands, has yet. Intact. Stephanie Strickland. ExTi

Simone Signoret, Beldam. Richard Murray Vaughan. Coast

Simone Weil: In Assisi. Edward Hirsch. BBASP

Simple [(For Langston Hughes)]. Naomi Long Madgett. GT

Simple ain't it? Genius Child. Kevin Powell. AmPoNex

Simple Autumnal. Louise Bogan. MoAmPo

—Simple child, A. Solstice for John. John Cope. GeoH

Simple child, dear brother Jim, A. We Are Seven. William Wordsworth. NAEL-6v2; NAEL-7v2; NOBRP; NPBRoP

Simple contact with a wooden spoon and the word, The. Words. Barbara Guest. AWPTFC; FTOS; OxBoAm

Simple flush of a toilet, The. Science of Forgetting, The. Brother Yao. BtF

Simple Gifts. Unknown. APN-2

Simple legs in silk. (LL) She lies, hip high. George Oppen. APT-2; PFTM-1

Simple Life, The. Philip Whalen. WANABP

Simple Like That. Wil'um Lee. InTrad

Simple lust is all my woe, A. Dennis Brutus. HBAPE

Simple Machines. Marianne Boruch. AmAlph

Simple nosegay! was that much to ask?, A. Troll's Nosegay, The. Robert Graves. OxBSo

Simple Outlines, Human Shapes. Irving Feldman. VCAP Fr. All of Us Here.

Simple outlines, human shapes, daily acts, plain poses. Irving Feldman. VCAP Fr. All of Us Here.

Simple Purification, The. Kabir. WoPoe, tr. by Robert Bly

Simple sentences. Helmut Heissenbüttel. GTCP, tr. by Reinhold Grimm

Simple Story, A [with music]. Gwen Harwood. BeAl; NOBAu

Simple Truth, The. Philip Levine. BeAl; CAP-8; NoP-4; NoP-5

Simple Truths. William Heyen. CAP-8

Simple Verses. José Martí. tr. by Elinore Randall and Seymour Resnick

   1. NAAPv.1

   5. NAAPv.1

   "I am an honest man." TCLAP, tr. by Elinore Randall

   "I know: from flesh." TCLAP, tr. by Elinore Randall

   "In the shadow of a wing." TCLAP, tr. by Elinore Randall

   "Lonely trembling soul can ache, The." TCLAP, tr. by Elinore Randall

Simplest and the Hardest, The. Margaret Lloyd. OPRER

Simplest / Words say the grass blade, The. Occurrences, The. George Oppen. APT-2

Simpleton, he squeezed the vastness, A. Bruckner. Rayne Mackinnon. EdScPo

Simplex Munditiis. Ben Jonson. See Sweet Neglect, The.

Simplicity. Sandra M. Gilbert. WaAnP

Simplicity. Henri Michaux. PML, tr. by Richard Ellmann

Simplicity and spotless innocence. (LL) John Milton. NOSC; WaAnP Fr. Paradise Lost.

Simplicity and Sweet Neglect. Ben Jonson. See Sweet Neglect, The.

Simplicity so graven hurts the sense. So Graven. Josephine Miles. NoAM

Simplify Me When I'm Dead. Keith Douglas. EdScPo; FaBoWar; NAMCP V.1; NoAM

Simplify Your Combination Therapy. Mark Wunderlich. NAPBL

Simplon Pass, The. William Wordsworth. CABP Fr. Prelude, The; Growth of a Poet's Mind [1805 version].

Simplon Pass, The. William Wordsworth. NPeEn

Simply by sailing in a new direction. Landfall in Unknown Seas. Allen Curnow. NoP-4; NoP-5

Simply I would sing for the time being. Interlude. Keidrych Rhys. AngWePo

Simply sit still, if you must, and breathe. I Still Can't Say the Word. Walter McDonald. LiTh

Simply that you've placed one gem in each puckered. Earliest Crows in Mineral. Jennifer Timoner. ICANM

Si-mu: Request for Furlough. Unknown. CCL1, tr. by Ezra Pound

Simultaneously. David Ignatow. AtGh

Simultaneously, as soundlessly. W. H. Auden. NAMCP V.1 Fr. Horae Canonicae.

Simultaneously, five thousand miles apart. Simultaneously. David Ignatow. AtGh

Sin. "Angelus Silesius." GePo Fr. Cherubical Wanderer, The.

Sin. David Gwenallt Jones. BBMWP, tr. by Joseph P. Clancy

Sin. Ben Scammell. NLP

Sin. Percy Bysshe Shelley. NPBRoP Fr. Peter Bell the Third.

Sin: "Tree bore the efflorescence of October apples, The." Carol Frost. PoDa

Sin (1). George Herbert. NoP-4; NoP-5; OxAEP-1; WaAnP

Sin, 1969. Afaa Michael Weaver. BtF

Sin and Death. John Milton. OBNV Fr. Paradise Lost.

Sin and Despair Have So Possess'd My Heart. Anne Vaughan Locke. CABP

Sin, Despair, and Lucifer. Phineas Fletcher. NOSC Fr. Locusts, or Appolyonists, The.

Sin duda está muy bien la revolución armada de las encías. Hostilidad. Gerardo Diego. RaW

Sin luces, ya nocturna toda, bárbara. Anulación de lo Peor. Jorge Guillén. RaW

Sin of Omission, The. Margaret Elizabeth Munson Sangster. ITBLP

Sin[ne] of self[e]-love possesseth all mine eye [or eie]. William Shakespeare. OxAEP-1 Fr. Sonnets.

Sin' they nailed him to the tree. (LL) Ballad of the Goodly Fere. Ezra Pound. ChIV-2; MoAmPo

Since 1619. Margaret Abigail Walker. NoP-4; NoP-5

Since Akkad, Since Elam, Since Sumer. Aimé Césaire. WoPoe, tr. by Gregson Davis

Since all that beat about in Nature's range. Constancy to an Ideal Object. Samuel Taylor Coleridge. NAEL-6v2; NOBRP

Since as in night's deck-watch ye show. John Marr. Herman Melville. APN-2

Since autumn attached itself to the humid streets of this city. Return 2. Tamara Kamenszain. MirDau, tr. by Roberta Gordenstein

Since before anyone remembers. Old Creek. Muso Soseki. EaWin, tr. by W. S. Merwin

Since Bonny-Boots Was Dead. Unknown. NPeEn

Since brass, nor stone, nor earth, nor boundless sea. William Shakespeare. AEP; NAEL-6v1; NAEL-7v1; NoP-5; NoSic; OxAEP-1; OxBSo; RaBo; TFi; TreFP Fr. Sonnets.

Since Cassius first did whet me against Cæsar. William Shakespeare. OxAEP-1 Fr. Julius Caesar.

Since certainly it is mine. (LL) Lilacs. Amy Lowell. APT-1; MoAmPo

Since coming to Tongsung Hermitage. Mountain Life. Pyungyang Ungee. BecRai, tr. by Kim Daljin, Kim Won-Chung and Christopher Merrill

Since, Coridon, you have a hart can pay. To a Gentleman that Courted Several Ladys. Poets of the Tixall Circle. EMWP

Since every quill is silent to relate. Monumental Memorial of Marine Mercy, A. Richard Steere. TCAPo

Since feeling is first. E. E. Cummings. GoPo; MoAmPo; NoP-4; NoP-5; WaAnP

Since first break of dawn the fiend. John Milton. NOSC Fr. Paradise Lost.

Since First I Saw Your Face. Unknown. OBEV

Since first my little one lay on my breast. Augusta Davies Webster. ViWPN; VWP Fr. Mother and Daughter.

Since first we met. Encounter. Mary Low. SurWo

Since he kissed them and put them there. (LL) Little Boy Blue. Eugene Field. BRP; ChAP; ITBLP; SoSe-8

Since he was the priest. Death of Anselmo Luna, The. Alberto A. Ríos. NAMCP V.2

Since his later history is so obscure, it's no wonder he is most remembered first bold steps. Matériel. Don McKay. NLPA

Since I abandoned and tied my soul to your sweet appearance and manners oh Sir, guide and light of my life, will I ever see you before I die? Cecco Nuccoli. CAGL, tr. by Jill Claretta Robbins

Since I am a man in love with the setting stars. (LL) Night Abraham Called to the Stars, The. Robert Bly. OxBoAm; PoCho

Since I am coming [or comming] to that holy room[e]. Hymn[e] to God My God, In My Sickness[e], A. John Donne. BASC; HeIP-4; NAEL-6v1; NAEL-7v1; NoP-4; NoP-5; NOSC; OxAEP-1; PBRV; SoSe-8; TFi

Since I am here at the river's side. Beside the Evening River. Ko Ŭn. CAMKP, tr. by Anthony, Brother of Taizé

Since I am the bookish, just like you, abuelita. Memoranda for Rosario. Maria Elena Caballero-Robb. ReBoTo

Since I do not hope to return ever. Ballata II: Last Song: from Exile. Guido Cavalcanti. WoPoe, tr. by George Sutherland Fraser

Since I do trust Jehova still. Bible, O.T. OBVE

Since I don't wake with her. Thin, Black Band, A. Sandor Csoori. VCWP

Since I emerged that day from the labyrinth. Labyrinth, The. Edwin Muir. MoBrPo

Since I got my cat Five White. Offering for the Cat, An. Mei Yao Ch'en. ColAnChi, tr. by Burton Watson

Since I have lived in the desert all summer I've learned. Since I Have Lived. Beckian Fritz Goldberg. AmAlph

Since I left home to seek official state. Poem for Yuan Zhen. Po Chü-i. CCL1, tr. by Arthur Waley

Since I lived a stranger in the City of Hsün-yang. Rain. Po Chü-i. BLT, tr. by Arthur Waley

Since I must love your north. To My Mountain. Kathleen Jessie Raine. EdScPo

Since I noo mwore do zee your feäce. Wife a-Lost, The. William Barnes. OBEV

Since I prefer rivers to regrets. Seine in Paris, The. Jean Tardieu. YaTCFP, *tr. by* David Kelley

Since I reached the charming age of puberty. Where Is the Life That Late I Led? Cole Porter. ReLy

Since I was a kid they've been choking me. Zombies Arise. Alexander Akao. OGAHCP, *tr. by* Boadiba and Jack Hirschman

Since I Was Thrown Inside. Nazim Hikmet. AF

Since i wrote the night sky down i've been out for. Roy Kiyooka. NLPA *Fr.* Pear Tree Pomes.

Since I'm Island-born home's as precise. Island, The. Milton Acorn. Coast

Since in a land not barren still. Love and Discipline. Henry Vaughan. SacPr

Since, in the loop of time this will return. Love's Parallel. Elizabeth Garrett. MFPA

Since it must be so. New-Courtier, The. Alexander Brome. BASC

As it was the eve of the 14th of July. Guillaume Apollinaire. PFTM-1

Since it's spring and raining. Pigeon Makes His Request, The. Issa. WED, *tr. by* Robert Bly

Since I've been in this colony I've written many a song. Flash Colonial Barman, The. William W. Coxon. NOBAu

Since I've decided to revolutionize my life. Eating Chocolate Ice Cream: Reading Mayakovsky. Barbara Guest. AHA

Since last the tutelary hearth. Christmas Family Reunion. Peter De Vries. NBLV

Since last we met, thou and thy horse, my dear. Henry Vaughan. AngWePo *Fr.* Invitation to Brecknock, An.

Since laws were made for ev'ry [*or* every] degree. John Gay. NAEL-6v1; NoP-5 *Fr.* Beggar's Opera, The.

Since, Lord, to thee / A narrow way and little gate. Holy Baptism (2). George Herbert. ChIV-2

Since Love is shivering. Sor Juana Inés de la Cruz. WPoS *Fr.* First Villancico, Written for the Nativity of Our Lord, Puebla, 1689, The.

Since man has been articulate. Every Thing. Harold Monro. MoBrPo

Since man with that inconstancy was born. To Alexis in Answer to His Poem Against Fruition. Aphra Behn. LW

Since man's life is nothing but a bit of action at a distance. Piano Solo. Nicanor Parra. PoetW; TCLAP, *tr. by* William Carlos Williams

Since Maria left me to go into another star. Autumn Lament. Charles Baudelaire. MotU, *tr. by* Keith Bosley

Since *metaphor* derives from *transferring*. Welcome to Ithaca. Rebecca Seiferle. ExTi

Since moonrise last evening I'm here like a fool sitting up. Up All Night. Theo Dorgan. IrLP

Since morning glories. Chiyojo. SoOfWa, *tr. by* Sam Hamill

Since my wife was born. Notes for the Legend of Salad Woman. Michael Ondaatje. NoAM

Since Naturally Black is Naturally Beautiful. Naturally. Audre Lorde. ISC

Since nothing actually exists except You. Questions. Mirza Asadullah Khan Ghalib. WED, *tr. by* Robert Bly

Since, O ye powers, ye have bestowed on me. Jane Barker. BASC

Since observed by Yours faithfully, God. (LL) Reply, A. *Unknown.* NBLV; OxBEV

Since of no creature living the last breath. Edna St. Vincent Millay. HeIP-4

Since one anthologist put in his book. Anthologistics. Arthur Guiterman. NBLV

Since our Country, our God—Oh, my Sire! Jephtha's Daughter. Lord Byron. ChIV-1

Since Persia fell at Marathon. Villanelle of Change. Edwin Arlington Robinson. WaAnP

Since Potiphar made you his overseer. Israel II. Charles Reznikoff. ChIV-1

Since Reverend Doctors now declare. Respectable Burgher, The. Thomas Hardy. ChIV-2; NoAM

Since rheumatic fever and obesity destroyed. Nightmares Fit to Arouse Misgivings. Mohamed Lasheen. AnVo, *tr. by* Mohamed Enani

Since Rose is a classic taste possessed. Beau Ideal, The. Jessie Pope. FaBoWar

Since She Gives So Little Pay. Steinmar. GePo, *tr. by* J. W. Thomas

Since she was lovelier than any of you. (LL) Blue Girls. John Crowe Ransom. APT-1; BrAP; ColAP; MoAmPo; NoAM; NoP-4; NoP-5; WeW-3

Since she whom[e] I loved [*or* lov'd *or* lovd] hath paid [*or* payd] her last debt. John Donne. BASC; FSCP; NAEL-6v1; NAEL-7v1; NOSC; PBRV *Fr.* Holy Sonnets.

Since that day. Abortion. Iman Mirsal. NAfrP, *tr. by* Clarissa C. Burt

Since that first morning when I crawled. Hornworm: Autumn Lamentation. Stanley Kunitz. AmFaPo; BodElec; ItP

Since that this thing we call the world. Epicurean Ode, An. John Hall. NOSC; NPeEn

Since the Conquest none of us. Conquest, The. Oliver St. John Gogarty. OBMV

Since the day of internment. Sasabune. NAAPv.2

Since the first toss of gale that blew. Valentine Ackland and Sylvia Townsend Warner. PoBW

Since the red hat vanished from our sight. (LL) Red Hat, The. Rachel Hadas. OxBoAm; RA; WaAnP

Since the siege and the assault upon Troy were finished. *Unknown.* WaAnP *Fr.* Sir Gawain and the Green Knight [Merwin Translation].

Since the siege and the assault was ceased at Troy. *Unknown.* NAEL-6v1; NAEL-7v1; NAWM-7v1 *Fr.* Sir Gawain and the Green Knight [Marie Borroff Translation].

Since the / Spirit's omnipresent, there's a difference. John Cage. APSN *Fr.* Diary: How to Improve the World (You Will Only Make Matters Worse).

Since the thunderbolt of disaster set our. Na'ili [*or* Yeni-Zada Mustafa Efendi]. OLP, *tr. by* Walter Andrews, Najaat Black and Mehmet Kalpakli

Since their dream has / come true. (LL) Passing. Langston Hughes. APSN; APT-2; OxBoAm; SAmP

Since Then. Yehuda Amichai. NRoS, *tr. by* Esther Raizen

Since Then. Dennis Joseph Enright. OBSV

Since then I was. Significance of a Water Animal, The. Ray A. Young Bear. HATNAP

Since there are depths. Though. Composition. Hugh Seidman. BodElec

Since There's No Help . . . R. P. Blackmur. APT-2

Since There's No Help. Michael Drayton. CABP; PoPoPo

Since there's no help, come let us kiss and part. Michael Drayton. AEP; BASC; ClHu; GSo; HeIP-4; NAEL-6v1; NAEL-7v1; NoP-5; OPOU; OxBSo; SoSe-8; TFi; WaAnP *Fr.* Idea.

Since this is the circumstance of life. Standing Near the Ghats Along the Ganges. William Kistler. WhBo

Since this morning he's gone through. Firestarter. Dorianne Laux. RoV

Since those we love and those we hate. W. E. Henley. OBMV *Fr.* Hawthorn and Lavender.

Since thou fayre soule, art warblinge to a spheare. Elegie Written by the Lady A. S. to the Countesse of London Derrye Supposyenge Hir to be Dead by Hir Long Silence, An. Lady Anne Harris Southwell. EMWP

Since thou hast viewed [*or* view'd] some Gorgon, and art grown. Double Rock, The. Henry King, Bishop of Chichester. NOSC

Since Thursday last the bare living-room. Bicycle. David Malouf. ArBi; BMAP

Since Tyndareos. Stesichoros. SaLy, *tr. by* Diane Rayor

Since wailing is a bud of causeful sorrow. Sir Philip Sidney. MakPoe *Fr.* Countesse of Pembroke's Arcadia, The.

Since we agreed to let the road between us. No Road. Philip Larkin. MoBrPo; OxAEP-2

Since we are told it we believe it's true. Surprise. Anthony Cronin. IrLP

Since we must soon be fed. Philosophy. Elsa Gidlow. PoBW

Since we stood on the back porch. Roy Kiyooka. NLPA *Fr.* Pear Tree Pomes.

Since we through war awhile must part. At Parting. Anne Ridler. FaBoWar; LW

Since we're not young, weeks have to do time. Adrienne Rich. WaAnP *Fr.* Twenty-one Love Poems.

Since when. Vespers. Ōkuma Kotomichi. EMJL, *tr. by* Haruo Shirane

Since yes you [were] once a child. Sappho. SaLy, *tr. by* Diane Rayor

Since you all will have singing, and won't be said nay. King's Own Regulars, The [And Their Triumphs Over the Irregulars]. *Unknown.* NAAPv.1

Since you and i forsook the rites of marriage. Roy Kiyooka. NLPA *Fr.* Pear Tree Pomes.

Since you are this way and they are that. Dreams of the One, The. Lőrinc Szabó. IQMS, *tr. by* Edwin Morgan

Since you ask, most days I cannot remember. Wanting to Die. Anne Sexton. ColAP; EMP; IJHIL; NoAM; OxBoAm; TRP; VCAP; WaAnP

Since you, Charmenion, come from Corinth. Martial. RomPo, *tr. by* Dorothea Wender

Since you dare Brave me, with a Rivals Name. To My Rival. "Ephelia." LW

Since you died, I notice. Metamorphosis. Caroline Sprague Smith. StAl

Since you fail to ponder, scarcely. *Unknown.* PriapPR *Fr.* Priapus Poems, The.

Since you have turned unkind. To a Lady Friend. W. H. Davies. MoBrPo

Since you set sail for the state of Min. Thinking of Retired Scholar Wu on the River. Chia Tao. CSKM, *tr. by* Mike O'Connor

Since you walked out on me. Lady of Miracles. Nina Cassian. StAl, *tr. by* Laura Schiff

Since you went away, oh. Added to a Letter Sent to a Traveler. Pao Ling-hui. ColAnChi, *tr. by* Anne Birrell and Jeanne Larsen

Since you will needs my hart possesse. Confession, A. *Poets of the Tixall Circle.* EMWP

Sincere and most Peruvian mechanics. Telluric and Magnetic. César Vallejo. PFTM-1

Sincere man am I, A. José Martí. NAAPv.1 *Fr.* Simple Verses.

Sincerity. Ágnes Nemes Nagy. VCWP, *tr. by* Hugh Maxton

Sine qua non of bed wetting. Air and Angels. Charles North. FTOS

Sinfonia Domestica. Jean Starr Untermeyer. MoAmPo

Sinfonia Eroica. Amy Levy. ViWPN

Sing a last song. John Montague. PBCIP *Fr.* Dead Kingdom, The.

Sing a song of critics. Valentine. Ernest Hemingway. IllVoic

Sing a Song of People. Lois Lenski. NOxBChV

Sing a song of rugby. Vive Le Sport. Harri Webb. TCAWP

Sing a song of sad young men. Ballad of the Sad Young Men, The. Fran Landesman. ReLy

Sing a song of sixpence. Mother Goose. OxBEV

Sing a song of wargames a pocket full of grass. Four and Twenty Soldiers. S. P. Shephard. BtF

Sing, Ballad-singer, raise a hearty tune. At Casterbridge Fair. Thomas Hardy.

Sing, Brothers, Sing! William Robert Rodgers. MoBrPo

Sing cuccu [*or* cuckoo]! Sing cuccu [*or* cuckoo] nu [*or* now]! (LL) Sumer Is Icumen [*or* Ycomen] In. *Unknown.* HeIP-4; OPOU; OxBEV

(Ne swik thu naver nu [*or* thou never now]!) (LL) NAEL-6v1; NoP-4; NoP-5; OWoS; UV; WaAnP

Sing goddamm, sing goddamm, DAMM. (LL) Ancient Music. Ezra Pound. AmWit; HeIP-4; NBLV; OBCoV; TCAPo; UV

Sing Goddess of the centrality of America. Central America. Jackson Mac Low. Eno

Sing, great river. Paper 18. Dominique Batraville. OGAHCP, *tr. by* Boadiba and Jack Hirschman

Sing his praises that doth keep. John Fletcher. OBEV *Fr.* Faithful Shepherdess, The.

Sing in me, Muse, and through me tell the story. Odyssey, The. Homer. NAWM-5v1; NAWM-7v1, *tr. by* Robert Fitzgerald

Sing lowly, foot slowly, oh, why should we chase. Sydney Thompson Dobell. STuOW *Fr.* Roman, The.

Sing lullaby [*or* lullabie] as women do[e]. Lullaby [*or* Lullabie] of a Lover, The. George Gascoigne. NAEL-6v1; PtR

Sing Me a Song. Robert Louis Stevenson. CABP

Sing me a song of the dead. Dead Man Asks for a Song, The. *Unknown.* WoPoe, *tr. by* Willard Trask

Sing me a song of the whirling wheel that paced the coming rain. Rain Race, The. Post Wheeler. ArBi

Sing me "Woe," you glades and Dorian water. Lament for Bion. Moschus. HePo, *tr. by* Barbara Hughes Fowler

Sing, Muse, the son of Maia and of Jove. *Unknown. Fr.* Homeric Hymns.

"Sing, my golden cock, I'll give thee grain!" Neidhart von Reuental. GePo

Sing, My Heart. Ted Koehler. ReLy

Sing Not for Others, But for Me. Lady Caroline Lamb. RWP

Sing of lusty foods. Kalamu ya Salaam. SpirFl *Fr.* New Orleans Haiku.

Sing on a brittle sea of glass! Morgan Llwyd. AngWePo *Fr.* 1648.

Sing out, my soul, thy songs of joy. Songs of Joy. W. H. Davies. MoBrPo

Sing, Poet, 'tis a merry world. Alexander Smith. NePenScot *Fr.* Glasgow.

Sing, Sing, Sing, Numen, Lumen, Numen. To Her Modest Mirth-Making Friend, Mr Robert Dover. Thomas Cole and Sibella Cole Dover. EMWP

Sing so dogs bark, oxen bolt. Singer with a Bad Voice, The. *Vietnamese Oral Tradition.* CaDao, *tr. by* John Balaban

Sing the Alpha forest gods. Walt Whitman. Edward Dahlberg. APT-2

Sing to Apollo, God of Day. John Lyly. NoSic *Fr.* Midas.

Sing to me, i say. sing to me of rivers. (LL) African Sleeping Sickness. Wanda Coleman. PmAP; WaAnP

'Sing to us Sappho!' cried the crowd. Michael Field. ViWPN

Sing together. Interlude. Rachel Beck. IaFF

Sing We and Chant It. Thomas Morley. NoSic

Sing we for love and idleness. Ezra Pound. AmWit; MoAmPo; TCAPo *Fr.* Ripostes of Ezra Pound.

Sing we now merily. Thomas Ravenscroft. PBRV

Sing what God doth, and do[o] what men may sing. (LL) To the Thrice-Sacred Queen Elizabeth. Mary Sidney Herbert, Countess of Pembroke. NALW; NoP-4; NoP-5; WaAnP

Sing, women o' the Earth. Mune Rune. Helen Adam. APT-2

Singapore. Mary Oliver. CAP-8; NIL-7

Singapore, July 4th. Sascha Feinstein. AmPoNex

Singer, The. Gerald William Barrax. ESEAA

Singer, The. Edward Dowden. OxBSo *Fr.* In the Garden.

Singer, The. Sadiq Sharshar. AnVo, *tr. by* Mohamed Enani

Singer, The. Diane Wakoski. HeIP-4

Singer, The. Chocolate Waters. SUP

Singer, The. Anna Wickham. MoBrPo

Singer Has Aged, The. Badr Shakir al-Sayyab. IrPoTo, *tr. by* Ibtisam Barakat

Singer is old and has forgotten, The. Maire Macrae's Song. Kathleen Jessie Raine. EdScPo

Singer sings and days go by, A. Weeping Singer, A. Hô Sugyông. EcSo, *tr. by* Youngju Ryu

Singer with a Bad Voice, The. *Vietnamese Oral Tradition.* CaDao, *tr. by* John Balaban

Singers Change, the Music Goes On, The. Linda Gregg. BAP-01; OxBoAm

Singers filled the tiny schoolhouse stage, The. State Song. Berta Hart Nance. TiP2

Singers of serenades, The. Mandoline. Paul Verlaine. OBMV, *tr. by* Arthur Symons

Singin' in the Rain. Arthur Freed. ReLy

Singin shoutin joinin fingers love chain. All Up in There. Derrin Maxwell. BRtP

Singing. Geoff Hattersley. NeBl

Singing. Carl Phillips. CAP-8

Singing, The. C. K. Williams. CAP-8

Singing about her head, as she rode by. (LL) Love Without Hope. Robert Graves. NAEL-6v2; NAEL-7v2; NoP-4; NoP-5; NOxBChV; NPeEn; OPOU; OxBEV; Spl

Singing Alone. Nancy Cox. MiVo

Singing Aloud. Carolyn Kizer. TAPaP

Singing Back the World. Dorianne Laux. P180

Singing Bones, The. Randolph Stow. BMAP

Singing, dancing—handsome actors entertain. On the Cold Food Festival, Entertaining at the Southern Estate—the Guests Were Li Chiu-ho, Ma Nan-yeh, Wei Tung-kao, Li Hu-ch'uan, Huang K'ung-ts'un, Li Lung-t'ang, and Hu Hu-shan. Li K'ai-hsien. ColAnChi, *tr. by* Jonathan Chaves

Singing & Doubling Together. A. R. Ammons. NoAM

Singing down the Breadfruit. Pauline Stewart. NOxBChV

Singing Drum, The. Frank Mkalawile Chipasula. NAfrP

Singing Flower, The. "Shu Ting." VCWP, *tr. by* Carolyn Kizer and Y. H. Zhao

Singing, flying, singing. Basho. EH, *tr. by* Robert Hass

Singing Girls (Written in Jest). Tu Fu [*or* Du Fu]. CrYelRi, *tr. by* Sam Hamill

Singing his name. Sweet Bread. Frank X. Walker. SpirFl

Singing in the Streets. Leonard Clark. NOxBChV

Singing in the Toyota. Dave Etter. IllVoic

Singing Lesson, The [*with music*]. David Wagoner. NoAM

Singing Lute, The. Ibn Arfa' Ra'suh. HiArP; NAWM-7v1, *tr. by* James T. Monroe

Singing Maid, The. *Unknown.* WaAnP

Singing my days. Passage to India. Walt Whitman. APN-1; NAAPv.1; NCAP

Singing of the Source of Holy Church. Wu Li. ColAnChi, *tr. by* Jonathan Chaves

Singing, planting rice. Basho. SoOfWa, *tr. by* Sam Hamill

Singing Queen, Where Are You? Pierre-Richard Narcisse. OGAHCP, *tr. by* Boadiba and Jack Hirschman

Singing School. Seamus Heaney.
  Constable Calls, A. ArBi; EmeKit
  Exposure. NPeEn; PBCIP; PNI; WaAnP

Singing the Mozart Requiem. Ingrid Wendt. FiBr

Singing to Tony Bennett's Cock. Victoria Redel. KGB

Singing, today I married my white girl. Epithalamion. Dannie Abse. OBWVE

Singing we ride over the field. Vasco [*or* Vasko] Popa. PoSu; WoPoe *Fr.* Blackbird's Field, The.

Singing with open mouths their strong melodious songs. (LL) I Hear America Singing. Walt Whitman. BLPJKO; HHAm; ITBLP; MoAmPo; NIL-7; SAmP; TFi; WeW-3

Singing woman moves upstream on the river of night, The. Woman Singing. Tsujii Takashi. PML, *tr. by* Robert Brady and Susanne Akemi Wegmüller

Singing-Girls in the Brazen Bird. Ho Hsun. CCL1, *tr. by* John Frodsham

Single and last carriage is ready for the journey, A. David Vogel. FIT, *tr. by* Robert Friend

Single bird sang, A. Bird. Yona Volach. DTA, *tr. by* Miriyam Glazer

Single Blossom, A. Mun Chônghui. EcSo, *tr. by* Catherine J. Kim

Single cart to the frontier, A. Mission to the Frontier. Wang Wei. CCL1, *tr. by* Jerome P. Seaton

Single clenched fist lifted and ready, The. Choose. Carl Sandburg. Spl; StAl

Single cloud envelops ten-thousand streamside pines, A. Han-shan Te-ch'ing. CSKM, *tr. by* Red Pine

Single Eye All Light, no Darkness, A. Laurence Clarkson.
  "Behold, the King of glory now is come." PBRV

Single fact is matter, The. Chronic Meanings. Bob Perelman. OxBoAm; PmAP

Single figure, A. Parrot Parted from Her Cage. Hsüeh T'ao [*or* Xue Tao]. CCL1, *tr. by* Jeanne Larsen

Single flow'r he sent me, since we met, A.   One Perfect Rose.   Dorothy Parker.   AmWit; APT-1; NAAPv.2; NALW; NAMCP V.1; NBLV; NIL-7; NIP-4; NoP-4; NoP-5; OBCoV

Single Gentleman.   Pablo Neruda.   ConPit, *tr.* by Clayton Eshleman

Single grain of rice falling—into the Great Barn, A. (LL)   Climbing the Ling-ying Terrace and Looking North.   Po Chü-i.   BLT; CCL1, *tr.* by Arthur Waley

Single leaf falls, A.   Ransetsu.   SoOfWa, *tr.* by Sam Hamill

Single man stands like a bird-watcher, A.   Mouth of the Hudson, The.   Robert Lowell.   VCAP

Single Most [*with music*].   Rae Armantrout.   OnScMo

Single Parent.   Connie Bensley.   BeAl

Single ripple starts from where he stood, A. (LL)   Heron, The.   Theodore Roethke.   APT-2; OWoS

Single rose-red tile, A.   Visiting Light.   Jean Earle.   TCAWP

Single Screw of Flesh, A.   Emily Dickinson.   APN-2

Single spot slides the trumpet's flare then stops, A.   Lost Fugue for Chet. Lynda Hull.   LaCa; SeSe

Single teardrop, A.   Azalea.   Kang Ŭn'gyo.   CAMKP, *tr.* by Tae Yang Kwak

Single thought which benefits and harms me, A.   Verses in Italian and French, Written by the Queen of Scots to the Queen of England.   Mary Stuart, Queen of Scots.   EMWP

Single true man, A.   For Myo's Departure for Shofuku-ji.   Muso Soseki. EaWin, *tr.* by W. S. Merwin

Single Urge, The.   Baron Wormser.   NevBe

Single wild goose climbs into the void, A. (LL)   Clear After Rain ("Autumn, cloud blades on the horizon.")   Tu Fu [*or* Du Fu].   BLT; CCL1, *tr.* by Kenneth Rexroth

Single yam leaf, A.   Kikaku.   SoOfWa, *tr.* by Sam Hamill

Sing-Song.   Christina Georgina Rossetti.

　Caterpillar, The.   FaBoVe

　City Mouse and the Garden Mouse, The.   NTCP

　Ferry Me across the Water.   TLR

　"Horses of the sea, The."   NTCP

　Let's Be Merry.   TLR

　Mix a Pancake.   NTCP

　(Precious Stones.)   ChAP

Singular goddess, brown as night, and wild.   Sed non satiata.   Charles Baudelaire.   SxFrPo, *tr.* by James McGowan

Singularity.   Allan Graham.   ICANM

Sinister.   Forrest Gander.   PoDa

Sink is choked with dirty plates, The.   Daedalus.   Stephen Knight.   TCAWP

Sinking.   Mark Bibbins.   PoDa

Sinking, The.   Faith Shearin.   SweBea

Sinking, below the star-several harps.   Old Poems.   David Shapiro.   KGB

Sinking Feeling, A.   Amy Gerstler.   BodElec

Sinking into sound grief.   Rebus Tact.   Ray DiPalma.   PmAP

Sinking of Clay City, The.   Robert Wrigley.   GifTon

Sinking of the *Titanic proceeds according to plan, The.*   Hans Magnus Enzensberger.   PoSu *Fr.* Sinking of the Titanic, The.

Sinking of the Titanic, The.   Hans Magnus Enzensberger.

　Sixteenth Canto.   PoSu

　Thirty-third Canto.   PoSu

　Twenty-ninth Canto.   PoSu

1. The Sinking.   Charles Reznikoff.   ColAP; NAAPv.2 *Fr.* Testimony.

Sinless Child, The.   Elizabeth Oakes-Smith.

　Insect Affection.   STuOW

　"'Tis the summer prime, when the noiseless air."   SWaP

Sinner Kissed an Angel, A.   Mack David.   ReLy

Sinner row to save your soul, / Hallelujah! (LL)   Michael Row the Boat Ashore.   *Unknown.*   APN-2; NAAPv.1; SSUS

Sinner Won't Die No More.   *Unknown.*   SSUS

Sin's Round.   George Herbert.   NOSC

Sin-Sick Soul, The.   *Unknown.*   SSUS

Sinverguenza.   Robinson Jeffers.   AmWaPo

Sion.   George Herbert.   ChIV-1

Sioux Woman Defends Her Children, The.   *Chippewa Oral Tradition.* NAAL-5

Sioux Women Gather Up Their Wounded, The.   *Chippewa Oral Tradition.* NAAL-5

　(Song of War.)   NAAPv.1

Sioux women, The.   Sioux Women Gather Up Their Wounded, The. *Chippewa Oral Tradition.*   NAAL-5

Sip a little.   Baby's Drinking Song.   James Kirkup.   NTCP

Sip of Coors makes children be, A.   Booze Turns Men into Women. Bernadette Mayer.   NYP2

Sir, after all that sweet cod.   Dafydd's Seagull and the West Wind.   Glyn Jones.   TCAWP

Sir Anthony Habberton, Justice and Knight.   Obiter Dicta.   Joseph Hilaire Pierre Belloc.   OBCoV

Sir Balaam.   Alexander Pope.   NPeEn *Fr.* Epistle III, to Allen Lord Bathurst.

Sir Beelzebub.   Dame Edith Sitwell.   MoBrPo; MoWP; NALW; OBCoV *Fr.* Façade.

Sir Brian had a battleaxe with great big knobs on.   Bad Sir Brian Botany. Alan Alexander Milne.   NOxBChV

Sir Charles into my chamber coming in.   Courting the Faerie Queen.   Margaret Lucas Cavendish, Duchess of Newcastle.   NOSC

Sir Christopher Wren.   Edmund Clerihew Bentley.   NBLV *Fr.* Clerihews.

Sir Christopher Wren.   Edmund Clerihew Bentley.   NBLV *Fr.* Clerihews.

Sir Fantasy.   Ssu-ma Hsiang-ju.   ColAnChi, *tr.* by Burton Watson

Sir *Frauncis* and *Sir Phillip* have noe Tombe.   Of Sir Frauncis Walsingham Sir Phillipp Sydney, and Sir Christopher Hatton, Lord Chancelor.   *Unknown.* PBRV

Sir Gawain and the Green Knight [Marie Borroff Translation].   *Unknown.* NAEL-6v1; NAEL-7v1; NAWM-7v1, *tr.* by Marie Borroff

Sir Gawain and the Green Knight [Merwin Translation].   *Unknown. tr.* by W. S. Merwin

　"Since the siege and the assault upon Troy were finished."   WaAnP, *tr.* by W. S. Merwin

Sir Gawain and the Green Knight [Middle English Text Selections].   *Unknown.*

　"Now rides this renk thurgh the ryalme of Logres."   NPeEn

Sir Gawaine and the Green Knight.   Yvor Winters.   NoAM

Sir Gelli Meurig.   Ronald Stuart Thomas.   AngWePo

Sir Gelli to R.S.   Roland Mathias.   AngWePo

Sir Gregory Nonsense's News from No Place.   John Taylor.

　"It was in June the eight and thirtieth day."   NOSC

Sir, How much do you need.   Follow Me.   Nada El-Hage.   PoArWo, *tr.* by Nathalie El-Hani

Sir Hudibras his passing worth.   Samuel Butler.   BASC; NAEL-6v1; NAEL-7v1 *Fr.* Hudibras.

Sir Hudson Lowe, Sir Hudson *Low.*   To Sir Hudson Lowe.   Thomas Moore. OBSV

Sir Humphry Davy.   Edmund Clerihew Bentley.   OxBEV *Fr.* Clerihews.

Sir, I am not a bird of prey.   Reply From His Coy Mistress, A.   Anne Finch. FFC

Sir, I Ham a very Bad Hand at Righting. (LL)   Tony Harrison.   CABP; HarvBoo; NAMCP V.2; NoP-4; NoP-5 *Fr.* School of Eloquence, The.

Sir, I have remained so overcome, that I can no longer suffer your attacks. Marino Ceccoli.   CAGL, *tr.* by Jill Claretta Robbins

Sir Isaac Newton.   *Unknown.*   WeW-3

Sir James Murray.   Edwin Morgan.   HarvBoo

Sir John Raynsford's Confession.   John Harington.   NoSic

Sir John, The Hero.   Sándor Petőfi. *tr.* by Watson Kirkconnell

　"Upon the shepherd-boy the summer sun."   IQMS, *tr.* by Watson Kirkconnell

Sir Joshua Reynolds.   Oliver Goldsmith.   OBCoV; OxBEV *Fr.* Retaliation.

Sir, laugh no more at Pliny and the rest.   Animal Weather-Forecasting. Thomas Lodge.   NoSic

Sir, more than kisses, letters mingle souls.   To Sir Henry Wotton.   John Donne. NoSic

Sir, no man's enemy, forgiving all.   Petition.   W. H. Auden.   NAEL-6v2; NAEL-7v2

Sir Nose D'VoidofFunk.   Thomas Sayers Ellis.   FuFl; NeAmPo

Sir, / not that we did not hear the noise.   What Her Girl Friend Said to Him. Kannan.   WoPoe, *tr.* by A. K. Ramanujan

Sir Patrick Spens [*or* Spence].   *Unknown.*   BrAP; ClHu; GoPo; MakPoe; NAEL-6v1; NAEL-7v1; NePenScot; NIL-7; NIP-4; NoP-4; NoP-5; NPeEn; OBEV; OBSP; OxBEV; PoPoPo; TFi; WaAnP; WeW-3

Sir Revel.   Samuel Rowlands.   NoSic; OBCoV

Sir, say no more.   Trumbull Stickney.   APN-2; NAAPv.2 *Fr.* Dramatic Fragments.

Sir Thomas Maitland's Satyr upon Sir Niel Laing.   Sir Thomas Maitland. NePenScot

Sir, though (I thank God for it) I do hate.   John Donne.   OBSV *Fr.* Satires.

Sir, though (I thank God for it) I do hate.   John Donne. *Fr.* Satires.

Sir, to a wise man, all the world's his soil.   Ben Jonson.   NAEL-7v1 *Fr.* Volpone.

Sir, to be short, in this expensive town.   John Oldham.   NOSC *Fr.* Satyr, A.

Sir Walter Ralegh to the Queen.   Sir Walter Ralegh.   NoSic

Sir Walter Ra[u]le[i]gh to His Son[ne].   Sir Walter Ralegh.   GSo; NAEL-6v1; NAEL-7v1; NoP-4; NoSic; NPeEn; OxBSo; WoPoe

　(Three Thinges There Bee That Prosper Up Apace.)   BrAP

　(Three Things There Be.)   NoP-4

Sir! when I flew to seize the bird.   Beau's Reply.   William Cowper.   DiBP

Sir, / Whether these lines do find you out.   Summons to Town, A.   Sir John Suckling.   NOSC

Sir William Dyer, Knight. Lady Catherine Dyer.
(Epitaph on Sir William Dyer.) NPeEn

My Dearest Dust: Epitaph on the Monument of Sir William Dyer at Colmworth, 1641. InoFa

Sir William Wallace. Henry the Minstrel (Blind Harry).
On Wallace's Track. DiBP

Sir, / You need no Parian or Egyptian stone. To Sir Henry Newton, upon His Re-edifying the Church of Charleton in Kent. Thomas Philipott. NOSC

Sir, you should notice me: I am the Man. Epitaph. Lascelles Abercrombie. MoBrPo

Siren. Jonathan Galassi. PoDa

Siren. Amy Gerstler. ExTi

Siren. Louise Glück. OxBoAm

Siren, The. Violet Fane. VWP

Siren, The. Alfonsina Storni. TANSG, *tr.* by Mark McCaffrey

Siren Bird, The. Henrietta Cordelia Ray. CBWP-3

Siren of Love, A. Asher Reich. NRoS, *tr.* by Esther Raizen

Siren sang, and Europe turned away, A. To the Western World. Louis Simpson. OxBoAm; TRP

Siren Song. Margaret Atwood. NIL-7; NIP-2; PoA 2002; WeW-3 *Fr.* Songs of the Transformed.

Siren waits thee, singing song for song, The. (LL) To Robert Browning. Walter Savage Landor. NoP-4; NoP-5

Sirena. Michael Drayton. OBEV

Sirens, The. Franz Kafka. MotU, *tr.* by Clement Greenberg

Sirens, The. John Streeter Manifold. MoBrPo

Sirens are those journeys, The. Wound-dresser's Dream, The. Pauline Stainer. NeBl

Sirens, rising, woke me; and the night, The. Moonlight Alert. Yvor Winters. PWW2

Sirens' Song, The. William Browne. OBEV *Fr.* Inner Temple Masque, The.

Sirhan Drinks His Coffee in the Cafeteria. Mahmoud Darwish. VCWP, *tr.* by Rana Kabbani

Sirius:. "H. D." NAAL-5 *Fr.* Walls Do Not Fall, The.

Sirji, do you recall that. Pro Bono Publico. Alamgir Hashmi. PML

Sirmione. James Wright. BodElec

Sirs—though we fail you—let us live. To Men. Anna Wickham. MoBrPo

Sirventes. Bertrans de Born. WoPoe, *tr.* by Paul Blackburn

Sis Boom Ba. Tina Darragh. FTOS

Sis co wet. Sis Boom Ba. Tina Darragh. FTOS

Sista. Dickie Bradley. OWABP

Sistah Flo. Terri L. Jewell. FiBr

Sister: "House, A. A car. Sweet things. Gold." Angela Agali. NeNiPo

Sister. Magali Alabaú. TANSG, *tr.* by Mary Jane Treacy

Sister. Langston Hughes. APSN

Sister. Karol Wojtyla. PML, *tr.* by Jerzy Peterkiewicz

Sister, A / asked me why. Explaining. Evan X. Hyde. OWABP

Sister, a sister calling. Gerard Manley Hopkins. FaBoVe *Fr.* Wreck of the Deutschland, The.

Sister Agnes Writes to Her Beloved Mother. Paul Durcan. OBCoV

Sister and mother and diviner love. To the One of Fictive Music. Wallace Stevens. APT-1; MoAmPo; NoP-4; TCAPo

Sister Ann Zita Shows Us the Foolishness of the Forbidden Books. Len Roberts. BodElec

Sister, Awake! *Unknown.* OBEV

Sister Cat. Frances Mayes. P180

Sister darling, ope the window, let the balmy air once more. Dying Girl, The. Mary Weston Fordham. CBWP-2

Sister Death. Penny Harter. TWW

Sister Dolly light the lamp, and the lamp light the road. White Marble Stone, The. *Unknown.* SSUS

Sister Emma, O you must come down to the mire. Down to the Mire. *Unknown.* WPoS

Sister Gone. William Barnes. OxBEV

Sister, I have come to take your place. Anna Andreyevna Akhmatova. ARWW, *tr.* by Catriona Kelly

Sister, I wish to be the waters. My Shattered Sister. Naomi Quinonez. FTtHH

Sister, I'm Sorry. Ayukawa Nobuo. PML, *tr.* by Leza Lowitz and Oketani Shogo

Sister Johnson's Speech. Maggie Pogue Johnson. CBWP-4

Sister Lakin and Lally. Dorothy Perry Thompson. SpirFl

Sister Lou. Sterling Allen Brown. APT-2; InoFa

Sister Margaret Clare. In the Middle of Priest Lake. Madeline DeFrees. ExTi

Sister married a sometime preacher addicted to silk suits and the chickenfat attentions of christian women. Eulogy for Sister. Opal Moore. FuFl

Sister Mary Appassionata Lectures the Bible Study Class: Homage to Onan. David Citino. UpMys

Sister Mary Appassionata Lectures the Eighth Grade Boys and Girls on the Nature of the Candle. David Citino. UpMys

Sister Mary Appassionata Lectures the Eighth Grade Boys and Girls: The Family Jewels. David Citino. UpMys

Sister Mary Appassionata Lectures the Folklore Class: Doctrines of the Strawberry. David Citino. UpMys

Sister Mary Appassionata Lectures the Home Ec Class: The Feast. David Citino. UpMys

Sister Mary Appassionata Lectures the Pre-Med Class. David Citino.
6. The Nature of Love. UpMys

Sister Mary Appassionata Lectures the Science Class: Fossils, Physics, Apple, Heart. David Citino. UpMys

Sister Mary Appassionata Proves to the Entomology Class That Woman and Man Descended from the Cricket. David Citino. UpMys

Sister Midnight. John James. Oth

Sister Muse, lament for my pain. Elegy on Reichenau. Walafrid Strabo. NAWM-7v1, *tr.* by Peter Godman

Sister of Mercy, The. Constance Naden. ViWPN; VWP

Sister on the Tracks, A. Donald Hall. GM

Sister once of weeds and a dark water that held still. Family Romance. Larry Levis. BodElec

Sister Rosy, you get to heaven before I go. Travel On. *Unknown.* SSUS

Sister saying—"Soon you'll be back in the ward—." In the Theatre. Dannie Abse. BloBone; NoAM; TCAWP

Sister, sister. What Danger We Court. Luci Tapahonso. ReEnLa

Sister, sister go to bed! Brother and Sister. Lewis Carroll. NOxBChV

Sister Songs. Francis Thompson.
"But lo! at length the day is lingered out." OBMV

Sister Swallow to Swinburne. Mary Holtby. UV

Sister, You Cannot Think a Baby Out! Irène Assiba d'Almeida. HAWP

Sister, you open. 1915 Interior. Clarence Major. OxAAAP

Sisters. Kimberly Ann Collins. InTrad

Sisters. Wendy Cope. ItWoWo

Sisters. Haunani-Kay Trask. ReEnLa

Sisters, The. Roy Campbell. NoP-4; NoP-5; OBMV

Sisters, The. Melissa Cannon. FFC

Sisters, The. George Crabbe. *Fr.* Tales of the Hall.

Sisters, The. Amy Lowell. NALW

Sisters, The. John Banister Tabb. APN-2

Sisters, The. Judith Wright. NALW

Sisters, do you know how it is? On one hand. Condition of Women, The. Hồ Xuân Huong. PoChi, *tr.* by John Balaban

Sisters Newyearsgift from Elizabeth to Mary a Happie Mother of Good Children, The. Elizabeth Cromwell. EMWP

Sisters, Now We Are the Path and the Light. Ko Chônghûi. EcSo, *tr.* by Catherine J. Kim

Sisters of Saida Manoubia, The. Sibyl James. FiBr

Sisters of Sexual Treasure, The. Sharon Olds. PBCAP

Sisters! sisters! who sent you here? Fire, Famine, and Slaughter. Samuel Taylor Coleridge. FaBoWar

Sisters / Where there is cold silence. To Black Women. Gwendolyn Brooks. IllVoic

Sisters-in-law are a tribe apart. 60. Taban lo Liyong. PML

Sistrum. Margaret Fuller. APN-1

Sit down / and I'll feed you. Ham and the Moon. Jesse Lee Kercheval. SweBea

Sit Down, You're Rockin' the Boat. Frank Loesser. ReLy

Sit, everyone, under the luxuriant laurel. Anyte. SaLy, *tr.* by Diane Rayor

Sit. Feast on your life. (LL) Love after Love. Derek Walcott. BeAl; PML; PtR; RaF; TWF; WhBo

Sit for a while on a stone. Thomas A. Clark. Oth

Sit here and guard the household. To My Dog, Swan. Dezső Kosztolányi. IQMS, *tr.* by Lydia Pasternak-Slater

Sit on the bed. I'm blind, and three parts shell. A Terre. Wilfred Owen. FaBoWar; PoWW

Sit separated by wire-meshed glass. Visiting Hours. John Alexander Frazier, Jr. BtF

Sit, she said. The wolf sat. Shake, she said. Manners. Pamela Alexander. ExTi

Sit the noon out, pale and lost in thought. Eugenio Montale. PoCho, *tr.* by Jonathan Galassi

Sit there and count your fingers. Lorenz Hart. *See* When I was very young.

Sita. Pathabhi. HotL, *tr.* by V. Narayana Rao

Sita was my classmate. Sita. Pathabhi. HotL, *tr.* by V. Narayana Rao

Site of My Grandfather's House, The. Dominador I. Ilio. ReBoTo

Site of the Indian Fights of 1871, Abilene. Naomi Shihab Nye. TiP2

Sith al that in this world hath ben in rerum natura. *Unknown.* OHMEL

Sith Cynthia is ascended to that rest. Emilia Lanier and Aemilia Bassano Lanyer. BASC; NoP-4; NoP-5 *Fr.* Salve Deus Rex Judaeorum.

Sith gone is my delight and only pleasure. Sextain. William Drummond of Hawthornden. NOSC

Sith my life from life is parted. Marie [*or* Mary] Magdalens Complaint at Christs Death. Robert Southwell. ChIV-2

Sits on her carefully made bed. Housewife, The. Ginger Andrews. SUP

Sitter Bitter. Miss Bitter. N. M. Bodecker. NTCP

Sittin' on the porch at night when all the tasks are done. Sittin' on the Porch. Edgar Albert Guest. ITBLP

Sitting, The. Medbh McGuckian. CABP; ModIr; PNI

Sitting Alone. Hurbak Myungjo. BecRai, *tr. by* Kim Daljin, Kim Won-Chung and Christopher Merrill

Sitting Alone. Mookam Choinul. BecRai, *tr. by* Kim Daljin, Kim Won-Chung and Christopher Merrill

Sitting alone (as one forsook). Vision, The. Robert Herrick. CavPo; PBRV

Sitting alone by the pond. Facing the Shadow. Jinkag Haesim. BecRai, *tr. by* Kim Daljin, Kim Won-Chung and Christopher Merrill

Sitting alone, hid in bamboo. Bamboo Lane House. Wang Wei. NDACCP, *tr. by* Gary Snyder

Sitting alone in recluse bamboo dark. Bamboo-Midst Cottage. Wang Wei. NDACCP, *tr. by* David Hinton

Sitting alone in the empty hall. Sitting Alone on an Autumn Night. Wang Wei. CrYelRi, *tr. by* Sam Hamill

Sitting Alone on an Autumn Night. Wang Wei. CrYelRi, *tr. by* Sam Hamill

Sitting Alone One Cold June Night Before an Empty Whiskey Bottle a Coffee Pot & an Oil Stove with a Window through which I Watched the Flames. James Koller. AHA

SITTING alone upon my thought, in melancholy mood. Edward, 17th Earl of Oxford De Vere. NoSic

Sitting, and ready to be drawn. Ben Jonson. NOSC *Fr.* Eupheme.

Sitting and Teaching at Night. Jinkag Haesim. BecRai, *tr. by* Kim Daljin, Kim Won-Chung and Christopher Merrill

Sitting at crossings and waiting for freights to pass, we have all noticed. Project for Freight Trains, A. David Young. GM

Sitting at her table, she serves. Nani. Alberto A. Ríos. MakPoe; SoSe-8; UnSA; WaAnP

Sitting at my desk, I concentrate. I Listen to Alice Walker on a Pocket Radio. Paulann Petersen. FiBr

Sitting at Night. Po Chü-i. TAL

Sitting at Night at an Old Inn in Silla. Yujŏng. BecRai, *tr. by* Kim Daljin, Kim Won-Chung and Christopher Merrill

Sitting at Night on the Front Porch. Charles Wright. ColAP; GeoHom

Sitting at Night with My Nephew Who Has Just Come from Afar. Su Tung-p'o. TAL

Sitting at table, or. Dialectique. Hugh Maxton. IrLP

Sitting at the bar. Hard-Boiled Egg. Jim Daniels. LiTh

Sitting between the sea and the buildings. Painter, The. John Ashbery. EmeKit; NoP-4; NoP-5; PoPoPo; YaYoPo

Sitting by a Bush in Broad Daylight. Robert Frost. ChIV-1

Sitting by the barbecue. Dinner Together. Diana Rivera. InvLad

Sitting by the inlet. Schizo de Picasso. Elin Llwyd Morgan. BBMWP, *tr. by* the author

Sitting by the streams that glide. Bible, *O.T. See* By the rivers of Babylon, there we sat down, yea, we wept, when [*or* then] we remembered Zion.

Sitting crosslegged on a wooden floor. Allen Ginsberg. WhBo

Sitting dead in Death Valley. Death Valley. Sorley MacLean. FaBoWar; NePenScot; PoAgWa

Sitting, facing the sun, eyes closed. I can hear the. Before the Snake. Nathaniel Tarn. ICANM

Sitting here alone, in peace. Private Sadness. Bob Kaufman. ISC

Sitting Idly. Karai Senryū. EMJL, *tr. by* Makoto Ueda

Sitting in mystic bamboo grove, back unseen. Wang Wei. NDACCP, *tr. by* Ezra Pound

Sitting in sunlight, the child. Eleven A.M. on My Day Off, My Sister Phones Desperate for a Babysitter. Sharon Hashimoto. OpBo

Sitting in the Doctor's Office the Next Day. Laura Boss. BRtP

Sitting in the first row, right hand on the small desk. Auditor. Gerardo Deniz. RMCMP, *tr. by* Mónica de la Torre

Sitting in the Grief House (250). Khwaja Shams-ad-din Muhammad Hafiz. WED, *tr. by* Robert Bly and Leonard Lewisohn

Sitting in the Sixth Grade at Ascension of Our Lord School in Cleveland, Ohio, Reading a Pamphlet Entitled "Possession in Iowa." David Citino. UpMys

Sitting in the tin-boarded doorframe of a dead house. (LL) Mugging. Allen Ginsberg. NAMCP V.2; NoAM

Sitting naked together. Rain Journal: London: June '65. Lee Harwood. AHA

Sitting on a shelf. Tomas Tranströmer. WoBe *Fr.* Haiku.

Sitting on a windowsill, swinging. Blue Moon. Mimi Khalvati. MFPA

Sitting on Farm Lawn on Sunday Afternoon. Robert Penn Warren. LPSFW

Sitting on the Brooklyn Bridge at night. Side 4. Víctor Hernández Cruz. PueRic

Sitting on the grass. In the Park. Judith Beveridge. BMAP

Sitting on the train. Conrail Wax Museum. Manuel Ulacia. RMCMP, *tr. by* Indran Amirthanayagam

Sitting on Top of Corpses. Miguel Hernández. WED, *tr. by* Robert Bly

Sitting Outside at the End of Autumn. Charles Wright. WaAnP

Sitting over words. Utterance. W. S. Merwin. BLT

Sitting Quietly: Written During My Illness. Po Chü-i. CCL1, *tr. by* Arthur Waley

Sitting shoulder to shoulder. Kim Roberts. AmPoNex *Fr.* Constellation x Frigidaire, The.

Sitting there nearly translucent You'll end up. Hoa Nguyen. WANABP

Sitting until the sun rises. At the Teahouse, 7 am. Holly Hughes. AmZen

Sitting up. (LL) First Trimester, The. Campbell McGrath. NeAmPo; UrbNat

Sitting Up Late with My Father, 1977. Franz Wright. AmAlph

Sitting, Wedding Morning. Tony Trigilio. AmZen

Sitting with Lester Young. Paul Zimmer. SeSe

Sitting with My Uncle. Marvin Francis. PoPra

Situation. Langston Hughes. APSN

Situation No. 7: The Poison Lover. David Citino. UpMys

Situation No. 9: The Corposant. David Citino. UpMys

Situation No. 13: City Hall. David Citino. UpMys

Situation No. 33: The Feast. David Citino. UpMys

Siv, With Ocean (Pacific). Ron Loewinsohn. ASA

Six. Caitríona O'Reilly. NIrP

6. Raúl Zurita. TCLAP, *tr. by* Jack Schmitt

6 A.M. All over the world. Rosemary. John A. Stone. BloBone

Six Apologies, Lord. Olena Kalytiak Davis. PLBUT

Six black ibis. Snapshots. Mary Oliver. PoCoUp

Six changeful years have vanished since I first. William Wordsworth. *Fr.* Prelude, The; Growth of a Poet's Mind [1850 version].

Six Characters from the *Heart Sutra*. Kazuaki Tanahashi. WhBo

Six Characters in Search of Something. Jamie McKendrick. NeBrP

Six charred leaves drift. Rea Nikonova. CRWP, *tr. by* Gerald Janecek

Six Choruses. Tu Fu [*or* Du Fu]. CrYelRi, *tr. by* Sam Hamill

Six Commissioned Texts. W. H. Auden.
    Ballad of Barnaby, The. OBNV

Six Cranes at Dusk. Henri Faust. YaYoPo

Six crock bowls the bride smashed. Angry Bride, The. *Unknown.* WoPoe, *tr. by* Kevin O'Rourke

Six decades gone and one to come. Juxtapositions. David Wright. NLP

Six directions which form a sheep, The. Kepler Considers the Dimensions of a Sheep. Linden Ontjes. PoDa

Six discs / with Decca. (LL) Be-Bop Boys. Langston Hughes. APSN; APT-2

Six Dream Songs. *Wintu Oral Tradition.* NAAPv.1
    Dandelion Puffs. NAAPv.1
    Minnows and Flowers. NAAPv.1
    Sleep. NAAPv.1
    Strange Flowers. NAAPv.1
    There Above. NAAPv.1
    You and I Shall Go. NAAPv.1

Six Families of Puerto Ricans. Terence Winch. FTtHH

Six feet by three feet patch. At the Center. Patricia Goedicke. PoDa

Six green plums bottoms. Wickson Plums. William Corbett. PmAP

Six Hermetic Songs. Michael Palmer.
    "There were nine grand pianos in my father's house." ASA

Six hours outstetched in the sun, yes. On a Theme from Julian's Chapter 20. Denise Levertov. UpMys

Six Household Appliances. Justin Quinn.
    2. Icebox. NIrP

Six in the morning, a weekday in May. Highland, 1955. Kevin Fitzpatrick. MiVo

Six Lectures in Verse. Czeslaw Milosz. *tr. by* the author and Leonard Nathan
    Lecture 5. GI, *tr. by* the author and Leonard Nathan

Six little ones fighting the wind down the path. Dylan Iorwerth. BBMWP *Fr.* Sand.

Six Local Poems. David Avidan. FIT, *tr. by* Robert Friend

Six long-headed jazzers play. (LL) Jazzonia. Langston Hughes. ColAP; NAAPv.2

Six masons are sitting and talking. Italian Masons. Sarah Barkan. Prolet, *tr. by* Amelia Glaser

Six Million, The. Naomi Replansky. InoFa

Six Minutes Writing. Kadija George. BRtP

Six monarch butterfly cocoons. Ars Poetica. Dana Levin. TAPaP

Six Movements for Portraits of Erzulie. Sandra McPherson. FTtHH

Six Nations Museum Onchiota, New York—January. Wendy Rose. HATNAP

Six/Nine/Forty-Four. David St. John. AmAlph

Six Nuns Die in Convent Inferno. Paul Durcan.
"We resided in a Loreto convent in the centre of Dublin city." ModIr

Six O'Clock. Trumbull Stickney. APN-2; OxBoAm

Six o'clock: the kitchen bulbs which blister. Ode to Suburbia. Eavan Boland. PBCIP

Six One-Line Film Scripts. Tom Andrews. P180

Six or seven rows of waves struggle landward. On the Oregon Coast. Galway Kinnell. NAMCP V.2; NoAM

Six Part Lust Story. Jonathan Fisher. PML

Six Poems of Loneliness. Enrique Lihn. VCWP, tr. by David Unger

Six Poems on Nothing. Gwyneth Lewis. HarvBoo

Six, seven years ago. He Makes a House Call. John A. Stone. BloBone

Six, Sex, Say. Barbara Hamby. PoDa

Six Small Fires. Paul Jenkins. OPRER

Six stone in weight and so disconsolate. Society Woman, The. Dezső Kosztolányi. IQMS, tr. by Peter Zollman

Six street ends come together here. Blue Island Intersection. Carl Sandburg. MoAmPo

Six Strings, The. Federico García Lorca. RaW, tr. by Donald Hall

Six Ten Sixty-Nine. Conyus. GT

Six Town Eclogues. Lady Mary Wortley Montagu.
Saturday: The Small-Pox. BrAP; NoP-5

6/20/97. Harvey Shapiro. KGB

Six Variations. Denise Levertov.
"Shlup, shlup, the dog." HeIP-4

Six Variations on Love. Víctor Terán. RMCMP, tr. by Donald Frischmann

Six Ways, The. Issa. EH, tr. by Robert Hass

Six Winter Privacy Poems. Robert Bly. CAP-8

Six Years Later. Joseph Brodsky. VCWP, tr. by Richard Wilbur

Six years the moon shone at mid-autumn. Mid-Autumn Moon. Su Tung-p'o. GifTon, tr. by Burton Watson

Six Young Men. Ted Hughes. OBWP; PoAgWa; PoWW

Six-Cornered Snowflake, The. John Frederick Nims.
"Not / above / a juggler's." PoA 2002

Six-cylinder car and two Fords in the middle of / the fields, A. Harvest. Blaise Cendrars. BLT, tr. by Monique Chefdor

"Sixpence a week," says the girl to her lover. Thomas Hardy. MoBrPo Fr. Satires of Circumstance in Fifteen Glimpses.

Sixteen Dead Men. William Butler Yeats. OBWP

1686–1802 / Toll taker at Dunk's Ferry, Pennsylvania. Alice. Gale Jackson. SpirFl

1648. Morgan Llwyd.
Excuse, The. AngWePo
Harvest, The. AngWePo
Spring, The. AngWePo
Summer, The. AngWePo
Winter, The. AngWePo

1619: exhausted, you appeared. Modern Love Poem, A. Candice Nicole Love. BRtP

1619. Virginia. Gale Jackson. BtF

1691. Tituba of Salem. Gale Jackson. BtF

Sixteen Poems in Eight Pairings. John Crowe Ransom.
(Conrad in Twilight.) FuPo
"Here lies a lady of beauty and high degree." APT-1; MoAmPo; NAAPv.2; NAMCP V.1; NoAM
"I have a grief." OxBoAm
Prelude to an Evening. MoAmPo
(Vanity of the Bright Young Men, The.) FuPo

1668. Dom Moraes. EmeKit

Sixteen Sonnets. Thomas A. Clark.
"As I walked out early." Oth
"Our boat touches the bank." Oth

Sixteen to the day, the first time. Into First. Ron Egatz. NevBe

Sixteen wasps against a fallen apple, hissing green. Poison, 1959. David Wojahn. PoDa

16 Year-Old Girl Who's Standing, A. Rudolph Muller. OGAHCP; PoCho, tr. by Boadiba and Jack Hirschman

16 years old. My Old Man. Charles Bukowski. CalPo; OxBoAm; PmAP

Sixteen years old and crooked. Meeting Mescalito at Oak Hill Cemetery. Lorna Dee Cervantes. PBCAP

Sixteenth Canto. Hans Magnus Enzensberger. PoSu Fr. Sinking of the Titanic, The.

6th Dance—Doing Things With Pencils—17–18 February 1964. Jackson Mac Low. PmAP Fr. Pronouns, The—A Collection of 40 Dances—For the Dancers.

Sixth Grade. Melanie Hope. WiU

Sixth Grade. Marie Howe. KGB

6th Grade—Our Lady of Pompeii. Vittoria Repetto. UnSA

Sixth Night: Waking, The. Muriel Rukeyser. PoCho

Sixth Ode: The Grottoes. Gustaf Sobin. WoBe

Sixth of January, The. David Budbill. GoPo

Sixth Song of the Holy Young Men. Unknown. APN-2 Fr. Mountain Chant, The.

Sixth Vertical Poetry. Roberto Juarroz.
"Bell is full of wind, The." VCWP

Sixties brought a clash of arms, The. Emancipation Day. Lizelia Augusta Jenkins Moorer. CBWP-3

Sixty percent of the universe's energy is missing. Beneath Cold Mountain. Michael Hannon. GeoHom

Sixty second / August. Maxine Chernoff. PmAP Fr. Japan.

67 Words with One Vowel and One Consonant. Christophe Tarkos. YaTCFP, tr. by Stacy Doris

63rd and Broadway. Reuben Jackson. ESEAA

Sixty-five years. Unpo Bun-Etsu. ZenPo, tr. by Takashi Ikemoto and Lucien Stryk

Sixty-one? I thought you were that back. Swallows of Salangan. Gloria Vando. TouFir

Sixty-Six. Philip Booth. BodElec

66°7' N/22°17' W. Peter Rafferty. NLP

Sixty-six years. Tendo-Nyojo. ZenPo, tr. by Takashi Ikemoto and Lucien Stryk

Six-year-old boy, The. Still I See in Front of Me. Ivan Matanov. PML, tr. by Lyudmila Kolechkova

Size of a Bed Sheet, The. Amy Dryansky. SweBea

Size of It, The. Timothy Liu. WiU

Size of This Universe, The. Randolph Healy. Oth

Sizing. Heather McHugh. ExTi

Sizing up an adversary is a matter of estimating his familiarity with pain. Battle at Horizon. Ben Marcus. HeMarv

Sizing up our present situation. Woman's Intuition, A. Ned Washington. ReLy

Skaian Gate, The. Geoffrey Scott.
"Hector, the captain bronzed, from simple fight." OBMV

Skara Brae. Michael Longley. PBCIP

Skate. Jean Valentine. CAP-8

Skateboard. Thom Gunn. MoASP

Skater, The. Hester Knibbe. TuT, tr. by Micheal O'Siadhail

Skater, The. Sir Charles G. D. Roberts. BrAP; IFF

Skaters, The. John Ashbery.
"These decibels / Are a kind of flagellation, an entity of sound." PmAP
"Wind thrashes the maple seed-pods, The." APSN

Skaters, The. John Gould Fletcher. MoAmPo

Skating north along the river. 47° 28' N, 19° 1' E. Michael Murphy. NIrP

Skating with Heather Grace. Thomas Lynch. BeAl

Skein. Silvia Eugenia Castillero. SPV, tr. by Jen Hofer

Skein, The. Emperor Wu of Han. CAP-8, tr. by Carolyn Kizer

Skeins o geese write a word. Skeins o Geese. Kathleen Jamie. GPPA; MoWP; NeBrP

Skeleton buried. Silly Ghost. Natalia Toledo. RMCMP, tr. by Alberto A. Ríos

Skeleton in Armor [or Armour], The. Henry Wadsworth Longfellow. APN-1; TreFP

Skeleton in the Cupboard, The. Dora Sigerson Shorter. VWP

Skeleton is hiding in the closet as it should, The. Everything in Its Place. Arthur Guiterman. AmWit; NBLV; OBCoV

Skeleton of stone was once a young girl, The. Young Girl, A. Waldo Williams. BBMWP, tr. by Anthony Conran

Skeleton of the Future, The. Hugh MacDiarmid. MoBrPo; OBMV

Skeleton of the Great Moa in the Canterbury Museum, Christchurch, The. Allen Curnow. BrAP

Skeleton of the moa on iron crutches, The. Skeleton of the Great Moa in the Canterbury Museum, Christchurch, The. Allen Curnow. BrAP

Skeleton of Winter. Joy Harjo. LoL

Skeleton Parade. Jack Prelutsky. NTCP

Skeletons are out tonight, The. Skeleton Parade. Jack Prelutsky. NTCP

Skeleton's Defense of Carnality, The. Jack Foley. ASA

Skeletons in this town are mostly, The. Fallen Women. Audrey Poetker-Thiessen. ACAMVP

Skellings to Frost, it's difficult. Frost to Skellings. Edmund Skellings. VisFro

Skengeh, A. Eena Mi Corner. Jean Binta Breeze. WaCA

Skeptic, The. Colette Inez. PA9/11

Skeptic, The. Clara Ann Thompson. CBWP-2

Sketch. Cecília Meireles. TCLAP, *tr.* by Luiz Fernández García

Sketch, A. Christina Georgina Rossetti. VWP

Sketch for an Aesthetic Project [*I believe now that love is half persistence, / A medium in which, from change to change, / Understanding may be gathered.*]. Jay Wright. GT

Sketch from the Campaign in the North, A. Vijay Seshadri. PoDa

Sketch in October. Tomas Tranströmer. VCWP, *tr.* by Robin Fulton

Sketch of a Fetish. Kim Kwang-kyu. PML, *tr.* by Anthony, Brother of Taizé

Sketch of the Frontier Woman. Claudia Lars. TCLAP, *tr.* by Donald D. Walsh

Sketches. Federico García Lorca. PFTM-1 *Fr.* Night (Suite for Piano and Poet's Voice).

Sketches for 13 Sonnets. Ebbe Borregaard. AHA

Sketches of Harlem. David Henderson. EGAG

Sketches of Natural History. Mary Howitt.
    Tobias's Dog. DiBP

Sketching in Barnstable. Carol Arber. PfS

Skialetheia Satire 5. Everard Guilpin.
    "What more variety of pleasures can." PBRV

Skiddaw House. David Scott. NLP

Skies ain't gonna cloud no mo'. Happiness Is Just a Thing Called Joe. E. Y. Harburg. ReLy

Skies are cold and hard; the dead lights trail, The. Departure, The. Trumbull Stickney. ColAP

Skies are cold; fierce tigers. Spending the Night at East Forest Temple. Lingche. CCL1, *tr.* by Stephen Owen

Skies gan scowl, o'ercast with misty clouds, The. George Gascoigne. ChIV-1 *Fr.* De Profundis.

Skies o'ercast and fierce winds blow, The. December. Josephine D. Henderson Heard. CBWP-4

Skies they were ashen and sober, The. Ulalume [*or* Ulalume—a Ballad]. Edgar Allan Poe. APN-1; NAAL-5; NAAPv.1; NCAP; OxBoAm; TCAPo

Skiing in a red and blue outfit. Chogyam Trungpa. WhBo

Skiing on Russian Christmas. Nora Dauenhauer. HATNAP

Skill is leaching from his hands, moment, The. Allegiance. Sheenagh Pugh. TCAWP

Skill originated in the West, The. Lines in Praise of a Self-Chiming Clock. Hsüan-yeh. ColAnChi, *tr.* by Jonathan D. Spence

Skill'd metrics. Lens. Steve Jonas. EGAG

Skilled to pull wires, he baffles Nature's hope. Boss, The. James Russell Lowell. NCAP

Skills. Celia de Fréine. NIrP, *tr.* by the author

Skim from curb to curb like regatta. Island Women of Paris, The. Rita Dove. LoL

Skimming / an asphalt sea. Sidewalk Racer Or, On the Skateboard, The. Lillian Morrison. NTCP

Skimming lightly, wheeling still. Shiloh (A Requiem). Herman Melville. AmWaPo; APN-2; CBCWP; ColAP; CtM; NAAPv.1; NoP-4; NoP-5; OBWP; OxBoAm; PCW; PoAgWa; TCAPo

Skimming the Ice. Tom Sexton. PoCoUp

Skin. Anthony Butts. AmPoNex

Skin. Linda Hogan. ReEnLa

Skin. Mary Leader. NAPBL

Skin. Ruth Padel. NeBrP

Skin. Marjorie Welish. PmAP

Skin: "Never mind the fantasy about the tweezers and the tongue." Brian Henry. AmPoNex; LegDan

Skin: "Back then it seemed that wherever a girl took off her clothes the police would find her." Lucia Maria Perillo. IllVoic; P180

Skin Canoes. Carolyn Forché. YaYoPo

Skin Color from the Sun. Daryl Ngee Chinn. LTA

Skin color marks me. Why I Wont Wear a Tatoo. Tracie Morris. BtF

Skin cracks like a pod, The. Blessing. Imtiaz Dharker. BeAl; MoWP

Skin Full. Lavinia Greenlaw. NoP-5

Skin is broken. The hotel breakfast china, The. John Ashbery. FTOS

Skin like the spathe of a broad white lily on the first morning it unfurls. (LL) Skin: "Back then it seemed that wherever a girl took off her clothes the police would find her." Lucia Maria Perillo. IllVoic; P180

Skin / Meat / BONES. Anne Waldman. PmAP

Skin meeting skin, we want to think. Touching Each Other's Surfaces. Carol Jane Bangs. NIP-4

Skin of Clouds. Thulani Davis. FTtHH

Skin of ice. Lyrics to the Tune "Fairy Grotto." Su Tung-p'o. WoPoe, *tr.* by Greg Whincup

Skin of the night bristling with stars. Night, I Know All About You. Yolanda Bedregal. TANSG, *tr.* by Carolyne Wright

Skin ripples over my body like moon-wooed water, The. Prison Song. Alan Dugan. PoA 2002; YaYoPo

Skin that is closed curtain. Poll. Ed Roberson. EGAG

Skin the glorious color of chicken fat. (LL) Out of Our Hands. Cathy Song. PoA 2002; UnSA

Skin these hands will also salve, The. (LL) Integrity. Adrienne Rich. ColAP; StAl

Skin you wore through cortisone years, The. Skin You Wore, The. Robert John Moore. Coast

Skinful of bowls, he bowls them. Second Glance at a Jaguar. Ted Hughes. BrAP; NAMCP V.2; NoAM

Skinned lab rabbit's blue cerebral lobes swimming in formaldehyde. Fourteen. David Wheatley. NIrP

Skinny frog. Issa. EMJL, *tr.* by Haruo Shirane

Skinny woman is beaten under the eaves, A. Study of Women's History 4, A. Ko Chônghûi. EcSo, *tr.* by Catherine J. Kim

Skinny-Dipping the Ganges. Ray McNiece. AmZen

Skins. Judith Wright. BMAP

Skin-sack, The. Mina Loy. NAMCP V.1 *Fr.* Love Songs to Joannes.

Skin-tight with longing, like dangerous girls. August. Esta Spalding. StAl

Skip, The. James Fenton. HarvBoo

Skip The Byuppie. Ted Joans. FTtHH

Skipper Ireson's Ride. John Greenleaf Whittier. APN-1; NAAPv.1; NCAP

Skipping. Jim Barnes. RWB

Skipping along the footpath. Wind Debates Asian Immigration, The. Peter Rose. BMAP

Skirt architecture softened. Josée Lapeyrère. SCFWP *Fr.* Skirt, The.

Skirt, The. Josée Lapeyrère. SCFWP, *tr.* by Serge Gavronsky

Skirting a scrub-pine forest there's a scent of snow in air. Patton. Lincoln Kirstein. PWW2

Skirting the river road, (my forenoon walk, my rest,). Dalliance of the Eagles, The. Walt Whitman. HeIP-4; NAAL-3; NAAPv.1; NoP-4; NoP-5; SAmP; TCAPo; TRP; WaAnP

Skirts. Gray Jacobik. PoDa

Skreak and skritter of evening gone, The. Autumn Refrain. Wallace Stevens. APT-1; OxBoAm

Skua flew into our heads in 1968. Southern Skua, The. Robert Adamson. BeAl

Skull. Douglas Burnet Smith. Coast

Skull. Edward Weismiller. YaYoPo

Skull of a Snowshoe Hare, The. Robert Wrigley. RoV

Skull of the Horse. Thomas McGrath. BodElec

Skull Ring, The. Chelsey Minnis. IIR

Skulls, The. Ivan Turgeniev. MotU, *tr.* by Isabel Florence Hapgood

Skunk, The. Seamus Heaney. NAEL-6v2; NAEL-7v2; NoP-4; NoP-5; StAl; WaAnP

Skunk Cabbage. Mary Oliver. WaAnP

Skunk Cabbage. Eric Ormsby. NoP-4; NoP-5

Skunk cabbage with its smug and opulent smell, The. Skunk Cabbage. Eric Ormsby. NoP-4; NoP-5

Skunk Hour [(*For Elizabeth Bishop*)]. Robert Lowell. BrAP; CAP-8; ColAP; EmeKit; HarvBoo; HeIP-4; IJHIL; MoAmPo; NAAL-5; NAMCP V.2; NIL-7; NIP-4; NoAM; NoP-4; NoP-5; OxBoAm; PoetW; PoPoPo; TFi; TRP; VCAP; WaAnP

Skunks fight under the house and keep us. Bureau 2. Josephine Miles. NALW

Sky. James Harms. NAPBL

Sky. Richard Katrovas. LTA

Sky. Takahashi Shinkichi. ZenPo, *tr.* by Takashi Ikemoto and Lucien Stryk

Sky. William Stafford. PoDa

Sky, The. April 5th. Vera Gheraducci. CItWP, *tr.* by Cinzia Sartini Blum and Lara Trubowitz

Sky, The. Mathemaku for Beethoven. Bob Grumman. AnSo

Sky, The. Ernesto Lumbreras. RMCMP, *tr.* by Rebecca Seiferle

Sky, The. Elizabeth Madox Roberts. MoAmPo

Sky above Garden St, The. Heart Attack. Adam Ziemianin. PML, *tr.* by Amelia Gregorek and Jerzy Gregorek

Sky above the roof's, The. Paul Verlaine. SxFrPo, *tr.* by Martin Sorrell

Sky above us was silent and empty, The. Yiddish Poets in America. Richard Chess. TaR

Sky, almond and chalk. Shadows Behind, Before. Ingrid de Kok. TSAP

Sky becomes one with its clouds, The. "Fisherman's Honor," The. Li Ch'ing-chao. WPoS, *tr.* by Jane Hirshfield

Sky Clears, The. *Unknown.* OBVE, *tr.* by Frances Densmore

Sky Diving. Ishmael Reed. FaoP

Sky drank in sparrows making lucid the oaks, The. Sky Drank In, The. Gillian Conoley. BAP-97

Sky Drank In, The. Gillian Conoley. BAP-97

Sky extends upwards for ninety thousand miles, The. Buddhist Monk Cut and Burned His Own Flesh to Make The Rains Stop—A Man From His Native Place Asked Me to Write a Poem to Send to Him, A. Hsü Wei. ColAnChi, *tr. by* Jonathan Chaves

Sky full of autumn. Autumn. Ngo Chi Lan. EaWin, *tr. by* M. S. Merwin, W. S. Merwin, Nguyen Ngoc Bich and Nguyen Ngoh Bich

Sky full of cymbals, of fiddles and lutes. Spring Joy Praising God. Catharina Regina von Greiffenberg. GePo, *tr. by* George C. Schoolfield

Sky Harbor. Norman Dubie. AmAlph

Sky has been dark, The. Youngest Daughter, The. Cathy Song. NoAM; WaAnP

Sky has Recovered, The. Louise Herlin. MFP, *tr. by* Martin Sorrell

Sky in Daduza Township, The. Bruce Weigl. AmAlph

Sky in the trees, the trees mixed up, The. Landscape at the End of the Century. Stephen Dunn. CAP-8

Sky is a dark bowl, the stars die and fall, The. *Unknown.* WoPoe *Fr.* Cannibal Hymn, The.

Sky is a piece of mind, The. Housekeeping in a Dream. Laura Kasischke. SweBea

Sky is an *overflowing willow*, The. Among its branches the sun is a golden oriole. Sky, The. Ernesto Lumbreras. RMCMP, *tr. by* Rebecca Seiferle

Sky is changed!—and such a change! Oh night, The. Lord Byron. NOBRP *Fr.* Childe Harold's Pilgrimage.

Sky is cloudy, yellowed by the smoke, The. In a London Drawingroom. "George Eliot." NPeEn

Sky is covered with stars, like a body with sores, The. Svetlana Kekova. ItGoST, *tr. by* Judith Hemschemeyer

Sky is green, ands there is no book to tell us what it means. It has. Engines of Gloom and Affection. John Yau. PmAP

Sky is hot and yellow, filled, The. Brides Come to Yuba City, The. Chitra Divakaruni. FTtHH; OpBo; UnSA

Sky is letting its blue eyes close, The. Lullaby. Attila József. IQMS, *tr. by* Vernon Watkins

Sky is low—the Clouds are mean, The. Emily Dickinson. MoAmPo

Sky is mine to admire, The. Museum Cashier, The. Yona Harvey. BtF

Sky is overcast and behind it an infinite regress, The. Within This Book, Called Marguerite. Marjorie Welish. FTOS; PmAP

Sky is strewn with stars, The. *Unknown.* WoPoe, *tr. by* Charles Simic

Sky is violet like no other hypnosis, The. Afterward, There Will Be a Hallway. Arielle Greenberg. LegDan

Sky Lark, The. John Clare. NPeEn

Sky, lazily disdaining to pursue, The. Georgia Dusk. Jean Toomer. APT-2; InGu; NAAL-5; NAAPv.2; NAMCP V.1; NoAM; NoP-4; NoP-5; OxBoAm

Sky Lies Blue—Like a Sea, The. Nikolai Alekseievich Klyuyev. TCRusP, *tr. by* John Glad

Sky low down in distant West, The. To Mary. Mary E. Tucker. CBWP-1

Sky My Husband, The. John Ash. NeBrP

Sky Nails. Jamie McKendrick. NeBrP

Sky of churning cogs and work without weekends, A. First Circle, The. S. K. Kelen. BMAP

Sky on this mountain. Water Lilies. Ralph J., Jr. Mills. IllVoic

Sky or an edge or a beach or a wall or a room or a, A. Nursery Rhyme. Kit Robinson. FTOS

Sky overpowering, grey; beneath it. Holland. Hendrik Marsman. TuT, *tr. by* Michael Longley

Sky Picture. Henrietta Cordelia Ray. CBWP-3

Sky possesses the moon, The. You're Mine, You! Edward Heyman. ReLy

Sky rumbles. Gathers. Rain. Virgil. EroLit *Fr.* Aeneid [*or* Eneados *or* Aeneis], The.

Sky Scrape / City Scape. Jane Yolen. SSCS

Sky so pale, and the trees, such frail things, The. la Promenade, A. Paul Verlaine. OBVE, *tr. by* Arthur Symons

Sky that blue is not a sad thing, A. Alba: Aberdeen. Cate Marvin. IIR

Sky that has never known sun, moon, or stars, A. Rear Porches of an Apartment Building, The. Maxwell Bodenheim. APT-1

Sky that is the limit is the one, The. Incomplete Scenario Involving What the Voice Said. Jane Mead. NAPBL

Sky that the seasons pass through, The. One Night I Count the Stars. Yun Tongju. CAMKP, *tr. by* Kay Richards and Steffen Richards

Sky the color of a wren's [*or* wrens] breath, A. At Chadwicks Bar and Grill. Lance Henson. HATNAP

Sky, The / could collapse this morning. Ernesto Lumbreras. RMCMP, *tr. by* Rebecca Seiferle

Sky, The / cries out. Hues of Electric Blue. Felicia L. Morgenstern. BtF

Sky turns, The. To the Tune "You Move in Fragrance." Li Ch'ing-chao. NDACCP, *tr. by* Kenneth Rexroth

Sky unrolls like a rug, The / unwelcoming, gun-grey. As Our Bodies Rise, Our Names Turn into Light. Charles Wright. NoP-5

Sky very blue. Raul Bopp. TCLAP *Fr.* Black Snake.

Sky was a somber cave of water, The. Rain Psalm. Leopoldo Lugones. TCLAP, *tr. by* Julie Schumacher

Sky was a street map with stars for, The. Ode. Elizabeth Alexander. GT; PoPoPo

Sky was battened down, The. On Galveston Beach. Barbara Howes. MoAmPo

Sky was carpeted with Italian flak. Crump!, The. Malta. John Forbes. NOBAu

Sky was low, the sounding rain was falling dense and dark, The. Late Passenger, The. Clive Staples Lewis. P180

Sky was red and the earth got hot, The. When One Is Feeling One's Way. Lawrence Joseph. KGB

Sky we bear on our shoulders, heaven-height, The. Sonnet. Karen Volkman. IAoNAP

Sky wears in a belt of clouds, The. Only for You. Else Lasker-Schüler. BBASP, *tr. by* Robert P. Newton

Sky will never be this gray—belly of a mallard, The. Explaining Current Events to a One-Year-Old. Martha Silano. RWB

Sky Will Resound, The. Frances Densmore. APT-1 *Fr.* Chippewa Music.

Sky with reddened eyelids foretells windy weather, The. Glory. Nikolai Kanchev. CSCBP, *tr. by* Georgi Belev and Lisa Sapinkopf

Sky-Blue Dress, The. Cathy Song. SweBea

Skye Boat Song. *Unknown.* BLPJKO

Sky-geese have gone, high away, The. Sky-geese have gone, The. Cho Myŏngni [*or* Myŏnghŭi]. SonAtl, *tr. by* Anthony, Brother of Taizé, Kim Fulton and Sunyoung Yi

Skykomish River Running. Richard Hugo. PoA 2002

Skylark. Basho. WoPoe; ZenPo, *tr. by* Takashi Ikemoto and Lucien Stryk

Skylark. Johnny Mercer. ReLy

Skylark / Have you anything to say to me? Skylark. Johnny Mercer. ReLy

Skylark school, The. Prince Shiki. SoOfWa, *tr. by* Sam Hamill

Skylark / Soaring—her young. Sora. ZenPo, *tr. by* Takashi Ikemoto and Lucien Stryk

Skylark, what prompts your silver song. Nature Poem. Adrian Mitchell. Spl

Skylarks and Fuji. Kusano Shimpei. PFTM-1

Skylark's melody is sealed in ice, The. Coronach. Tracey Herd. NeBl

Skylarks singing / The farmer. Issa. ZenPo, *tr. by* Takashi Ikemoto and Lucien Stryk

Skylight, The. Seamus Heaney. NoP-5; OxBSo *Fr.* Glanmore Revisited.

Skylike limpid eyes, The. Ezra Pound. MoAmPo; NAAPv.2 *Fr.* Hugh Selwyn Mauberley (Life and Contacts).

Skyline. Jean Toomer. NAAPv.2

Skyline of New York does not excite me, The. Review from Staten Island. Gloria C. Oden. GT

Skyline of New York is a splendid sight, The. It's So Peaceful in the Country. Alec Wilder. ReLy

Skylord. Linda Gregg. AFaM

Skymen coming down out the clouds land. Poem for Deep Thinkers, A. Imamu Amiri Baraka. APSN

Sky-piercing sword, gleaming cold. Zuian. ZenPo, *tr. by* Takashi Ikemoto and Lucien Stryk

Sky's as blue and black as ink, The. Calligram, 15 May 1915. Guillaume Apollinaire. OBWP, *tr. by* O. Bernard

Sky's face has turned dark, don't believe, The. Neshâtî. OLP, *tr. by* Walter Andrews, Najaat Black and Mehmet Kalpakli

Sky's not high, earth not solid. Seiho. ZenPo, *tr. by* Takashi Ikemoto and Lucien Stryk

Skyscraper. Carl Sandburg. HHAm

Skyscraper, skyscraper. Dennis Lee. SSCS

Skyscrapers. Star Black. PA9/11

Skyscrapers. Rachel Lyman Field. ChAP; NOxBChV; SSCS

Skywriting. Jamie Grant. EmeKit

Slain. T. W. H. Crosland. OBWP

Slain as they lay by the secret, slow. Year's "Casualties", A. Ambrose Bierce. PCW

Slam, Dunk, & Hook. Yusef Komunyakaa. ISC; MoASP

Slant of light that kind of silver light among the poplars that kind of sudden silence, A. Patrick Friesen. ACAMVP *Fr.* Clearing Poems.

Slanting both hands against her forehead. Song. Aubrey Thomas De Vere. IrLP

Slanting ray of evening light, A. Squire's Pew, The. Jane Taylor. PEW

Slanting wind, misty rain. Tune: "The Charm of a Maiden Singer;" Spring Thoughts. Li Ch'ing-chao and Jiaosheng Wang. ColAnChi

Slap in the Face of Public Taste, A. D. Burliuk, Aleksandr Kruchenykh, V. Mayakovsky *and* Viktor Khlebnikov.

Slap in the Face of Public Taste, A. PFTM-1

Slap of the screen door, flat knock. Dishwater. Ted Kooser. WaAnP

Slap on a frame. (LL) High Renaissance. George Starbuck. AmWit; NBLV

Slash my back with a sickle. Poem. Hô Sugyông. EcSo, *tr. by* Youngju Ryu

Slashed and dumped. (LL) Grauballe Man, The. Seamus Heaney. BrAP; NAMCP V.2; OxBEV; PoetW

Slate. Richard Murphy. PBCIP *Fr.* Battle of Aughrim, The.

Slate. Francis Ponge. YaTCFP, *tr. by* Simon Watson Taylor

Slate I picked from a nettlebed. Richard Murphy. PBCIP *Fr.* Battle of Aughrim, The.

Slate Quay: Felinheli. Peter Gruffydd. AngWePo

Slate roof. No Return. Hô Sugyông. EcSo, *tr. by* Youngju Ryu

Slate Roof Blues. Jessica Freeman. AnSo

Slate Street School. Ciaran Carson. CABP

Slate-gray waves of day. Sunset. John Cope. GeoH

Slattern. Kate Clanchy. MoWP

Slaughter. Susan Stewart. BodElec

Slave, The. "Ada." NAAPv.1

Slave Auction, The. Frances Ellen Watkins Harper. APN-2; ColAP; ISC; NAAPv.1; PCW

Slave Boat. Obu Udeozo. NeNiPo

Slave Cabin, Sotterly Plantation, Maryland, 1989. Lucille Clifton. LoL

Slave Girl's Farewell, The. "Ada." NAAPv.1

Slave in the Dismal Swamp, The. Henry Wadsworth Longfellow. TCAPo

Slave Mother, The. Frances Ellen Watkins Harper. NAAPv.1; WaAnP

Slave Mother, The: A Tale of the Ohio. Frances Ellen Watkins Harper. ColAP; NAAPv.1

Slave Ritual. Carolyn M. Rodgers. ISC

Slave Trade, The. Hannah More.
 "Strange power of song! the strain that warms the heart." NoP-4; NoP-5

Slavery. Hannah More. RWP; WoRP
 "No; they have heads to think, and hearts to feel." NPBRoP

Slavery. Jones Very. NCAP

Slaves are dragging the last, The. Rain. Leslie Ullman. YaYoPo

Slave's Dream, The. Henry Wadsworth Longfellow. NAAL-3; NAAL-5

Slaves' Outside Evening or Evening, Pal Mal Comic. Leslie Scalapino. Eno

Slaves to London, I'll deceive you. Song, A. Peter Anthony Motteux. NOSC

Slaveship[s]. Lucille Clifton. ESEAA; OPRER

Slave-Ships, The. John Greenleaf Whittier. TCAPo

Slavic poet sips his morning vodka, his mind, The. Georgi Borisov in Paris. John Balaban. TAPaP

Sld bar 1.99 + drnk. 'Merícn Fst Fd. Thom Tammaro. ReTh

Sled Burial, Dream Ceremony. James Dickey. NoP-4; NoP-5

Sledgehammer. John MacKenzie. Coast

Sleek, dark-suited. Elegist, The. Geoff Page. BMAP

Sleek mechanical dart: the syringe noses into the blue vein marking the target of me. D. A. Powell. LegDan; NeAmPo

Sleep. Mary Crockett Hill. AmPoNex

Sleep. Jane Holland. NeBl

Sleep. Sir Philip Sidney. *See* Sonnet 39: "Come Sleep! O sleep the certain knot of peace."

Sleep. Kenneth Slessor. BMAP

Sleep. Beth Tornes. MotU

Sleep. Yvor Winters. NAAPv.2 *Fr.* Magpie's Shadow, The.

Sleep. *Wintu Oral Tradition.* NAAPv.1 *Fr.* Six Dream Songs.

Sleep: "Nobody nowhere they've all gone home." Ajanta. HotL, *tr. by* V. Narayana Rao

Sleep, The. Elizabeth Barrett Browning. ChIV-1; OxAEP-2

Sleep a little, a little little, thou needest feel no fear or dread. Sleep-Song of Grainne over Dermuid, The. Eleanor Hull. IrLP

Sleep and Poetry. John Keats.
 "O for ten years, that I may overwhelm." NAEL-6v2; NAEL-7v2; NPBRoP

Sleep and rain, two gangsters. Lullaby. Alan Michael Parker. AmPoNex

Sleep and sleep well, little one. Sleep-song. *Unknown.* SonAtl, *tr. by* Leonard Allen, Alan Brierly and B. L. Surley

Sleep, Big Baby, sleep your fill. (LL) Lullaby, A: "Din of work is subdued, The." W. H. Auden. NAMCP V.1; NoAM

Sleep child in your cradle, I'm watching you. Child, You New Man. Malka Lee. Prolet, *tr. by* Amelia Glaser

Sleep, Christian warrior, sleep. To Rev. Thaddeus Saltus. Mary Weston Fordham. CBWP-2

Sleep drops its nets for monsters old as the flood. Sleep Drops Its Nets. Jean Valentine. YaYoPo

Sleep, grim Reproof; my jocund muse doth sing. John Marston. NoSic *Fr.* Satires.

Sleep, hungry folk, sleep. Lullaby for the Hungry, A. Muhammad Mahdi Al-Jawahiri. IrPoTo, *tr. by* Terri DeYoung

Sleep is a Deep and Many Voiced Flood. Robert Duncan. CLPP

Sleep is postponed. Counting Sheep. Hamish Brown. EdScPo

Sleep, King Jesus. Mary's Song. Charles Causley. OBCP

Sleep, kinsman thou to death and trance. Alfred Tennyson. NAEL-6v2; NAEL-7v2 *Fr.* In Memoriam A. H. H.

Sleep, little architect. It is your mother's wish. Lullaby. Joan Murray. OxBoAm; YaYoPo

Sleep, little sister, far from pain. Elegy in August. Robert McDowell. PoDa

Sleep, love sleep. (LL) Serenade: "Sleep, love sleep." Mary Weston Fordham. CBWP-2; SWaP

Sleep, love sleep. Serenade. Mary Weston Fordham. CBWP-2; SWaP

Sleep, my child; because of you. Night. Gabriela Mistral. WoPoe, *tr. by* Alice Jane McVan

Sleep, my darling, sleep. Cradle Song. Louis MacNeice. IrLP

Sleep, my favourite flannel shirt, wears thin, and shreds, and birdsong happens in the holes. Waking At The Mouth Of The Willow River. Don McKay. OpeFie

Sleep, my little one, sleep, my pretty / one, sleep. (LL) Alfred Tennyson. ChAP; NAEL-6v2; NAEL-7v2 *Fr.* Princess, The.

Sleep, my love, and peace attend thee. All Through the Night. *Unknown.* ITBLP

Sleep No More: Paris, Oct. 1792. William Wordsworth. NPBRoP *Fr.* Prelude, The; Growth of a Poet's Mind [1805 version].

Sleep of Adam, The. John Hejduk. ChIV-1

Sleep of Beasts, The. Peter Cooley. UrbNat

Sleep of my Lions, The. Douglas Livingstone. TSAP

Sleep of Palinurus, The. Virgil. WoPoe *Fr.* Aeneid [*or* Eneados *or* Aeneis], The.

Sleep of the Insomniac, The. William Virgil Davis. YaYoPo

Sleep on, and dream of Heaven awhile. Sleeping Beauty, The. Samuel Rogers. OxAEP-2

Sleep on, I lie at heaven's high oriels. Nirvana. John Hall Wheelock. MoAmPo

Sleep on in thy sunny sand-dunes and slumber in thy byways. Old Monterey. Charles Warren Stoddard. CalPo

Sleep on the ground. Taneda Santoka. CAoMJL1, *tr. by* Burton Watson

Sleep, our lord, and for thy peace. Night Song for a Child. Charles Williams. OBEV

Sleep (Second Version). Georg Trakl. GTCP, *tr. by* Robert Firmage

Sleep, Silence' Child. William Drummond of Hawthornden. NePenScot (Sonnet: "Sleep, silence' child, sweet father of soft rest.") NOSC

Sleep, silence, darkness, cool white air, and language. (LL) Kenneth Koch. NAMCP V.2; NoAM *Fr.* Days and Nights.

Sleep, sleep. (LL) I Want to Sleep. Jorge Guillén. RaW; WoPoe, *tr. by* James Wright and James Wright

Sleep, sleep, beauty bright. Cradle Song, A. William Blake. OBEV

Sleep sleep old sun, thou canst not have repast [*or* repassed]. Resurrection, Imperfect. John Donne. ChIV-2

Sleep Softly. John Macrae. NePenScot, *tr. by* Derick Thomson

Sleep softly...eagle forgotten...under the stone. Eagle That Is Forgotten, The. Vachel Lindsay. APT-1; MoAmPo

Sleep Song. John Fletcher. NOSC

Sleep soundly, dear poet. Evelina Shats. CRWP, *tr. by* Daniel Weissbort

Sleep soundly, dogs: the Dog Star and the Maid. *Unknown.* PriapPo *Fr.* Priapus Poems, The.

Sleep Spaces. Robert Desnos. SurPaPo, *tr. by* Mary Ann Caws *and* Jean-Pierre Cauvin

Sleep sweetly in your humble graves. Ode. Henry Timrod. CBCWP; ColAP; MakPoe; NAAPv.1

Sleep Walk. Christopher Buckley. SUP

Sleep well, my love, sleep well. Nightsong: City. Dennis Brutus. HBAPE; PoetW; WoPoe

Sleep will He give His beloved? Nirvana. Rosamund Marriott Watson. VWP

Sleep Writer, The. Maggie Anderson. PLBUT

Sleep you shipwrecked sailor! (LL) Brief Lessons in Eroticism 1. Gioconda Belli. ErotSp; TANSG, *tr. by* Steven F. White

Sleep your sleep softly, my darling, my love. Sleep Softly. John Macrae. NePenScot, *tr. by* Derick Thomson

Sleepe after our short light / One everlasting night. (LL) Catullus. NoSic; OBVE *Fr.* Carmina.

Sleeper. Amy Fusselman. HeMarv

Sleeper. Patricia Pogson. NLP

Sleeper. Ken Worpole. RSaN

Sleeper, The. Edgar Allan Poe. BrAP; NAAL-3; NCAP

Sleeper, The ("As Ann came in one summer's day.") Walter De la Mare. MoBrPo

Sleeper in the Valley, The. Arthur Rimbaud. OBWP; WoPoe, *tr. by* William Jay Smith

Sleeper in the Valley, The. Arthur Rimbaud. OBWP *Fr.* Eighteen-Seventy.

Sleepers. Branko Miljkovic. WoPoe, *tr. by* Charles Simic

Sleepers, The. Walt Whitman. NAAL-3

"I wander all night in my vision." AWTN

"Now what my mother told me one day as we sat at dinner together." BLT

Sleepers, The. Walt Whitman. APN-1 *Fr.* Leaves of Grass [1855 Version].

Sleepers Awake. Diana Fitzgerald Bryden. OpeFie

Sleepers humped down on the benches, The. Night Raid. Desmond Hawkins. PoWW

Sleepers rise, roll up. Sleepers Awake. Diana Fitzgerald Bryden. OpeFie

Sleeping. (LL) Weep [*or* Weepe] You No More [Sad Fountains]. *Unknown.* NoP-5; NOSC; NoSic; TFi

Sleeping armies of the living God, The. Death of Saul, The. Philip Levine. ChIV-1

Sleeping at last, the trouble and tumult over. Sleeping at Last. Christina Georgina Rossetti. NAEL-6v2; NAEL-7v2

Sleeping Beauty. Ai. NAMCP V.2

Sleeping Beauty, The. Hayden Carruth.

"Called him "Big Joe" yes and Joe Turner it was his name." GifTon

"Your dream: / The letters HIV appear." GifTon

Sleeping Beauty, The. Samuel Rogers. OxAEP-2

Sleeping Beauty, The. Dame Edith Sitwell.

1. OBMV

Sleeping Beauty, The: Variation of the Prince. Randall Jarrell. PoA 2002

Sleeping Compartment. Norman Alexander MacCaig. EmeKit

Sleeping Father. David Chin. InvLad

Sleeping Fury, The. Louise Bogan. NAAPv.2; NALW

Sleeping Heroes. Edward Richard Burton Shanks. OBMV

Sleeping in Pulil Hermitage. Jaewol Kyunghun. BecRai, *tr. by* Kim Daljin, Kim Won-Chung and Christopher Merrill

Sleeping in the Forest. Mary Oliver. CAP-8; PLBUT

Sleeping late. Buson. EH, *tr. by* Robert Hass

Sleeping Lord, The. David Jones.

"Does he cock his weather-ear, enquiringly." TCAWP

"Tawny-black sky-scurries." OBWVE

Sleeping Man Must Be Awakened to Be Killed, A. Erin Belieu. NeAmPo

Sleeping on. Pinwheel, A. Ōkuma Kotomichi. EMJL, *tr. by* Peter Flueckiger

Sleeping on Horseback. Po Chü-i. BLT, *tr. by* Arthur Waley

Sleeping on the Ceiling. Elizabeth Bishop. APT-2; OBGa

Sleeping on the Nail. Na Hûidôk. EcSo, *tr. by* Peter H. Lee

Sleeping Soundly Where LIzzie Borden Did. Vivian Shipley. LiTh

Sleeping, turning in turn like planets. Adrienne Rich. TRP; WaAnP *Fr.* Twenty-one Love Poems.

Sleeping with Artemis. Josh Bell. LegDan; PoDa

Sleeping with the Dictionary. Harryette Mullen. AWPTFC

Sleeping with the Fishes. Helen Ivory. BeAl

Sleepless. Tatamkulu Afrika. TSAP

Sleepless. Ch'in Kuan. CrYelRi, *tr. by* Sam Hamill

Sleepless. Eileen Myles. WiU

Sleepless again, / I get up. Reading Chinese Poetry before Dawn. Jane Hirshfield. WANABP

Sleepless as Prospero back in his bedroom. Darwin in 1881. Gjertrud Schnackenberg. NoAM; NoP-4; NoP-5

Sleepless at Crown Point. Richard Wilbur. WeW-3

Sleepless at Midnight. Juan Chi. CCL1, *tr. by* Michael Bullock and C. J. Chen

Sleepless, I stare. Broken Dark, The. Robert Earl Hayden. AWTN; GT

Sleepless Night, A. Philip Levine. BLT

Sleepless Night, A. Pak Inhwan. CAMKP, *tr. by* Scott Swaner

Sleepless Nights. Tu Fu [*or* Du Fu]. CrYelRi, *tr. by* Sam Hamill

Sleepless Nights. Marilyn Nelson Waniek. ISC

Sleepless nights, The. I Wish I Were in Love Again. Lorenz Hart. OBCoV

(You don't know that I felt good.) ReLy

Sleepless with cold commemorative eye. (LL) Dante Gabriel Rossetti. BrAP; GSo; NAEL-6v2; NAEL-7v2; NoP-4 *Fr.* House of Life, The.

Sleepless, with pleasure and expiring fears. Walter Savage Landor. NOBRP *Fr.* Gebir.

Sleeplessness. Michelle Boisseau. ExTi

Sleeplessness. Gerardo Diego. BLPSL, *tr. by* Rene de Costa, Rigas Kappatos and Eleni Paidoussi

Sleeplessness. Luigi Fontanella. NeIt, *tr. by* W. S. Di Piero

Sleeplessness. Homer. The sails tight. Osip Emilevich Mandelstam. ASA, *tr. by* Robert Tracy

Sleep'ry Sim of the Lamb-kill. Fray of Suport, The. *Unknown.* IBB

Sleep's dream / the nerve-flash in the blood. Subliminal. Lorine Niedecker. PFTM-1

Sleep's Underside. Melissa Kirsch. AWTN

Sleep's very dear to me, but being stone's. "Night" in the Medici Chapel. Michelangelo Buonarroti. WoPoe, *tr. by* William Jay Smith

Sleep-song. *Unknown.* SonAtl, *tr. by* Leonard Allen, Alan Brierly and B. L. Surley

Sleep-Song of Grainne over Dermuid, The. Eleanor Hull. IrLP

Sleepwalker, The / circling upon his star. Sleepwalker, The. Nelly Sachs. GTCP, *tr. by* Michael Hamburger

Sleepwalkers' Ballad. Federico García Lorca. STV; WeW-3, *tr. by* John Frederick Nims

Sleepwalking Ballad, The. Federico García Lorca. WoPoe, *tr. by* Michael Hartnett

Sleepwalking Soho. Stuart Dybek. IllVoic

Sleep-walking vapor, like a visitant ghost. Still Life. Anthony Hecht. AmWaPo; NoP-4; NoP-5; PWW2

Sleep-Worker, The. Thomas Hardy. OxBSo

Sleepy Giant, The. Charles Edward Carryl. NOxBChV

Sleepy lagoon, A. Sleepy Lagoon. Jack Lawrence. ReLy

Sleepy Sentinel, The. Rudyard Kipling. PoAgWa *Fr.* Epitaphs of the War [1914–1918].

Sleepy Time Gal. Joseph Reed Alden and Raymond B. Egan. ReLy

Sleet. Kang Ŭn'gyo. EcSo, *tr. by* Ann Y. Choi

Sleet. Norman Alexander MacCaig. OBCP

Sleet and rain, as if the pot were boiling. Bad Government. Kuan Hsiu. WoPoe, *tr. by* Jerome P. Seaton

Sleet falls. Sleet. Kang Ŭn'gyo. CAMKP, *tr. by* Tae Yang Kwak

Sleet. / Not refreshing like rain. Sleet. Kang Ŭn'gyo. EcSo, *tr. by* Ann Y. Choi

Sleigh Ride in July. Johnny Burke. ReLy

Sleigh, The. Sergey Aleksandrovich Yesenin. RusPo, *tr. by* Robert Arthur Douglas Ford

Slender as a needle. Awotunde Aworinde. PFTM-1 *Fr.* If a Suite in Praise of the Yoruba Oracle.

Slender bamboo is like a hermit, The. On a Painting by Wang the Clerk of Yen Ling. Su Tung-p'o. BLT, *tr. by* Kenneth Rexroth

Slender, delicate, soft jade. Slender Fingers. Chao Luan-luan. CCL1; NDACCP, *tr. by* Chung Ling and Kenneth Rexroth

Slender Fingers. Chao Luan-luan. CCL1; NDACCP, *tr. by* Chung Ling and Kenneth Rexroth

Slender grasses. Traveling at Night. Tu Fu [*or* Du Fu]. WoPoe, *tr. by* Greg Whincup

Slender Lad, The. *Unknown.* OBWVE, *tr. by* Kenneth Hurlstone Jackson

Slender line. Mariiane Mays. PoPra *Fr.* (HERO)neck: attempts at a portrait.

Slender plank above a waterhole, A. Founding of New Hampshire, The. Carl Rakosi. FTOS

Slender rays: a chord barely seen. New Moon. Tu Fu [*or* Du Fu]. ChinPo, *tr. by* Ye Weilian [*or* Yeh Wei-lien *or* Wai-lim Yip]

Slender vessel used for weddings, The. Adult Joy. Brenda Hillman. RoV

Slice, A / Of precious stone. Broken Tablets. Hsi Chou. CSKM, *tr. by* Paul Hansen

Slice of Moon, A. Ko Ŭn. CAMKP, *tr. by* David R. McCann

Slice of Wedding Cake, A. Robert Graves. BrAP; NAEL-6v2; NAEL-7v2

Slices of flesh made burnt offering. Laughing at Myself 2. Ching An. CSKM, *tr. by* Jerome P. Seaton

Slices of Knowledge. Henri Michaux. YaTCFP

"He who knows how to shave the razor, will know how to erase the." PFTM-1

"If your child has a trunk on its nose, be not afraid of elephants." YaTCFP, *tr. by* Rosemary Lloyd

Slicing my head off shaving I think of Charles I. Notes for a Revised Sonnet. Edward Pygge. OBCoV

Slick. Víctor Hernández Cruz. PueRic

Slicker. David Trinidad. BeDoSh

Slide Show, The. Barbara Einzig *and* Jerome Rothenberg. OnScMo

Slide soft, fair forth, and make a crystal plain. Sonnet. William Drummond of Hawthornden. NOSC; OxBSo

Slides by on grease. (LL) For the Union Dead. Robert Lowell. AmWaPo; BrAP; CAP-8; CBCWP; ColAP; EMP; FaBoA; HarvBoo; HeIP-4; NAAL-5; NAMCP V.2; NoAM; NoP-4; NoP-5; OBWP; OxBoAm; PoetW; PoPoPo; PtR; TFi; TRP; VCAP; WaAnP; WeW-3

Sliding. Sam Adams. AngWePo

Sliding from half-up the eucalyptus trees, the wild desert pigs practice flight. Border, The. Joanna Rawson. BodElec

Sliding window, The. Confession of My Images. Barbara Guest. AWPTFC

Slievenamon. Charles Joseph Kickham. IrLP

Slight as thou art, thou art enough to hide. To a Daisy. Alice Thompson Meynell. MoBrPo; SacPr; VWP

Slight unpremeditated Words are borne. Love's Witness. Aphra Behn. LW

Slight wind stirs grasses along the bank, A. Thoughts on a Night Journey. Tu Fu [*or* Du Fu]. TAPaP; WaAnP, *tr. by* Arthur Sze

Slighted Lady, The. Anna Wickham. LW

Slightest crack, The. Bliss. Jean Follain. YaTCFP, *tr. by* Stephen Romer

Slightest vacuum when the concrete-mixer stops, The. Michael Haslam. Oth *Fr.* Continual Song.

Slim and singing copper girl, A. Early Copper. Carl Sandburg. HeIP-4

Slim cunning hands at rest, and cozening eyes. Slim Cunning Hands. Walter De la Mare. NIL-7; NIP-4; WeW-3

Slim Greer. Sterling Allen Brown. NAAPv.2; NAMCP V.1

Slim in Atlanta. Sterling Allen Brown. APT-2; NAMCP V.1; NoP-4; NoP-5

Slim Lands a Job? Sterling Allen Brown. NAAPv.2

Slim / young fascist, A. On the Yard. Etheridge Knight. RaBo

Slime on the stones. Ryunosuke Akutagawa. CAoMJL1, *tr.* by Makoto Ueda

Slim—Stout. Sikong Tu. CCL1 *Fr.* Twenty-Four Modes of Poetry.

Sling me under the sea. Bones. Carl Sandburg. TCAPo

Slink back with me. Vipers, Flies, and Women of the Cloth. James Coleman. BtF

Slip, The. Wendell Berry. UpMys

Slip of loveliness, slim, seemly. In Praise of a Girl. Huw Morus. OBWVE, *tr.* by Gwyn Williams

Slip of the tong. (LL) Lapsus Linguae. Keith Preston. NBLV; OBCoV

Slipped away / This occasion becomes remembering. Slipped Away. Norman Fischer. WANABP

Slippery Ground. Daniel Simidor. OGAHCP, *tr.* by Boadiba and Jack Hirschman

Slippery twitch near my loafer, toy so. Red Salamander—Video Store Parking Lot. Mark DeFoe. UrbNat

Slipping in blood, by his own hand, through pride. To an Artist, to Take Heart. Louise Bogan. TRP

Slips. Medbh McGuckian. MoWP; NAMCP V.2

Slipshod writing, premature publication. Martial. RomPo, *tr.* by Peter Whigham

Slit in the earth, A. Persephone 2. Cynthia Cruz. IAoNAP

Slithergadee has crawled out of the sea, The. Slithergadee, The. Shel Silverstein. NBLV; OBCoV

Sliver of Sermon. Langston Hughes. APT-2

Slobodan Milosevic is a marvelous father. Marvelous Father. Dana Levin. PoChi

Sloe Gin. Seamus Heaney. PNI

Slop Barrel, The. Philip Whalen. PmAP

Slope of it. Body. Robert Creeley. FTOS

Slope woods' snows melt. Easter Sunday. Allen Ginsberg. FTOS

Slopes of the sun and vine, and thou dark stream. Pastoral. George Cabot Lodge. APN-2

Slope-shouldered, bellies before them. Nurses. Julia Darling. PoCu

Sloshy sounds and high wire maneuvers. Venus Preserved. Kenward Elmslie. NYP2

Sloth. V. B. Price. ICANM

Sloth, The. Theodore Roethke. ChAP; ItP; TRP

Slouch. Brendan Cleary. NeBl

Slouches towards Bethlehem to be born? (LL) Second Coming, The. William Butler Yeats. BLPJKO; BrAP; CABP; ChIV-2; ClHu; CtM; EMP; GI; HarvBoo; HeIP-4; IrV; MoBrPo; NAAL-3; NAEL-6v2; NAEL-7v2; NAMCP V.1; NIL-7; NIP-4; NoAM; NoP-4; NoP-5; OxAEP-2; OxBEV; PoPoPo; RaBo; RSR; SoSe-8; TFi; TRP; WaAnP; WoPoe

Slough. Sir John Betjeman. HarvBoo; MoBrPo; NAMCP V.1; NoAM; OxAEP-2

Slough of unamiable liars. Ezra Pound. NAMCP V.1 *Fr.* Cantos.

Sloughing off ribs. (LL) Eve's Striptease. Julia Kasdorf. ACAMVP; NeAmPo

Slow. Marvin Bell. MoASP

Slow. Robert Francis. APT-2

Slow. George Stanley. NLPA *Fr.* Mountains and Air.

Slow and reluctant, now I have waited. Taking Leave of Wang Wei. Meng Hao Jan. CCL1, *tr.* by Witter Bynner

Slow Animals Crossing. W. N. Herbert. NeBrP; StAl

Slow, blue shadows of the olive groves, The. Good Men. Roberta Spear. GeoHom

Slow by slow people come. Christmas Eve: Nuyorican Café. Miguel Algarin. PueRic

Slow clear. That More Simple Natural Time Tone Distortion. Tom Raworth. Oth

Slow coffee shop days where talk of the mine and reheated gossip are mixed. This is a Small Northern Town. Rosanna Deerchild. PoPra

Slow Curtain. John Wheelwright. APT-2

Slow Dance. David St. John. AmAlph

Slow Delight. Leopoldo Lugones. BLPSL, *tr.* by Rene de Costa, Rigas Kappatos and Eleni Paidoussi

Slow dirty tears. (LL) Walking Around. Pablo Neruda. PoetW; VCWP, *tr.* by W. S. Merwin

Slow dulcimer, gavotte and bow, in autumn. Impossible to Tell. Robert Pinsky. InoFa

Slow Fade to Black. Thomas Sayers Ellis. LegDan

Slow for the sake of flowers as they turn. Release. R. S. Gwynn. RA

Slow horses and fast women. (LL) Proust's Madeleine. Kenneth Rexroth. NAMCP V.1; NoAM; TRP

Slow hour to come in: the barman making, A. Let's Not Get Ahead of Ourselves. John Redmond. NIrP

Slow in the Wintry Morn, the struggling light. Emigrants, The. Charlotte Smith. RWP

Slow moves the pageant of a climbing race. Slow Through the Dark. Paul Laurence Dunbar. GSo; SacPr

Slow Night on Texas Street, A. James Kimbrell. NAPBL

Slow on the leash, / pallid the leash-men! (LL) Ezra Pound. APT-1; MoAmPo; NAAPv.2; NAMCP V.1; NoAM; NPeEn; OxBoAm; TRP; WeW-3 *Fr.* Ripostes of Ezra Pound.

Slow overture of rain, The. Mind. Jorie Graham. WaAnP

Slow Pacific Swell, The. Yvor Winters. APT-2; CalPo; ColAP; HarvBoo; NAMCP V.1

Slow pass the hours—ah, passing slow! Ballade Tragique à Double Refrain. Max Beerbohm. OBSV

Slow River. Czeslaw Milosz. FaoP, *tr.* by Renata Gorczynski

Slow, Slow, Fresh Fount [Keep Time with My Salt Tears]. Ben Jonson. *See* Echo's [*or* Eccho's] Song.

Slow, slow, fresh fount, keep time with my salt tears. Ben Jonson. NOSC *Fr.* Cynthia's Revels.

Slow Song for Mark Rothko. John Taggart. PFTM-2

Slow splashing splashing. Malay Figures. *Unknown.* EaWin, *tr.* by W. S. Merwin

Slow the limpid currents twining. Canzonet. Mary Robinson. NOBRP

Slow Through the Dark. Paul Laurence Dunbar. GSo; SacPr

Slow toiling upward from the misty vale. Nearing the Snow-Line. Oliver Wendell Holmes. APN-1

Slow train, A. Few travellers. If. Eleanor Maxted. NewEx

Slow vengeance, like a blood-hound at his heels. (LL) To the Earl of Oxford, Late Lord Treasurer. Jonathan Swift. FaBoWar; OBVE

Slow wand'ring came the sightless sire and she. Antigone and Oedipus. Henrietta Cordelia Ray. CBWP-3

Slow-grained slide to embed the blade, The. Wedding the Locksmith's Daughter. Robin Robertson. NeBrP

Slowing Down for Death. Hal Sirowitz. PA9/11

Slowly. James Reeves. NOxBChV

Slowly. . . / The Scarecrow. Garry Gay. CalPo

Slowly along the lamp-emblazoned street. John Gould Fletcher. PoA 2002 *Fr.* Irradiations.

Slowly an armchair turns on some sort of pedestal. Dogged Persistence. Molly Peacock. PfS

Slowly, and flake by flake . . . At the drifted fond. Winter Night: Mount Royal. Abraham Moses Klein. NoAM

Slowly, by the slimy wooden wharves. Chicago River. Jun Fujita. NAAPv.2

Slowly, carefully, I live. (LL) Clouded Sky. Miklós Radnóti. GifTon; HP, *tr.* by Stephen Berg, F. J. Marks, S. J. Marks and Steven Polgar

Slowly he moves. Boy on a Swing. Mbuyiseni Oswald Mtshali. NIL-7

Slowly he sways that head that cannot hear. Rattler, Alert. Brewster Ghiselin. WeW-3

Slowly he turns himself round and round. Dancing Bear, The. Rachel Lyman Field. NTCP

Slowly I Open My Eyes. Amy Gerstler. MotU; SUP

Slowly in three to four weeks. My Girlfriends. Erich Fried. AF, *tr.* by Georg Rapp

Slowly, it is dusk. Now and Then. Alice B. Fogel. CFP

Slowly, like a hot tear tracing the skin's folds. Doomsday. Maurya Simon. ExTi

Slowly Nan the window goes. Planter's Charm. Fay M. Yauger. TiP2

Slowly out of the sun-blackened landscape. (LL) Rivers and Mountains. John Ashbery. NoAM; TRP

(Slowly out into the sun-blackened landscape.) (LL) FTOS; NoP-4

Slowly / Over cedars. Gyodai. ZenPo, *tr.* by Takashi Ikemoto and Lucien Stryk

Slowly, silently, now the moon. Silver. Walter De la Mare. MoBrPo

Slowly, slowly. David Steinberg. PasH

Slowly, Slowly, Horses. Julianne Buchsbaum. LegDan

Slowly, Slowly Poem, The. Yüan Hung-tao. ColAnChi, *tr.* by Jonathan Chaves

Slowly, slowly, / the autumn draws to its close. Written on the Ninth Day of the Ninth Month of the Year Yi-you. T'ao Ch'ien. CCL1, *tr.* by William Acker

Slowly, Slowly Wisdom Gathers. Mark Van Doren. PoA 2002

Slowly the clock is ticking the long hours. Museum Piece. Iorwerth Cyfeilog Peate. BBMWP, *tr.* by Joseph P. Clancy

Slowly the moon is rising out of the ruddy haze.　Aware.　D. H. Lawrence. MoBrPo; NAMCP V.1; NoAM

Slowly the ocean-liner.　Ocean Liner.　Ko Changsu.　WoPoe, *tr. by* the author

Slowly the old stone building walls downtown dissolve.　Kenneth Irby. PFTM-2

Slowly the poison the whole blood stream fills.　Missing Dates.　William Empson.　HarvBoo; MakPoe; MoBrPo; NAMCP V.1; NoAM; NoP-5; NPeEn; OxBEV; StAl

Slowly the sea is parted from the sky.　North of Berwick.　Sydney Tremayne. EdScPo

Slowly the tide creeps up the sand.　Slowly.　James Reeves.　NOxBChV

Slowly the women file to where he stands.　Faith Healing.　Philip Larkin. ChIV-2; GI; NAMCP V.2; NoAM; OxBEV

Slowly the world freezes into me.　Ice.　Ágnes Nemes Nagy.　IQMS, *tr. by* Ila Egon

Slowly things get rich, as if underwater.　Slide Show, The.　Barbara Einzig *and* Jerome Rothenberg.　OnScMo

Slowly through the tomb-still streets I go.　Lover's Farewell, The.　James Clarence Mangan.　IrLP

Slowness of Belief in a Spiritual World, The.　Jones Very.　NCAP

Slow-rolling beauty.　Mountains of California: Part 2, The.　Al Young. GeoHom

Slug.　Robert Siegel.　PfSP

Slug in Woods.　Earle Birney.　NoP-4

Sluggard, The.　W. H. Davies.　OBMV

Sluggard, The.　Isaac Watts.　OxBEV; UV

Slugs.　Gillian Ferguson.　MFPA

Slum man they killed, the mountain man lives on, The. (LL)　Early Lynching. Carl Sandburg.　ChIV-2; MoAmPo

Slumber Did My Spirit Seal, A.　William Wordsworth.　BrAP; CtM; HeIP-4; InoFa; NAEL-6v2; NAEL-7v2; NOBRP; NoP-4; NoP-5; NPBRoP; NPeEn; OxBEV; PoPoPo; WeW-3 *Fr.* Lucy.

Slumbering Passion.　Josephine D. Henderson Heard.　CBWP-4

Slumming on Park Avenue.　Irving Berlin.　APT-1

Slumped on a chair, his body is an S.　Lavatory Attendant, The.　Wendy Cope. MoWP; UV

Slumped on a pallet of winter-withered grass.　Cross Cut.　Peter Davison. ColAP

Slumped under the impressive genitals.　Boston Common.　John Berryman. CBCWP

Slung in mid-air. (LL)　Girl at the Window.　Pinkie Gordon Lane.　FuFl; GT

Slung over a screen.　Buson.　SoOfWa, *tr. by* Sam Hamill

Slurp me up like biscuits pick up gravy.　Home Cookin.　Estelle E. Farley. BtF

Slutty.　Mark Bibbins.　LegDan

Sma' was I, amang brether o' mine.　David and Goliath.　P. Hately Waddell. ChIV-1

Small / & with intensely.　Parents.　Hilda Morley.　PmAP

Small Acts.　Thomas Centolella.　GiftTon; ViWalt

Small, and absurd, and hers: for once, not hers, unclassified. (LL)　Edna St. Vincent Millay.　APT-1; InoFa; NALW; NAMCP V.1 *Fr.* Sonnets from an Ungrafted Tree.

Small and emptied woman you lie here a thousand years dead.　In the Museum. Isabella Gardner.　SoSe-8

Small arena almost filled, The.　Event.　Kim Addonizio.　MoASP

Small as a soul he is on the mountain ledge. (LL)　Coma.　Mimi Khalvati. PoCu; Prnts

Small as he is he can nimbly dance.　Tune: "Hung Hsiu-hsieh" To a Flea. Yang Na.　ColAnChi, *tr. by* James I. Crump

Small bird, The.　North-East.　*Unknown*.　WoPoe, *tr. by* Seamus Heaney

Small birds flit under.　Stranger.　Tisa Bryant.　BtF

Small boat, a fishing rod, A.　Fisherman's Song, A.　Jinkag Haesim.　BecRai, *tr. by* Kim Daljin, Kim Won-Chung and Christopher Merrill

Small boat lurches, drifting, The.　Gwbert: Mackerel Fishing.　Sam Adams. TCAWP

Small Bodies That Cannot Be Healed.　Fathi Abdullah.　AnVo, *tr. by* Mohamed Enani

Small bold breed, and steady to the game.　Oppian of Apamea [*or* Pella]. DiBP *Fr.* Cynegetica.

Small boy is looking for his voice, The.　Boy Unable to Speak, The.　Federico García Lorca.　WED, *tr. by* Robert Bly

Small bundle of bones, small bundle of fingers, of plumpness, of heart.　Song for the Burial of Natalie Going.　Susan Wheeler.　ExTi

Small but floating high.　Yun Sŏndo.　CATKP *Fr.* Songs of Five Friends.

Small but splendid is.　Smell.　'Enayat Jaber.　PoArWo, *tr. by* Wen Chin Ouyang

Small Celandine, The.　William Wordsworth.　NPeEn

Small change, when we'are [*or* we are *or* we're] to bodies gone. (LL)　Ecstasy, The.　John Donne.　BASC; CABP; FSCP; NAEL-6v1; NAEL-7v1; NoP-4; NoP-5; OBEV; OxBEV; TFi; WaAnP

Small cherries sip delicately.　Red Sandalwood Mouth.　Chao Luan-luan. CCL1; NDACCP, *tr. by* Chung Ling and Kenneth Rexroth

Small Comfort.　Katha Pollitt.　P180

Small doses, effleurage will do.　Sea or Sky?　Medbh McGuckian.　PBCIP

Small Dream.　Fujii Sadakazu.　PFTM-2 *Fr.* Where is Japanese Poetry?

Small fact and fingers and farthest one from me.　Poem for Emily, A.　Miller Williams.　InGu; WeW-3

Small Farm, A.　Michael Hartnett.　PBCIP

Small Female Skull.　Carol Ann Duffy.　EmeKit; HarvBoo; MoWP

Small Fig Tree, A.　Donald Hall.　ChIV-2; GI

Small fish-boats / After what.　Kagami Shiko.　ZenPo, *tr. by* Takashi Ikemoto and Lucien Stryk

Small fists waving.　Baby Hilary, Sir Edmund, The.　Kathleen Leland Baker. NBLV

Small flames afloat in a blue duskfall, beneath trees.　Mercy.　David Baker. Vesp

Small Frogs Killed on the Highway.　James Wright.　NAMCP V.2; NoAM

Small Girl Brings an Injured Bird into the Surgery, A.　Michael O'Reilly. BloBone

Small girl leading a horse.　Painting on a T'ang Dynasty Water Vessel.　Bruce Weigl.　AmAlph

Small girls on trikes.　Christmas Day.　Roy Fuller.　OBCP

Small gleams on the bank. (LL)　Bog Queen.　Seamus Heaney.　NAMCP V.2; NoAM; RACG

Small gnats that fly.　One Hard Look.　Robert Graves.　MoBrPo

Small gray cloudy louse that nests in my beard, The.　James Keir Baxter. NoP-4

Small hawk flutters fiercely upright, The.　Skylord.　Linda Gregg.　AFaM

Small hills upon small hills: sungold sheen comes and goes.　Tune: "Beautiful Barbarians."　Wen T'ing-yün.　ChinPo, *tr. by* Ye Weilian [*or* Yeh Wei-lien *or* Wai-lim Yip]

Small Hotel, A.　Selima Hill.　NeBrP

Small Hours.　David Barber.　AmPoNex

Small house, the room, The. I walk in.　Leslie Kaplan.　SCFWP *Fr.* Livre des ciels, Le.

Small is the thought of "Fatherland."　Matriatism.　Charlotte Perkins Stetson Gilman.　CalPo

Small Joys.　May Sarton.　FFC

Small Light, A.　Cathy Song.　TRP

Small Lochs.　Norman Alexander MacCaig.　NePenScot

Small Lower-Middle-Class White Southern Male.　Rodney Jones.　OxBoAm

Small mean feats and regurgitation of memories made baby wild.　Carla Harryman.　BAP-04 *Fr.* Baby.

Small. Miniaturized, yet you insist.　Country of Dust, The.　Vahan Tekeyan. AF, *tr. by* Diana Der Hovanessian and Marzbed Margossian

Small Miracle, A.　Anabel Torres.　TANSG, *tr. by* Celeste Kostopulos-Cooperman

Small Miseries.　Letitia Elizabeth Landon.　VWP

Small Moon on the Shoulder of New York.　George Keithley.　UrbNat

Small Number, A.　Olena Kalytiak Davis.　NAPBL

Small Ode to a Black Cuban Boxer.　Nicolás Guillén.　TCLAP, *tr. by* Robert Marquez and David Arthur McMurray

Small old spaniel,—which had been Don Jose's, A.　Lord Byron.　DiBP *Fr.* Don Juan.

Small outfit of contemporary techno-wizards who've taken up digs, The.　Tyger Tyger.　Andrew Schelling.　WANABP

Small Pain, A.　Martha Rhodes.　LaCa

Small Park, A.　Yi Yuksa.　CAMKP, *tr. by* Kyung-Ja Chun

Small Passing.　Ingrid de Kok.　HAWP; TSAP

Small Patch of Ice, A.　Betsy Sholl.　PBCAP

Small Plane in Kansas.　Thom Gunn.　OtW

Small Pleasures.　Angela Shaw.　NeAmPo

Small Power.　Lynne Hugo.　PfS

Small Prayer.　Weldon Kees.　PoA 2002

Small Print.　Daphne Marlatt.　OpeFie

Small Purchase.　Bob Hicok.　AmAlph

Small Rains.　N. M. Bodecker.　Spl

Small, rounded woman sits next to me, A. She is gumming sunflower seeds. Addison Street.　David Wright.　ACAMVP

Small sad man with a hat, A.　John Montague.　PBCIP *Fr.* Dead Kingdom, The.

Small Secret Book, A.　Michael McClure.　PFTM-2

Small Secrets.　John Montague.　ModIr

Small Sentence to Drive Yourself Sane.　Lew Welch.　WhBo

Small service is true service while it lasts. To a Child [Written in Her Album]. William Wordsworth. Spl

Small Sins. Maram Masri. PoArWo, *tr. by* Amal Amireh

Small Song. A. R. Ammons. NAMCP V.2; NoAM

Small Square, The. Sophia De Mello Breyner. VCWP, *tr. by* Ruth Fainlight

Small swallow's nest under the eaves. Sleeping on the Nail. Na Hûidôk. EcSo, *tr. by* Peter H. Lee

Small things, like the turning of a key. Chimes. Michael Smith. PBCIP

Small Town. Rita Dove. AmAlph; GT

Small Town with One Road. Gary Soto. SoSe-8

Small, unimaginable, cold. (LL) Lint. Rita Dove. AmAlph; TRP

Small Variation. Octavio Paz. VCWP, *tr. by* Mark Strand

Small Vases from Hebron, The. Naomi Shihab Nye. CAP-8; PoArWo

Small, viewless Æronaut, that by the line. To the Insect of the Gossamer. Charlotte Smith. OxBSo

Small village that danced all night, The. And it's Morning. Keita Fodeba. SonAtl, *tr. by* Gregory Beaven, Kurt Ganzl, Saul Goode and Jim Yarris

Small vocabulary, A. Peter Riley. VaPo *Fr.* Excavations.

Small War, A. Leslie Norris.
Eden. ArBi

Small wax candles melt to light, The. Poor Women in a City Church. Seamus Heaney. BrAP

Small wheel, A. Watch Repair. Charles Simic. NAMCP V.2; NoP-4; NoP-5

Small, where I let you see me. Imperialism—The Dancing Do Not Die. Thomas Stanley. BtF

Small wind lightly, A. Count Carrots. Gerda Mayer. OBSP

Small wind whispers through the leafless hedge, The. Winter. John Clare. CenSon

Small Wire. Anne Sexton. InvLi

Small wonder / he's not been sighted all winter. Brock. Paul Muldoon. NoAM; NoP-4

Small Wooden Vessel, A. Pak Sôwbn. EcSo, *tr. by* Julie C. Park

Smaller, older *Girl at a Sewing Machine*, The. Two Hoppers. John Updike. PoSol

Smaller than the small. Canticle of the Void, The. Paul Murray. InvLi

Smaller—that Covered Vision—Here. (LL) Renunciation—is a piercing Virtue. Emily Dickinson. APN-2; NoP-4; NoP-5

Smallest sting can wound the breast of Love, The. (LL) To the Eolian Harp. Mary Robinson. CenSon; RWP

Small-mouth bass breaks water, gorged with spawn, The. (LL) After the Surprising Conversions. Robert Lowell. NAMCP V.2; NoAM; TRP

Smallpox, insurrection. Was her kingdom not ravaged enough already? Empress Shōtoku Invents Printing in 1770. Teresa D. Cader. ExTi

Small-town Gladys. David Campbell. BMAP

Smalltown Memorials. Geoff Page. BMAP

Smalltown Yala. *Unknown.* SonAtl, *tr. by* Alan Brierly, Brenda Ginever and Malcolm Ginever

Smart. Fěng Měng-lung. ColAnChi; WoPoe *Fr.* Mountain Songs.

Smart armadillo stays, The. Dead Armadillos. Gail White. UrbNat

Smart or stupid they circle the hook: their education. (LL) Why Fool Around? Stephen Dobyns. PML; PoDa

Smash Your Fist. Anabel Torres. TANSG, *tr. by* Celeste Kostopulos-Cooperman

Smeared with the gold of the opulent sun. (LL) Postcard from the Volcano, A. Wallace Stevens. APT-1; GPTC; NAMCP V.1; NoAM; PoCho; SAmP; WeW-3

Smears re-bop / sound. (LL) Neon Signs. Langston Hughes. APSN; PFTM-1

Smell. 'Enayat Jaber. PoArWo, *tr. by* Wen Chin Ouyang

Smell. William Carlos Williams. MoAmPo; OxBoAm; RaBo (ßSmell!) SAmP

Smell and Envy. Douglas Goetsch. P180

Smell of autumn / Heart longs. Basho. ZenPo, *tr. by* Takashi Ikemoto and Lucien Stryk

Smell of Coal Smoke, The. Les A. Murray. NOBAu

Smell of coffee and of newspapers, The. Camden, 1892. Jorge Luis Borges. ViWalt, *tr. by* Willis Barnstone

Smell of fermenting wine, The. Little Kitchen Song, A. Mun Chônghui. EcSo, *tr. by* Catherine J. Kim

Smell of gasoline. (LL) Moose, The. Elizabeth Bishop. NAAL-5; NALW; NoP-4; NoP-5; StAl; WaAnP

Smell of him went soon, The. Four Years. Pamela Gillilan. StAl

Smell of leather in the air, A. When it's hot / The. Still Life. Stratis Haviaras. MotU

Smell of piss guides us down the halls. Hospital State, The. Betsy Sholl. PBCAP

Smell of snow, stinging in nostrils as the wind lifts it from a beach, The. Crystal Lithium, The. James Schuyler. PmAP; VCAP

Smell of the heat is boxwood, The. To Daphne and Virginia. William Carlos Williams. APT-1

Smell sweet and blossom in their dust. (LL) James Shirley. BASC; FaBoWar; NPeEn; OBEV; OxBEV; PBRV; WoPoe *Fr.* Contention of Ajax and Ulysses, The.

Smells. Bei Dao. WoBe, *tr. by* Iona Man-Cheong and Eliot Weinberger

Smelly Gulf water waves beckon. Memory Waves. Quo Vadis Gex-Breaux. FuFl

Smike. Lucile Adler. ICANM

Smilax in our homes entwine, The. Christmas Eve. Lizelia Augusta Jenkins Moorer. CBWP-3

Smile. Reuben Jackson. BtF

Smile, A. Nikolai Kanchev. CSCBP, *tr. by* Georgi Belev and Lisa Sapinkopf

Smile, A. Tzu Yeh. CrYelRi; ErotSp, *tr. by* Sam Hamill

Smile, The. William Blake. PtR

Smile, The. Luciana Frezza. CItWP, *tr. by* Cinzia Sartini Blum and Lara Trubowitz

Smile fell in the grass, A. Night Dances, The. Sylvia Plath. AmFaPo; MoWP

Smile for Daddy. Elizabeth Bartlett. Prnts

Smile his lips, A. Richard Wagner. EroLit *Fr.* Tristan and Isolde.

Smile of public art—only a possibility—and its curious, The. Robin Blaser. NLPA *Fr.* Image-Nation.

Smile of the Goat has a meaning that few, The. Smile of the Goat, The. Oliver Herford. OBCoV

Smile of the Walrus is wild and distraught, The. Smile of the Walrus, The. Oliver Herford. OBCoV

Smile/rippling river of dance. Tune for a Teenage Niece. Eugene B. Redmond. OxAAAP

Smile / Show me that the seeds of your discontent. 450 Years of Selective Memory (Smile). Ken McManus. BRtP

Smile, smile / Blest isle! Lilliputian Ode on Their Majesties' Accession, A. Henry Carey. FaBoVe; NPeEn; OBCoV

Smile————>stop smiling. Disappearing Music for Face. Mieko Shiomi. WhBo

Smiled at me and said, Yeah honey I guess I sure am. (LL) Waiting on Elvis, 1956. Joyce Carol Oates. AllShUp; PoA 2002; SwNoth

Smiles grow a little sharper. he blames it on the bossanova. he writes his own new arrangements. (LL) *Tall and* thin *and young and lovely the* michael with kaposi's sarcoma *goes walking.* D. A. Powell. AmPoNex; LegDan

Smiling and haunted, to a dark morning. (LL) To the Snake. Denise Levertov. NAAL-5; PoA 2002

Smiling becomes. Smile, The. Luciana Frezza. CItWP, *tr. by* Cinzia Sartini Blum and Lara Trubowitz

Smiling Dawn, with diadem of dew, The. Poet's Ministrants, The. Henrietta Cordelia Ray. CBWP-3

Smiling, faces pressed against the stone. (LL) Salmon. Jorie Graham. FaoP; StAl

Smiling mouth and laughing eyn grey, The. Smiling Mouth [and Laughing Eyen Grey], The. Charles, Duc d' Orléans. NoP-4; NoP-5

Smiling Through. Reed Whittemore. BodElec

Smirr. W. N. Herbert. NeBrP

Smith makes me, A. Rudyard Kipling. NoAM *Fr.* Puck of Pook's Hill.

Smiths, The. E. G. Murphy. NOBAu

Smithville Tandem Bike, The. W. T. Goodge. ArBi

Smitten. Rod Mengham. VaPo

Smitten Purist, The. James Whitcomb Riley. VerBaPo

Smitten with sorrow, overcast with gloom. Roaming the East Field. Hsieh T'iao. ChinPo, *tr. by* Ye Weilian [*or* Yeh Wei-lien *or* Wai-lim Yip]

Smoke. Rubén Bonitaz Nuño. STV, *tr. by* John Frederick Nims

Smoke. Dorianne Laux. RoV

Smoke. Philip Levine. MakPoe

Smoke. Susan Mitchell. EmeKit

Smoke. Jacob Polley. BeAl

Smoke. Henry David Thoreau. NAAPv.1; NoP-4; NoP-5

Smoke. Smoke Rose. Itamar Ya'oz-kest. HP, *tr. by* Glenda Abramson

Smoke and nothing the breath of being. Living and Dying. Manuel González Prada. SpanPo, *tr. by* Kate Flores

Smoke and Steel. Carl Sandburg.
"Smoke of the fields in spring is one." MoAmPo

Smoke Animals. Rowena Bastin Bennett. CA

Smoke contending with smoke which will be maddest. Portrait of an Engine Driver. Bobi Jones. OBWVE, *tr. by* Joseph P. Clancy

Smoke from the train-gulf hid by hoardings blunders upward. Birmingham. Louis MacNeice. MoBrPo; OxAEP-2

Smoke Gets in Your Eyes. Otto Harbach. ReLy

Smoke of the fields in spring is one. Carl Sandburg. MoAmPo *Fr.* Smoke and Steel.

Smoke on, salt swamps. Do Not Have Pity. Aimé Césaire. NAWM-7v2, tr. by Gregson Davis

Smoke Painting. Yoko Ono. WhBo

Smoke Rose. Itamar Ya'oz-kest. HP, tr. by Glenda Abramson

Smoke seeps slowly under the door. 1st Lt. John R. Fox: Rain of Fire. Jabari Asim. BtF

Smoke should dry me well before I slept, The. (LL) John Davies of Hereford. NPeEn; OBCoV Fr. Scourge of Folly, The.

Smoke shrouds cold water, moonlight shrouds sand. Mooring at River Ch'in-Huai. Tu Mu. ChinPo, tr. by Ye Weilian [or Yeh Wei-lien or Wai-lim Yip]

Smoke still burns between us, The. Fire/Water Blues. Darrell Stover. BtF

Smoke twisting over the scorched ground. This Curious Involvement, a Dominant Species. John Seed. Oth

Smoke upon Smoke. Mehmet Salihoḡlu. NaPG, tr. by Talat Sait Halman

Smoke We Make Pictures Of, The. Cortney Davis. FiBr

Smoke-Blackened Smiths. Unknown. OBCoV

Smokehouse, The. Yusef Komunyakaa. NoP-4; NoP-5

Smokestacks, Chicago. Campbell McGrath. LiTh

Smokey the Bear Sutra. Gary Snyder. WhBo

Smokey's Getting Old. Jessica Tarahata Hagedorn. OpBo

Smokin' my pipe on the mountings, sniffin' the mornin'-cool. Screw-Guns. Rudyard Kipling. FaBoWar

Smoking. Elton Glaser. BAP-97; P180

Smoking. Ronald Wallace. SwNoth

Smoking and shaving and drinking the dry beer. (LL) Way of Life, A. Howard Nemerov. NIL-7; NIP-4

Smoking & juvenile obesity are not uncommon in unhappy people. Don't Let Me Eat Dinner. Jeni Olin. FreRad

Smoky mist weaves through cold mountain forests. To the Tune: Beautiful Barbarian. Li Po. CrYelRi, tr. by Sam Hamill

Smoky summer evening, The. Window, The. Dino Campana. STV, tr. by John Frederick Nims

Smooth Gnarled Crape Myrtle. Marianne Moore. APT-1

Smooth in the extreme when they turned around diurnal. Angélica Tornero. SPV, tr. by Jen Hofer

Smooth simple path! whose undulating line. To a Gravel Walk. William Mason. OBGa

Smooth smell of Manhattan taxis, The. Dance of the Infidels. Al Young. ESEAA; SeSe

Smoothing the holy surfaces. (LL) Planet Earth. Patricia K. Page. BeAl; IFF

Smoothness of onions infuriates him, The. Onion. Katha Pollitt. RaBo

Smudges of moon in the morning. Preparation for the Big Emptiness. Kapka Kassabova. StAl

Smuggled human hair from Mexico. David Wojahn. P180; PBCAP Fr. Mystery Train: A Sequence.

Smuggling you in. (LL) White Porch, The. Cathy Song. BeAl; NAAL-5; YaYoPo

Snack. Stefanie Marlis. AFaM

Snack—a small or hurried meal, variation of the Middle English snacchen, snap. Snack. Stefanie Marlis. AFaM

Snag. Rosanna Deerchild. PoPra

Snail, The. Vincent Bourne. NPeEn; OBVE, tr. by William Cowper

Snail—baring. Issa. IllVoic Fr. Issa: A Suite of Haiku.

Snail gets up, The. Issa. EH; NIL-7, tr. by Robert Hass

Snail is climbing up the window-sill, A. For a Five-Year-Old. Fleur Adcock. StAl

Snail is necessary the bindweed is necessary, The. Garden of the One, The. Salah Stétié. YaTCFP, tr. by Marilyn Hacker

Snail moves like a, The. Hedgehog. Paul Muldoon. NAMCP V.2; NoAM; PBCIP; WaAnP

Snail [or Snayl], The. Richard Lovelace. NPeEn

Snail Poem. Peter Orlovsky. BB

Snail pushes through a green, The. Considering the Snail. Thom Gunn. NAEL-6v2; NAEL-7v2; OxBEV; PtR; StAl

Snail River. James Bertolino. PoCoUp

Snails have made a garden of green lace, The. After Rain. Patricia K. Page. BrAP

Snail's Lesson, The. Priscilla Jane Thompson. CBWP-2

Snails spit glistening threads on my poor pansies, chewed to lace. Natural Woman. Judith Taylor. SUP

Snake [with music]. Dannie Abse. NoAM

Snake. D. H. Lawrence. AmFaPo; BrAP; CABP; ChAP; HarvBoo; HeIP-4; NAEL-6v2; NAEL-7v2; NAMCP V.1; NoAM; NoP-4; NoP-5; OxBEV; TFi; UV; WaAnP

Snake. Dan Pagis. WoPoe, tr. by Stephen Mitchell

Snake, The. Michael Collier. WaAnP

Snake, The. Emily Dickinson. ClHu; HeIP-4; NAAL-3; NALW; NAMCP V.1; NIP-4; NoAM; NoP-4; NoP-5; SAmP; SoSe-8; TFi; TRP; WaAnP; WeW-3; WoPoe

(Narrow Fellow in the Grass, A.) BLT; BrAP; ChAP; ColAP; CtM; NAAL-5; NAAPv.1; NIL-7; OxBoAm; PoPoPo

Snake, The. Kenneth Mackenzie. BrAP

Snake, The. Vance Palmer. NOBAu

Snake came to my water-trough, A. Snake. D. H. Lawrence. AmFaPo; BrAP; CABP; ChAP; HarvBoo; HeIP-4; NAEL-6v2; NAEL-7v2; NAMCP V.1; NoAM; NoP-4; NoP-5; OxBEV; TFi; UV; WaAnP

Snake can separate itself, The. Fear Of Snakes. Lorna Crozier. OpeFie

Snake Dance [(Hotevilla)]. Witter Bynner. NAAPv.2

Snake Dress, The. Pascale Petit. MoWP

Snake on D. H. Lawrence, The. N. J. Warburton. UV

Snake snatched, The. Horned Snake, The. Louis Oliver. HATNAP; NAAPv.2

Snake swam across the blue stream. Four Divine Animals. Takahashi Shinkichi. ZenPo, tr. by Takashi Ikemoto and Lucien Stryk

Snake that Dances, The. Charles Baudelaire. EroLit

Snakebread. Hans Arp. MotU, tr. by Walter Howell III

Snakebread is the rapture of snakes. Snakebread. Hans Arp. MotU, tr. by Walter Howell III

Snakeroot. J. L. Jacobs. AmPoNex

Snakes. A. K. Ramanujan. NoP-4; NoP-5; WaAnP

Snakes. Nikolai Alekseievich Zabolotsky. TCRusP, tr. by Denis Johnson and Kathy Lewis

Snakes. Crased with the cipher of certainty they had crossed over the yellow plants in the garden to drink the light. Ecstasy. María Baranda. RMCMP, tr. by Mónica de la Torre

Snakes of September, The. Stanley Kunitz. ColAP; WaAnP

Snap it on and the anchor scrapes. Setting. Joe Denham. OpeFie

Snap tempered tooth chips. Sawmill. Richard Kenney. NoP-4; NoP-5

Snaps of Immigration. Víctor Hernández Cruz. TouFir

Snapshot. Lajos Kassák. IQMS, tr. by Edwin Morgan

Snapshot. Steve Kowit. PML

Snapshot. Charles Tomlinson. NAMCP V.2

Snapshot, A. Li Po. CCL1, tr. by H. A. Giles

Snapshot of a Crab-Picker among Barrels Spilling Over, Apparently at the End of Her Shift. Dave Jeddie Smith. NoAM

Snapshot: West Philly. Kimmika L. H. Williams. BtF

Snapshots. Mary Oliver. PoCoUp

Snapshots. John Updike. NoP-4

Snapshots of a Daughter-in-Law. Adrienne Rich. MoWP; NAAL-5; NALW; NAMCP V.2; NIL-7; NIP-4; NoAM; NoP-4; NoP-5; PoPoPo; VCAP; WaAnP

Snapshots of the Chameleon Woman. Perla Schwartz. TANSG, tr. by Celeste Kostopulos-Cooperman

Snare me the soul of a dragon-fly. Miyoko San. Mary Fenollosa. NAAPv.1

Snatch. Lincoln Kirstein. AmWaPo; PWW2

Snatch out of time the passionate transitory. (LL) Hospital, The. Patrick Kavanagh. CABP; EmeKit; ModIr; NPeEn

Snatches of the Fool's songs. Catch, The. Sandy Feinstein. IaFF

Sneeze, A. Sŏ Chŏngju. VCWP, tr. by David R. McCann

Sneeze on [a] Monday, [You] sneeze for danger. Sneezing. Unknown. NBLV

Sneezing. Unknown. NBLV

Sniff for madness—you'll find ripped-up quartets. Stout Brahms. Bruce Berger. GeoH

Sniff of the real, that's, The. Autobiography. Thom Gunn. NoAM

Sniffed, dilating my nostrils. Elvin's Blues. Michael S. Harper. LoL

Sniper. Lucien Stryk. PWW2

Snipers. Roger McGough. RSaN

Snoad Hill Poems, The. Elaine Randell.

  "And if my light should." Oth

  "Hedge breaks out in bud, The." Oth

  "Its this familiar black line from the tops." Oth

  "Jetty, The." Oth

  "O house, o sloping field, o poplar trees whose tall arms salute." Oth

  "Our hands crushed." Oth

  "She had the stance of a snowdrop." Oth

  "Temperament is related to physique." Oth

  "Waiting." Oth

  "Walking towards the village." Oth

Snoblesse Oblige. Elizabeth Barrett Browning. STuOW Fr. Lady Geraldine's Courtship.

Snore in the foam: the night is vast and blind. Tristan da Cunha. Roy Campbell. MoBrPo

Snoring in New York. Edwin Denby.
  "New York, smog-dim under August." AHA
  "When I come, who is here? voices were speaking." AHA
Snoring of the storm in Melleray last night, The. Mount Melleray. Sean O
  Riordain. ModIr, tr. by Patrick Crotty
Snow. Adelaide Crapsey. APT-1
Snow. William Virgil Davis. YaYoPo
Snow. Walter De la Mare. OxAEP-2
Snow. Regina DeCormier-Shekejian. TWW
Snow. George Dillon. IllVoic
Snow. Vladimir Holan. StAl, tr. by Ian Milner and Jarmila Milner
Snow. Dulce Maria Loynaz. TANSG, tr. by Alan West
Snow. Louis MacNeice. HarvBoo; ModIr; NAMCP V.1; NoAM; NPeEn;
  OPOU; OxAEP-2; OxBEV; PNI; StAl
Snow. Jessemyn Meyerhoff. WhBo
Snow. Muso Soseki. EaWin, tr. by W. S. Merwin
Snow. William Robert Rodgers. ModIr
Snow. Maurya Simon. FiBr
Snow. Edward Thomas. OPOU
Snow: "Walking through a field with my little brother Seth." David Berman.
  P180
Snow: "It snowed. It snowed comfortably. No, that's not it. In the beginning, it
  snowed violently." Yi Chinmyŏng. EcSo, tr. by Carolyn U. So
Snow: "Over strip-raked iron rooves." Atanas Dalchev. SonAtl, tr. by Tamara
  Romanyk and Frederick Spencer
Snow: "Who affirms that crystals are alive?" John Davidson. EdScPo;
  NePenScot; NPeEn
Snow: "White is lying on top of the green, The." Jorge Guillén. RaW, tr. by
  Robert Bly
Snow: "White moths in crazy mobs." M. C. Richards. WhBo
Snow: "Today the snow is drifting." Philip Levine. ColAP; UrbNat; WaAnP
Snow: "Purpose of the blanket, The." Elizabeth Robinson. IIR
Snow, The. Yves Bonnefoy. YaTCFP, tr. by John Naughton
Snow, The. Emily Dickinson. MoW; SoSe-8; WHSW
Snow, The: "Snow is in the oak." Donald Hall. MoW
Snow [with music]. Charles Wright. CAP-8; ColAP; OxBoAm
Snow; a fear of dying. Matt Robinson. Coast
Snow and the Plum, The—1. Lu Mei-Po. TAPaP, tr. by Red Pine
Snow and the Plum, The—2. Lu Mei-Po. TAPaP, tr. by Red Pine
Snow and then rain. The roads are wet. A car. Edgar Bowers. VCAP Fr.
  Autumn Shade.
Snow astonishing their hammered faces. Prisoners of Saint Lawrence, The.
  Martín Espada. PoCho; TouFir
Snow at Rohatsu Sesshin. Muso Soseki. EaWin, tr. by W. S. Merwin
Snow bared the black lines of hedges in thorn. Wishes. Ger Killeen.
  AmPoNex
Snow besieges my plank door I crowd the stove at night. Han-shan Te-ch'ing.
  CSKM, tr. by Red Pine
Snow came down last night like moths, The. First Snow in Alsace. Richard
  Wilbur. AmWaPo; NoP-4; NoP-5; OBWP; PWW2
Snow Climbers. Steve Wiesinger. PasH
Snow closed the road. Nazim Hikmet. NaPG, tr. by Talat Sait Halman
Snow collects. Living at a Monastery, Sent to Chien Chang. Huai Ku.
  CSKM, tr. by Paul Hansen
Snow coming in parallel to the street. Grief. William Matthews. BeAl;
  CAP-8; PoCho
Snow Country Weavers. James Welch. HATNAP
Snow covers earth and sky everything is new. Han-shan Te-ch'ing. CSKM, tr.
  by Red Pine
Snow Day. Billy Collins. BAP-01
Snow Day. Rosanna Warren. MoW
Snow dissolv'd no more is seen, The. Horace. NAEL-6v1; NAEL-7v1 Fr.
  Odes.
Snow doesn't start its journey. Seeing Snow. Mun Chŏnghui. EcSo, tr. by
  Catherine J. Kim
Snow envelops the mountain house; the tree shadows darken, The. Reading a
  Book on a Winter Night. Kan Chazan. EMJL, tr. by Haruo Shirane
Snow fall on green leaves. Joanne Kyger. WANABP
Snow falling. Snowfall. Artis Bernard. NTCP
Snow falling and night falling fast, oh, fast. Desert Places. Robert Frost.
  APT-1; BrAP; HarvBoo; MoAmPo; NAAL-5; NAAPv.2; NAMCP V.1;
  NoAM; OxBoAm; SoSe-8; TRP
Snow falling around the man in the naked woods, The. White Heart of God,
  The. Jack Gilbert. BodElec
Snow Falling in the Pine Forest: Two Poems. Chŏng Ch'ŏl. tr. by Kevin
  O'Rourke
  "Snow falling in the pine forest." WoPoe, tr. by Kevin O'Rourke
  "Why does that pine tree stand." WoPoe, tr. by Kevin O'Rourke

Snow falls. A raven flies through it. Crossing. Pamela Alexander. AmAlph
Snow falls after it fell. Snow. Kim Suyŏng. CAMKP, tr. by Kevin O'Rourke
Snow falls deep; the forest lies alone, The. Gipsies [or The Gipsy Camp].
  John Clare. NoP-5
Snow falls on the mountain village. Myŏngok. CATKP, tr. by Peter H. Lee
Snow falls over Chagall's village in March. Snow over Chagall's Village.
  Kim Ch'unsu [or Chun-soo]. CAMKP, tr. by Anthony, Brother of Taizé
Snow falls so hard the neighbors' windows seem. Hangman. Philip Stephens.
  AmPoNex
Snow falls with, The. If You Listen. Rosemerry Wahtola Trommer. GeoH
Snow fell, and its power was multiplied, The. Russia 1812. Victor Hugo.
  FaBoWar; OBWP, tr. by Robert Lowell
Snow Fell Twice, the Sun Always Shone. Sakyong Mipham. WhBo
Snow fills the fields like milk. Mother: Dorcas Good, The. Nicole Cooley.
  NeAmPo
Snow fills the leaves that haven't blown. Quiet Earth, The. Heid E. Erdrich.
  AmPoNex
Snow flakes / I counted till they danced so. Emily Dickinson. MoW
Snow Garden. Muso Soseki. EaWin, tr. by W. S. Merwin
Snow Globe, The. Howard Nemerov. ItP
Snow had begun in the gloaming, The. First Snowfall [or Snow-Fall], The.
  James Russell Lowell. AmFaPo; MoW
Snow had buried Stuyvesant, The. Inauguration Day: January 1953. Robert
  Lowell. OxBSo
Snow had fallen many nights and days, The. End of the World, The. Gordon
  Bottomley. MoBrPo
Snow has covered the next line of tracks. Looking at New-Fallen Snow from a
  Train. Robert Bly. GM
Snow has gone from Zhongnan; spring is almost come, The. Passing Tianmen
  Street in Chang'an and Seeing a Distant View of Zhongnan Mountains. Po
  Chü-i. CCL1, tr. by Arthur Waley
Snow has melted now, The. January. Douglas Gibson. OBCP
Snow hurries / the strawberries. Jay Wright. ESEAA Fr. Love's Dozen.
Snow immaculate upon that mountain's brow!, The. (LL) Mount Shasta:
  "Behold the dread Mt. Shasta, where it stands." John Rollin Ridge.
  APN-2; CalPo
Snow in Condoland. Chase Twichell. PfSP
Snow in Europe. David Gascoyne. NPeEn
Snow in North Jersey. August Kleinzahler. BeAl
Snow in October. Alice Moore Dunbar-Nelson. InGu
Snow in the Suburbs. Thomas Hardy. MoBrPo; OBMV
Snow in Wrexham. Bryan Martin Davies. BBMWP, tr. by Elin ap Hywel
Snow is a mind. Revival. Steve Crow. HATNAP
Snow is a strange white word. On Receiving News of the War. Isaac
  Rosenberg. HarvBoo; MoBrPo; OBWP; OxAEP-2; PoWW
Snow Is Falling. Boris Leonidovich Pasternak. ChAP
Snow Is Falling. Tomas Tranströmer. WoBe, tr. by Robin Fulton
Snow is falling along the Boulevard. Snow in North Jersey. August
  Kleinzahler. BeAl
Snow is falling, snow is falling. Snow Is Falling. Boris Leonidovich
  Pasternak. ChAP
Snow is in the oak. Snow, The. Donald Hall. MoW
Snow is knee-deep in the courtyard, The. Cucumber, The. Nazim Hikmet.
  VCWP
Snow is melting, The. Issa. EH, tr. by Robert Hass
Snow is snowing, The. I've Got My Love to Keep Me Warm. Irving Berlin.
  ReLy
Snow is water. Snow. Dulce Maria Loynaz. TANSG, tr. by Alan West
Snow is weaving a soft, white, shroud, The. Dying Year, The. Clara Ann
  Thompson. CBWP-2
Snow is white on wood and wold, The. Kiss, The. Edith Nesbit. LW
Snow is witherin' off'n the' gress, T'. Drained Cup, The. D. H. Lawrence.
  FaBoVe
Snow Landscape, in a Glass Globe. Jean Valentine. CAP-8
Snow Lies Sprinkled on the Beach, The [with music]. Robert Bridges. NoAM
Snow lies there—ro' räni'!, The. Unknown. APN-2 Fr. Ghost-Dance Songs.
Snow Light, The [with music]. May Sarton. APT-2; NBLV
Snow Line. John Berryman. PoA 2002
Snow Lip. Iain Sinclair. Oth Fr. Ebbing of Kraft, The.
Snow Maiden, The. Bella Akhatovna Akhmadulina. TCRusP, tr. by Daniel
  Weissbort
Snow makes Monday as white. Notes on a Blizzard. Maxine W. Kumin.
  MoW
Snow Man, The. Wallace Stevens. AmFaPo; APT-1; ColAP; GoPo; HarvBoo;
  HeIP-4; IJHIL; MoW; NAAL-5; NAAPv.2; NAMCP V.1; NoAM; NoP-4;
  NoP-5; OxBoAm; PoA 2002; PoPoPo; SoSe-8; StAl; TCAPo; TRP;
  WaAnP; WeW-3
Snow Melting. Gjertrud Schnackenberg. StAl
Snow Monkey Argues with God, The. David Huddle. PfSP

Snow. No roofs this morning, alps, ominous message. Cold. Anne Stevenson. PfSP

Snow, not the rare snow of Jerusalem. Little Research in Snow, A. Gabriel Preil. FIT, *tr. by* Robert Friend

Snow obstructs my brushwood door with me inside alone. Han-shan Te-ch'ing. CSKM, *tr. by* Red Pine

Snow on a Mountain. Dom Moraes. NoP-4; NoP-5

Snow on a Southern State. James Dickey. LPSFW

Snow on Lotus Mountain. Liu Ch'ang-ch'ing. CCL1, *tr. by* Kenneth Rexroth

Snow on my ladder's rungs, The. Winter Regrets. Bill Knott. BodElec

Snow on Saddle Mountain, The. Miyazawa Kenji. ColAP; NoAM; OxBoAm; WaAnP, *tr. by* Gary Snyder

Snow on the Desert. Agha Shahid Ali. AmAlph

Snow, out over the elephant's rump. Landscape Winter. Anne Sexton. MoW

Snow out the window's light. B. P. Nichol. NLPA *Fr.* Inchoate Road.

Snow over Chagall's Village. Kim Ch'unsu [*or* Chun-soo]. CAMKP, *tr. by* Anthony, Brother of Taizé

Snow panels, ice pipes, house the afternoon. January of a Gnat, The. Carl Rakosi. APT-2; FTOS

Snow Party, The. Derek Mahon. HarvBoo; ModIr; NAMCP V.2; NPeEn; PBCIP; PNI; WaAnP

Snow Poem. Rodolfo Di Biasio. NeIt, *tr. by* Stephen Sartarelli

Snow Poem. Roger McGough. Spl

Snow, rocks darker than any shadow in the world. Undiscovered Country. James Longenbach. NAPBL

Snow settles over the night, A. Yun Sŏndo. CATKP *Fr.* Angler's Calendar, The.

Snow Signs. Charles Tomlinson. NoAM

Snow, Snow. Marge Piercy. MoW

Snow, snow over the whole land. Winter Night. Boris Leonidovich Pasternak. GPTC, *tr. by* Richard McKane

Snow Song. Henrietta Cordelia Ray. CBWP-3

Snow Songs. W. D. Snodgrass.
  "One. now another. one." InvLad

Snow Storm. Dunya Mikhail. IrPoTo, *tr. by* Liz Winslow

Snow Storm. Tu Fu [*or* Du Fu]. BLT; NDACCP, *tr. by* Kenneth Rexroth

Snow Storm, The. Mary Weston Fordham. CBWP-2

Snow sweeps through February. Poem in Three Parts. S. J. Marks. BodElec

Snow twirling night road. For a Moose. Denise Lassaw-Paljor. WhBo

Snow: II. C. K. Williams. NoP-4; NoP-5

Snow Valley. Muso Soseki. EaWin, *tr. by* W. S. Merwin

Snow was falling last night when I returned. Stain. Stuart Dybek. LiTh

Snow whispers about me, The. Falling Snow. Amy Lowell. ColAP

Snow White and the Seven Deadly Sins. R. S. Gwynn. SoSe-8

Snow White and the Seven Dwarfs. Anne Sexton. PoPoPo

Snow White was nude at her wedding, she's so white. Lessons from a Mirror. Thylias Moss. ESEAA; LTA; OxAAAP

Snow wind-whipt to ice. Winter. Richard Hughes. OBMV; OBWVE

Snow-Ball, The. Soame Jenyns. OBVE

Snow-Ball, The. Thomas Stanley. NPeEn

Snowbanks North of the House. Robert Bly. BodElec; CAP-8; RaBo

Snow-Bound [*or* Snow-Bound] [A Winter Idyl]. John Greenleaf Whittier. APN-1; ColAP; NAAL-3; NAAL-5; NAAPv.1; TCAPo; TFi
  Firelight. OBCP
  "Shut in from all the world without." NoP-5
  "Sun that brief December day, The." MoW
  Winter Night. CtM

Snowcone Vendor. Josaphat Robert Large. OGAHCP, *tr. by* Boadiba and Jack Hirschman

Snow-covered dead, The. Dead, The. José María Eguren. TCLAP, *tr. by* Iver Lofving

Snow-Day. Judith Baumel. KGB

Snowdonia after Chernobyl. BBMWP, *tr. by* Joseph P. Clancy

Snowdrop. Ted Hughes. HarvBoo

Snowdrop, The. Mary Weston Fordham. CBWP-2

Snowdrop of dogs, with ear of brownest dye. Sonnet: To Tartar, a Terrier Beauty. Thomas Lovell Beddoes. OxBSo

Snowdrops [*with music*]. Margiad Evans. OBWVE

Snowdrops. George MacBeth. OBCP

Snowdrops and Summer Snowflakes, Drooping. Reginald Shepherd. IaFF

Snowed. Some of Betty's Story Round 1850. Gale Jackson. SpirFl

Snowed-in cross within the woods, A. Woodland Cross, The. Endre Ady. IQMS, *tr. by* Anton N. Nyerges

Snowfall. Artis Bernard. NTCP

Snowfall, The [*with music*]. Gwerfyl Mechain. OBWVE, *tr. by* Kenneth Hurlstone Jackson

Snowfall; a Poem about Spring. James Wright. NoAM

Snowfall in March. For Lew Welch in a Snowfall. Gary Snyder. InoFa

Snowfall Is So Silent, The. Miguel de Unamuno. RaW, *tr. by* Robert Bly

Snowfall on a College Garden. Cecil Day Lewis. OBGa

Snow-Fiend, The. Anne Batten Cristall. RWP

Snowflake. First Snowflake. N. M. Bodecker. TLR

Snowflake Which Is Now and Hence Forever, The. Archibald MacLeish. NoP-4; NoP-5

Snow-Flakes. Henry Wadsworth Longfellow. APN-1; BrAP; CtM; ITBLP; MoW; NCAP; NoP-4; NoP-5; TCAPo

Snowflakes. Howard Nemerov. NAMCP V.2

Snowflakes. Clive Sansom. OBCP

Snowflakes flutter—butterflies chase flowers. Kim Yŏng. CATKP, *tr. by* Peter H. Lee

Snow-Flakes, The. Priscilla Jane Thompson. CBWP-2

Snowflakes were teeming down. Jerzy Ficowski. HP *Fr.* Assumption of Miriam from the Street in the Winter of 1942, The.

Snowflame. Kawai Suimei. CAoMJL1, *tr. by* Leith Morton

Snowman in a field. Roger McGough. Spl

Snowman in the yard is frozen hard, The. Let It Snow! Let It Snow! Let It Snow! Sammy Cahn. ReLy

Snowman Sniffles. N. M. Bodecker. TLR

Snowpoems. Dan Guillory.
  "Retinal burn of warm November light." IllVoic

Snows are fled away, leaves on the shaws, The. Diffugere Nives. A. E. Housman. AmFaPo

Snows are thaw'd, now grass new cloaths the earth. Horace. NPeEn *Fr.* Odes.

Snows dissolving, grass returns to meadow. Horace. WoPoe *Fr.* Odes.

Snows of February had buried Christmas, The. Christmas Robin, The. Robert Graves. ChrPo

Snows that glittered on the disk of Mars, The. Oliver Wendell Holmes. APN-1 *Fr.* Wind-Clouds and Star-Drifts.

Snow's thick froth scraped off by rain, The. After the Snow. Rayne Mackinnon. EdScPo

Snowstorm made the earth tremble, A. Winter Night. Boris Leonidovich Pasternak. WoPoe, *tr. by* Edwin Morgan

Snow-Storm [*or* Snowstorm], The. Ralph Waldo Emerson. APN-1; BrAP; ITBLP; MoW; NAAL-3; NAAPv.1; NCAP; NoP-4; NoP-5; OxBoAm; PoPoPo; TCAPo; TFi; TreFP; WaAnP

Snowy coats and snowy crests and beaks of blue jade. Egrets. Tu Mu. WoPoe, *tr. by* A. C. Graham

Snowy curtain / slides up the sky, A. Noon Office. James Schuyler. BodElec

Snowy Day, A. *Unknown.* OBWVE, *tr. by* H. Idris Bell

Snowy Egret. Bruce Weigl. UrbNat

Snowy morning, A. Basho. EH, *tr. by* Robert Hass

Snowy Owl. Matthew J. Spireng. PoCoUp

Snowy owl, storm cast from the arctic tundra. Snowy Owl near Ocean Shores. Duane Niatum. HATNAP

Snowy River. Liu Tsung-yüan. CrYelRi, *tr. by* Sam Hamill

Snowy Sky. Takahashi Shinkichi. ZenPo, *tr. by* Takashi Ikemoto and Lucien Stryk

Snowy white, the tar baby promised. Tar Baby on the Soapbox, The. Carole Boston Weatherford. BtF

Snub end of a dismal year. Reading Lao Tzu Again in the New Year. Charles Wright. PfSP; PoA 2002

Snub-nosed, bone-fingered, deft with engraving tools. Death the Painter. Anthony Hecht. NoP-4; NoP-5

Snub-nosed dog, to fat inclined, A. Christopher Smart. DiBP *Fr.* English Bull Dog, Dutch Mastiff, and Quail, The.

So. Citadel. Edward Kamau Brathwaite. VCWP

So? Leonard Nathan. PBCAP

So Abram rose, and clave the wood, and went. Parable of the Old Men and the Young, The. Wilfred Owen. ChIV-1; HarvBoo; RSaN

So all day long the noise of battle rolled. Alfred Tennyson. NIP-4; OBNV; OxAEP-2 *Fr.* Morte d'Arthur.

So all through Troy the men who had fled like panicked fawns. Homer. NAWM-7v1 *Fr.* Iliad, The.

So all within be livelier than before. (LL) Forerunners, The. George Herbert. AngWePo; FSCP; NAEL-6v1; NAEL-7v1; NoP-4; NoP-5; PBRV

So am I as the rich, whose blessed key. William Shakespeare. OxAEP-1 *Fr.* Sonnets.

So angels love and all the rest is dross. Platonic Love. Elizabeth Singer Rowe. BASC

So apparent, wanting so much that it bothers me. (LL) Rondeau at the Train Stop. Erin Belieu. GifTon; NeAmPo

So as I sit still on the porch. Letter Left On the Porch of the Kerouac House. Ray McNiece. AmZen

So autumn comes to an end with these few wet sad stains. Christmas East of the Blue Ridge. Charles Wright. LPSFW

So Bartas-like thy fine spun poems been. Anagram, An. *Unknown.* TCAPo

So Be It. Ruth Stone. ExTi

So be merry, so be dead. (LL)   All the hills and vales along.   Charles Hamilton Sorley.   MoBrPo; OBWP; OxAEP-2; PoWW

So Beautiful.   Indran Amirthanayagam.   OpBo

So beautiful? (LL)   Air Raid.   Sachiko Yoshihara.   CFP; GifTon, tr. by Naoshi Koriyama and Edward Lueders and Edward Lueders

So beautiful that couple.   So Beautiful.   Indran Amirthanayagam.   OpBo

So beautiful the lungs.   From "Songs of a Wanderer."   Aleksander Wat.   BLT

So, because you chose to follow me into the subtle sadness of night.   Giving Back the Flower.   Sarah Morgan Bryan Piatt.   APN-2; NAAPv.1

So, behind the heavy backyard orchard.   We Wondered about the Mellow Peaches.   Jack A. Mapanje.   HBAPE

So big in life, head like a chopping block.   Kookaburra.   Frieda Hughes.   NeBl

So bored we made a film of our lives.   Clownfish.   Lavinia Greenlaw.   MoWP

So Bring the Order for My Execution.   Faiz Ahmad Faiz.   VCWP, tr. by Agha Shahid Ali

So by sixteen we move in packs.   Deliberate.   Amy Uyematsu.   CalPo

So careful of the type? but no.   Alfred Tennyson.   BrAP; NAEL-6v2; NAEL-7v2; NAWM-7v2; NoP-5; NPeEn; WaAnP Fr. In Memoriam A. H. H.

So close I felt a rift in the air.   On Not Finding Frost's Grave in the Dark.   Bruce Weigl.   VisFro

So cold? (LL)   Warning, The.   Adelaide Crapsey.   APT-1; NAAPv.2; Spl; TCAPo

So cold and lost for ever evermore. (LL)   Dead before Death.   Christina Georgina Rossetti.   NAEL-6v2; NAEL-7v2; NALW

So covetous Ballaam with fond intent.   Abraham Cowley.   ChIV-1 Fr. Davideis.

So coy, pretending shyness. (LL)   Li Po.   CrYelRi; ErotSp Fr. Women of Yueh.

So cruel [or cruell or crewell] prison how could betide [or howe coulde betyde], alas.   Prison in Windsor Castle.   Henry Howard, Earl of Surrey.   NoSic

So Cruel Prison.   Henry Howard, Earl of Surrey.   See Prison in Windsor Castle.

So cruel prison how could betide, alas.   Henry Howard, Earl of Surrey.   CABP; NAEL-6v1; NAEL-7v1 Fr. Windsor Castle.

So dawn. A morcellation of the dark, the one.   A.M.: The Hopeful Monster.   Alice Fulton.   PfSP

So, Dear, your mother says you got a divorce.   Family Reunion—Aunt Vern's Two Cents.   Beth Gylys.   AmPoNex

So different, this man.   Marriage.   William Carlos Williams.   PoA 2002

So does the sun withdraw his beam[e]s.   On His Mistress Going from Home [Song].   Unknown.   NOSC

So don't tell me what to write. (LL)   Poet Is Not a Jukebox, A.   Dudley Randall.   BRtP; NoAM

So, driven to new shoes incessantly.   Lake, The.   Alphonse Marie Louis de Lamartine.   SxFrPo, tr. by A. M. and E. H. Blackmore

So Drunk Am I with the Night, the Air, and the Trees.   Mona Saudi.   PoArWo, tr. by Kamal Boullata

So drunk, I enfold the seas of forgetfulness.   So Drunk Am I with the Night, the Air, and the Trees.   Mona Saudi.   PoArWo, tr. by Kamal Boullata

So early it's still almost dark out.   Happiness.   Raymond Carver.   GoPo; PoA 2002; StAl

So elegant, so simple, yet thought.   Insulin Receptor.   H. J. Van Peenen.   BloBone

So fair thy vision that the night.   Milton.   John Banister Tabb.   APN-2

So faire, so fressh, so goodly on-to see.   Unknown.   OHMEL

So fairely mounted in fertile Soile.   On the Situation of Highbury.   Katherine Austen.   EMWP

So fallen! so lost! the light withdrawn.   Ichabod[!].   John Greenleaf Whittier.   APN-1; NAAL-3; NAAL-5; NAAPv.1; PoCho; TCAPo

So far, have managed, Not.   Small Number, A.   Olena Kalytiak Davis.   NAPBL

So Far Off and Yet Here.   C. D. Wright.   CAP-8

So. Farewell Krishna.   In Memoriam Krishna Menon.   E. J. Thribb.   OBCoV

So. Farewell / Then / Larry Parnes.   In Memoriam Larry Parnes ("Mr Parnes Shillings and Pence").   E. J. Thribb.   OBCoV

So Farwell. and If for Ever, Still for Ever Fare Ye Well.   Wang Wei.   CCL1, tr. by W. J. B. Fletcher

So first there's the chemo: three sticks, once a week.   Needles.   Lucia Maria Perillo.   IllVoic

So, forgetful Mahadeva.   Kamalākānta Bhaṭṭācārya.   SinGod, tr. by Rachel Fell McDermott

So forlorn am I.   Lady Izumi.   WoPoe, tr. by Steven D. Carter

So Foul Is Sin and Loathsome in Thy Sight.   Anne Vaughan Locke.   CABP

So, friends, every day so something.   Wendell Berry.   UpMys Fr. Manifesto: The Mad Farmer Liberation Front.

So from the bosom of darkness our days come roaring and gleaming.   Fragment: August 4, 1856.   Henry Wadsworth Longfellow.   TCAPo

So from the ground we felt that virtue branch.   Transfiguration, The.   Edwin Muir.   ChIV-2

So furze tell me what you mean and don't make such a rhubarb. (LL)   Poem of Medicine Puns.   Unknown.   ColAnChi; WoPoe, tr. by Victor H. Mair

So Gallantly Streaming: To the Poet.   Carter Ratcliff.   PA9/11

So Get Over It, Honey.   Belle Waring.   ExTi

So get up speed. So you're sick with fear again so what so what.   Denise Riley.   Oth Fr. Seven Strangely Exciting Lies.

So get you gone, Von Hügel, though with blessings on your head. (LL)   Vacillation.   William Butler Yeats.   NAMCP V.1; NoAM

So glad that your especial sperm.   Birthday, A.   Anne Rouse.   MFPA

So good luck came, and on my roof[e] did light.   Coming of Good Luck, The.   Robert Herrick.   NPeEn; OxBEV; Spl

So goodly wonne with her owne will beguyld. (LL)   Edmund Spenser.   HeIP-4; NoP-5 Fr. Amoretti.

So Graven.   Josephine Miles.   NoAM

So hand in glove.   Line Drive Caught by the Grace of God.   Linda Gregerson.   ExTi; MoASP

So hard to keep the body still, early photography studios.   Self-Portrait as a Drowned Man.   Jennifer Grotz.   NevBe

So hard to say I love you madly.   Love Song for Difficult Times.   Maria Elena Cruz Varela.   VCWP, tr. by Mairym Cruz-Bernal and Deborah Digges

So harmless and regal in the hieratic dark.   Jill Hartman.   PoPra

So have I seen ere this a silly fly.   Ludovico Ariosto.   DiBP Fr. Orlando Furioso.

So having ended, silence long ensewed.   Edmund Spenser.   MakPoe Fr. Faerie Queene, The.

So he came to write again.   Burning Hills.   Michael Ondaatje.   NoAM

So he was exiled from rome.   Ovid Twice Exiled.   Jerzy Ficowski.   PoSu, tr. by Frank J. Corliss, Jr. and Grazyna Sandel

So he'd be sure to see me, we came in late.   Versification of a Passage from Penthouse.   Andrew Hudgins.   AllShUp

So. / Hello then / Dali.   In Memoriam Salvador Dali.   E. J. Thribb.   OBCoV

So her close beauties further blaze her fame.   George Chapman.   OxBSo Fr. Coronet for His Mistress Philosophy, A.

So here comes this mf (excuse me).   Whole Truth So Help Me God—Also Known as the Gettin' Rid of Nigguz Business.   Lorena M. Craighead.   InTrad

So here I am again thinking of you—.   Mother Tongue.   Rebecca Seiferle.   ExTi

So here I am, in the middle way, having had twenty years.   T. S. Eliot.   TWF Fr. Four Quartets.

So here is the old buck.   Other World, The.   Robert Wrigley.   P180

So here the great man stood.   On the Porch at the Frost Place, Franconia, NH.   William Matthews.   VisFro

So, here, tied in that crooked line.   Chart Showing Rain, Winds, Isothermal Lines and Ocean Currents.   Louise Owen.   YaYoPo

So him at first De Nance commanded was to kill;.   Anne Dowriche.   PBRV; WaAnP Fr. French Historie, The.

So, how decisive a house is.   Domestic Poem.   Helen Dunmore.   MoWP

So how is life with your new bloke?   Attempt at Jealousy, An.   Craig Raine.   NoAM

So, how was I to know, when he invited.   Helen.   James Harrison.   NBLV

So I came. (LL)   Mary's Dream.   Van K. Brock.   AllShUp; SwNoth

So I came down the steps to Lenin.   Dorothy, Duchess of Wellington Wellesley.   OBMV Fr. Lenin.

So I did sit and eat. (LL)   Love (3): "Love bade me welcome: yet my soul drew back."   George Herbert.   BASC; BBASP; CABP; ChIV-3; ClHu; CtM; FaBoVe; FSCP; HeIP-4; InvLi; NAEL-6v1; NAEL-7v1; NoP-4; NoP-5; NOSC; NPeEn; OBEV; OBWVE; OxAEP-1; OxBEV; PBRV; PoPoPo; PtR; RaF; TFi; WeW-3

So I don't mind it raining. (LL)   Till the Clouds Roll By.   P. G. Wodehouse.   NAAPv.2; ReLy

So I dream nightly of an embarkation.   Allen Ginsberg.   CLPP Fr. Siesta in Xbalba.

So I experienced.   Robert Grenier.   FTOS Fr. Phantom Anthems.

So I fled into the thing for him.   Walter Lowenfels.   APT-2 Fr. Elegy in the Manner of a Requiem in Memory of D.H. Lawrence.

So I hand him half. (LL)   Now.   Christopher Gilbert.   GT; OxAAAP

So I have known this life.   Lollingdon Downs.   John Masefield.

So, I have seen a man killed!   Arthur Hugh Clough.   NPeEn Fr. Amours de Voyage.

So I Lost My Temper.   Rose Romano.   UnSA

So I may say.   Epitaph.   "H. D."   APT-1; NAAPv.2; NAMCP V.1; OxBoAm

So, I Remained Alone.   Anna Andreyevna Akhmatova.   TCRusP, tr. by Daniel Weissbort

So I Said I Am Ezra.   A. R. Ammons.   ColAP; NAAL-5; NAMCP V.2; NoAM; OxBoAm; WaAnP

So I said to her.   All Apologies to L. Cohen.   Simon Thompson.   PML

So I shall never hear from his own lips.   Donald Evans.   Witter Bynner.   APT-1

So I stay at home with a book. (LL)   Song of One of the Girls.   Dorothy Parker.   AmWit; NALW

So I stood by and watched.   Irina Mashinskaya.   CRWP, tr. by the author

So I took her to the riverside. Unfaithful Wife, The. Federico García Lorca. EroLit, *tr. by* Alan Bold

So I wait—bereft of 2,000 years and the bath of life. (LL) Marriage. Gregory Corso. NoP-4; NoP-5; PmAP; TRP

So I walk a little too fast. End of a Love Affair, The. Edward C. Redding. ReLy

So I walked her down to the river. Unfaithful Wife, The. Federico García Lorca. STV, *tr. by* John Frederick Nims

So I was past caring so many, too many men. Paragraph 36. Hayden Carruth. BodElec

So I went wrong. Revival. Arthur Hugh Clough. SacPr

So I would hear out those lungs. Buckdancer's Choice. James Dickey. HeIP-4; NAMCP V.2; NoAM; NoP-4; NoP-5

So I would rather drown, remembering. "H. D." APT-1 *Fr.* Flowering of the Rod, The.

So if all do their duty, they need not fear harm. (LL) William Blake. BrAP; HeIP-4; ItP; NAEL-6v2; NAEL-7v2; NAWM-7v2; NPBRoP; OxAEP-2; SoSe-8; TFi *Fr.* Songs of Innocence.

So if I lie, I'll know you're at my throat. (LL) Cousin Coat. Sean O'Brien. NeBrP; NoP-5

So I'le not feare the Judge, or thee. (LL) To His Conscience. Robert Herrick. ChIV-1; NAEL-6v1; NAEL-7v1; NoP-4; NoP-5; WaAnP

(So I'll not fear the judge or thee.) (LL) NAEL-6v1; NAEL-7v1; NoP-4; NoP-5; WaAnP

So I'll keep repeating in my mind. (LL) Look for the Silver Lining. B. G. DeSylva. ReLy; TCAPo

So I'm an alcoholic Catholic mother-lover. Jack Would Speak Through the Imperfect Medium of Alice. Alice Notley. PmAP

So I'm the only thing you care about? Dionne Brand. IFF *Fr.* Winter Epigrams.

So in every day there is breathe presence. Born. Brother Yao. BtF

So in hers am I buried this night. (LL) Barnabe Barnes. NoSic; NPeEn; WaAnP *Fr.* Parthenophil and Parthenophe.

So in Love. Cole Porter. ReLy

So in Pieria, from the wedded bliss. In Memory of Bryan Lathrop. Edgar Lee Masters. PoA 2002

So in whose folds. Directions to the Maze. Ken Harris. AnSo

So inferred. From the Novissimi. Giulia Niccolai. PFTM-2, *tr. by* Paul Vangelisti

So Inferred. Giulia Niccolai. CItWP, *tr. by* Cinzia Sartini Blum and Lara Trubowitz

So is it not with me as with that Muse. William Shakespeare. HeIP-4 *Fr.* Sonnets.

So is the vision of the day. (LL) Gods Wrote, The. Keorapetse Kgositsile. GT; OxAAAP

So it begins. Adam is in his earth. James Agee. APT-2 *Fr.* Sonnets.

So it came in a dream I was bound. Being. Adriann Roland Holst. TuT, *tr. by* Paula Meehan

So it came time. Mansion. A. R. Ammons. AmFaPo; OxBoAm

So it had to be—. Akhmatova. Deborah Digges. ExTi

So it is because. *Unknown.* ArkPo, *tr. by* Edwin A. Cranston

So it is whispered here and there. Lesson in a Picture, A. Sarah Morgan Bryan Piatt. NCAP

So it takes very little indeed: a brasserie. Edoardo Sanguineti. ItPo *Fr.* Reisebilder.

So it tries to reach her inside her mind. Silvana Colonna. ItPo, *tr. by* Gayle Ridinger

So it was. / I broke the copious curls upon my head. Elizabeth Barrett Browning. BrAP *Fr.* Aurora Leigh.

So, it's like this. Reading the I Ching. Raquel Chalfi. DTA, *tr. by* Karen Alkalay-Gut

So it's one of those bars, see. Plastic Cup, The. Kim Roberts. AmPoNex

So Jah Sey. Kendel Hippolyte. WaCA

So jealous of your beauty. Michael Field. VWP

So large, so over-the-top, so willing to expand and even in grief exalt. Whit for Whitman, A. David Mason. ViWalt

So late in my life, some things I have remembered. Childhood. Syl Cheney-Coker. NAfrP

So learned men in controversies spend. George Chapman. NOSC *Fr.* Tears of Peace, The or Euthymia Raptus.

So let it be. (LL) Parting Song, A. Felicia Dorothea Hemans. NPBRoP; VWP

So let's live—really live!—for love and loving. Catullus. *See* Lesbia / live with me.

So Let's Look at It Another Way. John Godfrey. PmAP

So like a harrow pin. Iron Spike. Seamus Heaney. BodElec; TRP

So like the smaller stars we rowed among.. (LL) Lotus Flowers, The. Ellen Bryant Voigt. CAP-8; WaAnP

So Little and So Much. John Oxenham. SacPr

So little Master Wagtail I'll bid you a 'Good-bye'. (LL) Little Trotty Wagtail. John Clare. BLPJKO; NOxBChV

So little there is of Life: of Letters, page on page! Rhapsody: Keeping Faith. István Vas. IQMS, *tr. by* George Szirtes

So live, that when thy summons comes to join. William Cullen Bryant. TreFP *Fr.* Thanatopsis.

So Long. Jayne Cortez. LW; OxAAAP

So Long. Langston Hughes. APSN; APT-2

So Long and Still No Mate. *Unknown.* CCL1, *tr. by* John Frodsham

So long as I am alive, love enlivens each day. Jelaluddin Rumi. NaPG, *tr. by* Talat Sait Halman

So long as it is our fate to be irked all our life let us just keep our heads up and take our irking with insouciant urbanity. (LL) Necessary Dirge, A. Ogden Nash. AmWit; APT-2

So long as this breath fills your nostrils. Mahadevi. WPoS

So long gone from life itself, so many things have changed. (LL) Immigrants in Our Own Land. Jimmy Santiago Baca. AF; UnSA

So long had life together been that now. Six Years Later. Joseph Brodsky. VCWP, *tr. by* Richard Wilbur

So long honey, don't ever come around again, I'm sick of you. Sonnet. Bernadette Mayer. OxBoAm

So long / is in the song. So Long. Langston Hughes. APSN; APT-2

So long lives this, and this gives life to thee. (LL) William Shakespeare. AEP; AmFaPo; BLPJKO; BrAP; CABP; ClHu; CtM; HeIP-4; ITBLP; MakPoe; NAEL-6v1; NAEL-7v1; NIL-7; NoP-5; NoSic; NPeEn; OBEV; OxBEV; OxBSo; PoPoPo; TFi; WaAnP; WeW-3 *Fr.* Sonnets.

So Long, Mary. George M. Cohan. ReLy

So long, sad times! Happy Days Are Here Again. Jack Yellen. ReLy

So long, silversides. To a Young Diver. Marilyn Taylor. PoA 2002

So long, / So far away. Afro-American Fragment. Langston Hughes. OxAAAP

219: So Long? Stevens. John Berryman. NAMCP V.2 *Fr.* Dream Songs.

So long to love / so long. (LL) So Long. Jayne Cortez. LW; OxAAAP

So long, visitor. Pablo Neruda. TAPaP *Fr.* Still Another Day.

So Love and Folly were in hell. (LL) Barley-Break , A. Sir John Suckling. BASC; CavPo

So. Magnus / Magnusson. Lines on the Award "Pipe Man of the Year" to Magnus Magnusson. E. J. Thribb. OBCoV

So many books! A temple, whose thick walls are built of books. Spirit Escapes, The. Pierre Reverdy. MotU, *tr. by* Michael Benedikt

So Many Books, So Little Time. Haki R. Madhubuti. BRtP

So many boulders have been cast at me. Solitude. Anna Andreyevna Akhmatova. ARWW, *tr. by* Catriona Kelly

So many bright words covered. Word. Zishe Vaynper. Prolet, *tr. by* Amelia Glaser

So many convolutions and not enough simplicity! To Marina. Kenneth Koch. NoAM

So many days spent tracking the desert. Argument, The. Christiane Jacox Kyle. YaYoPo

So Many Feathers. Jayne Cortez. ISC

So many flea bites. Issa. SoOfWa, *tr. by* Sam Hamill

So many kinds of sadness. Sotto Voce. M. Vasalis. TuT, *tr. by* Peter van de Kamp

So many kisses. Kisses that have pulled me. Kisses. Giancarlo Majorino. ItPo, *tr. by* Gayle Ridinger

So many mornings I awoke. Between Worlds. Adam Hill. Vesp

So many new crimes since then! Since Then. Dennis Joseph Enright. OBSV

So many people. After Sappho. Lee Ann Brown. IIR

So many people, not to speak of the dog. (LL) Taxis, The. Louis MacNeice. EmeKit; NPeEn; PNI

So many poems with kimonos. Another Kimono. Nancy Eimers. AtGh

So Many Summers. Norman Alexander MacCaig. HarvBoo

So many times / I walked and walked. By Forty-Sixth. Fernando D'Almeida. NAfrP, *tr. by* Faustine Boateng Gyima

So many times since antiquity. Lamenting the Civil War. Muso Soseki. EaWin, *tr. by* W. S. Merwin

So many traces. Louise Herlin. MFP, *tr. by* Martin Sorrell

So many traces, fragile monuments. So Many Traces. Louise Herlin. MFP, *tr. by* Martin Sorrell

So many want to be lifted by song and dancing. Dark Thing Inside the Day, A. Linda Gregg. BLT; OxBoAm

So many women are murdered because some man. Body Count. Leonard Nathan. PBCAP

So Mary died last night! To-day. Twilight. Amy Levy. VWP

So Mexicans Are Taking Jobs from Americans. Jimmy Santiago Baca. LTA; UnSA

So, midst the wither'd waste of life, those tears would flow to me. (LL) Stanzas for Music ("There's not a joy the world can give like that it takes away.") Lord Byron. NOBRP; NPeEn

So might you speak the world as who should know. Soldiers in Death. William Bronk. PWW2

So, Mind / You've decided to go on pilgrimage? Rāmprasād Sen. SinGod, *tr. by Rachel Fell McDermott*

So mine be your eyes!. (LL) To Morfydd. Lionel Pigot Johnson. MoBrPo; OBMV

So Miss Myrtle is going to marry? Charming Woman, The. Helen Selina Blackwood, Countess of Dufferin and Clandeboye. VWP

So Motown taught me all about men. Men worshipped. Patricia Smith. UnSA *Fr. Sweet Daddy.*

So mourn'd Pelides his late loss, so weighty were his moans. Homer. FaBoWar *Fr. Iliad, The.*

So much beauty home—flowers filled the house. To Send Far Away. Li Po. NDACCP, *tr. by David Hinton*

So much crap in my head. Doves. C. K. Williams. WaAnP

So much depends. Red Wheelbarrow, The. William Carlos Williams. APT-1; BLPJKO; BLT; BrAP; ChAP; ColAP; EMP; HarvBoo; HeiP-4; MoAmPo; NAAL-5; NAAPv.2; NAMCP V.1; NIL-7; NIP-4; NoAM; NoP-4; NoP-5; OxBoAm; SAmP; SoSe-8; TFi; TRP; TWF; WaAnP; WeW-3

So much for its stiff-quilled stoop. Kestrel. Peter Sanger. Coast

So much for Julia. Now we'll turn to Juan. Lord Byron. NPEEn *Fr. Don Juan.*

So much for the elves' wergild, the true governance. Geoffrey Hill. NAMCP V.2; NoAM; WoPoe *Fr. Mercian Hymns.*

So much gentleness from unknown men. Marina Boroditskaya. CRWP, *tr. by Ruth Fainlight*

So Much Happiness. Naomi Shihab Nye. BeAl; PLBUT

So much I have forgotten in ten years. Claude McKay. GT

So much it froze that the milky branches. Lied of the Fig Tree. René Char. YaTCFP, *tr. by Gustaf Sobin*

So much of life in the world is waiting, that. Witnessing the Launch of the Shuttle *Atlantis*. Howard Nemerov. OtW

So much of what we live goes on inside. Unsaid. Dana Gioia. WaAnP

So much red. Field of Red Tulips. Margot Scharpenberg. GTCP, *tr. by the author*

So much Summer. Emily Dickinson. SWaP

So much sweeter here than in other lands? (LL) Columbus Day. Jimmie Durham. HATNAP; LTA

So much time has gone by! Napoleon's house. Day We Visited New Orleans, The. Robert Bly. KGB

So much to load! Small Wooden Vessel, A. Pak Sŏwŏn. EcSo, *tr. by Julie C. Park*

So my heart flutters. On the Way to Durham, N.C. Kofi Awoonor. BrAP

So my mother begins. Nice Thing About Counting Stars, The. Dwight Okita. UnSA

So my old evil spirit can get a Greyhound Bus and ride. (LL) Me and the Devil Blues. Robert Johnson. APT-2; OxBoAm

So my pictures are in prison, instead of in the Zoo. (LL) Innocent England. D. H. Lawrence. NPEEn; OBCoV

So my soul can sing. (LL) Feeling Fucked/Up Up. Etheridge Knight. GT; PBCAP; RaBo

So name her Vivian. I, scarecrow Merlin—. Elegy for Mélusine from the Intensive Care Ward. Ramon Guthrie. APT-2

So narrow the crack whence came the voice. Words of the Poem, The. André Frénaud. YaTCFP, *tr. by Michael Sheringham*

So nothing is left of your agony. Talking to Jim. Walta Borawski. CAGL

So now I bid farewell to my barber. Leaving Paris. Todd Swift. OpeFie

So now I have confess'd that he is thine. William Shakespeare. HeiP-4; OxAEP-1 *Fr. Sonnets.*

So now i have to pack my forests. Leaving. Pamela Brown. BMAP

So now just suppose that someone wanted to know. Surgery. Kenneth Pitchford. CAGL

So now my summer task is ended, Mary. Percy Bysshe Shelley. NPBRoP *Fr. Laon and Cythna [Earlier version of The Revolt of Islam].*

So now the sun moves to die at mid-morning. Harvest of Hate. Wole Soyinka. AF

So Now You're Chicana. Carol Lem. GeoHom

So oft have I invok'd thee for my muse. William Shakespeare. AEP *Fr. Sonnets.*

So often artists have painted a woman. January 18, 1979. John Yau. OxBoAm

So often it has been displayed to us, the hourglass. Testament. Hayden Carruth. GifTon

So often true back then. One White Face in the Place, The. Sydney Lea. SwNoth

So on the first day of fall only not really because it's still early October you. Train Rides. Nikki Giovanni. InGu

So out of death, she breathes. Cleopatra. Adrianne Marcus. IaFF

So perfectly done and yet. Mac Wellman. HeMarv *Fr. Rat Minaret: Miniaturist-Divan, The.*

So pleasing a light. Robert Duncan. APSN *Fr. Passages.*

So plentiful, the babes-in-a-pot. *Unknown.* ColAnChi *Fr. Classic of Odes.*

So proper and polite. Night Is Young and You're So Beautiful, The. Irving Kahal and Billy Rose. ReLy

So put your nightdress on. Bedtime. Ian Hamilton Finlay. EdScPo

So quiet birds. Ambush. Yusef Komunyakaa. RoV

So quiet it was in that high, sun-steeped room. Nuremberg. Kenneth Slessor. BMAP

So rarely we lie. Eiléan Ní Chuilleanáin. IrLP *Fr. Rose Geranium, The.*

So Saint Michael. "H. D." NAAPv.2 *Fr. Tribute to the Angels.*

So sang he: and as meeting rose and rose. Dante Gabriel Rossetti. NAEL-6v2; OxBSo *Fr. House of Life, The.*

So sang the gallant glorious chronicle. Alfred Tennyson. OBGa *Fr. Princess, The.*

So say, This earth untouched is ruptured enough to grieve. (LL) Testimonial. Claudia Rankine. ExTi; NeAmPo

So saying, light-foot Iris passed away. Homer. OBVE *Fr. Iliad, The.*

So shaken as we are, so wan with care. William Shakespeare. OxAEP-1 *Fr. King Henry IV, Pt. I.*

So shall I live, the poet said, supposing. Ragged Sonnet: So Shall I Live. Leonard Nathan. IaFF

So she became a bird and bird-like danced. Procne. Peter Quennell. MoBrPo

So she came back into his house again. Edna St. Vincent Millay. ColAP; NALW *Fr. Sonnets from an Ungrafted Tree.*

So she can go on and on. Whereas before, she had to fasten. Pal Mal Comic, Or. Leslie Scalapino. Eno

So she moved into the hospital the last nine days. Lovebirds. Jo Shapcott. BeAl

So she must have been pleased with us,. "H. D." NAAPv.2; NALW *Fr. Tribute to the Angels.*

So she sat down. For P—Celtic: found text from Machen. Bill Griffiths. Oth

So she sd, if u lose me, u lose a good thing. Next Door. Laini Mataka. ISC

So, She wants to use me again, said my desk, because. Revolt. Maura Stanton. SUP

So shimmering fine it is and fair. (LL) Song: "I make my shroud but no one knows." Adelaide Crapsey. APT-1; NAAPv.2

So ships at anchor lie upon the sea. (LL) Sea Similized to Meadows and Pastures, The: the mariners; to Shepherds: the Mast, to a May-Pole: the Fish, to Beasts. Margaret Lucas Cavendish, Duchess of Newcastle. NoP-4; NoP-5

So shoots a star as doth my mistress glide. John Davies of Hereford. OxBSo *Fr. Wit's Pilgrimage.*

So shuts the marigold her leaves. William Browne. OBEV *Fr. Britannia's Pastorals.*

So silent I when Love was by. Anecdote. Dorothy Parker. IJHIL

So Simple. Mark Van Doren. APT-2

So sits enthroned in vegetable pride. Erasmus Darwin. OBGa *Fr. Botanic Garden, The.*

So slight a ritual can still remind. Apprehension. Jeremy Ingalls. YaYoPo

So smell those odours that do rise. To the Most Fair and Lovely Mistress Anne Soame, Now Lady Abdie. Robert Herrick. NOSC

So smelling their sweetness would be no theft. (LL) Unharvested. Robert Frost. APT-1; NAMCP V.1; SAmP

So smooth does the sun enter me. Alone in Belize. Shonda Buchanan. BRtP

So smooth, so sweet, so silv'ry is thy voice. Upon Julia's Voice. Robert Herrick. NPEEn; SoSe-8

So soft in the hemlock wood. Pastoral. Robert Silliman Hillyer. MoAmPo

So soon, so tired. So Soon. Mieke Tillema. TuT, *tr. by Joan McBreen*

So soon. Today, love, we. Tzu Yeh. WoPoe, *tr. by Jeanne Larsen*

So soon. Today, love, we. *Unknown.* ColAnChi *Fr. Midnight Songs.*

So soon—so without tomorrow. So Soon. Mieke Tillema. TuT, *tr. by Medbh McGuckian*

So spake the godlike power, and thus our sire. John Milton. NAEL-6v1 *Fr. Paradise Lost.*

So spake the [*or* th'] Archangel Michael; then paused. John Milton. NAEL-6v1 *Fr. Paradise Lost.*

So spake the Son of God, and Satan stood. John Milton. *Fr. Paradise Regained [or Regain'd].*

So spoke of the existence of things. George Oppen. NAMCP V.1 *Fr. Of Being Numerous.*

So squeezed, wince you I scream? I love you & hate. John Berryman. PoCho *Fr. Homage to Mistress Bradstreet.*

So stick up *Ivie* and the *Bays*. Henry Vaughan. ChrPo

Still the Tadpole cleaves the watery vale. Erasmus Darwin. STuOW *Fr. Temple of Nature; or, The Origin of Society, The.*

So strange to hear that song again tonight. Cruising with the Beach Boys. Dana Gioia. GeoHom; PoA 2002; RWPCtW; SwNoth

So strong you thump O terrible drums—so loud you bugles blow. (LL) Beat! Beat! Drums! Walt Whitman. CBCWP; FaBoWar; HeiP-4; NAAL-3; NAAL-5; NCAP; NoP-4; NoP-5; OBWP

So suddenly. Martha Anthony. InTrad

So sweet, all sweet—the body as the shyer. Sweet-Briar in Rose. Michael Field. VWP

So sweet, so golden. Christian Hofmann von Hofmannswaldau. GePo, *tr. by* Alexander Gode

So swim in the embassy pool in a tinkling breeze. Helene and Heloise. Glyn Maxwell. NeBrP

So ta–*dah*: here's the moment to which we've been brung. For the Pileated Woodpecker and Its Cousin, the Ivory-Billed, Who May or May Not Be Extinct. Lucia Maria Perillo. RoV

So take my vows and scatter them to sea. Sonnet for the End of a Sequence. Dorothy Parker. BrAP

So talks as it's most used to do. (LL) Christabel. Samuel Taylor Coleridge. NAEL-6v2; NAEL-7v2; NOBRP

So tell me about fever dreams. Poet Is Served Her Papers, The. Lorna Dee Cervantes. TouFir

So terrible a scold above the squat adobe. Magpie. Alan Michael Parker. AmPoNex

So Terrifyingly Melancholy. Hagiwara Sakutaro. PFTM-1

So that a colony will breed here. We Must Make a Kingdom of It. Gregory Orr. WaAnP

So that each. Aubade: Some Peaches, After Storm. Carl Phillips. CAP-8

So that each person may quickly find that. Johann Joachim Quantz's Five Lessons. William Sydney Graham. EmeKit; HarvBoo

So that I may been oon of hem at the day of doom that shulle be saved. (LL) Geoffrey Chaucer. NAEL-6v1; NAEL-7v1 *Fr.* Canterbury Tales, The.

So that I might see you. Gift, The. Edgar Silex. NAPBL

So that, / in the next myth. Daphne with Her Thighs in Bark. Eavan Boland. AFaM

So that is his mother. Born of Woman. Wisława Szymborska. GI

So That No Light Would Remain to Love Us. Rose Ausländer. GTCP, *tr. by* Reinhold Grimm

So that the vines burst from my fingers. Ezra Pound. APT-1; OBMV *Fr.* Cantos.

So That We Do Not Forget. Buland Al-Haidari. IrPoTo, *tr. by* Hussein Kadhim and Christopher Merrill

So that what must come to pass shall pass. (LL) Brute Image. John Ashbery. NoP-4; NoP-5

So that you should visit us no more. (LL) Dedication: "You whom I could not save." Czesław Miłosz. AF; BeAl; PoAgWa; WoPoe, *tr. by* the author

So the blues are again requiem. Paul Butterfield, Dead at 44. Robert Gibb. SwNoth

So / the body. 4/30/92 for Rodney King. Lucille Clifton. ESEAA

So the boy now nigratin' overseas. (LL) Calypso. Edward Kamau Brathwaite. BrAP; HarvBoo; NAMCP V.2

So. The cormorants have come home. Cormorants. Thomas O'Grady. Coast

So the fight went on, like an inextinguishable fire. Homer. CAGL *Fr.* Iliad, The.

So the lone Truffle, lodged beneath the earth. Erasmus Darwin. STuOW *Fr.* Temple of Nature; or, The Origin of Society, The.

So the Lord said: 'Eat this scroll'. Gwyneth Lewis. MoWP; NeBl *Fr.* Parables & Faxes.

So the man spread his blanket on the field. Tall Man Executes a Jig, A. Irving Layton. NoAM

So the men fought on like a mass of whirling fire. Homer. NAWM-7v1 *Fr.* Iliad, The.

So the mesenja arrived. Kulu. Seitlhamo Motsapi. TSAP

So the milk carton which used to wobble. They Are Planning to Cancel the School Milk Program to Fund a Tax Cut for the Middle Class. Liz Rosenberg. InvLad

So the rain falls. Cornkind. Frank O'Hara. CLPP

So the river—yes, the river; I have come to that at last. Emily Jane Pfeiffer. VWP *Fr.* Out of the Night.

So the sky wounded you, jagged at the heart. Daylights. Rosanna Warren. NoAM

So the soldier replied to the poet. Volunteer's Reply to the Poet, The. Roy Campbell. FaBoWar

So. The Spear-Danes in days gone by. *Unknown.* NoP-5 *Fr.* Beowulf [Heaney Translation].

So the thought can erect itself, like plywood battlements. (LL) Poem of Unrest, A. John Ashbery. OxBoAm; PoA 2002

So the Trojans held their watch that night but not the Achaeans. Homer. NAWM-7v1 *Fr.* Iliad, The.

So the villa, having learned its many skills. Madrid. Jay Wright. ESEAA

So the world became me. Secularist, The. Claudia Keelan. RoV

So the World Changes. Kofi Awoonor. VCWP

So the world offers itself in love. Sunday Park. Gwyneth Lewis. TCAWP

So the world runs on wheels, they used to say. Elizabethan Phrase, The. Philip Whalen. WANABP

So the world woos its children back for an evening kiss. (LL) Letters from a Father. Mona Van Duyn. NoP-4; NoP-5

So the years go by. Song for a Seed. Violeta Parra. TANSG, *tr. by* Bonnie Shepard

So then he wandered out into the street and began to testify. Prophet. Tom Clark. OxBoAm

So then the sunken heart was hauled up, nearly breaking. Poem That Was Once Called "Desperate" But Is Now Striving to Become the Perfect Love Poem. Richard Jackson. BAP-97

So there it is. Painting, The. Jack Hirschman. BodElec

So there stood Matthew Arnold and this girl. Dover Bitch, The. Anthony Hecht. AmWit; NBLV; NIL-7; NIP-4; NoP-5

So there we remained, completely alone. (LL) Say You Love Me. Molly Peacock. CFP; RaF

So there you are, in wispy veil and hat. Tea Party. Nancy Vieira Couto. PBCAP

So there's this episode of Mary Tyler Moore where Ted's trying to get a raise. Ted's Head. Rod Smith. Eno

So these are the Himalayas. Notes from a Nonexistent Himalayan Expedition. Wisława Szymborska. AmFaPo; ItP, *tr. by* Stanisław Barańczak *and* Clara Cavanagh and Clare Cavanagh

So these are the ropes. Rules of the Road, The. Carolyn Leigh. ReLy

So these were wed, and merrily rang the bells. Alfred Tennyson. STuOW *Fr.* Enoch Arden.

So they buried her, and turned home. Meadowsweet. Kathleen Jamie. MoWP; PoCu

So they canonized him by the name of Jem Crow! (LL) Thomas Ingoldsby. OBCoV; OBNV; OBSP *Fr.* Ingoldsby Legends, The.

So they change / themselves. (LL) Stations. Audre Lorde. BrAP; OxAAAP

So they get this and we're coming off some it's like and. Et in Leucadia Ego. Michael Davidson. PmAP

So they have got you down at last, omera. Omera. Marjorie Oludhe Macgoye. HBAPE

So they smashed that old man of Whitehaven. (LL) Limerick: "There was an Old Man of Whitehaven." Edward Lear. NPeEn; OxAEP-2

So they went, leaving a picnic-litter of talk. Party, The. William Robert Rodgers. PNI

So this is all of life! Whirling, singing. Pre-Memory. Nikolai Stepanovich Gumilyov. TCRusP, *tr. by* Denis Johnson and Kathy Lewis

So this is death. Jules Pascin. Mina Loy. HarvBoo

So this is, Jimmy, where we live. Urgent Letter, An. Hugh Maxton. PBCIP

So this is Kansas. Battle hymn. Rita D. Costello. RWB

So this is love. Squid. Michael C. Blumenthal. WaAnP

So This Is Love. Lorna Crozier. LW

So this is the fruit that made us all human. Apple, The. Bruce Guernsey. IllVoic

So this is the man you dreamt I had betrayed. Gwyneth Lewis. TCAWP *Fr.* Welsh Espionage.

So this is utopia, is it? Well. In a Copy of More's (or Shaw's or Wells's or Plato's or Anybody's) Utopia. Max Beerbohm. OBCoV

So this is what it means. Cain. Lucille Clifton. NAMCP V.2

So this is what it's like being a wife. Being a Wife. Selima Hill. BeAl; EmeKit

So this is what it's like when love. Gouge, Adze, Rasp, Hammer. Chris Forhan. P180

So this is what the afterlife is like! Man's Country. Daryl Hine. IllVoic

So this is women's work: folding. St Bride's. Kathleen Jamie. MoWP; NePenScot

So thou art come again, old black-winged night. To Night. Thomas Lovell Beddoes. CenSon

So through that unripe day you bore your head. Philip Larkin. NoAM

So through the night rode Paul Revere. Henry Wadsworth Longfellow. CA *Fr.* Tales of a Wayside Inn.

So thus he sorrowed till it was day and heard the foules sing, then somewhat he was comforted. David Jones. NAMCP V.1; NoAM *Fr.* In Parenthesis.

So tired! so weary. Catharine of Aragon. Eloise Bibb. CBWP-4

So to the sylvan lodge. John Milton. NAEL-6v1 *Fr.* Paradise Lost.

So Transparent Your Soul. Pedro Salinas. RaW, *tr. by* W. S. Merwin

So turbid though I am. Edith Jay Scovell. HarvBoo *Fr.* Water Images.

So unwarely was never no man caught [*or* cawght]. Sir Thomas Wyatt. OxBEV

So, up the steep side of the rugged hill. Jack and Jill. A. E. Housman. UV

So vast, our Goddess Night, she rises. *Unknown.* WoPoe *Fr.* Rig Veda.

So vast, our Goddess Night, she rises. *Unknown.* WoPoe *Fr.* Vedic Hymns.

So very sad. (LL) First Circle, The. Kofi Awoonor. BrAP; HBAPE; VCWP

So very still, even. Fukaku. SoOfWa, *tr. by* Sam Hamill

So was their sanctuary violated. Alfred Tennyson. *Fr.* Princess, The.

So we are taking off our masks, are we, and keeping. Homosexuality. Frank O'Hara. CAGL; PFTM-2; PoA 2002; WaAnP

So we begin to plan. Karen Alkalay-Gut. DTA *Fr.* Between Bombardments: A Journal.

So we came at last to meet, after the lights were out. John Hollander. VCAP *Fr.* Powers of Thirteen.

So, we got you in the heel. Goodnight, Achilles. Enrique Lihn. VCWP, *tr. by* Alastair Reid

So we march into the present. Rosemary Benét and Steven Vincent Benét. HHAm *Fr.* U.S.A.

So we made a boat to drown them. (LL) Song of Lies, A. Vincent Woods. BeAl; NIrP

So we move now. Sam Hamod. UnSA *Fr.* Moving.

So we must part, my body, you and I. Any Soul to Any Body. Cosmo Monkhouse. OxBEV

So we must say Goodbye, my darling. Goodbye. Alun Lewis. AngWePo; NAEL-6v2; NoP-4; NoP-5; OBWP; PoWW; TCAWP

So we pass our time together, calm and delighted. (LL) For My Son Noah, Ten Years Old. Robert Bly. GoPo; LoL; RaBo

So we wait on the verge of. Sequence. Kenneth Irby. FTOS

So we'd shine like dimes. (LL) Momma Sayings. Harryette Mullen. ISC; ItWoWo; TiP2

So We'll Go No More A-Roving. Lord Byron. BrAP; CABP; ChAP; ClHu; CtM; HeIP-4; IJHIL; MakPoe; NAEL-6v2; NAEL-7v2; NePenScot; NoP-4; NoP-5; NPeEn; OPOU; TFi; WoPoe
(We'll Go No More A-Roving.) NPBRoP; OBEV; WaAnP

So well that I can live without. Emily Dickinson. TCAPo

So/ Went this little pig from the mainland to the market. Louis Untermeyer. MoAmPo *Fr.* Mother Goose Up-to-Date.

So What. Quincy Troupe. PrTe

So what! A penis. To a Flasher. Dawn L. Hannaham. BtF

So what if clowns and gnomes. Golden Age, The. Artur Miedzyrzecki. PoSu

So what if I scar? White Paintings II (in parenthesis). Laura Mullen. RoV

So what if I'm fragile. Kite. Brian McCabe. EdScPo

So what if next year the deep pink burst. Perennial. Susan Hahn. IllVoic

So what, if the nurses on this particular shift. Going Under. Carl Phillips. OxAAAP

So what if you believe in angels. Practicing Eternity. Susan Elbe. FiBr

So what is faith if it is not. Geoffrey Hill. NAMCP V.2 *Fr.* Triumph of Love, The.

So, what more do you want from me? Return, The. Yevgeny Borisovich Rein. ItGoST, *tr. by* Judith Hemschemeyer

So, when he lost his temper, the Owl lost its life. (LL) Lewis Carroll. OBCoV; UV *Fr.* Alice's Adventures in Wonderland.

So when I offer me, a medium as. Dragonfly at My Windowpane. Wole Soyinka. NAMCP V.2

So, when she saw Narcissus wandering through the lonely countryside, Echo fell in love with him, and followed secretly in his steps. Ovid. EroLit *Fr.* Metamorphoses.

So when the Queen of Love rose from the Seas. To a Very Young Gentleman at a Dancing-School. Elizabeth Singer Rowe. EMWP

So when you see the desolating sacrilege spoken of by the prophet Daniel. William Butler Yeats. GI *Fr.* St. Matthew.

So where does one begin? Desert Storm. Kofi Anyidoho. PML

So where is that guy who left us piles. Mikhail Aizenberg. ItGoST, *tr. by* J. Kates

So where will the crowning text be? So Where. Claire Lejeune. YaTCFP, *tr. by* Judy Cockran and Renée Linkhorn

So while you bloom, adopt a more becoming demeanor. (LL) Marbod of Rennes. CAGL; EroLit *Fr.* Unyielding Youth, The.

So white and red on him in order growes. (LL) Richard Barnfield. CAGL; NoSic *Fr.* Affectionate Shepherd [*or* Shephearde], The.

So who in hell will he sell it to? (LL) Old Tai's Wine Shop. Li Po. CCL1; WoPoe, *tr. by* Elling O. Eide

So who of us. Vsevolod Nekrasov. ItGoST, *tr. by* Gerald Janecek

So who you be now. Foursomes. Marvin K. White. BRtP

So wide the wells of darkness sink. Fragmentary Stars. Léonie Adams. APT-2

So would this be how I'd remember my hands. Lament in Good Weather. Lucia Maria Perillo. ExTi

So write, before I die, " 'E liked it all!" (LL) Sestina of the Tramp-Royal. Rudyard Kipling. MakPoe; MoBrPo; WaAnP

So you alone are blessed with thought, free-thinking man. Golden Sayings. Gérard de Nerval. WoPoe, *tr. by* Richard Sieburth

So you are married, girl. It makes me sad. Epithalamium. Roy McFadden. IrLP; PNI

So you aren't Tolstoy or Saint Francis. So? Leonard Nathan. PBCAP

So you come with these maps in your head. Man Who Makes Brooms, The. Naomi Shihab Nye. LoL

So you fought for the Jews. To an Anti-Semite. Carl Rakosi. APT-2

So, you have gone my erstwhile glad boy. Ballygrand Widow. Deborah Randall. BeAl; NeBl

So you have swept me back. "H. D." NALW *Fr.* Eurydice.

So you may write this poem. (LL) Thrall. Carolyn Kizer. CAP-8; GifTon; StAl

So You Put the Dog to Sleep. Thomas Lux. SUP

So you try to catch the last ride. Coffee Table Blues. Duncan Mercredi. PoPra

So you wanna kill white people. Something easy for Ultra Black Nationalists. Kenneth Carroll. SpirFl

So you want to be a writer? Charles Bukowski. OxBoAm

So You Want to Hear the Blues. Grace Bauer. MiVo

So you were David's father. In Memoriam, Private D. Sutherland. Ewart Alan Mackintosh. PoWW

So you will presently my loving hands abjure. To This Book. Martin Opitz. GePo, *tr. by* George C. Schoolfield

So You Would Listen to Me. Laura Riesco. TANSG, *tr. by* Shaun Griffin and Emma Sepúlveda-Pulvirenti

So young, so pretty. Help is a Discotheque. Eddie Bell. BtF

So your daughter had a white dress, and once you saw. Stopwatch. Mary Ruefle. ExTi

So you're a horse girl, he says. Horse Girls. Tammy Armstrong. Coast

So you're a windmill. Vincente Huidobro. TCLAP *Fr.* Altazor.

So you've come to me now without knowing why. To Himself. Mark Strand. PoA 2002

So you've reached your thirty-eighth birthday. My Husband's Birthday. Josephine D. Henderson Heard. CBWP-4

Soaked into a paste fine breaker slant. Ken Edwards. Oth *Fr.* 3600 Weekends.

Soaked to the skin I peer through the drizzle, and I perceive. Hans Magnus Enzensberger. PoSu *Fr.* Sinking of the Titanic, The.

Soaking, The. Ivor Gurney. OxBEV

Soaking Up Sun. Tom Hennen. GoPo; IPoFL

Soap. Jane Coleman. ReTh

Soap. Im Yŏngjo. CAMKP, *tr. by* Edward W. Poitras

Soap. M. R. Peacocke. NLP

Soap. Gerald Stern. CAP-8; TaR

Soap Bubbles. Chrystos. ReTh

Soap is wet from the storm, The. After the Rain. Joseph Ceravolo. NYP2

Soap Suds. Louis MacNeice. EmeKit; ModIr; NAEL-6v2; NAEL-7v2; NPeEn

Soap-Pig, The. Paul Muldoon. PBCIP

Soaring. Kim Sŭnghŭi. EcSo, *tr. by* K. Kim Richards and Steffen Richards

Soaring again from the Leukadian Rock. Anacreon. SaLy, *tr. by* Diane Rayor

Soaring hawk from fist that flies, The. Lover Compareth Himself to the Painful Falconer, The. *Unknown.* NoSic

Sober Ghost. Michael Burkard. LaCa

Sober, Remaining. Hŏ Sugyŏng. EcSo, *tr. by* Youngju Ryu

Sobering thought, the idea of you stretched there, A. Derek Mahon. NAMCP V.2 *Fr.* Yellow Book, The.

Sobieski-Stuarts. Robert Crawford. EdScPo

Sobre él discurren con suavidad. Coral Bracho. RMCMP

Sobre la calle estamos. Puerta, La. Carlos Bousoño. RaW

Sobre la tierra amarga. Antonio Machado Ruiz. RaW *Fr.* Del Camino.

Sobre un camino. Duda. Víctor Terán. RMCMP

Sobre un Poema Nativo de las Islas Salomón que Comienza: "Tu Vergüenza Genital Es el Gramófono del Hombre Blanco." Gabriel Celaya. RaW

Social Band, The. *Unknown.* SSUS

Social Glass, The. Lizelia Augusta Jenkins Moorer. CBWP-3

Social Life, The. Lizelia Augusta Jenkins Moorer. CBWP-3

Social Note. Dorothy Parker. LW

Social Security. Terence Winch. P180

Social Worship. Bishop Richard Mant. SacPr

Socialist Manifesto for East Balgillo, The. W. N. Herbert. NePenScot

Socially-constituted objects include ourselves. Erin Mouré. NLPA *Fr.* Wittgenstein Letters to Mel Gibson's Braveheart, The.

Society. Tom Clark. PmAP

Society has quite forsaken all her wicked courses. William Schwenck Gilbert. OBSV *Fr.* Utopia Limited.

Society in my head, The. Sense of Responsibility, The. Harry Mathews. NYP2

Society upon the Stanislaus, The. Bret Harte. CalPo

Society Woman, The. Dezső Kosztolányi. IQMS, *tr. by* Peter Zollman

Sock, A. Sandra McPherson. MotU

Scope. Maria Manuela Margarido. HAWP, *tr. by* Julia Kirst

Socrates. Peter Johnson. PoDa *Fr.* Travels with Oedipus.

Soda Gong. Clark Coolidge. NYP2

Soda Jerk. Cynthia Rylant.
  Living in Cheston. HHAm

Soda pop. (LL) You Too? Me Too—Why Not? Soda Pop. Robert Hollander. NIL-7; NIP-4

Sodden weather of an early spring. Mizzle. Jay Parini. PfSP

Sodeynly affrayed, half wakyng, half slepyng. *Unknown.* OHMEL

Sodger laddie's socht a hoose, A. Under the Greenwood Tree. Hugh MacDiarmid. FaBoWar; OBVE

Sodgers, The. Alexander Scott. EdScPo

Sodium Light. Fergus Allen. NIrP

Sodom; or The Quintessence of Debauchery. John Wilmot, 2d Earl of Rochester. Song. EroLit

Sodomy. Orlando Ricardo Menes. PML

Soe well I love thee, as without thee I. Michael Drayton. NPeEn; PBRV

Soeur Louise de la Miséricorde (1674). Christina Georgina Rossetti. VWP

Sofa, The. William Cowper. *Fr.* Task, The.

Sofa, The. Medbh McGuckian. PBCIP; PNI

Sofa in the Forties, A. Seamus Heaney. EmeKit

Sofas, Fogs, and Cinemas, The. Rosemary Tonks. MoWP

Sofia. John Seed. Oth

Soft. Jennifer L. Shakan. BeDoSh

Soft as old silk. Loving You. Frances Horovitz. LW

Soft Black Eyes. Priscilla Jane Thompson. CBWP-2

Soft blushing flower! my bosom grieves. To a Llangollen Rose, the Day after It Had Been Given by Miss Ponsonby. Matilda Barbara Betham-Edwards. CenSon

Soft breeze! / Whispering trees! Strange Music. George Forrest and Robert Wright. ReLy

Soft drinks and hot music. Jukebox Saturday Night. Al Stillman. ReLy

Soft Echoes. Hsiao Kang. CCL1, *tr. by* Anne Birrell

Soft found a way to damn me undefended. James Vincent Cunningham. APT-2 *Fr.* Epigrams: A Journal.

Soft hangs the opiate in the brain. Opium Fantasy, An. Maria White Lowell. APN-2; NAAPv.1

Soft kisses may be innocent. Caution, The. Catherine Cockburn. LW

Soft lights, the companionship, the beers, The. James Vincent Cunningham. APT-2

Soft May mists are here again. May, 1972. James Schuyler. PoA 2002

Soft moon shimmers out. Kalamu ya Salaam. SpirFl *Fr.* New Orleans Haiku.

Soft moonlight shines upon the corner store. Night in Kolozsvár. Lajos Áprily. IQMS, *tr. by* Watson Kirkconnell

Soft murmur in the walnut leaf. Insect. Sándor Weöres. IQMS, *tr. by* Peter Zollman

Soft new grass is creeping o'er the graves, The. By the Potomac. Thomas Bailey Aldrich. PCW

Soft, our poem begins as vandals dreams. (LL) Vandals, Horses. Alan Michael Parker. NAPBL; PuP-23

Soft *quem quam* will be Scops the Owl, The. Acropolis. Lawrence Durrell. OxAEP-2

Soft rain. Mitsu Suzuki. WhBo

Soft ridge of cloud or mountain! which thou art. Malvern at a Distance. John Keble. OxBSo

Soft Sea washed around the House, A. Emily Dickinson. SAmP

Soft Snow. William Blake. SoSe-8

Soft, soft echoes of twilight eaves. Soft Echoes. Hsiao Kang. CCL1, *tr. by* Anne Birrell

Soft sound of his steps on the pier, The. Photograph of a Child, Japanese-American Evacuation, Bainbridge Island, Washington, March 30, 1942. James Masao Mitsui. OpBo

Soft stockings coddle them by day and nail-bossed leather shoes buttress them. Toenails. Jorge Luis Borges. MotU, *tr. by* Mildred Boyer

Soft Swimmer, Winter Swan. Robert Horan. YaYoPo

Soft Targets [*for Black Girls*]. Essex Hemphill. GT; OxAAAP

Soft through the silent air descend the feathery snow-flakes. Fragment: December 18, 1847. Henry Wadsworth Longfellow. APN-1; TCAPo

Soft Time of the Year, The. Hayden Carruth. PoCoUp

Soft, to your places, animals. Soft, To Your Places. Thomas Kinsella. HarvBoo

Soft toys that make to seem girls. Strip-tease. Lawrence Durrell. OxAEP-2

Soft wind of the vale. *Unknown.* NDACCP, *tr. by* Ezra Pound

Soft wind southwesterly, something like, A. Vermont Thaw. Robert Penn Warren. BodElec

Soft winds circle the mountain head. Whisky Lovers. *Vietnamese Oral Tradition.* CeDao, *tr. by* John Balaban

Soft you; a word or two before you go. William Shakespeare. OxAEP-1 *Fr.* Othello.

Softball at Julia Tutwiler Prison. R. T. Smith. MoASP

Soft-boiled egg is emptied, The. History Goes to Work. Elizabeth Garrett. MFPA; NeBl

Softly. Nighttime. René Crevel. CAGL, *tr. by* Michael Taylor

Softly along the road of evening. Nod. Walter De la Mare. MoBrPo

Softly and humbly to the Gulf of Arabs. Beach Burial. Kenneth Slessor. BrAP

Softly gliding I go. John Fletcher. NOSC *Fr.* Faithful Shepherdess, The.

Softly, in the dusk, a woman is singing to me. Piano. D. H. Lawrence. BrAP; CABP; GoPo; HarvBoo; HeIP-4; MoBrPo; NAEL-6v2; NAEL-7v2; NAMCP V.1; NIL-7; NoAM; NoP-4; NoP-5; OPOU; TFi; TRP; WeW-3

Softly now the day is dawning. Signal Gun, The. Mary E. Tucker. CBWP-1

Softly, O midnight Hours! Serenade. Aubrey Thomas De Vere. OBEV

Softly she breaks off. Buson. EMJL *Fr.* Spring Breeze on the Kema Embankment.

Softly, softly, the rhyme is running out. Rhyme Is Running Out,The. József Kiss. IQMS, *tr. by* Anthony Edkins

Softly the civilized. Raiders' Dawn. Alun Lewis. AngWePo; NPeEn; PoAgWa

Softly the linden grows green in the opening summer. Early Noon. Ingeborg Bachmann. AF, *tr. by* Mark Anderson

Soft-toned clock upon the stair chimed three, The. Dawn. Ella Higginson. SWaP

Soho Hospital for Women, The. Fleur Adcock. NAEL-6v2; NAEL-7v2; NoP-4; NoP-5

Sohrab and Rustum. Matthew Arnold. OBNV

"And night came down over the solemn waste." OxBEV

"Then Sohrab with his sword smote Rustum's helm." OBWP

Soil between balls of thumb and forefinger crumbled / falls. Skylarks and Fuji. Kusano Shimpei. PFTM-1

Soil is freshly dug, the half-faded wreaths of leaves, The. Heraclitus of Halicarnassus. WoPoe, *tr. by* Edwin Morgan

Soil now gets a rumpling soft and damp, The. Strong Are Saying Nothing, The. Robert Frost. APT-1

Soir après soir. Méditation du 8/5/85. Jacques Roubaud. YaTCFP

Soir venu, on se prépare un voyage, Le. Soir venu, Le. Claude Esteban. YaTCFP

Soirée. Ezra Pound. OBCoV

Sois sage, ô ma douleur . . . I don't. Michael Foley. PNI *Fr.* True Life Love Stories.

Soissons. Keith Douglas. NAMCP V.1; NoAM

67 mots d'une voyelle et d'une consonne. Christophe Tarkos. YaTCFP

Sojourn in the Whale. Marianne Moore. NALW

Sojourners, The. Bino A. Realuyo. ReBoTo

Sojun, What powers will you use to direct others? Mondo. Sojun Mel Weitsman and Zen Center Sangha. WhBo

Sokoya, I said, looking through. There Is No Word for Goodbye. Mary Tallmountain. HATNAP; LoL

Sol abre los labios y nos dice, El. Alfonso D'Aquino. RMCMP

Sol. Activa persiana. Sombras, Las. Jorge Guillén. RaW

Sol de la Muerte. José Luis Hidalgo. RaW

Sol de medianoche era más grande que el puente, sus rojos casi flama casi sangre, El. Liebre, La. Silvia Eugenia Castillero. SPV

Sol furioso de oro ciego, El. Naranja de luz abierta, La. Alfonso D'Aquino. RMCMP

Sol/o. Seitlhamo Motsapi. TSAP

Sol through white curtains shot a tim'rous ray. Alexander Pope. NPeEn *Fr.* Rape of the Lock, The: An Heroi-Comical Poem in Five Cantos.

Sol took his nightcap off and gazed. After the Storm. Henrietta Cordelia Ray. CBWP-3

Solace. Josephine D. Henderson Heard. CBWP-4

Solace. Margaret Abigail Walker. OxAAAP

Solace hast thou for pain! (LL) Dying Words of Stonewall Jackson, The. Sidney Lanier. APN-2; CBCWP; PCW

Solace to man's miseries. (LL) Lü-yi: Green Robe. *Unknown.* APSN; CCL1; NDACCP, *tr. by* Ezra Pound

Solange. Rashidah Ismaili. HAWP

Solar. Philip Larkin. NAMCP V.2

Solar Creation. Charles Madge. OBMV

Solar Eclipse, St. John's, Newfoundland. Carmelita McGrath. Coast

Solar Flare. Gu Cheng. WoBe *Fr.* Liquid Mercury.

Solar Myth. Genevieve Taggard. MoAmPo

Soldados se Duermen, Los. Rafael Alberti. RaW

Solde. Léon Damas. YaTCFP

Soldier, A. Sorrow Song. John Alexander Frazier, Jr. BtF

Soldier, A. Sir John Suckling. WaAnP

Soldier, A: His Prayer. Gerald Kersch. PLBUT

Soldier, The. John Clare. FaBoWar

Soldier, The. Gerard Manley Hopkins. FaBoWar

Soldier, The. "If I should die, think only this of me." Rupert Brooke. AmFaPo; CABP; EMP; FaBoWar; GSo; HeIP-4; InoFa; MoBrPo; NAEL-6v2; NAEL-7v2; NoP-4; NoP-5; OBEV; OBWP; PoA 2002; PoWW; TFi; UV; WaAnP

Soldier Addresses his Body, The.   Edgell Rickword.   PoWW

Soldier Bathing.   Frank Ormsby.   PNI *Fr.* Northern Spring, A.

Soldier boy, dark and tall, sat for a rest.   Break.   Colette Bryce.   NIrP

Soldier Boy's Dream, The.   Mary E. Tucker.   CBWP-1

Soldier from the Wars Returning.   A. E. Housman.   OBMV

Soldier, full of battles and renown, The.   Returned Soldier, The.   John Clare. FaBoWar

Soldier Going to the Field, The.   Sir William Davenant.   FaBoWar; OBWP

Soldier of the Legion lay dying in Algiers, A.   Bingen on the Rhine.   Caroline Elizabeth Norton.   TreFP

Soldier of Urbina, A.   Jorge Luis Borges.   PoetW, *tr.* by Alastair Reid

Soldier on the Marsh, A.   Andrew Hudgins.   CBCWP

Soldier passed me in the freshly fallen snow, A.   To a Conscript of 1940.   Sir Herbert Read.   OBWP; PoWW

Soldier, past full retreat, is marching out of the grave, The.   Go Ask the Dead.   Thomas McGrath.   AF

Soldier stood at the pearly gate.   *Unknown.*   FaBoWar

Soldier, there is a war between the mind.   Wallace Stevens.   AmWaPo; ColAP; NoAM; WaAnP *Fr.* Notes toward a Supreme Fiction.

Soldier: Twentieth Century.   Isaac Rosenberg.   PoWW

Soldier waits until he's called—then, A.   Alfonzo Prepares to Go Over the Top.   Rita Dove.   LoL

Soldier Who Crucified Jesus, The.   Martinus Nijhoff.   TuT, *tr.* by Desmond Egan

Soldiers.   Sutardji Calzoum Bachri.   WoPoe, *tr.* by Harry Aveling

Soldiers.   Patricia Blanco.   AFaM

Soldiers.   Padraic Fiacc.   PNI

Soldiers.   Giuseppe Ungaretti.   PFTM-1

Soldiers.   *Unknown.*   FaBoWar; PoAgWa

Soldiers: "Crossing the mountains."   Ucha Sakhltkhutsishvili.   PML, *tr.* by the author and Al Zolynas

Soldiers, The.   Occupation.   Suji Kwock Kim.   LegDan

Soldiers and poor, unable to rejoice. (LL)   Owl, The.   Edward Thomas.   AF; ChAP; NAEL-6v2; NAEL-7v2; NAMCP V.1; NIP-4; NoAM; NoP-4; NoP-5; OBWVE; OWoS; OxAEP-2; PoCho; TCAWP; TFi; TRP

Soldiers and stockbrokers.   Welcome.   Karen Press.   TSAP

Soldiers are citizens of death's grey land.   Dreamers.   Siegfried Sassoon.   GSo; MoBrPo; NAMCP V.1; NoAM

Soldiers Bathing.   Frank Templeton Prince.   MoBrPo; OBWP

Soldiers, behold, and captains, mark it well.   George Gascoigne.   FaBoWar *Fr.* Fruits of War, The.

Soldiers' Chorus from Faust.   *Unknown.*   NOBAu

Soldier's Death, The.   Anne Finch, Countess of Winchilsea. *See* Trail All Your Pikes.

Soldier's Dream, The.   Thomas Campbell.   OxAEP-2

Soldier's Farewell, A.   Robert Burns. *See* Silver Tassie, The.

Soldiers in Death.   William Bronk.   PWW2

Soldier's Letter, A.   Fitz-James O'Brien.   PCW

Soldiers never do die well.   Champs d'Honneur.   Ernest Hemingway.   AmWaPo; IllVoic; PoA 2002

Soldier's Rest.   Roque Dalton.   TCLAP, *tr.* by Richard Schaaf

Soldiers Sleep, The.   Rafael Alberti.   RaW, *tr.* by Rachel Benson

Soldier's Song.   Bálint Balassi.   IQMS, *tr.* by Joseph Leftwich

Soldier's Song.   *Unknown.*   APN-2, *tr.* by Stephen Return Riggs

Soldiers' Songs of the First World War.   *Unknown.*

"Bells of hell go ting-a-ling-a-ling, The."   OBCoV

I Don't Want to be a Soldier.   PoWW

"I have no pain, dear mother, now."   OBCoV

"Sure, a little bit of shrapnel fell from out the sky one day."   OBCoV

"Wash me in the water."   OBCoV

"We are Fred Karno's army."   OBCoV

Soldier's Tear, The.   Thomas Haynes Bayly.   STuOW

Soldiers, what finer worth.   Soldier's Song.   Bálint Balassi.   IQMS, *tr.* by Joseph Leftwich

Soldiers who wish to be a hero.   Soldiers.   *Unknown.*   FaBoWar; PoAgWa

Soldier's Wife, The.   Robert Southey.   FaBoWar

Sole listener, Duddon! to the breeze that played.   William Wordsworth.   CenSon *Fr.* River Duddon [A Series of Sonnets], The.

Sole of Dover.   William Loran Smith.   LaCa

Sole Positive of Night!   Ne Plus Ultra.   Samuel Taylor Coleridge.   WaAnP

Sole science to remain standing, The.   Story of Every Day, The.   Eugenio Montale.   ItPo, *tr.* by Gayle Ridinger

Sole watchman of the flying stars, guard me.   John Berryman.   ItP *Fr.* Eleven Addresses to the Lord.

Solea of the Simooms.   Will Alexander.

"Not some writhing in a tortuous canine province."   BAP-04

Soledad.   Brother Yao.   BtF

Soledad.   Robert Earl Hayden.   APT-2

Soledad. = f. Solitude, loneliness, homesickness; lonely retreat.   Adrienne Rich.   GeoHom *Fr.* Atlas of the Difficult World, An.

Soleil Cou Coupé.   Jennifer Moxley.   VaPo

Soleilland.   Edmond Jabès.   YaTCFP

Solemn moon-beams fall, soft dews distill, The.   Invocation to the Spirit Said to Haunt Wroxall Down.   Mary F. Johnson.   CenSon

Solemn plain-faced child stands gazing there, A.   Portrait, A.   Walter De la Mare.   NoAM

Solemn receptions given by death.   Two of the Festivals of Death.   João Cabral de Melo Neto.   TCLAP, *tr.* by W. S. Merwin

Solemn thing—it was—I said, A.   Emily Dickinson.   NALW

Solemne Long Enduring Passion, A.   Nicholas Breton.

"I have neither Plummes nor Cherries."   NPeEn

"Let mee thinke no more on thee."   NPeEn

"Wearie thoughts doe waite upon me."   NPeEn

Solemnly, mournfully, / Dealing its dole.   Curfew.   Henry Wadsworth Longfellow.   APN-1

Solfège parasite.   Camille Martin.   AnSo

Solicit not thy thoughts with matters hid.   John Milton.   NAWM-7v1 *Fr.* Paradise Lost.

Solid Ground.   Mary Beath.   ICANM

Solid houses in the mist, The.   New Year's.   Charles Reznikoff.   TaR

Solidarity Is the Name We Give to What We Cannot Hold.   Charles Bernstein.   OxBoAm

Soliloquy.   Oscar Hammerstein, II.   ReLy

Soliloquy.   Eugenio Montale.   ItPo, *tr.* by Gayle Ridinger

Soliloquy.   George Sewell.   OBGa

Soliloquy: "What folly to complain."   Ann Yearsley.   NOBRP

Soliloquy at Potsdam.   Peter Porter.   BrAP; NOBAu

Soliloquy of a Maiden Aunt.   Dollie Radford.   OxBEV

Soliloquy of the Danish Cloister.   Mike O'Connor.   WANABP

Soliloquy of the Night, The.   Mihály Vörösmarty.   IQMS *Fr.* Csongor and Tünde.

Soliloquy of the Solipsist.   Sylvia Plath.   HarvBoo

Soliloquy of the Spanish Cloister.   Robert Browning.   BrAP; FaBoVe; NAEL-6v2; NAEL-7v2; NIL-7; NIP-4; NoP-4; NoP-5; OxBEV; UV

Soliloquy: South Africa.   Arthur Nortje.   TSAP

Solitaire.   Conrad Potter Aiken.   ColAP

Solitaire.   George Hitchcock.   GifTon

Solitaire.   Amy Lowell.   MoAmPo; TCAPo

Solitary.   Lance Henson.   HATNAP

Solitary.   Samar Sen.   WoPoe, *tr.* by Pritish Nandy

Solitary, A.   Basho.   SoOfWa, *tr.* by Sam Hamill

Solitary, The.   Mary Barnard.   APT-2

Solitary, The.   Sara Teasdale.   MoAmPo

Solitary Carouse on a Day in Spring, A.   Li Po.   CCL1, *tr.* by Robert Kennaway Douglas

Solitary Confinement.   Robert Walker.   NOBAu

Solitary Crow.   Norman Alexander MacCaig.   NoP-4

Solitary dance on the windings of the red carpet, A.   Meeting.   Max Jacob.   YaTCFP, *tr.* by Mary Ann Caws *and* Jean-Pierre Cauvin

Solitary Falcon above the Buddha Hall of the Monastery of Universal Purity, A.   Mei Yao Ch'en.   WoPoe, *tr.* by Jonathan Chaves

Solitary fly, nice, and content, A.   All Soul's Day.   Willem Jan Otten.   TuT, *tr.* by Micheal O'Siadhail

Solitary life beside Chi River, A.   Chi River Gardens and Fields.   Wang Wei.   CrYelRi, *tr.* by Sam Hamill

Solitary Man.   Boris Hristov.   CSCBP, *tr.* by Georgi Belev and Lisa Sapinkopf

Solitary molar of a whore, The.   Cycle.   Gottfried Benn.   PFTM-1

Solitary peak stands alone—high, aloof, The.   35.   Shih Shu.   CSKM, *tr.* by James H. Sanford

Solitary Reaper, The.   William Wordsworth.   CABP; ClHu; HeIP-4; NAEL-6v2; NAEL-7v2; NOBRP; NoP-4; NoP-5; NPBRoP; OBEV; OxAEP-2; OxBEV; PoPoPo; SoSe-8; TFi; WaAnP; WeW-3

Solitary statues are introduced into the orchestra, while groups of statues are in the boxes.   Special Performance for Statues, A.   Miroslav Holub.   MotU, *tr.* by the author and Stuart Friebert

Solitary thoughts on death and other illegal mysteries carried off.   Bob Kaufman.   WhBo

Solitary winter lantern casts a feeble shadow, A.   Han-shan Te-ch'ing.   CSKM, *tr.* by Red Pine

Solitary Woodsman, The.   Sir Charles G. D. Roberts.   BrAP

Solitude.   Anna Andreyevna Akhmatova.   ARWW, *tr.* by Catriona Kelly

Solitude.   Dániel Berzsenyi.   IQMS, *tr.* by Watson Kirkconnell

Solitude.   Lord Byron. *See* Apostrophe to the Ocean.

Solitude.   Abraham Cowley. *See* Of Solitude.

Solitude.   Michael Cuddihy.   GifTon

Solitude.   Babette Deutsch.   LW

Solitude. Andreas Gryphius. GePo, *tr. by* George C. Schoolfield

Solitude. 'Enayat Jaber. PoArWo, *tr. by* Wen Chin Ouyang

Solitude. Helen Hunt Jackson. SWaP

Solitude. Eddie DeLange and Irving Mills. ReLy

Solitude. Mary Mollineux. NOSC

Solitude. Harold Monro. MoBrPo

Solitude. Charles Simic. CAP-8

Solitude. Tomas Tranströmer. WED, *tr. by* Robert Bly

Solitude. Ella Wheeler Wilcox. BRP; GoPo; SWaP; TCAPo

Solitude, and the rain, and the roads, The. (LL) Black Stone Lying on a White Stone. César Vallejo. PoCho; TCLAP; WED, *tr. by* Robert Bly and John Knoepfle

Solitude Dinner. Renée Gregorio. ICANM

Solitude Exercises. Iman Mersal. PoArWo, *tr. by* Khaled Mattawa

Solitude flared out, The. Lyn Hejinian. FTOS *Fr.* Person, The.

Solitude is turning dark. Magnet, The. Mario Benedetti. PML, *tr. by* Richard Zenith

Solitude of Glass, The. Yvor Winters. APT-2

Solitude, solitude so sought after . . . I love you. XXX. Dulce Maria Loynaz. TANSG, *tr. by* Alan West

Solitude that unmakes me one of men. Compensation. Robinson Jeffers. MoAmPo

Solitude: you must be very strong. Lines from the Testament. Pier Paolo Pasolini. VCWP, *tr. by* Norman MacAfee *and* Luciano Martinengo

Solitudes, The. Luis de Góngora y Argote. *tr. by* Edward E. Wilson

  "It was the flowery season of the year." SpanPo, *tr. by* Edward E. Wilson Wedding Hymn.

    "Come Hymen come, for here to thee we bring." SpanPo, *tr. by* Edward E. Wilson

Solo. Mary Elizabeth Coleridge. ViWPN; VWP

Solo. Anna Glazova. CRWP, *tr. by* Max Nemtsov

Sólo el oído del laberinto. Historia del laberinto, La. Veronica Volkow. RMCMP

Solo for Ear-Trumpet. Dame Edith Sitwell. MoBrPo

Solo for the Lone Intuition, A. Shakir Samawi. IrPoTo, *tr. by* Chuck Miller and Saadi A. Simawe

Solo for Two Voices. Octavio Paz. STV, *tr. by* John Frederick Nims

Solo for Voice 17 Song with Electronics (Relevant). John Cage. PFTM-2 *Fr.* Song Books.

Sólo la luna sospecha la verdad. No Existe el Hombre. Vicente Aleixandre. RaW

Solo Native. Thomas Lux. AmAlph

Solo or in the ride out gliding and. Barney Bigard. Suzanne Noguere. FFC

Solo Palabras. Magdalena Gomez. PueRic

Solo: The Good Blues. Dolores Kendrick. FFC

Solo with Chorus. Rose Fyleman. NOxBChV

Soloing. Philip Levine. OPRER

Soloists, The. Mingus Speaks: Found Poems. George Barlow. ISC

Solomon and Balkis. Robert Browning. ChIV-1

Solomon and the Witch. William Butler Yeats. ChIV-1; NoAM; WoPoe

Solomon Grundy. Mother Goose. NBLV

Solomon Grundy / Bored on Tuesday. Senilio Passes, Singing. Martin Bell. OBCoV

Solomon King of the Jews and the Queen of Sheba, Balkis. Solomon and Balkis. Robert Browning. ChIV-1

Solomon on the Vanity of the World. Matthew Prior. Knowledge.

  Home-Loving Dog, The. DiBP

Solomon Redivivus, 1886. Constance Naden. VWP *Fr.* Evolutional Erotics.

Solstice. Gerald Dawe. PNI

Solstice for John. John Cope. GeoH

Solstice moon rides within a ring of ice, The. On the Feast of Saint John the Evangelist. David Brendon Hopes. UpMys

Solstice Quipu. Arthur Sze. WANABP

Solstice / Surgery. A. Di Michele. AnSo

Solum Mihi Superest Sepulchrum. William Habington. ChIV-1; NOSC *Fr.* Castara.

Solution. George Oppen. NAMCP V.1

Solution, The. Bertolt Brecht. PoSu, *tr. by* Dereck Bowman

Solutions to the Problem, / Of course, wait. (LL) Dinner Guest: Me. Langston Hughes. LTA; NoP-5; SSLK

Solvent. Jason Christie. PoPra

Solvitur Acris Hiems. Horace. WoPoe *Fr.* Three Odes of Horace.

Soma. Suzanne Noguere. FFC

Soma haoma avestan haoma. Hymn to the Sacred Mushroom. Bob Cobbing. Oth

Somalia. Nancy Mercado. BRtP

Somber and hermetic, but approachable and of a divertingly theoretical bent. Actor, The. Tom Mandel. OnScMo

Somber empress. To Death, from the Genie of My Poetry. Delmira Agustini. TANSG, *tr. by* Mark McCaffrey

Somber Song. Almad Shamlu. PML, *tr. by Unknown*

Sombra que dibuja la luz, La. Natalia Toledo. RMCMP

Sombras, Las. Jorge Guillén. RaW

Sombre Moment, A. Oliver Goldsmith. STuOW *Fr.* Captivity, The.

Sombre [*or* Somber] and rich, the skies. By the Statue of King Charles [*or* I] at Charing Cross. Lionel Pigot Johnson. MoBrPo; OBEV; OBMV

Sombre the night is. Returning, We Hear the Larks. Isaac Rosenberg. HarvBoo; NAEL-6v2; NAEL-7v2; NAMCP V.1; NoAM; OBWP; PoWW; StAl

Sombreo Beach, Vancouver Island, BC. Carrie Boden. BeDoSh

Some Account of Anne Whitehead's Early Experience, as Written by Her Near Thirty Years Ago. Anne Greenwell. EMWP

Some act of *Love's* bound to rehearse. Ben Jonson. PBRV

Some Adventures of John Kennedy Jr. Dennis Cooper.

  In New York. ReTh

  In School. ReTh; WiU

Some anti- / blasphemy. Woo's People. Harold Carrington. EGAG

Some are & are going to my howinouse. 12th Horse Song of Frank Mitchell (Blue), The. Frank Mitchell. APSN; FTOS, *tr. by* Jerome Rothenberg

Some are bewildered in the maze of Schools. Alexander Pope. OBSV *Fr.* Essay on Criticism, An.

Some are plain lucky—we ourselves among them. Lost Soul, A. Jay Macpherson. BrAP; NoP-4; NoP-5

Some are pure business, land deals, receipts, a contract. You Sort Old Letters. Robert Penn Warren. BodElec

Some ask for envy'd pow'r; which publick hate. Juvenal. OBVE *Fr.* Satires.

Some autumn leaves a painter took. Sumach Leaves, The. Jones Very. ColAP

Some banks cropped close, and lawns smooth mown and green. Hill-Side Park, The. W. H. Davies. OBGa

Some Beasts. Pablo Neruda. TCLAP, *tr. by* James Wright and James Wright

Some believe the end will come in the form of a mathematical equation. Rider, The. Sarah Manguso. BAP-01

Some Biographical Data. Cees Buddingh'. TuT, *tr. by* Mary E. O'Donnell

Some bite off the others'. Vasco [*or* Vasko] Popa. PoSu; StAl *Fr.* Games.

Some blue flowers. Sweet Pain of It, The. Eileen Myles. Eno

Some broken. State of Nature, A. John Hollander. NIL-7

Some by their friends, more by themselves thought wise. John Dryden. ChIV-1; OBSV *Fr.* Absalom and Achitophel.

Some call Experience. (LL) I stepped from Plank to Plank. Emily Dickinson. SAmP; TCAPo

Some call that deep-deep bell. "H. D." NAAPv.2; NALW *Fr.* Tribute to the Angels.

Some can gaze and not be sick. A. E. Housman. OBSV; OxBEV

Some candle clear burns somewhere I come by. Candle Indoors, The. Gerard Manley Hopkins. ChIV-2; OxAEP-2

Some can't. (LL) Even with insects. Issa. ASA; EH, *tr. by* Robert Hass

Some celebration. / One by one they all left me. On the Carpet, Staring at Myself. Slavko Mihalic. PoSu, *tr. by* Peter Kastmiler

Some Compensation. Jay Parini. PfSP

Some Cool. Alice Fulton. AllShUp

Some creep came to my water trough. Snake on D. H. Lawrence, The. N. J. Warburton. UV

Some critic tried to put me down. Han-shan (Cold Mountain). BB, *tr. by* Gary Snyder

Some Day. Ivan Davidkov. CSCBP, *tr. by* Georgi Belev and Lisa Sapinkopf

Some Day. Darío Jaramillo Agudelo. BLPSL, *tr. by* Rene de Costa, Rigas Kappatos and Eleni Paidoussi

Some day I will go to Aarhus. Tollund Man, The. Seamus Heaney. CABP; ModIr; NAMCP V.2; NPeEn; PBCIP; PNI; WoPoe

Some day I will write a poem for you that will not mention the air or the night. Some Day. Darío Jaramillo Agudelo. BLPSL, *tr. by* Rene de Costa, Rigas Kappatos and Eleni Paidoussi

Some day I'm going to have a store. General Store. Rachel Lyman Field. ChAP

Some day in six inches of. Kenneth Rexroth. APSN; APT-2; NAAPv.2; NAMCP V.1 *Fr.* Love Poems of Marichiko, The.

Some day shall I be the one who let. Some Day Shall I Be. Jules Supervielle. MFP, *tr. by* Martin Sorrell

Some day we will be saying, "That was the time of the sun." Regretting the Earth. Jules Supervielle. YaTCFP, *tr. by* Patricia Terry

Some day when I'm awf'ly low. Way You Look Tonight, The. Dorothy Fields. ReLy

Some days after. At a Wine House near Taegu. Sŏ Chŏngju. CAMKP, *tr. by* David R. McCann

Some days ago I remarried. Marrying Again. Mei Yao Ch'en. ColAnChi, *tr.* by Burton Watson

Some days, although we cannot pray, a prayer. Prayer. Carol Ann Duffy. EdScPo; HarvBoo; MoWP; NeBrP; NePenScot; NoP-4; NoP-5; OxBSo; RWPCtW

Some days he lurched around. Riding Lesson. Robin Becker. NevBe

Some days he would wander around his attic-room. Wisdom of AE, The. Thomas McCarthy. PBCIP

Some days I am lonesome I want to talk to my mother. Grace Paley. TaR

Some days I do feel better. Then I know. Worst Fear, The. George MacBeth. OxBSo

Some days I feel myself ravaged. Hotwire. Leslie Ullman. PoA 2002

Some days in May, little stars. Long Branch Song, A. Robert Pinsky. NoP-4; NoP-5

Some Days in the City. Mark McMorris. IAoNAP

Some days, Parasdise seems just a stone's throw. Some Days, Paradise. Thomas O'Grady. Coast

Some days start already swung from rafters. Here and There. Ann Lauterbach. BodElec

Some days, the sky descends to the level of mid-thigh water. Some Days in the City. Mark McMorris. IAoNAP

Some define the happening. (LL) Native's letter. Arthur Nortje. BrAP; HBAPE; TSAP

Some depature from the norm. John Ashbery. FTOS

Some Details of Hebridean House Construction. Thomas A. Clark. GoPo

Some Die of Light. Simeon Dumdum. ReBoTo

Some distance in, a life fills. Last in before Dark. Jason Sommer. PoDa

Some dogs who sleep at night. Eulogy to a Hell of a Dame. Charles Bukowski. CalPo

Some dreams are like glass. Lake Has Swallowed the Whole Sky, The. Silvia Curbelo. TouFir

Some Dreams They Forgot. Elizabeth Bishop. ItP; NoAM

Some Early gardenists. William Mason. OBGa *Fr.* English Garden, The.

Some Enchanted Evening. Oscar Hammerstein, II. ReLy

Some Exaggerations. Mirza Asadullah Khan Ghalib. WED, *tr. by* Robert Bly

Some Experimental Passages of My Life, with Reflections upon Jacob's Words, Few and Evil Have the Days of the Years of My Life Been. Elizabeth Tipper. EMWP

Some eyes condemn the earth they gaze upon. Some Eyes Condemn. Edward Thomas. NoAM; OxBSo

Some fathers hate to read but love to. Short Talk on Reading. Anne Carson. OpeFie

Some fellers love to Tip-Toe Through the Tulips. Bidin' My Time. Ira Gershwin. ReLy

Some final questions. Phyllis Webb. NLPA *Fr.* Naked Poems.

Some folk think that poet. Disdirected, The. Louis Reyes Rivera. BRtP

Some folks transplant rice for wages. Farmer's Pride, The. *Unknown.* WoPoe, *tr. by* Nguyen Ngoc Bich

Some folks will tell you the blues is a woman. I'm a Fool to Love You. Cornelius Eady. P180

Some fools once were listening to a poet reading his poem. William Carlos Williams. TCAPo *Fr.* Kora in Hell.

Some for the Glories of This World; and some. Omar Khayyám. CABP; TRP *Fr.* Rubáiyát of Omar Khayyám [of Naishápúr], The.

Some Foreign Letters. Anne Sexton. MoAmPo

Some formula for sacred council as not to weep. Potter's Field. Prageeta Sharma. HeMarv

Some Frenchmen. John Updike. NBLV

Some Ghosts and Some Ghouls. Jay Macpherson. IFF *Fr.* Way Down, The.

Some Girls. Susanne Doyle. CalPo; FFC

Some girls are just prostitutes to the tinier pageantry of bees—sighing. Push the Feathered Glory. Jennifer Timoner. ICANM

Some glory in their birth, some in their skill. William Shakespeare. WaAnP *Fr.* Sonnets.

Some Glow on the Sill. Clark Coolidge. FTOS

Some glowing in the common blood. / Some specialness within. (LL) Of Robert Frost. Gwendolyn Brooks. NoAM; VisFro

Some go to lunch at midday. News, The. *Unknown.* RWPCtW

Some gold lies veiled behind each evening cloud. Hidden Essence. Henrietta Cordelia Ray. CBWP-3

Some Grand River Blues. Daniel David Moses. HATNAP

Some guy in the miserable convoy. Last Lie, The. Bruce Weigl. AF; AmWaPo

Some had forgotten how. (LL) School Among the Ruins, The. Adrienne Rich. AmWaPo; CAP-8

Some Harvard men, stalwart and hairy. Limerick. Edward Gorey. OBCoV

Some have no money. John Skelton. NAEL-7v1 *Fr.* Tunnyng [*or* Tunning] of Elynour [*or* Elinor] Rummyng [*or* Rumming], The.

Some have [*or* hae] meat and cannot [*or* canna] eat. Grace at Kirkudbright. Robert Burns. OxBEV

Some heaps of trash upon a vacant lot. Ambrose Bierce. APN-2 *Fr.* Devil's Dictionary, The.

Some horror routed them from their homes. Holy Innocents. David Brendon Hopes. UpMys

Some in a child would live, some in a book. Mary Elizabeth Coleridge. ViWPN

Some in Yarrow will tell it differently. Tree with a Hole in Our Front Yard, The. Leonard Neufeldt. ACAMVP

Some interiors keep their shade. Some Die of Light. Simeon Dumdum. ReBoTo

Some keep the Sabbath going to Church. Emily Dickinson. BLPJKO; HeIP-4; MoAmPo; TCAPo

Some kind, a prodigy, a maimed one. (LL) Geoffrey Hill. NAMCP V.2; NoAM; WoPoe *Fr.* Mercian Hymns.

Some Kind of Crazy. Major L. Jackson. FuFl; SpirFl

Some Kind of Thanks. Menna Elfyn. ATSWP, *tr. by* Robert Minhinnick

Some ladies smoke too much and some ladies drink too much and some ladies pray too much. Curl Up and Diet. Ogden Nash. OBCoV

Some Lapland Views. Christian Dotrement. PFTM-2, *tr. by* Pierre Joris

Some Last Questions. W. S. Merwin. NAMCP V.2; VCAP

Some leading thoroughfares of man. Herman Melville. APN-2; NCAP *Fr.* Clarel: A Poem and Pilgrimage in the Holy Land.

Some like cats, and some like dogs. Cats and Dogs. N. M. Bodecker. TLR

Some like them gentle and sweet. I Like Them Fluffy. Sir Alan Patrick Herbert. NBLV

Some Lines Finished Just Before Dawn at the Bedside of a Dying Student It Has Snowed All Night. Miller Williams. InGu

Some lonely men stand around this city. Statues. Karen Press. TSAP

Some lovers speak, when they their Muses entertain. Sir Philip Sidney. NAEL-6v1; NAEL-7v1; NoSic *Fr.* Astrophil and Stella.

Some loves are soft, others are rough. *Unknown.* NAAPv.2

Some lucky day each November great waves awake and are drawn. November Surf. Robinson Jeffers. CalPo

Some man unworthy to be possessor. Confined Love. John Donne. BASC

Some Mangled Dream Songs for Henry Who is Twenty-eight Years Dead and Past Caring. Tracey Herd. "Shadowed by your father." StAl

Some marring in the glass of the body. Shatter. Elizabeth Robinson. AmPoNex

Some may occasion snatch to carp,. Harp, The. Ralph Knevet. ChIV-2

Some meaning rain. Irritable Songs. Russell Atkins. EGAG

Some men break your heart in two. Experience. Dorothy Parker. AmWit

Some men never think of it. Flowers. Wendy Cope. NoP-4; NoP-5

Some men, some men. Chant for Dark Hours. Dorothy Parker. AmWit; ItWoWo

Some men to carriages aspire. Ballade of an Omnibus. Amy Levy. ViWPN

Some men wash their hands five times a day. Hygiene. Reginald Shepherd. ReTh

Some Metaphysics of Junior Wells. Sandra McPherson. SeSe

Some miles beyond the last reef's barricade. Offset, The. Wyatt Prunty. PfSP

Some, misbelieving and profane in love. Michael Drayton. AEP *Fr.* Idea.

Some moments stolen by a slave. Frozen Witness, The. Nick Piombino. FTOS

Some More Scruples Clear'd. Elizabeth Hincks. EMWP

Some mornings I wake up kicking like a frog. Original Face. Henri Cole. BeAl

Some names are ominous, wherein wise fate. Of St Stephen. Francis Quarles. NOSC

Some names there are that win the best applause. William Lloyd Garrison. Henrietta Cordelia Ray. CBWP-3

Some ne'er advance a judgment of their own. Alexander Pope. OBSV *Fr.* Essay on Criticism, An.

Some Nets. B. P. Nichol. FTOS

Some night under a pale moon and geraniums. Serenade. Adelia Prado. TANSG, *tr. by* Ellen Doré Watson

Some nights, / driving home from anywhere. Crossing Over. Raylene Hinz-Penner. ACAMVP

Some Nights I Love Everybody in Texas. Del Marie Rogers. TiP2

Some nights I sleep with my dress on. My teeth. Personals. C. D. Wright. AmAlph; PtR

Some nights, the girl heard scales scrape. Chivalry. John Lundberg. LiTh

Some nights the quiet is all wrong. A tape. Over *Voice of America.* Dennis Finnell. SwNoth

Some nineteen German planes, they say. Reprisals. William Butler Yeats. OBWP; PoWW

Some of Betty's Story Round 1850. Gale Jackson. SpirFl

Some of his messages were personal. Passed On. Bernard Spencer. FaBoWar

Some of the ears on the floor were pressed to the ground. (LL) Colonel, The. Carolyn Forché. AmWaPo; MakPoe; MotU; NAMCP V.2; OBWP; OxBoAm; PoAgWa; SoSe-8; WaAnP

Some of the girls are playing jacks. Narcissa. Gwendolyn Brooks. NTCP

Some of the things you may be wondering. Air War, The. Geoffrey Nutter. IAoNAP

Some of the time. Working with Mother. Myra Cohn Livingston. TLR

Some of their chiefs were princes of the land. John Dryden. OxBEV *Fr.* Absalom and Achitophel.

Some of them with staves. Basho. TAL

Some of These Days. Shelton Brooks. ReLy

Some of those pioneers who came. Long Gone to Texas. William D. Barney. TiP2

Some of us already older than Mozart was when death. Singing the Mozart Requiem. Ingrid Wendt. FiBr

Some of us are telling secrets. Late Night Radio. Aleda Shirley. ExTi

Some of us believe. Night Game, The. Robert Pinsky. TaR

Some of us flinch, some do not. (LL) Eulogy, The. Carol Muske-Dukes. InoFa; PBCAP

Some of us know. Intelligence Quotients. Dorothy Perry Thompson. SpirFl

Some of Us Wear Pink Triangles. Walta Borawski. CAGL

Some of what we do, we do. Love Poem with Toast. Miller Williams. PoDa

Some Old How. Sándor Petőfi. IQMS, *tr. by* Peter Zollman

Some old lady scarcely younger. *Unknown.* PriapPo *Fr.* Priapus Poems, The.

Some One. Walter De la Mare. TLR

Some one calls out, and some one else. Sick Men Sleeping. Kenneth Mackenzie. BMAP

Some one prepared this mighty show. Emily Dickinson. SAmP

Some Other Time. Betty Comden and Adolph Green. ReLy

Some part of the lyric wants to exclude. Some Part of the Lyric. Gregory Orr. TAPaP

Some patios won't allow the shadow of a maid. Scattered Light. Fanny Howe. FTOS

Some People. Rachel Lyman Field. ChAP; NTCP

Some People. Rita Ann Higgins. BeAl

Some People. A. K. Ramanujan. VCWP

Some People. Stephen Sondheim. ReLy

Some People Are about Jam. Sandra Maria Esteves. PueRic

Some people are getting so they think a poor girl. Julia A. Moore. VerBaPo *Fr.* Roll On, Time, Roll On.

Some people are like that. Let's Go Over It All Again. James Fenton. BeAl

Some people as they die grow fierce, afraid. Hereafter, The. Andrew Hudgins. RA

Some people / ascend out of our life, some people. Some People. Rolf Jacobsen. WED, *tr. by* Robert Bly

Some people can get a thrill. Some People. Stephen Sondheim. ReLy

Some people go their whole lives. Dream On. James Tate. BodElec; OxBoAm; PtR

Some people know what it's like. Some People. Rita Ann Higgins. BeAl

Some People Laugh, Some People Cry. Sri Sri.

    "Man walks on the bridge and gives away the change in his, A." HotL, *tr. by* V. Narayana Rao and A. K. Ramanujan

Some people need a lot of money. I'm Just a Lucky So-and-So. Mack David. ReLy

Some people should take a break. Have you ever. Mercy Flight. Anselm Berrigan. HeMarv

Some people terrified for their lives cut. Karen Alkalay-Gut. DTA *Fr.* Between Bombardments: A Journal.

Some people weren't meant to eat a New York Strip. Angel Finally Admits What She Knows to Lou Binkler of Bethany, Missouri, An. Catie Rosemurgy. AmPoNex

Some pimps wear summer hats. What? Langston Hughes. NBLV

Some poem with girls on hands and knees, but now. Trying to Sleep on My Father's Couch and Staring at the Fractured Plaster, I Recall. Tony Barnstone, Willis Barnstone *and* Haixin Xu. VisFro

Some Poems Aren't For You. Heather Sellers. LiTh

Some Poetry. Freda Downie. MoWP

Some prefer a glory of horsemen; warships. Sappho. STV

Some primal termite knocked on wood. Termite, The. Ogden Nash. AmWit

Some prowl sea-beds, some hurtle to a star. X-Ray. Dannie Abse. AngWePo; BloBone; PoA 2002

Some push us around, some curse us. *Unknown.* NAAPv.2

Some queen has left her mirror on the grass. Frozen Tarn. Catherine Fisher. TCAWP

Some Questions You Might Ask. Mary Oliver. BeAl; ColAP; OxBoAm; StAl

Some Quiet, Plain Poems. Robert Penn Warren.

    Holly and Hickory. LPSFW

    In Italian They Call the Bird *Civetta.* LPSFW

    In Moonlight, Somewhere, They Are Singing. LPSFW

    Well House, The. LPSFW

Some Reflections. Anne Finch, Countess of Winchilsea. ChIV-1

Some Remarks When Richard Hugo Came. William Stafford. PWW2

Some Reservation Valentines. Patricia Smith. ICANM

Some Ruthless Rhymes. Harry Graham.

    Tender-Heartedness. NBLV; NOxBChV

Some Saian sports my splendid shield. Archilochus. PoAgWa, *tr. by* Martin Litchfield West

Some said the northern window was bright. Hanu. CATKP, *tr. by* Peter H. Lee

Some San Francisco Poems. George Oppen.

    And Their Winter and Night in Disguise. APSN

    Anniversary Poem. APSN

    But So as by Fire. APT-2

    Impossible Poem, The. ASA

    Morality Play, A: Preface. APSN

    "Silver as / The needle's eye." FTOS

    Taste, The. FTOS

Some say an army of horsemen, others. Sappho. SaLy, *tr. by* Diane Rayor

Some say: look at what's happening behind the scenes. In the Limpid Air. Michel Houellebecq. YaTCFP, *tr. by* Mary Ann Caws *and* Jean-Pierre Cauvin

Some say that love is sweet as a rose. Candy. Mack David, Alex Kramer and Joan Whitney. ReLy

Some say that love's a little boy. W. H. Auden. NoP-5; StAl *Fr.* Twelve Songs.

Some say the radiance around the body. 11/10 Again. Lucille Clifton. GT

Some say the voices here meander. East Texas Blues. Mary Loving Blanchard. TiP2

Some say the world will end in fire. Fire and Ice. Robert Frost. APT-1; BrAP; BRP; ColAP; HeIP-4; MoAmPo; NAAL-5; NAAPv.2; NAMCP V.1; NoAM; OxBoAm; RaBo; SoSe-8; TFi; WaAnP

Some say the world will end in fire. Fire and Ice by Robert Frost: an early draft. Ron Overton. VisFro

Some say they saw the Bull. Brigomaglos, a Christian, Speaks. Frances Horovitz. MoWP

Some seek de Lord and they don't seek him right. Almost Over. *Unknown.* SSUS

Some shapes cannot be seen in a glass. Holding the Mirror Up to Nature. Howard Nemerov. PoA 2002

Some Sights Sometimes Seen and Seldom Seen. William Cole. TLR

Some silver-fingered fountain steals the world. (LL) Sonnet IV. E. E. Cummings. ChIV-1; MoAmPo

Some six-hundred thousand years after fire, what thinks. Easter Lesson, The. Jennifer Moxley. VaPo

Some Sixties. Ray Gonzalez. MiVo

Some slob tracked burning styrofoam across the dear sky's parlor. Beautiful American Poem, The. Josh Bell. RWB

Some slumbring thoughts possess'd my brain. Golden Island, The; or, the Darian Song. *Unknown.* EMWP

Some Solace, Some Yearning. William Henry Lewis. BtF

Some songs by women. Some Songs Women Sing. Peter Harris. ISC

Some Songs Women Sing. Peter Harris. ISC

Some sort of chronicler I am, mixing. Some Sort of Chronicler I Am. Lawrence Joseph. OxBoAm

Some spare relief. Fossil Garden, The. Emily Wilson. LegDan

Some Sparrows. Ernesto Trejo. PoCho

Some speak of ancestral emptiness. 92. Shih Shu. CSKM, *tr. by* James H. Sanford

Some Sporting Motifs. Maurice Riordan. NIrP

Some sports are odious, but. John Tranter. VaPo *Fr.* Blackout.

Some springs the mississippi rose up so high. Thulani Davis. SeSe

Some talk of Alexander, and some of Hercules. British Grenadiers, The. *Unknown.* FaBoWar

Some talke of Ganimede th' Idalian Boy. Richard Barnfield. CAGL

Some Tears. Kees Ouwens. TuT, *tr. by* Peter van de Kamp

Some Tentative Definitions 1. Kwame Dawes. WaCA

Some Tentative Definitions 11. Kwame Dawes. WaCA

Some Tentative Definitions 4. Kwame Dawes. WaCA

Some Tentative Definitions 7. Kwame Dawes. WaCA

Some Terms in Real Estate Defined. Richard Cecil. SUP

Some Terrify Lions [*or* Anna Matilda]. Robert Merry. STuOW

Some that have deeper digged love's mine [or myne] than [or then] I.   Love's Alchemy [or Alchemie].   John Donne.   BASC; NAEL-6v1; NAEL-7v1; NoP-4; NoP-5

Some there are who say that the fairest thing seen.   Sappho.   NAWM-7v1, tr. by Richmond Lattimore

Some Thing Black.   Jacques Roubaud. tr. by Rosmarie Waldrop
    Section V.   PFTM-2, tr. by Rosmarie Waldrop

Some things are best unsaid, and best unheard.   Answering Robert Frost.   Felix Stefanile.   VisFro

Some things are truly lost. Think of a sun-hat.   Mind-Reader, The.   Richard Wilbur.   NoAM

Some things I do not profess.   Abduction, The.   Stanley Kunitz.   CAP-8; WeW-3

Some things I have to say aren't getting said.   Bilingual Sestina.   Julia Alvarez.   ExTi; FFC; WaAnP

Some things that fly there be.   Emily Dickinson.   NCAP; NoP-5

Some things we do take up a lot more time.   Ode to Bill.   John Ashbery.   NoP-5

Some things you should forget.   But Bird.   Paul Zimmer.   AtGh; SeSe

Some think.   Dilection.   Ernst Jandl.   OnScMo, tr. by Anselm Hollo

Some think a fleet, a troop of horse.   Sappho.   PoAgWa, tr. by Martin Litchfield West

Some thought it was because of all the babies I suddenly seemed to be having.   Babies, The.   Sabrina Orah Mark.   LegDan

Some Thracian exults in an excellent shield.   Archilochus.   SaLy, tr. by Diane Rayor

Some three or four mile out of town.   Robert Lloyd.   OBGa

Some Time After.   Anne Ridler.   SacPr

Some time ago a soul, now erased, was mine.   Sweet Reliquaries, The.   Delmira Agustini.   TANSG, tr. by Mark McCaffrey

Some time now past in the autumnal tide.   Contemplations.   Anne Bradstreet.   ColAP; NAAL-3; NAAL-5; NAAPv.1; TCAPo

Some time when the river is ice ask me.   Ask Me.   William Stafford.   CAP-8; LoL; OxBoAm

Some / times.   5 Minutes, Mr. Salaam.   Kalamu ya Salaam.   SpirFl

Some to Conceit alone their taste confine.   Alexander Pope.   OxAEP-1 Fr. Essay on Criticism, An.

Some Towns of Texas.   Karle Wilson Baker.
    Austin.   TiP2

Some Trees.   John Ashbery.   FaoP; NAMCP V.2; YaYoPo

Some truths may pierce the spirit's deeper gloom.   Frederick Goddard Tuckerman.   APN-2 Fr. Sonnets.

Some Valiant Solider.   Unknown.   SSUS

Some Versions of Pastoral.   Steve McCaffery.   BAP-04

Some vex their souls with jealous pain.   On One Who Died Discovering Her Kindness.   John, Duke of Buckingham and Normandy Sheffield.   OBEV

Some Views Concerning the Proposed Site of a National Park.   Miyazawa Kenji.   WhBo

Some Walks With You.   John Hollander.   BodElec

Some walls enclosing furniture. (LL)   Key, The.   John Ormond.   AngWePo; TCAWP

Some war, I bomb their towns from five.   Some Remarks When Richard Hugo Came.   William Stafford.   PWW2

Some waves / a wave of now.   Latin and Soul for Joe Bataan.   Víctor Hernández Cruz.   PueRic

Some weep to find the Golden Pear.   Colored Blues Singer.   Countee Cullen.   OxBoAm

Some with sharp swords, to tell O most accursed!   Margaret Lucas Cavendish, Duchess of Newcastle.   PEW Fr. Fort or Castle of Hope, The.

Some without remote interview.   Shakeout.   Diane Ward.   FTOS

Some women love / to wait.   Stations.   Audre Lorde.   BrAP; OxAAAP

Some women marry houses.   Sarah Messer.   SweBea

Some women marry houses.   Housewife.   Anne Sexton.   NALW; WaAnP

Some women save their sanity with needles.   Mr. McGregor's Garden.   Medbh McGuckian.   PNI

Some would have you think the Pony Express.   Pony Express.   Stephen Dobyns.   SUP

Some years ago, ere time and taste.   Winthrop Mackworth Praed.   OBEV; OxAEP-2 Fr. Every Day Characters.

Some years back I worked a strip mine.   Lester Tells of Wanda and the Big Snow.   Paul Zimmer.   GoPo

Somebody Consoles Me with a Poem.   Sandor Csoori.   GifTon; TAPaP, tr. by Len Roberts and László Vértes

Somebody dies every four minutes.   Rapid Transit.   William Carlos Williams.   APT-1; OxBoAm

Somebody doubts it, so I have heard. (LL)   Unknown.   APN-2; NAAPv.1 Fr. Mountain Chant, The.

Somebody Else.   Jackie Kay.   BeAl; NeBl

Somebody from the enemy thought I was one of their own. (LL)   On the Amtrak from Boston to New York City.   Sherman Alexie.   NAMCP V.2; PoPoPo

Somebody has given my.   Proust's Madeleine.   Kenneth Rexroth.   NAMCP V.1; NoAM; TRP

Somebody is knocking at the door.   Christmas.   Dunya Mikhail.   IrPoTo, tr. by Liz Winslow

Somebody is shooting at something in our town.   Swarm, The.   Sylvia Plath.   NALW

Somebody Loves Me.   B. G. DeSylva and Ballard MacDonald.   ReLy

Somebody loves us all. (LL)   Filling Station.   Elizabeth Bishop.   NoP-4; NoP-5; PoetW; PtR; VCAP; WeW-3

Somebody said that it couldn't be done.   It Couldn't Be Done.   Edgar Albert Guest.   BRP; ITBLP

Somebody said when snubbed, "Is Damon so."   Diodes.   CAGL, tr. by Daryl Hine

Somebody / Somewhere.   S'what Up.   Joel Dailey.   AnSo

Somebody, Somewhere.   Frank Loesser.   ReLy

Somebody who knew him.   Unknown Forebear.   W. S. Merwin.   StAl

Somebody who should have been born.   Abortion, The.   Anne Sexton.   CAP-8

Somebody's husband raped you while you were supposed to be in the choir pounding a tambourine.   Goodness and the Salt of the Earth.   Thylias Moss.   MotU

Somebody's knockin' at th' door.   Collier's Wife, The.   D. H. Lawrence.   FaBoVe

Somebody's Mother.   Unknown.   ChAP

Somebody's welding.   Bus Poems, The.   Del Ray Cross.   FreRad

Someday, emerging at last from the violent insight.   Rainer Maria Rilke.   Fr. Duino Elegies, The [Stephen Mitchell Translation].

Someday he'll leave me: then what will I do? (LL)   How Lies Grow.   Maxine Chernoff.   IllVoic; PmAP; SUP

Someday I will leave this town and not look back.   Suture.   Mark Wunderlich.   AmPoNex

Someday I'll say: welcome.   Meeting, The.   José Hierro.   RaW, tr. by Rachel Benson

Someday I'll wake and hardly think of you.   Shorelines.   Howard Moss.   GoPo

Someday the phoebe bird will sing.   Occupant of the Hose.   Larissa Szporluk.   NeAmPo

Someday they'll bring you in.   Witness, The.   Ken Mikolowski.   PrTe

Someday they'll find me out, and my lavish hands.   Self-Portrait.   Charles Wright.   PoPoPo

Somehow I never stopped to notice.   His Costume.   Sharon Olds.   BAP-01

Somehow I really want to go.   Vsevolod Nekrasov.   ItGoST, tr. by Gerald Janecek

Somehow it got into my room.   My Life.   Joe Wenderoth.   BodElec; NAPBL; P180

Somehow myself survived the Night.   Emily Dickinson.   APN-2

Somehow, one expects.   Sadness of My Neighbors, The.   James Tate.   ItP

Somehow, somewhere / the clever dust slips in.   How It Begins / How It Ends.   Richard Blanco.   LegDan

Somehow the intentness of the whole.   Nut Castle.   John Ashbery.   VaPo

Somehow they are a lie. (LL)   Elemental.   D. H. Lawrence.   NoP-4; NoP-5

Somehow We Survive.   Dennis Brutus.   PLBUT

Someone.   Ruth Forman.   AmPoNex

Someone.   Miroslav Holub.   VCWP

Someone.   Dennis O'Driscoll.   InoFa; StAl

Someone.   Someone Will Take The Ball.   Nelly Sachs.   BBASP, tr. by Matthew Mead and Ruth Mead

Someone.   Nelly Sachs.   WPoS, tr. by Matthew Mead and Ruth Mead

Someone always likes to ride backwards.   Riding Backwards on a Train.   James Hoch.   PoDa

Someone anonymous in the anonymous throng.   Writing on a Tombstone.   J. C. Bloem.   TuT, tr. by Desmond Egan

Someone Asked the Publisher.   John Bingham Morton.   UV Fr. When We Were Very Silly.

Someone brought them to Palma.   Toward the Jurassic Age.   Claribel Alegría.   TCLAP, tr. by Carolyn Forché

Someone came knocking.   Someone [or Some One].   Walter De la Mare.   MoBrPo

Someone dancing inside us.   Advice.   Bill Holm.   RaBo

Someone Digging in the Ground.   Jelaluddin Rumi.   RaBo, tr. by Coleman Barks

Someone drove a two-by-four.   Child's Grave, Hale County, Alabama.   Jim Simmerman.   WeW-3

Someone dumped it here one night, locked.   '49 Merc, A.   Kurt Brown.   PoDa

Someone else cut off my head.   Bread.   Brendan Kennelly.   PBCIP

Someone else has made you say it. (LL) In Las Vegas. Katherine Lederer. IIR; LegDan

Someone else's life. Kapka Kassabova. BeAl

Someone explained once how the pieces of what we are. Concerning the Atoms of the Soul. John Glenday. NeBrP

Someone flips a lit match off the road. X and O. Arthur Sze. AmAlph

Someone gave the name, sometime, of pearly everlasting. (LL) Interrupted Meditation. Robert Hass. BAP-97; FaoP

Someone had been walking in and out. Origin of Baseball, The. Kenneth Patchen. APT-2; CLPP

Someone hands you an English thriller. This Is Bad. Gottfried Benn. WoPoe, tr. by Harvey Shapiro

Someone has remembered to dry the dishes. Red Lilies. Barbara Guest. FTOS; PmAP

Someone has shut the shining eyes, straightened and folded. Beside the Bed. Charlotte Mew. InoFa; MoBrPo

Someone has to sweep these million golden. Sweeping Heaven. Heid E. Erdrich. SweBea

Someone I flew with. Flying Dutchman, The. Walter McDonald. TiP2

Someone I know is dying at seventeen. Gray Fox, The. Gregory Orr. PfSP

Someone, if you pay the price, can hypnotize. Interview with an Alchemist in the New Age. Stephanie Brown. BodElec

Someone in Quaker meeting talks about greed and aggression. Greed and Aggression. Sharon Olds. RaBo

Someone in the garden murmurs all the day. Someone in the Garden. Mary Mapes Dodge. SWaP

Someone is always, always stepping out of line. (LL) Beware. Kenneth Fearing. APT-2; NAAPv.2

Someone Is Beating a Woman. Andrey Andreievich Voznesensky. VCWP, tr. by Jean Garrigue

Someone is dressing up for death today, a change of skirt or tie. Someone. Dennis O'Driscoll. InoFa; StAl

Someone is leaving town as clean smoke. Passing the Crematorium. Frank Ormsby. ModIr

Someone is locking out the stars and the yellow flowers. Old Man in a Moon Loft. T. Glynne Davies. OBWVE, tr. by the author

Someone Is Probably Dead. Marvin Bell. BodElec

Someone is shutting out the stars and the buttercups. Bailiff, The. T. Glynne Davies. BBMWP, tr. by Joseph P. Clancy

Someone is sitting in the red house. Small Town. Rita Dove. AmAlph; GT

Someone is waving a white handkerchief. Departure and Departure and. George Bruce. EdScPo

Someone lights a saxophone. Rapid Transit. Nzadi Z. Keita. BRtP

Someone might live. Dark Spaces: Thoughts on All Souls Day. John Knoepfle. IllVoic

Someone might think that because New Jersey is a relatively easy concept. Dinner in the Sun. Donald Berger. NAPBL

Someone [or Some One]. Walter De la Mare. MoBrPo

Someone produces frequent groans. Flowers ornament the walls. Carla Harryman. BAP-04 Fr. Baby.

Someone said in a dream, 'Flying's dead easy'. Mass. Mairi MacInnes. MoWP

Someone said my name in the garden. Out of Hiding. Li-Young Lee. NoP-5; PoDa

Someone said, "Our right hand is in the book. But the left has the / privilege of opening and closing." Book, The. Edmond Jabès. AF, tr. by Rosmarie Waldrop

Someone said the place had been the secret. On Lookout: Guadalupe River Ranch. William Virgil Davis. TiP2

Someone sits in a mountain gorge. Han-shan (Cold Mountain). GifTon, tr. by Red Pine

Someone, somewhere, is always starting trouble. Beware. Kenneth Fearing. APT-2; NAAPv.2

Someone sows someone. Vasco [or Vasko] Popa. PoSu Fr. Games.

Someone spoke to me last night. Dust. Dorianne Laux. SUP

Someone stirs above me. Night Flute, The. Beryle Williams. MiVo

Someone Talking to Himself. Richard Wilbur. HarvBoo

Someone that I belong to. Prisoner of Love. Clarence Gaskill and Leo Robin. ReLy

Someone throws stones at my roof, then. Revenge. Amado Nervo. TCLAP, tr. by Sue Standing

Someone to Watch over Me. Ira Gershwin. ReLy

Someone told me. Patrizia Cavalli. NeIt

Someone told me, Heraclitus. Callimachus. HePo, tr. by Barbara Hughes Fowler

Someone, turning in sleep. While the Wolf Walks the Edge of the Woods. Mary Sue Koeppel. AmZen

Someone was searching for a Form of Fire. Create Desire. Karen Volkman. KGB; NAPBL

Someone was writing this incredibly personal poem. Santa Monica. Charlie Smith. KGB

Someone we love, old friend, has telephoned. For William Stafford. Henry Taylor. PoA 2002

Someone who appeared. Surreal Love Life. Gene Frumkin. ICANM

Someone Who Knows My Heart. Kim Yŏngnang. CAMKP, tr. by Anthony, Brother of Taizé

Someone who well knew how she'd toss her chin. Loose Woman. X. J. Kennedy. WeW-3

Someone, whose morals need mending. Time's Betrayal. Herman Melville. NCAP

Someone will conquer them. (LL) Witter Bynner. NoP-4; NoP-5 Fr. Chinese Drawings.

Someone will consider something you do prolific. Estrella's Prophecies #47. David Baratier. AmPoNex

Someone will reap you like a field. To One Loved Wholly Within Wisdom. Genevieve Taggard. APT-2

Someone Will Take The Ball. Nelly Sachs. BBASP, tr. by Matthew Mead and Ruth Mead

Someone would like to have you for her child. Lullaby. Unknown. WoPoe, tr. by Kwabenia Nketia

Someone writes kike on. Being Jewish in a Small Town. Lyn Lifshin. UnSA

Someone yelled come home, but we were dancing in the night. (LL) Jungle Music. Warren Woessner. MiVo; SwNoth

Someone's absence you. Sofia. John Seed. Oth

Someone's Been Sending Me Flowers. Sheldon Harnick. ReLy

Someone's licked a finger, touched it to the mirror. Ghazal on signs of Love and Occupation. Philip Salom. BMAP

Someone's old parents in the desert on folding chairs. Giants. Jane Miller. ExTi

Someone's thinking about his mother tonight. Eternal Son, The. Li-Young Lee. RoV

Somer is i-comen in. Unknown. See Sumer is icumen in.

Somers Point. A. R. Ammons. PfSP

Somerset Maugham said a professional was someone who could do his best work. Churchyard. Robert Hass. MotU

Somerville Saturday Night. Ron Schreiber. PrTe

Something. Robert Creeley. CAP-8

Something. (LL) Jackson Mac Low. FTOS; PFTM-2; PmAP Fr. Pronouns, The—A Collection of 40 Dances—For the Dancers.

Something. Design. Mary Oliver. PoCoUp

Something, The. Charles Simic. BAP-97

Something About Being an Indian. Adrian C. Louis. UnSA

Something about pumpkins caused. What Brings Us Out. Naomi Shihab Nye. CAP-8

Something about Silence. Elizabeth Hincks. EMWP

Something about You. Jessica Tarahata Hagedorn. PmAP

Something breaks that won't be ignored. Necessity. Keith Ratzlaff. ACAMVP

Something Childish, but Very Natural. Samuel Taylor Coleridge. NPBRoP

Something Cool. Billy Barnes. ReLy

Something cracks every moment because. Brief Thoughts on Cracks. Miroslav Holub. PoSu, tr. by Ian Milner and Jarmila Milner

Something easy for Ultra Black Nationalists. Kenneth Carroll. SpirFl

Something Else. Paul Muldoon. ModIr

Something familiar / Something peculiar. Comedy Tonight. Stephen Sondheim. ReLy

Something for Easter. Robert Creeley. InvLad

Something for her lips. oh dare, oh share. something. Bernice Got Next to Isis. Leslie Simon. FFC

Something from an untidy Russian life. Katia Kapovich. CRWP, tr. by Richard McKane

Something Goes By. May Swenson. BodElec

Something goes wrong with my synthetic brain. Case for the Miners, The. Siegfried Sassoon. RSaN

Something hangs in back of me. Wings, The. Denise Levertov. APSN; NALW

Something Happened. Patricia Donegan. WhBo

Something has happened. Tomas Tranströmer. WoBe Fr. Haiku.

Something has happened to me. Kofi Awoonor. HBAPE

Something has happened to my name. Catalogue Army. Naomi Shihab Nye. ReTh

Something has reached out and taken in the beams of my eyes. All I Was Doing Was Breathing. Mirabai. WED; WoPoe; WPoS, tr. by Robert Bly

Something hurts me, on the side, do You see, my Lord? Something Hurt. Admiel Kosman. PML, tr. by Lisa Katz

Something I saw or thought I saw. On the Heart's Beginning to Cloud the Mind. Robert Frost. GM

Something I'm Not. Liz Lochhead. NePenScot

Something in the letter found in the box, and something just out there. Meditation Brought About by George Bogin's Translation of Jules Supervielle's Poem "The Sea." Michael Burkard. BodElec

Something in the water. Lorine Niedecker. AFaM; NAMCP V.1

Something / in the way these alleys twist and. Reggae Cat (for Boston Jack). Kendel Hippolyte. WaCA

Something in the world. Almost at the Horizon. Alan Williamson. FaoP

Something in their psyche insists on Elvis. Them and Us. Lucille Clifton. AllShUp

Something inspires the only cow of late. Cow in Apple Time, The. Robert Frost. MoAmPo

Something is always vanishing. Unearth. Mary Louise Sullivan. PfS

Something is bound to happen yet to my head. Thin Wire. Leo Vroman. TuT, tr. by Desmond Egan

Something is breaking loose. Fourteen. James A. Emanuel. OxAAAP

Something is going to go, baby. Cyril Connolly. OBCoV Fr. Where Engels Fears to Tread.

Something is happening. Dear Jesse Helms. Lucille Clifton. GifTon

Something is in the line and air along edges. Mountains. Alice Oswald. MFPA; StAl

Something is laying its hand on this hour. Life in the Comics. Jenny Mueller. IAoNAP

Something is pushing against my blood. Posthumous. Michael O'Loughlin. PBCIP

Something is taking its course. Harvest of War. Catherine Obianuju Acholonu. HAWP; NAfrP

Something is taking place. Robert Duncan. NAMCP V.2 Fr. Rites of Passage.

Something Like A. Blas de Otero. RaW, tr. by Hardie St. Martin

Something like a rabbit comes. Burning of Margaret Moone, The. Mary Doughtery Bartlett. ICANM

Something Like a Sonnet for Phillis Miracle Wheatley. June Jordan. NIL-7

Something Like Marriage. Joan Logghe. ICANM

Something Like That. Nicanor Parra. WoBe, tr. by Liz Werner

Something like volcanic ash wafted in air. Cabbage Butterfly, The. Henri Cole. UrbNat

Something More Obvious. Amanda R. Evans. BeDoSh

Something must be done right away. Song for Those Who Know. Hans Magnus Enzensberger. PoSu; VCWP, tr. by the author and Michael Hamburger

Something never quite returns when you want. Skipping. Jim Barnes. RWB

Something Nice. Jack Forbes. FTtHH

Something of a Departure. Paul Muldoon. IrLP; PBCIP

Something of glass about her, of dead water. Circe. Louis MacNeice. OBMV

Something of the Flowers. David Brendon Hopes. "If the flowers could ask me." UpMys

Something old and tyrannical burning there. Coal Fire in Winter, A. Thomas McGrath. ErotSp; GifTon; RaBo

Something one day occurr'd about a bill. George Crabbe. STuOW Fr. Tales of the Hall.

Something or Other. Ron Padgett. FTOS

Something or someone. A feeling. Ignis Fatuus. Yusef Komunyakaa. BAP-04

Something outside my window in the dark. Wind from a Wing, A. William Stafford. CAP-8

Something Remembered. Emilio Prados. RaW, tr. by Hardie St. Martin

Something removed roars in the ears of this house. Missing the Sea. Derek Walcott. OxBEV

Something said: You have nothing to fear. Heard by a Girl. Louise Bogan. APT-2

Something says find out. Drifter. Marilyn Nelson. BtF

Something stands here to peril our advance. Thomas Hardy. FaBoWar Fr. Dynasts, Part 2, The.

Something Starting Over. Thomas Hornsby Ferril. APT-2

Something startles me where I thought I was safest. This Compost. Walt Whitman. MoAmPo; NAAL-3; OBGa; PFTM-1

Something straight growing on the ground. Bamboo. Hagiwara Sakutaro. CAoMJL1, tr. by Hiroaki Sato

Something strange happened yesterday. After-Word. Ras Baraka. InTrad

Something strange I do not comprehend. Literature: The God, Its Ritual. Merrill Moore. FuPo

Something Terrible Something. Sam Cornish. BtF

Something There [author's tr. of his "Hors crâne seul dedans"]. Samuel Beckett. OxBEV

Something there is that doesn't love a wall. Mending Wall. Robert Frost. APT-1; BrAP; BRP; ChAP; ClHu; CtM; EMP; HarvBoo; HeIP-4; ITBLP; MoAmPo; NAAL-5; NAAPv.2; NAMCP V.1; NoAM; NoP-4; NoP-5; OxBoAm; PoPoPo; RaF; SAmP; SoSe-8; TCAPo; TFi; WeW-3

Something they said beside me. At the Cafe Door. Constantine P. Cavafy. CAGL, tr. by Edmund Keeley and Philip Sherrard

Something this foggy day, a something which. Christina Georgina Rossetti. NAEL-6v2 Fr. Later Life: A Double Sonnet of Sonnets.

Something to Live For. Billy Strayhorn. ReLy

Something to love, some tree or flow'r. Something to Love. Thomas Haynes Bayly. STuOW

Something to Remember You By. Howard Dietz. ReLy

Something to Say. Betsy Sholl. ExTi

Something told the wild geese. Something Told the Wild Geese. Rachel Lyman Field. ChAP; NTCP

Something uncertain moves. Again. Lenard D. Moore. GT

Something was killing sheep. Trust, The. Ellen Bryant Voigt. CAP-8

Something Whispered in the *Shakuhachi*. Garrett Kaoru Hongo. WhBo

Something you won't ever bring pressure to bear on. James Sutherland-Smith. NewEx

Something's familiar about that villain. Fathers, The. Elizabeth Holmes. P180

Something's Gotta Give. Johnny Mercer. ReLy

Sometime a while back it seemed real clear to me. Just Word Wranglin'. John Nelson. GeoH

Sometime around dusk moose lifts. Wife Hits Moose. Thomas Lux. StAl

Sometime at night you'll look for me. Song at a Late Hour. Olafs Stumbrs. PML, tr. by Inara Cedrins

Sometime busdriver. Sonatina of Peter Govender, beached. Douglas Livingstone. TSAP

Sometime during eternity / some guys show up. Sometime During Eternity. Lawrence Ferlinghetti. NoAM; NoP-4; NoP-5

Sometime during the night there are three mushrooms which are the. Moon Poem. Max Jacob. AF, tr. by Michael Brownstein

Sometime I fled the fire that me brent. Sir Thomas Wyatt. NoSic

Sometime in the '50s. Robert Frost, a visiting. Ghosts of Luxury, The. Bruce Cohen. VisFro

Sometime the world seems sad and lonely. Lonely World. Mrs. Henry Linden. CBWP-4

Sometimes. Jan Eijkelboom. TuT, tr. by Peter van de Kamp

Sometimes. Maggie Pogue Johnson. CBWP-4

Sometimes. Lilian Moore. TLR

Sometimes: "Sometimes God resembles a kitten." Ivan Metodiev. CSCBP Fr. Songs for Orphans Big and Small.

Sometimes a button. Sometimes a rat. (LL) Residue. Carlos Drummond de Andrade. GPTC; PoetW; VCWP, tr. by Mark Strand

Sometimes a child will bring it to consciousness. Lights Out. John Gilgun. AmZen

Sometimes a crumb falls. Luck. Langston Hughes. APT-2; OxBoAm; SAmP

Sometimes a horse pulled a wagon down the street. Childhood Around 1950, A. Alan Williamson. ASA; FaoP

Sometimes a lantern moves along the night. Lantern Out of Doors, The. Gerard Manley Hopkins. SacPr

Sometimes a man. How a Place Becomes Holy. Yehoshua November. IJHIL

Sometimes a Man Stands Up During Supper. Rainer Maria Rilke. BBASP; RaBo; WED, tr. by Robert Bly

Sometimes a man walks away from a window. Talking cure, The. Ingrid de Kok. TSAP

Sometimes / mesh of ideas. Dennis Brutus. HBAPE

Sometimes / A night funeral. Dead in There. Langston Hughes. APSN; NAMCP V.1

Sometimes a Voice 1. Don McKay. OpeFie

Sometimes a voice—have you heard this? Sometimes a Voice 1. Don McKay. OpeFie

Sometimes a woman will lie in sleep. Old Wives' Tale. Olga Broumas. FiBr

Sometimes a word will start it, like. Variant. John Ashbery. BodElec

Sometimes, all I want to be is the dreaming world. (LL) Sycamore Canyon Nocturne. Christopher Buckley. GeoHom; PfSP

Sometimes all night I kept vigil with men stripped of their flesh. Peter Blackman. RSaN Fr. My Song is for All Men.

Sometimes alone at night. Vanderdecken. Douglas Livingstone. TSAP

Sometimes an effluence rises. Scarcely. Alfonso Reyes. TCLAP, tr. by Samuel Beckett

Sometimes and always, with mixed feelings? (LL) At North Farm. John Ashbery. ColAm; HarvBoo; NAMCP V.2; OxBoAm; WaAnP

Sometimes, as a Child. Olga Broumas. YaYoPo

Sometimes, as young things will, she vexes me. Augusta Davies Webster. ViWPN Fr. Mother and Daughter.

Sometimes at night, when I sit and write. In the Night. Ella Wheeler Wilcox. SWaP

Sometimes at night when the heart stumbles and stops. Caesura. Kenneth Mackenzie. BeAl; BrAP; NOBAu; PoCu

Sometimes blood looks for an opening. Blood. William Olsen. LiTh

Sometimes by night I don't know why. Anne Carson. BodElec; OxBoAm; WoBe *Fr.* Truth About God, The.

Sometimes colored tears play. George Grosz. Else Lasker-Schüler. PFTM-1

Sometimes Damocles is less afraid that the sword may drop. Comic Look at Damocles, A. Bill Knott. BodElec

Sometimes / do you. Autumn End. Luu Trong Lu. SonAtl, *tr. by* Duong Thu Huong, Mrs. S. Goldenhall, S. Goldenhall, Elisa Joy Holland and Sally Yang

Sometimes, Doctor, I awake. Dario Villa. ItPo, *tr. by* Gayle Ridinger

Sometimes Even Parents Win. John Ciardi. NOxBChV

Sometimes, everywhere I look. Kabir. ErotSp, *tr. by* Sam Hamill

Sometimes farm granaries become especially beautiful when all the oats or wheat are gone. Warning to the Reader. Robert Bly. CAP-8

Sometimes fate takes. Needlework. Elaine Terranova. PoDa

Sometimes Feel. Pearse Hutchinson. ModIr

Sometimes Fred and I talk in bed. Philodendron Named Joan, A. Joan Jobe Smith. SUP

Sometimes frozen fanta is the best way to remember moving day. you should lift from. Try Book-ending Punctuation Vouchers. Nicole Markotić. PoPra

Sometimes God resembles a kitten. Ivan Metodiev. CSCBP *Fr.* Songs for Orphans Big and Small.

Sometimes God will drop a fit on you. Anne Carson. BodElec; WoBe *Fr.* Truth About God, The.

Sometimes grown-ups forget you're down there. Battered Toddler, Page B6. Ellen Doré Watson. OPRER

Sometimes he did this, sometimes he did that. (LL) Poem: "And if it snowed and snow covered the drive." Simon Armitage. HarvBoo; NeBrP; StAl

Sometimes he steps out with the class. Some Biographical Data. Cees Buddingh'. TuT, *tr. by* Mary E. O'Donnell

Sometimes he walked to occupy / his feet. Generations 2. Sam Cornish. GT

Sometimes he will break. I, the Neighbor Mr. Uskovich, Watch Every Morning Kenji Takezo Hold His Breath. Rick Noguchi. NeAmPo

Sometimes hidden from me. Wild Rose, The. Wendell Berry. UpMys

Sometimes I am brought so low. For Jude the Obscure. Peter Cooley. Vesp

Sometimes I am so lonely the phone. Phone Sex. Richard Tayson. WiU

Sometimes I call X nostalgia. Little Ode for X. Maura Stanton. IllVoic

Sometimes I carry the smell of moist hay from my childhood. Retro Lullaby. Beckian Fritz Goldberg. AmAlph

Sometimes / i close my eyes. Birth. Kelly Elaine Navies. BRtP

Sometimes I do despatch my heart. Michael Field. VWP

Sometimes I dress, with women sit. Matthew Green. NPeEn; OBCoV *Fr.* Spleen, The [Complete].

Sometimes I feel discouraged, and think my work's in vain. There Is a Balm in Gilead. *Unknown.* TCAPo

Sometimes I feel I've shacked up. Doing the Evolution Shuffle. Alice Fulton. PoA 2002

Sometimes I feel like a motherless child. *Unknown.* APN-2

Sometimes I feel like I will never stop. To Satch. Samuel Allen. FuFl; ISC; MoASP

Sometimes I feel like my money's gone to Heaven. Product of Evolution, I Invest in a Mutual Fund, A. Amanda Pecor. BodElec

Sometimes I get the feeling I've never. A. R. Ammons. NAMCP V.2 *Fr.* Strip.

Sometimes I get up at daybreak, thirsty. Murmur. Adelia Prado. TANSG, *tr. by* Ellen Doré Watson

Sometimes / I go about pitying myself. Song of the Thunders. *Unknown.* OBVE, *tr. by* Frances Densmore

Sometimes I Go about Pitying Myself. *Unknown.* RaBo; WoPoe, *tr. by* Robert Bly and Frances Densmore

Sometimes I go to the pornos. No God. Dennis Cooper. PmAP

Sometimes I had such fury I would choose. Mary Kröger. Louise Erdrich. UpMys

Sometimes I have spent hours face to face with a single stalk. Bamboo. Stephen Mitchell. WhBo

Sometimes I have wanted. Coat. Vicki Feaver. LW

Sometimes I hear haunted mouths. Few Picnics in Illinois, A. Maura Stanton. IllVoic

Sometimes I know the way. Absence. Charlotte Mew. MoBrPo

Sometimes I lie in wait. Full Face. Andrée Chedid. PoArWo, *tr. by* Lucy McNair

Sometimes I long to be the woodpile. Hunger for Something. Chase Twichell. BeAl

Sometimes I look at people & think Jesus what happened here. Para-Olympic Legacy, The. Jeni Olin. FreRad

Sometimes I must smell that sulphur pit. Sometimes. Jan Eijkelboom. TuT, *tr. by* Peter van de Kamp

Sometimes I plunge into the ocean, for a long time. Sometimes I Plunge into the Ocean . . . . Heberto Padilla. AF, *tr. by* Alastair Reid

Sometimes I prefer the stove's pilot light to the splendor of a fire. Shy Ones, The. Antonio Deltoro. RMCMP, *tr. by* Christian Viveros-Fauné

Sometimes I remember you, little Ruth. Little Ruth. Yehuda Amichai. VCWP, *tr. by* Benjamin Harshav *and* Barbara Harshav

Sometimes I sauntered from my lone abode. *Unknown.* CAGL *Fr.* Don Leon.

Sometimes I see churches. Winter Walking. Alfred Wellington Purdy. NoAM

Sometimes I see in my mind's eye a four or five. Gwendolyn Brooks. Anthony Walton. RD

Sometimes I see my spirit, swiftly unsheathed. Saddhu of Couva, The. Derek Walcott. BodElec

Sometimes I sit in the balcony. Symphony from the Balcony. Jared Angira. NAfrP

Sometimes I stop. Wongòl Poem. Emmanuel Eugene. OGAHCP, *tr. by* Boadiba and Jack Hirschman

Sometimes I stop on the street afraid. Materialism. Lőrinc Szabó. IQMS, *tr. by* Laurence James

Sometimes I think. On the Strength of All Conviction and the Stamina of Love. Jennifer Michael Hecht. GoPo

Sometimes I think of its bright cramped spaces. Dancing at Oakmead Road. Maura Dooley. NeBl

Sometimes I think you're. Everything You Own. Gerald Costanzo. GifTon

Sometimes I thought I might. Taking Calls in Freeport, NY. Colette Inez. NevBe

Sometimes I walk where the deep water dips. Frederick Goddard Tuckerman. APN-2; OxBoAm *Fr.* Sonnets.

Sometimes I wish that I his pillow were. Richard Barnfield. PBRV *Fr.* Cynthia, with Certain[e] Sonnets.

Sometimes I wish that I were Helen-fair. Poem. Lesbia Harford. NOBAu

Sometimes I wonder about the power of invention. Look Around. Brian Henry. IIR

Sometimes I would imagine you, standing outside in the dark. Satori. Nin Andrews. AmZen

Sometimes I'm Happy. Irving Caesar. ReLy

Sometimes I'm happy: la la la la la la la. Joy Sonnet in a Random Universe. Helen Chasin. NIL-7

Sometimes I'm Not Myself. Felix Morisseau-Leroy. OGAHCP, *tr. by* Boadiba and Jack Hirschman

Sometimes I'm startled to find myself. Way Animals Are, The. Leslie Ullman. TiP2

Sometimes in early June I am standing. It Arrives Suddenly and Carries Us Off As Usual. Marge Piercy. PasH

Sometimes in the dark I fear trampling. Fear of Subways. Maureen Seaton. FFC

Sometimes in the evening when love. Sometimes Mysteriously. Luis Omar Salinas. GeoHom

Sometimes in the over-heated house, but not for long. Fame. Charlotte Mew. HarvBoo; NPeEn; VWP

Sometimes, in the terrible. Understanding the Light. Elin ap Hywel. ATSWP, *tr. by* Robert Minhinnick

Sometimes it frightens me. Coincidence. Aida Gelbtrunk. MirDau, *tr. by* Roberta Gordenstein

Sometimes it seems almost beyond belief. Whirling Round the Sun. Suzanne Noguere. FFC

Sometimes it's difficult, isn't it, not to grow grim and rancorous. Necessary Dirge, A. Ogden Nash. AmWit; APT-2

Sometimes it's salt. Getting to Know Her. Jacqueline Berger. AmPoNex

Sometimes it's the flagrant accentuation. Jazz as Was. Al Young. ESEAA

Sometimes it's the zombie. Busy Days of My Nights, The. Bob Hicok. AmAlph

Sometimes love comes. Phenomenon, A. Job Degenaar. TuT, *tr. by* Aidan Sharkey

Sometimes my sister calls to say. Man in Miami, The. Kevin Prufer. LiTh

Sometimes my tongue wanders. In What Disappears. John Brandi. ICANM

Sometimes Mysteriously. Luis Omar Salinas. GeoHom

Sometimes, not often, it's true. Tatyana Milova. CRWP, *tr. by* Robert Reid

Sometimes / on Sunday afternoons. Understanding Light. Elin ap Hywel. BBMWP, *tr. by* the author

Sometimes pus / Sometimes a poem. Ibn Gabirol. Yehuda Amichai. AF, *tr. by* Assia Gutmann

Sometimes she climbed. Old Stone Age. Frances Angela. Prnts

Sometimes, she remembers, a chipped flint. Imago. Amy Clampitt. VCAP

Sometimes she turns around in the printed seasons and asks the time, or. Targets and Flowers (Begun with Lines from Breton). Garrett Caples. IIR

Sometimes super cool. Metaphor Crosses the Road, A. Martha McFerren. P180

Sometimes the dials on Anna's magnificent machinery would be set incorrectly. Geoff Ward. VaPo *Fr.* English Music.

Sometimes the Mind. Jane Mead. NAPBL

Sometimes the moon.   Homage to Robert Johnson.   David St. John.   SwNoth

Sometimes the mountain.   Witness.   Denise Levertov.   BLT; TWF

Sometimes the music's in the room.   Planxty Irwin.   David Brendon Hopes.   UpMys

Sometimes the night echoes to prideless wailing.   John Berryman.   NoAM *Fr.* Sonnets to Chris.

Sometimes the notes are ferocious.   Marginalia.   Billy Collins.   PoA 2002

Sometimes the rapid-fire channel switching is like eye music.   Grazing.   Ira Sadoff.   BodElec

Sometimes the sight of them.   Jar of Pens.   Robert Pinsky.   FaoP

Sometimes the weather goes on for days.   Mystery of Emily Dickinson, The.   Marvin Bell.   CAP-8; InvLad

Sometimes the wind.   Nothing.   Pak Chaesam.   CAMKP, *tr. by* David R. McCann and Jiwon Shin

Sometimes the words are so close I am.   Julia Alvarez.   FFC *Fr.* ("33").

Sometimes there has been enough writing.   Pickup.   Paul Allen.   ReTh

Sometimes there is steam in the apartment.   Celebration of Home Birth: November 15th, 1981, A.   Sandra Maria Esteves.   PueRic

Sometimes, they save people from drowning in the river.   Angels of Juárez, Mexico, The.   Ray Gonzalez.   TiP2; TouFir

Sometimes they were put in baskets, little nests.   Infanticide.   Pattiann Rogers.   CFP

Sometimes things don't go, after all.   Sometimes.   Sheenagh Pugh.   BeAl; GoPo; OPOU; PoCu; TCAWP

Sometimes to get their own back.   Years, The.   Tom Pow.   EdScPo

Sometimes too personal, sun, you.   Sun.   John Blight.   BMAP

Sometimes under my arm where I keep it warm.   My Gun Has So Many Places to Hide.   David Lazar.   LiTh

Sometimes under the night.   Equinox.   Susan Musgrave.   BrAP

Sometimes waking, sometimes sleeping.   Nestus Gurley.   Randall Jarrell.   HeIP-4; InGu

Sometimes walking late at night.   Butcher Shop.   Charles Simic.   AF

Sometimes We Close Our Eyes.   Marco Pantani.   ArBi

Sometimes we collide, tectonic plates merging.   Implications of One Plus One.   Marge Piercy.   PasH

Sometimes we dream of young brunettes.   In Praise of Robert Desnos.   Franck Venaille.   YaTCFP, *tr. by* Mary Ann Caws *and* Jean-Pierre Cauvin

Sometimes we fit together like the creamy.   It.   Sharon Olds.   MoWP

Sometimes when.   Each Happiness Ringed by Lions.   Jane Hirshfield.   ExTi

Sometimes when.   Greyhound.   Christopher Stahl.   BeDoSh

Sometimes when I feel bad.   If You Were the Only Girl in the World.   Clifford Grey.   ReLy

Sometimes when I see the bare arms of trees in the evening.   Bare Arms of Trees, The.   John Tagliabue.   GoPo

Sometimes, when I wonder what I'm like, underneath.   My First Weeks.   Sharon Olds.   BeAl

Sometimes, when I'm cooking in autumn.   Western Holly Stove.   Alison Townsend.   SweBea

Sometimes when I'm lonely.   Hope.   Langston Hughes.   TRP

Sometimes When It Rains.   Gcina Mhlophe.   HAWP; NAfrP

Sometimes when my eyes are red.   My Sad Self.   Allen Ginsberg.   BrAP; VCAP

Sometimes (/ when the night air feels *chevere*).   Oye Mundo/Sometimes.   Jesús Papoleto Meléndez.   UnSA

Sometimes when they passed I'd touch the glass.   Postmaster's Children, The.   Betsy Sholl.   PfS

Sometimes when time goes by.   Shape for It, A.   Michael Ryan.   PoA 2002

Sometimes, when we're lying after love.   Prayer.   Kim Addonizio.   RoV

Sometimes, when you're called a bastard.   When Something Happens.   James A., Jr. Randall.   SSLK

Sometimes where you get it they wrap it up in a.   Thing of Beauty, A.   W. S. Merwin.   OxBoAm

Sometimes while I sleep.   Edwin Honig.   NoAM *Fr.* To Restore a Dead Child.

Sometimes with one I love I fill myself with rage for fear I effuse unreturn'd love.   Sometimes with One I Love.   Walt Whitman.   APN-1; SAmP

Sometimes you almost get a punch in.   Shadowboxing.   James Tate.   MoASP

Sometimes you appear in the swampy twilight.   Meeting.   László Kálnoky.   IQMS, *tr. by* Kenneth McRobbie and Zita McRobbie

Sometimes you can hear the naked will.   Death on Columbus Day.   James Tate.   YaYoPo

Sometimes / you feel / like / a / bottle.   No Deposit.   Earle Thompson.   HATNAP

Sometimes you glimpse one.   Great Grandfathers.   Jane Duran.   MoWP

Sometimes you hear, fifth-hand.   Poetry of Departures.   Philip Larkin.   BeAl; BrAP; HeIP-4

Sometimes you just get tired.   Another day.   Rosamond S. King.   BtF

Sometimes you show yourself.   Epiphany.   Elsa Cross.   RMCMP; TAPaP, *tr. by* Margaret Sayers Peden

Sometimes your writing is a lush web of fine thoughts.   Lu Chi.   WoPoe *Fr.* Art of Writing, The.

Somewhat back from the village street.   Old Clock on the Stairs, The.   Henry Wadsworth Longfellow.   TreFP

Somewhat more splendid in dress, in a waistcoat work of a lady.   Arthur Hugh Clough.   FaBoVe *Fr.* Bothie of Tober-na-Vuolich, The [A Long-Vacation Pastoral].

Somewhere.   Robert Creeley.   NoAM

Somewhere.   Sneeze, A.   Sŏ Chŏngju.   VCWP, *tr. by* David R. McCann

Somewhere.   Stephen Sondheim.   ReLy

Somewhere, a cup tinkles in its saucer.   English Earthquake, The.   Eva Salzman.   MFPA

Somewhere / a girl.   First Blood.   Vegunta Mohana Prasad.   HotL, *tr. by* V. Narayana Rao

Somewhere a wolf spider dances on a white rock.   Always.   Brian Bartlett.   Coast

Somewhere afield here something lies.   Shelley's Skylark.   Thomas Hardy.   CABP

Somewhere around.   Tanka.   Shaku Chōkū.   CAoMJL1, *tr. by* Makoto Ueda

Somewhere at the side of the rough shape.   Nerve, The.   Glyn Maxwell.   BeAl

Somewhere beneath that piano's superb sleek black.   Piano, The.   D. H. Lawrence.   PtR; WeW-3

Somewhere between a bird's nest and a solar system whom did.   Station (4).   James Galvin.   GifTon

Somewhere between *Amazing Grace*.   Death of Chet Baker, The.   Miller Williams.   SeSe

Somewhere between faith and grace there is the footprint of logic lost.   Before.   Khaled Mattawa.   NeAmPo

Somewhere deep in the San Joaquin Valley.   Orchard of Figs in the Fall, An.   Diana García.   TouFir

Somewhere does the sky bend into itself.   Show Me a Rose.   John Godfrey.   FTOS

Somewhere Else.   Philip Whalen.   WANABP

Somewhere else, Charles and Furdnor.   From Birmingham to Bristol in a Boxcar.   Carole Boston Weatherford.   FuFl

Somewhere Holy.   Carl Phillips.   AmAlph

Somewhere I read that high and loe notes.   Comfort.   Maura Stanton.   SoSe-8

Somewhere in Africa.   Anne Sexton.   InoFa; NALW

Somewhere in all the time that's passed.   Way, The.   Robert Creeley.   WoBe

Somewhere in everyone's head something points toward home.   Shrinking Lonesome Sestina, The.   Miller Williams.   MakPoe

Somewhere in his body a blood-clot is moving.   Little Death.   Gwyn Thomas.   OBWVE, *tr. by* Joseph P. Clancy

Somewhere in my heart, it seems, an endless river flows.   Endless River Flows, An.   Kim Yŏngnang.   CAMKP, *tr. by* Anthony, Brother of Taizé

Somewhere in the community a person is belligerent, defensive.   Lisa Gill.   ICANM *Fr.* Letters to a Dead Trappist.

Somewhere / in the light above the womb.   My Grandfather Walks in the Woods.   Marilyn Nelson Waniek.   ESEAA

Somewhere in the middle, Sunday.   Wopko Jensma.   TSAP

Somewhere in the Midwest.   Crabapples.   Michael Van Walleghen.   IllVoic

Somewhere in the mountains.   Puerto Rico Made in Japan.   Jose Angel Figueroa.   PueRic

Somewhere in the next block.   Early Sunday Morning.   John A. Stone.   PoSol

Somewhere in the unknown world.   Quilting.   Lucille Clifton.   SweBea

Somewhere in the world my tree stands, for I know that every person.   Mail.   Sarah Kirsch.   AF, *tr. by* Wayne Kvam

Somewhere in there, in a gap between a taxi.   Short Wave.   George Szirtes.   RWPCtW

Somewhere / inside my head.   Taneda Santoka.   CAoMJL1, *tr. by* Burton Watson

Somewhere is the software to ID all.   Save As: Salvation.   Bill Knott.   BodElec

Somewhere it being yesterday.   Song of Mary, A.   Lucille Clifton.   NALW

Somewhere now she takes off the dress I am putting.   Palindrome.   Lisel Mueller.   WeW-3

Somewhere nowhere in Utah, a boy by the roadside.   Utah.   Anne Stevenson.   FaBoVe

Somewhere on the other side of this wide night.   Words, Wide Night.   Carol Ann Duffy.   NePenScot

Somewhere or Other.   Christina Georgina Rossetti.   FaBoVe; OxBEV

Somewhere out there the sea has shrugged its shoulders.   Severn Bore.   Catherine Fisher.   AngWePo; TCAWP

Somewhere outside your window.   Sense of Coolness, A.   Quincy Troupe.   GT

Somewhere So Lush.   Lee Upton.   AmAlph

Somewhere someone is traveling furiously toward you.   At North Farm.   John Ashbery.   ColAP; HarvBoo; NAMCP V.2; OxBoAm; WaAnP

Somewhere the deer lies on the ground, I think; I walk about. Hunter's Song. *Unknown.* APN-2, *tr. by* Albert S. Gatschet

Somewhere there figures a man. In uniform. He's not white. He. Kings' Daughters, Home for Unwed Mothers, 1948. C. D. Wright. InGu

Somewhere there has to be. Other Half of Me, The. Jack Lawrence. ReLy

Somewhere There's a Man. Roberto Juarroz. TCLAP, *tr. by* W. S. Merwin

Somewhere there's music. How High the Moon. Nancy Hamilton. ReLy

Somewhere under sand. Primitive Place. Mildred Weston. FFC

Somewhere—in desolate wind-swept space. Identity. Thomas Bailey Aldrich. TCAPo

Sominex. Dan Pagis. MotU, *tr. by* Stephen Mitchell

Somnambulist. Adele Ne Jame. PoArWo

Somnambulist Ballad. Federico García Lorca. SpanPo, *tr. by* Robert O'Brien

Somnolence of shoes, The. Saturday Afternoon. Sue Sinclair. Coast

Somnolent through landscapes and by trees. Permanent Tourists, The. Patricia K. Page. BrAP

Somonour was ther with us in that place, A. Geoffrey Chaucer. OBCoV *Fr.* Canterbury Tales, The.

Somtimes you have to say it. Fight Song. Deborah Garrison. BeAl

Somtyme the pryde of mye assured trothe. Argument, The. Sir Thomas Wyatt. SacPr

So—Murray to Byron in Italy. Kaleidoscope. G. K. Page. NoAM

Son. Pavel Grigoryevich Antokolsky. *tr. by* Bob Perelman and Shirley Rihner
"We are not always dependent on memory." TCRusP, *tr. by* Bob Perelman and Shirley Rihner
"You must dig in black ashes a long time." TCRusP, *tr. by* Bob Perelman and Shirley Rihner
"You share your mourning with all Moscow. There." TCRusP, *tr. by* Bob Perelman and Shirley Rihner

Son. Richard Jones. PoChi

Son. David McCord. NOxBChV

Son, A. Rudyard Kipling. NPeEn; PoAgWa *Fr.* Epitaphs of the War [1914–1918].

Son, The. Denise Levertov. NALW

Son, The. Frederic Ridgely Torrence. TCAPo

Son, The. Jones Very. NCAP

"Son, come tell me 'bout the meetin." Old and the New, The. Clara Ann Thompson. CBWP-2

Son et Lumière. Mark Todd. GeoH

Son, / Forgive me. Last Will and Testament. Thomas McGrath. PoChi

Son, I am going: the morning. Mitayo, The. Manuel González Prada. SpanPo, *tr. by* Kate Flores

Son, if you desert our war. *Unknown.* SLW, *tr. by* Marjolijn De Jager, Sayd Bahodin Majrouh and André Velter

Son of a sterile mother. Samson. Primo Levi. PML, *tr. by* Ruth Feldman

Son of Enops, Thestor next he smote, The. Homer. OBVE *Fr.* Iliad, The.

Son of Msippi. Henry Dumas. OxAAAP

Son of the Bone Speaks, The. Roger Gilbert-Lecomte. PFTM-1

Son of The House of a Thousand Chandeliers. Jennifer L. Knox. FreRad

Son of the ocean isle! England's Dead. Felicia Dorothea Hemans. NAEL-6v2; NAEL-7v2; NoP-4; NoP-5; WaAnP

Son singin. Imamu Amiri Baraka. FTOS *Fr.* Why's / Wise.

Son, we had violence in high school, too, even a shooting. Back in My Day. Steve Fay. LiTh

Sonata. Mark Cox. PoDa

Sonata. Alvaro Mutis. TCLAP, *tr. by* Sophie Cabot Black and Maria Negroni

Sonata of Love's History. Richard Jackson. MAAN

Sonatina. Rubén Darío. TCLAP, *tr. by* Lysander Kemp

Sonatina. Rubén Darío. SpanPo, *tr. by* John Crow

Sonatina in Yellow. Donald Justice. ColAP

Sonatina of Peter Govender, beached. Douglas Livingstone. TSAP

Son-Days [dayes]. Henry Vaughan. AngWePo; NOSC

Sonet. Mark Alexander Boyd. *See* Fra Bank to Bank, Fra Wood to Wood I Rin.

So'net 3. Paul Dutton. IFF

Sonet: "Fra bank [*or* banc] to bank [*or* banc], fra wood [*or* wod] to wood [*or* wod] I rin." Mark Alexander Boyd. *See* Fra Bank to Bank, Fra Wood to Wood I Rin.

Sonet: "Thocht Polibus, pisander, and with them." Alexander Montgomerie. NePenScot

Sonet. In Orknay. William Fowler. NePenScot

Sonet written in prayse of the brown beautie, A. George Gascoigne. PBRV

Sonetos del Amor Oscuro [Sonnets of Dark Love]. Federico García Lorca. *tr. by* David William Foster
"Ah secret voice of dark love! Ah bleating without wool! Ah wound! Ah prick of gall, sunken camellia!" CAGL, *tr. by* David William Foster
Night of Sleepless Love. CAGL, *tr. by* David William Foster
Poet Asks His Love About the Enchanted City of Cuenca, The. CAGL, *tr. by* David William Foster

Poet Asks His Love to Write to Him, The. CAGL, *tr. by* David William Foster

Poet Speaks the Truth, The. CAGL, *tr. by* David William Foster

Poet Speaks with Love by Telephone, The. CAGL, *tr. by* David William Foster

Sonnet of Sweet Weeping. CAGL, *tr. by* David William Foster

Song. Thomas Lovell Beddoes. *See* Old Adam, the Carrion Crow.

Song. Aphra Behn. *See* On Her Loving Two Equally.

Song. William Blake. *See* How Sweet I Roamed [*or* Roam'd] from Field to Field.

Song. Anne Brontë. PEW

Song. Robert Browning. *See* Pippa's Song.

Song. Robert Burns. *See* Ae Fond Kiss.

Song. Robert Burns. NOBRP

Song. Thomas Carew. *See* To My Inconstant Mistress [*or* Mistris].

Song. John Clare. NAEL-6v2; NAEL-7v2; OxBEV

Song. Hartley Coleridge. *See* She Is Not Fair to Outward View.

Song. Anne Collins. PEW *Fr.* Another Song Exciting to Spirituall Mirth.

Song. William Congreve. *See* Pious Selinda [*or* Celinda].

Song. William Congreve. *See* False Though She Be.

Song. William Congreve. IrLP

Song. Robert Creeley. *See* Song: "What I took in my hand."

Song. George Darley. *See* Song: "Sweet in her green dell the flower of beauty slumbers."

Song. Thomas Dekker *and others.* NOSC

Song. John Dryden. OxAEP-1

Song. Cornelius Eady. GT

Song. Ebenezer Elliott. OxAEP-2

Song. Thomas Flatman. InoFa

Song. Kath Fraser. LW

Song. Oliver Goldsmith. *See* When Lovely Woman Stoops to Folly.

Song. Oliver Goldsmith. IrLP

Song: To Amarantha, That She Would Dishevel Her Hair. Richard Lovelace. *See* To Amarantha, That She Would Dishevel[l] Her Hair[e].

Song. Richard Lovelace. *See* To Amarantha, That She Would Dishevel[l] Her Hair[e].

Song: To Lucasta, Going beyond the Seas. Richard Lovelace. *See* To Lucasta, [on] Going beyond the Seas.

Song. Richard Lovelace. *See* To Lucasta, [on] Going beyond the Seas.

Song: The Scrutiny. Richard Lovelace. NOSC

Song. Richard Lovelace. CavPo

Song. George Macdonald. NePenScot

Song. Philip Massinger. OxAEP-1

Song. John Milton. PBRV

Song. John Milton. *See* Sabrina Fair.

Song. John Milton. *See* Echo.

Song. Gabriela Mistral. WPoS, *tr. by* Langston Hughes

Song. Matthew Prior. *See* Ode, An: "Merchant, to secure his treasure, The."

Song. Primus St. John. GT

Song. Sir Walter Scott. NOBRP

Song. William Shakespeare. *See* Amiens's Song.

Song. William Shakespeare. *See* Country Song.

Song. William Shakespeare. *See* Dirge for Fidele.

Song. Alfred Tennyson. HeIP-4; OBGa

Song. Alfred Tennyson. *See* Now Sleeps the Crimson Petal.

Song. Anne Wharton. EMWP; LW

Song. William Wordsworth. *See* She Dwelt among the Untrodden Ways.

Song: "Absent from thee, I languish still." John Wilmot, 2d Earl of Rochester. NPeEn; OxBEV
(Return.) OBEV

Song: "After the eating, the drinking, the singing." Liu Yung. CrYelRi, *tr. by* Sam Hamill

Song: "Afternoon cooking in the fall sun." Robert Hass. ASA; LoL; NAMCP V.2

Song: "Age is when to a man." Samuel Beckett. ModIr *Fr.* Words and Music.

Song: "Ah, Dangerous Swain, tell me no more." LW

Song: "All, all of a piece throughout." John Dryden. WeW-3

Song: "All roocoogirls." Hans Andreus. TuT, *tr. by* Peter van de Kamp

Song: "Among the clamor the single shout." Blanca Wiethüchter. TANSG, *tr. by* Shaun Griffin and Emma Sepúlveda-Pulvirenti

Song: "And I thought over again." *Eskimo Oral Tradition.* NAAPv.1

Song: "April, April, / Laugh thy girlish laughter." Sir William Watson. OBEV

Song: "As F—at her Toilet sat." Margaret, Lady Godolphin. EMWP

Song: "As I walked out one evening." W. H. Auden. *See* As I Walked Out One Evening.

Song: "At night on my bed I longed for." Bible, *O.T.* WPoS *Fr.* Song of Solomon.

Song: "Balkis was in her marble town." Lascelles Abercrombie. MoBrPo *Fr.* Judith.

Song: "Because spring brings miserable green and painful red." Liu Yung. CrYelRi, *tr.* by Sam Hamill

Song: "Bells of Sunday rang us down, The." John Ciardi. PWW2

Song: "Beloved, it is morn!" Emily Hickey. SacPr

Song: "Boat is chafing at our long delay, The." John Davidson. OBEV

Song: "Both gloomy and dark was the shadowy night." Anne Batten Cristall. RWP

Song: "Bridge of my solitude." Emilio Prados. RaW, *tr.* by Robert Mezey

Song: "Bring from the craggy haunts of birch and pine." John Todhunter. IrV

Song: "By all love's soft, yet mighty powers." John Wilmot, 2d Earl of Rochester. BASC

Song: "By the rushy-fringèd bank." John Milton. OxBEV *Fr.* Comus; a Masque Presented at Ludlow Castle.

Song: "By vulgar Eros long misled." Sarah Ponsonby. PoBW

Song: "Chestnuts shine through the cloven rind, The." Thomas Bailey Aldrich. TreFP

Song: "Chloris, forbear a while." Henry Bold. NOSC

Song: "Come, fair one, be kind." George Farquhar. IrLP *Fr.* Recruiting Officer, The.

Song: "Come, let us dance and sing." Anne Batten Cristall. RWP

Song: "Come, let's grant joy to this heart of ours that founders in distress." Nedim. NaPG, *tr.* by Talat Sait Halman

Song: "Come, live with me and be my love." Cecil Day Lewis. NIP-4; OBMV; WaAnP *Fr.* Two Songs.

Song: "Come, my beloved." Bible, *O.T.* WPoS *Fr.* Song of Solomon, The.

Song: "Dearest [*or* Deerest] if I by my deserving." Mary Sidney Wroth, Countess of Montgomery. EMWP *Fr.* Pamphilia to Amphilanthus.

Song: "Dorinda's sparkling wit, and eyes." Charles, 6th Earl of Dorset Sackville. *See* On the Countess of Dorchester.

Song: "Eve descends with radiant streaks, The." Anne Batten Cristall. RWP

Song: "Fair Chloris in a pigsty lay." John Wilmot, 2d Earl of Rochester. NOSC

Song: "Fairest things are those which live, The." Mary Russell Mitford. NOBRP

Song: "Fall, leaves, fall; die, flowers, away;." Emily Jane Brontë. NPeEn

Song: "Farewell!—and never think of me." Letitia Elizabeth Landon. VWP

Song: "For her gait, if she be walking." William Browne. OBEV

(Sonnet.) NOSC

Song: "Give Isaac the nymph who no beauty can boast." Richard Brinsley Sheridan. IrLP *Fr.* Duenna, The.

Song: "Give me leave to rail at you." John Wilmot, 2d Earl of Rochester. NOSC

Song: "Go and catch a falling star." John Donne. BLPJKO; ClHu; FSCP; HeIP-4; NAEL-6v1; NAEL-7v1; NAWM-5v1; NIL-7; NIP-4; NoP-4; NoP-5; NOSC; NoSic; OBEV; OxAEP-1; PtR; SoSe-8; TFi; WaAnP; WoPoe

Song: "Go[e], lovely rose." Edmund Waller. BASC; CABP; ClHu; CtM; HeIP-4; NAEL-6v1; NAEL-7v1; NIL-7; NoP-4; NoP-5; NOSC; NPeEn; OBEV; OxAEP-1; OxBEV; PBRV; PoPoPo; SoSe-8; TFi; WaAnP; WeW-3; WoPoe

(Go, Lovely Rose!) ItP

Song: "Goe turne away those Cruell Eyes." Captain Henry Cooke and Barbara Syms. EMWP

Song: "Hang sorrow, cast away care." *Unknown.* NOSC

Song: "Hark! hark! the lark at heaven's gate sings." William Shakespeare. NOSC

Song: "Heap cassia, sandal-buds and stripes." Robert Browning. OBEV *Fr.* Paracelsus.

Song: "Her nose is like a satellite." William Logan. PoDa

Song: "Here's to the maiden [*or* maid] of bashful fifteen." Richard Brinsley Sheridan. *See* Drinking Song.

Song: "How many times do I love thee, dear?" Thomas Lovell Beddoes. NAEL-6v2 *Fr.* Torrismond.

Song: "I am dark, daughters of Jerusalem." Bible, *O.T.* WPoS *Fr.* Song of Solomon, The.

Song: "I carouse all night." Cho-yong. WoPoe, *tr.* by Okhee Yoo and Michael Stephens

Song: "I chuck my Bible in the parlour fire." Peter Redgrove. EmeKit

Song: "I dreamed my voice was an Anasazi pot." Demetria Martinez. ICANM

Song: "I have halted my horse by the tree of the doves." "St.-John Perse." YaTCFP, *tr.* by T. S. Eliot

Song: "I have heard the silvery note." Sándor Kisfaludy. IQMS, *tr.* by Anthony Edkins

Song: "I have so little sorrow." Patricia Jones. ISC

Song: "I led my Silvia to a grove." Aphra Behn. BASC

Song: "I made another garden, yea." Arthur William Edgar O'Shaughnessy. OBEV

Song: "I make my shroud but no one knows." Adelaide Crapsey. APT-1; NAAPv.2

Song: "I peeled bits of straw and I got switches too." John Clare. NAEL-6v2; NAEL-7v2

Song: "I prithee spare me, gentle boy." Sir John Suckling. CavPo

Song: "I tell thee, Charmion, could I time retrieve." William Congreve. IrLP

Song: "I want to sing: to be a flower." Rafael Alberti. RaW, *tr.* by Charles Guenther and Hardie St. Martin

Song: "I was asleep but my heart stayed awake." Bible, *O.T.* WPoS

Song: "I was so chill, and overworn, and sad." Anna Wickham. MoBrPo

Song: "I watered my horse at the Long Wall caves." Ch'en Lin. ColAnChi, *tr.* by Burton Watson

Song: "I Work with the shape." Michael McClure. ASA

Song: "If I were tortur'd with greensickness." Elizabeth Polwhele. EMWP

Song: "If she be not as kind as fair." Sir George Etherege. NOSC

Song: "If to your ear it wonder bring." Ben Jonson. OxBEV *Fr.* Key Keeper, The.

Song: "In the world are many roads I haven't walked, and I have pain." Yi Kyŏngnim. EcSo, *tr.* by Peter H. Lee

Song: "It is not now I learn." Louise Bogan. APT-2

Song: "It's the wine, this ache, this longing." Liu Yung. CrYelRi, *tr.* by Sam Hamill

Song: "Lark now leaves his wat'ry [*or* watery] nest, The." Sir William Davenant. *See* Lark Now Leaves His Watery [*or* Wat'ry] Nest.

Song: "Let it be forgotten, as a flower is forgotten." Sara Teasdale. MoAmPo; PoA 2002; TCAPo

Song: "Let not the sluggish sleep." William Byrd. SacPr

Song: "Linnet in the rocky dells, The." Emily Jane Brontë. RACG

(Linnet in the rocky dells, The.) VWP

(My Lady's Grave.) OxAEP-2

Song: "Listen: there was a goat's head hanging by ropes in a tree." Brigit Pegeen Kelly. ExTi; IllVoic *Fr.* Southern Review, The.

Song: "Longing, I watch the open window." Tzu Yeh. CrYelRi, *tr.* by Sam Hamill

Song: "Lord, when the sense of Thy sweet grace." Richard Crashaw. InvLi (Ecstasy, An.) OxAEP-1

Song: "Love a child is ever crying [*or* criing]." Mary Sidney Wroth, Countess of Montgomery. BASC; LW; NAEL-6v1; NAEL-7v1; NoP-4; NoP-5; NOSC; OxBEV *Fr.* Pamphilia to Amphilanthus.

Song: "Love a woman? You're [*or* Y'are] an ass." John Wilmot, 2d Earl of Rochester. NBLV; NOSC; WoPoe

Song: "Love is a green girl." Michael Stillman. TLR

Song: "Love, love today, my dear." Charlotte Mew. MoBrPo

Song: "Love still has something of the sea." Sir Charles Sedley. OxAEP-1; OxBEV

Song: "Love what art thou? A vain thought." Mary Sidney Wroth, Countess of Montgomery. NAEL-6v1; NAEL-7v1; NoP-4; NoP-5; WaAnP *Fr.* Urania.

Song: "Lovely hill-torrents are." Walter James Turner. MoBrPo

Song: "Mary leave thy lowly cot." John Clare. NPBRoP

Song: "Memory, hither come." William Blake. NAEL-6v2

Song: "Moth's kiss, first, The!" Robert Browning. OBEV *Fr.* In a Gondola.

Song: "My heart is like the failing hearth." Letitia Elizabeth Landon. NOBRP; NPBRoP *Fr.* Golden Violet, The.

Song: "My heart, my dove, my snail, my sail, my." Cynthia Zarin. NIL-7; NoP-4; NoP-5

Song: "My silks and fine array." William Blake. RACG

Song: "Never take her away." Vinícius de Moraes. WoPoe, *tr.* by Richard Wilbur

Song: "*Nigger-Lover* is a song, spat out." Cornelius Eady. ESEAA

Song: "No use to aim that sextant now." Reuel Denney. YaYoPo

Song: "Nothing ades to Loves fond fire." Elizabeth Wilmot, Countess of Rochester. EMWP; LW

Song: "Now and then there will arise." *Unknown.* OBVE, *tr.* by Frances Densmore

Song: "Now that Fate is dead and gone." Dame Edith Sitwell. MoBrPo

Song: "Now the moon is rising." Antonio Machado Ruiz. SpanPo, *tr.* by Kate Flores

Song: "Nymphs and Shepherds dance no more." John Milton. OxBEV *Fr.* Arcades.

Song: "O sing into my roundelay." Thomas Chatterton. OBEV

Song: "O sweet, sad, singing river." Henrietta Cordelia Ray. CBWP-3

Song: "O where does the dancer dance." Judith Wright. BrAP

Song: "Oh, baby, baby, baby dear." Edith Nesbit. PEW

Song: "Oh, dear! Oh, me! Oh, my!" Gregory Corso. BB

Song: "Oh for the wings of a dove." Agnes Mary Frances Robinson. VWP

Song: "Oh gentle Venus, ease a tarse." John Wilmot, 2d Earl of Rochester. EroLit *Fr.* Sodom; or The Quintessence of Debauchery.

Song: "O[h] me[e], the time is [*or* has] come to part." Mary Sidney Wroth, Countess of Montgomery. NOSC *Fr.* Pamphilia to Amphilanthus.

Song: "Oh roses for the flush of youth." Christina Georgina Rossetti. WaAnP

Song: "Oh say not that my heart is cold." Charles Wolfe. OxAEP-2

Song: "Old song with new words, An." Yen Shu. CrYelRi, tr. by Sam Hamill

Song: "On the Eastern Way at the city of Lo-yang." Sung Tzu-hou. WoPoe, tr. by Arthur Waley

Song: "Only the wanderer." Ivor Gurney. HarvBoo

Song: "Or love me less, or love me more." Sidney Godolphin. NOSC

Song: "O're [or O'er] the smooth enamel'd [or enameled or enamelld] green." John Milton. OBEV Fr. Arcades.

Song: "Phillis, let's shun the common fate." Sir Charles Sedley. NPeEn

Song: "Place in thy memory, dearest, A." Gerald Griffin. IrLP

Song: "Platinum fur and brass revolver shine." Michael McClure. BB

Song: "Pleading eyebrows, intoxicating eyes!" Ch'in Kuan. CrYelRi, tr. by Sam Hamill

Song: "Pursuing beauty, men descry." Thomas Southerne. NOSC

Song: "Quoth the Duchess of Cleveland to counselor Knight." John Wilmot, 2d Earl of Rochester. BASC

Song: "Rowan like a lip-sticked girl, A." Seamus Heaney. TRP

Song: "Sad was the day when my Willie did leave me." John Clare. NPBRoP

Song: "Scholar first my Love implor'd, A." Dorothea Du Bois. LW

Song: "Setting sun left my heart, The." Juan Ramón Jiménez. RaW, tr. by Ralph Nelson and Rita García Nelson

Song: "She has left me, my pretty." Sylvia Townsend Warner. MoBrPo

Song: "She lowers her fragrant curtain." Liu Yung. ErotSp, tr. by Sam Hamill

Song: "She sat and sang alway." Christina Georgina Rossetti. NAEL-6v2; NAEL-7v2

Song: "Shephard loveth thow me vell?" Jean Passerat. NPeEn; OBVE, tr. by William Drummond of Hawthornden

Song: "She's somewhere in the sunlight strong." Richard Le Gallienne. OBEV

Song: "Slanting both hands against her forehead." Aubrey Thomas De Vere. IrLP

Song: "Song tells us of our old way of living, The." John Ashbery. WaAnP

Song: "Stop all the clocks, cut off the telephone." W. H. Auden. CAGL; EMP; MoBrPo; OPOU Fr. Twelve Songs.

Song: "Streams that wind amid the hills, The." George Darley. IrLP Fr. Sylvia; or, The May Queen.

Song: "Strive not, vain Lover, to be fine." Richard Lovelace. CavPo

Song: "Summer is over upon the sea." Elizabeth Bishop. PoA 2002

Song: "Sun sets in night, and the stars shun the day, The." Royall Tyler. NAAL-3 Fr. Contrast, The.

Song: "Sunny shaft did I behold, A." Samuel Taylor Coleridge. OBEV Fr. Zapolya.

Song: "Sweet beast, I have gone prowling." W. D. Snodgrass. MoAmPo

Song: "Sweet in her green dell the flower of beauty slumbers." George Darley. OBEV

(Song.) OxAEP-2

Song: "Sweetest love, I do not go[e]." John Donne. HeIP-4; NAEL-7v1; NoP-4; NoP-5; NoSic; TFi

Song: "There never was." Carl Rakosi. BodElec

Song: "There's a beautiful woman in the north." Li Yen-nien. CrYelRi, tr. by Sam Hamill

Song: "This is a song for the speechless." Edward Hirsch. OPRER

Song: "Though regions farr divided." Aurelian Townshend. NOSC

Song: "Through springtime walks, with flowers perfumed." Anne Batten Cristall. RWP

(Through Springtime Walks.) NPBRoP

Song: "'Tis light to love thee living, girl, when hope is full and fair." Thomas Tod Stoddart. NOBRP Fr. Death-Wake, The; or, Lunacy.

Song: "To enter the real." Charles Tomlinson. WoBe

Song: "Tomorrow is Saint Valentine's Day." William Shakespeare. See Song: "Tomorrow is saint valentine's day."

Song: "Tomorrow is saint valentine's day." William Shakespeare. NoSic Fr. Hamlet.

Song: "Tossed midst life's terrific storms." Anne Batten Cristall. RWP

Song: "Turn, turn thy beauteous face away." Francis Beaumont and John Fletcher. NOSC Fr. Love's Cure.

Song: "Under the bronze leaves a colt was foaled." "St.-John Perse." YaTCFP, tr. by T. S. Eliot

Song: "Wandering in the still of eve." Anne Batten Cristall. RWP

Song: "Were I laid on Greenland's coast." John Gay. NAEL-6v1; NPeEn; OxBEV Fr. Beggar's Opera, The.

Song: "What a dainty life the milkmaid leads!" Thomas Nabbes. NOSC

Song: "What I took in my hand." Robert Creeley. PoA 2002

(Song.) FTOS

Song: "What mak's me so unnimbly ryse." Aurelian Townshend. OxBEV Fr. Albion's Triumph.

Song: "What means this strangeness now of late." Sir Robert Aytoun. NOSC

Song: "What voice is this, thou evening gale!" Joanna Baillie. RWP; WoRP

Song: "What's in the body you've forgotten." Robert Creeley. OnScMo

Song: "When, dearest, I but think on [or of] thee." OBEV

(Ensuing Copy the Late Printer Hath Been Pleased to Honour, by Mistaking It Among Those of the Most Ingenious and Too Early Lost Sir John Suckling, The.) NOSC

Song: "When I am dead, my dearest." Christina Georgina Rossetti. CABP; NAEL-6v2; NAEL-7v2; NoP-4; NoP-5; NPeEn; OBEV; OxAEP-2; ViWPN; VWP

(When I Am Dead [My Dearest].) TFi

Song: "When that I was and a little tiny boy." William Shakespeare. NoSic; OxAEP-1; TFi Fr. Twelfth Night.

Song: "When thy beauty appears." Thomas Parnell. IrLP; OBEV; OxAEP-1

Song: "Whenas [or When as] the Rye [or Rie] reach to the chin." George Peele. FaBoVe; NoSic; NPeEn; OxBEV; TFi Fr. Old Wives' [or Wife's] Tale, The.

Song: "Where is all the bright company gone." Dame Edith Sitwell. NALW

Song: "Where, O! where's the chain to fling." Letitia Elizabeth Landon. NOBRP Fr. Golden Violet, The.

Song: "Why Damon, why, why, why so pressing?" Mary Lee, Lady Chudleigh. LW

Song: "Why should your face so please me." Edwin Muir. EdScPo

Song: "Why so pale and wan, fond lover?" Sir John Suckling. BASC; CavPo; ClHu; HeIP-4; ITBLP; NAEL-6v1; NAEL-7v1; NBLV; NIL-7; NIP-4; NoP-4; NoP-5; NPeEn; OBEV; OxAEP-1; OxBEV; TFi; WaAnP Fr. Aglaura.

Song: "Winter skies are cold and low." Tzu Yeh. CrYelRi; ErotSp, tr. by Sam Hamill

Song: "Woman sits on her porch." Earle Thompson. HATNAP

Song: "Yellow coverlet, A." Rosanna Warren. ExTi; MakPoe; PfSP

Song: "Yellow dust drifts down the road to Ch'ang-an." Unknown. CrYelRi, tr. by Sam Hamill

Song: "Yi surta." Tom Leonard. Oth

Song: "You are as gold." "H. D." APT-1; MoAmPo; TCAPo

Song: "You are the sandstorm beneath my skin." Odia Ofeimun. NAfrP

Song: "You asked me to sing." Lorenzo Thomas. EGAG

Song: "You bound strong sandals on my feet." Sara Teasdale. PoBW

Song: "You, don't sing." Nakano Shigeharu. CAoMJL1, tr. by Miriam Silverberg

Song: "You wear the morning like your dress." Joseph Hilaire Pierre Belloc. OBEV

Song: "You wrong me, Strephon, when you say." "Ephelia." EMWP

First Song: "Doubt you to whom my Muse these notes intendeth [or entendeth]." Sir Philip Sidney. OxAEP-1 Fr. Astrophil and Stella.

Song 1: "Wild wing my notes, fierce passions urge the strain." Anne Batten Cristall. RWP Fr. Enthusiast, The. Songs of Arla.

Song 1 from "Three Songs from the 50's." Víctor Hernández Cruz. FTtHH

Song 2: "All night I weep[e], all day I cry, Ay me[e]." Mary Sidney Wroth, Countess of Montgomery. NOSC Fr. Pamphilia to Amphilanthus.

Second Song: "Have I caught my heav'nly jewel." Sir Philip Sidney. NoSic Fr. Astrophil and Stella.

Song No. 2: "I say. all you young girls waiting to live." Sonia Sanchez. FFC

Song No. 3: "Cain't nobody tell me any different." Sonia Sanchez. FFC; NOxBChV

Song 3: "Impassion'd strains my trembling lips rehearse." Anne Batten Cristall. RWP Fr. Enthusiast, The. Songs of Arla.

Song 3: "Surrounded by the gentle sound." Baldomero Garcilaso de la Vega. SpanPo, tr. by Frances Fletcher

Fourth Song: "Only joy, now here you are." Sir Philip Sidney. NAEL-6v1; NAEL-7v1; NoP-4; NoP-5; NoSic Fr. Astrophil and Stella.

Song 4: "Sweetest love return[e] again[e]." Mary Sidney Wroth, Countess of Montgomery. NAEL-6v1; NAEL-7v1 Fr. Pamphilia to Amphilanthus.

Eighth Song: "In a grove most rich of shade." Sir Philip Sidney. NoSic; PBRV Fr. Astrophil and Stella.

Ninth Song: "Go, my flock, go get you hence." Sir Philip Sidney. NoSic Fr. Astrophil and Stella.

Song 9. Harry Gilonis. Oth

Eleventh Song: "Who is it that this dark[e] night." Sir Philip Sidney. NAEL-6v1; NAEL-7v1; NoSic; OxAEP-1 Fr. Astrophil and Stella.

Song, A. George Darley. See It Is Not Beauty I Demand.

Song, A. George Farquhar. NOSC

Song[, A]: "Ask[e] me no more where Jove bestow[e]s." Thomas Carew. BASC; CavPo; ClHu; NAEL-6v1; NAEL-7v1; NoP-4; NOSC; OBEV; OxBEV; TFi

Song, A: "In the north there is a lovely woman." Li Yen-nien. ColAnChi, tr. by Anne Birrell

Song, A: "Lying is an occupation." Laetitia Pilkington. PEW

Song, A: "Morpheus, the humble god, that dwells." Sir John Denham. NOSC

Song, A: "No riches from his scanty store." Helen Maria Williams. WoRP

Song, A: On His Mistress. Sir Robert Aytoun. NOSC

Song, A: "Slaves to London, I'll deceive you."   Peter Anthony Motteux. NOSC

Song, A: "Strephon, your breach of faith and trust."   Laetitia Pilkington.   IrLP; LW; PEW

Song: A Lovely Girl Combing Her Hair.   Li Ho.   CCL1, *tr.* by John Frodsham

Song, The.   George Herbert. *See* Easter.

Song, The.   Balakrishna Sama.   PoetW

Song, The.   Jones Very.   APN-1

Song, The: "Beauty no more the subject be."   Thomas Nabbes.   NOSC

Song, The: "Beehive source."   Anne Baring.   HW

Song, The: "Drink and be merry, merry, merry boys."   Thomas Morton. NAAL-3

Song, The: "It's the tone, not the harp."   L. Tureski.   Prolet, *tr.* by Amelia Glaser

Song, The: "Oh, foully slighted Ethiope maid!"   Priscilla Jane Thompson. CBWP-2

Song, a poem of itself—the word itself a dirge, A.   Yonnondio.   Walt Whitman.   NAAL-3

Song About Benedek Virág.   Dezső Kosztolányi.   IQMS, *tr.* by Watson Kirkconnell

Song about Kőrösi Csoma.   Gyula Juhász.   IQMS, *tr.* by Watson Kirkconnell

Song about Myself, A.   John Keats.
  There Was a Naughty Boy.   OBCoV

Song about Soup, A.   Elin ap Hywel.   ATSWP, *tr.* by Robert Minhinnick

Song against Grocers, The.   G. K. Chesterton.   OBCoV

Song Against Natural Selection.   Edward Hirsch.   SUP

Song and Musick, Set by Mr. Eccles, and Sung by Mrs. Leveridge.   Delariviere Manley.   EMWP

Song and Poetry.   *Unknown.*   OBWVE, *tr.* by Gwyn Jones

Song and Story.   Ellen Bryant Voigt.   InGu

Song at a Late Hour.   Olafs Stumbrs.   PML, *tr.* by Inara Cedrins

Song at Graveside.   Ewald von Kleist.   GePo, *tr.* by George C. Schoolfield

Song at Midnight.   Lucille Clifton.   ErotSp; OxAAAP; UnSA

Song at the African Middle Class [*(for Augustinho Neto)*].   Molara Ogundipe-Leslie.   HBAPE

Song at the End of a Meal.   John Hollander.   TaR

Song Beside a Sippy Cup.   Jenny Factor.   P180; PoDa

Song Bewailing the Time of Christmas, So Much Decayed in England, A. *Unknown.*   NoP-4; NoP-5

  (Songe bewailinge the tyme of Christmas, So much decayed in Englande, A.) PBRV

Song Books.   John Cage.
  Solo for Voice 17 Song with Electronics (Relevant).   PFTM-2

Song: Boundless Space.   Sándor Weöres.   WoPoe, *tr.* by William Jay Smith

Song by Isbrand.   Thomas Lovell Beddoes.   OxBEV *Fr.* Death's Jest Book.

Song by the Shore, A.   Richard Hovey.   APN-2

Song by the Walls.   Wang Ch'ang-ling.   CCL1, *tr.* by Stephen Owen

Song. Celia singing.   Thomas Carew.   NPeEn

Song Composed in Time of the Civill Warr, when the Wicked Did Much Insult over the Godly, A.   Anne Collins.   EMWP

Song Cycle of Jacky, The.   Mudrooroo Narogin.
  Song Thirty-Four.   BMAP

Song Cycle of the Moon-Bone.   *Unknown.*   NOBAu, *tr.* by Ronald M. Berndt

Song: Dragons at Midnight.   Li Ho.   CCL1, *tr.* by John Frodsham

Song Embodying What I've Learned in Thirty-Five Years.   Dick Lourie.   PrTe

Song: Endimion Porter and Olivia.   Sir William Davenant.   NOSC; NPeEn

Song: Eternity of Love Protested.   Thomas Carew.   NOSC

Song for a Baby on Padre Island.   Mayme Evans.   TiP2

Song for a Birth or a Death.   Elizabeth Jennings.   HarvBoo

Song for a Dark Girl.   Langston Hughes.   InoFa; NAAL-5; NAAPv.2; NAMCP V.1; NoP-4; NoP-5; SAmP

Song for a Fallen Warrior.   *Unknown.*   AmWaPo; APN-2, *tr.* by John Mason Browne

Song for A Fishing Party.   Jonathan Odell.   NAAPv.1

Song for a Forgotten Shrine to Pan.   John Chipman Farrar.   YaYoPo

Song for a Girl.   John Dryden.   ErotSp

Song for a Play.   Dan Chiasson.   LegDan

Song for a Sea Tower.   Helen Adam.   EdScPo

Song for a Seed.   Violeta Parra.   TANSG, *tr.* by Bonnie Shepard

Song for a Suicide.   Langston Hughes.   OxAAAP

Song: For A' That and A' That.   Robert Burns. *See* For A' That and A' That ["Is there, for honest poverty"].

Song for a Thin Sister.   Audre Lorde.   OxWW

Song for a Young General.   Tu Fu [*or* Du Fu].   CrYelRi, *tr.* by Sam Hamill

Song for a Young Girl's Puberty Ceremony.   *Unknown.*   ChAP; ItWoWo, *tr.* by Frances Densmore

Song for All Seas, All Ships.   Walt Whitman.   APN-1

Song for Annie.   Harry Gilonis.   Oth

Song for Bringing a Child into the World.   *Seminole Oral Tradition.*   NAAPv.1

Song for February, A.   Thomas Given.   FaBoVe

Song for General Zhao.   Ts'en Shen.   CCL1, *tr.* by Stephen Owen

Song for Ghosts and for Those Now Gone.   Philippe Soupault.   YaTCFP, *tr.* by Mary Ann Caws *and* Jean-Pierre Cauvin

Song for Gwydion.   Ronald Stuart Thomas.   HarvBoo

Song for Ishtar.   Denise Levertov.   MoWP; NALW; NAMCP V.2; NoAM

Song for Late Autumn.   Master Naong.   BecRai, *tr.* by Kim Daljin, Kim Won-Chung and Christopher Merrill

Song for My Father, A.   Dimitris Tsaloumas.   PML

Song for My Lover.   Rafael Campo.
  Medical Student Learns Love and Death, A.   WiU
  Our Country of Origin.   WiU

Song for My Own Shadow.   Haewŏn.   BecRai, *tr.* by Kim Daljin, Kim Won-Chung and Christopher Merrill

Song for My Shadow, A.   Kim Pyŏngyŏn.   CATKP; WoPoe, *tr.* by Richard John Lynn

Song for Naomi.   Irving Layton.   IFF

Song for Occupations, A.   Walt Whitman.   APN-1 *Fr.* Leaves of Grass [1855 Version, Complete Text].

Song for Occupations, A.   Walt Whitman.
  "Will you seek afar off? you surely come back at last."   ChIV-1

Song for St Cecilia's Day, 1687, A.   John Dryden.   BASC; NAEL-6v1; NAEL-7v1; NoP-5; NOSC; OBEV; OxAEP-1; TFi; TreFP; WoPoe
  "Trumpet's loud clangor, The."   FaBoWar

Song for saint ein.   B. P. Nichol.   OpeFie

Song / for Sanna.   Olga Broumas.   PoBW

Song for Serpents, A.   Kysha N. Brown.   BtF

Song for Simeon, A.   T. S. Eliot.   ChIV-2

Song for Smooth Waters.   Haida.   CA

Song for Straphangers.   George Buchanan.   PNI

Song for the Cattle.   David Campbell.   NOBAu

Song for the Clatter-Bones.   Frederick Robert Higgins.   ChIV-1; OBMV

Song for the Dying.   *Seminole Oral Tradition.*   NAAPv.1

Song for the Falling Kingdom.   Li Po.   NDACCP, *tr.* by Ezra Pound

Song for the Heroes.   Alex Comfort.   MoBrPo

Song for "The Jacquerie."   Sidney Lanier.   NCAP

Song for the Last Act.   Louise Bogan.   NoP-4; NoP-5

Song for the Middle of the Night, A.   James Wright.   WeW-3

Song for the Moon.   Nazik al-Mala'ika.   BBASP, *tr.* by Christopher Middleton and Matthew Sorenson

Song for the Music in the Warsaw Ghetto.   Jacqueline Osherow.   TaR

Song for the New Order.   Lionel Abrahams.   TSAP

Song for the Rainy Season.   Elizabeth Bishop.   APT-2

Song for the Spirit of Natalie Going.   Susan Wheeler.   ExTi

Song for the Squeeze-Box.   Theodore Roethke.   NBLV

Song for the Sugar Cane.   Virgil Suárez.   AmPoNex

Song for the Sun That Disappeared behind the Rainclouds.   *Unknown.*   ChAP

Song for the unsung heroes who rose in the country's need, A.   Unsung Heroes, The.   Paul Laurence Dunbar.   AmWaPo; CBCWP

Song for the Workers, A.   Eliza Cook.   VWP

Song for the Year's End, A.   Louis Zukofsky.   TaR
  "I shall go back to my mother's grave after this war."   PWW2

Song for Those Who Know.   Hans Magnus Enzensberger.   PoSu; VCWP, *tr.* by the author, Hans Magnus Enzensberger and Michael Hamburger

Song for Three Dreams.   Chunghur Hyujung.   BecRai, *tr.* by Kim Daljin, Kim Won-Chung and Christopher Merrill

Song for Wei City, A.   Wang Wei.   TAL

Song Form.   Imamu Amiri Baraka.   ChAP

Song from *Mardi*.   Herman Melville.   APN-2

Song from Shakespeare's Cymbeline, A.   William Collins.   CABP

Song from the Bride of Smithfield.   Sylvia Townsend Warner.   MoBrPo

Song from the Coptic, A.   Johann Wolfgang von Goethe.   WoPoe, *tr.* by James Clarence Mangan

Song from The Indian Emperor.   John Dryden.   NoP-4; NoP-5

Song from the Occupation Time.   Ion Caraion.   AF, *tr.* by Marguerite Dorian *and* Elliott B. Urdang

Song from the Traffic.   Margaret Bell Houston.   TiP2

Song from Troilus and Cressida.   John Dryden.   NoP-4; NoP-5

Song gives birth to . . . The woman with white hair.   Song of Ancient Ways, The.   William Oandasan.   HATNAP

Song: Green Water, Singing Girl.   Li Ho.   CrYelRi, *tr.* by Sam Hamill

Song: I Want a Witness.   Michael S. Harper.   LTA

Song in a Graveyard.   Pak Tujin.   CAMKP, *tr.* by Edward W. Poitras

Song in Making of the Arrows, The.   John Lyly.   NoSic

Song in Sligo.   Jean Garrigue.   APT-2; OxBoAm

Song in Spite of Myself. Countee Cullen. ISC; ItP

Song in the Blood. Jacques Prévert. AF, *tr. by* Lawrence Ferlinghetti

Song in the Front Yard, A. Gwendolyn Brooks. CAP-8; ESEAA; NAMCP V.2; NoAM; NOxBChV; OxBoAm *Fr.* Street in Bronzeville, A.

Song in the Rock. *Navajo Oral Tradition.* NAAPv.1

Song in the Wood. John Fletcher. NOSC *Fr.* Little French Lawyer, The.

Song Inscribed on an Earthenware Vessel. *Unknown.* WoPoe, *tr. by* John L. Foster

Song Is Ended (But the Melody Lingers On), The. Irving Berlin. ReLy

Song is gone; the dance, The. Bora Ring. Judith Wright. NAMCP V.2; NoAM

Song is in the air. You and the Night and the Music. Howard Dietz. ReLy

Song Is You, The. Oscar Hammerstein, II. ReLy

Song: Lift-Boy. Robert Graves. OxAEP-2

Song. Love Arm'd [*or* Armed]. Aphra Behn. BASC; LW; NALW; NoP-4; NoP-5; NOSC; NPeEn; OBEV; OxAEP-1; OxBEV; PEW; WeW-3
   (Love in fantastick Triumph sat.) BrAP

Song: Love Lives Beyond the Tomb. John Clare. NoP-4; NoP-5

Song: Miss Penelope Burgess, Balling the Jack [*song*]. Thomas McGrath. MiVo

Song: Montrose. Charles Cotton. NOSC

Song of a Balloon in Search of Her Mom's balloon. Yi Hyangji. EcSo, *tr. by* Catherine J. Kim

Song of a Foolish Wife. *Unknown.* CATKP, *tr. by* Carolyn So

Song of a Hungarian Jacobin. Endre Ady. IQMS, *tr. by* Sir Maurice Bowra

Song of a Man in the Dark. Adonis. VCWP, *tr. by* Samuel Hazo

Song of a Man Who Has Come Through. D. H. Lawrence. HarvBoo; RaBo; TRP

Song of a Man Who Has Come Through. D. H. Lawrence.
   Song of a Man Who Has Come Through, The. RaBo; TRP

Song of a Man Who Has Come Through, The. D. H. Lawrence. RaBo; TRP *Fr.* Song of a Man Who Has Come Through.

Song of a Marriageable Girl. *Unknown.* WoPoe, *tr. by* Willard Trask

Song of a Middle-Aged Woman. Mun Chŏnghui. EcSo, *tr. by* Catherine J. Kim

Song of a Prisoner. Jack Spicer. APSN

Song of a Spirit. Ann Radcliffe. RWP

Song of a Thousand Empty Hands. Adele Ne Jame. PoArWo

Song of a Traveller, The. Robert Louis Stevenson. MoBrPo; OBEV
   (I Will Make You Brooches.) GoPo

Song of a Turf-sod. William A. Byrne. IrV

Song of a Young Lady to Her Ancient Lover, A. John Wilmot, 2d Earl of Rochester. BASC; NoP-4; NoP-5; NOSC; NPeEn; OxAEP-1; OxBEV; WaAnP

Song of Absinthe Granny, The. Ruth Stone. NALW

Song of an Arrowhead from Changping. Li Ho. CCL1, *tr. by* John Frodsham

Song of an Impossible Blue. Porfirio Barba-Jacob. *tr. by* Jeff Bingham and Juan Antonio Serna Servin
   Song of the Fleeting Day. CAGL, *tr. by* Jeff Bingham and Juan Antonio Serna Servin

Song of an Old Gray Wolf. *Unknown.* APN-2, *tr. by* Alfred Kroeber

Song of an Old Maid. *Unknown.* CATKP, *tr. by* Carolyn So

Song of Ancient Ways, The. William Oandasan. HATNAP

Song of Apollo. John Lyly. NoSic *Fr.* Midas.

Song of Apollo. Percy Bysshe Shelley. NAEL-6v2

Song of Arla, Written During Her Enthusiasm, A. Anne Batten Cristall. RWP

Song of Autumn, A. Joseph Ceravolo. NYP2

Song of Autumn I. Charles Baudelaire. NAWM-7v2, *tr. by* Carlyle Ferren MacIntyre

Song of Becoming. Fadwa Tuqan. AF, *tr. by* Naomi Shihab Nye

Song of Bekotsidi, The. *Unknown.* OBVE, *tr. by* Washington Matthews

Song of Bliss. Edmund Spenser. OBVE *Fr.* Faerie Queene, The.

Song of Blodeuwedd, The. *Unknown.* NoP-4; WoPoe, *tr. by* Robert Graves

Song of Braddock's Men, The. Stephen Tilden. AmWaPo

Song of Bullets, The. Jessica Tarahata Hagedorn. FiBr

Song of Cayetano's Circus, The [*tr. of Creole slave song*]. George Washington Cable. APN-2

Song of Ch'ang-kan. Li Po. WaAnP, *tr. by* Arthur Sze

Song of Ch'ang-Kan (Yueh-Fu), The. Li Po. ChinPo, *tr. by* Ye Weilian [*or* Yeh Wei-lien *or* Wai-lim Yip]

Song of Children in the Land of Ice Who Love the Sun. Kim Sŭnghŭi. CAMKP, *tr. by* Anthony, Brother of Taizé

Song of Ch'ŏngŭp. *Unknown.* CATKP, *tr. by* Peter H. Lee

Song of Ch'ŏyong. Ch'ŏyong. CATKP, *tr. by* Peter H. Lee

Song of Ch'ŏyong. *Unknown.* CATKP, *tr. by* Peter H. Lee

Song of Crede, Daughter of Guare, The. *Unknown.* IrLP, *tr. by* Kuno Meyer

Song of Cursive Calligraphy. Hsieh Chin. ColAnChi, *tr. by* Jonathan Chaves

Song of Dalliance, A. William Cartwright. NOSC

Song of Degrees, A. Howard Nemerov. TaR

Song of Departure, A. Li Ch'ing-chao. NDACCP,

Song of Derivations, A. Alice Thompson Meynell. CABP

Song of Devotion to the Forest [*after the pygmies of the Ituri Forest*]. David Henderson. GT

Song of Diamond Eyes, The. Franco Buffoni. ItPo, *tr. by* Gayle Ridinger

Song of Disillusionment, A. Hsi K'ang. CCL1, *tr. by* John Turner

Song of Earth. Uri Zvi Greenberg. FIT, *tr. by* Robert Friend

Song of Emigration. Felicia Dorothea Hemans. VWP

Song of Entertaining the Holy One. *Korean Oral Tradition.* CATKP, *tr. by* Peter H. Lee

Song of Esechia, The. John Hall. ChIV-1

Song of Everlasting Sorrow. Po Chü-i. WoPoe, *tr. by* Dore J. Levy

Song of Finis, The. Walter De la Mare. MoBrPo

Song of Fixed Accord. Wallace Stevens. SAmP

Song of Freedom, A. Roland A. Parks. OWABP

Song of Grass. Na Hǔidôk. EcSo, *tr. by* Peter H. Lee

Song of Green Mountain. *Unknown.* CATKP, *tr. by* Peter H. Lee

Song of Hiawatha, The. Henry Wadsworth Longfellow.
   Famine, The. TreFP
   Four Winds, The.
      "Honor be to Mudjekeewis!" UV
   Hiawatha's Childhood.
      "By the shores of Gitche[e] Gumee." NoP-5
   Hiawatha's Departure.
      "Heavy with the heat and silence." APN-1
   Hiawatha's Fasting. NAAPv.1
      "On the fourth day of his fasting." TCAPo
   Introduction. ColAP
   Picture-Writing. APN-1; NAAPv.1
   White Man's Foot, The.
      Hiawatha: The White Man's Foot. NCAP

Song of Honor [*or* Honour], The. Ralph Hodgson. MoBrPo

Song of Hungarrda, The. Ngunaitponi. NOBAu

Song of Igor's Campaign, The. *Unknown. tr. by* Harry Strickhausen
   "And in the mountains of Kiev, Sviatoslav." WoPoe, *tr. by* Harry Strickhausen

Song of Jonah in the Whale's Belly, The. Michael Drayton. ChIV-1

Song of Joys, A. Walt Whitman.
   "O the engineer's joys! to go with a locomotive!" HHAm

Song of "Kornél Esti", The. Dezső Kosztolányi. IQMS, *tr. by* Adam Makkai

Song of Krishna. Viswanatha Satyanarayana. HotL, *tr. by* V. Narayana Rao and David Shulman

Song of Krishna: The Fourth Song, Sung with Raga "Ramakari." Jayadeva. WoPoe *Fr.* Gita Govinda, The.

Song of Lasting Regret, The. Po Chü-i. ColAnChi, *tr. by* Paul W. Kroll

Song of Lawino. Okot P'Bitek.
   My Husband's Tongue Is Bitter. NAMCP V.2
   Woman with Whom I Share My Husband, The. NAMCP V.2; PoetW

Song of Lazarus, The. Alex Comfort.
   Notes for My Son. MoBrPo; RSaN

Song of Liang-chou. Wang Han. WaAnP, *tr. by* Arthur Sze

Song of Liberty, A. William Blake. NAEL-6v2; NAEL-7v2 *Fr.* Marriage of Heaven and Hell, The.

Song of Lies, A. Vincent Woods. BeAl; NIrP

Song of Lies on Sabbath Eve, A. Yehuda Amichai. PoSu, *tr. by* Chana Bloch

Song of Longing. Chŏng Ch'ŏl. CATKP, *tr. by* David R. McCann

Song of Manchan the Hermit, The. *Unknown.* IrV, *tr. by* Eleanor Hull

Song of Marke Anthony, A. John Cleveland. NPeEn

Song of Mary. No Hyegyông. EcSo, *tr. by* Ann Y. Choi

Song of Mary, A. Lucille Clifton. NALW

Song of Mehitabel, The. Don Marquis. AmWit; APT-1; OBCoV *Fr.* Archy and Mehitabel.

Song of Mercies, A. David Brendon Hopes.
   "Mercy on me Spirit." UpMys

Song of Milkanwatha, The. George A. Strong.
   Modern Hiawatha, The. OBCoV; UV

Song of Mount T'ai. Lu Chi. CrYelRi, *tr. by* Sam Hamill

Song of Mr Toad, The. Kenneth Grahame. NOxBChV *Fr.* Wind in the Willows, The.

Song of My Mountain Dwelling. Zhidun. CCL1, *tr. by* John Frodsham

Song of My People-Forest, People-Sea. Uri Zvi Greenberg. FIT, *tr. by* Robert Friend

Song of My Soul. Ralph Chubb. CAGL

Song of Myself. Walt Whitman. APN-1; HeIP-4; OxBoAm *Fr.* Leaves of Grass [1855 Version].

Song of Myself by Walt Whitman. Alex Rawls. AnSo

Song of Myself. Walt Whitman. MoAmPo; NAAL-3; NAAL-5; NAAPv.1
　"All truths wait in all things." ColAP
　"Alone far in the wilds and mountains I hunt." SAmP; WaAnP
　　"Runaway slave came to my house and stopt outside, The." HHAm
　"And as to you Death, and you bitter hug of mortality, it is idle to try to alarm me." ColAP
　"Big doors of the country barn stand open and ready, The." ColAP; ITBLP; WaAnP
　"Blind loving wrestling touch! Sheathed hooded sharptoothed touch!" CAGL
　"Call in the midst of the crowd, A." ColAP
　"Child said *What is the grass?* fetching it to me with full hands, A." ColAP; NoP-4; NoP-5; SAmP
　　"Child said *What is the grass?* fetching it to me with full hands, A." ITBLP
　"Dazzling and tremendous how quick the sun-rise would kill me." ColAP
　"Has any one supposed it lucky to be born?" ColAP; NAWM-7v2; WaAnP
　"Houses and rooms are full of perfumes, the shelves are crowded with perfumes." CAGL; ColAP
　"I am of old and young, of the foolish as much as the wise." NAWM-7v2
　"I am the poet of the Body and I am the poet of the Soul." BrAP; CAGL; ColAP; NAWM-7v2; WaAnP; WeW-3
　"I am the teacher of athletes." CAGL; ColAP
　"I believe a leaf of grass is no less than the journey-work of the stars." ColAP; SAmP; WaAnP
　"I believe in you my soul, the other I am must not abase itself to you." CAGL; ColAP; NoP-5
　"I celebrate myself, and sing myself." ColAP; FaBoVe; NAMCP V.1; NAWM-7v2; NCAP; NIL-7; NoAM; NoP-5; PoPoPo; RaBo; SAmP; TCAPo; WaAnP
　"I have heard what the talkers were talking, the talk of the beginning and the end." CAGL
　"I have said that the soul is not more than the body." ColAP
　"I know I have the best of time and space, and was never measured and will never be measured." ColAP; NAWM-7v2; NoAM
　"I think I could turn and live with animals, they are so placid and self-contained." NAWM-7v2; SAmP; WeW-3
　"Is this then a touch? . . . quivering me to a new identity." CAGL
　"Little one sleeps in its cradle, The." ColAP; SAmP; WaAnP
　"Negro holds firmly the reins of his four horses, the block swags underneath on its tied-over chain, The." NoP-5
　"Now I will do nothing but listen." SAmP
　"Past and present wilt—I have filled them, emptied them, The." CAGL; ColAP; NAWM-7v2
　"Pure contralto sings in the organloft, The." FaBoA
　"Space and Time! now I see it is true, what I guess'd at."
　　"I understand the large hearts of heroes." SAmP
　"Spotted hawk swoops by and accuses me, he complains of my gab and my loitering, The." AmFaPo; CAGL; ColAP; ItP; NAWM-7v2; NoP-5; SAmP; WaAnP
　"Stretch'd and still lies the midnight." ColAP
　"There is that in me—I do not know what it is—but I know it is in me." CAGL; ColAP; ItP
　"This is the meal pleasantly set . . . this is the meat and drink for natural hunger." CAGL
　"To be in any form, what is that?" CAGL
　"Trippers and askers surround me." CAGL; ColAP; NAWM-7v2
　"Twenty-eight young men bathe by the shore." CAGL; ColAP; CtM; NoP-4; NoP-5; SAmP; WaAnP
　"Walt Whitman, a kosmos, of Manhattan the son." ColAP; NAWM-7v2; NoP-4; NoP-5; SAmP; WaAnP
　"Who goes there? hankering, gross, mystical, nude." BrAP; CAGL; ColAP
　"Wild gander leads his flock through the cool night, The." ColAP
　"Would you hear of an old-time [*or* old-fashioned] sea fight?" SAmP
　"You sea! I resign myself to you also—I guess what you mean." CAGL
Song of Nature. Ralph Waldo Emerson. APN-1
Song of Obstacles. Louise Glück. LW *Fr.* Marathon.
Song of One of the Girls. Dorothy Parker. AmWit; NALW
Song of Pajaro. Jeff Tagami. OpBo
Song of Parting. Wang Po-ch'eng. CrYelRi, *tr. by* Sam Hamill
Song of Peace. Pak Illo. CATKP, *tr. by* Peter H. Lee
Song of Peach Tree Spring. Wang Wei. WoPoe, *tr. by* Tony Barnstone, Willis Barnstone *and* Haixin Xu, Willis Barnstone and Xu Haixin
Song of Pengya. Tu Fu [*or* Du Fu]. CCL1, *tr. by* Burton Watson
Song of Ptahhotep, The. Robert Bringhurst. GifTon
Song of Pursuit. Gabriel Zaid. TCLAP, *tr. by* Mónica Hernández-Cancio
Song of P'yŏngyang. *Unknown.* CATKP, *tr. by* Peter H. Lee
Song of P'yŏngyang without Refrain. *Unknown.* CATKP, *tr. by* Peter H. Lee

Song of Quavering, A. Jerome Rothenberg. FTOS
Song of Racquetball. David Allan Evans. MoASP
Song of Regret. Pan Chieh-yû. CCL1, *tr. by* Burton Watson
Song of Reply. Alda Merini. CItWP, *tr. by* Cinzia Sartini Blum and Lara Trubowitz
Song of Reproach. Ferenc Apáti. IQMS, *tr. by* Adam Makkai
Song of Repulse to a Vain Lover. *Makah Oral Tradition.* NAAPv.1
Song of Roland, The. *Unknown. tr. by* Frederick Goldin, Dorothy Leigh Sayers and Charles Hubert Sisson
　"Charles the King, our Emperor, the great." NAWM-5v1; NAWM-7v1, *tr. by* Frederick Goldin
　"In wrath and grief away the Paynims fly." OBWP
　"Marsilion sees his people's martyrdom." NAWM-5v1; NAWM-7v1, *tr. by* Frederick Goldin
　"Night passes on, and the bright day appears." NAWM-7v1, *tr. by* Frederick Goldin
　"Now Roland feels that he is at death's door." FaBoWar, *tr. by* Dorothy Leigh Sayers
　"Oliver's climbed upon a hilly crest." FaBoWar, *tr. by* Dorothy Leigh Sayers
　Roncevalles. WoPoe, *tr. by* Charles Hubert Sisson
　"They arm themselves with Saracen hauberks." NAWM-5v1; NAWM-7v1, *tr. by* Frederick Goldin
Song of Samuel Sweet, The. Charles Causley. OBNV
Song of Saul before His Last Battle. Lord Byron. ChIV-1
Song of Selling Flowers. Tsung Ch'en. ColAnChi, *tr. by* Jonathan Chaves
Song of Sequence. *Unknown. See* First Song of the Exploding Stick.
Song of Shem. James Philip McAuley. ChIV-1 *Fr.* Family of Love, The.
Song of skylark. Issa. IllVoic *Fr.* Issa: A Suite of Haiku.
Song of Slaves in the Desert. John Greenleaf Whittier. APN-1
Song of Smoke. Kevin Young. LegDan; P180
Song of Sŏdong. Mu, King of Paekche. CATKP, *tr. by* Peter H. Lee
Song of Solomon. Bible, *O.T.*
　Song. WPoS
Song of Solomon, The. Bible, *O.T.*
　Song of Solomon, The. OBGa
Song of Solomon, The. Bible, *O.T.*
　Song."Come, by beloved." WPoS
Song of Solomon, The. Bible, *O.T.*
　Song."I am dark, daughters of Jerusalem." WPoS
Song of Solomon, The. Bible, *O.T. tr. by* Barbara Mackay, Lady Scourie
　"As apple tree among the trees of wood." EMWP, *tr. by* Barbara Mackay, Lady Scourie
Song of Solomon, The [*or* The Song of Songs]. Bible, *O.T. tr. by* Willis Barnstone, Marcia Falk, Sam Hamill, Peter Jay and King James Version
　"Give me all the kisses of your mouth." ErotSp, *tr. by* Sam Hamill
　"How beautiful are thy feet with shoes." EroLit, *tr. by* King James Version
　"I am come into my garden, my sister, my spouse." EroLit, *tr. by* King James Version
　"I am come into my garden, my sister, my spouse." OBVE
　I Am the Rose of Sharon. OBVE
　"I was drowsy, but my heart was awake. Listen!" WoPoe, *tr. by* Peter Jay
　"My beloved spake, and said unto me." OPOU
　"Song of songs, which is Solomon's, The." OBVE
　"Sound of my lover, The." WoPoe, *tr. by* Marcia Falk
Song of Songs. Chiedu Ezeanah.
　4. NeNiPo
　5. NeNiPo
　"His silence in the middle of stones." NeNiPo
Song of Songs, The. Heinrich Heine. EroLit, *tr. by* Louis Untermeyer
Song of Songs, The. Ogden Nash. AmWit
Song of songs, which is Solomon's, The. Bible, *O.T.* OBVE *Fr.* Song of Solomon, The [*or* The Song of Songs].
Song of Sorrow, A. Mary Cameron. EMWP
Song of Spring, A. *Chippewa Oral Tradition.* APT-1 *Fr.* Chippewa Music.
Song of Summer. Paul Laurence Dunbar. APN-2
Song of Summer. Alexander MacDonald. *tr. by* Derick Thomson
　"Month of plants and of honey." NePenScot, *tr. by* Derick Thomson
Song of Summer. *Unknown.* NAWM-7v1, *tr. by* Jan Ziolkowski
Song of Surfing on the Bore. Cheng Hsieh. ColAnChi, *tr. by* Jonathan Chaves
Song of Surrender. Saleem Peeradina. Vesp
Song of Taking Leave. Emilio Prados. RaW, *tr. by* Robert Mezey
Song of the Aged Mother which shook the heavens with wrath, The. Vala; *or* The Four Zoas. William Blake.
Song of the Alaskero. *Unknown.* NAAPv.2
Song of the Alpine Hunter. Paul Van Ostaijen. TuT, *tr. by* Theo Dorgan

Song of the Andoumboulou.   Nathaniel Mackey.

  6.   FTOS

  7.   FTOS

  12. FTOS; OxAAAP

  15: Bedouin Wind. PFTM-2

  46. WoBe

  56. WoBe

  58. Eno; RD

  62. RD

  "One hand on her hip, one hand." OxAAAP

Song of the Andoumboulou: 15. Nathaniel Mackey. PFTM-2

Song of the Angels. Lizelia Augusta Jenkins Moorer. CBWP-3

Song of the Answerer. Walt Whitman. APN-1 *Fr.* Leaves of Grass [1855 Version].

Song of the Bald Eagle. *Unknown.* APN-2 *Fr.* Minnetare Songs.

Song of the Banana Man, The. Evan Jones. ItP

Song of the Barren Orange Tree. Federico García Lorca. AmFaPo; RaW, *tr. by* W. S. Merwin

Song of the Bear. *Unknown.* APN-2 *Fr.* Minnetare Songs.

Song of the Black Bear, The. *Unknown.* RaBo

Song of the Bowmen of Shu [1915]. Bunno [Wen Wang or King Wen]. FaBoWar; NDACCP; OBVE, *tr. by* Ezra Pound

Song of the Bowmen of Shu [1954]. Bunno [Wen Wang or King Wen]. NDACCP; OBVE, *tr. by* Ezra Pound

Song of the Breaking of the Willow. *Unknown.* ColAnChi, *tr. by* Burton Watson

Song of the Broad-Axe [*or* Broad-Ax]. Walt Whitman.

  "Beauty of wood-boys and wood-men their clear untrimmed faces, The." CA

  Broad-Ax, The. MoAmPo

Song of the Burning. David Wojahn. SwNoth

Song of the Butterfly, The. Frances Densmore. APT-1 *Fr.* Chippewa Music.

Song of the Captive Sioux Woman. *Chippewa Oral Tradition.* NAAL-5; NAAPv.2

Song of the Chattahoochee. Sidney Lanier. APN-2; ColAP; TCAPo

Song of the Chinchilla. Lisa Jarnot. LegDan

Song of the Coffin Close. Kenneth White. EdScPo

Song of the Comet. Yungch'ŏn, Master. CATKP, *tr. by* Peter H. Lee

Song of the Cook. Natasha Sajé. SweBea

Song of the Crow Pecking at My Scarred Donkey. Wang Yü-ch'eng. WoPoe, *tr. by* Jonathan Chaves

Song of the Crows. *Chippewa Oral Tradition.* NAAL-5; NAAPv.2

Song of the Cuban Blacks. Federico García Lorca. RaBo; WED, *tr. by* Robert Bly

Song of the Cycle. Charles Henry Crandall. ArBi

Song of the Dead Soldier, The. Christopher Logue. FaBoWar

Song of the Degrees, A. Ezra Pound. APT-1

Song of the Dogs, The. Sándor Petőfi. IQMS, *tr. by* George Sutherland Fraser

Song of the Dove, The. Alexander Robertson. APT-1

Song of the Dream Garden. Ikkyu Sojun. ErotSp, *tr. by* Sam Hamill

Song of the Dying Gunner A.A.1. Charles Causley. FaBoWar; PoWW

Song of the Earth. *Navajo Oral Tradition.* NAAPv.1

Song of the Eiffel Tower. David Shapiro. BodElec

Song of the Elk. *Unknown.* APN-2 *Fr.* Minnetare Songs.

Song of the English Bowmen. *Unknown.* FaBoWar

Song of the Eucharist, A. James Ryman. SacPr

Song of the Exposition. Walt Whitman.

  Muse in the New World, The. MoAmPo

Song of the Faithful, A. Michael Drayton. ChIV-1

Song of the Faithful Daughter Shiragiku. Ochiai Naobumi. CAoMJL1, *tr. by* Leith Morton

Song of the Fallen Deer. *Unknown.* OBVE, *tr. by* Frank Russell

Song of the Fisherman, The. Kao Shih. CCL1, *tr. by* Stephen Owen

Song of the Fleeting Day. Porfirio Barba-Jacob. CAGL *Fr.* Song of an Impossible Blue.

Song of the flute, O sister, is madness, The. Mirabai. WPoS

Song of the Ghost, The. Alfred Perceval Graves. IrV

Song of the Gong and Chimes. *Unknown.* CATKP, *tr. by* Peter H. Lee

Song of the Gourd. C. D. Wright. GPPA

Song of the Graves, The. *Unknown.* OBMV *Fr.* Black Book of Carmarthen, The.

Song of the Great Mind. Uri Zvi Greenberg. FIT, *tr. by* Robert Friend

Song of the Great Wind. Liu Pang. ColAnChi, *tr. by* Victor H. Mair

Song of the Great Wind. Liu Pang. CCL1, *tr. by* Burton Watson

Song of the Gun. *Unknown.* APN-2 *Fr.* Minnetare Songs.

Song of the Happy Shepherd, The. William Butler Yeats. NoAM

Song of the Hat-Raising Doll. John Mole. OBCoV *Fr.* Penny Toys.

Song of the Heavenly Horse. Li Po. CCL1, *tr. by* Elling O. Eide

Song of the Imprisoned Bird. Eliza Cook. VWP

Song of the Indian Maid. John Keats. OBEV *Fr.* Endymion: A Poetic Romance.

Song of the Indian Wars, The. John Gneisenau Neihardt.

  "Summer turned." GM

Song of the Initiate. Léopold Sédar Senghor. VCWP, *tr. by* Melvin Dixon

Song of the Insolent Air. Ch'i-chi. CSKM, *tr. by* Burton Watson

Song of the Juggler. Heberto Padilla. AF; BeAl, *tr. by* Andrew Hurley and Alastair Reid

Song of the Lenape Warriors Going against the Enemy, The. *Unknown.* APN-2, *tr. by* John Heckwelder

Song of the Little Miss by the Green Rill. *Unknown.* ChinPo, *tr. by* Ye Weilian [*or* Yeh Wei-lien *or* Wai-lim Yip]

Song of the Lotus-Eaters. Alfred Tennyson. OBEV

Song of the Lower Classes, The. Ernest Charles Jones. RSaN

Song of the Mad Prince, The. Walter De la Mare. CtM; MakPoe; NoAM; OxAEP-2

Song of the Magic Strings. Li Ho. CCL1, *tr. by* John Frodsham

Song of the Man of Green Hill, The. Kao Ch'i. ColAnChi, *tr. by* Jonathan Chaves

Song of the Messiah, The. John Gneisenau Neihardt.

  "In vain against the formless wolves of air." APT-1

Song of the Mischievous Dog, The. Dylan Thomas. OBCoV

Song of the Mock Turtle, The. Lewis Carroll. UV *Fr.* Alice's Adventures in Wonderland.

Song of the Modern Time. Eliza Cook. VWP

Song of the Moon. Priscilla Jane Thompson. CBWP-2

Song of the Oktahutchee. Alexander L. Posey. APN-2

Song of the Old Man. Richard Jones. IllVoic

Song of the Old Mother, The. William Butler Yeats. MoBrPo

Song of the Old Sword. Ch'i-chi. CSKM, *tr. by* Burton Watson

Song of the Open Road. Ogden Nash. APT-2

Song of the Open Road. Walt Whitman.

  "Earth expanding right hand and left hand, The." AmFaPo

  "Efflux of the soul is happiness, here is happiness, The." AmFaPo

  "I take to the open road." ArBi

Song of the Ospreys, The. *Unknown.* CCL1 *Fr.* Guan-ju.

Song of the Owl. *Unknown.* APN-2, *tr. by* Henry Wadsworth Longfellow

Song of the Palace of Ch'en. Kuan Hsiu. WoPoe, *tr. by* Jerome P. Seaton

Song of the Passion, A. Richard Rolle of Hampole. SacPr

Song of the Pearl-Fishers, The. Yüan Chĕn. CCL1, *tr. by* John A. Scott

Song of the Peasants in the Time of Yao. *Unknown.* CCL1, *tr. by* James Legge

Song of the Pestle. *Unknown.* CATKP, *tr. by* Peter H. Lee

Song of the Pheasant. *Unknown.* APN-2 *Fr.* Minnetare Songs.

Song of the Pigeon. *Unknown.* CATKP, *tr. by* Peter H. Lee

Song of the Pines. Po Chü-i. TAL

Song of the P'i-P'a. Po Chü-i. ChinPo, *tr. by* Ye Weilian [*or* Yeh Wei-lien *or* Wai-lim Yip]

Song of the Pleiades. *Pawnee Oral Tradition.* TCAPo

  (Song to the Pleiades.) NAAPv.2

Song of the Promise of the Buffalo. *Unknown.* APN-2 *Fr.* Hako, The.

Song of the Prophet. *Unknown.* APN-2 *Fr.* Mountain Chant, The.

Song of the Pure Land. Master Naong. CATKP, *tr. by* Pori Park

Song of the Rabbits Outside the Tavern, The. Elizabeth Jane Coatsworth. SoSe-8

Song of the Ransom of the Dark. Bruce Smith. BAP-04

Song of the Rider. Federico García Lorca. WoPoe, *tr. by* Edwin Honig

Song of the Rider ("Córdoba. / Distant and alone.") Federico García Lorca. WED, *tr. by* Robert Bly

Song of the Riders. Stephen Vincent Benét. MoAmPo *Fr.* John Brown's Body.

Song of the Rising Sun Dance. *Unknown.* APN-2 *Fr.* Mountain Chant, The.

Song of the Round Man. Michael Palmer. NAMCP V.2

Song of the Running Horse River, A: Presented on Saying Farewell to the Army Going on Campaign to the West. Ts'en Shen. ColAnChi, *tr. by* Daniel Bryant

Song of the Rushlight. Eliza Cook. VWP

Song of the Seaweed. Eliza Cook.

  Becalmed in the Tropics. STuOW; VerBaPo

Song of the Seeress. *Unknown.* NAWM-5v1

Song of the Self: The Grandmother. Alma Villanueva. HW

Song of the Shadows, The. Walter De la Mare. MoBrPo

Song of the Shirt, The. Thomas Hood. BRP

Song of the Silent Night. Aurelio Arturo. BLPSL, *tr. by* Rene de Costa, Rigas Kappatos and Eleni Paidoussi

Song of the Sky Loom. *Tewa Oral Tradition*. WoPoe, *tr.* by Herbert J. Spinden

Song of the Slave Girl, The. Fadil Azzawi. IrPoTo, *tr.* by Ralph Saverese and Saadi A. Simawe

Song of the Smoke, The. William Edward Burghardt DuBois. ISC; SSLK

Song of the snails on their way to a funeral. Jacques Prévert. MFP, *tr.* by Martin Sorrell

Song of the Son. Jean Toomer. InGu; ISC; MakPoe; NAAPv.2; NAMCP V.1; NIL-7; NIP-4; OxAAAP

Song of the Soul of Chicago. Sherwood Anderson. MotU

Song of the Spring Wind. Ch'i-chi. CSKM, *tr.* by Burton Watson

Song of the Stars. William Cullen Bryant. TreFP

Song of the Stars, The. *Unknown*. APN-2, *tr.* by Charles Godfrey Leland

Song of the Sterile Orange Tree. Federico García Lorca. SonAtl, *tr.* by Becca, Jenny Boarder, Thomas Boarder and Lisa Martin

Song of the Stone Drums. Han Yü. CCL1, *tr.* by Innes Herdan

Song of the Strange Woman. Leah Goldberg. FIT, *tr.* by Robert Friend

Song of The Suffering Servant, The. Bible, *O.T.* NAWM-5v1 *Fr.* Isaiah.

Song of the Sword. W. E. Henley.
   "I am the feast-maker." FaBoWar

Song of the Taste. Gary Snyder. WhBo

Song of the Third Generation. Julia Lisella. UnSA

Song of the Three Hundred Thousand Drunkards in the United States. William Bingham Tappan.
   "Onward! though ever in our march." VerBaPo

Song of the Thunders. *Unknown*. OBVE, *tr.* by Frances Densmore

Song of the Tölös. Hulü Chin. ColAnChi, *tr.* by Victor H. Mair

Song of the Tower of Skulls. Vasco [*or* Vasko] Popa. WoPoe, *tr.* by Anne Pennington

Song of the Train. David McCord. NTCP

Song of the Transportationist, The. *Unknown*. NOBAu

Song of the Traveler at Evening. Johann Wolfgang von Goethe. STV, *tr.* by John Frederick Nims

Song of the Trees. *Unknown*. OBVE, *tr.* by Frances Densmore

Song of the Ugly Maiden. Eliza Cook. VWP

Song of the Ungirt Runners, The. Charles Hamilton Sorley. MoBrPo; OBEV

Song of the Vermeil Phoenix. Tu Fu [*or* Du Fu]. TAL

Song of the Viet Boatman. *Unknown*. ColAnChi, *tr.* by Anne Birrell

Song of the Virgin Mary, The. Miles Coverdale. ChIV-2

Song of the War Wagons. Tu Fu [*or* Du Fu]. CrYelRi, *tr.* by Sam Hamill

Song of the War-Carts. Tu Fu [*or* Du Fu]. NDACCP, *tr.* by David Hinton

Song of the War-Chariots (Yueh-fu). Tu Fu [*or* Du Fu]. ChinPo, *tr.* by Ye Weilian [*or* Yeh Wei-lien *or* Wai-lim Yip]

Song of the Weasel. *Unknown*. APN-2 *Fr.* Minnetare Songs.

Song of the Western Countries. Georg Trakl. WED, *tr.* by Robert Bly

Song of the Wheel. Adam David Miller. FuFl

Song of the Wheel, A. Arthur H. Lawrence. ArBi

Song of the Wheel, The. George Lynde Richardson. ArBi

Song of the Whirlwind. Fenton Johnson. OxAAAP

Song of the White Man. *Unknown*. APN-2 *Fr.* Minnetare Songs.

Song of the Wife of a Gold Mountain Man. *Chinese Oral Tradition*. NAAPv.1

Song of the Wolves,The. Sándor Petőfi. IQMS, *tr.* by George Sutherland Fraser

Song of the Yellow Cedar Face, A. George Clutesi. HATNAP

Song of the Yodo River. Buson. EH, *tr.* by Robert Hass

Song of Troylus, The. Geoffrey Chaucer. NoP-4 *Fr.* Troilus and Criseyde [*or* Criseide].

Song of T'ung-ku. Tu Fu [*or* Du Fu]. CrYelRi, *tr.* by Sam Hamill

Song of Tuṣita Heaven. Wölmyŏng, Master. CATKP, *tr.* by Peter H. Lee

Song of Ullikummi, The. Charles Olson. PFTM-1

Song of Wandering Aengus, The. William Butler Yeats. BLPJKO; ChAP; CtM; IrLP; MoBrPo; NAMCP V.1; PtR; RaBo; TFi; WaAnP

Song of War. Kofi Awoonor. PoetW

Song of War. *Chippewa Oral Tradition*. *See* Sioux Women Gather Up Their Wounded, The.

Song of War, A. Li Po. TAL

Song of Welcome to the Bride of King Wen. *Unknown*. CCL1 *Fr.* Guan-ju.

Song of White Hair, A. Chuo Wen-chün. CCL1, *tr.* by Chung Ling and Kenneth Rexroth

Song of Winnie. Gwendolyn Brooks. ESEAA *Fr.* Winnie.

Song of Winter, A. Emily Jane Pfeiffer. OBWVE

Song of Winter, A. *Unknown*. IrV, *tr.* by Kuno Meyer

Song of Xiling Lake, A. Su Hsiao-hsiao. CCL1, *tr.* by Chung Ling and Kenneth Rexroth

Song of Yan, A. Ts'ao P'i. CCL1, *tr.* by John Frodsham

Song on Enduring the Cold. Ts'ao Ts'ao. CCL1; ColAnChi, *tr.* by Burton Watson

Song: On Her Loving Two Equally. Aphra Behn. NoP-5

Song on Leaving the Country Early in the Spring. Anne Batten Cristall. RWP

Song (On Seeing Dead Bodies Floating Off the Cape). Alun Lewis. NAEL-6v2; NoP-4; NoP-5; OBWP

Song on the End of the World, A. Czeslaw Milosz. FaoP; WoPoe *Fr.* Voices of Poor People.

Song on the Water. Thomas Lovell Beddoes. WoPoe *Fr.* Death's Jest Book.

Song on Youzhou Terrace. Chen Zi'ang. CCL1, *tr.* by Stephen Owen

Song Out of Season, A. May Probyn. VWP

Song: Persuasions to Enjoy. Thomas Carew. NOSC

Pious Selinda [*or* Celinda]. William Congreve. NPeEn
   (Song.) NBLV; OxBEV

Song Poem, The. Lenard D. Moore. SpirFl

Song (Poverty Parts Good Company, For an Old Scotch Air. Joanna Baillie. RWP

Song Set by John Farmer. *Unknown*. NoSic

Song Sung by Egistus and Clytemnestra. John Pickering. NoSic *Fr.* Horestes.

Song Taught to Joseph, The. Ray A. Young Bear. AF

Song tells us of our old way of living, The. Song. John Ashbery. WaAnP

Song that I came to sing remains unsung to this day, The. Song That I Came to Sing, The. Rabindranath Tagore. WoPoe

Song: The Railway Train. *Unknown*. NOBAu, *tr.* by George Taplin

Song: The Willing Mistriss. Aphra Behn. PEW

Song Thirty-Four. Mudrooroo Narogin. BMAP *Fr.* Song Cycle of Jacky, The.

Song to a Child. *Unknown*. WoPoe, *tr.* by Anthony Conran

Song to a Fair Young Lady, Going Out of the Town in the Spring. John Dryden. OBEV

Song to a Negro Wash-woman, A. Langston Hughes. NAAPv.2

Song to Alasdair Mac Colla, A. Dorothy Brown. EMWP

Song to Amoret, A. Henry Vaughan. NAEL-7v1

Song to be Shouted Out. Nissim Ezekiel. OBCoV *Fr.* Songs for Nandu Bhende.

Song to Be Sung by the Father of Infant Female Children. Ogden Nash. MoAmPo

Song to Be Written on a Wave. José Emilio Pacheco. STV, *tr.* by John Frederick Nims

Song to Bring Fair Weather. *Unknown*. WoPoe, *tr.* by Frances Densmore

Song to Celia. Sir Charles Sedley. OxBEV
   (To Celia.) OBEV

Song. To Celia ("Come my Celia, let us prove.") Ben Jonson. AEP; BrAP; NIL-7; NoP-4; NoP-5; NPeEn; OBVE; OxBEV; PoPoPo; TFi; WaAnP *Fr.* Volpone.

Song. To Celia ("Drink to me only with thine eyes.") Ben Jonson. AmFaPo; ClHu; NAEL-6v1; NAEL-7v1; NoP-4; NoP-5; NOSC; OxAEP-1; OxBEV; SoSe-8; TFi; UV; WaAnP
   (To Celia.) CtM; OBEV; OBVE

Song to Come, The. Doreen Baingana. BtF

Song to David, A. Christopher Smart. NAEL-6v1; NAEL-7v1; OBWVE
   "O David, highest in the list." NPeEn; OxBEV
   Strength. UV
   "Sublime – invention ever young." OBEV

Song to Erin [*with music*]. Mary Weston Fordham. CBWP-2

Song to Fidel. Ernesto "Che" Guevara. TCLAP, *tr.* by Gordon Brotherston and Edward Dorn

Song to Heaven. Uri Zvi Greenberg. FIT, *tr.* by Robert Friend

Song to Hymen: 1942. Anthony Richardson. PoWW

Song: To Mary. Charles Wolfe. *See* To Mary.

Song to Mithras, A. Rudyard Kipling. NoAM *Fr.* Puck of Pook's Hill.

Song. To My Inconstant Mistress. Thomas Carew. *See* To My Inconstant Mistress [*or* Mistris].

Song to Myself at Seventeen. Gerard Wozek. BeDoSh

Song to Onions. Roy, Jr. Blount. GoPo

Song to Promote Growth. *Unknown*. OBVE, *tr.* by Washington Matthews

Song to the Alpaca. Denise Y. Arnold. PoCoUp

Song to the Banyan. Virgil Suárez. AmPoNex

Song to the Creator. Hildegard von Bingen. WPoS, *tr.* by Barbara Newman

Song to the Men of England. Percy Bysshe Shelley. CABP; NAEL-6v2; NAEL-7v2; RSaN

Song to the Mother of the World. Suzanne Ironbiter. HW

Song to the Pleiades. *Pawnee Oral Tradition*. *See* Song of the Pleiades.

Song to the Trees and Streams. *Unknown*. APN-2 *Fr.* Hako, The.

Song to the Tune "Ting Feng Po." Liu Yung. WoPoe, *tr.* by Sam Hamill

Song to the Virgin Mary. András Vásárhelyi. IQMS, *tr.* by René Bonnerjea

Song. Tune, The Heavy Hours: "Balmy comforts that are fled, The." Anne Batten Cristall. RWP

Song Turning Back into Itself, The. Al Young.
   "Always it's either." OxAAAP

Song upon Miss Harriet Hanbury, Addressed to the Revd Mr Birt.   Sir Charles Hanbury Williams.   OBCoV

Song Wants to Be Light, The.   Federico García Lorca.   SpanPo, *tr. by* Rachel Benson and Robert O'Brien

Song with Words.   James Agee.   ChIV-1; MoAmPo

Song: Woo'd and married and a'.   Joanna Baillie.   NAEL-6v2; NAEL-7v2; NoP-4; NoP-5

Song Written at Sea in the First Dutch War (1665), the Night before an Engagement.   Charles, 6th Earl of Dorset Sackville.   OBEV; OBWP; OxAEP-1

   (Written at Sea, in the First Dutch War.)   NOSC

Songe 17: "Sun is set, and masked night, The."   Robert Sidney.   NoSic

Songe betwene the Quenes majestie and Englande, A.   William Birche.

Songe bewailinge the tyme of Christmas, So much decayed in Englande, A.   *Unknown. See* Song Bewailing the Time of Christmas, So Much Decayed in England, A.

Songe d'Athalie.   Stevie Smith.   OxBEV

Songe Made by Her Majestie and Songe before Her at Her Cominge from White Hall to Powles through Fleete Streete in Anno Domini 1588, A.   Queen of England Elizabeth I.   EMWP

Song-Maker.   Anita Endrezze.   HATNAP

Song-Maker, The.   Anna Wickham.   MoBrPo

Songs.   Steve Crow.
   "They say a man dies."   HATNAP

Songs.   Langston Hughes.   APT-2

Songs about Life and Brighter Things Yet.   Samuel Hoffenstein.   NBLV
   "Crickets chirping in the dark, The."   AmWit
   "Serpent has no feet or hands, The."   AmWit
   "Though Caesar stop a bunghole now."   AmWit

Songs and Chants.   *Unknown.* APN-2, *tr. by* John Wesley Powell

Songs are Thoughts, Sung Out with the Breath.   Orpingalik.   PFTM-1

Songs, but the bloody revolution goes unnoticed.   When People Rise from Cheese, Statement #1.   Duo Duo.   PFTM-2, *tr. by* John Rosenwald

Songs come at us first; and then the rhymed, The.   By Heart.   John Hollander.   NAMCP V.2

Songs for a Colored Singer.   Elizabeth Bishop.

Songs for Eve.   Archibald MacLeish.
   What the Serpent Said to Adam.   ChIV-1

Songs for My Father.   Yusef Komunyakaa.   FuFl
   [Excerpts].   InoFa

Songs for Nandu Bhende.   Nissim Ezekiel.
   Family.   OBCoV
   Song to be Shouted Out.   OBCoV

Songs for Orphans Big and Small.   Ivan Metodiev.
   Garden of Questions.   CSCBP, *tr. by* Georgi Belev and Lisa Sapinkopf
   River.   CSCBP, *tr. by* Georgi Belev and Lisa Sapinkopf
   Sometimes.   CSCBP, *tr. by* Georgi Belev and Lisa Sapinkopf
   Sonnet-Mantra of the Crickets.   CSCBP, *tr. by* Georgi Belev and Lisa Sapinkopf
   These Things from Words.   CSCBP, *tr. by* Georgi Belev and Lisa Sapinkopf
   "This crow is unlike the others."   CSCBP, *tr. by* Georgi Belev and Lisa Sapinkopf

Songs for the Four Parts of the Night.   Tohono O'odham.   WPoS, *tr. by* Frances Densmore

Songs for the Seasons: A Distant Collaboration.   William Shakespeare and Michael Stillman.   IaFF

Songs for the Sleepless.   Elaine Randell.
   "Tomorrow I shall."   Oth

Songs for Treating Sickness, Sung durring the Four Parts of the Night.   Tohono O'odham.
   "In the great night my heart will go out."   NAAPv.1, *tr. by* Frances Densmore
   No. 72. Brown Owls.   NAAPv.1; SWaP
   No. 73. In the Blue Night.   NAAPv.1
   No. 74. The Owl Feather.   NAAPv.1, *tr. by* Frances Densmore
   No. 75. They Come Hooting.   NAAPv.1, *tr. by* Frances Densmore
   No. 76. In the Dark I Enter.   NAAPv.1, *tr. by* Frances Densmore
   No. 77. His Heart Is Almost Covered with Night.   NAAPv.1, *tr. by* Frances Densmore
   No. 78. I See Spirit-Tufts of White Feathers.   NAAPv.1, *tr. by* Frances Densmore
   No. 79. Yonder Lies the Spirit Land.   NAAPv.1, *tr. by* Frances Densmore
   No. 80. Song of a Spirit.   NAAPv.1, *tr. by* Frances Densmore
   No. 81. We Will Join Them.   NAAPv.1, *tr. by* Frances Densmore
   No. 82. My Feathers.   NAAPv.1, *tr. by* Frances Densmore
   No. 83. The Women Are Singing.   NAAPv.1, *tr. by* Frances Densmore
   No. 84. I Am Going to See the Land.   NAAPv.1, *tr. by* Frances Densmore
   No. 85. I Run Toward Ashes Hill.   NAAPv.1, *tr. by* Frances Densmore
   No. 86. The Waters of the Spirits.   NAAPv.1, *tr. by* Frances Densmore
   "On the west side they are singing, the women hear it."   NAAPv.1, *tr. by* Frances Densmore
   "Sadly I was treated, sadly I was treated."   NAAPv.1, *tr. by* Frances Densmore

Songs from an Island.   Ingeborg Bachmann.   VCWP, *tr. by* Mark Anderson

Songs from Below.   Philippe Jaccottet.
   "It's easy to talk, and writing words on the page."   StAl, *tr. by* Derek Mahon

Songs from Cyprus.   "H. D."
   "Gather for festival."   MoAmPo
   "Where is the nightingale."   APT-1; MoAmPo

Songs from the Great Feast to the Dead.   *Unknown.* APN-2, *tr. by* Edward William Nelson

Songs from the Society of the Mystic Animals.   Richard Johnny John, Jerome Rothenberg *and* Ian Tyson.
   Two Songs About a Dead Person or a Mole—Whichever It Was.   PFTM-1

Songs in the Desert! songs of husky breath.   James Thomson.   SacPr

Songs of Abuse: To Stanislaus the Renegade.   Kofi Awoonor.   PML

Songs of an Other.   Robert Duncan.   PmAP

Songs of birds which leaps from leaf to leaf, The.   Canto de li Augei di Frunda in Frunda, Il.   Matteo Maria Boiardo.   WoPoe, *tr. by* Peter Russell

Songs of Conn the Fool, The.   Fannie Stearns Gifford.
   Moon Folly.   RACG

Songs of Degrees.   Louis Zukofsky.
   "William / Carlos / Williams / alive!"   PFTM-1

Songs of Depression.   Yang Wan-li. *tr. by* Jonathan Chaves
   "I don't feel like reading another book."   ColAnChi, *tr. by* Jonathan Chaves

Songs of Education.   G. K. Chesterton.
   Geography.   OBSV
   History.   OBSV

Songs of Experience.   William Blake.
   "Ah Sun-flower! weary of time."   NAEL-6v2; NAEL-7v2; NIP-4; NOBRP; NoP-4; NoP-5; NPBRoP; NPeEn; PoPoPo; TFi; WaAnP; WeW-3
   Angel, The.   RACG
   Chimney Sweeper, The.   BrAP; NAEL-6v2; NAEL-7v2; NAWM-7v2; NPBRoP
   Clod & the Pebble, The.   NAEL-6v1; NAEL-7v2; NoP-4; NoP-5; NPBRoP; NPeEn; OxAEP-2; OxBEV; TFi
   "Cruelty has a Human heart."   ChIV-1; NAEL-6v2; NAEL-7v2; NoP-4; NoP-5
   Earth's Answer.   ChIV-1; NAEL-6v2; NAEL-7v2; NAWM-7v2; NOBRP; NPBRoP
   (Fly, The.)   NOBRP; NOxBChV; NPBRoP; OxAEP-2
   Garden of Love, The.   ItP; NAEL-6v2; NAEL-7v2; NoP-4; NoP-5; NPBRoP; NPeEn; OBGa; OxAEP-2; OxBEV; PoPoPo; TFi; TRP
   (Hear the Voice.)   OBEV
   Holy Thursday [2].   BrAP; NAEL-6v2; NAEL-7v2; NOBRP; NoP-4; NoP-5; NPBRoP
   (Holy Thursday [Experience].)   NOxBChV
   Human Abstract, The.   NAEL-6v2; NAEL-7v2; NOBRP; NPBRoP; OxAEP-2
   Infant Sorrow.   IJHIL; NAEL-6v2; NAEL-7v2; NPBRoP; OxAEP-2; OxBEV; PoPoPo
   Introduction.   ChIV-1; NAEL-6v2; NAEL-7v2; NAWM-7v2; NOBRP; NoP-4; NoP-5; NPBRoP; NPeEn; OxBEV; TFi
   Lily, The.   NOBRP
   Little Fly.   NAEL-6v2; NAEL-7v2; NBLV
   Little Girl Found, The.   NOBRP
   Little Girl Lost, The.   NOBRP
   Little Vagabond, The.   NBLV; OBSV
   London.   BrAP; CABP; ClHu; HeIP-4; IJHIL; NAEL-6v2; NAEL-7v2; NAWM-7v2; NIL-7; NIP-4; NOBRP; NoP-4; NoP-5; NPBRoP; NPeEn; OxAEP-2; OxBEV; PoPoPo; TFi; TRP; WeW-3
   My Pretty Rose-Tree.   NAEL-6v2; NAEL-7v2; NOBRP; NPBRoP
   Nurse's Song.   NPBRoP; PtR
   Poison Tree, A.   NAEL-6v2; NAEL-7v2; NoP-4; NoP-5; NPBRoP; NPeEn; OxAEP-2; OxBEV; SoSe-8; TFi; WaAnP; WeW-3
   School-Boy, The.   OxAEP-2
   Sick Rose, The.   BrAP; CABP; ClHu; HeIP-4; NAEL-6v2; NAEL-7v2; NAWM-7v2; NIL-7; NIP-4; NOBRP; NoP-4; NoP-5; NPBRoP; NPeEn; OPOU; OxAEP-2; OxBEV; PoPoPo; SoSe-8; TFi; TRP; WaAnP; WeW-3
   To Tirzah.   NAEL-6v2; NAEL-7v2
   Tyger, The.   BBASP; BrAP; BRP; ChAP; ClHu; CtM; HeIP-4; ITBLP; MakPoe; NAEL-6v2; NAEL-7v2; NAWM-7v2; NIL-7; NIP-4; NOBRP; NoP-4; NoP-5; NOxBChV; NPBRoP; NPeEn; OBEV; OPOU; OxBEV; PoPoPo; SoSe-8; TFi; WaAnP; WHSW

Songs of Fairly Utter Despair.   Samuel Hoffenstein.
   "Now, alas, it is too late."   OBCoV

Songs of Five Friends. Yun Sŏndo. CATKP, *tr. by* Peter H. Lee
"Flowers bloom when it is warm." CATKP, *tr. by* Peter H. Lee
"How many friends have I? Count them." CATKP, *tr. by* Peter H. Lee
"Small but floating high." CATKP, *tr. by* Peter H. Lee
"They say the color of clouds is fine." CATKP, *tr. by* Peter H. Lee
"Why do flowers fade so soon." CATKP, *tr. by* Peter H. Lee
"You are not a tree." CATKP, *tr. by* Peter H. Lee
Songs of Flying Dragons. *Various authors.*
"Anxious only to fulfill the royal clause." CATKP, *tr. by* Peter H. Lee
"Because he loved men and sought their welfare." CATKP, *tr. by* Peter H. Lee
"Because his bright nature." CATKP, *tr. by* Peter H. Lee
"Because robbers poisoned the people." CATKP, *tr. by* Peter H. Lee
"Because the govenment burdened the people." CATKP, *tr. by* Peter H. Lee
"Because the wolves wrought havoc." CATKP, *tr. by* Peter H. Lee
"Brothers rebelled against one another, The." CATKP, *tr. by* Peter H. Lee
"Even though they were rebellious." CATKP, *tr. by* Peter H. Lee
"He battled against the king's enemy." CATKP, *tr. by* Peter H. Lee
"He did not boast of his natural gifts." CATKP, *tr. by* Peter H. Lee
"He had many to help him." CATKP, *tr. by* Peter H. Lee
"He hit the backs of forty tailed deer." CATKP, *tr. by* Peter H. Lee
"He opened the four borders." CATKP, *tr. by* Peter H. Lee
"He shot six roebucks." CATKP, *tr. by* Peter H. Lee
"He was consistent from beginning to end." CATKP, *tr. by* Peter H. Lee
"Heaven gave him courage and wisdom." CATKP, *tr. by* Peter H. Lee
"Heaven sent a genius." CATKP, *tr. by* Peter H. Lee
"His arrow was huge beyond compare." CATKP, *tr. by* Peter H. Lee
"His nature being one with Heaven." CATKP, *tr. by* Peter H. Lee
"It was a polo match played by royal order." CATKP, *tr. by* Peter H. Lee
"Kind and selfless to his brothers." CATKP, *tr. by* Peter H. Lee
"Korea's six dragons flew in the sky." CATKP, *tr. by* Peter H. Lee
"Many slandered him." CATKP, *tr. by* Peter H. Lee
"Millennium ago, A." CATKP, *tr. by* Peter H. Lee
"On Mount Chorae he struck two roebucks." CATKP, *tr. by* Peter H. Lee
"Seeing the bodies lying in heaps." CATKP, *tr. by* Peter H. Lee
"Seven pinecones." CATKP, *tr. by* Peter H. Lee
"Though he was busy with war." CATKP, *tr. by* Peter H. Lee
"Tree, whose roots are deep, The." CATKP, *tr. by* Peter H. Lee
"Upon receiving an old scholar." CATKP, *tr. by* Peter H. Lee
"Wishing to entrust him with a great task." CATKP, *tr. by* Peter H. Lee
"Your four ancestors never enjoyed peace." CATKP, *tr. by* Peter H. Lee
"Zealous to deliver the suffering people." CATKP, *tr. by* Peter H. Lee
Songs of Good Hope, The. Michele Leggott. VaPo
Songs of Innocence. William Blake. NAEL-7v2
Chimney Sweeper, The. BrAP; HeIP-4; ItP; NAEL-6v2; NAEL-7v2; NAWM-7v2; NPBRoP; OxAEP-2; SoSe-8; TFi
Cradle Song, A. OBCP
Divine Image, The. BBASP; ChAP; InvLi; NAEL-6v2; NAEL-7v2; NOBRP; NoP-4; NoP-5; NPBRoP; OxBEV; WaAnP
Dream, A. NOBRP
Echoing [*or* Ecchoing] Green, The. AmFaPo; NAEL-6v2; NAEL-7v2; NPBRoP; OxAEP-2
"Father, father, where are you going?" NoP-4; NoP-5; WaAnP
Holy Thursday [1]. BrAP; GoPo; NAEL-6v2; NAEL-7v2; NAWM-7v2; NOBRP; NoP-4; NoP-5; NPBRoP; NPeEn; TFi
(Holy Thursday [Innocence].) NOxBChV
Infant Joy. NPBRoP; OxAEP-2; PoPoPo
(Introduction.) NAEL-6v2; NAEL-7v2; NAWM-7v2; NOBRP; NoP-5; NPBRoP
Lamb, The. BrAP; ChIV-2; HeIP-4; ITBLP; NAEL-6v2; NAEL-7v2; NAWM-7v2; NIL-7; NIP-4; NOBRP; NoP-4; NoP-5; NPBRoP; OxAEP-2; PoPoPo; SoSe-8; TFi; TRP; WaAnP
(Laughing Song.) NPBRoP
Little Black Boy, The. AmFaPo; CABP; ChAP; HeIP-4; NAEL-6v2; NAEL-7v2; NAWM-7v2; NOBRP; NoP-4; NoP-5; OBEV; PoPoPo; TFi
Little Boy Found, The. NoP-4; NoP-5; WaAnP
Little Girl Found, The. NOBRP
Little Girl Lost, The. NOBRP
Night. ITBLP; OBEV
Nurse's Song. NAEL-6v2; NAEL-7v2; NPBRoP; RACG
On Another's Sorrow. InvLi; OxAEP-2
Piping Down the Valleys Wild. ChAP; ClHu; HeIP-4; NoP-4; NOxBChV; SoSe-8; TFi
(Reeds of Innocence.) OBEV
Shepherd, The. ChAP; NPBRoP
Spring. NOxBChV
"When the green woods laugh with the voice of joy." NBLV

Songs of Innocence. Attila József. IQMS, *tr. by* Thomas Kabdebo and Anton N. Nyerges
Songs of Joy. W. H. Davies. MoBrPo
Songs of My Soul. Juan Chi.
"Confucianist is versed in the Six Arts, The." ColAnChi
"Elder lives by the side of the river, An." ColAnChi
"Hibiscus grows lushly on the grave mounds, The." ColAnChi
"It is the middle of the night—I cannot sleep." ColAnChi
"Lucent dew congeals into frost, The." ColAnChi
"My steps lead me to a junction of three roads." ColAnChi
"Whether one is eminent or humble depends on Fate." ColAnChi
Songs of Rescue. Jacques Dupin.
"From a thread in space, endless and unbroken. Without unravelling." VCWP
Songs of Seven. Jean Ingelow.
Seven Time Six. Giving in Marriage. TreFP
Seven Times Three. Love. TreFP
Songs of Sorrow. Kofi Awoonor. HBAPE
Songs of Spirits. *Unknown.* APN-2, *tr. by* Jeremiah Curtin
Songs of the Arapaho. *Arapaho Oral Tradition.* APN-2 *Fr.* Ghost-Dance Songs.
Songs of the Fruits and Sweets of Childhood. Lorna Goodison. VCWP
Songs of the Kiowa. *Unknown.* APN-2 *Fr.* Ghost-Dance Songs.
Songs of the Kwakiutl Indians. *Unknown. tr. by* Franz Boas
Girl's Song, A. APN-2
Love Song. APN-2
Warsong of the Kwakiutl. APN-2
Songs of the Paiute. *Unknown.* APN-2 *Fr.* Ghost-Dance Songs.
Songs of the Psyche. Thomas Kinsella.
Songs of the Sacred Mysteries. *Unknown.* APN-2, *tr. by* Alfred Longley Riggs
Songs of the Sioux. *Sioux Oral Tradition.* APN-2 *Fr.* Ghost-Dance Songs.
Songs of the Squatters. Robert, Viscount Sherbrooke Lowe. NOBAu
"Commissioner bet me a pony, The—I won, The." NOBAu
"Gum has no shade, The." NOBAu
Songs of the Transformed. Margaret Atwood.
Rat Song. NIP-4
Siren Song. NIL-7; NIP-4; PoA 2002; WeW-3
Songs of the Valley. John Koethe. BAP-01
Songs to Joannes. Mina Loy. *See* Love Songs to Joannes.
Songs We Fought For, The. Walter McDonald. SwNoth
Song—Written at the North. Samuel Henry Dickson. APN-1
Sonido Ink(quieto). Brenda Cárdenas and Aidé Rodriguez. BRtP
Son[ne], The. George Herbert. AngWePo
Sonnent / les criées. Tahar Bekri. YaTCFP *Fr.* Retour en Tunisie.
Sonnet. William Browne. *See* Song: "For her gait, if she be walking."
Sonnet. Willem Kloos. TuT, *tr. by* Tony Curtis and Tony Curtis
Sonnet. John Milton. *See* When the Assault Was Intended to the City.
Sonnet. John Milton. *See* To Mr. Cyriack Skinner upon His Blindness.
Sonnet. John Milton. *See* To Cyriack Skinner.
Sonnet. John Milton. *See* To Mr. Lawrence.
Sonnet. John Milton. *See* On His Deceased Wife.
Sonnet. John Milton. *See* Sonnet: On the Religious Memorie of Mrs. Catherine Thomason My Christian Friend Deceas'd Decem. 1646.
Sonnet. Caroline Elizabeth Norton. IrLP
Sonnet: "Alexis, here she stayed; among these pines." William Drummond of Hawthornden. NOSC
(Spring Bereaved.) OBEV
Sonnet: "All we need is fourteen lines, well, thirteen now." Billy Collins. CAP-8; PoA 2002
Sonnet: "Alone, in mourning, wearing an archaic black gown." J. V. Foix. WoPoe, *tr. by* M. L. Rosenthal
Sonnet: "Amid these fragments of heroic days." James Russell Lowell. NCAP
Sonnet: "And so, as this great sphere (now turning slow)." Frederick Goddard Tuckerman. ColAP; WaAnP
Sonnet: "As in a duskie [*or* dusky] and tempestuous night." William Drummond of Hawthornden. NOSC; OxAEP-1
Sonnet: "As the dream a consciousness adored." Karen Volkman. IAoNAP
Sonnet: "Beauty of songs your absence I should not show." Bernadette Mayer. PmAP
Sonnet: "Blueness of the hour, The." Frank O'Hara. AHA
Sonnet: "Brown is the flat gestation of a maze." Karen Volkman. IAoNAP
Sonnet: "Caught—the bubble." Elizabeth Bishop. APT-2; WaAnP
Sonnet: "Crumbled rock of London is dripping under, The." Roy Fuller. PoA 2002

Sonnet: "Dost see how unregarded now." Sir John Suckling. BASC; CavPo; NOSC

Sonnet: "Farewell, Love." Sir Thomas Wyatt. AEP

Sonnet: "Five a.m. on East Fourteenth I'm out to eat." Tom Clark. AHA

Sonnet: "Give me a cottage on some Cambrian wild." Henry Kirke White. CenSon

Sonnet: "Here lies the noble flesh of Spartacus the knave." Daniel Casper von Lohenstein. GePo *Fr.* Arminius.

Sonnet: "How do I hate you? Let me count the ways." Stanley J. Sharpless. UV

Sonnet: "How many times night's silent queene her face." William Drummond of Hawthornden. NPeEn

Sonnet: "I am an honest man." Octavio Armand. TCLAP, *tr. by* Jason Shinder

Sonnet: "I am in need of music that would flow." Elizabeth Bishop. CtM; PoCu

Sonnet: "I dreamed the nymph that o'er my fancy reigns." Sir William Alexander, Earl of Stirling. NOSC *Fr.* Aurora.

Sonnet: "I had no thought of violets of late." Alice Moore Dunbar-Nelson. InGu

Sonnet: "I hate the Spring in parti-coloured vest." Mary Locke. CenSon

Sonnet: "I saw magic on a green country road." Michael Hartnett. PBCIP *Fr.* Thirteen Sonnets.

Sonnet: "I still shall smile and go my careless way." Mamie A. Richardson. LW

Sonnet: "I that erstwhile the world's sweet air did draw." George Wither. NOSC *Fr.* Shephe[a]rd's Hunting, The.

Sonnet: "I wandered out a while agone." George Wither. NOSC *Fr.* Fair Virtue, the Mistress of Philarete [Selections from anthologies].

Sonnet: "If it be night . . . ." Alec Brock Stevenson. FuPo

Sonnet: "If love is chaste, what bears adultery?" Sibylla Schwarz. GePo, *tr. by* George C. Schoolfield

Sonnet: "If there were any power in human love." Frances Anne Kemble. VWP

Sonnet: "Invisible in vernal pools." Michele Glazer. IAoNAP

Sonnet: "Lease of my leaving, heartfelt lack, what does." Karen Volkman. IAoNAP

Sonnet: "Lifting whither, cycle of the sift." Karen Volkman. IAoNAP

Sonnet: "Light-spring, oh sun, in light our wedding joys immure." Daniel Casper von Lohenstein. GePo *Fr.* Arminius.

Sonnet: "Love is a babe as you know and when you." Bernadette Mayer. OxBoAm

Sonnet: "Man talking to his ex-wife on the phone, A." Robert Hass. NAMCP V.2

Sonnet: "Master and the slave go hand in hand, The." Edwin Arlington Robinson. APN-2

Sonnet: "Morsels of my lifework: the story of a professional party hostess." D. A. Powell. NeAmPo

Sonnet: "My dream a drink with Lonnie Johnson we discuss the code." Ted Berrigan. NoAM *Fr.* Sonnets, The.

Sonnet: My Errors My Loves My Unlucky Star. Luís de Camões [*or* Camõens *or* Camoëns]. WoPoe, *tr. by* David Wevill

Sonnet: "My Galley Charged." Sir Thomas Wyatt. AEP; GSo

(My Galley [Charged with Forgetfulness].) NoP-5; WaAnP

Sonnet: "My God, where is that ancient heat towards Thee." George Herbert. NOSC

(Sonnet 1.) FSCP

Sonnet: "My love, if I write a song for you." Veronica Forrest-Thomson. EdScPo; HarvBoo; MoWP

Sonnet: "My meditation turns to thinking." Giorgio Baffo. EroLit, *tr. by* Wayland Young

Sonnet: "Never got, and never thought, and yet." Karen Volkman. IAoNAP

Sonnet: "Not if you crawled from there to here, you hear?" Eleanor Brown. BeAl

Sonnet: "Nothing was ever what it claimed to be." Karen Volkman. IAoNAP

Sonnet: "Now I see them sitting me before a mirror." Michael Palmer. HarvBoo; MakPoe

Sonnet: "Now the bat circles on the breeze of eve." Ann Radcliffe. CenSon

Sonnet: "Now you nerve. Flurred, avid as the raw." Karen Volkman. IAoNAP

Sonnet: "Nuns fret not at their convent's narrow room." William Wordsworth. BrAP; CenSon; GSo; NIL-7; NIP-4; NoP-4; OBEV

(Nuns Fret Not [at Their Convent's Narrow Room].) NoP-5; NPBRoP

Sonnet: "O thou who never harbored fear." Eloise Bibb. CBWP-4

Sonnet: "October's gold is dim—the forests rot." David Gray. OxAEP-2

Sonnet: "Of thee, kind boy, I ask no red and white." Sir John Suckling. BASC; CavPo; NoP-4; NoP-5; NOSC

Sonnet: "Oh! Death will find me, long before I tire." Rupert Brooke. NoP-4; NoP-5

(Sonnet: Death Will Find Me.) MoBrPo

Sonnet: "Oh for a poet—for a beacon bright." Edwin Arlington Robinson. APN-2; NCAP

Sonnet: "O[h]! for some honest lover's ghost." Sir John Suckling. BASC; CavPo; OxBEV

(Doubt of Martyrdom, A.) OBEV

Sonnet: "Premise, a solace—deciduous dress, A." Karen Volkman. IAoNAP

Sonnet: "Record is nothing, and the hero great." John Byrne Leicester Warren, 3d Baron De Tabley. OxBSo

Sonnet: "Scorn not the sonnet; critic, you have frowned." William Wordsworth. *See* Scorn Not the Sonnet [Critic, You Have Frowned].

Sonnet: "She took the dappled partridge flecked [*or* fleckt] with blood." Alfred Tennyson. NAEL-6v2

Sonnet: "Silver herring throbbed thick in my seine, The." Kenneth Leslie. IFF; OxBSo *Fr.* By Stubborn Stars.

Sonnet: "Sky we bear on our shoulders, heaven-height, The." Karen Volkman. IAoNAP

Sonnet: "Sleep, silence' child, sweet father of soft rest." William Drummond of Hawthornden. *See* Sleep, Silence' Child.

Sonnet: "Slide soft, fair forth, and make a crystal plain." William Drummond of Hawthornden. NOSC; OxBSo

Sonnet: "So long honey, don't ever come around again, I'm sick of you." Bernadette Mayer. OxBoAm

Sonnet: "Stranger, when o'er yon slant, warm field no cloud." Anna Seward. NOBRP

Sonnet: "Suns, she is all in all, I stood on a sea, The." İlhan Berk. NaPG, *tr. by* Talat Sait Halman

Sonnet: "Sure, Lord, there is enough in Thee to dry." George Herbert. NOSC

Sonnet: "Tell me[e] no more how fair[e] she[e] is." Henry King, Bishop of Chichester. OxBEV

Sonnet: "The long love." Sir Thomas Wyatt. *See* Long love that in my thought doth harbo[u]r, The.

Sonnet: "There are strange shadows fostered of the moon." Arthur Davison Ficke. TCAPo

Sonnet: "This ellipse, slip between seasons." Karen Volkman. IAoNAP

Sonnet: "This infant world has taken long to make." George Macdonald. SacPr

Sonnet: "This is for the afternoon we lay in the leaves." C. B. Trail. GoPo

Sonnet: "Thou poisonous laurel leaf, that in the soil." Frances Anne Kemble. SWaP

Sonnet: "Thousand apples you might put in your theories." Bernadette Mayer. PmAP

Sonnet 3: 'The sovereign beauty'. Edmund Spenser. AEP

Sonnet: "Tilt the placeless waver of this moving." Karen Volkman. IAoNAP

Sonnet: "To see a woman long oppressed by fear." Hayden Carruth. ErotSp *Fr.* Sonnets.

Sonnet: "To work away in art's traditional measure." Johann Wolfgang von Goethe. STV, *tr. by* John Frederick Nims

Sonnet: "Way the world is not, The." Bill Knott. PBCAP

Sonnet: "We often pass a night warm and intimate." Feng Chih. WoPoe, *tr. by* Ye Weilian [*or* Yeh Wei-lien *or* Wai-lim Yip]

Sonnet: "We will not whisper, we have found the place." Joseph Hilaire Pierre Belloc. MoBrPo

Sonnet: "Well, she told me I had an aura. 'What?' I said." Hayden Carruth. GifTon; StAl

Sonnet: "What is my lady like? thou fain would'st know." Frances Anne Kemble. SWaP

Sonnet: "What is this witness, the watching ages." Karen Volkman. IAoNAP

Sonnet: "When she walks by here." Petrarch. WoPoe, *tr. by* Nicholas Kilmer

Sonnet: "Winter deepening, the hay all in, The." Richard Wilbur. OxBSo

Sonnet: "Wisest of all men lies buried on this spot, The." Daniel Casper von Lohenstein. GePo *Fr.* Arminius.

Sonnet: "Women have loved before as I love now." Edna St. Vincent Millay. HeIP-4; NALW; NIL-7; PoA 2002

Sonnet: "Ye praise the humble: of the meek ye say." Sir Aubrey De Vere. SacPr

Sonnet: "You are the faintest freckles on the hide." Elinor Wylie. APT-1

Sonnet: "You jerk you didn't call me up." Bernadette Mayer. OxBoAm

Sonnet: "You know all those sonnets the ones where I said, I love you, well." Tom Devaney. AmPoNex

Sonnet: "You rose from our embrace and the small light spread." Hayden Carruth. ErotSp *Fr.* Sonnets.

Sonnet: "You were born; must die; were loved; must love." Stephen Spender. MoBrPo

Sonnet: "Your selfe the Sonne, and I the meltinge froste." Sir Arthur Gorges. OxBSo

Sonnet, The. Richard Watson Gilder. APN-2

Sonnet, The. Ella Wheeler Wilcox. APN-2

Sonnet, A: "O lovely O most charming pug." Marjory Fleming. NBLV

Sonnet; A Still Place. Barry Cornwall. NOBRP

Sonnet, A: "Two voices are there: one is of the deep." James Kenneth Stephen. CABP; UV

Sonnet, A: "When you see millions of the mouthless dead." Charles Hamilton Sorley. EdScPo; FaBoWar; NPeEn; OBWP; OxBSo; PoAgWa; PoWW

Sonnet Addressed to Henry III on the Death of Thulène, the King's Fool. Jean Passerat. WoPoe, tr. by Richmond Lattimore

Sonnet Addressed to My Mother. Mary Tighe. NoP-4

Sonnet Against Nuclear Weapons. Jane Miller. ExTi

Sonnet All of a Sudden, A. Félix Lope de Vega Carpio. SpanPo, tr. by Dorren Bell

Sonnet and Duet for Flapper and Poet. Alexander Pomerantz. Prolet, tr. by Amelia Glaser

Sonnet Around Stephanie. Lee Ann Brown. BAP-01

Sonnet at Three-Speed. J. Lorraine Brown. ArBi

Sonnet Composed on a Journey Homeward; the Author Having Received Intelligence of the Birth of a Son, 20 September 1796. Samuel Taylor Coleridge. OxBSo

(Composed on a Journey Homeward; the Author Having Received Intelligence of the Birth of a Son.) NPBRoP

[Sonnet] Conclusive. Mary Robinson. CenSon; RWP

44. Sonnet Conclusive. Mary Robinson. NPBRoP Fr. Sappho and Phaon.

Sonnet: Death Warnings. Francisco de Quevedo y Villegas. OxBEV; WoPoe, tr. by John Masefield

Sonnet: Death Will Find Me. Rupert Brooke. See Sonnet: "Oh! Death will find me, long before I tire."

Sonnet: England in 1819. Percy Bysshe Shelley. See England in 1819.

Sonnet for a Picture. Algernon Charles Swinburne. OxBSo; UV Fr. Heptalogia, The.

Sonnet for an SR-71. P. L. Delano. OtW

Sonnet for Christmas. Judith Wright. LW

Sonnet for July. Rosemerry Wahtola Trommer. GeoH

Sonnet for Minimalists. Mona Van Duyn. FFC; WeW-3

Sonnet for the End of a Sequence. Dorothy Parker. BrAP

Sonnet for the Season. Art Lange. PmAP

Sonnet 43. Eleanor Brown. MFPA

Sonnet IV. E. E. Cummings. ChIV-1; MoAmPo

Sonnet: [From the Italian of Dante.] Dante Alighieri to Guido Cavalcanti. Dante Alighieri. OBVE; WoPoe

Sonnet: How Life Too Is Sentimental. Gavin Ewart. StAl

Sonnet (III), The. John Addington Symonds. GSo

Sonnet in Primary Colors. Rita Dove. InoFa; PfS

Sonnet: In Time of Revolt. Rupert Brooke. OBCoV

Sonnet: Ingratitude. Anna Seward. CenSon

Sonnet Introductory. Mary Robinson. CenSon; RWP

1. Sonnet Introductory. Mary Robinson. NPBRoP Fr. Sappho and Phaon.

Sonnet is a moment's monument, A. Dante Gabriel Rossetti. BrAP; GSo; NAEL-6v2; NAEL-7v2; NIL-7; NoP-4; NoP-5 Fr. House of Life, The.

Sonnet is a world, where feelings caught, The. Sonnet (III), The. John Addington Symonds. GSo

Sonnet: Kamikaze: "Dawn and night of fighting, lovers like actual wars." Bernadette Mayer. FTOS

Sonnet: Lady, That in the Prime. John Milton. See Sonnet 9: "Ladie [or Lady], that in the prime of earliest youth."

Sonnet: Lift Not the Painted Veil. Percy Bysshe Shelley. CenSon; GSo; NOBRP

(Lift Not the Painted Veil.) NPBRoP

Sonnet Made upon the Groves near Merlou [or Merlow] Castle. Edward Herbert, 1st Baron Herbert of Cherbury. NOSC; NPeEn

Sonnet of a Gentleman. Alan Brownjohn. PML

Sonnet of Black Beauty. Edward Herbert, 1st Baron Herbert of Cherbury. NoP-5; NOSC

Sonnet of Sweet Complaint. Federico García Lorca. BLPSL, tr. by Rene de Costa, Rigas Kappatos and Eleni Paidoussi

Sonnet of Sweet Weeping. Federico García Lorca. CAGL Fr. Sonetos del Amor Oscuro [Sonnets of Dark Love].

Sonnet on a Family Picture. Thomas Edwards. CenSon

Sonnet on Chillon. Lord Byron. CenSon; GSo; NPBRoP

Sonnet on Famous and Familiar Sonnets and Experiences. Delmore Schwartz. TRP

Sonnet on Reading 'The Mountain Daisy' by Burns. Helen Maria Williams. NPBRoP

Sonnet [on the Death of Mr. Richard West]. Thomas Gray. BrAP; CenSon; NoP-4; OxBSo

(On the Death of Mr. Richard West.) GSo

Sonnet on the Death of the Man Who Invented Plastic Roses. Peter Meinke. PBCAP

Sonnet: On The Loss Of His Mistress. Sir Robert Aytoun. NOSC

Sonnet: On the Religious Memorie of Mrs. Catherine Thomason My Christian Friend Deceas'd Decem. 1646. John Milton. ChIV-2

(Sonnet.) OxAEP-1

Sonnet: On the River Tweed. Sir Robert Aytoun. NOSC

Sonnet one: "Supremely individual, flamboyant, proud." Arthur Nortje. TSAP

Sonnet: Political Greatness. Percy Bysshe Shelley. CenSon

Sonnet Reversed. Rupert Brooke. OxBSo

Sonnet Right off the Bat. Félix Lope de Vega Carpio. STV, tr. by John Frederick Nims

Sonnet sent to Blackness to Mr. John Welsch, by the Lady Culross, A. Elizabeth Melville, Lady Culross. EMWP

Sonnet 6. To the Torrid Zone. Helen Maria Williams. CenSon; NOBRP

(To the Torrid Zone.) NoP-4

Sonnet: Suppos'd to Be Written at Lemnos. Thomas Russell. NOBRP

Sonnet: Tattoo Tears. Sherman Alexie. PrTe; WaAnP

Sonnet 10: 'Unrighteous Lord of Love'. Edmund Spenser. AEP

Sonnet: That Sad and Joyful Dawn. Luis de Camões [or Camõens or Camoëns]. WoPoe, tr. by David Wevill

Sonnet: The Beautiful American Word, Sure. Delmore Schwartz. APT-2

Sonnet: The Ladies' Home Journal. Sandra M. Gilbert. See Ladies' Home Journal, The.

Sonnet: The Last Things. Gavin Ewart. OxBSo

Sonnet, to a Child. Wilfred Owen. NOxBChV

Sonnet to a Friend Who Asked How I Felt When the Nurse First Presented My Infant to Me. Samuel Taylor Coleridge. CenSon

Sonnet to a Negro in Harlem [with music]. Helene Johnson. APT-2; NIL-7; NIP-4; OxAAAP; SSLK

Sonnet: To a Portrait of Hart Crane. Allen Tate. GS

Sonnet to a Sonnet. Thomas Hood. CenSon

Sonnet to Britain. William Edmondstoune Aytoun. OxBSo

Sonnet to France On Her Present Exertions. Anna Laetitia Barbauld. RWP

Sonnet to Gath. Edna St. Vincent Millay. MoAmPo

Sonnet to Lake Leman. Lord Byron. CenSon; NPBRoP

Sonnet: To Mr. H. Lawes, on His Air[e]s. John Milton. See To Mr. H. Lawes On His Airs.

Sonnet to My First Born [with music]. Mary Weston Fordham. CBWP-2

Sonnet to My Mother. George Barker. OxBSo; RaBo

(To My Mother.) MakPoe; OxAEP-2; PoWW; PtR

Sonnet to Nothing. Thomas Beck. NOBRP

Sonnet to Sleep. John Keats. See To Sleep.

Sonnet: To Tartar, a Terrier Beauty. Thomas Lovell Beddoes. OxBSo

Sonnet to the Asshole. Paul Verlaine. CAGL, tr. by Alan Stone

Sonnet to the Imagination. Robin Becker. BodElec

Sonnet to the "Most Distinguished Chancellor" that Oxford Has Had. UV

Sonnet to the Noble Lady, the Lady Mary Wroth, A. Ben Jonson. NAEL-7v1; NoP-4; NoP-5

Sonnet to the River Lodon. Thomas, the Younger Warton. CenSon; OxBSo

(To the River Loden.) NPBRoP

Sonnet to the River Otter. Samuel Taylor Coleridge. CenSon; OxBSo

(To the River Otter.) NPBRoP

Sonnet, to the Same. Lord Byron. OxBSo

Sonnet to Twilight. Helen Maria Williams. CenSon Fr. Poems.

Sonnet to Valclusa. Thomas Russell. NOBRP

Sonnet to Vauxhall. Thomas Hood. NPeEn; OBCoV; OxBSo

Sonnet two: "I have drunk up nights and spent the days." Arthur Nortje. TSAP

Sonnet upon Sonnets, A. Robert Burns. GSo

Sonnet with Lock and Key. Jasper Bernes. IAoNAP

Sonnet Written at the Close of Spring [or Elegiac Sonnet]. Charlotte Smith. CenSon; RWP

(Written at the Close of Spring.) NAEL-6v2; NAEL-7v2; NPBRoP

Sonnet Written from an Eastern Apartment in the Bishop's Palace at Lichfield, Which Commands a View of Stowe Valley. Anna Seward. RWP

Sonnet Written in Keats' Endymion. Thomas Hood. NPBRoP

Sonnet. Written in the Church-Yard at Middleton in Sussex. Charlotte Smith. See Pressed by the Moon, Mute Arbitress of Tides.

Sonnet Written upon My Lord Admiral Seymour, A. John Harington. NoSic

Sonnet-Mantra of the Crickets. Ivan Metodiev. CSCBP Fr. Songs for Orphans Big and Small.

Sonnets. James Agee. MoAmPo

"Now stands our love on that still verge of day." APT-2

"So it begins. Adam is in his earth." APT-2

Sonnets. Hayden Carruth.

Sonnet. ErotSp

Sonnet. ErotSp

Sonnets. John Masefield.

"Is there a great green commonwealth of Thought." MoBrPo

Sonnets. George Santayana.
  Sonnet 3. APN-2; TCAPo
  Sonnet 5. APN-2
  Sonnet 25. APN-2
  Sonnet 43: The Candour of the gods is in thy gaze. APN-2
  Sonnet 48. APN-2
Sonnets. Anna Seward.
  "Behold that tree, in Autumn's dim decay." WoRP
  "On the fleet streams, the Sun, that late arose." WoRP
  "While one sere leaf, that parting autumn yields." WoRP
Sonnets. William Shakespeare.
  (Love's Not Time's Fool.) ITBLP
  Sonnet 1. HeIP-4; NAEL-6v1; NAEL-7v1; NoP-5; WaAnP
  Sonnet 2. HeIP-4; ItP; NoP-5; NoSic
  Sonnet 3. NAEL-6v1; NAEL-7v1; NoP-4; NoP-5
  Sonnet 5. AEP
  Sonnet 12. GSo; HeIP-4; NAEL-6v1; NAEL-7v1; NoP-5; NoSic; WoPoe
  Sonnet 15. AEP; CABP; ClHu; GSo; HeIP-4; NAEL-6v1; NAEL-7v1; NIL-7; NIP-4; NoP-5; NoSic; NPeEn; OBEV; OxAEP-1; OxBEV; OxBSo; PoPoPo; SoSe-8; TFi; TRP; WeW-3
  Sonnet 18. AEP; AmFaPo; BLPJKO; BrAP; CABP; ClHu; CtM; HeIP-4; ITBLP; MakPoe; NAEL-6v1; NAEL-7v1; NIL-7; NoP-5; NoSic; NPeEn; OBEV; OxBEV; OxBSo; PoPoPo; TFi; WaAnP; WeW-3
  Sonnet 19. HeIP-4; NAEL-6v1; NAEL-7v1; NoSic; OxAEP-1; PBRV
  Sonnet 20. CAGL; HeIP-4; NAEL-6v1; NAEL-7v1; NoP-4; NoP-5; NoSic; OxAEP-1; PBRV; WaAnP
  Sonnet 21. HeIP-4
  Sonnet 23. CABP; ItP; NoSic
  Sonnet 25. FaBoWar; GoPo; OxAEP-1
  Sonnet 27. AWTN; CAGL; HeIP-4; NoSic
  Sonnet 28. AWTN
  Sonnet 29. AEP; AmFaPo; BLPJKO; BrAP; GSo; HeIP-4; ITBLP; ItP; NAEL-6v1; NAEL-7v1; NoP-4; NoP-5; NoSic; OBEV; OPOU; OxAEP-1; PBRV; PoPoPo; TFi; WaAnP; WeW-3; WoPoe
  Sonnet 30. BrAP; CABP; ClHu; GSo; HeIP-4; NAEL-6v1; NAEL-7v1; NoP-5; NoSic; OBEV; OxAEP-1; PoPoPo; TFi; WaAnP
  Sonnet 31. OBEV
  Sonnet 33. NAEL-7v1; NIL-7; NIP-4; NoP-4; NoP-5; NoSic; OxAEP-1; TFi; WeW-3
  Sonnet 34. HeIP-4; OxAEP-1
  Sonnet 35. HeIP-4; NAEL-6v1; NAEL-7v1; NoP-5; NoSic; OxAEP-1; PBRV; RaF
  Sonnet 36. HeIP-4; PBRV
  Sonnet 37. GoPo
  Sonnet 40. HeIP-4; OxAEP-1
  Sonnet 41. OxAEP-1
  Sonnet 42. HeIP-4; OxAEP-1
  Sonnet 46. HeIP-4
  Sonnet 49. OxAEP-1
  Sonnet 50. OxAEP-1
  Sonnet 52. OxAEP-1
  Sonnet 53. NoSic; OBEV; OxAEP-1; OxBEV
  Sonnet 54. AEP; OBEV
  Sonnet 55. AEP; CABP; CtM; GSo; HeIP-4; NAEL-6v1; NAEL-7v1; NIL-7; NIP-4; NoP-4; NoP-5; NoSic; NPeEn; OxAEP-1; OxBSo; PBRV; WaAnP
  Sonnet 56. PBRV
  Sonnet 57. CAGL; NoSic; OBEV
  Sonnet 59. TreFP
  Sonnet 60. CABP; NAEL-6v1; NAEL-7v1; NIL-7; NIP-4; NoP-5; NoSic; NPeEn; OxAEP-1; OxBEV; OxBSo; PoPoPo; TFi; TreFP
  Sonnet 61. AWTN; CAGL
  Sonnet 62. OxAEP-1
  Sonnet 64. AEP; HeIP-4; NoSic; OxAEP-1; TreFP
  Sonnet 65. AEP; NAEL-6v1; NAEL-7v1; NoP-5; NoSic; OxAEP-1; OxBSo; RaBo; TFi; TreFP
  Sonnet 66. CABP; NoSic; OxAEP-1; PoPoPo; TFi; WeW-3
  Sonnet 70. OxAEP-1
  Sonnet 71. HeIP-4; InoFa; NAEL-6v1; NAEL-7v1; NoP-5; NoSic; OxAEP-1; TFi; WaAnP
  Sonnet 72. OxAEP-1
  Sonnet 73. AEP; BrAP; CABP; ClHu; HeIP-4; ItP; NAEL-6v1; NAEL-7v1; NIL-7; NIP-4; NoP-4; NoP-5; NoSic; OBEV; OxBSo; SoSe-8; TFi; WeW-3
  Sonnet 74. NAEL-6v1; NAEL-7v1; OxAEP-1; PBRV; WaAnP
  Sonnet 76. NoP-5; NoSic; OxAEP-1
  Sonnet 77. HeIP-4
  Sonnet 78. AEP

  Sonnet 80. CAGL; OxAEP-1
  Sonnet 81. OxAEP-1
  Sonnet 86. CABP; NoSic; OxAEP-1; OxBEV
  Sonnet 87. CAGL; NAEL-6v1; NAEL-7v1; NoP-5; NoSic; OBEV; OxAEP-1; TFi
  Sonnet 88. OxAEP-1
  Sonnet 89. OxAEP-1
  Sonnet 90. NoSic; OBEV; OxAEP-1; RaF
  Sonnet 91. WaAnP
  Sonnet 94. CABP; NAEL-6v1; NAEL-7v1; NIL-7; NoP-4; NoP-5; NoSic; NPeEn; OBEV; OxAEP-1; OxBEV; OxBSo; PBRV; TRP; WoPoe
  Sonnet 95. HeIP-4
  Sonnet 97. AEP; HeIP-4; NAEL-6v1; NAEL-7v1; NoP-5; NoSic; OBEV; OxAEP-1; TFi
  Sonnet 98. NAEL-6v1; NAEL-7v1; NoSic; OBEV; OxAEP-1
  Sonnet 99. OxAEP-1
  Sonnet 100. TreFP
  Sonnet 102. OBEV
  Sonnet 104. HeIP-4; NoSic; OBEV; OxAEP-1
  Sonnet 106. NAEL-6v1; NAEL-7v1; NoP-5; NoSic; OBEV; OxAEP-1; WoPoe
  Sonnet 107. NAEL-6v1; NAEL-7v1; NoP-5; NoSic; OxAEP-1
  Sonnet 108. PBRV; TreFP
  Sonnet 109. OBEV; OxAEP-1
  Sonnet 110. AEP; NAEL-6v1; NAEL-7v1; NoSic; OxAEP-1
  Sonnet 111. OxAEP-1
  Sonnet 116. AEP; BLPJKO; BrAP; CABP; ClHu; GSo; HeIP-4; NAEL-6v1; NAEL-7v1; NIL-7; NIP-4; NoP-5; NoSic; NPeEn; OBEV; OxAEP-1; OxBEV; OxBSo; PoPoPo; PtR; SoSe-8; TFi; TRP; WaAnP; WeW-3
  Sonnet 119. OxAEP-1
  Sonnet 120. OxAEP-1
  Sonnet 121. CAGL; NoSic; OxAEP-1; PBRV
  Sonnet 123. OxAEP-1
  Sonnet 124. NoSic; NPeEn; PBRV
  Sonnet 125. AEP; NoSic
  Sonnet 126. HeIP-4; NAEL-6v1; NAEL-7v1; NoP-5
  Sonnet 127. NAEL-6v1; NAEL-7v1; OxAEP-1
  Sonnet 128. NAEL-6v1; NAEL-7v1; OxAEP-1
  Sonnet 129. BrAP; CABP; ErotSp; HeIP-4; NAEL-6v1; NAEL-7v1; NIL-7; NIP-4; NoP-5; NoSic; NPeEn; OBEV; OxAEP-1; OxBEV; PBRV; PoPoPo; TFi; WoPoe
  Sonnet 130. AEP; CABP; HeIP-4; NAEL-6v1; NAEL-7v1; NIL-7; NIP-4; NoP-5; NoSic; OxAEP-1; OxBEV; PoPoPo; SoSe-8; TFi; WaAnP; WeW-3
  Sonnet 132. OxAEP-1; WaAnP
  Sonnet 133. OxAEP-1
  Sonnet 134. HeIP-4; OxAEP-1
  Sonnet 135. NAEL-6v1; NAEL-7v1; NoP-5; PBRV
  Sonnet 138. AmFaPo; CABP; HeIP-4; NAEL-6v1; NAEL-7v1; NoP-4; NoP-5; NoSic; NPeEn; OxAEP-1; OxBEV; PBRV; SoSe-8
  Sonnet 140. NoSic
  Sonnet 141. HeIP-4; OxAEP-1
  Sonnet 144. AEP; HeIP-4; NAEL-6v1; NAEL-7v1; NIL-7; NoP-5; OxBSo; PBRV
  Sonnet 146. BrAP; HeIP-4; NAEL-6v1; NAEL-7v1; NoP-4; NoP-5; OBEV; OxAEP-1; SacPr; TFi; WaAnP
  Sonnet 147. AEP; NAEL-6v1; NAEL-7v1; OxAEP-1
  Sonnet 150. OxAEP-1
  Sonnet 151. HeIP-4; NoSic; OxAEP-1; WaAnP
  Sonnet 152. HeIP-4
Sonnets: First Series, 1854–1860. Frederick Goddard Tuckerman.
  6. TCAPo
  7. APN-2; OxBoAm
  8. APN-2
  10. APN-2; GSo; NoP-4; OxBoAm; OxBSo
  12. OxBSo
  22. APN-2
Sonnets: Second Series, 1854–1860. Frederick Goddard Tuckerman.
  6. TCAPo
  7. APN-2; NoP-4; TCAPo
Sonnets: A Sequence on Profane Love. George Henry Boker.
  Sonnet 24. APN-2
  Sonnet 25. APN-2
  Sonnet 42. APN-2
  Sonnet 165. APN-2
  Sonnet 188. APN-2
  Sonnet 280. APN-2

Sonnets at Christmas. Allen Tate. APT-2
  "Ah, Christ, I love you rings to the wild sky." ChrPo
  "This is the day His hour of life draws near." ChrPo
Sonnets Attempted in the Manner of Contemporary Writers. Samuel Taylor
    Coleridge.
  On a Ruined House in a Romantic Country. CenSon
  "Pensive at eve on the hard world I mus'd [or mused]." CenSon
  To Simplicity. CenSon
Sonnets, Devotional and Memorial. Felicia Dorothea Hemans.
  Mountain Sanctuaries. CenSon
  Olive Tree, The. CenSon
Sonnets for Roberta (1954). John Hewitt.
  "How have I served you? I have let you waste." IrLP; PNI
  "If I had given you that love and care." PNI
Sonnets for Stan Gage (1945–1992). Sascha Feinstein. SeSe
Sonnets for the Novachord. "Ern Malley." BMAP
Sonnets from a Lock Box. Anna Hempstead Branch.
  "Around this rod my writhing self might twist." APT-1
  "I say that words are men and when we spell." APT-1; NALW
  "I used to think . . . number was fixed and still." APT-1
  "Into the void behold my shuddering flight,.." NALW
  "What witchlike spell weaves here its deep design." APT-1; NALW
Sonnets from an Ungrafted Tree. Edna St. Vincent Millay. NALW
  1. ColAP; NALW
  2. NALW
  3. NALW
  4. NALW
  5. NALW
  6. NALW
  7. NALW
  8. NALW
  9. NALW
  10. NALW
  11. NALW
  12. NALW
  13. NALW
  14. NALW
  15. NALW
  16. NALW
  17. APT-1; InoFa; NALW; NAMCP V.1
Sonnets from Greece. Trumbull Stickney. APN-1
  Mt. Lykaion. NAAPv.2
Sonnets from Scotland. Edwin Morgan.
  Coin, The. NePenScot
Sonnets from the Portuguese. Elizabeth Barrett Browning. CenSon
  Sonnet 1. CenSon; NoP-4; NoP-5; OBEV; OxAEP-2; PoPoPo
  Sonnet 2. CenSon
  Sonnet 3. CABP; CenSon; OBEV; OxAEP-2
  Sonnet 4. CenSon; OxAEP-2; VWP
  Sonnet 5. CenSon; LW; NALW; PEW; VWP
  Sonnet 6. CenSon; LW; OBEV; OxAEP-2; PtR
  Sonnet 7. CenSon
  Sonnet 8. CenSon; OxAEP-2
  Sonnet 9. CenSon
  Sonnet 10. CenSon; OxAEP-2
  Sonnet 11. CenSon
  Sonnet 12. CenSon
  Sonnet 13. CABP; CenSon; VWP; WaAnP
  Sonnet 14. CenSon; GSo; HeIP-4; LW; OBEV; OxAEP-2; OxBSo
  Sonnet 15. CenSon
  Sonnet 16. CenSon
  Sonnet 17. CenSon
  Sonnet 18. CenSon; OxBSo
  Sonnet 19. CenSon
  Sonnet 20. CenSon
  Sonnet 22. BrAP; CenSon; LW; NAEL-6v2; NAEL-7v2; NALW; OBEV
  Sonnet 21. CenSon; NAEL-6v2; NAEL-7v2; OxBSo
  Sonnet 23. CenSon
  Sonnet 24. CenSon
  Sonnet 25. CenSon
  Sonnet 26. CenSon
  Sonnet 27. CenSon
  Sonnet 28. CenSon; OxAEP-2
  Sonnet 29. CenSon; PEW
  Sonnet 30. CenSon
  Sonnet 31. CenSon

  Sonnet 32. CenSon; NAEL-6v2; NAEL-7v2
  Sonnet 33. CenSon
  Sonnet 34. CenSon
  Sonnet 35. CenSon
  Sonnet 36. CenSon
  Sonnet 37. CenSon
  Sonnet 38. CenSon; ITBLP; LW
  Sonnet 39. CenSon
  Sonnet 40. CenSon
  Sonnet 41. CenSon
  Sonnet 43. AmFaPo; BrAP; CABP; CenSon; GSo; HeIP-4; ITBLP; MakPoe;
    NAEL-6v2; NAEL-7v2; NALW; NIL-7; NIP-4; NoP-4; NoP-5; OPOU;
    OxAEP-2; OxBSo; PoPoPo; TFi; UV; VWP; WaAnP
  Sonnet 44. CenSon; LW; OxBSo
Sonnets from the Series Relating to Edgar Allan Poe. Sarah Helen Whitman.
  "If thy sad heart, pining for human love." NAAPv.1
  "On our lone pathway bloomed no earthly hopes." NAAPv.1
Sonnets of Laura.
  Absence. CenSon
  Reproach. CenSon
  Veil, The. CenSon
Sonnets on the Statue of Mary, Queen of Scots, in the Luxembourg Gardens,
    Paris. Joseph Brodsky. tr. by Bernard Meares
  "In my declining years, in a land beyond the ocean." TCRusP, tr. by Bernard
    Meares
  "Mary, the Scots are sots in any case." TCRusP, tr. by Bernard Meares
  "Part of the field, A. Trumpets sound and two men enter." TCRusP, tr. by
    Bernard Meares
  "That which ripped an amazed scream." TCRusP, tr. by Bernard Meares
  "Will a mouth that's muttered its goodbyes." TCRusP, tr. by Bernard Meares
  "With a simple, truly unrebellious pen." TCRusP, tr. by Bernard Meares
Sonnets. Frederick Goddard Tuckerman.
  "And two I knew, an old man and a boy." APN-2
  "But war his overturning trumpet blew." APN-2
  "How oft in schoolboy-days, from the school's sway." APN-2; NoP-4;
    OxBoAm
  "Let me give something!—as the years unfold." APN-2
  "Let me give something!—though my spring be done." APN-2
  "Nor strange it is, to us who walk in bonds." APN-2; TCAPo
  Series 2, Sonnet 16. APN-2
  Series 2, Sonnet 17. APN-2
  Series 2, Sonnet 18. APN-2; TCAPo
  Series 2, Sonnet 21. GSo
  Series 2, Sonnet 23. APN-2
  Series 2, Sonnet 30. APN-2
  Series 3, Sonnet 4. APN-2; NoP-5
  Series 3, Sonnet 5. APN-2; NoP-5
  Series 3, Sonnet 6. NoP-5
  Series 3, Sonnet 10. APN-2; OxBoAm
Sonnets: "Starry flower, the flower-like stars that fade, The." Frederick
    Goddard Tuckerman. APN-2; NAAPv.1
(Sonnet.) ColAP
Sonnets, The. Ted Berrigan.
  "Academy of the future is opening its doors, The." NYP2; PFTM-2
  "(Clarity! clarity!) a semblance of motion, omniscience." PFTM-2
  "Dear Margie, hello. It is 5:15 a.m." PmAP
  "Each tree stands alone in stillness." NYP2
  Final Sonnet, A. FTOS; PFTM-2; PmAP; WaAnP
  "In Joe Brainard's collage its white arrow." OxBoAm
  "It is a human universe: & I." PFTM-2
  "It is night. You are asleep. And beautiful tears." NYP2; PFTM-2
  "It's 8:54 a.m. in Brooklyn it's the 28th [or 26th] of July [and]." NYP2;
    OxBoAm; PmAP
  "On the 15th day of November in the year of the motorcar." NYP2
  "Poem upon the page is as massive as, The." PFTM-2
  Real Live. FTOS
  Sonnet I. FTOS; NYP2
  Sonnet III. FTOS
  Sonnet XXX. NYP2
  Sonnet XXXIV. FTOS
  Sonnet XXXV. FTOS
  Sonnet LV. FTOS; NYP2; PFTM-2
  Sonnet LIX. NYP2
  Sonnet 70. FTOS; OxBoAm
  Sonnet LXXVI. NYP2
  Sonnet. NoAM

Sonnets to Aurelia.   Robert Malise Bowyer Nichols.   OBMV

Sonnets to be Written from Prison.   Robert Adamson.

"O to be in the news again—now as fashion runs."   BMAP

Sonnets to Bothwell.   Mary Stuart, Queen of Scots. *tr. by Unknown*

"For him also I powrit out mony teiris."   NePenScot, *tr. by Unknown*

Sonnets to Chris.   John Berryman.

"Astronomies and slangs to find you, dear."   AWTN

"Great citadels whereon the gold sun falls."   WaAnP

"Sometimes the night echoes to prideless wailing."   NoAM

Sonnet 115.   WaAnP

Sonnets to Helen.   Pierre de Ronsard. *tr. by Humbert Wolfe*

"By looking too long on your perfect face."   EroLit

"When you are old, at evening candle-lit."   WoPoe, *tr. by Humbert Wolfe*

Sonnets to James Clarence Mangan.   David Wheatley.

1.   NIrP

6.   NIrP

9.   NIrP

12.   NIrP

14.   NIrP

Sonnets to Laura.   Petrarch. *tr. by Joseph Auslander, Bernard Bergonzi, Morris Gilbert Bishop, Robert M. Durling, Edward Fitzgerald, Charlotte Smith, Henry Howard, Earl of Surrey, John Millington Synge, Arturo Vivante and Sir Thomas Wyatt*

"Apollo, if the sweet desire is still alive that inflamed you beside."   NAWM-7v1, *tr. by Robert M. Durling*

"Blest be the day, and blest the month and year."   NAWM-5v1; NAWM-7v1, *tr. by Joseph Auslander*

"Clear, fresh, sweet waters, where she who alone seems lady."   NAWM-7v1, *tr. by Robert M. Durling*

Complaint of a Lover Rebuked.   HeIP-4; OBVE, *tr. by Henry Howard, Earl of Surrey*

Description of the Contrarious Passions in a Lover.   OBVE, *tr. by Sir Thomas Wyatt*

"Eyes that drew from me such fervent praise, The."   NAWM-5v1

"Father in heaven, after each lost day."   NAWM-5v1; NAWM-7v1, *tr. by Bernard Bergonzi*

Galley, The.   OBVE; OxBEV; WeW-3, *tr. by Sir Thomas Wyatt*

"Go, grieving rimes of mine, to that hard stone."   NAWM-5v1; NAWM-7v1, *tr. by Morris Gilbert Bishop*

"Great is my envy of you, earth, in your greed."   NAWM-5v1, *tr. by Morris Gilbert Bishop*

He is Jealous of the Heavens and the Earth.   MoBrPo, *tr. by John Millington Synge*

He Understands the Great Cruelty of Death.   OBMV; OxBEV; WoPoe, *tr. by John Millington Synge*

"In the years of her age the most beautiful."   OBMV, *tr. by John Millington Synge*

"It was the day when the sun's rays turned pale with grief for his."   NAWM-7v1, *tr. by Robert M. Durling*

"It was the morning of that blessed day."   NAWM-5v1

Laura Waits for Him in Heaven.   OBMV, *tr. by John Millington Synge*

"Long[e] love that in my thought do[e]th [*or* I] harbour [*or* harber *or* harbar], The."   NPeEn, *tr. by Sir Thomas Wyatt*

"Loose to the wind her golden tresses streamed."   CenSon; RWP, *tr. by Charlotte Smith*

(Love, That Doth Reign and Live Within My Thought.)   BrAP; GSo; NAEL-6v1; NAEL-7v1; NoP-4; NoP-5; WaAnP, *tr. by Henry Howard, Earl of Surrey*

Love's Fidelity.   NoSic; OxBSo, *tr. by Henry Howard, Earl of Surrey*

(My Galley.)   NAEL-6v1; WoPoe, *tr. by Sir Thomas Wyatt*

"My ship laden with forgetfulness passes through a harsh sea, at."   NAWM-7v1, *tr. by Robert M. Durling*

"Oh! place me where the burning noon."   RWP, *tr. by Charlotte Smith*

"She used to let her golden hair fly free."   NAWM-5v1; NAWM-7v1, *tr. by Morris Gilbert Bishop*

"When Simon received the high idea which, for my sake, put his."   NAWM-7v1, *tr. by Robert M. Durling*

"Ye vales and woods! fair scenes of happier hours."   RWP, *tr. by Charlotte Smith*

"You who hear in scattered rhymes the sound of those sighs with."   NAWM-7v1, *tr. by Robert M. Durling*

Sonnets to Orpheus.   Rainer Maria Rilke.

"O you lovers that are so gentle, step occasionally."   RaBo, *tr. by Robert Bly*

"This is the creature there has never been."   OBVE, *tr. by J. B. Leishman*

"To praise is the whole thing! A man who can praise."   WED, *tr. by Robert Bly*

"Where in what ever-blissfully watered gardens, upon what trees."   OBVE, *tr. by J. B. Leishman*

"Where praise already is is the only place Grief."   RaBo, *tr. by Robert Bly*

Sonnets to Some Sexual Organs.   Howard Phelps Putnam.   OxBoAm

Sonnets to the Left.   Chris Wallace-Crabbe.

Sonnet IV.   BMAP

Sonnets to the Seasons.   Hartley Coleridge.

November.   CenSon

Sonnets upon the Punishment of Death.   William Wordsworth.

"See the Condemned alone within his cell."   SacPr

Sonnet's Voice, The [(A Metrical Lesson by the Seashore)].   Theodore Watts-Dunton.   GSo

Sonnet—Silence.   Edgar Allan Poe.   ColAP; TCAPo

(Silence.)   APN-1; GSo; NCAP

Sonnet—To an American Painter Departing for Europe.   William Cullen Bryant. *See* To Cole, the Painter, Departing for Europe.

Sonnet—To Science.   Edgar Allan Poe.   NAAPv.1; NCAP; NoP-4; NoP-5; OxBSo; TCAPo

(To Science.)   APN-1; GSo

Sonnet-writing. To F. W. F.   Frederick William Faber.   CenSon

Sonny's Lettah.   Linton Kwesi Johnson.   RSaN

Sonny's Purple Heart.   Adrian C. Louis.   ReTh

Sonogram, The.   Paul Muldoon.   BeAl; NAMCP V.2; P180

Sonreír con la Alegre Tristeza del Olivo.   Miguel Hernández.   RaW

Sonrisas.   Pat Mora.   NIL-7; NIP-4

Son's a poor, wretched, unfortunate creature, The.   James Henry.   NPeEn

Sons and grandsons are dearest to one's heart. *Unknown.*   NAAPv.2

Sons Changed Into Stags, The.   József Erdélyi.   IQMS, *tr. by Watson Kirkconnell*

Sons d'un Cornet, Li. *Unknown.*   WoPoe, *tr. by Willard Trask*

Sons of al-'Abbās say, The: "Has Egypt been conquered?" Therefore reply to the sons of al-'Abbās: "The matter has already been accomplished."   Abū al-Qāsim Muhammad Ibn Hānī al-Andalusi.   HiArP, *tr. by James T. Monroe*

Sons of Art all med'cines tried, The.   John Dryden.   STuOW *Fr.* Threnodia Augustalis.

Sons of bitches.   Theory of Recruiting.   Regina Derieva.   CRWP, *tr. by Kevin Carey*

Sons of Martha, The.   Rudyard Kipling.   ChIV-2

Sons of Mary seldom bother, for they have inherited that good part, The.   Sons of Martha, The.   Rudyard Kipling.   ChIV-2

(Sons of Mary seldom bother, The.)   GI

Sons of War [*with music*].   Samih Al-Qasim.   FaBoWar, *tr. by Abdullah Al-Udhari*

Sons of War sometimes are known, The.   Evan Lloyd.   OBSV *Fr.* Methodist, The.

Sons of Whitman sons of Poe.   Adieu À Charlot.   Lawrence Ferlinghetti.   FTtHH

Sonsy Milkmaid, The.   Emily Jane Pfeiffer.   ViWPN

Sookey dead / Sookey dead-o.... (LL)   Ancestors.   Edward Kamau Brathwaite.   NoP-4; NoP-5

Soon.   Pamela Alexander.   ExTi

Soon.   James Harms.   NeAmPo

Soon.   Vikram Seth.   PML

(Soon after).   Tune: "Drunk in the East Wind."   Lu Chih.   ChinPo, *tr. by Ye Weilian [or Yeh Wei-lien or Wai-lim Yip]*

Soon after, he a crystal stream espying.   Ludovico Ariosto.   NoSic *Fr.* Orlando Furioso.

Soon and silently.   Peter Reading.   NewEx

Soon / come. (LL)   Nathaniel Mackey.   Eno; RD *Fr.* Song of the Andoumboulou.

Soon I shall take more.   Rotting Symbols.   Eileen Myles.   BodElec

Soon I'll be the age you are.   Anniversary.   William Greenway.   PoA 2002

Soon it will be thirteen years since the nightingale.   Letters from the Ming Dynasty.   Joseph Brodsky.   PoetW, *tr. by Derek Walcott*

Soon it will be twenty years.   Barcelona Days.   Jaime Manrique.   WiU, *tr. by Edith Grossman*

Soon kindled and soon spent, we that were the pick of many. (LL)   Old Woman's Lamentations, An.   François Villon.   MoBrPo; OBMV, *tr. by John Millington Synge*

Soon one more goes thither! (LL)   Exeunt Omnes.   Thomas Hardy.   FaBoVe; UV

Soon the last trains will be backed.   Last Trains, The.   C. G. Hanzlicek.   GM

Soon the rush-lights will go out in the flesh.   Prayer to Shadows on My Wall.   Mark McMorris.   IAoNAP

Soon we shall be truly wedded.   Some Old How.   Sándor Petőfi.   IQMS, *tr. by Peter Zollman*

Soon we shall plunge into the chilly fogs.   Song of Autumn I.   Charles Baudelaire.   NAWM-7v2, *tr. by Carlyle Ferren MacIntyre*

Sooner I may some fixed statue be.   On the Duke of Buckingham, Slain by Felton, the 23rd August, 1628.   Owen Felltham [*or* Feltham].   NOSC

Sooner or late—in earnest or in jest.   Rudyard Kipling.   OxBSo *Fr.* Land and Sea Tales.

Sooner or later the sun cracks rebecca. Fragment. Ray DiPalma. FTOS

Sooner tears than sleep this midnight. Wind's Lament, The. John Morris-Jones. OBWVE, *tr.* by Anthony Conran

Soonest Mended. John Ashbery. NAAL-5; NAMCP V.2; NoP-5; OxBoAm; PoetW; VCAP

Soote season, that bud and bloom forth brings, The. Soote Season, The. Petrarch. BrAP; NAEL-6v1; NAEL-7v1; NoP-4; NoP-5; NoSic; WaAnP
  (Soot season, that bud and bloom forth brings, The.) AEP
  (Soote season, that bud and blome furth bringes, The.) PBRV

Soothed by the murmurs on the sea-beat shore. To the Curlew. Helen Maria Williams. CenSon; WoRP

Sootie Joe. Melvin B. Tolson. OxBoAm

Sooty, swart smiths, smattered with smoke. Blacksmiths, The. *Unknown.* WoPoe, *tr.* by Wesli Court

Sophia! Antiphon for Divine Wisdom. Hildegard von Bingen. WPoS, *tr.* by Barbara Newman

Sophia. Joyce Rupp. HW

Sophia, / to you I come. Sophia. Joyce Rupp. HW

Sophie, Climbing the Stairs. Dolores Kendrick. ESEAA

Sophisticated Lady. Irving Mills and Mitchell Parish. ReLy

Sophoclean. Seamus Heaney. PoAgWa

Sor Juana's Last Dream. Gail Wronsky.
  "Be a child forever." PoChi

Sordello. Robert Browning.
  Sordello. OBGa

Sordid Scene. Edward Robert Bulwer-Lytton. STuOW *Fr.* Misery.

Sordid, unfeeling, reprobate, degraded, / Spiritless outcast! (LL) Friend of Humanity and the Knife Grinder, The. George Canning *and* John Hookham Frere. OBCoV; UV

Sore Throat, The. Aaron Kunin. IIR

Sore Thumb. Mara Bergman. PoCu

Sorrento Valley. John Koethe. OxBoAm

Sorrow. Aubrey Thomas De Vere. SacPr

Sorrow. D. H. Lawrence. InoFa; NAMCP V.1; NPeEn; OBMV

Sorrow. Mei Yao Ch'en. WoPoe, *tr.* by Kenneth Rexroth

Sorrow. Edna St. Vincent Millay. APT-1

Sorrow. Alfonsina Storni. TCLAP, *tr.* by Andrew Rosing

Sorrow: "White moon gleams through scudding, The." Chu Shu-chen. NDACCP, *tr.* by Kenneth Rexroth

Sorrow? A Great Ocean. Sándor Petőfi. IQMS *Fr.* Clouds, The.

Sorrow and Rapture. Maura Stanton. IllVoic

Sorrow for Spring. Li Ching. CCL1, *tr.* by Alan Ayling and Duncan Mackintosh

Sorrow is my own yard. Widow's Lament in Springtime, The. William Carlos Williams. APT-1; CtM; FTtHH; NAAL-5; NAMCP V.1; NoAM; SAmP; SoSe-8; TCAPo

Sorrow Is the Only Faithful One. Owen Dodson. OxAAAP

Sorrow is to be discarded. Meditation. Mary Sue Koeppel. AmZen

Sorrow / its outlines blurred. Tanka. Ishikawa Takuboku. CAoMJL1, *tr.* by Makoto Ueda

Sorrow lay upon my breast more heavily than winter clay. Desolation Is a Delicate Thing. Elinor Wylie. MoAmPo

Sorrow of Departure. Li Ch'ing-chao. NDACCP, *tr.* by Kenneth Rexroth

Sorrow of Mydath. John Masefield. MoBrPo

Sorrow of Sarajevo, The. Goran Simić. PoAgWa, *tr.* by David Harsent

Sorrow Since Sitting Bull, A. Christopher Gilbert. ESEAA

Sorrow, since you cannot make me. Sorrow Vanquished. Amado Nervo. TCLAP, *tr.* by Sue Standing

Sorrow Song. Lucille Clifton. BodElec; CFP

Sorrow Song. John Alexander Frazier, Jr. BtF

Sorrow Vanquished. Amado Nervo. TCLAP, *tr.* by Sue Standing

Sorrow Wakes Me. Hwang Insuk. EcSo, *tr.* by Peter H. Lee

Sorrowful Sea-Gull, The. Menella Bute Smedley. VWP

Sorrowful Shadow, The. Julio Herrera y Reissig. TCLAP, *tr.* by Andrew Rosing

Sorrows of an Abandoned Queen. Nguyễn Gia Thiều. *tr.* by Nguyen Ngoc Bich
  "You were a fool, Old Man of the Moon." WoPoe, *tr.* by Nguyen Ngoc Bich

Sorrows of Werther, The. William Makepeace Thackeray. NBLV; OBCoV

Sorrows play at the edge of these willow leaf curves. Willow Eyebrows. Chao Luan-luan. CCL1; NDACCP, *tr.* by Chung Ling and Kenneth Rexroth

Sorry, Hank. / Found out / The Hard / Way. Hank Mobley's. Cornelius Eady. SeSe

Sorry I am, my God, sorry I am. Sin's Round. George Herbert. NOSC

Sorry I'm late. I had to drive way out of my. Mrs. Eden in Town for the Day. Richard Howard. KGB

Sorry there's no more space. But date your reply. (LL) Letter from Pretoria Central Prison. Arthur Nortje. BrAP; HBAPE

Sort of a Song, A. William Carlos Williams. APT-1; NAAL-5; NoP-4; NoP-5; WoPoe

Sort of attachment to the family tree, A. Lilith, Adam's First Companion. Elina Wechsler. MirDau, *tr.* by Darrell Lockhart

Sortie, The. Miklós Zrínyi. IQMS, *tr.* by Thomas Kabdebo

Sorting clothes, I find our son's old. Good Will. Sharon Olds. CAP-8

Sorting Laundry. Elisavietta Ritchie. SoSe-8

Sorting out letters and piles of my old. Mementos, 1. W. D. Snodgrass. MoAmPo; NoP-4; NoP-5; OxBoAm; VCAP

Sorting Things Out. Wanda Barford. Prnts

Sorting Through. Liz Lochhead. StAl

Sory beverech [*or* beuerech] it is and sore it is abought [*or* a-bouth], A. Christ's Prayer in Gethsemane. *Unknown.* SacPr

S.O.S. Léon Damas. PFTM-1

So's Liberty. (LL) No Rack can torture me. Emily Dickinson. NALW; TCAPo

Sotto Voce. M. Vasalis. TuT, *tr.* by Peter van de Kamp

Sotto voce / cynics pass the word. But God is Silent / Psalm 114. Bible, *O.T.* InvLi; UpMys

Sottoportico San Zaccaria. Kenneth Rexroth. ErotSp

Sot-Weed Factor, The. Ebenezer Cook. TCAPo

Souffle. Pierre Reverdy. YaTCFP

Sought by the world, and hath the world disdained. Love's Ending. *Unknown.* NoSic

Souks were always empty, The. Liberators. Dennis Nurkse. PrTe

Soul. Alan Shapiro. PoA 2002

Soul, A. Christina Georgina Rossetti. NALW

Soul, The. Joseph Addison. TreFP *Fr.* Cato.

Soul, The. Ira Sadoff. BodElec

Soul, The: "Flame is full, The." Nedelcho Ganev. CSCBP, *tr.* by Georgi Belev and Lisa Sapinkopf

Soul a crystal is, the Godhead is its shine, The. "Angelus Silesius." GePo *Fr.* Cherubical Wanderer, The.

Soul against the state, The. Paavo Haavikko. WoPoe, *tr.* by Anselm Hollo

Soul and Body [*epigram*]. Friedrich von Logau. GePo, *tr.* by George C. Schoolfield

Soul and Body of John Brown, The. Muriel Rukeyser. CBCWP; MoAmPo

Soul and fire of windsongs must not be neutral, The. Killing Memory. Haki R. Madhubuti. IllVoic

Soul and Love, The. Albert Verwey. TuT, *tr.* by Tony Curtis and Tony Curtis

Soul and race. Here Where Coltrane Is. Michael S. Harper. CAP-8; ESEAA

Soul-animating strains—alas, too few! (LL) Scorn Not the Sonnet [Critic, You Have Frowned]. William Wordsworth. CenSon; GSo; HeIP-4; NoP-4; NoP-5; NPBRoP; OxBSo; WaAnP

Soul as a Body, The. Chard DeNiord. Vesp

Soul Call. *Unknown.* SonAtl, *tr.* by Caroline O'Sullivan and Anne Swann

Soul Food. Janice Mirikitani. OpBo

Soul has Bandaged moments, The. Emily Dickinson. NAAPv.1; NALW; OxBoAm; TRP

Soul in Space. Chase Twichell. AmZen

Soul Incense. Henrietta Cordelia Ray. CBWP-3

Soul is a beautiful thing, The. Three Days/out of Franklin. Víctor Hernández Cruz. PueRic

Soul is a prisoner, and body is its jail. Soul and Body. Friedrich von Logau. GePo, *tr.* by George C. Schoolfield

Soul is a region without definite boundaries, The. Terrain. A. R. Ammons. VCAP

Soul Keeping Company. Lucie Brock-Broido. AWPTFC

Soul like marcus bookstore and eso won. Soul Gestures in Spring. Michael Datcher. BtF

Soul, like the moon, The. Lal Ded. WoPoe; WPoS, *tr.* by Coleman Barks

Soul, little wandering friend. Emperor Hadrian on his Soul. Emperor Hadrian. WoPoe, *tr.* by Frederick Morgan

Soul Make a Path Through Shouting [*for Elizabeth Eckford / Little Rock, Arkansas, 1957*]. Cyrus Cassells. GifTon; GT; OPRER; UnSA

Soul Music. Baron Wormser. LTA; SwNoth

Soul Music: The Derry Air. Eamon Grennan. PBCIP

Soul of a Man, The. Ferenc Kazinczy. IQMS, *tr.* by Adam Makkai

Soul of a pebble on top of the mountain, The. Shakir Li'aibi. IrPoTo, *tr.* by Ralph Saverese and Saadi A. Simawe

Soul of my inner face, face of my race. Ernest Francisco Fenollosa. APN-2 *Fr.* East and West.

Soul of my soul, my joy, my crown, my friend! Katherine Philips. *See* Soule of my soule! my Joy, my crown, my friend!

Soul Roots. Felicia L. Morgenstern. BtF

Soul Says. Jorie Graham. PoPoPo

Soul, secure in her existence, smiles, The. Joseph Addison. TreFP *Fr.* Cato.

Soul selects her own Society, The. Emily Dickinson. APN-2; BrAP; HeIP-4; MoAmPo; NAAL-3; NAAL-5; NAAPv.1; NALW; NAMCP V.1; NAWM-7v2; NoAM; NoP-4; NoP-5; OxBoAm; OxWW; PoPoPo; SAmP; TCAPo; TFi

Soul Speaks, The. *Unknown.*
    "Beguines who hear these words." WPoS

Soul that hath a Guest, The. Emily Dickinson. APN-2

Soul that's fed on Nature is content, The. Nature's Uplifting. Henrietta Cordelia Ray. CBWP-3

Soul Train. Allison Joseph. AmPoNex; ExTi; SUP

Soul tries a thousand remedies in vain, The. Michelangelo Buonarroti. CAGL, *tr. by* James M. Saslow

Soul warmed in gutta-percha, A. Rubber Knight, The. Tom Ahern. OnScMo

Soul Woven of Shadows. Árpád Tóth. IQMS, *tr. by* Edmund Charles Blunden and J. G. Nichols

Soule, and Body. Margaret Lucas Cavendish, Duchess of Newcastle. PEW

Soule of my soule! my Joy, my crown, my friend! L'Amitié: To Mrs M Awbrey. Katherine Philips. BrAP
    (Soul of my soul, my joy, my crown, my friend!) NIL-7; NOSC

Soul[e] which doth with God unite, The. William Habington. ChIV-2 *Fr.* Castara.

Soule, which to Hell wast thrall. Faith Above Reason. William Drummond of Hawthornden. SacPr

Soulgroovin Ditty #7. Hannah Howard. BRtP

Soul-Hunter, The. Julia Ward Howe. SWaP *Fr.* Lyrics of the Street.

Souls. Dannie Abse. PLBUT

Souls. Michael McClure. Eno

77: Soul's Beauty. Dante Gabriel Rossetti. NAEL-7v2; OBEV; OxAEP-2 *Fr.* House of Life, The.

Soul's Courts, The. Henrietta Cordelia Ray. CBWP-3

Soul's Desire, The. *Unknown.* SacPr, *tr. by* Eleanor Hull

Soul's distinct connection, The. Emily Dickinson. SAmP

Soul's Groan to Christ for Succo[u]r, The. Edward Taylor. NAAL-3 *Fr.* God's Determinations [touching his Elect].

Souls have no value they are fox furs, The. Souls. Michael McClure. Eno

Soul's joy, bend not those morning stars from me. Sir Philip Sidney. NoP-4; NoP-5 *Fr.* Astrophil and Stella.

Souls Lake. Robert Fitzgerald. APT-2

Soul's Liberty. Anna Wickham. MoBrPo

Souls of Poets, The. Dickie Bradley. OWABP

Soul's Rialto hath its merchandise, The. Elizabeth Barrett Browning. CenSon *Fr.* Sonnets from the Portuguese.

Soul's Superior instants, The. Emily Dickinson. APN-2

Soul-troubled at the febrile ways of breath. For Hazel Hall, American Poet. Countee Cullen. APT-2

Sound Advice. *Unknown.* NBLV

Sound and Cerement. Nathaniel Mackey. BAP-04

Sound, and the imagination of the sound—a place, The. (LL) Triphammer Bridge. A. R. Ammons. ColAP; OxBoAm

Sound Bite. Frederick D'Aguiar. NeBrP; Oth

Sound bubbled up, The. Jah Music. Lorna Goodison. WaCA

Sound Check. Ted Pearson. Eno

Sound 8. Kang Ŭn'gyo. CAMKP, *tr. by* Tae Yang Kwak

Sound I Listened For, The. Robert Francis. APT-2

Sound Is Fading Away, The. Frances Densmore. APT-1 *Fr.* Chippewa Music.

Sound is forced [*or* forc'd], the notes are few, The. (LL) To the Muses. William Blake. HeIP-4; NAEL-6v2; NoP-4; NoP-5; OBEV

Sound is like rain, leaves, or sheets settling, The. (LL) Bats. Dave Jeddie Smith. NoAM; RoV; WaAnP

Sound is louder in paperbacks. Buckles. Joy Lahey. AnSo

SOUND is ProFound Sense. Kalamu ya Salaam. AnSo

Sound is sea: pattern lapping pattern. If we erase the air and slow the. Ronald Johnson. APSN *Fr.* Ark.

Sound Letter. Marina Boroditskaya. CRWP, *tr. by* Ruth Fainlight

Sound like a great big crowd. (LL) Morning After. Langston Hughes. NAMCP V.1; NBLV; NoAM; OBCoV

Sound like a rusty pump beneath our window, A. Blue Jay. Paul Lake. RA

Sound like I can hear this morning. Death Bells. Lightnin' Hopkins. APT-2

Sound of a bell. Buson. EH, *tr. by* Robert Hass

Sound of a saw. Buson. EH, *tr. by* Robert Hass

Sound of Birds at Noon, The. Dahlia Ravikovitch. VCWP

Sound of each other, rustling, The. Diana Hartog. NLPA *Fr.* Oasis.

Sound of gunfire—dilutes the bloody terror of revolution, The. Duo Duo. AF *Fr.* Thoughts and Recollections.

Sound of guns from beleaguered Donelson, The. Lines Written for Allen Tate on His Sixtieth Anniversary. Donald Davidson. FuPo

Sound of her silk skirt has stopped, The. Li Furen. Emperor Wu of Han. CCL1, *tr. by* Arthur Waley

Sound of Music, The. Oscar Hammerstein, II. ReLy

Sound of my lover, The. *Unknown.* WoPoe *Fr.* Song of Solomon, The [*or* The Song of Songs].

Sound of Night, The. Maxine W. Kumin. SoSe-8

Sound of Rain, The. Chu Yohan. CAMKP, *tr. by* Chong Bum Kim

Sound of rain, The. (LL) On Gay Wallpaper. William Carlos Williams. APT-1; MoAmPo

Sound of shoes going down to the grave in the dark, The. Shadow 1. Miyoshi Toyoichiro. GifTon, *tr. by* Naoshi Koriyama *and* Edward Lueders and Edward Lueders

Sound of Silence, The. Srirangam Narayana Babu. HotL, *tr. by* V. Narayana Rao

Sound of tears on the wind, The. Lament. Máire Mhac an tSaoi. ModIr, *tr. by* Patrick Crotty

Sound of the boy walking, The. New Year's Prayer: 1976. Sŏ Chŏngju. CAMKP, *tr. by* David R. McCann

Sound of the cylinder blade, The. Dehorning the Yearlings. LuAnn Keener. FiBr

Sound of the horse whips, softly, softly, crossing the river at night. On a Painting of Kenshin Attacking Shingen. Rai San'yo. EMJL, *tr. by* Haruo Shirane

Sound of the Mountain Bird. Paek Sŏk. CAMKP, *tr. by* Kyunghwan Choi

Sound of the rain, The. Richard Wright. APT-2

Sound of the Resurrected Dead Man's Footsteps (#2). Marvin Bell. TAPaP

Sound of the Sea, The. Henry Wadsworth Longfellow. ITBLP; TCAPo

Sound of the Taffy-Seller's Shears. Pak Chaesam. CAMKP, *tr. by* David R. McCann and Jiwon Shin

Sound of the waterfall awakens the mountain. Startled, a wild pheasant takes flight. Entering Chikso Falls. Ch'ŏn Yanghŭi. EcSo, *tr. by* Aimee N. Kwon

Sound of the waves in the silence, The. Yocheved Bat-Miriam. FIT, *tr. by* Robert Friend

Sound of the Wind That Is Blowing, The. J. Kitchener Davies. *tr. by* Joseph P. Clancy
    "Today / there came a breeze thin as the needle of a syringe." BBMWP; OBWVE, *tr. by* Joseph P. Clancy

Sound of Trees, The. Robert Frost. APT-1; NoAM

Sound of Water. Mary O'Neill. NTCP

Sound of water in the shallows has stopped and now dry music flows, The. Reply at an Unknown Place. Yi Hyangji. EcSo, *tr. by* Catherine J. Kim

Sound of words as they fall away from our mouths, The. Duet for a Chair and a Table. Jack Spicer. APSN

Sound on, thou dark unslumbering sea! Last Song of Sappho, The. Felicia Dorothea Hemans. VWP

Sound opens sound. Dissonance Royal Traveller. Barbara Guest. NYP2

Sound, sound forever, trumpet-calls of thought! Victor Hugo. SxFrPo, *tr. by* A. M. and E. H. Blackmore

Sound, Sound the Clarion. Sir Walter Scott. OxAEP-2 *Fr.* Old Mortality.

Sound Systems. Ronald Wallace. SwNoth

Sound the Flute! William Blake. NOxBChV *Fr.* Songs of Innocence.

Sound the loud timbrel o'er Egypt's dark sea! Sound the Loud Timbrel. Thomas Moore. ChIV-1

Sound trumpets, ho!—weigh anchor—loosen sail. Voyager's Song, The. Edward Coote Pinkney. APN-1

Sound variegated through beneath lit. Gyre's Galax. Norman Henry, II Pritchard. EGAG

Sound Waves. Fergus Allen. NIrP

Sound Waves. Mary Kinzie. FFC

Sounding / the criée. Return to Tunisia. Tahar Bekri. YaTCFP, *tr. by* Mary Ann Caws *and* Jean-Pierre Cauvin

Sounding the Name. Robert Kroetsch. BeAl

Soundings. Paula Gunn Allen. HATNAP

Soundless as dots—on a Disc of Snow. (LL) Safe in their Alabaster Chambers. Emily Dickinson. APN-2; NoP-5; OxBoAm; RaBo; TCAPo; WoPoe
    (Ah, what sagacity perished here!) (LL) NAAL-3; NAAL-5; NAWM-7v2; NIL-7; NoP-4; PoPoPo

Soundlessly, / the woman is falling. Loop. Fiona Tinwei Lam. IFF

Sounds. Lindley Williams Hubbell. APT-2

Sounds. Wassily Kandinsky. PFTM-1

Sounds, The. Into Still Air. Larry Smith. AmZen

Sounds, The. Gerald Stern. BodElec

Sounds are the sea, breaking out of sight, The. Birthday Party, The. Josephine Jacobsen. OxBoAm

Sounds Begin Again, The. Dennis Brutus. HBAPE

Sounds came sifting down. Earphones. Richard Church. RWPCtW

Sounds like big. Waking from a Nap on the Beach. May Swenson. NTCP

Sounds like prayer, sacrum. Each Bone of the Body. Frankie Paino. FaoP

Sounds of a Dreamer. James Berry. WaCA

Sounds of Ireland, The. Windharp. John Montague. PNI

Sounds / Of the Harlem night, The. Summer Night. Langston Hughes. APT-2

Sounds of the Resurrected Dead Man's Footsteps (#1). Marvin Bell. IaFF

Sounds of the Resurrected Dead Man's Footsteps (#3). Marvin Bell. Vesp

Sounds of the stream, The. Incomparable-Verse Valley. Muso Soseki. EaWin, tr. by W. S. Merwin

Sounds our parents heard echoing over, The. Strangers Like Us: Pittsburgh, Raleigh, 1945–1985. Gerald William Barrax. ISC

Sounds That Arrived, The. Milo De Angelis. NeIt, tr. by Lawrence Venuti

Soundtrack. Lawrence L. White. IAoNAP

Soundtrack. Kevin Young. LegDan

Soundtracks. Timothy Geiger. AmPoNex

Soundwaves. Andrew Sant. NOBAu

Soup. Tony Curtis. TCAWP

Soup. Carl Sandburg. HHAm

Soup, The. Gary Soto. NoP-4; NoP-5

Soup, The: "On the day of your scan, I make a soup." Peggy Penn. SweBea

Soup and Sherry. George Bruce. EdScPo

Soup and Slavery. Myra Schneider. Prnts

Soup and the Clouds, The. Charles Baudelaire. MotU, tr. by Edward K. Kaplan

Soup Kitchen. Betsy Sholl. ACAMVP; PBCAP

Soup Kitchen Song. Unknown. NOBAu

Soup so thick you could shake its hand, A. Scotch Broth. Robert Crawford. EdScPo

Sour fiend, go home and tell the Pit. Ghoul Care. Ralph Hodgson. MoBrPo

Sour Grapes. Derek Walcott. See Sea Grapes.

Sour smell, The. Getting in the Wood. Gary Snyder. NoAM

Source. Benjamin Péret. YaTCFP

Source, The. Jon Stallworthy. PML

Source, The. David Wagoner. VCAP

Source of the Singing, The. Marilyn Nelson Waniek. OxAAAP

Sources of the Delaware. Dean Young. BAP-01

Sourdough Mountain Lookout. Philip Whalen. BB

Sous-Entendu. Anne Stevenson. LW

South. Blaise Cendrars. BLT, tr. by Monique Chefdor

South. Aurora Levins Morales. PueRic

South. M. L. Williams. GeoHom

South, The. Emma Lazarus. APN-2; ColAP; NAAPv.1

South, The. Wang Chien. BLT, tr. by Arthur Waley

South America Mi Hija. Sharon Doubiago.
"Out the window, Colombia, out the window." PBCAP

South America, Take It Away! Harold Rome. ReLy

South American stories. Tangerine. Johnny Mercer. ReLy

South Bound: Facing North. Geraldine Monk. Oth

South Bronx appears on the TV screen, The. Getting Out Alive. Rosario Morales. PueRic

South Bronx Testimonial. Sandra Maria Esteves. UnSA

South Central: Notes toward a Shooting Script. Jasper Bernes. IAoNAP

South Coast Haiku. Laurie Duggan. BMAP Fr. Dogs.

South Country. Kenneth Slessor. BMAP

South Country, The. Joseph Hilaire Pierre Belloc. MoBrPo; OxAEP-2

South Dakota, August 1989. The buffaloes' deep red-brown. Everyone Was Drunk. Jean Valentine. LaCa

South, droops a tree. Jiu-mu: South, Droops a Tree. Unknown. CCL1, tr. by V. W. X.

South knows ruin and likes it, The. East Jesus. Kevin Young. FuFl

South, North, East, West, inland and seaboard, we will surely awake. (LL) To the States, To Identify the 16th, 17th, or 18th Presidentiad. Walt Whitman. NAAL-3; RaBo

South of house, north of house, all spring water. Guest, A. Tu Fu [or Du Fu]. ChinPo, tr. by Ye Weilian [or Yeh Wei-lien or Wai-lim Yip]

South of Hsien-yang. Rhymeprose on the Sword Gallery. Li Po. ColAnChi, tr. by Elling O. Eide

South of the Bridge on Seventeenth. Fifteen. William Stafford. CAP-8

South of the Line, inland from far Durban. Christmas Ghost-Story, A. Thomas Hardy. ChrPo; OBWP

South of the River, north of the River, wandering comfortless. Divided by the Han River. Yu Xuanji. CCL1, tr. by Genevieve Wimsatt

South of the river: to pluck lotus. South of the Yangtze. Unknown. ChinPo, tr. by Ye Weilian [or Yeh Wei-lien or Wai-lim Yip]

South of the Yangtze. Unknown. ChinPo, tr. by Ye Weilian [or Yeh Wei-lien or Wai-lim Yip]

South Parade Peddler. Louise Bennett. NAMCP V.2

South Ridge Zendo. Miriam Sagan. WANABP

South Rim: Big Bend National Park. Arthur M. Sampley. TiP2

South Sea Ballad, A. Edward Ward. OBCoV

South Shore (Aberystwyth), The. Bobi Jones. BBMWP, tr. by Anthony Conran

South Side. Robert Fitzgerald. APT-2

South Song. Bill Griffiths. Oth Fr. Building: The New London Hospital.

South, Southwest. William Burford. TiP2

South Texas Boxcar Blues. Chip Dameron. TiP2

South Wind. Tu Fu [or Du Fu]. BLT, tr. by Kenneth Rexroth

South wind blows open the folds of my dress, The. Spring Longing. Amy Lowell. APT-1

South wind brought a soft goddess, The. Rain. Nishiwaki Junzaburo. CAoMJL1, tr. by Hosea Hirata

South wind does not shed so great a cast, The. Callimachus. HePo Fr. Hecale.

South Yard, The. Chông Hwajin. EcSo, tr. by Julie C. Park

Southbound on the Freeway. May Swenson. NTCP

Southeast, and storm, and every weathervane. Hatteras Calling. Conrad Potter Aiken. ColAP; InGu

Southeast at low tide. Skiing on Russian Christmas. Nora Dauenhauer. HATNAP

Southeast the Peacock Flies. Unknown. CCL1, tr. by Burton Watson

Southeast wind brings the smell of Gulf, The. Subtropical. Jane Epton Seale. TiP2

Southern Birth. Kevin Powell. AmPoNex; InTrad

Southern Blues. Unknown. APT-1

Southern Blues, The. Big Bill Broonzy. GM

Southern Cop. Sterling Allen Brown. OxBoAm; SoSe-8

Southern Crescent Was on time, The. Andrew Hudgins. GM

Southern Cross. Herman Melville. TCAPo Fr. Clarel: A Poem and Pilgrimage in the Holy Land.

Southern Dawn. Pier Paolo Pasolini. VCWP, tr. by Norman MacAfee and Luciano Martinengo

Southern gentle lady. Langston Hughes. NAAL-5; NAMCP V.1 Fr. Three Songs about Lynching.

Southern Kyoto. Basho. EMJL, tr. by Haruo Shirane

Southern Literature. Andrew Hudgins. LPSFW

Southern Mansion. Arna Bontemps. APT-2; GT

Southern Night. D. H. Lawrence. NAMCP V.1

Southern Pacific. Carl Sandburg. GM

Southern Paiute Poetry. Unknown. APN-2, tr. by John Wesley Powell

Southern Press, The. Lizelia Augusta Jenkins Moorer. CBWP-3

Southern Pulpit, The. Lizelia Augusta Jenkins Moorer. CBWP-3

Southern Review, The. Brigit Pegeen Kelly.
Song. ExTi; IllVoic

Southern Road. Sterling Allen Brown. APT-2; InGu; NAMCP V.1; OxAAAP

Southern Road. Mwatabu Okantah. SeSe

Southern Road, The. Dudley Randall. GM

Southern Room Over the River, The. Su Tung-p'o. NDACCP, tr. by Kenneth Rexroth

Southern Scene, A. Priscilla Jane Thompson. CBWP-2

Southern Skua, The. Robert Adamson. BeAl

Southern Song. Margaret Abigail Walker. InGu

Southern trees bear a strange fruit. Strange Fruit. Lewis Allan. ReLy

Southern University, 1962. Kevin Young. SpirFl

Southern women have alabaster skin. Li Po. CrYelRi; ErotSp Fr. Women of Yueh.

Southern Work of Dr. and Mrs. L. M. Dunton. Lizelia Augusta Jenkins Moorer. CBWP-3

South-Folk in Cold Country. Li Po. NDACCP; OBVE, tr. by Ezra Pound

Southland Drive-In. James Applewhite. LPSFW

Southpaw. Maurice Riordan. NIrP

Southward from hence ten miles, where Derwent laves. Charles Cotton. OBGa Fr. Wonders of the Peak, The.

Southwest. Viktor Krivulin. TCRusP, tr. by Anna Barker and Daniel Weissbort

South-wind brings, The. Threnody. Ralph Waldo Emerson. APN-1; TCAPo

South-wind strengthens to a gale, The. Low Barometer. Robert Bridges. CABP; NoAM

Souvenir. Edwin Arlington Robinson. APT-1; NoAM

Souvenir. Paul Van Ostaijen. TuT, tr. by Tony Curtis and Tony Curtis

Souvenir, The. Dan Pagis. MotU, tr. by Stephen Mitchell

Souvenir, A / despite the rain. Merchant's Daughter. Thomas Meyer. AnSo

Souvenir de Monsieur Poop. Stevie Smith. MoWP; NALW; NAMCP V.1

Souvenir from Anywhere. Harryette Mullen. WANABP

Souvenir of the Manassah Ball. Lorenzo Thomas. RD

Souvenirs. Jessica Tarahata Hagedorn. ReBoTo

Sovereign beauty which I do admire, The. Edmund Spenser. AEP

Soviet Union, The. John Berryman. WaAnP

Sower, The. William Cowper. ChIV-2 Fr. Olney Hymns.

Sower, The.   Sir Charles G. D. Roberts.   BrAP

Sower, The.   Jones Very.   SacPr

Sower went forth to sow, A.   Parable of the Sower, The.   Stephen Mitchell. GI

Sown in dishonor!   Emily Dickinson.   ChIV-2

Soy Inés Tohmahtohlahkikt.   Presente.   Inés Hernández-Ávila.   ReEnLa

Soy la guardiana del Jardín Elíseo.   Jardín Elíseo.   Carmen Boullosa. RMCMP

Soybeans.   Thomas Alan Orr.   GoPo; IPoFL

Soyŏng Problems.   Yi Sang.   PFTM-1

Sozzled, Mo-tsu, after a silence, vouchsafed.   Scholars at the Orchid Pavilion. John Berryman.   HarvBoo

Space.   Verneda Sagay-Lights.   BtF

Space.   Maura Stanton.   OPRER

Space.   Urdeath.   August Stramm.   PFTM-1

Space, The.   Garden.   Ok-Ku Kang.   WhBo

Space. A Prose Poem Monologue.   Sekou Sundiata.   FaoP

Space & stars / reflected into sound.   Federico García Lorca.   PFTM-1 *Fr.* Night (Suite for Piano and Poet's Voice).

Space and Time! now I see it is true, what I guess'd at.   Walt Whitman. *Fr.* Song of Myself.

Space being(don't forget to remember)Curved.   E. E. Cummings.   NoAM

Space Between, The.   Elena Georgiou.   WiU

Space Between, The.   Edith Jay Scovell.   MoWP

Space between us, The.   Chasm.   Mary Gomez Parham.   OWABP

Space Heater, The.   Sharon Olds.   P180

Space in the lives of their friends, A. (LL)   Ishmael Reed. *See* In the lives of their friends.

Space instead of furniture.   Space Instead.   Jean Daive.   MFP, *tr. by* Martin Sorrell

Space is ample, east and west.   Unity.   Ralph Waldo Emerson.   TCAPo

Space is arched like a sail.   Svetlana Kekova.   CRWP, *tr. by* Ruth Fainlight

Space Memorabilia Auction, Superior Stamp and Coin, Beverly Hills, California. Joel Brouwer.   AmPoNex

Space Needle, The.   Roger Fanning.   NAPBL

Space Needle works like a pushpin, The.   Space Needle, The.   Roger Fanning. NAPBL

Space Parable.   Max Winter.   NeAmPo

Space Song.   Alfonso Cortes.   TCLAP, *tr. by* Thomas Merton

Space to the pad seems to be stocked, The.   Sketching in Barnstable.   Carol Arber.   PfS

Space was easier then, and time slower.   *Planisféria*, Map of the World, Lisbon, 1554.   Ellen Hinsey.   AmPoNex

Space with figure who holds the newspaper.   Doing.   Giancarlo Majorino. ItPo, *tr. by* Gayle Ridinger

Spacepod shrunk to microscopic, The.   Undetectable.   Justin Chin.   WiU

Spaces We Leave Empty.   Cathy Song.   YaYoPo

Spaceship drifting up, The.   Christmas.   Peter McDonald.   PNI

Space-vase ... the past is lioness to swallow.   Next Two Tablets, The.   Armand Schwerner.   BodElec

Spacious firmament on high, The.   Ode.   Joseph Addison.   ChIV-1; NPeEn; OxBEV

Spacious Firmament on High, The.   Joseph Addison. *See* Ode: "Spacious firmament on high, The."

Spacious firmament on high, The.   Bible, *O.T. See* Heavens declare the glory of God, The.

Spade.   Dan Chiasson.   PoCho

Spade, The.   George Wither.   NOSC *Fr.* Collection of Emblemes, Ancient and Moderne, A.

Spade.   Emile Verhaeren.   SonAtl, *tr. by* Gregory Beaven, Kurt Ganzl and Heather Goode

Spade and the Wreath, The.   George Wither.   NOSC *Fr.* Collection of Emblemes, Ancient and Moderne, A.

Spade, for labour stands. The ball with wings, The.   George Wither.   NOSC *Fr.* Collection of Emblemes, Ancient and Moderne, A.

Spain frightened you. Spain.   You Hated Spain.   Ted Hughes.   EmeKit

Spain! much more beautiful than Egypt!   Madrid.   Frank O'Hara.   FTOS

Spain [1937].   W. H. Auden.   AF; NAEL-6v2; NAEL-7v2; NAMCP V.1; NoP-4; NoP-5; OBWP

Spain: splendor.   Andalusian Landscape.   Aaron Kurtz.   Prolet, *tr. by* Amelia Glaser

Spain, Take Away This Cup from Me [España, Aparta de Mí Este Cáliz].   César Vallejo. *tr. by* Gordon Brotherston and Edward Dorn

    Mass.   StAl, *tr. by* Gordon Brotherston and Edward Dorn

Spain, Take [Away] This Cup from Me [España, Aparta de Mí Este Cáliz].   César Vallejo. *tr. by* Clayton Eshelman and Clayton Eshelman

    Mass.   TCLAP, *tr. by* Clayton Eshelman

    Short Prayer for a Loyalist Hero.   TCLAP, *tr. by* Clayton Eshelman

Spain, Take This Cup from Me.   TCLAP, *tr. by* Clayton Eshelman

Spain, Take This Cup from Me.   César Vallejo.   TCLAP *Fr.* Spain, Take [Away] This Cup from Me [España, Aparta de Mí Este Cáliz].

Span of Life, The.   Robert Frost.   SoSe-8 *Fr.* Ten Mills.

SpaNglisH.   Lissette Norman.   BRtP

Spaniard That Blighted My Life, The.   Billy Merson.   OBCoV

To *El Mingo* (with Whom I Share Eva Victoria and Anahi Paz).   Alicia Partnoy. CFP, *tr. by* Gail Wronsky

With a Little Notebook at the Met.   Cecilia Vicuña.   WANABP, *tr. by* Rosa Alcalá

SPA 100 Conversational Spanish.   Community College Revises Its Curriculum in Response to Changing Demographics, The.   Martín Espada.   LiTh

Spanish Dancer.   Oliver Reynolds.   TCAWP

Spanish Dancer.   Rainer Maria Rilke.   NAWM-7v2, *tr. by* Stephen Mitchell

Spanish Descent, The.   Daniel Defoe.

    "Word's gone out, and now they spread the main, The."   OBWP

Spanish Friar [*or* Fryar], The.   John Dryden.

    "'Twere well your judgments but in plays did range."   OBSV

Spanish Generosity.   Max Jacob.   CuPo

Spanish is the lovin' tongue.   Border Affair, A.   Charles Badger, Jr. Clark. APT-1

Spanish Jake.   Irving Caesar and Sammy Lerner.   ReLy

Spanish Jew's Tale: Azrael, The.   Henry Wadsworth Longfellow.   APN-1; TCAPo *Fr.* Tales of a Wayside Inn.

Spanish Jew's Tale: The Legend of Rabbi Ben Levi, The.   Henry Wadsworth Longfellow.   NCAP; TCAPo *Fr.* Tales of a Wayside Inn.

Spanish Lullaby.   Aaron Kurtz.   Prolet, *tr. by* Amelia Glaser

Spanish of Our Out-Loud Dreams, The.   Martín Espada.   PueRic

Spanish Peasant Boy.   Jane Duran.   Prnts *Fr.* Silences from the Spanish Civil War.

Spanner in the what? works.   Wopko Jensma.   TSAP

Spare, gen'rous Victor, spare the slave.   To a Lady: She Refusing to Continue a Dispute with Me.   Matthew Prior.   NoP-4; NoP-5

Spare not but play thee! (LL)   Thomas Lodge. *See* For your offence.

Spare radiance blooms, blooms again, expires, A.   Santa Fe Sky.   Ann Lauterbach.   OxBoAm

Spare then the person, and expose the vice.   Alexander Pope.   OBSV *Fr.* Epilogue to the Satires, in Two Dialogues.

Spare Tire (*the atheist's unmailed letter to god*).   Ivan Urquiza-Vicente.   Vesp

Spark.   Richard Lemm.   Coast

Spark, The.   Brenda Hillman.   FaoP

Spark Divine, A.   Sir Francis Hastings Doyle.   DiBP

Spark of Green.   Maria Luisa Spaziani.   CItWP, *tr. by* Cinzia Sartini Blum and Lara Trubowitz

Spark of Joy, The.   Colette Ni Ghallchóir.   NIrP, *tr. by* the author

Spark struck in secret under the stairs in dust, The.   Housefire.   Miranda Field. LegDan

Sparkles from the Wheel.   Walt Whitman.   NAAL-3; SAmP

Sparkling Beaches, The.   Raúl Zurita.   TCLAP, *tr. by* Jack Schmitt

Sparks from my heart rise.   Baqi.   OLP, *tr. by* Walter Andrews, Najaat Black and Mehmet Kalpakli

Sparrow.   Wendell Berry.   WaAnP

Sparrow.   Reginald Gibbons.   IllVoic

Sparrow.   Claudio Rodríguez.   RaW, *tr. by* Robert Mezey

Sparrow and Bird-Net Building.   Takahashi Shinkichi.   ZenPo, *tr. by* Takashi Ikemoto and Lucien Stryk

Sparrow dives from roof to ground.   Flight of the Sparrow.   Takahashi Shinkichi.   ZenPo, *tr. by* Takashi Ikemoto and Lucien Stryk

Sparrow has cut the day in half, The.   Position of the Sparrow, The.   Takahashi Shinkichi.   ZenPo, *tr. by* Takashi Ikemoto and Lucien Stryk

Sparrow Hills.   Robley, Jr. Wilson.   PBCAP

Sparrow in Withered Field.   Takahashi Shinkichi.   ZenPo, *tr. by* Takashi Ikemoto and Lucien Stryk

Sparrow is, A / his hunger organized.   Sparrow.   Wendell Berry.   WaAnP

Sparrow singing.   Buson.   EH, *tr. by* Robert Hass

Sparrow, you darling pet of my beloved.   Catullus.   NAWM-7v1 *Fr.* Carmina [Charles Martin Translation].

Sparrowhawk, soaring, I saw, A.   Taliesin.   Emyr Lewis.   ATSWP, *tr. by* Robert Minhinnick

Sparrows: "Like the poor, they are with us always."   Christopher Buckley. CalPo

Sparrow's always sleeping.   Sparrow and Bird-Net Building.   Takahashi Shinkichi.   ZenPo, *tr. by* Takashi Ikemoto and Lucien Stryk

Sparrows at the Airport, The.   Anthony Ostroff.   OtW

Sparrows dry hearts.   Pittancer, the.   Brian Catling.   VaPo

Sparrows / hop about casually.   My Heart.   Abd al-Rahim Salih al-Rahim. IrPoTo, *tr. by* Saadi A. Simawe and Daniel Weissbort

Sparrows in a Hillside Drift.   James Wright.   ColAP

Sparrows tired of chirping alight on the sloping roof. Chirping. Yi Kyŏngnim. EcSo, *tr. by* Peter H. Lee

Sparrows were feeding in a freezing drizzle. Because You Asked about the Line between Prose and Poetry. Howard Nemerov. OxBoAm; VCAP; WeW-3

Sparse season, the lean, The. Disconsolate Morning. Elizabeth Madox Roberts. APT-1

Spartan Mother, The. Benedek Virág. IQMS, *tr. by* Joseph Leftwich

Spasibo. Thanks. O.K.. (LL) Two Songs. Adrienne Rich. EmeKit; NIL-7

Spastic T-bars pivot and descend, The. (LL) T-Bar. Patricia K. Page. BrAP; NoAM

Spatial Spectacles. Sasha Steensen.
  "State of affairs is thinkable, eventually, A." Eno

Spatulate is the word *Glamour Magazine* uses. Personal History of Hands, A. Lori Jakiela. ReTh

Spawn of a profligate hog. Malediction, A. Peter Didsbury. BeAl

Spawn of Fantasies. Love Songs to Joannes. Mina Loy. NAAPv.2

Spawn of Fantasies. Mina Loy. NAMCP V.1 *Fr.* Love Songs to Joannes.

Speach of Love persuading men to learn Dancing, The. Sir John Davies. NPeEn *Fr.* Orchestra; or, A Poem[e] of Da[u]ncing.

Speak. Pierre Albert Jourdan. YaTCFP, *tr. by* Mary Ann Caws *and* Jean-Pierre Cauvin

Speak! William Wordsworth. OBEV

Speak. James Wright. NoP-4; NoP-5

Speak. Benjamin Zephaniah. Oth

Speak Again. Brian Staveley. IaFF

Speak! And I'll say what you are. 'Tis enough! Altogether I know you. Merits of Writers. Ferenc Kazinczy. IQMS, *tr. by* Watson Kirkconnell

Speak and tell us, our Ximena, looking northward far away. Angels of Buena Vista, The. John Greenleaf Whittier. AmWaPo

Speak, chrysanthemum, why do you you shun. An Minyŏng. CATKP, *tr. by* Peter H. Lee

Speak, daughter, speak; art speaking now? Demeter and Cora. Dora Greenwell. VWP

Speak earth and bless me with what is richest. Love Poem. Audre Lorde. NAMCP V.2; NoAM; PoBW

Speak easy, brother. Attempt at communication, An. Mafika Pascal Gwala. TSAP

SPEAK, gentlemen, what shall we do today?" Sir Revel. Samuel Rowlands. NoSic; OBCoV

Speak gently; it is better far. Speak Gently. G. W. Langford. UV

Speak in the voice of defense. The boar ran, I pulled a knife. (this is plum). Orange Tree Glistens, The. Malinda Markham. IAoNAP

Speak into water, a. Echo and A. Dan Beachy-Quick. IAoNAP

Speak Japanese to me, lover. When You Talk That Talk. Viki Radden. BtF

Speak Low. Ogden Nash. ReLy

Speak low to me, my Saviour, low and sweet. Comfort. Elizabeth Barrett Browning. SacPr

Speak low when you speak love. Speak Low. Ogden Nash. ReLy

Speak, Mistress Quaker, a parable waits from which. Invocation. Ann Lauterbach. OxBoAm

Speak not of passion, for my heart is tired. Sister of Mercy, The. Constance Naden. ViWPN; VWP

Speak [*or* Speke], Parrot. John Skelton.
  "Now, Parrot, my sweet bird, speak our yet once again." NoSic
  (Parrot's Complaint.) NPeEn
  Parrot's Soliloquy. NoSic

Speak out, speak, well. József Katona. IQMS *Fr.* Bánk the Palatine.

Speak out your secret, bellowing waves. Lines: Composed at the Old Temples of Maralipoor. Charles Timothy Brooks. APN-1

Speak roughly to your little boy. Lewis Carroll. NBLV; UV *Fr.* Alice's Adventures in Wonderland.

Speak! speak! thou fearful guest! Skeleton in Armor [*or* Armour], The. Henry Wadsworth Longfellow. APN-1; TreFP

Speak the Truth to the People. Mari E. Evans. FTtHH

Speak, thou jaded heart, defective heart. To a Bad Heart. Tim Reynolds. RaF

Speak to her heart. Ars Amoris. James Vincent Cunningham. WaAnP

Speak to Her Tenderly [*with music*]. Mary E. Tucker. CBWP-1

Speak to Me. Fanny Carrión de Fierro. TANSG, *tr. by* Sally Cheney Bell

Speak to me, aching heart: what. Midnight. Louise Glück. CAP-8

Speak to me. Take my hand. What are you now? Effort at Speech between Two People. Muriel Rukeyser. ItP; MoAmPo; NAAL-5; WaAnP

Speak when I have nothing to say. (LL) Lady Love. Paul Éluard. OBVE; SurPaPo; WoPoe, *tr. by* Samuel Beckett

Speak You Too. Paul Celan. PoetW, *tr. by* John Felstiner

Speaker in the Square, A. George Buchanan. PNI

Speakin' in general, I 've tried 'em all. Sestina of the Tramp-Royal. Rudyard Kipling. MakPoe; MoBrPo; WaAnP

Speaking. Simon J. Ortiz. NIL-7

Speaking. Michael Ryan. SoSe-8

Speaking about epics, mother. Louis Zukofsky. NAMCP V.1; PFTM-1; TaR *Fr.* Poem Beginning "The."

Speaking About My Cracked Sump. Andrew Waterhouse. BeAl; PoCu

Speaking as one Jew to another. Of Dogs and Ostriches. Eve Merriam. TaR

Speaking Hands. Elizabeth Woody. FiBr

Speaking in a state of fidelity to the subject, living flesh though it may. My Story. Carla Harryman. PmAP

Speaking Into the Candles. Medbh McGuckian. ModIr *Fr.* Porcelain Bells.

Speaking My Mind. Ch'i-chi. CSKM, *tr. by* Burton Watson

Speaking My Mind. Chung-ch'ang T'ung. CCL1, *tr. by* Burton Watson

Speaking of Gabriel. Rosario Castellanos. TANSG, *tr. by* Magda Bogin

Speaking of marvels, I am alive. Alive Together. Lisel Mueller. IllVoic

Speaking of Poetry. John Peale Bishop. APT-1; InGu

Speaking of sunsets. Never Again the Same. James Tate. BodElec

Speaking of Television. Phyllis McGinley.
  Robin Hood. OBSV

Speaking of the Poem. Christoph Meckel. GTCP, *tr. by* Reinhold Grimm

Speaking Other Than with Words. Luis Cernuda. RaW, *tr. by* Timothy Baland

Speaking Through White: For My Mother. Kyoko Mori. UnSA

Speaking with Hands. Luis J. Rodriguez. UnSA

Speaking Your Name. Alejandra Pizarnik. TANSG, *tr. by* Susan Bassnett

Speaks to spirits. Abu Salim, Healer. Rachel Tzvia Back. DTA

Spearman heard the bugle sound, The. Beth Gelert. William Robert Spencer. DiBP

Special Branch are after my neck, The. Everything to Declare. Frank Mkalawile Chipasula. NAfrP

Special Jurymen of England! who admire your country's laws. Damages, Two Hundred Pounds. William Makepeace Thackeray. OBSV

Special Performance for Statues, A. Miroslav Holub. MotU, *tr. by* the author and Stuart Friebert

Special Theory came to me, The. Naming the Living God. Kathleen Norris. InvLi; UpMys

Specialist is brought in to the Buddhist college to redirect, A. Office Feng Shui. Shin Yu Pai. WANABP

Specially for me, she had some breaded. Breaded Fish. A. K. Ramanujan. NoP-4; NoP-5

Species. Charles Boyle. EmeKit

Species Means Guilt. Bruce Andrews. PmAP

Species of Audibles. Saskia Hamilton. IIR

Specific Incendiaries of Springtime, The. Lisa Jarnot. VaPo

Specifically the rose window specifically the center. Sainte-Chapelle. John Taggart. FTOS

Specimen. Christopher Pilling. NLP

Specimens of Indian Songs. *Unknown*. APN-2, *tr. by* Lewis Cass

Speck Speaks, A. Adrian Mitchell. OBSP

Speck that would have been beneath my sight, A. Considerable Speck, A. Robert Frost. MoAmPo; SAmP

Speckled Hen's Morning Song to Biddy Early, The. Nancy Willard. FFC

Spectator ab Extra. Arthur Hugh Clough. OBCoV
  As I Sat at the Café. NBLV; OBCoV
  Le Diner. OBCoV; OBSV
  Parvenant. OBCoV

Spectator, The. Evan J. Thomas. AngWePo

Spectator's Guide to Contemporary Art. Phyllis McGinley.
  On the Farther Wall, Marc Chagall. OBSV
  Squeeze Play. OBCoV; OBSV

Spectators' murmur heralds them. Thunderbirds. Tony Dater. OtW

Spectators only on this bustling stage. Charles Churchill. OBSV *Fr.* Night; an Epistle to Robert Lloyd.

Specters. Jorge Fernández Granados. RMCMP, *tr. by* John Oliver Simon

Spectra. Witter Bynner.
  "If I were only dafter." TCAPo

Spectral Dues. Pimone Triplett. AmPoNex

Spectral Lovers. John Crowe Ransom. APT-1; HeIP-4

Spectre of the Rose, The. Luis de Góngora y Argote. *tr. by* Roy Campbell
  Allegory of the Brevity of Things Human. SpanPo; WoPoe, *tr. by* Roy Campbell

Spectrum. Aidan Carl Mathews. PBCIP

Spectrum Trench. Autumn. Nineteen-Sixteen. Dead Soldiers, The. Max Plowman. PoWW

Specula. Gauze in a halo of disinfectant. Depth of Field. Linda Bierds. ExTi

Speculate on anxiety, courtesy of midnight. Dissonances. Giusi Busceti. ItPo, *tr. by* Gayle Ridinger

Speculations. Marcel Duchamp. PFTM-1

Speculations on the Present through the Prism of the Past [*for Haruko*]. June Jordan. GT

Speculations on the Subject of Barabbas. Zbigniew Herbert. GI, *tr. by* John Carpenter *and* Bogdana Carpenter

Speculators, The. William Makepeace Thackeray. OBCoV; OBSV

Speech. Michel-Ange Hyppolite. OGAHCP, *tr. by* Boadiba and Jack Hirschman

Speech. Leopold Staff. PoSu, *tr. by* Adam Czerniawski

Speech. Henry Taylor. NBLV

Speech after long silence; it is right. After Long Silence. William Butler Yeats. HeIP-4; NAEL-6v2; NAEL-7v2; OBMV

Speech Against Stone. Charles Martin. RA

Speech Alone. Jean Follain. TAPaP, *tr. by* W. S. Merwin

Speech and Image: An African Tradition of the Surreal. Léopold Sédar Senghor. PFTM-1

Speech Before Harfleur, The. William Shakespeare. *See* Henry V at the Siege of Harfleur.

Speech for Psyche in the Golden Book of Apuleius. Ezra Pound. HarvBoo

Speech has crawled up a tree. Speech. Michel-Ange Hyppolite. OGAHCP, *tr. by* Boadiba and Jack Hirschman

Speech is a stream. Inga Kuznetsova. CRWP, *tr. by* Max Nemtsov

Speech of the Nymph. Anna Seward. NOBRP

Speech Poem. Laura Solórzano. SPV, *tr. by* Jen Hofer

Speech seems to us the main instrument of thought, emotion and action. Speech and Image: An African Tradition of the Surreal. Léopold Sédar Senghor. PFTM-1

Speech! Speech! Geoffrey Hill.
    "Age of mass consent: go global with her." RWPCtW

Speech to a Crowd. Archibald MacLeish. MoAmPo

Speech to the Young Speech to the Progress-Toward (Among Them Nora and Henry III). Gwendolyn Brooks. PLBUT

Speeches at the Barriers. Susan Howe.
    "Right or ruth." PmAP
    "Sabbath and sweet spices." PmAP
    "Twenty lines of / boughs bend into hindering." PmAP

Speechless, considering, feet well apart. Still Life in Garden. Rachel Hadas. ExTi

Speechless moment thins my blood, A. At the Havana Hilton. Sandra M. Castillo. TouFir

Speechless, speechless, you testify against us. (LL) On the Wall of a KZ-Lager. János Pilinszky. AF; HP; PoSu

Speechless: Upon the Marriage of Two Deaf and Dumb Persons. Philip Bourke Marston. OxBSo

Speechless[e] still, and never cry [*or* crie]. (LL) Epitaph on the Earl of Strafford. John Cleveland. BASC; NOSC; NPeEn; OxBEV

Speed, a Pastoral. John Forbes. BMAP

Speed and light, and what else is one to live for? Duesenberg, 1929. Herbert Morris. PoA 2002

Speed Ball. Yusef Komunyakaa. SeSe

Speed, bonnie boat, like a bird on the wing, Onward, the sailors cry! Skye Boat Song. *Unknown.* BLPJKO

Speed of Darkness, The. Muriel Rukeyser *and* Leif Sjoberg. APSN; APT-2; PFTM-2
    "My night awake." AWTN

Speed of horses, The. The steel of cars. Last Instrument, The. Johannes Göransson. FreRad

Speed of the punch. Homage to the Brown Bomber. Michael S. Harper. MoASP

Speedy dancing and the leaves Germany meet me at the elevator. Fred Wah. NLPA *Fr.* This Dendrite Map: Father / Mother Haibun.

Spell. Kate Clanchy. StAl

Spell. Harry Mathews. NYP2

Spell, A. *Unknown.* WoPoe *Fr.* Three Swedish Spells.

Spell, The. Molly Peacock. FFC

Spell, The: "You can almost see him, looking as if well." William Burford. TiP2

Spell against Predatory Animals. *Unknown.* WoPoe *Fr.* Three Swedish Spells.

Spell Against Sorrow. Kathleen Jessie Raine.

Spell against Twisting an Ankle. *Unknown.* WoPoe *Fr.* Three Swedish Spells.

Spell for a Daughter. Theresa Kishkan. IFF

Spell for Birth. Jeni Couzyn. HAWP

Spell for Jealousy. Jeni Couzyn. BrAP; HAWP

Spell for Sleeping, A. Alastair Reid. NOxBChV

Spell of Blazing Trees, The. Sa'adyya Muffareh. PoArWo, *tr. by* Mona Fayad

Spell of Creation. Kathleen Jessie Raine. PoCho

Spell of Weather, A. Eve Merriam. CA

Spell Spoken by Suppliant to Helios for Protection. Tom Sleigh. PoCho

Spell to Be Said After Illness. Jane Hirshfield. AFaM

Spell to Cure Barrenness. Jeni Couzyn. HAWP

Spell to Protect Our Love. Jeni Couzyn. HAWP

Spell to Soften the Hard Heart of a Woman. Jeni Couzyn. BrAP

Spellbinding image, A. De Pisis--Piacenza Papers. Franco Buffoni. ItPo, *tr. by* Gayle Ridinger

Spellbound. Emily Jane Brontë. NPeEn
    (Night is darkening round me, the.) VWP

Spelling [*with music*]. Margaret Atwood. NALW; NoAM

Spelling reformer indicted, A. Ambrose Bierce. APN-2; CalPo *Fr.* Devil's Dictionary, The.

Spells. Eva Salzman. BeAl

Spelt from Sibyl's Leaves. Gerard Manley Hopkins. NAMCP V.1; NPeEn; OxBEV; OxBSo

Spend the night on water, mist and rain chill. Autumn Evening on the Great Lake. Wang Ch'ang-ling. CCL1, *tr. by* Stephen Owen

Spende and god schall sende. Penny. *Unknown.* FaBoVe

Spending beyond their income on gifts for Christmas. Christmas Shopping. Louis MacNeice. OBCP

Spending hand that alway poureth [*or* powreth] out [*or* owte], A. Sir Thomas Wyatt. NoSic *Fr.* Satires.

Spending the Night. Scott Hightower. BeDoSh

Spending the Night at a Mountain Temple. Chia Tao. CCL1, *tr. by* Stephen Owen

Spending the Night at East Forest Temple. Lingche. CCL1, *tr. by* Stephen Owen

Spending these lonesome evenings. Why Was I Born? Oscar Hammerstein, II. ReLy

Spendthrift, disinherited and graceless, The. Remittance Man. Judith Wright. NoAM

Spenser's Ireland. Marianne Moore. NoAM

Spent a night in Pratt, Kansas. Dead Center. Alfred A. Yuson. ReBoTo

Spent purpose of a perfectly marvellous, The. In Favor of One's Time. Frank O'Hara. PoA 2002

Sperm Count. Steven Huff. NevBe

Spermal Chimney. Francis Picabia. PFTM-1

Sperrins surround it, the Faughan flows by, The. Claudy. James Simmons. PBCIP

Spes mea in Deo est. My Hope Is in God. *Unknown.* SacPr

Speshal Rikwes. Ahdri Zhina Mandiela. WaCA

Spesse Fiate Vegnonmi a la Mente. Dante Alighieri. WoPoe,

Spew out thy filth, thy flesh abjure. Instruction, The. Thomas Traherne. BASC

Sphere. A. R. Ammons.
    "I was pulling veronica out of the lawn when this hornet came." NoAM
    "There is a faculty or knack, smallish, in the mind that can turn." NoAM

Sphere. Jules Supervielle. MFP, *tr. by* Martin Sorrell

Sphere, The: "Their first time, they were wonderfully tender." Gray Jacobik. NevBe

Spheroid. Eggplant. Ibn Sara. WoPoe, *tr. by* Leticia Garza-Falcón and Christopher Middleton

Sphincter. Allen Ginsberg. NAMCP V.2

Sphinx. Van K. Brock. AllShUp; SwNoth

Sphinx. Robert Earl Hayden. GT

Sphinx, The. W. H. Auden. OxBSo *Fr.* Voyage, A.

Sphinx, The. Ralph Waldo Emerson. APN-1; TCAPo

Sphinx, The. Ivan Turgeniev. MotU, *tr. by* Isabel Florence Hapgood

Sphinx, The. Oscar Wilde.
    Fin-de-Siècle Cat. TriCat
    "How subtle-secret is your smile! Did you love none then? Nay, I know." MoBrPo

Sphinx slinks above the blond commotion, The. Lust. Star Black. KGB

Sphinxes. Sandra Hochman. YaYoPo

Spice and pungent air of the earth, The. Confession of Cleopas, The. Eric Pankey. GI

Spice of Life, The. Kalamu ya Salaam. SpirFl *Fr.* New Orleans Haiku.

Spicewood. Lizette Woodworth Reese. MoAmPo

Spider. William Virgil Davis. YaYoPo

Spider. Iwan Llwyd. ATSWP

Spider. Joan Swift. UrbNat

Spider: "How you like these threads, said white spider." Paul Muldoon and Gerald Stern. GPPA

Spider: "What I throw out to the world." Kang Ŭn'gyo. EcSo, *tr. by* Ann Y. Choi

Spider, The. Richard Eberhart. NoAM; PoA 2002

Spider, The. César Vallejo. RaBo; WED, *tr. by* Robert Bly

Spider and the Fly, The. Mary Howitt. ITBLP; UV

Spider, cork, pearl. In Portuguese. Adelia Prado. TCLAP, *tr. by* Marcia Kirinus

Spider Crystal Ascension. Charles Wright. VCAP

Spider don't faze me, mice, bats, no problem, but fish. Confessions of a Pisciphobe. Ruth Maassen. PfS

Spider, dropping down from twig, The. Natural History. Elwyn Brooks White. PtR

Spider expects the cold of winter, The. Spider, The. Richard Eberhart. NoAM; PoA 2002

Spider, from his flaming sleep. Little City. Robert Horan. YaYoPo

Spider Hangs Too Far from the Ground, The. Antonio Cisneros. TCLAP, tr. by William Rowe

Spider, if you had a voice. Basho. WED, tr. by Robert Bly

Spider, juiced crystal and Milky Way, drifts on his web through the night sky, The. Spider Crystal Ascension. Charles Wright. VCAP

Spider Lilies. Kitahara Hakushū. CAoMJL1, tr. by Leith Morton

Spider of Doubt. Pimone Triplett. AmPoNex

Spider, salute the Sun! No rancor show. Philosophy. Rubén Darío. SpanPo, tr. by Muna Lee

Spider sewed at Night, A. Emily Dickinson. NAAL-3; NALW

Spiders I Have Known. W. S. Merwin. MotU

Spiders' spun threads spread through curtains. Spiders' Spun Threads. Hsiao Kang. CCL1, tr. by Anne Birrell

Spiders started out to go with the wind on its pilgrimage, The. Broken, The. W. S. Merwin. MotU

Spied by our own eyes under the shadow of the mad locomotive riverbank sunset Frisco hilly tincan evening sitdown vision. (LL) Sunflower Sutra. Allen Ginsberg. GM; NAMCP V.2; PoPoPo; VCAP

Spiel of [the] Three Mountebanks. John Crowe Ransom. MoAmPo

Spies' March, The. Rudyard Kipling. FaBoWar

Spies whisper through my air condition units. Light Reading. Vassar Miller. FFC

Spies, you are lights in state, but of base stuff. On Spies. Ben Jonson. FaBoVe; NoP-4; NoP-5; NPeEn; WoPoe

Spik o' the Lan, The. Sheena Blackhall. EdScPo

Spiked thorns all over, and a thirty-foot wall. Ballad of the Government Granary Clerk. Ho Ching-ming. ColAnChi, tr. by Jonathan Chaves

Spilt Milk. Sarah Maguire. EmeKit; LW; MFPA; MoWP

Spin. Tracy Ryan. NeBl

Spin a coin, spin a coin. Queen Nefertiti. Unknown. TLR

Spin him like a top! (LL) Homage to My Hips. Lucille Clifton. CAP-8; NAMCP V.2; StAl; WaAnP

Spin in the roles we've saddled on each other, A. Conor O'Callaghan. NIrP Fr. Loose Change.

Spin my own shroud. (LL) "H. D." APT-1; NAMCP V.1 Fr. Walls Do Not Fall, The.

Spinal Cord. 'Aisha Arnaout. PoArWo, tr. by Mona Fayad

Spinazzola: Quella Cantina Là. Richard Hugo. PWW2

Spin-Cycle. Jane Holland. MFPA

Spindrift, crustacean patience. Swim in Co. Wicklow, A. Derek Mahon. NAMCP V.2

Spine doesn't give or arch to it, The. Not-loving. Sylvia Kantaris. LW

Spine has been tingled; the horn has been swoggled, The. Woolly Words. Robert N. Feinstein. NBLV

Spineless and eyeless we spend our days. Sea-Polyp, The. Julia Copus. NeBl

Spinner, seated near the window sash, The. Spinner, The. Paul Valéry. YaTCFP, tr. by Grace Schulman

Spinner, The. Nathan Alterman. FIT, tr. by Robert Friend

Spinner, The. Paul Valéry. YaTCFP, tr. by Grace Schulman

Spinning. May Muzaffar. PoArWo, tr. by Tahia Abdel Nasser

Spinning. Alfred Wellington Purdy. NoAM

Spinning Dharma Wheel. Takahashi Shinkichi. ZenPo, tr. by Takashi Ikemoto and Lucien Stryk

Spinning ritual into fusion. Breath. Daniel Gray-Kontar. BRtP

Spinning Song. Dame Edith Sitwell. MoBrPo

Spinning-Wheel, The. John Francis Waller. IrV

Spinoza. Jorge Luis Borges. TCLAP, tr. by Richard Howard and César Renert

Spinster. Sylvia Plath. LW; SoSe-8

Spinster near Gyöngyös displays, A. Unspeakable. Ferenc Faludi. IQMS, tr. by J. G. Nichols

Spinster Song: African-American Woman Guild. Angela Jackson. IllVoic

Spinster swats a worm on her tabletop, A. Aunt Sophie's Morning. James Tate. SUP

Spinster with a mouth like a dam and a heart, A. Lizzie. Nancy Vieira Couto. PBCAP

Spinster's Sweet-Arts, The. Alfred Tennyson.
  "Robby, git down wi'tha, wilt tha?" FaBoVe

Spiraling, the sparks. Nejati. OLP, tr. by Walter Andrews, Najaat Black and Mehmet Kalpakli

Spire, The. Ellen Bryant Voigt. NoAM

Spire cranes, The. Its statue is an aviary. Spire Cranes, The. Dylan Thomas. PoA 2002

Spirella lady sipped tea, The. Fitting. Pauline Prior-Pitt. Prnts

Spirit, The. Jones Very. NCAP

Spirit appeared to me, and said, A. Spirit Appeared to Me, A. Herman Melville. ChIV-1

Spirit came upon me in the night, A. After-State. Frederick William Faber. CenSon

Spirit Escapes, The [with music]. Pierre Reverdy. MotU, tr. by Michael Benedikt

Spirit from Perfecter Ages. Arthur Hugh Clough. OxAEP-2 Fr. Amours de Voyage.

Spirit Host Is Advancing, They Say, The. Arapaho Oral Tradition. NAAPv.2

Spirit in the sky. Spirit Song. Unknown. WoPoe, tr. by Stephen Berg

Spirit is lame and in the pale flesh, The. Landing Area. J. H. Prynne. PFTM-2

Spirit is too Blunt an Instrument, The. Anne Stevenson. ColAP; StAl

Spirit is treading the earth, A. Sick-Room, The. Maria White Lowell. NAAPv.1

Spirit lasts, but in what mode, The. Emily Dickinson. APN-2

Spirit Level. Anthony Conran. TCAWP

Spirit Level, The. David Barber. AmPoNex

Spirit moved upon the face of the waters, The. (LL) Reading the Bible Backwards. Eleanor Wilner. NoP-4; NoP-5

Spirit of '76, The. Friederike Mayröcker. PFTM-2, tr. by Anselm Hollo

Spirit of Bell Mountain, the Divinity of Grass Hut Cloister, The. Proclamation on North Mountain. K'ung Chih-kuei. CCL1, tr. by James Robert Hightower

Spirit of dreams, that when the dark hours steep. Invocation, To the Genius of Slumber Written Oct. 1787. Anna Seward. PEW

Spirit of evil, with which the earth is rife. Charles Johnston. CenSon

Spirit of God! descend upon my heart. Supplication, A. George Croly. SacPr

Spirit of God, The. Antiphon for the Holy Spirit. Hildegard von Bingen. WPoS, tr. by Barbara Newman

Spirit of light divine! Semele. Rose Terry Cooke. NAAPv.1

Spirit of light, whose eye unfolds. Ode Inscribed to the Infant Son of S.T. Coleridge, Esq. Mary Robinson. RWP

Spirit of Place: Great Blue Heron. William Stafford. PfSP

Spirit of Plato. Unknown. OBVE

Spirit of Poetry, The. Henry Wadsworth Longfellow. APN-1

Spirit of pure benevolence, descend. On the Slave-Trade. Isabella Lickbarrow. RWP

Spirit of spirits, who, through ev'ry part. Hymn to Na'a'yena, A. Sir William Jones. NOBRP

Spirit of the Age, The. Christopher Pearse Cranch. APN-1

Spirit of the Dancer. Lisa Elaine Johnson. BtF

Spirit of the Place, The. Tony Curtis. AngWePo

Spirit of the Staircase, The. Lavinia Greenlaw. NeBrP

Spirit Papers. Teresa D. Cader. ExTi

Spirit Pass'd Before Me, A. Lord Byron. ChIV-1

Spirit saith, come, The. Bible, N.T. EMWP Fr. Revelation of St. John the Divine.

Spirit sets about its task, but slowly, The. J. D. McClatchy. WiU Fr. First Steps.

Spirit, Silken Thread. Margot Ruddock. OBMV

Spirit Song. Unknown. WoPoe, tr. by Stephen Berg

Spirit sweats—the horizon's, The. Moochkap. Boris Leonidovich Pasternak. TCRusP, tr. by Bogdan Boychuk and Mark Rudman

Spirit! What art thou erecting. Poet's Ideal, The. Henrietta Cordelia Ray. CBWP-3

Spirit whose work is done—spirit of dreadful hours! Spirit Whose Work Is Done. Walt Whitman. CBCWP; NAAL-3; PCW

Spirited light! on the edge. Antiphon for the Angels. Hildegard von Bingen. WPoS, tr. by Barbara Newman

Spirits. Robert Bridges. OBEV

Spirits. Víctor Hernández Cruz. PueRic

Spirits are wafted along the roof &. Wintu Oral Tradition. NAAPv.1 Fr. Six Dream Songs.

Spirit's artery snapped, God's film snapped, The. Hand. Nishiwaki Junzaburo. CAoMJL1, tr. by Hosea Hirata

Spirit's Epilogue, The. John Milton. See Farewell of the Attendant Spirit.

Spirit's Mysteries, The. Felicia Dorothea Hemans. RWP

Spirits of children are remote and wise, The. Ode on the Whole Duty Of Parents. Frances Darwin Cornford. MoWP

Spirits of man's escapism. Armstrong and Aldrin on the Moon. William Richard Philip George. BBMWP, tr. by Richard Poole

Spirits of the dead lights. Jerome Rothenberg. PFTM-2 Fr. Khurbn.

Spirits of well-shot woodcock, partridge, snipe. Death of King George V. Sir John Betjeman. OxBEV

Spirits on the balcony at one A.M.. Origami. Jay Griswold. AtGh

Spirit's Return, A. Felicia Dorothea Hemans. NAEL-7v2

Spiritual: "How did you feel when you come out the wilderness?" William W. Cook. SpirFl

Spiritual, A. Paul Laurence Dunbar. SacPr

Spiritual Alchemy, The. "Angelus Silesius." GePo Fr. Cherubical Wanderer, The.

Spiritual Alphabet in Midsummer. Bruce Beasley.
　"This is the finger of God." AmAlph

Spiritual Ark And The Manna-Vessel, The. "Angelus Silesius." GePo Fr. Cherubical Wanderer, The.

Spiritual Athlete in an Orange Robe, The. Kabir. See Hopeful Spiritual Athlete, The.

Spiritual athlete often changes the color of his clothes, The. Hopeful Spiritual Athlete, The. Kabir. RaBo, tr. by Robert Bly

Spiritual Canticle. San Juan de la Cruz. SpanPo, tr. by John Frederick Nims

Spiritual Canticle, The. San Juan de la Cruz. STV, tr. by John Frederick Nims

Spiritual Chickens. Stephen Dobyns. StAl

Spiritual Geography. Kalamu ya Salaam. SpirFl Fr. New Orleans Haiku.

Spiritual Impregnation, The. "Angelus Silesius." GePo Fr. Cherubical Wanderer, The.

Spiritual Laws. Ralph Waldo Emerson. APN-1

Spiritual Meditation upon a Bee, A. Amey Hayward. EMWP

Spiritual Morning. Robin Becker. TaR

Spiritual, the carnal, are one, The. Dorothy, Duchess of Wellington Wellesley. OBMV Fr. Matrix.

Spiritual Wedding. Manuel Bandeira. TCLAP, tr. by Candace Slater

Spirituality vs. the Temporality, The. John Skelton. NAEL-6v1 Fr. Colin Clout.

Spit. A. R. Ammons. BodElec

Spit. C. K. Williams. TaR

Spit in my face ye [or you] Jew[e]s, and pierce my side. John Donne. BASC; WaAnP Fr. Holy Sonnets.

Spit in the shape of an ocean. Story Pillow, The. Dave Brinks. AnSo

Spit it out when sweet. Farewell, My Youth. Yi Sanghûi. EcSo, tr. by Jennifer M. Lee

Spit of sky, awash with Venetian gold, A. Sunset at Wellfleet. Jean Valentine. YaYoPo

Spit-cup, The. J-O-Y. James Richardson. RD

Spite made the architects put the front desk of the hotel. Hard Put. Catie Rosemurgy. AmPoNex

Spitfire! from BlackFleshMotors. Dance Bodies #1. Eugene B. Redmond. ISC

Spits of glitter in lowgrade ore. Conserving the Magnitude of Uselessness. A. R. Ammons. NoAM

Spitting in the Leaves. Maggie Anderson. PBCAP

Spittle beads as ice along. Wrong Way Will Haunt You, The. Sydney Lea. RA

Splash and spread. Milkstone. Shin Yu Pai. AmZen

Splash water on level ground. Pao Chao. ChinPo Fr. Weary Road, The.

Splashes of color on the cover. First Books. Andrea Hollander Budy. NevBe

Splashing—that is now stone. (LL) These. William Carlos Williams. APT-1; GPTC; MoAmPo; NAAPv.2; OxBoAm

Splat of bare feet on wet tile, The. Women's Locker Room. Marilyn Nelson Waniek. LTA

Splayed wide in a candid unshamable V. (LL) Letter, The: "If I remember right, his first letter." Andrew Motion. EmeKit; NeBrP

Spleen. Ernest Dowson. MoBrPo

Spleen. August Kleinzahler. PmAP

Spleen. Paul Verlaine. SxFrPo, tr. by Martin Sorrell

Spleen, Le. Joseph Warton. STuOW Fr. Ode against Despair.

Spleen LXXIX. Charles Baudelaire. NAWM-7v2,

Spleen LXXV. Charles Baudelaire. SxFrPo, tr. by James McGowan

Spleen LXXVI. Charles Baudelaire. SxFrPo, tr. by James McGowan

Spleen LXXVII. Charles Baudelaire. SxFrPo, tr. by James McGowan

Spleen LXXVIII. Charles Baudelaire. NAWM-7v2,

Spleen LXXVIII. Charles Baudelaire. SxFrPo, tr. by James McGowan

Spleen LXXXI. Charles Baudelaire. NAWM-7v2,

Spleen, The: A Pindaric Poem. Anne Finch, Countess of Winchilsea. NALW; NoP-4; NoP-5; NOSC; WaAnP
　Power of Spleen, The. NPeEn

Spleen, The [Complete]. Matthew Green.
　Epistle to Mr. Cuthbert Jackson, An. NoP-4; NoP-5
　"I always choose the plainest food." VerBaPo
　"Sometimes I dress, with women sit." NPeEn; OBCoV
　"To cure the mind's wrong bias, Spleen." NPeEn
　"When by its magic lantern Spleen." OxAEP-1

Splendid Bankrupt, The. Arthur A. Sykes. UV

Splendid body is private, and calls for more, The. Hymn. Rex Warner. RSaN

Splendid breasts. Ozaki Hosai. CAoMJL1, tr. by Makoto Ueda

Splendid Cheek emerges from the hawthorn muslins, The. Sunrise. Saint-Pol Roux. YaTCFP, tr. by Mary Ann Caws and Jean-Pierre Cauvin

Splendid coat that wrapped the favored son, The. Woman of Color. Constance Merritt. AmPoNex

Splendid Stags, The. József Erdélyi. IQMS, tr. by Thomas Land

Splendid Village, The. Ebenezer Elliott.
　"Village! thy butcher's son, the steward now." OBSV

Splendidly-shining darkness. Félix Lope de Vega Carpio. WoPoe Fr. Pentecost Castle, The.

Splendor and pride I celebrate. Angelo Politziano. WoPoe Fr. Tournament, The.

Splendor and ruin, sorrow and joy, long life or early death. Sick and Old, Same as Ever: A Poem to Figure It All Out. Po Chü-i. NDACCP, tr. by David Hinton

Splendor falls on castle walls, The. Alfred Tennyson. ClHu; CtM; HeIP-4; NAEL-6v1; NAEL-7v1; NoP-4; NoP-5; TFi Fr. Princess, The.

Splendor from the Splendid. Uri Zvi Greenberg. NRoS, tr. by Esther Raizen

Splendor in the Wind. Raúl Zurita. TCLAP, tr. by Jack Schmitt

Splendor of the world is just an empty dream, The. Retreat at Haein Temple. Daegak Euchon. BecRai, tr. by Kim Daljin, Kim Won-Chung and Christopher Merrill

Splendour falls on castle walls, The. Alfred Tennyson. See Splendor falls on castle walls, The.

Splendour of life so splendidly contained. Geoffrey Hill. NoAM Fr. Lachrimae; or Seven Tears Figured in Seven Passionate Pavans.

Splendour [orSplendor] Falls, The. Alfred Tennyson. ClHu; CtM; HeIP-4; NAEL-6v1; NAEL-7v1; NoP-4; NoP-5; TFi Fr. Princess, The.

Splendour recurrent. Unknown. OBVE Fr. Deer Sing.

Splinter. Silvia Eugenia Castillero. SPV, tr. by Jen Hofer

Splinter. Carl Sandburg. SoSe-8; Spl

Splinter, The. Fanny Howe.
　"See how this being at the neck and bowel." FaoP
　"Very pain it came first." FaoP

Splinter under nail. Spell to Cure Barrenness. Jeni Couzyn. HAWP

Splintered the crystal of identity. "H. D." NAAL-5 Fr. Walls Do Not Fall, The.

Splish splash, February-fill-the-dike. February. John Heath-Stubbs. OBCP

Split. George Held. ArBi

Split ears of morning earth green now. Lorca. Bob Kaufman. EGAG

Split the Lark—and you'll find the Music. Emily Dickinson. APN-2; ChIV-2; NoP-4; NoP-5; TCAPo

Split-second disaster. (LL) Meridian. Amy Clampitt. NAMCP V.2; NIL-7

Splitting from Jack Delaney's, Sheridan Square. Derek Walcott. GT

Splitting the void in half. Nanei. ZenPo, tr. by Takashi Ikemoto and Lucien Stryk

Splitting Wood Near Morris, Oklahoma on Robbie and Lesa McMurtry's Farm. Lance Henson. HATNAP

Splittings. Adrienne Rich. HarvBoo

Spofford Hall. Alison Stone. SwNoth

Spoils. Robert Graves. WeW-3

Spoils of Annwn, The. Unknown. WoPoe, tr. by Anthony Conran

Spoke Aug 19. Hannah Weiner.
　Seen Words. FTOS

Sponge. Fabio Morabito. RMCMP, tr. by Geoff Hargreaves

Sponge Boy. Stefi Weisburd. MAAN

Spontaneous Me. Walt Whitman. NAAL-3; NAAL-5

Spontaneous me, Nature. Spontaneous Me. Walt Whitman. NAAL-3; NAAL-5

Spontaneous momentum, A. Sheaf Mark. Ray DiPalma. FTOS

Spontaneous Monument. Meredith Walters. IIR

Spookism. Lamont B. Steptoe. FuFl

Spool, The. Ben Belitt. PWW2

Spoon, for instance, just, The. Simple Machines. Marianne Boruch. AmAlph

Spoon Maker's Daughter, The. Susan Utting. Prnts

Spoon of your head, The. Rain. John Ashbery. FTOS

Spoon River Anthology. Edgar Lee Masters.
　A. D. Blood. APT-1
　Amanda Barker. APT-1; NAMCP V.1; NoAM; OxBoAm
　Anne Rutledge. CBCWP; MoAmPo; NAMCP V.1; NoAM; OxBoAm; TFi
　Archibald Higbie. APT-1; OxBoAm
　Benjamin Pantier. APT-1
　"Butch" Weldy. APT-1
　Carl Hamblin. OBSV

Constance Hately. APT-1

Doctor Meyers. APT-1; IllVoic

Editor Whedon. APT-1; OBSV; OxBoAm

Elsa Wertman. NAAPv.1; NAMCP V.1; NoAM

Emily Sparks. APT-1

Fiddler Jones. IllVoic; NAMCP V.1; NoAM

Flossie Cabanis. APT-1

Hamilton Greene. NAAPv.1; NAMCP V.1; NoAM

Harry Williams. AmWaPo; APT-1

Henry C. Calhoun.
  "On the way to the grove you'll pass the Fates." TCAPo

Hill, The. ColAP; IllVoic; NAMCP V.1; NoAM; OxBoAm

Indignation Jones. APT-1

Judge Somers. OBSV

Justice Arnett. APT-1

Lucinda Matlock. IllVoic; MoAmPo; NoAM

Margaret Fuller Slack. APT-1; IllVoic; RACG

Minerva Jones. APT-1; IllVoic

Mrs. Benjamin Pantier. APT-1

Mrs. Meyers. APT-1; IllVoic

Oscar Hummel. APT-1

Petit, the Poet. ColAP; MoAmPo; NAMCP V.1; NoAM; TCAPo

Ralph Rhodes. APT-1

Reuben Pantier. APT-1

Serepta Mason. APT-1

Sexsmith the Dentist. GeoHom

Starved Rock. GeoHom

Trainor, the Druggist. APT-1; IllVoic

Unknown, The. NAAPv.1

Webster Ford. APT-1

Willie Metcalf. APT-1

Spoonful of Cocoa, A. Ishikawa Takuboku. CAoMJL1, tr. by Leith Morton

Spooning. David Mason. WaAnP

Spoons with Realistic Dead Flies on Them. Charles Simic. NAMCP V.2

Spoor bank, The. Jim Brodey. AHA Fr. Identikit.

Sportif. David McCord. See Ascot Waistcoat.

Sporting Acquaintances. Siegfried Sassoon. OxBSo

Sporting at fancie, setting light by love. Richard Barnfield. CAGL Fr. Cynthia, with Certain[e] Sonnets.

Sporting Beasley. Sterling Allen Brown. APT-2; NAMCP V.1

Sporting Life. Jack Spicer. OxBoAm

Sporting people, The. Free Fantasia: Tiger Flowers. Robert Earl Hayden. ESEAA

Sporting the Plaid. Chris Wallace-Crabbe. NOBAu

Sports and gallantries, the stage, the arts, the antics of dancers. Boats in a Fog. Robinson Jeffers. NAAPv.2; NoP-4; NoP-5; WaAnP

Sportsmen. Keith Douglas. See Aristocrats.

Sporus. Alexander Pope. OBSV; OxBEV Fr. Epistle to Dr. Arbuthnot.

S'posin'. Andy Razaf. ReLy

Spot her, but don't lock on her. How to Approach Your Lover's Wife. Amy Bottke. OPRER

Spot the Ball. Frank Ormsby. PBCIP; PNI

Spot which will be my grave, The. (LL) New Heavens for Old. Amy Lowell. APT-1; NAMCP V.1

Spotlights had you covered, The. Poem about Poems about Vietnam, A. Jon Stallworthy. NoAM

Spots. Estella Lauter. SweBea

Spots, The. Joel Brouwer. LegDan

Spots triumphed in the afternoon light, The. After the Rain. Kristina Rungano. HAWP

Spotted hawk swoops by and accuses me, he complains of my gab and my loitering, the. Walt Whitman. AmFaPo; CAGL; ColAP; ItP; NAWM-7v2; NoP-5; SAmP; WaAnP Fr. Song of Myself.

Spouse of Jesus Laments Her Heart's Flame, The. Friedrich Spee. GePo, tr. by George C. Schoolfield

Spraggy cod'll grow ni fatter, A. Fisherman's Rhyme. Unknown. FaBoVe

Sprawl is the quality. Quality of Sprawl, The. Les A. Murray. EmeKit; HarvBoo; NoP-4; NoP-5

Sprawl is the quality. Les A. Murray. UpMys Fr. Quality of Sprawl, The.

Sprawled belly-down on the damp planks. Bullhead. John Engels. MoASP

Sprawled in the pigsty. For a Young Artist. Robert Earl Hayden. NoAM

Sprawled on the crates and sacks in the rear of the truck. Green, Green Is El Aghir. Norman Cameron. NePenScot; NPeEn; OBWP

Sprawls across the centerline. Roadkill Coyote. Art Goodtimes. GeoH

Spray. Biddy Jenkinson. ModIr, tr. by Alex Osborne

Spray of pine-needles, A. Nullo. Jean Toomer. APT-2

Spraying the Potatoes. Patrick Kavanagh. CABP

Spray-painted across a garage door. Strange Fruit. Timothy Liu. WiU

Sprays of wisteria. Masaoka Shiki. CAoMJL1 Fr. Fifteen Haiku.

Spread. Leandro Katz. AHA

Spread a Little Happiness. Clifford Grey. ReLy

Spread beneath me it lies—lean upland. Flying Above California. Thom Gunn. CalPo

Spread eagle sheep legs wide. Mantanza to Welcome Spring. Jimmy Santiago Baca. PmAP

Spread, Table, Spread. George Peele. NoSic Fr. Old Wives' [or Wife's] Tale, The.

Spread their gay wings before the Throne, and smile. (LL) Epitaph on the Tombstone of a Child, the Last of Seven that Died Before. Aphra Behn. CABP; NOSC; OxBSo

Spreadeagled for sleep, godlike, on your back. Contrary Motion. Elizabeth Garrett. NeBl

Spreadeagled in the empty air / of existence. (LL) Constantly Risking Absurdity. Lawrence Ferlinghetti. CalPo; PmAP

Spreadin' Rhythm Around. Ted Koehler. ReLy

Spreading their legs between the rows. American Pylons. Kevin Durkin. PoDa

Spreading Wings on Wind. Simon J. Ortiz. HATNAP

Spree. Maxine W. Kumin. NoAM

Sprig of Moss, The. William McGonagall.
  "By taking the impressions of watch-cases he discovered, one day." VerBaPo

Spring. Winona Baker.
  "In the pocket." IFF

Spring! Basho. EH, tr. by Robert Hass

Spring. William Blake. NOxBChV Fr. Songs of Innocence.

Spring. Judith Ortiz Cofer. PueRic

Spring. Rubén Darío. SpanPo, tr. by Anita Volland

Spring. Ebenezer Elliott. OxAEP-2

Spring. Ferenc Faludi. IQMS, tr. by Donald Davie

Spring. Adelaida Gertsyk. ARWW, tr. by Catriona Kelly

Spring. Margherita Guidacci. CItWP, tr. by Cinzia Sartini Blum and Lara Trubowitz

Spring. Friedrich Hölderlin. WoPoe Fr. Seasons, The.

Spring. Iio Sogi. WoPoe, tr. by Steven D. Carter

Spring: "All the truth you'll ever be able to cull." Carl Dennis. PfSP

Spring: "Nothing is so beautiful as Spring." Gerard Manley Hopkins. BrAP; GoPo; GSo; MoBrPo; NAEL-6v2; NAEL-7v2; NAMCP V.1; NoAM; OBMV; TFi

Spring. Pinkie Gordon Lane. GT

Spring. Philip Larkin. MoBrPo

Spring. Hugo Majer. Spl

Spring: "To what purpose, April, do you return again?" Edna St. Vincent Millay. APT-1; MoAmPo; NAMCP V.1; NoP-4; NoP-5

Spring. Thomas Nashe. See Spring, the Sweet Spring.

Spring. Papyrus. Ezra Pound. APT-1; PFTM-1

Spring: "After the bitter weather." R. Williams Parry. BBMWP, tr. by Joseph P. Clancy

Spring. Rudaki. WoPoe, tr. by Geoffrey Squires

Spring. William Shakespeare. NAEL-6v1; NBLV; NIL-7; NIP-4; NoP-5; NoSic; OBEV; TFi Fr. Love's Labour's Lost.

Spring: "Willows tangle like silk threads." Shen Yüeh. CCL1, tr. by Anne Birrell

Spring: "This is what I saw—old snow on the ground." Charles Simic. PtR

Spring: "Spring afternoon, a lovely sky, bright sunshine, A." Daniel Simidor. OGAHCP, tr. by Boadiba and Jack Hirschman

Spring. Takahashi Shinkichi. ZenPo, tr. by Takashi Ikemoto and Lucien Stryk

Spring: "Let's not talk." Tracy K. Smith. PoDa

Spring. Tu Fu [or Du Fu]. TAL

Spring. Mary E. Tucker. CBWP-1

Spring: "Spring wind stirs my romantic heart, The." Unknown. CCL1, tr. by John Frodsham

Spring. Yun Söndo. CATKP Fr. Angler's Calendar, The.

Spring, The. Morgan Llwyd. AngWePo Fr. 1648.

Spring, The. Ellen Bryant Voigt. LPSFW

Spring, The: "Now that the Winter's gone, the earth hath lost." Thomas Carew. CavPo; NoP-4; NoP-5; PBRV

Spring, The: "Though you be absent here, I needs must say." Abraham Cowley. OxAEP-1 Fr. Mistress, The.

Spring 61. Lenore Kandel. BB

Spring after spring, I sat before my mirror. Boat of Stars. Li Ch'ing-chao. ErotSp, tr. by Sam Hamill

Spring afternoon, a lovely sky, bright sunshine, A. Spring. Daniel Simidor. OGAHCP, tr. by Boadiba and Jack Hirschman

Spring already short of breath, A.   Imaginary Crimes in a Real Garden. Russell Atkins.   EGAG

Spring and All.   William Carlos Williams.   APT-1; ChAP; ColAP; EMP; MakPoe; NAAL-5; NAAPv.2; NAMCP V.1; NoAM; OxBoAm; PoPoPo; TCAPo; TFi; TRP

    (Poem: "By the road to the contagious hospital.")   MoAmPo; PtR

Spring, and all over town.   Signs.   Wendy Mnookin.   UrbNat

Spring & Asura.   Miyazawa Kenji.   CAoMJL1, *tr. by* Hiroaki Sato

Spring and Fall [To a Young Child].   Gerard Manley Hopkins.   BrAP; CABP; ClHu; CtM; HeIP-4; InoFa; NAEL-6v2; NAEL-7v2; NAMCP V.1; NIL-7; NIP-4; NoAM; NoP-4; NoP-5; OPOU; PoPoPo; PtR; TFi; TRP; WaAnP

Spring / and for you, spring—isn't it spring?   Kukutis's Swallow's Hymn. Marcelijus Martinaitis.   TWW, *tr. by* Laima Sruoginis

Spring and Other Places.   David Chaloner.   VaPo

Spring and the Ashura.   Miyazawa Kenji.   PFTM-1

Spring and the girls are twirling batons.   Twirling.   Jane Flanders.   ItWoWo; PBCAP

Spring: another / joke.   C. K. Williams.   OnScMo

Spring appears, in which the earth, The.   Vigil of Venus, The.   *Unknown. tr. by* Thomas Stanley

Spring at Nant Dywelan.   Bobi Jones.   OBWVE, *tr. by* Joseph P. Clancy

Spring at Wu Ling.   Li Ch'ing-chao.   ErotSp, *tr. by* Sam Hamill

    (To the Tune: Spring at Wu Ling.)   CrYelRi

Spring at Yesan Station.   Sub-ok.   WPoS, *tr. by* Julie Pickering

Spring Azures.   Mary Oliver.   CAP-8

Spring being at her blessed carpentry, The.   Garden Chidings.   Louise Imogen Guiney.   SWaP

Spring Bereaved.   William Drummond of Hawthornden. *See* Sonnet: "Alexis, here she stayed; among these pines."

Spring Bereaved.   William Drummond of Hawthornden.   OBEV

Spring Bereaved 2.   William Drummond of Hawthornden.   OBEV

Spring blossoms, autumn moon.   To the Tune: Beautiful Lady Yu.   Li Yu [*or* Li Hou-Chu].   CrYelRi, *tr. by* Sam Hamill

Spring Blossoms into Flower.   *Unknown.*   CAoMJL1, *tr. by* Leith Morton

Spring breeze.   Buson.   EMJL *Fr.* Spring Breeze on the Kema Embankment.

Spring Breeze on the Kema Embankment.   Buson.   EMJL, *tr. by* Christopher Drake

"As I near my village, spring deepens."   EMJL, *tr. by* Christopher Drake

"Dandelions blooming in fives and threes."   EMJL, *tr. by* Christopher Drake

"From outside a hedge, a hen calls her chicks."   EMJL, *tr. by* Christopher Drake

"Home for three days."   EMJL, *tr. by* Christopher Drake

"I set out from my village three springs ago."   EMJL, *tr. by* Christopher Drake

"I went down the bank to pick fragrant plants."   EMJL, *tr. by* Christopher Drake

"I've learned how."   EMJL, *tr. by* Christopher Drake

"Long, long ago."   EMJL, *tr. by* Christopher Drake

"Old post town, two or three houses."   EMJL, *tr. by* Christopher Drake

"Old woman at the teahouse, The."   EMJL, *tr. by* Christopher Drake

"Raising my head, I make out my house in the twilight."   EMJL, *tr. by* Christopher Drake

"Road becomes three, The."   EMJL, *tr. by* Christopher Drake

"Rocks rising from the rushing water."   EMJL, *tr. by* Christopher Drake

"Softly she breaks off."   EMJL, *tr. by* Christopher Drake

"Spring breeze."   EMJL, *tr. by* Christopher Drake

"Springs passed."   EMJL, *tr. by* Christopher Drake

"Three whole days off."   EMJL, *tr. by* Christopher Drake

"Two men drink wine at the only table."   EMJL, *tr. by* Christopher Drake

"White plum blossoms."   EMJL, *tr. by* Christopher Drake

"Willow, The."   EMJL, *tr. by* Christopher Drake

Spring breezes blow, grasses bud.   Maiden Called Love, The.   Takeshima Hagaromo.   CAoMJL1, *tr. by* Leith Morton

Spring breezes erase the flowers.   Spring Evening on Pan Mountain.   Wang An-shih.   CrYelRi, *tr. by* Sam Hamill

Spring came.   Spring.   Rudaki.   WoPoe, *tr. by* Geoffrey Squires

Spring Can Really Hang You Up the Most.   Fran Landesman.   ReLy

Spring Chrysanthemums.   Ku Sang.   CAMKP, *tr. by* Kevin O'Rourke

Spring Cliff.   Muso Soseki.   EaWin, *tr. by* W. S. Merwin

Spring, Coast Range.   Kenneth Rexroth.   APT-2 *Fr.* Toward an Organic Philosophy.

Spring comes early to the gardens.   Green Jade Plum Trees in Spring.   Ouyang Hsiu.   NDACCP, *tr. by* Kenneth Rexroth

Spring comes in Dallas like a gunshot, like.   Early Warning.   Frederick Turner.   TiP2

Spring Comes to Chicago.   Campbell McGrath.   NeAmPo

Spring Comes to Murray Hill.   Ogden Nash.   AmWit; APT-2

Spring comes to rivers and lakes.   Four Seasons by the Rivers and Lakes.   Maeng Sasŏng.   CATKP, *tr. by* Peter H. Lee

Spring Comes to the Suburbs.   Phyllis McGinley.   APT-2

Spring comes, together with a rush of feelings.   On the Road: A Spring Day at Ling-Feng.   Ching An.   CSKM, *tr. by* Jerome P. Seaton

Spring Coming.   A. R. Ammons.   HeIP-4

Spring Dawn.   Meng Hao Jan.   ColAnChi, *tr. by* Elling O. Eide

Spring Dawn ("Spring sleep, not yet awake to dawn.")   Meng Hao Jan.   NDACCP, *tr. by* Gary Snyder

Spring Day.   John Ashbery.   ColAP

Spring Day.   Cho Chihun.   CAMKP, *tr. by* Kevin O'Rourke

Spring Day.   Yu Chien-wu.   ColAnChi, *tr. by* Victor H. Mair and Tsu-Lin Mei

Spring day, The.   Issa.   EH, *tr. by* Robert Hass

Spring Day: Thinking of Li Po.   Tu Fu [*or* Du Fu].   ChinPo, *tr. by* Ye Weilian [*or* Yeh Wei-lien *or* Wai-lim Yip]

Spring Does Not Flow Now, The.   Rosalía de Castro.   SpanPo, *tr. by* Muriel Kittel

Spring does not flow now, the stream is quite dry, The.   Spring Does Not Flow Now, The.   Rosalía de Castro.   SpanPo, *tr. by* Muriel Kittel

Spring Drawing 2.   Robert Hass.   CAP-8

Spring Dreams.   Meng Hao Jan.   CrYelRi, *tr. by* Sam Hamill

Spring dusk. (LL)   Village without bells, A.   Basho.   EH; NIL-7, *tr. by* Robert Hass

SPRING DUSK DARK SHORE.   Poem for Old Walt.   Lawrence Ferlinghetti.   ViWalt

Spring Ecstasy.   Lizette Woodworth Reese.   MoAmPo

Spring Ends.   Li Ch'ing-chao.   NDACCP,

Spring Equinox.   Peter Blue Cloud.   ChAP *Fr.* Within the Seasons.

Spring Evening.   Frederick Turner.   RA

Spring Evening on Pan Mountain.   Wang An-shih.   CrYelRi, *tr. by* Sam Hamill

Spring fades. Why should I suffer so much from homesickness?   Spring Fades.   Li Ch'ing-chao.   NDACCP, *tr. by* Kenneth Rexroth

Spring Fever.   Rosario Morales.   PueRic

Spring flowers, autumn moon: when to end?   Tune: "Beauty Yu."   Li Yü.   ChinPo, *tr. by* Ye Weilian [*or* Yeh Wei-lien *or* Wai-lim Yip]

Spring flowers, Autumn moons.   Plaint.   Chu Shu-chen.   NDACCP, *tr. by* Kenneth Rexroth

Spring flowers, autumn moon—when will you end?   Bella Donna Iu.   Li Yü.   NDACCP, *tr. by* William Carlos Williams

Spring Flowers Own, The.   Etel Adnan.   "Butterfly came to die, A."   PoArWo

Spring Forward.   Martin Steingesser.   PoCoUp

Spring Forward, Fall Back.   Alpay Ulku.   AmPoNex

Spring from the earth, food for our children. Give us good health. Let us grow up, and become ripe.   *Unknown.*   APN-2 *Fr.* Minnetare Songs.

Spring garden is *Irish* green, The.   British Garden, A.   Wes Magee.   OBGa

Spring goes, and the hundred flowers.   Rebirth.   Man Giac.   EaWin; WoPoe, *tr. by* W. S. Merwin and Nguyen Ngoc Bich

Spring going.   Basho.   EH, *tr. by* Robert Hass

Spring going.   Basho.   EMJL, *tr. by* Haruo Shirane

Spring / gradually taking form.   Basho.   EMJL

Spring groves: flowers, such charm.   Spring Song from "Tzu-Yeh" Songs of the Four Seasons.   *Unknown.*   ChinPo, *tr. by* Ye Weilian [*or* Yeh Wei-lien *or* Wai-lim Yip]

Spring hailstones would drive us.   Because of My Father's Job.   James Masao Mitsui.   NIL-7; OpBo; UnSA

Spring Harvest of Snow Peas.   Maxine Hong Kingston.   ASA

Spring Has Come.   Antonio Machado Ruiz.   SpanPo, *tr. by* Kate Flores

Spring has come again the snow has finally stopped.   Han-shan Te-ch'ing.   CSKM, *tr. by* Red Pine

Spring has darkened with activity, The.   Time and the Garden.   Yvor Winters.   APT-2; HarvBoo; MoAmPo; NoAM

Spring has returned. The earth is.   Spring Has Returned.   Rainer Maria Rilke.   WoPoe, *tr. by* Charles Haseloff

Spring has vanished.   End to Spring, An.   Tzu Yeh.   CrYelRi, *tr. by* Sam Hamill

Spring Homecoming.   Tu Fu [*or* Du Fu].   CrYelRi, *tr. by* Sam Hamill

Spring House.   Bernadette Mayer.   AHA

Spring in a Mountain Village.   Noin.   WoPoe, *tr. by* Steven D. Carter

Spring in London.   John Bingham Morton.   OBCoV

Spring in New Hampshire.   Claude McKay.   ChAP

Spring in Palo Duro Canyon.   Jerry Craven.   TiP2

Spring in Placitas.   Mary Doughtery Bartlett.   ICANM

Spring in the Bronx.   *Unknown.*   OBCoV

Spring in This World of Poor Mutts.   Joseph Ceravolo.   AHA; FTOS; NYP2

11. Spring in Toronto.   David McFadden.   NLPA

Spring is a Cat, The.   Yi Jang'hi.   WoPoe, *tr. by* Ko Changsu

Spring is a juice, a rejoicing, forcing. Sirventes. Bertrans de Born. WoPoe, *tr.* by Paul Blackburn

Spring is a-rising. Young Miracle Stag, The. László Nagy. IQMS, *tr.* by Adam Makkai

Spring is cheap, but clean of sky. Long after she used to. In the Clear Long After. Olena Kalytiak Davis. NAPBL; PoDa

Spring is come at last, my freens, cheer up, you sons of toil, The. Working Man, The. Ellen Johnston. VWP

Spring is early this year. Kenneth Rexroth. APSN *Fr.* Love Poems of Marichiko, The.

Spring is going, gone! Tune: "Memories of the South." Liu Yu Hsi. ColAnChi, *tr.* by Jiaosheng Wang

Spring is half gone since we parted. Tune: "Pure Serene Music." Li Yü. ColAnChi, *tr.* by Jiaosheng Wang

Spring Is Here. Lorenz Hart. ReLy

Spring is here / I'm a fool if I fall again. Fun to be Fooled. Ira Gershwin and E. Y. Harburg. ReLy

Spring is hidden in my studio. Fading Plum Blossoms. Li Ch'ing-chao. NDACCP, *tr.* by Kenneth Rexroth

Spring is like a perhaps hand. E. E. Cummings. NoP-4; NoP-5

Spring is not so beautiful there, The. Water-Front Streets. Langston Hughes. SAmP

Spring is short. Yosano Akiko. CAoMJL1, *tr.* by Janine Beichman

Spring is sprung. Spring in the Bronx. *Unknown*. OBCoV

Spring isn't ev'rything, it's true. Spring Isn't Everything. Ralph Blane and Harry Warren. ReLy

Spring Joy. Chu Shu-chen. NDACCP, *tr.* by Kenneth Rexroth

Spring Joy Praising God. Catharina Regina von Greiffenberg. GePo, *tr.* by George C. Schoolfield

Spring Landscape. Augusta Peaux. TuT, *tr.* by Tony Curtis and Tony Curtis

Spring lies abandoned. April and Silence. Tomas Tranströmer. WED, *tr.* by Robert Bly

Spring lingers on, The. Richard Wright. APT-2

Spring Longing. Amy Lowell. APT-1

Spring Love. Francis Ledwidge. IrLP

Spring mellows on the hill, but the sick wayfarer is suffering. Thought on My Sickness, A. Chunghur Hyujung. BecRai, *tr.* by Kim Daljin, Kim Won-Chung and Christopher Merrill

Spring Memorandum, A: Fort Knox. Robert Duncan. PWW2

Spring moon—. Basho. Spl

Spring moonrise—. Haiku. Lenard D. Moore. SpirFl

Spring Morning. D. H. Lawrence. MoBrPo

Spring Morning, A. Meng Hao Jan. CCL1, *tr.* by Witter Bynner

Spring Mountains. Niu Hsi-chi. CCL1, *tr.* by C. H. Kwock *and* Vincent McHugh and Vincent McHugh

Spring, my dear, The. Out of Tune. W. E. Henley. MoBrPo

Spring Night. Chu Shu-chen. NDACCP, *tr.* by Kenneth Rexroth

Spring Night. Hagiwara Sakutaro. PFTM-1

Spring Night. Richard Kell. IrLP

Spring Night. Sara Teasdale. MoAmPo

Spring Night at Bamboo Pavillion, Presenting a Poem to Subprefect Qian about His Staying for Good in Blue Field Mountains. Wang Wei. WoPoe, *tr.* by Tony Barnstone, Willis Barnstone *and* Haixin Xu, Willis Barnstone and Xu Haixin

Spring Night, Happy Rain. Tu Fu [*or* Du Fu]. CCL1, *tr.* by Florence Ayscough *and* Amy Lowell

Spring Night in Luoyang—Hearing a Flute. Li Po. CCL1, *tr.* by Burton Watson

Spring of the Steel Bar Window. No Ch'ŏnmyŏng. CAMKP, *tr.* by Mickey Hong

Spring of Work Storm. Joseph Ceravolo. FTOS

Spring omnipotent goddess thou dost. E. E. Cummings. NBLV

Spring on the Mountain. Hueung Powoo. BecRai, *tr.* by Kim Daljin, Kim Won-Chung and Christopher Merrill

Spring one hundred years ago. Spring. Takahashi Shinkichi. ZenPo, *tr.* by Takashi Ikemoto and Lucien Stryk

Spring Overflows the Pavilion. *Unknown*. CATKP, *tr.* by Peter H. Lee

Spring passing. Buson. EMJL, *tr.* by Haruo Shirane

Spring Passion. Yu Xuanji. CCL1, *tr.* by Genevieve Wimsatt

Spring Pastoral. Elinor Wylie. TCAPo

Spring Peepers. Joseph Bruchac. PoCoUp

Spring plain / Gulped. Yamei. ZenPo, *tr.* by Takashi Ikemoto and Lucien Stryk

Spring Poem, The. Dave Jeddie Smith. PoPoPo

Spring Pools. Robert Frost. APT-1; ColAP; CtM; NoAmP; OxBoAm

Spring quickly passes. Yosano Akiko. ErotSp, *tr.* by Sam Hamill

Spring rain. Basho. EH, *tr.* by Robert Hass

Spring Rain. Robert Hass. BodElec

Spring rain. Issa. EH, *tr.* by Robert Hass

Spring Rain. Li Shang-yin. ChinPo, *tr.* by Ye Weilian [*or* Yeh Wei-lien *or* Wai-lim Yip]

Spring Rain. Tu Fu [*or* Du Fu]. CCL1; WaAnP, *tr.* by Kenneth Rexroth

Spring rain! And as yet. Buson. TAL

Spring Report. Lionel Abrahams. TSAP

Spring returns to Peach Blossom River. Heading South. Tu Fu [*or* Du Fu]. CrYelRi, *tr.* by Sam Hamill

Spring, River, Flowers, Moon, Night. Zhang Ruoxu. CCL1, *tr.* by David Lattimore

Spring river tidal water. Spring, River, Flowers, Moon, Night. Zhang Ruoxu. CCL1, *tr.* by David Lattimore

Spring roses, autumn fruits, and summer grain. *Unknown*. PriapPo *Fr.* Priapus Poems, The.

Spring Scales. Darya Sukhovey. CRWP, *tr.* by Christopher Mattison

Spring Scene. Su Tung-p'o. TAL

Spring Scene. Tu Fu [*or* Du Fu]. ChinPo, *tr.* by Ye Weilian [*or* Yeh Wei-lien *or* Wai-lim Yip]

Spring scene finds me thinner still, The. Tune: "Joy of Returning to the Fields." Huang T'ing-chien. ColAnChi, *tr.* by James Robert Hightower

Spring sea rising, The. Buson. ASA; EH, *tr.* by Robert Hass

Spring sea, The. EMJL, *tr.* by Haruo Shirane

Spring sets the scene among. Crabapple Brook. Hsüeh T'ao [*or* Xue Tao]. CCL1, *tr.* by Jeanne Larsen

Spring Shade. Robert Fitzgerald. APT-2

Spring should be with us—but spring is a laggart. May Day, 1917. W. N. Ewer. RSaN

Spring sleep, not yet awake to dawn. Spring Dawn. Meng Hao Jan. NDACCP, *tr.* by Gary Snyder

Spring / slips / silent / snowdrops. Spring. Hugo Majer. Spl

Spring Smoke. Arthur Sze. MAAN

Spring Snow. Chŏng Chiyong. CAMKP, *tr.* by Anthony, Brother of Taizé

Spring Song. Lucille Clifton. IPoFL

Spring Song. Peter Fallon. PBCIP

Spring Song: "Young lass, A." Li Po. NDACCP, *tr.* by William Carlos Williams

Spring Song. Federico García Lorca. SpanPo, *tr.* by Rachel Benson and Robert O'Brien

Spring Song. William of Aquitaine. NAWM-7v1, *tr.* by Peter Dronke

Spring Song from "Tzu-Yeh" Songs of the Four Seasons. *Unknown*. ChinPo, *tr.* by Ye Weilian [*or* Yeh Wei-lien *or* Wai-lim Yip]

Spring Song of the Birds. James I, King of Scotland. OBEV

Spring South of the River. Tu Mu. CCL1, *tr.* by R. F. Burton

Spring stirs slowly, shuffles, hops. Season Song. Judith Nicholls. Spl

Spring Storm. Johanna Rayl. PasH

Spring storm shakes the old peach tree, A. Garden Note I, Los Altos. Janet Lewis. APT-2

Spring Strains. William Carlos Williams. APT-1; TCAPo

Spring Street Girl Friend (#8). C. D. Wright. GPPA

Spring Thaw. Yosano Akiko. CAoMJL1, *tr.* by Janine Beichman

Spring: the first morning when that one true block of sweet, laminar, complex scent arrives. From My Window. C. K. Williams. CAP-8

Spring. The golfball head. Bash on Basho: Six of the Best. Geoffrey Holloway. NLP

Spring the purple Violet. (LL) Upon Prue [*or* Prew], His Maid. Robert Herrick. NAEL-6v1; NAEL-7v1; NoP-4; NoP-5; NPeEn

Spring, the sweet spring, is the year's pleasant king. Thomas Nashe. NAEL-6v1; NoP-4; NoP-5; NoSic; TFi; WaAnP *Fr.* Summer's Last Will and Testament.

Spring Thoughts. Li Po. WoPoe, *tr.* by Elling O. Eide

Spring Thoughts Sent to Tzu-an. Yü Hsüan-chi. WoPoe, *tr.* by Geoffrey Waters

Spring Trances in the Control Emerald Night. Christopher Dewdney. "August a haze amniotic our dream aether and lens of distance. Tree sentinels in." FTOS

Spring Travel. Chia Tao. CSKM, *tr.* by Mike O'Connor

Spring Vacation, The. Derek Mahon. PNI

Spring View. Tran Nhan-tong. WoPoe, *tr.* by Nguyen Ngoc Bich

Spring View. Tu Fu [*or* Du Fu]. ColAnChi; NDACCP, *tr.* by Gary Snyder

Spring View. Tu Fu [*or* Du Fu]. WaAnP, *tr.* by Arthur Sze

Spring Vigil in the Imperial Chancellery. Tu Fu [*or* Du Fu]. ChinPo, *tr.* by Ye Weilian [*or* Yeh Wei-lien *or* Wai-lim Yip]

Spring was coming, brimful. Yellow Spring. Juan Ramón Jiménez. SpanPo, *tr.* by Angel Flores

Spring waters run north and south from here. To a Guest. Tu Fu [*or* Du Fu]. CrYelRi, *tr.* by Sam Hamill

Spring we don't see, The. Basho. EH, *tr.* by Robert Hass

Spring we went into the heat of lilacs. For My Father. Philip Schultz. TaR

Spring Will Be a Little Late This Year. Frank Loesser. ReLy

Spring Wind. Ho Hsun. CCL1, *tr.* by John Frodsham.

Spring wind in North Park. Tune: "Courtyard Full of Fragrance, The." Huang T'ing-chien. ColAnChi, *tr.* by James Robert Hightower.

Spring Wind on the Riverbank at Kema. Buson. EH, *tr.* by Robert Hass.

Spring wind raises fine dust from the road, The. Walk in the Country, A. Su Tung-p'o. NDACCP, *tr.* by Kenneth Rexroth.

Spring wind stirs my romantic heart, The. Spring. *Unknown.* CCL1, *tr.* by John Frodsham.

Spring winds buffet his straw cape. Old Farmer, The. Ch'i-chi. CSKM, *tr.* by Burton Watson.

Spring winds perfume the shop. Saying Good-bye in a Ch'in-ling Wineshop. Li Po. CrYelRi, *tr.* by Sam Hamill.

Springboard, The. Louis MacNeice. PoA 2002.

Springfield Mountain. *Unknown.* TCAPo.

Springfield, Virginia. Anne Rouse. StAl.

Springing, full-grown, from your own head, Athena? (LL) Carolyn Kizer. FFC; VCAP *Fr.* Pro Femina.

Springs. Nike Adesuyi. NeNiPo.

Spring's dewy hand on this fair summit weaves. Written in Farm Wood, South Downs, in May 1784. Charlotte Smith. RWP.

Spring's end: washing in clear water. Third Day of the Third Month at the Meandering River, The. Yu Ch'an. ChinPo, *tr.* by Ye Weilian [*or* Yeh Wei-lien *or* Wai-lim Yip].

Spring's Last Drop, The. Catherine Obianuju Acholonu. HAWP; NAfrP.

Springs passed. Buson. EMJL *Fr.* Spring Breeze on the Kema Embankment.

Spring's Path. Pak Chaesam. CAMKP, *tr.* by David R. McCann and Jiwon Shin.

Spring's source faced the springtime city, The. At the Stream's Source in Spring: A Party. Wang Ch'ang-ling. CCL1, *tr.* by Stephen Owen.

Spring's sun has just turned, the year's about to end. New Year's Eve. Yang Wen-li. WoPoe, *tr.* by Nancy Hodes and Tung Yuan-fang.

Spring's sweet attendant! modest simple flower. To a Violet. Susan Evance. CenSon.

Spring's Welcome. John Lyly. *See* Trico's Song.

Spring-Tide. *Unknown.* OBEV.

Springtime. Rubén Darío. TCLAP, *tr.* by Lysander Kemp.

Springtime. Nikki Giovanni. TLR.

Springtime. Norman Henry, II Pritchard. GT.

Springtime at Twilight. Michael S. Smith. PasH.

Springtime Cometh, The. E. Y. Harburg. ReLy.

Springtime flowers fill the mountains. Yi Hwang. CATKP *Fr.* Twelve Songs of Tosan.

Springtime in the Rockies, Lichen. Lew Welch. WhBo.

Springtime It Brings On the Shearing, The. E. J. Overbury. NOBAu.

Springtime Sleep. Meng Hao Jan. ChinPo, *tr.* by Ye Weilian [*or* Yeh Wei-lien *or* Wai-lim Yip].

Springtime sleep: too deep to know dawn. Springtime Sleep. Meng Hao Jan. ChinPo, *tr.* by Ye Weilian [*or* Yeh Wei-lien *or* Wai-lim Yip].

Springtime South of the Yangtze. K'o Chun. CrYelRi, *tr.* by Sam Hamill.

Springtime South of the Yangtze. Li Po. CrYelRi, *tr.* by Sam Hamill.

Springwater, Part 105. Bingxin. CFP, *tr.* by Michelle Yeh.

Sprinkle water wide / For the sparrow. Kikaku. ZenPo, *tr.* by Takashi Ikemoto and Lucien Stryk.

Sprinkler had come out on the road with a green hiss, The. Aridness of Air, The. Silvio Giussani. ItPo, *tr.* by Gayle Ridinger.

Sprinkles of rain. Wet Dream. Carlos Omar Gardinet. BRtP.

Sprinkling / sprinkling. Sprinkling. Hokko. NAAPv.2.

Sprinter from Carmarthen disgorges, The. Intercity, Swansea-London. Jon Dressel. TCAWP.

Sprites. Richard Jackson. VisFro.

Sprouting two small wings. (LL) Wingfoot Lake. Rita Dove. CAP-8; NAMCP V.2; PoPoPo.

Spsjpi. Cryptographiku for Wallace Stevens. Bob Grumman. AnSo.

Spun in some mighty wizard's brain. Invention. Robert Clarkson Tongue. ArBi.

Spunk Talking. Anne Rouse. BeAl; MFPA; NeBl.

Spur, The. William Butler Yeats. NAMCP V.1; OxAEP-2; WeW-3.

Spur of Love, The. Hugh MacDiarmid. OxBEV.

Spursknicksspursknicksspursknicksspursknicksspurskni. My Knicks Are Going to Beat Your Spurs—NBA Souvenir Bracelet 1999 for My Long Distance Love. Catherine Bowman. MoASP.

Spurt of Blood, The. Antonin Artaud. PFTM-1.

Spuyten Duyvil. Honor Moore. AtGh.

Spyrytual. Russell Atkins. EGAG.

Squabbling gods the fight forsake, The. Thomas Bridges. FaBoWar *Fr.* Homer Travestie.

Squad I. Tim Suermondt. PA9/11.

Squad in the Land, A. Hillel Omer. NRoS, *tr.* by Esther Raizen.

Squadrons swoop down, shrieking. Invaders from South of the Border Imperil Native Population. Charles Harper Webb. GeoHom.

Squads, platoons, and regiments, The. [Winter Sketches V]. Charles Reznikoff. PoA 2002.

Squalid street after squalid street. Great Industrial Centre, A. Edith Nesbit. VWP.

Squall, The. Milton Acorn. Coast.

Squall Line. Joan Houlihan. IAoNAP.

Square. Rob MacKenzie. Oth.

Square of the Holy Passion, gaze on the demonstrators. Natalya Gorbanevskaya. TCRusP, *tr.* by Daniel Weissbort.

Square, squat room (a cellar on promotion), A. W. E. Henley. NAEL-6v2; NAEL-7v2; NPeEn *Fr.* In Hospital.

Squarely face your. Alex Rawls. AnSo *Fr.* What's Your Sign?

Squares. Pierre Reverdy. PFTM-1.

Squares and Courtyards. Marilyn Hacker. WiU.

Squaring the Names. Diana García. TouFir.

Squarings. Seamus Heaney.

  "Annals say: when the monks of Clonmacnoise, The." EmeKit; ModIr; NoP-5; NPeEn; StAl.

  "Be literal a moment. Recollect." PoetW.

  "Boat that did not rock or wobble once, A." ModIr.

  "Deserted harbour stillness. Every stone." PoetW.

  "Roof it again. Batten down. Dig in." PoetW.

  "Visible sea at a distance from the shore, The." PoetW.

Squat man under the hoop, The. Winter Ball. August Kleinzahler. MoASP.

Squating / in front of perry's stick hall. Sting—a South Carolina Ave. Folk Tale. Harold Carrington. EGAG.

Squats on a toad-stool under a tree. Thomas Lovell Beddoes. OxBEV *Fr.* Death's Jest Book.

Squatter in the Foreground. Kenward Elmslie. FTOS.

Squaw-thorn, devilsclaw, and Joshua. Desert, Not Wastleand. Robert Burlingame. TiP2.

Squeak. Philip Dacey. SUP.

Squealing under city stone. Rapid Transit. James Agee. MoAmPo.

Squeeze. Abigail Child. FTOS.

Squeeze Play. Phyllis McGinley. OBCoV; OBSV *Fr.* Spectator's Guide to Contemporary Art.

Squeezes. Brian Patten. Spl.

Squid. Michael C. Blumenthal. WaAnP.

Squid seller's call, The. Basho. EH, *tr.* by Robert Hass.

Squint your eyes, listen and tremble. We Are the Heirs. Isaac Platner. Prolet, *tr.* by Amelia Glaser.

Squinting though eye-slits in our balaclavas. Crossing the Square. Grace Schulman. ExTi.

Squire nagged and bullied till I went to fight. Memorial Tablet. Siegfried Sassoon. PoWW.

Squire sat alone beside the board, The. Little Fay's Thanksgiving. Henrietta Cordelia Ray. CBWP-3.

Squire Squint, shooting at a pheasant. G. J. Blundell. UV.

Squire's Pew, The. Jane Taylor. PEW.

Squirrel chase in the bare trees. Year. Jenny Mueller. IAoNAP.

Srategies for Survival. Beryle Williams. AtGh.

Sri Nityananda Mandir (The Temple of Nityananda). Elsa Cross. TANSG, *tr.* by Patricia Dubrava.

Sssnnnwhufffffl? Loch Ness Monster's Song, The. Edwin Morgan. NePenScot; OPOU; StAl.

Ssssssoundcheck. Doggin the Rockman. Paul Beatty. InTrad.

Stabbed, clubbed, and slashed, I stand. Wound Man, The. D. A. Feinfeld. BloBone.

Stability. Tim Lilburn. OpeFie.

Stable Relationship, A. Tessa Ransford. EdScPo.

Stable-lamp is lighted, A. Christmas Hymn, A. Richard Wilbur. ChIV-2; ChrPo; OBCP.

Stack of summer suits makes a better emblem than a piano, A. Requirements for Suggesting Fats Waller. Connie Deanovich. AmPoNex.

Stackalee. *Unknown.* APN-2.

Stacked circles (rain down) say green it releases nothing. Bundled wires. Mark Bibbins. BAP-04 *Fr.* Blasted Fields of Clover Bring Harrowing and Regretful Sighs.

Stacking the Straw. Amy Clampitt. VCAP.

Stacks of paperbacks. From Where the Blues? Norman Henry, II Pritchard. EGAG.

Stadium, The. William Heyen. MoASP.

Staff Sgt. Edward A. Carter, Jr.: There and Back. Jabari Asim. BtF.

Staff slips from the hand, The. Outward. Louis Simpson. EmeKit.

Staffordshire Murderer, A. James Fenton. NeBrP.

Stag does not lay his side to sleep. Grania's Song to Diarmuid. *Unknown.* WoPoe, *tr.* by Frank O'Connor

Stag in blazing sun. Tomas Tranströmer. WoBe *Fr.* Haiku.

Stag lifts his nostrils to the morning, A. Scotland. Frederick Seidel. BodElec

Stag of Irisoda, The. Lajos Áprily. IQMS, *tr.* by Adam Makkai

Stag on the westward ridge, melodious. *Unknown.* WoPoe *Fr.* Sweeney Astray.

100 The Stag. Conor O'Callaghan. NIrP *Fr.* Loose Change.

Stag was very proud of his swiftness, The. Ballade 1. Eustache Deschamps. WoPoe, *tr.* by David Curzon and Jeffrey Fiskin

Stage and Screen, 1989. Carol Muske-Dukes. BodElec

Stage Duo. Kenward Elmslie. FTOS

Stage was set, the house was packed, The. Concert Party: Busseboom. Edmund Charles Blunden. FaBoWar

Stags from the foundry bugle from the front door. Trophy Homes. Bruce Berger. GeoH

Staid schizophrenic named Struther, A. Limerick. *Unknown.* NIP-4

Stain. Stuart Dybek. LiTh

Stain of blood that writes an island story, The. (LL) Landfall in Unknown Seas. Allen Curnow. NoP-4; NoP-5

Stain of the Sea, The (414). Khwaja Shams-ad-din Muhammad Hafiz. WED, *tr.* by Robert Bly and Leonard Lewisohn

Stained Glass Window. Adelia Prado. TCLAP, *tr.* by Marcia Kirinus

Stained-glass panels shed their red as in a chapel to endow. Snatch. Lincoln Kirstein. AmWaPo; PWW2

Stains of Stalin. Bill Berkson. NYP2

Staircase. Marina Ivanovna Tsvetayeva. ARWW, *tr.* by Catriona Kelly

Stairs are dark, the steps are high, The. Up in Mabel's Room. Kenneth Slessor. BMAP

Stairway, The. Stephen Dunn. CAP-8

Stairway is not, The. Jacob's Ladder, The. Denise Levertov. APSN; BrAP; ChIV-1; NAAL-5; PFTM-2

Stairway to Heaven. Robert Creeley. FTOS

Stairway to Paradise. B. G. DeSylva and Arthur Francis. TCAPo

Stalagmites in spring caves rise to more stalactites. Red Embankment. Tu Mu. ColAnChi, *tr.* by John M. Ortinau

Stale Spit is the Morning Train. Emyr Lewis. BBMWP *Fr.* Dawn.

Stalin Epigram, The. Osip Emilevich Mandelstam. AF; WoPoe, *tr.* by Clarence Brown *and* W. S. Merwin and W. S. Merwin

Stalin Moy Golubchik. "Sagittarius." OBCoV

Stalingrad: 1942. Norman Nicholson. RSaN

Stalin's Genius. Bruce Andrews. PmAP

Stalking. Where Seed Falls. Essex Hemphill. GT

Stalking before the lords of life, one came. Circumstance. John Townsend Trowbridge. APN-2

Stall Me Out. Paul Beatty. AmPoNex

Stall so tight he can't raise heels or knees, The. Bronco Busting, Event #1. May Swenson. APT-2

Stalled before my metal shaving mirror. Notes for a Sonnet. Edward Pygge. OBCoV

Stallion, The. Tudur Aled. OBWVE, *tr.* by Joseph P. Clancy

Stammering it fights to get. Lyric. Denise Riley. MoWP

Stamp, roar like our Russian poets, like Derzhavin. Ode for the Dancing Khlysty. Yury Ivask. TCRusP, *tr.* by Alla Burago and Burton Raffel

Stan Musial meets the Emperor of Japan. In a Motel in Louisiana I Watch the Pirates And the OJ Simpson Freeway Chase at the Same Time. Rick Campbell. LiTh

Stance. Kate Clanchy. BeAl

Stand above the steep precipice, and cry out into the rift. Welsh Language, The. Alan Llwyd. BBMWP, *tr.* by Joseph P. Clancy

Stand back, ye sleeping jacks at home. John Pickering. NoSic *Fr.* Horestes.

Stand by Me. Charles A. Tindley. InvLi

Stand by me, Death, lest these dark days. Three Pleas. Henry Treece. PoWW

Stand close around, ye Stygian set. Walter Savage Landor. NAEL-6v2; NoP-4; NoP-5; NPeEn; OBEV; OxAEP-2; OxBEV; TFi; WeW-3; WoPoe *Fr.* Pericles and Aspasia.

Stand fast, my child, and after all. Christopher Smart. ChIV-2 *Fr.* Hymns for the Amusement of Children.

Stand here at night in the shudder of the Elevated. All Death, All Love. Conrad Potter Aiken. InGu

Stand here, says the professional TV person. Telyric. Andrei Codrescu. PmAP

Stand in a field long enough, and the sounds. Becoming a Redwood. Dana Gioia. GeoHom; PfSP

Stand in a row and learn. (LL) Drunk in the Furnace, The. W. S. Merwin. NAMCP V.2; NoAM; NoP-4; NoP-5; WaAnP

Stand in the sun long enough to remember. Radiation. Margaret Gibson. AtGh

Stand like a beaten anvil, when thy dream. Anvil, The. Alfred Noyes. SacPr

Stand next to your bike, like that. Lesson, The. Claudia M. Reder. ArBi

Stand not uttering sedately. Epitaphium Citharistriae. Victor Gustave Plarr. NBLV

Stand of paper birches years and years, A. Refuge. Randy Blasing. PoA 2002

Stand off, daughter of the dusk. Gwendolyn Brooks. NALW *Fr.* Womanhood, The.

Stand off from me; be still your own. Love's Chord. Edward Dowden. IrLP

Stand off, physician! Let me frolic. On Melancholy. *Unknown.* NOSC

Stand on the highest pavement of the stair. La Figlia Che Piange. T. S. Eliot. APT-1; HarvBoo; HeIP-4; OxBEV; OxBoAm; PoA 2002; TCAPo

Stand on the sandy beach with your back to the sea. Mirror. Mieko Shiomi. WhBo

Stand [*or* Stond] who so list upon the slipper top[pe]. Seneca. NoSic; NPeEn; OBVE; OxBEV *Fr.* Thyestes.

Stand out, maids, and look on the land of Cynddylan. *Unknown.* OBWVE *Fr.* Elegy on Cynddylan, The.

Stand still. In the Fog. Lilian Moore. TLR

Stand Still. Jim Peterson. PoCoUp

Stand still, and I will read to thee. Lecture upon the Shadow, A. John Donne. NAEL-6v1; NAEL-7v1; NoSic

Stand still, and See. Betty Scott Stam. SacPr

Stand still. Places move within us. Big Rig the Baroque Sky. Tessa Rumsey. LegDan

Stand still. The trees ahead and bushes beside you. Lost. David Wagoner. GoPo; PoA 2002; TWF

Stand still, yet we will make him run. (LL) To His Coy Mistress. Andrew Marvell. AmFaPo; BASC; BrAP; CABP; ClHu; EroLit; ErotSp; FSCP; HeIP-4; NAEL-6v1; NAEL-7v1; NIL-7; NIP-4; NoP-4; NoP-5; NOSC; NPeEn; OBEV; OxAEP-1; OxBEV; PBRV; PoPoPo; TFi; TRP; UV; WaAnP; WoPoe

Stand! the ground's your own, my braves! Warren's Address at Bunker Hill [*or* to the American Soldiers]. John Pierpont. AmWaPo

Stand there just a moment. Moonlight Becomes You. Johnny Burke. ReLy

Stand there, manslaying spear; no longer drip. Anyte. SaLy, *tr.* by Diane Rayor

Stand to one side. No, over here with me. Venetian Interior, 1889. Richard Howard. VCAP

Stand Up! Stand Up for Jesus [*with music*]. George, Jr. Duffield. SacPr; TCAPo

Stand! Who goes there? John Lyly. NoSic; OBCoV *Fr.* Endimion.

Stand whoso list upon the slipper top. Stand Whoso List. Sir Thomas Wyatt. NAEL-7v1; NoP-4; NoP-5

Stand your ground, soul. Strong Beams. Mairtin O Direain. ModIr, *tr.* by Patrick Crotty

Standard Time. Ira Sadoff. BodElec

Standard Time: Novena for My Father. Dionisio D. Martinez. TouFir

Standing Alone. Tu Fu [*or* Du Fu]. NDACCP, *tr.* by David Hinton

Standing alone on a solitary peak. Ascending the Mountain. Bernard Tetsugen Glassman. WhBo

Standing alone on the highway. (Here Am I) Broken Hearted. Lew Brown. ReLy

Standing aloof in giant ignorance. To Homer. John Keats. NAEL-6v2; NAEL-7v2; NoP-4; NoP-5

Standing at dawn where Union and Burnside. Closer to Home. Floyd Skloot. UrbNat

Standing at Pasternak's Table, Peredelkino. James Ragan. TWW

Standing at the. Concentrating. Michael Hulse. PML

Standing at the baggage passing time. Waiting for a Ride. Gary Snyder. WANABP

Standing Between Two Ideas. Maurya Simon. InvLad

Standing Coffin. Tamura Ryuichi. AF, *tr.* by Christopher Drake

Standing corn is green, the wild in flower, The. Nunc Viridant Segetes. Sedulius Scottus. NAWM-5v1, *tr.* by Helen Waddell

Standing erect in the mire. Sketch of the Frontier Woman. Claudia Lars. TCLAP, *tr.* by Donald D. Walsh

Standing guests, a grotesque glade, The. Party, The. Margaret Avison. PoA 2002

Standing here in his muscle shirt at the bar. Redneck with Hair on His Back. Paul Ruffin. LiTh

Standing in her basement. Sequence. Peter E. Murphy. NevBe

Standing in ribbons, over our heads, for an hour. (LL) End of the Picnic. Francis Webb. BMAP; NOBAu

Standing in the Doorway, I Watch the Young Child Sleep. Sharon Hashimoto. OpBo

Standing in the hall against the / wall. Listening to Grownups Quarreling. Ruth Whitman. NTCP

Standing in the middle of a field: claw-footed. Bath, The. Ron Butler. EdScPo

Standing in your lofty tower. Kim Sujang. CATKP, tr. by Peter H. Lee

Standing in your same skin. Stranger in the Village. Lorelei Williams. BtF

Standing knee-deep in Oak Creek. Dog Days and Delta Nights. Franz Douskey. PasH

Standing Light Up. A. R. Ammons. PfSP

Standing Near the Ghats Along the Ganges. William Kistler. WhBo

Standing Stone. Ruth Bidgood. AngWePo

Standing Trains, The. Thomas McCarthy. ModIr

Standing under the greengrocer's awning. Hailstone, The. Peter Didsbury. NPeEn

Standing Up. Tomas Tranströmer.
  "It's been a hard winter, but summer is here and the fields." RaBo

Standing upon a hill of fancies high. Landscape, A. Margaret Lucas Cavendish, Duchess of Newcastle. NOSC

Standing with Chiyo-Ni. Pesha Gertler. FiBr

Standing, with your back turned, taut at work. Vista. Elizabeth Garrett. NeBl

Standing Worship. Dhabya Khamees. PoArWo, tr. by Clarissa C. Burt

Stands for hope. (LL) Marianne Moore. APT-1; ColAP; FTtHH; HarvBoo; NAAPv.2; NAMCP V.1; NoAM; NoP-4; NoP-5; OxBoAm; PoA 2002; PoPoPo Fr. Part of a Novel, Part of a Poem, Part of a Play.

Stands the moon, brilliant, cloudless. (LL) On this summer night. Chikako. WoPoe; WPoS, tr. by Edwin A. Cranston

Stand-To, The. Cecil Day Lewis. NoP-4; OBWP

Stanley, my ex, the painter. Summer Was Not Long Enough, The. Jean Valentine. LaCa

Stanley turrentine, you nut! yes, 'don't mess'. Suspect under Section A1 Special. Wopko Jensma. TSAP

Stanza 4. Ursula K. Le Guin. GoPo Fr. Coming of Age.

Stanza: "What, my Lord, shall I do with." Unknown. WoPoe, tr. by Lewis Turco

Stanzas: "Often rebuked, yet always back returning." Emily Jane Brontë. BrAP; CtM; NALW; OBEV; OxBEV; PEW; VWP

Stanzas: "When a man hath no freedom to fight for at home." Lord Byron. NBLV; NoP-4; NoP-5; OxAEP-2; TRP
  (When a Man Hath No Freedom to Fight for at Home.) NAEL-6v2; NAEL-7v2

Stanzas. Thomas Hood. NPeEn

Stanzas. John Keats. See In [a] Drear-nighted December.

Stanzas: "In this vain, busy world, where the good and the gay." Mary Robinson. WoRP

Stanzas: "Ah! think'st thou, Laura, then, that wealth." Charlotte Smith. NoP-4; NoP-5

Stanzas: "Oh, come to me in dreams, my love!" Mary Wollstonecraft Shelley. LW

Stanzas. Edgar Allan Poe. NCAP

Stanzas: "How often we forget all time, when lone." Edgar Allan Poe. APN-1

Stanzas 1–9: "Oh! lay me by yon peaceful stream." Unknown. RWP Fr. Aged Bard's Wish, The.

Stanzas 10–18: "Oh! wake the chace where I may hear." Unknown. RWP Fr. Aged Bard's Wish, The.

Stanzas 19–27: "Be thou, with snowy plumage soft." Unknown. RWP Fr. Aged Bard's Wish, The.

Stanzas 28–36: "Lift me, O you, whose arms are young!" Unknown. RWP Fr. Aged Bard's Wish, The.

Stanzas Against Forgetting. Guillaume Apollinaire. AF, tr. by Carolyn Forché

Stanzas for an Imaginary Garden. Octavio Paz. OBGa

Stanzas for Music ("There be none of Beauty's daughters.") Lord Byron. NAEL-6v2; NAEL-7v2; NPBRoP

Stanzas for Music ("There's not a joy the world can give like that it takes away.") Lord Byron. NOBRP; NPeEn

Stanzas from the Grande Chartreuse. Matthew Arnold. NAEL-6v2; NAEL-7v2

Stanzas Imitated From Psalm 119. Bible, O.T. ChIV-1, tr. by Thomas Warton, the Elder

Stanzas in Bloomsbury. Richard Howard. MakPoe

Stanzas in Mediation. David Buuck.
  "Geopolitical, The." Eno

Stanzas in Meditation. Gertrude Stein.
  "Full well I know that she is there." PoA 2002
  Part 3, Stanza 2. NoP-4; NoP-5
  Part 3, Stanza 5. NoP-4; NoP-5
  Part 5, Stanza 38. NoP-4; NoP-5
  Part 5, Stanza 63. NoP-4; NoP-5
  "She may count three little daisies very well." NoP-4; NoP-5
  Stanza 10. APT-1
  Stanza 83. NAMCP V.1; PoA 2002

"Thank you for hurrying through." PoA 2002

"Whole of this last end is to say which of two." PoA 2002

Stanzas of the Graves, The. Unknown.
  "Graves the rain makes wet and sleek, The." OBWVE

Stanzas on Charles Armitage Brown. John Keats. UV

Stanzas on the Death of Mrs Hemans. Letitia Elizabeth Landon. VWP Fr. New Monthly Magazine, 44 286–8.

Stanzas on the Psalms. Thomas Warton, the Elder. ChIV-1

Stanzas, Sexes, Seductions. Anne Carson. NAMCP V.2

Stanzas to Augusta ("Though the day of my destiny's over.") Lord Byron. NPBRoP

Stanzas to the Memory of the Late King. Felicia Dorothea Hemans. RWP

Stanzas to the River Po. Lord Byron. NPBRoP

Stanzas to the Speaker Asleep. Winthrop Mackworth Praed. OBSV

Stanzas Written in Dejection, Near Naples [or —December 1818, near Naples]. Percy Bysshe Shelley. ItP; NAEL-6v2; NAEL-7v2; NAWM-7v2; NoP-4; NoP-5; NPBRoP

Stanzas Written in London in 1773. Edward Williams.
  "Why, Cambria did I quit thy shore." AngWePo

Stanzas Written on the Road between Florence and Pisa. Lord Byron. BrAP; NAEL-6v2; NAEL-7v2

Stanzas Written Under Aeolus' Harp. Amelia Alderson Opie. NPBRoP

Staple Island Swing. Jen Hadfield. BeAl

Star. Chŏng Chiyong. CAMKP, tr. by Anthony, Brother of Taizé

Star, A. Federico García Lorca. PFTM-1 Fr. Night (Suite for Piano and Poet's Voice).

Star, The. Kathleen Jessie Raine. MoWP

Star, The. Jane Taylor. NOBRP; NOxBChV; NPBRoP; NTCP; OxBEV; UV (Twinkle Twinkle Little Star.) ChAP

Star, The. Clyde A. Wray. BtF

Star and Sea. William Peskett. PNI

Star Apocrypha. Christopher Buckley. PoDa

Star burns out over the tree tops, The. Aleksandr Semionovich Kushner. TCRusP, tr. by Daniel Weissbort

Star Child. Thomas Sayers Ellis. NeAmPo

Star crossed on its own limbs. O Hero Akimbo on the Mountains of To-morrow. George Barker. RSaN

Star Dust. Mitchell Parish. NAAPv.2; ReLy

Star exploding in the body, The. Cancer and Nova. Hyam Plutzik. AmFaPo

Star glide, a single frantic sullenness, a single financial grass greediness, A. Gertrude Stein. NAAPv.2; NAMCP V.1 Fr. Tender Buttons.

Star, / If you are. Christmas Tree, A. William Burford. SoSe-8

Star in a Stoneboat, A. Robert Frost. APT-1

Star Is Born in the Eagle Nebula, A. Marcia Southwick. PoDa

Star is gone, A! a star is gone! Fallen Star, The. George Darley. OBEV

Star light, star bright. Wishing Poem. Unknown. NTCP

Star looks down at me, A. Waiting Both. Thomas Hardy. MoBrPo

Star of Evening. Sappho. WoPoe, tr. by Paul Roche

Star of Free Will, The. Maria Luisa Spaziani.
  "I shall find in paradise that emaciated rose shoot." NeIt
  "Sunday in the provinces, a plaintive Norman bell-peal." NeIt
  "Traveling with too much baggage is not a good idea." NeIt

Star of the Evening. James M. Sayles. UV

Star of the North! though night winds drift. Fugitive Slave's Apostrophe to the North Star, The. John Pierpont. APN-1

Star over all. Christmas Tree. Laurence Smith. OBCP

Star Quilt. Roberta Hill Whiteman. NoAM

Star Song. Henrietta Cordelia Ray. CBWP-3

Star System, The. Richard Wilbur. NBLV Fr. Flippancies.

Star That Bids the Shepherd Fold, The. John Milton. NPeEn; OBEV Fr. Comus; a Masque Presented at Ludlow Castle.

Star that bringest home the bee. To the Evening Star. Thomas Campbell. NePenScot

Star that once, A. Yosano Akiko. CAoMJL1, tr. by Janine Beichman

Star Watcher, The. Peter Davison. WaAnP; YaYoPo

Star Whisper. Carol Rumens. StAl

Star-crowned solitude of thine oblivious hours!, The. (LL) To One in Bedlam. Ernest Dowson. GSo; MoBrPo; OBMV

Stare, The. Mun Chŏnghui. EcSo, tr. by Catherine J. Kim

Stare Decisis. Gale Nelson. OnScMo

Stare from your pillow into the sun. People of Unrest. Margaret Walker Alexander. GT

Star-filled seas are smooth to-night, The. A. E. Housman. MoBrPo Fr. Shropshire Lad, A.

Starfish. Lorna Dee Cervantes. TouFir

Starfish. Eric Ormsby. NoP-4; NoP-5

Starfish Waving to Me from the Sand. Matthew Rohrer. NAPBL

Star-Fix. Marilyn Nelson Waniek. ESEAA; LTA

Star-Gazer. Louis MacNeice. ModIr; NAEL-6v2; NAEL-7v2; NoP-4; NoP-5

Staring. Zhang Shuai. CCL1, tr. by Anne Birrell

Staring Aristogoras in the face. To Aristogoras. Meleager. CAGL, tr. by Daryl Hine

Staring at the Sea on the Day of the Death of Another. May Swenson. APT-2; NAMCP V.2; OxBoAm

Staring down the mountainous wall. Paredón. Ricardo Pau-Llosa. OPRER

Staring, you look for clues. Vanishing Point. Gary Metras. PasH

Stark Electric Jesus. Malay Roy Choudhury. PFTM-2

Stark Major. Hart Crane. FuPo

Stark naked. Tanka. Kanoko Okamoto. CAoMJL1, tr. by Makoto Ueda

Stark Weather. William Trowbridge. LiTh

Starlet. Fanny Howe. ExTi

Starlette. Chioma Okereke. BRtP

Starlight. Philip Levine. BeAl

Starlight Haven. Shirley Lim. UnSA

Starlight like Intuition Pierced the Twelve. Delmore Schwartz. ChIV-2

Starlight Night, The. Gerard Manley Hopkins. MoBrPo; NAEL-6v2; NAEL-7v2

Starlight Scope Myopia. Yusef Komunyakaa. AF; AmAlph; AmWaPo; MakPoe; NAMCP V.2; RoV

Starlight's intuitions pierced the twelve, The. Starlight like Intuition Pierced the Twelve. Delmore Schwartz. ChIV-2

Starling, The. John Heath-Stubbs. OWoS

Starling, The. Ruth Padel. NeBrP

Starling is my darling, although, The. Starling, The. John Heath-Stubbs. OWoS

Starling Migration, The. Jeffrey Skinner. PBCAP

Starry flower, the flower-like stars that fade, The. Sonnets. Frederick Goddard Tuckerman. APN-2; NAAPv.1

Starry hush, The. Dark Between, The. Philip Schultz. PoA 2002

Starry Night, The. Anne Sexton. ColAP; NAAL-5; NAMCP V.2; NoAM; VCAP

Stars. Agha Shahid Ali. FaoP

Stars. Emily Jane Brontë. AWTN; NAEL-6v2; NAEL-7v2; NALW

(Ah! Why, Because the Dazzling Sun.) VWP

Stars. Carl Sandburg. NOxBChV

Stars, The. Madison Cawein. APN-2

Stars, The. Lydia Huntley Sigourney. ColAP; TCAPo

Stars above, The. Poisonous Illusions. Abd al-Rahim Salih al-Rahim. IrPoTo, tr. by Saadi A. Simawe and Daniel Weissbort

Stars and grass. Weeds. James Dickey. BodElec

Stars and Planets. Norman Alexander MacCaig. OPOU

Stars and Stripes. Mary Weston Fordham. CBWP-2

Stars and Stripes fly high, The. Protest at Los Alamos, August 2000. Judith Strasser. RWB

Stars are a memory system, The. Notes on the Art of Memory. Diane Di Prima. SeSe

Stars are dredging, The. Richard Wright. APT-2

Stars are dropping thick as stones into the twiggy. Stars over the Dordogne. Sylvia Plath. PoA 2002

Stars are forth, the moon above the tops, The. Lord Byron. AmFaPo; TreFP Fr. Manfred.

Stars are gone out spark by spark, The. At Cockcrow. Lizette Woodworth Reese. SacPr

Stars are old and wise, The. Tonight they look. Very Young Man Speaks, A. Paul Tanaquil. YaYoPo

Stars are still on high, The. There's a Lull in My Life. Mack Gordon. ReLy

Stars are too many to count, The. Stars. Carl Sandburg. NOxBChV

Stars around the fair moon, The. Sappho. SaLy, tr. by Diane Rayor

Stars around the luminous moon—how soon they. Sappho. STV, tr. by John Frederick Nims

Stars at night, The. Ode to Bohemians. Ron Padgett. NYP2

Stars at Tallapoosa. Wallace Stevens. WoPoe

Stars Begin to Fall. Unknown. SacPr; SSUS

Stars being the visible past, The. (LL) On Being a Householder. Alan Dugan. NAMCP V.2; NoAM

Stars dead heroes in the sky, The. Offensive, The. Keith Douglas. PoWW

Stars Falling. Jay Parini. PfSP

Stars Fell on Alabama. Mitchell Parish. ReLy

Stars Go Over the Lonely Ocean, The. Robinson Jeffers. HarvBoo

Stars, gold specks, are piercing the dark leaves, The. At the Window in the Dark. Victor Hugo. SxFrPo, tr. by A. M. and E. H. Blackmore

Stars had the look of dogs to him sometimes. Star Watcher, The. Peter Davison. WaAnP; YaYoPo

Stars. I have confidence in my grandfather's building. (LL) Wild Night at Treweithan. Gwyn Williams. AngWePo; TCAWP

Stars moving from their summertime. Book, for Growing Old, The. Yves Bonnefoy. PoetW, tr. by Emily Grosholz

Stars of Night contain the glittering Day, The. Dying Words of Stonewall Jackson, The. Sidney Lanier. APN-2; CBCWP; PCW

Stars over snow. Night. Sara Teasdale. NOxBChV

Stars over the Dordogne. Sylvia Plath. PoA 2002

Stars scribble on our eyes the frosty sagas. Hart Crane. OtW Fr. Bridge, The.

Stars shine and go out. Hayyim Nahman Bialik. FIT, tr. by Robert Friend

Stars stand up in the air, The. Stars Stand Up, The. Unknown. IrLP; IrV, tr. by Eleanor Hull

Stars were strange lightbulbs, the moon was half, The. Alas, That Is the Name of Our Town; I Have Been Concealing It All This Time. Joshua Clover. NeAmPo

Stars wheel in purple, yours is not so rare. "H. D." APT-1; MoAmPo Fr. Let Zeus Record.

Star's Whole Secret, The. Mary Jo Bang. NAPBL

Star-Spangled. Michele Glazer. OPRER

Star-Spangled Banner, The. Francis Scott Key. AmWaPo; HHAm; NoP-4; UV

(Defence of Fort McHenry.) AmWaPo; NoP-4; OxBoAm

(Defence of Fort McHenry.) APN-1

Star-Struck Utopias of 2000. "Antler." PoCoUp; RWB

Start. Martin Sorescu. VCWP, tr. by Michael Hamburger

Start from death's slumbers to eternity. (LL) New Birth, The. Jones Very. APN-1; NCAP; OxBoAm; SacPr

Start from the dreamlike wilderness of life? (LL) Dreaming Child, The. Felicia Dorothea Hemans. NOBRP; NPBRoP

Start like pieces of string. Advice to the Orchestra. David Wagoner. NoAM

Start my good song. Song of "Kornél Esti", The. Dezső Kosztolányi. IQMS, tr. by Adam Makkai

Start not at her, who, in fantastic guise. Idiot Girl, The. Mary F. Johnson. CenSon

Start of a Late Autumn Novel. Tomas Tranströmer. MotU, tr. by Robert Bly

Start of Autumn: Hearing a Cicada While Sick in Bed. Ch'i-chi. CSKM, tr. by Burton Watson

Start over, all over again. (LL) Who Remains Standing? Andrée Chedid. CFP; HAWP; WoPoe, tr. by Mirène Ghossein and Samuel Haze

Start slowly and simply—warming up is crucial. Recreational Mathematics. Steve Wilson. AmPoNex

Star-Talk. Robert Graves. MoBrPo

Started as arr. Crow. Robert Grenier. PmAP

Starting a Pasture. Walter McDonald. TiP2

Starting at the center. Tables in Pictures. Diane Ward. FTOS

Starting Early from the Ch'u-ch'êng Inn. Po Chü-i. OBVE, tr. by Arthur Waley

(Starting Early.) BLT

Starting from Central Station. David Campbell.

(I Starting from Central Station.) BMAP

Starting from San Francisco. Lawrence Ferlinghetti. GM

Starting from Scratch. Ingrid Wendt. RWB; SweBea

Starting here, what do you want to remember? You Reading This, Be Ready. William Stafford. TWF

Starting in a long swale between the Sierras. Garrett Kaoru Hongo. GeoHom Fr. Cruising 99.

Starting in the upper left-hand corner, like a sail. (LL) For John Clare. John Ashbery. HarvBoo; MotU

Starting now the hours of the clock. Against the Laws. Friedrich Wilhelm Nietzsche. WoPoe, tr. by W. S. Merwin

Starting on the frosty path at dawn. Road Back, The. Pak Chaesam. CAMKP, tr. by David R. McCann and Jiwon Shin

Starting School. Annie Foster. NLP

Starting to Make a Tree. Roy Fisher. Fr. City.

Starting up behind them. All Souls'. Rita Dove. BAP-04

Starting with a projectile. Hungry Form. Caroline Bergvall. VaPo

Starting with Little Things. William Stafford. IPoFL

Starting-cry of a race, The. A name to conjure with. (LL) Geoffrey Hill. NAMCP V.2; NoAM; WoPoe Fr. Mercian Hymns.

Startle, and stare out. (LL) Psalm: "In the small beauty of the forest." George Oppen. APT-2; CalPo; HarvBoo; ItP; NAMCP V.1; OxBoAm; PFTM-2; PoCho; WoPoe

Startled into Life Like Fire. Charles Bukowski. PmAP

Startled stag, the blue-grey night, A. Dark Stag, The. Isabella Valancy Crawford. BrAP

Startling reality of things / Is my discovery every single day, The. "Startling Reality of Things," The. Fernando Pessoa. PFTM-1

"Startling Reality of Things," The. Fernando Pessoa. PFTM-1

Startling the cool gray depths of morning air. Fuji at Sunrise. Ernest Francisco Fenollosa. NAAPv.1

Star-Tribes, The. Aborigine Oral Tradition. NOBAu, tr. by Fred Biggs

Starts for a moment from its dust. (LL) Crows. Lizette Woodworth Reese. APT-1; TCAPo

Starvation. Ai. AFaM

Starvation was their legacy. Chilean People, The. Gareth Alban Davies. BBMWP, tr. by the author

Starved. Laura Riding Jackson. FuPo

Starved Rock. James Ballowe. IllVoic

Starved Rock. Edgar Lee Masters. GeoHom Fr. Spoon River Anthology.

Starwork. L. S. Asekoff. BodElec

Stasis in darkness. Ariel. Sylvia Plath. BrAP; ColAP; HeIP-4; NALW; NAMCP V.2; NoAM; NoP-4; NoP-5; VCAP

State, a state, oh! dungeon state indeed, A. Edward Taylor. ChIV-1 Fr. Preparatory Meditations Before My Approach to the Lord's Supper.

State, as if to stamp the final seal, The. William Wordsworth. NPBRoP Fr. Prelude, The; Growth of a Poet's Mind [1805 version].

State becomes statement, Petrarch, A. Refrain. Reginald Shepherd. RD

State Executive. Tanure Ojaide. PML

State Fair. David Riley Russell. TiP2

State Funeral. Thomas McCarthy. ModIr

State Occasion, A. Edward Edwin Foot. STuOW Fr. Christening the Prince.

State of affairs is thinkable, eventually, A. Sasha Steensen. Eno Fr. Spatial Spectacles.

State of Arkansas, The [see also The Arkansaw Traveler]. Unknown. APN-2

State of Butterfly. Ahmed Taha. NAfrP, tr. by Clarissa C. Burt

State of Nature, A. John Hollander. NIL-7

State of Preservation. Celeste Turner Wright. FFC

State of Seige. Teresa Calderón. TANSG, tr. by Celeste Kostopulos-Cooperman

State of the Nation, The. Kenneth Patchen. CLPP

State of the Union. Ben Friedlander. Eno

State of the Union. Alice Notley. BAP-04

State Poetry Day. Ronald Wallace. PBCAP

State Song. Berta Hart Nance. TiP2

State Street is lonely today. Aunt Jane Allen has driven her chariot to Heaven. Aunt Jane Allen. Fenton Johnson. OxAAAP

State Street's cold mingling. Chicago/3 Hours. PueRic

State Will Be Served Even By Poets, The. Julian Beck. PFTM-2

State you must dare not enter, A. Happiness. Stephen Dunn. StAl

Statecraft and Foresight have gone to their mountain council. Bowmen, The. Paavo Haavikko. WoPoe, tr. by Anselm Hollo

Stateless. Linda France. RSaN

Stately as a Galleon. Joyce Grenfell. OBCoV

Stately home where doves, in dovecotes, coo—, A. Owl Writes a Detective Story, The. Gavin Ewart. OBCoV

Stately Homes of England, The. Noël Coward. OBCoV

"Stately Homes of England, The." UV

Stately homes of England, The. Homes of England, The. Felicia Dorothea Hemans. NAEL-7v2; NOBRP; PEW; RWP; UV; ViWPN

Stately palace in which the queen dwells, The. Her Descending Down. Margaret Lucas Cavendish, Duchess of Newcastle. BASC; NOSC

Stately yon vessel sails adown the tide. Ship, The. Robert Southey. TreFP

State/meant. Imamu Amiri Baraka. BB

State-of-the-Art 'pataphysical poetry project arrives on the burning wings of a bona fide literary god, The. Darren Wershler-Henry. PoPra Fr. Ten Out of Ten, or, Why Poetry Criticism Sucks in 2003.

State's Claim That It Seeks in No Way to Deprive Indians of Their Rightful Share of Water, The. Simon J. Ortiz. ICANM

States of War. Maya Bejerano. DTA, tr. by Miriyam Glazer

States when they black out and lie there rolling when they turn, The. Falling. James Dickey. InGu; NoAM

Statesmanship. Ch'ungdam, Master. CATKP, tr. by Peter H. Lee

Statesmen. W. H. Auden. BeAl; OBCoV Fr. Shorts [1939–1947].

Statesmen, The. Ambrose Bierce. APN-2

Statesmen have known visions. And, not alone. Geoffrey Hill. UpMys Fr. Of Commerce and Society: Variations on a Theme.

Statesmen, in your exalted station know. Unknown. CAGL Fr. Don Leon.

Static. Mary Barnard. APT-2

Static. Barton Sutter. PoA 2002

Static Autumn. Yvor Winters. PoA 2002

Static, The. Lewis Warsh. FTOS

Station. Sharon Olds. PBCAP

Station (1). James Galvin. GifTon

Station (2). James Galvin. GifTon

Station (4). James Galvin. GifTon

Station. He.She.You.Me. Lawrence L. White. IAoNAP

Station Island. Seamus Heaney.
  "Black water. White waves. Furrows snowcapped." NAMCP V.2; NoAM
  "I had come to the edge of the water." NPeEn; PBCIP
  "Like a convalescent, I took the hand." NAEL-6v2; NAEL-7v2; NAMCP V.2; NoAM; NoP-5

Station platform scene. Tomas Tranströmer. WoBe Fr. Haiku.

Stationary Bicycle. Linda Pastan. ArBi

Stationery. Agha Shahid Ali. BeAl

Stations. Philip Booth. GM

Stations. Ted Hughes.
  "I can understand the haggard eyes." NoAM
  "Suddenly his poor body." NoAM
  "Whether you say it, think it, know it." NoAM
  "You are a wild look—out of an egg." NoAM

Stations. Audre Lorde. BrAP; OxAAAP

Stations of the Crux. Michael Savitz. FreRad

Stations Underground. U. A. Fanthorpe.
  Fanfare. MoWP; Prnts

Statistic. Michelle Parkerson. ISC

Statistics. Stephen Spender. MoBrPo

Statistics. Barrett Watten. PmAP

Statuary. John Ashbery. NoAM

Statuary Christ bleeds sweating grief, A. Bookbuying in the Tenderloin. Robert Hass. YaYoPo

Statue, The. Ivano Fermini. ItPo, tr. by Gayle Ridinger

Statue, The. Ella Higginson. SWaP

Statue, The. George Murray. PA9/11

Statue, The. Luz Maria Umpierre. PueRic

Statue and Birds. Louise Bogan. MoAmPo

Statue Horse. William Wordsworth. NPBRoP

Statue of a Libertine, The. Ron Padgett. AHA

Statue of Medusa, The. GS

Statue of the Dying Gladiator, The. Felicia Dorothea Hemans. RWP

Statue, The. Joseph Hilaire Pierre Belloc. OxAEP-2

Statues. Lisel Mueller. ExTi

Statues. Karen Press. TSAP

Statues, The. Laurence Binyon. OBEV

Statues, The. William Butler Yeats. NoAM; WeW-3

Statues with exposed hearts and barbed-wire crowns. Mud Vision, The. Seamus Heaney. PBCIP

Staunin noo aside his braw bress-haunled coffin. My Father. Duncan Glen. EdScPo

Stay, and behold; and see the greatest wonder. Essay upon Good-Friday, An. Anne King. EMWP

Stay Behind, The. Andrew Elliott. PNI

Stay! Beneath your feet is a wonder of women. On a Woman. Robert Williams. OBWVE, tr. by H. Idris Bell

Stay, Death. Not mine the Christus-wand. Herman Melville. APN-2; NCAP Fr. Clarel: A Poem and Pilgrimage in the Holy Land.

Stay, fairest Chari[e]ssa, stay and mark. Glowworm, The. Thomas Stanley. NOSC

Stay here, a little longer. Stay Here. Ingrid de Kok. TSAP

Stay here, fond youth, and ask no more. Against Fruition. Sir John Suckling. CavPo; NOSC

Stay Home. Wendell Berry. LPSFW

Stay in this world with me. Please. Laura Kasischke. NAPBL

Stay near me. Speak my name. Oh, do not wander. Midcentury Love Letter. Phyllis McGinley. LW

Stay near me—do not take thy flight! To a Butterfly. William Wordsworth. NPBRoP

Stay not, with lingering foot, O learner, here. Two Sonnets. Unknown. ArBi

Stay of your secure firm dry embrace, The. (LL) Hug, The. Thom Gunn. HarvBoo; NPeEn; StAl

Stay, passenger, and tend a tear. On a Hopeful Youth. Owen Feltham [or Feltham]. NOSC

'Stay!' said the child. The bird said, 'No'. Footprint on the Air, A. Naomi Lewis. NOxBChV

Stay: / will you go? Must you go? Sŏngjong, King of Chosŏn. CATKP, tr. by Peter H. Lee

Stay with me, God. The night is dark. Soldier, A: His Prayer. Gerald Kersch. PLBUT

Stay within yourself, Mind. Kamalākānta Bhattācārya. SinGod, tr. by Rachel Fell McDermott

Stayed by what was, and pulled by what would be. (LL) She. Theodore Roethke. NIL-7; StAl

Staying Alive. Denise Levertov.
At the Justice Department November 15, 1969. AmWaPo
"Went with some of my students to work in the People's."
"At 6 a.m. the ominous zooming, war-sound, of helicopters breaks into our sleep." ASA

Staying alive the boy on the screen is doing it. Breakdancing. Jorie Graham. BodElec

Staying at an inn. Basho. EH, tr. by Robert Hass

Staying at Ed's Place. May Swenson. VCAP

Staying by chance. Given to Wen Chao. Hui Ch'ung. CSKM, tr. by Paul Hansen

Staying in Luoxiang County for the Evening. Chen Zi'ang. CCL1, tr. by Stephen Owen

Staying in Touch. Bill Pearlman. ICANM

Staying up to eat and play all night. All the Stars Are Foxfire. Van K. Brock. AllShUp

Staying with a friend, you leave his mother's kitchen. In the Outhouse. Katherine Pierpoint. MFPA

Staying with Master Heng Chao at Roost of the Sages Monastery on Mount Lu. Wei Feng. CSKM, tr. by Paul Hansen

Staying Young. Bob Merrill. ReLy

Stayover at Chien-Teh River. Meng Hao Jan. ChinPo, tr. by Ye Weilian [or Yeh Wei-lien or Wai-lim Yip]

Stayover at Pei-Ku-Shan. Wang Wan. ChinPo, tr. by Ye Weilian [or Yeh Wei-lien or Wai-lim Yip]

Steadfastness. Sir Thomas Wyatt. FaBoVe; NoSic; OBEV
(Forget Not Yet.) AmFaPo; NAEL-6v1; NAEL-7v1; NoP-4; NoP-5; PoPoPo

Steady, the evening fades. Buffalo Evening. Robert Creeley. BodElec

Steady to the end. Dark Horses. Thomas O'Grady. Coast

Steadying, The. William Heyen. AmWaPo

Steak and Eggs. Bobby Byrd. ICANM

Steak Platter, A. Takamura Kotaro. CAoMJL1, tr. by Leith Morton

Steal Away to Jesus. Unknown. NoP-4; NoP-5
(Steal Away.) APN-2; ISC

Stealing. Carol Ann Duffy. EmeKit

Stealing from Your Mother. Dan Chiasson. LegDan

Stealing of Apollo's Cattle, The. Unknown. WoPoe Fr. Homeric Hymns.

Stealing the Genre. Carol Rumens. MoWP

Stealth-pirates of Cyberia. Blair Ewing. BRtP

Steam Engine; or, The Power of the Flame, The. Thomas Baker.
Death of Huskisson, The. STuOW
Great Western Days. STuOW
Lesson for the Proud, A. STuOW
Lord Stanhope's Steamer. STuOW; VerBaPo
On the Cork Packet, 1837. STuOW
Railway Boom, 1845, The. STuOW
Roses All the Way. STuOW
Vision. STuOW

Steam makes a dream-scene out of the sweating men. Matthea Harvey. IAoNAP Fr. Thermae.

Steam rises over my nose. Coffee. Wanda Coleman. BrAP; ISC

Steam Shovel. Charles Malam. NTCP

Steam: The Steamy Side. Julia A. Moore. See Ashtabula Disaster, The.

Steam was what she thought. Birthday. Christine Hume. AmPoNex

Steam whistle cleaves to the wind, The. Spring at Yesan Station. Sub-ok. WPoS, tr. by Julie Pickering

Steamboats, Viaducts, and Railways. William Wordsworth. CenSon; NAEL-6v2; NAEL-7v2

Steatopygous sky. Thoughts Drifting through the Fat Black Woman's Head While Having a Full Bubble Bath. Grace Nichols. MoWP

Steddefast cross, inmong alle other. William Herebert. SacPr

Stedfast and enduring bone, The. (LL) A. E. Housman. MoBrPo; SoSe-8 Fr. Shropshire Lad, A.

Steed bit his master, The. On a Clergyman's Horse Biting Him. Unknown. NBLV

Steed Bit His Master, The. Unknown. See On a Clergyman's Horse Biting Him.

Steekit, consecrat, fou o fire but fuel. Douglas Young. OBVE Fr. Kirkyaird by the Sea, The.

Steel. Lee Ranaldo. HeMarv

Steel Horse. Dana Gelinas. SPV, tr. by Jen Hofer

Steel sky's smashed to smithereens, A. Epitaph in Time of War. Marguerite Yourcenar. YaTCFP, tr. by Martin Sorrell

Steel Usurps the Forests; Silence Dethrones Dialogue. Bible, Apocrypha. HBAPE

Steel worker on the girder, The. Building of the Skyscraper, The. George Oppen. CalPo; OxBoAm

Steel Yourself. Siùsaidh NicNèill. EdScPo

Steele Glas, The. George Gascoigne.
"These knacks, my lord, I cannot call to mind." SacPr

Steelhead in the Whitehorse Rearing Pond. Joan Swift. PoCoUp

Steely vegetation burgeons and burgeons on, The. For that Reason We Are Also Not Obliged to Polish the Claws, Horns, and Weather Vanes. Hans Arp. MotU, tr. by Walter Howell III

Steep Acquisitions Motionless Fears. Gabriella Leto. CItWP, tr. by Cinzia Sartini Blum and Lara Trubowitz

Steep mountains. Tiger Valley. Muso Soseki. EaWin, tr. by W. S. Merwin

Steep slope hangs above, The. On Visiting Shorin Temple, Where Bodhidharma Once Lived. Soen. ZenPo, tr. by Takashi Ikemoto and Lucien Stryk

Steep valley overhung by trees, A. Plea for Peace. Frank Prewett. HATNAP

Steeplejack. Katherine Pierpoint. MFPA

Steeple-Jack, The. Marianne Moore. APT-1; ColAP; FTtHH; HarvBoo; NAAPv.2; NAMCP V.1; NoAM; NoP-4; NoP-5; OxBoAm; PoA 2002; PoPoPo Fr. Part of a Novel, Part of a Poem, Part of a Play.

Steer hither, steer your wingèd pines. William Browne. OBEV Fr. Inner Temple Masque, The.

Steerage. Albert Goldbarth. TaR

Steered straight into this century I see narrowboats. Homage to the Canal People. Andrew Sant. NOBAu

Steering my little boat towards a misty islet. Meng Hao Jan. NDACCP, tr. by William Carlos Williams

Stefansson: a walrus of a man. Stefansson Island. Philip Booth. SoSe-8

Stefansson Island. Philip Booth. SoSe-8

Stèidhichean Làidir. Derick Thomson. EdScPo

(Steingeröll) new signs putting. Tristan Tzara. PFTM-1 Fr. Poemes Negres.

Stele (1-2 c. B.C.). Denise Levertov. BodElec

Stele and my Sirens and mournful pitcher that hold. Erinna. HePo Fr. Epigrams.

Stele and my sirens and mournful urn. Erinna. SaLy, tr. by Diane Rayor

Stele for Lenz. Isabelle Hovald. OnScMo, tr. by Keith Waldrop

Stele for Wang Ziqiao. Ts'ai Yung. CCL1, tr. by Donald Holzman

Stella behold, and then begin t'indite. (LL) Sir Philip Sidney. NoSic; OxAEP-1 Fr. Astrophil and Stella.

Stella oft sees the very face of woe. Sir Philip Sidney. NAEL-6v1; NAEL-7v1; NoSic Fr. Astrophil and Stella.

Stella, since thou so right a Princess art. Sir Philip Sidney. NoP-4; NoP-5; OxAEP-1 Fr. Astrophil and Stella.

Stella, think not that I by verse seek fame. Sir Philip Sidney. NoP-4; NoP-5; NoSic; WaAnP Fr. Astrophil and Stella.

Stella to Dr Swift. Esther Johnson. IrLP

Stella, while now by honour's cruel might. Sir Philip Sidney. NAEL-6v1; NAEL-7v1 Fr. Astrophil and Stella.

Stellar dust has settled. Origin of Order, The. Pattiann Rogers. PoA 2002

Stellar Elements. Dan Beachy-Quick. IAoNAP

Stellar sea crawler, maw, The. Starfish. Eric Ormsby. NoP-4; NoP-5

Stella's Birthday, 1725. Jonathan Swift. CABP; IrLP

Stella's Birthday [1721]. Jonathan Swift. NAEL-6v1; OxAEP-1

Stella's Birthday ([March 13,] 1727). Jonathan Swift. NoP-4; NoP-5

Stella's Kiss. Sir Philip Sidney. NoSic

Stem of the Tree of Orestes. Jennifer Moxley. VaPo

Stenographers, The. Patricia K. Page. BrAP; HeIP-4; NALW; NAMCP V.2; NoAM

Stentor and Mourning. Alan Dugan. PWW2

Step Away from Them, A. Frank O'Hara. NAMCP V.2; OxBoAm; PtR; VCAP; WoPoe

Step or two inside the door, A. Murphy's Law. Alan Jenkins. OxBSo

Step out onto the planet. Lew Welch. WhBo

Step right up, come one, come all, don't. Unknown. PriapPo Fr. Priapus Poems, The.

Stepback, stepforward; it was that kind of rhythm. Frederick D'Aguiar. WaCA Fr. GDR.

Stephano Remembers. James Simmons. PBCIP; PNI

Stephen Smith, University of Iowa sophomore, burned what he said was his draft card. Of Late. George Starbuck. AmWaPo

Stephen to Lazarus. Clive Staples Lewis. ChIV-2; SacPr

Stepmother. Dinah Livingstone. Prnts

Stepmother, The. Tatiana Shcherbina. ItGoST, tr. by J. Kates

Stepping Aside. Andrée Chedid. HAWP, tr. by Harriet Zinnes

Stepping down from the blackberry bushes. Bogyman. Fleur Adcock. MoWP

Stepping down from the swing. Tune: "Rouged Lips." Li Ch'ing-chao. ColAnChi, tr. by Jiaosheng Wang

Stepping gingerly. Cat in the Snow. Aileen Fisher. NTCP

Stepping in the Same River. Karen Chamberlain. GeoH

Stepping into the field, sadness fills my deep heart. Love Lament. *Vietnamese Oral Tradition*. CaDao, *tr. by* John Balaban

Stepping Out. Michael Brownstein. FTOS

Stepping Out. Allen Fisher.
 Progressions of Spacetime: I. Oth
 Rims of Distinction: I. Oth
 Stepping Out: 2. Oth
 Stepping Out: I. Oth

Stepping out of my apartment building. Ordinance, The. Luis Cabalquinto. ReBoTo

Stepping Out of Poetry. Gerald Stern. GoPo

Stepping Out With Edvard Munch ("When from the other world you.") Elma van Haren. TuT, *tr. by* Anne Kennedy

Stepping Out With Edvard Munch ("When from the virile grave.") Elma van Haren. TuT, *tr. by* Medbh McGuckian

Stepping through snow. Oshio. NAAPv.2

Stepping to da Muse/Sic. Afua Cooper. WaCA

Stepping Westward. Denise Levertov. NALW

Stepping Westward. William Wordsworth. NPBRoP

Stepping-Stones, The. William Wordsworth. CenSon *Fr.* River Duddon [A Series of Sonnets], The.

Steps. Adivi Bapiraju. HotL, *tr. by* V. Narayana Rao

Steps. Kojo Laing. NAfrP

Steps. Bernadette Mayer. NYP2

Steps. Naomi Shihab Nye. CAP-8; ExTi

Steps. Frank O'Hara. CAP-8; PmAP; PtR

Steps in the Night. Mahmoud Darwish. VCWP, *tr. by* Denys Johnson-Davies

Steps, shops noses, ears, eyes steps. Steps. Bernadette Mayer. NYP2

Steps / steps. Steps. Adivi Bapiraju. HotL, *tr. by* V. Narayana Rao

Steps to the Temple. Richard Crashaw. SacPr *Fr.* Strage degli innocenti, La.

Steps were thorny, I climbed all the way down, silver-pointing my steps, The. From Revelation and Defeat. Georg Trakl. MotU, *tr. by* Stuart Friebert

Stereo Time with Booker Little. Rick Madigan. SeSe

Stereograph: 1903. Julie Fay. NAPBL

Sterile Dish, The. Lenka Valachová. SurWo, *tr. by* Katerina Pinosová

Sterile line glows, The. Poem for Claude. Ray DiPalma. FTOS

Sterling Brown. Ronald D. Palmer. BtF

Sterling Park. Del Ray Cross. FreRad

Sterling Williams has a nosebleed. Sterling Williams' Nosebleed. David Chin. InvLad

Sterling Williams' Nosebleed. David Chin. InvLad

Stern Daughter of the Voice of God! Ode to Duty. William Wordsworth. NAEL-6v2; NAEL-7v2; NOBRP; OBEV

Stern eyes of the soul are moved to smile, The. (LL) True to myself am I, and false to all. Mary Elizabeth Coleridge. ViWPN; VWP

Stern Miss Frugle always said. What Happened to Miss Frugle. Brian Patten. OBSP

Stern Truth. Letitia Elizabeth Landon. VWP

Sterricky. Mary Dalton. OpeFie

Stet. Peter Reading.
 "Dirty sex violence of TV." NeBrP

Stethoscope, The. Dannie Abse. BloBone

Steve's Commando Paintball, San Adriano, California. Joel Brouwer. AmPoNex

Steve's very beautiful. Six Part Lust Story. Jonathan Fisher. PML

Steveston. Daphne Marlatt.
 Ghost. BrAP

Stevie Wonder. Lyn'elle Patrice Chapman. BtF

Stevie wonder visited nambé, gave his harp. New Mex Hip. Anne MacNaughton. ICANM

Stewed and Fraught with Birds. Stephen Rodefer. VaPo

Stick and Hat. King Lẻ Thánh–tông. WoPoe, *tr. by* John S. Major

Stick of Incense, A. William Butler Yeats. ChIV-2

Stick stick call then, stick stick sticking, sticking with a chicken. Sticking in a extra succession, sticking in. Gertrude Stein. NAMCP V.1 *Fr.* Tender Buttons.

Stick-up. Jeni Olin. FreRad

Stick your patent name on a signboard. Hart Crane. GM; MoAmPo; NAAL-5; OxBoAm *Fr.* Bridge, The.

Sticking morphine in the arm and eating meat. (LL) Last Night in Calcutta. Allen Ginsberg. FTOS; NAMCP V.2; NoAM

Sticking with the situations provided. Trigger D'evolution. Randy Prunty. AnSo

Sticks. Thomas Sayers Ellis. LegDan; NAPBL

Sticks in one hand. U T'ak. CATKP, *tr. by* Peter H. Lee

Sticks-in-a-drowse droop over sugary loam. Cuttings. Theodore Roethke. APT-2; IPoFL; NAAL-5; NAMCP V.1; NoAM; OBGa; WaAnP

Stiff as a crustacean's carapace. Breakfast. Joe Denham. OpeFie

Stiff lines of the twigs, The. April. Charles Reznikoff. APT-2

Stiff, still features, The. (LL) Ezra Pound. NAMCP V.1; NoAM *Fr.* Cantos.

Stiff west wind blows another cloud of tear gas, A. Dispersal of It. Anne Waldman. AHA

Stiff with weapons, fighting back over the same ground. (LL) Thistles. Ted Hughes. FaBoVe; NAMCP V.2; NoAM; NPeEn; SoSe-8; WaAnP

Stiffen, not knowing what to do or say. (LL) Young Girls. Raymond Souster. BrAP; HeIP-4

Stifling atmosphere impelled me away from home to the sea. War Night 6. Ilan Sheinfeld. NRoS, *tr. by* Esther Raizen

Stigmata. Mitch Rayes. ICANM

Stike up, Gypsy, you have quaffed your wages. Ancient Gypsy, The. Mihály Vörösmarty. IQMS, *tr. by* Peter Zollman

Still. A. R. Ammons. OxBoAm

Still. Lucille Clifton. NAMCP V.2

Still. Andrew Greig. EdScPo

Still. Wisława Szymborska. AF, *tr. by* Robert A. Maguire

Still. Ronald Stuart Thomas. TCAWP

Still. James Wright. *See* Still, / I would leap too.

Still alive. Basho. EH, *tr. by* Robert Hass

Still—all things appear. Nothingness. T'aego, National Preceptor. CATKP, *tr. by* Peter H. Lee

Still, all was calm in heaven. Nor yet appeared. Robert Pollok. STuOW *Fr.* Course of Time, The.

Still and All. Burns Singer. HarvBoo

Still Another Day. Pablo Neruda. TAPaP
 #28. TAPaP, *tr. by* William O'Daly

Still are the cowslips from thy bosom springing. Felicia Dorothea Hemans. NPBRoP *Fr.* Records of the Spring of 1834.

Still as. Moon-Shadows. Adelaide Crapsey. APT-1

Still as a moth face on the water. Memory of Quiet. Rosalie Moore. APT-2

Still blooming on, when Summer-flowers all fade. Autumn Flowers. Jones Very. APN-1

Still breath on the summer breeze, A. Ghost Lights. H. Palmer Hall. TiP2

Still Burn. M. S. C. Okolo. NeNiPo

Still burning. (LL) Portrait, The. Stanley Kunitz. CAP-8; GoPo; InvLad; NAAPv.2; NAMCP V.1; PoCho; RaBo

Still, Citizen Sparrow. Richard Wilbur. ColAP; NoAM; TRP

Still clear, that morning his family moved. After a Friendship. Robert Minhinnick. AngWePo

Still clinging to your shirt. (LL) My Papa's Waltz. Theodore Roethke. AmFaPo; APT-2; BeAl; BrAP; CAP-8; ClHu; ColAP; EMP; HeIP-4; NAAL-5; NAMCP V.1; NBLV; NIL-7; NIP-4; NoAM; NoP-4; NoP-5; NOxBChV; OxBoAm; PoPoPo; RaBo; TFi; TRP; WaAnP

Still crowned by petals. (LL) Way of the Water-Hyacinth, The. Zawgee. AmFaPo; ItP, *tr. by* Lyn Aye

Still dark / The unknown bird sits on his usual branch. Five Flights Up. Elizabeth Bishop. OxBoAm

Still dark when we file like children out on the turf. Sydney Lea. Vesp

Still Do I Keep My Look, My Identity. Gwendolyn Brooks. IllVoic; OxBoAm *Fr.* Gay Chaps at the Bar.

Still do I love, still shed my innocent light, my Blood, for thee. (LL) Still Falls the Rain. Dame Edith Sitwell. BrAP; CABP; MoBrPo; MoWP; NAEL-6v2; NAEL-7v2; NAMCP V.1; NoAM; OBWP; PFTM-1; TFi; WaAnP

Still do the stars impart their light. Falsehood. William Cartwright. OBEV

Still drone of the time, The. What She Said. Patumanār. AWTN, *tr. by* A. K. Ramanujan

Still eight years my elder. This Poem Is for You, My Sister. Mona Lisa Saloy. FuFl

Still exhausted at dawn, she plays. She Calms the Savage Beast with Her Aubade. Grace Bauer. MiVo

Still explosions on the rocks, The. Shampoo, The. Elizabeth Bishop. APT-2; HarvBoo; OxBoAm; PtR; StAl; VCAP

Still Falls the Rain. Dame Edith Sitwell. BrAP; CABP; MoBrPo; MoWP; NAEL-6v2; NAEL-7v2; NAMCP V.1; NoAM; OBWP; PFTM-1; TFi; WaAnP

Still Gyte, Man? Stude I in yere claes. Still Gyte, Man? George Campbell Hay. EdScPo

Still had hair! (LL) For Emily (Dickinson). Maureen Owen. PmAP; ReTh

Still Here. Langston Hughes. SAmP

Still hovering round the fair at sixty-four. On an Amorous Old Man. David Mallet. NePenScot

Still, I am here. Pablo Neruda. GifTon, *tr. by* William O'Daly

Still I complain; I am complaining still. Edward Taylor. SacPr *Fr.* Preparatory Meditations Before My Approach to the Lord's Supper.

Still, I lay awake in the dark. Call, The. Robert Harris. BMAP

Still I Rise. Maya Angelou. BeAl

Still I See in Front of Me. Ivan Matanov. PML, *tr. by* Lyudmila Kolechkova

Still I toil. Joseph Cottle. STuOW *Fr.* Malvern Hills.

Still, / I would leap too.   Small Frogs Killed on the Highway.   James Wright. NAMCP V.2; NoAM

(Still.)   PoPoPo

Still in his mother's lap the baby Love played.   Meleager.   HePo, *tr. by* Barbara Hughes Fowler

Still in one body, locked and barred.   Prisons.   Lőrinc Szabó.   IQMS, *tr. by* Edwin Morgan

Still in sleeping bags, the promised delivery.   Bats.   Dave Jeddie Smith. NoAM; RoV; WaAnP

Still in the published city but not yet.   John Ashbery.   PmAP *Fr.* Flow Chart.

Still, in the stale cigarette smell.   Mother and Son.   Karen Swenson.   PoChi

Still in the taste.   Jerry Kilbride.   WhBo

Still is my love telling what is told. (LL)   William Shakespeare.   NoP-5; NoSic; OxAEP-1 *Fr.* Sonnets.

Still it is raining lightly.   Love Medicine, A.   Louise Erdrich.   HATNAP

Still / it was nice.   Still.   Lucille Clifton.   NAMCP V.2

Still, leagues beyond those leagues, there is more sea. (LL)   Dante Gabriel Rossetti.   ChIV-2; OBEV *Fr.* House of Life, The.

Still let my tyrants know, I am not doomed to wear.   Emily Jane Brontë. IJHIL; NoP-4; OBEV *Fr.* Prisoner, The. A Fragment.

Still Life.   Raymond Garlick.   AngWePo

Still Life.   Stratis Haviaras.   MotU

Still Life.   Anthony Hecht.   AmWaPo; NoP-4; NoP-5; PWW2

Still Life.   Lisa Jarnot.   VaPo

Still Life.   Sharan Strange.   GT

Still Life.   C. K. Williams.   PtR

Still Life: "After your letter arrived I left the oven on."   Madeline DeFrees. VisFro

Still Life: "Cello on the bed, A."   Georgi Rupchev.   CSCBP, *tr. by* Georgi Belev and Lisa Sapinkopf

Still Life: "Here in a summer full of dust."   Luljeta Lleshanaku.   WoBe, *tr. by* Henry Israeli

Still Life: "I shall not soon forget."   Thom Gunn.   NAMCP V.2; PoCho

Still Life in Garden.   Rachel Hadas.   ExTi

Still life: on a table, a white paper, A.   Déjeuner, Le.   Carol Snow.   AFaM

Still Life: The Table.   Theo Van Doesburg.   PFTM-1

Still Life: "There is a train, no, there are train."   Robin Behn.   AmAlph

Still Life: "Three old New Mexican men."   Keith Wilson.   ICANM

Still Life with Endings.   Ray Gonzalez.   TouFir

Still Life w/Influences.   Joyelle McSweeney.   LegDan

Still Life with Minnows.   Sherod Santos.   PfSP

Still life: "Woman is wild, The."   Ingrid de Kok.   TSAP

Still limping, she has come. She waits at the foot of the hill, doesn't.   Orpheus Meets Eurydice in the Underworld.   Sue Sinclair.   Coast

Still looking for a scoot-hole, Phemios the poet.   Michael Longley.   ModIr *Fr.* Odyssey.

Still much to read, but too late.   Charles Reznikoff.   NAAPv.2

Still must I hear?—shall hoarse Fitzgerald bawl.   English Bards and Scotch Reviewers [1812 version].   Lord Byron.

Still must I tamely.   Sigh, A.   Witter Bynner.   APT-1

Still night. The old clock Ticks.   Last Night in Calcutta.   Allen Ginsberg. FTOS; NAMCP V.2; NoAM

Still Night Thoughts.   Li Po.   ColAnChi; ItP, *tr. by* Burton Watson

Still, O Lord, for Thee I Tarry.   Charles Wesley.   SacPr

Still often, the silence ahead of me.   Signals.   Yvonne Cullen.   NIrP

Still old pond, The.   Basho.   NIL-7, *tr. by* Earl Miner

Still one more year of preparation.   Preparation.   Czeslaw Milosz.   WoPoe, *tr. by* the author and Robert Hass

Still onward winds the dreary way.   Alfred Tennyson.   NAEL-6v2; NAEL-7v2 *Fr.* In Memoriam A. H. H.

Still parleying, in earshot of his peers. (LL)   Terminus.   Seamus Heaney. NAMCP V.2; PoPoPo

Still seems to need. (LL)   Memories of a Lost War.   Louis Simpson. AmWaPo; OBWP; PWW2

Still singing. (LL)   Insects on a bough.   Issa.   EH; NIL-7, *tr. by* Robert Hass

Still Small Voice, The.   Abraham Moses Klein.   IFF

Still small voice unto, The.   Successful Summer, A.   David Schubert.   APT-2; ChIV-1

Still south I went and west and south again.   Prelude.   John Millington Synge. MoBrPo; OBMV

Still, still my eye will gaze long-fixed on thee.   Columbine, The.   Jones Very. ColAP; GSo; WaAnP

Still the loud death drum, thundering from afar.   Eighteen Hundred and Eleven, a Poem.   Anna Laetitia Barbauld.   NOBRP; RWP

Still the 'Messerschmitts' claw at the heart.   Hospital, The.   Boris Abramovich Slutsky.   TCRusP, *tr. by* Daniel Weissbort

Still the mighty mountains stand.   Epilogue to Alun Mabon.   John Ceiriog Hughes.   OBWVE, *tr. by* H. Idris Bell

Still the walls do not fall.   "H. D."   NAAL-5 *Fr.* Walls Do Not Fall, The.

Still the warm fingerprints.   Man Falls at Work, A.   Ber Grin.   Prolet, *tr. by* Amelia Glaser

Still, there was quite a decent turn-out really.   New Rock n Roll, The. Brendan Cleary.   NeBl

Still to Be Neat.   Ben Jonson. *See* Sweet Neglect, The.

Still to be neat, still to be dressed [*or* Drest].   Ben Jonson.   NAEL-6v1; NAEL-7v1; NIL-7; NoP-4; NPeEn; PoPoPo; TFi; WeW-3 *Fr.* Epicoene; or, The Silent Woman.

Still to my sight thy love doth rise.   To a Friend, Who Gave the Author a Reading Glass.   Elizabeth Moody.   PoBW

Still to survive in my immortal song. (LL)   Michael Drayton.   HeIP-4; NAEL-7v1; NIP-4; NoP-5; NOSC *Fr.* Idea.

Still today, sober and tenured as I can be.   Cleveland, Angels, Ogres, Trolls. David Citino.   UpMys

Still Waiting for My Winter Coat: A Sequence of Fragments.   Hipponax. WoPoe, *tr. by* Anselm Hollo

Still waiting for the pool to fill. (LL)   Audubon Drive, Memphis.   James Seay. AllShUp; SwNoth

Still was the night, Serene and Bright.   Michael Wigglesworth.   ColAP; NAAL-3; TCAPo *Fr.* Day of Doom, The [First Section].

Still was the night, serene and bright.   Michael Wigglesworth.   NAAPv.1 *Fr.* Day of Doom, The: Or, A Poetical Description of the Great and Last Judgment.

Still we are the same. . .Sideways. (LL)   Russian New Year.   Bill Berkson. NYP2; PmAP

Still Winter (Spring).   Charlie Smith.   PoDa

Still without Life.   Rosalie Moore.   CalPo; YaYoPo

Still your people and mine were tearing each other to pieces when we.   Letter to the Actor Charles Laughton concerning the Work on the Play "The Life of Galileo."   Bertolt Brecht.   PoSu, *tr. by* Michael Hamburger

Stillborn.   Jane Duran.   MFPA

Stillborn.   Sylvia Plath.   CAP-8

Stillborn Night.   Beth Brant.   ReEnLa

Stilled is the lute string after hours of song.   Orchid Door, The.   *Unknown.* WoPoe, *tr. by* Jean S. Grigsby

Stilled room to which I am called, A.   Call, The.   Dennis Haskell.   NOBAu

Still-Heart.   Frank Pearce Sturm.   OBMV

Still-Life.   Elizabeth Daryush.   MoWP; NPeEn; OxBEV

Still-Life.   Maurice Kenny.   UrbNat

Still-Life.   Tatiana Shcherbina.   ItGoST, *tr. by* J. Kates

Still-Life with Woodstove.   William W. Cook.   SpirFl

Stillness.   Basho.   EH, *tr. by* Robert Hass

Stillness.   Basho.   EMJL, *tr. by* Haruo Shirane

Stillness.   James Elroy Flecker.   MoBrPo

Stillness! Down the drinking ride.   Tunstall Forest.   Donald Davie.   OxBEV

Stillness is all in the key of that desolate sound, The. (LL)   Autumn Refrain. Wallace Stevens.   APT-1; OxBoAm

Stillness is highest act.   James McAuley.   BMAP *Fr.* Seven Days of Creation, The.

Stillness / not on the branch.   Exclamation.   Octavio Paz.   ChAP, *tr. by* Eliot Weinberger

Stillness, the Dancing, The.   Linda Bierds.   RoV

Stillness, The / of the wood.   Figures, The.   Robert Creeley.   CAP-8

Still—Volcano—Life, A.   Emily Dickinson.   NAAPv.1

Stilt Jack.   John Thompson.

9.   IFF

Stilts and Other Vehicles.   Richard Sale.   TiP2

Stilt-walker.   Susan Wicks.   Prnts

Stincher, The.   Jackie Kay.   NOxBChV

Sting, The.   Tom Paulin.   EmeKit

Sting—a South Carolina Ave. Folk Tale.   Harold Carrington.   EGAG

Sting Her Up!   Edward Young.   STuOW *Fr.* Imperium Pelagi, or, The Merchant.

Sting of Death, The.   Frederick George Scott.   SacPr

Stinging / gold swarms.   Sunset.   E. E. Cummings.   MoAmPo

Stings.   Sylvia Plath.   NALW

Stink and are thrown away. End fair enough. (LL)   On Spies.   Ben Jonson. FaBoVe; NoP-4; NoP-5; NPeEn; WoPoe

Stinking of chlorine and sweit, the sweirt recruits.   1941.   Robert Garioch. FaBoWar

Stinking Rose, The.   Sujata Bhatt.   HarvBoo

Stir of the world, the music of the mountain, The. (LL)   Fawn's Foster-Mother. Robinson Jeffers.   NAMCP V.1; NoAM

Stirring / a steering / a seedling, A.   Octavio Paz.   PFTM-2 *Fr.* Blanco.

Stirring of a feathering cloud, The.   Nature's Minor Chords.   Henrietta Cordelia Ray.   CBWP-3

Stirrups, leggings, a stainless.   Love Medley: Patrice Cuchulain.   Michael S. Harper.   CAP-8

Stirs its ashes and embers, its burnt sticks.   Old Age Gets Up.   Ted Hughes. NoAM

Stirs the Culprit—Life! (LL)   Surgeons must be very careful.   Emily Dickinson.   ItP; SAmP; TCAPo

Stitch.   Robert Budde.   PoPra

Stitches.   Debra Kang Dean.   NAPBL

Stitches.   Sinéad Morrissey.   NIrP

Stitches.   Takahashi Shinkichi.   ZenPo, tr. by Takashi Ikemoto and Lucien Stryk

Stitching.   Elin ap Hywel.   ATSWP, tr. by Robert Minhinnick

Stitching.   Katie Donovan.   NIrP

Stockade prisoners on hunger strike: Nani Mo Mite Inai Kokoro No Hi Ga Tsuzuki Kogen Natsu Takenawa.   Violet Kazue De Cristoforo.   CalPo

Stockdoves, The.   Andrew Young.   NePenScot

Stocking Up.   Sylvia Kantaris.   LW

Stoic, The.   Paul Muldoon.   GPPA

Stoic, The: For Laura Von Courten.   Edgar Bowers.   CalPo; PWW2

Stolen Away.   Joseph Ceravolo.   FTOS

Stolen Child, The.   William Butler Yeats.   NAEL-6v2; NAEL-7v2; NoP-4; NoP-5; WaAnP

Stolen Light.   Stewart Conn.   EdScPo

Stolen Moments.   Kim Addonizio.   CalPo

Stolen Visit, A.   Rosa Mulholland.   PoBW

Stolen White Girl, The.   John Rollin Ridge.   APN-2; NAAPv.1

Stolen world, glowing and benighted with vision, The.   Ian Patterson.   VaPo Fr. Hardihood.

Stomach of goat, crushed.   Salami.   Philip Levine.   TRP; WaAnP

Stompin' at the Savoy.   Andy Razaf.   ReLy

Stomping to the house.   To Kill Stray Dogs.   Mark Todd.   GeoH

Stomping with Pettit on the Battenkill.   Garrett Kaoru Hongo.   PfSP

Stond wel, Moder, under rode.   Unknown.   OHMEL

Stone.   Charles Simic.   CAP-8; ChAP

Stone: "When the stone fall that morning out of the johncrow sky."   Edward Kamau Brathwaite.   NAMCP V.2; PFTM-2; WaCA; WoBe

Stone, A.   Yves Bonnefoy.   VCWP, tr. by John Naughton

Stone, A / i saved.   Stanford M. Forrester.   AmZen

Stone, The.   Walter De la Mare.   WeW-3

Stone, The.   Wilfrid Wilson Gibson.   MoBrPo

Stone, The.   Another Stone in the Swamp.   Rumen Leonidov.   CSCBP, tr. by Georgi Belev and Lisa Sapinkopf

Stone, The.   Henry Vaughan.   ChIV-1

Stone, The.   Thomas Vaughan.   OBWVE

Stone and Fern.   Leslie Norris.   AngWePo

Stone and Light.   Shuntaro Tanikawa.   VCWP, tr. by Harold Wright

Stone and Sky.   Nikolay Novikov.   tr. by Daniel Weissbort

"In our world it's unusual."   TCRusP, tr. by Daniel Weissbort

Stone / and that hard.   Lorine Niedecker.   APT-2

Stone at dawn, A.   Easter Morning.   Amy Clampitt.   ChIV-2

Stone at the Bottom, The.   Manuel Ulacia.   VCWP, tr. by Reginald Gibbons

Stone at the Tip of the Tongue, A.   Oumarou Watta.   NAfrP

Stone bell tolls on the seabed, The.   August Sleepwalker, The.   Bei Dao.   PFTM-2, tr. by Bonnie S. McDougall

Stone, bronze, stone, steel, stone, oakleaves, horses' heels.   T. S. Eliot.   AmWaPo; OBWP Fr. Coriolan.

Stone by stone I pile.   Mark of Resistance, A.   Adrienne Rich.   PoA 2002

Stone Canyon Nocturne.   Charles Wright.   ColAP; GeoHom; NAMCP V.2; VCAP

Stone cries to stone.   Jerusalem.   James Fenton.   BeAl; HarvBoo

Stone Curlew, The.   Robert Adamson.   StAl

Stone doesn't repel the light, The.   Stone and Light.   Shuntaro Tanikawa.   VCWP, tr. by Harold Wright

Stone Dog, The.   King Lě Thánh-tông.   WoPoe, tr. by Nguyen Ngoc Bich

Stone Dolphin, The.   Fay Zwicky.   BMAP Fr. Three Songs of Love and Hate.

Stone Face.   Lola Ridge.   NAAPv.2

Stone Face Falls.   William Everson.   APT-2

Stone Face, The.   Harri Webb.   AngWePo

Stone falls, A.   Moving through Air.   Lewis Warsh.   AHA

Stone For A Statue.   Sarah Morgan Bryan Piatt.   NCAP

Stone for the sake of the souls of the slain birds sailing.. (LL)   Over Sir John's Hill.   Dylan Thomas.   AngWePo; NPeEn; TCAWP

Stone Free.   Jim Brodey.   AHA

Stone Fruit.   Lin Max.   FiBr

Stone Gullets.   May Swenson.   VCAP

Stone gullets among.   Stone Gullets.   May Swenson.   VCAP

Stone had skidded arc'd and bloomed into islands, The.   Calypso.   Edward Kamau Brathwaite.   BrAP; HarvBoo; NAMCP V.2

Stone in the Sand.   Coral Bracho.   RMCMP, tr. by Suzanne Jill Levine

Stone in the Swamp, A.   Rumen Leonidov.   CSCBP, tr. by Georgi Belev and Lisa Sapinkopf

Stone in the Water of Sanity, A.   Coral Bracho.   RMCMP, tr. by Suzanne Jill Levine

Stone in your face, The.   Ode to César Vallejo.   Pablo Neruda.   TCLAP, tr. by Stephen Tapscott

Stone is a mirror which works poorly, The.   Charles Simic.   VCAP

Stone of Patience.   Mimi Khalvati.   MFPA

Stone of the Arabian woman, The.   Shakir Li'aibi.   IrPoTo, tr. by Ralph Saverese and Saadi A. Simawe

Stone / On summer plain.   Masaoka Shiki.   ZenPo, tr. by Takashi Ikemoto and Lucien Stryk

Stone on the Hilltop, The.   Lu Yu.   ColAnChi, tr. by Burton Watson

Stone or Water.   André Du Bouchet.   YaTCFP, tr. by Hoyt Rogers

Stone Pond.   Ellen Bryant Voigt.   LPSFW

Stone relief I never tire of, A.   Spinning Dharma Wheel.   Takahashi Shinkichi.   ZenPo, tr. by Takashi Ikemoto and Lucien Stryk

Stone ruins of a monastery.   Tutelage.   Chase Twichell.   WANABP

Stone says that it covers here the white dog, The.   Tymnes.   HePo, tr. by Barbara Hughes Fowler

Stone Speech.   Charles Tomlinson.   NPeEn

Stone stands among new firs, The.   Standing Stone.   Ruth Bidgood.   AngWePo

Stone stood in her house, A.   Lionel Abrahams.   TSAP

Stone Stream.   Pou Kuksa.   BecRai, tr. by Kim Daljin, Kim Won-Chung and Christopher Merrill

Stone that God whets laws with, The.   Trinity.   Gerrit Achterberg.   TuT, tr. by Dennis O'Driscoll

Stone upon stone.   Farm in the Green Mountains, A.   Dave Etter.   VisFro

Stone upon stone, and man, where was he?   Pablo Neruda.   TCLAP Fr. Heights of Macchu Picchu, The.

Stone Verdict, The.   Seamus Heaney.   NAMCP V.2

Stone Wall.   Takahashi Shinkichi.   ZenPo, tr. by Takashi Ikemoto and Lucien Stryk

Stone Wall and Celebration.   János Pilinszky.   PoSu, tr. by Peter Jay

Stone Wall and Fiesta.   János Pilinszky.   IQMS, tr. by Adam Makkai

Stone walls are adorned with worthless decor.   Stone Walls.   Thich Tue Sy.   WhBo

Stone Will Talk, The.   Houda Al-Na'mani.   PoArWo

Stone within stone, and man, where was he?   Pablo Neruda.   VCWP Fr. Heights of Macchu Picchu, The.

Stone you let fall in me will not resile, The.   Edith Jay Scovell.   HarvBoo Fr. Water Images.

Stone-cutters fighting time with marble, you foredefeated.   To the Stone-Cutters.   Robinson Jeffers.   ColAP; MoAmPo; NAAL-5; OxBoAm

Stoned & / singing Indian scat.   River Still To Be Found, A.   Lawrence Ferlinghetti.   BB

Stoned by noon, I'd take the trail.   Marijuana.   Chase Twichell.   WANABP

Stonehenge.   Samuel Daniel.   NPeEn Fr. Musophilus; or, Defence of All Learning.

Stonemason wanted . . . he dared to want, A.   Tomb of the Imagination.   Miguel Hernández.   AF, tr. by Tom Jones

Stonepicker.   Frieda Hughes.   StAl

Stones.   Shirley Kaufman.   DTA

Stones (a miracle to mortal view), The.   Ovid.   OBVE Fr. Metamorphoses.

Stones and all the elements with thee, The.   Bible, O.T.   STuOW Fr. Paraphrase on the Book of Job, A.

Stones and Bones.   Christopher Reid.   NPeEn

Stones and Snow.   Homer.   OBVE Fr. Iliad, The.

Stones are time, The.   Village.   Octavio Paz.   TCLAP, tr. by Charles Tomlinson

Stone's finely wrought parable, The.   Stone in the Swamp, A.   Rumen Leonidov.   CSCBP, tr. by Georgi Belev and Lisa Sapinkopf

Stones huddled together on the ramparts and men lived off the moss of the stones, The.   Faction Du Muet.   René Char.   MotU, tr. by Thomas Merton

Stones in my Passway.   Robert Johnson.   APT-2

Stones inimic, The.   Reconnaissance Patrol.   August Stramm.   GTCP, tr. by Reinhold Grimm

Stones (Istanbul, Robert Smithson).   Ann Lauterbach.   AWPTFC

Stones must form a circle first not a wall.   First Rule.   Maurice Kenny.   HATNAP

Stones no longer interest me,The.   In the Roman Forum.   István Vas.   IQMS, tr. by Bruce Berlind

Stones of the desert town, The.   Lodging, The.   George Mackay Brown.   EdScPo

Stones of Time, The.   Kenneth Koch.   NAMCP V.2; NoAM Fr. Days and Nights.

Stones only, the disjecta membra of this Great House.   Ruins of a Great House.   Derek Walcott.   BrAP; PoPoPo

Stones Speak of an Earthless Sky.   Duane Niatum.   PoCoUp

Stones Where the Haft Rotted, The.   Meng Chiao.   CCL1, *tr. by* A. C. Graham

Stone-Throw.   Stratis Haviaras.   MotU

Stonewall Jackson.   Herman Melville.   NCAP

Stonewall Jackson's Way.   John Williamson Palmer.   CBCWP

Stony Grey Soil.   Patrick Kavanagh.   HarvBoo; ModIr

Stony Lonesome.   Langston Hughes.   SAmP

Stony lonesome reached out and grabbed me.   Dannemora Contraband.   Jackie Warren-Moore.   SpirFl

Stood among those lost trees / & moved only when I moved. (LL)   Thanks.   Yusef Komunyakaa.   AmAlph; CAP-8; OxBoAm

Stood off shrouded in his loneliness. (LL)   Watchmaker God.   Robert Lowell.   InvLi; SoSe-8

Stood on the porch in.   Allen Ginsberg.   WhBo

Stoop, and there it is.   Sikong Tu.   CCL1 *Fr.* Twenty-Four Modes of Poetry.

Stooping in the dooryard the boy saint picks up the body.   Miracles of St. Sebastian, The.   G. C. Waldrep.   LegDan

Stooping to pull up a weed.   Taproot.   Debra Kang Dean.   NAPBL

Stop all the clocks.   W. H. Auden.   *See* Song: "Stop all the clocks, cut off the telephone."

Stop all the clocks, cut off the telephone.   W. H. Auden.   CAGL; EMP; MoBrPo; OPOU *Fr.* Twelve Songs.

Stop. Along this path, in phrases of light.   Plainsong.   Carol Ann Duffy.   MoWP

Stop bleeding said the knife.   Bleeding.   May Swenson.   NALW

Stop, Christian passer-by!—Stop, child of God.   Epitaph.   Samuel Taylor Coleridge.   NAEL-6v2; NAEL-7v2; SacPr

Stop, cried the wolf to the lamb seven.   Failure.   Natan Zach.   FIT, *tr. by* Robert Friend

Stop!—for thy tread is on an Empire's dust!   NAEL-6v2; NAEL-7v2 *Fr.* Childe Harold's Pilgrimage.

Stop!—Gaze thro' this hushed gallery! The air.   Benjamin Paul Blood.   APN-2 *Fr.* Bride of the Iconoclasts, The.

Stop, let me have the truth of that!   Dîs Aliter Visum; or, Le Byron de Nos Jours.   Robert Browning.   NAEL-6v2

STOP LOOK LISTEN / as gate stripes swing down.   Philip Booth.   GM

Stop looking like a purse. How could a purse.   Toad.   Norman Alexander MacCaig.   EdScPo; HarvBoo

Stop, my Augustine, stop: ere you will God explain.   "Angelus Silesius."   GePo *Fr.* Cherubical Wanderer, The.

Stop, passenger! a wondrous tale to list.   Epitaph on Mr W—.   Felicia Dorothea Hemans.   ViWPN

Stop, shadow of my tricky fate.   In Containing a Thought Satisfied with Chaste Love.   Sor Juana Inés de la Cruz.   BLPSL, *tr. by* Rene de Costa, Rigas Kappatos and Eleni Paidoussi

Stop that Alabama bus I don't wanna ride.   Alabama Bus.   William Hairston.   WaAnP

Stop the car beside the litter bin.   Schiehallion.   Deric Bolton.   EdScPo

Stop this motherfucking Limo, says the King.   Elvis Moving a Small Cloud: The Desert Near Las Vegas, 1976.   David Wojahn.   AllShUp

Stop you my mouth with still still kissing me. (LL)   Sir Philip Sidney.   NAEL-6v1; NAEL-7v1; OxBSo *Fr.* Astrophil and Stella.

Stop your pretenses.   Sex Everywhere.   Srirangam Narayana Babu.   HotL, *tr. by* V. Narayana Rao

Stop! You're Breakin' My Heart.   Ted Koehler.   ReLy

Stopless wind, here are the columbine seeds I have.   Of Forced Sightes and Trusty Ferefulness.   Jorie Graham.   PoPoPo

Stopping at Amakusa Sea.   Rai San'yo.   EMJL, *tr. by* Haruo Shirane

Stopping at Night at Hsiang-yin.   Ch'i-chi.   CSKM, *tr. by* Burton Watson

Stopping before the steps, the young monk gushed.   Tung Chieh-yüan.   ColAnChi *Fr.* Master Tung's Western Chamber Romance.

Stopping By.   Laura Mullen.   IAoNAP

Stopping by Fields on a Snowy Afternoon.   Jane Rohrer.   ACAMVP

Stopping by Woods on a Snowy Evening.   Robert Frost.   APT-1; BLPJKO; BrAP; BRP; ChAP; ClHu; ColAP; EMP; HarvBoo; HeIP-4; ITBLP; MoAmPo; NAAL-5; NAAPv.2; NAMCP V.1; NIL-7; NIP-4; NoAM; NoP-4; NoP-5; NTCP; OxBoAm; PoPoPo; SAmP; SoSe-8; StAl; TFi; TRP; WaAnP

Stopping the diary.   Forget What Did.   Philip Larkin.   NAMCP V.2; NoAM

Stopping to Take Notes.   Michael Smith.   PBCIP

Stopwatch.   Mary Ruefle.   ExTi

Store dick lays a hand on your shoulder, The.   Shoplifting.   Baron Wormser.   ReTh

Stored in the attic, even in sleep.   To Atlas in the Attic.   Julie Agoos.   YaYoPo

Stores and filling stations prefer a roof.   Christmas Tree.   Stanley Cook.   OBCP

Stores were bright, and not too far from home, The.   From the Porch.   John Koethe.   MakPoe

Storied cliffs were the fortune I cast.   Han-shan (Cold Mountain).   GifTon, *tr. by* Red Pine

Storied Sonnet.   Ann Radcliffe.   CenSon

Stories.   J. Patrick Lewis.   NOxBChV

Stories.   Philip Schultz.   PoDa

Stories Are Made of Mistakes.   James Galvin.   TAPaP

Stories from the Tower.   Monica Ferrell.   LegDan

Stories I Tell My Daughter.   Deborah A. Miranda.   FiBr

Stories of Snow.   Patricia K. Page.   BrAP; NoP-4; NoP-5

Stories / would be braided in my hair, The.   Story Keeper.   Wendy Rose.   UnSA

Storing Memories.   Belinda Zubicueta Carmona.   TANSG, *tr. by* Celeste Kostopulos-Cooperman

Stork has one leg, A.   Legging Behind.   Ramy Ditzanny.   NRoS, *tr. by* the author

Storm.   Emily Dickinson.   NAAL-3

Storm.   "H. D."   APT-1

Storm: "Edges of slave ships are narrow and difficult for footing, The."   Brandon D. Johnson.   BtF

Storm.   Ágnes Nemes Nagy.   IQMS, *tr. by* Hugh Maxton

Storm.   Charles Wright.   MotU

Storm, A.   Nikolai Nikolaevich Morshen.   TCRusP, *tr. by* John Glad

Storm, The.   Sara Coleridge.   NOxBChV

Storm, The.   Walter De la Mare.   NOxBChV

Storm, The.   Richard Jones.   PoChi

Storm, The.   Adam Mickiewicz.   WoPoe, *tr. by* Vyt Bakaitis

Storm, The.   Eugenio Montale.   AF, *tr. by* William Arrowsmith

Storm, The.   Jirka Polak.   INSAB

Storm, The.   George Scarbrough.   LPSFW

Storm, The.   Margaret Stanley-Wrench.   LW

Storm, The: "Isn't there a man."   Mun Chônghui.   EcSo, *tr. by* Catherine J. Kim

Storm, an Endless Instant.   Boris Leonidovich Pasternak.   TCRusP, *tr. by* Bogdan Boychuk and Mark Rudman

Storm and Calm: Sent from Embden to M. Edw. Ma. and M. Tho. Ly, The.   Nicholas Murford.   NOSC

Storm at Sea.   Rumann, Son of Colman.   WoPoe, *tr. by* Frank O'Connor

Storm blew in last night and knocked out, A.   Window, The.   Raymond Carver.   BLT

Storm blew up so suddenly, The.   In Rough Weather.   Paul Lake.   RA

Storm Cellar, The.   Paul Ruffin.   TiP2

Storm clouds, thrown runes.   Cubs, The.   Pura López Colomé.   RMCMP, *tr. by* Forrest Gander

Storm Cone, The.   Rudyard Kipling.   NoAM

Storm Ending.   Jean Toomer.   APT-2

Storm Fear.   Robert Frost.   APT-1; ColAP; TCAPo

Storm from the Far Heights.   Sándor Weöres.   IQMS, *tr. by* Adam Makkai and Donald E. Morse

Storm has ended and death steps back, The.   On the Beach.   Tom Clark.   BodElec

Storm has started and they say it won't stop, The.   Subject of Our Lives, The.   Robin Becker.   PfS

Storm high.   Brown Rosellen.   FFC

Storm in the Black Forest.   D. H. Lawrence.   FaBoVe

Storm is coming because, The.   Kolob Canyon.   William Stafford.   PfSP

Storm is over, the land hushes to rest, The.   Robert Bridges.   OBMV

Storm is sweeping o'er the land, The.   Wild Night, A.   Julia Ward Howe.   ColAP

Storm on Mount Asama!   Basho.   WED, *tr. by* Robert Bly

Storm, park, and restless.   Christopher Street 1979.   Walter Holland.   CAGL

Storm Pattern.   Greg Pape.   PBCAP

Storm Sketches a Silver Margin, The.   Joyce Mansour.   YaTCFP, *tr. by* Mary Ann Caws *and* Jean-Pierre Cauvin

Storm splattering the tough magnolia, The.   Storm, The.   Eugenio Montale.   AF, *tr. by* William Arrowsmith

Storm / Storm / Let there be light on the weeping willow.   Dance.   Yamamura Bochō.   CAoMJL1, *tr. by* Leith Morton

Storm Surf.   Greg Pape.   MoASP

Storm Warnings.   Adrienne Rich.   NAAL-5; NIL-7; NIP-4; PtR; YaYoPo

Storm Windows.   Howard Nemerov.   VCAP

Stormalong!   *Unknown.*   FaBoVe

Storm-Beat Maid, The.   Joanna Baillie.   NPBRoP

Storm-Beaten.   Clara Ann Thompson.   CBWP-2

Storm-beaten old watch-tower, A.   Symbols.   William Butler Yeats.   OBMV

Storm—chestnuts / Race along.   Masaoka Shiki.   ZenPo, *tr. by* Takashi Ikemoto and Lucien Stryk

Storm-dances of gulls, the barking game of seals, The. Divinely Superfluous Beauty. Robinson Jeffers. HeIP-4; MoAmPo

Storm[e], The. John Donne. NAEL-6v1; NAEL-7v1; NoSic

Stormeys' dead that good old man—. Stormalong! *Unknown.* FaBoVe

Storming Column, The. John William DeForest. PCW

Stormpetrel. Richard Murphy. ModIr

Storm's still everywhere I step, The. Abbott's Lagoon. Dennis Schmitz. GeoHom

Storm-wearied Argo slept upon the water. Bayard Taylor. CAGL *Fr.* Hylas.

Stormy Lear. Ken Pobo. IaFF

Stormy Night. William Robert Rodgers. ModIr; PNI

Stormy Weather (Keeps Rainin' All the Time). Ted Koehler. ReLy

Stornelli and Strambotti. Agnes Mary Frances Robinson. VWP

Story. Eavan Boland. HarvBoo

Story. Dorothy Parker. AmWit

Story, A. Jane Hirshfield. BLT

Story, A. Jean Ingelow. VWP

Story, A. Li-Young Lee. LoL; RaBo

Story, The. Kevin Hart. BMAP

Story, The. Brendan Kennelly. BeAl

Story, The. Dan Pagis. PoSu, *tr. by* Stephen Mitchell

Story, The. Carly Sachs. BAP-04

Story About Chicken Soup, A. Louis Simpson. PoWW; UnSA

Story about the Body, A. Robert Hass. CAP-8; FaoP; OxBoAm; RaBo

Story After the Story, The. Marie Ponsot. ExTi

Story begins here, The. It was an afternoon. Story Begins Here, The. Carlos Sahagún. RaW, *tr. by* David Ignatow

Story comes apart near Gala's eyebrows, The. Hallucinogenic Bullfighter. Juan Felipe Herrera. BodElec

Story for Margarita. Rubén Darío. PtR, *tr. by* Maggie Dietz

Story for the Mother Tongue. Pimone Triplett. LegDan

Story goes, from evil, The. Alcaeus. SaLy, *tr. by* Diane Rayor

Story goes like this: the light, The. Juliana Spahr. NAPBL *Fr.* We.

Story Having to Do with Walt Whitman, A. Daisy Fried. ViWalt

Story I Like to Tell, The. Robin Becker. PBCAP

Story is simple, The. Linda. Jack Lawrence. ReLy

Story is true, The. (LL) Bresson's Movies. Robert Creeley. NoP-4; NoP-5; PmAP

Story Keeper. Wendy Rose. UnSA

Story of a Hotel Room. Rosemary Tonks. BeAl; LW; MoWP

Story of a Sound, The. Kim Chiha. CAMKP, *tr. by* David R. McCann

Story of a Story, The. Vasco [*or* Vasko] Popa. StAl, *tr. by* Anne Pennington

Story of a Well-made Shield, The. N. Scott Momaday. HATNAP

Story of Abraham, The. Alicia Ostriker. InvLi

Story of Augustus Who Would Not Have Any Soup, The. Heinrich Hoffmann. NBLV

Story of Bonnie and Clyde, The. Bonnie Parker. TiP2

Story of Canobie Dick, The. Libby Houston. OBSP

Story of Every Day, The. Eugenio Montale. ItPo, *tr. by* Gayle Ridinger

Story of Frankie . . . My Man, The. Archie Weller. BMAP

Story of How a Wall Stands, A. Simon J. Ortiz. HATNAP

Story of How the Monk Tripiṭaka of the Great Country of T'ang Brought back the Sūtras, The. *Unknown.* ColAnChi, *tr. by* Charles J. Wivell

Story of Joshua. Alicia Ostriker. ChIV-1

Story of Kepa Falekaono, The. *Unknown.* SonAtl, *tr. by* Marcia Gilchrist, I. Futa Helu, Helen Morton Lee, Daniel Longstaff, Okusi Mahina, Erica Mehrtens, Konai Thaman and Elizabeth Wood-Ellem

Story of Keys, The. Richard Garcia. TouFir

Story of Lovers Leap, The. Maggie Pogue Johnson. CBWP-4

Story of My Land, The. Brent MacLaine.

4. Birth Story. Coast

Story of My Life, The. Liz Rosenberg. PBCAP

Story of my skin, The. Autobiographical Poem. Elaine Equi. KGB

Story of Our Lives, The. Mark Strand. VCAP

Story of Phoebus and Daphne Applied, [etc.], The. Edmund Waller. NOSC

(Story of Phœbus and Daphne appli'd, The.) PBRV

Story of Rimini, The. Leigh Hunt.

Canto 3.

Lover's Exchange. STuOW

"Noble range it was, of many a rood, A." OBGa

"One day,—'twas on a summer afternoon." NOBRP

Paulo and Francesca. NPBRoP

What with This and That. STuOW

Story of Sound. Peter Makuck. NevBe

Story of Stonewall goes like this: On the night of Judy Garland's, A. Story of Stonewall, A. Maureen Seaton. ReTh

Story of the End of the Story, The. James Galvin. TAPaP

Story of the Eucharistic queer descended, The. To Be Christ is Not to Be Jesus Christ. Antonin Artaud. ConPit, *tr. by* Clayton Eshleman

Story of the Gadsbys, The. Rudyard Kipling.

(L'Envoi: "What is the moral? Who rides may read.") MoBrPo

Story of the Labyrinth, The. Veronica Volkow. RMCMP, *tr. by* Margaret Sayers Peden

Story of the Man Whose Tastes Were Too Refined. Charles Rafferty. AmPoNex

Story of Uriah, The. Rudyard Kipling. OxBEV

Story Often Told in Bars, A: The *Reader's Digest* Version. William Matthews. ReTh

Story Pillow, The. Dave Brinks. AnSo

Story So Far, The. John Clarke. UV

Story That Could Be True, A. William Stafford. NTCP; RaBo

Story: There was a cow in the road, struck by a semi, A. Difficult Body. Mark Wunderlich. NAPBL; Vesp

Story they tell, the people who dwell, A. Whiskey-Bomb Battle. Mayme Evans. TiP2

Story was almost too simple, The. Izu Dancer, The. Kimiko Hahn. CAP-8

Story was not born with Robbie Cox, The. Story, The. Brendan Kennelly. BeAl

Story We Know, The. Martha Collins. SoSe-8

Storyteller's face, The. One. Thomas Kinsella.

Storytime. Judith Nicholls. OBSP

Storyville Diary. Natasha Trethewey.

(Self) Portrait. RD

Stout Brahms. Bruce Berger. GeoH

Stove Problem, The. Elke Erb. OnScMo, *tr. by* Rosmarie Waldrop

Stove, The / In my mountain kitchen. Living in Poverty. Shi Zhiyuan. CSKM, *tr. by* Paul Hansen

Stow, birde, stow, stow! John Skelton. NoSic *Fr.* Magnificence.

Stowaway. Olive Senior. WaAnP

Stowe, the Gardens of the Rt. Hon. Richard Lord Viscount Cobham. Gilbert West.

Stowe, the Gardens of the Rt. Hon. Richard Lord Viscount Cobham. OBGa

Stowed away in a Montreal lumber room. O God! O Montreal! Samuel Butler. OBSV

Strage degli innocenti, La. Giovanni Giambattista.

Sospetto d'Herode.

Steps to the Temple. SacPr

Straggled soldier halted—stared at Him, The. Christ and the Soldier. Siegfried Sassoon. NoP-4; NoP-5

Strahan, Tonson, Lintot of the times. To Mr. Murray. Lord Byron. UV

Straight from the east the wind blows sharp with rain. April in Town. Lizette Woodworth Reese. APN-2

Straight from the heart. Love Is a Random Thing. George Marion, Jr. ReLy

Straight line, row of swimmers. Perpetual *Look* Physics: 17/5. Bernard Collin. YaTCFP, *tr. by* Mary Ann Caws *and* Jean-Pierre Cauvin

Straight remnant, of the spiry birchen bough. Elegiac Sonnet to a Mopstick. William Beckford. CenSon

Straight rye whiskey, 100 proof. Brooklyn Narcissus. Paul Blackburn. PmAP

Straight stone walks. Walking through Myoshin-Ji. Gary Snyder. WANABP

Straight Talk from Plain Women. Sherley Anne Williams. GT

Straight through the air my mooring line to you. (LL) Kenneth Leslie. IFF; OxBSo *Fr.* By Stubborn Stars.

Strait-Jackets, The. Pascale Petit. BeAl

Stampin' the bent, like the Angel o' Daith. Molecatcher. Albert D. Mackie. EdScPo

Strand at Lough Beg, The. Seamus Heaney. NAMCP V.2; NoAM; NPeEn; OBWP

Strand of Hair, A. Justin Quinn. NIrP

Strange. To a Fair Lady Playing with a Snake. Edmund Waller. CABP; NOSC

Strange Adventure. Rossana Ombres. NeIt

Strange, almost, how azaleas and dogwoods bloom together. Azaleas and Dogwoods. Cyd Adams. TiP2

Strange Altars. Margaret Gibson. AmZen

Strange and mysterious. That Thing. Fadhil Assultani. IrPoTo, *tr. by* Raghid Nahhas

Strange and slow work: they dug in turn. Well, The. Philip Salom. NOBAu

Strange are the paths of mankind in the night. Revelation and Decline. Georg Trakl. PFTM-1

Strange arrangement to comfort the heart—, A. Fragrant Hands. Faiz Ahmad Faiz. VCWP, *tr. by* Agha Shahid Ali

Strange Beasts. Beda Higgins. PoCu

Strange beauty, eight-limbed and eight-handed. Octopus. Arthur Clement Hilton. UV

Strange bed, whose recurrent dream we are, The. Hôtel de l'Univers et Portugal. James Merrill. PoA 2002

Strange Bird, A. Michael Dransfield. BMAP

Strange bird / His song remains secret. Youth. James Wright. OxBoAm

Strange Business. Jelaluddin Rumi. LoL, tr. by Coleman Barks

Strange calling; to play the minor effects, A. Foley Artist, The. Nick Drake. NeBl

Strange Case, The. Michael Ondaatje. EmeKit; StAl

Strange church smelled a bit 'high,' of censers, The. Geoffrey Hill. EmeKit Fr. Mercian Hymns.

Strange Country. Julie Parson-Nesbitt. MPUn

Strange, dear, but true, dear. So in Love. Cole Porter. ReLy

Strange Fits of Passion Have I Known ("Strange fits of passion have I known.") William Wordsworth. BrAP; NAEL-6v2; NAEL-7v2; NOBRP; OBEV Fr. Lucy.

Strange Flowers. Wintu Oral Tradition. NAAPv.1 Fr. Six Dream Songs.

Strange Fruit. Lewis Allan. ReLy

Strange Fruit. Joy Harjo. SeSe

Strange Fruit. Timothy Liu. WiU

Strange grows the river on the sunless evenings! Vesperal. Ernest Dowson. OBMV

Strange Hells. Ivor Gurney. FaBoWar

Strange Hurt. Langston Hughes. APT-2

Strange Meeting. Wilfred Owen. BrAP; FaBoWar; HarvBoo; HeIP-4; MakPoe; MoBrPo; NAEL-6v2; NAEL-7v2; NAMCP V.1; NoAM; NoP-4; NoP-5; OBWP; OxAEP-2; OxBEV; PoWW; TCAWP; TFi; WaAnP

Strange Meetings. Harold Monro.
  Flower Is Looking, A. MoBrPo
  If Suddenly a Clod of Earth. MoBrPo

Strange Metamorphosis of Poets. Howard Nemerov. NoP-5

Strange Music. George Forrest and Robert Wright. ReLy

Strange mysterious God visits the forest, A. Eternal Farewell. Ricardo Jaimes Freyre. TCLAP, tr. by Victor Tulli

Strange New Cottage in Berkeley, A. Allen Ginsberg. ASA

Strange news! a city full? will none give way. Sir John Suckling. ChIV-2; ChrPo

Strange now to think of you, gone without corsets & eyes, while I walk on the sunny pavement of Greenwich Village. Kaddish. Allen Ginsberg. OxBoAm; PmAP

Strange paradise, complete with worms. Ware Collection of Glass Flowers and Fruit, Harvard Museum, The. Mark Doty. HarvBoo

Strange Peak. Muso Soseki. EaWin, tr. by W. S. Merwin

Strange People, The. Louise Erdrich. PoPoPo

Strange power, I know not what thou art. To Memory. Mary Elizabeth Coleridge. ViWPN

Strange Power! I trust thy might; trust thou my constancy. (LL) Visionary, The. Emily Jane Brontë. NPeEn; OxBEV

Strange power of song! the strain that warms the heart. Hannah More. NoP-4; NoP-5 Fr. Slave Trade, The.

Strange race of critics, A. Antiphanes. WoPoe, tr. by Sam Hamill

Strange room, from this angle. Soho Hospital for Women, The. Fleur Adcock. NAEL-6v2; NAEL-7v2; NoP-4; NoP-5

Strange Shepherd, Set My Bellwether Free. Félix Lope de Vega Carpio. SpanPo, tr. by W. S. Merwin

Strange spirit with inky hair. Lion, The. Walter James Turner. MoBrPo

Strange that I did not know him then. Old Story, An. Edwin Arlington Robinson. MoAmPo; OxBoAm

Strange, / That in this nigger place. Aesthete [or Esthete] in Harlem. Langston Hughes. ColAP; WaAnP

Strange / that we wake. A. X. Nicholas. OxAAAP

Strange that your image should occur to me. Grudge, The. Dimitris Tsaloumas. BMAP

Strange the formation of Eely Race. Oppian [of Corycus]. NPeEn Fr. Halieutica.

Strange the formation of the eely race. William Diaper. OBVE Fr. Halieutica.

Strange things indeed Are seen in the sea-world. Nature of the Siren, The. Cynewulf. WoPoe, tr. by Richard Wilbur

Strange to behold, unmingled with surprize. On the Civilization of the Western Aboriginal Country. Philip Freneau. APN-1

Strange to reach Paradise without crossing Jordan. Strangeness of Dawn, The. R. Williams Parry. BBMWP, tr. by Anthony Conran

Strange to step straight into the beautiful dawn. Miraculous Dawn. R. Williams Parry. OBWVE, tr. by Joseph P. Clancy

Strange, tonight I've remembered. Beggar, The. Francisco Brines. RaW, tr. by Rachel Benson

Strange tropic warmth and hints of summer seas. (LL) Ethnogenesis. Henry Timrod. APN-2; PCW; TCAPo

Strange Type. Malcolm Lowry. NoP-4; NoP-5; NPeEn

Strange walkers! See their processional. Mushroom Gatherers, The. Adam Mickiewicz. OxBEV, tr. by Donald Davie

Strange was the way of my life—its paths were paths of wonder. Orphanhood. Hayyim Nahman Bialik. FIT, tr. by Robert Friend

Strange wind blows from somewhere, A. Memory of Underdevelopment. No Hyegyông. EcSo, tr. by Ann Y. Choi

Strangely assorted, the shape of song and the bloody man. Military Harpist, The. Ruth Pitter. NALW

Strangeness of Dawn, The. R. Williams Parry. BBMWP, tr. by Anthony Conran

Strangeness of Mountains after Rain, The. Jaewol Kyunghun. BecRai, tr. by Kim Daljin, Kim Won-Chung and Christopher Merrill

Stranger. Tisa Bryant. BtF

Stranger. Kerry Hardie. MoWP

Stranger. Elizabeth Madox Roberts. MoAmPo

Stranger, The. Charles Baudelaire. IJHIL, tr. by Louise Varese

Stranger, The. Gerald Locklin. OPRER

Stranger, The. W. S. Merwin. OxBoAm

Stranger, The. Gabriela Mistral. SpanPo, tr. by Kate Flores

Stranger, The. Aldo Palazzeschi. PFTM-1

Stranger. A curious hand touches the snow raising pigeons. Jungle Book. Tom Raworth. PFTM-2

Stranger and His Friend, The. James F. Montgomery. SacPr

Stranger at Home. James R. Lee. BtF

Stranger, behold the mighty Hector's tomb! Lord Orrery's Hector. Unknown. DiBP

Stranger, below the boulder rest your spent limbs. Anyte. SaLy, tr. by Diane Rayor

Stranger, captive in the lands of the West, will be mourned by a certain pulpit and throne, A. Mu'tamid, King of Seville. HiArP, tr. by James T. Monroe

Stranger, if thou hast learned [or learnt] a truth which needs. Inscription for the Entrance to a Wood. William Cullen Bryant. APN-1

Stranger, if you sail to the land of lovely dances, Mitylene. Nossis. SaLy, tr. by Diane Rayor

Stranger in Louisiana, The. Felicia Dorothea Hemans. RWP

Stranger in Paradise. George Forrest and Robert Wright. ReLy

Stranger in the Pumpkin, The. John Ciardi. NTCP

Stranger in the street, A. (LL) Sword of Surprise, The. G. K. Chesterton. MoBrPo; SacPr

Stranger in the Village. Lorelei Williams. BtF

Stranger, Stranger. Jorge de Lima. TCLAP, tr. by Luiz Fernández García

Stranger! Tell the people of Spoon River two things. Edgar Lee Masters. InoFa; NoAM Fr. New Spoon River, The.

Stranger, the bark you see before you says. Catullus. OBVE,

Stranger to a Small Child. Ben Scammell. NLP

Stranger to Love, Whoever Loves Not Thee. Félix Lope de Vega Carpio. SpanPo, tr. by Ian Fletcher

Stranger, when o'er yon slant, warm field no cloud. Sonnet. Anna Seward. NOBRP

Stranger, when you come to / Lakedaimon. Simonides. OBVE

Stranger whom I once knew well. Ringstead Mill. Margot Heinemann. RSaN

Strangers. Huda Ablan. PoArWo, tr. by Nathalie Handal and Ibrahim Muhawi

Strangers, The. Jones Very. APN-1

Strangers: An Essay. Jim Elledge. SwNoth

Strangers are people we haven't seen before. Conversations with Strangers. George Buchanan. PNI

Stranger's heart! Oh! wound it not!, The. Stranger's Heart, The. Felicia Dorothea Hemans. VWP

Stranger's Heart, The. Felicia Dorothea Hemans. VWP

Strangers Like Us: Pittsburgh, Raleigh, 1945–1985. Gerald William Barrax. ISC

Strangling women in the suburban bush. Das Kapital. Imamu Amiri Baraka. PFTM-2

Strapped at the center of the blazing wheel. Pilot from the Carrier, A. Randall Jarrell. PoWW

Strata. Roger Jones. TiP2

Strategic Air Command. Gary Snyder. AtGh

Strategy. Archilochus. WoPoe, tr. by Guy Davenport

Strategy. Gali-Danah Zinger. CRWP, tr. by the author and Ashraf Noor

Strategy maps are placed neatly on long tables. To an Unborn Child. Allan Cooper. AtGh

Stratis the Sailor by the Dead Sea. George Seferis. WoPoe, tr. by Rex Warner

Stravinsky in L.A. Elizabeth Alexander. AmPoNex

Straw Hat. Rita Dove. MAAN; NAAL-5 Fr. Thomas and Beulah.

Straw Hat in the Rain. Harry Akst and Lew Brown. ReLy

Straw in the street where I pass to-day. Straw in the Street. Amy Levy. VWP

Straw reed climbs the car antenna, A. Götterdämmerung. Rita Dove. ExTi

Straw sandal half sunk. Buson. EH, *tr. by* Yoel Hoffmann

Strawberries: "Strawberries when I first remember them are not red but blue, The." Margaret Atwood. OpeFie

Strawberries. W. S. Merwin. AmFaPo; NoP-4

Strawberries. Edwin Morgan. EdScPo; NoP-4; NoP-5

Strawberries when I first remember them are not red but blue, The. Strawberries. Margaret Atwood. OpeFie

Strawberry. Paisley Rekdal. LegDan

Strawberry, The. Maggie Pogue Johnson. CBWP-4

Strawberry Blond. Bill Berkson. NYP2

Strawberry blooms upon its lowly bed, The. To the Strawberry. Helen Maria Williams. CenSon; OxBSo; RWP

Strawberry Canyon Swimming Pool. Integrating the Strawberry Swimming Pool in 1998. Cecil Brown. FTtHH

Strawberry Picking. Alexander the Wild. NAWM-7v1, *tr. by* Peter Dronke

Strawberrying. Maurice Kenny. HATNAP

Strawberrying. May Swenson. NAMCP V.2; VCAP

Straws like tame lightnings lie about the grass. Summer Farm. Norman Alexander MacCaig. NePenScot; NoP-5; NPeEn; StAl; WaAnP

Stray Animals. James Tate. NAMCP V.2; NoAM

Stray bullet, A. Angel. Marisela Norte. GeoHom

Stray Dogs, Foaming. Thom Ward. AmPoNex

Stray Moth, Asleep. Joyce Peseroff. VisFro

Stray Paragraphs in February, Year of the Rat. Charles Wright. NAMCP V.2

Stray white lips, petals kissing middle distance between blue iris you. Daphne Marlatt. NLPA *Fr.* Touch to My Tongue.

Strayed Crab. Elizabeth Bishop. MotU *Fr.* Rainy Season; Sub-Tropics.

Strayed Reveller, The. Matthew Arnold. Strayed Reveller to Ulysses, The. OBEV

Straying Student, The. Austin Clarke. ModIr; NPeEn

Streak of world blurred charcoal and scarlet, the El slows. Window, The. Lynda Hull. ExTi

Streak, The. Julia Kasdorf. AmPoNex

Streaked and fretted with effort, the thick. Street, The. Robert Pinsky. NAAL-5; NoP-4; NoP-5

Stream, The. Edith Jay Scovell. HarvBoo *Fr.* Water Images.

Stream, The. Mona Van Duyn. VCAP; WaAnP

Stream at the House of the Luans, The. Pei Di and Wang Wei. CCL1 *Fr.* Wheel River.

Stream of It, The. Jane Hirshfield. FiBr

Stream of our Lady of Sorrows. Mission Dolores. Hoa Nguyen. WANABP

Stream of rain off metal awning. View Café, The. Jonathan Johnson. AmPoNex

Stream rills softly, The. The carp. Carp, The. *Vietnamese Oral Tradition.* CaDao, *tr. by* John Balaban

Stream runs clear to its stones, The. Painting, The. *Vietnamese Oral Tradition.* CaDao, *tr. by* John Balaban

Stream swirls, The. The wind moans in. Jade Flower Palace. Tu Fu [*or* Du Fu]. CCL1, *tr. by* Kenneth Rexroth

Stream was swift, and so cold, The. Captivity. Louise Erdrich. AmWaPo; HATNAP; NAMCP V.2; NoAM

Stream with Washerwomen. Jorge Guillén. RaW, *tr. by* Charles Guenther

Streambed, A / Winds between their solid trunks. Pine Whisk, The. Yu Chao. CSKM, *tr. by* Paul Hansen

Streamers. Sandra McPherson. VCAP

Streamers of crepe idling before doors. Epidemic. Charles Reznikoff. APT-2

Streamers of farewell. *Unknown.* NAAPv.2

Streaming down the sides, like fun in the sun, air in the air. (LL) Blue Is the Hero. Bill Berkson. AHA; NYP2

Streaming from the lamps below. In Memory of My Mother. Cathal McCabe. NIrP

Streaming into the heart. (LL) Exiles, The. Iain Crichton Smith. HarvBoo; NePenScot

Streaming rivulets draw back, sandflats emerge. Climbing a Tall Building on an Autumn Evening: I Gaze to Where the South River Touches the Shixing Road. Chang Chiu-ling. CCL1, *tr. by* Stephen Owen

Streamlet! methinks thy lot resembles mine. John F. M. Dovaston. CenSon

Streamline to instantaneous. Up to Speed. Rae Armantrout. AWPTFC

Streams. Derek Walcott. ItP

Streams are fettered, and with us as rare, The. Thomas Shipman. NOSC *Fr.* Frost, 1654, The: To Mr. W.L.

Streams in the Desert. Christine de Luca. EdScPo

Stream's Song, The. Lascelles Abercrombie. OBMV

Streams stop as ice: wind blanches the cloudbank. Spade. Emile Verhaeren. SonAtl, *tr. by* Gregory Beaven, Kurt Ganzl and Heather Goode

Streams that wind amid the hills, The. George Darley. IrLP *Fr.* Sylvia; or, The May Queen.

Street. Eiléan Ní Chuilleanáin. EmeKit

Street. Gary Soto. GeoHom

Street, The. James Russell Lowell. GSo

Street, The. Robert Pinsky. NAAL-5; NoP-4; NoP-5

Street Angel, The. K'o Chia Tsang. WoPoe, *tr. by* Kai-yu Hsu

Street Ballad. George Barker. GoPo

Street Corner College. Kenneth Patchen. APT-2; CLPP; MoAmPo

Street Country. Laura Solórzano. SPV, *tr. by* Jen Hofer

Street Cries. Sidney Lanier. To Richard Wagner. APN-2; NCAP

Street Demonstration. Margaret Abigail Walker. InGu

Street Fair: The Quartet. Marvin Bell. BodElec

Street Flower in Big D. Frances E. Neidhardt. TiP2

Street Funeral. Irving Layton. NIL-7

Street in Agrigento. Salvatore Quasimodo. WoPoe, *tr. by* Denis Devlin

Street in Bronzeville, A. Gwendolyn Brooks. Hunchback Girl: She Thinks of Heaven. ChAP

Kitchenette building. GT; NAAL-5; NoP-4; NoP-5; OxAAAP; PoPoPo

Mother, The. CAP-8; ESEAA; IllVoic; ISC; MoWP; NAAL-5; NALW; OxAAAP; OxBoAm; PoPoPo

Of De Witt Williams on His Way to Lincoln Cemetery. ESEAA; InoFa; NAMCP V.2; NoAM

Preacher: Ruminates behind the Sermon, The. InvLi

Sadie and Maud. BeAl; ESEAA; NAMCP V.2; NoAM; StAl; WaAnP

Song in the Front Yard, A. CAP-8; ESEAA; NAMCP V.2; NoAM; NOxBChV; OxBoAm

Vacant Lot, The. NAMCP V.2; NoAM; WaAnP

Street in country town at midnight time, A. Near the Front. Nathaniel Southgate Shaler. PCW

Street Instructions at the Crotch. Edward Field. CAGL

Street is pure black and there are no seasonal traces, The. Nocturne. Pierre Reverdy. MotU, *tr. by* Michael Benedikt

Street Is Waiting for the Night, The. Juan Ramón Jiménez. SpanPo, *tr. by* Lysander Kemp

Street lamp. Something missing. Drugstore. Mikhail Yeryomin. ItGoST, *tr. by* J. Kates

Street Lamps in Early Spring. Gwendolyn B. Bennett. NAAPv.2

Street Life. Alan Jenkins. PML

Street Music. Elizabeth Akers Allen. SWaP

Street Music. Greg Pape. PBCAP

Street Musicians. John Ashbery. PoPoPo

Street of Dreams. Sam M. Lewis. ReLy

Street Scenes: Houston. Sunshine Dickinson Ryman. "Matthew, Mark, Luke and John, / She chanted." TiP2

Street Song. Thom Gunn. HeIP-4

Street Song. Langston Hughes. APT-2

Street Song. Sylvia Plath. MiVo

Street there is in Paris famous, A. Ballad of Bouillabaisse, The. William Makepeace Thackeray. OBEV; OxAEP-2

Street threatened, The. Aerial, The. Reiner Kunze. PoSu, *tr. by* Ewald Osers

Street Yarn. Julia Ward Howe. SWaP *Fr.* Lyrics of the Street.

Streetcar Named Poetry, A. Yevgeny Aleksandrovich Yevtushenko. RusPo, *tr. by* Robert Arthur Douglas Ford

Streetcar That Lost Its Way, The. Nikolai Stepanovich Gumilyov. TCRusP, *tr. by* Denis Johnson and Kathy Lewis

Streetcleaner's Lament, The. Patricia Hubbell. SSCS

Streetcorner Church. Sharan Strange. InTrad

Streetlamps glow, The. Who Sez Thunderbirds Can't Fly. Gary Lilley. BtF

Streets. Henrik Nordbrandt. VCWP, *tr. by* Henrik Norbrandt *and* Alexander Taylor and Alexander Taylor

Streets 1. Paul Verlaine. SxFrPo, *tr. by* Martin Sorrell

Streets 2. Paul Verlaine. SxFrPo, *tr. by* Martin Sorrell

Streets, a garden. City Life. Jorge Guillén. RaW, *tr. by* Charles Guenther

Streets are quiet as a fall of snow, The. (LL) Big Parade, The. Stephen Knight. NeBl; TCAWP

Streets are waiting for a snow, The. Dundee. John Burnside. NePenScot

Streets, in a poor district. Power, the Enchanted World. George Oppen. FTOS

Streets of Air, The. Malcolm Cowley. PoA 2002 *Fr.* Blue Juniata.

Streets of Black and White. Ahmed Yamani. AnVo, *tr. by* Mohamed Enani

Streets of Ch'ang-an. Ch'u Kuang-hsi. ColAnChi, *tr. by* Burton Watson

Streets of Forbes, The. Jack McGuire. NOBAu

Streets of Laredo, The. Louis MacNeice. BaFoWar; OBWP

Streets of the roaring town. On a Soldier Fallen in the Philippines. William Vaughn Moody. AmWaPo

Streets of your glances, The. Vasco [*or* Vasko] Popa. PoSu *Fr.* Far Within Us.

Streets outside have ice on them, The.   My Grandfather Always Promised Us.   Liam Rector.   UrbNat

Streets shall be designed *Euro-Style* with 300-ft right-of-ways.   Perfect City Code.   Richard Blanco.   LegDan

Streets we live by fall away, The.   Potholes.   Linda Hogan.   UrbNat

Streets were clogged with garbage, The.   New Brooms, The.   Odia Ofeimun.   NAfrP

Street-traders were roaring and steaming, The.   Combustion Engine.   Katherine Pierpoint.   MFPA

Streetwalker Trying to Speak to Sojourner Truth, A.   Elaine Maria Upton.   BtF

Strength.   Helen Chasin.   YaYoPo

Strength.   Sikong Tu.   CCL1 *Fr.* Twenty-Four Modes of Poetry.

Strength.   Christopher Smart.   UV *Fr.* Song to David, A.

Strength of Fields, The.   James Dickey.   VCAP

Strengthened to live, strengthened to die for.   In Distrust of Merits.   Marianne Moore.   AmWaPo; APT-1; ColAP; MoAmPo; NAAL-5; NAAPv.2; OBWP

Strenuous Life, The.   Henry Sidgwick.   OBCoV

Strephon hath Fashion, Wit and Youth.   Elizabeth Taylor.   LW

Strephon kissed me in the spring.   Look, The.   Sara Teasdale.   APT-1; LW

Strephon to Celia. A modern Love-Letter.   Mary Leapor.   BrAP; RACG

Strephon, your breach of faith and trust.   Song, A.   Laetitia Pilkington.   IrLP; LW; PEW

Stretch a bow to the very full.   Lao Tzu.   CCL1 *Fr.* Way and Its Power, The.

Stretch cast out night's long,'d, The.   Lakefront, Cleveland.   Russell Atkins.   GT

Stretch of blue water between the shores in autumn, A.   Night Rain on the Rivers Hsiao and Hsiang.   Yi Illo.   CATKP, *tr. by* Peter H. Lee

Stretch of country woods, A.   Boiled Peanuts.   Eleanor Ross Taylor.   AFaM

Stretch of wall, The.   Volga Towns, The.   Johannes Bobrowski.   PoSu, *tr. by* Matthew Mead and Ruth Mead

Stretch out your hands to me.   Bei Dao.   AF, *tr. by* Bonnie S. McDougall

Stretch'd and still lies the midnight.   Walt Whitman.   ColAP *Fr.* Song of Myself.

Stretched out among the tumult of your voice lie diaries.   Rain My Wife, The.   Tracy Philpot.   IAoNAP

Stretched out I want to take him into me.   *Unknown.*   SLW, *tr. by* Marjolijn De Jager, Sayd Bahodin Majrouh and André Velter

Stretched Out in Solitude.   Belinda Zubicueta Carmona.   TANSG, *tr. by* Celeste Kostopulos-Cooperman

Stretched out on the sands of forgetting.   If Only the Horse Was Left to Its Solitude.   Abdel Kader El Janabi.   Eno, *tr. by* Pierre Joris

Stretched out under the oak, in the wood's new leaves.   Forest Murmurs.   Eduard Friedrich Mörike.   WoPoe, *tr. by* Randall Jarrell

Stretched-out.   Crickets, Green-faced.   Binyo Ivanov.   CSCBP, *tr. by* Georgi Belev and Lisa Sapinkopf

Stretches of the path are darker.   Lights of the Bigtop.   Garrett McDowell.   BtF

Stretching.   Robert Morgan.   WeW-3

Stretching before and after. (LL)   T. S. Eliot.   APT-1; HarvBoo; MoAmPo; NAAL-5 *Fr.* Four Quartets.

Stretching into the distance.   By the Sea.   Muso Soseki.   EaWin, *tr. by* W. S. Merwin

Stretching onward toward the sunset.   Old Mackenzie Trail, The.   William Lawrence Chittenden.   TiP2

Stretchmarks.   Elizabeth Bartlett.   MoWP

4. Stretto.   Don McKay.   NLPA *Fr.* Matériel.

Strew on her roses, roses.   Requiescat.   Matthew Arnold.   OBEV

Stricken Deer, The.   William Cowper.   NAEL-6v1; NAEL-7v1 *Fr.* Task, The.

Strictly personal.   Anna Mendelssohn.   VaPo

Strictly Speaking.   Debra Gregerman.   AmPoNex

Stride On.   Iswar Ballav.   SonAtl, *tr. by* Binil Aryal, Sunita Khadgi, Pallav Ranjan, Phoebe Ravenhall and Karuna Shashi

Striding, shuddering.   Lina Tibi.   PoArWo, *tr. by* Subhi Hadidi and Nathalie Handal

Striding up to his bed, you.   Confabulation.   John A. Stone.   BloBone

Strife is grown between Virtue and Love, A.   Sir Philip Sidney.   NAEL-6v1; NAEL-7v1; NoP-4; NoP-5 *Fr.* Astrophil and Stella.

Strike.   Aaron Rapoport.   Prolet, *tr. by* Amelia Glaser

Strike, The.   Shamsur Rahman.   SonAtl, *tr. by* Latifa Das, Harjeet Singh Gill, Jafor Iqbal and Peter Ramsey

Strike, churl; hurl, cheerless wind, then; heltering hail.   Hailstorm in May.   Gerard Manley Hopkins.   Spl

Strike of the Coal Miners.   Ber Grin.   Prolet, *tr. by* Amelia Glaser

'Strike Up the Band.   Ira Gershwin.   ReLy

Strikers in Hyde Park.   Louise Imogen Guiney.   APN-2

Striking Distance.   Tom French.   NIrP

Striking Distance.   Carole Satyamurti.   MoWP

String Diamond, The.   Arthur Sze.   AmAlph

String of Ordinary Words, A.   Maj Ragain.   AmZen

String of pearls is what I make, A.   Comet, The.   Gurajada Apparao.   HotL, *tr. by* V. Narayana Rao

Stringbeans.   Kay Lindsey.   BtF

Stringer's Field.   Roy McFadden.   PNI

Stringless bees.   Elegy for the Bee-god.   Selima Hill.   MoWP

Strings' Excitement, The.   W. H. Auden.   MoBrPo

Stringy, skittery, thistle-burred, rib-etched.   Harvesting the Cows.   Ellen Bryant Voigt.   CAP-8

Stringybark Cockatoo, The.   *Unknown.*   NOBAu

Strip.   A. R. Ammons.
43.   NAMCP V.2
"Wdn't it be silly to be serious, now."   BAP-97

Strip.   Lyrae Van Clief-Stefanon.   BRtP

Strip her first of home and family.   Out.   Eleanor Brown.   MFPA

Striped blouse in a clearing by Bazille, A.   Ceremony.   Richard Wilbur.   NAAL-5; NAMCP V.2; NoAM

Striped suit.   New Suit, The.   Nidia Sanabria de Romero.   ChAP, *tr. by* Arnaldo D. Larrosa and Naomi Shihab Nye

Stripper, The.   Anita Endrezze.   ReTh

Stripping and Putting On.   May Swenson.   WeW-3

Stripping Leaves from Sugarcane.   *Hawaiian Oral Tradition.*   NAAPv.1

Strips of adhesive tape criss-crossed the windowpane cutting.   After Fall, 1956.   Devorah Amir.   DTA, *tr. by* Miriyam Glazer

Strip-tease.   Lawrence Durrell.   OxAEP-2

Strip-Tease.   Gwyneth Lewis.   BBMWP, *tr. by* Joseph P. Clancy

Striptease.   Andrey Andreievich Voznesensky.   TCRusP, *tr. by* Daniel Weissbort

Strive not, vain Lover, to be fine.   Song.   Richard Lovelace.   CavPo

Strive, Wait, and Pray.   Adelaide Anne Procter.   TreFP

Strive: yet I do not promise.   Strive, Wait, and Pray.   Adelaide Anne Procter.   TreFP

Stroke.   Vincent Buckley.
"In the faint blue light."   BMAP

Stroke.   Arthur Ginsberg.   BloBone

Stroke ("He would get the gold.")   Hugh Seidman.   BodElec

Stroke ("Writhing.")   Hugh Seidman.   BodElec

Stroke the small silk with your whispering hands.   Geoffrey Hill.   NPeEn; OxBEV *Fr.* Apology for the Revival of Christian Architecture in England, An.

Strokes are pulses: from my shapely cloud, The.   Minor Van Gogh (He Speaks), A.   Alicia Ostriker.   RACG

Strokes of an Adult's Pencil.   Denizé Lauture.   OGAHCP, *tr. by* Boadiba and Jack Hirschman

Stroll on, thou dark not deep "blue" dandy, stroll.   Sea Replies to Byron, The.   G. K. Chesterton.   UV

Stroll to Parfondeval, A.   Remco Campert.   TuT, *tr. by* Theo Dorgan

Strolling one day, beyond the Kalends, on Mount Cyllene.   Austin Clarke.   ModIr *Fr.* Tiresias.

Stroll-Joy.   Johann Klaj.   GePo, *tr. by* George C. Schoolfield

Strolls.   A. R. Ammons.   PoA 2002

Strong and slippery / built for the midnight grass-party.   Peter.   Marianne Moore.   APT-1; NoP-4

Strong ankled, sun burned, almost naked.   Vitamins and Roughage.   Kenneth Rexroth.   CalPo; NoAM; OxBoAm

Strong Are Saying Nothing, The.   Robert Frost.   APT-1

Strong Beams.   Mairtin O Direain.   ModIr, *tr. by* Patrick Crotty

Strong Bond, The.   Juana de Ibarbourou.   TCLAP, *tr. by* Sophie Cabot Black, Linda Scheer and Maria Negroni

Strong Draughts of Their Refreshing Minds.   Emily Dickinson.   SWaP

Strong drink, hundred-year-old, A.   Soul Music: The Derry Air.   Eamon Grennan.   PBCIP

Strong enough to trust to. (LL)   Paper Nautilus, The.   Marianne Moore.   HarvBoo; MakPoe; NAAL-5; NAAPv.2; NALW; NAMCP V.1

Strong God which made the topmost stars.   Prophet Lost in the Hills at Evening, The.   Joseph Hilaire Pierre Belloc.   SacPr

Strong is the horse upon his speed.   Christopher Smart.   UV *Fr.* Song to David, A.

Strong Men.   Sterling Allen Brown.   ISC; ItP; NAAPv.2; NAMCP V.1; OxAAAP

Strong men came from the Eastern way.   And It Shall Come.   Albert Young.   RSaN

Strong men keep coming on, The.   Upstream.   Carl Sandburg.   MoAmPo

Strong Men, Riding Horses / Lester after the Western.   Gwendolyn Brooks.   GT

Strong Room of the House, The.   William Bronk.   APSN

Strong saturation of sea! O widely flown.   George Cabot Lodge.   APN-2

Strong Son of God, immortal Love.   Alfred Tennyson.   NAEL-6v2; NAEL-7v2; NAWM-7v2; SacPr *Fr.* In Memoriam A. H. H.

Strong spirit of pure steel, from autumn's metal cast.   Needle and Thread, The.   Pan Chao.   ColAnChi

Strong tendency towards silence, A.   Anselm Hollo.   PrTe *Fr.* Guests of Space.

Strong twin, the one with nothing, The.   Newly Born Twins.   Helen Farish.   BeAl

Strong Winds Below the Canyons.   Larry Kramer.   GeoHom

Strong with its cryptic American, / Its dated beauty. (LL)   Manhole Covers.   Karl Shapiro.   NAMCP V.2; NoAM

Strong without rage, without o'erflowing full. (LL)   Sir John Denham.   NAEL-6v1; NOSC; NPeEn *Fr.* Cooper's Hill.

Strong without rage, without o'er-flowing full. (LL)   Sir John Denham.   OxAEP-1; OxBEV *Fr.* Cooper's Hill.

Stronger Lessons.   Walt Whitman.   RaF

Stronger than alcohol, more great than song.   Ted Berrigan.   FTOS *Fr.* Sonnets, The.

Strongest parts of language are lonely, desolate women, singing, The.   Fragments to Overcome Silence.   Alejandra Pizarnik.   TANSG, *tr. by* Susan Bassnett

Strongest thing in the world, The.   Ring on the Finger.   Harold Rome.   ReLy

Strongly it bears us along in swelling and limitless billows.   Homeric Hexameter, The.   Samuel Taylor Coleridge.   OxAEP-2

Strongly worded to say on the subject. (LL)   Seascape.   Elizabeth Bishop.   ColAP; OxBoAm

Strong-shouldered mole.   Dead Mole, A.   Andrew Young.   NePenScot

Strontium descend des hauteurs du ciel bleu, Le.   Journaux Quotidiens.   Marguerite Yourcenar.   YaTCFP

Strophe.   "H. D."   MotU

Stroppy kippie moeketsi.   No dreams.   Wopko Jensma.   TSAP

Struck out of dim fluctuant forces and shock of electrical vapour.   Mathilde Blind.   VWP *Fr.* Ascent of Man, The.

Struck through such a dome.   Baroque Sunburst, A.   Amy Clampitt.   ColAP

Struck to the heart by this sad pageantry.   Percy Bysshe Shelley.   OxBEV *Fr.* Triumph of Life, The.

Struck, was I, not yet by Lightning.   Emily Dickinson.   NCAP

Structural Study of Myth, The.   Jerome Rothenberg.   FTOS

Structure of Rime XVIII.   Robert Duncan.   FTOS

Structure of Rime XXIII.   Robert Duncan.   FTOS

Structure of Rime, The.   Robert Duncan.
   "What of the structure of Rime? I said."   ASA

Structure of the soul, The.   States of War.   Maya Bejerano.   DTA, *tr. by* Miriyam Glazer

Structure, yes. You'd hardly say a house, A.   At the Flyfisher's Shack.   Sydney Lea.   RA

Struggle, The.   Toi Derricotte.   LTA; PBCAP

Struggle for Life.   Frigyes Karinthy.   IQMS, *tr. by* Peter Zollman

Struggle for the Border, The.   Dick Gallup.   AHA

Struggle for the Taal, The.   Breyten Breytenbach.   AF, *tr. by* Denis Hirson

Struggle to preserve once spoken words, The.   Art and Extinction.   Tony Harrison.   HarvBoo

Struggle-Road Dance.   Ahmos, II Zu-Bolton.   ISC

Struggling, like all Jews, to know the place where he lives. (LL)   And Cause His Countenance to Shine upon You: *Corpus Christi, Texas.*   Cynthia MacDonald.   AFaM; TiP2

Struggling Rill insensibly is grown, The.   William Wordsworth.   CenSon *Fr.* River Duddon [A Series of Sonnets], The.

Strugnell's Bargain.   Wendy Cope.   UV

Strugnell's Rubáiyát.   Wendy Cope.   UV

Strugnell's Sonnets.   Wendy Cope.
   6.   WaAnP

Strung along back elm.   Contentment.   J. B. Bryan.   ICANM

Strut and wiggle.   To Midnight Nan at Leroy's.   Langston Hughes.   NAAPv.2

Stubble Burning, The.   Sarah Ruden.   AmPoNex

Stubborn donkey, The.   Everyday.   Abd al-Rahim Salih al-Rahim.   IrPoTo, *tr. by* Ralph Saverese and Saadi A. Simawe

Stubbornly loving shadow of a star that was once our sun, The. (LL)   Prayer for a Future Beyond Ideology and War.   Kelly Cherry.   AtGh; RWB

Stuck.   Cheryl Clarke.   WiU

Stuck each summer at Bible camp.   Constipation.   Ronald Wallace.   SUP

Stuck in an unnamed place.   Space Between, The.   Elena Georgiou.   WiU

Stud, The.   Fred Voss.   SUP

Student, The.   Marianne Moore.   OxBoAm

Student, The.   *Unknown.*   OBMV, *tr. by* Frank O'Connor

Student all the way down, The.   Writing Class.   Stephen Berg.   TAPaP

Student and His Cat, The.   *Unknown. See* Pangur Bán.

Student, do the simple purification.   Simple Purification, The.   Kabir.   WoPoe, *tr. by* Robert Bly

Student Theme, The.   Ronald Wallace.   P180

Student who sat facing me on the Osaka express, A.   Lindley Williams Hubbell.   APT-2

Student's life is pleasant, The.   Student, The.   *Unknown.*   OBMV, *tr. by* Frank O'Connor

Student's Tale, The.   George Elliott Clarke.   OpeFie

Studied poverty of a moon roof, The.   Slips.   Medbh McGuckian.   MoWP; NAMCP V.2

Studied slouch of nouns, The.   Dementia.   John Cope.   GeoH

Studies.   Carlos Pellicer.   TCLAP, *tr. by* Donald Justice

Studies from the Antique.   Emily Jane Pfeiffer.   ViWPN

Studies in Classic American Literature.   Tony Lopez.   VaPo

Studies in Desire.   Pimone Triplett.   AmPoNex

Studies in Light.   Diane Di Prima.   PFTM-2

Studio, The (Homeage to Alice Neel).   Alicia Ostriker.   ExTi

Studio Up Over In Your Ear.   Al Young.   GT

Studley Park.   John Langhorne.   OBGa

Studs.   Michael S. Harper.   CAP-8; ESEAA

Studs and Rings: Favors of the Piercing Party.   D. A. Powell.   WiU

Study.   Tony Harrison.   CABP

Study, A.   Alice Thompson Meynell.   VWP

Study (A Soul), A.   Christina Georgina Rossetti.   VWP

Study in Aesthetics, The.   Ezra Pound.   APT-1; EMP

Study in Blue.   Evan Jones.   NOBAu

Study of Reading Habits, A.   Philip Larkin.   OBCoV

Study of Two Pears.   Wallace Stevens.   APT-1; BLT; NAMCP V.1; NoAM; OxBoAm

Study of Women's History 4, A.   Ko Chônghûi.   EcSo, *tr. by* Catherine J. Kim

Study of Women's History 6, A.   Ko Chônghûi.   EcSo, *tr. by* Catherine J. Kim

Study Peace.   Imamu Amiri Baraka.   APSN

Study the Way and never grow old.   37.   Shih Shu.   CSKM, *tr. by* James H. Sanford

Studying.   Primus St. John.   EGAG

Studying history.   History.   Juan Gelman.   TCLAP, *tr. by* Robert Marquez

Studying Horses.   Robert Kelly.   APSN

Studying in the Temple.   Daegak Euchon.   BecRai, *tr. by* Kim Daljin, Kim Won-Chung and Christopher Merrill

Studying Physics with My Daughter.   Jeanne Murray Walker.   WeW-3

Studying the Language.   Eiléan Ní Chuilleanáin.   EmeKit; NPeEn

Studying the Signs.   Allen Ginsberg.   FTOS

Studying Wu Wei, Muir Beach.   Jane Hirshfield.   AFaM; WANABP

Stuff.   Linda Gregg.   ExTi

Stuff of the moon.   Nocturne in a Deserted Brickyard.   Carl Sandburg.   APT-1; MoAmPo

Stuffed like a scarecrow, are these.   Funk Qualms.   John Wilkinson.   VaPo

Stuffed Owl, The.   William Wordsworth.   STuOW

Stuffed pink stocking, the neck.   One of the Strangest.   May Swenson.   APT-2; OWoS

Stuffed quail, A.   October Tune.   Joseph Brodsky.   VCWP, *tr. by* the author and Joseph Brodsky

Stuffy Turkey.   Dave Etter.   SeSe

Stumbling along a sidewalk clogged with snow.   Falcon.   Rachel Hadas.   ExTi

Stung by the tail of a scorpion.   Jet Plane.   Aloysius Michael Sullivan.   OtW

Stunned by Freedom.   Eva Svankmajerová.   SurWo, *tr. by* Katerina Pinosová

Stunned heat of noon. In shade, tan, silken cows.   Becune Point.   Derek Walcott.   PoA 2002

Stunned I Was Looking for Reasons.   Patrizia Cavalli.   CItWP, *tr. by* Cinzia Sartini Blum and Lara Trubowitz

Stunned in the stone light, laid among the lilies.   Ophelia.   Vernon Watkins.   TCAWP

Stupendious love! all saints astonishment.   Edward Taylor.   SacPr *Fr.* Preparatory Meditations Before My Approach to the Lord's Supper.

Stupid.   Paisley Rekdal.   LegDan

Stupid. But each of us took turns.   Landscape.   Michael Collier.   PfSP

Stupid Leander.   Colombine.   Paul Verlaine.   SxFrPo, *tr. by* Martin Sorrell

Stupidity.   Vegunta Mohana Prasad.   HotL, *tr. by* V. Narayana Rao

Stupidity Street.   Ralph Hodgson.   MoBrPo

Sturdy ploughman doth the soldier see, The.   Joseph Hall.   OBSV *Fr.* Virgidemiarum.

Sturgeon.   Karen Solie.   PoPra

Sturm und Drang narcissus, loose petals.   At the Freud Hilton.   Campbell McGrath.   AmPoNex

Stuttering Lover, The.   Fred Emerson Brooks.   VerBaPo

Stuttering rain at the window.   Sister Midnight.   John James.   Oth

Style.   Mark Cox.   SUP

Style.   Howard Nemerov.   NoAM; OxBoAm

Style is the water out of Homer.   Garden God, The.   Richard Eberhart.   OBGa

Style thee a most great fool, but no great man. (LL)   On Don Surly.   Ben Jonson.   NAEL-6v1; NAEL-7v1

Stylist, The.   Mary O'Donoghue.   NIrP

Styro.   Jim Carroll.   AHA

Styro.   Clark Coolidge.   PmAP

Styx.   Robert Duncan.   VCAP

Su Creek Pavilion.   Tai Shu-lun.   CCL1, tr. by Stephen Owen

Su follaje: la piedad de quien duerme un corazón entre abejas.   Sauce desbordado.   Ernesto Lumbreras.   RMCMP

Sub Contra.   Louise Bogan.   APT-2; WaAnP

Sub Shop Girl.   Afaa Michael Weaver.   SpirFl

Sub Umbra.   Leo Bradley.   OWABP

Sub Umbra Floreo.   Sharron K. Williams.   OWABP

Subalterns.   Elizabeth Daryush.   OBWP

Subaltern's Love-Song, A.   Sir John Betjeman.   BrAP; NoAM; OxAEP-2

Subalterns, The.   Thomas Hardy.   MoBrPo; NoAM

Subject / Matter.   Robin Becker.   RWB

Subject of Our Lives, The.   Robin Becker.   PfS

Subject of people unverifiable, The.   Patois.   Marianne Vitale.   HeMarv

Subject's always ostensible, The.   Retrievers in Translation.   Mark Doty.   AmAlph

Subjoined to the Yearly Bill of Mortality of the Parish of All Saints, Northampton, 1792.   William Cowper.   SacPr

Sublimated Mercury.   Alice Rahon.   SurWo, tr. by Myrna Bell Rochester

Sublimation.   Anne Michaels.
   "Once you called at midnight."   StAl

Sublimation, a new version of piety.   Report from the Field.   Dorothea Tanning.   PoCho

Sublime – invention ever young.   Christopher Smart.   OBEV Fr. Song to David, A.

Sublime is now, The.   Bad Time for the Sublime, A.   Kay Ryan.   OxBoAm

Subliminal.   Lorine Niedecker.   PFTM-1

Subliminal pre-sighting, A? Before I can say.   Dipper Territory.   James Aitchison.   EdScPo

Submarine.   Antonio Deltoro.   PML, tr. by John Oliver Simon

Submarine.   Brian Henry.   LegDan

Submarine Jaunt, A.   Edward Young.   STuOW Fr. Last Day, The.

Submission.   Clara Ann Thompson.   CBWP-2

Submit proposals force.   Alex Rawls.   AnSo Fr. What's Your Sign?

Subnarcosis.   Andrea Zanzotto.   ItPo, tr. by Gayle Ridinger

Substance and Shadow.   John Hewitt.   ModIr; PNI

Substance, Shadow, and Spirit ("Earth and heaven endure forever.")   T'ao Ch'ien.   ColAnChi, tr. by James Robert Hightower

Substance, Shadow, and Spirit ("Heaven and Earth endure and do not perish.")   T'ao Ch'ien.   CCL1, tr. by William Acker

Substance that stirs in my palm, The.   Ash.   Jayanta Mahapatra.   PoA 2002; VCWP

Substituted Poem of Laureate Quynh, The.   Unknown.   EaWin, tr. by W. S. Merwin and Nguyen Ngoc Bich

Substitution.   Elizabeth Barrett Browning.   SacPr

Subterranean.   Michael Hannon.   GeoHom

Subterranean Business.   Mark Ivey.   ICANM

Subterranean catacombs.   Turkish Bath in Ortamezar.   Ivan Teofilov.   CSCBP, tr. by Georgi Belev and Lisa Sapinkopf

Subterranean geography.   Elena Clementelli.   CItWP Fr. Etruscan Notebook.

Subterranean means underground.   Subterranean Night-Colored Magus.   DJ Renegade.   FuFl

Subterranean Night-Colored Magus.   DJ Renegade.   FuFl

Subterranean River Poem.   Svetlana Ivanova.   CRWP, tr. by Angela Livingstone

Subtle art of breathing, The.   Asha Bandele.   BtF

Subtle capering on a simple thought.   Fleadh Cheoil.   Pearse Hutchinson.   PBCIP

Subtle chain of countless rings, A.   Nature [1836].   Ralph Waldo Emerson.   APN-1

Subtle erratic vocation, A.   Cesare Greppi.   ItPo, tr. by Gayle Ridinger

Subtlest strain a great musician weaves, The.   Limitations.   Henrietta Cordelia Ray.   CBWP-3

Subtracted Words.   P. Inman.   FTOS

Subtraction Song.   Sally Keith.   LegDan

Subtropical.   Jane Epton Seale.   TiP2

Suburb of Long Suffering.   Mary Ruefle.   FaoP

Suburban.   John Ciardi.   NBLV

Suburban buddha, coffeehouse christ.   Mark S. Kuhar.   AmZen

Suburban Childhood, A.   Liz Rosenberg.   PBCAP

Suburban Crimes 3.   David Starkey.   LiTh

Suburban Lovers.   Bruce Dawe.   NOBAu

Suburban Song.   Elizabeth Riddell.   NOBAu

Suburbia.   David Ignatow.   PoCoUp

Suburbs on a Hazy Day.   D. H. Lawrence.   OBMV

Subverted Flower, The.   Robert Frost.   APT-1; ColAP; NoAM

Subway.   Miranda Field.   LegDan

Subway, The.   Edwin Denby.   APT-2; NYP2

Subway Face.   Langston Hughes.   APT-2

Subway flatters like the dope habit, The.   Subway, The.   Edwin Denby.   APT-2; NYP2

Subway in March, 5:45 P.M.   Maggie Nelson.   IIR

Subway Train.   Gottfried Benn.   GTCP, tr. by Michael Hamburger

Subway Train, The.   Leland B. Jacobs.   SSCS

Subway Wind.   Claude McKay.   APT-1

Subway Witnesses, The.   Lorenzo Thomas.   GT

Subways Are People.   Lee Bennett Hopkins.   HHAm

Success.   Cornelius Eady.   ISC

Success.   Norman Fischer.
   Monday, 3 December.   WANABP
   Saturday, 1 December.   WANABP
   Tuesday, 17 April.   WANABP

Success.   Emma Lazarus.   SWaP

Success is counted sweetest.   Emily Dickinson.   APN-2; ColAP; GoPo; HeIP-4; MoAmPo; NAAL-3; NAAL-5; NAAPv.1; NoP-4; NoP-5; OxBoAm; PoAgWa; PoPoPo; SAmP; TCAPo; TFi

Successful Summer, A.   David Schubert.   APT-2; ChIV-1

Successions, The.   Lee Bartlett.   ICANM

Successive Deaths.   Adelia Prado.   TANSG, tr. by Ellen Doré Watson

Such a Boat of Land.   Lamont B. Steptoe.   UnSA

Such a book must contain.   Introduction to My Anthology, An.   Marvin Bell.   TAPaP

Such a brightness.   Drizzle.   Cornelius Eady.   PfSP

Such a flow of language!   Rebecca Cutlet.   Bill Berkson.   PmAP

Such a fool as I am you had better ignore.   Usk, The.   Charles Hubert Sisson.   HarvBoo

Such a funny word.   Chalazion.   Allison Joseph.   NAPBL

Such a gentleman, lowering black wool.   In Kind.   Linda France.   NeBl

Such a gloomy day.   Meditation by the Xerox Machine.   Doris Safie.   PoArWo

Such a heart!   Love-Song, A.   Unknown.   IrLP, tr. by Brendan Kennelly

Such a howl went when I walked in.   Monkey House.   Betsy Sholl.   SUP

Such a Land.   Sŏ Chŏngju.   CAMKP, tr. by David R. McCann

Such a moon.   Buson.   WoPoe; ZenPo, tr. by Takashi Ikemoto and Lucien Stryk

Such a nice girl. Just what I wanted.   U. A. Fanthorpe.   MoWP Fr. Only Here for the Bier.

Such a Parcel of Rogues in a Nation.   Robert Burns.   NePenScot

Such a peculiar lot.   Fantasy of an African Boy.   James Berry.   RSaN

Such a prelate, I trow.   John Skelton.   OBSV Fr. Why Come Ye Not to Court.

Such a result so soon—and from such a beginning! (LL)   Hand-Mirror, A.   Walt Whitman.   NAAL-3; NAAPv.1; NAMCP V.1; PoPoPo

Such a series refuses the laundry and walks.   Jena Osman.   OnScMo Fr. Twelve Parts of Her.

Such a splendid place! The cedar and elm are whispering.   More about God (But with Some Reservations).   Victor Hugo.   SxFrPo, tr. by A. M. and E. H. Blackmore

Such a suprise to find icicles.   Overnight Winder: Texas.   William Virgil Davis.   TiP2

Such a Way to Go.   Martha Silano.   AmPoNex

Such a wizened creature.   Old Age.   Eliza Keary.   RSaN

Such accidents do happen.   Blues 2.   Barry Wallenstein.   SeSe

Such an itch and tickle of slow.   Stretching.   Robert Morgan.   WeW-3

Such an old hotel.   Old Hotel, The.   Kim Hyesun.   CAMKP, tr. by Jiwon Shin

Such an unlikely lady to teach Spanish.   Minnie Henderson.   Colleen Beeson.   TiP2

Such apples as once brought Atlanta down.   Unknown.   PriapPo Fr. Priapus Poems, The.

Such as she was, such as she would become. (LL)   Gift Outright, The.   Robert Frost.   BLPJKO; ColAP; FaBoA; HarvBoo; HHAm; MoAmPo; NAAL-5; NAMCP V.1; NoAM; NoP-4; NoP-5; OxBoAm; PoPoPo; TFi; TRP; WaAnP

Such beautiful, beautiful hands!   My Mother's Hands.   Ellen M. Huntington Gates.   ITBLP

Such brazen slatterns.   Dandelions.   Gerda Mayer.   Spl

Such Cloe is, and common as the air. (LL)   Cloe.   George, Baron Lansdowne Granville.   NIP-4; OxBEV

Such closets to search, such alcoves to importune! (LL)   Love in a Life.   Robert Browning.   NPeEn; OxBEV

Such counsels ye gave to me, O! (LL)   Edward [or Edward, Edward].
  Unknown. ClHu; NoP-4; OBEV; OxBEV; SoSe-8; TFi; TRP

  (Sic counseils ye gave to me, O.) (LL)   NoP-4; NPeEn

Such days as these there are before the spring.   Such Days as These.   Anna
  Andreyevna Akhmatova.   RusPo, *tr. by* Robert Arthur Douglas Ford

Such earnestness! such wear and tear.   Herman Melville. *Fr.* Clarel: A Poem
  and Pilgrimage in the Holy Land.

Such familiar space.   This House.   Robert Creeley.   BodElec

Such fruitless questions may not long beguile.   William Wordsworth.   CenSon
  Fr. River Duddon [A Series of Sonnets], The.

Such gaudy tulips raised [or rais'd] from dung. (LL)   Lady's Dressing Room,
  The.   Jonathan Swift.   NAEL-7v1; NoP-4; NoP-5; WaAnP

Such haukes, such hounds, and such a leman. (LL)   Three Ravens, The.
  Unknown. HeIP-4; OBEV; TFi

  (Such hawks, such hounds, and such a leman.) (LL)   NoP-4; NoP-5

  (Such hawks, such hounds, and such a lemman.) (LL)   NAEL-6v1; NAEL-
  7v1

Such is the death of struggle leaders.   Rosa Luxemburg.   Y. A. Rontsh.
  Prolet, *tr. by* Amelia Glaser

Such Is the Grief of the Grey-Haired Man.   *Unknown.* WoPoe *Fr.* Beowulf.

Such is the way of the world.   "St.-John Perse."   OBVE *Fr.* Anabasis.

Such is the wood-pigeon's song when the shower approaches.   Room in Space.
  René Char.   YaTCFP, *tr. by* W. S. Merwin

Such joy.   Sex.   David Baker.   PfSP

Such let me seem till such I be.   Mignon Aspiring to Heaven.   Johann
  Wolfgang von Goethe.   TreFP

Such marvellous ways to kill a man!   Bofors A. A. Gun, The.   Gavin Ewart.
  PoWW

Such men as sideling ride the ambling Muse.   Homer and the Brazen Head of
  Rumour.   George Chapman.   NOSC

Such men have lost all patriotic feeling. (LL)   Lamentations.   Siegfried
  Sassoon.   OBSV; OxAEP-2

Such passion for love coiled in my heart.   Archilochus.   SaLy, *tr. by* Diane
  Rayor

Such pretious perils for mankind! (LL)   Boethius.   NOSC; OBVE *Fr.*
  Consolation of Philosophy, The ("De Consolacione Philosophie").

Such proneness to sadness, such little fits.   They Call You Moody.   Ann
  Townsend.   LegDan

Such shameless bards we have; and yet 'tis true.   Alexander Pope.   OBSV *Fr.*
  Essay on Criticism, An.

Such silence falls. (LL)   Anna Andreyevna Akhmatova.   FaBoWar; PoetW *Fr.*
  In 1940.

Such silence / Snow tracing wings.   Masaoka Shiki.   ZenPo, *tr. by* Takashi
  Ikemoto and Lucien Stryk

Such stillness.   Basho.   WoPoe, *tr. by* Donald Keene

Such subtile filigranity and nobless of construccion.   "Wellcome, to the Caves
  of Artá!"   Robert Graves.   NBLV

Such such is life—. (LL)   Cold Are the Crabs.   Edward Lear.   NAEL-6v2;
  NAEL-7v2

Such Sweet Sorrow.   Elizabeth Delmore.   NLP

Such Tophet was; so looked the grinning fiend.   Tophet.   Thomas Gray.
  ChIV-1

Such violence. And such repose. (LL)   Tywater.   Richard Wilbur.   TRP;
  UpMys

Such warmth, such light, such love, and so much fear. (LL)   Boy at the
  Window.   Richard Wilbur.   GoPo; MoW; NAMCP V.2; OxBoAm; RaBo

Such wrong, as when a married man doth woo[e]. (LL)   Break of Day.   John
  Donne.   CtM; NAEL-6v1; NAEL-7v1; SoSe-8

Suck, The.   John Wieners.   FTOS

Suck, baby, suck, mother's love grows by giving.   Gipsy's Malison, The.
  Charles Lamb.   OxBSo

Suck / we'll suck bones.   Liberty.   Ernst Mirville.   OGAHCP, *tr. by* Boadiba
  and Jack Hirschman

Sudden a thought came like a full-blown rose.   John Keats.   EroLit *Fr.* Eve of
  St. Agnes, The.

Sudden Appearance of a Monster at a Window.   Lawrence Raab.   BLT; SUP

Sudden as a northeasterly.   Marriage, The.   Mary Dalton.   Coast

Sudden attack of aphasia, I hold my breath like smoke.   Alternative to Speech,
  An.   David Lehman.   WaAnP

Sudden blow, A! And she claims me for child.   Neither Innocence or
  Experience.   Dambudzo Marechera.   NAfrP

Sudden blow: a great bird lifts us, A.   Notion of Grace, A.   Brenda J. Moossy.
  PoArWo

Sudden blow: the great wings beating still, A.   Leda and the Swan.   William
  Butler Yeats.   BrAP; CABP; ClHu; EMP; EroLit; GSo; HarvBoo; HeIP-4;
  MoBrPo; NAEL-6v2; NAEL-7v2; NAMCP V.1; NAWM-7v2; NIL-7; NIP-
  4; NoAM; NoP-4; NoP-5; NPeEn; OWoS; OxAEP-2; OxBEV; OxBSo;
  PoPoPo; SoSe-8; TFi; TRP; WaAnP; WeW-3

Sudden chill, A / In our room my dead wife's.   Buson.   ZenPo, *tr. by* Takashi
  Ikemoto and Lucien Stryk

Sudden Discords in the Trumpets of Overdelayed Last Judgement, 1956.   Jack
  Lindsay.   RSaN

Sudden green gust from a roadside tree, A.   Express Train.   Ivan Tsanev.
  CSCBP, *tr. by* Georgi Belev and Lisa Sapinkopf

Sudden Journey.   Tess Gallagher.   NIL-7; NIP-4

Sudden Light.   Dante Gabriel Rossetti.   CABP; NoP-4; NoP-5; NPeEn;
  OxBEV

Sudden Movements.   Bob Hicok.   AmAlph

Sudden Rain in the Green Mountains, A.   Stephen Burt.   IIR

Sudden rain / Rows of horses.   Masaoka Shiki.   ZenPo, *tr. by* Takashi Ikemoto
  and Lucien Stryk

Sudden rain this afternoon.   Evening after Rain.   Tu Fu [or Du Fu].   CrYelRi,
  tr. by Sam Hamill

Sudden risk of birds, A.   David Helwig.   Coast *Fr.* On the Island.

Sudden sad mischance, A.   Looking-Glass for Men and Maids, A.   *Unknown.*
  BASC

Sudden shower.   Buson.   EH, *tr. by* Robert Hass

Sudden Shower.   John Clare.   OxAEP-2

Sudden shower / Cooling lava.   Sodo.   ZenPo, *tr. by* Takashi Ikemoto and
  Lucien Stryk

Sudden the desert changes.   Bridge-Guard in the Karroo.   Rudyard Kipling.
  OBWP

Sudden Tug of the Familiar, The.   Faye George.   PoDa

Sudden, unexpected movement; his hand, A.   Audible and Inaudible.   Yannis
  Ritsos.   AF, *tr. by* Minas Savas

Sudden wakin', a sudden weepin', A.   Man's Days.   Eden Phillpotts.   OBEV

Sudden, weightless, warm. (LL)   Apples on Champlain.   Richard Kenney.
  NoP-4; NoP-5

Suddening one day by myself.   Fence, The.   Heather McHugh.   FaoP

Suddenly.   Robin Blaser.   FTOS

Suddenly.   Semyon Isaakovich Kirsanov.   RusPo, *tr. by* Robert Arthur Douglas
  Ford

Suddenly.   Motoko Michiura.   CFP, *tr. by* Aoyami Miyuki, Leza Lowitz and
  Akemi Tomioka

Suddenly.   Al Young.   GT

Suddenly after a few years of abject misery, depression and paralysis.   Obvious,
  The.   Anna Couani.   BMAP

Suddenly, after the quarrel, while we waited.   Quarrel, The.   Conrad Potter
  Aiken.   MoAmPo; StAl

Suddenly, against the mountainous.   There's Not a Friend like the Lowly Jesus.
  William Anderson.   EGAG

Suddenly as the riot squad moved in, it was raining exclamation marks.   Belfast
  Confetti.   Ciaran Carson.   NPeEn; PNI

Suddenly at sunset Adam surprised us.   Trees of Ithaca, The.   Sa'di Yusuf.
  IrPoTo, *tr. by* Khaled Mattawa

Suddenly below my ankles.   Face.   No Hyegyông.   EcSo, *tr. by* Ann Y. Choi

Suddenly drawn in through the thick glass plate.   Charles Martin.   RA

Suddenly forgetting my illness one day.   Ishikawa Takuboku.   PoCho, *tr. by*
  Sanford Goldstein and Seishi Shinoda

Suddenly half in jest.   Album Leaf.   Stéphane Mallarmé.   OBVE, *tr. by* Keith
  Bosley

Suddenly his mouth filled with sand.   Death of a Poet.   Charles Causley.
  EmeKit

Suddenly his poor body.   Ted Hughes.   NoAM *Fr.* Stations.

Suddenly / I am the same age.   Suddenly.   Semyon Isaakovich Kirsanov.
  RusPo, *tr. by* Robert Arthur Douglas Ford

Suddenly I find out that my fingers.   Dali.   Mahmoud Sharaf.   AnVo, *tr. by*
  Mohamed Enani

Suddenly I knew how it was to be my uncle's Labrador retriever.   First Blow-
  Job.   Meg Kearney.   NevBe

Suddenly I saw the cold and rook-delighting heaven.   Cold Heaven, The.
  William Butler Yeats.   InoFa; IrLP; NAMCP V.1; NoAM; NPeEn

Suddenly I too see.   Against Poetry.   Sandra M. Gilbert.   PoA 2002

Suddenly I was stabbed from behind.   Maya Bejerano.   DTA *Fr.* Hymns of
  Job.

Suddenly I would like prison. (LL)   Now that the time seems all mine.
  Patrizia Cavalli.   Nelt; VCWP, *tr. by* Judith Baumel

Suddenly in the midst of a game of lotto with his sisters.   Louis Armstrong.
  Ernst Moerman.   SeSe

Suddenly into flowers more lovely than the white moon. (LL)   Train Journey.
  Judith Wright.   NoP-4; NoP-5

Suddenly it was clear to me.   Saint Animal.   Chase Twichell.   StAl

Suddenly, it's the way it was.   Hit squad.   Tatamkulu Afrika.   TSAP

Suddenly, like an arrow from the East.   Woodpecker.   Gerald Bullett.   OWoS

Suddenly my grandfather lifted up his nightie, I.   Lifting, The.   Sharon Olds.   CAP-
  8; InoFa; MoWP; NIL-7

Suddenly my father lifted up his nightie, I.   In the Hospital Near the End.
  Sharon Olds.   NIP-4

Suddenly night crushed out the day and hurled. Unreturning, The. Wilfred Owen. MoBrPo

Suddenly on a day in July. Giusi Busceti. ItPo, *tr.* by Gayle Ridinger

Suddenly one morning I woke up and I had ass-belly! Becoming a Buddha. Seido Ray Ronci. AmZen

Suddenly out of its stale and drowsy lair, the lair of slaves. Europe, the 72d and 73d Year of These States. Walt Whitman. TCAPo

Suddenly out of its stale and drowsy lair, the lair of slaves. Walt Whitman. APN-1 *Fr.* Leaves of Grass [1855 Version].

Suddenly Startled. Léopold Sédar Senghor. PoetW, *tr.* by Melvin Dixon

Suddenly startled at the fresh sound, the stabbing dagger. Suddenly Startled. Léopold Sédar Senghor. PoetW, *tr.* by Melvin Dixon

Suddenly the golden grove stopped. Golden Grove, The. Sergey Aleksandrovich Yesenin. RusPo, *tr.* by Robert Arthur Douglas Ford and R.A.D. Ford

Suddenly, the legs want a different sort of work. April. Cornelius Eady. ESEAA

Suddenly the statuary is upon us. Statue, The. George Murray. PA9/11

Suddenly the swallow's shadow reaped the glances of its nostalgia: / Noon. Origin of Landscape or the End of Mercy, The. Odysseus Elytis. VCWP

Suddenly the window will open. Return, The. Tadeusz Rózewicz. HP, *tr.* by Adam Czerniawski

Suddenly, the Yard Where Rice and Yeast Brew. Chŏng Hwajin. EcSo, *tr.* by Julie C. Park

Suddenly there were cherries. Transformation. Günter Grass. GTCP, *tr.* by Irmgard Hunt

Suddenly there were forms there. Horses. Gwyn Thomas. BBMWP; OBWVE, *tr.* by Joseph P. Clancy

Suddenly they all stopped talking about it. Yet I. John Ashbery. PFTM-2 *Fr.* Flow Chart.

Suddenly they came flying, like a long scarf of smoke. Thing, The. Theodore Roethke. APT-2

Suddenly to become John Benbow, walking down William Street. Metempsychosis. Kenneth Slessor. NOBAu

Suddenly wait against the moon's face. (LL) Wind has blown the rain away and blown, A. E. E. Cummings. HarvBoo; MoAmPo

Suddenly we're sons of Noah. From the Theater of Wine. Cyrus Cassells. GifTon

Suddenly / when I hear airplanes overhead. Porter. Marilyn Nelson Waniek. ESEAA

Suddenly while shaving, you looked in the mirror to discover that your canine teeth have grown remarkably long. Devil's Symbol, The. Haytham El-Shawwaf. AnVo, *tr.* by Mohamed Enani

Suddenly / (yet somehow expected). Thief in the Night, A. Jelaluddin Rumi. BBASP, *tr.* by Nasrollah Pourjavady and Peter Lamborn Wilson

Suddenly you felt it. And under the white. Roman Arbor, The. Ellen Hinsey. YaYoPo

Suddenness, The. Alicia Gaspar de Alba. FTtHH *Fr.* Elemental Journey: Anniversary Gift.

Sueden chance ded mak me mues, The. Lady Margaret Howard. EMWP

Sueño de los justos, El. Dana Gelinas. SPV

Sueño un sol misterioso, hoja de un viejo otoño. Sol de la Muerte. José Luis Hidalgo. RaW

Suffenus whom you know, the Witty. Catullus. OBVE,

Sufferance of her race is shown, The. Formerly a Slave. Herman Melville. APN-2

Suffering. Miroslav Holub. PoSu, *tr.* by Ian Milner and George Theiner

Suffering. Patricia K. Page. NoAM

Suffering envelops everything like dust on the floor below. Neighbors. Antonio Deltoro. RMCMP, *tr.* by Christian Viveros-Fauné

Suffering has settled like a sly disguise. Korean Woman Seated by a Wall, A. William Meredith. AmWaPo

Suffering The Sea Change: All My Pretty Ones. Lucinda Roy. GT

Suffice [*or* Suffise] they show [*or* shew] I lived [*or* liv'd], and loved [*or* lov'd] thee dear[e]. (LL) Samuel Daniel. GSo; NAEL-6v1; NAEL-7v1; NoP-5; NoSic; OBEV; PBRV; WaAnP *Fr.* Sonnets to Delia.

Sufficeth it to yow my joyes interred. Sir Walter Ralegh. PBRV

Suffused in April twilight. Redemption. Pauli Murray. GT

Sugar. Gertrude Stein. NAMCP V.1 *Fr.* Tender Buttons.

Sugar. Crystal Williams. RD

Sugar Cane. Grace Nichols. BeAl

Sugar Cane, The. James Grainger.
  Advice to Slave-Owners. STuOW
  Book 4. PoSl
  Crescendo. STuOW
  "Of composts shall the Muse disdain to sing?" VerBaPo
    Call to the Muse. STuOW
  Shame of France, The. STuOW

Sugar Loaf Hill. Nanao Sakaki. WhBo

Sugar Poem. Aurora Levins Morales. PueRic

Sugar-bank of sweet thoughts! Poet to a Poet. Salman al-Tajir. SonAtl, *tr.* by Abdul Kalam Azad

Sugarmother's Daughter Dreams. Patrice Vecchione. RaF

Sugar-Plum Tree, The. Eugene Field. ITBLP; NBLV

Suggested by a Picture of Peele Castle, in a Storm, Painted by Sir George Beaumont. William Wordsworth. *See* Elegiac Stanzas: Suggested by a Picture of Peele Castle, in a Storm, Painted by Sir George Beaumont.

Suggestion, A. Ismail. HotL, *tr.* by V. Narayana Rao

Suggestion from a Friend. Jane Kenyon. LoL *Fr.* Having It Out with Melancholy.

Suggestion of chill pervades the little bower, A. Tune: "Sand of Silk-Washing Brook." Ch'in Kuan. ColAnChi, *tr.* by Jiaosheng Wang

Su-guan [Translations]. *Unknown.* CCL1
  Plain Cap. CCL1, *tr.* by Arthur Waley
  White Cap, The. CCL1

Sui Veneris/The Poet of No Return. Ricardo M. de Ungria. ReBoTo

Suicide?! In Answer to the Question: Have You Ever Considered Suicide. Kate Rushin. PfS

Suicide. Lina Tibi. PoArWo, *tr.* by Subhi Hadidi and Nathalie Handal

Suicide: "As if a wood of oaks gave." Menke Katz. Prolet, *tr.* by Amelia Glaser

Suicide, The. Louis MacNeice. ModIr

Suicide, The. Jennifer Rose. PfS

Suicide applicant, A. Ant Dodger. Bill Knott. PBCAP

Suicide in the Trenches. Siegfried Sassoon. FaBoWar; PoAgWa; PoWW

Suicide is a duel with yourself. Sergey Chudakov. TCRusP, *tr.* by Daniel Weissbort

Suicide letters from strangers, stained pages stinking of fear. Accomplice. Peter Johnson. LiTh

Suicide Note. Janice Mirikitani. OxWW

Suicide of an Unemployed Person, The. Kodama Kagai. CAoMJL1, *tr.* by Leith Morton

Suicide on Pentwyn Bridge. Gillian Clarke. AngWePo

Suicide Rates, The. Lewis Warsh. AHA; FTOS

Suicide with Squirtgun. Tom Clark. PmAP

Suicide Year, The. Alice Anderson. AmPoNex

Suicides and Fools. S. P. Shephard. BtF

Suicide's Note. Langston Hughes. APT-2; NAMCP V.1; OxAAAP; PoPoPo; SAmP

Suilven. Andrew Young. EdScPo

Suilven and the Eagle. Gordon Bottomley.
  Eagle Song. MoBrPo

Suit, The. Seamus Heaney. PoA 2002

Suitable for a gentleman with medals. War Lord in the Early Evening. Patricia K. Page. NoAM

Suitcase is weary of being used, of hiding your clothes, The. Travelling Music. Philip Levine. MotU

Naked Poems. Phyllis Webb. NLPA
  Non Linear. NLPA
  Some final questions. NLPA
  Suite 1. NLPA
  Suite 2. NLPA
  Suite of Lies. NLPA

Suite 1. Phyllis Webb. NLPA *Fr.* Naked Poems.

Suite 2. Phyllis Webb. NLPA *Fr.* Naked Poems.

Suite for Augustus, A. Rita Dove.
  Planning the Perfect Evening. GT

Suite in the Ch'ing-p'ing Mode, A. Li Po. ColAnChi, *tr.* by Elling O. Eide

Suite of Lies. Phyllis Webb. NLPA *Fr.* Naked Poems.

Suite Repose. Carl Hancock Rux. SpirFl

Suitors lined up like sailors. Briar Rose Waltz. Cynthia Cruz. IAoNAP

Suitors watch Ulysses string the bow, The. Homer. OBVE *Fr.* Odyssey.

Sukey [*or* Suky], you shall be my wife. *Unknown.* TLR

Sukhanovo. Natalya Gorbanevskaya. AF, *tr.* by Daniel Weissbort

Suliko. *Unknown.* SonAtl, *tr.* by Dorli Meek and Tamara Romanyk

Sulking in the Seventies. Kris Hemensley. BMAP

Sullenness. Michael Field. VWP

Sulpicia. Michael Longley. OxBSo; RACG

Sultan of Light Years at Café Riche. To Naguib Mahfouz. Abdul Wahab Al-Bayati. IrPoTo, *tr.* by Farouk Abdel Wahab

Sultan of the Animals Is the Night, The. Fazil Hüsnü Daglarca. WoPoe, *tr.* by Ahmet Ö. Evin

Sultry Night, A. Boris Leonidovich Pasternak. TCRusP, *tr.* by Bogdan Boychuk and Mark Rudman

Sultry noon, not in the summer's prime, A. Carlos Wilcox. APN-1 *Fr.* Age of Benevolence, The.

Sum, A. Lewis Carroll. Spl

Sum speikis of lords, sum speikis of lairds. *Unknown*. IBB

Sumac in Ohio, The. James Wright. MotU

Sumach Leaves, The. Jones Very. ColAP

Sumer Is Icumen [*or* Ycomen] In. *Unknown*. HeIP-4; OPOU; OxBEV

(Cuckoo Song, The.) NAEL-7v1; NBLV; NoP-4; NoP-5; OBEV; OWoS; TFi; WaAnP

Summa is i-cumen in. Baccalaureate. David McCord. NBLV

Summary. Jaime Torres Bodet. TCLAP, *tr. by* Sonja Karsen

Summary for Alastor. Laura Riding Jackson. FuPo; WoPoe

Summary of Lord Lyttleton's 'Advice to a Lady', A. Lady Mary Wortley Montagu. OxBEV

Summer. Conrad Potter Aiken. NoAM

Summer. Frank Asch. NTCP

Summer. Luciana Frezza. CItWP, *tr. by* Cinzia Sartini Blum and Lara Trubowitz

Summer. Judah Ha-Levi. NAWM-7v1, *tr. by* William M. Davis

Summer. Friedrich Hölderlin. WoPoe *Fr.* Seasons, The.

Summer. David Oliveira. GeoHom

Summer. Dennis Saleh. GeoHom

Summer. *Unknown*. CCL1 *Fr.* Tzu Yeh Songs.

Summer. Judith Wright. HarvBoo *Fr.* Shadow of Fire: Ghazals, The.

Summer. Yun Söndo. CATKP *Fr.* Angler's Calendar, The.

Summer: "At evening the complaint of the cuckoo." Georg Trakl. WED, *tr. by* Robert Bly

Summer: "Fills the white enamel bucket, overflows." Maura Eichner. UpMys

Summer: "Flying curved to the wind shear-waters turn their bodies in the wave." Kay Boyle. MotU

Summer ("Good, it's hot.") Pascalle Monnier. YaTCFP, *tr. by* Cole Swensen

Summer: "I stroll on Madison in expensive clothes, sour." Edwin Denby. NYP2; OxBoAm

Summer: "It's the season of birdsong." Xuan Quynh. PoCho, *tr. by* Nguyen Ba Chung and Carolyn Forché

Summer: "On this long farm facing Rila Mountain." Binyo Ivanov. CSCBP, *tr. by* Georgi Belev and Lisa Sapinkopf

Summer: "She has done with silkworms and the fieldwork." *Unknown*. CCL1, *tr. by* John Frodsham

Summer: "Summer climbs the mountains." Aba Qunanbaev. SonAtl, *tr. by* Charles Carlsson, Nathan Lite and Dana Ziyasheva

Summer: "There is no breeze, sounds travel far in the dead air." Vern Rutsala. MotU

Summer ("These are the first fine days.") Pascalle Monnier. YaTCFP, *tr. by* Cole Swensen

Summer: "These hot afternoons "it's quite absurd" she whispered." Lee Harwood. AHA

Summer 1983. Mary Jo Salter. RA

Summer, A. Carl Phillips. AmAlph

Summer, The. Morgan Llwyd. AngWePo *Fr.* 1648.

Summer, The. Morgan Llwyd.

"What? summer now? divisions ring." PBRV

Summer, adieu. Ode to the End of Summer. Phyllis McGinley. NBLV

Summer after Last, The. Michael Burkard. LaCa

Summer afternoon. Stanford M. Forrester. AmZen

Summer Afternoon in Solon, Iowa. Stuart Dybek. PoDa

Summer Again. Yves Bonnefoy. VCWP, *tr. by* Lisa Sapinkopf

Summer airing / On one pole. Morikawa Kyoroku. ZenPo, *tr. by* Takashi Ikemoto and Lucien Stryk

Summer airing / Trying on a quilt. Kikaku. ZenPo, *tr. by* Takashi Ikemoto and Lucien Stryk

Summer, and a woman lowers her jug to the river. She bathes and sings the word "why." White Nile Elegy. Khaled Mattawa. NAPBL

Summer and dawn. It's Visitation Day. Summer and Dawn. Sándor Sík. IQMS, *tr. by* Watson Kirkconnell

Summer and Smoke. Manuel Vázquez Montalbán. RaW, *tr. by* Robert Mezey

Summer, and the long grass is a snare drum. Field-Mouse, The. Gillian Clarke. MoWP

Summer and Winter. Percy Bysshe Shelley. OxAEP-2

Summer at North Farm. Stephen Kuusisto. PoDa

Summer Begins Outside Dalhart, Texas. Mary Vanek. TiP2

Summer Birds and Flowers (2). Margaret Gibson. AmZen

Summer blew its little drifts of sound, The. Army of Occupation. Sarah Morgan Bryan Piatt. NCAP

Summer brought fireflies in swarms. Childhood. Sharan Strange. GT

Summer Bull. Valerie Gillies. EdScPo

Summer butterfly. Mitsu Suzuki. WhBo

Summer came and went leaving its traceries on his fall. Roy Kiyooka. NLPA *Fr.* Pear Tree Pomes.

Summer came too fast, The. Chocolate Confessions. Magdalena Gomez. PueRic

Summer Christmas in Australia, A. Douglas Brook Wheelton Sladen. OBCP

Summer climbs the mountains. Summer. Aba Qunanbaev. SonAtl, *tr. by* Charles Carlsson, Nathan Lite and Dana Ziyasheva

Summer Cloud, A. Waldo Williams. OBWVE, *tr. by* Joseph P. Clancy

Summer Cloud, A. Waldo Williams. BBMWP, *tr. by* Anthony Conran

Summer cold, A. No rash. No fever. Nothing. But a dozen times during the night I wake. Shade, The. C. K. Williams. BeAl; StAl

Summer comes. Magalu. Helene Johnson. APT-2

Summer comes, the Summer dies, The. Captive. Rose Terry Cooke. NAAPv.1

Summer comes to rivers and lakes. Maeng Sasŏng. CATKP *Fr.* Four Seasons by the Rivers and Lakes.

Summer Commentary, A. Yvor Winters. CalPo; OxBoAm

Summer Dawn. William Morris. GSo; OBEV; OxAEP-2; OxBEV

Summer Day, A. Robert Greacen. PNI

Summer Day, The. Mary Oliver. AmFaPo; BeAl; CAP-8; TWF

Summer Days in the Mountains. Li Po. CrYelRi, *tr. by* Sam Hamill

Summer dream beneath the tamarind tree?, The. (LL) Sonnet—To Science. Edgar Allan Poe. NAAPv.1; NCAP; NoP-4; NoP-5; OxBSo; TCAPo

Summer ends now; now, barbarous in beauty, the stooks [a]rise. Hurrahing in Harvest. Gerard Manley Hopkins. MoBrPo; NAEL-6v2; NAEL-7v2; OxBSo; SacPr

Summer Evening. Walter De la Mare. MoBrPo

Summer Evening, A.

"Toward the substation in the testing wind." BAP-97

Summer evenings, I was put. Catching the Scent. Anne Haines. PfS

Summer Evening's Meditation, A. Anna Laetitia Barbauld. NAEL-7v2

"'Tis now the hour." NPBRoP

Summer Eve's Vision, A. Maria Jane Jewsbury. VWP

Summer Farm. Norman Alexander MacCaig. NePenScot; NoP-5; NPeEn; StAl; WaAnP

Summer finally lies facedown. In Squire Park with M., Esquire. Julianne Buchsbaum. LegDan

Summer Fires of Mulanje Mountain. Edison Mpina. NAfrP

Summer Garden, The. Elena Ignatova. ItGoST, *tr. by* Sibelan Forrester

Summer grass. Basho. EH, *tr. by* Robert Hass

Summer grasses. Basho. SoOfWa, *tr. by* Sam Hamill

Summer grasses. Basho. Spl

Summer grasses. Basho. EMJL, *tr. by* Haruo Shirane

Summer grasses / All that remains. Basho. ZenPo, *tr. by* Takashi Ikemoto and Lucien Stryk

Summer grasses grow, The. Basho. TAL

Summer grew, broadened out. Peonies. Harry Edmund Martinson. WoPoe, *tr. by* Leif Sjöberg and William Jay Smith

Summer has come, healthy and free. Summer Has Come. *Unknown*. IrV, *tr. by* Kuno Meyer

Summer Heat. Edward Carpenter. CAGL *Fr.* Towards Democracy.

Summer Holiday. Robinson Jeffers. MoAmPo

Summer Home. Seamus Heaney. PBCIP

Summer I killed my pet chicken, The. Summer of the New Well. David Marlatt. AmPoNex

Summer I slept, The. My Cockroach Lover. Martín Espada. UrbNat

Summer I Was Sixteen, The. Geraldine Connolly. P180

Summer in England, 1914. Alice Thompson Meynell. SoSe-8

Summer in Killowen. Cathal McCabe. NIrP

Summer in Slumville. Angel González. RaW, *tr. by* Herbert Baird and William Stafford

Summer in the South. Paul Laurence Dunbar. GT

Summer Is a Poem by Ovid. Douglas G. Jones. NIP-4

Summer Is a-Comin' In. John Latouche. ReLy

Summer Is By. William Soutar. FaBoVe

Summer is dying in the purple and gold and russet. Hayyim Nahman Bialik. FIT, *tr. by* Robert Friend

Summer Is Ended. Christina Georgina Rossetti. NPeEn; OxBEV

Summer is fading. Afternoons. Philip Larkin. NPeEn; OxBEV; PoetW

Summer is happening above the heads of the dead. Blue Dome, The. Deborah Randall. NeBl

Summer is late, my heart. Touch Me. Stanley Kunitz. APT-2; BeAl; CAP-8; NAMCP V.1; NoP-4; NoP-5; PoDa; StAl

Summer is over and. Bashō, A Departure. Robert Hass. LoL

Summer is over on the island. To the Days Lost in August. Deborah Cummins. PoDa

Summer is over upon the sea. Song. Elizabeth Bishop. PoA 2002

Summer journeys to Niag'ra. Manhattan. Lorenz Hart. ReLy

Summer Lost. Harriet Hamilton King. VWP

Summer love was ever thus. Jean Bleakney. NIrP

Summer Me, Winter Me. Alan Bergman and Marilyn Bergman. ReLy

Summer meant peeling: peaches. Preserving, The. Kevin Young. GT

Summer Mist.   David Huerta.   RMCMP, *tr. by* Mark Schafer

Summer Mist, A.   Kitahara Hakushū.   CAoMJL1, *tr. by* Margaret Benton Fukasawa

Summer Morning.   Charles Simic.   GoPo; WaAnP

Summer Morning.   Louis Simpson.   GoPo

Summer Morning, A.   Rachel Lyman Field.   ChAP

Summer Morning, A.   Richard Wilbur.   NBLV; StAI

Summer mornings we.   Sherley Anne Williams.   GeoHom *Fr.* Iconography of Childhood, The.

Summer mountains.   Basho.   EMJL, *tr. by* Haruo Shirane

Summer, my dearest, turns again to the dark.   Two of Us Together, Each of Us Alone, The.   Yehuda Amichai.   FIT, *tr. by* Robert Friend

Summer nests uncovered by autumn wind, The.   Birds' Nests.   Edward Thomas.   OWoS

Summer Night.   BLT, *tr. by* Willis Barnstone

Summer Night.   Nathan Alterman.   FIT, *tr. by* Robert Friend

Summer Night.   Hayyim Nahman Bialik.   FIT, *tr. by* Robert Friend

Summer Night.   Susan Griffin.   WhBo

Summer Night.   Langston Hughes.   APT-2

Summer night.   Issa.   EH, *tr. by* Robert Hass

Summer Night.   Antonio Machado Ruiz.   WoPoe, *tr. by* Willis Barnstone

Summer Night.   Alfred Tennyson. *See* Now Sleeps the Crimson Petal.

Summer Night.   Tu Fu [*or* Du Fu].   TAL

Summer Night, A.   W. H. Auden.   NPeEn

Summer night is flying, The.   Flight.   Floyd Skloot.   PoDa

Summer Night, Riverside.   Sara Teasdale.   APT-1

Summer Night, The.   Friedrich Gottlieb Klopstock.   GePo, *tr. by* George C. Schoolfield

Summer night—a night whose wide-spread wings, A.   Infinite in the Skies, The.   Alphonse Marie Louis de Lamartine.   SxFrPo, *tr. by* A. M. and E. H. Blackmore

Summer Nights.   Paul Christensen.   TiP2

Summer nights I loved the cool pillow.   Screen Porch.   Frederick Marchant.   UrbNat

Summer Nights in Texas.   Grace Noll Crowell.   TiP2

Summer 1984.   Duncan Bush.   TCAWP

Summer Noon: 1941.   Yvor Winters.   ColAP

Summer Nostalgia.   Virginia E. Escandor.   ReBoTo

Summer, now we must live without your sweet weather.   Neidhart von Reuental.   GePo

Summer of Lost Rachel, The.   Seamus Heaney.   NIL-7

Summer of nineteen eighteen, The.   Bad Old Days, The.   Kenneth Rexroth.   NoAM

Summer of polio, they drained the pools, The.   I dreamed of Jehovah.   Letters from the Earth.   Rodney Jones.   InGu

Summer of 'sixty-three, sir, and Conrad was gone away.   Kentucky Belle.   Constance Fenimore Woolson.   CBCWP

Summer of strike and drought.   Summer 1984.   Duncan Bush.   TCAWP

Summer of the New Well.   David Marlatt.   AmPoNex

Summer or Its Ending.   Yehuda Amichai.   PoSu, *tr. by* Dennis Silk

Summer [*or* Sumer] is y-comen [*or* y-cumen] in.   *Unknown. See* Sumer is icumen in.

Summer passed through the cool rooms, violent.   Stone, A.   Yves Bonnefoy.   VCWP, *tr. by* John Naughton

Summer Poem, A.   Jayanta Mahapatra.   VCWP

Summer Rain.   Bob Grumman.   AnSo

Summer rain isn't here yet, The.   Language of Weather, The.   Ray A. Young Bear.   HATNAP

Summer Recital.   Cynthia S. Pederson.   MiVo

Summer Retreat: Pema Osel Ling.   Diane Di Prima.   AmZen

Summer river, The.   Yamaguchi Seishi.   CAoMJL1, *tr. by* Alfred H. Marks and Takashi Kodaira

Summer Seeming.   John Riley.   Oth

Summer set lip to earth's bosom bare.   Poppy, The.   Francis Thompson.   MoBrPo

Summer sets on the cities like a hen.   Mob, The.   Calvin C. Hernton.   OxAAAP

Summer Shower.   David McCord.   TLR

Summer Shower, The.   Thomas Buchanan Read.   TreFP

Summer Sketches.   Bessie Rayner Parkes.
   Lilian's Second Letter.   VWP

Summer sky / Clear after rain.   Masaoka Shiki.   ZenPo, *tr. by* Takashi Ikemoto and Lucien Stryk

Summer Solstice.   Alan Garner.   NOxBChV

Summer Solstice.   Dorothy Hewett.
   "Sunset flames over the city, The."   BMAP

Summer Solstice.   Enos D. Watts.   Coast

Summer Solstice, New York City.   Sharon Olds.   FaoP

Summer Song.   *Unknown.*   APN-2, *tr. by* Franz Boas

Summer Song, A.   Ernst Jandl.   GTCP, *tr. by* Reinhold Grimm

Summer Song, A.   George Peele. *See* Song: "Whenas [*or* When as] the Rye [*or* Rie] reach to the chin."

Summer Song ("Mirror Lake, The.")   Li Po.   NDACCP, *tr. by* William Carlos Williams

Summer Song I.   George Barker.   HarvBoo

Summer Storm.   Dana Gioia.   GoPo; OxBoAm; RA

Summer Storm.   Louis Simpson.   OxBSo

Summer Sun.   Robert Louis Stevenson.   MoBrPo

Summer sun ray, The.   Noon Walk on the Asylum Lawn.   Anne Sexton.   OBGa

Summer Sunday.   *Unknown.*   WoPoe, *tr. by* John Gardner

Summer. Sunset. Someone is playing.   Transient Barracks (1944).   Randall Jarrell.   PWW2

Summer Surprised Us.   Edward Hirsch.   PfSP

Summer swells like a fruit.   Heat.   Maura Dooley.   NeBl

Summer that I was ten, The.   Centaur, The.   May Swenson.   APT-2; ItP; NAMCP V.2

Summer the Beatles Went Over Seven Minutes on a Single, The.   Doyle Wesley Walls.   SwNoth

Summer, the Sacramento.   Muriel Rukeyser.   ASA

Summer, this is our flesh.   Seasons of the Soul.   Allen Tate.   FuPo

Summer thunder darkens, and its climbing.   Prometheus.   Charles Tomlinson.   HarvBoo

Summer Thunder, The.   Howard Moss.   OxBoAm

Summer Time on Bredon.   Hugh Kingsmill.   UV

Summer Triangle.   Derek Beaulieu.   PoPra

Summer turned.   John Gneisenau Neihardt.   GM *Fr.* Song of the Indian Wars, The.

Summer twilight, The. (LL)   Lower leaves of the trees, The.   Sone no Yoshitada.   AmFaPo; ItP, *tr. by* Kenneth Rexroth

Summer was dry, dry the garden.   On the Debt My Mother Owed to Sears Roebuck.   Edward Dorn.   TRP

Summer Was Not Long Enough, The.   Jean Valentine.   LaCa

Summer was over. (LL)   Mockingbird, The.   Charles Bukowski.   PmAP; WaAnP

Summer waves goodbye to the wayside.   Storm, an Endless Instant.   Boris Leonidovich Pasternak.   TCRusP, *tr. by* Bogdan Boychuk and Mark Rudman

Summer Wind.   William Cullen Bryant.   APN-1

Summer with its tint, The.   Marriage of Heaven and Hell in Española.   Joan Logghe.   ICANM

Summer with Monika.   Roger McGough.
   "Away from you."   OBCoV

Summer Words of [*or* for] a Sistuh [*or* Sister] Addict.   Sonia Sanchez.   WaAnP

Summer Worlds: A Mythic Landscape.   Askia Muhammad Touré.   FuFl

Summer-Camp Bus Pulls Away from the Curb, The.   Sharon Olds.   PLBUT

Summerfield.   Jim Barnes.   HATNAP *Fr.* Ex-Deputy Sheriff Remembers the Eastern Oklahoma Murderers, An.

Summerhouse Piano.   Sascha Feinstein.   AmPoNex

Summers and summers have come, and gone with the flight of the swallow.   Tantramar Revisited, The.   Sir Charles G. D. Roberts.   BrAP

Summer's Day, A.   Joanna Baillie.   WoRP

Summer's End.   Eve Merriam.   WhBo

Summer's last thunder: and from the treetops.   Smile, A.   Nikolai Kanchev.   CSCBP, *tr. by* Georgi Belev and Lisa Sapinkopf

Summer's Last Will and Testament.   Thomas Nashe.
   Adieu, Farewell, Earth's Bliss[e].   HeIP-4; NoP-4; NoP-5; NoSic; NPeEn; OxBEV; TFi; TRP

   Autumn.   NoSic

   Fair Summer Droops.   NoSic

   (In a Time of Pestilence.)   OBEV

   (In Time of Pestilence.)   WoPoe

   (Litany in Time of Plague, A.)   ClHu; CtM; InoFa; NAEL-6v1; NAEL-7v1; NIL-7; NIP-4; PoPoPo; SacPr

   (Spring.)   OBEV

   "Spring, the sweet spring, is the year's pleasant king."   NAEL-6v1; NoP-4; NoP-5; NoSic; TFi; WaAnP

Summer's Night, A.   Paul Laurence Dunbar.   APN-2; NAAPv.1; NoP-4; NoP-5

Summer's Night, A.   Antonio Machado Ruiz.   SpanPo, *tr. by* James Duffy

Summers of Vietnam.   Mary Kinzie.   IllVoic

Summertime.   George Gershwin.   ReLy

Summertime and the livin' is easy.   Summertime.   George Gershwin.   ReLy

Summertime Late Show.   Edwin Torres.   HeMarv

Summing Up.   Claribel Alegría.   LoL

Summit, A. Tu Fu [*or* Du Fu]. CrYelRi, *tr. by* Sam Hamill

Summit, The. Yi Yuksa. CAMKP, *tr. by* Kyung-Ja Chun

Summit Temple, The. Li Po. TAL

Summon now the kings of the forest. Mmenson. Edward Kamau Brathwaite. OPOU

Summon the Earth (the fair Astrea's gone). Elegy upon the Death of Mrs. A. Behn, the Incomparable Astrea, An. *Unknown.* EMWP

Summoned by conscious recollection, she. Misery and Splendor. Robert Hass. BeAl; OxBoAm; PtR; VCAP

Summoning artists to participate. For John F. Kennedy; His Inauguration. Robert Frost. BLPJKO

Summoning the Recluse. Lu Chi. CCL1, *tr. by* John Frodsham

Summoning the Recluse. Tso Ssu. CCL1, *tr. by* John Frodsham

Summons. Christian Morgenstern. WoPoe, *tr. by* David R. Slavitt

Summons. David Rivard. OPRER

Summons of the Soul, The. Ch'u Yüan. WoPoe, *tr. by* David Hawkes

Summons to Town, A. Sir John Suckling. NOSC

Sumo wrestler, The. Karai Senryū. EMJL, *tr. by* Makoto Ueda

Sumptuous Destitution. Anne Carson. NoP-5

Sumptuous, luxuriously illuminated ballroom; a multitude of cavaliers and ladies, A. Skulls, The. Ivan Turgeniev. MotU, *tr. by* Isabel Florence Hapgood

Sumthin, yes's. Pointless Objects Riddle, The. Wopko Jensma. TSAP

Sun. John Blight. BMAP

Sun. Morning. Vincente Huidobro. CuPo

Sun ("Headless man walks, lives, A.") Michael Palmer. "Lines through these words, The." PFTM-2

Sun ("Write this. We have burned all their villages.") Michael Palmer. APSN; CAP-8; FTOS; NAMCP V.2; PFTM-2

Sun. Henry Rowe. OBEV

Sun. Gary Soto. TRP

Sun: "Dead darkness falls." *Unknown.* SonAtl, *tr. by* Alan Brierly and F. Murphy

Sun. Valerie Worth. NOxBChV

Sun, The. Judah Al-Harizi. BLT, *tr. by* T. Carmi

Sun, The. Hugo Ball. PFTM-1

Sun, The. John Drinkwater. NTCP

Sun, The. Czeslaw Milosz. ChAP *Fr.* World, The.

Sun, The. (LL) My friend tree. Lorine Niedecker. APT-2; NAAPv.2

Sun, The. Sweet Brown Rice and Red Bones. Lamont B. Steptoe. SpirFl

Sun, The. Francis Thompson. MoBrPo *Fr.* Ode to the Setting Sun.

Sun, The. Walter James Turner. MoBrPo

Sun, The. Sun. Valerie Worth. NOxBChV

Sun, The. Benjamin Zephaniah. Oth

Sun, The: "Each day the gold sun comes over the hill." Georg Trakl. WED, *tr. by* Robert Bly

Sun above the hills raged in the height, The. Lot and His Daughters II. Alec Derwent Hope. ChIV-1

Sun and Fog Contested, The. Emily Dickinson. Spl

Sun and Moon. Cynewulf. WoPoe *Fr.* Riddles (Exeter Book).

Sun and Moon. Mary Kinzie. FFC

Sun and rain at work together. Red-Gold Rain, The. Sacheverell Sitwell. MoBrPo

Sun and spore: root and lightning. Island. Corsino Fortes. SonAtl, *tr. by* Jose Barros, Gunga Tavares and Krystyna Ziemba

Sun and the north wind observed a traveler, The. Phoebus and Boreas. Jean de La Fontaine. WoPoe, *tr. by* Marianne Moore

Sun and the Ocean, The. Gravestone, August 8, 1968, A. Paul Goodman. BodElec

Sun and the sea have erupted, sheet-lightning, The. Paradise Regained. Hendrik Marsman. TuT, *tr. by* Michael Longley

Sun as a Spinning Top (I), The. Francis Ponge. AF, *tr. by* Serge Gavronsky

Sun at midday, distinctly warm waves, The. Anesthesia of Red Flowers. Kitahara Hakushū. CAoMJL1, *tr. by* Leith Morton

Sun, beholding so as he does pass, The. On a Fair Lady, Looking in the Glass. Richard Leigh. NOSC

Sun blazing slowly in its last hour, The. Evening, An. Robert Mezey. GeoHom

Sun breaks over the eucalyptus. Marin-An. Gary Snyder. CalPo

Sun burning down on back and loins, penetrating the skin, bathing their flanks in sweat. Edward Carpenter. CAGL *Fr.* Towards Democracy.

Sun bursts through the window, The. Poet in the Kitchen. Margit Mikes. IQMS, *tr. by* Susanne K. Walther

Sun came, The. Rothko. Del Ray Cross. FreRad

Sun, come forth! Sun. Pak Tujin. CAMKP, *tr. by* Edward W. Poitras

Sun comes up. Sun, The: Day. Bert Schierbeek. PFTM-2, *tr. by* Charles McGeehan

Sun comes up, The. Losing My Mind. Stephen Sondheim. ReLy

Sun creeps under the caves. Reader, The. Janet Lewis. APT-2

Sun, dear Haemon, in its far domain, The. Antigone. Lajos Áprily. IQMS, *tr. by* Watson Kirkconnell

Sun descended on the top of the mountain, The. Who Can Understand This? László Mécs. IQMS, *tr. by* Kenneth Thomas

Sun descending in the west, The. William Blake. ITBLP; OBEV *Fr.* Songs of Innocence.

Sun disappears, The. Tomas Tranströmer. WoBe *Fr.* Haiku.

Sun does [*or* doth] arise, The. William Blake. AmFaPo; NAEL-6v2; NAEL-7v2; NPBRoP; OxAEP-2 *Fr.* Songs of Innocence.

Sun drew near to a full moon: wine and a drinking companion!, A. Hātim Ibn Sa'īd. HiArP, *tr. by* James T. Monroe

Sun drew off at last his piercing fires, The. Witchcraft: New Style. Lascelles Abercrombie. MoBrPo

Sun drops luridly into the west, The. Augusta Davies Webster. VWP *Fr.* Circe.

Sun frets, a fat wafer falling like a trap of failed mesh, The. Hole, Where Once in Passion We Swam. Dave Jeddie Smith. NoAM

Sun goes down, and over all, The. Low Tide on Grand Pré. Bliss Carman. BrAP; IFF

Sun goes down for hours, taking more of her along, The. Lady in the Pink Mustang, The. Louise Erdrich. HATNAP; OPRER; ReTh

Sun goes down, The. Evening in Terezin, An. Eva Schulzová. INSAB

Sun going down. Sundown Blues. Raymond R. Patterson. SeSe

Sun gone for a moment, air, The. Pentecost. Martha Collins. Vesp

Sun had begun in the gloaming, The. First Snow-fall, The. James Russell Lowell. ITBLP

Sun had reached, The. Ann Yearsley. NPBRoP *Fr.* On the Inhumanity of the Slave Trade.

Sun had stooped, his westward clouds to win. Nutting. John Clare. CenSon

Sun had thrown its noontide ray, The. Noon. Lysander. Anne Batten Cristall. RWP

Sun has come, I know, The. Sun, The. Walter James Turner. MoBrPo

Sun has its lunch, The. It loosens its belt. Dandelion Bone. Boris Hristov. CSCBP, *tr. by* Georgi Belev and Lisa Sapinkopf

Sun has risen across the Mayan hills, The. New Spirit, The. Glenn Godfrey. OWABP

Sun has rung, The. Summer. Dennis Saleh. GeoHom

Sun has set in the water's clear void, The. Near the Lizhou Ferry. Wen T'ing-yün. CCL1, *tr. by* Witter Bynner

Sun has sunk 'neath yonder distant hill, The. Belshazzar's Feast. Eloise Bibb. CBWP-4

Sun hath run his course through all the Signes, The. George Wither. PBRV *Fr.* Vox Pacifica.

Sun heaves up out of the sea, The. Two-day-old Grandchild. Fergus Allen. NIrP

Sun House. Haki R. Madhubuti. ESEAA

Sun hovering a mile above the edge, The. Infidelity. C. Dale Young. LegDan

Sun I worship, The. Lines. Yonejiro (Yone) Noguchi. NAAPv.2

Sun, / in her memory, The. Lost in the Desert. Clarence Major. FTOS

Sun in the mouth of the day. Envoi. Robley, Jr. Wilson. InvLad; PBCAP

Sun in the south ranges a winter heaven, The. South Side. Robert Fitzgerald. APT-2

Sun is a huntress young, The. Indian Summer Day on the Prairie, An. Vachel Lindsay. IllVoic

SUN IS A NEGRO, THE. Bob Kaufman. ISC

Sun is blazing and the sky is blue, The. Pink Dog. Elizabeth Bishop. NALW

Sun is blue and scarlet on my page, The. Falling Asleep over the Aeneid. Robert Lowell. MoAmPo

Sun is falling as the peasant girl, The. Village Saturday, The. Giacomo Leopardi. NAWM-7v2, *tr. by* Ottavio M. Casale

Sun is folding, cars stall and rise, The. New World, The. Imamu Amiri Baraka. NoAM; NoP-4; PmAP

Sun is in Capricorn, The. Joyce Mansour. HAWP, *tr. by* Carol Cosman

Sun is in mourning, The. Be like the sun. Possessed. Charles Baudelaire. ErotSp, *tr. by* Richard Howard

Sun is lord and god, sublime, serene, The. Lake of Gaube, The. Algernon Charles Swinburne. CABP; NAEL-6v2

Sun is on the crowded street, The. Letitia Elizabeth Landon. RWP *Fr.* Scenes in London.

Sun is rising, The. Healing Song. *Unknown.* OBVE, *tr. by* Frances Densmore

Sun is set, and masked night, The. Songe 17. Robert Sidney. NoSic (Sunn is set, and masked night, The.) PBRV

Sun is setting—has set—on the Spring-green Mountain, The. Retreat of Hsieh Kung, The. Li Po. NAAPv.2, *tr. by* Florence Ayscough and Amy Lowell

Sun is shining in my backdoor, The. Myself When I Am Real. Al Young. OxAAAP

Sun is shining, the grass is green, The. White Christmas. Irving Berlin. ReLy

Sun is sinking low, The. Deep Purple. Mitchell Parish. ReLy

Sun is warm, the sky is clear, The. Stanzas Written in Dejection, Near Naples [or —December 1818, near Naples]. Percy Bysshe Shelley. ItP; NAEL-6v2; NAEL-7v2; NAWM-7v2; NoP-4; NoP-5; NPBRoP

Sun it is an arrow, The. The moon it is a bow. Inscription on an Old Tomb at Guangling. Li Po. CCL1, tr. by Elling O. Eide

Sun kept setting—setting—still, The. Emily Dickinson. APN-2

Sun King Sulking. Peter Porter. PoA 2002

Sun Lengthens. Tu Fu [or Du Fu]. CCL1, tr. by Florence Ayscough and Amy Lowell

Sun lengthens; streams, hills glorious. Sun Lengthens. Tu Fu [or Du Fu]. CCL1, tr. by Florence Ayscough and Amy Lowell

Sun lights my hand writing, The. Sun On My Hand, The. Bert Voeten. TuT, tr. by James Simmons

Sun looks o'er the mountain fair, The. Pastoral, A. F. V. N. (Franklin Verzelius Newton) Painter. ArBi

Sun makes music as of old, The. Johann Wolfgang von Goethe. Fr. Faust.

Sun Mass. Kim Sŭnghŭi. CAMKP, tr. by Anthony, Brother of Taizé

Sun May Set, The. Catullus. NoSic; OBVE Fr. Carmina.

Sun moon stars rain. (LL) Anyone lived in a pretty how town. E. E. Cummings. BrAP; ChAP; ColAP; CtM; EMP; MoAmPo; NAAL-5; NAMCP V.1; NoP-4; NoP-5; OxBoAm; PoA 2002; PoPoPo; TFi; WaAnP

Sun now angles downward, and southward, The. Fear and Trembling. Robert Penn Warren. NAMCP V.1

Sun of Auschwitz, The. Tadeusz Borowski. AF, tr. by Larry Rafferty, Meryl Natchez and Tadeusz Pioro

Sun of Auschwitz, The. Tadeusz Borowski. HP, tr. by Tadeuszt Pióro

Sun of Death. José Luis Hidalgo. RaW, tr. by Hardie St. Martin

Sun of my soul, thou Saviour dear. John Keble. SacPr

Sun of Our Existence, The. Mrs. Henry Linden. CBWP-4

Sun, of whose terrain we creatures are, The. Solar Creation. Charles Madge. OBMV

Sun on boarded windows. Abandoned Outport. Tom Dawe. Coast

Sun on hillsides, wind on seas. Desolation. Unknown. OBWVE, tr. by Aneirin Talfan Davies

Sun On My Hand, The ("Sun lights my hand writing, The.") Bert Voeten. TuT, tr. by James Simmons

Sun On My Hand, The ("Writing with the sun on my hand.") Bert Voeten. TuT, tr. by Tony Curtis

Sun on the faces. On the knotted rocks. Muriel Rukeyser. GM

Sun on the windowsill. Stanford M. Forrester. AmZen

Sun on Your Shoulder, The. John Haines. PoDa

Sun opens its lips and says to us, The. Alfonso D'Aquino. RMCMP, tr. by Rebecca Seiferle

Sun plants a foot in the pasture, The. Goree. Niyi Osundare. HBAPE

Sun pours over me, The. Loneliness. Dhabya Khamees. PoArWo, tr. by Clarissa C. Burt

Sun / right in my eye. Charles Olson. NAMCP V.2

Sun rises at the southeastern corner, The. Mulberry by the Path. Unknown. WoPoe, tr. by Arthur Waley

Sun Rises from Water. Tu Fu [or Du Fu]. CCL1, tr. by Florence Ayscough and Amy Lowell

Sun rises from water East of plaited fence. Sun Rises from Water. Tu Fu [or Du Fu]. CCL1, tr. by Florence Ayscough and Amy Lowell

Sun rises going the rounds. Tatar Songs. Unknown. EaWin, tr. by W. S. Merwin

Sun rises in south east corner of things, The. Ballad of the Mulberry Road, A. Unknown. NDACCP, tr. by Ezra Pound

Sun rises in the ancient east, The. Ode to Governor Capper, An. J. P. Dunn. VerBaPo

Sun rises in the southeast corner, The. Ballad of the Mulberry Road. Unknown. ChinPo, tr. by Ye Weilian [or Yeh Wei-lien or Wai-lim Yip]

Sun rises on a professor gargling, The. Because it is morning. Garglers, The. Mark Cox. SUP

Sun rises over eastern seas, The. Six Choruses. Tu Fu [or Du Fu]. CrYelRi, tr. by Sam Hamill

Sun rises, The. Dawn of Freedom. Roland A. Parks. OWABP

Sun rising over the mountains, The. Right Cross, The. Philip Levine. MoASP

Sun Rising, The. John Donne. BASC; CABP; ClHu; FSCP; HeIP-4; NAEL-6v1; NAEL-7v1; NIL-7; NIP-4; NoP-4; NoP-5; NOSC; PoPoPo; TFi; WaAnP; WeW-3

(Sunne Rising, The.) BrAP; PBRV

Sun rose and ravens flew, The. Economics of Gererosity, The. Judyth Hill. ICANM

Sun rushed up the sky, The; the taxi flew. Parting as Descent. John Berryman. MoAmPo

Sun sank in the thunderous sky of the town, The. Marriage. Walter James Turner. NOBAu

Sun says she is there, The. White Deer, The. Jay Wright. ESEAA

Sun Serpent. Aimé Césaire. NAWM-7v2, tr. by Gregson Davis

Sun serpent: eye beguiling my eye. Sun Serpent. Aimé Césaire. NAWM-7v2, tr. by Gregson Davis

Sun set early on the forest, The. After the Wedding Party. Matthew Rohrer. ReTh

Sun sets as the moon, The. City of the Moon, The. Kenneth Rexroth.

Sun sets, bell sounds, the mist. Over King Yu Mountain with a Friend. Ching An. CSKM, tr. by Jerome P. Seaton

Sun sets brightly—but a ruddier glow, The. Wife of Asdrubal, The. Felicia Dorothea Hemans. ViWPN

Sun sets in night, and the stars shun the day, The. Royall Tyler. NAAL-3 Fr. Contrast, The.

Sun sets in the cold without friends, The. Dusk in Winter. W. S. Merwin. BLT; OxBoAm

Sun shines bright, but sadly, The. Autumn. Priscilla Jane Thompson. CBWP-2

Sun shines bright in the old Kentucky home, The. My Old Kentucky Home. Stephen Collins Foster. APN-2

Sun shines; by the mailbox, leaves, The. Matins. Louise Glück. MoWP

Sun shines easy, sun shines gay. Louis MacNeice. Fr. Autumn Journal.

Sun shines, The. Tommies in the Train. D. H. Lawrence. PoWW

Sun shows thin through hail, wallpaper-pale, and falls, The. Soft Swimmer, Winter Swan. Robert Horan. YaYoPo

Sun sinks low, The. I. Unknown. ColAnChi Fr. Midnight Songs.

Sun sinks—evening on the blue river, The. Meditation on the Past at White Emperor City. Chen Zi'ang. CCL1, tr. by Stephen Owen

Sun slides down behind brick dust, The. Urban Renewal. Yusef Komunyakaa. RoV

Sun smudge on the smoky water. Autumn. Archibald MacLeish. IllVoic

Sun sought thy dim bed and brought forth light, The. Africa. Claude McKay. APT-1; FTtHH; NAAL-5

Sun sticks like an aspirin in the sky, The. Good Friday, Alice Liddell. Nicole Cooley. AFaM

Sun still proud, the shadow still disdained, The. (LL) Follow Thy Fair Sun[ne] [Unhappy Shadow]. Thomas Campion. NoP-4; NoP-5; NOSC; NoSic

Sun still shines, The. After Tomasito's Departure. Thomas McGrath. PoChi

Sun Storm. Tsering Wangno Dhompa. WANABP

Sun, stun me, sustain me. On Looking into Henry Moore. Dorothy Livesay. BrAP

Sun, sweet girl, hath run his year-long race. First Birthday, The. Hartley Coleridge. CenSon

Sun, that brave man, The. Brave Man, The. Wallace Stevens. SAmP

Sun that brief December day, The. Snow-Bound [or Snow-Bound] [A Winter Idyl]. John Greenleaf Whittier. APN-1; ColAP; NAAL-3; NAAL-5; NAAPv.1; TCAPo; TFi

Sun that brief December day, The. John Greenleaf Whittier. MoW Fr. Snow-Bound [or Snow-Bound] [A Winter Idyl].

Sun that silvers all the buildings here, The. Here. Mark Strand. PfSP

Sun, The: Day. Bert Schierbeek. PFTM-2, tr. by Charles McGeehan

Sun the executioner the press of the masses, The. Day and Night. Aimé Césaire. NAWM-7v2, tr. by Gregson Davis

Sun the First. Odysseus Elytis. GifTon, tr. by Olga Broumas

Sun the moon the stars the polar ice caps and the ice cream cones, The. They Loved These Things Too. Lisa Jarnot. IIR

Sun, the moon, the stars, the seas, the hills and the plains, The. Higher Pantheism, The. Alfred Tennyson. CABP; InvLi

Sun This March, The. Wallace Stevens. APT-1; HarvBoo

Sun this, The. Tom Montag. AmZen Fr. Plain Poems: A Fairwater Daybook.

Sun trailing alongside. Bird, The. Michael Savitz. FreRad

Sun Underfoot Among the Sundews, The. Amy Clampitt. NoP-4; NoP-5; OxBoAm; StAl

Sun upon the Weirdlaw Hill, The. Dreary Change, The. Sir Walter Scott. NAEL-6v2

Sun used to shine while we two walked, The. Sun Used to Shine, The. Edward Thomas. VisFro

Sun was black with judgment, and the moon, The. Femina Contra Mundum. G. K. Chesterton. OxAEP-2

Sun was down, and twilight grey, The. In the Room. James Thomson. NePenScot; OxBEV

Sun was drooling on the skulls, The. . .Somewhere the stones of the Revelation wer consuming themselves. Ink. Abdel Kader El Janabi. Eno, tr. by Pierre Joris

Sun was following me, The. Cross, The. Yun Tongju. CAMKP, tr. by Kay Richards and Steffen Richards

Sun was shining on the sea, The. Lewis Carroll. CABP; ChAP; ITBLP; NAEL-6v2; NAEL-7v2; NoAM; OBSP; OxAEP-2; TFi *Fr.* Through the Looking-Glass.

Sun was slow in arriving that morning, The. Creation. Trinity Site, New Mexico. 5:30 A.M. July 16th, 1945. Benjamin Alire Sáenz. AtGh

Sun, when he enamels day, The. Praise of a Yellow Skin, The, or An Elizabeth in Gold. John Collop. NOSC

Sun, when it shines on traffic, has a look. Noon on Alameda Street. Hildegarde Flanner. CalPo

Sun with Issues. David Colosi. FTtHH

Sun woke me this morning loud, The. True Account of Talking to the Sun at Fire Island, A. Frank O'Hara. AmFaPo; EmeKit; NAMCP V.2; OxBoAm

Sun Worshiper. Fred Voss. SUP

Sun Yat Sen Comes to Lodi. Alan Chong Lau. FTtHH

Sun—a shadow of a magnitude, A. (LL) On Seeing the Elgin Marbles. John Keats. CenSon; GSo; NAEL-6v2; NAEL-7v2; NIL-7; NIP-4

Sun-a-shine, Rain-a-fall. Valerie Bloom. NOxBChV

Sunbathing. Nancy Travis. ISC

Sun-beams of thy face, The. (LL) Bible, *O.T.* EMWP; PEW *Fr.* Psalms.

Sun-beat, salt-scrubbed, sooty wooden boards, The. Watermarks. Geoffrey Cook. Coast

Sunburned eyes. Man Is Dead, A. Claire Gebeyli. PoArWo, *tr. by* Mona Takyeddine Amyuni

Sun-crossed. Cornelia Veenendaal. PfS

Sunday. Mário de Andrade. TCLAP, *tr. by* Jack E. Tomlins

Sunday. J. C. Bloem. TuT, *tr. by* Desmond Egan

Sunday. Jorge Carrera Andrade. TCLAP, *tr. by* Muna Lee

Sunday. Antonio Deltoro. RMCMP, *tr. by* Christian Viveros-Fauné

Sunday. Timothy Liu. NeAmPo

Sunday. Achy Obejas. WiU

Sunday. Carl Phillips. GT

Sunday. Primus St. John. ISC

Sunday: "It could have been the way the Southern." Angela Shannon. BtF

Sunday. Philippe Soupault. PFTM-1

Sunday. Kathleen Spivack. PfS

Sunday A.M. Not in Manhattan. John Hollander. PoSol

Sunday A.M. so early even FM crackles church service. In the Kingdom of Perpetual Repair. Kevin Stein. IllVoic

Sunday Afternoon. Rachel Hadas. PA9/11

Sunday Afternoon. Franz Wright. AmAlph

Sunday afternoon and the water. Fording the River. Seamus Deane. PBCIP; PNI

Sunday Afternoon at Fulham Palace. Elizabeth Spires. AtGh; CAP-8

Sunday afternoon in late September, one of the last, A. Sunday Afternoon at Fulham Palace. Elizabeth Spires. AtGh; CAP-8

Sunday Afternoons. Yusef Komunyakaa. InGu; NoP-4; NoP-5

Sunday afternoons. Coyote. Jim Linebarger. TiP2

Sunday and sunlight ashen on the Square. Self Unsatisfied Runs Everywhere, The. Delmore Schwartz. PoA 2002

Sunday, and the thin lull of evening. San Buenaventura. Maurina Sherman. GeoHom

Sunday at Hampstead. James Thomson.
  (In the Train.) OBEV

Sunday at the State Hospital. David Ignatow. RaBo

Sunday Baking. Gailmarie Pahmeier. SweBea

Sunday Bear-Baiting. Robert Crowley. DiBP

Sunday Brunch. Reuben Jackson. ISC

Sunday by the Combination. Langston Hughes. APT-2

Sunday Chicken. Gwendolyn Brooks. ColAP *Fr.* Notes from the Childhood and the Girlhood.

Sunday Chimes in the City. Louise Imogen Guiney. APN-2

Sunday Dinner, A. David Bottoms. PoDa

Sunday Dreamer's Guide to Yarrow, Missouri, A. Jim Barnes. HATNAP

Sunday Evening in the Common. John Hall Wheelock. MoAmPo

Sunday Greens. Rita Dove. AmAlph; GT

Sunday heavy potlid on the boiling blood. Tristan Tzara. PFTM-1 *Fr.* Approximate Man, The.

Sunday in Great Tew. Peter McDonald. ModIr; PNI

Sunday in the Park. William Carlos Williams. NoAM *Fr.* Paterson.

Sunday in the provinces, a plaintive Norman bell-peal. Maria Luisa Spaziani. NeIt *Fr.* Star of Free Will, The.

Sunday in the snow. Fall, The. Michael Anania. IllVoic

Sunday is wringing its discoloured hands. Mild Citizen. Glyn Maxwell. HarvBoo

Sunday lamb cracks in its fat, The. Mary's Song. Sylvia Plath. AFaM; ChIV-2

Sunday, late. The winter dark already coming down. Public Broadcast. Philip Booth. PoDa

Sunday Matinee. Sybil Kollar. FFC

Sunday Morning. Robert Grenier. PmAP

Sunday Morning: "Down the road someone is practising scales." Louis MacNeice. MoBrPo; NAEL-6v2; NAEL-7v2; NIP-4; OxAEP-2; WaAnP

Sunday Morning. Robert Minhinnick. TCAWP

Sunday Morning. David Ray. AllShUp

Sunday Morning. Anne Rouse. NeBl

Sunday Morning. Wallace Stevens. APT-1; BBASP; ColAP; EMP; HarvBoo; HeIP-4; MoAmPo; NAAL-5; NAAPv.2; NAMCP V.1; NAWM-7v2; NIL-7; NIP-4; NoAM; NoP-4; NoP-5; OxBoAm; PoA 2002; PoPoPo; SAmP; SoSe-8; TCAPo; TFi; TRP; WaAnP

Sunday morning. A summery. Figures, The. Robert Patrick Dana. PoDa

Sunday Morning Apples. Hart Crane. HarvBoo; ItP

Sunday morning at the marina. Common Prayer. Lynn Ungar. AFaM

Sunday Morning in Old San Juan. Julio Marzán. PueRic

Sunday Morning, 1950. Irene McKinney. PBCAP

Sunday Morning Services. Michael S. Smith. ArBi

Sunday Morning Through Binoculars. Eamon Grennan. PBCIP

Sunday Morning Walk. Vern Rutsala. NevBe

Sunday mornings I would reach. My Father's Hats. Mark Irwin. P180

Sunday News, The. Dana Gioia. WeW-3

Sunday night, 2:00 A.M. Night Call. George Young. BloBone

Sunday Papers. Charles Simic. WaAnP

Sunday Park. Gwyneth Lewis. TCAWP

Sunday Piece. Jules Laforgue. WoPoe, *tr. by* William Jay Smith

Sunday Shopping. George Scarbrough. PoDa

Sunday shuts down on this twentieth-century evening. Boy with His Hair Cut Short. Muriel Rukeyser. NALW; NAMCP V.2; NoAM; NoP-5

Sunday Skaters. Mary Jo Salter. MoASP

Sunday swallows edged the sky, The. Omnibus, The. Vera Bulich. ARWW, *tr. by* Catriona Kelly

Sunday, Tarzan in His Hammock. Lewis Buzbee. TWF

Sunday the Power Went Off, The. Duncan Bush. TCAWP

Sunday up the River. James Thomson.
  Gifts. OBEV
  Wine of Love, The. OBEV

Sunday Visit. Antigone Kefala. BMAP

Sunday was calm and airy. Stentor and Mourning. Alan Dugan. PWW2

Sunday Water. Phyllis Webb.
  "Ten white blooms on the sundeck." IFF

Sundays. Seitu J. Hart. BRtP

Sunday's bad. Why do you bother. Too Bad. Gig Ryan. NOBAu

Sundays of Satin-Legs Smith, The. Gwendolyn Brooks. SeSe

Sundays too my father got up early. Those Winter Sundays. Robert Earl Hayden. AmFaPo; APT-2; CAP-8; ChAP; ColAP; CtM; ESEAA; GoPo; ISC; MakPoe; NAAL-5; NAMCP V.2; NIL-7; NIP-4; NoAM; NoP-4; NoP-5; OxAAAP; OxBoAm; PoPoPo; RaBo; SoSe-8; SSLK; StAl; TFi; WaAnP; WeW-3

Sundays we cranked old bikes up hills. Eight-Mile Bike Ride, The. Philip Schultz. ArBi

Sunder me from my bones, O sword of God. Sword of Surprise, The. G. K. Chesterton. MoBrPo; SacPr

Sunderland Children, The. Alice Thompson Meynell. NALW

Sunderland Nights. Peter Armstrong. PML

Sundial. Gabriel Zaid. TCLAP, *tr. by* Adrian Hernandez

Sun-Dial, The. Adelaide Crapsey. APT-1; NAAPv.2

Sundial, The. Austin Dobson. OBGa

Sundial, The. Douglas Dunn. NPeEn

Sundown. Léonie Adams. MoAmPo

Sundown / at Walden Pond. Redwings. 3-4-00. Jack Collom. BAP-04

Sundown Blues. Raymond R. Patterson. SeSe

Sundown on the sand, and your shadow. Air Dagger. Jack Marshall. GeoHom

Sundown splendid and serene / Death, The. (LL) W. E. Henley. MoBrPo; OBEV *Fr.* Echoes.

Sundry Notes. Nguyễn Chí Thiện.
  "Party holds you down and you lie still, The." VCWP

Sunflakes. Frank Asch. NTCP

Sun-flames of springtime, The. March in Transylvania. Lajos Áprily. IQMS, *tr. by* Adam Makkai

Sunflower. Mack David. ReLy

Sunflower. Rolf Jacobsen. RaBo; WED, *tr. by* Robert Bly

Sunflower. Rolf Jacobsen. IJHIL, *tr. by* Olav Grinde

Sun-Flower, The. Dora Greenwell. EroLit; VWP
  (Sunflower, The.) PEW

Sunflower! gross of leaf and porous. Wild Sunflower. Yvor Winters. APT-2

Sunflower Sutra. Allen Ginsberg. GM; NAMCP V.2; PoPoPo; VCAP

Sunflowers are sprouting in the tropical livingroom. Quilt. George Elliott Clarke. OpeFie

Sunflowers at Prime. Tim Lilburn. OpeFie

Sunflowers, Wyoming. Deborah Slicer. RWB

Sung Impromptu. Yi Kyubo. CATKP, tr. by Kevin O'Rourke

Sung in a Graveyard. Anna Wickham. ItWoWo

Sun-god was reclining on a couch of rosy shells, The. Sunset Picture. Henrietta Cordelia Ray. CBWP-3

Sung's line and state. (LL) Wide, Ho? / A reed will cross its flow. Unknown. NDACCP; OBVE, tr. by Ezra Pound

Sun-Hunters, The. Mark O'Connor. NOBAu

Sunk in slate-gray plastic panels. Ancestral Echoes/Rap Music. Charles Lynch. SwNoth

Sunken Gardens (Huntington, IN), The. Shari Miller Wagner. ACAMVP

Sunken Gold. Eugene Lee-Hamilton. GSo

Sunken Sailor. Francis Claiborne Mason. YaYoPo

Sunken Ship, The. Salma Khadra Jayyusi. PoArWo, tr. by Suneet Chopra

Sunland. Edmond Jabès. YaTCFP, tr. by Keith Waldrop

Sunlicht still on me, you row'd in clood, The. At My Father's Grave. Hugh MacDiarmid. HarvBoo; InoFa; NePenScot

Sunlight. Seamus Heaney. BeAl; ModIr; WaAnP Fr. Mossbawn.

Sunlight alights and plays by my baby's sleeping head. For Baby. Kim Namjo. CAMKP, tr. by David R. McCann and Hyunjae Yee Sallee

Sunlight beings to fade. Longing. Li Po. CCL1, tr. by Arthur Cooper

Sunlight cast back enters the village lanes. Autumn Day. Geng Wei. CCL1, tr. by Stephen Owen

Sunlight climbs the snowpeak. Late October Camping in the Sawtooths. Gary Snyder. BLT

Sunlight dried the last small patches of moisture. In Ferrara. Ken Bolton and John Jenkins. BMAP

Sunlight folds back pages of quiet shadows. At Hans Christian Andersen's Birthplace, Odense, Denmark. Maurice Lindsay. EdScPo

Sunlight in a, The. At the Faucet of June. William Carlos Williams. APT-1

Sunlight in the alleys. There is always a window. Puzzle Pieces. Chana Bloch. ExTi

Sunlight on the Garden, The. Louis MacNeice. HarvBoo; NAEL-6v2; NAEL-7v2; NAMCP V.1; NoP-4; NoP-5; NPeEn; OxAEP-2; PNI; TRP; WaAnP; WoPoe

Sunlight on the ice sheet a shower of rain driven before it a rainbow then sun. Neanderthal Funeral. Martin Mooney. NIrP

Sunlight one Sunday afternoon, and dust. First Time at the Wheel. Kurt Brown. NevBe

Sun-light recedes on the mountains, in long gold shafts. Interlude. Maxwell Bodenheim. APT-1

Sunlight. Rustling blinds. Shadows, The. Jorge Guillén. RaW, tr. by Charles Guenther

Sunlight Showers Down in Sheets. Chông Hwajin. EcSo, tr. by Julie C. Park

Sunlight steams the river stones. Waterfall at Lu-shan. Li Po. CrYelRi, tr. by Sam Hamill

Sunlight streaming on Incense Stone kindles violet smoke. Viewing the Waterfall at Mount Lu. Li Po. ColAnChi, tr. by Burton Watson

(Sunlight streaming on Incense Stone kindles violet.) ChAP

Sunlight streams from the cloudless southern sky. Rifle Range: Louisiana. Charles E. Butler. PWW2

Sunlight strikes a glass of grapefruit juice. Morning in the Hospital Solarium. Sylvia Plath. BodElec

Sunlight was falling, The. A part. New Year's: A Short Pantoum. Greg Williamson. NoP-5

Sunlit clouds navigated, The. Badger, The. Gwynn Ap Gwilym. BBMWP, tr. by Grahame Davies

Sunn is set, and masked night, The. Robert Sidney. See Sun is set, and masked night, The.

Sunne may set and rise, The. Catullus. NoSic; OBVE Fr. Carmina.

Sunne Rising, The. John Donne. See Sun Rising, The.

Sunny Afternoon Dream, The. Giovanna Pollarolo. TANSG, tr. by Marjorie Agosin

Sunny afternoons. Sunny Afternoon Dream, The. Giovanna Pollarolo. TANSG, tr. by Marjorie Agosin

Sunny Disposish. Ira Gershwin. ReLy

Sunny Gale. Hugh MacDiarmid. FaBoVe

Sunny Prestatyn. John Davies. TCAWP

Sunny Prestatyn. Philip Larkin. NAMCP V.2; NoAM; OBCoV

Sunny shaft did I behold, A. Samuel Taylor Coleridge. OBEV Fr. Zapolya.

Sunny Side Up. Lew Brown, B. G. DeSylva and Ray Henderson. ReLy

Sunrise. Saint-Pol Roux. YaTCFP, tr. by Mary Ann Caws

Sunrise: "Blood stolen from my body before dawn." Yi Hyangji. EcSo, tr. by Catherine J. Kim

Sunrise 7:18, sunset 7:23: we are approaching that point. Daphne Marlatt. NLPA Fr. Touch to My Tongue.

Sunrise at the octagonal hut. At the Teahouse, 6 am. Holly Hughes. AmZen

Sunrise at the southeast corner. Mulberry up the Lane. Unknown. ColAnChi, tr. by Anne Birrell

Sunrise brightens my autumn window. Traveler's Pavilion. Tu Fu [or Du Fu]. CrYelRi, tr. by Sam Hamill

Sunrise Comes to Second Avenue. Thylias Moss. TRP

Sunrise on the River. Kalamu ya Salaam. SpirFl Fr. New Orleans Haiku.

Sunrise runs for Both, The. Emily Dickinson. SWaP

Sunrise Sequence. Unknown. NOBAu Fr. Dulngulg Song Cycle, The.

Sun-Rise: Sonnet, A. Ann Radcliffe. CenSon

Sunrise, Sunset. Sheldon Harnick. ReLy

Sunrise with Sea Monster. Charles North. FTOS; NYP2

Sunrising and sunsetting evermore. (LL) Another and another and another. James Henry. NPeEn; OxBEV

Sun's accomplice, the tree. / Maurice. (LL) Dusting. Rita Dove. AmAlph; ESEAA; HeIP-4; NAMCP V.2; PoA 2002

(Maurice.) (LL) NoP-4; PoPoPo

Sun's bright orb, declining all serene, The. William Falconer. OxAEP-1 Fr. Shipwreck, The.

Sun's Darling, The. Thomas Dekker and others.

(Song.) NOSC

Suns eye gleams on the burnt black prairie, The. Confluence. John Knoepfle. IllVoic

Sun's fair rays are shining, The. Yun Sŏndo. CATKP; WoPoe Fr. Angler's Calendar, The.

Suns in the Night of the Massacre. Aziz Samawi. IrPoTo, tr. by Alex Bellem

Sun's lying down, The. Little Love Kiss. Lenous Surprice. OGAHCP, tr. by Boadiba and Jack Hirschman

Suns of the world may stain when heaven's sun staineth. (LL) William Shakespeare. NAEL-7v1; NIL-7; NIP-4; NoP-4; NoP-5; NoSic; OxAEP-1; TFi; WeW-3 Fr. Sonnets.

Sun's return is magical, The. Carnival. Primus St. John. GT

Suns, she is all in all, I stood on a sea, The. Sonnet. İlhan Berk. NaPG, tr. by Talat Sait Halman

Sunset. Joseph Ceravolo. FTOS

Sunset ("Stinging / gold swarms.") E. E. Cummings. MoAmPo

Sunset. John Cope. GeoH

Sunset. Mary Weston Fordham. CBWP-2

Sunset. Juan Ramón Jiménez. SpanPo, tr. by Kate Flores

Sunset ("How beautiful the river is in spring.") Tu Fu [or Du Fu]. CrYelRi, tr. by Sam Hamill

Sunset ("Sunset glitters on the beads.") Tu Fu [or Du Fu]. BLT, tr. by Kenneth Rexroth

Sunset Along U.S. Highway 90 Between Langtry and Sanderson. David C. Yates. TiP2

Sunset and evening star. Crossing the Bar. Alfred Tennyson. BrAP; BRP; ChIV-2; ClHu; HeIP-4; InoFa; ITBLP; NAEL-6v2; NAEL-7v2; NoP-4; NoP-5; OBEV; SacPr; SoSe-8; TFi; TWF

Sunset and silence! A man: around him earth savage, earth broken. Plower, The. Padraic Colum. MoBrPo

Sunset at Twin Lake. Anita Endrezze. HATNAP

Sunset at Wellfleet. Jean Valentine. YaYoPo

Sunset. Blue peaks vanish in dusk. Snow on Lotus Mountain. Liu Ch'ang-ch'ing. CCL1, tr. by Kenneth Rexroth

Sunset by the lake. Lake Murry. Pinkie Gordon Lane. GT

Sunset fades, and from the little hill, The. Konstantin Iakovlevich Vanshenkin. TCRusP, tr. by Daniel Weissbort

Sunset fires the San Pedro Valley. Of Simple Intent. Pamela Uschuk. AtGh

Sunset flames over the city, The. Dorothy Hewett. BMAP Fr. Summer Solstice.

Sunset from Omaha Hotel Window. Carl Sandburg. APT-1

Sunset glitters on the beads. Sunset. Tu Fu [or Du Fu]. BLT, tr. by Kenneth Rexroth

Sunset in the Tropics. James Weldon Johnson. APT-1; NAMCP V.1 Fr. Down by the Carib Sea.

Sunset knocks the edge from the. Green Eyed Monsters of the Valley Dusk, The. Sherley Anne Williams. GeoHom

Sunset like the grasshopper flying. (LL) Ezra Pound. APT-1; OBMV Fr. Cantos.

Sunset nails the lip of a building. Harlem: Neo-Image. Kevin Powell. AmPoNex

Sunset of the City / Kathleen Eileen, A. Gwendolyn Brooks. GT

Sunset on Calvary. Unknown. NAEL-6v1; NAEL-7v1

Sunset on the Bayou. Sybil Pittman Estess. TiP2

Sunset on the River. Corinth Morter-Lewis. OWABP

Sunset Over Llŷn. Sion Aled. BBMWP, tr. by Grahame Davies

Sunset Picture. Henrietta Cordelia Ray. CBWP-3

Sunset pours its gold through jade-colored clouds. To the Tune: Eternal Joy. Li Ch'ing-chao. CrYelRi, *tr.* by Sam Hamill

Sunset Reverie. Edney Cain. OWABP

Sunset Stripping: Visiting L.A. Michael Lassell. WiU

Sunset: the blaze of evening burns. Hospital Evening. Gwen Harwood. EmeKit

Sunset, the cheapest of all picture-shows. Frederiksted, Dusk. Derek Walcott. NoAM

Sunset was thick with the feel of rain. Miscellaneous Poem on Rural Life. Liu Yin. ColAnChi, *tr.* by John Timothy Wixted

Sunsets. Carl Sandburg. MoAmPo

Sunset's moulded cloud, A. William Allingham. IrLP

Sunsetting giant climbs the sirens, A. Hungerdance, The. Menke Katz. Prolet, *tr.* by Amelia Glaser

Sunshine. Macel Aguilar. BeDoSh

Sunshine after Cloud. Josephine D. Henderson Heard. CBWP-4

Sunshine and shadow play amid the trees. July. Henrietta Cordelia Ray. CBWP-3

Sunshine on some ample lips. Dream of Mango. Rohan B. Preston. BtF

Sunstone. Octavio Paz. *tr.* by Eliot Weinberger
    "And the banquet, the exile, the first crime." PoetW, *tr.* by Eliot Weinberger
    "Better the crime, / the suicides of lovers, the incest committed." PoetW, *tr.* by Eliot Weinberger
    "Crystal willow, a poplar of water, A." WoPoe, *tr.* by Eliot Weinberger
    "Face I can see to see my face, A." WoPoe, *tr.* by Eliot Weinberger
    "Was it I making plans / for the summer—and for all the summers." PoetW, *tr.* by Eliot Weinberger

Sunstone. Octavio Paz.
    "All is transformed and is sacred." BLPSL, *tr.* by Rene de Costa, Rigas Kappatos and Eleni Paidoussi
    "I travel your body as I would travel the world." BLPSL, *tr.* by Rene de Costa, Rigas Kappatos and Eleni Paidoussi
    "Madrid, 1937, / in the Plaza del Angel the women." BLPSL, *tr.* by Rene de Costa, Rigas Kappatos and Eleni Paidoussi

Sunstroke. Blaga Dimitrova. CSCBP, *tr.* by Georgi Belev and Lisa Sapinkopf

Sun-Struck Eagle, The. Eleanor Percy Lee and Catherine Anne Warfield. SWaP

Sunstruck spray sifts back breakwater waves, A. Pavilion on the Pier, The. Byron Vazakas. APT-2

Sun-swept beaches with a light wind blowing. Unchanging, The. Sara Teasdale. APT-1

Sunt Lacrimae Rerum et Mentem Mortalia Tangunt. R. P. Blackmur. APT-2

Sunt Leones. Stevie Smith. GoPo; NAMCP V.1; NoAM

Sunworshippers. Cathy Song. NAMCP V.2

Super High. Evan X. Hyde. OWABP; PML

Superabundance, an excess, a plethora of greetings, A. For Your Birthday, Philip: And upon the Occasion of Becoming Abbot of the Hartford Street Zen Center. Joanne Kyger. WANABP

Superb and sole, upon a plumèd spray. Mocking Bird, The. Sidney Lanier. APN-2; TCAPo

Superhighway elegy in a pink convertible / It was 1956. Western CIV, 4 and 5. Joan Retallack. FTOS

Superior. Gerardo Deniz. RMCMP, *tr.* by Mónica de la Torre

Superior, as a singer from Lesbos to those of other lands. Sappho. SaLy, *tr.* by Diane Rayor

Superliminare. George Herbert. NOSC

Superman Is Dead. Rafael Campo. ReTh

Supermarket. Peter Meinke. PBCAP

Supermarket in California, A. Allen Ginsberg. BrAP; CAGL; FaBoA; GPTC; HeIP-4; MotU; NAAL-5; NAMCP V.2; NIL-7; NoAM; NoP-5; OxBoAm; PmAP; PtR; ReTh; TFi; WeW-3

Supernal. Alice Fulton. MAAN

Supernatural Love. Gjertrud Schnackenberg. MakPoe; NoAM; NoP-4; NoP-5; StAl; VCAP

97: A Superscription. Dante Gabriel Rossetti. BrAP; GSo; NAEL-6v2; NAEL-7v2; NoP-4 *Fr.* House of Life, The.

Superstition, more destructive still. Mary Robinson. RWP *Fr.* Progress of Liberty, The.

Superstitions. Maggie Pogue Johnson. CBWP-4

Superstition's Dream. John Clare.
    "That time was come, or seemed as it was come." NPBRoP

Supine the Wanderer lay. William Wordsworth. NOBRP *Fr.* Excursion, The.

Supper. Yousif al-Sa'igh. IrPoTo, *tr.* by Saadi A. Simawe

Supper. Andrew Hudgins. CAP-8

Supper: House Outside Town. Gennady Aygi. WoBe, *tr.* by Peter France

Supper Time. Irving Berlin. ReLy

Supper time / I should set the table. Supper Time. Irving Berlin. ReLy

Supple / slender. Tyger, Tyger. Isabel Meyrelles. SurWo, *tr.* by Penelope Rosemont

Supple Wreath of Myrtle, A. Robert Hass. RoV

Supplement of an Imperfect Copy of Verses of Mr. Will. Shakespeare's, by the Author, A. Sir John Suckling. CavPo

Supplementary to the account. Wrong Side of the Door, The. Ray DiPalma. FTOS

Suppliant, The. Georgia Douglas Johnson. NAAPv.2

Supplication. Constantine P. Cavafy. BLT, *tr.* by Rae Dalven

Supplication, A. George Croly. SacPr

Support act, The. Nigger and Some Poofters, A. Nigel Roberts. BMAP

Suppose an Eyes. Gertrude Stein. PFTM-1

Suppose, for instance. Text of Evening, The. Eric Tretheway. Coast

Suppose Gauguin had never seen Tahiti. Suppose the. Wheatfield Under Clouded Sky. Campbell McGrath. NeAmPo

Suppose he had been Tabled at thy Teates. Bible, *N.T.* ChIV-2; NOSC *Fr.* St. Luke.

Suppose he had been tabled at thy teats. Luke 11: Blessed Be the Paps Which Thou Hast Sucked. Richard Crashaw. NAEL-7v1

Suppose I can convince myself this world. Summons. David Rivard. OPRER

Suppose I Make a Timepiece of Humanity. Velemir Khlebnikov. AF, *tr.* by Paul Schmidt

Suppose it is Achilles to be told. Robert Kelly. WANABP *Fr.* Threads.

Suppose it is within a gate which open is open at the hour of closing summer that is to say so. Suppose an Eyes. Gertrude Stein. PFTM-1

Suppose one thing. For Those Who Always Fear the Worst. *Unknown.* NBLV

Suppose the dead can't help looking back. Crossing. Nin Andrews. AmZen

Suppose the stars. Yonejiro (Yone) Noguchi. CalPo

Suppose the stars. Yonejiro (Yone) Noguchi. NAAPv.2 *Fr.* Japanese Hokkus.

Suppose there is no heaven and no hell. All Souls'. Dana Gioia. StAl

Suppose there is something. Black Women with Jewish Names. James Coleman. BtF

Suppose we could see evil with such clarity we wouldn't hesitate. Theodicy. Kim Addonizio. LiTh

Suppose we could telephone the dead. Hotel de Dream. Jane Cooper. ExTi

Suppose you screeve? or go cheap-jack? Villon's Straight Tip to All Cross Coves. W. E. Henley. OxAEP-2

Suppose you slosh gin deep into a glass. Cheers. Charles McDonald. NLP

Suppose you telephone your own answering. Allan Kaprow. WhBo

Suppose you want to write. Adrienne Rich. LoL *Fr.* North American Time.

Suppose you were dreaming about your family. Benign Neglect / [West Point,] Mississippi, 1970. Primus St. John. EGAG

Suppose you're a solo native here. Solo Native. Thomas Lux. AmAlph

Supposed Dancer, The. Roy Fisher. HarvBoo

Supposed to Be Written By One On Whom the Death of an Excellent Woman Has Forced the Conviction of a Future State. Charles Tennyson Turner.
    1. CenSon

Supposed To Be Written by Werter. Charlotte Smith. CenSon; RWP

Supposing all the things on the playground. On a Cold Autumn Day. Bonnie Nims. TLR

Supposing that one walks out into the air. Kenneth Koch. OBCoV *Fr.* Fresh Air.

Supposing the wildlife became a person. Postcard Element in Winter, The. Charles North. NYP2

Supposing you were I and I were you. You, I, Love, Beauty, Earth. Rita Joe. Coast

Supremacy. Edwin Arlington Robinson. APN-2; NoAM

Supreme Hour, The. Viktor Aleksandrovich Sosnora. ItGoST, *tr.* by F. D. Reeve

Supreme love poet through the vale. Three English Poets and England. Waldo Williams. BBMWP, *tr.* by Anthony Conran

Supreme Savior of Sinners. Rāmprasād Sen. SinGod, *tr.* by Rachel Fell McDermott

Supremely individual, flamboyant, proud. Sonnet One. Arthur Nortje. TSAP

Supremes, The. Mark Jarman. GeoHom; SwNoth

Suprised by this turn of events. (LL) Man Then Suddenly Stops Moving, A. Alberto A. Ríos. NAMCP V.2; NoAM

Sur des traces oubliées, dans des lieux innommés. Sur des traces oubliées. Abdelwahab Meddeb. YaTCFP

Sur la route de san romano. André Breton. YaTCFP

Sur les pas de la lune. Philippe Jaccottet. YaTCFP

Sur mon dédain du monde. Par la fenêtre ouverte à demi. Léon Damas. YaTCFP

Sur nos têtes. Vertical. Michel Leiris. YaTCFP

SURcenSURE. Marcel Duchamp. PFTM-1

Sure, a little bit of shrapnel fell from out the sky one day. *Unknown.* OBCoV *Fr.* Soldiers' Songs of the First World War.

Sure he can sling that ball. This Is What Happens When You Let Hamlet Play Quarterback. Jack Conway. IaFF

Sure, if those Babel-builders had thought good. On the Babel-Builders. Francis Quarles. ChIV-1

Sure It was so. Man in those early days. Corruption. Henry Vaughan. NAEL-6v1; NAEL-7v1; NOSC

Sure Jo & I used to spend hours doin' it. Boys' Own. Brendan Cleary. NeBl

Sure John and I are more than quit. (LL) Epigram, An: "To John I ow'd great obligation." Matthew Prior. OBVE; OxBEV

Sure, Lord, there is enough in Thee to dry. Sonnet. George Herbert. NOSC

Sure, Saul as little looked to be a king. On Saul and David. Francis Quarles. ChIV-1

Sure the last end. Robert Blair. OxAEP-1 *Fr.* Grave, The.

Sure there are Poets which did never dream. Cooper's Hill. Sir John Denham. CABP; PBRV

Sure there are some differences. I'm no virgin. Self Portrait as Nancy Drew, Girl Sleuth. Kristy Nielsen. ReTh

Sure, there are times when one cries with acidity. To An Undiscerning Critic. Sir Arthur Conan Doyle. OBCoV

Sure there is lots of trouble. Up and Doing. Douglas Malloch. ITBLP

Sure thing / I'm a spirit! / see me becoming visible? Seven Songs and Song Pictures. *Unknown.* PFTM-1

Sure thou didst flourish once! and many springs. Timber, The. Henry Vaughan. OBEV

Sure, to the mansions of the blest. To a Bereaved Mother. John Quincy Adams. SacPr

Sure we have poets, that did never dream. Sir John Denham. *See* Sure there are Poets which did never dream.

Sure, You Can Ask Me a Personal Question. Iwan Llwyd. BBMWP, *tr. by* Grahame Davies

Surely! Sir Fantasy. Ssu-ma Hsiang-ju. ColAnChi, *tr. by* Burton Watson

Surely among a rich man's flowering lawns. William Butler Yeats. OBGa *Fr.* Meditations in Time of Civil War.

Surely God thought this would be a moment. Annunciation, The. David Starkey. Vesp

Surely he undertakes. Frank Templeton Prince. PoCho *Fr.* Not a *Paris Review* Interview.

Surely I heard a voice—surely my name. Dreams. Caroline Elizabeth Norton. NPBRoP

Surely, I suffer on your account. Once More to Lilla. Mihály Csokonai Vitéz. IQMS, *tr. by* Adam Makkai

Surely that moan is not the thing. Fog-Horn. W. S. Merwin. CAP-8

Surely the air must still have human warmth. Air. Jennifer Maiden. BMAP

Surely They're Just So Large. Irving Feldman. VCAP *Fr.* All of Us Here.

Surely they're just so large as their burdens allow. Irving Feldman. VCAP *Fr.* All of Us Here.

Surely this face—generic, blank. Reconstructed Face. Rachel Loden. LiTh

Surely you paused at this roadside oasis. Garage in Co. Cork, A. Derek Mahon. PBCIP

Surely You Remember. Dahlia Ravikovitch. VCWP

Surely you would not ask me to have known. Question to Life. Patrick Kavanagh. MoBrPo

Surf. Dylan Iorwerth. BBMWP *Fr.* Sand.

Surf. Lillian Morrison. NTCP

Surf. Kiyoko Nagase. ItWoWo, *tr. by* Kijima Hajime

Surf Motel, The. Stephen Knight. NeBl

Surf washed up its rows of green, The. Continent's Edge. Mark Wunderlich. WiU

Surface. Donald Hall. PfSP

Surface of the pond was mostly green, The. Lotus Flowers, The. Ellen Bryant Voigt. CAP-8; WaAnP

Surface removed, A. Or an "I" here, as in *I*. Applications of. Laura Mullen. IAoNAP

Surface, The. Jorie Graham. HarvBoo; NAMCP V.2; NoP-5

Surfaces. Harvena Richter. ICANM

Surfaces. Kay Ryan. ExTi

Surfaces serve. Surfaces. Kay Ryan. ExTi

Surfers. Robert Minhinnick. TCAWP

Surfing on the dance floor. Trickster 4 (for Sister Patra). Kwame Dawes. WaCA

Surge, The. Molly Peacock. PasH

Surge of spirit that goes with using an axe, The. Felling a Tree. Ivor Gurney. FaBoVe

Surged like language into my thumb. (LL) Horse: "First horse I ever saw, The." Michael Waters. NevBe; UrbNat

Surgeon's Knife, The. Eliza Cook. VWP

   "There are hearts—stout hearts,—that own no fear." VerBaPo

Surgeons must be very careful. Emily Dickinson. ItP; SAmP; TCAPo

Surgery. Kenneth Pitchford. CAGL

Surgery has cut me back. Privacy. Lionel Abrahams. TSAP

Surgical Moves. Rachel Wetzsteon. AmPoNex; ExTi

Surplice, The. David Scott. NLP

Surplus. Abigail Child. FTOS

Surplus. Rebecca Reynolds. AmPoNex

Surprise. Scott Cairns. UpMys

Surprise. Anthony Cronin. IrLP

Surprise in the Peninsula, A. Fleur Adcock. EmeKit; MoWP

Surprise, Surprise. *Unknown.* EroLit, *tr. by* Derek Parker

Surprise, they say in the dark. Lilies at Night. Beckian Fritz Goldberg. AmAlph

Surprised by joy—impatient as the Wind. Surprised by Joy. William Wordsworth. CABP; CenSon; GSo; NAEL-6v2; NAEL-7v2; NoP-4; NoP-5; NPBRoP; OxBSo; TFi

Surprising sunshine has ruled more than a hundred days. Frozen Drought. Peter Davison. MoW

Surprisingly easy to cook a meal now. Turning Fifty. Thomas William Shapcott. BMAP

Surreal Love Life. Gene Frumkin. ICANM

Surrealism, *n.* Psychic automatism in its pure state. André Breton. PFTM-1 *Fr.* Manifesto of Surrealism (1924).

Surrender. Amitiyah Elayne Hyman. BtF

Surrender. William Larsen. WhBo

Surrender. "Rachel." FIT, *tr. by* Robert Friend

Surrender, The. Henry King, Bishop of Chichester. NOSC

Surrender to Christ. Frederic William Henry Myers. SacPr

Surrendered Names. Gerald Vizenor. HATNAP

Surrendering the joys that they condemn. (LL) Geoffrey Hill. NAEL-6v2; NoAM; NoP-5 *Fr.* Lachrimae; or Seven Tears Figured in Seven Passionate Pavans.

Surrexit Dominus de sepulchro. (LL) Done is a battell [*or* battle] on the dragon blak [*or* black]. William Dunbar. NePenScot; NPeEn; OxBEV; SacPr

Surrey with the Fringe on Top, The. Oscar Hammerstein, II. ReLy

Surrogate Mothers. Andrea M. Wren. InTrad

Surrounded by bric-à-brac—mugs of stale coffee and old manuals—Lawrence works at his desk. Perl Poem. Leontia Flynn. NIrP

Surrounded by eunuchs and limp as a tissue. Martial. WoPoe *Fr.* Epigrams.

Surrounded by my shields, am. Song of the Self: The Grandmother. Alma Villanueva. HW

Surrounded by scientists in a faculty. Homage to the New World. Michael S. Harper. ESEAA

Surrounded by the gentle sound. Song 3. Baldomero Garcilaso de la Vega. SpanPo, *tr. by* Frances Fletcher

Surrounding boxes alarm you, The. Sojourners, The. Bino A. Realuyo. ReBoTo

Sursum Corda. Ralph Waldo Emerson. APN-1

Surveillances. Tom Paulin. PNI

Survey of Literature. John Crowe Ransom. AmWit; NBLV

Surveying Britain's battled coast. Servant of the House. "Sagittarius." UV

Surveyor climbs a stonewall into woods, The. Surface. Donald Hall. PfSP

Surveyor's Story, The. Fergus Allen. NIrP

Survival, The. Edmund Charles Blunden. OBEV; OBMV

Survival 1. Chiqui Vicioso. TANSG, *tr. by* Emma Jane Robinett

Survival 2. Chiqui Vicioso. TANSG, *tr. by* Emma Jane Robinett

Survival: Infantry. George Oppen. AmWaPo; FTOS; NAMCP V.1; PWW2

Survival Motion: Notice. Melvin E. Brown. ISC

Survivalist. Carolyne Wright. LiTh

Survivals. Ruth Behar. MirDau

Surviving. Gail Tremblay. FiBr

Surviving. James Welch. HATNAP

Surviving is keeping your eyes open. Portraits of Tudor Statesmen. U. A. Fanthorpe. EmeKit; OxBEV

Survivor. Mike Jenkins. TCAWP

Survivor. Roger McGough. OBCoV

Survivor, The. Thomas Dorsett. BloBone

Survivor, The [to B. V.]. Primo Levi. HP, *tr. by* Ruth Feldman

Survivor, The. Tadeusz Rózewicz. BeAl; HP; PoAgWa; PoSu, *tr. by* Adam Czerniawski

Survivor of that time, that place. (LL) Requiem: "No foreign sky protected me." Anna Andreyevna Akhmatova. AF; PoetW; WoPoe, *tr. by* Max Hayward and Stanley Kunitz

Survivor, Walking. Stephen Sandy. PoA 2002

Survivors. Sterling Plumpp. UrbNat

Survivors, The. Tracey Herd. BeAl; NeBl

Survivors will be human. (LL) Deathwatch. Michael S. Harper. NAAL-5; NAMCP V.2

Survivors—Found. Joan Murray. PLBUT

"Susaddah!" exclaimed Ibsen. Edmund Clerihew Bentley. OBCoV *Fr.* Clerihews.

Susan B.'s voice: We cannot retrace our steps, going forward may be the. Gertrude Stein. PFTM-2 *Fr.* Mother of Us All, The.

Susanna. Stephen Collins Foster. *See* Oh! Susanna.

Susanna and the Elders. Adelaide Crapsey. APT-1; NAAPv.2; OxBoAm; TCAPo

Susanna: girl and bride. Man-Fate, The. William Everson. NoAM

Susanna is drenched. Anne Portugal. SCFWP *Fr.* Bath, The.

Susannah [(*Time of the Gingham Rooster,* collage by Romare Bearden)]. Thulani Davis. GT

Susannah Bathing. Ödön Palasovszky. IQMS, *tr. by* Kenneth McRobbie

Susans. Susan Clements. UnSA

Sushi. Paul Muldoon. CABP

Susie Asado. Gertrude Stein. APT-1; ASA; NAAPv.2; NAMCP V.1; NoAM

Susie Wong was at the Starlight Haven. Starlight Haven. Shirley Lim. UnSA

Susie's galoshes. Galoshes. Rhoda Warner Bacmeister. NTCP

Susie's Lament for Johnny. Mihály Csokonai Vitéz. IQMS, *tr. by* Anthony Edkins

Suspect under section a1 special. Wopko Jensma. TSAP

Suspects his Constancy. Mary Robinson. CenSon; RWP

Suspend a violin with a long rope. Event for Late Afternoon. Mieko Shiomi. WhBo

Suspended Elegy, A. M. S. C. Okolo. NeNiPo

Suspended from / your animal form. Marvelous Beast. Patti Tana. PasH

Suspended in a sea of blue-gray slate. American Dreams. "Sapphire." AfrBLW

Suspended lion face. Solar. Philip Larkin. NAMCP V.2

Suspended / on the still surface of the night lake. Depth Sounding, Lake Windermere. Christopher Dewdney. OpeFie

Suspense. Emily Dickinson. MoAmPo; TCAPo

Suspense. D. H. Lawrence. MoBrPo

Suspensión de una obra. David Huerta. RMCMP

Suspension: Junior Wells on a Small Stage in a Converted Barn. Sandra McPherson. SeSe

Suspicion. Alejandra Pizarnik. TANSG, *tr. by* Susan Bassnett

Suspicion, a doubt, a jealousy, A. Medusa. Carol Ann Duffy. NAMCP V.2

5. The Suspicions of Joseph. Rainer Maria Rilke. WED *Fr.* Life of the Virgin Mary, The.

Suspiria. *Unknown.* OBEV

Suspiria Noctis. Henry Howard Brownell. APN-2

Susquehanna. Liz Rosenberg. GoPo

Sussex Street sleeps in mists of nickel moonlight. Night Flower. Geoffrey Lehmann. NOBAu

Sustain tomorrow's road. (LL) Survival, The. Edmund Charles Blunden. OBEV; OBMV

Sustains the hill's lost granite surge. (LL) Robert Penn Warren. OxBoAm; PoA 2002 *Fr.* Kentucky Mountain Farm.

Susu. R. Erica Doyle. BRtP

Susu we say when women put. Susu. R. Erica Doyle. BRtP

Suttee, The. Lydia Huntley Sigourney. NAAPv.1

Suture. Mark Wunderlich. AmPoNex

Suzan Osho's Visit. Muso Soseki. EaWin, *tr. by* W. S. Merwin

Suzan Oshos's Visit to My West Mountain Hut. Muso Soseki. EaWin, *tr. by* W. S. Merwin

Suzanne. Gerald Stern. NevBe

Suzanne takes you down [to]. Suzanne [Takes You Down]. Leonard Cohen. PML

Suzie Wong Doesn't Live Here. Diane Mei Lin Mark. ReTh

Suzy Wong's Been Dead a Long Time. Kitty Tsui. ReTh

Svidrigailov's Last Night. László Kálnoky. IQMS, *tr. by* Kenneth McRobbie and Zita McRobbie

Swallow. Cloud's Anchor, The. Ian Hamilton Finlay. NePenScot

Swallow, The. Abraham Cowley. OBEV; OxAEP-1

Swallow flies away, The. *Unknown.* ColAnChi *Fr.* Classic of Odes.

Swallow, my sister, O sister swallow. Itylus. Algernon Charles Swinburne. NPeEn; UV

Swallow nothing but light. (LL) Envoi: "Sun in the mouth of the day." Robley, Jr. Wilson. InvLad; PBCAP

Swallow the Lake. Clarence Major. ESEAA; FTOS; GT; OxAAAP; PmAP

Swallow Wings. Rosemary Catacalos. TiP2

Swallower. Beckian Fritz Goldberg. ExTi

Swallowing raindrops / clear from China. (LL) Prayer to the Pacific. Leslie Marmon Silko. NAMCP V.2; NoP-4; PoPoPo; WeW-3

Swallowing the dark truths at my sides. I Have Lost A Verse. Julia de Burgos. TANSG, *tr. by* Heather Rosario Sievert

Swallowing words in water. Rebis. Mitch Highfill. HeMarv

Swallows, The. Elizabeth Jane Coatsworth. TLR

Swallows and Tortoises. Neil Curry. NLP

Swallows carve lake wind. Skin Canoes. Carolyn Forché. YaYoPo

Swallows / In eaves of mansions. Buson. ZenPo, *tr. by* Takashi Ikemoto and Lucien Stryk

Swallows of Salangan. Gloria Vando. TouFir

Swamp Angel, The. Herman Melville. APN-2

Swamp Formalism. Lisa Jarnot. Eno

Swamps, marshes, borrow-pits and other. Culture as Exhibit. "Ern Malley." BMAP

Swan, The. Delmira Agustini. TANSG, *tr. by* Mark McCaffrey

Swan, The. Charles Baudelaire. WoPoe, *tr. by* Louis Simpson

Swan, The. Charles Baudelaire. SxFrPo, *tr. by* James McGowan

Swan, The. Mei-Mei Berssenbrugge. OpBo

Swan, The. Cynewulf. WoPoe *Fr.* Riddles (Exeter Book).

Swan, The. Rubén Darío. TCLAP, *tr. by* Lysander Kemp

Swan, The. Gunnar Ekelof.
   1. WED, *tr. by* Robert Bly

Swan, The. Jay Macpherson. NoP-4; NoP-5; WaAnP

Swan, The. Rainer Maria Rilke. NAWM-7v2; OWoS, *tr. by* Stephen Mitchell

Swan, The. William Robert Rodgers. PNI

Swan, The ("This clumsy living that moves lumbering.") Rainer Maria Rilke. WED, *tr. by* Robert Bly

Swan among the shadows is like snow, The. Leda. Rubén Darío. SpanPo, *tr. by* Dorren Bell

Swan and Shadow. John Hollander. NoP-4; NoP-5; OxBoAm; PoA 2002; VCAP

Swan at Edgewater Park, The. Ruth L. Schwartz. P180

Swan at Sheffield Park, The. David St. John. CAP-8

Swan Bathing, The. Ruth Pitter. MoBrPo

Swan dive, The. All the Natural Movements of the Soul. Olena Kalytiak Davis. LegDan

Swan existing, The. Voyage à l'Infini. Walter Conrad Arensberg. APT-1

Swan in the room! Swan in the room! Editing *The Gazette of the Infinite.* Michael Benedikt. MotU

Swan sail with her young beneath her wings, The. (LL) George Meredith. OxBEV; WaAnP *Fr.* Modern Love.

Swan Sequence, The. *Unknown.* WoPoe, *tr. by* Denis Goacher

Swans. Lawrence Durrell. MoBrPo

Swans. Yoshida Issui. CAoMJL1, *tr. by* Leith Morton

Swans, The. Rubén Darío. SpanPo, *tr. by* Dorren Bell

Swans, The. Clifford Dyment. TCAWP

Swans, The. Dame Edith Sitwell. BrAP

Swans' Book, The. Víctor Hernández Cruz. PueRic

Swans Mating. Michael Longley. PNI; StAl

Swans on the River Ayr. Mary Oliver. UrbNat

Swansea Bay. Julia Ann Hatton. AngWePo

Swansonville. Mary Lou Sanelli. IPoFL

Swarm. Nick Flynn. LegDan

Swarm is copulating in the blood, A. Babel. Giuseppe Ungaretti. PFTM-1

Swarm, The. Jorie Graham. NAMCP V.2

Swarm, The. Sylvia Plath. NALW

Swarming and resonant jungle, The. (LL) Allure of Forms, The. Coral Bracho. RMCMP; TAPaP, *tr. by* Mónica de la Torre

Swarming things swarm in the wall space as heavy, The. Akbar. John Kinsella. VaPo

Swart Italian with his breast of fur, The. Public Beach (Long Island Sound). Christopher Darlington Morley. NBLV

Swarte smeked smethes smatered with smoke. *Unknown.* CABP; FaBoVe; OBCoV

Swath. Federico García Lorca. PFTM-1 *Fr.* Night (Suite for Piano and Poet's Voice).

Swathed in silence I drop. Enid Shomer. OtW *Fr.* World Goes Black, The.

Swatted twice by the selfsame billboard. Colorado Desert Night. Sam Gardiner. NIrP

Swatting mosquitoes. Masaoka Shiki. CAoMJL1, *tr. by* Burton Watson

Sway. Henry Israeli. IIR

Sway. Louis Simpson. NoAM

Swaying, the trembling, The. In the Dark World. Haniel Long. APT-1

Swear. Virtual Reality. Charles Bernstein. FTOS

Swear by the olive in the God-kissed land. Land. Agha Shahid Ali. PoA 2002

Swear by what the sages spoke. Under Ben Bulben. William Butler Yeats. NAEL-6v2; NAEL-7v2; NAMCP V.1; NoAM; NoP-4; NoP-5

Sweat all over their faces. Workers in Love. Kavikondala Venkatarao. HotL, *tr. by* V. Narayana Rao

Sweat is a style of the body. John Tranter. NoAM *Fr.* Crying in Early Infancy.

Sweater, The. Gregory Orr. TRP

Sweater, The. Ivan Radoev. CSCBP, *tr. by* Georgi Belev and Lisa Sapinkopf

Sweater Weather: A Love Song to Language. Sharon Bryan. GoPo

Sweaters, The. Lucia Maria Perillo. UnSA

Sweating in the midnight snow. First Day of Spring, The. Pedro Juan Pietri. PueRic

Swedes. Edward Thomas. HarvBoo

Sweeney Agonistes. T. S. Eliot. APT-1
  "Well here again that don't apply." FaBoVe

Sweeney among the Nightingales. T. S. Eliot. APT-1; BrAP; HarvBoo; HeIP-4; NAEL-6v2; NAEL-7v2; NAMCP V.1; NoAM; NoP-4; NPeEn; OBMV; OxBEV; PoPoPo; TFi; WeW-3

Sweeney Astray. *Unknown. tr. by Austin Clarke and Seamus Heaney*
  My Dark Night Has Come Round Again. WoPoe, *tr. by Seamus Heaney*
  Trees of the Forest, The. WoPoe, *tr. by Austin Clarke*

Sweeney Redivivus. Seamus Heaney.
  Artist, An. PoetW
  Cleric, The. ModIr
  First Kingdom, The. PoetW
  Sweeney Redivivus. NoAM

Sweep. Rodney Jones. SUP

Sweep Me through Your Many-Chambered Heart. Diane Ackerman. NIL-7; NIP-4

Sweep the house clean. Love Song. William Carlos Williams. MoAmPo; SAmP

Sweep the mind. Field, The. Mary Barnard. APT-2

Sweep thy faint strings, Musician. Song of the Shadows, The. Walter De la Mare. MoBrPo

Sweeper collects dry leaves with his broom, The. Vasco [*or* Vasko] Popa. PoSu *Fr.* Raw Flesh.

Sweeper said Karanje had a temple, The. Karanje Village. Alun Lewis. TCAWP

Sweeping. Leslie Monsour. FFC

Sweeping Heaven. Heid E. Erdrich. SweBea

Sweeping past the florist's came the baby and the girl. Girl and Baby Florist Sidewalk Pram Nineteen Seventy Something. Kenneth Koch. NoP-4

Sweeping the Floor. Martha Rhodes. LaCa

Sweeping up, the turning out, The. (LL) Mr and Mrs Scotland Are Dead. Kathleen Jamie. EmeKit; MoWP

Sweet after showers, ambrosial air. Alfred Tennyson. NAEL-6v2; NAEL-7v2 *Fr.* In Memoriam A. H. H.

Sweet and calm the breezes stealing. Sabbath Bells. Josephine D. Henderson Heard. CBWP-4

Sweet and low, sweet and low. Alfred Tennyson. ChAP; NAEL-6v2; NAEL-7v2 *Fr.* Princess, The.

Sweet and merry sunshine makes the very churchyard fair, The. Thought, A [*or* Sunshine]. Eliza Cook. STuOW

Sweet and pleasant Sonnet, entitled: My mind to me a kingdom is, A. Sir Edward Dyer. *See* My Mind to Me a Kingdom Is.

Sweet and sly, you were all business when the old bent. Poem for Dizzy. Betty Adcock. InoFa

Sweet apple reddens on a high branch, The. Sappho. SaLy, *tr. by Diane Rayor*

Sweet are the ways of death to weary feet. Euripides. OBEV *Fr.* Medea.

Sweet Armida tooke this charge on hand, The. Torquato Tasso. OBVE *Fr.* Godfrey of Bulloigne; or, The Recoverie of Jerusalem [Gerusalemme Liberata].

Sweet as the tender fragrance that survives. Delia. Henry Wadsworth Longfellow. TCAPo

Sweet Auburn, loveliest village of the plain,. Deserted Village, The. Oliver Goldsmith. NAEL-6v1; NAEL-7v1; NoP-4; NoP-5; OxAEP-1; TFi

Sweet baby boy, accept a stranger's song. Mary Robinson. NPBRoP *Fr.* Ode Inscribed to the Infant Son of S.T. Coleridge, Esq.

Sweet, be not proud of those two eyes. To Dianeme. Robert Herrick. BASC; NOSC; OBEV

Sweet beast, I have gone prowling. Song. W. D. Snodgrass. MoAmPo

Sweet beats of jazz impaled on slivers of wind. Walking Parker Home. Bob Kaufman. OxAAAP

Sweet beguilings. Cheat, The. Joseph Beaumont. NOSC

Sweet bird, that sing'st away the early howres [*or* hours]. To a Nightingale. William Drummond of Hawthornden. OWoS

Sweet birds sang: *there is trouble in paradise today.* and we sweated each other away: shirtless. First Fugue. D. A. Powell. IIR

Sweet Bread. Frank X. Walker. SpirFl

Sweet Brown Rice and Red Bones. Lamont B. Steptoe. SpirFl

Sweet Bye and Bye. Ogden Nash. ReLy

Sweet Catullus's all-but-island, olive-silvery Sirmio! (LL) Frater Ave Atque Vale. Alfred Tennyson. NAEL-6v2; NoP-4; NoP-5

Sweet Chance, that led my steps abroad. Great Time, A. W. H. Davies. MoBrPo

Sweet cheat gone, The. (LL) Ghost, The ("Who knocks? I, who was beautiful.") Walter De la Mare. InoFa; MoBrPo

Sweet children amid the apple boughs. On the Picture of a Child. Henrietta Cordelia Ray. CBWP-3

Sweet Content. Thomas Dekker *and others. See* Happy Heart, The.

Sweet Corrall lips, where Nature's treasure lies. Richard Barnfield. CAGL *Fr.* Cynthia, with Certain[e] Sonnets.

Sweet Creatures, did you truely understand. To All Those Worthy Women, Who Have Any Desire to Live in Newfound-Land. Robert Hayman. IFF

Sweet Daddy. Patricia Smith.
  "So Motown taught me all about men. Men worshipped." UnSA

Sweet Darkness. David Whyte. TWF

Sweet daughter of a rough and stormy sire. Ode to Spring. Anna Laetitia Barbauld. OxAEP-1

Sweet day, so cool, so calm, so bright. Virtue [*or* Vertue]. George Herbert. AmFaPo; BASC; ClHu; FSCP; HeIP-4; NAEL-6v1; NAEL-7v1; NoP-4; NoP-5; NOSC; OBEV; OPOU; OxBEV; SoSe-8; TFi; TreFP; WaAnP

Sweet, deep sense of mystery filled the wood, A. In Cool, Green Haunts. Mahlon Leonard Fisher. WeW-3

Sweet Disorder in the Dress, A. Harry Hooton. NOBAu

Sweet disorder in the dress[e], A. Delight in Disorder. Robert Herrick. BASC; BrAP; CABP; CavPo; ClHu; ErotSp; HeIP-4; NAEL-6v1; NAEL-7v1; NIL-7; NIP-4; NoP-4; NoP-5; NOSC; NPeEn; OBEV; OxAEP-1; OxBEV; PBRV; TFi; TRP; TWF; WaAnP; WeW-3

Sweet Dog! now cold and stiff in death. Georgia Bailey Parrington. VerBaPo *Fr.* Elegy to a Dissected Puppy, An.

Sweet Dreams. Christian Wiman. AmPoNex

Sweet dreams form a shade. William Blake. OBCP *Fr.* Songs of Innocence.

Sweet dreams, sweet memories, sweet taste of earth. Cemetery Nights. Stephen Dobyns. CAP-8; StAl

Sweet earth, he ran and changed his shoes to go. Arrangements with Earth for Three Dead Friends. James Wright. NIL-7; NIP-4

Sweet Echo, sweetest Nymph, that livest unseen. John Milton. OBEV *Fr.* Comus; a Masque Presented at Ludlow Castle.

Sweet elfin music comes to me. Dream of Elfland, A. Henrietta Cordelia Ray. CBWP-3

Sweet enthusiast, on a rock reclin'd, The. Power of Love, The. Charlotte Dacre. NOBRP

Sweet especial rural scene. (LL) Binsey Poplars (Felled 1879). Gerard Manley Hopkins. NAEL-6v2; NAEL-7v2; NAMCP V.1; NoAM; PtR

Sweet, exclude me[e] not, nor be divided. Thomas Campion. BASC

Sweet flattery! then she loves but me alone. (LL) William Shakespeare. HeIP-4; OxAEP-1 *Fr.* Sonnets.

Sweet flocks, whose soft enamel's wing. Flying Fowl, and Creeping Things, Praise Ye the Lord. Isaac Watts. ChIV-1

Sweet Georgia Brown. Ben Bernie, Kenneth Casey and Maceo Pinkard. ReLy

Sweet Gifts. Baldomero Garcilaso de la Vega. SpanPo, *tr. by Edwin Morgan*

Sweet gifts, by me found something less than sweet. Sweet Gifts. Baldomero Garcilaso de la Vega. SpanPo, *tr. by Edwin Morgan*

Sweet, harmles[s] livers [*or* lives]! (on whose holy leisure). Shepherds [*or* Shepheards], The. Henry Vaughan. ChIV-2

Sweet Hour. Diane Gilliam Fisher. SweBea

Sweet Iesus of thy mercie, our pitifull praiers heare. Hymne of the Daie of Judgment, The. Lady Elizabeth Tyrwhit. EMWP

Sweet in her green dell the flower of beauty slumbers. Song. George Darley. OBEV

Sweet infancy! Rapture, The. Thomas Traherne. NOSC

Sweet inferno, gusting, funneled, A. Buffalo. Eugenio Montale. ArBi, *tr. by Jonathan Galassi*

Sweet is the death that taketh end by love. (LL) Petrarch. HeIP-4; OBVE *Fr.* Sonnets to Laura.

Sweet is the rose, but grows upon a brere. Edmund Spenser. ItP *Fr.* Amoretti.

Sweet is the whispering of that pine tree, goatherd. Theocritus. HePo *Fr.* Idylls.

Sweet is your antique body, not yet young. Sonnet, to a Child. Wilfred Owen. NOxBChV

Sweet it is to be a child. "Tabitha." FaBoVe

Sweet jazz, The. Long Marriage, The. Maxine W. Kumin. PoDa

Sweet jesus bleeding asshole no they cant. W. D. Snodgrass. BodElec *Fr.* Führer Bunker, The.

Sweet Jesus, let her save you, let her take. Prayer. Dorianne Laux. OPRER

Sweet jesus, superman. Note, Passed to Superman. Lucille Clifton. ReTh

Sweet joy befall thee! (LL) William Blake. NPBRoP; OxAEP-2; PoPoPo *Fr.* Songs of Innocence.

Sweet Killen Hill. Tom MacIntyre. *See* On Sweet Killen Hill.

Sweet lad, tender lad. Imitation of the Arabic. Alexander Sergeyevich Pushkin. CAGL, *tr. by Michael Green*

Sweet Levinsky in the night. Sweet Levinsky. Allen Ginsberg. NBLV

Sweet Lorraine. Mitchell Parish. ReLy

Sweet love, renew thy force; be it not said. William Shakespeare. PBRV *Fr.* Sonnets.

Sweet Lovers love the spring. (LL) William Shakespeare. NoSic; OBEV; TFi *Fr.* As You Like It.

Sweet lullabie, A. Nicholas Breton. RACG *Fr.* Arbor of Amorous Devises, The.

Sweet Maid. Bhartrihari. WoPoe, *tr.* by Barbara Stoler Miller

Sweet maid, you perform a singular feat. Sweet Maid. Bhartrihari. WoPoe, *tr.* by Barbara Stoler Miller

Sweet Marie-Anne, she thought. Paris Latin Quarter. Femi Osofisan. NAfrP

Sweet marmalade of kisses newly gather'd. Dissert, A. Margaret Lucas Cavendish, Duchess of Newcastle. PEW

Sweet / May / again. (LL) Locust Tree in Flower, The. William Carlos Williams. NAAPv.2; OxBoAm; Spl

Sweet Meat Has Sour Sauce. William Cowper. OBSV
(Sweet Meat has Sour Sauce, or The Slave-Trader in the Dumps.) NPBRoP

Sweet molasses. Sonya Brooks. InTrad

Sweet monster you hold death in your beak. Meetings. Paul Éluard. AF, *tr.* by Lloyd Alexander

Sweet mother, I cannot weave. Sappho. SaLy, *tr.* by Diane Rayor

Sweet Mother! rare in gifts of tenderness! To My Mother. Henrietta Cordelia Ray. CBWP-3

Sweet Mountains—Ye tell Me no lie. Emily Dickinson. NALW

Sweet mouth that offers for a taste, The. Sonnet 82. Luis de Góngora y Argote. BLPSL, *tr.* by Rene de Costa, Rigas Kappatos and Eleni Paidoussi

Sweet nature, give me holy dreams. At Nature's Shrine. Henrietta Cordelia Ray. CBWP-3

Sweet Neglect, The. Ben Jonson. NAEL-6v1; NAEL-7v1; NIL-7; NoP-4; NPeEn; PoPoPo; TFi; WeW-3 *Fr.* Epicoene; or, The Silent Woman.

Sweet nurslings of the vernal skies. Flowers of the Field. John Keble. SacPr

Sweet nymph, come to thy lover. *Unknown.* NoSic

Sweet Pain of It, The. Eileen Myles. Eno

Sweet pale girl—who begs. Sweet Pale Girl. Alfredo Espino. SonAtl, *tr.* by Eleanor Davidson

Sweet peace, where dost thou dwell? I humbly crave. Peace. George Herbert. NOSC; TreFP

Sweet Peril. George Macdonald. ITBLP

Sweet poet of the woods, a long adieu! On the Departure of the Nightingale. Charlotte Smith. RWP; WoRP

Sweet Poetess! as pensive oft I stray. To Mrs. Charlotte Smith. Martha Hanson. CenSon

Sweet Polly Oliver. *Unknown.* FaBoWar

Sweet Potato. Takahashi Shinkichi. ZenPo, *tr.* by Takashi Ikemoto and Lucien Stryk

Sweet Reader, Flanneled and Tulled. Olena Kalytiak Davis. BAP-01; NAPBL

Sweet Red Peppers, Sun-Drieds, the Hearts of Artichokes. Martha Silano. AmPoNex

Sweet Reliquaries, The. Delmira Agustini. TANSG, *tr.* by Mark McCaffrey

Sweet Ruin. Tony Hoagland. FaoP

Sweet run ends with the shutdown, The. At Summer's End. Jean Janzen. GeoHom

Sweet Saturday afternoons with nothing to do and it's spring-turning-into-. Dolce Far Niente. Fidelito Cortes. ReBoTo

Sweet, serene, sky-like flower. Richard Lovelace. CavPo

Sweet shift go slow go. Drew Milne. VaPo *Fr.* Bench Marks.

Sweet Silence after Bells! Christopher John Brennan. NOBAu

Sweet silver trumpets, / Jesus! (LL) When Sue Wears Red. Langston Hughes. APT-2; NAMCP V.1

Sweet Sixteen. Eunice De Souza. NAMCP V.2

Sweet soul, which now with heavenly songs dost tell. To the Marquess of Piscat's Soul. Henry Constable. NoSic

Sweet Soule of goodnesse, in whoe Saintlike brest. Double Acrostich on Mrs Svsanna Blvnt, A. Thomas Jordan. NPeEn

Sweet sounds, oh, beautiful music, do not cease! On Hearing a Symphony of Beethoven. Edna St. Vincent Millay. ItP; MoAmPo

Sweet sparrow, my lover's pet. Catullus. ErotSp, *tr.* by Sam Hamill

Sweet Spirit, comfort me! (LL) His Litany to the Holy Spirit. Robert Herrick. BASC; NOSC

Sweet Spring, thou turn'st with all thy goodly train. Spring Bereaved 2. William Drummond of Hawthornden. OBEV

Sweet spring, while others hail thy op'ning flowers. Farewell, for Two Years, to England, A. A Poem. Helen Maria Williams. RWP

Sweet Springs Palace, The. Yang Hsiung. CCL1, *tr.* by David Knechtges

Sweet springtime showers. Buson. SoOfWa, *tr.* by Sam Hamill

Sweet stream, that dost with equal pace. On His Mistress Drown'd [*or* Drowned]. Thomas Spratt. STuOW

Sweet stream, that winds through [*or* thro'] yonder glade. To a Young Lady. William Cowper. SacPr

Sweet Suffolk Owl. *Unknown.* NPeEn

Sweet Suffolk owl, so trimly dight. Sweet Suffolk Owl. *Unknown.* NPeEn

Sweet summer flowers were braided in her hair. Maniac, The. Agnes Strickland. CenSon

Sweet sweet sweet sweet sweet tea. Susie Asado. Gertrude Stein. APT-1; ASA; NAAPv.2; NAMCP V.1; NoAM

Sweet Talk. Ferreira Gullar. TCLAP, *tr.* by Renato Rezende

Sweet, thou art pale. Three Enemies, The. Christina Georgina Rossetti. SacPr

Sweet, though short, our. John Montague. PNI *Fr.* Dead Kingdom, The.

Sweet Time. Molly Peacock. FiBr

Sweet upland, to whose walks, with fond repair. To Hampstead. Leigh Hunt. CenSon

Sweet warrio[u]r, when shall I have peace with you? Edmund Spenser. OxBSo *Fr.* Amoretti.

Sweet was the song the Virgin sang. Virgin's Lullaby, The. *Unknown.* RSR

Sweet was the sound, when oft at evening's close. Oliver Goldsmith. NPeEn *Fr.* Deserted Village, The.

Sweet western wind, whose luck it is. To the Western Wind. Robert Herrick. OBEV

Sweet Will. Philip Levine. PoA 2002; VCAP

Sweet William. "Ern Malley." BMAP

Sweet William Blake. At Kenneth Rexroth's. Lawrence Ferlinghetti. WhBo

Sweet william, silverweed, sally-my-handsome. Spell for Sleeping, A. Alastair Reid. NOxBChV

Sweet, winsome May, coy, pensive fay. May. Henrietta Cordelia Ray. CBWP-3

Sweet Words on Race. Langston Hughes. LTA

Sweet words that take. Sweet Words on Race. Langston Hughes. LTA

Sweet-and-Twenty. William Shakespeare. *See* O[h] Mistress Mine.

Sweet-Briar in Rose. Michael Field. VWP

Sweetchile / dem will say dat. Revo Lyric. Kendel Hippolyte. WaCA

Sweete Saynt: Thow better canst declare to me. Henry Constable. PBRV

Sweet[e] Thames! [*or* Themmes] run[ne] softly, till I end my song. (LL) Prothalamion. Edmund Spenser. BrAP; NoSic; NPeEn; OBEV; OxAEP-1; OxBEV; TFi; WoPoe

Sweeter Far than the Harp, More Gold than Gold. Michael Field. OBMV

Sweeter than sour apples flesh to boys. Ted Berrigan. FTOS; OxBoAm *Fr.* Sonnets, The.

Sweetest love, I do not go[e]. Song. John Donne. HeIP-4; NAEL-7v1; NoP-4; NoP-5; NoSic; TFi
(Sweetest love, I do not go for weariness of thee.) FSCP

Sweetest love return[e] again[e]. Mary Sidney Wroth, Countess of Montgomery. NAEL-6v1; NAEL-7v1 *Fr.* Pamphilia to Amphilanthus.

Sweetest notes among the human heart-strings, The. Love Unexpressed. Constance Fenimore Woolson. APN-2

Sweetest of sweets, I thank you: when displeasure. Church-Music[k]. George Herbert. AmFaPo

Sweetest Saviour, if my soul. Dialogue, A. George Herbert. FSCP; NOSC; OBEV

Sweetgrass. Maurice Kenny. HATNAP

Sweet-Heart I come unto thee. No ring, no Wedding. *Unknown.* BASC

Sweetheart, I love you. Mean to Me. Roy Turk. ReLy

Sweetheart / when you break through. Diane Di Prima. BB

Sweetly breathed morning. Morning Thesis. Christiania Whitehead. NeBl

Sweetness. Stephen Dunn. StAl

Sweetness. Michael Savitz. FreRad

Sweetness, Always. Pablo Neruda. BeAl, *tr.* by Alastair Reid

Sweetness and wit, they are [*or* they're] but mummy, possessed. (LL) Love's Alchemy [*or* Alchemie]. John Donne. BASC; NAEL-6v1; NAEL-7v1; NoP-4; NoP-5

Sweetness of England, The. Elizabeth Barrett Browning. OxAEP-2 *Fr.* Aurora Leigh.

Sweetpeas turn blue as they die, The. I guess. March, The. Mary Ruefle. AmAlph

Sweit rois [*or* Sweet rose] of vertew [*or* virtue] and of gentilnes [*or* gentleness]. To a Lady[e]. William Dunbar. OBEV

Swell to the size of fruits bursting with seeds. (LL) Feathered Dancers. Kenward Elmslie. AHA; NYP2; PmAP

Swellfish eaten / He chants nembutsu. Tan Taigi. ZenPo, *tr.* by Takashi Ikemoto and Lucien Stryk

Swelling with boundless happiness. (LL) Evening in the Garden, Clear after Rain. Ch'u Ch'uang I. CCL1; WaAnP, *tr.* by Kenneth Rexroth

Swells in their cove, and smothers their sweet song. (LL) Seals at High Island. Richard Murphy. ModIr; PBCIP

Swept. Hayden Carruth. PoDa

Swept Away. László Kálnoky. IQMS, *tr.* by Kenneth McRobbie and Zita McRobbie

Swept by light the feet of that multitude seemed. Splendor in the Wind. Raúl Zurita. TCLAP, *tr.* by Jack Schmitt

Swept into limbo is the host. Ballad of Religion and Marriage, A. Amy Levy. NPeEn; ViWPN; VWP

Swept snow, Li Po. Lorine Niedecker. NAMCP V.1

Swept up by motley wings of love. Flying. Pedro Serrano. RMCMP, *tr. by* Geoff Hargreaves

Swerving east, from rich industrial shadows. Here. Philip Larkin. NAMCP V.2; NPeEn

S'what Up. Joel Dailey. AnSo

Swich fyn hath, lo, this Troilus for love! Geoffrey Chaucer. SacPr *Fr.* Troilus and Criseyde [*or* Criseide].

Swift [and] cold and deep. (LL) Charon's Cosmology. Charles Simic. PoPoPo; WaAnP

Swift as a spirit hastening to his task. Triumph of Life, The. Percy Bysshe Shelley. NAEL-6v2; NOBRP

Swift cloud, swift light, now dark, now bright, across the landscape played. Idyl of Harvest Time, An. John Townsend Trowbridge. APN-2

Swift, for him, I would have traveled. With only two or three stamens, masculine flowers burst. They rise from their own depths, glistening and moist. Loosely turning over, they bring themselves up under the sky midway between light and shadow. Voiceless they wilt. Sluggish they die. María Baranda. RMCMP, *tr. by* Mónica de la Torre

Swift has sailed into his rest. Swift's Epitaph. William Butler Yeats. OBVE

Swift heft wrench. Barefoot/Extinguish at Will. Dana Lisa Lustig. AnSo

Swift red flesh, a winter king, The. Hart Crane. MoAmPo; NAAL-5 *Fr.* Bridge, The.

Swift, The. René Char. YaTCFP, *tr. by* Patricia Terry

Swift Things Are Beautiful. Elizabeth Jane Coatsworth. ChAP

Swift through the yielding air I glide. Lark, The. *Unknown.* NOSC; OWoS

Swift was sweet on Stella. Us Poets. Franklin Pierce Adams. AmWit

Swift whose wings are too wide. Swift, The. René Char. YaTCFP, *tr. by* Patricia Terry

Swiftly re-light the flame,. "H. D." NALW *Fr.* Tribute to the Angels.

Swiftly riding past the willows. Tune: "Pure Serene Music" En Route to Po-shan. Hsin Ch'i-chi. ColAnChi, *tr. by* Jiaosheng Wang

Swiftly walk o'er the western wave. To Night. Percy Bysshe Shelley. NAEL-6v2; NAEL-7v2; TFi

Swiftly walking away. Mitsu Suzuki. WhBo

Swiftly We Fly. James Clarence Harvey. ArBi

Swiftness With Which Those Cities Fell, The. Dennis Nurkse. PrTe

Swifts. Ted Hughes. OWoS

Swifts. Philippe Jaccottet. VCWP, *tr. by* Derek Mahon

Swifts. Glyn Jones. AngWePo

Swifts at Evening. Jeffrey Harrison. UrbNat

Swift's Epitaph. William Butler Yeats. OBVE

Swifts turn in the heights of the air. Distances. Philippe Jaccottet. StAl; VCWP, *tr. by* Derek Mahon

Swim in Co. Wicklow, A. Derek Mahon. NAMCP V.2

Swim Right Up to Me. Katherine Pierpoint. MFPA

Swim? What will I do now, with my hands? (LL) As from a Quiver of Arrows. Carl Phillips. AmAlph; BtF; WaAnP; WiU

Swimmer. Robert Francis. APT-2; WeW-3

Swimmer, The. Brendan Kennelly. PBCIP; PML

Swimmer's Moment, The. Margaret Avison. BrAP

Swimmers, The. David Brendon Hopes. UpMys

Swimmers, The. Allen Tate. APT-2; FuPo; MoAmPo; NAAPv.2; NAMCP V.1; NoAM; NoP-5

Swimming. Carmen Horst. ACAMVP

Swimming By Night. James Merrill. ColAP; HarvBoo

Swimming Chenango Lake. Charles Tomlinson. NAMCP V.2; NoAM

Swimming in and through us like transparent fish. (LL) I Fail as a Dharma Teacher. Diane Di Prima. BB; WhBo

Swimming in the Flood. John Burnside. EmeKit

Swimming Pool. Myra Cohn Livingston. NOxBChV

Swimming Pool Ghost, The. Gillian Ferguson. MFPA

Swimming Pool, The. Thomas Lux. GoPo

Swimming Upstream. Aimée Grunberger. PoCoUp

Swimming with Seiger. Rick Agran. AmPoNex

Swinburne, old Swinburn, silly old Swinburne. Sister Swallow to Swinburne. Mary Holtby. UV

Swineherd. Eiléan Ní Chuilleanáin. EmeKit

Swineherd. Eiléan Ní Chuilleanáin. NPeEn

Swing. Ode to Singer. Paul Van Ostaijen. TuT, *tr. by* Peter van de Kamp

Swing, The. George Bowering. BrAP

Swing, The. Hwang O. CATKP, *tr. by* Chi-gyu Kim [*or* Kim Chonggil]

Swing, The. Robert Louis Stevenson. BLPJKO; ChAP; NOxBChV; NTCP; TLR

Swing dat hammer—hunh. Southern Road. Sterling Allen Brown. APT-2; InGu; NAMCP V.1; OxAAAP

Swing Shift Blues. Alan Dugan. BodElec

Swing Song, A. William Allingham. TLR

Swing, swing. Swing Song, A. William Allingham. TLR

Swing the bird over the brook. Snap the hood off and sing. Obedience / Intention to Hunt. Malinda Markham. IAoNAP

Swing up into the apple-tree. (LL) T. S. Eliot. NoAM; WeW-3 *Fr.* Landscapes.

Swinging doors of knocking-wood cowards: 8 for us. Esther Louise. BtF

Swinging Low. Carter Revard. NevBe

Swinging on a Star. Johnny Burke. ReLy

Swinging on the First Pitch. Dabney Stuart. MoASP

Switch. Sean O Riordain. ModIr; StAl, *tr. by* Patrick Crotty

Switch on lights yellow as the sun. City Midnight Junk Strains. Allen Ginsberg. OxBoAm

Switch on the Night. Ray Bradbury. OBSP

Switch sides with every jump. (LL) Flounder. Natasha Trethewey. OxAAAP; TWW

Switzerland. Matthew Arnold.

  Isolation: To Marguerite. BrAP; NAEL-6v2; NAEL-7v2

  (To Marguerite.) CABP; NoP-4; PoPoPo

  To Marguerite—Continued. BrAP; NAEL-6v2; NAEL-7v2; NoP-5; NPeEn; OxBEV; SoSe-8; WaAnP

Switzerland upon, A. Child's Birthday, A. Henry Rago. IllVoic

Switzer's Wife, The. Felicia Dorothea Hemans. RWP

Swollen belly of the hull. Boat Builder. Tammy Armstrong. Coast

Swollen river sang through the green hole, The. Arthur Rimbaud. OBWP *Fr.* Eighteen-Seventy.

Swoon of noon, a trance of tide, A. In a Bye-Canal. Herman Melville. APN-2; NCAP

Sword bites for peace, The. Another Voice. Richard Wilbur. UpMys

Sword in a Cloud of Light, A. Kenneth Rexroth. StAl *Fr.* Lights in the Sky are Stars, The.

Sword in his right hand, a stone in his left hand, A. Bronze David of Donatello, The. Randall Jarrell. InGu

Sword is a cold bride. Yuk!, The. Michael Foley. PNI *Fr.* True Life Love Stories.

Sword of God doth ever well, The. To Generall Cromwell. "Eliza." EMWP

Sword of Robert Lee, The. Abram Joseph Ryan. CBCWP; PCW

Sword of Surprise, The. G. K. Chesterton. MoBrPo; SacPr

Sword shall break the sword they say, The. Sadakichi. NAAPv.1 *Fr.* My Rubaiyat.

Swordfishtrombone. Tom Waits. PFTM-2

Swung torch scatters seeds, The. Night Piece. "Ern Malley." BMAP

Sx msg n fgy mrr. Train Phone Sext. Clive Holden. PoPra

Syama Mother's lap a-climbing. Najrul Islām. SinGod, *tr. by* Rachel Fell McDermott

Syama wakes on the cremation grounds. Najrul Islām. SinGod, *tr. by* Rachel Fell McDermott

Sybil. Rebecca Wolff. LegDan

Sybil, The. Virgil. OBVE *Fr.* Aeneid [*or* Eneados *or* Aeneis], The.

Sybil Sibelius! Yes, Belinda Brahms! Great Women Composers, The. Gavin Ewart. OBCoV

Sybilline. "Ern Malley." BMAP

Sycamore. Jessica Smucker Falcón. ACAMVP

Sycamore, The. Wendell Berry. LPSFW; UpMys

Sycamore Canyon Nocturne. Christopher Buckley. GeoHom; PfSP

Sycamore stood in the middle of our backyard. Sycamore. Jessica Smucker Falcón. ACAMVP

Sycamore stretches straight, The. Station. He.She.You.Me. Lawrence L. White. IAoNAP

Sy-che and the King. Li Po. CCL1, *tr. by* E. Powys Mathers

Sycophantic Fox and the Gullible Raven, The. Guy Wetmore Carryl. NBLV

Sydney. Robert Harris. NOBAu

Sydney Cove, 1788. Peter Porter. BrAP; NoAM

Sydney Highrise Variations, The. Les A. Murray.

  Flight from Manhattan, The. BMAP

Sydney Place. Sean Dunne.

  Beans. ModIr

  Bus Station, The. ModIr

  Dead Pianist, The. ModIr

  Lost Wife, The. ModIr

  Mobile, The. ModIr

  Night Sky, The. ModIr

  Old School, The. ModIr

  Poet Upstairs, The. ModIr

  Railings. ModIr

  Tea. ModIr

Syllables shaped around the darkening day's. Cancer Winter. Marilyn Hacker. RA

Syllabling. Sean O Riordain. ModIr, *tr. by* Patrick Crotty

Sylphs of the Seasons, The. Washington Allston.
   "And now, in accents deep and low." APN-1

Sylva. Abraham Cowley.
   To His Mistress. NOSC; OxAEP-1

Sylvae [*or* Silvae]. Publius Papinius Statius. *tr. by* W. G. Shepherd
   First of December, The. RomPo, *tr. by* W. G. Shepherd
   In Memory of His Father. RomPo, *tr. by* W. G. Shepherd
   Jocular Lines to Plotius Grypus. RomPo, *tr. by* W. G. Shepherd
   Thanksgiving to the Emperor Augustus Germanicus Domitianus. RomPo, *tr. by* W. G. Shepherd
   To Sleep. RomPo, *tr. by* W. G. Shepherd

Sylvester's Dying Bed. Langston Hughes. NAMCP V.1; NoAM; SAmP

Sylvia. Meic Stevens. BBMWP, *tr. by* the author

Sylvia. Do you remember still. To Sylvia. Giacomo Leopardi. NAWM-7v2, *tr. by* Ottavio M. Casale

Sylvia; or, The May Queen. George Darley.
   Song. IrLP
   "View like one of Fairy-land, A." NOBRP

Sylvia Plath is setting my hair. Female seer will burn upon this pyre, The. Elizabeth Alexander. SweBea

Sylvia the Fair. John Dryden. PoPoPo

Sylvia's Death. Anne Sexton. InoFa; NAAL-5; NALW

Sylvie and Bruno. Lewis Carroll.
   Mad Gardener's Song, The. WoPoe

Symbols. Christina Georgina Rossetti. NALW

Symbols. William Butler Yeats. OBMV

Symbols of Fertility. Audrey Poetker-Thiessen. ACAMVP

Symbols of Transformation. Ron Padgett. FTOS

Symmetron: You and Brother Will. Jack Rogow. IaFF

Sympathetic Portrait of a Child. William Carlos Williams. APT-1; NAMCP V.1

3. Sympathies. Oliver Wendell Holmes. APN-1 *Fr.* Wind-Clouds and Star-Drifts.

Sympathy: "I know what the caged bird feels, alas!" Paul Laurence Dunbar. APN-2; GT; IJHIL; NAAPv.1; NIL-7; NoP-4; NoP-5; SSLK; TCAPo

Sympathy. Viola Meynell. LW

Sympathy. Lizelia Augusta Jenkins Moorer. CBWP-3

Sympathy. Henry David Thoreau. CAGL

Sympathy, A Welcome, A. John Berryman. NoP-4

Sympathy and Envy. Katherine Lederer. LegDan

Symphonies. Herman Melville. APN-2 *Fr.* Clarel: A Poem and Pilgrimage in the Holy Land.

Symphony from the Balcony. Jared Angira. NAfrP

Symphony in Gray Major. Rubén Darío. SpanPo, *tr. by* Denise Levertov

Symphony in Yellow. Oscar Wilde. MoBrPo; NoAM; OPOU

Symphony No. 2. Daniil Kharms. AF, *tr. by* George Gibian

Symphony of the Hammers. Evaristo Ribera Chevremont. NAAPv.2

Symposium. Paul Muldoon. BeAl

Symptom Recital. Dorothy Parker. APT-1
   (Symptom.) LW

Symptoms. Sophie Hannah. MFPA

Synagogue in Prague. Alan Sillitoe. HP

Synchoresis. Godfrey Turner. OBCoV

Synchronized Swimming. Angela Sorby. AmPoNex

Syncopation, it has roused the nation to a red, red hot degree. (That's the Way) Dixieland Started Jazz. Shelton Brooks. ReLy

Syne nethir-mare he went quhare Pluto was. Robert Henryson. NePenScot *Fr.* Orpheus and Eurydice.

Syne went thai southwart in the land. John Barbour. NePenScot *Fr.* Bruce, The.

Syng a song of Saxons. Old-Saxon Fragment. *Unknown.* OBCoV

Synge we alle and seye we thus. *Unknown.* OHMEL

Synge's Chair. Maryhelen Snyder. ICANM

Synopsis of the Great Welsh Novel. Harri Webb. AngWePo; TCAWP

Syntactic and Verbal. Giulia Niccolai. CItWP, *tr. by* Cinzia Sartini Blum and Lara Trubowitz

Syntax. Wang Ping. PoDa

Syon lyes waste, and thy *Jerusalem.* Fulke, 1st Baron Brooke Greville. ChIV-1; NoSic *Fr.* Caelica.

Syren Songs. George Darley.
   Mermaidens' Vesper-Hymn, The. NAEL-6v2; NPeEn

Syringa. John Ashbery. APSN; GPTC; NoAM; VCAP

Syrinx. Amy Clampitt. NAMCP V.2; NoP-4; NoP-5

Syrinx. James Merrill. OxBoAm

Syros. Tomas Tranströmer. BLT, *tr. by* Leif Sjöberg and May Swenson

Syrup's up again. Maple Syrup Sonnet. Bernadette Mayer. NYP2

System. Tiziano Rossi. ItPo, *tr. by* Gayle Ridinger

System of high-chair government. that's still pay-for-view. we depend on mad. Verbatim begins with this decade's hit and miss. Nicole Markotić. PoPra

Syvatoslav had no use for comfort. Memorandum. Yunna Petrovna Moritz. TCRusP, *tr. by* Daniel Weissbort

Szondi. Ferenc Kölcsey. IQMS, *tr. by* Watson Kirkconnell

T

T.A.P.O.A.F.O.M. Thomas Sayers Ellis. BAP-01

T. E. Lawrence Poems, The. Gwendolyn MacEwen.
   Apologies. StAl
   Damascus. StAl
   Tall Tales. StAl

'T is not to honor thee by verse of mine. On Michael Angelo. Washington Allston. APN-1

T minus 60 seconds. Countdown. Ron Penoyer. OtW

T. R. Donald Hall. OxBoAm

T. S. Eliot. Robert Lowell. NoAM

T' undo, or be undone. (LL) Ulysses and the Siren [*or* Syren]. Samuel Daniel. NAEL-6v1; NoP-4; NoP-5; OBEV; OxAEP-1

'T was earliest morning in the early spring. Bird and the Bell, The. Christopher Pearse Cranch. APN-1

Ta Ta Cha Cha. Rita Dove. AmAlph

Ta te/ak'etik yorail ya x-ajk'otajik. Pedro Pérez Conde. RMCMP

Ta Tiopa Maza Win. Ta Tiopa Maza Win / Iron Door Woman. Wendy Rose. FiBr

Ta Tiopa Maza Win / Iron Door Woman. Wendy Rose. FiBr

Tab, The. Clark Coolidge. FTOS

Tabernacle. D. H. Lawrence. ChIV-1

Table. Richard Tillinghast. MAAN

Table, A. Gertrude Stein. NAAPv.2 *Fr.* Tender Buttons.

Table, The. Ray DiPalma. FTOS

Table, The. Lee Upton. AmAlph

Table and chair were overturned. Ballade of the Moment After. Paul Goodman. BodElec

Table and the Chair, The. Edward Lear. ITBLP

Table gleams, The. Yellow Room, The. Juan Felipe Herrera. TouFir

Table hurled itself, to our surprise, The. Lingard and the Stars. Edwin Arlington Robinson. OxBSo

Table in the Wilderness, A. Li-Young Lee. Vesp

Table is spread, the lamp glitters and sighs, The. Expected Guest, The. Sidney Keyes. PoWW

Table Manners: "Goops they lick their fingers, The." Frank Gelett Burgess. CalPo

Table means does it not my dear it means a whole steadiness, A. Gertrude Stein. NAAPv.2 *Fr.* Tender Buttons.

Table near the band, A. Music, Maestro, Please! Herb Magidson. ReLy

Table, son, is laid, The. House, The. Gabriela Mistral. BBASP; TCLAP, *tr. by* Doris Dana

Table Talk. Wallace Stevens. NoP-4; NoP-5

Tableau. Countee Cullen. BLPJKO; NAAPv.2

Table-Birds. Kenneth Mackenzie. BMAP; NOBAu

Tablecloths laid out, for his sons and grandsons, The. (LL) Cemetery in Punta Arenas. Enrique Lihn. TCLAP; VCWP, *tr. by* David Unger

¡Tablero de la mesa. Naturaleza Viva. Jorge Guillén. RaW

Tables in Pictures. Diane Ward. FTOS

Tables Turned, The. William Wordsworth. NAEL-6v2; NAEL-7v2; NOBRP; NoP-5

Tablets, The. Armand Schwerner.
   Tablet II. PFTM-2
   Tablet X. PFTM-2
   Tablet XV. PFTM-2
   Tablet XXVI.
      "He is not quite dead." PFTM-2; WoPoe

Tabloid News. Blythe Nobleman. ReTh

Taboo. Cherryl "Blue." Floyd-Miller. BtF

Tabula Rasa? Daryl Hine. BrAP

Tâche d'Espérance, La. Yves Bonnefoy. YaTCFP

Tacit. Thom Ward. AmPoNex

Tact. Paul Pascal. WeW-3

Tact. Edwin Arlington Robinson. NoAM

Tactics ("Licit tremendous unjust oxidized fancified notions tremulously.") Jen Hofer. Eno

Tactics ("Will not tolerate will expend offer known facts armed with knives.") Jen Hofer. Eno

Tadpole, it's not time yet to nag you. Upon Seeing an Ultrasound Photo of an Unborn Child. Thomas Lux. NevBe; SUP; WaAnP

Tae titly. *Unknown.* FaBoVe

Taedium. *Unknown.* CCL1 *Fr.* Cai-ge.

Taffy, the topaz-coloured cat. In Honour of Taffy Topaz. Christopher Darlington Morley. WHSW

Tag. Langston Hughes. APT-2

Taga for Mbaye Dyôb. Léopold Sédar Senghor. PFTM-1

Tagging. Maureen Seaton. ExTi; IllVoic

Tagus farewell, that westward with thy streams. In Spayn. Sir Thomas Wyatt. NoSic; OPOU

(Tagus fare well that westward with thy strems.) PBRV

Tahoe in August. Robert Hass. CalPo; NoP-4; NoP-5

Tahoe Nocturne. Sherod Santos. GeoHom

Taid's Grave. Gillian Clarke. OPOU

Taiga bore me, The. Taiga, The. Ivan Kharabarov. RusPo, *tr. by* Robert Arthur Douglas Ford

Taiga, The. Ivan Kharabarov. RusPo, *tr. by* Robert Arthur Douglas Ford

Taill of the Uponlandis Mous, and the Burges Mous. Robert Henryson. NePenScot *Fr.* Morall Fabillis of Esope the Phrygian, The.

Táin, The. *Unknown. tr. by* Thomas Kinsella
   Combat of Ferdia and Cúchulainn. WoPoe, *tr. by* Thomas Kinsella

Taino. Jose Angel Figueroa. PueRic

T'ain't No Sin to Dance Around in Your Bones. Edgar Leslie. ReLy

T'Ain't No Use. Herb Magidson. ReLy

T'ai-shan is a holy place, incomparable. Looking at Mount T'ai. Tu Fu [*or* Du Fu]. CrYelRi, *tr. by* Sam Hamill

Tak any brid, and put it in a cage. Geoffrey Chaucer. OWoS *Fr.* Canterbury Tales, The.

Tak tyme in tym, or tym will not be tane. Description of Tyme, A. Alexander Montgomerie. OxBEV

Take a big bite and let its jagged fumes pierce. Bite into the Onion. Marge Piercy. AFaM

Take a drink of water. Silent Room. Aaron Smith. PA9/11

Take a hammer to the amphora of soft Euphrates clay. Jack Gilbert. Campbell McGrath. NAPBL

Take a Hike. Jim Simmerman. PoA 2002

Take a Lamp and Wander Forth. *Unknown.* CCL1,

Take a large olive, stone it and then stuff it. Dish for a Poet, A. *Unknown.* OBCP

Take a long view from Mynydd Bach. Jeremy Hooker. AngWePo

Take a model of the world so big. Rescued Year, The. William Stafford. ColAP

Take a note and spin it around spin it around don't. Genie in the Jar, The. Nikki Giovanni. SeSe

Take a pen in your uncertain fingers. Pen, The. Muhammad Al-Ghuzzi. NAfrP, *tr. by* John Heath-Stubbs and May Jayyusi

Take a plane to London. Directions. Joseph Stroud. GoPo

Take a rib of light. Diorama. Jenny Mueller. IAoNAP

Take: A Roman Wedding. Alice Fulton. ExTi

Take a sheet of paper. How to Reach the Sun . . . on a Piece of Paper. Wes Magee. NOxBChV

Take a taxi and go fishing. Future Models May Have Infra-Red Sensors. Tom Raworth. Oth

Take all my loves, my Love, yea, take them all. William Shakespeare. HeIP-4; OxAEP-1 *Fr.* Sonnets.

Take all of me, pour out my life as wine. To a Woman. Helen Hay Whitney. PoBW

Take all the rest the sun goes round. (LL) On a Girdle. Edmund Waller. BASC; NoP-4; NOSC; OBEV; TFi

Take an eight-cylinder engine down to Mission Street and race the trains and lose. Mission Street Song. Jon Paul Fiorentino. PoPra

Take apart your cassock and make a coat. *Unknown.* CATKP, *tr. by* Peter H. Lee

Take as a sign of the rising wind the swelling sea. Aratus. HePo *Fr.* Phaenomena.

Take Away. Margot Ruddock. OBMV

Take away the whirlwind of hours. Siren, The. Alfonsina Storni. TANSG, *tr. by* Mark McCaffrey

Take back that Heart, you with such Caution give. To Lysander, on Some Verses Be Writ, and Asking More for His Heart. Aphra Behn. LW

Take Back Your Mink. Frank Loesser. ReLy

Take, cradled Nursling of the mountains, take. William Wordsworth. CenSon *Fr.* River Duddon [A Series of Sonnets], The.

Take dandelions first salad. Philip Whalen. WhBo

Take Detroit, where boys. Thinking American. Hayan Charara. AmPoNex; PrTe

Take down its ears first. Dismantling the Silence. Charles Simic. WaAnP

Take eat take glowing coal eat. Body and Soul: Poem for Two Readers. John Taggart. FTOS

Take Five of These. Julie Kalendek. OnScMo

Take from me my voice and I shall voiceless go. Ballad of a Shadow. Alice Oswald. MFPA

Take, gentle marble, to thy trust. Elegy upon His Tomb in Herndon-Hill Church, Erected by His Wife, Who Speaks, An. James Howell. OBWVE

Take Good Care of Yourself. Mark Wunderlich. NeAmPo; ReTh; WiU

Take Hands. Laura Riding Jackson. APT-2

Take heart, Ovid. No sentence. Paavo Haavikko. WoPoe *Fr.* Fifteen Epigrams in Praise of the Tyrant.

Take heart, the journey's ended. In the Town. *Unknown.* OBCP, *tr. by* Eleanor Farjeon

Take heed mine eyes, how you your look[e]s do[e] cast. Mary Sidney Wroth, Countess of Montgomery. BASC; NAEL-7v1; PEW *Fr.* Pamphilia to Amphilanthus.

Take heed of loving me[e]. Prohibition, The. John Donne. NOSC

Take him away, he's dead as they die. Obituary. Kenneth Fearing. IllVoic

Take home Thy prodigal child, O Lord of Hosts! Birthday Sonnet. Elinor Wylie. MoAmPo

Take in hand the cup of delusion. Drink On. Mary E. Tucker. CBWP-1

Take it from me kiddo. Poem, or Beauty Hurts Mr. Vinal. E. E. Cummings. FaBoA; HarvBoo; MoAmPo; NAAL-5; NAAPv.2; PFTM-1; TRP

Take it not back! the priceless gift. Invocation to the Muse. Henrietta Cordelia Ray. CBWP-3

Take it out in vile whisky, take it out. William Carlos Williams. FaBoA

Take it to the hoop, "magic" johnson. Poem for "Magic", A. Quincy Troupe. FTtHH; ISC

Take, Lord, this soul of furred unblemished worth. Epitaph for a Good Mouser. Anne Stevenson. Spl

Take me home. "H. D." APT-1; NAAL-5 *Fr.* Walls Do Not Fall, The.

Take me home. Plea, The. Calvin Forbes. BtF

Take Me in Your Arms, Miss Moneypenny-Wilson. Patrick Barrington. OBCoV

Take Me, Loneliness. Gzar Hantoosh. IrPoTo, *tr. by* Saadi A. Simawe and Ellen Doré Watson

Take me now while it's still early. Hour, The. Juana de Ibarbourou. TCLAP, *tr. by* Sophie Cabot Black

Take Me Out to the Ball Game. Jack Norworth. NAAPv.2; TCAPo

Take my hand / I'm a stranger in paradise. Stranger in Paradise. George Forrest and Robert Wright. ReLy

Take My Hand, Precious Lord. Thomas A. Dorsey. APT-2; ISC; NAAPv.2

Take My Life and Let It Be. Frances Ridley Havergal. SacPr

Take my spirit to Thee. (LL) Prayers. Henry Charles Beeching. OBEV; SacPr

Take, O Take Those Lips Away. William Shakespeare. NoSic; OBEV; TFi *Fr.* Measure for Measure.

Take off your clothes, my love! Paulus Silentiarius. ErotSp, *tr. by* Sam Hamill

Take, Oh, Take Those Lips Away. John Fletcher. NoP-4; NoP-5

Take, oh take those lips away. William Shakespeare. *See* Take, O take those lips away.

Take 1 for magic. City in You. Michael Hill. BtF

Take 1 green pepper and 2 tomatoes. Pour Commencer. Jon Stallworthy. NoAM

Take sackcloth of the darkest dye. Bible Defence of Slavery. Frances Ellen Watkins Harper. APN-2; NAAPv.1

Take severely ill, he is conscious only at brief intervals. Transmutation. Gael Turnbull. BeAl

Take Something like a Star. Robert Frost. *See* Choose Something like a Star.

Take strands of speech, faded and broken. Maker of Songs. Hazel Hall. FiBr

Take, take this cosse, atonys, atonys, my hert! Roundel. Charles, Duc d' Orléans. NPeEn

Take telegraph wires, a lonely moor. Telegraph Wires. Ted Hughes. NPeEn

Take that, damn you; and that! Mezzo Forte. William Carlos Williams. SAmP

Take the Bottle, and Ascend. Tu Mu. CCL1, *tr. by* Robert Morrison

Take the Hearts of Children. Sandra Maria Esteves. PueRic

Take the intellectual prig. Just How Low Can a Highbrow Go When a Highbrow Lowers His Brow? Ogden Nash. OxBoAm

Take the night Myron Stout shut his sure blind eyes. Baby Vallejo. David Rivard. SeSe

Take the thickest socks. Packing for the Future: Instructions. Lorna Crozier. OpeFie

Take the wide shovel down from your attic. Preparing for Snow. Mark Ivey. ICANM

Take Then, These. Charles Bernstein. FTOS

Take, then, your paltry Christ. To the Christians. Francis Lauderdale Adams. ChIV-2

Take Therefore That You May Have. "Angelus Silesius." GePo *Fr.* Cherubical Wanderer, The.

Take these who will as may be: I. Permit Me Voyage. James Agee. MoAmPo; YaYoPo

Take this city-filled. Abiquiu. Luis Lopez. GeoH

Take this fruit, these flowers, these branches and leaves. Green. Paul Verlaine. SxFrPo, *tr. by* Martin Sorrell

Take this Hammer. "Leadbelly." GM

Take this hammer, (huh!) carry it to the captain, (huh!). Take this Hammer. "Leadbelly." GM

Take this hammer—huh! *Unknown.* ISC

Take this kiss upon the brow! Dream within a Dream, A. Edgar Allan Poe. NCAP; OxBoAm; TCAPo

Take this man with an axe. Private, The. Robert Adamson. BMAP

Take this news to the Lakedaimonians, friend. For the Spartan Dead at Thermopylai (480 B.C.). Simonides. PoAgWa, *tr. by* Peter Jay

Take thou the world and all that will. (LL) Flesh and the Spirit, The. Anne Bradstreet. BASC; ChIV-2; NAAL-3; NAAPv.1; OxWW

Take time while time doth last. Song Set by John Farmer. *Unknown.* NoSic

Take two extra-old cabinet ministers and overtake them on the North Sea. Monologue with Its Wife. Gunnar Ekelof. WED, *tr. by* Robert Bly

Take two hundred soldiers. Hazel. Oliver Reynolds. FaBoWar

Take two photographs. King Kong Meets Wallace Stevens. Michael Ondaatje. BrAP; NIL-7

Take up the pen: fall into the net of law. Call to Arms. "Lu Hsün." WoPoe, *tr. by* William R. Schultz

Take up the song; forget the epitaph. (LL) To Inez Milholland. Edna St. Vincent Millay. NAAPv.2; NALW

Take up the White Man's burden. White Man's Burden, The. Rudyard Kipling. WaAnP

Take What He Gives You. "Anvari." WoPoe, *tr. by* Dick Davis

Take what he gives you, even if it's paltry. Take What He GIves You. "Anvari." WoPoe, *tr. by* Dick Davis

Take Wine. Li Po. CCL1, *tr. by* Elling O. Eide

Take ye heed, watch and pray: for ye know not when the time is. Mark 13:33. Jones Very. ChIV-2

Take your fill of intimate remorse, perfumed sorrow. Right to Grief, The. Carl Sandburg. IllVoic

Take your first steps in a Walker. Poem for the Children. Carolyn Beard Whitlow. FFC

Take your kids away, take them. Childish. Gerardo Deniz. PoChi; RMCMP, *tr. by* Mónica de la Torre

Take your moon face away. Caminando. Víctor Hernández Cruz. PFTM-2

Take Yourself to the Rose-Garden. Nedîm. OLP; WoPoe, *tr. by* Walter Andrews, Najaat Black and Mehmet Kalpakli

Take yourself to the rose-garden, it's the season. Take Yourself to the Rose-Garden. Nedîm. OLP; WoPoe, *tr. by* Walter Andrews, Najaat Black and Mehmet Kalpakli

Taken in. Soul Roots. Felicia L. Morgenstern. BtF

Take-Off. Peter Thorpe. OtW

Taking a Captive / 1984. Barney Bush. HATNAP

Taking a Chance on Love. Ted Fetter and John Latouche. ReLy

Taking a midday nap. Basho. EMJL, *tr. by* Haruo Shirane

Taking a nap. Basho. EH, *tr. by* Robert Hass

Taking a View of the Country from His Retirement [*or* Elegy 21]. William Shenstone.

     Goats and Botanists. STuOW

Taking a Watermelon as a Paradigm. Yi Yônju. EcSo, *tr. by* Yung-Hee Kim

Taking Calls in Freeport, NY. Colette Inez. NevBe

Taking coolness. Basho. EMJL, *tr. by* Haruo Shirane

Taking, giving back their lives. Field Hospital, The. Paul Muldoon. PNI

Taking hold, one's astray in nothingness. Kokai. ZenPo, *tr. by* Takashi Ikemoto and Lucien Stryk

Taking in Wash. Rita Dove. OxAAAP

Taking It Back. Dixie Salazar. UnSA

Taking Leave of a Friend. Li Po. ChinPo, *tr. by* Ye Weilian [*or* Yeh Wei-lien *or* Wai-lim Yip]

Taking Leave of a Friend. Li Po. CrYelRi, *tr. by* Sam Hamill

Taking Leave of a Friend ("Blue mountains to the north of the walls.") Li Po. NDACCP; PoCho; WaAnP, *tr. by* Ezra Pound

Taking Leave of Minister So Seyang. Hwang Chini. CATKP, *tr. by* Peter H. Lee

Taking Leave of Two Officials. Tu Fu [*or* Du Fu]. CrYelRi, *tr. by* Sam Hamill

Taking Leave of Wang Wei. Meng Hao Jan. CCL1, *tr. by* Witter Bynner

Taking Notice. Marilyn Hacker.

     "And I shout at Iva, whine at you. Easily." VCAP

     "If we talk, we're too tired to make love; if we." VCAP

     "In the Public Theater lobby, I wait for Marie." VCAP

     "No better lost than any other woman." NAMCP V.2

     "We work, play, don't cross-reference calendars." VCAP

Taking of Life Brings Serious Thoughts, The. *Unknown.* AmWaPo, *tr. by* Frank Russell

Taking of the Koppie, The. Uys Krige. FaBoWar

Taking Off Emily Dickinson's Clothes. Billy Collins. StAl

Taking Off My Clothes. Carolyn Forché. NAMCP V.2; NIL-7; NoAM

Taking off / my clothes. Desire. Connemara Wadsworth. PasH

Taking Pleasure in Myself. Hueung Powoo. BecRai, *tr. by* Kim Daljin, Kim Won-Chung and Christopher Merrill

Taking stock of what I have and what I haven't. I Got the Sun in the Morning. Irving Berlin. ReLy

Taking Tea with My Father and Mother. Pam Zinnemann-Hope. Prnts

Taking the air rifle from my son's hand. Cain. Irving Layton. BrAP

Taking the Census. Charles Robert Thatcher. NOBAu

Taking the Hands of Someone You Love. Robert Bly. TRP

Taking the Night-Train. John James Piatt. APN-2

Taking the Plunge. John Mole. NOxBChV

Taking the Soundings on Third Avenue. David Kherdian.

     "Couple that walked, The." UrbNat

     "Dogs on a leash." UrbNat

     "Hawthorne berries, The." UrbNat

     "In the autumn-come-winter park." UrbNat

     "Wind rips through the." UrbNat

     "Wing-set lone seagull, The." UrbNat

Taking Time to Grow. Mary Mapes Dodge. SWaP

Taking to myself, and would draw blood. (LL) My Mother Would Be a Falconress. Robert Duncan. FTOS; OxBoAm; RaBo; WoPoe

Taking Turns. Norma Farber. TLR

Taking us by and large, we're a queer lot. Sisters, The. Amy Lowell. NALW

Taking what is, and seeing it as it is. Vermeer. Howard Nemerov. GoPo

Takings. Gael Turnbull. Oth

Taklamakan. Kim Hyesun. EcSo, *tr. by* Youngju Ryu

Taku Skanskan. Paula Gunn Allen. HATNAP

Tal vez sólo haga falta. Hampstead Heath. Manuel Ulacia. RMCMP

Tale: "Children's poet's own child is dying, A." Georgi Belev. CSCBP, *tr. by* the author and Lisa Sapinkopf

Tale. Jennifer Rankin. BMAP

Tale, A. Louise Bogan. StAl

Tale, A. Ahmed Taha. AnVo, *tr. by* Mohamed Enani

Tale, A. Edward Thomas. OxBEV

Tale, A [Revised Version]. Edward Thomas. OxBEV

Tale Before the End of the World. Maurya Simon. AtGh

Tale I frame shall be found to tally. *Unknown.* OBVE *Fr.* Seafarer, The.

Tale I frame shall be found to tally, The. Seafarer, The. *Unknown.* OBVE, *tr. by* Michael Alexander

Tale is told of long ago, A. Song of the Yellow Cedar Face, A. George Clutesi. HATNAP

Tale of a Friar and a Shoemaker's Wife, A. Thomas Churchyard. NoSic

Tale of a Pony, The. Bret Harte. OBNV

Tale of Bananas, A. Víctor Hernández Cruz. PueRic

Tale of Custard the Dragon, The. Ogden Nash. ITBLP; MakPoe

Tale of Genji. Hugh Seidman. YaYoPo

Tale of Genji, The. Murasaki Shikibu. *tr. by* Edward Seidensticker

     "Warblers are today as long ago, The." WoPoe, *tr. by* Edward Seidensticker

Tale of Italy, A. Eloise Bibb. CBWP-4

Tale of Me, The. Eiléan Ní Chuilleanáin. Prnts

Tale of Red-Haired Motele, Mister Inspector, Rabbi Isaiah and Commissar Blokh, The. Iosif Pavlovich Utkin. TCRusP, *tr. by* Denis Johnson and Kathy Lewis

Tale of St. Petersburg, A. Alexander Sergeyevich Pushkin. WoPoe *Fr.* Bronze Horseman, The.

Tale of Sunlight, The. Gary Soto. CAP-8; NoAM

Tale of the Beginning of Friars and Cloisterers, A. William Warner. NoSic *Fr.* Albion's England.

Tale of the Oyster, The. Cole Porter. ReLy

Tale of the Reign of Terror, A. Caroline Anne Bowles Southey. DiBP *Fr.* Conte à mon chien.

Tale of the Sea, A. William McGonagall.

     "'Twas on the 8th April, on the afternoon of that day." VerBaPo

Tale of the Upland Mouse and the Burgess Mouse, The. Robert Henryson. *See* Taill of the Uponlandis Mous, and the Burges Mous.

Tale of Time. Robert Penn Warren. NAAPv.2

Tale That's Not a Tale, A. Binyo Ivanov. CSCBP, *tr. by* Georgi Belev and Lisa Sapinkopf

Talent and Friendship. Thomas Kinsella. HarvBoo *Fr.* Notes.

Talented Man, The. Winthrop Mackworth Praed. CABP
　(Letter, From a Lady in London to a Lady at Lausanne, A.) OBCoV

Tales. George Crabbe.
　Procrastination. NOBRP; NPBRoP

Tales of a Wayside Inn. Henry Wadsworth Longfellow.
　(Landlord's Tale: Paul Revere's Ride, The.) APN-1
　　"So through the night rode Paul Revere." CA
　Paul Revere's Ride [The Landlord's Tale]. AmWaPo; BLPJKO; BRP; ChAP; ColAP; HHAm; ITBLP; NAAPv.1; NOxBChV; OBNV; OxBoAm; TCAPo; TFi; WaAnP
　　"So through the night rode Paul Revere." CA
　Prelude: The Wayside Inn. APN-1
　Spanish Jew's Tale: Azrael, The. APN-1; TCAPo
　Spanish Jew's Tale: The Legend of Rabbi Ben Levi, The. NCAP; TCAPo

Tales of the Hall. George Crabbe.
　Delay has Danger. NOBRP
　　"Three weeks had past, and Richard rambles now." NPeEn
　Elder Brother, The.
　　Business Man's Lair, A. STuOW
　Sisters, The.
　　Bright Morning, A. STuOW
　　Invitation to the Waltz. STuOW
　William Bailey.
　　Baileys, The. STuOW

Taliban blew up the buddha, The. You can't blow up the buddha. Mark S. Kuhar. AmZen

Taliesin. Emyr Lewis. ATSWP, *tr. by* Robert Minhinnick

Taliesin 1952. Ronald Stuart Thomas. HarvBoo

Taliesin and the Mockers. Vernon Watkins. AngWePo

Talin of the Pasta Factory. Rossana Ombres. CItWP, *tr. by* Cinzia Sartini Blum and Lara Trubowitz

Talisman, A. Marianne Moore. MoAmPo

Talismans. Maudelle Driskell. AllShUp

Talk. Roo Borson. NIP-4

Talk. Terrance Hayes. LegDan

Talk. Murad Mikha'il. IrPoTo, *tr. by* Christina Coyle and Sadok Masliyah

Talk about cringing. Landmarks. Claude Wilkinson. BtF

Talk is of boats, sea-legs, The. Deep. Patricia Pogson. Prnts

Talk no more of the lucky escape of the head. On a Stone Thrown at a Very Great Man, But Which Missed Him. "Peter Pindar." NBLV

Talk of energy. Mayan sub-flower. Dangers of the Journey to the Happy Land. Joseph Ceravolo. NYP2

Talk of old families—last remains. Death of a Species. Anthony Conran. AngWePo

Talk Show, The. Albert Goldbarth. CAP-8; IllVoic; ReTh

Talk, talk, talk. . .talk, talk, talk. Ernst Mirville. OGAHCP, *tr. by* Boadiba and Jack Hirschman

Talk to me, *javas*, talk to me. Najrul Islām. SinGod, *tr. by* Rachel Fell McDermott

Talk we could have, The. Erin Mouré. NLPA *Fr.* Wittgenstein Letters to Mel Gibson's Braveheart, The.

Talked to my father again in a dream he seemed happy. Le Jazz Hot. Anselm Hollo. SeSe

Talkin' Trash. Elena Georgiou. WiU

Talking. Miguel Algarin. PueRic

Talking about Birds. *Vietnamese Oral Tradition.* CaDao, *tr. by* John Balaban

Talking About Boys. Lisa Glatt. SUP

Talking about ghosts. Things That Stand One's Hair on End. *Unknown.* EMJL, *tr. by* Edward Putzar

Talking about the chemical changes. Glow Worm. Vicki Feaver. MoWP; StAl

Talking About Things. Michael Ryan. YaYoPo

Talking backwards. (LL) Call It Fear. Joy Harjo. ICANM; NAAL-5

Talking Cure, The. Ingrid de Kok. TSAP

Talking Cure, The. Sherod Santos. LiTh

Talking Dust Bowl. Woody Guthrie. APT-2

Talking in bed ought to be easiest. Talking in Bed. Philip Larkin. NAEL-6v2; NAEL-7v2; NAMCP V.2; NoP-4; NoP-5; PoetW; PoPoPo

Talking of Ezra Pound and long-dead pantos. Robert Malise Bowyer Nichols. OBSV *Fr.* Fisbo.

Talking of poetry, hauling the books. In a Classroom. Adrienne Rich. LoL

Talking of Sharp Things. Frank Mkalawile Chipasula. HBAPE

Talking; seven steps, eight falls. Shishin-Goshin. ZenPo, *tr. by* Takashi Ikemoto and Lucien Stryk

Talking to Arlene. Peter Schjeldahl. MotU

Talking to God on the Seventh Day. Ruth L. Schwartz. BeAl

Talking to her, he knew it was the end. Hector. Valentin Iremonger. IrLP

Talking to Jim. Walta Borawski. CAGL

Talking to strange men on the subway. My Mother. John Wieners. BB; PmAP

Talking to the Birds. Brian Bartlett.
　2. to a northern gannet. Coast

Talking to the Family. John A. Stone. BloBone

Talking to Vladimir Mayakovsky. Ron Padgett. NYP2

Talking to You Afterwards. Peter Porter. BMAP

Talking with Soldiers. Walter James Turner. MoBrPo

Talks and talks. (LL) Age ("Most explicit—/ the sense of trap.") Robert Creeley. FTOS; PmAP

Tall and thin and young and lovely the michael with kaposi's sarcoma *goes walking.* D. A. Powell. AmPoNex; LegDan

Tall as a telephone pole and as old as the oldest house on. Roy Kiyooka. NLPA *Fr.* Pear Tree Pomes.

Tall as a village spire. Wireless at Night. *Unknown.* RWPCtW

Tall bamboos, The. Pei Di and Wang Wei. CCL1 *Fr.* Wheel River.

Tall camels of the spirit, The. World Without Objects Is a Sensible Emptiness, A. Richard Wilbur. MoAmPo; NoAM; PoA 2002; UpMys

The tall constructions facing the sun in the cloudless sky are visible from the room at the top of the landscape. These Tall Constructions. Dora Maar. YaTCFP, *tr. by* Mary Ann Caws *and* Jean-Pierre Cauvin

Tall dancer dances, The. Dancer, The. Joseph Campbell. OBMV

Tall Girl, The. John Crowe Ransom. OxBSo

Tall in a top hat. Situation No. 13: City Hall. David Citino. UpMys

Tall man and myself tonight, The. Grand Army Plaza. June Jordan. ISC

Tall Man Executes a Jig, A. Irving Layton. NoAM

Tall masts quiver'd as they lay afloat, The. Alfred Tennyson. STuOW *Fr.* Dream of Fair Women, A.

Tall Nettles. Edward Thomas. FaBoVe; MoBrPo; NPeEn; OxBEV

Tall plumes surmount a painted mask of death. (LL) Atavism. Elinor Wylie. NALW; PoA 2002

Tall stately plants with spikes and forks of gold. Frederick Goddard Tuckerman. OxBSo *Fr.* Sonnets: First Series, 1854–1860.

Tall Tale, A; or, A Moral Song. Phyllis Webb. BrAP

Tall Tales. Gwendolyn MacEwen. StAl *Fr.* T. E. Lawrence Poems, The.

Tall trees are full of sad wind, The. Ballad of the Orioles in the Fields. Ts'ao Chih. ColAnChi, *tr. by* Hans H. Frankel

Tall unpopular men. Dedication. Oliver St. John Gogarty. OBMV

Tall Weeds. W. S. Rendra. WoPoe, *tr. by* Burton Raffel

Tall Wood twins, The. Les A. Murray. NewEx

Tall yellow haired girl jogs smoothly past our windows, The. American Exercises. Patricia Goedicke. RWB

Talla ly li oh / Freedom a come oh! Freedom a Come Oh! *Unknown.* FaBoVe

Tallahassee. Aimee Nezhukumatathil. LiTh

Taller To-day. W. H. Auden. NPeEn

Taller to-day, we remember similar evenings. Taller To-day. W. H. Auden. NPeEn

Tallest peaks, The. At I-Chou, Climbing the Tower of Lung-Hsing Temple to View the High Northern Mountains. Chia Tao. CSKM, *tr. by* Mike O'Connor

Tallulah. James Matthew Legaré. APN-2

Tally. Josephine Miles. NoAM

Tally Stick, The. Jarold Ramsey. NIL-7; NIP-4

Talysarn. Brenda Chamberlain. OBWVE

Tam i' the Kirk. Violet Jacob. EdScPo; NePenScot

Tam Lin. *Unknown.* OBEV; OBNV

Tam o' Shanter; A Tale. Robert Burns. CABP; NAEL-6v2; NAEL-7v2; NePenScot; NoP-4; NoP-5; NPBRoP; PoEEn; OBNV; WaAnP

Tam o' the Lin was fu' o' pride. Tam O' the Lin. Joanna Baillie. RWP

Tamarind hangs its head, The. Airy Hall Icongraphy. Frederick D'Aguiar. Oth

Tambourine Tommy. Thomas Sayers Ellis. NAPBL

Tambourines. Langston Hughes. NOxBChV; SAmP

Tambourines / To glory! (LL) Tambourines. Langston Hughes. NOxBChV; SAmP

Tambov wolf is your comrade, A. Arrow in the Wall. Andrey Andreievich Voznesensky. RusPo, *tr. by* Robert Arthur Douglas Ford

Tamburā. Anuradha Mahapatra. FiBr, *tr. by* Paramita Banerjee and Carolyne Wright

Tamburlaine the Great. Christopher Marlowe.
　"And ride in triumph through Persepolis?" FaBoWar
　What Is Beauty? MakPoe

Tamburlaine the Great, Part 2.   Christopher Marlowe.
  "Bastardly boy, sprung from some coward's loins."   FaBoWar
  "Blacke is the beauty of the brightest day."   OxBEV
  "But now my boys, leave off, and list to me."   FaBoWar
  "Now fetch me out the Turkish concubines."   FaBoWar
Tame and Ferocious Animal, A.   Nancy Morejón.   TANSG, tr. by Joy
  Renjilian-Burgy
Tame Cat.   Ezra Pound.   APT-1
Tamed by *Miltown* we lie on Mother's bed;.   Man And Wife.   Robert Lowell.
  ColAP; VCAP
Tamer and Hawk.   Thom Gunn.   HarvBoo
Taming of the Shrew, The.   William Shakespeare.
  Rival Favourites.   DiBP
  "Thy gown? Why, ay. Come, tailor, let us see't."   OBCoV
Tamoxifen.   Alison Mosquera.   PoCu
Tamp 'em up solid.   Tamping Ties.   *Unknown.*   GM
Tamping Ties.   *Unknown.*   GM
Tan Chanteuse, The.   Carole Boston Weatherford.   FuFl
Tan Manhattan.   Andy Razaf.   ReLy
Tan Tien.   Mei-Mei Berssenbrugge.   OpBo
Tanagra! think not I forget.   Walter Savage Landor.   OBEV Fr. Pericles and
  Aspasia.
Tanana Valley.   Janice Gould.   FiBr
Tangerine.   Johnny Mercer.   ReLy
Tangerine Orchids.   Rachel Hadas.   PA9/11
Tangled Hair.   Lady Izumi.   WoPoe, tr. by Steven D. Carter
Tangled Hair.   Yosano Akiko. tr. by Sanford Goldstein and Seishi Shinoda
  "Thousand lines, A."   WoPoe, tr. by Sanford Goldstein and Seishi Shinoda
Tango.   Oliver Pitcher.   EGAG
Tango.   Ntozake Shange.   GT
Tango'd Love.   J. B. Bernstein.   PasH
Tank with pennies and nickels, nickel-and-diming "Lori the Seal" wishes for
  change.   Petition Hecate at the seal.   Jill Hartman.   PoPra
Tanka.   Sadakichi.   NAAPv.1
Tanka: "Month of rain ends—."   Lenard D. Moore.   SpirFl
Tanka: "After church meeting."   Lenard D. Moore.   SpirFl
Tanka: "Accidentally / having broken a teacup."   Ishikawa Takuboku.
  CAoMJL1, tr. by Makoto Ueda
Tanka: "All the young men I know."   Toki Zenmaro.   CAoMJL1, tr. by
  Makoto Ueda
Tanka: "As I gaze upon."   Kanoko Okamoto.   CAoMJL1, tr. by Makoto Ueda
Tanka: "As if in water."   Ishikawa Takuboku.   CAoMJL1, tr. by Makoto Ueda
Tanka: "Flower blooms, A."   Kanoko Okamoto.   CAoMJL1, tr. by Makoto
  Ueda
Tanka: "Having let flow."   Kanoko Okamoto.   CAoMJL1, tr. by Makoto Ueda
Tanka: "I work."   Ishikawa Takuboku.   CAoMJL1, tr. by Makoto Ueda
Tanka: "Ice rain coats berries."   Henry Beissel.   IFF
Tanka: "Imagining / the grassy ground not shown."   Shaku Chōkū.   CAoMJL1,
  tr. by Makoto Ueda
Tanka: "In sullen silence."   Toki Zenmaro.   CAoMJL1, tr. by Makoto Ueda
Tanka: "Innately reserved."   Kanoko Okamoto.   CAoMJL1, tr. by Makoto
  Ueda
Tanka: "Just for fun."   Ishikawa Takuboku.   CAoMJL1, tr. by Makoto Ueda
Tanka: "Like a white lotus."   Ishikawa Takuboku.   CAoMJL1, tr. by Makoto
  Ueda
Tanka: "No news of him."   Toki Zenmaro.   CAoMJL1, tr. by Makoto Ueda
Tanka: "Nothing / but reason."   Toki Zenmaro.   CAoMJL1, tr. by Makoto
  Ueda
Tanka: "Old Japan."   Toki Zenmaro.   CAoMJL1, tr. by Makoto Ueda
Tanka: "On the roadside."   Ishikawa Takuboku.   CAoMJL1, tr. by Makoto
  Ueda
Tanka: "Somewhere around."   Shaku Chōkū.   CAoMJL1, tr. by Makoto Ueda
Tanka: "Sorrow / its outlines blurred."   Ishikawa Takuboku.   CAoMJL1, tr. by
  Makoto Ueda
Tanka: "Stark naked."   Kanoko Okamoto.   CAoMJL1, tr. by Makoto Ueda
Tanka: "Ten years ago."   Kanoko Okamoto.   CAoMJL1, tr. by Makoto Ueda
Tanka: "Work on the impossible."   Toki Zenmaro.   CAoMJL1, tr. by Makoto
  Ueda
Tanks.   Rhyll McMaster.   NOBAu
Tannhauser.   Newman Levy.   AmWit
Tansy buttons, tansy.   Charles Olson.   APT-2; PmAP Fr. Maximus Poems, The.
Tant il gela que les branches laiteuses.   Lied du figuier.   René Char.   YaTCFP
Tantalized by wind, this flag that flies.   At the Grave of My Brother: Bomber
  Pilot.   William Stafford.   PWW2
Tantalos.   Paulus Silentiarius.   WoPoe, tr. by Dudley Fitts
Tantramar Revisited, The.   Sir Charles G. D. Roberts.   BrAP
Tantric Praise of the Goddess.   *Unknown.*   HW, tr. by Jalaja Bonheim

Tantum Ergo.   Richard Foerster.   Vesp
Tao.   *Vietnamese Oral Tradition.*   CaDao, tr. by John Balaban
Tao and Unfitness at Inistiogue on the River Nore.   Thomas Kinsella.   NPeEn;
  PBCIP
T'ao Ch'ien withdrew from all the world.   Tu Fu [or Du Fu].   CrYelRi Fr.
  Random Pleasures.
Tão delicados (mais que um arbusto) e correm.   Boi Vě os Homens, Um.
  Carlos Drummond de Andrade.   IPoFL
Tao is a low whisper coming from a shiny, The.   Tao Sequence, The.   Dave
  Brinks.   AnSo
Tao of Poetry, A.   Sam Hamill.
  "Each word carefully."   TAPaP
Tao Sequence, The.   Dave Brinks.   AnSo
Tao Te Ching.   Lao Tzu. tr. by Robert Henricks and Moss Roberts
  "Best be done before the last degree."   WoPoe, tr. by Moss Roberts
  "Boundless shaping Power, A."   WoPoe, tr. by Moss Roberts
  "Human beings are / soft and supple when alive."   ColAnChi, tr. by Victor H.
  Mair
  "Know masculinity, / Maintain femininity."   ColAnChi, tr. by Victor H. Mair
  "Large state is like a low-lying estuary, A."   ColAnChi, tr. by Victor H. Mair
  "Let there be a small state with few people."   ColAnChi, tr. by Victor H.
  Mair
  "Person of superior integrity, The."   ColAnChi, tr. by Victor H. Mair
  "Thirty spokes converge on a single hub."   ColAnChi, tr. by Victor H. Mair
  "To understand others is to be knowledgeable."   AmFaPo, tr. by Robert
  Henricks
  "Valley spirit never dies, The."   ColAnChi, tr. by Victor H. Mair
  "Way as "Way" bespoke is no true lasting way; The."   WoPoe, tr. by Moss
  Roberts
  "Ways that can be walked are not the eternal Way, The."   ColAnChi, tr. by
  Victor H. Mair
  "When thirty spokes join the wheel-hole."   WoPoe, tr. by Moss Roberts
  "Whenever all the world declares fair "fair.""   WoPoe, tr. by Moss Roberts
  "While you / Cultivate the soul and embrace unity."   ColAnChi, tr. by Victor
  H. Mair
  "Without going out-of-doors."   ColAnChi, tr. by Victor H. Mair
Taoist Huang Has Died of Alcoholism, The.   Shen Chou.   ColAnChi, tr. by
  Jonathan Chaves
Taoist Song.   Wang Yang-ming.   CrYelRi, tr. by Sam Hamill
Taoist Song: "Empty bag of skin filling with desire."   Teng Yu-pin.   CrYelRi,
  tr. by Sam Hamill
Taoist Song: "Heaven and hell are men's unhappy inventions."   Teng Yu-pin.
  CrYelRi, tr. by Sam Hamill
Taoist Song: "In white clouds, in green mountains."   Teng Yu-pin.   CrYelRi, tr.
  by Sam Hamill
Taormini.   John Henry, Cardinal Newman.   SacPr
Taos Pueblo Indians: 700 strong according to Bobby's last census.   Miguel
  Algarin.   PueRic
Tao-yao: Like the Slender Peach.   *Unknown.*   CCL1, tr. by V. W. X.
Tap.   Maggie Hannan.   NLP
Tap.   Alice Jones.   BloBone
Tap Dancing Lessons.   Gerald Locklin.   SUP
Tap Your Troubles Away.   Jerry Herman.   ReLy
Tape Mark.   Nanni Balestrini.   PFTM-2, tr. by Lawrence R. Smith
Tape, The.   Myra Cohn Livingston.   NTCP
Taped to the wall of my cell are 47 pictures: 47 black.   Idea of Ancestry, The.
  Etheridge Knight.   AF; ESEAA; InGu; ISC; NIP-4; OxAAAP; PBCAP;
  RaBo; StAl
Tapers in the great God's hall, The.   By Night.   Philip Jerome Cleveland.
  SacPr
Tapes.   Thomas Sayers Ellis.   AmPoNex
Tapestry.   Charles Simic.   VCAP
Tapestry of the Heart, The.   Jolanda Insana.   CItWP, tr. by Cinzia Sartini Blum
  and Lara Trubowitz
Tapestry Weaver, The.   Anson G. Chester.   ITBLP
Tapping in on your inner telephone life.   Wire Tap.   Miguel Algarin.   PueRic
Tapping, tapping the carved wooden fish.   Ancient Temple.   Cho Chihun.
  CAMKP, tr. by David R. McCann
Tap-Room, The.   Robert Tannahill.   NePenScot
Taproot.   Debra Kang Dean.   NAPBL
Taproots.   Dorothy Marie Rice.   FuFl
Taps have not been running, The.   Hamza Aweiwi, a Shoemaker in Hebron.
  Hayan Charara.   PrTe
Tar.   C. K. Williams.   AtGh; VCAP
Tar Baby on the Soapbox, The.   Carole Boston Weatherford.   BtF
Tara, Mother / Lift me out by the hair.   Kamalākānta Bhattācārya.   SinGod, tr.
  by Rachel Fell McDermott

Tara, this is why I call upon You. Tārinī Debī. SinGod, *tr. by* Rachel Fell McDermott

Tara, what more are You planning? Rāmprasād Sen. SinGod, *tr. by* Rachel Fell McDermott

Tara, You are Cintamayi, Full of Thought. Kumār Śambhucandra Rāy. SinGod, *tr. by* Rachel Fell McDermott

Tarahumara Indians have come down, The. Tarahumara Herbs. Alfonso Reyes. TCLAP, *tr. by* Samuel Beckett

Tarantella. Joseph Hilaire Pierre Belloc. BLPJKO; MoBrPo; OBMV; UV

Tarantino's languor and dreaming back. Aleksandra Petrova. CRWP, *tr. by* Dennis Silk

Tarantula of Love, The. William Fowler.
    "Upon this firthe, as on the sees of love." NePenScot

Tarantula rattling at the lily's foot, The. O Carib Isle! Hart Crane. APT-2; NoAM; OxBoAm; PFTM-1

Tarantulas on the Lifebuoy. Thomas Lux. AmAlph

Tarde caía, La. Víctor Terán. RMCMP

Tarde Cualquiera, Una. José Hierro. RaW

Tarde de Sol. Mary Gomez Parham. OWABP

Tarde está muriendo, La. Campo. Antonio Machado Ruiz. RaW

Tarde parda y fría, Una. Recuerdo Infantil. Antonio Machado Ruiz. RaW

Tarde se absorbe en tu silencio, La. Hiedra. Elsa Cross. RMCMP

Targeting me with your eyes, uplifed, two steps down. Wreckage is the only Answer. Barry MacSweeney. VaPo

Targets and Flowers (Begun with Lines from Breton). Garrett Caples. IIR

Tarpeia. Louise Imogen Guiney. NAAPv.1

Tarred road simmered in a blue haze. The reservoir was dry, The. Judgement. Ciaran Carson. PBCIP

Tarred rope's end of life burnt through his hands, The. Sunken Sailor. Francis Claiborne Mason. YaYoPo

Tarry a moment, happy feet. Statues, The. Laurence Binyon. OBEV

Tarry Awhile, Restless Bird. Walter Höllerer. GTCP, *tr. by* Irmgard Hunt

Tarry Flynn. Patrick Kavanagh. IPoFL; ModIr

Tartar Horse. Wei Ying-wu. CCL1, *tr. by* Marsha Wagner

Tartarus. Oliver Wendell Holmes. NCAP

Tarye no lenger; toward thyn herytage. Vox Ultima Crucis. John Lydgate. OBEV

(Tarye no longer; toward thyn herytage.) SacPr

Tarzan. Jaime Manrique. WiU

Tashlikh. Gerald Stern. TaR

Task, A. Czeslaw Milosz. AF, *tr. by* the author and Czeslaw Milosz

Task, The. William Cowper.
    Garden, The.
        Stricken Deer, The. NAEL-6v1; NAEL-7v1
        "Groans of nature in this nether world, The." NoP-5
    Sofa, The.
        Crazy Kate. NAEL-6v1; NAEL-7v1; NPBRoP
        Landscape Described, A. NAEL-6v1; NAEL-7v1
    Time-piece, The.
        On Slavery. BrAP
    Winter Evening, The.
        "Just when our drawing-rooms begin to blaze." NoP-4; NoP-5; NPBRoP; NPeEn
    Winter Evening, The: A Brown Study. NAEL-6v1; NAEL-7v1
    Winter Morning Walk, The.
        (Frolic in the Snow, A.) DiBP
        "Great princes have great playthings. Some have played." FaBoWar
    Winter Walk at Noon, The. NPeEn

Task, The. Denise Levertov. InvLi; UpMys

Task, The. Ruth Pitter. BeAl; MoBrPo

Task it was to found the Roman people. (LL) Virgil. NAWM-5v1; NAWM-7v1 *Fr.* Aeneid [*or* Eneados *or* Aeneis], The.

Task of Hope, The. Yves Bonnefoy. YaTCFP, *tr. by* John Naughton

Task[e] is easier to destroy, than [*or* then] build, The. (LL) Upon His Majesty's [*or* Majesties] Repairing of Paul's. Edmund Waller. BASC; PBRV

Tasmania. Vivian Smith. NOBAu

Tasmanian Scenes. Louisa Meredith. NOBAu

Tassajara, 1969. Diane Di Prima. BB

Tassajara, Early 1970's. Diane Di Prima. WANABP

Taste. Jennifer Maiden. BMAP

Taste. Pablo Neruda. ConPit, *tr. by* Clayton Eshleman

Taste, The. George Oppen. FTOS *Fr.* Some San Francisco Poems.

Taste for Tomorrow. Jayanta Mahapatra. VCWP

Taste his terror on my hands. (LL) John Montague. ModIr; NoP-4; NoP-5; PBCIP; PNI; StAl *Fr.* All Legendary Obstacles.

Taste of Life Going On, The. Opal Moore. FuFl

Taste of October on your shoulders, The. To Poetry. Carlos Pellicer. TCLAP, *tr. by* Alexandra Migoya

Taste of pomegranate, The. Persephone. Ziporah Hildebrandt. HW

Taste of Wild Cherry, The. Chris Forhan. NAPBL

Taste the unnecessary tears. Reading. Bei Dao. WoBe, *tr. by* Iona Man-Cheong and Eliot Weinberger

Tasted, the green cypress is bitter. Empty Purse. Tu Fu [*or* Du Fu]. CrYelRi, *tr. by* Sam Hamill

Tatale Swine. Kojo Laing. HBAPE

Tatale there rounding the fat woman that fried it. Tatale Swine. Kojo Laing. HBAPE

Tatar Anguish. Anna Barkova. ARWW, *tr. by* Catriona Kelly

Tatar anguish, anguish of the Volga. Tatar Anguish. Anna Barkova. ARWW, *tr. by* Catriona Kelly

Tatar Songs. Unknown. EaWin, *tr. by* W. S. Merwin

Tato—Reading at the Nuyorican Poets' Cafe. Miguel Algarin. PmAP

Tattered Hungarian tent, The. Driving with Dominic in the Southern Province We See Hints of the Circus. Michael Ondaatje. NAMCP V.2; NoP-5

Tattered Kaddish. Adrienne Rich. ColAP

Tattered outlaw of the earth, The. Donkey, The [1920 version]. G. K. Chesterton. WaAnP

Tattered rain. Wet Pain . . . Tread with Care. Leseko Rampolekeng. NAfrP

Tattered Sack, The. Devara Dasimayya. WoPoe, *tr. by* A. K. Ramanujan

Tattering of rain and then the regin, A. Darkling Summer, Ominous Dusk, Rumorous Rain. Delmore Schwartz. APT-2

Tatton Parachute Training School. Unknown. FaBoWar

Tattoo. Robert Budde. PoPra

Tattoo. Peter Johnson. LiTh

Tattoo. Liliane Welch. Coast

Tattoo, The. Peter Finch. TCAWP

Tattoo, The. Ania Walwicz. BMAP

Tattoo #47, "Happy Dragon." Paul Allen. ReTh

Tattoo, Corazon: Ritchie Valens, 1959. David Wojahn. PBCAP *Fr.* Mystery Train: A Sequence.

Tattoo of, A. Karai Senryū. EMJL, *tr. by* Haruo Shirane

Tattoo, or Henna. Odetta D. Norton. BtF

Tattoo Writing. Fawziyya Abu Khalid. CFP, *tr. by* Kamal Boullata

Tattooed Girl. Monica A. Hand. BtF

Tattooed Man, The. Robert Earl Hayden. NoAM

Tattooed on your arm. (LL) I Remember Haifa Being Lovely But. Lyn Lifshin. CFP; UnSA

Tattooing the Motherline. Krista Franklin. BRtP

Tattoos. J. D. McClatchy. BAP-01

Tattoos. Charles Wright. BodElec

Tattoos in the Water. Efraín Bartolomé. RMCMP, *tr. by* Asa Zatz

Tatuajes en el Agua. Efraín Bartolomé. RMCMP

Taught early that his mother's skin was the sign of error. Mr. Z. M. Carl Holman. SoSe-8

Taurean reaper of the wild apple field. Tattered Kaddish. Adrienne Rich. ColAP

Taut, industrious little drum. To His Pulse. Robert B. Shaw. PoA 2002

Tavarisch is a dirty word. Blue-pencilled. Stateless. Linda France. RSaN

Tavern Guitar Playing a *Jota* Today. Antonio Machado Ruiz. SpanPo, *tr. by* Charles Guenther

Tavern, The. Edwin Arlington Robinson. NCAP

Tavern's red lamp flickers as though it will choke and go out, The. Black Cove. Ch'ŏn Yanghŭi. EcSo, *tr. by* Aimee N. Kwon

Tawny are the leaves turned but they still hold. Antique Harvesters. John Crowe Ransom. MoAmPo

Tawny-black sky-scurries. David Jones. OBWVE *Fr.* Sleeping Lord, The.

Taxi Suite. Lew Welch.

Taxi, The. Amy Lowell. IJHIL; LW; MoAmPo; NAAPv.2; PoCho; WaAnP

Taxidermist, A. Jean Follain. BLT

Taxidermist at the Zoo, The. Ruth Anderson Barnett. UrbNat

Taxidermist is sitting / before the russet breasts, A. Taxidermist, A. Jean Follain. BLT

Taxing. Eileen Myles. BodElec

Taxing the Rain. Penelope Shuttle. MoWP

Taxis, The. Louis MacNeice. EmeKit; NPeEn; PNI

Taxman. George Mackay Brown. NePenScot

Taxonomy. Joy Katz. NeAmPo

Tay Bridge Disaster, The. William McGonagall. VerBaPo
    "Beautiful Railway Bridge of the Silv'ry Tay!" UV

Tayis Bank. Unknown. FaBoVe

Taylor's Arithmetic from One to Twelve. John Taylor.
    "10 Commandments, are the Law Divine." ChIV-1

Tayyib studies literature at Tel Aviv University. Transparent. Ronny Someck. Eno; IrPoTo, *tr. by* Vivian Eden

T-Bar. Patricia K. Page. BrAP; NoAM

Tchaikowsky (And Other Russians). Ira Gershwin. ReLy

Tchirek River. Tchirek Song (Northern Yueh-Fu). *Unknown.* ChinPo, *tr. by* Ye Weilian [*or* Yeh Wei-lien *or* Wai-lim Yip]

Tchirek Song (Northern Yueh-Fu). *Unknown.* ChinPo, *tr. by* Yeh Wei-lien *or* Wai-lim Yip]

Te Deum. Charles Reznikoff. ChIV-1; NAAPv.2; NAMCP V.1; OxBoAm

Te Martyrum Candidatus. Lionel Pigot Johnson. OBMV

Te miro en tu retrato. Hielo. Mónica Nepote. SPV

Te Saluer. Claude De Burine. YaTCFP

Tea. Ch'u Ch'uang I. CCL1; NDACCP, *tr. by* Kenneth Rexroth

Tea. Sean Dunne. ModIr *Fr.* Sydney Place.

Tea. Amy Uyematsu. WhBo

Tea at the Magdalene. Clara Silva. TANSG, *tr. by* Celeste Kostopulos-Cooperman

Tea at the Palaz of Hoon. Wallace Stevens. AmFaPo; APT-1; NAMCP V.1; OxBoAm; PoA 2002; WoPoe

Tea Dance. Wayne Koestenbaum. WiU

Tea flowers. Buson. EH, *tr. by* Robert Hass

Tea for the Emperor arrives on a tray. Princess Parade. Sarah Gorham. FFC

Tea for Two. Irving Caesar. ReLy

Tea for two / And two for tea. W. D. Snodgrass. BodElec *Fr.* Führer Bunker, The.

Tea for Two, before the War. No, No, Nanette. K. Schippers. TuT, *tr. by* Dennis O'Driscoll

Tea is one, wine another, women third. Women. Trần Tế Xu'o'ng. EaWin; WoPoe, *tr. by* W. S. Merwin and Nguyen Ngoc Bich

Tea Making. Antoinette Scudder. PoBW

Tea Merchant, The. H. C. Artmann. MotU, *tr. by* Stuart Friebert

Tea Mind. Chase Twichell. ExTi

Tea Party. Nancy Vieira Couto. PBCAP

Tea Party, The. Jean Earle. TCAWP

Tea Shop, The. Ezra Pound. HeIP-4

Teach it me, if you can,—forgetfulness! Love's Last Lesson. Letitia Elizabeth Landon. NAEL-7v2; RWP

Teach me, my God and King. Elixir [*or* Elixer], The. George Herbert. BASC; NoP-4; NoP-5; NOSC; SacPr

Teach Me Tonight. Sammy Cahn. ReLy

Teach the free man how to praise. (LL) In Memory of W. B. Yeats. W. H. Auden. AmFaPo; BrAP; GPTC; HeIP-4; MakPoe; MoBrPo; NAEL-6v2; NAEL-7v2; NAMCP V.1; NIL-7; NoAM; NoP-4; NoP-5; NPeEn; OxAEP-2; OxBoAm; TFi; TRP; WaAnP; WeW-3

Teach the kings sonne, who kings hym self shalbe. Mary Sidney Herbert, Countess of Pembroke. EMWP *Fr.* Psalms.

Teach Us to Number Our Days. Rita Dove. ESEAA; NoAM

Teachable Texts. Steve McCaffery. NLPA

Teacher asked Paul, A. Rain. Naomi Shihab Nye. CFP; P180

Teacher asks a question, The. Hand, The. Mary Ruefle. P180

Teacher, Jimmie's toe is bleedin'. Johnny's Pet Superstition. Clara Ann Thompson. CBWP-2

Teacher of Defeated Hebrew Language. Eitan Kalinski. NRoS, *tr. by* Esther Raizen

Teacher of standing, a poet, tells her class, *"Never put stars in your poems. . .",* A. Erasing Stars. Stephen Kuusisto. TAPaP

Teacher presents his teachings; students take them as their standards, The. Kuan Chung. ColAnChi *Fr.* Kuan Tzu.

Teacher said *inner truth,* The. Seven Postcards from Dover. Mary Ruefle. AmAlph

Teacher seated me at the table, The. Mississippi Girls, Plaited. Chelle Miko. RWB

Teachers of culture hate science but the teachers of science do not hate culture, The. Karl Shapiro. BodElec *Fr.* Bourgeois Poet, The.

Teachers taught her, The. Gertrude Stein. NOxBChV

Teaching a Stone to Talk. Annie Dillard.

"In the deeps are the violence and terror of which psychology has warned us." TWF

Teaching About Disease. Miroslav Holub. MotU, *tr. by* Dana Hábová and David Young

Teaching German Literature. Vincent Buckley. OBCoV

Teaching, Hurt. Hilda Raz. PfSP

Teaching My Husband to Swim. Lesley-Anne Bourne. Coast

Teaching Numbers. Gary Soto. NOxBChV

Teaching Poetry at Votech High, Santa Fe, the Week John Lennon Was Shot. Paula Gunn Allen. ReTh

Teaching Shakespeare. Tania Runyan. IaFF

Teaching the Ape to Write. James Tate. *See* Teaching the Ape to Write Poems.

Teaching the Ape to Write Poems. James Tate. OxBoAm

(Teaching the Ape to Write). BLT

Teaching the Children. Myra Sklarew. CFP

Teaching the first lesson and the last. School Among the Ruins, The. Adrienne Rich. AmWaPo; CAP-8

Tea-kettle / Hooked in mid-air. Hakuin. ZenPo, *tr. by* Takashi Ikemoto and Lucien Stryk

Team Effort. Bob Hicok. AmAlph

Team of Budweiser horses, The. 8-Ball at the Twilite. David Baker. ReTh

Teamster's Farewell, A. Carl Sandburg. IllVoic

Tear. Linda Hogan. ExTi

Tear. Thomas Kinsella. ModIr; NoP-4; NoP-5; OxBEV

Tear, The. Lord Byron. STuOW

Tear, The. Martin Sorescu. VCWP, *tr. by* Seamus Heaney and Joana Russell-Gebbett

Teardrop, A. Kim Hyesun. EcSo, *tr. by* Youngju Ryu

Tear[e], The. Richard Crashaw. NoP-5

Teares I could sonne have brought unto this hearse. Upon a Command to Write on My Father. Gertrude Aston Thimelby. EMWP

Tearing the hairy leeches from his throat. (LL) Thomas Lovell Beddoes. NPeEn; OxBEV *Fr.* Last Man, The.

Tearing the Page. Li-Young Lee. FaoP

Tearing Up the Tracks. Christopher Bursk. GM

Tea-rose tea-gown, etc., The. Ezra Pound. ColAP; HarvBoo; MoAmPo *Fr.* Hugh Selwyn Mauberley (Life and Contacts).

Tears. Buson. EH, *tr. by* Robert Hass

Tears. Lizette Woodworth Reese. MoAmPo

Tears: "There is a scream that binds my heart to." Saniyya Saleh. CFP, *tr. by* Kamal Boullata

Tears. Alena Synková. INSAB

Tears. Edward Thomas. NAEL-6v2; NAEL-7v2

Tears. Walt Whitman. APN-1

Tears and love for the Gray. (LL) Blue and the Gray, The. Francis Miles Finch. APN-2; CBCWP; CtM; PCW

Tears and recriminations don't cut no ice. Grievances. Philip Whalen. WANABP

Tears are streaming down my face. *Unknown.* SLW, *tr. by* Marjolijn De Jager, Sayd Bahodin Majrouh and André Velter

Tears beneath the earth, Heliodora, I give. Meleager. HePo, *tr. by* Barbara Hughes Fowler

Tears Fall in My Heart. Paul Verlaine. WoPoe, *tr. by* David Curzon

Tears Henry Shed for Poor Old Hemingway (235). John Berryman. OxBoAm *Fr.* Dream Songs.

Tears, idle tears, I know not what they mean. Alfred Tennyson. CABP; CtM; NAEL-6v2; NAEL-7v2; NIL-7; NIP-4; NoP-4; NoP-5; OxAEP-2; OxBEV; PoPoPo; TFi; TreFP *Fr.* Princess, The.

Tears in Sleep. Louise Bogan. MakPoe

Tears, in the end. For Men to Tell How Human Life Began Is Hard, For Who Himself Beginning Knew? Desire With Thee Still Longer to Converse Induced Me as New-Waked from Soundest Sleep Soft on the Flow'ry Herb I Found Me Laid in Balmy Sweat. Yi Sanghûi. EcSo, *tr. by* Jennifer M. Lee

Tears like a lover wept. (LL) In the Wilderness. Robert Graves. ChIV-2; MoBrPo

Tears of Peace, The or Euthymia Raptus. George Chapman.

Conclusio.

Peace of Death, The. NOSC

Teares of Peace, The.

Justice. NOSC

Learning ("So Learned Men in Controversies Spend"). NOSC

Peace Discovers the Poet. NOSC

Tears of the Dying. Walter Savage Landor. NPeEn

Tears of the Fatherland, Anno Domini 1636. Andreas Gryphius. GePo, *tr. by* George C. Schoolfield

Tears of the widower, when he sees. Alfred Tennyson. CAGL; NAEL-6v2; NAEL-7v2 *Fr.* In Memoriam A. H. H.

Tears soak her thin shawl. Palace Song. Po Chü-i. NDACCP, *tr. by* Gary Snyder

Tears! tears! tears! / In the night, in solitude, tears. Tears. Walt Whitman. APN-1

Tears that are shed and a breast that is burned Water and fire! / Things never joined save for matters of moment! Abū l-'Abbās Al-A'mā at-Tuṭīlī. HiArP, *tr. by* James T. Monroe

Tears, the firebursts and the vows, The. Cracked Looking Glass. Jean Garrigue. VCAP

Teased Pet, The. John Clare. DiBP *Fr.* Shepherd's [*or* Shepheards] Calendar, The.

Teasers, The. William Empson. HarvBoo

Teatro Amazonas, remnant, the. Ansel Talvikki. YaYoPo *Fr.* In Fragments, In Streams.

Tecendo a manhã. João Cabral de Melo Neto. IPoFL

Technicians, overseers, assistant. Lads, The. Dennis O'Driscoll. PML

Techniques of Mass Persuasion. Geoffrey O'Brien. PA9/11

Technologies. George Starbuck. YaYoPo

Technology of Spring, The. Lynn Emanuel. BodElec

Tedded hay, the first fruits of the soil, The. Keepsake, The. Samuel Taylor Coleridge. NPBRoP

Teddy. Leroy V. Quintana. LiTh

Teddy Bear, Teddy Bear. *Unknown.* NTCP

Teddy Bear's Picnic. Jimmy Kennedy. BLPJKO

Tedious rain over at last. Yun Sŏndo. CATKP *Fr.* Angler's Calendar, The.

Ted's Bar and Grill. Jim Daniels. ReTh

Ted's Head. Rod Smith. Eno

Ted's studio burnt down, with all his poems. Martial. WoPoe *Fr.* Epigrams.

Tee. Reuben Jackson. UnSA

Teed Off. John Nelson. GeoH

Teen Drowns in Rehabilitation Camp Days Before 17th Birthday, Questions Persist. Gaylord Brewer. AmPoNex

Teen Idols. Dennis Cooper. WiU

Teen idols are the best boys on the block. Teen Idols. Dennis Cooper. WiU

Teenage Interplanetary Vixens Run Wild on Bikini Beach. Allison Joseph. NAPBL

Teenage plankton luminously twitch, A. (LL) Watching the Dance. James Merrill. NIL-7; NIP-4

Teenagers. Ivan Teofilov. CSCBP, *tr. by* Georgi Belev and Lisa Sapinkopf

Teeter totters. Demockery. Ngoma. BRtP

Teeth. Miroslav Holub. MotU, *tr. by* Stuart Friebert

Teeth. Jackie Kay. EdScPo

Teeth. Spike Milligan. OPOU

Teeth and Gums. Mother Goose. NTCP

Teeth are a rather ridiculous inside remnant of the outside. Teeth. Miroslav Holub. MotU, *tr. by* Stuart Friebert

Teeth are bared, the mouth drawn tight, the face, The. Vera Inber. FaBoWar *Fr.* Pulkovo Meridian, The.

Teeth of flowers, hair of dew. I'm Going to Sleep. Alfonsina Storni. TCLAP, *tr. by* Andrew Rosing

Teeth sensitive to the sand. Basho. EH, *tr. by* Robert Hass

Tefillin. Yona Volach. DTA, *tr. by* Aryeh Cohen and Miriyam Glazer

TEHKARIHHOKEN! / Continue to listen! *Unknown.* APN-2 *Fr.* Ancient Rites of the Condoling Council.

Teilhard de Chardin Surfs the Internet. David Waltner-Toews. ACAMVP

Tel Aviv 1935. Leah Goldberg. FIT, *tr. by* Robert Friend

Tel le chant du ramier quand l'averse est prochaine—l'air se poudre de pluie. Chambre dans l'espace, La. René Char. YaTCFP

Telegram. Milo De Angelis. NeIt, *tr. by* Lawrence Venuti

Telegram from the Muse, A. William Matthews. PoA 2002

Telegraph Wires. Ted Hughes. NPeEn

Teleology. May Swenson. VCAP

Telephone call ran out in the night and glittered over the countryside ,A. Homewards. Tomas Tranströmer. WoPoe, *tr. by* Robin Fulton

Telephone Conversation. Wole Soyinka. NAMCP V.2; NoP-4; NoP-5; PoetW; WaAnP

Telephone poles, The. Donald Justice. StAl *Fr.* American Sketches (for William Carlos Williams).

Telephone Repairman. Joseph Millar. P180

Telephoning God. Gary Soto. PBCAP

Telescope. Sydney Lea. RA

Telesphere, The. Charles Olson. BodElec *Fr.* Maximus Poems, The.

Television aerials, Chinese characters. On Roofs of Terry Street. Douglas Dunn. NPeEn

Television as God. Tijan M. Sallah. NAfrP

Television is a herafter. Old Movies. Robley, Jr. Wilson. PoA 2002

Tell a wise person, or else keep silent. Holy Longing, The. Johann Wolfgang von Goethe. ItP; RaBo; WoPoe, *tr. by* Robert Bly

Tell all my mourners. Wake. Langston Hughes. OBCoV

Tell her I love. Poems for My Daughter. Horace Gregory. MoAmPo

Tell Her So. Mrs. Henry Linden. CBWP-4

Tell her to find her purse. (LL) Ghost in the Martini, The. Anthony Hecht. NoP-4; NoP-5

Tell her we still expose our bottoms. Messages. Jack A. Mapanje. HBAPE

Tell him it's all a lie. Learned Mistress, A. Frank O'Connor. IrLP

Tell him of apples, roads, friends. Escalade (Paul-Émile Borduas, 1905-1960). Peter Sanger. Coast

Tell him the tale is a lie! Learned Mistress, A. *Unknown.* OBMV, *tr. by* Frank O'Connor

Tell, if thou canst, the wondrous sight disclosed. Ovid. DiBP *Fr.* Metamorphoses.

Tell Me. Langston Hughes. APSN; SAmP

Tell me. Rāmprasād Sen. SinGod, *tr. by* Rachel Fell McDermott

Tell me. *Unknown.* WoPoe *Fr.* Bhagavad-Gita, The.

"Tell me a story." Bedtime Story. Lilian Moore. NTCP

Tell Me a Story. Robert Penn Warren. FuPo; ItP; NAAL-5; NAAPv.2 *Fr.* Audubon: A Vision.

Tell me a story, father, please. Natives of America, The. Ann Plato. TCAPo

Tell Me About It. Ruth Padel. MFPA

Tell me about the good things. How Long Has Trane Been Gone. Jayne Cortez. ISC

Tell me about yourself they. Word in Edgeways, A. Charles Tomlinson. CABP

Tell Me Again. Nigâr Hanim. ItWoWo; NaPG, *tr. by* Talat Sait Halman

Tell me again, Love, what is a wedding? Mark McMorris. IIR

Tell me another, my dear Sheherazade. Hooray for Hollywood. Thomas M. Disch. PoA 2002

Tell me, Antonio, do you remember the year '14. Evocation to Record a Music Box. Luis Rosales. RaW, *tr. by* Ralph Nelson and Rita García Nelson

Tell me bout da others. Lemmy Knows Two. Wopko Jensma. TSAP

Tell me, Comrade God, how can life, over this stretch. Tatiana Shcherbina. CRWP, *tr. by* Daniel Weissbort

Tell me, daughter, my pretty daughter. Cossante. Pero Meogo. WoPoe, *tr. by* Yvor Winters

Tell me, enigmatical man, whom do you love best, your. Stranger, The. Charles Baudelaire. IJHIL, *tr. by* Louise Varese

Tell me fair Nymph, who justly had design'd. To Orabella, Marry'd to an Old Man. Sarah Fyge Egerton. EMWP

Tell me, good Hobbinoll, what garres thee greete? Edmund Spenser. NAEL-6v1; NoP-5; OBEV *Fr.* Shepherd's Calender, The.

Tell me if ah seeing right. Poetry Jump-Up. John Agard. NOxBChV

Tell me if any get more than the lovers. . .in the dust. . .in the cool tombs. (LL) Cool Tombs. Carl Sandburg. APT-1; HeIP-4; MoAmPo; NAMCP V.1; NoAM; TCAPo; TFi

(In the dust . . . in the cool / tombs.) (LL) CBCWP; ColAP

Tell me if it is too far for you. Elegy for N. N. Czeslaw Milosz. BodElec; GPTC, *tr. by the author and Lawrence Davis

Tell Me If You Remember, Love. Antonio Machado Ruiz. RaW, *tr. by* Charles Guenther

Tell me I'm beautiful, and bring me flowers. Eleanor Brown. NeBl

Tell me, is love still a popular suggestion. I'm a Stranger Here Myself. Ogden Nash. ReLy

Tell me, is the rose naked. Pablo Neruda. GifTon *Fr.* Book of Questions, The.

Tell me it's wrong the scarlet nails my son sports or the toy store rings he clusters. Bedecked. Victoria Redel. MAAN

Tell me lies about Vietnam. (LL) To Whom It May Concern (Tell Me Lies about Vietnam). Adrian Mitchell. BeAl; FaBoWar; OBWP; RSaN

Tell me, Mama, what's a blessing? Blessing Over Bread, A. Dovid Seltzer. Prolet, *tr. by* Amelia Glaser

Tell me, men with wisdom gifted. Hiraeth. *Unknown.* OBWVE, *tr. by* Aneirin Talfan Davies

Tell me, Moon. Ivan Metodiev. CSCBP *Fr.* Songs for Orphans Big and Small.

Tell me my harte how wilte thow doe. Sir Arthur Gorges. NoSic

Tell me, my patient friends, awaiters of messages. Speech to a Crowd. Archibald MacLeish. MoAmPo

Tell me no more of constancy. Against Constancy. John Wilmot, 2d Earl of Rochester. NOSC; OxAEP-1

Tell me no more of Minds embracing Minds. No Platonic [or Platonique] Love. William Cartwright. NOSC; NPeEn

Tell me not, friend, you are unkind. Lucasta Replies to Lovelace. G. K. Chesterton. NPeEn

Tell me not here, it needs not saying. Tell Me Not Here [It Needs Not Saying]. A. E. Housman. NoAM; NPeEn; OxBEV

Tell me not, in mournful numbers. Psalm of Life, A. Henry Wadsworth Longfellow. AmFaPo; APN-1; BRP; ITBLP; ItP; NAAL-3; NAAL-5; NAAPv.1; TCAPo

Tell me not of a face that's fair. Resolve, The. Alexander Brome. NOSC; OBEV

Tell me not, Sweet, I am unkind. Lines Where Beauty Lingers. Franklin Pierce Adams. AmWit

Tell me not, Sweet, I am unkind[e]. To Lucasta, [on] Going to the War[re]s. Richard Lovelace. BASC; CABP; CavPo; ClHu; FaBoWar; NAEL-6v1; NAEL-7v1; NIL-7; NIP-4; NoP-4; NoP-5; NOSC; NPeEn; OBEV; OBWP; OxAEP-1; OxBEV; PBRV; PoPoPo; TFi; UV; WaAnP; WeW-3

Tell me not what too well I know. On Catullus. Walter Savage Landor. OBEV

Tell me now in what hidden way is. Ballad[e] of Dead Ladies, The. François Villon. OBVE, *tr. by* Dante Gabriel Rossetti

Tell me now is Love's day done? Tell Me Now. Oliver St. John Gogarty. IrLP

Tell me, O Wheelman, ere you ride away. Wheel Ethics. Charles Richards Dodge. ArBi

Tell me of thy heart's devotion. Whisper Words of Love to Me. Lizelia Augusta Jenkins Moorer. CBWP-3

Tell me, O[h] tell, what kind[e] of thing is wit. Ode: Of Wit. Abraham Cowley. NAEL-6v1; NAEL-7v1; NOSC

Tell me something. Adrienne Rich. PoPoPo

Tell me, Syama. Kamalākānta Bhattācārya. SinGod, tr. by Rachel Fell McDermott

Tell me, tell me. Do It Again. B. G. DeSylva. ReLy

Tell me, tell me, smiling child. Emily Jane Brontë. NALW

Tell me the stories of wanting are flowering. Promiscuity. Lisa Fishman. AmPoNex

Tell me, thou gentle shepherd swain. Roundelay Between Two Shepherds, A. Michael Drayton. NoP-4; NoP-5

Tell me thou safest end of all our woe. Anne Killigrew. See Tell me thou[gh] safest end of all our woe.

'Tell me, thou skilful shepherd's swain'. Michael Drayton. AEP

Tell me, thou Star, whose wings of light. World's Wanderers, The. Percy Bysshe Shelley. TreFP

Tell me thou[gh] safest end of all our woe. On Death. Anne Killigrew. ChIV-1

(Tell me thou safest end of all our woe.) PEW

Tell me, / Was Venus more beautiful. Venus Transiens. Amy Lowell. APT-1; NAAL-5; NAAPv.2; NALW; NAMCP V.1

Tell me we will drink water, and drink to me. John Tranter. VaPo Fr. Blackout.

Tell me, what are you doing now, Mind. Mahendranāth Bhattācārya. SinGod, tr. by Rachel Fell McDermott

Tell me, what binds us to some meaning. Sentimental Elegy, A. Arkadii Dragomoschenko. PFTM-2, tr. by Elena Balashova and Lyn Hejinian

Tell me / What can I do? Kamalākānta Bhattācārya. SinGod, tr. by Rachel Fell McDermott

Tell Me, What Have I Lost? Jelaluddin Rumi. WED, tr. by Robert Bly

Tell me what you see in it. Black Pine Tree in an Orange Light. Sylvia Plath. BodElec

Tell me what you're doing over here, John Gorham. John Gorham. Edwin Arlington Robinson. MoAmPo

Tell me whaur, in whit countrie. Ballat o the Leddies o Langsyne. François Villon. OBVE; OxBEV, tr. by Tom Scott

Tell me, where doth Whiteness grow. Whiteness, or Chastity. Joseph Beaumont. NOSC

Tell me where, in what country, where. Ballade. François Villon. STV, tr. by John Frederick Nims

Tell Me Where Is Fancy Bred. William Shakespeare. See Casket Song, A.

Tell me where is fancy [or Fancie] bred. William Shakespeare. NoSic; TFi Fr. Merchant of Venice, The.

Tell Me, Wight in the Broom. Unknown. NAEL-6v1

Tell me, woman, your parents, your name, your land. B. Calliteles. Antipater of Sidon. HePo, tr. by Barbara Hughes Fowler

Tell me, would you like to be my playmate? Would You Like to Play? Dezső Kosztolányi. IQMS, tr. by Thomas Kabdebo

Tell me, ye registers of fate. To the Same. Charlotte MacCarthy. PoBW

Tell me, you anti-saints, why glass. Upon Fairford Windows. Richard Corbet. NOSC

Tell me you Hate; and Flatter me no more. To J. G. "Ephelia." NOSC

Tell me[e] no more how fair[e] she[e] is. Sonnet. Henry King, Bishop of Chichester. OxBEV

Tell My Jesus "Morning." Unknown. SSUS

Tell Nimrod, he told me, "to return." Cancellation of a Construction Project. David Huerta. RMCMP, tr. by Mark Schafer

Tell the beads of the chromosomes like a rosary. Route. George Oppen. AF; APSN; APT-2

Tell the portly waitress to stay overtime and. Serving of Water, The. Tino Villanueva. TiP2

Tell the Truth. George Stanley. NLPA Fr. Mountains and Air.

Tell the wind. Small Sins. Maram Masri. PoArWo, tr. by Amal Amireh

Tell them. If You Are Asked. Olena Kalytiak Davis. LegDan

Tell them, because our fathers lied. (LL) Rudyard Kipling. HarvBoo; InoFa; NPeEn; PoAgWa; WoPoe Fr. Epitaphs of the War [1914–1918].

Tell Them I'm Struggling to Sing with Angels. David Meltzer. TaR

Tell them something you can live with. Cole Porter. Dionisio D. Martinez. TouFir

Tell them what you like. Tell them. Few Helpful Hints, A. Peter Sirr. ModIr

Tell Us, Josephine. Ron Padgett. FTOS

Tell us, Professor. Imre Madách. IQMS Fr. Tragedy of Man.

Tell us the story about the little boots. . . / The Llandeilo boots, because that is probably where. Little Boots, The. Dafydd Rowlands. BBMWP, tr. by Meic Stephens

Tell, what name beseems. Sadakichi. NAAPv.1 Fr. Tanka.

Tell where I lie. (LL) Ode on Solitude. Alexander Pope. HeIP-4; NAEL-6v1; NIL-7; NOSC; SacPr; WaAnP

Tell you a story—an' it's a fac'. Jack the Giant-Killer. James Whitcomb Riley. NOxBChV

Tell you? ha! who. Charles Olson. NoAM Fr. Maximus Poems, The.

Tell you I chill. Tunning of Elinour Rumming, The. John Skelton.

Tell you wonderful things. (LL) Wonderful Things. Ron Padgett. AHA; PmAP

Telling, The. Andrew Hudgins. RA

Telling About Coyote. Simon J. Ortiz. ICANM

Telling each other secrets. (LL) Venus's-flytraps. Yusef Komunyakaa. FaoP; PtR

Telling Fortunes. Alice Cary. SWaP

Telling it like it is, A. Poetry Became. Margaret Randall. ICANM

Telling Myself. Kay Ekevall. RSaN

Telling Part, The. Jackie Kay. Prnts

Telling the Bees. Carol Frost. CAP-8

Telling the Bees. Lizette Woodworth Reese. SWaP

Telling the Bees. John Greenleaf Whittier. APN-1; ColAP; NAAPv.1; NoP-4; NoP-5; OxBoAm; TCAPo

Telling the Time. Christine de Luca. EdScPo

Telling us this is home no more. (LL) Red Hills of Home. Chenjerai Hove. HBAPE; NAfrP

Tells us as much, and was never written with us in mind. (LL) Night, The Porch, The. Mark Strand. CAP-8; KGB

Telltale tit. You Worthless. Unknown. FaBoVe

Telluric and Magnetic. César Vallejo. PFTM-1

Telyric. Andrei Codrescu. PmAP

Temeraire, The. Herman Melville. APN-2; FaBoWar

Temper (1), The. George Herbert. NoP-4; NoP-5

Temperament is related to physique. Elaine Randell. Oth Fr. Snoad Hill Poems, The.

Temperaments, The. Ezra Pound. NAMCP V.1; NoAM; OBCoV

Temperance Army, The. Julia A. Moore.
  Anti-Bacchics 2. STuOW

Temperance Reform Clubs. Julia A. Moore.
  Anti-Bacchics 1. STuOW

Temperate. Joseph Somoza. ICANM

Temperature hotter than the sun, A. (LL) Demographics. Catherine Bowman. ExTi; SUP

Temperature is zero below, The. Glassworks. Margit Mikes. IQMS, tr. by Susanne K. Walther

Temperature now that farms project. Three Madrigals. John Ashbery. AHA

Tempered, annealed, the hard essence of autumn metals. Needle and Thread. Pan Chao. WoPoe, tr. by Richard Mather and Rob Swigart

Tempered, annealed, the hard essence of autumn metals. Needle and Thread. Pan Zhao. WPoS, tr. by Richard Mather

Tempered consonants of discipline, The. (LL) Teresa. Richard Wilbur. NoAM; UpMys

Tempest. Theodore H. Banks, Jr. YaYoPo

Tempest. Sekeena Shaben. PoArWo

Tempest on the plain of Lir. Storm at Sea. Rumann, Son of Colman. WoPoe, tr. by Frank O'Connor

Tempest, The. Stephen Corey. IaFF

Tempest, The. William Jay Smith. MoAmPo

Tempest, The. Marya Alexandrovna Zaturenska. MoAmPo

Tempest, The. William Shakespeare.
  Ariel's Song: "Come unto these yellow sands." NOSC; NoSic; NPeEn; OBEV; SoSe-8; TFi
  "Where should this Musick be? I'th'aire, or th'earth?" NPeEn
  "Dost thou forget." OxAEP-1
  Epilogue. ASA; UV
  "Full fathom [or fadom] five thy father lies." ClHu; NAEL-6v1; NoP-4; NoP-5; NoSic; OBEV; OxBEV; PoPoPo; TFi
  "Hast thou, spirit." OxAEP-1
  Magic. OxAEP-1; WaAnP
  (Sea Song, A.) NBLV; OBCoV
  To Dream Again. OxAEP-1
  "Where the bee sucks, there suck I." BLPJKO; NBLV; NoSic; OBEV; TFi
  (Where the Bee Sucks, There Suck I.) NAEL-6v1; NoP-4; NoP-5

Tempests pass through the air, as they pile up cloudbank on, The. Yearning for Winter. Karl Wilhelm Ramler. GePo, tr. by George C. Schoolfield

Template, The. John Ashbery. VaPo

Temple. Natalia Toledo. RMCMP, tr. by Alberto A. Ríos

Temple, The. OBMV, tr. by Arthur Waley

Temple bell / A cloud of cherry flowers. Basho. ZenPo, tr. by Takashi Ikemoto and Lucien Stryk

Temple bell ringing. Stanford M. Forrester. AmZen

Temple bell stops, The.   Basho.   WED; WoPoe, *tr. by* Robert Bly

Temple bell, The.   Yosano Akiko.   CAoMJL1, *tr. by* Janine Beichman

Temple buried in white clouds, A.   Mountain Temple.   Yi Tal.   CATKP, *tr. by* Peter H. Lee

Temple City Blvd. and Ellis Ln.   Carol Lem.   GeoHom

Temple in / Deep winter grove.   Tan Taigi.   ZenPo, *tr. by* Takashi Ikemoto and Lucien Stryk

Temple in spring is immaculate, as usual, The.   On the Death of the Most Reverend Priest.   Jinkag Haesim.   BecRai, *tr. by* Kim Daljin, Kim Won-Chung and Christopher Merrill

Temple Near Quang Tri, Not on the Map.   Bruce Weigl.   AmAlph

Temple of Chastity, The.   Mary Robinson.   CenSon; RWP

2. The Temple of Chastity.   Mary Robinson.   NPBRoP; STuOW *Fr.* Sappho and Phaon.

Temple of Eternal Light.   Muso Soseki.   EaWin, *tr. by* W. S. Merwin

Temple of Mars, The.   Geoffrey Chaucer.   NPEeN *Fr.* Canterbury Tales, The.

Temple of Nature; or, The Origin of Society, The.   Erasmus Darwin.
   Ae Fond Kiss, and Then.   STuOW
   Maiden Truffle, The.   STuOW

Temple of Su Wu, The.   Wen T'ing-yün.   CCL1, *tr. by* Witter Bynner

Temple of the animals has fallen into disrepair, The.   Temple of the Animals, The.   Robert Duncan.   CalPo; OxBoAm

Temple of the Mariposa.   Elizabeth Robinson.   ASA

Temple of Your Familiar.   Felicia L. Morgenstern.   BtF

Temple ruin.   Stanford M. Forrester.   AmZen

Templo.   Natalia Toledo.   RMCMP

Tempo.   Lauris Edmond.   BeAl

Temporada de Paraíso, Una.   José Luis Rivas.   RMCMP

Temporall Goods.   Robert Herrick.   SacPr

Temporarily in Oxford.   Anne Stevenson.   NoP-4; NoP-5

Temporary City.   Nijole Miliauskaite.   VCWP, *tr. by* Jonas Zdanys

Temporary Heart.   Michael Hannon.   GeoHom

Temporary Insanity.   Tanai Sanders.   BRtP

Temporary Language, A.   Larry Eigner.   PmAP

Temporary Losses.   Dionisio D. Martinez.   NAMCP V.2

Temporary Situation, A.   David St. John.   BodElec

Temps a Laissié, Le.   Charles, Duc d' Orléans.   WoPoe, *tr. by* Stanley Burnshaw

Tempt me no more; for I.   Cecil Day Lewis.   MoBrPo; OBMV *Fr.* Magnetic Mountain, The.

Temptation.   Salwa Al-Neimi.   PoArWo, *tr. by* Subhi Hadidi and Nathalie Handal

Temptation.   Nina Cassian.   AF; StAl, *tr. by* Andrea Deletant and Brenda Walker

Temptation.   Robert Herrick.   SacPr

Temptation.   Czeslaw Milosz.   GI, *tr. by* the author and Lillian Vallee

Temptation.   Bruce Weigl.   AmAlph

Temptation, The.   Nicole Brossard.   PFTM-2 *Fr.* Barbizon, The.

Temptations still nest in it like basilisks.   Dead Hand.   W. S. Merwin.   CAP-8

Tempted by the Classical on Returning from the Store at Twenty Below Zero.   Sydney Lea.   SwNoth

Tempter Disarmed, The.   John Milton.   NOSC *Fr.* Paradise Lost.

Tempus Fugit.   Richard Harteis.   OtW

Temujin Becomes Chingis Khan.   Unknown.   WoPoe *Fr.* Secret History of the Mongols, The.

10:30. A long and thin.   Breathless Storm.   Michael Burkard.   BodElec

Ten Cents a Dance.   Lorenz Hart.   ReLy

Ten comawndementis I haue broke.   All Ten Commandments I Have Broken.   *Unknown.*   SacPr

Ten commandments are between us.   Magdalene.   Marina Ivanovna Tsvetayeva.   GI, *tr. by* Michael M. Naydan and Slava Yastremski

10 Commandments, are the Law Divine.   John Taylor.   ChIV-1 *Fr.* Taylor's Arithmetic from One to Twelve.

Ten dancers glide.   Ballad of the Ten Casino Dancers.   Cecília Meireles.   TCLAP, *tr. by* James Merrill

Ten Days Leave.   W. D. Snodgrass.   MoAmPo; PWW2

10 Dead Friends.   Dennis Cooper.   WiU

Ten Definitions of Poetry.   Carl Sandburg.   MoAmPo

Ten fussy days running this temple all red tape.   Stephen Berg.   GifTon

Ten holy nights / Even tea.   Buson.   ZenPo, *tr. by* Takashi Ikemoto and Lucien Stryk

Ten, I kept saying, *I'm only ten.* (LL)   Flash Cards.   Rita Dove.   ESEAA; LoL; PoPoPo

Ten ii.   Laurie Duggan.   BMAP

Ten kinds of wolf are gone and twelve of rat.   Names.   William Matthews.   PfSP; PoCoUp

Ten Little Rembrandts.   Theodore Weiss.   NoAM

Ten Million Flames of Los Angeles, The.   Amy Uyematsu.   CalPo; GeoHom

Ten Mills.   Robert Frost.
   In Divés' Dive.   AmWit; GI
   Span of Life, The.   SoSe-8
   Wrights' Biplane, The.   AmWit; WeW-3

Ten o'clock train to New York, The.   Winter.   Ruth Stone.   InoFa; OxBoAm

Ten out of ten means you are dead. (LL)   Death Is a Matter of Mathematics.   Barry Amiel.   FaBoWar; PoWW

Ten Out of Ten, or, Why Poetry Criticism Sucks in 2003.   Darren Wershler-Henry.   PoPra

Ten Patients, and Another.   Rafael Campo.
   Jane Doe #2.   AmPoNex; WiU
   John Doe.   InoFa
   Kelly.   WiU
   Manuel.   WiU

Ten poems written in one month.   Valerio Magrelli.   NeIt

Ten Questions for Mona.   Matthew Zapruder.   IIR

Ten rains, and then snow, then more snow, then.   Ice Skating.   Greg Kuzma.   InvLad

10 Reasons Why I Fall in Love with Inaccessible Straight Boys Every Damn Time.   Richard Murray Vaughan.   Coast

Ten Seconds.   Rohan B. Preston.   WaCA

Ten Short Poems.   Juan Ramón Jiménez. *tr. by* James Wright
   "Dawn brings with it, The."   SpanPo; WoPoe, *tr. by* James Wright
   "To the bridge of love."   SpanPo; WoPoe, *tr. by* James Wright

Ten Songs.   W. H. Auden.
   Refugee Blues.   AmFaPo; BeAl; HP; OxAEP-2

Ten Songs, one solid block of agony.   John Berryman.   StAl *Fr.* Dream Songs.

Ten Still Lives.   Juan Felipe Herrera.   LiTh

Ten Suns Rise in the East, The.   Juan Chi.   WoPoe, *tr. by* Graham Hartill and Wu Fusheng

(10,000) brutal, beautiful years. (LL)   People of the Other Village, The.   Thomas Lux.   PoCho; StAl; SUP

Ten thousand rows of bamboo reach my door.   Bamboo Forest.   Master Naong.   BecRai, *tr. by* Kim Daljin, Kim Won-Chung and Christopher Merrill

Ten Thousand Sutras.   Sam Hamill.   ErotSp

Ten thousand things all hushed and silent, The.   On an Autumn Evening Listening to Reverend Yeh Play the Ch'in.   Ch'i-chi.   CSKM, *tr. by* Burton Watson

Ten thousand things in heaven and earth.   Sent to a Poetry Friend.   Ch'i-chi.   CSKM, *tr. by* Burton Watson

Ten thousand things wound my heart when you're before my eyes.   In Illness, Dismissing My Singing Girl.   Ssu-k'ung Shu.   ColAnChi, *tr. by* Burton Watson

Ten thousand trees.   On the Spot Where Shih-chia Tzu Sits in Meditation.   Ching An.   CSKM, *tr. by* Jerome P. Seaton

Ten thousand trees frozen, just about to crack.   Early Plum Blossoms.   Ch'i-chi.   CSKM, *tr. by* Burton Watson

Ten thousand years. (LL)   Above Pate Valley.   Gary Snyder.   GeoHom; NAMCP V.2; NoP-4; NoP-5; OxBoAm; StAl; TRP

Ten to One to No.   Joyce Mansour.   SurWo, *tr. by* Mary Beach

Ten Ways of Looking at P.B. Shelley.   Hugo Claus.   LWR, *tr. by* John M. Coetzee

Ten white blooms on the sundeck.   Phyllis Webb.   IFF *Fr.* Sunday Water.

Ten years ago.   Tanka.   Kanoko Okamoto.   CAoMJL1, *tr. by* Makoto Ueda

Ten Years Ago.   Alaric Alexander Watts.   TreFP

Ten years ago, beneath the Hotel Astoria.   Annus Mirabilis 1989.   Elaine Feinstein.   HP

Ten years ago it seemed impossible.   In Progress.   Christina Georgina Rossetti.   NAEL-6v2; NAEL-7v2

Ten years ago you died.   Remembering My Wife.   Su Tung-p'o.   ErotSp, *tr. by* Sam Hamill

Ten Years and More.   Miriam Waddington.   BrAP

Ten Years It Took.   Song Sun.   WoPoe, *tr. by* Virginia Olsen Baron and Chung Seuk Park

Ten years later.   Big Cars.   Wesley McNair.   PoA 2002

Ten years of loving loyalty.   On an Irish Retriever.   Frances Anne Kemble.   DiBP

Ten years of my life, spent at the window or beneath the lamp.   Song of Cursive Calligraphy.   Hsieh Chin.   ColAnChi, *tr. by* Jonathan Chaves

Ten years of whorehouse joy I'm alone now in the mountains.   Ikkyu Sojun.   WoPoe *Fr.* Four Poems.

Ten years old with my father.   Trails.   Patrick Williams.   PNI

Ten years since we were married, since we stood.   Long Finish.   Paul Muldoon.   HarvBoo

Ten years that the language is gone.   Antonin Artaud.   ConPit, *tr. by* Clayton Eshleman

Ten years together without yet a cloud.   Firelight.   Edwin Arlington Robinson.   NoAM

Tenant at Will, A.   Stuart Dischell.   PoCho

Tenant Of Wildfeld Hall, The.   Todd Swift.   OpeFie

Ten-Day Visitor, The.   *Unknown*.   SonAtl, *tr. by* Brenda Ginever, Malcolm Ginever, Badisa Macasi and Kgosi Puleng

Tender, and averse to killing. (LL)   Ode: To Miss Margaret Pulteney [Daughter of Daniel Pulteney, Esq., in the Nursery].   Ambrose Philips.   OxAEP-1; STuOW; UV

Tender Buttons.   Gertrude Stein.
   Apple.   MotU
   "Asparagus is a lean in a lean to hot."   NAAPv.2
   Box, A.   NAAPv.2
   Box, A.   MoWP
   Brown, A.   NAAPv.2; NAMCP V.1
   Carafe, that is a blind glass, A.   MoWP; NAAPv.2; NAMCP V.1
   Centre in a table, A.   NAMCP V.1
   Chicken.   NAAPv.2; NAMCP V.1
   Chicken.   NAMCP V.1
   Chicken.   NAAPv.2; NAMCP V.1
   Chicken.   NAMCP V.1
   Cloth, A.   TCAPo
   "Custard is this."   NAAPv.2
   Dog, A.   NAMCP V.1
   Eggs.   NAMCP V.1
   Frightful Release, A.   MotU; TCAPo
   Glazed glitter.   NAAPv.2
   Little Bit of Tumbler, A.   NAMCP V.1
   Little called Pauline, A.   NAMCP V.1
   Long Dress, A.   MoWP
   Long Dress, A.   NAAPv.2
   Milk.   MotU
   More.   TCAPo
   Mounted Umbrella, A.   MoWP; TCAPo
   Mutton.   NAMCP V.1
   Orange in.   NAAPv.2
   Peeled pencil, choke.   NAMCP V.1
   Piece fo Coffee, A.   NAMCP V.1
   Purse, A.   TCAPo
   Red Hat, A.   MoWP
   Rooms.
     "Act so that there is no use in a centre."   NAMCP V.1
   Sugar.   NAMCP V.1
   Table, A.   NAAPv.2
   This is this dress, aider.   NAAPv.2
   Waist, A.   NAAPv.2; NAMCP V.1
   "White hunter is nearly crazy, A."   NAAPv.2; NAMCP V.1

Tender fingers ran up my ankle.   Can I Tempt You to a Pond Walk?   James Schuyler.   PoA 2002

Tender floss of my flesh.   Close to Me.   Gabriela Mistral.   TANSG, *tr. by* Maria Giachetti [*or* Jacketti] and Maria Jacketti

Tender heart, hairy muscle.   Maria Luisa Spaziani.   NeIt

Tender infant, meek and mild, The.   Ballad.   Samuel Johnson.   OxAEP-1

Tender little Buddha.   Futures in Lilacs.   Robert Hass.   RoV

Tender, semi- / articulate flickers.   For My Mother: Genevieve Jules Creeley.   Robert Creeley.   TRP

Tendered.   Sandy Feinstein.   IaFF

Tender-Heartedness.   Harry Graham.   NBLV; NOxBChV *Fr.* Some Ruthless Rhymes.

Tenderitis.   Maxine Chernoff.   IllVoic

Tenderly.   Stephen Dobyns.   CAP-8

Tenderly.   Jack Lawrence.   ReLy

Tenderly, in those times, as though she fed.   Edna St. Vincent Millay.   NALW *Fr.* Sonnets from an Ungrafted Tree.

Tenderness.   Belinda Zubicueta Carmona.   TANSG, *tr. by* Celeste Kostopulos-Cooperman

Tenderness.   Stephen Dunn.   NIP-4

Tenderness I prize lightly from me remove!, The. (LL)   Mary Tighe.   NoP-4; RWP *Fr.* Psyche.

Tenderness of love is extraordinary, The.   Thanksgiving (1974).   Stefan Brecht.   CLPP

Tending Flowers.   Susan Spady.   FiBr

Tending the Graves.   Jennifer Strauss.   NOBAu

Tendons sewn together and the small bones, The.   Safe.   Linda Gregerson.   AmAlph

Tendril in the Mesh.   William Everson.
   "Daughter of earth and child of the wave be appeased."   NoAM

Tendril Love of Africa.   Molara Ogundipe-Leslie.   HAWP

Tendrils of Strength.   Locks.   Joy Dawson.   BtF

Tenebrae.   Suze Baron.   OGAHCP, *tr. by* Boadiba and Jack Hirschman

Tenebrae.   Paul Celan.   PoetW, *tr. by* John Felstiner

Tenebrae.   Paul Celan.   PoSu; VCWP

Tenebrae.   Geoffrey Hill.   HarvBoo

Tenebrae.   Juan Ramón Jiménez.   SpanPo, *tr. by* Alice Sternberg

Tenebrae.   Denise Levertov.   EMP; NoP-4; NoP-5

Tenebrae.   John Banister Tabb.   APN-2

Tenebris.   Angelina Weld Grimké.   APT-1; NAAPv.2; OxAAAP; OxBoAm

Tenebris Interlucentem.   James Elroy Flecker.   MoBrPo

Tenement house.   Masaoka Shiki.   CAoMJL1, *tr.* by Burton Watson

Tengan Osho's Visit to Erin-ji.   Muso Soseki.   EaWin, *tr.* by W. S. Merwin

Tennessee June.   Jorie Graham.   HarvBoo

Tennessee Waltz, The.   James Haug.   OPRER

Tennis.   Margaret Avison.   IFF

Tennis.   Pierre Drieu la Rochelle.   CuPo

Tennis Court Oath, The.   John Ashbery.   NAMCP V.2; NoAM

Tennis in the City.   Frank Higgins.   MoASP

Tennis Trophy.   John Frederick Nims.   PoA 2002

Tennyson's Poems.   Josephine D. Henderson Heard.   CBWP-4; SWaP

Tenochtitlán Blues.   Manuel Ulacia.   RMCMP, *tr.* by Indran Amirthanayagam

Tent marks in Mínan are worn away, The.   Labid.   WoPoe *Fr.* Mu'allaqat, The.

Tent on the Beach: [The Dreamer].   John Greenleaf Whittier.
   Tent on the Beach: [The Dreamer].   NCAP

Tent that is pitched at the base, A.   War.   Edgar Wallace.   OBWP

Tentacles, the brazen phiz whose glare, The.   Medusa.   Amy Clampitt.   VCAP

Tentative / as envoys to.   Beall Mountain Seasonal.   Linda Pastan.   PfSP

Tentative rap at the door would, A.   At the Stop.   Zinaida Bykova.   CRWP, *tr. by* Robert Reid

Tenth.9.   Roberto Juarroz.   PoetW, *tr. by* Mary Crow

Tenth day of the winter month November, The.   Memorandum of Martha Moulsworth, Widow, The.   Martha Moulsworth.   NAEL-7v1

Tenth day of the winter month November, The.   Memorandum of Martha Moulsworth Widdowe, The.   Martha Dorsett Prynne.   EMWP

Tenth Satire.   Juvenal.   *Fr.* Satires.

10th Untitled Poem.   Pedro Juan Pietri.   PueRic

Tenth Wedding Anniversary (July 3, 1994): Tsuki Oboro Totsugishi Yoru No Sora Datta.   Violet Kazue De Cristoforo.   CalPo

Tenth-Year Elegy.   Neal Bowers.   PoA 2002

Tenting on the Old Camp Ground.   Walter Kittredge.   NAAPv.1

Tents, *marquees*, and baggage-wagons.   Camp, The.   Mary Robinson.   NOBRP

Tenuous and Precarious.   Stevie Smith.   HarvBoo

Tenzone.   Ezra Pound.   PoA 2002 *Fr.* Contemporania.

Tenzo's Song.   Gillian Coote.   WhBo

Teodoro Luna's Two Kisses.   Alberto A. Ríos.   PoPoPo

Teorí de Fractales.   Alberto Blanco.   RMCMP

Teoría cuántica.   Alberto Blanco.   RMCMP

Teoría de conjuntos.   Alberto Blanco.   RMCMP

Teoría de la luz.   Alberto Blanco.   RMCMP

Teoría de Silencios.   Gabriel Celaya.   RaW

Teorías.   Federico García Lorca.
   "Agosto."   RaW

Tepidarium (warm room).   Matthea Harvey.   IAoNAP *Fr.* Thermae.

Tepozán.   Josué Ramírez.   RMCMP, *tr.* by Joan Lindgren

Terce.   W. H. Auden.   GI *Fr.* Horae Canonicae.

Tercer Mundo.   Christina Rivera-Garza.   SPV

Tercios del Muerte.   Gerry Gordon.   MiVo

Terence, this is stupid stuff.   A. E. Housman.   BrAP; CABP; HeIP-4; NAEL-6v2; NAEL-7v2; NAMCP V.1; NoAM; NoP-4; NoP-5; TFi *Fr.* Shropshire Lad, A.

Terentius Neo and wife. Their oval eyes.   Portrait of a Married Couple.   Margaret Scott.   NOBAu

Teresa.   R. T. Smith.   Vesp

Teresa.   Richard Wilbur.   NoAM; UpMys

Teresa lived in a personal black cube.   Anne Carson.   WoBe *Fr.* Truth About God, The.

Teresa of God.   Anne Carson.   WoBe *Fr.* Truth About God, The.

Terezin.   Hanuš Hachenburg.   INSAB

Terezin.   Mif.   INSAB

Terezin is full of beauty.   It All Depends on How You Look at It.   Miroslav Košek.   INSAB

Term, The.   Oni Buchanan.   LegDan

Termina diciendo.   Final de Pound, Un.   Tedi López Mills.   RMCMP

Terminal.   Thom Gunn.   CAGL; OxBEV

Terminal.   Karl Shapiro.   GM

Terminal Colloquy.   Charles Martin.   AtGh

Terminal Hip.   Mac Wellman.
   "Of Power, Money, Cheese, Real Estate, Conboberation, Hoohah."   FTOS

Terminal Resemblance. Louise Glück. InoFa

Terminally Ill. Anna Swirszczynska [or Swir]. PoSu

Termination. Fred Voss. SUP

Terminology was a science she wasn't at all sure of. Elizabeth Looks at Robert. Jo Shapcott. MoWP

Terminus. Seamus Heaney. NAMCP V.2; PoPoPo

Terminus. Peter Rose. BMAP

Terminus. Edith Wharton. APT-1

Terminus ("It is time to be old.") Ralph Waldo Emerson. APN-1; BrAP; GoPo; NCAP; TCAPo

Termite, The. Ogden Nash. AmWit

Terms. Kevin Stein. MAAN

Terms in Which I Think of Reality, The. Allen Ginsberg. AmFaPo

Terms of all kinds mellow with time, growing. Robert Pinsky. NoAM; PoA 2002 Fr. Essay on Psychiatrists.

Terpsichore [told] me. Korinna [or Corinna]. SaLy, tr. by Diane Rayor

Terre, La. Amina Saïd. YaTCFP

Terra Australis. James Philip McAuley. NOBAu

Terra Australis. Douglas Stewart. NOBAu

Terra Incognita. Joyce Sutphen. RWB

Terrace fronts the mountain, The. Yi Hwang. CATKP Fr. Twelve Songs of Tosan.

Terrace in the Snow, The. Su Tung-p'o. NDACCP, tr. by Kenneth Rexroth

Terraced Landscape. Ágnes Nemes Nagy. MotU, tr. by Hugh Maxton

Terrain. A. R. Ammons. VCAP

Terrain se rétrécit, Le. Hier, une lettre encore est arrivé à la fin. 67 mots d'une voyelle et d'une consonne. Christophe Tarkos. YaTCFP

Terre est bleue comme une orange, La. Paul Éluard. YaTCFP

Terre originelle. Anne Hébert. YaTCFP

Terri. Alan Wearne. BMAP Fr. Nightmarkets, The.

Terrible beauty is born, A. (LL) Easter 1916. William Butler Yeats. BrAP; HarvBoo; HeIP-4; IrV; NAEL-6v2; NAEL-7v2; NAMCP V.1; NAWM-7v2; NIL-7; NIP-4; NoAM; NoP-4; NoP-5; NPeEn; OBWP; OxAEP-2; PoPoPo; TFi; WaAnP

Terrible beds, soft beds, wily, elusive beds. Beds. Charlie Smith. BAP-97

Terrible child-bed hast thou had, my dear, A. William Shakespeare. OxAEP-1 Fr. Pericles.

Terrible Infant, A. Frederick Locker-Lampson. OBCoV

Terrible One, knowing their hearts, The. Cristina Campo. CItWP Fr. Tiger's Absence.

Terrible People, The. Ogden Nash. APT-2

Terrible, the rain. All night, rain. Trace, In Unison. Tess Gallagher. ExTi

Terrifying are the attent sleek thrushes on the lawn. Thrushes. Ted Hughes. TRP

Terror. Denise Levertov. MoWP

4. Terror and Love as Fugitives. Henry Rago. PoA 2002 Fr. Metaphor, The.

Terror and stillness and ebon-hued horror, night in its iciness. Midnight. Andreas Gryphius. GePo, tr. by George C. Schoolfield

Terror is more certain than all the rare desirable popular songs i know, A. Terror Is More Certain, A. Bob Kaufman. EGAG

Terror of the serene plane is in their eyes, The. About Eyes. Edwin Rolfe. OtW

Terror sat knitting quietly. We waited. Henry Rago. PoA 2002 Fr. Metaphor, The.

Terrorist, He Watches, The. Wisława Szymborska. PoSu

Terrorist Is Watching, A. Wisława Szymborska. WoPoe, tr. by Austin Flint

Terrorist, The. Sergey Stratanovsky. ItGoST, tr. by J. Kates

Terrorists of the last. I Am So in Love I Grow a New Hymen. Sandra Cisneros. IllVoic

Terrorizer of armies, Yaḥya ibn Dhī n-Nūn, The. (LL) Singing Lute, The. Ibn Arfaʿ Raʾsuh. HiArP; NAWM-7v1, tr. by James T. Monroe

Terrors of the In-Between. Paul Skyrm. AmZen

Teshuva: heading south. Hank Lazer. AnSo Fr. New Spirit, The.

Tesoro. Valerie Martínez. TouFir

Tess's Lament. Thomas Hardy. FaBoVe

Tess's Torch Song (I Had a Man). Ted Koehler. ReLy

Test. Nicanor Parra. PFTM-2, tr. by Miller Williams

Test. Kay Ryan. PoA 2002

Test of Atlanta 1979, The. June Jordan. ISC

Test 1 How to design freedom. How fine does the. Bernadette Mayer. AHA Fr. Moving.

Test Paper. Rolfe Humphries. APT-2

Testamant (Or, Homage to Walt Whitman). Erica Jong. ViWalt

Testament. Tudor Arghezi. AF, tr. by Andrei Bantas and Thomas Amherst Perry

Testament. Wendell Berry.
 1. UpMys
 2. UpMys
 4. UpMys

Testament. Hayden Carruth. GifTon

Testament. Roland Mathias. AngWePo

Testament. Felix Morisseau-Leroy. OGAHCP, tr. by Boadiba and Jack Hirschman

Testament. Saleem Peeradina. Vesp

Testament: "To my last technician." Anne Rouse. NeBrP

Testament, The. François Villon. tr. by Galway Kinnell
 "Now I think I hear the laments." NAWM-7v1, tr. by Galway Kinnell

Testament of Beauty, The. Robert Bridges.
 Book 3.
 "Art is the true and happy science of the soul." GS

Testament of Cresseid, The. Robert Henryson. NePenScot
 "O ladyis fair of Troy and Grece, attend." NPeEn
 "That samin tyme, of Troy the garnisoun." OxBEV

Testament of John Davidson, The. John Davidson.
 (Epilogue—the Last Journey.) EdScPo

Testament of Loss. Gloria C. Oden. ESEAA

Testifying to Beauty. Ronny Someck. IrPoTo, tr. by Vivian Eden

Testimonial. Rita Dove. CAP-8

Testimonial. Langston Hughes. APT-2

Testimonial. Harry Newman, Jr. GoPo

Testimonial. Claudia Rankine. ExTi; NeAmPo

Testimonies. Rosita Kalina. TANSG, tr. by Celeste Kostopulos-Cooperman

Testimonies. Rosita Kalina. MirDau, tr. by Roberta Gordenstein

Testimony. Seamus Heaney. PoAgWa

Testimony. Dan Pagis. PoSu, tr. by Stephen Mitchell

Testimony. Charles Reznikoff. NAAPv.2; PFTM-1
 4. NAAPv.2; OxBoAm
 3. The Immigrants. NAAPv.2
 2. The Job. ColAP; NAAPv.2
 1. The Sinking. ColAP; NAAPv.2

Testimony. Suzanne Wise. LegDan

Testimony of J. Robert Oppenheimer, The. Ai. AtGh

Testimony of Light, The. Carolyn Forché. AFaM; ExTi

Testimony: The United States (1901–1910) Recitative/The South. Charles Reznikoff. FTOS

Testing out the door-posts. Gregorio Scalise. ItPo, tr. by Gayle Ridinger

Testing, testing. Celia de Fréine. NIrP Fr. Price on My Head, A.

Testing the Confucian Ideal. Vietnamese Oral Tradition. CaDao, tr. by John Balaban

Testing-Tree, The. Stanley Kunitz. APT-2

Tête Pleine de Beauté, La. Pierre Reverdy. YaTCFP

Tête-à-Tête. Edwin Honig. NoAM

Tête-à-Tête. May Probyn. NPeEn; VWP

Tetélestai. Conrad Potter Aiken. APT-1; MoAmPo

Tethered horse, A. Buson. ChAP; EH, tr. by Robert Hass

Tethered Souls, The. Endre Ady. IQMS, tr. by Anton N. Nyerges

Tethy's Festival. Samuel Daniel.
 (Are They Shadows.) NoP-4; NoP-5
 Are They Shadows [That We See]? NOSC

Texas. Mei-Mei Berssenbrugge. PmAP

Texas. Caley O'Dwyer. TiP2

Texas. William Allen Ward. TiP2

Texas Autumn. Grace Noll Crowell. TiP2

Texas Boomer. John Collin Murphey. TiP2

Texas Chainsaw Massacre. Sherman Alexie. LiTh

Texas, / Child of the West. Texas. William Allen Ward. TiP2

Texas Corrido. Unknown. NAAPv.2

Texas Cowboy. Karle Wilson Baker. TiP2

Texas Eclogues. Frederick Turner. TiP2

Texas Memoranda. Lexie Dean Robertson. TiP2

Texas Poetry. Violette Newton. TiP2

Texas: Sesquicentennial. William Virgil Davis. TiP2

Texas Splendor. Janet Lowery. TiP2

Texas Sunrise, A. Jay Brannan. BeDoSh

Texas Trails. Norman H. Crowell. TiP2

Texas, unlike the rest of the West. Heart of Texas, The. James Cody. TiP2

Texian Call to Arms. Sam Houston.

Text and Commentary. Elke Erb. PFTM-2, tr. by Roderick Iverson

Text of Evening, The. Eric Tretheway. Coast

Text of necessity. Ingrid de Kok. TSAP

Text XXX. Josaphat Robert Large. OGAHCP, *tr.* by Boadiba and Jack Hirschman

Textbook. Im Yŏngjo. CAMKP, *tr.* by Edward W. Poitras

Textbook 10. Helmut Heissenbüttel. *tr.* by Pierre Joris
   Lesson 3. PFTM-2, *tr.* by Pierre Joris

Textbook of Poetry, 21, A. Jack Spicer. ASA

Textile 9. Marjorie Welish. VaPo

Textile 11. Marjorie Welish. VaPo

Textile 12. Marjorie Welish. VaPo

Textile 13. Marjorie Welish. VaPo

Textures. William Stafford. BodElec

Textures, The. Mary O'Donoghue. NIrP

Th' Attempt was brave, how happy your success. To Mrs. Manley. By the Author of Agnes de Castro. Catherine Cockburn. EMWP

Tha bùird is tàirnean air an uinneig. Hallaig. Sorley MacLean. EdScPo

Tha do stèidhichean làidir. Stèidhichean Làidir. Derick Thomson. EdScPo

Tha na fulmairean air Stac an Armainn. Coimhthional Hiort. Derick Thomson. EdScPo

Thalaba the Destroyer. Robert Southey.
   "Cold! cold! 'tis a chilly clime." NOBRP

Thalassa. Louis MacNeice. BrAP; WoPoe

Thalassa. José Luis Rivas. RMCMP, *tr.* by Alastair Reid

Thalassa. José Luis Rivas. RMCMP

Thamar and Amnon ("Moon turns in the sky, The.") Federico García Lorca. WED, *tr.* by Robert Bly

Thames from Cooper's Hill, The. Sir John Denham. OxAEP-1; OxBEV *Fr.* Cooper's Hill.

Thames nocturne of blue and gold, The. Impression du Matin. Oscar Wilde. MoBrPo; NAEL-6v2; NAEL-7v2; NoAM

Than a calm spin in a tomb of water. (LL) I Am Root. Claribel Alegría. PoetW; VCWP, *tr.* by Carolyn Forché

Than a human could play in a lifetime, to their graves. (LL) Pity the Bastards. Tom French. BeAl; NIrP

Than all men else, than thy self [*or* thyself] only less. (LL) To Ben Jonson. Thomas Carew. BASC; CavPo; NAEL-6v1; NAEL-7v1; NOSC

Than all the eastern sages knew. (LL) On the Emigration to America [and Peopling the Western Country]. Philip Freneau. ColAP; NAAL-3; NAAL-5; NAAPv.1; OxBoAm

Than all their timely descendants. (LL) Foundlings in the Yukon. A. K. Ramanujan. NAMCP V.2; PoetW

Than blood in the heart. (LL) Night: "Cold remote islands, The." Louise Bogan. APT-2; NAMCP V.1; NoP-4; NoP-5; WaAnP

Than by my threatenings [*or* threat'nings *or* threatnings] rest still innocent. (LL) Apparition, The. John Donne. BASC; FSCP; HeIP-4; NAEL-6v1; NAEL-7v1; NAWM-5v1; NoP-5; NoSic; OBEV; RaF; SoSe-8; TFi

Than Christ was a man. (LL) Consorting with Angels. Anne Sexton. MoWP; NALW

Than could whole seas of craw-fish soup. (LL) To a Young Lady, with Some Lampreys. John Gay. CABP; OBCoV

Than his picture, his shined shoes tied with twine. (LL) Clever and Poor. V. Penelope Pelizzon. AmPoNex; PoDa

Than I wished. (LL) Parachutes, My Love, Could Carry Us Higher. Barbara Guest. ASA; NYP2; OxBoAm

Than, if this noble kyng. John Skelton. PBRV *Fr.* Replycacion, A.

Than never to have loved at all. (LL) Alfred Tennyson. BrAP; CABP; CAGL; NAEL-6v2; NAEL-7v2; NAWM-7v2 *Fr.* In Memoriam A. H. H.

Than no illume at all. (LL) Those—dying then. Emily Dickinson. APN-2; NCAP

Than none at all. Provide, provide! (LL) Provide, Provide. Robert Frost. APT-1; ChIV-1; HarvBoo; NAMCP V.1; NoAM; NoP-4; NoP-5; OxBoAm; TFi; WeW-3; WoPoe

Than on real, live, weak creatures crushed by strong. (LL) Elizabeth Barrett Browning. PEW; VWP *Fr.* Casa Guidi Windows.

Than railroads, a soiled red-letter day. (LL) Sitting, The. Medbh McGuckian. CABP; ModIr; PNI

Than teach ten thousand stars how not to dance. (LL) You Shall Above All Things Be Glad and Young. E. E. Cummings. ColAP; NoAM; TWF

Than that I lose no more for Stella's sake. (LL) Sir Philip Sidney. NAEL-6v1; NAEL-7v1; NoSic *Fr.* Astrophil and Stella.

Than that it lived at all. Farewell. (LL) Epitaph on Elizabeth, L. H. Ben Jonson. NAEL-6v1; NIL-7; NIP-4; NoP-4; NoP-5; NOSC; OBEV

Than that which you / can do! (LL) Charles Olson. NAMCP V.2; NoAM; PmAP *Fr.* Maximus Poems, The.

Than that you should remember and be sad. (LL) Remember [Me]. Christina Georgina Rossetti. ChAP; GSo; InoFa; LW; NoP-4; NoP-5; OBEV; OxAEP-2; PEW; TFi; VWP; WaAnP

Than the strong man in his wrath. (LL) Cry of the Children, The. Elizabeth Barrett Browning. NAEL-7v2; OxAEP-2; ViWPN; VWP

Than the two hearts beating each to each! (LL) Meeting at Night. Robert Browning. BRP; CABP; FaBoVe; HeIP-4; ITBLP; NAEL-6v2; NAEL-7v2; OBEV; OPOU; OxBEV; SoSe-8; TFi

Than the wind goin' over my hand. (LL) Sea Love. Charlotte Mew. LW; MoBrPo; OxAEP-2; OxBEV

Than this fair park, from what it was before. (LL) On St. James's Park, as Lately Improved by His Majesty. Edmund Waller. BASC; NOSC; OBGa

Than this smart Misery. (LL) Of Course—I prayed. Emily Dickinson. APN-2; MoAmPo; TCAPo

Than those that to the earth with many tears they give. (LL) Dead, The. Jones Very. APN-1; NoP-4; NoP-5; OxBoAm; SacPr; TCAPo

Than to have people say when seen. (LL) Bird in a Gilded Cage, A. Arthur J. Lamb. NAAPv.2; TCAPo

Than to live not perfected. (LL) His Request to Julia. Robert Herrick. CavPo; NOSC

Than to sink among men. Inscription on a Bathing Vessel. *Unknown.* CCL1, *tr.* by James Legge

Than when I was a boy. (LL) I Remember, I Remember. Thomas Hood. ITBLP; NPBRoP; OxAEP-2; OxBEV; TFi; TreFP

Than write such hopeless rubbish as thy worst.. (LL) Sonnet, A: "Two voices are there: one is of the deep." James Kenneth Stephen. CABP; UV

Than young Hope in his sunniest hour hath known. (LL) Dreams: "Oh! That my young life were a lasting dream!" Edgar Allan Poe. NCAP; OxBoAm

Thanatopsis. William Cullen Bryant. APN-1; BRP; ColAP; NAAL-3; NAAL-5; NAAPv.1; NCAP; NoP-4; NoP-5; OBEV; OxBoAm; TCAPo; TFi
   "So live, that when thy summons comes to join." TreFP

Thanatos, Thy Praise I Sing. Michael Field. ViWPN

Thank God. Lousy in Center Field. James Tate. MoASP

Thank God for All. John Lydgate. SacPr

Thank god he stuck his tongue. Mostly Mick Jagger. Catie Rosemurgy. BAP-97

Thank God they're all gone. Nazis. Ira Sadoff. LTA; OPRER

Thank Heaven! the crisis. For Annie. Edgar Allan Poe. APN-1; ColAP; OBEV; TCAPo

Thank Heaven! the crisis. Edgar Allan Poe. STuOW *Fr.* For Annie.

Thank you for attending this tribute to love. Milena Jesenká. Edward Hirsch. BodElec

Thank You for Being You. Matthew Zapruder. NevBe

Thank you for hurrying through. Gertrude Stein. PoA 2002 *Fr.* Stanzas in Meditation.

Thank you for saying pathos instead of pathetic, keeping us the same size as before. Heather Ramsdell. IAoNAP *Fr.* Vague Swimmers.

Thank you for these tiny. Dusting. Marilyn Nelson Waniek. PfSP

Thank you, Mr Rason, for the Apples. E. G. Murphy. OBCoV

Thank You, My Fate. Anna Swirszczynska [*or* Swir]. BLT

Thank You, My Little Son. Meg Bateman. MoWP

Thank you, she says, we both needed that. Incident in a Filing Cupboard. Roddy Lumsden. PoDa

Thank you, whatever comes. And then she turned. Erat Hora. Ezra Pound. ItP

Thank you. You are too. (LL) My Erotic Double. John Ashbery. EMP; VCAP

Thank Your Father. Lew Brown, B. G. DeSylva and Ray Henderson. ReLy

Thankful soil manured and winter dressed, The. Shamed by the Creature. Mildmay Fane, 2d Earl of Westmorland. NOSC

Thankfulness. Adelaide Anne Procter. SacPr

Thanking Doctor Jen. Li K'ai-hsien. ColAnChi, *tr.* by Jonathan Chaves

Thankless too for peace. Samuel Taylor Coleridge. FaBoWar; PoAgWa *Fr.* Fears in Solitude [Written in April, 1798, during the Alarm of an Invasion].

Thankmeal our grace is given. Holy Sonnet. Robert Kelly. WhBo

Thanks. Yusef Komunyakaa. AmAlph; CAP-8; OxBoAm

Thanks a Lot, but No Thanks. Betty Comden and Adolph Green. ReLy

Thanks and a Plea to Mary. *Unknown.* FaBoVe

Thanks and blessing be. Grace. Rafael Jesús González. IPoFL

Thanks but no. I will do. Dianae Sumus in Fide. Biancamaria Frabotta. CItWP, *tr.* by Cinzia Sartini Blum and Lara Trubowitz

Thanks for Daisen Osho's Visit. Muso Soseki. EaWin, *tr.* by W. S. Merwin

Thanks for the Memory. Ralph Rainger and Leo Robin. ReLy

Thanks for the novel on Catherine the Great. Stick-up. Jeni Olin. FreRad

Thanks for the tree / between me & a sniper's bullet. Thanks. Yusef Komunyakaa. AmAlph; CAP-8; OxBoAm

Thanks for your of already some. Age of Correggio and the Carracci, The. Charles Bernstein. BodElec

Thanks in old age—thanks ere I go. Thanks in Old Age. Walt Whitman. SAmP

Thanks in Winter. Harri Webb. AngWePo

Thanks, my dear Richard; and, I pray thee, deign. George Crabbe. *Fr.* Tales of the Hall.

Thanks, Robert Frost. David Ray. VisFro

Thanks Sent to Taihei Osho. Muso Soseki. EaWin, *tr. by* W. S. Merwin

Thanks that we rise again from death and live. (LL) "H. D." APT-1; NALW *Fr.* Tribute to the Angels.

Thanks to a Spanish friend of mine the king of Spain had given me. Spanish Generosity. Max Jacob. CuPo

Thanks to life that has given me so much. Here's to Life. Violeta Parra. TCLAP, *tr. by* Joan Baez and James Upton

Thanks to rental movies. Things I can. Insides of Alfred Hitchcock, The. Alejandrino Hufana. ReBoTo

Thanks to Saint Matthew, who had been. Comrade Jesus. Sarah Norcliffe Cleghorn. APT-1

Thanks to the ear. Benediction. James Berry. OPOU

Thanks to the morning light. World-Soul, The. Ralph Waldo Emerson. APN-1; NCAP

Thanks to the Things. Rutger Kopland. VCWP, *tr. by* James Brockway

Thanksgibin' day am now at han'. Day befo' Thanksgibin', De. Maggie Pogue Johnson. CBWP-4

Thanksgiving. Martín Espada. PrTe; PuP-23

Thanksgiving. Mac Hammond. P180

Thanksgiving. Lizelia Augusta Jenkins Moorer. CBWP-3

Thanksgiving. Ed Ochester. SUP

Thanksgiving. Tracy Philpot. IAoNAP

Thanksgiving. Liz Rosenberg. PBCAP

Thanksgiving (1974). Stefan Brecht. CLPP

Thanksgiving—Christmas 2. Annie Dillard. UpMys *Fr.* Feast Days.

Thanksgiving—Christmas 3. Annie Dillard. UpMys *Fr.* Feast Days.

Thanksgiving Day. Lydia Maria Child. NTCP; WHSW (New-England Boy's Song about Thanksgiving Day, The.) APN-1; ColAP

Thanksgiving Dinner. Aileen Fisher. CA

Thanksgiving to God for His House, A. Robert Herrick. BASC; CavPo; NOSC

Thanksgiving to the Emperor Augustus Germanicus Domitianus. Publius Papinius Statius. RomPo *Fr.* Sylvae [*or* Silvae].

Thanksgivings, The. *Unknown.* APN-2, *tr. by* Harriet Maxwell Converse

Thankyou Note. Dannie Abse. TCAWP

Thank-You Note. Sarah Kirsch. MotU, *tr. by* Peter Spycher

Thar na slorruidheachd, thar a sneachda. Coin is madaidhean-allaidh. Sorley MacLean. EdScPo

Thass a funny title, Mr. Bones. John Berryman. CAP-8; ChIV-2 *Fr.* Dream Songs.

Thassyryans king, in peas with fowle desyre. Henry Howard, Earl of Surrey. *See* Assyrian [*or* Assyrians'] King in peace, with foul desire, The [*or* Th'].

That. Pierre Reverdy. YaTCFP, *tr. by* John Ashbery

That actual day. Anne Portugal. OnScMo, *tr. by* Norma Cole

That after horror that was us. Emily Dickinson. APN-2

That after Horror—that 'twas us. That after horror that was us. Emily Dickinson. APN-2

That afternoon I had been fishing alone. Dream of Retarded Children, A. Robert Bly. LoL

That all is well. (LL) Death Sunyata Chant: A Rite for Passing Over. Diane Di Prima. BB; WANABP

That all men would be cowards if they dare. Tales. George Crabbe.

That all these dyings may be life in death. (LL) Mortification. George Herbert. FSCP; NOSC

That all things should be mine. Amendment. Thomas Traherne. InvLi

That always passes away, and does not end. (LL) Juan Ramón Jiménez. SpanPo; WoPoe *Fr.* Ten Short Poems.

That an Immortal binds. (LL) Of Paul and Silas it is said. Emily Dickinson. ChIV-2; SacPr

That anxious way you have of closing doors. Possession. Caitríona O'Reilly. StAl

That any thing should be. Axle Song. Mark Van Doren. APT-2

That April Morning. Patricia Lasoen. TuT, *tr. by* Dennis O'Driscoll

That are so wondrous sweet and fair. (LL) Song: "Go[e], lovely rose." Edmund Waller. BASC; CABP; ClHu; CtM; HeIP-4; NAEL-6v1; NAEL-7v1; NIL-7; NoP-4; NoP-5; NOSC; NPeEn; OBEV; OxAEP-1; OxBEV; PBRV; PoPoPo; SoSe-8; TFi; WaAnP; WeW-3; WoPoe

That as all parts of it. Posited. James McMichael. GeoHom

That asks not happiness, but longs for rest! (LL) To Hope. Helen Maria Williams. CenSon; OxBSo

That August afternoon the family. State Funeral. Thomas McCarthy. ModIr

That August, reflections grew very bright. Swiftness With Which Those Cities Fell, The. Dennis Nurkse. PrTe

That axe that I hear. Buson. TAL

That bakeapples are not baked, or apples. What We Learned on the Highway Near St. John's. Jeanette Lynes. Coast

That bean flower O. *Unknown.* CCL1 *Fr.* Cai-ge [Translations].

That bears the coming harvest in its breast. (LL) Zulu Girl, The. Roy Campbell. NoP-4; NoP-5; OBMV; OxAEP-2

That bears the Human soul. (LL) There is No Frigate Like a Book. Emily Dickinson. APN-2; BRP; MoAmPo; OxBoAm; PtR; SAmP; SoSe-8

That bears the zodiac. (LL) Goose Fish, The. Howard Nemerov. HeIP-4; NAMCP V.2; NIL-7; NIP-4; NoAM; NoP-4; NoP-5

That Been to Me My Lives Light and Saviour. Susan Wheeler. ExTi

That being a good mother. Things No One Told Me. Opal Palmer Adisa. BtF

That bird flying for the first time. Sailor. Vincente Huidobro. TCLAP, *tr. by* David Guss

That bird named for the bird twice-size itelf. Woodpecker Finch. Robyn Schiff. LegDan

That bit of filth in dirty walls. Terezin. Hanuš Hachenburg. INSAB

That black drunken eye has become a tavern. Nef'i. OLP, *tr. by* Walter Andrews, Najaat Black and Mehmet Kalpakli

That black forest and the fire in earnest. (LL) Gretel in Darkness. Louise Glück. NoAM; NoP-4; NoP-5

That Black Girl Fulô. Jorge de Lima. TCLAP, *tr. by* Elizabeth Gordon

That board—you'd rave and rend them with your teeth. (LL) Question, A. John Millington Synge. MoBrPo; OBMV

That bony potbellied arrow, wing-pumping along. Cormorant in Its Element, The. Amy Clampitt. NoP-4; NoP-5

That bound and tied they fled. Ivano Fermini. ItPo, *tr. by* Gayle Ridinger

That Boxing Day morning, I would hear the familiar, far-off gowls and gulders. Beagles. Paul Muldoon. GPPA

That boy. Crush. Rigoberto González. BeDoSh

That boy last night is a pleasure I shall always store. (LL) Memory, A. Yi Chŏngbo. CATKP; WoPoe, *tr. by* Kevin O'Rourke

That brekis thair hairt and nocht the bettir. (LL) To luve unluvit it is ane pane. Alexander Scott. NePenScot; NPeEn; PBRV

That brings to maddening love, no soothing dream! (LL) Her Address to the Moon. Mary Robinson. CenSon; RWP

That by all bodies else obscures her name. (LL) Fulke, 1st Baron Brooke Greville. NoSic; NPeEn *Fr.* Caelica.

That came for the children. (LL) Seven Sorrows, The. Ted Hughes. NAEL-6v2; NAEL-7v2

That Can Not Be Taken Away From It. Carla Harryman. FTOS

That cancels the blackness of each image. (LL) Blank Sonnet. George Elliott Clarke. Coast; OpeFie

That "cannot be done," and you'll do it. (LL) It Couldn't Be Done. Edgar Albert Guest. BRP; ITBLP

That cannot long one fashion entertain. (LL) Michael Drayton. NAEL-6v1; NAEL-7v1; NOSC *Fr.* Idea.

That chair. Coup. Leonard Nathan. CalPo

That, chased by a covey of hunters, the fox. Altamira: What She Remembered. Linda Bierds. AmAlph

That child I was. Beginning Speech. Adonis. PoCho, *tr. by* John Heath-Stubbs and Lena Jayyusi *and* W. S. Merwin

That child will never lie in me, and you. Unknown Child, The. Elizabeth Jennings. MoWP

That childish thoughts such joys inspire. Thomas Traherne. BASC *Fr.* Third Century, The.

That Christmas, unlike others. Gifts. Lenard D. Moore. SpirFl

That civilisation may not sink. Long-Legged Fly. William Butler Yeats. NAEL-6v2; NAEL-7v2; NAMCP V.1; NoAM; NoP-4; NoP-5; NPeEn; WaAnP

That clock is ticking. Marie Lucille. Gwendolyn Brooks. TLR

That clouds have no intent. Yi Chono. CATKP, *tr. by* Peter H. Lee

That Cold Summer. Nin Andrews. BAP-97

That comes into and steadies my soul. (LL) Pangolin, The. Marianne Moore. APT-1; NAAPv.2; NAMCP V.1; NoAM; WaAnP

That constant Susannah. Susannah. Thulani Davis. GT

That conversation we were always on the edge. Adrienne Rich. NoAM *Fr.* Twenty-one Love Poems.

"That cop was powerful mean." Idiot, The. Dudley Randall. LTA

That Corner. Blanaid Salkeld. IrLP

That Corrugated Look To Water. Milton Acorn. Coast

That curse her when they come. (LL) Ralph Waldo Emerson. APN-1; NoP-4; NoP-5 *Fr.* Quatrains.

That Dada Strain. Jerome Rothenberg. FTOS; PFTM-2

That dared attack my Chesterton. (LL) Lion, The. Joseph Hilaire Pierre Belloc. MoBrPo; NBLV; WHSW

That dared attack my Chesterton. (LL) Lines to a Don. Joseph Hilaire Pierre Belloc. MoBrPo; OBSV

That darkesome cave they enter, where they find. Edmund Spenser. OxBEV *Fr.* Faerie Queene, The.

That Darkness—is about to pass. (LL) Presentiment—is that long Shadow—on the lawn. Emily Dickinson. APN-2; HeIP-4

That darts along her smile? (LL) Sympathetic Portrait of a Child. William Carlos Williams. APT-1; NAMCP V.1

That Day. Shin Kyŏngnim. CAMKP, *tr. by* David R. McCann

That day as guidons fluttered. Antonio López and Emily. James Gregory Smith. TiP2

That day, *Eke*, a lean spirit touched another spirit. Extended Relations (1). Uduma Kalu. NeNiPo

That day I lost everything. 22.6.1941. Ondra Lysohorsky. AF, *tr. by* Ewald Osers

That day in December I sat down. Miz Rosa Rides the Bus. Angela Jackson. IllVoic

That day she threw the goose over the roof. Grandma's Man. James Welch. NoAM

That day the albatross. Captain Amasa Delano's Dilemma. Yusef Komunyakaa. BodElec

That day the plains of Texas tilted north. Last Running, The. Jerry Craven. TiP2

That day the sails of the ship were torn. Lament for Tadhg Cronin's Children. Egan O'Rahilly. ModIr; PBCIP; WoPoe, *tr. by* Michael Hartnett

That day would skin a fairy. Dying Art, A. Derek Mahon. ModIr

That Dear Little Cat. D'Arcy Wentworth Thompson. NOxBChV

That death receives you. Amen. Alvaro Mutis. TCLAP, *tr. by* Sophie Cabot Black and Maria Negroni

That desire is quite over. Thinking of Love. Elizabeth Jennings. LW

That devour America. (LL) In Goya's greatest scenes we seem to see. Lawrence Ferlinghetti. CalPo; HeIP-4; NAMCP V.2; NoAM; PmAP

That dey road no pave. Road of the Dread, The. Lorna Goodison. VCWP

That dithyramb of ticky-tick, boom. Cheap Gas. Brenda Hillman. RoV

That does not see you. You must change your life. (LL) Archaic Torso of Apollo. Rainer Maria Rilke. NAWM-7v2; PtR; RaBo; TWF, *tr. by* Stephen Mitchell

That Dog with daisies for eyes. Dog of Art, The. Denise Levertov. NAMCP V.2; NoAM; WaAnP

That dolphin-torn, that gong-tormented sea. (LL) Byzantium. William Butler Yeats. HarvBoo; MoBrPo; NAEL-6v2; NAEL-7v2; NAMCP V.1; NAWM-7v2; NIL-7; NIP-4; NoAM; NoP-4; NoP-5; OxBEV; WaAnP

That don't scare me so much death of my guts. That don't Scare Me. Raymond Queneau. YaTCFP, *tr. by* Keith Waldrop

That dream, her eyes like rocks studded the high. Snow on a Mountain. Dom Moraes. NoP-4; NoP-5

That drew to a close sometime shortly after lunch. (LL) Lines Composed Over Three Thousand Miles From Tintern Abbey. Billy Collins. OxBoAm; WaAnP

That drop of sweat which is sliding down my mouth. Esprit d'Escalier. John Wheelwright. APT-2

That dry inhabitant of clay. Rufous-Crowned Sparrow Seen Loitering below Possum Kingdom Dam. William D. Barney. TiP2

That dying is what, to live, each has to do. (LL) Curiosity. Alastair Reid. SoSe-8; WaAnP

That each, who seems a separate whole. Alfred Tennyson. NAEL-6v2; NAEL-7v2 *Fr.* In Memoriam A. H. H.

That empty sack, my heart. A box of matches. (LL) What Every Woman Should Carry. Maura Dooley. NeBl; StAl

That enormous nose. (LL) Sidekicks. Ron Koertge. CalPo; P180

That Eureka of Archimedes out of his bath. Voluptuaries and Others. Margaret Avison. BrAP

That evening. Zoe and the Ghosts. Dieter Weslowski. InvLad

That Evening Pierre Insisted That I Had Two Roast Pigeons at Dinner. Lee Harwood. AHA

That evening Sinda thought she heard the drums. Dream, The. Robert Earl Hayden. ESEAA

That ever younger evening sky's pastel accord's. Harmonie du Soir. Stephen Yenser. PoDa

That every tongue says beauty should look so. (LL) William Shakespeare. NAEL-6v1; NAEL-7v1; OxAEP-1 *Fr.* Sonnets.

That Exploit of Yours. Ford Madox Ford. PoWW

That eye didn't stop Mr. Isaak. Man with the Glass Eye, The. Leonard Neufeldt. ACAMVP

That Face. Ralph Blane and Hugh Martin. ReLy

That fall, when we shared a phonograph. Year the Space Age Was Born, The. Floyd Skloot. SwNoth

That Falling. Jane Hirshfield. BodElec

That familiar curving hand. Letter. Sue Hubbard. Prnts

That fateful year I wished for you, flushed. Suicide Year, The. Alice Anderson. AmPoNex

That final newsreel of the war. John Montague. PNI *Fr.* Time in Armagh.

That fire that eats what it illuminates. (LL) Style. Howard Nemerov. NoAM; OxBoAm

That first day. Six Minutes Writing. Kadija George. BRtP

That first day, to break me in. Sky Nails. Jamie McKendrick. NeBrP

That first green night of their dreaming. Sixth Night: Waking, The. Muriel Rukeyser. PoCho

That first time. Dylan Iorwerth. BBMWP *Fr.* Sand.

That first winter. Cold War. Sara London. PoDa

That fixed the tilt of the wings. (LL) Perfect. Hugh MacDiarmid. NePenScot; NoP-4; OxBEV; WoPoe

That floral apron. (LL) Floral Apron, The. Marilyn Chin. LoL; SweBea

That flower unseen, that gem of purest ray. In a Churchyard. Richard Wilbur. HeIP-4; UpMys

That flowing water! That flowing water! *Unknown*. APN-2 *Fr.* Mountain Chant, The.

That flows through me to you in a continuous path. (LL) My Blood Brother. Frank Mkalawile Chipasula. HBAPE; PML

That flutter out of their lives. (LL) Poem: "Late butterflies gliding through the air." Timothy Liu. NeAmPo; TAPaP

That for seven *Lusters* I did never come. Robert Herrick. CavPo; PBRV

That fought with us upon Saint Crispin's day. (LL) William Shakespeare. FaBoWar; OxAEP-1 *Fr.* King Henry V.

That free love with bondage bound. (LL) William Blake. ChIV-1; NAEL-6v2; NAEL-7v2; NAWM-7v2; NOBRP; NPBRoP *Fr.* Songs of Experience.

That from the seed of men. Psalm. Peter Huchel. AF; AtGh, *tr. by* Daniel S. Simko

That gap between the Sunday papers and lunch. (LL) Against Coupling. Fleur Adcock. EmeKit; MoWP; NALW

That gaunt old man came first, his hair as white. Their Bodies. David Wagoner. EMP; PoA 2002

That girl so long ago walked, as they all did, shop girls. Bolt, The. Mary Kinzie. ExTi; PtR

That girl wears her hair in a chicken's tail. Across the Field of the Old Corporal. *Vietnamese Oral Tradition*. CaDao, *tr. by* John Balaban

That girl's breats distracted everyone at the baseball game. Carson Cistulli. FreRad *Fr.* Twenty-Six Friends, That's the Same as Your Age.

That glass was it filled with alcohol, water, or light. Flight. Franz Wright. AmAlph

That Glove. Mary E. Tucker. CBWP-1

That God is All, His shadow shows. (LL) Plaint. Ebenezer Elliott. OBEV; SacPr

That God Made. Will Heford. FTtHH

That God of ours, the Great Geometer. Grace to Be Said at the Supermarket. Howard Nemerov. SoSe-8

That gorgeous kite. Issa. EH, *tr. by* Robert Hass

That great blue oak. Basho. SoOfWa, *tr. by* Sam Hamill

That Great Wingless Bird. Adrian C. Louis. UnSA

That grudging man [can't hurt] you. Korinna [*or* Corinna]. SaLy, *tr. by* Diane Rayor

That had left so much unsaid. (LL) Local Poet, A. John Hewitt. ModIr; PNI

That half-death, / suckled big with our life. In Prague. Paul Celan. VCWP, *tr. by* Michael Hamburger

That handsaw marks time. Buson. SoOfWa, *tr. by* Sam Hamill

That Harp You Play So Well. Marianne Moore. MoAmPo

That harsh, irregular flame? (LL) Quarrel, The. Stanley Kunitz. APT-2; TaR

That has been hurting her. (LL) Proletarian Portrait. William Carlos Williams. BLT; OxBoAm; SAmP

That has no end. (LL) Near the Wall of a House. Yehuda Amichai. BBASP; PFTM-2, *tr. by* Chana Bloch

That has not been rent. (LL) Crazy Jane Talks with the Bishop. William Butler Yeats. CABP; NAEL-6v2; NAEL-7v2; NAMCP V.1; NoAM; NoP-4; NoP-5; OxAEP-2; PoPoPo; TRP

That has transfigured me. (LL) Lamentation of the Old Pensioner, The (1925 version). William Butler Yeats. TRP; WeW-3

That has yet to enter the language. (LL) Quoof. Paul Muldoon. FaBoVe; NAMCP V.2; NPeEn; PBCIP; PNI; StAl

That he is old and new a shade. (LL) Walter Savage Landor. NAEL-6v2; NoP-4; NoP-5; NPeEn; OBEV; OxAEP-2; OxBEV; TFi; WeW-3; WoPoe *Fr.* Pericles and Aspasia.

That he may sleep upon his hill again? (LL) Abraham Lincoln Walks at Midnight. Vachel Lindsay. APT-1; CBCWP; IllVoic; MoAmPo; NAAPv.2; TCAPo; TFi

That he might just snap again was part of it, blind himself, and, well, you're there. Twilight. Ralph Angel. BodElec

That he slew me to gratify his hatred. (LL) Edgar Lee Masters. APT-1; NAMCP V.1; NoAM; OxBoAm *Fr.* Spoon River Anthology.

That he will still require some waters to his blood. (LL) Christ's Passion. Abraham Cowley. ChIV-2; SacPr

That heard me whisper, "I am she!" (LL) Other Side of a Mirror, The. Mary Elizabeth Coleridge. NAEL-7v2; NALW; ViWPN; VWP

That here, obedient to their laws, we lie. (LL) Thermopylae. Simonides. OBVE; OBWP; WoPoe, *tr. by* William Lisle Bowles

That hick farmer's got my number. *Unknown*. PriapPo *Fr.* Priapus Poems, The.

That hid the shyest grape. (LL)   Monody: "To have known him, to have loved him." Herman Melville.   APN-2; NAAL-3; NAAPv.1; NoP-4; NoP-5; PoPoPo; TCAPo

That hideous overgrown toad again!   Dragon Slaying.   Zoltán Jékely.   IQMS, *tr. by George Szirtes*

That his daddy once tied up my garter for me! (LL)   Dark-Eyed Gentleman, The.   Thomas Hardy.   MoBrPo; NBLV

That his eyebrows were false—that his hair.   Maiden's Mistake, The.   Frances Sargent Osgood.   NAAPv.1

That history is an event.   Taku Skanskan.   Paula Gunn Allen.   HATNAP

That hobnailed goblin, the bobtailed Hob.   Dame Edith Sitwell.   NAMCP V.1; NoAM *Fr.* Façade.

That Holy Thing.   George Macdonald.   OBEV; SacPr *Fr.* Paul Faber, Surgeon.

That hoop-back man.   Compass of the Dying.   Laurence Lieberman.   IllVoic

That horn chased me.   Up on the Spoon.   Stanley Crouch.   SeSe

That hot September night, we slept in a single bed.   Girlfriends.   Carol Ann Duffy.   HarvBoo

That humor now, declines for age drawes on.   Thomas Churchyard.   PBRV *Fr.* Musicall Consort, A.

That hump of a man bunching chrysanthemums.   Old Florist.   Theodore Roethke.   APT-2

That I, all else defac'd, not envie Kinges. (LL)   Content and Resolute.   William Drummond of Hawthornden.   NPeEn; PBRV

That I am clo[a]th[e]d in holy robes for glory. (LL)   Huswifery.   Edward Taylor.   ColAP; InvLi; ITBLP; NAAL-3; NAAL-5; NAAPv.1; NIP-4; OxBoAm; SacPr; TCAPo; TFi

That I Can Do This Autumn.   Hong Yunsuk.   CAMKP, *tr. by Genell Y. Poitras*

That I did always love.   Emily Dickinson.   SacPr

That I have been an hour away. (LL)   Alfred Tennyson.   NAEL-6v2; NAEL-7v2 *Fr.* In Memoriam A. H. H.

That I have been in certain sad places.   Song of Reply.   Alda Merini.   CItWP, *tr. by Cinzia Sartini Blum and Lara Trubowitz*

That I have been looking.   Subway Face.   Langston Hughes.   APT-2

That I have loved my whole life! (LL)   At First She Came to Me Pure.   Juan Ramón Jiménez.   RaW; WED, *tr. by Robert Bly*

That I invent. A wild girl watches me from my inmost self / I am intact. (LL) Life is nothing but time.   Gloria Gervitz.   CFP; MirDau, *tr. by Stephen Tapscott*

That I love not, without I leave to love. (LL)   Sir Philip Sidney.   NAEL-6v1; NAEL-7v1 *Fr.* Astrophil and Stella.

That I might chisel a statue, line on line.   Statue, The.   Ella Higginson.   SWaP

That I might there present it—O! to Whom? (LL)   Question, The: "I dream'd that, as I wander'd by the way."   Percy Bysshe Shelley.   OBEV; OxBEV

That I shall never find him. (LL)   Mad Maid's Song, The.   Robert Herrick.   OBEV; RACG

That I shall never find my home. (LL)   Mower to the Glowworms [or Glow-Worms or Glo-Worms], The.   Andrew Marvell.   BASC; FSCP; NAEL-6v1; NAEL-7v1; NoP-4; NoP-5; NPeEn; PBRV; TFi

That I should love, and he should be ingrate. (LL)   To One That Asked Me Why I Loved J.G G.   "Ephelia."   EMWP; NOSC

That I went to warm my self in Lady Betty's Chamber.   To Their Excellencies the Lords Justices of Ireland, the Humble Petition of Frances Harris, Who Must Starve, and Die a Maid if It Miscarries.   Jonathan Swift.   OxBEV

That I would not persuaded be.   Service Is No Heritage.   Nicholas Breton.   NoSic

That if I dipped my hand the spawn would clutch it. (LL)   Death of a Naturalist.   Seamus Heaney.   NAMCP V.2; NoAM; OxBEV; WaAnP; WeW-3

That if the linen flapped too loud.   And Let Us Say.   Matthew Hollis.   BeAl

That I'm alive to tell you so. (LL)   Stella's Birthday ([March 13,] 1727).   Jonathan Swift.   NoP-4; NoP-5

That I'm lucky.   They All Think.   Giovanna Pollarolo.   TANSG, *tr. by Marjorie Agosin*

That I'm still here. (LL)   Full Indian Rope Trick, The.   Colette Bryce.   MoWP; NIrP

That in black ink my love may still shine bright. (LL)   William Shakespeare.   AEP; NAEL-6v1; NAEL-7v1; NoP-5; NoSic; OxAEP-1; OxBSo; RaBo; TFi; TreFP *Fr.* Sonnets.

That in the manage myself takes delight.   Sir Philip Sidney.   NAEL-6v1; NAEL-7v1; NoP-4; NoP-5 *Fr.* Astrophil and Stella.

That insect, without antennae, over its.   Crane, The.   Charles Tomlinson.   MoBrPo

That is fit home for Thee! (LL)   To the Cuckoo ("O blithe New-comer! I have heard.")   William Wordsworth.   NOBRP; NPBRoP; UV

That is fluent in even the wintriest bronze. (LL)   Sense of the Sleight-of-Hand Man, The.   Wallace Stevens.   MoAmPo; NoAM; OxBoAm; PoA 2002; WeW-3

That is most difficult. (LL)   To a Friend Whose Work Has Come to Nothing.   William Butler Yeats.   MoBrPo; OBMV; OxAEP-2; WoPoe

That is no country for old men. The young.   Sailing to Byzantium.   William Butler Yeats.   AmFaPo; BLPJKO; BrAP; CABP; ClHu; EMP; HarvBoo; HeIP-4; MoBrPo; NAEL-6v2; NAEL-7v2; NAMCP V.1; NAWM-7v2; NIL-7; NIP-4; NoAM; NoP-4; NoP-5; NPeEn; OBMV; OWoS; OxBEV; PoPoPo; RaBo; SoSe-8; TFi; WaAnP; WeW-3; WoPoe

That is not lovable? (LL)   It is night again.   Tzu Yeh.   EroLit; WoPoe, *tr. by Chung Ling and Kenneth Rexroth*

That is not the way.   Divorce 19th-century Style.   Colette Ni Ghallchóir.   NIrP, *tr. by the author*

That is reserved for his kind. (LL)   Hyaenas [or Hyenas], The.   Rudyard Kipling.   BrAP; NAEL-6v2; NAEL-7v2; OBSV

That is the dawn fairy.   Dawn Fairy, The.   Dunya Mikhail.   PoArWo, *tr. by Samira Kawar*

That is the glebe and this is the glissando. The future is nothing.   Codex.   Stephen Rodefer.   PmAP

That Is the Way.   Max Winter.   FreRad

That is their quality: not mercy, not mind, not goodness, but the beauty of God. (LL)   Birds and Fishes.   Robinson Jeffers.   NAAL-5; NoP-4; NoP-5; WaAnP

That is why we dedicate our books.   Books of the Dead, The.   Marta Kornblith.   MirDau, *tr. by Roberta Gordenstein*

That is, without a doubt, the decisive test. (LL)   In Trying Times.   Heberto Padilla.   AF; PoetW, *tr. by Andrew Hurley and Alastair Reid*

That it also comes this way, in parts. (LL)   Toys.   Carl Phillips.   CAP-8; ReTh

That it is a road.   Narihira.   WoPoe *Fr.* Ise Monogatari, The.

That it is she is only fair. (LL)   Roundelay Between Two Shepherds, A.   Michael Drayton.   NoP-4; NoP-5

That it is we who are important. (LL)   For a Coming Extinction.   W. S. Merwin.   EMP; GifTon; NAMCP V.2; PoPoPo; VCAP

That it seems as if she were still alive? (LL)   When she showed me her photograph.   Marjorie Agosin.   CFP; TANSG, *tr. by Celeste Kostopulos-Cooperman*

That it will never come again.   Emily Dickinson.   APN-2

That its sparkle may amuse you. (LL)   Lady, A.   Amy Lowell.   MoAmPo; TCAPo

That Jewish Crusader.   Diana Anhalt.   MirDau

That Journeys Are Good.   Jelaluddin Rumi.   RaBo; WED, *tr. by Robert Bly*

That joy[e]s so ripe, so little keep[e]. (LL)   To Amarantha, That She Would Dishevel[l] Her Hair[e].   Richard Lovelace.   CABP; CavPo; NIL-7; NoP-4; NoP-5; OBEV

That Justice is a blind goddess.   Justice.   Langston Hughes.   NAAPv.2

That keep him rich and orphaned and beloved? (LL)   Illiterate, The.   William Meredith.   EMP; NoP-4; NoP-5; OxBSo; PoA 2002; VCAP

That kill, that kill, that kill. (LL)   Elm.   Sylvia Plath.   NAMCP V.2; NoAM; NoP-4; NoP-5; OxBoAm

That kindles my mother's fire! (LL)   Wife of Usher's Well, The.   *Unknown*. MakPoe; NAEL-6v1; NAEL-7v1; NePenScot; NoP-4; NoP-5; NPeEn; OBEV; OxAEP-1; TFi

That kingfisher jewelling upstream.   Kingfisher.   Norman Alexander MacCaig.   NoP-4; NoP-5

That Kings for such a Tomb would wish to die. (LL)   On Shakespear[e].   John Milton.   BrAP; CABP; NAEL-6v1; NAEL-7v1; NoP-4; NoP-5; NOSC; PoPoPo

That knows—it cannot see. (LL)   Difference between Despair, The.   Emily Dickinson.   NAAL-3; TCAPo

That labor / a face to remember in wonder.   Sappho.   OBVE

That landlike slept along the deep. (LL)   Alfred Tennyson.   NAEL-6v2; NAEL-7v2 *Fr.* In Memoriam A. H. H.

That last afternoon.   Jack's Last Words.   Stephen Kessler.   GeoHom

That last night we passed quietly, my brother and I.   Voice of Col. Von Stauffenberg Rising from Purgatory, The.   Donald Justice.   PoA 2002

That lead from Thirty————even to Forty-eight. (LL)   Thirty-eight: Addressed to Mrs H—y.   Charlotte Smith.   NALW; PEW

That leaves look[e] pale, dreading the winter's near [or neere]. (LL)   William Shakespeare.   AEP; HeIP-4; NAEL-6v1; NAEL-7v1; NoP-5; NoSic; OBEV; OxAEP-1; TFi *Fr.* Sonnets.

That light, reflected, but makes darkness plain. (LL)   In Dispraise of the Moon.   Mary Elizabeth Coleridge.   PEW; ViWPN

That little jukebox right over there.   I'd Give a Dollar for a Dime.   Andy Razaf.   ReLy

That little Negro's married and got a kid.   Sister.   Langston Hughes.   APSN

That little pretty [or prettie] bleeding part.   To His Savior [or Saviour]. The New Years [or yeers] Gift.   Robert Herrick.   ChIV-2; NAEL-6v1

(That liv'd so sweetly) dead, so sweet a Grave! (LL)   Music[k]'s Duel[l].   Richard Crashaw.   NAEL-7v1; NPeEn

That living there I never could look up. (LL)   Glory Trumpeter, The.   Derek Walcott.   GT; NAEL-6v2; NAEL-7v2; NoP-4; NoP-5; SeSe

That look of attention.   Young Mothers 1.   Sharon Olds.   EMP

That look you roll.   To the Lighthouse.   Yvonne Cullen.   NIrP

That loosiana swamp dog put some funny stuff. Chuck Man. Wanda Coleman. SUP

That Love is all there is. Emily Dickinson. TCAPo

That love of mine for him had waxen wings—. Comet, The. Maria Luisa Spaziani. Nelt, *tr. by* Beverly Allen

That love to her I cast away. (LL) Disdain Returned. Thomas Carew. BASC; CavPo

That lovely climbing vine, so fresh. Conversation with a Japanese Student. Eleanor Wilner. GifTon

That lover of a night. Crazy Jane on God. William Butler Yeats. RACG

That Lucky Old Sun. Haven Gillespie. ReLy

That Lucy's eyes surveyed [*or* survey'd]. (LL) William Wordsworth. BrAP; NAEL-6v2; NAEL-7v2 *Fr.* Lucy.

That made our human hearts their homes. (LL) Poems: "I think that I shall never read." Thomas M. Disch. PoA 2002; UV

That made the oleander's leaves tremble. (LL) I-5 Incident. Juan Delgado. AmPoNex; GeoHom

That made them what they were! (LL) Transformations. Thomas Hardy. BrAP; TRP

That Man. Reginald Shepherd. WiU

That man came shouting, I am a chief. Satire. *Unknown.* WoPoe, *tr. by* Sir Arthur Grimble

That man, I wish him well. I wish him grass. (LL) Removal from Terry Street, A. Douglas Dunn. FaBoVe; NoP-4; NoP-5; NPeEn; StAl

That man is pleasing and worthy of praise who shuns vice and always. Pacifico Massimi. CAGL *Fr.* Hecateleguim.

That man is truly blessed who never strays. Paraphrase on the Psalms of David. Bible, *O.T.*

That man of old has already ridden. Yellow Crane Tower. Ts'ui Hao. CCL1, *tr. by* Stephen Owen

That man standing there, who is he? Johann Wolfgang von Goethe. WoPoe *Fr.* Journey in Winter.

That man walks along weeping. Narration. George Seferis. PoetW, *tr. by* Edmund Keeley and Philip Sherrard

That mandarin did it all on this bed with mirrors. Bed with Mirrors. Gonzalo Rojas. TCLAP, *tr. by* Christopher Maurer

That many friends had opened long ago. (LL) Mr Flood's Party. Edwin Arlington Robinson. AmFaPo; APT-1; ClHu; ColAP; HeIP-4; MoAmPo; NAAL-5; NAAPv.1; NAMCP V.1; NIL-7; NIP-4; NoAM; NoP-4; NoP-5; OxBoAm; SoSe-8; TCAPo; TFi; TRP; WaAnP; WeW-3

That March night I remember how we heard. Hare, The. Gillian Clarke. TCAWP

That marks each of us so differently. (LL) Invocation: "This August night, raccoons." Jane Hirshfield. BodElec; GeoHom

That matter of the murder is hushed up. Cenci, The. Percy Bysshe Shelley.

That mayden mylde hir childe dide kepe. *Unknown.* OHMEL

That me alone you lov'd, you once did say. Catullus. OBVE

That mind—the small one—is soft, like a pullet. Song of the Great Mind. Uri Zvi Greenberg. FIT, *tr. by* Robert Friend

That Moment. Ted Hughes. UV *Fr.* Crow.

That moon which the sky never saw. Jelaluddin Rumi. EaWin, *tr. by* Talat Sait Halman and W. S. Merwin

That More Simple Natural Time Tone Distortion. Tom Raworth. Oth

That morn[e] which saw me made a Bride. Upon a Maid That Died [*or* Dyed] the Day She Was Married [*or* Married]. Meleager. OBVE, *tr. by* Robert Herrick

That Morning. Ted Hughes. HarvBoo

That morning. Man Lying in a Hallway. Huw Jones. TCAWP

That morning, daylight was the same. Approach of War, The. Ellen Hinsey. AmPoNex

That morning early I ran through briars. Nun Takes the Veil, A. Bernard O'Donoghue. ModIr

That morning she stood in the kitchen. Rouge. Ann Townsend. ExTi

That morning the sun trespassed. White Dwarf. Gerry LaFemina. AmPoNex

That morning, while driving to his job. First Zen Abbess of America, The. Nathaniel Tarn. WANABP

That morning you found your lights on. Adagio. Gerald William Barrax. GT

That morning you took the wind. Portrait of Woman in Long Black Dress / Aurelia. Juan Felipe Herrera. TouFir

That Mountain Far Away. *Unknown.* CA, *tr. by* Herbert Joseph Spinden

That my face was not handsome. Mirror, The. Dafydd ap Gwilym. WoPoe, *tr. by* Daniel Huws

That my old bitter heart was pierced in this black doom. Grey Eye Weeping, A. Egan O'Rahilly. OBMV, *tr. by* Frank O'Connor

That name: D'VoidofFunk. Sir Nose D'VoidofFunk. Thomas Sayers Ellis. FuFl; NeAmPo

That Nature Is a Heraclitean Fire and of the Comfort of the Resurrection. Gerard Manley Hopkins. FaBoVe; NAEL-7v2; NoP-4; NoP-5; PFTM-1

That needed bronze to lock them, bronze or stone. (LL) Substance and Shadow. John Hewitt. ModIr; PNI

That neither fame nor love might wanting be. To Sir Henry Cary. Ben Jonson. NoP-4; NoP-5; NOSC

That never yet drowned me. (LL) Our Bog is Dood. Stevie Smith. NAEL-6v2; NAEL-7v2; NAMCP V.1; NBLV; NIL-7; WeW-3

That new thing! (LL) Little Girl, My String Bean, My Lovely Woman. Anne Sexton. AFaM; NAAL-5

That nibbles at the soul. (LL) This World Is Not Conclusion. Emily Dickinson. APN-2; NAAL-3; NAAPv.1; NCAP; TCAPo

That Night. Victor Hugo. SxFrPo, *tr. by* A. M. and E. H. Blackmore

That night, all night, he lay on his back. Unguentarium. Elizabeth Garrett. NeBl

That night an eagle swooped down from the skies onto Sophocles' house. Death of Sophocles, The. Anna Andreyevna Akhmatova. PoetW, *tr. by* Max Hayward and Stanley Kunitz

That night at Trafalgar! (LL) Thomas Hardy. MoBrPo; OBMV *Fr.* Dynasts, The.

That night he told me everything. Unspeakable Wounds of War, The. Maisha Baton. ICANM

That night I dipped [*or* laved *or* washed] my hands in your breasts. (LL) Key of Water, The. Octavio Paz. VCWP; WoPoe, *tr. by* Elizabeth Bishop

That night machines stood in the dark. Instrument. Gerrit Achterberg. TuT, *tr. by* Peter van de Kamp

That night the house. Lighthouse. Gerard Woodward. EmeKit

That night the moon drifted over the pond. Prediction, The. Mark Strand. CAP-8; NAMCP V.2; NoP-4; NoP-5; VCAP

That night, the roof flew, singing. Wave, The. Fatima Lim-Wilson. AmPoNex

That night / the scarecrow came into the cèilidh-house. Scarecrow. Derick Thomson. EdScPo

That night the whole world mingled. Certain Evening, A. G. K. Chesterton. OxAEP-2

That night the wind stirred in the forsythia bushes. Crossroads in the Past. John Ashbery. BAP-01

That Night They All Gathered on the Highest Tower. Jovan Hristic. GI, *tr. by* Charles Simic

That Night We Were Ravenous. John Steffler. Coast

That night when joy began. W. H. Auden. SoSe-8 *Fr.* Five Songs.

That night when you were hungry, the smoke. Bag Lady's Body in the Financial District, A. Arthur Powers. RWB

That night you looked like a little androgyne in your silk tie. Man Who Killed Himself to Avoid August, The. Maureen Seaton. ExTi

That night your great guns, unawares. Channel Firing. Thomas Hardy. BrAP; CABP; HarvBoo; HeIP-4; NAEL-6v2; NAEL-7v2; NAMCP V.1; NIL-7; NIP-4; NoAM; NoP-4; NoP-5; OxAEP-2; OxBEV; PoAgWa; PoPoPo; PoWW; SoSe-8; TFi; WaAnP

That, nightly. To Break, to Ride. Carl Phillips. AmAlph

That no fair woman will, wonder not why. Catullus. OBVE

That no grisly ghost may glide in its shadow.. (LL) William Langland. NAEL-6v1; NAEL-7v1 *Fr.* Vision of Piers Plowman, The.

That no man yet could in the bible find. Erat Quaedam Mulier. Lady Mary Cheke. EMWP

That none beguiled be by time's quick flowing. Love's Clock. Sir John Suckling. NOSC

That none of you can understand? (LL) Where Art Is a Midwife. Tom Paulin. ModIr; NPeEn

That nose is out of drawing. With a gasp. Algernon Charles Swinburne. OxBSo; UV *Fr.* Heptalogia, The.

That note comes clear, like water running clear. Piano Tuner's Wife, The. Karl Shapiro. NAMCP V.2; NoAM

That note you hold, narrowing and rising, shakes. For Sidney Bechet. Philip Larkin. NoP-4; NoP-5

That now to them dost all thy substance give. (LL) Lost, The ("Fairest day that ever yet has shone, The.") Jones Very. APN-1; NoP-4; NoP-5

That numinous healer who preached Saturnalia and paradox. Say-but-the-Word Centurion Attempts a Summary, The. Les A. Murray. UpMys

That odor in the world? (LL) Mock Orange. Louise Glück. CAP-8; MakPoe; NAMCP V.2; NoAM; OxBoAm; PoPoPo; VCAP

That Old Black Magic. Johnny Mercer. ReLy

That old black magic has me in its spell. That Old Black Magic. Johnny Mercer. ReLy

That Old Devil Called Love. Doris Fisher and Allan Roberts. ReLy

That old FB eye. FB Eye Blues, The. Richard Wright. APT-2

That Old Feeling. Lew Brown. ReLy

That "old last act"! / And yet sometimes. Adrienne Rich. NIP-4 *Fr.* Two Songs.

That old lonely lovely way of living. For the Old Highlands. Douglas Young. EdScPo

That old man—tramping down Flatbush Avenue. To Walt Whitman. Richard Fein. ViWalt

That Old-Time Religion. Peter Didsbury. NeBrP

That once the gentle mind of my dead wife. William Ellery Leonard. APT-1 *Fr.* Two Lives.

That once was mine! what woman taught you this? (LL) Alfred Tennyson. NAEL-6v2; NAEL-7v2 *Fr.* Princess, The.

That one long year we moved. We Still Have Basketball, Sara. Lisa Olstein. MoASP

That one might have for an honest living. (LL) Among My Friends. Robert Duncan. CLPP; HarvBoo

That one seems to me to be like the gods, the man whosoever sits facing you. Sappho. EroLit, *tr. by* John D. Winkler

That opens and shuts. (LL) My way is in the sand flowing. Samuel Beckett. ModIr; YaTCFP, *tr. by* the author

That Orpheus Calliops sonne who stayde the running brooke. Seneca. OBVE *Fr.* Medea.

That our own houses show as strange when we come back in the dawn! (LL) Dykes, The. Rudyard Kipling. HarvBoo; OBWP

That our senses lie and our minds trick us is true, but in general. Advice to Pilgrims. Robinson Jeffers. APT-1

That Pain has ceased to mock, to mar. End of "Pain", The. Amanda Ros. VerBaPo

That painting next to the brocaded drapery. Alcohol. Raymond Carver. LaCa

That peachtree so frail. *Unknown.* ColAnChi *Fr.* Classic of Odes.

That pearl-of-great-price. (LL) "H. D." APT-1; NAMCP V.1 *Fr.* Walls Do Not Fall, The.

That people celebrate it by forgetting its name. (LL) At the Un-National Monument along the Canadian Border. William Stafford. BrAP; HeIP-4

That people ought to be. (LL) James Kenneth Stephen. FaBoA; OBCoV *Fr.* England and America.

That perishes at the heart'. (LL) Bitter Withy, The. *Unknown.* NoP-4; NoP-5

That person's name escapes me now. When Seasons Pass. Pak Inhwan. CAMKP, *tr. by* Scott Swaner

That Phatom Phil, the master of them all, has come and gone, but will return, and all is well. (LL) Art Review. Kenneth Fearing. APT-2; NAAPv.2

That place. And I Think it Yours. Gael Turnbull. EdScPo

That place at the eastern end of wide stretching plains. Homesickness. Chŏng Chiyong. CAMKP, *tr. by* Anthony, Brother of Taizé

That Place Isn't Far. Na Hûidôk. EcSo, *tr. by* Peter H. Lee

That plump little chorus. Sanderlings. Roland Mathias. TCAWP

That poem I didn't write. Leah Goldberg. FIT, *tr. by* Robert Friend

That poets are far rarer births than kings. To Elizabeth, Countess of Rutland. Ben Jonson. NoP-4; NoP-5

That points at him amazed. (LL) Full Moon and Little Frieda. Ted Hughes. HarvBoo; NPeEn; OPOU; StAl

That posts dwell at times in water and, lifeless themselves. Post Heads. Johanna Kruit. TuT, *tr. by* Eamon Grennan

That pretty girl. Issa. EH, *tr. by* Robert Hass

That Prince, who may doe nothing but what's just. King and No King, A. Robert Herrick. PBRV

That profound waiting time. Karin Boye. SonAtl, *tr. by* Stephen Alexandersson, Max Griffin and Trudi Hindle

That promised corn but ripened into men. (LL) Year 1812, The. Adam Mickiewicz. OBVE; OBWP; WoPoe, *tr. by* Donald Davie

That Pull from the Left. Louise Erdrich. NoAM

That quiet man with the hoe is a beast. Inmate, An. Peter Kocan. NOBAu

That rabbit's foot I carried in my left pocket. Sybilline. "Ern Malley." BMAP

That ragged vagabond, snow, brings. Intruder. Alison Bielski. AngWePo

That rain-strewn night in the woods, the chorus, chorus. Chorus. David Wagoner. MiVo

That Rank Bed. Nadine Brummer. Prnts

That reach through [*or* thro'] nature, molding [*or* moulding] men. (LL) Alfred Tennyson. CABP; NAEL-6v2; NAEL-7v2; NAWM-7v2 *Fr.* In Memoriam A. H. H.

That red-shafted flicker in the woods. Purpose of Design Is to Make the Whole Greater Than the Sum of Its Parts, The. Michele Glazer. IAoNAP

That rides the glorious cherubim. (LL) To Find[e] God. Robert Herrick. InvLi; NoP-4; NoP-5

That road / got no people. Federico García Lorca. PFTM-1 *Fr.* Night (Suite for Piano and Poet's Voice).

That romantic star. Federico García Lorca. PFTM-1 *Fr.* Night (Suite for Piano and Poet's Voice).

That rose slowly toward[s] me, watching. (LL) Pike. Ted Hughes. BrAP; HeIP-4; NAEL-6v2; NAEL-7v2; NAMCP V.2; NoP-4; NoP-5; NPeEn; OxBEV; WaAnP

That rotting breath was cider. Nes From Nowhere. John Lucas. RSaN

That row of icicles along the gutter. Beyond Words. Robert Frost. Spl; WeW-3

That runs on and on at its own sweet will. (LL) Sweet Will. Philip Levine. PoA 2002; VCAP

That sad and joyful dawn. Sonnet: That Sad and Joyful Dawn. Luis de Camões [*or* Camöens *or* Camoëns]. WoPoe, *tr. by* David Wevill

That sail in cloudless light. Sea Grapes. Derek Walcott. TRP

That sail in cloudless light. Derek Walcott. *See* That sail which leans on light.

That sail which leans on light. Sea Grapes. Derek Walcott. PoetW (That sail in cloudless light.) TRP

That samin tyme, of Troy the garnisoun. Robert Henryson. OxBEV *Fr.* Testament of Cresseid, The.

That Saturday Without a Car. Stephen Dunn. WaAnP

That sculptor we knew, the passionate-eyed son of a quarryman. Artist, An. Robinson Jeffers. HarvBoo

That scything wind has cut the rich corn down. John Knox. Iain Crichton Smith. EdScPo

That season when the leaf deserts the bole. October 1. Karl Shapiro. MoAmPo

That second time they hunted me. Italian in England, The. Robert Browning. OBNV

That seemed hard frozen: may it happen for you. (LL) Sometimes. Sheenagh Pugh. BeAl; GoPo; OPOU; PoCu; TCAWP

That separate rights are lost in mutual love. (LL) Rights of Woman, The. Anna Laetitia Barbauld. BrAP; CABP; NAEL-6v2; NAEL-7v2; NoP-4; NoP-5; PEW; WaAnP; WoRP

That shadow my likeness that goes to and fro seeking a livelihood, chattering, chaffering. That Shadow My Likeness. Walt Whitman. APN-1

That Shady Crab. *Unknown.* CCL1 *Fr.* Gan-tang [Translations].

That she is beautiful is not delight. Augusta Davies Webster. ViWPN *Fr.* Mother and Daughter.

That she that makes me sin, awards me pain. (LL) William Shakespeare. HeIP-4; OxAEP-1 *Fr.* Sonnets.

That she was glad to sit down. What the Uneducated Old Woman Told Me. Christopher Reid. NeBrP

That she will move from mourning into morning. (LL) Sonnet to My Mother. George Barker. OxBSo; RaBo

That she would grow again. (LL) Countee Cullen. APT-2; MoAmPo; SSLK *Fr.* Four Epitaphs.

That shipwrecked [*or* shipwrackt] vessel which th' Apostle bore. Upon His Majesty's [*or* Majesties] Repairing of Paul's. Edmund Waller. BASC; PBRV

That Silent Evening. Galway Kinnell. StAl

That since you would save none of me, I bury some of you. (LL) Funeral[l], The. John Donne. FSCP; HeIP-4; NAEL-6v1; NAEL-7v1; NAWM-5v1; NoP-4; NoP-5; OBEV; TFi

That Sindhi boy is keen on you. Mrs. Biswas of Maryland on the Phone. Reetika Vazirani. AmPoNex

That sleeping drifts towards, death illuminates. (LL) Way, The. William Bronk. BeAl; StAl

That slide would be halted. Rollercoaster. Cris Cheek. Oth

That small girl crouched. Eavesdropper, The. Jane O. Wayne. InvLad

That snail. Buson. ChAP

That somber greens—ferns, conifers, cycads—flittered. Ecosystem. Anna Rabinowitz. PoDa

That some day death who has us all for jest. Augusta Davies Webster. VWP *Fr.* Mother and Daughter.

That sonnofa bitch! Variety Show, 1984. Hwang Jiwoo. CAMKP, *tr. by* Young-Jun Lee and Scott Swaner

That sound of his is like a boat with black sails. Listening to a Cricket in the Wainscoting. Robert Bly. InvLad

That splash like brackish tears into our cap. (LL) Tony Harrison. NAEL-6v2; NAEL-7v2; NAMCP V.2 *Fr.* School of Eloquence, The.

That spring he was fourteen. By the Rivers. Shirley Kaufman. GifTon; TAPaP

That spring was late. We watched the sky. Neighbours. Gillian Clarke. TCAWP

That spring we wondered at the fierce display. Al-Khamasin. Michael Murphy. NIrP

That sputter of rain, flipping the hedgerows. Shower, A. Amy Lowell. PoBW

That stand upon the threshold of the new. (LL) Of the Last Verses in the Book. Edmund Waller. BASC; NoP-4; NoP-5; NOSC; NPeEn; OxBEV; PoPoPo; SacPr

That star I now see. Star and Sea. William Peskett. PNI

That still keeps on insisting it is there. (LL) Elevator Music. Henry Taylor. GoPo; P180

That still my Syrinx' lips I kiss. (LL) John Lyly. NoSic; NPeEn *Fr.* Midas.

That stone in the stream looks like a turtle. Fisherman at Byolam. Muyong Sooyon. BecRai, *tr.* by Kim Daljin, Kim Won-Chung and Christopher Merrill

That story which the bold Sir Bedivere. Alfred Tennyson. NAEL-6v2; NAEL-7v2 *Fr.* Idylls of the King.

That strange flower, the sun. Gubbinal. Wallace Stevens. NAAPv.2

That Strangest is of all; yet brought to pass. (LL) Salutation [*or* Salutations], The. Thomas Traherne. NoP-4; NoP-5; SacPr

That street washed with violet. Last Trams. Kenneth Slessor. BMAP

That street where midnight. Monk's World. Imamu Amiri Baraka. NAMCP V.2

That strong god whose touch made Dante tremble. Modern Love. Anne Ridler. SacPr

That substitute teacher in art, you could tell she was strange. Wearing Dad's White Shirt Backwards. Rick Agran. AmPoNex

That sultry afternoon the world went strange. One Tuesday in Summer. James McAuley. BMAP

That summer bird its oft-repeated note. Wryneck's Nest, The. John Clare. CenSon

That summer I went to Woodstock. Woodstock. Jan-Mitchell Sherrill. ReTh

That summer, in a small glass booth. Praise of Italian Chip-Shops. W. N. Herbert. NeBl

That summer in Culpeper, all there was to eat was white. Nineteen. Elizabeth Alexander. GT; InTrad; PoPoPo

That summer my best friend Matt and I manned. Salem, Indiana, 1983. Richard Newman. LiTh

That summer the women sat on their porches. Misguided Angels. Gale Renée Walden. ReTh

That summer they had cars, soft roofs crumpling. Them. Kim Addonizio. RoV

That summer they took off a corner of the cemetery. Hard Surface Road. Michael Chitwood. MotU

That summer with a thousand Julys. For the Last Summer. Robert Wrigley. SwNoth

That sun that breathed love's fire into my youth. Dante Alighieri. NAWM-5v1 *Fr.* Divina Commedia.

That Sunday at the zoo I understood the child. Family Group, The. Madeline DeFrees. PoChi

That Sunday nothing big moved. Ophelia. Alice Friman. IaFF

That Sunday, on my oath, the rain was a heavy overcoat. Mary Hynes. Anthony Raftery. IrLP

That sway from mood to mood the willing mind! (LL) Poet, The. William Cullen Bryant. NAAL-3; NCAP

That terra-cotta waitress. Villa Restaurant, The. Derek Walcott. WeW-3

That terrible day my heart took a blow that nearly killed. Starlet. Fanny Howe. ExTi

That Thanksgiving my mother made me sit. When My Sister Was Fifteen. Rita D. Costello. BeDoSh

That that mind perceives how to fly alone. Allen Fisher. Oth *Fr.* Emergent Manner.

That that part of me is dripping. *Unknown.* PriapPo *Fr.* Priapus Poems, The.

That the earth be made safer for men, and more stable. *Unknown.* APN-2 *Fr.* Hardening of the World, and the First Settlement of Men, The.

That the glass would melt in heat. Glass of Water, The. Wallace Stevens. MoAmPo

That the Great Angell-blinding light should shrinke. Richard Crashaw. SacPr *Fr.* Strage degli innocenti, La.

That the great work not falter but go on. (LL) Fable of the War, A. Howard Nemerov. AmWaPo; OBWP; PWW2

That the mere glimpse of a plain cap. *Unknown.* CCL1 *Fr.* Su-guan.

That the Muses have no more fervent. Person's Tale, The. U. A. Fanthorpe. NoP-4

That the Science of Cartography Is Limited. Eavan Boland. EMP; HarvBoo; NAEL-7v2; NoP-4; NoP-5

That the Theocritan pick-up has been versed. Rabbiters: A Pastoral, The. John Kinsella. NeBl

That the transactions would end. Beauty and the Beast. Gillian Conoley. BodElec; RoV

That the world / is going. C. K. Williams. OnScMo

That then I scorn [*or* skorne] to change my state with kings. (LL) William Shakespeare. AEP; AmFaPo; BLPJKO; BrAP; GSo; HeIP-4; ITBLP; ItP; NAEL-6v1; NAEL-7v1; NoP-4; NoP-5; NoSic; OBEV; OPOU; OxAEP-1; PBRV; PoPoPo; TFi; WaAnP; WeW-3; WoPoe *Fr.* Sonnets.

That there should never be air. Roses. Barbara Guest. NoP-4; NoP-5

That there was doubt about these things. (LL) Dialogue. Adrienne Rich. NIL-7; TWF

That there was later on. Nothing That Is, The. Ralph Angel. BodElec

That therewith my song is broken. (LL) Sir Philip Sidney. NoSic; PBRV *Fr.* Astrophil and Stella.

That they are brown, no man will dare to say. Her Eyes. Helen Hunt Jackson. PoBW; TCAPo

That they might come back unceasingly. Sikong Tu. CCL1 *Fr.* Twenty-Four Modes of Poetry.

That they were at the beach—aeolotropic series. Leslie Scalapino. "Playing ball—so it's like paradise, not because it's in the past, we're on a." BodElec

That thin little boy. Emigrant's Son, The. Luis Andrade Silva. NAfrP; *tr.* by Don Burness

That Thing. Fadhil Assultani. IrPoTo, *tr.* by Raghid Nahhas

That thirst for living day to day. While Watching Sunset. Ch'oe Sûngja. EcSo, *tr.* by Mickey Hong

That thou art blam'd shall not be thy defect. William Shakespeare. OxAEP-1 *Fr.* Sonnets.

That thou hast her, it is not all my grief[e]. William Shakespeare. HeIP-4; OxAEP-1 *Fr.* Sonnets.

That thou hast kept thy love, increased thy will. To the Same [Sir Thomas Roe]. Ben Jonson. BASC

That thou mayst fit thyself against thy fall. (LL) Church Monuments. George Herbert. BASC; NAEL-6v1; NAEL-7v1; NOSC; NPeEn; TRP

That thou may'st know me[e], and I'll turn[e] my face. (LL) Good Friday [*or* Goodfriday], 1613. Riding Westward. John Donne. BASC; BBASP; BrAP; ChIV-2; FSCP; NAEL-6v1; NAEL-7v1; NoP-4; NoP-5; NOSC; PBRV; SacPr; TFi; WaAnP

That thou wilt scorn me for my very love. (LL) Oh! craven, craven! while my brothers fall. George Henry Boker. APN-2; PCW

That though thine absence starve me, I wish not thee. (LL) Storm[e], The. John Donne. NAEL-6v1; NAEL-7v1; NoSic

That throng my hiddenness. (LL) What would I do without this world faceless incurious. Samuel Beckett. ModIr; NoAM; YaTCFP, *tr.* by the author

That time I did not save Warsaw, nor Prague later. Natalya Gorbanevskaya. TCRusP, *tr.* by Daniel Weissbort

That time I thought I was in love. Each from Different Heights. Stephen Dunn. StAl

That time / in the sun. When Sun Came to Riverwoman. Leslie Marmon Silko. ReEnLa

That time my grandmother dragged me. Weakness, The. Toi Derricotte. GT; LTA

That time of drought the embered air. Drought Year. Judith Wright. NAMCP V.2; NoAM

That time of evening, weightless and disparate. Blackwater Mountain. Charles Wright. NAMCP V.2

That time of year thou may'st in me behold. William Shakespeare. AEP; BrAP; CABP; CIHu; HeIP-4; ItP; NAEL-6v1; NAEL-7v1; NIL-7; NIP-4; NoP-4; NoP-5; NoSic; NPeEn; OBEV; OxBSo; SoSe-8; TFi; WeW-3 *Fr.* Sonnets.

That time of year you may in me behold. Winter Twilight, Glowing Black and Gold, The. Delmore Schwartz. NoAM

That time was come, or seemed as it was come. John Clare. NPBRoP *Fr.* Superstition's Dream.

That told the history of my lost people. (LL) Belonging. Rafael Campo. AmPoNex; WiU

That tomorrow a new walk is a new walk. (LL) Corsons Inlet. A. R. Ammons. ColAP; InGu; NAAL-5; NAMCP V.2; NoAM; NoP-4; NoP-5; OxBoAm; VCAP; WaAnP

That tom-tom talked. Tom-Tom Talk. Suze Baron. OGAHCP, *tr.* by Boadiba and Jack Hirschman

That top-secret flight at night. Lights. Ernesto Cardenal. TCLAP, *tr.* by Jonathan Cohen

That trembles in the ripples. (LL) Li Po. CrYelRi; ErotSp *Fr.* Women of Yueh.

That Trinacria was made one part of Italy. To Frederick V, by the Grace of God . . . Bathsua Pell Makin. EMWP

That truth whose name alone so utterly absorbs poor Pontius Pilate. (LL) Jesus Before Pilate. René Daumal. GI; MotU, *tr.* by Katharine Washburn

That Tsugunobu. Karai Senryū. EMJL, *tr.* by Makoto Ueda

"That turn'll get her," I said. Toujours la Politesse. Ezra Pound. OBVE

That tyrant, is she not persuaded by the tears. Baqi. OLP, *tr.* by Walter Andrews, Najaat Black and Mehmet Kalpakli

That unction sweet, which lulls the bleeding breast! (LL) Resolves to Take the Leap of Leucata. Mary Robinson. CenSon; RWP

That used to mark America's dangerous shores. (LL) Boy with Book of Knowledge. Howard Nemerov. NoP-4; NoP-5

That Van Gogh's ear, set free. What Is Worth Knowing? Sujata Bhatt. NeBrP

That very day. William Wordsworth. NAEL-6v2; NAEL-7v2 *Fr.* Prelude, The; Growth of a Poet's Mind [1850 version].

That Virtue but that body grant to us. (LL) Sir Philip Sidney. NAEL-6v1; NAEL-7v1; NoP-4; NoP-5 *Fr.* Astrophil and Stella.

That virtuous is, when the reward's away. (LL) To Sir Henry Cary. Ben Jonson. NoP-4; NoP-5; NOSC

That wail! 'tis prophecy. Oh, hush! be still. Birth Wail, The. Henrietta Tindal. VWP

That wan and sickly droops upon her breast! (LL) Samuel Taylor Coleridge. CenSon; GSo *Fr.* Effusions.

That wand[e]reth lightly. (LL) George Peele. ChIV-1; NoSic; NPeEn; OxBEV

That wants himself[e] is poor[e] indeed. (LL) Grasshopper, The [To My Noble Friend Mr Charles Cotton: Ode]. Richard Lovelace. BASC; CavPo; NAEL-6v1; NAEL-7v1; NoP-4; NoP-5; NOSC; OBEV; TFi; WaAnP

That was a different time. Güler's Hours of Love. Necati Cumalı. NaPG, *tr. by* Talat Sait Halman

That was a joyous day in Rheims of old. Joan of Arc, in Rheims. Felicia Dorothea Hemans. RWP; ViWPN

That was all then. Dead Weight of the Land, The. Tedi López Mills. RMCMP, *tr. by* Esther Allen

That Was Before I Met You. P. G. Wodehouse. ReLy

That was enough. You Called Me *Corazón*. Sandra Cisneros. AmFaPo; RaF

That was my very soul that stole to the lips in our kissing. Kiss, The. Plato. STV, *tr. by* John Frederick Nims

That was not a reminder of the end. (LL) Sonnet: Death Warnings. Francisco de Quevedo y Villegas. OxBEV; WoPoe, *tr. by* John Masefield

That Was Summer. Marci Ridlon. NTCP

That was the best moment of the monk's life. Burning Oneself to Death. Takahashi Shinkichi. ZenPo, *tr. by* Takashi Ikemoto and Lucien Stryk

That was the day that went too far. Day. Colette Bryce. NIrP

That was the day they killed the Son of God. Killing, The. Edwin Muir. GI

That was the moment when, without. Short History of the Bourgeoisie. Hans Magnus Enzensberger. VCWP, *tr. by* the author, Hans Magnus Enzensberger and Michael Hamburger

That was the summer I used *The Duino Elegies*. Collaboration, The. Tony Hoagland. SUP

That was the summer the bleeding stopped. How to Catch a Ghost in a Jar. Cynthia Cruz. IAoNAP

"That was the thrush's last good-night," I thought. Edward Dowden. OxBSo *Fr.* In the Garden.

That was the top of the walk, when he said. Gypsy, The. Ezra Pound. NPeEn

That was the year I drove around all the time. Invention of Pittsburgh, The. Maggie Anderson. PBCAP

That was when I knew I was in trouble, the increments. Scales, The. Phyllis Stowell. AFaM

That watches and receives. (LL) Tables Turned, The. William Wordsworth. NAEL-6v2; NAEL-7v2; NOBRP; NoP-5

That watery light, so undervalued. Of the Light. John Ashbery. NAMCP V.2

That wavering Reason lends, in life's long darkling way. (LL) Written near a Port on a Dark Evening. Charlotte Smith. CenSon; NoP-4; NoP-5

That way. (LL) Insects. Issa. WED; WoPoe, *tr. by* Robert Bly

That way look, my Infant, lo! Kitten and [the] Falling Leaves, The. William Wordsworth.

That we are ruined by the thing we kill. (LL) Australia 1970. Judith Wright. HarvBoo; MakPoe; NoAM

That we confront. (LL) Route. George Oppen. AF; APSN; APT-2

That we have wrought him, stone-deaf and stone-blind. (LL) February Afternoon. Edward Thomas. NAMCP V.1; NoAM; PoWW

That we know you, terrible joy. (LL) Matins. Denise Levertov. BrAP; NoAM

That we lift, as chaff lifts, toward God. (LL) Mennonites. Julia Kasdorf. ACAMVP; NeAmPo; PBCAP

That weren't to be trusted. (LL) Castration. Nigel Jenkins. AngWePo; TCAWP

That what. Dream Thief. Nathaniel Mackey. GT

That when we live no more we may live ever. (LL) To My Dear and Loving Husband. Anne Bradstreet. AmFaPo; BASC; BrAP; ColAP; ErotSp; HeIP-4; ITBLP; LW; NAAL-3; NAAL-5; NAAPv.1; NIL-7; NIP-4; NoP-4; NoP-5; NOSC; OxBEV; OxBoAm; OxWW; PEW; SacPr; TCAPo; TFi; WaAnP; WeW-3

That which abandoned me. To See Secretary Shu-Yun Off at the Hsieh T'iao Tower at Hsuan-Ch'eng. Li Po. ChinPo, *tr. by* Ye Weilian [*or* Yeh Wei-lien *or* Wai-lim Yip]

That which existed last night is and isn't. Finnish Tango. Hans Magnus Enzensberger. GTCP, *tr. by* Reinhold Grimm

That which has forsaken me. Farewell Dinner for My Uncle Li Yun, the Collator, at Xie Tiao's Tower in Xuan Prefecture. Li Po. CCL1, *tr. by* Elling O. Eide

That which has life inevitably dies. Three Dirges: Written in Imitation of an Ancient Funeral Song. T'ao Ch'ien. CCL1, *tr. by* Gladys Yang, Yang Xianyi, *and* Hu Shiguang

That which her slender waist confined. On a Girdle. Edmund Waller. BASC; NoP-4; NOSC; OBEV; TFi

That Which Hovers. Lara Ramsey. RWB

That which is, being the only answer. Question and Answer. Kathleen Jessie Raine. MoBrPo

That Which Is Enough for Love. Luis Cernuda. CAGL, *tr. by* Rick Lipinski

That which is, for example. Bicycle, The. Stan Rice. ArBi

That Which Is Fugitive, That Which Is Medicinally Sweet or Alterable to Gold, That Which Is Substantiated by Unscientific Means. Valerie Wohlfeld. YaYoPo

That which is in part, finding its whole again throughout the universe. (LL) Tortoise Shout. D. H. Lawrence. NAEL-6v2; NAEL-7v2; PFTM-1

That which is most lost. Undoing, The. Elizabeth Robinson. Eno

That which makes milk can't. Breasts. Gary Snyder. WANABP

That which ripped an amazed scream. Joseph Brodsky. TCRusP *Fr.* Sonnets on the Statue of Mary, Queen of Scots, in the Luxembourg Gardens, Paris.

That which the mouth cannot utter. Stone at the Tip of the Tongue, A. Oumarou Watta. NAfrP

That which then was ours, my love. Don't Ask Me for That Love Again. Faiz Ahmad Faiz. PoetW; VCWP, *tr. by* Agha Shahid Ali

That Which We Call a Rose. Michael Dransfield. NOBAu

That which we call reality is that. Corals and Shells. William Bronk. APSN

That which we dare invoke to bless. Alfred Tennyson. CABP; NAEL-6v2; NAEL-7v2; NAWM-7v2; SacPr *Fr.* In Memoriam A. H. H.

That while he lived never thought of death. (LL) Fulke, 1st Baron Brooke Greville. CABP; NOSC; NoSic *Fr.* Caelica.

That whiskey will cook the egg. Bar. Langston Hughes. APSN

That whispers in my ear: alas, alas? (LL) Mark Strand. NAMCP V.2; NoP-4; NoP-5 *Fr.* Dark Harbor.

That whistles in the wind. (LL) Lucy Gray; or, Solitude. William Wordsworth. NAEL-6v2; NAEL-7v2; NOBRP; OxAEP-2; WaAnP

That white cloud in its contrast. Patrizia Cavalli. NeIt

That Whitsun, I was late getting away. Whitsun Weddings, The. Philip Larkin. BeAl; HeIP-4; NAMCP V.2; NoAM; NoP-4; NoP-5; OxAEP-2

That whole morning we were full of joy. Interlude of Joy. George Seferis. PoetW, *tr. by* Edmund Keeley and Philip Sherrard

That will go on after me. (LL) Lament for the Makers. W. S. Merwin. InoFa; PoA 2002

That will let me go adrift. (LL) Lightness. Meg Bateman. EdScPo; NePenScot; StAl, *tr. by* the author

That will not state—its sting. (LL) If you were coming in the Fall. Emily Dickinson. PtR; SoSe-8; TCAPo

That Willowwood should hold her wandering! (LL) Dante Gabriel Rossetti. NAEL-6v2; OxBSo *Fr.* House of Life, The.

That winged word. (LL) Twenty Years Hence. Walter Savage Landor. NAEL-6v2; NAEL-7v2

That wink of time when I was happy still. Winter Noon. Umberto Saba. STV, *tr. by* John Frederick Nims

That Winter. Ruth Stone. GPTC

That winter I stopped loving the President. Suite for Augustus, A. Rita Dove.

That winter love spoke and we raised no objection, at. Jig. Cecil Day Lewis. IrLP

That winter, the dead could not be buried. Leningrad Cemetery, Winter of 1941. Sharon Olds. NIL-7; NIP-4

That winter the stairs were always unlit. Confinement. Ann Sansom. NeBl

That winter was cold—Lord yes. Conkerbells. Mary Dalton. OpeFie

That with this bright believing band. Impercipient, The. Thomas Hardy. NAEL-6v2; NAEL-7v2

That witnessing presence. (LL) Witness. Denise Levertov. BLT; TWF

"That woman there is almost dead." Rat, The. W. H. Davies. OBWVE

That won my heart in my greener years. (LL) Green River. William Cullen Bryant. APN-1; TCAPo

That would, at least, have been an honest way to die. (LL) Ophelia's Confession. Tracey Herd. BeAl; StAl

That would be enough. (LL) What Would I Do White? June Jordan. LTA; UnSA

That would be waving and that would be crying. Waving Adieu, Adieu, Adieu. Wallace Stevens. NoP-4; NoP-5

That would help you imagine how much of the reservation she had tattooed across her skin? (LL) Sonnet: Tattoo Tears. Sherman Alexie. PrTe; WaAnP

That, woven, it lifts itself through itself: balloon light. (LL) Weaving the Morning. João Cabral de Melo Neto. IPoFL; TCLAP, *tr. by* Galway Kinnell

That wren. Issa. EH, *tr. by* Robert Hass

That year he found himself without a job. Days of 1908. Constantine P. Cavafy. WoPoe, *tr. by* James Merrill

That year it was like everyone i knew fell out of a tree, hurt. You Can't Go Back to Sleep. T. Cole Rachel. BeDoSh

That year of the cloud, when my marriage failed. River Road. Stanley Kunitz. NoAM

That year they fought in the snow. Rostov. George Sutherland Fraser. PoWW

That year we hardly slept, waking like inmates. Getting Out. Cleopatra Mathis. SoSe-8

That you and I, and you,. Anniversary. Davi Walders. MPUn

That you are right. (LL) You Are Right. Cathryn Essinger. PoA 2002; PoDa

That you belong to the 'folk', sonny-boy, had you not better show us. Piece of Advice, A. Gyula Illyés. IQMS, *tr.* by Adam Makkai

That you need a drink, a cigarette, a cup of coffee. (LL) Hell: "I died & went to Hell & it was nothing like L.A." Steve Kowit. CalPo; SUP

"That you two have problems." (LL) Wayman in Love. Tom Wayman. NIL-7; NIP-4

That you were once unkind, befriends me now. William Shakespeare. OxAEP-1 *Fr.* Sonnets.

That young man my father. (LL) Guild, The. Sharon Olds. PoA 2002; RaBo

That your honour's petitioners (dealers in rhymes). To the Right Hon. Henry Pelham. Edward Moore. OBSV

That zephyr every year. Spring Bereaved. William Drummond of Hawthornden. OBEV

Thatch House. Tu Fu [*or* Du Fu]. NDACCP, *tr.* by David Hinton

Thatched House. Yi Yuksa. CAMKP, *tr.* by Kyung-Ja Chun

Thatched Hut, The. Tu Fu [*or* Du Fu]. CrYelRi, *tr.* by Sam Hamill

Thatched roof rings like heaven where mice, The. Byre. Norman Alexander MacCaig. EdScPo

Thatcher, A. Judith Kazantzis. RSaN

Thatcher is someone who makes a roof, A. Thatcher, A. Judith Kazantzis. RSaN

That's All. Lawrence Joseph. PBCAP

That's all that I remember. (LL) Incident. Countee Cullen. APT-2; ChAP; NAAL-5; NAAPv.2; NAMCP V.1; NoAM; NoP-4; NoP-5; NOxBChV; NTCP; PoPoPo; PtR; SSLK

That's enough of that, Mr Bones. *Some* lady you make. John Berryman. EMP; VCAP *Fr.* Dream Songs.

That's Entertainment. Howard Dietz. ReLy

That's Good, That's Enough. Judyth Hill. ICANM

That's him: head reared above the Babelic ramp. Csontváry. László Nagy. IQMS, *tr.* by Geroge Gömöri and Kenneth McRobbie

That's how billboards give up their promises. Midnight Reports. Lynda Hull. SwNoth

That's how it was: I turned my sickroom glances. To Await Arrival. Bella Akhatovna Akhmadulina. CRWP, *tr.* by Catriona Kelly

That's How We Are. Andrea Zanzotto. GPTC, *tr.* by Ruth Feldman and Brian Swann

That's how we distinguish a man from a woman, or from. Histories of Bodies. Mariko Nagai. PuP-23

That's it—I love that fawn. Shmuel HaNagid. ErotSp, *tr.* by Harris Lenowitz and Jerome Rothenberg

That's Jack. Jack. Charles Henry Ross. NOxBChV; Spl

That's me, arguing for another effort. Appomattox. Terese Svoboda. ExTi

That's memory, the wood that goes into your house, this paper, his cross, the cedar chest of a bride who is buried in a box of pine. (LL) Wood. Patricia Y. Ikeda. MotU; WhBo

That's my last Duchess painted on the wall. My Last Duchess. Robert Browning. AmFaPo; BrAP; CABP; ClHu; CtM; HeIP-4; ITBLP; MakPoe; NAEL-7v2; NAWM-7v2; NIL-7; NIP-4; NoP-4; NoP-5; NPeEn; OxBEV; PoPoPo; SoSe-8; TFi; TRP; WaAnP

That's my son! That's my son! (LL) Edgar Lee Masters. NAAPv.1; NAMCP V.1; NoAM *Fr.* Spoon River Anthology.

That's My Style. Peggy Lee. ReLy

That's My Weakness Now. Bud Green and Sam H. Stept. ReLy

That's not a man in pain. Short Lexicon of Torture in the Eighties, A. Edward Hirsch. VCAP

That's not even it. Recitation. Ellease Southerland. GT

That's Not in My Job Description. Paul Beatty. NeAmPo

That's not scratching you hear. It's writing. (LL) Poem to Line My Casket with, Ramona. Josh Bell. IIR; LegDan

That's pretty much what they will do. (LL) Poem for Players, A. Al Young. LTA; OxAAAP

That's right, there's a clear spot in me, and in you. Mirrored. Giancarlo Majorino. ItPo, *tr.* by Gayle Ridinger

That's the main thing. (LL) Housewife. Anne Sexton. NALW; WaAnP

That's the moment I always think of—when the. Moment the Two Worlds Meet, The. Sharon Olds. NAMCP V.2

That's the only image. Wall, A. Charles Simic. NAMCP V.2

That's the prison. San Quentin 1968. Robert Peterson. GeoHom

That's the trouble around here. Loose Shoes. Charles Bernstein. FTOS

(That's the Way) Dixieland Started Jazz. Shelton Brooks. ReLy

That's the way for Billy and me. (LL) Boy's Song, A. James Hogg. NOxBChV; OBEV; OxAEP-2

That's the way it is, he said. For Heiner Muller: Part 3. Safaa Fathy. AnVo, *tr.* by Mohamed Enani

That's the Way, Uh Huh, Uh Huh, I Liked It. Anthony R. Vigil. AmPoNex

That's what he did, on a stage and in public. Sawing His Wife in Half. Dafydd Rowlands. BBMWP, *tr.* by Meic Stephens

That's what I said. (LL) Song of the Mad Prince, The. Walter De la Mare. CtM; MakPoe; NoAM; OxAEP-2

That's what I was doing on a Wednesday morning. Keeping Track. Maurya Simon. GeoHom

That's what love is like. The whole river. Crossing Over. William Meredith. NoAM

That's what misery is. Poetry Is a Destructive Force. Wallace Stevens. APT-1; RaBo

That's what they call us, those icky guys. Foolish Earthlings. Ron Koertge. SUP

That's what we went for, Holly and I. Carnies. Debra Allbery. PBCAP

That's when I left the south. (LL) Musician Talks about "Process," The. Rita Dove. ESEAA; PoDa

That's when I saw a whole series of things. Final Manuscript. Giannina Braschi. TANSG, *tr.* by Alan West

That's when the Indians left. (LL) Thanksgiving. Martín Espada. PrTe; PuP-23

That's where Lyle Wilson went, wearing his Mariners. Land of Lincoln. Angela Sorby. AmPoNex

That's where your father. Witness. Bruce Beasley. AmAlph

That's why I want to. (LL) Chronic Meanings. Bob Perelman. OxBoAm; PmAP

That's why societies usedta throw us away/ or sell us/ or. It's Not so Good to be Born a Girl/ Sometimes. Ntozake Shange. SSLK

That's why they are so obsequious. (LL) Blood or Color. Marjorie Welish. FTOS; OnScMo

That's Why They Call Me "Shine." Cecil Mack. ReLy

That's your freedom—bootleg whiskey. Two Countries. Tadeusz Borowski. AF, *tr.* by Larry Rafferty, Meryl Natchez *and* Tadeusz Pioro

T'have hit the wavering [*or* wav'ring] form, or given [*or* giv'n] this thing a name! (LL) Adam Posed. Anne Finch, Countess of Winchilsea. ChIV-1; NoP-4; NoP-5

Thaw. Edward Thomas. MoBrPo; OxAEP-2; OxBEV; Spl

Thaw, The. Marianne Wolfe. GifTon

Thawing earth, The. What We Feared. Judith Ortiz Cofer. PueRic

The / Attic once. Conch from Sicily, A. Alfred Corn. NoP-5

The / children have a society of their own. John Cage. APSN *Fr.* Diary: How to Improve the World (You Will Only Make Matters Worse).

The. Corner. Of. Carla Harryman. BAP-04 *Fr.* Being.

Death of nothing, funeral of Gaius!, The. (LL) Lean Gaius, who was thinner than a straw. Lucilius. OBVE; WoPoe, *tr.* by Peter Porter

Rain sounded just like that, he said, on the roofs there, The. (LL) Nineteen. Elizabeth Alexander. GT; InTrad; PoPoPo

The / the ledger survived. Ledger, The. Robert Kroetsch. NLPA

The / the / the / he. Makeme. *Unknown.* SonAtl, *tr.* by Lester Browne, Rob Holden and Myrna Teirrel

The / Voice of Jesus I. Rush singing. Louis Zukofsky. NAMCP V.1 *Fr.* Poem Beginning "The."

Theare be great Prince, such as will tell you howe. Samuel Daniel. PBRV *Fr.* Epistle. To Prince Henrie].

Theater Impressions. Wisława Szymborska. VCWP

Theater Music. Takehisa Kosugi. WhBo

Theater treat it set threat. Twenties 3. Jackson Mac Low. WhBo

"Theatre." Anne-Marie Albiach. MFP, *tr.* by Martin Sorrell

Theatre. Remco Campert. TuT, *tr.* by Theo Dorgan

Theatre, The. Remco Campert. TuT, *tr.* by Desmond Egan

Theatrical Venus. George Buchanan. PNI

Theatrum Mundi. Günter Kunert. GTCP, *tr.* by Reinhold Grimm

Thebais [*or* Thebaid]. Publius Papinius Statius. *tr.* by Norman Austin, Walter Harte, William S. Lewis, Ruth Morse and Alexander Pope

   Book 10. RompPo, *tr.* by Norman Austin and Ruth Morse

Thee, dear friend, a brother soothes. To Rhea. Ralph Waldo Emerson. APN-1

Thee for my recitative. To a Locomotive in Winter. Walt Whitman. BrAP; GM; MoAmPo; NAAL-3; NCAP; NoAM; NoP-4; NoP-5

Thee, God, I come from, to Thee go. Gerard Manley Hopkins. SacPr

Thee Pompey thy past deeds by turns infest. Lucan. OBVE *Fr.* Civil War [Bellum Civile] *or* Pharsalia.

Thee, Queen of Shadows!—shall I still invoke. To Fancy. Charlotte Smith. OxBSo

Thee, Thee, Only Thee. Thomas Moore. IrLP

Thee too, modest tressèd maid. Moon. Henry Rowe. OBEV

Thee, Trade! I first—who boast no store. Edward Young. STuOW *Fr.* Imperium Pelagi, or, The Merchant.

Thee we adore, O hidden Saviour, thee. Saint Thomas Aquinas. SacPr, *tr.* by F. R. Woodford

Thee will I love, my God and King. Robert Bridges. SacPr

Theft. Karen Volkman. AmPoNex

Theft's hour—the bus. Late Bus (After a Series of Hold-Ups). Russell Atkins.
  LTA

Their ancient, glittering eyes, are gay. (LL) Lapis Lazuli. William Butler
  Yeats. BrAP; CABP; HeIP-4; NAEL-6v2; NAEL-7v2; NAMCP V.1;
  NAWM-7v2; NoAM; NoP-4; NoP-5; TFi

Their Ardour kindles all the Grecian Pow'rs. Homer. OBVE *Fr.* Iliad, The.

Their barbarism did not assuage the grief. Retreat of Ita Cagney, The.
  Michael Hartnett. PBCIP

Their bar-stools have slouched them too early. Slouch. Brendan Cleary.
  NeBl

Their Beginning. Constantine P. Cavafy. CAGL, *tr. by* Edmund Keeley and
  Philip Sherrard

Their Behaviour. Dennis Brutus. HBAPE

Their Bodies. David Wagoner. EMP; PoA 2002

Their bones in one mad dance. (LL) Horse, The: "They spoke of the horse
  alive." Philip Levine. AtGh; VCAP

Their bones not even picked for souvenirs. (LL) From Colony to Nation.
  Irving Layton. BrAP; NIL-7

Their bodies come with me, women writers. Women's Work. Gillian Clarke.
  MoWP

Their boon is life forever freed from toil. Pindar. BLPJKO *Fr.* Olympian
  Odes, The.

Their breasts protected by hard metal disks. (LL) Man in Space. Billy
  Collins. BeAl; CAP-8

Their brown, harmless flack. Sparrows at the Airport, The. Anthony Ostroff.
  OtW

Their center blocks out and the ball. Good "D." James McKean. MoASP

Their cheeks were fresh and tender. Civil Song. Pier Paolo Pasolini. VCWP,
  tr. by Norman MacAfee *and* Luciano Martinengo

Their childhoods must have come and gone. For the Bullies of West Morris
  High. Steven Cramer. PoA 2002

Their colons fed with mucus, brains with lies. Monologue. Gottfried Benn.
  AF, *tr. by* Christopher Middleton

Their cry may be heard at eventide. Wild Geese, The. Gareth Alban Davies.
  BBMWP, *tr. by* the author

Their departures hence and die. (LL) Upon the Loss[e] of His Mistresses.
  Robert Herrick. BASC; CavPo; NAEL-6v1; NAEL-7v1; NOSC

Their enemies have delivered themselves to destruction. (LL) Incantation.
  Czeslaw Milosz. PtR; VCWP, *tr. by* the author and Robert Pinsky

Their essences of lilies and of roses. (LL) Thoughts After Ruskin. Elma
  Mitchell. EdScPo; MoWP; NPeEn; StAl

Their faces, safe as an interior. Middle-Aged, The. Adrienne Rich.
  OxBoAm; PoPoPo

Their father played the banjo. Rough Boys. Sam Adams. TCAWP

Their feet on London, their heads in the grey clouds. Whit Monday. Louis
  MacNeice. ChIV-1

Their first time, they were wonderfully tender. Sphere, The. Gray Jacobik.
  NevBe

Their footless dance. Robert Penn Warren. NAAL-5; NAAPv.2 *Fr.* Audubon:
  A Vision.

Their footsteps borrow silence from the snow. (LL) Persephone. Michael
  Longley. NPeEn; PBCIP

Their forces were about three kilometers from our front lines. Bottle of Suze,
  A. Pablo Picasso. PFTM-1

Their garden has a silent tall stone-wall. Caserta Garden. Richard Wilbur.
  OBGa

Their generals are already poring over maps. (LL) W. H. Auden. BeAl;
  OBCoV *Fr.* Shorts [1939–1947].

Their ground they stil made good. Homer. OBVE *Fr.* Iliad, The.

Their guilt / is not so very different from ours. Their Behaviour. Dennis
  Brutus. HBAPE

Their hands upon their hearts. (LL) Could man be drunk for ever. A. E.
  Housman. NAEL-6v2; OBMV

Their Hats Is Always White. Jim Elledge. SwNoth

Their hats to a queen? (LL) Queen of the Blues. Gwendolyn Brooks.
  NALW; SeSe

Their heels slapped their bumping mules. Merchants from Cathay. William
  Rose Benét. MoAmPo

Their Height in Heaven comforts not. Emily Dickinson. APN-2

Their hooves through the moonlight. (LL) John Montague. ModIr; PBCIP;
  PNI *Fr.* Great Cloak, The.

Their horns are pure baroque. Rams. Alasdair Maclean. EdScPo

Their illicit pleasure has been fulfilled. Their Beginning. Constantine P.
  Cavafy. CAGL, *tr. by* Edmund Keeley and Philip Sherrard

Their jeans sparkled, cut off. After School, Street Football, Eighth Grade.
  Dennis Cooper. WiU

Their last pages are transparent. Lace Makers, The. Stanley Moss. PoA
  2002

Their laughter like a sprinkling of salt. Herring Girls, The. Derick Thomson.
  NePenScot

Their laughter pelting down on us like trash. (LL) At the Movie: Virginia,
  1956. Ellen Bryant Voigt. LPSFW; LTA; NoAM

Their lips upon each other's lips are laid. Speechless: Upon the Marriage of
  Two Deaf and Dumb Persons. Philip Bourke Marston. OxBSo

Their Lonely Betters. W. H. Auden. NAEL-6v2; NAEL-7v2; NoAM; NoP-5;
  OBGa

Their men took them to flat-footed milltowns. Desert Flowers. Jeanne Bryner.
  SweBea

Their music marvelous, though sad, and strange. (LL) Town Dump, The.
  Howard Nemerov. NIL-7; WaAnP

Their name is Legion, grinning from afar. Athenians' Answer, The. Elizabeth
  Singer Rowe. BASC

Their nation was no mother to them. Around the Campfire. Nathan Alterman.
  NRoS, *tr. by* Esther Raizen

Their necks and their dark heads lifted into a dawn. Loons Mating. David
  Wagoner. BLT

Their necks make, narrowing the sky. (LL) I Was Sleeping Where the Black
  Oaks Move. Louise Erdrich. CAP-8; HATNAP; NoP-4; NoP-5; PoPoPo

Their new landlord was a handsome man. Deserter, A. Charles Reznikoff.
  TRP

Their ochre clings to the stone. (LL) Ts'ai Chi'h. Ezra Pound. NoP-4;
  NoP-5

Their ordeal over, now the only trouble. Half a Double Sonnet. Mary Jo
  Salter. MakPoe

Their out of bounds bedroom. Out of Bounds. Priscilla Borthwick. Prnts

Their Patients. Robert Pinsky. NoAM *Fr.* Essay on Psychiatrists.

Their Philistinism Considered. Robert Pinsky. NoAM *Fr.* Essay on
  Psychiatrists.

Their ravish'd spirits did possess. (LL) Ode, upon a Question Moved, Whether
  Love Should Continue Forever?, An. Edward Herbert, 1st Baron Herbert
  of Cherbury. BASC; OxAEP-1; OxBEV

Their Rectitude Their Beauty. Donald Davie. HarvBoo

Their red lamps make a childlike stab. Billie's Blues. Alfred Corn. CAGL

Their roofs and floors unstaved, the houses. Diptych. Dewi Stephen Jones.
  BBMWP, *tr. by* Joseph P. Clancy

Their salt wet life erased, eroded, only. Consider the Lillies of the Sea. Anne
  Porter. APT-2

Their sense is with their senses all mixed in. George Meredith. NAEL-6v2;
  NoP-4; NoP-5 *Fr.* Modern Love.

Their separate, discontinuous lanterns. (LL) Blue Ridge. Ellen Bryant Voigt.
  LPSFW; NoAM

Their Seriousness, with Further Comparisons. Robert Pinsky. NoAM *Fr.*
  Essay on Psychiatrists.

Their Sex Life. A. R. Ammons. OBCoV; OxBoAm

Their shadow dims the sunshine of our day. Birds of Prey. Claude McKay.
  APT-1

Their sin-sick souls by him shall be recured. (LL) Thomas Campion. InvLi;
  SacPr

Their souls became cold. Sappho. SaLy, *tr. by* Diane Rayor

Their souls parchment dry, brittle, they came. Ethiopian Apocalypse of Don,
  The. Norman Weinstein. WaCA

Their spades grafted through the variably-resistant soil. Geoffrey Hill.
  EmeKit *Fr.* Mercian Hymns.

Their Speech, Compared with Wisdom and Poetry. Robert Pinsky. NoAM;
  PoA 2002 *Fr.* Essay on Psychiatrists.

Their spinning and experienced bodies. (LL) Soul Train. Allison Joseph.
  AmPoNex; ExTi; SUP

Their squints and stammers disappeared. Children, The. Robert Minhinnick.
  AngWePo

Their strong foundations laid by God's right hand! (LL) New World, The.
  Jones Very. APN-1; OxBoAm

Their supply-lines cut, / The leaves go down to defeat. Alatus. Richard
  Wilbur. UpMys

Their tautology. Erin Mouré. NLPA *Fr.* Wittgenstein Letters to Mel Gibson's
  Braveheart, The.

Their Thoughts Cling to Everything They See on the Way. Allen Afterman.
  NOBAu

Their time past, pulled down. Burning the Christmas Greens. William Carlos
  Williams. APT-1; ChrPo; NAAL-5; NAMCP V.1; NoAM

Their vast, shady, turned-down brim. (LL) Exchanging Hats. Elizabeth
  Bishop. NIL-7; OxBoAm

Their voices are thin as lines of rain. Spring Peepers. Joseph Bruchac.
  PoCoUp

Their voices heard, I stumble suddenly, remembering. One More New Botched
  Beginning. Stephen Spender. NoAM

Their Wedding Journey. Henry Cuyler Bunner.
  "Dear Mother." VerBaPo

Their youth was poor and barren as the land. Banquet. Ruth Bidgood. TCAWP

Theirs is the house whose windows—every pane. On the Asylum Road. Charlotte Mew. MoBrPo; VWP

Theirs was not the peaceful death-bed. Two Smothered Children. Marion Albina Bigelow. VerBaPo

Thelmon and Carmel; An Irregular Poem. Anne Batten Cristall. RWP

Thelonious. Reuben Jackson. ESEAA

Thelonious Monk dies. 17:II:82. David Meltzer. SeSe

Thelonius. Afaa Michael Weaver. BtF; FuFl

Them. Kim Addonizio. RoV

Them always fair. (LL) Thomas Hardy. NoAM; OBMV Fr. At Casterbridge Fair.

Them and Us. Lucille Clifton. AllShUp

Them mounted in magazines. Or stuffed. (LL) How to Write Anglo-Welsh Poetry. John Davies. AngWePo; TCAWP

Them only with / spring. (LL) O sweet spontaneous. E. E. Cummings. IPoFL; NAAL-5; NAAPv.2; NAMCP V.1; NoAM; RaBo; TCAPo

Them that's got shall get. God Bless the Child. Arthur Herzog, Jr. and Billie Holiday. ReLy

Them/There. John Ash. HarvBoo

Them & [uz]. Tony Harrison. NoP-4; NoP-5

Theme for English B. Langston Hughes. APT-2; ColAP; FaBoA; NAMCP V.1; NIL-7; NIP-4; NoAM; NoP-4; NoP-5; PoPoPo; PtR; SSLK; WaAnP

Theme of yesterday's poet, The. Poetry That Is Life. Almad Shamlu. PML, tr. by Unknown

Themes for women. Elizabeth Bartlett. StAl

Themselves, they marry, they raise their kind. (LL) Sheep Child, The. James Dickey. CAP-8; EmeKit; NAMCP V.2; NoAM; VCAP

Then. Lawrence Joseph. PBCAP

Then. Roddy Lumsden. NeBl

Then. Gail Mazur. ExTi

Then. Edwin Muir. OxBEV; PoA 2002

Then Achilles. Homer. WoPoe Fr. Iliad, The.

Then all the nations of birds lifted together. Season of Phantasmal Peace, The. Derek Walcott. EmeKit; GPTC; NAMCP V.2; PoetW; PoPoPo; VCWP

Then / an awakened citron. Ana Istarú. TANSG, tr. by Mary Jane Treacy

Then and after were no use to me, nor the desire to make permanent. Grove at Nemi, The. Susan Mitchell. ExTi

Then and Now. James Laughlin. PmAP

Then and now rivers and mountains have no certain lot. Tune: "Butterflies Lingering over Flowers." Nara Singde. ColAnChi, tr. by David McCraw

. . . Then, as if he would have sold. John Donne. PBRV Fr. Satire 4.

Then as they spake, unraised his head. Homer. DiBP Fr. Odyssey.

Then, at 3 A.M. I see her bend. Intensive Care. Carol Muske-Dukes. PBCAP

Then Ball, my cut-tailed cur, and I begin to play. Dancing Dog, The. Michael Drayton. DiBP

Then[,] blessing all, "Go, children of my care!" Alexander Pope. NAEL-6v1; NAEL-7v1; NPeEn Fr. Dunciad, The.

Then came I to the shoreless shore of silence. Conrad Potter Aiken. OxBoAm Fr. Preludes for Memnon; or, Preludes to Attitude.

Then came the cry of "Call all hands on deck!" John Masefield. MoBrPo Fr. Dauber.

Then came the year of fires. Years, The. Catherine Davis. FFC

Then came to pass what Merlin spoke of long before. Layamon. NAEL-7v1 Fr. Brut, The.

Then cautiously she pushed the cellar door. Edna St. Vincent Millay. NALW Fr. Sonnets from an Ungrafted Tree.

Then, certanlye, scho tuke me be the hand. Sir David Lyndsay. NePenScot Fr. Dreme, The.

Then cherish pity, lest you drive an angel from your door. (LL) William Blake. BrAP; GoPo; NAEL-6v2; NAEL-7v2; NAWM-7v2; NOBRP; NoP-4; NoP-5; NPBRoP; NPeEn; TFi Fr. Songs of Innocence.

Then chiefly lives. (LL) Virtue [or Vertue]. George Herbert. AmFaPo; BASC; ClHu; FSCP; HeIP-4; NAEL-6v1; NAEL-7v1; NoP-4; NoP-5; NOSC; OBEV; OPOU; OxBEV; SoSe-8; TFi; TreFP; WaAnP

Then colors rose through the leaves in light. Gertrude Stein Rides the Town Down El. Tom Postell. EGAG

Then come my God, and hap what will. (LL) To God ("Come to me God; but do not come.") Robert Herrick. CavPo; RSR

Then did he to the throng around. Kingdom of Heaven Compared to a Grain of Mustard-Seed, The. Henry Vaughan. ChIV-2

Then down the brave man lay with his bolster. Unknown. WaAnP Fr. Beowulf [Heaney Translation].

Then draw your curtains, and begin the dawn. (LL) Lark Now Leaves His Watery [or Wat'ry] Nest. Sir William Davenant. OxBEV; TFi

Then drew near unto him all the publicans and sinners. Bible, N.T. NAWM-5v1 Fr. St. Luke.

Then El Presidente. Noche, Una. Michael Palmer. WoBe

Then everyone disappearing into the houses. (LL) TV. Rodney Jones. BeAl; IllVoic; ReTh

Then, everything slept. Cry, The. Larry Levis. NevBe

Then fall, and with an art of falling, to a state of shelter. Peter Riley. VaPo Fr. Excavations.

Then first he form'd th' immense and solid Shield. Homer. OBVE Fr. Iliad, The.

Then first with locks dishevelled and bare. Barnabe Barnes. NoSic; NPeEn; WaAnP Fr. Parthenophil and Parthenophe.

Then flit not from this heavenly boy. (LL) Robert Southwell. See Then flit[t] not from this heavenly boy[e].

Then for / twelve years. Low Volume. Reiner Kunze. PoSu, tr. by Michael Hamburger

Then forth issued (great goddess) great Dame Nature. Edmund Spenser. AEP

Then from the teeming Filth, and putrid Heap. Oppian [of Corycus]. NPeEn Fr. Halieutica.

Then from their poverty they rose. Ordinary Women, The. Wallace Stevens. NAAPv.2

Then Frome (a nobler flood) the Muses doth implore. Michael Drayton. NOSC Fr. Polyolbion [or Poly-Oobion].

Then Gabriel sent down a dream that I stood. Gjertrud Schnackenberg. StAl Fr. Gilded Lapse of Time, A.

Then gan this crafty couple to devise. Edmund Spenser. NoSic Fr. Mother Hubbard's Tale.

Then God said to me, Stop. Tree, The. Frank Gaspar. UrbNat

Then grave Clarissa graceful wav'd her fan. Alexander Pope. NPeEn; OxBEV Fr. Rape of the Lock, The: An Heroi-Comical Poem in Five Cantos.

Then hark again! The human hunt begun. Edward Robert Bulwer-Lytton. DiBP Fr. Arthur.

Then hate me when thou wilt; if ever, now. William Shakespeare. NoSic; OBEV; OxAEP-1; RaF Fr. Sonnets.

Then Herod, when he saw that he had been tricked by the wise men. Julia Hartwig. GI Fr. St. Matthew.

Then Hope took hold of a horn of Deus tu conversus vivificabis nos. William Langland. NAEL-6v1; NAEL-7v1 Fr. Vision of Piers Plowman, The.

Then I am pensive—I hastily walk away fill'd with the bitterest envy. (LL) When I Peruse the Conquer'd Fame. Walt Whitman. APN-1; SAmP

Then I answered: Yea. (LL) Christina Georgina Rossetti. NoP-4; NoP-5; ViWPN Fr. Old and New Year Ditties.

Then I dreamed I chose. Purple Blouse. Dan Chiasson. PoCho

Then I finally understood that the angel. Expulsion. Lisa Sewell. AmPoNex

Then I got on the train, very late. London Welsh v. Bridgend. John Powell Ward. TCAWP

Then I heard the bomber call me in. Little Friend. Unknown. WoPoe

Then I Saw What the Calling Was. Muriel Rukeyser. ColAP

Then I sign an armmistice, I listen to the voices. Biography. Mariella Bettarini. CItWP, tr. by Cinzia Sartini Blum and Lara Trubowitz

Then I stand up on my hassock and say sing that. Pretext. Stephen Rodefer. PmAP

Then I took the poem in my hand and walked out. Scarecrow Eclogue. Srikanth Reddy. LegDan

Then I woke up, the shuffle of images still with me. Portishead Suite. Rick Barot. NeAmPo

Then if I think about it. Dario Villa. ItPo, tr. by Gayle Ridinger

Then I'll Be Tired of You. E. Y. Harburg. ReLy

Then I'll bear the torch and the needle. Fanny Howe. FaoP Fr. Passion, The.

Then in her triumph spoke the Fairy Queen. Percy Bysshe Shelley. NAEL-7v2 Fr. Queen Mab.

Then, in the form of a white rose, the host. Dante Alighieri. NAWM-5v1 Fr. Divina Commedia.

Then, in the scale of Pricks, 'tis plain. John Wilkes. EroLit Fr. Essay on Woman.

Then in the scalloped leaves of the plane tree. Black Series. Brenda Hillman. BodElec

Then in we went to the garden glorious. Pastime of Pleasure, The. Stephen Hawes. OBGa

Then indeed into all our fluttering hearts. Virgil. FaBoWar Fr. Aeneid [or Eneados or Aeneis], The.

Then into solemn thought I passed once more. (LL) William Wordsworth. NAEL-6v2; NAEL-7v2 Fr. Prelude, The; Growth of a Poet's Mind [1850 version].

Then it is this simple. I felt the unordinary romance of. Dionne Brand. PoBW Fr. Hard Against the Soul.

Then it was dusk in Illinois, the small boy. First Song. Galway Kinnell. NAMCP V.2; NoP-4; NoP-5

Then Jane says: there is an invisible threat between. Heroine. Carol Muske-Dukes. AmAlph

Then Jesus was led up by the Spirit into the wilderness to be tempted by the devil.   Czeslaw Milosz.   GI *Fr.* St. Matthew.

Then Job spoke and cursed his day and chanted and said.   *Unknown.*   WoPoe *Fr.* Job.

Then lacked [*or* lack'd *or* lackt] I matter, that enfeebled [*or* infeebled] mine. (LL)   William Shakespeare.   CABP; NoSic; OxAEP-1; OxBEV *Fr.* Sonnets.

Then, land!—then, England! oh, the frosty cliffs.   Elizabeth Barrett Browning.   NAEL-6v2; NAEL-7v2 *Fr.* Aurora Leigh.

Then leave old regret.   Moral Poem, A.   James Vincent Cunningham.   APT-2

Then leave the future to thy sons, / Carolina! (LL)   Carolina.   Henry Timrod.   APN-2; CBCWP; PCW

Then Lelex rose, an old experienced man.   Ovid.   OBVE *Fr.* Metamorphoses.

Then let us boast of ancestors no more.   Daniel Defoe.   OBSV *Fr.* True-born Englishman, The.

Then let[t] us live companions without strife. (LL)   Mary Sidney Wroth, Countess of Montgomery.   NoP-4; NoP-5 *Fr.* Pamphilia to Amphilanthus.

Then live, my strength, anchor of weary ships.   To Grimold, Abbot of St. Gall.   Hrabanus Maurus.   CAGL, *tr. by* Helen Waddell

Then live with me and be my love. (LL)   Two Songs.   Cecil Day Lewis.   NAMCP V.1; NoP-4; NoP-5

Then live with me and be my love. (LL)   Cecil Day Lewis.   NIP-4; OBMV; WaAnP *Fr.* Two Songs.

Then live with me[e] and be my Love. (LL)   Passionate Shepherd to His Love, The.   Christopher Marlowe.   BLPJKO; ClHu; HeIP-4; ITBLP; MakPoe; NAEL-6v1; NAEL-7v1; NBLV; NIL-7; NIP-4; NoP-5; NoSic; OBEV; OxAEP-1; OxBEV; TFi; TRP; WaAnP; WeW-3; WoPoe

Then looks at me and says, "I know." (LL)   Experts, The.   Jack Myers.   BodElec; TiP2

Then love is sin, and let me sinful be. (LL)   Sir Philip Sidney.   NoP-4; NoP-5; NoSic *Fr.* Astrophil and Stella.

Then might I see upon a white horse set.   Sonnet 14.   Edmund Spenser.   ChIV-2

Then move not, while my prayers' effect I take. (LL)   William Shakespeare.   OxAEP-1; SoSe-8 *Fr.* Romeo and Juliet.

"Then, must it be."   Elizabeth Barrett Browning.   NALW *Fr.* Aurora Leigh.

Then must the Jew be mercifull.   William Shakespeare.   OxBEV *Fr.* Merchant of Venice, The.

Then my father's rain-filled room.   *Zuni Oral Tradition.*   NAWM-7v2 *Fr.* Shalako.

Then Nicholas spoke: "My King, most kind to me."   János Arany.   IQMS *Fr.* Toldi.

Then, O blind one, you will see again! (LL)   Chorus of the Stars.   Nelly Sachs.   BBASP; PFTM-1, *tr. by* Michael Roloff

Then Old Man spoke to the people.   Wahsah Zeh (War Dance)—As Long as the Grass.   Joseph Bruchac.   AtGh

Then one day the gray rags vanish.   Fence, The.   Louise Erdrich.   NAMCP V.2

Then one of the students with blue hair and a tongue stud.   America.   Tony Hoagland.   FaoP; StAl

Then one of the twelve, called Judas Iscariot.   Bible, *N.T.*   NAWM-5v1 *Fr.* St. Matthew.

Then Oothoon waited silent all the day and all the night.   William Blake.   NPeEn *Fr.* Visions of the Daughters of Albion.

Then out of the night.   *Unknown.*   NoP-5 *Fr.* Beowulf [Heaney Translation].

Then out spake brave Horatius.   Thomas Babington Macaulay, 1st Baron Macaulay.   CABP; TreFP *Fr.* Lays of Ancient Rome.

Then owl.   Dark.   Hoa Nguyen.   WANABP

Then pallid death at last will with his icy hand.   Beauty's Transitoriness.   Christian Hofmann von Hofmannswaldau.   GePo, *tr. by* George C. Schoolfield

Then powdered up with phlegm, and rheum that's salt. (LL)   Margaret Lucas Cavendish, Duchess of Newcastle.   BrAP; PEW

Then pushed her over the edge into the river. (LL)   Traveling Through the Dark.   William Stafford.   BrAP; CAP-8; ColAP; HeIP-4; NAMCP V.2; NoAM; OxBoAm; SoSe-8; StAl; TRP; WaAnP; WeW-3

Then rash Patroclus with new fury glows.   Homer.   FaBoWar *Fr.* Iliad, The.

Then rising in his Rage above the Shores.   Homer.   OBVE *Fr.* Iliad, The.

Then Sang Moses.   Bible, *O.T.*   OBWP *Fr.* Exodus.

Then sang Moses and the children of Israel this song.   Bible, *O.T.*   OBWP *Fr.* Exodus.

Then, say not Man's imperfect, Heaven in fault.   John Wilkes.   EroLit *Fr.* Essay on Woman.

Then Sense, I fear[e], will be a me[e]re dull Fool[e]. (LL)   Imagination.   Margaret Lucas Cavendish, Duchess of Newcastle.   BASC; NOSC

Then she stands still, smiling above flowers. (LL)   Young Girl with a Pitcher Full of Water, A.   David Wagoner.   NAMCP V.2; NoAM

Then since within this wide great Universe.   Edmund Spenser.   NPeEn *Fr.* Faerie Queene, The.

Then Sohrab with his sword smote Rustum's helm.   Matthew Arnold.   OBWP *Fr.* Sohrab and Rustum.

Then spoke the Spirit of the Earth.   William Ellery Channing.   TCAPo *Fr.* Earth Spirit, The.

Then sprang up first the golden age, which of itself maintained.   Ovid.   NAEL-6v1; NAEL-7v1 *Fr.* Metamorphoses.

Then suddenly his brain became the sound.   Raymond Tong.   NewEx

Then swallowed up, of View. (LL)   I've known a Heaven, like a Tent.   Emily Dickinson.   GoPo; NCAP

Then tall Hektor of the shining helm answered her: "All these."   Homer.   AmFaPo *Fr.* Iliad, The.

Then tell, O[h] tell, how thou didst murder [*or* murther] me. (LL)   When Thou Must Home.   Propertius.   BrAP; NoP-4; NoP-5; NoSic; NPeEn; OxAEP-1; OxBEV; WoPoe, *tr. by* Thomas Campion

Then the air was a brutal architecture of sugar.   Everlasting Quail.   Sam Witt.   NeAmPo

Then the Ermine.   Marianne Moore.   PoA 2002

Then the long sunlight lying on the sea.   Insusceptibles, The.   Adrienne Rich.   HeIP-4

Then the Lord answered Job out of the whirlewind, and sayd.   Bible, *O.T.*   OBVE; WoPoe *Fr.* Job.

Then the Lord answered Job out of the whirlwind.   Bible, *O.T.*   InvLi *Fr.* Job.

Then the mailman came and.   9.1.59: II.   Pablo Picasso.   CLPP, *tr. by* Paul Blackburn

Then the Master.   Henry Wadsworth Longfellow.   NAAL-3 *Fr.* Building of the Ship, The.

Then the mighty Lord Maxfield over the mountains fleeth.   *Unknown.*   NoSic *Fr.* Scot[t]ish Field[e].

Then the old fruit-and-vegetable economy dried up and blew away but self-defense gave us a way.   Craig Watson.   Eno *Fr.* Home Guard.

Then the Pharisees went and took counsel how to entangle him in his talk.   Desanka Maksimovic.   GI *Fr.* St. Matthew.

Then the Provost he uprose.   William Edmonstoune Aytoun.   OBWP *Fr.* Edinburgh after Flodden.

Then the pulse.   Burial Practice.   Srikanth Reddy.   LegDan

Then the tall shade, in drooping linens veiled.   John Keats.   OxBEV *Fr.* Fall of Hyperion, The; A Dream.

Then there is this civilising love of death, by which.   Ignorance of Death.   William Empson.   NAMCP V.1; NoAM

Then, / there was a horizon of blue women.   Man-Myth: Puberty.   Jean-Baptiste Tati-Loutard.   SonAtl, *tr. by* Gregory Beaven and Kurt Ganzl

Then there was the rose I fell in love with.   Elena Ignatova.   CRWP, *tr. by* Daniel Weissbort

Then they are young and on vacation, their camera.   Alex Kuo.   FTtHH *Fr.* Lives in Dreadful Wanting.

Then they moved the whole camp.   *Unknown.*   WoPoe *Fr.* Secret History of the Mongols, The.

Then they set spur to horse.   *Unknown.*   WoPoe *Fr.* Excerpts from *The Poem of the Cid.*

Then they went away too.   Hans Faverey.   WoBe *Fr.* Eighteen Poems.

Then they will call-up the Little Prince.   Military Call-up.   Meir Wieseltier.   NRoS, *tr. by* Esther Raizen

Then thick as locusts black'ning the ground.   Alexander Pope.   NPeEn *Fr.* Dunciad, The.

Then this light flipped in the rowboats.   Werner Herzog 68 / Iowa City 88.   Ann Lauterbach.   ExTi

Then this the whom say Neville.   Waves Broke on the Shore, The.   Jackson Mac Low.   OnScMo

Then, though we[e] do[e] not know, we love. (LL)   Hymn: "Lord, when the wise men came from far[r]."   Sidney Godolphin.   NPeEn; RSR; SacPr

Then to admire some beached whales.   Ode to Election Day.   Anselm Berrigan.   HeMarv

Then to th' extremest heat of fight he did his valour turn.   Homer.   FaBoWar *Fr.* Iliad, The.

Then, to the starboard, a lilac-paced synchrony.   Mathemaku No. 17.   Bob Grumman.   AnSo

Then Trystan and Gwalchmai went to Arthur.   Trystan and Esyllt.   *Unknown.*   OBWVE, *tr. by* Gwyn Jones

Then up the ladder of the earth I climbed.   Pablo Neruda.   TCLAP *Fr.* Heights of Macchu Picchu, The.

Then up three winding stairs my feet were brought.   Philip Freneau.   NAAL-3 *Fr.* House of Night, The.

Then very gently the earth grows a mane, swivels maneuvering its.   Bucolic.   Aimé Césaire.   VCWP

Then wake to weep. (LL)   Mutability ("Flower that smiles today, The.")   Percy Bysshe Shelley.   NAEL-6v2; NoP-4; NoP-5

Then watch her spread her wings and soar. (LL)   Flight: "Mother blackbird I've been feeding, The."   Sarah Wardle.   BeAl; PoCu

Then we had just the pink carpet, the drugs kicking in, the flat soda.   Mud.   Mark Bibbins.   WiU

Then we have work to do. (LL) Jelaluddin Rumi. RaBo; WoPoe *Fr.* Three Quatrains.

Then we plyed by guess. Log Written by an Unkown Hand in the. Christine Hume. IAoNAP

Then we'll sing of Lydia Pinkham. Lydia Pinkham. *Unknown.* OBCoV

Then, what do you say to the poem of Mizpah? Dialogue between Father and Daughter. Robert Browning. OBCoV

Then what have I to do with thee? (LL) William Blake. NAEL-6v2; NAEL-7v2 *Fr.* Songs of Experience.

Then what is it I am. Your Words, My Answers. Burns Singer. HarvBoo

Then, what is life? I cried. (LL) Triumph of Life, The. Percy Bysshe Shelley. NAEL-6v2; NOBRP

Then why did I have to make. *Unknown.* NAAPv.2

Then why do they sneer at me? (LL) Jew, The. Isaac Rosenberg. ChIV-1; MoBrPo

Then will thou go and leave me here? Valediction. Sir Robert Aytoun. NOSC

Then with my white sails and bad luck. Sibyl. Robert Adamson. BMAP

Then would I make thee read, but to despight thee. (LL) Michael Drayton. NOSC; WaAnP *Fr.* Idea.

Then you will be practically unconscious without positively having to go. (LL) Thoughts about the Person from Porlock. Stevie Smith. NAEL-6v2; NAEL-7v2; NAMCP V.1; NoAM; NoP-4; NoP-5

Then you'll hear the horn they blow. *Unknown. See* Michael row the [*or* de] boat ashore.

Then you're so rude!—when people call. Rude Ranger Rebuked. Caroline Anne Bowles Southey. DiBP

Thence passing forth, they shortly do arrive. Edmund Spenser. NAEL-6v1; NAEL-7v1; OBGa *Fr.* Faerie Queene, The.

Thenmy of liff decayer of all kynde. Sir Thomas Wyatt. FaBoVe

Theocritus: A Villanelle. Oscar Wilde. WaAnP

Theodicy. Kim Addonizio. LiTh

Theodore and Honoria, From [Fables Ancient and Modern from] Boccace. John Dryden.
  Disdain Punished. NOSC

Theogony. Hesiod. *tr. by* Charles Doria and Richmond Lattimore
  Great Father Eating His Children, The. RaBo
  Vision. WoPoe, *tr. by* Charles Doria

Theological. Dick Lourie. PrTe

Theology. Sherman Alexie. NeAmPo

Theology. Paul Laurence Dunbar. SacPr

Theology. Jane Hirshfield. WANABP

Theology. Ted Hughes. NAEL-6v2; NAEL-7v2; NoAM; NoP-4; NoP-5

Theology. Richard Newman. Vesp

Theology of Doubt, The. Scott Cairns. UpMys

Theology of Hair, The. Menna Elfyn. BBMWP, *tr. by* Elin ap Hywel

Theology of Jonathan Edwards, The. Phyllis McGinley. MoAmPo

Theophia. Edward Benlowes.
  Pleasures of Retirement, The. NOSC

Theorem. Walter Conrad Arensberg. APT-1

Theoretical People. Paul Hoover. IllVoic

Theorist Has No Samba!, The. Edwin Torres. BAP-04

Theory, A. Charles Simic. ChAP

Theory and Practice in Poetry. Eleanor Wilner. TAPaP

Theory has it the word came first. But you always. Nesting of Layer Protocols. Kit Robinson. FTOS

Theory My Natural Brown Ass. Sonnet L'Abbé. OpeFie

Theory of a Good Death. Maria Negroni. PoCho, *tr. by* Anne Twitty

Theory of Curve. Christopher Gilbert. LTA

Theory of Fractals. Gustavo V. Segade. RMCMP

Theory of Light. Alberto Blanco. RMCMP, *tr. by* Gustavo V. Segade

Theory of Pursuit: there is no me minus you. Halt (Naïve). Dan Beachy-Quick. IAoNAP

Theory of Recruiting. Regina Derieva. CRWP, *tr. by* Kevin Carey

Theory of Silences. Gabriel Celaya. RaW, *tr. by* Robert Mezey

Theory of the Flower, The. Michael Palmer. HarvBoo

Theory of Tragedy. Joseph Duemer. BodElec

Theory on Extinction or what happened to the dinosaurs? Kenneth Carroll. AmPoNex; SpirFl

THEORY X: People are naturally lazy. Managing the Common Herd: Two Approaches for Senior Management. Julie O'Callaghan. BeAl

Ther bloweth a cold wynd to-day, to-day. *Unknown.* OHMEL

Ther is a chielde, a heuenly childe. James Ryman. SacPr

Ther is no rose of swych vertu. Rose That Bore Jesu, The. *Unknown.* NPeEn

Ther saugh I first the derke ymaginyng. Geoffrey Chaucer. PoAgWa *Fr.* Canterbury Tales, The.

Ther was also a Nonne, a Prioresse. Geoffrey Chaucer. BrAP; NPeEn *Fr.* Canterbury Tales, The.

Therapies. Julio Cortázar. MotU, *tr. by* Paul Blackburn

Therapist, The. Leanne O'Sullivan. NIrP

Therapist's Comment, The. Jenny Hamlett. Prnts

Therapy. Giovanna. SurWo, *tr. by* Myrna Bell Rochester

Therapy. John Wright. BloBone

Therapy junkie because. Hot House. Rick Zand. MAAN

There. Etel Adnan.
  "In the green escape of my palace, over a bridge, under a." PoArWo

There. Ray Gonzalez. TouFir

There. Philip Mead. BMAP

There. Caroline Natzler. Prnts

There. Gertrude Stein. OxBoAm *Fr.* Book Concluding with As A Wife Has a Cow a Love Story, A.

"There," / He said. John Hancock. Lee Bennett Hopkins. HHAm

There a bowl of ambrosia. Sappho. SaLy, *tr. by* Diane Rayor

There Above. *Wintu Oral Tradition.* NAAPv.1 *Fr.* Six Dream Songs.

There all the golden codgers lay. News for the Delphic Oracle. William Butler Yeats. NoAM

There all the happy souls that ever were. Pleasures of Heaven, The. Ben Jonson. TreFP

There always is a noise when it is dark! In the Night. James Stephens. OBMV

There among puddles of sewage in Sabra and Shatilah. You don't Kill Babies Twice. Dahlia Ravikovitch. NRoS, *tr. by* Esther Raizen

There an old man sat serene. Scott's Dogs at Melrose Abbey. Arthur Henry Hallam. DiBP

There once was a may, and she lo'ed na men. Lady Grisel Baillie. *See* There was an a May and she lo'ed na men.

There are a few things. Yet to Come. Luke E. Ramirez. OWABP

There are a few things yet you haven't heard of. Imre Madách. IQMS *Fr.* Tragedy of Man.

There are ads in all the papers. Military Life, The. Harold Rome. ReLy

There are afternoons in jazz. Art of Benny Carter, The. Al Young. OxAAAP

There are all things reflected here, yet all. Well, The. Bernard Raymund. YaYoPo

There are always questions. Post Scriptum. Mark Todd. GeoH

There are always the poor. Soliloquy at Potsdam. Peter Porter. BrAP; NOBAu

There are always ties of responsibility. Transportation. Karen Alkalay-Gut. DTA

There are answers in the ponds at night. Pond in the Woods, A. Thomas Rain Crowe. AmZen

There are artifacts from every period here. Tour of Ein Kerem, A. David Curzon. GI

There are at least one hundred billion galaxies in the universe. Sense of Proportion, The. Stephen Mitchell. WhBo

There are bare places. Bare Places. Douglas Burnet Smith. Coast

There are birds. Landscape with Yellow Birds. Shuntaro Tanikawa. PoetW, *tr. by* Harold Wright

There are birds that are parts of speech, bones. Hardin County. Charles Wright. LPSFW

There are black guards slamming cell gates. Jimmy Santiago Baca. LTA

There are blows in life, so powerful. . .I don't know! Black Heralds, The. César Vallejo. PoCho, *tr. by* Rebecca Seiferle

There are blows in life so violent—don't ask me! Black Riders, The. César Vallejo. RaBo; WED, *tr. by* Robert Bly
  (There are blows in life so violent—I can't answer!) AF

There are bog-people in the foundations. Foundations, The. Jennifer Maiden. BMAP

There are brightest apples on those trees. Fertile Muck, The. Irving Layton. NoAM

There are cemeteries that are lonely. Nothing but Death. Pablo Neruda. WED, *tr. by* Robert Bly

There are christs spiked against trees. There Is Life. Breyten Breytenbach. VCWP, *tr. by* Breyten Breytenbach

There are constantly, she told him further, lions in the village. Henri Michaux. GPTC; MotU *Fr.* I Am Writing to You from a Far-Off Country.

There are countless tons of rock above his head. Idris Davies. TCAWP *Fr.* Gwalia Deserta.

There are days in which I wake up beautiful. Natalia. Natalia Toledo. RMCMP, *tr. by* Alberto A. Ríos

There are days when the dead will have nothing to do with us. Tending the Graves. Jennifer Strauss. NOBAu

There are days when you go. Studying Wu Wei, Muir Beach. Jane Hirshfield. AFaM; WANABP

There are ecstatic rituals every do-good deity knows. Shiva's Prowess. Maurya Simon. ErotSp

There are even silences, prosecutors. Tap. Maggie Hannan. NLP

There are exact arrangements. Mimikòs. Luigi Fontanella. NeIt, tr. by Michael Palma

There are few moments of silence. Heartland. Linda Hogan. UrbNat

There are few of us now, soon. For Eli Jacobson. Kenneth Rexroth. RaBo

There are few stars north of the Milky Way. Watching a Lonely Wild Goose at Nightfall. Hsiao Kang. CrYelRi, tr. by Sam Hamill

There are five thousand of us here. Estadio Chile. Víctor Jara. TCLAP, tr. by Joan Jara

There are flowers now, they say, at Alamein. El Alamein. John Jarmain. FaBoWar

There are four kinds of men who'll get no fee from me. Khosravani. WoPoe, tr. by Dick Davis

There are four men mowing down by the Isar. Youth Mowing, A. D. H. Lawrence. MoBrPo; NAMCP V.1; NoAM

There are great advantages to having been dead. Gwyneth Lewis. NeBl

There are great puddles of blood on the world. Song in the Blood. Jacques Prévert. AF, tr. by Lawrence Ferlinghetti

There are hearts—stout hearts,—that own no fear. Surgeon's Knife, The. Eliza Cook. VWP

There are hearts—stout hearts,—that own no fear. Eliza Cook. VerBaPo Fr. Surgeon's Knife, The.

There are hermit souls that live withdrawn. House by the Side of the Road, The. Sam Walter Foss. BRP; ITBLP

There are (I scarce can think it, but [I] am told). First Satire of the Second Book of Horace [Imitated], The. Alexander Pope.

There are / in the back of the mind. Up Yonder in the Meadow of Children. Brita Bergland. OnScMo

There are in this rude stunning tide. Happiness. John Keble. TreFP

There are just not enough. Living Space. Imtiaz Dharker. NeBl

There are just so many years. Turning Pro. Ishmael Reed. SoSe-8

There are knocks in life so hard. . .I don't know! Black heralds, The. César Vallejo. BeAl, tr. by Gordon Brotherston and Edward Dorn

There are ladders. Relics. Barbara Baldwin. FiBr

There are lakes in our region. Inventions. William Scammell. NLP

There are lights soft as milk striking. Winter Fires. David St. John. AmAlph

There are limits to brotherly love, as I've observed more than once. There Are Limits to Brotherly Love. John Gwyn Griffiths. BBMWP, tr. by Richard Poole

There are lonely cemeteries. Only Death. Pablo Neruda. ConPit; PFTM-1, tr. by Clayton Eshleman

There are long kilometers. From Now Until Chile. Emma Sepúlveda-Pulvirenti. TANSG, tr. by Shaun Griffin

There are lots of fellows think that they're in love. When a Fellow's on the Level with a Girl That's on the Square. George M. Cohan. ReLy

There are many and more. Many and More. Maya Angelou. LW

There are many beginnings. Thicket of Time. David Chaloner. VaPo

There are many cumbersome ways to kill a man. Five Ways to Kill a Man. Edwin Brock. BeAl

There are many dead in the brutish desert. Hamish Henderson. EdScPo; PoWW; RSaN Fr. Elegies for the Dead in Cyrenaica.

There are many intricate pieces of workmanship. Richard Eberhart. PWW2 Fr. Aesthetics after War.

There are many minds in circulation. One Life to Live. Ira Gershwin. ReLy

There are many monsters that a glassen surface. Octopus, The. James Merrill. CAP-8

There are many more Good Fridays. Unkept Good Fridays. Thomas Hardy. GI

There Are Many Pathways to the Garden. Philip Lamantia. ASA

There Are Many Things I Want to Tell You. Indran Amirthanayagam. OpBo

There Are Many Traps in the World. Ferreira Gullar. TCLAP, tr. by Renato Rezende

There are many Washingtons. Which Washington? Eve Merriam. NTCP

There are many ways of saying Chinese. Address. Adrienne Su. AmPoNex

There are many ways to die. Robert Penn Warren. CBCWP; MoAmPo Fr. Kentucky Mountain Farm.

There are many who say that a dog has his day. Song of the Mischievous Dog, The. Dylan Thomas. OBCoV

There are men and women huddled in rooms tonight. Absence. Bob Hicok. PoDa

There are men so crazy from not having something. Family Man, The. William Loran Smith. LaCa

There are more functions to a freezing plant. Post Mortem. Wole Soyinka. PoetW

There are more stars in the universe. Size of This Universe, The. Randolph Healy. Oth

There are more ways to abandon a child. True Names of Birds, The. Susan Goyette. Coast; OpeFie

There are mountains on this earth. Glistening, The. Deema K. Shehabi. PoArWo

There are nights as soft as fur on a foal. Watching Shoah in a Hotel Room in America. Adam Zagajewski. VCWP, tr. by Renata Gorczynski, Benjamin Ivry and C. K. Williams

There are no accidents, or so. What Could Hold Us. Heather McHugh. NIP-4

There are no bolts that do not exactly. Kirkwall Auction Mart. David Scott. NLP

There are no centers but the circle exists. Carla Faesler Bremer. SPV, tr. by Jen Hofer

There are no crosses. Charles Tomlinson. See There are no crosses / on the Hopi graves. They lie.

There are no crosses / on the Hopi graves. They lie. Death in the Desert, A. Charles Tomlinson. ICANM

(There are no crosses.) CABP

There Are No Doors. Olga Orozco. BLPSL, tr. by Rene de Costa, Rigas Kappatos and Eleni Paidoussi

There are no dry bones. Bones of My Father, The. Etheridge Knight. BodElec; OxAAAP

There are no girls among us now with small high breasts. We Are So Fond of One Another, Because Our Ailments Are the Same. Winfield Townley Scott. ICANM

There are no gospel singers. Downtown Boom. Lorenzo Thomas. RD; TiP2

There are no handles upon a language. Languages. Carl Sandburg. APT-1; ColAP

There are no houses no trees there is no body. Humidity. C. D. Wright. AmAlph

There are no leaders to lead us to honour, and yet without leaders we sally. Spies' March, The. Rudyard Kipling. FaBoWar

There are no pacts. Angelo Lumelli. ItPo, tr. by Gayle Ridinger

There are no perfect waves. William Carlos Williams. APT-1

There are no rocks. Geography: a Song. Howard Moss. OBCoV

There are no ships in the. Bypass, The. Conor O'Callaghan. NIrP

There are no simple explanations. No Simple Explanations. Jayne Cortez. GT

There are no small ones. Puritans. Elaine Equi. PmAP

There are no stars to-night. My Grandmother's Love Letters. Hart Crane. BeAl; GPTC; NAAPv.2; NoAM; NoP-4; NoP-5; OxBoAm; PtR; WaAnP

There are no words here. Hooded Legion, The. Gerald McCarthy. AmWaPo

There are no words in me for Gaza, for what i saw. Diana Brandt. ACAMVP

There are no words left for. Roy Kiyooka. NLPA Fr. Pear Tree Pomes.

There are notes to lightning in my bedroom. Star Quilt. Roberta Hill Whiteman. NoAM

There are of course tho' we don't see them. Postscripts 2. Dennis Brutus. HBAPE

There are old drunks among the tenements. Griots Who Know Brer Fox, The. Colleen J. McElroy. OxAAAP

There are only so many words. Janet Fisher. MFPA

There are owls tonight at Dôl-y-garreg-wen. Nant yr Eira. Will Ifan. BBMWP, tr. by Joseph P. Clancy

There are passionate love affairs, often between. Leslie Kaplan. SCFWP Fr. Règne.

"There are people so dumb," my father said. Plain Talk. William Jay Smith. MoAmPo

There are, perhaps, whom passion gives a grace. Aged Lover Discourses in the Flat Style, The. James Vincent Cunningham. NoAM

There are places in this world where. Somewhere Holy. Carl Phillips. AmAlph

There are places in Wales I don't go. Reservoirs. Ronald Stuart Thomas. AngWePo

There are places where the eye can starve. Those Graves in Rome. Larry Levis. PoDa

There Are Points of Silence Circling the Heart. Roberto Juarroz. TCLAP, tr. by W. S. Merwin

There are portraits and still-lifes. Paring the Apple. Charles Tomlinson. TRP

There are ribald interventions. Palinode. "Ern Malley." BMAP

There are rivers of oranges, sweet. There Are Rivers of Oranges. James Tipton. GeoH

There are rooms that know you, rooms you know. Rooms. Brian Henry. LegDan

There are rows of bottles against the glass;. Small-town Gladys. David Campbell. BMAP

There are, said my old philosophy professor, two kinds. On the Nature of Desire. David Lehman. PfSP

There are sea and sky about me. Midnight. Louisa Sarah Bevington. PEW

There are secrets. Leaving Winston-Salem. Toneka Nathene Bonitto-Burwell. BtF

There are shades of light. Felled Shadows. Terri L. Jewell. FiBr

There are similarities / I notice: that the hills. Journey to the Interior. Margaret Atwood. BrAP

There are so few photographs of him. Grandfather's Cap, My. David St. John. MoASP

There are so many islands. And Yet. Patricia Goedicke. ExTi

There are so many kinds of awful men. Rondeau Redoublé. Wendy Cope. HarvBoo

There are so many kinds of riches. Best Things in Life Are Free, The. Lew Brown, B. G. DeSylva and Ray Henderson. ReLy

There are so many photographs of that curve of rocky beach. Imagining Point Dume. Diane Wakoski. GeoHom

There are some blows in life so hard...I don't know! (LL) Black Messengers, The. César Vallejo. PoetW; TCLAP, tr. by Rachel Benson

There are some blows in life so hard...I don't know! Black Messengers, The. César Vallejo. PoetW; TCLAP, tr. by Rachel Benson

There are some days the happy ocean lies. Seascape. Stephen Spender. NoP-4; NoP-5

There are some qualities—some incorporate things. Sonnet—Silence. Edgar Allan Poe. ColAP; TCAPo

There are some questions one should know by heart. Postscript. Henri Coulette. CalPo

There are some tiny obvious details in human life. Against Surrealism. James Wright. MotU

There are stories told by the elderly. Old Stories. Rita Joe. Coast

There are strange hells within the minds war made. Strange Hells. Ivor Gurney. FaBoWar

There are strange shadows fostered of the moon. Sonnet. Arthur Davison Ficke. TCAPo

There are strange things done in the midnight sun. Cremation of Sam McGee, The. Robert W. Service. BRP; IFF; OBCoV; OBNV; TCAPo; WaAnP

There are strange trees in that pale field. Forest of the Dead, The. James Griffyth Fairfax. PoWW

There are strangers above me, below me and all around me and we are all. Path to the Milky Way Leads Through Los Angeles, The. Joy Harjo. NAMCP V.2; StAl

There are sunsets I would've. Lilac. Brad Daugherty. BeDoSh

There are sunsets who whisper a good-by. Sunsets. Carl Sandburg. MoAmPo

There are the Alps. What is there to say about them? On the Fly-Leaf of Pound's Cantos. Basil Bunting. HarvBoo; NAMCP V.1; NoAM

There are the bruises on your arms. Lacrosse. Gary Margolis. MAAN

There are things. Of Being Numerous. George Oppen.

There are things best not set down in books. Road to Patmos, The. John Ennis. PBCIP

There Are Things I Must Realise You Can No Longer Do. Chrissie Gittins. PoCu

There are things tonight I've never known. Hilo: First Night Back. Garrett Kaoru Hongo. LoL

There are things we need words for. No Title. Sam Gardiner. NIrP

There are things which you gave me. Kleptomaniac. Polly Clark. NeBl

There are those to whom place is unimportant. Rose, The. Theodore Roethke. APT-2; TRP

There are those to whom place is unimportant. Theodore Roethke. TRP Fr. North American Sequence.

There are those who can leave love or take it. I Fall in Love Too Easily. Sammy Cahn. ReLy

There are those who think the tandem is the instrument sublime. Shovelin' Coal. Tony Pranses. ArBi

There are thow who grow. Knocker, A. Zbigniew Herbert. PoSu, tr. by Czeslaw Milosz

There are three. Accident in a Naked Place. Kim Hunter. RD

There are three suppositions. the first, it's not amiss to number them: there is no more. I shall not name it. Jacques Roubaud. PFTM-2 Fr. Some Thing Black.

There are times in one's life which one cannot forget. Mr. Billings of Louisville. Eugene Field. NBLV

There are times when we men write. Three Poems on Death. Carlos Bousoño. RaW, tr. by Charles Guenther

There are too many similes for bed. Love Poem. Erin Belieu. TAPaP

There are too many skateboards here, too many. Ding Repair. Peter Gizzi. VaPo

There are too many waterfalls here; the crowded streams. Questions of Travel. Elizabeth Bishop. ColAP; HarvBoo; OxBoAm

There are truths you Americans need to be told. James Russell Lowell. OBSV Fr. Fable for Critics, A.

There are two bears that near us we should allow to dwell. Two Bears, The. Lillian E. Curtis. VerBaPo

There are two bends in the road, and an unexpected dip. Pont y Caniedydd. Alun Llywelyn-Williams. OBWVE, tr. by Joseph R. Clancy

There are two choirs, one poised in space. Songs of the Valley. John Koethe. BAP-01

There are two extremes of love. One Night Stand. Kenward Elmslie. FTOS

There are two kinds of intelligence: one acquired. Two Kinds of Intelligence. Jelaluddin Rumi. TWF, tr. by Coleman Barks

There are two kinds of people, soldiers and women. Postfeminism. Brenda Shaughnessy. AmPoNex; LegDan

There are two men. Two Men. Andrew Lansdown. NOBAu

There are two men in the world, who. Eternal Three, The. Tove Ditlevsen. WoPoe, tr. by Inga Allwood, Martin Allwood and John Hollander

There Are Two Worlds. Larry Levis. BodElec

There are white flowers on the water. (LL) "H. D." APT-1; MoWP; NAAPv.2; NAMCP V.1 Fr. Tribute to the Angels.

There are who say the sonnet's meted maze. John F. M. Dovaston. CenSon

There are who separate the eternal light. One in All, The. Margaret Fuller. SWaP

There are whole blocks in New York. Summer Morning. Louis Simpson. GoPo

There are, whose blood. John Armstrong. STuOW Fr. Art of Preserving Health, The.

There are wolves in the next room waiting. Wolves, The. Allen Tate. APT-2; NAAPv.2; OxBoAm

There are women. Sad Song. Laura Kasischke. PuP-23

There are women locked in my joints. I Walk in the History of My People. Chrystos. UnSA

There Are Words. Gael Turnbull. Oth

There are words that coast alongside thought. Valerio Magrelli. ItPo, tr. by Gayle Ridinger

There are worms in the dark recesses of my gut. Parasites. John Gwyn Griffiths. BBMWP, tr. by Richard Poole

There are worse things than having behaved foolishly in public. Things. Fleur Adcock. IJHIL; StAl

There aren't many. Inventory of Places Propitious for Love. Angel González. VCWP, tr. by Steven Ford Brown and Revuelta Gutierrez

There be none of Beauty's daughters. Stanzas for Music. Lord Byron. NAEL-6v2; NAEL-7v2; NPBRoP

There be the greyhounds! lo'k! an' there's the heäre! Heäre, The. William Barnes. DiBP

There be three things seeking my death. Prayer for the Speedy End of Three Great Misfortunes. Unknown. OBMV, tr. by Frank O'Connor

There be two men of all mankind. Two Men. Edwin Arlington Robinson. AmWit

There Blooms No Bud in May. Walter De la Mare. MoBrPo

There, blossoming once again, like blown. Fourteen Irises for J. L. Gustaf Sobin. WoBe

There blows a colde wynd todaye, todaye. Unknown. SacPr

There breathes no being but has some pretence. Poesy. Oliver Wendell Holmes. TreFP

There, breathless, with his digging nails he clung. Lord Byron. OxAEP-2 Fr. Don Juan.

There broke into my cell last night. Hayim Lenski. FIT, tr. by Robert Friend

There But for the Grace. Wisława Szymborska. TWF, tr. by Magnus J. Krynski and Robert A. Maguire

There by some wrinkled stones round a leafless tree. Twelve, The. Allen Tate. APT-2; ChIV-2

There, by the curb. Oil Slick. Judith Thurman. SSCS

There came a Day at Summer's full. Renunciation. Emily Dickinson. APN-2; MoAmPo; NAAL-3

There came a dove, an Easter dove. My Easter Dove. Henrietta Cordelia Ray. CBWP-3

There came a man across the moor. Master and Guest. Mary Elizabeth Coleridge. ViWPN; VWP

There came a Wind like a Bugle. Emily Dickinson. APN-2; NAAL-3; NAWM-7v2; SAmP

There came gray stretches of volcanic plains. In Death Valley. Edwin Markham. APN-2

There came this bright young thing. As for the Quince. Nuala Ni Dhomhnaill. MoWP; PBCIP, tr. by Paul Muldoon

There cedars dark, the osier, and the pine. Philip Freneau. NAAL-3 Fr. House of Night, The.

There chanced to meet together in an inn. Epigram. John Taylor. NOSC

There Charon stands, who rules the dreary Coast. Virgil. OBVE Fr. Aeneid [or Eneados or Aeneis], The.

There Cintheus sat twynklyng upon his harpe stringis. John Skelton. NPeEn Fr. Garland [or Garlande or Garlands] of Laurel[l], The.

There come to me. Pause. Octavio Paz. STV, tr. by John Frederick Nims

There comes a little space between the south. Depression in Winter. Jane Kenyon. LoL

There comes a moment in her veins. More Lovely than Antiquity. Witter Bynner. NoP-4; NoP-5

There comes a time to rusticate the numbers. The way the birds, jug.   Karen Volkman.   NAPBL

There comes an hour when begging stops.   Emily Dickinson.   NCAP

There comes Emerson first, whose rich words, every one.   James Russell Lowell.   APN-1; NAAPv.1; OxBoAm; TCAPo *Fr.* Fable for Critics, A.

There comes ———, for instance; to see him's rare sport.   James Russell Lowell.   TCAPo *Fr.* Fable for Critics, A.

There comes Philothea, her face all aglow.   James Russell Lowell.   TCAPo *Fr.* Fable for Critics, A.

There comes Poe, with his raven, like Barnaby Rudge.   James Russell Lowell.   APN-1; OxBoAm; TCAPo *Fr.* Fable for Critics, A.

There died a myriad.   Ezra Pound.   AmWaPo; HarvBoo; InoFa; MoAmPo; NPEEn; OxBoAm; PoAgWa; TRP; WaAnP *Fr.* Hugh Selwyn Mauberley (Life and Contacts).

There, done. I watched it once again.   Listener of Bats.   Laure-Anne Bosselaar.   PoDa

There dwelt a farmer in the west.   Treacherous Towser.   Thomas Yalden.   DiBP

There dwelt a farmer in the west.   Thomas Yalden.   DiBP

There existed a person, not a woman or a boy, being in the first part of life.   Semantic Limerick According to Dr. Johnson's Dictionary (Edition of 1765), The.   Gavin Ewart.   OBCoV

There existed an adult male person who had lived a relatively short time.   Semantic Limerick According to the Shorter Oxford English Dictionary (1933), The.   Gavin Ewart.   OBCoV

There Exists.   Jacques Dupin.   YaTCFP, *tr.* by Stephen Romer

There exists something that fits nowhere.   Gunnar Ekelof.   WED *Fr.* Variations.

There exists somewhere, for a reader who is absent but impatiently awaited.   There Exists.   Jacques Dupin.   YaTCFP, *tr.* by Stephen Romer

There, far away.   Marin Georgiev.   CSCBP *Fr.* Memory.

There fared a mother driven forth.   House of Christmas, The.   G. K. Chesterton.   ChrPo; MoBrPo; SacPr

There, figured and pre-figured in the nothing-transfiguring wheel. (LL)   Figured Wheel, The.   Robert Pinsky.   NAMCP V.2; NoAM

There go Adem and Eve—I see.   Poems from Subway to Work.   Peter Orlovsky.   CLPP

There go the grownups.   Lazy Thought, A.   Eve Merriam.   SSCS

There go the storeyed liners.   Navigation.   Ronald Stuart Thomas.   HarvBoo

There God is dwelling too. (LL)   William Blake.   BBASP; ChAP; InvLi; NAEL-6v2; NAEL-7v2; NOBRP; NoP-4; NoP-5; NPBRoP; OxBEV; WaAnP *Fr.* Songs of Innocence.

There goes a queen!   Queen, A.   Bella Akhatovna Akhmadulina.   TCRusP, *tr.* by Daniel Weissbort

There goes my young intended.   He Was Too Good to Me.   Lorenz Hart.   ReLy

There Goes the Bride.   M. Loncar.   AmPoNex

There goes the Wapiti.   Wapiti, The.   Ogden Nash.   TLR

There, good night, darling! now, I fain would sleep. (LL)   Crazed.   Mary E. Tucker.   CBWP-1; RACG

There grew two olives, closest of the grove.   Homer.   OBVE *Fr.* Odyssey.

There grows one in the human brain. (LL)   William Blake.   NAEL-6v2; NAEL-7v2; NOBRP; NPBRoP; OxAEP-2 *Fr.* Songs of Experience.

There had been a cricket in the basement.   Overture.   A. V. Christie.   NAPBL

There had been the logos. A long long time ago.   Draft 55: Quiptych.   Rachel Blau DuPlessis.   BAP-04

There had to be a way of making a building talk.   Memorial.   Yvonne Cullen.   NIrP

There has been a death in the street.   Community.   Sally Roberts Jones.   AngWePo

There has been a light snow.   In a Train.   Robert Bly.   InvLad

There has been / Another death.   To W. C. W. M. D.   Alfred Kreymborg.   PoA 2002

There has been extravagance in speech.   Stitches.   Sinéad Morrissey.   NIrP

There Has Been More Than Beginning and End to Face.   Joan Murray.   YaYoPo

There has not been for a long time a spring.   Slow River.   Czeslaw Milosz.   FaoP, *tr.* by Renata Gorczynski

There have been a thousand raggy, draggy dances.   Baltimore Buzz.   Noble Sissle.   ReLy

There have been plates but no appetite.   Museum, The.   Wisława Szymborska.   PoSu, *tr.* by Magnus F. Krynski

There have never been men crazier than these.   Gregorio Scalise.   ItPo, *tr.* by Gayle Ridinger

There he glowed on me.   Elizabeth Barrett Browning.   NAEL-6v2; NAEL-7v2 *Fr.* Aurora Leigh.

There he goes as usual.   If You Hadn't—But You Did.   Betty Comden and Adolph Green.   ReLy

There he goes / Have you ever seen such perfection?   Meet the Beat of My Heart.   Mack Gordon.   ReLy

There he moved, cropping the grass at the purple canyon's lip.   Horse Thief, The.   William Rose Benét.   MoAmPo

There he stands with his bucket.   Twenty Million Buckets.   Bert Ward.   RSaN

There he stood, quite suddenly.   Gauguin's White Horse.   Vicki Hearne.   GS

There I go again shoving my wheelbarrow.   Ordinary Evening, An.   Noelle Kocot.   LegDan

There! I have lock'd the door.   Real Comfort.   Mary Stanley Bunce Dana.   SWaP

There I was / at the top of the walnut tree.   I Thought Back and.   Ann Stanford.   PoChi

There I was midsummer skating on a lake.   Trendelenburg Position.   M. Wyrebek.   AmPoNex

There I was standing on the shore of a small lake in the Muskokas.   David McFadden.   NLPA

There / In any obscure corner.   I Considered Myself.   Youssri Hassaan.   AnVo, *tr.* by Mohamed Enani

There in her moonlit chamber she is dreaming of him still.   In Her Moonlit Chamber.   Wen T'ing-yün.   CCL1, *tr.* by Glen Baxter

There, in that bed so closely curtained round.   Written in a Sick Chamber.   Samuel Rogers.   NOBRP

There, in that lost.   Salter's Gate.   Anne Stevenson.   PfSP

There, in the corner, staring at his drink.   Docker.   Seamus Heaney.   BrAP; HeIP-4

There in the fragrant pines and the cedars dusk and dim. (LL)   Walt Whitman.   APN-1; CBCWP; ColAP; InoFa; MoAmPo; NAAL-3; NAAL-5; NAAPv.1; NAMCP V.1; NCAP; NIL-7; NoP-4; NoP-5; OxBoAm; PCW; PoPoPo; SAmP; TCAPo; TFi; WaAnP *Fr.* Memories of President Lincoln.

There, in the high part of the land.   There, in the High Part.   Antonio Machado Ruiz.   RaW, *tr.* by Robert Bly

There, in the Promised Land.   Child is Born, A.   Elina Wechsler.   MirDau, *tr.* by Darrell Lockhart

There in the slick streets.   Confession #1.   Ryan Van Cleave.   NevBe

There Is a Balm in Gilead.   *Unknown.*   TCAPo

There is a bareness in the images.   Substance and Shadow.   John Hewitt.   ModIr; PNI

There is a bird in the poplars.   Metric Figure.   William Carlos Williams.   MoAmPo

There is a bird that hangs head-down and cries.   Thirst.   Genevieve Taggard.   APT-2

There is a bitter river.   Bitter River, The.   Langston Hughes.   NAMCP V.1

There Is A Boundary.   Anna Andreyevna Akhmatova.   TCRusP, *tr.* by Daniel Weissbort

There is a boundary in the heart's land.   There Is A Boundary.   Anna Andreyevna Akhmatova.   TCRusP, *tr.* by Daniel Weissbort

There is a boy who sits outside my window.   Audre's Son.   John Alexander Frazier, Jr.   BtF

There is a bright posy on the edge of the quay.   Shining Posy, The.   Anthony Raftery.   IrLP, *tr.* by Eleanor Hull

There is a brook in the mountains.   Mountain Spring, A.   Ch'u Ch'uang I.   CCL1; NDACCP; WaAnP, *tr.* by Kenneth Rexroth

There Is a Caterpillar That Makes a Very Complicated Hammock.   Clark Coolidge.   NYP2

There is a change—and I am poor.   Complaint, A.   William Wordsworth.   NPBRoP

There is a Charm no vulgar mind can reach.   On the Luxembourg Gallery.   Washington Allston.   APN-1

There is a coal-black Angel.   Swamp Angel, The.   Herman Melville.   APN-2

There is a coldness I do not want.   What Is Kept.   Linda Gregg.   BodElec

There is a creator called God.   Dante Gabriel Rossetti.   OBCoV

There Is a Dead Poet Alive.   Yasser Musa.   OWABP

There is a difference it used to make.   Custom.   Carl Phillips.   AmAlph

There is a dish to hold the sea.   John Davidson.   MoBrPo *Fr.* New Year's Eve.

There is a drear and lonely tract of hell.   Supremacy.   Edwin Arlington Robinson.   APN-2; NoAM

There is a drought, the farmers have a hard time finding food.   Following the Rhymes of Shao-pao Huang's Poem on Being Moved while Visiting the Farmers.   Yang Shih-ch'i.   WoPoe, *tr.* by Jonathan Chaves

There is a drunk on Main Avenue, slumped.   Song-Maker.   Anita Endrezze.   HATNAP

There is a duck lost at sea when.   First Bookshelf.   Patty Seyburn.   LegDan

There is a face in the honeysuckle—eyes.   Man in the Honeysuckle, The.   David Campbell.   BMAP

There is a faculty or knack, smallish, in the mind that can turn.   A. R. Ammons.   NoAM *Fr.* Sphere.

There is a faltering crimson by the wall.   Day Before Spring, The.   Lizette Woodworth Reese.   SWaP

There is a flower I wish to wear.   Hearts-Ease.   Walter Savage Landor.   OxBEV

There is a flower that bees prefer.   Purple Clover.   Emily Dickinson.   MoAmPo

There is a flower that blooms out of season. Ensnaring Flower of Psalms. Rossana Ombres. NeIt

There is a flower, the Lesser Celandine. Small Celandine, The. William Wordsworth. NPeEn

There is a fork in a branch. Perch, The. Galway Kinnell. PML; PoDa

There is a fountain filled with blood. William Cowper. SacPr *Fr.* Olney Hymns.

There is a fountain, to whose flowery side. Poetical Happiness. Frederick Tennyson. CenSon

There is a garden in her face. William Cole. AmWit *Fr.* Uncoupled Couplets.

There is a garden where lilies. Eutopia. Francis Turner Palgrave. OBGa

There is a girl dragging heavy. Ritual Girl. Frank Mkalawile Chipasula. HBAPE

There is a girl you like so you tell her. Courtship. Mark Strand. PoPoPo

There is a god in whom I do not believe. God the Eater. Stevie Smith. NAMCP V.1

There is a God that carves to each his own. (LL) Bible, *O.T.* BASC; NoP-4; NoP-5; NPeEn; PEW *Fr.* Psalms.

There is a goddess and I know her. Her hands are not clean. Apotheosis of the Kitchen Goddess 2. Teresa Noelle Roberts. HW; IPoFL

There is a great amount of poetry in unconscious. Critics and Connoisseurs. Marianne Moore. APT-1; BrAP; NAAPv.2; NAMCP V.1; NoAM; OxBoAm

There is a great river this side of Stygia. River of Rivers in Connecticut, The. Wallace Stevens. APT-1; FaBoA; NAMCP V.1

There is a greater charm to me. *Unknown.* VerBaPo

There is a green spell stolen from Birmingham;. Death at Winson Green, A. Francis Webb. BMAP

There is a grey thing that lives in the tree-tops. Stephen Crane. APN-2

There is a hawk that is picking the birds out of our sky. Shiva. Robinson Jeffers. NoAM

There is a heaven, for ever, day by day. Theology. Paul Laurence Dunbar. SacPr

There is a hit list. Intermission from Sunday. Pedro Juan Pietri. PueRic

There Is a House. Lamont B. Steptoe. OxAAAP

There is a hush now while the hills rise up. Fishing in the Keep of Silence. Linda Gregg. BodElec; GoPo

There is a joy, which angels well may prize. Social Worship. Bishop Richard Mant. SacPr

There is a key. Gertrude Stein. MotU; OxBoAm *Fr.* Book Concluding with As A Wife Has a Cow A Love Story, A.

There is a kind of love called maintenance. Atlas. U. A. Fanthorpe. BeAl

There is a knot in the middle of my head. Glimpse, A. John Wieners. FTOS

There Is a Lady Sweet and Kind. Thomas Ford. HeIP-4; NoP-4; NoP-5; NOSC; OBEV

There is a language before. Mute Prophets. Nicholas Samaras. OPRER

There Is a Last, Solitary Coach. David Vogel. HP, *tr. by* A. C. Jacobs

There is a last, solitary coach about to leave. There Is a Last, Solitary Coach. David Vogel. HP, *tr. by* A. C. Jacobs

There is a light seed grain inside. Jelaluddin Rumi. IJHIL, *tr. by* Coleman Barks

There Is a Light That Shrouds the Whole Field. Francisco Brines. RaW, *tr. by* Rachel Benson

There is a little glass boy. "From Your Depths and Kneeling . . ." Teresa Calderón. TANSG, *tr. by* Celeste Kostopulos-Cooperman

There is a little lightning in his eyes. Of Robert Frost. Gwendolyn Brooks. NoAM; VisFro

There is a lobster in the ocean. Pretty Beads. Dick Gallup. AHA

There is a loud noise of Death. To Dear Daniel. Samuel Greenberg. APT-1

There is a love that tumbles like a stream. Philip Jerome Cleveland. SacPr

There is a map of the city which shows the brdige that was never built. Turn Again. Ciaran Carson. BeAl

There is a mathematical illusion that, if performed correctly makes two. Prodigal Son in His Own Words, The: The Bees. Dionisio D. Martinez. NAMCP V.2

There is a melody for which I would surrender. Fantasy. Gérard de Nerval. WoPoe, *tr. by* Geoffrey Wagner

There is a middleaged man, Tim Flanagan. Middleaged Man, The. Louis Simpson. BodElec

There is a modesty in nature. In the small. Precision, The. Linda Gregg. PoDa

There is a mole on Ahmad's cheek that draws all those who. Mole, The. Al-Muntafil. RaBo, *tr. by* Robert Bly

There is a moment blind with light, split by the hum. Icarus in November. Alec Brock Stevenson. FuPo

There is a moment of separation. Before I Was Born. Lewis Warsh. PA9/11

There is a morn by men unseen. Emily Dickinson. NALW

There is a mountain and a wood between us. Separation. Walter Savage Landor. NPeEn

There is a movie called "She's Gotta Have It." Wild is the Wind. Travis Nichols. IIR

There is a music to this sadness. Tonight I Can Almost Hear the Singing. Silvia Curbelo. TouFir

There is a mystic splendour that one feels. There is a Mystic Splendour. Raymond Barrow. OWABP

There is a new family at our reunion. Reunion. Sarah Cortez. TiP2

There is a new instantism > a language of tangent =. Theorist Has No Samba!, The. Edwin Torres. BAP-04

There is a new person in the world today. New Person, A. John Ridland. CalPo

There is a node. There, one day. Prospecting. Margaret Avison. GPPA

There is a pain—so utter. Emily Dickinson. APN-2; NCAP

There is a painting by Lucas Cranach. Official Love Story. Linda Gregg. BodElec

There is a painting of it: an eighteenth-century miniature from the Kangra School of India. Painting. Jane Hirshfield. ExTi

There is a parrot imitating spring. Parsley. Rita Dove. AmAlph; CAP-8; EMP; ESEAA; LoL; NAAL-5; NAMCP V.2; NIL-7; NoAM; NoP-4; NoP-5; PoPoPo; VCAP; WaAnP

There is a path no vulture's eye hath seen. Anne Bradstreet. WPoS *Fr.* Vanity of All Worldly Things, The.

There is a people of dreams driving. Sea Dreams. Rosita Copioli. CItWP, *tr. by* Cinzia Sartini Blum and Lara Trubowitz

There is a place at the center of earth. Crossings. Linda Hogan. BodElec

There is a place between an owl. Owl Village. Alice Oswald. MoWP

There Is a Place in Distant Seas. Richard, Archbishop Whately. NOBAu

There is a place that some men know. Cross, The. Allen Tate. ChIV-2; MoAmPo

There is a place where Contrarities are equally True. William Blake. NOBRP *Fr.* Milton.

There is a pleasure in the pathless woods. Lord Byron. OxAEP-2 *Fr.* Childe Harold's Pilgrimage.

There is a precise instant in time. Midway. Robert Desnos. PFTM-1

There is a question. Elegy. Max Winter. NeAmPo

There is a quiet spirit in these woods. Spirit of Poetry, The. Henry Wadsworth Longfellow. APN-1

There is a reason why the compass needle. Abilene, TX: We Pull Out For New England. Robert A. Fink. TiP2

There is a record. Prayer for Continuation. Susan Griffin. AtGh

There / is a revolution. Roots. Mawiyah Kai el-Jamah Bomani. BtF

There is a road through the canyon. Mark Strand. CAP-8; NAMCP V.2 *Fr.* Dark Harbor.

There is a scream that binds my heart to. Tears. Saniyya Saleh. CFP, *tr. by* Kamal Boullata

There is a scud of cloud. Gun Emplacement: Sundown. Jeremy Ingalls. YaYoPo

There is a secret room. John Montague. ModIr; PNI *Fr.* Great Cloak, The.

There is a section in my library for death. Tomes. Billy Collins. KGB

There is a shapeliness in grief. Persephone's Notes. Caroline Finkelstein. PfS

There is a ship that sails the sea. When My Ship Comes In. Gustave Kahn. ReLy

There is a sighing in the wood. Silent, The. Jones Very. NCAP

There is a silence of deep gathered eve. Onycha. Michael Field. ViWPN

There is a silence where hath been no sound. Silence. Thomas Hood. GSo; OBEV; OxBSo

There is a silent beat in between the drums. Bob Kaufman. WhBo

There is a singer everyone has heard. Oven Bird, The. Robert Frost. APT-1; GSo; HeIP-4; ItP; NAAL-5; NAAPv.2; NAMCP V.1; NoAM; NoP-4; NoP-5; OWoS; OxBoAm; TCAPo; WaAnP

There is a small wrought-iron balcony. Desire. David St. John. FaoP

There is a Smile of Love. Smile, The. William Blake. PtR

There is a solitude in seeing you. Lightning. Witter Bynner. APT-1

There is a song, there is a moaning in the song. Baby at the Bottom of the River. W. S. Rendra. WoPoe, *tr. by* Harry Aveling

There is a source of intention in joy. Sadness of Water, The. Paul Claudel. YaTCFP, *tr. by* James Lawler

There is a spell, for instance. "H. D." APT-1; NAMCP V.1 *Fr.* Walls Do Not Fall, The.

There is a sphere, a secret sphere. Inner Realm, The. Priscilla Jane Thompson. CBWP-2

There is a stone in the air. Peru Eye, the Heart of the Lamp. Clark Coolidge. APSN

There is a strange, solemn, silent, graceless. David Ferry. FaBoA

There is a stream, I name not its name. Arthur Hugh Clough. FaBoVe *Fr.* Bothie of Tober-na-Vuolich, The [A Long-Vacation Pastoral].

There is a street in Cairo, full of sin and shame. Shari Wag El Burka. *Unknown.* FaBoWar

There is a strong wall about me to protect me. Love Song. Mary Carolyn Davies. LW

There is a Supreme God in the ethnological section. Homage to the British Museum. William Empson. MoBrPo; NPeEn; OxBEV

There is a sway that comes soon after. To a Stranger (At the End of a Caboose). Laura Jensen. GM

There is a table in the back where she opens. Waitress. Jason Shinder. ReTh

There is a tale. Simonides. SaLy, *tr.* by Diane Rayor

There is a tall grey cliff before mine eyes. R. W. Emerson. Rose Terry Cooke. NAAPv.1

There is a tall long-sided dame. Samuel Butler. OBSV *Fr.* Hudibras.

There is a temper of atmosphere which prevents rain. Dennis Phillips. FTOS *Fr.* Twenty Questions.

There is a thing which in the light. Candle, A. Sir John Suckling. BASC

There is a Thorn—it looks so old. Thorn, The. William Wordsworth. NAEL-7v2; NPBRoP

There is a tide in the affairs of men. William Shakespeare. ITBLP *Fr.* Julius Caesar.

There is a timbre of voice. Echoes. Audre Lorde. NoP-4; NoP-5

There is a train. Loco. Jane Holland. MFPA

There is a train inside this iris. Iris. David St. John. AmAlph; MakPoe

There is a train, no, there are train. Still Life. Robin Behn. AmAlph

There is a tranquil star. Federico García Lorca. PFTM-1 *Fr.* Night (Suite for Piano and Poet's Voice).

There is a tree by day. Tenebris. Angelina Weld Grimké. APT-1; NAAPv.2; OxAAAP; OxBoAm

There is a tree native in Turkestan. Note on Local Flora. William Empson. OxAEP-2; OxBEV

There is a tribe of invisible men. Invisible Men, The. Nakasuk. RaBo, *tr.* by Edward Field

There is a truce . . . O lovers, tell. Truce, The. Stella Gibbons. LW

There is a vale which none hath seen. Rumors from an Aeolian Harp. Henry David Thoreau. APN-1

There is a very life in our despair. Lord Byron. NOBRP *Fr.* Childe Harold's Pilgrimage.

There is a voice inside the body. Man Lost by a River, A. Michael C. Blumenthal. RaBo

There is a Void, outside of Existence, which if entered into. Jerusalem. William Blake.

There is a votive X tattered like a chewed card. Gypsy Summer. Noelle Kocot. LegDan

There is a war in the distance. Waves in August. M. S. Merwin. OxBoAm

There is a way to sew wings on arms. Ekaterina Vlasova. CRWP, *tr.* by Peter France

There is a white cliff, sea-worn, temple-scarred. Sappho's Leap. Howard Baker. APT-2

There is a whole world involved in me. Martyn Crucefix. NewEx

There is a willow grows aslant a brook. William Shakespeare. OxAEP-1 *Fr.* Hamlet.

There is a wolf in me...fangs pointed for tearing gashes. Wilderness. Carl Sandburg. RaBo

There is a word that never. Etel Adnan. PoArWo *Fr.* Indian Never Had a Horse, The.

There is a yearning in me to touch your face. Imani's Song. Alison Morris. BtF

There is a Zone whose even Years. Emily Dickinson. APN-2; NCAP

There is always a sound. Linda Zisquit. DTA *Fr.* Unopened Letters.

There is always the other one. Judy Travaillo Variations, The. Michael Anania. IllVoic

There is an ancient silence changed into a statue. Theory of Silences. Gabriel Celaya. RaW, *tr.* by Robert Mezey

There is an ancient story. My Father's Story. Priscilla Jane Thompson. CBWP-2

There IS an animal syntax, thin blue skrim over. Note to Skip on Max and Maxine, A. Bill Lavender. AnSo

There is an awful quiet in the air. Prayer. Hartley Coleridge. GSo

There is an egg in the middle of things. Man Who Loved White Chocolate, The. Robert Kelly. PFTM-2

There is an embalmer who operates. Embalmer. Rossana Ombres. NeIt

There Is an Error at the Heart of Desire. Chard DeNiord. PfSP

There is an evening coming in. Going. Philip Larkin. WoPoe

There is an excuse for expecting success there is an excuse. Gertrude Stein. OxBoAm *Fr.* Book Concluding with As A Wife Has a Cow a Love Story, A.

There is an I in space, I am, space. Another Day on the Pilgrimage. Peter Gizzi. VaPo

There is an inn, a merry old inn. Man in the Moon Stayed up To Late, The. John Ronald Reuel Tolkien. OBSP

There is another heaven and earth beyond the world of men. (LL) Conversations in the Mountains. Li Po. RaBo; TAL, *tr.* by Robert Payne

There is another Loneliness. Emily Dickinson. APN-2

There is another word above this one; or outside of this one. Gary Snyder. BB

There is another world above this one; or outside of this one. Gary Snyder. PoA 2002 *Fr.* Through the Smoke Hole.

There is, at times, an evening sky. Vincent Ogé. George Boyer Vashon. APN-2

There is but one, and that one ever. (LL) Easter ("Rise heart; thy Lord is risen. Sing his praise.") George Herbert. NAEL-6v1; NOSC

There is but one, and that one ever. (LL) Easter ("I got me flowers to straw [*or* strew *or* strow] Thy [*or* the] way.") George Herbert. OBEV; OxBEV

There Is But One True Friend. John Fitzgerald. BBMWP, *tr.* by Joseph P. Clancy

There is castle by the Eastern Sea. Song of the Comet. Yungch'ŏn, Master. CATKP, *tr.* by Peter H. Lee

There is Celilo. She-Who-Watches . . . The Names are Prayer. Elizabeth Woody. OPRER

There is darkness in the house tonight, and the moon. Cute Petite. Barry MacSweeney. VaPo

There is death enough in Europe without these. Dead Ponies. Brenda Chamberlain. OBWVE

There is delight in singing, though none hear. To Robert Browning. Walter Savage Landor. NoP-4; NoP-5

There is downpour, always. Diesel to Yesterday. John Tripp. AngWePo

There is everything in his eyes. Dog, The. Susan Fromberg Schaeffer. PoCoUp

There is fern and frost, a gethering of small birds melting song in the underbrush. Daphne Marlatt. BrAP; NLPA *Fr.* Touch to My Tongue.

There is freedom too, a peculiar kind. Meanwhile, in Rwanda. Patricia Smith. SpirFl

There is from the legs in sleep an exhalation of the light, along the tops of the thighs. Kenneth Irby. PFTM-2 *Fr.* Three Sets of Three.

There is Hawthorne, with genius so shrinking and rare. James Russell Lowell. TCAPo *Fr.* Fable for Critics, A.

There is hope for man. Ballad of a Little Lamp. René Depestre. YaTCFP, *tr.* by Joan Dayan

There is illness left in my body still. Sound of the Taffy-Seller's Shears. Pak Chaesam. CAMKP, *tr.* by David R. McCann and Jiwon Shin

There is in his daughter's gaze. Portrait. David St. John. PoDa

There is in life no blessing like affection. Bonds of Affection. Letitia Elizabeth Landon. TreFP

There is in the idea of christ. I Spit on the Innate Christ. Antonin Artaud. ConPit, *tr.* by Clayton Eshleman

There is, it seems, no poppy seed so old. Poppy Heads. Neil Curry. NLP

There is joy. Welcome Morning. Anne Sexton. GoPo

There is Law for Fire. Seasons of Fire, The. Billy Marshall-Stoneking. NOBAu

There Is Life. Breyten Breytenbach. VCWP, *tr.* by Breyten Breytenbach

There is little inspiration. Tempest. Sekeena Shaben. PoArWo

There is love to begin with, early love. Themes for women. Elizabeth Bartlett. StAl

There is Lowell, who's striving Parnassus to climb. James Russell Lowell. NAAPv.1; TCAPo *Fr.* Fable for Critics, A.

There is many a country. Love. Bekes Jr. IrPoTo, *tr.* by Muhamad Tawfiq Ali

There is moonrise under your fingernail—. Guiffre's Nightmusic. Thomas McGrath. SeSe

There is more than glass between the snow and the huge roses. (LL) Snow. Louis MacNeice. HarvBoo; ModIr; NAMCP V.1; NoAM; NPeEn; OPOU; OxAEP-2; OxBEV; PNI; StAl

There is, mother, a place in the world called Paris. Good Sense. César Vallejo. PoetW, *tr.* by Clayton Eshleman

There is motherhood. Leaning into the Tilt. Virginia McGuire. FiBr

There Is Music Going Down the Stairs. Ali Mansour. AnVo, *tr.* by Mohamed Enani

There is my country under glass. At the Tourist Centre in Boston. Margaret Atwood. BrAP

There is naught for thee by thy haste to gain. Created, The. Jones Very. APN-1; InvLi

There is neither beginning nor end to the imagination. William Carlos Williams. CLPP *Fr.* Kora in Hell.

There is no. John Cage. WhBo

There is no beauty. World I See, The. Mari E. Evans. OxAAAP

There is no beauty in New England like the boats. Product. George Oppen. HarvBoo

There is no better way to know us. Modest Proposal, A. Ted Hughes. CABP

There is no bidding me farewell. None. Duo Duo. PoetW, *tr.* by Maghiel van Crevel

There is no breeze, sounds travel far in the dead air.   Summer.   Vern Rutsala.   MotU

There is no caring less.   Fix.   Alice Fulton.   PoDa

There is no chapel on the day.   Oscar Wilde.   NoAM *Fr.* Ballad of Reading Gaol, The.

There is no city as old as a river.   Thoughts on Johannesburg's Centenary.   Lionel Abrahams.   TSAP

There is no debauchery worse than thought.   Contribution on Pornography, A.   Wisława Szymborska.   PoSu, *tr.* by Adam Czerniawski

There is no eighty-eighth storey.   Shape of Things, The.   Lavinia Greenlaw.   MFPA

There is no faith; the mountain stands within.   Faith.   Jones Very.   SacPr

There is no fence.   Sojin Takei.   NAAPv.2

There is no fire of the crackling boughs.   Glenaradale.   Walter Chalmers Smith.   OBEV

There Is No Forgetting (Sonata).   Pablo Neruda.   ConPit, *tr.* by Clayton Eshleman

There is No Frigate Like a Book.   Emily Dickinson.   APN-2; BRP; MoAmPo; OxBoAm; PtR; SAmP; SoSe-8

There is no future in virtue. A woman.   According to Ovid.   Bin Ramke.   PoA 2002

"There is no God," the foolish saith.   Elizabeth Barrett Browning.   SacPr *Fr.* Cry of the Human, The.

There is no God, the wicked saith.   Arthur Hugh Clough.   BrAP; CABP; NoP-4; NPeEn; OxBEV; SacPr; WaAnP *Fr.* Dipsychus [and the Spirit].

There is no grammar for the language of the dead.   Language of the Dead, The.   Thomas McGrath.   BodElec

There is no great and no small.   History.   Ralph Waldo Emerson.   APN-1

There is no greater crime than leaving.   Bertolt Brecht.   StAl, *tr.* by Frank Jones

There is no happiness on earth!   Dialogue No. 5.   Dmitry Aleksandrovich Prigov.   ItGoST, *tr.* by Robert Reid

There is no happy life.   Love's Matrimony.   William Cavendish, Duke of Newcastle.   NOSC

There is no hope.   Idea Vilariño.   CFP; TANSG, *tr.* by Louise B. Popkin

There is no house.   White Hotel.   Carol Potter.   PfS

There is no kindness in me here. I ache to be kind, but the weather.   February.   Sinéad Morrissey.   NIrP

There Is No Land Yet.   Laura Riding Jackson.   ChIV-1

There is no language but "reconstructed" imaged parentheses back into.   Statistics.   Barrett Watten.   PmAP

There is no language for the present time.   Sulking in the Seventies.   Kris Hemensley.   BMAP

There is no Life or Death.   Mina Loy.   OxBoAm

There is no limit to the number of times.   From Father to Son.   Emyr Humphreys.   AngWePo; OBWVE; TCAWP

There is no lord within my heart.   Shrine, The.   Sara Teasdale.   APT-1

There is no magic when we meet.   After Love.   Sara Teasdale.   APT-1

There is no mirror in Mirissa.   House on a Red Cliff.   Michael Ondaatje.   NoP-5

There is no mistaking it.   Accident, The.   Tatamkulu Afrika.   TSAP

There is no more silence on the plains of the moon.   Night After Bushfire.   Judith Wright.   BMAP

There is no music now in all Arkansas.   Variations for Two Pianos.   Donald Justice.   EmeKit

There Is No Natural Religion.   William Blake.   NAEL-6v2; NAEL-7v2

There is no need for me to keep a skull on my desk.   Memento Mori.   Billy Collins.   EmeKit

There is no need for Pain Lord.   Breyten Prays for Himself.   Breyten Breytenbach.   PoetW; VCWP, *tr.* by Denis Hirson

There is no need to personify the wound.   Poem for Central America.   Hilary Booth.   SurWo

There is no needle without piercing point.   Death.   *Unknown.*   RaBo

"There is no one . . . ."   Edith Södergran.   WPoS, *tr.* by Stina Katchadourian

There is no one among men that has not a special failing.   Madly Singing in the Mountains.   Po Chü-i.   BLT; WoPoe, *tr.* by Arthur Waley

There is no one here.   Matisse: "The Red Studio."   W. D. Snodgrass.   GS

There is no one in the abandoned encampment to inform us of the beloved ones, so from whom will we seek information about their condition?   Abū Āmir Ahmad Ibn Shuhayd.   HiArP, *tr.* by James T. Monroe

There is no one in this world who has time.   "There is no one . . . ."   Edith Södergran.   WPoS, *tr.* by Stina Katchadourian

There Is No Opera like "Lohengrin."   John Wheelwright.   OxBoAm

There is no other girl, bridegroom, like this.   Sappho.   SaLy, *tr.* by Diane Rayor

There is no other life. (LL)   Why Log Truck Drivers Rise Earlier Than Students of Zen.   Gary Snyder.   GeoHom; LoL

There is no outside.   Moving Object.   Jean Day.   FTOS

There is no perfect.   Exits from Elmina Castle: Cape Coast, Ghana.   Toi Derricotte.   BtF

There is no pigment in blue feathers.   Bluebird in Cutleaf Beech.   Wendy Wilder Larsen.   KGB

There is no place in this dark.   Radiant Silhouette II.   John Yau.   OpBo

There is no point in work.   Work.   D. H. Lawrence.   OBMV

There is no Raynard fox. Just foxes.   Gods, The.   Les A. Murray.   WoPoe

There is no real edge to anything.   Jody Aliesan.   FiBr

There Is No Real Peace in the World.   Douglas Crase.   BodElec; OxBoAm

There is no reason for amazement: surely one always knew that cultures decay, and life's end is death. (LL)   Purse-Seine, The.   Robinson Jeffers.   AmFaPo; NAAPv.2; NAMCP V.1; NoAM; NoP-4; NoP-5; WeW-3

There is no rest beside this stream, no love.   Peach Blossom Stream.   Chou Pang-yen.   CrYelRi, *tr.* by Sam Hamill

There is no ripple on the world.   Paul S. Piper.   AmZen

There is no road here—not even a path.   Lake Baskunchak.   Andrey Alekseievich Amalrik.   TCRusP, *tr.* by John Glad

There is no science of separation.   Tristia.   Ger Killeen.   AmPoNex

There is no sense that I should write a line.   To Cynthia.   Sir Francis Kynaston.   NOSC

There is no silence but when danger comes. (LL)   Becoming a Redwood.   Dana Gioia.   GeoHom; PfSP

There is no sky today. Echoes of birds.   Counterparts.   Stephen Dobyns.   PoA 2002

There is no stray bullet, sirs.   For Mohammed Zeid, Age 15.   Naomi Shihab Nye.   P180

There is no such thing.   On the Death of Philip Whalen.   Mark S. Kuhar.   AmZen

There is no such thing as a dada lecture.   Tristan Tzara.   Edward Hirsch.   BodElec

There is no there there anywhere.   Localism or t/here.   Juliana Spahr.   LegDan

There is no umbrella.   To Carlos Drummond de Andrade.   João Cabral de Melo Neto.   TCLAP, *tr.* by Guy Pacitti

There is no vehicle out. (LL)   Ordinance on Arrival.   Naomi Lazard.   BLT; P180

There is no way I can crank a dial.   Lexicon of Exile.   Aleida Rodríguez.   CalPo

There is no way to show it.   Threads.   Russell Leong.   WhBo

There is no wherefore, there is a command of song.   Eduardo Milán.   RMCMP, *tr.* by Roberto Tejada

There is no wolf, of course.   Where the Wolf Sings.   Mary Low.   SurWo

There is no word for goodbye. (LL)   There Is No Word for Goodbye.   Mary Tallmountain.   HATNAP; LoL

There Is No Word for Goodbye.   Mary Tallmountain.   HATNAP; LoL

There Is No Word for Sex in Taglog.   Noel Mateo.   ReBoTo

There is none. And this means today.   Consolation.   David Rivard.   SwNoth

There is none, no none but I.   Sir Robert Aytoun.   NOSC

There is Not and There Will Never Be So Much.   Gabriella Leto.   CItWP, *tr.* by Cinzia Sartini Blum and Lara Trubowitz

There is not in the wide world a valley so sweet.   Meeting of the Waters, The.   Thomas Moore.   ItP

There is not much that I can do.   At the Railway Station, Upway.   Thomas Hardy.   PtR

There Is Nothin' like a Dame.   Oscar Hammerstein, II.   ReLy

There is nothing but water in the holy pools.   How Much Is Not True.   Kabir.   RaBo, *tr.* by Robert Bly

There is nothing for you to say. You must.   Learning a Dead Language.   W. S. Merwin.   TAPaP

There is nothing here. (LL)   At the Well.   Paul Blackburn.   APSN; PFTM-2

There is Nothing in Vain.   Eliza Cook.   Thought, A.   STuOW

There is nothing left of the beat.   Cassation on a Theme by Jacques Dupin.   Harry Mathews.   NYP2

There is nothing more to say. (LL)   House on the Hill, The.   Edwin Arlington Robinson.   APN-2; CtM; MakPoe; MoAmPo; NAAPv.1; NCAP; OxBoAm

There is nothing there at the top of the valley.   To See if Something Comes Next.   Jack Gilbert.   BodElec

There is nothing to remember but flight. The owl's eyes spoke.   Thermal Signatures.   Sam Witt.   IAoNAP

There is one grief worse than any other.   Daughter.   Ellen Bryant Voigt.   StAl

There is one season of the year.   Indian Summer.   Olga Fiodorovna Berggolts.   TCRusP, *tr.* by Daniel Weissbort

There is one sin: to call a green leaf grey.   Ecclesiastes.   G. K. Chesterton.   ChIV-1; MoBrPo

There is one story and one story only.   To Juan at the Winter Solstice.   Robert Graves.   HarvBoo; MoBrPo; NAEL-6v2; NAEL-7v2; NAMCP V.1; NoAM; NoP-4; NoP-5; NPeEn; RaBo; WaAnP

There is only one.   Culture.   Alfred Kreymborg.   APT-1

There Is Only One Almighty. Mariella Bettarini. CItWP, *tr. by* Cinzia Sartini Blum and Lara Trubowitz

There is our herd of cars stopped. Bison Crossing Near Mt. Rushmore. May Swenson. GoPo

There is pain in my heart. Neidhart von Reuental. GePo

There Is Power in a Union. Joe Hill. HHAm

There is revenge—writing. To Everyone. Velemir Khlebnikov. TCRusP, *tr. by* Kathy Lewis and Bob Perelman

There is room in the world for more pleasure. Live and Let Live. Eliza Cook. STuOW

There is sand where the tracks were. Tearing Up the Tracks. Christopher Bursk. GM

There is smoke above the hawks in the hall of the king. *Unknown.* FaBoWar *Fr.* Treachery of Asmund, The.

There is so little that is close and warm. Debris of Life and Mind. Wallace Stevens. SAmP

There is so much violence yet to be done. And They Were Both Right. Kapka Kassabova. StAl

There is some goggling and conversation coming from the box. Outrigger. Charles Bernstein. PFTM-2

There is something about dropping a line into the unseen. Old Women Fishing from Bridges. Darrell Bourque. Vesp

There is something / about sugarcane. Sugar Cane. Grace Nichols. BeAl

There is something after all of pleasure. At the Window. "Rachel." FIT, *tr. by* Robert Friend

There is something dense, united, settled in the depths. Unity. Pablo Neruda. ConPit, *tr. by* Clayton Eshleman

There is something down there and you want it told. (LL) Dark Pines under Water. Gwendolyn MacEwen. BeAl; BrAP

There is something I want. 25th Anniversary. Linda Pastan. FaoP

There is something in the autumn that is native to my blood. Vagabond Song, A. Bliss Carman. BRP; IFF; TCAPo

There is something out in the dark that wants to correct us. Against Certainty. Jane Hirshfield. WANABP

There is something which I dread. Fear of Madness, The. Lucretia Davidson. TCAPo

There is subtle sad aggression. Performance Test. Prageeta Sharma. HeMarv

There is sun in the mirror, my head in the trees. Riverbed, The. Vona Groarke. MFPA; NIrP

There is that in me—I do not know what it is—but I know it is in me. Walt Whitman. CAGL; ColAP; ItP *Fr.* Song of Myself.

There Is the Body Lying in State. Joshua Clover. AmPoNex

There is the death of the car, which was quiet and signifies little, ticking gently in a field of snow. Car Has Fallen from a Bridge, A. Kevin Prufer. LegDan

There Is the Fire. Valentine Penrose. SurWo, *tr. by* Roy Edwards

There is the fire it burns and I am the water í drown. There Is the Fire. Valentine Penrose. SurWo, *tr. by* Roy Edwards

There is the loneliness of peopled places. Solitude. Babette Deutsch. LW

There is the mourning dish of salt outside. One Thousand Days, The. Lucie Brock-Broido. AWPTFC

There is the old pond! Basho. NIL-7, *tr. by* John Thomas Bryan

There is the one who turns. Chiapas. Gary Soto. NoAM

There is the persistence of song. (LL) Persistence of Song, The. Howard Moss. GoPo; NoP-4; NoP-5

There is the trap that catches noblest spirits, that caught—they say—God, when he walked on earth. (LL) Shine, Perishing Republic. Robinson Jeffers. APT-1; CalPo; ColAP; HarvBoo; NAAL-5; NAMCP V.1; NoAM; NoP-4; NoP-5; OxBoAm; PoPoPo; TFi; WaAnP

There is the voice of confinement in the pine cone. There. Ray Gonzalez. TouFir

There is the western gate, Luke Havergal— / Luke Havergal. (LL) Luke Havergal. Edwin Arlington Robinson. APN-2; MoAmPo; NAAL-5; NAAPv.1; NAMCP V.1; NoAM; OxBoAm; TCAPo; TFi

There is the woman. Radio. Cornelius Eady. ESEAA

There is the world, we say, and mean a kind. Way, The. William Bronk. BeAl; StAl

There is this desire to resurrect. We Never Should Have Stopped at Pussy Island. Matthew Rohrer. LegDan

There is this edge where shadows. Call It Fear. Joy Harjo. ICANM; NAAL-5

There is, / to rid of us morning. Whitman Again. John Judson. ViWalt

There is too much pain. Lines Scribbled on an Envelope. Madeleine L'Engle. SacPr

There is war. (LL) Poem for the Young White Man Who Asked Me How I, An Intelligent, Well-Read Person Could Believe in the War Between Races. Lorna Dee Cervantes. FTtHH; PBCAP; PoPoPo

(But in this country / there is war.) (LL) LTA; UnSA

There is wind where the rose was. Autumn. Walter De la Mare. NPeEn

There isn't any death. There Isn't Any Death. Perry Brass. CAGL

There it all was: the gaslamp, drugstore. Viktor Aleksandrovich Sosnora. ItGoST, *tr. by* Maia Tekses

There It Is. Jayne Cortez. BRtP

There it was, word for word. Poem That Took the Place of a Mountain, The. Wallace Stevens. NAMCP V.1; TWF

There Lackethe Somethynge Stylle. Thomas Chatterton. OxAEP-1 *Fr.* Aella; a Tragycal Enterlude.

There lasts a wind which I remember, burning. Street in Agrigento. Salvatore Quasimodo. WoPoe, *tr.* by Denis Devlin

There Lena rested but a breathing spell. Albery Allson Whitman. NAAPv.1 *Fr.* Octoroon, The.

There lie the black mountains. *Unknown.* APN-2 *Fr.* Mountain Chant, The.

There lies a somnolent lake. In the Past. Trumbull Stickney. ColAP

There lies afar behind a western hill. Town without a Market, The. James Elroy Flecker. MoBrPo

There liv'd a wife in Whistle Cockpen. Will Ye Na Can Ye Na Let Me Be. *Unknown.* FaBoVe

There liv'd, as Authors tell, in Days of Yore. Geoffrey Chaucer. OBVE *Fr.* Canterbury Tales, The.

There Lived a King. William Schwenck Gilbert. OBCoV *Fr.* Gondoliers, The.

There lived a king in Thule. King in Thule, The. Johann Wolfgang von Goethe. STV, *tr. by* John Frederick Nims

There lived a wife at Usher's Well. Wife of Usher's Well, The. *Unknown.* MakPoe; NAEL-6v1; NAEL-7v1; NePenScot; NoP-4; NoP-5; NPeEn; OBEV; OxAEP-1; TFi

There lived four sisters in a tower by the sea. Song for a Sea Tower. Helen Adam. EdScPo

There lived in Gothic days, as legends tell. Edwin, The Minstrel. James Beattie. OxAEP-1

There lived in Munich a poor, weakly youth. Sprig of Moss, The. William McGonagall.

There may be some places the sun. Into the Light. Pattiann Rogers. PoCoUp

There may be streets that have their sorrow. Broadway Melody. Arthur Freed. ReLy

There may be trouble ahead. Let's Face the Music and Dance. Irving Berlin. ReLy

There may have been a boy. Last Train, The. Linda Pastan. GM

There might be found the flowing grace. My Welsh Home. John Morgan. AngWePo

There must be a place where the whole of it all comes right. Hoping It Might Be So. Kit Wright. StAl

There must be a schoolgirl deep inside there, stuttering. High Altitude Photo of Hiroshima (Circa 1944). Kent Johnson. AtGh

There must be at least one pome to a pear tree in all. Roy Kiyooka. NLPA *Fr.* Pear Tree Pomes.

There must be forgiveness. Suicides and Fools. S. P. Shephard. BtF

There must be one thing that makes you shiver. Death of Isadora Duncan, The. Dionisio D. Martinez. TouFir

There Must Be Somethin' Better Than Love. Dorothy Fields. ReLy

There must have been a moment after the expulsion. Long Story. Stephen Dobyns. CAP-8

There, my lad, lie the Articles. Scene from a Play, Acted at Oxford, Called "Matriculation." Thomas Moore. OBSV

There never was. Song. Carl Rakosi. BodElec

There never yet was honest man. Loving and Beloved. Sir John Suckling. CavPo; NAEL-6v1; NAEL-7v1

There never yet was woman made. Woman's Constancy. Sir John Suckling. CavPo

There now he lives in everlasting joy. Edmund Spenser. CAGL *Fr.* Faerie Queene, The.

There now, where the first crumb. Solitude. Charles Simic. CAP-8

There often wanders one, whom better days. William Cowper. NAEL-6v1; NAEL-7v1; NPBRoP *Fr.* Task, The.

There on Sirius. Federico García Lorca. PFTM-1 *Fr.* Night (Suite for Piano and Poet's Voice).

There on the horizon. African Poem. Agostinho Neto. PoetW, *tr. by* W. S. Merwin

There on the sun-hot stone. Lizard, The. Lydia Pender. NOxBChV

There once the walls. Tale, A. Edward Thomas. OxBEV

There once was a bard of Hong Kong. Limerick. Gerard Benson. OBCoV

There once was a bull named the Duke of Buccleuch. Duke Of Buccleuch, The. J. A. Phelp. NOBAu

There once was a girl from St. Paul. Limerick. *Unknown.* NIP-4

There once was a girl named Jenny. Saga of Jenny, The. Ira Gershwin. ReLy

There once was a leaf with all its lines. There Once Was a Leaf. Robert Desnos. MFP, *tr. by* Martin Sorrell

There Once Was a Man. Richard Adler and Jerry Ross. ReLy

There once was a man who said, "God."   Idealism.   Ronald Arbuthnott Knox.   NBLV; OxBEV

There once was a Marquis de Sade.   De Sade.   John Fuller.   NBLV

There Once Was a Puffin.   Florence Page Jaques.   NTCP

There Once Was a Spinster of Ealing.   *Unknown.*   NIP-4

There once was a witch of Willowby Wood.   Rowena Bastin Bennett.   ChAP   *Fr.* Witch of Willowby Wood, The.

There once were some people called Sioux.   American Indian, The.   *Unknown.*   NBLV

There plenty of reason for making an exchange. (LL)   Gertrude Stein.   MoWP; TCAPo *Fr.* Tender Buttons.

There reigns a prince, whose hand the sceptre claims.   Joel Barlow.   TCAPo   *Fr.* Vision of Columbus, The.

There rests a shade above yon town.   Factory, The.   Letitia Elizabeth Landon.   NPBRoP

There rolls the deep where grew the tree.   Alfred Tennyson.   NAEL-6v2; NAEL-7v2; WaAnP *Fr.* In Memoriam A. H. H.

There runs a road by Merrow Down.   Rudyard Kipling.   NOxBChV *Fr.* Just-So Stories.

There s a dance or two.   Mehitabel's Song.   Don Marquis.   GoPo

There sandy seems the golden sky.   Cliff Dwelling, A.   Robert Frost.   APT-1

There sat down, once, a thing on Henry's heart.   John Berryman.   BrAP; CAP-8; HarvBoo; NAAL-5; NAMCP V.2; NoP-4; NoP-5; OxBoAm; VCAP *Fr.* Dream Songs.

There sate the Seniors of the Trojan Race.   Homer.   OBVE *Fr.* Iliad, The.

There seems no reason he should've died. His hands.   Dead Christ.   Andrew Hudgins.   RA; UpMys

There shall always be the Church and the World.   T. S. Eliot.   SacPr

There shall be no more land, say fish. (LL)   Heaven.   Rupert Brooke.   MoBrPo; NPeEn; OxBEV

There she is! There she is!   Ain't She Sweet?   Jack Yellen.   ReLy

There she looms on the golden path.   Returning.   Victor Vroomkoning.   TuT, *tr. by* Ruth Hooley

There! She says and.   Game Trail, The.   Mark Todd.   GeoH

There she sits, cross-legged.   Night Ride On 21.   Mustafa Ziyalan.   PML, *tr. by the author*

There she took her lover to sea.   Long Nook.   John Wieners.   FTOS

There she was, for centuries, the big.   Muse, The.   Eleanor Wilner.   GifTon

There sinks the nebulous star we call the Sun.   Alfred Tennyson. *Fr.* Princess, The.

There still would seem to be a way. (LL)   Unforgiven, The.   Edwin Arlington Robinson.   APT-1; ItP

There sunk the greatest, nor the worst of men.   Lord Byron.   NAEL-6v2; NAEL-7v2 *Fr.* Childe Harold's Pilgrimage.

There the ash-tree leaves do vall.   Leaves a-Vallen.   William Barnes.   NPeEn

There the black river, boundary to hell.   Southern Road, The.   Dudley Randall.   GM

There the blue-green gums are a fringe of remote disorder.   Envoi.   James McAuley.   BMAP

There the deer stands with morning on the hilltop.   Crystal Moment.   Edward Weismiller.   YaYoPo

There the folk museum alone lies in its embers.   Anna Gorenko.   CRWP, *tr. by* Peter France

There the true Silence is, self-conscious and alone. (LL)   Silence.   Thomas Hood.   GSo; OBEV; OxBSo

There the voluptuous nightingales.   Percy Bysshe Shelley.   OWoS *Fr.* Prometheus Unbound.

There, / the whisper.   Celan.   James Brasfield.   PoDa

There there. No place like home. (LL)   Lonely Tylenol.   Peter Gizzi.   ReTh; VaPo

There, there where those black spruces crowd.   Ragged Island.   Edna St. Vincent Millay.   ColAP; NoP-4; NoP-5; WaAnP

There they are.   Blackstone Rangers, The.   Gwendolyn Brooks.   ESEAA; NAMCP V.2; NoAM

There they are again. It's after dark.   Black Riviera, The.   Mark Jarman.   GeoHom

There they are / drooping over the breakfast plates.   Anne Sexton.   OxBoAm *Fr.* Furies, The.

There they go, down to the fatal ship.   Cythera.   David Ferry.   GS

There they go. Slowly they saunter.   April in the Old Park.   Anna Hajnal.   IQMS, *tr. by* Daniel Gerard Hoffman

There they stand, on their ends, the fifty faggots.   Fifty Faggots.   Edward Thomas.   MoBrPo; PoWW

There they were.   Seals, The.   Pauline Stainer.   NeBl

There they were, right before my eyes: it was terrible and at the same.   Fable.   Eugenio de Andrade.   VCWP, *tr. by* Alexis Levitin

There they were. The notes clipped. Short, spread out. Deathless and.   Carla Harryman.   BAP-04 *Fr.* Baby.

There though where they / were regardless.   Degree Four.   Nathaniel Mackey.   ESEAA

There, through the long, long summer hours.   June.   William Cullen Bryant.   TreFP

There / to the right of venus.   If I Go All the Way Without You Where Would I Go!   Ntozake Shange.   FaoP

There: / township music of Soweto reverberates.   Fatherless Townships.   Abiyah.   BRtP

There, tyrant passion finds a glorious tomb! (LL)   Bower of Pleasure, The.   Mary Robinson.   CenSon; RWP

There u guys go.   Astig.   Eric Fructuoso.   ReBoTo

There wanders many a lighted star.   North Star, The.   John Morris-Jones.   OBWVE, *tr. by* Anthony Conran

There was a battle fought of late.   To His Mother.   John Harington.   NoSic

There was a boy whose name was Jim.   Jim Who Ran Away from His Nurse, and Was Eaten by a Lion.   Joseph Hilaire Pierre Belloc.   NOxBChV; OBSP; OxAEP-2

There was a boy;—ye knew him well, ye cliffs.   William Wordsworth.   NAEL-6v2; NAEL-7v2; NOBRP *Fr.* Prelude, The; Growth of a Poet's Mind [1850 version].

There Was a Castle.   Vivian Lamarque.   CItWP, *tr. by* Cinzia Sartini Blum and Lara Trubowitz

There was a cat in Egypt, in Egypt, in Egypt.   Cat, The.   Rose Fyleman.   NOxBChV

There was a certain Mr. Great Man, for whom.   Hymn to the Virtue of Wine.   Liu Ling.   CCL1, *tr. by* Richard B. Mather

There Was a Child Went Forth.   Walt Whitman.   APN-1 *Fr.* Leaves of Grass [1855 Version].

There was a child went forth every day.   There Was a Child Went Forth.   Walt Whitman.   NAAL-5; NAAPv.1; PtR; SAmP

There was a child went forth every day.   Walt Whitman.   APN-1 *Fr.* Leaves of Grass [1855 Version].

There was a city.   Forward March.   Gerwyn Williams.   BBMWP, *tr. by the author and* Richard Poole

There was a common wall between the fence of our Elementary School.   To Enjoy the Horror.   Fawziyya Abu Khalid.   PoArWo, *tr. by* Farouk Mustafa

There was a contest.   Peaches.   Siv Cedering Fox.   PBCAP

There was a dance at the black school.   Bent Tones.   C. D. Wright.   AmAlph

There was a day when the sea overflowed.   Great Wave, The.   Sŏ Chŏngju.   CAMKP, *tr. by* David R. McCann

There was a delicate white mole.   Code, The.   Robert Morgan.   PoDa

There was a feast that night.   Banquet, The.   Letitia Elizabeth Landon.   TreFP

There was a frost.   Frozen Greenhouse, The.   Thomas Hardy.   OBGa

There was a garden.   Dylan Iorwerth.   BBMWP *Fr.* Sand.

There was a gather'd stillness in the room.   My Mother.   William Bell Scott.   GSo

There was a ghost at our wedding.   Kiss, The.   Chana Bloch.   FaoP

There was a great battle Saturday morning.   Battle of Argoed Llwyfain, The.   Taliesin.   OBWVE, *tr. by* Anthony Conran

There was a great Marxist called Lenin.   Progress.   Robert Conquest.   OBCoV

There was a guy who.   Side 18.   Víctor Hernández Cruz.   PueRic

There was a hag who kept two chambermaids.   Hag and the Slavies, The.   Jean de La Fontaine.   OBVE, *tr. by* Edward Marsh

There was a hardware shop in Main Street sold.   Didn't He Ramble.   James Simmons.   PNI

There was a house I wanted to run away from. Could I? (LL)   Chapter One.   Stephanie Brown.   BodElec; SUP

There Was a King.   *Unknown.*   NBLV

There was a knight, / A rich man of great might.   Dog and the Adder, The.   *Unknown.*   DiBP

There was a lady lived in a hall.   Two Red Roses across the Moon.   William Morris.   UV

There Was a Little Girl.   Henry Wadsworth Longfellow.   BRP

There was a little girl, she had a little curl.   There Was a Little Girl.   Henry Wadsworth Longfellow.   BRP

There was a little man.   *Unknown.*   OBCoV *Fr.* Advertising Rhymes.

There was a little turtle.   Little Turtle, The.   Vachel Lindsay.   BLPJKO; NOxBChV; NTCP; OBSP

There was a little woman, as I've heard tell.   Doubt as to Identity.   *Unknown.*   DiBP

There was a man and his shadow.   Shadow, The.   Nathan Alterman.   FIT, *tr. by* Robert Friend

There was a man here, Samian born, but he.   Ovid.   NAWM-5v1 *Fr.* Metamorphoses.

There was a man in the land of Ur.   Services.   Carl Rakosi.   ChIV-1

There was a man in The Land of Uz whose name was Job.   Job.   Bible, *O.T.*   NAWM-5v1, *tr. by* King James Version, New Revised Standard Version and R. P. Scheindlin

There was a man lived quite near us.   Man with the Wooden Leg, The.   Katherine Mansfield.   FaBoWar

There was a man of Carcassone. Wife of Carcassone, The. A. G. Prys-Jones. TCAWP

There was a man spent seven years in hell's circles. Political. Rita Dove. FFC

There was a man suspended from a nose. To a Nose. Francisco de Quevedo y Villegas. SpanPo, *tr. by* James Edward Tobin

There was a man who didn't know what was his. Man Who Didn't Know What Was His, The. Robert Bly. PML

There was a man who found two leaves and came indoors holding them out saying to his parents that he was a tree. Fall, The. Russell Edson. MotU; OxBoAm

There was a man who married a maid. She laughed as he led her home. I Love My Love. Helen Adam. EdScPo

There was a man who studied the art of disappearing. Parable, A. Li K'ai-hsien. ColAnChi, *tr. by* Jonathan Chaves

There was a man who watched the river flow. Cranes of Ibycus, The. Emma Lazarus. APN-2; NAAPv.1

There was a man who won a beautiful woman. Slighted Lady, The. Anna Wickham. LW

There was a man with tongue of wood. Stephen Crane. MoAmPo

There was a month I called May. When I buried it in papers, passion. Seasons. Safaa Fathy. PoArWo, *tr. by* S. V. Atalla

There was a most odious Yak. Yak, The. Theodore Roethke. BLPJKO

There was a mountain, over its black roots [the deer]. Papago. CA

There was a mute noise. The air of wheat when it allows itself. In the Distance. Silvio Giussani. ItPo, *tr. by* Gayle Ridinger

There Was a Naughty Boy. John Keats. OBCoV *Fr.* Song about Myself, A.

There was a neutrino from Kent. Particle Limericks. Alan Robert Wilson. IFF

There was a pattering in the rafters, mother. Dialogue. James McAuley. BMAP

There was a person. Revenge Fable. Ted Hughes. RaF

There was a plastic cup of iced coffee. Red Lipstick on a Straw. Michael Melo. ReBoTo

There Was a Prince. *Hungarian Oral Tradition.* IQMS, *tr. by* Joseph Leftwich

There was a Prince, in days of yore. There Was a Prince. *Hungarian Oral Tradition.* IQMS, *tr. by* Joseph Leftwich

There was a Puerto Rican man who. Man Who Came to the Last Floor, The. Víctor Hernández Cruz. PueRic

There was a queen that fell in love with a jolly sailor. Sailor and the Shark, The. Paul Fort. OBMV, *tr. by* Frederick York Powell

There was a Raja, pious-minded, just. *Unknown.* TAL *Fr.* Mahabharata, The.

There was a river overhung with trees. In a Notebook. James Fenton. NeBrP; NPeEn

There was a roaring in the wind all night. Resolution and Independence. William Wordsworth. NAEL-6v2; NAEL-7v2; NOBRP; NoP-4; NoP-5; OxAEP-2; TFi

There was a roaring in the wind all night. William Wordsworth. ITBLP; WoPoe *Fr.* Resolution and Independence.

There was a rose called Guy de Maupassant. Roses. Gerald Stern. GPPA

There was a saint once. Parable. Carl Phillips. AmAlph; CAP-8

There Was a Saviour. Dylan Thomas. ChIV-2; NAEL-6v2; NAEL-7v2

There was a Serpent who had to sing. Serpent, The. Theodore Roethke. NOxBChV

There was a shepherd's dochter. Knight and Shepherd's Daughter, The. *Unknown.* NoP-4; NoP-5

There was a sojourner in Ying who intoned "White Snows." Li Po. ColAnChi *Fr.* Poems in an Old Style.

There Was a Song. Gerald William Barrax. GT

There Was a Sound of Revelry by Night. Lord Byron. FaBoWar; OBWP; OxAEP-2; TFi *Fr.* Childe Harold's Pilgrimage.

There was a sound of revelry by night. Lord Byron. FaBoWar; OBWP; OxAEP-2; TFi *Fr.* Childe Harold's Pilgrimage.

There was a speedboat ploughing up Lough Erne. Enniskillen. David Morley. NLP

There was a Stag, did in the Forest lye. Hunting of a Stag, The. Margaret Lucas Cavendish, Duchess of Newcastle. EMWP

There was a stillness about the games, afternoons. Home Team. James Applewhite. LPSFW

There was a stunted handpost just on the crest. Near Lanivet, 1872. Thomas Hardy. NoAM

There was a sunlit absence. Seamus Heaney. BeAl; ModIr; WaAnP *Fr.* Mossbawn.

There was a sunny interlude. Reasons for the Beginning. Milo De Angelis. ItPo, *tr. by* Gayle Ridinger

There was a taed wha thocht sae lang. Philosophic Taed, The. William Soutar. EdScPo; NePenScot

There was a taut dryness all that summer. Lyric Afterwards, A. Tom Paulin. PNI

There was a tide-mark on the jetty which. Landfall, The. John Blight. BMAP

There was a time. To My Daughter. Keorapetse Kgositsile. GT

There was a time for discoveries. Voyage West. Archibald MacLeish. APT-1

There was a time her door was never closed. Her Door. Mary Leader. GoPo

There was a time I might have cried. Muffled Cry, A. Marjorie Oludhe Macgoye. HAWP

There was a time, in Esher's peaceful grove. William Mason. OBGa *Fr.* Heroic Epistle to Sir William Chambers, An.

There was a time in former years. She Hears The Storm. Thomas Hardy. NAEL-6v2; NAEL-7v2

There was a time in my life when. Old Neighborhood, The. Gerald Costanzo. OPRER

There was a time, poor phrensied maid. To a Maniac. Amelia Alderson Opie. NOBRP

There was a time when Eucritus and I were going. Theocritus. HePo *Fr.* Idylls.

There was a time when I could fly. I swear it. I, Icarus. Alden Nowlan. BrAP; NOxBChV

There was a time when I thought sweeter than the quiet. Wild Man Comes to the Monastery, The. *Unknown.* RaBo

There was a time when I would magnify. Elegy for an Unknown Soldier. James Keir Baxter. BrAP

There was a time when I wouldn't. Raven's Revenge. Tyler Doherty. WANABP

There was a time when meadow, grove, and stream. Ode: Intimations of Immortality from Recollections of Early Childhood. William Wordsworth. BrAP; HeIP-4; NAEL-6v2; NAEL-7v2; NAWM-7v2; NOBRP; NoP-4; NoP-5; NPeEn; OBEV; OxBEV; PoPoPo; TFi; TRP; WaAnP

There was a time when peace at evening. Progress. Violet Helen Friedlaender. RWPCtW

There Was a Time When the Only Worth. Dennis Brutus. VCWP

There was a tumult in the city. Independence Bell—July 4, 1776. *Unknown.* HHAm

There was a weasel lived in the sun. Gallows, The. Edward Thomas. MoBrPo; NAMCP V.1; NoAM

There was a wee bit wifukie was comin' frae the fair. Infallible Doussiekie. Alexander Geddes. DiBP

There was a wee cooper who lived in Fife. Wee Cooper of Fife, The. *Unknown.* NePenScot

There was a whispering in my hearth. Miners. Wilfred Owen. MoBrPo; OBWVE; OxAEP-2

There was a woman in Ithaca. Toast. Leonard Nathan. BLT

There was a woman lived in Winston-Salem. I. J. Brittain. VerBaPo *Fr.* Tragedy of Ida Ball Warren and Samuel Christie, The.

There was a woman who had lost her husband. Widow and the Soldier or: The Measure of a Woman's Inconstancy and Lust, The. Phaedrus. RomPo, *tr. by* Eugene O'Connor

There was a woman who hit her head. Gift, The. Lucille Clifton. CAP-8

There was a wood, a witches' wood. Witches' Wood, The. Mary Elizabeth Coleridge. VWP

There was a young belle of old Natchez. Requiem. Ogden Nash. NoP-4; NoP-5

There was a young fellow named Cholmondeley. Nomenclaturik. Harry Hearson. OBCoV

There was a young guy from Gloucester. Sometimes Even Parents Win. John Ciardi. NOxBChV

There Was a Young Lady of Niger. Cosmo Monkhouse. NBLV; TLR

There was a Young Lady of Parma. Limerick. Edward Lear. OBCoV

There was a young lady of Portugal. Limerick. Edward Lear. OBCoV

There was a young lady of Rheims. Moonshine. Walter De la Mare. OBCoV

There was a young lady of Riga. Limerick. Cosmo Monkhouse. NIL-7

There was a young lady of Riga. *Unknown.* NIL-7

There was a young lady of Tottenham. Limerick. *Unknown.* WeW-3

There was a young maid who said, "Why." Limerick. *Unknown.* SoSe-8

There was a young man who said, Damn! Determinism. Maurice Evan Hare. OBCoV

There was a young person whose history. Limerick. Edward Lear. OBCoV

There was aince an auld body o' Sydney. Limerick. *Unknown.* OBCoV

There was also a nun, a prioress. Geoffrey Chaucer. DiBP *Fr.* Canterbury Tales, The.

There was always an official to please. Chinese Man in Smyrna, A. Sharon Olinka. BRtP

There was always someone snuffing it. Passing On. Menna Elfyn. ATSWP, *tr. by* Robert Minhinnick

There was an a May and she lo'ed na men. Were Ne My Hearts Light I Wad Dye. Lady Grisel Baillie. EMWP

(There ance was a may, and she lo'ed na men.) OBEV

(There was ance a may, and she lo'ed na men;.) CABP; LW

There was an ancient sage philosopher. Samuel Butler. NOSC *Fr.* Hudibras.

There was an apple tree in the yeard. Nostos. Louise Glück. CAP-8

There was an archdeacon who said. Limerick. *Unknown.* OBCoV

There was an avenue. Pulling the Ivy. Julia Copus. MFPA

There was an inchworm on the curb, one end stuck to the curb and the. David McFadden. NLPA

There was an old fellow of Kaber. Limerick. Philip Larkin. OBCoV

There was an old lady of Chertsey. Limerick. Edward Lear. OBCoV

There was an old Lady of Winchelsea. Limerick. Edward Lear. OBCoV

There was an old man at the bank today. Fourth Street, San Rafael. Bill Berkson. NYP2

There was an old man from Darjeeling. Old Man from Darjeeling. *Unknown.* NTCP

There Was an Old Man in a Tree. Edward Lear. CABP; NoP-4; NoP-5

There was an old man of Calcutta. Arthur. Ogden Nash. AmWit; NoP-4

There was an old man of [*or* from] Peru / Who dreamt [*or* dreamed] he was eating his shoe. Limerick. *Unknown.* SoSe-8

There was an old man of Thermopylae. Limerick. Edward Lear. OxAEP-2

There was an old man of Toulouse. Limerick. Edward Lear. OBCoV

There was an Old Man of Whitehaven. Limerick. Edward Lear. NPeEn; OxAEP-2

There was an Old Man on some rocks. Limerick. Edward Lear. OxBEV

There was an old man said, "I fear." Shubble, The. Walter De la Mare. OBCoV

There was an Old Man who forgot. Edward Lear. NOxBChV

There was an old man who screamed out. Limerick. Edward Lear. NPeEn; OxAEP-2; OxBEV

There Was an Old Man Who Supposed. Edward Lear. *See* Limerick: "There was an Old Man who supposed."

There was an Old Man who supposed. Limerick. Edward Lear. NAEL-6v2; NAEL-7v2

There was an old man whose despair. Limerick. Edward Lear. OBCoV

There was an old man with a beard. John Clarke. UV

There Was an Old Man With a Beard. Edward Lear. NoP-5; NOxBChV; NPeEn; OPOU; TLR

(Old Man with a Beard.) NTCP

There was an Old Person of Basing. Limerick. Edward Lear. NPeEn; OxAEP-2

There was an old person of Bow. Limerick. Edward Lear. OxAEP-2

There was an old Rabbi of Ur. Dear Sir. Walter De la Mare. OBCoV

There was an old soldier. Homeless Vets. S. P. Shephard. BtF

There was an old status quo. Crow and the Fox, The. Reed Whittemore. BodElec

There Was an Old Woman Named Piper. William Jay Smith. TLR

There was an old woman of Clare. Cat's Second Song, The. Nancy Willard. FFC

There was an old woman / Went blackberry picking. Berries. Walter De la Mare. MoBrPo

There was an old woman who never was wed. Ballad of an Old Woman. Frank A. Collymore. NOxBChV

There was ance a may, and she lo'ed na men;. Lady Grisel Baillie. *See* There was an a May and she lo'ed na men.

There was another boy, who might have had. Ovid. CAGL *Fr.* Metamorphoses.

There was another one then. You had almost forgotten. (LL) Animals. Miller Williams. BeAl; P180

There was Chapel and Prayer Meeting and Dorcas and Children's Meeting. Gwladys Rhys. W. J. Gruffydd. BBMWP, *tr. by* Robert Minhinnick

There was Dai Puw. He was no good. On the Farm. Ronald Stuart Thomas. NoP-4; NoP-5; NPeEn; OxBEV; TCAWP

There was earth inside them, and. Paul Celan. PoetW, *tr. by* John Felstiner

There was earth inside them, and. Paul Celan. PoSu

There was Fire in Vancouver. Sinéad Morrissey. MFPA

There was heard a song on the chiming sea. Song of Emigration. Felicia Dorothea Hemans. VWP

There was in danger desperate delight. Aging Poet, on a Reading Trip to Dayton, Visits the Air Force Museum and Discovers There a Plane He Once Flew, The. Richard Snyder. OtW

There was misery. Elegy That Was Never Finished, An. José Ángel Valente. RaW, *tr. by* Hardie St. Martin

There was nae hand there to see! (LL) Ballad of the Were-Wolf, A. Rosamund Marriott Watson. ViWPN; VWP

There was never a sound beside the wood but one. Mowing. Robert Frost. APT-1; ColAP; HarvBoo; ITBLP; NAAL-5; TRP; WaAnP

There was no good solution. Polish Knot, The. Tomasz Jastrun. AF, *tr. by* Michael March and Jaroslaw Anders

There was no one in him. Everything and Nothing. Jorge Luis Borges. PoetW, *tr. by* Anthony Kerrigan

There was no secret. Full Indian Rope Trick, The. Colette Bryce. MoWP; NIrP

There was not loveliness nor fortune there. Shirley Barker. YaYoPo

There was not one who did not think of home. (LL) Conquerors. Henry Treece. OBWVE; TCAWP

There was nothing but darkness, and midnight. Edward Robert Bulwer-Lytton. STuOW *Fr.* Count Rinaldo Rinaldi.

There was once a country. . .I left it as a child. Emigrée, The. Carol Rumens. BeAl

There was once a hog theater where hogs performed, had men been hogs. Performance at Hog Theater, A. Russell Edson. PmAP; PoCho

There was once a man who went down on his knee to ask a woman to marry him. Crumble-Knees, The. Russell Edson. SUP

There was once a woman whose father over the years had become an ox. Ox, The. Russell Edson. RaBo

There was once an angel who had a neighbor, and this neighbor was ambitious. Lyn Hejinian. FaoP *Fr.* Book of a Thousand Eyes, The.

There was one I recognised in a train. Just a Product of a Certain Situation. Steve Griffiths. AngWePo

There was only a wild world bare of trees. Barrenness. T. H. Parry-Williams. BBMWP, *tr. by* Richard Poole

There was only one book in our home. Books as Answer. Haki R. Madhubuti. FuFl

There was only one home. Commandments. Judith Hemschemeyer. FiBr

There was only one problem—the steepness of the hill. Mark Rudman. ArBi *Fr.* Rider.

There was rain falling as I walked through the quiet streets. Birth-Hour. Lindley Williams Hubbell. YaYoPo

There was rain this morning. Sacrifice. Melanie Hope. WiU

There was set before me a mighty hill. Stephen Crane. APN-2

There was something I can't bring myself. Poem. Denis Johnson. OPRER

There was something poignant in. Kaczynski. Jeffrey Clapp. LiTh

There was such brilliance lifting off the sea, its aquamarine strip. Denise Riley. Oth *Fr.* Seven Strangely Exciting Lies.

There was such speed in her little body. Bells for John Whiteside's Daughter. John Crowe Ransom. APT-1; BrAP; ColAP; FuPo; HarvBoo; HeIP-4; InGu; MakPoe; MoAmPo; NAAPv.2; NAMCP V.1; NIL-7; NIP-4; NoAM; NoP-4; NoP-5; OxBoAm; TFi; WaAnP; WeW-3

There was that business in Siberia, in '19. Soviet Union, The. John Berryman. WaAnP

There was that guy. Trying to Remember People I Never Really Knew. William Childress. AmWaPo

There was the cottage blazing. Fire! Willy Bal. WoPoe, *tr. by* Yann Lovelock

There was the Dog Man again today. One Man's Family. Rosemary Catacalos. FTtHH

There was the knife and the broken syringe. Torn. C. Dale Young. LegDan

There was the noise like when the men in droves. New Year Behind the Asylum. David Constantine. BeAl

There was the shield of another language. In the Museum of the Word (Henri Matisse). Ann Lauterbach. AWPTFC

There was the sky, starless and vast. Night Picnic. Charles Simic. BAP-01

There was the solitary palm, or scattered clumps. In Times and Places. Umberto Piersanti. NeIt, *tr. by* Stephen Sartarelli

There was the tree the day they planted. Tree, A. Mark Irwin. PoCoUp

There was this head had this mouth he kept shooting off. Mouth, The. Ciaran Carson. ModIr; PNI

There was this hidden grin. Grin, A. Ted Hughes. EmeKit

There was this king sitting in his gairden a' alane. Oor Hamlet. Adam McNaughtan. EdScPo

There was this poet. On the Poet Coming of Age. Lorna Dee Cervantes. TouFir

There was this pond in the village. Pond, The. Mervyn Morris. PML

There was time for the audience of the fish. Epistle of the Shipwreck. María Baranda. RMCMP, *tr. by* Mónica de la Torre

There was vain time when my fingers could shape the world. Gypsy in the Condemned Cell, A. Mihály Babits. IQMS, *tr. by* Peter Zollman

There was too much, always, then too little. Time. Louise Glück. BAP-01; PtR

There was upon the sill a pencil mark. Edna St. Vincent Millay. NALW *Fr.* Sonnets from an Ungrafted Tree.

There wasn't much else we could do. Shooting the Dogs. Philip Hodgins. BMAP

There watched a cur before the miser's gate. George Crabbe. DiBP *Fr.* Dealer and the Clerk, The.

There we go in cars, did you guess we wore sandals? Way of Being, A. Barbara Guest. FTOS

There we two, content, happy in being together, speaking little, perhaps not a word. (LL) Glimpse, A. Walt Whitman. APN-1; RaBo

There we were that beautiful line, synchronized as. Kilgore Rangerette Whose Life Was Ruined, The. Cynthia MacDonald. TiP2

There we were. Two women, who I think still. 21 East 10th, 2BR, WBF, EIK. Robyn Selman. WiU

There went a warrior's funeral through the night. Peasant Girl of the Rhone, The. Felicia Dorothea Hemans. RWP

There went a widow woman from the outskirts of the city. Cruse of Tears, The. A Russian Legend. Emily Jane Pfeiffer. ViWPN

There were. There Were Those I Loved. Emperor Gotoba. WoPoe, *tr.* by Howard S. Levy

There were assembled, so the papers say. Old Boatman, The. R. Williams Parry. BBMWP, *tr.* by Anthony Conran

There were bells on the hill. Till There Was You. Meredith Willson. ReLy

There were bizarre beginnings in old lands for the making of me. Dark Blood. Margaret Abigail Walker. NALW

There were cathedrals falling out of your eyes. Bicycle Poem. Noelle Kocot. IIR

There were days when the Korean checkerboard was set in a woman's way. Study of Women's History 6, A. Ko Chônghûi. EcSo, *tr.* by Catherine J. Kim

There were distinctive. Language of Love. Rae Armantrout. PmAP

There were fifteen men in green. David Campbell. BMAP

There were five men walking down the street, when suddenly. Five Men. Cole Heinowitz. FreRad

There were ghosts that returned to earth to hear his phrases. Large Red Man Reading. Wallace Stevens. APT-1; NAAPv.2; NAMCP V.1

There were ladies, they lived in a bower. Mary [*or* Marie] Hamilton [Version from Motherwell's Manuscript]. *Unknown.* NoP-4

There were little farmhouses there they. Path to the White Moon, The. John Ashbery. PtR

There were lots of them. Olga Zondberg. CRWP, *tr.* by Daniel Weissbort

There were many *don'ts*: pirates, maidens, deer. In Henry Carlile's *Writing 213*. Martha Silano. AmPoNex

There were mornings following rain. Morning, A. Douglas Livingstone. TSAP

There were never strawberries. Strawberries. Edwin Morgan. EdScPo; NoP-4; NoP-5

There were nights too when only a radish. When the Time Comes. Michael Teig. IIR

There were nine grand pianos in my father's house. Michael Palmer. ASA *Fr.* Six Hermetic Songs.

There Were No Deer in the Thicket. David Biespiel. AmPoNex

There were no leaders, but they were first. Dog Fox Field. Les A. Murray. BMAP

There were no lines of violent diamonds, blinding light. Madwoman in the Park, The. Dame Edith Sitwell. PFTM-1

There were no markets in Watts. Speaking with Hands. Luis J. Rodriguez. UnSA

There were no men and women then at all. Then. Edwin Muir. OxBEV; PoA 2002

There were no poems that year. For Imelda. James Simmons. PNI

There were no undesirables or girls in my set. Commander Lowell. Robert Lowell. NAMCP V.2

There were none of my blood in this battle. Wildwest. Archibald MacLeish. AmWaPo

There were once two cats of Kilkenny. Cats of Kilkenny, The. *Unknown.* ChAP

There were other forms. Other Forms of Slaughter. Catherine Obianuju Acholonu. HAWP; HBAPE

There were other forms of slaughter. (LL) Other Forms of Slaughter. Catherine Obianuju Acholonu. HAWP; HBAPE

There were other separations, and so many of them. Homer. ModIr *Fr.* Odyssey.

There were roses, first. Laszlo. Frieda Hughes. NeBl

There were rules. On Growing Up the Darker Berry. Harriet Jacobs. ISC

There were snakes in the. I Remember Haifa Being Lovely But. Lyn Lifshin. CFP; UnSA

There were so many books. she had to separate them to avoid being. Reading. Joanne Burns. BMAP

There were some dirty plates. Last Words of My English Grandmother, The. William Carlos Williams. APT-1; InoFa; NAMCP V.1; PtR; RaBo; SAmP

There Were Some Summers. Thomas Lux. AmAlph

There were the roses, in the rain. Act, The. William Carlos Williams. PtR; SAmP

There were these enormous Canadas, shaved and bedridden. O Canada! G. C. Waldrep. LegDan

There Were Those I Loved. Emperor Gotoba. WoPoe, *tr.* by Howard S. Levy

There were three at one table; the pot-bellied judge. Old Veteran and Napoleon, The. János Garay. IQMS, *tr.* by Watson Kirkconnell

There were three cherry trees once. Three Cherry Trees, The. Walter De la Mare. OBGa

There were three girls in the Kalmoe house. No-More-Daughters's. Ko Ŭn. CAMKP, *tr.* by Kevin O'Rourke

There were three in the meadow by the brook. Code, The. Robert Frost. OBNV

There were three little owls in a wood. Limerick. *Unknown.* OBCoV

There were three ravens [*or* rauens *or* crows] sat on a tree. Three Ravens, The. *Unknown.* HeIP-4; OBEV; TFi

(There were three Ravens sat on a tree.) NoP-4; NoP-5

There were three sailors of Bristol city. Little Billee. William Makepeace Thackeray. OxAEP-2

There were tiny flames in her eyes. Epitaph on a Living Woman. Angelina Weld Grimké. APT-1

There were twa sisters [sat] in a bower [*or* bour *or* bowr]. Binnorie; or, The Two Sisters. *Unknown.* OBEV

There were two extra hooks of a worrying nature. Bargain with the Watchman. Eva Salzman. MFPA

There were two royal children. *Unknown.* GePo

There were two surprises for us. At Ynysddu. Graham Thomas. AngWePo

There were two thousand queens last night at the Flamingo. Last Night at the Flamingo. John Iozia. CAGL

There weren't any curtains in my parent's house. Bare Windows. Martha Rhodes. ExTi

There, when they thought they saw in well sought Books. Sir William Davenant. PBRV *Fr.* Gondibert Book 2

There, where at eve I sought a bed. Pressgang, The. Tu Fu [*or* Du Fu]. CCL1, *tr.* by H. A. Giles

There where the angels weave the sky. Archangel Cathedral. Olga Postnikova. CRWP, *tr.* by Richard McKane

There where the course is. At Galway Races. William Butler Yeats. WoPoe

There where the deepe did show his sandy flore. Bible, *O.T.* OBVE

There, where the rusty iron lies. Rooks. Charles Hamilton Sorley. MoBrPo

There where you see a green valley. World, The. Czeslaw Milosz. *tr.* by the author

There Where You Sleep. Francisco Segovia. RMCMP, *tr.* by Michael Wiegers

There will be a going back to the laws. (LL) There Will Be a Talking. Michael Hartnett. BeAl; PBCIP

There will be a rusty gun on the wall, sweetheart. A. E. F. Carl Sandburg. MoAmPo

There will be a talking of lovely things. There Will Be a Talking. Michael Hartnett. BeAl; PBCIP

There will be bluebells growing under the big trees. Bluebells for Love. Patrick Kavanagh. IrLP

There will be more of this. For Hans Keller. Craig Raine. NoP-5

There will be no deafening noise. No hornblow of thunder. Update on the Last Judgment. Ellen Hinsey. PoA 2002

There will be no monograms on our skulls. Rebellion against the North Side. Naomi Shihab Nye. WeW-3

There will be no other end of the world. (LL) Czeslaw Milosz. FaoP; WoPoe *Fr.* Voices of Poor People.

There will be rose and rhododendron. Elegy before Death. Edna St. Vincent Millay. BrAP

There will be the cough before the silence, then. Dictum: For a Masque of Deluge. W. S. Merwin. YaYoPo

There will come soft rains and the smell of the ground. There Will Come Soft Rains. Sara Teasdale. AmWaPo; APT-1; WaAnP

There Will Never Be Another You. Mack Gordon. ReLy

There, with ten Rembrandts. Ten Little Rembrandts. Theodore Weiss. NoAM

There would be bolts and violet circumferences. Baroque Cell, A. David Huerta. RMCMP, *tr.* by Mark Schafer

There would be room for me. (LL) Grandmother, a Caribbean Indian, Described by My Father. Yvonne Sapia. NIL-7; UnSA

There, wrapped in his own roars, the lone airman. Raider, The. William Robert Rodgers. MoBrPo

There ye gang, ye daft. Grace of God and the Meth-Drinker, The. Sydney Goodsir Smith. NePenScot

There you are again. To Marie Osmond. Jack Skelley. SwNoth

There you are, my love, in front of me. Moment of Love, A. Awwad Nasir. IrPoTo, *tr.* by Ralph Saverese and Saadi A. Simawe

There you are, snow filling the air. Porch in Snow. Joanna Klink. LegDan

There you go again. Jeepneyfying. Noel Mateo. ReBoTo

There you go, it's everywhere. Shopping for Midnight. G. E. Murray. ReTh

There! You shed a ray. He Wrote the History Book. Marianne Moore. APT-1

There you were in your purple vestments. Miraculous Grass. Nuala Ni Dhomhnaill. ModIr, *tr. by* Seamus Heaney

There—but for the clutch of luck—go I. Death by Heroin of Sid Vicious, The. Paul Durcan. BeAl; NPeEn

There—but for the clutch of luck—go we all. (LL) Death by Heroin of Sid Vicious, The. Paul Durcan. BeAl; NPeEn

There'd be, if Adam hadn't sold our stock. What Might Have Been. Giuseppe Gioacchino Belli. WoPoe, *tr. by* Anthony Burgess

Therefore. (LL) Susanna and the Elders. Adelaide Crapsey. APT-1; NAAPv.2; OxBoAm; TCAPo

Therefore also divine. (LL) Printer's Error, The. Aaron Fogel. OxBoAm; P180

Therefore do thou, stiff-set Northumberland. Imitation. Joseph Hilaire Pierre Belloc. OBCoV

Therefore God becomes as we are, that we may become as he is. (LL) There Is No Natural Religion. William Blake. NAEL-6v2; NAEL-7v2

Therefore John read how that thou wouldst. Anna Trapnell. ChIV-2 *Fr.* Cry of a Stone, A [*or* The].

Therefore myself is that one only thing. Christina Georgina Rossetti. PEW *Fr.* Thread of Life, The.

Therefore Philippi saw once more the Roman battalions. Virgil. APT-2 *Fr.* Georgics.

Therefore release me and depart on your way. (LL) Whoever You Are Holding Me Now in Hand. Walt Whitman. APN-1; CAGL; NAAL-3

Therefore say no more at first. (LL) Mary Sidney Wroth, Countess of Montgomery. NAEL-6v1; NAEL-7v1; NoP-4; NoP-5; WaAnP *Fr.* Urania.

Therefore [*or* Therfore] that he may raise the Lord throws down. (LL) Hymn[e] to God My God, In My Sickness[e], A. John Donne. BASC; HeIP-4; NAEL-6v1; NAEL-7v1; NoP-4; NoP-5; NOSC; OxAEP-1; PBRV; SoSe-8; TFi

Therefore the Oxford party went off to adorn for the dinner. Bothie of Toberna-Vuolich, The [A Long-Vacation Pastoral]. Arthur Hugh Clough.

Therefore we moun singen, *Deo Gracias!*. (LL) Adam Lay Ybounden [*or* I-bounden]. *Unknown.* ChIV-2; NoP-5; TFi; TRP; WeW-3

Therefore, when thou wouldst pray, or dost thine alms. Right Use of Prayer, The. Sir Aubrey De Vere. SacPr

Therefore, who doeth work rightful to do. *Unknown.* TAL *Fr.* Bhagavad-Gita, The.

Therefore your halls, your ancient colleges. Lines on Cambridge of 1830. Alfred Tennyson. OxBSo

There—leaving out a Man. (LL) It's easy to invent a Life. Emily Dickinson. APN-2; TCAPo

There'll be no more. Finished. Kate Llewellyn. NOBAu

There'll be no town-going today. Million Futures of Late, A. Christine Hume. IAoNAP

There'll be time enough to sleep. (LL) A. E. Housman. CABP; HarvBoo; MoBrPo; NoP-4; NoP-5 *Fr.* Shropshire Lad, A.

There'll soon be. Karai Senryū. EMJL, *tr. by* Makoto Ueda

Thereof be therefore heedful. Prayer for His Wife and Children, Written in Newgate. George Wither. SacPr

There're Not Many Birds in the Village Now. Gu Cheng. WoBe *Fr.* Liquid Mercury.

There's a barrel-organ caroling across a golden street. Barrel-Organ, The. Alfred Noyes. BRP; MoBrPo

There's a barrier between. Left Eye. Brenda Hillman. ASA

There's a beautiful woman in the north. Song. Li Yen-nien. CrYelRi, *tr. by* Sam Hamill

There's a better shine. Lorine Niedecker. APT-2

There's a bird perched on my shoulder. Bird. Ágnes Nemes Nagy. PoSu, *tr. by* Bruce Berlind

There's a black and white photo of Elvis. Audubon Drive, Memphis. James Seay. AllShUp; SwNoth

There's a body inside the body. Soul as a Body, The. Chard DeNiord. Vesp

There's a Breathless Hush. Noel Petty. UV

There's a breathless hush in the Close tonight. Vitaï Lampada. Sir Henry John Newbolt. FaBoWar; OBWP; UV

There's a breathless hush in the Close tonight. There's a Breathless Hush. Noel Petty. UV

There's a Breathless Hush on the Centre Court. Stanley J. Sharpless. UV

There's a bright, golden haze on the meadow. Oh, What a Beautiful Mornin'! Oscar Hammerstein, II. ReLy

There's a caliche pit not far from here. Dove at Sundown. Catherine Bowman. MoASP

There's a ceremony for everything. Move to liquid, A. Matt Robinson. Coast

There's a certain beekeeper I've fallen in love with. His hair smells. *BZZZZZZZ.* Amy Gerstler. PmAP

There's a certain point each evening when I have to put on some really soul-shattering rock-and-roll music. There's a Certain Point Each Evening. James Tate. MotU

There's a certain Slant of light. Emily Dickinson. APN-2; BrAP; ColAP; HeIP-4; MoAmPo; NAAL-3; NAAL-5; NAAPv.1; NALW; NAMCP V.1; NAWM-7v2; NCAP; NoAM; NoP-4; NoP-5; OxBoAm; PoPoPo; SAmP; SoSe-8; TCAPo; TFi

There's a cinnamon tree that grows on the Moon. Raisa Moroz. CRWP, *tr. by* Max Nemtsov

There's a class of men (and women) who are always on their guard. Men Who Come Behind, The. Henry Lawson. NOBAu

There's a clock in my chest that ticks a lifetime. Bloody Clock, A. Kim Hyesun. EcSo, *tr. by* Youngju Ryu

There's a colleen fair as May. Pearl of the White Breast. *Irish Oral Tradition.* IrV, *tr. by* George Petrie

There's a country at my shoulder. Country at My Shoulder, The. Moniza Alvi. MoWP

There's a daisy nodding. Within the Dome. Ron Padgett and James Schuyler. AHA

There's a dear little plant that grows in our isle. Green Little Shamrock of Ireland, The. Andrew Cherry. IrV

There's a diner in Garden City. Garden City Diner: Loving Back. Sherry Craven. TiP2

There's a disco ball. New Boogaloo. Willie Perdomo. BRtP

There's a doctor livin' in your town. Doctor, Lawyer, Indian Chief. Paul Francis Webster. ReLy

There's a fabulous story. Place Where the Rainbow Ends, The. Paul Laurence Dunbar. SacPr

There's a famous seaside place called Blackpool. Lion and Albert, The. Marriott Edgar. OBNV

There's a feeling comes a stealing. You're a Grand Old Flag. George M. Cohan. NAAPv.2; ReLy

There's a fierce gray Bird, with a bending beak. John Neal. APN-1 *Fr.* Battle of Niagara, The.

There's a fire / in the Architectural! Big Fire at the Architectural College, The. Andrey Andreievich Voznesensky. CLPP, *tr. by* Anselm Hollo

There's a fire in the vestry beyond hope. Self-Portrait at Fifty-Three. Bruce Weigl. AmAlph

There's a girl in Rio de Janeiro. I, Yi, Yi, Yi, Yi (I Like You Very Much). Mack Gordon. ReLy

There's a goblin as green. Goblin, The. Jack Prelutsky. TLR

There's a god on each side. *Unknown.* APN-2 *Fr.* Mountain Chant, The.

There's a grandfather's clock in the hall, watch it closely, The. The minute hand stands still, then it jumps, and in between jumps there is no-Time. There's a Grandfather's Clock in the Hall. Robert Penn Warren. NAMCP V.1; NoAM; NoP-4; NoP-5

There's a half hour towards dusk when flies. In the Attic. Donald Justice. OxBoAm

There's a Hand that Nails Down. Milo De Angelis. ItPo, *tr. by* Gayle Ridinger

There's a horse on the fridge. Coloring. Mark DeCarteret. AmPoNex

There's a huge hullabaloo in my lotus heart. Mahendranāth Bhattācārya. SinGod, *tr. by* Rachel Fell McDermott

There's a lady—an earl's daughter; she is proud and she is noble. Elizabeth Barrett Browning. STuOW *Fr.* Lady Geraldine's Courtship.

There's a land in the West where nature is blessed. Home on the Range. *Unknown.* GoPo

There's a land that bears a world-known name. Eliza Cook. STuOW

There's a land they call astutely. Okato-Otaia. Sándor Petőfi. IQMS, *tr. by* Anton N. Nyerges

There's a land with a heart of silicon. San José: A Poem. Cynthia Gomez. FTtHH

There's a liddle fact of hishdory vitch few hafe oondershtand. Charles Godfrey Leland. APN-2 *Fr.* Hans Breitmann as a Politician.

There's a life awaiting on a rocky coast. It is Everywhere. Jean Toomer. GT

There's a line of Verlaine's that I'm not going to remember again. Limits (or Good-byes). Jorge Luis Borges. PoetW; TCLAP, *tr. by* Alan Dugan

There's a little fear piercing. Mistaken Identity. Lewis Warsh. BodElec

There's a little low hut by the river side. Picture, A. B. P. Shillaber. TreFP

There's a lodger lives on the first floor. Cornucopia. Christopher Pearse Cranch. APN-1

There's a long-legged girl. Pickin Em Up and Layin Em Down. Maya Angelou. NBLV

There's a Lull in My Life. Mack Gordon. ReLy

There's a magnet in the desert earth. Desert Center. Margaret Erwin Schevill. ASA

There's a man goin' 'round takin' names. Angel of Death, The. *Unknown.* SacPr

There's a man I know who feigns deafness. Man Who Feigns Deafness, The. Nguyễn Khuyến. WoPoe, *tr. by* Nguyen Ngoc Bich

There's a man, I really believe, compares with. Sappho. STV

There's a man I really believe's in heaven. Sappho. WeW-3

There's a man in my dream. In the Crevices of Night. Gloria Vando. TouFir

There's a Man in My Life. George Marion, Jr. ReLy

There's a man with a Nose. Ambrose Bierce. APN-2 *Fr.* Devil's Dictionary, The.

There's a Meeting Here To-Night. *Unknown.* NAAPv.1; SSUS

There's a merry brown thrush sitting up in the tree. Lucy Larcom. NOxBChV

There's a Miracle Going On in the Ashes. Carlos Bousoño. RaW, *tr. by* Lewis Hyde

There's a mission, no doubt, for the mole in the dust. Eliza Cook. STuOW *Fr.* There is Nothing in Vain.

There's a mouse house. I Wouldn't. John Ciardi. TLR

There's a mystery. Gin. David St. John. AmAlph; CAP-8

There's a naked bug at Cold Mountain [*after* Han-shan]. Han-shan (Cold Mountain). BB; WoPoe, *tr. by* Gary Snyder

There's a patch of old snow in a corner. Patch of Old Snow, A. Robert Frost. WeW-3

There's a path that leads to Nowhere. Path that Leads to Nowhere, The. Corinne Roosevelt Robinson. ITBLP

There's a place between two stands of trees where the grass grows uphill. Adrienne Rich. ExTi; LoL; WaAnP *Fr.* Not Somewhere Else, But Here.

There's a place for us. Somewhere. Stephen Sondheim. ReLy

There's a precise moment in time. Mid-way. Robert Desnos. GPTC, *tr. by* Carole Frankel and William Kulik

There's a quaint little place they call Lullaby Town. Lullaby Town. John Irving Diller. ITBLP

There's a reid lowe in yer cheek. Sang. Robert MacLellan. EdScPo

There's a revolution going on. Lozenge. Hoa Nguyen. WANABP

There's a road we know. My Wheel and I. Alberto A. Bennett. ArBi

There's a Sampson lying, sleeping in the land. Black Sampson, The. Josephine D. Henderson Heard. CBWP-4; SWaP

There's a saying old. Someone to Watch over Me. Ira Gershwin. ReLy

There's a scandal in the neighborhood. He's a Cousin of Mine. Cecil Mack. ReLy

There's a screen of arabesque between us and them. Arabesque. Ahmed Taha. NAfrP, *tr. by* Clarissa C. Burt

There's a seat right next to me. Brain on Ice. Michael Warr. UnSA

There's a serpent, namely, drinking. Social Glass, The. Lizelia Augusta Jenkins Moorer. CBWP-3

There's a shuffle in the thin fall morning. 8 O'Clock Defeat, Approximately. Chris O. Cook. FreRad

There's a sickness in me. During. Invisible Dreams. Toi Derricotte. PuP-23

There's a Small Hotel. Lorenz Hart. ReLy

There's a song in the air! Christmas Carol, A. Josiah Gilbert Holland. SacPr

There's a stage play by Naomi Wallace, called *the inland sea*. West Nile Crow. Marvin Francis. PoPra

There's a straw in the manger and babies in danger. Colin Gibson. RSR

There's a tattoo of a tiny gun on my hand symbolic of the tiny wars. Tattoo. Peter Johnson. LiTh

There's a thread you follow. It goes among. Way It Is, The. William Stafford. TWF

There's a time each year that we always hold dear. In the Good Old Summer Time. Ren Shields. NAAPv.2

There's a tortoise-man on TV. His skin. Blue. Elin ap Hywel. BBMWP, *tr. by* the author

There's a tortoise-man on TV. His skin's. Blue. Elin ap Hywel. ATSWP, *tr. by* Robert Minhinnick

There's a trade you all know well. Overlander, The. *Unknown.* NOBAu

There's a vastness out there. Alone. Aled Lewis Evans. BBMWP, *tr. by* Peter Finch

There's a village and there's no village. Prelude to 'Blood and Ash'. Justinas Marcinkevičius. SonAtl, *tr. by* Terese Gustiene, Justinas Marcinkevičius, Dorli Meek, Tamara Romanyk and Alfredas Zalys

There's a volcano snow-capped in the air some twenty miles. Resort. George Oppen. FTOS

There's a wanderer, there's a wanderer, his name is Tzu-mei. Seven Songs Written while Living at T'ung-ku in 759. Tu Fu [*or* Du Fu]. ColAnChi, *tr. by* Geoffrey Waters

There's a whimsey in my noddle, there's a maggot in my brain. Problem, A. Carolyn Wells. SWaP

There's a whirlwind cutting up the Thames. London, 1792. Emyr Lewis. ATSWP, *tr. by* Robert Minhinnick

There's a whisper down the field where the year has shot her yield. Envoi. Rudyard Kipling. OBEV

There's a woman like a dew-drop, she's so purer than the purest. Robert Browning. OBEV *Fr.* Blot in the 'Scutcheon, A.

There's a woman who resembles a phrase. She has a spot of. Vegetable Calendar. Silvio Giussani. ItPo, *tr. by* Gayle Ridinger

There's a wonderful story. Angel's Message, The. Clara Ann Thompson. CBWP-2

There's a word for what we do. Devotions in Confidence. Margot Schilpp. AmPoNex

There's a yellow rose of Texas that I am going to see. Yellow Rose of Texas, The. *Unknown.* TCAPo

There's a zoo in Grandma's pocket. Grandma's Zoo. Dorothy Molloy. NIrP

There's always a headscarf stooped. Glasgow 1956. Gerald Mangan. EdScPo

There's always a joke. Dylan Iorwerth. BBMWP *Fr.* Sand.

There's always been this dream that reasons, shearing off. Maritime. Reginald Shepherd. AmPoNex

There's always something sepulchral. What Did You Come to See. Bruce Beasley. AmAlph

There's always the illusion the museum I carry. New House. Geraldine Connolly. SweBea

There's an arch in your heart. Isla Mujeres. Lorna Dee Cervantes. TouFir

There's an early memory that I carry around. My Father's Back. Edward Hirsch. VCAP

There's an inn in Indiana with a very good clientele. Ladies Who Sing with a Band, The. George Marion, Jr. ReLy

There's an Irishman, Arthur O'Shaughnessy. On the Poet, Arthur O'Shaughnessy—. Dante Gabriel Rossetti. OBCoV

There's an island not so tropical. Spreadin' Rhythm Around. Ted Koehler. ReLy

There's an ordinary woman whom the English call "the Queen." English Queen, The. Henry Lawson. NOBAu

There's an Unknown River in Soweto. Zindzi Mandela. NAfrP

There's antimony, arsenic, aluminium, selenium. Elements, The. Tom Lehrer. UV

There's been a change of more than silhouette. (LL) Grim Sisters, The. Liz Lochhead. CABP; MoWP

There's been a Death, in the Opposite House. Emily Dickinson. APN-2; InoFa; SAmP; SoSe-8

"There's been an accident," they said. Mr. Jones. Harry Graham. UV

There's been an eagle on a nickel. Fact. Langston Hughes. APSN; OxBoAm; PFTM-1

There's blood between us, love, my love. Convent Threshold, The. Christina Georgina Rossetti. NALW; NoP-4; NoP-5; VWP

There's blues in the night. (LL) Blues in the Night. Johnny Mercer. APT-2; ReLy

There's classic and there's quaint. Richard Wilbur. UpMys *Fr.* Objects.

There's force to this cold sun, makes beard stubble stand shinily. William Carlos Williams. TCAPo *Fr.* Kora in Hell.

There's fox creeps creeps. You-hu: There's Fox. *Unknown.* CCL1, *tr. by* Arthur Cooper

There's heaven above, and night by night. Johannes Agricola in Meditation. Robert Browning. SacPr

There's Holmes, who is matchless among you for wit. James Russell Lowell. TCAPo *Fr.* Fable for Critics, A.

There's holy holy people. Capel Calvin. Idris Davies. AngWePo

There's in my mind a woman. In Mind. Denise Levertov. NAAL-5; NALW

There's just no accounting for happiness. Happiness. Jane Kenyon. BeAl; PoA 2002; PoDa

There's just one fellow. I'm Just Wild about Harry. Noble Sissle. ReLy

There's just one thing I want to ask ya: how come. Who Knows Where the Time Goes? Michael Brownstein. AHA

"There's light ahead!" Hope ever cries. Hope Deferred. Clara Ann Thompson. CBWP-2

There's lightning in the sky. Dancing with Rex. Beth Cuthand. ReEnLa

There's little in taking or giving. Coda. Dorothy Parker. AmWit; APT-1

There's little joy in life for me. On the Death of Anne Brontë. Charlotte Brontë. VWP

There's machinery in the butterfly. Horrid Voice of Science, The. Vachel Lindsay. PoA 2002

There's Magic in the Air. Ira Gershwin. NAAPv.2

There's Malichevsky, Rubinstein, Arensky, and Tchaikowsky. Tchaikowsky (And Other Russians). Ira Gershwin. ReLy

There's more in words than I can teach. Loving and Liking [Irregular Verses Addressed to A Child]. Dorothy Wordsworth. SacPr; WoRP

There's music in the old bones yet. (LL) Song for the Clatter-Bones. Frederick Robert Higgins. ChIV-1; OBMV

There's Nae Luck about the House. Jean Adams. NePenScot

There's Nae Luck about the House. William Julius Mickle. OxAEP-1

There's never been a poet where I live. Apple from Walt Whitman, An. Eric Torgerson. ViWalt

There's No Business Like Show Business. Irving Berlin. ReLy

There's no comfort inside me, only a small. Beehive Cell. Richard Murphy. OxBSo

There's no dew left on the daisies and clover. Songs of Seven. Jean Ingelow.

There's no excitement, news or anything. Imre Madách. IQMS *Fr.* Tragedy of Man.

There's no helping. Tune: "New Bounty of Royalty." Li Yü. ColAnChi, *tr.* by Jiaosheng Wang

There's no keeping back spring. Tune: "Magnolia Flower." Ou-yang Hsiu. ColAnChi, *tr.* by James Robert Hightower

There's no modesty, Todorov. To a French Structuralist. David Kirby. BLT

There's no Nepenthe, now, on earth for me. (LL) Nepenthe. Charlotte Smith. NoP-4; NoP-5

There's no oblivion—but in death alone! (LL) To the South Downs. Charlotte Smith. CenSon; NPBRoP

There's no occasion for knocking at an out-of-the-way door. Tune: "Partridge Sky" I Rejoice to Meet a Friend Visting at My Rustic Study. Ch'iao Lai. ColAnChi, *tr.* by Jiaosheng Wang

There's no other discipline for the student. Twelve More Songs for Master Jikong. Baekoon Kyunghan. BecRai, *tr.* by Kim Daljin, Kim Won-Chung and Christopher Merrill

There's no overdoing. Elegy of Our Times. Eugenio Montale. ItPo, *tr.* by Gayle Ridinger

There's no poet quite like you, Li Po. To Li Po on a Spring Day. Tu Fu [*or* Du Fu]. CrYelRi, *tr.* by Sam Hamill

There's No Rigor Like the Old Rigor 2. Ira Sadoff. BodElec

There's no sense in listening to it, except. Getting the News. Helen Chasin. YaYoPo

There's no such thing as leading apes in hell. (LL) Married State, A. Katherine Philips. BASC; NAEL-7v1

There's No To-Morrow. Anne Finch, Countess of Winchilsea. NIL-7

There's no way I'm going to write about. Child Dancing, The. Gwendolyn MacEwen. BrAP

There's no way out. In the Suburbs. Louis Simpson. CAP-8; TRP

There's not a chance now that I might recover. Scar, The. John Hewitt. PNI

There's Not a Friend like the Lowly Jesus. William Anderson. EGAG

There's not a joy the world can give like that it takes away. Stanzas for Music. Lord Byron. NOBRP; NPeEn

There's not a nook within this solemn Pass. Trosachs, The. William Wordsworth. OBEV

There's not a nude in a museum. Cohabiting. Stephen Dunn. CAP-8

There's nothing. Clearing. Lawson Fusao Inada. WhBo

There's nothing grieves me, but that age should haste. Michael Drayton. NOSC; WaAnP *Fr.* Idea.

There's nothing I can't find under there. Pillow. Li-Young Lee. NAMCP V.2

There's nothing I couldn't forgive. (LL) What the Water Knows. Sam Hamill. BodElec; WANABP

There's nothing in me My Lord. Bible, *O.T.* AHA *Fr.* Psalms [David Rosenberg Adaption].

There's nothing left for me. Among My Souvenirs. Edgar Leslie. ReLy

There's nothing over there. After Yes. James Harms. AmPoNex

There's nothing to love in this. Warmth. Joseph Ceravolo. NYP2

There's nothing truer than fake fruit, let's say. Edoardo Cacciatore. ItPo *Fr.* Full Powers: Five Warning Signs.

There's nothing wrong with. Lies We Tell Ourselves. Marj Hahne. BRtP

There's one called "Wild." Tubes. Terry Wolverton. WiU

There's one I miss. A little questioning maid. Augusta Davies Webster. ViWPN; VWP *Fr.* Mother and Daughter.

There's one thing to think of when you're blue. Sunny Side Up. Lew Brown, B. G. DeSylva and Ray Henderson. ReLy

There's only these few. George Stanley. NLPA *Fr.* Mountains and Air.

There's our candle, on the bedstand still. Love Lamp. W. D. Snodgrass. CAP-8

There's our street, let's say. Sergey Gandlevsky. ItGoST, *tr.* by Philip Metres

There's parties ad yer meets about. Albert Chevalier. UV *Fr.* Sich a Nice Man Too!

There's sanity in your scissored hair. Sion Eirian. BBMWP *Fr.* Adolescent Experiences.

There's silence between one page and another. Valerio Magrelli. NeIt

There's snow in every street. Winter. John Millington Synge. OBMV

There's so little sweetness in the music I hear now. Homage: Doo-Wop. Joseph Stroud. GoPo

"There's someone at the door," said gold candlestick. Green Candles. Humbert Wolfe. MoBrPo

There's something about being an Indian. Something About Being an Indian. Adrian C. Louis. UnSA

There's something in a flying horse. William Wordsworth. NPBRoP *Fr.* Peter Bell.

"There's something in the air," he said. Two Voices. Edmund Charles Blunden. OBWP

There's something in the air that you can sense. On Such a Night As This. Marshall Barer. ReLy

There's something inside of my heart that cries. Give Me a Heart to Sing To. Ned Washington. ReLy

There's something religious in the way we sit. Having Our Tea. Bobi Jones. BBMWP, *tr.* by Joseph P. Clancy

There's something uncertain about the rock. Land at the World's End, The. Brian Swann. PoCoUp

There's something we call a game show with all kinds of dings and glitches. Tagging. Maureen Seaton. ExTi; IllVoic

There's still on the rim of night (having been in it) which is (in night). Leslie Scalapino. ExTi *Fr.* New Time.

There's such a stillness, Lord. Glimpse of God. Tatamkulu Afrika. TSAP

There's Such an Evening. Na Hûidôk. EcSo, *tr.* by Peter H. Lee

There's teuch sauchs growin' i' the Reuch Heuch Hauch. Sauchs in the Reuch Heuch Hauch, The. Hugh MacDiarmid. NAMCP V.1; NoAM

There's the obese three-quarters moon of Aquinas. Ars Poetica: A Stone Soup. Norman Dubie. TAPaP

There's the sea, far beyond the yellow hills. August Moon. Cesare Pavese. AF, *tr.* by William Arrowsmith

There's the wonderful love of a beautiful maid. Love. *Unknown.* SoSe-8

There's this much space between me and. Stowaway. Olive Senior. WaAnP

There's too much light in my life. Merk. Eileen Myles. WiU

There's War or There's Peace. Claire Malroux. YaTCFP, *tr.* by Marilyn Hacker

There's where we'll meet and we'll never part no more. (LL) Carry Me Back to Old Virginny. James A. Bland. APN-2; TCAPo

Theresa of Avila surely had a gold thimble. Things of This World. Anna Kamienska. GI, *tr.* by David Curzon and Grażyna Drabik

Theresienstadt's Hospital. *Unknown, fr. Terezin Concentration Camp.* INSAB

Theris, the old man who lived by his fish traps. Leonidas of Tarentum. WoPoe, *tr.* by Kenneth Rexroth

Theris, thrice-old, who got his living from. Leonidas of Tarentum. HePo, *tr.* by Barbara Hughes Fowler

Thermae. Matthea Harvey. IAoNAP
　Apodyterium (dressing room). IAoNAP
　Calidarium (hot room). IAoNAP
　Frigidarium (cold room). IAoNAP
　Laconicum (sweating room). IAoNAP
　Palaestra (athletics room). IAoNAP
　Tepidarium (warm room). IAoNAP
　Vestibulum (entrance hall). IAoNAP

Thermal Signatures ("I sing a place called Newborn.") Sam Witt. IAoNAP

Thermal Signatures ("There is nothing to remember but flight. The owl's eyes spoke.") Sam Witt. IAoNAP

Thermal Stair, The. William Sydney Graham. HarvBoo

Thermodynamics. Arthur Sze. WANABP

Thermometer. Giovanni Singleton. BtF

Thermometer of Happiness. Shehata El-Iryaan. AnVo, *tr.* by Mohamed Enani

Thermopylae. Simonides. OBVE; OBWP; WoPoe, *tr.* by William Lisle Bowles

Thermopylai's dead. Simonides. SaLy, *tr.* by Diane Rayor

Thermos, The. Arthur Sze. PoChi

THESCRIBESPACKEDCAPITALSACROSSTHEPAGE. Scribes, The. Suzanne Noguere. FFC

These. William Carlos Williams. APT-1; GPTC; MoAmPo; NAAPv.2; OxBoAm

These accents seem their own defence. (LL) Some Trees. John Ashbery. FaoP; NAMCP V.2; YaYoPo

These acres, always again lost. Lost Acres. Robert Graves. NoAM

These Americans I see. 13 November 1983. Lee Cataldi. BMAP

These apples. Paul Dermée. CuPo

These Are All My Father's Children. *Unknown.* SSUS

These are amazing: each. Some Trees. John Ashbery. FaoP; NAMCP V.2; YaYoPo

These are arrows that murder sleep. Song of Crede, Daughter of Guare, The. *Unknown.* IrLP, *tr.* by Kuno Meyer

These are calamitous times we're living through. Modern Times. Nicanor Parra. AF, *tr.* by Miller Williams

These are dissenters. Imre Madách. IQMS *Fr.* Tragedy of Man.

These are for me. (LL) Letitia Elizabeth Landon. NOBRP; NPBRoP *Fr.* Golden Violet, The.

These are Lilacs. Nijole Miliauskaite. VCWP, *tr.* by Jonas Zdanys

These are my countries, my forests. Nightsong. Thamnaret. WoPoe, *tr.* by Ronald Perry

These are my father's shoes. Father's Shoes. Tyehimba Jess. BtF

These are my murmur-laden shells that keep. On Some Shells Found Inland. Trumbull Stickney. APN-2

These are names to haunt our dreams. Names. Medora C. Addison. YaYoPo

These, are not brayed of Tongue. (LL) Soul has Bandaged moments, The. Emily Dickinson. NAAPv.1; NALW; OxBoAm; TRP

These Are Not Brushstrokes. Cyrus Cassells. GT

These are not the lines that came to me. Lines Lost among Trees. Billy Collins. BAP-97

These are our skirts. Gospel. Keith Ratzlaff. ACAMVP

These are the absolute top of the line. Mangosteens. Daniel Hall. NoP-4

These are the birds who nest. Chances. Taylor Graham. CalPo

These are the bosses of Rome; take a good look. Bosses of Rome, The. Giuseppe Gioacchino Belli. PoCho, tr. by Miller Williams

These are the Daemons that pervert the power. Robert Southey. NAEL-7v2 Fr. Joan of Arc.

These are the days of the horrible headlines. Peter Reading. StAl Fr. Going On.

These are the facts. The uncle, the elder brother, the squire. Arthur Hugh Clough. FaBoVe Fr. Amours de Voyage.

These are the few who love her as she is. Few, The. J. M. Edwards. BBMWP, tr. by Robert Minhinnick

These are the fields where rain has marched. History of Rain, The. Conor O'Callaghan. NIrP

These are the first citizens of contingency. Robert Pinsky. NoAM Fr. Essay on Psychiatrists.

These are the first days of fall. The wind. How To Like It. Stephen Dobyns. CAP-8; SUP

These are the first fine days. Summer. Pascalle Monnier. YaTCFP, tr. by Cole Swensen

These are the gardens of the Desert, these. Prairies, The. William Cullen Bryant. APN-1; ColAP; NAAL-3; NAAL-5; NCAP; TCAPo

These are the gardens of the Desert, these. William Cullen Bryant. ITBLP Fr. Prairies, The.

These are the holes—only holes. Elbow in Dumberland, An. Edwin Torres. HeMarv

These are the little shoes that died. Little Shoes That Died, The. Mary Gilmore. NOBAu

These are the long weeks. The weeks. Petition. Brigit Pegeen Kelly. ExTi

These are the men from México's boot, the ones. Penny Men. Rigoberto González. GeoHom

These are the mornings the Angel of Brazil blesses and steams my windows. Coffee. David St. John. MotU

These are the names of the horses. Muybridge. Linda Bierds. AmAlph

These are the Nights that Beetles love. Emily Dickinson. NCAP

These are the nights we dreamed of. Middle Years, The. Walter McDonald. GoPo

These are the original monies of the earth. Cabinet of Seeds Displayed, A. Howard Nemerov. NoP-5

These are the ravens of my soul. These Are the Ravens. William Everson. CalPo

These are the same hands that stroke my head in fever. Sugarmother's Daughter Dreams. Patrice Vecchione. RaF

These are the seductive voices of the night; the Sirens, too, sang that way. Sirens, The. Franz Kafka. MotU, tr. by Clement Greenberg

These are the strings of the Aegean lyre. Sonnets from Greece. Trumbull Stickney. APN-1

These Are the Sweet Girls. Anabel Torres. TANSG, tr. by Celeste Kostopulos-Cooperman

These are / the sweet girls / who go to the matinée. These Are the Sweet Girls. Anabel Torres. TANSG, tr. by Celeste Kostopulos-Cooperman

These are the things you saw and heard, these are the things you did, this is your record, / you. (LL) 1933. Kenneth Fearing. APT-2; FTtHH

These are the trees chopped down, chopped in a day. Down. Mark Abley. IFF

These are the two unarguable facts. Jewish. Dick Lourie. PrTe

These are the ultimate highlands. Lines. Sara Teasdale. APT-1

These are the vague demands you make on me. Sybil. Rebecca Wolff. LegDan

These are the voices of the pastors calling. Old Lutheran Bells at Home, The. Wallace Stevens. NoAM

These are the word wounds. Daniela Gioseffi. AtGh Fr. Last Fire Feast, The.

These are thrity carved stones. Playing the Goldberg Variations on Sunday Morning. Bill Holm. MiVo

These are times when their faith in gods. From Florrie Abraham Witness, December 1972. Jack A. Mapanje. HBAPE

These are what I will remember. Images of John (1967–92). Danton R. Remoto. ReBoTo

These are your lips. Vasco [or Vasko] Popa. PoSu Fr. Far Within Us.

These, as they change, Almighty Father! these. James Thomson. CABP Fr. Seasons, The.

These, as they change, Almighty Father! these. James Thomson. InvLi; TreFP Fr. Seasons, The.

These as they clack in the wind. In the Pea Patch. Maxine W. Kumin. AFaM; CAP-8

These bangs not yet reaching my eyes. Ch'ang-Kan Village Song. Li Po. NDACCP, tr. by David Hinton

These barrows of the century-darkened dead. Prehistoric Burials. Siegfried Sassoon. MoBrPo

These be / Three silent things. Triad. Adelaide Crapsey. APT-1; InoFa; OxBoAm; TCAPo

These beasts are four fathoms long, but perfectly gentle. Hydrodamalis Gigas. John Glenday. NeBrP

These beasts will not do. Send New Beasts. Joe Wenderoth. BodElec; LegDan

These became part of that child who went forth every day, and who now goes, and will always go forth every day. (LL) There Was a Child Went Forth. Walt Whitman. NAAL-5; NAAPv.1; PtR; SAmP

These bent rusted nails embedded in. Roy Kiyooka. NLPA Fr. Pear Tree Pomes.

These berries, with their choices, come to earth. Aeschyleans, The. Bernadette Mayer. FTOS

These birds are all the wedding dresses of the world. Banns. Don Domanski. Coast

These birds pursue their errands. Anthem. Anthony Hecht. PoA 2002

These Bones. T. H. Parry-Williams. OBWVE, tr. by H. Idris Bell

These branches. Naito Joso. ZenPo, tr. by Takashi Ikemoto and Lucien Stryk

These calm days of September with their sun. Harvest Time. Olav H. Hauge. WED, tr. by Robert Bly

These chaste / words go out. Any Nest I Can't Sleep in Should Be Burned. Christopher Davis. AmPoNex

These clothes don't fit. Running Hares. Tessa Rose Chester. MFPA

These coastal bogs, before they settle. Green. Amy Clampitt. PfSP

These Current Events. Kimiko Hahn. PrTe

These Days: "Whatever you have to say, leave." Charles Olson. APT-2; RaBo; TWF

These days. Sunday Skaters. Mary Jo Salter. MoASP

These days. Lifelong farewell. Idea Vilariño. TANSG, tr. by Louise B. Popkin

These days are not crying days. Days Gone By. Gu Cheng. WoBe, tr. by Joseph R. Allen

These days / I wear my robe half-open. Half-Open. Patricia Donegan. WhBo

These days in my friend's house. Days of 1994. James Merrill. OxBoAm

These days / lifting myself up. August Third. May Sarton. GoPo

These days obscure but cannot do thee wrong. (LL) Rosina Alcona to Julius Brenzaida. Judith Wright. InoFa; NALW

These days steal everything. Thief Stole This Poem, A. Allen Ginsberg. BodElec

These days the silence is immense. Silence Now, The. May Sarton. FiBr

These days the system is state of the art—scrims of smoke. At the Crematorium, My Son Asks Why We're All Wearing Black. Mark Cox. NevBe

These days, what comes from your mouth. Non Sequitur. Margot Schilpp. AmPoNex

These days whenever I stay away too long. Home. Frederick D'Aguiar. NeBrP

These dead astronauts cannot decay. Everlasting Astronauts, The. Tom Buchan. EdScPo

These decibels / Are a kind of flagellation, an entity of sound. John Ashbery. PmAP Fr. Skaters, The.

These demonstrations of the one God. Mountains of California: Part 1, The. Al Young. GeoHom

These difficulties—flamboyant tide, modest red berries. Boy Sleeping. Ann Lauterbach. PmAP

These downpours of my Cuban childhood. Aguacero. Virgil Suarez. PoDa

These drugstore windows. Crêpe de Chine. Mark Doty. FaoP

These eyes, [deare Lord], once brandons of desire. For the Magdalene. William Drummond of Hawthornden. ChIV-2

These feet and hands, two pelvises, this movement. Upon a Drawing. István Vas. IQMS, tr. by Daniel Gerard Hoffman

These fell miasmic rings of mist, with ghoulish menace bound. Prejudice. Georgia Douglas Johnson. NAAPv.2

These fields can never be. At Gettysburg. Linda Pastan. CFP

These figures moving in my rhyme. Two Figures. N. Scott Momaday. NoP-4; NoP-5

These first days of summer are like the pail. Summer Surprised Us. Edward Hirsch. PfSP

These flat and leathery leaves. Ars Poetica. Jane Hirshfield. BodElec

These flower forms vary to me in ways I can't say yet. Shiny Jewel Eye. Lee Ann Brown. VaPo

These flowers are I, poor Fanny Hurd. Voices from Things Growing in a Churchyard. Thomas Hardy. FaBoVe

These flowers unlock a heart I hadn't known. Tangerine Orchids. Rachel Hadas. PA9/11

These Foolish Things (Remind Me of You). Eric Maschwitz. ReLy

These foreign laws of God and man. (LL) Laws of God, the Laws of Man, The. A. E. Housman. CAGL; MoBrPo; NPeEn; OBSV

These fought in any case. Ezra Pound. AmWaPo; HarvBoo; HeIP-4; InoFa; MoAmPo; NPeEn; OBWP; OxBoAm; PoAgWa; PoWW; TRP; WaAnP *Fr.* Hugh Selwyn Mauberley (Life and Contacts).

These furies frying thus, yet thus were not content. Admiralls Being Slaine, They Likewise . . . , The. Anne Dowriche. EMWP

These giant grape hyacinths. In the Garden By the Sea: Easter. Kelly Cherry. LPSFW

These gifts to Aphrodite. Callimachus. HePo, *tr. by* Barbara Hughes Fowler

These graves make a grammar. Bilbao Churchyard. Bobi Jones. ATSWP, *tr. by* Robert Minhinnick

These Green Paths. Jeannette Miller. TANSG, *tr. by* Paula Vega

These Green-Going-to-Yellow. Marvin Bell. UrbNat

These have crimes accounted been[e]. (LL) Ben Jonson. AEP; BrAP; NIL-7; NoP-4; NoP-5; NPeEn; OBVE; OxBEV; PoPoPo; TFi; WaAnP *Fr.* Volpone.

These hearts were woven of human joys and cares. Rupert Brooke. SoSe-8

These hills were once mountains. Temporary Heart. Michael Hannon. GeoHom

These hips are big hips. Homage to my hips. Lucille Clifton. CAP-8; NAMCP V.2; StAl; WaAnP

These hollow truncated cones of wicker into mud. Two Varieties of the Bitter Orange. J. L. Jacobs. AmPoNex

These hot afternoons "it's quite absurd" she whispered. Summer. Lee Harwood. AHA

These huge teachable slangy people. Poem Americans Are Going to Have to Memorize Soon, A. Clarence Major. EGAG

These I can explain. (LL) In the Kitchen before Dinner. Jane Rohrer. ACAMVP; BodElec

These I singing in spring collect for lovers. These I Singing in Spring. Walt Whitman. APN-1

These, in the day when heaven was falling. Epitaph on an Army of Mercenaries. A. E. Housman. FaBoWar; NAEL-6v2; NAEL-7v2; NAMCP V.1; NoP-4; NoP-5; NPeEn; OxBEV; PoAgWa; SoSe-8; WaAnP

These inner city alleyways connect us. Alley Games 6/The Ascension. Ira B. Jones. BtF

These just-ripe, perfectly packaged blackberries. Plan, The. Jack Turner. BAP-97

These knacks, my lord, I cannot call to mind. George Gascoigne. SacPr *Fr.* Steele Glas, The.

These labor days, when shirking hardly looks like working. Back to Town. John Hollander. NAMCP V.2; NoAM

These labouring wits, like paviours, mend our ways. Edward Young. OBSV *Fr.* Epistles to Mr. Pope.

These lacustrine cities grew out of loathing. These Lacustrine Cities. John Ashbery. NAMCP V.2
    (These lacustrine cities grew out of loathing.) FTOS

These lagoons, these watercourses. Craze Field, The. Les A. Murray. UpMys

These Last Days. Katie Donovan. NeBl

These lazy spring days. Buson. SoOfWa, *tr. by* Sam Hamill

These lectures afford me a great pleasure. Lectures on Love, The. Edward Hirsch. PuP-23

These lights grew out of signs. Apprentice, The. Gerard Malanga. AHA

These lips of Mr. Tunis Flood are cornflower. Postmortem. Maurice Kilwein Guevara. AmPoNex

These little limbs [*or* limmes]. Salutation [*or* Salutations], The. Thomas Traherne. NoP-4; NoP-5; SacPr

These locusts by day, these crickets by night. Wallace Stevens. PoA 2002 *Fr.* Things of August.

These lovely groves of fountain-trees that shake. Golden Bough. Elinor Wylie. MoAmPo

These market-dames, mid-aged, with lips thin-drawn,. Thomas Hardy. NoAM; OBMV *Fr.* At Casterbridge Fair.

These massed grey shadows. Mothball Fleet: Benicia, California. John Haines. PWW2

[These] meetings in dreams. Yakamochi. TAL, *tr. by* Arthur Waley

These men are on their feet, not all day long. Driftwood and Seacoal. Andrew Crozier. Oth

These men died with the wrong names. Dying with the Wrong Name. Sam Hamod. UnSA

These men? In their dented felt hats. Colors of Desire, The. David Mura. LoL

These men lying here were carrying honors to Apollo. Simonides. PoCho, *tr. by* Burton Raffel

These men, / these proud black men. Tuskegee Airfield. Marilyn Nelson Waniek. ESEAA; GT; OtW

These messages are secret, the initials. Personal Column. Tom Paulin. PNI

These mountains: blackness, silence, and snow. Birth. Georg Trakl. WED, *tr. by* Robert Bly

These mountains, only one language can lift them. Welsh and Wales. Waldo Williams. BBMWP, *tr. by* Anthony Conran

These naked girls really love animals. Pastoral with Internet Porn. Jennifer L. Knox. FreRad

These nights we fear the aspects of the moon. Full Moon: New Guinea. Karl Shapiro. APT-2; PWW2

These nights when first. August Nights. Jean Janzen. GeoHom

These no-man's-lands. Poem-Object. André Breton. PFTM-1

These nymphs that I would perpetuate. Afternoon of a Faun, The. Stéphane Mallarmé. NAWM-7v2, *tr. by* Henry Weinfield

These older towns die. Poema para los Californios Muertos. Lorna Dee Cervantes. NAMCP V.2; PoPoPo

These pages, crumbling under my fingers. Old Photograph Album. Linda Pastan. TaR

These peaks gather like snowy swords. At Waterfall Temple. Chang K'o-chiu. CrYelRi, *tr. by* Sam Hamill

These pearls of thought in Persian gulfs were bred. In a Copy of Omar Khayyám. James Russell Lowell. NCAP

These people on the road—why they've gone out. Gates. Georgi Borisov. CSCBP, *tr. by* Georgi Belev and Lisa Sapinkopf

These pines / stand for it. Nightfall. C. Robert Lloyd. ICANM

These Poems. John Jarmain. FaBoWar

These poems do not live: it's a sad diagnosis. Stillborn. Sylvia Plath. CAP-8

These poems don't amount. Leaf Huts and Snow Houses. Olav H. Hauge. WED, *tr. by* Robert Bly

These poems, these poems. These Poems, She Said. Robert Bringhurst. TAPaP

These pools that, though in forests, still reflect. Spring Pools. Robert Frost. APT-1; ColAP; CtM; NoAM; OxBoAm

These [*or* Thise] rioteres [*or* riotoures] thre[e] of which[e] I tell[e]. Geoffrey Chaucer. NPeEn; OBNV *Fr.* Canterbury Tales, The.

These roads will take you into your own country. Book of the Dead, The. Muriel Rukeyser. APT-2

These sea slugs. Issa. EH, *tr. by* Robert Hass

These secretly are going to some place. Grand Central, with Soldiers, in Early Morning. Howard Nemerov. AmWaPo

These seven houses have learned to face one another. On a Painting by Patient B of the Independence State Hospital for the Insane. Donald Justice. NoAM

These shape the creature that is I. (LL) Long Live the Weeds. Theodore Roethke. NoAM; PoA 2002

These sibilants aren't the right sound. Sleeplessness. Michelle Boisseau. ExTi

These songs in my ears are enough. Long Distance. Max Winter. NeAmPo

These stanzas are done. (LL) Gertrude Stein. NAMCP V.1; PoA 2002 *Fr.* Stanzas in Meditation.

These statues on the grass will not grow old. May in My Lai. Menna Elfyn. ATSWP, *tr. by* Robert Minhinnick

These Strangers, In a Foreign World. Emily Dickinson. SAmP

These summer days I carry images of stone. Phenomenology of Stones, The. Thomas McCarthy. PBCIP

These, surely, are the unwholesomest whores of all. Yorkville. James Schuyler. AHA

These Tall Constructions. Dora Maar. YaTCFP, *tr. by* Mary Ann Caws *and* Jean-Pierre Cauvin

These tall lilies, color. Lilies, The. Richard Emil Braun. NoAM

These temp'rall goods God (the most Wise) commends. Temporall Goods. Robert Herrick. SacPr

These ten-year-olds all want other names. Lunch with Girl Scouts. Sharon Bryan. ReTh

These Things from Words. Ivan Metodiev. CSCBP *Fr.* Songs for Orphans Big and Small.

These things, our things. Things. Gloria Fuertes. RaW, *tr. by* Philip Levine

These thousand peaks cut off the flight of birds. River Snow. Liu Tsung-yüan. ColAnChi; NDACCP, *tr. by* Gary Snyder

These to me are beautiful people. Preference. Elinor Wylie. APT-1

These Too Are Our Elders. Jack A. Mapanje. HBAPE; NAfrP

These tracings from a world that's dead. To Violet. Basil Bunting. PoA 2002

These Trees in Particular. Susan Stewart. AmAlph

These Two. Harriet Monroe. IllVoic

These two tales I tell of myself and the life I led. John Hollander. VCAP *Fr.* Powers of Thirteen.

These unseen gravestones, and the darker dead. (LL) In a Churchyard. Richard Wilbur. HeIP-4; UpMys

These unshaped islands, on the sawyer's bench. New Zealand. James Keir Baxter. NoP-4; NoP-5

These verses weare made By Michaell Drayton Esquier Poett Lawreatt the night before hee dyed. Michael Drayton. NPeEn; PBRV

These Vietnamese women might as well be Jesus and we with our crusty. Ritual. Crystal Williams. RD

These watches. Ticking, still. Each hour is cold. Seven Paintings By Brueghel. Anne Simpson. OpeFie

These were my neighbors. It's a big group prose. Greg Williamson. NoP-5

These were not the average "contented" cows. Cows in Trouble. Steve Martin. MotU

These were the same horses. (LL) She Had Some Horses. Joy Harjo. HATNAP; LoL

These wings, these lights, this shoal of angels. Shrimp Boats, Biloxi. Campbell McGrath. AmPoNex

These winter days. Skeleton of Winter. Joy Harjo. LoL

These winter trees charcoaled against bare sky. First Lesson: Winter Trees. Michael Waters. NevBe

These women all. Women. ------ Heath. NoSic

These women crying in my head. Three Emily's, The. Dorothy Livesay. BrAP; NALW

These women live in roots darkness. Circumcising Pandora. Mirlande Jean-Gilles. BtF

These Women Plunder My Husband. *Unknown*. WoPoe *Fr.* Gathasaptasati, The.

These wood-shadows, timid, patient. These wood-shadows. Philippe Jaccottet. VCWP, *tr. by* Derek Mahon

These words appall and daunt them all. Michael Wigglesworth. NAAL-3 *Fr.* Day of Doom, The [First Section].

These words are dedicated to those who died. Irena Klepfisz. TaR *Fr.* Bashert.

These Words Are for You, Grandmother. Jean Janzen. ACAMVP

These words have no imagination. Simple Like That. Wil'um Lee. InTrad

These words seem to be rehearsing. Roy Kiyooka. NLPA *Fr.* Pear Tree Pomes.

These—saw Visions. Emily Dickinson. SWaP

These—the bright symbols of man's hope and fame. Stars, The. Madison Cawein. APN-2

149. Thesis. Peter Riley. VaPo *Fr.* Excavations.

Thespia, bearing a beautiful race, stranger-loving, Muse-beloved. Korinna [*or* Corinna]. SaLy, *tr. by* Diane Rayor

Thessalian. Winifred Bryher. PoA 2002

They. Venus Khoury-Gata. PoArWo, *tr. by* Lucy McNair

"They." Siegfried Sassoon. NAEL-6v2; NAEL-7v2; NoP-4; NoP-5; OBSV; OBWP

They. Shin Kyŏngnim. CAMKP, *tr. by* Kevin O'Rourke

They all are asleep, below. Juan Ramón Jiménez. *See* They are all asleep, below.

They all but cry out. Olga Zondberg. CRWP, *tr. by* Daniel Weissbort

They all came by today. Garage Sale. Brian Henry. AmPoNex

They all came, some wore sentiments. Other Tradition, The. John Ashbery. FTOS; PmAP

They all climbed up on a high board-fence. Nine Little Goblins, The. James Whitcomb Riley. NOxBChV

They All Laughed. Ira Gershwin. APT-2; ReLy

They all muddy the water that it may seem deep. Friedrich Wilhelm Nietzsche. WoPoe *Fr.* Zarathustra.

They All Save One Last Squirt. John Steffler. Coast *Fr.* Grey Islands, The.

They all see the same movies. Powwow. W. D. Snodgrass. SoSe-8

They All Think. Giovanna Pollarolo. TANSG, *tr. by* Marjorie Agosin

They all want to break at some point. Breaking Points. Eamon Grennan. ModIr

They all were looking for a king. George Macdonald. OBEV; SacPr *Fr.* Paul Faber, Surgeon.

They also serve who only stand and wait. (LL) On His Blindness. John Milton. BLPJKO; CABP; ChIV-2; CtM; GSo; HeIP-4; ITBLP; ItP; NAEL-6v1; NIL-7; NoP-4; NOSC; NPeEn; OBEV; OxBSo; PoPoPo; SacPr; SoSe-8; TFi; TRP; WaAnP; WeW-3

They always had me. Ophelia Speaks. Tracy Youngblom. IaFF

They amputated / Your hips from my loins. Pity, A. We Were Such a Good Invention. Yehuda Amichai. FIT, *tr. by* Robert Friend

They and all would resume what I have told them. (LL) Walt Whitman. CAGL; ColAP *Fr.* Song of Myself.

They and I. Xavier Villaurrutia. CAGL, *tr. by* Fanny Arango-Ramos and William Keeth

They and I are civilized. (LL) Heritage. Countee Cullen. APT-2; ColAP; HeIP-4; MoAmPo; NAAL-5; NAAPv.2; NAMCP V.1; NoAM; NoP-4; NoP-5; PoPoPo; SSLK

They appeared two but they were one thing only. Gentleman and the Lady, The. Vivian Lamarque. CItWP, *tr. by* Cinzia Sartini Blum and Lara Trubowitz

They applaud at the periods and sigh. Poet's Shuffle, The. Calvin Forbes. GT; LTA

They are a gift I have wanted again. Horses in Snow. Roberta Hill Whiteman. NoAM

They are all asleep, below. Road. Juan Ramón Jiménez. WED, *tr. by* Robert Bly

(They all are asleep, below.) RaW

They are all dying. Death as History. Jay Wright. ESEAA

They Are All Falling around Me. Bernice Reagon. FuFl

They are all gone away. House on the Hill, The. Edwin Arlington Robinson. APN-2; CtM; MakPoe; MoAmPo; NAAPv.1; NCAP; OxBoAm

They Are All Gone into the World of Light! Henry Vaughan. BASC; CABP; InoFa; NAEL-6v1; NAEL-7v1; NoP-4; NoP-5; NOSC; NPeEn; PBRV; PoPoPo; RSR; TFi; WaAnP; WoPoe

(Friends Departed.) OBEV

They are an unknown universe ever since. Link. Mehmet Yardımcı. NaPG, *tr. by* Talat Sait Halman

They are and suffer; that is all they do. W. H. Auden. NAMCP V.1

They are as fierce as tigers, rude as bears. (LL) Common People, The. Rowland Watkyns. AngWePo; BASC

They are assembled, astounded, bewildered. Rainer Maria Rilke. GI

They are at table. Last Supper, The. Jacques Prévert. CLPP, *tr. by* Lawrence Ferlinghetti

They are bodies left unburied. Rondeau. Cheryl Clarke. FFC

They are bringing back the bones of Che Guevara. Y, The. Brenda Hillman. MoASP

They are burning a boat on the beach. Decommissioning. Katrina Porteous. NeBl

They are burying my nanny. A poor. Nanny Tanya. Yevgeny Borisovich Rein. ItGoST, *tr. by* Judith Hemschemeyer

They Are Coming? Josephine D. Henderson Heard. CBWP-4

They are Coming. Filippo Tommaso Marinetti. PFTM-1

They are creatures lacking malice. (LL) Geometry Class. Mark Bibbins. AmPoNex; WiU

They are cutting down the great plane-trees at the end of the gardens. Trees Are Down, The. Charlotte Mew. ChIV-2; MoBrPo; MoWP; OxAEP-2; VWP

They are cutting up into pieces. It Took One Hundred Years. Malika O'Lahsen. HAWP; WoPoe, *tr. by* Eric Sellin

They are extremely rare. (LL) Frog, The. Joseph Hilaire Pierre Belloc. ChAP; NOxBChV; NTCP

They are falling all around me. They Are All Falling around Me. Bernice Reagon. FuFl

They are fast in their cars. In the Shadow of Fire. Frieda Hughes. NeBl

They are finished with sex. This Is How the Magician Produces a Dove out of the Hat. Mohamed Metwalli. AnVo, *tr. by* Mohamed Enani

They are formidable, the wild geese, in their numbers. 337,000, December, 2000. Aaron Fogel. BAP-04

They are gathering hay. The truck rolls slowly. Haying. Wyatt Prunty. PfSP

They are going to some point true and unproven. (LL) Geometry. Rita Dove. HeIP-4; NAMCP V.2; PtR

They are heard as a choir of seven. Pleiades, The. Mary Barnard. APT-2

They are in their element. (LL) Aquarium du Trocadéro. Duncan Bush. AngWePo; TCAWP

They are killing me tonight, they are murdering me tonight. On the State-sanctioned Murder of Shaka Sankofa. Suheir Hammad. BRtP

They are lang deid, folk that I used to ken. Elegy. Robert Garioch. EdScPo; NePenScot; NPeEn

They are light as flakes of dandruff with scrawny legs. Crabs. Marge Piercy. NBLV

They are like figures held in some glass ball. Children Walking Home from School through Good Neighborhood. Donald Justice. CAP-8; NIL-7; NIP-4

They are like those crazy women. At Pegasus. Terrance Hayes. AmPoNex

They are listening to what he hears. They ar long ago. Frost's Last Lecture: A Tape: His Audience—1963. William Olsen. VisFro

They are made to stand side by side. Poor Houses, The. Ed Roberson. GT

They are making a crèche at the Saturday morning classes. Crib, The. Robert Finch. OBCP

They are more delicate even than shrubs and they run. Ox Looks at Man, An. Carlos Drummond de Andrade. IPoFL; PoetW; PtR; TCLAP, *tr. by* Mark Strand

They are my secret food. Children's Letters, The. Dorothy Livesay. NALW

They are names. (LL) September 11, 1973. Emma Sepúlveda-Pulvirenti. CFP; TANSG, *tr. by* Shaun Griffin

They are no lords, no marquesses or dukes. Shrimps. Nguyễn Văn Lạc. WoPoe, *tr. by* Huỳnh Sanh Thông

They are no trophies of the sun. (LL) Praise for an Urn. Hart Crane. MoAmPo; NAAPv.2; NoAM; WeW-3

They are not dead, they are not dead! Argonauts, The. D. H. Lawrence. NoAM

They are not here. And we, we are the Others. Absent, The. Edwin Muir. GPTC; NAMCP V.1; NoAM

They are not lilacs, though. Jacaranda. Carol Muske-Dukes. AmAlph

They Are Not Long. Ernest Dowson. *See* Vitae Summa Brevis Spem Nos Vetat Incohare Longam.

They are not long, the weeping and the laughter. Vitae Summa Brevis Spem Nos Vetat Incohare Longam. Ernest Dowson. CABP; NoP-4; NoP-5; NPeEn; OBEV; OxBEV; TFi

They are often. Lattice at "Split." Tina Darragh. FTOS

They are ordinary, here. The man, lying in the metal bed. Act One. Danusha Laméris de Garza. IaFF

They Are Planning to Cancel the School Milk Program to Fund a Tax Cut for the Middle Class. Liz Rosenberg. InvLad

They are plump. Gathering the Wild Figs—Vizcaina, Gomera. Emilia Paredes. AFaM; IPoFL

They are potted at night, pink, and packed. Heavenly. David Baker. Vesp

They are pounded into the earth. It Is This Way with Men. C. K. Williams. RaBo; VCAP

They are rattling breakfast plates in basement kitchens. Morning at the Window. T. S. Eliot. OxBEV; PoA 2002; TCAPo

They are riding away from whatever might have been. Shooting Script, A. Seamus Heaney. BodElec

They are 7 in number, just 7. Seven, The. *Unknown.* WoPoe, *tr. by* Jerome Rothenberg

They are shaking their wings and hooting. (LL) Frances Densmore and Tohono O'odham. NAAPv.1; SWaP *Fr.* Songs for Treating Sickness, Sung durring the Four Parts of the Night.

They are slowly emptying the Armory. Matthew Brady Speaks of Whitman. Matthew Graham. ViWalt

They are small enough to find and care for a tiny stone. Her Body. Daniel Halpern. BAP-97

They are so cowardly and stupid. Romance for the Wild Turkey, A. Paul Zimmer. P180

They are so like. Dolls. David St. John. AmAlph

They are stalking humming birds. It Is a German Honeymoon. Kenneth Rexroth. APT-2

They are stones. Words. Catherine Fisher. TCAWP

They are taking all my letters, and they. Dishonest Mailmen, The. Robert Creeley. OxBoAm

They are talking of trepanning the Indian starling. Starling, The. Ruth Padel. NeBrP

They are terribly white. Cyclamens. Michael Field. ViWPN; VWP

They Are the Same. Priscilla Jane Thompson. CBWP-2

They are, the surfaces, gorgeous: a master, The. Gorgeous Surfaces. Thomas Lux. AmAlph

They are the watchful eyes of future generations. (LL) Answer, The. Bei Dao. AF; PFTM-2, *tr. by* Bonnie S. McDougall

They are there. Dogs on the Cliffs, The. Michael Burkard. BodElec

They are there just the same. Wheels of the Trains, The. W. S. Merwin. GM

They are thin. Women Who Love Angels. Judith Ortiz Cofer. TouFir

They are turning people into hulks of mud. Latest News. David Craig. RSaN

They are unholy who are born. Wild Plum. John Orrick. APT-1

They are very small, my neighbors. Minotaur Next Door, The. Greg Pape. PBCAP

They are waiting for it, waiting all their lives. Grass and the Sin, The. Larissa Szporluk. AmPoNex

They are waiting for me somewhere beyond Eden Rock. Eden Rock. Charles Causley. NoP-4; NoP-5; NPeEn; StAl

They are, we know, an acquired taste. Olives. Catharine Savage Brosman. PoDa

They are weighing the babies again on color television. Video Cuisine. Maxine W. Kumin. NoAM

They are young. Old Women, The. Naomi Long Madgett. OxAAAP

They arm themselves with Saracen hauberks. *Unknown.* NAWM-5v1; NAWM-7v1 *Fr.* Song of Roland, The.

They arrive. Sirhan Drinks His Coffee in the Cafeteria. Mahmoud Darwish. VCWP, *tr. by* Rana Kabbani

They arrive, always, unexpected. Yiddish Muses, The. Jacqueline Osherow. TaR

They ask her. Shower of Secret Things, The. Nathaniel Mackey. PmAP

They ask me to remember. Why some people be mad at me sometimes. Lucille Clifton. ESEAA

They ask why I still bother coming back. Interior, An. Paul Farley. NeBrP

They asked me how I knew. Smoke Gets in Your Eyes. Otto Harbach. ReLy

They asked that man for his time. In Trying Times. Heberto Padilla. AF; PoetW, *tr. by* Andrew Hurley and Alastair Reid

They await / War, and the news. George Oppen. AmWaPo *Fr.* Of Being Numerous.

They beat me different ways. Beatings. Joan Larkin. WiU

They bespoke doomsday and they meant it by. Geoffrey Hill. UpMys *Fr.* Funeral Music.

They bide their time off serpentine. Ancient Monuments. John Ormond. AngWePo; OBWVE

They blaze, between my eyes, the wick-twist and the intermediate hierarchy of an image this afternoon. Angélica Tornero. SPV, *tr. by* Jen Hofer

They bring in the knife, they show you. Angels, The. Cleopatra Mathis. ExTi

They bring me gifts, they honour me. If They Honoured Me, Giving Me Their Gifts. Michael Field. OBMV

They brought her to the hospital. Aunt Lil. Paul Zweig. BodElec

They brought him in on a stretcher from the world. Grandfather. Derek Mahon. OxBSo

They brought in the brine-crusted drift-wood. Drift-Wood. Clara Ann Thompson. CBWP-2

They brought me to the waters of the spirits. Tohono O'odham. NAAPv.1 *Fr.* Songs for Treating Sickness, Sung durring the Four Parts of the Night.

They bubble up to the surface of our memory. They. Venus Khoury-Gata. PoArWo, *tr. by* Lucy McNair

They built the front, upon my word. Building of a New Church, The. *Unknown.* HHAm

They burn the radio and listen to the blues. John Tranter. NoAM *Fr.* Crying in Early Infancy.

They burn you. Hitchhikers, The. Diane Wakoski. NoAM

They burnt their last witch in CONNECTICUT. Connecticut. Fitz-Greene Halleck.

They call all experience of the senses *mystic,* when the experience / is considered. Mystic. D. H. Lawrence. BLT

They call him the Dog. Brother Ben. John Rybicki. AmPoNex

They call me and I go. Complaint. William Carlos Williams. SAmP

They call me from there. Calling, The. Luis Palés Matos. BLPSL, *tr. by* Rene de Costa, Rigas Kappatos and Eleni Paidoussi

They call me Ghede. The butts. Ghede Poem. Nathaniel Mackey. PmAP

They call, no date. I'll Walk Alone. Sammy Cahn. ReLy

They call this "Black North." Names. Gerald Dawe. PNI

They call you Lady Luck. Luck, Be a Lady. Frank Loesser. APT-2; ReLy

They Call You Moody. Ann Townsend. LegDan

They called forth the train whistle at midnight. Nocturno de Washington. Pablo Medina. BodElec

They called her a cat. What They Said. Tanure Ojaide. HBAPE

They called it Annandale—and I was there. How Annandale Went Out. Edwin Arlington Robinson. APT-1; GSo; MoAmPo; NAMCP V.1; NoAM; SoSe-8

They called us. Charm, The. Rita Dove. OxAAAP

They came along. So That No Light Would Remain to Love Us. Rose Ausländer. GTCP, *tr. by* Reinhold Grimm

They came at night with their flashlights. Minutes of Hasiba, The. Holger Teschke. FaBoWar, *tr. by* Margitt Lehbert

They came back, a well known face. This Beach Can Be Dangerous. Allen Curnow. HarvBoo

They came back from the bush-haunts. Arrivants. Musaemura Bonus Zimunya. HBAPE; NAfrP

They came by the thousands into the square, eyeballs bulging. Playing the Part. Nina Nyhart. PfS

They came down from the ridge. Dunbar, 1650. Sidney Keyes. FaBoWar

They came drowned in the afternoon to the blue house on the wharf of brown broadcloth cafes. Epitafio. Ece Ayhan. WoPoe, *tr. by* Murat Nemet-Nejat

They came for the water. Homesteaders. Rosemary Catacalos. TiP2

They came from around the globe to change the shape of the globe. In Praise of the Seattle Coalition. Eliot Katz. BRtP

They came from far and wide. Portia. Kathleen Kirk. IaFF

They came from the arterial streets. Survivor. Mike Jenkins. TCAWP

They came from the terror and tumult. Exodus. Jaime Torres Bodet. TCLAP, *tr. by* Sonja Karsen

They came in search of hopes. Refugees. Patrick Sylvain. OGAHCP, *tr. by* Boadiba and Jack Hirschman

They came in to the little town. We Are Going. Oodgeroo of the tribe Noonuccal. BMAP; NOBAu

They came out of the sun undetected. Raid, The. William Everson. NoAM; OtW; PWW2

They came, since there are certain matters, and you gentlemen have / only yourselves to blame. December 14, 1979: A Poetry Reading. Stanislaw Baranczak. AF, *tr. by* Magnus J. Krynski

They came that morning, in gowns of pale green and white. Abstraction. Eleanor Wilner. ExTi

They came to rearrange the dust and shadows. Night Vision of the Gulf War. Dale Jacobson. AmWaPo

They came to the door because he was small or went to some church. Book of the Dead Man #58, The. Marvin Bell. OPRER; TaR

They came to the lodge door. Wolf "Aunt." Maurice Kenny. HATNAP

They came with a fury. Flight of the Itzás. Chilam Balam. WoPoe, *tr. by* Christopher Sawyer-Lauçanno

They can break the night like glass. What I Know About Owls. Paul Zimmer. PfSP

They can shake their boodies but they can't shake *you*. (LL) Blues Don't Change, The. Al Young. ESEAA; GT

They can suit whomever man's intestines can. (LL) Summer: "I stroll on Madison in expensive clothes, sour." Edwin Denby. NYP2; OxBoAm

They cannot steal, thou giv'st so much. (LL) To Saxham. Thomas Carew. BASC; CavPo

They can't live on their own. Eagles at Dollywood. Stephen Powers. RWB

They Can't Take That Away from Me. Ira Gershwin. ReLy

They carried a shadow in the soul's place. In the Darkness of the Other. Clara Silva. TANSG, *tr. by* Celeste Kostopulos-Cooperman

They carried her above us. As we walked. Dream of Christopher Columbus, The. Juan Felipe Herrera. TouFir

They carry their long, heavy bosoms inside old sweaters and wear examples. Thrift Shop Ladies. Jennifer M. Pierson. ReTh

They choke cities like snowstorms. Blonde White Women. Patricia Smith. GT; UnSA

They choose paths. Let Them Choose Paths. Odia Ofeimun. HBAPE

They climbed on sketchy ladders towards God. Cathedral Builders. John Ormond. GoPo; NoP-4; NoP-5; TCAWP

They Closed Her Eyes. Gustavo Adolfo Bécquer. SpanPo, *tr. by* Muriel Kittel

They come and are pressed. People of Olives. Nidaa Khoury. DTA, *tr. by* Karen Alkalay-Gut

They come as a boon and a blessing to men. *Unknown.* OBCoV *Fr.* Advertising Rhymes.

They come as couriers of Heaven: their feet. Three Elements, The. Madison Cawein. APN-2

They come back now, those nights my friend and I. Hitting Golfballs off the Bluff. Jeffrey Harrison. MoASP

They come, beset by riddling hail. Thomas Hardy. FaBoWar *Fr.* Dynasts, The.

They come down on their snowmobiles for the last time. End of Human Reign on Bashan Hill, The. Bernadette Mayer. FTOS

They come from the mountains, from the lowlands, from the desert. Parade of the Fallen. Hayim Hefer. NRoS, *tr. by* Esther Raizen

They Come Humming. Sharon Chmielarz. MiVo

They come in at night, leave in the early morning. Men of Terry Street. Douglas Dunn. WaAnP

They come in off the sea peaceable masters. Constable's Clouds for Keats. Stanley Plumly. BodElec

They come in white livery bringing the sun. Robed Heart, The. Elizabeth Spires. ExTi

They come like the ghosts of horses, shyly. Pit Ponies, The. Leslie Norris. ChAP

They come running. August 6, 1950. Tōge Sankichi. AtGh, *tr. by* Richard H. Minear

They come to resemble Buddhas. Hamburger. August Kleinzahler. PmAP

They come without siren-song or any ushering. To Eat To-day. Nancy Cunard. RSaN

They continue. The trains keep on passing. Trains, The. Sarina Helfgott. MirDau, *tr. by* Celeste Kostopulos-Cooperman

They coughed into the Aquarius wind. Redundant Miners. Mogg Williams. RSaN

They could be reservoirs for water. Angelo Lumelli. ItPo, *tr. by* Gayle Ridinger

They Couldn't Compare to You. Cole Porter. ReLy

They couldn't understand why the drover cried. Drover's Boy, The. Ted Egan. NOBAu

They cross from Glasgow to a black city. Settlers. Tom Paulin. PNI

They cross the yard. Louise Glück. NALW *Fr.* Dedication to Hunger.

They cut off his left arm / and his right arm. National Hero, The. Gojko Djogo. AF, *tr. by* Michael March *and* Dušan Puvaić

They cut off my hot water. Tatiana Shcherbina. CRWP, *tr. by* Daniel Weissbort

They dance the world as. John Cage. APSN *Fr.* Diary: How to Improve the World (You Will Only Make Matters Worse).

They danced by the light of the moon. (LL) Owl and the Pussy-Cat [*or* Pussycat], The. Edward Lear. BLPJKO; BRP; CABP; ChAP; CtM; NBLV; NoP-4; NoP-5; NOxBChV; NPeEn; NTCP; OBCoV; OBSP; OWoS; TFi; TLR; TriCat; WaAnP; WoPoe

They danced in the moon on nights. Moon Dance (Listen Sylvia). Tony Nduka Otiono. NeNiPo

They decide to exchange heads. Kinky. Denise Duhamel. AmPoNex

They demanded in loud voices. Roll Call of Bones, The. César Vallejo. AF; WED, *tr. by* Robert Bly

They demonize the ripples. Saints. Lana C. Williams. BtF

They descend upon us in the Douz graveyard. Sisters of Saida Manoubia, The. Sibyl James. FiBr

They descended into hell after injustice. Miners. Branko Miljkovic. WoPoe, *tr. by* Charles Simic

They destroyed the famous and wealthy. Ibycus. STV, *tr. by* Diane Rayor

They did not come to be heroes and legends. One Million Men Marching 2. Bernard Keller. BtF

They did not come to claim you back. Helen Todd: My Birthname. Sandra McPherson. LoL

They did not intend to distinguish between the essence. Yellow Book, The. Muriel Spark. EdScPo

They did not know. Dawn Dissolves the Monsters. Paul Éluard. AF, *tr. by* Lloyd Alexander

They did not know this face. Job. Elizabeth Sewell. ChIV-1

They did the deed of darkness. You and I Saw Hawks Exchanging the Prey. James Wright. NoAM

They Didn't Get Me. Alma Villanueva. UnSA

They didn't have much trouble. Teaching the Ape to Write Poems. James Tate. OxBoAm

They didn't want me around. Only Cherries? Kenneth Patchen. RaF

They died, these two. These Two. Harriet Monroe. IllVoic

They Do Not Have to Nest in Your Hair: A Tribute to Ron Brown. Carolyn Joyner. BtF

They do not know how to search for the World-Adorner. Hayâlî. OLP, *tr. by* Walter Andrews, Najaat Black and Mehmet Kalpakli

They do not live in the world. Animals, The. Edwin Muir. ChIV-1; CtM; HeIP-4; MoBrPo

They do not sleep nights. Legend of the Albino Farm. Erin Belieu. NeAmPo

They do not talk of Myrddin on the bridge at Beddgelert. Dinas Emrys. Brian Morris. AngWePo

They do not think whom they souse with spray. (LL) Walt Whitman. CAGL; ColAP; CtM; NoP-4; NoP-5; SAmP; WaAnP *Fr.* Song of Myself.

They do those things so well in France. (LL) Pig's-Eye View of Literature, A. Dorothy Parker. APT-1; BrAP

They dogged him all one afternoon. On the Way to the Mission. Duncan Campbell Scott. BrAP

They done took Cordelia. Stony Lonesome. Langston Hughes. SAmP

They don't build houses like that any more. Verandahs. Robert Francis Brissenden. NOBAu

They don't come along every day. Look out! There's a big one. (LL) My Philosophy of Life. John Ashbery. BodElec; OxBoAm

They don't have to have that. They don't Have to Have That Look. David Rattray. WoPoe

They don't Have to Have That Look. David Rattray. WoPoe

They don't hold grudges. First Monday Scottsboro Alabama. Tom Weatherly. EGAG

They don't live long. Basho. EH, *tr. by* Robert Hass

They don't notice. Issa. EH, *tr. by* Robert Hass

They don't plow, nor do they sow. Birds. Alexander Gerov. CSCBP, *tr. by* Georgi Belev and Lisa Sapinkopf

They don't want to stop. They can't stop. Demographics. Catherine Bowman. ExTi; SUP

They dragged you from [the] homeland. Strong Men. Sterling Allen Brown. ISC; ItP; NAAPv.2; NAMCP V.1; OxAAAP

They drank. They ate. They smoked. Igor Khomin. TCRusP, *tr. by* Daniel Weissbort

They drive me mad, those rosy lips, forever prattling. Dioscorides. HePo *Fr.* Epigrams.

They drove to Grado in a borrowed car. Wedding Day, The. V. Penelope Pelizzon. AmPoNex

They drove to the Market with ringing pockets. Hamnavoe Market. George Mackay Brown. EmeKit; NePenScot

They drove us out. Exodus. Horst Bienek. AF

They eat beans mostly, this old yellow pair. Bean Eaters, The. Gwendolyn Brooks. AFaM; AmFaPo; ESEAA; HeIP-4; HHAm; MoWP; NAAL-5; NALW; NAMCP V.2; NoP-4; NoP-5; PoPoPo; TRP; WaAnP; WeW-3

They eat only metal oatmeal and go barefoot in the spring muds. Their women are. Pontoon. Kit Robinson. FTOS

They Eat Out. Margaret Atwood. NAMCP V.2; NoAM

They end their flight. Buson. EH, *tr. by* Robert Hass

They ended parle, and both addressed for fight. John Milton. OBWP *Fr.* Paradise Lost.

They enter without calling by the false door. Burdens. Laura Riesco. TANSG, *tr. by* Shaun Griffin and Emma Sepúlveda-Pulvirenti

They entered the fiery furnace. Six Million, The. Naomi Replansky. InoFa

They err who think it glorious to subdue. John Milton. FaBoWar *Fr.* Paradise Regained [*or* Regain'd].

They explained to me the bloody bandages. Past-Lives Therapy. Charles Simic. StAl

They fed the bonfire chips, chair legs. Butane, Kerosene, Gasoline. Ann Townsend. NAPBL

They Feed They Lion. Philip Levine. CalPo; CAP-8; ItP; NAMCP V.2; NoAM; NoP-4; NoP-5; OxBoAm; StAl; VCAP

They feed they Lion and he comes. (LL) They Feed They Lion. Philip Levine. CalPo; CAP-8; ItP; NAMCP V.2; NoAM; NoP-4; NoP-5; OxBoAm; StAl; VCAP

They fell asleep but not for long, for soon. Callimachus. HePo *Fr.* Hecale.

They felt how far beyond the scope. Herman Melville. TCAPo *Fr.* Clarel: A Poem and Pilgrimage in the Holy Land.

They Fle from Me That Sometyme Did Me Seke. Sir Thomas Wyatt. *See* Lover Showeth How He Is Forsaken of Such as He Sometime Enjoyed, The.

They Flee From Me. Sir Thomas Wyatt. *See* Lover Showeth How He Is Forsaken of Such as He Sometime Enjoyed, The.

They fle[e] from me that sometime [*or* sometyme] did me se[e]k[e]. Lover Showeth How He Is Forsaken of Such as He Sometime Enjoyed, The. Sir Thomas Wyatt. CABP; ClHu; HeIP-4; MakPoe; NoSic; NPeEn; OxBEV; TFi; TRP

They flung many quinces toward the chariot. Stesichoros. SaLy, *tr.* by Diane Rayor

They fluttered off like withered souls of men. (LL) Pity of the Leaves, The. Edwin Arlington Robinson. APN-2; MoAmPo

They fold me up into myself. Twilight (Between Dog and Wolf). Olga Orozco. SurWo, *tr.* by Natalie Kenvin

They force you to crawl, these mountains. Escape Journey, 1988. Choman Hardi. BeAl

They Fought South of the Wall. *Unknown.* ColAnChi, *tr.* by Burton Watson

They found her unresponsive in the street. Rafael Campo. AmPoNex; WiU *Fr.* Ten Patients, and Another.

They found him in a phone booth, huddled. Clark Kent, Naked. Fred Moramarco. PML

They found him in the fields and called him back to music. Bunk Johnson Blowing. Muriel Rukeyser. SeSe

They Found Him Sitting in a Chair. Horace Gregory. MoAmPo

They found in his chest a lamp of roses and a moon. Mahmoud Darwish. VCWP

They found the world's new structure was a binary. Saltcoats Structuralists, The. Robert Crawford. NeBrP

They fuck you up, your mum and dad. This Be The Verse. Philip Larkin. NAMCP V.2; NoAM; NoP-5; NPeEn; PoetW; PoPoPo; StAl

They gathered around and told him not to do it. Noah. Roy Daniells. GoPo

They gave him a finger, but he took the whole hand. King Saul and I. Yehuda Amichai. PoSu, *tr.* by Assia Gutmann

They Gave Him Vinegar and Gall (Matt. 27) and Wine Mingled with Myrrh (Mark 15). Francis Quarles. NOSC

They gave them a rifle of the Mauzer model. To Wither Like Weeds in an Easterly Wind. Arye Sivan. NRoS, *tr.* by Esther Raizen

They get drunk, these Great-Sledmakers. Their copper mugs. Great-Sledmakers, The. Kenneth Patchen. MotU

They give a man a taste for death. (LL) Some can gaze and not be sick. A. E. Housman. OBSV; OxBEV

They give you a number. Hotel Room. Blaga Dimitrova. CSCBP, *tr.* by Georgi Belev and Lisa Sapinkopf

They go at it in the backseat of our car. We Take the New Young Couple Out to Dinner. Carol Tufts. PasH

They go upstairs. Gaze, The. Gu Cheng. WoBe, *tr.* by Joseph R. Allen

They got him in the end, of course. Walt Whitman at the Reburial of Poe. Nicholas Christopher. ViWalt

They got them fades now listening. Revolutionary Thoughts. Crystal Williams. BtF

They grew in beauty, side by side. Graves of a Household, The. Felicia Dorothea Hemans. NOBRP; NPBRoP; RWP; TreFP

They grow on the sides of the mountain. In Wild Iris Time. Jerry Martien. GeoHom

They grow over the Yangtze, the plum rains. Nisei: Second Generation Japanese-American. James Masao Mitsui. GifTon; OpBo

They had a happy childhood on the banks of the Hudson. Room 5600. Ernesto Cardenal. CLPP, *tr.* by Jonathan Cohen

They had a verb. I Held the Vein, But Death. Dennis Phillips. FTOS

They had been married in Italy in May. Charles Reznikoff. NAAPv.2 *Fr.* Testimony.

They had begun to whisper. Move. Lucille Clifton. MakPoe

They had chosen their deaths and marrtyrdom. Witness, Susanna Dickinson, The. Violette Newton. TiP2

They had come to see the salmon lunging and leaping. Excursion of the Speech and Hearing Class, The. David Wagoner. VCAP

They had crew cuts then, puffed cheeks like kids. Blues for Zoot. Sascha Feinstein. AmPoNex

They had faces open to whoever passed. Penniless Lovers. Eugenio de Andrade. VCWP, *tr.* by Alexis Levitin

They had gardens, they had mornings in those days! (LL) Carlos Drummond de Andrade. ChAP; VCWP

They had grown up together,—he and she. Albery Allson Whitman. NAAPv.1 *Fr.* Octoroon, The.

They had made love early in the high bed. Honeycomb, The. Pauline Stainer. NeBl; StAl

They had me laid out in a white. April Fools' Day. Yusef Komunyakaa. GT

They had never had one in the house before. Bronzeville Woman in a Red Hat. Gwendolyn Brooks. NALW

They had questioned him for hours. Campaign. Ciaran Carson. PNI

They had stolen my soul away! (LL) Romance. Walter James Turner. MoBrPo; NOBAu; NOxBChV; OBMV

They had supposed their formula was fixed. White Troops Had Their Orders but the Negroes Looked Like Men. Gwendolyn Brooks. NAAL-5

They hail you as their morning star. Men. Dorothy Parker. APT-1

They Hanged Him, I Said Dismissively. Dennis Brutus. VCWP

They have a little Odor—that to me. Emily Dickinson. TCAPo

They have been driven insane by history. Loyalty. Harvey Shapiro. TaR

They have been gone so long now, your. Mama. Rohan B. Preston. AmPoNex

They have breasts shaped. When I Look at Wifredo Lam's Paintings. Jayne Cortez. SurWo

They have broken every one. (LL) Gone, Gone Again. Edward Thomas. OxAEP-2; PoWW

They have built red factories along Lake Michigan. Charles Reznikoff. NAAPv.2

They have carved you into a stone face, Tom Mooney. Stone Face. Lola Ridge. NAAPv.2

They have closed the prison where they had you. Ringing Words. Mary Kinzie. FFC

They have coarse features, their hands are deft and accustomed to a hammer and nails, to wood and iron. Passion of Our Lord Painted By an Anonymous Hand from the Circle of Rhenish Masters, The. Zbigniew Herbert. GI, *tr.* by Adam Czerniawski

They have emptied the heart of Westport. Westport House, Portrush. James Simmons. PBCIP

They have given the orchard back to itself again. Deserted Orchard. Frances Mary Frost. YaYoPo

They have gone into the gray hills quilled with birches. Mined Country. Richard Wilbur. PWW2

They have no graves as yet. (LL) Elegy in a Country Churchyard. G. K. Chesterton. FaBoWar; MoBrPo; OBWP

They have not sown, and feed on bitter fruit. (LL) Black Man Talks of Reaping, A. Arna Bontemps. APT-2; ColAP; NAAPv.2; SSLK; WaAnP

They have [*or* They've *or* Th' have] left Thee naked, Lord, O[h] that they had! Upon the Body of Our Blessed Lord, Naked and Bloody. Richard Crashaw. NOSC

They have put my bed beside the unpainted screen. Last Poem. Po Chü-i. CCL1, *tr.* by Arthur Waley

They have shared still late October. Shipping Forecast, Donegal. Sean Street. RWPCtW

They have taken his horse and plume. Eagle Youth. Karle Wilson Baker. OtW

They have taken the gable from the roof of clay. Swedes. Edward Thomas. HarvBoo

They have the corner. Women, The. Joseph Ceravolo. FTOS

They have the faces of / no-one. (LL) Animals in That Country, The. Margaret Atwood. NALW; NoAM

They have thought upon this log. Turtles. Robert Siegel. PfSP

They have turned, and say that I am dying. That. I Substitute For The Dead Lecturer. Imamu Amiri Baraka. BrAP

They Have Turned the Church Where I Ate God. Gary Gildner. PBCAP

They have weighed man whitened with chalk. They Have Weighed. Joyce Mansour. SurPaPo, *tr.* by Mary Ann Caws *and* Jean-Pierre Cauvin

They have yarns / Of a skyscraper so tall they had to put hinges. Carl Sandburg. MoAmPo *Fr.* People, Yes, The.

They hear[e] and see, and sigh, and then they break[e]. (LL) Lowest trees have top[p]s, the ant[e] her gall. Sir Edward Dyer. NoSic; NPeEn

They hear Thee not, O God! nor see. Ezekiel. John Greenleaf Whittier. ChIV-1

They heated hatchet blades over gas fires in roadside workshops and. While the Record Plays. Gyula Illyés. PFTM-1

They hold no loyalties to the star-crossed lovers. Teaching Shakespeare. Tania Runyan. IaFF

They hung the lambs and cut their white throats. Blood. Gift, The. Andrew Hudgins. UpMys

They Hunt the Night. Kofi Anyidoho. NAfrP

They hunt, the velvet tigers in the jungle.　India.　Walter James Turner.　MoBrPo

They hurry through the forest suitcases in hand.　Six Small Fires.　Paul Jenkins.　OPRER

They improve everything, pork chops to soup.　Song to Onions.　Roy, Jr. Blount.　GoPo

They in the sea being burnt, they in the burnt ship drowned [or drown'd]. (LL)　Burnt Ship, A.　John Donne.　FaBoWar; OBWP

They just elected me Pope.　Poems of the Pope, The.　Nicanor Parra.　VCWP, tr. by Edith Grossman

They kick and flail like crabs on their backs.　One for All Newborns.　Thylias Moss.　OxAAAP

They Kill Us.　Ron Schreiber.　PrTe

They Killed the Lad.　Robert Ivanovich Rozhdestvensky.　TCRusP, tr. by Daniel Weissbort

They kneel on the slanting floor.　Foot-Washing, The.　George Ella Lyon.　OxWW

They knew how your good looks.　Miraculous Mandarin, The.　Deborah Tall.　PoDa

They knew that they were naked, and ashamed.　Serpent, The.　Jones Very.　NCAP

They knew you once, O beautiful and wise. (LL)　Conrad Potter Aiken.　ItP; OxBoAm Fr. Discordants.

They know how to live.　They and I.　Xavier Villaurrutia.　CAGL, tr. by Fanny Arango-Ramos and William Keeth

They know me not, but mourn with me. (LL)　Alfred Tennyson.　NAEL-6v2; NAEL-7v2 Fr. In Memoriam A. H. H.

They know us by our lips. They know the proverb.　Cups.　Gwen Harwood.　EmeKit; HarvBoo

They laid this stone trap.　Empty Church, The.　Ronald Stuart Thomas.　AngWePo; EmeKit

They laugh as I hey farm boy.　Han-shan (Cold Mountain).　ColAnChi, tr. by Red Pine

They laughed at one I loved.　Innocence.　Patrick Kavanagh.　ModIr

They Lay Dying Side by Side.　Anna Swirszczynska [or Swir].　PoSu

They lean against the cooling car, backs pressed.　Discovery of the Pacific, The.　Thom Gunn.　HeIP-4

They lean over the path.　Orchids.　Theodore Roethke.　ColAP; HarvBoo; TRP; WaAnP

They learned to turn off the gravity in an auditorium.　Childhood Stories.　Matthew Rohrer.　LegDan; NAPBL

They left me alone, stranded on a bald mountain.　On Bald Mountain.　A. Kadir.　NaPG, tr. by Talat Sait Halman

They left my hands like a printer's.　Blackberries.　Yusef Komunyakaa.　CAP-8

They lie in parallel rows.　Display of Mackerel, A.　Mark Doty.　AmAlph

They lie in their long hair, with brown faces.　Tombs of the Hetaerae.　Rainer Maria Rilke.　GPTC, tr. by Edward Snow

They lift / Out of the maternal watery blue lines.　Curlews [Lift].　Ted Hughes.

They lift their half-closed eyes out of the grammar.　Dead Language Lesson.　A. E. Stallings.　PoA 2002

They lift their skirts like blinds across your eyes. (LL)　In Memoriam.　Michael Longley.　ModIr; PNI

They locked us out without a cause—.　Glorious Strike of the Builders, The.　Unknown.　FaBoVe

They look at each other dully.　Vasco [or Vasko] Popa.　PoSu Fr. Quartz Pebble, The.

They look like big dogs badly drawn, drawn wrong.　Wolves in the Zoo.　Howard Nemerov.　NoAM

They looked at each other.　Stranger at Home.　James R. Lee.　BtF

They love me not, who at my table eat.　Harvest, The.　Jones Very.　SacPr

They Loved These Things Too.　Lisa Jarnot.　IIR

They made me a director.　Director, The.　Edmund George Valpy Knox.　OBCoV

They made me fireman at first, because 12 men missed the ship in Yokohama.　Ship in Yokohama, The.　Gary Snyder.　MotU

They made the chamber sweet with flowers and leaves.　Pause, A.　Christina Georgina Rossetti.　VWP

They made the good king pass.　King Tut in America.　Kwadwo Opoku-Agyemang.　NAfrP

They made their grim, sad faces and went out.　Death of the Polar Explorers.　Gabriel Gbadamosi.　HBAPE

They make it sound easy: some disjointed.　Fradel Schtok.　Irena Klepfisz.　TaR

They make love in his first language.　Las Flores para una Niña Negra.　Demetrice A. Worley.　SpirFl

They make the stars of bone. (LL)　Some Last Questions.　W. S. Merwin.　NAMCP V.2; VCAP

They married us when they put.　Drafted.　Su Wu.　WaAnP, tr. by Kenneth Rexroth

They may get better.　Lynching for Skip James, A.　Rudy Bee Graham.　EGAG

They may tell you the god is broken.　Osiris.　Jane Hirshfield.　BodElec

They measured you like a cup of meal. This much.　Blood Ties.　Thelma Seto.　TWW

They met at the Tagansky subway station.　Igor Khomin.　TCRusP, tr. by Daniel Weissbort

They might not need me—yet they might.　Emily Dickinson.　Spl

They might say, a white bird in the snow.　Stream of It, The.　Jane Hirshfield.　FiBr

They must have buried him away from the lake.　Idols.　Witter Bynner.　APT-1

They must have known that we escaped—if only.　Double Crossing.　Eva Salzman.　MFPA

They must to keep their certainty accuse.　Leaders of the Crowd, The.　William Butler Yeats.　MoBrPo; OxAEP-2

They mutilate they torment each other.　Voice, A.　Tadeusz Rózewicz.　BLT, tr. by Czeslaw Milosz

They named this stretch of river Postwar.　River.　Carlos Sahagún.　RaW, tr. by David Ignatow

They nearly made it.　Bleaklow.　Pauline Stainer.　NeBl

They never come back, though I loved them well.　Ballad of the Bird-Bride.　Rosamund Marriott Watson.　ViWPN; VWP

They Never Grew Old.　Judith Ortiz Cofer.　PueRic

They never left / the walled garden of their arms.　Waltz Poem of Those in Love and Inseparable Forever.　Miguel Hernández.　AF, tr. by Timothy Baland

They never read their Hedylos, nor could.　Renaissance Drunk, A.　George Evans.　PmAP

They never take the rouble. (LL)　Travel.　Julio Cortázar.　MotU; TCLAP, tr. by Paul Blackburn

They only find a medicine [or Med'cine] for the itch. (LL)　No Platonic [or Platonique] Love.　William Cartwright.　NOSC; NPeEn

They operate from elsewhere.　Juncos.　William Stafford.　OWoS

They owned their passiveness. (LL)　Subalterns, The.　Thomas Hardy.　MoBrPo; NoAM

They part at the edge of substance.　Stele (1-2 c. B.C.).　Denise Levertov.　BodElec

They parted aff careerin / Fu'blythe that night. (LL)　Halloween.　Robert Burns.　NOBRP; TreFP

They pass me.　Queue.　Tatamkulu Afrika.　TSAP

They pass me by like shadows, crowds on crowds.　Street, The.　James Russell Lowell.　GSo

They played with the pebble.　Vasco [or Vasko] Popa.　PoSu Fr. Quartz Pebble, The.

They please me not—these solemn songs.　Choice, A.　Paul Laurence Dunbar.　OxBoAm

They pointed me out on the highway, and they said.　Traveller [or Traveler], The.　John Berryman.　GM; OxBoAm; PoA 2002

They pose the portrait outside.　Vignette.　Natasha Trethewey.　RD

They preen beside puddles.　Guide to Urban Birds, A.　David B. Axelrod.　UrbNat

They pull off his ears.　Decomposition with Laughter.　Homero Aridjis.　TCLAP, tr. by Jerome Rothenberg

They put a mask on Haiti's face.　Mardi Gras.　Paul Laraque.　OGAHCP, tr. by Boadiba and Jack Hirschman

They put her together out of this and that.　Muse of Satire, The.　Mary Kinzie.　PoA 2002

They put Us far apart.　Emily Dickinson.　APN-2

They Receive Instructions Against Chile.　Pablo Neruda.　AF

They received from on high the divine voice.　Cabalists, The.　Angelina Muñiz Huberman.　MirDau, tr. by Aurora Camacho

They rendezvous each night, at ten.　Love Birds.　Paul Henry.　TCAWP

They Return.　Jay Macpherson.　PoA 2002 Fr. Way Down, The.

They rise, they walk again. (LL)　Heaven of Animals, The.　James Dickey.　CAP-8; ColAP; EmeKit; HeIP-4; InGu; InoFa; NAMCP V.2; NoAM; StAl; TRP; VCAP; WaAnP; WoPoe

They roar / Out of the river tunnels.　Rumble, A.　Virginia Schonborg.　SSCS

They rode north.　Blackie Thinks of His Brothers.　Stanley Crouch.　GT; OxAAAP

They rose up in a twinkling cloud.　Stockdoves, The.　Andrew Young.　NePenScot

They roused him with muffins—they roused him with ice.　Lewis Carroll.　NAEL-6v2; NAEL-7v2; OxAEP-2 Fr. Hunting of the Snark, The.

They ruined our lives.　We Should Remember.　Kaloji Narayana Rao.　HotL, tr. by V. Narayana Rao

They rush from Beds with giddy heads.　Michael Wigglesworth.　TCAPo Fr. Day of Doom, The [First Section].

They Said.　Lucy Larcom.　TCAPo

They Said.　Reg Saner.　AmWaPo

They said I had to have it. It was an instrument.　Will Campbell Displays His Craniotribe.　H. J. Van Peenen.　BloBone

They Said I Was a Crying Bride.　Alberto A. Ríos.　PoDa

They said it would be a feast.　Santa Rita Massacre, 1837.　Victoria Edwards Tester.　ICANM

They said, "Listen class attention before sorting."　They Said.　Reg Saner.　AmWaPo

They said / that the only reason.　Momma in Red.　Karen Williams.　BRtP

They said, the friends at Padua.　That's How We Are.　Andrea Zanzotto.　GPTC, *tr. by* Ruth Feldman and Brian Swann

They said the war was over.　Discreet Prayer, A.　Dionisio D. Martinez.　TouFir

They said there was a woman in the hills.　Women Are Not Gentlemen.　Harley Matthews.　NOBAu

They said to my grandmother: "Please do not be bitter."　Bitter Fruit of the Tree.　Sterling Allen Brown.　NoP-4; NoP-5; OxBoAm

They said we was nowhere.　Chanson d'Outre Tombe.　Philip Whalen.　BB

They said, "You are no longer a lad."　Battle Won Is Lost.　Phillip William George.　HHAm

They sat down one in front of the other.　Genesis (Chapter 7, Verse 5).　Manuela Fingueret.　MirDau, *tr. by* Roberta Gordenstein

They sat in even rows.　Miss Clement's Second Grade.　Maryfrances Cusumano Wagner.　UnSA

They sat like a disarmament proposal.　Memo About the Green Oranges, A.　Carol Rumens.　MoWP

They saw the young girls twisting their strings, Goulburn Island.　*Unknown*.　NOBAu *Fr.* Goulburn Island Song Cycle.

They saw their mamas put one foot out.　Little Girls Posing All Dressed Up.　Clarence Major.　BodElec

They saw you behind your muzzle much more clearly.　To a Farmer Who Hung Five Hawks on His Barbed Wire.　David Wagoner.　NoAM

They Say.　TAPaP

They Say.　Suze Baron.　OGAHCP, *tr. by* Boadiba and Jack Hirschman

They say a child with two mouths is no good.　Pantoun for Chinese Women.　Shirley Lim.　FiBr

They say a man dies.　Steve Crow.　HATNAP *Fr.* Songs.

They say: but cattle near.　Christmas.　John Frederick Nims.　ChrPo

They say dream visits.　Myŏngok.　CATKP, *tr. by* Peter H. Lee

They say "he need (present) enemy (plural)."　Transformations.　Jack Spicer.　FTOS

They say / human blood.　They Say.　Suze Baron.　OGAHCP, *tr. by* Boadiba and Jack Hirschman

They say I am excitable! How could.　King of Owls, The.　Louise Erdrich.　NoAM

They say I am robbing myself.　Garden of Friendship, The.　Frances Sargent Osgood.　PoBW

They say I don't love life.　Danila Stoyanova.　CSCBP, *tr. by* Georgi Belev and Lisa Sapinkopf

They say Ideal beauty cannot enter.　Hiram Powers' "Greek Slave."　Elizabeth Barrett Browning.　GS; NALW; ViWPN

They say I'm a beast.　Loose Women.　Sandra Cisneros.　IllVoic

They say, interpret it your own way, Christ is born. (LL)　Eclogue for Christmas, An.　Louis MacNeice.　NAMCP V.1; NoAM; OBMV

They say into your early life romance came.　Sophisticated Lady.　Irving Mills and Mitchell Parish.　ReLy

They say it comes from our Indian side.　Blessing Poem.　Demetria Martinez.　ICANM

They say it is waiting for more, the snow.　Snow Signs.　Charles Tomlinson.　NoAM

They say it's the iron in the blood that resists transformation.　Cannibal Women in the Avocado Jungle of Death.　Maureen Seaton.　ExTi

They Say It's Wonderful.　Irving Berlin.　ReLy

They say La Jac Brite Pink Skin Bleach avails not.　Government Injunction [Restraining Harlem Cosmetic Co.].　Josephine Miles.　OxBoAm

They say, little beast, little creator, the elders say.　First Prayer for the Hottentotsgod.　Breyten Breytenbach.　AF, *tr. by* Denis Hirson

They Say My Verse Is Sad: No Wonder.　A. E. Housman.　NAMCP V.1; NoAM

They say of me, and so they should.　Neither Blood Nor Bowed.　Dorothy Parker.　AmWit

They Say She Is Lovely.　Lőrinc Szabó.　IQMS, *tr. by* Susanne K. Walther

They Say She Is Veiled.　Judy Grahn.　HW

They say she used to be 'fine'.　Ashy Gal.　Baba Lukata.　BtF

They say she was sixteen when the angel of annunciation came to her.　Song of Mary.　No Hyegyông.　EcSo, *tr. by* Ann Y. Choi

They say souls of the dead.　Birds in the Graveyard.　Helon Habila.　NeNiPo

They say that an accident.　For the Death of a Monk.　Muso Soseki.　EaWin, *tr. by* W. S. Merwin

They Say That Black People . . . .　Patricia Smith.　GT

They say that black people.　They Say That Black People . . . .　Patricia Smith.　GT

They say that every idle word.　Idle Words.　Walter Savage Landor.　OBSV

They say that God lives very high.　Child's Thought of God, A.　Elizabeth Barrett Browning.　InvLi

They say that Hope is happiness.　Lord Byron.　NAEL-6v2; NAEL-7v2

They say that in some Gower glen.　Bone Prison, The.　E. Howard Harries.　AngWePo

They say that once Leda found.　Sappho.　SaLy, *tr. by* Diane Rayor

They say that poets should keep their tongue in check.　Paranoia.　Leonard Nolens.　TuT, *tr. by* Michael O'Loughlin

They Say that the Plants Do Not Speak.　Rosalía de Castro.　SpanPo, *tr. by* Kate Flores

They say that the plants do not speak, nor the brooks, nor the birds.　They Say that the Plants Do Not Speak.　Rosalía de Castro.　SpanPo, *tr. by* Kate Flores

They Say That Time Assuages.　Emily Dickinson.　APN-2

They say that "Time assuages."　They Say That Time Assuages.　Emily Dickinson.　APN-2

They say that you were blind, yet from the shore.　Homer.　George Campbell Hay.　EdScPo

They say the color of clouds is fine.　Yun Sŏndo.　CATKP *Fr.* Songs of Five Friends.

They say the first dream Adam our father had.　Adam's Dream.　Edwin Muir.　NoP-4; NoP-5

They say the ice will hold.　Farewell, The.　Edward Field.　P180

They say the Phoenix is dying, some say dead.　News of the Phoenix.　Arthur James Marshall Smith.　IFF

They say the roads of Sanso are steep.　Leave-taking Near Shoku.　Li Po.　NDACCP, *tr. by* Ezra Pound

They say the roads to Shu.　To See a Friend Off to Shu.　Li Po.　ChinPo, *tr. by* Ye Weilian [*or* Yeh Wei-lien *or* Wai-lim Yip]

They say the sea is cold, but the sea contains.　Whales Weep Not!　D. H. Lawrence.　NAMCP V.1; NoAM

They say the souls of poets.　Souls of Poets, The.　Dickie Bradley.　OWABP

They say the war is over. But water still.　Redeployment.　Howard Nemerov.　AmWaPo; OBWP; PoWW

They say there is.　*Unknown*.　TAL

They say there is a hollow, safe and still.　Frances Ridley Havergal.　SacPr *Fr.* Thoughts of God, The.

They say there lives.　Wakayama Bokusui.　CAoMJL1, *tr. by* Donald Keene

They say they are saving to move to Los Angeles. (LL)　Anne Carson.　OxBoAm; WoBe *Fr.* Truth About God, The.

They Say You're Staying in a Mountain Temple.　Tu Fu [*or* Du Fu].　CCL1, *tr. by* Burton Watson

They sculpted stone.　Arcana 4: The Emperor.　Veronica Volkow.　RMCMP, *tr. by* Margaret Sayers Peden

They see a bird that is bright in both beak and feather.　Translation.　Matthea Harvey.　IAoNAP

They seem hundreds of years away.　Breughel.　Seamus Heaney.　IPoFL; PNI *Fr.* Mossbawn.

They seem too pale for these cloud-breached days.　Clothes, The.　Julia Copus.　NeBl

They seemed to all take off.　Departures.　Linda Pastan.　GoPo

They seize the young girls of the western tribes, with their swaying.　*Unknown*.　NOBAu *Fr.* Goulburn Island Song Cycle.

They seized him while his friends were asleep.　Last Day.　Martinus Nijhoff.　TuT, *tr. by* Desmond Egan

They sell good beer at Haslemere.　West Sussex Drinking Song.　Joseph Hilaire Pierre Belloc.　MoBrPo

They sent him back to her. The letter came.　Not to Keep.　Robert Frost.　AmWaPo

They sent me a salwar kameez.　Presents from My Aunts in Pakistan.　Moniza Alvi.　MFPA

They sent me to gather the cresses, which lie.　*Unknown*.　CCL1 *Fr.* Guan-ju.

They serve revolving saucer eyes.　Ex-Queen Among the Astronomers, The.　Fleur Adcock.　MoWP; NAEL-6v2; NAEL-7v2; NALW; NoP-4; NoP-5

They set out to bring Beethoven.　Bringers of Beethoven, The.　Reiner Kunze.　PoSu, *tr. by* Gordon Brotherston and Gisela Brotherston

They settle out from their curfew.　How Things Bear Their Telling.　Ann Lauterbach.　ExTi

They settled their tent pegs here.　Pioneers.　Lillian M. Fisher.　HHAm

They shall find him ware an' wakin', as they found him long ago! (LL)　Drake's Drum.　Sir Henry John Newbolt.　FaBoWar; OBMV; UV

They Shall Know.　Kofi Awoonor.　VCWP

They Shall Look on Him.　Michael Field.　VWP

They shall never sound in slavery. (LL)　Minstrel Boy, The.　Thomas Moore.　ChAP; FaBoWar; OxAEP-2

They shall not return to us, the resolute, the young.　Mesopotamia.　Rudyard Kipling.　HarvBoo; PoWW

They shall sink under water. Cities, The. George Russell. OBMV

They shaped their souls on anvils of righteousness. For the Calvinists. Ben Howard. PoA 2002

They shook the green leaves down. Magic Fox. James Welch. HATNAP; NoAM

They shorten tedious nights. (LL) Now Winter Nights Enlarge. Thomas Campion. NAEL-7v1; NoP-4; NoP-5; NPeEn; OxAEP-1; OxBEV; PBRV; PtR

They should have slept, would have. Lynching, The. Thylias Moss. GT

They should let it go by. (LL) Women. Louise Bogan. APT-2; MoAmPo; NAAPv.2; NALW; NAMCP V.1; NoAM; WoPoe

They shoulder each other in old houses, these windows. Sadness of Windows, The. Carole Glasser Langille. Coast

They Shout Out the Price of Salt. Ammuvanar. WoPoe, tr. by George L. Hart III

They shout out the price of salt harvested from the salt flats. They Shout Out the Price of Salt. Ammuvanar. WoPoe, tr. by George L. Hart III

They showed up for awhile and they died. Showing. Liam Rector. TRP

They shut me up in Prose. Emily Dickinson. APN-2; FaBoVe; NAAPv.1; NALW; NCAP; NoP-4; NoP-5; OxBoAm

They shut the road through the woods. Way Through The Woods, The. Rudyard Kipling. BrAP; ChAP; HarvBoo; NAMCP V.1; NoAM; NOxBChV; OBEV; OxAEP-2; WHSW; WoPoe

They sing of Mary and Martha. Mary, don't You Weep. Honorée Fanonne Jeffers. BtF

They sing their dearest songs. During Wind and Rain. Thomas Hardy. HarvBoo; InoFa; NAEL-6v2; NAEL-7v2; NIL-7; NoP-4; NoP-5; NPeEn; OxBEV; TFi; TRP

They sing this song on all the radios. No Pasarán. Aaron Kurtz. Prolet, tr. by Amelia Glaser

They sit in a row. Fury of Overshoes. Anne Sexton. NIP-4

They sit in a row. Anne Sexton. NIL-7 Fr. Furies, The.

They sit in the bright cafe. Inventing My Parents. Susan Bartels Ludvigson. PoSol

They sit next to each other on the rose plastic bench. Couple Having Breakfast in the Deli, The. Jeanette I. Winthrop. PfS

They sit on top of everything. (LL) Elders Are Gods, The. Tijan M. Sallah. BRtP; NAfrP

They sleep, the mountain crags and gullies. Fragment 58: Night and Sleep. Alcman. WoPoe, tr. by Rosanna Warren

They slept in a circle around my body and my daughter. (LL) Sharon Olds. See Dark circle around my body and my daughter.

They slew by night. Félix Lope de Vega Carpio. WoPoe Fr. Pentecost Castle, The.

They slid like seals from sleep. Like Seals from Sleep. Kevin Faller. IrLP

They smell of Corycian saffron, of a. Martial. RomPo, tr. by Peter Whigham

They snarl Over Spain like cur-dogs over a bone, then look at each other. Sinverguenza. Robinson Jeffers. AmWaPo

They sought it with thimbles, they sought it with care. Lewis Carroll. OxAEP-2 Fr. Hunting of the Snark, The.

They sought to put us away like. They Hunt the Night. Kofi Anyidoho. NAfrP

They speak through my wounds. Creatures preach to St Francis, The. Pauline Stainer. MoWP

They spill from the tiniest shoes. Her Three Unborn Baby Boys. Menke Katz. Prolet, tr. by Amelia Glaser

They splay at a bend of the road, rifles slung, the. Spool, The. Ben Belitt. PWW2

They spoke of the horse alive. Horse, The. Philip Levine. AtGh; VCAP

They sprint eight feet and—. Ringed Plover by a Water's Edge. Norman Alexander MacCaig. NoP-4

They stack bright pyramids of goods and gather. Avenue. Robert Pinsky. TaR

They stand around. They reach into the offing. Justin Quinn. NIrP

They stand in the clearing of Kingfisher Flat. High Embrace, The. William Everson. GeoHom

They stand there and chat near the breakwater. Women. İlhan Berk. NaPG, tr. by Talat Sait Halman

They stand there weeping in the stained daylight. Fresco: Departure for an Imperialist War. Thomas McGrath. AF

They stare back into an increate future. Photographs of Old New York. Alfred Corn. PoA 2002

They still love you, Elvis. They want your hair, stories about your. Come Back, Elvis, Come Back to Holyoke. Mary A. Koncel. ReTh

They stood so still the leafless trees. Spring Landscape. Augusta Peaux. TuT, tr. by Tony Curtis and Tony Curtis

They strike mine eyes, but not my heart. (LL) Ben Jonson. NAEL-6v1; NAEL-7v1; NIL-7; NoP-4; NPeEn; PoPoPo; TFi; WeW-3 Fr. Epicoene; or, The Silent Woman.

They stuck pigs in the throat. Might I not have done. Work. Gyula Illyés. RaBo, tr. by William Jay Smith

(They stuck pigs in the throat.) PFTM-1

They stumbled down their barracks steps. Playing the Flute for the TMR Class. Jane Epton Seale. MiVo

They suffer, and I catch only the surface. I Am a Cameraman. Douglas Dunn. EmeKit; StAl

They swagger through the village like Capulets. Young Men of Blackburn, The. Dennis O'Donnell. EdScPo

They swallow clouds. Buson. EH, tr. by Robert Hass

They swarm in and unpack right. Bad Birds. William Trowbridge. UrbNat

They tagged you an illiterate, those idle bureaucrats. Yannis Ritsos. PFTM-2 Fr. Second Series.

They take advantage—the soldiers need clothes. Se Aprovechan. Irving Feldman. GS

They take them out in the morning. Five Men. Zbigniew Herbert. PoSu, tr. by Peter Dale Scott

They talk about it for a year. Building the Compost. Helena Minton. PfS

They talk of short-lived pleasure—be it so—. Mutation. William Cullen Bryant. NCAP

They taste good to her. (LL) To a Poor Old Woman. William Carlos Williams. BLT; ColAP; NAAPv.2; OxBoAm; WaAnP

They tax our policy and call it cowardice. William Shakespeare. FaBoWar Fr. Troilus and Cressida.

They tear Alele's tongue out. Frank Etienne. OGAHCP Fr. Cockfight Marathon.

They tell me how it was, and how time. Scars. William Stafford. AmFaPo

They Tell Me I Am Lost. Maurice Kenny. HATNAP

They tell me I live on a cloud. Tame and Ferocious Animal, A. Nancy Morejón. TANSG, tr. by Joy Renjilian-Burgy

They tell me: "Man." From a Talk. Yevgeny Aleksandrovich Yevtushenko. CLPP, tr. by Anselm Hollo

They tell me that over there the beaches are black. They Tell Me That Over There. André Breton. YaTCFP, tr. by Mary Ann Caws and Jean-Pierre Cauvin

They tell me that the Arena in Verona is the most beautifully preserved. Magnificence. James Wright. BodElec

They tell me that the "little horror" have fled the face of the earth. Unknown. SLW, tr. by Marjolijn De Jager, Sayd Bahodin Majrouh and André Velter

They tell me that the sun. Port Townsend Poems. Pinkie Gordon Lane. BtF

They tell me 'tis decided; you depart. Lord Byron. NOBRP Fr. Don Juan.

They tell that on St. Bernard's mount. Dog of St. Bernard's, The. Caroline Fry. DiBP

They tell us to forget. Melvin B. Tolson. NAAPv.2 Fr. Dark Symphony.

They tethered my soul upon a rope. Tethered Souls, The. Endre Ady. IQMS, tr. by Anton N. Nyerges

They that have power [or pow'r or powre] to hurt[e], and will do[e] none. William Shakespeare. CABP; NAEL-6v1; NAEL-7v1; NIL-7; NoP-4; NoP-5; NoSic; NPeEn; OBEV; OxAEP-1; OxBEV; OxBSo; PBRV; TRP; WoPoe Fr. Sonnets.

They that in play can do the thing they would. Robert Bridges. NoAM Fr. Growth of Love, The.

They That Wash on Monday. Mother Goose. NBLV

They That Wash on Thursday. Paul Muldoon. EMP

They think / I am stronger than I am. Naming Power. Wendy Rose. OxWW

They think I'm an animal in the water. Strokes of an Adult's Pencil. Denizé Lauture. OGAHCP, tr. by Boadiba and Jack Hirschman

They thought: Human! Marina Ivanovna Tsvetayeva. TCRusP Fr. Poems to Blok.

They throw in Drummer Hodge, to rest. Drummer Hodge. Thomas Hardy. BrAP; FaBoWar; HarvBoo; NAEL-6v2; NAEL-7v2; NAMCP V.1; NoAM; NoP-4; NoP-5; OBWP; OxAEP-2; WeW-3

They told her she had very special spaces. Awakening. Elizabeth Abbot. ICANM

They told her she would have to kill the dog. Veterinary Student, The. Jennifer Markell. PfS

They told me, Francis Hinsley, they told me you were hung. Evelyn Waugh. OBCoV Fr. Loved One, The.

They told me God came to Pius. In the Dark. Patrick Williams. PNI

They Told Me, Heraclitus. Brian Fore. UV

They Told Me, Heraclitus. Guy Hanlon. UV

They told me, Heraclitus, they told me you were dead. Heraclitus. William Johnson Cory. OBEV; OxAEP-2; UV

They told me, Heraclitus, they told me you were dead. They Told Me, Heraclitus. Brian Fore. UV

They told me, Heraclitus, they told me you were dead. They Told Me, Heraclitus. Guy Hanlon. UV

They told me poems must be. On Poems. Rudolph Smith. OWABP

They told me that when I was taken. At Mornington. Gwen Harwood. GPTC

They told me the. Pistachio Ice Cream. Annemarie Jacir. PoArWo

They told me, when I lived, because my art. Ancient Revisits, An. Laura Riding Jackson. APT-2

They told me you had been to her. Lewis Carroll. NPeEn *Fr.* Alice's Adventures in Wonderland.

They told my cousin Rowena not to marry. Family Secrets. Toi Derricotte. OxAAAP; SpirFl

They took a tire tool to his head. Jim Barnes. HATNAP *Fr.* Ex-Deputy Sheriff Remembers the Eastern Oklahoma Murderers, An.

They took all that was child. Al Wat Kind Is. Ingrid de Kok. HAWP

They took my flock away. Should I care? I have nothing to do now. Saturn Declining. Sándor Weöres. IQMS, *tr. by* Alan Dixon

They took my glasses and laid them. Touch Me Not. Ann Townsend. LegDan

They took off / and tricolor flags came out of their assholes. Nungesser und Coli Sind Verreckt. Benjamin Péret. AF, *tr. by* Keith Hollaman

They took off their clothes 1000 nights. Undressing, The. Carol Frost. CAP-8

They took quickly, they took hugely. Marina Ivanovna Tsvetayeva. AF *Fr.* March.

They took the stallion out into the field. Further. Nedelcho Ganev. CSCBP, *tr. by* Georgi Belev and Lisa Sapinkopf

They trod the streets and squares where now I tread. London Poets. Amy Levy. PEW; ViWPN

They Unite Naked. Jorge Gaitán Durán. BLPSL, *tr. by* Rene de Costa, Rigas Kappatos and Eleni Paidoussi

They used to tell me. Brother, Can You Spare a Dime? E. Y. Harburg. APT-2; NAAPv.2; ReLy

They used to use that circular rack to hang up clothes. Man Who Hanged Himself, The. Martin Birnbaum. Prolet, *tr. by* Amelia Glaser

They visited Robert Frost's grave and came back. Poetry's Beginning. Gail Hosking Gilberg. VisFro

They waited beneath the cold December snows. Embertide in Advent. David Middleton. PoDa

They waited for the man stretched out across the road to wake up. Heavier. Pierre Reverdy. YaTCFP, *tr. by* John Ashbery

They wake with horror, and dare sleep no more. (LL) John Dryden. BASC; FaBoWar *Fr.* Annus Mirabilis.

They walk around a corner at the back of town. War of the Roses, The. Michael Dransfield. BMAP

They walk into us. Fallen. Kate Schmitt. IJHIL

They wander in deep woods, in mournful light. Fields of Sorrow, The. Ausonius. WoPoe, *tr. by* Helen Waddell

They wanted from us. Ars Poetica. Eleanor Wilner. TAPaP

They wanted me to tell the truth. What They Wanted. Stephen Dunn. BodElec

They watched the pilgrims leave for Santiago. Part of the Crowd That Day. Ken Smith. BeAl

They wear. *Unknown.* WoPoe *Fr.* Two Pantuns.

They wear big felt hats. Church Ladies. Nancy Travis. ISC

They weave time in the variegated. Mysteries of Touch, The. Coral Bracho. RMCMP, *tr. by* Mónica de la Torre

They went to sea in a Sieve, they did. Eat Your Heart Out, Edward Lear! Roger Woddis. UV

They went to sea in a sieve, they did. Jumblies, The. Edward Lear. CABP; NAEL-6v2; NAEL-7v2; NOxBChV; TFi; UV

They went with axe and rifle, when the trail was still to blaze. Western Wagons. Rosemary Benét *and* Stephen Vincent Benét. HHAm

They went with songs to the battle, they were young. Laurence Binyon. FaBoWar *Fr.* For the Fallen.

They wept for the violet-wreathed [lady's]. Simonides. SaLy, *tr. by* Diane Rayor

They were a close family of giant otters. Giant Otters. Jackson Mac Low. FTOS

They Were Alone in the Winter. Luci Tapahonso. ItWoWo

They were always there, at the end of the garden or elsewhere. At Evening. Anthony Thwaite. OxBEV

They were at play, she and her cat. Femme et Chatte. Paul Verlaine. OBVE, *tr. by* Arthur Symons

They were born together, lived together. Martha and Mary. Gabriela Mistral. GI, *tr. by* Doris Dana

They were both still. Lamentations. Louise Glück. VCAP

They were but gourds for earth to drink therefrom. Ikeja, Friday, Four O'Clock. Wole Soyinka. PoetW

They were convinced that our scent. More Than We Dared. Hayan Charara. PrTe

They were crushed by a gigantic meteor. Theory on Extinction or what happened to the dinosaurs? Kenneth Carroll. AmPoNex; SpirFl

They were difficult to find. It was summer so. Like a Fire in a Fire. Mary Jo Bang. NAPBL

They were gestures out of a movie, I tell you. Hours Musicians Keep, The. Aleda Shirley. SwNoth

They were gliding down the river. They Were Gliding. Ruth Lepson. PfS

They were green paths in the placid time of the needle. These Green Paths. Jeannette Miller. TANSG, *tr. by* Paula Vega

They were his victory in old age. Claude Monet's Water Landscapes. Liliane Welch. Coast

They were in a big circle. Knights of the White Camellia and Deacons of Defense. Yusef Komunyakaa. LPSFW

They were introduced in a grave glade. Introduction, The. Louis MacNeice. IrLP; PNI

They were introduced in a green grave. (LL) Introduction, The: "They were introduced in a grave glade." Louis MacNeice. IrLP; PNI

They were just playing, lady and cat. Woman and Cat. Paul Verlaine. WoPoe, *tr. by* Felicity Bast

They were kings, after all. Magi, The. Jeffrey Fiskin. GI

They were lovely in the quartz and jasper sand. Starfish. Lorna Dee Cervantes. TouFir

They were never handsome and often came. Sidekicks. Ron Koertge. CalPo; P180

They were nil. Heritage. Mahdi Muhammad Ali. IrPoTo, *tr. by* Salaam Yousif

They were not the abandoned ones. Hansel and Gretel. Barbara Noel-Scott. Prnts

They were on location in the hills above a small California town and before. Motion Pictures: 15. Barbara Guest. BodElec

They were once like us, like we were. Rocks Along the Coast, The. Jerry Martien. GeoHom

They were partakers of a strange taste. At the hour when. Deflection Toward the Relative Minor. Forrest Gander. OPRER

They were shocked to see me, or so it looked. Visitant, The. Fergus Allen. NIrP

They were summoned from the hillside. Keep the Home Fires Burning (Till the Boys Come Home). Lena Guilbert Ford. NAAPv.2

They were supposed to be fixed by today, now that they're hardly needed—though they will be again. Screens. Barry Silesky. IllVoic

They were talking on the telephone about a low, drawn out light with blackness to it. Connecting Light. Susan Michie. Prnts

They were the choicest ones, full of life. . .their voice has grown silent. Ones Living by Their Virtue Say, The. Uri Zvi Greenberg. NRoS, *tr. by* Esther Raizen

They were the strong nudes of a forgotten. Anagram Born of Madness at Czernowitz, 12 November 1920. Norman Dubie. BodElec

They were, those people, a kind of solution. (LL) Constantine P. Cavafy. *See* Those people were a kind of solution.

They were wine suede with just a thin strap. Shoes, The. Lola Haskins. PfS

They were women then. Alice Walker. CFP *Fr.* In These Dissenting Times.

They weren't so bright, or clean, or clever. Robert Penn Warren. FuPo *Fr.* Promises.

They Who Are Poor. Attila József. IQMS, *tr. by* Vernon Watkins

They who in folly or mere greed. Where Are the War Poets? Cecil Day Lewis. NAMCP V.1; NoP-4; NoP-5; OBWP

They will be floating from my mouth like doves. 365 Poems. Ann Stanford. TAPaP

They will be without arms like God. Hummingbirds. Norman Dubie. BodElec

They will call him brave. (LL) Penelope. Dorothy Parker. FaBoWar; PoAgWa

They will catch me. On Hearing the Airlines Will Use a Psychological Profile to Catch Potential Skyjackers. Stephen Dunn. OtW; SUP

They will fit, she thinks. Marriage, The. Anne Stevenson. NALW

They will never come, neither from here, nor from there. Self-Defeating Poem, The. Fadil Azzawi. IrPoTo, *tr. by* the author

They will not ask us: have you sinned? Anatoly Steiger. TCRusP, *tr. by* Paul Schmidt

They will not be the same next time. The sayings. Saying Goodbye to Very Young Children. John Updike. PoA 2002

They will not hush, the leaves a-flutter around me, the beech leaves old. (LL) Madness of King Goll, The. William Butler Yeats. NAEL-6v2; NAEL-7v2

They will not stop me. Refusal. Colette Ni Ghallchóir. NIrP, *tr. by* the author

They will perhaps. Love Poem. Norman Henry, II Pritchard. GT

They will probably come just after the New Year. Three Magi, The. Stanislaw Baranczak. GI

They will remain[e], and so thou canst not die. (LL) Samuel Daniel. NoSic; PBRV *Fr.* Sonnets to Delia.

They will tumble down from the rooftops. Judgement Day. Odia Ofeimun. HBAPE

They will wash all my kisses and fingerprints off you. Poem Ended by a Death. Fleur Adcock. NAEL-6v2; NAEL-7v2; NoP-4; NoP-5

They without message, having read. Typists. Patricia K. Page. NALW

They wondered why the fruit had been forbidden. W. H. Auden. ChIV-1

They won't have time to change their mind! (LL) Hospital Soliloquy, A. Rose Terry Cooke. NAAPv.1; SWaP

They won't let railways alone, those yellow flowers. Ragwort. Anne Stevenson. OPOU

They won't say: when the walnut tree shook in the wind. In Dark Times. Bertolt Brecht. PoAgWa, *tr.* by Humphrey Milnes

They would ask him. Big Bad Art Thing, The. Carter Ratcliff. KGB

They would bar your way in the street. Invaders, The. Bernard Spencer. FaBoWar

They would have invited him gladly. *Unknown.* WoPoe *Fr.* Excerpts from *The Poem of the Cid.*

They would leave. Final Solution: Jobs, Leaving. Simon J. Ortiz. PFTM-2

They would like / to put the tick and flea collar. No Hatchet Job. Luz Maria Umpierre. PueRic

They would say that she of the neck like a duiker's. On Reading an Archeological Article. Molara Ogundipe-Leslie. HBAPE

They wring their hands, their caitiff-hands. Michael Wigglesworth. NAAL-3 *Fr.* Day of Doom, The [First Section].

They'd been warned. Drowning in Wheat. John Kinsella. PoA 2002

They'd eaten every one. (LL) Lewis Carroll. CABP; ChAP; ITBLP; NAEL-6v2; NAEL-7v2; NoAM; OBSP; OxAEP-2; TFi *Fr.* Through the Looking-Glass.

They'd latch the screendoors [*or* screen doors]. Sunday Afternoons. Yusef Komunyakaa. InGu; NoP-4; NoP-5

They'll be here soon, they've already been called. Ceremony. Georgi Rupchev. CSCBP, *tr.* by Georgi Belev and Lisa Sapinkopf

They'll Carry—Him! (LL) I Can Wade Grief. Emily Dickinson. APN-2; ColAP; HeIP-4

They'll say, "She must be from another country." Imtiaz Dharker. StAl

They'll soon be flying to Mars, I hear. Progress. Samuel Hoffenstein. OBCoV

They'll tell you when you're growing up. Gabachos in the Photograph, The. Bobby Byrd. ICANM

They're a curious lot, Manet's scandalous. Luncheon on the Grass. Carl Phillips. AmFaPo

They're afraid of me. For Medgar Evers. David Ignatow. LTA

They're almost gone. Misconstrued, The. Bruce Berger. GeoH

They're altogether otherworldly now. Grandparents. Robert Lowell. ColAP; NAMCP V.2; WaAnP

They're at that stage where so much desire streams between them, so much frank need and want. Love: Beginnnings. C. K. Williams. OxBoAm; StAl

They're becoming the same, Welsh ice and spring frost. Welsh Ice. Menna Elfyn. ATSWP, *tr.* by Robert Minhinnick

They're big for toads, lumpy. Tropical Toads. Randall Maggs. Coast

They're both convinced. Love at First Sight. Wisława Szymborska. BeAl, *tr.* by Stanislaw Barańczak *and* Clare Cavanagh

They're bringing them home, now, too late, too early. (LL) Homecoming. Bruce Dawe. BMAP; EmeKit

They're complaining from the pulpit, with an energy undue. New View of Sunday Cycling, A. *Unknown.* ArBi

They're dying on me! They've lived. Death of a Pair of Shoes. Jorge Guillén. RaW, *tr.* by Philip Levine

They're Either Too Young or Too Old. Frank Loesser. ReLy

They're Family Men. Ellen Bass. AtGh

They're gonna throw you, get off. (LL) Riding Lesson. Henry Taylor. GoPo; NBLV

They're insignificant when not in use. Stick and Hat. King Lệ Thánh-tông. WoPoe, *tr.* by John S. Major

They're Leaving with a Bridle Round the Neck. Mercedès F. Guignard. *tr.* by Boadiba and Jack Hirschman

"One morning just like that they arrive." OGAHCP, *tr.* by Boadiba and Jack Hirschman

They're marked men. Their park is like an open prison. Kevin Crossley-Holland. NewEx

They're nice—one would never dream of going over. Healthy Spot, A. W. H. Auden. OxBoAm

They're no heroes. People, The. Donald Evans. BBMWP, *tr.* by Gillian Clarke

They're only boys / who used to frolic and play. Song of Becoming. Fadwa Tuqan. AF, *tr.* by Naomi Shihab Nye

They're Putting a New Door In. Brian Kim Stefans. BAP-04

They're really here, spreading their ideas. Bad Aliens. Noelle Kocot. LegDan

They're selling postcards of the hanging. Desolation Row. Bob Dylan. OxBoAm

They're taking down a tree at the front door. Learning by Doing. Howard Nemerov. WeW-3

They're taller than me. Spring Harvest of Snow Peas. Maxine Hong Kingston. ASA

They're Tearing Up the Old Graveyard. Kobena Eyi Acquah. NAfrP

They're tearing up the old graveyard. They're Tearing Up the Old Graveyard. Kobena Eyi Acquah. NAfrP

They're tearing up the street. All holyroadz home. Mark S. Kuhar. AmZen

They're the dead ends. You and the Tijuana Mule. Rigoberto González. GeoHom

They're throwing a party upstairs. Party, The. Donald Finkel. OPRER

They're treated with curare. Liliane Giraudon. SCFWP *Fr.* Poem with Incense Paper.

They're used to carrying it in fine milled gold. Manuscript. Angelina Muñiz Huberman. MirDau, *tr.* by Aurora Camacho

They're waiting to be murdered. Old Couple. Charles Simic. PoPoPo

They're with O'Leary in the grave. (LL) September 1913. William Butler Yeats. HarvBoo; IrV; NAEL-6v2; NAEL-7v2; NAMCP V.1; NoAM

They've closed the forest trail. This new one's lower. Wolf's Road, The. Stanley Noyes. ICANM

They've cut down the old sugar maple. Sawdust. Jane Shore. PfSP

They've finally admitted that trying to save oil-soaked. Star Is Born in the Eagle Nebula, A. Marcia Southwick. PoDa

They've got me down as manic. Holding the Holy Card. J. Patrick Lewis. IJHIL

They've got the whole of death never. Vanished, The. Marie-Claire Bancquart. MFP, *tr.* by Martin Sorrell

They've let me walk with you. Visit, The. Ian Hamilton. NPeEn

They've paid the last respects in sad tobacco. Padraic O'Conaire—Gaelic Storyteller. Frederick Robert Higgins. OBMV

They've put the park bench. Notes for the Park Keeper. Peter Bland. OBGa

They've said the art of poetry resembles. Marriage in the Nineties, A. Alfred Corn. WiU

They've taken it apart. Three-Inch Reflector. Caroline Caddy. BMAP

They've taken the great elm down. Neighbor's Elm, The. Robert Ayres. UrbNat

They've taken thee out of the simple soil. Negro Spiritual. Claude McKay. APT-1

Thi cat sits at ma French windies. Three Year Ode, A. W. N. Herbert. RSaN

Thich Nhat Hanh said, There are enough Zen centers. We need more Zen corners. Zen Corners. Michael Wenger. WhBo

Thick at the schoolgate are the ones. Soul Make a Path Through Shouting. Cyrus Cassells. GifTon; GT; OPRER; UnSA

Thick crust, coarse-grained as limestone rough-cast, A. Churning Day. Seamus Heaney. ModIr

Thick darkness broodeth o'er the world. Past, The. Sarah Helen Whitman. TCAPo

Thick fog. Garden of Shanah. Sara Riwka Erlich. MirDau, *tr.* by Auristela Xavier

Thick throng the snow-flakes, the evening is dreary. Julia Ward Howe. SWaP *Fr.* Lyrics of the Street.

Thicket of deadly nightshade, The. Latvian Autumn, The. Johannes Bobrowski. PoSu

Thicket of Time. David Chaloner. VaPo

Thicket's in the thick of what, The. Scared Cows. Douglas Messerli. FTOS

Thicknesses of victor decreased: blanket->sheet->floss, The. Until no material would do. D. A. Powell. NeAmPo

Thick-rushing, like an ocean vast. Remembered Music. James Russell Lowell. APN-1

Thief, The. Stanley Kunitz. MoAmPo

Thief, The. Dorianne Laux. ErotSp; ExTi; PasH

Thief, The. Alden Nowlan. RaBo

Thief and Samaritan. James Keir Baxter. HarvBoo

Thief became the rabbi, The. Structural Study of Myth, The. Jerome Rothenberg. FTOS

Thief in the Night, A. Jelaluddin Rumi. BBASP, *tr.* by Nasrollah Pourjavady and Peter Lamborn Wilson

Thief Stole This Poem, A. Allen Ginsberg. BodElec

Thief, you dare to laugh and even. *Unknown.* PriapPo *Fr.* Priapus Poems, The.

Thigh-deep in sedge and marigolds. Other Side, The. Seamus Heaney. PNI

Thin. Caitríona O'Reilly. NIrP

Thin and crippled and sweet and humorous, A. March Blizzard. John Tagliabue. GoPo

Thin are the night-skirts left behind. Insomnia. Dante Gabriel Rossetti. AWTN

Thin as a sheet his mother came to him. John Berryman. CAP-8 *Fr.* Dream Songs.

Thin, Black Band, A. Sandor Csoori. VCWP

Thin brown-haired girl pouts, A. Strip. Lyrae Van Clief-Stefanon. BRtP

Thin grass bends on the breezy shore. Night Thoughts While Traveling. Tu Fu [or Du Fu]. CrYelRi, tr. by Sam Hamill

Thin leaves wave on the *wu-t'ung* tree beside the well. Lonely Night in Early Autumn. Po Chü-i. TAL

Thin lips can make a music. Redivivus. Donald Davidson. FuPo

Thin little leaves of wood fern, ribbed and toothed. Frederick Goddard Tuckerman. APN-2; NoP-5 *Fr.* Sonnets.

Thin Mary sits there. Winter Angel. Ágnes Nemes Nagy. PoSu, tr. by Hugh Maxton

Thin mist, A. Fireflies. José Gorostiza. TCLAP, tr. by Rachel Benson

Thin neon light spills on the hands in the tubs, The. Night Shift at the Fruit Cannery. Ilze Mueller. CFP

Thin peeling of an orange, impertinent, The. My Kingdom Is of This World. Audrey Poetker-Thiessen. ACAMVP

Thin priest, emphatic in black, A. In Torrett, Minorca. Norman Kreitman. EdScPo

Thin red faced pimpled boy, A. Walking into King Sooper after Two-Week Retreat. Allen Ginsberg. WhBo

Thin silver disc moon shredded at the bottom edge is. Leslie Scalapino. PfS *Fr.* Sight.

Thin sliver of november moon over maclean park. Roy Kiyooka. NLPA *Fr.* Pear Tree Pomes.

Thin steel in paired lines, forever mated, cuts. North Philadelphia, Trenton, and New York. Richmond Lattimore. APT-2

Thin wet sky, that yellows at the rim, A. Marshlands. Emily Pauline Johnson. SWaP

Thin wickedly intricate, The. Dark Area. Russell Atkins. GT

Thin Wire. Leo Vroman. TuT, tr. by Desmond Egan

Thine elder that I am, thou must not cling. Sweeter Far than the Harp, More Gold than Gold. Michael Field. OBMV

Thine eyes I love, and they, as pitying me. William Shakespeare. OxAEP-1; WaAnP *Fr.* Sonnets.

Thine eyes shall see the light of distant skies. To Cole, the Painter, Departing for Europe. William Cullen Bryant. ColAP; TCAPo

Thine Eyes Still Shined. Ralph Waldo Emerson. ColAP

Thine is a strain to read amongst the hills. To [or the Poet] Wordsworth. Felicia Dorothea Hemans. NPBRoP; RWP

Thine Own. Josephine D. Henderson Heard. CBWP-4; SWaP

Thine own reflection in Eternity! (LL) Aspiration. Adah Isaacs Menken. CBWP-1; ViWPN

Thine was a brain of nature's finest mould. Charles Sumner. Henrietta Cordelia Ray. CBWP-3

Thing. Elin ap Hywel. BBMWP, tr. by the author

Thing, The. Theodore Roethke. APT-2

Thing About Joe Sullivan, The. Roy Fisher. HarvBoo

Thing about playing solitaire, The. Playing Solitaire. Thulani Davis. GT

Thing about the dove was how he cried in, The. Inkspot, The. Paul Muldoon and Gerald Stern. GPPA

Thing could barely stand, The. Yet taken. Bull Calf, The. Irving Layton. BrAP

Thing I must somehow forget. (LL) To His Love. Ivor Gurney. InoFa; MakPoe; NAEL-7v2; NAMCP V.1; NoP-4; NoP-5; NPeEn; OBWP; PoAgWa; PoWW

Thing itself is in that, The. (LL) Firebombing, The. James Dickey. AmWaPo; OBWP; PWW2

Thing Language. Jack Spicer. APSN; FTOS; OxBoAm *Fr.* Language.

Thing long forgotten. Masaoka Shiki. ZenPo, tr. by Takashi Ikemoto and Lucien Stryk

Thing must End, The. I am no boy! I am. Sonnet: In Time of Revolt. Rupert Brooke. OBCoV

Thing not done, The. Deutschland. Hugh Maxton. PBCIP

Thing of Beauty, A. W. S. Merwin. OxBoAm

Thing of it was, The. After the Fact: To Ted Bundy. Robert Phillips. LiTh

Thing or Two about Childhood, A. Yury Iofe. TCRusP, tr. by John Glad

Thing to draw with compasses, The. Circles. Harry Behn. CA

Thing to remember, The. Imperative. Scott Cairns. UpMys

Thing Was Moving, The. Charles Olson. NAMCP V.2

Thing would have vanished by the time he got there, The. (LL) Oldest Living Thing in L.A., The. Larry Levis. P180; UrbNat

Things: "There are worse things than having behaved foolishly in public." Fleur Adcock. IJHIL; StAl

Things: "Things are the mind's mute looking-glass." Walter De la Mare. PoA 2002

Things. Gloria Fuertes. RaW, tr. by Philip Levine

Things. Geoffrey Holloway. NLP

Things. Bob Perelman. PmAP

Things, The. Conrad Potter Aiken. WeW-3

Things are as usual mute. Why Are Seaman Always Miserable? Zahrah Youssri. AnVo, tr. by Mohamed Enani

Things are happening. Daily. Translation of Raimundo Luz, The: My Farewell. Scott Cairns. UpMys

Things Are Looking Up. Ira Gershwin. ReLy

Things are the mind's mute looking-glass. Things. Walter De la Mare. PoA 2002

Things, As They Are. Dianne Edenfield Edwards. ICANM

Things break down in different ways. Entropic Villanelle. Thomas M. Disch. RA

Things bygone engender nothing but unbearable sorrow. Tune: "Sand Washed by Waves." Li Yü. ColAnChi, tr. by Jiaosheng Wang

Things concentrate at the edges; the pond-surface. Marginalia. Richard Wilbur. PoA 2002

Things don't forget. Roberto Carifi. PML, tr. by Oonagh Stransky

Things exist alone. Moon and Hare. Takahashi Shinkichi. ZenPo, tr. by Takashi Ikemoto and Lucien Stryk

Things Forbidden. *Unknown.* NoSic

Things glisten. Roof tiles rise. City. Angel González. VCWP, tr. by Steven Ford Brown and Revuelta Gutierrez

Things harness me here. I long. Lucy's Letter. James Berry. FaBoVe

Things have an admirable life. Valerio Magrelli. ItPo, tr. by Gayle Ridinger

Things have come to a pretty pass. Let's Call the Whole Thing Off. Ira Gershwin. ReLy

Things he has been spared, The. Donald Davie. NAMCP V.2 *Fr.* In the Stopping Train.

Things he timidly imagined as a schoolboy, The. Passing Through. Constantine P. Cavafy. CAGL, tr. by Edmund Keeley and Philip Sherrard

Things I Didn't Know I Loved. Nazim Hikmet. AF; AmFaPo; GPTC; VCWP, tr. by Randy Blasing and Mutlu Konuk

Things I Miss, The. Paula Yup. WhBo

Things I used to like, The. It Might As Well Be Spring. Oscar Hammerstein, II. ReLy

Things like littlenecks. Spring Night. Hagiwara Sakutaro. PFTM-1

Things live there, held still in glass cases, The. Reflections on a Visit to the Burke Museum, University of Washington, Seattle. Gail Tremblay. HATNAP

Things Made by Iron. D. H. Lawrence. Spl

Things may not be as then. (LL) Colonel's Soliloquy, The. Thomas Hardy. FaBoWar; OBWP

Things My Brother and I Could Do. Robert Bly. InvLad

Things My Grandfather Must Have Said. Mark Cox. SUP

Things No One Told Me. Opal Palmer Adisa. BtF

Things of August. Wallace Stevens.
"These locusts by day, these crickets by night." PoA 2002

Things of earth are not objects, The. A. R. Ammons. NAMCP V.2 *Fr.* Tombstones.

Things of my younger years. Beaches. Zachary Scott Robbins. BtF

Things of the Blind. Paz Molina. TANSG, tr. by Steven F. White

Things of the World, The. Robert Sargent. PoA 2002

Things of This World. Anna Kamienska. GI, tr. by David Curzon and Grażyna Drabik

Things One Would Like to Send Away. *Unknown.* EMJL, tr. by Edward Putzar

Things present but as a tale. (LL) One We Knew. Thomas Hardy. NAEL-6v2; NAEL-7v2

Things sinister with things sublime / Alike dissolving. (LL) Going and Staying. Thomas Hardy. NAMCP V.1; NoAM

Things swim. View from the Bathysphere. Peter Rafferty. NLP

Things That Are Lost. Kerry Hardie. MoWP

Things that enter by way of silence are beginning to come into the room. Interior. Gilberto Owen. MotU, tr. by Mark Strand

Things That Go Bump in the Night. *Unknown.* NTCP

Things That Grow. Hazel Hall. NAAPv.2

Things That Have Escaped Me. Jesse Lee Kercheval. SUP

Things that make a life to please, The. Happy Life, A. Martial. OBVE, tr. by Sir Richard Fanshawe

Things that make a soldier great and send him out to die, The. Things that Make a Soldier Great, The. Edgar Albert Guest. NIL-7

Things that make the happier life, are these, The. Martial. Epigram XLVII, Book X. Ben Jonson. OBVE

Things That Matter, The. Edith Nesbit. VWP

Things that our hearts wish to say to our girls, The. Word from the Gray Soldiers. Hillel Omer. NRoS, tr. by Esther Raizen

Things That Stand One's Hair on End. *Unknown.* EMJL, tr. by Edward Putzar

Things the Bigger the Better. *Unknown.* EMJL, tr. by Edward Putzar

Things the Smaller the Better. *Unknown.* EMJL, tr. by Edward Putzar

Things they did together, no one knew, The. 1904. Frederick Morgan. WeW-3

Things to Do.   James Schuyler.   OxBoAm

Things to Do Around San Francisco.   Gary Snyder.   OxBoAm

Things to Do in Holland.   Beau Sia.   HeMarv

Things to Do in the Bible.   Elaine Equi.   IllVoic

Things to Do in Valley of the Dolls (The Movie).   David Trinidad.   WiU

Things to Think.   Robert Bly.   PLBUT

Things touching each other sounds materials furrowed.   Angélica Tornero. SPV, *tr.* by Jen Hofer

Things turn mortal at twilight.   La Naval De Manila: Selim Sot as a Modern Political Observer.   Eric Gamalinda.   ReBoTo

Things We Did Last Summer, The.   Sammy Cahn.   ReLy

Things We Dreamt We Died For.   Marvin Bell.   PoA 2002

Things we love we have to learn to leave alone, The. (LL)   Woman with Flower.   Naomi Long Madgett.   GT; OxAAAP

Things went downhill.   When I Moved into the Neighborhood.   Carl Mayfield. ICANM

Things will be different.   In the Next Galaxy.   Ruth Stone.   BeAl; StAl

Things You Can't Do in Albuquerque or Santa Fe, #11.   Bobby Byrd.   TiP2

Things you had no right to do, the things you should have done, The.   Words from Robert W. Service.   Charles North.   NYP2

Things you need to live, the people, The.   Need.   Dionisio D. Martinez.   FaoP

Think about it.   Miracles.   Carol Muske-Dukes.   AmAlph; ExTi

Think about pools. (LL)   Tricks With Mirrors.   Margaret Atwood.   BrAP; NIP-4

Think about St. Joan without.   Evolution of Appetite.   Kelleen Zubick. OPRER

Think[e] all but one, and me in that one Will. (LL)   William Shakespeare. NAEL-6v1; NAEL-7v1; NoP-5; PBRV *Fr.* Sonnets.

Think as I think, said a man.   Stephen Crane.   IJHIL; WeW-3

Think Back.   Gerry Gomez Pearlberg.   WiU

Think Eight.   Todd Colby.   HeMarv

Think how unspeakably sweet.   Asclepiades.   ErotSp, *tr.* by Sam Hamill

Think in ways you've never thought before.   Things to Think.   Robert Bly. PLBUT

Think it enough for me to [*or* t'] have had thy love. (LL)   John Donne. CABP; FSCP; NAEL-6v1; NAEL-7v1; NoSic; NPeEn; OxAEP-1 *Fr.* Elegies.

Think not I have not heard.   Menses.   Edna St. Vincent Millay.   APT-1; BrAP; RACG

Think not, O man that dwells herein.   Upon the New Building at Appleton. Thomas Fairfax, Baron Fairfax of Cameron.   NOSC

Think not this paper comes with vain pretense.   Epistle from Mrs. Yonge to Her Husband.   Lady Mary Wortley Montagu.   NAEL-6v1; NAEL-7v1; NALW; NoP-4; NoP-5; NPeEn

Think, now: if you have found a dead bird.   Advice to a Discarded Lover. Fleur Adcock.   StAl

Think of a queen mole who is unequivocal.   Sexual Jealousy.   Carol Frost. CAP-8; PfSP

Think of cushions on a sofa.   All Sweet Things, Like Forgiveness, Are a Falling.   Juanita Brunk.   ACAMVP

Think of him as uninjured, barely disturbed. (LL)   Little Exercise.   Elizabeth Bishop.   ColAP; MoAmPo

Think of it in Beijing.   Butterfly Effect, The.   Harry Humes.   BAP-97

Think of it starting out this way: in profile.   Continent as the Letter M, The. Douglas Crase.   OxBoAm

Think of Slavery.   Imamu Amiri Baraka.   NAMCP V.2 *Fr.* Why's / Wise.

Think of that only when they think of me. (LL)   When the Sword of Sixty Comes Nigh His Head.   Firdowsi.   OBVE; WoPoe, *tr.* by Basil Bunting

Think of that statue open in the heart of the city.   Mónica Nepote.   SPV, *tr.* by Jen Hofer

Think of the boat departing from the quay, slowly leaving the shore.   Little Soul.   Valérie-Catherine Richez.   YaTCFP, *tr.* by Michael Tweed

Think of the Buddhist monks.   Poet's Heart, The.   Richard Jones.   GifTon

Think of the children in Baghdad.   Karen Alkalay-Gut.   DTA *Fr.* Between Bombardments: A Journal.

Think of the storm roaming the sky uneasily.   Little Exercise.   Elizabeth Bishop.   ColAP; MoAmPo

Think of the Words.   Marianne Boruch.   AmAlph

Think of this: that under the earth.   Deep Mining.   Irene McKinney.   PBCAP

Think of those Chinese monks' tales.   Inspiration.   Jane Hirshfield. WANABP

Think of those naturals who started right off blowing horn.   Ambition.   Bruce Berger.   GeoH

Think of those old, enduring connections.   Family Is All There Is, The. Pattiann Rogers.   NIP-4

Think of what you're losing.   I Won't Dance.   Dorothy Fields.   ReLy

Think of your age, old man.   Homo Erectus, Cerne Abbas.   Mercer Simpson. TCAWP

Think on him: bound.   Ariel.   Eva Hooker.   IaFF

Think sad thoughts of other days.   Song of the Palace of Ch'en.   Kuan Hsiu. WoPoe, *tr.* by Jerome P. Seaton

Think thou and act; to-morrow thou shalt die.   Dante Gabriel Rossetti.   ChIV-2; OBEV *Fr.* House of Life, The.

Think what the demotic droplet felt.   Processional.   James Merrill.   PoDa

Think While You Are Alive.   Kabir. *See* To Be a Slave of Intensity.

Think with your body.   Poem.   Víctor Hernández Cruz.   PueRic

Thinker Between the Bronze Shield and the Human Flesh, The.   Salah Niyazi. IrPoTo, *tr.* by Melissa Brown and Saadi A. Simawe

Thinking.   Jorie Graham.   BAP-97; ExTi

Thinking, A child's hand. The child's hand. (LL)   Flood Year.   Judith Wright. NAMCP V.2; NoAM

Thinking about air conditioning's Willis Carrier.   Man with the Hoe, The.   Les A. Murray.   UpMys

Thinking about all the eavesdroppers.   Roy Kiyooka.   NLPA *Fr.* Pear Tree Pomes.

Thinking about Bill, Dead of AIDS.   Miller Williams.   NIL-7

Thinking About Cows at Ten O'Clock in the Morning, Abilene.   Naomi Shihab Nye.   TiP2

Thinking about him.   Ono no Komachi.   WoPoe, *tr.* by Donald Keene

Thinking American.   Hayan Charara.   AmPoNex; PrTe

Thinking around things that edge me into.   Crack, The.   Clark Coolidge. PmAP

Thinking he walked on air, he.   Ravenna Bridge.   Leslie Norris.   AngWePo

Thinking he was asking about race, I told him I was black.   Origins.   Forrest Hamer.   GeoHom

Thinking how thin the glutton's skeleton.   Poem About Death, A.   Burns Singer.   EdScPo

Thinking I'd better be prepared when I went.   Spit.   A. R. Ammons.   BodElec

Thinking in terms of one.   Counting.   Philip Larkin.   PoetW

Thinking "In the beginning was the—(*What??*)."   What the Lovers in the Old Songs Thought.   John Hollander.   BAP-01

Thinking of a Friend.   Carl Mayfield.   ICANM

Thinking of a Monk of Flower Summit on Mount T'ien-t'ai.   Ch'i-chi. CSKM, *tr.* by Burton Watson

Thinking of a Relation between the Images of Metaphors.   Wallace Stevens. SAmP

Thinking of Death and Dogfood.   Maxine W. Kumin.   ItP

Thinking of East Mountain ("It's forever since I faced East Mountain.")   Li Po. NDACCP, *tr.* by David Hinton

Thinking of her had saddened me at first.   Celandine.   Edward Thomas. TCAWP

Thinking of Holland.   Memory of Holland.   Hendrik Marsman.   TuT, *tr.* by Michael Longley

Thinking of Impoverished Ancients.   T'ao Ch'ien.   GifTon, *tr.* by David Hinton

Thinking of Lady Yang at Midnight.   *Unknown*.   WoPoe, *tr.* by Jean S. Grigsby

Thinking of Li Po.   Tu Fu [*or* Du Fu].   CrYelRi, *tr.* by Sam Hamill

Thinking of Love.   Elizabeth Jennings.   LW

Thinking of Mr D.   Thomas Kinsella.   NoAM

Thinking of My Brother in Shantung on the Ninth Day of the Ninth Moon. Wang Wei.   TAL

Thinking of My Brothers on a Moonlit Night.   Tu Fu [*or* Du Fu].   TAL

Thinking of My Family on an Autumn Day.   Yang Wen-li.   WoPoe, *tr.* by Nancy Hodes and Tung Yuan-fang

Thinking of my father.   At the Nuclear Rally.   Laura Boss.   UnSA

Thinking of My Little Boy.   Tu Fu [*or* Du Fu].   ColAnChi; WoPoe, *tr.* by David Lattimore

Thinking of new ways to kill you.   Lily Pond.   Vicki Feaver.   EmeKit

Thinking of rain clouds that rose over the city.   St. Vincent's.   W. S. Merwin. CAP-8; VCAP

Thinking of Red.   Linda Bierds.   AmAlph

Thinking of Retired Scholar Wu on the River.   Chia Tao.   CSKM, *tr.* by Mike O'Connor

Thinking of Someone.   "Hsiung Hung."   CFP, *tr.* by Chung Ling and Kenneth Rexroth

Thinking of the Lost World.   Randall Jarrell.   NAAL-5; NAMCP V.2; NoAM; StAl

Thinking of you.   Love Notes.   Jennifer Strauss.   BMAP

Thinking of you, and all that was, and all.   Christina Georgina Rossetti. OxBSo *Fr.* Monna Innominata.

Thinking of You, Hiroshima.   Betsy Sholl.   PBCAP

Thinking of you, I think of the *coureurs de bois*.   Coureurs de Bois.   Douglas Le Pan.   BrAP

Thinking of you, in autumn night.   Autumn Night: A Letter Sent to Ch'iu. Wei Ying-wu.   ChinPo, *tr.* by Ye Weilian [*or* Yeh Wei-lien *or* Wai-lim Yip]

Thinking only of their vow that they would crush the Tartars.   Turkestan. Ch'en Tao.   WoPoe, *tr.* by Witter Bynner

Thinking the Alps.   Michael Davidson.   PmAP

Thinking they'd fledged too soon. Bluetits. Ruth Smith. Prnts

Thinking this morning of Susan. Presences. Lauris Edmond. PoCu

Thinking we were safe—insanity! Story of a Hotel Room. Rosemary Tonks. BeAl; LW; MoWP

Thinks even her acne. Japanese Figures 2. *Unknown.* EaWin, tr. by W. S. Merwin

Thinks it's all junk these days, the routine. Elm Tree on Lafayette Street, The. Rod Kessler. OPRER

Think'st Thou to Seduce Me Then. Thomas Campion. NAEL-7v1; OxAEP-1; NAEL-6v1

Think'st thou to seduce me then with words that have no meaning? Think'st thou to seduce me then. Thomas Campion. NAEL-7v1; OxAEP-1

Thin-Legged Lover. Kate Mullen. PfS

Thinnest meal on the slightest isle, The. Produce, Produce. Susan Wheeler. KGB

Thinnest sliver of moon, and caterpillars, A. Peony Lover. Lee Ann Roripaugh. AmPoNex

Thir riveris and thir watteris kepit war. Virgil. OxBEV Fr. Aeneid [or Eneados or Aeneis], The.

Third, A. Moishe Nadir. Prolet, tr. by Amelia Glaser

Third Avenue in sunlight. Nature's error. Third Avenue in Sunlight. Anthony Hecht. OxBoAm; VCAP

Third Avenue is a vacant lot with a Desert Air sign. Silent Globe. Debra Gregerman. AmPoNex

Third Body. Beckian Fritz Goldberg. AmAlph

Third Body, A. Robert Bly. BeAl; LoL

Third Century, The. Thomas Traherne.
  On News. OBEV
  "That childish thoughts such joys inspire." BASC

Third Cycle of Love Poems. George Barker.
  Shut the Seven Seas against Us. MoBrPo

Third Day. Thomas Traherne. ChIV-1 Fr. Meditations on the Six Days of the Creation.

Third Day, The. Phillis Levin. BBASP

Third Day of the Third Month at the Meandering River, The. Yu Ch'an. ChinPo, tr. by Ye Weilian [or Yeh Wei-lien or Wai-lim Yip]

Third Epistle to Timothy. Paul Muldoon. NoP-5

Third Eye, The. Jay Macpherson. IFF

Third Farming Poem. Brenda Coultas. HeMarv

Third generation timetable. Day-Long Day. Tino Villanueva. TiP2

Third Light, The. Michael Longley. PNI

3rd Light Poem: For Spencer, Beate, & Sebastian Holst—12 June 1962. Jackson Mac Low. PFTM-2

Third Maisie Poem. Daniel Nester. IIR

Third month, eleventh day. How I Felt Pawning My Coat: Shown to Ch'oe Chongbon. Yi Kyubo. CATKP, tr. by Kevin O'Rourke

Third month in T'ientsin, The. Li Po. ChinPo, tr. by Ye Weilian [or Yeh Wei-lien or Wai-lim Yip]

Third movement. Kurt Schwitters. PFTM-1 Fr. Ur Sonata.

Third one crooked the second one leaning, The. Bamboo Garden. Muso Soseki. EaWin, tr. by W. S. Merwin

Third person. (LL) Ghazal of the Better-Unbegun. Heather McHugh. ExTi; FaoP

Third Possibility, A. Wendell Berry. UpMys

Third Psalm. Anne Sexton. NALW Fr. O Ye Tongues.

Third Sermon on the Warpland, The. Gwendolyn Brooks. SeSe

Third Sex, The. Patricia Young. BrAP

Third Shell, The. David Meltzer. PFTM-2 Fr. Hero/Lil.

Third Shift. Anthony Walton. NAPBL

Third Stair, Seventh Stair, Landing. Jane Mead. SweBea

Third Street Promenade; Full Moon, Sunday Night, Santa Monica. Al Young. WhBo

Third, third, third–the rule I learned. Rule of Thirds, The. Jack Coulehan. BloBone

Third Time Wandering to Cloud Sluice Peak. Ching An. CSKM, tr. by Jerome P. Seaton

3rd Untitled Poem. Pedro Juan Pietri. PueRic

Third Warning Sign: An Endless Surprise. Edoardo Cacciatore. ItPo Fr. Full Powers: Five Warning Signs.

Third World. Christina Rivera-Garza. SPV, tr. by Jen Hofer

Third World Calling. Lawrence Ferlinghetti. BB

Thirsis a youth of the inspired train. Edmund Waller. *See* Thyrsis, a youth of the inspired train.

Thirst. Thurayya Al-Urayyid. PoArWo, tr. by Farouk Mustafa

Thirst. Arthur Rimbaud. WoPoe, tr. by Michael O'Brien

Thirst. Genevieve Taggard. APT-2

Thirst. Cecilia Vicuña. WANABP, tr. by Rosa Alcalá

Thirst. Mark Wunderlich. AmPoNex

Thirst for green, because too long deprived, A. Vega. Lawrence Durrell. OxAEP-2

Thirst for Knowledge, A. Diana Hartog. NLPA Fr. Oasis.

Thirst for the Sea. Magda Portal. TANSG, tr. by Shaun Griffin and Emma Sepúlveda-Pulvirenti

Thirst / is. Thirst. Cecilia Vicuña. WANABP, tr. by Rosa Alcalá

Thirst is no thing and yet it cruel can torment you. "Angelus Silesius." GePo Fr. Cherubical Wanderer, The.

Thirst of the crowd, The. We laid the surfer down. Joshua Beckman. LegDan

Thirst of Turtles, The. Thomas Lux. AmAlph

Thirsty. Dionne Brand. GPPA

Thirsty and pale, her face lowered in concentration. Cleaning the Elephant. Henri Cole. BeAl

Thirsty Earth soaks up the Rain, The. Drinking. Abraham Cowley. NPeEn; OBEV; OBVE; OxAEP-1; OxBEV, tr. by Abraham Cowley

Thirsty Fish, The. Kabir. WED, tr. by Robert Bly

Thirteen. Jimmy Santiago Baca. FaoP

13. Linh Dinh. BAP-04

13. Jennifer Murphy. BRtP

Thirteen. Ronald Wallace. PBCAP

13/1/78. George Stanley. NLPA Fr. Mountains and Air.

13 June 1994. Virginia Cerenio. ReBoTo

13 November 1983. Lee Cataldi. BMAP

Thirteen Propositions against Trivial Love. David Huerta. RMCMP, tr. by Mark Schafer

Thirteen Sonnets. Michael Hartnett.
  Sonnet. PBCIP

Thirteen Steps and the Thirteenth of March. Douglas Dunn. InoFa; NoP-4; NoP-5 Fr. Elegies.

Thirteen Ways of Looking at a Blackbird. Wallace Stevens. APT-1; BrAP; ChAP; ColAP; HeIP-4; NAAL-5; NAAPv.2; NAMCP V.1; NoAM; NoP-4; NoP-5; OWoS; OxBoAm; PoPoPo; PtR; SAmP; TCAPo; TFi

Thirteen Ways of Looking at a Hoover. Anthony Conran. TCAWP

Thirteen Years. Erin Mouré. NIL-7

Thirteen years ago, before bulk barns and. Change, The. A. A. Hedge Cole. ReEnLa

Thirteen years / Or haply less, I might have seen, when first. William Wordsworth. OxAEP-2 Fr. Prelude, The; Growth of a Poet's Mind [1805 version].

13ChildrenRushdownaStreet. Yi Sang. CAMKP Fr. Crow's-Eye View.

Thirteen's no age at all. Thirteen is nothing. Portrait of a Girl with Comic Book. Phyllis McGinley. APT-2

Thirteenth Bard's Song, The. James Hogg. NePenScot Fr. Queen's Wake, The.

13th day of November in that 1917th year, The. In the Paul Guillaume Gallery. Pierre Albert-Birot. CuPo

13th Horse Song of Frank Mitchell, The. María Sabina. PFTM-1

13th Letter, The. Jolivette Anderson. BRtP

Thirteenth Ode. Sekeena Shaben. PoArWo

30th Year Dream. Gregory Corso. BodElec

Thirty Bob a Week. John Davidson. CABP; NePenScot; NPeEn; OxBEV

Thirty East Forty-Second Street. Alan Davies. FTOS

30 55. Michael Haslam. Oth Fr. Continual Song.

31st day of August 1914, The. Little Car, The. Guillaume Apollinaire. YaTCFP, tr. by Ron Padgett

34.57. Carson Cistulli. FreRad Fr. Twenty-Six Friends, That's the Same as Your Age.

34. Chapter of the Prophet Isaiah, The. Abraham Cowley. ChIV-1

34th Merzgedicht in Memoriam Kurt Schwitters. Jackson Mac Low. PFTM-2

30 Miles from J-Town. Amy Uyematsu. GeoHom

Thirty minutes until feeding time in the cathouse at the Granby. David McFadden. NLPA

31. Catullus. AmFaPo, tr. by Peter Whigam

3600 Weekends. Ken Edwards.
  Lexically. Oth

Thirty soldiers, exhausted and grim-faced. T. Gwynn Jones. BBMWP Fr. Pro Patria.

Thirty spokes converge on a single hub. Lao Tzu. ColAnChi Fr. Tao Te Ching.

Thirty Tanka. Tachibana Akemi. tr. by Burton Watson
  Happiness Is When.
  "Happiness is when." WoPoe, tr. by Burton Watson

Thirty thousand feet of solid Cumberland. (LL) To the River Duddon. Norman Nicholson. NLP; NoP-4; NoP-5

32 Positions of Love, The. Paul Eluard and Andre Breton. PFTM-1 Fr. Immaculate Conception, The.

32s. 6d. for the chattels of Robert Hod, fugitive, Michaelmas 1230 at York. Alan Halsey. Oth Fr. Robin Hood Book, A.

Thirty white horses upon a red hill. Teeth and Gums. Mother Goose. NTCP

Thirty Years After. János Vajda. IQMS, *tr.* by Dorren Bell

Thirty years ago: gulls keen in the blue. Woman, A. Robert Pinsky. WeW-3

Thirty years ago, Marseilles lay burning in the sun, one day. Plato's Dog. John A. Scott. BMAP

Thirty Years On. Charles Hobday. RSaN

Thirty Years Rising. Olena Kalytiak Davis. AmPoNex; LegDan

38, The. Ted Joans. WeW-3

Thirty-eight: Addressed to Mrs H—y. Charlotte Smith. NALW; PEW

38 Phoenix Street. Thomas Kinsella. ModIr *Fr.* One.

Thirty-Eighth Year, The. Lucille Clifton. OxWW

Thirty-eighth year, The. Thirty-Eighth Year, The. Lucille Clifton. OxWW

Thirty-Five Miles to a Traffic Light. David Budbill. AmZen

35 Sonnets. Fernando Pessoa.
   "When in the widening circle of rebirth." ItP, *tr.* by Susan M. Brown and Edwin Honig

35,000 feet above Saskatchewan. B. P. Nichol. NLPA *Fr.* Inchoate Road.

Thirty-nine Haiku. Masaoka Shiki.
   Haiku. CAoMJL1, *tr.* by Burton Watson

Thirty-nine years in exile. My Tibetanness. PML

Thirty-six years, to the day, after our wedding. Pattern, The. Michael Longley. BeAl

Thirty-some years ago, hitchhiking. Memory of Wilmington. Galway Kinnell. OPRER

Thirty-third Canto. Hans Magnus Enzensberger. PoSu *Fr.* Sinking of the Titanic, The.

33. Julia Alvarez.
   Sonnet 1. FFC
   Sonnet 42. FFC

Thirty-three, goodbye. Happy Birthday. Frank Bidart. VCAP

Thirty-year-old man in a highly-thought-of group home, A. Beautiful Eyes. Louise Grassi Whitney. PfS

This. Yvonne Cullen. NIrP

This abacus of days. This withdrawal. This closing out. (LL) Autumn Cancer. Kerry Hardie. BeAl; PoCu

This acolyte of the western valley bows deeply. To Master Monk Nangjee. Great Master Wonhyo. BecRai, *tr.* by Kim Daljin, Kim Won-Chung and Christopher Merrill

This admirable gadget, when it is. Gyroscope. Howard Nemerov. NAMCP V.2; NoAM

This advanced frontier. Charles Tomlinson. WoBe *Fr.* Zipangu.

This Advent moon shines cold and clear. Advent. Christina Georgina Rossetti. RSR

This adventure had Arthur of handsels first. *Unknown.* NAEL-6v1; NAEL-7v1; NAWM-7v1 *Fr.* Sir Gawain and the Green Knight [Marie Borroff Translation].

This ae nighte [*or* ean night], this ae nighte. Lyke-Wake Dirge, The [*or* A]. *Unknown.* EMWP; NoP-4; NPeEn; OBEV; OxBEV; SacPr; TFi; WeW-3; WoPoe

This afternoon is grey and sad. Tropic Afternoon. Rubén Darío. SonAtl, *tr.* by Eleanor Davidson

This afternoon it rains as never before; and I. Down to the Dregs. César Vallejo. TCLAP, *tr.* by James Wright and James Wright

This afternoon, my treasure, when I talked with you. Pleaure Given by Suspicion with the Rhetoric of Crying, The. Sor Juana Inés de la Cruz. BLPSL, *tr.* by Rene de Costa, Rigas Kappatos and Eleni Paidoussi

This afternoon was the colour of water falling through sunlight. September, 1918. Amy Lowell. NAAL-5; NAAPv.2

This all happened before. David Lee. GifTon *Fr.* Driving and Drinking.

This almost bare tree is racing. November through a Giant Copper Beech. Edwin Honig. NoAM

This Amber Sunstream. Mark Van Doren. APT-2

This ancient silver bowl of mine, it tells of good old times. On Lending a Punch-Bowl. Oliver Wendell Holmes. TreFP

This and That. Elke Erb. OnScMo, *tr.* by Rosmarie Waldrop

This angel clung to boats. Fanny Howe. FaoP *Fr.* Passion, The.

This angel, who mediates between us. Angel, The. Galway Kinnell. NoAM

This apotheosis crushes me. Outcries. Hélène d'Oettingen. CuPo

This armless boy will ruin me. (LL) Cornelius Whur. STuOW; VerBaPo *Fr.* Armless Artist, The.

This astonishing delay, the everyday, takes place. (LL) Geese, The. Jorie Graham. MoWP; NoP-5; WaAnP

This Atomising of Things. Pauline Stainer. MoWP

This August night, raccoons. Invocation. Jane Hirshfield. BodElec; GeoHom

This August's Phloxes. Gennady Aygi. WoBe, *tr.* by Peter France

This autumn. Basho. EH, *tr.* by Robert Hass

This autumn / Sitting in my chair. That I Can Do This Autumn. Hong Yunsuk. CAMKP, *tr.* by Genell Y. Poitras

This Be the Verse. Philip Larkin. NAMCP V.2; NoAM; NoP-5; NPeEn; PoetW; PoPoPo; StAl

This Beach Can Be Dangerous. Allen Curnow. HarvBoo

This beast was fashioned well; it prowls. Around Us, Dawning. Wole Soyinka. NAMCP V.2

This beauteous form assures a piteous mind. (LL) John Donne. BASC; HeIP-4; NAEL-6v1; NAEL-7v1; NOSC; OxAEP-1 *Fr.* Holy Sonnets.

This bed thy center [*or* centre] is, these walls, thy sphe[a]re. (LL) Sun Rising, The. John Donne. BASC; CABP; ClHu; FSCP; HeIP-4; NAEL-6v1; NAEL-7v1; NIL-7; NIP-4; NoP-4; NoP-5; NOSC; PoPoPo; TFi; WaAnP; WeW-3

This before Trotsky and Breton. Make-Up. Maurice Kilwein Guevara. TouFir

This began somewhere. Essay on Language. Wanda Coleman. PmAP

This being Cambridge, he too. Accountant, The. Michael C. Blumenthal. PoDa

This biplane is the shape of human flight. Robert Frost. AmWit; WeW-3 *Fr.* Ten Mills.

This bird that a cat sprang loose in the house. More Joy in Heaven. Howard Nemerov. NoAM

This bit of polished marble—this. Bit of Marble, A. Clinton Scollard. APN-2

This Black Rich Country. A. R. Ammons. LPSFW

This blessing love gives again into our arms. (LL) After Making Love We Hear Footsteps. Galway Kinnell. BeAl; CAP-8; ColAP; EMP; NAAL-5; NAMCP V.2; NIL-7; NIP-4; NoAM; NoP-4; NoP-5; PasH; RaBo; VCAP; WaAnP

This bloody town's a bloody cuss. Bloody Orkneys, The. Hamish Blair. EdScPo

This blue / is nothing but elastic. Prose of the World Order. Jean Day. BAP-04

This blue stone. Blue Rock, The. Sojourner Kincaid Rolle. GeoHom

This Body. Michael Cuddihy. GifTon

This Body. Maurina Sherman. GeoHom

This body at night is the sound of the swaying creak of trees as they sink their roots to the river bank. This Body. Maurina Sherman. GeoHom

This body deemed machine—not daemon flesh. Soma. Suzanne Noguere. FFC

This body here feminine that hangs like a distant drop. To a Woman to a Path. Valentine Penrose. SurWo, *tr.* by Roland Penrose

This body of mine has lived a lot of years. Composed Playfully on New Year's Day. Yi Kyubo. CATKP, *tr.* by Kevin O'Rourke

This body won't pollute. Sekioku-Seikyo. ZenPo, *tr.* by Takashi Ikemoto and Lucien Stryk

This bone once moved a hand. Rune-Maker, The. Frederick Feirstein. RA

This book by any yet unread. To My Dear Children. Anne Bradstreet. BASC; NAAL-3; PtR

This Book is for Magda. Lew Welch. BB

This book is my link with father. At the South Pole. Jean Earle. Prnts

This book says that his form is the same as anarchy in that it is a faculty or. Picasso and Anarchism. Leslie Scalapino. FTOS

This book, this page, this harebell laid to rest. In Our Tenth Year. Simon Armitage. OxBSo

This boy listening eagerly to his friend. Mark Jarman. LiTh *Fr.* Unholy Sonnets.

This boy with the eyes of an owl. Cultivation of Orchids, The. Dionisio D. Martinez. TouFir

This brand of soap has the same smell as once in the big. Soap Suds. Louis MacNeice. EmeKit; ModIr; NAEL-6v2; NAEL-7v2; NPeEn

This Breach of Promise of Marriage! (LL) William Schwenck Gilbert. NAEL-6v2; NAEL-7v2 *Fr.* Trial by Jury.

This Bread I Break. Dylan Thomas. ChIV-2; GI; TRP

This Bridge Across. Christopher Gilbert. ESEAA; GT

This bridge of moon on bended knee above us. Paradise. Jill Alexander Essbaum. NAPBL

This brief effusion I indite. First-Rate Wife, The. Cornelius Whur. STuOW

This bright harvest moon. Basho. SoOfWa, *tr.* by Sam Hamill

This Bronze Censer. Pao Chao. CCL1, *tr.* by John Frodsham

This bronze censer, from a famous master of Luoyang. This Bronze Censer. Pao Chao. CCL1, *tr.* by John Frodsham

This brown woman's voice. Nina Simone. Lance Jeffers. SeSe

This burning behind my eyes as I open a door. Defeated. Robert Bly. StAl

This butterfly escaped, it seems. Tune: "Tsui-chung T'ien" To the Giant Butterfly. Wang Ho-ch'ing. ColAnChi, *tr.* by James I. Crump

This Can't Be Love. Lorenz Hart. ReLy

This carpenter hadde wedded newe a wyf. Geoffrey Chaucer. NPeEn *Fr.* Canterbury Tales, The.

This cash crop nation boasts one bridge. Here and There. Max Winter. FreRad

This Catching of Breath at the Top. Robert J. Gibbs. Coast

This cavernous apartment is ours on four months' good will. Five O'Clock Opera. Lavinia Greenlaw. MFPA

This celestial seascape, with white herons got up as angels. Seascape. Elizabeth Bishop. ColAP; OxBoAm

This change I feel puzzles me. Like Someone in Love. Johnny Burke. ReLy

This chapel that you gaze at, these stern tombs. Ruins of Time, The. Luis de Góngora y Argote. WoPoe, tr. by Robert Lowell

This child is an angel. Angel. Maxine Scates. PBCAP

This chirping. Sound of Birds at Noon, The. Dahlia Ravikovitch. VCWP

This city, Budapest, smells of violets in the spring as do mesdames along the promenade. Gyula Krúdy. IQMS, tr. by John Lukacs

This city, builded on more hills than Rome was. Scottish Renaissance in Glasgow, The: 1935. Naomi Mitchison. EdScPo

This city is beauty. Thirsty. Dionne Brand. GPPA

This city is made of stone, of blood, and fish. Anchorage. Joy Harjo. HATNAP; LTA; OPRER

This city where they raped and beat you. Cityscape. Mary Crow. LiTh

This city's architecture is characterised by the colonnades. New Year's Eve. Lavinia Greenlaw. MFPA

This clerk-work, this first January chore. New Diary, A. Dannie Abse. AngWePo; NoAM

This clock. Clock. Valerie Worth. TLR

This Close. Dorianne Laux. ExTi

This clumsy living that moves lumbering. Swan, The. Rainer Maria Rilke. WED, tr. by Robert Bly

This cold winter night. Buson. SoOfWa, tr. by Sam Hamill

This collision of teeth, of tongues and lips. First Kiss. April Lindner. GoPo

This color, its pure absence. Embarkation for Cythera. Lorenzo Thomas. EGAG

This Compost. Walt Whitman. MoAmPo; NAAL-3; OBGa; PFTM-1

This conscious attempt to see is producing sensations of. Lyn Hejinian. PfS Fr. Sight.

This Consciousness that is aware. Emily Dickinson. InoFa; NAAL-3; NAAPv.1

This Contradiction of Passion. Susan Goyette. OpeFie

This Corruptible. Elinor Wylie. MoAmPo

This cosmic. Hearing a Mozart Duo at 36,000 Feet. Ruth Whitman. PfS

This could be. Dinakdakan. Maria Luisa B. Aguilar-Cariño. ReBoTo

This could be Scotland: a crag and far below. Old Folsom Prison. William Matthews. OPRER

This could be the mind's antechamber. Faith Healers. Anne Rouse. NeBrP

This could have been a novel but it's a poem instead. Novel. Fred Moramarco. SUP

This country might have. Right On: White America. Sonia Sanchez. ISC

This country needs more noble men. This Country's Needs. Mrs. Henry Linden. CBWP-4

This crazy man has escaped the world. Wang Chiu-ssu. WoPoe Fr. After Reading the Poems of Master Han Shan.

This crescent's arc is. Kalamu ya Salaam. SpirFl Fr. New Orleans Haiku.

This cross is the most sublime. Coventry Cathedral. István Vas. IQMS, tr. by Geroge Gömöri and Clive Wilmer

This cross-tree here. Cross-tree, The. Robert Herrick. CavPo; ChIV-2

This crow is unlike the others. Ivan Metodiev. CSCBP Fr. Songs for Orphans Big and Small.

This Crusty Fragment. Marsden Hartley. APT-1

This Curious Involvement, a Dominant Species. John Seed. Oth

This Dai adjusts his slipping shoulder-straps. David Jones. AngWePo Fr. In Parenthesis.

This Damsell was not famous for the place. Arthur Golding. PBRV Fr. Ovid's Metamorphoses Book 6.

This dancer's stance slapped solely f'r th'effect. Square. Rob MacKenzie. Oth

This dark autumn. Basho. SoOfWa, tr. by Sam Hamill

This darksome burn, horseback brown. Inversnaid. Gerard Manley Hopkins. FaBoVe; MoBrPo; NoAM; NPeEn; SacPr; TFi

This dawn I completely lost my face. March of Dawn, The. Yi Hyangji. EcSo, tr. by Catherine J. Kim

This Day. Denise Levertov. UpMys

This day and age we're living in. As Time Goes By. Herman Hupfeld. ReLy

This day I saw ane endless muir. Wire, The. Robert Garioch. NePenScot

This day I will my thankes sure now declare. On the 30th of June to God. Lady Jane Cavendish. EMWP

This day is called the Feast of Crispian. William Shakespeare. BLPJKO Fr. King Henry V.

This day is Yours Great Charles! and in this War. To the King; Upon His Taking of Leicester. Robert Herrick. CavPo

This day, like all days. Last Chance for the Tarzan Holler. Thylias Moss. ExTi

This day, purified to nude, could be the past. Two Photographs. Phyllis Thompson. ICANM

This day so lonely. Kim Namjo. CAMKP Fr. Love's Cursive.

This day, so many years ago a day. Anniversary with Agave Plants. Margherita Guidacci. CItWP, tr. by Cinzia Sartini Blum and Lara Trubowitz

This day, whate'er the fates decree. Stella's Birthday ([March 13,] 1727). Jonathan Swift. NoP-4; NoP-5

This day winding down now. Author's Prologue. Dylan Thomas. ChIV-1

This day writhes with what? The lecturer. Ultimate Poem Is Abstract, The. Wallace Stevens. PoA 2002

This day's a riddle; for the God that made. Upon the Day of Our Saviour's Nativity. Francis Quarles. NOSC

This Dead Relationship. Katherine Pierpoint. EmeKit; StAl

This death you have nourished is too orderly. Medbh McGuckian. ModIr Fr. Porcelain Bells.

This Dendrite Map: Father / Mother Haibun. Fred Wah. NLPA

    Father / Mother Haibun #4. NLPA; OpeFie

    Father / Mother Haibun #5. IFF; NLPA

    Father / Mother Haibun #11. NLPA; OpeFie

This desert is a plateau of light. Language of Fossils, The. Anita Endrezze. HATNAP

This desolate valley is crowded with thieves. Crossing the Valley. Fadil Azzawi. IrPoTo, tr. by Ralph Saverese and Saadi A. Simawe

This difficult, tedious, painful enterprise. (LL) Lament: "Your dying was a difficult enterprise." Thom Gunn. CAGL; GPTC; InoFa

This dirty—little—Heart. Emily Dickinson. NCAP

This disease is an evil bound upon the day. Sophocles. EroLit Fr. Lovers of Achilles, The.

This divine October morning. Sorrow. Alfonsina Storni. TCLAP, tr. by Andrew Rosing

This Do in Remembrance of Me. Horatius Bonar.

    "Here, O my Lord, I see Thee face to face." SacPr

This docile one inter. Emily Dickinson. APN-2

This dog standing in the middle of the street. Real-Life Drama, A. Michael Collier. WaAnP

This door you might not open, and you did. Bluebeard. Edna St. Vincent Millay. APT-1; NAAPv.2

This downhill path is easy, but there's no turning back. (LL) Amor Mundi. Christina Georgina Rossetti. NoP-4; NoP-5; PEW; RACG

This dread is like a calm. Winter Holding off the Coast of North America. N. Scott Momaday. ColAP

This dream is not a map. Exploring the Dark Content. Harryette Mullen. OxAAAP

This dream of water—what does it harbor? I See Chile in My Rearview Mirror. Agha Shahid Ali. AmAlph; NAMCP V.2; NoP-4

This dream the world is having about itself. Vocation. William Stafford. CAP-8

This dream was either a prophesy or not. Dream, A. Anna Andreyevna Akhmatova. TCRusP, tr. by Daniel Weissbort

This dry night nothing unusual. War Horse, The. Eavan Boland. PBCIP

This Durgling was a dual personage. Delivered at the Knighting of Lord Durgling by Great Bruce-Jean. Jean Toomer. GT

This early May morn when there is none to wed. (LL) Cherry Trees, The. Edward Thomas. NAEL-6v2; NAEL-7v2; OBWP; Spl

This earth. Bill Neidjie. NOxBChV

This earth flails its environs. Outer Layers of Nervousness, The. Alan Davies. FTOS

This earth gave us. California, 1852. Sharyn Jeanne Skeeter. ISC

This Earth, My Brother. Kofi Awoonor. VCWP

This Earth our mighty Mother is, the Stones. Ovid. NPeEn Fr. Metamorphoses.

This Edward in the Aprill of his age. Michael Drayton. CAGL Fr. Piers Gaveston [1619].

This elderly gentleman. Hat. Tomasz Jastrun. AF, tr. by Daniel Bourne

This elderly poet, unpublished for five decades. Ashes, The. Carolyn Kizer. BAP-01

This ellipse, slip between seasons. Sonnet. Karen Volkman. IAoNAP

This endless gray-roofed city, and each heart. London Despair. Frances Darwin Cornford. OBMV

This England never did, nor never shall. William Shakespeare. OxAEP-1 Fr. King John.

This Englishwoman. Stevie Smith. NALW; NAMCP V.1

This entire / horror shew. IV. Steve Jonas. EGAG

This entire volume. (LL) Drawing. George Oppen. APT-2; PFTM-1

This evening, fear and grief grabbed me again. How Can I Turn Off This Engine Now? Christopher Davis. LiTh

This evening holds her breath. Winter Night. Cecil Day Lewis. PoA 2002

This evening I pace chambers where I sought. In the King's Rooms. Timothy Steele. RA

This evening, I sat by an open window. Happy Birthday, A. Ted Kooser. PoCho

This evening / Is the only evening. Alan Davies. Eno Fr. Pain.

This evening it's raining, and my picture of you is raining. The day falls open in my memory. You walked in. It's Raining. Vicente Aleixandre. RaW, tr. by Robert Bly

This evening only the lonely ones come and go upon. On the White Wall. Paek Sŏk. CAMKP, tr. by Kyunghwan Choi

This evening stroll deserves a poem. Essay, An. Semezdin Mehmedinović. PML, tr. by Antonela Glavinic and Kathleen Jamie

This evening, the sturdy Levis. Notice. Steve Kowit. BLT

This evening Venus places newly. Evening Star. Francisco Segovia. RMCMP, tr. by Michael Wiegers

This Evening When I Spoke to You. Sor Juana Inés de la Cruz. SpanPo, tr. by Muriel Kittel

This evening when I spoke to you, my dear. This Evening When I Spoke to You. Sor Juana Inés de la Cruz. SpanPo, tr. by Muriel Kittel

This fabulous shadow only the sea keeps. (LL) At Melville's Tomb. Hart Crane. APT-2; HarvBoo; InoFa; MoAmPo; NAAL-5; NAMCP V.1; NoAM; NoP-4; NoP-5; OxBoAm; PoA 2002; WaAnP

This face had no use for light, took none of it. Made Shine. Josephine Miles. NoAM

This fall morning is pretty much. Improvisation for the Stately Dwelling, An. A. R. Ammons. BodElec

This fall / the advertisement in the newspaper. Advertisement. Tedi López Mills. RMCMP, tr. by C. M. Mayo

This Familiarity. Eli Clare. PfS

This family portrait. Portrait of a Family. Carlos Drummond de Andrade. TCLAP, tr. by Virginia de Araújo

This far I know: We will all singularly choose where to lie down. Nuclear Winter. Nicholas Samaras. AtGh

This far in. Pleasure. Carl Phillips. BAP-04

This far out in the country no one is talking. Starting a Pasture. Walter McDonald. TiP2

This fear brings the war back—then it seemed. Former WWII Paratrooper Dreams of Suicide, 1977, A. Marianne Burke. RWB

This feast-day of the sun, his altar there. Dante Gabriel Rossetti. NoP-4; NoP-5 Fr. House of Life, The.

This fellow, perfect in men's eyes. Ikuo-Joun. ZenPo, tr. by Takashi Ikemoto and Lucien Stryk

This Fevers Me. Richard Eberhart. APT-2

This field they've contracted. Dreaming Over a Page. Lewis Warsh. AHA

This final drouth of penitential tears? (LL) John Sutter. Yvor Winters. MoAmPo; NAMCP V.1; NoAM

This first fallen snow. Basho. SoOfWa, tr. by Sam Hamill

This flesh you have loved. Kenneth Rexroth. APSN; APT-2 Fr. Love Poems of Marichiko, The.

This flood thus stained fairer streames. (LL) Bible, N.T. NOSC; SacPr Fr. St. Luke.

This flying angel's torrent cry. Eastern Tempest. Edmund Charles Blunden. MoBrPo

This Fog. Alan Feldman. PoDa

This, for my soul's peace, have I heard from Thee. Unknown. TAL Fr. Bhagavad-Gita, The.

This Form of Life Needs Sex. Allen Ginsberg. CLPP

This frightened, horny boy. Romance. Paul Zimmer. ReTh

This frog is more gifted. Swimming Upstream. Aimée Grunberger. PoCoUp

This fucking town's a fucking cuss. Oh! Fucking Halkirk. Unknown. FaBoWar

This fugitive between the Earth and Sky. Prelude. Tu Fu [or Du Fu]. TAL

This Garden Being: The Hanging of Books. Clark Coolidge. FTOS

This garden does not take my eyes. Garden, The. James Shirley. NOSC

This garden, stone-white: starwort, star aster, wisteria (the yearning earth). this. Syliva Legris. PoPra Fr. Negative Garden.

This garden too pleasant. Concert. Helen G. Quigless. EGAG

This garment I give you. Be Brothers. Ifi Amadiume. HAWP

This garment with the thin white stripes. Village Near a Church, A. Aliyah Abdul-Salaam. AnVo, tr. by Mohamed Enani

This Gate. Beau Beausoleil. Eno

This gentleman of cultivated virtue. Gardening Chrysanthemums, I Think of [T'ao] Yüan-Ming. Ishikawa Jōzan. WoPoe, tr. by Jonathan Chaves

This ghoul-haunted woodland of Weir. (LL) Ulalume [or Ulalume—a Ballad]. Edgar Allan Poe. APN-1; NAAL-5; NAAPv.1; NCAP; OxBoAm; TCAPo

This gift of story. Heron-Woman. Marjorie M. Evasco. ReBoTo

This girlchild was born as usual. Barbie Doll. Marge Piercy. BrAP; NIL-7; NIP-4; WaAnP

This gives support to insects. Jackson Mac Low. PmAP Fr. Pronouns, The—A Collection of 40 Dances—For the Dancers.

This glacier that creaks. Light of the Blade, The. André Du Bouchet. YaTCFP, tr. by Paul Auster

This god who has gaped ever since we created him. Lost. Orkhan Muyassar. BBASP, tr. by Samuel Hazo and Lena Jayyusi and W. S. Merwin

This grandson of fishes holds inside him. Evolution from the Fish. Robert Bly. NoAM

This great Grandmother of all creatures bred. Edmund Spenser. NoSic Fr. Faerie Queene, The.

This grey-haired spinster, Catharine Plouffe. Catharine Plouffe. Susan Frances Harrison. IFF

This Grizzly. Reg Saner. PoCoUp

This had happened before: rain that began. Flood. Claudia Emerson. PoDa

This handless clock stares blindly from its tower. Clock in the Square, A. Adrienne Rich. HeIP-4

This hand-to-mouth, pert, rapid, nineteenth century. James Russell Lowell. TCAPo Fr. Our Own—Progression F.

This handwriting wears itself away. Valerio Magrelli. NeIt

This happy place with all delights abounds. James Thomson. UV Fr. On Beauty [or Beauety].

This hare which scampers into age and death. Dürer's 'Young Hare'. Norah Hill. Prnts

This harpie with dry red curls. Red Dust. Philip Levine. NoAM

This has happened before. Mere Pleasure of Flying, The. Jane Duran. MFPA

This has nothing / to do with. Conjugation of the Paramecium, The. Muriel Rukeyser. NAMCP V.2

This he said to american poetry. Eastward Ho! A Succession. David Bromige. FTOS

This heap betrays me: please, Priapus, say. Unknown. PriapPo Fr. Priapus Poems, The.

This Heart of Mine. Arthur Freed. ReLy

This highest scholar in the school of sin. Sir Francis Hubert. NOSC Fr. Life and Death of Edward II, The.

This hill has been standing in my heart a long time. Antistrophe. Giacomo Leopardi. WoPoe, tr. by Robert Bringhurst

This holy night in open forum. Office Party. Phyllis McGinley. ChrPo; OBSV

This holy season, fit to fast and pray. Edmund Spenser. WaAnP Fr. Amoretti.

This horrible but superb painting. Parable of the Blind, The. William Carlos Williams. SAmP

This horrible but superb painting. William Carlos Williams. SAmP Fr. Pictures from Brueghel.

This hot day swept away. Basho. SoOfWa, tr. by Sam Hamill

This hot summer wind. When the Camel Is Dust It Goes through the Needle's Eye. Anne Stevenson. Prnts

This hot tide of blood. Yosano Akiko. CAoMJL1, tr. by Janine Beichman

This Hour. Sharon Olds. BeAl

This Hour and What Is Dead. Li-Young Lee. InoFa

This hour is made of iron grates where the underground. Michelangelo Coviello. ItPo Fr. Well of Clouds, The.

This hour of the star. Deep Rock. Jeffrey Renard Allen. RD

This hour was set the time for heaven's descent. Twilit Revelation. Léonie Adams. MoAmPo

This Houre Her Vigill. Valentin Iremonger. ModIr

This House. Robert Creeley. BodElec

This house has been far out at sea all night. Wind. Ted Hughes. HarvBoo; NAEL-6v2; NAEL-7v2; NoP-4; NoP-5

This house is a wreck said the children. Sad Children's Song, The. Grace Paley. SoSe-8; TaR

This house is closed to neighbors. Wayfarers, The. Yusuf Al-Khal. PFTM-2, tr. by Sargon Boulus and Samuel Hazo

This house, pitched now. Distances, The. Henry Rago. IllVoic

This house, September, and a woman. Second-Born Son: Lines for Walt Whitman Composed on Nantucket Island. Gary Miranda. ViWalt

This Humanist whom no beliefs constrained. James Vincent Cunningham. APT-2 Fr. Epigrams: A Journal.

This hurt has beat so long. Stillborn. Jane Duran. MFPA

This hush, my pollen—the ordinary grace in the buds. Ars Poetica. Dana Levin. TAPaP

This I beheld, or dreamed it in a dream. Opportunity. Edward Rowland Sill. APN-2

This I do, being mad. Siege. Edna St. Vincent Millay. APT-1

This, I guess, is. Issa. EMJL, tr. by Haruo Shirane

This I had not expected. One December Night. Denise Levertov. BodElec

This I know, how love begins to be. Albrecht von Johannsdorf. GePo

This—I mean whatever comes to mind when you read this. Sermon on Language. Robert Kelly. WhBo

This I Whisper. Horehound Stillpoint. BeDoSh

This I write, mix ink with tears. Sadi. WoPoe, *tr. by* Basil Bunting

This ignorance upon my tongue. On Reading Aloud My Early Poems. John Williams. WeW-3

This image is alive with my longing for you. Robert Glück. WiU *Fr.* Visit, The.

This indecent procession of the undead. Mannequins. Daniel Mark Epstein. ReTh

This infant world has taken long to make. Sonnet. George Macdonald. SacPr

This institution / perhaps one should say enterprise. Marriage. Marianne Moore. APT-1; ColAP; MoWP; NAAPv.2; NALW; OxBoAm

This introspective exile here today. Desmond O'Grady. PBCIP *Fr.* Lines in a Roman Schoolbook.

This is a beautiful day. I sit down into it, the eucalyptus leaves fly down and up. Thank-You Note. Sarah Kirsch. MotU, *tr. by* Peter Spycher

This is a big girl's pink poem. Pink Poem. Jackie Warren-Moore. SpirFl

This Is a Blessing, This Is a Curse. Chard DeNiord. PfSP

This is a bridgeless blues. Two Fishing Villages. Ellease Southerland. GT

This is a busy corner. Near Roscoe and Coldwater. Amy Uyematsu. OpBo

This is a damned inhuman sort of war. Unseen Fire. Ralph Nixon Currey. OBWP; PoWW

This is a day rain hangs above water. To Keep the Spirits. Jo Whitehorse Cochran. FiBr

This is a day to celebrate can- / openers, those lantern-jawed long-tailed. Cast Off, The. Marge Piercy. NAMCP V.2; NoAM

This is a drowned man's tomb. Sail on, stranger. Epitaph, An. Theodoridas. PoCho, *tr. by* Burton Raffel

This is a field book. John Giorno. AHA *Fr.* Birds.

This is a fine mess. Rāmprasād Sen. SinGod, *tr. by* Rachel Fell McDermott

This is a fine romance! (LL) Fine Romance, A. Dorothy Fields. OBCoV; ReLy

This is a glove. Village of Reason, The. Michael Palmer. PtR

This is a good place for those things to wait. Railway Signals. Sheenagh Pugh. TCAWP

This is a good place to begin. Beginner, The. Lyn Hejinian. VaPo

This is a hard life you are living. Album. Josephine Miles. APT-2; CalPo; ColAP

This is a hill that holds the church up. Burning Graves at Netherton, The. Roy Fisher. Oth

This is a hurtful thing, when your memory fails you. Geography. Adisa Vera Beatty. FuFl

This is a journey into sight, sound, pain. Jump Black Honey Jump Black. Malkia Amala Cyril. InTrad

This is a litany of lost things. Litany, The. Dana Gioia. BAP-97; Vesp

This Is a Love. Efraín Huerta. TCLAP, *tr. by* Todd Dampier

This is a love poem to our family. Flowers. Julie Fay. NAPBL

This is a love that began. This Is a Love. Efraín Huerta. TCLAP, *tr. by* Todd Dampier

This is a message to those who live here not to worry excessively. *Unknown.* NAAPv.2

This is a morning to say something. Morning to Remember, A; or, E Pluribus Unum. Edward Dorn. NoAM

This Is a Photograph of Me. Margaret Atwood. BrAP; NALW; NAMCP V.2; NoAM; NoP-4; NoP-5

This is a place of ease. Pastoral. Marion Strobel. PoA 2002

This is a poem about the itch. History. Tracy K. Smith. LegDan

This Is a Poem for the Dead. Michael Ryan. YaYoPo

This is a poem like a suitcase. Wedding Preparations in the Country. David St. John. AmAlph

This is a poem to my son Peter. Peter Meinke. PBCAP

This is a portrait. Here one can. Grandpapa. Harry Graham. OBCoV

This is a precise place on your grandfather's farm a hard place by that you mean you stumbled on it. Patrick Friesen. ACAMVP *Fr.* Clearing Poems.

This is a project as overwrought. Changing Address Books. Michael S. Glaser. UnSA

This is a public service announcement. Heralds of the Hurricane. Sandy Baldwin. AnSo

This is a quiet sector of a quiet front. Letter from Aragon, A. John Cornford. OBWP

This is a rugged land, a wild land, nature's country. Birth of a Nation. Milton Arana. OWABP

This is a scene where a singer. Singer, The. Sadiq Sharshar. AnVo, *tr. by* Mohamed Enani

This is a season of holding back. Drought. Joan I. Siegel. PoCoUp

This is a sight that Wordsworth never knew. View from an Airplane at Night, over California, The. Bruce Bawer. RA

This is a small boy. Reading a Story to My Child. Primus St. John. PoChi

This is a small northern town. Rosanna Deerchild. PoPra

This is a song an epithalamium it is also. Couples. Kate Jennings. BMAP

This is a song for the genius child. Genius Child. Langston Hughes. PoPoPo

This is a song for the speechless. Song. Edward Hirsch. OPRER

This is a spirit poem. This Poem. Shirley Bradley LeFlore. SpirFl

This is a spray the Bird clung to. Misconceptions. Robert Browning. OBEV

This is a story I have heard. Kamasutra Sutra. Harryette Mullen. WANABP

This is a story Jung would understand. Candelaria and the Sea Turtle. Gladys Cardiff. HATNAP

This is a story my father told to me. *Tsa'lagi* Council Tree. Gladys Cardiff. HATNAP

This is a straight-forward choice between. Having Read Up on the Subject. Jane Holland. NeBl

This is a strange country. Strange Country. Julie Parson-Nesbitt. MPUn

This is a strange seder. Seder, The. Enid Dame. UnSA

This is a street at war. Britain Street: Saint John, New Brunswick. Alden Nowlan. Coast

This is a symbol of beauty (you continue). "H. D." NAAPv.2; NALW; NAMCP V.1 *Fr.* Tribute to the Angels.

This is a temple the state built with great effort. Abandoned Princess, The. *Korean Oral Tradition.* CATKP, *tr. by* Peter H. Lee

This is a wild land, country of my choice. Rocky Acres. Robert Graves. NoAM

This is a word we use to plug. Variations on the Word *Love*. Margaret Atwood. LW; NoAM

This is about the summer and the wheels of sleep. Salt Pork, The. Robert Clayton Casto. HeIP-4

This is addressed to you, Stanislaus, wherever you are. Songs of Abuse: To Stanislaus the Renegade. Kofi Awoonor. PML

This is addressed to you—A century later. Silence. Vitalina Tkhorzhevskaya. CRWP, *tr. by* Daniel Weissbort

This is all I like now, the museum. The scaredusty cleanness of the objects. Walk at the Museum, A. Ágnes Nemes Nagy. MotU, *tr. by* Hugh Maxton

This is all still something of a mystery. More Rain. David Baker. LiTh

This is all that I saw, and all I know of the battle. (LL) Arthur Hugh Clough. NPeEn; OxAEP-2 *Fr.* Amours de Voyage.

This is alone Life, Joy, Empire, and Victory. (LL) Prometheus Unbound. Percy Bysshe Shelley. NAEL-6v2; NAEL-7v2; NOBRP

This is America, son. Letter to an Unconceived Son. Tyehimba Jess. BRtP

This is an age in which imagination. Covenant. Jorie Graham. AWPTFC

This is an age of anxiety. Choice. Liu K'o-hsiang. PML, *tr. by* Michelle Yeh

This is an age-old story. Sinner Kissed an Angel, A. Mack David. ReLy

This is an American flag. American Flag. Jack Anderson. AHA

This is an old and very cruel god. Vicarious Atonement. Richard Aldington. MoBrPo

This is an old fiction of reliability. Affections Must Not. Denise Riley. MoWP

This is an open poem. Open Poem. Melinda Goodman. WiU

This is an urgent call. Urgent Call, An. Dunya Mikhail. WoBe, *tr. by* Liz Winslow

This is Anacreon's grave. Here lie. Antipater of Sidon. WoPoe, *tr. by* Robin Skelton

This is as far from home as you can get. Walk, The. William Scammell. NLP

This is as much of the ocean as we ever wanted. Sandbox. 1952.—*Homage to Joseph Cornell.* Laura Mullen. IAoNAP

This Is Bad. Gottfried Benn. WoPoe, *tr. by* Harvey Shapiro

This is because I am spiteful. You see, I hate. Cassandra. William Dickey. YaYoPo

This is before I'd read Nietzsche. Before Kant or Kierkegaard, even before Whitman and Yeats. Gas Station, The. C. K. Williams. CAP-8; VCAP

This is Bohemia, lady. Exit, Pursued by a Bear. Kathleen Kirk. IaFF

This is Campidojo, whaur Titus ran. Campidoglio. Robert Garioch. OBVE

This is Charing Cross. Ford Madox Ford. FaBoWar *Fr.* Antwerp.

This is civilization. Summer Night. Susan Griffin. WhBo

This is dedicated to Merry Clayton, Fontella Bass, Vonetta. Black Back-Ups, The. Kate Rushin. ReTh

This is eternity. (LL) What Are Years? Marianne Moore. HarvBoo; ItP; MoAmPo; NAMCP V.1; NoAM; NoP-4; NoP-5; OxBoAm; SoSe-8

This is far too rich for poetry. Beyond Poetry. Shakuntala Hawoldar. HAWP

This is for Elsa, also known as Liz. Invocation. Marilyn Hacker. ExTi; PuP-23; WiU

This is for him, the writer, him I term. Poem Recalls the Poet, The. Glyn Maxwell. NeBrP

This Is for Megan. Polly Brown. PfS

This is for ntozake. Something about You. Jessica Tarahata Hagedorn. PmAP

This is for the afternoon we lay in the leaves. Sonnet. C. B. Trail. GoPo

This is for the brothers—who aint here. For the Brothers Who Aint Here. Ras Baraka. InTrad

This is for the daughter. Cleopatra Mathis. ExTi *Fr.* Lessons.

This is for the men and women. Isalutu. Askhari. InTrad

This is for the woman with one black wing. Sonnet in Primary Colors. Rita Dove. InoFa; PfS

This is he, who, felled by foes. Worship. Ralph Waldo Emerson. APN-1

This is how he made her fall. Romance. Ann Sansom. MFPA; NeBl

This is how I felt. Love # 49. Reuben Jackson. BtF

This is how I learned. Wayne Koestenbaum. WiU *Fr.* Erotic Collectibles.

This is how I was found. Ariadne, waiting. Cynthia Cruz. IAoNAP

This is how I was given to the world. (LL) Poem on the First Day of School. Peter Cooley. NevBe; PoA 2002

This Is How It Comes. R. T. Smith. LiTh

This is how it happened. Rusks. Rita Dove. PfSP

This is how it was. At the Movie: Virginia, 1956. Ellen Bryant Voigt. LPSFW; LTA; NoAM

This is how it was. Lilac preoccupations. Grey Dawn. Julio Herrera y Reissig. TCLAP, *tr.* by Andrew Rosing

This is how it's done. Rough Music. Deborah Digges. ExTi

This is how, one sunrise, we cut down them canoes. Derek Walcott. NAMCP V.2; WaAnP *Fr.* Omeros.

This is how, perhaps. Petit Mal. Richard Foerster. Vesp

This is how the body can move. Dance. Sandy Shreve. IFF

This Is How the Magician Produces a Dove out of the Hat. Mohamed Metwalli. AnVo, *tr.* by Mohamed Enani

This is how they make rain, the raw. Rain Dance. Susan Wicks. MFPA; MoWP

This is how you live when you have a cold heart. Lamium. Louise Glück. HarvBoo; StAl

This is Imagination's nuclear-free zone. Radio Caliban. Peter Porter. RWPCtW

This is in the wind. Unswerving Marine. Carl Rakosi. FTOS

This is innocent. Teenage. Blossom. Tinderbox. Ruth Padel. NeBrP

THIS IS IT and so: so long. P.O.E. Lincoln Kirstein. APT-2; PoWW; PWW2

This is it / grey, great. Work, No Light. Reed Bye. AHA

This is Italian. Here. Gardens of the Villa D'Este, The. Anthony Hecht. ColAP; OBGa

This is joye, this is true pleasure. Verses by the Princess Elizabeth, Given to Lord Harington, of Exton, Her Preceptor. Elizabeth, Queen of Bohemia. EMWP

This Is Just a Fairy Tale. Jane R. Ransom. PfS

This is just a place. In Memoriam Mae Noblitt. A. R. Ammons. ItP

This is just about light, how suddenly. Physics of Sudden Light, A. Alberto A. Ríos. TAPaP

This Is Just to Say. Erica-Lynn Gambino. GoPo

This Is Just to Say. William Carlos Williams. APT-1; BrAP; ChAP; GoPo; HarvBoo; HeIP-4; NAAL-5; NAAPv.2; NAMCP V.1; NIL-7; NIP-4; NoAM; NoP-4; NoP-5; OPOU; OxBoAm; PoPoPo; TRP; WaAnP

This is Kypris' place; it ever pleases her. Anyte. SaLy, *tr.* by Diane Rayor

This is made. House Cap. Bernadette Mayer. FTOS

This is my age. Fin-de-Siècle Identikit. Pierre Joris. PFTM-2

This is my book, in my hand. Emyr Lewis. BBMWP *Fr.* Dawn.

This is my cap. Inventory. Günter Eich. AF, *tr.* by David Young

This is my father. My Wicked Wicked Ways. Sandra Cisneros. ItWoWo; WaAnP

This is my last affair. (LL) Last Affair: Bessie's Blues Song. Michael S. Harper. ESEAA; FuFl

This Is My Letter to the World. Emily Dickinson. APN-2; HeIP-4; NAAL-3; NAAL-5; NAAPv.1; NALW; NoAM; OxWW; SAmP; TCAPo; WaAnP

This is my mother's childhood home, my own. This Shade. Susanne Doyle. FFC

This is my mother's last garden. Dill. Keith Ratzlaff. ACAMVP

This is my page for English B. (LL) Theme for English B. Langston Hughes. APT-2; ColAP; FaBoA; NAMCP V.1; NIL-7; NIP-4; NoAM; NoP-4; NoP-5; PoPoPo; PtR; SSLK; WaAnP

This is my play's [or playes] last scene, here heavens appoint. John Donne. BASC; FaBoVe *Fr.* Holy Sonnets.

This is my portrait of Joanna—since the split. Seed-Picture, The. Medbh McGuckian. ModIr; PNI

This Is My Rock. David McCord. NTCP; TLR

This Is My Son's Song: *"Ungie, Hi Ungie"*. Michael S. Harper. CAP-8

This is my testament, the voice of one. Caradog Prichard. BBMWP *Fr.* Earthly Turmoil.

This is my third Cold Food Festival. Rain During the Cold Food Festival. Su Tung-p'o. CrYelRi, *tr.* by Sam Hamill

This is my work so. Ann Bell. FaBoVe

This is neither the time nor the place for singing of. Some Walks With You. John Hollander. BodElec

This is no baby skin—. Brown Rosellen. FFC

This Is No Case of Petty Right or Wrong. Edward Thomas. PoWW

This is no joke. She is fat and happy in the U.S.A. The kind of woman. Fat in America. Heid E. Erdrich. AmPoNex

This is no mountain. Gods Are Here, The. Jean Toomer. APT-2; OxBoAm

This is no proper route for middle-age. Stringer's Field. Roy McFadden. PNI

This is no rune nor riddle. "H. D." APT-1 *Fr.* Tribute to the Angels.

This is no rune nor symbol. "H. D." *See* This is no rune nor riddle.

This is no time for a child to be born. Risk of Birth, The. Madeleine L'Engle. SacPr

This is not a dance. Large Room with Wood Floor. Clarence Major. GT

This is not a riot policeman. Karen Press. TSAP

This is Not a Small Voice. Sonia Sanchez. InGu; SpirFl

This is not a small voice / you hear. (LL) This is Not a Small Voice. Sonia Sanchez. InGu; SpirFl

This is not about her but she is an example in this. At this show of kindness the person begins to cry. Heather Ramsdell. IAoNAP *Fr.* Vague Swimmers.

This is not about romance and dream. C. T. at the Five Spot. Thulani Davis. SeSe

This is not bad. Man Listening to Disc. Billy Collins. OxBoAm

This Is Not Death. Humbert Wolfe. MoBrPo

This is not exactly what I mean. World and I, The. Laura Riding Jackson. APT-2; ColAP; HarvBoo; NAAPv.2; OxBoAm

This is not first love. Anniversary. Gary Metras. PasH

This Is Not Her. Joaquín Pasos. BLPSL, *tr.* by Rene de Costa, Rigas Kappatos and Eleni Paidoussi

This is not her, it is the wind. This Is Not Her. Joaquín Pasos. BLPSL, *tr.* by Rene de Costa, Rigas Kappatos and Eleni Paidoussi

This is not I. I had no body once. Naked Girl and Mirror. Judith Wright. NALW

This is not in German, nor in the tongue. Beethoven's Old Age. István Vas. IQMS, *tr.* by Daniel Gerard Hoffman

This Is Not Love's Offering. Shaun Griffin. PoDa

This is not my home. How did I get so far from water? It must. Elizabeth Bishop. MotU *Fr.* Rainy Season; Sub-Tropics.

This is not passion, but with pleasure. Ruth Says. Andrew Greig. EdScPo

This is not tenderness: the lilacs hanging in the rain. Lilacs, The. Anne Simpson. Coast

This Is Not the Place Where I was Born. Miguel Piñero. PueRic

This is not the West, this is. Look. Sarah Messer. LegDan

This is not winter: where is the crisp air. California Winter. Edward Rowland Sill. APN-2

This is not you? These phrases are not you? Conrad Potter Aiken. MoAmPo *Fr.* Preludes for Memnon; or, Preludes to Attitude.

This is only a most piteous pretense of sleep! (LL) Beside the Bed. Charlotte Mew. InoFa; MoBrPo

This is our last dance together. There Will Never Be Another You. Mack Gordon. ReLy

This is our lot if we live so long and labour unto the end. Old Men, The. Rudyard Kipling. OBSV

This is plenty. This is more than enough. (LL) September Song. Geoffrey Hill. EMP; FaBoWar; HarvBoo; HP; NAEL-6v2; NAEL-7v2; NAMCP V.2; NoAM; NoP-4; NoP-5; NPeEn; OBWP; OxBEV; StAl

This is prettiest of all, it is very pretty. (LL) Pretty. Stevie Smith. NAEL-6v2; NAEL-7v2; NAMCP V.1; NoAM; NoP-4

This is simple enough: I am seated. Seated in a Chinese Painting, He Speaks. Netta Gillespie. AmZen

This is so far asea from the plateau. Marikudo in Kalibo, 1979. Dominador I. Ilio. ReBoTo

This is Still Life. Marla Jernigan. AnSo

This is such a day: the sun is dazzling twice as before. Jelaluddin Rumi. NaPG, *tr.* by Talat Sait Halman

This is Sunday. Mary O'Donoghue. NIrP

This is sung at dawn. Natalya Gorbanevskaya. CFP, *tr.* by Gerald S. Smith

This is Tarsus, one place like anyplace else. Francine's Room. Louise Erdrich. NoAM

This is that dream i wake from. Powell (officer charged with the beating of rodney king). Lucille Clifton. RACG

This Is the Army, Mr. Jones. Irving Berlin. ReLy

This is the arsenal. From floor to ceiling. Arsenal at Springfield, The. Henry Wadsworth Longfellow. NoAM

This is the barrow of grizzled Maronis, on which you see. Antipater of Sidon. HePo, *tr.* by Barbara Hughes Fowler

This is the beauty of being alone. Stray Animals. James Tate. NAMCP V.2; NoAM

This is the beginning of my terrorist notebook all terrorism. My Terrorist Notebook. Lisa Jarnot. Eno

This is the black day when. Dark Morning, The. Thomas Merton. PoA 2002

This is the black sea-brute bulling through wave-wrack. Leviathan. W. S. Merwin. ChIV-1; NoAM

This Is the Body, Consoling Itself. Sue MacLeod. Coast

This is the body in solitude. This Is the Body, Consoling Itself. Sue MacLeod. Coast

This is the bricklayer; hear the thud. Sanctuary. Elinor Wylie. MoAmPo; NAAPv.2

This is the camping ground. Struggle-Road Dance. Ahmos Zu-Bolton, II. ISC

This is the Chapel: here, my son. Clifton Chapel. Sir Henry John Newbolt. OBEV

This is the chapter of. Prism, A: Wet With Wars. Sinan Antoon. IrPoTo, *tr. by* the author

This is the charm that will protect you, the charm. Spell Spoken by Suppliant to Helios for Protection. Tom Sleigh. PoCho

This is the child in a buff-colored coat with a foxtail collar. Grossdaadi's Funeral. Julia Kasdorf. NeAmPo

This is the city of great doges hidden. Edgar Lee Masters. TCAPo *Fr.* Chicago.

This is the city of lost things, thrown away. Emyr Lewis. BBMWP *Fr.* Freedom.

This is the city of three leaves. Tripoli. Nadia Tuéni. PoArWo

This is the corrido about the. New Corrido of Laredo. *Unknown.* NAAPv.2

This is the creature I am! Iron Horse. Allen Ginsberg.

This is the creature there has never been. Rainer Maria Rilke. OBVE *Fr.* Sonnets to Orpheus.

This is the cripples' hour on Seventh Avenue. Seventh Avenue. Muriel Rukeyser. NoAM

This is the curse. Write. (LL) Curse for a Nation, A. Elizabeth Barrett Browning. NALW; ViWPN

This is the day His hour of life draws near. Allen Tate. ChrPo *Fr.* Sonnets at Christmas.

This is the day, the cock has crowed. Good Friday. Kathleen Jessie Raine. BBASP

This is the day when, under beneficent skies. Good Sunday. John Lucas. RSaN

This is the debt I pay. Debt, The. Paul Laurence Dunbar. ColAP; NAAPv.1

This is the dress rehearsal. After Minor Surgery. Linda Pastan. EMP; PoA 2002

This is The Dust. Pneumoconiosis. Duncan Bush. AngWePo; TCAWP

This is the Earth that God made. That God Made. Will Heford. FTtHH

This is the earth? Then. White Rose, The. Louise Glück. CAP-8

This is the easy time, there is nothing doing. Wintering. Sylvia Plath. MoW; NALW

This is the end of him, here he lies. Epitaph. Amy Levy. NPeEn; PEW

This is the farmer sowing his corn. This Is the House that Jack Built. Mother Goose. NPeEn

This is the female form. Walt Whitman. ErotSp *Fr.* I Sing the Body Electric.

This is the festival; we will inter hope. Tyrant, The. Faiz Ahmad Faiz. AF, *tr. by* Naomi Lazard

This is the field where the battle did not happen. At the Un-National Monument along the Canadian Border. William Stafford. BrAP; HeIP-4

This is the field you did not come to, this. To the Lost Child. Brigit Pegeen Kelly. YaYoPo

This is the finger of God. Bruce Beasley. AmAlph *Fr.* Spiritual Alphabet in Midsummer.

This is the first of the themes, the lecturer said. Bach Fugue. Barker Fairley. IFF

This is the first poem. There was none. First Poem, The. Mark Van Doren. APT-2

This is the first time I've seen a song. Hard Song. J. Eirian Davies. BBMWP, *tr. by* Sion Eirian

This is the flat with its absence of curtains. In Residence: A Worst Case View. Sean O'Brien. OBCoV

This is the flower of the World. (LL) In Back of the Real. Allen Ginsberg. HeIP-4; PtR

This is the forest primeval. The murmuring pines and the hemlocks. Henry Wadsworth Longfellow. APN-1; NAAPv.1; NoP-4; TCAPo; UV *Fr.* Evangeline: A Tale of Acadie.

This is the forest primeval. The murmuring pines and the hemlocks. Henry Wadsworth Longfellow. NoP-5 *Fr.* Evangeline: A Tale of Acadie.

This is the garden: colours come and go. Sonnet IV. E. E. Cummings. ChIV-1; MoAmPo

This is the germinal spot of gathering green. Dreaming Bean, The. Katherine Pierpoint. MoWP

This is the gift I thank Medusa for. (LL) Muse as Medusa, The. May Sarton. HW; NALW

This is the gift my son gave me. Peacock of Motherhood, The. Anna Jackson. BeAl

This is the girl's first nightclub, in Juarez. In Juarez. Susan Wheeler. IFF

This is the good child. As Soft and as Pink as a Nursery. Eleanor Wilner. PoChi

This is the Green Man. No Problem, But Not Easy. Michael Harlow. BeAl

This is the green wherein a river chants. Sleeper in the Valley, The. Arthur Rimbaud. OBWP; WoPoe, *tr. by* William Jay Smith.

This is the hall of broken limbs. Guide to the Other Gallery. Dana Gioia. RA; WaAnP

This is the heart's thorn: the red rinse of memory. Fugue for Phantoms. Robin Robertson. NeBrP

This is the heart's world. This is the land. Eastward in Eastanalle. George Scarbrough. LPSFW

This is the heat that seeks the flaw in everything. Tennessee June. Jorie Graham. HarvBoo

This is the hour I love: the in-between. Women, The. Eavan Boland. MoWP; NAMCP V.2

This is the hour of magic, when the Moon. Hour of Magic, The. W. H. Davies. MoBrPo

This is the hour the pale and neutral moon. Dust of Silence. Oliver Pitcher. EGAG

This is the house destroyed by Jack. Berlin Wall Tune, The. Joseph Brodsky. AF, *tr. by* Joseph Brodsky

This is the House that Jack built. Political House that Jack Built, The. William Hone. NOBRP

This is the House that Jack Built. Mother Goose. NPeEn

This is the house that Jack built. House That Jack Built, The. Mother Goose. OxBEV

This is the house where Jesse White. Lowery Cot. Leonard Alfred George Strong. MoBrPo

This is the huge dream of us that we are heroes. Flowers of Politics, I, The. Michael McClure. CalPo

This is the island named Misfortune. Weepers, The. Isabel Nathaniel. TiP2

This is the key to my happiness. Key, The. Richard Jones. GifTon

This is the knife with a handle of horn. House That Jack Built, The. *Unknown.* NBLV

This is the lair of the landlady. Landlady, The. Margaret Atwood. NALW

This is the last picture of me. Last Picture, The. Philip Dacey. PoDa

This is the last prayer in the book. No Heaven. David St. John. FaoP

This is the lay of Ike. John Berryman. OxBoAm *Fr.* Dream Songs.

This Is the Life. Louis MacNeice. NoAM

This is the light of the mind, cold and planetary. Moon and the Yew Tree, The. Sylvia Plath. BBASP

This is the light we dream in. Negatives. Charles Wright. PoA 2002

This is THE MAN—all shaven and shorn. William Hone. OBCoV *Fr.* Political House that Jack Built, The.

This Is the Map. Rodger Kamenetz. TaR

This is the meal pleasantly set . . . this is the meat and drink for natural hunger. Walt Whitman. CAGL *Fr.* Song of Myself.

This is the metre Columbian. Metre Columbian, The. *Unknown.* UV

This is the midnight—let no star. Storm Cone, The. Rudyard Kipling. NoAM

This is the moment the *sigl-di-gwt*. Beginning to Forget. Gwyneth Lewis. ATSWP, *tr. by* Robert Minhinnick

This is the Month, and this the happy morn. On the Morning of Christ's Nativity. John Milton. BASC; ChrPo; NAEL-6v1; NAEL-7v1; NoP-4; NoP-5; PBRV; WaAnP

This is the month of warm days. Potatoes. Linda Hogan. AFaM; IPoFL

This is the month of sunrise skies. Lucy Larcom. TCAPo *Fr.* November.

This is the most audacious landscape. The gangster's. Alloy. Muriel Rukeyser. NAMCP V.2; NoAM

This is the obligatory Southern poem. *Southland* Drive-In. James Applewhite. LPSFW

This is the ocean. Relict. Emily Wilson. LegDan

This is the oldest book. Ordovician Fossil Algae. Lindley Williams Hubbell. APT-2

This is the one moment. Don't Worry 'Bout Me. Ted Koehler. ReLy

This is the one song everyone. Margaret Atwood. NIL-7; NIP-4; PoA 2002; WeW-3 *Fr.* Songs of the Transformed.

This is the only thing as large as that. I regret I am not the physical giant. Realism. Tom Mandel. PmAP

This is the part where. Ben Hur. Joe Weil. BRtP

This is the part where after a few minutes. Rapt. Irene McKinney. PBCAP

This Is the Place to Wait. Horace Gregory. MoAmPo *Fr.* Passion of M'Phail, The.

This is the place / Where far from the unholy populace. In a Meadow. John Swinnerton Phillimore. OBEV

This is the poem. Poem for Têt. Ted Sexauer. WhBo

This Is the Poem I Never Meant to Write. Colleen J. McElroy. FTtHH

This is the point where I shall stick my arrow.   Dance with Nothing On, with Nobody Around, A.   Mas-oud Shouman.   AnVo, *tr. by* Mohamed Enani

This is the right gift for a poet.   Empress Receives the Head of a Taiping Rebel, The.   Sarah Gorham.   FFC

This is the rotten-breathed forest.   Raul Bopp.   TCLAP *Fr.* Black Snake.

This is the sadness of the sea.   Sadness of the Sea, The.   William Carlos Williams.   ColAP

This is the second month of the year I turn thirty-seven.   February.   Lisa Lewis.   BodElec

This is the shame of the woman whose hand hides.   Shame.   Vern Rutsala.   OPRER

This is the ship of pearl, which, poets feign.   Oliver Wendell Holmes.   APN-1; ColAP; CtM; ITBLP; NAAL-3; NAAPv.1; NCAP; NoP-4; NoP-5; OxBoAm; TCAPo; TFi; WaAnP *Fr.* Autocrat of the Breakfast Table, The.

This is the silence of astounded souls.   (LL)   Crossing the Water.   Sylvia Plath.   BrAP; CAP-8

This is the sin against the Holy Ghost.   Unpardonable Sin, The.   Vachel Lindsay.   ChIV-2

This is the solid-looking quagmire.   Liberal, or Innocent by Definition.   James Philip McAuley.   NOBAu

This is the song for a soldier.   Come Back Clean.   Ella Wheeler Wilcox.   VerBaPo

This is the song of a dadaist.   Chanson Dada.   Tristan Tzara.   PFTM-1

This is the song of Mehitabel.   Don Marquis.   AmWit; APT-1; OBCoV *Fr.* Archy and Mehitabel.

This is the sort of place you might arrive at after a long journey.   Ferns and the Night.   John Ash.   HarvBoo

This is the south. I look for evidence.   New Orleans.   Joy Harjo.   HATNAP

This is the spot where Jack Johnson.   Boxing Day.   Yusef Komunyakaa.   ISC

This is the spread of wings.   "H. D."   WoPoe *Fr.* Helen in Egypt.

This is the State above the Law.   Death-Bed, A.   Rudyard Kipling.   OxBEV; PoWW

This is the story of a man and woman.   Listen. This Is the Noise of Myth.   Eavan Boland.   ModIr

This is the story of the men who stole chicken soup after it was.   If Chickens Could Talk.   Víctor Hernández Cruz.   PueRic

This is the story told to me.   To Keep from Shouting Something.   Honorée Fanonne Jeffers.   BtF

This is the sweet work of Erinna, not much, of course.   Asclepiades.   HePo, *tr. by* Barbara Hughes Fowler

This is the tale of the man.   Ticonderoga: A Legend of the West Highlands.   Robert Louis Stevenson.   OBNV

This is the taste of the.   Islandis.   Víctor Hernández Cruz.   TouFir

This is the temple of the Lord.   Do Not Trust in These Deceptive Words.   Sydney Lea.   Vesp

This is the terminal: the light.   At the San Francisco Airport.   Yvor Winters.   CalPo; HeIP-4; NIL-7; NIP-4; OxBoAm

This is the time lean woods shall spend.   Sundown.   Léonie Adams.   MoAmPo

This is the time of year.   Armadillo, The.   Elizabeth Bishop.   APT-2; BrAP; ColAP; NAAL-5; NAMCP V.2; NIL-7; NoAM; NoP-4; NoP-5; VCAP; WaAnP

This is the time of year.   William Carlos Williams.   SAmP

This is the time of year / the lengthening dark appears.   In Lakeview Cemetery.   Christian Wiman.   AmPoNex

This is the time, when most divine to hear.   Religious Musings.   Samuel Taylor Coleridge.

This is the time when you can begin to die.   Written in Rain.   Blas de Otero.   RaW, *tr.* by Hardie St. Martin

This is the tree of earthly delights.   Tree of Earthly Delights.   Nancy Morejón.   TANSG, *tr. by* Joy Renjilian-Burgy

This Is the Trouble of the World.   *Unknown.*   SSUS

This is the true land of fairy tales.   Return of the Native.   Elizabeth Brewster.   Coast

This is the twentieth century.   First on TV, A.   David Ignatow.   RaBo

This is the urgency: Live!   Second Sermon on the Warpland, The.   Gwendolyn Brooks.   FuFl

This is the voice of mine own steadfast will.   (LL)   Sister of Mercy, The.   Constance Naden.   ViWPN; VWP

This / is the way.   Way, The.   Catherine Obianuju Acholonu.   NAfrP

This is the way a row of official tulips.   Vera Pavlova.   CRWP, *tr. by* Derek Walcott

This is the way it begins: the small.   Overture.   Linda Pastan.   MiVo

This is the way of it, wide world over.   Way of It, The.   Ella Wheeler Wilcox.   LW

This is the way that autumn came to the trees.   When Autumn Came.   Faiz Ahmad Faiz.   PLBUT; PoetW, *tr. by* Naomi Lazard

This is the way to start a sentence about startling a sentence. Here is the.   Wait.   Charles Bernstein.   PmAP

This is the weather of change.   Turning Thirty, I Contemplate Students Bicycling Home.   Rita Dove.   AmAlph; ArBi; ESEAA

This is the weather the cuckoo likes.   Weathers [*or* Weather].   Thomas Hardy.   MoBrPo; OBMV

This is the West.   Imperial Hotel.   Nakano Shigeharu.   CAoMJL1, *tr. by* Miriam Silverberg

This is the Wheel of Dreams.   Carriers of the Dream Wheel.   N. Scott Momaday.   ColAP; WaAnP

This is the wind, the wind in a field of corn.   Wind.   James Fenton.   BeAl; NAEL-6v2; NAEL-7v2; NeBrP

This is the work of the hammer: to break us open.   Sledgehammer.   John MacKenzie.   Coast

This is the world.   Map.   Linda Hogan.   ExTi

This is the world we wanted.   Gretel in Darkness.   Louise Glück.   NoAM; NoP-4; NoP-5

This is the year that squatters evict landlords.   Imagine the Angels of Bread.   Martín Espada.   PrTe; TouFir

This is the year the old ones.   September 1961.   Denise Levertov.   NAMCP V.2

This is the year you fall in.   Magellan Street, 1974.   Maxine W. Kumin.   GoPo

This is the young man, two cars ahead.   Accident, The.   Liz Rosenberg.   PBCAP

This is thi.   Tom Leonard.   NePenScot; NPeEn *Fr.* Unrelated Incidents.

This is this dress, aider.   Gertrude Stein.   NAAPv.2 *Fr.* Tender Buttons.

This is thy hour O Soul, thy free flight into the wordless.   Clear Midnight, A.   Walt Whitman.   AWTN; SAmP; Spl

This is time's.   Dandelion.   Neil Curry.   NLP

This is too good for words. I lie here naked.   Fritz.   Gerald Stern.   MiVo

This is too tall, dark wave of soul.   Rodin's "Gates of Hell."   Jane Greer.   FFC

This is too tight; loosen it a little. I pray.   Annie Dillard.   UpMys *Fr.* Deathbeds.

This is true: it really happened. Honest.   TV Movie.   Jack Turner.   PoA 2002

This is unclean: to eat turbots on Tuesdays.   Peter Reading.   BeAl *Fr.* Going On.

This Is What Happens When You Let Hamlet Play Quarterback.   Jack Conway.   IaFF

This is what I cannot remember.   July, 1949.   Ron Rash.   RWB

This Is What I Wanted to Sign Off With.   Alden Nowlan.   PoCu; StAl

This is what it was: Sometime in the recent but until now unrecorded past.   Meat Epitaph, The.   Michael Benedikt.   MotU

This is what the afternoons of our first youth were like.   Memory.   Roque Dalton.   BLPSL, *tr.* de Costa, Rigas Kappatos and Eleni Paidoussi

This is what the professor wrote home, listen.   Substituted Poem of Laureate Quynh, The.   *Unknown.*   EaWin, *tr.* by W. S. Merwin and Nguyen Ngoc Bich

This is what will happen.   Keeping Track of the Serpents.   Víctor Hernández Cruz.   TouFir

This is where he sought God.   Llanrhaeadr Ym Mochnant.   Ronald Stuart Thomas.   AngWePo

This is where he washed to shore.   Glass Man, The.   Scott Cairns.   UpMys

This is where I am unborn. (LL)   Stray Animals.   James Tate.   NAMCP V.2; NoAM

This is where I came from.   Ideal, The.   James Fenton.   BeAl

This is where I learned it. After pounding.   Two Poems.   Rosario Castellanos.   PFTM-2, *tr. by* Magda Bogin

This is where I work. I live a little further to the east.   Thirty East Forty-Second Street.   Alan Davies.   FTOS

This is where my recklessness has gotten me.   Memo, Who Loved Motorcycles.   Luis Miguel Aguilar.   PML, *tr. by* Robert Jones

This is where the People take tea.   In a Chain-Store Cafeteria.   Paul Grano.   NOBAu

This is where the serpent lives, the bodiless.   Auroras of Autumn, The.   Wallace Stevens.   APT-1

This Is Where We Laid Him to Rest.   Chirikure Chirikure.   PML, *tr. by* Haba Musengezi

This is why we read: this same tragedy.   I Took by the Throat the Circumcised Dog.   Chad Davidson.   IaFF

This is X who has all her own teeth.   Teeth.   Jackie Kay.   EdScPo

This is you at the speed of light. (LL)   Disappearances, The.   Vijay Seshadri.   BeAl; StAl

This is your growing seed. Woman, rejoice. (LL)   Annunciation.   Primo Levi.   AF; GI, *tr. by* Ruth Feldman

This island, garlanded with wild woods.   Archilochus.   OBVE

This Island Liv'd in Peace full many a Day.   Ruine of this Island, The.   Margaret Lucas Cavendish, Duchess of Newcastle.   EMWP

This isn't a piece written in leisure at the sea. I've talked.   No Surprises.   Rochelle Mass.   Eno

This isn't a very good poem. You don't Want to Hear a Poem, Do You? Don Weinstock. SUP

This isn't Italy where even. Elsewhere. Lynn Emanuel. BodElec

This isn't right and I'm not going to throw it. (LL) Football: "I take the snap from center, fake to the right, fade back." Louis Jenkins. MoASP; P180; RaBo

This isn't the end. It simply. Morning Star. C. D. Wright. TAPaP

This isn't the wind in the willows. Music in the Age of Iron. Alberto Blanco. CLPP, *tr. by* Julian Palley

This itch of scribbling has no end, no ease. Author's Quietus, The. Henry Carey. FaBoVe

This? it's my Lounge Lizard look, very. Up. Bill Kushner. ReTh

This johnny / is Mr Strong from Strongtown. Celo Kalagoe. SonAtl, *tr. by* Nancy Gallas, Janet Leake, Julian Maka'a, Amber Rawlins and Albert Wendt

This june 3. And it Came to Pass. C. D. Wright. TAPaP

This juxtaposition of events without. Ken Edwards. Oth *Fr.* Five Nocturnes, after Derek Jarman.

This Kansas boy who never knew the sea. Kansas Boy. Ruth Lechlitner. PoA 2002

This keeps my hands. Bracelets. William Strode. NOSC

This kiss. Mary. Lucille Clifton. BBASP

This knave came in where he knew she'd be. *Unknown.* EroLit *Fr.* Riddles (Exeter Book).

This knife is as long as my wife in the pool. Cuauhtemoc. Frank Lima. BodElec

This laboring through what is still undone. Swan, The. Rainer Maria Rilke. NAWM-7v2; OWoS, *tr. by* Stephen Mitchell

This labour will be welcome, honoured Friend! (LL) William Wordsworth. NAEL-6v2; NAEL-7v2 *Fr.* Prelude, The; Growth of a Poet's Mind [1850 version].

This ladies' room fluorescence will not be ignored. Midnight Vapor Light Breakdown. Betsy Sholl. LTA

This Lady and Her Beautiful Window. Michel Deguy. PFTM-2, *tr. by* Clayton Eshleman

This lady and her beautiful window. This Lady and Her Beautiful Window. Michel Deguy. PFTM-2, *tr. by* Clayton Eshleman

This lady in her wheel chair has been left. Sea World. Eric Berlin. OPRER

This lady of the West Country? (LL) Epitaph, An: "Here lies a most beautiful lady." Walter De la Mare. MoBrPo; OBEV

This Land. Ian Mudie. NOBAu

This Land. Sasha Steensen. Eno

This land is my block and my people. Song of Devotion to the Forest. David Henderson. GT

This land lies low toward the Gulf, a ridge. Louisiana Sea of Faith, The. Dave Jeddie Smith. LPSFW

This land like a mirror turns you inward. Dark Pines under Water. Gwendolyn MacEwen. BeAL; BrAP

This land: / The hills, round under straw. George Oppen. APT-2; PFTM-1

This Land's No Joy. Nguyễn Chí Thiện. VCWP, *tr. by* Huynh Sanh Thông

This land's salvation. (LL) My Blackness Is the Beauty of This Land. Lance Jeffers. ISC; OxAAAP

This lassitude. (LL) Nocturnal Visits. Claribel Alegría. CFP; TANSG; VCWP, *tr. by* Darwin Flakoll

This Last Pain. William Empson. HarvBoo; MoBrPo; NoAM; NPeEn

This lazy prince of tennis balls and lutes. Navigator. May Sarton. PWW2

This let me further add, that nature knows. Ovid. OBVE *Fr.* Metamorphoses.

This letter has been sent to you for good luck. The. Chain Mail. Elliot Fried. SUP

This license certifies. Poetic License. Ron Padgett. OxBoAm

This Life. Rita Dove. GT

This Life a Theater. Palladas. NIP-4, *tr. by* Robert Bland

This life a theatre we well may call. This Life a Theater. Palladas. NIP-4, *tr. by* Robert Bland

This life is most jolly. (LL) William Shakespeare. NoSic; OBEV *Fr.* As You Like It.

This life, which seems so fair. Madrigal. William Drummond of Hawthornden. NOSC

This lifeless construction. Doll Believers, The. Clarence Major. PoChi

This life's a play, said Shakespeare; they're the truest words he spoke. I'm Mighty Glad I'm Living and That's All. George M. Cohan. ReLy

This Lime-Tree Bower My Prison. Samuel Taylor Coleridge. HeIP-4; NAEL-6v2; NAEL-7v2; NoP-5; NPBRoP; OBGa; OxAEP-2

This line of black ants. Issa. WED, *tr. by* Robert Bly

This little attraction takes up no room and deals with only. Weighing-machine, The. Pierre McOrlan. MFP, *tr. by* Martin Sorrell

This little Babe so few dayes olde. Robert Southwell. *See* Come to your heaven, you [*or* yowe] heavenly choirs [*or* quires].

This little Grave embraces. Epitaph on the Duke of Buckingham. *Unknown.* BASC; NPeEn; PBRV

This Little House Is Sugar. Langston Hughes. NTCP

This Little Pig Went to Market. Mother Goose. OxBEV

This little pool in the air is. Rearview Mirror. Robert Morgan. PoA 2002

This little rill that, from the springs. Rivulet, The. William Cullen Bryant. APN-1

This Little, Silent, Gloomy Monument. Epitaph on the Tombstone of a Child, the Last of Seven that Died Before. Aphra Behn. CABP; NOSC; OxBSo

This little time the breath and bulk of being. James Agee. APT-2

This Living Hand, Now Warm and Capable. John Keats. AmFaPo; NoP-5; TRP

(This Living Hand.) NoP-4; NPBRoP; PoPoPo

(To Fanny Brawne.) WoPoe

This lobster flown in from Maine to Houston. Lobster, The. Cynthia MacDonald. AFaM

This lobster's not a lobster but the telephone. Paul Muldoon. NAMCP V.2 *Fr.* 7, Middagh Street.

This lonely beautiful word. La Chapelle. 92nd Division. Ted. Rita Dove. AmAlph

This lonely hill has always been so dear. Infinite, The. Giacomo Leopardi. NAWM-7v2, *tr. by* Ottavio M. Casale

This lonely oak. Oak, The. Aleksandr Semionovich Kushner. TCRusP, *tr. by* Daniel Weissbort

This long valley caught. Pomegranate. Jean Janzen. GeoHom

This loud morning / sensed a small cry in. Third World Calling. Lawrence Ferlinghetti. BB

This loved Philology. (LL) Word made Flesh is seldom, A. Emily Dickinson. APN-2; ChIV-2; NAAL-3; NALW; TCAPo

This lovely day will lengthen into ev'ning. I'll Remember April. Patricia Johnston and Don Raye. ReLy

This lovely flower fell to seed. Countee Cullen. APT-2; MoAmPo; SSLK *Fr.* Four Epitaphs.

This lovely, sweet, and beauteous Fairy Queen. Pastime of the Queen of Fairies, The. Margaret Lucas Cavendish, Duchess of Newcastle. BASC; NAEL-6v1

This Lunar Beauty. W. H. Auden. MoBrPo; NAMCP V.1; NPeEn; OBMV

This Lydian earth covers Amyntor, Philip's son. Anyte. SaLy, *tr. by* Diane Rayor

This Mahādeva is a great white dog. Walking with the God. Gwyneth Lewis. HarvBoo

This man, blind and honored. Forces. Jean Valentine. LaCa

This man escaped the dirty fates. Flyer's Fall. Wallace Stevens. SAmP

This man is o so. Item. E. E. Cummings. MoAmPo

This man knew out the secret ways of love. Ezra Pound. APT-1 *Fr.* Ripostes of Ezra Pound.

This man measures my waste like substance abuse. High Speed. Debra Gregerman. AmPoNex

This man with my own face. (LL) Cleaving, The. Li-Young Lee. OpBo; RoV

This Manes alive once was a slave; now dead. Anyte. SaLy, *tr. by* Diane Rayor

This mania of knowing I am an angel. Exile. Alejandra Pizarnik. TCLAP, *tr. by* Frank Graziano and María Rosa Fort

This man's metallic; at a sudden blow. "George Eliot." LW *Fr. from* Felix Holt, the Radical.

This many are the days. *Zuni Oral Tradition.* NAWM-7v2 *Fr.* Shalako.

This mast, new-shaved, through whom I rive the ropes. Choosing a Mast. Roy Campbell. NoP-4

This matted and glossy photo of Yesenin. James Harrison. BodElec *Fr.* Letters to Yesenin.

This meal-white snow. Snow. Walter De la Mare. OxAEP-2

This Measure. Léonie Adams. MoAmPo

This melancholy moment will remain. Philosopher's Conquest, The. Mark Strand. OxBoAm

This Message Will Self-Destruct in Sixty Seconds. Martin Ross. PA9/11

This mild child's not turned her face. Honour. Ceri Wyn Jones. BBMWP, *tr. by* Robert Minhinnick

This moment, this minute. My Shining Hour. Johnny Mercer. ReLy

This moment yearning and thoughtful sitting alone. This Moment Yearning and Thoughtful. Walt Whitman. APN-1

This monstrosity called life. (LL) Poetry Reading. Anna Swirszczynska [*or* Swir]. BLT; TAPaP, *tr. by* Czeslaw Milosz and Leonard Nathan

This monument will outlast metal and I made it. Horace. WoPoe *Fr.* Odes.

This morn ere yet had rung the matin peal. On a Frightful Dream. John Codrington Bampfylde. CenSon

This Morning. Raymond Carver. PML

This morning. Introit. Paul Murray. BBASP

This morning. At the Shore. Mary Oliver. PoCoUp

This Morning. Michael Rosen. NOxBChV

This Morning. Kristina Rungano. HAWP; NAfrP

This morning. Suck, The. John Wieners. FTOS

This morning, at waterside, a sparrow flew. Look and See. Mary Oliver. BeAl

This morning, between two branches of a tree. Dependencies, The. Howard Nemerov. VCAP

This morning finches come. Perspective. David Huddle. PfSP

This morning, flew up the lane. John Crowe Ransom. *See* This morning, there flew up the lane.

This morning I can't seem to get out of bed. Han Yü. CCL1 *Fr.* Autumn Thoughts.

This morning I found. Fall. Jane Mead. LaCa

This morning I heard persistent and angry blows on a carpet. In the Yard of the Policlinic. Vladimir Holan. AF, *tr. by* C. G. Hanzlicek and Dana Habova

This morning I steel my eyes open so horror can not seal them. 1619. Virginia. Gale Jackson. BtF

This morning I visited the place where we lay. This Morning. Kristina Rungano. HAWP; NAfrP

This morning in a car off Sunset the sky. Entity of Its Word, An. Sam Pereira. BodElec

This morning it is. And So It Begins Again. Edward Hirsch. RoV

This morning, it is raining. Rain. Danton R. Remoto. ReBoTo

This morning / laughing together. Auspicious Arrival of Yung T'ao. Chia Tao. CSKM, *tr. by* Mike O'Connor

This morning my father looks out of the window, rubs his nose. This Morning. Michael Rosen. NOxBChV

This morning of the small snow. Charles Olson. NoAM *Fr.* Maximus Poems, The.

This morning our boat left the. This Morning Our Boat Left. *Unknown.* NDACCP, *tr. by* Kenneth Rexroth

This morning she bought green 'methi'. Another Woman. Imtiaz Dharker. EmeKit

This morning that would've meant. *Bienvenido* Poem for Sophie. Sandra Cisneros. TiP2

This morning / the hawk / rose up. Hawk. Mary Oliver. NAAL-5; NAMCP V.2; OWoS

This morning the hibiscus is in bloom, so I stayed in bed late. Will. L. S. Asekoff. KGB

This morning, there flew up the lane. Lady Lost. John Crowe Ransom. MoAmPo

(This morning, flew up the lane.) NoP-4; NoP-5

This morning/ there is a woman giving a sermon/ Her voice trembles over the. On the Uptown Lexington Avenue Express: Martin Luther King Day 1995. Duriel Harris. SpirFl

This morning there was another one in the mail. Postcards from the Maginot Line. W. S. Merwin. MotU

This morning they came like the dying. Redwing Blackbirds. Fred Dings. PoDa

This morning, timely rapt with holy fire. On Lucy, Countess of Bedford. Ben Jonson. BASC; NAEL-7v1; NOSC

This morning view / is very plain: thou art. Our Father. James Schuyler. ChIV-2

This morning wakes. Liquid City. Lorenzo Thomas. TiP2

This morning was something. A little snow. This Morning. Raymond Carver. PML

This morning we escort Sharon. Going Home. Patricia Pogson. NLP

This morning we find dead earthworms in the dining room again. First Trimester, The. Campbell McGrath. NeAmPo; UrbNat

This morning we shall spend a few minutes. Money. Howard Nemerov. VCAP; WeW-3

This morning, when a woman walks home. On the Otis Redding Bridge. Judson Mitcham. SwNoth

This morning, when I heard the crows. Crows, The. David McCord. MoAmPo

This morning while waiting for you to wake. INRI. Melanie Hope. WiU

This morning with a blue flame burning. Poem for Trapped Things, A. John Wieners. BB; PmAP

This mortal coil. Robert Fleming. BtF

This moth caught in the room tonight. Lying Awake. W. D. Snodgrass. MoAmPo

This moth saw brightness. Issa. EH, *tr. by* Robert Hass

This motley piece to you I send. Matthew Green. NoP-4; NoP-5 *Fr.* Spleen, The.

This motly piece to you I send. Spleen, The [Complete]. Matthew Green.

This motor won't start. Electroconvulsive Therapy. Elspeth Cameron Ritchie. BloBone

This mouse that in my absence haunts the room. Mouse, The. John Frederick Nims. PfSP

This much I have: an urban space . . . Impressive. Asphalt Musings. Carl Hancock Rux. HeMarv

This much I know, I walked through the scraggly wood. Suzanne. Gerald Stern. NevBe

This much, O heaven—if I should brood or rave. Prayer in Darkness, A. G. K. Chesterton. MoBrPo

This much-praised general made such a cock of things. General's Plaque, The. Hồ Xuân Hương. FaBoWar, *tr. by* Graeme Wilson

This music has lasted since the world began. Aegean, The. Maria Luisa Spaziani. NeIt, *tr. by* Beverly Allen

This music is the country you lost. Flamenco Guitar. Ruth L. Schwartz. WiU

This must be the month when someone decided. In This January. Susan Goyette. OpeFie

"This must have been her bedroom, Mr. Choi." Counting the Children. Dana Gioia. RA

This never-ended searching for the eyes. Egg-and-Dart. Robert Finch. IFF

This new and gorgeous garment, majesty. William Shakespeare. OxAEP-1 *Fr.* King Henry IV, Pt. II.

This new kind of metal will not suffer. Christianite. William Stafford. NoAM

This new map, unrolled, smoothed. We Change the Map. Kerry Hardie. NIrP

This new year scarce would serve me, so farewell. (LL) Upon Dr. Davies's British Grammar. James Howell. AngWePo; OBWVE

This nigger too should be in history. Memo: For the Race Orators. Sterling Allen Brown. InGu

This night begins in scraps—blue velvet. When Night Meets Thread and Needle and Lies Down among the Bedclothes. Sue MacLeod. Coast

This Night: For Walt Whitman. Robert Bly. ViWalt

This night is pure and clear as thrice refinèd silver. Fountains. Sacheverell Sitwell. MoBrPo

This night, one of those clouded. Waking Here. Scott Cairns. UpMys

This night presents a play, which publick rage. Prologue to Hugh Kelly's *A Word to the Wise.* Samuel Johnson. NPeEn; OxAEP-1

This night shall thy soul be required of thee. Scorpion. Stevie Smith. NPeEn; OxAEP-2

This night there are no limits to what may be given. Jelaluddin Rumi. WoPoe, *tr. by* Coleman Barks and John Moyne

This night tonight is cold. Janet Campbell. EMWP

This night unacquainted. Re: Robert. Larkin Higgins. VisFro

This night we're drinking beer a pint. Terms. Kevin Stein. MAAN

This, no song of an ingénue. Ballade at Thirty-Five. Dorothy Parker. AmWit; APT-1

This notebook in which he used to sketch. Milk. Maurice Riordan. ModIr; NIrP

This now is yours. I seek another place. (LL) Bluebeard. Edna St. Vincent Millay. APT-1; NAAPv.2

This ocean, humiliating in its disguises. Jack Spicer. APSN; FTOS; OxBoAm *Fr.* Language.

This Octopus Exploits Women. James Fenton. NoAM

This old fence will speak its piece. Feste and the Fence Post. Daniel Williams. IaFF

This Old Man. Jackie Sheeler. BRtP

This old notebook I write in was my father's. Ursula K. Le Guin. GoPo *Fr.* Coming of Age.

This old village. Basho. EH, *tr. by* Robert Hass

This Old Woman. Mongane Wally Serote. NAfrP

This old woman, stalking up the street. This Old Woman. Mongane Wally Serote. NAfrP

This once we will vanquish violence. For Teen-Age Boys Murdered in Texas: The Refusal to Dramatize Bloodlust. Kelly Cherry. LPSFW

This One. T. H. Parry-Williams. BBMWP, *tr. by* Emyr Humphreys

This one cartouche surrenders. To the Soviet Embalmers. Rod Mengham. VaPo

This one goes out. Dedicated to the Domestics. Nzadi Z. Keita. BtF

This one goes out to you who wrote so many for me. Sun with Issues. David Colosi. FTtHH

This one guy who had recently been brought in. Nursing Home, 3rd Shift. David Craig. UpMys

This one lie down on grass. Astrologer Predicts at Mary's Birth, The. Lucille Clifton. NALW

This one request I make to him that sits the clouds above. Love and Debt Alike Troublesome. Sir John Suckling. CavPo

This one shows me standing by the Delaware. Tashlikh. Gerald Stern. TaR

This one steps into an outsize pair of wings. Poem for a Younger Son. William Scammell. NLP

This one was no philanthropist. For the Grave of a Peace-Loving Man. Hans Magnus Enzensberger. VCWP, *tr. by the author* and Michael Hamburger

This one was put in a jacket.   Counting the Mad.   Donald Justice.   InGu; NIP-4; NoP-4; NoP-5; TRP

This onion-dome holds all intricacies.   Greenwich Observatory.   Sidney Keyes.   MoBrPo

This only grant me, that my means may lie [*or* lye].   Of Myself [*or* My Self].   Abraham Cowley.   BASC

This open book. . .my open coffin. (LL)   Reading Myself.   Robert Lowell.   NAMCP V.2; VCAP; WaAnP

This or that or some such thing chuck when talking.   Hank Lazer.   AnSo *Fr.* New Spirit, The.

This oriental country, year after year.   Fan from Korea, A.   Chu Yün-ming.   ColAnChi, *tr. by* Jonathan Chaves

This orphaned house. Its needs, its presences.   House.   Ellen Bryant Voigt.   LPSFW

This page will be no less a riddle.   John 1:14 (1969).   Jorge Luis Borges.   GI, *tr. by* Norman Thomas Di Giovanni

This pair of skin gloves is sixty-six years old.   Skins.   Judith Wright.   BMAP

This palace was once magnificent.   At Ch'ang-men Palace.   Li Po.   CrYelRi, *tr. by* Sam Hamill

This pale winter the wisteria looks like an empty.   Wisteria.   Eloise Klein Healy.   GeoHom

This Passover or the Next I Will Never Be in Jerusalem.   Hilton Obenzinger.   FTtHH

This person never came to pass.   Evelyn Cavallo.   Muriel Spark.   MoWP

This phalanx of pines, these demi-fountains.   Martial.   Thom Gunn.   OBGa, *tr. by* Peter Porter

This picnic table's carefully etched.   Eighties Meditation.   Kay Murphy.   SwNoth

This pines.   This That and Then.   Douglas Messerli.   FTOS

This place full of contradiction.   Daphne Marlatt.   NLPA *Fr.* Touch to My Tongue.

This place has no nakedness.   Wilderness.   Faye George.   PoCoUp

This place is called an island of immortals.   *Unknown.*   NAAPv.2

This place is so remote people call it Nowhere.   Irrelevant and Useless.   David Budbill.   AmZen

This place of wild land.   Beyond the World.   Muso Soseki.   EaWin, *tr. by* W. S. Merwin

This Place Rumored to Have Been Sodom.   Robert Duncan.   CAGL; CalPo (This Place Rumored to Have Been Sodom.)   GPTC

This Place Rumored to Have Been Sodom.   Robert Duncan. *See* This Place Rumored to Have Been Sodom.

This place, these bounds.   Goodland.   *Unknown.*   SonAtl, *tr. by* Vince Akland and Tracey Yuan

This place up in Charlotte called Chuck's where I.   Waiting on Elvis, 1956.   Joyce Carol Oates.   AllShUp; PoA 2002; SwNoth

This place's quality is not its former nature.   Judith Wright.   HarvBoo *Fr.* Shadow of Fire: Ghazals, The.

This plant, so exceptional since its flower never lasts more than a few hours.   This Plant, So Exceptional.   Jean Follain.   MotU, *tr. by* Mary Feeney and William Matthews

This plate of fois gras.   Pleasures of the Flesh.   Anne Barrows.   AFaM

This Plot, which fail'd for want of common Sense.   John Dryden.   NPeEn *Fr.* Absalom and Achitophel.

This ploughman dead in battle slept out of doors.   Private, A.   Edward Thomas.   TCAWP

This Poem.   Ruth Forman.   SpirFl

This Poem.   Barbara Leslie Jordan.   ExTi; PoDa

This Poem.   Shirley Bradley LeFlore.   SpirFl

This Poem.   Constance Urdang.   PBCAP

This poem by Rupert Brookeborough.   Written Answer, A.   Tom Paulin.   ModIr

This poem intentionally left blank.   Charles Bernstein.   NoP-5

This poem is a letter to tell you that I.   Transformations.   Joy Harjo.   HATNAP

This poem is a prayer candle.   Jimmy Santiago Baca.   ICANM *Fr.* Healing Earthquakes.

This poem is about the strength and sadness of potatoes.   Potatoes.   David Donnell.   NIP-4

This poem is being written in the dark.   Poem Composed During a Brownout.   Fidelito Cortes.   ReBoTo

This poem is concerned with language on a very plain level.   Paradoxes and Oxymorons.   John Ashbery.   FTOS; HeIP-4; NAMCP V.2; NoAM; NoP-5; PmAP; PoPoPo

This poem is dangerous: it should not be left.   This Poem.   Elma Mitchell.   BeAl; PoCu

This Poem Is for Bear.   Gary Snyder.   PFTM-2 *Fr.* Myths and Texts.

This Poem Is for Deer.   Gary Snyder.   GeoHom *Fr.* Myths and Texts.

This Poem Is for You, My Sister.   Mona Lisa Saloy.   FuFl

This poem isn't a nation. A nation of trees pulped and bleached into something we are bound.   Vernal Conifer Seance.   Jason Christie.   PoPra

This poem isn't an intricate theory years in the making.   Accomplice, The.   David Clewell.   PoDa

This poem should have started.   Between Acts.   Janice Lowe.   InTrad

This poet describes carbon paper, how it lies flat.   Salad Days.   Susan Musgrave.   NoAM

This pool, the quiet sky.   March Evening.   Leonard Alfred George Strong.   MoBrPo

This Poor Man.   W. J. Gruffydd.   OBWVE, *tr. by* Gwyn Jones

This Poor Man.   W. J. Gruffydd.   BBMWP, *tr. by* Anthony Conran

This poring over your *Grand Cyrus*.   On A Romantic Lady.   Mary Monck.   RACG

This portrait captures Thaumareta's form—it renders.   Nossis.   SaLy, *tr. by* Diane Rayor

This portrait which I treasure so.   Epigram: Likeness, The.   Martial.   RomPo, *tr. by* Brian Hill

This present that constantly fails.   Demand.   Piera Oppezzo.   CItWP, *tr. by* Cinzia Sartini Blum and Lara Trubowitz

This printed face doesn't see.   Philip Whalen.   WANABP *Fr.* Epigrams & Imitations.

This profound piety is my own country.   My Country.   Jaime Torres Bodet.   TCLAP, *tr. by* Sonja Karsen

This proud scepter which now severed.   *Unknown.*   PriapPo *Fr.* Priapus Poems, The.

This Quiet Dust.   John Hall Wheelock.   MoAmPo

This quiet Dust was Gentlemen and Ladies.   Cemetery, A.   Emily Dickinson.   MoAmPo

This quiet morning light.   To Mark Anthony in Heaven.   William Carlos Williams.   SAmP; TCAPo

This quiet roof, bestirred with pigeon plumes.   Graveyard by the Sea, The.   Paul Valéry.   STV, *tr. by* John Frederick Nims

This racer of the watry plain.   Catullus.   OBVE.

This ragged shining.   Few Last Lines of Laundry, A.   Eamon Grennan.   PoA 2002

This Railway Station.   Allan M. Laing.   UV

This rather tall Indian man shot me in a dream.   Action-Packed Sonnet.   Prageeta Sharma.   HeMarv

This reckless flight, where is this bound to take us?   Imre Madách.   IQMS *Fr.* Tragedy of Man.

This reverend shadow cast that setting sun.   Upon Bishop Andrewes's [*or* Andrewes His] Picture before His Sermons.   Richard Crashaw.   NOSC

This ritzy vista includes the money.   Love Poem.   John Forbes.   BMAP

This River.   Annette Allen.   MPUn

This River Here.   Carmen Tafolla.   TiP2

This road.   Basho.   EH; NIL-7, *tr. by* Robert Hass

This road.   Basho.   EMJL, *tr. by* Haruo Shirane

This road our blithe-heart elders knew.   Lyric on the Lyric, A.   Lizette Woodworth Reese.   APN-2

This rock-hewn seat in a favourite corner.   His Favourite Seat.   Deborah Randall.   NeBl

This Roman road—eye's axis.   Bike Ride on a Roman Road.   Alice Oswald.   NeBrP

This Room.   John Ashbery.   ItP; OxBoAm

This Room and Everything in It.   Li-Young Lee.   CAP-8; IllVoic; NAAL-5; OpBo; RoV

This room is breaking out.   This Room.   Imtiaz Dharker.   BeAl

This room is dead; the occupant has gone.   Not at Home.   Elizabeth Jennings.   BeAl

This room is reserved for wandering Jews.   For the Wandering Jews.   Philip Schultz.   TaR

This room is so wide and empty.   At Munsoo Temple.   Daegam Tanyon.   BecRai, *tr. by* Kim Daljin, Kim Won-Chung and Christopher Merrill

This rose tree is not made to bear.   Envy.   Charles Lamb and Mary Lamb.   WoRP

This royal throne of kings, this scepter'd isle.   William Shakespeare.   UV; WaAnP

This royall Throne of Kings, this sceptred Isle.   William Shakespeare.   OxBEV

This rubber pump in my hand sighs, pants, and wheezes.   Anaesthetist, The.   Anne Rouse.   NeBrP; PoCu

This rude contraption, two plain boards.   Robert Frost's Writing Desk.   David Graham.   VisFro

This ruined temple.   Basho.   SoOfWa, *tr. by* Sam Hamill

This rumble—we've heard it before. Low, distant, deep, and secret.   August, Beirut, 1982.   Mahmoud Darwish.   Eno, *tr. by* Ibrahim Muhawi

This rust-infested cage with worn-out brakes.   Lines on a Van's Dereliction.   Douglas Houston.   TCAWP

This sacred urn holds the ashes of the Queen of Navarre.   Anne Seymour Dudley, Jane Seymour and Margaret Seymour.   EMWP *Fr.* Hecatodistichon.

This sadness. (LL)   Garden, The: "I couldn't do it again."   Louise Glück.   NoP-4; NoP-5

This said, divine Talthybius he call'd, and bad him haste. Homer. FaBoWar *Fr.* Iliad, The.

This said, he reacht to take his sonne. Homer. OBVE *Fr.* Iliad, The.

This said, she twirled the thread on an ugly spool. Seneca. RomPo *Fr.* Apocolocyntosis.

This said, the restles generall through the darke. Christopher Marlowe. PBRV *Fr.* Lucan's Pharsalia Book 1.

This salt. Ode to Salt. Pablo Neruda. TCLAP, *tr.* by Margaret Sayers Peden

This same moon hangs over Fu-chou. Moonlit Night. Tu Fu [*or* Du Fu]. CrYelRi, *tr.* by Sam Hamill

This sea will never die, neither will it ever grow old. Middle of the World. D. H. Lawrence. NoAM; WoPoe

This season always makes me think of peace. Begging for Change in Winter. Rafael Campo. MoW

This sense of space. Jeannette Miller. TANSG, *tr.* by Paula Vega

This sense of space, mine, familiar. This sense of space. Jeannette Miller. TANSG, *tr.* by Paula Vega

This Shade. Susanne Doyle. FFC

This shadow at my shoulder doesn't shed. Climbing. Jennifer Maiden. BMAP

This she? no, this is Diomed's Cressida. William Shakespeare. OxAEP-1 *Fr.* Troilus and Cressida.

This Shining Moment in the Now. David Budbill. AmZen

This shining that us showers. *Unknown.* WoPoe *Fr.* Doomsday, the Mysteries.

This shop in a little road I know is like a grubby sweet left. Hairdresser's, The. Pierre McOrlan. MFP, *tr.* by Martin Sorrell

This should be a eulogy without words. Eulogy. Amichai Israeli. NRoS, *tr.* by Esther Raizen

This silence at the sea's edge, so late in the afternoon. About Time. Laurens Vancrevel. TuT, *tr.* by Anne Kennedy

This silent girl who loves a man who leaves. (LL) Last Night: "When the sun sets, and he walks." Chryss Yost. CalPo; PoDa

This silken wreath, which circles in mine arm. Upon a Ribbon [*or* Ribband]. Thomas Carew. NOSC

This sitting on a case, this fact sans face. (LL) Time: "How long for the small yellow flowers." Robert Creeley. BodElec; ICANM

This skirt's in the style. Hsüeh T'ao [*or* Xue Tao]. WoPoe *Fr.* Trying on New-Made Clothes: Three Poems.

This slow one. (LL) Tortoise-Shell. D. H. Lawrence. FaBoVe; NAEL-6v2; NAEL-7v2; OxAEP-2

This small repast, with her I love. Contentment, to a Friend. Charlotte MacCarthy. PoBW

This smell is the point at which the landscape dissolves, ceases to be a landscape and becomes something else. (LL) Autobiography: "First thing I can remember is a blue line, The. This was on the left." Margaret Atwood. MotU; OpeFie

This Smoking World. Graham Lee Hemminger. NBLV

This soft October. Reserved Sacrament. James Schuyler. BodElec

This solemn altar. (LL) Altar. Marilyn Chin. NAMCP V.2; PoPoPo

This solitary fretwork. Final Tree. Gabriela Mistral. TCLAP, *tr.* by Doris Dana

This song explodes. *Unknown.* SonAtl, *tr.* by R. Mossen

This sonnet. Note. Joan Brossa. StAl, *tr.* by Arthur Terry

This sort of position uncomfortable allows me to speak. Reading Postures 3. Marcella Durand. IIR

This sound I can hear. Monk. Gaston Neal. BtF

This space so clear and blue. Windows. Frank O'Hara. BodElec

This Spanish Christ that hasn't lived. Miguel de Unamuno. RaW *Fr.* Dead Christ Lying in the Church of Santa Clara (Church of the Cross) in Palencia, The.

This speech all Troyans did applaud, who from their traces losde. Homer. OBVE *Fr.* Iliad, The.

This spoke, a huge wave tooke him by the head. Homer. OBVE *Fr.* Odyssey.

This spoonful of chocolate tapioca. Thinking of the Lost World. Randall Jarrell. NAAL-5; NAMCP V.2; NoAM; StAl

This spring as it comes bursts up in bonfires green. Enkindled Spring, The. D. H. Lawrence. NAMCP V.1; NoAM

This spring is going, too. New Music, A. Haniel Long. APT-1

This squalid dome of soot-obscuréd glass. This Railway Station. Allan M. Laing. UV

This stalk of day-old bread. Three-Course Meal for the New Year, A. Myra Sklarew. TaR

This still mountain night is not still. Earth Screaming. Esther Iverem. GT

This stone is a forehead where dreams groan. Federico García Lorca. RaW

This stone, with not unpardonable pride. Epitaph. John Sparrow. OBCoV

This story is not true. Stesichoros. SaLy, *tr.* by Diane Rayor

This story was told to me by another traveller. Margaret Atwood. NALW *Fr.* Circe / Mud Poems.

This strange thing must have crept. Fork. Charles Simic. CAP-8; ChAP; ColAP; NAMCP V.2; PoPoPo; TRP; WaAnP; WeW-3

This string upon my harp was best beloved. Harmonics. William Vaughn Moody. AmFaPo; APN-2

This stripper is dancing. 'Round Killar. Eric Dyer. BloBone

This stupid world. Issa. EH, *tr.* by Robert Hass

This summer I caught handfuls of wind. Handfuls of Wind. Laila Halaby. PoArWo

This summer, most friends out of town. Missoula Softball Tournament. Richard Hugo. MoASP

This summer, reading the history of the Jews of Spain. Crypto-Jews, The. Robin Becker. ExTi; OPRER; TaR

This Summer's Sky. Bertolt Brecht. PoSu, *tr.* by Michael Hamburger

This Sun. John Rybicki. AmPoNex

This sun was mine and yours; we shared it. Our Sun. George Seferis. AF

This sunday morning breaks blue clear, in st paul de vence. In Jimmy's Garden. Quincy Troupe. GT

This sunken-eyed moment wobbling. Christmas in Biafra (1969). Chinua Achebe. ChrPo

This suspense is killing me. Love Me or Leave Me. Gustave Kahn. ReLy

This tale is doon, and God save al the route [*or* rowte]! (LL) Geoffrey Chaucer. NAEL-6v1; NAEL-7v1 *Fr.* Canterbury Tales, The.

This tells of wolf and lamb who drank. Wolf and the Lamb, The. Marie de France. NAEL-7v1, *tr.* by Harriet Spiegel

This That and Then. Douglas Messerli. FTOS

This that at night keeps flashing. Eugenio Montale. PFTM-1

This that I give you now. Bread. Stanley Burnshaw. APT-2

This that is washed with weed and pebblestone. Figurehead, The. Léonie Adams. APT-2; OxBoAm

This that you see, this colorful pretense. On Her Portrait. Sor Juana Inés de la Cruz. WoPoe, *tr.* by Robert Mezey

This, the last ornament among the peers. Joseph Hilaire Pierre Belloc. OBSV

This the mortared stone. Prolegomenon to a Theodicy, A. Kenneth Rexroth.

This: the nagging way. Mortal Roundness. Clarence Major. EGAG

Then buddy is the blue routine. My Buddy. Richard Hugo. SeSe

This thing happens in mid-summer. Purest Rage, The. Charles Baxter. SwNoth

This thing of palpitations and. Crushin. StacyLynn. BtF

This thing the night flashes. Little Testament. Eugenio Montale. PoetW, *tr.* by Robert Lowell

This thing we learn from others. Ingrid de Kok. TSAP

This thin-lipped king with his helmeted head. To President Bush at the Start of the Gulf War. Robert Bly. RaBo

This, this is what I love, and what is this? George Macdonald. SacPr

This Time. Michael Palmer. NAMCP V.2

This time his father takes him. Father's Day. Gloria Vando. TouFir

This time, I have left my body behind me, crying. Trying to Pray. James Wright. BBASP; WaAnP

This time I won't permit the blue. Patrizia Cavalli. NeIt; VCWP, *tr.* by Judith Baumel

This time I'm wide awake, and. Out-of-Body Experience. Jim Crenner. PoDa

This time it is no dream. After twenty-three years away. Going Back to the Convent. Madeline DeFrees. TAPaP

This time it's true, as much as I remember. New York, 1927. Anne Marie Macari. NevBe

This time I've realized the essence. Rāmprasād Sen. SinGod, *tr.* by Rachel Fell McDermott

This time, Kali. Rāmprasād Sen. SinGod, *tr.* by Rachel Fell McDermott

This time no one's looking for love. Twilight at a Little Harbor. Chairil Anwar. PoetW, *tr.* by Burton Raffel

This time of year The North goes by, bird. Chair in the Meadow, The. William Stafford. BodElec

This time the dead man will see them in Hell. (LL) Book of the Dead Man #58, The. Marvin Bell. OPRER; TaR

This time the hold up man didn't know a video-sound camera hidden up in a corner. Fragment. C. K. Williams. InoFa

This time the mycorrhizal infection. World Truffle. Sarah Lindsay. BeAl; PoDa

This time there was no beak. Pile of Feathers. Gerald Stern. LoL

This to the crown and blessing of my life. Letter to Daphnis, A. Anne Finch, Countess of Winchilsea. EMWP; LW; MakPoe; NALW; PEW

This tomb Damis built for his courageous horse. Anyte. HePo *Fr.* Epigrams.

This tomcat cuts across the. Tomcat. James Keir Baxter. BeAl

This, too. Karen Press. TSAP

This too is an experience of the soul. Isis Wanderer. Kathleen Jessie Raine. NALW

This too is one of them. (LL) Old Man's Lazy, The. Peter Blue Cloud. HATNAP; LTA

This Tooth. Lee Bennett Hopkins. TLR

This top is the pitch of the world. Girls. Lauris Edmond. ArBi; BeAl

This torment of love. Describes Rationally the Irrational Effects of Love. Sor Juana Inés de la Cruz. SpanPo, tr. by Samuel Beckett

This town has docks where channel boats come sidling. Arrivals, Departures. Philip Larkin. MoBrPo

This tranquil vault, assuming files of doves. Graves by the Sea, The. Paul Valéry. WoPoe, tr. by John Finlay

This treasure is the best, of all those gifts the grain. Upon the Birth of a Young and Highly Desired Son. Christian Weise. GePo, tr. by George C. Schoolfield

This tree is God's challah. God's Body. Sara Klugman. HW

This triangle of water athirst. Love with No Letup. Antonin Artaud. YaTCFP, tr. by Mary Ann Caws and Jean-Pierre Cauvin

This trip. Taneda Santoka. CAoMJL1, tr. by Burton Watson

This Troilus in armes gan hir streyne. Geoffrey Chaucer. EroLit Fr. Troilus and Criseyde [or Criseide].

This tuft that thrives on saline nothingness. Air Plant, The. Hart Crane. MoAmPo

This tumultuous life is nothing for me but the sound of a. Michelangelo Coviello. ItPo Fr. Caravaggio.

This twisted and bitter figure. Black Thorn, The. J. Eirian Davies. BBMWP, tr. by Sion Eirian

This unphilosophic sight. To a Lady's Countenance. Elinor Wylie. NALW

This urge, wrestle, resurrection of dry sticks. Cuttings (later). Theodore Roethke. APT-2; CAP-8; NAAL-5; NAMCP V.1; NoAM; OBGa; TRP; VCAP; WaAnP

This useless clairvoyance. Flash Point. Lorenzo Thomas. AnSo

This vale—my daily haunt—is a delight. Shepherds and Flocks. Victor Hugo. SxFrPo, tr. by A. M. and E. H. Blackmore

This valley: as if a huge, dull, primordial axe. Grim Town in a Steep Valley. Thomas Lux. AmAlph

This Version of Love. Dorothy Hewett. BMAP

This version of the starving artist. Bela. Gerald Stern. BodElec

This very day, a little while ago, you lived. Dead on the War Path. Unknown. FaBoWar, tr. by Herbert J. Spinden

This very moment, love. (LL) Aubade: "Cold snap. Five o'clock." Richard Kenney. NoP-4; NoP-5

This victim from a lukewarm pigs' redoubt. Unknown. PriapPo Fr. Priapus Poems, The.

This village clings to rock like a swallow's nest to the eaves. This and That. Elke Erb. OnScMo, tr. by Rosmarie Waldrop

This virginal long-living lovely day. Stéphane Mallarmé. SxFrPo, tr. by A. M. and E. H. Blackmore

This vision of a face, radiant and full of beauty. Marbod of Rennes. CAGL; EroLit Fr. Unyielding Youth, The.

This voice an older friend has kept. Isaiah by Kerosene Lantern Light. Robert Harris. ChIV-1; NOBAu

This Wall has heard many prayers. Paratroopers are Weeping, The. Hayim Hefer. NRoS, tr. by Esther Raizen

This warl's a tap-room owre and owre. Tap-Room, The. Robert Tannahill. NePenScot

This war's dead heroes, who has seen them? Heroes. Kathleen Jessie Raine. FaBoWar

This was a dream. (LL) In Winter in my Room. Emily Dickinson. APN-2; NAAL-3; NALW; NCAP; NoAM

This was a new catechism, a new testament. Sitting in the Sixth Grade at Ascension of Our Lord School in Cleveland, Ohio, Reading a Pamphlet Entitled "Possession in Iowa." David Citino. UpMys

This was a Poet—It is That. Emily Dickinson. APN-2; NAAL-3; NAAL-5; NAAPv.1; NCAP; OxBoAm; TCAPo

This was a private crime; but you shall hear. Juvenal. BASC Fr. Satires.

This was a time, when only the dead. Introduction. Anna Andreyevna Akhmatova. PFTM-1

This was a world of white lines, a game. Poem for Pancho Gonzales. Leroy V. Quintana. ICANM

This was all roses, here, where an overblown house crowns. Until Words Turn to Moss. C. D. Wright. AmAlph

This was gruesome—fighting over a ham sandwich. Another Insane Devotion. Gerald Stern. CAP-8

This was Mr Bleaney's room. He stayed. Mr Bleaney. Philip Larkin. NPeEn; OxBEV; PoPoPo; TRP; UV

This was more like it, looking up to find a burlapped fawn. Stoic, The. Paul Muldoon. GPPA

"This was Mr. Strugnell's room," she'll say. Mr. Strugnell. Wendy Cope. UV

This was not experience. Painted Cup, The. Michael Palmer. FTOS

This was not to be expected. Seaman, 1941. Molly Holden. PoAgWa

This was our first line of defense. It held. Ferniehirst Castle. Richard Hugo. NoAM

This was the eerie mine of souls. Orpheus, Eurydice, Hermes. Rainer Maria Rilke. WoPoe, tr. by Franz Wright

This was the first Thanksgiving with my wife's family. Thanksgiving. Martín Espada. PrTe; PuP-23

This was the last I'd trouble the ducks this season. Late Season. Sydney Lea. WaAnP

This was the moment when Before. BC:AD. U. A. Fanthorpe. OBCP; OxBEV

This was the real England, that still lives on, a fading tapestry. Geoff Ward. VaPo Fr. English Music.

This was the salty taste of glory. Wallace Stevens. FaBoWar Fr. Phases.

This was the surplus childhood, held as cheap! Sunderland Children, The. Alice Thompson Meynell. NALW

This was the table. Its surface, its legs. Ghost, The. Ágnes Nemes Nagy. PoSu, tr. by Bruce Berlind

This was the time of their heaviest migration. No Matter What, After All, and That Beautiful Word So. Hayden Carruth. BeAl

This was the woman; what now of the man? George Meredith. NAEL-6v2 Fr. Modern Love.

This was the young Camonus; this his face. Martial. RomPo, tr. by Brian Hill

This water droplet, charity of the air. Man Seeking Experience Enquires His Way of a Drop of Water, The. Ted Hughes. OxAEP-2

This watery vague how vast! This misty globe. On the Bay. Richard Watson Gilder. APN-2

This way I salute you. City Johannesburg. Mongane Wally Serote. NAfrP; TSAP

This way of writing I observed by some. Satire. Unknown. BASC

This way, that way? Polar Cub. Judith Nicholls. NOxBChV

This way, this way, come and hear. John Fletcher. NOSC Fr. Little French Lawyer, The.

This wedding in Lawrence. Blanca's Red Lips. Gloria Vando. TouFir

This weighty machine. Army, The. Hagiwara Sakutaro. CAoMJL1, tr. by Hiroaki Sato

This wet evening, in a lost age. (LL) Mountain over Aberdare, The. Alun Lewis. AngWePo; TCAWP

Which I write now. Inheritance. George Bruce. EdScPo

This while we are abroad. Ode Written in the Peak[e], An. Michael Drayton. NOSC

This white explosion of water plunges down. Falls of Falloch, The. Sydney Tremayne. EdScPo

This whole town is sand. Even the cypress. Tallahassee. Aimee Nezhukumatathil. LiTh

This wild team rushes at a savage pace. If I Have to Yield My Bones. Milán Füst. IQMS, tr. by Paul Tabori

This will be the last ditch to fall. Capital. John Tripp. AngWePo

This will go too, this curve of shore. Slate Quay: Felinheli. Peter Gruffydd. AngWePo

This will happen. Born into a World Knowing. Susan Griffin. PoChi; WhBo

This wind begun to knead the Grass. Emily Dickinson. See Wind begun to knead the Grass, The.

This wind from Fife has cruel fingers, scooping. Double Life. Norman Alexander MacCaig. EdScPo

This wind is easy, the moon pleasant. Song: Green Water, Singing Girl. Li Ho. CrYelRi, tr. by Sam Hamill

This Wind That Loiters. Odysseus Elytis. WoPoe, tr. by Edmund Keeley and Philip Sherrard

This wine is really awful. Quality of Wine. Hayden Carruth. BodElec

This Winter's Night. Margaret Chula. AFaM

This woman cannot live more than one year. Where I? Robinson Jeffers. OxBSo

This woman vomiting her. Sonia Sanchez. UnSA

This woman's fingernails. There Is No Real Edge to Anything. Jody Aliesan. FiBr

This wondrous art in the human realm. To a Pyrotechnist. Chao Meng-fu. ColAnChi, tr. by Jonathan Chaves

This won't be a political poem, brothers. Only Democracy (in the Middle East), The. Rami Saari. PML, tr. by Lisa Katz

This work and it was not finished? (LL) View from the Window, The. Ronald Stuart Thomas. NoP-4; NoP-5

This work proceeds, he will not wish for more. (LL) William Wordsworth. NAEL-6v2; NAEL-7v2 Fr. Prelude, The; Growth of a Poet's Mind [1850 version].

This world. Lal Ded. WPoS

This World. Sarah Morgan Bryan Piatt. NCAP

This World. Malvina Reynolds. ASA

This World Fares as a Fantasy. John Gower.
  "Of fantasye is all oure fare." SacPr

This World Is All a Fleeting Show. Thomas Moore. SacPr

This world is gradually becoming a place. John Berryman. NAMCP V.2; NoAM *Fr.* Dream Songs.

This World Is Not Conclusion. Emily Dickinson. APN-2; NAAL-3; NAAPv.1; NCAP; TCAPo

This world of day and night. Our Baby is a Living Prayer. Ko Chônghûi. EcSo, *tr.* by Catherine J. Kim

This world of dew. Issa. SoOfWa, *tr.* by Sam Hamill

This world of dew's. Issa. EMJL, *tr.* by Haruo Shirane

This World, Poor Thing. N. Revathi Devi. HotL, *tr.* by V. Narayana Rao and A. K. Ramanujan

This worlde is full of variaunce. Duplicity of Women, The. John Lydgate. WaAnP

This world's a dream, so why. Rising Drunk on a Spring Day. Li Po. CrYelRi, *tr.* by Sam Hamill

This world's dead weight and cycle on your back. (LL) Night Sweat. Robert Lowell. HarvBoo; OxBoAm

This world's just mad enough to have been made. Creation Myth on a Moebius Band. Howard Nemerov. OBCoV

This would be a bewildering way unless we had a guide. William Langland. NAEL-6v1; NAEL-7v1 *Fr.* Vision of Piers Plowman, The.

This year. These Green-Going-to-Yellow. Marvin Bell. UrbNat

This Year. Abubakar Othman. NeNiPo

This year again the bruise-colored oak. Seeing the Bones. Maxine W. Kumin. NoAM

This Year, before It Ends. Eve Langley. NOBAu

This year, before it ends, holds out time as a weight to us. This Year, before It Ends. Eve Langley. NOBAu

This year I tried on voices just like hats. Paula Cunningham. NIrP *Fr.* Dog Called Chance, A.

This year I was excited to find the. Three Recent Trips to the Golden Past: East Village, Clarksdale Mississippi, Athens. Dick Lourie. PrTe

This year Marie drives back and forth. Migration. Tony Hoagland. BeAl; PoCho

This year, maybe, do you think I can graduate? Deferred. Langston Hughes. APSN; APT-2

This year on, forever. Issa. SoOfWa, *tr.* by Sam Hamill

This year we are making. Margaret Atwood. PoetW *Fr.* Four Small Elegies.

This year we've lived in stone. Vines, The. William Greenway. PoDa

This Year's Drive to Appomattox. Eleanor Ross Taylor. CBCWP

This, you were sure, whatever happened. Pair of Shoes, A. Theodore Weiss. NoAM

This youth too long has heard the break. Tale, A. Louise Bogan. StAl

This zoo of smoky dragons now swarming from our best brains. (LL) Dragon-Watching in St. Louis. Carter Revard. OtW; UrbNat

Thise olde gentil Brito[u]ns in hir dayes. Geoffrey Chaucer. NAEL-6v1 *Fr.* Canterbury Tales, The.

Thistle. Vona Groarke. NIrP

Thistle. Roy Scheele. MotU

Thistle rises and forever will, The. (LL) Hugh MacDiarmid. NAEL-6v2; NAEL-7v2 *Fr.* Drunk Man Looks at the Thistle, A.

Thistledown's flying Though the winds are all still, The. Autumn. John Clare. BBASP; WeW-3

Thistles. Ted Hughes. FaBoVe; NAMCP V.2; NoAM; NPeEn; SoSe-8; WaAnP

Thistles. Takahashi Shinkichi. ZenPo, *tr.* by Takashi Ikemoto and Lucien Stryk

Thistles bloomed in the vast moonlit. Thistles. Takahashi Shinkichi. ZenPo, *tr.* by Takashi Ikemoto and Lucien Stryk

Thistles climb the thatch, The. Forever. Clearances, The. Iain Crichton Smith. NePenScot

Thistle's Grown aboon the Rose, The. Allan Cunningham. NePenScot

Tho' grief and fondness in my breast rebel. Samuel Johnson. NPeEn *Fr.* London: A Poem in Imitation of the Third Satire of Juvenal.

Tho' he be nae mine, as I am his. (LL) Mary's Song. Marion Angus. EdScPo; LW

Tho' I'm no Catholic. Catholic Bells, The. William Carlos Williams. SAmP

Tho' men say thou bring'st the Spring.. (LL) Swallow, The. Abraham Cowley. OBEV; OxAEP-1

Tho' the days are long. I'll See You in My Dreams. Gustave Kahn. ReLy

Tho they in flames bright as your eyes expire. (LL) What makes me write my dearest Freind you aske. Hester Wyat. EMWP; FaBoVe

Tho when as chearelesse night ycovered had. Edmund Spenser. NAEL-6v1; NAEL-7v1 *Fr.* Faerie Queene, The.

Thocht Polibus, pisander, and with them. Sonet. Alexander Montgomerie. NePenScot

Thomalin, since Thirsil nothing has to leave thee. To Thomalin. Phineas Fletcher. NOSC

Thomas and Beulah. Rita Dove.
  Dusting. NAAL-5; NoP-5; WaAnP
  Event, The. NAAL-5; NAMCP V.2
  Straw Hat. MAAN; NAAL-5

Thomas at Chickamauga. Kate Brownlee Sherwood. PCW

Thomas Campion. William Cole. AmWit *Fr.* Uncoupled Couplets.

Thomas Carlyle. Dorothy Parker. NALW *Fr.* Pig's-Eye View of Literature, A.

Thomas Hardy. Walter De la Mare. NoAM

Thomas Hardy. Norman Dubie. AmAlph

Thomas Hardy and A. E. Housman. Max Beerbohm. NBLV

Thomas Jefferson. Lorine Niedecker. HarvBoo; NAMCP V.1

Thomas lay on the Huntlie bank. Thomas the Rhymer [or Rimer]. *Unknown.* OBEV

Thomas mouths. Gandhabba #5. Tom Weatherly. EGAG

Thomas Müntzer. Jeffrey Wainwright. HarvBoo

Thomas Rhymer [and the Queen of Elfland]. *Unknown. See* Thomas the Rhymer.

Thomas Rymer. *Unknown. See* Thomas the Rhymer [or Rimer].

Thomas the Rhymer. *Unknown.* OBEV; TFi
  (Thomas Rhymer [and the Queen of Elfland].) NPeEn

Thomas the Rhymer [or Rimer]. *Unknown.* OBEV
  (Thomas Rymer.) NePenScot

Thomas, the vagrant piper's son. Louis Untermeyer. MoAmPo *Fr.* Mother Goose Up-to-Date.

Thompson's Lunch Room—Grand Central Station. Amy Lowell. APT-1 *Fr.* Towns in Colour.

Thonah! Thonah! / There is a voice above. *Unknown.* APN-2; TCAPo *Fr.* Mountain Chant, The.

Thong. Joel Dailey. AnSo

Thor Heyerdahl, a stolid. Thor Heyerdahl's Mother. Jan Erik Vold. PML, *tr.* by the author

Thor Heyerdahl's Mother. Jan Erik Vold. PML, *tr.* by the author

Thoreau. Timothy Liu. AmPoNex; GifTon; OPRER

Thoreau's Eyes: Two Poems for Kazuaki Tanahashi. Michael McClure. WANABP

Thorn, The. William Wordsworth. NAEL-7v2; NPBRoP
  "Before you up the mountain go." VerBaPo
  Poet Reveals All, The. STuOW

Thorn grows flat against the flank of Calton Hill. Robin Robertson. EdScPo *Fr.* Camera Obscura.

Thorn grows flat against the flank of Calton Hill. Flags of Autumn from Camera Obscura. Robin Robertson. EdScPo

Thorn Merchant's Mistress, The. Yusef Komunyakaa. RACG

Thorn that grew in her coat, The. Behind the House. Mahmoud Sharaf. AnVo, *tr.* by Mohamed Enani

Thorns of the iron fence. Kyokusui. NAAPv.2

Thorny Gaps Suddenly Moving. Fatma Kandil. PoArWo, *tr.* by Khaled Mattawa

Thoroughfares await them. Michele Leggott. VaPo

Thorow. Susan Howe. APSN
  "Cannot Be." NAMCP V.2
  "Elegiac western Imagination." NAMCP V.2
  "Gabion / Parapet." NAMCP V.2

Those ancient Greeks. Unexpected Manna. Gary H. Holthaus. GifTon

Those are my best days, when I shake with fear. (LL) John Donne. BASC; ChIV-2; NAEL-7v1; NOSC; WaAnP *Fr.* Holy Sonnets.

Those are the features, those the smiles. Lines, Written on Seeing My Husband's Picture, Painted When He Was Young. Anna Sawyer. LW

Those autumns my parents slept. Dream of Glass Bangles, A. Agha Shahid Ali. OpBo

Those black silk pajamas. Black Silk Pajamas. Danton R. Remoto. ReBoTo

Those blessèd structures, plot and rhyme. Epilogue. Robert Lowell. HarvBoo; NAAL-5; NAMCP V.2; NoAM; NoP-4; NoP-5; OxBoAm; PoetW; PoPoPo; StAl; VCAP; WaAnP

Those boys that ran together. Lucille Clifton. OxAAAP

Those breathing Tokens of your kind regard. Liberty [*sequel to* Gold and Silver Fishes in a Vase]. William Wordsworth.

Those cells, burning, doubling, splitting out of their skins. (LL) Louise Erdrich. *See* We see, burning, doubling, splitting out of its skin.

Those / Concerning whom they have never spoken and thought never to speak. Psychiatrist's Song. Louise Bogan. NAAPv.2

Those days are now. William Wordsworth. OxAEP-2 *Fr.* Prelude, The; Growth of a Poet's Mind [1805 version].

Those days we slept in a trumpet. Music for Brass. Günter Grass. AF, *tr.* by Christopher Middleton

Those doors through my soul knock about. Memory of My Private Childhood. Eunice Odio. TCLAP, *tr.* by Suzanne Jill Levine

Those—dying then. Emily Dickinson. APN-2; NCAP

Those eyes of mine in nineteen-ten.   1910.   Federico García Lorca.   PtR, *tr. by* Greg Simon and Steven F. White

Those eyes that [*or which*] set my fancy on a fire.   Conquest [*or His Lady's Might*].   Philippe Desportes.   NoSic, *tr. by* Unknown

Those falling blossoms.   Moritake.   SoOfWa, *tr. by* Sam Hamill

Those famous men of old, the Ogres.   Ogres and Pygmies.   Robert Graves.   NAMCP V.1; NoAM

Those final, fall evenings: my father.   Pegasus the Winged Horse.   Alan Robert Wilson.   Coast

Those first days, making love above your father's study.   My Funny Valentine.   Chris Greenhalgh.   NeBl

Those five or six young guys.   Blues.   Derek Walcott.   EMP

Those four black girls blown up.   American History.   Michael S. Harper.   ESEAA; NAAL-5; NAMCP V.2; NoAM; PoPoPo

Those glances rain down arrows on the country.   Nejati.   OLP, *tr. by* Walter Andrews, Najaat Black and Mehmet Kalpakli

Those gone are day by day remote.   *Unknown.*   ChinPo.   *tr. by* Ye Weilian [*or* Yeh Wei-lien *or* Wai-lim Yip]

Those Graves in Rome.   Larry Levis.   PoDa

Those great sea-horses bare their teeth and laugh at the dawn. (LL)   High Talk.   William Butler Yeats.   FaBoVe; RaBo

Those great sweeps of snow that stop suddenly six feet from the house.   Snowbanks North of the House.   Robert Bly.   BodElec; CAP-8; RaBo

Those green summer afternoons.   Storm Cellar, The.   Paul Ruffin.   TiP2

Those greetings! those goodbyes!   Kennedy Airport.   Aaron Kramer.   OtW

Those groans men use.   Mutes, The.   Denise Levertov.   BeAl; CAP-8; ErotSp; NALW; OxBoAm

Those hands, which heav'n like to a curtain spread.   Crucified.   Francis Quarles.   NOSC

Those hands which you so clapt [*or clapped*], go now and wring.   Upon the Lines and Life of the Famous Scenic Poet, Master William Shakespeare.   Hugh Holland.   AngWePo; OBWVE

Those hills and away. (LL)   Young Wife's Lament.   Brigit Pegeen Kelly.   CFP; IllVoic

Those hours that with gentle work did frame.   William Shakespeare.   AEP *Fr.* Sonnets.

Those i love are sometimes white.   Imani Tolliver.   BtF

Those I love scattered away, poor.   Winter Night.   Po Chü-i.   NDACCP, *tr. by* David Hinton

Those in the vegetable rain retain.   Stories of Snow.   Patricia K. Page.   BrAP; NoP-4; NoP-5

Those laden lilacs / at the lawn's end.   Lilacs, The.   Richard Wilbur.   CAP-8

Those long black tresses.   Fujiwara noTeika.   WoPoe, *tr. by* Steven D. Carter

Those long uneven lines.   MCMXIV.   Philip Larkin.   FaBoWar; HarvBoo; NAEL-6v2; NAEL-7v2; NAMCP V.2; NoAM; NoP-4; NoP-5; OBWP; OxAEP-2; PoAgWa

Those many dark nights in our wedding house.   Susquehanna.   Liz Rosenberg.   GoPo

Those men who love the *crwth* and harp.   Song and Poetry.   *Unknown.*   OBWVE, *tr. by* Gwyn Jones

Those men with dollars on the mind.   Gamble.   Linda Hogan.   HATNAP

Those milestones, always.   Tomas Tranströmer.   WoBe *Fr.* Haiku.

Those moon-gilded dancers.   Gay, The.   George Russell.   OBMV

Those Mornings.   Robert Kinsley.   IPoFL

Those mornings were thick with Benedictine incense.   1965.   Frankie Paino.   AmPoNex

Those neck-pointing out full bodylength and calling.   Gulls.   Jorie Graham.   AWPTFC; BAP-01

Those nymphs, I want to capture them.   Afternoon of a Faun, The.   Stéphane Mallarmé.   WoPoe, *tr. by* Louis Simpson

Those of us still left.   Welsh-speaking Welsh, The.   Gwyn Thomas.   BBMWP, *tr. by* the author

Those Paperweights with Snow Inside.   Molly Peacock.   RA

Those people were a kind of solution. (LL)   Waiting for the Barbarians.   Constantine P. Cavafy.   AF; BLT; PoAgWa; PtR, *tr. by* Edmund Keeley and Philip Sherrard

(They were, those people, a kind of solution.) (LL)   PFTM-1; StAl

Those perennial apparitions.   Cormorants.   John Kinsella.   OWoS

Those poor, arthritically swollen knees.   With Her.   Czeslaw Milosz.   GI, *tr. by the author* and Robert Hass

Those pretty [*or petty*] wrongs that liberty commits.   William Shakespeare.   OxAEP-1 *Fr.* Sonnets.

Those quaint old worn-out words!   Antiques.   Walter De la Mare.   PoA 2002

Those quiet little feet in the reflected room.   Cesare Greppi.   ItPo, *tr. by* Gayle Ridinger

Those Rainy Mornings.   Frank Mkalawile Chipasula.   HBAPE

Those smells making you remember again.   Smells.   Bei Dao.   WoBe, *tr. by* Iona Man-Cheong and Eliot Weinberger

Those speckled trout we glimpsed in a pool last year.   Two Fish.   Katha Pollitt.   NIL-7; NIP-4

Those spirits which we Animal do call.   Of the Animal Spirits.   Margaret Lucas Cavendish, Duchess of Newcastle.   PEW

Those streets amid opacity she and Robertson heard.   Pronoun Woven.   Derek Beaulieu.   PoPra

Those sultry nights we used to pass outdoors.   Amos Niven Wilder.   YaYoPo *Fr.* Battle-Retrospect.

Those supposedly *in the know* about *moments*.   Defining Moment.   Liz Ahl.   RWB

Those that could not be even these.   Metempsychosis of the Dog.   Alfonso D'Aquino.   RMCMP, *tr. by* Rebecca Seiferle

Those three women winding wool may have.   Madeline DeFrees.   FiBr *Fr.* Figures for a Carrousel.

Those transparent Dacca gauzes.   Dacca Gauzes, The.   Agha Shahid Ali.   BeAl; NAMCP V.2; NIL-7; NoP-4; NoP-5

Those tulip-cheeked ones—what they dared do in the garden!   Nejati.   OLP, *tr. by* Walter Andrews, Najaat Black and Mehmet Kalpakli

Those twenty-six letters filling the blackboard.   Elegy with a Chimneysweep Falling Inside It.   Larry Levis.   AmAlph

Those two are gone who walked upright on two legs.   Leopard in Eden, The.   Gail White.   FFC

Those Two Boys.   Franklin Pierce Adams.   OBCoV

Those Various Scalpels.   Marianne Moore.   PtR

Those Walks We Took.   David Wright.   NLP

Those walks we took I shall not take.   Those Walks We Took.   David Wright.   NLP

Those we love die like birds.   Lament.   Mai Sayigh.   CFP, *tr. by* Charles Doria and Salma Khadra Jayyusi

Those Were the Days.   Lee Adams.   ReLy

Those were the days.   Mother, a Young Wife Leans to Sew.   Geraldine Connolly.   SweBea

Those were the days.   Energy in Sweden.   Kenneth Koch.   NoP-4; NoP-5

Those Which Were Pomp and Delight.   Pedro Calderón de la Barca.   WoPoe, *tr. by* Katherine Washburn

Those who.   Petty Bourgeoisie, The.   Roque Dalton.   TCLAP, *tr. by* Richard Schaaf

Those who are beautiful.   Robert Kelly.   APSN

Those who cannot love the heavens or the earth.   Chaff, The.   W. S. Merwin.   CAP-8

Those who can't find anything to live for.   Basic Con, The.   Lew Welch.   CalPo; OxBoAm

Those Who Carry.   Anna Kamienska.   GI, *tr. by* David Curzon and Grażyna Drabik

Those who carry grand pianos / to the tenth floor.   Those Who Carry.   Anna Kamienska.   GI, *tr. by* David Curzon and Grażyna Drabik

Those who come by me passing.   Attention.   Sa'di Yusuf.   ItP, *tr. by* Khaled Mattawa

Those who crawl are the freest!   Home-Study Course in Freedom.   Radoi Ralin.   CSCBP, *tr. by* Georgi Belev and Lisa Sapinkopf

Those Who Do Not Dance.   Gabriela Mistral.   WPoS, *tr. by* Maria Giachetti [*or* Jacketti]

Those who give ear to the heart of the night.   Nocturne.   Rubén Darío.   SpanPo, *tr. by* Kate Flores

Those who go forth with weapons to the war of their people.   Splendor from the Splendid.   Uri Zvi Greenberg.   NRoS, *tr. by* Esther Raizen

Those who have not been chosen for any higher call.   From the Admonitions of St. Theresa of Avila.   István Vas.   IQMS, *tr. by* George Szirtes

Those, who in quarrels interpose.   John Gay.   *Fr.* Fables: First Series.

Those Who Love.   Cyprian Norwid.   WoPoe, *tr. by* Jerzy Peterkiewicz, Burns Singer and Jon Stallworthy

Those Who Love.   Sara Teasdale.   GoPo; LW

Those who love the most.   Those Who Love.   Sara Teasdale.   GoPo; LW

Those who loved freedom.   One Kind of Freedom Speaks.   Erich Fried.   AF, *tr. by* Georg Rapp

Those Who Make Paths.   Catherine Fisher.   TCAWP

Those who painted my portrait painted me.   Nef'i.   OLP, *tr. by* Walter Andrews, Najaat Black and Mehmet Kalpakli

Those who refused to meet.   Vera Pavlova.   CRWP *Fr.* Letter from Memory.

"Those who speak know nothing:."   Philosophers: Lao-Tzu, The.   Po Chü-i.   BLT, *tr. by* Arthur Waley

Those who speak know nothing.   Laozi.   Po Chü-i.   CCL1, *tr. by* Arthur Waley

Those who widened the Panama Canal.   Roque Dalton.   AF

Those Who Wrestle with the Angel for Us.   Brigit Pegeen Kelly.   OtW

Those whose houses were burned.   Margaret Atwood.   PoetW *Fr.* Four Small Elegies.

Those who've been to war love maps.   Maps.   Bruce Guernsey.   IllVoic

Those Winter Sundays.   Robert Earl Hayden.   AmFaPo; APT-2; CAP-8; ChAP; ColAP; CtM; ESEAA; GoPo; ISC; MakPoe; NAAL-5; NAMCP V.2; NIL-7; NIP-4; NoAM; NoP-4; NoP-5; OxAAAP; OxBoAm; PoPoPo; RaBo; SoSe-8; SSLK; StAl; TFi; WaAnP; WeW-3

Those Women. *Unknown.* WoPoe *Fr.* Gathasaptasati, The.

Those women. *Unknown.* WoPoe *Fr.* Gathasaptasati, The.

Those [*or* These] words were uttered as in [*or* in a] pensive mood. William Wordsworth. CenSon

Those young gamogues. Sterricky. Mary Dalton. OpeFie

Thou. Anne Carson. NLPA *Fr.* Glass Essay, The.

Thou and I, my noble wheel. Bicycle and I, The. *Unknown.* ArBi

Thou art gone, and for ever! (LL) Sir Walter Scott. CtM; NOBRP; NPeEn; OxAEP-2 *Fr.* Lady of the Lake, The.

Thou art indeed just, Lord, if I contend. Thou Art Indeed Just, Lord. Gerard Manley Hopkins. BrAP; InvLi; MoBrPo; NAEL-6v2; NAEL-7v2; NAMCP V.1; NoAM; NoP-4; NoP-5; SacPr; TFi; WaAnP

Thou art love's victim; and must die. Richard Crashaw. EroLit *Fr.* Hymn to the Name and Hono[u]r of the Admirable Saint[e] Teresa, A.

Thou art not near me, but I see Thine eyes. I Love Thee. Josephine D. Henderson Heard. CBWP-4

Thou art not, Penshurst, built to envious show. To Penshurst. Ben Jonson. BASC; CABP; NAEL-6v1; NAEL-7v1; NoP-4; NoP-5; NOSC; OxBEV; PBRV; TFi; WaAnP

Thou Art the Sky. Rabindranath Tagore. OBMV *Fr.* Gitanjali.

Thou art the star for which all evening waits. Aldebaran at Dusk. George Sterling. TCAPo

Thou art the Way. I Am the Way. Alice Thompson Meynell. OBMV

Thou art; there is no stay but in Thy love. Rock, The. Jones Very. InvLi

Thou art to all lost love the best. To the Willow-Tree. Robert Herrick. OBEV

Thou art weary, weary, weary. Witch's Chant, A. James Hogg. NOBRP

Thou as laborious, as thy master kind. Nicolas Boileau-Despéaux. OBGa *Fr.* Epistle to My Gardener.

Thou bay-crowned living One that o'er the bay-crowned Dead art bowing. Elizabeth Barrett Browning. VWP

Thou bearst the bottle, I the bag (oh Lord). Bottle, The. Ralph Knevet. ChIV-2

Thou beauteous off-spring of a syre as fair. On a Sunbeam. Thomas Heyrick. NOSC

Thou Black, wherein all colours are compos'd. Another Sonnet to Black It Self [*or* Itself]. Edward Herbert, 1st Baron Herbert of Cherbury. NoP-5

Thou bleedest, my poor Heart! and thy distress. Samuel Taylor Coleridge. CenSon; GSo *Fr.* Effusions.

Thou Blind Man's Mark. Sir Philip Sidney. HeIP-4; NAEL-6v1; NAEL-7v1

Thou blind man's mark, thou fool's self-chosen snare [*Wr.* considered Sonnet CIX *of* Astrophil *and* Stella]. Thou Blind Man's Mark. Sir Philip Sidney. HeIP-4; NAEL-6v1; NAEL-7v1

Thou blossom bright with autumn dew. To the Fringed Gentian. William Cullen Bryant. APN-1

Thou brimming river, full, how full. Detroit River. Constance Fenimore Woolson. APN-2

Thou Canst Not Boast of Fortune's Store. Richard Brinsley Sheridan. IrLP *Fr.* Duenna, The.

Thou canst not die whilst any zeal[e] abound. Samuel Daniel. NoSic *Fr.* Sonnets to Delia.

Thou canst not prove that thou art body alone. Ancient Sage, The. Alfred Tennyson. SacPr

Thou comest! all is said without a word. Elizabeth Barrett Browning. CenSon *Fr.* Sonnets from the Portuguese.

Thou comest, Autumn, heralded by the rain. Autumn. Henry Wadsworth Longfellow. APN-1

Thou cursed cock, with thy perpetual noise. On a Cock at Rochester. Sir Charles Sedley. NOSC; NPeEn; OBCoV

Thou daughter of the royal line. Ninth Canticle, The. George Wither. ChIV-1

Thou dearest object of my fondest love. Ardelia to Flavia, an Epistle. Charlotte Lennox. PoBW

Thou Didst Delight My Eyes. Robert Bridges. MoBrPo

Thou Didst Say Me. Miriam Waddington. BrAP

Thou doggèd Cineas, hated like a dog. Sir John Davies. DiBP *Fr.* Epigrams.

Thou dost establish—and our hearts receive—. John Addington Symonds. CAGL *Fr.* Love and Death: A Symphony.

Thou dost not heed my lay. (LL) Mother to Her Waking Infant, A. Joanna Baillie. CABP; NoP-5; WaAnP; WoRP

Thou dost reign on high. O Come to My Heart, Lord Jesus. Emily E S Elliott. SacPr

Thou dravest love from thee, who dravest Me. (LL) Hound of Heaven, The. Francis Thompson. CABP; ChIV-2; InvLi; MoBrPo; NAEL-6v2; NAEL-7v2; OBMV; SacPr; TFi

Thou ermined judge, pull off that sable cap! *Unknown.* CAGL *Fr.* Don Leon.

Thou fair-hair'd [*or* fair-haired] angel of the evening. To the Evening Star. William Blake. GSo; NAEL-6v2; NAEL-7v2; NoP-4; NoP-5; NPeEn; TFi

Thou far-fled pasture, long evanished scene. John Clare. NPBRoP *Fr.* Helpstone.

Thou first and worst disturber of man's rest. (LL) On a Cock at Rochester. Sir Charles Sedley. NOSC; NPeEn; OBCoV

Thou flimsy, showy, melancholy weed. (LL) To the Poppy. Anna Seward. CenSon; WoRP

Thou fool who treatest with the sword, and not. Liberty to M. le Diplomate. Sydney Thompson Dobell. OxBSo

Thou foolish bird, of feathers proud. On a Peacock. Thomas Heyrick. OWoS

Thou Gaia Art I. Heide Göttner-Abendroth. HW

Thou hadst breathed joy in earth and in thy kind. (LL) To Christina Rossetti. Michael Field. NAEL-7v2; VWP

Thou happy, happy elf! Parental Ode to My Son, Aged Three Years and Five Months, A. Thomas Hood. OBCoV

Thou happy, happy elf! Thomas Hood. OBCoV *Fr.* Domestic Poems.

Thou hast a charmed cup O Fame! Woman and Fame. Felicia Dorothea Hemans. ViWPN; VWP

Thou hast a sister by the mother's side. William Shakespeare. OxAEP-1 *Fr.* Antony and Cleopatra.

Thou hast been where the rocks of coral grow. Diver, The. Felicia Dorothea Hemans. TreFP

Thou hast been wrong'd, I think old age. Old Age. Caroline Clive. VWP

Thou hast begun well, Roe, which stand well too. To Sir Thomas Roe. Ben Jonson. BASC

Thou Hast Blessed the Work of His Hands. Bin Ramke. RoV

Thou hast done well, perhaps. Dark Side, The. Adelaide Anne Procter. SacPr

Thou hast filled me a golden cup. To Christina Rossetti. Dora Greenwell. VWP

Thou hast loved and thou hast suffer'd! To a Wandering Female Singer. Felicia Dorothea Hemans. ViWPN; VWP

Thou hast made me, and shall thy work[e] decay? John Donne. GSo; InvLi; NAEL-6v1; NAEL-7v1; NoP-4; NoP-5; NOSC; OxAEP-1 *Fr.* Holy Sonnets.

Thou hast not left the rough-barked tree to grow. I Was Sick and in Prison. Jones Very. ColAP; SacPr

Thou hast thy calling to some palace-floor. Elizabeth Barrett Browning. CenSon; OxAEP-2; VWP *Fr.* Sonnets from the Portuguese.

Thou hast thy record in the monarch's hall. Memorial of Mary, The. Felicia Dorothea Hemans. CenSon

Thou hermit, haunter of the lonely glen. Sand Martin, The. John Clare. NPeEn

Thou hide thy face? (LL) Speak. James Wright. NoP-4; NoP-5

Thou ill-formed offspring of my feeble brain. Author to Her Book, The. Anne Bradstreet. BASC; BrAP; ColAP; EMWP; MakPoe; NAAL-3; NAAL-5; NAAPv.1; NALW; NoP-4; NoP-5; OxBoAm; TCAPo; WaAnP

Thou in the garden, I in paradise. (LL) To Amanda Walking in the Garden. N. Hookes. NOSC; OBGa

Thou Joy of my Life. Sidney Godolphin. OxBEV

Thou king of terrors with thy gastly eyes. Fig for Thee, Oh! Death, A. Edward Taylor. NAAL-3

Thou knowest my praise of nature most sincere. William Cowper. NAEL-6v1; NAEL-7v1 *Fr.* Task, The.

Thou knowst I lov'd thee well. Martin Parker. PBRV *Fr.* Cupid's Wrongs Vindicated.

Thou large-brained woman and large-hearted man. To George Sand: A Desire. Elizabeth Barrett Browning. NAEL-6v2; NAEL-7v2; NALW; PoBW; VWP

Thou leadest, O God! All's well with Thy troopers that follow. (LL) Wild Ride, The. Louise Imogen Guiney. ColAP; RACG; TCAPo

Thou little friend who, in my heart. Lost Friend, A. Henry Charles Leonard. DiBP

Thou lovely sorceress of the witching night. To the Moon. Anna Maria Jones. CenSon

Thou Lovest Me. Josephine D. Henderson Heard. CBWP-4

Thou mastering me. Wreck of the Deutschland, The. Gerard Manley Hopkins. NAMCP V.1; NoAM; OxAEP-2; OxBEV; WaAnP

Thou mastering me. Gerard Manley Hopkins. NPeEn *Fr.* Wreck of the Deutschland, The.

Thou mayst love on, through love's eternity. (LL) Elizabeth Barrett Browning. CenSon; GSo; HeIP-4; LW; OBEV; OxAEP-2; OxBSo *Fr.* Sonnets from the Portuguese.

Thou mighty gulf, insatiate cormorant. John Marston. NoSic *Fr.* Scourge of Villainy [*or* Villanie], The.

Thou monstrous gilt and rainbow-tinted thing. New Organ, The. Josephine D. Henderson Heard. CBWP-4

Thou only Good! Eternal All! Samuel Davies. SacPr

Thou, paw-paw-paw; thou, glurd; thou, spotted. Adam's Task. John Hollander. NAMCP V.2; NIL-7; NIP-4; NoP-4; NoP-5; OxBoAm; WoPoe

Thou Pleiad of the lyric world. Adelina Patti. Adah Isaacs Menken. CBWP-1

Thou poisonous laurel leaf, that in the soil. Sonnet. Frances Anne Kemble. SWaP

Thou readest, but each lettered word can give. Eye and Ear, The. Jones Very. APN-1

Thou retir'st to endless rest. (LL) Grasshopper, The. Abraham Cowley. BASC; NOSC; OBVE; OxAEP-1

Thou saidst that I alone thy Heart cou'd move. Catullus. OBVE

Thou sai'st I swore I lov'd thee best. Variety, The. John Dancer. NOSC

Thou, sand's dance, knots and thousands. This is Still Life. Marla Jernigan. AnSo

Thou seest the Hills candied with Snow. Horace. OBVE Fr. Odes.

Thou seest, we are not all alone unhappie. William Shakespeare. OxBEV Fr. As You Like It.

Thou shalt be judge how I do spend my time [or tyme]. (LL) Sir Thomas Wyatt. NoSic; NPeEn; OBSV; OBVE Fr. Satires.

Thou shalt have one God only; who. Latest Decalogue, The. Arthur Hugh Clough. BrAP; CABP; ChIV-1; NAEL-6v2; NAEL-7v2; NoP-4; NoP-5; NPeEn; OBSV; OxBEV; SacPr; TFi; WeW-3; WoPoe

Thou shalt not be the fool of loss. (LL) Alfred Tennyson. CtM; NAEL-6v2; NAEL-7v2 Fr. In Memoriam A. H. H.

Thou shalt not laugh in this leaf, Muse, nor they. John Donne. OBSV Fr. Satires.

Thou shalt the mountain move; be strong in me. Mountain, The. Jones Very. NCAP

Thou show'st thy beauty unto all the men. Wasted. Mary Elizabeth Coleridge. ViWPN

Thou silent herald of Time's silent flight! To the Sun-Dial. John Quincy Adams. APN-1

Thou snowy farm[e] with thy five tenements! Elinda's [or Ellinda's] Glove. Richard Lovelace. NOSC; CavPo

Thou sorrow, venom elf[e]. Upon a Spider Catching a Fly. Edward Taylor. ColAP; NAAPv.1; NoP-4; NoP-5; OxBEV; OxBoAm; TCAPo; WaAnP

Thou still unravished [or unravish'd] bride of quietness. Ode on a Grecian Urn. John Keats. BLPJKO; BrAP; ClHu; HeIP-4; MakPoe; NAEL-6v2; NAEL-7v2; NAWM-7v2; NIP-4; NOBRP; NoP-5; NPBRoP; OBEV; OxBEV; TFi; WaAnP

Thou stranger, which for Rome in Rome here seekest. Joachim Du Bellay. OBVE Fr. Ruins of Rome.

Thou Swell. Lorenz Hart. ReLy

Thou that loved once now loves no more. Answer, The. Sir Robert Aytoun. NOSC

Thou, that where Freedom's sacred fountains play. Sonnet to France On Her Present Exertions. Anna Laetitia Barbauld. RWP

Thou thing of years departed! Image in Lava, The. Felicia Dorothea Hemans. CABP; NOBRP

Thou two-faced year, Mother of Change and Fate. 1492. Emma Lazarus. APN-2; NAAPv.1; OxBoAm; SWaP

Thou vexed Atlantic, who hast lately seen. To Mrs. Hayley, On her Voyage to America. 1784. William Hayley. CenSon

Thou walkest with me as the spirit-light. Mathilde Blind. ViWPN Fr. Love in Exile.

Thou wast all that [or that all] to me, love. To One in Paradise. Edgar Allan Poe. NCAP; OBEV; OxBoAm

Thou Were My Ain Thing, An. Allan Ramsay. OxAEP-1

Thou wert the morning star among the living. To Stella. Plato. OBVE, tr. by Percy Bysshe Shelley

Thou which art I, ('tis nothing to be so[e]). Storm[e], The. John Donne. NAEL-6v1; NAEL-7v1; NoSic

Thou who didst hang upon a barren tree. Long Barren. Christina Georgina Rossetti. ViWPN

Thou who dost all my worldly thoughts employ. Verses Written on Her Death-bed at Bath to Her Husband in London. Mary Monck. LW

Thou who hast slept all night upon the storm. To the Man-of-War Bird. Walt Whitman. APN-1

Thou who never canst err, for Thyself art the Way. Night Journey. Alfred Noyes. SacPr

Thou, who with all the poet's genuine rage. Richard Polwhele. NOBRP Fr. Unsex'd Females, The.

Thou, who wouldst wear the name. Poet, The. William Cullen Bryant. NAAL-3; NCAP

Thou, whom the former precepts have. Superliminare. George Herbert. NOSC

Thou! whose impassion'd face. Picture of Sappho, The. Caroline Elizabeth Norton. VWP

Thou with thy Savior art in endless bliss. (LL) In Memory of My Dear Grandchild Anne Bradstreet Who Deceased June 20, 1669, Being Three Years and Seven Months Old. Anne Bradstreet. InoFa; NAAL-3

Thou wouldst not part thy spoil. To 'A Certain Rich Man'. Alice Thompson Meynell. ChIV-2

Thou wretched man, whom I discover, borne. George Chapman. NOSC Fr. Tears of Peace, The.

Thou wretched thing of blood. John Webster. OxBEV Fr. Duchess of Malfi, The.

Thou wringest, with thy invisible hand, the foam. Wind, The. Thomas Holley Chivers. APN-1

Thou youngest virgin-daughter of the skies. To the Pious Memory of the Accomplished [or Accomplisht] Young Lady, Mrs. Anne Killigrew, [Excellent in the Two Sister-Arts of Poesie and Painting. An Ode]. John Dryden. BrAP; CABP; NAEL-6v1

Though a seeker since my birth. Garland of Precepts, A. Phyllis McGinley. NBLV

Though age at my elbow has taken his stand. Public Spirit of the Women, The. Unknown. NAAPv.1

Though aging and abused still half benign. Red Lights of Plenty, The. Tony Harrison. RSaN

Though all men should desert you. In a Late Hour. James McAuley. BMAP

Though all of you consort now underground. (LL) In Memoriam Francis Ledwidge. Seamus Heaney. NAMCP V.2; NoAM

Though all the buddhas. Kyunyŏ, Great Master. CATKP Fr. Eleven Poems on the Ten Vows of the Universally Worthy Bodhisattva.

Though All the Fates Should Prove Unkind. Henry David Thoreau. TCAPo

Though all the lower world should ransacked be. Chapter IV. Elizabeth Singer Rowe. PEW

Though all thy gestures and discourses be. Innocent III, The. Abraham Cowley. BASC

Though / Already / Perhaps / However. One Size Fits All: a Critical Essay. David Lehman. OBCoV

Though authors are a dreadful clan. I Missed His Book, but I Read His Name. John Updike. NoP-4; NoP-5

Though beauty be the mark of praise. Elegy, An. Ben Jonson. NoP-4; NoP-5; OBEV

Though buds still speak in hints. Field-Glasses. Andrew Young. EdScPo

Though Caesar falling, shew'd no sign of fear. Caesar and Brutus. Anne Finch, Countess of Winchilsea. EMWP

Though Caesar stop a bunghole now. Samuel Hoffenstein. AmWit Fr. Songs about Life and Brighter Things Yet.

Though Clock, / To tell how night draw[e]s hence, I've none. His Grange, or Private Wealth. Robert Herrick. BASC; CavPo

Though countless as the Grains of Sand. Boethius. OBVE Fr. Consolation of Philosophy, The ("De Consolacione Philosophie").

Though cruel seas like mountains fill the bay. Apple Island. Robert Graves. EmeKit

Though day is just breaking. Angling, a Day. Galway Kinnell. MoASP

Though faithful to a proverb we regard. Robert Bloomfield. DiBP Fr. Farmer's Boy, The.

Though frost and snow locked [or lock'd] from mine eyes. To Saxham. Thomas Carew. BASC; CavPo

Though giving pleasure to many. Roger McGough. NewEx

Though he is dead now and his miracle. Robert Wilson. Michael Collier. OPRER

Though he looks almost exactly the way. Peace Studies. Lynne McMahon. ExTi

Though he was busy with war. Various authors. CATKP Fr. Songs of Flying Dragons.

Though he was young, Kao. At Hu-k'ou, Mourning for Kao Po-tsu. Ching An. CSKM, tr. by Jerome P. Seaton

Though her lips are redder than the raspberries. (LL) Berry Picking. Irving Layton. HeIP-4; NIP-4; NoP-4; NoP-5

Though her mother told her. Leda and the Swan. Oliver St. John Gogarty. IrLP

Though here no towering mountain-steep. Our Island Home. Charles Timothy Brooks. APN-1

Though his wit and talent did not fail. Trial of Renard, The. Unknown. NAWM-7v1, tr. by Patricia Terry

Though I am an ugly clay pot. Kim Namjo. CAMKP Fr. Love's Cursive.

Though I Am Young [and Cannot Tell]. Ben Jonson. NoP-4; NoP-5; WaAnP

Though I be strange, sweet friend, be thou not so. Court Lady Addresses Her Lover, A. Edward, 17th Earl of Oxford De Vere. NoSic

Though I get home how late, how late! Return, The. Emily Dickinson. MoAmPo

Though I go to you. Ono no Komachi. WoPoe, tr. by Helen Craig McCullough

Though I have the gift of tongues. Word, The. Alden Nowlan. BrAP

Though I have touched her flesh of moons. Modern Craft. Hart Crane. CAGL

Though I know that we meet ev'ry night. With a Song in My Heart. Lorenz Hart. ReLy

Though I look like you. Hand Me Down Blues. Calvin Forbes. GT

Though I love this travelling life and yearn. Rooms. Kathleen Jamie. MoWP

Though I must live here, and by force. To My Mistress[e] in My Absence. Thomas Carew. NOSC

Though I sang in my chains like the sea. (LL) Fern Hill. Dylan Thomas. AmFaPo; AngWePo; BrAP; CABP; ChAP; ClHu; EMP; GPTC; HarvBoo; HeIP-4; IPoFL; MoBrPo; NAEL-6v2; NAEL-7v2; NAMCP V.2; NIL-7; NIP-4; NoAM; NoP-4; NoP-5; OBWVE; PoPoPo; SoSe-8; TCAWP; TFi; TRP; WaAnP

Though I Speak with the Tongues of Men and Angels. Bible, *N.T.* BLPJKO *Fr.* First Corinthians.

Though I think I'd like to go to France. On a Trip. Hagiwara Sakutaro. CAoMJL1, *tr. by* Hiroaki Sato

Though I thy Mithridates were. James Joyce. NoAM

Though I'm just a wood Priapus. *Unknown.* PriapPo *Fr.* Priapus Poems, The.

Though I'm left without a penny. Never Gonna Dance. Dorothy Fields. ReLy

Though I'm modest as most. Available Now: Archaic Torsos of Both Sexes. Gregory Orr. PoA 2002

Though in my heart. Lady Otomo no Sakanoé. ArkPo, *tr. by* Edwin A. Cranston

Though in should flags. Clark Coolidge. AHA

Though in them he heard the weird symmetry. It Didn't Begin with Horned Owls Hooting at Noon. Kevin Stein. IllVoic

Though it all floods back to you. Massive Stoner. Michael Savitz. FreRad

Though it is not cold. Little Travel Story, A. David Oliveira. GeoHom

Though it may look like (*Write* it!) like disaster. (LL) One Art. Elizabeth Bishop. AmFaPo; APT-2; BLPJKO; BrAP; CAP-8; EMP; HarvBoo; IJHIL; MakPoe; NAAL-5; NALW; NAMCP V.2; NoAM; NoP-4; NoP-5; OxBoAm; PoetW; PoPoPo; SoSe-8; StAl; VCAP; WaAnP

Though it were ten thousand mile! (LL) Red, Red Rose, A. Robert Burns. BrAP; ChAP; CtM; GoPo; HeIP-4; ITBLP; NAEL-6v2; NAEL-7v2; NePenScot; NIL-7; NIP-4; NOBRP; NoP-4; NoP-5; NPBRoP; NPeEn; OxAEP-2; OxBEV; PoPoPo; TFi; UV; WaAnP

Though it's a fickle age. Ain't Misbehavin'. Andy Razaf. ReLy

Though it's common belief. How I Got Born. Cornelius Eady. FuFl

Though it's far away will you follow me down. Far Rockaway. Iwan Llwyd. ATSWP, *tr. by* Robert Minhinnick

Though its map is drenched with watery names. Moon, The. Martha Silano. AmPoNex

Though I've an Olympic swimmer's chest. Lines to His New Instructress. Maurice Riordan. NIrP

Though jealous exclusion may tremble to own us. Envoy. May Kendall. ViWPN

Though king-bred rage, with lawless uproar rude. Samuel Taylor Coleridge. CenSon

Though leaves are many, the root is one. Coming of Wisdom with Time, The. William Butler Yeats. HarvBoo; SoSe-8

Though loath to grieve. Ode, Inscribed to W. H. Channing. Ralph Waldo Emerson. AmWaPo; APN-1; ColAP; NAAL-3; NAAPv.1; NCAP; NoP-4; NoP-5; OxBoAm; TCAPo; WaAnP

Though love has grown cold. Sadakichi Hartmann. NAAPv.1 *Fr.* Tanka.

Though many men had passed the ford, not one. Fight with a Water-Spirit. Norman Cameron. OxBSo

Though my little daughter owns an Ideal farmyard. Ideal. Carol Muske-Dukes. AmAlph

Though my mother was already two years dead. Long Distance II. Tony Harrison. PoCu; StAl

Though my position is of low degree. Porter's Love Song to a Chambermaid, A. Andy Razaf. ReLy

Though my small incomes never can afford. Jane Colman Turell. TCAPo *Fr.* Invitation Into the Country, In Imitation of Horace, An.

Though my stomach is still in Alabama pig / pens. (LL) King: April 4, 1968. Gerald William Barrax. ESEAA; GT

Though naked trees seem dead to sight. Hopeless Desire Soon Withers and Dies. A. W. NoSic

Though never claimed by us within my hearing. (LL) Swimmers, The. Allen Tate. APT-2; FuPo; MoAmPo; NAAPv.2; NAMCP V.1; NoAM; NoP-5

Though night after night. Takuan. ZenPo, *tr. by* Takashi Ikemoto and Lucien Stryk

Though no blossoms cluster. Mrs. Mary Furman Weston Byrd. Mary Weston Fordham. CBWP-2

Though not human, the dead language of the insect. Pendulum, The. Norman Dubie. AmAlph

Though now and then your problems fall. When in Rome (I Do As the Romans Do). Carolyn Leigh. ReLy

Though on the day your hard blue eyes met mine. Heritage. Dorothea MacKellar. NOBAu

Though our envoy, Su Wu, is gone, body and soul. Temple of Su Wu, The. Wen T'ing-yün. CCL1, *tr. by* Witter Bynner

Though our thoughts often, we ourselves. Charles Reznikoff. APT-2

Though poverty's no stain. Anna Petrovna Bunina. ARWW, *tr. by* Sibelan Forrester

Though prejudice perhaps my mind befogs. I Think I Know No Finer Things than Dogs. Hally Carrington Brent. ITBLP

Though pretty, it rarely worked, lining seduction. Carpe Diem. Rodney Jones. LPSFW

Though, Priapus, you're stuck with a well-stiffened cock. *Unknown.* PriapPo *Fr.* Priapus Poems, The.

Though regions far [*or* farr] divided. Song: "Though Regions Farr Divided." Aurelian Townshend. NOSC

Though seven times, or seventy times seven. Women of Jericho, The. Phyllis McGinley. ChIV-1

Though she couldn't know it at the time. Civil War, The. Stephanie Farrow. FiBr

Though she is deaf. Peter Levitt. WhBo

Though she was born late in their lives. Autobiography in Third Person. Betsy Sholl. ACAMVP

Though sick, I rise at dawn. Poem for Mr. Li in Early Spring. Tu Fu [*or* Du Fu]. CrYelRi, *tr. by* Sam Hamill

Though since thy first sad entrance by Just Abel's blood. Death. Henry Vaughan. AngWePo

Though skilled in Latin and in Greek. To a New England Poet. Philip Freneau. NAAL-3

Though splinted a controlling thumb. Oiled Sweater. John Wilkinson. VaPo

Though stands low on the mountain. Autumn Aspens: Cumbres Pass. Reg Saner. PoCoUp

Though starlings imitate me. Michael Henry. NewEx

Though still she kept the form and voice of Mentor. (LL) Odyssey, The. Homer. NAWM-5v1; NAWM-7v1, *tr. by* Robert Fitzgerald

Though storms and tempest mark thy gloomy reign. Written in a Winter's Morning. Mrs. B. Finch. CenSon

Though sun rubbed honey slow. By the Nape. Sandra Alcosser. ExTi

Though Tennyson the Poet King. James Madison Bell. CBCWP *Fr.* Poem Entitled the Day and the War, A.

Though Tennyson, the poet king. James Madison Bell. CBCWP *Fr.* Poem Entitled the Day and the War, A.

Though that was not what Berkeley meant at all. (LL) Fountain, The. Donald Davie. NoP-4; NoP-5

Though the Clerk of the Weather insist. Pebbles. Herman Melville. NCAP

Though the cunning of the Indian and the Zulu's thirst for blood. Claflin's Alumni. Lizelia Augusta Jenkins Moorer. CBWP-3

Though the day of my destiny's over. Stanzas to Augusta. Lord Byron. NPBRoP

Though the little clouds ran southward still, the quiet autumnal. Autumn Evening. Robinson Jeffers. ChAP

Though the nuns had dubbed us Crusaders. Hurley High. Paul Zarzyski. SwNoth

Though the road lead nowhere. Song of Degrees, A. Howard Nemerov. TaR

Though the road turn at last. Prisoners. Denise Levertov. NoAM; VCAP

Though the time seemed. brken promises. Sibby Anderson-Thompkins. InTrad

Though the unseen may vanish, though insight fails. Plain Song for Comadre, A. Richard Wilbur. NoP-5

Though the walkers walk alone. Path, The. Konstantin Iakovlevich Vanshenkin. TCRusP, *tr. by* Daniel Weissbort

Though the willows bent down to shelter us where we played. Doll. Josephine Miles. FTtHH; NALW

Though the world fall apart, surely ye shall prevail. (LL) Carthusians. Ernest Dowson. NAEL-6v2; NAEL-7v2

Though the world has slipped and gone. Lullaby. Dame Edith Sitwell. NALW

Though the Xhosa owned the coast. From the Mouth of the Gxara. Carole Boston Weatherford. BtF

Though there are wild dogs. Orpheus and Eurydice. Geoffrey Hill. TRP

Though they say it's great to see a beauty. Beauty, A. Kim Suyŏng. CAMKP, *tr. by* Young-Jun Lee

Though this body, I know. Kino Sadamaru. EMJL, *tr. by* Burton Watson

Though this frame should die and die. Chŏng Mongju. CATKP, *tr. by* Richard Rutt

Though this might take me a little time. (LL) More Loving One, The. W. H. Auden. ItP; OxBoAm

Though thousands traipse round Wordsworth's Lakeland shrine. Remains. Tony Harrison. FaBoVe

Though to the vilest things beneath the moon. Arthur Hugh Clough. OxBSo *Fr.* Blank Misgivings of a Creature Moving About in Worlds Not Realized.

Though to think / Rejoiceth me. Love Song. Margot Ruddock. OBMV

Though truth be guild in any mould, and talents all for use. Morgan Llwyd. AngWePo *Fr.* 1648.

Though unable to imagine. Mezuzah. Alan Shapiro. TaR

Though we thought it, Doña Carolina did not die.　Dream of Husbands, A.　Alberto A. Ríos.　NoAM

Though with no lily [*or* lilie], stay with me! (LL)　Cock-crowing.　Henry Vaughan.　BASC; NAEL-7v1; NPeEn; PBRV

Though you be absent here, I needs must say.　Abraham Cowley.　OxAEP-1 *Fr.* Mistress, The.

Though you do anything, he thinks no ill. (LL)　William Shakespeare.　CAGL; NoSic; OBEV *Fr.* Sonnets.

Though you fled the Capital for the woods.　Remembering Priest Quang Tri.　Doan Van Kham.　WoPoe, *tr. by* Nguyen Ngoc Bich

Though you had never possessed me.　One O'Clock at Night.　Mina Loy.　OxBoAm

Though you have never possessed me.　Three Moments in Paris.　Mina Loy.　PFTM-1

Though you in your hermitage.　To My Father Norman Alone in the Blue Mountains.　Jack Lindsay.　NOBAu

Though you made me think.　*Unknown.*　WoPoe *Fr.* Kokin Shu.

Though you've decided that our love is wrong.　Guilty.　Gustave Kahn.　ReLy

Though I seem straunge sweete freende be thou not so.　Anne Vavasour Field.　EMWP

Thought.　D. H. Lawrence.　OxBEV

Thought.　Ahmad Nadeem Qasmi.　WoPoe, *tr. by* Raja Changez Sultan

Thought ("Of obedience, faith, adhesiveness.")　Walt Whitman.　HHAm

Thought, A.　Eliza Cook.　STuOW *Fr.* There is Nothing in Vain.

Thought, The.　Edward Herbert, 1st Baron Herbert of Cherbury.　AngWePo

Thought, The.　Michael Palmer.　WoBe

Thought, The.　William Brighty Rands.　OBEV

Thought, A [*or* Sunshine].　Eliza Cook.　STuOW

Thought about holy skirts—to tune of "*Wheels are growing on rose*".　Holy Skirts.　Else Von Freytag-Loringhoven.　PFTM-1

Thought about *my* place in the long war, A.　Gambier.　Joe Osterhaus.　AmPoNex; NAPBL

Thought at Walden, A.　Henrietta Cordelia Ray.　CBWP-3

Thought beneath so slight a film, The.　Emily Dickinson.　TCAPo

Thought bounded / rigid edges glued.　Crossing.　Diane Ward.　FTOS

Thought clambers up.　William Carlos Williams.　NAMCP V.1 *Fr.* Paterson.

Thought flashed 'cross a kindly mind, A.　Kindly Deed, A.　Priscilla Jane Thompson.　CBWP-2

Thought for a Lonely Death-Bed, A.　Elizabeth Barrett Browning.　ViWPN

Thought from an Italian Poet.　Felicia Dorothea Hemans.　RWP

Thought from Ruddigore, A.　William Schwenck Gilbert.　OBCoV *Fr.* Ruddigore.

Thought, I love thought.　Thought.　D. H. Lawrence.　OxBEV

Thought looking out on thought.　Opening of Eyes.　Laura Riding Jackson.　OxBoAm

Thought o' Mary Morison, The. (LL)　Mary Morison.　Robert Burns.　NePenScot; OBEV

Thought of a Briton on the Subjugation of Switzerland.　William Wordsworth.　*See* Thought[s] of a Briton on the Subjugation of Switzerland.

Thought of a dear friend: 1:54 a.m.　Captain's Log.　Todd Colby.　HeMarv

Thought of Death, A.　Thomas Flatman.　NOSC

Thought of Lake Ontario, A.　Henrietta Cordelia Ray.　CBWP-3

Thought of mother haunts my memory, The.　Mother.　Kristina Rungano.　HAWP

Thought of our past years in me doth breed, The.　William Wordsworth.　SacPr *Fr.* Ode: Intimations of Immortality from Recollections of Early Childhood.

Thought on My Sickness, A.　Chunghur Hyujung.　BecRai, *tr. by* Kim Daljin, Kim Won-Chung and Christopher Merrill

Thought thrusts up, homely as a hyacinth.　Marilyn Hacker.　PoA 2002 *Fr.* Paragraphs from a Day-Book.

Thought went up my mind today, A.　Emily Dickinson.　TCAPo

Thought-Fox, The.　Ted Hughes.　BrAP; HeIP-4; MakPoe; NAMCP V.2; NoAM; NoP-5; NPeEn; StAl; WaAnP

Thoughts.　Maggie Pogue Johnson.　CBWP-4

Thoughts.　Jacqueline Kennedy Onassis.　BLPJKO

Thoughts.　Amanda Ros.　VerBaPo

Thoughts.　Tu Fu [*or* Du Fu].
　1.　NDACCP, *tr. by* David Hinton

Thoughts about Sari's Jump.　Devorah Amir.　DTA, *tr. by* Miriyam Glazer

Thoughts about the Person from Porlock.　Stevie Smith.　NAEL-6v2; NAEL-7v2; NAMCP V.1; NoAM; NoP-4; NoP-5

Thoughts After Ruskin.　Elma Mitchell.　EdScPo; MoWP; NPeEn; StAl

Thoughts and Recollections.　Duo Duo. *tr. by* Gregory Lee and John Cayley
　When the People Stand Up out of the Hard Cheese.　AF

Thoughts arise endlessly.　Daichi.　ZenPo, *tr. by* Takashi Ikemoto and Lucien Stryk

Thoughts Before Dawn.　John Balaban.　AmWaPo

Thoughts Breathing in a Blizzard.　"Antler."　PoCoUp

Thoughts came to him like long lines of freight, The.　Yehuda Amichai.　FIT, *tr. by* Robert Friend

Thoughts drifting through the fat black woman's head while having a full bubble bath.　Grace Nichols.　MoWP

Thoughts During an Air Raid.　Stephen Spender.　MoBrPo

Thoughts during Sickness.　Felicia Dorothea Hemans.　Remembrance of Nature.　NPBRoP

Thought's End.　Léonie Adams.　MoAmPo

Thoughts from a 747.　Dana Gilkes.　BtF

Thoughts from a Bar Stool.　Deirdre May.　BRtP

Thoughts from Underground.　Margaret Atwood.　BrAP

Thoughts in a Black Taxi.　Sinéad Morrissey.　MFPA

Thoughts in a Garden.　Andrew Marvell. *See* Garden, The.

Thoughts in Exile.　Su Tung-p'o.　NDACCP, *tr. by* Kenneth Rexroth

Thoughts in Midnight Hours.　Fanny Crosby.　SWaP

Thoughts in Night Quiet.　Li Po.　NDACCP, *tr. by* David Hinton

Thoughts in Separation.　Alice Thompson Meynell.　OxBSo

Thoughts in the Library.　Mihály Vörösmarty.　IQMS, *tr. by* Hymen H. Hart

Thoughts march.　Ear Injured by Hearing Things, An.　Steve Jonas.　EGAG

Thought[s] of a Briton on the Subjugation of Switzerland.　William Wordsworth.　UV

(Thought of a Briton on the Subjugation of Switzerland.)　CABP

Thoughts of a dry brain in a dry season. (LL)　Gerontion.　T. S. Eliot.　APT-1; ColAP; NAAL-5; NAAPv.2; NAMCP V.1; NoAM; NPeEn; OxAEP-2; TCAPo; TFi; WaAnP

Thoughts of a Solitary Farmhouse.　Franz Wright.　AmAlph

Thoughts of a Young Girl.　John Ashbery.　WaAnP

Thoughts of Boyhood.　John Lloyd.　AngWePo

Thoughts of Death.　Sterling Allen Brown.　PtR

Thoughts of God, The.　Frances Ridley Havergal.
　"They say there is a hollow, safe and still."　SacPr

Thoughts of Phena.　Thomas Hardy.　HarvBoo; NoP-4; NPeEn

Thoughts on a Bird.　Ch'ŏn Yanghũi.　EcSo, *tr. by* Aimee N. Kwon

Thoughts on a Night Journey.　Tu Fu [*or* Du Fu].　TAPaP; WaAnP, *tr. by* Arthur Sze

Thoughts on Eyes Growing Dim: Presented to Chŏn Iji.　Yi Kyubo.　CATKP, *tr. by* Kevin O'Rourke

Thoughts on Happiness.　Francis Homfray.　AngWePo

Thoughts on Innocence.　Olga Nolla.　TANSG, *tr. by* Paula Vega

Thoughts on Johannesburg's Centenary.　Lionel Abrahams.　TSAP

Thoughts on my sick-bed.　Dorothy Wordsworth.　NAEL-7v2; PEW

Thoughts on One's Head.　William Meredith.　VCAP

Thoughts on the Works of Providence.　Phillis Wheatley.　ColAP; InvLi; NAAL-3; NAAL-5
　"As reason's pow'rs by day our God disclose."　SacPr

Thoughts standing still, like.　Tomas Tranströmer.　WoBe *Fr.* Haiku.

Thoughts that burned and glowed within, The. (LL)　Fire of Drift-Wood, The.　Henry Wadsworth Longfellow.　APN-1; ITBLP; MakPoe; NAAL-3; NCAP; OxBoAm

Thoughts that do often lie too deep for tears. (LL)　Ode: Intimations of Immortality from Recollections of Early Childhood.　William Wordsworth.　BrAP; HeIP-4; NAEL-6v2; NAEL-7v2; NAWM-7v2; NOBRP; NoP-4; NoP-5; NPeEn; OBEV; OxBEV; PoPoPo; TFi; TRP; WaAnP

Thoughts, Traveling at Night.　Tu Fu [*or* Du Fu].　NDACCP, *tr. by* David Hinton

Thoughts While Broadcasting.　Ronald Frankau.　RWPCtW

Thoughts While Walking.　Rachel Wetzsteon.　ExTi

Thousand, A / Peaks arise in cold azure.　Sent to Zen Master Yun-Shui.　Chien Chang.　CSKM, *tr. by* Paul Hansen

Thousand apples you might put in your theories.　Sonnet.　Bernadette Mayer.　PmAP

Thousand bees were tensing, A.　Arbor 1937, The.　Susan Stewart.　ExTi

Thousand bones carry, now call home. (LL)　Quivira City Limits.　Kevin Young.　FuFl; NeAmPo

Thousand Character Classic, The.　Zhou Xingsi.
　Extracts.　CCL1, *tr. by* Elijah Coleman Bridgman

Thousand Chinese Dinners, A.　Robert Mezey.
　"From a thousand Chinese dinners, one cookie."　RaBo

Thousand Cranes, A.　Dale Ritterbusch.　AmWaPo

Thousand days great Beelzebub and Pope his son and fool, A.　Morgan Llwyd.　AngWePo *Fr.* 1648.

Thousand days of their lives. (LL)　Envelope, The.　Maxine W. Kumin.　CFP; NALW

Thousand doves, A.　*Unknown.*　WoPoe *Fr.* Two Pantuns.

Thousand guileless sheep have bled, A.　Song from the Bride of Smithfield.　Sylvia Townsend Warner.　MoBrPo

Thousand Hairy Savages, A.　Spike Milligan.　NBLV

Thousand Killed, A. Bernard Spencer. FaBoWar; OBWP

Thousand lines, A. Yosano Akiko. WoPoe *Fr.* Tangled Hair.

Thousand Marionettes, A. Sydney March. BtF

Thousand Martyrs, A. Aphra Behn. *See* Thousand Martyrs I Have Made, A.

Thousand Martyrs I Have Made, A. Aphra Behn. NPeEn
  (Thousand Martyrs, A.) NoP-4; NoP-5

Thousand miles and two world wars, A. Phoenix. Elizabeth Kay. Prnts

Thousand minstrels woke within me. Monadnoc. Ralph Waldo Emerson.

Thousand minutes came out of the tottering state, A. After Mahler. Ann
  Lauterbach. BAP-04

Thousand mountains without a bird, A. Liu Tsung-yüan. NDACCP, *tr. by*
  Kenneth Rexroth

Thousand mountains—no bird's flight, A. River Snow. Liu Tsung-yüan.
  ChinPo, *tr. by* Ye Weilian [*or* Yeh Wei-lien *or* Wai-lim Yip]

Thousand peaks: no more birds in flight, A. River Snow. Liu Tsung-yüan.
  NDACCP, *tr. by* David Hinton

Thousand strands, A. Yosano Akiko. ErotSp, *tr. by* Sam Hamill

Thousand streets of London gray, The. Sheep and the Goat, The. George
  Macdonald. SacPr

Thousand, ten thousand thoughts, A. Deathbed Song. Chunghur Hyujung.
  BecRai, *tr. by* Kim Daljin, Kim Won-Chung and Christopher Merrill

Thousand things, and yet nothing, The. Thinking of Impoverished Ancients.
  T'ao Ch'ien. GifTon, *tr. by* David Hinton

Thousand thousand worlds, A. To Show You All, on the First Morning of the
  Year. Ching An. CSKM, *tr. by* Jerome P. Seaton

Thousand times travelling over these fields, A. Millennium. Patricia Beer.
  HarvBoo

Thousand torments wait on love, A. Thousand Torments, A. Mary Robinson.
  NPBRoP

Thousand years from now, A. Extermination of the Jews, The. Marvin Bell.
  TaR

Thousand years, with God (the Scriptures say), A. On the Life of Man.
  Francis Quarles. ChIV-2

Thousands and thousands of hushed years ago. Silence. James Whitcomb
  Riley. GSo

Thousands arrive when a bird's about to fly. Gwyneth Lewis. NeBl

Thousands, lately, have asked me about my hair. Making a Statement. Dave
  Jeddie Smith. RoV

Thousands of images have suddenly brightened in the emptiness. Duo Duo.
  AF, *tr. by* Gregory Lee and John Cayley

Thousands of women hold me. Snapshots of the Chameleon Woman. Perla
  Schwartz. TANSG, *tr. by* Celeste Kostopulos-Cooperman

Thousands to sleep. (LL) Will You Be as Hard? Douglas Hyde. IrLP;
  OBMV, *tr. by* Augusta, Lady Gregory

Thow art pretty but unconstant. Lines in the Corner of a Manuscript.
  Unknown. FaBoVe

Thracian filly, why do you. Anacreon. SaLy, *tr. by* Diane Rayor

Thracian poet's song gets trees, rocks, The. Ovid. WoPoe *Fr.* Metamorphoses.

Thrall. Carolyn Kizer. CAP-8; GifTon; StAl

Thrash away, you'll hev to rattle. James Russell Lowell. AmWaPo *Fr.* Biglow
  Papers, The.

Thrasher. Karen Solie. OpeFie

Thrasher in the Willow by the Lake, The. Robert Pack. ColAP

Thrashing Doves, The. Jack Kerouac. PmAP

Thraso. Samuel Rowlands. NoSic

Thrawn water? Aye, owre thrawn to be aye thrawn! By Wauchopeside. Hugh
  MacDiarmid. OxAEP-2

Thread. Yousif al-Sa'igh. IrPoTo, *tr. by* Chuck Miller and Saadi A. Simawe

Thread. Catherine Lucy Czerkawska. LW

Thread of Life, The. Christina Georgina Rossetti.
  Aloof. OBEV
  (Verse I.) PEW
  Verse II. PEW
  Verse III. PEW

Thread of white maggots, A. Thread. Yousif al-Sa'igh. IrPoTo, *tr. by* Chuck
  Miller and Saadi A. Simawe

Thread pendulums. Olga's House. Natalia Toledo. RMCMP, *tr. by* Alberto
  A. Ríos.

Thread Suns. Paul Celan. BBASP; OBVE; VCWP, *tr. by* Michael Hamburger

Thread suns / above the grey-black wilderness. Thread Suns. Paul Celan.
  BBASP; OBVE; VCWP, *tr. by* Michael Hamburger

Thread the Needle. *Unknown.* FaBoVe

Thread the needle thread the needle. Thread the Needle. *Unknown.* FaBoVe

Threading Frost. *Unknown.* CATKP, *tr. by* Peter H. Lee

Threading the Miles. Alfred Encarnacion. OpBo

Threading the palm, a web of little lines. Signs. Gjertrud Schnackenberg.
  PoA 2002; StAl; VCAP

Threads. Robert Kelly.
  11. WANABP
  12. WANABP
  20. WANABP

Threads. Russell Leong. WhBo

Threads our hands in blindness spin, The. Overruled. John Greenleaf
  Whittier. NCAP

Threadsuns / over the grayblack wasteness. Paul Celan. PoetW, *tr. by* John
  Felstiner

Threat of the Sick. Breyten Breytenbach. PoetW, *tr. by* Denis Hirson

Threat'ning clouds of yesternight, The. While the Choir Sang. Priscilla Jane
  Thompson. CBWP-2

Three. Anne Carson. NLPA *Fr.* Glass Essay, The.

Three ("Once upon a time there would be the bluest bitch of the pack.") Jen
  Hofer and Ofelia Perez Sepúlveda. SPV

Three: "Your shaved head on my thigh." Lavinia Greenlaw. NeBrP

III: "As if dead the buried text." Danielle Collobert. MFP, *tr. by* Martin
  Sorrell

Three. Carolyn Kizer. BrAP; FTtHH; NALW *Fr.* Pro Femina.

3 A.M. Lauris Edmond. BeAl

Three A.M. Eternal. Reginald Shepherd. WiU

3 A.M. Kitchen: My Father Talking. Tess Gallagher. LaCa

Three a.m. smoke rises from underground. Poe Story, A. Anthony Butts.
  AmPoNex

Three American Women and a German Bayonet. Winfield Townley Scott.
  PWW2

Three Amoretti. Rick Barot. NeAmPo

Three ancient men in Bethlehem's cave. Mystic Magi, The. Robert Stephen
  Hawker. OBCP

Three Angels. Bob Dylan. RaBo

37: Three around the Old Gentleman. John Berryman. NAMCP V.2 *Fr.*
  Dream Songs.

Three, at the most four days later. Glads. Carl Phillips. CAP-8

Three blind mice, see how they run! Mother Goose. OxBEV

Three blue king. Feasting with Etang a Hundred Times Around. Al Robles.
  ReBoTo

Three Bodies. Anna Swirszczynska [*or* Swir]. PoChi, *tr. by* Czeslaw Milosz
  and Leonard Nathan

Three boots from Great Lakes stumble arm-in-arm. Tattoos. J. D. McClatchy.
  BAP-01

Three Bridges. Corey Marks. LegDan

Three Bridges. Sa'di Yusuf. IrPoTo, *tr. by* Khaled Mattawa

Three Cantos of a Poem of Some Length. Ezra Pound.
  3. TCAPo

Three Cherry Trees, The. Walter De la Mare. OBGa

Three Churches. Patricia Y. Ikeda. MotU

Three Companions, The. W. H. Auden. *See* Epilogue: "'O where are you
  going?' said reader to rider."

Three Cows in Hamra Street. Nasri Hajjaj. Eno, *tr. by* Ibrahim Muhawi

Three cups of wine a prudent man may take. Benefits and Abuse of Alcohol,
  The. Eubulus. NBLV, *tr. by* Richard Cumberland

3D. José Craveirinha. SonAtl, *tr. by* Martin Balas and Sophia Balas

3D Matchmove Artist, The. Kit Robinson. BAP-04

Three days. I Starve My Belly for a Sublime Purpose. Anna Swirszczynska
  [*or* Swir]. BLT

Three days after the lightning hit it / or the beat, check this, I can play around it.
  Some Nets. B. P. Nichol. FTOS

Three days before he died the hospital called me. Tongues. Philip Martin.
  NOBAu

Three days of rest. Sun is in Capricorn, The. Joyce Mansour. HAWP, *tr. by*
  Carol Cosman

Three Days/out of Franklin. Víctor Hernández Cruz. PueRic

Three days through sapphire seas we sailed. Bay Fight, The. Henry Howard
  Brownell. PCW

Three days we had. First Thanksgiving. Myra Cohn Livingston. HHAm

Three "Dharma Poems." Diane Di Prima. WANABP; WhBo

Three Dirges: Written in Imitation of an Ancient Funeral Song. T'ao Ch'ien.
  CCL1, *tr. by* Gladys Yang and Yang Xianyi

Three Dreams in Chiang-ling. Yüan Chên. CrYelRi, *tr. by* Sam Hamill

Three Elegiac Poems. Wendell Berry.
  "He goes free of the earth." UpMys
  "I stand at the cistern in front of the old barn." UpMys

Three Elements, The. Madison Cawein. APN-2

Three Emily's, The. Dorothy Livesay. BrAP; NALW

Three Enemies, The. Christina Georgina Rossetti. SacPr

Three English Poets and England. Waldo Williams. BBMWP, *tr. by* Anthony
  Conran

Three Epigrams. Theodore Roethke. NBLV
   Mistake, The. OBCoV
   Pipling. OBCoV
Three Epitaphs on John Hewet and Sarah Drew. Alexander Pope. NIP-4
Three Evenings in a Life. Adelaide Anne Procter. VWP
Three Excerpts. André Breton. PFTM-1 *Fr.* Manifesto of Surrealism (1924).
Three Fates, The. Rosemary Dobson. BMAP
Three Fish. Bruce Weigl. AmAlph
Three Flags. Murad Mikha'il. IrPoTo, *tr. by* Christina Coyle and Sadok Masliyah
Three Floors. Stanley Kunitz. LoL
Three floors up, I fall. Living Near the Plaza of Thieves. Leslie Ullman. PBCAP
Three folds of the cloth, yet one only napkin is there. Sacred Trinity, The. *Unknown.* IrV, *tr. by* Eleanor Hull
Three for Bear. Aimé Césaire. PFTM-1
Three for Children. Thom Gunn.
   Aquarium, The. NOxBChV
   Cannibal. NOxBChV
Three for the Road. E. San Juan, Jr. ReBoTo
Three xlvii. Laurie Duggan. BMAP
Three Found Poems. Laurie Duggan.
   Hearts (1983). BMAP
Three Fragments. Bertolt Brecht. PFTM-1
Three friends were with him at the Élysée. That Night. Victor Hugo. SxFrPo, *tr. by* A. M. and E. H. Blackmore
Three from the Market. Sandra McPherson. AFaM
   From the Market. IPoFL
Three Ghostesses. *Unknown.* OBCoV
   (Three Little Ghostesses.) NOxBChV
Three Gifts. Vincent Woods. NIrP
Three Goals, The. David Budbill. GoPo
Three Gypsies. Shalin Hai-Jew. UnSA
Three Gypsy Songs. *Unknown. tr. by* Anselm Hollo
   "It's you puts the green sprig in my hatband." WoPoe, *tr. by* Anselm Hollo
   "Moon shines on valley." WoPoe, *tr. by* Anselm Hollo
   "See the great vultures." WoPoe, *tr. by* Anselm Hollo
Three herrings. Herrings and Birch Trees. Jude Stéfan. YaTCFP, *tr. by* Edward Lucie-Smith
Three Holy Kings, The. Rainer Maria Rilke. ChrPo, *tr. by* Edward Snow
Three hours ago he blundered up the trench. Working Party, A. Siegfried Sassoon. AF
Three hours chain-smoking words. In the Evening. Adrienne Rich. WaAnP
Three Hours; or, The Vigil of Love. Sarah Josepha Buell Hale.
   First Hour.
      "Blessing on the printer's art!, A." SWaP
Three Houses. Padraic Fallon.
   Gurteen. ModIr
Three Hunchbacks, The. *Unknown.* NAWM-7v1, *tr. by* Ned Dubin
365 Poems. Ann Stanford. TAPaP
337,000, December, 2000. Aaron Fogel. BAP-04
Three hundred womanly states of the Eiffel Tower are frozen, The. César Vallejo. ConPit, *tr. by* Clayton Eshleman and Jorge Guzman
Three Hymns for Aphrodite. V. B. Price. ICANM
Three images of dying stick in my mind like morbid transfers. Bruce Beaver. NOBAu *Fr.* Letters to Live Poets.
Three Kalis appeared in Daksinesvar. Śyāmāpad Basu Rāy. SinGod, *tr. by* Rachel Fell McDermott
Three Kinds of Life Answerable to the Three Powers of the Soul. John Davies. SacPr
Three kings. Bethlehem. Marina Ivanovna Tsvetayeva. GI, *tr. by* Nina Kossman
Three Kings, The. Henry Wadsworth Longfellow. ChIV-2; ChrPo
Three Kings came riding from far away. Three Kings, The. Henry Wadsworth Longfellow. ChIV-2; ChrPo
Three Kings of Bethlehem, The. Attila József. IQMS, *tr. by* Istvan Fekete
Three Kings of Orient. John Henry Hopkins, Jr. *See* We Three Kings of Orient Are.
Three Ladies, The. Lawrence Kearney. ArBi
Three landlords, stupid ones; cut each in two. Recipe for a Warsaw Novel. Cyprian Norwid. WoPoe, *tr. by* Jerzy Peterkiewicz, Burns Singer and Jon Stallworthy
Three Legged Chairs. Lamont B. Steptoe. OxAAAP
Three little ghostesses. Three Ghostesses. *Unknown.* OBCoV
Three Little Ghostesses. *Unknown. See* Three Ghostesses.
Three Little Girls. Kate Greenaway. NOxBChV

Three little girls were sitting on a rail. Three Little Girls. Kate Greenaway. NOxBChV
Three little ponies who didn't like their hay. Three Ponies. Arthur Guiterman. BLPJKO
Three little unexpected children. Triplets. Howard Dietz. ReLy
Three Little Words. Bert Kalmar and Harry Ruby. ReLy
Three little words *teshuvah* turn toward you no more. Hank Lazer. AnSo *Fr.* New Spirit, The.
Three Madrigals. John Ashbery. AHA
Three Magi, The. Stanislaw Baranczak. GI
Three mares. Danila Stoyanova. CSCBP, *tr. by* Georgi Belev and Lisa Sapinkopf
Three Marys at Castle Howard, in 1812 and 1837, The. Ebenezer Elliott. SacPr
Three measures of breadth I take. Measures. Adam Drinan. EdScPo
Three men are fully clothed, long sleeves, The. Edward Hopper's Nighthawks, 1942. Joyce Carol Oates. PoSol
Three men came talking up the road. Night Piece. John Streeter Manifold. MoBrPo
Three men coming down the winter hill, The. Winter Landscape. John Berryman. GS; HarvBoo; MoAmPo; OxBoAm
Three Men in a Tent. Marilyn Nelson Waniek. ESEAA
Three men / laughing. Little Crisis Framed in My Window. Christopher Davis. AmPoNex
Three Men of Gotham. Thomas Love Peacock. OBEV; OxAEP-2
Three men sit on a stoop. Three men. Christopher Nickelson. BtF
Three merry men, and three merry men. George Peele. NoSic *Fr.* Old Wives' [*or* Wife's] Tale, The.
Three million years later, they found her. Lucy, *Lucie.* Peter Garner. IFF
Three Mirrors, The. Edwin Muir. NoAM
Three Modes of History and Culture. Imamu Amiri Baraka. BrAP; ESEAA; OxAAAP; PmAP
Three Moments in Paris. Mina Loy. PFTM-1
Three Moral Tales. Emmanuel Hocquard. YaTCFP, *tr. by* Michael Palmer
Three mothers, The. Mongane Wally Serote. TSAP
Three nights in a row. Hound Song. Donald Finkel. P180
Three nights running I have been to see it. Ghost Ship. Tom French. NIrP
Three nights you lay in our house. Wake. Tess Gallagher. InoFa; StAl
Three Notes Toward Definitions. Timothy Steele.
   2. Of Faith. PoA 2002
Three Observations on Belief. Tarin Towers. AmPoNex
"Three Observations on the Zombie Culture." Dolores Kendrick.
   26th Person, The. GT
3 o'clock. Playing the Messiah. Jean Binta Breeze. MoWP
Three O'Clock Love Song. Michael S. Harper. GT
Three Octets. Osip Emilevich Mandelstam. RusPo, *tr. by* Robert Arthur Douglas Ford
Three Odes of Horace. Horace. *tr. by* Louis MacNeice
   Solvitur Acris Hiems. WoPoe, *tr. by* Louis MacNeice
Three of us afloat in the meadow by the swing. Pirate Story. Robert Louis Stevenson. NOxBChV
Three old ladies in an apple tree. Ballad of Old Women & of How They Are Constrained To Simulate Youth In Order To Avoid Shocking the Young. Norman Talbot. NOBAu
3 Old Men at Separate Tables. Charles Bukowski. PML
Three old men in a scrawny rain. Ivan Metodiev. CSCBP *Fr.* Songs for Orphans Big and Small.
Three old New Mexican men. Still Life. Keith Wilson. ICANM
Three or four hours unconscious there. (LL) Milk for the Cat. Harold Monro. MoBrPo; OBMV
Three or four young sylph women. Kuan Hsiu. CCL1, *tr. by* Edward H. Schafer
Three pairs of dimpled arms, as white as snow. Angels in the House, The. *Unknown.* TreFP
Three Panels Depending on the Heart. Timothy Donnelly. LegDan
3 Pictograms From The Interior of BC. Fred Wah. OpeFie
Three Pieces of Candy. Anna Swirszczynska [*or* Swir]. PoChi, *tr. by* Czeslaw Milosz and Leonard Nathan
Three pine masts lodged in the clay of the pining sailors. These Trees in Particular. Susan Stewart. AmAlph
Three Pleas. Henry Treece. PoWW
3 poems. Aleksei Eliseievich Kruchyonykh. PFTM-1 *Fr.* Pomade.
Three Poems. Michael Lassell. WiU
Three Poems. Robert James Waller. TiP2
Three Poems 1989. Larry Eigner. PFTM-2
3 Poems for Benedetta Barzini. Gerard Malanga. AHA
Three Poems for Violin. Barbara Nickel. ACAMVP

Three Poems in Memory of Mamá (Grandmother). Judith Ortiz Cofer.
  Cold as Heaven. ExTi
Three Poems of the Atomic Bomb. Dame Edith Sitwell.
  Dirge for the New Sunrise. MoBrPo
Three Poems on Death. Carlos Bousoño. RaW, *tr. by* Charles Guenther
Three Poems on Friendship. Khwaja Shams-ad-din Muhammad Hafiz. *tr. by*
  Dick Davis
  "Desire's destroyed my life; what gifts have I." WoPoe, *tr. by* Dick Davis
  "Each friend turned out to be an enemy." WoPoe, *tr. by* Dick Davis
  "My friend, hold back your heart from enemies." WoPoe, *tr. by* Dick Davis
Three poets, in three distant ages born. Lines Printed under the Engraved
  Portrait of Milton [In Tonson's Folio of the "Paradise Lost"]. John
  Dryden. OxAEP-1
Three Point Five Nine. Patricia Young. BrAP
Three Ponies. Arthur Guiterman. BLPJKO
Three Posthumous Poems. W. H. Auden. CAGL
  Aubade. CAGL
  Glad. CAGL
  Minnelied. CAGL
Three practical farmers from back of the dale. Shepherds' Carol. Norman
  Nicholson. OBCP
Three prisoners—the biggest black. O My Name It Is Sam Hall. Randall
  Jarrell. PWW2
Three Puddocks, The. William Soutar. FaBoVe
Three/Quarters Time. Nikki Giovanni. CA
Three Quatrains. Edwin Arlington Robinson. NCAP
Three Quatrains. Jelaluddin Rumi. *tr. by* Coleman Barks and John Moyne
  "Let the lover be disgraceful, crazy." RaBo, *tr. by* Coleman Barks
  "Never too many fish in a swift creek,.." RaBo
  "Night full of talking that hurts, A." RaBo; WoPoe, *tr. by* Coleman Barks
  and John Moyne
Three Ravens. Jamie Meyerhoff. WhBo
Three Ravens, The. *Unknown.* HeIP-4; OBEV; TFi
Three Recent Trips to the Golden Past: East Village, Clarksdale Mississippi,
  Athens. Dick Lourie. PrTe
Three rivers join in the wilds of Chu. Sailing Down the Han. Wang Wei.
  CrYelRi, *tr. by* Sam Hamill
Three rocks, a few burnt pines, an abandoned chapel. George Seferis. WoPoe
  Fr. Mythistorima.
Three rompers run together, hand in hand. To ———. Wilfred Owen.
  OxBSo
Three Roses, The. Walter Savage Landor. NAEL-6v2
Three Ruba'iyat. Abdul Wahab Al-Bayati. IrPoTo, *tr. by* Carolina
  Hotchandani and Najat Rahman
Three sang of love together: one with lips. Triad, A. Christina Georgina
  Rossetti. NAEL-6v2; NAEL-7v2; NALW
Three Sets of Three. Kenneth Irby.
  "There is from the legs in sleep an exhalation of the light, along the tops of
  the thighs." PFTM-2
Three ("She is of the continent, around her everything is light and I observe her
  atop the slab in the image of her body.") Ofelia Perez Sepúlveda. SPV,
  tr. by Jen Hofer
Three Shops, The. Francis Ponge. WED, *tr. by* Robert Bly
Three Silences. Rachel Hadas. RA
Three silent women at the kitchen table. Anne Carson. NLPA *Fr.* Glass Essay,
  The.
Three Sisters, The. Arthur Davison Ficke. TCAPo
Three slender ones whereon the whole Earth swings. Early Irish Triads.
  Unknown. IrV, *tr. by* Alfred Perceval Graves
Three Small Parables for My Poet Friends. Stanley Kunitz. OxBoAm
Three Small Rooms. Colin Morton.
  "In this empty room we gather." IFF
Three Snakes, Strawberry Canyon, Berkeley. Ray Gonzales. FTtHH
Three Songs. Thom Gunn.
  Baby Song. AmFaPo; BeAl
Three Songs. Rachel Wetzsteon. RA
Three Songs. Rachel Wetzsteon. RA
Three Songs about Lynching. Langston Hughes.
  Silhouette. NAAL-5; NAMCP V.1
Three Songs for *King Leir*. Ann Lauinger.
  Cordeilla. IaFF
  Edgar. IaFF
  Leir. IaFF
Three Songs of Love and Hate. Fay Zwicky.
  Stone Dolphin, The. BMAP
Three Songs of Mary. Madeleine L'Engle.
  O Simplicitas. OBCP
Three Sorts of Serpents Do Resemble Thee. Michael Drayton. PtR *Fr.* Idea.

Three Stanzas. Johann Wolfgang von Goethe. WoPoe *Fr.* Journey in Winter.
Three Star Final. Conrad Potter Aiken. PWW2
Three Stars. Robert Desnos. SurPaPo, *tr. by* Mary Ann Caws and Jean-Pierre
  Cauvin
Three stars, five stars rise over the hill. *Unknown.* NDACCP *Fr.* Shao and the
  South.
Three States and Three Kingdoms. Alberto Blanco. RMCMP, *tr. by* Joan
  Lindgren
Three Storks Restaurant. Nazim Hikmet. NaPG, *tr. by* Talat Sait Halman
Three strange men came to the inn. Lady Comes to an Inn, A. Elizabeth Jane
  Coatsworth. MoAmPo
Three Strolls. Alice Notley. AHA
Three Summers since I chose a maid. Farmer's Bride, The. Charlotte Mew.
  CABP; LW; MoBrPo; MoWP; NALW; NoP-4; NoP-5; RACG; VWP
Three sunbursts spin, enigmatic energies. David Schloss. PoA 2002 *Fr.*
  Figures in the Carpets.
Three sunrises. Gabi. Maria Luisa B. Aguilar-Cariño. ReBoTo
Three Swedish Spells. *Unknown. tr. by* Siv Cedering Fox
  Spell, A. WoPoe, *tr. by* Siv Cedering Fox
  Spell against Predatory Animals. WoPoe, *tr. by* Siv Cedering Fox
  Spell against Twisting an Ankle. WoPoe, *tr. by* Siv Cedering Fox
3:10 A.M. I get up and go to the kitchen. I see it while looking for a glass of
  water. Knife Gets Bigger, A. Chông Hwajin. EcSo, *tr. by* Julie C. Park
Three Tests for Darwin Duke. Jane Holland. MFPA
Three that end the same way. St. Anzas VI. B. P. Nichol. FTOS
Three then came forward out of darkness, one. Road, The. Conrad Potter
  Aiken. MoAmPo
Three thing[e]s there be[e] that prosper up apace. Sir Walter Ra[u]le[i]gh to
  His Son[ne]. Sir Walter Ralegh. GSo; NAEL-6v1; NAEL-7v1; NoP-4;
  NoSic; NPeEn; OxBSo; WoPoe
Three Thinges There Bee That Prosper Up Apace. Sir Walter Ralegh. *See* Sir
  Walter Ra[u]le[i]gh to His Son[ne].
Three Things [*fr.* Words for Music Perhaps]. William Butler Yeats. OBMV
Three Things Come Without Seeking. *Unknown.* NePenScot, *tr. by* Iain
  Crichton Smith
Three things come without seeking. Three Things Come Without Seeking.
  Unknown. NePenScot, *tr. by* Iain Crichton Smith
Three things make earth unquiet. Servant When He Reigneth, A. Rudyard
  Kipling. ChIV-1
Three things stopped him in his stride. Buddha, Birdbath, Hanging Plant.
  Peter Skrzynecki. PML
Three things there be in Mans opinion deare. Fulke, 1st Baron Brooke
  Greville. NOSC; NoSic; SacPr *Fr.* Caelica.
Three Things to Remember. William Blake. OWoS *Fr.* Auguries of
  Innocence.
Three Tides. Brendan Kennelly. ModIr *Fr.* Cromwell.
Three times a night it woke you. Coal Train. Jay Parini. GM
Three times a year the nightmare comes again. Triolets for Ken. Christopher
  Wiseman. IFF
Three times he crossed our way where with me went. Old Man Pondered.
  John Crowe Ransom. MoAmPo
Three times I saw him face to face. Antinous. Mikhail Alekseievich Kuzmin.
  CAGL, *tr. by* Michael Green
Three times the carline grain'd and rifted. Lucky Spence's Last Advice. Allan
  Ramsay. NePenScot
Three times to the world's end I went. Edge, The. Rosemary Dobson.
  NOBAu
Three To's and an Oi. Heather McHugh. ExTi
Three Trees. Wanda Coleman. BrAP
Three turkeys fair their last have breathed. Melancholy Lay, A. Marjory
  Fleming. NBLV
321738. Kiren Shoman. OWABP
Three Undated Fragments. John Keats.
  "O grant that like to Peter I." ChIV-2
Three Visions of Imperial Rome. John Addington Symonds.
  Midnight at Baiae. CAGL
Three Ways of Looking at God. Robin Robertson. StAl
Three Ways of Recovering a Body. Helen Dunmore. MoWP; StAl
Three wee bit puddocks. Three Puddocks, The. William Soutar. FaBoVe
Three weeks gone and the combatants gone. Vergissmeinnicht. Keith
  Douglas. EdScPo; FaBoWar; GoPo; HarvBoo; NAEL-6v2; NAEL-7v2;
  NAMCP V.1; NoAM; NoP-4; NoP-5; NPeEn; OBWP; OxBEV; PoAgWa;
  PoWW; SoSe-8; StAl; WoPoe
Three weeks had past, and Richard rambles now. George Crabbe. NPeEn *Fr.*
  Tales of the Hall.
Three weeks had past, and Richard rambles now. George Crabbe. NOBRP *Fr.*
  Tales of the Hall.
Three weeks past my father's death. After-Image. Linda Bierds. ExTi

Three whole days off. Buson. EMJL *Fr.* Spring Breeze on the Kema Embankment.

Three wide / Funnels raked aft, and the masts slanted, The. George Oppen. APT-2; PFTM-1

Three wise men looked equivocally, The. Magi, The. Ramon Guthrie. GI

Three wise men of Gotham. Mother Goose. Spl

Three Wise Old Women. Elizabeth T. Corbett. NOxBChV; OBSP

Three wise old women were they, were they. Three Wise Old Women. Elizabeth T. Corbett. NOxBChV; OBSP

Three Woodchoppers. Robert Francis. TRP

Three woodchoppers walk up the road. Three Woodchoppers. Robert Francis. TRP

Three words in my dictionary. Three Little Words. Bert Kalmar and Harry Ruby and Harry Ruby. ReLy

Three Written Poems, Unconnected. Marianne Vitale. HeMarv

Three Year Ode, A. W. N. Herbert. RSaN

Three years ago, in the afternoons. Sitting Outside at the End of Autumn. Charles Wright. WaAnP

Three Years from Sorrento. Dorothy Belle Flanagan. YaYoPo

Three years old, she didn't talk. Learning to Speak. Eli Clare. PfS

Three Years She Grew [in Sun and Shower]. William Wordsworth. BrAP; NAEL-6v2; NAEL-7v2; NoP-5; NPBRoP *Fr.* Lucy.

Three-Card Monte. Malena Mörling. AmPoNex

Three-Coloured Banner. János Pilinszky. PoSu, *tr. by* Peter Jay

Three-Course Meal for the New Year, A. Myra Sklarew. TaR

Three-fold terror of love; a fallen flare, The. Mother of God, The. William Butler Yeats. BBASP; ChIV-2; ChrPo

  (Three-fold terror of love, The.) GI

Three-fold terror of love, The. William Butler Yeats. *See* Three-fold terror of love; a fallen flare, The.

Three-foot-long sword that can split a feather, The. At the Moment of My Death. Chŏnggam, Great Master. CATKP, *tr. by* Peter H. Lee

Three-Headed Womon Song. Wanda Coleman. RD

Three-Inch Reflector. Caroline Caddy. BMAP

Three-Liners. Nina Gorlanova. CRWP, *tr. by* Daniel Weissbort

Threesome. Dora Teitelboim. Prolet, *tr. by* Amelia Glaser

Three-Step Waterfall. Muso Soseki. EaWin, *tr. by* W. S. Merwin

Three-Toed Sloth, The. Fleur Adcock. OBCoV

Threissa, someone's knocking at the door. Procuress, The. Herodas. HePo, *tr. by* Barbara Hughes Fowler

Threnodia Augustalis. John Dryden.

  Faculty at Work, The. STuOW

Threnody: "South-wind brings, The." Ralph Waldo Emerson. APN-1; TCAPo

Threnody: "What, what, what / What's the news from Swat?" George Thomas Lanigan. NBLV

Threnody: "What's your story Atlanta/ America?" Kalamu ya Salaam. BtF

Threnody for Sunrise ("Please, when you ask me in this dream.") Richard Cecil. BodElec

Threnody for Sunset ("It's five o'clock. Someone's taped my name out.") Richard Cecil. BodElec

There are long lines that. Queue. Rashidah Ismaili. HAWP

Thresholds of tolerance. Lionel Abrahams. TSAP

Thrice bless'd are they, who feel their loneliness. Melchizedek. John Henry, Cardinal Newman. SacPr

Thrice Toss[e] These Oaken Ashes in the Air [*or* Ayre]. Thomas Campion. OxBSo; PoCho; TFi; WeW-3

Third Vertical Poetry. Roberto Juarroz.

  "Lamp lit, A." VCWP

Thrift. Cornelius Eady. LTA

Thrift alone for meaning ceases. We Forego Mimicry. Ray DiPalma. FTOS

Thrift Shop Ladies. Jennifer M. Pierson. ReTh

Thrillsville. Julianne Buchsbaum. LegDan

Thro' the thick vagueness of the vaporous night. Edward Robert Bulwer-Lytton. *Fr.* Misery.

Throat, The. Wild Flower. Maurice Kenny. PoCoUp

Throat is, The. Sore Throat, The. Aaron Kunin. IIR

Throat puckered like crepe. My Body. Joan Larkin. WiU

Throat Song: The Whirling Earth. Wendy Rose. HATNAP

Throbbings. Jamil B. Holway. NAAPv.2, *tr. by* George Dimitri Selim

Throbs for the Instructress. Pedro López-Adorno. BRtP

Throbs with vain pangs, here will I love to rest. (LL) Written in Autumn. Mary Tighe. CenSon; OxBSo

Throe upon the features, A. Emily Dickinson. TCAPo

Throes. Anthony Thwaite. PoCu

Thrombosis Trombone. Thomas Lux. BodElec

Throne of Grace, The. Kathleen Norris. UpMys

Throned in splendor, deathless, O Aphrodite. Sappho. NAWM-7v1, *tr. by* Richmond Lattimore

Throned, yet adoring! (LL) Day of Judg[e]ment, The; an Ode [Attempted in English Sapphic]. Isaac Watts. ChIV-2; NoP-4; NoP-5; OBEV; OxBEV (Shout the Redeemer.) NoP-4; NoP-5; NPeEn

Throng of hand-casts. Cactuses. Jean-Joseph Rabéarivelo. SonAtl, *tr. by* Audrey Cooper, W. Ender and Celia Martin

Thronging the heart. Residues: Thronging the Heart. Gael Turnbull. Oth

Through a black and gold day, while the bright elm leaves. Witness, The. Eve Triem. PWW2

Through a few splinters of. Han-shan Te-ch'ing. WoPoe *Fr.* Mountain Living.

Through a hospital window. In a Hospital Garden. Randall Jarrell. OBGa

Through a red prairie. (LL) Last Quatrain of the Ballad of Emmett Till, The. Gwendolyn Brooks. ESEAA; NAAL-5; NAMCP V.2

Through a Slit in the Tent. Carole Glasser Langille. Coast

Through a two-way telescope of time. Aerolingual Poet of Prey. Eugene B. Redmond. SpirFl

Through a Window-Light. Sofiya Parnok. ARWW, *tr. by* Catriona Kelly

Through all the city's streets there poured a flood. Gathering of the Grand Army, The. Charlotte L. Forten Grimke. AmWaPo

Through all the evening. Borderlands. Louise Imogen Guiney. TCAPo

Through all the fates of earth, through every spell that works on man its spleen. To Ausonius. Paulinus of Nola. CAGL, *tr. by* Jack Lindsay

Through all the pomp of kingdoms still he shines. Homer. NOSC *Fr.* Iliad, The.

Through all this granite land. Lorine Niedecker. FTOS *Fr.* Lake Superior.

Through Alpine meadows soft-suffused. Stanzas from the Grande Chartreuse. Matthew Arnold. NAEL-6v2; NAEL-7v2

Through an infernal [blank] and sea. Where Were You. Ethan Paquin. LegDan

Through bruised reeds my boat thrusts. Safaddan. Ruth Bidgood. TCAWP

Through brute nature upward rising. Winged Sphinx. Margaret Fuller. TCAPo

Through cardamom flower beds. Enemies. Sa'di Yusuf. IrPoTo, *tr. by* Khaled Mattawa

Through cigar smoke, through. Through the Smoke. István Vas. IQMS, *tr. by* George Szirtes

Through Clouds, Their Whispers. Martha Rhodes. NAPBI.

Through congoed leaves of. Kalamu ya Salaam. SpirFl *Fr.* New Orleans Haiku.

Through dark ravines of cloud the dawning broke. Austin Clarke. *Fr.* Vengeance of Fionn, The.

Through dark tenements and fallen temples. Dialectical Materialism. Bruce Weigl. AmAlph

Through deir dus'. (LL) Memphis Blues. Sterling Allen Brown. APT-2; InGu; NAMCP V.1

Through different streets that are all alike we walk down toward the docks. Night Meeting. Thomas McGrath. BodElec

Through Eden took their solitary way. (LL) John Milton. NAWM-5v1; NAWM-7v1 *Fr.* Paradise Lost.

Through every night we hate. Mothers, Daughters. Shirley Kaufman. PoChi

Through fear of sharp and bitter pain. King's Last Farewell to the World, The. *Unknown.* BASC

Through fields that were part of no earthly estate. (LL) Tarry Flynn. Patrick Kavanagh. IPoFL; ModIr

Through frost and snow and sunlight. Brian Patten. NewEx

Through frozen rice fields. Basho. SoOfWa, *tr. by* Sam Hamill

Through glades and glooms! Oh fair! Oh, sad! Collins. Lionel Pigot Johnson. OxAEP-2

Through her forced, abnormal quiet. Quakerdom (The Formal Call). Charles Graham Halpine. IrLP

Through high still air. (LL) Mid-August at Sourdough Mountain Lookout. Gary Snyder. ColAP; FaoP; LoL; NoP-4; OxBoAm; VCAP; WaAnP

Through infinite immensity. (LL) I'm happiest when most away. Emily Jane Brontë. NAEL-6v2; NAEL-7v2

Through it / over young women's abdomens tense. Stethoscope, The. Dannie Abse. BloBone

Through lane or black archway. Young Woman of Beare, The. Austin Clarke. ModIr; NAMCP V.1; NoAM

Through lenses the world opens. Microscope. Gwyn Thomas. BBMWP; OBWVE, *tr. by* Joseph P. Clancy

Through lonely motel walls. Oh, Atonement. Bruce Weigl. MAAN

Through me come into the city full of pain. Dante Alighieri. WoPoe *Fr.* Divina Commedia (Selections from Anthologies, in English).

Through miles of green cornfields that lusty. Constance Fenimore Woolson. SWaP *Fr.* Two Women.

Through mud, fouled nuts, black grime. Removing the Plate of the Pump on the Hydraulic System of the Backhoe. Gary Snyder. LoL

Through my window, asphalt rooftops, cyclone. Letter Home from Brooklyn. Enid Shomer. UrbNat

Through nights of slanting rain. Ripeness Is All. Peter Viereck. PWW2

Through Paris lay my readiest path, and there. William Wordsworth. NPBRoP *Fr.* Prelude, The; Growth of a Poet's Mind [1805 version].

Through paths of pleasant thought I ran. Reason and Faith. Cecil Frances Alexander. SacPr

Through pearly deeps of sky, cloud-mountains rose. Sky Picture. Henrietta Cordelia Ray. CBWP-3

Through Persia raving. CXXXIX. Pita Amor. TANSG, *tr.* by Shaun Griffin and Emma Sepúlveda-Pulvirenti

Through Ruddy Orchards. Mary Oliver. SoSe-8

Through salt marsh, grassy channel where the shark's. Tide Turning. John Frederick Nims. IllVoic

Through scant pride to be so put out! Geoffrey Hill. UpMys *Fr.* Metamorphoses.

Through seas of dreams and seas of phantasies. Nirvâna. Sidney Lanier. NCAP

Through sepia air the boarders come and go. Landlady, The. Patricia K. Page. BrAP

Through sere trees and beheaded. August Rain, after Haying. Jane Kenyon. ExTi

Through snow / Lights of homes. Buson. ZenPo, *tr.* by Takashi Ikemoto and Lucien Stryk

Through space, in the cold. Determination of Time. Alena Nádvorníková. SurWo

Through springtime walks, with flowers perfumed. Song. Anne Batten Cristall. RWP

Through storms you reach them and from storms are free. Enviable Isles, The. Herman Melville. NCAP

Through summer air. Flight. Jorge Guillén. BLT, *tr.* by Reginald Gibbons

Through tall bamboo the mossy path. Spring Homecoming. Tu Fu [*or* Du Fu]. CrYelRi, *tr.* by Sam Hamill

Through that pure virgin shrine. Night, The. Henry Vaughan. BASC; ChIV-2; FSCP; NAEL-6v1; NAEL-7v1; NoP-4; NoP-5; NPeEn; OBEV; OBWVE; OxAEP-1; OxBEV; TFi

Through that window—all else being extinct. Room, The. Conrad Potter Aiken. APT-1; InGu; MoAmPo

Through the ample open door of the peaceful country barn. Farm Picture, A. Walt Whitman. BLT; TRP

Through the bending twigs of the coral grove. (LL) Coral Grove, The. James Gates Percival. APN-1; ColAP

Through the black, rushing smoke-bursts. Matthew Arnold. OBEV *Fr.* Empedocles on Etna.

Through the blinds, it must have been the streetlamp [*or* searchlight] I saw. Landing, The. J. D. McClatchy. OxBoAm

Through the bound cable strands, the arching path. Hart Crane. NAAL-5 *Fr.* Bridge, The.

Through the broad bright land. (LL) Song of the Ungirt Runners, The. Charles Hamilton Sorley. MoBrPo; OBEV

Through the bruised unbalanced waves? (LL) Late Night Ode. Horace. PfSP; WaAnP; WiU; WoPoe, *tr.* by J. D. McClatchy

Through the bustle and commotion. Illusions. Llion Jones. BBMWP, *tr.* by Geriant Løvgreen

Through the cambered flesh of clover and wild carrot. (LL) Flitting, The. Medbh McGuckian. PBCIP; PNI

Through the cheap iron gate and its mythic. Night Shift, after Drinking Dinner, Container Corporation of America, 1972. Kevin Stein. IllVoic

Through the clotted street and down. Nocturne. Ellen Bryant Voigt. UrbNat

Through the crawl space. Tattoo #47, "Happy Dragon." Paul Allen. ReTh

Through the cut poplar I can spot. Height. Nedelcho Ganev. CSCBP, *tr.* by Georgi Belev and Lisa Sapinkopf

Through the dark city. (LL) Great Figure, The. William Carlos Williams. HeIP-4; NAAPv.2; NAMCP V.1; NoAM; SAmP

Through the Dark Sod—as Education. Emily Dickinson. NALW

Through the deep shadows of the darkening years. Charlotte Brontë. Paul Hamilton Hayne. APN-2

Through the dusky purple glimmer. Anita and Giovanni. Henrietta Cordelia Ray. CBWP-3

Through the front gate. *Unknown.* ColAnChi *Fr.* Midnight Songs.

Through the garbled signals. Heirlooms. Geoffrey Philp. WaCA

Through the gate, where nowhere and night begin. At the Airport. Howard Nemerov. OtW

Through the green grass. Cantiga de Amigo. Pero Meogo. WoPoe, *tr.* by Keith Bosley

Through the Half-Opened Window. Léon Damas. YaTCFP, *tr.* by Mary Ann Caws and Jean-Pierre Cauvin

Through the hole in the hut's wall. Deserter, The. Ai. BodElec

Through the host with this the goddess ran. Homer. FaBoWar *Fr.* Iliad, The.

Through the house what busy joy. First Tooth, The. Charles Lamb and Mary Lamb. WoRP

Through the lands low-lying, fast and free. Moonlight Ride, A. Harriet Hamilton King. VWP

Through the laurel branches. Casida of the Dark Doves. Federico García Lorca. WoPoe, *tr.* by Edwin Honig

Through the lit crystal of the cup. (LL) Autumn. Roy Campbell. MoBrPo; OBMV

Through the Long Night. Edward Carpenter. CAGL *Fr.* Towards Democracy.

Through the Looking-Glass. Lewis Carroll.
Humpty Dumpty's Poetic Recitation. NPeEn
(Humpty Dumpty's Recitation.) OBSP
(Humpty Dumpty's Song.) OBCoV
Jabberwocky. AmFaPo; BrAP; BRP; CABP; CaBP; ChAP; ClHu; CtM; HeIP-4; ITBLP; NAEL-6v2; NAEL-7v2; NBLV; NoAM; NoP-4; NoP-5; NOxBChV; NTCP; OBSP; OxAEP-2; OxBEV; TFi; TRP; UV
Walrus and the Carpenter, The. CABP; ChAP; ITBLP; NAEL-6v2; NAEL-7v2; NoAM; OBSP; OxAEP-2; TFi
Welcome Queen Alice. UV
White Knight's Song, The. BrAP; NAEL-6v2; NAEL-7v2; NoAM; NoP-4; NoP-5; TFi; UV

Through the Metidja to Abd-el-Kadr. Robert Browning. WoPoe

Through the narrow aisles of pain. (LL) Solitude. Ella Wheeler Wilcox. BRP; GoPo; SWaP; TCAPo

Through the open French window the warm sun. Still-Life. Elizabeth Daryush. MoWP; NPeEn; OxBEV

Through the orange glow of taillights, I crossed. In the Black Camaro. David Bottoms. ReTh

Through the root power flashes unseen. Root. Miklós Radnóti. ConPit, *tr.* by Clayton Eshleman and Gyula Kodolanyi

Through the screened window. Double Helix. Sean Thomas Dougherty. AmPoNex

Through the slits of my eyes a perambulator passes. Sun, The. Hugo Ball. PFTM-1

Through the slow succeeding ages. Only Way, The. W. N. Ewer. FaBoWar

Through the small opening in the boarded wall. Autobiographical Response from a Provincial Wasteland (in Reply to a New Year's Greeting Sent with a Bouquet). Elizaveta Shakhova. ARWW, *tr.* by Catriona Kelly

Through the Smoke. István Vas. IQMS, *tr.* by George Szirtes

Through the Smoke Hole. Gary Snyder.
1. PoA 2002

Through the sod—an anchor, a cross of rust. (LL) Daffodils. Ted Hughes. NAEL-7v2; NoP-5

Through the soft evening air enwinding all. Italian Music in Dakota. Walt Whitman. APN-1

Through the strait gate of passion. Paradise Re-entered. D. H. Lawrence. ChIV-2

Through the supermarket aisles I push a cart. Shopping. Agi Mishol. DTA, *tr.* by Tsipi Keller

Through the tentflap, across the air mattress, up over my shoulderblade. Chott. J. D. McClatchy. PfSP

Through the tobacco haze. Blew It. Michael Castro. SeSe

Through the upper right-hand corner of things, to say grace. (LL) Reunion. Charles Wright. CAP-8; OxBoAm

Through the vast crowded wards, thousands came round. Freedom. Anthony Thwaite. OxBSo

Through the viridian (and black of the burnt match). Virgo Descending. Charles Wright. ColAP; TRP; WaAnP

Through the wide, grey loft window. Village Life, A. Derek Walcott. GT

Through the winding lanes where willows lean. Ballads of the Wheel. Clinton Scollard. ArBi

Through the Window of the All-Night Restaurant. Nicholas Christopher. P180

Through the winter's cold. Crocuses and Crown-of-Thorns. Enos D. Watts. Coast

Through the years of happiness and hardships. Blockade Swallow, The. Olga Fiodorovna Berggolts. TCRusP, *tr.* by Daniel Weissbort

Through These Halls. Judy Jordan. AmPoNex

Through this toilsome world, alas! I Shall Not Pass This Way Again. *Unknown.* ChAP

Through this window, thin rivers. Housework. Joan Larkin. WiU

Through Time's Segments. István Vas. IQMS, *tr.* by Daniel Gerard Hoffman

Through traffic, honking and off-course, direction veering. Coming to You. Daphne Marlatt. PoBW

Through traffic, honking and off-course, direction veering. Daphne Marlatt. NLPA *Fr.* Touch to My Tongue.

Through tranquil years they watched the changes. Clearing for the Plough. Ernest G. Moll. NOBAu

Through weathered wood dark. Kalamu ya Salaam. SpirFl *Fr.* New Orleans Haiku.

Through what long heaviness, assayed in what strange fire. Carthusians. Ernest Dowson. NAEL-6v2; NAEL-7v2

Through which one may not put one's hands to touch. (LL) Prisms. Laura Riding Jackson. APT-2; ColAP

Through wild and tangled forests. On the Mississippi. Hamlin Garland. APN-2

Through winter streets to steer your course aright. Trivia; or, The Art of Walking the Streets of London. John Gay.

Throughout Heaven and Earth, whatever lives. Tu Fu [or Du Fu]. NDACCP Fr. Thoughts.

Throughout the field I find no grain. Winter in Durnover Field. Thomas Hardy. MoBrPo

Throughout the night the trees paraded. Wood, The. Geraint Jarman. BBMWP, tr. by Peter Finch

Throughout the winter, we once believed, they hid. Chimney Swifts. Mark Jarman. PfSP

Throughout the world, if it were sought. Honesty. Sir Thomas Wyatt. NoSic

Throw away thy rod. Discipline. George Herbert. FSCP; NAEL-6v1; NAEL-7v1; NoP-4; NoP-5; OBEV; OxAEP-1

Throw away thy wrath. (LL) Discipline. George Herbert. FSCP; NAEL-6v1; NAEL-7v1; NoP-4; NoP-5; OBEV; OxAEP-1

Throw Hannibal on the scales, how many pounds. Juvenal. OBVE Fr. Satires.

Throw me a quince. Unknown. ColAnChi Fr. Classic of Odes.

Throw open the window. Our Sunday Rest. Don Aminado. TCRusP, tr. by John Glad

Throw within a stone, thrust through the void within, force force within. Stone-Throw. Stratis Haviaras. MotU

Throw Yourself Like Seed. Miguel de Unamuno. PLBUT; RaBo; RaW, tr. by Robert Bly

Throwback, The. Paul Muldoon. PoA 2002

Throwing her arms around her dear father. Anyte. SaLy, tr. by Diane Rayor

Throwing Out at / of (Com)pare (Dis)pair, A. Tina Darragh. FTOS

Throwing Out My Father's Dictionary. Moniza Alvi. MoWP; Prnts

Throwing Out the Flowers. Gwendolyn Brooks. ColAP Fr. Notes from the Childhood and the Girlhood.

Thrown between me and the sky. (LL) Once, I knew a fine song. Stephen Crane. APN-2; IJHIL

Thrown from the world. (LL) Revelation in the Mother Lode. George Evans. AF; PmAP

Thrown in the moon-glade by the palm. (LL) Herman Melville. APN-2; NCAP Fr. Clarel: A Poem and Pilgrimage in the Holy Land.

Thrown off-center. Theory of Curve. Christopher Gilbert. LTA

Thrown out of a third story window on acid late spring. Assembling My Shepherd. Tessa Rumsey. LegDan

Thrush before Dawn, A. Alice Thompson Meynell. MoBrPo

Thrush how beautifully she sings, The. (LL) Going Without Saying. Bernard O'Donoghue. BeAl; PoCu

Thrush in the syringa sings, A. Basil Bunting. HarvBoo; WoPoe

Thrush is singing on the walnut tree, A. Die Zauberflöte. Rosamund Marriott Watson. ViWPN

Thrush is tapping a stone, A. Dawn. Gordon Bottomley. MoBrPo

Thrush, linnet, stare and wren. In Glencullen. John Millington Synge. OBMV

Thrushes. Ted Hughes. TRP

Thrushes flying under the lake. Nightingales singing underground. Pewter. Jack Gilbert. BodElec

Thrust upon by a softly-swinging wind. (LL) Weather-Cock Points South, The. Amy Lowell. APT-1; NALW; NoP-4; NoP-5; OxBoAm

Thud, thud, all the sores go blind. View From a Porch. Thomas Lux. AmAlph

Thule, the period of cosmography. Wonders. Unknown. NPeEn

Thulène is dead, my lord. I saw his funeral. Sonnet Addressed to Henry III on the Death of Thulène, the King's Fool. Jean Passerat. WoPoe, tr. by Richmond Lattimore

Thumb is this fat Flemish innkeeper, with a lewd, grumbling temper, The. Five Fingers of the Hand, The. Aloysius Bertrand. MotU, tr. by James Weeks

Thumb, loose tooth of a horse. Bestiary for the Fingers of My Right Hand. Charles Simic. P180

Thumbprint, A. Moon. Katie Donovan. NIrP

"Thumbs in the thumb-place." Mitten Song, The. Marie Louise Allen. NTCP

Thumb-sized birds in gaudy greens. Inside the Hummingbird Aviary. David Huddle. PfSP

Thumb's-length landscape, A: Snow, on a hill. Snow Landscape, in a Glass Globe. Jean Valentine. CAP-8

Thumping heart, The. Hospital Interiors. Giovanni Raboni. ItPo, tr. by Gayle Ridinger

Thunder, The: Perfect Mind. Nag Hammadi Library.
   "Look upon me." HW
   "Sent from the Power." WPoS

Thunder & the flaw of their great quarrel, The. John Berryman. VCAP Fr. Dream Songs.

Thunder blossoms gorgeously above our heads. Storm Ending. Jean Toomer. APT-2

Thunder Can Break. Christopher Okigbo. HBAPE

Thunder can split the mountain, The. Yi Hwang. CATKP Fr. Twelve Songs of Tosan.

Thunder floats. Unknown. SonAtl, tr. by Alex Bishop, Lorna MacIntosh and Misty Plummer

Thunder grumbles, drops, thuds, breaking. Standing Light Up. A. R. Ammons. PfSP

Thunder heard—speak to ourselves. John Tranter. VaPo Fr. Blackout.

Thunder mutters louder and more loud, The. John Clare. NPeEn

Thunder of the Rain God. House in Taos, A. Langston Hughes. APT-2

Thunder, Perfect Mind, The. Unknown.
   "I was sent forth from the power." PFTM-1

Thunder Storm. Mary F. Johnson. CenSon

Thunder Storm. George Keithley. PasH

Thunder / Voices of drowned. Tan Taigi. ZenPo, tr. by Takashi Ikemoto and Lucien Stryk

Thunderbirds. Tony Dater. OtW

Thunderbirds flying. Shagoon 1–4. Andrew Hope III. FTtHH

Thunderbolt—eyes wide, A. Mumon-Ekai. ZenPo, tr. by Takashi Ikemoto and Lucien Stryk

Thundered in her skull for evermore! (LL) In the Children's Hospital. Hugh MacDiarmid. BrAP; NAEL-6v2; NAEL-7v2

Thundering sea, why in savage storm did you plunge. Leonidas of Tarentum. HePo, tr. by Barbara Hughes Fowler

Thunderstorm. Sam Mitchell. NOBAu, tr. by George von Brandenstein

Thunder-Storm, A. Emily Dickinson. APN-2; NCAP; WeW-3

Thunderstorm breaks up, The. Prince Shiki. SoOfWa, tr. by Sam Hamill

Thung joo Kwa yaa na povi sah. Gia's Song. Nora Naranjo-Morse. ReEnLa

Thursday. Víctor Hernández Cruz. PueRic

Thursday. Thomas James Jones. BBMWP, tr. by Jon Dressel

Thursday. Edna St. Vincent Millay. AmWit; PoA 2002

Thursday. Miklós Radnóti. IQMS, tr. by John Wain

Thursday. William Carlos Williams. APT-1

Thursday Afternoon: Life Is Sweet. Holly Iglesias. SweBea

Thursday Before New Yeares Day (Being on the Satterdy) the Maide, by Councell of One, On. She Trustid Well, Excussid Herself on This Wise to Milord, The. Marie Collyn. EMWP

Thursday Poem. DJ Renegade. FuFl

Thus. . . / He now begins his wakefulness. State of Butterfly. Ahmed Taha. NAfrP, tr. by Clarissa C. Burt

Thus Achelous ends; his audience hear. Ovid. NOSC Fr. Metamorphoses.

Thus all men's pleas the Judge with ease. Michael Wigglesworth. NAAL-3 Fr. Day of Doom, The [First Section].

Thus all that day, they spent in divers talke. Sir John Harington. PBRV Fr. Ariosto's Orlando Furioso Book 34.

Thus all the year I mourn. (LL) I Walked [or Walkt or Walk'd] the Other Day to Spend My Hour. Henry Vaughan. BASC; FSCP; NAEL-6v1

Thus am I mine own prison. Everything. Christina Georgina Rossetti. PEW Fr. Thread of Life, The.

Thus at the panting Dove a Falcon flies. Homer. OBVE Fr. Iliad, The.

Thus been they parted, Arthur on his way. Edmund Spenser. OBNV Fr. Faerie Queene, The.

Thus began a beautiful summer day. (LL) Beginning of a Beautiful Day (A Symphony), The. Daniil Kharms. AF; MotU, tr. by George Gibian

Thus began / Outrage from lifeless things; but Discord first. John Milton. NAEL-6v1; NAWM-7v1 Fr. Paradise Lost.

Thus Bonny-boots the birthday celebrated. John Holmes. NPeEn

Thus briefly sketched [or sketch'd] the sacred rights of man. On Mr. Paine's Rights of Man. Philip Freneau. NAAL-3; NAAL-5; NAAPv.1
   (Thus briefly sketched the sacred RIGHTS OF MAN.) ColAP

Thus, by turns, the leaders suffered the wounds of war. Lucan. RomPo Fr. Civil War [Bellum Civile] or Pharsalia.

Thus charg'd he; nor Argicides denied. Homer. OBVE Fr. Odyssey.

Thus Criticks, of less Judgment than Caprice. Alexander Pope. See Thus critics, of less judgment than caprice.

Thus critics, of less judgment than caprice. Alexander Pope. BrAP Fr. Essay on Criticism, An.

Thus Damon sung—What though unknown to praise. Taking a View of the Country from His Retirement [or Elegy 21]. William Shenstone.

Thus did a nameless and immortal hand. On a Bas-relief of Pelops and Hippodameia. Mary Elizabeth Coleridge. ViWPN

Thus does the new moon lie cradled in earth. Sic transit gloria mundi. Skip Fox. AnSo

Thus does the sun. Sic transit. Skip Fox. AnSo

Thus ebbs and flows the current of her sorrow. William Shakespeare. NoSic Fr. Rape of Lucrece, The.

Thus / Egyptians roam about, as roam hippo-.   December 31.   Ahmed Taha. NAfrP, *tr. by* Clarissa C. Burt.

Thus every dream secretly and small inscribes its letters.   Dreams Are Also Wounds.   Breyten Breytenbach.   VCWP, *tr. by* André Brink

Thus every one before the Throne.   Michael Wigglesworth.   TCAPo *Fr.* Day of Doom, The [First Section].

Thus everyone before the throne.   Michael Wigglesworth.   NAAL-3 *Fr.* Day of Doom, The [First Section].

Thus far I did come laden with my sin.   John Bunyan.   SacPr *Fr.* Pilgrim's Progress, The.

Thus far, my friend, have we retraced the way.   William Wordsworth. NPBRoP *Fr.* Two-Part Prelude, The.

Thus far, O Friend! have we, though leaving much.   William Wordsworth. NAEL-6v2; NAEL-7v2 *Fr.* Prelude, The; Growth of a Poet's Mind [1850 version].

Thus far, O Friend! have we, though leaving much.   William Wordsworth. *Fr.* Prelude, The; Growth of a Poet's Mind [1805 version].

Thus far this figure still remains unchanged. (LL)   Contribution to Statistics, A. Wisława Szymborska.   PtR; TWF, *tr. by* Stanislaw Barańczak and Clara Cavanagh and Clare Cavanagh

Thus far was right, the rest belongs to Heav'n. (LL)   Epistle to Dr. Arbuthnot. Alexander Pope.   NAEL-6v1; NAEL-7v1; NoP-4; NoP-5; OxAEP-1; TFi

Thus fell the King, who yet surviv'd the state.   Virgil.   OBVE *Fr.* Aeneid [*or* Eneados *or* Aeneis], The.

Thus feverish fancies floated in my brain.   *Unknown*.   CAGL *Fr.* Don Leon.

Thus Freud deposed about our infant state.   In the Beginning.   Howard Nemerov.   BodElec

Thus hath his death rais'd up this soule of mine. (LL)   Fulke, 1st Baron Brooke Greville.   CABP; NOSC; NoSic; NPeEn; PBRV *Fr.* Caelica.

Thus have I made up.   Very Short Sutra on the Meeting of the Buddha and the Goddess, The.   Rick Fields.   WhBo

Thus having been, that thou shouldst cease to be. (LL)   To Wordsworth.   Percy Bysshe Shelley.   CenSon; NAEL-6v2; NAEL-7v2; NoP-4; NoP-5; NPBRoP; NPeEn

Thus he addressed the cornfield.   Before a Cornfield.   Gottfried Benn. WoPoe, *tr. by* Harvey Shapiro

Thus he doth find of all mankind.   Michael Wigglesworth.   NAAL-3 *Fr.* Day of Doom, The [First Section].

Thus / Hides the.   George Oppen.   APT-2; PFTM-1

Thus I awoke, as God's my witness, when I lived in Cornhill.   William Langland.   NAEL-6v1; NAEL-7v1 *Fr.* Vision of Piers Plowman, The.

Thus I awoke, God knows, when I lived in Cornhill.   William Langland. WoPoe *Fr.* Vision of Piers Plowman, The.

Thus I Find My Legs.   Pam Rehm.   OnScMo

Thus I have written this poem on a jet seat in mid Heaven. (LL)   Kral Majales. Allen Ginsberg.   BB; PFTM-2

Thus long my grief has kept me dumb.   Threnodia Augustalis.   John Dryden.

Thus mayest thou ever, evermore rejoice! (LL)   Dejection: An Ode.   Samuel Taylor Coleridge.   BrAP; HeIP-4; NAEL-6v2; NAEL-7v2; NAWM-7v2; NOBRP; NoP-4; NoP-5; NPBRoP; NPeEn; OxAEP-2; PoPoPo; TFi; WaAnP

Thus much he prayed, and thence away he went.   Ludovico Ariosto.   NoSic *Fr.* Orlando Furioso.

Thus my brother.   Jamal Juma'h.   IrPoTo *Fr.* Letters to My Brother.

Thus Neptune rous'd these men.   Homer.   FaBoWar *Fr.* Iliad, The.

Thus, not the thing held in memory, but this.   On the Uncountable Nature of Things.   Ellen Hinsey.   StAl

Thus now I leave my love in fortunes {handes / bandes}.   Sir Walter Ralegh. PBRV *Fr.* Fortune Hath Taken The Away My Love.

Thus o'er his art indignant Rubens reared.   Rubens.   Washington Allston. APN-1

Thus on a bank, upon a summer's day.   Pups and the Alligator, The.   "Peter Pindar."   DiBP

Thus poor thieves suffer when the greater 'scape. (LL)   Michael Drayton. NoP-4; NoP-5 *Fr.* Idea.

Thus said The Lord in the Vault above the Cherubim.   Last Chantey, The. Rudyard Kipling.   MoBrPo

Thus saying, from her husband's hand her hand.   John Milton. *See* To whom thus also th' Angel last repli'd.

Thus saying rose / The monarch, and prevented all reply.   John Milton.   NOSC *Fr.* Paradise Lost.

Thus set them *ope*. (LL)   I Am the Door [*or* Doore].   Richard Crashaw. NAEL-6v1; NAEL-7v1

Thus shall they lie, and wail, and cry.   Michael Wigglesworth.   NAAL-3 *Fr.* Day of Doom, The [First Section].

Thus she had lain.   Africa.   Maya Angelou.   NIL-7; NIP-4

Thus should have been our travels.   Over 2000 Illustrations and a Complete Concordance.   Elizabeth Bishop.   APT-2; HarvBoo; NAMCP V.2; NoAM; OxBoAm; PoetW; VCAP

Thus spoke the lady underneath the tree.   Colonel Fantock.   Dame Edith Sitwell.   MoBrPo; OBMV

Thus spring begins: old.   Issa.   SoOfWa, *tr. by* Sam Hamill

Thus the Mayne Glideth.   Robert Browning.   OBEV *Fr.* Paracelsus.

Thus the ride of Sin. (LL)   Black riders came from the sea.   Stephen Crane. APN-2; NAAPv.1; NoP-4; NoP-5

Thus the tale ended. (LL)   Skeleton in Armor [*or* Armour], The.   Henry Wadsworth Longfellow.   APN-1; TreFP

Thus, therefore, he who feels the fiery dart.   Lucretius.   EroLit *Fr.* De Rerum Natura (On the Nature of Things).

Thus they in lowliest plight repentant stood.   John Milton. *Fr.* Paradise Lost.

Thus to Glaucus spake / Divine Sarpedon, since he did not find.   Homer. NPeEn; OBVE *Fr.* Iliad, The.

Thus was my love, thus was my Ganymed.   Richard Barnfield.   CAGL *Fr.* Cynthia, with Certain[e] Sonnets.

Thus with imagin'd way our swift scene flies.   William Shakespeare. OxAEP-1 *Fr.* King Henry V.

Thus you lived your life without regret.   Irina Ratushinskaya.   CRWP, *tr. by* C. J. K. Arkell

Thwack of an ax, The.   Buson.   SoOfWa, *tr. by* Sam Hamill

Thwarted.   Priscilla Jane Thompson.   CBWP-2

Thweet Poethy! let me *lithp* forthwith.   Smitten Purist, The.   James Whitcomb Riley.   VerBaPo

Thy ax shall harm it not. (LL)   Woodman, Spare That Tree.   George Pope Morris.   BRP; TCAPo

Thy beauty haunts me heart and soul.   Moon, The.   W. H. Davies.   MoBrPo

Thy best its best, Please God, thy best its best. (LL)   Cardinal Newman. Christina Georgina Rossetti.   NAEL-6v2; NAEL-7v2

Thy Better Self.   Jones Very.   TCAPo

Thy birth, thy beauty, nor thy brave attire.   George Gascoigne.   NAEL-6v1

Thy bosom is endeared with all hearts.   William Shakespeare.   OBEV *Fr.* Sonnets.

Thy Brother's Blood.   Jones Very.   APN-1

Thy care be first the various gifts to trace.   Thomas Tickell.   DiBP *Fr.* Fragment of a Poem on Hunting, A.

Thy cheek is pale with thought, but not from woe.   Sonnet, to the Same.   Lord Byron.   OxBSo

Thy Church has long been becoming the Fossil of a Faith.   James Thomson. SacPr *Fr.* Doom of a City, The.

Thy curate's place, thy fruitful wife.   Jonathan Swift.   UV *Fr.* Parson's Case, The.

Thy fabulous provinces belong. (LL)   Philomela.   John Crowe Ransom.   APT-1; FuPo; NoAM; OBSV

Thy Fields, propitious Pales, I rehearse.   Virgil.   *Fr.* Georgics.

Thy fingers make early flowers of.   E. E. Cummings.   MoAmPo

Thy flesh to earth, thy soul to God.   General B. F. Butler.   Ambrose Bierce. CBCWP

Thy flow'r afloat, goolden zummer clote! (LL)   Clote, The.   William Barnes. FaBoVe; NPeEn

Thy foes had girt thee with their dread array.   Last Banquet of Antony and Cleopatra, The.   Felicia Dorothea Hemans.   RWP

Thy forests, Windsor! and thy green retreats.   Alexander Pope.   OxAEP-1 *Fr.* Windsor-Forest [*or* Windsor Forest].

Thy glass will show thee how thy beauties wear.   William Shakespeare.   HeIP-4 *Fr.* Sonnets.

Thy God, thy life, thy Cure. (LL)   Peace.   Henry Vaughan.   FSCP; OBEV; OxAEP-1; OxBEV; RSR; TFi; WeW-3

Thy going smileth in me over.   Encounter.   August Stramm.   PFTM-1

Thy gown? Why, ay. Come, tailor, let us see't.   William Shakespeare.   OBCoV *Fr.* Taming of the Shrew, The.

Thy Heart.   *Unknown*.   OBCoV

Thy heart is in the upper world, where fleet the chamois bounds.   Chamois Hunter's Love, The.   Felicia Dorothea Hemans.   RWP; VWP

Thy human frame, my glorious Lord, I spy.   Edward Taylor.   ChIV-1 *Fr.* Preparatory Meditations Before My Approach to the Lord's Supper.

Thy husband to a banquet goes with me.   Ovid.   CABP; NoSic *Fr.* Elegies.

Thy life has touched the edges of my life.   My Spirit's Complement.   Henrietta Cordelia Ray.   CBWP-3

(Thy life hath touched the edges of my life.)   TCAPo

Thy love thou sentest oft to me.   Contrast, A.   James Russell Lowell.   NCAP

Thy lovely saints do bring Thee love.   Christina Georgina Rossetti.   SacPr *Fr.* Christ Our All in All.

Thy mansion is the Christian's heart.   William Cowper.   ChIV-2 *Fr.* Olney Hymns.

Thy mercy, Lord, Lord now thy mercy show.   Bible, *O.T.*   EMWP; PEW *Fr.* Psalms.

Thy mercy on Thy People, Lord! (LL)   Recessional.   Rudyard Kipling. BrAP; BRP; CABP; InvLi; MoBrPo; NAEL-6v2; NAEL-7v2; NAMCP V.1; NoAM; NoP-4; NoP-5; NPeEn; OBEV; OxAEP-2; OxBEV; TFi; UV; WaAnP

Thy mind which voluntary doubts molest. Lines Contributed to Hawkesworth's "The Rival." Samuel Johnson. NPeEn

Thy nature, and Thy name is Love.. (LL) Wrestling Jacob. Charles Wesley. OBEV; OxAEP-1

Thy nearness our forgiving cure. (LL) Broken Dark, The. Robert Earl Hayden. AWTN; GT

Thy Otway's sorrows, and lament his fate! (LL) To the River Arun ("On thy wild banks, by frequent torrents worn.") Charlotte Smith. CenSon; RWP

Thy place is changed; thou art the same. (LL) Alfred Tennyson. NAEL-6v2; NAEL-7v2; NoP-5 *Fr.* In Memoriam A. H. H.

Thy praise or dispraise is to me alike. To Fool or Knave. Ben Jonson. NoP-4; NoP-5

Thy pride upon a ring? (LL) Come, Gorgo, put the rug in place. Michael Field. ViWPN; VWP

Thy restless feet now cannot go. Christ Crucified. Richard Crashaw. OBEV

Thy sacred dew: protect them with thine influence. (LL) To the Evening Star. William Blake. GSo; NAEL-6v2; NAEL-7v2; NoP-4; NoP-5; NPeEn; TFi

Thy sacred law, O God. On God's Law. Francis Quarles. ChIV-1

Thy satin vesture richer is than looms. Copa de Oro (The California Poppy). Ina Coolbrith. ASA

Thy sheep with thee. (LL) And do they so? Henry Vaughan. BASC; SacPr

Thy sleep makes ridiculous. (LL) Humble-Bee, The. Ralph Waldo Emerson. APN-1; NAAPv.1; NCAP

Thy soul within such silent pomp did keep. Quiet Soul, A. John Oldham. OBEV

Thy spirit ere our fatal loss. Alfred Tennyson. CAGL *Fr.* In Memoriam A. H. H.

Thy summer voice, Musketaquit. Two Rivers. Ralph Waldo Emerson. APN-1; NCAP

Thy summer's day was long, but couldst thou think. 1802. Mary Tighe. CenSon

Thy tablet glimmers to the dawn. (LL) Alfred Tennyson. InoFa; NAEL-6v2; NAEL-7v2; NoP-5 *Fr.* In Memoriam A. H. H.

Thy throne, to Thee the rent in happiness. (LL) Edward Taylor. NAAL-3; NAAL-5; NAAPv.1 *Fr.* Preparatory Meditations Before My Approach to the Lord's Supper.

Thy trivial harp will never please. Ralph Waldo Emerson. NAAPv.1; NCAP *Fr.* Merlin.

Thy various works, imperial queen, we see. On Imagination. Phillis Wheatley. NAAPv.1; NoP-5; OxWW; RWP

Thy victory is in the heart. Victoria. Henry Van Dyke. SacPr

Thy voice is on the rolling air. Alfred Tennyson. CAGL; HeIP-4; NAEL-6v2; NAEL-7v2; NoP-5 *Fr.* In Memoriam A. H. H.

Thy voice prevails—dear friend, my gentle friend! Spirit's Return, A. Felicia Dorothea Hemans. NAEL-7v2

Thy voice, slow rising like a spirit, lingers. Percy Bysshe Shelley. NPBRoP

Thy way, not mine, O Lord. Thy Way, Not Mine. Horatius Bonar. SacPr

Thy weary feet have pressed once more thy native soil. Welcome Home. Josephine D. Henderson Heard. CBWP-4

Thy worn out heart will break at last, / My Mary! (LL) To Mary. William Cowper. NPBRoP; UV

Thyestes. Seneca. *tr. by* Abraham Cowley, Sir Matthew Hale, Jasper Heywood, Andrew Marvell and Sir Thomas Wyatt

"Climb at court for me that will." OBVE, *tr. by* Andrew Marvell

"Let him that will, ascend the tottering seat." OBVE, *tr. by* Sir Matthew Hale

"Let who so lyst with mighty mace to raygne." OBVE, *tr. by* Jasper Heywood

"O yee, whome lorde of lande and waters wyde." OBVE, *tr. by* Jasper Heywood

"Stand [*or* Stond] who so list upon the slipper top[pe]." NoSic; NPeEn; OBVE; OxBEV, *tr. by* Sir Thomas Wyatt

"Upon the slippery tops of human[e] state." BASC; OBVE, *tr. by* Abraham Cowley

Thyrsis. Matthew Arnold. NAEL-6v2; NAEL-7v2; NoP-4; NoP-5; OBEV; WaAnP

Thyrsis, a youth of the inspired train. Story of Phoebus and Daphne Applied, [etc.], The. Edmund Waller. NOSC

(*Thirsis* a youth of the inspired train.) PBRV

Thyrsis, sleep'st Thou? *Unknown.* NoSic

Thyrsis, sleep'st thou? Holla! Let not sorrow stay us. Thyrsis, Sleep'st Thou? *Unknown.* NoSic

Ti. Melvin B. Tolson. APT-2 *Fr.* Libretto for the Republic of Liberia.

Ti dxíta guidiladi miati. Dxiibi Guidxa. Natalia Toledo. RMCMP

Tía Olivia Serves Wallace Stevens a Cuban Egg. Richard Blanco. NAPBL

Tiananmen / Is broad and clean. Tiananmen. James Fenton. InoFa

Tiara. Mark Doty. MakPoe; WaAnP

Tibetan lamas say. Check Up. Patricia Donegan. WhBo

Tibia, tarsal, skull, and shin. Elegy for a Cave Full of Bones. John Ciardi. PWW2

Tichborne's Elegy. Chidiock Tichborne. AmFaPo; HeIP-4; InoFa; NIL-7; NoP-4; NoP-5; NoSic; PoPoPo; TFi; WeW-3

(Elegy: "My Prime of Youth Is But a Frost of Cares.") WaAnP; WeW-3

(On the Eve of His Execution.) WoPoe

Ticker. Amy Fusselman. HeMarv

Tickets for a Prayer Wheel. Annie Dillard.

"You go down the hall." UpMys

Ticking minutes shed their sound, The. Consolations Before an Affair, Upper West Side. Noelle Kocot. BAP-01

Tickle Rhyme, The. Ian Serraillier. NTCP; Spl

Ticklish Moments. Pedro Serrano. RMCMP, *tr. by* Geoff Hargreaves

Ticonderoga: A Legend of the West Highlands. Robert Louis Stevenson. OBNV

Tidal River, The. Edith Jay Scovell. HarvBoo *Fr.* Water Images.

Tidal wave over-runs the island, A. Wedding, A. Nadir Hussein. PML

Tide be runnin' the great world over. Sea Love. Charlotte Mew. LW; MoBrPo; OxAEP-2; OxBEV

Tide ebbs, The. Beachhead. Samuel Menashe. PWW2

Tide gone out for good, The. Death of Irish, The. Aidan Carl Mathews. PBCIP

Tide in the River, The. Eleanor Farjeon. NOxBChV

Tide Line Garden. W. S. Merwin. BodElec

Tide of Battle Turns, The. Homer. NAWM-7v1 *Fr.* Iliad, The.

Tide Rises, the Tide Falls, The. Henry Wadsworth Longfellow. APN-1; BrAP; CtM; ITBLP; NAAPv.1; OxBAm; PoPoPo

Tide Turning. John Frederick Nims. IllVoic

Tide-Reach. Roland Mathias.

Laus Deo. AngWePo

Tides. Helen Hunt Jackson. LW

Tides, The. Michael Klein. WiU

Tidings. Czeslaw Milosz. BodElec, *tr. by* Lillian Vallee

Tie, The. William Heyen. GM

Tie a bandage over his eyes. Rebel, A. John Gould Fletcher. MoAmPo

Tie the Strings to my Life, My Lord. Emily Dickinson. SacPr

Tie up my bones and walk them away. *Unknown.* SonAtl

Tiempo de bailar los árboles. Pedro Pérez Conde. RMCMP

Tiempo es un espejo en que te miras, El. Agua Desatándose. Luis Rosales. RaW

Tiempo hubo para la audiencia de los peces. Epístola del náufrago. María Baranda. RMCMP

Tiempo Mezquino. Claudio Rodríguez. RaW

Tiempo se ha ido recorriendo como si se hubiera trasroscado, El. Noria, La. Pedro Serrano. RMCMP

Tien manieren om P.B. Shelley te zien. Hugo Claus. LWR

Tierra de Nadie. José Ángel Valente. RaW

Tierra prometida, La. Jorge Fernández Granados. RMCMP

Ties. Eluned Phillips. BBMWP, *tr. by* Gillian Clarke

Tiff Belt Parley. David Thomas Roberts. AnSo

Tiff, The [*or* The Interview]. Robert Merry. STuOW

Tig. *Unknown.* FaBoVe

Tiger, The. Joseph Hilaire Pierre Belloc. MoBrPo

Tiger, The. Laura Riding Jackson. MoWP

Tiger, The. Marie Laurencin. CuPo

Tiger Christ unsheathed his sword. For the One Who Would Take Man's Life in His Hands. Delmore Schwartz. MoAmPo

Tiger comes to mind, A. The twilight here. Other Tiger, The. Jorge Luis Borges. TCLAP, *tr. by* Norman Thomas Di Giovanni

Tiger in me I know late, not burning bright, The. Tiger, The. Laura Riding Jackson. MoWP

Tiger in the tiger-pit, The. Lines for an Old Man. T. S. Eliot. RaBo

Tiger Lady. Miguel Algarín. PueRic

Tiger Lily. Alfred Kreymborg. APT-1

Tiger moth, now another and another another, A. (LL) Dusk: "Before the dusk grows deeper." Joseph Ceravolo. NYP2; OxBoAm

Tiger, on the other hand, is kittenish and mild, The. Tiger, The. Joseph Hilaire Pierre Belloc. MoBrPo

"Tiger, strolling at my side." Triumph of Sensibility. Sylvia Townsend Warner. MoBrPo

Tiger Valley. Muso Soseki. EaWin, *tr. by* W. S. Merwin

Tigerish. Cahit Zarifoǧlu. NaPG, *tr. by* Talat Sait Halman

Tiger-Lilies. Michael Field. ViWPN

Tiger's Absence. Cristina Campo. *tr. by* Cinzia Sartini Blum and Lara Trubowitz

"Ah that the Tiger." CItWP, *tr. by* Cinzia Sartini Blum and Lara Trubowitz

Canon 4. CItWP, *tr. by* Cinzia Sartini Blum and Lara Trubowitz

Tigers Know from Birth. Anne Wilkinson. IFF

(My Bones Predict.) BrAP

Tight Corners. David Bromige.
 "He thought it humanity's lot for ever to be persuading a huge rock up a
   mountainside." FTOS

Tighten. Hadewijch II. WPoS

Tighter, me boys! One half-twist on that screw. Iago to His Torturers. R. S.
 Gwynn. IaFF

Tightly-folded bud. Born Yesterday. Philip Larkin. NoP-5

Tightness and the nilness round that space, The. From the Frontier of Writing.
 Seamus Heaney. BrAP; CABP; ModIr; PoetW; PoPoPo

Tightrope Wedding, The. Michael Laskey. BeAl

Tijeras, Las. Fabio Morabito. RMCMP

Til Death Do Us Part. Kalamu ya Salaam. SpirFl Fr. New Orleans Haiku.

Tilde impar, La. Dolores Dorantes. SPV

Tilden Park. Alison Deming. UrbNat

Tile is loose for splendid feet, A. Stepping Out. Michael Brownstein. FTOS

Tiles. Witter Bynner. APT-1; TCAPo

Till a moment ago we were "Mister" and "Miss." My Darling, My Darling.
 Frank Loesser. ReLy

Till all sweet gums and juices flow. Prince's Progress, The. Christina
 Georgina Rossetti.

Till both our heads were in his aureole. (LL) Dante Gabriel Rossetti. NAEL-
 6v2; OxBSo Fr. House of Life, The.

Till bright as blood the peachstone showed. (LL) Peachstone. Dannie Abse.
 AngWePo; WeW-3

'Till cheerless on their path the night descends. (LL) Languid, and sad, and
 slow. William Lisle Bowles. CenSon; NAEL-6v2

Till cherry-ripe themselves do[e] cry. (LL) There is a garden in her face.
 Thomas Campion. BASC; BrAP; HeIP-4; NAEL-6v1; NAEL-7v1; NOSC;
 NPeEn; PBRV; TFi

 (Till "Cherry ripe!" themselves do cry.) (LL) NoP-4; NoP-5

Till dreadful[l] death do [c]ease my doleful[l] state? (LL) Pillar [or Piller]
 perished [or pearisht] is whe[a]rto I le[a]nt, The. Sir Thomas Wyatt.
 NoSic; OBVE; OxBEV; PBRV

Till earth restores her sons to heaven again. (LL) I Was Sick and in Prison.
 Jones Very. ColAP; SacPr

Till eight days like any happy fly. Course of a Life, The. Yehuda Amichai.
 BBASP, tr. by Chana Bloch

Till Evening. Jakov Steinberg. FIT, tr. by Robert Friend

Till ev'n his beams sing, and my music[k] shine. (LL) Christmas. George
 Herbert. ChrPo; NOSC

Till God calls you away. (LL) Unquiet Grave, The. Unknown. CABP; HeIP-
 4; NoP-4; NoP-5; TFi; WeW-3; WoPoe

Till her fingers are stiff with cold. Poor Woman. Hŏ Nansŏrhŏn. CATKP, tr.
 by Peter H. Lee

Till human voices wake us, and we drown. (LL) Love Song of J. Alfred
 Prufrock, The. T. S. Eliot. AmFaPo; APT-1; BrAP; ClHu; ColAP; EMP;
 GPTC; HarvBoo; HeIP-4; IJHIL; MakPoe; MoAmPo; NAAL-5; NAAPv.2;
 NAEL-6v2; NAEL-7v2; NAMCP V.1; NAWM-7v2; NIL-7; NoAM; NoP-4;
 NoP-5; NPeEn; OxAEP-2; OxBEV; OxBoAm; PoA 2002; PoPoPo; SoSe-8;
 TCAPo; TFi; TRP; WaAnP; WeW-3; WoPoe

Till I become accustomed to the dark. (LL) When I too long have looked upon
 your face. Edna St. Vincent Millay. HeIP-4; MoWP

Till I have made my valiant mistress yield. (LL) To His Coy Mistress. Sir
 Robert Aytoun. NOSC; WaAnP

Till I reach heaven [or heav'n] and, much more, thee. (LL) Affliction (4).
 George Herbert. CABP; NOSC

'Till in the rising tide the exhausted sufferer dies. (LL) Written on the Sea
 Shore.—October, 1784. Charlotte Smith. CenSon; RWP

Till it could come no more. (LL) At the Seaside [or Sea-Side]. Robert Louis
 Stevenson. NTCP; TLR; WHSW

Till life divine re-animate[s] his dust. (LL) On the Death of the Rev. Mr.
 George Whitefield [1770]. Phillis Wheatley. ColAP; NAAL-3; NAAL-5;
 NAAPv.1; SacPr; WaAnP

Till life's last hour, with Phaon's self decays! (LL) Describes Phaon. Mary
 Robinson. CenSon; RWP

Till Love and Fame to nothingness do sink. (LL) When I Have Fears [That I
 May Cease to Be]. John Keats. BrAP; CABP; CenSon; GSo; HeIP-4;
 NAEL-6v2; NAEL-7v2; NIL-7; NIP-4; NoP-4; NoP-5; NPBRoP; OBEV;
 PoPoPo; TFi; WaAnP; WoPoe

Till my bad angel fire my good one out. (LL) William Shakespeare. AEP;
 HeIP-4; NAEL-6v1; NAEL-7v1; NIL-7; NoP-5; OxBSo; PBRV Fr. Sonnets.

Till my feet, cloven too, take hold on hell? (LL) World, The. Christina
 Georgina Rossetti. NALW; PEW; ViWPN

Till no one. Wopko Jensma. TSAP

Till now / I've not been able to imagine. Inna Kulishova. CRWP, tr. by
 Daniel Weissbort

Till that her blush taught me my shame to see. (LL) Sir Philip Sidney.
 NAEL-6v1; NAEL-7v1; NoSic Fr. Astrophil and Stella.

Till the Clouds Roll By. P. G. Wodehouse. NAAPv.2; ReLy

Till the day I die, I shall never leave her beauty's sun. Muhibbi. NaPG, tr. by
 Talat Sait Halman

Till the gossamer thread you fling catch somewhere, O my soul. (LL) Noiseless
 Patient Spider, A. Walt Whitman. APN-1; BLT; BrAP; ColAP; CtM;
 HeIP-4; ITBLP; MoAmPo; NAAL-3; NAAL-5; NAAPv.1; NCAP; NIL-7;
 NoP-4; NoP-5; OxBoAm; PoPoPo; SAmP; TCAPo; TFi; WaAnP; WoPoe

Till the lamp flickers, and the memory fails. (LL) Holy Tide, The. Frederick
 Tennyson. OBEV; SacPr

Till the rough-gem moon. Lady Otomo no Sakanoé. ArkPo, tr. by Edwin A.
 Cranston

Till the slow daylight pale. Sun-Flower, The. Dora Greenwell. EroLit; VWP

Till There Was You. Meredith Willson. ReLy

Till they are incandescent. (LL) Her Lips Are Copper Wire. Jean Toomer.
 APT-2; GT; NAAPv.2; NAMCP V.1; NoAM

Till thy wished smile thy mother's pangs o'erpay. (LL) To a Little Invisible
 Being Who Is Expected Soon to Become Visible. Anna Laetitia Barbauld.
 NAEL-6v2; NAEL-7v2; WoRP

Till twelve years' [or yeres'] age, how Christ His childhood spent. Christ[e]'s
 Childhood[e]. Robert Southwell. ChIV-2

Till we make our own land holy. Robert Kelly. WhBo Fr. Flowers of
 Unceasing Coincidence, The.

Till When Will We Sleep after the Whore. Ronny Someck. IrPoTo, tr. by
 Vivian Eden

Tilling the field. Buson. EH, tr. by Robert Hass

Tilt, The. Kim Roberts. AmPoNex Fr. Constellation Frigidaire, The.

Tilt the placeless waver of this moving. Sonnet. Karen Volkman. IAoNAP

Tilth. Robert Graves. OBSV

Tilts, Point Lance, The. Agnes Walsh. Coast

Tim Finnegan [or Finnigin or Finigan] liv'd in Walkin [or lived in Walker]
 Street. Finnegan's Wake. Unknown. NBLV

Timbalero—if you don't know. Timbalero. Julia Maier. BRtP

Timber, The. Henry Vaughan. OBEV

Time. Mary Ursula Bethell. OBGa

Time. (LL) Anne Carson. OxBoAm; WoBe Fr. Truth About God, The.

Time. Tom Clark. BodElec

Time: "How long for the small yellow flowers." Robert Creeley. BodElec;
 ICANM

Time: "There was too much, always, then too little." Louise Glück. BAP-01;
 PtR

Time. George Herbert. NAEL-6v1; NAEL-7v1

Time. Dulce Maria Loynaz. TANSG, tr. by Alan West

Time. Jasper Mayne. OBEV

Time. Adelia Prado. TANSG, tr. by Ellen Doré Watson

Time 5. Yi Kyŏngnim. EcSo, tr. by Peter H. Lee

Time: A Poem. Henry Kirke White.
 Britannia Rejecta. STuOW

Time After Time. Sammy Cahn. ReLy

Time Allotted, The. Ingeborg Bachmann. PFTM-2, tr. by Jerome Rothenberg

Time and again I have to love you. Hans Faverey. WoBe Fr. Eighteen Poems.

Time and again I've longed for adventure. All the Things You Are. Oscar
 Hammerstein, II. ReLy

Time and again, time and again I tie. Edge, The. Louise Glück. HarvBoo

Time and again we're cut down to size. Martin Sorrell. NewEx

Time and again, with my hand. Robinson. Karl Krolow. GTCP, tr. by
 Reinhold Grimm

Time and Grief. William Lisle Bowles. OBEV
 ("O Time! who know'st a lenient hand to lay.") GSo

Time and Light. Jim Powell.
 "Now in the tight trench you go." CalPo

Time and Materials. Robert Hass. RoV

Time and Music. Janet Lewis. FFC

Time and the bell have buried the day. T. S. Eliot. WaAnP Fr. Four Quartets.

Time and the Garden. Yvor Winters. APT-2; HarvBoo; MoAmPo; NoAM

Time and the Response, The. Nathan Alterman. NRoS, tr. by Esther Raizen

Time, and thy charms, thou fanciest will redeem. To a Young Lady, Purposing
 to Marry a Man of Immoral Character in the Hope of his Reformation.
 Anna Seward. CenSon

Time between us stretches out, The. Black Winter. Frank Stewart. AmWaPo

Time Break. Everett Hoagland. FuFl

Time brought me many another friend. Not Yet. Mary Elizabeth Coleridge.
 PoBW

Time Bum. Jordan Davis. HeMarv

Time came for him to be released, The. Exile. Stephen Dobyns. OPRER

Time can [or will] say nothing but I told you so. Villanelle. W. H. Auden.
 MoBrPo

Time comes when a majority of those you remember, A. Titanic, The. Witter
 Bynner. APT-1

Time Comes When You Are Facing Him, The. David Ignatow. PoDa

Time comes when you no longer can say: my God, A. Your Shoulders Hold Up the World. Carlos Drummond de Andrade. PoetW, *tr.* by Mark Strand

Time couldn't take away our words but place changed them. Dyke View Berry Farm. Leonard Neufeldt. ACAMVP

Time does not bring relief; you all have lied. Sonnet 2. Edna St. Vincent Millay. HarvBoo; HeIP-4; LW; NAAPv.2; OxBSo; PLBUT; WaAnP

Time draws near the birth of Christ, The. Alfred Tennyson. ChrPo; NAEL-6v2; NAEL-7v2; NAWM-7v2; RSR; SoSe-8 *Fr.* In Memoriam A. H. H.

Time even for the grass hut. Basho. EMJL, *tr.* by Haruo Shirane

Time flies by like a great whale. Ted Berrigan. FTOS *Fr.* Sonnets, The.

Time flies, hope flags, life plies a wearied wing. Christina Georgina Rossetti. OxBSo *Fr.* Monna Innominata.

Time flits away, time flits away, lady. Variation on Ronsard. Thomas Sturge Moore. OBMV

Time for a walk. Muso Soseki. EaWin, *tr.* by W. S. Merwin

Time for Blushing, A. Fergus Allen. IrLP

Time for Dejection. Hamda Khamees. PoArWo, *tr.* by Joseph T. Zeidan

Time for Guns, A. Darryl Holmes. InTrad

Time for the wood, the clay. Kept. Louise Bogan. APT-2

Time for toil has passed, and night has come, The. Bringing Our Sheaves with Us. Elizabeth Akers. TreFP

Time for Trees to Dance. Pedro Pérez Conde. RMCMP, *tr.* by Michael Wiegers

Time, Give Me the Secret. Juan Ramón Jiménez. RaW, *tr.* by Ralph Nelson and Rita García Nelson

Time has been that these wild solitudes, The. Winter Piece, A. William Cullen Bryant. APN-1; ColAP

Time has brought about great changes. Scraps of Time. Mrs. Henry Linden. CBWP-4

Time has come to devote myself to my hiker's stick, The. On Receiving My Letter of Termination. Yüan Hung-tao. ColAnChi, *tr.* by Jonathan Chaves

Time has no spectacle more stern and strange. Lower New York. George Cabot Lodge. APN-2

Time has not laid. Plait of Hair, The. Alice V. Stuart. PoBW

Time has not quenched your beauty. Much of your bygone prime. Rufinus. HePo, *tr.* by Barbara Hughes Fowler

Time Heals All Wounds—But One. Vernon Rowe. BloBone

Time Heals Everything. Jerry Herman. ReLy

Time heals ev'rything. Time Heals Everything. Jerry Herman. ReLy

Time heals not: it extends a sorrow's scope. James Vincent Cunningham. WoPoe *Fr.* Epigrams.

Time, Hope, and Memory. Thomas Hood. TreFP

Time I bought that cheap jackknife, The. Memoir of the Cosmopolite Who Stayed Home. Ron McFarland. RWB

Time I dropped your almost body down, The. Lost baby poem, The. Lucille Clifton. AmFaPo; BeAl; CAP-8; ESEAA; InoFa; ISC; OxAAAP; WaAnP

Time I went to church I sat, The. Mr. Rockefeller's Hat. Helen Smith Bevington. AmWit

Time in Armagh. John Montague.
  Welcoming Party, A. PNI

Time in the brain cells swearing like a nail bomb. Killing Time #2. Simon Armitage. BeAl

Time is, The. Anger. Robert Creeley. PFTM-2

Time is a mirror in which you see yourself. Loosening Water. Luis Rosales. RaW, *tr.* by Ralph Nelson and Rita García Nelson

Time is a thing. Epilogue. Stephen Spender. MoBrPo

Time is come I must depart[e], The. Aucthour Maketh Her Wyll and Testament, The. Isabella Whitney. EMWP; NoP-4

Time is filled with beginners. You are right. Now. Lyn Hejinian. FaoP *Fr.* Fatalist, The.

Time is hunger, space is cold. Great Prayer. Alfonso Cortes. TCLAP, *tr.* by Thomas Merton

Time is my debtor for my years untold. (LL) Long Time a Child. Hartley Coleridge. CenSon; NPBRoP; NPeEn; OxBSo

Time is not remote when I, The. Jonathan Swift. NPeEn; OxAEP-1; OxBEV *Fr.* Verses on the Death of Dr. Swift, D.S.P.D, Occasioned by Reading a Maxim in Rochefoucauld.

Time is the feather'd thing. Time. Jasper Mayne. OBEV

Time I've Lost in Wooing, The. Thomas Moore. AmFaPo; NAEL-6v2; NAEL-7v2; NOBRP

Time like the receptions of a child's piano. Reconciliation, The. Archibald MacLeish. MoAmPo

Time may come, when to remember, A. Fatherland in the Heights. Gyula Illyés. IQMS, *tr.* by Vernon Watkins

Time Now Please. Adriann Roland Holst. TuT, *tr.* by Paula Meehan

Time of Cherries, A. Suzanne Burrows. Prnts

Time of day: a dim dream, probably. Yards of Sarajevo, The. Richard Hugo. AF

Time of fear, a time of dread, A. Time of Fear, A. Sándor Petőfi. IQMS, *tr.* by George F. Cushing

Time of fools is coming. Untitled. Aleksandar Ristovic. BeAl, *tr.* by Charles Simic

Time of green spring winds returns, The. Springtime South of the Yangtze. Li Po. CrYelRi, *tr.* by Sam Hamill

Time of joy, A. Each city was a big family united by fear. At the Gates of Aerea. René Char. BAP-04; MotU, *tr.* by Franz Wright

Time of loving and fluttering has not yet come, The. Land Stretching Up to the Sky, A. Nada El-Hage. PoArWo, *tr.* by Nathalie El-Hani

Time of Roses. Thomas Hood. OBEV

Time of Turtles. Grace Perry. NOBAu

Time of vigils comes, alas to blight, The. Verse of Darkness, The. Jenő Dsida. IQMS, *tr.* by Watson Kirkconnell

Time of white violets; and on the slopes. Convent in '45, The. Maria Luisa Spaziani. NeIt, *tr.* by Beverly Allen

Time of year has grown indifferent, The. Man Whose Pharynx Was Bad, The. Wallace Stevens. OxBoAm

Time on My Hands. Harold Adamson and Mack Gordon. ReLy

Time Once Again. Mark McMorris. IAoNAP

Time only/. Opting for Early Retirement. Tom Leonard. Oth

Time Out. Maurice Riordan. BeAl; EmeKit; ModIr

Time Out: "We will put Time to sleep on that warm hill." Genevieve Taggard. ASA

Time passes—a false light. (LL) Closed car—closed in glass. George Oppen. APT-2; PFTM-1

Time Passing, Beloved. Donald Davie. HarvBoo; NoP-4; NoP-5

Time Past, A. Denise Levertov. NAMCP V.2; NoAM

Time, Place, and Parenthood. Hayden Carruth. PoChi

Time, Please. Adriann Roland Holst. TuT, *tr.* by Sean Dunne

Time present and time past. T. S. Eliot. APT-1; HarvBoo; MoAmPo; NAAL-5 *Fr.* Four Quartets.

Time Presses Me. Lee Ranaldo. HeMarv

Time, Real and Imaginary. Samuel Taylor Coleridge. OBEV

Time Recover'd. Thomas Stanley. OBVE

Time Signature. Linda Andrews. MiVo

"Time stands still." Unbeseechable, The. Frances Darwin Cornford. MoBrPo

Time stays, they said. We go. Ancient Ones, The: Betátakin. Janet Lewis. APT-2

Time stood still. Grandmother, The. Claribel Alegría. TANSG, *tr.* by Darwin Flakoll

Time Swept Up. Vasco [or Vasko] Popa. PoSu *Fr.* Raw Flesh.

Time, Temperature. Jim Daniels. LTA

Time that brings [or bringes] all things to light. Epitaph. Thomas Morton. NOSC

Time, that gives to music life. Time and Music. Janet Lewis. FFC

Time that is moved by little fidget wheels. Five Bells. Kenneth Slessor. BrAP; NOBAu

Time that passes between my mother and me, The. Time That Passes, The. Agnes Walsh. Coast

Time there was I hated this old chair, A. Turning a Fresh Eye. Lillias Scott Forbes. EdScPo

Time ticks away the centre of my pride. Empty Glen, The. R. Crombie Saunders. EdScPo

Time To Be Up, Marie, Young Sleepyhead. Pierre de Ronsard. STV, *tr.* by John Frederick Nims

Time to Hear Ourselves Think. Dick Allen. PoDa

Time to love, and a time to hate; a time of war, and a time of peace, A. (LL) Bible, *O.T.* BLPJKO; NAWM-5v1; OBVE *Fr.* Ecclesiastes.

"Time to put off the world and go somewhere." Beggar to Beggar Cried. William Butler Yeats. NoAM; OxAEP-2

Time to Shine. Hamda Khamees. PoArWo, *tr.* by Joseph T. Zeidan

Time to tell you things are well, A. Snow Country Weavers. James Welch. HATNAP

Time to Tickle a Lizard, The. Lizard, The. Theodore Roethke. NOxBChV

Time to wipe away the slime. Now. Margaret Abigail Walker. OxAAAP

Time Travel. Nick Piombino. FTOS

Time Traveler's Potlatch. Philip Lamantia. CLPP

Time turned inside out. Olga Ivanova. CRWP, *tr.* by Jenefer Coates

Time wants to show you a different country. It's the one. Gift, The. William Stafford. ItP

Time was, and that was termed the time of Gold. Joseph Hall. OBSV *Fr.* Virgidemiarum.

Time was away and she was here. (LL) Meeting Point. Louis MacNeice. ModIr; NPeEn; PNI

Time was away and somewhere else. Meeting Point. Louis MacNeice. ModIr; NPeEn; PNI

Time was, ere yet in these degenerate days. Lord Byron. NPBRoP *Fr.* English Bards and Scotch Reviewers [1810 version].

Time was God judged. In the Days of Socrates. Friedrich Hölderlin. PFTM-1

Time was, I sat upon a lofty stool. Literary Reminiscences. Thomas Hood. OxBSo

Time was the apple Adam ate. Original Sequence. Philip Booth. ChIV-1

Time was when his half million drew. Bewick Finzer. Edwin Arlington Robinson. MoAmPo

Time was, when we were sow'd, and just began. Ovid. NPeEn *Fr.* Metamorphoses.

Time wasted and time spent. Times, The. Charles Madge. OBMV

Time we rightfully called ours, when breakfast was toast, A. Feeding Frenzy. Holly Iglesias. SweBea

Time, while it beauty's pow'r impairs. To a Friend, Fearful of Being Forgotten in Absence. Eliza Cobbe, Lady Tuite. PoBW

Time will come, after insomnias and strayings, The. Ballad for Dialectical Materialism. Ivan Radoev. CSCBP, *tr.* by Georgi Belev and Lisa Sapinkopf

Time will come, The. Love after Love. Derek Walcott. BeAl; PML; PtR; RaF; TWF; WhBo

Time will say nothing but I told you so. If I Could Tell You. W. H. Auden. HarvBoo; OxBoAm; WaAnP

Time with his scythe honed fine. Hay Fever. Alec Derwent Hope. NoAM

Time with Stevie Wonder in It. Christopher Gilbert. SwNoth

Time, wouldst thou hurt us? Never shall we grow old. Double Fortress, The. Alfred Noyes. SacPr

Time, You Old Gypsy Man. Ralph Hodgson. MoBrPo

Time, you thief, who love to get. Max Beerbohm. UV

Time you won your town the race, The. A. E. Housman. BrAP; ChAP; CtM; HeIP-4; InoFa; MoBrPo; NAEL-6v2; NAEL-7v2; NAMCP V.1; NIP-4; NoAM; NoP-4; NoP-5; PtR; SoSe-8; TFi; TRP; WaAnP; WeW-3 *Fr.* Shropshire Lad, A.

Time Zones. Jane Duran. MFPA

Timely Hint, A. Sydney Thompson Dobell. STuOW *Fr.* Roman, The.

Time-piece, The. William Cowper. *Fr.* Task, The.

Timer. Tony Harrison. EmeKit; HarvBoo; NAMCP V.2 *Fr.* School of Eloquence, The.

Times. Tom Weatherly. SeSe

Times. Lola Haskins. LiTh

Times, The. Charles Churchill. "Is a son born into this world of woe?" OBSV

Times, The. Charles Madge. OBMV

Time's Betrayal. Herman Melville. NCAP

Times come round again, The. To a Military Rifle, 1942. Yvor Winters. MoAmPo; PWW2

Time's come up pearls—let us wander. Time's Come Up Pearls. Sándor Weöres. IQMS, *tr.* by Adam Makkai and Donald E. Morse

Times followed one another. Came a morn. Elizabeth Barrett Browning. NAEL-6v2; NAEL-7v2 *Fr.* Aurora Leigh.

Time's Fool. Ruth Pitter. MoBrPo

Time's fool, but not heaven's: yet hope not for any return. Time's Fool. Ruth Pitter. MoBrPo

Times [or Tymes] Go[e] By Turn[e]s. Robert Southwell. ChIV-1; NoSic

Times Go by Turns. Richard Verstegan. SacPr

Times Gone By. János Vajda. IQMS, *tr.* by Jess Perlman

Times have changed. Anything Goes. Cole Porter. APT-1; ReLy

Times have changed, there is not left to us, The. Allen Tate. PoA 2002

Times Like This. Richard Jones. GifTon

Time's Muteness. Gareth Alban Davies. BBMWP, *tr.* by Joseph P. Clancy

Time's passed as if its screw got crossed. Treadmill. Pedro Serrano. RMCMP, *tr.* by Geoff Hargreaves

Times Square. Alter Brody. TaR

Times Square Water Music. Amy Clampitt. UrbNat

Time's Whirligig, Or, The Blue-New-Made-Gentleman Mounted. Humphrey Willis. NOSC

Timetable. Kate Clanchy. EdScPo

Timid grace sits trembling in her eye, A. Charles Lamb. GSo

Timid Lover. Countee Cullen. ColAP

Tímidos, Los. Antonio Deltoro. RMCMP

Timing. Anne Rouse. NeBl

Timoleon. Herman Melville. APN-2

Timon, for you exist no more. Callimachus. HePo, *tr.* by Barbara Hughes Fowler

Timon of Athens. William Shakespeare. Misanthropos. DiBP

"O blessed breeding sun! draw from the earth." OxAEP-1

"Put up thy gold: go on,—here's gold,—go on." OxAEP-1

Timon's Villa. Alexander Pope. NPeEn; OxBEV *Fr.* Epistle IV to Richard Boyle, Earl of Burlington.

Timor Mortis. *Unknown.* NoP-4; NoP-5; SacPr

Timor mortis conturbat me. (LL) Lament for the Makaris [or Makars or Makers]. William Dunbar. InoFa; MakPoe; NePenScot; NoP-4; NoP-5; OBEV; OxBEV; WaAnP

Timor mortis conturbat me. (LL) Timor Mortis. *Unknown.* NoP-4; NoP-5; SacPr

Timoshenko. Sidney Keyes. OBWP

Timothy. Timothy Steele. RA

Tin bath once brimmed with daughters, The. Things. Geoffrey Holloway. NLP

Tin Frog, The. Russell Hoban. Spl

Tin Roof. Michael Ondaatje. "Oh Rilke, I want to sit down calm like you." BrAP

Tin shack, where my baby sleeps on his back. Everything: Eloy, Arizona, 1956. Ai. BodElec

Tin Wash Dish, The. Les A. Murray. BMAP

Tina and Seth met in the midst of an overcrowded militarism. Histoire. Harry Mathews. NIP-4; OxBoAm; PmAP

Tina speaks to her friend on the phone. Motor Oil Queen. Cheryl Burke. WiU

Tind friends, I pray extuse me. New Baby, The. Fred Emerson Brooks. VerBaPo

Tinder. Seamus Heaney. OxAEP-2

Tinderbox. Ruth Padel. NeBrP

Tinfoil. Joyce Mansour. MFP; YaTCFP, *tr.* by Martin Sorrell

Tingle: / a shaft must be imagined to. Getting Warm. Rae Armantrout. FTOS

Tinian. Friedrich Hölderlin. *tr.* by David Gascoyne "Pleasant to wander." WoPoe, *tr.* by David Gascoyne

Tinily a star goes down. Iain Crichton Smith. StAl

Tinker, Come Bring Your Solder. Mary Mapes Dodge. SWaP

Tinker, come bring your solder. Tinker, Come Bring Your Solder. Mary Mapes Dodge. SWaP

Tinker's Wife. Patrick Kavanagh. NoAM

Tinkling treble, / Rolling bass. Dream Boogie: Variation. Langston Hughes. APSN; NAMCP V.1; OxBoAm; SSLK

Tinnitus. Karen McCosker. NevBe

Tin-roofed shacks, The. Ruby Red's Migrant Camp. Wilma Elizabeth McDaniel. GeoHom

Tinsel Marie; The Coora Flower. Gwendolyn Brooks. ESEAA *Fr.* Children Going Home.

Tint I cannot take—is best, The. Emily Dickinson. APN-2; MoAmPo

Tintern Abbey. William Wordsworth. *See* Lines Composed a Few Miles above Tintern Abbey on Revisiting the Banks of the Wye During a Tour, July 13, 1798.

Tintoret peignit sa fille morte, Le. Pomme Rouge, La. Jean Follain. YaTCFP

Tintoretto painted his dead daughter. Red Apple, The. Jean Follain. YaTCFP, *tr.* by Serge Gavronsky

Tintype of a Private in the Fifteenth Georgia Infantry. Paul Horgan. CBCWP

Tiny Bird, A. *Vietnamese Oral Tradition.* CaDao, *tr.* by John Balaban

Tiny bird with red feathers, A. Tiny Bird, A. *Vietnamese Oral Tradition.* CaDao, *tr.* by John Balaban

Tiny dew reinvigorates the tiny grass, The. Margherita Guidacci. CItWP *Fr.* Meditations and Maxims.

Tiny fish. Idyl. John James. Oth

Tiny fish enjoy themselves, The. Little Fish. D. H. Lawrence. Spl

Tiny hut in a world of plants, A. Han-shan Te-ch'ing. CSKM, *tr.* by Red Pine

Tiny joys, joys like a lizard's tail. "Rachel." FIT, *tr.* by Robert Friend

Tiny man!, A. Tiny Man, The. Ivan Radoev. CSCBP, *tr.* by Georgi Belev and Lisa Sapinkopf

Tiny Man, The. Ivan Radoev. CSCBP, *tr.* by Georgi Belev and Lisa Sapinkopf

Tiny moon as small and white as a single jasmine flower, A. White Blossom, A. D. H. Lawrence. MoBrPo

Tiny petals of the mountain ash, The. (LL) Frederick Goddard Tuckerman. APN-2; GSo; NoP-4; OxBoAm; OxBSo *Fr.* Sonnets: First Series, 1854–1860.

Tiny radiance in a dark place, A. (LL) Toad. Norman Alexander MacCaig. EdScPo; HarvBoo

Tiny sun, A. In the Ashtray. Vasco [or Vasko] Popa. VCWP, *tr.* by Anne Pennington

Tip for Saturday, A. Francis Webb. BMAP

Tip, The. Belle Waring. PBCAP

Tip the barmaid in tight jeans. Las Girlfriends. Sandra Cisneros. TiP2

Tip their mouths open to the sky. Small Vases from Hebron, The. Naomi Shihab Nye. CAP-8; PoArWo

Tipped goblets, the blue herons. Glory Monster. Sandra Alcosser. PfSP

Tipped wing fans spread, tail a shut fan dangled. (LL) Waterbird. May Swenson. NoP-4; NoP-5; OxBoAm

Tippi in a pea-green suit and pin-heels. Weekend in Bodega Bay, A. Caitríona O'Reilly. NIrP

Tipping down from above the clouds at Athens. Athens and Jerusalem. Rose Drachler. TaR

Tips his hat. (LL) Rita Dove. MAAN; NAAL-5 *Fr.* Thomas and Beulah.

Tips waves up big dipper fires. Wonderful. Ania Walwicz. BMAP

Tiptoe on wall-top, head in. Wild Cherry. Nigel Jenkins. TCAWP

Tip-Toe Tail. Dixie Willson. NTCP

Tire burns in an empty square, The. Demonstration. Hanan Mikha'il. CFP, *tr. by* Kamal Boullata

Tire Hangs in the Woods, The. Dave Jeddie Smith. CAP-8

Tire tracks words lost in lost snow today. Generic Elbows. Bernadette Mayer. FTOS

Tired. Basho. EH, *tr. by* Robert Hass

Tired. Fenton Johnson. APT-1; OxAAAP; TCAPo

Tired. Doris Fisher and Allan Roberts. ReLy

Tired and Unhappy, You Think of Houses. Delmore Schwartz. APT-2; ItP; MoAmPo

Tired as I Can Be. Bessie Jackson. FaBoVe; GoPo

Tired Hunter, The. Gabriel Preil. FIT, *tr. by* Robert Friend

Tired i count the ways in which it determines my life. ISM, The. Wanda Coleman. OxAAAP; PmAP

Tired Lizi Tired. Lindiwe Mabuza. HAWP

Tired Man, The. Suliaman El-Hadi. SpirFl

Tired nature's sweet restorer, balmy Sleep! Edward Young. OxAEP-1 *Fr.* Night Thoughts.

Tired of all things—with even hope put by. Valley, The. Alphonse Marie Louis de Lamartine. SxFrPo, *tr. by* A. M. and E. H. Blackmore

Tired of chewing. Street Funeral. Irving Layton. NIL-7

Tired of him and forgets. (LL) Turn of Privacy, The. Rick Noguchi. AmPoNex; NeAmPo

Tired of my writing brush, I gazed out the window. Night Duty in the Palace, Dreaming of a Hsien-yu Temple. Po Chü-i. CrYelRi, *tr. by* Sam Hamill

Tired of the life I lead. Tired. Doris Fisher and Allan Roberts. ReLy

Tired of waiting for me. Tongues in My Mouth. Demetrice A. Worley. SpirFl

Tired of women. Cristina Peri Rossi. TANSG *Fr.* Evohé.

Tired river took shelter in the shade, The. Calm, The. Dulce Maria Loynaz. TANSG, *tr. by* Alan West

Tired Tim. Walter De la Mare. NTCP

Tired [*or* Tyr'd *or* Tir'd] with all these, for restful[l] death I cry. Sonnet 66. William Shakespeare. CABP; NoSic; OxAEP-1; PoPoPo; TFi; WeW-3 *Fr.* Sonnets.

Tired with dull grief, grown old before my day. 1916 Seen from 1921. Edmund Charles Blunden. NoP-4; NoP-5

Tired Woman, The. Anna Wickham. MoBrPo

Tireder than usual I got up. Personal. Peter Rafferty. NLP

Tireless Sculptor, The. Henrietta Cordelia Ray. CBWP-3; SWaP

Tires chew into the soft. Mud Season. Mark Todd. GeoH

Tires Stacked in the Hallways of Civilization. Martín Espada. InvLad

Tiresias. Austin Clarke.
   "Strolling one day, beyond the Kalends, on Mount Cyllene." ModIr

Tiresias in the City of Heroes. Karen Press.

Tiresias Remembers. TSAP

Tiresias Remembers. Karen Press. TSAP *Fr.* Tiresias in the City of Heroes.

Tiring of cans and paper soups. Blueberry City. Virginia Hamilton Adair. AFaM

Tirocinium; or, A Review of Schools. William Cowper.
   "Father, who designs his babe a priest, The." OBSV
   "To you, then, tenants of life's middle state." OBSV
   "Would you your son should be a sot or dunce." OBSV

Tiruppavai, The. Andal.
   "O sister of wealth." WPoS
   "O you who guard over." WPoS
   "We rose before dawn." WPoS

'Tis a dull sight. Old Song. Edward Fitzgerald. OBEV; OxAEP-2

'Tis a fair tree, the almond tree; there spring. Death in the Flower. Letitia Elizabeth Landon. RWP

'Tis a lesson you should heed. Try, Try Again. T. H. Palmer. ChAP; ITBLP

'Tis a Little Thing. Sir Thomas N. Talfourd. TreFP

'Tis a new life—thoughts move not as they did. New Birth, The. Jones Very. APN-1; NCAP; OxBoAm; SacPr

'Tis a sad land, that in one day. Death. Henry Vaughan. ChIV-1

'Tis a strange mystery, the power of words! Power of Words, The. Letitia Elizabeth Landon. VWP

'Tis a time for much rejoicing. Emancipation. Priscilla Jane Thompson. CBWP-2

'Tis all that Heav'n allows.. (LL) Love And Life. John Wilmot, 2d Earl of Rochester. NPeEn; OBEV; OxBEV

'Tis an old dial, dark with many a stain. Sundial, The. Austin Dobson. OBGa

'Tis April again in my garden, again the grey stone-wall. To Francis Jammes. Robert Bridges. NPeEn; OxBSo

Tis better to be vile than vile esteemed. William Shakespeare. CAGL; NoSic; OxAEP-1; PBRV *Fr.* Sonnets.

'Tis but a phantom of the weary brain. Life for a Life. Mary E. Tucker. CBWP-1

'Tis Christmas weather, and a country house. George Meredith. NAEL-6v2; WaAnP *Fr.* Modern Love.

'Tis customary as we part. Emily Dickinson. LW

'Tis dead night round about: Horror [*or* Horrour] doth creep[e]. Lamp[e], The. Henry Vaughan. ChIV-2

'Tis done! Dread Winter spreads his latest glooms. James Thomson. OxAEP-1 *Fr.* Seasons, The.

'Tis dreadful! Aisle of a Temple, The. William Congreve. OxAEP-1

'Tis eight o'clock,—a clear March night. Idiot Boy, The. William Wordsworth. NOBRP; NPBRoP; OBNV

'Tis fine to see the Old World, and travel up and down. America for Me. Henry Van Dyke. ChAP

'Tis first the true and then the beautiful. Precedence. Horatius Bonar. SacPr

'Tis folly to be wise. (LL) Ode on a Distant Prospect of Eton College. Thomas Gray. NAEL-6v1; NAEL-7v1; NoP-4; NoP-5; OxAEP-1

'Tis hard to say, if greater want of skill. Essay on Criticism, An. Alexander Pope. NAEL-6v1; NAEL-7v1; TFi

'Tis his one hope: all else that round his life. Infatuation. Frederick Goddard Tuckerman. NCAP

'Tis, in good truth, a most wonderful thing. Sir William Davenant. NOSC

'Tis know, at least it should be, that throughout. Lord Byron. NOBRP *Fr.* Beppo; a Venetian Story.

'Tis known, at least it should be, that throughout. Beppo; a Venetian Story. Lord Byron. OBNV; OBSV

'Tis late and cold; stir up the fire. John Fletcher. OxAEP-1 *Fr.* Lover's Progress, The.

'Tis Lent, the holy time of fast and prayer. Easter Light, The. Clara Ann Thompson. CBWP-2

'Tis light to love thee living, girl, when hope is full and fair. Thomas Tod Stoddart. NOBRP *Fr.* Death-Wake, The; or, Lunacy.

'Tis little I— could care for Pearls. Emily Dickinson. WPoS

'Tis made by Nothing now again[e]. (LL) And He Answered Them Nothing. Richard Crashaw. ChIV-2; SacPr

'Tis men who say that through all hurt and pain. Augusta Davies Webster. ViWPN; VWP *Fr.* Mother and Daughter.

'Tis Midnight. *Unknown.* NTCP

'Tis midnight! and pale Melancholy stands. Written at the Couch of a Dying Parent. Eliza Cook. CenSon

'Tis Midnight, and the setting sun. 'Tis Midnight. *Unknown.* NTCP

'Tis morning; and the sun, with ruddy orb. William Cowper. *Fr.* Task, The.

'Tis near the morning watch, the dim lamp burns. Morning Watch, The. Jones Very. APN-1

'Tis near the time. I'm glad 'tis getting late. Achsa W. Sprague. SWaP *Fr.* Poet, The.

Tis night: the grape-juice mantles high. Reason Fair, A (Liangzhou Song). Wang Han. CCL1, *tr. by* H. A. Giles

'Tis night; the mercenary tyrants sleep. Robert Southey. CenSon

" 'Tis no sin for a man to labour in his vocation." Ballad of Villon and Fat Madge, The. François Villon. OBVE

'Tis not a coat of gray or shepherd's life. To John Donne. Sir Henry Wotton. NoSic

'Tis not by brooding on delight. Marcus Curtius. Oliver St. John Gogarty. OBMV

Tis not enough for one that is a wife. Chorus. Elizabeth Cary, Countess of Falkland. EMWP

'Tis not for man to trifle: life is brief. Only One Life. *Unknown.* TreFP

'Tis not how long we have to live. Anacreontic. John Thelwall. NOBRP

'Tis not how witty, nor how free. Upon Kind[e] and True Love. Aurelian Townshend. NOSC; WaAnP

'Tis not that Dying hurts us so. Emily Dickinson. APN-2

'Tis not that I am weary grown. Upon [His] Leaving His Mistress. John Wilmot, 2d Earl of Rochester. BASC; NBLV; NOSC

'Tis now clear[e] day: I see a rose. Search, The. Henry Vaughan. ChIV-2

'Tis now, since I sat[e] down before. Love's Siege. Sir John Suckling. NPeEn
   ('Tis now, since I sate down before.) CavPo

'Tis now the hour. Anna Laetitia Barbauld. NPBRoP *Fr.* Summer Evening's Meditation, A.

'Tis now the hour of mirth, the hour of love. Maria Gowen Brooks. APN-1 *Fr.* Zophïel or, the Bride of Seven.

'Tis of a gallant Yankee ship that flew the stripes and stars. Yankee Man-of-War, The. *Unknown.* TCAPo

'Tis of my country that I would endite. Homme Moyen Sensuel, L'. Ezra Pound.

'Tis on October thirty-first. Hallowe'en. Lizelia Augusta Jenkins Moorer. CBWP-3

'Tis Opposites—entice. Emily Dickinson. TCAPo

'Tis passed!—the sultry tyrant of the south. Summer Evening's Meditation, A. Anna Laetitia Barbauld. NAEL-7v2

'Tis said. Heavenly Questions. Ch'u Yüan. ColAnChi, *tr.* by Victor H. Mair

'Tis said, as Cupid danced [*or* danc't] among. How Roses Came Red. Robert Herrick. SoSe-8

'Tis said but a name is friendship. Lines to Mrs. Isabel Peace. Mary Weston Fordham. CBWP-2

'Tis said that faith declines; believe it not;. Faith, Hope, and Charity Are the Prospects of Manhood. Leigh Hunt. ChIV-2

'Tis said that to the brow of yon fair hill. Tradition of Oker Hill in Darley Dale, Derbyshire, A. William Wordsworth. OxBSo

'Tis said there were no thought of hell. Heaven and Hell. Francis Thompson. SacPr

'Tis Sixty Years Since. Maurice Lindsay. EdScPo

'Tis so appalling—it exhilarates. Emily Dickinson. NCAP

'Tis starving makes it fat. (LL) Mine Enemy is growing old. Emily Dickinson. RaBo; RaF

Tis strang. Dialogue betwixt Man, and Nature, A. Margaret Lucas Cavendish, Duchess of Newcastle. PBRV

'Tis strange how much is mark'd on memory. History of the Lyre, A. Letitia Elizabeth Landon. VWP

Tis strange my Theseus, that these lovers speake of. William Shakespeare. OxBEV *Fr.* Midsummer Night's Dream, A.

'Tis strange that he Unborn, ere he saw Light. Some Experimental Passages of My Life, with Reflections upon Jacob's Words, Few and Evil Have the Days of the Years of My Life Been. Elizabeth Tipper. EMWP

'Tis strange to think, if we could fling aside. Mask of Gaiety, The. Letitia Elizabeth Landon. VWP

'Tis summer eve, when heaven's ethereal bow. Thomas Campbell. TreFP *Fr.* Pleasures of Hope, The.

'Tis summer time on Bredon. Summer Time on Bredon. Hugh Kingsmill. UV

'Tis sweet to hear the watch-dog's honest bark. Lord Byron. DiBP *Fr.* Don Juan.

'Tis the middle of night by the castle clock. Christabel. Samuel Taylor Coleridge. NAEL-6v2; NAEL-7v2; NOBRP

'Tis the season when Nature awakes from her sleep. Easter; or, Spring-Time. Lizelia Augusta Jenkins Moorer. CBWP-3

'Tis the summer prime, when the noiseless air. Elizabeth Oakes-Smith. SWaP *Fr.* Sinless Child, The.

'Tis the voice of the Lobster: I heard him /declare declare. Lewis Carroll. OBCoV; UV *Fr.* Alice's Adventures in Wonderland.

'Tis the voice of the [*or* a] sluggard; I heard him complain. Sluggard, The. Isaac Watts. OxBEV; UV

'Tis the week before Christmas and every night. For the Children or the Grown-ups? *Unknown.* OBCP

Tis the yeares midnight, and it is the dayes. John Donne. *See* 'Tis the year's midnight, and it is the day's.

'Tis the year's midnight, and it is the day's. Nocturnal[l] upon Saint Lucy's [*or* S. Lucy's *or* S. Lucies] Day, Being the Shortest Day, A. John Donne. BASC; CABP; NAEL-6v1; NAEL-7v1; NoP-4; NoP-5; NOSC; OxAEP-1; TFi

(Tis the yeares midnight, and it is the dayes.) NPeEn; OxBEV; PBRV

'Tis time this heart should be unmoved. On This Day I Complete My Thirty-sixth Year. Lord Byron. BrAP; CAGL; NAEL-6v2; NAEL-7v2; NoP-4; NoP-5; NPBRoP; NPeEn; OBWP

'Tis Time to conclude; for I make it a Rule. Conclusion of a Letter to the Rev. Mr. C———, The. Mary Barber. CABP

'Tis to Create. Lord Byron. NPBRoP

'Tis to yourself I speak; you cannot know. Yourself. Jones Very. APN-1; OxBoAm

'Tis true, dear[e] Ben, thy just chastizing [*or* chastising] hand. To Ben Jonson. Thomas Carew. BASC; CavPo; NAEL-6v1; NAEL-7v1; NOSC

'Tis true I weepe, I sigh, I wring my hands. Eleanora Wyatt Finch. EMWP

'Tis true, 'tis day, what though it be? Break of Day. John Donne. CtM; NAEL-6v1; NAEL-7v1; SoSe-8

'Tis true—yet 'tis no pity that 'tis true. James Kirke Paulding. APN-1 *Fr.* Backwoodsman, The.

'Tis very hard when men forsake. Jack Hall. Thomas Hood. NOBRP

'Tis very sure God walks in mine. (LL) My Garden. Thomas Edward Brown. OBEV; OBGa; UV

'Tis want of sense that makes us poor. (LL) To the Same Purpos[e]. Thomas Traherne. NoP-4; NoP-5

'Tis war again, and I am glad 'tis so. John Dryden. FaBoWar *Fr.* Conquest of Granada, The.

'Tis Washington's health—fill a bumper around. Toast to Washington, A. Francis Hopkinson. NAAPv.1

'Tis Well to Wake the Theme of Love. Eliza Cook. VWP

'Tis well to woo, 'tis well to wed. Building upon the Sand. Eliza Cook. TreFP

Tis well you think me truly one of those. To John Keats. Leigh Hunt. CenSon

'Tis what they say. Red Man's Wife, The. *Unknown.* IrLP, *tr.* by Douglas Hyde

'Tis wretchedness too much to be cast down. Sir Francis Hubert. ChIV-1 *Fr.* Egypt's Favorite.

Tishah B'Ov / 1952. David Meltzer. TaR

Tísica. Diana García. TouFir

Tisza, The. Sándor Petőfi. IQMS, *tr.* by Watson Kirkconnell

Titan! to whose immortal eyes. Prometheus. Lord Byron. OxAEP-2

Titanic. David R. Slavitt. GoPo

Titanic, reincarnate, now a cauldron, The. Titanic, Reincarnate, The. Kim Hyesun. CAMKP, *tr.* by Jiwon Shin

Titanic, The. Witter Bynner. APT-1

Titanic, The. *Unknown.* APT-1

Tita's Poem. Aurora Levins Morales. PueRic

Tithonus. Alfred Tennyson. CABP; NAEL-6v2; NAEL-7v2; NAWM-7v2; NoP-4; NoP-5; NPeEn; OxBEV

Titivate: cosmetic task. Tabula Rasa? Daryl Hine. BrAP

Title conveyed, seal set. Clause for a Covenant. Constance Carrier. APT-2

Title divine—is mine! Emily Dickinson. APN-2; NAAPv.1; NALW; OxBoAm; TCAPo

Title of This Poem Was Lost, The. Pedro Juan Pietri. PueRic

Titled. Tom Ahern. OnScMo

Titty Mary, you know I gwine follow. Gwine Follow. *Unknown.* SSUS

Titty 'Ritta die like-a Lazarus Die. I Want to Die Like-A Lazarus Die. *Unknown.* SSUS

Titty wainscott n' all th'droppin's. Elder Dubb. Edwin Torres. HeMarv

Titus Andronicus. William Shakespeare. Roman Hunting. DiBP

Titus the brave and valorous gallant. Sir John Davies. NoSic *Fr.* Epigrams.

Titwillow. William Schwenck Gilbert. NoP-4; NoP-5

Tiva's Tapestry: La Llorona. Linda Hogan. FTtHH

Tizzy Boost. Bruce Andrews. "Appetizers'." FTOS

Tjanting. Ron Silliman. "Not this. / What then?" PmAP

Tlingit Concrete Poem. Nora Dauenhauer. NIP-4

TM. Ulli Freer. Oth

To. To Linda. Guillaume Apollinaire. CuPo

To———: "O thou unknown disturber of my rest." Mary Bryan. CenSon

To———: "O timeless guest!—so soon returned art thou." Mary Bryan. CenSon

To ———: "Had I a man's fair form, then might my sighs." John Keats. CenSon; OxAEP-2

To———: "Ah, wherefore, lonely, to and fro." Herman Melville. NCAP

To———, Sleeping. Adah Isaacs Menken. PoBW

To ———: "Three rompers run together, hand in hand." Wilfred Owen. OxBSo

To———: "'Twas eve; the broadly shining sun." Edward Coote Pinkney. APN-1

To ———: "Vainly my heart had with thy sorceries striven." Sarah Helen Whitman. APN-1; NAAPv.1; TCAPo

To———. Ulalume: A Ballad. Edgar Allan Poe. *See* Ulalume [*or* Ulalume—a Ballad].

To———: "Lo! dreary Winter, howling o'er the waste." Ann Yearsley. CenSon

To———: "One word is too often profaned." Percy Bysshe Shelley. OBEV; OxAEP-2; TFi

To —. With the Following Poem [*preface to* The Palace of Art]. Alfred Tennyson. NOBRP

To —: "Music, when soft voices die." Percy Bysshe Shelley. HeIP-4; NAEL-6v2; NAEL-7v2; OBEV; OxAEP-2; OxBEV; TFi

(Music, When Soft Voices Die.) NPBRoP

To a Bad Heart. Tim Reynolds. RaF

To a Beauty, White, Pure, and Constant. Abu Bakr ibn Abd al-Malik Ibn Quzman. WoPoe, *tr.* by Leticia Garza-Falcón and Christopher Middleton

To a Bereaved Mother. John Quincy Adams. SacPr

To a Blind Mother. Gilbert Ruddock. BBMWP, *tr.* by Mike Jenkins

To a Blockhead. Alexander Pope. NBLV

To a Boon Companion. Oliver St. John Gogarty. OBMV

To a Boy. Nancy Morejón. TANSG, *tr.* by Joy Renjilian-Burgy

To a Brook Near the Village of Corston. Robert Southey. NPBRoP

To a Bull Moose. Eugene O'Neill. UV

To a Butterfly. Menke Katz. Prolet, *tr.* by Amelia Glaser

To a Butterfly ("I've watched you now a full half-hour.") William Wordsworth. NPBRoP

To a Butterfly ("Stay near me—do not take thy flight!") William Wordsworth. NPBRoP

To a Calvinist in Bali. Edna St. Vincent Millay. NAMCP V.1; NoAM

To a Cape Ann Schooner. John Greenleaf Whittier. OxBSo

To a Cat. John Keats. CenSon; OxBSo; TriCat
  (To Mrs. Reynolds's Cat.) NPBRoP

To a Certain Cantatrice. Walt Whitman. AmFaPo

To a Certain Civilian. Walt Whitman. CBCWP; FaBoWar

To 'A Certain Rich Man'. Alice Thompson Meynell. ChIV-2

To a Chameleon. Marianne Moore. APT-1; NoP-5

To a Child. Judith Wright. BMAP

To a Child in Death. Charlotte Mew. ChIV-2; MoBrPo

To a Child of Quality, Five Years Old, the Author Suppos'd Forty. Matthew Prior. OBEV; OxBEV

To a Child Running with Outstretched Arms in Canyon de Chelly. N. Scott Momaday. HATNAP

To a Child Trapped in a Barber Shop. Philip Levine. NoAM

To a Child [Written in Her Album]. William Wordsworth.
  (Written in an Album.) Spl

To a Coal Miner in Madrid, New Mexico. Luis Lopez. GeoH

To a Common Prostitute. Walt Whitman. MoAmPo

To a Comrade in Arms. Alun Lewis. MoBrPo

To a Conscript of 1940. Sir Herbert Read. OBWP; PoWW

To a Crucifix. Anna Wickham. MoBrPo

To a Cuckoo at Coolanlough. Medbh McGuckian. PBCIP

To a Daisy. Alice Thompson Meynell. MoBrPo; SacPr; VWP

To a Dark Girl. Gwendolyn B. Bennett. ColAP; WaAnP

To a Daughter at Fourteen Forsaking the Violin. Carole Oles. WeW-3

To a Daughter Leaving Home. Linda Pastan. ArBi; ItWoWo; NIL-7; NIP-4

To a Dead Friend. Agnes Mary Frances Robinson. PoBW

To a Dead Lady. Antonio Cisneros. TCLAP, *tr.* by Maureen Ahern and David Tipton

To a Deceased Friend. Priscilla Jane Thompson. CBWP-2

To a Departed Spirit. Felicia Dorothea Hemans. RWP

To a Distant Scene. Felicia Dorothea Hemans. NPBRoP *Fr.* Records of the Spring of 1834.

To a Dog Injured in the Street. William Carlos Williams. SAmP

To a Drunken Guest. CATKP, *tr.* by Peter H. Lee

To a Face in a Crowd. Robert Penn Warren. FuPo

To a Fair Lady Playing with a Snake. Edmund Waller. CABP; NOSC

To a Fallen Walnut Tree. Dávid Baróti Szabó. IQMS, *tr.* by Watson Kirkconnell

To a Farmer Who Hung Five Hawks on His Barbed Wire. David Wagoner. NoAM

To a Fat Lady Seen from the Train. Frances Darwin Cornford. MoBrPo; OBMV; OxBEV; UV; WeW-3

To a Fellow Monk. Jaewol Kyunghun. BecRai, *tr.* by Kim Daljin, Kim Won-Chung and Christopher Merrill

To a Fish. Leigh Hunt. NBLV; NPeEn *Fr.* Fish, the Man, and the Spirit, The.

To a Fisherman with the Present of a Knife. Naomi Mitchison. EdScPo

To a Flasher. Dawn L. Hannaham. BtF

To a French Structuralist. David Kirby. BLT

To a Friend. Matthew Arnold. NAEL-6v2

To a Friend. William Lisle Bowles. CenSon

To a Friend. Hartley Coleridge. CenSon
  (Friendship.) OBEV

To a Friend. Joseph Rodman Drake. APN-1

To a Friend. Im Öngnyŏng. CATKP, *tr.* by Chi-gyu Kim [*or* Kim Chonggil]

To a Friend. Li Po. CrYelRi, *tr.* by Sam Hamill

To a Friend. Pyŏn Wŏngyu. CATKP, *tr.* by Peter H. Lee

To a Friend. Charlotte Smith. RWP

To a Friend and Fellow Poet. Hugh MacDiarmid. NePenScot

To a Friend Bound East. Wen T'ing-yün. CCL1, *tr.* by Witter Bynner

To a Friend, Fearful of Being Forgotten in Absence. Eliza Cobbe, Lady Tuite. PoBW

To a Friend, Who Gave the Author a Reading Glass. Elizabeth Moody. PoBW

To a Friend Who Sent Me Some Roses. John Keats. CenSon

To a Friend, Who Thinks Sensibility a Misfortune. Anna Seward. CenSon

To a Friend Who Wouldn't Bother to Strain His Noodleboard Because Even So It Is Hard to Go Hunting When Your Rifle Is Blunt and Love Is Soft as an Old Blanket. Jacob Glatstein. PFTM-1

To a Friend Whose Work Has Come to Nothing. William Butler Yeats. MoBrPo; OBMV; OxAEP-2; WoPoe

To a Friend Whose Work Has Come to Triumph. Anne Sexton. CAP-8; OtW

To a friend with osteoporosis. Elizabeth Smither. PoCu

To a Gardener. Robert Louis Stevenson. OBGa

To a Gentleman that Courted Several Ladys. *Poets of the Tixall Circle.* EMWP

To a Golden-Haired Girl in a Louisiana Town. Vachel Lindsay. MoAmPo

To a Goose [*or* Gosse]. Robert Southey. CenSon

To a Gravel Walk. William Mason. OBGa

To a Guest. Tu Fu [*or* Du Fu]. CrYelRi, *tr.* by Sam Hamill

To A. H. James M. Whitfield. APN-2

To A.H.B. Margaret Witter Fuller. PoBW

To a Haggis. Robert Burns. FaBoVe; NePenScot
  (Address to a Haggis.) AmFaPo

To a hamster the property of plastic. White. Ronaldo V. Wilson. BtF

To a Hermit in the Mountains. Hsü Pen. ColAnChi, *tr.* by Jonathan Chaves

To a Hermit Thrush. Adelaide Crapsey. APT-1

To a Hooligan Girl. Lajos Kassák. IQMS, *tr.* by Michael Kitka

To a Kill-Joy. Wang Ji. CCL1, *tr.* by H. A. Giles

To a Lady[e]. William Dunbar. OBEV

To a Lady. John Gay. OBEV

To a Lady. Francisco de Terrazas. BLPSL, *tr.* by Rene de Costa, Rigas Kappatos and Eleni Paidoussi

To a Lady Asking Him How Long He Would Love Her. Sir George Etherege. OBEV

To a Lady Combing Her Hair. Juan de Tassis y Peralta, Count of Villamediana. BLPSL, *tr.* by Rene de Costa, Rigas Kappatos and Eleni Paidoussi

To a Lady Friend. W. H. Davies. MoBrPo

To a Lady in a Garden. Edmund Waller. NPeEn

To a Lady Making Love. Lady Mary Wortley Montagu. LW

To a Lady on the Rise of Morn. Anne Batten Cristall. RWP

To a Lady: She Refusing to Continue a Dispute with Me. Matthew Prior. NoP-4; NoP-5

To a Lady That Desired I Would Love Her. Thomas Carew. BASC; CavPo

To a Lady, Who Desired Me Not To Be in Love with Her. John, Baron Cutts Cutts. NOSC

To a Lady, Who Was a Great Talker. Elizabeth Moody. PoBW

To a Lady with Child that Asked [*or* Ask'd] an Old Shirt. Richard Lovelace. BASC; NOSC

To a Lady's Countenance. Elinor Wylie. NALW

To a Late Local Environmentalist. Jane Epton Seale. TiP2

To a Lily. James Matthew Legaré. APN-2

To a Little Colored Boy. Priscilla Jane Thompson. CBWP-2

To a Little Invisible Being Who Is Expected Soon to Become Visible. Anna Laetitia Barbauld. NAEL-6v2; NAEL-7v2; WoRP

To a Living Author: "Your comedy I've read, my friend." *Unknown.* NBLV

To a Llangollen Rose, the Day after It Had Been Given by Miss Ponsonby. Matilda Barbara Betham-Edwards. CenSon

To a Locomotive in Winter. Walt Whitman. BrAP; GM; MoAmPo; NAAL-3; NCAP; NoAM; NoP-4; NoP-5

To a lodge that stood. William Wordsworth. STuOW *Fr.* Vaudracour and Julia.

To a Lofty Beauty, from Her Poor Kinsman. Hartley Coleridge. OxAEP-2

To a Louse [On Seeing One on a Lady's Bonnet at Church]. Robert Burns. FaBoVe; NAEL-6v2; NAEL-7v2; NePenScot; NOBRP

To a Loved One. Mary Weston Fordham. CBWP-2

To a Man Dying on His Feet. William Carlos Williams. APT-1

To a Man Who is Rob Southland. Nia Francisco. HATNAP

To a Maniac. Amelia Alderson Opie. NOBRP

To a Mathematician. Jan Kochanowski. WoPoe, *tr.* by Jerzy Peterkiewicz and Burns Singer

To a Military Rifle, 1942. Yvor Winters. MoAmPo; PWW2

To a Mistress Dying. Sir William Davenant. *See* Lover and Philosopher.

To a Monk. Buhyu Sunsoo. BecRai, *tr.* by Kim Daljin, Kim Won-Chung and Christopher Merrill

To a Monk Asking About Zen. Chimi Sucho. BecRai, *tr.* by Kim Daljin, Kim Won-Chung and Christopher Merrill

To a Moth that Drinketh of the Ripe October. Emily Jane Pfeiffer. ViWPN

To a Mountain Daisy [On Turning One Down, with the Plough, in April—1786]. Robert Burns. NPBRoP

To a mountain village. Spring in a Mountain Village. Noin. WoPoe, *tr.* by Steven D. Carter

To a Mouse; On Turning Her up in Her Nest, with the Plough, November, 1785. Robert Burns.   BRP; CABP; FaBoVe; HeIP-4; NAEL-6v2; NAEL-7v2; NePenScot; NoP-4; NoP-5; NPBRoP; NPeEn; OxAEP-2; OxBEV; TFi; UV; WaAnP

To a Mousse.   W. N. Herbert.   NeBl

To a Musician.   George Wither.   SacPr

To a New England Poet.   Philip Freneau.   NAAL-3

To a newspaper carelessly left there. *Good dog.* (LL)   Dog's Death.   John Updike.   GoPo; P180

To a Nightingale.   William Drummond of Hawthornden.   OWoS

To a Nightingale.   Charlotte Smith.   CenSon; OxBSo; RWP

2. To a northern gannet.   Brian Bartlett.   Coast *Fr.* Talking to the Birds.

To a Nose.   Francisco de Quevedo y Villegas.   SpanPo, *tr. by* James Edward Tobin

To a Nun.   John Ormond.   NoP-4

To a Pair of Legs.   Francisco de Terrazas.   BLPSL, *tr. by* Rene de Costa, Rigas Kappatos and Eleni Paidoussi

To a Persian Boy in the Bazaar at Smyrna.   Bayard Taylor.   CAGL

To a Pessimist.   Ronald Arbuthnott Knox.   OBCoV

To a Piano.   Mary Elizabeth Coleridge.   OxBSo

To a Poet.   Ágnes Nemes Nagy.   PoSu, *tr. by* Bruce Berlind

To a Poet a Thousand Years Hence.   James Elroy Flecker.   MoBrPo

To a Poet (the Pearl).   Gus Blaisdell.   ICANM

To a Poetess.   Jim Carroll.   AHA

To a Poor Old Woman.   William Carlos Williams.   BLT; ColAP; NAAPv.2; OxBoAm; WaAnP

To a President.   Walt Whitman.   NAAL-3

To a Proud Beauty.   "Ephelia."   PEW

To a Pyrotechnist.   Chao Meng-fu.   ColAnChi, *tr. by* Jonathan Chaves

To a Randy Old Woman.   Horace.   EroLit *Fr.* Epodes.

To a Rejected Sonnet.   William Ewart Gladstone.   CenSon

To a Rich Man.   Phineas Fletcher. *See* Against a Rich Man Despising Poverty.

To a Sad Daughter.   Michael Ondaatje.   NoAM

To a Sea Eagle.   Hugh MacDiarmid.   MoBrPo

To a Seaman Dead on Land.   Kay Boyle.   PoA 2002

To a Shade.   William Butler Yeats.   NAEL-6v2; NAEL-7v2

To a Shy Girl at a Party.   Ken Morrice.   EdScPo

To a Sigh.   Mary Robinson.   CenSon; RWP

38. To a Sigh.   Mary Robinson.   NPBRoP *Fr.* Sappho and Phaon.

To a Skylark.   Percy Bysshe Shelley.   BrAP; BRP; NAEL-6v2; NAEL-7v2; NOBRP; NoP-4; NoP-5; NPBRoP; OBEV; OWoS; OxAEP-2; TFi; WaAnP

To a Snail.   Marianne Moore.   APT-1; NALW; NAMCP V.1; OxBoAm; PoPoPo

To a Snowflake.   Francis Thompson.   MoBrPo; SacPr

To a soft, oleaginous mutta. (LL)   Arthur.   Ogden Nash.   AmWit; NoP-4

To a Solemn Musick.   Edward Young.   STuOW *Fr.* Imperium Pelagi, or, The Merchant.

To a Song of Sappho Discovered in Egypt.   Leonora Speyer.   APT-1

To a Spaniel.   Walter Savage Landor.   DiBP

To a Sparrow.   T. E. Nicholas.   BBMWP, *tr. by* Joseph P. Clancy

To a Sparrow.   William Carlos Williams.   OWoS

To a Squirrel at Kyle-Na-No.   William Butler Yeats.   ChAP

To a Steam Roller.   Marianne Moore.   APT-1; MoAmPo; NAMCP V.1; NoP-5; OxBoAm; PoPoPo

To a Stranger.   Edward Carpenter.   CAGL *Fr.* Towards Democracy.

To a Stranger.   Walt Whitman.   APN-1; OxBoAm; SAmP

To a Stranger (At the End of a Caboose).   Laura Jensen.   GM

To a Swallow.   Euenus.   OBVE, *tr. by* John Peale Bishop

To a Talkative Guest.   Po Chü-i.   CCL1, *tr. by* Arthur Waley

To a Terrorist.   Stephen Dunn.   RaF

To a Thesaurus.   Franklin Pierce Adams.   AmWit; NBLV

To a thirteen-year-old sleeping.   Last Thing I Say, The.   Marvin Bell.   PoChi

To a Traitor.   *Unknown.*   WoPoe, *tr. by* Willard Trask

To a Traveler.   Lionel Pigot Johnson.   MoBrPo

To a Traveler.   Su Tung-p'o.   NDACCP, *tr. by* Kenneth Rexroth

To a Tropic Reef.   Hugh Fuller.   OWABP

To a Very Young Gentleman at a Dancing-School.   Elizabeth Singer Rowe.   EMWP

To a Vine-clad Telegraph Pole.   Louis Untermeyer.   MoAmPo

To a Violet.   Susan Evance.   CenSon

To a Voyager.   Mohammed Dib.   YaTCFP, *tr. by* Ronnie Scharfman

To a Wandering Female Singer.   Felicia Dorothea Hemans.   ViWPN; VWP

To a Wanton: "In vain[e], fair[e] sorceress[e], thy eyes speak[e] charms." William Habington.   NOSC *Fr.* Castara.

To a War Correspondent.   Star Black.   KGB

To a Waterfowl.   William Cullen Bryant.   APN-1; ColAP; CtM; ITBLP; NAAL-3; NAAL-5; NAAPv.1; NCAP; NoP-4; NoP-5; OWoS; OxBoAm; SoSe-8; TFi; WaAnP

To a Waterfowl.   Donald Hall.   BodElec

To a Western Boy.   Walt Whitman.   APN-1

To a woman. (LL)   Elizabeth Barrett Browning.   NAEL-6v2; NAEL-7v2 *Fr.* Aurora Leigh.

To a Woman.   Helen Hay Whitney.   PoBW

To a Woman to a Path.   Valentine Penrose.   SurWo, *tr. by* Roland Penrose

To a Worthy Friend, Who Often Objects the Coldnesse of the Winter in Newfound-Land.   Robert Hayman.   IFF

To a Young Ass.   Samuel Taylor Coleridge.   OxAEP-2 *Fr.* Effusions.

To a Young Diver.   Marilyn Taylor.   PoA 2002

To a Young Girl Leaving the Hill Country.   Arna Bontemps.   GT

To a Young Lady.   William Cowper.   DiBP

To a Young Lady, Purposing to Marry a Man of Immoral Character in the Hope of his Reformation.   Anna Seward.   CenSon

To a Young Lady That Desired a Verse of My Being Servant One Day and Mistress Another.   Elizabeth Tipper.   EMWP; NOSC *Fr.* Pilgrim's Viaticum; or, The Destitute, But Not Forlorn.

To a Young Lady, with Some Lampreys.   John Gay.   CABP; OBCoV

To a Young Lady's Dog.   Thomas Blacklock.   DiBP

To a Young Widow.   Po Chü-i.   CrYelRi, *tr. by* Sam Hamill

To a Young Writer.   Yvor Winters.   APT-2

To Abbot Min the Compassionate.   Tu Fu [*or* Du Fu].   CrYelRi, *tr. by* Sam Hamill

To abcs and from rimbaud.   Camille Martin.   AnSo

To accept this vale.   One Strategy for Loving the World.   Mona Van Duyn.   ExTi

To Account Rendered.   John Dryden.   STuOW *Fr.* Don Sebastian.

To adam.   Thandiwe Shiphrah.   BtF

To Afaa Michael S. Weaver.   Major L. Jackson.   FuFl

To after-Times thy Wit. (LL)   To the Virginian Voyage.   Michael Drayton.   BASC; NOSC; OBEV

To Ailsa Rock.   John Keats.   CenSon

To Alchemists.   Ben Jonson.   BASC

To Alexis in Answer to His Poem Against Fruition.   Aphra Behn.   LW

To Alexis in Answer to His Poem Against Fruition. Ode.   Aphra Behn.   BrAP; NOSC

To Alfred Gwyer.   Joseph Gwyer.   VerBaPo

To Alice Dunbar.   Paul Laurence Dunbar.   NAAPv.1

To all my length. (LL)   To Earthward.   Robert Frost.   APT-1; MoAmPo; NAMCP V.1; NoAM; NoP-4; OxBoAm; PtR; RaBo; TRP; WaAnP

To all things light gives force; God dwells Himself in light.   "Angelus Silesius." GePo *Fr.* Cherubical Wanderer, The.

To all things there is an appointed time, and a time to everie purpose under the heaven.   Bible, *O.T. See* To everything there is a season.

To All Those Worthy Women, Who Have Any Desire to Live in Newfound-Land.   Robert Hayman.   IFF

To All Us Sansei Who Wanted to Be Westside.   Amy Uyematsu.   GeoHom

To All Virtuous Ladies in General.   Emilia Lanier and Aemilia Bassano Lanyer.   BASC

To all who carve their love on a picnic table.   Open Letter from a Constant Reader.   Mona Van Duyn.   OxBoAm

To all you ladies now at land.   Song Written at Sea in the First Dutch War (1665), the Night before an Engagement.   Charles, 6th Earl of Dorset Sackville.   OBEV; OBWP; OxAEP-1

To Allen Ginsberg & Co.   Luciana Frezza.   CItWP, *tr. by* Cinzia Sartini Blum and Lara Trubowitz

To allow himself to be properly held.   Man Who Closed Shop, The.   Stephen Dunn.   NIP-4

To Almystrea.   Mary Lee, Lady Chudleigh.   EMWP

To Almystrea, on her Divine Works.   Elizabeth Thomas.   EMWP

To Althea, from Prison.   Richard Lovelace.   BASC; CavPo; CtM; ITBLP; ItP; NAEL-6v1; NAEL-7v1; NIL-7; NoP-4; NoP-5; NOSC; NPeEn; OBEV; OxBEV; PBRV; TFi; WaAnP

To Amanda Walking in the Garden.   N. Hookes.   NOSC; OBGa

To Amarantha, That She Would Dishevel[l] Her Hair[e].   Richard Lovelace.   CABP; CavPo; NIL-7; NoP-4; NoP-5; OBEV

(Song: To Amarantha, That She Would Dishevel Her Hair.)   CABP; NOSC (Song.)   CavPo

To Amine.   James Clarence Mangan.   OBEV

To amuse His Royal Majesty he will change water into wine.   Žito the Magician.   Miroslav Holub.   PoSu; WoPoe, *tr. by* Ian Milner and George Theiner

To an admiring Bog! (LL)   I'm Nobody! Who are you?   Emily Dickinson.   AmFaPo; APN-2; ChAP; HeIP-4; ItP; NAAPv.1; NALW; NBLV; NoP-5; OBCoV; OxBoAm; PoPoPo; SAmP; TCAPo

To an Adolescent Weeping Willow.   Marvin Bell.   CAP-8

To an American Painter Departing for Europe. William Cullen Bryant. *See* To Cole, the Painter, Departing for Europe.

To an American Poet Just Dead. Richard Wilbur. NBLV

"To an Amiable Child." Babette Deutsch. APT-2

To an Ancient Tune. Chu Tun-ju. CrYelRi, *tr. by* Sam Hamill

To an Ancient Tune. *Unknown.* CrYelRi, *tr. by* Sam Hamill

To an Ancient Tune. Yao K'uan. CrYelRi, *tr. by* Sam Hamill

To an Angel in the House. John Sparrow. OBCoV

To an Angry Bee. John Clare. CenSon

To an Anthologist. Theodore Roethke. PoA 2002

To an Anti-Semite. Carl Rakosi. APT-2

To an Artist, to Take Heart. Louise Bogan. TRP

To an Athlete Dying Young. A. E. Housman. BrAP; ChAP; CtM; HeIP-4; InoFa; MoBrPo; NAEL-6v2; NAEL-7v2; NAMCP V.1; NIP-4; NoAM; NoP-4; NoP-5; PtR; SoSe-8; TFi; TRP; WaAnP; WeW-3 *Fr.* Shropshire Lad, A.

To an Audience. John Koethe. BAP-04

To an Author. Philip Freneau. ColAP

To an Author who Loved Truth More than Fame. Bessie Rayner Parkes. VWP

To an English Boy: "Beautiful boy, flower fair." Hilary. EroLit, *tr. by* John Boswell

To an English Boy: "Hail, fair youth, who seeks no bribe." Hilary. CAGL, *tr. by* John Boswell

To an Exeter City Cocktail Waitress. Jon Veinberg. GeoHom

To an Hour-Glass. John Clare. CenSon

To an Immortal Solitude Where We Now Pitch Our Stately Tent. Tahsin Saraç. NaPG, *tr. by* Talat Sait Halman

To an Inconstant One. Sir Robert Aytoun. OBEV

To an Infant. Mary Weston Fordham. CBWP-2

To an Intra-Mural Rat. Marianne Moore. APT-1

To An Old Black Woman, Homeless and Indistinct. Gwendolyn Brooks. ESEAA

To an Old, Deaf, and Blind Monk. Jungkwan Ilson. BecRai, *tr. by* Kim Daljin, Kim Won-Chung and Christopher Merrill

To an Old Friend. Nadia Hazboun Reimer. PoArWo

To an Old Jaundiced Woman. William Carlos Williams. APT-1

To an Old Lady. William Empson. NoAM; OxAEP-2; OxBEV

To an Old Philosopher in Rome. Wallace Stevens. APT-1; ColAP; NAMCP V.1; NoAM

To an Old Tune. Hsin Ch'i-chi. NDACCP, *tr. by* Kenneth Rexroth

To an Outstanding Elder. Buhyu Sunsoo. BecRai, *tr. by* Kim Daljin, Kim Won-Chung and Christopher Merrill

To an Unborn Child. Allan Cooper. AtGh

To an Undiscerning Critic. Sir Arthur Conan Doyle. OBCoV

To an Unknown Poet. Carolyn Kizer. OPRER

To Ancestry. John Thelwall. CenSon

To and / back and forth. To And. Robert Creeley. OxBoAm

To Anita. Sonia Sanchez. ISC

To Anna Matilda. Robert Merry. NOBRP

To Anne Frank. Rosita Kalina. MirDau, *tr. by* Roberta Gordenstein

To Annie. Mary E. Tucker. CBWP-1

To Another Housewife. Judith Wright. NALW

To Answer Your Question. Bruce Berger. MiVo

To Antenor. Katherine Philips. EMWP

To Anthea, Who May Command Him Anything. Robert Herrick. BASC; NOSC; OBEV; OxBEV

To Any Reader. Robert Louis Stevenson.

"As from the house your mother sees." NePenScot

To any watch they keep? (LL) Neither Out Far Nor In Deep. Robert Frost. APT-1; BrAP; NAMCP V.1; NoAM; NoP-4; NoP-5; OxBoAm; TRP; WeW-3; WoPoe

To Ararat; all men are Noah's sons. (LL) Still, Citizen Sparrow. Richard Wilbur. ColAP; NoAM; TRP

To Aretha Franklin from Sparkle. Amina Baraka. BRtP

To Aristius Fuscus. Horace. OBVE,

To Aristogoras. Meleager. CAGL, *tr. by* Daryl Hine

To arms, to arms! my jolly grenadiers. Song of Braddock's Men, The. Stephen Tilden. AmWaPo

To Artemisia.—'Tis to her we sing. Mary Leapor. PEW *Fr.* Essay on Friendship.

To Arthur de Noé Walker. Walter Savage Landor. OxBSo

To ascend? How? Song of a Man in the Dark. Adonis. VCWP, *tr. by* Samuel Hazo

To ask the hard question is simple. Question, The. W. H. Auden. OxAEP-2

To Aspasia. Susanna Highmore Duncombe. PoBW

To Atlas in the Attic. Julie Agoos. YaYoPo

To Aunt Rose. Allen Ginsberg. CLPP; ColAP; NAMCP V.2; NoAM; NoP-4; NoP-5; OxBoAm; PmAP; TaR; WaAnP

To Aurelius. Catullus. CAGL, *tr. by* Eugene O'Connor

To Aurelius and Furius. Catullus. CAGL, *tr. by* Eugene O'Connor

To Ausonius. Paulinus of Nola. CAGL, *tr. by* Jack Lindsay

To Autumn. William Blake. NAEL-6v2; NAEL-7v2

To Autumn: "Season of mists and mellow fruitfulness!" John Keats. BrAP; CABP; ClHu; CtM; HeIP-4; ITBLP; MakPoe; NAEL-6v2; NAEL-7v2; NAWM-7v2; NIL-7; NIP-4; NOBRP; NoP-4; NoP-5; NPBRoP; NPeEn; OBEV; OxAEP-2; OxBEV; PoPoPo; PtR; RaBo; SoSe-8; TFi; TRP; WaAnP; WeW-3

To avoid being laughed at during the day. (LL) Small Town. Rita Dove. AmAlph; GT

To Await Arrival. Bella Akhatovna Akhmadulina. CRWP, *tr. by* Catriona Kelly

To B. P. Aleksandr Semionovich Kushner. TCRusP, *tr. by* Daniel Weissbort

To B.R. Haydon, with a Sonnet Written on Seeing the Elgin Marbles. John Keats. CenSon

To banish the less I find my chief relief. (LL) Henry Howard, Earl of Surrey. CABP; NAEL-6v1; NAEL-7v1 *Fr.* Windsor Castle.

To Bayard Taylor. Sidney Lanier. NCAP

To be. Orange Tree, The. Ben Belitt. APT-2

To Be. Marvin Bell. BodElec

To be a Jew in the Twentieth Century. Muriel Rukeyser. NALW; PoCho; TaR *Fr.* Letter to the Front.

To be a mountain you have to climb alone. Silver Star. William Stafford. TWF

To be a mouse. Preferably a field mouse. Or a garden mouse—. Aleksander Wat. AF

To be a poet and not know the trade. Sanctity. Patrick Kavanagh. NoP-4; NoP-5; StAl

To Be a Slave of Intensity. Kabir. RaBo, *tr. by* Robert Bly

(Think While You Are Alive.) WED

To be a stranger in a strange land. Thinking of My Brother in Shantung on the Ninth Day of the Ninth Moon. Wang Wei. TAL

To Be a Woman. Shakuntala Hawoldar. HAWP

To be a woman. To Be a Woman. Shakuntala Hawoldar. HAWP

To be able to see every side of every question. Edgar Lee Masters. APT-1; OBSV; OxBoAm *Fr.* Spoon River Anthology.

To be alive then. Ronald Stuart Thomas. BeAl *Fr.* Counterpoint.

To be alone in a strange place in spring. Child, The. Judith Wright. BMAP

To be always carrying. Immigrants. Debra Kang Dean. NAPBL

To be announced. Nicolás Guillén. PFTM-1 *Fr.* Daily Daily, The.

To be blessed, throat, eye and knucklebone. (LL) Truth the Dead Know, The. Anne Sexton. ColAP; FTtHH; ItP; MoAmPo; NAMCP V.2; NoAM; NoP-4; NoP-5; VCAP

To be blown into fragments. your flesh. How Europe Underdeveloped Africa. Edward Kamau Brathwaite. WoBe

To be born! (LL) Eclogue: "Men talking, The." George Oppen. APT-2; FTOS

To be born is to want—is it that simple? Hated Rats, The. Nguyen Binh Khiem. WoPoe, *tr. by* Nguyen Ngoc Bich

To be buried in times of war. Michael Ondaatje. NAMCP V.2 *Fr.* Buried.

To be but to be a crow with claws vicious enough. Barbarian. Mohammed Khaïr-Eddine. PFTM-2, *tr. by* Pierre Joris

To be carried / Good luck of skin. If I Yes. Olga Broumas. GifTon

To Be Carved on a Stone at Thoor Ballylee. William Butler Yeats. NAMCP V.1; NoAM; NoP-4; NoP-5

To be Christ is not to be Jesus Christ. Antonin Artaud. ConPit, *tr. by* Clayton Eshleman

To be cocked like a rifle, the hand. To Live in the Land of Israel. Arye Sivan. NRoS, *tr. by* Esther Raizen

To Be Famous Isn't Decent. Boris Leonidovich Pasternak. TCRusP, *tr. by* Kathy Lewis and Bob Perelman

To be famous isn't decent, there's. To Be Famous Isn't Decent. Boris Leonidovich Pasternak. TCRusP, *tr. by* Kathy Lewis and Bob Perelman

To Be Held. Ron Schreiber. PrTe

TO BE / Immortal. Dawn, The. Charles North. NYP2

To be in any form, what is that? Walt Whitman. CAGL *Fr.* Song of Myself.

To Be in Love. Gwendolyn Brooks. GT

To be in my life, it is your duty. Guest, The. Sheenagh Pugh. TCAWP

To be in not to be. Robert Kelly. WhBo *Fr.* Flowers of Unceasing Coincidence, The.

To be in the book. To figure in the book of questions, to be part of it. Edmond Jabès. PFTM-1 *Fr.* Book of Questions, The.

To be in the way, belonging. To wait. Hunt, The. Sophie Cabot Black. NevBe

To be: let me bash out praises—pass the tambourine. (LL) Way we live, The. Kathleen Jamie. NeBrP; StAl

To be long silent was my thought. *Unknown.* GePo

To Be of Use. Marge Piercy. GoPo; IPoFl; TWF

To be or not to be. Brian G. Gilmore. SpirFl

To be / or not to be / That is not the question. I Want to Be Bad. Lew Brown, B. G. DeSylva and Ray Henderson. ReLy

To be or not to be! That is the question. Lord Byron. OBCoV *Fr.* Don Juan.

To be, or not to be, that is the question. William Shakespeare. OxAEP-1; OxBEV; TreFP; UV; WaAnP *Fr.* Hamlet.

To be pleased and to please. (LL) Why Do You Feel Differently. Gertrude Stein. ItWoWo; PFTM-1

To be put on the train and kissed and given my ticket. Observation Car. Alec Derwent Hope. NAMCP V.1; NoAM

To Be Read above the Castle-Gate, When His Princely Highness Rode in to His Marriage Bed. Simon Dach. GePo, *tr. by* George C. Schoolfield

To Be Said Over and Over Again. György Petri. VCWP, *tr. by* Geroge Gömöri and Clive Wilmer

To Be Seventeen Again. Violeta Parra. TANSG, *tr. by* Shaun Griffin and Emma Sepúlveda-Pulvirenti

To be seventeen again. To Be Seventeen Again. Violeta Parra. TANSG, *tr. by* Shaun Griffin and Emma Sepúlveda-Pulvirenti

To be simply like thin flesh without skin. Declaration of Hate. Efraín Huerta. TCLAP, *tr. by* Todd Dampier

To be so held by brittleness, shapeliness. Soul Says. Jorie Graham. PoPoPo

To be soldiers together and allies. Franco Buffoni. ItPo, *tr. by* Gayle Ridinger

To be Sung on the Fourth of July. Wyatt Prunty. RA

To be that weak lonely figure. How People Do. Imamu Amiri Baraka. EGAG

To be the opening act. Opening Act. Jayne Cortez. EGAG

To be thought an outcast in my beloved country. Inna L'vovna Lisnyanskaya. ItGoST, *tr. by* Judith Hemschemeyer

To be untangled from these mother's bones.. (LL) With Child. Genevieve Taggard. MoAmPo; NAAPv.2

To Be with the Dead. Manuel González Prada. SpanPo, *tr. by* Kate Flores

To be with the dead. To Be with the Dead. Manuel González Prada. SpanPo, *tr. by* Kate Flores

To be with you is my desire. January Hangover. Pedro Pietri. BRtP

To be woo'd and married at a'! (LL) Song: Woo'd and Married and A'. Joanna Baillie. NAEL-6v2; NAEL-7v2; NoP-4; NoP-5

To be written. 9/11/01. Pierre Joris. Eno

To be Young, Gifted, and Black. Weldon J., Jr. Irvine. ISC

To be your beadsman now that was your knight. (LL) George Peele. NIP-4; NoP-4; NoP-5; NPeEn; OxBEV; TFi *Fr.* Polyhymnia.

To Beachey, 1912. Carl Sandburg. OtW

To bear, to nurse, to rear. Jean Ingelow. TreFP *Fr.* Songs of Seven.

To bear your life you need accompaniment. In Your Own Sweet Time. Alane Rollings. IllVoic

To beat real iron out, to work the bellows. (LL) Forge, The. Seamus Heaney. NAEL-6v2; NAEL-7v2; NoP-4; NoP-5; OxAEP-2; WaAnP

To become a bodhisattva. Maxim for a Man of Virtue. Jinkag Haesim. BecRai, *tr. by* Kim Daljin, Kim Won-Chung and Christopher Merrill

To become a tree. Antonio Porta. ItPo *Fr.* Essences.

To Become Unconscious. Ebony Page. BRtP

To Beethoven. Sidney Lanier. NCAP

To begin I cut fine silk of Ch'i. Song of Regret. Pan Chieh-yû. CCL1, *tr. by* Burton Watson

To begin with, none of your neighbors began here. Starting from Scratch. Ingrid Wendt. RWB; SweBea

To begin with something not already caught. How Late Desire Looks. Katrina Roberts. NAPBL

To Belinda. Johann Wolfgang von Goethe. STV, *tr. by* John Frederick Nims

To Belshazzar. Lord Byron. ChIV-1

To Ben Jonson. Thomas Carew. BASC; CavPo; NAEL-6v1; NAEL-7v1; NOSC

To Beth On Her Forty-Second Birthday. Jane Chambers. PoBW

To better the condition of humanity. Our Club Work. Mrs. Henry Linden. CBWP-4

To Black Women. Gwendolyn Brooks. IllVoic

To Blossoms. Robert Herrick. BrAP; NAEL-6v1; NOSC; OBEV; TreFP

To board the train for Toronto and glance over at the other. City Lights. Roo Borson. BeAl

To Boccaccio. Thomas Russell. OxBSo

To Bodhidharma. Tenshin Reb Anderson. WhBo

To braid the locks of the dark. Night Hair. Raquel Chalfi. DTA, *tr. by* Karen Alkalay-Gut

To brave and to know the unknown. Unknown, The. John Davidson. MoBrPo

To break earth's sleep at all? (LL) Futility. Wilfred Owen. HarvBoo; MoBrPo; NAEL-6v2; NAEL-7v2; NAMCP V.1; NoAM; NoP-4; NoP-5; NPeEn; OBWP; PoAgWa; TCAWP; WaAnP

To Break, to Ride. Carl Phillips. AmAlph

To breakfast on a light-blue tablecloth, smelling of milk. Gyula Krúdy. IQMS, *tr. by* John Lukacs

To breakfast on stale rum sardines and peas. (LL) Eye-Opener. Malcolm Lowry. NoP-4; NoP-5

To breathe and stretch one's arms again. Slow Song for Mark Rothko. John Taggart. PFTM-2

To Breisach, Taken by That Supremely Celebrated Hero, Bernhard, Duke of Saxony. Georg Rudolph Weckherlin. GePo, *tr. by* George C. Schoolfield

To bring one chrysanthemum. Beside a Chrysanthemum. Sŏ Chŏngju. CAMKP; VCWP, *tr. by* David R. McCann

To Bring the Dead to Life. Robert Graves. MoBrPo

To bring the honey to the wind. (LL) Tragic Mary Queen of Scots, The. Michael Field. LW; OBMV

To broaden into boundless day. (LL) Alfred Tennyson. NAEL-6v2; NAEL-7v2; NAWM-7v2; NoP-5; WaAnP *Fr.* In Memoriam A. H. H.

To Brooklyn Bridge. Hart Crane. AmFaPo; ChIV-1; ClHu; ColAP; EMP; FaBoA; HarvBoo; MakPoe; MoAmPo; NAAL-5; NAAPv.2; NoP-4; OxBoAm; PoPoPo; TFi; TRP *Fr.* Bridge, The.

To build something human with it. (LL) Night Vision. Lucille Clifton. BodElec; GifTon; UnSA

To build up a world out of strange books. George Stanley. NLPA *Fr.* Mountains and Air.

To Buonaparte. *Unknown.* NOBRP

To burn at least one thing they once owned: she tears. Many Are Called. Rick Barot. LegDan

To burn in this immense torpidity. (LL) Mummy Invokes His Soul, The. Michael Field. NPeEn; OxBSo; VWP

To burn the bridge. Here's a Match. Krissi Banzon. BeDoSh

To burn, to smolder with the jeweled incendiary coal. Smokestacks, Chicago. Campbell McGrath. LiTh

To burst into fulfillment's desolate attic. (LL) Deceptions. Philip Larkin. HarvBoo; OxAEP-2

To Caelia. Richard Duke. NOSC

To California Where Rhymes Fail. Margaret Rozga. RWB

To call, in the harsh morning, sleep-stupid faces through the daily gate. (LL) Birmingham. Louis MacNeice. MoBrPo; OxAEP-2

To call it a wet dream would be too barren. Nocturne, Aubade, and Vesper. James Wright. BodElec

To call me back into our helpless tribe. (LL) Words for My Daughter. John Balaban. PoChi; RaBo; SUP

To calm the anxious breast, to close the streaming eye. (LL) To Sleep. Charlotte Smith. CenSon; NAEL-6v2; NAEL-7v2; RWP

To Canaan: A Puritan War-Song. Oliver Wendell Holmes. PCW

To Captain Hungry. Ben Jonson. FaBoWar

To Carelessness. Kenneth Koch. PWW2

To Carlos Drummond de Andrade. João Cabral de Melo Neto. TCLAP, *tr. by* Guy Pacitti

To carry home on your back. (LL) Small passing. Ingrid de Kok. HAWP; TSAP

To Castara, *Being to Take a Journey*: "What's death more than a departure; the dead go." William Habington. NOSC *Fr.* Castara.

To Castara, upon an Embrace. William Habington. NPeEn *Fr.* Castara.

To catch the first sweet drop, but none came down. (LL) Man of the House, The. David Wagoner. NAMCP V.2; NoAM

To Catch the Moon. Chu Yohan. CAMKP, *tr. by* Chong Bum Kim

To catch the spirit in its wayward flight. Self-Mastery. Henrietta Cordelia Ray. CBWP-3; SWaP

To Cattraeth's vale in glitt'ring row. Aneirin. OBVE *Fr.* Gododdin, The.

To celebrate the need of comrades. (LL) In Paths Untrodden. Walt Whitman. APN-1; CAGL; NAAPv.1; TCAPo

To Celia. Ben Jonson. *See* Song. To Celia.

To Celia. Sir Charles Sedley. *See* Song to Celia.

To Celia Pleading Want of Merit. Thomas Stanley. NOSC

To Celia, upon Love's Ubiquity. Thomas Carew. CavPo

To Celinda. Elizabeth Singer Rowe. BASC; PEW

To Censorious Courtling. Ben Jonson. NOSC

To chain me down he takes charge of the chains. *Unknown.* SLW, *tr. by* Marjolijn De Jager, Sayd Bahodin Majrouh and André Velter

To Charles Diodati. John Milton. OxBSo, *tr. by* William Cowper

To Charles Roux, of Switzerland. Nathaniel Parker Willis. APN-1

To Charlotte Cushman. Eliza Cook. VWP

To Charlotte von Stein. Johann Wolfgang von Goethe. STV, *tr. by* John Frederick Nims

To Chatterton. John Keats. CenSon

To Chloe, who for His Sake Wished Herself Younger. William Cartwright. *See* To Chloe, Who Wished Herself Young Enough for Me.

To Chloe, Who Wished Herself Young Enough for Me. William Cartwright. NOSC; OxAEP-1

(To Chloe, who for His Sake Wished Herself Younger.) OBEV

To Chloris. Sir Charles Sedley. OBEV

To Christ. William Alabaster. NoSic; OxBSo

To Christ Crucified. Miguel de Guevara. SpanPo, *tr. by* Ian Fletcher

To Christ Our Lord. Galway Kinnell. HeIP-4

To Christina Rossetti. Michael Field. NAEL-7v2; VWP

To Christina Rossetti. Dora Greenwell. VWP

To circle their wagons? (LL) Why Do So Few Blacks Study Creative Writing? Cornelius Eady. GT; LTA; OxAAAP

To civilize with graver notes our wits again. (LL) Ode to Master [*or* Mr.] Anthony Stafford to Hasten Him into the Country, An. Thomas Randolph. BASC; NOSC; OBEV

To claim, at a dead party, to have spotted a grackle. Lying. Richard Wilbur. MakPoe; OxBoAm

To claim my attention and consume me. (LL) When My Grandmother Said "Pussy." Carole Bernstein. AmPoNex; UnSA

To clarify and allow. Reason, The. Eric Pankey. GI

To Clemena. Elizabeth Thomas. PoBW

To Clement Edmonds, on His *Caesar's Commentaries* Observed, and Translated. Ben Jonson. NOSC

To Clements' Ferry. Josephine D. Henderson Heard. CBWP-4; SWaP

To Cleone. Elizabeth Singer Rowe. PoBW

To climb and descend steps. Walker in Prague. Vitězslau Nezval. AF, *tr. by* Ewald Osers

To climb these stairs again, bearing a tray. Kaleidoscope, The. Douglas Dunn. OxBSo

To climb to thee. (LL) Pearl, The. Matth. 13:45. George Herbert. BASC; ChIV-2; FSCP; NOSC; OxBEV

To Cloe. George, Baron Lansdowne Granville. NBLV; OxBEV

To Cloe. Martial. NBLV, *tr. by* Thomas Moore

To Close. William Carlos Williams. SAmP

To clothe the fiery thought. Ralph Waldo Emerson. Spl; TCAPo *Fr.* Quatrains.

To Coelia. Charles Cotton. OBEV

To Cole, the Painter, Departing for Europe. William Cullen Bryant. ColAP; TCAPo

(Sonnet—To an American Painter Departing for Europe.) NAAL-3; OxBoAm

(To an American Painter Departing for Europe.) APN-1

To Colindra. Elizabeth Thomas. LW

To come again into the place of revolutionary. California. Hayden Carruth. TAPaP

To come back from the sweet South, to the North. Italia, Io Ti Saluto! Christina Georgina Rossetti. VWP

To Come! / Come! / Come! (LL) Drum. Langston Hughes. APT-2; MoAmPo; NAMCP V.1

To conceive death as death. Death as Death. Laura Riding Jackson. NAMCP V.1

To Conscripts. Alice Thompson Meynell. SacPr

To consecrate the flicker, not the flame. (LL) George Crabbe. Edwin Arlington Robinson. APN-2; MoAmPo; NoP-4; NoP-5

To cook women. How To Cook Women. Takagi Kyozo. PML, *tr. by* James Kirup and Michio Nakano

To copulate and to rain, they remind me of the willow's white night. Reunion of Cellos. Ernesto Lumbreras. RMCMP, *tr. by* Rebecca Seiferle

To Cotton Mather, from a Quaker. Thomas Maule. TCAPo

To course across more kindly waters now. Dante Alighieri. NAWM-7v1 *Fr.* Divine Comedy, The (Mandelbaum Translation).

To cover it, spilt water on the place. (LL) Ovid. CABP; OBVE *Fr.* Elegies.

To cover your shame. Mr. White Discoverer. Amelia Blossom Pegram. HAWP

To covet fetters, though they golden bee. (LL) Edmund Spenser. BrAP; NAEL-6v1; NoP-4 *Fr.* Amoretti.

To crown her head, and bosom[e] fill. (LL) Gallery, The. Andrew Marvell. BASC; NoP-4; PBRV

To crucify. (LL) De Souza Prabhu. Eunice De Souza. FaBoVe; NAMCP V.2

To cry or see one cry is rather embarrassing to see: between crying and. Water of Tears, The. Francis Ponge. AF, *tr. by* Beth Archer

To cultivate in ev'ry noble mind. To the Rev. Dr. Thomas Amory on Reading His Sermons on Daily Devotion. Phillis Wheatley. SacPr

To Cupid. Joanna Baillie. LW

To cure myself of wanting Cuban songs. My Voice. Rafael Campo. AmPoNex

To cure the mind's wrong bias, Spleen. Matthew Green. NPeEn *Fr.* Spleen, The [Complete].

To cut an animal tongue, to turn the body. Compendium Notes. Malinda Markham. IAoNAP

To Cynthia. Sir Francis Kynaston. NOSC

To Cyriack Skinner. John Milton. OBEV

(Sonnet.) NOSC; OxAEP-1

(Cyriack, Whose Grandsire.) NoP-4; NoP-5

To D——, Dead by Her Own Hand. Howard Nemerov. PoA 2002

To Daffodils [*or* Daffadills]. Robert Herrick. BASC; NoP-4; NOSC; OBEV; OxAEP-1; PtR; TFi; TreFP

To Daisies, Not to Shut So Soon[e]. Robert Herrick. OBEV

To Dame—Augustin nun on her curious gum-work. Jane Barker. EMWP

To Damon. To Inquire of Him if He Cou'd Tell Me by the Style, Who Writ Me a Copy of Verses that Came to Me in an Unknown Hand. Aphra Behn. EMWP

To D'Annunzio: Lines from the Sea. Robert Malise Bowyer Nichols. OBMV

To Dante [*or* Sonnet: Guido Cavalcanti to Dante Alighieri]. Guido Cavalcanti. OBVE, *tr. by* Percy Bysshe Shelley

To Daphne and Virginia. William Carlos Williams. APT-1

To David. Dan Clurman. WhBo

To de new Jerusalem. (LL) Blow Your Trumpet, Gabriel. *Unknown.* APN-2; SSUS

To Dean-bourn, a Rude River in Devon, by Which Sometimes He Lived. Robert Herrick. PBRV

(Dean Bourn, a Rude River in Devon, by Which Sometimes He Lived.) CavPo

To Dear Daniel. Samuel Greenberg. APT-1

To Death. Johann Wilhelm Ludwig Gleim. GePo, *tr. by* George C. Schoolfield

To Death. Oliver St. John Gogarty. OBMV

To Death. Mary Tighe. CenSon; NPBRoP

To Death. Anne Finch, Countess of Winchilsea. NoP-4; NoP-5

To Death, from the Genie of My Poetry. Delmira Agustini. TANSG, *tr. by* Mark McCaffrey

To Della Crusca. The Pen. Hannah Cowley. NOBRP

To Dennis Brutus. Kofi Awoonor. HBAPE

To Dependence. Charlotte Smith. CenSon

To Derek Mahon. Michael Longley. CABP

To Derek Walcott. R. Gerallt Jones. BBMWP, *tr. by* the author

To Detraction I Present My Poesie. John Marston. NoSic *Fr.* Scourge of Villainy [*or* Villanie], The.

To Dian, Queen of Earth, and Heaven, and Hell. (LL) To Homer. John Keats. NAEL-6v2; NAEL-7v2; NoP-4; NoP-5

To Diana. Elisaveta Kulman. ARWW, *tr. by* Catriona Kelly

To Dianeme ("Show [*or* Shew] me thy feet; show [*or* shew] me thy legs, thy thighs.") Robert Herrick. CavPo; NOSC

To Dianeme ("Sweet, be not proud of those two eyes.") Robert Herrick. BASC; NOSC; OBEV

To die. Not About Death. Bulat Shalvovich Okudzhava. RusPo, *tr. by* Robert Arthur Douglas Ford

To Die. Sándor Weöres. IQMS, *tr. by* Edwin Morgan

To die. And be born as an inspector of playgrounds for tiny tots. Olga Zondberg. CRWP, *tr. by* Daniel Weissbort

To die and know it. This is the Black Widow, death. (LL) Mr. Edwards and the Spider. Robert Lowell. ColAP; HarvBoo; HeIP-4; NAAL-5; NoP-4; NoP-5; TFi

To die be given us, or attain! Resignation. Matthew Arnold.

To die, but far away. Roberto Juarroz. VCWP *Fr.* Ninth Vertical Poetry.

To die . . . To fall like a drop. Antonio Machado Ruiz. WED *Fr.* Moral Proverbs and Folk Songs.

To dig. As they bury the dead. Bell Hooks. WhBo

To Diodorus, Dorotheus, Callicrates et al. Meleager. CAGL, *tr. by* Daryl Hine

To dip, alas, into some unseemlier world. (LL) Old Mansion. John Crowe Ransom. FuPo; HeIP-4

To Disgrace of Price. (LL) Publication—is the Auction. Emily Dickinson. APN-2; GoPo; NAAL-3; NAAPv.1; NALW; NCAP; NoP-4; NoP-5; OxBoAm; TCAPo

To distant men, who must go there, or die. (LL) Sea-Shore. Ralph Waldo Emerson. APN-1; ColAP

To Dives. Joseph Hilaire Pierre Belloc. ChIV-2; OBSV

To do all I'd want to do. (LL) Lover's Prize, A. Countess de Die Beatrice. EroLit; NAWM-7v1, *tr. by* Peter Dronke

To do as Adam did. Ronald Johnson. FTOS *Fr.* Ark.

To do celestial chores. (LL) Countee Cullen. APT-2; HeIP-4; NAAPv.2; NAMCP V.1; NIL-7; NIP-4; SSLK; TRP *Fr.* Four Epitaphs.

To do less would be nothing but dishonesty. (LL) Peter. Marianne Moore. APT-1; NoP-4

To do something very common, in my own way. (LL) Valediction Forbidding Mourning, A. Adrienne Rich. BrAP; NAAL-5; NAMCP V.2; NoAM; NoP-4; NoP-5; OxBoAm; WaAnP

To do the wronged [*or* wrong'd] Corinna right for thee. (LL) Imperfect Enjoyment, The. John Wilmot, 2d Earl of Rochester. BASC; NAEL-7v1; NoP-5

To do with ego, guilt, ambition, or even money. (LL) Cormorant in Its Element, The. Amy Clampitt. NoP-4; NoP-5

To do with love. (LL) This Room and Everything in It. Li-Young Lee. CAP-8; IllVoic; NAAL-5; OpBo; RoV

To do without what blood remained these wounds. (LL) A Terre. Wilfred Owen. FaBoWar; PoWW

To Doctor Bale. Barnabe Googe. NoSic

To Doctor Empiric[k]. Ben Jonson. WoPoe

(To Doctor Empirick.) NoP-4

To Dr. Jonathan Swift. Alexander Pope. OxAEP-1 *Fr.* Dunciad, The.

To Dr Moore, in Answer to a Poetical Epistle Written by Him in Wales. Helen Maria Williams. WoRP

France 1792. NPBRoP

To doe me harme, content to doe amisse? (LL) Fulke, 1st Baron Brooke Greville. NoSic; PtR *Fr.* Caelica.

To Don Juan Baz. Mary E. Tucker. CBWP-1

To Dora W[ordsworth]; *On Being Asked By Her Father to Write in Her Album.* Charles Lamb. OxBSo

To Dorothy. Marvin Bell. CAP-8; InvLad; VCAP

To draw down Gods, and lift the soul to Heaven! (LL) To the Fragment of a Statue of Hercules, Commonly Called the Torso. Samuel Rogers. CenSon; GS

To draw no envy, Shakespeare, on thy name. To the Memory of My Beloved, the Author Mr [*or* Master] William Shakespeare: And What He Hath Left Us. Ben Jonson. BASC; BrAP; HeIP-4; InoFa; NAEL-6v1; NAEL-7v1; NoP-4; NoP-5; NOSC; OxAEP-1; PoPoPo

To draw the boat safe, high at the cottage shore. (LL) Crossing the Loch. Kathleen Jamie. EdScPo; MoWP

To dream about tremors is a salt dream. Fisher Towers. Jenny Mueller. IAoNAP

To Dream Again. William Shakespeare. OxAEP-1 *Fr.* Tempest, The.

To Dreams. Mary Julia Young. CenSon

To drift with every passion till my soul. Hélas! Oscar Wilde. CAGL; GSo; MoBrPo; NAEL-6v2; NAEL-7v2

To Drink. Jane Hirshfield. PasH

To Drink. Philippe Soupault. SurPaPo, *tr. by* Mary Ann Caws and Jean-Pierre Cauvin and Patricia Terry

To drink its water. Ingrid de Kok. TSAP

To drown the ancient sorrows. Mountain Drinking Song. Li Po. CrYelRi, *tr. by* Sam Hamill

To dwell a weeping hermit there! (LL) How Sleep the Brave. William Collins. CABP; OBEV; OxAEP-1; TFi

To E. Fitzgerald. Alfred Tennyson. NPeEn

To E. S. Salomon. Ambrose Bierce. CBCWP; PCW

To Each His Own. Ray Evans and Jay Livingston. ReLy

To each new storm which frets the angry main. (LL) Written at Scarborough. Mary Tighe. CenSon; NPBRoP; WaAnP

To Earthward. Robert Frost. APT-1; MoAmPo; NAMCP V.1; NoAM; NoP-4; OxBoAm; PtR; RaBo; TRP; WaAnP

To Easter Island and the presences. Introduction: My Themes. Pablo Neruda. GifTon, *tr. by* William O'Daly

To Eat a Pie and to Have It—I. To Eat a Pie and to Have It. Jaan Kaplinski. StAl, *tr. by* Hildi Hawkins

To eat mutton cold and cut blocks with a razor. (LL) Oliver Goldsmith. NPeEn; OxBEV *Fr.* Retaliation.

To eat the world's due, by the grave and thee. (LL) William Shakespeare. HeIP-4; NAEL-6v1; NAEL-7v1; NoP-5; WaAnP *Fr.* Sonnets.

To Eat To-day. Nancy Cunard. RSaN

To Echo. Anna Maria Jones. CenSon

To Edward Alleyn. Ben Jonson. NOSC

To Edward Dahlberg. Jack Kerouac. WhBo

To Edward FitzGerald. Robert Browning. NAEL-6v2

To Edward Thomas. Alun Lewis. PoWW

To Electra ("I dare not ask a kiss[e].") Robert Herrick. OBEV

To Elinda. Richard Lovelace. CavPo

To Elinor Wylie ("Oh, she was beautiful in every part!") Edna St. Vincent Millay. NAAPv.2

To Elizabeth Barrett Browning. Bessie Rayner Parkes. VWP

To Elizabeth Barrett Browning, in 1851. Dora Greenwell. PoBW; VWP

To Elizabeth Barrett Browning, in 1861. Dora Greenwell. PoBW; VWP

To Elizabeth, Countess of Rutland. Ben Jonson. NoP-4; NoP-5

To Elsie. William Carlos Williams. AmFaPo; APT-1; NAAL-5; NAAPv.2; NAMCP V.1; OxBoAm; PoPoPo; StAl

To embalm my father's corse; What? will he die? (LL) John Donne. FSCP; NoSic *Fr.* Elegies.

To embark sleepily. Without Pity. Elizabeth Willis. IIR

To embrace you forever. (LL) Kenneth Rexroth. APSN; APT-2 *Fr.* Love Poems of Marichiko, The.

To Emerge from a Woman Is to Become Separate. Homero Aridjis. TCLAP, *tr. by* W. S. Merwin

To emerge from a woman is to become separate. To Emerge from a Woman Is to Become Separate. Homero Aridjis. TCLAP, *tr. by* W. S. Merwin

To Emily Dickinson. Hart Crane. ColAP; NIL-7; NIP-4; NoAM; NoP-4; NoP-5; OxBoAm

To End Her Fear. John Freeman. OBMV

To Enjoy the Horror. Fawziyya Abu Khalid. PoArWo, *tr. by* Farouk Mustafa

To enrich the earth I have sowed clover and grass. Enriching the Earth. Wendell Berry. InGu; WaAnP

To enter that queer niteclub, you step over the spot: sexworker stabbed. [Coda & discography]. D. A. Powell. LegDan

To enter the real. Song. Charles Tomlinson. WoBe

To Eros. Wilfred Owen. CAGL

To Eros. Alfonsina Storni. TANSG, *tr. by* Mark McCaffrey

To Eros. Alfonsina Storni. PoCho, *tr. by* Kay Short

To Err Is Human. Robert Bloomfield. DiBP *Fr.* Farmer's Boy, The.

To err is human, I heard you say. Was That the Human Thing to Do? Joe Young. ReLy

To escape conscription. It was in the air! (LL) Rudyard Kipling. InoFa; WoPoe *Fr.* Epitaphs of the War [1914–1918].

To escape God who is burning, / untended. (LL) Anne Carson. BodElec; WoBe *Fr.* Truth About God, The.

To Etan: An Israeli Child from the Kibbutz Ma'oz Hayim. Fadwa Tuqan. CFP, *tr. by* Kamal Boullata

To Etna's scorching sands my Phaon flies! Sappho's Conjectures. Mary Robinson. CenSon; RWP

To Etna's scorching sands my Phaon flies! Mary Robinson. NPBRoP *Fr.* Sappho and Phaon.

To Eugene P. Loveman. Alexander Bergman. AmWaPo

To Eva. Jacqueline Osherow. TaR

To Everlasting Oblivion. John Marston. NoSic *Fr.* Scourge of Villainy [*or* Villanie], The.

To every hill crest. Wanderer's Night Song. Johann Wolfgang von Goethe. WoPoe, *tr. by* Peter Viereck

To every woman a happy ending. (LL) Barbie Doll. Marge Piercy. BrAP; NIL-7; NIP-4; WaAnP

To Everyone. Velemir Khlebnikov. TCRusP, *tr. by* Kathy Lewis and Bob Perelman

To Everything There Is a Season. Bible, *O.T.* BLPJKO; NAWM-5v1; OBVE *Fr.* Ecclesiastes.

To everything there is a season. Bible, *O.T.* BLPJKO; NAWM-5v1; OBVE *Fr.* Ecclesiastes.

To Evoke Posterity. Robert Graves. HarvBoo; NPeEn

To excuse oneself from table. It Being Forbidden. Martha Rhodes. KGB; NAPBL

To experiment on my heart? (LL) Kenneth Rexroth. APSN; APT-2 *Fr.* Love Poems of Marichiko, The.

To explore the nature of rain I opened the door because inside the workings of language clear vision is impossible. Rosmarie Waldrop. PmAP *Fr.* Inserting the Mirror.

To F——. Edgar Allan Poe. APN-1

To Fancy. Martha Hanson. CenSon

To Fancy. Charlotte Smith. OxBSo

To Fannie. Mary E. Tucker. CBWP-1

To Fanny Brawne. John Keats. *See* This Living Hand, Now Warm and Capable.

To Fat Boy, the Bomb. Henry Braun. BodElec

To Father. Mary E. Tucker. CBWP-1

To Favonius. Edmund Bolton. NoSic

To fear himself, and love all human kind [*or* humankind]. (LL) Hymn to Intellectual Beauty. Percy Bysshe Shelley. HeIP-4; NAEL-6v2; NAEL-7v2; NOBRP; NoP-4; NoP-5; NPBRoP

To feast our eyes is sweet. (LL) Sound Bite. Frederick D'Aguiar. NeBrP; Oth

To feed ez they hev fed me. (LL) James Russell Lowell. APN-1; NCAP *Fr.* Biglow Papers, The.

To feed on that, which to disused [*or* disus'd] tast[e]s seem[e]s tough. (LL) John Donne. FSCP; OxAEP-1; PBRV *Fr.* Elegies.

To feel and speak the astonishing beauty of things—earth, stone and water. Beauty of Things, The. Robinson Jeffers. APT-1; PoA 2002

To fend for the bony goats and the crying children. (LL) Village, The. Marina Gashe. CFP; HAWP

To Ferencz Liszt. Mihály Vörösmarty. IQMS, *tr. by* Alan Dixon

To Ferrara as to the world. / Nikolaus Mardruz. (LL) Nikolaus Mardruz to his Master Ferdinand, Count of Tyrol, 1565. Richard Howard. NoP-4; NoP-5

To fertilize some other ground. (LL)   Floating Island at Hawkshead.   Dorothy Wordsworth.   NPeEn; PEW

To fiddle-faddle in a minor key. (LL)   Ambrose Bierce.   AmWit; APN-2 *Fr.* Devil's Dictionary, The.

To fight aloud, is very brave.   Emily Dickinson.   GoPo; ItP

To fill the catalogue of human woes.. (LL)   Ode: "I hate that drum's discordant sound."   John Scott of Amwell.   NIP-4; OxAEP-1

To fill up half the *Orb* of *Round Eternity*. (LL)   Abraham Cowley.   CABP; PBRV *Fr.* Pindarique Odes.

To finally know.   Onitsura.   SoOfWa, *tr. by* Sam Hamill

To finally pull the plug on the word machine.   Poem for Writers, A.   Lee Harwood.   Oth

To find beyond death / Bridgeport, Ohio. (LL)   In Response to a Rumor that the Oldest Whorehouse in Wheeling, West Virginia, Has Been Condemned.   James Wright.   CAP-8; NAMCP V.2; NoAM; OxBoAm; VCAP

To find me now will cost you everything. (LL)   Whitman.   Larry Levis.   ReTh; ViWalt

To find out the temperature, she tosses a cup of water into the air.   Alakanak Break-Up.   Mei-Mei Berssenbrugge.   PmAP

To find out what it really means. (LL)   Introduction to Poetry.   Billy Collins.   BeAl; OxBoAm; P180

To find the Western path.   Morning.   William Blake.   WoPoe

To find they have flown away? (LL)   Wild Swans at Coole, The.   William Butler Yeats.   HeIP-4; MoBrPo; NAEL-6v2; NAEL-7v2; NAMCP V.1; NoAM; NoP-4; NoP-5; NPeEn; OWoS; PoPoPo; SoSe-8; TFi

To find[e] out *death* but missest *life* at hand. (LL)   Vanity [*or* Vanitie] (1).   George Herbert.   BASC; FSCP; NoP-4; NoP-5; NOSC

To Fine Lady Would-Be.   Ben Jonson.   NoP-4; NOSC

To Flaxman.   William Blake.   PtR

To Flight.   S. Conant Foster.   ArBi

To fling my arms wide.   Dream Variation[s].   Langston Hughes.   APT-2; ISC; ITBLP; NoP-4; NoP-5; OxAAAP; OxBoAm; SAmP; SSLK

To float in the space between.. (LL)   Idea of Ancestry, The.   Etheridge Knight.   AF; ESEAA; InGu; ISC; NIP-4; OxAAAP; PBCAP; RaBo; StAl

To float.—The swimmer floats, the lover sleeps. (LL)   Swimmer.   Robert Francis.   APT-2; WeW-3

To float you must float from within.   Trapeze.   Larissa Szporluk.   PoDa

To Flossie.   William Carlos Williams.   SAmP

To Flush, My Dog.   Elizabeth Barrett Browning.   DiBP

To flutter—and the Bird is on the Wing. (LL)   Omar Khayyám.   TRP; UV *Fr.* Rubáiyát of Omar Khayyám [of Naishápúr], The.

To fold the clothes. No matter who lives.   I Stop Writing the Poem.   Tess Gallagher.   GoPo

To follow, to seek, to be with her dear dead son. (LL)   Come Up from the Fields Father.   Walt Whitman.   AmWaPo; APN-1; CBCWP; FaBoWar; HHAm; MoAmPo; OBWP; SAmP

To Fool or Knave.   Ben Jonson.   NoP-4; NoP-5

To force the pace and never to be still.   Poet, Lover, Birdwatcher.   Nissim Ezekiel.   BrAP

To Ford Madox Ford in Heaven.   William Carlos Williams.   ColAP

To forget.   Isabel Meyrelles.   SurWo, *tr. by* Jean R. Longland

To Forget?   Lőrinc Szabó.   IQMS *Fr.* Cricket Music.

To Forget the Image.   Michel Deguy.   PFTM-2, *tr. by* Clayton Eshleman

To Fortuna Parvulorum.   Anthony Hecht.   OxBoAm

To Fortune.   Robert Herrick.   CavPo

To frame her cloudy prison for the soul! (LL)   Autumn: "I saw old Autumn in the misty morn."   Thomas Hood.   OBEV; OxAEP-2

To Francis Jammes.   Robert Bridges.   NPeEn; OxBSo

To Frederick V, by the Grace of God . . .   Bathsua Pell Makin.   EMWP

To Freedom.   Joseph Hucks.   CenSon

To Freedom.   Ágnes Nemes Nagy.   PoSu, *tr. by* Bruce Berlind

To freighted ships[,] baffled in wind and blast. (LL)   "H. D."   APT-1; MoAmPo *Fr.* Let Zeus Record.

To Friends Behind a Frontier.   Tomas Tranströmer.   WoPoe, *tr. by* Robin Fulton

To Friendship.   Charlotte Smith.   RWP

To Friend-Tree of Counted Days.   René Char.   YaTCFP, *tr. by* William Carlos Williams

To G.   *Unknown.*   EroLit, *tr. by* John Boswell

To G., her singular rose.   To G.   *Unknown.*   EroLit, *tr. by* John Boswell

To gather Paradise. (LL)   I dwell in Possibility.   Emily Dickinson.   APN-2; HeIP-4; NAAPv.1; NALW; NAMCP V.1; NAWM-7v2; NCAP; NIL-7; NoAM; OxBoAm; TCAPo; WaAnP

To gaze with envy on their gloomy rest. (LL)   Pressed by the Moon, Mute Arbitress of Tides.   Charlotte Smith.   CenSon; NALW

To gem the vanquished heart he scorned to save. (LL)   To the Muses.   Mary Robinson.   CenSon; RWP

To General Pershing.   Hilton Ross Greer.   TiP2

To Generall Cromwell.   "Eliza."   EMWP

To Genevieve Taggard Who Called Me Traitor in a Poem.   Max Eastman.   APT-1

To gentle, pleasant strains.   Ted Berrigan.   BodElec

To George Romney, Esq.   William Cowper.   OxBSo

To George Sand: A Desire.   Elizabeth Barrett Browning.   NAEL-6v2; NAEL-7v2; NALW; PoBW; VWP

To George Sand: A Recognition.   Elizabeth Barrett Browning.   NAEL-6v2; NAEL-7v2; NALW; PEW; PoBW; VWP

To George Sand on her Interview with Elizabeth Barrett Browning.   Isa Blagden.   VWP

To Germany.   Charles Hamilton Sorley.   MoBrPo

To Germany.   Georg Rudolph Weckherlin.   GePo, *tr. by* George C. Schoolfield

To Get Clear.   J. P. Ward.   AngWePo

To get home? (LL)   Song: "My heart, my dove, my snail, my sail, my."   Cynthia Zarin.   NIL-7; NoP-4; NoP-5

To get out of this and go back home!   Return, The.   T'ao Ch'ien.   ColAnChi, *tr. by* James Robert Hightower

To get recruits for Pain, I use.   Cupid.   Bernard O'Dowd.   NOBAu

To get to the Med on the dream map of Berkeley.   Caffe Mediterraneum.   John Oliver Simon.   ASA

To Giovan Battista Buoninsegni.   Angelo Poliziano.   CAGL *Fr.* Greek Epigrams.

To give a cup of water; yet its draught.   'Tis a Little Thing.   Sir Thomas N. Talfourd.   TreFP

To give employment to the artisan. (LL)   Lord Finchley.   Joseph Hilaire Pierre Belloc.   NBLV; NoAM; OxAEP-2

To give is the white hand.   Michael McClure.   WANABP *Fr.* Touching the Edge: Dharma Devotions.

To give it away, give it up, before they take it from us.   Montezuma.   Diane Di Prima.   BB

To give me its bright plumes, they shot a jay.   Flaw, A.   Michael Field.   ViWPN; VWP

To give the people a break.   Why God Invented the Cold.   Catie Rosemurgy.   AmPoNex

To give to romantic passersby. (LL)   Li Po.   CrYelRi; ErotSp *Fr.* Women of Yueh.

To give us comfort through the lonely dark. (LL)   Douglass.   Paul Laurence Dunbar.   CBCWP; GSo; NAAPv.1; WaAnP

To glad the heart, and save from harm. (LL)   Lament of the Flowers, The.   Jones Very.   APN-1; ColAP

To Gluttony and Guzzling, that fastidious gourmet.   Leonidas of Tarentum.   HePo, *tr. by* Barbara Hughes Fowler

To go back where we came from. (LL)   Belle Isle, 1949.   Philip Levine.   ColAP; NAMCP V.2; VCAP; WaAnP

To go home and wear shorts forever.   Dream of Wearing Shorts Forever, The.   Les A. Murray.   EmeKit

To go there: do not fall asleep, your forehead.   Neighborhood of Make-Believe, The.   Thomas Lux.   LaCa

To Go Through Life Is to Walk Across a Field.   S. J. Marks.   BodElec

To go to Lvov. Which station.   To Go to Lvov.   Adam Zagajewski.   AmFaPo, *tr. by* Renata Gorczynski

To Go with Shih K'o's Painting of an Old Man Tasting Vinegar.   Huang T'ing-chien.   ColAnChi, *tr. by* Burton Watson

To go with the old grey Widow-maker? (LL)   Rudyard Kipling.   HarvBoo; NAMCP V.1; RACG *Fr.* Puck of Pook's Hill.

To God.   Tatamkulu Afrika.   TSAP

To God.   Ivor Gurney.   OxBEV

To God ("Come to me God; but do not come.")   Robert Herrick.   CavPo; RSR

To God ("Do with me, God! as Thou didst deal with John.")   Robert Herrick.   ChIV-2

To God ("God's undivided, One in Persons Three.")   Robert Herrick.   SacPr

To God ("If any thing delight me for to print.")   Robert Herrick.   SacPr

To God: an Anthem, Sung in the Chapel at White-Hall, Before the King.   Robert Herrick.   ChIV-1

To God be the glory, great things he hath done!   Fanny Crosby.   SacPr

To God the highest glory.   Song of the Angels.   Lizelia Augusta Jenkins Moorer.   CBWP-3

To God the Holy Ghost.   Henry Constable.   NoSic

To God: to illuminate all men. Beginning with Skid Road.   Psalm III.   Allen Ginsberg.   ChIV-1

To goldenhaired Phoibos whom Leto bore.   Sappho.   SaLy, *tr. by* Diane Rayor

To Grandmother on Her Going.   Gail Tremblay.   HATNAP

To grass, or leaf, or fruit, or wall.   Snail, The.   Vincent Bourne.   NPeEn; OBVE, *tr. by* William Cowper

To green Nature, not the world, the poet belongs.   Propaganda of the Poet, The.   R. Williams Parry.   BBMWP, *tr. by* Anthony Conran

To Greet a Letter-Carrier.   William Carlos Williams.   SAmP

To Grimold, Abbot of St. Gall. Hrabanus Maurus. CAGL, *tr. by* Helen Waddell

To groom one another, to smooth the other's skin. (LL) In April. Richard Kenney. WaAnP; YaYoPo

To guard my body from the blight of age. Vision: Second Poem of Wandering Immortals. Kuo P'o. CCL1, *tr. by* Graeme Wilson

To H. John Wieners. FTOS

To H. C., Six Years Old. William Wordsworth. NPBRoP

To H.N. David Mura. UnSA

To Halley's Comet. Lionel Abrahams. TSAP

To Hampstead ("Sweet upland, to whose walks, with fond repair.") Leigh Hunt. CenSon

To Hampstead ("Winter has reached thee once again at last.") Leigh Hunt. CenSon
(Written During the Author's Imprisonment, November 1814.) NPBRoP

To hang his pants on while he slept. (LL) Museum Piece. Richard Wilbur. NIL-7; NIP-4; TRP

To Harriet ("Whose is the love that, gleaming through the world.") Percy Bysshe Shelley. NPBRoP *Fr.* Queen Mab.

To Have and Have Not. Karen Solie. PoPra

To have been held down in a park. Rimbaud Having a Bath. Robert Adamson. BMAP

To have blocked off from each other these two persons unable even to shake hands is a great crime. (LL) Yi Sang. CAMKP; PFTM-1 *Fr.* Crow's-Eye View.

To Have Done with the Judgment of God. Antonin Artaud. *tr. by* Clayton Eshleman and Norman Glass
"I learned yesterday." PFTM-2, *tr. by* Clayton Eshleman and Norman Glass

To have escaped Hitler and come to this. To the Parents of a Childhood Friend, a Suicide. Judith Baumel. TaR

To have it out or not? that is the question. C. A. W. UV

To have known him, to have loved him. Monody. Herman Melville. APN-2; NAAL-3; NAAPv.1; NoP-4; NoP-5; PoPoPo; TCAPo

To have lived [*or* liv'd] eminent in a degree. Upon the Death of My Ever Desired Friend Doctor [*or* Dr] Donne Dean of Paul's. Henry King, Bishop of Chichester. BASC

To have missed the plane. To have never fit his body. To Have and Have Not. Karen Solie. PoPra

To have reached. Tiger Lily. Alfred Kreymborg. APT-1

To have seen you exactly, once. Art of Translation, The. Adrienne Rich. BodElec

To Have the Whole Air! Theodore Roethke. IPoFL

To have to go to bed by day? (LL) Bed in Summer. Robert Louis Stevenson. BLPJKO; BRP; NBLV

To have waited at least a moment to see what was already there. (LL) One Train May Hide Another. Kenneth Koch. GPTC; NAMCP V.2; OxBoAm

To have white bouquets. Pearl. Irène Hamoir. SurWo, *tr. by* Myrna Bell Rochester

To Have without Holding. Marge Piercy. NIL-7; NIP-4

To hawks we're a woodland insect. Complicated Shadows. Stephen Corey. PasH

To Hayden Carruth on His Eightieth Birthday. Sam Hamill. WANABP

To hear a cart go jolting down the street. (LL) Shell, The. James Stephens. IrV; MoBrPo

To hear all night the goods trains coming and leaving. (LL) Spilt Milk. Sarah Maguire. EmeKit; LW; MFPA; MoWP

To hear with eyes belongs to love's fine wit. (LL) William Shakespeare. CABP; ItP; NoSic *Fr.* Sonnets.

To Heaven. Robert Herrick. ChIV-2

To Heaven. Ben Jonson. BASC; ChIV-2; InvLi; NAEL-6v1; NAEL-7v1; NOSC; NPeEn; SacPr; TRP

To Helen. Helen Smith Bevington. AmWit

To Helen ("Helen, thy beauty is to me.") Edgar Allan Poe. APN-1; BrAP; BRP; ClHu; ColAP; CtM; HeIP-4; NAAL-3; NAAL-5; NAAPv.1; NIP-4; NoP-4; NoP-5; OBEV; OxBoAm; PoPoPo; PtR; TCAPo; TFi; WaAnP; WeW-3

To Helen ("I saw thee once—once only—years ago.") Edgar Allan Poe. NAAPv.1

To Helen of Troy (N.Y.). Peter Viereck. WeW-3

To Helene. George Darley. NOBRP

To Hell and Back, with Cake. Safiya Henderson-Holmes. UnSA

To hell, my love, with you! (LL) Indian Summer. Dorothy Parker. NIL-7; NIP-4

To Help the Monkey Cross the River. Thomas Lux. AmAlph

To Henry Darnley, King of Scots. George Buchanan. NePenScot, *tr. by* Robert Crawford

To Henry James. Robert Louis Stevenson. OBCoV

To Her Father, with Some Verses. Anne Bradstreet. NAAL-3; NAAL-5; NAAPv.1; NALW

To Her Husband, on New Year's Day 1651. Gertrude Aston Thimelby. EMWP

To her let us garlands bring. (LL) William Shakespeare. NoSic; WaAnP *Fr.* Two Gentlemen of Verona, The.

To Her Lover's Complaint. Jane Barker. NPeEn

To Her Modest Mirth-Making Friend, Mr Robert Dover. Thomas Cole and Sibella Cole Dover. EMWP

To Her of Whom They Dream. Paul Éluard. AF, *tr. by* Lloyd Alexander

To Her Sea-faring Lover. *Unknown.* OBEV

To herald in another year. January. Henrietta Cordelia Ray. CBWP-3

To Hermes. Alfred Corn. CAGL; WiU

To Hersa. Forceythe Willson. APN-2

To Hilda Dancing. John Bingham Morton. OBCoV

To Him That Was Crucified. Walt Whitman. ChIV-2

To him who in the love of Nature holds. Thanatopsis. William Cullen Bryant. APN-1; BRP; ColAP; NAAL-3; NAAL-5; NAAPv.1; NCAP; NoP-5; OBEV; OxBoAm; TCAPo; TFi

To Himself. Paul Fleming. GePo, *tr. by* George C. Schoolfield

To Himself. Andreas Gryphius. GePo, *tr. by* George C. Schoolfield

To Himself. Giacomo Leopardi. NAWM-7v2, *tr. by* Ottavio M. Casale

To Himself. Mark Strand. PoA 2002

To His Book[e]. Martial. OBVE, *tr. by* Robert Herrick

To His Booke. Edmund Spenser. NAEL-6v1; NAEL-7v1 *Fr.* Shepherd's Calender, The.

To His Book[e] ("Have I not blessed [*or* blest] thee? Then go forth; nor fear.") Robert Herrick. BASC

To His Book[e] ("Make haste away, and let one be.") Robert Herrick. NOSC

To His Books. Henry Vaughan. BASC

To His Book's End. Robert Herrick. NAEL-6v1; NAEL-7v1

To his club-footed child said Lord Stipple. Limerick. Edward Gorey. OBCoV

To His Conscience. Robert Herrick. ChIV-1; NAEL-6v1; NAEL-7v1; NoP-4; NoP-5; WaAnP

To His Coy Love, A Canzonet. Michael Drayton. NOSC; PBRV

To His Coy Mistress. Sir Robert Aytoun. NOSC; WaAnP

To His Coy Mistress. Andrew Marvell. AmFaPo; BASC; BrAP; CABP; ClHu; EroLit; ErotSp; FSCP; HeIP-4; NAEL-6v1; NAEL-7v1; NIL-7; NIP-4; NoP-4; NoP-5; NOSC; NPeEn; OBEV; OxAEP-1; OxBEV; PBRV; PoPoPo; TFi; TRP; UV; WaAnP; WoPoe

To His Dead Body. Siegfried Sassoon. NAMCP V.1; NoAM

To His Dear Friend, Bones. Jay Parini. WaAnP

To His Dying Brother, Master William Herrick. Robert Herrick. CavPo; NOSC

To His Ever-Loving God. Robert Herrick. OxBEV

To His Excellency General Washington. Phillis Wheatley. AmWaPo; NAAL-3; NAAL-5; NAAPv.1

To his extreme annoyance, tempted him. (LL) On Lady Poltagrue, a Public Peril. Joseph Hilaire Pierre Belloc. MoBrPo; OBCoV

To His Forsaken Mistress. Sir Robert Aytoun. OBEV

To His Friend. George Turberville. AEP

To His Friend in Absence. Walafrid Strabo. CAGL, *tr. by* Helen Waddell

To His Friend P. of Courting, Traveling, Dicing, and Tennis. George Turberville. NoSic

To His Honoured and Most Ingenious Friend Mr. Charles Cotton. Robert Herrick. NOSC

To His Importunate Mistress. Peter De Vries. NBLV; NIL-7; NIP-4

To His Importunate Mistress. Paul Griffin. UV

To his kennel in the dark. (LL) Hunchback in the Park, The. Dylan Thomas. AngWePo; MoBrPo; NAEL-6v2; NAEL-7v2; NAMCP V.2; NoAM; NoP-4; NoP-5; OxBEV; TCAWP

To His Lady. Henry VIII, King of England. NoSic

To His Love. Ivor Gurney. InoFa; MakPoe; NAEL-7v2; NAMCP V.1; NoP-4; NoP-5; NPeEn; OBWP; PoAgWa; PoWW

To His Love. *Unknown.* NoP-4; NoP-5

To his Love that sent him a Ring wherein was gravde, / Let Reason rule. George Turberville. PBRV

To His Love When He Had Obtained Her. Sir Walter Ralegh. NoSic

To His Lute. William Drummond of Hawthornden. NOSC
("My lute, be as thou wert when thou didst grow.") GSo

To His Mistress. Abraham Cowley. NOSC; OxAEP-1 *Fr.* Sylva.

To His Mistress. John Wilmot, 2d Earl of Rochester. OBEV

To His Mistress Going to Bed. John Donne. BASC; FSCP; NAEL-6v1; NAEL-7v1; NoP-4; NoP-5; NoSic; PBRV *Fr.* Elegies.

To His Mistress[es] ("Help[e] me! help[e] me! now I call.") Robert Herrick. ErotSp

To His Mistris Going to Bed. John Donne. *See* To His Mistress Going to Bed.

To His Mother. John Harington. NoSic

To His Peculiar Friend Master Thomas Shapcott, Lawyer. Robert Herrick. NOSC

To His Pulse. Robert B. Shaw. PoA 2002

To his retired friend, an Invitation to Brecknock. Henry Vaughan. "Town believes thee lost, and didst thou see, The." PBRV

To His Savior [or Saviour]. The New Years [or yeers] Gift. Robert Herrick. ChIV-2; NAEL-6v1

To His Saviour. Robert Herrick. SacPr

To His Saviour, a Child; a Present, by a Child. Robert Herrick. ChIV-2

To His Scribe Adam. Geoffrey Chaucer. See Chaucer's Wordes unto Adam, his Owne Scriveyn.

To His Skeleton. Richard Wilbur. UpMys

To His Sleeping Mistress. John Fletcher. NOSC

To His Son Benedict Hoskyns. John Hoskyns. NOSC

To His Son [or Sonne], Vincent Corbet[t]. Richard Corbet. NOSC; OxAEP-1

To his stinking slum. (LL) Kingfisher. Norman Alexander MacCaig. NoP-4; NoP-5

To his two little girls. (LL) Star-Fix. Marilyn Nelson Waniek. ESEAA; LTA

To His Watch. Gerard Manley Hopkins. MoBrPo

To His Wife. Fyodor Ivanovich Tyutchev. OxBEV, tr. by Henry Gifford and Charles Tomlinson

To His Wife, for Striking Her Dog. Sir John Harington. WaAnP (On Striking His Wife's Dog.) DiBP

To hit my sister with it, but I didn't know this. (LL) Childhood Stories. Matthew Rohrer. LegDan; NAPBL

To l / hitch. Hand Game. Frances Boyle. IFF

To hold a damaged sparrow. With No Experience in Such Matters. Stephen Dunn. ItP

To hold a shadow in your hands the longest time. Battle at the Edge of the Falls. César Moro. BLPSL, tr. by Rene de Costa, Rigas Kappatos and Eleni Paidoussi

To hold an avalanche off. (LL) Man With Night Sweats, The. Thom Gunn. CABP; CalPo; HarvBoo; PoPoPo

To Homer. John Keats. NAEL-6v2; NAEL-7v2; NoP-4; NoP-5

To honey and bread old purity could love. (LL) My dreams, my works must wait till after hell. Gwendolyn Brooks. NoP-4; NoP-5; WaAnP

To Honora Sneyd [sonnet]. Anna Seward. CenSon; PoBW

To honour all their deaths, who for her bleed. (LL) Sir Philip Sidney. NAEL-6v1; NAEL-7v1; NIL-7; NIP-4 Fr. Astrophil and Stella.

To Hope. Charlotte Smith. RWP

To Hope. Mihály Csokonai Vitéz. IQMS, tr. by Watson Kirkconnell

To Hope. Helen Maria Williams. CenSon; OxBSo

To horse! to horse! my coal-black steed. Lord Byron. STuOW Fr. Deformed Transformed, The.

To Hou Xi. Han Yü. CCL1, tr. by Stephen Owen

To Hsuan-Ch'eng, Past Hsin-Lin-P'u, Toward Pan-Ch'iao. Hsieh T'iao. ChinPo, tr. by Ye Weilian [or Yeh Wei-lien or Wai-lim Yip]

To Human Skin. Cheryl Savageau. TWW

To Hungarian Youth. Dávid Baróti Szabó. IQMS, tr. by Matthew Mead and Ruth Mead

To hurt the Negro and avoid the Jew. University. Karl Shapiro. APT-2; PoA 2002

To Il y a. Hélène d'Oettingen. CuPo

To Imagination. Emily Jane Brontë. VWP

To impossible challenges. Toast in Response. André Frénaud. YaTCFP, tr. by Mary Ann Caws and Jean-Pierre Cauvin

To indicate is to / turn off in a world. Data. Joseph Ceravolo. BodElec

To Inez Milholland. Edna St. Vincent Millay. NAAPv.2; NALW

To Intellectual Detachment. Allen Tate. FuPo

To Ireland in the Coming Times. William Butler Yeats. IrV; NAMCP V.1; NoAM

To Iron-Founders and Others. Gordon Bottomley. OBEV; OBMV

To Isa Sleeping. Thomas Holley Chivers. APN-1

To Isle of Wight. Dave Jeddie Smith. InGu

To J. G. "Ephelia." NOSC

To J.G. on the News of His Marriage. "Ephelia." LW

To J. H. Reynolds, Esq. John Keats. Epistle to J.H. Reynolds. NPBRoP

To J—Y Colonna. Gérard de Nerval. WoPoe, tr. by Richard Sieburth

To János Arany. Sándor Petőfi. IQMS, tr. by Madeline Mason

To János Arany in Answer to His Poem "Cosmopolitan Poetry." Gyula Reviczky. IQMS, tr. by Madeline Mason

To Jane: The Invitation. Percy Bysshe Shelley. NAEL-6v2; NPBRoP; NPeEn (Invitation, The.) OBEV

To Jane: The Recollection. Percy Bysshe Shelley. NPBRoP

To Jane with a Guitar. Percy Bysshe Shelley. NPBRoP

To Janet, on Galileo. Honor Moore. PfS

To Jerusalem, 1990. Myra Shapiro. OPRER

To Jesus on His Birthday. Edna St. Vincent Millay. ChIV-2; HeIP-4

To John Ashbery. Tom Clark and Lewis Warsh. AHA

To John Ashbery. Frank O'Hara. AHA

To John Ashbery on Szymanowski's Birthday. Frank O'Hara. BodElec

To John Donne ("Who shall doubt, Donne, where [or whe'er] I a poet be[e].") Ben Jonson. NoP-4; NoP-5

To John Donne ("Donne, the delight of Phoebus, and each Muse.") Ben Jonson. NAEL-6v1; NAEL-7v1

To John Donne. Sir Henry Wotton. NoSic (To John Donne from Mr Henry Wotton.) NOSC

To John Donne from Mr Henry Wotton. Sir Henry Wotton. See To John Donne.

To John I ow'd great obligation. Epigram, An. Matthew Prior. OBVE; OxBEV

To John Keats. Leigh Hunt. CenSon

To John Keats, Poet, at Springtime [or Spring Time]. Countee Cullen. BrAP; OxBoAm; PtR

To John Reed. Max Eastman. APT-1

To join [or joyn] with them, who here confer. His Offering, with the Rest, at the Sepulcher. Robert Herrick. ChIV-2

To Josh Gibson (Legendary Slugger of the Old Negro Baseball League). George, Jr. Mosby. ISC

To Juan at the Winter Solstice. Robert Graves. HarvBoo; MoBrPo; NAEL-6v2; NAEL-7v2; NAMCP V.1; NoAM; NoP-4; NoP-5; NPeEn; RaBo; WaAnP

To Judge Faolain, Dead Long Enough: A Summons. Linda McCarriston. FaoP; LoL

To Judge Han Chuo at Yangzhou. Tu Mu. CCL1, tr. by A. C. Graham

To Judgement: An Assay. Jane Hirshfield. AmZen

To Julia de Burgos. Julia de Burgos. TCLAP, tr. by Grace Schulman

To Julia ("Julia, when thy Herrick dies.") Robert Herrick. NOSC

To jump off in the midst of the sea, rise again, nod to me, shout, and laughingly dash with your hair. (LL) Walt Whitman. ColAP; NAWM-7v2; NoAM Fr. Song of Myself.

To justify—Despair. (LL) It was not Death, for I stood up. Emily Dickinson. APN-2; NAAL-3; NAAL-5; NAAPv.1; OxBoAm; SAmP; TCAPo

To justify the Dream. (LL) I reckon—when I count at all. Emily Dickinson. APN-2; MoAmPo; NIL-7; NIP-4; NoP-4; NoP-5; OxBoAm; TCAPo

To justify your faith at last. (LL) Any Husband to Many a Wife. Emily Jane Pfeiffer. ViWPN; VWP

To Juventius. Catullus. CAGL, tr. by Frank O. Copley

To Kalon. Ezra Pound. PoA 2002

To Karl Marx. William Soutar. RSaN

To Keep a True Lent. Robert Herrick. SacPr

To keep from ending. Story of the End of the Story, The. James Galvin. TAPaP

To Keep from Shouting Something. Honorée Fanonne Jeffers. BtF

To keep him with us, feasts are not enough. Bartók. László Nagy. IQMS, tr. by Adam Makkai

To Keep My Love Alive. Lorenz Hart. ReLy

To keep our metaphysics warm. (LL) Whispers of Immortality. T. S. Eliot. APT-1; NAMCP V.1; NoAM; OBMV; OxAEP-2

To keep silent when nothing can be said. Ralph Adamo. AnSo Fr. Bicameralization, The.

To keep the blue wave dancing in its prison. (LL) Self-Portrait in Tyvek(TM) Windbreaker. James Merrill. NAMCP V.2; OxBoAm

To keep the soul serene even when the way is. Bring Roses and Cardamom (2.3). Horace. WED, tr. by Robert Bly

To Keep the Spirits. Jo Whitehorse Cochran. FiBr

To keep things whole. (LL) Keeping Things Whole. Mark Strand. CAP-8; HeIP-4; ItP; NAMCP V.2; OxBoAm; PoPoPo; VCAP

To keep your marriage brimming. Word to Husbands, A. Ogden Nash. OBCoV

To Kengai Osho of Engaku-ji. Muso Soseki. EaWin, tr. by W. S. Merwin

To Kill a Deer. Carol Frost. CAP-8; MoASP

To kill a language is to kill a people. Frost is All Over, The. Pearse Hutchinson. PBCIP

To Kill Stray Dogs. Mark Todd. GeoH

To kindle fire so that flame. What Man Can Do on This Planet. László Kálnoky. IQMS, tr. by Geroge Gömöri

To Kiss a Forehead Is to Erase Worry. Marina Ivanovna Tsvetayeva. TCRusP, tr. by John Glad

To kiss his sweet explaining lips. (LL) Here. Grace Paley. BAP-01; BeAl; GoPo

To kiss upon thy lips a stainless fame. (LL) To George Sand: A Desire. Elizabeth Barrett Browning. NAEL-6v2; NAEL-7v2; NALW; PoBW; VWP

To know he still is warm tho' I am cold. (LL) After Death. Christina Georgina Rossetti. NAEL-6v2; NAEL-7v2; NALW

To know just how He suffered—would be dear. Emily Dickinson. NCAP

To Know Me? Jolanda Insana. CItWP, *tr. by* Cinzia Sartini Blum and Lara Trubowitz

To know the final failure of the poet? (LL) Heartless Art, The. Tony Harrison. NoP-4; NoP-5

To / know whether or not art is overcome. John Cage. APSN *Fr.* Diary: How to Improve the World (You Will Only Make Matters Worse).

To Kosciusko. John Keats. CenSon

To L. H. B. Katherine Mansfield. FaBoWar

To Lady Elizabeth Foster, from Georgiana, Duchess of Devonshire, When She Was Apprehensive of Losing Her Eyesight–1796. Georgiana Cavendish, Duchess of Devonshire. PoBW

To Lallie. Amy Levy. PoBW; ViWPN

To Larra with Some Violets. Luis Cernuda. RaW, *tr. by* James Wright

To Laura. Henrietta Cordelia Ray. CBWP-3

To lead back to splendour. (LL) Ezra Pound. APSN; APT-1; NAAPv.2; NAMCP V.1; PFTM-2 *Fr.* Cantos.

To learn how to die. *Unknown.* SoOfWa, *tr. by* Sam Hamill

To learn that. Stunned by Freedom. Eva Svankmajerová. SurWo, *tr. by* Katerina Pinosová

To learn the scriptures is easy. Lal Ded. WPoS

To leave yet to stay, and by staying to leave. Sonnet 61. Félix Lope de Vega Carpio. BLPSL, *tr. by* Rene de Costa, Rigas Kappatos and Eleni Paidoussi

To Lena I've been partial. I have been. Albery Allson Whitman. NAAPv.1 *Fr.* Octoroon, The.

To let the warm Love in! (LL) Ode to Psyche. John Keats. NAEL-6v2; NAEL-7v2; NOBRP; NoP-4; NoP-5; NPBRoP; OBEV; OxAEP-2; TFi

To let them feel they're not quite as nice as they might be. (LL) English Are So Nice!, The. D. H. Lawrence. NAMCP V.1; NoP-4; NoP-5; PoPoPo; RaBo

To Leven Water. Tobias Smollett. OBEV

To Levine on the Day of Atonement. Robert Mezey. TaR

To Li Po ("When the cold wind visits you from the corners of the earth.") Tu Fu [*or* Du Fu]. TAL

To Li Po ("Floating cloud follows the sun, The.") Tu Fu [*or* Du Fu]. NDACCP, *tr. by* William Carlos Williams

To Li Po on a Spring Day ("Po, the unrivalled poet.") Tu Fu [*or* Du Fu]. TAL

To Li Po on a Spring Day ("There's no poet quite like you, Li Po.") Tu Fu [*or* Du Fu]. CrYelRi, *tr. by* Sam Hamill

To Li Po on a Winter Day. Tu Fu [*or* Du Fu]. CrYelRi, *tr. by* Sam Hamill

To Liberty. Ágnes Nemes Nagy. IQMS, *tr. by* Ila Egon

To Liberty. Mary Robinson. OxBSo

To lie on these beaches for another summer. Late August on the Lido. John Hollander. YaYoPo

To Life. Lizette Woodworth Reese. TCAPo

To life upon these shores. (LL) Middle Passage. Robert Earl Hayden. APT-2; CAP-8; ColAP; NAAL-5; NAMCP V.2; NoAM; OxAAAP; OxBoAm; TRP; VCAP; WaAnP

To lift her over the threshold, and let her in at the door. (LL) Witch, The. Mary Elizabeth Coleridge. CABP; NAEL-7v2; NALW; PoBW; ViWPN; VWP

To Light. Linda Hogan. HATNAP

To light the dark. Litany. Elise Paschen. FFC

To Lighten Heavy Loads. Aua. IFF *Fr.* Magic Words.

To Linda. Guillaume Apollinaire. CuPo

To linger till ninety, like Landor. (LL) Obit on Parnassus. F. Scott Fitzgerald. AmWit; NBLV

To live and die for thee. (LL) To Anthea, Who May Command Him Anything. Robert Herrick. BASC; NOSC; OBEV; OxBEV

To live and not to be thine own. Thine Own. Josephine D. Henderson Heard. CBWP-4; SWaP

To live in court among the crew is care. To His Friend P. of Courting, Traveling, Dicing, and Tennis. George Turberville. NoSic

To live in mankind, far, far more...than to live in a name. (LL) Eagle That Is Forgotten, The. Vachel Lindsay. APT-1; MoAmPo

To Live in the Land of Israel. Arye Sivan. NRoS, *tr. by* Esther Raizen

To Live in This World Again. Joanne Kyger. WANABP

To live in Wales. Welsh Wordscape, A. Peter Finch. AngWePo

To live in Wales is to be conscious. Welsh Landscape. Ronald Stuart Thomas. NoP-4; NoP-5; TCAWP

To Live Merrily, and To Trust to Good Verses. Robert Herrick. BASC; CavPo; NOSC

To live one's life is no stroll in the park. (LL) Hamlet. Boris Leonidovich Pasternak. GI; WoPoe, *tr. by* Nina Kossman

To live simply on this earth. (LL) Summer Morning. Charles Simic. GoPo; WaAnP

To live to die to die to live to be to. Just Asking. Carl Hancock Rux. BtF

To live with him, and sing in endles[s] morn of light[!]. (LL) At a Solemn Music[k]. John Milton. HeIP-4; OBEV; SacPr

To live with me and be. Covenant. Douglas Crase. WaAnP

To live with thee and be thy Love. (LL) Nymph's [*or* Nimphs] Reply to the [Passionate] Shepherd [*or* Sheepheard], The. Sir Walter Ralegh. AEP; AmFaPo; BrAP; CABP; ClHu; HeIP-4; NAEL-6v1; NAEL-7v1; NBLV; NIL-7; NIP-4; NoP-4; NoP-5; NoSic; NPeEn; PoPoPo; RACG; TFi; TRP; UV; WaAnP; WeW-3

To live within a cave—it is most good. Salve! Thomas Edward Brown. OBEV

To live without him: liked [*or* lik'd] it not, and died [*or* di'd]. (LL) Upon the Death of Sir Albert Morton's Wife. Sir Henry Wotton. BASC; NPeEn; OBEV; OxBEV; PBRV; WeW-3

To living virtues turns the deadly vices. George Chapman. OxBSo *Fr.* Coronet for His Mistress Philosophy, A.

To Lizbie Browne. Thomas Hardy. FaBoVe; OxAEP-2

To London once my stepps [*or* steps] I bent. London Lickpenny. *Unknown.* OBSV

To Look at Any Thing. John Moffitt. TWF

To look at the moon. (LL) Funeral Rites. Seamus Heaney. ModIr; PBCIP; PoetW

To look at the river made of time and water. Ars Poetica. Jorge Luis Borges. PtR; TCLAP, *tr. by* W. S. Merwin

To look at your face. *Your beautiful face.* (LL) Electricity. Lavinia Greenlaw. MoWP; NeBrP

To look back and say, a flash, a white flash sparkled. (LL) Fundamental Project of Technology, The. Galway Kinnell. AtGh; CAP-8

To Look Out Once from High Windows. Sinéad Morrissey. MFPA

To look up slowly. Nearing Long Moons. J. L. Jacobs. AmPoNex

To loosen with all ten fingers held wide and limber. Moss-Gathering. Theodore Roethke. BLT

To Lord Byron. Gyula Juhász. IQMS, *tr. by* J. G. Nichols

To lose a lodging, yet to find the sky. To a Dead Friend. Agnes Mary Frances Robinson. PoBW

To lose one's faith—surpass. Emily Dickinson. TCAPo

To Louisa M[artin], Whom I Used to Call "Monkey." Charles Lamb. NPBRoP

To Love. Edmund Gardner. CenSon

To Love. Boris Leonidovich Pasternak. TCRusP, *tr. by* Bogdan Boychuk and Mark Rudman

To Love a Stranger. Sibby Anderson-Thompkins. InTrad

To Love a Woman. Ed. Hoornik. TuT, *tr. by* Mary E. O'Donnell

To love a woman is to escape from death. To Love a Woman. Ed. Hoornik. TuT, *tr. by* Mary E. O'Donnell

To love and never seek compassion. (LL) Fulke, 1st Baron Brooke Greville. NoP-4; NoP-5 *Fr.* Caelica.

To love / Is. Is. Fazil Hüsnü Daglarca. NaPG, *tr. by* Talat Sait Halman

To Love Is. Alicia Ostriker.

    3. FiBr

To love is to remove the face. Crowd. Cole Swensen. OnScMo

To love me also in silence with thy soul. (LL) Elizabeth Barrett Browning. CenSon; NAEL-6v2; NAEL-7v2; OxBSo *Fr.* Sonnets from the Portuguese.

To love my own, my body. On This Earth. Juanita Brunk. ACAMVP

To love so well the world that we may believe, in the end, in God. (LL) Robert Penn Warren. NoP-4; NoP-5; VCAP *Fr.* Island of Summer.

To Love That Well. Janice Townley Moore. IaFF

To love that well which thou must leave ere long. (LL) William Shakespeare. AEP; BrAP; CABP; ClHu; HeIP-4; ItP; NAEL-6v1; NAEL-7v1; NIL-7; NIP-4; NoP-4; NoP-5; NoSic; NPeEn; OBEV; OxBSo; SoSe-8; TFi; WeW-3 *Fr.* Sonnets.

To love, to go in endless thunder. To Love. Boris Leonidovich Pasternak. TCRusP, *tr. by* Bogdan Boychuk and Mark Rudman

To love, to love, to love, to love always, with all. I Love, You Love. Rubén Darío. BLPSL, *tr. by* Rene de Costa, Rigas Kappatos and Eleni Paidoussi

To love you in shadow as in the light. Glass, The. Edwin Morgan. HarvBoo

To love your country. Prelude. Marilyn Chin. LoL

To Lucasta. Richard Lovelace. CavPo

To Lucasta, from Prison. Richard Lovelace. BASC; CavPo

To Lucasta, [on] Going beyond the Seas. Richard Lovelace. OBEV; OxAEP-1

    (Song: To Lucasta, Going beyond the Seas.) NOSC

    (Song.) CavPo

To Lucasta, [on] Going to the War[re]s. Richard Lovelace. BASC; CABP; CavPo; ClHu; FaBoWar; NAEL-6v1; NAEL-7v1; NIL-7; NIP-4; NoP-4; NoP-5; NOSC; NPeEn; OBEV; OBWP; OxAEP-1; OxBEV; PBRV; PoPoPo; TFi; UV; WaAnP; WeW-3

To Lucia Playing on Her Lute, Another. Samuel Pordage. NOSC

To Luck. W. S. Merwin. PoA 2002

To Lucy, Countess of Bedford, with Mr. Donne's Satires. Ben Jonson. NAEL-6v1; NAEL-7v1

(To Lucy, Countesse of Bedford, with Mr. Donnes Satyres.) PBRV

To Lucy, Countesse of Bedford, with Mr. Donnes Satyres. Ben Jonson. *See* To Lucy, Countesse of Bedford, with Mr. Donne's Satires.

To Lydia. Horace. *See* Ode 1.25: Ribald Romeos Less and Less Berattle ("Parcius iunctas quatiunt fenestras").

To Lysander, on Some Verses Be Writ, and Asking More for His Heart. Aphra Behn. LW

To Madam Bhen. "Ephelia." EMWP

To Maecenas. Phillis Wheatley. NAAL-5; WaAnP

To Magistrate Zhang. Wang Wei. CCL1, *tr. by* Jerome P. Seaton

To Mainz! Ursula Krechel. GTCP, *tr. by* Irmgard Hunt

To make a bit of music. Ode: In a Few Hours. Hans Lodeizen. TuT, *tr. by* Eamon Grennan

To make a delta praise for the poets ah. (LL) For the Poets. Jayne Cortez. InoFa; PmAP

To make a final conquest of all me. Fair Singer, The. Andrew Marvell. FSCP; NoP-4; NoP-5

To Make a Long Story Short. Nicanor Parra. WoBe, *tr. by* Liz Werner

To Make a Poem in Prison. Etheridge Knight. AF

To make a poet black, and bid him sing! (LL) Yet Do I Marvel. Countee Cullen. AmFaPo; APT-2; BrAP; InvLi; NAAL-5; NAAPv.2; NAMCP V.1; NIL-7; NoAM; NoP-5; SSLK; WaAnP

To make a prairie it takes a clover and one bee. Emily Dickinson. HeIP-4; NBLV; TCAPo

To make a start. William Carlos Williams. NAMCP V.1; NoAM *Fr.* Paterson.

To Make a Talisman. Olga Orozco. TCLAP, *tr. by* Stephen Tapscott

To make it into history. (LL) It Took One Hundred Years. Malika O'Lahsen. HAWP; WoPoe, *tr. by* Eric Sellin

To make itself secure. (LL) Reassurance, The. Thom Gunn. NPeEn; StAl

To make layers. Time and Materials. Robert Hass. RoV

To make love with a stranger is the best. Unclaimed. Vikram Seth. PML

To make me *deaf*, and mend my *sight*. (LL) Stella's Birthday, 1725. Jonathan Swift. CABP; IrLP

To make my grave. (LL) Cross-tree, The. Robert Herrick. CavPo; ChIV-2

To make One's Toilette—after Death. Emily Dickinson. TCAPo

To make quick way I'll leap o'er heavy blocks. John Dryden. OBSV *Fr.* Absalom and Achitophel, Part 2.

To make seas. (LL) Mawu of the Waters. Abena Busia. HAWP; NAfrP

To make some bread you must have dough. One, Two, Three—Gough! Eve Merriam. NTCP

To make sorbet with campari, for a party. I am peeling four pink grapefruit. Natasha Sajé. PoDa

To make sure I was noticing. (LL) On Being Asked to Write a Poem Against the War in Vietnam. Hayden Carruth. AmWaPo; PoAgWa

To make that curve of the water. Curve of the Water. Hilda Morley. PmAP

To make the cherry red! (LL) Nevertheless. Marianne Moore. HarvBoo; NAAPv.2; NoP-4; NoP-5; SoSe-8

To make the child in your own image is a capital crime. Karl Shapiro. BodElec *Fr.* Bourgeois Poet, The.

To make this condiment, your poet begs. Salad, A. Sydney Goodsir Smith. NBLV

To Mal Waldron and everyone and I stopped breathing. (LL) Day Lady Died, The. Frank O'Hara. CAP-8; EMP; InoFa; ItP; NAMCP V.2; NoAM; NoP-4; NoP-5; OxBoAm; PFTM-2; PmAP; RaBo; SwNoth; TRP; VCAP; WaAnP

To Mani Leyb. Shifre Vays. Prolet, *tr. by* Amelia Glaser

To many a flute of Arcady. (LL) Alfred Tennyson. CAGL; NAEL-6v2; NAEL-7v2; NAWM-7v2 *Fr.* In Memoriam A. H. H.

To Marcus Aurelius. Zbigniew Herbert. VCWP, *tr. by* Czeslaw Miosz and Peter Dale Scott

To Margot Heinemann. John Cornford. OBWP

To Marguerite. Matthew Arnold. *See* To Marguerite—Continued.

To Marguerite—Continued. Matthew Arnold. BrAP; NAEL-6v2; NAEL-7v2; NoP-5; NPeEn; OxBEV; SoSe-8; WaAnP *Fr.* Switzerland.

To Marie Osmond. Jack Skelley. SwNoth

To Marina. Kenneth Koch. NoAM

To Mark Anthony in Heaven. William Carlos Williams. SAmP; TCAPo

To Mars, a Prayer for Peace. Janus Pannonius. IQMS, *tr. by* Anthony Barrett

To Marthe. Bill Bathurst. AHA

To Mary. William Cowper. NPBRoP; UV

(My Mary.) OBEV

To Mary. Mary E. Tucker. CBWP-1

To Mary. Charles Wolfe. IrLP; OBEV

(Song: To Mary.) OxAEP-2

To Mary Ann Lamb, the Author's Best Friend and Sister. Charles Lamb. *See* If From My Lips Some Angry Accents Fell.

To Mary, Lady Wroth ("Madam[e], had all antiquity [*or* antiquitie] been lost.") Ben Jonson. NOSC

To Mary Pickford—Moving Picture Actress. Vachel Lindsay. IllVoic

To Mary Unwin. William Cowper. CenSon; OBEV

To mask a King in weeds. (LL) Ralph Waldo Emerson. Spl; TCAPo *Fr.* Quatrains.

To Master Groggy, From Afar. Dōyaku Sensei, Master Artery. EMJL, *tr. by* Haruo Shirane

To Master Monk Nangjee. Great Master Wonhyo. BecRai, *tr. by* Kim Daljin, Kim Won-Chung and Christopher Merrill

To Mastres Margery Wentworthe. John Skelton. *See* To Mistress Margery Wentworth.

To May. Jane West. CenSon

To me, fair friend, you never can be old. William Shakespeare. HeIP-4; NoSic; OBEV; OxAEP-1 *Fr.* Sonnets.

To me how wildly pleasing is that scene. Gypsy's Evening Blaze, The. John Clare. CenSon

To me it seems. Sappho. SaLy, *tr. by* Diane Rayor

To me, *lion* was sun on a wing. Eve Names the Animals. Susan Donnelly. NIL-7

To me, love is the flame. Şeyh Galib. OLP, *tr. by* Walter Andrews, Najaat Black and Mehmet Kalpakli

To me, Muscovites are sweethearts out of old stories. Bulat Shalvovich Okudzhava. ItGoST, *tr. by* Ronnie Apter and Mark Herman

To me nothing seems as splendid nor as praiseworthy. Unknown. GePo

To me, one silly task is like another. Cassandra. Louise Bogan. APT-2; MoAmPo; NALW; NAMCP V.1

To me. Somewhere they are building. My Lady Carries Stones. Nick Piombino. FTOS

To me that man seems like a god in heaven. Catullus. NAWM-7v1 *Fr.* Carmina [Charles Martin Translation].

To me the sound of falling rain. Sounds. Lindley Williams Hubbell. APT-2

To me there is more relevance in your single flight. Welsh Homer. Cliff James. AngWePo

To me, to love is no go. Music That Makes Me Dance. Bob Merrill. ReLy

To me tomorrow constantly deny it. (LL) Ovid. CABP; NoSic *Fr.* Elegies.

To me what she so rarely did with you. (LL) Yeah Yeah Yeah. Roddy Lumsden. EdScPo; NeBl

To me, whom in their lays the shepherds call. Mark Akenside. OBGa *Fr.* Inscriptions.

To me—who since childhood went on my way. Time. Adelia Prado. TANSG, *tr. by* Ellen Doré Watson

To me, your beauty, breathstop-young. To me, your beauty. Unknown. SonAtl, *tr. by* Alois Berma and Mick Henson

To Meadows [*or* Meddowes]. Robert Herrick. BASC; NOSC; NPeEn; OBEV; PBRV

To measure long journeys. (LL) Tour Guide: La Maison des Esclaves. Melvin Dixon. ESEAA; OxAAAP

To Meath of the pastures. Drover, A. Padraic Colum. MoBrPo; OBMV

To meet a bad lad on the African waste. African Lion, The. A. E. Housman. NOxBChV

To meet so enabled a Man! (LL) He preached upon "Breadth" till it argued him narrow. Emily Dickinson. NAWM-7v2; SacPr

To Melancholy. Susan Evance. CenSon

To Melancholy. Written on the Banks of the Arun, October 1785. Charlotte Smith. CenSon; RWP

To Memory. Mary Elizabeth Coleridge. ViWPN

To Men. Anna Wickham. MoBrPo

To Meng Hao-jan. Li Po. ColAnChi, *tr. by* Stephen Owen

To Mercy, Pity, Peace and Love. William Blake. BBASP; ChAP; InvLi; NAEL-6v2; NAEL-7v2; NOBRP; NoP-4; NoP-5; NPBRoP; OxBEV; WaAnP *Fr.* Songs of Innocence.

To merely uncover the depths of love. Travelogue. Lewis Warsh. BodElec

To Mertill Who Desired Her to Speak to Clorinda of His Love. Elizabeth Taylor. EMWP

To Michal. Lucille Clifton. ExTi

To middle age I loved the Way. In Retirement at Zhongnan. Wang Wei. CCL1, *tr. by* Jerome P. Seaton

To Midnight Nan at Leroy's. Langston Hughes. NAAPv.2

To Military Progress. Marianne Moore. NAAPv.2

To Minerva. Thomas Hood. NBLV

To Miss C—on Being Desired To Attempt Writing a Comedy. Charlotte Smith. RWP

To Miss Sophia Headle. Dorothea Primrose Campbell. PoBW

To Mistress [*or* Maystres] Isabell Pennell. John Skelton. NoSic; NPeEn; OBEV *Fr.* Garland [*or* Garlande *or* Garlands] of Laurel[l], The.

To Mistress [*or* Maystres] Margaret Hussey. John Skelton. NAEL-6v1; NBLV; NoP-4; NoP-5; NoSic; OBEV; OxBEV; TFi; WaAnP *Fr.* Garland [*or* Garlande *or* Garlands] of Laurel[l], The.

To Mistress Margery Wentworth. John Skelton. OBEV *Fr.* Garland [*or* Garlande *or* Garlands] of Laurel[l], The.

To mock the barbarous triumphs of despair! (LL) Sappho Discovers her Passion. Mary Robinson. CenSon; RWP

To mock the riddle corpses round Bapaume. (LL) Blighters. Siegfried Sassoon. NAMCP V.1; NoAM; OxBEV; PoWW

To moralize the state, they drag out a man. Morning's News, The. Wendell Berry. UpMys

To Morfydd. Lionel Pigot Johnson. MoBrPo; OBMV

To Morning. William Blake. OxAEP-2

To mortal eyes, you, Hope, do seem. To Hope. Mihály Csokonai Vitéz. IQMS, *tr. by* Watson Kirkconnell

To Mother. Keorapetse Kgositsile. GT

To Mother Luddwels Cave and Spring. Martha, Lady Giffard. EMWP

To mount the wheel with perfect grace. Wooing the Bicycle. Grace Duffie Boylan. ArBi

To Mr [S.T.] C[olerid]ge. Anna Laetitia Barbauld. *See* To Mr. S. T. Coleridge.

To Mr. Gay, Who Wrote Him a Congratulatory Letter on the Finishing His House. Alexander Pope. NPeEn; OBGa

To Mr. Hayley, on Receiving Some Elegant Lines from Him. Charlotte Smith. RWP

To Mr. Lawrence. John Milton. OBEV
  (Sonnet.) NOSC; OxAEP-1
  (To Edward Lawrence.) PBRV

To Mr. Murray. Lord Byron. UV

To Mr. S. T. Coleridge. Anna Laetitia Barbauld. CABP; NoP-4; WoRP
  (To Mr [S.T.] C[olerid]ge.) NOBRP
  (To Mr Coleridge.) NPBRoP

To Mr. Blanchard, the Celebrated Aeronaut in America. Philip Freneau. APN-1

To Mr Coleridge. Anna Laetitia Barbauld. *See* To Mr. S. T. Coleridge.

To Mr. Cyriack Skinner upon His Blindness. John Milton. NOSC; NPeEn
  (Sonnet.) OxAEP-1

To Mr. George Herbert. John Donne. OBVE

To Mr. H. Lawes On His Airs. John Milton. NoP-4; NoP-5
  (Sonnet: To Mr. H. Lawes, on His Air[e]s.) NOSC

To Mr. Henry Cary, On the Publication of his Sonnets. Anna Seward. CenSon

To Mr. Henry Lawes. Katherine Philips. NoP-4; NoP-5

To Mr. Hobs: "Vast *Bodies* of *Philosophie*." Abraham Cowley. BASC *Fr.* Pindarique Odes.

To Mr. Maunder Maunder, Professional Poet. Genevieve Taggard. APT-2

To Mr. Opie, On His Having Painted for Me the Picture of Mrs Twis. Amelia Alderson Opie. RWP

To Mrs B. from a Lady Who Had a Desire to See Her, and Who Complains on the Ingratitude of Her Fugitive Lover. *Unknown*. EMWP

To Mrs. Charlotte Smith. Martha Hanson. CenSon

To Mrs. Hayley, on her Voyage to America. 1784. William Hayley. CenSon

To Mrs. K———, On Her Sending Me an English Christmas Plum-Cake at Paris. Helen Maria Williams. WoRP

To Mrs. G. Charlotte Smith. RWP

To Mrs M. A. at Parting. Katherine Philips. NAEL-6v1; NAEL-7v1

To Mrs. Reynolds's Cat. John Keats. *See* To a Cat.

To Mrs. W. on Her Excellent Verses. Aphra Behn. EMWP

To Mrs. Will H. Low. Robert Louis Stevenson. NPeEn

To Mrs. M.A. Upon Absence. Katherine Philips. PoBW

To Mrs. Manley. By the Author of Agnes de Castro. Catherine Cockburn. EMWP

To Mrs. Manley, upon Her Tragedy Call'd The Royal Mischief. Mary Pix. EMWP

To Mrs. Norton. Frances Anne Kemble. VWP

To Mrs S. F. on Her Poems. Mary Pix. EMWP

To Ms. Ann. Lucille Clifton. ESEAA

To Music, to Becalm His Fever. Robert Herrick. OBEV

To mute and to material things. Sir Walter Scott. OBEV *Fr.* Marmion.

To my affections what a slave am I? Verses by my Mother in Her Own Hand. Amy Hammond. EMWP

To my aunt blanche. Praise song. Lucille Clifton. P180

To My Beloved. R. G. Ka. Prolet, *tr. by* Amelia Glaser

To My Bones. Zoltán Jékely. IQMS, *tr. by* George Szirtes

To My Book. Ben Jonson. FaBoVe; NAEL-6v1; NAEL-7v1

To My Books. Caroline Elizabeth Norton. CenSon

To My Brother ("O, thou art far away from me—dear boy!") Mary Bryan. CenSon

To My Brother ("Oh transient sorrows, light as morning dews.") Mary Bryan. NPBRoP

To My Brother ("Once in our customed walk a wounded bird.") Mary Bryan. CenSon

To My Brother: "Do you recall the fancies of many years ago." Letitia Elizabeth Landon. NPBRoP

To My Brother: Killed: Hammont Wood: October, 1918. Louise Bogan. AmWaPo

To My Brother Miguel. César Vallejo. PoetW; TCLAP, *tr. by* John Knoepfle and James Wright

To My Child. Barry Cornwall. CenSon

To My Children. Karen Gershon. ItWoWo

To My Children. Charlotte Smith. NPBRoP

To My Cousin, Ching-yuan, Twelfth Month, 403. T'ao Ch'ien. CrYelRi, *tr. by* Sam Hamill

To My Craft. Ágnes Nemes Nagy. IQMS, *tr. by* Hugh Maxton

To my creel and stack-net island. O.H.M.S. Ian Hamilton Finlay. EdScPo

To My Cycle. Adriel Vere. ArBi

To My Daughter. N. Balamani Amma. CFP, *tr. by* N. Balamani Amma

To My Daughter. Keorapetse Kgositsile. GT

To My Daughter. Margit Mikes. IQMS, *tr. by* Susanne K. Walther

To My Daughter Catherine on Ashwednesday 1645, Finding Her Weeping at Prayers, Because I Would Not Consent to Her Fasting. Katherine Thimelby Aston. EMWP

To My Dead Brother. Clara Ann Thompson. CBWP-2

To My Dear and Loving Husband. Anne Bradstreet. AmFaPo; BASC; BrAP; ColAP; ErotSp; HeIP-4; ITBLP; LW; NAAL-3; NAAL-5; NAAPv.1; NIL-7; NIP-4; NoP-4; NoP-5; NOSC; OxBEV; OxBoAm; OxWW; PEW; SacPr; TCAPo; TFi; WaAnP; WeW-3

To My Dear and Most Worthy Friend, Mr. Isaac Walton. Charles Cotton. NPeEn

To My Dear Children. Anne Bradstreet. BASC; NAAL-3; PtR

To My Dear Friend Mr Congreve [on His Comedy Called "The Double-Dealer"]. John Dryden. NPeEn; OxAEP-1

To my dear wife. Last Will and Testament, A. John Winstanley. FaBoVe; OBSV

To My Dog, Swan. Dezső Kosztolányi. IQMS, *tr. by* Lydia Pasternak-Slater

To my dream land I go. City, The. Meirion MacIntyre Huws. BBMWP, *tr. by* Geriant Løvgreen

To My Eldest Brother, With the British Army in Portugal. Felicia Dorothea Hemans. RWP

To My Excellent Lucasia, On Our Friendship. Katherine Philips. BASC; LW; NALW; NoP-4; NoP-5; NOSC; NPeEn; OxBEV; PBRV; PEW; PoBW

To My Father. John Berryman. PoPoPo

To My Father. Tony Curtis. AngWePo; TCAWP

To My Father. Henrietta Cordelia Ray. CBWP-3

To My Father Norman Alone in the Blue Mountains. Jack Lindsay. NOBAu

To My Fellow Artists. Christopher Logue. RSaN

To My First Teacher. Tenshin Reb Anderson. WhBo

To My First White Hairs. Wole Soyinka. OPOU

To my firstborn land, in the south. Firstborn Land, The. Ingeborg Bachmann. GTCP, *tr. by* Irmgard Hunt and Daniel Huws

To my Friend, Jerina. Lucille Clifton. ESEAA

To My Friend (With an Identity Disc). Wilfred Owen. CAGL

To My Friends Against Poetry. Jane Barker. BASC

To My Friends and Critics. Julia A. Moore.
  Poet is Scornful, The. STuOW

To my friends. When I'm dead. Legacy. Ludwig Heinrich Christoph Hölty. SonAtl, *tr. by* Kurt Ganzl and Markus Jaigirder

To My Heavenly Charmer. Martha Sansom. LW

To My Husband. "Eliza." EMWP; LW; PBRV

To My Husband—December 1844. Margaret Moffette Lea Houston. TiP2

To My Inconstant Mistress [*or* Mistris]. Thomas Carew. CavPo; NoP-4; OBEV; TFi
  (Song.) NoP-4
  (Song. To My Inconstant Mistress.) NoP-5; WaAnP

To My Infant Daughter. Yvor Winters. IllVoic
  "Alas, that I should be." WoPoe

To My Ingenious and Worthy Friend William Lowndes, Esq. John Gay. OBSV

To my jumbled shadows. I Present Myself to the World. Amina Saïd. PoArWo, *tr. by* Lucy McNair

To My Lady Morland at Tunbrige [*or* Tunbridge]. Aphra Behn. PoBW

To My Lady of Poetry. Alfonsina Storni. PoCho, *tr. by* Kay Short

To my last period. Lucille Clifton. BeAl; NAMCP V.2; PoCu

To my last technician. Testament. Anne Rouse. NeBrP

To My Least Favorite Reviewer. Howard Nemerov. OBCoV

To My Little Girl. Shakuntala Hawoldar. CFP; HAWP

To My Little Radio. Bertolt Brecht. RWPCtW, *tr. by* John Willett

To my Lord Biron's Tune of—Adieu Phillis. Katherine Philips. NPeEn

To My Love. Kjell Hjern. PML, *tr. by* Leif Sjöberg and William Jay Smith

To My Love, Combing Her Hair. Yehuda Amichai. BeAl, *tr.* by Chana Bloch and Stephen Mitchell

To my lover I want to sacrifice it all. *Unknown.* SLW, *tr.* by Marjolijn De Jager, Sayd Bahodin Majrouh and André Velter

To My Lyre. Eliza Cook. VWP

To My Mistress[e] in My Absence. Thomas Carew. NOSC

To my most dearely-loved friend Henery Reynolds Esquire, of Poets and Poesie. Michael Drayton. PBRV

To My Most Honord Cosen, Mrs Somerset on the Unjust Censure Past Upon My Poore Marcelia. Frances Boothby. EMWP

To My Mother. Anna Adams. Prnts

To My Mother. George Barker. *See* Sonnet to My Mother.

To My Mother. Wendell Berry. GoPo; PoA 2002

To My Mother. Simeon Dumdum. ReBoTo

To My Mother. Mary Weston Fordham. CBWP-2

To My Mother. Edgar Allan Poe. NAAPv.1

To My Mother. Henrietta Cordelia Ray. CBWP-3

To my mother, / and to my mother's monument. Message. Rosario Ferré. TANSG

To My Mountain. Kathleen Jessie Raine. EdScPo

To My Much Esteemed Friend on Her Play Call'd Fatal-Friendship. Lady Sarah Piers. EMWP

To My Muse. Agnes Mary Frances Robinson. VWP

To My Niece Dorothy, a Sleepless Baby. Dorothy Wordsworth. CABP

To My Noble Friend Master William Browne: Of the Evil Time. Michael Drayton. CABP

To My Old Friend Lee. Chunghur Hyujung. BecRai, *tr.* by Kim Daljin, Kim Won-Chung and Christopher Merrill

To My Old Poems. Kenneth Koch. PoA 2002

To My Old Schoolmaster. John Greenleaf Whittier. ColAP

To My Own Face. Caroline Lindsay. VWP

To My Own Heart. Maria Jane Jewsbury. VWP

To My Pen. Mary Julia Young. CenSon

To my prowd foe thus, sister, humblie saye. Virgil. OBVE *Fr.* Aeneid [*or* Eneados *or* Aeneis], The.

To My Rival. Thomas Carew. OxBSo

To My Rival. "Ephelia." LW

To My Shtetl Years. Yosl Grinshpan. Prolet, *tr.* by Amelia Glaser

To My Sister. Olga Fiodorovna Berggolts. TCRusP, *tr.* by Daniel Weissbort

To My Sister. William Wordsworth. MakPoe; NPBRoP

To My Soldier Son. Zseni Várnai. IQMS, *tr.* by Peter Zollman

To My Son. Mun Chônghui. EcSo, *tr.* by Catherine J. Kim

To My Son. David Shapiro. OxBoAm

To My Son, Abbas. Khurshid-Banu. SonAtl, *tr.* by Betty Blair, Azer H. Hasret and Mehmet Kara

To My Soul. Jean Valentine. YaYoPo

To my true king I offered free from stain. Jacobite's Epitaph, A. Thomas Babington Macaulay, 1st Baron Macaulay. OBEV

To My Twenties. Kenneth Koch. EMP; NoP-5

To My Twin Sister Who Died at Birth. Kathleene West. GifTon

To My Venerable Friend, the President of the Royal Academy. Washington Allston. APN-1

To my wash-stand. Louis Zukofsky. APT-2; NAMCP V.1; OxBoAm *Fr.* 29 Songs.

To My Wife. James Vincent Cunningham. VCAP

To My Wife: "Anterooms keep nice and cool with you." Oktay Rifat. NaPG, *tr.* by Talat Sait Halman

To My Worthy Friend Mr. Peter Lely [*or* Lilly]. Richard Lovelace. BASC; CavPo; GS; NOSC

To My Young Lover. Jane Barker. BASC; LW

To My Younger Brother. Tu Fu [*or* Du Fu]. CrYelRi, *tr.* by Sam Hamill

To Myself. Abba Kovner. AF, *tr.* by Shirley Kaufman

To Myself. Kenneth Slessor. BMAP

To Naguib Mahfouz. Abdul Wahab Al-Bayati. IrPoTo, *tr.* by Farouk Abdel Wahab

To Napoleon. Dániel Berzsenyi. IQMS, *tr.* by Adam Makkai

To Nature. Samuel Taylor Coleridge. NPBRoP; OxBSo

To Nature. Emily Jane Pfeiffer.
  "If we be fools of chance, indeed, and tend." ViWPN
  "O Nature! thou whom I have thought to love." ViWPN

To Ned. Herman Melville. APN-2; NAAL-3; TCAPo

To New York. Léopold Sédar Senghor. PoetW; WoPeo, *tr.* by Melvin Dixon

To Night. Thomas Lovell Beddoes. CenSon

To Night. Percy Bysshe Shelley. NAEL-6v2; NAEL-7v2; TFi
  (Night.) OBEV

To Night. Charlotte Smith. NAEL-6v2; NAEL-7v2

To Night. Joseph Blanco White. GSo; OBEV; OxAEP-2
  (Night and Death.) CenSon

To no believable blue I turn my eyes. Sylvia Townsend Warner. OxBSo *Fr.* Astrophysics.

To No One in Particular. Marvin Bell. TAPaP

To Novella, on Her Saying Deridingly, that a Lady of Great Merit, and Fine Address, Was Bred in the Old Way. An Epigram. Mary Barber. NIL-7

To Nysus. Sir Charles Sedley. OBSV

To obtain the value. 2 Pages, 122 Words on Music and Dance. John Cage. APT-2

To O. E. A. Claude McKay. GT

To Oenone ("What conscience, say, is it in thee.") Robert Herrick. OBEV

To Old Age. Kenneth Koch. PoCho

To Old Age. Walt Whitman. Spl

To Olga. Alena Synková. INSAB

To Olive. Lord Alfred Bruce Douglas. OBEV

To Olivia. Francis Thompson. MoBrPo

To One Afflicted with Adolescence. Anna Cascella. CltWP, *tr.* by Cinzia Sartini Blum and Lara Trubowitz

To One Black, and Not Very Handsome, Who Expected Commendation. Edward Herbert, 1st Baron Herbert of Cherbury. NOSC

To one full sound and silently. Man with Three Friends, The. Dora Greenwell. SacPr

To One in Bedlam. Ernest Dowson. GSo; MoBrPo; OBMV

To one in love with solitude and song. (LL) Echoes. Emma Lazarus. APN-2; GSo; NAAPv.1

To One in Paradise. Edgar Allan Poe. NCAP; OBEV; OxBoAm

To one it is a piece of ground. What is a Garden? Reginald Arkell. OBGa

To one kneeling down no word came. In a Country Church. Ronald Stuart Thomas. HarvBoo

To One Loved Wholly Within Wisdom. Genevieve Taggard. APT-2

To One Persuading a Lady to Marriage. Katherine Philips. *See* Answer to Another Persuading a Lady to Marriage, An.

To One That Asked Me Why I Loved J.G. "Ephelia." EMWP; NOSC; PEW
  (To One that Asked Me Why I Lov'd J.G.) LW

To one that persuades me to leave the Muses. Elizabeth Singer Rowe.
  "Forgo the charming Muses! No, in spite." PEW

To One Who Died in a Garret in Cardiff. Huw Menai. AngWePo

To One Who Has Been Long in City Pent. John Keats. CenSon

To one who lonely sees the springtime close. Shaken, They Cling Again. Li Yu [*or* Li Hou-Chu]. CCL1, *tr.* by John Turner

To One Who Sleepeth. Mary E. Tucker. CBWP-1

To One Who Would Make a Confession. Wilfrid Scawen Blunt. GSo

To Open. Antonio Porta. PFTM-2, *tr.* by Paul Vangelisti

To open (like an Albertine), to flower. (LL) To Smithereens. Vona Groarke. MoWP; NIrP

To Orabella, Marry'd to an Old Man. Sarah Fyge Egerton. EMWP

To Orestes. Elizabeth Singer Rowe. PEW

To origin, which is another patch of sun. Roy Fisher. VaPo *Fr.* Cut Pages, The.

To Osbert Sitwell. Cyril Connolly. OBCoV

To others / Only heaven. Luck ("Sometimes a crumb falls.") Langston Hughes. APT-2; OxBoAm; SAmP

To Our Blessed Lady. Henry Constable. NoSic

To Our Blessed Lord upon the Choice of His Sepulchre. Richard Crashaw. NOSC
  (Upon Our Saviour's Tomb[e] Wherein Never Man Was Laid.) ChIV-2; NPeEn

To Our Cosmeticians. Dzvinia Orlowsky. PfS

To our house in the street down town. (LL) Samuel Brown. Phoebe Cary. APN-2; NAAPv.1

To our mother, maimed. American Rain. Marilyn Chin. OpBo

To our theme. The man who has stood on the Acropolis. Lord Byron. OBSV *Fr.* Don Juan.

To our vaulting into enormous rooms. (LL) Ourstory. Carole Satyamurti. BeAl; MoWP

To Out of the whale's mouth. (LL) Of This Cloth Doll Which. Michael Palmer. NoP-4; NoP-5

To Ovid. Elena Ignatova. ItGoST, *tr.* by Sibelan Forrester

To own our own at last. (LL) White Lady. Lucille Clifton. ESEAA; SUP

To Oxford [*sonnet*]. Thomas Russell. CenSon

To: Oxon. Marey Waller. EMWP

To P. J. (2 Yrs Old Who Sed Write a Poem for Me in Portland, Oregon). Sonia Sanchez. CA
  (To P.J.) NOxBChV

To Pál Ányos. Ábrahám Barcsay. IQMS, *tr.* by Adam Makkai

To Paint a Water Lily. Ted Hughes. CABP

To paint the summer morning. (LL) London's Summer Morning. Mary Robinson. NAEL-7v2; RWP; WoRP

To Pallas, Theris, cunning of hand, dedicated. Leonidas of Tarentum. HePo, *tr.* by Barbara Hughes Fowler

To Pallas, three girls, all of an age, skilled as the spider. Antipater of Sidon. HePo, *tr.* by Barbara Hughes Fowler

To palm them back to living. (LL) Cannery Town in August. Lorna Dee Cervantes. NAMCP V.2; NoAM

To Pan three brothers hung up these tools of the trade. Antipater of Sidon. HePo, *tr.* by Barbara Hughes Fowler

To Papaji. Nina Wise. WhBo

To Paradise. (LL) Fever 103°. Sylvia Plath. NAMCP V.2; NoAM; OxBoAm; PoA 2002; VCAP

To Paris that was once her owne though now it be not so. Ovid. OBVE *Fr.* Heroides.

To part no more forever. (LL) Michael Wigglesworth. ColAP; NAAL-3 *Fr.* Day of Doom, The [First Section].

To pass all men's believing. (LL) Ezra Pound. AmWit; MoAmPo; TCAPo *Fr.* Ripostes of Ezra Pound.

To pass the hours away. (LL) Cows. James Reeves. NOxBChV; NTCP

To Paterson. (LL) William Carlos Williams. NAMCP V.1; NoAM *Fr.* Paterson.

To Patriarch Sun at Hua-yang Grotto. Li Te-yü. ColAnChi, *tr.* by Edward H. Schafer

To Paul Robeson, Opus No. 3. Percy Johnston. EGAG

To Peace. Richard Watson Dixon. OxAEP-2

To Peace. Suzanne Gardinier. AmPoNex

To Penshurst. Ben Jonson. BASC; CABP; NAEL-6v1; NAEL-7v1; NoP-4; NoP-5; NOSC; OxBEV; PBRV; TFi; WaAnP

To Percy Shelley. Leigh Hunt. CenSon

To Perilla. Robert Herrick. NOSC

To perish, or to live? (LL) Final Inch, The. Emily Dickinson. APN-2; NCAP

To perish—of Delight. (LL) It might be lonelier. Emily Dickinson. APN-2; SAmP; TCAPo

To Persecuted Foreigners. Penina Moise and Edward N. Calisch. SWaP

To Persephone. Harold Vinal. YaYoPo

To Pete Atkin: A Letter from Paris. Clive James.
"Weather's cleared, The. We're filming at Versailles." OBSV

To Petronius Arbiter. Oliver St. John Gogarty. OBMV

25. To Phaon. Mary Robinson. NPBRoP *Fr.* Sappho and Phaon.

To Phaon ("Can'st thou forget, O! Idol of my soul!") Mary Robinson. CenSon; RWP

To Phaon ("Oh! I could toil for thee o'er burning plains.") Mary Robinson. CenSon; RWP

To Phaon ("Why art thou changed? O Phaon! tell me why?") Mary Robinson. CenSon; RWP

To Phil Dow, in Oregon. Robert Hass. BodElec

To Philip Whalen, 1999. Diane Di Prima. WANABP

To Phryne. Owen Feltham [*or* Feltham]. NOSC

To Phylocles, Inviting Him to Friendship. "Ephelia." NOSC

To Pi Ssu Yao. Tu Fu [*or* Du Fu]. BLT; NDACCP, *tr.* by Kenneth Rexroth

To pile like Thunder to its close. Emily Dickinson. APN-2; NCAP

To P.J. Sonia Sanchez. *See* To P. J. (2 Yrs Old Who Sed Write a Poem for Me in Portland, Oregon).

To Play Pianissimo. Lola Haskins. MiVo

To play the school games with the others. (LL) Picnic, The: "It is the picnic with Ruth in the spring." John Logan. NevBe; TRP

To pluck the sun down into the dead sea. (LL) And, the last day being come, Man stood alone. Trumbull Stickney. APN-2; NoP-4

To Poetry. Nazik al-Mala'ika. IrPoTo, *tr.* by Ferial J. Ghazoul

To Poetry. Carlos Pellicer. TCLAP, *tr.* by Alexandra Migoya

To point a moral, or adorn a tale. (LL) Juvenal. FaBoWar; OBWP; OxBEV *Fr.* Vanity of Human Wishes, The; The Tenth Satire of Juvenal [Imitated].

To poll their tops that seek such change and gape for joy. (LL) Doubt of Future Foes. Queen of England Elizabeth I. NAEL-6v1; NAEL-7v1; NALW; NoP-4; NoP-5; NoSic

(To poll their tops that seek such change or gape for future joy.) (LL) NoP-4; PEW

To poll their tops that seek such change or gape for future joy. (LL) Queen of England Elizabeth I. *See* To poll their tops that seek such change and gape for joy.

To practice for Eternity. (LL) Bearded Oaks. Robert Penn Warren. APT-2; ColAP; EMP; FuPo; InGu; MoAmPo; NAAL-5; NAMCP V.1; NoAM; NoP-4; NoP-5; PoA 2002

To practice noticing. Reasons to Meditate. Lisa Cullen. WhBo

To Praise. Ellen Bass. FiBr

To praise is the whole thing! A man who can praise. Rainer Maria Rilke. WED *Fr.* Sonnets to Orpheus.

To pray you open your whole self. Eagle Poem. Joy Harjo. HATNAP; NAAL-5; WeW-3

To prepare the body. Ikebana. Cathy Song. YaYoPo

To President Bush at the Start of the Gulf War. Robert Bly. RaBo

To pretend that I'm enjoying. (LL) Iceberg Theory, The. Gerald Locklin. BeAl; GoPo

To Professor Byrd Prillerman. Maggie Pogue Johnson. CBWP-4

To prove that we're still here. (LL) Al Young. OxAAAP; UnSA

To pull the metal splinter from my palm. Gift, The. Li-Young Lee. BodElec; CAP-8; LoL; NAMCP V.2; OpBo; RaBo; RoV; TWF; UnSA

To put all hands into the water. Dolores Dorantes. SPV, *tr.* by Jen Hofer

To put on shoes and be sophisticated. Ode to Language. Robert Kelly. PFTM-2; SeSe

To put on the dumb blue blazer of your death. (LL) How It Is. Maxine W. Kumin. InoFa; NALW; NAMCP V.2; NoAM

To put the black well-fashioned yewship. Alexander MacDonald. NePenScot *Fr.* Clanranald's Galley.

To Queen Elizabeth. Mary Sidney Herbert, Countess of Pembroke. *See* To the Thrice-Sacred Queen Elizabeth.

To Queen Elizabeth. Jane Seager. EMWP

To Quilca: A Country-house of Dr. Sheridan, in No Very Good Repair, Where the Author and Some of His Friends Spent a Summer in the Year 1725. Jonathan Swift. IrV

To R. B. Gerard Manley Hopkins. OxAEP-2

To R. K. James Kenneth Stephen. NBLV; UV

To Raise the Blind on Purpose. Stephanie Sallaska. SUP

To range, deep-wrapt, along a heavenly height. To Bayard Taylor. Sidney Lanier. NCAP

To read it well: that is, to understand. (LL) To the Reader ("Pray thee, take care, that tak'st my book[e] in hand.") Ben Jonson. BASC; NoP-4; NoP-5

To read my book[e], the virgin shy [*or* shie]. To His Book[e]. Martial. OBVE, *tr.* by Robert Herrick

To read my next instalment. (LL) Out-Patients. Carole Satyamurti. PoCu; StAl

To read our few poets. Ode. Hugh Maxton. PBCIP

To Reason. Carl Dennis. PoA 2002

To refind the horse. Hallucinatory Sunset, with Sons. Vicente Gerbasi. SonAtl, *tr.* by Eleanor Davidson

To remember with tears! (LL) Four Ducks on a Pond. William Allingham. IrV; OxAEP-2

To rend me and redeem. (LL) Bone-Flower Elegy. Robert Earl Hayden. APT-2; NAMCP V.2; NoAM

To replay agonies was the necessary terror. Daughter-Mother-Maya-Seeta. Reetika Vazirani. NAPBL

To Restore a Dead Child. Edwin Honig.
1925. NoAM

To Retiredness. Mildmay Fane, 2d Earl of Westmorland. NOSC

To Return to the Urges Unconscious of their Beginnings. Pham Tien Duat. AmFaPo, *tr.* by Kevin Bowen and Ngo Vinh Hai

To Rev. Thaddeus Saltus. Mary Weston Fordham. CBWP-2

To Rhea. Ralph Waldo Emerson. APN-1

To Richard Wagner. Sidney Lanier. APN-2; NCAP *Fr.* Street Cries.

To Rilke. Denise Levertov. UpMys

To rise. Sandor Csoori. VCWP

To rise from the table. Table, The. Lee Upton. AmAlph

To Robert Baron. Arthur Johnston. NePenScot, *tr.* by Robert Crawford

To Robert Browning. Walter Savage Landor. NoP-4; NoP-5

To Robert Louis Stevenson. W. E. Henley. MoBrPo

To Robert Lowell and Osip Mandelstam. Frederick Seidel. BodElec

To roll his mare among the trampled lilies. (LL) Zebras, The. Roy Campbell. MoBrPo; OxBSo

To Rome Entombed in Her Ruins. Francisco de Quevedo y Villegas. SpanPo, *tr.* by Kate Flores

To Roosevelt. Rubén Darío. PFTM-1; TCLAP, *tr.* by Lysander Kemp

To root from the earth all such insolent vermin. (LL) Burrowing Yankees. *Unknown.* AmWaPo; NAAPv.1

To Rosamond. Geoffrey Chaucer. NoP-4; NoP-5

To Rosania (now Mrs Montague) Being With Her, 25th September 1652. Katherine Philips. PoBW

To Rose. Roberta Hill. ReEnLa

To Rosemounde. Geoffrey Chaucer. WaAnP

To Roses in the Bosom[e] of Castara. William Habington. NOSC; OBEV *Fr.* Castara.

To row aboot his corse. (LL) Under the Greenwood Tree. Hugh MacDiarmid. FaBoWar; OBVE

To Rowntrees one morning. Chocolate Soldier. Ian Duhig. NeBrP

To Russian Women. Olga Ivanova. CRWP, *tr.* by Jenefer Coates

To S.C. Robert Louis Stevenson. NePenScot

To S. M., a Young African Painter. Phillis Wheatley. ColAP; MakPoe; NAAL-3; NAAL-5; NAAPv.1; NoP-4; NoP-5

To S. R. Crockett. Robert Louis Stevenson. *See* Blows the Wind Today.

To S.V. György Petri. VCWP, *tr.* by Geroge Gömöri and Clive Wilmer

To sail on wings of corrugated iron's. Swinging Low. Carter Revard. NevBe

To sail the entire length of a body. Brief Lessons in Eroticism 1. Gioconda Belli. ErotSp; TANSG, *tr.* by Steven F. White

To St. Augustine. "Angelus Silesius." GePo *Fr.* Cherubical Wanderer, The.

To St John Baptist. Henry Constable. ChIV-2; NoSic

To St Mary Magdalen. Henry Constable. PBRV

To St Mary Magdalen. Henry Constable. ChIV-2; NoSic

To Saint Margaret. Henry Constable. NoSic

To St. Michael the Archangel. Henry Constable. ChIV-2

To St. Peter and St. Paul. Henry Constable. NoSic

To Sallie, Walking. Sterling Allen Brown. GT

To Sally. John Quincy Adams. APN-1

To Satch. Samuel Allen. FuFl; ISC; MoASP (American Gothic.) OxAAAP

To save lives. (LL) Conception: "Death did not come to my mother." Josephine Miles. CalPo; ColAP; OxBoAm

To save my heart, veins. After Heart-Bypass Surgery, Another Ritual for Continuing Struggle. Ralph Salisbury. RWB

To Saxham. Thomas Carew. BASC; CavPo

To say it once held daisies and bluebells. Broken Bowl, The. James Merrill. PoA 2002

To say less. (LL) Souvenir de Monsieur Poop. Stevie Smith. MoWP; NALW; NAMCP V.1

To scare myself with my own desert places. (LL) Desert Places. Robert Frost. APT-1; BrAP; HarvBoo; MoAmPo; NAAL-5; NAAPv.2; NAMCP V.1; NoAM; OxBoAm; SoSe-8; TRP

To Science. Edgar Allan Poe. *See* Sonnet—To Science.

To scream for help through a horn. (LL) February in Sydney. Yusef Komunyakaa. ESEAA; InGu; NAMCP V.2

To See a Friend Off. Wang Wei. CCL1; ChinPo, *tr.* by Ye Weilian [*or* Yeh Wei-lien *or* Wai-lim Yip]

To See a Friend Off to Shu. Li Po. ChinPo, *tr.* by Ye Weilian [*or* Yeh Wei-lien *or* Wai-lim Yip]

To see a strange [*or* quaint] outlandish fowl. Bounty of Our Age, The. Henry Farley. NOSC

To see a woman long oppressed by fear. Hayden Carruth. ErotSp *Fr.* Sonnets.

To see a world in a grain of sand. Auguries of Innocence. William Blake. OxAEP-2; TFi

To see both blended in one flood. Upon the Infant Martyrs. Richard Crashaw. NoP-4; NoP-5; NPeEn

To see herself tonight. (LL) Brown Girl Dead, A. Countee Cullen. GT; InoFa

To See if Something Comes Next. Jack Gilbert. BodElec

To See Meng Hao-Jan Off to Yang-Chou. Li Po. ChinPo, *tr.* by Ye Weilian [*or* Yeh Wei-lien *or* Wai-lim Yip]

To see my father. Golden State. Frank Bidart. NoAM

To see myself, to set the darkness echoing. (LL) Personal Helicon. Seamus Heaney. BrAP; NPeEn; WaAnP

To See Ol' Booker T. Maggie Pogue Johnson. CBWP-4

To See Secretary Shu-Yun Off at the Hsieh T'iao Tower at Hsuan-Ch'eng. Li Po. ChinPo, *tr.* by Ye Weilian [*or* Yeh Wei-lien *or* Wai-lim Yip]

To see the charcoal. Saitō Mokichi. CAoMJL1, *tr.* by Amy Vladek Heinrich

To see the cherry hung with snow. (LL) A. E. Housman. BrAP; ChAP; ClHu; MakPoe; MoBrPo; NAEL-6v2; NAEL-7v2; NAMCP V.1; NoAM; NoP-4; NoP-5; PoPoPo; SoSe-8; TFi; WaAnP; WeW-3 *Fr.* Shropshire Lad, A.

To See the Hours of Fever. Gustavo Adolfo Bécquer. SpanPo, *tr.* by John Crow

To see the hours of fever. To See the Hours of Fever. Gustavo Adolfo Bécquer. SpanPo, *tr.* by John Crow

To see the house you were born in. I Stopped in Tupelo, Elvis. Van K. Brock. AllShUp

To see the land I love. (LL) Night Journey. Theodore Roethke. AmFaPo; BeAl; GM; GoPo

To see the lark, delighted, dare. Bernard [*or* Bernart] de Ventadour *or* Ventadorn. STV

To see the Moscow-bound express withdraw. Poetry of Motion, The. Raymond Garlick. AngWePo

To see the universe. Lord Brain. Bruce Beasley. AmAlph

To see them go by drowning in the river. Eli, Eli. Judith Wright. BMAP; GI

To see those eyes. Philadelphia: Spring, 1985. Sonia Sanchez. ESEAA; FuFl

To see / to hear. Nazim Hikmet. NaPG *Fr.* Letters to Taranta Babu.

To seek a place with less inclement weather. (LL) Two Fish. Katha Pollitt. NIL-7; NIP-4

To seek our way of thinking. Light in One's Blood, The. Gemino H. Abad. ReBoTo

To seem the stranger lies my lot, my life. To Seem the Stranger. Gerard Manley Hopkins. ItP

To Selah. George Elliott Clarke. OpeFie

To Send Far Away. Li Po. NDACCP, *tr.* by David Hinton

To Send to Tu Fu as a Joke. Li Po. ColAnChi, *tr.* by Elling O. Eide

To shade and fiber, milk and memory. (LL) James Merrill. NAMCP V.2; NoAM; NoP-4; NoP-5; OxBoAm; VCAP *Fr.* Book of Ephraim, The.

To shadows and delusions here. (LL) Indian Burying Ground, The. Philip Freneau. ColAP; NAAL-3; NAAPv.1; NoP-4; NoP-5; OxBoAm; TCAPo; TFi

To Shakespeare. Nina Nikolaevna Berberova. TCRusP, *tr.* by John Glad

To Shakspeare. Frances Anne Kemble. SWaP

To shell and eat you, I brought all kinds of condiments. Grill, to grill and eat you. Fish and Sauce. No Hyegyông. EcSo, *tr.* by Ann Y. Choi

To shew their sharpnesse. (LL) Homer. NPeEn; OBVE *Fr.* Iliad, The.

To shield her from despair. (LL) Angel in Blythburgh Church, An. Peter Porter. NoP-4; NoP-5

To shove this chair away from here. To Sit, to Stand, to Kill, to Die. Attila József. AF, *tr.* by John Batki

To show that still she lives. (LL) Harp That Once through Tara's Halls, The. Thomas Moore. CABP; NAEL-6v2; NAEL-7v2

To show the laboring [*or* lab'ring] bosom's deep intent. To S. M., a Young African Painter. Phillis Wheatley. ColAP; MakPoe; NAAL-3; NAAL-5; NAAPv.1; NoP-4; NoP-5

To Show to My Sons. Lu Yu. ColAnChi, *tr.* by Burton Watson

To Show You All, on the First Morning of the Year. Ching An. CSKM, *tr.* by Jerome P. Seaton

To shroud me from my proper scorn. (LL) Alfred Tennyson. NAEL-6v2; NAEL-7v2 *Fr.* In Memoriam A. H. H.

To shun the heaven [*or* heav'n] that leads men to this hell! (LL) William Shakespeare. BrAP; CABP; ErotSp; HeIP-4; NAEL-6v1; NAEL-7v1; NIL-7; NIP-4; NoP-5; NoSic; NPeEn; OBEV; OxAEP-1; OxBEV; PBRV; PoPoPo; TFi; WoPoe *Fr.* Sonnets.

To Sidmouth and Castlereagh. Percy Bysshe Shelley. NAEL-6v2; NAEL-7v2

To sigh, and sing at liberty—like thee! (LL) To a Nightingale. Charlotte Smith. CenSon; OxBSo; RWP

To signal *yes yes yes*. (LL) Glow Worm. Vicki Feaver. MoWP; StAl

To Silence. Alice Thompson Meynell. VWP

To Simplicity. Samuel Taylor Coleridge. CenSon *Fr.* Sonnets Attempted in the Manner of Contemporary Writers.

To simulate the burning of the heart. Patrizia Cavalli. NeIt; VCWP, *tr.* by Judith Baumel

To Simulate the Burning of the Heart, the Humiliation. Patrizia Cavalli. CItWP, *tr.* by Cinzia Sartini Blum and Lara Trubowitz

To sing of wars, of captain[e]s, and of kings. Prologue, The. Anne Bradstreet. BASC; BrAP; EMWP; NAAL-3; NAAL-5; NAAPv.1; NALW; NoP-4; NoP-5; OxBoAm; PEW; TCAPo

To sing with the loudest voice. (LL) On the Tattered Edges. Amina Saïd. HAWP; NAfrP, *tr.* by Eric Sellin

To sing you / one song. Pruzzian Elegy. Johannes Bobrowski. AF

To Single Women. Ch'ôn Yanghûi. EcSo, *tr.* by Aimee N. Kwon

To sin's a vice in nature, and we find. Daniel Defoe. OBSV *Fr.* More Reformation.

To Siôn Lloyd: the Mother's Advice to Her Heir. Catherin Owen Llwyd. EMWP

To Sir Francis Brian. Sir Thomas Wyatt. NoSic *Fr.* Satires.

To Sir Henry Cary. Ben Jonson. NoP-4; NoP-5; NOSC

To Sir Henry Goodyere. Ben Jonson. NOSC

To Sir Henry Newton, upon His Re-edifying the Church of Charleton in Kent. Thomas Philipott. NOSC

To Sir Henry Savile [upon His Translation of Tacitus]. Ben Jonson. BASC

To Sir Henry Vane the Younger. John Milton. PBRV

To Sir Henry Wotton ("Here's no more news, than virtue, I may as well.") John Donne. OxAEP-1

To Sir Henry Wotton ("Sir, more than kisses, letters mingle souls.") John Donne. NoSic

To Sir Hudson Lowe. Thomas Moore. OBSV

To Sir John Wentworth, Upon His Curiosities and Courteous Entertainment at Summerly in Lovingland. Mildmay Fane, 2d Earl of Westmorland. OBGa

To Sir Philip Sidney's Soul. Henry Constable. *See* On the Death of Sir Philip Sidney.

To Sir Thomas Roe. Ben Jonson. BASC

To Sir Toby. Philip Freneau. NAAL-3; NAAPv.1; NoP-4; NoP-5; WaAnP

To Sisters on a Walk in the Garden, after a Shower. Jane Johnston Schoolcraft. NAAPv.1

To sit on the moon. (LL) Witches' Ride, The. Karla Kuskin. NOxBChV; TLR

To sit on the veranda of a hotel in Jerusalem. Letter. Yehuda Amichai. VCWP

To sit people on gas-stove jets. Mother-in-Law of the Marquis de Sade, The. Jennifer Maiden. NOBAu

To sit silent. Otomo no Tabito. TAL

To Sit, to Stand, to Kill, to Die. Attila József. AF, tr. by John Batki

To sit upon her belly warm. Jack Frost. Fay Zwicky. BMAP

To Sleep. Lord Alfred Bruce Douglas. GSo

To Sleep. John Keats. ItP; NIP-4; OBEV; OxBSo
(Sonnet to Sleep.) NAEL-6v2; NAEL-7v2

To Sleep. Charlotte Smith. CenSon; NAEL-6v2; NAEL-7v2; RWP

To Sleep. Publius Papinius Status. RomPo Fr. Sylvae [or Silvae].

To Sleep I give my powers away. Alfred Tennyson. CtM; NAEL-6v2; NAEL-7v2 Fr. In Memoriam A. H. H.

To slice through Buddhas, Patriarchs. Daito. ZenPo, tr. by Takashi Ikemoto and Lucien Stryk

To Smile with the Joyful Sadness of the Olive Tree. Miguel Hernández. RaW, tr. by Timothy Baland

To Smithereens. Vona Groarke. MoWP; NIrP

To sob, pressing oneself against the officer's greatcoat. Elena Ignatova. CRWP, tr. by Daniel Weissbort

To So-kin of Rakuyō, ancient friend, Chancellor of Gen. Exile's Letter. Li Po. APT-1; CCL1; NDACCP, tr. by Ezra Pound

To Solitude. Alice Cary. APN-2

To Solitude. Mihály Csokonai Vitéz. IQMS, tr. by Edmund Charles Blunden

To Some Ladies. John Keats. STuOW

To Some Young Communists from an Older Socialist. Naomi Mitchison. RSaN

To Someone Who Insisted I Look up Someone. X. J. Kennedy. OBCoV

To Somes / from incarceration, Taunton State Hospital, 1972. Children of the Working Class. John Weiners. BB

To speak in a flat voice. Speak. James Wright. NoP-4; NoP-5

To speak of maculate beauty, it is this. Maculate Beauty. Karl Kirchwey. PoDa

To Speak of My Influences. Jean Garrigue. LW

To Speak of Woe That Is in Marriage. Robert Lowell. CAP-8; NAMCP V.2; NoAM; WaAnP

To speak out for me. (LL) First They Came for the Jews. Pastor Niemoller. BeAl; HP; PoAgWa, tr. by Unknown

To speak the truth, although believed too late. (LL) Upon the Saying That My Verses Were Made by Another. Anne Killigrew. BASC; CABP; EMWP; NALW; PEW

To Spencer. George Turberville. NoSic

To spend even one moment grieving about this world. Deciding Not to Go to India (147). Khwaja Shams-ad-din Muhammad Hafiz. WED, tr. by Robert Bly and Leonard Lewisohn

To spread the azure canopy of heaven. William Henry Drummond. OxBSo

To Spring. William Blake. NAEL-6v2; NAEL-7v2; OBEV

To Spring. Mihály Fazekas. IQMS, tr. by Watson Kirkconnell

To Spring. Charlotte Smith. RWP

To stain the stiff dishonoured shroud. (LL) Sweeney among the Nightingales. T. S. Eliot. APT-1; BrAP; HarvBoo; HeIP-4; NAEL-6v2; NAEL-7v2; NAMCP V.1; NoAM; NoP-4; NPeEn; OBMV; OxBEV; PoPoPo; TFi; WeW-3

To stand here in the wings of Europe. On a Return from Egypt. Keith Douglas. NoP-4; NoP-5

To stand my little gray wren a drink. (LL) Genius: "Two old dancing shoes my grandfather." Philip Levine. CalPo; NoAM

To stand on the parcel of land where the saint. Simone Weil: In Assisi. Edward Hirsch. BBASP

To stand upon the river-bank. Discontent. Han Yü. CCL1, tr. by H. A. Giles

To stare at nothing is to learn by heart. Night, The Porch, The. Mark Strand. CAP-8; KGB

To start somewhere. Weather They Were Written In, The. Kathy Fagan. PuP-23

To start with, grapple your opponent 'round. Strato. CAGL, tr. by Daryl Hine

To start with there is the shell of a castle that rises. Along a Cliff. David Wheatley. NIrP

To stay good currency with your heart solvent. Lesssons in Survival. Peter Scupham. PoCu

To stay our minds on and be staid. (LL) Choose Something like a Star. Robert Frost. APT-1; BLPJKO; MoAmPo

To stay the season of a mind. (LL) Massacre, October '66. Wole Soyinka. AF; NAMCP V.2

To steady my heart I say these words, to keep me. Strange Altars. Margaret Gibson. AmZen

To Stella. Plato. OBVE, tr. by Percy Bysshe Shelley

To strengthen whilst one stands. (LL) Goblin Market. Christina Georgina Rossetti. BrAP; NAEL-6v2; NAEL-7v2; NALW; NOxBChV; OBNV; OxAEP-2; OxBEV; ViWPN; VWP; WaAnP

To strict Rapunzel to let down her hair. (LL) Ivory Tower, The. Allen Tate. APT-2; OxBoAm

To strive, to seek, to find, and not to yield. (LL) Ulysses. Alfred Tennyson. AmFaPo; BLPJKO; BrAP; CABP; ClHu; CtM; HeIP-4; MakPoe; NAEL-6v2; NAEL-7v2; NAWM-7v2; NIL-7; NIP-4; NoP-4; NoP-5; NPeEn; OxAEP-2; OxBEV; PoPoPo; SoSe-8; TFi; TRP; WaAnP; WeW-3

To stub an oar on a rock where none should be. Basking Shark. Norman Alexander MacCaig. NePenScot

To such a state have I been brought by your mischief, my Lesbia. Catullus. NAWM-7v1 Fr. Carmina [Charles Martin Translation].

To suffer for this land, to live for it and aid. Encouragement. János Batsányi. IQMS, tr. by Matthew Mead and Ruth Mead

To sulk upon my mother's breast. (LL) William Blake. IJHIL; NAEL-6v2; NAEL-7v2; NPBRoP; OxAEP-2; OxBEV; PoPoPo Fr. Songs of Experience.

To survive? (LL) Anchorage. Joy Harjo. HATNAP; LTA; OPRER

To survive things have to be blunted. Blunting, The. Richard Eberhart. BodElec

To swerve from village chapel to a town's. Visitor's Book, 8, The. John Davies. TCAWP

To Swim, to Believe. Maxine W. Kumin. CAP-8; MoASP; PoCho

To Sylvia. Giacomo Leopardi. NAWM-7v2, tr. by Ottavio M. Casale

To T.A.R.H. Stephen Spender. CAGL

To TS Eliot. Abdul Wahab Al-Bayati. IrPoTo, tr. by Carolina Hotchandani and Najat Rahman

To take a Part of mine. (LL) Polwart on the Green. Allan Ramsay. NPeEn; OxBEV

To take a woman in your arms. It's Easy. Lee Cataldi. BMAP

To take the darkness in. Crowdoll. L. S. Asekoff. BodElec

To take the field. (LL) Bit of Brass, A. Padraic Fallon. ModIr; NPeEn

To take the measure. Measure, The. Peter Levitt. WhBo

To take the wrong road. Little Infinite Poem. Federico García Lorca. RaBo; WED, tr. by Robert Bly

To take up the word again. Mónica Nepote. SPV, tr. by Jen Hofer

To take us sick, that sound would not take thee? (LL) Pursuit[e], The. Henry Vaughan. AngWPo; NOSC; SacPr

To talk about trees. (LL) Adrienne Rich. ExTi; LoL; WaAnP Fr. Not Somewhere Else, But Here.

To talk alone, at the threshold, with already-gone, has-been, to-be- / announced. To be your own legend. Notebook, Two. Edmond Jabès. AF, tr. by Rosmarie Waldrop

To talk to each other. (LL) Little. Dorothy Aldis. NTCP; WHSW

To talk with someone. Antonio Machado Ruiz. WED Fr. Moral Proverbs and Folk Songs.

To Tan Ch'iu. Li Po. TAL

To Tania. Alda do Espírito Santo. SonAtl, tr. by Simon Lewis and Krystyna Ziemba

To Tanya at Christmas. Wendell Berry. UpMys

To tedious Hell this body with its muddy feet in my mind! (LL) Menses. Edna St. Vincent Millay. APT-1; BrAP; RACG

To tell of Prodigies, and cause affright. (LL) Virgil. NPeEn; OBVE Fr. Aeneid [or Eneados or Aeneis], The.

To tell the world my proper name. Ralph Erskine. SacPr Fr. Believer's Riddle, The.

To tell us about aliens like you. (LL) Angel. Ruth Padel. MFPA; NeBrP

To tell what others were, came down? (LL) Epicurean Ode, An. John Hall. NOSC; NPeEn

To tell you from the start, I have lost him whose hand and eye are gentle. He Whose Hand and Eye Are Gentle. Unknown. OBWVE, tr. by Kenneth Hurlstone Jackson

To that deliberate progress. (LL) Considering the Snail. Thom Gunn. NAEL-6v2; NAEL-7v2; OxBEV; PtR; StAl

To that I am on my way running. (LL) Song for a Young Girl's Puberty Ceremony. Unknown. ChAP; ItWoWo, tr. by Frances Densmore

To that invisible element which claimed. Invisible Element, The. István Vas. IQMS, tr. by George Szirtes

To that lov'd bowl my spoon by instinct flies. (LL) Joel Barlow. NAAL-3; NAAPv.1; OxBoAm; TCAPo Fr. Hasty Pudding, The [complete text].

To that other. (LL) "H. D." NALW; NAMCP V.1; NoAM Fr. Tribute to the Angels.

To that sweet thief [or theefe] which sourl[e]y robs from me. (LL) William Shakespeare. HeIP-4; NAEL-6v1; NAEL-7v1; NoP-5; NoSic; OxAEP-1; PBRV; RaF Fr. Sonnets.

To the Accuser Who Is the God of This World. William Blake. See Epilogue: "Truly my Satan thou art but a dunce."

To the Air of a Pibroch. Duncan Ban MacIntyre. NePenScot Fr. Last Farewell to the Hills.

To the Almighty on his radiant throne. Anne Finch, Countess of Winchilsea. ChIV-1 *Fr.* Pindaric Poem, A.

To the Angel Spirit of the Most Excellent Sir Philip Sidney. Mary Sidney Herbert, Countess of Pembroke. NAEL-7v1

To the apostles of history. Aleksey Petrovich Tsvetkov. TCRusP

To the arms of brown people. (LL) Black Hair. Gary Soto. CAP-8; MoASP; UnSA

To the audience hall the worthy banished minister was recalled. Master Chia. Li Shang-yin. ColAnChi, *tr.* by James J. Y. Liu

To the Author of Agnes de Castro. Delariviere Manley. EMWP

To the Autumnal Moon. Samuel Taylor Coleridge. CenSon *Fr.* Effusions.

To The Barbarian. Else Lasker-Schüler. PFTM-1

To the Bartholdi Statue. Ambrose Bierce. APN-2

To the Bat. Ann Radcliffe. CenSon

To the Beloved. Alice Thompson Meynell. VWP

To the Bicycle. John Gibbens. ArBi

To the Blessed Sacrament. Henry Constable. NoSic

To the Blessed Virgin. William Alabaster. NoSic

To the Body: "Creation's and Creator's crowning good." Coventry Patmore. CABP *Fr.* Unknown Eros, The.

To the boy who comes in summer the country. Goat God, The. Cesare Pavese. WoPoe, *tr.* by William Arrowsmith

To the bridge of love. Juan Ramón Jiménez. SpanPo; WoPoe *Fr.* Ten Short Poems.

To the Building Trade. Matthew Sweeney. ModIr

To the Cambro-Britons [*or* Britans], and their Harp[e], his Ballad of Agincourt. Michael Drayton. BASC

To the capital / Snow-clouds forming. Basho. ZenPo, *tr.* by Takashi Ikemoto and Lucien Stryk

To the Child Elis. Georg Trakl. WoPoe, *tr.* by Robert Firmage

To the Child That Never Was. Emma Sepúlveda-Pulvirenti. TANSG, *tr.* by Shaun Griffin

To the Children. Gabriela Mistral. SpanPo, *tr.* by Kate Flores

To the Christians: "Take, then, your paltry Christ." Francis Lauderdale Adams. ChIV-2

To [*or* In Honour of] the City of London. William Dunbar. OBEV "Above all rivers thy river hath renown." OPOU

To the Cloud Juggler. Hart Crane. HarvBoo

To the Clouds. Susan Evance. CenSon

To the Coming of the Decade. Simone Waight. OWABP

To the Conference. Mrs. Henry Linden. CBWP-4

To the Countess of A—. Written on the Anniversary of Her Marriage. Charlotte Smith. RWP

To the Countess of Bedford ("Madam, / Reason is our soul's left hand, Faith her right.") John Donne. NOSC

To the cove of my breasts your forehead will return. Ana Istarú. TANSG, *tr.* by Shaun Griffin and Emma Sepúlveda-Pulvirenti

To the Creator of My Bones. Anna Hajnal. IQMS, *tr.* by Jeannette Nichols

To the Critic. Michael Drayton. NOSC

To the Cuckoo. Michael Bruce. OBEV

To the Cuckoo. F. H. Townsend. UV

To the Cuckoo ("O blithe New-comer! I have heard.") William Wordsworth. NOBRP; NPBRoP; UV

To the curator of the museum, to the exhibition of the fathers. Seersucker Suit. Deborah Digges. PoCho

To the Curlew. Helen Maria Williams. CenSon; WoRP

To the Dandelion. James Russell Lowell. NAAL-3

To the Day-Dreamer. Mihály Vörösmarty. IQMS, *tr.* by Hymen H. Hart and Watson Kirkconnell

To the Days. Adrienne Rich. AmFaPo; BeAl; LoL *Fr.* Not Somewhere Else, But Here.

To the Days Lost in August. Deborah Cummins. PoDa

To the Dead. Frank Bidart. MakPoe

To the Death. Gerallt Lloyd Owen. BBMWP, *tr.* by Gillian Clarke

To the Death of Mirrors. Nancy Joyce Peters. SurWo

To The Delicately (Winter) Coming On. Icy Rose. Anne Waldman. AHA

To the Department of Motor Vehicles. Anonymous. Susan Love Fitts. IJHIL

To the Detracter. Robert Herrick. PBRV

To the Diaspora. Gwendolyn Brooks. NAAL-5; NIL-7

To the dim light and the large circle of shade. Sestina: Of the Lady Pietra degli Scrovigni. Dante Alighieri. MakPoe; NPeEn; OBVE, *tr.* by Dante Gabriel Rossetti

To the Distant One. Po Chü-i. TAL

To the Dregs. Betsy Sholl. ExTi

To the Eagle. Mary Weston Fordham. CBWP-2

To the Earl of Egremont. Charlotte Smith. RWP

To the Earl of Oxford, Late Lord Treasurer. Jonathan Swift. FaBoWar; OBVE

To the Earl of Warwick, on the Death of Mr. Addison. Thomas Tickell. OxAEP-1

To the East and to the West. Walt Whitman. APN-1

To the East, whitish winds on my allotted boundary lines. Angélica Tornero. SPV, *tr.* by Jen Hofer

To the Echo of Tihany. Mihály Csokonai Vitéz. IQMS, *tr.* by Adam Makkai

To the Eminent Scholar and Meddler. Kofi Awoonor. HBAPE

To the Emperor. Theodore Prodromos. WoPoe, *tr.* by Jack Lindsay

To the Emperor's Messenger. Muso Soseki. EaWin, *tr.* by W. S. Merwin

To the end, to the end, they remain. (LL) For the Fallen. Laurence Binyon. NPeEn; OBEV; OBWP

To the Enemies. Vladimir Holan. AF, *tr.* by C. G. Hanzlicek and Dana Habova

To the Eolian Harp. Mary Robinson. CenSon; RWP

14. To the Eolian Harp. Mary Robinson. NPBRoP *Fr.* Sappho and Phaon.

To the Evening Star. William Blake. GSo; NAEL-6v2; NAEL-7v2; NoP-4; NoP-5; NPeEn; TFi

To the Evening Star. Thomas Campbell. NePenScot

To the Evening Star: Central Minnesota. James Wright. NAAL-5

To the Excellent Mrs. Anne Owen. Katherine Philips. NOSC

To the Excellent Orinda. "Philo-Philippa." BASC

To the Fair Clarinda [*or* Clorinda], Who Made Love to Me, Imagin'd [*or* Imagined] More than Woman. Aphra Behn. BASC; CABP; EMWP; NALW; NIL-7; NoP-4; NoP-5; PEW; PoBW; WaAnP

To the fallen heart that does not cease to fall.. (LL) Wild Bees. James Keir Baxter. NoP-4; NoP-5

To the falling London rain. (LL) London Rain. Louis MacNeice. NoP-4; NoP-5

To the Far Corners of Fractured Worlds. Susan Griffin. GifTon

To the Fates. Friedrich Hölderlin. NAWM-7v2, *tr.* by Christopher Middleton

To the Father of Me. Lamont B. Steptoe. OxAAAP

To the Father through the features of men's faces. (LL) As Kingfishers Catch Fire. Gerard Manley Hopkins. MoBrPo; NAEL-6v2; NAEL-7v2; NAMCP V.1; NoP-4; NoP-5; NPeEn; OxAEP-2

To the Fifteen of Piazzale Loreto. Salvatore Quasimodo. AF, *tr.* by Jack Bevan

To the Film Industry in Crisis. Frank O'Hara. GPTC; OxBoAm

To the First Slave Ship. Lydia Huntley Sigourney. ColAP

To the Four Courts, Please. James Stephens. MoBrPo

To the Fragment of a Statue of Hercules, Commonly Called the Torso. Samuel Rogers. CenSon; GS

To the free skies unpent and glad and strong. (LL) To a Locomotive in Winter. Walt Whitman. BrAP; GM; MoAmPo; NAAL-3; NCAP; NoAM; NoP-4; NoP-5

To the French of the Second Empire. Arthur Rimbaud. OBWP *Fr.* Eighteen-Seventy.

To the Fringed Gentian. William Cullen Bryant. APN-1

To the Garden the World. Walt Whitman. ChIV-1

To the Gardin att O: [Owthorpe] 7:th. Lucy Hutchinson. EMWP

To the Gentlewoman of Llanarth Hall. Evan Thomas. OBWVE, *tr.* by Gwyn Jones

To the German People. Friedrich Hölderlin. WoPoe, *tr.* by Robert Bly

To the ghostly garden to the laurel mute. Autumn Garden. Dino Campana. STV, *tr.* by John Frederick Nims

To the God of Duality, only with metaphors. In Xóchitl in Cuícatl. Ernesto Cardenal. PFTM-2, *tr.* by Carlos Altschul and Monique Altschul

To the Gods the Shades Flavinus of the Cavalry Regiment. David Wright. NLP

To the Good Thief. Saunders Lewis. OBWVE, *tr.* by Gwyn Morgan

To the grace of the make-believe bed. (LL) Ted Berrigan. FTOS; NYP2; PFTM-2 *Fr.* Sonnets, The.

To the Grasshopper. Richard Lovelace. *See* Grasshopper, The [To My Noble Friend Mr Charles Cotton: Ode].

To the Grasshopper and the Cricket. Leigh Hunt. CenSon; GSo; OxBSo (Grasshopper and the Cricket, The.) OxAEP-2

To the Great City of Moscow, as He Was Leaving June 25, 1636. Paul Fleming. GePo, *tr.* by George C. Schoolfield

To the hall, to the hall. Leveller's Rant, The. Alexander Brome. BASC

To the Harbormaster. Frank O'Hara. OxBoAm; VCAP

To the Harvest Moon. William Stanley Roscoe. CenSon

To the head bobbing in the gunsight. Line. Milo De Angelis. NeIt, *tr.* by Lawrence Venuti

To the Heart. Tadeusz Rózewicz. PoSu, *tr.* by Victor Contoski

To the Heavens above us. Astrologer's Song, An. Rudyard Kipling. MoBrPo

To the High Court of Parliament ("Where's probity in this.") Geoffrey Hill. NAMCP V.2

To the High Court of Parliament ("Who could outbalance poised.") Geoffrey Hill. OxBEV

To the highest bidder. Highest Bidder, The. Witter Bynner. TCAPo

To the Holy Spirit. Yvor Winters. MoAmPo

To the honorable Senate and House. Belinda's Petition. Rita Dove. PtR

To the Honourable Mr. Erskine. Samuel Taylor Coleridge. CenSon *Fr.* Effusions.

To the Horizon. Michael Savitz. FreRad

To the Hungarian Nation. Matthew Arnold. OxBSo

To the Hungarian People. János Edrosi Sylvester. IQMS, *tr. by* Adam Makkai

To the Hungarians: "Oh you, once mighty Hungary, gone to seed." Dániel Berzsenyi. IQMS, *tr. by* Adam Makkai

To the Hungarians: "Seas of Sorrow boil with a rage, Magyar, The." Dániel Berzsenyi. IQMS, *tr. by* Adam Makkai

To the idealistic killers. Lionel Abrahams. TSAP

To the Immortal Memory and Friendship of That Noble Pair, Sir Lucius Cary and Sir H. [*or* Henry] Morison. Ben Jonson. BASC; CABP; NAEL-6v1; NAEL-7v1; NoP-4; NoP-5; NOSC; PBRV

It Is Not Growing Like a Tree. WaAnP

(Noble Nature, The.) TreFP

(Part of an Ode, A.) OBEV

To the Infant Martyrs. Richard Crashaw. ChIV-2; NAEL-6v1; NAEL-7v1; NoP-4; NoP-5

To the Insect of the Gossamer. Charlotte Smith. OxBSo

To the interior, limbs folded. Nocturne. Valerie Martínez. TouFir

To the King and Queen[e], upon Their Unhappy Distances. Robert Herrick. BASC

To the King; Upon His Com[m]ing with His Army into the West. Robert Herrick. CavPo

To the King; Upon His Taking of Leicester. Robert Herrick. CavPo

To the Kinges Most Excellent Majestye. Lady Anne Harris Southwell. EMWP

To the Lacedemonians. Allen Tate. NoAM

To the Ladies. Mary Lee, Lady Chudleigh. BrAP; CABP; NALW; NIL-7; PEW

To the Lady Anne, Countess of Dorset. Emilia Lanier.

"To you I dedicate this work of grace." NOSC

To the Lady Arabella. Emilia Lanier. NOSC

To The Lady Lucie, Countesse of Bedford. Samuel Daniel. PBRV

To the Lady Margaret, Countess [*or* Countesse] of Cumberland. Samuel Daniel. NOSC

To the Lady Margaret Ley. John Milton. OBEV

To the Lady May. Aurelian Townshend. OxBEV

To the Lady with a Book. *Unknown.* IrLP, *tr. by* Frank O'Connor

To the Late William Jerdan. Eliza Cook. VWP

To the Latin Lover I Left at the Candy Store. Magdalena Gomez. PueRic

To the legion of the lost ones, to the cohort of the damned. Gentlemen-Rankers. Rudyard Kipling. FaBoWar

To the Lighthouse. Yvonne Cullen. NIrP

To the lights and the long street curving. (LL) Soho Hospital for Women, The. Fleur Adcock. NAEL-6v2; NAEL-7v2; NoP-4; NoP-5

To the Looking-Glass world it was Alice that said. Lewis Carroll. UV *Fr.* Through the Looking-Glass.

To the Lord General Cromwell. John Milton. NAEL-6v1; NoP-5; NOSC; WaAnP

(To the Lord General Cromwell, on the Proposals of Certain Ministers at the Committee for the Propagation of the Gospel.) GSo

(To the Lord Generall Cromwell May 1652.) PBRV

To the Lord General Cromwell, on the Proposals of Certain Ministers at the Committee for the Propagation of the Gospel. John Milton. *See* To the Lord General Cromwell.

To the Lord Generall Cromwell May 1652. John Milton. *See* To the Lord General Cromwell.

To the Lord Love. Michael Field. OBMV

To the Lords of Convention 'twas Claver'se who spoke. Sir Walter Scott. UV *Fr.* Doom of Devorgoil, The.

To the Lost Child. Brigit Pegeen Kelly. YaYoPo

To the majestic assembly of buddhas. Kyunyŏ, Great Master. CATKP *Fr.* Eleven Poems on the Ten Vows of the Universally Worthy Bodhisattva.

To the Man after the Harrow. Patrick Kavanagh. ModIr; WaAnP

To the Man Holding a Sickle. Pak Sŏwôn. EcSo, *tr. by* Julie C. Park

To the Man Inside. Carl Rakosi. BodElec

To the Man Saying "Come on Seis" at Hollywood Park. David Hayward. MoASP

To the Man-of-War Bird. Walt Whitman. APN-1

To the Marquess of Piscat's Soul. Henry Constable. NoSic

To the Marquis of Graham on His Marriage. *Unknown.* OBSV

To the medicine / man. (LL) Horned Snake, The. Louis Oliver. HATNAP; NAAPv.2

To the Memory of a Comrade. Hillel Omer. NRoS, *tr. by* Esther Raizen

To the Memory of John Keats. John Clare. CenSon

To the Memory of Mr Oldham. John Dryden. BASC; BrAP; NAEL-6v1; NAEL-7v1; NIL-7; NIP-4; NoP-4; NoP-5; NOSC; NPeEn; OxAEP-1; OxBEV; PoPoPo; TFi; TRP; WaAnP

To the Memory of My Beloved, the Author Mr [*or* Master] William Shakespeare: And What He Hath Left Us. Ben Jonson. BASC; BrAP; HeIP-4; InoFa; NAEL-6v1; NAEL-7v1; NoP-4; NoP-5; NOSC; OxAEP-1; PoPoPo

"I, therefore, will begin. Soul of the age!" WaAnP

To the Memory of My Dear and Ever Honored Father Thomas Dudley Esq. Who Deceased July 31, 1653, and of His Age 77. Anne Bradstreet. NAAL-3

To the Men of Kent (October, 1803). William Wordsworth. OBWP

To the Mercy Killers. Dudley Randall. SoSe-8

To the miller himsel', and his three bonny daughters. (LL) Farewell: "Farewell to the bushy clump close to the river." John Clare. NoP-4; NoP-5

To the mind's briefer and more desert place. (LL) Twelve, The. Allen Tate. APT-2; ChIV-2

To the mini-skirted customs official who with sibyl-dove eyes. Edoardo Sanguineti. ItPo *Fr.* Reisebilder.

To the moaning and the groaning of the bells. (LL) Bells, The. Edgar Allan Poe. APN-1; BRP; ChAP; IJHIL; ITBLP; NAAPv.1; TCAPo; TFi; TreFP

To the Mock-Bird. Mary Weston Fordham. CBWP-2

To the Mocking-Bird. Richard Henry Wilde. APN-1

To the Moment Last Past: "O whither dost thou flye? Cannot my vow." William Habington. OxBSo *Fr.* Castara.

To the Monk Dúc Son at Thanh-phong Monastery. King Trăn Thái-Tông. AWTN, *tr. by* Huỳnh Sanh Thông

To the Monk Wu-hsia on the Occasion of His Editing the Lotus Sutra. Mo Shih-lung. ColAnChi, *tr. by* Jonathan Chaves

To the Moon. Paul Fleming. GePo, *tr. by* George C. Schoolfield

To the Moon. Johann Wolfgang von Goethe. STV, *tr. by* John Frederick Nims

To the Moon. Anna Maria Jones. CenSon

To the Moon. Percy Bysshe Shelley. OxAEP-2

To the Moon. Charlotte Smith. CenSon; RWP

To the Moon. Song Ikp'il. CATKP, *tr. by* Chi-gyu Kim [*or* Kim Chonggil]

To The Moon. Dávid Baróti Szabó. IQMS, *tr. by* Adam Makkai

To the Moon. Helen Maria Williams. NoP-4

To the Moon. Yvor Winters. APT-2

To the Moon, 1969. Babette Deutsch. OtW

To the Moon and Back. William Plomer. OBCoV

To the mooring of starting out, that day so long ago. (LL) Soonest Mended. John Ashbery. NAAL-5; NAMCP V.2; NoP-5; OxBoAm; PoetW; VCAP

To the Most Excellently Accomplished Mrs. Katherine Philips. Henry Vaughan. CABP

To the Most Fair and Lovely Mistress Anne Soame, Now Lady Abdie. Robert Herrick. NOSC

To the Most Illustrious and Most Hopeful[l] Prince, Charles, Prince of Wales. Robert Herrick. BASC

To the much-tossed Ulysses, never done. Ulysses. Robert Graves. NoAM

To the Muse. Denise Levertov. APSN

To the Muse. Caitríona O'Reilly. NIrP

To the Muses. William Blake. HeIP-4; NAEL-6v2; NoP-4; NoP-5; OBEV

To the Muses. Mary Robinson. CenSon; RWP

39. To the Muses. Mary Robinson. NPBRoP *Fr.* Sappho and Phaon.

To the Naiad of the Arun. Charlotte Smith. CenSon; RWP

To the Name Above Every Name, the Name of Iesvs a Hymn. Richard Crashaw. FSCP

To the Natural World: at 37. Genevieve Taggard. APT-2

To the New World. Claudia Keelan. BodElec

To the New Year. Michael Drayton. NOSC

To the New Year. Priscilla Jane Thompson. CBWP-2

To *The New York Times*: Your health editor. Man Who Beat Up Homosexuals Reported to Have AIDS Virus. Richard Howard. NAMCP V.2

To the Nightingale. Jorge Luis Borges. PoCho, *tr. by* Alastair Reid

To the Nightingale. John Milton. OWoS

To the Nightingale. Anne Finch, Countess of Winchilsea. NALW

To the Noblest and Best of Ladies, the Countess of Denbigh. Richard Crashaw. NAEL-6v1; NAEL-7v1

(Letter from Mr Crashaw to the Countess of Denbigh, Against Irresolution and Delay in Matters of Religion, A.) NOSC

(Letter to the Countess of Denbigh.) NOSC

(To the Noblest and best of Ladyes, the Countesse of Denbigh. Perswading her to Resolution in Religion, and to render her selfe without further delay into the Communion of the Catholick Church.) PBRV

To The Noblest and best of Ladyes, the Countesse of Denbigh. Perswading her to Resolution in Religion, and to render her selfe without further delay into the Communion of the Catholick Church. Richard Crashaw. *See* To the Noblest and Best of Ladies, the Countess of Denbigh.

To the north, the cold and its broken jasmine. Island in the Earth. Sara de Ibáñez. TCLAP, *tr. by* Inés Probert.

To the Oaks of Glencree. John Millington Synge. InoFa; MoBrPo

To the Ocean. Thomas Hood. CenSon

To the Ocean. S. J. Marks. BodElec

To the ocean now I fly. John Milton. OBEV; OxAEP-1 *Fr.* Comus; a Masque Presented at Ludlow Castle.

To the Old Reverend Monk, Hwasung. Soyo Taeneung. BecRai, *tr. by* Kim Daljin, Kim Won-Chung and Christopher Merrill

To the One of Fictive Music. Wallace Stevens. APT-1; MoAmPo; NoP-4; TCAPo

To the One Upstairs. Charles Simic. StAl

To the one who sets a second place at the table anyway. Years of Solitude. Dionisio D. Martinez. PtR

To the Owl. Thomas Russell. CenSon

To the Pale Poets. Ray Durem. OxAAAP

To the Palmetto State, in the year seventy three. Southern Work of Dr. and Mrs. L. M. Dunton. Lizelia Augusta Jenkins Moorer. CBWP-3

To the Parents of a Childhood Friend, a Suicide. Judith Baumel. TaR

To the People of a Small Town in Ohio, Who As I Approach Them on the Street, Are Afraid That This Black Man Is Going to Do Them Harm. William Henry Lewis. BtF

To the Phiz an Ode. Allan Ramsay. NePenScot

To the Pious Memory of the Accomplished [*or* Accomplisht] Young Lady, Mrs. Anne Killigrew, [Excellent in the Two Sister-Arts of Poesie and Painting. An Ode]. John Dryden. BrAP; CABP; NAEL-6v1

  (Ode to the Pious Memory of the Accomplished Young Lady, Mrs. Anne Killigrew.) OBEV

To the placid supreme in the sweep of his reign. (LL) Man-of-War Hawk, The. Herman Melville. APN-2; OWoS

To the Poet Coleridge. Mary Robinson. NAEL-7v2; NPBRoP; WaAnP

To The Poets. Ábrahám Barcsay. IQMS, *tr. by* Adam Makkai

To the Poets: To Make Much of the World. George Oppen. BodElec

To the Police Officer Who Refused to Sit in the Same Room as My Son because He's a "Gang Banger." Luis J. Rodriguez. IllVoic

To the Poor. Anna Laetitia Barbauld. NoP-4; NoP-5

To the Poppy [*sonnet*]. Anna Seward. CenSon; WoRP

To the Powers of Desolation. Genevieve Taggard. APT-2

To the Principal and Professors of the University of St Andrews, on their Superb Treat to Dr Samuel Johnson. Robert Fergusson. NePenScot

To the Prussians of England. Ivor Gurney. RSaN

To the Queen of Inconstancy, Regina Collier, in Antwerp. Katherine Philips. PEW

To the Queen of the British Government. Mrs. Henry Linden. CBWP-4

To the Queen[e], Entertain[e]d at Night by the Countess[e] of Anglesey. Sir William Davenant. NOSC

To the Queen's Most Excellent Majesty. Emilia Lanier and Aemilia Bassano Lanyer. NAEL-7v1 *Fr.* Salve Deus Rex Judaeorum.

To the railroad tracks at the bottom of summer. Dog-God. Robin Becker. ExTi

To the Rattlesnake. Vaida Stewart Montgomery. TiP2

To the Reader. Charles Baudelaire. NAWM-7v2, *tr. by* Robert Lowell

To the Reader. Charles Baudelaire. SxFrPo, *tr. by* James McGowan

To the Reader. Charles Baudelaire. WoPoe, *tr. by* Stanley Kunitz

To the Reader ("Pray thee, take care, that tak'st my book[e] in hand.") Ben Jonson. BASC; NoP-4; NoP-5

To the Reader. Elizabeth Jane Leon. EMWP

To the Reader. Rowland Watkyns. BASC

To the Reader, in Vindication of This Book. Elizabeth Bradford. EMWP

To the Reader of These Sonnets. Michael Drayton. NAEL-6v1; NAEL-7v1; NOSC *Fr.* Idea.

To the Readers. Han Yong'un [*or* Yongwun]. CAMKP, *tr. by* Sammy Solberg

To the Readers. Maria Luisa Spaziani. CItWP, *tr. by* Cinzia Sartini Blum and Lara Trubowitz

To the readers of our New First Unexpected. D. Burliuk, Aleksandr Kruchenykh, V. Mayakovsky and Viktor Khlebnikov. PFTM-1 *Fr.* Slap in the Face of Public Taste, A.

To the Readers Who Write to Me. Daria Menicanti. CItWP, *tr. by* Cinzia Sartini Blum and Lara Trubowitz

To the real world of her kitchen. (LL) Changeling, The. Judith Ortiz Cofer. NIL-7; TouFir

To the Red Lory. John Shaw Neilson. NOBAu

To the rest of us. (LL) Riot Act, April 29, 1992. Ai. CAP-8; ESEAA; NIL-7

To the Rev. Dr. Thomas Amory on Reading His Sermons on Daily Devotion. Phillis Wheatley. SacPr

To the Reverend Bagam. Muyong Sooyon. BecRai, *tr. by* Kim Daljin, Kim Won-Chung and Christopher Merrill

To the Rev. Mr. Powell. Christopher Smart. OBWVE

To the Rev. [*or* Reverend] W. L. Bowles. Samuel Taylor Coleridge. CenSon *Fr.* Effusions.

To the right. Well, The. Padma Sachdev. CFP, *tr. by* Iqbal Masud

To the Right Hon. and Right Revd. Fredrick, Earl of Bristol, Bishop of Derry, Etc., Etc. Ann Yearsley. RWP

To the Right Hon. Henry Pelham. Edward Moore. OBSV

To the Right Honorable, the Lady Mary, Countess of Pembroke. Samuel Daniel. NAEL-6v1

To the Right Honourable Charles Lord Halifax [one of the Lords Justices appointed by his Majesty]. Ambrose Philips.

  Salute to Property. STuOW

To the Right Honourable the Lord *Windsor*. William Habington. ChIV-2 *Fr.* Castara.

To the Right Honourable William, Earl of Dartmouth. Phillis Wheatley. NAAL-5; NAAPv.1; NALW; OxBoAm

To the right the summer dawn wakes the leaves and the mists. Ruts. Arthur Rimbaud. MotU, *tr. by* Louise Varese

To the Right Worshipful Lady Her Most Dear Mother, the Lady Prudentia Munda, the True Pattern of Piety and Virtue, C. M. Wisheth Increase of Happiness. Constantia Munda. EMWP

To the Right Worshipful, My Singular Good Frend, Master Gabriell Harvey, Doctor of the Lawes. Edmund Spenser. NoSic *Fr.* Commendatory Sonnets.

To the Right Worshipfull, My Singular Good Friend, Master Gabriel Harvey, Doctor of the Lawes. Edmund Spenser. NoSic

To the River Arun ("Be the proud Thames of trade the busy mart!") Charlotte Smith. RWP

To the River Arun ("On thy wild banks, by frequent torrents worn.") Charlotte Smith. CenSon; RWP

To the River Cherwell. William Lisle Bowles. CenSon

To the River Duddon. Norman Nicholson. NLP; NoP-4; NoP-5

To the River Itchin. William Lisle Bowles. *See* To the River Itchin, near Winton.

To the River Itchin, near Winton. William Lisle Bowles. CenSon; NAEL-6v2; OxBSo

  (To the River Itchin.) NPBRoP

To the River Loden. Thomas, the Younger Warton. *See* Sonnet: To the River Lodon.

To the River Otter. Samuel Taylor Coleridge. *See* Sonnet to the River Otter.

To the River Tweed. William Lisle Bowles. CenSon

To the River Wenbeck. William Lisle Bowles. CenSon

To the Roaring Wind [*also incl. in* "Primordia"]. Wallace Stevens. TCAPo

To the Roman Forum. Kenneth Koch. NAMCP V.2

To the Rose upon the Rood of Time. William Butler Yeats. NAMCP V.1; NoAM

To the Royal Society: "Philosophy the great and only Heir." Abraham Cowley. BASC *Fr.* Pindarique Odes.

To the Same. Leigh Hunt. CenSon

To the Same. Charlotte MacCarthy. PoBW

To the Same [Celia]. Ben Jonson. EroLit; NOSC *Fr.* Volpone.

To the Same; Enquiring Why I Wept. Mary Masters. PoBW

To the Same [My Dear Sister, Mrs S.]: The Tears. William Hammond. NOSC

To the same purpose: he, not long before. To the Same Purpos[e]. Thomas Traherne. NoP-4; NoP-5

To the Same [Robert, Earl of Salisbury] [Upon the Accension of the Treasurership to Him]. Ben Jonson. NOSC

To the Same [Sir Thomas Roe]. Ben Jonson. BASC

To the scullery, and down to the back room. (LL) Ancestor. Thomas Kinsella. ModIr; NPeEn; OxBEV; PBCIP

To the seagull. Ode to the Seagull. Pablo Neruda. GPTC, *tr. by* Margaret Sayers Peden

To the Shade of Burns. Charlotte Smith. NoP-4; NoP-5; WaAnP

To the Shade of Po Chü-I. William Carlos Williams. HarvBoo

To the ship I carried statues. I Carried Statues. Ágnes Nemes Nagy. PoSu

To the side of the road. (LL) Old Flame, The. Robert Lowell. ItP; NoAM

To the side of their own lives. (LL) Afternoons. Philip Larkin. NPeEn; OxBEV; PoetW

To the Singing Girl Named Luu. Nguyễn Khuyến. WoPoe, *tr. by* Nguyen Ngoc Bich

To the singing, to the drums. (LL) Eagle-Feather Fan, The. N. Scott Momaday. NoP-4; NoP-5

To the Six Million. Irving Feldman. TaR

To the sky. (LL) Draft of a Reparations Agreement. Dan Pagis. HP; PoSu; WoPoe, *tr. by* Stephen Mitchell

To the Snake. Denise Levertov. NAAL-5; PoA 2002

To the Sour[e] Reader. Robert Herrick. NBLV; NoP-4; NoP-5

To the South. Maurice Thompson. CBCWP

To the South Downs. Charlotte Smith. CenSon; NPBRoP

To the South: "Journey to Italy began in your youth, The." Christine Casson. NevBe

To the south there is a dragon living in a mountain pool. Tu Fu [or Du Fu]. CCL1 *Fr.* Seven Songs Written During the Qianyuan Era While Staying at Tonggu District.

To the southwest I look at Mount Lu. Dalei Riverbank. Pao Chao. CCL1, *tr.* by Kang-i Sun Chang

To the Soviet Embalmers. Rod Mengham. VaPo

To the Spider. Thomas Russell. CenSon

To the Stars. Andreas Gryphius. GePo, *tr.* by George C. Schoolfield

To the state of West Virginia. Story of Lovers Leap, The. Maggie Pogue Johnson. CBWP-4

To the States. Walt Whitman. TCAPo

To the States, To Identify the 16th, 17th, or 18th Presidentiad. Walt Whitman. NAAL-3; RaBo

To the Station. Carla Willard. PfS

To the Statue on the Capitol. John James Piatt. APN-2
  (To the Statue on the Capitol: Looking Eastward at Dawn.) GS

To the Stone-Cutters. Robinson Jeffers. ColAP; MoAmPo; NAAL-5; OxBoAm

To the Stork. Mihály Tompa. IQMS, *tr.* by Yakov Hornstein

To the Strawberry. Helen Maria Williams. CenSon; OxBSo; RWP

To the strenuous work of vanishing. (LL) Heroin. Bob Hicok. AmPoNex; BAP-97

To the Sun. Ingeborg Bachmann. GPTC, *tr.* by Peter Filkins

To the Sun. Tom Sleigh. UrbNat

To the Sun of the War. Rafael Alberti. RaW, *tr.* by Rachel Benson

To the Sun-Dial. John Quincy Adams. APN-1

To the sunk sun, the far, surrendered sea. (LL) Ebbtide at Sundown. Michael Field. OxBSo; VWP

To the Superhuman Adelmund, When She Would Undo the Kiss Already Done. Philipp von Zesen. GePo, *tr.* by George C. Schoolfield

To The Supreme Commander, Sirian Forces. Day on the Planet, A. Brian Morse. NOxBChV

To the Swallow. Euenus. OBVE, *tr.* by William Cowper

To the table down at Mory's, to the place where Louis dwells. Whiffenpoof Song. Ted. B. Galloway, Meade Minnigerode and George S. Pomeroy. TCAPo

To the temple, singing. (LL) In the Suburbs. Louis Simpson. CAP-8; TRP

To the Terrestrial Globe. William Schwenck Gilbert. NBLV

To the thatched hut on the topmost peak. Seeking a Hermit on West Mountain and Not Finding Him. Ch'iu Wei. CCL1, *tr.* by John Minford

To the Thoughtful Reader. William Meredith. NoAM

To the Thrice-Sacred Queen Elizabeth. Mary Sidney Herbert, Countess of Pembroke. NALW; NoP-4; NoP-5; WaAnP
  (To Queen Elizabeth.) PBRV

To the Tormentors. Lewis Morris. DiBP

To the Torrid Zone. Helen Maria Williams. *See* Sonnet 6. To the Torrid Zone.

To the Translator. Sir Walter Ralegh. PBRV

To the Tune "A Floating Cloud Crosses Enchanted Mountain." Huang O. WoPoe, *tr.* by Chung Ling and Kenneth Rexroth

To the Tune "A Spray of Flowers" (Not Giving In to Old Age). Kuan Han-ch'ing. WoPoe, *tr.* by Stephen Owen

To the Tune: Beautiful Barbarian. Li Po. CrYelRi, *tr.* by Sam Hamill

To the Tune: Beautiful Barbarian. *Unknown.* CrYelRi, *tr.* by Sam Hamill

To the Tune: Beautiful Barbarian. Wei Chuang. CrYelRi, *tr.* by Sam Hamill

To the Tune: Beautiful Lady Yu. Li Yu [or Li Hou-Chu]. CrYelRi, *tr.* by Sam Hamill

To the Tune: Boat of Stars. Li Ch'ing-chao. *See* Boat of Stars.

To the Tune: Bodhisattva's Headdress. Li Ch'ing-chao. CrYelRi, *tr.* by Sam Hamill

To the Tune: Butterflies Love Flowers. Li Ch'ing-chao. *See* Butterflies Love Flowers.

To the Tune "Clear Peace Happiness." Li Ch'ing-chao. NDACCP, *tr.* by Kenneth Rexroth

To the Tune: Drunk in Flower Shadows. Li Ch'ing-chao. CrYelRi, *tr.* by Sam Hamill

To the Tune: Eternal Joy. Li Ch'ing-chao. CrYelRi, *tr.* by Sam Hamill

To the Tune: Happiness Approaches. Li Ch'ing-chao. CrYelRi, *tr.* by Sam Hamill

To the Tune: In the Hills. Hsueh Chao-yun. CrYelRi, *tr.* by Sam Hamill

To the Tune "Intoxicated with Shadows of Flowers." Yü Ch'ing-tsĕng. EroLit, *tr.* by Chung Ling and Kenneth Rexroth

To the Tune: Lips Painted Red. Li Ch'ing-chao. CrYelRi, *tr.* by Sam Hamill

To the Tune: Magnolia Blossoms. Li Ch'ing-chao. CrYelRi, *tr.* by Sam Hamill

To the Tune "Meeting Happiness." Li Yü. WoPoe, *tr.* by Arthur Sze

To the Tune "Moon Over West River." Yang Shen. ColAnChi, *tr.* by Jonathan Chaves

To the Tune of The Coventry Carol. Stevie Smith. WoPoe

To the Tune: Partridge Sky. Li Ch'ing-chao. CrYelRi, *tr.* by Sam Hamill

To the Tune: Partridge Sky. Li Ch'ing-chao. CrYelRi, *tr.* by Sam Hamill

To the Tune: Plum Blossoms. Li Ch'ing-chao. *See* Plum Blossoms.

To the Tune: Sands of the Washing Stream. Li Ch'ing-chao. *See* Washing Stream, The.

To the Tune: Sands of the Washing Stream. Li Ch'ing-chao. CrYelRi, *tr.* by Sam Hamill

To the tune "Soaring Clouds." Huang O. EroLit

To the Tune: Southern Song. Wen T'ing-yün. CrYelRi, *tr.* by Sam Hamill

To the Tune: Spring at Wu Ling. Li Ch'ing-chao. *See* Spring at Wu Ling.

To the Tune "The Bodhisattva's Headdress." Li Ch'ing-chao. NDACCP, *tr.* by Kenneth Rexroth

To the Tune "The Drunken Young Lord." *Unknown.* WoPoe, *tr.* by C. H. Kwock and Vincent McHugh

To the Tune "The Fair Maid of Yu." Chiang Chieh. NDACCP, *tr.* by Kenneth Rexroth

To the Tune "The River Is Red." Ch'iu Chin. ItWoWo, *tr.* by Chung Ling and Kenneth Rexroth

To the Tune: The Water Clock. Wen T'ing-yün. CrYelRi, *tr.* by Sam Hamill

To the Tune: The Wine Spring: "Eternal autumn rain—evening sounds." Li Hsun. CrYelRi; ErotSp, *tr.* by Sam Hamill

To the Tune: The Wine Spring: "Rain falls on fallen flowers." Li Hsun. CrYelRi; ErotSp, *tr.* by Sam Hamill

To the Tune "You Move in Fragrance." Li Ch'ing-chao. NDACCP, *tr.* by Kenneth Rexroth

To the Unconstant Cynthia: a Song. Sir Robert Howard and John Dryden. NOSC

To the University. Alicia D'Anvers. NOSC *Fr.* Academia; or The Humours of the University of Oxford.

To the University of Cambridge, in New-England. Phillis Wheatley. NAAL-3; NAAPv.1; TCAPo

To the Unnamed Buddhist Nun Who Burned Herself to Death on the Night of June 3, 1966. Diane Di Prima. BB

To the Unseeable Animal. Wendell Berry. UpMys

To the Veterans of the Abraham Lincoln Brigade. Genevieve Taggard. AmWaPo; NAAPv.2

To the veterans of the Blue and the Gray. Old Fort Phantom Hill. Larry Chittendon. TiP2

To the Victims of Mauthausen. Maria Luisa Spaziani. CItWP, *tr.* by Cinzia Sartini Blum and Lara Trubowitz

(To the Virgin). Maria De' Medici. WPoS, *tr.* by Laura Anna Stortoni *and* Mary Prentice Lillie

To the Virgin Mary. Andreas Gryphius. WoPoe, *tr.* by Christopher Benfey

To the Virginian Voyage [*ode*]. Michael Drayton. BASC; NOSC; OBEV
  (Ode. To the Virginian Voyage.) NAEL-6v1; NAEL-7v1

To the Virgins, to Make Much of Time. Robert Herrick. BASC; BrAP; CavPo; ClHu; CtM; HeIP-4; ITBLP; NAEL-6v1; NAEL-7v1; NBLV; NIL-7; NIP-4; NoP-4; NoP-5; NOSC; NPeEn; OBEV; OxAEP-1; OxBEV; PoPoPo; PtR; SoSe-8; TFi; UV; WaAnP

To the Virgins, to Make the Most of Time. Gavin Ewart. OBCoV

To the Visions of Fancy. Ann Radcliffe. CenSon

To the Voice of Kathleen Ferrier. Yves Bonnefoy. YaTCFP, *tr.* by Mary Ann Caws and Jean-Pierre Cauvin

To the Water Nymphs, Drinking at the Fountain. Robert Herrick. NAEL-6v1

To the Western Wind. Robert Herrick. OBEV

To the Western World. Louis Simpson. OxBoAm; TRP

To the Wheel. Charles E. Pratt. ArBi

To the Wheel of Progress. Mrs. Henry Linden. CBWP-4

To the White Bird of the Tropic. Helen Maria Williams. CenSon

To the Wife of a Non-interventionist Statesman (March 1938). Edgell Rickword. RSaN

To the willow. Basho. ZenPo, *tr.* by Takashi Ikemoto and Lucien Stryk

To the Willow-Tree. Robert Herrick. OBEV

To the wind she says, "They have eaten me alive." (LL) In the Park. Gwen Harwood. BMAP; NIL-7

To the Winds. Ann Radcliffe. RWP

To the Wine Treasurer of the Circuit Mess. Horace Smith. UV

To the wineglass, weary of holding wine. (LL) Happiness. Jane Kenyon. BeAl; PoA 2002; PoDa

To the Winter Aphrodite. Michael Field. VWP

To the Wissahiccon. Frances Anne Kemble. APN-1

To the Woman in Bond Street Station. Edward Weismiller. PWW2

To the World We Must Appear. Heinrich Heine. WoPoe, *tr.* by Francis C. Golffing

To the world we must appear. To the World We Must Appear. Heinrich Heine. WoPoe, *tr.* by Francis C. Golffing

To thee, dear Paris, Lord of my Desires. Paraphrase on Oenone to Paris, A. Aphra Behn. EMWP

To thee, fair freedom! I retire. Written at [*or* in] an Inn at Henley. William Shenstone. OBEV; OxAEP-1; OxBEV

To thee obeyeth all the East as far as Ganges goes. Ovid. OBVE *Fr.* Metamorphoses.

To thee, sweet Fop, these lines I send. Bounce to Fop. Alexander Pope. DiBP

To Their Excellencies the Lords Justices of Ireland, the Humble Petition of Frances Harris, Who Must Starve, and Die a Maid if It Miscarries. Jonathan Swift. OxBEV

To their long home the greatest princes go. Upon a Funeral. Sir John Beaumont. NOSC

To Their Most Excellent Majesty of Great Brittaines Monarchy. Mary Fage. EMWP

To their ssh of vapors and their vowel ooo. (LL) January of a Gnat, The. Carl Rakosi. APT-2; FTOS

To them who crossed the flood. Inscription. Herman Melville. PCW

To them, yes, every pane! (LL) On the Asylum Road. Charlotte Mew. MoBrPo; VWP

To Theodorus et al. Rhianos. CAGL, *tr. by* Daryl Hine

To these bare fields, built at today's expense. (LL) Pyrography. John Ashbery. HarvBoo; VCAP

To these whom death again did wed. Epitaph Upon Husband and Wife Who Died and Were Buried Together, An. Richard Crashaw. OBEV; OxAEP-1

To things good to eat, and green, and lovely. (LL) Apotheosis of the Kitchen Goddess 2. Teresa Noelle Roberts. HW; IPoFL

To think / I must be alone. Moonshine. Richard Murphy. IrLP

To Think of Time. Walt Whitman. APN-1 *Fr.* Leaves of Grass [1855 Version, Complete Text].

To think of time. . . .to think through the retrospection. Walt Whitman. APN-1 *Fr.* Leaves of Grass [1855 Version, Complete Text].

To think of you is blue as if strolling. Azure Because of You. Eduardo Carranza. BLPSL, *tr. by* Rene de Costa, Rigas Kappatos and Eleni Paidoussi

To think so many battles have been fought. Surplice, The. David Scott. NLP

To think that this meaningless thing was ever a rose. Summer Is Ended. Christina Georgina Rossetti. NPeEn; OxBEV

To think to know the country and not know. Hillside Thaw, A. Robert Frost. AmFaPo

To This Book. Martin Opitz. GePo, *tr. by* George C. Schoolfield

To this bridge the pale river and flickers away in images of blue. Summer, the Sacramento. Muriel Rukeyser. ASA

To this, great hector said. Homer. FaBoWar *Fr.* Iliad, The.

To this grove of dying poplars. Autumn. Gabriela Mistral. SpanPo, *tr. by* Muriel Kittel

To this long pelt over the back of a chair. (LL) Otter, An. Ted Hughes. NAMCP V.2; NoAM

To this, speech already aspires. Dream-Work, The. Harry Mathews. NYP2

To this sweet and pretty air. Art of Love, The. Arnaut Daniel. NAWM-7v1, *tr. by* Frederick Goldin

To Thomalin. Phineas Fletcher. NOSC

To Thomas Palmer [on His Book *The Sprite of Trees and Herbs*]. Ben Jonson. NoSic

To Those Born Later. Bertolt Brecht. AF; GTCP, *tr. by* Erich Fried, Ralph Manheim and John Willett

  1. AF; PLBUT, *tr. by* Erich Fried, Ralph Manheim and John Willett

  2. AF, *tr. by* Erich Fried, Ralph Manheim *and* John Willett and John Willett

  3. AF, *tr. by* Erich Fried, Ralph Manheim *and* John Willett and John Willett

To those fair isles where crimson sunsets burn. Toussaint L'Ouverture. Henrietta Cordelia Ray. CBWP-3; SWaP

To those fixed on white. People. Jean Toomer. GT

To those who dwell in realms of day. (LL) Auguries of Innocence. William Blake. OxAEP-2; TFi

To those who have fashioned it. (LL) "H. D." APT-1; HarvBoo *Fr.* Flowering of the Rod, The.

To those who say we are burning the pages. (LL) Or Anything Resembling It. Michael Palmer. BodElec; CAP-8; WoBe

To throw that faint thin line upon the shore! (LL) George Meredith. GSo; NAEL-6v2; NAEL-7v2; NoP-4; NoP-5; NPeEn; OxAEP-2; OxBEV; TFi *Fr.* Modern Love.

To Thyrza. Lord Byron. CAGL

To Time. Mary Julia Young. CenSon

To Time Past. Anna Seward. RWP *Fr.* Llangollen Vale.

To tinge his verse as with his own heart's blood. (LL) Poet and Botanist. Constance Naden. ViWPN; VWP

To Tirzah. William Blake. NAEL-6v2; NAEL-7v2 *Fr.* Songs of Experience.

To Toussaint L'Ouverture. William Wordsworth. CenSon; NPBRoP

To Trace from Hebrew. Ece Ayhan. PFTM-2, *tr. by* Murat Nemet-Nejat

To trace the Kilmansegg pedigree. Miss Kilmansegg and Her Precious Leg. Thomas Hood.

To travel high summer. Sierra Cup. Reg Saner. PoCoUp

To Tray—Stolen. Mary Russell Mitford. DiBP

To tread those blest paths which before I writ. (LL) Passionate Man['.]s Pilgrimage, The. Sir Walter Ralegh. ChIV-2; NoP-5; NoSic; NPeEn; OxBEV; TFi

To tremble in prayer and trepidation. Revelation, The. Stanley Crouch. SeSe

To Tu Fu. Li Po. TAL

To Tu Fu from Shantung. Li Po. CrYelRi, *tr. by* Sam Hamill

To turn a stone. High Noon at Los Alamos. Eleanor Wilner. AtGh; NoP-4; NoP-5

To Turn Back. John Haines. TRP

To turn my soul nesh! (LL) In the Pantry. Hugh MacDiarmid. NAMCP V.1; NoAM

To Two of My Characters. John Updike. PoDa

To Tyranny. John Thelwall. CenSon

To unbalance. To keep over, accidentally, or submit to the pressure of gravity. To plummet in worth, especialy currency. Fall. Conor O'Callaghan. NIrP

To Understand Flight. Malinda Markham. IAoNAP

To understand her, you must imagine. Denise Levertov. UpMys *Fr.* Showings, The: Lady Julian of Norwich, 1342-1416.

To understand others is to be knowledgeable. Lao Tzu. AmFaPo *Fr.* Tao Te Ching.

To Urania. Joseph Brodsky. AF, *tr. by* the author and Joseph Brodsky

To Vahine (Painted by Gaugin). Enrique Molina. BLPSL, *tr. by* Rene de Costa, Rigas Kappatos and Eleni Paidoussi

To Valenton: Impressions circa 1947. Liliane Richman. TWW

To veil the saintly face. Counterfable of Orpheus. Marie-Claire Bancquart. MFP, *tr. by* Martin Sorrell

To Venus. Horace. OBVE,

To Vera, Who Asked a Song. Edith Nesbit. PoBW

To Vernon Lee. Amy Levy. VWP

To vex thy soul with these unjust alarms. To Orestes. Elizabeth Singer Rowe. PEW

To Violet. Basil Bunting. PoA 2002

To Violets. Robert Herrick. OBEV

To Virgil. Helen Dunmore. BeAl

To Virgil [*or* Vergil]. Alfred Tennyson. NAEL-6v2

To W. C. W. M. D. Alfred Kreymborg. PoA 2002

To W. L. Esq. While He Sung a Song to Purcell's Music. Samuel Taylor Coleridge. CenSon

To W. P. George Santayana. TCAPo

To W. R. W. E. Henley. *See* Madam Life's A Piece in Bloom.

To W. S. M. Arthur W. Monroe. APN-2

To W.S.—On his Wonderful Toys. Walter Davies. NOxBChV

To wake to the reassurance of grey stone streets. Greeting, Not Greeting. Angus Calder. EdScPo

To Waken an Old Lady. William Carlos Williams. OxBoAm; SoSe-8; WeW-3

To Wales once more, though not on holiday now. Louis MacNeice. ModIr *Fr.* Autumn Sequel.

To walk in the sun. Curfew Breakers, The. Samuel Chimsoro. NAfrP

To walk on air. (LL) Beethoven, Opus 111. Amy Clampitt. NAMCP V.2; NIP-4; NoP-4; NoP-5

To walk with sober step, to raise the eyebrow. Joachim Du Bellay. WoPoe *Fr.* Regrets.

To Walker Evans. James Agee. APT-2

To Walt Whitman. Richard Fein. ViWalt

To Walt Whitman on America's Birthday. Roger Mitchell. ViWalt

To Wang Lun. Li Po. CCL1, *tr. by* David Young

To Waning Day, To the Wide Round of Shadow. Dante Alighieri. STV, *tr. by* John Frederick Nims

To want is there to be where I am not. Sower, The. Jones Very. SacPr

To warm life passing singing with the grace. Ants. Ramón López Velarde. TCLAP, *tr. by* Samuel Beckett

To watch you walk. Song of Smoke. Kevin Young. LegDan; P180

To water and eternity. (LL) Across the Swamp. Olav H. Hauge. RaBo; WED; WoPoe, *tr. by* Robert Bly

To We Who Were Saved by the Stars. Lorna Dee Cervantes. TouFir

To weep there! (LL) William Shakespeare. NoSic; TFi *Fr.* Twelfth Night.

To Wei Pa, a Retired Scholar. Tu Fu [*or* Du Fu]. NDACCP, *tr. by* Kenneth Rexroth

To Welcome a Changeling. Colleen J. McElroy. FiBr

To welcome the new-livery'd year. (LL) On a Bank [*or* Banck] as I Sat[e] [a-]Fishing; a Description of the Spring. Sir Henry Wotton. AmFaPo; BASC; NOSC

To western woods and lonely plains. On the Emigration to America [and Peopling the Western Country]. Philip Freneau. ColAP; NAAL-3; NAAL-5; NAAPv.1; OxBoAm

To what intent or purpose was Man made. As Concerning Man. Alexander Radcliffe. NOSC; OBSV

To what it could never understand as being the human shore. (LL) Death of John Berryman,The. William Dickey. BAP-97; InoFa

To what purpose, April, do you return again? Spring. Edna St. Vincent Millay. APT-1; MoAmPo; NAMCP V.1; NoP-4; NoP-5

To what shall I liken this high and desolate hill? Gao Tang Rhapsody, The. Sung Yu. CCL1, *tr. by* Arthur Waley

To which I have attuned my breathing for so many years. (LL) Anniversary. Judith Ortiz Cofer. PueRic; TouFir

To which the whole creation moves. (LL) Alfred Tennyson. NAEL-6v2; NAEL-7v2 *Fr.* In Memoriam A. H. H.

To which they can't admit they can never be admitted. (LL) Misery and Splendor. Robert Hass. BeAl; OxBoAm; PtR; VCAP

To Whistler, American. Ezra Pound. FaBoA; PoA 2002

To Whittier. Josephine D. Henderson Heard. CBWP-4

To whoever is not listening to the sea. Poet's Obligation, The. Pablo Neruda. TWF, *tr. by* William Ward Ayer

To whoever is not listening to the sea. Poet's Obligation. Pablo Neruda. PoetW; VCWP, *tr. by* Alastair Reid

To Whom. Peter Klappert. YaYoPo

To Whom Else. George Barker. HarvBoo

To Whom Else Can We Fly? Giles, the Younger Fletcher. SacPr

To Whom it may concern. Judith Johnson Sherwin. YaYoPo

To Whom It May Concern (Tell Me Lies about Vietnam). Adrian Mitchell. BeAl; FaBoWar; OBWP; RSaN

To whom now, Pyrrha, art thou kind? Horace. OBVE

To whom the Tempter impudent replied. John Milton. ChIV-2 *Fr.* Paradise Regained [*or* Regain'd].

To whom the wingèd hierarch replied. John Milton. NOSC *Fr.* Paradise Lost.

To whom thus also th' Angel last repli'd. John Milton. OxAEP-1 *Fr.* Paradise Lost.

To whom with healing words Adam replied. John Milton. NOSC *Fr.* Paradise Lost.

To whomever taught me the word *dickhead*. Dickhead. Tony Hoagland. MAAN

To whose chest I give my five senses. Man Who Offers Me His Chest, The. Hala Mohammad. PoArWo, *tr. by* Cornelia Al-Khaled

To William Camden. Ben Jonson. BASC; NAEL-6v1; NAEL-7v1; NOSC; NPeEn

To William Carlos Williams. Galway Kinnell. NoAM

To William Drummond of Hawthornden. Mary, of Morpeth Oxlie. EMWP

3. To William Meredith. John Berryman. PoA 2002 *Fr.* Four Dream Songs.

To William Roe ("When Nature bids us leave to live, 'tis late.") Ben Jonson. NOSC

To William Wordsworth. Samuel Taylor Coleridge. NPBRoP

To William Wordsworth [1817 version]. Samuel Taylor Coleridge. NAEL-6v2; NAEL-7v2

To win the war and be killed. Self-Repeating Poem. Sybren Polet. LWR, *tr. by* John M. Coetzee

To windward midnight glowed, iridium sheen. Ice. Alan Gould. NOBAu

To Winter. Amelia Alderson Opie. CenSon

To wipe the sleep grains from my eyes or rub. Grandmother's Spit. Andrew Hudgins. CAP-8

To wit, the lever said. Lorine Niedecker. PFTM-1

To Wither Like Weeds in an Easterly Wind. Arye Sivan. NRoS, *tr. by* Esther Raizen

To witness, to / enter this. Blue. William Heyen. InoFa

To Women. Richard Hugo. NIP-4

To Women, as Far as I'm Concerned. D. H. Lawrence. NPeEn; RaBo

To women in contemporary voice and dislocation. Re-reading Jane. Anne Stevenson. NALW

To wood and field. (LL) Snow-Flakes. Henry Wadsworth Longfellow. APN-1; BrAP; CtM; ITBLP; MoW; NCAP; NoP-4; NoP-5; TCAPo

To [*or* the Poet] Wordsworth. Felicia Dorothea Hemans. NPBRoP; RWP

To Wordsworth. Percy Bysshe Shelley. CenSon; NAEL-6v2; NAEL-7v2; NoP-4; NoP-5; NPBRoP; NPeEn

To work away in art's traditional measure. Sonnet. Johann Wolfgang von Goethe. STV, *tr. by* John Frederick Nims

To World War Two. Kenneth Koch. BAP-01; OxBoAm; PWW2

To wound myself upon the sharp edges of the night? (LL) Taxi, The. Amy Lowell. IJHIL; LW; MoAmPo; NAAPv.2; PoCho; WaAnP

To wrestle with the angel—Art. (LL) Art: "In placid hours well-pleased we dream." Herman Melville. AmFaPo; APN-2; BrAP; ColAP; NAAL-3; NAAPv.1; NCAP

To write down all I contain at this moment. Moment, The. Kathleen Jessie Raine. MoWP

To write more. To speak more. To whom? To Write More. Jaan Kaplinski. TAPaP, *tr. by* the author, Sam Hamill and Riina Tamm

To write of Sol in his exaltation. Robert Copland. NoSic *Fr.* High Way to the Spital House, The (Hye Way to the Spyttell Hous, The).

To write the country. Diana Helen Melhem. PoArWo *Fr.* Country.

To write threescore: this is the second of our reign [*or* raigne]. (LL) Anniversary [*or* Anniversarie], The. John Donne. BASC; FSCP; NoP-4; NoP-5; NoSic; TFi; WeW-3

To yeeld the sinne her everlasting doome. (LL) Fulke, 1st Baron Brooke Greville. ChIV-1; NoSic *Fr.* Caelica.

To yet more boastful visions of despair. (LL) Recalling War. Robert Graves. AF; BrAP; HarvBoo; NAMCP V.1; NoAM; OBWP; PoWW

To you, a poet, glorious, heaven-born. Love Sonnets of Proteus, The. Wilfrid Scawen Blunt.

To you, fine wine in gold cup. Pao Chao. ChinPo *Fr.* Weary Road, The.

To you gave Sense, Good-humour, and a Poet. (LL) Epistle [II,] to a Lady[: Of the Characters of Women]. Alexander Pope. CABP; NAEL-6v1; NAEL-7v1; WaAnP

To you I brought sun and fire. . .as bows. Iraqi Sorrows. Aziz Samawi. IrPoTo, *tr. by* Alex Bellem

To you I dedicate this work of grace. Emilia Lanier. NOSC *Fr.* To the Lady Anne, Countess of Dorset.

To You: "I love you as a sheriff searches for a walnut." Kenneth Koch. P180

To You, My Beloved Ssuma Ch'ien. Mun Chônghui. EcSo, *tr. by* Catherine J. Kim

To you, my lord, a gold goblet of vintage wine. Goblet of Wine, A. Pao Chao. CCL1, *tr. by* John Frodsham

To you, my purs, and to noon other wight. Geoffrey Chaucer. NAEL-6v1; NAEL-7v1; NoP-4; NoP-5

To you that lyfe possess grete troubles do befall. Emma Foxe. EMWP

To you, then, tenants of life's middle state. William Cowper. OBSV *Fr.* Tirocinium; or, A Review of Schools.

To your enterprise foretold. (LL) *Unknown.* NAEL-6v1; NAEL-7v1; NAWM-7v1 *Fr.* Sir Gawain and the Green Knight [Marie Borroff Translation].

To your judgement which will be just. (LL) Epistle to a Patron, An. Frank Templeton Prince. HarvBoo; OxBEV

To your life's final borders. Looking at Childhood. Andrée Chédid. YaTCFP, *tr. by* Rosemary Lloyd

To your owne bents dispose you: you'le be found. William Shakespeare. FaBoVe *Fr.* Winter's Tale, The.

To your question: why are my private parts. *Unknown.* RomPo *Fr.* Priapean Corpus, The.

To Youth. Josephine D. Henderson Heard. CBWP-4

To youth alone the mad, impassioned measure. Eternal Controversy, The. Dean B. Lyman, Jr. YaYoPo

To youths, who hurry thus away. On a Painted Woman. Percy Bysshe Shelley. NBLV

To Yuan Chen. Po Chü-i. CrYelRi, *tr. by* Sam Hamill

To Zhang Xu. Li Qi. CCL1, *tr. by* Stephen Owen

Toad. Norman Alexander MacCaig. EdScPo; HarvBoo

Toad. Takahashi Shinkichi. ZenPo, *tr. by* Takashi Ikemoto and Lucien Stryk

Toad, The. Juan José Arreola. MotU, *tr. by* W. S. Merwin

Toad grabbed a fly in its mouth, A. *Unknown.* CATKP, *tr. by* Kevin O'Rourke

Toad! It looks like, The. Issa. EH, *tr. by* Robert Hass

Toad the power mower caught, A. Death of a Toad, The. Richard Wilbur. BrAP; NAAL-5; NAMCP V.2; NoAM; PoA 2002; PtR

Toadfish. Stephen Perry. MiVo

Toads. Philip Larkin. BeAl; NoAM; OxAEP-2; SoSe-8

Toads Revisited. Philip Larkin. OxAEP-2

Toady toady min yoself. Digging Sing, A. *Unknown.* FaBoVe

To-and-Fro of Saint Theresa. Alfonso Reyes. WoPoe, *tr. by* Samuel Beckett

Toast. Stéphane Mallarmé. WoPoe, *tr. by* Frederick Morgan

Toast. Stéphane Mallarmé. SxFrPo, *tr. by* A. M. and E. H. Blackmore

Toast. Thomas McCarthy. PBCIP

Toast. Leonard Nathan. BLT

Toast en réponse. André Frénaud. YaTCFP

Toast in Response. André Frénaud. YaTCFP, *tr. by* Mary Ann Caws and Jean-Pierre Cauvin

Toast to 2,000, A. Richard Percival Lister. OBCoV

Toast to Washington, A. Francis Hopkinson. NAAPv.1

Toasted susie is my ice-cream. (LL) Preciosilla. Gertrude Stein. NAAPv.2; NAMCP V.1

Toaster, A / A plate. Ode to the Yard Sale. Gary Soto. WaAnP

Toaster, The. William Jay Smith. NOxBChV

Toasting my back I lean on the sunny rail. (LL) Thinking of My Little Boy. Tu Fu [*or* Du Fu]. ColAnChi; WoPoe, *tr. by* David Lattimore

Toasting Song. S. Conant Foster. ArBi

Tobacco crumbs, vases and fringes. (LL) Bean Eaters, The. Gwendolyn Brooks. AFaM; AmFaPo; ESEAA; HeIP-4; HHAm; MoWP; NAAL-5; NALW; NAMCP V.2; NoP-4; NoP-5; PoPoPo; TRP; WaAnP; WeW-3

Tobacco Pickers. Kočo Racin. SonAtl, *tr. by* Broz Koneski

Tobacco Shop, The. Álvaro de Campos. GPTC, *tr.* by Richard Zenith

Tobacco stains from your beautiful fingers, The. And I wish I did not feel like your mother. (LL) Rendezvous. Edna St. Vincent Millay. APT-1; NALW; OxBoAm

Tobacco Warehouse Blues. Houston A. Baker, Jr. SeSe

Tobera. Jeff Tagami. OpBo

Tobias's Dog. Mary Howitt. DiBP *Fr.* Sketches of Natural History.

Tobong Mountain. Pak Tujin. CAMKP, *tr.* by Edward W. Poitras

Toccata of Galuppi's, A. Robert Browning. FaBoVe; NAEL-6v2; NAEL-7v2; NoP-5; UV

Toco la piedra fundamental del año. Vértigo. Pedro Serrano. RMCMP

Toda la noche de la tierra. Orilla de la Noche. José Luis Hidalgo. RaW

Today. As Soon As It's Here It's Gone But So What. Emilie Buchwald. MiVo

Today. Today We Will Not Be Invisible Nor Silent. Victoria Lena Manyarrows. UnSA

Today. Pak Mogwŏl [*or* Mokwŏl]. CAMKP *Fr.* Nature of Gravel, The.

Today. Sunday. Primus St. John. ISC

Today. Sarcophagus. Pauline Stainer. NeBl

Today: "I won't be sitting shiva." Shifre Vays. Prolet, *tr.* by Amelia Glaser

Today a brown duck with a green head. Allen Fisher. Oth *Fr.* Stepping Out.

Today, a coed with a black eye. Style. Mark Cox. SUP

Today a field of pumpkins. Sassafras. Barbara Guest. FTOS

Today a fine old face has gone under the soil. Kathleen Jessie Raine. EdScPo *Fr.* Eileann Chanaidh.

To-day a rude brief recitative. Song for All Seas, All Ships. Walt Whitman. APN-1

Today about love we'll say some truths. Merlin. Gerardo Deniz. RMCMP, *tr.* by Mónica de la Torre

Today as I hang out the wash I see them again, a code. Geese, The. Jorie Graham. MoWP; NoP-5; WaAnP

Today as I ride down Twenty-fifth Street I smell honeysuckle. June Fourth. Gerald Stern. PoA 2002

Today as the news from Selma and Saigon. Monet's "Waterlilies." Robert Earl Hayden. AmFaPo; GT

Today, as usual, the mind goes hunting for a word. Once Again the Mind. Faiz Ahmad Faiz. AF, *tr.* by Naomi Lazard

Today / as we flew the kites. History. John Burnside. BeAl; PoAgWa

Today at Lord's the second test began. Cricket. Dafydd Rowlands. BBMWP, *tr.* by Meic Stephens

Today at the Publix with my daughters. Song for the Sugar Cane. Virgil Suárez. AmPoNex

Today, Braddock Avenue's a parade. Technology of Spring, The. Lynn Emanuel. BodElec

Today, brother, I am at home writing. Letter to Spencer. George Scarbrough. LPSFW

Today— but before today too—. Love Says. Daria Menicanti. CItWP, *tr.* by Cinzia Sartini Blum and Lara Trubowitz

Today, *catorce de julio.* 14 de julio. Sandra Cisneros. WaAnP

Today, Cheng, I touched your face. Prisoner, The. Keith Douglas. HarvBoo

Today, dear heart, but just today. Her Answer. John Bennett. ITBLP

Today Delight's Fair Ship. Félix Lope de Vega Carpio. SpanPo, *tr.* by William M. Davis

Today delight's fair ship. Today Delight's Fair Ship. Félix Lope de Vega Carpio. SpanPo, *tr.* by William M. Davis

Today Eurydice played. You All Know the Story of the Two Lovers. Carlota Caulfield. TANSG, *tr.* by Chris Allen

Today / Everlasting passing apparent imperceptible. Mina Loy. NAMCP V.1 *Fr.* Love Songs to Joannes.

Today / Hark! Heaven sings! On Christmas Day to My Heart. Clement Paman. ChrPo; NOSC; RSR

Today has it all, sunshine. Gwyn Williams. OBWVE *Fr.* Aspects of Now.

Today I am going to tell about the field. Battlesfield, The. Angel González. RaW, *tr.* by Herbert Baird and William Stafford

Today I am, I don't know how. I Have Plenty of Heart. Miguel Hernández. RaW; WED, *tr.* by Robert Bly

Today I am modest like an animal. Esther Raab. FIT, *tr.* by Robert Friend

Today I am simply in pain. (LL) I Am Going to Talk About Hope. César Vallejo. TCLAP; WED, *tr.* by Robert Bly

Today I am walking in woods. Beginning, A. Richard Jones. IllVoic

Today I began anew. Warp is Even, The: Taut Vertical Loops Between Our Father and the Earth. Luci Tapahonso. ICANM

Today I bring you cold chrysanthemums. Between Seasons. Li-Young Lee. TRP

Today I chopped back irises. Clearing Away. Andrew Taylor. BMAP

Today, I dedicate this to you: you are long. Every Day, Matilde. Pablo Neruda. GifTon, *tr.* by William O'Daly

Today I don't know what to do with the Earth. Voyages. Jules Supervielle. MFP, *tr.* by Martin Sorrell

Today I dreamed all day. I dreamed. Rauf Parfi. SonAtl, *tr.* by Hafiz Boboyorov, Tanju Cataltepe, Akram Tairovich Khabibullaev and Shawn Lyons

Today I drove through a cloud of leaves. Hands in the Wind. Ted Kooser. UrbNat

Today I followed my servant, Hestia, down the dusty path. Learning to Walk Alone. Judith Ortiz Cofer. PueRic

Today I found the right fruit for my prime. Kumquat for John Keats, A. Tony Harrison. BeAl; NoP-4; NoP-5; WaAnP

Today I get this letter from you and the sun. Tom Clark. PmAP *Fr.* You.

Today I hate that I was born. Desert Cry, A. Magdalena Gomez. PueRic

Today I have drunk the sun through every pore. Intact Pitcher. Yolanda Bedregal. TANSG, *tr.* by Carolyne Wright

Today I have finished a work outlasting bronze. Horace. PoCho *Fr.* Odes.

Today I have turned thirty-two. For My Birthday. Attila József. IQMS, *tr.* by Istvan Fekete

Today I inhabit the Día de la Virgen. Miracle Country. Dana Gelinas. SPV, *tr.* by Jen Hofer

Today I learned the *coora* flower. Coora Flower, The. Gwendolyn Brooks. IllVoic; NAAL-5; NIL-7; NoP-4

Today I learned the *coora* flower. Gwendolyn Brooks. ESEAA *Fr.* Children Going Home.

Today I like life much less. César Vallejo. TCLAP, *tr.* by Clayton Eshleman

Today I met you, son of a Spanish exile. Jane Duran. Prnts *Fr.* Silences from the Spanish Civil War.

Today I parted from my love. So Long and Still No Mate. *Unknown.* CCL1, *tr.* by John Frodsham

Today I pass the time reading. Japan. Billy Collins. CAP-8; FaoP; NoP-5

Today I picked up. Seven Stones. Marjorie Agosin. TANSG, *tr.* by Cola Franzen

Today I saw a thing of arresting poignant beauty. Snow in October. Alice Moore Dunbar-Nelson. InGu

Today I saw black men. Men, The. UnSA

Today I see what my father saw. Road Trip. Alma Stacey Allen. PfS

Today I stayed home. Day at Home, A. Zoya Ezrokhi. CRWP, *tr.* by Daniel Weissbort

Today I stopped / I call my niece to tell her I'm through. Healing Logic, A. M. Wyrebek. AmPoNex

Today I think. Digging. Edward Thomas. MoBrPo

Today I turn thirteen and quit the 4-H club for good. Chicken Bucket. Jennifer L. Knox. FreRad

Today I wake having swung, naked, in London. Here and There. Ann Lauterbach. PmAP

Today, I want to know how your Fall works. To the People of a Small Town in Ohio, Who As I Approach Them on the Street, Are Afraid That This Black Man Is Going to Do Them Harm. William Henry Lewis. BtF

Today I was caught alone in a summer storm. Judith Wright. HarvBoo *Fr.* Shadow of Fire: Ghazals, The.

Today I watched a woman by the water. Levee: Letter to No One, The. Lorna Dee Cervantes. TouFir

Today / I will b. Epitaph for Willie or Little Black Poet with No Future. Sibby Anderson-Thompkins. InTrad

Today I woke up again. Panorama 2. Romelia Alarcón de Folgar. TANSG, *tr.* by Alison Ridley

Today I'd like to climb the difference. Hades in Manganese. Clayton Eshleman. APSN

Today, if the breath of breeze. Any Lover to Any Beloved. Faiz Ahmad Faiz. RaF; WoPoe, *tr.* by Naomi Lazard

Today I'll wear a cool summer coat. My Soul's Wardrobe. Sharon Dolin. PoCoUp

Today I'm a proper king's daughter. Irina Shostakovskaya. CRWP, *tr.* by Daniel Weissbort

Today I'm going into town to give away what's left. What's Left. Jack Myers. BodElec

Today I'm thinking of St. Paul—St. Paul. What Light Destroys. Andrew Hudgins. UpMys

Today, I'm wearing new love. Poem # 3. Sybil J. Roberts. BtF

Today, I'm your queen. Sonnet for July. Rosemerry Wahtola Trommer. GeoH

Today in hazy San Francisco, I face seaward. We Are Americans Now, We Live in the Tundra. Marilyn Chin. FiBr; NIL-7; OPRER; UnSA

Today, in the war-torn state, the nightly news. Nightly News, The. Daniel Anderson. AmPoNex

Today is a day like any other. Watch of Time. Magda Portal. TANSG, *tr.* by Shaun Griffin and Emma Sepúlveda-Pulvirenti

Today Is a Day of Great Joy. Víctor Hernández Cruz. LoL; PueRic

Today is everybody's favorite day of the week. Everybody. Mark Levine. AmPoNex

Today Is Not the Day. Audre Lorde. AfrBLW

Today is summer's day. Poem with Incense Paper. Liliane Giraudon. SCFWP, *tr. by* Serge Gavronsky

Today is Sunday. In Memoriam. Léopold Sédar Senghor. PoetW, *tr. by* Melvin Dixon

Today Is the First Day of the Rest of My Life. Richard Maltby, Jr. ReLy

Today is the last day of winter. *Unknown.* NAAPv.2

Today is washday. My mother. Days of My Mother, The. Laurel Mills. SweBea

Today is your. April Fool Birthday Poem for Grandpa. Diane Di Prima. CLPP; FTtHH

Today, it came to me. How you, my friends. To My Fellow Artists. Christopher Logue. RSaN

Today it rains all over the world and we are two. Angel in the Deluge. Rosario Murillo. CLPP, *tr. by* Alejandro Murguía

Today it seems plausible that myth alone could. Basket with Blue Ox. Nance Van Winckel. RoV

Today it's going to cost us twenty dollars. How Things Work. Gary Soto. NAMCP V.2; NoAM

Today I've felt the. Embrace. Dulce Maria Loynaz. TANSG, *tr. by* Alan West

Today I've invented a man. Wine from Bordeaux. Sujata Bhatt. AtGh

Today, lonely for my father, I saw. My Father's Wedding. Robert Bly. NAMCP V.2; NoAM; RaBo

Today, / love compromised my character. Kim Namjo. CAMKP *Fr.* Love's Cursive.

Today, my poetry has exacted a confession from me. (LL) Manifesto on Ars Poetica. Frank Mkalawile Chipasula. HBAPE; NAfrP; PML

Today no anxious arms crowd the counters. Strike, The. Shamsur Rahman. SonAtl, *tr. by* Latifa Das, Harjeet Singh Gill, Jafor Iqbal and Peter Ramsey

Today no-one has come to inquire. Agape. César Vallejo. TCLAP, *tr. by* Gordon Brotherston and Edward Dorn

Today on the field and on the footpath. Power of Song, The. Euros Bowen. BBMWP, *tr. by* the author

Today on the lip of a bowl in the backyard. Caterpillar, The. Miller Williams. InGu

Today outside your prison I stand. Message from the Wanderer, A. William Stafford. BrAP

Today Rakan, riding an iron horse. Rakan-Keinan. ZenPo, *tr. by* Takashi Ikemoto and Lucien Stryk

Today saw the last of my Spanish shampoo. Empty Song, The. Liz Lochhead. EdScPo

Today she parades her shape like swellings of song. Portrait of a Pregnant Woman. Bobi Jones. OBWVE, *tr. by* Joseph P. Clancy

Today, the angel of dread, invisible. Angel of Dread, The. Miklós Radnóti. ConPit; PFTM-1, *tr. by* Clayton Eshleman and Gyula Kodolanyi

Today the bass booming. Lemons. Gail Martin. SweBea

Today the ghetto knows a different fear. Fear. Eva Picková. INSAB; ItWoWo

Today the grave is bright for me. Alfred Tennyson. NAWM-7v2 *Fr.* In Memoriam A. H. H.

Today the leaves cry, hanging on branches swept by wind. Course of a Particular, The. Wallace Stevens. APT-1

To-day the lot caved in upon me. Page from a Diary. Desmond O'Grady. NoAM

Today the 'sigl-di-gwt'. Gwyneth Lewis. BBMWP *Fr.* Language Murderer, The.

Today the sixth of june. Nigeria in the Year 1999. Catherine Obianuju Acholonu. HBAPE

Today the snow is drifting. Snow. Philip Levine. ColAP; UrbNat; WaAnP

Today the sunlight is the paint on lead soldiers. Toyland. Roy Fisher. HarvBoo; NPeEn

Today / the Valley. No Trespassing (Private Beach). Katayoon Zandvakili. AmPoNex

Today the windy Italian air was clean as the air of Montauk. Postcard to Walt Whitman from Siena. Stanley Moss. ViWalt

Today then, her head is thudding. Dionne Brand. OpeFie *Fr.* Every Chapter of the World.

Today there are hands I love. Song for Ghosts and for Those Now Gone. Philippe Soupault. YaTCFP, *tr. by* Mary Ann Caws and Jean-Pierre Cauvin

Today / there came a breeze thin as the needle of a syringe. J. Kitchener Davies. BBMWP; OBWVE *Fr.* Sound of the Wind That Is Blowing, The.

To-day there have been lovely things. Vision. May Thielgaard Watts. LW

Today there is the kind of sunshine old men love. Soaking Up Sun. Tom Hennen. GoPo; IPoFL

Today there've been moments. For a Daughter Gone Away. Brendan Galvin. GM

Today, Tom, I followed the tractor ruts north. Cranes on the Seashore. Linda Gregerson. AmAlph

Today, Tuesday, I decided to move on. Malcolm Mooney's Land. William Sydney Graham. NePenScot; NPeEn

Today Tutu Is Beating the Same Burru As Me. Lebert Bethune. GT

Today Was a Bad Day Like TB. Chrystos. UnSA

Today was a day of fragments. Mouvance. Sue Standing. UrbNat

Today we have marking of folders. Yesterday. Marking of Folders. Anne Anderton. UV

Today we have naming of parts. Yesterday. Henry Reed. AmFaPo; BrAP; FaBoWar; MoBrPo; NAEL-6v2; NAEL-7v2; NoP-4; NoP-5; OxBEV; PoPoPo; RaBo; SoSe-8; TFi; UV; WaAnP *Fr.* Lessons of the War.

Today we lynched a Negro, here in Alabama. Done a Good Job. Y. A. Rontsh. Prolet, *tr. by* Amelia Glaser

Today We Will Not Be Invisible Nor Silent. Victoria Lena Manyarrows. UnSA

Today we woke up to a revolution of snow. Snow Day. Billy Collins. BAP-01

Today when I came underneath the spell. Lőrinc Szabó. IQMS *Fr.* Cricket Music.

Today will be the day of what we both said. (LL) West-Running Brook. Robert Frost. APT-1; MoAmPo; NoP-4; NoP-5

Today with the north wind. Petty Time. Claudio Rodríguez. RaW, *tr. by* Robert Mezey

Today, you span the far mountains. Driving to Katoomba. Merlinda Bobis. ReBoTo

Today you would find your distant sad shire. For Wilfred Owen. Freda Downie. StAl

Today, your being so considerate. Bagatelle. HSü Ling. CCL1, *tr. by* Anne Birrell

To-day's house makes to-morrow's road. Survival, The. Edmund Charles Blunden. OBEV; OBMV

Today's Market-in-the-Loop finds the poet. Commerce and the Man. Ricardo M. de Ungria. ReBoTo

Today's Meditation. Antonio Machado Ruiz. AF; WED, *tr. by* Robert Bly

Today's News. Elizabeth Alexander. InTrad; ISC; OxAAAP

Today's sadness is different from yesterday's. Sad Sestina. Robin Becker. BodElec

Today's white fog won't rise above the tree-tops. Judith Wright. HarvBoo *Fr.* Shadow of Fire: Ghazals, The.

Todd. Stewart Conn. EdScPo; NePenScot

Todo cambia de estado en la materia. Tres estados y los tres reinos, Los. Alberto Blanco. RMCMP

Todo el mundo back to his side. (LL) *Navidad*, St. Nicholas Ave. Alfred Corn. NoP-4; NoP-5

Todo final borra los rastros de su trama. Carta. Tedi López Mills. RMCMP

Todo quiere ser agua. Agua desdichada, El. Efraín Bartolomé. RMCMP

Todo se desmorona como cucharada de sal en la entropía de la comida. Prurito. Pedro Serrano. RMCMP

Todos duerman, abajo. Ruta. Juan Ramón Jiménez. RaW

Toe upon [*or* after] toe, a snowing flesh. Nude Descending a Staircase. X. J. Kennedy. NIP-4; PoA 2002

To-Em-Mei's "The Unmoving Cloud." T'ao Ch'ien. NDACCP, *tr. by* Ezra Pound

Toenails. Jorge Luis Borges. MotU, *tr. by* Mildred Boyer

Toe'osh; a Laguna Coyote Story. Leslie Marmon Silko. NAMCP V.2; NoAM

Tofu that's shown up overnight in this house is frightening, The. Vegetarian Physics. David Clewell. P180

Together again. (LL) Equinox 1980. Peter Davison. NoP-4; NoP-5

Together Again ("I behold her there.") Victor Vroomkoning. TuT, *tr. by* Anne Kennedy

Together Again ("You get these thoughts in melancholy Autumn.") Victor Vroomkoning. TuT, *tr. by* James Simmons

Together, babe, we could have had the world sewn up. Olive Senior. NewEx

Together eternity and death threaten me. Patrizia Cavalli. NeIt

Together I am supplicant. I am bride. (LL) To Swim, to Believe. Maxine W. Kumin. CAP-8; MoASP; PoCho

Together in infinite shade. Too Much Coffee. Edwin Arlington Robinson. MoAmPo

Together in this grave lie Benjamin Pantier, attorney at law. Edgar Lee Masters. APT-1 *Fr.* Spoon River Anthology.

Together, their snouts full of soil, they hope this and are ruthless in their waiting. (LL) Sexual Jealousy. Carol Frost. CAP-8; PfSP

Together twists their threads, and yet draws hers the longer.. (LL) Dialogue betwixt Time and a Pilgrim[e], A. Aurelian Townshend. NPeEn; OxBEV

Together, we drink; the mountain flowers open. Drinking with a Friend, Among the Mountains. Li Po. CCL1, *tr. by* Jerome P. Seaton

Together we explore my inner landscape on the screen. Scan. Pat Borthwick. PoCu

Together We Know Happiness. *Unknown.* NAAPv.2, *tr. by* Florence Ayscough and Amy Lowell

Together, we will not get through this. (LL) My Life: "Somehow it got into my room." Joe Wenderoth. BodElec; NAPBL; P180

Together Wherever We Go. Stephen Sondheim. ReLy

Together with my stones. Shibboleth. Paul Celan. PoetW, *tr. by* Michael Hamburger

"Toil! toil! toil!" Wandering Jew, The. Eloise Bibb. CBWP-4

Toilet, The. Alexander Pope. OxAEP-1; OxBEV *Fr.* Rape of the Lock, The: An Heroi-Comical Poem in Five Cantos.

Toiling in Town now is "horrid." In Town. Austin Dobson. MakPoe

Toiling stallions, winding road. Si-mu: Request for Furlough. *Unknown.* CCL1, *tr. by* Ezra Pound

Toishan Song, A. *Unknown.* WoPoe, *tr. by* Gary Gach and C. H. Kwock and Vincent McHugh

Token. Alison Bielski. AngWePo

Token Enabler. Anselm Berrigan. BAP-04

Token woman gleams like a gold molar in a toothless mouth, The. Token Woman, The. Marge Piercy. NALW

Token Woman, The. Marge Piercy. NALW

Toki-no-Ge (Satori Poem). Muso Soseki. EaWin, *tr. by* W. S. Merwin

Told to the Missionary. George R. Sims. DiBP

Toldi. János Arany. *tr. by* Watson Kirkconnell

  Canto 1.

    "As on an autumn night a herdman's fire." IQMS, *tr. by* Watson Kirkconnell

  Canto 11.

    "River seemed a broad stream, fenced with folk, The." IQMS, *tr. by* Watson Kirkconnell

  Canto 12.

    "Then Nicholas spoke: "My King, most kind to me."" IQMS, *tr. by* Watson Kirkconnell

  Canto 5.

    "Day to the reedy marsh had closed her eye." IQMS, *tr. by* Watson Kirkconnell

  Canto 6.

    "As if a nest of hornets rose to sting." IQMS, *tr. by* Watson Kirkconnell

  Canto 8.

    "My brother's done for, by all human law." IQMS, *tr. by* Watson Kirkconnell

Toledo. Roy Campbell. MoBrPo

Toll the bell, fellow. Red Cow Is Dead, The. Elwyn Brooks White. NBLV

Tollund Man. Hugo Claus. TuT, *tr. by* Peter van de Kamp

Tollund Man, The. Hugo Claus. PFTM-2, *tr. by* Theo Hermans

Tollund Man, The. Seamus Heaney. CABP; ModIr; NAMCP V.2; NPeEn; PBCIP; PNI; WoPoe

Tolly Masters sat on the porch. Tolly Masters. Brenda Black White. TiP2

Toltec, The. Ana Castillo. IllVoic

Toltecs. Eloise Klein Healy. SUP

Toltecs were wise, The. *Unknown.* CA

Tom Bowling. Charles Dibdin. OxAEP-1

Tom Brokaw is a beautiful person. Tom Brokaw. Jeni Olin. FreRad

Tom Clark and I went out to Greenwich. Larry Fagin. AHA *Fr.* Parade of the Caterpillars, The.

Tom Deadlight. Herman Melville. APN-2; NCAP

Tom Farley. Colin Thiele. NOBAu

Tom Fool at Jamaica. Marianne Moore. APT-1

Tom o' Bedlam's Song. *Unknown.* BASC; NoP-4; NoP-5; NPeEn; TFi

  (Loving Mad Tom.) WeW-3

  (Mad Tom's Song.) PtR

Tom Passey's Child. Maggie Hannan. NLP

Tom Punsibi's Letter to Dean Swift. Thomas Sheridan. NPeEn

Tom Thumb the Great. Henry Fielding.

  Revenge. DiBP

Tom used spit for lubricant and fucked me. David Trinidad. WiU *Fr.* Eighteen to Twenty-One.

Tom, will you let me love you in your restaurant? Litany. Carolyn Creedon. BodElec

Tomás. Luis Lopez. GeoH

Tomar de nuevo la palabra. Mónica Nepote. SPV

Tomato. Tatyana Milova. CRWP *Fr.* Erotic Fruit.

Tomato. Obu Udeozo. NeNiPo

Tomato is so vulgar and so lustful. Tatyana Milova. CRWP *Fr.* Erotic Fruit.

Tomato Ketchup. *Unknown. See* On Tomato Ketchup.

Tomatoes. Stephen Dobyns. CAP-8

Tomatoes grow large this year, though it is the mirrors which hold us to their architecture, The. Successions, The. Lee Bartlett. ICANM

Tomb. Stéphane Mallarmé. SxFrPo, *tr. by* A. M. and E. H. Blackmore

Tomb/ A hollow hateful world. Agamemnon's Tomb. Sacheverell Sitwell. OBMV

Tomb, bend / To autumn wind—. Basho. ZenPo, *tr. by* Takashi Ikemoto and Lucien Stryk

Tomb of Charles Baudelaire, The. Stéphane Mallarmé. SxFrPo, *tr. by* A. M. and E. H. Blackmore

Tomb of Edgar Allan Poe, The. Stéphane Mallarmé. SxFrPo, *tr. by* A. M. and E. H. Blackmore

Tomb of Edgar Poe, The. Stéphane Mallarmé. NAWM-7v2, *tr. by* Henry Weinfield

Tomb of Hegeso, The. Mihály Babits. IQMS, *tr. by* Watson Kirkconnell

Tomb of Heracles, The. James McAuley. BMAP *Fr.* Hero and the Hydra, The.

Tomb of Ilaria Giunigi, The. Edith Wharton. APN-2

Tomb of Sir Lawrence Tanfield obiit 30 Ap. 1625 erected by Lady Tanfield 1628. Lady Elizabeth Tanfield. *See* Epitaph for Sir Lawrence Tanfield.

Tomb of the Imagination. Miguel Hernández. AF, *tr. by* Tom Jones

Tomb of the Kings, The. Anne Hébert. WoPoe, *tr. by* A. Poulin, Jr.

Tombs of the Hetaerae. Rainer Maria Rilke. PFTM-1

Tombs of the Hetaerae. Rainer Maria Rilke. GPTC, *tr. by* Edward Snow

Tombstones. A. R. Ammons.

  1. NAMCP V.2

  11. NAMCP V.2

  19. NAMCP V.2

  27. NAMCP V.2

  29. NAMCP V.2

Tombstones in the Starlight. Dorothy Parker.

  Actress, The. AmWit

Tomcat. James Keir Baxter. BeAl

Tomes. Billy Collins. KGB

Tommies in the Train. D. H. Lawrence. PoWW

Tommorow. Amal Dunqul. NAfrP, *tr. by* Sharif Elmusa and Thomas G. Ezzy

Tommy. Rudyard Kipling. CABP; FaBoWar; MoBrPo; NoP-4; NoP-5; OBWP; OxAEP-2; UV

Tommy is three and when he's bad. Red Roses. Anne Sexton. EmeKit

Tommy was ruled by his father and mother. King Tommy's Rise and Fall. Ella Wheeler Wilcox. ArBi

Tomorrow. Anna Laetitia Barbauld. PEW

Tomorrow: "Tomorrow / we are." David Budbill. AmZen

Tomorrow. Langston Hughes. APSN

Tomorrow: "Tomorrow I will start to be happy." Dennis O'Driscoll. PoA 2002

Tomorrow. John Henry Mackay. CAGL, *tr. by* Hubert Kennedy

To-morrow. John Masefield. MoBrPo

Tomorrow. E. Ethelbert Miller. ISC

Tomorrow I will start to be happy. Tomorrow. Dennis O'Driscoll. PoA 2002

Tomorrow again will shine the sun. Tomorrow. John Henry Mackay. CAGL, *tr. by* Hubert Kennedy

Tomorrow, and Tomorrow, and Tomorrow. William Shakespeare. SoSe-8 *Fr.* Macbeth.

To-morrow, and to-morrow, and to-morrow. William Shakespeare. WaAnP *Fr.* Macbeth.

Tomorrow autumn will come. Dead in a Bereft Horah. Yekhi'el Khazak. NRoS, *tr. by* Esther Raizen

Tomorrow I shall. Elaine Randell. Oth *Fr.* Songs for the Sleepless.

Tomorrow I shall wake to welcome him. (LL) Félix Lope de Vega Carpio. OxBSo; UpMys; WoPoe *Fr.* Lachrimae; or Seven Tears Figured in Seven Passionate Pavans.

Tomorrow Is Another Day. Gustave Kahn. ReLy

Tomorrow is saint valentine's day. William Shakespeare. NoSic *Fr.* Hamlet.

Tomorrow may be. Tomorrow. Langston Hughes. APSN

Tomorrow morning I will take a shower. Valerio Magrelli. NeIt

Tomorrow night. Untitled. Lauren Anita Arrington. BtF

To-morrow shall be my dancing day. *Unknown.* ChrPo *Fr.* My Dancing Day.

Tomorrow, since I have so few. Rooster. James Tate. WaAnP

Tomorrow the Past Comes. Ion Caraion. AF, *tr. by* Marguerite Dorian and Elliott B. Urdang

Tomorrow / they will clothe me in ashes at dawn. Shadow of Days to Come. Alejandra Pizarnik. TANSG, *tr. by* Susan Bassnett

Tomorrow those who hunger for my love will be satisfied. *Unknown.* SLW, *tr. by* Marjolijn De Jager, Sayd Bahodin Majrouh and André Velter

Tomorrow [*or* To morrow] to fresh woods, and pastures new. (LL) Lycidas. John Milton. AmFaPo; BASC; BrAP; CABP; ClHu; InoFa; MakPoe; NAEL-6v1; NAEL-7v1; NIL-7; NoP-4; NoP-5; NOSC; NPeEn; OBEV; OxAEP-1; OxBEV; PBRV; PoPoPo; TFi; WaAnP

Tomorrow, Tomorrow. Derek Walcott. PoetW

Tomorrow, tomorrow, we have tomorrow. Yun Sŏndo. CATKP *Fr.* Angler's Calendar, The.

Tomorrow / we are. Tomorrow. David Budbill. AmZen

Tomorrow, We'll Dance in America. James Harms. AmPoNex

Tomorrow, when the meadows grow. Victor Hugo. SxFrPo, *tr.* by A. M. and E. H. Blackmore

Tomorrow Will Be the Same Day. Abdellatif Laâbi. YaTCFP, *tr.* by Pierre Joris

Tomorrow will be Tuesday. Survival 2. Chiqui Vicioso. TANSG, *tr.* by Emma Jane Robinett

Tomorrow Will Really Be Sunday. Ron Schreiber. PrTe

Tomorrow you will live, you always cry. Procrastination. Martial. OBVE, *tr.* by Abraham Cowley

Tomorrow / you will walk toward other evenings. History. Heberto Padilla. AF, *tr.* by Alastair Reid

Tomorrows. James Merrill. AmWit

Tomorrow's Child. Rubin Alves. TWF

Tomorrow's Hope. Bob Lapierre. OGAHCP, *tr.* by Boadiba and Jack Hirschman

Tomorrows reactivate somnolence. Of Promises and Prophecy. Steve Chimombo. HBAPE

Tompkins Sq. Branches With Snowy Arms. Lewis Ellingham. AHA

Tompkins Square Park's a mess of shopping carts. Given in Person Only. Mark Wunderlich. WiU

Tom-Tom Talk. Suze Baron. OGAHCP, *tr.* by Boadiba and Jack Hirschman

Tonal Embryology. Folade Mondisa Speaks. BRtP

Tone Poem. Oliver Reynolds.
  Bestiary. TCAWP
  Eous. TCAWP

Tone, The. Judson Crews. ICANM

Tongue, The. Zbigniew Herbert. BeAl, *tr.* by Czeslaw Milosz

Tongue, call out. Rāmprasād Sen. SinGod, *tr.* by Rachel Fell McDermott

Tongue Graft Variations. Syliva Legris. *Fr.* Negative Garden.

Tongue in the mouth, A. Liliane Giraudon. SCFWP *Fr.* Poem with Incense Paper.

Tongue lashing. Tonguing. Greg S. Tate. ISC

Tongue mist lip boat brown gull hill town bed. Music at the Heart of Thinking 52. Fred Wah. OpeFie

Tongue of the waves tolled in the earth's bell, The. Want Bone, The. Robert Pinsky. ASA

Tongue shapes and molds sound. Speech, The. Not Sense. Gail Tremblay. WeW-3

Tongue that mothered such a metaphor, The. Hogwash. Robert Francis. NIL-7; NIP-4; TRP

Tongue Tied. Jaime Jacinto. ReBoTo

Tongue we all, bards Welsh, Ta! (LL) Cywydd o Fawl. Harri Webb. AngWePo; TCAWP

Tongue, what are you doing up there in space. Say. Beckian Fritz Goldberg. PfS

Tongueless man gets his land took, The. (LL) Tony Harrison. HarvBoo; NAEL-6v2; NAEL-7v2; RSaN *Fr.* School of Eloquence, The.

Tongues. Philip Martin. NOBAu

Tongues in My Mouth. Demetrice A. Worley. SpirFl

Tongue-tied in Black and White. Michael S. Harper. ESEAA

Tonguing. Greg S. Tate. ISC

Tonight, a beautiful redhead. Undertaker's Daughter Feels Neglect, The. Thylias Moss. ESEAA

Tonight a half-moon. O-mei Mountain Moon. Li Po. CrYelRi, *tr.* by Sam Hamill

Tonight a man with AIDS called. Grief. Ruth L. Schwartz. AmPoNex

Tonight, after a rain. Longing for Eternal Life, The. Liz Rosenberg. PBCAP

Tonight at *Antony and Cleopatra.* Between the Acts. Elise Paschen. IllVoic

Tonight at Eight. Sheldon Harnick. ReLy

Tonight, grave sir, both my poor[e] house and I. Inviting a Friend to Supper. Ben Jonson. BASC; BrAP; ItP; NAEL-6v1; NAEL-7v1; NoP-4; NoP-5; NOSC; NPeEn; PBRV; WaAnP

Tonight / he is understanding Canada. Understanding Canada. Peter Sirr. PBCIP

Tonight he's playing the Black Orchid. Black Orchid. David Jauss. SeSe

Tonight—I am alone in the night. Marina Ivanovna Tsvetayeva. AWTN *Fr.* Insomnia.

Tonight I buy my son a mountain bike. At the Crossroads. Mary Scott. ArBi

Tonight I Can Almost Hear the Singing. Silvia Curbelo. TouFir

Tonight I Can Write. Pablo Neruda. *See* Tonight I Can Write the Saddest Lines.

Tonight I Can Write the Saddest Lines. Pablo Neruda. PoetW; TCLAP, *tr.* by W. S. Merwin

  (Tonight I Can Write.) PtR

Tonight I curl my tongue around the uncertain. Uncertain Geometry. Rita D. Costello. BeDoSh

Tonight I do the bidding of a ghost. House by the Sea, The. Elizabeth Stoddard. SWaP

Tonight I have a date. Serenade for Two Poplars, A. Esther Raab. FIT, *tr.* by Robert Friend and Shimon Sandbank

Tonight I hunger so. Wave-Won. Emily Pauline Johnson. SWaP

Tonight I light the candles of my eyes in the lee. Rhyme for Halloween, A. Maurice Kilwein Guevara. TouFir

Tonight, I look, thunderstruck. Note on my Son's Face, A. Toi Derricotte. ISC

Tonight I resurrected from the dead. Turn and Turn About. Eva Gerlach. TuT, *tr.* by Eamon Grennan

Tonight I saw myself in the dark window as. Mirror Image. Louise Glück. StAl

Tonight I walk home through the park. Recovery. M. Wyrebek. AmPoNex

Tonight I want to say something wonderful. For the Sleepwalkers. Edward Hirsch. IllVoic; SUP

Tonight I watch my father's hair. Two Postures beside a Fire. James Wright. HeIP-4

Tonight / I will have to search. Scream! Nesta Wyn Jones. BBMWP, *tr.* by Robert Minhinnick

Tonight I wore my bright red suit. Love Poem to an Avocado from a Tomato. Yumi Thomas. FTtHH

Tonight I'll walk the razor along your throat. Punk Pantoum. Pamela Stewart. ReTh

Tonight I'm downhearted. Are You Lonesome Tonight? Roy Turk. ReLy

Tonight / In my neighborhood HEB where español is le langue. Dangereux avril. Teresa Palma Acosta. TiP2

Tonight in the cold I know most of the living are waiting. Elegy for the Nightbound. Anthony Cronin. PBCIP

Tonight I've watched. Sappho. AWTN, *tr.* by Mary Barnard

Tonight, leaning at the window. In the Steps of the Moon. Philippe Jaccottet. YaTCFP, *tr.* by Edward Lucie-Smith

Tonight, moon over Fu-chou. Moonlit Night. Tu Fu [*or* Du Fu]. ChinPo, *tr.* by Ye Weilian [*or* Yeh Wei-lien *or* Wai-lim Yip]

Tonight my brother, in heavy boots, is walking. This Hour and What Is Dead. Li-Young Lee. InoFa

Tonight my children hunch. It Out-Herods Herod. Pray You, Avoid It. Anthony Hecht. AF; NAMCP V.2; NIP-4; NoAM

Tonight of Yesterday. Vona Groarke. NIrP; StAl

Tonight, on holiday in Oxford, Bach's Magnificat. Magnificat! Michael S. Glaser. OPRER

Tonight our bodies lie unused like clothes flung. Aviation. Elaine Feinstein. MoWP

Tonight our cat, Tahi, who lately lost. Buried Stream, The. James Keir Baxter. HarvBoo

Tonight our heaven is an estuary. Pearls. Alan Gould. NOBAu

Tonight, Sally and I are making stuffed / grapeleaves. Leaves. Sam Hamod. UnSA

Tonight she is sitting by a window. Old Woman, The. Iain Crichton Smith. WoPoe

Tonight the lights went out. Melba Street. Deena November. IJHIL

Tonight the moon hovers in the sky. Modern English. Jeffery Conway. WiU

Tonight the moon's sunk into the city. Moon in the streets, The. Patrick Friesen. ACAMVP

Tonight / the nightmare was very condensed. Intermittent. Yousif al-Sa'igh. IrPoTo, *tr.* by Chuck Miller and Saadi A. Simawe

Tonight the Sky Is My Begging Bowl. Sina Queyras. IFF

Tonight the tenement smells of oysters. Ecstasy of St Saviour's Avenue, The. Neil Rollinson. EmeKit

To-night the very horses springing by. Winter Evening. Archibald Lampman. BrAP; NIL-7

Tonight the whooping moan of invading blues. Drying Spit Blues. Jayne Cortez. EGAG

Tonight the wind gnaws. Christmas Landscape. Laurie Lee. OBCP

Tonight the winds begin to rise. Alfred Tennyson. NAEL-6v2; NAEL-7v2; NAWM-7v2 *Fr.* In Memoriam A. H. H.

Tonight the workmen. Distance. David Wojahn. YaYoPo

Tonight there must be people who are getting what they want. September. Jennifer Michael Hecht. PLBUT

Tonight they need to be both host and stranger. Familiar Story. Alan Shapiro. NIP-4

Tonight, they tell me you died. Joe Williams at the Blue Note/Chicago, 1955; March 30 1999. Sam Hamod. FTtHH

Tonight they will shoot off fireworks. Factory Town on the 4th of July. Susan Jelus. RWB

Tonight ungathered let us leave. Alfred Tennyson. ChrPo; NAEL-6v2; NAEL-7v2 *Fr.* In Memoriam A. H. H.

Tonight / we are talking about dreams and science. Rain on Snow. Leigh Hancock. FiBr

Tonight, we make up our own legends. Beginning of Things, The. Fatima Lim-Wilson. ReBoTo

Tonight we talk about ammo. Ammo. Liz Ahl. LiTh

Tonight we wait for the alarm. Karen Alkalay-Gut. DTA *Fr.* Between Bombardments: A Journal.

Tonight, what sort of night.   Song of the Viet Boatman.   *Unknown.* ColAnChi, *tr.* by Anne Birrell

Tonight when I knelt down next to our cat, Zooey.   Wild Gratitude.   Edward Hirsch.   IllVoic; WaAnP

Tonight when the sea runs like a sore.   Voyage to Labrador.   GS

Tonight / while shampooing my hair.   Patricia Donegan.   WhBo

Tonight with Bold Desire.   Amelia Rosselli.   CItWP, *tr.* by Cinzia Sartini Blum and Lara Trubowitz

Tonight with wine being poured.   Jelaluddin Rumi.   RaBo *Fr.* Four Quatrains.

Tonight You Being From Me.   Aonghas MacNeacail.   EdScPo

Tonight you too / Are rushed.   Issa.   ZenPo, *tr.* by Takashi Ikemoto and Lucien Stryk

Tonight, you will not tire.   All-Night Diner, The.   Markham Johnson.   ReTh

Tonight's howler blinds.   Hating.   Kate Fetherston.   MAAN

Tonio told me at catechism.   Purpose of Altar Boys, The.   Alberto A. Ríos.   FTtHH

Tonite I walked out of my red apartment door on East tenth street's dusk.   Mugging.   Allen Ginsberg.   NAMCP V.2; NoAM

Tonite in need of you.   Morning Song and Evening Walk.   Sonia Sanchez.   InGu

Tonite, thriller was.   Beware: Do Not Read This Poem.   Ishmael Reed.   NIP-4 (Tonite, *thriller* was / abt an ol woman, so vain she.)   GT

Tonite, *thriller* was / abt an ol woman, so vain she.   Ishmael Reed.   *See* Tonite, thriller was.

Tontine.   Scott Hightower.   PA9/11

Tonto is dead, Tonto is dead, Tonto is dead.   Late Lamented Wind, Burned in Indignation, The.   Bob Kaufman.   EGAG

Tonton Macoutes Steal Dreams.   Bobby Medard.   OGAHCP, *tr.* by Boadiba and Jack Hirschman

Tony Went to the Bodega but He Didn't Buy Anything.   Martín Espada.   PueRic

Tony's father left the family.   Tony Went to the Bodega but He Didn't Buy Anything.   Martín Espada.   PueRic

Too Bad.   Gig Ryan.   NOBAu

Too Close for Comfort.   Jerry Bock, Larry Holofcener and George David Weiss.   ReLy

Too crossover, too, love. (LL)   Avalanche.   Quincy Troupe.   PFTM-2; SpirFl

Too. Darkly he rose, and then I slept. (LL)   True Account of Talking to the Sun at Fire Island, A.   Frank O'Hara.   AmFaPo; EmeKit; NAMCP V.2; OxBoAm

Too Darn Hot.   Cole Porter.   ReLy

Too far for you to see.   Welsh Hill Country, The.   Ronald Stuart Thomas.   AngWePo

Too far off, too faded: we do not see.   Wartime Photos of My Father.   David Wojahn.   MAAN

Too green the springing April grass.   Spring in New Hampshire.   Claude McKay.   ChAP

Too happy Time dissolves itself.   Emily Dickinson.   APN-2

Too heavy! (LL)   Guarded Wound, The.   Adelaide Crapsey.   APT-1; NAAPv.2

Too Heavy.   Julia Darling.   PoCu

Too immense for imagination, just big enough for boredom.   Wonderful Whale, The.   Eve Merriam.   YaYoPo

Too Late.   Scythinus.   WoPoe,

Too Late.   Tu Mu.   CCL1, *tr.* by H. A. Giles

Too late, alas! . . . I came to find.   Too Late.   Tu Mu.   CCL1, *tr.* by H. A. Giles

Too Late for a Husband.   *Unknown.*   WoPoe, *tr.* by Nguyen Ngoc Bich

Too late for love, too late for joy.   Christina Georgina Rossetti.   OBEV *Fr.* Prince's Progress, The.

Too lazy even to move a feather fan.   Summer Days in the Mountains.   Li Po.   CrYelRi, *tr.* by Sam Hamill

Too Lazy to Be Ambitious.   Ryokan.   IPoFL

Too little.   Door, The.   Charles Tomlinson.   OxBEV

Too Many Names.   Pablo Neruda.   VCWP, *tr.* by Alastair Reid

Too many nights.   Apology.   Elizabeth Spires.   FFC

Too Many Rings Around Rosie.   Irving Caesar.   ReLy

Too many speak of whip-poor-wills.   Against Whitman.   Ira Sadoff.   ViWalt

Too many summers out of the way of a trowel.   Lawn Roller, The.   Robert Layzer.   OBGa

Too Many Times.   Eman Mersaal.   AnVo, *tr.* by Mohamed Enani

Too many times I simply cannot think.   Skinny-Dipping the Ganges.   Ray McNiece.   AmZen

Too many waves to mark two more or three. (LL)   Old Woman.   Iain Crichton Smith.   EdScPo; HarvBoo; NePenScot; OxBEV

Too Marvelous for Words.   Johnny Mercer.   ReLy

Too Much Coffee.   Edwin Arlington Robinson.   MoAmPo

Too much have I been a mere man.   Self-Transformation.   Willem Kloos.   TuT, *tr.* by Desmond Egan

Too much history.   Town on the Ten Dollar Note, The.   Laurie Duggan.   BMAP

Too much of Europe, here transplanted o'er.   Joel Barlow.   APN-1 *Fr.* Columbiad, The.

Too Much to Ask.   Jien.   WoPoe, *tr.* by Howard S. Levy

Too much to ask.   Too Much to Ask.   Jien.   WoPoe, *tr.* by Howard S. Levy

Too nearly join'd to sickness, toils, and pains.   Philip Freneau.   TCAPo *Fr.* House of Night, The.

Too noble, Rick said.   Too Noble.   Daniel Hughes.   PoCho

Too often working, or caught in the pincer.   Fo'c'sle Dreams.   Joe Denham.   OpeFie

Too old for you as you for me. (LL)   To Chloe, Who Wished Herself Young Enough for Me.   William Cartwright.   NOSC; OxAEP-1

Too old to carry arms and fight like the others—.   Report from the Besieged City.   Zbigniew Herbert.   AF, *tr.* by John Carpenter and Bogdana Carpenter

Too prosaic, didactic.   I Can't Write a Poem about Class Rage.   Erin Belieu.   TAPaP

Too proud to sue! too tender to resign! (LL)   To Phaon ("Oh! I could toil for thee o'er burning plains.")   Mary Robinson.   CenSon; RWP

Too sad is the grief in my heart.   Elegy for His Daughter Ellen.   Goronwy Owen.   OBWVE, *tr.* by George Burrow

Too solemn for day, too sweet for night.   William Sidney Walker.   OBEV

Too soon. (LL)   Riding the "A."   May Swenson.   APT-2; GM; OxBoAm

Too soon, alas! too soon I plunged into the world with tone and clang.   Désillusion.   Lady Jane Francesca Wilde.   VWP

Too soon put up for the wind that blew it down.   City.   Michael Smith.   PBCIP

Too soon the mother states with jealous fear.   Joel Barlow.   AmWaPo *Fr.* Columbiad, The.

Too sound for waking and for dreams too deep. (LL)   Not for That City.   Charlotte Mew.   ChIV-2; HarvBoo; MoBrPo; VWP

Too talented to give a hot damn.   Dave Oliphant.   TiP2 *Fr.* Beaumont: Class Reunion.

Too tart the fruit it brought! (LL)   Shut Out That Moon.   Thomas Hardy.   NAMCP V.1; NoAM

Too tremulously fine! (LL)   Kiss, The: "Greatest bliss, The."   Charlotte Dacre.   CABP; NOBRP; WaAnP

Too volatile, am I? too voluble? too much a word-person?   Ghazal of the Better-Unbegun.   Heather McHugh.   ExTi; FaoP

Too weak am I to pray, as some have prayed.   Preparation.   William Johnson Cory.   OxBSo

Too young for congregating in the praying corner at church.   At Fifty.   Vivian Shipley.   ExTi

Too young to have known the meaning of sorrow.   Silent at Her Window.   Wang Ch'ang-ling.   ColAnChi; CrYelRi, *tr.* by Sam Hamill

Too Young to Know.   Cornelius Eady.   PfSP; WaAnP

Took / Two snowdrops to fall off the world.   Potter.   Michael O'Reilly.   BloBone

Too-Late Born, The.   Archibald MacLeish.   MoAmPo
(Silent Slain, The.)   BrAP

Tools.   Thomas Rain Crowe.   AmZen

Tools: An Ode.   Andrew Hudgins.   PML

Tools of my father's art: old radios.   On Air.   Gillian Clarke.   RWPCtW

Toome Road, The.   Seamus Heaney.   StAl

Tooms 4.   Donald Revell.   RoV

Toot, Toot, Tootsie! (Good-bye).   Gustave Kahn.   ReLy

Toothache.   Maxine Chernoff.   SUP

Toothpuller Who Wanted to Turn a Mouth into a Grinding Machine, The.   Francisco de Quevedo y Villegas.   WoPoe, *tr.* by Willis Barnstone

Too-well-done.   Nursery Song.   Anna Wickham.   NOxBChV

Top Hat, White Tie, and Tails.   Irving Berlin.   ReLy

Top of the World, The.   Yves Bonnefoy.   VCWP, *tr.* by John Naughton

Top Stories.   Brigitte Byrd.   LiTh

Top Ten of American Poetry.   Nanao Sakaki.   WhBo

Topeka . . . Junction City.   Poet at the Train Museum.   Linda Pastan.   GM

Tophet.   Thomas Gray.   ChIV-1

Topiary.   Maurice Riordan.   NIrP

Topiary Rooster.   Chase Twichell.   WANABP

Topics.   James Merrill.
Casual Wear.   BeAl; NIP-4

Toplight hammered down by shadowless noon.   Alfred Corn.   VCAP *Fr.* Call in the Midst of the Crowd, A.

Topografía.   Josué Ramírez.   RMCMP

Topography.   Sharon Olds.   GoPo; OxBoAm; WaAnP

Topography.   Maureen Owen.   PrTe

Topography.   Josué Ramírez.   RMCMP, *tr.* by Joan Lindgren

Topophilia.   Mary Ruefle.   BAP-97

Topos. Jane Miller. GifTon

Topple down[e] headlong. (LL) William Shakespeare. OxAEP-1; OxBEV *Fr.* King Lear.

Topple the house down, wind. Nocturne. Lizette Woodworth Reese. PoBW

Toppled wine-cup, A. Bits of Reminiscence. "Shu Ting." VCWP, *tr. by* Carolyn Kizer and Y. H. Zhao

Tops of the hibiscus trees, The. Pei Di and Wang Wei. CCL1 *Fr.* Wheel River.

Tops of the higher peaks, The. Blues. Kenneth Rexroth. NAMCP V.1

Tops were sign enough, The. Potato Blight. David Lindley. NLP

Topsell's Beasts. Julia Copus. MoWP

Toque de queda: Curfew in Lawrence. Martín Espada. PueRic

Tor House. William Everson. APT-2

Tor House. Robinson Jeffers. APT-1

Torah Braids. Tamara Kamenszain. MirDau, *tr. by* Roberta Gordenstein

Torch. Aleida Rodríguez. FaoP

Torch, The. Walt Whitman. SAmP

Torch I carry is handsome, The. Guess I'll Hang My Tears Out to Dry. Sammy Cahn. ReLy

Tore us down to the human. (LL) Blackbottom. Toi Derricotte. BtF; GT; LTA; OxAAAP; PBCAP

Torment by appetite. Reminder. Michael Ryan. PoCho

Torn. C. Dale Young. LegDan

Torn between griefs, which grief shall I lament. Sophocles. APT-1; OBVE *Fr.* Women of Trachis.

Torn by screaming steel. (LL) Winter Warfare. Edgell Rickword. FaBoWar; OBWP; PoWW

Torn feet and cursed earth. Buna. Primo Levi. AF, *tr. by* Ruth Feldman and Brian Swann

Torn from their grasp, and bleeding as they part. (LL) Hannah More. NoP-4; NoP-5 *Fr.* Slave Trade, The.

Torn hillside with its crooked hands, The. Description of Some Confederate Soldiers, A. Randall Jarrell. CBCWP

Torn Ones, The. John Wilkinson. VaPo

Tornados. Thylias Moss. GT; MakPoe

Torpor of trivial things. Summer in Slumville. Angel González. RaW, *tr. by* Herbert Baird and William Stafford

Torque. David Rivard. PBCAP

Torrent, The. Edwin Arlington Robinson. APN-2

Torrent of light and river of the air. Galaxy, The. Henry Wadsworth Longfellow. OxBSo

Torrismond. Thomas Lovell Beddoes.
    Song. NAEL-6v2

Torso, The / Passages 18. Robert Duncan. CAGL; HarvBoo; OxBoAm; PmAP

Torso, The. Robert Duncan. CAGL *Fr.* Passages.

Tortillas. Margie Norris. AFaM

Tortoise. Nina Gabrielian. CRWP, *tr. by* Peter France

Tortoise and Badger. Cheryl Clarke. FFC

Tortoise I see on a lotus-flower resting, A. Snapshot, A. Li Po. CCL1, *tr. by* H. A. Giles

Tortoise Shout. D. H. Lawrence. NAEL-6v2; NAEL-7v2; PFTM-1

Tortoise-Shell. D. H. Lawrence. FaBoVe; NAEL-6v2; NAEL-7v2; OxAEP-2

Torture. Paul Engle. PoA 2002 *Fr.* Images of China.

Torture Boy at the Easter Confest, Repentance Creek. Beckian Fritz Goldberg. MAAN

Torture Chamber. Enrique Lihn. PoetW; VCWP, *tr. by* Mary Crow

Torture chamber is not like anything, The. Footnote to the Amnesty Report on Torture. Margaret Atwood. NAMCP V.2; NoAM

Torture of the beloved is no punishment, The. Ahmed Dâi. OLP, *tr. by* Walter Andrews, Najaat Black and Mehmet Kalpakli

Torture, that we pray it may be mild. Beanstalk, Meditated Later, The. Judith Wright. NoAM

Tortured, The. May Sarton. FFC

Tortured body, lie at rest alone. Unknown Man in the Morgue. Merrill Moore. MoAmPo

6. Tortured by Kahlil Gibran. David McFadden. NLPA

Tortured mullet served the Roman's pride, The. On a Vase of Gold-Fish. Charles Tennyson Turner. NPeEn

Tory, a Puppy. Mortimer Collins. DiBP

Tory Pledges. Thomas Moore. OBSV

Toscanità. Dino Campana. MotU, *tr. by* Charles Wright

Toss not my soul, O Love, 'twixt hope and fear. *Unknown.* NoSic

Toss the bouquet. (LL) Atomic Bride. Thomas Sayers Ellis. BAP-97; IIR; LegDan; NeAmPo

Toss your gay heads. At April. Angelina Weld Grimké. GT

Tossed midst life's terrific storms. Song. Anne Batten Cristall. RWP

Tossed on the stormy waves of time. "I Was a Stranger and Ye Took Me In." Mary E. Tucker. CBWP-1

Tossed out of the dream. Blaga Dimitrova. CSCBP *Fr.* Forbidden Sea.

Tossing a crimson ball. Anacreon. SaLy, *tr. by* Diane Rayor

Tossing his mane of snows in wildest eddies and tangles. Earliest Spring. William Dean Howells. OBEV

To-ta Ti-om. Peter Blue Cloud. HATNAP

Total darkness / The light's off in the kitchen. Inna Kulishova. CRWP, *tr. by* Daniel Weissbort

Totalled. Peter McDonald. PNI

Totem. Eamon Grennan. ModIr

Totem. Léopold Sédar Senghor. PML; PoetW, *tr. by* Melvin Dixon

Totem Banking. Barry MacSweeney. VaPo

Totemic fuse of non-events is rising like a fume, The. Totem Banking. Barry MacSweeney. VaPo

Totems. Christine Ama Ata Aidoo. HAWP

T'other day, as Apollo sat pitching his darts. Feast of the Poets, The. Leigh Hunt.

Tou Wan Speaks to Her Husband Liu Sheng. Rita Dove. ESEAA

Toucan, The. Pyke, Jr. Johnson. NTCP

Touch. Eugene Gloria. ReBoTo

Touch. Thom Gunn. HarvBoo

Touch, A. Michael Longley. IrLP

Touch base with. Alex Rawls. AnSo *Fr.* What's Your Sign?

Touch,—for there is a Spirit in the woods. (LL) Nutting. William Wordsworth. NAEL-6v2; NAEL-7v2; NOBRP; WaAnP

Touch Him! Samuel Bamford. NOBRP

Touch It. Robert Mezey. CalPo; GeoHom

Touch me. Unconditionals #3. Viki Akiwumi. InTrad

Touch Me. Stanley Kunitz. APT-2; BeAl; CAP-8; NAMCP V.1; NoP-4; NoP-5; PoDa; StAl

Touch Me Not. Ann Townsend. LegDan

Touch me, touch me. Grass Fingers. Angelina Weld Grimké. APT-1; NAAPv.2

Touch of cold in the Autumn night, A. Autumn. Thomas Ernest Hulme. NPeEn

Touch of Your Lips, The. Ray Noble. ReLy

Touch *them* with gold, *they'll turn to what you please.* (LL) Epigram: "Midas, they say, possessed the art of old." "Peter Pindar." NIL-7; NIP-4

Touch to My Tongue. Daphne Marlatt. NLPA
    Climbing the canyon even as. NLPA
    Coming to you. NLPA
    Coming up from underground. NLPA
    Down the season's avenue. NLPA
    Eating. NLPA
    Healing. NLPA
    Hidden ground. NLPA
    Houseless. NLPA
    In the dark of the coast. BrAP; NLPA
    Kore. NLPA
    Prairie. NLPA
    This place full of contradiction. NLPA
    Where we went. NLPA
    Yes. NLPA

Touch was all. Memo. Leslie Ullman. YaYoPo

Touch Wood. Helen Foley. LW

Touch wood, be humble, never dare to say. Touch Wood. Helen Foley. LW

Touché. Jessie Redmond Fauset. NAAPv.2

Touched. Olga Broumas. GifTon

Touched. Elizabeth Dodd. AmPoNex

Touched with a Feeling of Our Infirmities. Cecil Frances Alexander. SacPr

Touches belonging to the ascent of the brother. Evening Walk, An. J. H. Prynne. PFTM-2

Touching and melting. / Nowhere. (LL) Night Dances, The. Sylvia Plath. AmFaPo; MoWP

Touching Each Other's Surfaces. Carol Jane Bangs. NIP-4

Touching Ezekiel his workman's hand. Jesus. James Philip McAuley. ChIV-2

Touching my face. Remembering Miller. Kay Smith. Coast

Touching the Edge: Dharma Devotions. Michael McClure.
    34. WANABP
    46. WANABP
    98. WANABP
    99. WANABP

Touching the River. Tom French. NIrP

Touching the tulips was a shyness. Tulips. Medbh McGuckian. PNI

Touching You Underwater. Stephen J. Lyons. PasH

Touching your goodness, I am like a man. Illiterate, The. William Meredith. EMP; NoP-4; NoP-5; OxBSo; PoA 2002; VCAP

Touchingly alike, old man, old dog. Difference, The. Elizabeth Delmore. NLP

Tougaloo Blues. Kelly Norman Ellis. SpirFl

Tough Guy of London, The. Kojo Gyinaye Kyei. EmeKit

Tough hair like dead. Vacant Lot. Yvor Winters. APT-2

Tough hand closes gently on the load, The. Man Carrying Bale. Harold Monro. MoBrPo

Tough / New. Saturday. Philip Whalen. WhBo

Toughest gal I ever did see. Kissie Lee. Margaret Abigail Walker. NALW; RaF

Toughness indoor people have, The. Birthday Card to My Mother. Philip Appleman. GoPo

Toujours. Guillaume Apollinaire. YaTCFP

Toujours la Politesse. Ezra Pound. OBVE

Toujours / Nous irons plus loins sans avancer jamais. Toujours. Guillaume Apollinaire. YaTCFP

Toujours pour la première fois. André Breton. YaTCFP

Tour de France. Michael Cantor. ArBi

Tour Guide: La Maison des Esclaves. Melvin Dixon. ESEAA; OxAAAP

Tour: "Near a shrine in Japan he'd swept the path." Carol Snow. P180

Touris, white man, wipin his face. Song of the Banana Man, The. Evan Jones. ItP

Tourism in the Late 20th Century. Silvia Curbelo. BodElec

Tourist, as he views the place, The. Taliesin Williams. AngWePo Fr. Cardiff Castle.

Tourist came in from Orbitville, A. Southbound on the Freeway. May Swenson. NTCP

Tourist Country. William Stafford. NoAM

Tourist dame, A. Miss Tourist. Lord Kitchener. PML

Tourist from Syracuse, The. Donald Justice. NAMCP V.2; NoAM; OxBoAm; VCAP

Tourist, spare the avid glance. Attic Landscape, The. Herman Melville. NCAP

Tourist Stricken at the Uffizi. Richard Outram. IFF

Tourist Weather. Silvia Curbelo. TouFir

Tourists. Sherman Alexie. NAMCP V.2

Tourists. Yehuda Amichai. PoSu, tr. by Glenda Abramson and Tudor Parfitt

Tourists. Howard Moss. NoP-4; NoP-5; OBCoV

Tourist's Unconcern, A: Paris, Dec. 1791. William Wordsworth. NPBRoP Fr. Prelude, The; Growth of a Poet's Mind [1805 version; Selections from Anthologies].

Tourists / Wonder. Edible World, The. David Bromige. FTOS

Tournament, The. Angelo Politziano. tr. by Guy Davenport
"Splendor and pride I celebrate." WoPoe, tr. by Guy Davenport

Tourniquet tight, spade vein rising, I must have done it. In the Park. Tom Sleigh. MAAN

Touro Synagogue. Ruth Whitman. TaR

Tours. Charles David Wright. AmAlph

Tous ces morts. Ombres 1. Habib Tengour. YaTCFP Fr. Au pays des morts.

Tous ces morts. Ombres 2. Habib Tengour. YaTCFP Fr. Au pays des morts.

Tous ces morts. Ombres 3. Habib Tengour. YaTCFP Fr. Au pays des morts.

Tous ces morts. Ombres 10. Habib Tengour. YaTCFP Fr. Au pays des morts.

Toussaint L'Ouverture. Henrietta Cordelia Ray. CBWP-3; SWaP

Toussaint, the most unhappy man of men! To Toussaint L'Ouverture. William Wordsworth. CenSon; NPBRoP

Tout les Matins du Monde. Peter Gizzi. VaPo

Toute douceur toute ironie se rassemblaient. À la voix de Kathleen Ferrier. Yves Bonnefoy. YaTCFP

Toute la ville est entrée dans ma chambre. Horizon. Philippe Soupault. YaTCFP

Toute vie qui doit poindre. Toute Vie. René Char. YaTCFP

Toutes les choses de la terre. Anne Perrier. YaTCFP

Toutes les haleines (me mentais-je). Toutes les haleines. Claire Malroux. YaTCFP

Tovu-Vavohu. Manuela Fingueret. MirDau, tr. by Roberta Gordenstein

Tow Head on his skateboard. Skateboard. Thom Gunn. MoASP

Toward a different shore. (LL) Claiming the Dust. Jean Janzen. ACAMVP; GeoHom

Toward a mist upon the water. On Seeing Wang Leave for the South. Liu Ch'ang-ch'ing. CCL1, tr. by Witter Bynner

Toward a Personal Semantics. June Jordan. EGAG

Toward a Portrait of the Undocumented. Javier Omar Huerta. RWB

Toward an Organic Philosophy. Kenneth Rexroth.
Spring, Coast Range. APT-2

Toward Arcturus—and returning as suddenly. (LL) Mind Is an Ancient and Famous Capital, The. Delmore Schwartz. APT-2; NAMCP V.2; NoAM

Toward calm and shady places. Frances Densmore. APT-1 Fr. Chippewa Music.

Toward Ch'ang-an. Tune: "Merriment Before the Palace Hall." Chang K'o-chiu. ChinPo, tr. by Ye Weilian [or Yeh Wei-lien or Wai-lim Yip]

Toward dusk. There's Such an Evening. Na Hûidôk. EcSo, tr. by Peter H. Lee

Toward evening it ends. Day's overtures. Rain Near Heart Lake. Reg Saner. PoCoUp

Toward evening on East Hill gazing. View of the Wilds. Wang Ji. CCL1, tr. by Stephen Owen

Toward Guinea: For Larry Neal, 1937–1981. Houston A., Jr. Baker. ISC

Toward Mena. David Thomas Roberts. AnSo

Toward morning around seven. Irina Ermakova. CRWP, tr. by Daniel Weissbort

Toward Myself. Leah Goldberg. FIT, tr. by Robert Friend

Toward sunset, at a great height. (LL) Heart of Autumn. Robert Penn Warren. APT-2; ColAP; FuPo; InGu; WaAnP

Toward that same church, which he forgot. (LL) Sometimes a Man Stands Up During Supper. Rainer Maria Rilke. BBASP; RaBo; WED, tr. by Robert Bly

Toward the city's bright towers. (LL) It Was Fever That Made the World. Jim Powell. NIP-4; SwNoth

Toward the Corner. Laura Riding Jackson. NOxBChV

Toward the end of her life she said that the. Berthe Morisot. Anne Waldman. PmAP

Toward the end of May, the air in southern Ohio is filling with fragrances. Sumac in Ohio, The. James Wright. MotU

Toward the Jurassic Age. Claribel Alegría. TCLAP, tr. by Carolyn Forché

Toward the laughter we no longer. To Mother. Keorapetse Kgositsile. GT

Toward the person who has died. Dying Away. William Meredith. NAMCP V.2; NoAM

Toward the substation in the testing wind. Geoffrey Nutter. BAP-97 Fr. Summer Evening, A.

Toward Toba Palace. Buson. EMJL, tr. by Haruo Shirane

Toward what force on the beach. Coastal. Valerie Martínez. AmPoNex

Toward which all hungers leap, all pleasures pass. (LL) Baroque Wall-Fountain in the Villa Sciarra, A. Richard Wilbur. ColAP; GS; NoP-4; NoP-5; OBGA; OxBoAm; VCAP

Toward which you lend no part! (LL) El Hombre. William Carlos Williams. NAAPv.2; SAmP; StAl

Toward Winter. Unknown. WoPoe, tr. by Thomas Kinsella

Toward world's end, through the bare. Magi, The. Louise Glück. GI; HarvBoo; PoA 2002

Towards a Beginning. Silvio Giussani. ItPo, tr. by Gayle Ridinger

Towards a New Resolve. Pak Inhwan. CAMKP, tr. by Scott Swaner

Towards Abraham's Bosom. Amelia Blossom Pegram. HAWP

Towards Curing AIDS. Rafael Campo. BloBone; NeAmPo

Towards dawn / taxis / idle, The. Girandole. Gustaf Sobin. APSN

Towards Democracy. Edward Carpenter.
Summer Heat. CAGL
Through the Long Night. CAGL
To a Stranger. CAGL

Towards evening time. Conductor, The. Dezső Kosztolányi. IQMS, tr. by Leslie A. Kery

Towards Lillers. Ivor Gurney. NAEL-6v2; NoP-4

Towards Springtime. Ágnes Nemes Nagy. IQMS, tr. by Ila Egon

Towards Sunset at Camino Cielo. Maurina Sherman. GeoHom

Towards that we gravitate. (LL) Homage to Issac Newton. János Pilinszky. IQMS; StAl, tr. by Peter Jay

Towards the Land of the Composer. Francis Webb. BMAP

Towards the Last Spike. Edwin John Pratt.
"Road itself was like a stream that men, The." BrAP

Towards the Mind. Milo De Angelis. ItPo, tr. by Gayle Ridinger

Towards the New Millennium. Zoltán Jékely. IQMS, tr. by George Szirtes

Towards the songs' pretended sea. (LL) Legacy. Imamu Amiri Baraka. ColAP; NAMCP V.2; NoAM

Towards the Vanishing Point. David Lehman. PmAP

Towards thy bright beams I turn my swimming eyes. Charlotte Smith. RWP

Towards your hand. Dandelion. Frigyes Karinthy. IQMS, tr. by Peter Zollman

Towboat is freckled with rust. What's it doing here so far / inland?, The. Sketch in October. Tomas Tranströmer. VCWP, tr. by Robin Fulton

Tower. David Biespiel. NAPBL

Tower, The. William Butler Yeats. NAMCP V.1; NoAM

Tower by the Yangtze River, A. Tu Mu. CCL1, tr. by R. F. Burton

Tower, no ivy, I. The wind was powerless, A. Hecuba's Testament. Rosario Castellanos. STV, tr. by John Frederick Nims

Tower of Babel, The.   Guillaume de Salluste Du Bartas.   NoSic *Fr.* Divine Weeks and Works, The.

Tower of Babel, The.   Laurance Wieder.   ChIV-1

Towering Alps, the haughty Appenine, The.   Philip Freneau.   TCAPo *Fr.* House of Night, The.

Towering is that southern mountain.   *Unknown.*   ColAnChi *Fr.* Classic of Odes.

Towering rocks rending the sky asunder.   Wandering Round Mount Taiping.   K'ung Chih-kuei.   CCL1, *tr.* by John Frodsham

Towers, The.   José María Eguren.   TCLAP, *tr.* by Iver Lofving

Towery city and branchy between towers.   Duns Scotus's Oxford.   Gerard Manley Hopkins.   CABP; NAEL-6v2; NAEL-7v2; NoAM; OBMV; OxAEP-2

Town.   Marie-Claire Bancquart.   MFP, *tr.* by Martin Sorrell

Town a Bird Sanctuary, The.   Jan Eijkelboom.   TuT, *tr.* by Peter van de Kamp

Town, a town.   George Oppen.   APT-2; PFTM-1

Town again, trailing your legs and crying!, The. (LL)   Wild Swans.   Edna St. Vincent Millay.   HarvBoo; MoAmPo; MoWP; OWoS

Town and Country.   Arthur Waugh.   ArBi

Town believes thee lost, and didst thou see, The.   Henry Vaughan.   PBRV *Fr.* To his retired friend, an Invitation to Brecknock.

Town, / branches over the river.   Kaunas 1941.   Johannes Bobrowski.   AF

Town Clerk, The.   Mark DeCarteret.   AmPoNex

Town does not exist, The.   Starry Night, The.   Anne Sexton.   ColAP; NAAL-5; NAMCP V.2; NoAM; VCAP

Town Dump, The.   Howard Nemerov.   NIL-7; WaAnP

Town Eclogue, A.   "Peter Pindar."   OBCoV *Fr.* Bozzy and Piozzi.

Town Garden, A.   Tony Lucas.   OBGa

Town hall squatting / on its elephant legs, / come again. (LL)   Freedom Fighter.   Antigone Kefala.   BMAP; ItWoWo

Town has opened to the sun, The.   Bombardment.   D. H. Lawrence.   FaBoWar

Town History, 1917.   David Huddle.   PBCAP

Town I was born in was destroyed by shells, The.   Yehuda Amichai.   PoSu *Fr.* Patriotic Songs.

Town in which my capacity for thought is, The.   O Magdalen!   Oskar Pastior.   OnScMo, *tr.* by Christopher Middleton

Town is old and very steep, The.   Ken.   Charlotte Mew.   VWP

Town is still, The.   Bombing.   Paul Rodenko.   TuT, *tr.* by Mary E. O'Donnell

Town is tilted toward the stream, The.   Sunday Dreamer's Guide to Yarrow, Missouri, A.   Jim Barnes.   HATNAP

Town less, A.   Sherley Anne Williams.   GeoHom *Fr.* Iconography of Childhood, The.

Town lies in the Valley, A.   Quiet Town, The.   Richard Dehmel.   GTCP, *tr.* by Reinhold Grimm

Town Meeting.   Gary Margolis.   RWB

Town of Finding Out About the Love of God.   Anne Carson.   PLBUT *Fr.* Life of Towns, The.

Town on the Ten Dollar Note, The.   Laurie Duggan.   BMAP

Town or poem, I don't care how it looks. Old woman.   White Center.   Richard Hugo.   NAMCP V.2

Town the wealthy come to, not overly, The.   Jeffers Country.   Sherod Santos.   GeoHom

Town visitor's easy talk flows in an endless stream, The.   To a Talkative Guest.   Po Chü-i.   CCL1, *tr.* by Arthur Waley

Town was proud of the town's gardens, The.   Flowers.   Dennis Joseph Enright.   OBGa

Town wasn't much, The.   Jungle Warfare.   Jack Spicer.   APSN

Town where I was born is surrounded by hills, The.   Town Where I Was Born, The.   John Barnie.   TCAWP

Town where I was born, Radautz, in the county of Bukovina, The.   Souvenir, The.   Dan Pagis.   MotU, *tr.* by Stephen Mitchell

Town Where I Was Born, The.   John Barnie.   TCAWP

Town without a Market, The.   James Elroy Flecker.   MoBrPo

Town-Meeting, A.M., The.   John Trumbull.   TCAPo *Fr.* M'Fingal.

Town's aflame with summer heat, The.   Tokuo.   ZenPo, *tr.* by Takashi Ikemoto and Lucien Stryk

Towns in Colour.   Amy Lowell.
    Thompson's Lunch Room—Grand Central Station.   APT-1

Toxicity.   Erin Mouré.   BeAl

Toy, The / become the aesthetic archetype.   Brancusi's Golden Bird.   Mina Loy.   APT-1; HarvBoo; MoWP; NAAPv.2; NAMCP V.1

Toye-Voye.   Esther Shumyatsher.   Prolet, *tr.* by Amelia Glaser

Toyland.   Roy Fisher.   HarvBoo; NPeEn

Toy-maker made a toy wife and a toy child. He made a toy house and some toy years, A.   Toy-Maker, The.   Russell Edson.   PmAP

Toy-Maker, The.   Russell Edson.   PmAP

Toys.   Gemino H. Abad.   ReBoTo

Toys.   Carl Phillips.   CAP-8; ReTh

Toys, The.   Coventry Patmore.   OBEV; OxAEP-2; SoSe-8 *Fr.* Unknown Eros, The.

Toys and rose The zoo body zigzags.   How Spring Comes.   Alice Notley.   PmAP

Toys I had, soldiers of lead and a sword of tin.   Tropical Childhood.   Salomon De la Selva.   NAAPv.2

Toys in a Field.   Yusef Komunyakaa.   FaoP

Toys Talk of the World, The.   Katharine Pyle.   NOxBChV

Tŷ'r Ysgol.   T. H. Parry-Williams.   BBMWP, *tr.* by Joseph P. Clancy

Trace, In Unison.   Tess Gallagher.   ExTi

Trace of shadow veils the light of the sun, A.   Emotion.   Ts'ao Chih.   CCL1, *tr.* by John Frodsham

Traceless, no more need to hide.   Suian.   ZenPo, *tr.* by Takashi Ikemoto and Lucien Stryk

Traces.   Beau Beausoleil.   Eno

Traces a letter.   Ana Belén López Pulido.   SPV, *tr.* by Jen Hofer

Traces/Renown/Shades/Urns/Life(s)/Epoch/Zenith.   Habib Tengour.   PFTM-2 *Fr.* Empedocles' Sandal.

Traces. Then things themselves are not names.   Notes About My Face.   Michael Burkard.   BAP-01

Tracing of an Evening.   David Shapiro.   PmAP

Track.   Tomas Tranströmer.   GPTC; WED, *tr.* by Robert Bly
    (Tracks.)   BLT

Track was hot, the lanes were hard and black, The.   Elegy for the Hurdler.   Randall Mann.   BeDoSh

Tracking the Siuslaw Man.   Jim Barnes.   HATNAP

Tracks.   Tomas Tranströmer. *See* Track.

Tracks.   Tomas Tranströmer.   StAl, *tr.* by Robin Fulton

Tracks of Longing.   Sion Aled.   BBMWP, *tr.* by Grahame Davies

Tracks of rain and light linger in.   Romance Moderne.   William Carlos Williams.   APT-1

Tract.   William Carlos Williams.   InoFa; MoAmPo; NAAPv.2; NAMCP V.1; NoAM; SAmP

Tract houses.   Piece of the Loot, A.   Wang the Zealot.   CCL1, *tr.* by C. H. Kwock and Vincent McHugh

Tractatus.   Derek Mahon.   ModIr

Tractor.   Ted Hughes.   OxAEP-2

Tractor stands frozen—an agony, The.   Tractor.   Ted Hughes.   OxAEP-2

Tractor, The.   Isfoel.   BBMWP, *tr.* by Joseph P. Clancy

Tractor-trailer carrying two dozen crushed automobiles overtakes a tractor-trailer carrying a dozen new, A.   Sheffield Ghazal 4: Driving West.   Galway Kinnell.   NAMCP V.2

Tracy and Joe.   Lisa Lewis.   SUP

Trade Show.   Miles A. Coon.   NevBe

Trade Winds.   John Masefield.   OBMV

Trader I am to the African shore, A.   Sweet Meat Has Sour Sauce.   William Cowper.   OBSV

Tradition.   William Wordsworth.   CenSon *Fr.* River Duddon [A Series of Sonnets], The.

Tradition, The.   Assata Shakur.   BRtP

Tradition/Abstraction.   Mendi Lewis Obadike.   RD

Tradition and Change.   Nora Naranjo-Morse.   ReTh

Tradition of Oker Hill in Darley Dale, Derbyshire, A.   William Wordsworth.   OxBSo

Traditional.   Traditional Post-Modern Neo-HooDoo Afra-Centric Sister in a Purple Head Rag Mourning Death and Cooking.   Michelle T. Clinton.   SpirFl

Traditional Post-Modern Neo-HooDoo Afra-Centric Sister in a Purple Head Rag Mourning Death and Cooking.   Michelle T. Clinton.   SpirFl

Traditional Tune.   Muriel Rukeyser.   TaR

Traffic interlude: Descent from the Tower.   Douglas Livingstone.   TSAP

Traffic jamming at.   New York City.   Michael Castro.   UrbNat

Traffic Misdirector.   Pedro Juan Pietri.   PueRic

Traffic was heavy coming off the bridge.   History of My Stupidity, The: Volume 3, Chapter 5.   Edward Hirsch.   RoV

Traffic's been worse than ever this year, The.   Flyover Elegies.   Gwyneth Lewis.   MFPA

Tragedy.   George Russell.   MoBrPo

Tragedy, A.   Théophile Julius Henry Marzials.   VerBaPo

Tragedy, Colette said, is that one, The.   After 65.   Richard Howard.   BAP-01; OxBoAm

Tragedy of Dido, The.   Christopher Marlowe.
    "What is't, sweet wag, I should deny thy youth?"   CAGL

Tragedy of Ida Ball Warren and Samuel Christie, The.   I. J. Brittain.
    "There was a woman lived in Winston-Salem."   VerBaPo

Tragedy of Man. Imre Madách. *tr.* by Iain MacLeod
  "Adam, I think I'm going to be a mother." IQMS, *tr.* by Iain MacLeod
  "And you, Lucifer, standing there aloof." IQMS, *tr.* by Iain MacLeod
  "Be strong, brother!" IQMS, *tr.* by Iain MacLeod
  "I'm tired of these grim wastes of snow and ice." IQMS, *tr.* by Iain MacLeod
  "It's hard to say, John, but I need some money." IQMS, *tr.* by Iain MacLeod
  "It's kind of you to let me come alone." IQMS, *tr.* by Iain MacLeod
  "Let them be! Get out!" IQMS, *tr.* by Iain MacLeod
  "Now, this is it, the toilsome journey's end." IQMS, *tr.* by Iain MacLeod
  "Tell us, Professor." IQMS, *tr.* by Iain MacLeod
  "There are a few things yet you haven't heard of." IQMS, *tr.* by Iain MacLeod
  "There's no excitement, news or anything." IQMS, *tr.* by Iain MacLeod
  "These are dissenters." IQMS, *tr.* by Iain MacLeod
  "This reckless flight, where is this bound to take us?" IQMS, *tr.* by Iain MacLeod
  "Very ground dissolves beneath my feet, The." IQMS, *tr.* by Iain MacLeod
  "You see the fellow with the scarlet sash?" IQMS, *tr.* by Iain MacLeod
Tragedy of the leaves, The. Charles Bukowski. CalPo; SUP
Tragedy of Valentinian, The. John Fletcher.
  God Lyaeus, Ever Young. OBEV
  Hear, Ye Ladies [That Despise]. OBEV
  (Love's Emblems.) NOSC
  (Sleep Song.) NOSC
Tragedy. Reconsidered. Carla Harryman. BAP-04 *Fr.* Baby.
Tragic Hero. Eleanor Brown. MFPA
Tragic Love. Walter James Turner. OBMV
Tragic Mary Queen of Scots, The. Michael Field. LW; OBMV
Tragic Mary Queen of Scots, II, The. Michael Field. OBMV
Tragic Mulatto is Neither, The. Michael C. Ladd. BRtP
Tragicall Epigram, A. Sir John Harington. PBRV
Trahison fidèle. Victor Segalen. YaTCFP
Tràighean. Sorley MacLean. EdScPo
Trail All Your Pikes. Anne Finch, Countess of Winchilsea. OPOU
  (Soldier's Death, The.) PoAgWa
Trail Breakers. James Henry Daugherty.
  "Pack train, stage coach, pony express, climb over the mountain passes." HHAm
Trail, The. Myra Stillborn. ArBi
Trail the edge of your robe wherever it pleases, and add more drunkenness to your intoxication. Ibn Bājja. HiArP, *tr.* by James T. Monroe
Trail you down the hall—issue. Disembodied Voices of Women, The. Craig Arnold. NAPBL
Trailer parks, projects, Circle K parking lots. Happy As I Am. Steve Orlen. LiTh
Trailer Trash. Alison Pelegrin. RWB
Trailing a wake of heady odors, what slim. Horace. WoPoe *Fr.* Odes.
Trailing her father, bearing his hand axe. Goose. Richard Emil Braun. NoAM
Trailing pen draws out a seismograph, The. Cryptogram, The. David Lindley. NLP
Trails. Patrick Williams. PNI
Trails of it like trout-streaks skid. Morning Light at Wanship, Utah. Dave Jeddie Smith. BodElec
Trails that wander and writhe and bend. Texas Trails. Norman H. Crowell. TiP2
Train. Georgi Belev. CSCBP, *tr.* by the author and Lisa Sapinkopf
Train. Donald Justice. GM
Train. Jennifer Snyder. BodElec
Train Dogs, The. Emily Pauline Johnson. IFF
Train has just come to a stop, The. South. Blaise Cendrars. BLT, *tr.* by Monique Chefdor
Train in the Desert—1916. Christopher Buckley. GM
Train is A-Comin'. *Unknown.* CA
Train is a-comin', oh yes. Train is A-Comin'. *Unknown.* CA
Train is right on time, The. From the Provinces. Ben Scammell. NLP
Train Journey. Judith Wright. NoP-4; NoP-5
Train Leaving. Hô Sugyông. EcSo, *tr.* by Youngju Ryu
Train moves through the Guadarrama, The. Rainbow at Night. Antonio Machado Ruiz. AF; BLT; WED, *tr.* by Robert Bly
Train passes by and night flowers fall, A. Train Leaving. Hô Sugyông. EcSo, *tr.* by Youngju Ryu
Train passing in the night, slightly shaking the structure, The. Peter Riley. VaPo *Fr.* Excavations.
Train Phone Sext. Clive Holden. PoPra
Train Ride. Ruth Stone. OxBoAm

Train Ride. John Wheelwright. OxBoAm
Train Rides. Nikki Giovanni. InGu
Train Rising Out of the Sea. John Ashbery. ColAP
Train scarcely slackens speed, The. Hans Faverey. WoBe *Fr.* Eighteen Poems.
Train she rides is sixteen coaches long. David Wojahn. GM; PBCAP *Fr.* Mystery Train: A Sequence.
Train shot through the dark, The. Return. Seamus Deane. PBCIP; PNI
Train sneaks through farm country, The. Example, An. M. Wyrebek. AmPoNex
Train Station Zoetrope. Geoffrey Nutter. IAoNAP
Train Stops at Healy Fork, The. John Haines. BLT
Train tears along, I'm on my way, The. Lapiade, Opus 3. Ödön Palasovszky. IQMS, *tr.* by Kenneth McRobbie
Train that carried me there was a chip, The. Chip City. Linda France. MFPA
Train, The! The twelve o'clock for paradise. Harold Monro. MoBrPo *Fr.* Week-End.
Train Tune. Louise Bogan. GM
Train was going downwards very slowly, The. Dream, A. Evan Jones. NOBAu
Train whistles punctual as a clock, The. English-Speaking Persons Will Find Translations. Michael S. Glaser. UnSA
Train Wreck, 1890: My Grandmother Lies Down with the Dead. T. R. Hummer. GM
Trained tenderly by Heaven and Earth. Contrast, A. Menella Bute Smedley. VWP
Training Horses. Jack Myers. MAAN
Training on the Peninsula. Brian Turner. ArBi
Trainor, the Druggist. Edgar Lee Masters. APT-1; IllVoic *Fr.* Spoon River Anthology.
Trains. William Scammell. NLP
Trains, The. Sarina Helfgott. MirDau, *tr.* by Celeste Kostopulos-Cooperman
Trains are stopp'd, the Mighty Chiefs of Flame, The. Thomas Baker. STuOW *Fr.* Steam Engine; or, The Power of the Flame, The.
Trains go towards the fast bridge where in the darkness the. Towards a Beginning. Silvio Giussani. ItPo, *tr.* by Gayle Ridinger
Train's going to that town, The. Going out of Town. N. Revathi Devi. HotL, *tr.* by V. Narayana Rao
Trains!, The, Trains hugged by the tunnels, The. Invitation to a Voyage. Max Jacob. CuPo
Trainwrecked Soldiers. John Frederick Nims. GM
Traitor. Allison Joseph. IllVoic; SUP
Traitor. Pat Stodghill. TiP2
Traitor's skull, we shall drink out of it, The. To a Traitor. *Unknown.* WoPoe, *tr.* by Willard Trask
Trajeron las lluvias otra vida. Monzón. Elsa Cross. RMCMP
Trakl. Johannes Bobrowski. GTCP, *tr.* by Michael Hamburger
Trakl. Norman Dubie. BodElec
Tram bore along, my eyes, The. Marked Ones, The. Gyula Illyés. IQMS, *tr.* by John Brander and John Wilkinson
Trame, La. Pierre Reverdy. YaTCFP
Tramp. Frank Mkalawile Chipasula. HBAPE
Tramp. Richard Hughes. MoBrPo
Trampling. Miguel Algarin. PueRic
Trampwoman's Tragedy, A. Thomas Hardy. NAEL-6v2; NAEL-7v2; OBNV
Trams. Dame Edith Sitwell. NOxBChV
Tramstop swarms with schooligans, their brand, A. Election Eve, with Cat. Alex Skovron. BMAP
Tramway climbs from Merthyr to Dowlais, The. Deluge 1939, The. Saunders Lewis. OBWVE, *tr.* by Gwyn Morgan
Trance. "H. D." APT-1
Trance Event. Robert Desnos. PFTM-1
Tranced creature: no rhyme or ringing words. Gazelle, The. Rainer Maria Rilke. PoCho, *tr.* by Robin Robertson
Tranches de savoir. Henri Michaux.
  "Si votre enfant a une trompe sur le nez, ne soyez pas effrayé par les éléphants." YaTCFP
Trane. Edward Kamau Brathwaite. NAMCP V.2
Trane. / Trane. / History Love Scream Oh. Am/Trak. Imamu Amiri Baraka. PmAP
Trang Tu's legendary wife is very much the modern woman. Woman's Heart, A. *Vietnamese Oral Tradition.* CaDao, *tr.* by John Balaban
Tranquil Miracle, The. Lőrinc Szabó. IQMS *Fr.* Cricket Music.
Tranquil Night. Luís De León. SpanPo, *tr.* by Edwin Morgan
Tranquil Repose. Sikong Tu. CCL1 *Fr.* Twenty-Four Modes of Poetry.
Tranquil surface where a spinnaker moves, A. Seaside Cemetery, The. Paul Valéry. YaTCFP, *tr.* by Derek Mahon
Trans Canada. Francis Reginald Scott. BrAP
Transcanadian. Robert Hedin. GifTon

Transcendent beauty molders midst the earth! Elegy on a Young Lady. Anne Batten Cristall. RWP

Transcendental, The. Sikong Tu. CCL1 *Fr.* Twenty-Four Modes of Poetry.

Transcircularities. Quincy Troupe. PrTe

Transcription of Organ Music. Allen Ginsberg. ItP

Transfer. Ingrid de Kok. TSAP

Transfer of Title. María Rivera. SPV, *tr. by* Jen Hofer

Transfiguration. Ralph Chubb. CAGL

Transfiguration. Jack Hirschman. CLPP

Transfiguration. John Wright. BloBone

Transfiguration of the Rain. Jorge Carrera Andrade. TCLAP, *tr. by* Michael Surman

Transfiguration, The. Edwin Muir. ChIV-2

Transformable Prophecy. Angela Jackson. IllVoic

Transformation. Jeni Couzyn. HAWP

Transformation. Günter Grass. GTCP, *tr. by* Irmgard Hunt

Transformation. Adria Klinger. PasH

Transformation and Escape. Gregory Corso. PFTM-2

Transformation Text on Mahāmaudgalyāyana Rescuing His Mother from the Underworld. *Chinese Oral Tradition.* ColAnChi, *tr. by* Victor H. Mair

Transformation Text on the Boy Shun's Extreme Filial Piety. *Chinese Oral Tradition.* ColAnChi, *tr. by* Richard W. Bodman

Transformations. Thomas Hardy. BrAP; TRP

Transformations. Joy Harjo. HATNAP

Transformations. Tadeusz Rózewicz. ChAP, *tr. by* Czeslaw Milosz

Transformations. Jack Spicer. FTOS

Transformations of Aisha: Aisha's Birth and Death in the Magical Rituals Inscribed in Cuneiform on the Nineveh Tablets. Abdul Wahab Al-Bayati. IrPoTo, *tr. by* Farouk Abdel Wahab

Transformations of Livy. Zbigniew Herbert. PoetW, *tr. by* Bogdana Carpenter and John Carpenter

Transgressing the Real. Robert Duncan. APSN *Fr.* Passages.

Transhumant stars; and the shepherd bending. Book, for Growing Old, The. Yves Bonnefoy. YaTCFP, *tr. by* Richard Pevear

Transient Barracks (1944). Randall Jarrell. PWW2

Transient Hotel Sky at the Hour of Sleep. Martín Espada. ReTh

Transient Servitude. Haroldo de Campos. *tr. by* Edwin Morgan "De sol a sol." PFTM-2, *tr. by* Edwin Morgan

Transit. Prageeta Sharma. HeMarv

Transit. Richard Wilbur. NIL-7

Transition #2. Sabah As-Sabah. InTrad

Transits. Sharan Strange. InTrad

Translated from the American. Sherman Alexie. UnSA

Translated from the European. Anna Gorenko. CRWP, *tr. by* Peter France

Translated from the German or the Bosnian. Max Jacob. GPTC, *tr. by* John Ashbery

Translating Birdsong. Jean Sprackland. MoWP

Translation. Gillian Clarke. MoWP

Translation. Matthea Harvey. IAoNAP

Translation. Rika Lesser. KGB; PoA 2002

Translation. Nicholas Samaras. YaYoPo

Translation from Walter von der Vogelweide, A. Walther von der Vogelweide. MoBrPo, *tr. by* John Millington Synge

Translation of Lines by Benserade. Isaac de Benserade. WoPoe, *tr. by* Samuel Johnson

Translation of "Pax Bello Potior." *Unknown.* NOBRP, *tr. by Unknown*

Translation of Raimundo Luz, The: My Amusing Despair. Scott Cairns. UpMys

Translation of Raimundo Luz, The: My Farewell. Scott Cairns. UpMys

Translation of Raimundo Luz, The: My Good Luck. Scott Cairns. UpMys

Translation of Raimundo Luz, The: My Imitation. Scott Cairns. UpMys

Translation of Raimundo Luz, The: My Incredulity. Scott Cairns. UpMys

Translation of the Psalms of David, A. Bible, *O.T. tr. by* Christopher Smart Psalm 58. NoP-4; NoP-5, *tr. by* Christopher Smart Psalm 114. NoP-5, *tr. by* Christopher Smart

Translations. Adrienne Rich. OxBoAm

Translations from Martial. Robert Louis Stevenson. OBGa

Translator tried to lay bare, The. Lesson in Translation, A. Gabriel Preil. FIT, *tr. by* Robert Friend

Transmigration. Bruce Berger. GeoH

Transmutation. Julia de Burgos. TANSG, *tr. by* Heather Rosario Sievert

Transmutation ("Boy is amazed to see his father home from work in the afternoon with a bandaged finger, A.") Gael Turnbull. BeAl

Transmutation ("Every evening a mother makes up another episode of the same story for her son.") Gael Turnbull. BeAl

Transmutation ("It was as if she couldn't know herself. Only other persons could do that.") Gael Turnbull. BeAl

Transmutation ("Taken severely ill, he is conscious only at brief intervals.") Gael Turnbull. BeAl

Transom Over Death's Door, A. Jennifer Moxley. VaPo

Transparencies. Bruce Bond. Vesp

Transparent. Ronny Someck. Eno; IrPoTo, *tr. by* Vivian Eden

Transparent Life, The. Luigi Fontanella. NeIt, *tr. by* W. S. Di Piero

Transparent Man, The. Bernard Bador. ConPit, *tr. by* Clayton Eshleman

Transparent Woman. Donna Henderson. FiBr

Transplanting rice / He pisses. Yayu. ZenPo, *tr. by* Takashi Ikemoto and Lucien Stryk

Transplanting Song. *Korean Oral Tradition.* CATKP, *tr. by* Peter H. Lee

Transport of the Dead. Gaylord Brewer. Vesp

Transportation. Karen Alkalay-Gut. DTA

Transporter. Oni Buchanan. LegDan

Transposition of Clermont, The. Les A. Murray. EmeKit

Trans-Relational Love Poem. Caroline Crumpacker. IIR

Trans-Siberian Express, The. Don Paterson. EdScPo

Transylvania, 1919. Sabrina Orah Mark. LegDan

Trap Door. Vitĕzslau Nezval. PFTM-1

Trapeze. Larissa Szporluk. PoDa

Trapeze artists and human cannonballs, fourth. Night. Tony Towle. AHA

Trapped. Adelaide Crapsey. APT-1; OxBoAm

Trapped in a dismal marsh, he told his troops. All Except Hannibal. Robert Graves. EmeKit

Trapped like Cordelia's heart, tongue-tied inside. Speak Again. Brian Staveley. IaFF

Trapped Wind. Geoff Ward. VaPo

Trapping Fairies. Frank Gelett Burgess. OBCoV

Trapping fairies in West Virginia. Trapping Fairies. Frank Gelett Burgess. OBCoV

Tras de la reja abierta entre los muros. Cementerio en la Ciudad. Luis Cernuda. RaW

Trash. Kenneth Irby. PFTM-2

Trash. Linda Smukler. WiU

Trash Talker, The. Howard Rambsy II. BRtP

Trashmen Shaking Hands with Hubert Humphrey at the Opening of Apache Plaza Shopping Center, Suburban Minneapolis, August 1963, The. David Wojahn. PBCAP *Fr.* Mystery Train: A Sequence.

Traslación de dominio. María Rivera. SPV

Trastevere: A Dedication. Edwin Denby. NYP2

Traumerei. David Shapiro. BodElec

Travel. Julio Cortázar. MotU; TCLAP, *tr. by* Paul Blackburn

Travel: After a Death. Jane Kenyon. FFC

Travel North: The Rules. Jane Epton Seale. TiP2

Travel Note. Albert Huffstickler. TiP2

Travel Notes. John Riley. Oth

Travel On. *Unknown.* SSUS

Travel on the seas of silence. Na Hermila Limón. Natalia Toledo. RMCMP, *tr. by* Alberto A. Ríos

Travel Poem. Diane Di Prima. WANABP

Travel through evenings without memories with memories. Goran's Whispers. Nathalie Handal. PoArWo

Travel with Grief—Goodbye to Joy. Nguyễn Chí Thiện. VCWP, *tr. by* Huynh Sanh Thông

Traveler. Valerie Martínez. TouFir

Traveler. Antonio Porta. ItPo, *tr. by* Gayle Ridinger

Traveler, The. Vachel Lindsay. MoAmPo

Traveler, The. Duane Niatum. HATNAP

Traveler, a traveler, Zimei his name, A. Tu Fu [*or* Du Fu]. CCL1 *Fr.* Seven Songs Written During the Qianyuan Era While Staying at Tonggu District.

Traveler at Night Writes His Thoughts, A. Tu Fu [*or* Du Fu]. CCL1, *tr. by* Florence Ayscough and Amy Lowell

Traveler came from far away, A. In the Key of Farewell. Pao Ling-hui. CCL1, *tr. by* Anne Birrell

Traveler endures countless tribulations, A. Climbing Stone Drum Mountain. Hsieh Ling-yün. CrYelRi, *tr. by* Sam Hamill

Traveler is a prey to endless sorrows, The. On Climbing Stone Drum Mountain, Near Shangshu. Hsieh Ling-yün. CCL1, *tr. by* John Frodsham

Traveler, rest. The time of man runs on. In Blue-Stocking Hollow. Donald Davidson. FuPo

Traveler's Companion. Bill Berkson. AHA

Traveler's Life, A. Sung Fang-hu. CrYelRi, *tr. by* Sam Hamill

Travelers long on the road. At the Point. Robert Mezey. GeoHom

Traveler's Pavilion. Tu Fu [*or* Du Fu]. CrYelRi, *tr. by* Sam Hamill

Travelers perhaps, / but I am not sure of finding. Nuclear Umbrella. Heberto Padilla. AF, *tr. by* Alastair Reid

Traveler's sadness, A. At Ni-Yang Inn. Chia Tao. CSKM, *tr. by* Mike O'Connor

Traveling as a Family. Carlos Drummond de Andrade. TCLAP, *tr. by* Virginia de Araújo

Traveling at Night. Tu Fu [*or* Du Fu]. WoPoe, *tr. by* Greg Whincup

Traveling Boy. William Meredith. YaYoPo

Traveling Gospel. Cynthia Cruz. IAoNAP

Traveling Highway 101. California Dreaming. Carol Lem. GeoHom

Traveling / old armor. Ransetsu. ZenPo, *tr. by* Takashi Ikemoto and Lucien Stryk

Traveling Onion, The. Naomi Shihab Nye. AFaM; CAP-8; IPoFL; LoL

Traveling Out, The. Lucile Adler. ICANM

Traveling this high. Basho. SoOfWa, *tr. by* Sam Hamill

Traveling through the dark I found a deer. Traveling Through the Dark. William Stafford. BrAP; CAP-8; ColAP; HeIP-4; NAMCP V.2; NoAM; OxBoAm; SoSe-8; StAl; TRP; WaAnP; WeW-3

Traveling Through the Yard. Rae Armantrout. OxBoAm

Traveling Valise. Marjorie Agosin. MirDau, *tr. by* Laura Nakazawa

Traveling with Cats on a Snowy Evening. Gail White. VisFro

Traveling with too much baggage is not a good idea. Maria Luisa Spaziani. NeIt *Fr.* Star of Free Will, The.

Traveller Has Regrets, The. George Sutherland Fraser. EdScPo

Traveller on the Flaminian Way. Martial. RomPo, *tr. by* Olive Pitt-Kethley

Traveller [*or* Traveler], The. John Berryman. GM; OxBoAm; PoA 2002

Traveller, The. Guillaume Apollinaire. WoPoe, *tr. by* Rachel Blau

Traveller, The. C. J. Dennis. NOBAu

Traveller take heed for journeys undertaken in the dark of the year. October Journey. Margaret Walker Alexander. GT

Traveller, the highway my guide, A. James Vincent Cunningham. APT-2

Traveller, The; or, A Prospect of Society. Oliver Goldsmith.
Britain. NPeEn

Traveller, traveller. Jules Supervielle. MFP, *tr. by* Martin Sorrell

Traveller, traveller, accept you must go back. Traveller, traveller. Jules Supervielle. MFP, *tr. by* Martin Sorrell

Traveller who walks a temperate zone, A. Against Romanticism. Kingsley Amis. NAMCP V.2; NoAM

Traveller, you must set out. Wole Soyinka. NAMCP V.2 *Fr.* Idanre and Other Poems (1967).

Travellers, The. Eva Gore-Booth. PoBW

Travellers came, after the long day's ride, The. Blinkered Mind, The. Amy Witting. NOBAu

Travel[l]er's Curse after Misdirection[, The]. Robert Graves. MoBrPo; NBLV; OBCoV

Traveller's Song. Hugo von Hofmannsthal. WoPoe, *tr. by* Robert Bly

Travelling. Simon J. Ortiz. NAAL-5 *Fr.* Poems from the Veterans Hospital.

Travelling, a man met a tiger, so . . . Good Taste. Christopher Logue. OBSP

Travelling Music. Philip Levine. MotU

Travelling Northward. Tu Fu [*or* Du Fu]. BLT; CCL1; NDACCP, *tr. by* Kenneth Rexroth

Travelling Post Office, The. Andrew Barton Paterson. NOBAu

Travelling to Gleis-Binario. Andrew Taylor.
Goethe and Brentano. BMAP

Travelling, / where darkness hauls the world. Tanks. Rhyll McMaster. NOBAu

Travelogue. Lewis Warsh. BodElec

Travelogue for Exiles. Karl Shapiro. MoAmPo

Travelors poor Tombes thes. avoide and flee. When Hee Was Come to the Other Side of the Contrye, of the Gergesenes, There Mett Him Two: Possessed with Devils Coming Out of the Tombes. Eleanor Touchet Davies. EMWP

Travels in the South. Simon J. Ortiz. UnSA

Travels of a Latter-Day Benjamin of Tudela. Yehuda Amichai.
"I am a solitary man, not a democracy." PoSu

Travels of Mu, Son of Heaven, The. *Unknown.* CCL1, *tr. by* Cheng Te-k'un
"Hills and mountains come into view." CCL1, *tr. by* Cheng Te-k'un
"O, Yellow Pond." CCL1, *tr. by* Cheng Te-k'un

Travels. The jet takes off. Eyes are closed, breathing deep. *Om mani padme hum.* Glorious Ruins. Tomislav Longinovic. PML

Travels with Oedipus. Peter Johnson.
Socrates. PoDa

Travis Brown saw the light of day. Ballad of a Bombardier from Texas. Goldie Capers Smith. TiP2

Tray—A Hero. Robert Browning. DiBP

Tray of Eggs, A. Michael Laskey. BeAl

Tray, the Exemplar. John Gay. DiBP *Fr.* Fables: First Series.

Treacherous sea, The. (LL) Fife Tune. John Streeter Manifold. FaBoWar; NBLV; NOBAu

Treacherous Towser. Thomas Yalden. DiBP

Treachery of Asmund, The. *Unknown.* tr. by W. H. Auden and Paul B. Taylor
"There is smoke above the hawks in the hall of the king." FaBoWar, *tr. by* W. H. Auden and Paul B. Taylor

Treacle. Paul Farley. NeBrP

Tread lightly, she is near. Requiescat. Oscar Wilde. GoPo; IrV; MoBrPo

Tread not the earth where lies her youthful form. Mrs. E. Cohrs Brown. Mary Weston Fordham. CBWP-2

Tread soft, for if you wake this knight alone. Epitaph on the Monument of Sir William Strode. William Strode. NOSC

Tread softly! all the earth is holy ground. Christina Georgina Rossetti. WPoS *Fr.* Later Life: A Double Sonnet of Sonnets.

Tread softly because you tread on my dreams. (LL) He Wishes for the Cloths of Heaven. William Butler Yeats. BLPJKO; ChAP; GoPo; MoBrPo; NAMCP V.1; NoAM; OBEV; PtR

Tread softly here! Go reverently and slow! Vimy Ridge. John Oxenham. SacPr

Treading the path to nobler ends. Love's Farewell. Edmund Waller. OxBSo

Treading through the half-light of ivy. New Gravity. Robin Robertson. StAl

Tread-mighty monster, fearsome and ferocious. Double-decker. Gilbert Ruddock. BBMWP, *tr. by* the author

Treadmill. Pedro Serrano. RMCMP, *tr. by* Geoff Hargreaves

Treason doth never prosper. Sir John Harington. *See* Treason doth never prosper [*or* Treason never prospers]; what's the reason?

Treason doth never prosper [*or* Treason never prospers]; what's the reason? Of Treason. Sir John Harington. NoSic; NPeEn; OBCoV; OxBEV; PBRV; SoSe-8

Treason's Choice. Philip Hammial. BMAP

Treasure: "Ax heads and sledges, musket balls and elixir bottles." Mark Cox. NevBe

Treasure. Elin ap Hywel. ATSWP, *tr. by* Robert Minhinnick

Treasure, The. U Tam'si Tchicaya. PFTM-2, *tr. by* Pierre Joris

Treasure at the heart of the rose, The. Rose, The. Gabriela Mistral. WPoS, *tr. by* Langston Hughes

Treasure I sought. My Treasure. John Oxenham. SacPr

Treasure Island. Robert Louis Stevenson.
Pirate Ditty. NPeEn

Treasure Lies In the Cornerstone, The. "Angelus Silesius." GePo *Fr.* Cherubical Wanderer, The.

Treasure not so the forlorn days. Behind the Line. Edmund Charles Blunden. OxBEV

Treasures and Glories of Life, The. Manuel González Prada. SpanPo, *tr. by* Kate Flores

Treasures and glories of life, The. Treasures and Glories of Life, The. Manuel González Prada. SpanPo, *tr. by* Kate Flores

Treat. / A somewhat favorable determination. *Unknown.* ColAnChi *Fr.* I Ching [*or* The Book of Changes *or* The Classic of Changes].

Treat. / The small fox is on the point of crossing the stream and wetting its tail: there is nothing for which this is favorable. *Unknown.* ColAnChi *Fr.* I Ching [*or* The Book of Changes *or* The Classic of Changes].

Treated shabbily / by fleas, by flies. Issa. ZenPo, *tr. by* Takashi Ikemoto and Lucien Stryk

Treatise of Monarchy, A. Fulke, 1st Baron Brooke Greville.
Of Nobility.
"For as the harmony which sense admires." NOSC
Of Peace.
"Peace is the next in order, first in end." NOSC

Treatise of Religion, A. Fulke, 1st Baron Brooke Greville.
"What is the chain which draws us back again." SacPr

Treaty of Human Learning, A. Fulke, 1st Baron Brooke Greville.
"Mind of man is this world's true dimension, The." NOSC

Treblinka. Michael Hamburger. HP

Trece intenciones contra el amor trivial. David Huerta. RMCMP

Tree. Zulaykha Abu-Risha. PoArWo, *tr. by* Clarissa C. Burt

Tree: "Man in love with a tree goes to live with him awhile before getting married, A." Juan Carlos Galeano. PML, *tr. by* Delia Poey

Tree. Stratis Haviaras. MotU

Tree. Jane Hirshfield. CalPo

Tree. Andrew Hudgins. InvLad

Tree, A. Fadhil Assultani. IrPoTo, *tr. by* Saadi A. Simawe

Tree, A. Mark Irwin. PoCoUp

Tree, The. Dorothy Auchterlonie. NOBAu

Tree, The. Frank Gaspar. UrbNat

Tree, The. Alfred Kreymborg. APT-1

Tree, The. Ezra Pound. HarvBoo

Tree and the Lady, The. Thomas Hardy. MoBrPo

Tree at my window, window tree. Tree at My Window. Robert Frost. APT-1; MoAmPo; NAMCP V.1; NoAM

Tree bore the efflorescence of October apples, The. Sin. Carol Frost. PoDa

Tree by the river, The.   Tree of Fire.   Adonis.   VCWP, *tr.* by Samuel Hazo

Tree enters and says with a bow, A.   Lesson, The.   Miroslav Holub.   PoSu, *tr. by* Ian Milner and Jarmila Milner

Tree Falling in a Vacant Forest, The.   Linda Gregg.   ExTi

Tree frog places all its trust in the willow that tows it, The.   Tree Frog, The.   René Char.   MotU, *tr.* by Franz Wright

Tree Frog, The.   René Char.   MotU, *tr.* by Franz Wright

Tree grew inside my head, A.   Tree Within, A.   Octavio Paz.   TCLAP, *tr.* by Eliot Weinberger

Tree grew under your hand one day, The.   Lines for a Painter.   Anthony Cronin.   PBCIP

Tree grows old in the tree, it is summer, The.   Yves Bonnefoy.   VCWP

Tree has entered my hands, The.   Ezra Pound.   MoAmPo; NOxBChV *Fr.* Ripostes of Ezra Pound.

Tree in December.   Melville Cane.   MoAmPo

Tree in Winter.   Emily Dickinson.   NOxBChV

Tree is a tree, The.   Out of the Winter-Tree Into the Spring-Tree.   Hwang Jiwoo.   CAMKP, *tr.* by Young-Jun Lee and Scott Swaner

Tree is happy because it is scarcely sentient, The.   Fatality.   Rubén Darío.   TCLAP, *tr.* by Lysander Kemp

Tree is stripped, The.   Form in Void.   Ikkyu Sojun.   ZenPo, *tr.* by Takashi Ikemoto and Lucien Stryk

Tree nymphs, daughters of River, ambrosial.   Moiro.   SaLy, *tr.* by Diane Rayor

Tree of Diana.   Alejandra Pizarnik. *tr.* by Susan Bassnett

"I gave the surge of myself to the dawn."   TANSG, *tr.* by Susan Bassnett

Tree of Earthly Delights.   Nancy Morejón.   TANSG, *tr.* by Joy Renjilian-Burgy

Tree of Fire.   Adonis.   VCWP, *tr.* by Samuel Hazo

Tree of Knowledge, The.   Edwin Emanuel Bradford.   Equality.   VerBaPo

Tree of Knowledge, The.   Abraham Cowley.   ChIV-1

Tree of Knowledge, The.   Lizelia Augusta Jenkins Moorer.   CBWP-3

Tree of knowledge was the tree of reason, The.   Contraband.   Denise Levertov.   BLT

Tree of life my soul hath seen, The.   Christ the Apple-Tree.   *Unknown.*   TCAPo

Tree of Life, The.   Margaret Holley.   PoA 2002

Tree of nothing matters grew red leaves then dropped them confetti-like, The.   Triptych.   Jim Elledge.   IllVoic

Tree of the Great Peace, The.   *Iroquois Oral Tradition.*   NAAPv.1

Tree rows in orchards are capable of patterns. What, The.   Lyn Hejinian.   FTOS *Fr.* My Life.

Tree stands on a pike-top, The.   Lone Tree.   Lismaco Chavarría.   SonAtl, *tr.* by Carole Gibson and Anne Swann

Tree still bends over the lake, The.   Winter.   Sheila Wingfield.   LW; MoWP

Tree Stillness.   Karen L. Mitchell.   GT

Tree, take my girdle.   Ezili Impending.   Rachel E. Harding.   BtF

Tree Telling of Orpheus, A.   Denise Levertov.   APSN; MiVo

Tree that lingers at the window is just sixteen, The.   What Parents Do Not Yet Know.   Kay Boyle.   PoChi

Tree the intact, The.   Some Lapland Views.   Christian Dotremont.   PFTM-2, *tr.* by Pierre Joris

Tree the tempest with a crash of wood, The.   On a Tree Fallen Across the Road (To Hear Us Talk).   Robert Frost.   GoPo

Tree toad loved a she-toad, A.   Tree Toad.   *Unknown.*   NTCP

Tree trembles, A.   Woods.   Kang Ŭn'gyo.   EcSo, *tr.* by Ann Y. Choi

Tree was shaken from the inside, The.   Not Falling.   Lynne McMahon.   ExTi

Tree we plant will, when its boughs are grown, The.   *Unknown.*   CAGL *Fr.* Don Leon.

Tree, whose roots are deep, The.   *Various authors.*   CATKP *Fr.* Songs of Flying Dragons.

Tree with a hole in our front yard, The.   Leonard Neufeldt.   ACAMVP

Tree Within, A.   Octavio Paz.   TCLAP, *tr.* by Eliot Weinberger

Treeback.   *Unknown.*   SonAtl, *tr.* by Ian Bevan, Nancy Gallas, Kurt Ganzl, Lorna MacIntosh, Bill Matthews and Tai Walker

Treefrog winks without springing.   Drawings of the Song Animals.   Duane Niatum.   HATNAP

Tree-leaves labour up and down.   Nobody Comes.   Thomas Hardy.   NAMCP V.1

Tree-mother.   Baobab.   Alvin Aubert.   FuFl

Trees.   Fleur Adcock.   OBGa

Trees.   Joyce Kilmer.   APT-1; BRP; ChAP; ITBLP; PoA 2002; TCAPo; UV

Trees.   Ágnes Nemes Nagy.   PoSu, *tr.* by Bruce Berlind

Trees.   Cheryl Savageau.   TWW

Trees, The: "Trees are coming into leaf, The."   Philip Larkin.   BeAl; HarvBoo; NoAM; NoP-4; NoP-5; OPOU

Trees, The.   Adrienne Rich.   EmeKit

Trees are a mane of shaken yellow, The.   Pool.   Pedro Serrano.   RMCMP, *tr.* by Geoff Hargreaves

Trees are cages for them: water holds its breath.   Stars and Planets.   Norman Alexander MacCaig.   OPOU

Trees are coming into leaf, The.   Trees, The.   Philip Larkin.   BeAl; HarvBoo; NoAM; NoP-4; NoP-5; OPOU

Trees Are Down, The.   Charlotte Mew.   ChIV-2; MoBrPo; MoWP; OxAEP-2; VWP

TREES ARE ELEPHANTS' HEADS, THE.   Michael McClure.   PFTM-2 *Fr.* Ghost Tantras.

Trees are hopelessly overstylized, the sycamores, The.   Self-Portrait, Jackson.   James Kimbrell.   NAPBL

Trees are in their autumn beauty, The.   Wild Swans at Coole, The.   William Butler Yeats.   HeIP-4; MoBrPo; NAEL-6v2; NAEL-7v2; NAMCP V.1; NoAM; NoP-4; NoP-5; NPeEn; OWoS; PoPoPo; SoSe-8; TFi

Trees are never the same, The.   Return, The.   Thomas McGrath.   GifTon

Trees are tall, but the moon small, The.   Hide and Seek.   Robert Graves.   NTCP

Trees are uncurling their first, The.   Married Love.   Liz Rosenberg.   NIL-7

Trees are very high in the wan signal-beam, for whose slow, The.   David Jones.   TCAWP *Fr.* In Parenthesis.

Trees' black hair electric, The.   February Evening in Boston, 1971.   Denise Levertov.   TaR

Trees descend, image of love, The.   Edith Jay Scovell.   HarvBoo *Fr.* Water Images.

Trees, drowned in the gray snow.   Idea of Russia, The.   Viktor Krivulin.   TCRusP, *tr.* by Anna Barker and Daniel Weissbort

Trees full of snipers, the new kind, The.   War.   Lorine Niedecker.   FTOS

Trees Green the Quiet Sun.   Larry Eigner.   PmAP

Trees hold against, The.   Annuals.   Daniel Halpern.   PfSP

Trees in groves / Kine in droves.   Saadi.   Ralph Waldo Emerson.   APN-1

Trees in the forest fall and, falling, find.   Some Compensation.   Jay Parini.   PfSP

Trees in the Garden.   D. H. Lawrence.   MoBrPo; NoP-4; NoP-5; WaAnP

Trees in the old days used to stand.   Carentan O Carentan.   Louis Simpson.   AmWaPo; OBWP; PWW2; WoPoe

Trees in the wood lifeless.   Little Sunlight, A.   Takahashi Shinkichi.   ZenPo, *tr.* by Takashi Ikemoto and Lucien Stryk

Trees inside are moving out into the forest, The.   Trees, The.   Adrienne Rich.   EmeKit

Trees, Late in the Season.   Willem Kloos.   TuT, *tr.* by Desmond Egan

Trees, late in the season, bare.   Trees, Late in the Season.   Willem Kloos.   TuT, *tr.* by Desmond Egan

Trees, like great jade elephants, The.   John Gould Fletcher.   MoAmPo *Fr.* Irradiations.

Trees like ominous old men are shaking, The. (LL)   Soissons.   Keith Douglas.   NAMCP V.1; NoAM

Trees like Tassels—hit—and swung, The.   Emily Dickinson.   NCAP

Trees make their mark on the sky, The.   Palms.   June Sylvester.   PasH

Trees of Ithaca, The.   Sa'di Yusuf.   IrPoTo, *tr.* by Khaled Mattawa

Trees of the Forest, The.   *Unknown.*   WoPoe *Fr.* Sweeney Astray.

Trees on the hospital lawn, The.   University Hospital, Boston.   Mary Oliver.   CAP-8

Trees on the other side of the river.   River and Bridge.   Meena Alexander.   RWB

Trees seem to sweat in the dark.   Night-time.   Mongane Wally Serote.   TSAP

Trees seen now whose roots touch.   Trees Seen Now.   Antler.   WhBo

Trees shading trees, mist-smoke weaves.   Tune: "Beautiful Barbarians."   Li Po.   ChInPo, *tr.* by Ye Weilian [*or* Yeh Wei-lien *or* Wai-lim Yip]

Trees that Change Our Lives.   Gary Soto.   PasH

Trees That Come Undone within a Sphere of Fog.   Francis Ponge.   YaTCFP, *tr.* by Lee Fahnestock

Trees, The! They pierce us, they pack the distance tight.   Tom Montag.   AmZen *Fr.* Plain Poems: A Fairwater Daybook.

Trees thick and full gathering pure.   After Kuo Chu-Pu's Poems.   T'ao Ch'ien.   PoChi, *tr.* by David Hinton

Trees twinkle.   Tomato.   Obu Udeozo.   NeNiPo

Trees, up to their waists in earth, The.   Flood.   John McAuliffe.   NIrP

Trees were hung with marzipan, The.   Such Sweet Sorrow.   Elizabeth Delmore.   NLP

Trees were like bubblyjocks, The.   Sunny Gale.   Hugh MacDiarmid.   FaBoVe

Trees were moving.   Emilio Villa.   ItPo *Fr.* Words.

Trees were taller than the night, The.   Robber, The.   Walter James Turner.   MoBrPo

Tremble, oh my gravemound.   Basho.   SoOfWa, *tr.* by Sam Hamill

Trembling, across the plain my course I held.   Philip Freneau.   TCAPo *Fr.* House of Night, The.

Trembling I sit day and night. My friends are astonished at me.   William Blake.   NPBRoP; WaAnP *Fr.* Jerusalem.

Trembling I write my dream, and recollect.   Philip Freneau.   NAAL-3; TCAPo *Fr.* House of Night, The.

Trembling the spectres glide, and plaintive vent.   Homer.   OBVE *Fr.* Odyssey.

Trembling train clings to the leaning wall, The.   Moonrise in the Rockies.   Ella Higginson.   SWaP

Trembling with engines, gulping oil, the river.   Anthony Cronin.   PBCIP *Fr. R.M.S. Titanic.*

Tremendous assertion.   Erin Mouré.   NLPA *Fr.* Wittgenstein Letters to Mel Gibson's Braveheart, The.

Tremor, The.   Jack Hirschman.   BodElec

Tremors.   Stewart Conn.   BeAl

Tremulous word, a lingering hand, the burning, A.   Taking the Night-Train.   John James Piatt.   APN-2

Trench Poets.   Edgell Rickword.   FaBoWar

Trenches, The.   Frederic Manning.   NOBAu; PoWW

Trendelenburg Position.   M. Wyrebek.   AmPoNex

31 du mois d'août 1914, Le.   Petite Auto, La.   Guillaume Apollinaire.   YaTCFP

Tres Ciudades.   Federico García Lorca.

     Malagueña.   RaW

Tres ("Es del continente, alrededor de ella todo es luz y yo la observo sobre la plancha en la imagen de su cuerpo.")   Ofelia Perez Sepúlveda.   SPV

Tres estados y los tres reinos, Los.   Alberto Blanco.   RMCMP

Tres ("Había una vez la perra más azul de la manada.")   Ofelia Perez Sepúlveda.   SPV

Tres Poemas Sobre la Muerte.   Carlos Bousoño.   RaW

Trespasser in my own house.   Portrait.   Constance Urdang.   OPRER

Trespasses.   Nujoum Al-Ghanim. *tr. by* Clarissa C. Burt

     "I don't know how I lost my amulets."   PoArWo, *tr. by* Clarissa C. Burt

Tretis [*or* Book] of the Tua Mariit Wemen [*or* Two Married Women] and the Wedo[w] [*or* Widow], The.   William Dunbar.

     Widow Has Buried Her Second Husband, The.   RACG

Triad.   Adelaide Crapsey.   APT-1; InoFa; OxBoAm; TCAPo

Triad, A.   Christina Georgina Rossetti.   NAEL-6v2; NAEL-7v2; NALW

Triage.   Lisel Mueller.   IllVoic

Triage.   Margot Schilpp.   AmPoNex; PoDa

Triage.   Larissa Szporluk.   NeAmPo

Trial.   Ruth Padel.   MFPA

Trial, A.   Murder.   Yury Timofeievich Galanskov.   TCRusP, *tr. by* Olive Dehn

Trial by Jury.   William Schwenck Gilbert.

     When I, Good Friends, Was Called to the Bar.   NAEL-6v2; NAEL-7v2

Trial Desert.   Jean Grosjean.   YaTCFP, *tr. by* Mary Ann Caws *and* Jean-Pierre Cauvin *and* Patricia Terry

Trial of Endurance, A.   Ludovico Ariosto.   DiBP *Fr.* Orlando Furioso.

Trial of Renard, The.   *Unknown.*   NAWM-7v1, *tr. by* Patricia Terry

Trial Separation.   Marie Harris.   PfS

Trial, The.   Zbigniew Herbert.   AF, PoetW *tr. by* John Carpenter *and* Bogdana Carpenter

Trials of a Tourist.   Anne Tibble.   NBLV

Trials of the Poet.   Andrée Chédid.   YaTCFP, *tr. by* Rosemary Lloyd

Trials that the Saviour bore have paved the golden way, The.   Benefits of Sorrow.   Lizelia Augusta Jenkins Moorer.   CBWP-3

Triangle.   L. Miller.   Prolet, *tr. by* Amelia Glaser

Triangle, Comb.   No Hyegyông.   EcSo, *tr. by* Ann Y. Choi

Triangle, Mirror.   No Hyegyông.   EcSo, *tr. by* Ann Y. Choi

Triangular Legs.   Sir Alan Patrick Herbert.   NBLV

Triangulation.   Daryl E. Jones.   TiP2

Tribal Chant.   Carol Lee Sanchez.   ReEnLa

Tribal Marks.   Saundra Sharp.   SpirFl

Tribal Memories.   Robert Duncan.   APSN *Fr.* Passages.

Tribe forsook you, The.   Nightmare 1.   Abdul Maqsoud Abdul Karim.   NAfrP, *tr. by* Clarissa C. Burt

Tribunal, The.   Chris Wallace-Crabbe.   ChIV-2

Tribune's Visitation, The.   David Jones.

     "I have a word to say to you as men and as a man speaking to."   TCAWP

Tributary.   Leonard Nolens.   TuT, *tr. by* Michael O'Loughlin

Tributary Stream.   William Wordsworth.   CenSon *Fr.* River Duddon [A Series of Sonnets], The.

Tribute.   Eloise Bibb.   CBWP-4

Tribute to a Lost Steamer.   Mary Weston Fordham.   CBWP-2

Tribute to a Mohogany Cutter.   J. Alexander Bennett.   OWABP

Tribute to Capt. F. W. Dawson.   Mary Weston Fordham.   CBWP-2

Tribute to Chief Joseph, A.   Duane Niatum.   AmWaPo

Tribute to Duke.   Sarah Webster Fabio.   FTtHH

Tribute to Neruda the Poet Collector of Seashells.   William Carlos Williams.   NAAPv.2

Tribute to the Angels.   "H. D."
     24.   NALW; NAMCP V.1; NoAM
     25.   NALW; NAMCP V.1
     26.   NALW; NAMCP V.1
     27.   NALW; NAMCP V.1
     28.   MoWP; NAAPv.2; NALW; NAMCP V.1
     29.   APT-1; HW; MoWP; NAAPv.2; NALW; NAMCP V.1; PFTM-1
     30.   APT-1; MoWP; NAAPv.2; NAMCP V.1
     31.   NAAPv.2; NAMCP V.1
     32.   NAAPv.2
     33.   NAAPv.2
     34.   NAAPv.2
     35.   NAAPv.2; NALW
     36.   NAAPv.2; NALW; NAMCP V.1; NoAM
     37.   NAAPv.2; NALW; NAMCP V.1
     38.   NAAPv.2; NALW; NAMCP V.1
     39.   NAAPv.2; NALW; NAMCP V.1
     40.   APT-1
     41.   NAAPv.2; NALW; NAMCP V.1
     42.   NAAPv.2; NALW
     43.   APT-1; NALW
     "Bitter, bitter jewel."   NALW
     "Hermes Trismegistus."   NALW
     "I can not invent it,."   NALW
     "I John saw. I testify."   NALW
     "In the field-furrow."   APT-1
     "Invisible, indivisible Spirit."   APT-1
     "New sensation, A."   APT-1
     "Now polish the crucible."   NALW
     "O swiftly, re-light the flame."   NALW
     "Swiftly re-light the flame,."   NALW
     "What is the jewel colour?"   NALW
     "Your walls do not fall, he said."   NALW

Tribute to the Bride and Groom, A.   Priscilla Jane Thompson.   CBWP-2

Trick, A.   Steve Kowit.   SUP

Trick, The.   John Mole.   NOxBChV

Trick, The.   Mark Wunderlich.   WiU

Trick, he said, is to look not at all, The.   Beekeeper.   Barbara J. Orton.   NeAmPo

Trick Noir.   Brian Teare.   LegDan

Trick or Treat.   John Frederick Nims.   IllVoic

Trickle Drops.   Walt Whitman.   APN-1; NAAL-3; NAAL-5; NAAPv.1

Trickle drops! my blue veins leaving!   Trickle Drops.   Walt Whitman.   APN-1; NAAL-3; NAAL-5; NAAPv.1

Trickle of sand on the grave's edge, A.   Ad Infinitum.   Joan Aronsten.   NOBAu

Tricks for the Barmaid.   Roddy Lumsden.   NeBl

Tricks With Mirrors.   Margaret Atwood.   BrAP; NIP-4

Trickster 1 (for Winston Rodney).   Kwame Dawes.   WaCA

Trickster 2 (for Lee "Scratch" Perry).   Kwame Dawes.   WaCA

Trickster 4 (for Sister Patra).   Kwame Dawes.   WaCA

Trickster Rabbit.   Roland Legiardi-Laura.   FTtHH

Tricky Margaret.   Mary Macleod.   EMWP

Trico's Song.   John Lyly.   NoSic *Fr.* Alexander and Campaspe.

Tricycles.   Francisco Aragon.   InoFa

Trident, in nightmare, The.   Peace Plan: Meditation on the 9 Stages of "Peacemaking" as Tribute to Senator Claiborne Pell: 1997.   Michael S. Harper.   PuP-23

Tries a nosedive, kamikaze.   Baby Random.   Belle Waring.   PBCAP

Trifles.   George Farquhar.   OBCoV

Trifling song you shall hear, A.   Trifles.   George Farquhar.   OBCoV

Trigger D'evolution.   Randy Prunty.   AnSo

Trilce.   César Vallejo.
     Trilce.   PFTM-1

Trillium.   Louise Glück.   MoWP; StAl

Trilobite trilobites. (LL)   Ounce code orange.   Clark Coolidge.   NYP2; WhBo

Trilobytes.   Kent Johnson.   AtGh

Trilogy.   Del Ray Cross.   FreRad

Trilogy for X.   Louis MacNeice.
     And Love Hung Still.   MoBrPo

Trilogy of Passion.   Johann Wolfgang von Goethe.   STV, *tr. by* John Frederick Nims

Trilogy of the Man in Black.   Awwad Nasir.   IrPoTo, *tr. by* Saadi A. Simawe *and* Daniel Weissbort

Trilogy of Travel.   Abd al-Karim Kassid.   IrPoTo, *tr. by* Chuck Miller *and* Saadi A. Simawe

Trim, thou are right!—'Tis sure that I.   Death in the Kitchen.   Thomas Hood.
  NPeEn
Trinity.   Gerrit Achterberg.   TuT, *tr. by* Dennis O'Driscoll
Trinity.   Michael Field.   VWP
Trinity Place.   Phyllis McGinley.   AmWit; MoAmPo; SoSe-8
Trinity, The.   William Langland.   SacPr *Fr.* Vision of Piers Plowman, The.
Trinker im Frühling, Der.   Li Po.   CCL1, *tr. by* Hans Bethge
Trio.   Kimberly Ann Collins.   InTrad
Trio for Two Cats and a Trombone.   Dame Edith Sitwell.   NAEL-6v2 *Fr.*
  Façade.
Triolet.   Wendy Cope.   OBCoV
Triolet for the Amphetamine Afflicted.   Susan McCaslin.   IFF
Triolet: "He came in."   Jack London.   ASA
Triolets for Ken.   Christopher Wiseman.   IFF
Trip, Dharma Trip, Sangha Trip, The.   Bob Kaufman.   WhBo
Trip on Mount T'ai-P'ing.   K'ung Chih-kuei.   ChinPo, *tr. by* Ye Weilian [*or*
  Yeh Wei-lien *or* Wai-lim Yip]
Trip Through the Mind Jail, A.   Raul Salinas.   FaBoA
Trip to Delphi.   Alice Friman.   RWB
Trip to Paris and Belgium, A.   Dante Gabriel Rossetti.
  Antwerp to Ghent.   NPeEn
  "Constant keeping-past of shaken trees."   NPeEn
Trip west, The.   Vague Poem.   Elizabeth Bishop.   BAP-01
Triphammer Bridge.   A. R. Ammons.   ColAP; OxBoAm
Triple Benison, The.   Henrietta Cordelia Ray.   CBWP-3
Triple Feature.   Denise Levertov.   NoP-4; NoP-5
Triple Fool, The.   John Donne.   FSCP; NOSC; SoSe-8
  (Triple Foole, The.)   PBRV
Triple Foole, The.   John Donne. *See* Triple Fool, The.
Triple Great Grandpa.   Tragic Mulatto is Neither, The.   Michael C. Ladd.
  BRtP
Triple Overtime.   Lucinda Roy.   GT
Triplets.   Howard Dietz.   ReLy
Tripoli.   Peter A. Sanders.   FaBoWar
Tripoli.   Nadia Tuéni.   PoArWo
Trippers and askers surround me.   Walt Whitman.   CAGL; ColAP; NAWM-
  7v2 *Fr.* Song of Myself.
Trips.   Nikki Giovanni.   CA
Triptych.   Jim Elledge.   IllVoic
Triptych.   Beatrix Gates.   WiU
  Cathy.   WiU
  Homeless.   WiU
  Ron.   WiU
Triptych.   Christopher Pilling.   NLP
Triptych.   D. A. Powell.   WiU
Triptych of Reflection.   Inna L'vovna Lisnyanskaya.   CRWP, *tr. by* Ruth
  Fainlight
Tristan and Isolde.   Richard Wagner. *tr. by* Alfred Forman
  "Smile his lips, A."   EroLit, *tr. by* Alfred Forman
Tristan da Cunha.   Roy Campbell.   MoBrPo
Tristan had no choice.   Heinrich von Veldeke.   GePo
Tristan Tzara.   Edward Hirsch.   BodElec
Tristesse de l'Eau.   Paul Claudel.   YaTCFP
Tristia.   Ger Killeen.   AmPoNex
Tristia.   Osip Emilevich Mandelstam.   WoPoe, *tr. by* James Greene
Tristia.   Osip Emilevich Mandelstam.
  Tristia.   PFTM-1
Tristia.   Ovid. *tr. by* Peter Green and David R. Slavitt
  Book 1.   RomPo, *tr. by* Peter Green
  Book 3. *tr. by* David R. Slavitt
    "Friend of the arts and artists, scholar, generous patron."   WoPoe, *tr. by*
    David R. Slavitt
  Book 5. *tr. by* David R. Slavitt
    "I have been looking these pages over, my dearest wife."   WoPoe, *tr. by*
    David R. Slavitt
Tristia.   Charles Hubert Sisson.   HarvBoo
Tristitia Ante.   Maurice Gilliams.   TuT, *tr. by* Sean Dunne
Tristium.   Ovid.
  "And here I wish my soul died with my breath."   OBVE
  "And on this day, which poets unto thee."   OBVE
Tristram lies sick to death.   Tristram's End.   Laurence Binyon.   OBMV
Tristram's End.   Laurence Binyon.   OBMV
Tri-toned whistle of the night train, The.   Santa Fe Railroad, The.   Charles
  Tomlinson.   ICANM
Triumph, The.   Ben Jonson. *See* Her Triumph.
Triumph—may be of several kinds.   Emily Dickinson.   TCAPo

Triumph! My Jesus has! Triumph! His empire gained!   15th Kühl-Psalm, The.
  Quirinus Kuhlmann.   GePo, *tr. by* George C. Schoolfield
Triumph of Achilles, The.   Louise Glück.   OxBoAm
Triumph of Charis, The.   Ben Jonson. *See* Her Triumph.
Triumph of Dullness, The.   Alexander Pope.   NAEL-6v1; NAEL-7v1; NPeEn
  Fr. Dunciad, The.
Triumph of Life, The.   Percy Bysshe Shelley.   NAEL-6v2; NOBRP
  "As in that trance of wondrous thought I lay."   NPeEn
  "Struck to the heart by this sad pageantry."   OxBEV
Triumph of Love.   John Hall Wheelock.   MoAmPo
Triumph of Love, The.   Geoffrey Hill.
  "So what is faith if it is not."   NAMCP V.2
Triumph of Sensibility.   Sylvia Townsend Warner.   MoBrPo
Triumph of Superstition, The. Raphael and Ianthe.   Anne Batten Cristall.   RWP
Triumph of the Church, The.   Phineas Fletcher.   SacPr
Triumph of the Whale, The.   Charles Lamb.
  "Io! Paean! Io! sing."   OxAEP-2
Triumph of Time, The.   Algernon Charles Swinburne.
  I Will Go Back to the Great Sweet Mother.   NAEL-6v2
Triumph of Vice, The.   Alexander Pope.   NPeEn; OBSV *Fr.* Epilogue to the
  Satires, in Two Dialogues.
Triumph or the tomb, The. (LL)   Charleston.   Henry Timrod.   AmWaPo;
  APN-2; CBCWP; ColAP; OxBoAm; PCW; TCAPo
Triumphal March.   Rubén Darío.   SpanPo, *tr. by* Charles Guenther
Triumphal March.   T. S. Eliot.   AmWaPo; OBWP *Fr.* Coriolan.
Triumphant Demons stand, and Angels start.   Heart's Abysses, The.   Walter
  Savage Landor.   OBSV
Triumphant was the burst of rapt'rous joy.   Thomas Baker.   STuOW *Fr.* Steam
  Engine; or, The Power of the Flame, The.
Triumphing chariots, statues, crownes of bayes.   William Drummond of
  Hawthornden.   NOSC *Fr.* Urania, or Spiritual Poems.
Triumphing over Death, and Chance, and thee O Time. (LL)   On Time.   John
  Milton.   OBEV; SacPr
Triumphs of Nature, The.   Samuel Boyse.   OBGa *Fr.* Triumphs of Nature, The.
Triumphs of Nature, The.   Samuel Boyse.
  Triumphs of Nature, The.   OBGa
Triune, shaping, restless power.   Sistrum.   Margaret Fuller.   APN-1
Trivia; or, The Art of Walking the Streets of London.   John Gay.
  "Be sure observe where brown Ostrea stands."   OxBEV
  (Of the Weather.)   NPeEn
Troades.   Seneca. *tr. by* John Wilmot, 2d Earl of Rochester
  After Death Nothing Is.   OBVE, *tr. by* John Wilmot, 2d Earl of Rochester
  (Seneca's Troas. Act 2. Chorus.)   OxBEV, *tr. by* John Wilmot, 2d Earl of
  Rochester
Trŏchĕe trĭps frŏm lŏng tŏ shŏrt.   Metrical Feet.   Samuel Taylor Coleridge.
  NIL-7; NIP-4
Troilus and Cressida.   John Dryden.
  (Song from Troilus and Cressida.)   NoP-4; NoP-5
Troilus and Cressida.   William Shakespeare.
  "And is it true that I must go from Troy?"   OxAEP-1
  "Have you seen my cousin?"   OxAEP-1
  "Peace, you ungracious clamours! peace, rude sounds!"   OxAEP-1
  "They tax our policy and call it cowardice."   FaBoWar
  "This she? no, this is Diomed's Cressida."   OxAEP-1
  "What! are my deeds forgot?"   OxAEP-1
  "You are for dreams and slumbers, brother priest."   OxAEP-1
Troilus and Criseyde [*or* Criseide].   Geoffrey Chaucer. *tr. by* Burton Raffel and
  Selden Rodman
  (Cantus Troili.)   NoP-5
  Complaint of Troilus, The.   OBEV
  Conclusion.   WoPoe, *tr. by* Burton Raffel and Selden Rodman
  "Double sorwe of Troilus to tellen, The."   MakPoe
  Love Unfeigned.   OBEV
  Song of Troylus, The.   NoP-4
  "Swich fyn hath, lo, this Troilus for love!"   SacPr
  "This Troilus in armes gan hir streyne."   EroLit
  (Troilus's Song.)   NAEL-7v1
  "Wrath, as I bigan yow for to seye, The."   OxBEV
Troilus's Song.   Geoffrey Chaucer. *See* Song of Troylus, The.
Trois harengs.   Harengs et bouleaux.   Jude Stéfan.   YaTCFP
Trois leçons de morale.   Emmanuel Hocquard.   YaTCFP
Trois Petits Tours et Puis . . .   Marie Ponsot.   ExTi
Trojan Women.   Seneca.   RomPo, *tr. by* Anthony James Boyle
Trolley Song, The.   Ralph Blane and Hugh Martin.   ReLy
Trolling for Blues.   Richard Wilbur.   PoA 2002
Troll's Nosegay, The.   Robert Graves.   OxBSo
Trombone Solo.   Eliza Cook.   STuOW

Trombone Solo. Stoddard King. NBLV

Trompe l'oeil. Tracy Ryan. NeBl

Trompe L'Oeil in Winter. Mary Ann Samyn. AmPoNex

Troop home to silent grots and caves. George Darley. NAEL-6v2; NPeEn *Fr.* Syren Songs.

Troop ship, The. Isaac Rosenberg. OxBEV; PoWW

Troop ship whistles once; I still waver, The. Colonial Troops Transport, The. *Vietnamese Oral Tradition.* CaDao, *tr. by* John Balaban

Troop Train. Karl Shapiro. AmWaPo; APT-2; OxBoAm; PWW2; WaAnP

Troopers are riding, are riding by, The. Romance. Charles Reznikoff. NAAPv.2

Troparion. Kassiane. WPoS, *tr. by* Liana Sakelliou

Trope Market. Jackson Mac Low. PmAP

Trophies of pain I've gathered. whose sorrow. For H.D. Diane Di Prima. PmAP

Trophy Homes. Bruce Berger. GeoH

Tropic Afternoon. Rubén Darío. SonAtl, *tr. by* Eleanor Davidson

Tropic green days, red. Kalamu ya Salaam. SpirFl *Fr.* New Orleans Haiku.

Tropic Love. Olive Senior. WaAnP

Tropical Afternoon. Rubén Darío. TCLAP, *tr. by* Lysander Kemp

Tropical Childhood. Salomon De la Selva. NAAPv.2

Tropical Death. Grace Nichols. InoFa; NAMCP V.2

Tropical nights. Boston Beguine, The. Sheldon Harnick. ReLy

Tropical plants fringe the sea. At this resort. Ingrid de Kok. TSAP

Tropical Toads. Randall Maggs. Coast

Tropical Town. Salomon De la Selva. NAAPv.2

Tropicalia. Margaret Haley. YaYoPo

Trópico. Nicholas Christopher. PoCho

Tropics in New York, The. Claude McKay. APT-1; GT; MakPoe; NAAPv.2; NAMCP V.1; NoAM; OxBoAm

Tropics vanish, and meseems that I, The. Robert Louis Stevenson. NePenScot

Tropics, why did you give me. Wishes. Carlos Pellicer. TCLAP, *tr. by* Donald Justice

Trosachs, The. William Wordsworth. OBEV

Troth. Michael Davidson. FTOS

Trotsky in Mexico. Dmitry Vasil'evich Bobyshev. ItGoST, *tr. by* Michael Van Walleghen

Trotsky's dead. My strays. Letters from an Exile. Valerie Duff. OPRER

Troubadour Love. Olga Nolla. TANSG, *tr. by* Paula Vega

Trouble. Kiki Wainwright. OGAHCP, *tr. by* Boadiba and Jack Hirschman

Trouble enters our house. Trouble. Kiki Wainwright. OGAHCP, *tr. by* Boadiba and Jack Hirschman

Trouble Is a Man. Alec Wilder. ReLy

Trouble I've Seen, The. Fred Hampton Jr. BRtP

Trouble of a book is first to be, The. Troubles of a Book, The. Laura Riding Jackson. HarvBoo; MoWP; NAMCP V.1

Trouble of the World, The. *Unknown.* SSUS

Trouble was they left her too much alone, The. Poemectomy. John Dickson. IllVoic

Trouble with comparing a poet with a radio is that radios don't develop scar tissue, The. Sporting Life. Jack Spicer. OxBoAm

Trouble with home-made armour, The. Children in Armour. Geoffrey Adkins. FaBoWar

Trouble with me, The. Growing Up. Jason Shinder. MAAN

Trouble with Spain. Charles Bukowski. SUP

Trouble with the Light, The. Pedro Salinas. RaW, *tr. by* W. S. Merwin

Trouble with you is you're not, The. How the Last Act Begins. Chana Bloch. ExTi

Troubled Awakening. Magdalena Gomez. PueRic

Troubled midnight and the noon's repose, The. (LL) La Figlia Che Piange. T. S. Eliot. APT-1; HarvBoo; HeIP-4; OxBEV; OxBoAm; PoA 2002; TCAPo

Troubled tale that fills me with grief, A. (LL) Song on Enduring the Cold. Ts'ao Ts'ao. CCL1; ColAnChi, *tr. by* Burton Watson

Troubles with the Soul at Morning Calisthenics. Anna Swirszczynska [*or* Swir]. BLT

Troubling the water? (LL) Brilliance. Mark Doty. BeAl; PoCu

Troubling the Water. Yusef Komunyakaa. OxBoAm

Trouncer, the Foxes Foe. Robert Bloomfield. DiBP *Fr.* Farmer's Boy, The.

Trousseau. Vona Groarke. MFPA

Trout, The. John Montague. ModIr; NoP-4; NoP-5; PBCIP; PNI; StAl *Fr.* All Legendary Obstacles.

Trout Quintet, The. Frank O'Hara. BodElec

Trout seem to learn that danger. Observations and Experiments. Annie Dillard. UpMys

Troy. Edwin Muir. HarvBoo

Troy. Maher Sabry. AnVo, *tr. by* Mohamed Enani

Truant, A. Mike Jenkins. TCAWP

Truant! You love me not–the reason this. We Can Love But Once. Charlotte Dacre. RWP

Truants, The. Walter De la Mare. MoBrPo

Truce. Paul Muldoon. FaBoWar; PBCIP; PNI

Truce. Louis Untermeyer. STuOW

Truce, The. Stella Gibbons. LW

Truce, gentle love, a parley now I crave. Michael Drayton. NoSic *Fr.* Idea.

Truck, The. John A. Stone. BloBone

Trucker leans on his horn down below, A. Work Song. Robyn Selman. TaR

Trucker, The. Will Dyson. NOBAu

Truckin'. Ted Koehler. ReLy

Trucks carried 40 000 blacks to the southern edge of the desert. Dispossessed words. Karen Press. TSAP

True Account of Talking to the Sun at Fire Island, A. Frank O'Hara. AmFaPo; EmeKit; NAMCP V.2; OxBoAm

True and earthy prayer, The / of salami. (LL) Salami. Philip Levine. TRP; WaAnP

True and Obscure Definitions of *Fly*, Domestic and Otherwise. Christine Hume. IAoNAP

True, and yet true that I must Stella love. (LL) Sir Philip Sidney. NAEL-6v1; NAEL-7v1; NoSic *Fr.* Astrophil and Stella.

"True Arab knows how to catch a fly in his hands," A. Naomi Shihab Nye. UnSA

True Blue Lou. Sam Coslow and Leo Robin. ReLy

True Bride, The. Amy Gerstler. PmAP

True daughters of Lilith, night demons. Summer Night. Hayyim Nahman Bialik. FIT, *tr. by* Robert Friend

True, Debby was pure as Weber Bread. Two Timer. Juan Delgado. TouFir

True Descenders. James Kimbrell. AmPoNex; NAPBL

True Dream, A. Elizabeth Barrett Browning. NALW

True Friend, The. Ann Plato. SWaP

True genius, but true woman! dost deny. To George Sand: A Recognition. Elizabeth Barrett Browning. NAEL-6v2; NAEL-7v2; NALW; PEW; PoBW; VWP

True happiness had no localities. Happiness. Robert Pollok. TreFP

True Heroism. *Unknown.* ITBLP

True Illumination Is Habitude. Sam Hamill. AmZen

True Knight [*or* True Knighthood], The. Stephen Hawes. OBEV *Fr.* Pastime of Pleasure, The.

True Knowledge. Bishop Richard Mant. SacPr

True Life Love Stories. Michael Foley.
  "Ah no, ah no, they weren't all gross and slow." PNI
  "*Sois sage, ô ma douleur . . .* I don't." PNI
  "Sword is a cold bride. Yuk!, The." PNI

True Love. Kathleen Norris. UpMys

True Love. Sharon Olds. BodElec; StAl

True Love. Jeremy Young. IrLP

True Love, A. Nicholas Grimald. OBEV

True love in every moment praises God. Mechthild von Magdeburg. WPoS

True Maid, A. Matthew Prior. NAEL-6v1; NAEL-7v1; NIP-4; NPeEn; WaAnP

True Man, A. Attila József. IQMS, *tr. by* Edwin Morgan

True Man is the source, he being the Poetic Genius, The. (LL) All Religions Are One. William Blake. NAEL-6v2; NAEL-7v2

True Measure of Life, The. Philip James Bailey. TreFP

True name is not the one that gilds portals, illustrates proceedings, The. Hidden Name. Victor Segalen. BBASP, *tr. by* Nathaniel Tarn

True Names of Birds, The. Susan Goyette. Coast; OpeFie

True obedience. Onitsura. SoOfWa, *tr. by* Sam Hamill

True path is shadowy and still, far away and hard to find, The. Natsume Soseki. CAoMJL1, *tr. by* Burton Watson

True poesy is not in words. Pastoral Poesy. John Clare. NAEL-7v2

True Relation of their Practice at Oxford Town when there an Act is, A. Alicia D'Anvers. EMWP *Fr.* Oxford-Act, The.

True shape of death and power.. (LL) To a Military Rifle, 1942. Yvor Winters. MoAmPo; PWW2

True Story, A. Marvin Bell. BodElec

True Story Ending in False Hope, A. Pearse Hutchinson. PBCIP

True Story of Snow White, The. Bruce Bennett. ReTh

True storyteller is a, The. *Unknown.* CA

True Texan wears the Lone Star in his heart, A. True Texan, A. Peggy Zuleika Lynch. TiP2

True Thomas lay o'er yond grassy [*or* on Huntlie] bank. Thomas the Rhymer. *Unknown.* OBEV; TFi

True Thomas on earth was never seen.. (LL) Thomas the Rhymer. *Unknown.* OBEV; TFi

True to myself am I, and false to all. Mary Elizabeth Coleridge. ViWPN; VWP

True to our God, true to our native land. (LL)   Lift Every [*or* Ev'ry] Voice and Sing.   James Weldon Johnson.   APT-1; InGu; ISC; TCAPo

(True to our native land.) (LL)   ISC; OxAAAP

True to our native land. (LL)   James Weldon Johnson. *See* True to our God, true to our native land.

True Use of Music, The.   Charles Wesley.   SacPr

True We Are Two Grown Men.   Ed Roberson.   GT

True we are two grown men.   True We Are Two Grown Men.   Ed Roberson. GT

True Western Summer.   Hildegarde Flanner.   APT-2

True-blue the salmon—from his sally.   No Place Like Home.   Llawdden.   OBWVE, *tr. by* Gwyn Jones

True-born Englishman, The.   Daniel Defoe.

"Breed's described, The: Now, Satire, if you can."   OBSV

"In their religion they are so unev'n."   OBSV

"Then let us boast of ancestors no more."   OBSV

"Wherever God erects a house of prayer."   OBSV

True-hearted, whole-hearted, faithful and loyal.   Frances Ridley Havergal.   SacPr

Truelove, his hound so good.   Murder Will Out.   *Unknown.*   DiBP

Trueman, whom for sagacious nose we hail.   Fox Hunt, The.   Henry Brooke.   DiBP

Truest Poetry Is the Most Feigning, The [or, Ars Poetica for Hard Times].   W. H. Auden.   WaAnP

Truffled green green turtle liver.   Menus.   Blaise Cendrars.   GPTC, *tr. by* Ron Padgett

Truganinny.   Wendy Rose.   HATNAP

Truisms, The.   Louis MacNeice.   OBSV; PNI

Truly.   Ingeborg Bachmann.   PoSu

Truly alone muley.   Times.   SeSe

Truly Great.   W. H. Davies.   OBMV

Truly Great, The.   Stephen Spender. *See* I Think Continually of Those Who Were Truly Great.

Truly, he lived in dark times.   Brecht.   Heiner Müller.   GTCP, *tr. by* Reinhold Grimm

Truly I have lost weight, I *have*.   Skeleton's Defense of Carnality, The.   Jack Foley.   ASA

Truly, I live in dark times!   To Those Born Later.   Bertolt Brecht.   AF; GTCP, *tr. by* Erich Fried, Ralph Manheim and John Willett and John Willett

Truly in the east / The white bean.   Song to Promote Growth.   *Unknown.*   OBVE, *tr. by* Washington Matthews

Truly lawn brawn fawn dawn. (LL)   Song Beside a Sippy Cup.   Jenny Factor.   P180; PoDa

Truly my Satan thou art but a dunce.   William Blake.   WeW-3 *Fr.* Gates of Paradise, The.

Truly now.   *Unknown.*   WoPoe *Fr.* Popul Vuh, The.

Truly there is no beauty in Fort Worth, no song.   Beauty is Elsewhere.   Boyce House.   TiP2

Trumpet, The.   Felicia Dorothea Hemans.   TreFP

Trumpet, The.   Edward Thomas.   MoBrPo

Trumpet like a sharp plow, A.   Untitled.   Bei Dao.   WoBe, *tr. by* Iona Man-Cheong and Eliot Weinberger

Trumpet of Judgement, The.   Victor Hugo.   SxFrPo, *tr. by* A. M. and E. H. Blackmore

Trumpet of Liberty, The.   *Unknown.*   NOBRP

Trumpet Player.   Langston Hughes.   BrAP

Trumpet, Shout, Carry!   Velemir Khlebnikov.   TCRusP, *tr. by* Kathy Lewis and Bob Perelman

Trumpet Voluntary in Praise of My Four Children.   Alvaro Cardona-Hine.   ICANM

Trumpets, The.   Jorge de Lima.   TCLAP, *tr. by* Luiz Fernández García

Trumpet's loud clangor, The.   John Dryden.   FaBoWar *Fr.* Song for St Cecilia's Day, 1687, A.

Trumpets, trams, cars backfiring, screeching brakes.   Days of April '43.   George Seferis.   PoetW, *tr. by* Edmund Keeley and Philip Sherrard

Trumpet's voice hath roused the land, The.   Trumpet, The.   Felicia Dorothea Hemans.   TreFP

Trumpet's voice, loud and authoritative, The.   Reasons for Attendance.   Philip Larkin.   NAMCP V.2; PoPoPo

Trundled from / the strangeness of the sea.   Sea-Elephant, The.   William Carlos Williams.   SAmP

Trunks budded and scarred.   Coal Age.   Emily Wilson.   LegDan

Trunks of birches, like scrolls.   A. Velichansky.   TCRusP, *tr. by* Daniel Weissbort

Truro.   Rose Solari.   AmPoNex

Tru's god Lizi.   Tired Lizi Tired.   Lindiwe Mabuza.   HAWP

Truss cuts early Autumn's blue plane, The.   Mechanics.   Sally Keith.   LegDan

Trust.   Lizette Woodworth Reese.   SWaP

Trust, The.   Ellen Bryant Voigt.   CAP-8

Trust Me.   Jean Valentine.   LaCa

Trust me, I have not earned your dear rebuke.   Christina Georgina Rossetti.   OxBSo *Fr.* Monna Innominata.

Trust me. The world is run on a shoestring.   Hard Times.   John Ashbery.   NoAM

Trust never to another's hand.   Elfrida.   László Arany.   IQMS, *tr. by* Watson Kirkconnell

Trust Thou Thy Love.   John Ruskin.   OBEV

Trust thrust first tinder kindling grown.   Burnt Sienna.   Norman Henry, II Pritchard.   GT

Trusted the servile womb to breed free men? (LL)   Advice to Young Ladies.   Alec Derwent Hope.   NAMCP V.1; NoAM; NoP-4; NoP-5

Trusting Jesus.   Frances Ridley Havergal.   SacPr

Trusting steel.   Bryce Milligan.   TiP2

Trusty Lydia, The.   Martial.   DiBP *Fr.* Epigrams.

Truth: "Breast / nursery."   *Unknown.*   SonAtl, *tr. by* Abdul Kalam Azad

Truth.   Geoffrey Chaucer.   NoP-4; NoP-5

Truth.   Josephine D. Henderson Heard.   CBWP-4

Truth.   Kim Chiha.   CAMKP, *tr. by* Kevin O'Rourke

Truth.   George Russell.   MoBrPo

Truth.   Jean Valentine.   BodElec

Truth, The.   Randall Jarrell.   AmWaPo

Truth, The.   Frankie Paino.   AmPoNex; FaoP

Truth? A pebble of quartz? For once, then, something. (LL)   For Once, Then, Something.   Robert Frost.   APT-1; NAMCP V.1; NoAM; OxBoAm

Truth About God, The.   Anne Carson.

By God.   BodElec; OxBoAm; WoBe

(Deflect.)   WoBe

Flexion of God.   BodElec

God Coup, The.   BodElec; WoBe

God Fit, The.   BodElec; WoBe

God Stiff.   WoBe

God's Beloveds Remain True.   WoBe

God's Bouquet of Undying Love.   WoBe

God's Christ Theory.   OxBoAm; WoBe

God's Handiwork.   BodElec

God's Justice.   OxBoAm; WoBe

God's List of Liquids.   OxBoAm; WoBe

God's Mother.   OxBoAm; WoBe

God's Name.   BodElec; WoBe

God's Woman.   OxBoAm; WoBe

God's Work.   BodElec; OxBoAm; WoBe

Grace That Comes by Violence, The.   WoBe

"My religion makes no sense."   BodElec; OxBoAm; WoBe

Teresa of God.   WoBe

Wolf God, The.   WoBe

Truth About Karen, The.   Kenneth Carroll.   ISC

Truth about Northern Lights, The.   Christine Hume.   IAoNAP

Truth at Last.   Edward Rowland Sill.   APN-2

Truth at Last, The.   Fred Chappell.   WoPoe

Truth be told, I do not want to forget.   Native Guard.   Natasha Trethewey.   LegDan

Truth Hall.   Muso Soseki.   EaWin, *tr. by* W. S. Merwin

Truth I do not stretch or shove, The.   Dog, The.   Ogden Nash.   Spl

Truth: I Have Five Fingers on Each Hand!   Imad Fouad.   AnVo, *tr. by* Mohamed Enani

"Truth in the cups" men say, dear youth.   Theocritus.   CAGL *Fr.* Idylls.

Truth Is, The.   Linda Hogan.   HATNAP; ItWoWo; LTA

Truth—is as old as God.   Emily Dickinson.   MoAmPo

Truth is, I envy them.   Tornados.   Thylias Moss.   GT; MakPoe

Truth is I loved it, The.   Addiction.   Sheryl St. Germain.   IllVoic

Truth is love and love is truth.   Mendacity.   Alfred Edgar Coppard.   OBMV

Truth is not precision but evidence.   Lyn Hejinian.   PFTM-2 *Fr.* Oxota: A Short Russian Novel.

Truth of dependent origination tells me, The.   Kyunyŏ, Great Master.   CATKP *Fr.* Eleven Poems on the Ten Vows of the Universally Worthy Bodhisattva.

Truth of truth was being missed, The. The one who was thinking.   Pieces O'six—XVIII.   Jackson Mac Low.   FTOS

Truth Put It.   Marianne Vitale.   HeMarv

Truth Suppressed, The.   Lizelia Augusta Jenkins Moorer.   CBWP-3

Truth the Dead Know, The.   Anne Sexton.   ColAP; FTtHH; ItP; MoAmPo; NAMCP V.2; NoAM; NoP-4; NoP-5; VCAP

Truth You Carry Is Very Dark, The.   Alfred B. Spellman.   EGAG

Truthful James to the Editor.   Bret Harte.   APN-2

Truth-loving Persians do not dwell upon.   Persian Version, The.   Robert Graves.   EMP; NAMCP V.1; NoAM; NoP-4; NoP-5; OBWP; StAl; WeW-3

Try a Little Tenderness.   Jimmy Campbell, Reginald Connelly and Harry Woods.   ReLy

Try and Make It.   Han-shan (Cold Mountain).   BB; CCL1; NDACCP, *tr. by* Gary Snyder

Try and make it to Cold Mountain. (LL)   Try and Make It.   Han-shan (Cold Mountain).   BB; CCL1; NDACCP, *tr. by* Gary Snyder

Try book-ending punctuation vouchers.   Nicole Markotić.   PoPra

Try / Delivery.   Forest Utilization.   Anthony Barnett.   OnScMo

Try to avoid inhaling the laden air. (LL)   Lovers of the Poor, The.   Gwendolyn Brooks.   CAP-8; ESEAA; IllVoic; LTA; NoAM

Try to be done now.   Silence Afterwards, The.   Rolf Jacobsen.   WED, *tr. by* Robert Bly

Try to Cover Your Shivering Shoulders.   Irina Ratushinskaya.   AF

Try to cover your shivering shoulders in rags of the oldest.   Try to Cover Your Shivering Shoulders.   Irina Ratushinskaya.   AF

Try to keep them, poet.   When They Come Alive.   Constantine P. Cavafy.   CAGL, *tr. by* Edmund Keeley and Philip Sherrard

Try to Praise the Mutilated World.   Adam Zagajewski.   BeAl; PLBUT; StAl, *tr. by* Clare Cavanagh

Try to see the spring here.   Letter.   Sarah Ruden.   AmPoNex

Try to think that love's not around.   Angel Eyes.   Earl Brent.   ReLy

Try Tropic.   Genevieve Taggard.   APT-2; MoAmPo

Try, try again.. (LL)   Try, Try Again.   T. H. Palmer.   ChAP; ITBLP

Try, Try Again.   T. H. Palmer.   ChAP; ITBLP

Trying Again.   Dahlia Ravikovitch.   VCWP

Trying for some.   Writing the Poem.   Gary H. Holthaus.   TAPaP

Trying on a hat in the shop.   Dangerous Hats.   Richard Garcia.   TouFir

Trying on New-Made Clothes: Three Poems.   Hsüeh T'ao [*or* Xue Tao]. *tr. by* Jeanne Larsen
    1.   WoPoe, *tr. by* Jeanne Larsen
    2.   WoPoe, *tr. by* Jeanne Larsen
    3.   WoPoe, *tr. by* Jeanne Larsen

Trying so hard.   Sunbathing.   Nancy Travis.   ISC

Trying To.   Wendy Barker.   InoFa

Trying to.   Hut Poem #1.   Jonathan Greene.   WhBo

Trying to Make Music.   David Wagoner.   BAP-04

Trying to open locked doors with a sword, threading.   Sojourn in the Whale.   Marianne Moore.   NALW

Trying to Pray.   James Wright.   BBASP; WaAnP

Trying to protect his students' innocence.   History Teacher, The.   Billy Collins.   SUP

Trying to Raise the Dead.   Dorianne Laux.   RoV

Trying to Remember People I Never Really Knew.   William Childress.   AmWaPo

Trying to Sleep After Studying Color Photos of Goma.   Monifa Atungaye Love.   BtF

Trying to Sleep on My Father's Couch and Staring at the Fractured Plaster, I Recall.   Tony Barnstone, Willis Barnstone and Haixin Xu.   VisFro

Trying to speak means flailing with.   Winged Words.   Rachel Hadas.   FFC

Trying to Talk with a Man.   Adrienne Rich.   AtGh

Trying to understand the words.   Bird-Language.   W. H. Auden.   OWoS

Tryma.   David R. Slavitt.   PoDa

Tryma is a nutlike drupe, A.   Tryma.   David R. Slavitt.   PoDa

Try-Outs, The.   Sharon Olds.   PoDa

Tryst.   Olga Broumas.   WiU

Tryst.   Lavinia Greenlaw.   BeAl

Tryst.   Duvvuri Ramireddy.   HotL, *tr. by* V. Narayana Rao

Tryst: "My eyes transfixed on the road, I strained in their light to see."   Yahya Kemal [Beyatlı].   NaPG, *tr. by* Talat Sait Halman

Tryst [*or* Trysting Place], The.   William Soutar.   EdScPo; NePenScot; NPeEn

Tryst, The.   Harriet Prescott Spofford.   SWaP

Tryst, The.   Mary E. Tucker.   CBWP-1

Tryst, The.   *Unknown*.   OBWVE, *tr. by* Joseph P. Clancy

Trystan and Esyllt.   *Unknown*.   OBWVE, *tr. by* Gwyn Jones

Ts'ai Chi'h.   Ezra Pound.   NoP-4; NoP-5

Tsa'lagi Council Tree.   Gladys Cardiff.   HATNAP

Tsar sits on his throne as if he sat on bones, The.   Svetlana Kekova.   CRWP, *tr. by* Ruth Fainlight

Tsiek tsiek and again tsiek tsiek.   Mu-Lan.   *Unknown*.   WoPoe, *tr. by* Hans H. Frankel

Tsitsa.   Kofi Anyidoho.   NAfrP

Tsu Mei is early dead. Chang Yu.   Reading the Poems of an Absent Friend.   Ou-yang Hsiu.   NDACCP, *tr. by* Kenneth Rexroth

Tsuneko—Psychiatric Medications Clinic.   Susan Kolodny.   OPRER

Ttest.   Lee Ranaldo.   HeMarv

Tu as écrit: Me voici, fidèle à l'écho de ta voix, taciturne, inexprimé..   Trahison fidèle.   Victor Segalen.   YaTCFP

Tu as les yeux pers des champs de rosées.   Gaston Miron.   YaTCFP *Fr.* Marche à l'amour, La.

Tu Corazón, una Naranja Helada.   Miguel Hernández.   RaW

Tu cuerpo es la noche.   Forma.   Elsa Cross.   RMCMP

Tu Do Street.   Yusef Komunyakaa.   AmAlph; AmWaPo; CAP-8; LTA; NAMCP V.2; OxBoAm; SwNoth

Tu es celui.   Autre, L'.   André Velter.   YaTCFP

Tu m'as dit si tu m'écris.   Lettre.   Blaise Cendrars.   YaTCFP

Tú me llevas, conciencia plena, deseante dios.   Conciencia Plena.   Juan Ramón Jiménez.   RaW

Tu vergüenza genital es el gramófono del hombre blanco.   Sobre un Poema Nativo de las Islas Salomón que Comienza: "Tu Vergüenza Genital Es el Gramófono del Hombre Blanco."   Gabriel Celaya.   RaW

Tu viens souvent avec ton oiseau sur le poing.   Tu viens souvent.   Franck André Jamme.   YaTCFP

Tub with no bottom, A.   Buson.   EH, *tr. by* Robert Hass

Tube Ride to Martha's.   Matthew Sweeney.   ModIr

Tube, The.   W. C. W. Watching Presley's Second Appearance on The Ed Sullivan Show: Mercy Hospital, Newark, 1956.   David Wojahn.   AllShUp; SwNoth

Tube Time.   Eve Merriam.   TLR

Tubes.   Terry Wolverton.   WiU

Tubman Strong.   Darryl Holmes.   InTrad

Tubs of / memory.   Roof Garden.   James Schuyler.   OBGa

Tuckanuck.   George Cabot Lodge.   APN-2

Tuckett. Bill Tuckett. Telegraph operator, Hall's Creek.   Morse.   Les A. Murray.   NoP-4; NoP-5

Tucking up your dress.   Little Hand.   Larry Fagin.   AHA

Tudor indeed is gone and every rose.   Ezra Pound.   WoPoe *Fr.* Cantos.

Tuesday.   Lisa Robertson.   OpeFie

Tuesday, 17 April.   Norman Fischer.   WANABP *Fr.* Success.

Tuesday, June 4, 1991.   Billy Collins.   PoDa

Tuesday Morning, Loading Pigs.   David Lee.   P180

Tuesday Night Affair.   Sandra Turner Bond.   ISC

Tuesday 9:00 AM.   Denver Butson.   P180

Tuesday Shaman.   Maurice Kilwein Guevara.   TouFir

Tuesday, torrential downpours blackened.   ArabInnocents.   Joanna Kadi.   PoArWo

Tuesdays we always have fish.   Spring House.   Bernadette Mayer.   AHA

Tuft of Flowers, The.   Robert Frost.   APT-1; MoAmPo; NAAPv.2

Tuft of Kelp, The.   Herman Melville.   APN-2

Tug against the river.   George Oppen.   APT-2; PFTM-1

Tug with bright streets at lonely lights like his. (LL)   Flying at Night.   Ted Kooser.   OtW; PBCAP

Tugboat outside, The.   Remark, The.   Oliver Pitcher.   EGAG

Tugged Hand, The.   W. H. Davies.   TCAWP

Tugged out of bed by a dream.   Near Dawn.   Eric Tretheway.   PfSP

Tugging at containment.   I Swear to You, That Ship Never Sunk in Middle-Passage!   Lawrence S. Cumberbatch.   EGAG

Tuglik's Song.   Tuglik.   WoPoe, *tr. by* Stephen Berg

Tugs like the gravity that drags it back to earth. (LL)   Calf.   Katrina Porteous.   BeAl; NeBl

Tugs were pulling the ship out to sea, The.   Girl on the Quay at Rio, The.   T. H. Parry-Williams.   BBMWP, *tr. by* Richard Poole

Tukuaho: what a bastard.   Story of Kepa Falekaono, The.   *Unknown*.   SonAtl, *tr. by* Marcia Gilchrist, I. Futa Helu, Helen Morton Lee, Daniel Longstaff, Okusi Mahina, Erica Mehrtens, Konai Thaman and Elizabeth Wood-Ellem

Tulip.   Penny Harter.   TWW

Tulip.   Humbert Wolfe.   MoBrPo

Tulip Bed, The.   William Carlos Williams.   OBGa

Tulip / Girl's breasts.   Healers.   Natalia Toledo.   RMCMP, *tr. by* Alberto A. Ríos

Tulip, just opened, had offered to hold, A.   Butterfly's Dream, The.   Hannah Flagg Gould.   SWaP

Tulip Merchant, The.   Aloysius Bertrand.   MotU, *tr. by* James Weeks

Tulip or Turnip.   Don George.   ReLy

Tulip or turnip, rosebud or rhubarb.   Tulip or Turnip.   Don George.   ReLy

Tulip / Senos de niña.   Curanderas.   Natalia Toledo.   RMCMP

Tulip shits on the lawn, The.   Flower Piece.   Gerhard Rühm.   PFTM-2, *tr. by* Rosmarie Waldrop

Tulip Time in Sing Sing.   P. G. Wodehouse.   ReLy

Tulip Tree.   Sacheverell Sitwell.   MoBrPo

Tulips.   Mark Halperin.   PoDa

Tulips.   Medbh McGuckian.   PNI

Tulips.   Sylvia Plath.   NAMCP V.2; NoP-4; NoP-5; WeW-3

Tulips.   Mieke Tillema.   TuT, *tr. by* Joan McBreen

Tulips are too excitable, it is winter here, The.   Tulips.   Sylvia Plath.   NAMCP V.2; NoP-4; NoP-5; WeW-3

Tulips I do not love, they seem. Tulips. Mieke Tillema. TuT, *tr.* by Joan McBreen

Tulips, like Americans. Considering Tulips. Mieke Tillema. TuT, *tr.* by Medbh McGuckian

Tullynoe: Tête-à-Tête in the Parish Priest's Parlour. Paul Durcan. BeAl; ModIr; NPeEn; OBCoV

Tulum Saw the Coming. Alan Napier. AtGh

Tumble me down, and I will sit. To Fortune. Robert Herrick. CavPo

Tumbled out of heaven. Blue Day Journey, The. Gwyn Jones. OBWVE

Tumbler, The. Ludovico Ariosto. DiBP *Fr.* Orlando Furioso.

Tumblers. Jongleurs. Ring-a-rosies. *Stet!*. (LL) Wheels within Wheels. Seamus Heaney. ArBi; ModIr

Tumbleweed that leaves its root and stock, The. Ts'ao Chih. CCL1, *tr.* by John Frodsham

Tumbling Dice. Rachel Loden. SwNoth

Tumbling from some far-flung cloud. Love, Like Water. Julia Copus. BeAl; MoWP

Tumbling in big solitary drops. Sexual Water. Pablo Neruda. ConPit; PFTM-1, *tr.* by Clayton Eshleman

Tumbling, pausing, leaping, knocking together. Metaphysic of Snow. Donald Finkel. PoA 2002

Tumult of my fretted mind, The. Self-Analysis. Anna Wickham. MoBrPo

Tumult, weeping, many new ghosts. Snow Storm. Tu Fu [*or* Du Fu]. BLT; NDACCP, *tr.* by Kenneth Rexroth

Tumultuous Plenty in the Heavens. Sorley MacLean. EdScPo, *tr.* by Iain Crichton Smith

Tunbridge Wells. John Wilmot, 2d Earl of Rochester. OBSV

Tundra's Edge. John Burnside. EdScPo

Tune. Robert Kelly. FTOS

Tune, The. Yousif al-Sa'igh. IrPoTo, *tr.* by Saadi A. Simawe

Tune: "A Riverside Town." Su Tung-p'o. ColAnChi, *tr.* by Jiaosheng Wang

Tune: "A Thousand Autumns." Huang T'ing-chien. ColAnChi, *tr.* by James Robert Hightower

Tune: "Airing Inmost Feelings." Li Ch'ing-chao. ColAnChi, *tr.* by Jiaosheng Wang

Tune: "Always Having Fun." Su Tung-p'o. ColAnChi, *tr.* by James Robert Hightower

Tune: "As If in a Dream." Nara Singde. ColAnChi, *tr.* by David McCraw

Tune: "Beating Silk Floss." Li Yü. ColAnChi, *tr.* by Jiaosheng Wang

Tune: "Beautiful Barbarians." Li Po. ChinPo, *tr.* by Ye Weilian [*or* Yeh Wei-lien *or* Wai-lim Yip]

Tune: "Beautiful Barbarians." Wen T'ing-yün. ChinPo, *tr.* by Ye Weilian [*or* Yeh Wei-lien *or* Wai-lim Yip]

Tune: "Beauty Yu." Li Yü. ChinPo, *tr.* by Ye Weilian [*or* Yeh Wei-lien *or* Wai-lim Yip]

Tune: "Bells in the Rain." Liu Yung. ChinPo, *tr.* by Ye Weilian [*or* Yeh Wei-lien *or* Wai-lim Yip]

Tune: "Bells Ringing in the Rain." Liu Yung. ColAnChi, *tr.* by Jiaosheng Wang

Tune: "Butterflies Lingering over Flowers." Nara Singde. ColAnChi, *tr.* by David McCraw

Tune: "Butterflies Lingering over Flowers." Su Tung-p'o. ColAnChi, *tr.* by Jiaosheng Wang

Tune: "Calming Windswept Waves." Su Tung-p'o. ColAnChi, *tr.* by Jiaosheng Wang

Tune: "Charming Nien-Nu." Su Tung-p'o. ChinPo, *tr.* by Ye Weilian [*or* Yeh Wei-lien *or* Wai-lim Yip]

Tune: "Ch'ing-P'ing Song." Huang T'ing-chien. ChinPo, *tr.* by Ye Weilian [*or* Yeh Wei-lien *or* Wai-lim Yip]

Tune: "Courtyard Full of Fragrance, The." Huang T'ing-chien. ColAnChi, *tr.* by James Robert Hightower

Tune: "Dream Song." Li Ch'ing-chao. ChinPo, *tr.* by Ye Weilian [*or* Yeh Wei-lien *or* Wai-lim Yip]

Tune: "Dreaming of Southland" Thinking of Someone. Liu Shih. ColAnChi, *tr.* by Kang-i Sun Chang

Tune: "Drunk in Fairyland." Ou-yang Hsiu. ColAnChi, *tr.* by James Robert Hightower

Tune: "Drunk in the East Wind." Lu Chih. ChinPo, *tr.* by Ye Weilian [*or* Yeh Wei-lien *or* Wai-lim Yip]

Tune: "Eight Beats of a Kan-chou Song." Liu Yung. ColAnChi, *tr.* by James J. Y. Liu

Tune: Eternal Longing. *Unknown.* ColAnChi *Fr.* Four *Tz'u* from Tun-huang.

Tune: Eternal Longing. *Unknown.* ColAnChi *Fr.* Four *Tz'u* from Tun-huang.

Tune: Eternal Longing. *Unknown.* ColAnChi *Fr.* Four *Tz'u* from Tun-huang.

Tune: "Fisherman's Pride." Li Ch'ing-chao. ColAnChi, *tr.* by Jiaosheng Wang

Tune for a Flute. Ivan Davidkov.

  1. CSCBP, *tr.* by Georgi Belev and Lisa Sapinkopf

Tune for a Teenage Niece. Eugene B. Redmond. OxAAAP

Tune: "Four Pieces of Jade." Kuan Han-ch'ing. ChinPo, *tr.* by Ye Weilian [*or* Yeh Wei-lien *or* Wai-lim Yip]

Tune: "Fragrance Fills the Courtyard." Su Tung-p'o. ColAnChi, *tr.* by James Robert Hightower

Tune: "Full Court of Fragrance." Yao Sui. ChinPo, *tr.* by Ye Weilian [*or* Yeh Wei-lien *or* Wai-lim Yip]

Tune: "Gathering Mulberry Leaves." Ou-yang Hsiu. ColAnChi, *tr.* by James Robert Hightower

Tune: "Hairpin Phoenix." Lu Yu. ChinPo, *tr.* by Ye Weilian [*or* Yeh Wei-lien *or* Wai-lim Yip]

Tune: "Happily Flitting Oriole." Wu Li. ColAnChi, *tr.* by Jonathan Chaves

Tune: "Happiness Approaches." Ch'in Kuan. ColAnChi, *tr.* by Jiaosheng Wang

Tune: "Heaven-Cleansed Sands." Ma Chih-yüan. ColAnChi, *tr.* by Victor H. Mair

Tune: "Hung Hsiu-hsieh" To a Flea. Yang Na. ColAnChi, *tr.* by James I. Crump

Tune: "Immortal at the Riverbank." Ch'en Yü-yi. ColAnChi, *tr.* by Jiaosheng Wang

Tune: "Immortal by the River." Su Tung-p'o. ColAnChi, *tr.* by James Robert Hightower

Tune: "Immortal by the River." Su Tung-p'o. ChinPo, *tr.* by Ye Weilian [*or* Yeh Wei-lien *or* Wai-lim Yip]

Tune: "Joy of Encounter." Li Yü. ColAnChi, *tr.* by Jiaosheng Wang

Tune: "Joy of Encounter." Li Yü. ColAnChi, *tr.* by Jiaosheng Wang

Tune: "Joy of Eternal Union." Li Ch'ing-chao. ColAnChi, *tr.* by Jiaosheng Wang

Tune: "Joy of Returning to the Fields" ("Evening rain drips on the steps.") Huang T'ing-chien. ColAnChi, *tr.* by James Robert Hightower

Tune: "Joy of Returning to the Fields" ("Spring scene finds me thinner still, The.") Huang T'ing-chien. ColAnChi, *tr.* by James Robert Hightower

Tune: "Magnolia Flower." Ou-yang Hsiu. ColAnChi, *tr.* by James Robert Hightower

Tune: "Magnolia Flowers." Li Ch'ing-chao and Jiaosheng Wang. ColAnChi

Tune: Magpie on the Branch. *Unknown.* ColAnChi *Fr.* Four *Tz'u* from Tun-huang.

Tune: "Memories of the South." Li Yü. ColAnChi, *tr.* by Jiaosheng Wang

Tune: "Memories of the South." Liu Yu Hsi. ColAnChi, *tr.* by Jiaosheng Wang

Tune: "Memories of the South." Po Chü-i. ColAnChi, *tr.* by Jiaosheng Wang

Tune: "Merriment Before the Palace Hall." Chang K'o-chiu. ChinPo, *tr.* by Ye Weilian [*or* Yeh Wei-lien *or* Wai-lim Yip]

Tune: "Moon of the Western River." Hsin Ch'i-chi. ChinPo, *tr.* by Ye Weilian [*or* Yeh Wei-lien *or* Wai-lim Yip]

Tune: "New Bounty of Royalty." Li Yü. ColAnChi, *tr.* by Jiaosheng Wang

Tune: "Nien-nu Is Charming." Chu Tun-ju. ColAnChi, *tr.* by James Robert Hightower

Tune: "On the Trail of Sweet Incense." Li Ch'ing-chao. ColAnChi, *tr.* by Jiaosheng Wang

Tune: "Partridge Sky." Li Ch'ing-chao. ColAnChi, *tr.* by Jiaosheng Wang

Tune: "Partridge Sky." Su Tung-p'o. ColAnChi, *tr.* by Jiaosheng Wang

Tune: "Partridge Sky" At Po-shan Monastery. Hsin Ch'i-chi. ColAnChi, *tr.* by Jiaosheng Wang

Tune: "Partridge Sky" For a Friend. Hsin Ch'i-chi. ColAnChi, *tr.* by Jiaosheng Wang

Tune: "Partridge Sky" I Rejoice to Meet a Friend Visting at My Rustic Study. Ch'iao Lai. ColAnChi, *tr.* by Jiaosheng Wang

Tune: "Perfumed Garden." Ch'in Kuan. ColAnChi, *tr.* by Jiaosheng Wang

Tune: "Picking Mulberry Seeds" Written on a Wall en route to Po-shan. Hsin Ch'i-chi. ColAnChi, *tr.* by Jiaosheng Wang

Tune: "Po Pu-tuan" Fat Couple. Wang Ho-ch'ing. ColAnChi, *tr.* by James I. Crump

Tune: "Po Pu-tuan" Long-Haired Little Dog. Wang Ho-ch'ing. ColAnChi, *tr.* by James I. Crump

Tune: "Prince Lan-Ling." Chou Pang-yen. ChinPo, *tr.* by Ye Weilian [*or* Yeh Wei-lien *or* Wai-lim Yip]

Tune: "Pure Serene Music." Chang Yen. ColAnChi, *tr.* by Jiaosheng Wang

Tune: "Pure Serene Music." Li Yü. ColAnChi, *tr.* by Jiaosheng Wang

Tune: "Pure Serene Music" En Route to Po-shan. Hsin Ch'i-chi. ColAnChi, *tr.* by Jiaosheng Wang

Tune: "Pure Serene Music" Rural Life. Hsin Ch'i-chi. ColAnChi, *tr.* by Jiaosheng Wang

Tune: "Rapt with Wine, Loudly Singing; Joy in Spring's Coming." Kuan Yün-shih. ColAnChi, *tr.* by Richard John Lynn

Tune: "River Town." Su Tung-p'o. ColAnChi, *tr.* by James Robert Hightower

Tune: "Rouged Lips." Ch'in Kuan. ColAnChi, *tr.* by Jiaosheng Wang

Tune: "Rouged Lips." Li Ch'ing-chao. ColAnChi, *tr.* by Jiaosheng Wang

Tune: "Rouged Lips." Wang Kuo-wei. ColAnChi, *tr.* by Jiaosheng Wang

Tune: "Rouged Lips" Rain Just Over on the Night of the Lantern Preview.   Wu Wen-ying.   ColAnChi, *tr. by* Jiaosheng Wang

Tune: "Sand of Silk-Washing Brook."   Ch'in Kuan.   ColAnChi, *tr. by* Jiaosheng Wang

Tune: "Sand of Silk-Washing Brook" ("Faded hibiscus and its leaves.")   Wang Kuo-wei.   ColAnChi, *tr. by* Jiaosheng Wang

Tune: "Sand of Silk-Washing Brook" ("Hazy mountain temple hides away behind the setting sun, A.")   Wang Kuo-wei.   ColAnChi, *tr. by* Jiaosheng Wang

Tune: "Sand of Silk-Washing Brook."   Yen Shu.   ColAnChi, *tr. by* Jiaosheng Wang

Tune: "Sand of Silk-Washing Brook" A Reminiscence.   Wu Wen-ying.   ColAnChi, *tr. by* Jiaosheng Wang

Tune: "Sand of Silk-Washing Brook" In Memoriam.   Nara Singde.   ColAnChi, *tr. by* Jiaosheng Wang

Tune: "Sand Washed by Waves."   Li Yü.   ColAnChi, *tr. by* Jiaosheng Wang

Tune: "Sand Washed by Waves."   Li Yü.   ColAnChi, *tr. by* Jiaosheng Wang

Tune: "San-fan Yü-lou Jen."   *Unknown.*   ColAnChi, *tr. by* James I. Crump

Tune: "Sheep on the Mountain Slope."   Chang Yang-hao.   ChinPo, *tr. by* Ye Weilian [*or* Yeh Wei-lien *or* Wai-lim Yip]

Tune: "Sheep on the Mountain Slope."   Liu Chih.   ChinPo, *tr. by* Ye Weilian [*or* Yeh Wei-lien *or* Wai-lim Yip]

Tune: "Shua Hai-erh" Country Cousin at the Theater.   Tu Shan-fu.   ColAnChi, *tr. by* James I. Crump

Tune: "Sky-Pure Sand."   Ma Chih-yüan.   ChinPo, *tr. by* Ye Weilian [*or* Yeh Wei-lien *or* Wai-lim Yip]

Tune: "Song of Clear River."   Ma Chih-yüan.   ChinPo, *tr. by* Ye Weilian [*or* Yeh Wei-lien *or* Wai-lim Yip]

Tune: Spring at Wu Ling.   Li Ch'ing-chao.   ColAnChi, *tr. by* Jiaosheng Wang

Tune: "Spring in the Ch'in Garden."   Hsin Ch'i-chi.   ColAnChi, *tr. by* James Robert Hightower

Tune: "Spring in the Jade House."   Yen Shu.   ColAnChi, *tr. by* James Robert Hightower

Tune: "Spring in the Painted Hall."   Ch'in Kuan.   ColAnChi, *tr. by* Jiaosheng Wang

Tune: "Sumuche Dancers."   Fan Chung-yen.   ColAnChi, *tr. by* James Robert Hightower

Tune: "The Beauty of Yü."   Li Yü.   ColAnChi, *tr. by* Jiaosheng Wang

Tune: "The Bodhisattva Foreigner."   Wei Chuang.   ColAnChi, *tr. by* John Timothy Wixted

Tune: "The Bodhisattva's Golden Headdress."   Hsin Ch'i-chi.   ColAnChi, *tr. by* Jiaosheng Wang

Tune: "The Charm of a Maiden Singer;" Spring Thoughts.   Li Ch'ing-chao and Jiaosheng Wang.   ColAnChi

Tune: "The Crow's Nocturnal Cry."   Li Yü.   ColAnChi, *tr. by* Jiaosheng Wang

Tune: "The Dark Clouds of Ch'u" Visiting the Rainy Crag Alone.   Hsin Ch'i-chi.   ColAnChi, *tr. by* Jiaosheng Wang

Tune: "The Diviner."   Li Chih-yi.   ColAnChi, *tr. by* Victor H. Mair

Tune the Old Cow Died Of, The.   Norman Nicholson.   EmeKit

Tune: "Thinking of the Imperial Capital."   Wei Chuang.   ColAnChi, *tr. by* John Timothy Wixted

Tune thy music[ke] to thy heart [*or* hart].   Heart's Music.   Thomas Campion.   OBEV

Tune: "Traveler Welcoming the Immortal."   Chang K'o-chiu.   ChinPo, *tr. by* Ye Weilian [*or* Yeh Wei-lien *or* Wai-lim Yip]

Tune: "Treading on Fragrant Grass."   Yen Shu.   ColAnChi, *tr. by* Jiaosheng Wang

Tune: "Trimming the Silver Lamp."   Fan Chung-yen.   ColAnChi, *tr. by* James Robert Hightower

Tune: "Tsui-chung T'ien" To the Giant Butterfly.   Wang Ho-ch'ing.   ColAnChi, *tr. by* James I. Crump

Tune: "Unbroken."   Chang K'o-chiu.   ChinPo, *tr. by* Ye Weilian [*or* Yeh Wei-lien *or* Wai-lim Yip]

Tune: "Vast Virtue."   Kuan Han-ch'ing.   ChinPo, *tr. by* Ye Weilian [*or* Yeh Wei-lien *or* Wai-lim Yip]

Tune: "Walk on the Imperial Street."   Fan Chung-yen.   ChinPo, *tr. by* Ye Weilian [*or* Yeh Wei-lien *or* Wai-lim Yip]

Tune: "Water Mode Song."   Su Tung-p'o.   ColAnChi, *tr. by* James Robert Hightower

Tune: "Winds of Falling Plums."   Ma Chih-yüan.   ChinPo, *tr. by* Ye Weilian [*or* Yeh Wei-lien *or* Wai-lim Yip]

Tune with no more substance than the air, A.   Elevator Music.   Henry Taylor.   GoPo; P180

Tune: "Wu Yeh-erh" Twitting the Teller of Tall Tales.   *Unknown.*   ColAnChi, *tr. by* James I. Crump

Tuned to 104.6 on the FM.   Household Gods.   Jim Elledge.   SwNoth

Tuneful poet, Britain's glory.   Mutual Congratulations of the Poets Anna Seward and Hayley, The.   Richard Porson.   OBSV

Tune's image holding in the line, The.   (LL)   Anew 20.   Louis Zukofsky.   APT-2; NAAPv.2

Tune-Up.   Carl Dennis.   PfSP

T'ung Pass.   Chang Yang-hao.   WoPoe, *tr. by* Sam Hamill

Tungeei, that was her native name.   Captain Cook.   *Aborigine Oral Tradition.*   NOBAu, *tr. by* Percy Mumbulla

Tunnel, The.   Nicanor Parra.   GPTC; TCLAP, *tr. by* W. S. Merwin

Tunnel, The.   Muriel Rukeyser.
   Ceiling Unlimited.   OtW

Tunnel, The.   Mark Strand.   HeIP-4

Tunnel angels crouched in the olive trees spinning the dust of.   About the Extinction Of.   A. Di Michele.   AnSo

Tunnel, but the roof is green and some light, A.   Black Road Over Which Green Trees Grow.   Thomas Lux.   AmAlph

Tunnel, The.   Hart Crane.   MoAmPo; NAAL-5; OxBoAm *Fr.* Bridge, The.

Tunnels.   Yusef Komunyakaa.   AmAlph

Tunning of Elinour Rumming, The.   John Skelton.
   "Instead of coin and money."   NoSic

Tunnyng [*or* Tunning] of Elynour [*or* Elinor] Rummyng [*or* Rumming], The.   John Skelton.
   "Some have no money."   NAEL-7v1

Tunstall Forest.   Donald Davie.   OxBEV

Turbaned / polychrome.   Mandap.   Elsa Cross.   RMCMP, *tr. by* Margaret Sayers Peden

Turbia dicción.   Malva Flores.
   "Siempre que algo se muere."   RMCMP

Turbid Diction.   Malva Flores. *tr. by* Jen Hofer
   "Whenever something dies."   RMCMP, *tr. by* Jen Hofer

Turbulence and Tongue.   Anthony Barnett.   Oth

Turbulent Water, The.   *Unknown.*   TAL

Turf Song.   Sterling Plumpp.   GT

Turf-Stacks.   Louis MacNeice.   OBMV

Turgid itch and the perfume of death.   Fear and the Monkey.   William S. Burroughs.   PFTM-2

Turgid lines of footnote.   (LL)   My Ambition.   James Laughlin.   GifTon; PoA 2002

Turkestan.   Ch'en Tao.   WoPoe, *tr. by* Witter Bynner

Turkey in the Straw.   *Unknown.*   TCAPo

Turkey People.   Brynn Noelle Saito.   FTtHH

Turkeys.   John Clare.   FaBoVe

Turkeys in August.   Gray Jacobik.   UrbNat

Turkeys Observed.   Seamus Heaney.   OWoS

Turkeys wade the close to catch bees, The.   Turkeys.   John Clare.   FaBoVe

Turkish Bakery, The.   O Cham.   CATKP, *tr. by* Peter H. Lee

Turkish Bath in Ortamezar.   Ivan Teofilov.   CSCBP, *tr. by* Georgi Belev and Lisa Sapinkopf

Turkish. Belly-dancer. Sexy tricks.   Automedon.   EroLit, *tr. by* Kenneth McLeish

Turkish government allowes no Law, The.   Fulke, 1st Baron Brooke Greville.   WaAnP *Fr.* Caelica.

Turmoil, The.   Sorley MacLean.   HarvBoo

Turn.   Andrée Chedid.   PoArWo, *tr. by* Lucy McNair

Turn, The.   Robert Creeley.   FTOS

Turn Again.   Ciaran Carson.   BeAl

Turn again, turn again, turn once again.   Carrousel Tune.   Tennessee Williams.   NBLV

Turn and Turn About.   Eva Gerlach.   TuT, *tr. by* Eamon Grennan

Turn back, Uma.   Kamalākānta Bhattācārya.   SinGod, *tr. by* Rachel Fell McDermott

Turn from that road's beguiling ease; return.   Sea's Wash in the Hollow of the Heart, The.   Denise Levertov.   LW

Turn, good wooden horses, round.   Wooden Horses.   Paul Verlaine.   NAWM-7v2, *tr. by* Carlyle Ferren MacIntyre

Turn inside out turn me.   Request.   Shuntaro Tanikawa.   VCWP, *tr. by* Harold Wright

Turn me every which way, three-cornered God.   Lucky Strikes.   Ron Padgett.   FTOS

Turn not [to] the prophet's page, O Son! He knew.   For The Holy Family, by Michelangelo, in the National Gallery.   Dante Gabriel Rossetti.   SacPr

Turn of Privacy, The.   Rick Noguchi.   AmPoNex; NeAmPo

Turn off that charm.   Remind Me.   Dorothy Fields.   ReLy

Turn off the wireless.   W. H. Auden and Christopher Isherwood.   RWPCtW *Fr.* Ascent of F6, The.

Turn off the wireless; we are tired.   W. H. Auden and Christopher Isherwood.   RWPCtW *Fr.* Ascent of F6, The.

Turn on my tongue, O Spanish verse; confirm.   Ewigkeit.   Jorge Luis Borges.   WoPoe, *tr. by* Richard Wilbur

Turn On the Heat.   Lew Brown, B. G. DeSylva and Ray Henderson.   ReLy

Turn on the prudent Ant thy heedless eyes.   Paraphrase.   Samuel Johnson.   ChIV-1

Turn-on (with most of a line by Spicer). Del Ray Cross. FreRad

Turn on Your Side and Bear the Day to Me. George Barker. HarvBoo

Turn Right Next Corner / *The Biggest Little Town in Kansas.* Allen Ginsberg. FTOS *Fr.* Wichita Vortex Sutra.

Turn sharp right off the forestry track. Favourite Stretch of Disused Railway, A. Tom Pow. EdScPo

Turn, sinner, turn today, / Turn sinner, turn O! Turn, Sinner, Turn O! *Unknown.* SSUS

Turn Thanks to Miss Mirry. Lorna Goodison. NAMCP V.2

Turn the other cheek when your brother. Nonresistance, or love Mennonite style. Diana Brandt. ACAMVP

Turn to right, turn to left. Witches' Spells. Madeleine Edmondson. NTCP

Turn to sugar in our mouths. (LL) Potatoes. Linda Hogan. AFaM; IPoFL

Turn to yon vale beneath, whose tangled shade. Bower of Pleasure, The. Mary Robinson. CenSon; RWP

Turn to yon vale beneath, whose tangled shade. Mary Robinson. NPBRoP *Fr.* Sappho and Phaon.

Turn towards the end, be a leaf dying. Jakov Steinberg. FIT, *tr. by* Robert Friend

Turn, turn, my wheel! Turn round and round. Kéramos. Henry Wadsworth Longfellow. APN-1

Turn, turn thy beauteous face away. Francis Beaumont and John Fletcher. NOSC *Fr.* Love's Cure.

Turn your head, look, the light is turning yellow. Villanelle at Sundown. Donald Justice. OxBoAm

Turnabout. Linda Pastan. NIP-4

Turncoat, The. Priscilla Jane Thompson. CBWP-2

Turn'd to that dirt from whence he sprung. (LL) Satirical Elegy on the Death of a Late Famous General, A. Jonathan Swift. NBLV; NPeEn; OBSV; WaAnP

Turned down the gas in the hall. (LL) Death in Leamington. Sir John Betjeman. MakPoe; NoP-4; NoP-5; OxAEP-2

Turned from the camera's eye, hovering. Postcard from Okemah, A. Terrance Hayes. LegDan

Turned from the "eau-forte." Ezra Pound. *Fr.* Hugh Selwyn Mauberley (Life and Contacts).

Turned into a weapon. (LL) Objection to Being Stepped On, The. Robert Frost. NBLV; OBCoV

Turned into a white blade, which fell. (LL) Hawk. Mary Oliver. NAAL-5; NAMCP V.2; OWoS

Turned to stone. Bread to Stone. Joy Kogawa. IFF

Turned violet as its shadow. (LL) Ant Hill, The. Cynthia Zarin. NoP-4; NoP-5

Turnes all the spirits of Man into desire. (LL) Fulke, 1st Baron Brooke Greville. NoP-4; NoP-5 *Fr.* Caelica.

Turning, The. Janet Paisley. EdScPo

Turning a Fresh Eye. Lillias Scott Forbes. EdScPo

Turning and turning in the widening gyre. Second Coming, The. William Butler Yeats. BLPJKO; BrAP; CABP; ChIV-2; ClHu; CtM; EMP; GI; HarvBoo; HeIP-4; IrV; MoBrPo; NAAL-3; NAEL-6v2; NAEL-7v2; NAMCP V.1; NIL-7; NIP-4; NoAM; NoP-4; NoP-5; OxAEP-2; OxBEV; PoPoPo; RaBo; RSR; SoSe-8; TFi; TRP; WaAnP; WoPoe

Turning away abruptly, out of respect. (LL) Variations on a Text by Vallejo. Donald Justice. CAP-8; NAMCP V.2; NoAM; VCAP

Turning back from the end. In Memory. Bei Dao. WoBe, *tr. by* Iona Man-Cheong and Eliot Weinberger

Turning Fifty. Thomas William Shapcott. BMAP

Turning into an Oak Tree. Cindy Goff. LaCa

Turning it over, considering, like a madman. John Berryman. NoAM *Fr.* Dream Songs.

Turning of the car. Luigi Fontanella. NeIt

Turning of the Year, The. Delaina Thomas. OpBo

Turning Pro. Ishmael Reed. SoSe-8

Turning Prose into Poetry. Bernadette Mayer. NYP2

Turning their backs on the sabbath. Kirkintilloch Revisited. Gerald Mangan. EdScPo

Turning Thirty, I Contemplate Students Bicycling Home. Rita Dove. AmAlph; ArBi; ESEAA

Turning those many lefts and rights. House of Memories. Ch'oe Sûngja. EcSo, *tr. by* Mickey Hong

Turning to sponge a flank. Eureka. Maureen Duffy. PoBW

Turning to you, my name—. Recognized Futures. Lisa Suhair Majaj. UnSA

Turning Year, The. Su Tung-p'o. NDACCP, *tr. by* Kenneth Rexroth

Turning your back, you button your blouse. That's new. Changing What We Mean. Eloise Klein Healy. WiU

Turnip Field. John Thompson. Coast

Turnips Are. B. P. Nichol. IFF

Turnover. Profit. Readies. Cash. Loot. Dough. Income. Stash. Making Money. Carol Ann Duffy. RSaN

Turns. Tony Harrison. NAEL-6v2; NAEL-7v2; NAMCP V.2 *Fr.* School of Eloquence, The.

Turns at the Dance. Diana García. TouFir

Turns in the waking west and goes to sleep. (LL) Hart Crane. MoAmPo; NoAM; OxBoAm *Fr.* Bridge, The.

Turnspit Taught, The. John Gay. DiBP *Fr.* Fables: Second Series.

Turnstile, The. William Barnes. NPeEn; OxBEV

Turnus and the Courser. Virgil. OBVE *Fr.* Aeneid [*or* Eneados *or* Aeneis], The.

Turnus and the Stone. Virgil. OBVE *Fr.* Aeneid [*or* Eneados *or* Aeneis], The.

Turnus and the Wanton Courser. Virgil. OBVE *Fr.* Aeneid [*or* Eneados *or* Aeneis], The.

Turnus Summons His Allies, Aeneas Is "Perturbit wyth Gret Thochtis." Virgil. OBVE *Fr.* Aeneid [*or* Eneados *or* Aeneis], The.

Turo, Rescuer of the Sun and Moon. *Unknown. tr. by* Keith Bosley

"One son of God, The." WoPoe, *tr. by* Keith Bosley

Turquoise pool rose up to meet us, The. Summer I Was Sixteen, The. Geraldine Connolly. P180

Turtle. Yousif al-Sa'igh. IrPoTo, *tr. by* Chuck Miller and Saadi A. Simawe

Turtle. Peter Blue Cloud. HATNAP

Turtle: "Who would be a turtle who could help it?" Kay Ryan. CalPo

Turtle, A. Robert Bly. MotU

Turtle, The. William Carlos Williams. EmeKit; PtR; RaBo; SAmP

Turtle Blessing. Penny Harter. TWW

Turtle Dove, The. Geoffrey Hill. OxBEV

Turtle entered our house, A. Turtle. Yousif al-Sa'igh. IrPoTo, *tr. by* Chuck Miller and Saadi A. Simawe

Turtle Head Stupa. Muso Soseki. EaWin, *tr. by* W. S. Merwin

Turtle lives 'twixt plated decks, The. Turtle, The. Ogden Nash. NAAPv.2; NoP-4; NoP-5; SoSe-8

Turtle Soup. Marilyn Chin. LoL

Turtles. Robert Siegel. PfSP

Turtles Hatching. Mark O'Connor. NOBAu

Turvy-Topsy. Paul Groves. TCAWP

Tus palabras queman. Varas. Veronica Volkow. RMCMP

Tuscaloosa: Riversong. Honorée Fanonne Jeffers. RD

Tuscan cypresses. Cypresses. D. H. Lawrence. NAEL-6v2; NAEL-7v2

Tuscan Olives. Agnes Mary Frances Robinson. VWP

Tuscan, that wanderest through the realms of gloom. Dante. Henry Wadsworth Longfellow. NCAP

Tuscarora. Jan Heller Levi. PfS

Tuskegee Airfield [*for the Tuskegee Airmen*]. Marilyn Nelson Waniek. ESEAA; GT; OtW

Tuskegee Experiment. Mohammed Sadiq. SeSe

Tusks that clashed in mighty brawls, The. On the Vanity of Earthly Greatness. Arthur Guiterman. AmWit; APT-1; HeIP-4

Tut-tut! give back the flags—how can you care. Confederate Flags, The. Ambrose Bierce. AmWaPo; CBCWP

Tutelage. Chase Twichell. WANABP

Tutelar of the Place, The. David Jones.

"Queen of the differentiated sites, administratrix of the." AngWePo; TCAWP

Tuti's Ice Cream. Chairil Anwar. PoetW, *tr. by* Burton Raffel

Tutor who tooted a flute, A. Limerick. Carolyn Wells. SoSe-8

Tutto è Sciolto. James Joyce. OBMV

Tutumantu is like hopscotch, kwani-kwani is like hide-and-seek. Comprehensive. Carol Ann Duffy. RSaN

Tuya Es la Hacienda. León Felipe. RaW

Tu-zhi: Hares. *Unknown.* CCL1, *tr. by* Arthur Cooper

T.V. John Forbes. BMAP

TV. Rodney Jones. BeAl; IllVoic; ReTh

TV Dinner. Michael Warr. BRtP

TV in Black and White. Gary Soto. ReTh; RWB

TV is presocial, like Men. Anne Carson. NAMCP V.2 *Fr.* TV Men.

TV Men. Anne Carson.

Lazarus. WaAnP

"TV is presocial, like Men." NAMCP V.2

TV Movie. Jack Turner. PoA 2002

TV set, stirring itself, confides, The. Visitor's Book, 9, The. John Davies. TCAWP

Twa bodachs, I mind, had a threep ae day. Mercy o' Gode. Pittendrigh Macgillivray. EdScPo

Twa Corbies, The. *Unknown.* NePenScot; NoP-5; NPeEn; OBEV; OWoS; OxBEV

(Two Ravens, The.) SoSe-8

Twa Warlds. Duncan Glen. EdScPo

'Twas a battle of States. Battle of Gettysburg, The. Edgar Lee Masters. CBCWP

'Twas a cloudless morn and the sun shone bright. Cherokee, The. Mary Weston Fordham. CBWP-2

'Twas a new feeling—something more. Did Not. Thomas Moore. IrLP

'Twas a night like this. Little White Lies. Walter Donaldson. ReLy

Twas a pause in the hip hop. Club House. Janice Lowe. InTrad

'Twas a summer evening. Robert Southey. *See* It was a summer [*or* summer's] evening.

'Twas a time when Europe was rejoiced. William Wordsworth. NPBRoP

'Twas a tough task, believe it, thus to tame. Upon Dr. Davies's British Grammar. James Howell. AngWePo; OBWVE

'Twas at the royal feast, for Persia won. Alexander's Feast; or, The Power of Music [*or* Musique]. John Dryden. NAEL-6v1; NAEL-7v1; TFi; WaAnP

'Twas at the silent, solemn hour. William and Margaret. David Mallet. OxAEP-1

'Twas brillig, and the slithy toves. Lewis Carroll. AmFaPo; BrAP; BRP; CABP; ChAP; ClHu; CtM; HeIP-4; ITBLP; NAEL-6v2; NAEL-7v2; NBLV; NoAM; NoP-4; NoP-5; NOxBChV; NTCP; OBSP; OxAEP-2; OxBEV; TFi; TRP; UV *Fr.* Through the Looking-Glass.

'Twas but a dream!—I saw the stag leap free. Arabella Stuart. Felicia Dorothea Hemans. NPBRoP; RWP

'Twas Christmas Eve and bitter cold. Dark Christmas on Wildwood Road, The. Morris Gilbert Bishop. ChrPo

'Twas Crisis—All the length had passed. Emily Dickinson. InoFa

'Twas eve in sunny Italy. Tale of Italy, A. Eloise Bibb. CBWP-4

'Twas eve; the broadly shining sun. To ———. Edward Coote Pinkney. APN-1

'Twas ever thus from childhood's hour! Disaster. Charles Stuart Calverley. NBLV

'Twas fifty quatrains: and from unknown strands. Fifty Quatrains. Michael Field. VWP

'Twas here my summer paused. Emily Dickinson. APN-2

'Twas in a neighbouring land what time. Caroline Anne Bowles Southey. DiBP *Fr.* Conte à mon chien.

'Twas in a Paris café that first I found him. Just a Gigolo. Julius Brammer. ReLy, *tr. by* Irving Caesar and Leonello Casucci

'Twas in heaven pronounced, and 'twas muttered in hell. Riddle, A. Catherine Maria Fanshawe. NOBRP; OxBEV

'Twas in the mazes of a wood. Savage of Aveyron, The. Mary Robinson. RWP

'Twas in the middle of the night. Mary's Ghost. Thomas Hood. NPBRoP

'Twas in the prime of summer time. Dream of Eugene Aram [the Murderer], The. Thomas Hood. NPBRoP

'Twas in the year two thousand and one. Last Man, The. Thomas Hood. NPBRoP

'Twas like a Maelstrom, with a notch. Final Inch, The. Emily Dickinson. APN-2; NCAP

'Twas mercy brought me from my *Pagan* land. On Being Brought from Africa to America. Phillis Wheatley. ColAP; FaBoA; ISC; NAAL-3; NAAL-5; NAAPv.1; NALW; NoP-4; NoP-5; OxBEV; OxBoAm; RWP; SacPr

Twas Mulga Bill, from Eaglehawk, that caught the cycling craze. Mulga Bill's Bicycle. Andrew Barton Paterson. ArBi

'Twas nobly thought, and worthy-still. Poetical Question concerning the Jacobites, sent to the Athenians, A. Elizabeth Singer Rowe. BASC

'Twas not for some calm blessing to receive. Her Muffe. Richard Lovelace. PBRV

'Twas on a Holy Thursday, their innocent faces clean. William Blake. BrAP; GoPo; NAEL-6v2; NAEL-7v2; NAWM-7v2; NOBRP; NoP-4; NoP-5; NPBRoP; NPeEn; TFi *Fr.* Songs of Innocence.

'Twas on a lofty vase's side. Ode on the Death of a Favo[u]rite Cat, Drowned in a Tub [*or* Bowl] of Gold Fishes. Thomas Gray. BrAP; ClHu; CtM; ItP; NAEL-6v1; NAEL-7v1; NBLV; NoP-5; OBCoV; OxBEV; TFi; WaAnP

Twas on a Monday morning. Charlie is my Darling. James Hogg. NePenScot

'Twas on a summer noon, in Stainsford mead. My Ox Duke. John Dyer. NPeEn

'Twas on the 8th April, on the afternoon of that day. William McGonagall. VerBaPo *Fr.* Tale of the Sea, A.

'Twas on the shores that round our coast. Yarn of the *Nancy Bell*, The. William Schwenck Gilbert. TFi; UV

'Twas only a passing thought, my love. Only a Thought. Charles MacKay. STuOW

'Twas Rollog, and the Minim Potes. *Unknown.* UV

'Twas said of Greece two thousand years ago. Colonial Nomenclature. John Dunmore Lang. NOBAu

'Twas such a big surprise to see you. Welcome to My Dream. Johnny Burke. ReLy

'Twas Summer and the sun was mounted high. Ruined Cottage, The. William Wordsworth. NAEL-6v2; NAEL-7v2; NoP-4; NoP-5; NPBRoP

'Twas sunset's hallow'd time—and such an eve. James Kirke Paulding. APN-1 *Fr.* Backwoodsman, The.

'Twas sunset's hour, the glorious day. Exile's Reverie, The. Mary Weston Fordham. CBWP-2

'Twas the angel of death that to us downward flew. In Memoriam of E. B. Clark. Lizelia Augusta Jenkins Moorer. CBWP-3

'Twas the angel of Eden, to Adam he said. Dedication Day Poem. Lizelia Augusta Jenkins Moorer. CBWP-3

'Twas the dream of a God. Ireland. Dora Sigerson Shorter. OBEV

'Twas the horse thief, Andy Regan, that was hunted like a dog. Father Riley's Horse. Andrew Barton Paterson. NOBAu

'Twas the night before Christmas. Visit from St Nicholas, A. Clement Clarke Moore. APN-1; BLPJKO; BRP; ChAP; ChrPo; NTCP; OBCP; OxBoAm; TCAPo; TFi

'Twas the voice of the Wanderer, I heard her exclaim. Wanderer, The. Stevie Smith. NALW

'Twas thereupon. Arch, The. Herman Melville. NCAP

'Twas warm—at first—like Us. Emily Dickinson. APN-2; InoFa; NAWM-7v2; NCAP; SoSe-8

'Twas when the spousal time of May. Coventry Patmore. OxAEP-2 *Fr.* Angel in the House, The.

'Twas whispered in Heaven, 'twas muttered in Hell. Enigma. Catherine Maria Fanshawe. OBCoV

'Twas yesterday; 'twas long ago. Where Home Was. Augusta Davies Webster. ViWPN

Twasinta's Seminoles; Or Rape of Florida. Albery Allson Whitman.
  "Have I not seen the hills of Candahar." APN-2
  "Is manhood less because man's face is black?" APN-2

Twats in the Ops Room. *Unknown.* FaBoWar

Tweed and Till. *Unknown.* NPeEn
  (Says Tweed tae Till.) FaBoVe
  (Two Rivers, The.) OBEV

Tweedledee and Tweedledoom. Ogden Nash. OBCoV

Twelfth Birthday. Rachel Hadas. PoA 2002

12th Dance—Getting Leather by Language—21 February 1964. Jackson Mac Low. PmAP *Fr.* Pronouns, The—A Collection of 40 Dances—For the Dancers.

Twelfth day of Christmas, The. Twelve Days of Christmas, The. *Unknown.* ChrPo

12 East Scott Street. Elise Paschen. IllVoic

Twelfth Floor West. Marilyn Hacker. ExTi; NAMCP V.2

12th Horse Song of Frank Mitchell (Blue), The. Frank Mitchell. APSN; FTOS, *tr. by* Jerome Rothenberg

Twelfth Man, The. Iftiqar Arif. PML, *tr. by* Brenda Walker and Andrea Deletant

Twelfth Morning; or What You Will. Elizabeth Bishop. APT-2

Twelfth Night. Phyllis McGinley. APT-2

Twelfth Night. Peter Scupham. OBCP

Twelfth Night. Elinor Wylie. ChrPo; SacPr

Twelfth Night. William Shakespeare.
  Clown's Song, The. NoSic; TFi
  (Come Away, Come Away, Death.) NoP-4; NoP-5
  (Dirge.) OBEV
  (Feste's Song.) NBLV
  "I see you what you are: you are too proud." OxAEP-1
  "If Music be the food of love, play on." WaAnP
  (O mistress mine, where are you roaming?) BrAP
  "O[h] mistress mine, where are you roaming?" AEP; ClHu; NAEL-6v1; NBLV; NoP-4; NoP-5; NoSic; TFi; WoPoe
  Song. NoSic; OxAEP-1; TFi
  (Sweet-and-Twenty.) OBEV
  (When That I Was and a Little Tiny Boy.) CtM; NoP-4; NoP-5

Twelfth of July, The. Patrick Kavanagh. ModIr

Twelfth of July, the voice of Ulster speaking, The. Twelfth of July, The. Patrick Kavanagh. ModIr

Twelfth Song of the Holy Young Men. *Unknown.* APN-2 *Fr.* Mountain Chant, The.

Twelfth Song of the Thunder. *Unknown.* APN-2 *Fr.* Mountain Chant, The.

Twelve. Rossana Ombres. NeIt

Twelve, The. Aleksandr Aleksandrovich Blok. *tr. by* Anselm Hollo
  "Making tracks." WoPoe, *tr. by* Anselm Hollo

Twelve, The. Allen Tate. APT-2; ChIV-2

Twelve Articles. Jonathan Swift. NBLV; OBCoV

Twelve Bar Bessie. Jackie Kay. BeAl; NeBl

Twelve children, twelve gray geese in starched. Handbell Choir, The. Jane Flanders. PBCAP

Twelve Days of Christmas, The. *Unknown.* ChrPo

Twelve Faces of the Emerald. Dan Pagis. WoPoe, *tr. by* Stephen Mitchell

Twelve Gates. Lorenzo Thomas. EGAG

Twelve good friends. Peter and John. Elinor Wylie. MakPoe; MoAmPo

Twelve Lies, The. Jelaluddin Rumi. WED, *tr. by* Robert Bly

Twelve Lines about the Burning Bush. Melech Ravitch. BBASP, *tr. by* Ruth Whitman

Twelve Minutes. J. C. Hall. InoFa

Twelve months a year. Thank You Father. Yu Jian. PML, *tr. by* Ron Padgett and Wang Ping

Twelve More Songs for Master Jikong. Baekoon Kyunghan. BecRai, *tr. by* Kim Daljin, Kim Won-Chung and Christopher Merrill

Twelve O'Clock. Carolyn Kizer. ExTi

Twelve o'clock. / Along the reaches of the street. Rhapsody on a Windy Night. T. S. Eliot. HeIP-4

Twelve O'Clock Chant. Leonard Cohen. IFF

12 October. Myra Cohn Livingston. NTCP

Twelve Parts of Her. Jena Osman.
   8. OnScMo
   9. OnScMo
   10. OnScMo

Twelve people, most of us strangers, stand in a room. Eating the Pig. Donald Hall. BodElec

Twelve Poems. Larry Fagin. AHA

12 second poem. Trasi Johnson. InTrad

Twelve, small as six. Broken Moon. Carole Satyamurti. BeAl; MoWP

Twelve Songs. W. H. Auden.
   Fish in the Unruffled Lakes. MoBrPo
   (Funeral Blues.) NoP-5; StAl
   Roman Wall Blues. FaBoWar
   "Some say that love's a little boy." NoP-5; StAl
   Song. CAGL; EMP; MoBrPo; OPOU
   (Stop all the clocks.) NIL-7

Twelve Songs of Tosan. Yi Hwang. CATKP, *tr. by* Richard Rutt

Twelve Stones. Chapter 1: Prologue. Yuasa Hangetsu. CAoMJL1, *tr. by* Leith Morton

12,000 Years Is Not Too Long. Carol Cullar. TiP2

Twelve turns of the rail on walls of emerald. Walls of Emerald, The. Li Shang-yin. CCL1, *tr. by* A. C. Graham

Twelve years ago I made a mock. School and Schoolfellows. Winthrop Mackworth Praed. OxAEP-2

Twelve years ago, i met. For Gwendolyn Brooks. Quraysh Ali Lansana. BRtP

Twelve-year-old looks fetching in his prime, A. Strato. CAGL, *tr. by* Daryl Hine

Twenties 3. Jackson Mac Low. WhBo

Twenties 27. Jackson Mac Low. PmAP

Twenties 26. Jackson Mac Low. PmAP

20th Century, The. Lesley Dauer. NAPBL

Twentieth Century Children. Beckian Fritz Goldberg. AmAlph

Twentieth Century Children (2). Beckian Fritz Goldberg. AmAlph

Twentieth Century Children (5): Blood-Kissing. Beckian Fritz Goldberg. AmAlph

Twentieth Century Fresco. Sándor Weöres. IQMS, *tr. by* Adam Makkai

Twentieth year is well-nigh past, The. To Mary. William Cowper. NPBRoP; UV

Twentieth-Century Blues. Kenneth Fearing. IllVoic

Twentieth-Century Love. George M. Cohan. ReLy

20 July 1994. Virginia Cerenio. ReBoTo

Twenty Billion Light Years of Loneliness. Shuntaro Tanikawa. PoetW, *tr. by* Harold Wright

Twenty Golden Years Ago. James Clarence Mangan. OxBEV

Twenty lines of / boughs bend into hindering. Susan Howe. PmAP *Fr.* Speeches at the Barriers.

Twenty Little Engines. James Keir Baxter. NOxBChV

Twenty little engines. Twenty Little Engines. James Keir Baxter. NOxBChV

Twenty men crossing a bridge. Metaphors of a Magnifico. Wallace Stevens. TCAPo

Twenty Million Buckets. Bert Ward. RSaN

Twenty months out of the womb. Standing in the Doorway, I Watch the Young Child Sleep. Sharon Hashimoto. OpBo

20 Questions. Alan Bernheimer. BAP-04

Twenty Questions. Dennis Phillips.
   Five. FTOS

Twenty sparrows / on. Breakfast. William Carlos Williams. SAmP

20-200 on 737. Heather McHugh. NIP-4

Twenty Years. Đỗ Tấn Xuân. WoPoe, *tr. by* Nguyen Ngoc Bich

Twenty years a pilgrim. Seiken-Chiju. ZenPo, *tr. by* Takashi Ikemoto and Lucien Stryk

Twenty Years After. János Vajda. IQMS, *tr. by* Neville Masterman

Twenty years ago today, your death changed. Speaking Through White: For My Mother. Kyoko Mori. UnSA

Twenty years are gone. Palinode. Oliver St. John Gogarty. OBMV

Twenty Years From Auschwitz, Bergen-Belsen and Other Camps. Luisa Futuransky. MirDau, *tr. by* Celeste Kostopulos-Cooperman

Twenty years have fled before your bitterness. Widow. Bryan Martin Davies. BBMWP, *tr. by* Elin ap Hywel

Twenty Years Hence. Walter Savage Landor. NAEL-6v2; NAEL-7v2

Twenty years. I still remember. Pit, The. Lucien Stryk. AmWaPo

Twenty Years in the Wadi. Dan Pagis. NRoS, *tr. by* Esther Raizen

Twenty Years Later, to a Friend. Andrea Potos. FiBr

20 Years of Grant Applications and State College Jobs. Christopher Buckley. GeoHom

28. Philip Levine. GeoHom

Twenty-eight Indian Patriarchs. Patriarch Peaks. Muso Soseki. EaWin, *tr. by* W. S. Merwin

Twenty-eight young men bathe by the shore. Walt Whitman. CAGL; ColAP; CtM; NoP-4; NoP-5; SAmP; WaAnP *Fr.* Song of Myself.

25th Anniversary. Linda Pastan. FaoP

Twenty-First Century, Farewell. Todd James Pierce. RWB

Twenty-First. Night. Monday. Anna Andreyevna Akhmatova. RaBo, *tr. by* Jane Kenyon

Twenty-first, The. Night. Monday. Poem. Anna Andreyevna Akhmatova. RusPo, *tr. by* Robert Arthur Douglas Ford

25. Lawrence Ferlinghetti. CLPP

Twenty-Five Laments for Iraq. Robert Minhinnick. HarvBoo

25 Mesostics Re and Not Re Mark Tobey. John Cage. PmAP

Twenty-five people. Dolores Kendrick. GT *Fr.* "Three Observations on the Zombie Culture."

Twenty-five years ago I lied. Broken Silence. Louis M. Abbey. BloBone

Twenty-four hours can go so fast. Some Other Time. Betty Comden and Adolph Green. ReLy

Twenty-four Logics in Memory of Lee Hickman. Michael Palmer. BodElec

Twenty-Four Modes of Poetry. Sikong Tu. CCL1, *tr. by* H. A. Giles

29 Poems. Louis Zukofsky.
   "Cocktails / and signs of." APT-2
   Ferry. APT-2
   "Not much more than being." APT-2
   Two Dedications: Tibor Serly. APT-2

29-77-02. Artur Miedzyrzecki. PoSu

29 Songs. Louis Zukofsky.
   In Arizona. TRP
   "In that this happening." APT-2
   "To my wash-stand." APT-2; NAMCP V.1; OxBoAm

Twenty-ninth Canto. Hans Magnus Enzensberger. PoSu *Fr.* Sinking of the Titanic, The.

21. Lawrence Ferlinghetti. CLPP

21 East 10th, 2BR, WBF, EIK. Robyn Selman. WiU

Twenty-one Love Poems. Adrienne Rich. NAMCP V.2
   "Dark lintels, the blue and foreign stones, The." NALW; NoAM
   "Every peak is a crater. This is the law of volcanoes." NALW; NoAM
   Floating Poem, Unnumbered, The. EroLit; NALW; NoAM; WaAnP
   "I wake up in your bed. I know I have been dreaming." ErotSp; NoAM; TRP
   "No one's fated or doomed to love anyone." PoBW
   "Rain on the West Side Highway." WaAnP
   "Rules break like a thermometer, The." WaAnP
   "Since we're not young, weeks have to do time." WaAnP
   "Sleeping, turning in turn like planets." TRP; WaAnP
   "That conversation we were always on the edge." NoAM
   "Your small hands, precisely equal to my own." TRP

Twenty-seven Props for a Production of *Eine Lebenszeit*. Timothy Donnelly. LegDan

27th Dance—Walking—22 March 1964. Jackson Mac Low. FTOS *Fr.* Pronouns, The—A Collection of 40 Dances—For the Dancers.

27/10/76. George Stanley. NLPA *Fr.* Mountains and Air.

26th Person, The. Dolores Kendrick. GT *Fr.* "Three Observations on the Zombie Culture."

Twenty-Six Friends, That's the Same as Your Age. Carson Cistulli.
   47.57. FreRad
   42.24. FreRad
   34.57. FreRad

Twenty-Six Ways of Looking at a Blackman. Raymond R. Patterson. ESEAA

23 October 1992. Virginia Cerenio. ReBoTo

23rd Psalm, The: "Lord is my Shepherd, I have all I need, The." Bobby McFerrin. HW

23rd Street Runs into Heaven. Kenneth Patchen. APT-2

Twenty-third Flight. Earle Birney. HeIP-4

.22. Joy Lahey. AnSo

22.6.1941. Ondra Lysohorsky. AF, *tr. by* Ewald Osers

Twenty-two Quatrains on Receiving the Obituary Notice for my Son Shih-Chü. T'ang Hsien-tsu. *tr. by* Jonathan Chaves

    "My son, you loved telling the story of Prince Nata." ColAnChi, *tr. by* Jonathan Chaves

Twenty-Year Marriage. Ai. CAP-8; GT; NAMCP V.2; NoAM; WaAnP

'Twere blessed to have seen. (LL) I've seen a Dying Eye. Emily Dickinson. APN-2; NAAL-3; NAAPv.1; NCAP

'Twere well your judgments but in plays did range. John Dryden. OBSV *Fr.* Spanish Friar [*or* Fryar], The.

Twice. Christina Georgina Rossetti. OBEV; VWP

Twice as high as the clothes-line. Wireless Aerial, The. Edward Storey. RWPCtW

Twice Forty months in wedlock I did stay. On the Death of My First and Dearest Child, Hector Philips. Katherine Philips. InoFa; NAEL-6v1; NAEL-7v1

Twice having seen your shingled heads adorable. Evening on Lesbos. Edna St. Vincent Millay. PoBW

Twice I bow before my friend's picture. Wind Burial. Hwang Tonggyu. CAMKP, *tr. by* Kevin O'Rourke

Twice in my quickly disappearing forties. Year's End. Marilyn Hacker. NAMCP V.2; WiU

Twice now this morning I am wakened by full-throated geese. Colin Morton. IFF *Fr.* Hortus Urbanus / Urban Garden.

Twice or thrice had I loved thee. Air[e] and Angels. John Donne. BASC; NAEL-6v1; NAEL-7v1

Twice the fangs strike your brain. Walt Whitman at Timber Creek. Randall R. Freisinger. ViWalt

Twice the Man. Aidan Rooney-Céspedes. NIrP

Twice, three times. Paavo Haavikko. WoPoe *Fr.* Fifteen Epigrams in Praise of the Tyrant.

Twice Times Then Is Now. Ibn Hazm al-Andalusi. OBVE; WoPoe, *tr. by* Omar S. Pound

Twickenham [*or* Twicknam] Garden. John Donne. BASC; OBGa

Twig of willow. (LL) Counting-out Rhyme. Edna St. Vincent Millay. NOxBChV; SoSe-8

Twigs stiffen / the fingers. Sense. Rae Armantrout. FTOS

Twilight. Ralph Angel. BodElec

Twilight. Louisa Sarah Bevington. PEW

Twilight. Ch'en Yün. WoPoe, *tr. by* Henry Hart

Twilight. D. H. Lawrence. OBMV

Twilight. Amy Levy. VWP

Twilight. Philippe Soupault. SurPaPo, *tr. by* Mary Ann Caws and Jean-Pierre Cauvin and Patricia Terry

Twilight. Margit Szécsi. IQMS, *tr. by* Agnes Arany-Makkai

Twilight. Yi Yuksa. CAMKP, *tr. by* David R. McCann

Twilight—and you. Beso, El. Angelina Weld Grimké. NAAPv.2

Twilight: After Haying. Jane Kenyon. GoPo

Twilight at a Little Harbor. Chairil Anwar. PoetW, *tr. by* Burton Raffel

Twilight (Between Dog and Wolf). Olga Orozco. SurWo, *tr. by* Natalie Kenvin

Twilight by the plantation. John Moat. NewEx

Twilight comes down the mountains to. Night in the Villa by the River. Tu Fu [*or* Du Fu]. TAL

Twilight comes over the monastery garden. Twilight Comes. Wang Wei. NDACCP, *tr. by* Kenneth Rexroth

Twilight falls; I soften the dusting feathers, The. Sappho. James Wright. NoAM

Twilight heavens are flushed with gathering light, The. Red Sunsets, 1883, The. Mathilde Blind. ViWPN

Twilight hours are always gruff and gory. Oblivion. Ahmet Muhip Dıranas. NaPG, *tr. by* Talat Sait Halman

Twilight in the Garden. Wang Wei. WaAnP, *tr. by* Jay Parini

Twilight in the Library. John Tripp. TCAWP

Twilight in West Virginia: Six O'Clock Mine Report. Irene McKinney. PBCAP

Twilight is here, soft breezes bow the grass. In Exile. Emma Lazarus. APN-2; NAAPv.1

Twilight is spacious, near things in it seem far. Miracles. Conrad Potter Aiken. MoAmPo; TCAPo

Twilight Musings. Mary Weston Fordham. CBWP-2

Twilight of eternal day, The. (LL) Alfred Tennyson. BrAP; CABP; HeIP-4; NAEL-6v2; NAEL-7v2; NAWM-7v2; NoP-5; WaAnP *Fr.* In Memoriam A. H. H.

Twilight of the Outward Life. Hugo von Hofmannsthal. WoPoe, *tr. by* Peter Viereck

Twilight on Union Street. Donald Davidson. FuPo

Twilight over the field is blurred. Edge, The. Andrey Andreievich Voznesensky. RusPo, *tr. by* Robert Arthur Douglas Ford

Twilight Polka Dots. Barbara Guest. NoP-4; NoP-5; NYP2; PmAP

Twilight Seduction. Yusef Komunyakaa. SeSe

Twilight Song. Kang Ŭn'gyo. EcSo, *tr. by* Ann Y. Choi

Twilight Time. Samuel Palmer. NPBRoP

Twilight Time. Floyd Skloot. MiVo

Twilight Under Pine Ridge. Robert Mezey. GeoHom

Twilight's Last Gleaming. Arthur W. Monks. NIP-4

Twilit Revelation. Léonie Adams. MoAmPo

'Twill soon be sunrise. Down the valley waiting. Lakeward. Trumbull Stickney. APN-2

Twin Barrel Bucky: A Kingston 12 Dub, The. Brian Meeks. WaCA

Twin brothers slept on thin cots near a furnace. Basement Tale, A. Brian Bartlett. Coast

Twin Flames. James Broughton. PasH

Twin memory, we all seek it. David St. John. GeoHom *Fr.* Of the Remembered.

Twin stars through my purpling pane. Dusk. Angelina Weld Grimké. APT-1; NAAPv.2

Twin streaks twice higher than cumulus. Vapor Trails. Gary Snyder. AtGh

Twining her fingers through. Satyr, Cunnilinguent: To Herman Melville. Charles Martin. RA

Twinkle, twinkle, little star. Star, The. Jane Taylor. NOBRP; NOxBChV; NPBRoP; NTCP; OxBEV; UV

Twinkle Twinkle Little Star. Jane Taylor. *See* Star, The.

Twins. Robert Graves. OBCoV

Twins, The. Robert Browning. FaBoVe

Twins, The. Karl Shapiro. MoAmPo

Twins, The. James Stephens. RaBo

Twins, The. Mona Van Duyn. VCAP

Twirling. Jane Flanders. ItWoWo; PBCAP

Twirling an angry necklace on her fingers under. Between. Christian Karlson Stead. PoetW

Twirling your blue skirts, traveling the sward. John Crowe Ransom. *See* Twirling your blue skirts, travelling the sward.

Twirling your blue skirts, travelling the sward. Blue Girls. John Crowe Ransom. APT-1; BrAP; ColAP; MoAmPo; NoAM; NoP-4; NoP-5; WeW-3

(Twirling your blue skirts, traveling the sward.) FuPo

Twist, The. Alfred B. Spellman. EGAG; ISC

Twist of cloth on the flat stones, A. Desmond O'Grady. PBCIP *Fr.* Dark Edge of Europe, The.

Twist of hair, A. *Unknown.* SonAtl, *tr. by* Lee Bledisloe and Alex Burgin

Twisting brass, key of G, tenement stoned. East Fifth Street (N.Y.). Bob Kaufman. EGAG

Twisting out of fevered sheets. Ophelia, in Winter. Judith H. Montgomery. IaFF

Twisting tendril, A. Richard Wright. APT-2

Twitched in her belly, or he raised a fist. Figlio Maggiore. Robert Fitzgerald. NoP-4; NoP-5

Twitching in the cactus. Deathwatch. Michael S. Harper. NAAL-5; NAMCP V.2

'Twixt Carrowbrough Edge and Settlingstones. Old Skinflint. Wilfrid Wilson Gibson. OBMV

'Twixt Cup and Lip. Mark Hollis. NBLV

Twixt devil and deep sea, man hacks his caves. Arachne. William Empson. OBMV

Twixt Kings and Subjects ther[e]'s this mighty odds. Difference Betwixt King and Subjects, The. Robert Herrick. BASC

Twixt the Girthhead and Langwoodend. Lads of Wamphray, The. *Unknown.* IBB

'Twixt women's love, and men's will ever be[e]. (LL) Air[e] and Angels. John Donne. BASC; NAEL-6v1; NAEL-7v1

#2. Lawrence Ferlinghetti. PoDa

Two, The. Hugo von Hofmannsthal. GTCP, *tr. by* Walter Kaufmann

Two, The. Philip Levine. CAP-8

Two. Carolyn Kizer. FFC; VCAP *Fr.* Pro Femina.

Two Ajaxes Compared to Oxen, The. Homer. OBVE *Fr.* Iliad, The.

2 am. Dorianne Laux. SUP

2 a.m.: moonlight. The train has stopped. Track. Tomas Tranströmer. GPTC; WED, *tr. by* Robert Bly

(Night, two o'clock: moonlight. The train has stopped.) BLT

2 a.m.: moonlight. The train has stopped. Tracks. Tomas Tranströmer. StAl, *tr. by* Robin Fulton

2:00 A.M., time of the hedgehog that. Bad Luck with the Second Throw. Durs Grünbein. GTCP, *tr. by* Reinhold Grimm

Two and One. Richard Chess. TaR

Two Apes of Brueghel, The. Wisława Szymborska. WoPoe, *tr. by* Sharon Olds

Two April Mornings, The.　William Wordsworth.　NAEL-6v2; NAEL-7v2; NPBRoP

Two are embracing, a strange act.　Two Are Embracing.　John Gwyn Griffiths. BBMWP, *tr.* by Richard Poole

Two Armies.　Stephen Spender.　OBWP

Two armies covered hill and plain.　Music in Camp.　John Reuben Thompson. CBCWP

Two Artists, The.　Constance Naden.　ViWPN; VWP

Two autumns. (LL)　I go.　Buson.　ChAP; EH, *tr.* by Robert Hass

Two Backgrounds.　Edith Wharton.　APN-2

Two bad actors canonized by ballads.　Villon/Leadbelly.　Yusef Komunyakaa. LPSFW

Two basins, one rising from the other.　Roman Fountain.　Rainer Maria Rilke. GS, *tr.* by Edward Snow

Two battered at the Red Lamp Hitting the bars.　Journey, The.　Emmy Bridgwater.　SurWo

Two Bears, The.　Lillian E. Curtis.　VerBaPo

Two Beautiful Creatures.　Promise Ogochukwu Okekwe.　NeNiPo

2 Blinds & a Bittern.　Michele Glazer.　IAoNAP

Two bodies that unite naked.　They Unite Naked.　Jorge Gaitán Durán. BLPSL, *tr.* by Rene de Costa, Rigas Kappatos and Eleni Paidoussi

Two Boys, The.　Mary Lamb.　WoRP

Two boys uncoached are tossing a poem together.　Catch.　Robert Francis. RaBo

Two boys, whose birth beyond all question springs.　Charles Churchill.　OBSV *Fr.* Prophecy of Famine, The.

Two bricklayers are setting the walls of a cellar.　Bricklayer's Lunch Hour, The. Allen Ginsberg.　MotU

Two bronzes, but they were passing bronze before.　Two Wrestlers.　Robert Francis.　MoASP

Two Brothers in a Field of Absence.　Cynthia MacDonald.　NIP-4

Two brothers once, of merry mood.　Obey Your Parents.　William Bingham Tappan.　VerBaPo

Two carousing hawk moths, their wings like nervous silk.　Inna L'vovna Lisnyanskaya.　ItGoST, *tr.* by Judith Hemschemeyer

Two Centuries in One Day.　Eloise Klein Healy.　GeoHom

Two Cherokee Songs of Friendship.　*Unknown.*　APN-2, *tr.* by Samuel L. Mitchill

Two Christs were at Golgotha.　Early Lynching.　Carl Sandburg.　ChIV-2; MoAmPo

Two Cigarettes in the Dark.　Paul Francis Webster.　ReLy

Two coffees in the Español, the last.　Conrad Potter Aiken.　APT-1; NoAM *Fr.* Preludes for Memnon; or, Preludes to Attitude.

Two cops who are really famous actors.　In Your Dream after Falling in Love. Richard Hugo.　BodElec

Two Countries.　Tadeusz Borowski.　AF, *tr.* by Larry Rafferty, Meryl Natchez and Tadeusz Pioro

Two Countries.　José Martí.　TCLAP, *tr.* by Elinore Randall

Two Couples.　Debra Bruce.　FFC

Two crags, and a pair of quarries, both closed down. (LL)　Llyn y Gadair.　T. H. Parry-Williams.　BBMWP; OBWVE, *tr.* by Anthony Conran

Two crones were giving a whipping to a drunkard in the fog.　Drunken Merchant, The.　Milán Füst.　IQMS, *tr.* by Jess Perlman

Two crows walk down the road.　Pasolini.　Robert Glück.　WiU

Two crutches.　Premature Elegy.　Buland Al-Haidari.　IrPoTo, *tr.* by Hussein Kadhim and Christopher Merrill

Two Cures for Love.　Wendy Cope.　OBCoV

Two dayes now in that sea he sayled has.　Edmund Spenser.　NoSic *Fr.* Faerie Queene, The.

Two days ago in Rafi'ah.　As We Were Marching.　Aharon Shabtai.　WoBe, *tr.* by Peter Cole

Two days ago they were playing the piano.　Malvolio in San Francisco.　Jack Gilbert.　YaYoPo

Two days ago with dancing glancing hair.　My Friend.　Christina Georgina Rossetti.　InoFa

Two days' rain. The minute it stops, I'm out.　EFT.　Roberta Swann.　PoCoUp

Two Dedications: Tibor Serly.　Louis Zukofsky.　APT-2 *Fr.* 29 Poems.

Two dogs stuck together. The male lifts one leg.　Brief Entanglements. Richard Garcia.　TouFir

Two donkeys stand.　Donkeys in Anantapur.　Ismail.　HotL, *tr.* by V. Narayana Rao

Two Doors.　Hwang Insuk.　EcSo, *tr.* by Peter H. Lee

Two Dreams, The.　Giovanni Boccaccio.　OBGa, *tr.* by Algernon Charles Swinburne

Two Ember Days in Alabama.　Andrew Hudgins.　RA

Two Epilogues: "Cleanness of the path."　Gennady Aygi.　WoBe, *tr.* by Peter France

Two Evangelists.　Robert A. West.　PoA 2002

Two eyes, the cathedral's spires look black.　One Tourist's Cologne.　Hal Colebatch.　NOBAu

Two feet deep.　Ajo Lily.　Peggy Shumaker.　PoCoUp

Two Figures.　N. Scott Momaday.　NoP-4; NoP-5

Two figures face each other.　Greeting Shekinah.　Lynn Gottlieb.　HW

Two Figures in Dense Violet Night.　Wallace Stevens.　MoAmPo

Two Fires, The.　Judith Wright.　MoBrPo

Two Fish.　Katha Pollitt.　NIL-7; NIP-4

Two Fishing Villages.　Ellease Southerland.　GT

Two floods I read of; water, and of wine.　On the Two Great Floods.　Francis Quarles.　ChIV-1

Two flowers in a letter.　Kenneth Rexroth.　APSN *Fr.* Love Poems of Marichiko, The.

Two foot-companions once in deep discourse.　Nimmers, The.　John Byrom. OxAEP-1

Two Formal Elegies.　Geoffrey Hill.　NAMCP V.2

Two forms of darkness are there. One is Night.　Doubt.　Mary Elizabeth Coleridge.　NALW; ViWPN

Two freezing winters, and one summer's heat.　From a Sick Poetesse to Mrs St George on Her Feeding the Swans.　*Poets of the Tixall Circle.*　EMWP

Two from Israel.　Dom Moraes.
　Rendezvous.　NoP-4; NoP-5

2G (Another Millennium Poem).　C. Leigh McInnis.　BRtP

Two Gardens.　Walter De la Mare.　OBGa

Two gardens see!—this, of enchanted flowers.　Two Gardens.　Walter De la Mare.　OBGa

Two Garnett brothers who run the Shell station here, The.　Sweep.　Rodney Jones.　SUP

Two Generations.　Leonard Alfred George Strong.　OBMV

Two Gentlemen of Verona, The.　William Shakespeare.
　(Silvia.)　OBEV
　"Who is Silvia? what is she."　NoSic; WaAnP

Two Girls.　Suzanne Gardinier.　KGB; NeAmPo

Two girls discover.　Secret, The.　Denise Levertov.　PtR

Two girls on a ditch bank.　Fishing.　Paula McLain.　AmPoNex

Two Girls Singing.　Iain Crichton Smith.　EdScPo; NePenScot

Two girls walk to the river bank.　La Llorona.　Juan Delgado.　GeoHom

Two Grandmas.　Stanley H. Barkan.　UnSA

Two green-webbed chairs.　Children Playing Checkers at the Edge of the Forest.　Adrienne Rich.　WeW-3

Two Guitars.　Víctor Hernández Cruz.　PueRic; TouFir

Two guitars were left in a room all alone.　Two Guitars.　Víctor Hernández Cruz.　PueRic; TouFir

Two hands upon the breast.　Labor and Rest.　Dinah Maria Mulock.　TreFP

Two Hangovers.　James Wright.
　"I slouch in bed."　EmeKit
　I Try to Waken and Greet the World Once Again.　EmeKit

Two Headmistresses.　*Unknown.*　OBCoV

Two heaps of clothes by an old stump.　Nicholas by the River.　Nance Van Winckel.　RoV

Two Hearts Divided.　R. Williams Parry.　OBWVE, *tr.* by Joseph P. Clancy

Two, Hers and Mine.　Susan Griffin.　PoChi

Two Historians.　J. E. Thorold Rogers.　OBCoV

Two hollow eyes follow a cat's crie.　Mac Wellman.　FTOS *Fr.* Hollowness.

Two homecomings sustained my life.　Homecomings.　Pablo Neruda.　GifTon, *tr.* by William O'Daly

Two Hoppers.　John Updike.　PoSol

Two Horses and a Dog.　James Galvin.　GifTon

Two horses stand in a yellow light.　Adrienne Rich.　BodElec

Two hours out of Nairobi, distance.　Windowseat.　Sandra Meek.　OtW

Two hulks on Hudson's stormy bosom lie.　Philip Freneau.　TCAPo *Fr.* British Prison Ship, The.

Two Hundred and Sixty-Five Words.　Sophie Hannah.　HarvBoo

Two Hundred and Twenty-Eighth Chorus.　Jack Kerouac.　PmAP *Fr.* Mexico City Blues.

287 Cafe, Dumas, Texas.　Some Nights I Love Everybody in Texas.　Del Marie Rogers.　TiP2

211th Chorus.　Jack Kerouac.　PFTM-2; PmAP *Fr.* Mexico City Blues.

Two hundred men and eighteen killed.　James Henry.　WaAnP

209 Canal.　Richard Howard.　OxBoAm

270 The birches are worn out by mirrors.　My Final Agonies.　Benjamin Péret. PFTM-1

Two hundred years ago Issa heard the morning birds.　What Issa Heard.　David Budbill.　TAPaP

Two Ice Storms.　Charles Behlen.　TiP2

Two images of love: one, a child artisan's, abstract.　Six Movements for Portraits of Erzulie.　Sandra McPherson.　FTtHH

Two in a Room. Viktor Krivulin. TCRusP, *tr.* by Anna Barker and Daniel Weissbort

Two in Bed. Abram Bunn Ross. NTCP

Two in the Campagna. Robert Browning. ItP; NAEL-6v2; NAEL-7v2; NoP-4; NoP-5; NPeEn; OxAEP-2; OxBEV; TFi

Two Infinities. Edward Dowden. GSo

Two Iowa Farmers. Natalie Goldberg. FiBr

Two Irish yews, prickly green, poisonous. Gate Lodge. Richard Murphy. PBCIP

Two jays came down my street. Jays, The. John Heath-Stubbs. NOxBChV

Two kids in baggy jeans. Hoagie Scam, The. Jim Daniels. SUP

Two kinds in the Saturday crowd. Hollis Street Square, Halifax. John Steffler. BeAl

Two Kinds of Intelligence. Jelaluddin Rumi. TWF, *tr.* by Coleman Barks

Two Kinds of Miracles. Jelaluddin Rumi. WED, *tr.* by Robert Bly

Two Kinds of Welsh Bards. Endre Ady. IQMS, *tr.* by Neville Masterman

Two ladies walked on the soft green grass. Dream of Comparison, A. Stevie Smith. MoWP

Two lands at last connected. Ode to the Severn Bridge. Harri Webb. TCAWP

Two Legs Sat Upon Three Legs. Mother Goose. NTCP

Two legs sat upon three legs. Two Legs Sat Upon Three Legs. Mother Goose. NTCP

Two Lines from Paul Celan. Mark Halperin. GifTon

Two Little Girls. Fawziyya Abu Khalid. PoArWo, *tr.* by Farouk Mustafa

Two little girls, one fair, one dark. Lost Children, The. Randall Jarrell. OxBoAm

Two little princesses, The. Palace Cook's Tale. Joan Aiken. NOxBChV

Two Lives. William Ellery Leonard.
Indian Summer. APT-1
"That once the gentle mind of my dead wife." APT-1

Two long had lov'd, and now the nymph desir'd. There's No To-Morrow. Anne Finch, Countess of Winchilsea. NIL-7

Two Look at Two. Robert Frost. MoAmPo

Two Lorries. Seamus Heaney. EMP; NoP-5

Two lovers face one another. Slow Curtain. John Wheelwright. APT-2

Two lovers in an Irish wood at dusk. Story. Eavan Boland. HarvBoo

Two lovers to a midnight meadow came. Amateurs of Heaven, The. Howard Nemerov. SoSe-8

Two Loves. Lord Alfred Bruce Douglas. CAGL

Two Loves Found Refuge. Francis Saltus Saltus.
"Two loves found refuge in my happy heart." VerBaPo

Two loves found refuge in my happy heart. Francis Saltus Saltus. VerBaPo *Fr.* Two Loves Found Refuge.

Two loves I have of comfort and despair [*or* dispaire]. William Shakespeare. AEP; HeIP-4; NAEL-6v1; NAEL-7v1; NIL-7; NoP-5; OxBSo; PBRV *Fr.* Sonnets.

Two mad men and to mad men what poetry is. Incorporation of Sophia's Cereal, The. Bernadette Mayer. NYP2

Two magpies under the cypresses, The. What Birds Were There. William Everson. NoAM

Two Masks Unearthed in Bulgaria. William Meredith. BodElec

Two Meditations. Rosario Castellanos. PFTM-2, *tr.* by Julian Pulley

Two Memories. Hugh MacDiarmid. EdScPo

Two Men. Andrew Lansdown. NOBAu

Two Men. Edwin Arlington Robinson. AmWit

Two men appear on a tractor. Poem about the Future. Hans Magnus Enzensberger. PoSu, *tr.* by Michael Hamburger

Two men drink wine at the only table. Buson. EMJL *Fr.* Spring Breeze on the Kema Embankment.

Two men embrace on the billboard, their faces. Simplify Your Combination Therapy. Mark Wunderlich. NAPBL

Two men filched pumpkins from the grocery display. Theft. Karen Volkman. AmPoNex

Two men sat roasting in their blue suits, The. Inspiration. James Tate. BodElec; OxBoAm

Two men smiled into each other's eyes, The. (LL) Episode of Hands. Hart Crane. CAGL; NIL-7

Two Men, Two Grapefruits. Donna Masini. KGB

Two men were dragging a cart through the woods. Duke and I 2, The. Charles Ducal. TuT, *tr.* by Desmond Egan

Two Mesostics Re Merce Cunningham. John Cage. PFTM-2

Two Mice, The. Robert Henryson. *See* Taill of the Uponlandis Mous, and the Burges Mous.

Two minutes long it pitches through some bar. Elvis Presley. Thom Gunn. AllShUp

Two minutes' silence was cut to one, The. Armistice Day '77, Honiton. John Tripp. TCAWP

Two Monkeys, The. John Gay. OBCoV

Two Months Married. Aidan Carl Mathews. PBCIP

2 Months Rent Due and 1 Bag of Rice. Luci Beach. ReEnLa

Two mules stand in front of the brick wall of a warehouse. Mule Team and Poster. Donald Justice. VCAP

Two Musicians, The. Henrietta Cordelia Ray. CBWP-3

Two nails, The. (LL) Mirror, The. Michael Davitt. BeAl; PBCIP, *tr.* by Paul Muldoon

Two Names. Betty Scott Stam. SacPr

Two Noble Kinsmen, The. John Fletcher and William Shakespeare.
Bridal Song, A. NOSC; NoSic
(Dirge of the Three Queens.) OBEV

Two o'clock on a Saturday afternoon in November. Matinee. Susan Clements. UnSA

2 o'clock: strong moonlight, few stars. (LL) Track. Tomas Tranströmer. GPTC; WED, *tr.* by Robert Bly

Two, of course there are two. Death and Co. Sylvia Plath. EmeKit

Two of Napoleon's grenadiers. Grenadiers, The. Heinrich Heine. FaBoWar, *tr.* by Unknown

Two of the Festivals of Death. João Cabral de Melo Neto. TCLAP, *tr.* by W. S. Merwin

Two of Them, The. Hugo von Hofmannsthal. STV, *tr.* by John Frederick Nims

Two of us sharing a single pair of shoes, The. (LL) Fĕng Mĕng-lung. ColAnChi; WoPoe *Fr.* Mountain Songs.

Two of Us Together, Each of Us Alone, The. Yehuda Amichai. FIT, *tr.* by Robert Friend

Two old dancing shoes my grandfather. Genius. Philip Levine. CalPo; NoAM

Two Old Kings, The. John Byrne Leicester Warren, 3d Baron De Tabley. OBEV

Two on one moped, leather-coated. Old in Overijssel. René van Riessen. TuT, *tr.* by Robert Greacen

Two or three men would go. Pig Killing Day. Donald Evans. BBMWP, *tr.* by Gillian Clarke

Two Pages of Szondi, The. János Arany. IQMS, *tr.* by Adam Makkai

2 Pages, 122 Words on Music and Dance. John Cage. APT-2

Two Pantuns. *Unknown. tr.* by R. J. Wilkinson and R. O. Winstedt
"They wear." WoPoe, *tr.* by R. J. Wilkinson and R. O. Winstedt
"Thousand doves, A." WoPoe, *tr.* by R. J. Wilkinson and R. O. Winstedt

Two People : 1. Yi Sang. CAMKP, *tr.* by Edward Mack

Two People : 2. Yi Sang. CAMKP, *tr.* by Edward Mack

Two Photographs. Phyllis Thompson. ICANM

Two pieces of ornamental stone, of identical size. Banat Museum. Elke Erb. OnScMo, *tr.* by Rosmarie Waldrop

Two play with a stone. Stone in the Sand. Coral Bracho. RMCMP, *tr.* by Suzanne Jill Levine

Two plum trees, The. Buson. EH, *tr.* by R. H. Blyth

Two Poems. Rosario Castellanos. PFTM-2, *tr.* by Magda Bogin

Two Poems. T. H. Parry-Williams. BBMWP, *tr.* by Richard Poole

Two Poems. Andrey Andreievich Voznesensky. VCWP, *tr.* by Patricia Blake and William Jay Smith

Two Poems about the First Battles. Yehuda Amichai. NRoS, *tr.* by Esther Raizen

Two Poems for Black Relocation Centers. Etheridge Knight.
Poem for Black Relocation Centers, A. ESEAA

Two Poems for My Son, Ali. Abdul Wahab Al-Bayati. IrPoTo, *tr.* by Carolina Hotchandani and Najat Rahman

Two Poems for the God Given. Robert Sund. WhBo

2 Poems on the Same Theme. Michael Burkard. BodElec

Two Poems Written While Drunk. T'ao Ch'ien. CCL1, *tr.* by Yang Xianyi, Gladys Yang and Hu Shiguang

Two Postures beside a Fire. James Wright. HeIP-4

Two Princes, The. Michael Stillman. IaFF

Two Prison Poems. Ho Chi Minh. PoetW, *tr.* by Burton Raffel

Two Quarters, Two Nickels, and the Jacket of the One Album He Ever Recorded—*America Welcomes Home the Desert Sax*—Are in the Open Felt-Lined Case On the Platform of the Astor Place Subway Station: Gulf War 1. Chuck Wachtel. PrTe

Two Quartz Pebbles. Vasco [*or* Vasko] Popa. PoSu *Fr.* Quartz Pebble, The.

Two Rain Songs (Papago). Winged Serpent. IPoFL

Two Ramages for Old Masters. Robert Bly. BodElec

Two Ravens, The. *Unknown. See* Twa Corbies, The.

Two Red Roses across the Moon. William Morris. UV

Two Rivers. Ralph Waldo Emerson. APN-1; NCAP

Two Rivers. Hilary Llewellyn-Williams. AngWePo; TCAWP

Two Rivers, The. *Unknown. See* Tweed and Till.

Two roads diverge, each in a yellow smog. Other-Directed. Turner Cassity. PoA 2002

Two roads diverge in South Gyle Industrial Estate. What You Get. Leontia Flynn. NIrP

Two roads diverged in a wood. Robert Frost Discovers Another Road Not Taken. X. J. Kennedy. VisFro

Two roads diverged in a yellow wood. Road Not Taken, The. Robert Frost. APT-1; BLPJKO; BrAP; ChAP; CtM; EMP; HarvBoo; HeIP-4; ITBLP; MoAmPo; NAAL-5; NAAPv.2; NAMCP V.1; NIL-7; NIP-4; NoAM; NoP-4; NoP-5; OxBoAm; PoPoPo; SAmP; SoSe-8; StAl; TCAPo; TFi; TRP; WaAnP

Two robed sheep, their spindly legs. Choreograph of the Robed Sheep. Maryhelen Snyder. ICANM

Two roses I gave the therapist. Two and One. Richard Chess. TaR

Two rows of cabbages. In the Ambulance. Wilfrid Wilson Gibson. FaBoWar

Two scenes lie before us. In the first. Nouns of Assemblage. Stephen Dobyns. BodElec

Two Seabirds. *Unknown*. WoPoe *Fr.* Wanderer and the Seafarer, The.

Two seas our eyes beheld—one dark, one light. From Green Mountain. William Reed Huntington. APN-2

Two Seconds. Marie-Dominique Massoni. SurWo, *tr.* by Myrna Bell Rochester

Two shadows now, north from the translucent. Alba, With a Refrain from the Provençal. *Unknown*. WoPoe, *tr.* by Tim Reynolds

Two shall be born the whole world wide apart. Fate. Carolyn Wells. SWaP

Two Sisters, The. *Aborigine Oral Tradition*. NOBAu, *tr.* by Manoowa

Two sisters who had no brother. Brotherless Sisters. *Unknown*. WoPoe, *tr.* by Charles Simic

Two Sleepy People. Frank Loesser. ReLy

Two Smothered Children. Marion Albina Bigelow. VerBaPo

Two snails are on their way. Song of the snails on their way to a funeral. Jacques Prévert. MFP, *tr.* by Martin Sorrell

Two soluble aspirins spore in this glass, their mycelia. Spilt Milk. Sarah Maguire. EmeKit; LW; MFPA; MoWP

Two songs. Louisa Sarah Bevington.
   With the Tide: A Cry of Weakness. PEW

Two Songs. Cecil Day Lewis. NAMCP V.1; NoAM; NoP-4; NoP-5
   "I've heard them lilting at loom and belting." OBMV
   Song. NIP-4; OBMV; WaAnP

Two Songs. Adrienne Rich. NIP-4 *Fr.* Two Songs.

Two Songs. Adrienne Rich. EmeKit; NIL-7
   "That "old last act"! / And yet sometimes." NIP-4

Two Songs. NIP-4

Two Songs About a Dead Person or a Mole—Whichever It Was. Richard Johnny John, Jerome Rothenberg *and* Ian Tyson. PFTM-1 *Fr.* Songs from the Society of the Mystic Animals.

Two Songs for Hendrix. James McManus. RWB

Two Songs of a Blacksmith. Aaron Kurtz. Prolet, *tr.* by Amelia Glaser

Two Songs of Advent. Yvor Winters. APT-2; NAAPv.2

Two Songs of Peace. Yehuda Amichai. AF, *tr.* by Assia Gutmann

Two Songs of Queen Anne Boleyn. Dame Edith Sitwell. BrAP

Two Songs on the Economy of Abundance. James Agee. MoAmPo

Two Sonnets. Charles Hamilton Sorley. MoBrPo

Two Sonnets. *Unknown*. ArBi

Two Sonnets on Fame. John Keats.
   On Fame. CenSon

Two sons are gone. Later Still. Philip Levine. ColAP; WaAnP

Two spiral stairs we climb to bed together. Philip Gross. NewEx

Two Spring Charms. *Unknown*. WoPoe, *tr.* by James Wright

Two springs, I filled our rooms with chirping fleets. Rehab. Richard Katrovas. PoDa

Two Standards. Elise Paschen. OPRER; ReEnLa

Two Stars, The. W. H. Davies. MoBrPo

Two Statues. Pauline Hawkesworth. Prnts

Two sticks and an apple. London Bells. *Unknown*. OPOU

Two Stories. Ron Overton. PrTe

Two stories high above Saturn St. For My Mother. Doris Brett. NOBAu

Two Strangers, The. Manuel A. Viray. ReBoTo

Two streams: one dry, one poured all night by our beds. Interrogation, The. Li-Young Lee. PoPoPo

Two Streams, The. Oliver Wendell Holmes. APN-1

Two strong impulses: One. Jelaluddin Rumi. RaBo *Fr.* Four Quatrains.

Two Studies in Idealism: Short Survey of American and Human History. Robert Penn Warren. CBCWP

Two Suffering Men. Eugene Hirsch. BloBone

Two summers? Epochs, then, of ice. Return to Harmony 3. Agha Shahid Ali. BAP-97

Two Sundays before Lent. (LL) Gracey Nugent. Turlough Carolan. IrLP; OxBEV, *tr.* by Austin Clarke

Two survived the flood. Stones and Bones. Christopher Reid. NPeEn

Two Swedish Riddles. *Unknown*. *tr.* by Siv Cedering Fox
   Nettle. WoPoe, *tr.* by Siv Cedering Fox
   New Moon, The. WoPoe, *tr.* by Siv Cedering Fox

Two sweethearts courted happily for quite a while. Some of These Days. Shelton Brooks. ReLy

Two swimmers wrestled on the spar. Emily Dickinson. TCAPo

Two Tales of Clumsy. Gjertrud Schnackenberg.
   "When Clumsy harks the gladsome ting-a-lings." NoAM

Two telephones all morning giving each other hell. Cash Positive. Peter McDonald. PNI

2 Termite Skyscrapers. *Unknown*. SonAtl, *tr.* by M. J. Bormann, Alan Brierly and Saul Goode

Two things a man's built for, killing and you-know-what. Two Studies in Idealism: Short Survey of American and Human History. Robert Penn Warren. CBCWP

Two things remained constant. Old Light, The. Moses Glyn Jones. BBMWP, *tr.* by Mike Jenkins

Two Thoughts of Death. Christina Georgina Rossetti. ViWPN

2000. Dave Jeddie Smith. CAP-8

Two Thousand and Two. Catherine Hunter. PoPra

Two thousand feet above the torrent's clattering sibilance. Night Out, A. Douglas Houston. TCAWP

2500 years Before Proust. Time. Tom Clark. BodElec

2527th Birthday of the Buddha. Yusef Komunyakaa. WhBo

MMDCCXIII½. Lorenzo Thomas. WhBo

2032. Mark Strand. OxBoAm

2002. Mark Strand. OxBoAm

2212 West Flower Street. Michael Collier. LiTh

Two thousand years ago the Master Tsuang Tsi. Dream of Tsuang Tsi, The. Lőrinc Szabó. IQMS, *tr.* by Adam Makkai

Two Timer. Juan Delgado. TouFir

Two Tokyos. Shuntaro Tanikawa. PoetW, *tr.* by Harold Wright

Two Tongue-Pointing (Satirical) Songs. *Unknown*. NOBAu

Two Tramps in Mud Time. Robert Frost. APT-1; MoAmPo; NAMCP V.1; NoAM; OxBoAm; SAmP

Two Trees. Grace Schulman. ExTi

Two Trees. Ellen Bryant Voigt. CAP-8; InGu

Two Trinities. Kenneth Mackenzie. BrAP

Two Truths. Helen Hunt Jackson. LW

II:II. Geoffrey Nutter. IIR

Two / Two cigarettes in the dark. Two Cigarettes in the Dark. Paul Francis Webster. ReLy

Two universes mosey down the street. Walking the Dog. Howard Nemerov. BeAl; GoPo

Two Variations on a Theme. Carl Rakosi. APT-2

Two Variations on a Theme by Kobayashi. Larry Levis. BodElec

Two Varieties of the Bitter Orange. J. L. Jacobs. AmPoNex

Two Vietnam Poems: (1966). Bill Knott. PBCAP

Two Views of Two Ghost Towns. Charles Tomlinson. NAMCP V.2; NoAM

Two Villages. Grace Paley. FaBoWar

Two virtues ride, by stallion, by nag. Death of Myth-making, The. Sylvia Plath. PoA 2002

Two Voices. Edmund Charles Blunden. OBWP

Two Voices. Diana Der Hovanessian. TWW

Two voices are there: one is of the deep. Sonnet, A. James Kenneth Stephen. CABP; UV

Two Voices are there; one is of the sea. Thought[s] of a Briton on the Subjugation of Switzerland. William Wordsworth. UV

2 Ways of Crossing the Creek. Red Hawk. PoDa

Two weeks across a strange sea. Katori Maru, October 1920. James Masao Mitsui. OpBo

Two weeks before. Damp Hips of the Women, The. Elisabeth Harvor. Coast

Two went to pray? o rather say. Two Went Up into the Temple To Pray. Richard Crashaw. ChIV-2

Two Went Up into the Temple To Pray. Richard Crashaw. ChIV-2

Two wheels to roll along the w A. Logocyclogram. Audrey Hughes. ArBi

Two Witches. Robert Frost.
   Witch of Coös, The. APT-1; NoAM; PoA 2002

Two Women. Carol Rumens. MoWP

Two Women. Constance Fenimore Woolson.
   One. SWaP
   Other, The. SWaP

Two women. Easy together in the twilight, and I. Convolvulus Tricolor. Leslie Adrienne Miller. SweBea

Two Women Knitting. Mrinal Pande. CFP, *tr.* by the author and Arlene Zide

Two women, seventies, hold hands. Day Trip. Carole Satyamurti. OPOU

Two women sit at a table by a window. Light breaks. After Twenty Years. Adrienne Rich. TRP

Two World Wars—no, we never saw those days, The. Shadows. Nesta Wyn Jones. BBMWP, *tr. by* Anthony Conran

Two Worlds. Richard Watson Gilder. GS

Two Worlds. Julia Older. TWW

Two worlds there are. One you think. Cleaning the Well. Fred Chappell. InGu

Two Wrestlers. Robert Francis. MoASP

Two yearling deer. Midsummer. Sam Hamill. WANABP

Two years hence. When I'm ready. My Moral Life. Mark Halliday. SUP

Two Years Later. John Wieners. PmAP; RaBo

Two years we spent. Woods, The. Derek Mahon. PBCIP

Two young guys. Tremor, The. Jack Hirschman. BodElec

Two young ones fed, bathèd, zippered, read to and sung to, The. Asleep. Time Out. Maurice Riordan. BeAl; EmeKit; ModIr

Two-blood passion man. Sounds of a Dreamer. James Berry. WaCA

Two-colored cloud-eyes. Na Tacha. Natalia Toledo. RMCMP

Two-day-old Grandchild. Fergus Allen. NIrP

Two-Faced Too. *Unknown.* OBWVE, *tr. by* Glyn Jones

Two-natured, loving my world. Comb and the Mirror, The. Elizabeth Spires. FFC

Two-Part Prelude, The. William Wordsworth. NPBRoP

TWO's a couple. Four on a Sidewalk. *Unknown.* CA

'Twould ring the bells of Heaven. Bells of Heaven, The. Ralph Hodgson. MoBrP; OBEV

Two-year-old boy, A. This Is My Son's Song: *"Ungie, Hi Ungie".* Michael S. Harper. CAP-8

Two-Year-Old Has Had a Motherless Week, The. Karl Shapiro. WeW-3

Tyger, The. William Blake. BBASP; BrAP; BRP; ChAP; ClHu; CtM; HeIP-4; ITBLP; MakPoe; NAEL-6v2; NAEL-7v2; NAWM-7v2; NIL-7; NIP-4; NOBRP; NoP-4; NoP-5; NOxBChV; NPBRoP; NPeEn; OBEV; OPOU; OxBEV; PoPoPo; SoSe-8; TFi; WaAnP; WHSW *Fr.* Songs of Experience

Tyger, Tyger. Isabel Meyrelles. SurWo, *tr. by* Penelope Rosemont

Tyger Tyger. Andrew Schelling. WANABP

Tyger Tyger burning bright. William Blake. BBASP; BrAP; BRP; ChAP; ClHu; CtM; HeIP-4; ITBLP; MakPoe; NAEL-6v2; NAEL-7v2; NAWM-7v2; NIL-7; NIP-4; NOBRP; NoP-4; NoP-5; NOxBChV; NPBRoP; NPeEn; OBEV; OPOU; OxBEV; PoPoPo; SoSe-8; TFi; WaAnP; WHSW *Fr.* Songs of Experience

Tying my heart to her by those rich chain[e]s. (LL) Description of Cooke-ham [*or* Cookham], The. Emilia Lanier and Aemilia Bassano Lanyer. BASC; CABP; NAEL-6v1; NAEL-7v1; NoP-4; NoP-5; PBRV; WaAnP

Tyler scuffs oak leaves to frisk. Nothing Happened. Belle Waring. PBCAP

Tyler was no Whig at all & after his term's end. Jackson Mac Low. APSN *Fr.* Presidents of the United States of America, The.

Type of the antique Rome! Rich reliquary. Coliseum, The. Edgar Allan Poe. APN-1

Typesetter had changed "Gelato" to "Zealot", The. Message to Mary Ferrari in Jo'Burg. Donna Brook. PrTe

Typhoon Thrum. Nicole Brossard. OpeFie, *tr. by* Robert Majzels and Erin Mouré

Typical Dioscuric body above the Heliconian mediocrity of this line. Muse. Gerardo Deniz. RMCMP, *tr. by* Mónica de la Torre

Typing the Letters. John A. Scott. BMAP

Typists. Patricia K. Page. NALW

Tyrannic Love. John Dryden.

 Epilogue to *Tyrannic[k] Love.* OBCoV

Tyranny of Choice. Elizabeth Garrett. NeBl; StAl

Tyranny of fuel, The. Up & down, round & round, merrygoround. Acrospiracal Meanderings in a Tongue of the Time. Chris Torrance. Oth

Tyranny of Love, The. Mary Robinson. CenSon; RWP

Tyrant, The. Faiz Ahmad Faiz. AF, *tr. by* Naomi Lazard

Tyrant in Sleep, Naught Differeth from a Common Man, A. Timothy Kendall. NoSic

Tyrant inspires small poems, The. Paavo Haavikko. WoPoe *Fr.* Fifteen Epigrams in Praise of the Tyrant.

Tyrant, why [*or* whie] swell'st thou thus. Bible, *O.T.* BASC; PBRV *Fr.* Psalms.

 (Tyrant, why swel'st [*or* swell'st] thou thus. Bible, *O.T.* NAEL-7v1; NoSic; OBVE)

Tyrants created my pleasurable madness. Crazy Satan. Murad Mikha'il. IrPoTo, *tr. by* Christina Coyle and Sadok Masliyah

Tyre of the farther West! be thou too warned. John Keble. SacPr *Fr.* Lyra Apostolica.

Tyre, the. Simon Armitage. NeBrP

Tyrian dye why do you wear. Abraham Cowley. NOSC; OxAEP-1 *Fr.* Sylva.

Tyrone is a junior in my creative writing class. Mouse, The. Gary Blankenburg. TWF

Tywater. Richard Wilbur. TRP; UpMys

Tzu Yeh Songs. *Unknown.*

 Autumn. CCL1, *tr. by* Burton Watson

 Fragrance Comes from the Scent I Wear, The. CCL1, *tr. by* Burton Watson

 Summer. CCL1, *tr. by* Burton Watson

 Winter. CCL1, *tr. by* Burton Watson

U

"u", "je", "r", "r", "im", "a", "finally." Douglas Oliver. Oth

U r n / u r n / u r n. Garden Poem. Ian Hamilton Finlay. OBGa

U.S.A. Rosemary Benét and Stephen Vincent Benét.

 "So we march into the present." HHAm

U.S.A. Court of No Appeal, The. George Edward Tait. BRtP

U.S. 1946 King's X. Robert Frost. NIP-4

U.S. Sailor with the Japanese Skull, The. Winfield Townley Scott. APT-2; ICANM; OxBoAm

U / Triple. Chances of Magic, The. Keith Waldrop. OnScMo

Uascán. Ciaran Berry. PML

UBI AMOR IBI OCULUS EST. (LL) Ezra Pound. APSN; APT-1 *Fr.* Cantos.

Ugliest little boy. Life of Lincoln West, The. Gwendolyn Brooks. NoAM

Ugly as a jackass. Tune: "Po Pu-tuan" Long-Haired Little Dog. Wang Ho-ch'ing. ColAnChi, *tr. by* James I. Crump

Ugly Child, The. Elizabeth Jennings. NOxBChV

Ugly creatures, ugly grunting creatures. Suffering. Miroslav Holub. PoSu, *tr. by* Ian Milner and George Theiner

Ugly Duckling, The. Luis Lloréns Torres. NAAPv.2

Ugly Heart, The. Martha Anthony. InTrad

Ugly Poem. Carmen Horst. ACAMVP

Ugly season of putrifying buzzards, An. Emilio Villa. ItPo *Fr.* Words.

Ugly Step Sister, The. Denise Duhamel. SweBea

Ugly your uproar at my side. *Unknown.* EMWP

Ugolino. Dante Alighieri. OxBEV *Fr.* Divina Commedia (Selections from Anthologies, in English).

Uguisu sing in the blossoming trees. Kenneth Rexroth. APT-2 *Fr.* Love Poems of Marichiko, The.

Uguisu sleeps in the bamboo grove, The. Kenneth Rexroth. APSN *Fr.* Love Poems of Marichiko, The.

Uh huh, uh huh, my jefitos. That's the Way, Uh Huh, Uh Huh, I Liked It. Anthony R. Vigil. AmPoNex

Uh-uh-uh / i thought i saw lady day in the park today but. Park mole. Merilene M. Murphy. BtF

Ukulele Music. Peter Reading.

 "Life is too black as he paints it and "Reading's nastiness sometimes."" StAl

Ulalume [*or* Ulalume—a Ballad]. Edgar Allan Poe. APN-1; NAAL-5; NAAPv.1; NCAP; OxBoAm; TCAPo

 (To———. Ulalume: A Ballad.) NAAL-3

Ulcerated tooth keeps me awake, there is. Letters from a Father. Mona Van Duyn. NoP-4; NoP-5

Ulisses and the Syren. Samuel Daniel. *See* Ulysses and the Siren [*or* Syren].

Ulrich von Hutten's Song. Ulrich von Hutten. GePo, *tr. by* Catherine Winkworth

Ulster Twilight, An. Seamus Heaney. PBCIP

Ulster Unionist Walks the Streets of London, An. Tom Paulin. PNI

Ultima Ratio. Friedrich Georg Jünger. UpMys; WoPoe, *tr. by* Les A. Murray

Ultima Ratio Reagan. Howard Nemerov. AF

Ultima Ratio Regum. Stephen Spender. AF; FaBoWar; NoP-4; NoP-5; OBWP; PoWW

Ultima Thule. Thomas Lux. AmAlph

Última Tierra en el Destierro. Jorge Guillén. RaW

Ultimate. G. K. Chesterton. SacPr

Ultimate, The. George Washington and the Loss of His Teeth. Diane Wakoski. PFTM-2

Ultimate Antientropy, The. Theodore Weiss. NoAM

Ultimate Argument. Ion Caraion. AF, *tr. by* Marguerite Dorian and Elliott B. Urdang

Ultimate Luxury Woman, The. Virgil Mihaiu. PML, *tr. by* Liviu Bleoca and Adam J. Sorkin and Irina Grigorescu Pan

Ultimate Poem Is Abstract, The. Wallace Stevens. PoA 2002

Ultimate Poem, The. Emmett Williams.

 Rose is a Rose is a Rose is a Rose. PFTM-2

 Rose is a Violin is a Codpiece. PFTM-2

 What. PFTM-2

Ultimate Tao is nameless, The. Presented to the Taoist Paragon Mao. Cheng Huan. ColAnChi, *tr. by* Edward H. Schafer

Ultimately it does not matter how he died—. Mozart's Death. Richard Foerster. MiVo

Ultimately the air. From Disaster. George Oppen. APT-2; NAMCP V.1

Ultimatum: Kid to Kid. Langston Hughes. NOxBChV

Ultra Sound. Penelope Shuttle. PoCu

Ultrasound. Kathleen Jamie. StAl

Ultrasound. Maria Luisa Spaziani. CItWP, tr. by Cinzia Sartini Blum and Lara Trubowitz

Ultrasound at 13 Weeks. Kona Macphee. BeAl

Ulumbo, a Cat. Rutger Kopland. VCWP, tr. by James Brockway

Ulysse tue les prétendants près d'un fragile bol de lait. Retour d'Ulysse. Marie-Claire Bancquart. YaTCFP

Ulysses. Gwendolyn Brooks.
    Religion. OxWW

Ulysses. Robert Graves. NoAM

Ulysses. James Joyce.
    "Bronze by gold heard the hoofirons, steelyringing." PFTM-1

Ulysses. Umberto Saba. WoPoe, tr. by Stephen Sartarelli

Ulysses. Alfred Tennyson. AmFaPo; BLPJKO; BrAP; CABP; ClHu; CtM; HeIP-4; MakPoe; NAEL-6v2; NAEL-7v2; NAWM-7v2; NIL-7; NIP-4; NoP-4; NoP-5; NPeEn; OxAEP-2; OxBEV; PoPoPo; SoSe-8; TFi; TRP; WaAnP; WeW-3

Ulysses and the Siren [or Syren]. Samuel Daniel. NAEL-6v1; NoP-4; NoP-5; OBEV; OxAEP-1
    (Ulisses and the Syren.) OxBEV

Ulysses Describes His Visit to the Underworld. Homer. WaAnP Fr. Odyssey.

Ulysses Embroidered. Miriam Waddington. NIL-7

Ulysses Insults over the Cyclops. Homer. NOSC Fr. Odyssey.

Ulysses Invokes the Dead. Homer. NOSC Fr. Odyssey.

Ulysses kills the suitors close to a fragile bowl of milk. Return of Ulysses. Marie-Claire Bancquart. YaTCFP, tr. by Martin Sorrell

Ulysses Reunited with Penelope. Homer. NOSC; OBVE Fr. Odyssey.

Uma Worshipping Shiva (On a Kangra miniature). Elsa Cross. TANSG, tr. by Patricia Dubrava

Umberto / Always worked hard. In the Winter. Sir Osbert Sitwell. OBGa

Umbilical Cord. Ellyn Maybe. AmPoNex

Umbra. Lloyd Addison. EGAG

Umbra. Dana Goodyear. PoDa

Umbra Vitae. Georg Heym. GTCP, tr. by Christopher Middleton

Umbrella / And a raincoat, An. Conversation. Buson. NTCP

Umm, I can't eat, Grandma. South Yard, The. Chông Hwajin. EcSo, tr. by Julie C. Park

Umpteen hundred and eternity. (LL) Carol for the Last Christmas Eve. Norman Nicholson. NOxBChV; OBCP

Un. Dennis Lee.
    "In wreck, in dearth, in necksong." OpeFie

Un Extraño. Tess Gallagher. ExTi

Un is okay. Zen Americana. Paula Gunn Allen. PoPoPo

Un Marin naufrageé (de Doncastre). George Du Maurier. OBCoV

Un pneumatic cross avec suctiondiscs topped avec thistle-tire . . . s'il vous plaît. (LL) Café du Dôme. Else Von Freytag-Loringhoven. APT-1; SurPaPo

Una a Una Desmonté las Piezas de Tu Alma. Gerardo Diego. RaW

Unable to divide love from hunger. (LL) Banking Potatoes. Yusef Komunyakaa. NoP-4; NoP-5

Unable to move. Karen Alkalay-Gut. DTA Fr. Between Bombardments: A Journal.

Unable to Sleep in Frost's Bed in Franconia. Marvin Bell. VisFro

Unable to sleep, or pray, I stand. Ice Storm. Robert Earl Hayden. APT-2; ESEAA

Unable to stand. Ryunosuke Akutagawa. CAoMJL1, tr. by Makoto Ueda

Unable to stop its growth. Going Home. Janice Gould. FiBr

Unaccompanied Suite. Barbara Winder. MiVo

Unaccountable Lapses. Rosmarie Waldrop. WoBe Fr. Hölderlin Hybrids.

Unaccountable trip, The. God Knows Why. Unknown. SonAtl, tr. by Alan Brierly, M. Ellison and Saul Goode

Unacknowledged Legislator. Harryette Mullen. RD

Un-American Investigators. Langston Hughes. HHAm

Un-American Women, The. John Tranter. BMAP

Unanswered. Yannis Ritsos. AF, tr. by Edmund Keeley

Unanswered Letter. Tess Gallagher. NIP-4

Unarmed Combat. Henry Reed. BrAP; NAEL-6v2 Fr. Lessons of the War.

Unassuming curve, An. Matisse, Cut Outs. Trasi Johnson. BtF

Unattained, The. Elizabeth Oakes-Smith. NAAPv.1

Unavoidable violence. What We Learned. Fanny Howe. FTOS

Unawakened, sweet / women. (LL) Belly Dancer. Diane Wakoski. NALW; NoAM

Unaware of illusion or enlightenment. Genko. ZenPo, tr. by Takashi Ikemoto and Lucien Stryk

Unaware of the dangers above the small neighborhood pond. On Transportation. Benjamin Paloff. UrbNat

Unbeginning, The. Brenda Hillman. RoV

Unbelief. Phoebe Cary. SacPr

Unbelievable as an antique ritual. Ceremony by the Sea, A. Richard Eberhart. PWW2

Unbeliever, The. Elizabeth Bishop. NAAL-5; NoAM

Unbending Prayer. René Char. AF

Unbeseechable, The. Frances Darwin Cornford. MoBrPo

Unbidden, yours; a way to offer praise. (LL) Translation. Rika Lesser. KGB; PoA 2002

Unborn. John Le Gay Brereton. NOBAu

Unborn Child, An. Derek Mahon. BeAl; CABP; PNI; WoPoe

Unbosoming. Michael Field. NAEL-7v2; VWP

Unbosoming, The. Olena Kalytiak Davis. LegDan

Unbridled licentiousness with no holds barred. Reading Pornography in Old Age. Howard Nemerov. NAMCP V.2; NoAM

Unbruised. Tom Ahern. OnScMo

Unburn the boat, rebuild the bridge. Recension Day. Duncan Forbes. BeAl

Uncalled. Madison Cawein. TCAPo

Uncertain Battle, The. David Gascoyne. PoWW

Uncertain Geometry. Rita D. Costello. BeDoSh

Uncertain Oneiromancy. Denise Levertov. MakPoe

Uncertain which, in ocean or in air. (LL) John Milton. NIL-7; NIP-4 Fr. Paradise Lost.

Uncertainty of the Poet, The. Wendy Cope. OPOU

Unchangeable indeclinable in cold currency in words. Poem Stalin, The. Adriano Spatola. PFTM-2, tr. by Paul Vangelisti

Unchanged. Michael McClure. WANABP

Unchanged within, to see all changed without. Duty Surviving Self-Love. Samuel Taylor Coleridge. NPeEn

Unchanging, The. Sara Teasdale. APT-1

Unchristian Jacobin whoever. Ode to a Jacobin. Unknown. UV

Uncircumcised, The. (LL) Czeslaw Milosz. HP; PoSu; VCWP Fr. Voices of Poor People.

Uncivil sickness, hast thou no regard. Henry Constable. OxBSo Fr. Diana.

Unclaimed. Vikram Seth. PML

Uncle. Julia Kasdorf. PBCAP

Uncle: "Sam was a family embarrassment." Ellie McDonald. EdScPo

Uncle Alfred's Long Jump. Gareth Owen. OBSP

Uncle Ananias. Edwin Arlington Robinson. MoAmPo; NIP-4

Uncle Bill had been there. Almost Going. David Huddle. PBCAP

Uncle Charles: A Home Movie. J. Bernlef. TuT, tr. by Peter van de Kamp

Uncle Devereux would blend to the one color. (LL) My Last Afternoon with Uncle Devereux Winslow. Robert Lowell. GPTC; NoP-4; NoP-5

Uncle Eggplant. Jeffrey McDaniel. SUP

Uncle Fenster's Grave. Roger Jones. TiP2

Uncle Good Intentions. Susie Silook. FTtHH

Uncle Harry at the La Brea Tar Pits. Ruth Whitman. TaR

Uncle Hussein mails his underwear. Holy Water. Hayan Charara. AmPoNex

Uncle Ike's Holiday. Priscilla Jane Thompson. CBWP-2

Uncle Iv Surveys His Domain from His Rocker. Jonathan Williams. NBLV

Uncle Jacob often told us. Frances Ellen Watkins Harper. NAAPv.1 Fr. Aunt Chloe.

Uncle Jim. Countee Cullen. GT

Uncle Jimmie's Yarn. Priscilla Jane Thompson. CBWP-2

Uncle Jimmy flies in from Hollywood. Quill Holler Waller. Joan Self. FTtHH

Uncle of mine who died of resurrection (Borges), An. Coast, The. Gonzalo Rojas. PML, tr. by John Oliver Simon

Uncle Rube on the Race Problem. Clara Ann Thompson. CBWP-2

Uncle Rube to the Young People. Clara Ann Thompson. CBWP-2

Uncle Rube's Defense. Clara Ann Thompson. CBWP-2

Uncle Seagram. Gwendolyn Brooks. See Merle; Uncle Seagram.

Uncle Time. Dennis Scott. PML

Uncle Tom ("Within— / The beaten pride.") Langston Hughes. SAmP

Uncle with Landscape—Kansas, 1954. Benjamin Vogt. RWB

Uncle Yair, against a white ceramic wall in my mother's kitchen. Nightingale of Uncle Yair, The. Devorah Amir. DTA, tr. by Linda Zisquit

Unclean spirits cry out in the body, The. Guest Ellen at the Supper for Street People, The. David Ferry. NIP-4

Unclean, unclean: my Lord, undone, all vile. Edward Taylor. NAAL-3 Fr. Preparatory Meditations Before My Approach to the Lord's Supper.

Unclenched, armless, silk and rough love that breaks all rocks. (LL) There Was a Saviour. Dylan Thomas. ChIV-2; NAEL-6v2; NAEL-7v2

Uncles. Nikky Finney. ISC

Uncle's First Rabbit. Lorna Dee Cervantes. NoAM

Uncloistered Virtue. John Milton. NOSC Fr. Paradise Lost.

Unconcerned, The: Song. Thomas Flatman. NOSC

Unconditionals #3. Viki Akiwumi. InTrad

Unconquered Air, The. Florence Earle Coates. OtW

Unconscious / came a beauty to my. Unconscious Came a Beauty. May Swenson. APT-2; NAMCP V.2; VCAP

Unconsciously. Ken Edwards. Oth

Uncontrollable mystery on the bestial floor, The. (LL) Magi, The. William Butler Yeats. ChIV-2; GI; HarvBoo; NAMCP V.1; NoAM; NPeEn; OxAEP-2; PoA 2002; TRP

Uncountable tiny pebbles. On the Beach. Jane Hirshfield. ExTi

Uncoupled Couplets. William Cole.

    Algernon Charles Swinburne. AmWit

    Robert Herrick. AmWit

    Robert Herrick. AmWit

    Thomas Campion. AmWit

    William Shakespeare. AmWit

Uncreation, The. Robert Pinsky. NAMCP V.2

Uncurl the sheet of vellum and there. Skin. Mary Leader. NAPBL

"Und now Ladies und Gentlemun, *Der Peedles!*." David Wojahn. PBCAP *Fr.* Mystery Train: A Sequence.

Undated dreams: the sea at Heringsdorf. Dreams in German. David Martin. NOBAu

Undeciphered but surmised. (LL) Elegy Just in Case. John Ciardi. AmWaPo; PWW2

Undenominational. Sir John Betjeman. SacPr

Under a Blossoming Plum Tree. David Biespiel. NAPBL

Under a Border-Fortress. Wang Ch'ang-ling. CCL1, *tr.* by Witter Bynner

Under a burning tropic sun. Color Sergeant, The. James Weldon Johnson. GT

Under a ceiling high Christmas tree. Filipino Boogie. Jessica Tarahata Hagedorn. UnSA

Under a Certain Little Star. Wisława Szymborska. PoetW; VCWP, *tr.* by Magnus J. Krynski and Robert A. Maguire

Under a Full Moon. Merle Woo. FiBr

Under a futile Torah. Both Your Mothers. Jerzy Ficowski. HP; PoSu, *tr.* by Keith Bosley

Under a gentle blue sky. Cricketer, The. Kashyap Bhattacharya. PML

Under a Hat Rim. Carl Sandburg. APT-1

Under a low sky. Silence. William Carlos Williams. SAmP

Under a night sky growing bright with stars. (LL) Lufthansa. John Tranter. BMAP; NOBAu

Under a ragged loincloth. Akera Kanko. EMJL, *tr.* by Burton Watson

Under a rain of blows, the heart. Heart Escaping. László Kálnoky. IQMS, *tr.* by Kenneth McRobbie and Zita McRobbie

Under a ruined mill. (LL) Old Woman, The. Joseph Campbell. IrV; MoBrPo

Under a shower of pear blossoms. Kyerang. CATKP, *tr.* by Peter H. Lee

Under a sky, in a garden, there are serious women and beautiful men, were talking. Sailed. Aaron Shurin. FTOS

Under a sky the color of pea soup. Marge Piercy. IPoFL; TWF *Fr.* Laying Down the Tower.

Under a Soprano Sky. Sonia Sanchez. FuFl

Under a splintered mast. Talisman, A. Marianne Moore. MoAmPo

Under a spreading chestnut tree. Village Blacksmith, The. Henry Wadsworth Longfellow. APN-1; BRP; UV

Under a starry sky I was taking a walk. Temptation. Czeslaw Milosz. GI, *tr.* by the author and Lillian Vallee

Under a tent of stars a lonely man. Romance to Night, A. Georg Trakl. AF, *tr.* by Daniel Simko

Under / a thin coat of dust. Pomegranates. Jane Hirshfield. AFaM

Under a tree, I'd constructed a rough shed made of planks in which I'd put a table. Why I Became a Saint. Oliver Cadiot. YaTCFP, *tr.* by Cole Swensen

Under a vast black sky sparkling with tomorrow's ashes. Diana Hartog. NLPA *Fr.* Oasis.

Under a white coverlet of snow. January. John Heath-Stubbs. OBCP

Under a Wing. Fedya Filkova. CSCBP, *tr.* by Georgi Belev and Lisa Sapinkopf

Under an Impure Star. Armanda Guiducci. CItWP, *tr.* by Cinzia Sartini Blum and Lara Trubowitz

Under apparel, apparel lies. One Self. Laura Riding Jackson. HarvBoo

Under bare Ben Bulben's head. William Butler Yeats. WeW-3 *Fr.* Under Ben Bulben.

Under Ben Bulben. William Butler Yeats. NAEL-6v2; NAEL-7v2; NAMCP V.1; NoAM; NoP-4; NoP-5

    "Irish poets, learn your trade." OxAEP-2

    "Under bare Ben Bulben's head." WeW-3

Under black yews that protect them. Owls. Charles Baudelaire. OWoS, *tr.* by Richard Howard

Under bright city lights. Underground. Conrad Kent Rivers. SeSe

Under bright moonlight. Illusions. Tzu Yeh. CrYelRi, *tr.* by Sam Hamill

Under Cancer. John Hollander. NAMCP V.2

Under cherry trees / There are. Issa. ZenPo, *tr.* by Takashi Ikemoto and Lucien Stryk

Under clouds birds sail. Fishermen from Ma Yuan. "Lucebert." TuT, *tr. by* Peter van de Kamp

Under Cover. Abbie Huston Evans. APT-1

Under darkness of stars our son flies. War in Bosnia, The. Walter McDonald. OtW

Under everything, everything. Source of the Singing, The. Marilyn Nelson Waniek. OxAAAP

Under Flag. Myung Mi Kim. AmWaPo

Under glass: glass dishes that [*or* which] changed. Fundamental Project of Technology, The. Galway Kinnell. AtGh; CAP-8

   (Under glass: glass dishes that changed.) BodElec

Under God's violent unsleeping eye. Difference. T. Harri Jones. OBWVE

Under Her Crib. Marcia Pelletiere. OPRER

Under her gown the girl is. Only Daughter, The. Laura Riding Jackson. FuPo

Under her solemn fillet saw the scorn. (LL) Days. Ralph Waldo Emerson. APN-1; ColAP; HeIP-4; NAAL-3; NAAPv.1; NCAP; NoP-4; NoP-5; OxBoAm; TCAPo; TFi

Under his Cross[e]. (LL) Hymn[e] to God the Father, A. Ben Jonson. BrAP; InVLi; NoP-4; NoP-5; NOSC; OxAEP-1; SacPr

Under his persistent look I closed my eyes. Student who sat facing me on the Osaka express, A. Lindley Williams Hubbell. APT-2

Under House Arrest. Dennis Brutus. AF

Under it out toward the island. (LL) Henry's Understanding. John Berryman. NAMCP V.2; NoAM; OxBoAm; PoCho; WoPoe

Under its spreading bankruptcy. Splendid Bankrupt, The. Arthur A. Sykes. UV

Under mercury light the little pup strives. A sinister shadow ducks under the curb. John Godfrey. FTOS

Under My Breath. Anne Waldman. BodElec

Under my feet the moon. Brimming Water. Tu Fu [*or* Du Fu]. CCL1; NDACCP, *tr.* by Kenneth Rexroth

Under my house. Issa. EH, *tr.* by Robert Hass

Under my ribcage a live coal. Woman Is Running for Her Life, A. Sheila Demetre. FiBr

Under my skin there lives a caged beast. Dancer. Martinus Nijhoff. TuT, *tr. by* Desmond Egan

Under my window-ledge the waters race. Coole Park and Ballylee, 1931. William Butler Yeats. NoAM; OBGa; OBMV

Under pines. Seeking but Not Finding the Recluse. Chia Tao. CSKM, *tr.* by Mike O'Connor

Under pressure Mick tells me one. Blue Days. Rita Dove. ExTi

Under rinsed thunderclouds. At the Nu'uanu Reservoir Pool. Phyllis Thompson. ICANM

Under Sedation. Alec Derwent Hope. BMAP

Under spring stars. Ophelia. Richard Hedderman. IaFF

Under striped flutter of awnings, they have come. Renoir. Rosanna Warren. GS

Under that embrace of wild saplings held fast. Wreck in the Woods. Dave Jeddie Smith. NAMCP V.2; RoV

Under that tamarind tree. Martyred Tamarind, The. Alberto Ferreira Gomes. NAfrP, *tr.* by Gerald M. Moser

Under the afterglow. Tune: "Winds of Falling Plums." Ma Chih-yüan. ChinPo, *tr.* by Ye Weilian [*or* Yeh Wei-lien *or* Wai-lim Yip]

Under the Apple Tree. Diana Rivera. InvLad

Under the arch of a million sighs. Chattels. Celia de Fréine. NIrP, *tr.* by the author

Under the arch of Life, where love and death. Dante Gabriel Rossetti. NAEL-7v2; OBEV; OxAEP-2 *Fr.* House of Life, The.

Under the azure sky. Lover's Song, A. Goran. IrPoTo, *tr.* by Abdul Kadir Said Ferhadi

Under the Big Top. Ted Genoways. PoDa

Under the blossom that hangs on the bough. (LL) William Shakespeare. BLPJKO; NBLV; NoSic; OBEV; TFi *Fr.* Tempest, The.

Under the Bram Bush. *Unknown.* FaBoVe

Under the bright disc the frog's blood was much brighter. Cutting Sod-Land. George Scarbrough. LPSFW

Under the bronze crown. Baroque Wall-Fountain in the Villa Sciarra, A. Richard Wilbur. ColAP; GS; NoP-4; NoP-5; OBGa; OxBoAm; VCAP

Under the bronze leaves a colt was foaled. Song. "St.-John Perse." YaTCFP, *tr.* by T. S. Eliot

Under the carpet, wrinkling to fulfillment. (LL) Harriet ("Repeating fly, blueback, thumbthick—so gross, A.") Robert Lowell. NoP-4; NoP-5

Under the centre of the sky. Death Song. *Unknown.* APN-2, *tr.* by Henry Rowe Schoolcraft

Under the cloudy cliff, near the temple door. On Basho's "Frog." Sengai Gibon. ZenPo, *tr.* by Takashi Ikemoto and Lucien Stryk

Under the cobbled bridge the white swans float. Swans on the River Ayr. Mary Oliver. UrbNat

Under the cold eyes, the cat eyes of those young. To Some Young Communists from an Older Socialist. Naomi Mitchison. RSaN

Under the concrete benches. Weed Puller. Theodore Roethke. NAMCP V.1

Under the copper-clad latticework of the power plant. Power Plant, The. Julianne Buchsbaum. LegDan

Under the cypresses the air is still. Life of Intimate Fleeing, A. Robert Kelly. FTOS

Under the dawn I wake my two-wheel friend. On a Bicycle. Yevgeny Aleksandrovich Yevtushenko. ArBi, tr. by Peter Levi and Robin Milner-Gulland

Under the day's crust a half-eaten child. Pied Piper, The. John Ashbery. YaYoPo

Under the death of winter's leaves he lies. Metho Drinker. Judith Wright. BMAP

Under the dogwood the bicycles are blue. Blue Bicycles. Charles Fishman. ArBi

Under the Drumlin. David Brendon Hopes. UpMys

Under the dusty print of hobnailed boot. Country Press. Rosemary Dobson. NOBAu

Under the earth's green bed. (LL) Chernobyl. Mary Jo Salter. AtGh; FFC

Under the Edge of February. Jayne Cortez. EGAG

Under the Eildon Tree. Sydney Goodsir Smith.
(Elegy 5.) EdScPo

Under the evening moon. Issa. EH; ChAP, tr. by Robert Hass

Under the Eyes. Tom Paulin. PNI

Under the fig tree it is October. Bertha Beninu. Natalia Toledo. RMCMP, tr. by Alberto A. Ríos

Under the fire escape, crouched, one knee in cinders. Desk, The. David Bottoms. WeW-3

Under the flowering chinaberry. Chinaberry Trees, The. Andrew Hudgins. LPSFW

Under the French horns of a November afternoon. Man in Blue, A. James Schuyler. FTOS; PmAP; WaAnP

Under the fucking truck, chum. Generals Ride in Cars. Unknown. FaBoWar

Under the great cold lakes, under the midmost. Midland. Mark Van Doren. APT-2

Under the green lamp-light her letter there. Letter of a Mother. Robert Penn Warren. MoAmPo

Under the Greenwood Tree. Hugh MacDiarmid. FaBoWar; OBVE

Under the greenwood tree. William Shakespeare. NoSic; OBEV Fr. As You Like It.

Under the harsh light, scolded by the Book. Exorcism. Dorothy Nimmo. Prnts

Under the hemlocks Fancy came. On the Concord River. Henrietta Cordelia Ray. CBWP-3

Under the Hill. Richard Eberhart. PoA 2002

Under the Hill. Daryl Hine. MakPoe

Under the hive-like dome the stooping haunted readers. British Museum Reading Room, The. Louis MacNeice. BrAP; GoPo; MoBrPo

Under the Ice. Stewart Conn. NePenScot

Under the image of Buddha. Issa. EH, tr. by Robert Hass

Under the Light, yet under. Emily Dickinson. FaBoVe; NAAPv.1; NCAP

"Under the Lime Tree." Walther von der Vogelweide. GePo

Under the lime-tree, on the daisied ground. Walther von der Vogelweide. OBVE

Under the linden. Walther von der Vogelweide. EroLit, tr. by Alan Bold

Under the Linden Tree. Unknown. EroLit Fr. Carmina Burana.

Under the Lindentree. Walther von der Vogelweide. WoPoe, tr. by Michael Benedikt

Under the lindentree. Under the Lindentree. Walther von der Vogelweide. WoPoe, tr. by Michael Benedikt

Under the long dark boughs, like jewels red. Cherry Robbers. D. H. Lawrence. MoBrPo

Under the maples at moonrise. Robert Penn Warren. LPSFW Fr. Some Quiet, Plain Poems.

Under the Microscope. Slavko Mihalic. PoSu, tr. by Charles Simic

Under the Mirabeau Bridge the Seine / Flows and [or with] our love[s]. Mirabeau Bridge, The. Guillaume Apollinaire. OBVE

Under the Mirabeau Bridge there flows the Seine. Mirabeau Bridge. Guillaume Apollinaire. WoPoe, tr. by Richard Wilbur

Under the mountain, as when first I knew. Frederick Goddard Tuckerman. APN-2 Fr. Sonnets.

Under the naked hoe of the moon. Peter Huchel. GTCP, tr. by Reinhold Grimm

Under the narrenga tree, Warrior, Bhaskar. Warrior, Bhaskar! Sivudu. HotL, tr. by V. Narayana Rao

Under the neon sign he stands. Drive-In, The. R. S. Gwynn. RA

Under the net of our kisses. (LL) Pablo Neruda. PasH; WoPoe Fr. Red Bird.

Under the new pond-dam. Looking Before and After. Carter Revard. HATNAP

Under the Ninth Sky. Georg Nikolic. IllVoic

Under the non-moon, in the watery tint. As in the Small Gaps Between Minutes. Gillian Conoley. RoV

Under the Oak Table. Colleen J. McElroy. GT; OxAAAP

Under the olives, in whose night they sleep. (LL) Table-Birds. Kenneth Mackenzie. BMAP; NOBAu

Under the parabola of a ball. How to Kill. Keith Douglas. HarvBoo; NPeEn; PLBUT; PoAgWa; PoWW

Under the pines I questioned the boy. Looking for a Recluse but Failing to Find Him. Chia Tao. ColAnChi, tr. by Burton Watson

Under the rain's broken fingers. (LL) Elements of San Joaquin, The. Gary Soto. GeoHom; PBCAP

Under the red Korean banner. Inupiat Christmas Pageant, The. Peggy Shumaker. PBCAP

Under the roof and the roof's shadow turns. Merry-go-round, The. Rainer Maria Rilke. WeW-3, tr. by C. F. MacIntyre

Under the Roof of Memory. Peter Davison. InoFa

Under the roof of the Fountain House. Anna Andreyevna Akhmatova. PFTM-2 Fr. Poem without a Hero.

Under the running tap that are not the hands of a child. (LL) Soap Suds. Louis MacNeice. EmeKit; ModIr; NAEL-6v2; NAEL-7v2; NPeEn

Under the sagging clotheslines of crepe paper. Best Slow Dancer, The. David Wagoner. NoAM; VCAP

Under the same roof. Basho. EMJL, tr. by Haruo Shirane

Under the Scorpion's Heart. Margot Schilpp. AmPoNex

Under the separated leaves of shade. Man Meets a Woman in the Street, A. Randall Jarrell. NoP-4; NoP-5

Under the shade of the riverbank snow lingers on; the moon is shining on the snow. Snowflame. Kawai Suimei. CAoMJL1, tr. by Leith Morton

Under the shadow of that wing. (LL) To a Child in Death. Charlotte Mew. ChIV-2; MoBrPo

Under the shadow of the gloomy night. Prologue. Samuel Rowlands. NOSC

Under the Sign of Walt Whitman. Gray Jacobik. ViWalt

Under the sky that deafened from listening for rain. (LL) Drought, The. Gary Soto. NAMCP V.2; NoAM

Under the sloped snow. As Children Together. Carolyn Forché. NoAM; OxWW

Under the Sod. Colette Ni Ghallchóir. NIrP, tr. by the author

Under the sovereign crests of dead volcanoes. On a Bougainvillaea Vine at the Summer Palace [or in Haiti]. Barbara Howes. MoAmPo

Under the spreading gooseberry bush. Village Burglar, The. Unknown. GoPo

Under the Stairs. Frank Ormsby. PBCIP

Under the stars / In the space of night. Under the Stars. Anne B. Murray. CFP

Under the stars the great wise Worm lay dead;. Fafnir. Alec Derwent Hope. BMAP

Under the sunrise the mountains. Robert Bringhurst. PoCoUp Fr. Dogen.

Under the Surface. Frances Ridley Havergal. SacPr

Under the thin smoke of winter. Evening Bells near a Temple. Ma Chih-yüan. CrYelRi, tr. by Sam Hamill

Under the thunder-dark, the cicadas resound. Dark Summer. Louise Bogan. APT-2; ItP

Under the too white marmoreal Lincoln Memorial. March 1, The. Robert Lowell. AmWaPo; PoetW; PoPoPo

Under the umbrella of concrete, yesterday, we laughed at tomato for its carelessness. Kitasono Katsue. CAoMJL1

Under the Vulture-Tree. David Bottoms. GifTon

Under the Walls of Ping City. Li Ho. CCL1, tr. by John Frodsham

Under the water like a bar of light. (LL) Swans Mating. Michael Longley. PNI; StAl

Under the water tower at the edge of town. To the Evening Star: Central Minnesota. James Wright. NAAL-5

Under the Waterfall. Thomas Hardy. NAEL-6v2; NAEL-7v2; NoP-4; NoP-5

Under the wheels of a hearse. (LL) Empty House. Yüan Chěn. CrYelRi; ErotSp, tr. by Sam Hamill

Under the white man's menace, out of time. (LL) Outcast. Claude McKay. APT-1; NAAPv.2; NAMCP V.1; OxAAAP

Under the white sheet of history. (LL) Real Thing, The. Eiléan Ní Chuilleanáin. ModIr; MoWP

Under the white silence of the great gumtree avenue. Finished Gentleman, A. Geoffrey Dutton. NOBAu

Under the wide and starry sky. Requiem. Robert Louis Stevenson. BRP; MoBrPo; NBLV; NePenScot; OBEV; OxBEV; TFi; WaAnP

Under the Williamsburg Bridge. Galway Kinnell. UrbNat

Under the Willows. James Russell Lowell.
  "May is a pious fraud of the almanac." APN-1; TCAPo
Under the wind. Jean Daive. MFP, *tr.* by Martin Sorrell
Under the wind I saw. Under the wind. Jean Daive. MFP, *tr.* by Martin
  Sorrell
Under the windblown sea. Oman. Gu Cheng. WoBe, *tr.* by Joseph R. Allen
Under the Window: Ouro Prêto. Elizabeth Bishop. VCAP
Under this bright moon. Issa. SoOfWa, *tr.* by Sam Hamill
Under this heap of stones interred lies. Upon Stephen Stoned. Sir John
  Suckling. ChIV-2
Under this stone doth lie. Epitaph upon Thomas, Lord Fairfax, An. George,
  2d Duke of Buckingham Villiers. NOSC
Under this stone / Lies a Reverend Drone. Epitaph upon That Profound and
  Learned Casuist, the Late Ordinary of Newgate, An. Thomas Brown.
  OBSV
Under this stone, reader, survey. On Sir John Vanbrugh [Architect]. Abel
  Evans. NPeEn
Under this stone, what lies? Evergreen, The. John Frederick Nims. APT-2
Under thudding cattle. Parts of a Thornbush, The. *Unknown.* SonAtl, *tr.* by
  Alan Brierly, Saul Goode and S. Wendo
Under Voice, The. Jean Valentine. BodElec; CAP-8; ExTi
Under walls white as a birch forest the ferns of paintings grow. In an. Painter.
  Zbigniew Herbert. AF, *tr.* by John Carpenter and Bogdana Carpenter
Under water, her limed hands spread the basest ligature, each. Simone
  Signoret, Beldam. Richard Murray Vaughan. Coast
Under what beechen shade, or silent oak. Sonnet; A Still Place. Barry
  Cornwall. NOBRP
Under Which Lyre: A Reactionary Tract for the Times. W. H. Auden.
  AmWit; MoBrPo; OxBoAm
Under Willows. Christina Georgina Rossetti. VWP
Under yonder beech-tree single on the green-sward [*Longer vers. (1878)*].
  Love in the Valley. George Meredith. OBEV
Under you, over you, on you. Ah. Robin Blaser. FTOS
Under your illkempt yellow roses. Delia Rexroth. Kenneth Rexroth.
  NAMCP V.1; OxBoAm
Under your love's burden. My Soul Sinks. Hayyim Nahman Bialik. FIT, *tr.*
  by Robert Friend
Under your Milky Way. Return of the Goddess [Artemis]. Robert Graves.
  PoA 2002
Underfoot rotten boards, forest rubble, bones. Remains of an Indian Village.
  Alfred Wellington Purdy. BrAP
Undergoing: Jewish General Hospital, Montreal 6:35 a.m. Fraser Sutherland.
  Coast
Undergone swamp ticket relative. Twenties 26. Jackson Mac Low. PmAP
Underground. May Kendall. ViWPN; VWP
Underground. Conrad Kent Rivers. SeSe
Underneath (1). Jorie Graham. BodElec
Underneath (2). Jorie Graham. BodElec
Underneath (3). Jorie Graham. BodElec
Underneath (7). Jorie Graham. BodElec
Underneath an old oak tree. Raven, The. Samuel Taylor Coleridge.
  NOxBChV
Underneath, her voice is. Duets. Caitríona O'Reilly. NIrP
Underneath Oblivion. Yannis Ritsos. AF, *tr.* by Minas Savas
Underneath Our Skirts. Katie Donovan. NeBl
Underneath the Archers *or* What's All This about Walter's Willy? Kit Wright.
  OBCoV
Underneath the photograph. Informant, The. Eiléan Ní Chuilleanáin. ModIr
Underneath the tree on some. Like They Say. Robert Creeley. OxBoAm
Underneath this blanket of snow. Night in the Ashes. Agnes Walsh. Coast
Underneath this greedy stone. Epitaph on Erotion. Martial. RomPo, *tr.* by
  Leigh Hunt
Underneath this myrtle shade. Epicure, The. Anacreon. OxAEP-1, *tr.* by
  Abraham Cowley
Underneath this sable hearse [*or* herse]. On the Countess Dowager of
  Pembroke. William Browne. BASC; TFi
  (Underneath this sable hearse.) NoP-4
  (Underneth this Marble Hearse.) NPeEn
Underneth this Marble Hearse. William Browne. *See* Underneath this sable
  hearse [*or* herse].
Underpants / Lying limp, shapeless. Transfiguration. John Wright. BloBone
Undersong of terrible holy joy, An. (LL) Old Women, The. George Mackay
  Brown. EdScPo; NoP-4; NoP-5; WaAnP
Understand. (LL) Maybe Then. Idea Vilariño. CFP; TANSG, *tr.* by Louise
  B. Popkin
Understand that they were sitting just inside the door. State of the Nation, The.
  Kenneth Patchen. CLPP
Understanding. István Vas. IQMS, *tr.* by Godfrey Turton
Understanding Canada. Peter Sirr. PBCIP

Understanding Each Other. Linda Noel. ReEnLa
Understanding is all, my mother would tell me. Dreaming Up Mother. Robert
  Adamson. BMAP
Understanding *King Lear*. Stephen Corey. IaFF
Understanding Light. Elin ap Hywel. BBMWP, *tr.* by the author
Understanding the Light. Elin ap Hywel. ATSWP, *tr.* by Robert Minhinnick
Understanding the *Ramayana*. Sujata Bhatt. HarvBoo
Understanding the Universe. John Frederick Nims. PfSP
Understory. Pamela Alexander. ExTi
Undertakers. Robert Johnstone. PNI
Undertaker's Daughter Feels Neglect, The. Thylias Moss. ESEAA
Undertaking, The. John Donne. NAEL-6v1; NAEL-7v1
  (Undertaking or Platonic Love, The.) FSCP
Undertaking in New Jersey, The. George Oppen. GPTC; OxBoAm
Undertaking or Platonic Love, The. John Donne. *See* Undertaking, The.
Underwater eyes, an eel's. Otter, An. Ted Hughes. NAMCP V.2; NoAM
Underwear. Lawrence Ferlinghetti. EmeKit
Underworld spreads in our ears, The. Oskar Loerke. GTCP *Fr.* At the Edge of
  the Great City.
Undesirable you may have been, untouchable. September Song. Geoffrey
  Hill. EMP; FaBoWar; HarvBoo; HP; NAEL-6v2; NAEL-7v2; NAMCP
  V.2; NoAM; NoP-4; NoP-5; NPeEn; OBWP; OxBEV; StAl
Undetectable. Justin Chin. WiU
Undine. Nicole Cooley. AmPoNex
Undiscouraged. Friedrich Wilhelm Nietzsche. WoPoe, *tr.* by Robert Bly
Undiscovered Country. James Longenbach. NAPBL
Undo me; naked, unbidden, at Night's muted birth. (LL) Wole Soyinka.
  WaAnP; WoPoe *Fr.* Idanre and Other Poems (1967).
Undoing, The. Elizabeth Robinson. Eno
'Undress me! Undress me!' you said. Oliver Reynolds. TCAWP *Fr.* Tone
  Poem.
Undressing, The. Carol Frost. CAP-8
Undressing Aunt Frieda. Richard Michelson. UnSA
Undressing for Li Po. Carl Phillips. WiU
Undulating grace. Woman. Alaide Foppa. TANSG, *tr.* by Celeste
  Kostopulos-Cooperman
Unduly elected body of our elders, An. Elegy for Yards, Pounds, and Gallons.
  David Wagoner. PoA 2002
Undying One, The. Caroline Elizabeth Norton.
  (Wealth Is Not Happiness.) TreFP
Unearth. Mary Louise Sullivan. PfS
Unearthing / my valentine, An. Louis Zukofsky. APSN *Fr.* A.
Unearthly lightning of presage. Epiphany. Robert Fitzgerald. ChrPo; PoCho
Unearthly word, The. Baying, The. James Bertolino. UrbNat
Uneasy poetry looking for an alternative. For Heiner Muller: Poem 1. Safaa
  Fathy. AnVo, *tr.* by Mohamed Enani
Unemployed and lazy, I wander around the village. Tu Fu [*or* Du Fu].
  CrYelRi *Fr.* Random Pleasures.
Unemployed Mami. Willie Perdomo. InTrad
Unemployed sky above the clouds, The. First Rock and Roll Song of 1970,
  The. Pedro Juan Pietri. ReTh
Unending loneliness from which others drink, The. Six Poems of Loneliness.
  Enrique Lihn. VCWP, *tr.* by David Unger
Unequal Fetters, The. Anne Finch, Countess of Winchilsea. BrAP; OxBEV
Uneven rows of hedges. Paul Verlaine. SxFrPo, *tr.* by Martin Sorrell
Uneven tilde, The. Dolores Dorantes. SPV, *tr.* by Jen Hofer
Unexpected Adventure, An. Amy Gerstler. SUP
Unexpected interest made him flush, The. Episode of Hands. Hart Crane.
  CAGL; NIL-7
Unexpected Manna. Gary H. Holthaus. GifTon
Unexpected Meeting. Wisława Szymborska. VCWP
Unexpected Pleasure, An. *Unknown.* UV
Unexpected Visit. Fleur Adcock. BrAP
Unexpectedly, from the outside. Joanne Kyger. AHA
Unexplained. Bird, A. Sheila Wingfield. MoWP; StAl
Unexploded ordinance carries instructions. Kristi Garboushian. AmWaPo *Fr.*
  Ribbon on Hell's Tree, The.
Unexpressed. Adelaide Anne Procter. SacPr
Unfailing Friend, The. Joseph Scriven. SacPr
  (What a Friend We Have in Jesus.) TCAPo
Unfailingly they escape. I go. Ark. Gerardo Deniz. RMCMP, *tr.* by Mónica
  de la Torre
Unfair to Men. *Unknown.* OBWVE, *tr.* by Gwyn Jones
Unfair to Women. *Unknown.* OBWVE, *tr.* by Gwyn Jones
Unfaithful Lover, The. Charlotte Dacre. RWP
Unfaithful Married Woman, The. Federico García Lorca. GPTC, *tr.* by Rolfe
  Humphries

Unfaithful Wife, The.   Federico García Lorca.   WoPoe, *tr. by* Michael Hartnett

Unfaithful Wife, The.   Federico García Lorca.   ErotSp, *tr. by* Sam Hamill

Unfaithful Wife, The.   Federico García Lorca.   STV, *tr. by* John Frederick Nims

Unfaithful Wife, The.   Federico García Lorca.   EroLit, *tr. by* Alan Bold

Unfaithful Wife, The.   Nuala Ni Dhomhnaill.   ModIr, *tr. by* Paul Muldoon

Unfallen Love.   John Milton.   NOSC

Unfalsifying sun, on this sick scene. (LL)   Keeping Their World Large. Marianne Moore.   PWW2; WaAnP

Unfamiliar warble 9 times more, An.   Retirement.   Joanne Kyger.   WANABP

Unfed dragons—take good care old friend. (LL)   Dreaming of Li Po ("Death at least gives separation repose.")   Tu Fu [*or* Du Fu].   NDACCP; WoPoe, *tr. by* David Hinton

Unfettered at last, a traveling monk.   Manan.   ZenPo, *tr. by* Takashi Ikemoto and Lucien Stryk

Unfinished Exile.   Fabio Doplicher.   NeIt, *tr. by* Stephen Sartarelli

Unfinished Letter to My Lady.   Dániel Berzsenyi.   IQMS, *tr. by* Peter Zollman

Unfinished Life Story.   Gerardo Diego.   RaW, *tr. by* Ralph Nelson

Unfinished Race, The.   Norman Cameron.   OxBSo

Unfinished Sewing, The.   Evdokiya Rostopchina.   ARWW, *tr. by* Catriona Kelly

Unfold, unfold! take in his light.   Revival, The.   Henry Vaughan.   InvLi

Unfolding moments.   Stretched Out in Solitude.   Belinda Zubicueta Carmona. TANSG, *tr. by* Celeste Kostopulos-Cooperman

Unforeseen, The.   Amy Gerstler.   MotU

Unforgettable.   Irving Gordon.   ReLy

Unforgettable / That's what you are.   Unforgettable.   Irving Gordon.   ReLy

Unforgiven, The.   Edwin Arlington Robinson.   APT-1; ItP

Unforgiving as the course of justice.   Holding My Beads.   Grace Nichols. ItWoWo

Unforseen camp-follower of not just our war, The. (LL)   Casualties, The. John Pepper Clark Bekedermo.   HBAPE; PLBUT

Unfortunate Coincidence.   Dorothy Parker.   AmWit; LW; NoP-4; NoP-5; OxBoAm

Unfortunate Damsel, The.   Mrs. Fleetwood Habergham.   LW

Unfortunate Gentleman, The.   Cornelius Whur.   STuOW

"In a dark and trying hour."   VerBaPo

Unfortunate human disorder, The.   Han-shan (Cold Mountain).   ColAnChi, *tr. by* Red Pine

Unfortunate Occurrence at Cwm-Cadno.   A. G. Prys-Jones.   AngWePo

Unfriendly friendly universe.   Child Dying, The.   Edwin Muir.   PoWW; WoPoe

Unfunny uncles who insist.   Exchanging Hats.   Elizabeth Bishop.   NIL-7; OxBoAm

Unfurl the banners to the breeze.   Texian Call to Arms.   Sam Houston.   TiP2

Ungag our souls!! Unstrangle our souls!! Unsmother our souls!!   "Antler." CLPP *Fr.* Factory.

Ungar's Harangue.   Herman Melville.   TCAPo *Fr.* Clarel: A Poem and Pilgrimage in the Holy Land.

Ungraciously, under.   Basho.   SoOfWa, *tr. by* Sam Hamill

Ungrateful Citizens, The.   John Ash.   NeBrP

Ungrateful Country, if thou e'er forget.   William Wordsworth.   SacPr *Fr.* Ecclesiastical Sonnets.

Ungrateful Garden, The.   Carolyn Kizer.   BrAP

Unguarded lies the wishing Maid.   Song and Musick, Set by Mr. Eccles, and Sung by Mrs. Leveridge.   Delariviere Manley.   EMWP

Unguentarium.   Elizabeth Garrett.   NeBl

Unhappie [*or* Unhappy] Light.   Madrigal.   William Drummond of Hawthornden.   NOSC

Unhappily I'm married. (LL)   Shades of Night, The.   A. E. Housman.   NBLV; OBCoV; UV

Unhappy about some far off things.   Stars Go Over the Lonely Ocean, The. Robinson Jeffers.   HarvBoo

Unhappy and at home. (LL)   Tollund Man, The.   Seamus Heaney.   CABP; ModIr; NAMCP V.2; NPeEn; PBCIP; PNI; WoPoe

Unhappy at being delayed at the Yangtze.   In the Mountains.   Wang Po. CrYelRi, *tr. by* Sam Hamill

Unhappy Dido burns, and in her rage.   NAEL-7v1 *Fr.* Aeneid [*or* Eneados *or* Aeneis], The.

Unhappy fate: that you have died.   Song at Graveside.   Ewald von Kleist. GePo, *tr. by* George C. Schoolfield

Unhappy He.   Rubén Darío.   SpanPo, *tr. by* Muna Lee

Unhappy he who his inner sphinx one day.   Unhappy He.   Rubén Darío. SpanPo, *tr. by* Muna Lee

Unhappy Kukutis in the Potato Patch.   Marcelijus Martinaitis.   TWW, *tr. by* Laima Sruoginis

Unhappy Love.   Sándor Kisfaludy. *tr. by* Watson Kirkconnell

"As the suffering hart confounded."   IQMS, *tr. by* Watson Kirkconnell

Unhappy pedophiles, cease your inane.   *Unknown.*   CAGL, *tr. by* Daryl Hine

Unhappy Pen, and ill-accepted lines.   Samuel Daniel.   NoP-5 *Fr.* Sonnets to Delia.

Unhappy Phaeton's splendidious sire.   Virgo, August.   John Taylor.   NOSC

Unhappy they, who by their duty led.   Mary Lee, Lady Chudleigh.   PEW *Fr.* Ladies Defence, The: Or, The Bride-Woman's Counsellor Answer'd: A Poem in Dialogue Between Sir John Brute, Sir William Loveall, Melissa, and a Parson.

Unhappy [*or* Unhappie] Verse, the witness[e] of my unhappy [*or* unhappie] state.   Iambicum Trimetrum.   Edmund Spenser.   NPeEn; OBEV

Unhappy woman's but a slave at large. (LL)   Essay on Woman, An.   Mary Leapor.   BrAP; NAEL-7v1

Unharnessed, the white horse ambles along.   Georgy Vladimirovich Ivanov. TCRusP, *tr. by* Daniel Weissbort

Unharvested.   Robert Frost.   APT-1; NAMCP V.1; SAmP

Unheard helicopter chop.   Don McKay.   NLPA *Fr.* Matériel.

Unhistoric Story, The.   Allen Curnow.   BrAP

Unhistorical Events.   Bob Kaufman.   CLPP; EGAG

Unholy Sonnet ("Breath like a house fly batters the shut mouth.")   Mark Jarman.   WaAnP *Fr.* Unholy Sonnets.

Unholy Sonnet ("He loads his weapons, but the Lord God sees him.")   Mark Jarman.   LiTh *Fr.* Unholy Sonnets.

Unholy Sonnet ("This boy listening eagerly to his friend.")   Mark Jarman. LiTh *Fr.* Unholy Sonnets.

Unholy Sonnets.   Mark Jarman.

  1.   P180

  4.   PoDa

"God like a kiss, God like a welcoming."   InvLi

Unholy Sonnet.   WaAnP

Unholy Sonnet.   LiTh

Unholy Sonnet.   LiTh

Unholy Spring.   John Godfrey.   FTOS

Unhurried as a snake I saw Time glide.   On Time.   Richard Hughes.   MoBrPo

Unhurt, like him, your charms I'll hear. (LL)   Farewell to Worldly Joys, A. Anne Killigrew.   BASC; CABP

Unica Zurn's Loam Bowl.   A. Di Michele.   AnSo

Unicorn stood, like a king in a dream, The.   Unicorn, The.   Emile Victor Rieu. OBSP

Unicorn, The.   Gertrud Kolmar.   GTCP, *tr. by* Henry A. Smith

Unicorn, The.   Ruth Pitter.   MoBrPo

Unicorn, The.   Emile Victor Rieu.   OBSP

Unicorn, The.   John Smith.   Coast

Unidentified Flying Object on an Errand of Love.   Mihangel Morgan. BBMWP, *tr. by* Martin Davis

Uniform, The.   Marvin Bell.   MAAN

Uniformed in grey that so ill-suits.   Plagiarist, The.   Bruce Berger.   GeoH

Uni-Gym, The.   Anne Rouse.   NeBl

Unimaginative, The.   Madison Cawein.   APN-2

Uninscribed Monument on One of the Battlefields of the Wilderness, An. Herman Melville.   CBCWP

Unintended.   Susan Moon.   FiBr

Uninvited, The.   Dorothy Livesay.   NoP-4

Uninvited woman, An.   Kim Namjo.   CAMKP *Fr.* Love's Cursive.

Union.   Emily Dickinson.   FaBoA

Union.   Annie Foster.   NLP

Union, The.   Ifi Amadiume.   HAWP

Union libre, L'.   André Breton.   YaTCFP

Union of Two, The.   Haki R. Madhubuti.   ISC; SpirFl

Union Square.   Lori Shine.   IIR

Unit.   Mary Elizabeth Fullerton.   NOBAu

United bolt and screw.   Mac Wellman.   HeMarv *Fr.* Rat Minaret: Miniaturist-Divan, The.

United Flight 608.   Leonard Nathan.   OtW

United Fruit Co.   Pablo Neruda.   TCLAP, *tr. by* Jack Schmitt

United Fruit Co., The.   Pablo Neruda.   WED, *tr. by* Robert Bly

United keeps for ever. (LL)   Knot, The.   Henry Vaughan.   BASC; RSR

United States.   John Keble.   SacPr *Fr.* Lyra Apostolica.

United States of America, The.   Lisa Jarnot.   Eno

United States of America rose at dawn this morning after a restless, The.   Good Morning America.   Frank Lima.   PA9/11

United States, The.   Johann Wolfgang von Goethe.   FaBoA, *tr. by* Robert Bly

United States themselves are essentially the greatest, The.—Walt Whitman. Top Ten of American Poetry.   Nanao Sakaki.   WhBo

United we stand and shake the chains heard round the world. (LL)   Back to Town.   John Hollander.   NAMCP V.2; NoAM

Units of Measurement.   Blaga Dimitrova.   CSCBP, *tr. by* Georgi Belev and Lisa Sapinkopf

Unity.   Fazil Hüsnü Dağlarca.   RaBo, *tr. by* Tâlat S. Halman

Unity.   Ralph Waldo Emerson.   TCAPo

Unity. Pablo Neruda. ConPit, *tr.* by Clayton Eshleman

Universal Favorite, The. Carolyn Wells. NBLV

Universal *is* the particular, The. (LL) Hugh MacDiarmid. BrAP; NAEL-6v2; NAEL-7v2; NoP-4; NoP-5 *Fr.* In Memoriam James Joyce.

Universal Prayer, The [Deo Opt. Max.]. Alexander Pope. InvLi; NoP-4; NoP-5

Universe is forever falling apart, The. Destruction. Takahashi Shinkichi. AtGh; ZenPo, *tr.* by Takashi Ikemoto and Lucien Stryk

Universe is large: to be eccentric, The. One's Country. Jonathan Griffin. Oth

Universe is Part of Ourselves, The. Robin Blaser. FTOS

Universe is sad, The. Resonance. Ruth Stone. BodElec; OxBoAm

Universe—is still, The. (LL) He fumbles at your Soul. Emily Dickinson. APN-2; LW; NAAL-3; NCAP; TCAPo; TRP

Universe / keeps them turning turning. Photograph. Lucille Clifton. OxAAAP

Universe of heated molecules, just above their bodies, The. (LL) Miniaturist, The. Maurice Kilwein Guevara. AmPoNex; TouFir

Universe of the Rose. Chimako Tada. VCWP, *tr.* by Kirsten Vidaeus

Universe, so whole within my mind, The. (LL) Flaw, A. Michael Field. ViWPN; VWP

Universe trembles before him, The. (LL) Destruction. Takahashi Shinkichi. AtGh; ZenPo, *tr.* by Takashi Ikemoto and Lucien Stryk

University. Karl Shapiro. APT-2; PoA 2002

University Hospital, Boston. Mary Oliver. CAP-8

University is waiting to honor him, The. James Baldwin, 1924–1987. Alvin Aubert. FuFl

Unjust, Imperial Heaven's way. Ying from "The Nine Declarations." Ch'u Yüan. ChinPo, *tr.* by Ye Weilian [*or* Yeh Wei-lien *or* Wai-lim Yip]

Unjust steals [*or* stole] the just's umbrella, The. (LL) Rain It Raineth, The. Charles Synge Christopher Bowen, Baron Bowen. NBLV; NTCP

Unjustly I've imposed upon my friends. Greg Williamson. NoP-5

Unjustly Punished Child. Sharon Olds. PBCAP

Unkept Good Fridays. Thomas Hardy. GI

Unkindness. George Herbert. NOSC

Unknowing, The. Linda Gregg. ExTi

Unknown, The. John Davidson. MoBrPo

Unknown, The. Edgar Lee Masters. NAAPv.1 *Fr.* Spoon River Anthology.

Unknown Also Attracts Cowards, The. Gloria Fuertes. RaW, *tr.* by Philip Levine

Unknown Child, The. Elizabeth Jennings. MoWP

Unknown Citizen, The. W. H. Auden. BrAP; HeIP-4; NAMCP V.1; NBLV; NIP-4; OBSV; SoSe-8; TRP

Unknown Dead, The. Henry Timrod. AmWaPo; PCW

Unknown Eros, The. Coventry Patmore.

    Arbor Vitae. OxBEV

    Departure. OBEV

    Farewell, A. OBEV

    (Magna Est Veritas.) NPeEn; OBEV; OxBEV

    To the Body. CABP

    Toys, The. OBEV; OxAEP-2; SoSe-8

Unknown Female Corpse. Rudyard Kipling. PoWW *Fr.* Epitaphs of the War [1914–1918].

Unknown Forebear. W. S. Merwin. StAl

Unknown Girl in the Maternity Ward. Anne Sexton. NoAM

Unknown God, The. George Russell. MoBrPo

Unknown guest in passing, An. Little Odes on Mount Star. Chŏng Ch'ŏl. CATKP, *tr.* by Peter H. Lee

Unknown Land. Rex Ingamells.

    "We who are called Australians have no country." NOBAu

Unknown Love. ADNAN Özer. NaPG, *tr.* by Talat Sait Halman

Unknown Man in the Morgue. Merrill Moore. MoAmPo

Unknown man, The. Fadil Azzawi. IrPoTo, *tr.* by Saadi A. Simawe

Unknown road still marching, The. (LL) March in the Ranks Hard-Prest, and the Road Unknown, A. Walt Whitman. AmWaPo; CBCWP; NAAL-3; PCW

Unknown, She Was My Favorite Shape. Paul Éluard. NAWM-7v2, *tr.* by Lloyd Alexander

Unknown, she was my favorite shape. Unknown, She Was My Favorite Shape. Paul Éluard. NAWM-7v2, *tr.* by Lloyd Alexander

Unknown Shores. Théophile Gautier. WoPoe, *tr.* by D. M. Thomas

Unknown Soldier, The. Alun Lewis. MoBrPo

Unknown Soldiers. Edgar Lee Masters. InoFa; NoAM *Fr.* New Spoon River, The.

Unknown Voice, An. Carlos German Belli. TCLAP, *tr.* by Maureen Ahern and David Tipton

Unknown voice told me, An. Unknown Voice, An. Carlos German Belli. TCLAP, *tr.* by Maureen Ahern and David Tipton

Unknown World, The. György Sárközi. IQMS, *tr.* by Watson Kirkconnell

Unlearning English. Michael Melo. ReBoTo

Unless God of his goodness grants us a truce. (LL) William Langland. NAEL-6v1; NAEL-7v1 *Fr.* Vision of Piers Plowman, The.

Unless is too blade. Clark Coolidge. AHA *Fr.* Ing.

Unless it trembled with the strings. (LL) Romance. Edgar Allan Poe. APN-1; NCAP

    (Did it not tremble with the strings!) (LL) NAAL-3; NAAPv.1

Unless there was time, and eternity's plenty. (LL) Mystery of Emily Dickinson, The. Marvin Bell. CAP-8; InvLad

Unless they love you. (LL) Cascando. Samuel Beckett. IrLP; ModIr

Unless You Are a Horse. Robert Hershon. PrTe

Unless you are mad with love for me. *Unknown.* SLW, *tr.* by Marjolijn De Jager, Sayd Bahodin Majrouh and André Velter

Unlettered. Edward J. Ingebretsen. VisFro

Unlike almost everything. Near the Desert Test Sites. Sherod Santos. GeoHom

Unlike are we, O princely Heart! Elizabeth Barrett Browning. CABP; CenSon; OBEV; OxAEP-2 *Fr.* Sonnets from the Portuguese.

Unlike flying or astral projection, walking through walls is a. Walking through a Wall. Louis Jenkins. RaBo

Unlike, for Example, the Sound of a Riptooth Saw. Thomas Lux. AmAlph

Unlike my friend John I like the painting entitled. 2 Poems on the Same Theme. Michael Burkard. BodElec

Unlike talk, like prayer, this mist unravels. God's Cutt-Off TV Screen's Vanishing Mirror Seems an Unshared Point. Christopher Davis. Vesp

Unlike the hawk he has no dream of height. Sea Owl. Dave Jeddie Smith. RoV

Unlike the heroes of each ancient race. Lord Byron. NOBRP *Fr.* Corsair, The.

Unlikely Obbligato of Andersonstown. Kit Wright. OBCoV

Unlived life is light, so light, The. Quotations for a Winter Evening. David Jauss. PoA 2002

Unloading hell behind him step by step. (LL) Rear-Guard, The. Siegfried Sassoon. MoBrPo; NAEL-6v2; NAEL-7v2; NAMCP V.1; NoAM; OBWP; PoWW; WaAnP

Unloved I love, unwept I weep. Reason. Charlotte Brontë. VWP

Unmarked Stop in Front of Westmond General Store, Westmond, Idaho. Jonathan Johnson. AmPoNex

Unmarried Clergy, The. Brian Merriman. IrLP *Fr.* Midnight Court, The.

Unmoved by cricket song of thee or me. (LL) Cricket, The. Frederick Goddard Tuckerman. APN-2; NAAPv.1; NCAP; TCAPo

Unmoving, it presents itself in a thousand shapes. Untitled. Pou Kuksa. BecRai, *tr.* by Kim Daljin, Kim Won-Chung and Christopher Merrill

Unnamed. David Chaloner. VaPo

Unnatural Light. Peter Meinke. UrbNat

Unnoticed. Miklós Radnóti. PoChi, *tr.* by Stephen Berg, S. J. Marks and Steven Polgar

Unnumbered suppliants crowd preferment's gate. Juvenal. OBSV *Fr.* Vanity of Human Wishes, The; The Tenth Satire of Juvenal [Imitated].

Uno está solo frente a esto: haciendo máscaras. Eduardo Milán. RMCMP

Unopened Letters. Linda Zisquit.

    "Because passion is the absence we speak." DTA

    "Because passion is the silence we share." DTA

    "There is always a sound." DTA

Unorthodox and impractical one not led. Hoa Nguyen. WANABP

Unpardonable Sin, The. Vachel Lindsay. ChIV-2

Unperturbed at the battle. Kamalākānta Bhattācārya. SinGod, *tr.* by Rachel Fell McDermott

Unpetal the flower of me. To Life. Lizette Woodworth Reese. TCAPo

Unpleasantness During a Memorial Service. Arye Sivan. NRoS, *tr.* by Esther Raizen

Unpleasing to a married ear! (LL) William Shakespeare. NAEL-6v1; NBLV; NIL-7; NIP-4; NoP-5; NoSic; OBEV; TFi *Fr.* Love's Labour's Lost.

Unpliable / Own. (LL) Offspring. Naomi Long Madgett. GT; OxAAAP; SoSe-8

Unplumbed [*or* unplumb'd], salt, estranging sea, The. (LL) Matthew Arnold. BrAP; NAEL-6v2; NAEL-7v2; NoP-5; NPeEn; OxBEV; SoSe-8; WaAnP *Fr.* Switzerland.

Unpod / the bag. Woman Turns Herself into a Fish, The. Eavan Boland. WaAnP

Unpredicted voices of our kind, The. (LL) Two Girls Singing. Iain Crichton Smith. EdScPo; NePenScot

Unprofessionals, The. U. A. Fanthorpe. PoCu; StAl

Unprofitablenes. Henry Vaughan. NAEL-7v1; NOSC

Unprofitably pleasing, and unsound. Mary Sidney Wroth, Countess of Montgomery. BASC *Fr.* Pamphilia to Amphilanthus.

Unpublished Man, The. Rafael Pérez Estrada. PML, *tr.* by Steven J. Stewart

Unpurged images of day recede, The. Byzantium. William Butler Yeats. HarvBoo; MoBrPo; NAEL-6v2; NAEL-7v2; NAMCP V.1; NAWM-7v2; NIL-7; NIP-4; NoAM; NoP-4; NoP-5; OxBEV; WaAnP

Unquiet Bed, The. Dorothy Livesay. BrAP

Unquiet Grave, The. *Unknown.* CABP; HeIP-4; NoP-4; NoP-5; TFi; WeW-3; WoPoe

Unraveled a spine of blood. (LL) Graciela. Gary Soto. NAMCP V.2; NoAM

Unraveling Ravel is no longer a secret. Ravel: Bolero. Al Young. SpirFl

Unraveling wins out: I leave my home, The. Leaving. Tiziano Rossi. ItPo, *tr. by* Gayle Ridinger

Unreachable father, when we were first. Matins. Louise Glück. InvLi; MoWP

Unreal Dwelling: My Years in Volcano, The. Garrett Kaoru Hongo. OpBo

Unreal tall as a myth. Bear on the Delhi Road, The. Earle Birney. BrAP; HeIP-4; NoAM; NoP-4; NoP-5

Unreasonable lenses refract the. Prairie Houses. Barbara Guest. PmAP

Unreasonable ryche manne, An. Of unsaciable purchasers. Robert Crowley. PBRV

Unrecognized, long after he has died. (LL) Counterfeiter, The. Greg Williamson. AmPoNex; RA

Un-Red Deer, The. Charles Hubert Sisson. HarvBoo

Un-red deer, The. Un-Red Deer, The. Charles Hubert Sisson. HarvBoo

Unreeling itself across the eletric billboard. Hair. Nina Iskrenko. ItGoST, *tr. by* Patrick Henry, John High and Katya Olmsted

Unrelated Incidents. Tom Leonard.

   "This is thi." NePenScot; NPeEn

Unrelenting Flood. William Matthews. BodElec

Unremarkable at first, this infant. Tom Passey's Child. Maggie Hannan. NLP

Unrepeatable, ever-present mirage. Hills, The. Ivan Teofilov. CSCBP, *tr. by* Georgi Belev and Lisa Sapinkopf

Unrepentant. Brandel France de Bravo. OPRER

Unreturning, The. Wilfred Owen. MoBrPo

Unreturning, The: "Blue is my sky peter." Alfred Goldsworthy Bailey. Coast

Unreturning Spring, The. Laurence Binyon. CABP

Unrighteous Mammon (Luke 16:9). Ernesto Cardenal. GI, *tr. by* Robert Pring-Mill

Unripe grapes. People of Grapes. Nidaa Khoury. PoArWo, *tr. by* Linda Zisquit

Unromantic Awakening, An. Priscilla Jane Thompson. CBWP-2

Unsaid. Dana Gioia. WaAnP

Unseals her earth, and lifts love in its shower. (LL) Broken Tower, The. Hart Crane. APT-2; ColAP; MoAmPo; NAAPv.2; NAMCP V.1; NoAM; NoP-4; OxBoAm; PoPoPo; WaAnP

Unseen Fire. Ralph Nixon Currey. OBWP; PoWW

Unseen Spirits. Nathaniel Parker Willis. APN-1; TreFP

Unseen, unknown, I here alone complain. Mary Sidney Wroth, Countess of Montgomery. NAEL-6v1; NAEL-7v1

Unsent. Tu Mu. NDACCP, *tr. by* David Hinton

Unsent Letter 4: Last Take. Carol Muske-Dukes. *See* Last Take.

Unsettled Motorcyclist's Vision of His Death, The. Thom Gunn. PoA 2002

Unsex'd Females, The. Richard Polwhele.

   "Alas! in every aspiration bold." NOBRP

   "Thou, who with all the poet's genuine rage." NOBRP

Unsheathing of the great knife of parting, The. (LL) Dead Child Speaks, A. Nelly Sachs. HP; PoSu

Unsigned architecture of loneliness, The. Last. Donald Revell. RoV

Unspeakable. Ferenc Faludi. IQMS, *tr. by* J. G. Nichols

Unspeakable Wounds of War, The. Maisha Baton. ICANM

Unspent. *Unknown.* SonAtl, *tr. by* Abdul Kalam Azad and Eric Howarth

Unspoken. Judith Ortiz Cofer. PueRic

Unspoken creed. Fearless Rider. Jim Clawson. ArBi

Unsquandered, sure and quiet as a root. Emily's Words. Leslie Monsour. FFC

Unstable dream[e] [*or* dreme], according [*or* accordyng] to the place. Sir Thomas Wyatt. OxBSo

Unsteady Yellow. Tess Gallagher. InvLad

Unstring the harp. Ann Lauinger. IaFF *Fr.* Three Songs for *King Leir.*

Unstring the silk in one continuous thread. (LL) Acanthus. Arthur Sze. AmAlph; BAP-04

Unstrung Lyre, The. Eric Pankey. PoDa

Unsubscriber, The. Bill Knott. PoCho

Unsung Heroes, The. Paul Laurence Dunbar. AmWaPo; CBCWP

Unsupported by reason's enigma. Scheherazade. John Ashbery. FaoP

Unsuspected Blackcurrant river rolls. Blackcurrant River. Arthur Rimbaud. SxFrPo, *tr. by* Martin Sorrell

Unswept, The. Sharon Olds. ASA

Unswerving Marine. Carl Rakosi. FTOS

Unthrifty loveliness, why dost thou spend. Ellen McGrath Smith. IaFF *Fr.* Shaken.

Unthronged Oracle, The. Laura Riding Jackson. OxBoAm

Untie my fatted lamb strange shepherd. Sonnet 188. Félix Lope de Vega Carpio. BLPSL, *tr. by* Rene de Costa, Rigas Kappatos and Eleni Paidoussi

Untie my tongue. Muse of fiery ABC. Autumn Prelude. Andrey Andreievich Voznesensky. RusPo, *tr. by* Robert Arthur Douglas Ford

Untied of all binding knots. Mistress of My Own Being. Ifi Amadiume. HAWP

Until a shiny providence comes. (LL) Yi Sang. CAMKP; PFTM-1 *Fr.* Crow's-Eye View.

Until after Labor Day. He just lays there. (LL) Rhode Island. William Meredith. NoP-4; NoP-5

Until deaf-dumb bullet self-improved comi-tragic time. After MLK: the marksman marked leftover kill. Lloyd Addison. EGAG

Until Eternity. (LL) Bustle in a House, The. Emily Dickinson. HeIP-4; NAAL-3; NAAL-5; NAAPv.1; NoP-4; NoP-5; SacPr; SAmP

Until, gasping with appreciative racism, both together sink into the unrevealed glory of sexism. (LL) Histoire. Harry Mathews. NIP-4; OxBoAm; PmAP

Until He Comes. Trasi Johnson. InTrad

Until he died we thought our neighbor dull. Future Debris. Heid E. Erdrich. AmPoNex

Until he named the horse. Naming the Animals. Lisel Mueller. IllVoic

Until he notices his mistake. (LL) Cartoon Physics, Part 1. Nick Flynn. BeAl; LegDan; NAPBL; P180; PoDa

Until his heart will break. (LL) Blue Water. Li Po. CrYelRi; ErotSp, *tr. by* Sam Hamill

Until I asked her to please stop doing it and was astonished to find that she not only could. My Mother's Lips. C. K. Williams. EmeKit

Until I could remember that I set her on fire. Lighter Fluid. Rodger Kamenetz. LiTh

Until *I* fall into coma. (LL) John Berryman. EMP; VCAP *Fr.* Dream Songs.

Until I Saw the Sea. Lilian Moore. NTCP

Until I'm covered and there's only one smell, / One word. (LL) Burning Shit at An Khe. Bruce Weigl. AF; AmWaPo

Until Manuel. Life of an Echo, The. Judith Ortiz Cofer. PueRic

Until mind and sweetgum are the same thing. Zen Sky. John Gilgun. AmZen

Until my friends abducted me. Sympathy and Envy. Katherine Lederer. LegDan

Until New Spring or Death. Árpád Tóth. IQMS, *tr. by* Madeline Mason

Until others mix our ashes. (LL) Pentecost: "Neither the sorrows of afternoon, waiting in the silent house." Dana Gioia. PoDa; Vesp

Until Peonies Bloom. Kim Yŏngnang. CAMKP, *tr. by* Anthony, Brother of Taizé

Until the blunting of time. (LL) Unprofessionals, The. U. A. Fanthorpe. PoCu; StAl

Until the day. I Get a Kick Out of You. Cole Porter. APT-1

   (My story is much too sad to be told.) ReLy

Until the destruction of language. (LL) Permanently. Kenneth Koch. NoP-4; NoP-5; OxBoAm; PmAP; PoA 2002

Until the duck's short legs. Kim Ku. CATKP, *tr. by* Peter H. Lee

Until the Real Thing Comes. Sammy Cahn and Mann Holiner. ReLy

Until the sound of the open ocean grows and the voice. (LL) What the End Is For. Jorie Graham. AtGh; NoP-4; PoPoPo

Until the sun sinks into a green. Anatoly Steiger. TCRusP, *tr. by* Paul Schmidt

Until the torches deaden at the bedroom door. (LL) Speaking of Poetry. John Peale Bishop. APT-1; InGu

Until the valve, tought as tripe, came right. (LL) Heart. David Scott. BeAl; PoCu

Until today. On the table. Experiments in the Impersonal. Steve Wilson. AmPoNex

Until words turn to moss. C. D. Wright. AmAlph

Until you can correct and heal yourself. Sadi. WoPoe, *tr. by* Dick Davis

Until you change your mind. Pantoumstone for a Dying Breed. Beth Lisick. AmPoNex

Until you have looked at something so long. Makings of Happiness, The. Ronald Wallace. PBCAP

Until your source dries up. Song of Grass. Na Hûidôk. EcSo, *tr. by* Peter H. Lee

Untitled: "First thought in my head waking up was, oh no." Robin Pickering. BeDoSh

Untitled: "Goddamn you, sliding around under." Mandy Kahn. FTtHH

Untitled: "I don't get." Christopher Nickelson. BtF

Untitled: "In the living room sit the men." Phillina Sun. FTtHH

Untitled: "I've traveled eight thousand miles." Baekoon Kyunghan. BecRai, *tr. by* Kim Daljin, Kim Won-Chung and Christopher Merrill

Untitled: "Number 1 bus jerks to a stop at Mass. Ave., The." Eli Goodwin. BtF

Untitled One. Kwan Booth. BtF

Untitled: "Remember our ecstatic parade." Robert N. Casper. IIR

Untitled: "Tomorrow night." Lauren Anita Arrington. BtF

Untitled: "Trumpet like a sharp plow, A." Bei Dao. WoBe, *tr. by* Iona Man-Cheong and Eliot Weinberger

Untitled: "Unmoving, it presents itself in a thousand shapes." Pou Kuksa. BecRai, *tr. by* Kim Daljin, Kim Won-Chung and Christopher Merrill

Untitled: "We are two straw dolls." Mohamed Metwalli. AnVo, *tr. by* Mohamed Enani

Untitled. Aleksandar Ristovic. BeAl, *tr. by* Charles Simic

Untitled. Cecilia Vicuña. WANABP, *tr. by* Eliot Weinberger

Untitled 2. Ch'oe Sûngja. EcSo, *tr. by* Mickey Hong

Untitled (April '91). Michael Palmer. BodElec

Untitled Blues; After a Photograph by Yevgeni Yevtushenko. Yusef Komunyakaa. ESEAA; GT; UnSA

Untitled Concrete Poem. Eugen Gomringer. GTCP, *tr. by* Reinhold Grimm

Untitled (February 2000). Michael Palmer. BAP-01

Unto all generations of the faithful heart. (LL) Lee in the Mountains. Donald Davidson. CBCWP; FuPo

Unto all life of mine may die! (LL) Richard Crashaw. OBEV; WoPoe *Fr.* Flaming Heart, The.

Unto all life of mine may die [*or dy*]. (LL) Flaming Heart, The. Richard Crashaw. NAEL-6v1; NAEL-7v1

Unto empty pockets. (LL) I Am Raftery [*or Raferty*]. Anthony Raftery. IrV; WoPoe, *tr. by* Douglas Hyde

Unto no body my woman saith she had rather a wife be [*or bee*]. Catullus. OBVE; WoPoe, *tr. by* Sir Philip Sidney

Unto the boundless Ocean of thy beauty [*or beautie*]. Samuel Daniel. NoP-4; NoP-5 *Fr.* Sonnets to Delia.

Unto the gates of hell. Song of Esechia, The. John Hall. ChIV-1

Unto the Person Kind there came. Mother Doorstep. Victor James Daley. NOBAu

Unto the queen of the gods, into whose hands are committed. Hymn to Ishtar. Ashur-Nasir-Pal, King of Assyria. HW

Unto the saints with sad complaints. Michael Wigglesworth. NAAL-3 *Fr.* Day of Doom, The [First Section].

Unto the thinking of the thought divine. (LL) George Santayana. APN-2; TCAPo *Fr.* Sonnets.

Unto this process briefly compiled. John Skelton. NoSic *Fr.* Magnificence.

Unto Us a Child is Born. William Dunbar. ChIV-2

Unto Us a Son Is Given. Alice Thompson Meynell. SacPr

Untold Want, The. Walt Whitman. MoAmPo

Untouched, the door swings open before us, and—*voilà!*—we're in the produce section. Man I Love and I Shop at Jewel, The. Jim Elledge. IllVoic; ReTh

Untoward. Ann Lauterbach. BodElec

Untransmittable and moving eastward. Taizan Maezumi. WhBo

Untrimming the Tree. John N. Morris. ChrPo

Unum est Necessarium. Agnes Mary Frances Robinson. VWP

Unusual Autumn, An. Dahlia Ravikovitch. DTA, *tr. by* Chana Bloch

Unusual saint of this age, The. Soap. Im Yŏngjo. CAMKP, *tr. by* Edward W. Poitras

Unusual View of the Town. J. P. Ward. AngWePo

Unusually the window panes are tinted gray. Repetition. Eman Mersaal. AnVo, *tr. by* Mohamed Enani

Unuttered Prayer. Josephine D. Henderson Heard. CBWP-4

Unwatched, the garden bough shall sway. Alfred Tennyson. OBGa *Fr.* In Memoriam A. H. H.

Unweary'd watch their list'ning Leaders keep, Th'. Homer. OBVE *Fr.* Iliad, The.

Unweathered stone beneath a rigid mane. Sonnet: To a Portrait of Hart Crane. Allen Tate. GS

Unwelcome. Mary Elizabeth Coleridge. OBEV; VWP

Unwelcome child. Child Compassion, The. Margot Ruddock. OBMV

Unwept, unhonour'd [*or unhonoured*], and unsung. (LL) Sir Walter Scott. ITBLP; NePenScot; OxBEV; SoSe-2; TFi *Fr.* Lay of the Last Minstrel, The.

Unwind my riddle. Stephen Crane. APN-2

Unwinged Ones, The. Ogden Nash. OtW

Unwittingly. John Burnside. StAl

Unworn. Dan Beachy-Quick. LegDan

Unworthy, since thou hast decreed. To the Queen of Inconstancy, Regina Collier, in Antwerp. Katherine Philips. PEW

Unwritten Law. Louise Glück. BodElec

Unwritten whorls on a spire lead a mollusk forward to build its celestial course, its factory, The. Sea. Valerie Wohlfeld. YaYoPo

Unyielding Youth, The. Marbod of Rennes. *tr. by* John Boswell
"Horace composed an ode about a certain boy." CAGL; EroLit, *tr. by* John Boswell
"This vision of a face, radiant and full of beauty." CAGL; EroLit, *tr. by* John Boswell

Up. Margaret Atwood. NoP-4; NoP-5

Up. Bill Kushner. ReTh

Up. Nigel Wells. AngWePo

Up after Illness, I Watch the Idle Clouds. Ch'i-chi. CSKM, *tr. by* Burton Watson

Up ahead, First Class. United Flight 608. Leonard Nathan. OtW

Up ahead, I know, he felt it stirring in himself already, the glance. Orpheus and Eurydice. Jorie Graham. OxBoAm; VCAP

Up All Night. Theo Dorgan. IrLP

Up and Doing. Douglas Malloch. ITBLP

Up and down. Hummingbird at Dawn. Catharino James Elijio. OWABP

Up and down I go, my stock. Lawrence Sail. NewEx

Up and down the lawn he walks with cycling hands. Gardener, The. Craig Raine. UV

Up and down the one way streets. Zebra. Natasha Trethewey. TWW

Up and down the wide wooden stairways. My Sixth Grade Sex Life: Milne Elementary, New Orleans. Brad Richard. BeDoSh

Up and down this red clay route. Late Summer News. Dorothy Barresi. SwNoth

Up and swallowed Bryan's Bryaness. (LL) Lion, The. Ogden Nash. TLR; WHSW

Up, black, striped and damasked like the chasuble. Skunk, The. Seamus Heaney. NAEL-6v2; NAEL-7v2; NoP-4; NoP-5; StAl; WaAnP

Up close, at the place. J. W. Hackett. NIL-7

Up country, her husband is working late. One Life. Andrew Motion. HarvBoo

Up Early. Kit Robinson.
"Intent to consider." FTOS

Up East, they do not think much. Texas Poetry. Violette Newton. TiP2

Up / from Msippi I grew. Son of Msippi. Henry Dumas. OxAAAP

Up from the bronze, I saw. Roman Fountain. Louise Bogan. APT-2; NoP-4; NoP-5

Up from the Grave He Arose. Robert Lowry. SacPr

Up from the meadows rich with corn. Barbara Frietchie. John Greenleaf Whittier. AmWaPo; APN-1; CBCWP; ColAP; HHAm; ITBLP; NCAP; OxBoAm; PCW; TFi

Up from the South, at break of day. Sheridan's Ride. Thomas Buchanan Read. APN-2; CBCWP; PCW

Up from the trawlers in the fishdock they walk to my house. Morning Call. Richard Murphy. ModIr

Up from the valley. August Town. Bob Stewart. WaCA

Up from the valley, ten children working the fields. Woman Who Weeps. Ellen Bryant Voigt. CAP-8; OPRER

Up from the Wreck Conjuring Montana Sonnet. Steven Davenport. RWB

Up half-known roads. (LL) Send-Off, The. Wilfred Owen. HarvBoo; MoBrPo; NPeEn; OBWP; OBWVE; OxBEV; PoWW; TCAWP

Up he stands. Rooster, The. Abu'l Qasim As'ad ibn Billita. WoPoe, *tr. by* Leticia Garza-Falcón and Christopher Middleton

Up here in the land of the hot dog stand. South America, Take It Away! Harold Rome. ReLy

Up here, there's no hurry. Alicia Gaspar de Alba. FTtHH *Fr.* Elemental Journey: Anniversary Gift.

Up here, where no Indian was ever meant to be. Airplane. Sherman Alexie. OtW

Up in Jackson County they have. Jutaculla Rock. Robert Morgan. LPSFW

Up in Mabel's Room. Kenneth Slessor. BMAP

Up in some cleft in the hills. Nameless Woman. No Ch'ŏnmyŏng. CAMKP, *tr. by* David R. McCann

Up in the Air. Allan Ramsay. OxBEV

Up in the Air. Greg Williamson. AmPoNex

Up in the air and down! (LL) Swing, The. Robert Louis Stevenson. BLPJKO; ChAP; NOxBChV; NTCP; TLR

Up in the attic. As I Play the Flute. Cho Chihun. CAMKP, *tr. by* Kyung-Ja Chun

Up in the heavenly saloon. Arizona Nature Myth. James Michie. FaBoA

Up in the mornin', out on the job. That Lucky Old Sun. Haven Gillespie. ReLy

Up in the Morning Early. Robert Burns. OPOU

Up into the Clouds Music. Li Po. ColAnChi, *tr. by* Elling O. Eide

Up late, reading alone. Night Seasons. Stephen Kuusisto. TAPaP

Up Madison, down Park. I Walk a Little Faster. Carolyn Leigh. ReLy

Up my backside a core of charcoal does its slither. I have completed my feast and. In Front of a Large Number of People. John Godfrey. FTOS

Up on Partickhill. Birds of Passage. Valerie Thornton. EdScPo

Up on the mountains where I live. Pwllderi. Dewi Emrys James. BBMWP, *tr. by* Elin ap Hywel

Up on the mountaintop the chambermaid puts. Loss. Judith Herzberg. TuT, *tr. by* Joan McBreen

Up on the Roof. Maura Dooley. NeBl

Up on the Spoon. Stanley Crouch. SeSe

Up on their brooms the Witches stream.   Ride-by-Nights, The.   Walter De la Mare.   ChAP

(Up on Top of a Rainbow) Sweepin' the Clouds Away.   Sam Coslow.   ReLy

Up! quit thy bower.   Joanna Baillie.   NAEL-6v2; NAEL-7v2; NoP-4

Up Rising.   Robert Duncan.   APSN; NAMCP V.2 *Fr.* Passages.

Up rushed a band, with compasses and scales.   Philip Freneau.   NAAL-3 *Fr.* House of Night, The.

Up stand / six.   Menage, The.   Carl Rakosi.   FTOS

Up tails all! (LL)   Kenneth Grahame.   NOxBChV; NTCP; WHSW *Fr.* Wind in the Willows, The.

Up Tchoupitoulas Nom de Guerre.   Jessica Freeman.   AnSo

Up the airy mountain.   Fairies, The.   William Allingham.   NOxBChV; OBEV; TFi

Up the crag.   Weapons.   Anna Wickham.   MoBrPo

Up the hillside beyond the road's.   Glimpses.   Christopher Gilbert.   GT

Up the moss-grown.   Horse, The.   Georgi Borisov.   CSCBP, *tr. by* Georgi Belev and Lisa Sapinkopf

Up the Noran Water.   Shy Geordie.   Helen B. Cruickshank.   EdScPo

Up the ravine the sun was choking with dust.   Emotion on the windows from the. Saturated.   Aaron Shurin.   FTOS

Up the reputable walks of old established trees.   Campus on the Hill, The.   W. D. Snodgrass.   NoAM

Up the river there's a college.   Tulip Time in Sing Sing.   P. G. Wodehouse.   ReLy

Up the road.   Apple Core.   Clarence Major.   GT

Up There.   Ruth Stone.   ExTi

Up there on the mountain road, the fireworks.   Blue Ridge.   Ellen Bryant Voigt.   LPSFW; NoAM

Up there—or down here.   Lorca Variations (XXVIII), The.   Jerome Rothenberg.   PFTM-2

Up they go, yawning.   1915.   Roger McDonald.   NOBAu

Up this green woodland ride let's softly rove.   Nightingale's Nest, The.   John Clare.   NAEL-7v2; NPeEn

Up those Museum steps you came.   To Lallie.   Amy Levy.   PoBW; ViWPN

Up through the buttercup meadow the children lead.   Cormorant, The. Rosanna Warren.   PfSP

Up Thru the Years.   Anne Waldman.   AHA

Up to my hotel window.   Window.   Meirion MacIntyre Huws.   BBMWP, *tr. by* Geriant Løvgreen

Up to Speed.   Rae Armantrout.   AWPTFC

Up to summer grass.   Yamaguchi Seishi.   CAoMJL1, *tr. by* Alfred H. Marks and Takashi Kodaira

Up to the bed by the window, where I be lyin'.   Old Shepherd's Prayer. Charlotte Mew.   MoBrPo

Up to the top of the haunted turf.   Louis Untermeyer.   MoAmPo *Fr.* Mother Goose Up-to-Date.

Up to those heights where angels rest.   Perfect Orchestra, The.   Henrietta Cordelia Ray.   CBWP-3

Up, Up, Home & Away.   John Forbes.   NOBAu

Up! up! my friend, and quit your books.   Tables Turned, The.   William Wordsworth.   NAEL-6v2; NAEL-7v2; NOBRP; NoP-5

Up with the lark in the first flush of morning.   Morning Ride.   *Unknown.* ArBi

Up Yonder in the Meadow of Children.   Brita Bergland.   OnScMo

Upanishads, The.   *Unknown. tr. by* Stephen Mitchell and Patrick Olivelle Mantreya Upanishad, The.

   "I am I, but also the other."   WoPoe, *tr. by* Patrick Olivelle

Up-Beat.   Langston Hughes.   APT-2

Upcheringe of the Messe, The.   Luke Sheperd.
   "Who hath not knowne or herd."   PBRV

Update on the Last Judgment.   Ellen Hinsey.   PoA 2002

Update, The.   Adam Yauch.   WhBo

Up-flaring through your nerves, you know the flash.   Lőrinc Szabó.   IQMS *Fr.* Cricket Music.

Upgrade, past snow-tangled bramble, past.   Sila.   Robert Penn Warren. NoP-4

Upheaval's stone garden.   Indian Peaks, Colorado.   Reg Saner.   PoCoUp

Uphill [*or* Up-Hill].   Christina Georgina Rossetti.   BrAP; CABP; CtM; NAEL-6v2; NAEL-7v2; NALW; NoP-4; NoP-5; OBEV; PEW; PoPoPo; SacPr; TFi; WaAnP; WeW-3

Uphold Me.   Karen Gershon.   LW

Upkeep.   Miriam Goodman.   UnSA

Upland Shepherd, as reclined he lies, The.   Sea View, The.   Charlotte Smith. CenSon; NAEL-7v2

Uplift a thousand voices full and sweet.   Ode Sung at the Opening of the International Exhibition.   Alfred Tennyson.   STuOW

Upon a Black Twist Rounding the Arm of the Countess of Carlile.   Robert Herrick.   CavPo

Upon a Booke Written at the Beginning of the Parliament 1640.   Anna Norman Ley.   EMWP

Upon a Bookseller.   John Oldham.   BASC

Upon a broken world. (LL)   September, 1918.   Amy Lowell.   NAAL-5; NAAPv.2

Upon a Child.   Robert Herrick.   OBEV

Upon a Child That Died [*or* Dyed].   Robert Herrick.   NoP-4; NoP-5; WaAnP (Epitaph Upon a Child that Died.)   OBEV

Upon a Cloak [*or* Cloke] Lent Him by Mr. J. Ridsley.   Henry Vaughan.   BASC
   "Here, take again thy sackcloth! and thank heaven."   AngWePo

Upon a Command to Write on My Father.   Gertrude Aston Thimelby.   EMWP

Upon a dark, light, gloomy, sunshine day.   Messe of Nonsense, A.   *Unknown.* NOSC

Upon a Dead Man's Head.   John Skelton.   WoPoe
   (Upon a Dead Man's Head, that was Sent to Him from an Honorable Gentlewoman for a Token.)   CABP

Upon a Dead Man's Head, that was Sent to Him from an Honorable Gentlewoman for a Token.   John Skelton.   *See* Upon a Dead Man's Head.

Upon a Drawing.   István Vas.   IQMS, *tr. by* Daniel Gerard Hoffman

Upon a Friend's Pet Cat, Being Sick.   John Winstanley.   TriCat

Upon a Funeral.   Sir John Beaumont.   NOSC

Upon a hill, after the sun has set. (LL)   Only until this cigarette is ended. Edna St. Vincent Millay.   HeIP-4; NAAPv.2

Upon a hill he turned.   Soldier's Tear, The.   Thomas Haynes Bayly.   STuOW

Upon a Joynted Ring.   Francellina Stapleton.   EMWP

Upon a little dappled nag, whose mane.   William Tennant.   NOBRP *Fr.* Anster Fair.

Upon a lonely desert beach.   Haunted Beach, The.   Mary Robinson. NPBRoP; RWP

Upon a Maid That Died [*or* Dyed] the Day She Was Married [*or* Married]. Meleager.   OBVE, *tr. by* Robert Herrick

Upon a mouth-organ. (LL)   Der Blinde Junge.   Mina Loy.   APT-1; HarvBoo; NAMCP V.1

Upon a Quarter Million.   Lorna Goodison.   WaCA

Upon a quarter million.   Upon a Quarter Million.   Lorna Goodison.   WaCA

Upon a Rare Voice.   Owen Felltham [*or* Feltham].   NOSC

Upon a Ribbon [*or* Ribband].   Thomas Carew.   NOSC

Upon a road / which forks.   Indecision.   Víctor Terán.   RMCMP, *tr. by* Donald Frischmann

Upon a Sacrament. (LL)   Light exists in Spring, A.   Emily Dickinson.   APN-2; ITBLP; NCAP

Upon a simmer Sunday morn.   Holy Fair, The.   Robert Burns.   OBSV

Upon a Spider Catching a Fly.   Edward Taylor.   ColAP; NAAPv.1; NoP-4; NoP-5; OxBEV; OxBoAm; TCAPo; WaAnP

Upon a time, before the faery broods.   Lamia.   John Keats.   NAEL-6v2; NAEL-7v2; NoP-5

Upon a time, before the faery broods.   John Keats.   NOBRP *Fr.* Lamia.

Upon a Wasp Chilled [*or* Child] with Cold.   Edward Taylor.   NAAL-3; NAAL-5; NAAPv.1; OxBEV

Upon an obscure night.   Obscure Night of the Soul, The.   San Juan de la Cruz. OBMV, *tr. by* Arthur Symons

Upon an Unhandsome Gentlewoman, who made Love unto him.   Richard Corbet.   BASC

Upon Appleton House [To My Lord Fairfax].   Andrew Marvell.   BASC; NAEL-7v1
   "And now to the ab[b]lyss I pass."   PBRV
   "At the demolishing, this seat."   NOSC
   "From that blest bed the hero came."   OBGa
   Garden, A.   OBEV

Upon Arch-bishop Laud, Prisoner in the Tower. 1641.   *Unknown.*   PBRV

Upon Ben Jo[h]nson.   Robert Herrick.   NoP-4; NoP-5

Upon Ben Johnson [*or* Jonson].   Edmund Waller.   NOSC

Upon Bishop Andrewes's [*or* Andrewes His] Picture before His Sermons. Richard Crashaw.   NOSC

Upon Castara's *Departure*.   William Habington.   NOSC *Fr.* Castara.

Upon Christ's Nativity or Christmas.   Rowland Watkyns.   OBWVE

Upon Closing the Book.   Armanda Guiducci.   CItWP, *tr. by* Cinzia Sartini Blum and Lara Trubowitz

(Upon Defacing of Whitehall.   Martin Parker.   NOSC; PBRV)

Upon Dr. Davies's British Grammar.   James Howell.   AngWePo; OBWVE

Upon Entering the Priesthood: A Warning.   Jinkag Haesim.   BecRai, *tr. by* Kim Daljin, Kim Won-Chung and Christopher Merrill

Upon Fairford Windows.   Richard Corbet.   NOSC

Upon Finding a Black Woman's Door Sprayed with Swastikas, I Tell Her This Story of Hands.   Kevin Stein.   SwNoth

Upon Finding Dying: An Introduction, by L. E. Sissman, Remaindered at ıs. Louis Edward Sissman. NoP-4

Upon Good-Friday, I will fast while I may. Charm. *Unknown.* EMWP

Upon Himselfe Being Buried. Robert Herrick. PBRV

Upon his frustrate and unhopeful quest. Fragment from "The Maladjusted: A Tragedy." Morris Gilbert Bishop. NBLV

Upon His Majesty's [*or* Majesties] Repairing of Paul's. Edmund Waller. BASC; PBRV

Upon His Picture. Thomas Randolph. BASC

Upon his red silk rugs. (LL) Dog Parted from Her Master. Hsüeh T'ao [*or* Xue Tao]. CCL1; WoPo, *tr. by* Jeanne Larsen

Upon His Spaniel[l] Tracie [*or* Tracy]. Robert Herrick. DiBP

Upon His Unconstant Mistress. Sir Robert Aytoun. NOSC

Upon His Verses. Robert Herrick. NAEL-6v1; NAEL-7v1

Upon Israel and upon the rabbis. Kaddish. Charles Reznikoff. TaR

Upon It They Gently Reflect. Coral Bracho. RMCMP, *tr. by* Suzanne Jill Levine

Upon Jack and Jill: Epigram. Robert Herrick. NAEL-6v1; NAEL-7v1

Upon Julia's Arctics. Bert Leston Taylor. NBLV

Upon Julia's Breasts. Robert Herrick. NoP-4; NoP-5; WaAnP

Upon Julia's Clothes. Robert Herrick. BASC; BrAP; CABP; CavPo; ClHu; HeIP-4; NAEL-6v1; NAEL-7v1; NBLV; NIL-7; NIP-4; NoP-4; NoP-5; NOSC; OBEV; OxAEP-1; OxBEV; PoPoPo; TFi; TRP; UV; WaAnP; WeW-3; WoPoe

Upon Julia's Clothes. Edmund George Valpy Knox. UV

Upon Julia's Haire Fill'd with Dew. Robert Herrick. PBRV

Upon Julia's Petticoat. Robert Herrick. CavPo

Upon Julia's Voice. Robert Herrick. NPeEn; SoSe-8

Upon Kind[e] and True Love. Aurelian Townshend. NOSC; WaAnP

Upon Kissing You after You Vomited. Haiku. James Shea. IIR

Upon learning that the mother wrote verses. Soirée. Ezra Pound. OBCoV

Upon [His] Leaving His Mistress. John Wilmot, 2d Earl of Rochester. BASC; NBLV; NOSC

Upon Leaving the Parole Board Hearing. Conyus. GT

Upon Listening to the Flute. Pak P'aengnyŏn, Sin Sukchu, Sŏng [*or* Sung] Sammun, Yi Kae and Yi Sŏkhyŏng. CATKP, *tr. by* Peter H. Lee

Upon Love. Sir Robert Aytoun. NOSC

Upon mica screens, candles flicker deep shadows. Ch'ang-O. Li Shang-yin. ChinPo, *tr. by* Ye Weilian [*or* Yeh Wei-lien *or* Wai-lim Yip]

Upon Mr. Hopton's Death. Henry Halswell. NOSC

Upon Mr Thomas Murrays Fall. Sir Robert Aytoun. NePenScot

Upon my chest the Cross of the Knights' Order. Letter about Horror, A. Milán Füst. IQMS, *tr. by* Jess Perlman

Upon My Lady Carlile's Walking in Hampton Court Garden. Sir John Suckling. *See* Upon My Lady Carlisle's Walking in Hampton Court Garden.

Upon My Lady Carlisle's Walking in Hampton Court Garden. Sir John Suckling. NoP-5

   (Upon My Lady Carlile's Walking in Hampton Court Garden.) CavPo

Upon my lap my sovereign sits. Lullaby. Richard Verstegan. OBEV

Upon My Lord Winchilsea's Converting the Mount in His Garden to a Terrace. Anne Finch, Countess of Winchilsea. OBGa

Upon my return to America, Josephine. Return. Carolyn Forché. BodElec

Upon Nothing. John Wilmot, 2d Earl of Rochester. NOSC; OBSV; OxAEP-1; OxBEV

Upon one day as I did mourn full sore. Elizabeth Melville, Lady Culross. ChIV-1 *Fr.* Ane Godly Dream.

Upon one side there are two spots of red. (LL) Sleeper in the Valley, The. Arthur Rimbaud. OBWP; WoPoe, *tr. by* William Jay Smith

Upon our anguish for each other's sake! (LL) Oh, my belovèd, have you thought of this. Edna St. Vincent Millay. HeIP-4; LW

Upon Our Saviour's Tomb[e] Wherein Never Man Was Laid. Richard Crashaw. *See* To Our Blessed Lord upon the Choice of His Sepulchre.

Upon Overhearing Tagalog. Fatima Lim-Wilson. AmPoNex

Upon Platonic Love: To Mistress Cicely Crofts, Maid of Honour. Sir Robert Aytoun. NOSC

Upon Prudence Baldwin Her Sickness[e]. Robert Herrick. BASC

Upon Prue [*or* Prew], His Maid. Robert Herrick. NAEL-6v1; NAEL-7v1; NoP-4; NoP-5; NPeEn

   (Upon Prue, His Maid.) NoP-4

Upon Reading Chuang Tzu. Chunggwan, Great Master. CATKP, *tr. by* Peter H. Lee

Upon Reading Tagore's "The Gardener." Han Yong'un [*or* Yongwun]. CAMKP, *tr. by* Sammy Solberg

Upon Reading Tu Fu's Poetry. Kwŏn P'il. CATKP, *tr. by* Richard John Lynn

Upon Receipt of a Pound of Coffee in 1863. Mary E. Tucker. CBWP-1

Upon receiving an old scholar. *Various authors.* CATKP *Fr.* Songs of Flying Dragons.

Upon Seeing an Ultrasound Photo of an Unborn Child. Thomas Lux. NevBe; SUP; WaAnP

Upon som honest[e] thing [*or* thyng] whil[e] that I drinke [*or* drynke]. (LL) Geoffrey Chaucer. NAEL-6v1; NAEL-7v1; WaAnP *Fr.* Canterbury Tales, The.

Upon Stephen Stoned. Sir John Suckling. ChIV-2

Upon that night, when fairies light. Halloween. Robert Burns. NOBRP; TreFP

Upon the arid shoulder. Giacomo Leopardi. WoPoe *Fr.* Broom, The; or, The Flower of the Desert.

Upon the Asse That Bore Our Saviour. Richard Crashaw. ChIV-2

Upon the beach are thousands of crabs; they are. Crustaceans. Roy Fuller. NoAM

Upon the Birth of a Young and Highly Desired Son. Christian Weise. GePo, *tr. by* George C. Schoolfield

Upon the Body of Our Blessed Lord, Naked and Bloody. Richard Crashaw. NOSC

   (On Our Crucified Lord, Naked and Bloody.) NAEL-6v1

Upon the Book and Picture of the Seraphical Saint Teresa. Richard Crashaw. OBEV; WoPoe *Fr.* Flaming Heart, The.

Upon the Burning of Our House July 10th, 1666. Anne Bradstreet. *See* [Here Follows Some] Verses upon the Burning of Our House [July 10th, 1666. Copied Out of a Loose Paper].

Upon the Circumcision. John Milton. ChIV-2

Upon the Crucifix. William Alabaster. NoSic

Upon the Day of Our Saviour's Nativity. Francis Quarles. NOSC

Upon the Death of My Deare and Lovely Daughter J. P. Jane Pulter, Baptized May 1 1625 and Died Oct 8 1646 Aet. 20. Hester Lee Pulter. EMWP

Upon the Death of My Ever Desired Friend Doctor [*or* Dr] Donne Dean of Paul's. Henry King, Bishop of Chichester. BASC

Upon the Death of Sir Albert Morton's Wife. Sir Henry Wotton. BASC; NPeEn; OBEV; OxBEV; PBRV; WeW-3

Upon the Double Murther of King Charles I. Katherine Philips. BASC; NAEL-7v1

Upon the Duke of Buckingham. *Unknown.* BASC

Upon the ecstatic diving board the diver. Lone Bather. Abraham Moses Klein. HeIP-4

Upon the Ensigns of Christ's Crucifying. William Alabaster. NoSic

Upon the eyes, the lips, the feet. Extreme Unction. Ernest Dowson. MoBrPo; OBMV

Upon the grass no longer hangs the dew. Hay making. Joanna Baillie. OxAEP-2

Upon the Grave of a Beggar. Timothy Kendall. NoSic

Upon the Graving of Her Name upon a Tree in Barnelmes Walks. Katherine Philips. PBRV

Upon the Heavenly Scarp. Abraham Moses Klein. PoA 2002 *Fr.* Psalter of Avram Haktani, The.

Upon the Hill and Grove at Bilbrough. Andrew Marvell. BASC

Upon the Horrid Plot Discovered by Harlequin the Bishop of Rochester's French Dog. Jonathan Swift. DiBP

Upon the Image of Death. Robert Southwell. NOSC

   "Before my face the picture hangs." NoSic

Upon the Imprisonment of His Sacred Majesties that Unparaleld Prince King Charles the First. Hester Lee Pulter. EMWP

Upon the Infant Martyrs. Richard Crashaw. NoP-4; NoP-5; NPeEn

Upon the jade steps white dews grow. Yu Chieh Yuan (Jade Steps Grievance, Yueh-fu). Li Po. ChinPo, *tr. by* Ye Weilian [*or* Yeh Wei-lien *or* Wai-lim Yip]

Upon the King's Return from Flanders, 1695. Henry Hall. NOSC

Upon the LD Saying KT Could Be Sad in Her Company. Katherine Thimelby Aston. EMWP

Upon the Lines and Life of the Famous Scenic Poet, Master William Shakespeare. Hugh Holland. AngWePo; OBWVE

Upon the Loss[e] of His Little Finger. Thomas Randolph. NOSC

Upon the Loss[e] of His Mistresses. Robert Herrick. BASC; CavPo; NAEL-6v1; NAEL-7v1; NOSC

Upon [*or* up on] the mountain my Lord spoke. Every [*or* Ev'ry] Time I Feel the [*or* de] Spirit. *Unknown.* APN-2

Upon the mournful death of our late Soveraign Lord Charles the first, King of England, etc. Rowland Watkyns. BASC

Upon the Much Lamented Death of the Right Honourable, the Lady Elizabeth Langham. Bathsua Pell Makin. EMWP

Upon the Necessity and Benefite of Learning Written in the Beginning of a Common Place Booke Belonging to W. B. a Young Scholler. Anna Norman Ley. EMWP

Upon the New Building at Appleton. Thomas Fairfax, Baron Fairfax of Cameron. NOSC

Upon the Nipples of Julia's Breast. Robert Herrick. ErotSp; NAEL-6v1; NAEL-7v1; NOSC

Upon the patch of earth that clings. Public Aid for Niagara Falls. Morris Gilbert Bishop. NBLV

Upon the Plymouth shore the wild rose blooms. Wild Rose of Plymouth, The. Jones Very. APN-1

Upon the Poet of His Time, Ben Jonson: His Honoured Friend and Father. James Howell. NOSC

Upon the Poet's Photograph. Philip Whalen. WANABP *Fr.* Epigrams & Imitations.

Upon the Saying That My Verses Were Made by Another. Anne Killigrew. BASC; CABP; EMWP; NALW; PEW

Upon the shepherd-boy the summer sun. Sándor Petőfi. IQMS *Fr.* Sir John, The Hero.

Upon the slippery tops of human[e] state. Seneca. BASC; OBVE *Fr.* Thyestes.

Upon the Sudden Restraint of the Earl[e] of Somerset, Then Falling from Favor [*or* Favour]. Sir Henry Wotton. NOSC; NPeEn; OxBEV

(Earle of Somerset.) PBRV

Upon the threshold of the mind? (LL) Alfred Tennyson. NAEL-6v2; NAEL-7v2; NAWM-7v2 *Fr.* In Memoriam A. H. H.

Upon the Troublesome Times. Robert Herrick. CavPo

Upon the twist and the shrug of the road. (LL) Slow Animals Crossing. W. N. Herbert. NeBrP; StAl

Upon the walls of Munkács. Exile of Rákóczi, The. *Unknown.* IQMS, *tr. by* Watson Kirkconnell

Upon the work of Walter Landor. Dorothy Parker. NALW *Fr.* Pig's-Eye View of Literature, A.

Upon their quivering wings. (LL) Fairyland [*or* Fairy-Land]. Edgar Allan Poe. APN-1; NAAL-3; OxBoAm

Upon this firthe, as on the sees of love. William Fowler. NePenScot *Fr.* Tarantula of Love, The.

Upon this ground how well grows barrenness. (LL) Of the Reed That the Jews Set in Our Saviour's Hand. William Alabaster. NoSic; NPeEn

Upon this marble bust that is not I. To Inez Milholland. Edna St. Vincent Millay. NAAPv.2; NALW

Upon Tyburn tree! (LL) John Gay. NAEL-6v1; NoP-5 *Fr.* Beggar's Opera, The.

Upon Wedlock and Death of Children. Edward Taylor. ColAP; NAAL-3; NAAL-5; NAAPv.1; NoP-4; NoP-5; SacPr; TCAPo

Upon what terms, with how much left unsaid. (LL) Middle-Aged, The. Adrienne Rich. OxBoAm; PoPoPo

Upon year end, reflect over the home. Estrella's Prophecies #18. David Baratier. RWB

Upon Your Leaving. Etheridge Knight. GT

Upone Tabacco. Sir Robert Aytoun. WaAnP

Upper arm rested on the stove, sweating, An. Mad Man. Steve Wilson. LiTh

Upper Broadway. Adrienne Rich. ItWoWo

Upper Chamber, An. Frances Bannerman. OBEV

Upper chamber in a darkened house, An. Frederick Goddard Tuckerman. APN-2; GSo; NoP-4; OxBoAm; OxBSo *Fr.* Sonnets: First Series, 1854–1860.

Upper Family. Maxwell Bodenheim. AmWit

Upper Marlboro. Kenneth Carroll. SpirFl

Upper Peninsula Landscape with Aunts. Pamela Gemin. SweBea

Upper slopes are busy with the cricket. Thom Gunn. NoAM *Fr.* Misanthropos.

Upper slopes are busy with the cricket, The. Elegy on the Dust. Thom Gunn. NoAM

Upraised arm, fist clenched, ready to hit, The. Crime Against Nature. Minnie Bruce Pratt. WiU

Uprearing from the thrashed. Where the Deer Go. Dabney Stuart. PoCoUp

Uprising of the 20,000, The. *Unknown.* NAAPv.2

Uproar, An / a spruce-green sky, bound in iron. Butterfly, The. Margaret Avison. BrAP

Uprooted tree leaves / behind it a hole in the ground, An. Jeremy Cronin. AF

Uprose the King of Men with speed. Descent of Odin, The. Thomas Gray. OxAEP-1

Upside Down Basket, The. Alan Chong Lau. UnSA

Upside Down Picture, An. Mahdi Muhammad Ali. IrPoTo, *tr. by* Salaam Yousif

Upstairs Jenny crashed her car & became a living corpse, Jake sold grass. Charnel Ground, The. Allen Ginsberg. BB; BodElec

Upstairs on the third floor. Bottled [New York]. Helene Johnson. APT-2

Upstate. Simon J. Ortiz. LTA

Upstate. Derek Walcott. GT; OPRER

Upstood upstaffed passing sinuously away over an airy arch. Christophe Russell Atkins. EGAG

Upstream. Carl Sandburg. MoAmPo

Upturn. Anne-Marie Fyfe. Prnts

Upturning with a band. William Wordsworth. NPBRoP *Fr.* Prelude, The; Growth of a Poet's Mind [1805 version].

Upupup! The light percussive. Airborne. Elizabeth Garrett. MFPA

Upward in motion with wet wind. (LL) Wales Visitation. Allen Ginsberg. APSN; BB; ColAP; VCAP

Upward Look, An. James Merrill. CAP-8; NAMCP V.2; PoPoPo

Ur / mit / mals. Volcanic tuff. Tina Darragh. FTOS

Ur Sonata. Kurt Schwitters.

"Third movement." PFTM-1

Urals post-master, this is your. Ode. Barry MacSweeney. Oth

Urania. Burleigh Muttén. HW

Urania, or Spiritual Poems. William Drummond of Hawthornden.

"Astrea in this time." NOSC

"Triumphing chariots, statues, crownes of bayes." NOSC

Uranium. Robert Morgan. AtGh

Uranium Ore. Thomas Meyer. AnSo

Uranne. Mary Weston Fordham. CBWP-2

Urban. Oliver Davies. AngWePo

Urban Convalescence, An. James Merrill. ColAP; NAAL-5

Urban Gallery. Rachel Wetzsteon. AmPoNex; NeAmPo

Urban Indians, Pioneer Square, Seattle. Gail Tremblay. FiBr

Urban Legend. Lucia Maria Perillo. RoV

Urban Love Poem. Marilyn Chin. FaoP

Urban Love Songs. Wing Tek Lum. OpBo

Urban Pastoral. Babette Deutsch. MakPoe

Urban Poem. Douglas Goetsch. AmPoNex; UrbNat

Urban Renewal. Major L. Jackson.

16. BAP-04

Urban Renewal. Yusef Komunyakaa. RoV

Urban Renewal 12. Major L. Jackson. IIR

Urban Tree. Alexander Gerov. CSCBP, *tr. by* Georgi Belev and Lisa Sapinkopf

Urbane man, composed, aware, An. Like Father. Herbert Williams. AngWePo

Urceus Exit. Austin Dobson. OBEV *Fr.* Rose-Leaves.

Urchin saw a rose—a dear. Rosebud in the Heather. Johann Wolfgang von Goethe. STV, *tr. by* John Frederick Nims

Urdeath. August Stramm. PFTM-1

Urge me no more! nor think, because I seem. Matilda Barbara Betham-Edwards. CenSon

Urge me no more to sing. I am not able. Satire on the Rebellion, A. Alexander Brome. BASC

Urge to wander is, The. Leaving. Rae Armantrout. FTOS

Urgent Call, An. Dunya Mikhail. WoBe, *tr. by* Liz Winslow

Urgent Letter, An. Hugh Maxton. PBCIP

Urgent letter that I try to write, The. Night Letter. Stanley Kunitz. AF

Urgent sounds the all. Rio. Joel Dailey. AnSo

Urging Her of a Promise. Ben Jonson. NAEL-7v1 *Fr.* Celebration of Charis in Ten Lyric[k] Pieces [*or* Peeces], A.

Uriel. Ralph Waldo Emerson. APN-1; NAAL-3

Uriel. William Force Stead.

How Infinite Are Thy Ways. OBMV

Urination is the major accomplishment of engineering. Ode to the Urge. Ricardo Castillo. PML, *tr. by* Robert Jones

Urine-stained quilt, A. Buson. EH, *tr. by* Takashi Hass

Urn. Takahashi Shinkichi. ZenPo, *tr. by* Takashi Ikemoto and Lucien Stryk

Urn was heavy, small but so heavy, The. His Ashes. Sharon Olds. InoFa

Urna de otras reliquias. Perfumista, La. Jorge Fernández Granados. RMCMP

Ursa Major ("Bear mother / gives suck to the stars.") Federico García Lorca. PFTM-1 *Fr.* Night (Suite for Piano and Poet's Voice).

Us. Anne Sexton. MPUn

Us all on sore cement was we. Pigs. Les A. Murray. StAl

Us, and nowhere but you to be. (LL) America. Robert Creeley. MakPoe; UnSA; WaAnP

Us-folks is purty pore—but Ma. Dubious "Old Kriss," A. James Whitcomb Riley.

Us po' Black boys. Window Shopping. Lamont B. Steptoe. SpirFl

Us Poets. Franklin Pierce Adams. AmWit

Us Two. Nina Cassian. PoSu, *tr. by* Nina Cassian

Use of Poetry, The. Michael Ryan. BodElec

Use to be eye would be laying there. Change. Quincy Troupe. PML

Use your mental eye. Nīlkantha Mukhopādhyāy. SinGod, *tr. by* Rachel Fell McDermott

Used Book Store. Charles Simic. CAP-8

Used to be, fellows would ask if you were married. Sweaters, The. Lucia Maria Perillo. UnSA

Used to be you could / touch your eyes. Gigabyte Me—How Much RAM in Your Summer of Love? Edwin Torres. HeMarv

Used to hang and brush their bosoms? I feel chilly and grown old. (LL) Toccata of Galuppi's, A. Robert Browning. FaBoVe; NAEL-6v2; NAEL-7v2; NoP-5; UV

Used together: seasons, books, a piece of music. Kind of Loss, A. Ingeborg Bachmann. PoetW, tr. by Mark Anderson

(Used together: seasons, books, a piece of music. Ingeborg Bachmann. AF; VCWP)

Useful. Elin ap Hywel. ATSWP, tr. by Robert Minhinnick

Useful, The. Jean Follain. TAPaP, tr. by W. S. Merwin

Useless to relate how I've strained my eyes. Cast Away. Christopher Pilling. NLP

Useless Valentines / Are better. Valentine, A. Jack Spicer. APSN

Uses of Poetry. Winfield Townley Scott. PoA 2002

Uses of the Dog, The. Virgil. DiBP Fr. Georgics.

Using salal leaves for money. Rolls-Royce Dreams. Ginger Andrews. GoPo

Using [the] gun mounts. Toys in a Field. Yusef Komunyakaa. FaoP

Using words this way. Millennial Polka. Alicia Ostriker. ExTi

Usk, The. Charles Hubert Sisson. HarvBoo

Usonian Journals 2000. Adrienne Rich. PrTe

Usquebaugh. Wendy Cope. UV

Usual Immigrant Uncle Poem, The. Askold Melnyczuk. OPRER

Usual is there, The. Landscape with Saxophonist. Thylias Moss. ESEAA

Usual Suspects, The. Reginald Harris. BRtP

Usually at the helipad. Prisoners. Yusef Komunyakaa. AmAlph

Usually it is night. After Edward Hopper. Lawrence Raab. PoSol

Usually late, the distinguished season. Sapphics. Daryl Hine. PoA 2002

Usurers, The. Nicolás Guillén. PFTM-1

Usury drove my parents from the house. Poem About Myself. George P. Elliott. ASA

Ut pictura . . . The disconcerting lips. Fan, The. Eugenio Montale. AF, tr. by William Arrowsmith

Utah. Anne Stevenson. FaBoVe

Utah Jazz, The. Rick Higgerson. MAAN

Utilitarian View of the Monitor's Fight, A. Herman Melville. AmWaPo; APN-2; ColAP; NAAL-3; NAAPv.1; NCAP

Utilities Advertisement in the Wake of Three Mile Island. Gary Metras. AtGh

Utitia'q's Song. Inuit Oral Tradition. AWTN, tr. by Franz Boas and Brian Swann

Utitia' q's Song. Unknown. APN-2, tr. by Franz Boas

Utopia. Richard Greene. Coast

Utopia Anglicized. William Schwenck Gilbert. OBSV Fr. Utopia Limited.

Utopia Limited. William Schwenck Gilbert.

Utopia Anglicized. OBSV

Utopian Melodies. Stephen Dobyns. PoA 2002

Utrillo on the wall. A nun is climbing. Mental Hospital Sitting-Room, A. Elizabeth Jennings. MoWP

Utter aloneness—. Buson. SoOfWa, tr. by Sam Hamill

Utterance. Donald Davidson. FuPo

Utterance. W. S. Merwin. BLT

Uttering cries that are almost human. (LL) American Poetry. Louis Simpson. FaBoA; NAMCP V.2; NoAM; WaAnP

Utterly secret. I know you, black swan. (LL) Music of Colours—White Blossom. Vernon Watkins. AngWePo; TCAWP

Utterly unlike the snow. (LL) First Sight. Philip Larkin. NTCP; PtR

Utterly wrapped up in themselves. (LL) Lecture Upon the Bat, A. Caitríona O'Reilly. MoWP; NIrP

U-turn. Joy Lahey. AnSo

Uuuuuuuuu. Dope. Imamu Amiri Baraka. APSN

V

V. Tony Harrison. NAMCP V.2

V. B. Nimble, V. B. Quick. John Updike. NoP-4; NoP-5; OBCoV

V. B. Wigglesworth wakes at noon. V. B. Nimble, V. B. Quick. John Updike. NoP-4; NoP-5; OBCoV

V. Innocentia Veritas Viat Fides Circumdederunt me inimici mei. Sir Thomas Wyatt. NAEL-6v1

V. N. and C, I, The. Maggie Pogue Johnson. CBWP-4

Vacancy in the Park. Wallace Stevens. SAmP

Vacancy in which, apparently, A. All is Emptiness, And I Must Spin. Thomas Kinsella. PBCIP

Vacancy instead of you, A. Elena Kostyleva. CRWP, tr. by Max Nemtsov

Vacant circumstance of love, The. (LL) More Lovely than Antiquity. Witter Bynner. NoP-4; NoP-5

Vacant Lot. Dudley Randall. NoAM

Vacant Lot. Yvor Winters. APT-2

Vacant Lot, The. Gwendolyn Brooks. NAMCP V.2; NoAM; WaAnP Fr. Street in Bronzeville, A.

Vacant parade grounds swept by the winter wind. Exile. Anthony Hecht. TaR

Vacant shuttles / Weave the wind. I have no ghosts. T. S. Eliot. UV Fr. Gerontion.

Vacation. Rita Dove. OtW; SpirFl

Vacation. William Stafford. BLT

Vacation, 1969. Dorothy Barresi. SwNoth

Vacation, The. Wendell Berry. GoPo

Vacillation. William Butler Yeats. NAMCP V.1; NoAM

"Must we part, Von Hügel, though much alike." OBMV

"My fiftieth year had come and gone." RaBo

Vacuous monochrome of a watery day. Mechanical-landscape-poem. Ion Minulescu. SonAtl, tr. by Chris Constantinescu, Dio Marescu, Phoebe Ravenhall and Helen Wilson

Vacuum, The. Howard Nemerov. NIL-7; NIP-4; StAl

Vacuum's one lung stiffens, aged, The. Poetry Despises Your Attempts at Domesticity. Juliana Baggott. SweBea

Vagabond is a newcomer, A. Vagabond, A. James Tate. NoAM

Vagabond Song, A. Bliss Carman. BRP; IFF; TCAPo

Vagabond, The. Robert Louis Stevenson. OxAEP-2

Vagabonds. Langston Hughes. SAmP

Vagos en una esquina blanca. Ernesto Lumbreras. RMCMP

Vague Poem. Elizabeth Bishop. BAP-01

Vague Swimmers. Heather Ramsdell.

"In repetition, minor violences grew more blunt and less precise." IAoNAP

"New flaws. Food rotting within a safe context. First the food." IAoNAP

"Now place your hand on her back. Now struggle and shove him off." IAoNAP

"Thank you for saying pathos instead of pathetic, keeping us the same size as before." IAoNAP

"This is not about her but she is an example in this. At this show of kindness the person begins to cry." IAoNAP

Vagueness comes over everything, A. Fog. Amy Clampitt. MakPoe

Vain Advice, The. Catherine Cockburn. LW

Vain and Careless. Robert Graves. NOxBChV

Vain Wish, A. Philip Bourke Marston. GSo

Vainglory in Snailhorn. Tune: "Fragrance Fills the Courtyard." Su Tung-p'o. ColAnChi, tr. by James Robert Hightower

Vainglory on terra firma. Three for the Road. E. San Juan, Jr. ReBoTo

Vainly I dug for a perfect sky. Muso Soseki. ZenPo, tr. by Takashi Ikemoto and Lucien Stryk

Vainly my heart had with thy sorceries striven. To ———. Sarah Helen Whitman. APN-1; NAAPv.1; TCAPo

Vajdahunyad. Ferenc Kazinczy. IQMS, tr. by Watson Kirkconnell

Vala; or The Four Zoas. William Blake.

"What is the price of Experience? Do men buy it for a song." RSaN

Vale. Rolando Hinojosa. TiP2

Vale from Carthage. Peter Viereck. MoAmPo; PWW2; WoPoe

Vale of My Youth, The. Will Ifan. BBMWP, tr. by Elin ap Hywel

Vale of Tear[e]s, A. Robert Southwell. NoSic

Vale there is, enwrapped [or enwrapt] with dreadful[l] shades, A. Vale of Tear[e]s, A. Robert Southwell. NoSic

Valediction. Sir Robert Aytoun. NOSC

Valediction. Clare Rossini. BAP-97

Valediction, A: Forbidding Mourning. John Donne. AmFaPo; BASC; BrAP; CABP; FSCP; HeIP-4; NAEL-6v1; NAEL-7v1; NIL-7; NoP-4; NoP-5; NOSC; NPeEn; OxBEV; PBRV; PoPoPo; SoSe-8; TFi; WaAnP; WeW-3

"Our two soules therefore, which are one." UV

Valediction, A (Liverpool Docks). John Masefield. OBMV

Valediction, A: of Weeping. John Donne. BASC; FSCP; HeIP-4; NAEL-6v1; NAEL-7v1; NoP-4; NoP-5; NOSC; WeW-3

Valediction Forbidding Mourning, A. Adrienne Rich. BrAP; NAAL-5; NAMCP V.2; NoAM; NoP-4; NoP-5; OxBoAm; WaAnP

Valediction of the Book, A. John Donne. NoP-4; NoP-5

Valediction to My Contemporaries. Horace Gregory. MoAmPo

Valediction—To My Father. Eddy Van Vliet. VCWP, tr. by John Van Tiel

Valedictory Sonnet to the River Duddon. William Wordsworth. See After-Thought.

Valentine. Wendy Cope. NoP-4; NoP-5

Valentine: "Not a red rose or a satin heart." Carol Ann Duffy. BeAl; EdScPo

Valentine. Donald Hall. NTCP

Valentine. Ernest Hemingway. IllVoic

Valentine, A. Robert Graves. FuPo

Valentine, A. Jack Spicer. APSN

Valentine, A. Priscilla Jane Thompson. CBWP-2

Valentine, A. Elizabeth Trefusis. LW Fr. Valentine, A.

Valentine, A. Elizabeth Trefusis.
  Valentine, A. LW
Valentine, The. Mary Weston Fordham. CBWP-2
Valentine Delivered by a Raven. Tess Gallagher. ExTi
Valentine for Ben Franklin Who Drives a Truck in California, A. Diane
  Wakoski. NoAM
Valentine for Matthew Arnold, A. William Logan. PoA 2002
Valentine to Sherwood Anderson, A. Gertrude Stein. NoAM; PFTM-1
  (Idem the Same.) APT-1; NAAPv.2; NAMCP V.1
Valentine's Day. Larry Fagin. AHA *Fr.* Parade of the Caterpillars, The.
Valentine's Day. Kenneth May. SeSe
Valentino's Hair. Yvonne Sapia. TRP
Valerie and I were only going to take a sip. First Drink. Susan Browne.
  NevBe
Valiant-for-Truth's Song. John Bunyan. *See* Pilgrim Song, The.
Valiantly—that too. Taneda Santoka. CAoMJL1, *tr. by* Burton Watson
Valiant's Song. John Bunyan. *See* Pilgrim Song, The.
Vallejo. Maggie Nelson. HeMarv
Valley, The. Alphonse Marie Louis de Lamartine. SxFrPo, *tr. by* A. M. and
  E. H. Blackmore
Valley, The. Agnes Mary Frances Robinson. VWP
Valley, After Blossoms, The. Jeanette Lynes. Coast
Valley Bleeds with Roman Rust, The. Osip Emilevich Mandelstam. TCRusP,
  tr. by John Glad
Valley bleeds with roman rust, The. Valley Bleeds with Roman Rust, The.
  Osip Emilevich Mandelstam. TCRusP, *tr. by* John Glad
Valley Candle. Wallace Stevens. SAmP
Valley divides the meagre miracle, The. (LL) Haddock Fishermen. George
  Mackay Brown. NoP-4; NoP-5
Valley floors. Collage for Richard Davis—Two Short Forms, A. De Leon
  Harrison. EGAG
Valley from the river shore withdrawn, A. Thomas Campbell. NPBRoP *Fr.*
  Gertrude of Wyoming.
Valley of Dry Bones, The. *Unknown.* WoPoe *Fr.* Ezekiel.
Valley of the Shadow of the Dogs. Lisa Jarnot. VaPo
Valley of the Usk, exactly mid-distant. Eros. John Powell Ward. RWPCtW
Valley of Unrest, The. Edgar Allan Poe. APN-1; NAAL-3
Valley of Zapata, The. Veronica Volkow. RMCMP, *tr. by* Margaret Sayers
  Peden
Valley Prince. Mervyn Morris. WaCA
Valley Spirit never dies, The. Valley Spirit never dies, The. Lao Tzu. HW,
  tr. by Arthur Waley
Valley spirit never dies, The. Lao Tzu. ColAnChi *Fr.* Tao Te Ching.
Valley Spirit never dies, The. Lao Tzu. CCL1 *Fr.* Way and Its Power, The.
Valley Wind, The. *Unknown.* CCL1 *Fr.* Gu-feng [Translations].
Valley-Folk. Fred Cogswell. Coast
Valleys crack and burn, the exhausted plains, The. Mahratta Ghats, The. Alun
  Lewis. AngWePo; OBWVE; PoWW; TCAWP
Valorous Vine. Barbara Guest. AWPTFC
Vals, El. Vicente Aleixandre. RaW
Valse Triste. Sándor Weöres. IQMS, *tr. by* W. Arthur Boggs
Valuably, the tune unwinds us! with, ah! Military Ball, A. Frank O'Hara.
  BodElec
Value Added in Smashing a German Roach on the Bathroom Door, The. Luis
  Cabalquinto. ReBoTo
Vampire, The. Rudyard Kipling. OxBEV
Vampire Finch. Robyn Schiff. LegDan
Vampire outlaw of the milky way. (LL) I Am a Cowboy in the Boat of Ra.
  Ishmael Reed. CalPo; ESEAA; NIL-7; NIP-4
Vampiro Nox. Marianne van Hirtum. SurWo, *tr. by* Guy Flandre and Peter
  Wood
Vampyre, The. Edward Robert Bulwer-Lytton.
  "I found a corpse, with golden hair." VerBaPo
Van Dieman's Land. *Unknown.* NOBAu
Van Diemen's Land. Allen Afterman. NOBAu
Van Gogh. Fadhil Assultani. IrPoTo, *tr. by* Raghid Nahhas
Van Gogh. Yi Sanghŭi. EcSo, *tr. by* Jennifer M. Lee
Van Gogh would paint the landscape. In Hayden's Collage. Michael S.
  Harper. ESEAA
Van Gogh's Ear. Ismail. HotL, *tr. by* V. Narayana Rao
Van Horn. Steven Tye Culbert. TiP2
Van Leeuwenhoek: 1675. Linda Bierds. AmAlph
Van Lingle Mungo. Dave Frishberg. ReLy
Van Winkle. Hart Crane. MoAmPo; NAAPv.2 *Fr.* Bridge, The.
Vancouver Lights. Earle Birney. BrAP
Vandals, The. Alan Michael Parker. LegDan; NeAmPo
Vandals are dreaming, wolves are dreaming, The. Vandals, Horses. Alan
  Michael Parker. NAPBL; PuP-23

Vandals Dying, The. Alan Michael Parker. LegDan
Vandals, Horses. Alan Michael Parker. NAPBL; PuP-23
Vandals in the Garden. Alan Michael Parker. NAPBL
Vanderdecken. Douglas Livingstone. TSAP
Vandunk's Four Humours, in Quality and Quantity. Richard Brathwaite [*or*
  Brathwait]. NOSC
Vane, young in yeares, but in sage counsell old. To Sir Henry Vane the
  Younger. John Milton. PBRV
Vanessa's Bower. Medbh McGuckian. MoWP
Vanguard of liberty, ye Men of Kent. To the Men of Kent (October, 1803).
  William Wordsworth. OBWP
Vanish in the gymnopaedia. (LL) Vitamins and Roughage. Kenneth Rexroth.
  CalPo; NoAM; OxBoAm
Vanished, The. Marie-Claire Bancquart. MFP, *tr. by* Martin Sorrell
Vanished day. Achilleus to Odysseus. Gig Ryan. VaPo
Vanished house that for an hour I knew, A. Souvenir. Edwin Arlington
  Robinson. APT-1; NoAM
Vanished under clearing skies. (LL) On the Spirit of the Heart as Moon-Disk.
  Kojijū. WoPoe; WPoS, *tr. by* Edwin A. Cranston
Vanished Work. Hans Magnus Enzensberger. VCWP, *tr. by* the author and
  Michael Hamburger
Vanishes in the obscurer town. (LL) Herman Melville. APN-2; NCAP *Fr.*
  Clarel: A Poem and Pilgrimage in the Holy Land.
Vanishing. Roddy Lumsden. EdScPo
Vanishing, The. Lewis Carroll. OxAEP-2 *Fr.* Hunting of the Snark, The.
Vanishing Lung Syndrome. Miroslav Holub. VCWP
Vanishing Point. Gary Metras. PasH
Vanishing Point. Jeni Olin. FreRad
Vanishing Spring Moves to Regret. Yu Xuanji. CCL1, *tr. by* Genevieve
  Wimsatt
Vanitas. James Frank Dobie. TiP2
Vanitas Vanitatum. John Webster. *See* Burial, The.
Vanitatum Vanitas. Ferenc Kölcsey. IQMS, *tr. by* Watson Kirkconnell
Vanity. Birago Diop. WoPoe, *tr. by* Ulli Beier and Gerald Moore
Vanity [*or* Vanitie] (1). George Herbert. BASC; FSCP; NoP-4; NoP-5; NOSC
Vanity of All Worldly Things, The. Anne Bradstreet. ChIV-1
Vanity of All Worldly Things, The. Anne Bradstreet.
  "There is a path no vulture's eye hath seen." WPoS
Vanity of Existence, The. Philip Freneau. TCAPo
Vanity of Human Wishes, The; The Tenth Satire of Juvenal [Imitated]. Juvenal.
  CABP; MakPoe; NAEL-6v1; NAEL-7v1; NoP-4; NoP-5; OxAEP-1;
  OxBEV; TFi; UV; WaAnP; WoPoe, *tr. by* Samuel Johnson
  "Enlarge my Life with Multitude of Days." OxBEV, *tr. by* Samuel Johnson
  "In full-blown Dignity, see Wolsey stand." OxBEV, *tr. by* Samuel Johnson
  "On what foundation stands the warrior's pride." FaBoWar; OBWP; OxBEV,
    tr. by Samuel Johnson
  Scholar's Life, The. NPEeN; OBSV, *tr. by* Samuel Johnson
  "Unnumbered suppliants crowd preferment's gate." OBSV, *tr. by* Samuel
    Johnson
  "Where then shall Hope and Fear their objects find?" OxBEV, *tr. by* Samuel
    Johnson
Vanity of men, The. Issa. SoOfWa, *tr. by* Sam Hamill
Vanity of National Grandeur, The. John Thelwall. CenSon
Vanity of Spirit. Henry Vaughan. NOSC
Vanity of the Blue Girls, The. John Crowe Ransom. *See* Blue Girls.
Vanity of the Bright Young Men, The. John Crowe Ransom. FuPo
Vanity of the World, The. Siôn Cent. OBWVE, *tr. by* Joseph P. Clancy
Vanity of vanities, saith the Preacher, vanity of vanities; all is vanity. Bible,
  O.T. NAWM-5v1 *Fr.* Ecclesiastes.
Vanity, saith the preacher, vanity! Bishop Orders His Tomb at Saint Praxed's
  Church, The. Robert Browning. BrAP; CABP; HeIP-4; NAEL-6v2;
  NAEL-7v2; NAWM-7v2; NoP-4; NoP-5; NPEeN; TFi
Vanity, vanity, all is vanity. Ha! Original Sin! Ogden Nash. NBLV
Vanity, Wisconsin. Maxine Chernoff. SUP
Vanna White's Bread Pudding. Michael Pettit. ReTh
Vanzetti's Ghost. Yosl Grinshpan. Prolet, *tr. by* Amelia Glaser
Vapor Trail Reflected in the Frog Pond. Galway Kinnell. AF; OBWP; VCAP
Vapor Trails. Gary Snyder. AtGh
Vaporetto founders in green slush, The. Gorey at the Biennale. Martin
  Johnston. BMAP
Vaporized. Shadow. Stephanie Strickland. AtGh
Varas. Veronica Volkow. RMCMP
Variable. Joshua Sylvester. NOSC
Variant. John Ashbery. BodElec
Variant on the Songs of the East and West Gates. Ts'ao Ts'ao. WoPoe, *tr. by*
  David Lattimore
Variation. Bill Berkson. NYP2

Variation 3 (On Love and More). Lello Voce. *tr. by* Gayle Ridinger
"Your eyes stolen." ItPo, *tr. by* Gayle Ridinger

Variation and Reflection on a Theme by Rilke (The Book of Hours, Book 1, Poem 7). Denise Levertov. UpMys

Variation on a Theme by Rilke. Denise Levertov. StAl

Variation on a Theme of Baudelaire. David Ricks. PoA 2002

Variation on a Theme of Wallace Stevens. John Burnside. WaAnP

Variation on Belloc's "Fatigue". Wendy Cope. UV

Variation on Heraclitus. Louis MacNeice. NAMCP V.1; NoAM

Variation on Ronsard. Thomas Sturge Moore. OBMV

Variation on the Word *Sleep.* Margaret Atwood. AmFaPo; BeAl

Variations. Gunnar Ekelof.
    5. WED, *tr. by* Robert Bly
    6. WED, *tr. by* Robert Bly

Variations. Randall Jarrell. WoPoe

Variations. Hédi Kaddour. YaTCFP, *tr. by* Marilyn Hacker

Variations. Hédi Kaddour. YaTCFP

Variations. Maurice Scully. Oth

Variations Done for Gerald Van De Wiele. Charles Olson. APT-2; NoAM; NoP-4; NoP-5

Variations for the Piano. Siv Cedering. MiVo

Variations for Two Pianos. Donald Justice. EmeKit

Variations for Two Voices. Roberta Hill Whiteman. HATNAP

Variations of Greek Themes. *Various authors.*
    Mighty Runner, A. AmWit, *tr. by* Edwin Arlington Robinson

Variations on a Fragment by Trumbull Stickney. John Hollander. NAMCP V.2; NoP-4; NoP-5

Variations on a Poem by Reznikoff. Louis Simpson. BodElec

Variations on a Text by Vallejo. Donald Justice. CAP-8; NAMCP V.2; NoAM; VCAP

Variations on a Theme by Justice. Paul Mariani. PfSP

Variations on a Theme by William Carlos Williams. Kenneth Koch. AmWit; NAMCP V.2; NBLV; NIL-7; NIP-4; NoAM; NoP-4; NoP-5; OxBoAm; PmAP; PoPoPo; WaAnP

Variations on an Air Composed on Having to Appear in a Pageant as Old King Cole. G. K. Chesterton.
    Old King Cole ("Me clairvoyant"). UV

Variations on the Word *Love.* Margaret Atwood. LW; NoAM

Varied Carol, The. David Graham. ViWalt

Varied theme it utters, A. Eliza Cook. VerBaPo *Fr.* Lines Among the Leaves.

Variegated tremor, The. Charles Tomlinson. WoBe *Fr.* Zipangu.

Variety, The. John Dancer. NOSC

Variety of animals, said Khlebnikov, The. Olga Zondberg. CRWP, *tr. by* Daniel Weissbort

Variety Show, 1984. Hwang Jiwoo. CAMKP, *tr. by* Young-Jun Lee and Scott Swaner

Variety Theater Manifesto, The. Filippo Tommaso Marinetti.
    Futurism Wants to Transform the Variety Theater into a Theater of Amazement, Record-setting, and Body-madness. PFTM-1

Various instants I'm not with you. Robert Johnstone. PNI *Fr.* Every Cache.

Various members of the hierarchy move, The. Morning Letter, A. Robert Duncan. PoA 2002

Various multitudes contained by the loves of my love, The. Anselm Berrigan. HeMarv; IIR

Various nostalgias: rock, scissor, and paper. Towards the Vanishing Point. David Lehman. PmAP

Various Readings of an Illegible Postcard. Christine Hume. AmPoNex

Various Songs of Leisure. Jungkwan Haean. BecRai, *tr. by* Kim Daljin, Kim Won-Chung and Christopher Merrill

Varium et Mutabile. Sir Thomas Wyatt. NoSic
    (Is It Possible.) CABP; NoP-4; NoP-5; WaAnP

Varsity Drag, The. Lew Brown, B. G. DeSylva and Ray Henderson. ReLy

Varus, whom I chanced to meet. Catullus. OBVE

Vary, re-vary; tune and tune again. Variable. Joshua Sylvester. NOSC

Vas en Afrique! Back to Africa! the butcher we used to / patronize in the rue Cadet market. Racists. C. K. Williams. LTA

Vase of Perfume, The. Chang Wu-chien. BLPJKO, *tr. by* Gertrude Laughlin Joerissen

Vase of the Universe, The. Edwin Torres. HeMarv

Vase, The. Hans Faverey. WoBe *Fr.* Eighteen Poems.

Vashti. Frances Ellen Watkins Harper. NALW

Vast and grey, the sky. Desolate Field, The. William Carlos Williams. APT-1

Vast *Bodies* of *Philosophie.* Abraham Cowley. BASC *Fr.* Pindarique Odes.

Vast mild melancholy splendid. Canberra in April. J. R. Rowland. NOBAu

Vast Ocean of light, whose rayes surround. Phineas Fletcher. *See* Ocean of Light.

Vast ocean of light, whose rays surround. Ocean of Light. Phineas Fletcher. NOSC

(Vast Ocean of light, whose rayes surround.) PBRV

Vast Parnassus never knew thy face, The. To My Muse. Agnes Mary Frances Robinson. VWP

Vast Problem Still Obscure. Siri von Reis. PoDa

Vast sky. Condor. David Tokuyu Reid-Marr. WhBo

Vast, tremulous. I Sent Thee Late. Louis Zukofsky. APT-2

Vate y vato. Juan Martínez, Juan Nadie, Juan Todos. Heriberto Yépez. RMCMP

Vaticinio. Nanni Cagnone. *tr. by* Gayle Ridinger
    Book Three: On Preparation. ItPo, *tr. by* Gayle Ridinger
    Fifth Book: On Limitation. ItPo, *tr. by* Gayle Ridinger

Vaudracour and Julia. William Wordsworth.
    Experiment that Failed, An. STuOW

Vaulting Ambition. William Shakespeare. OxAEP-1 *Fr.* Macbeth.

Vauxhall was grey she needed blocks of. Robert Sheppard. Oth *Fr.* Empty Diaries/Twentieth Century Blues 24.

Vecinos. Antonio Deltoro. RMCMP

Vectors: Aphorisms and Ten-Second Essays. James Richardson.
    "It's so much easier to get further from home than nearer that all men become travelers." PoDa

Vectors: Forty-five Aphorisms and Ten-second Essays. James Richardson. BAP-01

Vedantist, The. Sri Sri. HotL, *tr. by* V. Narayana Rao

Vedic Hymns. *Unknown. tr. by* Peter Dent, Edwin Gerow, Frederick Morgan, F. Max Muller and Raimundo Panikkar
    Rig Veda.
       Creation Hymn. WoPoe, *tr. by* Frederick Morgan
       Dawn Has Arisen, Our Welfare Is Assured. WoPoe, *tr. by* Raimundo Panikkar
       Hymn to Night. WoPoe, *tr. by* Peter Dent and Edwin Gerow
       "May the wind blows sweetness." WoPoe, *tr. by* Raimundo Panikkar

Veering and wheeling free in the open. (LL) Harbor, The. Carl Sandburg. APT-1; ColAP; NAMCP V.1

Vega. Lawrence Durrell. OxAEP-2

Vega over the rim of the Val Verzasca. John Peck. HarvBoo

Vegetable Air, The. Cathy Song. NoAM

Vegetable Calendar. Silvio Giussani. ItPo, *tr. by* Gayle Ridinger

Vegetable Garden, The. Wyatt Prunty. OBGa

Vegetable Love. Diane Lockward. SweBea

Vegetables / and jewelry, rightly displayed. For Instance. Robert McAlmon. PoA 2002

Vegetables make love above the tenors. Nancy Talley. IPoFL

Vegetal Animus. Francisco Segovia. RMCMP, *tr. by* Michael Wiegers

Vegetarian Physics. David Clewell. P180

Veil. János Pilinszky. IQMS, *tr. by* Peter Jay

Veil. Marjorie Welish. OnScMo; PmAP

Veil, The. Elizabeth Cobbold. CenSon *Fr.* Sonnets of Laura.

Veil not thy mirror, sweet Amine. To Amine. James Clarence Mangan. OBEV

Veil of death hath fallen, The. To a Deceased Friend. Priscilla Jane Thompson. CBWP-2

Veil of haze protects this, A. City Afternoon. John Ashbery. HeIP-4; NIP-4

Veil of If, The. Molly Peacock. FiBr

Veiled Lady, The. Maura Stanton. BodElec

Veils of Prayer. Ralph Angel. BodElec

Veil's removed, the gaudy, flimsy veil, The. Anna Maria Smallpiece. CenSon

Veils would fall from our eyes, we would know everything, The. (LL) Lifting, The. Sharon Olds. CAP-8; InoFa; MoWP; NIL-7

Vein of sapphires, A. Mahadevi. WoPoe; WPoS, *tr. by* Jane Hirshfield

Vein under my skin, A. Butterflies of Anxiety. Najaat Al-Udwany. PoArWo, *tr. by* Moulouk Berry and Ali Farghaly

Veins All Dried Up. Fatma Kandil. PoArWo, *tr. by* Khaled Mattawa

Velasquez took a pliant knife. Castilian. Elinor Wylie. ColAP

Veld Eclogue: The Pioneers, A. Roy Campbell. OBSV

Veldt Village. Dark Laughter. Melvin B. Tolson. EGAG

Velocity Among the Ruins of Angel Republic. Andrew Zawacki. LegDan

Velocity of Money. Allen Ginsberg. NIL-7

Velocity with which they write, The. Movie Actors Scribbling Letters Very Fast in Crucial Scenes. Jean Garrigue. OxBoAm

Velvet Blanket. Marlon D. Satchell. InTrad

Velvet ground we now with pleasure tread, The. Abbé Jacques de Lille. OBGa *Fr.* Gardens, The.

Velvet Hand, The. Phyllis McGinley. OBCoV

Velvet odor, scarlet brocade. Poem to Ophelia. Kate Horsley. ICANM

Velvet Shoes. Elinor Wylie. MoAmPo; NAAPv.2; WHSW

Vending Machine. Hans Magnus Enzensberger. PoSu, *tr. by* the author

Veneer. Vona Groarke. NIrP

Venerating Senses Save Us. Jonathan Griffin. Oth

Veneris Venefica Agrestis. Lucio Piccolo. OBVE, *tr. by* Charles Tomlinson

Venetia. Adah Isaacs Menken. CBWP-1

Venetian Air. Thomas Moore. GoPo

Venetian Interior, 1889. Richard Howard. VCAP

Venetian Nocturne. Agnes Mary Frances Robinson. VWP

Venetian Pastoral, by Giorgone, in the Louvre, A ("Water, for anguish of the solstice:—nay.") [*rev. vers.*]. Dante Gabriel Rossetti. GS

Venetian Vespers, The. Anthony Hecht.

   3. PoA 2002

Vengeance of Fionn, The. Austin Clarke.

   "Through dark ravines of cloud the dawning broke."
   Flower-Quiet in the Rush-Strewn Sheiling. IrLP

Vengeance: "Once on a night of sparkling sin." Shmuel Kreyter. Prolet, *tr. by* Amelia Glaser

Vengeance was once her nation's lore and law. Watkwenies. Duncan Campbell Scott. BrAP

Vengeance will sit above our faults; but till. Ode. John Donne. SacPr

Vengeful across the cold November moors. Pity of the Leaves, The. Edwin Arlington Robinson. APN-2; MoAmPo

Vengo de la sombra. Mira. Canción de Despedida. Emilio Prados. RaW

Veni Coronaberis. Geoffrey Hill. NoP-4; NoP-5

Veni Creator. Czeslaw Milosz. BeAl, *tr. by* the author and Robert Pinsky

Veni Creator Spiritus. Charlemagne and Hrabanus Maurus. SacPr, *tr. by* John Dryden

Venice. Henry Wadsworth Longfellow. APN-1

Venice. Herman Melville. APN-2

Venice Beach: Brief Song. Dorothy Barresi. SeSe; SwNoth

Venice: "Enormous clock at the sandy mansion, An." Anna Glazova. CRWP *Fr.* Cities.

Venice Lost. Günter Kunert. GTCP, *tr. by* Reinhold Grimm

Venice portrait: he, The. Humanist, The. Geoffrey Hill. UpMys

Venice, Unaccompanied. Monica Youn. IIR

Venipuncture. John Graham-Pole. BloBone

Venison. Karen Chase. NIL-7

Venni-Vach Revisited. Richard Hall.

   "How oft, ere morning lit the eastern steep." AngWePo

Vent agite doucement, à l'entour du Palais des Eaux, les fleurs embaumées des nénuphars, Le. Ivresse d'Amour. Li Po. CCL1, *tr. by* Judith Gautier

Vent caresse les affiches, Le. Cinéma-palace. Philippe Soupault. YaTCFP

Ventanas Pintadas. Gloria Fuertes. RaW

Ventriloquist's breath, The. Iron Lung. Lavinia Greenlaw. MFPA

Ventriloquy. Andrew Zawacki. IAoNAP

Ventriloquy / is the mother tongue. Attention. Rae Armantrout. PmAP

Venturing Out. *Vietnamese Oral Tradition.* CaDao, *tr. by* John Balaban

Venus ("Open sesame / by day.") Federico García Lorca. PFTM-1 *Fr.* Night (Suite for Piano and Poet's Voice).

Venus and Adonis. Bartholomew Griffin. NoSic

Venus and Adonis. Ovid. NAWM-7v1 *Fr.* Metamorphoses.

Venus and Adonis [Complete Text *and* Selections from Anthologies]. William Shakespeare.

   "All swoln with chasing, down Adonis sits." EroLit

   (Death of Adonis, The.) NoSic

   Venus with Adonis' and Hounds. DiBP

Venus and Cupid. Mark Alexander Boyd. *See* Fra Bank to Bank, Fra Wood to Wood I Rin.

VENUS, and young Adonis sitting by her. Venus and Adonis. Bartholomew Griffin. NoSic

Venus de Milo. Gottfried Keller. WoPoe, *tr. by* John Peck

Venus de Milo. Charles Marie René Leconte de Lisle. GS, *tr. by Unknown*

Venus Goes After Anchises. *Unknown.* OBVE *Fr.* Homeric Hymns.

Venus Hottentot, The. Elizabeth Alexander. ESEAA; InTrad

Venus, let me never see. (LL) Lady Who Offers Her Looking-Glass to Venus, The. Matthew Prior. NPeEn; OBEV; OxBEV

Venus of Laussel. Patricia Monaghan. HW

Venus of Milo, The. Henrietta Cordelia Ray. CBWP-3

Venus of the Louvre. Emma Lazarus. APN-2; GS; NAAPv.1; OxBoAm

Venus Preserved. Kenward Elmslie. NYP2

Venus Pudica stands, bent. Where her hand is. Lady at the Castle, The. John Hollander. NoAM

Venus, take my votive glass. Lady Who Offers Her Looking-Glass to Venus, The. Matthew Prior. NPeEn; OBEV; OxBEV

Venus Tells Anchises the Story of Aurora and Tithonus. *Unknown.* OBVE *Fr.* Homeric Hymns.

Venus the gleaming goddess. Virgil. NAWM-5v1; NAWM-7v1 *Fr.* Aeneid [*or* Eneados *or* Aeneis], The.

Venus! to thee, the Lesbian Muse shall sing. Sappho's Prayer to Venus. Mary Robinson. CenSon; RWP

Venus Transiens. Amy Lowell. APT-1; NAAL-5; NAAPv.2; NALW; NAMCP V.1

Venus with Adonis' and Hounds. William Shakespeare. DiBP *Fr.* Venus and Adonis [Complete Text *and* Selections from Anthologies].

Venus's Looking-Glass. Christina Georgina Rossetti. NALW

Venus's-flytraps. Yusef Komunyakaa. FaoP; PtR

Verandahs. Robert Francis Brissenden. NOBAu

Verano y Humo. Manuel Vázquez Montalbán. RaW

Verb, The. Nedelcho Ganev. CSCBP, *tr. by* Georgi Belev and Lisa Sapinkopf

Verbal gun shots. Reggie Timpson. BtF

Verbatim begins with this decade's hit and miss. Nicole Markotić. PoPra

Verde queen toe quires verde. Romance Somnambulo by Garcia Lorca. Federico García Lorca. AnSo, *tr. by* Alex Rawls

Verdict of Stone, A. Tanure Ojaide. NAfrP

Verge. James Schuyler. AHA

Verge bore the remnants of his shearings, The. Grandfather's Rockery. David Woo. OpBo

Vergine bella. Geoffrey Hill. PoetW

Vergine bella—it is here that I require. Vergine bella. Geoffrey Hill. PoetW

Vergissmeinnicht. Keith Douglas. EdScPo; FaBoWar; GoPo; HarvBoo; NAEL-6v2; NAEL-7v2; NAMCP V.1; NoAM; NoP-4; NoP-5; NPeEn; OBWP; OxBEV; PoAgWa; PoWW; SoSe-8; StAl; WoPoe

Verily. Ingeborg Bachmann. GTCP, *tr. by* Irmgard Hunt

Verily / The sky clears. Sky Clears, The. *Unknown.* OBVE, *tr. by* Frances Densmore

Veritable night, The. Rigamarole. William Carlos Williams. APT-1

Verlaine. Marilyn Hacker. PML, *tr. by* Hédi Kaddour

Verlaine. Richard Hovey. APN-2

Verlaine. Edwin Arlington Robinson. APN-2; NCAP

Verlaine Dying. David Wheatley. NIrP

Verlaine? He stands erect there on the grass. Verlaine. Marilyn Hacker. PML, *tr. by* Hédi Kaddour

Vermeer. Stephen Mitchell. GI

Vermeer. Howard Nemerov. GoPo

Vermeer. Tomas Tranströmer. WED, *tr. by* Robert Bly

Vermeer's Paint. Bobi Jones. ATSWP, *tr. by* Robert Minhinnick

Vermin. William Matthews. BAP-97; OxBoAm

Verminous aeronaut, leaflight turkey, kite. Egyptian Kites. Rex Warner. OWoS

Vermont. Hayden Carruth.

   "Republicans? We've got a few. In fact." GifTon

Vermont. Dan Chiasson. LegDan

Vermont. David Huddle. AmWaPo

Vermont Apollinaire. William Corbett. PmAP

Vermont Ballad: Change of Season. Robert Penn Warren. ColAP

Vermont Has a High Suicide Rate. Richard Donze. BloBone

Vermont: Spring Rains. Edward Weismiller. YaYoPo

Vermont Thaw. Robert Penn Warren. BodElec

Vernal breeze returns to refresh, The. Tune: "The Beauty of Yü." Li Yü. ColAnChi, *tr. by* Jiaosheng Wang

Vernal Conifer Seance. Jason Christie. PoPra

Vernal Equinox. Amy Lowell. APT-1; NAAPv.2

Vernal Equinox. Ruth Stone. MoAmPo

Vernon. Richard Garcia. SUP

Vernon of brick smokestacks, of circuitous. Vernon. Richard Garcia. SUP

Veronica, a Double Life. Kim Chôngnan. EcSo, *tr. by* Peter H. Lee

Vers l'arbre-frère aux jours comptés. René Char. YaTCFP

Versailles. Michael Gizzi. OnScMo

Versailles. Adrienne Rich. OBGa

Verse: "Past ruin'd [*or* ruined] Ilion Helen lives." John Lyle Donaghy. OBEV

Verse: "Past ruin'd Ilion." Walter Savage Landor. *See* Ianthe.

Verse: "What should we know." Oliver St. John Gogarty. OBMV

Verse, a breeze mid blossoms straying. Youth and Age. Samuel Taylor Coleridge. OBEV

Verse for First. Tseverin Furey. NevBe

Verse I. Christina Georgina Rossetti. *See* Aloof.

Verse II. Christina Georgina Rossetti. PEW *Fr.* Thread of Life, The.

Verse III. Christina Georgina Rossetti. PEW *Fr.* Thread of Life, The.

Verse of Darkness, The. Jenö Dsida. IQMS, *tr. by* Watson Kirkconnell

Verse Translator. John Frederick Nims. PoA 2002

Verses: "Clean is the autumn wind." Li Po. TAL

Verses. Lady Mary Wortley Montagu. CABP

Verses: "I am monarch of troubles a host." Maria Jane Jewsbury. VWP

Verses: "I am old, sick and lonely." Su Tung-p'o. TAL

Verses: "Written so long ago, I didn't even." Marina Ivanovna Tsvetayeva. MoWP, *tr. by* Elaine Feinstein

Verses: "You who come from the old village." Wang Wei. TAL

Verses: "Poor fellow, what is it to you." Sir Charles Hanbury Williams. OBWVE

Verses about Music. Elena Ignatova. *tr. by* Sibelan Forrester

"Italian Marcello, you breathe a much sweeter air." ItGoST, *tr. by* Sibelan Forrester

Verses Addressed to the Imitator of the First Satire of the Second Book of Horace. Lady Mary Wortley Montagu.

"When God created thee, one would believe." BrAP

Verses Against the Inconsequence of Men's Taste and Strictures. Sor Juana Inés de la Cruz. SpanPo, *tr. by* Muriel Kittel

Verses by my Mother in Her Own Hand. Amy Hammond. EMWP

Verses by the Princess Elizabeth, Given to Lord Harington, of Exton, Her Preceptor. Elizabeth, Queen of Bohemia. EMWP

Verses Design'd by Mrs. A. Behn to be Sent to a Fair Lady. Aphra Behn. PoBW

Verses Expressing the Feelings of a Lover [*sonnet*]. Sor Juana Inés de la Cruz. SpanPo, *tr. by* Samuel Beckett

Verses for a First Birthday. George Barker. MoBrPo

Verses for an Album. Charles Lamb. *See* In My Own Album.

Verses Found in His Bible in the Gatehouse at Westminster. Sir Walter Ralegh. *See* Authours Epitaph, Made by Himself, The.

Verses from the Shepherd's Hymn. Richard Crashaw. OBEV

Verses in Baretti's Commonplace Book. Samuel Johnson. OxAEP-1

Verses in Italian and French, Written by the Queen of Scots to the Queen of England. Mary Stuart, Queen of Scots. EMWP

Verses / Inviting Mrs. C—to Tea on a public Fast-day During the American War. Anna Seward. PEW

Verses Made by a Catholic in Praise of Campion That Was Executed at Tyburn for Treason, As Is Made Known by the Proclamation. *Unknown.* NoSic

Verses Made by Sappho, Done from the Greek by Boyleau, and from the French by a Lady of Quality. Sappho. EMWP

Verses made by Sir Walter Raleigh the Night before he was Beheaded. Sir Walter Ralegh. *See* Passionate Man['s] Pilgrimage, The.

Verses Made for the Women Who Cry Apples, etc. Jonathan Swift. IrV

Verses Made the Night before He Died [*or* Dyed]. Sir Walter Ralegh. *See* Even Such Is Time.

Verses Made the Night before His Beheading. Sir Walter Ralegh. *See* Authours Epitaph, Made by Himself, The.

Verses Occasioned by the Sudden Drying Up of St. Patrick's Well. Jonathan Swift.

"Wretched Ierne! with what grief I see." OBSV

Verses of a True Hungarian Patriot, The. *Unknown.* IQMS, *tr. by* René Bonnerjea and Earl M. Herrick

Verses on the Death of Dr. Swift, D.S.P.D, Occasioned by Reading a Maxim in Rochefoucauld. Jonathan Swift. NAEL-6v1; NAEL-7v1; NoP-5

"Here shift the scene, to represent." OxBEV

"Perhaps I may allow, the Dean." OxBEV

"Time is not remote when I, The." NPeEn; OxAEP-1; OxBEV

Verses on the Death of Sir James Hunter Blair. Robert Burns. STuOW

Verses on the Prospect of Planting Arts and Learning in America. George Berkeley. *See* On the Prospect of Planting Arts and Learning in America.

Verses Put into a Lady's Prayer-Book. John Wilmot, 2d Earl of Rochester. NOSC

Verses Sent to Mr Bevil Higgons, on His Sickness and Recovery from the Small-pox, in the Year 1693. Catherine Cockburn. EMWP

Verses to my Heart's-Sister. Henrietta Cordelia Ray. CBWP-3

Verses Written by a Gentlewoman upon the Jaylors Conversion. Anne Dowriche. EMWP

Verses Written by Alis Daughter of Gryffydd Son of Iefan When Her Father Asked Her What Sort of Husband She Would Like. Alis Ferch Gruffyd ab Ieuan ap Lleywelyn Fychan. EMWP

Verses Written by Mrs. Hutchinson. Lucy Hutchinson. BASC; NOSC

Verses Written during the War, 1756–1763. Thomas Osbert Mordaunt. (Call, The.) OBEV

Verses Written in the Spring. Anne Batten Cristall. RWP

Verses Written on Her Death-bed at Bath to Her Husband in London. Mary Monck. LW

Verses Written the Night before His Execution. Sir Walter Ralegh. *See* Even Such Is Time.

Versicle, A. James Clarence Harvey. ArBi

Versification of a Passage from Penthouse. Andrew Hudgins. AllShUp

Verso Libre. Nick Carbó. NAPBL

Vertical. Michel Leiris. YaTCFP

Vertical. Michel Leiris. YaTCFP, *tr. by* Cole Swensen

Vertical Poetry. Roberto Juarroz.

"Bottom of things is neither life nor death, The." VCWP

Vertigo. Michael Murphy. NIrP

Vértigo. Pedro Serrano. RMCMP

Vertigo. Pedro Serrano. RMCMP, *tr. by* Geoff Hargreaves

Vertigo. Anne Stevenson. PoDa

Vertigo. Andrew Zawacki. IIR; LegDan

Very brief. Basho. EH, *tr. by* Robert Hass

Very cautiously. Cleaning. Karel Soudijn. TuT, *tr. by* Peter van de Kamp

Very dear though it was I have bought you. Michelangelo Buonarroti. WoPoe, *tr. by* W. S. Merwin

Very due that being each one dwells. Narrow Path, The. Norman Henry, II Pritchard. GT

Very empty cubic, blue room. No windows. No door frames. Colors. Fortunato Depero. PFTM-1

Very few can. Pecan, The Toucan, The. Robert Williams Wood. NBLV

Very few people know where they will die. Deathplace, A. Louis Edward Sissman. NoP-4; NoP-5; PoDa

Very fine conga of sweat, A. I See Chano Pozo. Jayne Cortez. PmAP

Very fine is my valentine. Very Valentine, A. Gertrude Stein. FTtHH

Very Fine Lines. Britton Wilkie. AHA

Very floor of our existence as a couple, The. Very Floor of Our Existence, The. June Billings Safford. PasH

Very gently it began to rain. (LL) Cows at Night, The. Hayden Carruth. GifTon; PoA 2002

Very ground dissolves beneath my feet, The. Imre Madách. IQMS *Fr.* Tragedy of Man.

Very high this mountain. Muso Soseki. EaWin, *tr. by* W. S. Merwin

Very Like a Whale. Ogden Nash. APT-2; GPTC

Very little snail, A. What Do I See. Gertrude Stein. ItWoWo; PFTM-1

Very often when you are striving. Would-be Critic, The. Mrs. Henry Linden. CBWP-4

Very Old, The. Ted Kooser. PBCAP

Very old are the woods. All That's Past. Walter De la Mare. OBMV

Very old hotel, A. A hotel that at night lies curled up like a cat by the river. Very Old Hotel, A. Kim Hyesun. EcSo, *tr. by* Youngju Ryu

Very Old Man. James Henry. OxBEV

Very pain it came first. Fanny Howe. FaoP *Fr.* Splinter, The.

Very Real Story, A. Julio Cortázar. TCLAP, *tr. by* Paul Blackburn

Very Rich Hours, The. Nick Drake. BeAl; NeBl

Very Sad Conversation at Night, A. Anna Swirszczynska [*or* Swir]. PoSu

Very Short Poem. Raymond Souster. IFF

Very Short Sutra on the Meeting of the Buddha and the Goddess, The. Rick Fields. WhBo

Very Simply Topping Up the Brake Fluid. Simon Armitage. NeBrP

Very small children in patched clothing, The. Study in Aesthetics, The. Ezra Pound. APT-1; EMP

Very Soft Shoes. Marshall Barer. ReLy

Very soon the Yankee teachers. Frances Ellen Watkins Harper. NAAPv.1; NALW *Fr.* Aunt Chloe.

Very Strong Stomach Has Mr. Luke, A. Manuel González Prada. SpanPo, *tr. by* William M. Davis

Very strong stomach has Mr. Luke, A. Very Strong Stomach Has Mr. Luke, A. Manuel González Prada. SpanPo, *tr. by* William M. Davis

Very Thought of You, The. Ray Noble. ReLy

Very True Confessions. Sidney Burris. SwNoth

Very Valentine, A. Gertrude Stein. FTtHH

Very Young Man Speaks, A. Paul Tanaquil. YaYoPo

Vesey, of verse the judge and friend. Florio: A Tale, and The Bas-bleu; or, Conversation. Hannah More. RWP

Vesica Piscis. Coventry Patmore. SacPr

Vesperal. Ernest Dowson. OBMV

Vespers: "I don't wonder where you are anymore." Louise Glück. HarvBoo

Vespers: "In your extended absence, you permit me." Louise Glück. CAP-8; OxBoAm

Vespers: "Now it is evening, the light rushes to fall." Peter Cooley. Vesp

Vespers. Amy Lowell. NAAPv.2

Vespers. Alan Alexander Milne.

"Hush! Hush! Whisper who dares!" UV

Vespers. Ōkuma Kotomichi. EMJL, *tr. by* Haruo Shirane

Vespertilia. Rosamund Marriott Watson. ViWPN

Vespertilio. Linda Bierds. AmAlph; ExTi

Vessel. Sandra Kohler. FiBr *Fr.* Ars Poetica Feminae.

Vessel, The. C. K. Williams. TaR

Vessels of mercy, prepared unto glory! Frances Ridley Havergal. SacPr

Vest of Myrtle, The. Mary Robinson. *See* 13. She Endeavours to Fascinate Him.

Vesta. John Greenleaf Whittier. SacPr

Vestal Virgin, The.   Eloise Bibb.   CBWP-4

Vesta's Father.   Julia Kasdorf.   PBCAP

Vestibulum (entrance hall).   Matthea Harvey.   IAoNAP *Fr.* Thermae.

Vestigia.   Bliss Carman.   BrAP

Vesuvius at Home. (LL)   Volcanoes be in Sicily.   Emily Dickinson.
    NAAPv.1; NALW; OxWW

Vete.   Cultures.   Gloria Anzaldúa.   UnSA

Veteran.   Fanny Howe.   OxBoAm

Veterans.   Aleksey Shelvakh.   PML, *tr. by* J. Kates

Veterans of the Wars.   Edgar Lee Masters.   CBCWP

Veterinary Student, The.   Jennifer Markell.   PfS

Via Crucis.   Herman Melville.   APN-2; NCAP *Fr.* Clarel: A Poem and
    Pilgrimage in the Holy Land.

Via, et Veritas, et Vita.   Alice Thompson Meynell.   SacPr

Via Margutta.   Maria Luisa Spaziani.   NeIt, *tr. by* Beverly Allen

Via Negativa.   Ronald Stuart Thomas.   InvLi; StAl

Viajar por los mares del silencio.   Na hermila limón.   Natalia Toledo.
    RMCMP

Viaje.   Antonio Deltoro.   RMCMP

Viande de boucherie par Loti.   Jude Stéfan.   YaTCFP

Viareggio.   Günter Eich.   MotU, *tr. by* David Walker

Viatica.   Andrew Zawacki.
    "One of me stuttered and one."   LegDan

Vibora breve.   Alfonso D'Aquino.   RMCMP

Vibrant naive Naabeeho women.   Modern on the Surface.   Nia Francisco.
    HATNAP

Vibration Society.   Bill Berkson.   AHA

Vicar, The.   George Crabbe.   OBSV *Fr.* Borough, The.

Vicar, The.   Winthrop Mackworth Praed.   OBEV; OxAEP-2 *Fr.* Every Day
    Characters.

Vicar of Bray, The.   *Unknown.*   OBSV; OxBEV

Vicar of Wakefield, The.   Oliver Goldsmith.
    Elegy on the Death of a Mad Dog, An.   NBLV; OBNV; OxAEP-1; TFi
    (Mad Dog, The.)   DiBP
    (Song.)   OxAEP-1
    When Lovely Woman Stoops to Folly.   CABP; NoP-4; NoP-5; NPeEn;
        OxBEV; TFi
    (Woman.)   OBEV

Vicarious.   Amy Lowell.   NAAPv.2

Vicarious Atonement.   Richard Aldington.   MoBrPo

Vices of Men, The.   Joyce Mansour.   SurPaPo, *tr. by* Mary Ann Caws and
    Jean-Pierre Cauvin

Vices of men, The.   Vices of Men, The.   Joyce Mansour.   SurPaPo, *tr. by*
    Mary Ann Caws and Jean-Pierre Cauvin

Vices of the Modern World.   Nicanor Parra.   CLPP, *tr. by* Jorge Elliott

Vice's Song, The.   John Pickering.   NoSic *Fr.* Horestes.

Vicious Circle.   Marsha Prescod.   LW

Vicious winter finally yields, The.   W. D. Snodgrass.   NoP-5 *Fr.* Heart's
    Needle.

Vickery's Mountain.   Edwin Arlington Robinson.   MoAmPo

Vicki and Daphne.   Cheryl Clarke.   WiU

Vicksburg.   Paul Hamilton Hayne.   PCW

Victim Number 48.   Mahmoud Darwish.   VCWP

Victim, The.   Thom Gunn.   SwNoth

Victims of the demon dance.   For All Unwed Mothers.   Robert Fleming.   ISC

Victims, The.   Sharon Olds.   NIL-7; SoSe-8

Victoire.   Guillaume Apollinaire.
    Listen to the sea.   PFTM-1

Victor, The.   Lajos Áprily.   IQMS, *tr. by* Watson Kirkconnell

Victor, The.   Louis Untermeyer.   STuOW

Victor alone you were not—'twas the Age's Soul, that of Freedom.   To
    Napoleon.   Dániel Berzsenyi.   IQMS, *tr. by* Adam Makkai

Victor Dog, The.   James Merrill.   NAMCP V.2; NoAM; NoP-4; NoP-5

Victor Garibaldi.   Melvin B. Tolson.   GT

Victor Jara of Chile.   Adrian Mitchell.   RSaN

Victor Record Catalog.   David Schubert.   APT-2

Victoria.   Henry Van Dyke.   SacPr

Victoria Market.   Francis Brabazon.   NOBAu

Victoria Markets Recollected in Tranquility, The.   Furnley Maurice.   NOBAu

Victoria Station.   Luigi Fontanella.   NeIt, *tr. by* Michael Palma

Victorian Family Photograph.   Kit Wright.   OBCoV

Victorian Hangman Tells His Love, A.   Bruce Dawe.   NoAM

Victorian Idyll, A.   David Wagoner.   NoAM

Victorian mothers instructed their daughters, ahem.   Victoria's Secret.   Charles
    Martin.   RA

Victoria's Secret.   Charles Martin.   RA

Victories of Love, The.   Coventry Patmore.
    Music of Forefended Spheres, The.   NPeEn

Victories of mind, The.   War.   Ebenezer Elliott.   FaBoWar

Victory, The.   Anne Stevenson.   BeAl

Victory Arches.   Yosano Tekkan.   CAoMJL1, *tr. by* Leith Morton

Victory at Guernica, The.   Paul Eluard and Andre Breton.   SurPaPo, *tr. by*
    Mary Ann Caws *and* Jean-Pierre Cauvin

Victory Bonfire.   Ruth Pitter.   RSaN

Victory Burlesk, The.   Margaret Atwood.   MotU

Victory Calypso.   Egbert Moore.   OBCoV

Victory comes late.   Emily Dickinson.   APN-2; SWaP

Victory Obtained by Blake over the Spaniards, in the Bay of Santa Cruz in the
    Island of Teneriffe, 1657.   Andrew Marvell.
    "For Santacruze the glad fleet takes her way."   FaBoWar

Victory of Samothrace, The.   Rubén Darío.   GS, *tr. by Unknown*

Victory to Yogendra's Wife, Great Illusion!   Anthony Säheb.   SinGod, *tr. by*
    Rachel Fell McDermott

Victory, Victoria, My Beautiful Whisper.   Luis J. Rodriguez.   FaoP

Vida.   Vicente Aleixandre.   RaW

Vida de una mujer cucapá, La.   Heriberto Yépez.   RMCMP

Vida del agua.   Pabellón.   Elsa Cross.   RMCMP

Vida que Uno Lleva, La.   Gabriel Celaya.   RaW

Vida Urbana.   Jorge Guillén.   RaW

Vida va despacio, pisa tibio y mojado, La.   Sentido de la Sopa, El.   Gabriel
    Celaya.   RaW

Video, The.   Fleur Adcock.   StAl

Video Blues.   Mary Jo Salter.   P180; WaAnP

Video Box: 25, The.   Edwin Morgan.   EmeKit

Video Cuisine.   Maxine W. Kumin.   NoAM

Video Mama.   Jack Ridl.   SwNoth

Video Victim.   Luis H. Francia.   ReBoTo

Vie du scarabée, Le.   Franck André Jamme.
    "Et le paon repartait se pavaner seul dans le parc."   YaTCFP

Viejas Locas.   Harryette Mullen.   TiP2

Viejo.   Jean-Claude Martineau.   OGAHCP, *tr. by* Boadiba and Jack Hirschman

Viejo y barbudo sol, buen sol soldado.   Al Sol de la Guerra.   Rafael Alberti.
    RaW

Viejo y el Sol, El.   Vicente Aleixandre.   RaW

Viens, nous pénétrerons le secret du flot clair.   Rançon, La.   René[e] Vivien.
    YaTCFP

Vier Takte vor K time then before.   Pierre Joris.   PFTM-2 *Fr.* Winnetou Old.

Vierge Moderne.   Edith Södergran.   ItWoWo; PFTM-1, *tr. by* Stina
    Katchadourian

Viernes Santo / Good Friday.   Francisco X. Alarcón.   GeoHom

Vies Manquées.   Edith Nesbit.   VWP

Viet Kong.   William Trowbridge.   ReTh

Vietnam.   Clarence Major.   HHAm; PoAgWa

Vietnam Memorial, The.   Washington.   Gerwyn Williams.   BBMWP, *tr. by* the
    author and Richard Poole

Vietnam war drags on, the.   Newscast, The.   Ian Hamilton.   FaBoWar;
    NPeEn; PoAgWa

View.   Rae Armantrout.   AWPTFC

View, A.   James Schuyler.   BodElec

View, A.   Mona Van Duyn.   VCAP

View, all ye eyes above, this sight which flings.   Edward Taylor.   NOSC *Fr.*
    Preparatory Meditations Before My Approach to the Lord's Supper.

View Café, The.   Jonathan Johnson.   AmPoNex

View from a Cab, The.   Henry Taylor.   NBLV

View From a Porch.   Thomas Lux.   AmAlph

View from a Suburban Window.   Phyllis McGinley.   AmWit

View from an Airplane at Night, over California, The.   Bruce Bawer.   RA

View from Cortona, A.   Richard Hugo.   AF

View from Heron Tower.   Wang Chih-huan.   CrYelRi, *tr. by* Sam Hamill

View from Skates in Berkeley, The.   Quincy Troupe.   UnSA

View from the Bathysphere.   Peter Rafferty.   NLP

View from the Corner.   Samuel Allen.   SSLK

View from the Roof, Waverly Place.   Cornelius Eady.   InvLad

View from the Window, The.   Ronald Stuart Thomas.   NoP-4; NoP-5

View like one of Fairy-land, A.   George Darley.   NOBRP *Fr.* Sylvia; or, The
    May Queen.

View Mee, Lord.   Thomas Campion.   SacPr

View of a Pig.   Ted Hughes.   OxAEP-2; OxBEV

View of Christ's Kingdom, A.   William Williams. *tr. by* Gwyn Jones and Lewis
    Saunders
    Marriage in Eden, The.   OBWVE

View of the Blue Sea.   Ts'ao Ts'ao.   ChinPo, *tr. by* Ye Weilian [*or* Yeh Wei-
    lien *or* Wai-lim Yip]

View of the Library of Congress from Paul Laurence Dunbar High School [*for Doris Craig and Michael Olshausen*]. Thomas Sayers Ellis. FuFl; GT

View of the Wilds. Wang Ji. CCL1, *tr. by* Stephen Owen

View of Things, A. Edwin Morgan. HarvBoo

View with a Grain of Sand. Wisława Szymborska. BLT, *tr. by* Stanislaw Barańczak and Clare Cavanagh

Viewed in this way / her voice. Elsewhere, Things Tend. Claudia Rankine. AmPoNex

Viewing Mona Lisa. Angela Martin. FTtHH

Viewing the Body. W. D. Snodgrass. CAP-8; InoFa

Viewing the Three Lakes. Hsieh T'iao. ChinPo, *tr. by* Ye Weilian [*or* Yeh Wei-lien *or* Wai-lim Yip]

Viewing the Waterfall at Mount Lu. Li Po. ColAnChi, *tr. by* Burton Watson

Viewless, through heaven's vast vault your course ye steer. To the Winds. Ann Radcliffe. RWP

Viewpoint. Tessa Ransford. EdScPo

Vigil. Jocelyn Emerson. IAoNAP

Vigil. Blair Gibb. Prnts

Vigil. Ken Harris. AnSo

Vigil. Juan Ramón Jiménez. SpanPo, *tr. by* Willis Barnstone

Vigil. Cecília Meireles. TCLAP, *tr. by* James Merrill

Vigil, The. Ralph Angel. MAAN

Vigil at a Missile Silo, A. Mark Sanders. AtGh

Vigil: Dwindle. Robin Behn. AmAlph

Vigil of Aiden, The. Thomas Holley Chivers.
     "In the Rosy Bowers of Aiden." STuOW

Vigil of Rizpah, The. Felicia Dorothea Hemans. CenSon

Vigil of Venus, The. *Unknown. tr. by* Thomas Stanley
     "Goddesse bade the nymphs remove, The." OBVE
     "Love he to morrow, who lov'd never." OBVE

Vigil Strange I Kept on the Field One Night. Walt Whitman. APN-1; BrAP; CAGL; CBCWP; ColAP; HeIP-4; MoAmPo; NAAL-3; NAAPv.1; NoP-4; NoP-5; OBWP; PCW; PoPoPo; TCAPo; WaAnP

Vigilance. André Breton. SurPaPo, *tr. by* Jean-Pierre Cauvin and Mary Ann Caws and Jean-Pierre Cauvin

Vigilance. André Breton. YaTCFP

Vigilante Man. Woody Guthrie. APT-2

Vignette. Natasha Trethewey. RD

Viking. Brett Rutherford. OtW

Vilage is a circle, A. Village, A. Roland Jooris. TuT, *tr. by* Peter van de Kamp

Vile, and deformed by sin I stand. Human and Divine. Phoebe Cary. SacPr

Vile cur, why will you late and soon. Epode 6. Horace. DiBP *Fr.* Epodes.

Vile World. Simon Rae. UV

Villa at the Foot of Mount Chungnan. Wang Wei. ChinPo, *tr. by* Ye Weilian [*or* Yeh Wei-lien *or* Wai-lim Yip]

Villa d'Este. Edwin Denby. OBGa

Villa Fidelia. Michael Murphy. NIrP

Villa Restaurant, The. Derek Walcott. WeW-3

Village. Jean Earle. AngWePo

Village. Octavio Paz. TCLAP, *tr. by* Charles Tomlinson

Village, A. Roland Jooris. TuT, *tr. by* Peter van de Kamp

Village, The. George Crabbe.
     "No longer truth, though shown in verse, disdain." OxAEP-1
     Village Life. NAEL-7v1

Village, The. Marina Gashe. CFP; HAWP

Village, The. Dafydd Rowlands. BBMWP, *tr. by* Meic Stephens

Village, The. Ronald Stuart Thomas. HarvBoo

Village After Sunset, The. James Applewhite. LPSFW

Village Blacksmith, The. Henry Wadsworth Longfellow. APN-1; BRP; UV

Village Burglar, The. *Unknown.* GoPo

Village by the River. Tu Fu [*or* Du Fu]. CCL1, *tr. by* Jerome P. Seaton

Village Choir, The. *Unknown.* UV

Village Cricket. William Blake. NPBRoP *Fr.* Island in the Moon, An.

Village cur, of snappish race, A. John Gay. DiBP *Fr.* Fables: First Series.

Village dogs and ours, elate and brave, The. Jean Ingelow. DiBP *Fr.* Brothers, and a Sermon.

Village elders gather on the porch of the Rama temple, The. Other Tongue, The. Dasu Sriramulu. HotL, *tr. by* V. Narayana Rao

Village festival is really worth seeing, The. Watching a Village Festival. Yang Wan-li. ColAnChi, *tr. by* Jonathan Chaves

Village is straddled on both sides, The. Eglwys Newydd. John Tripp. AngWePo

Village Life. George Crabbe. NAEL-7v1 *Fr.* Village, The.

Village Life, A [*(for John Robertson)*]. Derek Walcott. GT

Village life, and every care that reigns. George Crabbe. NAEL-7v1 *Fr.* Village, The.

Village Maid, The. Mary F. Johnson. CenSon

Village maid was leaving home, with tears her eyes were wet, A. Heaven Will Protect the Working-Girl. Edgar Smith. ReLy

Village mill echoes, The. Farmhouse: Three Poems. Yi Kyubo. CATKP, *tr. by* Kevin O'Rourke

Village mill echoes, The. Yi Kyubo. CATKP *Fr.* Farmhouse: Three Poems.

Village Musings. Cornelius Whur.
     Poet Questions the Ant, The. STuOW

Village Mystery. Elinor Wylie. APT-1

Village named Little-Plum-Tree, A. Issa. EH, *tr. by* Robert Hass

Village Near a Church, A. Aliyah Abdul-Salaam. AnVo, *tr. by* Mohamed Enani

Village Night. Gyula Juhász. IQMS, *tr. by* Anthony Edkins

Village Noon; Mid-Day Bells. Merrill Moore. MoAmPo

Village Notary's Journey to Buda, A. József Gvadányi. *tr. by* Watson Kirkconnell
     On the Dress of the Hungarians. IQMS, *tr. by* Watson Kirkconnell

Village of Fochriw grunts among the higher hills, The. Idris Davies. AngWePo *Fr.* Gwalia Deserta.

Village of Reason, The. Michael Palmer. PtR

Village Patriarch, The. Ebenezer Elliott.
     "Five rivers, like the fingers of a hand." NOBRP

Village Revisited. Elwyn Brooks White. AmWit

Village Saturday, The. Giacomo Leopardi. NAWM-7v2, *tr. by* Ottavio M. Casale

Village Snow, Sitting at Night. Po Chü-i. NDACCP, *tr. by* David Hinton

Village Spa. Phyllis McGinley. OBCoV

Village! thy butcher's son, the steward now. Ebenezer Elliott. OBSV *Fr.* Splendid Village, The.

Village where they ring, A. Basho. TAL

Village with a thousand eaves. Buson. EH, *tr. by* Robert Hass

Village without bells, A. Basho. EH; NIL-7, *tr. by* Robert Hass

Village Woman. Margaret Gillies Brown. EdScPo

Village woman brings her five-year-old son, The. Ballad of Selling a Child. Wang Chiu-ssu. ColAnChi, *tr. by* Jonathan Chaves

Villagers all, this frosty tide. Kenneth Grahame. RSR *Fr.* Wind in the Willows, The.

Villagers who gather round. Spiel of [the] Three Mountebanks. John Crowe Ransom. MoAmPo

Villages Like Ghosts. Ivan Davidkov. CSCBP, *tr. by* Georgi Belev and Lisa Sapinkopf

Villages like ghosts will chase each other through the foggy fields. Villages Like Ghosts. Ivan Davidkov. CSCBP, *tr. by* Georgi Belev and Lisa Sapinkopf

Villain, The. W. H. Davies. AngWePo; MoBrPo

Villanelle: "Time can [*or* will] say nothing but I told you so." W. H. Auden. MoBrPo

Villanelle: "Crack is moving down the wall, The." Weldon Kees. StAl *Fr.* Five Villanelles.

Villanelle: "Every day our bodies separate." Marilyn Hacker. MakPoe

Villanelle: "It is the pain, it is the pain, endures." William Empson. HarvBoo; NAMCP V.1; NoAM; TRP; UV; WaAnP

Villanelle: "I've lost her now, my turtle-dove." Jean Passerat. WaAnP, *tr. by* Jay Parini

Villanelle VI. Judith Barrington. FFC

Villanelle at Sundown. Donald Justice. OxBoAm

Villanelle for the Middle of the Night. Jacqueline Osherow. MakPoe

Villanelle from a Sentence in a Poet's Brief Biography. Jacqueline Osherow. ExTi; WaAnP

Villanelle: Late Summer. Marilyn Hacker. WaAnP

Villanelle of Change. Edwin Arlington Robinson. WaAnP

Villanelle of His Lady's Treasures. Ernest Dowson. MakPoe

Villanelle of Marguerites. Ernest Dowson. MoBrPo

Villanelle of the Poet's Road. Ernest Dowson. OBMV

Ville de Nice, La. Kenneth Koch. AmWit

Villeggiature. Edith Nesbit. LW; PEW

Villon. Basil Bunting.
     "Remember, imbeciles and wits." NPeEn; OxBEV

Villon/Leadbelly. Yusef Komunyakaa. LPSFW

Villon's Straight Tip to All Cross Coves. W. E. Henley. OxAEP-2

Vimalakirti. Takahashi Shinkichi. ZenPo, *tr. by* Takashi Ikemoto and Lucien Stryk

Vimalakirti, Vaishali. Vimalakirti. Takahashi Shinkichi. ZenPo, *tr. by* Takashi Ikemoto and Lucien Stryk

Vimy Ridge. John Oxenham. SacPr

Vin du Masque. Kitasono Katsue. CAoMJL1, *tr. by* John Solt

Vincent. Peter Meinke. LiTh

Vincent Corbet[t], farther known[e]. Elegy upon the Death of His Own Father, An. Richard Corbet. NOSC

Vincent Ogé. George Boyer Vashon. APN-2

Vincent Watchman was shot. Pay Up or Else. Luci Tapahonso. ReTh

Vine a la Catedral porque dijeron que aquí encontraría a un tal Pedro. Ficción y las Cosas, La. Josué Ramírez. RMCMP

Vine, The. Robert Herrick. CavPo; EroLit; NAEL-6v1; NAEL-7v1; NoP-4; NoP-5

Vinegar of Cruelty. Kim Suyŏng. CAMKP, tr. by Young-Jun Lee

Vines. Pamela Alexander. AmAlph

Vines, The. William Greenway. PoDa

Vines grow up, around the coverlet. Dream of Frida, A. Judyth Hill. ICANM

Viney, go put on de kittle, I got one o' mastah's chickens. (LL) Accountability. Paul Laurence Dunbar. APN-2; NAAPv.1

Vineyard of My Beloved, The. Priscilla Jane Thompson. CBWP-2

Vineyard Place in My Care, A. Saunders Lewis. BBMWP, tr. by D. Myrddin Lloyd

Vino, Primero, Pura. Juan Ramón Jiménez. RaW

Vintage. Brendan Kennelly. ModIr Fr. Cromwell.

Vintage. Karen McKinnon. ICANM

Viola, cello, double bass, the distances. Kinds of Blue #41 Far Hills. Don McKay. OpeFie

Viola Recalls. Chris Terrio. IaFF

Viola, to Olivia. Mary Makofske. IaFF

Violante has commanded me to write. Sonnet All of a Sudden, A. Félix Lope de Vega Carpio. SpanPo, tr. by Dorren Bell

Viola's Song. Sir William Davenant. NOSC

Violence. Wendy Bishop. LiTh

Violence. Robert Lowell. NoAM

Violence, The. Gillian Conoley. MAAN

Violence of Oneness, The. Norman Fischer. Eno

Violence of Pronoun, The. Primus St. John. EGAG

Violence of the mind is the violence of god, The. Imamu Amiri Baraka. EGAG

Violent burning for prodigious beauty, A. Michelangelo Buonarroti. CAGL, tr. by James M. Saslow

Violent contrariety of men and days; calm. Geoffrey Hill. FaBoWar Fr. Mystery of the Charity of Charles Péguy, The.

Violent luck and a whole sample and even then quiet, A. Gertrude Stein. NAMCP V.1 Fr. Tender Buttons.

Violent order is disorder; and, A. Connoisseur of Chaos. Wallace Stevens. NAAPv.2; PFTM v.1

Violent storm, A. Abiding Mountain. Muso Soseki. EaWin, tr. by W. S. Merwin

Violently, because the acres were not smoothed with topsoil, she wrenches. Refusal. Carol Frost. PfSP

Violently vulnerable neck, The. (LL) Portraits of Tudor Statesmen. U. A. Fanthorpe. EmeKit; OxBEV

Violet. Arthur Symons.

  5. At Seventeen. OxBSo

Violet, The. Johann Wolfgang von Goethe. STV, tr. by John Frederick Nims

Violet, The. Jane Taylor. WoRP

Violet in the deepest green, A. Violet, The. Johann Wolfgang von Goethe. STV, tr. by John Frederick Nims

Violet loves a sunny bank, The. Proposal. Bayard Taylor. TreFP

Violets, Daffodils. Elizabeth Jane Coatsworth. TLR

Violets for Your Furs. Tom Adair. ReLy

Violin devil image on. Emmett Williams. PFTM-2 Fr. Ultimate Poem, The.

Violin which is following me, A. Conspiracy. Jack Spicer. APSN; CalPo

Violinist tamed the birds, The. Inside the Fence: Tule Lake Internment Camp. Kim R. Stafford. GifTon

Violins complain. Autumn Song. Paul Verlaine. WoPoe, tr. by Louis Simpson

Violins float in the sky. Europe, Late. Dan Pagis. HP, tr. by Stephen Mitchell

Violins tickling. Stephanie Koufman. PfS

Viper Light. Barbara Leslie Jordan. ExTi

Viper, The. Joseph Hilaire Pierre Belloc. NoAM

Viper, The. Nicanor Parra. TCLAP, tr. by W. S. Merwin

Vipers, Flies, and Women of the Cloth. James Coleman. BtF

Vir nullâ non donandus lauro. (LL) Winthrop Mackworth Praed. OBEV; OxAEP-2 Fr. Every Day Characters.

Vire will wind in other shadows. Saint-Lô. Samuel Beckett. NPeEn

Virgen de Plástico. Gloria Fuertes. RaW

Virgidemiarum Book 5. Joseph Hall.

  "Hous-keping's dead, *Saturio:* wot'st thou where?" PBRV

Virgidemiarum. Joseph Hall.

  "Gentle squire would gladly entertain, A." NoSic

  Olden Days, The. OBSV

  "Pardon, ye groaning ears; need will it out." NoSic

  "Sturdy ploughman doth the soldier see, The." OBSV

  "When Gullion died (who knows not Gullion?)." NoSic

  "Who doubts? The laws fell down from heaven's height." OBSV

Virgil, who brought great Aeneas to Laurentian lands. Publius Papinius Statius. RomPo Fr. Sylvae [or Silvae].

Virgin, The. Ruth Herschberger. OxBoAm

Virgin, The. Laura Riding Jackson. ChIV-2

Virgin and Child, by Hans Memmeling, A; in the Academy of Bruges. Dante Gabriel Rossetti. CenSon

Virgin at heart, A. Lost Daughter. Magdalena Gomez. PueRic

Virgin Forest, The. Aimé Césaire. SurPaPo, tr. by Clayton Eshleman and Annette Smith

Virgin Martyr, The. Ada Cambridge. NOBAu

Virgin Mary by the fire?, The. (LL) Joseph. G. K. Chesterton. ChIV-2; ChrPo

Virgin Mary, daughter of your Son. Dante Alighieri. NAWM-7v1 Fr. Divine Comedy, The (Mandelbaum Translation).

Virgin Mary, The. Unknown. OBWVE, tr. by Joseph P. Clancy

Virgin of the vestal flame. Vestal Virgin, The. Eloise Bibb. CBWP-4

Virgin of Troy, the days were well with thee. Studies from the Antique. Emily Jane Pfeiffer. ViWPN

Virgin, sing the Virgin Huntress. Ode 1.21. Horace. OBVE Fr. Odes.

Virginal, A. Ezra Pound. ColAP; MoAmPo; NAAPv.2; NIL-7; NIP-4; TCAPo Fr. Ripostes of Ezra Pound.

Virginal, vibrant, and beautiful dawn, The. Stéphane Mallarmé. NAWM-7v2, tr. by Henry Weinfield

Virginal, Vivid, Beautiful, Will This Be. Stéphane Mallarmé. WoPoe, tr. by Louis Simpson

Virginal, vivid, beautiful, will this be. Virginal, Vivid, Beautiful, Will This Be. Stéphane Mallarmé. WoPoe, tr. by Louis Simpson

Virginia. T. S. Eliot. FaBoA Fr. Landscapes.

Virginia Portrait. Sterling Allen Brown. GT; OxAAAP

Virginia Reel. Charles Wright. LPSFW

Virginia Woolf committed suicide in 1941 when the German bombing. Doubt. Fanny Howe. BAP-01

Virginia Woolf has Mrs. Dalloway stop. Fear No More. David Case. IaFF

Virginian Arcady. Anne Rouse. NeBl

Virginians of the Valley, The. Francis Orrery Ticknor. PCW

Virginia's writing her diary. Bloomsbury Snapshot. Connie Bensley. OBCoV

Virgin-Mother stood at distance (there), The. Observation. Robert Herrick. ChIV-2

Virgins, The. Derek Walcott. SoSe-8

Virgins are like the fair flower in its lustre. John Gay. NIL-7 Fr. Beggar's Opera, The.

Virgin's Lullaby, The. Unknown. RSR

Virgo, August. John Taylor. NOSC

Virgo Descending. Charles Wright. ColAP; TRP; WaAnP

Virgo Poem, The: Ouspensky Addresses a Congress of Virgoes. Charles Stein. AHA

Virtual Particles. Frank Wilczek. NBLV

Virtual Reality. Charles Bernstein. FTOS

Virtually whole they perceive it and name it Anagallis tenella. Allen Fisher. Oth Fr. Emergent Manner.

Virtue [or Vertue]. George Herbert. AmFaPo; BASC; ClHu; FSCP; HeIP-4; NAEL-6v1; NAEL-7v1; NoP-4; NoP-5; NOSC; OBEV; OPOU; OxBEV; SoSe-8; TFi; TreFP; WaAnP

Virtue: "All the houses are white." Cynthia Huntington. PoDa

Virtue alone can never die. but lives to. Hannah Taylor. FaBoVe

Virtue and compassion. No Gain. Muso Soseki. EaWin, tr. by W. S. Merwin

Virtue conceal'd within our breast. Jonathan Swift. OBVE

Virtue, dear friends, needs no 'defense.' Ode 1.22. Horace. OBVE Fr. Odes.

Virtue in a rear cup. Ode to the Seasons. Unknown. CATKP, tr. by Peter H. Lee

Virtue may choose the high or low degree. Alexander Pope. NPeEn; OBSV Fr. Epilogue to the Satires, in Two Dialogues.

Virtue may unlock hell, or even. Francis Thompson. MoBrPo Fr. Judgment in Heaven, A.

Virtue of Slovenliness, The. Geoffrey Holloway. NLP

Virtue Protests [or Epistle to Lord Byron]. Joseph Cottle. STuOW Fr. Expostulatory Epistle to Lord Byron, An.

Virtue was the sunset creeping in the grass. Lines on a Platonic Friendship. Daryl Hine. IllVoic

Virtue's branches wither, virtue pines. Thomas Dekker and others. NoSic Fr. Old Fortunatus.

Virtue's Goal Is God. "Angelus Silesius." GePo *Fr.* Cherubical Wanderer, The.

Virus². Jackie Kay. MFPA

Virus, The. Britton Wilkie. AHA

Virus nibbled the delicacy of my father's brain, A. In Hospital-land. Gillian Ferguson. MFPA

Visibility. Maura Stanton. BodElec

Visibility of Spirits, The. Laura Kasischke. SweBea

Visibility Trigger, The. Edward Kamau Brathwaite. WoBe

Visible Baby, The. Peter Redgrove. EmeKit

Visible, invisible. Jellyfish, A. Marianne Moore. ItP; NAAPv.2

Visible sea at a distance from the shore, The. Seamus Heaney. PoetW *Fr.* Squarings.

Vision. Delmira Agustini. TCLAP, *tr. by* Karl Kirchwey

Vision. Thomas Baker. STuOW *Fr.* Steam Engine; or, The Power of the Flame, The.

Vision. Harry Crosby. APT-2

Vision. James Devaney. NOBAu

Vision. Hesiod. WoPoe *Fr.* Theogony.

Vision. Robert Penn Warren. APT-2

Vision. May Thielgaard Watts. LW

Vision, A. John Clare. NAEL-6v2; NAEL-7v2; OxBEV

Vision, A. William Butler Yeats.
  All Souls' Night. OxAEP-2

Vision, The ("Methought I saw (as I did dream[e] in bed).") Robert Herrick. NOSC

Vision, The ("Sitting alone (as one forsook).") Robert Herrick. CavPo; PBRV

Vision (2). Sherman Alexie. UnSA

Vision V. William Browne. *See* 5.

Vision by Sweetwater. John Crowe Ransom. HarvBoo; OxBoAm

Vision from the Blue Window. Ernesto Cardenal. VCWP

Vision of a haloed host, The. Ultimate. G. K. Chesterton. SacPr

Vision of Beasts, A. John Heath-Stubbs. ChIV-1

Vision of Beauty, A. Ben Jonson. BASC; NOSC

Vision of Christ that thou dost see, The. William Blake. ChIV-2 *Fr.* Everlasting Gospel, The.

Vision of Columbus, The. Joel Barlow.
  "There reigns a prince, whose hand the sceptre claims." TCAPo

Vision of Eve, The. Henrietta Cordelia Ray. CBWP-3

Vision of Hiroshima. Oscar Hahn. TCLAP, *tr. by* Sandy McKinney

Vision of Judgement, A. Robert Southey.
  George III Enters Paradise. STuOW

Vision of Judgment, The. Lord Byron. NAEL-6v2
  "At length with jostling, elbowing, and the aid." OBSV
  Vision of Judgment, The. NPBRoP; NPeEn; OBSV; OxAEP-2

Vision of Judgment, The ("Saint Peter sat by the celestial gate.") Lord Byron. NPBRoP; NPeEn; OBSV; OxAEP-2 *Fr.* Vision of Judgment, The.

Vision of MacConglinne, The. MacConglinne. IrV, *tr. by* Kuno Meyer

Vision of Moonlight, A. Henrietta Cordelia Ray. CBWP-3

Vision of Myself, A. Hugh MacDiarmid. OxBEV

Vision of Niamh, The. Eva Gore-Booth. PoBW

Vision of Noah, The. May Kendall. VWP

Vision of Piers Plowman, The. William Langland. *tr. by* George Economou
  "Barones an burgeises and bondemen als." FaBoVe
  Confession of Gluttony. NAEL-6v1; NAEL-7v1
  Dreamer Meets Conscience and Reason. NAEL-6v1; NAEL-7v1
  "Envy with heavy heart asked for shrift." NAEL-6v1; NAEL-7v1
  Et Incarnatus Est. SacPr
  (Field of Folk, The.) NAEL-6v1; NAEL-7v1; NoP-5
  (Gluttony in the Ale-house.) NPeEn
  Incarnation, The. OBEV
  Piers Plowman Shows the Way to Saint Truth. NAEL-6v1; NAEL-7v1
  ""It is a kynde knowyng," quod she, "that kenneth in thine herte."" OxBEV
  Plowing of Piers's Half-acre, The. NAEL-6v1; NAEL-7v1
  (Prologue.) NPeEn; OxBEV
  "Thus I awoke, God knows, when I lived in Cornhill." WoPoe, *tr. by* George Economou
  Trinity, The. SacPr
  "Wool-chafed and wet-shoed I went forth after." NAEL-6v1; NAEL-7v1, *tr. by* Ethelbert Talbot Donaldson

Vision of Rahoon, A. John McAuliffe. NIrP

Vision of St. Michael and St. John, The. Jeremy Ingalls. YaYoPo

Vision of Salt & Water: Elijah's Horn. J. J. Blickstein. Vesp

Vision of Sir Launfal, The. James Russell Lowell.
  Prelude to Part the First. APN-1

Vision of Spring in Winter, A. Algernon Charles Swinburne. NPeEn

Vision of Sunday in Heaven, A. Victor James Daley. ChIV-2

Vision of the Graces, The. Edmund Spenser. NoSic *Fr.* Faerie Queene, The.

Vision of the Night, The. Philip Freneau. NAAL-3 *Fr.* House of Night, The.

Vision of Your Body. Daisy Zamora. LoL, *tr. by* Dinah Livingston

Vision: Second Poem of Wandering Immortals. Kuo P'o. CCL1, *tr. by* Graeme Wilson

Vision Shadows. Simon J. Ortiz. NAAL-5

Vision Test, The. Mona Van Duyn. FFC

Vision that appeared to me, A [*or* The]. Vision of MacConglinne, The. MacConglinne. IrV, *tr. by* Kuno Meyer

Vision upon the Fairy Queen, A. Sir Walter Ralegh. *See* Vision upon This Concei[p]t of the Faerie [*or* Faery] Queen[e], A.

Vision upon This Concei[p]t of the Faerie [*or* Faery] Queen[e], A. Sir Walter Ralegh. NoSic *Fr.* Commendatory Verses to Edmund Spenser's Fairy Queen.

Vision will come—the Truth be revealed—but, The. Vision. Robert Penn Warren. APT-2

Visionary, The [*see also* Julian M. and A. G. Rochelle *and* The Prisoner]. Emily Jane Brontë. NPeEn; OxBEV

Visionary theme!—a gorgeous shade!, A. (LL) Rejects the Influence of Reason. Mary Robinson. CenSon; RWP

Visions. William Browne.
  5. OBEV
  6. OxBSo
  (Vision V.) NOSC

Visions. Elsa Cross. TANSG, *tr. by* Patricia Dubrava

Visions. William Stafford. NoAM

Visions and Interpetations. Li-Young Lee. NIP-4

Visions Appear to her in a Dream. Mary Robinson. CenSon; RWP

40. Visions Appear to Her in a Dream. Mary Robinson. NPBRoP *Fr.* Sappho and Phaon.

Visions of Arthur. René Ricard. AHA

Visions of beauty, of light, and of love. Dreams of Beauty. Adah Isaacs Menken. CBWP-1

Visions of Jesus. Jerome Rothenberg. APSN

Visions of Mexico While at a Writing Symposium in Port Townsend, Washington. Lorna Dee Cervantes. NoAM

Visions of the Daughters of Albion. William Blake. CABP; NAEL-6v2; NAEL-7v2; NPBRoP
  "Infancy! fearless, lustful, happy, nestling for delight." OxAEP-2
  "Moment of desire! the moment of desire! the virgin, The." ErotSp; OxBEV
  "Then Oothoon waited silent all the day and all the night." NPeEn
  "With what sense is it that the chicken shuns the ravenous hawk?" OxBEV

Visions you never saw, The. Grandfather. Lance Henson. HATNAP, *tr. by* Lance Henson

Visit. Gerald William Barrax. GT

Visit. Tu Fu [*or* Du Fu]. NDACCP, *tr. by* William Carlos Williams

Visit, A. Anna Swirszczynska [*or* Swir]. CFP; PoSu, *tr. by* Czeslaw Milosz and Leonard Nathan

Visit, The: "Mary, more than quite contrary, bars the door." Lesley Duncan. EdScPo

Visit, The: "We were at the camp, it must have been." Wesley McNair. PoDa

Visit, The. NLP

Visit, The. Mary Bryan.
  "Here, said my guide." NPBRoP

Visit, The. Ralph Waldo Emerson. APN-1

Visit, The. Robert Glück.
  "Famous monk dropped to this knees before a giant image and cried, A." WiU
  "Odd to close my eyes during the day and open them at night." WiU
  "This image is alive with my longing for you." WiU

Visit, The. Ian Hamilton. NPeEn

Visit, The. Ibn Hazm al-Andalusi. WoPoe, *tr. by* Leticia Garza-Falcón and Christopher Middleton

Visit, The. Gene Shuford. TiP2

Visit, The. Toon Tellegen. TuT, *tr. by* Peter van de Kamp

Visit from Mr. Fox, A. *Unknown.* ChAP

Visit from St Nicholas, A. Clement Clarke Moore. APN-1; BLPJKO; BRP; ChAP; ChrPo; NTCP; OBCP; OxBoAm; TCAPo; TFi

Visit of the Gods, The [*ad. fr. the German of* Schiller]. Samuel Taylor Coleridge. OBVE

Visit of the Hawk. David Huddle. PfSP

Visit to Castletown House, A. Michael Hartnett. PBCIP

Visit to Fadin. Eugenio Montale. MotU, *tr. by* Charles Wright

Visit to Merlin, The. Edmund Spenser. NAEL-6v1; NAEL-7v1 *Fr.* Faerie Queene, The.

Visit to the British Museum. Frances Horovitz. MoWP

Visit to the Cities of Cheese, A. Margaret Johnson. OnScMo

Visit to the Hermit Ts'ui. Ch'ien Ch'i. NDACCP, tr. by Kenneth Rexroth

Visit to the House of the Poet—Nicaragua, 1987—Homage to Rubén Darío on His Birthday, A. Thomas McGrath. BodElec

Visit to the Palace of Venus. Irene Young. HW

Visit to the Village, A. Michael Smith. PBCIP

5. Visit to the Zoo, A. David McFadden. NLPA

Visit to Turk's Head Pub. Manuel Ulacia. RMCMP, tr. by Indran Amirthanayagam

Visita al Turk's Head Pub. Manuel Ulacia. RMCMP

Visitación. Mónica Nepote. SPV, tr. by Jen Hofer

Visitant, The. Fergus Allen. NIrP

Visitant, The. Theodore Roethke. TRP

Visitant Eclogue. John Kinsella. NeBl

Visitation. Jaime Jacinto. ReBoTo

Visitation. Max Jacob. YaTCFP, tr. by Moishe Black and Maria Green

Visitation. Max Jacob. YaTCFP

Visitation. Mónica Nepote. SPV, tr. by Jen Hofer

Visitation. Adriann Roland Holst. TuT, tr. by Paula Meehan

Visitation, The. Brigit Pegeen Kelly. YaYoPo

Visitation, The. Jan Owen. NOBAu

Visitation Rites. Jack Myers. ArBi

Visitations. Lawrence Durrell. MoBrPo Fr. Eight Aspects of Melissa.

Visited the jumping Jack, who moves all by himself. Diary Entry, January Seven. Elke Erb. OnScMo, tr. by Rosmarie Waldrop

Visiting. Alan Jenkins. NeBrP

Visiting conductor, A. Simple Story, A. Gwen Harwood. BeAl; NOBAu

Visiting Couple Kissing and Halved Onion. Greg Williamson. NoP-5

Visiting Dr Swift. Thomas Parnell and Alexander Pope. OBCoV

Visiting Emily Dickinson's Grave with Robert Francis. Robert Bly. MotU

Visiting Father. Juan Delgado. TouFir

Visiting Father and Friends. Allen Ginsberg. TaR

Visiting Hour. Stewart Conn. StAl

Visiting Hour. Lynda Hull. LaCa

Visiting Hour (Repatriation Hospital). Michael Dransfield. BMAP

Visiting Hours. John Alexander Frazier, Jr. BtF

Visiting Hours Are Over. Chana Bloch. PoA 2002

Visiting hours are over. Open Heart. Sekou Sundiata. SpirFl

Visiting Hsiang-Chi Monastery. Wang Wei. WoPoe, tr. by Eva Shan Chou

Visiting Jesus. Martin Birnbaum. Prolet, tr. by Amelia Glaser

Visiting Light. Jean Earle. TCAWP

Visiting My Gravesite: Talbott Churchyard, West Virginia. Irene McKinney. PBCAP

Visiting My Old Hut in Late Spring. Muso Soseki. EaWin, tr. by W. S. Merwin

Visiting New York. Sarah Rosenblatt. AmPoNex

Visiting Pai-an Pavilion. Hsieh Ling-yün. CrYelRi, tr. by Sam Hamill

Visiting the graves. Issa. EH, tr. by Robert Hass

Visiting the graves. Basho. EH, tr. by Robert Hass

Visiting the Graves. Ellen Bryant Voigt. LPSFW

Visiting the Hermit Cheng. Po Chü-i. TAL

Visiting the Monastery at Lung-men. Tu Fu [or Du Fu]. CrYelRi, tr. by Sam Hamill

Visiting the Mountain Hermitage of a Monk at Gan-hua Monastery. Wang Wei. CrYelRi, tr. by Sam Hamill

Visiting the Recluse Cheng. Po Chü-i. NDACCP, tr. by David Hinton

Visiting the Site of One of the First Churches My Grandfather Pastored. T. Crunk. YaYoPo

Visiting the West Bank. S. V. Atalla. PoArWo

Visiting Zan, Abbot of Dayun. Tu Fu [or Du Fu]. CCL1, tr. by Kenneth Rexroth

Visiting Zomba Plateau. Jack A. Mapanje. NAfrP

Visitor. Aleksandr Aleksandrovich Blok. TCRusP, tr. by Geoffrey Thurley

Visitor. Ingrid de Kok. TSAP

Visitor, A. Lewis Carroll. OBCoV

Visitor, A. Idea Vilariño. TANSG, tr. by Louise B. Popkin

Visitor, The. Anna Andreyevna Akhmatova. TCRusP, tr. by Daniel Weissbort

Visitor, The. W. H. Davies. OBWVE

Visitor, The. Carolyn Forché. OPOU

Visitor comes from Hungary as from outer space, A. Commonwealth, Common Poverty. Gloria Vando. TouFir

Visitor in Marl, A. Emily Dickinson. APN-2; TCAPo

Visitors. Tu Fu [or Du Fu]. BLT, tr. by Kenneth Rexroth

Visitors. Unknown. SonAtl, tr. by Alan Brierly

Visitor's Book, 8, The. John Davies. TCAWP

Visitor's Book, 9, The. John Davies. TCAWP

Visitor's Memories, The. Sandor Csoori. ConPit, tr. by Clayton Eshleman and Gyula Kodolanyi

Visitors to the Black Belt. Langston Hughes. NAAL-5

Visits from the Seventh. Sarah Arvio.
Mirrors. KGB

Visits of condolence is all we get from them. Tourists. Yehuda Amichai. PoSu, tr. by Glenda Abramson and Tudor Parfitt

Visored may, The. Portrait of My Father as the Boy of Winander. Jenny Mueller. IAoNAP

Víspera, La. José Ángel Valente. RaW

Vista. Faiz Ahmad Faiz. VCWP, tr. by Agha Shahid Ali

Vista. Elizabeth Garrett. NeBl

Vista Vert. David Chaloner. VaPo

Vita Nova. Louise Glück. NAMCP V.2; NoP-5

Vita Nuova, La. Dante Alighieri.
"Love and the gentle heart are one thing." NAWM-7v1, tr. by Dino Cervigni and Edward Vasta

Vitae Summa Brevis Spem Nos Vetat Incohare Longam. Ernest Dowson. CABP; NoP-4; NoP-5; NPeEn; OBEV; OxBEV; TFi
(Envoy: "They are not long, the weeping and the laughter.") MoBrPo
(They Are Not Long.) NAEL-6v2; NAEL-7v2

Vitaï Lampada. Sir Henry John Newbolt. FaBoWar; OBWP; UV

Vital, arrogant, fatal, dominant X, The. (LL) Motive for Metaphor, The. Wallace Stevens. APT-1; BrAP; MoAmPo; NAMCP V.1; OxBoAm

Vital spark of heavenly [or heav'nly] flame! Ode: The Dying Christian to His Soul. Alexander Pope. ChIV-2; SacPr

Vitamins and Roughage. Kenneth Rexroth. CalPo; NoAM; OxBoAm

Vitex in swamp ground. Ezra Pound. APT-1

Vive Le Sport. Harri Webb. TCAWP

Vivía en una casa. Ventanas Pintadas. Gloria Fuertes. RaW

Vivian, Take 57. BtF

Viviane est Viviane, oui. Emmanuel Hocquard. YaTCFP Fr. À Noël.

Viviane is Viviane, yes. Emmanuel Hocquard. OnScMo; YaTCFP Fr. At Christmas.

Vivid grass with visible delight, The. Castaways, The. Claude McKay. APT-1

Vivid summers of my kidhood were. James Brown. Linwood M. Ross. InTrad

Vivre L'Orange. Hélène Cixous.
"I urgency, I begged. Give me your dish, I said, icy." VCAP

Vixen. W. S. Merwin. GPTC

Vixen woman, The. Harold Monro. OBMV Fr. Natural History.

Vixi Puellis Nuper Idoneus. Sir Thomas Wyatt. See Lover Showeth How He Is Forsaken of Such as He Sometime Enjoyed, The.

V-J Day. John Ciardi. OtW; PWW2

Vladimirov was appointed. Safety Pins (excerpts). Radoi Ralin. CSCBP, tr. by Georgi Belev and Lisa Sapinkopf

Vlamertinghe. Edmund Charles Blunden. NoP-4; OBWP

V-Letter. Karl Shapiro. IllVoic; NoAM

Vocabulary. Ariel Dorfman. AF, tr. by Ariel Dorfman and Edith Grossman

Vocabulary of Dearness. Naomi Shihab Nye. CAP-8

Vocal texts evoke. Tom Weatherly. EGAG

Vocation. William Stafford. CAP-8

Vocational Guidance, with Special Reference to the Annunciation of Simone Martini. Richard Howard. BodElec

Vodka, whisky, gin. Scotch. Red wine, cognac. Loudmouth Soup. Thomas Lux. LaCa

Vodou Headwashing Ceremony. Andy Young. AnSo

VOG. Ron Silliman.
Compliance Engineering. BAP-04

Voice. Zbigniew Herbert. PoSu, tr. by Czeslaw Milosz

Voice. Ron Padgett. OxBoAm

Voice: "World put back on its." Jacqueline Risset. OnScMo, tr. by Jennifer Moxley

Voice. Ann Sansom. NeBl

Voice. Susan Wicks. MFPA

Voice, A. Yves Bonnefoy. YaTCFP, tr. by Hoyt Rogers

Voice, A. Tadeusz Rózewicz. BLT, tr. by Czeslaw Milosz

Voice, A. Lina Tibi. PoArWo, tr. by Subhi Hadidi and Nathalie Handal

Voice, A. Unknown. CA

Voice, A. Loneliness. Telly Wong. WhBo

Voice, A: "Voice hidden in midair, The." Ch'oe Sûngja. EcSo, tr. by Mickey Hong

Voice, The. May Muzaffar. PoArWo, tr. by Tahia Abdel Nasser

Voice and Address. Michael Palmer. FTOS; PmAP

Voice, because of its austerity, will often cause dust to rise, The. Recursus. Michael Palmer. APSN

Voice calling from the trees, A. Surprise. Scott Cairns. UpMys

Voice changed to a vinyl disc, a black larynx, A. New Release, A. Alice Fulton. AllShUp

Voice cried out in the wilderness, A. Trickster 2 (for Lee "Scratch" Perry). Kwame Dawes. WaCA

Voice fell, like a falling star, A / Excelsior! (LL) Excelsior. Henry Wadsworth Longfellow. BRP; GoPo; NAAL-3; OBSP; STuOW; TCAPo; UV

Voice for the Sirens, A. Maura Stanton. YaYoPo

Voice from the dark is calling me, A. Divorce. Anna Wickham. MoBrPo; NALW

Voice from the Dead, A. Mbuyiseni Oswald Mtshali. PML

Voice from the Factories, A. Caroline Elizabeth Norton. VWP *Fr.* Voice from the Factories, A.

Voice from the Factories, A. Caroline Elizabeth Norton.
"Fondly familiar is the look she gives." NPBRoP
Voice from the Factories, A. VWP

Voice from the Well [of Life Speaks to the Maiden], The. George Peele. NoSic

Voice hidden in midair, The. Voice, A. Ch'oe Sŭngja. EcSo, *tr.* by Mickey Hong

Voice is large, the man is small, The. Frog, A. Friedrich von Logau. GePo, *tr.* by George C. Schoolfield

Voice is never enough, The. Maysoun Saqr Al-Qasimi. PoArWo *Fr.* Morning of Every Sin, The.

Voice of Col. Von Stauffenberg Rising from Purgatory, The. Donald Justice. PoA 2002

Voice of Conscience, The. Murad Mikha'il. IrPoTo, *tr.* by Christina Coyle and Sadok Masliyah

Voice of Earth Mediums. Philip Lamantia. CLPP

Voice of Memory in Exile, from a Home in Ashes, The. William Gilmore Simms. AmWaPo

Voice of my beloved, The! behold, he cometh leaping upon the mountains, skipping upon the hills. Bible, *O.T.* BLPJKO

Voice of Pride: shout of blaring trumpets. Paul Verlaine. SxFrPo, *tr.* by Martin Sorrell

Voice of Spring, The. Felicia Dorothea Hemans. RWP

Voice of the drum slowly unravels, The. Poet, The. Clotaire Saint-Natus. OGAHCP, *tr.* by Boadiba and Jack Hirschman

Voice of the flute, The. Pei Dei and Wang Wei. CCL1 *Fr.* Wheel River.

Voice of the last cricket, The. Splinter. Carl Sandburg. SoSe-8; Spl

Voice of the Negro, The. Lizelia Augusta Jenkins Moorer. CBWP-3

Voice of the season talking to the oxen, The. (LL) You Will Forget. Chenjerai Hove. HBAPE; NAfrP; PLBUT

Voice of the Swallow, Flittering, Calls to Me, The. *Unknown.* WoPoe, *tr.* by John L. Foster

Voice of the swallow, flittering, calls to me, The. Voice of the Swallow, Flittering, Calls to Me, The. *Unknown.* WoPoe, *tr.* by John L. Foster

Voice of the Wheat, The. Jack Lindsay. RSaN

Voice of Things, The. Thomas Hardy. HarvBoo

Voice of water as it flows and falls, The. Lament for Passenger Pigeons. Judith Wright. HarvBoo

Voice on horseback, The. I listen to the breaths, the salivation. I listen to the. Speech Poem. Laura Solórzano. SPV, *tr.* by Jen Hofer

Voice on the winds, A. To Morfydd. Lionel Pigot Johnson. MoBrPo; OBMV

Voice out of the Sabbaths, A. Derek Walcott. WeW-3

Voice peals in this end of night, A. Thrush before Dawn, A. Alice Thompson Meynell. MoBrPo

Voice said, "Hurl her down!,"The. Lovely Shall Be Choosers, The. Robert Frost. MoAmPo

Voice said We are at War, The. Second World War, The. Elizabeth Jennings. ItWoWo

Voice that beautifies the land!, The. *Unknown.* APN-2 *Fr.* Mountain Chant, The.

Voice that came out of her, The. Callas. Edward Field. BodElec

Voice that would reach you, Hunter, must speak, The. To Roosevelt. Rubén Darío. PFTM-1; TCLAP, *tr.* by Lysander Kemp

Voice, The. Thomas Hardy. HarvBoo; InoFa; NAEL-6v2; NAEL-7v2; NAMCP V.1; NoAM; NoP-4; NoP-5; NPeEn; OxAEP-2; OxBEV; TFi

Voiceless, The. Oliver Wendell Holmes. APN-1 *Fr.* Autocrat of the Breakfast Table, The.

Voiceless, without a voice, seeking areas of consciousness without you. Epode. "H. D." MotU

Voices. Frances Bellerby. MoWP

Voices. Wanda Coleman. BrAP

Voices. Nora Dauenhauer. HATNAP

Voices. Sumaiya El-Sousy. PoArWo, *tr.* by Atef Abu-Seif and Nathalie Handal

Voices. Primo Levi. AF, *tr.* by Ruth Feldman

Voices. Wisława Szymborska. PoSu, *tr.* by Magnus F. Krynski

Voices: "When I hear my lover singing, I sing, too." F. D. Reeve. PoDa

Voices: "Yes, this is my voice." Nesta Wyn Jones. BBMWP, *tr.* by Anthony Conran

Voices (an Excerpt). Antonio Porchia. TAPaP, *tr.* by W. S. Merwin

Voices Are Coming Up, The. Frances Payne Adler. FiBr

Voices are crying an unknown name in the sky. (LL) Epistle to Be Left in the Earth. Archibald MacLeish. APT-1; MoAmPo

Voices at the Window. Sir Philip Sidney. *See* Eleventh Song: "Who is it that this dark[e] night."

Voices: be quiet. go away. Wanda Coleman. CalPo

Voices dabbed on the outhouse walls. Things, As They Are. Dianne Edenfield Edwards. ICANM

Voices fade as he walks. Sweet Dreams. Christian Wiman. AmPoNex

Voices from the Other World. James Merrill. CAP-8; VCAP

Voices from Things Growing in a Churchyard. Thomas Hardy. FaBoVe

Voices moving about in the quiet house. Falling Asleep. Siegfried Sassoon. MoBrPo

Voices mute for ever, or since yesterday, or just stilled;. Voices. Primo Levi. AF, *tr.* by Ruth Feldman

Voices of death are sounding. Death of Antoñito el Camborio. Federico García Lorca. SpanPo, *tr.* by Robert O'Brien

Voices of Poor People. Czeslaw Milosz.
Poor Christian Looks at the Ghetto, A. HP; PoSu; VCWP, *tr.* by the author
Song on the End of the World, A. FaoP; WoPoe, *tr.* by Tony Milosz

Voices of the Rain. Henrietta Cordelia Ray. CBWP-3

Voices play at will. Under a Wing. Fedya Filkova. CSCBP, *tr.* by Georgi Belev and Lisa Sapinkopf

Voices, single row of nights. They Shall Know. Kofi Awoonor. VCWP

Voici mûrs, ces fruits d'un ombrageux destin, Les. Nocturne. "St.-John Perse." YaTCFP

Voicing Deepest Thoughts. Yu Xuanji. CCL1, *tr.* by Genevieve Wimsatt

Void inside us, The. Void, The. G. M. Muktibodh. WoPoe, *tr.* by Vinay Dharwadker

Void has collapsed upon the earth, The. Zekkai Chushin. ZenPo, *tr.* by Takashi Ikemoto and Lucien Stryk

Void in Form. Ikkyu Sojun. ZenPo, *tr.* by Takashi Ikemoto and Lucien Stryk

Void Only. Kenneth Rexroth. WhBo *Fr.* Silver Swan, The.

Void, The. G. M. Muktibodh. WoPoe, *tr.* by Vinay Dharwadker

Voiler la sainte face. Contrefable d'Orphée. Marie-Claire Bancquart. YaTCFP

Voir Dire. Elise Paschen. PoDa

Voix, Une. Yves Bonnefoy. YaTCFP

Volcanic Ash. Peter Sears. UrbNat

Volcanic smoke of Mount Aso, The. Afterimages. Takahashi Shinkichi. ZenPo, *tr.* by Takashi Ikemoto and Lucien Stryk

Volcanic tuff. Tina Darragh. FTOS

Volcano. Ivan Van Sertima. CA

Volcano has snow on top, concealing. Dangers of Looking Back, The. Cynthia MacDonald. AFaM

Volcano is dark and suddenly thunder, The. Volcano is Dark, The. Malcolm Lowry. CLPP

Volcano is Dark, The. Malcolm Lowry. CLPP

Volcano rumbles, The. Kilimanjaro. Hélène d'Oettingen. CuPo

Volcanoes, The. José Santos Chocano. TCLAP, *tr.* by Andrew Rosing

Volcanoes be in Sicily. Emily Dickinson. NAAPv.1; NALW; OxWW

Volga Towns, The. Johannes Bobrowski. PoSu, *tr.* by Matthew Mead and Ruth Mead

Volière, La. Saint-Pol Roux. YaTCFP

Volkswagen parked in the gap, The. Ireland. Paul Muldoon. PBCIP

Volpone, childless, rich, feigns sick, despairs. Ben Jonson. NAEL-7v1 *Fr.* Volpone.

Volpone. Ben Jonson. NAEL-7v1

Volpone. Ben Jonson. NAEL-7v1, *tr.* by Ben Jonson
(Carmina V and VII [To the Same].) OBVE
"Good morning to the day; and, next, my gold." OxBEV
"I feare, I shall begin to grow in love." OxBEV
(To Celia.) OxAEP-1
Song. To Celia. AEP; BrAP; NIL-7; NoP-4; NoP-5; NPeEn; OBVE; OxBEV; PoPoPo; TFi; WaAnP
To the Same [Celia]. EroLit; NOSC

Voluntaries. Ralph Waldo Emerson. APN-1; CBCWP
[In an Age of Fops and Toys]. NAAPv.1

Voluntary Servitude. Mark Wunderlich. LegDan

Volunteer, The. Herbert Asquith. OBWP

Volunteers. Hilda Raz. ExTi

Volunteers, The. Charles MacKay.
Challenge, A. STuOW

Volunteer's Fairy Tale, A. Fred Moramarco. PML

Volunteer's Reply to the Poet, The. Roy Campbell. FaBoWar

Volupté est la plus puissante sensation que nous ayons de la vitesse, La. Malcolm de Chazal. YaTCFP *Fr.* Sens plastique (1948).

Voluptuaries and Others. Margaret Avison. BrAP

Von Aschenbach thinks as the tide comes in. Death in Venice. Jim Wilson. EdScPo

Voracious Time, uprooting all, consumes it. Seneca. RomPo, *tr. by* Marcus Wilson

Vorkuta. Horst Bienek. AF

Vote for Lunn. *Unknown.* FaBoVe

Vote, The. Del Ray Cross. FreRad

Vote, The. Ralph Knevet. FaBoWar; NOSC

Votive Candles. Nick Carbó. NeAmPo

Voucher. Michael Portnoy. HeMarv

Voudou Mama. Mawiyah Kai el-Jamah Bomani. BtF

Vow. Nina Nyhart. PfS

Vow 2. Pam Rehm. IIR

Vow, A. Allen Ginsberg. CLPP; OBWP

Vow, The. Anthony Hecht. TaR

Vow, The. Galway Kinnell. VCAP

Vowels. Arthur Rimbaud. SxFrPo, *tr. by* Martin Sorrell

Vowels and consonants into neat stacks. (LL) Dance of the Letters. Vince Gotera. FTtHH; OpBo

Vowels of Another Language, The. Thomas M. Disch. PoA 2002

Vows. Shirley Kaufman. TaR

Vows are vain. No suppliant breath. William Habington. NOSC *Fr.* Castara.

Vox Angelica. Timothy Liu. NeAmPo; WiU

Vox Pacifica. George Wither. "*Sun* hath run his course through all the Signes, The." PBRV

Vox Ultima Crucis. John Lydgate. OBEV

Voy a Correr por la Sombra. Juan Ramón Jiménez. RaW

Voyage. Antonio Deltoro. RMCMP, *tr. by* Christian Viveros-Fauné

Voyage, A. W. H. Auden. Sphinx, The. OxBSo

Voyage, The. Charles Baudelaire. NAWM-7v2, *tr. by* Charles Henri Ford

Voyage, The: "At first I was overly cautious, procedure being all-important." Charles Wright. MotU

Voyage à l'Infini. Walter Conrad Arensberg. APT-1

Voyage of Life, The. Thomas Cole. "As the broad mountain where the shadows flit." APN-1

Voyage on the Thames, The. Alexander Pope. OxAEP-1 *Fr.* Rape of the Lock, The: An Heroi-Comical Poem in Five Cantos.

Voyage to Cythera, A. Charles Baudelaire. SxFrPo, *tr. by* James McGowan

Voyage to Cythera, A. Charles Baudelaire. WoPoe, *tr. by* Frederick Morgan

Voyage to Labrador. GS

Voyage to Marryland, A; or, The Ladies Dressing Room. Mary Evelyn. EMWP

Voyage to the Isle of Love, A. Aphra Behn. Dream, The. RACG

Voyage to the Moon ("Wanderer in our skies.") Archibald MacLeish. OtW

Voyage West. Archibald MacLeish. APT-1

Voyage within you, on the fabled ocean. Terra Australis. James Philip McAuley. NOBAu

Voyager. Ken Morrice. EdScPo

Voyager, The. Guillaume Apollinaire. CuPo

Voyager's Song, The. Edward Coote Pinkney. APN-1

Voyages. Hart Crane. APT-2; CAGL; NAAPv.2; NAMCP V.1; NoAM; NoP-5 "And yet this great wink of eternity." ColAP; MoAmPo; OxBoAm; RaBo; TRP; WaAnP; WoPoe "Infinite consanguinity it bears." AmFaPo; ColAP "Meticulous, past midnight in clear rime." ColAP; NAAL-5 "Where icy and bright dungeons lift." ColAP; MoAmPo "Whose counted smile of hours and days, suppose." ColAP

Voyages. Jules Supervielle. MFP, *tr. by* Martin Sorrell

Voyaging. Charles Baudelaire. SxFrPo, *tr. by* James McGowan

Voyce of Anne Askewe out of the 54. Psalme of David, Called, Deus in Nomine Tuo, The. Anne Askew. EMWP

Voyelles. Arthur Rimbaud. WoPoe, *tr. by* F. Scott Fitzgerald

Voyeur. Sandra M. Castillo. LiTh

Voyeur. David Moolten. BloBone

Voyeur, The. Dana Gioia. MAAN

Voyeur's Dream. Barney Bush. HATNAP

Voyez ce mulet là, Musieu Bainjo. Musieu Bainjo. *Unknown.* SSUS

Voz de la Gente. Jimmy Santiago Baca. PmAP

V's Farmhouse. Lisa Fishman. AmPoNex

Vu de ce côté-ci ("De l'horizon il se.") Anne Portugal. YaTCFP

Vu de ce côté-ci ("Vu de ce côté-ci.") Anne Portugal. YaTCFP

Vuelo. Pedro Serrano. RMCMP

Vuelvo al Cielo Mis Ojos. Emilio Prados. RaW

Vuillard Interior. Elise Partridge. IFF

Vulcan Forges the Shield of Achilles. Homer. OBVE *Fr.* Iliad, The.

Vulgar of manner, overfed. Owed to New York. Byron Rufus Newton. NBLV

Vulgar paw-prints on the BMW. Carmel. Dennis Schmitz. GeoHom

Vulnerability. Fedya Filkova. CSCBP, *tr. by* Georgi Belev and Lisa Sapinkopf

Vulture. Robinson Jeffers. APT-1; NAMCP V.1; NoAM

Vulture. X. J. Kennedy. OWoS

Vulture, The. Joseph Hilaire Pierre Belloc. OWoS

Vulture eats between his meals, The. Vulture, The. Joseph Hilaire Pierre Belloc. OWoS

Vulture ravishes a rabbit, The. Gold talons. Appetite, the Great Painting. Nance Van Winckel. RoV

Vultures. Margaret Atwood. OWoS

Vultures, The. David Diop. WoPoe, *tr. by* Ulli Beier and Gerald Moore

Vultures Grow Impatient, The. Amina Saïd. HAWP; NAfrP, *tr. by* Eric Sellin

Vultures grow impatient, The. Vultures Grow Impatient, The. Amina Saïd. HAWP; NAfrP, *tr. by* Eric Sellin

Vulture's very like a sack, The. Vulture. X. J. Kennedy. OWoS

Vultures—in the Midst of War. Shaku Chōkū. CAoMJL1, *tr. by* Makoto Ueda

Vulva Operetta. Jessica Tarahata Hagedorn. ReBoTo

W

W. James Reeves. NOxBChV; NTCP

W / A / L / WHITMAN. [Walt Whitman]. Edwin Honig. ViWalt

W.C. Fields in French Light. Rochelle Owens. "It is for me poetry." PFTM-2

W. C. W. Watching Presley's Second Appearance on The Ed Sullivan Show: Mercy Hospital, Newark, 1956. David Wojahn. AllShUp; SwNoth

W. H. Louise Imogen Guiney. APN-2

W. L. M. K. Francis Reginald Scott. BrAP

W/outRomans / (Niew Yorc & Sun in hydra). Orgasm 0. Steve Jonas. EGAG

W. resteth here, that quick could never rest. Excellent Epitaffe of Syr Thomas Wyat, An. Henry Howard, Earl of Surrey. NPeEn

W. W. Imamu Amiri Baraka. HeIP-4

Wa ta se Na ka mo ni, Vietnam Memorial. Ray A. Young Bear. *See* Wadasa Nakamoon, Vietnam Memorial.

Wabash Cannonball, The. Delmore Brothers. GM

Wad be my queen, wad be my queen. (LL) O[h] Wert Thou in the Cauld Blast. Robert Burns. FaBoVe; NePenScot; NoP-4; NoP-5; NPeEn; OxAEP-2; PoPoPo

Wadasa Nakamoon, Vietnam Memorial. Ray A. Young Bear. HATNAP (Wa ta se Na ka mo ni, Vietnam Memorial.) AmWaPo

Wade in the water. New Miz Praise de Lawd, The. Nicole Breedlove. InTrad

Wade in this spirit, work, water, code. Five Note Range of Sorrow. Honorée Fanonne Jeffers. AnSo

Wade / through black jade. Fish, The. Marianne Moore. APT-1; BrAP; ColAP; EMP; GPTC; MoAmPo; NAAPv.2; NAMCP V.1; NoAM; NoP-4; NoP-5; OxBoAm; WaAnP

Wade's Hoggers. Debbra Palmer. FiBr

Wading through it. Buson. EH, *tr. by* Robert Hass

Wading up Brunigill's rush. October, Isle of Skye. Carter Revard. NoP-4

Waes-hael for [the] knight and [the] dame! King Arthur's Waes-hael. Robert Stephen Hawker. OBEV

Wag ballock wag. *Unknown.* FaBoVe

Wagers. Marilyn Hacker. RA

Wages of art, The! A month in an ex-fort on Puget Sound. White in the Woods. Jan Clausen. RWB

Wages of Love. C. D. Wright. CAP-8

Wages of sin is death. These words run, The. AIDS, Among Other Things. Peter Kocan. ChIV-2

Waggin' O' Our Dog's Tail, The. Norman Macleod. DiBP

Wagon Full of Thunder. Louis Oliver. HATNAP

Wagon is going to the woods, The. The woods. Where Is the Wagon Going? Meret Oppenheim. SurWo, *tr. by* Catherine Schelbert

Wagon stopped before the house, A; she heard. Edna St. Vincent Millay. NALW *Fr.* Sonnets from an Ungrafted Tree.

Wagons clang and horses cry. Song of the War Wagons. Tu Fu [*or* Du Fu]. CrYelRi, *tr. by* Sam Hamill

Wahiawa is still. Leaving. Cathy Song. NoAM

Wahsah Zeh (War Dance)—As Long as the Grass. Joseph Bruchac. AtGh

Wai', Mister Mackright, an' 'e yedde what Satan say. Wait, Mr. Mackright. *Unknown.* SSUS

Wai', my brudder, better true believe. My Body Rock 'Long Fever. *Unknown.* SSUS

Wai', poor Daniel, He lean on de Lord's side. Lean on the Lord's Side. *Unknown.* SSUS

Wail of Heights, The. Wafaa' Lamrani. PoArWo, *tr. by* Richard McKane and Tahia Abdel Nasser

Wail of the Divorced. Mary E. Tucker. CBWP-1

Wail of the Waiter, The. Marcus Clarke. NOBAu

Wail, wail, Ah for Adonis! He is lost to us, lovely Adonis! Lament for Adonis. Bion. WaAnP, *tr. by* John Addington Symonds

Wailed for the golden years. (LL) Percy Bysshe Shelley. HeIP-4; NAEL-6v2; NAEL-7v2 *Fr.* Hellas.

Wailer. Kim Sünghŭi. EcSo, *tr. by* K. Kim Richards and Steffen Richards

Wailing. Abd al-Rahim Salih al-Rahim. IrPoTo, *tr. by* Saadi A. Simawe and Daniel Weissbort

Wailing a state which can no comfort give. (LL) Mary Sidney Wroth, Countess of Montgomery. NAEL-6v1; NAEL-7v1

Wailing "don't be cruel." (LL) On the Elvis Mailing List. Neal Bowers. AllShUp; SwNoth

Wailing, wailing, wailing, the wind over land and sea. Rizpah. Alfred Tennyson. NPeEn

(Wailing, wailing, wailing, the wind over the land and sea.) RACG

Wailing wind doth not enough despair, The. Awake. Mary Elizabeth Coleridge. ViWPN

Wain upon the northern steep, The. Astronomy. A. E. Housman. NoP-4; NoP-5; OBWP

Waist, A. Gertrude Stein. NAAPv.2; NAMCP V.1 *Fr.* Tender Buttons.

Wait. Charles Bernstein. PmAP

Wait! *Unknown.* WoPoe *Fr.* Popul Vuh, The.

Wait, A.
    "Old anorak green." Oth

Wait a minute, Death. Rāmprasād Sen. SinGod, *tr. by* Rachel Fell McDermott

Wait a moment, Death. Tāpas Rāy. SinGod, *tr. by* Rachel Fell McDermott

Wait for evening. Become Becoming. Li-Young Lee. FaoP

Wait for the moonlight. Ryokan. EMJL, *tr. by* Burton Watson

Wait here, and I'll be back, though the hours divide. Three Star Final. Conrad Potter Aiken. PWW2

Wait Mister. Which way is home? Music Swims Back to Me. Anne Sexton. ColAP; MiVo; VCAP

Wait, Mr. Mackright. *Unknown.* SSUS

Wait somewhere to be burnt. (LL) Time Past, A. Denise Levertov. NAMCP V.2; NoAM

Wait Till You See Her. Lorenz Hart. ReLy

Wait to scatter. Spring. Iio Sogi. WoPoe, *tr. by* Steven D. Carter

Wait until this year's plums. Plum Crazy. Kate Sontag. SweBea

Waiter, Please. *Unknown. See* Limerick: "Epicure, Dining at Crewe, An."

Waitin for Jimmy Reed. Nightclub, A: on the Jacksboro Highway. Robert Trammell. TiP2

Waitin on Summer. Ruth Forman. SpirFl

Waiting. Raymond Carver. GoPo

Waiting. Cho Chihun. CAMKP, *tr. by* Kyung-Ja Chun

Waiting. W. E. Henley. NAEL-6v2; NAEL-7v2; NPeEn *Fr.* In Hospital.

Waiting. "Isolation of exile is a gutted, The." Arthur Nortje. HBAPE; TSAP

Waiting. Elaine Randell. Oth *Fr.* Snoad Hill Poems, The.

Waiting. Rayaprolu Subbarao. HotL, *tr. by* V. Narayana Rao

Waiting. Jean Valentine. YaYoPo

Waiting. William Carlos Williams. SAmP

Waiting. Donald Woods. CAGL

Waiting: "After the fervor." Shirley Kaufman. TAPaP

Waiting at Cerbere. Sylvia Townsend Warner. MoWP

Waiting beside my father's bed, watching the pleated sleep, the small breathing. Bedside. Diana O'Hehir. InoFa

Waiting Both. Thomas Hardy. MoBrPo

Waiting brief for milkmaid mornstar and worldrise. (LL) Anglo Saxon Street. Earle Birney. HeIP-4; NIL-7

Waiting for a Ride. Gary Snyder. WANABP

Waiting for a spirit to trouble the water. River Steamer, The. Edith Jay Scovell. HarvBoo

Waiting for a traffic break. Traffic interlude: Descent from the Tower. Douglas Livingstone. TSAP

Waiting For Breakfast, While She Brushed Her Hair. Philip Larkin. NoAM

Waiting for Claude is an all-day affair. Waiting for Claude. Philip Whalen. AHA

Waiting for Icarus. Muriel Rukeyser. OtW; OxBoAm

Waiting for me. For Her Lover. Lady Ishikawa. AHA

Waiting for My Love. Nŭngun. CATKP, *tr. by* Peter H. Lee

Waiting for Robinson. Roberta Hill Whiteman. HATNAP

Waiting for sleep at the air roots. Ivano Fermini. ItPo, *tr. by* Gayle Ridinger

Waiting for the Barbarians. Constantine P. Cavafy. FaBoWar, *tr. by* Edmund Keeley

Waiting for the Barbarians. Constantine P. Cavafy. GPTC; WoPoe, *tr. by* Edmund Keeley and Philip Sherrard

Waiting for the Barbarians. Constantine P. Cavafy. AF; BLT; PoAgWa; PtR, *tr. by* Edmund Keeley and Philip Sherrard

Waiting for the elevated train. Armitage Street. David Hernandez. UnSA

Waiting for the end, boys, waiting for the end. Just a Smack at Auden. William Empson. MoBrPo; OBCoV

Waiting for the End of Time. Kelly Cherry. LPSFW

Waiting for the flesh that dies. (LL) Bull, The. Ralph Hodgson. MoBrPo; OBMV

Waiting for the Invasion. Barbara Kingsolver. AtGh

Waiting for the keys. La Berline Arrētée Dans la Nuit. O. V. de L. Milosz. GifTon, *tr. by* Kenneth Rexroth

Waiting for the Results of a Pregnancy Test. Maria Gillan. BRtP

Waiting for the Storm. Timothy Steele. MakPoe

Waiting for weeks till the last one is ready to run, they. Turtles Hatching. Mark O'Connor. NOBAu

Waiting for what? Taneda Santoka. CAoMJL1, *tr. by* Burton Watson

Waiting for when the sun an hour or less. In Santa Maria del Popolo. Thom Gunn. HarvBoo; NPeEn

Waiting for whose hands to pick it up. (LL) Karl Shapiro. BodElec; IllVoic *Fr.* Bourgeois Poet, The.

Waiting for you. For You. Prince Otsu. AHA

Waiting, I rest in the waiting gate. Lich Gate, The. Clayton Eshleman. PmAP

Waiting Laughters. Niyi Osundare.
    "And the snake says to the toad." NAfrP

Waiting Lists, The. Jackie Kay. NeBl

Waiting on Elvis, 1956. Joyce Carol Oates. AllShUp; PoA 2002; SwNoth

Waiting Room. U. A. Fanthorpe. PoCu

Waiting room, The. Michelle Grangaud. SCFWP, *tr. by* Serge Gavronsky

Waiting Room in August, A. Julia Darling. PoCu

Waiting Rooms. Howard Nemerov. PoA 2002

Waiting to leave all day I hear the words. Gates, The. Muriel Rukeyser. BodElec

Waiting to whimper or for Messiah. In the Jury Room, in Pain. Paul Goodman. BodElec

Waiting up, he's deep in Angels and Archangels. Learning the Angels. Rennie McQuilkin. PoDa

Waiting Wife. Marcella Siegel. TiP2

Waiting with lowered voice. Jacques Dupin. VCWP

Waiting-rooms. David Vogel. FIT, *tr. by* Robert Friend

Waitress. Jason Shinder. ReTh

Waitress's Kid, The. Peggy Shumaker. PBCAP

Waits in unhope. (LL) Thomas Hardy. HarvBoo; NAMCP V.1; NoAM *Fr.* In Tenebris.

Waka. Lindley Williams Hubbell. APT-2

Wake. Tess Gallagher. InoFa; StAl

Wake. Langston Hughes. OBCoV

Wake. Yekhi'el Khazak. NRoS, *tr. by* Esther Raizen

Wake. Giuseppe Ungaretti. WoPoe, *tr. by* George Garrett

Wake. Kevin Young. OxAAAP

Wake, baillie, wake! the crafts are out. Winding-up Time. Jean Ingelow. VWP

Wake, eat, and drink, evacuate, and sleep. (LL) Human Life. Matthew Prior. OBCoV; OxBEV

Wake for Papa Montero. Nicolás Guillén. PFTM-1

Wake! For the Sun, who scattered into flight. Rubáiyát of Omar Khayyám [of Naishápúr], The. Omar Khayyám. NAEL-6v2; NAEL-7v2; NoP-4; NoP-5; TRP, *tr. by* Edward Fitzgerald

Wake, friend, from forth thy lethargy; the drum. Ben Jonson. FaBoWar *Fr.* Epistle to a Friend, to Persuade Him to the Wars, An.

Wake me up at eleven, she says. I want to watch the news, she. Shooting, Killing, Drug Busts, Cover-Ups, Fuck-Ups, Lighter Sides, Weather, and Sports. Bruce Jackson. AmPoNex

Wake Not for the World-heard Thunder. A. E. Housman. NoAM

Wake, O my soul; awake, and raise. Hymn, An. Phineas Fletcher. NOSC

Wake of Plenty, The. Roy Scheele. MotU

Wake: the silver dusk returning. A. E. Housman. CABP; HarvBoo; MoBrPo; NoP-4; NoP-5 *Fr.* Shropshire Lad, A.

Wake to find everything black. Negative. Kevin Young. LegDan

Wake up at six o'clock. We're out to sea. Painting It In. Anne Stevenson. PfSP

Wake Up (Call). Bill Berkson. AHA

Wake Up, Jacob. *Unknown.* SSUS

Wake up, Jacob, day is a-breaking, I'm on my way. Wake Up, Jacob. *Unknown.* SSUS

Wake up, my heart, get out of bed. Priest in the Sabbath Dawn Addresses His Somnolent Mistress, A. Peter Didsbury. EmeKit

Wake Up, My Little Pretties. Liza Jessie Peterson. BRtP

Wake up, Syama, wake up, Syama! Najrul Islām. SinGod, *tr. by* Rachel Fell McDermott

Wake up. The alarm of my clock says 6:30. Hey. Allan Kaplan. AHA

Wake up, wake up, Mother! Dāśarathi Rāy. SinGod, *tr. by* Rachel Fell McDermott

Wake up Woman! Arise to the Day's Toil. Assumpta Acam-Oturu. HAWP

Wake up, / you'll need your wits about you. Mrs. Adam. Kathleen Norris. PoA 2002

Wake Up, Yousif. Yousif al-Sa'igh. IrPoTo, *tr. by* Ralph Saverese and Saadi A. Simawe

Waked [*or* Wak'd] by the Gospel's Powerful Sound [*with music*]. Samson Occom. TCAPo

Wakeful in the Township. Elizabeth Riddell. NOBAu

Wakeful they lie. (LL) Counting the Beats. Robert Graves. HarvBoo; OxAEP-2; WeW-3; WoPoe

Wakening. Robert Melançon. YaTCFP, *tr. by* Philip Stratford

Wakening, The. *Unknown.* OBEV

Waking. Anne Simpson. IFF

Waking. Tristan Tzara. AF

Waking. Sheila Wingfield. StAl

Waking, The. Galway Kinnell. BodElec

Waking, The. Theodore Roethke. OxBoAm

Waking, The ("I wake to sleep, and take my waking slow.") Theodore Roethke. AmFaPo; APT-2; BrAP; HeIP-4; IJHIL; ITBLP; MakPoe; MoAmPo; NAAL-5; NAMCP V.1; NIL-7; NIP-4; NoAM; NoP-4; NoP-5; OxBoAm; PoPoPo; RaBo; StAl; TFi; VCAP; WaAnP; WeW-3; WoPoe

Waking at the Middle of Nowhere. Reg Saner. PoCoUp

Waking At The Mouth Of The Willow River. Don McKay. OpeFie

Waking Early Sunday Morning. Robert Lowell. HarvBoo; NAMCP V.2; OxBoAm; VCAP

Waking from a Nap. Chungji. BecRai, *tr. by* Kim Daljin, Kim Won-Chung and Christopher Merrill

Waking from a nap. Richard Wright. NoP-5

Waking from a Nap on the Beach. May Swenson. NTCP

Waking from Sleep. Robert Bly. NoP-4; NoP-5

Waking from violence: the surgeon's probe left in the foot. For a Friend in Travail. Adrienne Rich. NAAL-5

Waking Here. Scott Cairns. UpMys

Waking himself. Sixty-Six. Philip Booth. BodElec

Waking in March. Philip Levine. CalPo

Waking in silence and, through tilted blinds. Window at Key West, A. Honor Moore. KGB; WiU

Waking in the Blue. Robert Lowell. AmFaPo; MoAmPo; NAMCP V.2

Waking Intuitively. Quintus Catulus. WoPoe, *tr. by* Janet Lembke

Waking intuitively in the rosegray light of rising sun. Waking Intuitively. Quintus Catulus. WoPoe, *tr. by* Janet Lembke

Waking is this easy. Aubade. Marilyn Chin. NIP-4

Waking, months after I leave the jungle. Ansel Talvikki. YaYoPo *Fr.* In Fragments, In Streams.

Waking on a Summer Morning. Mary Oliver. PoCoUp

Waking / on the train, I thought. Venice, Unaccompanied. Monica Youn. IIR

Waking Up. Yolanda Palis. ReBoTo

Waking up in the same skin isn't enought. Mirages. Kapka Kassabova. StAl

Waking up over the candy store together. First Early Mornings Together. Robert Pinsky. ColAP; WaAnP

Waking Up Twice. Jack Anderson. PasH

Wakonda! Talako! deathonic turkey gobbling in the soft-. Gregory Corso. BB

Wal I got a gal. On a Kazoo. Dennis Lee. IFF

Walam Olum; or, Red Score [of the Lenâpé], The [*or* The Wallam Olum; The Red Score or Painted History of the Lenni Lenape]. *Unknown.*
  "After the rushing waters had subsided the Lenape of the turtle were close together, in hollow houses, living together there." APN-2
  "After the Seizer there were ten chiefs, and there was much warfare south and east." OBVE
  "At first in that place, at all times, above the earth." APN-2
  "Great land and a wide land was the east land, A." OBVE; TCAPo
  "Long ago there was a mighty snake, and beings evil to men." APN-2

Waldeinsamkeit. Ralph Waldo Emerson. APN-1

Walden. William Ellery Channing. APN-1

Walden [prose work]. Henry David Thoreau.
  "Life in us is like the water in the river, The." GoPo

Wales. David Gwenallt Jones. BBMWP, *tr. by* Joseph P. Clancy

Wales 1937. R. Williams Parry. BBMWP, *tr. by* Joseph P. Clancy

Wales '99. Donald Evans. BBMWP, *tr. by* Gillian Clarke

Wales Re-visited. Harry Guest. TCAWP

Wales Visitation. Allen Ginsberg. APSN; BB; ColAP; VCAP

Walk, A. Raymond Carver. GM

Walk, A. Hwang Insuk. EcSo, *tr. by* Peter H. Lee

Walk, A. Rainer Maria Rilke. RaBo; WED, *tr. by* Robert Bly

Walk, The. Oni Buchanan. BAP-04

Walk, The. Ethan Gilsdorf. OPRER

Walk, The. Thomas Hardy. NAEL-6v2; NAEL-7v2; NPeEn; OxBEV

Walk, The. William Scammell. NLP

Walk After Rain. Douglas Burnet Smith. Coast

Walk along back of the library. Seven Skins. Adrienne Rich. NAMCP V.2

Walk Along the Old Tracks, A. Robert Kinsley. GoPo

Walk at the Museum, A. Ágnes Nemes Nagy. MotU, *tr. by* Hugh Maxton

Walk by the Water, A. Charlotte Smith. NPBRoP

Walk fast in snow, in frost walk slow. Winter Wise. *Unknown.* Spl

Walk in, kind Saviour, / No man can hinder me! No Man Can Hinder Me. *Unknown.* SSUS

Walk in Late Summer, A. Theodore Roethke. APT-2

Walk in the Country, A. Su Tung-p'o. NDACCP, *tr. by* Kenneth Rexroth

Walk in the Rain. Polly Clark. NeBl

Walk Like Freedom. Carolyn M. Rodgers. OxAAAP

Walk me down to the wharf. Derek Walcott. NAMCP V.2 *Fr.* Omeros.

Walk, my love. Entanglement. Caitlin Maude. IrLP, *tr. by* Gabriel Fitzmaurice

Walk On. Sheena Blackhall. EdScPo

Walk on again walk on. *Unknown.* ChinPo, *tr. by* Ye Weilian [*or* Yeh Wei-lien *or* Wai-lim Yip]

Walk on by how much you were undone. Think Eight. Todd Colby. HeMarv

Walk on the Moon. N. Scott Momaday. OtW

Walk onto the dark stage dressed for a funeral. Members of the Orchestra, The. Kevin Hart. NOBAu

Walk out into the fields without looking behind you. Magic Broom, The. Marcia Southwick. PfSP

Walk Softly. *Unknown.* TCAPo

Walk softly, my sister. Padded Steps/Sister Song (a litany). Quo Vadis Gex-Breaux. FuFl

Walk the horses down the hill. When the Lease Is Up. Weldon Kees. NoP-5

Walk toward Love, The. Gaston Miron. YaTCFP, *tr. by* Mary Ann Caws and Jean-Pierre Cauvin

Walk up, walk up, my bonny boys. R.H. Ellis. FaBoWar *Fr.* Ode to St Crispin's Day.

Walk warily! Remember, sister, we are. Under Sedation. Alec Derwent Hope. BMAP

Walk with the Beautiful and with the Grand. Beautiful, The. E. H. Burrington. TreFP

Walk with the sun. Dream Song. Lewis Alexander. WHSW

Walked with no one. On the Sunny Side of the Street. Dorothy Fields. ReLy

Walker, The. Arturo Giovannitti. APT-1

Walker Evans in Bridgeport. Bill Zavatsky. PrTe

Walker in Prague. Vítězslav Nezval. AF, *tr. by* Ewald Osers

Walker, It Is Your Footsteps. Antonio Machado Ruiz. SpanPo, *tr. by* Kate Flores

Walker, it is your footsteps. Walker, It Is Your Footsteps. Antonio Machado Ruiz. SpanPo, *tr. by* Kate Flores

Walkin' Around. Pablo Neruda. PFTM-1, *tr. by* Jerome Rothenberg

Walkin' My Baby Back Home. Roy Turk. ReLy

Walkin' the Dog. Shelton Brooks. ReLy

Walking. Temporary City. Nijole Miliauskaite. VCWP, *tr. by* Jonas Zdanys

Walking a Field into Evening. Larry Smith. AmZen

Walking a short lane. Drunkard, A. Fei Ma. PML, *tr. by* Zhang Cuo

Walking Alone by the Riverbank Seeking Flowers. Tu Fu [*or* Du Fu]. CCL1, *tr. by* Stephen Owen

Walking alone in a multitude of loves when morning's light. Marriage of a Virgin, The. Dylan Thomas. ChIV-2

Walking Alone in Late WInter. Jane Kenyon. MoW

Walking along a little path. While Visiting on the South Stream the Taoist Priest Chang. Liu Ch'ang-ch'ing. CCL1, *tr. by* Witter Bynner

Walking along a river bank in an antiquated universe. Pulling in the Reins. Yoshimasu Gōzō. PFTM-2, *tr. by* Richard Arno

Walking along a road. Road, The. Shin Kyŏngnim. CAMKP, *tr. by* Anthony, Brother of Taizé

Walking [*or* Talking] along in this not quite prose way. Near. William Stafford. CAP-8

Walking along patchmake st. one day years ago. Dear Mozart. Reed Bye. AHA

Walking along the Sea of Galilee. Dovid Knut. TCRusP, tr. by John Glad

Walking among my own this windy morning. Spring Vacation, The. Derek Mahon. PNI

Walking Around. Pablo Neruda. RaBo; WED, tr. by Robert Bly

Walking Around. Pablo Neruda. PoetW; VCWP, tr. by W. S. Merwin

Walking Around. Pablo Neruda. TCLAP, tr. by Ben Belitt

Walking Around ("It happens that I am tired of being a man.") Pablo Neruda. ConPit, tr. by Clayton Eshleman

Walking around in the park. Toads Revisited. Philip Larkin. OxAEP-2

Walking around, wasting time. (LL) Moon and the flowers, The. Issa. EH; NIL-7, tr. by Robert Hass

Walking Around Watching the Miners Digging. Tachibana Akemi. EMJL, tr. by Burton Watson

Walking at Leisure. Wang Wei. TAL

Walking at leisure we watch laurel flowers falling. Walking at Leisure. Wang Wei. TAL

Walking at Night. Philip Salom. BMAP

Walking at Night. Brian Swann. PoCoUp

Walking at night on asphalt campus. Death News. Allen Ginsberg. BB

Walking Away. Cecil Day Lewis. BeAl

Walking backwards along shore. I am open. Michael Datcher. BtF

Walking beside the Kamogawa, Remembering Nansen and Fudo and Gary's Poem. Philip Whalen. BB

Walking Buddha. Barbara Guest. FTOS

Walking by the Cliffside Dyeworks. Robert Carnevale. UnSA

Walking by the river, the morning cold. River Walk. John Stuart Williams. AngWePo

Walking by the waters. In my country. Jackie Kay. MFPA; NeBl; NeBrP; StAl

Walking Down a Mountain. Ko Un. WhBo

Walking Down Park. Nikki Giovanni. OxAAAP

Walking down the beach, I took your arm. Cemetery Reef. Elizabeth Spires. CAP-8

Walking Down the Road. Adrienne Rich. NIL-7; NIP-4

Walking early morning light. Jojopan. Art Goodtimes. GeoH

Walking Fields at Night South of Hampton, Iowa. Steve Gehrke. AmPoNex

Walking Home. Gjertrud Schnackenberg. WeW-3

Walking home from school one afternoon. Walking Home. Gjertrud Schnackenberg. WeW-3

Walking in Gardens. Dylan Thomas. OBGa

Walking in gardens by the sides. Walking in Gardens. Dylan Thomas. OBGa

Walking in the children's park. Lines for a Hindi Poet. Bahadur Tejani. PML

Walking in the rain. Steve Sanfield. WhBo

Walking inland, inland, inland. Oxaitoq's Song. Inuit Oral Tradition. ErotSp, tr. by Sam Hamill

Walking into King Sooper after Two-Week Retreat. Allen Ginsberg. WhBo

Walking into the shadows, walking alone. Lee in the Mountains. Donald Davidson. CBCWP; FuPo

Walking north toward the point, I come on a dead seal. Dead Seal [near McClure's Beach], The. Robert Bly. CAP-8

Walking On: A Declaration of Wholeness. Saddi Khali. BtF

Walking on dishes. Buson. SoOfWa, tr. by Sam Hamill

Walking on the crusty surface, coming back. Studies in Classic American Literature. Tony Lopez. VaPo

Walking on Water. James Dickey. ChIV-2

Walking out of the "big E." Before the Stuff Comes Down. Gary Snyder. HeIP-4

Walking Parker Home. Bob Kaufman. OxAAAP

Walking Past the Dugout of Felix McKittrick. Robert Burlingame. TiP2

Walking past the Ritz a girl may be sitting on the last step crying. Part of the Effect of the Public Scene Is to Importune the Passing Viewer. Erin Belieu. AmPoNex

Walking Road, The. Richard Hughes. OBMV

Walking south down Broadway. February Ice Years. Melinda Goodman. WiU

Walking swiftly with a dreadful duchess. Infelice. Stevie Smith. LW

Walking the Baby to the Liquor Store. Michael Van Walleghen. IllVoic

Walking the Dog. Howard Nemerov. BeAl; GoPo

Walking the Dog. John Wright. BloBone

Walking the earth in all the changing. Late Summer. Ruth L. Schwartz. AmPoNex

Walking the heaved cement sidewalk down Main Street. Fog-Talk. Philip Booth. BodElec

Walking the path. Peter Levitt. WhBo

Walking the Plateau. Lupenga Mphande. NAfrP

Walking the railroad-right-of-way. Portobello. M. Travis Lane. Coast

Walking the shore that day, each reaches down. Sea Washes Sand Scours Sea. Tom Vander Ven. PoDa

Walking the streets, we watch the people stare. Urban Indians, Pioneer Square, Seattle. Gail Tremblay. FiBr

Walking this field I remember. Premonition, The. Theodore Roethke. HarvBoo

Walking this winter beach alone. Token. Alison Bielski. AngWePo

Walking through a field with my little brother Seth. Snow. David Berman. P180

Walking through a Wall. Louis Jenkins. RaBo

Walking through Myoshin-Ji. Gary Snyder. WANABP

Walking through wet wheat an ocean of mercury after. Iain Sinclair. Oth Fr. Ebbing of Kraft, The.

Walking to Cootehill. John Engels. PfSP

Walking to cure myself of the gun-proud. Arboretum. Alison Deming. LiTh

Walking to Martha's Vineyard. Franz Wright. AmAlph

Walking to my room from the park. Weeping, The. Jack Hirschman. BodElec

Walking to Philip's downhill in the rain. South Ridge Zendo. Miriam Sagan. WANABP

Walking to Sleep. Richard Wilbur. VCAP

Walking to the Cattle Place. Les A. Murray.
  Death Words. UpMys

Walking to your place for a love feast. Same Inside, The. Anna Swirszczynska [or Swir]. BLT

Walking towards the house, the terraces. Sestina in Time of Winter. Patrick Anderson. PoA 2002

Walking towards the village. Elaine Randell. Oth Fr. Snoad Hill Poems, The.

Walking up the driftwood beach at day's end. Flood Year. Judith Wright. NAMCP V.2; NoAM

Walking, when the Lake of the Air is Blue with Spring. J. S. Harry. BMAP

Walking with him was like walking somehow in shadow. Miracle of F6/18, The. Leontia Flynn. NIrP

Walking with Others. Jelaluddin Rumi. WED, tr. by Robert Bly

Walking with the God. Gwyneth Lewis. HarvBoo

Walking with you and another lady. Dream of Jealousy, A. Seamus Heaney. NoP-4; NoP-5

Walking Wounded. Vernon Scannell. OBWP

Walking-Mort, The. Djuna Barnes. APT-1

Walks everywhere now. He's afraid of fast cars. Tourists. Sherman Alexie. NAMCP V.2

Walkways, The. John Ashbery. BodElec

Wall, A. Andrew Motion. NeBrP

Wall, A. Charles Simic. NAMCP V.2

Wall, The. Witter Bynner. APT-1

Wall, The. Michel Deguy. YaTCFP, tr. by Clayton Eshleman

Wall, The. Zbigniew Herbert. AF, tr. by John Carpenter and Bogdana Carpenter

Wall, The. Calvin C. Hernton. EGAG

Wall, The. Eve Merriam. TaR

Wall, The: "I see a wall; but unwhole." Karol Wojtyla. SonAtl, tr. by Massimo Ceresa, Favorita '68 and Pyotr Vincent

Wall between Us, The. Mark Vinz. VisFro

Wall Calendar. Dan Pagis. VCWP, tr. by Tsipi Keller

Wall, The: For october 3, 1990. Reiner Kunze. GTCP, tr. by Reinhold Grimm

Wall in the Woods, A: Cummington. Richard Wilbur. PfSP

Wall is massive, of solid stone, hard, finished. Wall, The. Michel Deguy. YaTCFP, tr. by Clayton Eshleman

Wall, no! I can't tell whar he lives. Jim Bludso of the Prairie Belle. John Milton Hay. APN-2

Wall of Dreams (2). Ahmed Taha. NAfrP, tr. by Clarissa C. Burt

Wall of flies, A. Hand, The. Bernard Bador. ConPit, tr. by Clayton Eshleman

Wall of Genesis, The. Ahmed Taha. AnVo, tr. by Mohamed Enani

Wall of hopelessness. Tomas Tranströmer. WoBe Fr. Haiku.

Wall round my boyhood, Foel Drigarn, Carn Gyfrwy, Tal Mynydd. Preseli. Waldo Williams. BBMWP, tr. by Anthony Conran

Wall / They were driven everywhere. Wall, The. Calvin C. Hernton. EGAG

Wallace Stevens says Money is a kind of poetry. So I offer to trade him Tennes-. Money. Bob Perelman. FTOS

Wallace Stevens would've loved your poem. Ralph Adamo. AnSo Fr. Bicameralization, The.

Walled Garden. Dorothy, Duchess of Wellington Wellesley. OBGa

Wallet stolen, so we must end our stay. Note of Thanks, A. Wyatt Prunty. RA

Wallet, the hide of a goat, tough and untanned, a stick, A. Leonidas of Tarentum. HePo, tr. by Barbara Hughes Fowler

Walloping Window-Blind, The.   Charles Edward Carryl.   GoPo; NBLV *Fr.* Davy and the Goblin.

Wallowing in this bloody sty.   Drunken Fisherman, The.   Robert Lowell.   ChIV-2

Wallpaper.   Julia Alvarez.   BodElec

Wallpaper of Mr. R. K., The.   Max Jacob.   MotU, *tr.* by Andrei Codrescu

Wallpapering to Patsy Cline.   Judith Sornberger.   FiBr

Walls, The.   Douglas Goetsch.   AmPoNex

Walls are built with, The.   Some Details of Hebridean House Construction. Thomas A. Clark.   GoPo

Walls Do Not Fall, The.   "H. D."
   "Amen."   WPoS
   "Evil was active in the land."   HarvBoo; NAAL-5
   "In me (the worm) clearly."   APT-1; NAMCP V.1
   "In no wise is the pillar-of-fire."   WPoS
   "Let us, however, recover the Sceptre."   HarvBoo
   "Now my right hand."   APT-1; NAAL-5
   "O heart, small urn."   APT-1
   "O, Sire, is this the path?"   NAAL-5
   "Or anywhere."   NAAL-5
   "Presence was spectrum-blue, The."   APT-1
   "Sirius:."   NAAL-5
   "Splintered the crystal of identity."   NAAL-5
   "Still the walls do not fall."   NAAL-5
   "Take me home."   APT-1; NAAL-5
   "There is a spell, for instance."   APT-1; NAMCP V.1
   "We have had too much consecration."   NAMCP V.1
   "When in the company of the gods."   APT-1
   "Yet we, the latter-day twice-born."   APT-1

Walls have gooseflesh, The.   don't say it. Lionel Abrahams.   TSAP

Walls . . . iridescent with eyes.   Fifth-Floor Window, The.   Lola Ridge.   APT-1; NAAPv.2

Walls of Bois-de-Chene Shacks, The.   Carlo Résil.   OGAHCP, *tr.* by Boadiba and Jack Hirschman

Walls of Emerald, The.   Li Shang-yin.   CCL1, *tr.* by A. C. Graham

Walnut and Lily.   Douglas Oliver.   Oth

Walnut, peach and plum—hacked down. (LL)   Thoreau.   Timothy Liu. AmPoNex; GifTon; OPRER

Walrus and the Carpenter, The.   Lewis Carroll.   CABP; ChAP; ITBLP; NAEL-6v2; NAEL-7v2; NoAM; OBSP; OxAEP-2; TFi *Fr.* Through the Looking-Glass.

Walrus stretches forth a wrinkled hand, The.   Kingfisher's Boxing Gloves, The. James Fenton.   NoAM

Walrus Tusk from Alaska, A.   Alfred Corn.   MakPoe

Walsingham; or, the Pupil of Nature.   Mary Robinson.   RWP

Walt.   Ted Hughes.   NoP-4

Walt Disney wants you to have his child.   Revisionist History: Magic Kingdom. Robert Wynne.   RWB

Walt, I Salute You!   Lynn Emanuel.   MAAN; ViWalt

Walt, my old classmates who write poems.   Crossing Walt Whitman Bridge. Daniel Gerard Hoffman.   ViWalt

Walt, the Wounded.   W. S. Di Piero.   ViWalt

Walt, Walt, when you've a moment.   Your Sister.   Michael Dennis Browne. ViWalt

Walt Whitman.   Emanuel Carnevali.   PoA 2002

Walt Whitman.   Edward Dahlberg.   APT-2

Walt Whitman: "But do you really want to see Whitman's house instead of Roosevelt's?"   Juan Ramón Jiménez.   ViWalt; WED, *tr.* by Robert Bly

[Walt Whitman]: "W / A / L / WHITMAN."   Edwin Honig.   ViWalt

Walt Whitman: "Master-songs are ended, and the man, The."   Edwin Arlington Robinson.   APN-2; NCAP; TCAPo; ViWalt

Walt Whitman: "He is simply chopping wood in my front yard."   Wang Yin. ViWalt, *tr.* by Cheng Baolin and Richard Terrill

Walt Whitman, a kosmos, of Manhattan the son.   Walt Whitman.   ColAP; NAWM-7v2; NoP-4; NoP-5; SAmP; WaAnP *Fr.* Song of Myself.

Walt Whitman, an American, one of the roughs, a kosmos.   Walt Whitman. *See* Walt Whitman, a kosmos, of Manhattan the son.

Walt Whitman and the Birds.   Eugenio de Andrade.   ViWalt, *tr.* by Alexis Levitin

Walt Whitman at Bear Mountain [' . . . *life which does not give the preference to any other life, of any previous period, which therefore prefers its own existence . . .* '].   Louis Simpson.   TRP; ViWalt

Walt Whitman at Pfaff's: A Fantasy.   Phil Tabakow.   ViWalt

Walt Whitman at the Irish Festival, Syracuse, New York: Four Snapshots. Shane Seely.   ViWalt

Walt Whitman at the Reburial of Poe.   Nicholas Christopher.   ViWalt

Walt Whitman at Timber Creek.   Randall R. Freisinger.   ViWalt

Walt Whitman Bathing.   David Wagoner.   ViWalt

Walt Whitman, brother to brothers and brother to sisters.   Whitman's Grass. Martin Bell.   ViWalt

Walt Whitman Encounters the Cosmos with the Cats of New York.   Gail White. ViWalt

Walt Whitman has come to visit me in Ohio.   Walt Whitman in Ohio. Jonathan Cohen.   ViWalt

Walt Whitman has just walked into the room.   To Walt Whitman on America's Birthday.   Roger Mitchell.   ViWalt

Walt Whitman I lay on the grass today.   Memorials.   Suzanne Gardinier. ViWalt

Walt Whitman in Alabama.   Jake Adam York.   ViWalt

Walt Whitman in Hell.   T. R. Hummer.   ViWalt

Walt Whitman in New Orleans, 1848.   David Citino.   ViWalt

Walt Whitman in Ohio.   Jonathan Cohen.   ViWalt

Walt Whitman in the Car Lot, Repo or Used.   Gillian Conoley.   ViWalt

Walt Whitman in the Civil War Hospitals.   David Ignatow.   ViWalt

Walt Whitman is wearing mirrored sunglasses.   Walt Whitman in the Car Lot, Repo or Used.   Gillian Conoley.   ViWalt

Walt Whitman shakes. This game belongs to him. (LL)   Defending Walt Whitman.   Sherman Alexie.   AmPoNex; ViWalt

Walt Whitman's Brain Dropped on Laboratory Floor.   Thomas Lux.   ViWalt

Walter de la Mare Tells the Listener about Jack and Jill.   Louis Untermeyer. MoAmPo *Fr.* Mother Goose Up-to-Date.

Walter Parmer.   Greg Williamson.   RA

Walter Savage Landor.   Dorothy Parker.   NALW *Fr.* Pig's-Eye View of Literature, A.

Waltz.   Dame Edith Sitwell.   MoWP *Fr.* Façade.

Waltz against the Mountains.   Thomas Hornsby Ferril.   APT-2

Waltz, The.   Vicente Aleixandre.   RaW, *tr.* by Robert Bly

Waltz for Debby.   Gene Lees.   ReLy

Waltz of the Twenty-Year-Olds, The.   Louis Aragon.   FaBoWar, *tr.* by Malcolm Cowley and Rolfe Humphries

Waltz Poem of Those in Love and Inseparable Forever.   Miguel Hernández. AF, *tr.* by Timothy Baland

Waly, Waly [Love Be Bonny].   *Unknown.*   NOSC; OBEV; TFi

Wan leafs shak' atour us like the snaw, The.   Hugh MacDiarmid.   NAEL-6v2; NAEL-7v2 *Fr.* Drunk Man Looks at the Thistle, A.

Wand, A.   Inga Kuznetsova.   CRWP, *tr.* by Max Nemtsov

Wand is swaying in the peace, A.   Wand, A.   Inga Kuznetsova.   CRWP, *tr.* by Max Nemtsov

Wanda when are you gonna wear your hair down.   Wanda Why Aren't You Dead.   Wanda Coleman.   BrAP

Wanda Why Aren't You Dead.   Wanda Coleman.   BrAP

Wanda's Blues.   Jane Cooper.   SeSe

Wanda's daddy was a railroadman, she was his little wife.   Wanda's Blues. Jane Cooper.   SeSe

Wander Luís.   Carolyne Wright.   MAAN

Wander, my troubled soul, sigh mid the night thy pain.   Elegy.   Anne Batten Cristall.   RWP

Wander through the house in the wee hours.   Moonlight.   Kim Caldwell. ReEnLa

Wanderer and the Seafarer, The.   *Unknown. tr.* by John Updike
   Two Seabirds.   WoPoe, *tr.* by John Updike

Wanderer in our skies.   Voyage to the Moon.   Archibald MacLeish.   OtW

Wanderer in the Night of the World, A.   N. V. M. Gonzalez.   ReBoTo

Wanderer reaches home with joy, The.   First-Born, A.   Kong Rong.   CCL1, *tr.* by H. A. Giles

Wanderer, The.   W. H. Auden.   HarvBoo; NAMCP V.1; NoAM; WaAnP; WeW-3; WoPoe

Wanderer, The.   Stevie Smith.   NALW

Wanderer, The.   *Unknown.*   NAWM-5v1, *tr.* by Charles William Kennedy

Wanderer, The.   William Wordsworth. *Fr.* Excursion, The.

Wanderer, The: A Rococo Study.   William Carlos Williams. Paterson—the Strike.   TCAPo

Wanderers, The.   Robert Browning.   OBEV *Fr.* Paracelsus.

Wanderers, The.   Robert Williams Buchanan.   OxBSo

Wanderer's Bouquet.   Sŏ Chŏngju.   CAMKP; WoPoe, *tr.* by David R. McCann

Wanderer's Dog, The.   Sir Walter Scott.   DiBP

Wanderer's mind, A.   Early Spring at the Capital, Sent to the Honorable Kuan. Hsi Chou.   CSKM, *tr.* by Paul Hansen

Wanderer's Night Song.   Johann Wolfgang von Goethe.   WoPoe, *tr.* by Peter Viereck

Wanderer's Song, A.   John Masefield.   MoBrPo

Wandering.   Muso Soseki.   EaWin, *tr.* by W. S. Merwin

Wandering amid the horrors of the night.   Written When the Mind Was Oppressed.   Anne Batten Cristall.   RWP

Wandering beside rivers, I remember my home.   By Yangtze and Han.   Tu Fu [or Du Fu].   CrYelRi, *tr.* by Sam Hamill

Wandering by the heave of the town park, wondering. On the Closing of Millom Ironworks. Norman Nicholson. RSaN

Wandering Ch'ing-Ling Strea in Nan-Yang. Li Po. NDACCP, *tr.* by David Hinton

Wandering Curves. Keith Waldrop. PmAP

Wandering has been my way. Poem for My Brother Returning to My Farm. Tu Fu [*or* Du Fu]. CrYelRi, *tr.* by Sam Hamill

Wandering, in autumn, the woods of boyhood. Robert Penn Warren. TRP *Fr.* Promises.

Wandering in the evening beside Shinobazu pond. Withered Lotus. Yosano Tekkan. CAoMJL1, *tr.* by Leith Morton

Wandering in the still of eve. Song. Anne Batten Cristall. RWP

Wandering Islands, The. Alec Derwent Hope. HarvBoo

Wandering Jew, The. Eloise Bibb. CBWP-4

Wandering Jew, The. Robert Mezey. TaR

Wandering late by morning seas. Shelley's Vision. Herman Melville. APN-2

Wandering on Mount Tiantai. Sun Ch'o. CCL1, *tr.* by Burton Watson

Wandering Round Mount Taiping. K'ung Chih-kuei. CCL1, *tr.* by John Frodsham

Wandering to the other, wandering. Robin Blaser. NLPA *Fr.* Image-Nation.

Wanderings on a Heavenly Body. László Kálnoky. IQMS, *tr.* by Kenneth McRobbie and Zita McRobbie

Wands. Veronica Volkow. RMCMP, *tr.* by Margaret Sayers Peden

Waning August Moon. Roberta Hill. ReEnLa

Waning Honeymoon, The. William Whitehead. DiBP

Waning of the Harvest Moon, The. John Wieners. PmAP

Wanne mine eyhnen misten. How Death Comes. *Unknown.* WaAnP

Want back my thick tongued. What Do You Want? Brenda Leifso. IFF

Want Bone, The. Robert Pinsky. ASA

Want of You, The. Angelina Weld Grimké. NAAPv.2

Want of You, The. Ivan Leonard Wright. SoSe-8

Want, predation, sleep. Mary Kinzie. FFC

Want quickens wit: Want's pupils needs must work. Theocritus. OBVE *Fr.* Idylls.

Want sang and sang on my street today. My New York Street Sings. Esther Shumyatsher. Prolet, *tr.* by Amelia Glaser

Want to be with children. Kyotaro Komuro. NAAPv.2

Want to see you. Private Thoughts. Clyde A. Wray. BtF

Wanted. Josiah Gilbert Holland. ITBLP; SacPr

Wanted. Mercedes Roffé. TANSG, *tr.* by Kathryn Kopple

Wanted: Men. AD. Kenneth Fearing. NAAPv.2

Wanted, wanted: Dolores Haze. Vladimir Vladimirovich Nabokov. APT-2 *Fr.* Lolita.

Wanting a myth for blowing up the gods. Collective Invention, The. Chris Wallace-Crabbe. BMAP

Wanting one good organic line. Sam Hamill. WhBo

Wanting someone who looked natural. Persephone. Susan Wicks. MoWP

Wanting To. Jan G. Elburg. TuT, *tr.* by Peter van de Kamp

Wanting to Die. Anne Sexton. ColAP; EMP; IJHIL; NoAM; OxBoAm; TRP; VCAP; WaAnP

Wanting to say things. My Father's Song. Simon J. Ortiz. HATNAP; NIL-7

Wanting You. Terra Hunter. PasH

Wanton troopers riding by, The. Nymph Complaining for the Death of Her Faun [*or* Fawn], The. Andrew Marvell. BASC; HeIP-4; NAEL-6v1; NAEL-7v1; RACG

Wanton Wife of Bath, The. *Unknown.*

"In *Bath* a wanton wife did dwell." PBRV

Wants my son. White Lady. Lucille Clifton. ESEAA; SUP

Wants of Man, The. John Quincy Adams. APN-1

Wants to be finished waiting in the car. He ate his pear. Alcoholic's Son at Ten, The. Kathleen Peirce. PBCAP

Wapiti, The. Ogden Nash. TLR

War. André Breton. AF, *tr.* by Mary Ann Caws and Jean-Pierre Cauvin

War. Michael Brownstein. FTOS

War. Ebenezer Elliott. FaBoWar

War. Hedd Wyn. BBMWP, *tr.* by Gillian Clarke

War. Miguel Hernández. AF; RaBo

War. Max Jacob. AF, *tr.* by Michael Brownstein

War. Lorine Niedecker. FTOS

War. Aharon Shabtai. PoCho, *tr.* by Peter Cole

War. Edgar Wallace. OBWP

War against the Trees, The. Stanley Kunitz. NAMCP V.1

War, The. Frank O'Hara. BodElec

War against War in South Africa. W. T. Stead.

"Now that war is in the air, e'en the parson in his lair." FaBoWar

War and Alienation: London and Wales, 1793–4. William Wordsworth. NPBRoP *Fr.* Prelude, The; Growth of a Poet's Mind [1805 version].

War and greed stop food. Poem. Hugh Seidman. BodElec

War and Hell. Ernest Crosby.

"Hail to the hero!" FaBoWar

"I am a great inventor, did you but know it." FaBoWar

War Ballad. Andrey Andreievich Voznesensky. WoPoe, *tr.* by Stanley Moss

War begets Poverty. Edward Fitzgerald. FaBoWar

War between England and the United States! Iterating Sonnet. Leigh Hunt. OxBSo

War Blinded. Douglas Dunn. NePenScot; OBWP

War broke out in autumn at the empty border, The. Yehuda Amichai. PoSu *Fr.* Patriotic Songs.

War Cabinet, The. Myrddin ap Dafydd. BBMWP, *tr.* by Richard Poole

War Cat. Dorothy Leigh Sayers. TriCat

War Dance. Miidhu. NOBAu, *tr.* by George von Brandenstein

War Dance. *Unknown.* APN-2, *tr.* by George Catlin

    Approaching Dance, The. APN-2

    Eh-Ros-ka, the Warrior's Dance. APN-2

    Ha-Kon-E-Crase, the Eagle Dance. APN-2

    Wa-Sissica, the War Song. APN-2

War Diaries. Sami Mahdi. IrPoTo, *tr.* by Ferial J. Ghazoul

War Ending, The. Medbh McGuckian. NAMCP V.2

War Games. Connie Bensley. FaBoWar

War Has Been Given a Bad Name. Bertolt Brecht. BeAl; HP; PoAgWa; PoSu, *tr.* by John Willett

War Horse, The. Eavan Boland. PBCIP

War in Bosnia, The. Walter McDonald. OtW

War in Fife, The. Sydney Goodsir Smith. NePenScot *Fr.* Armageddon in Albyn.

War in the Air, The. Howard Nemerov. ColAP; EMP; OtW; PWW2; VCAP

War is fought by soldiers in machines, The. Apology. Richard Cecil. BodElec

War Is Kind. Stephen Crane. AmWaPo; APN-2; FaBoWar; NAAPv.1; NoP-4; NoP-5; OBWP; RaBo; TCAPo; WaAnP

War is no longer declared. Every Day. Ingeborg Bachmann. CFP; PoSu, *tr.* by Daniel Huws

War is no longer declared. Every Day. Ingeborg Bachmann. StAl, *tr.* by Peter Filkins

War is no longer declared. Every Day. Ingeborg Bachmann. GTCP, *tr.* by Reinhold Grimm and Irmgard Hunt

War Is Over, The. Ben Doyle. LegDan

War is the angry man waving his desperate. War-and-Peace. George Buchanan. PNI

War is the mistress of enormity. Joshua Sylvester. FaBoWar

War isn't on yet, though all the toys of battle are ready, The. Outdoor Chums in the Forest. Ann Townsend. ExTi

War Lament: "Autumn flowers." *Unknown.* CrYelRi, *tr.* by Sam Hamill

War Lament: "Every plant is burnt yellow." *Unknown.* CrYelRi, *tr.* by Sam Hamill

War, Like. Hans Magnus Enzensberger. GTCP, *tr.* by Reinhold Grimm

War Lord in the Early Evening. Patricia K. Page. NoAM

War Lullaby. Dora Teitelboim. Prolet, *tr.* by Amelia Glaser

War Memoir, A. Arnold Rattenbury. RSaN

War Memories. Xenophanes. WoPoe, *tr.* by Theodore Blanchard

War Memory, A. Lizette Woodworth Reese. AmWaPo

War Music. Christopher Logue.

    "Battle swayed, The." FaBoWar

    "Fate's sister, fortune, favours those." FaBoWar

    "See how that royal fights." FaBoWar

War Night 6. Ilan Sheinfeld. NRoS, *tr.* by Esther Raizen

War of the Roses, The [*for* Premier Bjelke-Petersen]. Michael Dransfield. BMAP

War of words is done, The. Battle. John Davidson. CABP

War Photograph. Kate Daniels. CFP

War Photographer. Carol Ann Duffy. EdScPo

War Photographers, The. Frank Ormsby. PNI

War pleased me to know of my interest, The. War, The. Frank O'Hara. BodElec

War Poet. Sidney Keyes. FaBoWar; NoP-4; NoP-5; PoWW; WaAnP

War Poetry. Kate Clanchy. StAl

War Resisters' Song. Thomas McGrath. AtGh

War separated, The. Friends, The. Bertolt Brecht. PoSu, *tr.* by Michael Hamburger

War shook the land where Levi dwelt. Field of Glory, The. Edwin Arlington Robinson. MoAmPo

War Song. *Unknown.* AmWaPo, *tr.* by Ruth Underhill

War Song, A. Bertrans de Born. FaBoWar,

War Song of Dinas Vawr, The. Thomas Love Peacock. CABP; FaBoWar; NAEL-6v2; NOBRP; NPeEn; OxAEP-2 *Fr.* Misfortunes of Elphin, The.

War Song of the Saracens. James Elroy Flecker. MoBrPo *Fr.* Hassan.

War Songs. *Unknown.* APN-2, *tr. by* Henry Rowe Schoolcraft

War Songs. *Unknown.* APN-2, *tr. by* Alfred Longley Riggs

War South of the Great Wall. Li Po. NDACCP, *tr. by* David Hinton

War Stories. Harvey Shapiro. PWW2

War, the hospitals—he was away, The. Inheritance, The. James Aitchison. EdScPo

War the Source of Riches. *Unknown.* NOBRP

War to end them all, The. Firebell for Peace. Joyce Lee. NOBAu

War was her life, with want and the wild air. Yorkshire Wife's Saga. Ruth Pitter. NALW

War was weary long, The. Campaigning. John William DeForest.

War Works Hard, The. Dunya Mikhail. WoBe, *tr. by* Liz Winslow

War-and-Peace. George Buchanan. PNI

Warbler sings, The. Basho. SoOfWa, *tr. by* Sam Hamill

Warblers are today as long ago, The. Murasaki Shikibu. WoPoe *Fr.* Tale of Genji, The.

War-carts clatter and creak. Song of the War-Carts. Tu Fu [*or* Du Fu]. NDACCP, *tr. by* David Hinton

War-chariots rumble. Song of the War-Chariots (Yueh-Fu). Tu Fu [*or* Du Fu]. ChinPo, *tr. by* Ye Weilian [*or* Yeh Wei-lien *or* Wai-lim Yip]

Ward, The. George MacBeth. EdScPo

Ward, and still in bonds, one day, A. Regeneration. Henry Vaughan. BASC; ChIV-1; FSCP; NAEL-6v1; NAEL-7v1; NoP-4; NoP-5

Ward is quiet, the mothers delivered, The. First Day, The. Elizabeth Spires. CAP-8

Ward Mouth. Pat Borthwick. PoCu

Ward Mouth knows everybody's business, The. Ward Mouth. Pat Borthwick. PoCu

Ward 6. Tanure Ojaide. HBAPE

Warden Said to Me the Other Day, The. Etheridge Knight. InGu; LTA; PBCAP; SoSe-8

Wardrobe, a mirror, a chair, A. Entresol. Jaime Sabines. TCLAP, *tr. by* Claudine-Marie D'Angelo

Wardrobes. Nicolette Golding. Prnts

Ware Collection of Glass Flowers and Fruit, Harvard Museum, The. Mark Doty. HarvBoo

Ware, ware, snares for hares. Tu-zhi: Hares. *Unknown.* CCL1, *tr. by* Arthur Cooper

Warhol at Wetlands. John Kinsella. NeBl

Wariness of the ship resting there, The. Manes P. Aground Off Fort Dufferin, The. Robert J. Gibbs. Coast

Waring. Robert Browning. NPeEn

Warlike Angels, The. Rafael Alberti. AF, *tr. by* Geoffrey Connell

Warm and friendly and without challenge. (LL) How to Watch Your Brother Die. Michael Lassell. CAGL; WiU

Warm ashes of the word, The. Cuncta Semper. Rodolfo Di Biasio. NeIt, *tr. by* Stephen Sartarelli

Warm, cheap snow, lightly wind-twirled, A. Still Winter (Spring). Charlie Smith. PoDa

Warm day for November, and we, A. Towards Sunset at Camino Cielo. Maurina Sherman. GeoHom

Warm east winds blow. Great Springtime. Ko Ŭn. CAMKP, *tr. by* Anthony, Brother of Taizé

Warm Invitation, A. Yüan Chiu-ts'ai. WoPoe, *tr. by* Henry Hart

Warm, living flowers. Evaporations. Ani Ilkov. CSCBP, *tr. by* Georgi Belev and Lisa Sapinkopf

Warm night fallen night. Condemned. Philippe Soupault. AF, *tr. by* Eden Paul

Warm night of Mozambique. Let My People Go. Noémia da Sousa. HAWP, *tr. by* Jacques-Noël Gouat

Warm plantains and chilled light radishes. Rogers in Italy. Frank O'Hara. FTOS

Warm rain and soft breeze by turns. Li Ch'ing-chao. NDACCP,

Warm rains and gentle winds. Butterflies Love Flowers. Li Ch'ing-chao. ErotSp, *tr. by* Sam Hamill

Warm rosebuds below, The. (LL) World-Soul, The. Ralph Waldo Emerson. APN-1; NCAP

Warm slipperiness of us in the car's backseat. Door Thrown Open to Daisies. Rick Agran. AmPoNex

Warm sun is failing, the bleak wind is wailing, The. Autumn: A Dirge. Percy Bysshe Shelley. TreFP

Warm to the Cuddly-toy Charm of a Koala Bear. Gavin Ewart. EmeKit

Warm tree. Live Oak. David Tokuyu Reid-Marr. WhBo

Warmer. Martha Collins. UrbNat

Warmest kiss, The. Fullness. Latasha Natasha Diggs. BRtP

Warmest welcome, at an inn, The. (LL) Written at [*or* in] an Inn at Henley. William Shenstone. OBEV; OxAEP-1; OxBEV

Warming Her Pearls. Carol Ann Duffy. BeAl; EdScPo; MakPoe; MoWP; NAMCP V.2; NeBrP; NePenScot; NoP-4; NoP-5; PoBW

Warmly wrapped. Basho. EMJL, *tr. by* Haruo Shirane

Warmness. Anabel Torres. TANSG, *tr. by* Celeste Kostopulos-Cooperman

Warmth. Joseph Ceravolo. NYP2

Warmth of cows, The. Carol, A. Donald Hall. ChrPo

Warmth of the wind-break wall, The. Louise Herlin. MFP, *tr. by* Martin Sorrell

Warmth of the wind-break wall, The. Warmth of the Wind-break Wall, The. Louise Herlin. MFP, *tr. by* Martin Sorrell

Warmth, The. Petar Alipiev. CSCBP, *tr. by* Georgi Belev and Lisa Sapinkopf

Warner Bros. Newest Thriller *Valentine.* Jeni Olin. FreRad

Warning. Text and Commentary. Elke Erb. PFTM-2, *tr. by* Roderick Iverson

Warning. Jenny Joseph. MoWP; StAl

Warning ("Daddy, / don't let your dog.") [*see also* "Warning: Augmented"]. Langston Hughes. PFTM-1

Warning. Tadeusz Różewicz. PoSu, *tr. by* Magnus F. Krynski

Warning. Nikolai Alekseievich Zabolotsky. TCRusP, *tr. by* Daniel Weissbort

Warning, A. Adam Lindsay Gordon. STuOW *Fr.* Ye Wearie Wayfarer.

Warning, A. Grace Paley. TaR

Warning, The. Adelaide Crapsey. APT-1; NAAPv.2; Spl; TCAPo (Cinquain: A Warning.) WeW-3

Warning, The. Robert Creeley. CAP-8

Warning, The. Henry Wadsworth Longfellow. APN-1; ChIV-1; NCAP; PCW; TCAPo

Warning: Augmented [*see also* "Warning ('Daddy, / don't let your dog')"]. Langston Hughes. APT-2

Warning drums have ended all travel. Moonlit Night Thinking of My Brothers. Tu Fu [*or* Du Fu]. NDACCP, *tr. by* David Hinton

Warning to Children. Robert Graves. NoP-4; NoP-5; NOxBChV; NPeEn; OxBEV; TWF

Warning to One. Merrill Moore. MoAmPo

Warning to the Reader. Robert Bly. CAP-8

Warning to Young Bright Sisters / White AM. Culture 101A. Michelle T. Clinton. InTrad

Warnings. Nicanor Parra. AF, *tr. by* Miller Williams

Warp is Even, The: Taut Vertical Loops Between Our Father and the Earth. Luci Tapahonso. ICANM

Warpath Song. *Unknown.* AmWaPo, *tr. by* Maurice Boyd

Warping bandstand reminds you of the hard rage, The. Return to La Plata, Missouri. Jim Barnes. HATNAP

Warping night air having brought the boom, The. Barred Owl, A. Richard Wilbur. NAMCP V.2

War-planes have been at it all day long. No Hands. Gillian Clarke. TCAWP

Warren Pryor. Alden Nowlan. BrAP

Warren's Address at Bunker Hill [*or* to the American Soldiers]. John Pierpont. AmWaPo

Warring sighs and groans I'll wage thee. (LL) Ae Fond Kiss. Robert Burns. NAEL-6v2; NePenScot; NPBRoP; OBEV

Warrior, Bhaskar! Sivudu. HotL, *tr. by* V. Narayana Rao

Warrior so bold and a virgin so bright, A. Alonzo the Brave and the Fair Imogine. Matthew Gregory Lewis. NOBRP; NPBRoP

Warrior! whose image on thy tomb. Effigies, The. Felicia Dorothea Hemans. NOBRP

Warrior Womb. Lenina Nadal. BRtP

Warrior wombs at night. Warrior Womb. Lenina Nadal. BRtP

Warriors and chiefs! should the shaft or the sword. Song of Saul before His Last Battle. Lord Byron. ChIV-1

Warrior's Lament, A. Nnamdi Olebara. PoAgWa, *tr. by* Chinweizu

Warrior's Tale, A. Sandra Alcosser. LiTh

Warru. Jack Davis. BMAP

Wars 1. Sinan Anton. IrPoTo, *tr. by* the author

War's killing ground? (LL) In the Casbah. Salma Khadra Jayyusi. CFP; PoArWo, *tr. by* Charles Doria

Wars of Imperialism. John Foulcher. NOBAu

Wars, The. Howard Moss. VCAP

Warscape, with Lovers. Marilyn Krysl. LiTh

Warsong of the Kwakiutl. *Unknown.* APN-2 *Fr.* Songs of the Kwakiutl Indians.

Wartburg, 1521–22, The. Timothy Steele. RA

Wartime Dawn, A. David Gascoyne. NPeEn

Wartime Photos of My Father. David Wojahn. MAAN

Was a bird; and the song was wordless; the singing will never be done. (LL) Everyone Sang. Siegfried Sassoon. MoBrPo; NAEL-6v2; NAEL-7v2; NAMCP V.1; NoAM; NoP-4; NoP-5; NPeEn; OBEV; OBWP; OPOU; StAl; WaAnP

Was a declaration of war. (LL) Question of Climate, A. Audre Lorde. NAMCP V.2; NoAM

Was almost eighteen years old. Herbie. David Alpaugh. OPRER

Was always there, its existence seldom. Template, The. John Ashbery. VaPo

Was as good a gun. She. Mary Dalton. OpeFie

Was balanced on the edge of the platform. Diver, The. Christopher Merrill. MoASP

Was banging the doors of the shed in the yard. (LL) Esyllt. Glyn Jones. AngWePo; OBWVE

Was dead and is alive. Amen. (LL) Task, The. Ruth Pitter. BeAl; MoBrPo

Was dirt. Floor, The. Yolanda Palis. ReBoTo

Was Elizabeth Siddal in a bath. Ophelia. Christopher Pilling. NLP

Was enough to carry me thru. (LL) Remember my little granite pail? Lorine Niedecker. APT-2; NAAPv.2

Was Ever Heart Like Mine? Edward Taylor. SacPr Fr. Preparatory Meditations Before My Approach to the Lord's Supper.

Was faithful unto death, and shamed the Devil. (LL) Lying. Richard Wilbur. MakPoe; OxBoAm

Was fluttering its wings. (LL) Bird, A. Sheila Wingfield. MoWP; StAl

Was for 300 or maybe 400 years. (LL) Toe'osh; a Laguna Coyote Story. Leslie Marmon Silko. NAMCP V.2; NoAM

Was full of dead bees. (LL) Story about the Body, A. Robert Hass. CAP-8; FaoP; OxBoAm; RaBo

Was hardly a Titan. He stood. Hyperion. Leslie Norris. TCAWP

Was he English, or French? Dead Turk, A. Li Kuang-t'ien. WoPoe, tr. by Kai-yu Hsu

Was he gone for good? Or only an hour? Louise could never tell. Night Falling Fast. Mary Jo Bang. PoDa

Was He Married? Stevie Smith. NoAM

Was healed, took up his bed and walked away. (LL) Seamus Heaney. NoP-5; OxBSo Fr. Glanmore Revisited.

Was heaven sent. (LL) Little Lyric (Of Great Importance). Langston Hughes. APT-2; NBLV; OBCoV

Was here before us, knew we would come, and sees beyond us. (LL) Adrienne Rich. NALW; NoAM Fr. Twenty-one Love Poems.

Was I an accident, Mommy? Unintended. Susan Moon. FiBr

Was I asleep? I think more about sleep. Falstaff's Dream. Jackson Wheeler. IaFF

Was I going to have such thoughts too. Did I Fall in Love? Orban Veli Kanik. NaPG, tr. by Talat Sait Halman

Was I no more than some fairy being. Last Poem: Goodbye to My Garden. Yuan Mei. GifTon, tr. by Jerome P. Seaton

Was I Not Made for Love? Unknown. CCL1, tr. by John Frodsham

Was it a blast to the balls dear brother. Black Poet Leaps to His Death, A. Etheridge Knight. BodElec

Was it a dream, or did I see it plain. Edmund Spenser. NIP-4; OxBSo Fr. Amoretti.

Was it a mountain wavering on the rim. Hagar. Rosanna Warren. ExTi

Was it a phoney coin that let. Back End of the Horse, The. Paul Groves. TCAWP

Was it a vision, or a waking dream? I heard her voice before I saw. Irish for No, The. Ciaran Carson. PNI

Was it because you'd wear. "To an Amiable Child." Babette Deutsch. APT-2

Was it D + 10 or D + 12 we caught. Frank Ormsby. PNI Fr. Northern Spring, A.

Was it for this. William Wordsworth. NPeEn Fr. Prelude, The; Growth of a Poet's Mind [1805 version].

Was it for this. William Wordsworth. NPBRoP Fr. Two-Part Prelude, The.

Was it for this I uttered prayers. Grown-up. Edna St. Vincent Millay. AmWit; NAAPv.2; NAMCP V.1; NoAM

Was it her eyes? Barbies, Las. Madeline Alviso. BeDoSh

Was it I making plans / for the summer—and for all the summers. Octavio Paz. PoetW Fr. Sunstone.

Was it in Tahiti? I Remember You. Johnny Mercer. ReLy

Was it Jonathan Edwards who'd repeat, continually. Jacqueline Osherow. PoDa Fr. Scattered Psalms.

Was it *my* wrist contused in the sarcophagic groove. Anastylosis. Carol Moldau. ICANM

Was It Not Curious? Stevie Smith. OxBEV

Was It One of the Long Hunters of Kentucky who Discovered Boone at Sunset? Robert Penn Warren. LPSFW

Was it perhaps in an imagined frame. Vision. Delmira Agustini. TCLAP, tr. by Karl Kirchwey

Was it some Spirit, Sheridan! that breathed. Samuel Taylor Coleridge. CenSon

Was it Some Sweet Device of Faery Land. Charles Lamb. CenSon

Was it something uncleaved, clean-cut you wanted? There's No Rigor Like the Old Rigor 2. Ira Sadoff. BodElec

Was it the ghoul in you that craved sex. Lady Macbeth, Afterward. Edwin Romond. IaFF

Was it the lazy haze of the summer afternoon. Restoration, A. Brendan Kennelly. IrLP

Was it the proud full sail[e] of his great verse. William Shakespeare. CABP; NoSic; OxAEP-1; OxBEV Fr. Sonnets.

Was it wind off the dumps. Summer Home. Seamus Heaney. PBCIP

Was it yesterday. Haiku: "Was it yesterday." Sonia Sanchez. FFC

Was Jesus Chaste? or did he. William Blake. ChIV-2 Fr. Everlasting Gospel, The.

Was Jesus Humble? or did he. William Blake. ChIV-2 Fr. Everlasting Gospel, The.

Was just that I was leaving home and my folks were growing old. (LL) Christmas at Sea. Robert Louis Stevenson. ChrPo; NePenScot

Was lout, son of lout, by old lout, and was da to a lout! (LL) Blue Blood. James Stephens. MoBrPo; OBCoV; OBMV

Was made for him, to tyrannize upon. (LL) Hunting of the Hare, The. Margaret Lucas Cavendish, Duchess of Newcastle. BASC; FaBoVe; NAEL-7v1; NOSC

Was made the Lady of the May. (LL) Nicholas Breton. NoSic; OBEV Fr. Honourable Entertainment Given to the Queen's Majesty in Progress at Elvetham, 1591, The.

Was my bones[. As I gave them]. What She Wanted. Ron Koertge. SUP

Was my soul, my body, my mind. What They Wanted. Victor H. Bausch. RaF

Was Nature always a snob. Miami Beach. Howard Moss. BodElec

Was never discussed, only frozen dinners. Housekeeping. Virginia Chase Sutton. SweBea

Was nevir in Scotland hard nor sene. Unknown. NePenScot

Was no more than his due who brought good news from Ghent. (LL) How They Brought the Good News from Ghent to Aix. Robert Browning. NAEL-6v2; NAEL-7v2; OBSP; UV

Was not the lost dauphin, though handsome was only. Robert Penn Warren. NAAL-5; NAMCP V.1 Fr. Audubon: A Vision.

Was not the lost dauphin, though handsome was only. Audubon: A Vision. Robert Penn Warren. APT-2

Was one that kept his word. (LL) Because I liked you better. A. E. Housman. CAGL; NPeEn; OxBEV

Was only an etiquette, a habit of speech not spoken. House Style, The. Elizabeth Macklin. KGB

Was Physiognomy. (LL) Spider sewed at Night, A. Emily Dickinson. NAAL-3; NALW

Was prettier than that of Robinson Crusoe. (LL) Infancy. Carlos Drummond de Andrade. BeAl; TCLAP, tr. by Elizabeth Bishop

Was sitting Astoria kitchen chair about to vote mayoral primary. When the Skyline Crumbles. Eliot Katz. PA9/11

Was startled there. (LL) Raiders' Dawn. Alun Lewis. AngWePo; NPeEn; PoAgWa

Was taken and carried to Canada. (LL) Bars Fight [August 28, 1746]. Lucy Terry. AmWaPo; NAAPv.1; WaAnP

Was that a leaf or a bird. In Muddy Waters. Larry Smith. AmZen

Was that sticky infusion, that rank flavor of blood, that poetry, by which I lived? (LL) Bear, The. Galway Kinnell. CAP-8; MakPoe; StAl; TRP; VCAP; WaAnP

Was That the Human Thing to Do? Joe Young. ReLy

Was that the wind? she said. Moment, A. John Todhunter. IrLP

Was that the year the water froze. History of My Father's House, The. Vona Groarke. MFPA

Was that young faithful heart. (LL) Casabianca. Felicia Dorothea Hemans. BRP; NAEL-6v2; NAEL-7v2; NOBRP; NoP-5; NPBRoP; NPeEn; RWP; ViWPN; VWP

Was the clock ticking. (LL) "H. D." NALW; NAMCP V.1 Fr. Tribute to the Angels.

Was the forgetful kingdom of death. (LL) Janet Waking. John Crowe Ransom. APT-1; ColAP; FuPo; InGu; MoAmPo; NoAM; PtR; WaAnP

Was the founder! (LL) Fit of Rhyme against Rhyme, A. Ben Jonson. NoP-4; NoP-5; PBRV

Was the mist becoming rain. (LL) Lost Heifer, The. Austin Clarke. ModIr; WoPoe

Was the nightingale killed in the groves? Nightingale, The. Euros Bowen. BBMWP, tr. by R. Gerallt Jones

Was the one he kept sailing home to? (LL) Odysseus. W. S. Merwin. NoP-4; NoP-5

Was the only thing I had. (LL) Homecoming. Langston Hughes. SAmP; TRP

Was the silkiest day of the young year. Day He Died, The. Ted Hughes. OxAEP-2

Was / the sky. Mariiane Mays. PoPra Fr. (HERO)neck: attempts at a portrait.

Was there another Troy for her to burn? (LL) No Second Troy. William Butler Yeats. HarvBoo; NAEL-6v2; NAEL-7v2; NAMCP V.1; NoAM; NoP-5; OxAEP-2; TFi; WaAnP; WeW-3

Was there one moment when the woman. Striking Distance. Carole Satyamurti. MoWP

Was this His coming! I had hoped to see. Ave Maria Gratia Plena. Oscar Wilde. ChIV-2

Was This the Face. Christopher Marlowe. BLPJKO *Fr.* Doctor Faustus.

Was this the face that launched a thousand ships? Christopher Marlowe. BLPJKO *Fr.* Doctor Faustus.

Was this Thy Passover. Christopher. Sydney E. Jerrold. SacPr

Was wild and welling at the source. (LL) Headwaters. N. Scott Momaday. ICANM; NoP-4; NoP-5; WaAnP

Was wrapped like *panettone* in Italian tinfoil. (LL) Sailing Home from Rapallo. Robert Lowell. InoFa; PoetW; PoPoPo

Was you at de hall las' night. Leap Yeah Party, De. Maggie Pogue Johnson. CBWP-4

Wash me in the water. *Unknown.* OBCoV *Fr.* Soldiers' Songs of the First World War.

Wash of surf guitar rolls, A. Teenage Interplanetary Vixens Run Wild on Bikini Beach. Allison Joseph. NAPBL

Wash over her, wet light. Woman Death. Hazel Hall. APT-1

Wash—Smelt. Sikong Tu. CCL1 *Fr.* Twenty-Four Modes of Poetry.

Washboard Wizard. Marilyn Nelson. BtF

Washday Battles. Geoffrey Summerfield. NOxBChV

Washed ashore. Repulse Bay. Marilyn Chin. OpBo

Washed by the rain, dust and grime are laid;. Starting Early from the Ch'u-ch'êng Inn. Po Chü-i. OBVE, *tr. by* Arthur Waley

Washed her body. Is Beautiful. Kiren Shoman. OWABP

Washed into the doorway. Guest, The. Wendell Berry. UpMys

Washerwoman. Carl Sandburg. IllVoic

Washerwoman, The. Mary Weston Fordham. CBWP-2

Washerwoman, The. Veronica Volkow. VCWP, *tr. by* Forrest Gander

Washerwoman is a member of the Salvation Army, The. Washerwoman. Carl Sandburg. IllVoic

Washing Dishes Late at Night. Kathleen Norris. UpMys

Washing hangs upon the line, A. Songs for a Colored Singer. Elizabeth Bishop.

Washing Kai in the sauna. Bath, The. Gary Snyder. CAP-8; FaoP; NAMCP V.2; PmAP; VCAP

Washing machine was chuffing, The. Long After Heine. Gwen Harwood. HarvBoo

Washing Stream, The. Li Ch'ing-chao. ErotSp, *tr. by* Sam Hamill
(To the Tune: Sands of the Washing Stream.) CrYelRi

Washing the Cow's Skull. David C. Yates. TiP2

Washing the hoe. Buson. EH, *tr. by* Yoel Hoffmann

Washing the saucepans. Issa. EH, *tr. by* Robert Hass

Washing Your Hair. Lucia Cordell Getsi. IllVoic

Washing-Day. Anna Laetitia Barbauld. BrAP; NAEL-7v2; PEW; WoRP

Washington. Gerwyn Williams. BBMWP, *tr. by* the author and Richard Poole

Washington Etude. Elizabeth Alexander. NAPBL

Washington Park. Gerald Costanzo. UrbNat

Washington Square: August Afternoon. Oliver Pitcher. EGAG

Washington Square Park and a Game of Chess. Christopher Stanard. SpirFl

Washington, the brave, the wise, the good. Inscription at Mount Vernon. *Unknown.* HHAm

Washington was calm, murderous, neo-classical. After I Seized the Pentagon. Robert Hass. YaYoPo

Wa-Sissica, the War Song. *Unknown.* APN-2 *Fr.* War Dance.

Wasn't this a queer thing? I stood with your mother. Queer Thing, A. Nancy Keesing. NOBAu

Wasn't this the site, asked the historian. House and Land. Allen Curnow. BrAP

Wasp. Bobi Jones. ATSWP, *tr. by* Robert Minhinnick

WASP Woman Visits a Black Junkie in Prison, A. Etheridge Knight. LaCa

Wasps, The. David Constantine. StAl

Wasps, The. Homer. OBVE *Fr.* Iliad, The.

Wasps between my bare toes crawl and tickle; black. Sant' Angelo d'Ischia. Edwin Denby. NYP2

Wasps' Nest. Mary Ruefle. AmAlph

Wassaile, The. Robert Herrick. PBRV

Wassailing Song. *Unknown.* OBCP

Waste. David Chaloner. VaPo

Waste. Grahame Davies. BBMWP, *tr. by* the author

Waste. Harry Graham. OBCoV; UV

Waste land at Station 14, The. Douglas Livingstone. TSAP

Waste Land Limericks. Wendy Cope. HarvBoo; PoCho

Waste Land, The. T. S. Eliot. APT-1; CABP; MoAmPo; NAAL-5; NAAPv.2; NAEL-6v2; NAEL-7v2; NAMCP V.1; NAWM-7v2; NoAM; NoP-4; NoP-5; OxAEP-2; OxBoAm; TCAPo; TFi; WaAnP
1. The Burial of the Dead. NPeEn
4. Death by Water. NPeEn; OBVE; OxBEV
3. The Fire Sermon. HarvBoo
2. A Game of Chess. HarvBoo
5. What the Thunder Said.
"When lovely woman stoops to folly and." UV

Waste reels out the daylight corpus. Half-Done, Half-Turn. Jon Gill Bentley. ICANM

Waste remains, the waste remains and kills, The. (LL) Missing Dates. William Empson. HarvBoo; MakPoe; MoBrPo; NAMCP V.1; NoAM; NoP-5; NPeEn; OxBEV; StAl

Waste Sonata. Sharon Olds. BeAl

Wasted. Mary Elizabeth Coleridge. ViWPN

Wasted. June Jordan. IJHIL

Wasted Day, A. Frances Darwin Cornford. MoBrPo

Wasted Days. Oscar Wilde. CAGL

Wasted years, the wasted years, The. Henry E. G. Rope. SacPr

Wasteland. Games at the Hour of the Desert. Manuela Fingueret. MirDau, *tr. by* Roberta Gordenstein

Wasteland—Gazing Far Away. Tu Fu [*or* Du Fu]. CCL1, *tr. by* Florence Ayscough and Amy Lowell

Wasting Game, The. Philip Gross.
"I'm fat, look, *fat*." StAl

Wasting my breath to cry hooly and fairly! (LL) Hooly and Fairly. Joanna Baillie. RACG; WoRP

Wasting Time. Opal Palmer. FaBoVe

Wat a joyful news, Miss Mattie. Colonization in Reverse. Louise Bennett. NAMCP V.2; OBCoV

Wat last year at Sang-kan's headwaters. War South of the Great Wall. Li Po. NDACCP, *tr. by* David Hinton

Wat ye what my Minnie did. Robert Burns. EroLit

Watch, The. Frances Darwin Cornford. MoBrPo; PtR

Watch. Amanda Dalton. NeBl *Fr.* Room of Leaves.

Watch, The. Gwyneth Lewis. ATSWP, *tr. by* Robert Minhinnick

Watch, The. Marge Piercy. BeAl

Watch. Giuseppe Ungaretti. FaBoWar, *tr. by* Patrick Creagh

Watch a red setter stretch and sink in cloud. (LL) Broken Home, The. James Merrill. BrAP; ColAP; EMP; GPTC; NAAL-5; NAMCP V.2; NoAM; NoP-4; NoP-5; PoPoPo

Watch and the Dogs, The. Homer. OBVE *Fr.* Iliad, The.

Watch for a scorpion, my friend, under every stone. Praxilla. SaLy, *tr. by* Diane Rayor

Watch it—you'll bump / Your heads. Issa. ZenPo, *tr. by* Takashi Ikemoto and Lucien Stryk

Watch long enough, and you will see the leaf. Conrad Potter Aiken. OxBoAm *Fr.* Preludes for Memnon; or, Preludes to Attitude.

Watch of Time. Magda Portal. TANSG, *tr. by* Shaun Griffin and Emma Sepúlveda-Pulvirenti

Watch out for Gullah woman. Gullah Women. Melvin E. Lewis. BtF

Watch out for the bloke astride the horse. Millet's *The Gleaners.* Matt Simpson. RSaN

Watch out, the pearl in the depth of future centuries. I Speak in All Ages. René Daumal. YaTCFP, *tr. by* Mary Ann Caws *and* Jean-Pierre Cauvin

Watch over every part of Mr. Y's body about. Manodharma with Mr. Y. Takehisa Kosugi. WhBo

Watch over me from heaven while within my arms I hold my boy. Angelo Poliziano. CAGL *Fr.* Greek Epigrams.

Watch Repair. Charles Simic. NAMCP V.2; NoP-4; NoP-5

Watch the. To a Butterfly. Menke Katz. Prolet, *tr. by* Amelia Glaser

Watch. The trees hook the sky. What We Say in New Mexico. Mary Doughtery Bartlett. ICANM

Watch them be themselves. At Shedd Aquarium. Robyn Schiff. LegDan

Watch these elders. They always come at night. These Too Are Our Elders. Jack A. Mapanje. HBAPE; NAfrP

Watch thou and fear; to-morrow thou shalt die. Dante Gabriel Rossetti. ChIV-2 *Fr.* House of Life, The.

Watch upon my wrist, The. W. H. Auden. AmWit *Fr.* Shorts I.

Watch-Dog's Honest Bark, The. Lord Byron. DiBP *Fr.* Don Juan.

Watched by every human love. (LL) Lullaby: "Lay your sleeping head, my love." W. H. Auden. EMP; HarvBoo; ItP; NAEL-6v2; NAEL-7v2; NAMCP V.1; NoAM; NoP-4; NoP-5; OxAEP-2; OxBEV; StAl; TFi; WaAnP; WeW-3

Watched with the cruel watching of the stars. In Her Prison. Sarah Morgan Bryan Piatt. NCAP

Watched you / & you were turning, turning. Journey, 1966. Anselm Hollo.

PmAP

Watcher, The. James Stephens. MoBrPo; OBEV

Watcher, The. Clara Ann Thompson. CBWP-2

Watchers. Robert Pack. PfSP

Watching a Dance Rehearsal in a Calgary Theatre with a Concrete Floor. Suzette Mayr. PoPra

Watching a Dance Rehearsal in a Calgary Theatre with a Concrete Floor 2. Suzette Mayr. PoPra

Watching a different sea. July. Marion Lomax. NeBl

Watching a Lonely Wild Goose at Nightfall. Hsiao Kang. CrYelRi, tr. by Sam Hamill

Watching a mallard, just beyond. At Present I Am Working as a Security Guard. Edison Dupree. OPRER

Watching a man vomit on the sidewalk. Play It Again, Salmonella. Jeffrey McDaniel. AmPoNex; SUP

Watching a thousand smiles. Discovery. Víctor Hernández Cruz. PueRic

Watching a Village Festival. Yang Wan-li. ColAnChi, tr. by Jonathan Chaves

Watching all those sexy Czechs. Act, The. William Scammell. RSaN

Watching alone by the ancient city wall. Thinking of Lady Yang at Midnight. Unknown. WoPoe, tr. by Jean S. Grigsby

Watching Ants Play Soccer in Central Park. Anthony Piccione. UrbNat

Watching baseball. Baseball Canto. Lawrence Ferlinghetti. MoASP

Watching buzzards. Crazy Boys. Beverly McLoughland. HHAm

Watching "Dark Circle." Denise Levertov. AtGh; UpMys

Watching Dogwood Blossoms Fall in a Parking Lot Off Route 46. August Kleinzahler. PoA 2002

Watching for Dolphins. David Constantine. HarvBoo; StAl

Watching for the time of day. (LL) Clock-A-Clay. John Clare. NAEL-6v2; NAEL-7v2

Watching love stories on TV. Gay Love and the Movies. Ralph Pomeroy. CAGL

Watching Rushcutters' bright bayful of masts and coloured keels. Angels' Weather. Bruce Beaver. BMAP

Watching Shoah in a Hotel Room in America. Adam Zagajewski. VCWP, tr. by Renata Gorczynski, Benjamin Ivry and C. K. Williams

Watching TV. Joanne Kyger. WANABP

Watching Tennis. John Heath-Stubbs. OxBSo

Watching the Dance. James Merrill. NIL-7; NIP-4

Watching the dark my spirit rose in flood. Bach and the Sentry. Ivor Gurney. HarvBoo

Watching the Distances. Tu Fu [or Du Fu]. CrYelRi, tr. by Sam Hamill

Watching the famous eruption of a volcano on Heimaey, Iceland. Reprieve, The. Hans Magnus Enzensberger. PoSu, tr. by Michael Hamburger

Watching the haar move in. Anstruther. John Burnside. EdScPo

Watching the Hearse. Charles Simic. BodElec

Watching the Late Day Clear after Snowfall. Chia Tao. CSKM, tr. by Mike O'Connor

Watching the Mayan Women. Luisa Villani. P180

Watching the Men Walk. Nance Van Winckel. PoDa

Watching the moon. Lady Izumi. HW, tr. by Mariko Aratani and Jane Hirshfield

Watching the moon. Lady Izumi. WPoS

Watching the New Moon, I Compose These Verses to Show to My Fellow-Travelers, Stranded with Me. Ho Hsun. CCL1, tr. by John Frodsham

Watching the Planes Come In at La Guardia. John Frederick Nims. OtW

Watching the Rain at Hoeduk Inn. Chungji. BecRai, tr. by Kim Daljin, Kim Won-Chung and Christopher Merrill

Watching the shied core. As Bad as a Mile. Philip Larkin. OxBEV

Watching the Swinging. Li K'ai-hsien. tr. by Jonathan Chaves

"Colorful frames are erected beside the Yellow River, The." ColAnChi, tr. by Jonathan Chaves

Watching the underlife idle by. On Becoming a Mermaid. Lorna Goodison. NAMCP V.2

Watching the Wheat. John Jones. AngWePo

Watching the world disappear as if on a journey of no return. (LL) Things I Didn't Know I Loved. Nazim Hikmet. AF; AmFaPo; GPTC; VCWP, tr. by Randy Blasing and Mutlu Konuk

Watching Trains. Joanna Fuhrman. AmPoNex

Watching, watching from the shore. Shipwreck. Rosalie Moore. CalPo; YaYoPo

Watching You. Simon J. Ortiz. HATNAP

Watching you in the mirror I wonder. Mirror, The. Louise Glück. CAP-8; OxBoAm

Watchmaker God. Robert Lowell. InvLi; SoSe-8

Watchman, What of the First First Lady? Ogden Nash. AmWit

Watchman! What of the night? John Oxenham. SacPr

Water. Mary Anne Cartelli. MotU

Water: "Water understands / Civilization well, The." Ralph Waldo Emerson.

OxBoAm

Water. Boat's Blueprint, The. Ian Hamilton Finlay. NePenScot

Water. Philip Larkin. EmeKit; NAMCP V.2

Water. Robert Lowell. HeIP-4; NoP-4; NoP-5

Water. Leslie Norris. AngWePo; OBWVE

Water. Francis Ponge. GPTC, tr. by Beth Archer

Water. Ann Taylor. NOxBChV

Water and Fire. José Rizal. WoPoe, tr. by Nick Joaquín

Water and Light. Noah Blaustein. MoASP

Water and Marble. Patricia K. Page. IFF

Water and stone and wind. (LL) Wind and Water and Stone. Octavio Paz. ItP; TCLAP, tr. by Mark Strand

Water and the Rock, The. Fred Cogswell. Coast

Water and Wine [epigram]. Friedrich von Logau. GePo, tr. by George C. Schoolfield

Water are we, you say, and yourselves fire. Water and Fire. José Rizal. WoPoe, tr. by Nick Joaquín

Water Babies, The. Charles Kingsley. Young and Old. GoPo; OxAEP-2

Water between us becoming a river, The. (LL) Jamaica, October 18, 1972. Shara McCallum. AmPoNex; BtF

Water Birds. Cynthia Harper. TiP2

Water bubbles! Water bubbles! Rain Man. Drahomira Vandas. SurWo, tr. by Guy Ducornet

Water Buffalo. Yusef Komunyakaa. AmAlph

Water Bug and the Shadows, The. Unknown. OBVE, tr. by Frances Densmore

Water bug is drawing the shadows, The. Water Bug and the Shadows, The. Unknown. OBVE, tr. by Frances Densmore

Water by the pier glows green, The. Night-Mullins River. Colville N. Young. OWABP

Water: City Wildlife and Greenery. Alfred Corn. UrbNat

Water, cold, and sweet, and pure. Xenophanes. Louis Zukofsky. APT-2

Water colour country. Here the hills. Tasmania. Vivian Smith. NOBAu

Water emerges, a rich decoration, The. Cattails Along Red River. Joy Lahey. AnSo

Water falls white on the white. Joni Mitchell. Joseph Hutchison. SwNoth

Water fills the balconies. People wave from the window, flower tops drown and are useless. We Folded the Hours and Set Them in the Rain. Malinda Markham. IAoNAP

Water / flower. (LL) Something in the water. Lorine Niedecker. AFaM; NAMCP V.1

Water, for anguish of the solstice:—nay. Venetian Pastoral, by Giorgone, in the Louvre, A. Dante Gabriel Rossetti. GS

Water from the Lamp Bottle. James Applewhite. LPSFW

Water from the Well. Duriel Harris. BRtP

Water hollowed the stone, The. Wind and Water and Stone. Octavio Paz. ItP; TCLAP, tr. by Mark Strand

Water Images. Edith Jay Scovell.
Stream, The. HarvBoo
Tidal River, The. HarvBoo
Well, The. HarvBoo

Water in a Gourd. Chŏng Hwajin. EcSo, tr. by Julie C. Park

Water in its silence of roots. Gloria Gervitz. RMCMP Fr. Migrations.

Water is always the same. Kenneth Rexroth. WhBo Fr. Heart's Garden, the Garden's Heart, The.

Water is hard in the well, The. Roland Mathias. AngWePo Fr. Tide-Reach.

Water is heavy silver over stone. What Any Lover Learns. Archibald MacLeish. OxBoAm

Water is Manhattan. Thursday. Víctor Hernández Cruz. PueRic

Water is preeminent and gold, like a fire. Pindar. PoCho Fr. Olympian Odes, The.

Water is so clear and so calm, The. Fish Cove. Blaise Cendrars. BLT, tr. by Monique Chefdor

Water, is taught by thirst. Emily Dickinson. NCAP

Water Island. Howard Moss. NoP-4

Water. / Lakes and rivers. He Na Tye Woman. Paula Gunn Allen. HW

Water Lilies. Ralph J., Jr. Mills. IllVoic

Water Man, The. Mary Dalton. OpeFie

Water: no matter how much, there is still not enough. Fountains in the Sea. Martin Sorescu. VCWP, tr. by Seamus Heaney and Joana Russell-Gebbett

Water of Tears, The. Francis Ponge. AF, tr. by Beth Archer

Water of the Flowery Mill (II), The. Jerome Rothenberg. FTOS

Water of the river goes fleeing from itself, The. Futile Flight, Futile Fugue. Dulce Maria Loynaz. TANSG, tr. by Alan West

Water on the Moon. Stephanie Norgate. PoCu

Water pouring from clouds. Unknown. EaWin, tr. by J. Moussaieff Masson and W. S. Merwin

Water pours down in order to swallow us. Traveller's Song. Hugo von Hofmannsthal. WoPoe, tr. by Robert Bly

Water / Skidding down platforms of stone. Waking on a Summer Morning. Mary Oliver. PoCoUp

Water smokes, the bulrushes, The. Dead Landscape. Attila József. WoPoe, *tr. by* Edwin Morgan

Water Song. Steve Crow. HATNAP

Water Song. Afaa Michael Weaver. ISC

Water Song, The. Glenna Luschei. GeoHom

Water spiders dissemble the light and spillage. Bride of Long Division, The. Christopher Howell. RoV

Water Spilt. Pao Chao. CCL1, *tr. by* John Frodsham

Water spilt on level ground. Water Spilt. Pao Chao. CCL1, *tr. by* John Frodsham

Water stain nibbles at the side of a woman's mouth, A. Scroll. Lee Upton. AmAlph

Water still flows. Illegitimate Things. William Carlos Williams. MoAmPo

Water tank above the trees, and then the town, The. Failed Memory Exercise. Rodney Jones. LPSFW

Water that can't be muddied, The. Clear Valley. Muso Soseki. EaWin, *tr. by* W. S. Merwin

Water that died on the wheel, The. Perpetual Motion. Gerardo Diego. RaW, *tr. by* Ralph Nelson

Water the horses at a breach in the Great Wall. Horses at a Breach in the Great Wall. Ch'en Lin. ChinPo, *tr. by* Ye Weilian [*or* Yeh Wei-lien *or* Wai-lim Yip]

Water the Horses at a Breach in the Great Wall. *Unknown.* ChinPo, *tr. by* Ye Weilian [*or* Yeh Wei-lien *or* Wai-lim Yip]

Water to the horizon. Late in the Day, Gazing Out from a River Pavilion. Chia Tao. CSKM, *tr. by* Mike O'Connor

Water travels a long shot. Water Song. Steve Crow. HATNAP

Water trickles into the ear: a stream snaking across the oasis. Diana Hartog. NLPA *Fr.* Oasis.

Water turns / a long way down over the raw stone, The. You Are Happy. Margaret Atwood. TRP

Water understands / Civilization well, The. Water. Ralph Waldo Emerson. OxBoAm

Water USA. Clarence Major. EGAG

Water was too cold for us, The. (LL) Water. Robert Lowell. HeIP-4; NoP-4; NoP-5

Water washed, the water rose, The. Fisherman, The. Johann Wolfgang von Goethe. STV, *tr. by* John Frederick Nims

Water Wheel, The. Antonio Machado Ruiz. SpanPo, *tr. by* James Duffy

Water Wheel, The ("Afternoon arrived, The.") Antonio Machado Ruiz. WED, *tr. by* Robert Bly

Water, White Cotton, and the Rich Man. Martín Espada. PueRic

Water Woman. Catherine Obianuju Acholonu. HAWP

Waterbird. May Swenson. NoP-4; NoP-5; OxBoAm

Waterbirds on / River islands! *Unknown.* CCL1 *Fr.* Guan-ju.

Waterborne. Linda Gregerson. BAP-01

Water-burn. Michael Longley. StAl

Water-clock marks dawn, The. Going to the Palace with a Friend at Dawn. Tu Fu [*or* Du Fu]. CrYelRi, *tr. by* Sam Hamill

Water-Colour of Venice, A. Lawrence Durrell. MoBrPo

Water-drawing rites. Basho. SoOfWa, *tr. by* Sam Hamill

Waterfall. Seamus Heaney. HeIP-4

Waterfall. Gareth Owen. Spl

Waterfall [*or* Water-Fall], The. Henry Vaughan. AngWePo; NAEL-6v1; NAEL-7v1; NoP-4; NoP-5; NOSC; OBWVE; OxAEP-1; SacPr; WaAnP (Water-fall, The.) FSCP; PBRV

Waterfall. Greg Williamson. RA

Waterfall, The. John Keble. Lyra Innocentium. SacPr

Waterfall, The. Michael Longley. BeAl

Waterfall, The / Is frozen. Cold presses. Staying with Master Heng Chao at Roost of the Sages Monastery on Mount Lu. Wei Feng. CSKM, *tr. by* Paul Hansen

Waterfall at Lu-shan. Li Po. CrYelRi, *tr. by* Sam Hamill

Waterfall: "Creek's easy purr, The." Bruce Berger. NevBe

Waterfall gown with water- / fowl sleekness embroidered so as to rise. Chanel N° 5. Robyn Schiff. LegDan

Waterfall plunges in mist, The. Country Scene. Hồ Xuân Hương. TAPaP, *tr. by* John Balaban

Waterford crystal smuggled from the Republic into Paisley's turf. Christmas, Belfast. Robert Coles. BloBone

Waterfowl Descending. Sam Witt. NeAmPo

Waterfowl, the cedar brakes, The. Lake Austin Diorama. John Collin Murphey. TiP2

Waterfowl their mates are calling. *Unknown.* CCL1 *Fr.* Guan-ju.

Waterfront Bars. Keith Wilson. AmWaPo

Water-Front Streets. Langston Hughes. SAmP

Watergaw, The. Hugh MacDiarmid. FaBoVe; HarvBoo; NAEL-6v2; NePenScot; NPeEn

Water-Hen, The. Violet Jacob. EdScPo

Watering Horses at a Long Wall Hole. *Unknown.* ColAnChi, *tr. by* Anne Birrell

Watering place of the long-tailed stars, The. (LL) Burning Shewolf. Vasco [*or* Vasko] Popa. PFTM-2; VCWP, *tr. by* Charles Simic

Watering the Horse. Robert Bly. StAl

Watering the New Lawn. Michael S. Smith. PasH

Water-Lilies. John Clare. WoPoe

Water-Lilies. Sara Teasdale. MoAmPo

Water-lilies on the meadow stream. Water-Lilies. John Clare. WoPoe

Water-Lily, The. D. M. Black. EdScPo

Waterloo Sunset. Ted Berrigan and Ron Padgett. AHA

Waterloo was the beginning; all the bridges of the world led to. Love Under the Rain. Abdul Wahab Al-Bayati. IrPoTo, *tr. by* Farouk Abdel Wahab

Waterloo! Waterloo! Waterloo! dismal plain! Victor Hugo. WoPoe *Fr.* Expiation.

Watermarks. Geoffrey Cook. Coast

Watermelon and Zen students. Peter Levitt. WhBo

Watermelon Man. Katie Donovan. NIrP

Watermelons. Charles Simic. OxBoAm; VCAP

Waterpot. Grace Nichols. RSaN

Water's Chant, The. Philip Levine. GeoHom

Waters darken, The. The continent vanishes. (LL) I See Chile in My Rearview Mirror. Agha Shahid Ali. AmAlph; NAMCP V.2; NoP-4

Waters from cold springs. Orchards in July. Zbigniew Machej. BLT

Waters have broken. Now your body's slow, The. Birth Day. Andrew Waterman. PML

Waters of Kunming Pool, The. Autumn Meditation: 7. Tu Fu [*or* Du Fu]. CCL1, *tr. by* Stephen Owen

Waters of Life, The. Humbert Wolfe. MoBrPo

Waters rippled, gleamed and fell, The. At the Cascade. Henrietta Cordelia Ray. CBWP-3

Water's surface trembles delicately, The. Hidden Path, The. Chông Hwajin. EcSo, *tr. by* Julie C. Park

Watershed. Robert Penn Warren. OxBoAm; PoA 2002 *Fr.* Kentucky Mountain Farm.

Watershed, The. Alice Thompson Meynell. VWP

Waterwings. Cathy Song. NoAM

Watery waste the sinful world has grown, A. Judah Ha-Levi. SWaP *Fr.* On the Voyage to Jerusalem.

Watkwenies. Duncan Campbell Scott. BrAP

Watteau, a Dream. Emile Nelligan. WoPoe, *tr. by* David Rattray

Watts. Conrad Kent Rivers. OxAAAP

Wauken by nicht, and bydand on some boon. Portrait of Mary Stuart, Holyrood. Lewis Spence. EdScPo

Wave. Mark Jarman. PfSP

Wave, The. Witter Bynner. APT-1

Wave, The. Fatima Lim-Wilson. AmPoNex

Wave, The. Virgil. PoDa, *tr. by* Robert Pinsky

Wave and the Dune, The. May Swenson. OxBoAm

Wave Falling on the Beach, A. Lawrence Goeckel. ICANM

Wave hits and troughs, The. How I'll Live Then. Sibyl James. FiBr

Wave in the round of the port-hole. Party on Shipboard. George Oppen. APT-2; PFTM-1

Wave Symphony, The. Arthur Davison Ficke. PoA 2002 *Fr.* Four Japanese Paintings.

Wave withdrawing, The. Dover Beach—a Note to That Poem. Archibald MacLeish. BrAP

Wave ye, dark tresses! clustering or apart. Not Gone Yet. John Swanwick Drennan. IrLP

Wavelength. Jane Holland. NeBl

Wavering. Denise Levertov. PmAP

Wavering blue floor. Campagna. John Peck. HarvBoo

Waverley. Sir Walter Scott. Hie Away, Hie Away. OxAEP-2

Waverly Pen, The. *Unknown.* OBCoV *Fr.* Advertising Rhymes.

Wavers, a candle's shadow, at the end. (LL) Legal Fiction. William Empson. HarvBoo; NoAM; NoP-4; NoP-5

Waves: "I have swum too far." Robin Robertson. P180

Waves, The. Marcia Southwick. PfSP

Waves break against the shore with the force, The. Waves, The. Marcia Southwick. PfSP

Waves Broke on the Shore, The. Jackson Mac Low. OnScMo

Waves claw, The. On The Beach. John Corben. Spl

Waves come—the large fourth wave, The. On the Oregon Coast. Robert Bly. BodElec

Waves forever move, The. Sisters, The. John Banister Tabb. APN-2

Waves in August. M. S. Merwin. OxBoAm

Waves know rocks by foam and recklessness, The. Merl. Jean Toomer. GT

Waves, like ridges of plow'd land, are high, The. Sea Similized to Meadows and Pastures, The: the Mariners, to Shepherds: the Mast, to a May-Pole: the Fish, to Beasts. Margaret Lucas Cavendish, Duchess of Newcastle. NoP-4; NoP-5

Waves of the sea, fathomless, pearls submerged in the sea. Song of the Pearl-Fishers, The. Yüan Chěn. CCL1, *tr.* by John A. Scott

Waves Sifting Sand. Po Chü-i.
    "One anchorage of sand appears as another dissolves away." NDACCP, *tr.* by David Hinton

Waves the short two-by-four. Painting Drunken Twilight. George Barlow. GT

Waves want / to be wheels. Surf. Lillian Morrison. NTCP

Waves which have kept me from reaching you, The. (LL) To the Harbormaster. Frank O'Hara. OxBoAm; VCAP

Wave-shaped dune is still, The. Wave and the Dune, The. May Swenson. OxBoAm

Wave-Won. Emily Pauline Johnson. SWaP

Waving a gaudy flag it loves and curses. (LL) Desertmartin. Tom Paulin. BeAl; ModIr; NPeEn; PBCIP; PNI

Waving Adieu, Adieu, Adieu. Wallace Stevens. NoP-4; NoP-5

Waving good-bye. (LL) Field Poem. Gary Soto. PBCAP; WaAnP

Waving Good-Bye. Gerald Stern. GoPo; PoA 2002

Waving of the Corn, The. Sidney Lanier. APN-2

Wax-white— / Floor, ceiling, walls. Amy Lowell. APT-1 *Fr.* Towns in Colour.

Waxes and wanes. (LL) Lunar Baedeker. Mina Loy. APT-1; OxBoAm

Waxing Poetic on Marvin. Gordon Chambers. InTrad

Waxwings. Robert Francis. APT-2; BLT; RaBo

Waxwings. Milton Kessler. InvLad

Way, The. Catherine Obianuju Acholonu. NAfrP

Way, The. William Bronk. BeAl; StAl

Way, The. Robert Creeley. WoBe

Way, The. Ngodup Paljor. WhBo

Way a Child Might Believe, The. Olga Broumas. ArBi

Way a crow, The. Dust of Snow. Robert Frost. APT-1; ChAP; NAAPv.2; NAMCP V.1; OxBoAm; PtR; SAmP; SoSe-8; WaAnP; WeW-3

Way a Ghost Dissolves, The. Richard Hugo. NoAM; NoP-4; NoP-5

Way a tired Chippewa woman, The. Hush. David St. John. CalPo; FaoP

Way a woman keeps her house, The. Gliding Toward the Lamps. Matthew Rohrer. NeAmPo

Way a word, feathering air, may outlast a building, The. Five Panels. Mark Irwin. PoDa

Way and Its Power, The. Lao Tzu. CCL1, *tr.* by Arthur Waley

Way Animals Are, The. Leslie Ullman. TiP2

Way as "Way" bespoke is no true lasting way; The. Lao Tzu. WoPoe *Fr.* Tao Te Ching.

Way Back Then. Fergus Allen. IrLP

Way back / to the yes yes y'alls. Asian Am Anthem, An. Thien-bao Thuc Phi. BRtP

Way cat fur comes in cool from the night, The. Passing House, The. Beckian Fritz Goldberg. AmAlph

Way Down, The. Jay Macpherson.
    Some Ghosts and Some Ghouls. IFF
    They Return. PoA 2002

Way down among Brazilians. Coffee Song (They've Got an Awful Lot of Coffee in Brazil), The. Bob Hilliard. ReLy

Way down Souf whar de lillies grow. To See Ol' Booker T. Maggie Pogue Johnson. CBWP-4

Way Down South in Dixie. Song for a Dark Girl. Langston Hughes. InoFa; NAAL-5; NAAPv.2; NAMCP V.1; NoP-4; NoP-5; SAmP

Way down there, in the doll's house, the unborn suddenly came of age. Anesthesia. Antonio Deltoro. RMCMP, *tr.* by Christian Viveros-Fauné

Way down upon de Swanee ribber [*or* river]. Old Folks at Home. Stephen Collins Foster. APN-2

Way Down Yonder in New Orleans. Henry Creamer. ReLy

Way he made that corpse dance, The. Infantry Assault. Doug Anderson. AmWaPo

Way he pushes deeper, The. Pole Boat at Honey Island. Sandra Alcosser. PoDa

Way He'd Like It, The. Al Zolynas. SUP

Way her silky garments undulate, The. Charles Baudelaire. SxFrPo, *tr.* by James McGowan

Way home's left implicit, the beauty being to cause the same answer, The. Home Avenue. C. S. Giscombe. RD

Way I, A. Jacques Roubaud. YaTCFP, *tr.* by the author

Way I can carry a canary on my finger through the house, The. Bedtime Story. Beckian Fritz Goldberg. AmAlph

Way I hear it, Chinese fortune cookies, The. Fortune Cookie Blues. Amy Uyematsu. LTA

Way I learned, The. Shérdi. Sujata Bhatt. NeBrP

Way I must enter, The. Lady Izumi. WPoS

'Way in de middle ob de air. (LL) Ezekiel Saw de [*or* the] Wheel. *Unknown.* APN-2; NoP-4; NoP-5
    ('Way up in the middle o' the air.) (LL) NoP-4; NoP-5

Way is like an empty vessel, The. Lao Tzu. CCL1 *Fr.* Way and Its Power, The.

Way is long and dreary, The. Pilgrims, The. Adelaide Anne Procter. SacPr

Way It Goes, The. Vona Groarke. NIrP

Way it is in fall, the moon a diamond, The. You Know. Valerie Graham. PfS

Way it is now, The. Charles Bukowski. GoPo

Way It Is, The. William Stafford. TWF

Way It Must Be, The. Enrique Molina. TCLAP, *tr.* by Naomi Lindstrom

Way Light Bends, The. William Daniel Ehrhart. AtGh

Way Lorene and I went back, The. Need Increasing Itself by Rounds. Kathleen Peirce. PBCAP

Way love rests upon coincidence, The. On Leaving the Artists' Colony. Bruce Bawer. RA

Way of Being, A. Barbara Guest. FTOS

Way of Geometry, The. Choice. David Bromige. FTOS

Way of It, The. Ella Wheeler Wilcox. LW

Way of Life, A. Howard Nemerov. NIL-7; NIP-4

Way of Pain, The. Wendell Berry. UpMys

Way of Tet, The. Bruce Weigl. AF; AmAlph

Way of the Water, The. Johanna Kruit. TuT, *tr.* by Peter van de Kamp

Way of the Water-Hyacinth, The. Zawgee. AmFaPo; ItP, *tr.* by Lyn Aye

Way of the world as it is, The. Alone at Night. Kwŏn P'il. GifTon, *tr.* by Sung-Il Lee

Way of the World, The. William Congreve. NAEL-6v1

Way of Words, The. Martha Elizabeth. TiP2

Way on back in the reign of Mrs. Duke. Drawing Hands. Greg Williamson. AmPoNex

Way Out, A. Fleur Adcock. MoWP

Way Out, The. Jeni Couzyn. HAWP

'Way out in Western Texas, where the Clear Fork's waters flow. Cowboys' Christmas Ball, The. William Lawrence Chittenden. TiP2

Way out is through fire, The. Way Out, The. Jeni Couzyn. HAWP

Way Out of the Wood, The.
    "I crossed." YaYoPo

Way sailors sing, The. Nothing of All That. Jan G. Elburg. TuT, *tr.* by Pat Boran

Way she played the piano, The. October 23, 1983. June Jordan. SeSe

Way that can be told of is not an Unvarying Way, The. Lao Tzu. CCL1 *Fr.* Way and Its Power, The.

Way the ball, The. Jump Shooter, The. Dennis Trudell. MoASP

Way the blacksmith begins by knowing, The. Green Field, The. Robin Behn. AmAlph

Way the Cards Fall, The. Yusef Komunyakaa. GT

Way the dog trots out the front door, The. Dharma. Billy Collins. OxBoAm

Way the dying hear things, I don't know, The. Way the Dying Hear Things, The. Marianne Boruch. AmAlph

Way the incense gripped, The. Father of My Father. Lawson Fusao Inada. UnSA

Way the water goes is blink blink blink, The. Intruder in a Set Scene. Norman Alexander MacCaig. NePenScot

Way the world is not, The. Sonnet. Bill Knott. PBCAP

Way the world works is like this, The. Advice to a First Cousin. Alberto A. Ríos. NAAL-5; NIL-7

Way they do, The. Loo-wit. Wendy Rose. HATNAP

Way they wait there, The. Rubbish Bags. Victor Vroomkoning. TuT, *tr.* by Dennis O'Driscoll

Way things move sometimes, The. If You Need a Reason. Silvia Curbelo. BodElec

Way things, The. Performance Sequence. Rick London. Eno

Way this poem is filled with trees, and birds, The. (LL) Singapore. Mary Oliver. CAP-8; NIL-7

Way those poems were more than familiar, The. Radnoti Quarantine: Razglednicas. John Kinsella. VaPo

Way Through The Woods, The. Rudyard Kipling. BrAP; ChAP; HarvBoo; NAMCP V.1; NoAM; NOxBChV; OBEV; OxAEP-2; WHSW; WoPoe

Way to Cold Mountain, The. Han-shan (Cold Mountain). CCL1; NDACCP, *tr.* by Gary Snyder

Way To Do It, The. Mary Mapes Dodge. SWaP

Way to hump a cow is not, The.   E. E. Cummings.   AmWit; NoAM

Way to the Temple, The.   Wang Wei.   CrYelRi, *tr. by* Sam Hamill

Way up here, where sky comes close.   In the Sierras.   Al Young.   CalPo

'Way up in the middle o' the air. (LL)   *Unknown. See* 'Way in de middle ob de air.

Way was long, the wind was cold, The.   Sir Walter Scott.   OxAEP-2 *Fr.* Lay of the Last Minstrel, The.

Way . . . way back . . . nine hills away.   Nostalgia.   Musa Ćatim Ćatić.   SonAtl, *tr. by* Merica Delic and Ziva Pecavar

Way We Live, The.   Vicki Feaver.   BeAl

Way we live, The.   Kathleen Jamie.   NeBrP; StAl

Way we move, funk groove, The.   Way We Move, The.   Tony Medina.   BRtP

Way We Were, The.   Alan Bergman and Marilyn Bergman.   ReLy

Way which thou so well hast learn'd below, The. (LL)   To the Pious Memory of the Accomplished [*or* Accomplisht] Young Lady, Mrs. Anne Killigrew, [Excellent in the Two Sister-Arts of Poesie and Painting. An Ode].   John Dryden.   BrAP; CABP; NAEL-6v1

Way You Look Tonight, The.   Dorothy Fields.   ReLy

Way you move, The.   Futile Poem, A.   Remco Campert.   TuT, *tr. by* Theo Dorgan

Way you see it first is through, The.   Secret Garden, The.   Eleanor Wilner.   GifTon

Way you will live before what comes next, The. (LL)   Starting from Scratch.   Ingrid Wendt.   RWB; SweBea

Wayfarer / Perceiving the pathway to truth, The.   Stephen Crane.   APN-2; MoAmPo

Wayfarer, The.   Pak Mogwŏl [*or* Mokwŏl].   CAMKP, *tr. by* Kevin O'Rourke

Wayfarer, The.   Padraic Pearse.   IrV

Wayfarer's path lies beyond the lonely cloud, The.   Sending off My Fellow Monk Hae.   Baggok Choneung.   BecRai, *tr. by* Kim Daljin, Kim Won-Chung and Christopher Merrill

Wayfarers, The.   Yusuf Al-Khal.   PFTM-2, *tr. by* Sargon Boulus and Samuel Hazo

Wayman in Love.   Tom Wayman.   NIL-7; NIP-4

Wayne's College of Beauty, Santa Cruz.   David Swanger.   GeoHom

Ways and whims.   DDD.   Bruce Andrews.   FTOS

Way's not for the blind.   Tozan-Gyoso.   ZenPo, *tr. by* Takashi Ikemoto and Lucien Stryk

Ways of heaven are mysterious, The.   Lament.   T'ao Ch'ien.   CrYelRi, *tr. by* Sam Hamill

Ways of Talking.   Ha Jin.   PoA 2002

Ways off, someone is singing as he walks, A.   Fantasie Metropolitan.   Janet Holmes.   ExTi

Ways that can be walked are not the eternal Way, The.   Lao Tzu.   ColAnChi *Fr.* Tao Te Ching.

Wayward Son, The.   Mrs. Henry Linden.   CBWP-4

Wayworn: wide sleepless eyes. A night scene enters.   Hearing a Startled Bird During Stayover at Chin-Ch'ang Pavilion.   Li Shang-yin.   ChinPo, *tr. by* Ye Weilian [*or* Yeh Wei-lien *or* Wai-lim Yip]

Wayzgoose, The.   Roy Campbell.
   "Attend my fable if your ears be clean."   OBSV

Wdn't it be silly to be serious, now.   A. R. Ammons.   BAP-97 *Fr.* Strip.

We.   Ryn Gargulinski.   ArBi

We.   Janeya K. Hisle.   BtF

We.   Juliana Spahr.
   "Story goes like this: the light, The."   NAPBL

We / a hambone people.   Hambone Gospel, A.   Lamont B. Steptoe.   OxAAAP

We accept no givens: from here on illusion.   Furious Clarity, A.   Gabriel Zaid.   TCLAP, *tr. by* George McWhirter

We advance! (LL)   Dark Symphony.   Melvin B. Tolson.   ColAP; SSLK

We ain't got nowheres to run to.   (LL)   Warden Said to Me the Other Day, The.   Etheridge Knight.   InGu; LTA; PBCAP; SoSe-8

We all are standing.   Gambling.   Dora Teitelboim.   Prolet, *tr. by* Amelia Glaser

We all assume that Oscar said it. (LL)   Dorothy Parker.   NALW; NAMCP V.1 *Fr.* Pig's-Eye View of Literature, A.

We All Conspire.   Mario Benedetti.   TCLAP, *tr. by* Sophie Cabot Black and Maria Negroni

We all expected to see you lame.   Pain.   Dionisio D. Martinez.   OPRER

We all have our faults. Mine is trying to write poems.   Singing Aloud.   Carolyn Kizer.   TAPaP

We all know that things look strange in the night.   Stranger. They look.   Never-Dead, The.   Anna Couani.   BMAP

We all know why you have come back home with no.   Making Our Clowns Martyrs.   Jack A. Mapanje.   HBAPE; NAfrP

We all look at corpses.   It's a Dog's Life.   Bruce A. Jacobs.   BtF

We all look on with anxious eyes.   When Father Carves the Duck.   Ernest Vincent Wright.   NTCP

We all loved our comrade although he'd done wrong. (LL)   Cowboy's Lament, The.   *Unknown.*   APN-2; ChAP; FaBoA

We all remember school, of course.   Timetable.   Kate Clanchy.   EdScPo

We all say it.   "N" Word, The.   Mona Lisa Saloy.   FuFl

We all walked under God.   God.   Boris Abramovich Slutsky.   TCRusP, *tr. by* Daniel Weissbort

We all wanted to see it when it came.   Wide-Eyed.   William D. Barney.   TiP2

We also like blown cloud.   Kuan-Yin Shan: Mother-of-Mercy Mountain.   Mike O'Connor.   WANABP

We always had choices.   Bound.   Odetta D. Norton.   BtF

We always knew there was no Orpheus in Ireland.   Irish Poetry.   Eavan Boland.   PoDa

We anchor the boat alongside a hazy island.   Night on the Great River.   Meng Hao Jan.   NDACCP, *tr. by* Kenneth Rexroth

We and They.   Rudyard Kipling.   NAMCP V.1; NoAM *Fr.* Debits and Credits.

We answer by the third ring.   Reception.   Traci Paris.   ICANM

We approached the shore. Once more.   Thomas Kinsella.   PBCIP *Fr.* One.

We are a crystal zoo.   John Cotton.   NewEx

We are a little crazier now, and less sober, and some joy has risen out of us. . .it was so glad to be gone.   Hawk, The.   Jelaluddin Rumi.   WED, *tr. by* Robert Bly

We are a multitude of contradictions.   From Fanon.   Sandra Maria Esteves.   PueRic

We are a symphony of scissors.   Collage.   Shara McCallum.   NAPBL

We are *all* / bargaining with heaven.   Gustave Thibon, How Simone Weil Appeared to Me/4.   Stephanie Strickland.   ExTi

We are all 44 at a fine point in this place.   5th Tuesday.   John Berryman.   BodElec

We are all friends who have lived our childhood.   Second Half of Our Lives, The.   Sarah Rosenblatt.   AmPoNex

"We are all jugs," the potter said; and, when I smiled, he added: "You."   Earthen Jugs.   Gabriela Mistral.   SpanPo, *tr. by* Kate Flores

We are all mothers.   Liberation.   Abena Busia.   HAWP; PoetW

We are always surprised that pears survive.   Diana Brebner.   IFF *Fr.* Golden Lotus, The.

We are Americans Now, We Live in the Tundra.   Marilyn Chin.   FiBr; NIL-7; OPRER; UnSA

We are among those who came to be moths.   Hayâlî.   OLP, *tr. by* Walter Andrews, Najaat Black and Mehmet Kalpakli

We are angry sisters.   Angry sisters.   Christopher Nickelson.   BtF

We are apart; the city grows quiet between us.   At Night.   Sara Teasdale.   APT-1

We are as.   Soldiers.   Giuseppe Ungaretti.   PFTM-1

We are as clouds that veil the midnight moon.   Mutability.   Percy Bysshe Shelley.   NAEL-6v2; NAEL-7v2

We are at a party that doesn't love us. Finally the party lets the mask.   Below Freezing.   Tomas Tranströmer.   VCWP, *tr. by* Robert Bly

We are becalmed in haze.   Copula.   John Cope.   GeoH

We are being told of the greatness.   I Am.   Imamu Amiri Baraka.   FuFl

We are betrayed by what is false within. (LL)   George Meredith.   NAEL-6v2; OBEV *Fr.* Modern Love.

We are born with dreams in our hearts.   Immigrants in Our Own Land.   Jimmy Santiago Baca.   AF; UnSA

We are both different.   Enheduanna and Goethe.   Amal Al-Juburi.   PoArWo, *tr. by* Salih J. Altoma

We are both from the center of the continent.   Lakota Sister/Cherokee Mother.   Victoria Lena Manyarrows.   UnSA

We are breath of drop of rain.   Gods Wrote, The.   Keorapetse Kgositsile.   GT; OxAAAP

We are burning / in our heads.   Poet Recognizing the Echo of the Voice, A.   Diane Wakoski.   NIP-4

We are but warriors for the working-day.   William Shakespeare.   FaBoWar *Fr.* King Henry V.

We are children of the sun.   Children of the Sun.   Fenton Johnson.   TCAPo

We are clean for them now, as naked-clean as they are.   Snake Dance.   Witter Bynner.   NAAPv.2

We are come in a stone boat.   One of Us.   Kathleen Jamie.   GPPA

We are coming, even going.   Kath Walker.   Lionel Fogarty.   VaPo

We are committed to candor and openness.   Utilities Advertisement in the Wake of Three Mile Island.   Gary Metras.   AtGh

We are complicating.   Shred.   Hoa Nguyen.   WANABP

We are desire hidden in the love-crazed call.   Neshâtî.   OLP, *tr. by* Walter Andrews, Najaat Black and Mehmet Kalpakli

We are Diana's virgin-train.   On a Picture Painted by Herself [*or* Her self], Representing Two Nymphs [*or* Nimphs] of Diana's, One in a Posture to Hunt, the other Bath[e]ing.   Anne Killigrew.   BASC; NOSC

We Are Easily Reduced.   HeidiLynn Nilsson.   NeAmPo

We are encircled by large grieving women.   Large Grieving Women.   Slavko Mihalic.   PoSu, *tr. by* Charles Simic

We Are Equals. Gwendoline C. Konie. HAWP

We are fatherless daughters. Lonely Women. Kysha N. Brown. BRtP

We are feral rare. Les Americains. Diane Di Prima. Eno

We are finished, yet still. My Country Weeps. Andreas Gryphius. WoPoe, *tr. by John Peck*

We are flying white air. The most pioneering. Flying, Reflying, Farming. Richard Hugo. OtW

We are Fred Karno's army. *Unknown.* OBCoV *Fr.* Soldiers' Songs of the First World War.

We are girls of differnt ages. W. H. Auden. UV *Fr.* Dog beneath the Skin, The.

We Are Going. Fanny Crosby. SWaP

We Are Going [for Grannie Coolwell]. Oodgeroo of the tribe Noonuccal. BMAP; NOBAu

We Are Going to Be Here Now. Primus St. John. GT

We are going to see the rabbit. Alan Brownjohn. NOxBChV

We Are Going to Shoot at the Heart. Anna Swirszczynska [*or* Swir]. PoSu

We are going, we are going. We Are Going. Fanny Crosby. SWaP

We are in Louisiana now. Exile's Letter (Or: An Essay on Assimilation). Marilyn Chin. OpBo

We are in over your head. Inside Job, An. Brendan Galvin. PoCoUp

We Are in the Fields. Peter Finch. AngWePo

We are ladies. For My D.C. Girlfriends. Michelle Calhoun Green. BtF

We are left, finally, to decide why. Snow. William Virgil Davis. YaYoPo

We are like the dead. What the Gypsy Said to Her Children. Judith Ortiz Cofer. OxWW; UnSA

We Are Like These Things. Madeline Gleason. ASA

We Are Listening. Diane Ackerman. PoA 2002

We Are Living. Brendan Kennelly. BeAl

We are made of newspaper and smoke. Urban Poem. Douglas Goetsch. AmPoNex; UrbNat

We are made pure by power. We Are Made. Juan Felipe Herrera. PfSP

We are making a good world, we are making a good day. Prayer upon Cutting down the Sacred Tree. *Unknown.* APN-2, *tr. by* John G. Bourke.

We Are Many. Pablo Neruda. VCWP, *tr. by* Alastair Reid

We are more than ever surrounded by ants, says her letter. Henri Michaux. GPTC *Fr.* I Am Writing to You from a Far-Off Country.

We are near. (LL) Tenebrae. Paul Celan. PoSu; VCWP

We are near, Lord. Tenebrae. Paul Celan. PoSu; VCWP

We are no other than a moving row. Omar Khayyám. CABP *Fr.* Rubáiyát of Omar Khayyám [of Naishápúr], The.

We are not a chrysalis but. Residents of the Cocoon, The. Kazuko Shiraishi. WoBe, *tr. by* Samuel Grolmes and Yumiko Tsumura

We are not always dependent on memory. Pavel Grigoryevich Antokolsky. TCRusP *Fr.* Son.

We are not as small as we appear to be. Bohol's Tarsier Population. Clovis L. Nazareno. ReBoTo

We are not born yet, and everything's crystal under our feet. California Dreaming. Charles Wright. CAP-8

We are not lovers. Man and Wife. Anne Sexton. CAP-8

We are not loving women, having lived long. Leavetaking. Ingrid de Kok. TSAP

We are not near enough to love. Insincere Wish Addressed to a Beggar, An. Mary Elizabeth Coleridge. NPeEn; PEW; VWP

We are not responsible for your lost or stolen relatives. We Are Not Responsible. Harryette Mullen. PrTe

We are not slaves. Vera Pavlova. CRWP *Fr.* Letter from Memory.

We are not slaves of Süleymân, nor the captives. Hayretî. OLP, *tr. by* Walter Andrews, Najaat Black and Mehmet Kalpakli

We Are Not Vegetarians. Miek Coccia. BeDoSh

We are now on an adventure of RIGHTLY APPLYING our VIGOROUS. Descartes and the Splendor of *a Real Drama of* Everyday Life. In Six Parts. Joanne Kyger. AHA

We are nowhere near as calm as we probably appear. Robert John Moore. Coast *Fr.* Golden Book of Bovinities, The.

We are on the roof today. Philosophical Emancipation, The. Rafael Zepeda. SUP

We are ourselves but carriers. Life. For a Woman with Child. James Vincent Cunningham. APT-2

We are pressed, pressed on each other. George Oppen. NAMCP V.1 *Fr.* Of Being Numerous.

We are raindrop women. Raindrop Women. Mariahadessa Ekere Tallie. BtF

We are ravenous after our. Pizza and Pretense. Nerissa S. Balce. ReBoTo

We are reading the story of our lives. Story of Our Lives, The. Mark Strand. VCAP

We are running. Lucille Clifton. PLBUT

We are sailing on a charming bay. Tracey Herd. NeBl *Fr.* Mystery of the Missing Century, The.

We are satisfied, if you are; but why did I die? (LL) Losses. Randall Jarrell. AmFaPo; AmWaPo; BrAP; OtW; PoA 2002

We Are Seven. William Wordsworth. NAEL-6v2; NAEL-7v2; NOBRP; NPBRoP
  "I met a little cottage Girl." UV

We are sheepskin coats. Burrowing moles: born stupid. Velemir Khlebnikov. TCRusP *Fr.* Laundress, The.

We are sighing, for time is flying. Class Song of '91. Eloise Bibb. CBWP-4

We are sitting here at a corner table at the. Ristorante San Marco, The. Mary Ferrari. AHA

We are slowly. Erosion. Linda Pastan. NIP-4

We Are So Fond of One Another, Because Our Ailments Are the Same. Winfield Townley Scott. ICANM

We are sorry to inform you. In Answer to Your Query. Naomi Lazard. NBLV

We are sorry we cannot use the enclosed. Form Rejection Letter. Philip Dacey. SUP

We are standing under the wall. Our youth has been taken off like a. Wall, The. Zbigniew Herbert. AF, *tr. by* John Carpenter and Bogdana Carpenter

We are statues of ourselves, stiffened eulogies. Robert Sheppard. Oth *Fr.* Empty Diaries/Twentieth Century Blues 24.

We are still together, are we not, wondering if. (LL) Driven by a Strange Desire. Mónica de la Torre. IIR; LegDan

We are talking about the plane. When They Know. Ruth L. Schwartz. AmPoNex

We are ten. My First Riot: Bronx, NYC. Safiya Henderson-Holmes. UnSA

We are ten miles from sea, in a parking lot. Kendall Gulls. Ricardo Pau-Llosa. UrbNat

We are the blues. Funk Lore. Imamu Amiri Baraka. UnSA

We are the clan of willows. Willow. Elizabeth Delmore. NLP

We are the dawn marauders. Seagull. Brian McCabe. EdScPo

We are the desperate. Vagabonds. Langston Hughes. SAmP

We are the dwarfed birches. Dwarf Birches. Yevgeny Aleksandrovich Yevtushenko. TCRusP, *tr. by* Peter Levi and Robin Milner-Gulland

We are the fools of time and terror: Days. Lord Byron. AmFaPo *Fr.* Manfred.

We Are the Heirs. Isaac Platner. Prolet, *tr. by* Amelia Glaser

We are the hollow men. Hollow Men, The. T. S. Eliot. APT-1; BrAP; MoAmPo; NAAL-5; NAEL-7v2; NoP-5; OBMV; OxBoAm; WaAnP

We are the inheritors. We hide here. Ghost Stations. Carole Satyamurti. RSaN

We are the last that there are anywhere. For Easter Island or Another Island. William Dickey. YaYoPo

We are the Little Folk, we, etc. (LL) Rudyard Kipling. NAMCP V.1; NoAM *Fr.* Puck of Pook's Hill.

We are the Mejnûn of our age, we dwell in the wilderness. Nisâyî. OLP, *tr. by* Walter Andrews, Najaat Black and Mehmet Kalpakli

We Are the Music Makers. Arthur William Edgar O'Shaughnessy. *See also* Ode: "We are the music-makers."

We are the music-makers. Ode. Arthur William Edgar O'Shaughnessy. OBEV

We are the people in the meadows. Summer Song, A. Ernst Jandl. GTCP, *tr. by* Reinhold Grimm

We are the poor children, come out to see the sights. Carol of the Poor Children, The. Richard Middleton. OBCP

We are the silent poets of the night. 1st Poem for Cuba. Sandra Maria Esteves. PueRic

We are the smiling comfortable homes. Homes. Charlotte Perkins Stetson Gilman. SWaP

We are the snake hidden in the staff. Na'ili [*or* Yeni-Zada Mustafa Efendi]. OLP, *tr. by* Walter Andrews, Najaat Black and Mehmet Kalpakli

We are the stars that sing. Passamaquoddy Song of the Stars. Rita Joe. Coast

We are the stars which sing. Song of the Stars, The. *Unknown.* APN-2, *tr. by* Charles Godfrey Leland

We are the tired warriors worn down by defeat after defeat. Not the Fear of Shivering. Gülten Akın Cankoçak. NaPG

We are the Vagabonds that sleep. Ballade of the Outcasts. Stuart Merrill. APN-2

We are the Writing on the Wall. Dolores Kendrick. FFC

We Are the Young Magicians. Ruth Forman. AmPoNex

We are they who come faster than fate. James Elroy Flecker. MoBrPo *Fr.* Hassan.

We are thine, O Love, being in thee and made of thee. Lascelles Abercrombie. OBEV *Fr.* Emblems of Love.

We are things of dry hours and the involuntary plan. Gwendolyn Brooks. GT; NAAL-5; NoP-4; NoP-5; OxAAAP; PoPoPo *Fr.* Street in Bronzeville, A.

We are those two natural and nonchalant persons. (LL) Behold This Swarthy Face. Walt Whitman. APN-1; NAAPv.1

We are titled against the constellations.   Salting the Brae.   Martin Mooney.   NIrP

We are travelling west of Alice Springs, and Sam is at the wheel.   West of Alice.   W. E. Harney.   NOBAu

We are truly fed up.   Voice of Earth Mediums.   Philip Lamantia.   CLPP

We are two straw dolls.   Untitled.   Mohamed Metwalli.   AnVo, tr. by Mohamed Enani

We are upon the Scheldt. We know we move.   Dante Gabriel Rossetti.   NPeEn Fr. Trip to Paris and Belgium, A.

We are very polite to each other.   Unexpected Meeting.   Wisława Szymborska.   VCWP

We are visitors into.   Meditating on Star Light While Traveling Highway.   Anita Endrezze.   HATNAP

We are walking our very public attraction.   History of Sexual Preference, A.   Robin Becker.   BodElec; ExTi

We are waltzing now into the moonlit morning.   Waltz against the Mountains.   Thomas Hornsby Ferril.   APT-2

We are what we hear. A well known singer died.   Langaig.   Richard Hugo.   CAP-8

We are wrapped around each other.   What Saves Us.   Bruce Weigl.   AmWaPo

We are your grandparents.   Thirst.   Arthur Rimbaud.   WoPoe, tr. by Michael O'Brien

We Asked.   Malak' Abd al-Aziz.   HAWP, tr. by Pamela Vittorio

We asked . . . / Keep the pearls in the shells.   We Asked.   Malak' Abd al-Aziz.   HAWP, tr. by Pamela Vittorio

We asked, what is this? It rustled. We dug a hole.   Experiments Lasted Through the Winter, The.   Sabrina Orah Mark.   LegDan

We Assume: On the Death of Our Son, Reuben Masai Harper.   Michael S. Harper.   CAP-8; GT; NAMCP V.2; OxAAAP

We assume / that in 28 [or twenty-eight] hours.   We Assume: On the Death of Our Son, Reuben Masai Harper.   Michael S. Harper.   CAP-8; GT; NAMCP V.2; OxAAAP

We ate lunch, rmember? and I paid the check.   Waterloo Sunset.   Ted Berrigan and Ron Padgett.   AHA

We ate our breakfast lying on our backs.   Breakfast.   Wilfrid Wilson Gibson.   FaBoWar; OBMV

We athletes who, with sternest discipline.   Golden Road to Barcelona: 1992, The.   Martin Fagg.   UV

We banter / back and forth.   Perfecto Flores.   Jimmy Santiago Baca.   TRP

We begged him to teach us Spanish.   Piñon Nuts.   Dixie Salazar.   UnSA

We begin kissing.   Nostalgia.   Charles Rossiter.   PasH

We believe books and music.   Anatoly Steiger.   TCRusP, tr. by John Glad

We ben chapmen lyght of fote.   Chapmen.   Unknown.   FaBoVe

We biked along the Amstel heading south.   Along the River.   Ad Zuiderent.   ArBi, tr. by James S. Holmes

We Billion Cheered.   Glyn Maxwell.   StAl

We bore down on the ship at sea's edge.   Homer.   WoPoe Fr. Odyssey, The.

We borrowed the loan of Kerr's big ass.   Kerr's Ass.   Patrick Kavanagh.   ModIr

We both might wonder what you're doing here.   Communion.   Sarah Maguire.   MFPA

We bought from Laotian refugees a cloth.   Absorption of Rock.   Maxine Hong Kingston.   OpBo

We break off a branch of poplar catkins.   All Year Long.   Unknown.   NDACCP, tr. by Kenneth Rexroth

We breathe in, we do not think.   Thought, The.   Michael Palmer.   WoBe

We bring news.   Ityopia phase-in.   Seitlhamo Motsapi.   TSAP

We broke out of our dream into a clearing.   Stephano Remembers.   James Simmons.   PBCIP; PNI

We brought him in from between the lines: we'd better have let him lie.   Only a Boche.   Robert W. Service.   BrAP

We brushed the dirt off, held it to the light.   Edwin Morgan.   NePenScot Fr. Sonnets from Scotland.

We buried Madaza.   From the Outside.   Mafika Pascal Gwala.   NAfrP

We burn cities.   To Fat Boy, the Bomb.   Henry Braun.   BodElec

We bury and dig each other up.   Bury and Dig.   Minnie Bruce Pratt.   PoBW

We call it a grain of sand.   View with a Grain of Sand.   Wisława Szymborska.   BLT, tr. by Stanisław Barańczak and Clare Cavanagh

We called the statue.   Niyi Osundare.   HBAPE Fr. Moonsongs.

We came back late from visiting.   Konstantin Iakovlevich Vanshenkin.   TCRusP, tr. by Daniel Weissbort

We came down above the houses.   Deaths and Engines.   Eiléan Ní Chuilleanáin.   ModIr

We came during those years.   Norman Rosten.   YaYoPo

We came out alone, under the aspens; wanted.   Politicisation of the North Wind, The.   David Morley.   NLP

We came out to a clearing in the rain.   Illusion, The.   F. D. Reeve.   VisFro

We came to unexpected latitudes.   Sighting the Slave Ship.   Pauline Stainer.   NeBl

We came where the salmon were so many.   That Morning.   Ted Hughes.   HarvBoo

We came with the children up out of the Métro.   Gobelins.   Ellen Bryant Voigt.   InGu

We can cry now. After centuries of holding.   Returning the Water.   Angela Shannon.   BtF

We can endure the eyes.   At the Jewish Museum.   Linda Pastan.   TaR

We can go by that door a dozen times.   Strong Room of the House, The.   William Bronk.   APSN

We can lay no claim to the stars.   Black Blot, The.   Hedd Wyn.   BBMWP, tr. by Gillian Clarke

We can look into the stove tonight.   Burning Oneself Out.   Adrienne Rich.   BodElec

We Can Love But Once.   Charlotte Dacre.   RWP

We Can Say That.   Tony Curtis.   TCAWP

We can string words on a line.   Naum Korzhavin.   TCRusP, tr. by John Glad

We can tell already.   Two Months Married.   Aidan Carl Mathews.   PBCIP

We cannot bear to roast a book.   Parental Critic, The.   Keith Preston.   NBLV

We cannot celebrate with doleful Music.   For Both of You, the Divorce Being Final.   John Hollander.   YaYoPo

We cannot go to the country.   Raleigh Was Right.   William Carlos Williams.   NIL-7; NIP-4; NoAM; PoA 2002; WaAnP; WoPoe

We cannot hear each other speak. (LL)   Alfred Tennyson.   NAEL-6v2; NAEL-7v2 Fr. In Memoriam A. H. H.

We cannot know his legendary head.   Archaic Torso of Apollo.   Rainer Maria Rilke.   NAWM-7v2; PtR; RaBo; TWF, tr. by Stephen Mitchell

We cannot lie on our back.   Long road, The.   Mongane Wally Serote.   TSAP

We cannot recognize a single face. (LL)   Brides Come to Yuba City, The.   Chitra Divakaruni.   FTtHH; OpBo; UnSA

We cannot tell now.   Unknown.   ArkPo, tr. by Helen Craig McCullough

We cannot walk like Byron among Ayasoluk's ruined.   Pleasure of Ruins, The.   J. D. McClatchy.   PoA 2002

We can't complain.   Middle Class Blues.   Hans Magnus Enzensberger.   VCWP, tr. by the author and Michael Hamburger

We can't go on like this: be truthful, empty.   Eduardo Milán.   RMCMP, tr. by Roberto Tejada

We can't help being thirsty.   Jelaluddin Rumi.   LoL

We can't hide! We recognize ourselves! (LL)   Walt, I Salute You!   Lynn Emanuel.   MAAN; ViWalt

We can't keep it out. It keeps on filling your room. (LL)   Virgo Descending.   Charles Wright.   ColAP; TRP; WaAnP

We Can't Let You Broadcast That.   Norman Long.
    "Now the BBC once wrote to me and said 'Dear Norman Long'."   RWPCtW

We can't play these roles anymore.   Suggestion, A.   Ismail.   HotL, tr. by V. Narayana Rao

We can't take our eyes off the young.   Tightrope Wedding, The.   Michael Laskey.   BeAl

We can't write ourselves into eternal life.   Witness.   David Ignatow.   PoA 2002

We carved our names.   Elegy.   Chang Chi.   CrYelRi, tr. by Sam Hamill

We caught fireflies.   Ruth.   Norman J. Loftis.   SpirFl

We caught the tread of dancing feet.   Harlot's House, The.   Oscar Wilde.   ItP; MoBrPo; NAEL-6v2; NAEL-7v2; NoAM

We chanced in passing by that afternoon.   Black Cottage, The.   Robert Frost.   CBCWP

We Change the Map.   Kerry Hardie.   NIrP

We charge through the skies of disillusion.   Song at the African Middle Class.   Molara Ogundipe-Leslie.   HBAPE

We clawed through Paris.   Sphinxes.   Sandra Hochman.   YaYoPo

We climb the slopes of life with throbbing heart.   Aspiration.   Henrietta Cordelia Ray.   CBWP-3

We climbed the hill to look over our land.   Our Land.   Yannis Ritsos.   AmFaPo, tr. by Edmund Keeley

We climbed the Sass Maor's snowy finery.   December 1972: First Winter Ascension of the Sass Maor.   Liliane Welch.   Coast

We climbed the steps of air with motor roaring.   Flying.   Florence Ripley Mastin.   OtW

We close the door, shut out all sound, this is a ritual. We open the current.   Computers Are Poets Too.   Mererid Puw Davies.   BBMWP, tr. by the author

We come in peace from the third planet.   First Men on Mercury, The.   Edwin Morgan.   EdScPo; NePenScot

We come now to the space which is boy-shaped.   At Sixteen.   Ann Darr.   LW

We come to this country.   To be Sung on the Fourth of July.   Wyatt Prunty.   RA

We come unnoticed from the barrios.   Place Without Shame, A.   David Baraza.   FTtHH

We commit what we do not commit.   Homage to Issac Newton.   János Pilinszky.   IQMS; StAl, tr. by Peter Jay

We could be here. This is the valley. Small Town with One Road. Gary Soto. SoSe-8

We could count the times we went for a walk. End of the Affair, The. James Simmons. PBCIP

We could have crossed the road but hesitated. Interrogation, The. Edwin Muir. NPeEn; PoWW

We Could Have Met. Lee Cataldi. BMAP

We could hitch the Horses of Instruction. Comet. Matthew Rohrer. NAPBL

We could never really say what it is like. This Hour. Sharon Olds. BeAl

We could not pause, while yet the noontide air. Obsequies of Stuart. John Randolph Thompson. CBCWP

We could point to the poem and say "that map." John Tranter. BMAP *Fr.* Alphabet Murders, The.

We could say. Imagination in flight: an improvisational duet. Harriet Jacobs. SpirFl

We could stand the world if it were hard all over. (LL) Across the Bay. Donald Davie. CABP; NAMCP V.2; NoAM

We could stream through the eye of a needle. (LL) Railway Children, The. Seamus Heaney. BrAP; OPOU

We could weep for him. Bodo. Thomas Lux. OPRER

We could wipe away a fly. Jungle Café, The. Gary Soto. NoAM

We couldn't get near the bathroom. Slutty. Mark Bibbins. LegDan

We count the broken lyres that rest. Oliver Wendell Holmes. APN-1 *Fr.* Autocrat of the Breakfast Table, The.

We crept in the tall grass and slept till noon. (LL) 1916 Seen from 1921. Edmund Charles Blunden. NoP-4; NoP-5

We crept up, watched a black. How Shall We Sing the Lord's Song in a Strange Land? Andrew Hudgins. UpMys

We cross over the distant Ching-men. Crossing Ching-Men to See a Friend Off. Li Po. ChinPo, *tr. by* Ye Weilian [*or* Yeh Wei-lien *or* Wai-lim Yip]

We cross the river narrows. Parting. Li Po. CrYelRi, *tr. by* Sam Hamill

We cross the river over dark waves. Rain on the River [1970]. Lu Yu. NDACCP, *tr. by* Kenneth Rexroth

We crossed the Styx. Descent. Esther Jansma. BeAl, *tr. by the author and* James Brockway

We curve along the edge of civilization. Rincón. Sandra M. Castillo. TouFir

We cycled on the water. No one thought. Hampton Lock. Dave McClure. ArBi

We dance a carnival ride. I Am Dancing with My Mennonite Father. Anna Ruth Ediger Baehr. ACAMVP

We dance in death's face. Kalamu ya Salaam. SpirFl *Fr.* New Orleans Haiku.

We daughters of foreign women. Naturalization Papers. Myriam Moscona. CFP, *tr. by* Cynthia Steele

We deemed the secret lost, the spirit gone. Flaxman. Margaret Fuller. APN-1

We descend on horses onto the battleground. Impromptu. Tu Fu [*or* Du Fu]. CrYelRi, *tr. by* Sam Hamill

We dial a recording. October Marriage. Dennis Nurkse. PA9/11

We did not anticipate you, you bright ones. Letter to a Future Generation. Gwendolyn MacEwen. BrAP

We did not know the first thing about. Thinking about Bill, Dead of AIDS. Miller Williams. NIL-7

We did our duty. We Have Done Our Duty. Yehuda Amichai. GPTC; VCWP, *tr. by* Benjamin Harshav and Barbara Harshav

We did our living in the kitchen. Still-Life with Woodstove. William W. Cook. SpirFl

"We did sums at school, Mummy." Halfway Street, Sidcup. Fleur Adcock. Spl

We did the thing that he projected. Joseph Hilaire Pierre Belloc. FaBoWar *Fr.* Modern Traveller, The.

We did things more dulcet, more marionette. Karen Volkman. IAoNAP; NeAmPo

We didn't appreciate it! Incomers. Gareth Alban Davies. BBMWP, *tr. by the author and* Mike Jenkins

We didn't deny the obvious. Obvious, The. Jeffrey McDaniel. AmPoNex

We didn't have this and we didn't have that. C. D. Wright. InGu *Fr.* Just Whistle.

We didn't know. About Poems. Evan X. Hyde. OWABP

We didn't sleep / Three nights we sat up. What We Did After My Mother's Mastectomy. Lisa Glatt. AmPoNex

We didn't want to be white—or did we? Struggle, The. Toi Derricotte. LTA; PBCAP

We died because the shift kept holiday. (LL) Rudyard Kipling. InoFa; WoPoe *Fr.* Epitaphs of the War [1914–1918].

We dine at Adorno and return to my Beauvoir. Platonic Love. Curt Anderson. PoA 2002

We disagree to disagree, we divide, we differ. Difficulty That Is Marriage, The. Paul Durcan. IrLP

We dismount; I give you wine. Seeing Someone Off. Wang Wei. CCL1, *tr. by* Burton Watson

We dissolve—away from daytime, away from the sun. Twilight. Margit Szécsi. IQMS, *tr. by* Agnes Arany-Makkai

We do not care if you were. Ben Webster: "Did You Call Her Today?" Ron Welburn. SeSe

We Do Not Know How to Say Goodbye. Anna Andreyevna Akhmatova. TCRusP, *tr. by* Daniel Weissbort

We do not know how to say goodbye. We Do Not Know How to Say Goodbye. Anna Andreyevna Akhmatova. TCRusP, *tr. by* Daniel Weissbort

We do not mean to complain. We know how it is. Petition for Replenishment. C. D. Wright. AmAlph

We do not play on Graves. Emily Dickinson. NIL-7; NIP-4

We do this at least once a year. River at Night. Conor O'Callaghan. NIrP

We docked at noon in the port of Veracruz. We wore our Russian furs. Gloria Gervitz. MirDau *Fr.* Yiskor.

We don't [*or* dont] cry—Tim and I. Emily Dickinson. NAAPv.1

We don't fall in love: it rises through us. In Defence of Adultery. Julia Copus. StAl

We don't know the ponderous. Tom Montag. AmZen *Fr.* Plain Poems: A Fairwater Daybook.

We / don't know, you know, / we / don't know, do we?, / what / counts. (LL) Zürich, the Stork Inn. Paul Celan. BBASP; HP, *tr. by* Michael Hamburger

We don't lack people here on the Northern coast. Amusing Our Daughters. Carolyn Kizer. VCAP

We don't need the cup of pleasure. Nev'î. OLP, *tr. by* Walter Andrews, Najaat Black and Mehmet Kalpakli

We don't understand it. (LL) Poems We Can Understand. Paul Hoover. PmAP; WaAnP

We don't wear it in sacred amulets on our chests. Our Own Land. Anna Andreyevna Akhmatova. StAl, *tr. by* Richard McKane

We drank while half the stars came out for us. Songs We Fought For, The. Walter McDonald. SwNoth

We dream, don't we. Life Within an Egg. Kim Sǔnghǔi. EcSo, *tr. by* K. Kim Richards and Steffen Richards

We drew a circle that took him in! (LL) Outwitted. Edwin Markham. CalPo; MoAmPo; NAAPv.1

We drew a line with chalk rock across blacktop in the afternoon. Playing for Love. Amanda R. Evans. BeDoSh

We drift around the bend, silent, paddles over gunwales. Pamela Alexander. AmAlph *Fr.* Foxlight.

We drink in the mountains while the flowers bloom. Drinking Together. Li Po. NDACCP, *tr. by* William Carlos Williams

We drink whiskey. Rocking Horse and the Lady, The. Pak Inhwan. CAMKP, *tr. by* Scott Swaner

We drive between lakes just turning green. Driving through Minnesota during the Hanoi Bombings. Robert Bly. InoFa

We drive to water. Bluegrass. Jean Nordhaus. PfSP

We drove past farms, the hills terraced with sheep. Travel: After a Death. Jane Kenyon. FFC

We drove towards the city. Industrial City. Antigone Kefala. BMAP

We dust the walls. Aus Einem April. Frank O'Hara. HarvBoo

We each wanted our own story, my father and I. Essential Story, The. Charlie Smith. PoA 2002

We eat / bread & stewed sausage. Taste. Jennifer Maiden. BMAP

We Encounter Nat King Cole as We Invent the Future. Joy Harjo. ReTh

We entered from the north. David Brendon Hopes. UpMys *Fr.* Five Neo-Platonic Commentaries.

We Europeans. Our way of life. Lionel Abrahams. TSAP

We examine today not sacked cities, but sacked lives. Archaeology of Divorce, The. Patricia Storace. FFC

We exist by what is half true. Cape Breton in Autumn. David Helwig. Coast

We fail, and white men call us faggots till the end of / the earth. (LL) Poem for Black Hearts, A. Imamu Amiri Baraka. NAMCP.V.2; SSLK; WaAnP

We feel that we are greater than we know. (LL) William Wordsworth. CenSon; NPBRoP *Fr.* River Duddon [A Series of Sonnets], The.

We fell on the chair. Hilbert's Program. Milo De Angelis. NeIt, *tr. by* Lawrence Venuti

We filled our ears with so much noise that. Americans in 1933–4–5–6–7–8–, Etc. Merrill Moore. FaBoA

We find in the East Indies stars there be. Of Stars. Margaret Lucas Cavendish, Duchess of Newcastle. NOSC

We finish washing love away. (LL) Hickie, The. Liz Lochhead. LW; MoWP

We finished clearing the last. Above Pate Valley. Gary Snyder. GeoHom; NAMCP.V.2; NoP-4; NoP-5; OxBoAm; StAl; TRP

We first lay down among flowers. Elegy. Ikkyu Sojun. ErotSp, *tr. by* Sam Hamill

We first saw fire on the tragic slopes. Aisne, The (1914–15). Alan Seeger. AmWaPo

We Fish. Herman Melville. WHSW

We fish, we fish, we merrily swim.　We Fish.　Herman Melville.　WHSW

We fished up the Atlantic Cable one day between the Barbadoes and the Tortugas.　Cable Ship, The.　Harry Edmund Martinson.　WED, *tr. by* Robert Bly

We flame the river.　Burning the Water Hyacinth.　Audre Lorde.　AFaM

We fly forwards.　Look Back into the Future.　Andrey Andreievich Voznesensky.　PFTM-2, *tr. by* Anselm Hollo

We Folded the Hours and Set Them in the Rain.　Malinda Markham.　IAoNAP

We fools are pleased enough.　Market's Closing.　Shin Kyŏngnim.　CAMKP, *tr. by* David R. McCann

We forced our faces.　Being There.　Thomas Sayers Ellis.　AmPoNex

We Forego Mimicry.　Ray DiPalma.　FTOS

We forget, praising his lotus feet, that he named his son Rahula: "Fetter" or "Impediment."　Identifying with the Buddha.　Charles Harper Webb.　Vesp

We forget where we came from. Our Jewish.　Jews in the Land of Israel.　Yehuda Amichai.　PoSu

We forgot to clear your grave, so we stood.　On the Anniversary Of Your Death.　Karen L. Mitchell.　GT

We fought in 1917.　'Strike Up the Band.　Ira Gershwin.　ReLy

We Fought South of the City Wall.　*Unknown.*　CCL1, *tr. by* Anne Birrell

We fought south of the city wall.　We Fought South of the City Wall.　*Unknown.*　CCL1, *tr. by* Anne Birrell

We found a mouse in the chalk quarry today.　Anne and the Field-Mouse.　Ian Serraillier.　NOxBChV

We found a place for the mess tent and a place.　Setting-Up Camp.　Jonathan Gefen.　NRoS, *tr. by* Esther Raizen

We found ambition caked around his heart.　Post Mortem.　Sinéad Morrissey.　NIrP

We four.　Manifest Destiny.　Suheir Hammad.　PoArWo

We from the black sun of fear.　Chorus of the Dead.　Nelly Sachs.　PFTM-1

We gather at the ship's unlit front deck.　Mighty Tropicale Orchestra, The.　Sean Harvey.　SeSe

We gather our bones from many places, look for.　Corn Children.　Carol Lee Sanchez.　HW

We gather where the weeping willow waves.　Decoration Day.　Josephine D. Henderson Heard.　CBWP-4

We gave a helping hand to grass.　Helping Hand, A.　Miroslav Holub.　PoSu, *tr. by* George Theiner

We get our danger from the lord. (LL)　Etymological Dirge.　Heather McHugh.　ExTi; FaoP

We get to it through troughs and rainbows.　Enlli.　Christine Evans.　TCAWP

We get up at six with him and build a fire.　He Considers the Birds of the Air.　Karl Kirchwey.　GI

We give life only to what we hate. (LL)　Destiny.　Rosario Castellanos.　CFP; TANSG, *tr. by* George Bogin

We give them our lives.　Landing Pattern.　Philip Appleman.　GoPo

We Go Away at Home.　Jack Myers.　TiP2

We go, in winter's biting wind.　Diehards, The.　Ruth Pitter.　OBGa

We go, Miletos, dear fatherland, spurning.　Anyte.　SaLy, *tr. by* Diane Rayor

We go no more to Calverly's.　Calverly's.　Edwin Arlington Robinson.　APT-1; NAAPv.1; NAMCP V.1; NoAM

We go on a business trip.　H. C. ten Berge.　TuT *Fr.* Lusitanian Variant, The.

We Go Out Together.　Kenneth Patchen.　MoAmPo

We go out together into the staring town.　We Go Out Together.　Kenneth Patchen.　MoAmPo

We go over to see the head of a woman.　Balance and Beauty.　Clarence Major.　FTOS

We go through life this way.　Valerio Magrelli.　ItPo, *tr. by* Gayle Ridinger

We go up a foreigner's steps.　We Pass through a Foreigner's House.　Boadiba.　OGAHCP, *tr. by* the author and Jack Hirschman

We go up twenty-five strong.　1st Lt. Vernon J. Baker: Hero on the Hill.　Jabari Asim.　BtF; FuFl

We got nuff jackass rope! (LL)　Independance.　Louise Bennett.　FaBoVe; NAMCP V.2

We got ready and showed our home.　Scattered Congregation, The.　Tomas Tranströmer.　RaBo; VCWP; WED, *tr. by* Robert Bly

We got seats high behind home plate.　Kingdome 1974, The.　George Bowering.　BrAP

We got sunlight on the sand.　There Is Nothin' like a Dame.　Oscar Hammerstein, II.　ReLy

We got them the hard way.　Tapes.　Thomas Sayers Ellis.　AmPoNex

We gotta.　Survival Motion: Notice.　Melvin E. Brown.　ISC

We gotta make a film of this, Jack.　Script Conference.　John Hartley Williams.　EmeKit

We greet thee now open this festal morn.　Greeting.　Henrietta Cordelia Ray.　CBWP-3

We greet you now, Diana.　To Diana.　Elisaveta Kulman.　ARWW, *tr. by* Catriona Kelly

We grow accustomed to the Dark.　Emily Dickinson.　GoPo; SAmP

We grow together.　Sister.　Karol Wojtyla.　PML, *tr. by* Jerzy Peterkiewicz

We had a back-to-nature weekend because our household robots went on a religious retreat.　Solvent.　Jason Christie.　PoPra

We had a bower among the beans.　Bower among the Beans, The.　Emily Jane Pfeiffer.　ViWPN

We had a country to keep.　Inheritance.　Gerallt Lloyd Owen.　BBMWP, *tr. by* Gillian Clarke

We had a female Passenger who came.　September 1, 1802.　William Wordsworth.　OxBSo

We had already left him. I walked the ice.　Dante Alighieri.　OxBEV *Fr.* Divina Commedia (Selections from Anthologies, in English).

We had an old door.　Virtue of Slovenliness, The.　Geoffrey Holloway.　NLP

We had as our platoon commander one.　Officers and Gentlemen Down Under.　John Brookes.　FaBoWar

We had been flying all day long at one hundred fucking feet.　Twats in the Ops Room.　*Unknown.*　FaBoWar

We had been in the tall grass for hours.　At Midsummer.　Norman Dubie.　NoAM

We had been looking at an idol in a glass case.　After.　Shirley Kaufman.　InoFa

We had been school-mates,—she and I.　Imogene.　Eloise Bibb.　CBWP-4

We had expected everything but revolt.　Nightmare Number Three.　Stephen Vincent Benét.　MoAmPo

We had gathered for the love-feast on the time appointed.　Who Is My Neighbor?　Josephine D. Henderson Heard.　CBWP-4

We had many problems set us when Coolgardie was a camp.　Smiths, The.　E. G. Murphy.　NOBAu

We had more than.　Words.　Vern Rutsala.　WeW-3

We had never seen black cockatoos, though in the park.　Shadow of War, 1941.　Thomas William Shapcott.　BMAP

We had our towers too, a large.　Yeats at Athenry Perhaps.　Padraic Fallon.　ModIr

We had ridden long and were still far from the inn;.　Sleeping on Horseback.　Po Chü-i.　BLT, *tr. by* Arthur Waley

We had sat up all night hearing it roar, the mere.　Morning in the Islands.　John Hollander.　ColAP

We had stayed up all night, my friends and I, under hanging mosque lamps.　Filippo Tommaso Marinetti.　PFTM-1 *Fr.* Manifesto of Futurism, The.

We had this stuff that Wayne found in the shed.　Cro-Kill.　Anthony Lawrence.　NOBAu

We hae a dog that wags his tail.　Waggin' O' Our Dog's Tail, The.　Norman Macleod.　DiBP

We hammered him to the cross. His fingers grabbed.　Soldier Who Crucified Jesus, The.　Martinus Nijhoff.　TuT, *tr. by* Desmond Egan

We harden like trees, and like rivers are cold. (LL)　Lover, The; a Ballad.　Lady Mary Wortley Montagu.　NAEL-6v1; NAEL-7v1; NoP-4; NoP-5; OxBEV; PEW

"We Hardly."　Richard Huelsenbeck.　PFTM-1

We hardly had gotten the man's pants down.　"We Hardly."　Richard Huelsenbeck.　PFTM-1

We hated them mad rocks, yes.　Mad Moll And Crazy Betty.　Mary Dalton.　OpeFie

We have / a map of the universe.　Wings.　Miroslav Holub.　PoSu, *tr. by* Ian Milner and George Theiner

We have a soul at times.　Few Words on the Soul, A.　Wisława Szymborska.　PoDa, *tr. by* Stanislaw Baranczak and Clare Cavanagh

We have a stove in the big hall all right, but can't get it warm.　Stove Problem, The.　Elke Erb.　OnScMo, *tr. by* Rosmarie Waldrop

We have all been in rooms.　Adultery.　James Dickey.　CAP-8

We have all seen them circling pastures.　Under the Vulture-Tree.　David Bottoms.　GifTon

We have always heard music.　And sometimes i hear this song in my head.　Harriet Jacobs.　SpirFl

We have always known that you wanted us. (LL)　Helmsman, The.　"H. D."　GPTC; OxBoAm

We have become beautiful without even knowing it. (LL)　Nightclub.　Billy Collins.　FaoP; GoPo; SUP

We have been believers believing in the black gods of an old.　We Have Been Believers.　Margaret Abigail Walker.　BRtP

We have been everywhere, suddenly.　Universe is Part of Ourselves, The.　Robin Blaser.　FTOS

We have been helping with the cake.　Day before Christmas.　Marchette Chute.　NTCP

We Have Been Here Before.　Morris Gilbert Bishop.　AmWit

We have been here before, but we are lost.　Wet Camp.　Alberto A. Ríos.　NAAL-5

We have been rewarded with a great intimacy; we are allowed to know.　Justice.　Ben Marcus.　HeMarv

We Have Chosen a Timely Day.　*Unknown.*　ColAnChi, *tr. by* Anne Birrell

We have chosen a timely day. We Have Chosen a Timely Day. *Unknown.*
ColAnChi, *tr. by* Anne Birrell

We have climbed the mountain. Here in Katmandu. Donald Justice. HeIP-4

We have come / at the mercy of winds. Prayer to Eshbu-Elegba. Jeffrey
Renard Allen. RD

We have come, have come, have come, have come. Ode to Yangji. *Unknown.* CATKP,
tr. by Peter H. Lee

We have come thus far, my brothers. We have already laid our plans. Taking of
Life Brings Serious Thoughts, The. *Unknown.* AmWaPo, *tr. by* Frank
Russell

We have come to the edge of the woods. Jacklight. Louise Erdrich. CAP-8;
HATNAP; NIL-7; WeW-3

We have come to your shrine to worship. Plea for Mercy, A. Kwesi Brew.
WoPoe

We have disconcerted / The revolutions with our prayers. Resistance. Horst
Bienek. AF

We Have Done Our Duty. Yehuda Amichai. VCWP, *tr. by* Benjamin Harshav
and Barbara Harshav

We Have Done Our Duty. Yehuda Amichai. GPTC, *tr. by* Barbara Harshav
and Benjamin Harshav and Barbara Harshav

We have done what we wanted. Coming to This. Mark Strand. VCAP

We have dropped out of the other schools. Wayne's College of Beauty, Santa
Cruz. David Swanger. GeoHom

We have erased each letter. Life As a Book That Has Been Put Down. John
Ashbery. FTOS

We Have Even Lost our Tongues! Ifi Amadiume. HAWP

We have floated to the surface of Monet's pond. Frank Ormsby. ModIr *Fr.*
Paris Honeymoon, A.

We have for many years been bored. Pen-guin. The Sword-fish, The. Robert
Williams Wood. NBLV

We have forgotten Paris, and his fate. Helen Grown Old. Janet Lewis.
APT-2

We have gone out in boats upon the sea at night. Passage over Water. Robert
Duncan. NAMCP V.2; NoAM

We have grown a tree of knowledge, "Worthy Claflin" is the name. Tree of
Knowledge, The. Lizelia Augusta Jenkins Moorer. CBWP-3

We have had too much consecration. "H. D." NAMCP V.1 *Fr.* Walls Do Not
Fall, The.

We have heard of the undimmed air. Icarium Mare. Richard Wilbur. UpMys

We have here, she said, only one sun in the month, and for only a little while.
Henri Michaux. GPTC; MotU *Fr.* I Am Writing to You from a Far-Off
Country.

We have kept the miracle. I will not be here. (LL) In the Deep Museum.
Anne Sexton. BrAP; MoAmPo; WaAnP

We have known such joy as a child knows. We Have Known. Marvin Bell.
PoChi

We Have Lived and Loved Together. Charles Jefferys. ITBLP

We have lived as ectoplasm. Coda. "Ern Malley." BMAP

We have lived like civilized people. Silent Piano, The. Louis Simpson.
EmeKit

We have lost our way back home. Road, The. Abd al-Rahim Salih al-Rahim.
IrPoTo, *tr. by* Saadi A. Simawe and Daniel Weissbort

We have lost the old tongue, and with it. Old Tongue, The. Herbert Williams.
AngWePo; TCAWP

We have loved the self, each other, and the rounded slope. Epithalamium, An.
Joan Murray. YaYoPo

We have memorized America. Of History and Hope. Miller Williams. InGu;
RWB

We have never been able to write without triggering an incarnation of the soul.
Revolt Against Poetry. Antonin Artaud. ConPit, *tr. by* Clayton Eshleman

We have Never Loved. Sam Cornish. OxAAAP

We have never parted in almost seventy years. Song for My Own Shadow.
Haewŏn. BecRai, *tr. by* Kim Daljin, Kim Won-Chung and Christopher
Merrill

We Have Never Seen the Sky Light Up. Darryl Holmes. InTrad

We have never seen the sky light up. We Have Never Seen the Sky Light Up.
Darryl Holmes. InTrad

We have no heart for the fishing—we have no hand for the oar. Dykes, The.
Rudyard Kipling. HarvBoo; OBWP

We have no prairies. Bogland. Seamus Heaney. HeIP-4; NAMCP V.2;
NoAM; PBCIP; PNI; PoetW; PoPoPo

We have no time to stand and stare. (LL) Leisure. W. H. Davies. AngWePo;
GoPo; MoBrPo; OBEV; OBMV; TFi

We Have No Unknown Soldiers. Yehuda Amichai. NRoS, *tr. by* Esther
Raizen

We have not forgotten you but here they have you pretend to work. Letter to a
Cretan Flute-Maker. Justin Vitiello. UnSA

We have not known thee as we ought. Thomas Benson Pollock. SacPr

We Have Not Long to Love. Tennessee Williams. PoA 2002

We have nothing to grasp but such implausible fire. Just that. (LL) Truth, The.
Frankie Paino. AmPoNex; FaoP

We have only one noun. Not Only the Eskimos. Lisel Mueller. GoPo

We have our moments. In the Madonna Dell' Orto. Peter Rafferty. NLP

We have our problems, / too, with you. (LL) High to Low. Langston Hughes.
APT-2; PoPoPo

We have plenty of matches in our house. Love Poem. Ron Padgett. NYP2

We have read and argued fiercely. After Endless Discussions. Ishikawa
Takuboku. CAoMJL1, *tr. by* Leith Morton

We have sat here in too many poetry readings. Welcome, Major Poet! Sean
O'Brien. NoP-5

We have scarcely time to tell thee. James McIntyre. VerBaPo *Fr.* English
Poets.

We have seen heaven. Shin Tongyŏp. CAMKP *Fr.* Kŭm River.

We have seen her / the world over. "H. D." APT-1; HW; MoWP; NAAPv.2;
NALW; NAMCP V.1; PFTM-1 *Fr.* Tribute to the Angels.

We have seen sand frothing like the sea. Sand. John Jarmain. FaBoWar

We have seen what simplicity can do. Temple of the Mariposa. Elizabeth
Robinson. ASA

We have served our day. Rudyard Kipling. HarvBoo *Fr.* Epitaphs of the War
[1914–1918].

We have set out from here for the sublime. Prospects. Anthony Hecht. ItP

We have settled on either side of a bridge, under arches. Mind the Gap.
Maura Dooley. BeAl

We have slept in. Message on Cape Cod, The. Afaa Michael Weaver. GT;
PBCAP

We have sold our shadow. Geometrical Place. Günter Eich. AF, *tr. by* David
Young

We Have Some Urgent Messages. Kate Clanchy. EdScPo

We have struck the regions wherein we are keel or reef. Zone. Louise Bogan.
APT-2

We have talent. People call us. To Pi Ssu Yao. Tu Fu [*or* Du Fu]. BLT;
NDACCP, *tr. by* Kenneth Rexroth

We have tales full of tragic knights. In a magic land. Fadil Azzawi. IrPoTo,
tr. by Saadi A. Simawe

We have the body of a woman, an arch over the ground. It Is Not. Valerie
Martínez. TouFir

We have the myrtle's breath around us here. Imelda. Felicia Dorothea
Hemans. RWP

We have the whole day to drive to Santa Fe. Vintage. Karen McKinnon.
ICANM

We have to believe that he despises women, and doesn't hide it. Sadistic
Judith. Claude Cahun. YaTCFP, *tr. by* Mary Ann Caws and Jean-Pierre
Cauvin

We have to discard the past. Past. Pablo Neruda. VCWP, *tr. by* Alastair Reid

We have to talk. In the Open Air. Gwyneth Lewis. ATSWP, *tr. by* Robert
Minhinnick

We have travelled many miles to find this bed. Bed, The. Moniza Alvi.
MFPA

We have watched for long. D-Hour. Lawrence Okezie Chibueze Anene.
NeNiPo

We have welded the towbar. Meadow, The. Peter Fallon. IPoFL; PBCIP

We have wintered in the poems of John Thompson. Winter Marsh. Andrew
Steeves. Coast

We haven't spoken of it since the early days. Ashes. Annie Foster. NLP

We hear her in the square. At two o'clock. Speaker in the Square, A. George
Buchanan. PNI

We hear too late or not too late. (LL) Christmas Trees. Geoffrey Hill.
ChrPo; UpMys

We heard people were standing. Depression. Isabel Joshlin Glaser. HHAm

We heard the rumbling drum song. Blooming in the Valley, A. Garrett
McDowell. FuFl

We heard the thrushes by the shore and sea. In Kerry. John Millington Synge.
IrLP; MoBrPo

We heard they would jump from buildings. What We Heard About the
Japanese. Rachel Rose. BAP-01

We held the last stone wall—when day was red—. Dragon's Breath. Hervey
Allen. YaYoPo

We hitched up the mare and we buckled her down. Four of July. Robert
Newton Peck. CA

We hold each other. We hold each other tight. (LL) On the Back of a
Photograph. János Pilinszky. PoSu; StAl, *tr. by* Peter Jay

"We hold our flat shields, we wear our jerkins of hide." Hymn to the Fallen.
Unknown. FaBoWar; OBWP, *tr. by* Arthur Waley

We hold these truths to be self-evident. Decoy. John Ashbery. OxBoAm

We Hope For Patrons. Kovur Kilar. WoPoe, *tr. by* George L. Hart III

We hope for patrons. We Hope For Patrons. Kovur Kilar. WoPoe, *tr. by*
George L. Hart III

We humans talk. Dogs. Hamish Brown. EdScPo

We hunted the mad bastard. As It Should Be. Derek Mahon. EmeKit

We hunted the wren for Robin the Bobbin. Hunting the Wren. *Unknown.* FaBoVe

We hustle hard as the rest of the folk me and my baby. Everything Happens to (Monk and) Me. Brenda Marie Osbey. BodElec

We invented these trees and mountains, that long gash. Wilderness. Vern Rutsala. UrbNat

We invite maybe fire or six authors here every spring. Half-Dead. David Kirby. LiTh

We is gathahed hyeah, my brothahs. Ante-Bellum Sermon, An. Paul Laurence Dunbar. APN-2

We joined hands. (LL) My Woman's Transparence. Amina Saïd. HAWP; NAfrP, *tr.* by Eric Sellin

We Just Couldn't Say Good-bye. Harry Woods. ReLy

We keep forgetting the gods. And if we happened to remember. Requiem on Poros. Yannis Ritsos. VCWP, *tr.* by Edmund Keeley

We keep our quilts in closets and do not dance. Mennonites. Julia Kasdorf. ACAMVP; NeAmPo; PBCAP

We keep the shutters drawn all afternoon. Galveston. Isabel Nathaniel. TiP2

We kept war in the kitchen. Dream of the Evil Servant. Reetika Vazirani. NAPBL

We kill what we love. What's left. Destiny. Rosario Castellanos. CFP; TANSG, *tr.* by George Bogin

We knew how to order. Just the dash. Gwendolyn Brooks. IllVoic *Fr.* Gay Chaps at the Bar.

We knew no other jobs. During Recess. Giovanna Pollarolo. TANSG, *tr.* by Marjorie Agosin

We knew so much; when her beautiful eyes could lighten. Sagacity. William Rose Benét. MoAmPo

We knew we had our man when his limp switched. Our Man. Ben Doyle. LegDan

We know, Doctor Williams, you and I. Letter to William Carlos Williams, A. George Young. BloBone

We know each other too long. Two Iowa Farmers. Natalie Goldberg. FiBr

We know it's to San Francisco. Miss Chang is Missing. Adrienne Su. PoDa

We know nothing. Death of Guillaume Apollinaire, The. Tristan Tzara. YaTCFP, *tr.* by Mary Ann Caws and Jean-Pierre Cauvin

We know our parents make us by our hands. (LL) Genetics. Sinéad Morrissey. BeAl; MoWP; NIrP

We know poetical poetry the common dangers. Basho 2. Cees Nooteboom. TuT, *tr.* by Michael O'Loughlin

We know so little about what matters. Nature of Suffering, The. Amy Gerstler. ExTi

We know that our master has left us for the day. (LL) Waking from Sleep. Robert Bly. NoP-4; NoP-5

We know the Rocket's upward whizz. Bonfires, The. Rudyard Kipling. NPeEn

We know the story. Generation. Rae Armantrout. FTOS

We know there must be consciousness in things. Astragaloi. Mark Jarman. PoCho

We know this is not life. Baize Queens. Jane Holland. NeBl

We know this story: how his daddy died of drink. David Wojahn. PBCAP *Fr.* Mystery Train: A Sequence.

We know where deepest lies the snow. Song. Anne Brontë. PEW

We Kurds are God's freedom lovers. God's Freedom Lovers. Ahmed Herdi. IrPoTo, *tr.* by Muhammad Ali

We lack the courage to be where we are. Edwin Arlington Robinson. NCAP

We laugh and we well might weep with the Ballads of George R. Sims. (LL) Ballad of George R. Sims, The. Sir John Betjeman. OBCoV; UV

We laughed. Second Class Citizen. Jennifer Lagier. UnSA

We Laughed at Him. Chinua Achebe. PFTM-2

We laughed at him our. We Laughed at Him. Chinua Achebe. PFTM-2

We lay on the couch by the window, almost asleep. Truce. Louis Untermeyer. STuOW

We lay red roses on his grave. Paul Laurence Dunbar. Robert Earl Hayden. ESEAA; GT; InoFa; NoP-4; NoP-5

We learned the Whole of Love. Emily Dickinson. APN-2

We leave the bed where your fingers. Desire. Kim Ports. PasH

We leave the things of earth. Driving in a Snowstorm, King Salmon to Naknek. Richard Dauenhauer. GifTon

We leave the well-beloved place. Alfred Tennyson. TreFP *Fr.* In Memoriam A. H. H.

We leave thy courts to-day. Farewell to Allen University. Josephine D. Henderson Heard. CBWP-4

We left before I had time. Back Seat of My Mother's Car, The. Julia Copus. IFF; MFPA; NeBl; StAl

We left slowly. The night was pale. We Left Slowly. Hayim Hefer. NRoS, *tr.* by Esther Raizen

We left the freighter moored off Zanzibar. Surveyor's Story, The. Fergus Allen. NIrP

We left the horses in the draw. Season of Loss, A. Jim Barnes. HATNAP

We left the western island to live among strangers. Search, The. John Hewitt. PNI

We let fire rip, we blacken the pale-gold acres. Burning Off. Geoffrey Dutton. NOBAu

We librarians went to Baja last weekend and sat in the sun. Chapter One. Stephanie Brown. BodElec; SUP

We lie at night. Insomnia. Justin Quinn. NIrP

We lie before the fire after love. Old Moon With Her Youth In Her Arms. Gale Swiontkowski. PasH

We lie together in the grass. Sun on Your Shoulder, The. John Haines. PoDa

We lift the curtain of the past to-day. Lincoln. Henrietta Cordelia Ray. CBWP-3

We listened to the music. Sunday Visit. Antigone Kefala. BMAP

We / little children in our shifts. Clap Your Hands for Herod. Josef Hanzlik. OBCP, *tr.* by Ian Milner

We live amidst hills of desolate. South Bronx Testimonial. Sandra Maria Esteves. UnSA

We live among objects in the light of them their arrangement is our history. Letters for a Document. Lee Bartlett. ICANM

We live between the covers of books. My Wales? Gerwyn Williams. BBMWP, *tr.* by the author and Richard Poole

We live by not being... By being we die. Summary. Jaime Torres Bodet. TCLAP, *tr.* by Sonja Karsen

We live by tunneling for we are people. Short Talk on Orchids. Anne Carson. OpeFie

We live down here. Framing. Michael Davidson. FTOS

We live here to eat. Biological Light. Primus St. John. GifTon

We Live in a Cage. William J. Harris. GT

We live in a modern society. Husbands and wives don't grow. Archipelago of Kisses, The. Jeffrey McDaniel. LegDan

We live in a small island stone nation. Without. Donald Hall. PoA 2002

We live in the egg. In the Egg. Günter Grass. AF

We live in the narrow bed of our flesh. Hygiene of the Soul, The. Zbigniew Herbert. MotU, *tr.* by Czeslaw Milosz

We live in the shadows of dogs and horses. We Sing in Our Sleep. We Converse with the Dead in Our Dreams. Philip Whalen. AHA

We live, not feeling the ground under our feet. Osip Emilevich Mandelstam. PFTM-1

We live on a hillside. What Keeps. C. D. Wright. TAPaP

We live on the third world from the sun. Number three. China. Bob Perelman. FTOS; PFTM-2

We live our lives as wanderers. Old Dust. Li Po. CrYelRi, *tr.* by Sam Hamill

We live—sometimes. Natalya Gorbanevskaya. CRWP, *tr.* by Daniel Weissbort

We live to some purpose, daughter. Failing in the Presence of Ants. Gary Soto. CAP-8; PoA 2002

We live under. Nevada Red Blues. Adrian C. Louis. AtGh

We live; we live in squalor. And so? It had to be. André Marie de Chénier. WoPoe, *tr.* by David Curzon and Jeffrey Fiskin

We lived deep in a land of optative moods. From the Canton of Expectation. Seamus Heaney. ModIr

We lived east of east L.A. / La Puente. La Puente. Elsa Rediva E'der. ReBoTo

We lived next door to the bootlegger, and were lucky. The. Autobiography. Joy Harjo. LTA

We lived north of the future, days opened. Dancing in Odessa. Ilya Kaminsky. LegDan

We lived our little drama. Stars Fell on Alabama. Mitchell Parish. ReLy

We loaf and lounge, usual intolerance. Essays on Excess and Escape. Gaylord Brewer. LiTh

We locked the cars and looked at the sea. Night Crossing in Ice. Randall Maggs. Coast

We long for the quiet. Immaculate Lives. Cathy Song. SweBea

We look up into the stars, stitch in the constellations. Night Bird, The. Larry Kramer. GeoHom

We looked for your ghosts here, Hamlet. Helsinore, Denmark. Maurya Simon. IaFF

We lose—because we win. Emily Dickinson. HeIP-4

We love and talk. Our Second Night. Viki Radden. BtF

We love each other so deeply. Ev'ry Time We Say Good-bye. Cole Porter. ReLy

We love the daylight. *Unknown.* WoPoe *Fr.* Rune Poem, The.

We love the things we love for what they are. (LL) Hyla Brook. Robert Frost. APT-1; CtM; NAMCP V.1; TCAPo

We love to squeeze bananas. Squeezes. Brian Patten. Spl

We loved as friends now twenty years and more:. Change, The. Henry King, Bishop of Chichester. NOSC

We loved each other and were ignorant. (LL) After Long Silence. William Butler Yeats. HeIP-4; NAEL-6v2; NAEL-7v2; OBMV

We loved our bodies nine years old. Something More Obvious. Amanda R. Evans. BeDoSh

We lying by seasand, watching yellow. We Lying by Seasand. Dylan Thomas. PoA 2002

We made love on a winter afternoon. Winter Poem. Frederick Morgan. GoPo

We made love. Then she cleaned. Equality. Hal Sirowitz. KGB

We made our high bed in the low chapel. Airing the Chapel. Sylvia Kantaris. LW

We make more fuss of ballads than of blueprints. Engineers' Corner. Wendy Cope. OBCoV

We make our meek adjustments. Chaplinesque. Hart Crane. APT-2; HeIP-4; NAAL-5; NAAPv.2; NAMCP V.1; NoAM; OxBoAm

We make ourselves a place apart. Revelation. Robert Frost. ChIV-2

We make three summer months of heat. (LL) Song: "Winter skies are cold and low." Tzu Yeh. CrYelRi; ErotSp, tr. by Sam Hamill

We many men from Mauritania see. Blackamoors, The. Rowland Watkyns. AngWePo

We married for acceptance; to stall the nagging. My Second Marriage to My First Husband. Alice Fulton. EmeKit

We may come out into the October reality, Imagination. Patrick Kavanagh. ModIr Fr. Great Hunger, The.

We mean to thrash these Prussian Pups. Unknown. PoWW

We Meet Again. Valerie Gillies. EdScPo

We meet again. Encounter. Marion Strobel. LW

We Meet at Morn, My Dog and I. Hardwick Drummond Rawnsley. DiBP

We meet in a room underground. Subterranean Business. Mark Ivey. ICANM

We meet only. Father and Son. DJ Renegade. BtF

We meet / To part again. Farewell to Master Yu Chao. Wen Chao. CSKM, tr. by Paul Hansen

We meet. We fall in love. Looking for Another Version. Kathleen Aguero. PfS

We Met. Thomas Haynes Bayly. TreFP

We met. Marriage, A. Ronald Stuart Thomas. BeAl; TCAWP

We Met. Mary E. Tucker. CBWP-1

We met, and memory flew to joys and tears. We Met. Mary E. Tucker. CBWP-1

We met at nine. I Remember It Well. Alan Jay Lerner. ReLy

We met on an evening in July. Ground Zero. Sharon Doubiago. AtGh

We met on Charles Bridge, it was snowing. Old Priest, The. Vladimir Holan. PoSu, tr. by George Theiner

We met on the stone bridge. Creation Night. Harry Edmund Martinson. WED, tr. by Robert Bly

We met that grey dull evening on the east shore. Drunken Lyricist, The. Gerry Cambridge. EdScPo

We met the British in the dead of winter. Meeting the British. Paul Muldoon. EmeKit; NAMCP V.2; NoAM; NoP-4; NoP-5; PNI

We met / them. Issues. Christine Ama Ata Aidoo. HAWP

We met— 'twas in a crowd— and I thought he/ would shun me;. We Met. Thomas Haynes Bayly. TreFP

We met up in Parliament Square by the left-hand lion. No Dice. Annie Foster. NLP

We met when time to both was young. Dream Fears. Bessie Rayner Parkes. PoBW

We might have coupled. Mina Loy. NAMCP V.1 Fr. Love Songs to Joannes.

We might have died by now. Horse on a Fence. George Evans. PmAP

We might have guessed it would end in argument. Portrait of the Artist, A. Thomas Kinsella. HarvBoo

We mind not now the merits of our kind. Sir Charles Sedley. OBSV Fr. Happy Pair, The.

We miss Her, not because We see. Emily Dickinson. SWaP

We miss you Ozzie. (LL) TV in Black and White. Gary Soto. ReTh; RWB

We mourn the broken things, chair legs. Housekeeping. Natasha Trethewey. SweBea

We mourn to-day o'er our sister dead. Resting. Josephine D. Henderson Heard. CBWP-4

We move back to my father's home. 12 East Scott Street. Elise Paschen. IllVoic

We moved house. Peacetime. Tom Paulin. FaBoWar

We moved into a house with 6 rooms: the Bedroom. Map Room, The. Joshua Clover. BAP-97; NeAmPo

We moved to Greenville. Eye of the Tornado. James Hoggard. TiP2

We must always return. News of the World. Meena Alexander. BRtP

We Must Be Assured That a Fine Poet Will Be Born, Even after Fifteen Years. Ali Mansour. AnVo, tr. by Mohamed Enani

We must be kind. Don't Let's Be Beastly to the Germans. Noël Coward. ReLy

We must buy coal. Song of Children in the Land of Ice Who Love the Sun. Kim Sŭnghŭi. CAMKP, tr. by Anthony, Brother of Taizé

We Must Die Because We Have Known Them. Rainer Maria Rilke. RaBo, tr. by Stephen Mitchell

We must die because we have known them. Die. We Must Die Because We Have Known Them. Rainer Maria Rilke. WED, tr. by Robert Bly

We must fulfill this golden time. While We're Young. William Engvick. ReLy

We must have done this thousands of times. Springtime at Twilight. Michael S. Smith. PasH

We must have nurtured multitudes to be left so alone. Epochs. Juan Gelman. TCLAP, tr. by Robert Marquez and Elinore Randall

We must look at the harebell as if. Hugh MacDiarmid. BrAP; NAEL-6v2; NAEL-7v2; NoP-4; NoP-5 Fr. In Memoriam James Joyce.

We Must Make a Kingdom of It. Gregory Orr. WaAnP

We must not quarrel, whatever we do. Her Word of Reproach. Sarah Morgan Bryan Piatt. NCAP

We must pass like smoke or live within the spirit's fire. Immortality. George Russell. OBMV

We must read The Kalevala, before we forget. Origin Charm Against Uncertain Injuries. Ansel Talvikki. NeAmPo

We must remember again the tribal pride. Saraband. Austin Hummell. AmPoNex

We must see, we must know. Slop Barrel, The. Philip Whalen. PmAP

We must try to rid evil of our character, the president says. Violence, The. Gillian Conoley. MAAN

We navigate snow not ours. Another Ode to Salt. Danielle Legros Georges. BtF

We Need a God Who Bleeds Now. Ntozake Shange. FaoP; HW

We need no runners here. Booze is law. Harlem, Montana. James Welch. HATNAP

We Need—please read this and see if you. Norman Henry Pritchard, II. EGAG

We never asked to be mysterious. It's in the Blood. Nellie Wong. FTtHH

We never believed in safety. For Jan as the End Draws Near. Carolyn Kizer. GeoHom

We never come to understand. We Never Come. Francisco Segovia. RMCMP, tr. by Michael Wiegers

We never danced. Charleston, South Carolina. Christopher Nickelson. BtF

We never did finish our conversation. To David. Dan Clurman. WhBo

We never had any doubt the world would end. Tale Before the End of the World. Maurya Simon. AtGh

We never half believed the stuff. James Wetherell. Edwin Arlington Robinson. MoAmPo

We never knew his head and all the light. Archaic Torso of Apollo. Rainer Maria Rilke. WoPoe, tr. by Edward Snow

We Never Know. Yusef Komunyakaa. AmAlph; OxBoAm; WhBo

We never meet, yet we meet day by day. Thoughts in Separation. Alice Thompson Meynell. OxBSo

We never questioned why they were. Caddo Mounds, The. Violette Newton. TiP2

We Never Should Have Stopped at Pussy Island. Matthew Rohrer. LegDan

We Never Stopped Crossing Borders. Luis J. Rodriguez. UnSA

We never stopped crossing borders. We Never Stopped Crossing Borders. Luis J. Rodriguez. UnSA

We now lament not, but congratulate. John Donne. NOSC Fr. Of the Progress of the Soul: The Second Anniversary.

We offer the prince a smile. To the Death. Gerallt Lloyd Owen. BBMWP, tr. by Gillian Clarke

We often pass a night warm and intimate. Sonnet. Feng Chih. WoPoe, tr. by Ye Weilian [or Yeh Wei-lien or Wai-lim Yip]

We only live between. For Sheridan. Robert Lowell. PoetW

We open the street door. Same Month They Bombed Cambodia, The. Amy Uyematsu. OpBo

We ourselves are aged. Struggle for the Taal, The. Breyten Breytenbach. AF, tr. by Denis Hirson

We outgrow love like other things. Emily Dickinson. SoSe-8

We pack a radio to relax. Pietá. Martyn Crucefix. PML

We park and stare. A full sky of the stars. Death of the Sheriff, The. Robert Lowell. MoAmPo

We part not with thee at this meeting day. (LL) Sir Walter Ralegh. See We[e] part not with the[e] at this meeting day.

We pass the flayed carcass of a cow. Man from Changi, The. Graeme Hetherington. NOBAu

We Pass through a Foreigner's House. Boadiba. OGAHCP, tr. by the author and Jack Hirschman

We passed a day on Mosel river. Mosel, The. Caroline Clive. PoBW

We passed each other, turned and stopped for half an hour, then went our way. On the Road to the Sea. Charlotte Mew. PoBW

We passengers ride backward on the train. Outbound. Greg Williamson. NoP-5

We pause between sense and foolishness, / And live. (LL) Because of Clothes. Laura Riding Jackson. APT-2; OxBoAm

We pick off dots like runners, between. Static, The. Lewis Warsh. FTOS

We picked flints. Tinder. Seamus Heaney. OxAEP-2

We pin dates to shadows. Borders, Cages and Walls. Homero Aridjis. PoCoUp, tr. by George McWhirter

We planned to keep your first toys. His Toys. Michael Dennis Browne. SUP

We Play at Paste. Emily Dickinson. PtR

We played by the water, ran barefoot. Perdita's Song. Annie Finch. IaFF

We plough [orplow] and sow—we're so very, very low. Song of the Lower Classes, The. Ernest Charles Jones. RSaN

We praise Love the limiter. (LL) Je t'adore. Thomas Kinsella. NAMCP V.2; NoAM

We praise only you. We cringe with shame like crumbs. Prayer. Afsar. HotL, tr. by V. Narayana Rao

We pray to life's source, Mary. Virgin Mary, The. Unknown. OBWVE, tr. by Joseph P. Clancy

We prepare / the meal together. Soul Food. Janice Mirikitani. OpBo

We pressed our faces. Train Stops at Healy Fork, The. John Haines. BLT

(We) Promenade. Sharon Kraus. PA9/11

We promise letters and send postcards. Letter Following. Aidan Carl Mathews. PBCIP

We pull off. Apollo. Elizabeth Alexander. ExTi; PoA 2002

We put a prop beneath the sagging bough. Wild Cherry, The. Malcolm Lowry. NoP-4; NoP-5

We put down our popguns. Looking for Choctaw. Yusef Komunyakaa. LPSFW

We put him on the roof and we painted him blue. Pedalling Man, The. Russell Hoban. NOxBChV

We put this water among this meall. Charm to Destroy the Male Child of the Laird of Parkis. Isabel Gowdie. EMWP

We rake the past, down to an ounce of wants. Squatter in the Foreground. Kenward Elmslie. FTOS

We ran from a home. Flight. Suji Kwock Kim. PoCho

We reach the promised land. Story of Joshua. Alicia Ostriker. ChIV-1

We real cool. We. We Real Cool. Gwendolyn Brooks. AmFaPo; CAP-8; EMP; ESEAA; FuFl; HeIP-4; HHAm; IllVoic; ItP; MakPoe; NAAL-5; NALW; NAMCP V.2; NIL-7; NoP-4; NoP-5; OxAAAP; OxBoAm; PoA 2002; PoPoPo; RaBo; SoSe-8; TFi; TRP; WaAnP; WeW-3

We really didn't see it. Three Snakes, Strawberry Canyon, Berkeley. Ray Gonzales. FTtHH

We received thee warmly—kindly—though we knew thou wert a quiz. OBCoV Fr. American's Apostrophe to Boz, The.

We reconstruct lives in the intensive. Clan Meeting: Births and Nations: A Blood Song. Michael S. Harper. NoAM

We remove a hand. Ted Berrigan. BodElec

We resided in a Loreto convent in the centre of Dublin city. Paul Durcan. ModIr Fr. Six Nuns Die in Convent Inferno.

We return to the apartment. Dream of the Closeness of Venus, A. James ("Jim.") Grabill. AtGh

We return with stumbling feet. Chiedu Ezeanah. NeNiPo Fr. Song of Songs.

We rise at sunrise. Song of the Peasants in the Time of Yao. Unknown. CCL1, tr. by James Legge

We rise from the snow where we've. Selective Service. Carolyn Forché. StAl

We Rise on Sun Beams and Fall in the Night. Allen Ginsberg. CLPP

We rise up early and. Anna Speaks of the Childhood of Mary Her Daughter. Lucille Clifton. NALW

We roam the streets at night, lovers. Walking at Night. Philip Salom. BMAP

We rock and grunt, grunt and / shine. (LL) Song for Ishtar. Denise Levertov. MoWP; NALW; NAMCP V.2; NoAM

We rode a day, from east, from west. Friends. Helen Hunt Jackson. PoBW

We rode hard, and brought the cattle from bushy springs. Proud Riders. Harold Lenoir Davis. APT-2

We rode summer on ten speeds. Woolworth's Poem, The. Quraysh Ali Lansana. IllVoic

We rose before dawn. Andal. WPoS Fr. Tiruppavai, The.

We rose like a phoenix. Amryl Johnson. Oth Fr. Rainbow Dragon Trilogy.

We run the dangercourse. We Walk the Way of the New World. Haki R. Madhubuti. ESEAA

We said there'd be a celebration. Bread and Wine. Nina Cassian. AWTN, tr. by Andrea Deletant and Brenda Walker

We sail out of season into an oyster-gray wind. Crossing the Atlantic. Anne Sexton. NoAM

We sailed in the Ark. New Noah, The. Adonis. AF, tr. by Abdullah Al-Udhari

We sat across the table. Friend, The. Marge Piercy. NALW

We sat / in big / chairs. 56 Westervelt. Maggie Nelson. AmPoNex

We sat in the commons, my eyes scrunched against the smoke. For the New York City Poet Who Informed Me that Few People Live This Way. Jeff Gundy. IllVoic

We sat on metal card chairs at the edge. Green plastic rugs hid the dirt workers flung up when they dug the hole. Ritual. Stephen Berg. PfSP

We sat on the cliff-head. H. Michael Palmer. BodElec

We sat there, her tiny audience. Mom Did Marilyn, Dad Did Fred. Jack Myers. ReTh

We sat together at one summer's end. Adam's Curse. William Butler Yeats. NAEL-6v2; NAEL-7v2; NAMCP V.1; NoAM; NoP-4; NoP-5; WeW-3

We sat under a rotunda, so the smallest sound reverberated, came back historic. Warrior's Tale, A. Sandra Alcosser. LiTh

We sat up late, talking. Red and the Black, The. Norman Alexander MacCaig. BeAl

We sat within the farm-house old. Fire of Drift-Wood, The. Henry Wadsworth Longfellow. APN-1; ITBLP; MakPoe; NAAL-3; NCAP; OxBoAm

We sate down and wept by the waters. By the Rivers of Babylon We Sat Down and Wept. Lord Byron. ChIV-1

We saved enough tinfoil. Last Good War—and Afterward, The. Isabel Joshlin Glaser. HHAm

We saw a town by the track in Colorado. Holding the Sky. William Stafford. GM

We saw it all. We saw the souvenir shops, and sitting. Niagara Falls. Alan Dugan. PoA 2002

We saw not when we moved therein? (LL) Alfred Tennyson. NAEL-6v2; NAEL-7v2 Fr. In Memoriam A. H. H.

We saw that sky. Blackness. Place of Fire. Johannes Bobrowski. PoSu

We saw the brows of countries, worthy of crowns. Seafarers. Georg Heym. WoPoe, tr. by Christopher Benfey

We saw the flames raise the night. Evening Star, The. Pablo Antonio Cuadra. TCLAP, tr. by Ann McCarthy de Zavala and Grace Schulman

We saw the swallows gathering in the sky. George Meredith. OxBEV; WaAnP Fr. Modern Love.

We saw thee, O stranger, and wept! Stranger in Louisiana, The. Felicia Dorothea Hemans. RWP

We saw this great movie last night. Culture Drift. Anne Waldman. AHA

We Say. Reginald Gibbons. BodElec

We say a heart breaks—like. We Say. Reginald Gibbons. BodElec

We say he is dead; ah, the word is too somber. Not Dead, but Sleeping. Clara Ann Thompson. CBWP-2

We say, "It rains." An unbelievable age! Hath the Rain a Father? Jones Very. ChIV-1

We say that a loon, most graceful and dark. Woman Gave Me a Red Star to Wear on My Headband, A. Jimmie Durham. HATNAP

We say tree. Afterwords. Dan Gerber. WhBo

We scoured the secret places of the creek. Moules à la Marinière. Elizabeth Garrett. MFPA

We see a forest and say. Whoever Finds a Horseshoe. Osip Emilevich Mandelstam. PFTM-1

We see her hand in her lap. "H. D." APT-1; MoWP; NAAPv.2; NAMCP V.1 Fr. Tribute to the Angels.

We see in authors, too stiff to recant. John Donne. NOSC Fr. Of the Progress of the Soul: The Second Anniversary.

We see them in old films. Emigrants. Janet Caird. EdScPo

We see them not—we cannot hear. Are They Not All Ministering Spirits? Robert Stephen Hawker. OxAEP-2

We send you home to a grave on Stone Tower Mountain. Weeping for Ying Yao. Wang Wei. CCL1, tr. by Burton Watson

We separate the fragments from the whole. (LL) Love in the Classroom. Al Zolynas. BLT; LTA; TWF

We shall. (LL) Near-Johannesburg Boy, The. Gwendolyn Brooks. ESEAA; FuFl; IllVoic

We shall arrive, / to see, soon. (LL) Bend in the River. Simon J. Ortiz. HATNAP; PoPoPo

We shall be called harsh names by men unborn. Contemporary. Hortense King Flexner. PoA 2002

We shall find out. (LL) Old Fools, The. Philip Larkin. EmeKit; HarvBoo

We shall go mad no doubt and die that way. (LL) Cool Web, The. Robert Graves. BrAP; HarvBoo; NAEL-6v2; NAEL-7v2; NAMCP V.1; NoAM; OxBEV; WoPoe

We shall have everything we want and there'll be no more dying. Ode to Joy. Frank O'Hara. PmAP; WaAnP

We shall love tomorrow. Love Tomorrow. Talat Sait Halman. NaPG, tr. by Talat Sait Halman

We shall not always plant while others reap. From the Dark Tower. Countee Cullen. APT-2; BrAP; ColAP; MakPoe; NAAPv.2; WaAnP

We shall not ever meet them bearded in heaven. On the Death of Friends in Childhood. Donald Justice. ColAP; NAMCP V.2; OxBoAm

We shall not lift our eyes towards the heavens. Song of Earth. Uri Zvi Greenberg. FIT, *tr. by* Robert Friend

We shall o'ersweep the grave to meet—Farewell! (LL) Arabella Stuart. Felicia Dorothea Hemans. NPBRoP; RWP

We shall overcome! September 11, 1973. Emma Sepúlveda-Pulvirenti. CFP; TANSG, *tr. by* Shaun Griffin

We shall sleep-out together through the dark. Ararat. Charles Tomlinson. NoP-4; NoP-5

We shall walk in the snow. (LL) Velvet Shoes. Elinor Wylie. MoAmPo; NAAPv.2; WHSW

We shape our self. Working Together. David Whyte. TWF

We share a habit of accepting hospitality. Umbra. Dana Goodyear. PoDa

We share all these disappointments of failing. Autumn Thoughts, Sent Far Away. Po Chü-i. NDACCP, *tr. by* David Hinton

We share now a pigeon's flight. Butt Cast in the Sea, A. Cemal Süreya. NaPG, *tr. by* Talat Sait Halman

We share this: that vanishing figure. Illusions. Sally Roberts Jones. AngWePo

We shared our supper with the flames. Supper. Andrew Hudgins. CAP-8

We sharing children, visit near mocking. By Accident, Blinked. Lionel Fogarty. VaPo

We shipped him at the Sandwich Isles. Whaler's Pig, The. Edwin James Brady. NOBAu

We should cultivate our different tastes. Cultivation. Mrs. Henry Linden. CBWP-4

We should have been galloping on horses, their hoofprints. Water-burn. Michael Longley. StAl

We should have seen it coming back. Dark Days, The. Greg Williamson. NeAmPo

We should not be lying here! (LL) Edgar Lee Masters. InoFa; NoAM *Fr.* New Spoon River, The.

We Should Remember. Kaloji Narayana Rao. HotL, *tr. by* V. Narayana Rao

We shouldered like pigs along the rail to try. Returned to Frisco, 1946. W. D. Snodgrass. PWW2

We Show You That Death as a Dancer. Hamish Henderson. PoWW

We shut the red judge in a bronze jar. Red Judge, The. D. M. Black. EmeKit

We sing a hymn to Artemis, for it is. Callimachus. HePo *Fr.* Hymns.

We Sing in Our Sleep. We Converse with the Dead in Our Dreams. Philip Whalen. AHA

We sing praise of him who died. Thomas Kelly. SacPr

We sit, a threesome in the car. Threesome. Dora Teitelboim. Prolet, *tr. by* Amelia Glaser

We sit at the table and that is grace. November and Aunt Jemima. Thylias Moss. TRP

We sit beside the Mississippi. Making Poems; on the road in Minneapolis. Sekou Sundiata. SpirFl

We sit here, talking of Barea and Lorca. Conversation in Gibraltar 1943. Charles Causley. PoWW

We sit in a circle around First Sergeant. Hand to Hand. Bruce Weigl. MotU

We sit in the womanless car. Four Men in a Car. Philip Dacey. PML

We sit on a bench & look at the raked rocks. Early Romance, Japanese Garden (*In the Heart of the City*). Michele Glazer. IAoNAP

We sit on a green bench in Harrison Railroad Park. Dreams in Harrison Railroad Park. Nellie Wong. CFP; OpBo

We sit on barstools. Whitman on the Beach. Mark Bibbins. WiU

We sit outside. Death of Dr. King. Sam Cornish. OxAAAP

We sit together among. Drinking Wine with a Mountain Hermit. Li Po. CrYelRi, *tr. by* Sam Hamill

We six pile in, the engine churning ink. Nigger Song: An Odyssey. Rita Dove. OxAAAP

We slept on the edge of town, in the last building. After Eden. Rachel Tzvia Back. DTA

We slipped, trampled, tripped. Leaving Mother, 1954. John Graham-Pole. BloBone

We smell on certain people as they pass. (LL) Urban Poem. Douglas Goetsch. AmPoNex; UrbNat

We smiled together. Gardens. Neil Curry. OBGa

We soaped our hands. Working Tobacco. Janet Kauffman. ACAMVP

We sound like crying bullheads. Voices. Nora Dauenhauer. HATNAP

We speak the language. No. We Can Say That. Tony Curtis. TCAWP

We speak with voices. Teilhard de Chardin Surfs the Internet. David Waltner-Toews. ACAMVP

We spend our morning. Memory of Elena, The. Carolyn Forché. LoL; NAMCP V.2; NoAM

We split a pill in two and walked in the Luxembourg Gardens until some gendarmes appeared on the side of a small hill and told us to leave. White Nights. Lewis Warsh. KGB

We spoke / at all. (LL) Night-Blooming Cereus, The. Robert Earl Hayden. APT-2; ESEAA; ItP

We spread torn quilts and blankets. Picnic, an Homage to Civil Rights, The. Afaa Michael Weaver. ISC; LTA; PoPoPo

We stand at the bedroom window. Occasions. Michael Murphy. NIrP

We stand in the rain in a long line. What Work Is. Philip Levine. BeAl; CAP-8; EmeKit; ItP

We stand on marble here, the way he stood. At the Robert Frost Memorial. William Stafford. VisFro

We stand together. John Montague. ModIr; PBCIP; PNI *Fr.* Dead Kingdom, The.

We stare together. Birth Room, The. Dennis Nurkse. NevBe

We stars, we stars. Chorus of the Stars. Nelly Sachs. BBASP; PFTM-1, *tr. by* Michael Roloff

We started home, my son and I. Jaan Kaplinski. BLT; GifTon; PoChi; WoPoe, *tr. by* the author, Sam Hamill and Riina Tamm

We started our house midway through the Cultural Revolution. Building. Gary Snyder. BB

We started speaking. Meeting, The. Katherine Mansfield. LW

We Startle Things. Beth Baruch Joselow. Eno

We startled each other. She was peering. Goddess, The. M. R. Peacocke. NLP

We step out on the green rectangle. On the Tennis Court at Night. Galway Kinnell. MoASP

We stepped into the lift. The two of us, alone. Meeting in a Lift. Vladimir Holan. PML; StAl, *tr. by* Ian Milner and Jarmila Milner

We Still Have Basketball, Sara. Lisa Olstein. MoASP

We still have funerals. Black Tax. Nzadi Z. Keita. BtF

We stood at the back door. And the Trains Go On. Philip Levine. GM

We stood at the edge. Jews Speak in Heaven, The. Gary Catalano. NOBAu

We stood before a great hill. Beneath the Stars. Vytautas Bloze. PML, *tr. by* Jonas Zdanys

We stood beside the unreal. Animal House Shape of God. Christine Hume. IIR

We stood by a pond that winter day. Neutral Tones. Thomas Hardy. CABP; HeIP-4; MoBrPo; NAEL-6v2; NAEL-7v2; NAMCP V.1; NoAM; NoP-4; NoP-5; NPeEn; TFi; WaAnP

We stood here in the coupledom of us. Land Love. Douglas Dunn. NePenScot

We stood, my mother and I. Two Statues. Pauline Hawkesworth. Prnts

We stood on the rented patio. Summer Storm. Dana Gioia. GoPo; OxBoAm; RA

We stood solemn, clad in tailored black clothing. *Nuestro* Marine. Elaine Romero. RWB

We stood up before day. In the Dordogne. John Peale Bishop. APT-1; OBWP; PoWW

We stretch under a black, starred sky. Mouse, The. *Unknown.* SonAtl, *tr. by* Peter A. Easton, Kathleen Hill and Jim Schneider

We strike at night. Creed of a Graffiti Writer, The. Steven Bonafide Rojas. BRtP

We stripped in the first warm spring night. Belle Isle, 1949. Philip Levine. ColAP; NAMCP V.2; VCAP; WaAnP

We strolled at night through the gardens. Park of the Dead. Gerrit Komrij. TuT, *tr. by* Peter van de Kamp

We study other languages, the signs and mirrors. Good Omen. Lewis Warsh. BodElec

We study the paper, fingers. Whole Wheat, Decaf Black, a Morbid Curiosity. David Citino. UpMys

We suffered drought, months without rain. In Praise of Rain. Tu Fu [*or* Du Fu]. CrYelRi, *tr. by* Sam Hamill

We Survived Them. Anna Swirszczynska [*or* Swir]. AF, *tr. by* Czeslaw Milosz

We swam in the rain-filled gully. Rain Ditch. Pinkie Gordon Lane. ISC

We swam naked to the blue pond's shore. Blue Pond at Berkovitsa. Vladimir Levchev. CSCBP, *tr. by* Georgi Belev and Lisa Sapinkopf

We swing ungirded hips. Song of the Ungirt Runners, The. Charles Hamilton Sorley. MoBrPo; OBEV

We take emerald to Bugojno, then the opal route. Cycles of Donji Vakuf. Tony Harrison. FaBoWar

We take long trips. Jelaluddin Rumi. LoL

We take shelter from the monsoon rains. Baked Oysters Rockefeller. Marjorie M. Evasco. ReBoTo

We take the direct shot. Highway 5. Fleda Brown Jackson. PoDa

We Take the New Young Couple Out to Dinner. Carol Tufts. PasH

We talk / And my joy tonight. Rains. Nike Adesuyi. NeNiPo

We talk of a friend. Skimming the Ice. Tom Sexton. PoCoUp

We talk of light things you and I in this. Father and Daughter. Sonia Sanchez. FFC; GT

We talked [*or* talk'd] with open heart, and tongue. Fountain, The. William Wordsworth. NPBRoP; OxAEP-2

We talked poetic tactics. Once-in-a-Lifetime, Never-to-Be-Repeated, A. Emyr Lewis. BBMWP, *tr.* by the author

We talked till late. Geometry. Jenni Daiches. EdScPo

We talked together in the Yongshou Temple. Letter, The. Po Chü-i. CCL1, *tr.* by Arthur Waley

We tend not to argue among ourselves. On the "Unusual" Lifestyle of the Cucapá Indians as Recorded by R. W. Hardy, British Lieutenant, While Exploring the Gulf of California. Heriberto Yépez. RMCMP, *tr.* by Harry Polkinhorn

We, that did nothing study but the way. Renunciation, A. Henry King, Bishop of Chichester. OBEV

We, the naturally hopeful. Appeal to the Grammarians. Paul Violi. BAP-04; OxBoAm

We, the rescued. Chorus of the Rescued. Nelly Sachs. PoSu

We (they, now) protect autumn from a cough of a man suffering from truth cancer. For Heiner Muller: Poem 2. Safaa Fathy. AnVo, *tr.* by Mohamed Enani

We think of lukewarm water, hope to get in it. (LL) Gwendolyn Brooks. GT; NAAL-5; NoP-4; NoP-5; OxAAAP; PoPoPo *Fr.* Street in Bronzeville, A.

We think of you as already dead. (LL) Last suppers, I fancy, are always wide-screen. Gwyneth Lewis. NeBl; StAl

We think of you before dawn. At the Threshold of the Moon. Gigi Maria Ross. BtF

We think our loved ones pull us under. On the Waterfront. Michael Foley. PNI

We think to create festivals. Poem. Antonio Machado Ruiz. WoPoe, *tr.* by John Dos Passos

We think you know the secret places. Mitigation. Kate Clanchy. EdScPo

We, this whole people, have been clamorous. Samuel Taylor Coleridge. NPBRoP *Fr.* Fears in Solitude [Written in April, 1798, during the Alarm of an Invasion].

We thought at first, this man is a king for sure. Blue Blood. James Stephens. MoBrPo; OBCoV; OBMV

We thought that love was over. We Just Couldn't Say Good-bye. Harry Woods. ReLy

We thought that they were gone. Survivors—Found. Joan Murray. PLBUT

We thought that Winter with his hungry pack. On the Occurrence of a Spell of Arctic Weather in May, 1858. Paul Hamilton Hayne. APN-2

We three kings all orient are. We Three Kings. *Unknown.* FaBoVe

We Three Kings of Orient Are. John Henry, Jr. Hopkins. ChrPo

(Three Kings of Orient.) APN-2

We tied branches to our helmets. Camouflaging the Chimera. Yusef Komunyakaa. AmAlph

We To America. James Weldon Johnson. APT-1

We told them the myths about others. Port, The. Bernadette Mayer. FTOS

We too, we too, descending once again. Too-Late Born, The. Archibald MacLeish. MoAmPo

We took our baskets to the blue mountain at dawn. Instructing Fellow Buddhists after Picking Brackens. Chungji. BecRai, *tr.* by Kim Daljin, Kim Won-Chung and Christopher Merrill

—We took our work, and went, you see. Recreation. Jane Taylor. OBCoV; PEW; WoRP

We took the children down for an hour's outing. Household Cavalry, Llanstephan. Sally Roberts Jones. TCAWP

We took their orders and are dead. (LL) Inscription for a War. Alec Derwent Hope. BMAP; NoP-4; NoP-5; WaAnP

We took turns at laying. Tremors. Stewart Conn. BeAl

We touch fingertips. Snow Climbers. Steve Wiesinger. PasH

We Travel Like Other People. Mahmoud Darwish. AF *Fr.* Poems after Beirut.

We travel like other people, but we return to nowhere. As if travelling. Mahmoud Darwish. AF *Fr.* Poems after Beirut.

We traveled down to see your house. Failed Tribute to the Stonemason of Tor House, Robinson Jeffers. James Tate. OxBoAm

We trot hand-in-hand in the morning. Pre-Teen Trot. Helen Adam. ASA

We trust and fear, we question and believe. Our Limitations. Oliver Wendell Holmes. NCAP

We try a new drug, a new combination. Back. Jane Kenyon. IJHIL

We tunnel through your noonday out to you. Ants, The. William Empson. OxBSo

We turn aside from everything. Birthday Wishes to a Minister of the Gospel. Lizelia Augusta Jenkins Moorer. CBWP-3

We turn from treasons, we shall accomplish these. (LL) Blood is Justified, The. Muriel Rukeyser. StAl; YaYoPo

We turn off the light. December 15th. Vera Gheraducci. CItWP, *tr.* by Cinzia Sartini Blum and Lara Trubowitz

We turned to fire when the water hit. Bathers, The. Lorenzo Thomas. EGAG

We Two. Sarah Morgan Bryan Piatt. NAAPv.1

We Two Boys Together Clinging. Walt Whitman. APN-1

We two were sweethearts. Just Friends. Sam M. Lewis. ReLy

We two women's eyes meet. Triangle, Mirror. No Hyegyông. EcSo, *tr.* by Ann Y. Choi

We unstrung necklaces into two glass bowls. Into Perfect Spheres Such Holes Are Pierced. Catherine Barnett. PoCho

We used to like talking about grief. Ways of Talking. Ha Jin. PoA 2002

We used to look for satellites. Astronomy. M. L. Williams. GeoHom

We used to meet at the Three Storks Restaurant in Prague. Three Storks Restaurant. Nazim Hikmet. NaPG, *tr.* by Talat Sait Halman

We used to sleep, you remember. Barn, The. "Rachel." FIT, *tr.* by Robert Friend

We used to spend the spring together. Most Beautiful Girl in the World, The. Lorenz Hart. ReLy

We used to tell each other erotic stories. Sleepless Nights. Marilyn Nelson Waniek. ISC

We utilise everyone. (LL) Welcome to the New Consciousness. Leseko Rampolekeng. NAfrP; PML

We wake to a world invisibly tangled up in threads. Every Winged Fowl of the Air. Colette Bryce. NIrP

We wake; we wake the day. Indian Singing in 20th Century America. Gail Tremblay. HATNAP; LTA; ReEnLa

We walk alone on the beach. We Are Like These Things. Madeline Gleason. ASA

We walk down a red clay road in Texas. Pecans. Paul Foreman. TiP2

We walk from streetlight to streetlight. Anna. Patrick Friesen. NLPA

We walk in under the empty tower, snow. KZ. Carolyne Wright. RoV

We walk on lava. After the Missionaries. Michael Chitwood. PoA 2002

We Walk the Way of the New World. Haki R. Madhubuti. ESEAA

We walk through a yellow-ocher adobe house. Silence, The. Arthur Sze. WhBo

We walk to the garden where the old rhubarb flourishes. After Rain. Allan Cooper. Coast

We walk to the top of São Francisco. Wander Luís. Carolyne Wright. MAAN

We Walk Towards a Land. Mahmoud Darwish. VCWP, *tr.* by Rana Kabbani

We walk towards a land not of our flesh. We Walk Towards a Land. Mahmoud Darwish. VCWP, *tr.* by Rana Kabbani

We walked across a frozen river in Manchuria. Expatriates. David Woo. OpBo

We walked and blinked at sunlight on the snow. Winter Sonnet. Linda Beatrice Brown. GT

We walked [*or* walk'd] along, while bright and red. Two April Mornings, The. William Wordsworth. NAEL-6v2; NAEL-7v2; NPBRoP

We walked the track by the Branch College. Her First Jew. Joan Logghe. ICANM

We wander in the bleak silence. Automobile, The. Vladislav Felitsianovich Khodasevich. TCRusP, *tr.* by Daniel Weissbort

We wander in the stifling heat. Shadow in Stone. Janice Mirikitani. OpBo

We wander now who marched before. Old Soldier. Padraic Colum. OBMV

We Want More Say. John Beecher. InGu

We want to work-we must not die! (LL) Fear. Eva Picková. INSAB; ItWoWo

We want what is real. We want what is real. Don't deceive us. *Unknown.* APN-2 *Fr.* Minnetare Songs.

We wanted Li Wing. Lapsus Linguae. Keith Preston. NBLV; OBCoV

We watch. Enemies. Charlotte Zolotow. HHAm

We watched from the house. I Was Sleeping Where the Black Oaks Move. Louise Erdrich. CAP-8; HATNAP; NoP-4; NoP-5; PoPoPo

We watched [*or* watch'd] her breathing thro' night. Death-Bed, The. Thomas Hood. InoFa; OBEV; TreFP

We wear the mask that grins and lies. We Wear the Mask. Paul Laurence Dunbar. AmFaPo; APN-2; ISC; NAAPv.1; NIL-7; NIP-4; NoP-4; NoP-5; OxAAAP; OxBoAm; PoPoPo; SacPr; SSLit; TCAPo

We Wear this Flesh. Harvest. Stephen Caldwell Wright. BtF

We weep that our heroes have died. Saba. Henry Dumas. OxAAAP

We welcomed him home, the headmaster. Community School. Sheikh Selman. IrPoTo, *tr.* by Muhamad Tawfiq Ali

We went down the long curved hill. La Route Jackman. Alfred Goldsworthy Bailey. Coast

We went north / to escape winter. Indian Song: Survival. Leslie Marmon Silko. WaAnP

We went on the trolley. Late 20th Century: Spring. Jerry Martien. GeoHom

We went out. Shout, The. Simon Armitage. NoP-5

We went there on the train. *They had big barges that they towed.* Protocols. Randall Jarrell. AmWaPo

We went to Oldshoremore. Itinerary. Edwin Morgan. HarvBoo; OBCoV

We went to Pumpkin Point. My Tenth Birthday. Robert Adamson. BMAP

We went to vote in our democracy. Poisonfield. Glyn Maxwell. HarvBoo

We went to what houses stars at the sea's edge, brilliant day. Daphne Marlatt. NLPA *Fr.* Touch to My Tongue.

We went upstairs in a canoe. I kept catching my paddle in the banisters. Canoeing, The. Russell Edson. MotU

We Went Westward o social telepathy at the. Hannah Weiner. FTOS *Fr.* Spoke Aug 19.

We were a people taut for war; the hills. Welsh History. Ronald Stuart Thomas. OBWVE

We were a tribe, a family, a people. Scotland 1941. Edwin Muir. CABP; EdScPo; NePenScot

We were a whole army underground. As Hour and Year Collapsed. Joe Wenderoth. LegDan; NAPBL

We Were a Whole Army Underground. Joe Wenderoth. BodElec

We were a whole army underground. We Were A Whole Army Underground. Joe Wenderoth. BodElec

We were able to notice that each one in a way carried a bundle, they were. Bundles for Them. Gertrude Stein. PFTM-1

We were all sitting round the table. Christmas Dinner. Michael Rosen. OBCP

We were alone one night on a long. Once in the 40s. William Stafford. GoPo

We were alone together. Adolescence. Juan Ramón Jiménez. WED, *tr. by* Robert Bly

We were apart; yet, day by day. Matthew Arnold. BrAP; NAEL-6v2; NAEL-7v2 *Fr.* Switzerland.

We were at the back of the back of the bus. Collaboration: Between Countries. Anthony Caleshu. NIrP

We were at the camp, it must have been. Visit, The. Wesley McNair. PoDa

We were bored with them. Inventing Stasis. Bernadette Mayer. AHA

We were born in the light. Twentieth Century Children. Beckian Fritz Goldberg. AmAlph

We were born / in the time of the first perfected machine guns;. Dialectic. Victor Serge. AF, *tr. by* James Brook

We were brought up to believe. Brief Thoughts on Floods. Miroslav Holub. PoSu, *tr. by* Ian Milner and Jarmila Milner

We were building a fort. Stranger, The. Gerald Locklin. OPRER

We were children once long ago, dear, you and I. You Never Knew About Me. P. G. Wodehouse. ReLy

We were consigned. Continuous Time. Milo De Angelis. NeIt, *tr. by* Lawrence Venuti

We were crowded in the cabin. Ballad of the Tempest. James Thomas Fields. TreFP

We were dancing—it must have. American Smooth. Rita Dove. CAP-8

We were doing laundry. November 22, 1983. Sherman Alexie. ReTh

We were drinking coffee (of course) when in walks. Peoria. M. Loncar. NAPBL

We were drinking for free, bumming beers. Class A, Salem, the Rookie League. Gary Fincke. MoASP

We were driving down the Kennedy having a great time guessing old groups. Ice. Maureen Seaton. IllVoic

We were enclosed. Catherine of Siena (Saint Catherine). WPoS *Fr.* Prayer 20.

We were fancydancing, you see. Powwow Polaroid. Sherman Alexie. UnSA

We were forgetting how to look, learning how to read. (LL) First Reader. Billy Collins. PoA 2002; TWF

We were forty miles from Albany. E-ri-e, The. *Unknown*. TCAPo

We were gestures of the ocean once. Secret in the Roar, The. Luis H. Francia. ReBoTo

We were going single file. Bummer, A. Michael Casey. PoAgWa

We were going toward nothing. Eye Like a Strange Balloon Mounts Toward Infinity, The. Mary Jo Bang. BAP-04

We were good, good and obedient. We Were Good, Good and Obedient. Sandor Csoori. VCWP, *tr. by* Len Roberts and László Vértes

We were growing old. He was the leaves, I was the flowering spring. Voice, A. Yves Bonnefoy. YaTCFP, *tr. by* Hoyt Rogers

We were halfway through July. Handsome afternoon! On the Banks of the Duero. Antonio Machado Ruiz. STV, *tr. by* John Frederick Nims

We were having fun, that devil Hermione and I. Asclepiades. EroLit, *tr. by* Kenneth McLeish

We were in a room that was once an attic. Amiel's Leg. Thomas Lux. LaCa

We were in the middle of something big. Motel Story. Maggie Nelson. AmPoNex

We were just camping out. First thirty-seven years, The. Karen Press. TSAP

We were just re-entering the city limits of Québec. Cure, The. Aidan Rooney-Céspedes. NIrP

We were killing pigs when the Yanks arrived. Testimony. Seamus Heaney. PoAgWa

We were loading a boar, a goddam mean big sonofabitch. Loading a Boar. David Lee. TAPaP

We were looking another way. Sudden Discords in the Trumpets of Overdelayed Last Judgement, 1956. Jack Lindsay. RSaN

We were looking for a basement to live in. Memories of Marriage. Enrique Lihn. TCLAP, *tr. by* John Felstiner

We were looking for a paradise, a place. Catch, The. Rebecca Seiferle. ExTi

We were low on petrol. Driving to the Hospital. Kate Clanchy. BeAl

We were many in the room. Bewilderment. Georgi Rupchev. CSCBP, *tr. by* Georgi Belev and Lisa Sapinkopf

We were mistaken, I think. Regalia Figure. Carl Phillips. NAPBL

We were mistaken. The Queen never. Corrections. Thomas Heise. LegDan

We were never formally introduced. My Noiseless Entourage. Charles Simic. CAP-8

We were never invited to his house. My Rich Uncle, Whom I Only Met Three Times. Marge Piercy. UnSA

We were no good as murderers, we were clowns. (LL) Stephano Remembers. James Simmons. PBCIP; PNI

We were not even moving. No one was moving. On the Eve of Our Mutually Assured Destruction. C. D. Wright. AtGh

We Were Not Expecting the Prince To-day. Muriel Spark. EdScPo

We were not raised to look in. You Were Never Miss Brown to Me. Sherley Anne Williams. GT

We were on a train to Cork. She was seven. Journey, The. Leanne O'Sullivan. NIrP

We were playing on the green together. "Is It Nothing to You?" May Probyn. OBEV; SacPr

We were riding through frozen fields in a wagon at dawn. Encounter. Czeslaw Milosz. ASA; BodElec; ChAP; GPTC; PoetW; StAl; WoPoe, *tr. by the author and Lillian Vallee*

We were sitting in a small room. Now Winter Nights. Robert Hass. BodElec

We were sitting in the gun-room, and the long-persistent snow. Old Rocket. Knight Horsfield. DiBP

We were so poor I had to take the place of the bait in the mousetrap. We Were So Poor. Charles Simic. MotU; StAl; VCAP

We were sorting soybeans. Morcels: Between the Lines. Theresa Hak Kyung Cha. ASA

We were spinning ourselves into a rare dessert. With Cheerful Speed. Tanya Larkin. FreRad

We were supposed to do a job in Italy. What He Thought. Heather McHugh. OxBoAm; P180; PtR; WaAnP

We were talking about poetry. Garden, The. Dorianne Laux. AtGh

We were talking about the great things. Great Things Have Happened. Alden Nowlan. BeAl

We were the first steamer in the fat that spring. On the Ice. Gordon Rodgers. Coast

We were The Hottentot Venus. Boys in Dresses. Yusef Komunyakaa. CAP-8

We Were Three. Claribel Alegría. AF; TCLAP, *tr. by* Carolyn Forché

We were thrown into the sea. First Horses, 1519. Victoria Edwards Tester. ICANM

We were together since the War began. Rudyard Kipling. HarvBoo; NPeEn *Fr.* Epitaphs of the War [1914–1918].

We were translations. Artists, The. Gearóid Mac Lochlainn. NIrP, *tr. by the author*

We were trying to put the roots back. Re-Rooting. Denise Levertov. UpMys

We were two pretty babes, the youngest she. Childhood Fled. Charles Lamb. CenSon

We were two women of one generation. (LL) Adrienne Rich. TRP; WaAnP *Fr.* Twenty-one Love Poems.

We were very tired, we were very merry. Recuerdo. Edna St. Vincent Millay. APT-1; ChAP; EMP; ItP; NAAL-5; NAAPv.2; NAMCP V.1; NoAM; PoA 2002

We were waiting at the station. Parting Kiss, The. Josephine D. Henderson Heard. CBWP-4

We were walking down Central downtown. Teddy. Leroy V. Quintana. LiTh

We were walking to your funeral, eleven friends. Julio Campal. Gerardo Diego. RaW, *tr. by* Robert Mezey

We were warned about frost, yet all day the summer. Early Frost. Leslie Norris. AngWePo

We were wrong to think. Form. Heather McHugh. OxBoAm

We were young, we were merry, we were very very wise. Unwelcome. Mary Elizabeth Coleridge. OBEV; VWP

We weren't waiting for anything to happen. Then. Gail Mazur. ExTi

We wet the dry discs. Painting with My Daughter. Ann Elizabeth Hostetler. ACAMVP

We who are called Australians have no country. Rex Ingamells. NOBAu *Fr.* Unknown Land.

We who are here present thank the Great Spirit that we are here to praise Him. Thanksgivings, The. *Unknown*. APN-2, *tr. by* Harriet Maxwell Converse

We who are responsible for living. Without Histories. Blanca Wiethüchter. TANSG, *tr. by* Shaun Griffin and Emma Sepúlveda-Pulvirenti

We who had known the desert's grit and granite. Exodus. Charles Reznikoff. ChIV-1

We who have always looked with tolerant irony. Prayer for the End of the Century, A. Heberto Padilla. VCWP

We Who Have Loved. Corinne Roosevelt Robinson. LW

We who have won from the primeval wood. To Karl Marx. William Soutar. RSaN

We who must act as handmaidens. Muse of Water, A. Carolyn Kizer. FFC; VCAP

We who play under the pines. Song of the Rabbits Outside the Tavern, The. Elizabeth Jane Coatsworth. SoSe-8

We who stung stone know how our toil bathed us in ash, while the lilies of the land. Harmony. Tom Postell. EGAG

We who were alive, held you in arms, welcomed you to table, to. Sic Transit. Skip Fox. AnSo

We Who Were Born. Eiluned Lewis. AngWePo

We who were born. We Who Were Born. Eiluned Lewis. AngWePo

We Who Were Executed. Faiz Ahmad Faiz. PoetW, *tr. by* Agha Shahid Ali

We who with songs beguile your pilgrimage. James Elroy Flecker. OBMV; UV *Fr.* Golden Journey to Samarkand, The.

We, whose fathers are hidden. Our Fathers. Ta'Lease Niche Cleveland. BRtP

We, whose lungs fill with the sweetness of day. Child of Europe. Czeslaw Milosz. AF, *tr. by* Jan Darowski

We will all have to just hang on for awhile. One Coat of Paint. John Ashbery. OxBoAm

We will be brought to recognize. Rising. Nzadi Z. Keita. BtF

We will be passing the telephone booths soon. Nonplussed. Ken Bolton. BMAP

We will call today. Michael Palmer. APSN

We will have to get down on all fours and eat the grasses of the cemeteries forever. (LL) Little Infinite Poem. Federico García Lorca. RaBo; WED, *tr. by* Robert Bly

We will have to go away, said the girls in the circus. Circus, The. Kenneth Koch. OxBoAm

We will it so / and so it is / past all accident. (LL) Ivy Crown, The. William Carlos Williams. ItP; NAAPv.2; NAMCP V.1; NoAM

We will kill our love. We Are Going to Shoot at the Heart. Anna Swirszczynska [*or* Swir]. PoSu

We will learn. Scar. Lucille Clifton. CAP-8

We will march thro' the valley in peace. We Will March Through the Valley. *Unknown.* SSUS

We will meet again. (LL) Animals, The. W. S. Merwin. VCAP; WaAnP

We will mention it. We will remember and mention. Alicia Kozameh. MirDau *Fr.* Saltos Sobre El Exilio.

We will never remember dying. Births. Pablo Neruda. BeAl, *tr. by* Stephen Mitchell

We will not whisper, we have found the place. Sonnet. Joseph Hilaire Pierre Belloc. MoBrPo

We Will Now Hear the Word of God from Each of Our Beloved Chaplains. Daniel Berrigan. UpMys

We will put Time to sleep on that warm hill. Time Out. Genevieve Taggard. ASA

We will see more passing than any. Nostalgia. Christopher Buckley. SeSe

We will sing a song. Songs from the Great Feast to the Dead. *Unknown.* APN-2, *tr. by* Edward William Nelson

We will sit all day on a bench in the sun watching the spider monkeys. Monkey Hill. Stan Rice. PoCho

We will use all gently, my lord. First Player's Monologue, The. Richard Hedderman. IaFF

We will yet see The Other Days. Other Days, The. Hayim Hefer. NRoS, *tr. by* Esther Raizen

We wish a drove of weasels transmuted into horses. *Unknown.* APN-2 *Fr.* Minnetare Songs.

We wish only to bury our dead. Shorn. Wole Soyinka. PoetW *Fr.* Funeral in Soweto.

We wish to bury our dead. Now, a funeral. Funeral Sermon, Soweto. Wole Soyinka. VCWP

We wish to the new child. For C. K. at His Christening. Daniel Lawrence Kelleher. BLPJKO

We with our Fair pitched among the feathery clover. Individualist Speaks, The. Louis MacNeice. OBMV

We woke near midnight. Eruption: Pu'u Ō'ō. Garrett Kaoru Hongo. LoL

We women here all live with tightened throats. Henri Michaux. GPTC *Fr.* I Am Writing to You from a Far-Off Country.

We women, / We sisters. We. Janeya K. Hisle. BtF

We wonder what the horoscope did show. Shakespeare. Henrietta Cordelia Ray. CBWP-3

We Wondered about the Mellow Peaches. Jack A. Mapanje. HBAPE

We won't come back. You come too. (LL) My Test Market. Rachel Loden. CalPo; PoDa; VisFro

We work here together. Pine Planters, The. Thomas Hardy. FaBoVe

We work, play, don't cross-reference calendars. Marilyn Hacker. VCAP *Fr.* Taking Notice.

We worked nights as machine operators. Making America Strong. Fred Voss. StAl

We worshipped dark. Black and White. Machiraju Savithri. HotL, *tr. by* V. Narayana Rao

We would climb the highest dune. With Kit, Age 7, at the Beach. William Stafford. CAP-8; PoCho; RaBo

We would meet in secret under. After diana died. Asha Bandele. BRtP

We wouldn't have a T.V. set for years. Certified Public Accountant recalls the Early 1950s, The. Robert A. Fink. TiP2

We Write. Siva Reddy. HotL, *tr. by* V. Narayana Rao and A. K. Ramanujan

We write them there forever. (LL) Walt Whitman: "Master-songs are ended, and the man, The." Edwin Arlington Robinson. APN-2; NCAP; TCAPo; ViWalt

We writhe in a star-net. Fish in the Net. János Pilinszky. IQMS, *tr. by* Adam Makkai

We younger kids were playing. Debt is Paid, A. A. Van Jordan. BtF

Weak is the sophistry, and vain the art. Describes the Fascinations of Love. Mary Robinson. CenSon; RWP

Weak Poet, The. David Shapiro. BodElec

Weak survive!, The. Song Against Natural Selection. Edward Hirsch. SUP

Weak with nice sense, the chaste MIMOSA stands. Erasmus Darwin. NOBRP *Fr.* Botanic Garden, The.

Weakened by loss of blood Robin's last act was to slash his sword. Alan Halsey. Oth *Fr.* Robin Hood Book, A.

Weakness. Alden Nowlan. StAl

Weakness, The. Toi Derricotte. GT; LTA

Weakness, The. Bernard O'Donoghue. ModIr; NoP-4

Weak-winged is song. Ode Recited at the Harvard Commemoration (July 21, 1865). James Russell Lowell. APN-1; CBCWP; OBWP; PCW

Wealth. Ralph Waldo Emerson. APN-1

Wealth and honor in life were dew on the grass leaf. Su Tung-p'o. WoPoe *Fr.* Roadside Flowers, Three Poems with Introduction.

Wealth came by water to this farmless island. Delos. Bernard Spencer. NoAM

Wealth in the deep of the rose, The. Rose, The. Gabriela Mistral. SpanPo, *tr. by* Kate Flores

Wealth Is Not Happiness. Caroline Elizabeth Norton. TreFP

Weaning of Furniture-Nutrition. Juan Felipe Herrera. BodElec

Weapon shapely, naked, wan. Song of the Broad-Axe [*or* Broad-Ax]. Walt Whitman.

Weapon that comes down as still, A. John Pierpont. APN-1 *Fr.* Word from a Petitioner.

Weapons. Anna Wickham. MoBrPo

Weapons are the tools of violence. Lao Tzu. WaAnP, *tr. by* Stephen Mitchell

Weapons Training. Bruce Dawe. OBCoV

Wear dark glasses in the rain. Adultery. Carol Ann Duffy. EmeKit

Wear my colored stripes. Dare to Be Different. Venus Harris. BRtP

Wear the heart like a home. Confederacy. Elise Paschen. FFC

Wear thou this fresh green garland this one day. Garland for Advancing Years, A. William Bell Scott. GSo

Wear white and bring an offering. Vodou Headwashing Ceremony. Andy Young. AnSo

Weare I a Kinge I coulde commande content. Edward, 17th Earl of Oxford De Vere. *See* Poem: "Were I a king, I could command content."

Weareth the leaden hue seen in the eyes of the blind. (LL) Fragment: December 18, 1847. Henry Wadsworth Longfellow. APN-1; TCAPo

Wearie thoughts doe waite upon me. Nicholas Breton. NPeEn *Fr.* Solemne Long Enduring Passion, A.

Wearied of its own turning. Burning Wheel, The. Aldous Leonard Huxley. ChIV-1

Wearily, drearily. In Prison. William Morris. FaBoWar

Weariness. Mary E. Tucker. CBWP-1

Weariness of life that has no will, The. Everyman. Siegfried Sassoon. MoBrPo

Wearing. Beau Beausoleil. Eno

Wearing a copy of the canvas. Hemingway's Hat. Vicki Feaver. MoWP

Wearing a floppy hat. Three Poems. Robert James Waller. TiP2

Wearing Achilles' Armour, Patroclus, along with the Myrmidons, Attacks the Trojans. Homer. OBVE *Fr.* Iliad, The.

Wearing an eighteen-year old boyish face. Road to Corruption, The. Pak Nohae. CAMKP, *tr. by* Scott Swaner

Wearing an overcoat on August heat. Bag Woman. Dudley Randall. NoAM

Wearing Dad's White Shirt Backwards. Rick Agran. AmPoNex

Wearing hemp clothes in the coldest winter. Cho Sik. CATKP, *tr. by* Peter H. Lee

Wearing her yellow rubber slicker. Myrtle. Ted Kooser. InvLad

Wearing my yellow straw hat. My Yellow Straw Hat. Lessie Jones Little. TLR

Wearing of the Green, The. Dion Boucicault. IrV

Wearing that same black dress. Women You Are Accustomed To, The. Lucille Clifton. ErotSp; GT

Weary already, weary miles to-night. Match with the Moon, A. Dante Gabriel Rossetti. NPeEn; OxBEV

Weary and destitute Farewell! I f you were to send me winter clothes, I do no know what return I could make. Meng Jiangnü at the Long Wall. *Unknown.* CCL1, *tr. by* Arthur Waley

Weary Blues, The. Langston Hughes. BrAP; ColAP; EMP; FaBoA; HarvBoo; ISC; NAAPv.2; NAMCP V.1; NoAM; NoP-4; NoP-5; OxBoAm; PoPoPo; SAmP

Weary of all this wordy strife. Catholic Love. Charles Wesley. SacPr

Weary of all who come with words, words but no language. From March 1979. Tomas Tranströmer. StAl, *tr. by* Robin Fulton

Weary Road, The. Pao Chao. *tr. by* Ye Weilian [*or* Yeh Wei-lien *or* Wai-lim Yip]

  "Do you not see the riverside grass." ChinPo, *tr. by* Ye Weilian [*or* Yeh Wei-lien *or* Wai-lim Yip]

  "Do you not see the young men off to war." ChinPo, *tr. by* Ye Weilian [*or* Yeh Wei-lien *or* Wai-lim Yip]

  "Splash water on level ground." ChinPo, *tr. by* Ye Weilian [*or* Yeh Wei-lien *or* Wai-lim Yip]

  "To you, fine wine in gold cup." ChinPo, *tr. by* Ye Weilian [*or* Yeh Wei-lien *or* Wai-lim Yip]

Weary silence bends. How Much a Word Could Help. "Zelda." NRoS, *tr. by* Esther Raizen

Weary sun, The. Fisherman, The. Yunna Petrovna Moritz. TCRusP, *tr. by* Daniel Weissbort

Weary the cry of the wind is, weary the sea. Sorrow of Mydath. John Masefield. MoBrPo

Weary traveler, who, all night long, The. Storied Sonnet. Ann Radcliffe. CenSon

Weary way-wanderer, languid and sick at heart. Soldier's Wife, The. Robert Southey. FaBoWar

Weary wild geese who came. Fujiwara noTeika. WoPoe, *tr. by* Steven D. Carter

Weary with reading and with meditation. Storm and Calm: Sent from Embden to M. Edw. Ma. and M. Tho. Ly, The. Nicholas Murford. NOSC

Weary with toil, I haste me to my bed. William Shakespeare. AWTN; CAGL; HeIP-4; NoSic *Fr.* Sonnets.

Weary, worn, and sorrow-laden. Storm-Beaten. Clara Ann Thompson. CBWP-2

Weasel. Lyubomir Levchev. CSCBP, *tr. by* Georgi Belev and Lisa Sapinkopf

Weather. Michael Burkard. BodElec

Weather. Hettie Jones. PrTe

Weather. Archibald MacLeish. *See* Cook County.

Weather. Eve Merriam. TLR

Weather. Linda Pastan. GoPo

Weather. May Swenson. FTtHH

Weather buffets our houses in armour all night. Gales. Anne Stevenson. Spl

Weather Forecast. Sion Aled. BBMWP, *tr. by* Grahame Davies

Weather forecast that snow would fall from the sky, The. Wherein space is constructed that matter may reside in. Michele Glazer. IAoNAP

Weather in my head, The. Degrees. Kevin Young. AmPoNex

Weather in place of God. Tempted by the Classical on Returning from the Store at Twenty Below Zero. Sydney Lea. SwNoth

Weather is fright'ning, The. Isn't This a Lovely Day (To Be Caught in the Rain?). Irving Berlin. ReLy

Weather left me raw, The. How to Change a Flat. Leslie Anne McIlroy. AmPoNex

Weather of Olympus, The. Robert Graves. OBCoV

Weather of this winter night, my mistress, The. Childlessness. James Merrill. ColAP

Weather, peddle our goods and die into the future. (LL) Crypto-Jews, The. Robin Becker. ExTi; OPRER; TaR

Weather Report. Brenda Coultas. HeMarv

Weather Report. Charles Tomlinson. HarvBoo

Weather Seems Different, The. Eliot Katz. PA9/11

Weather Signs. Aratus. HePo *Fr.* Phaenomena.

Weather They Were Written In, The. Kathy Fagan. PuP-23

Weather was fine, The. They took away his teeth. John Berryman. HarvBoo *Fr.* Dream Songs.

Weather wonderful—cannot go out in daylight. Honeymoon Postcard. Paul Durcan. OBCoV

Weather-Cock Points South, The. Amy Lowell. APT-1; NALW; NoP-4; NoP-5; OxBoAm

  (Weathervane Points South, The.) NAAPv.2

Weathered bones. Basho. EH, *tr. by* Robert Hass

Weathered raft I saw myself. Nathaniel Mackey. FTOS; OxAAAP *Fr.* Song of the Andoumboulou.

Weathered skeleton, A. Basho. SoOfWa, *tr. by* Sam Hamill

Weathering. Fleur Adcock. BeAl

Weathering. Alastair Reid. EdScPo

Weathering Out. Rita Dove. AmAlph; CFP; ESEAA; NAMCP V.2; NoAM

Weatherman for Boston ponders whether, *I'd bet not.* Evening forecast for the region, The. Nick Laird. NIrP

Weathers [*or* Weather]. Thomas Hardy. MoBrPo; OBMV

Weather's cast away its cloak, The. Temps a Laissié, Le. Charles, Duc d' Orléans. WoPoe, *tr. by* Stanley Burnshaw

Weather's cleared, The. We're filming at Versailles. Clive James. OBSV *Fr.* To Pete Atkin: A Letter from Paris.

Weather's on its way to us. What There Is, Today. Tracy Philpot. IAoNAP

Weathervane Points South, The. Amy Lowell. *See* Weather-Cock Points South, The.

Weave a carpet for me, Bodil. Carpet, The. Olav H. Hauge. WED, *tr. by* Robert Bly

Weave for me. Dyeing. Mabel Tobrise. NAfrP

Weave like a web in the air / Divinely superfluous beauty. (LL) Divinely Superfluous Beauty. Robinson Jeffers. HeIP-4; MoAmPo

Weave the warp, and weave the woof. Curse upon Edward, The. Thomas Gray. OBEV

Weave us a song of many threads. Weaver. Sandra Maria Esteves. PueRic

Weaver. Sandra Maria Esteves. PueRic

Weaver at rest, The. (LL) Task, The. Denise Levertov. InvLi; UpMys

Weaver Bird, The. Kofi Awoonor. HBAPE

Weavers Song, The. Thomas Deloney. PBRV

Weaving a garland long ago. Anacreon. ErotSp, *tr. by* Sam Hamill

Weaving the Morning. João Cabral de Melo Neto. IPoFL; TCLAP, *tr. by* Galway Kinnell

Web, The. Pierre Reverdy. YaTCFP, *tr. by* Mary Ann Caws and Jean-Pierre Cauvin and Patricia Terry

Web outside the window filled, The. Spider. William Virgil Davis. YaYoPo

Webern. Christopher Pilling. NLP

Webster Ford. Edgar Lee Masters. APT-1 *Fr.* Spoon River Anthology.

Webster was much possessed by death. Whispers of Immortality. T. S. Eliot. APT-1; NAMCP V.1; NoAM; OBMV; OxAEP-2

We'd all had a bit too much that night when you brought out. Sea-Cucumber, The. Martin Johnston. BMAP

We'd better leave him in the sump, he said. (LL) Mending Sump. Kenneth Koch. NAMCP V.2; NoAM; VisFro

We'd found an old Boche dug-out, and he knew. Wilfred Owen. FaBoWar *Fr.* Sentry, The.

We'd found the old Boche dug-out, and he knew. Sentry, The. Wilfred Owen. PoWW

We'd gained our first objective hours before. Counter-Attack. Siegfried Sassoon. MoBrPo; OxAEP-2; PoWW

We'd moved out. You'd stayed behind alone. Before the Brain Surgery. Paula Tatarunis. BloBone

We'd rather have the iceberg than the ship. Imaginary Iceberg, The. Elizabeth Bishop. MoAmPo

We'd shucked our shirts. Adolescence. Rebecca Gordon. FiBr

We'd sip our water and wait till supper came. Loose Change. Andrew Hudgins. UpMys

We'd walked into the small warm shed. Witness. William Heyen. CAP-8

Weddin' a woo a clog an' a shoe, A. Weddings. *Unknown.* FaBoVe

Wedding. Ruth Forman. OxAAAP

Wedding: "Inside the womb-like darkness." No Hyegyông. EcSo, *tr. by* Ann Y. Choi

Wedding. Alice Oswald. BeAl; MFPA; MoWP; NeBrP

Wedding, A. Nadir Hussein. PML

Wedding, A. W. B. Keckler. IIR

Wedding, A. James Tate. NoAM

Wedding, The. Alfonso D'Aquino. RMCMP, *tr. by* Rebecca Seiferle

Wedding, The. Franz Wright. MotU

Wedding Banquet. Diana O'Hehir. AFaM

Wedding Bells Are Breaking Up That Old Gang of Mine. Irving Kahal and Willie Raskin. ReLy

Wedding Day. Seamus Heaney. OxAEP-2

Wedding Day. Mark Levine. AmPoNex; BAP-01

Wedding Day, The. V. Penelope Pelizzon. AmPoNex

Wedding Feast, The. Edgar Lee Masters. ChIV-2

Wedding Gifts. Adrienne Su. NAPBL

Wedding in Hanover. Lorna Goodison. GT

Wedding in the Courthouse, The. Kathleen Norris. MPUn

Wedding Morn. D. H. Lawrence. MoBrPo

Wedding night / Graciela bled lightly. Graciela. Gary Soto. NAMCP V.2; NoAM

Wedding Party. Allison Joseph. AmPoNex; ExTi; MPUn

Wedding Party. William R. Lafleur. WhBo

Wedding Preparations in the Country. David St. John. AmAlph

Wedding Ring, The. Zinaida Nikolayevna Gippius. ARWW, *tr.* by Catriona Kelly

Wedding Song. Patricia Storace. FFC

Wedding Song: "Where the bridesmaid waits in the vestibule." Mary Louise Sullivan. PfS

Wedding the Locksmith's Daughter. Robin Robertson. NeBrP

Wedding Vow, The. Sharon Olds. MPUn

Wedding-Journey of a Princess, The. *Unknown.* CCL1 *Fr.* Que-chao [Translations].

Wedding-Ring. Denise Levertov. CAP-8; NIL-7

Weddings. *Unknown.* FaBoVe

Weddings of flowers take place upon the stigma, The. Pollen unfastens when aurora begins, and in a moment life redeems itself and then withdraws. María Baranda. RMCMP, *tr.* by Mónica de la Torre

Wedge inside your ease, The. Education by Degrees. Clarence Major. EGAG

Wednesday. Marvin Bell. VCAP

Wednesday. Lisa Robertson. VaPo

Wednesday Night Prayer Meeting. Jay Wright. ISC

Wednesday of Holy Week, 1940. Kenneth Rexroth. ChIV-1

Wednesday on a barge. Poems from Saint Pelagia Prison. Philippe Soupault. AF, *tr.* by Eden Paul

Wednesday, west of Sheridan, sky. Sunflowers, Wyoming. Deborah Slicer. RWB

Wee bird sang in the wasteland, A. Louis Notari. SonAtl, *tr.* by Favorita '68 and Anne Swann

Wee cock sparra sat on a tree, A. Wee Cock Sparra, The. Hugh Frater and Duncan Macrae. EdScPo

Wee Cooper of Fife, The. *Unknown.* NePenScot

Wee Falorie Man, The. *Unknown.* FaBoVe

Wee jenny wren she lays sixteen, The. Wee Jenny Wren, The. *Unknown.* FaBoVe

Wee Jenny Wren, The. *Unknown.* FaBoVe

Wee Lassie's First Luve, The. George Francis Savage-Armstrong. IrV

Wee leave Creete Country; and our sayls unwrapped uphoysing. Virgil. OBVE *Fr.* Aeneid [*or* Eneados *or* Aeneis], The.

Wee, modest, crimson-tipped flow'r. To a Mountain Daisy [On Turning One Down, with the Plough, in April—1786]. Robert Burns. NPBRoP

We[e] part not with the[e] at this meeting day. (LL) Sir Walter Ra[u]le[i]gh to His Son[ne]. Sir Walter Ralegh. GSo; NAEL-6v1; NAEL-7v1; NoP-4; NoSic; NPeEn; OxBSo; WoPoe

(We part not with thee at this meeting day.) (LL) GSo; NoP-4

Wee, sleeket [*or* sleekit], cow'rin' [*or* cowran], tim'rous beastie. To a Mouse; On Turning Her up in Her Nest, with the Plough, November, 1785. Robert Burns. BRP; CABP; FaBoVe; HeIP-4; NAEL-6v2; NAEL-7v2; NePenScot; NoP-4; NoP-5; NPBRoP; NPeEn; OxAEP-2; OxBEV; TFi; UV; WaAnP

Wee Willie Winkie rins [*or* runs] through the town. Willie Winkie. William Miller. OxBEV

Weed. Paula Gunn Allen. FiBr

Weed, The. Genevieve Taggard. APT-2

Weed grass weed root. Zai-shan: Weed Grass. *Unknown.* CCL1, *tr.* by Man Wong

Weed, moss-weed. Sea Iris. "H. D." APT-1

Weed Puller. Theodore Roethke. NAMCP V.1

Weeding. Michael Hamburger. OBGa

Weeds. James Dickey. BodElec

Weeds as Partial Survivors. Alan Dugan. YaYoPo

Weeds loom. Woman. Georgi Belev. CSCBP, *tr.* by the author and Lisa Sapinkopf

Week after her wedding I watch the Kentucky Derby, A. Louisa's Wedding. Tracy Philpot. AmPoNex

Week after my father died, A. Beyond Harm. Sharon Olds. BeAl

Week after our child was born, A. New Mother. Sharon Olds. PasH

Week after Your Death, A. Robert Bly. NAMCP V.2

Week ago, when I had finished, A. Vikram Seth. NoP-5 *Fr.* Golden Gate, The.

Week End Bid I. John Wheelwright. AmWit

Week End Bid II. John Wheelwright. AmWit

Week in August you come home, The. Family Reunion. Maxine W. Kumin. AFaM; GoPo

Week in the Life of the Ethnically Indeterminate, A. Elena Georgiou. WiU

Week is dealt out like a hand, The. Hope. Randall Jarrell. MoAmPo

Week of terse speaking is nearly done, A. Big guns go boom! (for Mark Prejsnar). Dana Lisa Lustig. AnSo

Week the first baby died, The. Caustic Soda. Liz Houghton. Prnts

Week-End. Harold Monro.
  "Train, The! The twelve o'clock for paradise." MoBrPo

Weekend at Home. John Pook. AngWePo

Week-End by the Sea. Edgar Lee Masters. MoAmPo

Weekend Equestrian, The. Afaa Michael Weaver. GT

Weekend in Bodega Bay, A. Caitríona O'Reilly. NIrP

Weekly Agenda of Love. M. Sami Aşar. NaPG, *tr.* by Talat Sait Halman

Weeks after the solstice. Migrants by Night. W. S. Merwin. BodElec

Weeks go by, The. I shelve them. Firstborn. Louise Glück. HarvBoo

Weeks go quickly by, The. Things We Did Last Summer, The. Sammy Cahn. ReLy

Weeksville Women. Elouise Loftin. ISC

Weep, ah weep love's losing, love's with its dwelling-place. Imr el Kais. TAL *Fr.* Mu'allaqat, The.

Weep, Children of Israel. Thomas Moore. ChIV-1

Weep No More. John Fletcher. OBEV; OxAEP-1 *Fr.* Queen of Corinth, The.

Weep no more, Marta. Happy Morning. *Unknown.* SSUS

Weep not because this child hath died so young. On the Death of Mistress Mary Prideaux. William Strode. NOSC

Weep not, Korea! Long, Long Autumn Nights. Oguma Hideo. CAoMJL1, *tr.* by David G. Goodman

Weep Not To-Day. Robert Bridges. OBMV

Weep not, weep not. Go Down Death (A Funeral Sermon). James Weldon Johnson. ISC; OxAAAP; SacPr

Weep, weep for him, the Man of God. Weep, Children of Israel. Thomas Moore. ChIV-1

Weep with me, all you that read. Epitaph on S. P. [*or* Salomon Pavy], a Child of Queen Elizabeth's Chapel. Ben Jonson. NAEL-6v1; NAEL-7v1; NOSC; OBEV; OxBEV

Weep, you may weep, for you may touch them not. (LL) Greater Love. Wilfred Owen. MoBrPo; NAMCP V.1; NoAM; TFi

Weep you no more, sad fountains. Weep [*or* Weepe] You No More [Sad Fountains]. *Unknown.* NoP-5; NOSC; NoSic; TFi

(Weepe you no more sad fountaines.) NPeEn; OxBEV

Weep You No More, Sad Fountains. *Unknown. See* Weep [*or* Weepe] You No More [Sad Fountains].

Weepe for the dead, for they have lost this light. On Himselfe. Robert Herrick. NOSC

Weep[e] not, my wanton, smile upon my knee. Robert Greene. NoSic; OxAEP-1 *Fr.* Menaphon.

Weepe you no more sad fountaines. *Unknown. See* Weep you no more, sad fountains.

Weeper, The. Richard Crashaw. *See* Saint Mary Magdalene *or* The Weeper.

Weeper, The. Richard Crashaw. FSCP

Weepers, The. Isabel Nathaniel. TiP2

Weepies, The. Paul Muldoon. NoAM; PNI

Weeping, The. Jack Hirschman. BodElec

Weeping and Kissing. Sir Edward Sherburne. NOSC

Weeping for the Zen Master Boyan. Chia Tao. CCL1, *tr.* by Stephen Owen

Weeping for Ying Yao. Wang Wei. WoPoe, *tr.* by Tony Barnstone, Willis Barnstone and Xu Haixin

Weeping for Ying Yao. Wang Wei. CCL1, *tr.* by Burton Watson

Weeping Headstones of the Isaac Becketts, The. Paul Durcan. PBCIP

Weeping over battle, many new ghosts. Facing the Snow. Tu Fu [*or* Du Fu]. CCL1, *tr.* by Stephen Owen

Weeping Singer, A. Hô Sugyông. EcSo, *tr.* by Youngju Ryu

Weeping: the food he eats. Louis Zukofsky. APSN *Fr.* A.

Weeping Woman. Denise Levertov. AF; AmWaPo

Weeps every eye. (LL) Shrewd star, who crudes our naming: you should be flame. Karen Volkman. IAoNAP; NAPBL; NeAmPo

Weeps out of western country something new. Birth in a narrow room, The. Gwendolyn Brooks. NoP-4; NoP-5

Weft of leafless spray, A. November. William Dean Howells. APN-2

Wei Wind. *Unknown. tr.* by Ezra Pound
  Pedlar. OBVE, *tr.* by Ezra Pound

Wei-chi (Not yet across the stream). *Unknown.* ColAnChi *Fr.* I Ching [*or* The Book of Changes *or* The Classic of Changes].

Weigh me the fire; or canst thou find. To Find[e] God. Robert Herrick. InvLi; NoP-4; NoP-5

Weighing the ste[a]dfastness and state. Man. Henry Vaughan. OBEV

Weighing-machine, the. Pierre McOrlan. MFP, *tr.* by Martin Sorrell

Weight. Jay Schneiders. OPRER

Weight Belt. Jeffery Conway. WiU

Weight of Sleep, The. W. S. Merwin. MotU

Weight of stones, of thoughts. Philippe Jaccottet. VCWP

Weight of Sweetness, The. Li-Young Lee. RaBo

Weight of the moment: immeasurable, the weight, The. Taste of Wild Cherry, The. Chris Forhan. NAPBL

Weill, gin they arena deid, it's time they were. (LL) Elegy: "They are lang deid, folk that I used to ken." Robert Garioch. EdScPo; NePenScot; NPeEn

Wein Geist. Charles Godfrey Leland. APN-2

Weingarten Travel Blessing, The. *Unknown.* GePo, *tr. by* Carroll Hightower

Weird as Puppets. Paul Verlaine. SxFrPo, *tr. by* Martin Sorrell

Weird containing stillness of the neighborhood, The. Pause. Eamon Grennan. NIL-7

Weird Dances. Juan Chi. CCL1, *tr. by* Michael Bullock and C. J. Chen

Weird dances are performed in the north street. Weird Dances. Juan Chi. CCL1, *tr. by* Michael Bullock and C. J. Chen

Weird hour. It's not. Sundial. Gabriel Zaid. TCLAP, *tr. by* Adrian Hernandez

Weird sister. In Salem. Lucille Clifton. ESEAA

Weird stuff this. Elizabeth Bletsoe. NewEx

Wel, who shal thise hornes blowe. *Unknown.* OHMEL

Welcome. David Hernandez. UnSA

Welcome. Micheal O'Siadhail. IrLP

Welcome. Karen Press. TSAP

Welcome, baby, to the world of swords. News of a Baby. Elizabeth Riddell. ItWoWo

Welcome back, Mr. K: Love of My Life. Welcome Back, Mr. Knight: Love of My Life. Etheridge Knight. LaCa; PBCAP; RaBo

Welcome / Black beetle. Harri Gwynn. BBMWP *Fr.* Creature, The.

Welcome, brave gallant, with those locks so fair. Periwig, A. Rowland Watkyns. NOSC

Welcome dear book, souls Joy, and food! The feast. H. Scriptures. Henry Vaughan. ChIV-2

Welcome dear chaos. Michael McClure. WANABP *Fr.* Plum Stones.

Welcome Eumenides. Eleanor Ross Taylor. InGu; NALW

Welcome Home. Josephine D. Henderson Heard. CBWP-4

Welcome, maids of honor. To Violets. Robert Herrick. OBEV

Welcome, Major Poet! Sean O'Brien. NoP-5

Welcome Morning. Anne Sexton. GoPo

Welcome, most welcome to our Vow[e]s and us. To the King; Upon His Com[m]ing with His Army into the West. Robert Herrick. CavPo

Welcome, o Supernatural One, o Swimmer. Prayer to the Sockeye Salmon. *Unknown.* WoPoe; WPoS, *tr. by* Jane Hirshfield

Welcome, pale Primrose! starting up between. Primrose, The. John Clare. CenSon

Welcome, proud lady. (LL) Sir Walter Scott. CABP; NAEL-6v2; NAEL-7v2; NePenScot; NOBRP; OBEV; OxBEV; RACG; TFi *Fr.* Heart of Midlothian, The.

Welcome Queen Alice. Lewis Carroll. UV *Fr.* Through the Looking-Glass.

Welcome, stranger! glad I greet thee. To Don Juan Baz. Mary E. Tucker. CBWP-1

Welcome the dawn. (LL) Nightingales. Robert Bridges. MoBrPo; OBEV; OBMV; TFi

Welcome thou safe retreate! William Habington. ChIV-1; NOSC *Fr.* Castara.

Welcome to ESL 100, English Surely Latinized. English con Salsa. Gina Valdés. CalPo

Welcome to Hiroshima. Mary Jo Salter. AmWaPo; AtGh; NIL-7; NIP-4; RA

Welcome to Hon. Frederick Douglass. Josephine D. Henderson Heard. CBWP-4

Welcome to Ithaca. Rebecca Seiferle. ExTi

Welcome to My Dream. Johnny Burke. ReLy

Welcome to the lascivious Court of Wei. First-born. Fergus Allen. NIrP

Welcome to the New Consciousness. Leseko Rampolekeng. NAfrP; PML

Welcome to Thomas Mann. Attila József. IQMS, *tr. by* Vernon Watkins

Welcome to Wales. John Tripp. AngWePo

Welcome to you. Ordinance on Arrival. Naomi Lazard. BLT; P180

Welcome, wild Northeaster! Ode to the Northeast Wind. Charles Kingsley. OxAEP-2

Welcome, woods crowned with sparse remains of green. Autumn. Alphonse Marie Louis de Lamartine. SxFrPo, *tr. by* A. M. and E. H. Blackmore

Welcoming Party, A. John Montague. PNI *Fr.* Time in Armagh.

Welcoming the Dawn. Oliver Wendell Holmes. DiBP

Welcum, illustrat Ladye, and oure Quene! Alexander Scott. NePenScot *Fr.* New Yeir Gift to the Quene Mary, quhen scho come first Hame, 1562, Ane.

Welkin's wind, way unhindered. Wind, The. Dafydd ap Gwilym. OBWVE, *tr. by* Joseph P. Clancy

Well? (LL) Trapped. Adelaide Crapsey. APT-1; OxBoAm

Well. Kim Chiha. CAMKP, *tr. by* David R. McCann

Well, The. Rose Ausländer. GTCP, *tr. by* Irmgard Hunt

Well, The. Yves Bonnefoy. VCWP, *tr. by* John Naughton

Well, The. Howard Phillips Lovecraft. APT-1

Well, The. Jay Macpherson. BrAP; NoP-4

Well, The. Bernard Raymund. YaYoPo

Well, The. Padma Sachdev. CFP, *tr. by* Iqbal Masud

Well, The. Philip Salom. NOBAu

Well, The. Edith Jay Scovell. HarvBoo *Fr.* Water Images.

Well, The. Ted Sexauer. WhBo

We'll all be Penelopes then. Spinster Song: African-American Woman Guild. Angela Jackson. IllVoic

Well and. Trapped. Adelaide Crapsey. APT-1; OxBoAm

We'll be home once more. (LL) Resurrection. Vladimir Holan. PoSu; StAl, *tr. by* George Theiner

We'll Be Together Again. Frankie Laine. ReLy

Well charged, halfway between generations. Poem 2 (for Duckie Simpson of Black Uhuru). Audrey Ingram-Roberts. WaCA

Well, comrade president, what is there left to say? Homage to Salvador Allende. Edward Palmer Thompson. RSaN

We'll dance again the saraband! (LL) Witch's Ballad, The. William Bell Scott. OBEV; RACG

We'll dance and sing / "Noel Noel." (LL) Little tree / little silent Christmas tree. E. E. Cummings. NTCP; OBCP

Well, Emily Sparks, your prayers were not wasted. Edgar Lee Masters. APT-1 *Fr.* Spoon River Anthology.

Well, first of all, just which God do you mean? Another Voice. Victor Hugo. SxFrPo, *tr. by* A. M. and E. H. Blackmore

Well, folks, and how. Archipelago, The. John Ashbery. BodElec

We'll Gather Lilacs. Ivor Novello. ReLy

Well girl, goodbye. To my last period. Lucille Clifton. BeAl; NAMCP V.2; PoCu

We'll give to idleness. (LL) To My Sister. William Wordsworth. MakPoe; NPBRoP

We'll Go No More A-Roving. Lord Byron. *See* So We'll Go No More A-Roving.

We'll go no more a-roving by the light of the moon. W. E. Henley. MoBrPo *Fr.* Echoes.

Well has thou spoken and yet not taught. Emily Jane Brontë. VWP

Well he came home from the war. Swordfishtrombone. Tom Waits. PFTM-2

Well, her book, anyway. The Kunitz volume. Anna Akhmatova Spends the Night on Miami Beach. John Balaban. GifTon

Well here again that don't apply. T. S. Eliot. FaBoVe *Fr.* Sweeney Agonistes.

Well, here I am in the *Centre Daily Times.* News Update. John Balaban. AF

Well here we are again jumping up and down. Proud Shore For Legends, A. Nicki Jackowska. RSaN

Well House, The. Robert Penn Warren. LPSFW *Fr.* Some Quiet, Plain Poems.

Well how do you like this lava flow? Some Views Concerning the Proposed Site of a National Park. Miyazawa Kenji. WhBo

Well, I am here, and all this brunt is past. Ben Jonson. NAEL-7v1 *Fr.* Volpone.

Well, I forget the rest. (LL) Memorabilia. Robert Browning. NAEL-6v2; NAEL-7v2; NoP-4; NoP-5; NPeEn; OxBEV; PoPoPo

Well I have and in fact. On Being Asked to Write a Poem Against the War in Vietnam. Hayden Carruth. AmWaPo; PoAgWa

Well, I may now receive, and die: my sin. John Donne. OBSV *Fr.* Satires.

Well I Remember How You Smiled. Walter Savage Landor. NAEL-6v2 *Fr.* Ianthe.

Well I remember in my boyish hours. Thoughts of Boyhood. John Lloyd. AngWePo

Well, I said to the missus that something pretty odd. Visitant Eclogue. John Kinsella. NeBl

Well I skated toward a star. Bonneville. Jenny Mueller. IAoNAP

Well I want all you women folks to fall in line. Dirty Dozens, The. Speckled Red (Rufus Perryman). FTtHH

Well, I was at the dresser. Just How It Happened. Priscilla Jane Thompson. CBWP-2

Well, if a King's a lion, at the least. Alexander Pope. OBSV *Fr.* First Epistle of the First Book of Horace Imitated, The.

Well; if ever I saw such another man since my mother bound my head. Mary the Cook-Maid's Letter to Dr. Sheridan. Jonathan Swift. NPeEn

Well! If the Bard was weather-wise, who made. Dejection: An Ode. Samuel Taylor Coleridge. BrAP; HeIP-4; NAEL-6v2; NAEL-7v2; NAWM-7v2; NOBRP; NoP-4; NoP-5; NPBRoP; NPeEn; OxAEP-2; PoPoPo; TFi; WaAnP

Well! if the Bard was weatherwise, who made. Letter to Sara Hutchinson. Samuel Taylor Coleridge. NPBRoP

Well, *if* you must know all the facts, I was merely reading a pamphlet. Visitor, A. Lewis Carroll. OBCoV

Well is he born, that may behold you ever. (LL) Edmund Spenser. NoP-5; OxBSo *Fr.* Amoretti.

Well, Is it Going to Budge, the Beast? Elke Erb. OnScMo, *tr. by* Rosmarie Waldrop

Well, it really hurts, to think of him going away. London, Greater London (After *Satire III*). John Holloway. WoPoe

Well, it's been a disappointing day. Health Forecast, The. Roger McGough. PoCu

Well it's half-past. Nearly Nowhere. Catherine Walsh. Oth

Well, it's partly the shape of the thing. Limerick. *Unknown.* SoSe-8

Well it's six o'clock in Oakland. Oakland Blues. Ishmael Reed. CalPo

Well, just a momentary good idea as your form. It Certainly Was Divine Running into You. Joanne Kyger. WANABP

Well may my Book come forth like Public [*or* Publique] Day. To the Most Illustrious and Most Hopeful[l] Prince, Charles, Prince of Wales. Robert Herrick. BASC

Well may that kisse be sweet that's giv'n t' a sleek. Sir Richard Fanshawe. OBVE *Fr.* Il Pastor Fido.

Well may you question the degree of falsehood. Aviary. Medbh McGuckian. MoWP

Well meaning readers! you that come as friends [*or* freinds]. Flaming Heart, The. Richard Crashaw. NAEL-6v1; NAEL-7v1

Well met Neighbour. Martin Parker.
"Whither away good neighbour." PBRV

Well might the ancients deem a grove to be. Prospect of a Landscape, Beginning with a Grove, The. Jane Barker. BASC

Well, mother, tomorrow night. 2-26-91. Roland Flint. PoCho

We'll never see the result. Refraction. If It Is True What Is Said of the Work. Heather Ramsdell. IAoNAP

Well, not exactly blind; I knew of her. Blind Date with the Muse. Stephen Dunn. NevBe

Well, now I'm lost in fog. Not metaphorically. This Fog. Alan Feldman. PoDa

Well O.K., he was wrong. David Guest. Martin Bell. RSaN

Well of blackness, all defiling. Contents of an Ink-bottle, The. Mary Elizabeth Coleridge. VWP

Well of Clouds, The. Michelangelo Coviello. *tr. by* Gayle Ridinger
"This hour is made of iron grates where the underground." ItPo, *tr. by* Gayle Ridinger

Well, Old Flame, the fire's out. Static. Barton Sutter. PoA 2002

Well, on the day I was born. Have You Anything to Say in Your Defense? César Vallejo. PoetW; RaBo, *tr. by* James Wright

We'll pay for it, we'll pay for it! (LL) Scotland: "It was a day peculiar to this piece of the planet." Alastair Reid. EdScPo; NePenScot

Well, read my cheek, and watch my eye. Lines of Life. Letitia Elizabeth Landon. NOBRP; NPBRoP; NPeEn

We'll see if it is, said Rivera.. (LL) I Paint What I See. Elwyn Brooks White. AmWit; NBLV

Well, she told me I had an aura. "What?" I said. Sonnet. Hayden Carruth. GifTon; StAl

Well silently overflowing. Paul Reps. WhBo

Well, since I became a lesbian. Beatrix Gates. WiU *Fr.* Triptych.

We'll smoke a couple cigarettes. Spring Scales. Darya Sukhovey. CRWP, *tr. by* Christopher Mattison

Well so, Hotgun he say. Hotgun on the Death of Yadeka Harjo. Alexander L. Posey. NAAPv.2

Well, so that is that. Now we must dismantle the tree. W. H. Auden. ChrPo; MoBrPo; OBCP *Fr.* For the Time Being; a Christmas Oratorio.

Well, some may hate and some may scorn. Emily Jane Brontë. VWP

Well, son de story of my life. Favorite Slave's Story, The. Priscilla Jane Thompson. CBWP-2; RACG

Well, son, I'll tell you. Mother to Son. Langston Hughes. AmFaPo; BLPJKO; ChAP; ISC; NAAL-5; NTCP; SAmP; TWF; WaAnP; WoPoe

Well, spring overflows the land. Lorine Niedecker. NAAPv.2; NAMCP V.1

We'll stay until ice begins. Styro. Jim Carroll. AHA

Well, sure, it's only. I Visit the Twenty-four Coin-op Church of Elvis. Fleda Brown Jackson. AllShUp

Well, sure, we both popped. My One Brother. Mary Dalton. OpeFie

Well, Teddy, I have found you. Lost Teddy Bear, The. Maggie Pogue Johnson. CBWP-4

Well the cat started actin funny. Earthquake Blues. Ishmael Reed. FTtHH

Well—the links are broken. Woman's Last Word, A. Adelaide Anne Procter. VWP

Well, the white asters. First Cold. A. R. Ammons. PfSP

Well then. Shumeekuli, The. Andrew Peynetsa. PFTM-2, *tr. by* Dennis Tedlock

Well then, how can I let you go away? (LL) Ah, yes, to your misfortune. Patrizia Cavalli. NeIt; VCWP, *tr. by* Judith Baumel

Well then; I now do plainly see. Abraham Cowley. BASC; NoP-4; NoP-5; NOSC; OBEV; OxAEP-1; PBRV *Fr.* Mistress, The.

Well, Then Let Slip the Masks. Gillian Eve Hanscombe and Suniti Namjoshi. PoBW

Well, then let slip the masks. Well, Then Let Slip the Masks. Gillian Eve Hanscombe and Suniti Namjoshi. PoBW

Well then, the promised [*or* promis'd] hour is come at last. To My Dear Friend Mr Congreve [on His Comedy Called "The Double-Dealer"]. John Dryden. NPeEn; OxAEP-1

Well there are many ways of being held prisoner. Anne Carson. NAMCP V.2 *Fr.* Glass Essay, The.

Well, there I was, trudgin' along to. Meeting the Master. Thomas Gannon. ViWalt

Well there's no end of things to do. Things My Brother and I Could Do. Robert Bly. InvLad

Well they are gone, and here must I remain. This Lime-Tree Bower My Prison. Samuel Taylor Coleridge. HeIP-4; NAEL-6v2; NAEL-7v2; NoP-5; NPBRoP; OBGa; OxAEP-2

Well they'd made up their minds to be everywhere because. W. S. Merwin. *See* Well they'd made up their minds to be everywhere because why not.

Well they'd made up their minds to be everywhere because why not. Last One, The. W. S. Merwin. NoAM
(Well they'd made up their minds to be everywhere because.) ChAP

Well, [*or* So] this bird comes, and under his wing is a crutch. Bird, The. Moyshe-Leyb Halpern. OxBoAm, *tr. by* John Hollander

"Well, this is where I go down to the river." Heat. Kenneth Mackenzie. BMAP

Well, though it seems. Liddell and Scott. Thomas Hardy. OBCoV

Well, though the bow's unbent, the wound bleeds on. (LL) Petrarch. NAWM-5v1; NAWM-7v1 *Fr.* Sonnets to Laura.

Well, thrill. That's their story. (LL) Freely Espousing. James Schuyler. FTOS; NoP-4; NoP-5

Well, to start with. Jonah and the Whale. Gareth Owen. OBSP

Well to that heart might his these absent greetings pour! (LL) Lord Byron. NAEL-6v2; NAEL-7v2 *Fr.* Childe Harold's Pilgrimage.

Well, twirl my turban! Man alive! Mister Five by Five. Don Raye. ReLy

"Well Uncle Ike! This beats me." Uncle Ike's Holiday. Priscilla Jane Thompson. CBWP-2

Well Water. Randall Jarrell. NAAL-5; PoCho; VCAP

Well we can go. Poem for Cocksuckers, A. John Wieners. CAGL

Well, we either do it or we don't, as the pigeon said to the loaf of bread. Sunrise with Sea Monster. Charles North. FTOS; NYP2

Well, we went down town a-shopping. Christmas Rush, The. Clara Ann Thompson. CBWP-2

Well, well, 'tis true. Plain Dealing. Alexander Brome. NOSC

Well, well, well, well, well,. She Loves Me. Sheldon Harnick. ReLy

Well, well, you's cum at las'. People's Literary, De. Maggie Pogue Johnson. CBWP-4

Well what's up, que pasa and a big hello. Hip Hop Bop. Jabari Asim. InTrad

Well, when all is said and done. Epilogue. George Russell. MoBrPo

Well, when I was courting. You Have No Horses. *Teton Sioux Oral Tradition.* NAAPv.2

Well, while wild roses grew around your head. . At the Grave. Yi Kyŏngnim. EcSo, *tr. by* Peter H. Lee

Well, World, you have kept faith with me. He Never Expected Much. Thomas Hardy. NAEL-6v2; NAEL-7v2; NAMCP V.1; NoAM

We'll worship Jesus / When jesus do. When We'll Worship Jesus. Imamu Amiri Baraka. APSN

Well worth Predecessors, and Fathers by name. Ditties Lamentation for the cruelty of this age. *Unknown.* BASC

Well ya got trouble, my friend, right here. Ya Got Trouble. Meredith Willson. ReLy

Well, you can't say. Sweet Sixteen. Eunice De Souza. NAMCP V.2

Well, you just have to read and get involved. On the Road. Clark Coolidge. NYP2

Well you know I wonder, it could be. Short Talk on the Sensation of Aeroplane Takeoff. Anne Carson. OpeFie

Well You Needn't. Dave Etter. SeSe

Well, You Needn't. Karen Volkman. PoDa

Well, you wake up in the mornin', hear the ding dong ring. "Leadbelly." GM

Well-Aimed Tear, The [*or* To Della Crusca]. Hannah Cowley. STuOW

Well-Bred Woman, A. Mervyn Taylor. BRtP

"Wellcome, to the Caves of Artá!" Robert Graves. NBLV

Well-dressed couple haggle, The. Knowingness. John Hughes. PNI

Wellfleet. Timothy Liu. AmPoNex

Wellfleet Whale, The. Stanley Kunitz. CAP-8; NoAM

Welling water—to which I add these tears, The. (LL) Stream, The. Mona Van Duyn. VCAP; WaAnP

Wellington. Charles Harpur. NOBAu

Well-Known Elizabethan Double Entendre, A. Pamela Alexander. YaYoPo

Well-rested can, The. (LL) Insomnia. Cornelius Eady. AWTN; ESEAA

Well-shadow'd landskip, fare ye well. Sir John Suckling. CavPo

Wellspring, The. Sharon Olds. BodElec

Well-uh Bird, Bird, Bird, Bird is the Word. David Wojahn. PBCAP *Fr.* Mystery Train: A Sequence.

Well-wrought this wall-stone which fate has broken. Ruin, The. *Unknown.* WoPoe, *tr. by* Michael O'Brien

Wels a Fish that Lives on the Bottom, The. Sarah Kirsch. PFTM-2, *tr. by* Wayne Kvam

Wels a fish that lives on the bottom, The. Wels a Fish that Lives on the Bottom, The. Sarah Kirsch. PFTM-2, *tr. by* Wayne Kvam

Welsh and Wales. Waldo Williams. BBMWP, *tr. by* Anthony Conran

Welsh Ballad, A. Edmwnd Prys. OBWVE, *tr. by* Gwyn Williams

Welsh Espionage. Gwyneth Lewis.
  Advice on Adultery. MFPA; NeBrP
  "So this is the man you dreamt I had betrayed." TCAWP
  "Welsh was the mother tongue, English was his." MoWP

Welsh Hill Country, The. Ronald Stuart Thomas. AngWePo

Welsh History. Ronald Stuart Thomas. OBWVE

Welsh Homer. Cliff James. AngWePo

Welsh Ice. Menna Elfyn. ATSWP, *tr. by* Robert Minhinnick

Welsh Incident. Robert Graves. OBSP; OxBEV; WaAnP

Welsh is a mad language; there are no words in it. Language Difficulty. Ann Drysdale. TCAWP

Welsh Landscape. Ronald Stuart Thomas. NoP-4; NoP-5; TCAWP

Welsh Language, The. Alan Llwyd. BBMWP, *tr. by* Joseph P. Clancy

Welsh Love Letter. Michael Burn. TCAWP

Welsh Testament, A. Ronald Stuart Thomas. TCAWP

Welsh Valley Cinema, 1930s. Dannie Abse. TCAWP

Welsh was the mother tongue, English was his. Gwyneth Lewis. MoWP *Fr.* Welsh Espionage.

Welsh Wordscape, A. Peter Finch. AngWePo

Welshman at St. James' Park, A. Ronald Stuart Thomas. AngWePo

Welshman in Exile Speaks, The. T. Harri Jones. AngWePo; OBWVE

Welsh-speaking Welsh, The. Gwyn Thomas. BBMWP, *tr. by the author*

We'n you see a man in woe. "Hullo!" Sam Walter Foss. VerBaPo

Wendell Phillips. Henrietta Cordelia Ray. CBWP-3

Wenn nur ein Traum das Dasein ist. Trinker im Frühling, Der. Li Po. CCL1, *tr. by* Hans Bethge

Went—and ne'er returned again! (LL) Hope. Emily Jane Brontë. NoP-4; NoP-5

Went dicing on my bike. African Boog. Allen Fisher. Oth

Went down to the yards. Long Track Blues. Sterling Allen Brown. GM

Went home and put a bullet through his head. (LL) Richard Cory. Edwin Arlington Robinson. APN-2; ChAP; ColAP; CtM; IJHIL; MoAmPo; NAAL-5; NAAPv.1; NAMCP V.1; NCAP; NoP-4; NoP-5; OxBoAm; PoPoPo; PtR; TCAPo; TFi; WaAnP

Went into a shoestore to buy a pair of shoes. Sale. Josephine Miles. APT-2

Went on cutting bread and butter. (LL) Sorrows of Werther, The. William Makepeace Thackeray. NBLV; OBCoV

Went out last night, had a great big fight. Prove It on Me Blues. Gertrude "Ma." Rainey. NAAPv.2

Went to see the *there* that was, for me, full. Story for the Mother Tongue. Pimone Triplett. LegDan

Went up a year this evening! Emily Dickinson. WeW-3

Wept, to behold a brighter goddess there! (LL) Determines to Follow Phaon. Mary Robinson. CenSon; RWP

We're a couple of swells; we stop at the best hotels. Couple of Swells, A. Irving Berlin. OBCoV; ReLy

We're afraid of sun and hope for rain. Volcanic Ash. Peter Sears. UrbNat

Were all the peaks of Gwynedd. Welsh Love Letter. Michael Burn. TCAWP

We're all uproarious, Philip and I and his. Reaching Around. Judith Moffett. ViWalt

We're babes on Broadway. Babes on Broadway. Ralph Freed. ReLy

Were becoming less sane. Growing Days, The. Rick Alley. AmPoNex

Were beth they biforen us weren. *Unknown.* NoP-5

We're Caribbean islands. Caribbean Islands. Michel-Ange Hyppolite. OGAHCP, *tr. by* Boadiba and Jack Hirschman

We're down to an anvil and conch. Heirlooms. Walter McDonald. RWB

We're eager to look like the manufacture of chocolate. Two Seconds. Marie-Dominique Massoni. SurWo, *tr. by* Myrna Bell Rochester

Were fading and all wars were done. (LL) Dark Hills, The. Edwin Arlington Robinson. MoAmPo; NAMCP V.1; NoAM

We're fed up with national colors! Project: Flag. Tadeusz Borowski. AF, *tr. by* Larry Rafferty, Meryl Natchez and Tadeusz Pioro

We're flattered they come so close. Animal Song. Heather McHugh. WaAnP

We're foot—slog—slog—slog—sloggin' over Africa. Boots. Rudyard Kipling. BRP; MoBrPo

We're French and Indian like the war. Like the Trails of Ndakinna. Cheryl Savageau. TWW

We're Frightfully BBC. Western Brothers.
  "Connected with County, and landed estates." RWPCtW

We're gan' tyek hor off, th' morn. Charlie Douglas. Katrina Porteous. NeBl

We're gathered in the backroom of the co-op mill. On a Winter's Night. Shin Kyŏngnim. CAMKP, *tr. by* Anthony, Brother of Taizé

We're going to need the minister. Minister. Anne Stevenson. InoFa

Were he composer, he would surely write. Portrait of the Boy as Artist. Barbara Howes. MoAmPo

We're heading where the light is draining. After the Rain. Anne Marie Macari. MotU

We're here because we're here. Because We're Here. *Unknown.* FaBoWar

We're here to cover the cracks. Wallpapering to Patsy Cline. Judith Sornberger. FiBr

We're hoping to be arrested. Street Demonstration. Margaret Abigail Walker. InGu

Were I a Flower. Ok-Ku Kang. WhBo

Were I a general of olden times. Mikhail Alekseievich Kuzmin. CAGL, *tr. by* Michael Green

Were I a king, I could command content. Poem. Edward, 17th Earl of Oxford De Vere. NoSic
  (Weare I a Kinge I coulde commande content.) NPeEn; PBRV

"Were I as Base as Is the Lowly Plain." Joshua Sylvester. GSo; NoSic
  (Ubique.) OBEV

Were I employ'd a garden to contrive. Samuel Gilbert. OBGa *Fr.* Florist's Vade-Mecum, The.

Were I idiom and. While. Bruce Andrews. FTOS

Were I laid on Greenland's coast. John Gay. NAEL-6v1; NPeEn; OxBEV *Fr.* Beggar's Opera, The.

Were I that wandering citizen whose city is the world. English Graves, The. G. K. Chesterton. FaBoWar

Were I to build a bamboo hut on the ice. Spring Overflows the Pavilion. *Unknown.* CATKP, *tr. by* Peter H. Lee

Were I to send word. *Unknown.* ArkPo, *tr. by* Helen Craig McCullough

Were I to tear out my tongue and. Liliane Giraudon. SCFWP *Fr.* Poem with Incense Paper.

Were I (who to my cost already am). Satire [*or* Satyre *or* Satyr] against [Reason and] Mankind, A. John Wilmot, 2d Earl of Rochester. BASC; NOSC; OBSV

Were I (who to my cost already am). John Wilmot, 2d Earl of Rochester. CABP; NPeEn; OxBEV *Fr.* Satire [*or* Satyre *or* Satyr] against [Reason and] Mankind, A.

Were I (who to my cost already am). Satire against Reason and Mankind, A. Grace Buchanan Sherwood. NoP-4

Were it not for / Cries in snow. Chiyojo. ZenPo, *tr. by* Takashi Ikemoto and Lucien Stryk

Were it not for making a living, which is rather a nouciance. (LL) Introspective Reflection. Ogden Nash. NBLV; OBCoV

Were it not strange that by the tideless sea. Travellers, The. Eva Gore-Booth. PoBW

Were it possible to say. Alexandria. Mongane Wally Serote. NAfrP

Were it sweet. Issa. EH, *tr. by* R. H. Blyth

Were lives of ease, dear Namesake, ours. Martial. RompO, *tr. by* Peter Whigham

We're living different lives, she says, as she unbuttons. No Guarantee. Craig Crist-Evans. MAAN

Were lost, if that were addle. (LL) Proper New Ballad Entitled [*or* Intituled] The Fairies' [*or* Faeryes] Farewell, or God-a-Mercy Will, A. Richard Corbet. BASC; NOSC; OxBEV; PBRV

"We're married," said Eddie. Newlyweds, The. John Updike. OBCoV

We're married, they say, and you think you have won me. Bridal Veil, The. Alice Cary. TCAPo

Were Ne My Hearts Light I Wad Dye. Lady Grisel Baillie. EMWP
  (Werena My Heart Licht I Wad Dee.) OBEV

We're Not Going to Malta. Richard Blanco. LegDan

Were not the one dead, turned to their affairs. (LL) Out, Out—. Robert Frost. AmFaPo; APT-1; ColAP; HarvBoo; HeIP-4; InoFa; ItP; NAAL-5; NAMCP V.1; OxBoAm; SoSe-8; TCAPo; TRP; WaAnP

We're Not Well Here. Abiodun Oyewole. BRtP

We're Off to See the Wizard (The Wonderful Wizard of Oz). E. Y. Harburg. ReLy

We're on Sorrow Watch engulfed by Scorpion Bowls. Good Night, All You Ships at Sea, You. Jim Behrle. FreRad

We're on the street. Door, The. Carlos Bousoño. RaW, *tr. by* Charles Guenther

We're out in my father's boat and he's fishing. Day at the Seaside, A. John Glenday. NeBrP

We're passing the whole summer, all of us. Pastoral. Geoffrey Nutter. IAoNAP

We're queer folks here. Just Folks. Edgar Albert Guest. ITBLP

We're riding home from *Godspell*, which most people. Good News/Bad News. Betsy Sholl. PfS

We're snug as a bug in a heated house. Quatrain. Adriann Roland Holst. TuT, *tr. by* Sean Dunne

We're so fed up with the Southland. Jump for Joy. Paul Francis Webster. ReLy

We're Staying at the Castlemount, Western Esplanade. M. R. Peacocke. NLP

We're talking different kinds of vulnerability here. Icicles Round a Tree in Dumfriesshire. Ruth Padel. MoWP

Were the Bees. Andy Weaver.
1. PoPra
2. PoPra
3. PoPra
4. PoPra
5. PoPra

Were the best of all my days. (LL) Animals. Frank O'Hara. GoPo; HarvBoo; StAl

We're the D-Day Dodgers, out in Italy. Ballad of the D-Day Dodgers. Hamish Henderson. RSaN

We're the healthy, happy heathens, the Men Who Ride for Fun. Men Who Ride for Fun, The. Walter G. Kendall. ArBi

Were the last days of our antithesis! (LL) Labyrinth, The. Jorge Luis Borges. PoetW; WoPoe, *tr. by* John Updike

Were there amongst us bridegrooms and brides. Heralds of New Jerusalem. Ayin Tur-Malka. NRoS, *tr. by* Esther Raizen

Were there no limits to my lust. To His Importunate Mistress. Paul Griffin. UV

Were there such an end as destination. Leaving. T. Crunk. YaYoPo

Were they then that are what they are now. (LL) A. R. Ammons. NAAL-5; NAMCP V.2 *Fr.* Garbage.

We're through with making love, right? Nothing Happened. Smile. HotL, *tr. by* V. Narayana Rao

We're together again. Measuring Apollo. Luke Icarus Simon. PML, *tr. by* the author

We're told how the great mazy world we wander. Understanding the Universe. John Frederick Nims. PfSP

Were toward Eternity. (LL) Because I could not stop for Death. Emily Dickinson. APN-2; BrAP; BRP; ClHu; ColAP; CtM; HelP-4; ITBLP; MoAmPo; NAAL-3; NAAL-5; NAAPv.1; NALW; NAMCP V.1; NAWM-7v2; NIL-7; NIP-4; NoAM; NoP-4; NoP-5; OxBoAm; PoPoPo; SAmP; SoSe-8; TFi; TRP; TWF; WaAnP; WeW-3

We're turning back the clocks tonight. Standard Time: Novena for My Father. Dionisio D. Martinez. TouFir

We're walking down Grant, through Chinatown. Playing for Time. Christopher Buckley. SeSe

Were we able to tell. Sadakichi. NAAPv.1 *Fr.* Tanka.

Were we not fine. American Indian Art: Form and Tradition. Diane Di Prima. BB

We're wed to one eternity. (LL) Invite to Eternity, An. John Clare. NAEL-6v2; NAEL-7v2

We're wonderful one times one. (LL) If everything happens that can't be done. E. E. Cummings. SoSe-8; WeW-3

Were you a string of beads. the elder daughter of Lady Otomo no Sakanoé. ArkPo, *tr. by* Edwin A. Cranston

Were you apprenticed to a fortune teller? Mikhail Alekseievich Kuzmin. CAGL, *tr. by* Michael Green

Were you ever down, not a cent in your pockets? For Services Rendered. F. G. Butterfield. FaBoWar

Were you (I suppose) expecting. My Man Caliban! James Richardson. RD

Were You There. *Unknown.* SacPr

"Were you there when they crucified my Lord?" APN-2

Were you there when they crucified my Lord? Were You There. *Unknown.* SacPr

Were you there when they crucified my Lord? *Unknown.* APN-2 *Fr.* Were You There.

Were You There When They Crucified My Lord? *Unknown.* APN-2

Were you to ask me what I'd wish to be. Sŏng [*or* Sung] Sammun. CATKP, *tr. by* Peter H. Lee

Were you to go to the fire of the Guidance on the side of Mount Sinai, you could take all the knowledge and light you wish. Muhammad ibn Ghalib al-Rusafi. HiArP, *tr. by* James T. Monroe

Werena My Heart Licht I Wad Dee. Lady Grisel Baillie. *See* Were Ne My Hearts Light I Wad Dye.

Were't aught to me I bore the canopy. Sonnet 125. William Shakespeare. AEP; NoSic *Fr.* Sonnets.

Werner Herzog 68 / Iowa City 88. Ann Lauterbach. ExTi

Wernher von Braun. Tom Lehrer. OBCoV

Werther had a love for Charlotte. Sorrows of Werther, The. William Makepeace Thackeray. NBLV; OBCoV

Wes. Boss Communication. Mari E. Evans. SeSe

We's invited down to brudder Browns. Krismas Dinnah. Maggie Pogue Johnson. CBWP-4

West, The. Alphonse Marie Louis de Lamartine. SxFrPo, *tr. by* A. M. and E. H. Blackmore

West, The. Michael Longley. PBCIP

West, The (Fourth Version). Georg Trakl. GTCP, *tr. by* Robert Firmage

West Coast Indian. George Clutesi. HATNAP

West Country, The. Alice Cary. APN-2; SWaP

West End Perk, The. James Bridie. EdScPo

West from the Capital's crowded throng. Constance Fenimore Woolson. SWaP *Fr.* Two Women.

West Gate Ballad. *Unknown.* CCL1, *tr. by* Anne Birrell

West Indian Primer. Elizabeth Alexander. NIL-7

West Kansas full moon. Directions in Our Blood. Barney Bush. HATNAP

West Nile Crow. Marvin Francis. PoPra

West of Alice. W. E. Harney. NOBAu

West of Hut. Tu Fu [*or* Du Fu]. CCL1, *tr. by* Florence Ayscough and Amy Lowell

West of hut grow bamboo-shoots; I open another door. West of Hut. Tu Fu [*or* Du Fu]. CCL1, *tr. by* Florence Ayscough *and* Amy Lowell

West of Murray, just off 641. In Memory of the Boys of Dexter, Kentucky. Joe Bolton. AmPoNex

West of my hut, I grow mulberry. Tu Fu [*or* Du Fu]. CrYelRi *Fr.* Random Pleasures.

West of the golden sky. Up into the Clouds Music. Li Po. ColAnChi, *tr. by* Elling O. Eide

West of the painted bridge. Beating the Heat at Jade Lake. Ching An. CSKM, *tr. by* Jerome P. Seaton

West Paddocks. Arthur Davies. NOBAu

West Pitch at the Falls. Marsden Hartley. APT-1

West provokes the East, The. The iron arm. Ernest Francisco Fenollosa. APN-2 *Fr.* East and West.

West Side—corn tortillas for a penny each. Allí Por La Calle San Luis. Carmen Tafolla. TiP2

West, so they say, is the home of the jay, The. Forty-five Minutes from Broadway. George M. Cohan. ReLy

West Strand Visions. James Simmons. ModIr; PBCIP

West Sussex Drinking Song. Joseph Hilaire Pierre Belloc. MoBrPo

West Texas. Bettye Hammer Givens. TiP2

West Texas Mid-Century. Roxy Gordon. TiP2

West Texas Rain Journal. Candice Favilla. ExTi

West Texas Suicide. Lillian Wright. TiP2

West Wall. W. S. Merwin. RaBo

West West. Bruce Andrews. FTOS

West Willow. Reginald Shepherd. AmPoNex; IllVoic

West Wind. Mary Oliver.
Poem 12. PoCoUp

West Wind, The. John Masefield. CABP; MoBrPo

West Wind Ferries Grief, The. Li Ching. CCL1, *tr. by* Alan Ayling and Duncan Mackintosh

West wind sets the dragon rippling over the flag. Dragon. Ruth Bidgood. AngWePo

Westering. Seamus Heaney. HarvBoo

Western Approaches, The. Howard Nemerov. ColAP

Western Capital is disordered and lawless, The. Seven Sorrows. Wang Ts'an. ColAnChi

Western CIV, 4 and 5. Joan Retallack. FTOS

Western clouds, hill above hill. Ch'iang Village. Tu Fu [*or* Du Fu]. CrYelRi, *tr. by* Sam Hamill

Western Course: a cicada's voice singing, The. On the Cicada: In Prison. Lo Pin-wang. ColAnChi, *tr. by* Stephen Owen

Western Emigrant, The. Lydia Huntley Sigourney. SWaP

Western Holly Stove. Alison Townsend. SweBea

Western Landscape. Louis MacNeice. ModIr

Western Patriarch's doctrine is transplanted!, The. Dogen. ZenPo, *tr. by* Takashi Ikemoto and Lucien Stryk

Western Peak. Master Naong. BecRai, *tr. by* Kim Daljin, Kim Won-Chung and Christopher Merrill

Western ranch is just a branch of Nowhere Junction to me, A. Buttons and Bows. Ray Evans and Jay Livingston. ReLy

Western sun withdraws the shortened day, The. James Thomson. NAEL-6v1; NAEL-7v1 *Fr.* Seasons, The.

Western Trail Cook, 1880. Sharyn Jeanne Skeeter. ISC

Western Wagons. Rosemary Benét *and* Stephen Vincent Benét and Stephen Vincent Benét. HHAm

Western Wall, The. Shirley Kaufman. TaR

Western Wind. *Unknown.* ClHu; HeIP-4; NAEL-6v1; NAEL-7v1; NIL-7; NoP-4; NoSic; OPOU; PoPoPo; SoSe-8; TFi; WeW-3; WoPoe
(Lover in Winter Plaineth for the Spring, The.) OBEV
(Westron Wind[e], When Will Thou Blow.) NIP-4

Western wind has blown but a few days, The. Cranes, The. Po Chü-i. CCL1; OBVE; OWoS, *tr. by* Arthur Waley

Wester[n] wind, when will [*or* wilt] thou blow. Western Wind. *Unknown.* ClHu; HeIP-4; NAEL-6v1; NAEL-7v1; NIL-7; NoP-4; NoSic; OPOU; PoPoPo; SoSe-8; TFi; WeW-3; WoPoe
(Westron winde, when will thou blow.) WaAnP
(Westron wynde when wyll thow [*or* thou] blow.) FaBoVe; NoP-5; NPeEn

Westminster Bridge. William Wordsworth. *See* Composed upon Westminster Bridge, September 3, 1802.

Westphalian Song. *Unknown.* OBVE, *tr. by* Samuel Taylor Coleridge

Westport House, Portrush. James Simmons. PBCIP

Westron Wind[e], When Will Thou Blow. *Unknown. See* Western Wind.

Westron winde, when will thou blow. *Unknown. See* Wester[n] wind, when will [*or* wilt] thou blow.

Westron wynde when wyll thow [*or* thou] blow. *Unknown. See* Wester[n] wind, when will [*or* wilt] thou blow.

West-Running Brook. Robert Frost. APT-1; MoAmPo; NoP-4; NoP-5

Westward over Lotus Mountain. Li Po. BLT

Westwood, sitting sadly by himself. Charles MacKay. STuOW *Fr.* Man's Heart, A.

Wet air, rain oncoming. Infidelities. James McCorkle. PoDa

Wet almond-trees, in the rain. Bare Almond-Trees. D. H. Lawrence. FaBoVe

Wet Bodies. Franz Douskey. PasH

Wet Camp. Alberto A. Ríos. NAAL-5

Wet Casements. John Ashbery. NAMCP V.2; OxBoAm

Wet centre is bottomless, The. (LL) Bogland. Seamus Heaney. HeIP-4; NAMCP V.2; NoAM; PBCIP; PNI; PoetW; PoPoPo

Wet Day. James McAuley. BMAP

Wet Day, A. Andrew Young. NePenScot

Wet Dream. Carlos Omar Gardinet. BRtP

Wet Earth. Ramón López Velarde. TCLAP, *tr. by* Samuel Beckett

Wet Evening in April. Patrick Kavanagh. BeAl; OPOU

Wet Feet. Jackie Hardy. NeBl

Wet green velvet scums the swimming pool, A. Frog in the Swimming Pool, The. Debora Greger. NoP-4

Wet ground, suddenly black. (LL) Laying the Dust. Denise Levertov. BrAP; MoWP

Wet Hair: If Now His Mother Should Come. Robert Penn Warren. NoAM *Fr.* Penological Study: Southern Exposure.

Wet hands work quickly, cartilage shines into light. To Understand Flight. Malinda Markham. IAoNAP

Wet leaf that clings to the threshold, A. (LL) Liu Ch'e. Emperor Wu of Han. APT-1; NDACCP; OBVE, *tr. by* Ezra Pound

Wet leaves along the threshold of the mid-day. Love Rockets. Jim Carroll. AHA

Wet Oak. Angela Shannon. BtF

Wet Pain . . . Tread with Care. Leseko Rampolekeng. NAfrP

Wet sand raven tracks. Ray McNiece. AmZen

Wet sheet and a flowing sea, A. Sea-Song, A. Allan Cunningham. OxAEP-2

Wet streets, black trees, a gold leaf smacked. Debra Bruce. FFC *Fr.* ("The Light They Make").

Wet, this is instantly mud country, and then as suddenly. In the Country of the Black Pig. Christopher Hope. EmeKit

Wet trees hung above the walks, The. Empty House, The. William Dean Howells. APN-2

Wet with morning dew. Basho. SoOfWa, *tr. by* Sam Hamill

Wet your lungs with wine—the dogstar rises. Alcaeus. SaLy, *tr. by* Diane Rayor

Wet-ash light. In Tornado Weather. Judith Kerman. P180

Wetlands out back of the supermarket. Evolution on 38th Street. Jack Brannon. UrbNat

We've all been. Dust Truck Blues. Iwan Llwyd. BBMWP, *tr. by* Geriant Løvgreen

We've all got history on our hands. Tatiana Bek. CRWP, *tr. by* Robert Reid

We've always thought / Knowledge is naught. Varsity Drag, The. Lew Brown, B. G. DeSylva and Ray Henderson. ReLy

We've been out for an hour. Fishing with Elvis. Dabney Stuart. AllShUp

We've been taught for two thousand years. Late Twentieth-Century Prayer, A. Ernest Sandeen. WeW-3

We've called ourselves adults for ages now. Goldminers' Waltz, The. Aleksandr Arkadevich Galich. TCRusP, *tr. by* Gerry Smith

We've come, the woman calls out, to listen. Melancholy. David Keller. UrbNat

We've Come This Far. Mona Lisa Saloy. FuFl

We've come to the place. Arrival. Patricia Dienstfrey. ASA

We've fought with many men acrost the seas. Fuzzy-Wuzzy. Rudyard Kipling. MoBrPo

We've got one day here, and not another minute. New York, New York. Betty Comden and Adolph Green. ReLy

We've got the cholera in camp—it's worse than forty fights. Cholera Camp. Rudyard Kipling. FaBoWar

We've got this cheese down here to give away. Capitalist Poem #36. Campbell McGrath. NAPBL

We've heard and heard, and finally believe. Diary, The. Johann Wolfgang von Goethe. STV, *tr. by* John Frederick Nims

We've just been introduced. Shall We Dance? Oscar Hammerstein, II. ReLy

We've made an art of it. Waiting Room in August, A. Julia Darling. PoCu

We've missed that for years, not so much. Time to Hear Ourselves Think. Dick Allen. PoDa

We've our business to attend Day's duties. Bending the Bow. Robert Duncan. HarvBoo

We've perfected the disappearing trick. Conor O'Callaghan. NIrP *Fr.* Loose Change.

We've / poisoned our food, polluted our air. John Cage. APSN *Fr.* Diary: How to Improve the World (You Will Only Make Matters Worse).

We've returned to autumn again; summer. Word for Summer, A. George Seferis. AF

We've Solved the Problem. Bernadette Mayer. FTOS

We've traveled long together. Verses to my Heart's-Sister. Henrietta Cordelia Ray. CBWP-3

We've trod the maze of error round. George Crabbe. OBEV *Fr.* Reflections.

We've yet to cohabit. For some we simply arrive and leave parties. Alan Wearne. BMAP *Fr.* Nightmarkets, The.

Wha daur meddle wi' me? Little Jock Elliot. *Unknown.* IBB

Wha Fe Call I'. Valerie Bloom. FaBoVe

Wha kens on whatna Bethlehems. Innumerable Christ, The. Hugh MacDiarmid. HarvBoo; OxAEP-2

Wha Me Mudder Do. Grace Nichols. NOxBChV

Wha wadna be in love. Maggie Lauder. Francis Sempill. NePenScot

Wha?? Wha dem say? Dem say dem wan fi know what is reggae? Reggae. Vejay Steede. WaCA

Wha wrong wid Mary dry-foot bwoy. Dry-Foot Bwoy. Louise Bennett. NAMCP V.2

Whacher. Anne Carson. NLPA *Fr.* Glass Essay, The.

Whacher, / Emily's habitual spelling of this word. Anne Carson. NLPA *Fr.* Glass Essay, The.

Whae dae ye think ye ur? (LL) Arraheids. Kathleen Jamie. EdScPo; GPPA

Whale. William Rose Benét. MoAmPo

Whale billows. At Iku's Embarkation for Yuan China. Muso Soseki. EaWin, *tr. by* W. S. Merwin

Whale Breathing: Bartlett Cove, Alaska. Bill Holm. MiVo

Whale hunt, The. Jacques Prévert. MFP, *tr. by* Martin Sorrell

Whale, improbable as lust, The. Tall Tale, A; or, A Moral Song. Phyllis Webb. BrAP

Whale in the Web, The. Bill O'Daly. GifTon

Whale / is a room, The. In a Blind Garden. David Shapiro. ChIV-1

Whale Spouting. Takamura Kotaro. WoPoe, *tr. by* James Kirkup and Akiko Takemoto

Whaler's Pig, The. Edwin James Brady. NOBAu

Whaler's Rhyme. *Unknown.* NOBAu

Whales. Morton Marcus. GeoHom

Whales / Bellowing dawn. Gyodai. ZenPo, *tr. by* Takashi Ikemoto and Lucien Stryk

Whales fall slowly to the ocean floor. Joy Addict, The. James Harms. NAPBL; NeAmPo

Whales Weep Not! D. H. Lawrence. NAMCP V.1; NoAM

Whales. We're going to hunt whales. Whale hunt, The. Jacques Prévert. MFP, *tr. by* Martin Sorrell

Whaling backdoor of Texarkana, The. Blue Texarkana. Glenn Stokes. EGAG

Whaling for continents coveted deep in the south. Unhistoric Story, The. Allen Curnow. BrAP

Whaling Song, A. John Osborn. TCAPo

Wha'll buy [my] caller herrin'? Caller Herrin'. Carolina Oliphant, Baroness Nairne. WoRP

Whan Cnut Cyng the Witan wold enfeoff. Beoleopard; or, The Witan's Whail. *Unknown.* OBCoV

Whan I on the rode see. *Unknown.* OHMEL

Whan I remembre agayn. John Skelton. NPeEn

Whan I see on rode. *Unknown.* OHMEL

Whan I thenke on the rode. *Unknown.* OHMEL

Whan I thenke thynges three. *Unknown.* OHMEL

Whan I was come ayeyn into the place. Geoffrey Chaucer. NPeEn *Fr.* Parlement of Foules, The.

Whan men beth muriest at her mele. *Unknown.* OHMEL

Whan that April[le] with his[e] shoures [*or* showres] so[o]te. Geoffrey Chaucer. NAEL-6v1; NAEL-7v1; NoP-5; WaAnP *Fr.* Canterbury Tales, The.

Whan that the Knight [*or* Knyght] had[de] thus his tale yto[o]ld. Geoffrey Chaucer. NAEL-6v1; NAEL-7v1 *Fr.* Canterbury Tales, The.

Whan the nyghtengale syngeth the wodes waxen grene. *Unknown.* OHMEL

Whan the turf is thy tour. *Unknown.* OHMEL

Whan they han goon nat fully half a mile. Geoffrey Chaucer. OxBEV *Fr.* Canterbury Tales, The.

Whapmagoostui. Charles Fishman. PoCoUp

What? Langston Hughes. NBLV

What. Emmett Williams. PFTM-2 *Fr.* Ultimate Poem, The.

What a bankruptcy! How. Bertolt Brecht. FaBoA

What a beautiful day for a wedding in May! For Me and My Gal. E. Ray Goetz and Edgar Leslie. ReLy

What a Boy Does Not Say. Christopher Bursk. MAAN

What a charming thing's a battle! Isaac Bickerstaffe. OBCoV; PoAgWa *Fr.* Recruiting Serjeant, The.

What a consoling poem this will be if the roadside. Shadows. Richard Jackson. SeSe

What a cost to be pure! did e'er strike your mind. Refining Fire. Lizelia Augusta Jenkins Moorer. CBWP-3

What a dainty life the milkmaid leads! Song. Thomas Nabbes. NOSC

What a delight that summer, page after page. Poem for Harry Houdini. Leroy V. Quintana. ICANM

What a dream I had last night! Kamalākānta Bhaṭṭācārya. SinGod, *tr. by* Rachel Fell McDermott

What a fad it is for poets. Twenty-First Century, Farewell. Todd James Pierce. RWB

What a Friend We Have in Jesus. Joseph Scriven. *See* Unfailing Friend, The.

What a friend we have in Jesus. Unfailing Friend, The. Joseph Scriven. SacPr

What a girl called "the dailiness of life." Well Water. Randall Jarrell. NAAL-5; PoCho; VCAP

What a grand time was the war! World War II. Langston Hughes. APT-2; PoPoPo

What a great battle you and I have fought. Marriage, The. Anna Wickham. ItWoWo

What a grudge I am bearing the earth. Petrarch. MoBrPo *Fr.* Sonnets to Laura.

What a host you are, Mancinus. Martial. OBVE

What a joke! Rāmprasād Sen. SinGod, *tr. by* Rachel Fell McDermott

What a joy to climb into bed. Presidents. Michael Heffernan. EmeKit

What a Little Girl Had on Her Mind. Ibaragi Noriko. WoPoe, *tr. by* Ikuko Atsumi and Kenneth Rexroth

What a little girl had on her mind was. What a Little Girl Had on Her Mind. Ibaragi Noriko. WoPoe, *tr. by* Ikuko Atsumi and Kenneth Rexroth

What a Little Moonlight Can Do. Joe Heithaus. SeSe

What a lonely town this is for me. Wedding Bells Are Breaking Up That Old Gang of Mine. Irving Kahal and Willie Raskin. ReLy

What a Man, What a Moon. Anna Couani. BMAP

What a man, what a moon, what a fish, what a chip, what a block. What a Man, What a Moon. Anna Couani. BMAP

What a miracle. Karai Senryū. EMJL, *tr. by* Makoto Ueda

What a mixup, what a mess. Ain't That the Way It Goes? Roy Turk. ReLy

What a modern age, modern age, modern age. Twentieth-Century Love. George M. Cohan. ReLy

What a moon. Issa. IllVoic *Fr.* Issa: A Suite of Haiku.

What a mouth has to do with the opening in a door. I hid a. Meshes. Elizabeth Robinson. AmPoNex

What a Perfect Combination. Irving Caesar, Bert Kalmar *and* Harry Ruby *and* Harry Ruby. ReLy

What a place for a garden. Proposed Elegy for Hart Crane. Merrill Gilfillan. AHA

What a Poet Does. Chana Bloch. FaoP

What a relief to be speaking again, restored. Comment on My Host, A. Mark Solomon. OPRER

What a silence, when you are here. What. Relationship. János Pilinszky. IQMS; StAl, *tr. by* Peter Jay

What a strain it is to be evil. (LL) Mask of Evil, The. Bertolt Brecht. PoSu; WoPoe, *tr. by* Hoffman Reynolds Hays

What a strange thing! Issa. EH, *tr. by* Robert Hass

What a strong little sucker you are! First Beating. Lorna Dee Cervantes. TouFir

What a sublime end of one's body, what an enskyment; what a life after death. (LL) Vulture. Robinson Jeffers. APT-1; NAMCP V.1; NoAM

What a sweet smell rises. Laying the Dust. Denise Levertov. BrAP; MoWP

What a thrill. Cut. Sylvia Plath. CAP-8; EmeKit; MoWP; NAMCP V.2

What a Trying Time. *Unknown.* SSUS

What a wall! Play No Ball. Gerard Benson. NOxBChV

What a wonderful bird the frog are! Frog, The. *Unknown.* NBLV; NOxBChV; NTCP

What a wonderful dumb story of America: country boy. Johnny B. Goode. James Seay. SwNoth

What a world / Where lotus flowers. Issa. ZenPo, *tr. by* Takashi Ikemoto and Lucien Stryk

What about all this writing? Young Love. William Carlos Williams. APT-1

What about his feelings—. Beginning by Value. Christopher Gilbert. GT

What about that girl in first grade? The one who hopped up on her desk. Mark Rudman. TaR *Fr.* Rider.

What about the grass? (LL) Some Questions You Might Ask. Mary Oliver. BeAl; ColAP; OxBoAm; StAl

What about the people who came to my father's office. Questions, The. Robert Pinsky. ColAP; NAMCP V.2; NoAM

What aeons passed without a count or name. Highway, The. Edwin John Pratt. BrAP

What age is this? What times are now? Time's Whirligig, Or, The Blue-New-Made-Gentleman Mounted. Humphrey Willis. NOSC

What ails my heart, that in my breast. When We Cannot Sleep. George Wither. SacPr

What ails my senses thus to cheat? London in July. Amy Levy. PoBW

What am I after all but a child, pleas'd with the sound of my own name? repeating it over and over. What Am I After All. Walt Whitman. OPOU

What am I? Ah, you know it. Constance Naden. VWP *Fr.* Evolutional Erotics.

What am I? and from whence?—I nothing know. Edward Young. SacPr *Fr.* Night Thoughts.

What am I but the creature Thou hast made? Oliver Wendell Holmes. *Fr.* Wind-Clouds and Star-Drifts.

What Am I Chasing! Hala Mohammad. PoArWo, *tr. by* Cornelia Al-Khaled

What am I doing, here, in New England? Deliverance. Salomon De la Selva. NAAPv.2

What am I doing reading. Music Appreciation. Floyd Skloot. MiVo

What am I forgetting? George Stanley. NLPA *Fr.* Mountains and Air.

What am I missing? Black River, The. C. S. Giscombe. RD

What am I? Nosing here, turning leaves over. Wodwo. Ted Hughes. BrAP; HarvBoo; NAMCP V.2; NoAM; WoPoe

What am I suppose to do. You Send Me: Bertha Franklin, December 11, 1964. E. Ethelbert Miller. SpirFl

What am I supposed to do. Noon Talk at Georgia's Coffee Shop. Allison Joseph. BtF

What America did you have when Charon quit poling his ferry and you got out on a smoking bank and stood watching the boat disappear on the black waters of Lethe? (LL) Supermarket in California, A. Allen Ginsberg. BrAP; CAGL; FaBoA; GPTC; HeIP-4; MotU; NAAL-5; NAMCP V.2; NIL-7; NoAM; NoP-5; OxBoAm; PmAP; PtR; ReTh; TFi; WeW-3

What amuses you in the sound. Pongnim, Prince. CATKP, *tr. by* Peter H. Lee

What an abyss. Expatriation. Mahdi Muhammad Ali. IrPoTo, *tr. by* Salaam Yousif

What? an English sparrow sing? Did You Ever Hear an English Sparrow Sing? Bertha Johnston. ITBLP

"What an old lady," says my friend. Dogs of New York, The. Lee Meitzen Grue. UrbNat

What Any Lover Learns. Archibald MacLeish. OxBoAm

What aperture brings me air salted with cries of an ancient corrida. (LL) Minotaur at Supper, The: Spare the Noritake and the Spode. D. A. Powell. IAoNAP; WiU

What are days for? Days. Philip Larkin. NPeEn; OxAEP-2; OxBEV; PoetW; WaAnP; WoPoe

What Are Folks Made Of [(*diff. vers.*)]. Mother Goose. UV

What Are Heavy? Christina Georgina Rossetti. Spl

What are little boys made of, made of? What Are Folks Made Of. Mother Goose. UV

What! are my deeds forgot? William Shakespeare. OxAEP-1 *Fr.* Troilus and Cressida.

What are stars, but hieroglyphics of God's glory writ in lightning. Apollo. Thomas Holley Chivers. APN-1

What are the bugles blowin' for? said Files-on-Parade. Danny Deever. Rudyard Kipling. BRP; FaBoWar; InoFa; MoBrPo; NAEL-6v2; NAEL-7v2; NAMCP V.1; NoAM; NPeEn; OxBEV; TFi

What are the islands to me. Islands, The. "H. D." MoAmPo; TCAPo

What are the people like there? How do they live? Them/There. John Ash. HarvBoo

What are the sights of our town! Folklore. Les A. Murray. PML

What are the suburbs made of? Nursery Rhyme. Gavin Ewart. UV

What are the things that grow here? Homeland. Ogaga Ifowodo. NeNiPo

What are these "perks" for American business executives I keep reading about in my newspaper? East-West Dialog 2002. Mark Pawlak. PrTe

What are these songs. Anew 10. Louis Zukofsky. NAAPv.2

What are these that glow from afar. Christina Georgina Rossetti. SacPr

What are these thou lovest? Vanity. On Her Vanity. Wilfrid Scawen Blunt. GSo

What are these women up to? They've gone and strung. Deodand, The. Anthony Hecht. NAMCP V.2; NoAM

What are they, the white roses. Mark Doty. AmAlph Fr. Fog Argument.

What are they waiting for? 1977. Jeffrey McDaniel. LaCa

What are to me those honours or renown. Last Words on Greece. Lord Byron. CAGL

What are we coming to. We're Not Well Here. Abiodun Oyewole. BRtP

What are we first? First, animals; and next. George Meredith. CABP; NoP-4; NoP-5 Fr. Modern Love.

What are we men indeed? Grim torment's habitation. Human Misery. Andreas Gryphius. GePo, tr. by George C. Schoolfield

What are We Playing at? Andrée Chedid. HAWP, tr. by Mirène Ghossein and Samuel Hazo

What are we *really?* Pain's return address. Misery. Andreas Gryphius. WoPoe, tr. by Christopher Benfey

What are we waiting for, assembled in the forum? Waiting for the Barbarians. Constantine P. Cavafy. AF; BLT; PoAgWa; PtR, tr. by Edmund Keeley and Philip Sherrard

(What are we waiting for, gathered in the market-place?) FaBoWar

What are we waiting for, gathered in the market-place? Waiting for the Barbarians. Constantine P. Cavafy. FaBoWar, tr. by Edmund Keeley

What are we waiting for, gathered in the market-place? Constantine P. Cavafy. *See* What are we waiting for, assembled in the forum?

What are we waiting for: packed in the forum? Waiting for the Barbarians. Constantine P. Cavafy. GPTC; WoPoe, tr. by Edmund Keeley and Philip Sherrard

What Are Years? Marianne Moore. HarvBoo; ItP; MoAmPo; NAMCP V.1; NoAM; NoP-4; NoP-5; OxBoAm; SoSe-8

What are you able to build with your blocks? Block City. Robert Louis Stevenson. AmFaPo; NTCP

What are you doing?. Something Goes By. May Swenson. BodElec

What are you doing in our street among the automobiles, horse? Charles Reznikoff. WoPoe

What are you doing out here. Somers Point. A. R. Ammons. PfSP

"What are you looking at?" the farmer said. Evening Primrose, The. Christopher Pearse Cranch. APN-1

What are you sad about? Phyllis Webb. NLPA Fr. Naked Poems.

What are you saying to me? Love-Charm Song. *Chippewa Oral Tradition.* NAAL-5; NAAPv.2

What are you thinking? For One Must Want / To Shut the Other's Gaze. Jorie Graham. BodElec

What are you thinking, that you speak no word? Thomas Hardy. FaBoWar Fr. Dynasts, The.

What are you? what new device, you who hurry in such a random. Richard Crashaw. PBRV Fr. Bulla.

What are you—banded one? (LL) Pool, The. "H. D." APT-1; HarvBoo; NAMCP V.1

What art thou, love? Whence are those charms. Jacob Allestry. NOSC

What art thou, Mignon, child of mystery? Mignon. Henrietta Cordelia Ray. CBWP-3

What Art thou, oh! thou new-found pain? On Desire. A Pindarick. Aphra Behn. EMWP

What art thou, Spleen, which ev'ry thing dost ape? Spleen, The: A Pindaric Poem. Anne Finch, Countess of Winchilsea. NALW; NoP-4; NoP-5; NOSC; WaAnP

What ash rises high. Testimonies. Rosita Kalina. TANSG, tr. by Celeste Kostopulos-Cooperman

What ash rises up haughtily. Testimonies. Rosita Kalina. MirDau, tr. by Roberta Gordenstein

What aspect bore the Man who roved or fled. William Wordsworth. CenSon Fr. River Duddon [A Series of Sonnets], The.

What astonishing contact, old man, your hands establish with our own! Hands. Victor Serge. AF, tr. by James Brook

What awful pageants crowd the evening sky! Written September 1791, During a Remarkable Thunder Storm, in which the Moon Was Perfectly Clear, While the Tempest Gathered in Various Directions Near the Earth. Charlotte Smith. CenSon

What beasts and angels practice I ignore. Little Ode. Paul Goodman. PoA 2002

What beauteous form beneath a marble veil. On an Unfinished Statue. George Santayana. APN-2

What became of the dear. What Became. Wesley McNair. PoA 2002

What beckoning [*or* beck'ning] ghost, along the moonlight shade. Elegy to the Memory of an Unfortunate Lady. Alexander Pope. OBEV

What Becomes Us. Sharon Mesmer. HeMarv

What began as an urge to satisfy. Lovers' Duet. Wendy Lee. PasH

What Begins Bitterly Becomes Another Love Poem. G. C. Waldrep. LegDan

What behooves us? (LL) Adrienne Rich. GeoHom; WaAnP Fr. Atlas of the Difficult World, An.

What bird so sings, yet so does wail? John Lyly. NoSic Fr. Alexander and Campaspe.

What bird unknown. Shore Bird. Brewster Ghiselin. APT-2

What Birds Were There. William Everson. NoAM

What bliss it would be to die. Josée Lapeyrère. SCFWP Fr. Apples.

What bliss to be alive this morn. Puncture Near Wittedrif. Gus Ferguson. ArBi

What bloody man is that? He can report. William Shakespeare. FaBoWar Fr. Macbeth.

What blust'ring noise now interrupts my sleep. William Drummond of Hawthornden. NOSC Fr. Forth Feasting.

What bone shall speak for me? (LL) Meditation on a Bone. Alec Derwent Hope. BrAP; NoAM; WoPoe

What *Booker* doth prognosticate. Martin Parker. PBRV

What boots it that thy steps to distant shores. Elizabeth Cobbold. CenSon Fr. Sonnets of Laura.

What booty gave the German War? Booty from the German War. Friedrich von Logau. GePo, tr. by George C. Schoolfield

What Bottom Said When He Came Home. Eva Hooker. IaFF

What bowery dell with fragrant breath. Ann Radcliffe. RWP Fr. Mysteries of Udolpho, The.

What bread does one eat? (LL) American Sublime, The. Wallace Stevens. FaBoA; OxBoAm

What bright soft thing is this? Tear[e], The. Richard Crashaw. NoP-5

What Brings Us Out. Naomi Shihab Nye. CAP-8

What bring[s] you, sailor, home from the sea. Luck. Wilfrid Wilson Gibson. OBMV

What buck last cattle lap form pits. Leaving Rattle Bar. Clark Coolidge. FTOS

What built a world may sure repair a state. (LL) To Mr. Henry Lawes. Katherine Philips. NoP-4; NoP-5

What bursts in the very moment of bursting is image. On the Nature of the Iconic. Gustaf Sobin. WoBe

What business, this? What reason should we give. *Unknown.* RomPo Fr. Priapean Corpus, The.

What can a yellow glove mean in a world of motorcars and. Yellow Glove. Naomi Shihab Nye. LoL; PoArWo

What can be said of the unspeakable that has not already been unsaid. 20 Questions. Alan Bernheimer. BAP-04

What can he do poor man? Myth of Myself. Sri Sri. HotL, tr. by V. Narayana Rao and A. K. Ramanujan

What can I do in Poetry. Departure of the Good Daemon, The. Robert Herrick. BASC; NPeEn

What can I do, now there's nothing to say? Night on the Boulevard. Lőrinc Szabó. IQMS, tr. by Laurence James

What can I do when I hate my city, Kalamazoo? Acceptance Speech. Elizabeth Kerlikowske. SUP

What can I give thee back, O liberal. Elizabeth Barrett Browning. CenSon; OxAEP-2 Fr. Sonnets from the Portuguese.

What can I give you, my lord, my lover. Gift, The. Sara Teasdale. LW

What can I learn from the hummingbird. After the Storm, August. Gail Mazur. ExTi

What can I say? I've even forgotten how. Stitches. Debra Kang Dean. NAPBL

What can I say to you, darling. Poem Without a Single Bird in It, A. Jack Spicer. BodElec

What can I tell you? Though your quarry. Rune. Paul Muldoon. NewEx

What Can Stop This. Donald Revell. PoDa

What can the mutineers hear from the hold? Last Look at the Mutineers, A. Matthew Rohrer. AmPoNex

What can they do. Low Road, The. Marge Piercy. BeAl; TWF

What can we, a small natoin adrift, beg of mighty Britannia? One For Miss Pardo's Travel Diary. Mihály Vörösmarty. IQMS, tr. by Adam Makkai

What can we do, how can we help! Sadakichi. NAAPv.1 Fr. My Rubaiyat.

What can we say to our children? (LL) Sad Children's Song, The. Grace Paley. SoSe-8; TaR

What can you do after Easter? Catholic. Fanny Howe. BAP-04

What can you see in yonder bay. Thomas Jeffrey Llewelyn Prichard. AngWePo Fr. Land Beneath the Sea, The.

What Cannot Be. John Addington Symonds. CAGL

What Cannot Be Kept. Reginald Shepherd. GT

What care I, so they stand the same. Merops. Ralph Waldo Emerson. APN-1

What Care I Though the World Reprove. *Unknown.* NOSC

What care I who makes the laws of a nation? Let Me Sing and I'm Happy. Irving Berlin. ReLy

What care our Drunken Dames to whom they spread? Juvenal. OxBEV *Fr.* Satires.

What care the Dead, for Chanticleer. Emily Dickinson. APN-2

What cause have we, asham'd to stand. Fruit of Sin, or a Lamentation for England, The. Julea Palmer. EMWP

What chance / Sweet dreamlike chance. I Won't Sell His Love. Fadwa Tuqan. AF, *tr. by* Mounah Aikhouri and Hamid Algar

What child could resist the sweet sting. Aim. Bruce Bond. LiTh

What children can solve the equation of loveliness. My Children. Lance Jeffers. OxAAAP

What Chord Did She Pluck. Steve Kowit. BLT

What chord did she pluck in my soul. What Chord Did She Pluck. Steve Kowit. BLT

What chorus? Eduardo Milán. RMCMP, *tr. by* Roberto Tejada

What Christ Said. George Macdonald. SacPr

What clicks and rattles coloured strings of plastic curtains all the afternoon. Denise Riley. Oth *Fr.* Seven Strangely Exciting Lies.

What Colour's a Man. Zelma Jex. OWABP

What Comes after Because. Kelli Russell Agodon. RWB

What cometh here from west to east a-wending? Death Song, A. William Morris. NAEL-6v2

What comforts him is a clear understanding. Prince of Aquitania, in His Torn-down Tower, The. Jaime Gil de Biedma. RaW, *tr. by* Lewis Hyde

What common language to unravel? Paterson: The Falls. William Carlos Williams. APT-1; ColAP

What conscience dictates to be done. Hymn. Alexander Pope. SacPr

What conscience, say, is it in thee. To Oenone. Robert Herrick. OBEV

What Could Happen. Dorianne Laux. BodElec; GeoHom; RoV

What Could Hold Us. Heather McHugh. NIP-4

What could I do. Unrepentant. Brandel France de Bravo. OPRER

What could my father do? My Father Went to Funerals. Howard Nelson. RaBo

What could my mother be. What He Said. Cempulappeyanirar. WoPoe, *tr. by* A. K. Ramanujan

What could my sweet Andean Rita of rush and blackberries. Dead Idyll. César Vallejo. BLPSL, *tr. by* Rene de Costa, Rigas Kappatos and Eleni Paidoussi

What could we say to you. Or Else. Heather McHugh. InoFa

What country is it that I see. Affairs of Memory. Teresa Calderón. TANSG, *tr. by* Celeste Kostopulos-Cooperman

What country woman bewitches your mind. Sappho. SaLy, *tr. by* Diane Rayor

What counts in any action. Dario Villa. ItPo, *tr. by* Gayle Ridinger

What creature's this with his short hairs. Character of a Roundhead, The. *Unknown.* NOSC; WaAnP

What creeps in. At general Electric, where they eat their/young. Robert Farr. SpirFl

What crops the region will bear. Virgil. IPoFL *Fr.* Georgics.

What crowding thoughts around me wake. To Mrs. K———, On Her Sending Me an English Christmas Plum-Cake at Paris. Helen Maria Williams. WoRP

What crowds by envied power, the wish of all. Juvenal. OBVE *Fr.* Satires.

What Cunning Can Express. Edward, 17th Earl of Oxford De Vere. NoSic

What Danger We Court. Luci Tapahonso. ReEnLa

What dark and terrible shadow is swaying in the wind?. Easter at Christmas. Alun Lewis. PoWW

What day did you come down from that former place. Rejoicing that the Zen Master Pao Has Arrived from Dragon Mountain. Liu Ch'ang-ch'ing. ColAnChi, *tr. by* Burton Watson

What day is it today? The way I live. Extract from a Diary. János Pilinszky. PoSu, *tr. by* Peter Jay

What day was it she slid. Birth of Venus. Constance Urdang. PoA 2002

What death? John Webster. OxBEV *Fr.* Duchess of Malfi, The.

What desire lurks. Nanni Cagnone. ItPo *Fr.* Vaticinio.

What did he do except lie. Banneker. Rita Dove. ESEAA; NAAL-5; NoAM; OxAAAP

What did I see in you? King, hero, saint. Lőrinc Szabó. IQMS *Fr.* Cricket Music.

WHAT DID LEONEL RUGAMA SAY? Report on the Protest in Front of the United States Embassy by the Pino Grande Movement, A. Daisy Zamora. CLPP, *tr. by* Barbara Paschke

What did she know. After Burying Her Son, A Mother Speaks. Mark Pawlak. GifTon

What did that girl on the playground mean. Traitor. Allison Joseph. IllVoic; SUP

What did the day bring? Letter from a Coward to a Hero. Robert Penn Warren. MoAmPo

What Did the Nazi Send His Wife? Bertolt Brecht. FaBoWar, *tr. by Unknown*

What did the Old Doctor do. 5.8.1942 / In Memory of Janusz Korczak. Jerzy Ficowski. HP, *tr. by* Keith Bosley

What did they know of reverence. Sankey Hymns. Alan Riach. EdScPo

What did they think they did when they killed Charlemagne Peralte and Benoit Batraville. What Did They Think They Did? Frank Fouché. OGAHCP, *tr. by* Boadiba and Jack Hirschman

What did we in all honesty expect? Notes Toward a Poem of Revolution. Diane Di Prima. Eno

What did we wish from you? Fennel. David Lindley. NLP

What Did You Come to See. Bruce Beasley. AmAlph

What did you do in those days. Conversation with a Survivor. Erich Fried. BeAl, *tr. by* Stuart Hood

What Did You Do Yesterday? Yi Hyangji. EcSo, *tr. by* Catherine J. Kim

What did you expect. Dear Nobody's Business. James Galvin. WaAnP

What did you hear? Advent; a Carol. Patric Dickinson. OBCP

What did you mean when you called me benighted. You are Mad: and I Mean It! Phumzile Zulu. HAWP

What difference does it make whether you've seen them yourself, stiff and cold at the bottom of the railway embankment. What Difference Does it Make. Erica Pedretti. MotU, *tr. by* Franz Wright

What different dooms our birthdays bring! Thomas Hood. OBCoV *Fr.* Miss Kilmansegg and Her Precious Leg.

What dire offense from amorous [or am'rous] causes springs. Rape of the Lock, The: An Heroi-Comical Poem in Five Cantos. Alexander Pope. CABP; NAEL-6v1; NAEL-7v1; NAWM-7v2; NoP-4; NoP-5; OBNV; WaAnP

What direction will you take when the universe collapses. you who when you go must go someplace. D. A. Powell. NAPBL

What discord of violin, strangled by the soul. Horizon Burns, The. Ernesto Lumbreras. RMCMP, *tr. by* Rebecca Seiferle

What do all those Buddhas *mean.* Replacement Buddhas. Joanne Kyger. WANABP

What do caterpillars do? Caterpillars. Aileen Fisher. TLR

What Do I Have, That You Seek Out My Friendship? Félix Lope de Vega Carpio. SpanPo, *tr. by* Kate Flores

What do I have, that you seek out my friendship? What Do I Have, That You Seek Out My Friendship? Félix Lope de Vega Carpio. SpanPo, *tr. by* Kate Flores

What do I have, when I contemplate this. Eleanor Brown. NeBl

What Do I Know. Giovanna. SurWo, *tr. by* Myrna Bell Rochester

What do I know. What Do I Know. Giovanna. SurWo, *tr. by* Myrna Bell Rochester

What Do I Know of Journey. David Meltzer. UnSA

What do I know of journey. What Do I Know of Journey. David Meltzer. UnSA

What do I owe the years, that I should bring. Years, The. Ina Coolbrith. CalPo

What Do I See. Gertrude Stein. ItWoWo; PFTM-1

What Do I Want? Madduri Nageshbabu. HotL, *tr. by* V. Narayana Rao

What do I wish? No more than what I have. Out of Horace. James Wright. NOSC

What do the long years bring us. Retrospection. Henrietta Cordelia Ray. CBWP-3

What do they matter now, the deprivations. Page to Commemorate Colonel Suárez, Victor at Junín, A. Jorge Luis Borges. PoetW, *tr. by* Alastair Reid

What do they sing, the last birds. Last Songs. Galway Kinnell. VCAP

What do they think has happened, the old fools. Old Fools, The. Philip Larkin. EmeKit; HarvBoo

What do we ask of ourselves? (LL) Astronauts. Robert Earl Hayden. ESEAA; OtW

What do we do with the body, do we. As from a Quiver of Arrows. Carl Phillips. AmAlph; BtF; WaAnP; WiU

What Do We Geese Wear For Clothes? *Unknown.* OWoS, *tr. by* W. D. Snodgrass

What do we know about the efficacy of medicine? Medicine. Wang Shih-chieng. ColAnChi, *tr. by* Richard John Lynn

What Do We Love When We Love? Gonzalo Rojas. BLPSL, *tr. by* Rene de Costa, Rigas Kappatos and Eleni Paidoussi

What do we love when we love, my God: the terrible light of life. What Do We Love When We Love? Gonzalo Rojas. BLPSL, *tr. by* Rene de Costa, Rigas Kappatos and Eleni Paidoussi

What do we praise?—Sunsets, and open fires. Test Paper. Rolfe Humphries. APT-2

What do we want to give each other as we park under the sign. Chinese Dragons. David Bottoms. GifTon

What Do Women Want? Kim Addonizio. BeAl

What Do Women Want? Mary Jo Salter. FFC; RA

What do you aim at? Or have you grown deaf and dumb? Mississippi. Milán Füst. IQMS, *tr. by* István Tótfalusi

What do you call it, bobsled champion, and you, too, Olympic roller-coaster ace. Twentieth-Century Blues. Kenneth Fearing. IllVoic

What do you consider your mission in life? Questionnaire. Gunnar Ekelof. WED, *tr. by* Robert Bly

What do you expect if you are always. Wet Feet. Jackie Hardy. NeBl

What do you make of that odd one by the door. Floor Scrapers. Daniel Tobin. NAPBL

What do you paint, when you paint on a wall? I Paint What I See. Elwyn Brooks White. AmWit; NBLV

What do you say about that cypress body that hunts the heart? Revânî. OLP, *tr. by* Walter Andrews

What do you say to the mother. Ring of Irony, The. Diane Wakoski. NIL-7

What do you scrawl. Love. Georgi Belev. CSCBP, *tr. by* the author and Lisa Sapinkopf

What do you see beside the road. Trash. Kenneth Irby. PFTM-2

What do you think of my life. In Praise of Spring. Chŏng Kŭgin. CATKP, *tr. by* Peter H. Lee

What do you think of the USA—NRA—TVA? Conga. Betty Comden and Adolph Green. ReLy

"What do *you* think?" The question my head. J. D. McClatchy. WiU *Fr.* First Steps.

What Do You Want? Brenda Leifso. IFF

What Do You Want: A Meaningful Dialogue, or a Satisfactory Talk? Ogden Nash. OBCoV

What do you want from me? Town Clerk, The. Mark DeCarteret. AmPoNex

What do you want from me? Eye to Eye. Alexander Gerov. CSCBP, *tr. by* Georgi Belev and Lisa Sapinkopf

What do you want to be when you grow up? Vermin. William Matthews. BAP-97; OxBoAm

What does a girl do? Girl, that's up to you. (LL) Mythology. Marilyn Hacker. NoAM; ReTh

What does a man do. Tyehimba Jess. BtF

What does he do with them all, the old king. Elegy for Drowned Children. Bruce Dawe. BMAP; NOBAu

What does he think? Question for the Frankfurt School, A. Heberto Padilla. TCLAP, *tr. by* Andrew Hurley and Alastair Reid

What does it feel like to be this shroud. White Dress, The. Lynn Emanuel. SUP

What does it matter? (LL) To Lallie. Amy Levy. PoBW; ViWPN

What does it matter. Doe, The. Patrick Phillips. NevBe

What does it take to make a day? Day, A. William Leroy Stidger. SoSe-8

What does love look like? Shape of Death, The. May Swenson. APT-2

What does not change / is the will to change. Kingfishers, The. Charles Olson. APSN; HarvBoo; OxBoAm; VCAP

What does not exist cannot be. Way of the Water, The. Johanna Kruit. TuT, *tr. by* Peter van de Kamp

What does one do. What Does One Do. Roland Jooris. TuT, *tr. by* Peter van de Kamp

What Does One Write When the World Starts to Disappear? Sujata Bhatt. FiBr

'What does she dream of'. Charlotte Brontë. PEW

What does she dream of, lingering all alone. 'What does she dream of'. Charlotte Brontë. PEW

What Does the Body Dream at Rest? Russell Leong. WhBo

What does the cloudy future hold. Prophecy, The. József Bajza. IQMS, *tr. by* Judith Kroll

What does the horse give you. Horse. Louise Glück. NALW

What Does the Political Scientist Know? Artur Miedzyrzecki. PoSu

What does the river know of its own bed. Olga Martynova. CRWP, *tr. by* Elaine Feinstein

What does the spring wind have in mind. Song of the Spring Wind. Ch'i-chi. CSKM, *tr. by* Burton Watson

What does the "u" mean in "gradual"? "u", "je", "r", "r", "im", "a", "finally." Douglas Oliver. Oth

What does the world with its lung of ocean breathe. Paul Verlaine at the Grave of Lucien Létinois. Bin Ramke. OPRER

What doest thou here, Elijah? Ghost of Abel, The. William Blake. ChIV-1

What drove young Joseph to interpret dreams. Yehuda Amichai. FIT, *tr. by* Robert Friend

What eagle can beho[u]ld her sunbright[e] eye. Sir John Davies. NoSic *Fr.* Gulling[e] Sonnets, The.

What earth is like—as round. Worsted Heather. Jody Gladding. YaYoPo

What effect has your new son had on your writing life? Richard Jones. PoChi

What else can he do but behave like a hero. *Unknown.* SLW, *tr. by* Marjolijn De Jager, Sayd Bahodin Majrouh and André Velter

What else can we do. What are We Playing at? Andrée Chedid. HAWP, *tr. by* Mirène Ghossein and Samuel Hazo

What else can you do but fight? *Unknown.* SLW, *tr. by* Marjolijn De Jager, Sayd Bahodin Majrouh and André Velter

What else have I to spur me into song? (LL) Spur, The. William Butler Yeats. NAMCP V.1; OxAEP-2; WeW-3

What else in this dark world turns true? Astronomer Works Nights: A Parable of Science, The. Bin Ramke. YaYoPo

What Else *(Part 2)*. Walter Abish. OnScMo

What empties a name of its substance. Emmanuel Hocquard. OnScMo; YaTCFP *Fr.* At Christmas.

What end did she meet, O my God, what end? Deep Are the Wells. Dezső Kosztolányi. IQMS, *tr. by* Egon F. Kunz

What endures? Not the arranged. Still Life. Sharan Strange. GT

What eucharist of air and bland. Wonder Bread. Alice Fulton. ExTi

What ever happened to fair dealing. Class. Fred Ebb. ReLy

What Every Woman Should Carry. Maura Dooley. NeBl; StAl

What exists of you I have spread thin and think of when. Distance. Adisa Vera Beatty. FuFl

What fair pomp have I spied of glittering ladies. What Fair[e] Pomp[e]. Thomas Campion. NoSic

What Fair[e] Pomp[e]. Thomas Campion. NoSic

What fall amounts to is really a cold infusion. End of Fall, The. Francis Ponge. WED, *tr. by* Robert Bly

What fills the whisper and. Hadrian's Lane. Ray DiPalma. FTOS

What fish feel. Basho. EH, *tr. by* Robert Hass

What foes are there without not suddenly. Head of Medusa on a Rotella of Michelangelo da Caravaggio, in the Gallery of the Grand Duke of Tuscany, The. GS, *tr. by Unknown*

What folly is this, to keep with danger. Sunday Bear-Baiting. Robert Crowley. DiBP

What folly to complain. Soliloquy. Ann Yearsley. NOBRP

What fools they are to believe the angels. Imagining Their Own Hymns. Brigit Pegeen Kelly. IllVoic

What for? Catullus. WoPoe, *tr. by* Charles Martin

What for Do I Live Then. Boris Vian. YaTCFP, *tr. by* Rosemary Lloyd

What Freedom Said. Georgi Borisov. CSCBP, *tr. by* Georgi Belev and Lisa Sapinkopf

What Frenzy Has of Late Possess'd the Brain. Sir Samuel Garth. NBLV

What Friendship is, Ardelia show. Friendship Between Ephelia and Ardelia. Anne Finch, Countess of Winchilsea. NALW; NoP-4; NoP-5; PoBW

What from this barren being do we reap? Lord Byron. NOBRP *Fr.* Childe Harold's Pilgrimage.

What full, sad sounds, the noise that you were making. Resurrection of a Mouse. David J. Rothman. GeoH

What fun to be able to purr. Catlike. Kate Y. A. Bone. EdScPo

What gathers in this sky. Elm. Robert Hass. BodElec

What generations could have dreamed. Pedestrian. George Oppen. NAMCP V.1

What gifts shall we bring in worship. Nativity. Craig Powell. NOBAu

What God Is. Robert Herrick. NOSC

What god is proud. Geriatric. Ronald Stuart Thomas. TCAWP

What Goes Around Comes Around, or The Proof is in the Pudding. Cheryl Clarke. FFC

What goes on inside those ambulance boxes. Let Me In. Judith Baumel. TaR

What good are children anyhow? Children. Carolyn Kizer. PoChi

What good are words I say to you? Time After Time. Sammy Cahn. ReLy

What good does it do anyone. Idea of Housework, The. Dorianne Laux. SweBea

What good is sitting alone in your room? Cabaret. Fred Ebb. ReLy

What good luck! Issa. EH, *tr. by* Robert Hass

What grass not yellowed? *Unknown.* ChinPo, *tr. by* Ye Weilian [*or* Yeh Wei-lien *or* Wai-lim Yip]

What great genius invented the waiting room? Waiting Rooms. Howard Nemerov. PoA 2002

What Greece, when learning flourished, only knew. John Dryden. NOSC *Fr.* Silent Woman to the University of Oxford, The.

What guile [*or* guyle] is this, that those her golden tresses. Edmund Spenser. BrAP; NAEL-6v1; NoP-4 *Fr.* Amoretti.

What Gyges so golden has doesn't matter to me. Archilochus. SaLy, *tr. by* Diane Rayor

What had been lost was heavenly. Presence, The. Pier Paolo Pasolini. ItPo, *tr. by* Gayle Ridinger

What had you been thinking about. Tennis Court Oath, The. John Ashbery. NAMCP V.2; NoAM

What Happened? John Wieners. FTOS

What happened earlier I'm not sure of. Say You Love Me. Molly Peacock. CFP; RaF

What happened, happened once. So now it's best.   Stolen Moments.   Kim Addonizio.   CalPo

What Happened Here Before.   Gary Snyder.   APSN

What happened? / The ninth night is over.   Kamalākānta Bhaṭṭācārya.   SinGod, *tr. by* Rachel Fell McDermott

What happened there, it was not much.   Robert Penn Warren.   LPSFW *Fr.* Some Quiet, Plain Poems.

What happened to Barabbas.   Speculations on the Subject of Barabbas. Zbigniew Herbert.   GI, *tr. by* John Carpenter *and* Bogdana Carpenter

What Happened to Miss Frugle.   Brian Patten.   OBSP

What happened to your green hair.   For the Stepford Girl Groups.   MiVo

What happened was my last breath fell back.   Whitman's Confession: In the Cleft of Eternity.   Beckian Fritz Goldberg.   ViWalt

What Happens.   Erich Fried.   BeAl, *tr. by* Stuart Hood

What Happens.   Tadeusz Różewicz.   AF, *tr. by* Robert A. Maguire

What happens is, the kind of snow that sweeps.   For a Lost Child.   William Stafford.   InoFa

What happens next is a complete surprise. (LL)   Dearborn North Apartments Chicago, Illinois.   Lola Haskins.   P180; PoDa

What happens to a dream deferred?   Langston Hughes.   APSN; APT-2; BrAP; GT; HeIP-4; NAMCP V.1; NIL-7; NIP-4; NoP-4; NoP-5; OxBoAm; RaBo; SAmP; SSLK; WaAnP *Fr.* Lenox Avenue Mural.

What happens to laughter.   Sándor Petőfi.   IQMS *Fr.* Clouds, The.

What happens / to the leaves after.   Roses, Late Summer.   Mary Oliver.   NIL-7

What happens when an old black man.   Thrift.   Cornelius Eady.   LTA

What happier fortune can one find.   Exile.   Frank O'Connor.   IrLP

What happy, secret fountain.   Dwelling-Place, The.   Henry Vaughan.   NOSC

What has been brought to a finish.   Disturbing the Sallies Forth.   Clark Coolidge.   FTOS

What has been particularly lacking in my life up to now is.   Simplicity.   Henri Michaux.   PML, *tr. by* Richard Ellmann

What has gotten into the bus driver.   Bus Driver, The.   Hédi Kaddour.   PML; YaTCFP, *tr. by* Marilyn Hacker

What has happened here in Zuveliskes?   Silly Spring.   Marcelijus Martinaitis.   TWW, *tr. by* Laima Sruoginis

What has happened over here?   Looking Through a French Photographer's Portrayal of Rajasthan with Extensive Use of Orange Filters.   Sujata Bhatt.   MoWP

What Has Happened to Lulu?   Charles Causley.   OBSP

What has happened to Lulu, mother?   What Has Happened to Lulu?   Charles Causley.   OBSP

What has happened to the stars? What thief, thin-soled.   Between the Moon and the Sun.   Dave Jeddie Smith.   BodElec

What has just happened between the lovers.   Waking, The.   Galway Kinnell.   BodElec

What has made you close your eyes.   Promise.   Francisco Segovia.   RMCMP, *tr. by* Michael Wiegers

What has that face got to do with that.   In Imitation.   Larry Eigner.   FTOS

What has this bugbear death to frighten man.   Lucretius.   NPeEn; OBVE *Fr.* De Rerum Natura (On the Nature of Things).

What has to happen for a tree to sing?   For the Tree to Sing...   Vladimir Alekseievich Soloukhin.   TCRusP, *tr. by* Daniel Weissbort

What Has Yet to Be Sung.   Malkia Amala Cyril.   AfrBLW

What hasn't happened.   Song / for Sanna.   Olga Broumas.   PoBW

What haunts me is a farmhouse among trees.   Landscape with Figures.   Frank Ormsby.   PBCIP

What have I gained? A little charity?   What Have I Gained?   Augusta, Lady Gregory.   IrLP

What have I got that the others ain't.   Honey in the Honeycomb.   John Latouche.   ReLy

What have I learned but.   What Have I Learned.   Gary Snyder.   LoL; TWF

What, have I thus betrayed my liberty?   Sir Philip Sidney.   NAEL-6v1; NAEL-7v1; NoP-4; NoP-5 *Fr.* Astrophil and Stella.

What Have We All—a Soliloquy of Essences.   Marsden Hartley.   APT-1

What Have We Done.   Gary Daniel.   OGAHCP, *tr. by* Boadiba *and* Jack Hirschman

What have we given him? Just a grave! (LL)   Grave in Hollywood Cemetery, Richmond, A.   Margaret Junkin Preston.   CBCWP; PCW

What have we here, a little daisy alongside the footpath, hmm.   Flower's Escape.   Ron Padgett.   NYP2

What have you done with the garden that was entrusted to you? (LL)   Wind, One Brilliant Day, The.   Antonio Machado Ruiz.   RaBo; WED, *tr. by* Robert Bly

What have you kept looking for.   Fine Day.   Ivan Tsanev.   CSCBP, *tr. by* Georgi Belev *and* Lisa Sapinkopf

What he can. (LL)   Darwin.   Lorine Niedecker.   APSN; APT-2

What he had in his hand seemed to be the handle.   Chance Encounter with a Wounded Man Playing a Theremin.   Dara Wier.   MAAN

What he liked in her voice.   Narcissus.   Gerda Mayer.   LW

What He Said.   Cempulappeyanirar.   WoPoe, *tr. by* A. K. Ramanujan

What He[e] Suffered.   Ben Jonson.   NAEL-7v1 *Fr.* Celebration of Charis in Ten Lyric[k] Pieces [*or* Peeces], A.

What He Thought.   Heather McHugh.   OxBoAm; P180; PtR; WaAnP

What he wants he can't say. Seven o'clock and the hill back lit.   Hardened Arm, The.   Michael Chitwood.   MotU

What heart could have thought you?   To a Snowflake.   Francis Thompson.   MoBrPo; SacPr

What heartache—ne'er a hill!   From the Flats.   Sidney Lanier.   APN-2; NoP-4; NoP-5

What heaven-entreated [*or* heaven-besiegèd *or* heav'n-beseiged] heart is this?   To the Noblest and Best of Ladies, the Countess of Denbigh.   Richard Crashaw.   NAEL-6v1; NAEL-7v1

(What heav'n-intreated HEART is This?)   PBRV

What heav'n-intreated HEART is This?   Richard Crashaw. *See* What heaven-entreated [*or* heaven-besiegèd *or* heav'n-beseiged] heart is this?

What Her Absence Means.   Christy Brown.   IrLP

What Her Friend Said.   Kollan Alici.   WoPoe, *tr. by* A. K. Ramanujan

What Her Girl Friend Said to Him.   Kannan.   WoPoe, *tr. by* A. K. Ramanujan

What Her Girl-Friend Said.   Peruñcattan.   WoPoe, *tr. by* A. K. Ramanujan

What here redeems us? Surely.   Tantum Ergo.   Richard Foerster.   Vesp

What here you see in deceiving tints.   On Her Portrait.   Sor Juana Inés de la Cruz.   SpanPo, *tr. by* Kate Flores

What Hiawatha Probably Did.   *Unknown.*   NBLV

What high rewards by little pain is won. (LL)   To St Mary Magdalen.   Henry Constable.   ChIV-2; NoSic

What homage will be paid to a beauty built to last.   Adrienne Rich.   NAAL-5 *Fr.* Atlas of the Difficult World, An.

What hope, what hope, what hope.   Wipp Protest.   Carol Merrill.   ICANM

What horrid sin condemned the teeming Earth.   On Tobacco.   Charles Cotton.   OBSV

What horror to awake at night.   Lorine Niedecker.   APT-2; NAAPv.2; NAMCP V.1

What House Would You Build For Me.   Yves Bonnefoy.   WoPoe, *tr. by* Galway Kinnell *and* Richard Pevear

What house would you build for me.   What House Would You Build For Me.   Yves Bonnefoy.   WoPoe, *tr. by* Galway Kinnell *and* Richard Pevear

What, However, is the discretion of left to your?   Oskar Pastior.   OnScMo, *tr. by* Rosmarie Waldrop

What hurrying human tides, or day or night!   Broadway.   Walt Whitman.   NAAL-3

What I Am.   Terrance Hayes.   BtF

What i am given to "see" lies half-hidden.   Roy Kiyooka.   NLPA *Fr.* Pear Tree Pomes.

What I am trying to say is this: from now on we must enter the poem from its blindspot.   Entering Poetic Blindspots.   Brian Schorn.   OnScMo

What I Believe.   Michael C. Blumenthal.   PLBUT

What I did, I won't excuse, except.   Unreal Dwelling: My Years in Volcano, The.   Garrett Kaoru Hongo.   OpBo

What I Disliked About the Pleistocene Era.   Patty Seyburn.   LegDan

What I do mind is going four to not to. (LL)   Believe me, sir, I'd like to spend whole days.   Martial.   OBVE; RomPo, *tr. by* James Vincent Cunningham

What I do to the grass, does to my thoughts and me. (LL)   Mower's Song, The.   Andrew Marvell.   BASC; CtM; NAEL-6v1; NAEL-7v1; NOSC

What I don't understand is the beauty.   Rothko's Yellow.   Dean Young.   IllVoic

What I dreamed was.   Yosano Akiko.   CAoMJL1, *tr. by* Janine Beichman

What I drink is not hot, not sweet.   Natalya Gorbanevskaya.   CRWP, *tr. by* Daniel Weissbort

What I expect from the day.   Early November.   Ursula Krechel.   GTCP, *tr. by* Reinhold Grimm

What I forgot to mention was the desultory.   Postscript to an Elegy.   Gibbons Ruark.   PoA 2002

What I get I bring home to you.   Wild Strawberries.   Helen Dunmore.   BeAl

What I give that man, some other woman takes.   Hopping Toad Blues.   Raymond R. Patterson.   SeSe

What i have been given to do will bear.   Roy Kiyooka.   NLPA *Fr.* Pear Tree Pomes.

What I have from 1956 in one instant at the Holiday.   Scene from the Movie *Giant.*   Tino Villanueva.   ReTh

What I have written / I have written. (LL)   What I Have Written I Have Written.   Peter Porter.   BMAP; NOBAu

What I Have Written I Have Written.   Peter Porter.   BMAP; NOBAu

What I Heard at the Discount Department Store.   David Budbill.   RaBo; TRP

What I Heard on the Radio Today.   Marc J. Straus.   BloBone

What I hope (when I hope) is that we'll.   To the Dead.   Frank Bidart.   MakPoe

What I in her am grieved to want. (LL)   Elegy, An: "Though beauty be the mark of praise."   Ben Jonson.   NoP-4; NoP-5; OBEV

What I know. Body and Soul. Luciana Notari. CItWP, *tr. by* Cinzia Sartini Blum and Lara Trubowitz

What I Know About Owls. Paul Zimmer. PfSP

What I Know Now. Linda France. MFPA *Fr.* On the Game.

What I know of you I take. Weight Belt. Jeffery Conway. WiU

What I Learned from My Mother. Julia Kasdorf. ACAMVP; AmPoNex; GoPo; PBCAP; SweBea

What I Learned From the Movies. Joan Jobe Smith. SUP

What I learned on this past trip. Clippings. Kimiko Hahn. ExTi

What I Leave to My Son. Du Tử' Lê. WoPoe, *tr. by* Nguyen Ngoc Bich

What I Like. Alice Fulton. WeW-3

What I like about the women in Hopper's paintings. For Edward Hopper, from the Floor. Lucia Maria Perillo. ExTi

What I love about dormice is their size. View of Things, A. Edwin Morgan. HarvBoo

What I love—the tall clock of thermals, blackbacks. Staple Island Swing. Jen Hadfield. BeAl

What I mean by too much metaphor and simile. (LL) Very Like a Whale. Ogden Nash. APT-2; GPTC

What I remember about that day. Eviction. Lucille Clifton. NTCP

What I remember are the tapestry edges. Stitching. Elin ap Hywel. ATSWP, *tr. by* Robert Minhinnick

What I remember didn't happen. Date With Robbe-Grillet, A. Elaine Equi. PmAP

What I remember is the ebb and flow of sound. Sound I Listened For, The. Robert Francis. APT-2

What I Remember the Writers Telling Me When I Was Young. William Meredith. PoDa

What I Said. Norman Stock. PA9/11

What I Saw. Robert Duncan. NAMCP V.2

What I Saw. Zbigniew Herbert. AF, *tr. by* John Carpenter and Bogdana Carpenter

What I saw was just one eye. Bird at Dawn, The. Harold Monro. MoBrPo

What I Saw When I Had Crossed the Lake. Hsieh Ling-yün. CCL1, *tr. by* John Frodsham

What I say is when I plan my future. Blue Book 18 Pages 1–4. Steve Benson. FTOS

What I shall leave thee, none can tell. To His Son [*or* Sonne], Vincent Corbet[t]. Richard Corbet. NOSC; OxAEP-1

What I Tell Him. Simon J. Ortiz. ChAP

What I throw out to the world. Spider. Kang Ŭn'gyo. EcSo, *tr. by* Ann Y. Choi

What I took in my hand. Song. Robert Creeley. PoA 2002

What I took to be a man in a white beard. Blue Skies, White Breasts, Green Trees. Gerald Stern. BodElec

What I want. Hour of Life, An. Jean-Paul Nyunai. SonAtl, *tr. by* Kurt Ganzl, Christophe Mirambeau, Aliko Songolo and Kenneth Wilburn

What I Want Is. C. G. Hanzlicek. GoPo

What I want is to see your face. Jelaluddin Rumi. ErotSp, *tr. by* Coleman Barks

What I Want to Make for You. Natasha Sajé. SweBea

What I want to remember is a street. Street. Gary Soto. GeoHom

What I Want You to See Is She When Not Here As in Now. Rachel Zucker. IAoNAP

What I was and what I am. (LL) Christ Triumphant. *Unknown.* NPeEn; SacPr; WeW-3

What I was doing with my white teeth exposed. Dog, The. Gerald Stern. BeAl; WeW-3

What I was reaching for. Under the Scorpion's Heart. Margot Schilpp. AmPoNex

What I wished you before, but harder. (LL) Writer, The. Richard Wilbur. CAP-8; NAMCP V.2; NoAM; PoPoPo; SoSe-8

What I Would Do. Marc Petersen. P180

What I would give you now. Love Poem, Later. Judith McCombs. FiBr

What I would not give for this century, were it only to change! Song from the Occupation Time. Ion Caraion. AF, *tr. by* Marguerite Dorian and Elliott B. Urdang

What I Wouldn't Do. Dorianne Laux. ExTi

What *I'd* call home. Quarreling with Robert Frost. Michael S. Glaser. VisFro

What If a Much of a Which of a Wind. E. E. Cummings. HarvBoo; MoAmPo; NAAL-5; PoA 2002

What if I didn't shoot the old lady. Beautiful Wreckage. William Daniel Ehrhart. AmWaPo

What if I do go armed? she said. Arms and the Woman. Dorothea MacKellar. NOBAu

What if I own more paper clips than I'll ever use in this. James Harrison. BodElec *Fr.* Letters to Yesenin.

What if I said I wanted. However. Jane Mead. NAPBL

What if my soul is left to me? Her Blindness in Grief. Sarah Morgan Bryan Piatt. NAAPv.1

What if small birds are peppering the sky. It Is Winter, I Know. Merrill Moore. MoAmPo

What if society became so obsessed with the stars. Star-Struck Utopias of 2000. "Antler." PoCoUp; RWB

What if the heart does not pale as the body wanes. Getting Ready. Jack Gilbert. BodElec

What if this present were the world's last night? John Donne. BASC; HeIP-4; NAEL-6v1; NAEL-7v1; NOSC; OxAEP-1 *Fr.* Holy Sonnets.

What if this road, that has held no surprises. What If This Road. Sheenagh Pugh. BeAl

What if, with my life half over. Id. Harry Clifton. PBCIP

What if you only had one scene to work with, say the nativity or the annunciation. Sacristy. Rachel Zucker. IAoNAP

What / if you were. How Everything Adores Being Alive. Mary Oliver. BeAl

What in all of heaven could have prompted her to go. Hymn to Him, A. Alan Jay Lerner. ReLy

What In Fire Did I, Firelover, Starter of Fires, Love? Lisa Jarnot. VaPo

What, in July's honey heat, do you weep for, poor goy. Mariya Galina. CRWP, *tr. by* Daniel Weissbort

What in our lives is burnt. August 1914. Isaac Rosenberg. HarvBoo; NPeEn; OBWP; OxBEV; PoAgWa

What influence they cast, and their effects. (LL) Discourse of Beasts, A. Margaret Lucas Cavendish, Duchess of Newcastle. BASC; PEW

What inspires me? On the Verge of the Path. Barbara Guest. OxBoAm

What is a Garden? Reginald Arkell. OBGa

What is a good prince? He is the sheepdog who puts the wolves to flight. De Principe Bono et Malo. Sir Thomas More. PBRV

What is a home? A guarded space. Home, A. Susan Coolidge. SWaP

What is a Jew in solitude? Yom Kippur 1984. Adrienne Rich. NoAM; PfS; TaR

What is a kiss? Language Event Two. Robert Desnos. PFTM-1

What Is a Man? Waldo Williams. BBMWP, *tr. by* Emyr Humphreys

What is a sonnet? 'T is [*or* 'Tis] the pearly shell. Sonnet, The. Richard Watson Gilder. APN-2

What is a woman that you forsake her. Rudyard Kipling. HarvBoo; NAMCP V.1; RACG *Fr.* Puck of Pook's Hill.

What is Africa to me. Heritage. Countee Cullen. APT-2; ColAP; HeIP-4; MoAmPo; NAAL-5; NAAPv.2; NAMCP V.1; NoAM; NoP-4; NoP-5; PoPoPo; SSLK

What is already dead. (LL) Women of Dan Dance with Swords in Their Hands to Mark the Time When They Were Warriors, The. Audre Lorde. MoWP; NALW; NoAM

What is ambition? 'tis unrest, defeat! Ambition. Henrietta Cordelia Ray. CBWP-3

What is an antipoet. Test. Nicanor Parra. PFTM-2, *tr. by* Miller Williams

What Is an Epigram? Samuel Taylor Coleridge. NIL-7; NIP-4

What is an epigram? a dwarfish whole. What Is an Epigram? Samuel Taylor Coleridge. NIL-7; NIP-4

What is Beautiful. Jay Wright. GT

What Is Beauty? Christopher Marlowe. MakPoe *Fr.* Tamburlaine the Great.

What is beauty, saith my sufferings, then? Christopher Marlowe. MakPoe *Fr.* Tamburlaine the Great.

What is beheld through glass seems glass. Prisms. Laura Riding Jackson. APT-2; ColAP

What is better than leaving a bar. Swing Shift Blues. Alan Dugan. BodElec

What Is Black? Mary O'Neill. NTCP

What is broken opened. Human Universe, The. Valerie Martínez. TouFir

What is clear kills what's unclear in order to be clear. What is clear is a shameless imperialism. Between May and June. Kim Chôngnan. EcSo, *tr. by* Peter H. Lee

What is failure? When the maiden. Failure. Henrietta Cordelia Ray. CBWP-3

"What is funny?" you ask, my child. Anatomy of Humor, The. Morris Gilbert Bishop. NBLV

What is green in me. Stepping Westward. Denise Levertov. NALW

What is happening to me now that loved faces. Childhood in Jacksonville, Florida. Jane Cooper. ExTi

What is he, this lordling, that cometh from the fight. Who is This that Cometh from Edom? William Herebert. ChIV-1; SacPr

What is her vanishing point? Gwyneth Lewis. NeBl

What Is History? 1. Ko Chônghûi. EcSo, *tr. by* Catherine J. Kim

What is hope? Tomorrow's Child. Rubin Alves. TWF

What Is Hoped For. James Laughlin. WhBo

What is, is not; and what is not, yet is. Believing Mind, The. Seng-ts'an. CCL1, *tr. by* Graeme Wilson

What is it about a Great Northern boxcar. Great Northern. Dave Etter. GM

What is it about women in water. Renoir's Bathers. Julie Moulds. AmPoNex

What is it all for, this poetry. August 22, 1939. Kenneth Rexroth. TAPaP

What is it? An airplane at dawn. No. Yehuda Amichai. FaBoWar, *tr. by* Barbara Harshav and Benjamin Harshav

What is it, fool, in the tall stars you'd find. Astrologer, The. Sir Thomas More. WoPoe, *tr. by* James Vincent Cunningham

What is it for, now that dividing neither. Wall in the Woods, A: Cummington. Richard Wilbur. PfSP

What is it, inside them and undeniable. King's Men, The. William Heyen. PoA 2002

What is it made of? Guilt. Blame. Sometimes. Finger. Jackie Kay. NeBrP

What is it makes thy sound unto my ear. Shell, The. Thomas Holley Chivers. TCAPo

What is it men in women do require? William Blake. ErotSp; NoP-4; NoP-5; OxBEV; WoPoe *Fr.* Several Questions Answered.

What is it our mammas bewitches. Written for My Son, and Spoken by Him at His First Putting on Breeches. Mary Barber. CABP

What is it that always rearranges. Mutability. Rachel Hadas. ExTi

What is it that glitters so clear and serene. Water. Ann Taylor. NOxBChV

What is it that love said when it spoke? Letter. Dhabya Khamees. PoArWo, *tr. by* Clarissa C. Burt

What is it that shoots from the mountains so high. Fire. Ann Taylor. NOxBChV

What is it that winds about over the world. Air. Ann Taylor. NOxBChV

What is it that's cover'd so richly with green. Earth. Ann Taylor. NOxBChV

What is it, then between us. From the Boat. Patricia Goedicke. ExTi

What is it to grasp. Grasshoppers. Roland Mathias. TCAWP

What is it to grow old? Growing Old. Matthew Arnold. NAEL-6v2; NPeEn

What is it when your man sits on the floor. Thief, The. Dorianne Laux. ErotSp; ExTi; PasH

What Is Kept. Linda Gregg. BodElec

What is left. Nzadi Z. Keita. BtF

What is Left and by Now Reduced to Little. Gabriella Leto. CItWP, *tr. by* Cinzia Sartini Blum and Lara Trubowitz

What is left to make us try? (LL) Winter Drive. James Philip McAuley. BMAP; PoA 2002

What Is Left to Say. Lisel Mueller. PoA 2002

What is life after all but a dream? Best of Life Is But, The. Li Po. CCL1, *tr. by* H. A. Giles

What is life, I ponder. Chu Ŭisik. CATKP, *tr. by* Peter H. Lee

What is living? Finding a great hall. What Is a Man? Waldo Williams. BBMWP, *tr. by* Emyr Humphreys

What Is Love? Eleanor Hull. IrLP

What is love, what is it? *Unknown.* CATKP, *tr. by* Peter H. Lee

What is Man? Richard Chenevix Trench. SacPr

What is memory? A palace? The belly of the mind? Of absence a dream? Rosmarie Waldrop. WoBe *Fr.* Hölderlin Hybrids.

What is memory? what makes a body glow. Maestro. Ilya Kaminsky. LegDan

What is more transcendent. Yun Sŏndo. CATKP *Fr.* Angler's Calendar, The.

What Is Moving. Takahashi Shinkichi. ZenPo, *tr. by* Takashi Ikemoto and Lucien Stryk

What is my lady like? thou fain would'st know. Sonnet. Frances Anne Kemble. SWaP

What is needed is a technique. Midston House. David Schubert. OxBoAm

What Is Not Mine. Hamda Khamees. PoArWo, *tr. by* Joseph T. Zeidan

What is not rooted in static. Bluesman's Blues, A. Lenard D. Moore. ISC

What is not there that one is missing. Somewhere Else. Philip Whalen. WANABP

What is our innocence. What Are Years? Marianne Moore. HarvBoo; ItP; MoAmPo; NAMCP V.1; NoAM; NoP-4; NoP-5; OxBoAm; SoSe-8

What Is Our Life? Sir Walter Ralegh. NAEL-7v1; NoSic; SoSe-8 (On the Life of Man.) NAEL-6v1

What is our life? a play of passion. What Is Our Life? Sir Walter Ralegh. NAEL-7v1; NoSic; SoSe-8

What is our life on earth? Remembering Min Ch'e. Su Tung-p'o. NDACCP, *tr. by* Kenneth Rexroth

What is pink? A rose is pink. Christina Georgina Rossetti. ChAP

What Is Poetry. John Ashbery. HarvBoo

What is pornography? What is dream? American River Sky Alcohol Father. Jean Valentine. CAP-8; ExTi; LaCa

What is questionable in the production of a text, its evidence. Erin Mouré. NLPA *Fr.* Wittgenstein Letters to Mel Gibson's Braveheart, The.

What is so strange about a tree alone in an open field? Hunting Pheasants in a Cornfield. Robert Bly. TRP

What is success of life I pray? Life's Success. James Martineau. OWABP

What Is Terrible. Roy Fuller. PoWW

What is that island, say you, stark and black—. Redwing. R. P. Blackmur. APT-2

What is that up yonder I see? I Want To Join the Band. *Unknown.* SSUS

What is the boy now, who has lost his ball. Ball Poem, The. John Berryman. ChAP; MoAmPo; NoAM

What is the cause, why states, that war and win. Fulke, 1st Baron Brooke Greville. FaBoWar

What is the chain which draws us back again. Fulke, 1st Baron Brooke Greville. SacPr *Fr.* Treatise of Religion, A.

What is the current that makes machinery. Gertrude Stein. MoWP; NAAPv.2 *Fr.* Tender Buttons.

What is the curse. Necessity. E. Y. Harburg. ReLy

What is the end of fame? 'Tis but to fill. Lord Byron. OBCoV *Fr.* Don Juan.

What is the head. Some Last Questions. W. S. Merwin. NAMCP V.2; VCAP

"What is the jewel colour?" "H. D." NALW *Fr.* Tribute to the Angels.

What is the keyboard. They Come Humming. Sharon Chmielarz. MiVo

What is the life. Careers. Imamu Amiri Baraka. TRP

What is the love of shadowy lips. Illusion. George Russell. IrLP

What Is the Matter With Me? *Unknown.* NDACCP, *tr. by* Kenneth Rexroth

What is the Meaning Hung from that Depend. Lyn Hejinian. OxBoAm *Fr.* My Life.

What is the name of King Ringang's daughter? Beauty Rohtraut. Eduard Friedrich Mörike. OBVE, *tr. by* George Meredith

What is the opposite of nuts? Richard Wilbur. NOxBChV

What is the opposite of *nuts?*. What is the opposite of nuts? Richard Wilbur. NOxBChV

What is the person? Is it hope? Person, The. Charles Hubert Sisson. HarvBoo

What is the price of Experience? Do men buy it for a song. William Blake. RSaN *Fr.* Vala; or The Four Zoas.

What is the purpose of visits to me twice since you've died? Grandmother. Grace Cavalieri. UnSA

What is the scope of the experience of sex—we talked about that. Lyn Hejinian. FaoP *Fr.* Oxota: A Short Russian Novel.

What is the summer. Summer Lost. Harriet Hamilton King. VWP

What is the Word. Samuel Beckett. OxBEV

What is the *World?* A great *Exchange* of ware. Francis Quarles. PBRV *Fr.* Pentelogia.

What is the world, and what is life. Hymn. William Williams. AngWePo

What is the world at night-time. First Nightmare Waking. Nicholas Samaras. NevBe

What is the world, O soldiers? Napoleon. Walter De la Mare. NPeEn; OxBEV; Spl; WoPoe

What is theirs. (LL) After Making Love. Stephen Dunn. EMP; PoA 2002

What Is There For Us? Jacqueline Johnson. BtF

What is there in my heart that you should sue. Félix Lope de Vega Carpio. OxBSo; UpMys; WoPoe *Fr.* Lachrimae; or Seven Tears Figured in Seven Passionate Pavans.

"What is there in the mountains?" you ask—. Poem Written in Answer to His Majesty's Question: "What Is There in the Mountains?" T'ao Hung Ching. ColAChn, *tr. by* Stephen Owen

What is there that we can do or say. Poem, A. Ezekiel Mphahlele. AF

What Is There to Say? E. Y. Harburg. ReLy

What is there to write. P.S. I Love You. Johnny Mercer. ReLy

What is this Death, ye deep read sophists, say? Philip Freneau. TCAPo *Fr.* House of Night, The.

What is this familiar power, I wondered. Of Marilyn, and Marijuana. Kenneth Rosen. NevBe

What is this Holy Spirit? Pentecost. David Craig. UpMys

What is this life if, full of care. Leisure. W. H. Davies. AngWePo; GoPo; MoBrPo; OBEV; OBMV; TFi

What is this power? (LL) Breath of Nature, The. Chuang Tzu. BBASP; WaAnP, *tr. by* Thomas Merton

What is this room. We Are Living. Brendan Kennelly. BeAl

What is this? said God. The obstinacy. Echoes. Ronald Stuart Thomas. OxAEP-2

What is this that I have heard? Dawn Has Yet to Ripple In. Melville Cane. MoAmPo

What Is This Thing Called Love? Cole Porter. ReLy

What is this weakness that washes over me as I sort through *the blues*. Blues. Christine Wiesenthal. IFF

What is this witness, the watching ages. Sonnet. Karen Volkman. IAoNAP

What is Thought but Won't Hold Still. Clark Coolidge. FTOS

What is thought that is not free? Free Thought. Algernon Charles Swinburne. NPeEn

What is to be born already fidgets in the stem. Christmas Card, After the Assassinations, A. Mona Van Duyn. ChrPo

What is translation? On a platter.   On Translating "Eugene Onegin."   Vladimir Vladimirovich Nabokov.   APT-2

What is true / is what seems.   Moon River.   Joe Wenderoth.   NAPBL

What is true knowledge?—Is it with keen eye.   True Knowledge.   Bishop Richard Mant.   SacPr

What is Truth? Says Pilate.   Louis MacNeice.   RSaN

What is whole has no face.   What.   Parśvanatha.   Robert Bringhurst.   GifTon

What Is Woman?   Mrs. Henry Linden.   CBWP-4

What Is Worth Knowing?   Sujata Bhatt.   NeBrP

What is wrought in the forge of the living and life.   Khwaja Shams-ad-din Muhammad Hafiz.   TAL Fr. Odes.

What is your plaster Doctor?   Christmas Rhyme: North Tyrone.   Unknown.   FaBoVe

What is your substance, whereof are you made.   William Shakespeare.   NoSic; OBEV; OxAEP-1; OxBEV Fr. Sonnets.

What isn't water in us must be bone.   Suffering The Sea Change: All My Pretty Ones.   Lucinda Roy.   GT

What Issa Heard.   David Budbill.   TAPaP

What is't, sweet wag, I should deny thy youth?   Christopher Marlowe.   CAGL Fr. Tragedy of Dido, The.

What is't you mean, that I am thus approach'd.   Sarah Fyge Egerton.   CABP

What It Comes Down To.   Tim Seibles.   TiP2

What it felt like to have been earth. (LL)   Geology, A.   Brenda Hillman.   AWPTFC; GeoHom

What it is all about.   Hans Faverey.   WoBe Fr. Eighteen Poems.

What it is all about? (LL)   Civilian and Soldier.   Wole Soyinka.   AF; PoetW

What It Means to be Avant-Garde.   Lee Bartlett.   ICANM

What it must be like to be an angel.   Parents.   William Meredith.   NAMCP V.2

What it showed was always the same.   Night Mirror, The.   John Hollander.   VCAP

What It Takes.   John Godfrey.   FTOS

What it took to be a woman in this life. (LL)   Exit.   Rita Dove.   AmAlph; ExTi

What it was, and it might serve me in a time when jests are few. (LL)   Rudyard Kipling.   NPeEn; PoAgWa Fr. Epitaphs of the War [1914–1918].

What It Was Like the Night Cary Grant Died.   Eloise Klein Healy.   WiU

What It's Like to Be a Black Girl (For Those of You Who Aren't).   Patricia Smith.   UnSA

What It's Like To Be Alive.   Deryn Rees-Jones.   BeAl

What I've Learned in My Travels.   Tom Clark and Lewis Warsh.   AHA

What Jenny Knows.   Jackie Kay.   NOxBChV

What Johnny Told Me.   John Ciardi.   TLR

What jungles he swung out of into the imagination.   Gorilla Gorilla.   Bruce Dawe.   NoAM

What, Kaiser dead? The heavy news.   Kaiser Dead.   Matthew Arnold.   DiBP

What Keeps.   C. D. Wright.   TAPaP

What Keeps Animals Sane?   Douglas Goetsch.   PA9/11

What keeps the full weight of my foot.   Cedar Waxwing, The.   Carole Oles.   PfSP

What killed that kangaroo-doe, slender skeieton.   River Bend.   Judith Wright.   BMAP

What kind of a person would kill Black children?   Test of Atlanta 1979, The.   June Jordan.   ISC

What kind of constant racket.   Tractor, The.   Isfoel.   BBMWP, tr. by Joseph P. Clancy

What Kind of Fool Am I?   Leslie Bricusse and Anthony Newley.   ReLy

What kind of fool am I.   What Kind of Fool Am I?   Leslie Bricusse and Anthony Newley.   ReLy

What kind of honey does a bee get from a thistle?   At Lac en Coeur.   Louis Dudek.   NLPA

What kind of love is this when she.   Anniversary Soak.   Paul Groves.   TCAWP

What kind of lover have you made me, mother.   La Dulce Culpa.   Cherríe Moraga.   FiBr

What kind of lovers could they have been.   Coosaponakeesa (Mary Mathews Musgrove Bosomsworth), Leader of the Creeks, 1700–1783.   Rayna Green.   AmWaPo

What Kind of Mistress He Would Have.   Robert Herrick.   CavPo

What kind of pain is it.   Wish.   Maggie Nelson.   AmPoNex

What kind of phantom is the ship?   Comprehension Questions.   Christine Hume.   LegDan

What kind of Pushkin am I.   Vsevolod Nekrasov.   ItGoST, tr. by Gerald Janecek

What Kind of Times Are These.   Adrienne Rich.   ExTi; LoL; WaAnP Fr. Not Somewhere Else, But Here.

What lady would not love a shepherd swain? (LL)   Robert Greene.   NoSic; RACG Fr. Greene's Mourning Garment.

What large, dark hands are those at the window.   Love On the Farm.   D. H. Lawrence.   CABP; MoBrPo; NAEL-6v2; NAEL-7v2; NAMCP V.1; NoAM; NoP-4; NoP-5

What lay under the midden the.   Roy Kiyooka.   NLPA Fr. Pear Tree Pomes.

What leaves us trembling in an empty house.   Shale.   Vona Groarke.   MFPA

What length of verse can serve brave Mopsa's good to show?   Sir Philip Sidney.   NoP-4; NoP-5 Fr. Countesse of Pembroke's Arcadia, The.

What Lies Beneath.   Shara McCallum.   SweBea

What Light Destroys.   Andrew Hudgins.   UpMys

What linking of soul to the halcyons of the afternoon!   Aegean Melancholy.   Odysseus Elytis.   VCWP

What lips my lips have kissed, and where, and why.   Sonnet 43.   Edna St. Vincent Millay.   APT-1; GoPo; HeIP-4; MakPoe; MoAmPo; NIP-4; OPOU; OxBoAm; WaAnP

What lively lad most pleasured me.   Last Confession, A.   William Butler Yeats.   NIP-4

What loud wave-motioned hooves awaken.   Blue Horses, The.   James McAuley.   BMAP

What love I when I love Thee, O my God?   George Macdonald.   SacPr

What lovely aftermath.   Butterfly.   Nelly Sachs.   PoCho, tr. by Matthew Mead and Ruth Mead

What lovely things / Thy hand hath made.   Scribe, The.   Walter De la Mare.   OBMV

What Luck.   Tadeusz Różewicz.   HP, tr. by Adam Czerniawski

What luck I can pick.   What Luck.   Tadeusz Różewicz.   HP, tr. by Adam Czerniawski

What Made Kabir a Servant.   Kabir.   WED, tr. by Robert Bly

What made the man kill this bear?   Bear on Main Street, The.   Dan Gerber.   PoDa

What made the place a landscape of despair.   Claus von Stauffenberg.   Thom Gunn.   OBWP

What make ole Satan da follow me so?   Hold Your Light.   Unknown.   SSUS

What makes a fire burn.   Fire.   Judy Brown.   TWF

What makes a knave a child of God.   Samuel Butler.   OBSV Fr. Hudibras.

What makes a man? Ruby, carbuncle, beryl.   Pericles, Prince of Tyre: A Commentary.   Reginald Shepherd.   IaFF

What makes Argia different from other cities is that it has earth instead of air.   Italo Calvino.   MotU Fr. Invisible Cities.

What makes it all bearable.   Fermi Lab: Sisyphus of Quarks.   Pearl Andelson Sherry.   PoA 2002

What makes life worth living is here in this land.   In This Land.   Mahmoud Darwish.   BeAl, tr. by Sabri Hafiz and Sarah Maguire

What makes me write my dearest Freind you aske.   Hester Wyat.   EMWP; FaBoVe

What makes the gopher leave his hole.   Eagle and Me, The.   E. Y. Harburg.   ReLy

What makes us rove that starlit corridor.   Science Fiction.   Kingsley Amis.   NAMCP V.2; NoAM

What Maks Makems.   Tom Pickard.   Oth

What mak's me so unnimbly ryse.   Aurelian Townshend.   OxBEV Fr. Albion's Triumph.

What Man Can Do on This Planet.   László Kálnoky.   IQMS, tr. by Geroge Gömöri

What man has made of man? (LL)   Lines Written in Early Spring.   William Wordsworth.   NAEL-6v2; NAEL-7v2; NOBRP; NPBRoP; SacPr

What Man Might Kill.   Cortney Davis.   PfS

What, many times I musing ask'd, is Man.   What is Man?   Richard Chenevix Trench.   SacPr

What marching men of Buffalo.   Vachel Lindsay.   AmWit Fr. Niagara.

What marvels smiles the morning-earth.   Stefan George.   GTCP, tr. by Irmgard Hunt

What Mary knew was just.   From a Woman's Life.   Maura Eichner.   UpMys

What masque of what old wind-withered New-Year.   For Spring, by Sandro Botticelli, in the Accademia of Florence.   Dante Gabriel Rossetti.   GS

What matter if I grow like this.   Twelve Songs of Tosan.   Yi Hwang.   CATKP, tr. by Richard Rutt

What Matters.   Teresa Porzecanski.   MirDau, tr. by Roberta Gordenstein

What matters here is (can a fish live).   Nanni Balestrini.   PFTM-2 Fr. Instinct of Self-Preservation, The.

What matters is the renewing and long running kinship.   Union of Two, The.   Haki R. Madhubuti.   ISC; SpirFl

What mean those Amorous Curles of Jet?   In Imitation of Horace.   Aphra Behn.   NOSC

What meanes this strangeness now of late.   Sir Robert Aytoun.   See What means this strangeness now of late.

What means my God? Why dost present to me.   Man's Natural Infirmity.   John Day.   InvLi

What means the mist opaque that veils these eyes.   Reproaches Phaon.   Mary Robinson.   CenSon

What means the mist opaque that veils these eyes? Mary Robinson. NPBRoP *Fr.* Sappho and Phaon.

What means this host of advancing. Advance of Education, The. Josephine D. Henderson Heard. CBWP-4

What means this strangeness now of late. Song. Sir Robert Aytoun. NOSC (What meanes this strangeness now of late.) NePenScot

What means this vast assemblage here. Dedication Day. Maggie Pogue Johnson. CBWP-4

What meant our careful parents so to wear,. Philippians 1.23. Francis Quarles. ChIV-2

What memory keeps fresh, frames unspoken. Small Joys. May Sarton. FFC

What metaphor could possibly convey. Signs on the Table, The. Amanda Berenguer. TANSG, *tr. by* Louise B. Popkin

What Michaelmas collision'f penis-waggle existentialism, eugenics. Category Mistakes in Biochemistry. Rob MacKenzie. Oth

What Might Have Been. Giuseppe Gioacchino Belli. WoPoe, *tr. by* Anthony Burgess

What Might Have Been. Kate Y. A. Bone. EdScPo

What more could I, a young man, want. (LL) Eating Alone. Li-Young Lee. CAP-8; NAAL-5; NAMCP V.2; TRP; WeW-3

What more variety of pleasures can. Everard Guilpin. PBRV *Fr.* Skialetheia Satire 5.

What moved me, was the way your hand. Lament. Dorothy Livesay. BrAP

What moves that lonely man is not the boom. Hermit, The. W. H. Davies. MoBrPo

What Mr. Cogito Thinks About Hell. Zbigniew Herbert. GPTC; VCWP; WoPoe, *tr. by* Bogdana Carpenter and John Carpenter

What Mr. Cogito Thinks About Hell. Zbigniew Herbert. MotU, *tr. by* Stuart Friebert

What must a man do in this house. Blues for the Nightowl. Elton Glaser. PBCAP

What must be studied. The winter trees. Trees. Ágnes Nemes Nagy. PoSu, *tr. by* Bruce Berlind

What must they have grown to now. Sean Dunne. ModIr *Fr.* Sydney Place.

What must we do, in a country lost already. Communist Poem, 1935. Valentine Ackland. RSaN

What must you do? Writing a Curriculum Vitae. Wisława Szymborska. PoSu, *tr. by* Grazyna Drabik

What My Child Learns of the Sea. Audre Lorde. GT

What My Father Believed. Robert Wrigley. RoV

What my hand follows on your body. Beneath My Hand and Eye the Distant Hills, Your Body. Gary Snyder. NAAL-5

What, my Lord, shall I do with. Stanza. *Unknown.* WoPoe, *tr. by* Lewis Turco

What My Mother Taught Me. Shara McCallum. BtF

What My Teachers Taught Me I Try to Teach My Students. Maura Eichner. UpMys

What mystery pervades a well! Emily Dickinson. NAAL-3; NAAPv.1; NCAP

What name do I have for you? Just Walking Around. John Ashbery. PtR

What nedeth these thretning wordes and wasted wynde? Sir Thomas Wyatt. OBVE

What need you, being come to sense. September 1913. William Butler Yeats. HarvBoo; IrV; NAEL-6v2; NAEL-7v2; NAMCP V.1; NoAM

What needs complaints. Comfort to a Youth That Had Lost His Love. Robert Herrick. OBEV

What needs my *Shakespear[e]* for his honour'd [or honoured or honored] Bones. On Shakespear[e]. John Milton. BrAP; CABP; NAEL-6v1; NAEL-7v1; NoP-4; NoP-5; NOSC; PoPoPo

What needst *thou* ask, or I reply? Sydney, Lady Morgan Owenson. RWP *Fr.* Lay of an Irish Harp, or Metrical Fragments, The.

What needst thou have more covering than [or then] a man? (LL) John Donne. BASC; FSCP; NAEL-6v1; NAEL-7v1; NoP-4; NoP-5; NoSic; PBRV *Fr.* Elegies.

What, never filled? Be thy lips screwed so fast. Isaiah 66.11. Francis Quarles. ChIV-1

What new element before us unborn in nature? Is there a new thing under the sun? Allen Ginsberg. CLPP *Fr.* Plutonian Ode.

What new element before us unborn in nature? Is there a new thing under the Sun? Allen Ginsberg. AtGh

What new woman is this? Whistling Woman. Al Zolynas. PML

What No One Could Have Told Them. C. D. Wright. GPPA; PoChi

What none, that dare in hand to take a pen. Injured Prince Vindicated, or, A Scurrilous and Detracting Pamphlet Answered, An. Elinor James. BASC

What nonsense they talk who complain of a War. War the Source of Riches. *Unknown.* NOBRP

What now / what now dumb nigger damn near dead. Another Poem for Me (after Recovering from an O.D.). Etheridge Knight. LaCa; OxAAAP

What nudity is beautiful as this. Portrait of a Machine. Louis Untermeyer. MoAmPo

What nymph should I admire, or trust. Question, to Lisetta, The. Matthew Prior. OBEV

What of my fourth grade teacher at Reynolds Elementary. Major L. Jackson. BAP-04 *Fr.* Urban Renewal.

What of the beauty that these hands have held. Since There's No Help . . . . R. P. Blackmur. APT-2

What of the faith and fire within us. Men Who March Away. Thomas Hardy. OBWP; PoWW

What of the night? I spent it in X. World as I Found It, The. Lawrence L. White. IAoNAP

What of the structure of Rime? I said. Robert Duncan. ASA *Fr.* Structure of Rime, The.

What of this house with massive walls. Widows' House, The. Sarah Orne Jewett. APN-2

'What of vile dust?' the preacher said. Praise of Dust, The. G. K. Chesterton. MoBrPo

What offspring other men have got. Upon His Verses. Robert Herrick. NAEL-6v1; NAEL-7v1

What on Earth deserves our Trust? Epitaph on her Son *H. P.* at St. Syth's Church [where her body also lies Interred]. Katherine Philips. CABP; MakPoe; NoP-4; NoP-5; NOSC; PBRV; PEW

What on this wide earth. Potato, The. Lillian E. Curtis. VerBaPo

What Once I Was. Sir Thomas Wyatt. WaAnP

What one wants from a letter is not an answer. Giving Way. Johanna Kruit. TuT, *tr. by* Medbh McGuckian

What one wants of course is the clothes to contain one which. Latticed Culotte and Starry Blouse. Alice Notley. AHA

What other men sometimes have thought they've seen. (LL) Ted Berrigan. FTOS; OxBoAm *Fr.* Sonnets, The.

What others doth discourage and dismay. To His Coy Mistress. Sir Robert Aytoun. NOSC; WaAnP

What painter has not with a careless smutch. Accident in Art. Richard Hovey. APN-2

What Parents Do Not Yet Know. Kay Boyle. PoChi

What part of my holiest and most beautiful feelings. Benedetto Varchi. CAGL, *tr. by* James J. Wilhelm

What passing-bells for these who die as cattle? Anthem for Doomed Youth. Wilfred Owen. AF; BrAP; CABP; CAGL; ClHu; FaBoWar; GPTC; GSo; HarvBoo; HeIP-4; InoFa; MoBrPo; NAEL-6v2; NAEL-7v2; NAMCP V.1; NoAM; NoP-4; NoP-5; NPeEn; OBEV; OBWP; OxBEV; PoPoPo; SoSe-8; StAl; TCAWP; TFi; WaAnP; WeW-3

What penetrated your life—acid spectacle encrusted in the site of spasm. Angélica Tornero. SPV, *tr. by* Jen Hofer

What people they were! Their boxers the strongest! Bertolt Brecht. FaBoA

What pictures now shall wanton fancy bring? On Winter. Mary Leapor. PEW

What pleasure can a bannish'd creature have. Mary Sidney Wroth, Countess of Montgomery. EMWP *Fr.* Pamphilia to Amphilanthus.

What pleasure have great princes. Quiet Life, The. William Byrd. NoSic

What pleasures have great princes? These: to know. Pleasure of Princes, The. Alec Derwent Hope. BrAP

What plucky sperm invented Mrs. Gale? New World Symphony, A. Kit Wright. NBLV

What potions have I drunk of Siren tears. William Shakespeare. OxAEP-1 *Fr.* Sonnets.

What powerful Spirit lives within! Hymn upon St. Bartholomew's Day, An. Thomas Traherne. SacPr

What price happiness? Wrap Your Troubles in Dreams. Ted Koehler. ReLy

What prompted her. Ishikawa Takuboku. PoCho, *tr. by* Sanford Goldstein and Seishi Shinoda

What pull did that leaping flame. Snow Maiden, The. Bella Akhatovna Akhmadulina. TCRusP, *tr. by* Daniel Weissbort

What Really Goes on in the College of Cardinals. *Unknown.* CAGL, *tr. by* James J. Wilhelm

What reason first imposed thee, gentle name. Family Name, The. Charles Lamb. CenSon

What remains haunting are not the crematory flames. Some Solace, Some Yearning. William Henry Lewis. BtF

What remains of the suicide's voice is the last conversation. Elegy. Edgar Silex. NAPBL

What rich profusion here. Manoah Bodman. APN-1 *Fr.* Oration on Death, An.

What rituals are in Benares? Sonnet Around Stephanie. Lee Ann Brown. BAP-01

What ruse of vision. Bear, The. N. Scott Momaday. HATNAP

What sacrifice so great! Mother's Love, A. Josephine D. Henderson Heard. CBWP-4

What saies my brother? William Shakespeare. OxBEV *Fr.* Measure for Measure.

What! Salomon! such words from you. To E. S. Salomon. Ambrose Bierce. CBCWP; PCW

What saved us? what for? (LL) "H. D." AF; AmWaPo; APT-1; HarvBoo; NAAL-5; NAMCP V.1; NoP-4; NoP-5; NPeEn; OBWP *Fr.* Walls Do Not Fall, The.

What Saves Us. Bruce Weigl. AmWaPo

What Say. John Godfrey. FTOS

What say the Bells of San Blas. Bells of San Blas, The. Henry Wadsworth Longfellow. APN-1

What say you, critic, now you have become. Camelus Saltat. George Meredith. OxBSo

What seas what shores what grey rocks and what islands. Marina. T. S. Eliot. APT-1; CABP; HeIP-4; NAEL-6v2; NAEL-7v2; NPeEn; OxBEV

What Secret Cravings of the Blood. Nelly Sachs. PoSu, *tr. by* Michael Hamburger

What seemed to have bothered him the most, after it was done. False Arrest. Cornelius Eady. LTA

What Seeps In. Devorah Amir. DTA, *tr. by* Miriyam Glazer

What seer is this. Ode on the Twentieth Century. Henrietta Cordelia Ray. CBWP-3

What serious students with their busied brains. Epigram LXVII: Time, the Interpreter. Hugh Crompton. NOSC

What shall divide me now? Sideshow. John Wilkinson. VaPo

What shall he have that killed the deer? William Shakespeare. NoSic *Fr.* As You Like It.

What shall I do? not to be Rich or Great. In Emulation of Mr Cowleys Poem Call'd The Motto. Mary Astell. EMWP; NOSC

What shall I do to be for ever known. Motto, The. Abraham Cowley. NOSC

What shall I do with this absurdity. Tower, The. William Butler Yeats. NAMCP V.1; NoAM

What shall I put in my experimental trousseau? Instructions to Her Next Husband. Judith Taylor. SUP

What shall I say, because talk I must? Yellow Flower, The. William Carlos Williams. HarvBoo

What shall I say, my Lord? With what begin? Edward Taylor. ChIV-2 *Fr.* Preparatory Meditations Before My Approach to the Lord's Supper.

What shall I say to Walt Whitman tonight? Centennial For Whitman. Richard Eberhart. ViWalt

What shall I say to You, Sankari? Mahendranāth Bhattācārya. SinGod, *tr. by* Rachel Fell McDermott

What shall I wear to sleep in alone? Yosano Akiko. WoPoe *Fr.* Channel Boat, The.

What shall the world do with its children? Romans Angry about the Inner World. Robert Bly. WaAnP

What shall we be, sweet, you and I. These Bones. T. H. Parry-Williams. OBWVE, *tr. by* H. Idris Bell

What shall we do for Love these days? Lascelles Abercrombie. MoBrPo *Fr.* Emblems of Love.

What shall we do for the striking seamen? What Shall We Do for the Striking Seamen? *Unknown.* HHAm

What shall we do for timber? Kilcash. *Unknown.* OBMV, *tr. by* Frank O'Connor

What shall we do with a murder of crows. Crows. Carole Glasser Langille. IFF

What shall we say to the lovers of freedom. Wallace Stevens. FaBoWar *Fr.* Phases.

What share have I at their festive board? Adam Lindsay Gordon. STuOW *Fr.* Ashtaroth: A Dramatic Lyric.

What she and I had between us once, America. John Hollander. VCAP *Fr.* Powers of Thirteen.

What she holds is the unimaginable. Pietà. Mariève Rugo. PfS

What she petitioned for was never. Denise Levertov. UpMys *Fr.* Showings, The: Lady Julian of Norwich, 1342-1416.

What She Said. Maturai Eruttalan Centamputan. WoPoe, *tr. by* A. K. Ramanujan

What She Said. Kaccipettu Nannakaiyar. WoPoe,

What She Said. Kallatanar. WoPoe, *tr. by* A. K. Ramanujan

What She Said. Mamalatan. WoPoe, *tr. by* A. K. Ramanujan

What She Said. Patumanār. AWTN, *tr. by* A. K. Ramanujan

What she said to her companion. Bihari. WoPoe *Fr.* Satasai, The.

What She Said to Her Girl-Friend. Maturaikkataiayattar Makan Vennakan. WoPoe, *tr. by* A. K. Ramanujan

What she thought was. Keith Abbott. WhBo

What She Wanted. Ron Koertge. SUP

What ship is that you're enlisted upon? Old Ship of Zion, The [Maryland version]. *Unknown.* SSUS

What should be the title of a king. Too, how also to include. What happened when. James Sherry. FTOS *Fr.* In Case.

What should happen is. Side 21. Víctor Hernández Cruz. PueRic

What Should I Call This? Floating Metonymy 5. Kim Sŭnghŭi. EcSo, *tr. by* K. Kim Richards and Steffen Richards

What should I do! Unhappy Kukutis in the Potato Patch. Marcelijus Martinaitis. TWW, *tr. by* Laima Sruoginis

What should I say. Sir Thomas Wyatt. NoSic

What Should I Say. Sir Thomas Wyatt. NoP-4; NoP-5

What should one. Picture of J. T. in a Prospect of Stone, The. Charles Tomlinson. NoP-4; NoP-5; NPeEn; WaAnP

What should there be in Christ to give offense? William Alabaster. OxBEV

What should we be without the sexual myth. Men Made out of Words. Wallace Stevens. APT-1

What should do we know. Verse. Oliver St. John Gogarty. OBMV

What sign do you make, O Swan, with your curved neck. Swans, The. Rubén Darío. SpanPo, *tr. by* Dorren Bell

What so true as night come fused. Darkling Thrums. Clark Coolidge. NYP2

What Soft—Cherubic Creatures. Emily Dickinson. APN-2; MoAmPo; NALW; TCAPo

What somehow echo through the clanging of the town bells. Gyula Krúdy. IQMS, *tr. by* John Lukacs

What Song the Syrens Sang. Eleanor Brown. MFPA

What song will ever be so sorrowful. Angelo Poliziano. CAGL *Fr.* Favola di Orfeo.

What songs should rise, how constant, how divine! (LL) Thoughts on the Works of Providence. Phillis Wheatley. ColAP; InvLi; NAAL-3; NAAL-5

What soon enough we would know? (LL) Bearer of Evil Tidings, The. Robert Frost. NoAM; SAmP

What soothes the angry snail? Eine Kleine Snailmusik. May Sarton. NBLV

What sorrow. (LL) Brilliant Sad Sun. William Carlos Williams. HarvBoo; NAAPv.2

What soul hath struck its need of melody. Incompleteness. Henrietta Cordelia Ray. CBWP-3

What sound awakened me, I wonder. Deserter, The. A. E. Housman. OBMV

What sounds like the broadcast of snow itself. Radio. Antony Dunn. RWPCtW

What sower has walked over the Earth. Sunflower. Rolf Jacobsen. IJHIL, *tr. by* Olav Grinde

What sower walked over earth. Sunflower. Rolf Jacobsen. RaBo; WED, *tr. by* Robert Bly

What sphinx of cement and aluminum bashed open their skulls and ate up their brains and imagination? Allen Ginsberg. BB; CLPP *Fr.* Howl.

What spirit can lift you up, to that immortall praise. Michael Drayton. PBRV *Fr.* Polyolbion [*or* Poly-Oobion].

What stalked the room was never envy. Minotaur. Carl Phillips. AmAlph

What started out as a study in naturalism. How to Live in the Elegy. Tracy Philpot. AmPoNex

What stays specific in age when much else fades. Has Faded in Part But Magnificent Also Late for RC / Mirrors. Robert Grenier. PmAP

What, still alive at twenty–two. Poem, after A. E. Housman. Hugh Kingsmill. UV

What strange pleasure do they get who'd / wipe whole worlds out. This Book is for Magda. Lew Welch. BB

What strange unusual prodigy is here,. On the Strange Apparitions at Christ's Death. Henry Colman. ChIV-2

What stripling now thee discomposes. Horace. OBVE,

What substance had Euridice. Kathleen Jessie Raine. NALW

What sudden blaze of song. Christmas Day. John Keble. RSR

What suits with Sappho, Phoebus suits with thee! (LL) Her Last Appeal to Phaon. Mary Robinson. CenSon; RWP

What? summer now? divisions ring. Morgan Llwyd. PBRV *Fr.* Summer, The.

What summer proposes is simply happiness. Tahoe in August. Robert Hass. CalPo; NoP-4; NoP-5

What sunken splendor in the Eastern skies. To the Statue on the Capitol. John James Piatt. APN-2

What Sunni Say. Elouise Loftin. EGAG

What Surprises Him. Dinty Moore. MAAN

What sweet children! Snow Storm. Dunya Mikhail. IrPoTo, *tr. by* Liz Winslow

What sweet relief the showers to thirsty plants we see. True Love, A. Nicholas Grimald. OBEV

What swimmers. We cannot leave lie. Larking. Karen Solie. OpeFie

What syllable are you seeking. To the Roaring Wind. Wallace Stevens. TCAPo

What tears in eyes now. Marina Ivanovna Tsvetayeva. PoAgWa

What That Street Is Called. Yelena Shwarts. VCWP, *tr. by* Michael Molnar

What that street is called—you can read it on the sign. What That Street Is Called. Yelena Shwarts. VCWP, *tr. by* Michael Molnar

What the bad news was. Meaningful Love. John Ashbery. VaPo

What the billboard. Elvis for the Ages, An. Lynne McMahon. AllShUp

What the Birds Said. John Greenleaf Whittier. APN-1; OxBoAm

What the Body Told. Rafael Campo. AmPoNex; BloBone; NeAmPo; WiU

What the Bullet Sang. Bret Harte. APN-2; CalPo; OBEV

What the Chairman Told Tom. Basil Bunting. BrAP; EmeKit; NAMCP V.1; NoP-4

What the Citizens of Corpus, Rockport, Palacios, or Bryan Need. Paul Christensen. TiP2

What the Dark Proposes. Charles Martin. PfSP

What the Dead Do. Jackie Graves. BRtP

What the Dead Fear. Kim Addonizio. SUP

What the Deal, Son? Kevin Powell. BRtP

What the deil hae we got for a King. Allan Cunningham. NePenScot

What the devil is his gripe. Owl. Sŏ Chŏngju. WoPoe, tr. by Kevin O'Rourke

What the Doctor Said. Raymond Carver. EmeKit

What the Dog Perhaps Hears. Lisel Mueller. MiVo

What the Donkey Saw. U. A. Fanthorpe. OBCP

What the End Is For. Jorie Graham. AtGh; NoP-4; PoPoPo

What the fine rain does not hide and cannot wash away. Complected. Teri Ellen Cross. BRtP

What the goddamn hell are you talking about, boy. How I Wrote It. David Dooley. TRP

What the Gypsy Said to Her Children. Judith Ortiz Cofer. OxWW; UnSA

What the hell am i doing anyway? California. Gerald Locklin. CalPo

What the Japanese Perhaps Heard. Rachel Rose. BAP-01

What the Light Teaches. Anne Michaels.

"Language is the house with lamplight in its windows." StAl

What the Listener Thinks. Unknown. RWPCtW

What the Living Do. Marie Howe. BeAl; ExTi; PoCho; PoDa

What the Lovers in the Old Songs Thought. John Hollander. BAP-01

What the Men Talk About When the Women Leave the Room. Dionisio D. Martinez.

"Room itself, The. The women. The absence of women." NoP-4; NoP-5

What the Motorcycle Said. Mona Van Duyn. NIL-7; NIP-4

What the mouth sings, the soul must learn to forgive. What the Water Knows. Sam Hamill. BodElec; WANABP

What the Music Wants. Gustaf Sobin. PmAP

What the Oracle Said. Shara McCallum. BRtP

What the other listener thinks. What the Listener Thinks. Unknown. RWPCtW

What the poet is searching for. Antonio Machado Ruiz. WED Fr. Moral Proverbs and Folk Songs.

What the river says, that is what I say. (LL) Ask Me. William Stafford. CAP-8; LoL; OxBoAm

What the Serpent Said to Adam. Archibald MacLeish. ChIV-1 Fr. Songs for Eve.

What the Shadow Said in the Presence of the Poem. Abd al-Karim Kassid. IrPoTo, tr. by Chuck Miller and Saadi A. Simawe

What the Sonnet Is. Eugene Lee-Hamilton. GSo

What the Spider Heard. Weldon Kees. NoP-5

What the sun burns up of it, the moon puts back. (LL) Plague of Dead Sharks. Alan Dugan. NoAM; PtR

What the swift mind beholds at every turn. (LL) Pity me not because the light o of day. Edna St. Vincent Millay. MoAmPo; OxBoAm

What the Train Ran Over. Lucy Larcom. SWaP

What the Uneducated Old Woman Told Me. Christopher Reid. NeBrP

What the vandals will do. After the Poem Who Knows. Alan Michael Parker. NAPBL

(After the poem who knows.) PoDa

What the Voice Sees. Catherine Hunter. PoPra

What the Water Knows. Sam Hamill. BodElec; WANABP

What the Women Told Me. E. Ethelbert Miller. GT

What their number is, be pined [or pin'd]. (LL) Ben Jonson. EroLit; NOSC Fr. Volpone.

What then remains, but, waiving each extreme. John Dryden. BASC Fr. Religio Laici.

What there is of it. Poem With Two Seasons Right Now. S. J. Marks. BodElec

What There Is, Today. Tracy Philpot. IAoNAP

What there's been of winter moves away. Buddy Holly. David Wojahn. SwNoth

What these can only memorize and mumble. (LL) Grandeur of Ghosts. Siegfried Sassoon. MoBrPo; OBMV

What they are doing makes their garden feel like a big room. Scissors Ceremony, The. Michael Longley. EmeKit

What they conceal. (LL) Ralph Waldo Emerson. NAAPv.1; NCAP Fr. Merlin.

What They Did by Lamplight. Kimberly M. Blaeser. SweBea

What They Do to You in Distant Places. Marvin Bell. MoASP

What they eats in Rome. (LL) When in Rome. Mari E. Evans. ESEAA; SoSe-8

What they felt then: isn't it / sweeter than every secret. Mary at Peace with the Risen Lord. Rainer Maria Rilke. GI

What they felt was this: Isn't it. Rainer Maria Rilke. WED Fr. Life of the Virgin Mary, The.

What they had at their window was earth's own shadow. Center. Josephine Miles. OxBoAm

What they had in common went beyond the I'm cool-are-you. Alice Fulton. AllShUp Fr. Give: A Sequence Reimagining Daphne & Apollo.

What They Left Behind. J. D. McClatchy. OxBoAm

What they really say is, let them die, / and the children too. (LL) So Mexicans Are Taking Jobs from Americans. Jimmy Santiago Baca. LTA; UnSA

What They Said. Tanure Ojaide. HBAPE

What they think is it's the twists and turns of politics. Electra. György Petri. VCWP, tr. by Geroge Gömöri and Clive Wilmer

What They Wanted. Victor H. Bausch. RaF

What They Wanted. Stephen Dunn. BodElec

What thing did I love that walks the street. Contemporary Muse, The. Edgell Rickword. OBSV

What thing is that, nor felt nor seen. Riddle: On a Kiss, A. William Strode. NOSC

What thing shall be held up to woman's beauty? Lascelles Abercrombie. MoBrPo Fr. Emblems of Love.

What Things Are Called. Erich Fried. AF, tr. by Georg Rapp

What think you I take my pen in hand to record? What Think You I Take My Pen in Hand? Walt Whitman. APN-1

What this driver knew of touch. Touch. Eugene Gloria. ReBoTo

What tho', Valclusa, the fond Bard be fled. Sonnet to Valclusa. Thomas Russell. NOBRP

(What though, Valclusa, the fond Bard be fled.) CenSon

What Thomas an Buile Said in a Pub. James Stephens. MoBrPo

(What Tomas Said in a Pub.) NoAM

What thou lovest well remains. Ezra Pound. OxBoAm; RaBo; WaAnP; WoPoe Fr. Cantos.

What though, for showing truth to flatter'd [or flattered] state. Written on the Day That Mr. Leigh Hunt Left Prison. John Keats. CenSon

What though my shorts are threadbare. Philip Whalen. WANABP Fr. Epigrams & Imitations.

What though the rain weeps down the pane. On Rainy Days. Unknown. ArBi

What though the rosebuds from my cheek. Departed Youth. Hannah Cowley. CABP

What though they conquer us? Witter Bynner. NoP-4; NoP-5 Fr. Chinese Drawings.

What though, Valclusa, the fond Bard be fled. Thomas Russell. See What tho', Valclusa, the fond Bard be fled.

What though, while the wonders of nature exploring. To Some Ladies. John Keats. STuOW

What though your eyes be stars, your hair be night. To One Black, and Not Very Handsome, Who Expected Commendation. Edward Herbert, 1st Baron Herbert of Cherbury. NOSC

What thoughts I have of you tonight, Walt Whitman, for I walked down the sidestreets under the trees with a headache self-conscious looking at the full moon. Supermarket in California, A. Allen Ginsberg. BrAP; CAGL; FaBoA; GPTC; HeIP-4; MotU; NAAL-5; NAMCP V.2; NIL-7; NoAM; NoP-5; OxBoAm; PmAP; PtR; ReTh; TFi; WeW-3

What time I was your one best bet. Horace. See While, Lydia, I was lov'd of thee.

What time the gifted lady took. Dorothy Parker. NALW; NAMCP V.1 Fr. Pig's-Eye View of Literature, A.

What times are these. Leaf, Treeless for Bertolt Brecht, A. Paul Celan. AF, tr. by Michael Hamburger

What to do with salvias? In the Park. Peter Jones. OBGa

What to make of them, the professors. Autumnal Sketch, An. August Kleinzahler. PmAP

What to say when the spider. Elegy in a Spider's Web. Laura Riding Jackson. PFTM-1

What to start with? Finding a Horseshoe. Osip Emilevich Mandelstam. RusPo, tr. by Robert Arthur Douglas Ford

What told us that the day was over? Canciones. Kenneth Zamora Damacion. OPRER

What Tomas Said in a Pub. James Stephens. See What Thomas an Buile Said in a Pub.

What trifling coil do we poor mortals keep. Human Life. Matthew Prior. OBCoV; OxBEV

What troubles you, wild sleepyhead? Narcissus to Echo. Edgar Bogardus. YaYoPo

What up, brother? the white teen with dreadlocks. Question. A. Van Jordan. BRtP

What use for words at all? (LL) I do not call it his sign. Mahadevi. WoPoe; WPoS, tr. by Jane Hirshfield

What use to suffer in labor, give birth to children, if she. Diotimus. HePo Fr. Epigrams.

What used to be. Change, The. Samuel Chimsoro. NAfrP

What value to me the seven kinds of treasures. Longing for His Son, Furuhi. Yamanoé no Okura. WoPoe, tr. by Helen Craig McCullough

What varying sounds from yon gray pinnacles. Church Bells, The. Bishop Richard Mant. SacPr

What voice. Basho. ASA; EH, tr. by Robert Hass

What voice is this, thou evening gale! Song. Joanna Baillie. RWP; WoRP

What was all the talk about? Dream Vision, A. Yvor Winters. NAAPv.2

What was blood. Written in Blood. Sue Owen. PoA 2002

What was happening in the kitchen awfully. Forensics. Ben Doyle. LegDan

What was he after there at Machrihanish. McTaggart. Kenneth White. EdScPo

What was he doing, the great god Pan. Musical Instrument, A. Elizabeth Barrett Browning. BrAP; CABP; NAEL-6v2; NoP-4; NoP-5; NPeEn; OBEV; PEW; PoPoPo; ViWPN; VWP

What was her beauty in our first estate. She. Richard Wilbur. NIL-7

What was her blondness like, I can't remember. What Was Her Blondness Like. Gyula Juhász. IQMS, tr. by Adam Makkai

What was her name. Who Was Mary Shelley? Lorine Niedecker. OxBoAm

What was i doing anyway. On extending the olive branch to my own self. Harriet Jacobs. SpirFl

What was I doing here, haunting the dead? Barcelona. Alan Jenkins. NeBrP

What was I thinking of when I threw one of my. Peaches. Paul Muldoon and Gerald Stern. GPPA

What was Inez supposed to do for. Rape. Jayne Cortez. GT; PmAP

What was it brought you, Seligenstadter. Memling. Roland Mathias. AngWePo

What was it drove me to insist on sleds. Snow-Day. Judith Baumel. KGB

What was it I saw at the top. Heaven. Eleni Sikelianos. IIR

What was it? What was it? Woman as Market. Muriel Rukeyser. NoAM

What was it you said again there by the river. Jackie Kay. NeBrP Fr. Other Lovers.

What Was Life. Idea Vilariño. TANSG, tr. by Louise B. Popkin

What was life. What Was Life. Idea Vilariño. TANSG, tr. by Louise B. Popkin

What Was My Choice? Fawzi Karim. IrPoTo, tr. by Chuck Miller and Saadi A. Simawe

What Was Not Conceivable. Fatima Mahmoud. PoArWo, tr. by Khaled Mattawa

What Was Solomon's Mind? Geoffrey Scott. OBMV

What was that sound we heard. Why Must You Know? John Wheelwright. APT-2; OxBoAm

What was the need like driving rain. Round. Robert Pinsky. OxBoAm

What was the use of not leaving it there where it would hang what. Gertrude Stein. MoWP; TCAPo Fr. Tender Buttons.

What Was There to Bring Me to Delight But to Love and Be Loved? Paisley Rekdal. LegDan

What way does the Wind come? What way does he go? Address to a Child during a Boisterous Winter Evening. Dorothy Wordsworth. WoRP

What we all. Joseph Jarman. EGAG

What we announced here at the Institute. Re: The Tobacco Institute. Ron Overton. PrTe

What We Believe. Charles Harper Webb. Vesp

What we below could not see, Winter pass. (LL) Thaw. Edward Thomas. MoBrPo; OxAEP-2; OxBEV; Spl

What we call the beginning is often the end. T. S. Eliot. BeAl Fr. Four Quartets.

What we came here to find. Finding My Old Battalion Command Post. William Daniel Ehrhart. AmWaPo

What we charge upon. Eat them for us. Unknown. APN-2 Fr. Minnetare Songs.

What we come round to. Epitaph for the Western Intelligentsia. Richard Allen. NOBAu

What We Could Do. William Trowbridge. SUP

What We Did After My Mother's Mastectomy. Lisa Glatt. AmPoNex

What We Didn't Tell the Medic. Ken Babstock. OpeFie

What we don't forget is what we don't say. Anger Sweetened. Molly Peacock. FFC

What We Feared. Judith Ortiz Cofer. PueRic

What we got stuck with. Flesh Tones. Richmond Lattimore. PoA 2002

What we have becomes. Anniversary, An. Wendell Berry. UpMys

What we have here is a mechanic who reads Nietzsche. One of the Citizens. Rodney Jones. InGu

What we have lost. Duriel Harris. SpirFl

What We Heard About the Japanese. Rachel Rose. BAP-01

What We Learned. Fanny Howe. FTOS

What We Learned on the Highway Near St. John's. Jeanette Lynes. Coast

What We Leave Behind. Elmaz Abinader. PoArWo

What we live / before the light is turned off. Quotidian, The. Claudia Rankine. AmPoNex

What We Lost. Eavan Boland. HarvBoo

What we love, can't see. Geology, A. Brenda Hillman. AWPTFC; GeoHom

What we mistook for flight. Reunion. T. Crunk. YaYoPo

What we must accept as we journey through the world. Lament for the Evanescence of Life, A. Yamanoé no Okura. WoPoe, tr. by Helen Craig McCullough

What We Need Words For. Rebecca Seiferle. PoChi; TAPaP

What we perceive is corpulent, well-dressed. Capitalization of "Clue", The. Ray Ragosta. OnScMo

What we reminded you of you are already forgetting. David Constantine. NewEx

What we run on our treadmills towards is four TVs. Winter, Voyeurism. William Olsen. MAAN

What We Say in New Mexico. Mary Doughtery Bartlett. ICANM

What we shall not perhaps get over, we. Luck. Carl Phillips. AmAlph

What We Teach at Claflin. Lizelia Augusta Jenkins Moorer. CBWP-3

What we to-day prize and most fondly cherish. Instability. Henrietta Cordelia Ray. CBWP-3

What We Want. Linda Pastan. FaoP

What we want is a model of the universe. Model of the Universe, A. Norman Fischer. WhBo

What we, when face to face we see. Arthur Hugh Clough. ChIV-2; SacPr

What weak remonstrance!—how I joy to find. Elizabeth Cobbold. CenSon Fr. Sonnets of Laura.

What well-heeled knuckle-head, straight from the unisex. Old Malediction, An. Horace. NoAM; OBCoV; WoPoe, tr. by Anthony Hecht

What went ye out to see? a shaken reed? John. Jones Very. ChIV-2

What were the secrets that we didn't tell? In 1969. Katharyn Howd Machan. SwNoth

What Were They Like? Denise Levertov. HeIP-4; NIP-4; OBWP; PoAgWa

What were they like as schoolboys? Long on themes. Poets. X. J. Kennedy. OPRER

What were they talking about? Ah yes, the end! Hans Magnus Enzensberger. PoSu Fr. Sinking of the Titanic, The.

What were this human. Woman. Ina Coolbrith. FTtHH; NAAPv.1

What were we fighting about? Gold. Gurajada Apparao. HotL, tr. by V. Narayana Rao

What were we playing? Was it prisoner's base? Running. Richard Wilbur. MoASP

What Were You Patching? Ruth Lisa Schechter. UnSA

What we've come for is the Comet. Comet and Treefrog. Jarold Ramsey. PoCoUp

What, what, what / What's the news from Swat? Threnody. George Thomas Lanigan. NBLV

What Will Be Your Destiny? Caroline Gilman. SWaP Fr. Oracles for Youth.

What will become her earliest memory. Older Child, The. Kimiko Hahn. CAP-8

What will become of these, the drab, the harsh. Final reductions. M. R. Peacocke. NLP

What will become of us, Nathalie. You in my memory, I in. Farewell. Enrique Lihn. BLPSL, tr. by Rene de Costa, Rigas Kappatos and Eleni Paidoussi

What will call out to us then. If the Silence Should Suddenly Return. Ekaterina Iosifova. CSCBP, tr. by Georgi Belev and Lisa Sapinkopf

What Will Come of This? Jenö Dsida. IQMS, tr. by Adam Makkai

What will Iraq catch as she travels by sea for a thousand years? Incomplete Anthem. Fadhil Assultani. IrPoTo, tr. by the author and Richard McKane

What will see us through, a certain calm. Elizabethan and Nova Scotian Music. Charles North. NYP2; PmAP

What will suffice for a true-love knot? Even the rain? Ghazal. Agha Shahid Ali. AmAlph

What will survive of us is love. (LL) Arundel Tomb, An. Philip Larkin. BeAl; BrAP; ItP; NAMCP V.2; NoP-4; NoP-5; OxAEP-2; WaAnP

What will the mood of the sky be? Yun Söndo. CATKP Fr. Angler's Calendar, The.

What will the next years teach? (LL) Figlio Maggiore. Robert Fitzgerald. NoP-4; NoP-5

What will you do, love, when I am going. What Will You Do, Love? Samuel Lover. IrLP

What will you do with your shovel, Dai. Idris Davies. RSaN

What will your landlady think of me. Passion at Forty. Jane Barnes. PfS

What wind there was. River in Dusk. Joanna Klink. IAoNAP

What winds around your feet. Sea Chanty. Suzanne Lummis. CalPo

What wings of a wild bird covered his back? Does Anyone Know Where Roque Dalton Spent His Final Night? Gaspar Aguilera Díaz. PML, *tr. by* John Oliver Simon

What winter floods, what showers of spring. Emily Jane Brontë. OxBEV

What wisdom and beauty his Sermon on the Mount. Gloss to Matthew V 27–28. Alec Derwent Hope. GI

What witch are you, that entangles our hearts. Na'ili [*or* Yeni-Zada Mustafa Efendi]. OLP, *tr. by* Walter Andrews, Najaat Black and Mehmet Kalpakli

What witchlike spell weaves here its deep design. Anna Hempstead Branch. APT-1; NALW *Fr.* Sonnets from a Lock Box.

What with the Italian. Portrait of Silverio Franconetti. Federico García Lorca. SpanPo, *tr. by* Rachel Benson and Robert O'Brien

What with This and That. Leigh Hunt. STuOW *Fr.* Story of Rimini, The.

What wonder, Percy, that with jealous rage. To Percy Shelley. Leigh Hunt. CenSon

What wonder strikes the curious, while he views. Ants, The. John Clare. OxBSo

What word have you, interpreters, of men. Of Heaven Considered as a Tomb. Wallace Stevens. PoA 2002

What words are these have fallen from me? Alfred Tennyson. NAWM-7v2 *Fr.* In Memoriam A. H. H.

What words must rush in. Cesare Greppi. ItPo, *tr. by* Gayle Ridinger

What Work Is. Philip Levine. BeAl; CAP-8; EmeKit; ItP

What works best / is the mile walk down Sleepy Hollow. Right of Way. Barry Sternlieb. GM

What would he make of it? we wondered. If keir hardie was the man on the moon. Paul Summers. RSaN

What would *housework* mean. Dictionary for the New Century. Kimberly M. Blaeser. SweBea

What would I do? Christina Georgina Rossetti. NOxBChV

What Would I Do White? June Jordan. LTA; UnSA

What would I do without this world faceless incurious [*Author's own English vers. of his* "Que ferais-je sans ce monde sans visage sans questions"]. Samuel Beckett. ModIr; NoAM; YaTCFP, *tr. by* the author

What Would I Give? Christina Georgina Rossetti. NPeEn

What would I have you do? I'll tell you, kinsman. Advice to a Reckless Youth. Ben Johnson. TreFP

What would Jung make of such levitation? My Son Shows Me a Photograph of Michael Jordan Performing a Slam Dunk. Louis Phillips. ReTh

What would my mother say if she could see. Domestic Humiliation. Allison Joseph. SweBea

What would she put in it? If She Only Had One Minute. Kay Ryan. ExTi

What would the blank, pared People say. What Would They Say? Alfonsina Storni. SonAtl, *tr. by* Rebecca Allan and Lisa Martin

What would the dead want from us. For Andrew Wood. James Fenton. NAMCP V.2

What would the self. Chemise. Kay Ryan. CalPo

What Would They Say? Alfonsina Storni. SonAtl, *tr. by* Rebecca Allan and Lisa Martin

What would this Man? Now upward will he soar. Alexander Pope. HeIP-4 *Fr.* Essay on Man, An.

What would we talk about before? I ask; what of, when we had. When We Meet Again. Giovanna Pollarolo. TANSG, *tr. by* Marjorie Agosin

What would you buy? (LL) Dream-Pedlary. Thomas Lovell Beddoes. OBEV; OxAEP

What would you do inside me? Hive. Nick Flynn. LegDan

What would you give for one of the old yellow streetcars. Stepping Out of Poetry. Gerald Stern. GoPo

What would you have? Your gentleness shall force. William Shakespeare. OxAEP-1 *Fr.* As You Like It.

What wouldn't you give for something Foolish. When Everything Is Goneril. Lee Patton. IaFF

What wouldst thou have? a King, a Lord, a Knight. Anabaptist, The. Rowland Watkyns. BASC

What Yo' Gwine to [*or* t'] Do When Yo' [*or de*] Lamp Burn Down? *Unknown.* APN-2

What, you are stepping westward?—"Yea." Stepping Westward. William Wordsworth. NPBRoP

What you can see. Steve Jonas. EGAG

What You Can't See. Karen Chase. SeSe

What you could not see in a face. (LL) Everything passes and vanishes. William Allingham. NPeEn; OxBEV; WaAnP

What you did to the blues. Blues for Bird. Linda France. NeBl

What you don't trust to stone. Eternal Moment. Sándor Weöres. IQMS, *tr. by* Edwin Morgan

What You Find in the Woods. James Longenbach. NAPBL

What You Get. Leontia Flynn. NIrP

What you give me is. Love Poem. Denise Levertov. NIL-7

What you have heard is true. I was in his house. Colonel, The. Carolyn Forché. AmWaPo; MakPoe; MotU; NAMCP V.2; OBWP; OxBoAm; PoAgWa; SoSe-8; WaAnP

What you knew of me. Eugenio Montale. PLBUT, *tr. by* Jonathan Galassi

What you love in me. Woman, The. Shakuntala Hawoldar. HAWP

What you may cluster 'round the knees of space. To the Cloud Juggler. Hart Crane. HarvBoo

What you mean to say about the film is that. Over Coffee. Bob Hicok. AmPoNex

What you need to know. Magic Carpet, The. Maurice Kilwein Guevara. TouFir

What you say deadens your legs. Enjoyment Body. Jonathan Cott. AHA

What you see is what you get. Landing. Sandy Shreve. IFF

What You Should Know to Be a Poet. Gary Snyder. APSN; OxBoAm; PFTM-2

What you thought it would be. (LL) Apple. Susan Stewart. AmAlph; BAP-01

What you want is for the tiger to eat me. Side 22. Víctor Hernández Cruz. PueRic

What you'd imagine the sound of. Capelin Scull. Michael Crummey. Coast

What young Raw Muisted Beau Bred at his Glass. Horace. NPeEn, *tr. by* Allan Ramsay

What your look meant then. (LL) Watergaw, The. Hugh MacDiarmid. FaBoVe; HarvBoo; NAEL-6v2; NePenScot; NPeEn

What you're reading (if you're reading me) are the effects. Edoardo Sanguineti. ItPo *Fr.* Scartabello.

What you've heard is true—I've gone to Thessilonika. Demas, in Love with This Present World. Kristin Fogdall. PoDa

Whate'er is Born of Mortal Birth. William Blake. NAEL-6v2; NAEL-7v2 *Fr.* Songs of Experience.

Whate'er my darkness be. Tenebrae. John Banister Tabb. APN-2

Whate'er we leave to God, God does. Inspiration. Henry David Thoreau. APN-1; ColAP; NCAP; OxBoAm

Whatever. Wes "Scoop." Nisker. WhBo

Whatever Became Of: Freud? Edward Field. BodElec

Whatever city or country road. Double Elegy. Michael S. Harper. ESEAA; NAMCP V.2; NoAM; WaAnP

Whatever clime we travel or explore. Evan Evans. AngWePo *Fr.* Love of Our Country, The.

Whatever constitutes. Act of Love, The. Robert Creeley. CAP-8

Whatever exists is now. What Is Not Mine. Hamda Khamees. PoArWo, *tr. by* Joseph T. Zeidan

Whatever force insatiable death has, how much power. On the Death of the Noble and Gentle Woman, Lady Joanna Kelley. Elizabeth Jane Leon. EMWP

Whatever Happened? Philip Larkin. OxBSo

Whatever Happened to Conway Twitty? Tim Thorne. BMAP

WHATEVER happened to the elephant. Hurrah for Thunder. Christopher Okigbo. HBAPE

Whatever happens with us, your body. Adrienne Rich. EroLit; NALW; NoAM; WaAnP *Fr.* Twenty-one Love Poems.

Whatever he had done was not quite right. Case Study. Nissim Ezekiel. PML

Whatever he has done. Man Running. Richard Wilbur. OxBoAm

Whatever he needs, he has or doesn't. Summer-Camp Bus Pulls Away from the Curb, The. Sharon Olds. PLBUT

Whatever he says. Karai Senryū. EMJL, *tr. by* Makoto Ueda

Whatever I was able to acquire in my life by way of acts visible to all, that is, to win my own transparency, I owe to a kind of special courage Poetry gave me: to be wind for the kite and kite for the wind, even when the sky is missing. Odysseus Elytis. GifTon *Fr.* Anoint the Ariston.

Whatever it is, I shouldn't hesitate. *Unknown.* PriapPo *Fr.* Priapus Poems, The.

Whatever it is, it bothers me all the time. (LL) Laguna Blues. Charles Wright. NAMCP V.2; PoPoPo; WaAnP

Whatever it is, it must have. American Poetry. Louis Simpson. FaBoA; NAMCP V.2; NoAM; WaAnP

Whatever it is, it's a passion. Love in America. Marianne Moore. NIL-7

Whatever it is that puts the dipper in my hand. Origin. Robin Behn. AmAlph

Whatever it was she had so fiercely fought. Karl Shapiro. ChIV-1 *Fr.* Adam and Eve.

Whatever it was to you. For Walt Whitman. Patricia Goedicke. ViWalt

Whatever Light. Stephen Corey. IaFF

Whatever lives must meet its end. Drinking Alone in the Rainy Season. T'ao Ch'ien. CrYelRi, *tr. by* Sam Hamill

Whatever Lola Wants (Lola Gets). Richard Adler and Jerry Ross. ReLy

Whatever Lola wants, Lola gets. Whatever Lola Wants (Lola Gets). Richard Adler and Jerry Ross. ReLy

Whatever the bird is, is perfect in the bird. Birds. Judith Wright. NoP-4

Whatever the cost. *Unknown.* ArkPo, *tr. by* Helen Craig McCullough

Whatever they wanted for their sons. Déjà Vu. Shirley Kaufman. DTA

Whatever was else or less. Road, The. Robert Creeley. BodElec

Whatever went wrong, that week, was more than weather. Hairline Fracture, A. Amy Clampitt. NoAM

Whatever Will Be, Will Be (Que Sera, Sera). Ray Evans and Jay Livingston. ReLy

Whatever wisdom sleep with thee. (LL) Alfred Tennyson. CABP; NAEL-6v2; NAEL-7v2 *Fr.* In Memoriam A. H. H.

Whatever you can do. Johann Wolfgang von Goethe. RaBo

Whatever you have to say, leave. These Days. Charles Olson. APT-2; RaBo; TWF

Whatever You Say Say Nothing. Seamus Heaney. OBWP

Whatever You Want. Angel González. VCWP, *tr. by* Steven Ford Brown and Revuelta Gutierrez

What'll I Do? Irving Berlin. ReLy

What's a boy to do, both shoes caught in the tar. Crossing the Road. Walter McDonald. PML

What's become of those small black signs, image and suggestion. Inn of Angels, The. Giampiero Neri. ItPo, *tr. by* Gayle Ridinger

What's become of Waring. Waring. Robert Browning. NPeEn

"What's beyond making love?" A true question. Green Place, A. Honor Moore. FFC

What's de Use ob Wukin in de Summer Time at All. Maggie Pogue Johnson. CBWP-4

What's death more than a departure; the dead go. William Habington. NOSC *Fr.* Castara.

What's Going On. Lavinia Greenlaw. NoP-5

What's going on here? Flypaper. Theodore Weiss. BodElec

What's going on in my garden? Who can explain. *Unknown.* PriapPo *Fr.* Priapus Poems, The.

What's going on this May morning on the hillsides? Ascension Thursday. Saunders Lewis. BBMWP, *tr. by* Gwyn Williams

What's going to be the end for both of us—God? Twelve Lines about the Burning Bush. Melech Ravitch. BBASP, *tr. by* Ruth Whitman

What's Going to Happen to the Tots? Noël Coward. NBLV

What's Good for the Soul is Good for Sales. Richard Wilbur. NBLV *Fr.* Flippancies.

What's happened to your beautiful dress. Orbit. Gig Ryan. BMAP

What's Happening. Jayne Cortez. PrTe

What's his offense? Two Variations on a Theme. Carl Rakosi. APT-2

What's in a Name? Christina Georgina Rossetti. FaBoVe

What's in a Name? Some Letter I Always Forget. Ogden Nash. AmWit

What's in a name? What's in a name? Fame. Josephine D. Henderson Heard. CBWP-4

What's in the body you've forgotten. Song. Robert Creeley. OnScMo

What's in the brain[e] that in[c]k may character. William Shakespeare. PBRV; TreFP *Fr.* Sonnets.

What's It For. Pamela Stewart. ExTi

What's it like? You take it from me. Capper Kaplinski at the North Side Cue Club. Hayden Carruth. MoASP

What's it you're howling, siren-telephone. Tatiana Shcherbina. CRWP, *tr. by* Daniel Weissbort

What's Left. Kerry Hardie. BeAl; NIrP

What's left. Vision of Rahoon, A. John McAuliffe. NIrP

What's Left. Jack Myers. BodElec

What's left but this to say of any war? (LL) *Vale* from Carthage. Peter Viereck. MoAmPo; PWW2; WoPoe

What's left for me to say? God. Olga Popova. ItGoST, *tr. by* J. Kates

What's left is the tiny gold glove. Amateur Night. Natasha Trethewey. OxAAAP

What's left now is what happened long before. Thirty Years After. János Vajda. IQMS, *tr. by* Dorren Bell

What's left of you hanging in the rooms. What's Left of You. Daria Menicanti. CItWP, *tr. by* Cinzia Sartini Blum and Lara Trubowitz

What's left, what's left of love. Hopeless Eveningsong. Leonidas Malenis. SonAtl, *tr. by* George Emba, Maria Henson, Elpida Kyriakide and Eleftherios Papaleontiou

What's Lost. Michael Crummey. Coast

What's lovelier / than your shoulders? Vera Pavlova. CRWP *Fr.* Letter from Memory.

What's Mo' Temptin' to de Palate? Maggie Pogue Johnson. CBWP-4

What's my name? What am I? Anon. Conor O'Callaghan. NIrP

What's new? Prophet's Lantern, The. David Lehman. KGB

What's new? I'm still in Illinois. Letter to Friends East and West. Albert Goldbarth. IllVoic

What's Not in the Heart. Abba Kovner. AF, *tr. by* Shirley Kaufman

What's on this May morning in the hills? Ascension Thursday. Saunders Lewis. OBWVE, *tr. by* Gwyn Morgan

What's playing at the Roxy? Frank Loesser. ReLy

What's so drastic in the Germans. By Fire or Flood. David Lindley. NLP

What's So Funny 'bout Peace, Love and Understanding. Robert Long. SwNoth

What's that bird, Mr Long? Geoffrey Lehmann. BMAP *Fr.* Ross's Poems.

What's that?! hisses my wife. Amplified Dog. Charles Harper Webb. SUP

What's that in which good housewives take delight. *Unknown.* EroLit *Fr.* Kitty's Atalantis for the year 1766.

What's That Smell in the Kitchen? Marge Piercy. NBLV; NIL-7; NIP-4

"What's that?" the boy asks his mother, pointing to the flag. Giulia Niccolai. ItPo *Fr.* Frisbees '88.

What's the attraction of age that makes. Attractions. Alexander Shurbanov. PML, *tr. by* Ewald Osers

What's the best thing in the world? Best Thing in the World, The. Elizabeth Barrett Browning. VWP

What's the best thing in the world? Best, The. Elizabeth Barrett Browning. OxBEV

What's the difference if I'm aged. *Unknown.* PriapPo *Fr.* Priapus Poems, The.

What's the fault of the poor mind? Kamalākānta Bhattācārya. SinGod, *tr. by* Rachel Fell McDermott

What's the fault of the poor mind? Rāmprasād Sen. SinGod, *tr. by* Rachel Fell McDermott

What's the French for "fiddle-de-dee"? For "Fiddle-De-De." John Hollander. P180

What's the lord's vast wealth. Issa. SoOfWa, *tr. by* Sam Hamill

What's the matter. Dickery Dean. Dennis Lee. TLR

What's the merriest burial ground? Sándor Petőfi. IQMS *Fr.* Clouds, The.

What's the name of this game we're playing? Stop! You're Breakin' My Heart. Ted Koehler. ReLy

What's the name of this town. I Arrived in that Town, Everyone Greeted Me and I Recognized no One. When I Was Going to Read My Verses, the Devil, Hidden Behind a Tree, Called Out to Me Sarcastically and Filled My Hands with Newspaper Clippings. J. V. Foix. PFTM-1

What's the News? William Sydney Graham. FaBoWar

What's the news? Sweet Bye and Bye. Ogden Nash. ReLy

What's the news, my bold. What's the News? William Sydney Graham. FaBoWar

What's the plaint against me, watchman? *Unknown.* PriapPo *Fr.* Priapus Poems, The.

What's the purpose of the thing? Whose idea. Wishbone USA. Joyce Sutphen. RWB

What's the text today for reading. Morning. Louisa Sarah Bevington. PEW

What's the use. As Long As I Live. Ted Koehler. ReLy

What's the use of all that noise and money? (LL) In a Tangle of Cliffs. Hanshan (Cold Mountain). BB; CCL1; NDACCP, *tr. by* Gary Snyder

What's the use of all this I ask you your fever your sobbing. Machinery. David Huerta. RMCMP, *tr. by* Mark Schafer

What's this? A dish for fat lips. Shape of the Fire, The. Theodore Roethke. VCAP

What's this morn's bright eye to me. Morning Hymn. Joseph Beaumont. SacPr

What's this? What does the anger of the gods ordain? *Unknown.* PriapPo *Fr.* Priapus Poems, The.

What's white is cloud, and blue, mountain. For Sanje, a Hermit. Daegak Euchon. BecRai, *tr. by* Kim Daljin, Kim Won-Chung and Christopher Merrill

What's wrong with American literature? Question and Answer. William Carlos Williams. HarvBoo

What's wrong with this What's Wrong with this Picture picture. What's Wrong. Geoff Ward. VaPo

What's your pet name? Collective noun? Crash of rhinos, A. Paisley Rekdal. LegDan

What's Your Sign? Alex Rawls.

   April 19, 1999. AnSo

   August 29, 1999. AnSo

   December 31, 1999. AnSo

   February 18, 1999. AnSo

   January 1, 1999. AnSo

   July 10, 1999. AnSo

   June 9, 1999. AnSo

   March 12, 1999. AnSo

   May 26, 1999. AnSo

   November 20, 1999. AnSo

   October 1, 1999. AnSo

   September 25, 1999. AnSo

What's your story Atlanta/ America? Threnody. Kalamu ya Salaam. BtF

What's Your Story, Morning Glory. Jack Lawrence and Paul Francis Webster. ReLy

What's your story, morning glory.   What's Your Story, Morning Glory.   Jack Lawrence and Paul Francis Webster.   ReLy

What's Your Take.   Jayne Cortez.   PrTe

Whatso men sayn.   Men Only Pretend.   *Unknown.*   WaAnP

Whatsume'er the failings on his part.   Charles Dickens.   FaBoVe *Fr.* Great Expectations.

Wheat.   Ishihara Yoshiro.   IPoFL

Wheat cock up their shoulders and turn away, The.   Pulling in the Nets.   C. Mikal Oness.   GeoHom

Wheat fields blaze, wide waving plains, The.   Grain Burning Far Away.   Thomas Lux.   AmAlph

Wheat grows from the earth.   Gu Cheng.   WoBe *Fr.* Liquid Mercury.

Wheatfield Under Clouded Sky.   Campbell McGrath.   NeAmPo

Wheat-miners.   Michael Field.   ViWPN

Wheel.   Michael Palmer.   BodElec

Wheel, The.   Wendell Berry.   RSR; UpMys

Wheel, The.   Edwin Muir.   NAMCP V.1; NoAM

Wheel, The.   Molly Peacock.   RA

Wheel Building.   Kate Taylor.   PfS

Wheel Ethics.   Charles Richards Dodge.   ArBi

Wheel of the quivering Meat, The.   Jack Kerouac.   PFTM-2; PmAP *Fr.* Mexico City Blues.

Wheel Revolves, The.   Kenneth Rexroth.   NAMCP V.1; NoAM

Wheel River.   Pei Di and Wang Wei.
  Bank of the Magnolias, The.   CCL1, *tr.* by Michael Bullock and C. J. Chen
  Cove of the Wall of Meng, The.   CCL1, *tr.* by Michael Bullock and C. J. Chen
  Deer Enclosure, The.   CCL1, *tr.* by Michael Bullock and C. J. Chen
  Hermitage of the Bamboos, The.   CCL1, *tr.* by Michael Bullock and C. J. Chen
  Hill of Huazi, The.   CCL1, *tr.* by Michael Bullock and C. J. Chen
  Hill of the Hatchet-Leaved Bamboos.   CCL1, *tr.* by Michael Bullock and C. J. Chen
  Lake Yi.   CCL1, *tr.* by Michael Bullock and C. J. Chen
  Magnolia Enclosure, The.   CCL1, *tr.* by Michael Bullock and C. J. Chen
  Path of the Ashtrees, The.   CCL1, *tr.* by Michael Bullock and C. J. Chen
  Stream at the House of the Luans, The.   CCL1, *tr.* by Michael Bullock and C. J. Chen

Wheelchair Butterfly, The.   James Tate.   NAMCP V.2; NoAM

Wheelchair child, The.   Jerry Kilbride.   WhBo

Wheeling and wheeling above the woods.   Hawk Above Felindre, The.   Alan Llwyd.   BBMWP, *tr.* by Joseph P. Clancy

Wheelmen's Song.   Will M. Carleton.   ArBi

Wheels: "My brother kept."   Jim Daniels.   P180

Wheels.   Douglas Livingstone.   TSAP

Wheels.   Sarah Rabkin.   RaF

Wheels are growing on rose-bushes.   Affectionate.   Else Von Freytag-Loringhoven.   PFTM-1

Wheels hurry onward, onward, The.   Cartload of Shoes, A.   Abraham Sutskever.   HP, *tr.* by David G. Roskies

Wheels jammed and flaming on a metal sea. (LL)   V-J Day.   John Ciardi.   OtW; PWW2

Wheels line up, pretty right, right, The.   Cattle Loading.   Gordon Mackay-Warna.   NOBAu, *tr.* by George von Brandenstein

Wheels of Jagannatha, The.   Sri Sri.   HotL, *tr.* by V. Narayana Rao

Wheels of the train were a runner's heartbeat, The.   White Bears: Tolstoy at Astapovo.   Linda Bierds.   AmAlph

Wheels of the Trains, The.   W. S. Merwin.   GM

Wheels within Wheels.   Seamus Heaney.   ArBi; ModIr

Wheesht, wheesht, my foolish hert.   Wheesht, Wheesht.   Hugh MacDiarmid.   OxAEP-2

Whelmed by my exalted moon.   Yun Söndo.   CATKP *Fr.* Angler's Calendar, The.

When.   Sharon Olds.   AtGh

When a Beau Goes In.   Gavin Ewart.   OBWP

When a Beautiful Woman Gets on the Jutiapa Bus.   Belle Waring.   EmeKit; PBCAP

When a Beggar Beholds You.   *Unknown.*   BLPJKO, *tr.* by Gertrude Laughlin Joerissen

When a bird flies out.   Bird and man.   *Unknown.*   SonAtl, *tr.* by Serone Bell, Andy Cox and Patricia Jabbeh Wesley

When a boy, serious and standing.   Photograph of a Boy.   Carlos Sahagún.   RaW, *tr.* by David Ignatow

When a brass sun staggers above the sky.   Tramp.   Richard Hughes.   MoBrPo

When a chile gets to be thirteen.   Mystery.   Langston Hughes.   APT-2

When a crowd of cares.   Aneirin.   NePenScot *Fr.* Gododdin, The.

When a disciple asked of Lu Chü how.   Sage in Unison, The.   Harold Stewart.   NOBAu

When a dream gets kicked around. (LL)   Langston Hughes.   APSN; APT-2; OxBoAm; SSLK *Fr.* Lenox Avenue Mural.

When a dream is born in you.   Pinch of Salt, A.   Robert Graves.   MoBrPo

When a Fellow's on the Level with a Girl That's on the Square.   George M. Cohan.   ReLy

When a fish.   *Unknown.*   SonAtl, *tr.* by Silvana Woods

When a Friend Dies.   Marge Piercy.   HeIP-4

When a friend dies, part.   When a Friend.   Stephen Dobyns.   BeAl

When a girl meets a boy.   How About You.   Ralph Freed.   ReLy

When a girl's in love with someone.   Who?   Oscar, II Hammerstein and Otto Harbach.   ReLy

When a gust from above plays—with the sea.   Foam.   T. Arfon Williams.   BBMWP, *tr.* by Emyr Lewis

When a guy calls your jazz show.   You and Them.   Patty Seyburn.   AmPoNex

When a half-crazed woman stepped aboard.   Madame Butterfly.   David Moolten.   BloBone

When a heavy cart.   Buson.   SoOfWa, *tr.* by Sam Hamill

When a man has grown a body.   Simple Truths.   William Heyen.   CAP-8

When a man hath no freedom to fight for at home.   Stanzas.   Lord Byron.   NBLV; NoP-4; NoP-5; OxAEP-2; TRP

When a man walks in the forest and lifts his voice there.   Song of My People-Forest, People-Sea.   Uri Zvi Greenberg.   FIT, *tr.* by Robert Friend

When a monk looks at the green mountain.   At the Zendo.   Jinkag Haesim.   BecRai, *tr.* by Kim Daljin, Kim Won-Chung and Christopher Merrill

When a Negro comes in question you may watch the Southern press.   Southern Press, The.   Lizelia Augusta Jenkins Moorer.   CBWP-3

When a new child comes.   At Terezin.   Teddy.   INSAB

When a new world is born, the old.   Rattle.   Peter Blue Cloud.   HATNAP

When a Poet is Born.   Stefan Tsanev.   CSCBP, *tr.* by Georgi Belev and Lisa Sapinkopf

When a poet is weak.   Weak Poet, The.   David Shapiro.   BodElec

When a puppet kicks the bucket, a black spider weaves a white web around the stage.   Funeral, The.   Miroslav Holub.   MotU, *tr.* by Dana Hábová and David Young

When a shepherd dies, his death is no different from Galen's.   Elegy to Aisha, An.   Abdul Wahab Al-Bayati.   IrPoTo, *tr.* by Farouk Abdel Wahab

When a ship passes at night on the Clyde.   Ships.   Douglas Dunn.   EdScPo

When a storm turns the corner, she wonders where to look.   When Ships Sail Too Close.   Lynn Davies.   Coast

When a stream ran across my path.   Herb-Garden, The.   Charles Hubert Sisson.   HarvBoo

When a tree falls.   My Philosophy.   Dan Nielsen.   SUP

When a whale rolls ashore.   Life Forms.   Robin Becker.   BodElec

When a Woman Feels Alone.   May Sarton.   HW

When A Woman Gets Blue.   Norman Jordan.   ISC

When a woman is without love.   Love's Cursive.   Kim Namjo.   CAMKP, *tr.* by David R. McCann and Hyunjae Yee Sallee

When a woman looks up at you with a twist about her eyes.   Made to Order Smile, The.   Paul Laurence Dunbar.   GT

When Abraham Lincoln was shoveled into the tombs, he forgot the copperheads and the assassin.   Cool Tombs.   Carl Sandburg.   APT-1; HeIP-4; MoAmPo; NAMCP V.1; NoAM; TCAPo; TFi
  (When Abraham Lincoln was shoveled into the tombs, he forgot the.)   ColAP

When Adam dalf and Eve span.   *Unknown.*   NPeEn

When Adam delf [*or* dalf]/ and Eve span.   Pointless Pride of Man, The.   *Unknown.*   FaBoVe

When Adam found his rib was gone.   Lady's-Maid's Song, The.   John Hollander.   OxBoAm

When Adam walked in Eden young.   A. E. Housman.   ChIV-1

When Africa Speaks.   Jude Chudi Okpala.   BtF

When after a long silence one picks up the pen.   Mark Strand.   CAP-8 *Fr.* Dark Harbor.

When after muchos años.   Wild West Workshop Poem.   Anselm Hollo.   PmAP

When, after storms that woodlands rue.   Requiem[:] for Soldiers Lost in Ocean Transports, A.   Herman Melville.   APN-2

When afternoon.   You.   Lucile Adler.   ICANM

When age hath made me what I am not now.   Upon His Picture.   Thomas Randolph.   BASC

When air's chill north his noisome frosts shall blow.   Hesiod.   NOSC *Fr.* Georgics of Heisod, The.

When *Alexander* entred phrygian land.   E. D. in Commendation of the Author and His Choise.   "E. D."   EMWP

When Alexander Pope strolled in the city.   Mr. Pope.   Allen Tate.   APT-2; ColAP; FuPo; NAMCP V.1; NoAM

When all else fails.   After Fighting for Hours.   Kate Gleason.   BAP-97

When all have forsaken me here.   Lord's Arrival, The.   Endre Ady.   IQMS, *tr.* by Anton N. Nyerges

When all her brothers in the house.   Killary.   Herbert Trench.   IrV

When all her robes are gone. (LL) Madrigal: "My Love in her attire doth show her wit." *Unknown.* HeIP-4; NAEL-6v1; NIP-4; OBEV; TFi

When all is done, and my last word is said. When All Is Done. Paul Laurence Dunbar. SacPr; TCAPo

When all is over and you march for home. Spoils. Robert Graves. WeW-3

When all is ruin once again. (LL) To Be Carved on a Stone at Thoor Ballylee. William Butler Yeats. NAMCP V.1; NoAM; NoP-4; NoP-5

When all is said and done. Home. Dennis O'Driscoll. BeAl

When all mankind are free. (LL) *Unknown.* APN-2; CBCWP

When All My Five and Country Senses See. Dylan Thomas. MoBrPo; NAMCP V.2; NoAM; PoA 2002

When all the altar lights were dead. Resurrection. Alfred Noyes. SacPr

When all the others were away at Mass. Seamus Heaney. BeAl; BLT; InoFa; ItP; NoP-5; PML; PNI *Fr.* Clearances.

When all the over-work of life. Christina Georgina Rossetti. VWP

When all the women in the transport. Pigtail. Tadeusz Różewicz. BeAl; HP; PoSu, *tr. by* Adam Czerniawski

When all the world is a hopeless jumble. Over the Rainbow. E. Y. Harburg. NAAPv.2; ReLy

When all the world would keep a matter hid. Fabulists, The. Rudyard Kipling. OxBEV

When all the *World's* a *Riddle,* why not I? (LL) Elizabeth Tipper. EMWP; NOSC *Fr.* Pilgrim's Viaticum; or, The Destitute, But Not Forlorn.

When all this *All* doth passe from age to age. Fulke, 1st Baron Brooke Greville. NoSic; PtR *Fr.* Caelica.

When all this is over, said the swineherd. Swineherd. Eiléan Ní Chuilleanáin. EmeKit; NPeEn

When All Thy Mercies. Joseph Addison. SacPr

When all was quiet and serene, a storm broke out at the dead. Riot, A. Mrs. Henry Linden. CBWP-4

When all were dreaming but Pastheen Power. Song of the Ghost, The. Alfred Perceval Graves. IrV

When all your world of beauty's [*or* Beautie's] gone. (LL) To Dianeme ("Sweet, be not proud of those two eyes.") Robert Herrick. BASC; NOSC; OBEV

When America closes for the night. Promises. Richard Shelton. GifTon

When Americans say a man. Language Lesson 1976. Heather McHugh. ItP

When an archer is shooting for nothing. Need to Win, The. Chuang Tzu. BLT, *tr. by* Thomas Merton

When an early Autumn walks the land. Early Autumn. Johnny Mercer. ReLy

When an effigy cries. Miraculous Image. Miranda Field. LegDan

When an irresistible force such as you. Something's Gotta Give. Johnny Mercer. ReLy

When anger spreads in the breast. Sappho. SaLy, *tr. by* Diane Rayor

When answers took no airships, walked a while. (LL) Gwendolyn Brooks. ColAP; PtR *Fr.* Notes from the Childhood and the Girlhood.

When approaching my father. Wildlife. Karen Williams. BRtP

When April with its sweet showers. Geoffrey Chaucer. *See* Whan that April[le] with his[e] shoures [*or* showres] so[o]te.

When are the children all happy and gay? Christmas Times. Maggie Pogue Johnson. CBWP-4

When are we going to see each other at last? (LL) Henri Michaux. GPTC; MotU *Fr.* I Am Writing to You from a Far-Off Country.

When as in the silks my Julia goes. Robert Herrick. *See* Whenas in silks my Julia goes.

When as Mans life, the light of humane lust. Fulke, 1st Baron Brooke Greville. CABP; NOSC; NoSic *Fr.* Caelica.

When as the chill charocco blows. Thomas Bonham. OBEV

When as the Nightingall chanted her Vesper. John Cleveland. NPeEn

When as the prince of Angels puffed with pride. To St. Michael the Archangel. Henry Constable. ChIV-2

When As the Rye Reach to the Chin. George Peele. *See* Song: "Whenas [*or* When as] the Rye [*or* Rie] reach to the chin."

When asked her opinion. Cowboy Film. Tom Matthews. PNI

When Asked to Lie Down on the Altar. Eleanor Wilner. TaR

When at break of day at a riverside. Piano and Drums. Gabriel Okara. NIP-4

When at Collatium this false lord arrived. William Shakespeare. NoSic *Fr.* Rape of Lucrece, The.

When at last he was well enough to take the sun. Leg in a Plaster Cast, A. Muriel Rukeyser. MoAmPo

When at last the prow crunches on sand. Voyager. Ken Morrice. EdScPo

When / At the close of war. I Say, Mr. A. Samuel Allen. SeSe

When at the first I took my pen in hand. John Bunyan. FaBoVe *Fr.* Author's Apology for His Book, The.

When Athens all the Graecian state did guide. John Dryden. NOSC *Fr.* Oedipus.

When August and the sultry summer's drouth. Valley, The. Agnes Mary Frances Robinson. VWP

When August was finally done, his. My Heart. Laura Kasischke. AmPoNex

When Autumn Came. Faiz Ahmad Faiz. PLBUT; PoetW, *tr. by* Naomi Lazard

When autumn comes, my orchard trees alone. Art and Life. Agnes Mary Frances Robinson. OxBSo; VWP

When autumn rains flatten sycamore leaves. Gary Soto. NoAM *Fr.* Elements of San Joaquin, The.

When avarice enslaves the mind. Negro Boy, The. David Samwell. AngWePo

When awful darkness and silence reign. Dong with a Luminous Nose, The. Edward Lear. NOxBChV; OxAEP-2; OxBEV

When Babe Ruth points, the whole table stops eating. What is it, Babe. Babe Ruth Pointing. Timothy Kelly. MotU

When Baby's cries grew hard to bear. L'Enfant Glacé. Harry Graham. NBLV; OBCoV

When Bad Angels Love Women. Julie Moulds. AmPoNex

When Barbarians overran the city. Thatched Hut, The. Tu Fu [*or* Du Fu]. CrYelRi, *tr. by* Sam Hamill

When beauty breaks and falls asunder. Juan's Song. Louise Bogan. NoP-4; NoP-5; OxBoAm

When beechen buds begin to swell. Yellow Violet, The. William Cullen Bryant. NAAL-3

When Bells stop ringing—Church—begins. Emily Dickinson. APN-2

When Bess, the landlord's black-eyed. Bess. Linda Pastan. GoPo

When Bill was a lad he was terribly bad. Those Two Boys. Franklin Pierce Adams. OBCoV

When Bird died, I didn't mind. Filling the Gap. Lawson Fusao Inada. FTtHH; OpBo

When bird passes on. Masahide. ZenPo, *tr. by* Takashi Ikemoto and Lucien Stryk

When Bishop Berkeley said "there was no matter." Lord Byron. NOBRP *Fr.* Don Juan.

When bitter passion stirred the earth. Cuillin, The. Rayne Mackinnon. EdScPo

When blessed Marie [*or* Mary] wip'd her Saviours [*or* Saviour's] feet. Mary [*or* Marie] Magdalene. George Herbert. SacPr

When bored by the drone of the wedlocked pair. Sacred and Profane Love, or, There's Nothing New under the Moon Either. Peter De Vries. NBLV; OBCoV

When both hands of the town clock stood at twelve. Village Noon; Mid-Day Bells. Merrill Moore. MoAmPo

When boys played women's parts, you'd think the stage. Epilogue to "The Parson's Wedding." Thomas Killigrew. NOSC

When "Brad" is lying naked, or rather naked is lying. My Last Hustler. Richard Howard. NAMCP V.2

When breezes are soft and skies are fair. William Cullen Bryant. ITBLP *Fr.* Green River.

When breezes are soft and skies are fair. Green River. William Cullen Bryant. APN-1; TCAPo

When Britain first, at heaven's command. David Mallet and James Thomson. OBWP; TreFP; WaAnP *Fr.* Alfred: A Masque.

When Britain really ruled the waves. William Schwenck Gilbert. NAEL-6v2 *Fr.* Iolanthe.

When British Freedom for an happier land. Samuel Taylor Coleridge. CenSon *Fr.* Effusions.

When buck fever struck. You don't Know What Happened When You Froze. Ansel Talvikki. NeAmPo

When Buddhist liberation no longer liberates. Deathbed Song. Soyo Taeneung. BecRai, *tr. by* Kim Daljin, Kim Won-Chung and Christopher Merrill

When butterflies dance around the house in the East. Dream of a Butterfly, The. Hurbak Myungjo. BecRai, *tr. by* Kim Daljin, Kim Won-Chung and Christopher Merrill

When by its magic lantern Spleen. Matthew Green. OxAEP-1 *Fr.* Spleen, The [Complete].

When by me in the dusk my child sits down. John Berryman. ColAP *Fr.* Homage to Mistress Bradstreet.

When by mistake you miss. Your Own Image. Michael Ryan. YaYoPo

When by the labour of my 'ands. Half-Ballad of Waterval. Rudyard Kipling. FaBoWar

When by thy scorn[e], O murderess[e] [*or* murd'ress *or* murdress], I am dead. Apparition, The. John Donne. BASC; FSCP; HeIP-4; NAEL-6v1; NAEL-7v1; NAWM-5v1; NoP-5; NoSic; OBEV; RaF; SoSe-8; TFi

When by Zeus relenting the mandate is revoked. Phoebus with Admetus. George Meredith. OBEV

When Caesar saw his army prone to war. Lucan. NoSic *Fr.* Civil War [Bellum Civile] *or* Pharsalia.

When came the last, sad word, *Farewell!.* (LL) Memory, A. Adah Isaacs Menken. CBWP-1; NAAPv.1; ViWPN

When Catrin was a small child. Foghorns. Gillian Clarke. TCAWP

When chapman [or chapmen] billies leave the street. Tam o' Shanter; A Tale. Robert Burns. CABP; NAEL-6v2; NAEL-7v2; NePenScot; NoP-4; NoP-5; NPBRoP; NPeEn; OBNV; WaAnP

When cherry flowers begin to blow. Yuki. Mary Fenollosa. NAAPv.1

When children are dying all around you. Shakespeare's Eyebrows. Sylvia Adams. IaFF

When children play the livelong day. Children in Slavery. Eliza Lee Cabot Follen. SWaP

When children slap their father's face. Robert Desnos. PFTM-1

When chill November's surly blast. Man Was Made to Mourn, a Dirge. Robert Burns. TreFP

When Christ from Heaven comes down straightway. For the Company Underground. Francis MacNamara. NOBAu

When civil fury [or dudgeon] first grew high. Samuel Butler. BASC; CABP; NAEL-6v1; NAEL-7v1 Fr. Hudibras.

When civilization was European. Racine. Frederick Seidel. OxBoAm

When Cleomira disbelieves. Force of Love, The. Samuel Jones. NPeEn

When Clifford wasn't back to camp by nine. After the Wilderness. Andrew Hudgins. CBCWP

When Clumsy harks the gladsome ting-a-lings. Gjertrud Schnackenberg. NoAM Fr. Two Tales of Clumsy.

When, Coelia, must my old day set. To Coelia. Charles Cotton. OBEV

When Cromwell "slighted" Kenilworth. State of Preservation. Celeste Turner Wright. FFC

When Cupid first instructs his darts to fly. Prophecy of Famine, The. Charles Churchill.

When Dad and Mother discovered one another. Come Fly with Me. Sammy Cahn. ReLy

When Daddy and Mum got quite plastered. Limerick. Unknown. OBCoV

When Daddy Cums from Wuk. Maggie Pogue Johnson. CBWP-4

When Daffadils begin to peere. William Shakespeare. See When daffodils begin to peer.

When Daffodils Begin to Peer. William Shakespeare. NoP-4; NoSic; OxAEP-1; TFi; UV; WaAnP Fr. Winter's Tale, The.

When daisies pied and violets Blue. William Shakespeare. NAEL-6v1; NBLV; NIL-7; NIP-4; NoP-5; NoSic; OBEV; TFi Fr. Love's Labour's Lost.

When Daniel Boone goes by, at night. Daniel Boone. Rosemary Benét and Stephen Vincent Benét and Stephen Vincent Benét. APT-2

When darkness crept and grew. Under the Hill. Richard Eberhart. PoA 2002

When darkness is darkest, and sorrow most sorrow. (LL) Window Just Over the Street, The. Alice Cary. PoBW; SWaP

When darkness settles itself. Within the Seasons. Peter Blue Cloud. HATNAP

When Dasies pied, and Violets blew. William Shakespeare. See When daisies pied and violets Blue.

When dawn hennas her hands with the blood. Hayâlî. OLP, tr. by Walter Andrews, Najaat Black and Mehmet Kalpakli

When de Saints Go Ma'chin' Home. Sterling Allen Brown. NAAPv.2

When de stars begin to fall! (LL) Stars Begin to Fall. Unknown. SacPr; SSUS

When, dearest, I but think on [or of] thee. Song. OBEV

When Death Came. Adam Zagajewski. VCWP, tr. by Renata Gorczynski

When death comes / like the hungry bear in autumn. When Death Comes. Mary Oliver. WaAnP

When death crawls by night. Panama. Patrick Sylvain. InTrad

When death dances in. Last Rites. David Citino. UpMys

When Death to Either Shall Come. Robert Bridges. OBEV

When descends on the Atlantic. Seaweed. Henry Wadsworth Longfellow. APN-1; ColAP

When desire blinds the mind with delusion and dust, O thou holy one, thou wakeful, come with thy light and thy thunder. (LL) Rabindranath Tagore. ItP; PtR Fr. Gitanjali.

When despair for the world grows in me. Peace of Wild Things, The. Wendell Berry. BeAl; GoPo; InGu; IPoFL; PLBUT

When Dey 'Listed Colored Soldiers. Paul Laurence Dunbar. CBCWP

When Diana, late at night. Unknown. WoPoe Fr. Carmina Burana.

When did my head become an ancient cow's sacred head? Takahashi Mutsuo. PFTM-2 Fr. Self-Portraits.

When did she know, when did she know it. Lucille Clifton. ExTi

When did the garden with its banked flowers. Death's Blue-Eyed Girl. Linda Pastan. InoFa

When did we drift into each other's arms. Envoi: Waking After Snow. David Baker. PasH

When did you start your tricks. Mosquito, The. D. H. Lawrence. NPeEn

When Dinah's careless eye was grown too lavish. On Dinah. Francis Quarles. ChIV-1

When dis ya bass-line drop. One Song. Geoffrey Philp. WaCA

When do I see thee most, beloved one? Dante Gabriel Rossetti. NAEL-6v2 Fr. House of Life, The.

When Dobbin and Robin, unharnessed from the plow. Circus-Postered Barn, The. Elizabeth Jane Coatsworth. MoAmPo

When does the soul leave the body? For My Mother. Ellen Bryant Voigt. NIP-4; StAl

When / Don / Pasquito arrived at the seaside. Dame Edith Sitwell. PFTM-1 Fr. Façade.

When doome of Peeres and Judges fore-appointed. Tragicall Epigram, A. Sir John Harington. PBRV

When down the deep-six I'll be stored. Who'll Ferry Love to the Yonder Shore. László Nagy. IQMS, tr. by Adam Makkai

When Durer drew Apollo, he placed him in a light- / er colored field surround by a golden. Durer's Apollo. Darrell Bourque. Vesp

When Earth's last picture is painted, and the tubes are twisted and dried. L'Envoi. Rudyard Kipling. BRP

When Eddie had his second birthday. Eddie and the Birthday. Michael Rosen. NOxBChV

When e'er we enter life's open field. Ambition. Maggie Pogue Johnson. CBWP-4

When Egypt said, "Exterminate." Retribution. Lizelia Augusta Jenkins Moorer. CBWP-3

When Eire first rose from the dark-swelling flood. Eire. William Drennan. IrV

When Eliot died it made him seem human. New Year's Eve Poem 1965. Peter Levi. OxEAP-2

When Euclid started out to measure Hades. Hades and Euclid (first version). Harry Edmund Martinson. WED, tr. by Robert Bly

When Eve first saw the glistering day. Song with Words. James Agee. ChIV-1; MoAmPo

When every one to pleasing pastime hies. Mary Sidney Wroth, Countess of Montgomery. BASC; PBRV Fr. Pamphilia to Amphilanthus.

When every pedal stroke's a bore. Puritan against the Wind. Gus Ferguson. ArBi

When every pencil meant a sacrifice. Warren Pryor. Alden Nowlan. BrAP

When everything but love was spent. Winter Tenement. Malcolm Cowley. APT-2

When Everything Is Goneril. Lee Patton. IaFF

When Evil-Doing Comes Like Falling Rain. Bertolt Brecht. AF, tr. by John Willett

When Faith and Love which parted from thee never. Sonnet: On the Religious Memorie of Mrs. Catherine Thomason My Christian Friend Deceas'd Decem. 1646. John Milton. ChIV-2

When famas go on a trip, when they pass the night in a city. Travel. Julio Cortázar. MotU; TCLAP, tr. by Paul Blackburn

When far-spent night persuades each mortal eye. Sir Philip Sidney. NoSic Fr. Astrophil and Stella.

When Fat Women Fear Famine. Brenda J. Moossy. PoArWo

When Father Carves the Duck. Ernest Vincent Wright. NTCP

When Fergus drew his favourite blade. William Malveisin. NePenScot Fr. Fergus of Galloway: Knight of King Arthur.

When finally one gives up all hope of personal exaltation. Poetry Is a Weapon Loaded with the Future. Gabriel Celaya. RaW, tr. by Robert Mezey

When First. Edward Thomas. NoAM

When first, descending from the moorlands. Extempore Effusion upon the Death of James Hogg. William Wordsworth. NAEL-6v2; NAEL-7v2; NPBRoP

When first described imperfectly. Erections. Erin Belieu. ExTi

When first I came here I had hope. When First. Edward Thomas. NoAM

When first I learned the ABC of love. John Davies of Hereford. OxBSo Fr. Wit's Pilgrimage.

When first I saw you in the curious street. German Prisoners. Joseph Lee. FaBoWar

When first I took to cutlass, blunderbuss and gun. Ballad of O'Bruadir, The. Frederick Robert Higgins. OBMV

When first I walked here I hobbled. Seekonk Woods, The. Galway Kinnell. NoAM

When first I was courtin' sweet Rosie O'Grady. Irish Song [Rosie O'Grady]. Noël Coward. NBLV; OBCoV

When first mine eyes beheld your princely name. Michael Drayton. NoSic Fr. England's Heroical Epistles.

When first my lines [or verse] of heavenly [or heav'nly] joy[e]s made mention. Jordan (2). George Herbert. BASC; CABP; FSCP; NAEL-6v1; NAEL-7v1; NOSC; OBWVE; PBRV; SacPr

When first the college rolls receive his name. Juvenal. NPeEn; OBSV Fr. Vanity of Human Wishes, The; The Tenth Satire of Juvenal [Imitated].

When first the unflowering Fern-forest. Darwinism. Agnes Mary Frances Robinson. VWP

When first the world grew dark to me. Cross-Road Epitaph, A. Amy Levy. VWP

When first this canvas felt Giorgione's hand. On the Concert. Trumbull Stickney. APN-2

When first thou camest, gentle, shy and fond. Mother's Heart, The. Caroline Elizabeth Norton. NPBRoP

When first thou didst entice to thee my heart. Affliction (1). George Herbert. BASC; FSCP; NAEL-6v1; NAEL-7v1; NoP-4; NoP-5; NOSC

When first thou didst even from the grave. Disorder and Frailty. Henry Vaughan. ChIV-1

When first thou on me, Lord, wrought'st thy sweet print. Ebb and Flow, The. Edward Taylor. InvLi

When first under fire an' you're wishful to duck. Rudyard Kipling. FaBoWar Fr. Young British Soldier, The.

When fishes flew and forests walked. Donkey, The. G. K. Chesterton. ChIV-2; GI; MoBrPo; OBEV

When five year old Pito fell out the sixth floor. Lil' Pito. Sandra Maria Esteves. PueRic

When flighting time is on, I go. Birdcatcher, The. Ralph Hodgson. MoBrPo

When for the Thorns with which I long, too long. Coronet, The. Andrew Marvell. BASC; BrAP; FSCP; NAEL-6v1; NAEL-7v1; NoP-4; NoP-5; NOSC; PBRV; SacPr

When for Weeks the Sea is Flat. Rick Noguchi. MoASP

When forty winters shall besiege thy brow. William Shakespeare. HeIP-4; ItP; NoP-5; NoSic Fr. Sonnets.

When forty winters shall besiege thy brow. Ellen McGrath Smith. IaFF Fr. Shaken.

When forty years come round. At Forty. Yevgeny Aleksandrovich Yevtushenko. RusPo, tr. by Robert Arthur Douglas Ford

When foxes eat the last gold grape. Escape. Elinor Wylie. MoAmPo

When Frank was drowning in the River Po. About the Shipwrecked Frandus. Janus Pannonius. IQMS, tr. by Iain MacLeod

When Freedom, from her mountain height. American Flag, The. Joseph Rodman Drake. APN-1; BRP

When Friendship or Love our sympathies move. Tear, The. Lord Byron. STuOW

When from our better selves we have too long. William Wordsworth. AmFaPo Fr. Prelude, The; Growth of a Poet's Mind [1805 version].

When from remote lands the wind rose. Spinning. May Muzaffar. PoArWo, tr. by Tahia Abdel Nasser

When from the frigid North into the woods. Times Gone By. János Vajda. IQMS, tr. by Jess Perlman

When from the gates of Paradise fair Eve. Vision of Eve, The. Henrietta Cordelia Ray. CBWP-3

When from the other world you. Stepping Out With Edvard Munch. Elma van Haren. TuT, tr. by Anne Kennedy

When from the river there's no longer. Liliane Giraudon. SCFWP Fr. Poem with Incense Paper.

When from the virile grave. Stepping Out With Edvard Munch. Elma van Haren. TuT, tr. by Medbh McGuckian

When from the world, I shall be tane. To My Husband. "Eliza." EMWP; LW; PBRV

When frost will not suffer to dike and to hedge. Thomas Tusser. NoSic Fr. Five Hundred Points of Good Husbandry.

When Gabriel (no blest spirit more kind or fair). Abraham Cowley. NOSC Fr. Davideis.

When gathering shells cast upwards by the waves. Chrysalis, A. Emily Jane Pfeiffer. ViWPN

When geometric diagrams and digits. "Novalis." WoPoe, tr. by Robert Bly

When Gerty goes a-wheeling half the people in the place. When Gerty Goes A-Wheeling. Manley H. Pike. ArBi

When getting my nose in a book. Study of Reading Habits, A. Philip Larkin. OBCoV

When glowing Phoebus quits the weeping earth. Mary Tighe. CenSon

When God at first made man. Pulley, The. George Herbert. BASC; BBASP; BrAP; ChIV-1; FSCP; HeIP-4; InvLi; NAEL-6v1; NAEL-7v1; NoP-4; NoP-5; NOSC; OBEV; OxAEP-1; TFi; WaAnP

When God closes a door, there are no windows. What My Mother Taught Me. Shara McCallum. BtF

When God / created. Black Cryptogram. Michael S. Harper. OxAAAP

When God created thee, one would believe. Lady Mary Wortley Montagu. BrAP Fr. Verses Addressed to the Imitator of the First Satire of the Second Book of Horace.

When God Lets My Body Be. E. E. Cummings. MoAmPo; WaAnP

When God made the angels, a man made me. Celestial, The. Elizabeth Spires. CAP-8

When God makes a great Man he intends all others to crush him. Arthur Hugh Clough. OBSV Fr. Amours de Voyage.

When God was learning to draw the human face. Two Masks Unearthed in Bulgaria. William Meredith. BodElec

When golden sunbeams gleam athwart the sky. At Eventide. James Clarence Harvey. ArBi

When Goldie the golden eagle escaped from the Zoo. Goldie Sapiens. P. J. Kavanagh. OBCoV

When Good Queen Elizabeth Governed the Realm. Joseph Stansbury. NAAPv.1

When good St. David, as old writs record. In Honour of St. David's Day. Unknown. OBWVE

When Grampa dies. Heart. Cheryl Savageau. PfS

When Grandmamma fell off the boat. Indifference. Harry Graham. NBLV

When great Nature sighs, we hear the winds. Breath of Nature, The. Chuang Tzu. BBASP; WaAnP, tr. by Thomas Merton

When groping farms are lanterned up. Country God, A. Edmund Charles Blunden. MoBrPo

When Gullion died (who knows not Gullion?). Joseph Hall. NoSic Fr. Virgidemiarum.

When Gwen heard at last. In Memoriam. W. J. Gruffydd. OBWVE, tr. by R. Gerallt Jones

When Han declining lost its grasp of power. Poem of Sorrow. Ts'ai Yen. CCL1, tr. by John Frodsham

When hands are joined and head bows in the dark. (LL) Penal Law. Austin Clarke. ModIr; OxBEV

When, hardly moving, you decorate night's hush. Waters of Life, The. Humbert Wolfe. MoBrPo

When have I known a boy. Girl on the Land, The. Alice Thompson Meynell. VWP

When he appears a block away, you know. Man Who Tried to Rape You, The. Erin Belieu. AmPoNex

When he asked me that. How Are You? Carole Satyamurti. StAl

When He Believed Himself to Be a Young Girl Lifting the Skin of the Water. Juan Felipe Herrera. TouFir

When he breathed his last breath it was he. Moment of My Father's Death, The. Sharon Olds. NIP-4

When he breathed his last breath, it was he. Exact Moment of His Death, The. Sharon Olds. NAMCP V.2

When he brings home a whale. Naughty Boy. Robert Creeley. HeIP-4; NAMCP V.2; NoAM

When He Comes He Is Neither Sun Nor Shade: a China Doll. D. A. Powell. IAoNAP

When he dances latin. El Jibarito Moderno. Miguel Algarin. PueRic

When he did read how did we flock to hear. Thomas Vaughan. AngWePo Fr. On The Death of an Oxford Proctor.

When he entered. Marxist to Liberals, A. David Lindley. NLP

When he finally put. Kiss, The. Marie Howe. ExTi; FaoP

When he found Laertes alone on the tidy terrace, hoeing. Homer. ModIr Fr. Odyssey.

When he gets off work at Packard, they meet. Two, The. Philip Levine. CAP-8

When he gives me a light he has to kneel down. Sarah Kirsch. PFTM-2 Fr. Kite-Flying.

When he got out of bed the world had changed. Drainage, The. Peter Didsbury. StAl

When he got up that morning everything was different. Journey, A. Edward Field. BLT

When he grew pale, and his voice trembled. Memory, A. Marceline Desbordes-Valmore. WoPoe, tr. by Louis Simpson

When he had made sure there were no survivors in his house. Michael Longley. ModIr; NPeEn Fr. Odyssey.

When he lends [or leads] any poet[s] about the town. (LL) Wits, The; A Session[s] of the Poets. Sir John Suckling. BASC; CABP

When he likened the cemetery to a herd of sheep. Flute, The. Oktay Rifat. WoPoe, tr. by Talat Sait Halman

When he looked at her, he invariably felt. Looking at Her. Alan Brownjohn. OxBSo

When he looks at me. Frog. Issa. WoPoe, tr. by Conrad Totman

When He Met Julia, He Greeted Her Thus. Bálint Balassi. IQMS, tr. by Adam Makkai

When he phoned the next morning from another state. Voir Dire. Elise Paschen. PoDa

When he pushed his bush of black hair off his brow. Sicilian Cyclamens. D. H. Lawrence. NAMCP V.1; NoAM

When he reaches for a photo of old times. Traveler. Antonio Porta. ItPo, tr. by Gayle Ridinger

When he returned from the meadow he said. Meadow, The. Susan Stewart. AmAlph

When he returned from there. Airman. Mariya Stepanova. CRWP, tr. by Richard McKane

When he said Mary, she did not at once. Contemplations of Mary. Roy McFadden. PNI

When He Said "Soul." Hwang Insuk. EcSo, tr. by Peter H. Lee

When he says to you. Did-You-Come-Yets of the Western World, The. Rita Ann Higgins. StAl

When he sets out across ranges of winter sea. (LL) Islandman. Brenda Chamberlain. AngWePo; OBWVE

When he shuts the door against his day-to-day, "June, I'm home." Man I Love and I Have a Typical Evening the Night Richard M. Nixon Dies, The. Jim Elledge. ReTh

When he sit, he sit on what he ain't got—almost. (LL) Frog, The. *Unknown*. NBLV; NOxBChV; NTCP

When he sits staring in at the flames in the range. Asperger Child. Tom French. NIrP

When he stands in the judgement place. Stone Verdict, The. Seamus Heaney. NAMCP V.2

When he the nation's heart had won. Presidents, The. Lizelia Augusta Jenkins Moorer. CBWP-3

When he walked through town, the wing-shot bird he'd hidden. Author of American Ornithology Sketches a Bird, Now Extinct, The. David Wagoner. BLT

When he was drowning. Perseverance. Jas. Mardis. TiP2

When he was far away from those evenings. Franco Buffoni. ItPo, *tr. by* Gayle Ridinger

When he was shot he toppled to the ground. Shot Who? Jim Lane! Merrill Moore. MoAmPo

When he was small, when he would fall. Vladimir Vladimirovich Nabokov. PWW2

When he was starting out, still green. Counterfeiter, The. Greg Williamson. AmPoNex; RA

When he was young and gift-strong. (LL) John Berryman. NAMCP V.2; NoAM *Fr.* Dream Songs.

When he wasn't working, on his days off, his father liked to spend his. Light. Peter Markus. AmPoNex

When He Went Away. Marcelle Ferry. SurWo, *tr. by* Myrna Bell Rochester

When he went away. When He Went Away. Marcelle Ferry. SurWo, *tr. by* Myrna Bell Rochester

When he who adores thee has left but the name. Pro Patria Mori. Thomas Moore. OxAEP-2

When he, who is the unforgiven. Unforgiven, The. Edwin Arlington Robinson. APT-1; ItP

When he whose empire is in clouds saw Hector bent to wage. Homer. NOSC *Fr.* Iliad, The.

When He Would Have His Verses Read. Robert Herrick. BASC; CavPo; NOSC

When Heaven in mercy gives thy prayers return. Hezekiah's Display. John Keble. ChIV-1

When he'd looked hard at all the monsters. When He'd Looked Hard. Eugène Guillevic. YaTCFP, *tr. by* Hoyt Rogers

When Hee Was Come to the Other Side of the Contrye, of the Gergesenes, There Mett Him Two: Possessed with Devils Coming Out of the Tombes. Eleanor Touchet Davies. EMWP

When Helen Keller Spoke. George Jay Smith. ViWalt

When Henri Toussaints. Henri Toussaints. Cheryl Savageau. TWW

When her dear bosom clips. Dog Star, The. William Drummond of Hawthornden. DiBP

When Her Father a Widower Asked What She Would Say to His Intention of Marrying a Young Girl. Alis Ferch Gruffyd ab Ieuan ap Lleywelyn Fychan. EMWP

When *Hercules* did use to spin. Weavers Song, The. Thomas Deloney. PBRV

When Hilda does the Highland reel. To Hilda Dancing. John Bingham Morton. OBCoV

When his beloved died. Eyes, The. Don Paterson. EdScPo

When his boat snapped loose. Long Boat, The. Stanley Kunitz. CAP-8

When His Excellency Prince Norodom Chantaraingsey. Dead Soldiers. James Fenton. AF; FaBoWar; NAMCP V.2; NoAM; NoP-4; NoP-5; OBWP

When his hour for death had come. Osceola. Walt Whitman. NAAL-3

When his lover died. Eyes, The. Antonio Machado Ruiz. BeAl, *tr. by* Willis Barnstone

When Hitler was the devil. Silent Generation, The. Louis Simpson. OxBoAm

When hope forms a bud of prayer. My Listener. Chase Twichell. WANABP

When human beings found out about death. Dog Was Crying Tonight in Wicklow Also, A. Seamus Heaney. PoA 2002

When I a verse shall make. His Prayer to Ben Jonson. Robert Herrick. BASC; NAEL-6v1; NAEL-7v1; NoP-4; NoP-5; NOSC

When I am alone. Antonio Machado Ruiz. WED *Fr.* Moral Proverbs and Folk Songs.

When I am alone I am happy. Waiting. William Carlos Williams. SAmP

When I am an old woman I shall wear purple. Warning. Jenny Joseph. MoWP; StAl

When I Am Asked. Lisel Mueller. GoPo; PoA 2002

When I am bored I climb the attic stairs. We're Staying at the Castlemount, Western Esplanade. M. R. Peacock. NLP

When I Am Dead. Emma Alice Browne. TreFP

When I am dead, and Doctors know not why. Damp[e], The. John Donne. NOSC

When I am dead and gone. (LL) A. E. Housman. MoBrPo; WeW-3 *Fr.* Shropshire Lad, A.

When I am dead and over me bright April. I Shall Not Care. Sara Teasdale. APT-1; MoAmPo; TCAPo

When I am dead and thou wouldst try. *Unknown*. NOSC

When I am dead, I hope it may be said. On His Books. Joseph Hilaire Pierre Belloc. MoBrPo; NBLV; WeW-3

When I am dead, my dearest. Song. Christina Georgina Rossetti. CABP; NAEL-6v2; NAEL-7v2; NoP-4; NoP-5; NPeEn; OBEV; OxAEP-2; ViWPN; VWP

When I am dead with you, fastened up, enameled. Modulation. Robert Clinton. PoDa

When I am deprived of your touch, what is the point of living? I Who Have Nothing. Běkes. IrPoTo, *tr. by* Abdul Kadir Said Ferhadi

When I am gone. Epitaph, An. Josephine D. Henderson Heard. CBWP-4

When I am grown to man's estate. Looking Forward. Robert Louis Stevenson. NBLV

When I am grown up I shall go and stoop digging clams. *Unknown*. APN-2 *Fr.* Songs of the Kwakiutl Indians.

When I am hungry. Mahadevi. WPoS

When I am living in the Midlands. South Country, The. Joseph Hilaire Pierre Belloc. MoBrPo; OxAEP-2

When I Am 19 I Was a Medic. D. F. Brown. AmWaPo

When I am no one. (LL) Wish for a Young Wife. Theodore Roethke. NAAL-5; NAMCP V.1; NoAM; NoP-4; NoP-5; WaAnP

When I am old. Grand Diva. Thandiwe Shiphrah. BtF

When I am old I might. At the Center, Creator Hourglass. Eliza Kelley. RWB

When I am riding round the ring no longer. Circus-Rider to Ringmaster. Thomas Hardy. RACG

When I am sad and weary. Celia Celia. Adrian Mitchell. OPOU

When I am sitting at my desk I have feelings. Boat, A. Jordan Davis. HeMarv

When I am the sky. Cancion. Denise Levertov. NALW

When I am with you, we stay up all night. Jelaluddin Rumi. IJHIL, *tr. by* Coleman Barks

When I Arrive. Fazil Hüsnü Daglarca. NaPG, *tr. by* Talat Sait Halman

When I arrived some clansmen had already come. Wood-Cutter, The. Lupenga Mphande. HBAPE

When I ask what things they fear. Fears of the Eighth Grade. Toi Derricotte. GT; LiTh

When I asked him about. Slave Ritual. Carolyn M. Rodgers. ISC

When I attained enlightenment. Testimony of J. Robert Oppenheimer, The. Ai. AtGh

When I awaken into the dream. Opal Trees, The. David St. John. RoV

When I awoke with cold. Coffee. James Vincent Cunningham. MoAmPo

When I become Jack Johnson. (LL) Dream of the Ring: The Great Jack Johnson, A. George Barlow. ESEAA; MoASP

When I beheld the Poet blind, yet bold. On Mr Milton's "Paradise Lost." Andrew Marvell. BASC; CABP; FSCP; NOSC

When I behold a forest spread. Robert Herrick. *See* When I behold a forrest spread.

When I behold a forrest spread. Art above Nature, to Julia. Robert Herrick. NOSC

(When I behold a forest spread.) CABP

When I behold how black, immortal ink. Ezra Pound. MoAmPo *Fr.* Ripostes of Ezra Pound.

When I behold the havoc and the spoil. George Wither. NOSC *Fr.* Collection of Emblemes, Ancient and Moderne, A.

When I behold the heavens as in their prime. Anne Bradstreet. OxBoAm *Fr.* Contemplations.

When I behold the skies aloft. Coventry Patmore. NAEL-6v2; NAEL-7v2 *Fr.* Angel in the House, The.

When I bethink me on that speech whilere. Edmund Spenser. *See* When I bethinke me on that speech whyleare.

When I bethinke me on that speech whyleare. Edmund Spenser. NoSic; NPeEn *Fr.* Faerie Queene, The.

When I bethought me well, under the restless sun. Henry Howard, Earl of Surrey. ChIV-1 *Fr.* Paraphrase of Part of the Book of Ecclesiates, A.

When I bid my wad—forty bucks—on a helmet. Space Memorabilia Auction, Superior Stamp and Coin, Beverly Hills, California. Joel Brouwer. AmPoNex

When i blow open green bottles. Nighttrains. Jayne Cortez. PFTM-2

When I bought bubble gum. Why We Bombed Haiphong. Jonathan Holden. ReTh

When I brood on Germany in the night. Night Thoughts. Heinrich Heine. WoPoe, *tr. by* Mark Rudman

When I built upon sand. Foundations. Leopold Staff. PoSu, *tr.* by Adam Czerniawski

When I but hear her sing, I fare. Upon a Rare Voice. Owen Felltham [*or* Feltham]. NOSC

When I Buy Pictures. Marianne Moore. APT-1; ColAP

When I called the children from play. For the Father of Sandro Gulotta. Janet Lewis. APT-2

When I came in that night I found. Surprise in the Peninsula, A. Fleur Adcock. EmeKit; MoWP

When I came into the world the war was endin'. End of the War, The. Ioan Alexandru. FaBoWar, *tr.* by Brenda Walker and Andrea Deletant

When I came with you that first time. 2 am. Dorianne Laux. SUP

When I cannot sleep, I stroke you. Manon Reassures Her Lover. Martha Elizabeth. PasH

When I cannot stand. Another Woman. Nina Iskrenko. CRWP, *tr.* by Stephanie Sandler

When I can't comprehend. They'll say, "She must be from another country." Imtiaz Dharker. StAl

When I can't face myself. People of the Earth 8. Ko Chônghûi. EcSo, *tr.* by Catherine J. Kim

When I carefully consider the curious habits of dogs. Meditatio. Ezra Pound. ItP

When I carry my little son in the cold. Poem. Thomas McGrath. GifTon

When I come back to my father's house,. Galway Kinnell. RaBo *Fr.* Memories of My Father.

When I come down to sleep death's endless night. My City. James Weldon Johnson. NAAPv.1

When I come home in old age, something holds me back. Returning to My Hometown. Chimi Sucho. BecRai, *tr.* by Kim Daljin, Kim Won-Chung and Christopher Merrill

When I come out of the bathroom. Animals. Sharon Thesen. BeAl

When I come, who is here? voices were speaking. Edwin Denby. AHA *Fr.* Snoring in New York.

When I consider every thing that grows. William Shakespeare. AEP; CABP; ClHu; GSo; HeIP-4; NAEL-6v1; NAEL-7v1; NIL-7; NIP-4; NoP-5; NoSic; NPeEn; OBEV; OxAEP-1; OxBEV; OxBSo; PoPoPo; SoSe-8; TFi; TRP; WeW-3 *Fr.* Sonnets.

When I consider how my light is spent. View from a Suburban Window. Phyllis McGinley. AmWit

When I Consider How My Light Is Spent. John Milton. *See* On His Blindness.

When I consider Life and its few years. Tears. Lizette Woodworth Reese. MoAmPo

When I consider the many hours spent. Lament of a Subwayite. Eugene O'Neill. UV

When I consider what you mean to me. Sonnet 4. Ronald David Laing. EdScPo

When I contemplate all alone. Alfred Tennyson. NAEL-6v2; NAEL-7v2 *Fr.* In Memoriam A. H. H.

When I couldn't he always discussed things. Action Would Kill It / A Gamble. Robert Adamson. BMAP

When I decide I shall assemble you. Identity. Elizabeth Jennings. MoWP

When I die. Lover of Rain in an Inkwell, The. Ghada al-Samman. PoArWo, *tr.* by Miriam Cooke and Richard McKane

When I die, I want your hands on my eyes. Pablo Neruda. BeAl *Fr.* 100 Love Sonnets.

When I die I will return to seek. Inscription. Sophia De Mello Breyner. StAl, *tr.* by Richard Zenith

When I die, make me a beautiful wake. Testament. Felix Morisseau-Leroy. OGAHCP, *tr.* by Boadiba and Jack Hirschman

When I die tomorrow. For Some Future Day. Hans Andreus. TuT, *tr.* by Peter van de Kamp

When I Died. Jo Shapcott. StAl

When I died they washed me out of the turret with a hose. (LL) Death of the Ball Turret Gunner, The. Randall Jarrell. AmWaPo; BrAP; ClHu; ColAP; EMP; HarvBoo; HeIP-4; InGu; InoFa; MoAmPo; NAAL-5; NAMCP V.2; NIL-7; NIP-4; NoAM; NoP-4; NoP-5; OBWP; OtW; OxBoAm; PoAgWa; PoPoPo; PoWW; PtR; PWW2; SoSe-8; TFi; VCAP; WaAnP

When I disappear for a few. Wife Of. Vicki L. Reitenauer. FiBr

When I discover that the substance of the beautiful is a certain rhythm. George Santayana. TCAPo *Fr.* Normal Madness.

When I do count the clock that tells the time. William Shakespeare. GSo; HeIP-4; NAEL-6v1; NAEL-7v1; NoP-5; NoSic; WoPoe *Fr.* Sonnets.

When I don't feel well, I wander among. Sandro Penna. CAGL, *tr.* by John McRae

When I draw the magnificent Dutch girl. Rembrandt—Self Portrait. Gregory Corso. BB

When I drive cab / I am moved by strange whistles and wear a hat. Lew Welch. BB

When I 'ear my daughter scream in the night. Legend of the Baker and Her Daughter, The. Mihangel Morgan. BBMWP, *tr.* by Martin Davis

When I eat alone, I am alone. Ballad of the Solitary Diner. Todd Swift. OpeFie

When I enter, the hotel looks like a huge mushroom on a hilltop, divided. Children on Top of the Hill. No Hyegyông. EcSo, *tr.* by Ann Y. Choi

When I enter through the hatch of memory. Growing Up Haunted. Marge Piercy. TaR

When I entered through the pine grove, the pine grove. Road. No Ch'ônmyông. CAMKP, *tr.* by Mickey Hong

When I Fall in Love. Edward Heyman. ReLy

When I feel like a drag queen. Inner Bloke. Joanne Limburg. NeBl

When I find myself among a laughing tribe. Emergency Kit. Tanure Ojaide. EmeKit

When I first reached this country. Thoughts from Underground. Margaret Atwood. BrAP

When I first saw a woman after childbirth. Ishtar. Judith Wright. NALW; NAMCP V.2; NoAM

When I First Saw Snow. Gregory Djanikian. UnSA

When I first saw you break through. Drowned Sailor, The. Judith Ortiz Cofer. PueRic

When I first sharpened a. Poem for George Miles. Dennis Cooper. WiU

When I first was brought to light. Eleanora Wyatt Finch. EMWP

When I form a fist. Fists. Peter Finch. TCAWP

When I fought the dog we almost danced. All I Did For Him. Paul Muldoon and Gerald Stern. GPPA

When I found her in the bathing pool. Bihari. ErotSp, *tr.* by Sam Hamill

When I gaze at the sun. Moment Please, A. Samuel Allen. FuFl; SSLK

When I get home from a day's shopping in a city street. Edna's Hymn. Barry Humphries. NOBAu

When I get nervous, it's so hard not to. Have You Ever Faked an Orgasm? Molly Peacock. RA

When I get to be a composer. Daybreak in Alabama. Langston Hughes. FaBoA

When I go. After Grave Deliberation. Elizabeth Flynn. NBLV

When I go away from you. Taxi, The. Amy Lowell. IJHIL; LW; MoAmPo; NAAPv.2; PoCho; WaAnP

When I go back to earth. Answer, The. Sara Teasdale. PoA 2002

When I go down by the sandy shore. Sea Joy. Jacqueline Kennedy Onassis. BLPJKO

When I go down to Wales for the long bank holiday. I'r Hen Iaith a'i Chaneuon. Ian Duhig. ModIr

When I go fishing I bring with me a cellophane bag, usually a carrot bag. Fisherman's Pants, The. Thomas Lux. MotU

When I go / Guard my tomb well. Issa. ZenPo, *tr.* by Takashi Ikemoto and Lucien Stryk

When I go out, I switch off the light. Precepts for City Living. Vladimir Burich. TCRusP, *tr.* by Daniel Weissbort

When I go out to my garden. Extracted. Aleida Rodríguez. FaoP, *tr.* by the author

When I go[e] musing all alone. Robert Burton. NOSC *Fr.* Anatomy of Melancholy, The.

When I, Good Friends, Was Called to the Bar. William Schwenck Gilbert. NAEL-6v2; NAEL-7v2 *Fr.* Trial by Jury.

When I, good friends, was called to the bar. William Schwenck Gilbert. NAEL-6v2; NAEL-7v2 *Fr.* Trial by Jury.

When I got back to base. I Am Sad. Le Ngoc Hiep. WoPoe, *tr.* by John Balaban and T. L. Nguyen

When I Got My First Tattoo I Was. Jennifer Bartlett. ICANM

When I got there the dead opossum looked like. Behaving Like a Jew. Gerald Stern. BodElec; InvLad; LoL; TaR

When I got to the airport I rushed up to the desk. Race, The. Sharon Olds. InvLad; OxBoAm; RaBo

When I got up this mornin', I heard the old Southern whistle blow. Southern Blues, The. Big Bill Broonzy. GM

When I grew up I went away to work. Whores. Margaret Abigail Walker. NALW

When I grew up there were 4 elements, seed stayed where you planted it. Makes Them Wild. Susan Bright. TiP2

When I Grow Up. Hugo Williams. EmeKit

When I Grow Up. William Wise. ChAP

When I grow up. When I Grow Up. William Wise. ChAP

When I grow up, I plan to keep. Plans. Maxine W. Kumin. TLR

When I grow up I want to have a bad leg. When I Grow Up. Hugo Williams. EmeKit

When I had journeyed half our life's way. Dante Alighieri. NAWM-7v1 *Fr.* Divine Comedy, The. (Mandelbaum Translation).

When I had money, money, O! Money. W. H. Davies. OBEV; OBMV

When I had no roof I made. Samurai Song. Robert Pinsky. OxBoAm

When I had reached the base.   Across the Jarbok.   Gerrit Achterberg.   TuT, *tr. by* Dennis O'Driscoll

When I have borne in memory what has tamed.   William Wordsworth.   OBEV

When I have crossed [*or* crost] the bar. (LL)   Crossing the Bar.   Alfred Tennyson.   BrAP; BRP; ChIV-2; ClHu; HeIP-4; InoFa; ITBLP; NAEL-6v2; NAEL-7v2; NoP-4; NoP-5; OBEV; SacPr; SoSe-8; TFi; TWF

When I have fears that I.   Do Sink.   George Bowering.   NLPA

When I have fears that I may cease to be.   When I Have Fears [That I May Cease to Be].   John Keats.   BrAP; CABP; CenSon; GSo; HeIP-4; NAEL-6v2; NAEL-7v2; NIL-7; NIP-4; NoP-4; NoP-5; NPBRoP; OBEV; PoPoPo; TFi; WaAnP; WoPoe

When I have heard small talk about great men.   Grandeur of Ghosts.   Siegfried Sassoon.   MoBrPo; OBMV

When I have seen by Time's fell hand defac'd [*or* defaced].   William Shakespeare.   AEP; HeIP-4; NoSic; OxAEP-1; TreFP *tr.* Sonnets.

When I have you, the passions of love make me stay awake.   Jelaluddin Rumi.   NaPG, *tr. by* Talat Sait Halman

When I hear laughter from a tavern door.   Wilfrid Scawen Blunt.   OBMV *Fr.* Esther [a Young Man's Tragedy].

When I hear my lover singing, I sing, too.   Voices.   F. D. Reeve.   PoDa

When I hear shocking news, I will faint.   What I Learned From the Movies.   Joan Jobe Smith.   SUP

When I hear that serenade in blue.   Serenade in Blue.   Mack Gordon.   ReLy

When I hear the guttural throatcall.   Nightsweats.   Richard Tayson.   AmPoNex; WiU

When I heard at the close of the day how my name had been receiv'd with plaudits in the capitol, still it was not a happy night for me that follow'd.   When I Heard at the Close Of The Day.   Walt Whitman.   APN-1; GoPo; NAAL-3; NoAM

When I Heard the Learn'd Astronomer.   Walt Whitman.   BrAP; BRP; ChAP; ColAP; MoAmPo; NAAL-3; NAAL-5; NAAPv.1; NoP-4; NoP-5; OxBoAm; PoPoPo; SoSe-8; WaAnP; WeW-3

When I heard the voice on the telephone.   Call, The.   Carol Muske-Dukes.   WaAnP

When I hoked there, I would find.   Terminus.   Seamus Heaney.   NAMCP V.2; PoPoPo

When I hold the prison warden's face underwater.   Hate Crimes.   Joanne Lowery.   LiTh

When I hug you tight at bedtime.   Unspoken.   Judith Ortiz Cofer.   PueRic

When I hurry down the mountain.   Leaving the Mountain.   Baggok Choneung.   BecRai, *tr. by* Kim Daljin, Kim Won-Chung and Christopher Merrill

When I kiss you in all the folding places.   Muse.   Jo Shapcott.   NeBrP; StAl

When I Know the Power of my Black Hand.   Lance Jeffers.   ISC

When I landed in the republic of conscience.   From the Republic of Conscience.   Seamus Heaney.   BodElec

When I last rade down Ettrick. (LL)   Ettrick.   Lady John Scott.   LW; SoSe-8

When I lay me down to sleep.   Insomnia the Gem of the Ocean.   John Updike.   NBLV

When I lean down to stir the bathwater.   Jane Duran.   NewEx

When I leap through the flung open windows of your dance.   Picadilly or Paradise.   John Yau.   BodElec

When I Leapt over Tower Bridge.   Sir John Collings Squire.   UV

When I learned that my parents were returning.   Machine That Cried, The.   Michael Hofmann.   NeBrP

When I leave my body in this world.   When I Leave My Body.   Rohan B. Preston.   BtF

When I left my home on Tuesday, October 25, I.   Birthing.   Cornelius Eady.   FuFl

When I lie down to sleep dream the Wishing Well it rings.   I Am a Victim of Telephone.   Allen Ginsberg.   NBLV

When I lie where shades of darkness.   Fare Well.   Walter De la Mare.   NoP-4; NoP-5; OBEV; OxBEV

When I lift your letter out of the mailbox.   Correspondence.   Judith Ortiz Cofer.   PueRic

When I listen for the sound of.   Patrizia Cavalli.   ItPo, *tr. by* Gayle Ridinger

When I lit the sparkler.   Spark of Joy, The.   Colette Ni Ghallchóir.   NIrP, *tr. by* the author

When I lived down in Devonshire.   Autobiographical Fragment.   Kingsley Amis.   OBCoV

When I lived in Milan the Duomo was thirty years younger.   Duomo, The.   Maria Luisa Spaziani.   NeIt, *tr. by* Beverly Allen

When I lived in Naples there was always a beggar woman at the gate of my palace.   Beggar Woman of Naples, The.   Max Jacob.   MotU; PoCho, *tr. by* John Ashbery

When I look at my elder sister now.   Elder Sister, The.   Sharon Olds.   CAP-8; NIL-7; NIP-4

When I look at the falling leaves.   Poem.   Marina Ivanovna Tsvetayeva.   RusPo, *tr. by* Robert Arthur Douglas Ford

When I look at the sky now, I look at it for you.   Before She Died.   Karen Chase.   P180

When I Look at Wifredo Lam's Paintings.   Jayne Cortez.   SurWo

When I look back upon my former race.   Path of the Just, The.   John Henry, Cardinal Newman.   SacPr

When I look back upon my life nigh spent.   Prayer, A.   George Macdonald.   SacPr

When I look forth at dawning, pool.   Nature's Questioning.   Thomas Hardy.   BrAP

When I look in the mirror.   Hopelessness.   Li Ch'ing-chao.   BLT, *tr. by* Kenneth Rexroth

When I look out, I see no hope for change.   My Spiritual State.   Mirza Asadullah Khan Ghalib.   WED, *tr. by* Robert Bly and Sunil Dutta

When I looked into the clear water.   By the Water.   Jinkag Haesim.   BecRai, *tr. by* Kim Daljin, Kim Won-Chung and Christopher Merrill

When I looked under the hedge.   Basho.   EH, *tr. by* Robert Hass

When I looked up, the black man was there.   Pride.   Jackie Kay.   NeBl

When I lost my job.   Good Ole Days, The.   Harriet Wilkes Washington.   BtF

When i lost my teeth.   Eating habits of the old man.   Alan Chong Lau.   WhBo

When I love (as some have told).   Hymn to the Graces, A.   Robert Herrick.   NOSC

When I made you, I loved you.   Retreating Wind.   Louise Glück.   CAP-8

When i make love to you.   For Willyce.   Patricia Parker.   PoBW

When I meet a monk.   Motto.   Yüan Mei.   WoPoe, *tr. by* Jerome P. Seaton

When I meet the morning beam.   A. E. Housman.   MoBrPo; SoSe-8 *Fr.* Shropshire Lad, A.

When I Met Him Approaching.   *Arapaho Oral Tradition.*   NAAPv.2

When I misbehaved as a child.   Bad Pilgrim Room, The.   Jeffrey McDaniel.   SUP

When I move your body.   Anatomy Lesson.   Jack Coulehan.   BloBone

When I Moved into the Neighborhood.   Carl Mayfield.   ICANM

When I must come to you, O my God, I pray.   Prayer to Go to Paradise with the Donkeys, A.   Francis Jammes.   GPTC; WoPoe, *tr. by* Richard Wilbur

When I observed that life had turned away its head and I became assured beyond doubt that death would seize me.   Abū Āmir Ahmad Ibn Shuhayd.   HiArP, *tr. by* James T. Monroe

When I open my legs to let you seek.   Return, The.   Molly Peacock.   PasH; RA

When I open the door a bit.   Moonlit Night.   Kim Namjo.   CAMKP, *tr. by* David R. McCann and Hyunjae Yee Sallee

When I opened the door.   Aware.   Denise Levertov.   NAMCP V.2

When I opened the window.   Where I Live.   Günter Eich.   GTCP, *tr. by* David Young

When I parted from my Good.   Friedrich von Hausen.   GePo

When I Passed in the Afternoon.   Laura Riesco.   TANSG, *tr. by* Shaun Griffin and Emma Sepúlveda-Pulvirenti

When i pat this floor with my tap.   Jayne Cortez.   ISC

When I pause, anemones fall on the month of December.   Year's End.   Frank Lima.   BodElec

When I pay close attention to my senses I become immobile.   Starfish Waving to Me from the Sand.   Matthew Rohrer.   NAPBL

When I peruse the conquer'd fame of heroes and the victories of mighty generals, I do not envy the generals.   When I Peruse the Conquer'd Fame.   Walt Whitman.   APN-1; SAmP

When I placed a stone on my tongue, a friend told me.   Lisa Gill.   ICANM *Fr.* Letters to a Dead Trappist.

When I play on my fiddle in Dooney.   Fiddler of Dooney, The.   William Butler Yeats.   NBLV; OxAEP-2

When I play roulette.   I May Be Wrong (But I Think You're Wonderful).   Harry Ruskin.   ReLy

When I put her out, once, by the garbage pail.   Geranium, The.   Theodore Roethke.   EmeKit; WeW-3

When I put my finger to the hole they've cut for a dimmer switch.   Loaf, The.   Paul Muldoon.   BeAl

When I ran, it rained. Late in the afternoon.   Between the Wars.   Robert Hass.   VCAP

When I ran to snatch the wires off our roof.   Powerline Incarnation, The.   Les A. Murray.   NAMCP V.2

When I reached his place.   It Was All Very Tidy.   Robert Graves.   NPeEn

When I Read Shakespeare.   D. H. Lawrence.   NoAM; OBCoV

When I read the article about phenobarbital.   Intelligence Quotient, The.   Deborah Harding.   SUP

When I recall that place.   Is It Not Strange?   Elizabeth Delmore.   NLP

When I recall you—as I often do.   Eleanor Brown.   NeBl

When I remember her light-sensitive skin.   My Mother's Skin.   Pascale Petit.   PoCu

When I remember Jiangnan.   Hangzhou.   Po Chü-i.   CCL1, *tr. by* Marsha Wagner

When I remember Jiangnan.   Wu.   Po Chü-i.   CCL1, *tr. by* Marsha Wagner

When I remember plain heroic strength. To the Prussians of England. Ivor Gurney. RSaN

When I remember you—beyond all accounting—O my mother? (LL) Lenox Hill. Agha Shahid Ali. AmALP; NAMCP V.2; NoP-5

When I return from the land of exile and silence. Poem of Return. Jofre Rocha. NAfrP, tr. by Don Burness

When I returned from lovers' lane. Kimono, The. James Merrill. CAP-8; ColAP; WaAnP

When I returned to my home town. Race. Karen Gershon. HP

When I returned to the hive I was one. Lost Bee, The. Phillis Levin. RA

When I revolve in my remembrance. Epitaph of Sir Griffith ap Rhys, The. Unknown. AngWePo

When I right the overturned ash can. My Father's Singing. Marc J. Sheehan. MiVo

When I rise up. Wendell Berry. UpMys Fr. Prayers and Sayings of the Mad Farmer.

When I rode south at twenty. Rio Grande Hills. Berta Hart Nance. TiP2

When I rolled three 7's. Situation. Langston Hughes. APSN

When I saw birches in Wasienki Park. Robert Frost in Warsaw. Peter Meinke. VisFro

When I saw my father for the last time, we both did the same thing. Terminal Resemblance. Louise Glück. InoFa

When I saw my mother's head on the cold pillow. Keine Lazarovitch, 1870-1959. Irving Layton. NIP-4

When I saw my son's heart blown up in bland black and white on the sonogram screen. Heart, The. C. K. Williams. PoCu

When I saw that clumsy crow. Night Crow. Theodore Roethke. NAAL-5

When I saw the dark clouds, I wept, O Dark One, I wept at the dark clouds. Clouds, The. Mirabai. WED, tr. by Robert Bly

When I saw the grapefruit drying, cherry [or cherries] in each centre lying. Reproof Deserved; or After the Lecture. Sir John Betjeman. OBCoV

When I saw the world had died away / the plants, the human race and all. Three Fragments. Bertolt Brecht. PFTM-1

When I saw you under the apple tree. First Love. Shimazaki Toson. CAoMJL1, tr. by Leith Morton

When I say I believe that women have a soul and that its substance contains two. Lawn of Excluded Middle. Rosmarie Waldrop. FTOS

When I see a bird in a cage. Thoughts on a Bird. Ch'ôn Yanghûi. EcSo, tr. by Aimee N. Kwon

When I see a brave building. Building. Gwendolyn Brooks. BRtP

When I see a couple of kids. High Windows. Philip Larkin. HarvBoo; NAEL-6v2; NAEL-7v2; NAMCP V.2; NoAM; PoetW; PoPoPo

When I see a wheel I long to make it turn. When I See a Wheel. Hwang Tonggyu. CAMKP, tr. by Anthony, Brother of Taizé

When I see birches bend to left and right. Birches. Robert Frost. AmFaPo; APT-1; BrAP; FaBoVe; HarvBoo; HeIP-1; ITBLP; MoAmPo; NAAL-5; NAAPv.2; NAMCP V.1; NoAM; NoP-4; NoP-5; OxBoAm; PoPoPo; SAmP; SoSe-8; TCAPo; TFi; TRP; WaAnP

When I see buildings in a town together. Mr. Frost Goes South to Boston. Firman Houghton. UV

When I see driven nails I think of the hammer and the hand. Box, The. Mark Turpin. ASA

When I see lobster pots the sea has mangled. Wrecked Creeves. Katrina Porteous. NeBl

When I see the lark stir her wings for joy. Can Vei La Lauzeta Mover. Bernard [or Bernart] de Ventadour [or Ventadorn]. APSN, tr. by Paul Blackburn

When I see the red maple. All the People Who Are Now Red Trees. Martín Espada. TouFir

When I see the searchlights splitting the moonlight. Searchlights. Kenneth Mackenzie. BMAP

When I see your face, the stones start spinning! Great Wagon, A. Jelaluddin Rumi. ErotSp, tr. by Coleman Barks

When I Set Out for Lyonnesse. Thomas Hardy. MoBrPo

When I sit alone on the floor, my anxieties arrive. Sitting Alone. Hurbak Myungjo. BecRai, tr. by Kim Daljin, Kim Won-Chung and Christopher Merrill

When I Sleep, Then I See Clearly. J. V. Foix. PFTM-1

When I some antique jar behold. To a Lady. John Gay. OBEV

When I speak now. Volcano. Ivan Van Sertima. CA

When I spread out my hand here today. Sitting by a Bush in Broad Daylight. Robert Frost. ChIV-1

When I squeeze through the narrow sluice of grief. Descent. Robyn Selman. TaR

When i stand around among poets. Lucille Clifton. OxAAAP

When I stand in the center of that man's madness. Reflection by a Mailbox. Stanley Kunitz. PWW2

When I stand on the shore, I wonder where you are. Villanelle VI. Judith Barrington. FFC

When I stand under the willow-tree. Vicarious. Amy Lowell. NAAPv.2

When I stand with these three. Hostages, The. Muriel Rukeyser. AF

When I start my fast driving. Unknown. EroLit Fr. Experiences as a Taxi-driver in Venezuela.

When I started wanting. Tzu Yeh. WoPoe, tr. by Jeanne Larsen

When I started wanting. Unknown. ColAnChi Fr. Midnight Songs.

When I stepped homeward to my hill. Home-coming. Léonie Adams. MoAmPo

When i stepped off the plane i knew i was home. Part Four: Rebirth. Sonia Sanchez. PfS

When I survey [or survay] the bright. William Habington. BASC; NPeEn; OBEV; OxBEV Fr. Castara.

When I survey the wondrous cross. Hymn. Isaac Watts. OxAEP-1; SacPr

When I Survey the Wondrous Cross. Isaac Watts. See also Hymn: "When I survey the wondrous cross."

When I take my girl to the swimming party. One Girl at the Boys Party, The. Sharon Olds. OxBoAm

When I Take My Sugar to Tea. Irving Kahal and Pierre Norman. ReLy

When I take off my glasses, these eyes are dark magnets. Leonard Commits Redeeming Adulteries with All the Women in Town. Louise Erdrich. UpMys

When I take you out tonight with me. Surrey with the Fringe on Top, The. Oscar Hammerstein, II. ReLy

When I taught you. To a Daughter Leaving Home. Linda Pastan. ArBi; ItWoWo; NIL-7; NIP-4

When I Think About America Sometimes (I Think of Ralph Kramden). Dorothy Barresi. ExTi; ReTh

When I Think About the Past. Hô Sugyông. EcSo, tr. by Youngju Ryu

When I Think About Why. Unknown. WoPoe, tr. by Virginia Olsen Baron and Chung Seuk Park

When I think about why. When I Think About Why. Unknown. WoPoe, tr. by Virginia Olsen Baron and Chung Seuk Park

When I think back now how my dad. Some Poems Aren't For You. Heather Sellers. LiTh

When I think how far the onion has traveled. Traveling Onion, The. Naomi Shihab Nye. AFaM; CAP-8; IPoFL; LoL

When I think of me. Ontology. Rutger Kopland. TuT, tr. by Seamus Deane

When I think of my youth I feel sorry not for myself. Mind-Body Problem. Katha Pollitt. KGB; OxBoAm

When I think of the alleys in my hometown. Loneliness of a Wayfarer, The. Great Master Hyecho. BecRai, tr. by Kim Daljin, Kim Won-Chung and Christopher Merrill

When I think of the house. Summer. David Oliveira. GeoHom

When I think of the long history of the self. Whole Self, The. Naomi Shihab Nye. PoArWo

When I think of the man who lived in the house. 2212 West Flower Street. Michael Collier. LiTh

When I think of the many people. Against Writing about Children. Erin Belieu. PoChi

When I think of those mothers giving up. After Reading Reznikoff. Kate Daniels. ExTi

When I think of Tom. Hello, Young Lovers. Oscar Hammerstein, II. ReLy

When I think of what I know about America. My Country. Tony Hoagland. SUP

When I think of you. Lady Izumi. ErotSp, tr. by Sam Hamill

When I think of your tail-bone, the tart sweetness. Lifelong. Sharon Olds. ExTi

When I think that Allen Ginsberg (b. 1926). My Dad Versus Ginsberg. Sion Eirian. BBMWP, tr. by Robert Minhinnick

When I think that you're the one girl I adore. Thank Your Father. Lew Brown, B. G. DeSylva and Ray Henderson. ReLy

When I think you gone, abruptly. Black Mood. Rosalía de Castro. WeW-3

When I think you're somewhere yonder. Black Mood. Rosalía de Castro. STV, tr. by John Frederick Nims

When I thought about him. Resist Confinement. Joette Harland-Watts. InTrad

When I thought about you, some tears came to mind. Some Tears. Kees Ouwens. TuT, tr. by Peter van de Kamp

When I too long have looked upon your face. Edna St. Vincent Millay. HeIP-4; MoWP

When I try makin' money. I Never Felt Better. Ralph Blane and Hugh Martin. ReLy

When I try to get the habit of doing what I should. My Heart Is a Hobo. Johnny Burke. ReLy

When I turn the ceiling light on. Self-Portrait. Gerald Stern. TaR

When I turned to look back. What Is Moving. Takahashi Shinkichi. ZenPo, tr. by Takashi Ikemoto and Lucien Stryk

When I used to stay at my brother's. Weather. Michael Burkard. BodElec

When I wait. Dance. Yi Sanghûi. EcSo, tr. by Jennifer M. Lee

When I wake alone in a drone of planes. Gulf. Marion Lomax. NeBl

When I wake I find it is late in the autumn. Given Day, A. W. S. Merwin. NAMCP V.2

When I wake in. Frame of Fear. Unoma Nguemo Azuah. NeNiPo

When I wake now it's below ocherous, saw-ridged. Fall River. David Rivard. PBCAP

When I wake the rain's falling. Taxing the Rain. Penelope Shuttle. MoWP

When I walk into the Pez Dorado I am always sad. Pez Dorado. Ann Spanel. PfS

When I walk, or look from my window. Crimea. Vladimir Vladimirovich Mayakovsky. RusPo, tr. by Robert Arthur Douglas Ford

When I walk the path this morning. Homeplace, The. Lenard D. Moore. GT

When I was a baby. Meditations on Stevie. Gordon Chambers. InTrad

When I was a baby. Good Luck Gold. Janet S. Wong. NOxBChV

When I was a beggarly boy. Aladdin. James Russell Lowell. TCAPo

When I was a Bermudian child. Hurricane Season. Edwina Trentham. AtGh

When I was a blonde I. First Corinthians at the Crossroads. Bruce Dawe. NoAM

When I was a boy. Two Songs of a Blacksmith. Aaron Kurtz. Prolet, tr. by Amelia Glaser

When I was a Boy. Alun Llywelyn-Williams. BBMWP, tr. by Joseph P. Clancy

When I was a boy desiring the title of man. George. Dudley Randall. NoAM

When I was a boy, my father drove us once. How Passion Comes to Matter. Donald Revell. RoV

When I was a boy there was a wondrous region. When I Was a Boy. Pennar Davies. BBMWP, tr. by Joseph P. Clancy

When I was a boy they came in blackness. Lascars, The. Peter Thomas. AngWePo

When I was a child. King: April 4, 1968. Gerald William Barrax. ESEAA; GT

When I was a child. Autobiographia Literaria. Frank O'Hara. OxBoAm; PtR

When I was a child. Message of the Rain, The. Norman H. Russell. ChAP

When I was a child and the soft flesh was forming. Song for Gwydion. Ronald Stuart Thomas. HarvBoo

When I was a child and thought as a child, I put. Wandering Jew, The. Robert Mezey. TaR

When I was a child, hawthorn. Hawthorn at Digiff. Ruth Bidgood. TCAWP

When I was a child, I came to worship tigers with a passion. Dreamtigers. Jorge Luis Borges. PtR, tr. by Alastair Reid

When I was a child I knew red miners. Childhood. Margaret Abigail Walker. NoP-4; NoP-5

When I was a child I saw. To a Child. Judith Wright. BMAP

When I was a child my father every morning. World as Will and Representation, The. Robert Hass. RoV

When I was a connoisseuse of slugs. Connoisseuse of Slugs, The. Sharon Olds. LW

When I was a goldfish you never noticed me. Sleeping with the Fishes. Helen Ivory. BeAl

When I was a kid. Me against the World. Charles Bukowski. OxBoAm

When I Was a Kid in Nueva York. Alvin Delgado. IJHIL

When I was a kid, still in short trousers. Three Tests for Darwin Duke. Jane Holland. MFPA

When I was a lad up in Flintshire. Liverpool. Grahame Davies. BBMWP, tr. by the author

When I was a little girl. Growing Up Italian. Maria Gillan. UnSA

When I was a medical student. Origin of Music, The. Dannie Abse. BloBone

When I was a teenager. Uncle Eggplant. Jeffrey McDaniel. SUP

When I was a young man courting the girls. September Song. Maxwell Anderson. ReLy

When I was about eight, I once stabbed somebody, another kid, a little girl. Blades. C. K. Williams. CAP-8

When I was almost forty. Golden Bells. Po Chü-i. BLT; CCL1, tr. by Arthur Waley

When I Was at My Most Beautiful. Ibaragi Noriko. ItWoWo, tr. by Aoyami Miyuki and Leza Lowitz

When I was born. Day's Ration, The. Ralph Waldo Emerson. APN-1

When I was born. (LL) Wonder. Thomas Traherne. BASC; NAEL-6v1; NAEL-7v1; NoP-4; NoP-5; NPeEn; OxBEV; WaAnP

When I was born a million stars. With Me. Oscar Williams. YaYoPo

When I was born I was hardened and human. Train. Jennifer Snyder. BodElec

When I was born in a world of sin. G. K. Chesterton on His Birth. A. E. Housman. NBLV

When I was born in the large house by the sea. Poem of a Distant Childhood. Noémia da Sousa. HAWP, tr. by Allan Francovich and Kathleen Weaver

When I was born on Amman Hill. Collier, The. Vernon Watkins. OBWVE; TCAWP

When I was born, one of the crooked. Seven-Sided Poem. Carlos Drummond de Andrade. PoetW; TCLAP; VCWP, tr. by Elizabeth Bishop

When I was born they christened me plain Samuel Johnson Brown. That's Why They Call Me "Shine." Cecil Mack. ReLy

When I was born, you waited. Jane Kenyon. LoL Fr. Having It Out with Melancholy.

When I was born, you waited. Having It Out with Melancholy. Jane Kenyon. EMP; ExTi; IJHIL; PoA 2002

When I was but thirteen or so. Romance. Walter James Turner. MoBrPo; NOBAu; NOxBChV; OBMV

When I Was Christened. David McCord. OBCoV Fr. Perambulator Poems, I-VII.

When I Was Conceived. Michael Ryan. NevBe

When I was dead, my spirit turned. At Home. Christina Georgina Rossetti. VWP

When I was down beside the sea. At the Seaside [or Sea-Side]. Robert Louis Stevenson. NTCP; TLR; WHSW

When I was dropped out of my mother. Wingless. Sándor Weöres. IQMS, tr. by Adam Makkai and Donald E. Morse

When I was eight, I was forced south. Old Tongue. Jackie Kay. EdScPo

When I Was Fair and Young. Queen of England Elizabeth I. NIP-4; NoSic

When I was fair and young and favour graced me. Queen of England Elizabeth I. See When I was fair and young, then favour graced me;.

When I was fair and young, then favour graced me;. When I Was Fair and Young. Queen of England Elizabeth I. NIP-4; NoSic

(When I was fair and young and favour graced me.) NIL-7

(When I was fair and young, then favor graced me.) NoP-4; NoP-5

When I was farthest away from my children. My Aunt and the Sun. Michael Burkard. BodElec

When i was five i thought heaven was located. Diana Brandt. ACAMVP

When I was five my brother and I made poison. Making Poison. Margaret Atwood. MotU

When I was five, we lived in Tesuque. Cherries. Joe Lamb. RaBo

When I was five years old. Gwendolyn Brooks. ESEAA Fr. Children Going Home.

When I was forced from Stella ever dear. Sir Philip Sidney. NAEL-6v1; NAEL-7v1 Fr. Astrophil and Stella.

When I was forty the stocktaker came. On My Fortieth Birthday. John Tripp. AngWePo

When I was forty-five I lay for hours. Forty-Five. Hayden Carruth. GoPo

When I was four my father went to Scotland. Truth, The. Randall Jarrell. AmWaPo

When I was four years old my mother led me to the park. Beggar Woman. Charles Reznikoff. OxBoAm

When I was girl by Nilus stream. Witch, The. Adelaide Crapsey. APT-1; NAAPv.2

When I Was Growing Up. Nellie Wong. OxWW; UnSA

When I was home de. Po' Boy Blues. Langston Hughes. ColAP; NAMCP V.1

When I was in fifth grade. Day 1: Portrait of the Artist, Small-kid Time. R. Zamora-Linmark. ReBoTo

When I was in high school, I wanted to be an actress. Soap Bubbles. Chrystos. ReTh

When I was just a little girl. Whatever Will Be, Will Be (Que Sera, Sera). Ray Evans and Jay Livingston. ReLy

When I was just a tiny tot, with tousled head. Raggedy Ann. Anne Caldwell. ReLy

When I was kneehigh to a tabletop. Snipers. Roger McGough. RSaN

When I was little and brown. Welcome. David Hernandez. UnSA

When I was little and he was riled. James Merrill. OxBSo Fr. Five Old Favorites.

When I was little, I thought the word loin. Lineage. Jeffrey McDaniel. LegDan

When I was made the magistrate. Magistrate. Chŏng Ch'ŏl. WoPoe, tr. by Graeme Wilson

When I was no one yet. Song: Boundless Space. Sándor Weöres. WoPoe, tr. by William Jay Smith

When I was once in Baltimore. Sheep. W. H. Davies. MoBrPo; NPeEn

When I was one-and-twenty. A. E. Housman. ChAP; HeIP-4; ITBLP; ItP; MoBrPo; NAEL-6v2; NAEL-7v2; NAMCP V.1; NoAM; TFi; WaAnP Fr. Shropshire Lad, A.

When I Was Prettiest in My Life. Ibaragi Noriko. CFP; WoPoe, tr. by Naoshi Koriyama and Edward Lueders

When I was Saul, and sat among the cloaks. St. Paul. Thomas Merton. ChIV-2

When I was set in that field. Praying. Cynthia Cruz. IAoNAP

When I was seventeen. Elkhart, Indiana. Todd Davis. ACAMVP

When I was seventeen. It Was a Very Good Year. Ervin Drake. ReLy

When I was Shakespeare. As If. Jim Peterson. IaFF

When I was sick and lay a-bed. Land of Counterpane, The. Robert Louis Stevenson. BLPJKO; ChAP; NBLV; NTCP; PtR; TLR; WHSW

When i was six years old. Cuz' mama played jazz. Daniel Gray-Kontar. SpirFl

When I was small. Clean. Ann Turner. SSCS

When I was small and they talked about love I laughed. Child's Story, The. Elizabeth Jennings. HarvBoo

When I was still a child. Poem. Lesbia Harford. NOBAu

When I was ten. American Son. Mitsuye Yamada. UnSA

When I was ten my mother, having sold. Year of the Foxes, The. David Malouf. NOBAu

When I was thirteen. Tarzan. Jaime Manrique. WiU

When I Was Three. Richard Edwards.

When I was three I had a friend. When I Was Three. Richard Edwards. Spl

When I was three, I told a lie. Stincher, The. Jackie Kay. NOxBChV

When I was told once, long ago, to write an essay on. Antenor. Alan Riach. EdScPo

When i was torn by war. Wars 1. Sinan Anton. IrPoTo, tr. by the author

When I was twelve we'd visit my aunt's friend. Randall Jarrell. StAl Fr. Lost World, The.

When I was twenty I walked past. Trees that Change Our Lives. Gary Soto. PasH

When I was twenty inches long. New-Born Baby's Song, The. Frances Darwin Cornford. MoWP; NIL-7

When I was very young. Little Girl Blue. Lorenz Hart. APT-2
  (Sit there and count your fingers.) ReLy

When I was very young. Charles Upton. CLPP Fr. Panic Grass.

When I was very young indeed. Little Cavalier, A. Lucy Larcom. SWaP

When I was wicked an' a prone to sin. You Must Be Pure and Holy. Unknown. SSUS

When I was writing my love poems, which sprouted from me. Pablo Neruda. WED Fr. Letter to Miguel Otero Silva, in Caracas.

When I Was Young. Alun Llywelyn-Williams. OBWVE, tr. by Gwyn Williams

When i was young. Proper Schooling, A. Aonghas MacNeacail. EdScPo

When i was young. Sarah Pelham. FaBoVe

When i was young. Call of Poetry. Sri Sri. HotL, tr. by V. Narayana Rao

When i was young. Beautiful Person, The. Ssu-ma Hsiang-ju. CCL1, tr. by John A. Scott

When I was young, a questing child. Spectator, The. Evan J. Thomas. AngWePo

When I was young all the gossip was. Treasure. Elin ap Hywel. ATSWP, tr. by Robert Minhinnick

When I was young and full of faith. Hesitating Veteran, The. Ambrose Bierce. CBCWP; PCW

When I was young and had no money to spend. Growing Old (2). Yüan Mei. WoPoe, tr. by Arthur Waley

When I was young and shiny as an apple in the good Lord's garden. Love Poem 1990. Peter Meinke. P180

When I was young and simple. I Never Do Anything Twice (Madam's Song). Stephen Sondheim. ReLy

When I was young I believed in intellectual conversation. In the men's room(s). Marge Piercy. BeAl

When I was young, I did not fit in. Returning to Fields and Gardens (1). T'ao Ch'ien. WaAnP, tr. by Arthur Sze

When I was young I little Thought. Unknown. EMWP

When I was young I looked high and low for a father. For His Father. William Meredith. PoA 2002

When I was young I studied hard and thirsted after knowledge. Chain Store Daisy. Harold Rome. ReLy

When I was young / I was my father's daughter. Me? Nirasana Kavulu. HotL, tr. by V. Narayana Rao

When I was young, just starting at our game. To My Least Favorite Reviewer. Howard Nemerov. OBCoV

When I was young, my graying father frowned. To the Emperor. Theodore Prodromos. WoPoe, tr. by Jack Lindsay

When I was young, my world was disharmonious. Returning to My Fields and Gardens. T'ao Ch'ien. CrYelRi, tr. by Sam Hamill

When I was young they had already been. Walk Along the Old Tracks, A. Robert Kinsley. GoPo

When I was young, unapt for use of man. Prayer to Hymen. Unknown. NOSC

When I was young, with sharper sense. Summer Commentary, A. Yvor Winters. CalPo; OxBoAm

When I was younger. Pastoral. William Carlos Williams. APT-1; SAmP

When I wash the soles of my feet. Ozaki Hosai. CAoMJL1, tr. by Donald Keene

When I watch my two boys, Walter and Robert, at play. I Am as Happy as a Queen on Her Throne. Mrs. Henry Linden. CBWP-4

When I watch the living meet. A. E. Housman. HarvBoo; MoBrPo; NoP-4; NoP-5; NPeEn Fr. Shropshire Lad, A.

When I watch you. Miss Rosie. Lucille Clifton. ESEAA

When I Went Out. Karla Kuskin. NTCP

When I went out to kill myself, I caught. Saint Judas. James Wright. GI; NAMCP V.2

When I wer still a bwoy, an' mother's pride. False Friends-like. William Barnes. NPeEn; OxBSo

When I were just a little lad, right small. Pulling the Chain. Simon Rae. UV

When I Woke, Everything Was the Same but Different. Olive M. Ritch. PoCu

When I woke up I was in a forest. The dark. Trillium. Louise Glück. MoWP; StAl

When I work outdoors all day, every day, as I do now, in the fall. This Shining Moment in the Now. David Budbill. AmZen

When I worked in the mill. If I Loved You. Oscar Hammerstein, II. ReLy

When I Would Die. Josephine D. Henderson Heard. CBWP-4

When I would sing of crooked streams and fields. Song, The. Jones Very. APN-1

When i would speak of other things. (LL) ISM, The. Wanda Coleman. OxAAAP; PmAP

When I write a novel in Vegas, I ask myself what other people will think. In Las Vegas. Katherine Lederer. IIR; LegDan

When I wrote of the women in their dances and wildness, it. Muriel Rukeyser. See When I wrote of the women in their dances and wildness, [it was a mask].

When I wrote of the women in their dances and wildness, [it was a mask]. Poem as Mask, The. Muriel Rukeyser. APT-2; NAAL-5; NALW; NAMCP V.2
  (When I wrote of the women in their dances and wildness, it.) OxWW

When Ibn Batutta, Arabian traveller. Ballad of the Dogs. Lars Gustafsson. WoPoe, tr. by Philip Martin

When ice on the pond is three feet thick. Unknown. CCL1 Fr. Tzu Yeh Songs.

When icicles by silver eaves. Winter Fairyland in Vermont. Francis P. Osgood. WeW-3

When icicles hang by the wall. William Shakespeare. ClHu; MakPoe; NAEL-6v1; NIL-7; NIP-4; NoP-4; NoP-5; OBEV; OxBEV; TFi; TRP; WaAnP; WeW-3 Fr. Love's Labour's Lost.

When icicles hang by the wall. Songs for the Seasons: A Distant Collaboration. William Shakespeare and Michael Stillman. IaFF

When idle in a poor Welsh mining valley. Rebel's Progress. Tom Earley. OBWVE

When I'm a little older. My Plan. Marchette Chute. WHSW

When I'm a quarter-inch off. I Blame It On Him. Len Roberts. PML

When I'm big, you say. Ice Cream. Ronny Someck. IrPoTo, tr. by Vivian Eden

When I'm bored with work. Polestar. K. Psaila. SonAtl, tr. by Xenia Broughton, Dorli Meek, Steven Ostermann, Emma Priest and Tamara Romanyk

When I'm drowned in days and gone. Who'll Bear Love. László Nagy. SonAtl, tr. by Helen Bell, Vasy Geza, Adam Horvath, Nike Koos, Zsuzsanna Rozsafalvi and Zsofia Zachar

When I'm eating this I want food. I mean what I say because. Realism. Carla Harryman. PmAP

When I'm Killed. Robert Graves. FaBoWar

When I'm killed, don't think of me. When I'm Killed. Robert Graves. FaBoWar

When I'm Not Near the Girl I Love. E. Y. Harburg. ReLy

When I'm not playing solitaire. don't Get Around Much Anymore. Bob Russell. ReLy

When I'm ready to think of something else, finally. Portrait of a Child. Corey Marks. LegDan

When I'm walking through the park. Oh! What It Seemed to Be. Bennie Benjamin, Frankie Carle and George David Weiss. ReLy

When in a deep depression of the self. Ragged Sonnet: When in a Deep Depression. Leonard Nathan. IaFF

When in a snap the hinge. Upon Closing the Book. Armanda Guiducci. CItWP, tr. by Cinzia Sartini Blum and Lara Trubowitz

When in danger or in doubt. Sound Advice. Unknown. NBLV

When, in disgrace with fortune and men's eyes. William Shakespeare. AEP; AmFaPo; BLPJKO; BrAP; GSo; HeIP-4; ITBLP; ItP; NAEL-6v1; NAEL-7v1; NoP-4; NoP-5; NoSic; OBEV; OPOU; OxAEP-1; PBRV; PoPoPo; TFi; WaAnP; WeW-3; WoPoe Fr. Sonnets.

When in My Pilgrimage. Unknown. ChIV-2

When in my pilgrimage I reach. When in My Pilgrimage. Unknown. ChIV-2

When, in our turn, we show to them a Man. (LL) Christ in the Universe. Alice Thompson Meynell. MoBrPo; OxAEP-2; VWP

When in Rome. Mari E. Evans. ESEAA; SoSe-8

When in Rome (I Do As the Romans Do). Carolyn Leigh. ReLy

When, in that final week. Evil Days, The. Boris Leonidovich Pasternak. GI, *tr. by* Nina Kossman

When in the bag thy hops the rustic treads. Christopher Smart. STuOW *Fr.* Hop-Garden, The.

When in the chronicle of wasted time. William Shakespeare. NAEL-6v1; NAEL-7v1; NoP-5; NoSic; OBEV; OxAEP-1; WoPoe *Fr.* Sonnets.

When in the company of the gods. "H. D." APT-1 *Fr.* Walls Do Not Fall, The.

When, in the dream factory. Paula Cunningham. NIrP *Fr.* Dog Called Chance, A.

When in the dusk a summer day had died. Tisza, The. Sándor Petőfi. IQMS, *tr. by* Watson Kirkconnell

When in the empty city a siren blasts through the stop-go then gone the. Ear Training. Sekou Sundiata. SpirFl

When, in the gloomy mansion of the dead. Foresees her Death. Mary Robinson. CenSon; RWP

When, in the gloomy mansion of the dead. Mary Robinson. NPBRoP *Fr.* Sappho and Phaon.

When in the heat of the first night of summer. My Beloved Compares Herself to a Pint of Stout. Paul Durcan. EmeKit; StAl

When in the night I await her coming. Muse, The. Anna Andreyevna Akhmatova. WoPoe, *tr. by* Stanley Burnshaw

When in the skillfully welded chest. Simonides. SaLy, *tr. by* Diane Rayor

When in the sun the hot red acres smoulder. Zulu Girl, The. Roy Campbell. NoP-4; NoP-5; OBMV; OxAEP-2

When in the throes of suicide. Anna Andreyevna Akhmatova. PoetW, *tr. by* Max Hayward and Stanley Kunitz

When in the widening circle of rebirth. Fernando Pessoa. ItP *Fr.* 35 Sonnets.

When in the wrought chest. Danae and Perseus. Simonides. WoPoe, *tr. by* Richmond Lattimore

When, in these gardens, in February. Consideration. Bryan Martin Davies. BBMWP, *tr. by* Elin ap Hywel

When in your gardens entrance you provide. Rene Rapin. OBGa *Fr.* Of Gardens.

When infant Reason first exerts her sway. On Education, December 1789. Elizabeth Bentley. WoRP

When Isaac watched his father strain back. Abraham's Madness. Bink Noll. ChIV-1

When Isis was bitten by the asp in the Jemez Mountains. Isis in the Heart. Rudolfo Anaya. ICANM

When Israel came from Egypt's coast. Bible, *O.T.* OBVE

When Israel came from Egypt's coast. Bible, *O.T.* NoP-5 *Fr.* Translation of the Psalms of David, A.

When Israel did depart th' Egyptians from among. Psalm 114. Bible, *O.T.* NoP-5, *tr. by Unknown*

When Israel, of the Lord Beloved. Sir Walter Scott. ChIV-1

When Israel sate by Babel's stream and wept. Lute of Afric's Tribe, The. Albery Allson Whitman. APN-2

When Israel was in Egypt's land. Let My People Go. *Unknown.* APN-2

When Israel's ruler on the royal bed. Hymn to the Supreme Being. Christopher Smart. ChIV-1

When Isr'el, freed from Pharoh's hand. Psalm 114. Bible, *O.T.* NoP-5, *tr. by* Isaac Watts

When it all comes true. Quiet Thing, A. Fred Ebb. ReLy

When it comes. Robert Creeley. NAMCP V.2; WoBe *Fr.* Life and Death.

When it comes back to teach you. Joy. Thomas Centolella. GifTon

When it comes to poets. Yadoyano Meshimori. EMJL, *tr. by* Burton Watson

When it comes to sea cliffs. Fulmars. Robert W. Service. EdScPo

When It Happened. Hilda Schiff. HP

When it is finally ours, this freedom, this liberty, this beautiful. Frederick Douglass. Robert Earl Hayden. CBCWP; ESEAA; ISC; NIL-7; NIP-4; OxAAAP; PoPoPo; PtR; VCAP

When it is impossible to write a word. When It Is Impossible. Jacques Dupin. YaTCFP, *tr. by* Mary Ann Caws and Jean-Pierre Cauvin

When it is past—the golden moment—gone! Lost Opportunities. Henrietta Cordelia Ray. CBWP-3

When it makes a man mad all the days of his life? (LL) Song: "I peeled bits of straw and I got switches too." John Clare. NAEL-6v2; NAEL-7v2

When it rain five days an' de skies turned dark as night. Backwater Blues. Bessie Smith. NAAPv.2

When it rains, and I go over my papers and end up. Great Moments. Gabriel Celaya. RaW, *tr. by* Robert Mezey

When it rains I dance alone. When I Sleep, Then I See Clearly. J. V. Foix. PFTM-1

When it was I first encountered you. Mikhail Alekseievich Kuzmin. CAGL, *tr. by* Michael Green

When it was my turn to sit beside the old poet. Once, in Santa Fe. Raylene Hinz-Penner. ACAMVP

When it was spring in Spain. When It Was Spring. Emilio Prados. RaW, *tr. by* Robert Mezey

When It's All Over. Myra Schneider. PoCu

When it's free, oh Haiti's going to be beautiful. Haiti Tomorrow. Jean-Claude Martineau. OGAHCP, *tr. by* Boadiba and Jack Hirschman

When it's hot. Summer. Frank Asch. NTCP

When it's ninety in the shade. Drive a Tractor. *Unknown.* NBLV

When it's time. Listening. Aileen Fisher. NTCP

When it's time for the Sacrifice. Bible Lesson. Harvey Shapiro. TaR

When it's time to move, he takes me for a walk. Room 40. Oni Buchanan. LegDan

When Jacob rolled the stone off the well. Biblical Meditations. Yehuda Amichai. WoPoe, *tr. by* Barbara Harshav and Benjamin Harshav

When Jane felt well enough for me to leave her. Porcelain Couple, The. Donald Hall. BAP-97; CAP-8

When Janis Joplin died. Fans. Baron Wormser. SwNoth

When Jesus commanded us to love our neighbour. D. H. Lawrence. GI

When Jesus was leaving this sin-accursed land. Whoso Gives Freely, Shall Freely Receive! Josephine D. Henderson Heard. CBWP-4

When Jill complain[e]s to Jack for want of meat[e]. Upon Jack and Jill: Epigram. Robert Herrick. NAEL-6v1; NAEL-7v1

When John Donne dropped to sleep all around him slept. Elegies. Hugh Maxton. PBCIP

When John Henry was a little boy. *Unknown.* HHAm

When John Henry was a little fellow. John Henry. *Unknown.* NAAPv.2

When Johnny comes marching home again. When Johnny Comes Marching Home. Patrick Sarsfield Gilmore. CBCWP; HHAm; NAAPv.1

When Joseph was an old man. Cherry-Tree Carol, The. *Unknown.* SacPr

When joy surprises me, I ripen. Quatrains for Joy. Muhammad Al-Ghuzzi. NAfrP, *tr. by* John Heath-Stubbs and May Jayyusi

When Judas, his betrayer. Zbigniew Herbert. GI *Fr.* St. Matthew.

When Judas writes the history of solitude. Sacrifice, The. Frank Bidart. InoFa; VCAP

When Julius Fabricius, Sub-Prefect of the Weald. Land, The. Rudyard Kipling. MoBrPo

When June came back from Spain in '66. Les Fils (Sons). Beverly Matherne. TWW

When, just as they are. Void in Form. Ikkyu Sojun. ZenPo, *tr. by* Takashi Ikemoto and Lucien Stryk

When Kennedy. Arthur Thinks on Kennedy. Myra Cohn Livingston. HHAm

When kiss spells contradiction it spills an ocean of open clothes. Karen Volkman. IIR

When Kukutis falls asleep. Kukutis's Sinful Spirit. Marcelijus Martinaitis. TWW, *tr. by* Laima Sruoginis

When lads have done with labor. A. E. Housman and a Few Friends. Humbert Wolfe. UV

When Lalement and de Brébeuf, brave souls. Brébeuf and His Brethren. Francis Reginald Scott. IFF

When last I heard your nimble fingers play. To Lucia Playing on Her Lute, Another. Samuel Pordage. NOSC

When last I saw thee, I did not[t] thee see. Mary Sidney Wroth, Countess of Montgomery. PEW *Fr.* Pamphilia to Amphilanthus.

When Last We Parted. Catherine Maria Fanshawe. LW

When late (grave Palmer) these thy graffs [*or* grafts] and flowers. To Thomas Palmer [on His Book *The Sprite of Trees and Herbs*]. Ben Jonson. NoSic

When late I attempted your pity to move. Expostulation, An. Isaac Bickerstaffe. OBCoV

When late the trees were stript by winter pale. On Bathing. Thomas, the Younger Warton. OxBSo

When latest Autumn spreads her evening veil. To Melancholy. Written on the Banks of the Arun, October 1785. Charlotte Smith. CenSon; RWP

When Laura was born, Ceri watched. Video, The. Fleur Adcock. StAl

When Laurens van der Post one night. Silence of the Stars, The. David Wagoner. PoDa

When lavish Phoebus pours out melted gold. Edward Benlowes. NOSC *Fr.* Theophia.

When Lazarus. Waking. Sheila Wingfield. StAl

When Learning's Triumph o'er her barb'rous [*or* barbarous] Foes. Prologue Spoken by Mr[.] Garrick at the Opening of the Theatre in Drury Lane, 1747. Samuel Johnson. NAEL-6v1; NAEL-7v1; NoP-4; NoP-5; OxAEP-1

When leaves fall and cold winds come. (LL) Lines: "When the lamp is shattered [*or* shatter'd]." Percy Bysshe Shelley. NAEL-7v2; OBEV; OxBEV

When leaving the primrose, bayberry dunes, seaward. Constant, The. A. R. Ammons. WeW-3

When legislators keep the law. Latter-Day Warnings. Oliver Wendell Holmes. NCAP

When Letty had scarce pass'd her third glad year. Letty's Globe. Charles Tennyson Turner. NPeEn; OBEV; OxBEV; OxBSo

When Life his lusty course began. Goblet, The. Bayard Taylor. TreFP

When Life's realities the Soul perceives. Anna Seward. CenSon

When light burns from the sea. Buddha of Sôkkuram, The. Shirley Kaufman. GifTon

When light bursts in at the window. Blind Man, The. Fazil Abdulovich Iskander. ItGoST, tr. by Avril Pyman

When Light returns to face the Earth anew. Friedrich Hölderlin. WoPoe Fr. Seasons, The.

When like the rising day. Gerald Griffin. OBEV Fr. Eileen Aroon.

When Lilacs Last in the Dooryard Bloom'd. Walt Whitman. APN-1; CBCWP; ColAP; InoFa; MoAmPo; NAAL-3; NAAL-5; NAAPv.1; NAMCP V.1; NCAP; NIL-7; NoP-4; NoP-5; OxBoAm; PCW; PoPoPo; SAmP; TCAPo; TFi; WaAnP Fr. Memories of President Lincoln.

When lions mate they disappear for days. Honeymoon. Alice Friman. MPUn

When little boys grown patient at last, weary. Allen Tate. FuPo

When little heads weary have gone to their bed. Plumpuppets, The. Christopher Darlington Morley. ChAP

When little matchsticks of rain bounce off drenched fields, an. Frog, The. Francis Ponge. BLT, tr. by Beth Archer

WHEN, lo, by break of morning. Unknown. NoSic

When Loneliness Is a Man. Yusef Komunyakaa. AWTN; OxAAAP

When lonely feelings chill the meadows of your mind. You Must Believe in Spring. Jacques Demy. ReLy, tr. by Alan Bergman, Marilyn Bergman and Michel Legrand

When long ago Liang's prince was in his glory. Ruined Terrace, The. Kao Shih. CCL1, tr. by Stephen Owen

When longing for you. Ono no Komachi. ArkPo, tr. by Helen Craig McCullough

When, looking on the present face of things. October, 1803. William Wordsworth. CenSon

When loose-strife, in flower, line. When to Slap a Woman. Paul Violi. PmAP

When, Lord, I seeke to shew thy praises, then. Edward Taylor. TCAPo Fr. Preparatory Meditations Before My Approach to the Lord's Supper.

When Louis came home to the flat. Meet Me in St. Louis, Louis. Andrew B. Sterling. NAAPv.2

When love gushed out. Incontinence. Susan Hahn. IllVoic

When love is gone. (LL) Night Has a Thousand Eyes, The. Francis William Bourdillon. BRP; OBEV

When Love its utmost vigour does imploy. Lucretius. NPeEn; OxBEV Fr. De Rerum Natura (On the Nature of Things).

When love was structured, so was verse—both fit. Good Old Days, The. Barbara Fried. NBLV

When Love with unconfinèd wings. To Althea, from Prison. Richard Lovelace. BASC; CavPo; CtM; ITBLP; ItP; NAEL-6v1; NAEL-7v1; NIL-7; NoP-4; NoP-5; NOSC; NPeEn; OBEV; OxBEV; PBRV; TFi; WaAnP

When Lovely Woman. Phoebe Cary. APN-2; UV

When Lovely Woman. Mary Demetriadis. UV

When lovely woman stoops to folly. When Lovely Woman. Mary Demetriadis. UV

When Lovely Woman Stoops to Folly. Oliver Goldsmith. CABP; NoP-4; NoP-5; NPeEn; OxBEV; TFi Fr. Vicar of Wakefield, The.

When lovely woman stoops to folly and. T. S. Eliot. UV Fr. Waste Land, The.

When lovers' lips from kissing disunite. Kiss of Betrothal, The. Charles Tennyson Turner. CenSon

When Love's Perished. Dambudzo Marechera. NAfrP

When low and heavy sky weighs like a lid. Spleen LXXVIII. Charles Baudelaire. SxFrPo, tr. by James McGowan

When Lucifer was lowliest in Heaven. Two Names. Betty Scott Stam. SacPr

When ma baby shouts in church. Lena Lovelace. Melvin B. Tolson. GT

When Ma Rainey. Ma Rainey. Sterling Allen Brown. APT-2; ISC; NAAPv.2; NAMCP V.1; OxAAAP

When Maggy Gangs Away. James Hogg. CABP; NPBRoP

When maidens such as Hester die. Hester. Charles Lamb. OBEV

When maize stands more than ten feet high. Hey, Boys! Up Go We! Unknown. NOBAu

When Malindy Sings. Paul Laurence Dunbar. APN-2; CtM; ISC; NAAPv.1

When man has conquered space. Earth's Bondman. Betty Page Dabney. OtW

When Mark Deloach Ruled the World. Dominique Parker. SpirFl

When Mary on her wedding day. Sister Gone. William Barnes. OxBEV

When Mary Rand. Uncle Alfred's Long Jump. Gareth Owen. OBSP

When May entered the Black Current off Kinkazan Island. Whale Spouting. Takamura Kotaro. WoPoe, tr. by James Kirkup and Akiko Takemoto

When meeting a bear, say. Unknown. WoPoe Fr. Three Swedish Spells.

When memory's fabled daughter. Notes for a History of Poetry. David Daiches. PoA 2002

When men a dangerous disease did 'scape. To Doctor Empiric[k]. Ben Jonson. WoPoe

When men are belligerent or crude. Spunk Talking. Anne Rouse. BeAl; MFPA; NeBl

When men see Hanshan. Try and Make It. Han-shan (Cold Mountain). BB; CCL1; NDACCP, tr. by Gary Snyder

When men shall find[e] thy flower [or flow'r], thy glory pass[e]. Samuel Daniel. AEP; NAEL-6v1; NAEL-7v1; NoP-4; NoP-5; NoSic; OBEV Fr. Sonnets to Delia.

When men straighten their shoulders and go by. Nocturne: The Eternal. Xavier Villaurrutia. GifTon, tr. by Eliot Weinberger

When men were all asleep the snow came flying. London Snow. Robert Bridges. MoBrPo; NoAM; OxAEP-2; TFi

When mice with wings can wear a human face. (LL) Bat, The. Theodore Roethke. APT-2; ChAP

When Mickey Mantle died. Players. E. Ethelbert Miller. SpirFl

When midnight comes a host of dogs and men. Badger. John Clare. NoP-4; NoP-5; NPeEn; PoPoPo; WaAnP

When midst the summer-roses the warm bees. Calder Campbell. CenSon

When Missus O'Leary's cow kicked the lantern. Put the Blame on Mame. Doris Fisher and Allan Roberts. ReLy

When Moling refused to revive the dead child. Touching the River. Tom French. NIrP

When morning gilds the skies. Unknown. SacPr, tr. by Edward Caswall

When morning has come, all the chief priests and elders of the people. Bible, N.T. NAWM-5v1 Fr. St. Matthew.

When Morrice views his prostrate peas. On a Fine Crop of Peas Being Spoiled by a Storm. Henry Jones. OBGa

When Moses an' his soldiers. He's Jus' de Same Today. Unknown. InvLi

When most impeach'd stands least in thy control. (LL) William Shakespeare. AEP; NoSic Fr. Sonnets.

When Mother died. Routine Things Around the House, The. Stephen Dunn. CAP-8; MAAN

When mother divorced you, we were glad. She took it and. Victims, The. Sharon Olds. NIL-7; SoSe-8

When mothers weep and fathers richly proud. Confirmation, The. Karl Shapiro. APT-2

When Mr. Croxford. At the St. Louis Institute of Music. Ronald Wallace. SUP

When Mr. Dennis does well play. Julia A. Moore. VerBaPo Fr. Grand Rapids Cricket Club, The.

When Mr. Apollinax visited the United States. Mr. Apollinax. T. S. Eliot. PoA 2002

When Mrs Gorm (Aunt Eloise). Opportunity. Harry Graham. OBCoV

When mum, who never quit the Party. Left Rites. Hylda Sims. Prnts

When "Music, Heavenly Maid," was very young. Music. Christopher Pearse Cranch. APN-1

When my blood flows calm as a purling river. Communism. Ella Wheeler Wilcox. SWaP

When my breast labors with oppressive care,. Paraphrase of the Latter part of the Sixth Chapter of St. Matthew, A. James Thomson. ChIV-2

When my brother hogs. Blanket Hog. Paul B. Janeczko. TLR

When my brother talks to me. My Brother. Chavali Bangaramma. HotL, tr. by V. Narayana Rao

When my brother Tommy. Two in Bed. Abram Bunn Ross. NTCP

When My Car Broke Down. John Brehm. PoDa

When my cat preens in dusty sunlight. Elegy Residence on Earth. Robert Hass. BodElec

When my children need my help. (LL) Elena. Pat Mora. NIL-7; UnSA

When my cousin Josie played the piano. On Fourteen Maple Street. Barbara Winder. MiVo

When my daughter makes bread, a cloud of flour. Bread. Sharon Olds. SweBea

When My Dead Father Called. Robert Bly. GoPo; MAAN

When my devotions could not pierce. Denial[l]. George Herbert. BASC; FSCP; NAEL-6v1; NAEL-7v1; NoP-4; NoP-5; NPeEn; PBRV

When my doctors thought. I Used to Go to Church. G. E. Patterson. PoDa

When My Dog Died. Freya Littledale. NTCP

When my ex-wife found magnetic north. Beginning of the End, The. Roddy Lumsden. NeBl

When my eyes rove in search of recognition. Sentimental Education. Rachel Hadas. RA

When my father. My Father's House. Sam Cornish. AllShUp

When my father died I saw a narrow valley. Strawberries. W. S. Merwin. AmFaPo; NoP-5

When my father dies and comes back as a dog. Benevolence. Tony Hoagland. BeAl

When my father dozes off beside me i become my father. Yi Sang. CAMKP; PFTM-1 *Fr.* Crow's-Eye View.

When my father had been dead a week. White Apples. Donald Hall. LoL

When my friend is away from me, I am depressed. Meeting, The. Kabir. WED, *tr. by* Robert Bly

When my grandfather Louie came here, from Chicago. World Above Suffering, A. Albert Goldbarth. TaR

When my grandfather stepped from the boat. Gallery. Albert Goldbarth. RWB; TaR

When my grandfather was about fifty, he fell sick. Charles Reznikoff. NAMCP V.1 *Fr.* Early History of a Writer.

When my grandmother and I shopped for clothes. Girl in the Boy's Dressing Room, The. Jody Helfand. BeDoSh

When My Grandmother Said "Pussy." Carole Bernstein. AmPoNex; UnSA

When my grave is broke up again[e]. Relic, The. John Donne. BASC; FSCP; HeIP-4; NAEL-6v1; NAEL-7v1; NoP-4; NoP-5; NOSC; TFi; WaAnP

When my hair just began to cover my forehead. Song of Ch'ang-kan. Li Po. WaAnP, *tr. by* Arthur Sze

When my hair was first in bangs. Ballad of Long Bank, The. Li Po. WoPoe, *tr. by* Elling O. Eide

When my hair was first trimmed across my forehead. Long Banister Lane. Li Po. NDACCP, *tr. by* William Carlos Williams

When my hands, arms, and head grew larger there was at one point a. Fred Wah. NLPA *Fr.* This Dendrite Map: Father / Mother Haibun.

When my heart asked for a way free, it was led into this lightless room. Killarney Clary. GeoHom

When my heart settles. Romance of Love. *Unknown.* BLPSL, *tr. by* Rene de Costa, Rigas Kappatos and Eleni Paidoussi

When my house was bare of skins and pots of meal. Hungry Master and Hungry Cat. Abu Shamaqmaq. TriCat

When my husband. Ten Years and More. Miriam Waddington. BrAP

When my last sunset is under a cloud. When I Am Dead. Emma Alice Browne. TreFP

When my life is done, let my body be left exposed to the wind. Wind Burial 1. Hwang Tonggyu. CAMKP, *tr. by* Anthony, Brother of Taizé

When my life was thrifty, thrifty. Shearing, The. *Unknown.* OBWVE, *tr. by* Glyn Jones

When my love swears that she is made of truth. William Cole. AmWit *Fr.* Uncoupled Couplets.

When my love swear[e]s that she is made of truth. William Shakespeare. AmFaPo; CABP; HeIP-4; NAEL-6v1; NAEL-7v1; NoP-4; NoP-5; NoSic; NPeEn; OxAEP-1; OxBEV; PBRV; SoSe-8 *Fr.* Sonnets.

When my lover sent his palanquin for me. Palanquin, The. Devulapalli Krishna Sastri. HotL, *tr. by* V. Narayana Rao

When my lover touches me, what I feel in my body. Louise Glück. LW *Fr.* Marathon.

When my mind can find no way to rest. Autumn River in Burning Tears. Pak Chaesam. CAMKP, *tr. by* David R. McCann and Jiwon Shin

When my mother died I was very young. William Blake. BrAP; HeIP-4; ItP; NAEL-6v2; NAEL-7v2; NAWM-7v2; NPBRoP; OxAEP-2; SoSe-8; TFi *Fr.* Songs of Innocence.

When my mother finally left her body. Legacy. Joan Larkin. WiU

When my mother knew why her treatment wasn't working. Marriage, A. Anne Stevenson. MoWP

When my mother left Mexico, soldiers commandeered the train, forcing the passengers to get off and wait for the next one. Mi Mamá, the Playgirl. Richard Garcia. InoFa; SUP

When my mother passed on I was forty-four. Bova. Mary O'Donoghue. NIrP

When my o'erlay was white as the foam o' the lin. Song (Poverty Parts Good Company, For an Old Scotch Air. Joanna Baillie. RWP

When my older brother. Rain, The. Zbigniew Herbert. PoetW, *tr. by* Bogdana Carpenter and John Carpenter

When My Poem Appeared. Estha Weiner. NevBe

When, my quiet scientific friend. Divorce and Mr. Circe. David Gewanter. NAPBL

When My Ship Comes In. Gustave Kahn. ReLy

When my shoulders shook. Lesson, The. Kevin Hearle. PoCu

When my sister died, I cried a great deal. Successive Deaths. Adelia Prado. TANSG, *tr. by* Ellen Doré Watson

When My Sister Was Fifteen. Rita D. Costello. BeDoSh

When my stomach bulges, I hurl wild whoops. Bill Greenwell. NewEx

When my thought goes out to you, it is perfumed. Autumn Verses. Rubén Darío. BLPSL, *tr. by* Rene de Costa, Rigas Kappatos and Eleni Paidoussi

When my time comes. Me. Chairil Anwar. PoetW, *tr. by* Burton Raffel

When my wife disappeared. Missing. Moniza Alvi. NeBl

When my wife left home. Yakamochi. ErotSp, *tr. by* Sam Hamill

When my words were wheat. Words. Mahmoud Darwish. VCWP, *tr. by* Rana Kabbani

When Natalia Ginzburg died, the papers of her region declared. Poem for Natalia Ginzburg. Anita Helle. OPRER

When Nature, at our awaking, sometimes proposes to us. Prairie, The. Francis Ponge. AF, *tr. by* Beth Archer

When Nature bids thee from the world retire. Philip Freneau. TCAPo *Fr.* House of Night, The.

When Nature bids us leave to live, 'tis late. To William Roe. Ben Jonson. NOSC

When Nature dreamt of making bores. Epigram: On Sir Roger Phillimore. *Unknown.* NBLV

When Nature made her chief work, Stella's eyes. Sir Philip Sidney. NAEL-6v1; NAEL-7v1; NIL-7; NIP-4 *Fr.* Astrophil and Stella.

When neither can hinder the other. (LL) John Dryden. NAEL-6v1; NAEL-7v1; NIL-7; NIP-4 *Fr.* Marriage à la Mode.

When news came that your mother'd. Kin. Michael S. Harper. OxAAAP

When night drifts along the streets of the city. Solitaire. Amy Lowell. MoAmPo; TCAPo

When night finally fades, when false dreams cease to be worshipped. Gutenberg Inscription. Mihály Vörösmarty. IQMS, *tr. by* Peter Zollman

When Night is almost done. Emily Dickinson. AWTN

When night meets thread and needle and lies down among the bedclothes. Sue MacLeod. Coast

When night stirred at sea. Planter's Daughter, The. Austin Clarke. IrLP; ModIr; NAMCP V.1; NPeEn; OxBEV

When night's black mantle could most darknes[s] prove. Mary Sidney Wroth, Countess of Montgomery. BASC; CABP; MakPoe; NAEL-6v1; NAEL-7v1; NoP-5 *Fr.* Pamphilia to Amphilanthus.

When night-time bars me in. Snowdrops. Margiad Evans. OBWVE

When Noah left the Ark, the animals. Kingfisher, The. John Heath-Stubbs. NOxBChV

When none of this interests me I distort my jaw. Each Sentence Is Into the Fast. Joe Wenderoth. BodElec

When Nothing Entices Nothing. Pierre Alféri. YaTCFP, *tr. by* Chet Wiener

When ocean-clouds over inland hills. Misgivings. Herman Melville. APN-2; NAAL-3; NCAP; OxBoAm; TCAPo

When of thy loves, and happy heavenly dreams. Lines. Frances Anne Kemble. VWP

When Old Tai goes down below. Old Tai's Wine Shop. Li Po. CCL1; WoPoe, *tr. by* Elling O. Eide

When old women say, it smells of snow. Northern Exposure. Charles Simic. NAMCP V.2

When on a cold day with deep snow. *Unknown.* CATKP, *tr. by* Wen Hsia-min

When on a summer dawn the birds start calling. Silence. Stefan Brecht. CLPP

When on life's ocean first I spread my sail. On Hearing of the Intention of a Gentleman to Purchase the Poet's Freedom. George Moses Horton. APN-1

When on my bed the moonlight falls. Alfred Tennyson. InoFa; NAEL-6v2; NAEL-7v2; NoP-5 *Fr.* In Memoriam A. H. H.

When on my sick bed I languish. Thought of Death, A. Thomas Flatman. NOSC

When on the Marge of Evening. Louise Imogen Guiney. ColAP

When on the marge of evening the last blue. When on the Marge of Evening. Louise Imogen Guiney. ColAP

When on the wane, you are always impatient to wax. To the Moon. Song Ikp'il. CATKP, *tr. by* Chi-gyu Kim [*or* Kim Chonggil]

When, on withering into life, smoke. On Fire. David Morley. NLP

When once the soul is ready to depart, sir. Sadi. WoPoe, *tr. by* Dick Davis

When once they find[e] her flower [*or* flowre], her glory pass[e]. (LL) Samuel Daniel. NoP-4; NoP-5; NoSic *Fr.* Sonnets to Delia.

When one deaf person meets another. Conversation of the Deaf, The. Bobi Jones. BBMWP, *tr. by* Joseph P. Clancy

When one gets there, the frigidaire in a corner is. Leslie Kaplan. SCFWP *Fr.* L'Excès-L'usine.

When One Has Lived a Long Time Alone. Galway Kinnell.
   "When one has lived a long time alone / one likes alike the pig, who brooks no deferment." LoL
   "When one has lived a long time alone / one wants to live again among men and women." StAl

When one has lived a long time alone / one likes alike the pig, who brooks no deferment. Galway Kinnell. LoL *Fr.* When One Has Lived a Long Time Alone.

When one has lived a long time alone / one refrains from swatting the fly. When One Has Lived a Long Time Alone. Galway Kinnell.

When one has lived a long time alone / one wants to live again among men and women. Galway Kinnell. StAl *Fr.* When One Has Lived a Long Time Alone.

When One Is Feeling One's Way. Lawrence Joseph. KGB

When one is lonely (and You). W. H. Auden. CAGL *Fr.* Three Posthumous Poems.

When One Loves Tensely. Don Marquis. NBLV

When one was on the cursed tree to die. They Gave Him Vinegar and Gall (Matt. 27) and Wine Mingled with Myrrh (Mark 15). Francis Quarles. NOSC

When Orion straddled his apex of sky. White Land, The. Roberta Hill Whiteman. HATNAP

When Orpheus turned. Orpheus. Linda Pastan. MiVo

When other lips and other eyes. Self-Evident. James Robinson Planché. OBCoV

When others more decorous. Lion's Teeth. Rebecca Hoogs. PoDa

When others run to windows or out of doors. Part for the Whole. Robert Francis. PoA 2002

When our beasts low in their stalls. James Philip McAuley. ChIV-1 *Fr.* Family of Love, The.

When our brother Fire was having his dog's day. Brother Fire. Louis MacNeice. AF; NAMCP V.1; NoAM

When our circus finally collapsed the train stopped on thin rails seven. Decisions, The. Rick Bursky. ReTh

When our heads are bowed with woe. Hymn. Henry Hart Milman. SacPr

When our movement is due to that of the window. Lyn Hejinian. PfS *Fr.* Sight.

When our son was a few weeks old he had bronchial trouble. Sonnet: How Life Too Is Sentimental. Gavin Ewart. StAl

When our two souls stand up erect and strong. Elizabeth Barrett Browning. BrAP; CenSon; LW; NAEL-6v2; NAEL-7v2; NALW; OBEV *Fr.* Sonnets from the Portuguese.

When our women go crazy, they're scared there won't be. When Our Women Go Crazy. Julia Kasdorf. NeAmPo; PBCAP; SweBea

When out at Shellbrook, round by stile and tree. Shellbrook. William Barnes. OxBEV

When out of the woods He came. (LL) Ballad of Trees and the Master, A. Sidney Lanier. APN-2; ChIV-2; ColAP; ITBLP; TCAPo

When over the flowery, sharp pasture's. Flowers by the Sea. William Carlos Williams. APT-1; MoAmPo; NAMCP V.1; NoAM

When Oxford gave thee two degrees in art. Epitaph. Mrs. Boughton. EMWP

When Pallas and golden-sandaled Hera saw Maeonis. Rufinus. HePo, *tr. by* Barbara Hughes Fowler

When Parliament passed the Onion Act of 1707. Postmodern Maturity. Tony Towle. KGB

When passing from nature to being. Vladimir Holan. PFTM-2 *Fr.* Night with Hamlet, A.

When passing from nature to being. Night with Hamlet, A. Vladimir Holan. ConPit, *tr. by* Clayton Eshleman, Frantisek Galan and Michael Heim

When Pat came over the hill. Whistlin' Thief, The. Samuel Lover. IrV

When pavements were blown up, exposing wires. Epilogue to a Human Drama. Stephen Spender. AF

When peace brought the men back. Longview, Texas. Cyd Adams. TiP2

When peace, like a river, attendeth my way. It Is Well with My Soul. Horatio G. Spafford. SacPr

When pears hang green on the garden wall. UV

When pensive on that portraiture I gaze. Sonnet on a Family Picture. Thomas Edwards. CenSon

When people are starving, they go inside. This is the only way. Woman with the Screw in Her Mouth Speaks, The. Sheri Hostetler. ACAMVP

When people call this beast to mind. Elephant, The. Joseph Hilaire Pierre Belloc. BLPJKO

When People Rise from Cheese, Statement #1. Duo Duo. PFTM-2, *tr. by* John Rosenwald

When people were being killed. Air Raid. Sachiko Yoshihara. CFP; GifTon, *tr. by* Naoshi Koriyama and Edward Lueders

When Petula Clark sang "Downtown," I wished I. Meet the Supremes. David Trinidad. SwNoth

When Phoebus looks through Aries on the spring. Christopher Smart. STuOW *Fr.* Hop-Garden, The.

When pigeons returned. Absent, The. May Muzaffar. PoArWo, *tr. by* Tahia Abdel Nasser

When pimps out of loneliness cry. Sliver of Sermon. Langston Hughes. APT-2

When plum / Blooms—. Issa. ZenPo, *tr. by* Takashi Ikemoto and Lucien Stryk

When poetry walked the live, spring wood. Kingcups. Sacheverell Sitwell. MoBrPo

When poets beg acceptance for their lines. Fit Music. Lorenzo Thomas. AHA

When poets print their works, the scribbling crew. To My Ingenious and Worthy Friend William Lowndes, Esq. John Gay. OBSV

When Polly lived back in the old deep woods. Stranger. Elizabeth Madox Roberts. MoAmPo

When poppies tear themselves away. Silence. Slavko Janevski. WoPoe, *tr. by* Charles Simic

When President Reagan visited Baltimore. Glass Canyons. David Romtvedt. UrbNat

When—presto—turf and trees are green. Bernard [*or* Bernart] de Ventadour [*or* Ventadorn]. STV

When Prez plays the blues. For Lady and Prez. Theodore A. Harris. BRtP

When primroses are out in Spring. Days Too Short. W. H. Davies. MoBrPo

When print on paper tells, in the time's affairs. To Genevieve Taggard Who Called Me Traitor in a Poem. Max Eastman. APT-1

When proof of Einsten's Glaswegian birth. Alba Einstein. Robert Crawford. NeBrP

When Psyche, Who Is Life, Descends Among the Shades. Osip Emilevich Mandelstam. WoPoe, *tr. by* James Greene

When Psyche, who is life, descends among the shades. When Psyche, Who Is Life, Descends Among the Shades. Osip Emilevich Mandelstam. WoPoe, *tr. by* James Greene

When Pym last night descended into hell. On Pym. William Drummond of Hawthornden. NOSC

When Raging Love. Henry Howard, Earl of Surrey. NoSic

When raging [*or* ragyng] love with extreme pain [*or* payne]. When Raging Love. Henry Howard, Earl of Surrey. NoSic

When rain like metal tips bounces off the sodden pastures. Frog, The. Francis Ponge. WED, *tr. by* Robert Bly

When rain-washed coils of mountain appear in the sky. Strangeness of Mountains after Rain, The. Jaewol Kyunghun. BecRai, *tr. by* Kim Daljin, Kim Won-Chung and Christopher Merrill

When Rebel Tam was in the pit. Rebel Tam. Joe Corrie. RSaN

When red hath set the beamless sun. Sir Walter Scott. DiBP *Fr.* Marmion.

When relatives came from out of town. Blackbottom. Toi Derricotte. BtF; GT; LTA; OxAAAP; PBCAP

When roads are covered with ice. Popryshchin. Nikolai Alekseievich Zabolotsky. TCRusP, *tr. by* Daniel Weissbort

When roaring gloom surged inward and you cried. To His Dead Body. Siegfried Sassoon. NAMCP V.1; NoAM

When Robert Frost came barding down to Hartford. Blue Plate Tea Room: Sestina, The. John Ridland. VisFro

When Robert Frost passed this stand of birch. Unlettered. Edward J. Ingebretsen. VisFro

When Robert Frost recited "The Gift Outright." January 20. David Lehman. VisFro

When Robert Frost set down a poetic whim. Frost and His Enemies. Robert Bly. VisFro

When Robert Frost walked. Dark and Deep. Norbert Krapf. VisFro

When Robert Graves got involved. Robert Graves. Gavin Ewart. NoAM

When Ron and Lisa split up, she took a job. From Now On. James Harms. AmPoNex

When rosy plumelets tuft the larch. Alfred Tennyson. NAEL-6v2; NAEL-7v2 *Fr.* In Memoriam A. H. H.

When round the earth the Father's hands. Rest. George Macdonald. SacPr

When rule and era passed away. Herman Melville. APN-2 *Fr.* Clarel: A Poem and Pilgrimage in the Holy Land.

When Sam goes back in memory. Sam. Walter De la Mare. MoBrPo

When Saturdays were blue. Blue. Bryan Martin Davies. BBMWP, *tr. by* Elin ap Hywel

When science starts to be interpretive. Self-Protection. D. H. Lawrence. NoP-4; NoP-5

When sea caps rush to shore. José Martí. NAAPv.1 *Fr.* Simple Verses.

When seasons' images pass out of sight and mind. Friedrich Hölderlin. WoPoe *Fr.* Seasons, The.

When Seasons Pass. Pak Inhwan. CAMKP, *tr. by* Scott Swaner

When sedentary and when peripatetic. (LL) Bear, The. Robert Frost. MoAmPo; NoAM

When Sengai put brush to paper. Circle, Triangle, Square. Shin Yu Pai. AmZen

When senselessness has pounded you around on the ropes. In celebration of surviving. Chuck Miller. GoPo

When shall I behold again the cold limbed bare breasted. Return. Archibald MacLeish. APT-1

When shall I see the half-moon sink again. End of Another Home Holiday. D. H. Lawrence. OxAEP-2

When she and I. Gas Station Attendant. Brian G. Gilmore. SpirFl

When she and I hid. In the Secret House of Night. Jorge Teillier. BLPSL, *tr. by* Rene de Costa, Rigas Kappatos and Eleni Paidoussi

When she approached you on the street. Admonition. Tzu Yeh. CrYelRi, *tr. by* Sam Hamill

When she begins to comprehend it. (LL) To a Child of Quality, Five Years Old, the Author Suppos'd Forty. Matthew Prior. OBEV; OxBEV

When she came to visit me, I turned my face to the wall. Pediatrics. Carol Muske-Dukes. PBCAP

When she cannot be sure. Woman Alone, A. Denise Levertov. BodElec; MoWP

When She Can't Sleep. Judith Sornberger. FiBr

When she died no face turned pale, no lips trembled. Elegy for a Woman of No Importance. Nazik al-Mala'ika. ItWoWo, tr. by Chris Knipp and Mohammed Sadiq

When she dreams, she dreams. Mission Poem. Tarin Towers. AmPoNex; PuP-23

When she is [or she's] embraced [or embrac'd] and open to most men. (LL) John Donne. BASC; FSCP; NAEL-6v1; NAEL-7v1; NoP-4; NoP-5; NOSC; OxBSo; PBRV; WaAnP Fr. Holy Sonnets.

When She Laughs. Judith Sornberger. HW

When she married years ago. Italian Garden, The. William Carlos Williams. OBGa

When she marries that man at eighteen, his workers line the tracks. Night in Gracie's Face. Jayne Anne Phillips. MotU

When She Opens the Door. Leo Romero. ICANM

When she rises in the morning. Gloire de Dijon. D. H. Lawrence. NAMCP V.1; NoAM; WaAnP

When she showed me her photograph. Marjorie Agosin. CFP; TANSG, tr. by Celeste Kostopulos-Cooperman

When she sits at the kitchen table. She. Christopher Gilbert. OxAAAP

When she snoozes. Lullaby for Suzanne. Michael Stillman. TLR

When she stopped by, just passing, on her way back from picking up the kids at school. Lover, The. C. K. Williams. OxBoAm

When she stopped on the sidewalk. In Simili Materia. Timothy Russell. P180

When she tells him about the lump in her breast. In a Duplex Near the San Andreas Fault. Dionisio D. Martinez. NoP-4; NoP-5

When she walks by here. Sonnet. Petrarch. WoPoe, tr. by Nicholas Kilmer

When shearing comes, lay down your drums. Whaler's Rhyme. Unknown. NOBAu

When she'd squeezed what she could. Queen Bee. Dilya Rose. EdScPo

When Sherman's March was over. Iris. Herman Melville. NCAP

When Ships Sail Too Close. Lynn Davies. Coast

When silence is a small quick word. Not Body. Jennifer Grotz. LegDan

When Simon received the high idea which, for my sake, put his. Petrarch. NAWM-7v1 Fr. Sonnets to Laura.

When / Sir / Beelzebub called for his syllabub in the hotel in Hell. Dame Edith Sitwell. MoBrPo; MoWP; NALW; OBCoV Fr. Façade.

When Sister Maria told us to cut. Window of Our Soul. Len Roberts. NevBe

When Sister sent Joe to the nurse's office. God's Blessing. Len Roberts. BodElec

When skies are gentle, breezes bland. Land, The. Victoria Mary Sackville-West. OBGa

When skies were dark. Great Day. Edward Eliscu and Billy Rose. ReLy

When skilful traders first set up. After the Small Pox. Mary Jones. PEW

When sleep comes down to seal the weary eyes. (LL) Ere Sleep Comes Down to Soothe the Weary Eyes. Paul Laurence Dunbar. APN-2; ColAP

When Slow October Changes Color. Umberto Piersanti. NeIt, tr. by Stephen Sartarelli

When smoke stood up from Ludlow. A. E. Housman. MoBrPo Fr. Shropshire Lad, A.

When snow like sheep lay in the fold. In Memory of Jane Fraser [or Frazer]. Geoffrey Hill. NAEL-6v2; NAEL-7v2; NAMCP V.2; NIL-7; NoAM; UpMys

When snow / Stays in the street on garbage cans. Aliens. John Peale Bishop. InGu

When some beloved voice that was to you. Substitution. Elizabeth Barrett Browning. SacPr

When some beloveds, 'neath whose eyelids lay. Bereavement. Elizabeth Barrett Browning. SacPr

When somebody loves you. All the Way. Sammy Cahn. ReLy

When someone cries, after making love spills. My God, Why Are You Crying? Molly Peacock. PasH

When someone in virginia. Ozymandias. Tom Raworth. Eno

When someone wakens with grace, so simple. Eugenio de Luelmo. Claudio Rodríguez. RaW, tr. by Philip Levine

When Something Happens. James A., Jr. Randall. SSLK

When sorrow and sleep both bind him. Unknown. WoPoe Fr. Wanderer and the Seafarer, The.

When sorrow (using mine own fire's might). Sir Philip Sidney. NAEL-6v1; NAEL-7v1 Fr. Astrophil and Stella.

When sorrows had begirt me round. For Deliverance from a Fever. Anne Bradstreet. NAAL-3; NAAPv.1; NALW

When soul and body feed, one sees. On a Theme from Nicolas of Cusa. Clive Staples Lewis. SacPr

When Spanky goes. Basketball. Nikki Giovanni. NOxBChV

When splendent Sol, which riseth in the East. Dream[e], The [or A]. Rachel Speght. BASC; EMWP

When Spoon River became a ganglion. Edgar Lee Masters. NoAM Fr. New Spoon River, The.

When spring comes, people have many things to do. Spring on the Mountain. Hueung Powoo. BecRai, tr. by Kim Daljin, Kim Won-Chung and Christopher Merrill

When spring returns with western gales. Whaling Song, A. John Osborn. TCAPo

When stars are hid in the western wave, dimmed at dawn. Cynewulf. WoPoe Fr. Phoenix, The.

When Statesmen gravely say, "We must be realistic." W. H. Auden. BeAl; OBCoV Fr. Shorts [1939–1947].

When storms arise. Hymn. Paul Laurence Dunbar. SacPr

When storms swoop down from the far heights. Storm from the Far Heights. Sándor Weöres. IQMS, tr. by Adam Makkai and Donald E. Morse

When straightening up, I saw the blue sea and sails. (LL) Gift: "Day so happy, A." Czeslaw Milosz. BeAl; PoCho; TWF; WhBo, tr. by the author

When suddenly. Ascent, The. Max Winter. FreRad

When suddenly I am old, and start to wear purple. (LL) Warning. Jenny Joseph. MoWP; StAl

When suddenly in the middle of a life arrives a word never before pronounced. Word, A. Alvaro Mutis. TCLAP, tr. by Sophie Cabot Black and Maria Negroni

When suddenly you wake to shouts and music. Leaving the West Coast. Christopher Buckley. CalPo

When suddenly, you're hit with good health. Patrizia Cavalli. ItPo

When Sue Wears Red. Langston Hughes. APT-2; NAMCP V.1

When summer ended. Emplumada. Lorna Dee Cervantes. NoAM; PBCAP

When summer's heat hath done his part. Aestas. Joshua Sylvester. NOSC

When Sun Came to Riverwoman. Leslie Marmon Silko. ReEnLa

When sun goes home. Taking Turns. Norma Farber. TLR

When Sunny Gets Blue. Jack Segal. ReLy

When Sunny gets blue. When Sunny Gets Blue. Jack Segal. ReLy

When Susanna Jones wears red. When Sue Wears Red. Langston Hughes. APT-2; NAMCP V.1

When Susan's work was done, she'd [or she would] sit. Old Susan. Walter De la Mare. MoBrPo

When Suzy Was. Kelvin Corcoran. Oth

When swelling buds their od'rous foliage shed. John Philips. OxAEP-1 Fr. Cyder.

When tenderness. Silence. Eugenio de Andrade. VCWP, tr. by Alexis Levitin

When that april with his sure as soot the draft of March has pierced it to the root. Ron Silliman. OnScMo Fr. Paradise.

When that century fell into step beside me, I could not tell which century it was. Terraced Landscape. Ágnes Nemes Nagy. MotU, tr. by Hugh Maxton

When that everybody's legal twin Mrs Trio. Circus Nerves and Worries. Kenward Elmslie. NYP2

When that fallen leaf of a girl. Like. Cathleen Calbert. PoDa

When that humble-headed elder, the sea, gave his wide. End of the Picnic. Francis Webb. BMAP; NOBAu

When that I was and a little tiny boy. William Shakespeare. NoSic; OxAEP-1; TFi Fr. Twelfth Night.

When that Master Masons twelve gathered presently. Wife of Master Mason Clement, The. Hungarian Oral Tradition. IQMS, tr. by Adam Makkai

"When that my sweet son was thirty winter old,." 'O, My Heart Is Woe'. Unknown. ChIV-2

When that repentant tears hath cleansed clear from ill. Henry Howard, Earl of Surrey. ChIV-1 Fr. Paraphrase of Part of the Book of Ecclesiates, A.

When that rich soul[e] which to her heaven is gone. John Donne. NAEL-6v1; NAEL-7v1 Fr. Anatomy [or Anatomie] of the World, An: The First Anniversary.

When that shall fade, my verse distills your truth. (LL) William Shakespeare. AEP; OBEV Fr. Sonnets.

When That with Tragic Rapture Moses Stood. Cynthia Ozick. TaR

When that with tragic rapture Moses stood on the edge and ledge. When That with Tragic Rapture Moses Stood. Cynthia Ozick. TaR

When the air is a sharpened blade. Felling of a Tree, The. Jennifer Rahim. CFP

When the air is rushing past us, and our ride has just begun. Song of the Wheel, A. Arthur H. Lawrence. ArBi

When the apple tree blooms. Moon and Apple. Rolf Jacobsen. WED, tr. by Robert Bly

When the Assault Was Intended to the City. John Milton. OxBSo (Sonnet.) OxAEP-1

When the autumnal rivers receive the shadow. Take the Bottle, and Ascend. Tu Mu. CCL1, tr. by Robert Morrison

When the autumn's breezes. Mr. Edward Fordham. Mary Weston Fordham. CBWP-2

When the bad angel loves. When Bad Angels Love Women. Julie Moulds. AmPoNex

When the badger glimmered away. Badgers, The. Seamus Heaney. ModIr

When the battle was over. César Vallejo. PoCho; WED Fr. España, Aparta de me Este Caliz.

When the beautiful young man drowned. Death of Antinoüs. Mark Doty. PoA 2002

When the bells justle in the tower. A. E. Housman. OxBEV

When the bike dropped it jammed. What We Didn't Tell the Medic. Ken Babstock. OpeFie

When the bird of sleep. Insomnia. Abu Amir ibn al-Hammarah. WoPoe, tr. by Cola Franzen

When the birds of spring again are singing. Harvest and Spring. Dic Jones. BBMWP, tr. by the author

When the black herds of the rain were grazing. Lost Heifer, The. Austin Clarke. ModIr; WoPoe

When the black snake. Black Snake, The. Mary Oliver. NAMCP V.2

When the blackberries hang. August. Mary Oliver. NAMCP V.2

When the blind is raised. Ashikaga Tadayoshi's Palace. Muso Soseki. EaWin, tr. by W. S. Merwin

When the body becomes Your mirror. Mahadevi. WPoS

When the boy's head, full of red torment. Lice-Seekers. Arthur Rimbaud. SxFrPo, tr. by Martin Sorrell

When the boys went to one neighbor's farm to ask him if they might pick some of his apples. Boys Go to Ask a Neighbor for Some Apples, The. Jim Heynen. MotU

When the breath of twilight blows to flame the misty skies. By the Margin of the Great Deep. George Russell. OBEV

When the breeze inflates your two robes of silk. When a Beggar Beholds You. Unknown. BLPJKO, tr. by Gertrude Laughlin Joerissen

When the breeze of a joyful dawn blew free. Recollections of The Arabian Nights. Alfred Tennyson. OBGa

When the bride and groom. Drunkard Promise, A. Stephanie Williams. AnSo

When the bronze annals of the oak-tree close. (LL) Advice to a Prophet. Richard Wilbur. AtGh; GPTC; HarvBoo; MoAmPo; NoP-4; NoP-5; OBWP; OxBoAm; UpMys; VCAP

When the buds began to burst. Three Roses, The. Walter Savage Landor. NAEL-6v2

When the bumblebees ride their black motorcycles down to the. Black Leather Because Bubmlebees Look Like It. Diane Wakoski. P180

When the burnt flesh is finally at rest. Annotations of Auschwitz. Peter Porter. BrAP; HP

When the bush warbler. Shoha. SoOfWa, tr. by Sam Hamill

When the call comes, be calm. How to Watch Your Brother Die. Michael Lassell. CAGL; WiU

When the Camel Is Dust it Goes Through the Needle's Eye. Anne Stevenson. Prnts

When the car gave up the ghost outside Lahore. When the Car Gave Up the Ghost. Fergus Allen. NIrP

When the car stopped. Autozobop. Boadiba. OGAHCP, tr. by the author and Jack Hirschman

When the census is taken, of course. Taking the Census. Charles Robert Thatcher. NOBAu

When the century dragged, like a great wheel stuck at dead center. Robert Penn Warren. Fr. Promises.

When the charms of spring awaken, awaken, awaken. Listen to the Mocking Bird. Septimus Winner. TCAPo

When the children are asleep and our old bed. Hell to Pay. Susanne Doyle. CalPo; FFC

When the children fight in the car. Gathas. Robert Aitken. WhBo

When the chilled dough of his flesh went in an oven. Tony Harrison. InoFa; NAEL-6v2; NAEL-7v2; NAMCP V.2 Fr. School of Eloquence, The.

When the city becomes a vast prison. Condition. Mahdi Muhammad Ali. IrPoTo, tr. by Salaam Yousif

When the city snores in blood-shot eyes. Rooftop Piper. David Hernandez. IllVoic

When the Clapper hits the Bell. (LL) Belmans Song, A. Thomas Ravenscroft. NPeEn; PBRV

When the clouds lift, he'll glimpse the miles-off sea. (LL) Kanheri Caves. Dom Moraes. NoP-4; NoP-5

When the clouds' swoln bosoms echo back the shouts of the many and strong. Thomas Hardy. ChIV-1; NAMCP V.1; NoAM Fr. In Tenebris.

When the cock crows. Lazy Man, The. Unknown. WoPoe, tr. by Ulli Beier and Bakare Gbadamosi

When the cold wind visits you from the corners of the earth. To Li Po. Tu Fu [or Du Fu]. TAL

When the cold-blooded are proved right. Little Wrongs. Fanny Howe. Eno

When the Corsican Chief, with a view to degrade. To Buonaparte. Unknown. NOBRP

When the crickets. Louis Zukofsky. APT-2

When the cry goes up. Sergey Chudakov. TCRusP, tr. by Daniel Weissbort

When the cuckoo cries. April. Pak Mogwŏl [or Mokwŏl]. CAMKP, tr. by Kevin O'Rourke

When the dark is wise to us, what is memory. Small Hours. David Barber. AmPoNex

When the Day Comes. Mirza Asadullah Khan Ghalib. WED, tr. by Robert Bly and Sunil Dutta

When the day comes my son looks through me. Fathers and Sons. Peter Cooley. MAAN

When the day fades away into twilight. Time on My Hands. Harold Adamson and Mack Gordon. ReLy

When the day students left school on late afternoons in winter. Shops. Jean Follain. MotU, tr. by Mary Feeney

When the day train in May. Nostalgia. No Ch'ŏnmyŏng. CAMKP, tr. by Mickey Hong

When the daylight came Enkidu got up and cried to Gilgamesh, "O my brother, such a dream I had last night. Unknown. CAGL Fr. Epic of Gilgamesh, The.

When the dead man hears thunder, he things someone is speaking. Book of the Dead Man (#13), The. Marvin Bell. Vesp

When the dead man itches, he thinks he has picked up a splinter. Book of the Dead Man #43, The. Marvin Bell. GifTon

When the dead rise in movies they're hideous. Night of the Living, Night of the Dead. Kim Addonizio. RoV

When the Dean said we could not cross campus. Sharon Olds. See Dean of the University said, The.

When the dividend's set, I can say without doubt. Contract Mucker, The. Wilson H. Thomson. IFF

When the doctor runs out of words and still. Body Mutinies, The. Lucia Maria Perillo. IllVoic

When the dogstar is aglow. Garden Calendar. N. M. Bodecker. TLR

When the door between the worlds opened. Red Water. Dana Levin. AmPoNex

When the door opened. In austin reigns a bald-headed queen. Pat LittleDog. TiP2

When the drifting rain on the window-pane streams over the pattering ledge. Old Road Map, The. Arthur Waugh. ArBi

When the eagle soared clear through a dawn distilling of emerald. Crow and the Birds. Ted Hughes. HarvBoo

When the east wind leaves that curl. Nedim. OLP, tr. by Walter Andrews, Najaat Black and Mehmet Kalpakli

When the enemy went after my father he spared no weapon. Returning from the Enemy, Part 6. June Jordan. CFP

When the enthusiasm / of our time. Before the Scales, Tomorrow. Otto René Castillo. AF, tr. by Barbara Paschke and David Volpendesta

When the Euxine goddess with astonished eyes. André Marie de Chénier. WoPoe Fr. Hermes.

When the Eye of Day Is Shut. A. E. Housman. NPeEn

When the Famous Black Poet speaks. Passing. Carl Phillips. BtF; PoPoPo

When the feet of the rain tread a dance on the roofs. Gipsy-Night. Richard Hughes. OBWVE

When the female railway clerk. Nissim Ezekiel. OBCoV Fr. Poems in the Greek Anthology Mode.

When the fierce north wind with his airy forces. Day of Judg[e]ment, The; an Ode [Attempted in English Sapphic]. Isaac Watts. ChIV-2; NoP-4; NoP-5; OBEV; OxBEV

When the fighters slow down, moving towards each other. Late Round. Kim Addonizio. MoASP

When the fires found their way up over the Laguna hills. Good Water. Patty Seyburn. AmPoNex

When the first patches of snow. Execution of Memory, The. Jerzy Ficowski. HP, tr. by Keith Bosley

When the flush of a new-born sun fell first on Eden's green and gold. Conundrum of the Workshops, The. Rudyard Kipling. MoBrPo

When the foreman whistled. Field Poem. Gary Soto. PBCAP; WaAnP

When the forests have been destroyed their darkness remains. Asians Dying, The. W. S. Merwin. AmWaPo; NAMCP V.2; PoPoPo; VCAP; WaAnP

When the French, to their shame. Zaragoza Clubs. SWaP Fr. Homenajes de Gratitud.

When the frost is on the punkin and the fodder's in the shock. When the Frost Is on the Punkin. James Whitcomb Riley. APN-2; BRP; ITBLP

When the Frosts Cover Them. Rosalía de Castro. SpanPo, tr. by Muriel Kittel

When the frosts cover them. When the Frosts Cover Them. Rosalía de Castro. SpanPo, tr. by Muriel Kittel

When the full moon comes. Song of the Cuban Blacks. Federico García Lorca. RaBo; WED, tr. by Robert Bly

When the gas-lamps are lighted, when twilight grows grey. Ballade of the Devout Husband, The. Arthur Waugh. ArBi

When the god, needing something, decided to become a swan. Leda. Rainer Maria Rilke. RaBo, *tr. by* Robert Bly

When the god of the river. Ovid. WoPoe *Fr.* Metamorphoses.

When the gods give both, a man shouldn't complain. (LL) Energy in Sweden. Kenneth Koch. NoP-4; NoP-5

When the Gods Put on Meter. Cal Bedient. BAP-01

When the Grain Is Golden and the Wind Is Chilly, Then It Is the Time to Harvest. Nick Carbó. NeAmPo

When the grandfathers and shell-shocked bachelors. Holding the Line. Tom French. NIrP

When the grass in Yen is still jade thread. Spring Thoughts. Li Po. WoPoe, *tr. by* Elling O. Eide

When the great acacias spread upon the sky. In the Courtyard of the Servants. Ferenc Jankovich. IQMS, *tr. by* Madeline Mason

When the great bell / Booms over the Portland stone urn, and. City. Sir John Betjeman. HarvBoo

When the Great Bird soars. Great Bird, The. Li Po. CrYelRi, *tr. by* Sam Hamill

When the great universe hung nebulous. 'Egoisme à Deux'. Louisa Sarah Bevington. VWP

When the Greek sea. Sometimes, as a Child. Olga Broumas. YaYoPo

When the green woods laugh with the voice of joy. William Blake. NBLV *Fr.* Songs of Innocence.

When the grey lake-water rushes. Solitary Woodsman, The. Sir Charles G. D. Roberts. VWP

When the gunner spoke in his sleep the hut was still. Gunner, The. Francis Webb. BMAP

When the hangman's bored he turns dangerous. November. Tomas Tranströmer. WoBe, *tr. by* Robin Fulton

When the heart bursts into flame. Jelaluddin Rumi. EaWin, *tr. by* Talat Sait Halman and W. S. Merwin

When the heart is hard and parched up, come upon me with a shower of mercy. Rabindranath Tagore. ItP; PtR *Fr.* Gitanjali.

When the Heavenly Jewel reign period was about to end and the Iranian wished to rebel. Iranian Whirling Girls. Yüan Chěn. ColAnChi, *tr. by* Victor H. Mair

When the heavens with stars are gleaming. For Who? Mary Weston Fordham. CBWP-2

When the hedgerows are sweet with bloom and bud. Flying Wheel, The. Ernest De Lancey Pierson. ArBi

When the horny god saw someone. *Unknown.* PriapPo *Fr.* Priapus Poems, The.

When the horny god was feted. *Unknown.* PriapPo *Fr.* Priapus Poems, The.

When the hot din of red trams at noon. Alley of Flowers, The. Chitra Divakaruni. FiBr

When the Hounds of Spring. Algernon Charles Swinburne. NAEL-6v2; NAEL-7v2; OBEV; OxBEV; TFi; WeW-3 *Fr.* Atalanta in Calydon.

When the hounds of spring are on winter's traces. William Cole. AmWit *Fr.* Uncoupled Couplets.

When the hounds of spring are on winter's traces. Algernon Charles Swinburne. NAEL-6v2; NAEL-7v2; OBEV; OxBEV; TFi; WeW-3 *Fr.* Atalanta in Calydon.

When the hour is here. Tomas Tranströmer. WoBe *Fr.* Haiku.

When the hysterical vision strikes. Baroque Exterior. "Ern Malley." BMAP

When the ice fell through, there was plenty of time. Midnight Run. Jonathan Johnson. AmPoNex

When the immutable accidents of birth. God Hunger. Michael Ryan. BodElec

When the king of the jungle first wakes up, he thinks. Sunday, Tarzan in His Hammock. Lewis Buzbee. TWF

When the king of Yueh returned. Remembering Ancient Days in Yueh. Li Po. CrYelRi, *tr. by* Sam Hamill

When the Kingdom Comes. Jill Alexander Essbaum. NAPBL

When the Kye Comes Hame. James Hogg. NPBRoP

When the lad for longing sighs. A. E. Housman. MoBrPo *Fr.* Shropshire Lad, A.

When the lamp is shattered [*or* shatter'd]. Lines. Percy Bysshe Shelley. NAEL-7v2; OBEV; OxBEV

When the language of the mountain. Mother tongue. Celia de Fréine. NIrP, *tr. by* the author

When the last day comes. Last Day, The. Kevin Hart. BMAP

When the last Flavius, drunk with fury, tore. Juvenal. OBVE *Fr.* Satires.

When the last mine closed. Sinking of Clay City, The. Robert Wrigley. GifTon

When the last newspaper is printed and the ink is faded and dried. Freedom in Peril. "Sagittarius." UV

When the Lease Is Up. Weldon Kees. NoP-5

When the Leather Is a Whip. Martín Espada. LiTh

When the lieutenant of the Guardia de Asalto. On the Murder of Lieutenant José del Castillo by the Falangist Bravo Martinez, July 12, 1936. Philip Levine. AmWaPo; WaAnP

When the light falls, it falls on her. When the Light Falls. Stanley Kunitz. MoAmPo

When the light from the narrow window falls on their last. Proserpine. Caitríona O'Reilly. NIrP

When the light of a burning element is refracted and diffracted. Very Fine Lines. Britton Wilkie. AHA

When the lily established herself in the. Water-Lily, The. D. M. Black. EdScPo

When the lion was young. Lord Byron. STuOW *Fr.* Deformed Transformed, The.

When the literary journal. Poet, The. Gerrit Komrij. TuT

When the little bluebird. Let's Do It, Let's Fall in Love. Cole Porter. ReLy; UV

When the little devil, panic. Of You. Norman Alexander MacCaig. PoCu

When the long-fingered leaves of the sycamore. Bearing Witness. Ellen Bass. LiTh

When the loons cry. New Hampshire. Howard Moss. GoPo

When the lover. Vow, The. Galway Kinnell. VCAP

When the man comes home he takes off his hat. Small Light, A. Cathy Song. TRP

When the man in the window seat. Experts, The. Jack Myers. BodElec; TiP2

When the map blossomed green. Elemental Journey: Anniversary Gift. Alicia Gaspar de Alba.

When the mar / when the mar / the marshymorasswamps. Henri Michaux. PFTM-1

When the master. Hut in Harmony. Muso Soseki. EaWin, *tr. by* W. S. Merwin

When the master lived a king and I a starving hutted slave. Lance Jeffers. SSLK

When the master sits at ease. Friend Cato. Anna Wickham. MoBrPo

When the Master was calling the roll. Anseo. Paul Muldoon. ModIr; NAMCP V.2; NPeEn; PNI

When the mellow moon begins to beam. Man I Love, The. Ira Gershwin. ReLy

When the Midnight Choo-Choo Leaves for Alabam'. Irving Berlin. ReLy

When the mind begins to see the lies it loves. Thrillsville. Julianne Buchsbaum. LegDan

When the monkeys howl, I know that dawn has broken. I Follow the Jinzhu Torrent. Hsieh Ling-yün. CCL1, *tr. by* John Frodsham

When the Monuments. Funso Aiyejina. NAfrP

When the monuments to our past. When the Monuments. Funso Aiyejina. NAfrP

When the moon. Winter Moon Haiku. Thomas Rain Crowe. AmZen

When the Moon Isn't Shining. L. Miller. Prolet, *tr. by* Amelia Glaser

When the moon sails out. Moon Sails Out, The. Federico García Lorca. AmFaPo, *tr. by* Robert Bly

When the moon's splendour shines in naked heaven. To His Friend in Absence. Walafrid Strabo. CAGL, *tr. by* Helen Waddell

When the morning hymn. Wonder-Teacher, The. Cynthia Ozick. TaR

When the morning was waking over the war. Among Those Killed in the Dawn Raid Was a Man Aged a Hundred. Dylan Thomas. OxBSo

When the mosquito death approaches. (LL) How to Kill. Keith Douglas. HarvBoo; NPeEn; PLBUT; PoAgWa; PoWW

When the motorcade rolled to a halt, Quang Duc. 2527th Birthday of the Buddha. Yusef Komunyakaa. WhBo

When the mouse died, there was a sort of pity. Death of a Whale. John Blight. BMAP

When the movie ends and the lights come on, the audience is puzzled. Corpse and Mirror III. John Yau. ReTh

When the movies were 35¢. Imitation of Life. Afaa Michael Weaver. UnSA

When the neat white. Duck. Valerie Worth. NTCP

When the NEHI Strawberry pop bottle cap. NEHI Strawberry Down-and-Away. Luis Lopez. GeoH

When the new teacher said. How the New Teacher Got Her Nickname. Brian Patten. NOxBChV

When the night comes in and the darkness becomes a staff. Growing Toward the Earth. Luis Rosales. RaW, *tr. by* Ralph Nelson and Rita García Nelson

When the night falls. Karai Senryū. EMJL, *tr. by* Makoto Ueda

When the night has already turned. At This Juncture. Blanca Wiethüchter. TANSG, *tr. by* Shaun Griffin and Emma Sepúlveda-Pulvirenti

When the night hour trembles in the steeple, that's when it's fine to look at the moon. Moonlight. Aloysius Bertrand. MotU, *tr. by* James Weeks

When the nightingale in the leaves. Love Song. Jaufré Rudel. NAWM-7v1, *tr. by* Roy Rosenstein and George Wolf

When the nightingale to his mate. *Unknown.* APT-1; OBVE; OxBoAm; WeW-3 *Fr.* Langue d'Oc.

When the Nomads Come Over the Hill. James Tate. WaAnP

When the Norn Mother saw the Whirlwind Hour. Lincoln, the Man of the People. Edwin Markham. MoAmPo

When the old man rubbed my back. Bear Fat. Linda Hogan. AFaM

When the one I love takes the cup of wine. Fish in Deep Water, The (144). Khwaja Shams-ad-din Muhammad Hafiz. WED, *tr. by* Robert Bly and Leonard Lewisohn

When the only sound in the empty street. Love for Sale. Cole Porter. ReLy

When the Osages captured you at the stream. I Will Bring You Twin Grays. Marla Big Boy. ReEnLa

When the others have gone, we row out to the island. Rainbearers. Vona Groarke. NIrP

When the owl hoots. Yi Chŏngbo. CATKP, *tr. by* Wen Hsia-min

When the ox-horn sounds in the buried hills. Second Psalm: The Signals. W. S. Merwin. GifTon

When the pale moon hides and the wild wind wails. Wolf, The. Georgia Roberts Durston. TLR

When the Parachute Does Not Open. Yevgeny Mikhailovich Vinokurov. TCRusP, *tr. by* Daniel Weissbort

When the parade horse horses through the parade. Ble. Oskar Pastior. OnScMo, *tr. by* Rosmarie Waldrop

When the peach ripens to a rosy bloom. Morning-Glory, The. Sarah Helen Whitman. ColAP

When the pen that motto drew. (LL) Long Neglect Has Worn Away. Emily Jane Brontë. NoP-4; NoP-5

When the People Stand Up out of the Hard Cheese. Duo Duo. AF *Fr.* Thoughts and Recollections.

When the pequi fruit blossomed. Mehinaku Girl in Seclusion, A. Cathy Song. OpBo

When the Pilgrims. First Thanksgiving, The. Jack Prelutsky. NTCP

When the pistol muzzle oozing blue vapour. Ted Hughes. UV *Fr.* Crow.

When the plunging hoofs were gone. (LL) Listeners, The. Walter De la Mare. ClHu; HeIP-4; MoBrPo; NoAM; NoP-4; NoP-5; NOxBChV; OBEV; OBMV; OBSP; OxAEP-2; SoSe-8; TFi

When the pods went pop on the broom, green broom. Runnable Stag, A. John Davidson. OBEV

When the Portuguese arrived. Portuguese Mistake. Oswald de Andrade. TCLAP, *tr. by* Flavia Vidal

When the Present has latched its postern behind my tremulous stay. Afterwards. Thomas Hardy. HarvBoo; ItP; MoBrPo; NAMCP V.1; NoP-4; NoP-5; OxAEP-2; OxBEV; PoPoPo; TFi; WoPoe

When the professor tells his class. Dennis Cooper. ReTh; WiU *Fr.* Some Adventures of John Kennedy Jr.

When the radiant morn of creation broke. Song of the Stars. William Cullen Bryant. TreFP

When the rain an the breeze an the storm an the sun. Quaco Sam. *Unknown.* FaBoVe

When the rain began to fall, he rolled back. Savior, The. Louise Erdrich. UpMys

When the rain of God falls down. Rain. Dunya Mikhail. PoArWo, *tr. by* Nathalie Handal and Samira Kawar

When the rains are in season and the wind sets fair. Tune: "Shua Hai-erh" Country Cousin at the Theater. Tu Shan-fu. ColAnChi, *tr. by* James I. Crump

When the rains came I was, for my own purposes. Three Bridges. Corey Marks. LegDan

When the rains came, it was cold at night. After Culloden. Alasdair Maclean. EdScPo

When the rattlesnake bit, I lay. Poisoned Man, The. James Dickey. CAP-8

When the realm of living runs out. Kyunyŏ, Great Master. CATKP *Fr.* Eleven Poems on the Ten Vows of the Universally Worthy Bodhisattva.

When the red, red robin. When the Red, Red Robin Comes Bob, Bob, Bobbin' Along. Harry Woods. ReLy

When the Red, Red Robin Comes Bob, Bob, Bobbin' Along. Harry Woods. ReLy

When the Regime commanded that books with harmful knowledge. Burning of the Books, The. Bertolt Brecht. PoSu, *tr. by* John Willeh

When the rice fields lie fallow. Harmony in the Kingdom. *Vietnamese Oral Tradition.* CaDao, *tr. by* John Balaban

When the rich pass proudly by. Poem. Wang Fan-chih. CrYelRi, *tr. by* Sam Hamill

When the ring gleamed white and your chair hugged the edge of it. Change of Address. Kathleen Fraser. CalPo

When the river is muddy. Yun Sŏndo. CATKP *Fr.* Angler's Calendar, The.

When the Roman Empire, like an overcooked. Sausage Parade, The. Martha Silano. PoDa

When the roofs of cars are themselves a fiery. Early, Late. Philip Fried. PA9/11

When the Rooms. Johannes Bobrowski. PoSu, *tr. by* Matthew Mead and Ruth Mead

When the rooms are deserted. When the Rooms. Johannes Bobrowski. PoSu, *tr. by* Matthew Mead and Ruth Mead

When the rooster jumps up on the windowsill. Cuba, 1962. Ai. ESEAA

When the Sabbath was declining, just at twilight's mystic hour. In Memoriam. Susan Eugenia Bennett. Mary Weston Fordham. CBWP-2

When the sad ruins of that face. Question and Answer, The. Thomas Beedome. NOSC

When the Saints Go Marchin' [*or* Marching] In. *Unknown.* TCAPo

When the salt water burns. Burn. Mary Dalton. Coast

When the Samurai walked into battle. String of Ordinary Words, A. Maj Ragain. AmZen

When the sea's to the west. Sea to the West. Norman Nicholson. BeAl

When the Second World War began. Charles Reznikoff. HP *Fr.* Holocaust.

When the Septentrion of the First Heaven. Dante Alighieri. NAWM-5v1 *Fr.* Divina Commedia (Selections from Anthologies, in English).

When the shade threatened with the fatal decree. Stéphane Mallarmé. SxFrPo, *tr. by* A. M. and E. H. Blackmore

When the sheen on tall summer grass is pale. Gazelles, The. Thomas Sturge Moore. OBMV

When the sheep are in the fauld, and the kye [*or* cows] at hame. Auld Robin Gray. Lady Anne Barnard (*née Lindsay*). OBEV; OxBEV

When the shimmer of the moonlight now descends. Summer Night, The. Friedrich Gottlieb Klopstock. GePo, *tr. by* George C. Schoolfield

When the shoals of plankton. Shooting Whales. Mark Strand. ColAP

When the shoe strings break. Blues, The. Langston Hughes. TLR

When the sirens don't blast the air. North Brunswick Street Lullaby. John McAuliffe. NIrP

When the sky blinks. Let's try something. Del Ray Cross. FreRad

When the sky darkens. Veils of Prayer. Ralph Angel. BodElec

When the sky fell, the earth turned blue. Nuclear Winter. Edward Nobles. P180

When the Skyline Crumbles. Eliot Katz. PA9/11

When the snake bit. Snake. Dannie Abse. NoAM

When the snow falls the flakes. Dance, The. William Carlos Williams. NAAL-5

When the soul sought refuge in the place of rest. Self-Discipline. George Russell. MoBrPo

When the spent sun throws up its rays on cloud. Acceptance. Robert Frost. GSo

When the squall comes running down the bay. Squall, The. Milton Acorn. Coast

When the stern god. Mythic Fragment. Louise Glück. NoAM

When the stone fall that morning out of the johncrow sky. Stone. Edward Kamau Brathwaite. NAMCP V.2; PFTM-2; WaCA; WoBe

When the storm / Rose, and the snow rolled on in ocean-waves. Samuel Rogers. DiBP *Fr.* Italy.

When the storms of life are raging. Stand by Me. Charles A. Tindley. InvLi

When the streetcar stalled on Joy Road. On the Birth of Good and Evil During the Long Winter of '28. Philip Levine. CAP-8

When the sultry air is ripped by a wind. Hope for a Miracle. György Sárközi. IQMS, *tr. by* Roy Fuller

When the Summer fields are mown. Aftermath. Henry Wadsworth Longfellow. APN-1; NAAL-3; NAAPv.1; PoPoPo

When the Sun Comes Out. Ted Koehler. ReLy

When the sun comes out. When the Sun Comes Out. Ted Koehler. ReLy

When the sun comes up we work. Ground-Thumping Song. *Unknown.* ColAnChi, *tr. by* Burton Watson

When the sun decides. You Stand There Fishing. Angie Estes. GeoHom

When the sun is high in the afternoon sky. In the Wee Small Hours of the Morning. Bob Hilliard. ReLy

When the sun is hot, it is burning. Drought. J.G. Mocoancoeng. WoPoe, *tr. by* Philip Bryant and Mongane Wally Serote

When the sun routinely sets. Waning August Moon. Roberta Hill. ReEnLa

When the sun sets, and he isn't home, she walks. Last Night. Chryss Yost. CalPo; PoDa

When the sun sets, the sky is inky dark. Elegy for Myself. Ki Joon. GifTon, *tr. by* Sung-Il Lee

When the sun shouts and people abound. Summer Holiday. Robinson Jeffers. MoAmPo

When the sun shuts down her cantina. Dry World. Dieter Weslowski. InvLad

When the sun strikes a tall dead tree. Baalbeck. Nadia Tuéni. PoArWo

When the sun turns gray and I become tired. Driven by a Strange Desire. Mónica de la Torre. IIR; LegDan

When the sun was a child's breath above the Earth. D. Jeffrey McDaniel. NeAmPo

When the sun's on the mountain. Why Snow Is White. Dafydd Iwan. BBMWP, *tr.* by Geriant Løvgreen

When the sun's whiteness closes around us. Map, The. Gary Soto. NoAM; WaAnP

When the surf licks with its tongues. Marsden Hartley. APT-1

When the sword of sixty comes nigh his head. Firdowsi. OBVE; WoPoe, *tr.* by Basil Bunting

When the swordsman fell in Kurosawa's *Seven Samurai*. Heroic Simile. Robert Hass. VCAP

When the synchrotron was being built. Almagest, Last Letter to Zakarias. Siv Cedering Fox. PBCAP

When the tea is brought at five o'clock. Milk for the Cat. Harold Monro. MoBrPo; OBMV

When the third summer freed us from restraint. William Wordsworth. NAEL-6v2; NAEL-7v2 *Fr.* Prelude, The; Growth of a Poet's Mind [1850 version].

When the three horsemen rode in. Landscape with 3 People. Lee Harwood. AHA

When the throb of her voice was cut off, I drove. On Re-recording Mozart. Susan Wicks. OxBSo

When the Time Comes. Michael Teig. IIR

When the Towers Fell. Galway Kinnell. AmWaPo

When the train came shrieking down. What the Train Ran Over. Lucy Larcom. SWaP

When the Tree Bares. Conrad Potter Aiken. MoAmPo

When the tree bares, the music of it changes. Conrad Potter Aiken. MoAmPo *Fr.* Seven Twilights.

When the trees began to calcify, and the birds to coalesce with the branches. Dream. Georgi Belev. CSCBP, *tr.* by the author and Lisa Sapinkopf

When the trumpet blared everything. United Fruit Co. Pablo Neruda. TCLAP, *tr.* by Jack Schmitt

When the trumpet sounded, it was. United Fruit Co., The. Pablo Neruda. WED, *tr.* by Robert Bly

When the Tules Are Peppered with Red-winged Blackbirds. Lin Max. FiBr

When the twenty-two clocks chime eight o'clock in almost perfect unison. (LL) Clocks. Sinéad Morrissey. MoWP; NIrP

When the tyrant is young. Everyone waits. Paavo Haavikko. WoPoe *Fr.* Fifteen Epigrams in Praise of the Tyrant.

When the unforgettable sad face comes to mind. Sister, I'm Sorry. Ayukawa Nobuo. PML, *tr.* by Leza Lowitz and Oketani Shogo

When the Vacation Is Over for Good. Mark Strand. AtGh

When the verdict / was read. After the Verdict. Tony Medina. SpirFl

When the voices of children are heard on the green. William Blake. NAEL-6v2; NAEL-7v2; NPBRoP; RACG *Fr.* Songs of Innocence.

When the voices of children are heard on the green / And whisperings [*or* whisprings] are in the dale. William Blake. NPBRoP; PtR *Fr.* Songs of Experience.

When the wafer dissolves on my tongue, won-. Devolution. Molly Peacock. FFC

When the wall between her and ghost. John Montague. ModIr *Fr.* Dead Kingdom, The.

When the warl's couped soon' as a peerie. Moonstruck. Hugh MacDiarmid. NAEL-6v2

When the watchman falls asleep. Rose of Time, The. Bei Dao. WoBe, *tr.* by Iona Man-Cheong and Eliot Weinberger

When the water-clock sounds three times, I realize it's midnight. Night in the Palace with Ch'ien Hui. Po Chü-i. NDACCP, *tr.* by David Hinton

When the wells of song were sweet. Concise History of Music, A. Thomas M. Disch. OxBoAm

When the white flame in us is gone. Dust. Rupert Brooke. MoBrPo

When the white flame of verses. Garden of Theophrastus, The. Peter Huchel. AF, *tr.* by Daniel Simko

When the white wave of a glory that is hardly I. Sinfonia Domestica. Jean Starr Untermeyer. MoAmPo

When the wild turnip. Issa. SoOfWa, *tr.* by Sam Hamill

When the wind. Michel Deguy. BBASP, *tr.* by Clayton Eshleman

When the wind blows the air inside. Rock in the Garden Allows People In, The. Malinda Markham. IAoNAP

When the wind came up that day. Let Go of It. Cindy Day Roberts. LaCa

When the wind invades the treetops. Urban Gallery. Rachel Wetzsteon. AmPoNex; NeAmPo

When the wind is in the east. Mother Goose. FaBoVe

When the wind works against us in the dark. Storm Fear. Robert Frost. APT-1; ColAP; TCAPo

When the winter chrysanthemums go. Basho. EH, *tr.* by Robert Hass

When the wintry winds are blowing. California, Here I Come. B. G. DeSylva and Al Jolson. ReLy

When the Wise Woman wears the crown. Let Wisdom Wear the Crown: Hymn for Gaia. Elsa Gidlow. HW

When the wolf moon howls, when the juncos. David Brendon Hopes. UpMys *Fr.* Advent Sequence.

When the woman in the purple trousers. Rough-Cut Head. Keith Ratzlaff. ACAMVP

When the words rustle no more. Stillness. James Elroy Flecker. MoBrPo

When the world dissolves in its own chemicals. Prayer for a Future Beyond Ideology and War. Kelly Cherry. AtGh; RWB

When the world ends. Dance, The. Cornelius Eady. GT

When the world ends. Transformable Prophecy. Angela Jackson. IllVoic

When the world finally ends. Baseball. Paul Hoover. MoASP

When the World Is Burning. Ebenezer Jones. OBEV

When the world takes over for us. Lear. William Carlos Williams. NAAL-5; PoA 2002

When the world turns completely upside down. Wild Peaches. Elinor Wylie. APT-1; ColAP; NAAPv.2; NALW; NAMCP V.1; OxBoAm; TCAPo

When the world was created wasn't it like this? Anniversary. Joy Harjo. CFP; PoDa

When the world's folk, one day of freedom. Labourer, The. Iolo Goch. OBWVE, *tr.* by Gwyn Williams

When the worst thing happens. Unprofessionals, The. U. A. Fanthorpe. PoCu; StAl

When the young brown-haired. Camps, The. Hayden Carruth. GifTon

When the young have grown tired. For Thomas Moore. James Simmons. PBCIP

When the young husband picked up his friend's pretty wife. When the Young Husband. Donald Hall. CAP-8; OxBoAm

When Thee (O holy sacrificed Lamb). To the Blessed Sacrament. Henry Constable. NoSic

When their eyes opened, it was more than morning. Making Camp. David Wagoner. VCAP

When their lordships asked Bacon. Edmund Clerihew Bentley. OBCoV *Fr.* Clerihews.

When there are so many we shall have to mourn. In Memory of Sigmund Freud. W. H. Auden. NAMCP V.1; NoAM; OxBoAm

When there comes a flower to the stingless nettle. Blue Jacket, The. Marion Angus. NePenScot

When there is love. Pyramus & Thisbe. Devin Johnston. IIR

When there is no more life. Triage. Larissa Szporluk. NeAmPo

When there is too much to say. Silent as Roses. Gillian Ferguson. NeBl

When there's a hint of spring, and the first crocus. Why Is This Night Different from All Other Nights? Nadine Brummer. Prnts

When there's no one about in the Quad. (LL) Idealism. Ronald Arbuthnott Knox. NBLV; OxBEV

When there's nothing left to wait for. Liliane Giraudon. YaTCFP,

When there's nothing left to wait for. Liliane Giraudon. SCFWP *Fr.* Poem with Incense Paper.

When these acknowledgments were left unpaid. (LL) William Wordsworth. NAEL-6v2; NAEL-7v2 *Fr.* Prelude, The; Growth of a Poet's Mind [1850 version].

When they ask us to visualize. In Dreams. Patricia Pogson. NLP

When they bare the iron hand. (LL) Martyr, The. Herman Melville. CBCWP; ColAP; NCAP; TCAPo

When they begin the beguine. Begin the Beguine. Cole Porter. ReLy

When they bowed. Understanding the *Ramayana*. Sujata Bhatt. HarvBoo

When they came to the tomb. Third Day, The. Phillis Levin. BBASP

When they cast our words. Intellectual, The. Yury Timofeievich Galanskov. TCRusP, *tr.* by Olive Dehn

When They Come Alive. Constantine P. Cavafy. CAGL, *tr.* by Edmund Keeley and Philip Sherrard

When they come for you no bigger than a piece of fruit. Brinkwomanship. Leontia Flynn. NIrP; StAl

When they confess that they have lost the penial bone. God Bless America. John Fuller. OBSV

When they entered through the back door. Morning They Shot Tony Lopez, Barber and Pusher Who Went Too Far, 1958, The. Gary Soto. PBCAP

When they gave you to me you were redolent. Birth. Elizabeth Bartlett. MoWP

When they go to death—they are singing. Before the Attack. Semyon Petrovich Gudzenko. TCRusP, *tr.* by Denis Johnson and Shirley Rihner

When they had won the war. Inner Part, The. Louis Simpson. PLBUT; RaBo

When They Have Lost. Cecil Day Lewis. MoBrPo

When they hear. Children's Children. Sterling Allen Brown. APT-2

When they in throngs a safe retirement seek. William Diaper. OBVE *Fr.* Halieutica.

When they kiss. Former Love, a Lover of Form, A. Carol Muske-Dukes. BodElec

When They Know. Ruth L. Schwartz. AmPoNex

When they mourn you over there. Tell Me About It. Ruth Padel. MFPA

When they moved into the house it was winter. Gardener. Dom Moraes. OBGa

When they plow their fields. Patacara. WPoS

When they removed the bandages. Judgment. Eleanor Wilner. ExTi

When they returned home from exile. Charter Flight into the Past, A. Hans Sahl. GTCP, tr. by Reinhold Grimm

When They Robbed Me of My Name. Nora Strejilevich. MirDau, tr. by Celeste Kostopulos-Cooperman

When they say Don't I know you? Art of Disappearing, The. Naomi Shihab Nye. LoL

When they say 'Go on, play your little girl'. Self-Portrait as a Warao Violin. Pascale Petit. BeAl

When they sent the robot camera down. Robot Camera. Robert Johnstone. PNI

When they shot you. For F. M. Who Did Not Get Killed Yesterday on 57th Street. Malena Mörling. AmPoNex

When they smile and they smile. Yoruba Love. Molara Ogundipe-Leslie. HAWP

When / they speak of my death. Notes for a Poem from the Middle Passage of Years. Lamont B. Steptoe. SpirFl

When they stop poems. Today Is a Day of Great Joy. Víctor Hernández Cruz. LoL; PueRic

When they surfaced to drink. Self-Creation. André Frénaud. YaTCFP, tr. by Michael Sheringham

When they tell me that my body. Donor. Lucille Clifton. FuFl

When They Told Me I Felt the Cold. Gustavo Adolfo Bécquer. SpanPo, tr. by Dorren Bell

When they told me I felt the cold. When They Told Me I Felt the Cold. Gustavo Adolfo Bécquer. SpanPo, tr. by Dorren Bell

When they told us we could have each other. Hands. Angela Shannon. BtF

When they took us to the shower I saw. Death Camp. Irena Klepfisz. TaR

When they turned off the lights, I felt like laughing. Footfalls of a Great Criminal, The. César Vallejo. ConPit, tr. by Clayton Eshleman

When they use elbow or arm boards to. Louis Zukofsky. APSN Fr. A.

When they were wild. Birth. Louise Erdrich. NoP-4; NoP-5

When things are bad, there's nothing to do but Practice. Buddhist Ruminations. Unknown. WhBo, tr. by Diane Di Prima

When things go wrong, as they sometimes will. Don't Quit. Edgar Albert Guest. TWF

When things go wrong it's rather tame. Blame the Vicar. Sir John Betjeman. SacPr

When thirty spokes join the wheel-hole. Lao Tzu. WoPoe Fr. Tao Te Ching.

When this world began. Somebody Loves Me. B. G. DeSylva and Ballard MacDonald. ReLy

When this yokel comes maundering. Plot Against the Giant, The. Wallace Stevens. SAmP

When those who can never again forgive themselves. Muriel Rukeyser. PoA 2002 Fr. Night-Music.

When thou art done thy toil, anew art born. Settler, The. Jones Very. SacPr

When thou art old there's grief enough for thee. (LL) Robert Greene. NoSic; OxAEP-1 Fr. Menaphon.

When thou choosest a wife, think not only of thyself. Marriage Market, The. Martin Farquhar Tupper. STuOW

When thou dost take this sacred book into thy hand. On the Bible. Thomas Traherne. ChIV-1

When thou hast spent the ling[e]ring day in pleasure and delight. Gascoigne's [or Gascoygnes] Good-Night. George Gascoigne. NoSic

When thou must home to shades of underground [or under ground]. When Thou Must Home. Propertius. BrAP; NoP-4; NoP-5; NoSic; NPeEn; OxAEP-1; OxBEV; WoPoe, tr. by Thomas Campion

When thou, poor[e] excommunicate. To My Inconstant Mistress [or Mistris]. Thomas Carew. CavPo; NoP-4; OBEV; TFi

When thou shalt be dispos'd to set me light. William Shakespeare. OxAEP-1 Fr. Sonnets.

When thou the choice of Nature's wealth hast scanned. To Sir John Wentworth, Upon His Curiosities and Courteous Entertainment at Summerly in Lovingland. Mildmay Fane, 2d Earl of Westmorland. OBGa

When thou thy youth shalt view. To Phryne. Owen Felltham [or Feltham]. NOSC

When thou to my true-love [or true love] com'st. Westphalian Song. Unknown. OBVE, tr. by Samuel Taylor Coleridge

WHEN Thraso meets his friend, he swears by God. Thraso. Samuel Rowlands. NoSic

When through night's veil they continue to seep, stars. Stars. Agha Shahid Ali. FaoP

When through the North a fire shall rush. Day of Judgement. Henry Vaughan. ChIV-2

When thy beauty appears. Song. Thomas Parnell. IrLP; OBEV; OxAEP-1

When thy bright beams, my Lord, do strike mine eye. Edward Taylor. NAAL-3; NAAL-5; NAAPv.1; TCAPo Fr. Preparatory Meditations Before My Approach to the Lord's Supper.

When time has made you wrinkled, sore and slow. Long Way After Ronsard, A. James Simmons. PBCIP

When time--irreversible--begins to doze. Patrizia Vicinelli. ItPo, tr. by Gayle Ridinger

When Tina Turner sings. Mighty Blood, The. A. Anthony Vessup. BtF

When, to check, I swung my headlamp from the coal. Canary. William Heyen. PfSP

When to Her Lute Corinna [or Corrina] Sings. Thomas Campion. NAEL-7v1; NoP-4; NoP-5; NoSic; WaAnP

When to Love's influence woman yields. Elizabeth Trefusis. LW Fr. Valentine, A.

When, to my deadly [or deadlie] pleasure. Sir Philip Sidney. NPeEn

When to my eyes. Midnight. Henry Vaughan. ChIV-2

When to my house you come, dear Dean. Tom Punsibi's Letter to Dean Swift. Thomas Sheridan. NPeEn

When to my native land. William Wordsworth. NPBRoP Fr. Prelude, The; Growth of a Poet's Mind [1805 version].

When to Slap a Woman. Paul Violi. PmAP

When to the common rest that crowns our days. Ages, The. William Cullen Bryant. APN-1

When to the powers beneath. Homer. WaAnP Fr. Odyssey.

When to the sessions of sweet silent thought. William Shakespeare. BrAP; CABP; ClHu; GSo; HeIP-4; NAEL-6v1; NAEL-7v1; NoP-5; NoSic; OBEV; OxAEP-1; PoPoPo; TFi; WaAnP Fr. Sonnets.

When to thy haunts two kindred spirits flee. (LL) O Solitude! If I Must With Thee Dwell. John Keats. AmFaPo; CenSon; IJHIL

When Tom and Elizabeth took the farm. Magpies, The. Denis Glover. BeAl

When Tomorrow Is Too Long. Tanure Ojaide. HBAPE

When Torrid Rhymes with Forehead. Ray DiPalma. FTOS

When, towards morning, faces. New Year's Letter in Warsaw, A. Andrey Andreievich Voznesensky. TCRusP, tr. by Daniel Weissbort

When trembling voice brings forth that I do Stella love. (LL) Sir Philip Sidney. NAEL-6v1; NAEL-7v1; NoSic Fr. Astrophil and Stella.

When troubles get me. Touch of Your Lips, The. Ray Noble. ReLy

When trout swim down Great Ormond Street. Conrad Potter Aiken. NoAM Fr. Priapus and the Pool.

When true lovers meet in Mayfair, so the legends tell. Nightingale Sang in Berkeley Square, A. Eric Maschwitz. ReLy

When two Evangelists shall seem to vary. On The Gospel. Francis Quarles. ChIV-2

When two plates of earth scrape along each other. Quake Theory. Sharon Olds. PBCAP

When twofold silence was the song of love. (LL) Dante Gabriel Rossetti. BrAP; GSo; NAEL-6v2; NAEL-7v2; NoP-4; NoP-5 Fr. House of Life, The.

When tyrants' crests and tombs of brass are spent. (LL) William Shakespeare. NAEL-6v1; NAEL-7v1; NoP-5; NoSic; OxAEP-1 Fr. Sonnets.

When Ulysses braved the wine-dark sea. Making the Move. Paul Muldoon. NoAM

When unborn, my mother minced. Raw Fish and Vegetables. Takahashi Shinkichi. ZenPo, tr. by Takashi Ikemoto and Lucien Stryk

When Uncle Fenster died. Uncle Fenster's Grave. Roger Jones. TiP2

When vain desire at last and vain regret. Dante Gabriel Rossetti. BrAP; GSo; NAEL-6v2; NAEL-7v2 Fr. House of Life, The.

When Venus first did see. Adonis. Theocritus. NoSic; NPeEn, tr. by Theocritus and Unknown

When Venus her Adonis found. Death of Adonis, The. Philip Ayres. OBVE

When Venus her Adonis found. Death of Adonis, The. Theocritus. NPeEn, tr. by Philip Ayres

When Vulcan forged the bolts of Jove. Origins of Naval Artillery. Thomas Dibdin. FaBoWar

When walking out one morning. Ballad of the Two Left Hands. Douglas Dunn. RSaN

When war's red banner trailed along the sky. Robert G. Shaw. Henrietta Cordelia Ray. CBWP-3

When was I unfaithful to you? Hwang Chini. CATKP, tr. by Peter H. Lee

When We Are Apart. Yüan Chên. CrYelRi, tr. by Sam Hamill

When we are dead, some Hunting-boy will pass. Statue, The. Joseph Hilaire Pierre Belloc. OxAEP-2

When we are driving through the border towns. Out of Exile. John Burnside. EdScPo

When we are old one night an the moon. Prayer for a Marriage. Steve Scafidi. GoPo

When we assemble here to worship God. Walk Softly. Unknown. TCAPo

When we came down from the country, we were strangers to the sea. Down from the Country. John Blight. BMAP

When We Cannot Sleep. George Wither. SacPr

When we carried you, Siân, that winter day. Burial Path. Ruth Bidgood. AngWePo

When we caught lice in third grade. Squaring the Names. Diana García. TouFir

When we climbed the slopes of the cutting. Railway Children, The. Seamus Heaney. BrAP; OPOU

When we come to that dark house. Dame Edith Sitwell. OBMV Fr. Sleeping Beauty, The.

When we could have met. the elder daughter of Lady Otomo no Sakanoé. ArkPo, tr. by Edwin A. Cranston

When we decided on the Japanese. Choose Your Garden. Erin Belieu. ExTi

When we die we will know where we go. (LL) Gathering the Wild Figs— Vizcaina, Gomera. Emilia Paredes. AFaM; IPoFL

When We Do Meet Again. Unknown. SSUS

When we do trace out nature's laws. James McIntyre. VerBaPo Fr. Potato Bug Exterminators.

When we drove up to the curb the woman. On Earth. Olga Broumas. BodElec

When we entered the bazaars. Fall, The. Malak' Abd al-Aziz. HAWP, tr. by Pamela Vittorio

When we first heard from blocks away. In. Andrew Hudgins. CAP-8

When we first rade down Ettrick. Ettrick. Lady John Scott. LW; SoSe-8

When we for age could neither read nor write. Of the Last Verses in the Book. Edmund Waller. BASC; NoP-4; NoP-5; NOSC; NPeEn; OxBEV; PoPoPo; SacPr

When we fought the Yankees and annihilation was near. Jubilation T. Cornpone. Johnny Mercer. OBCoV

When we found your father's Playboys. First Sex. Richard Tayson. WiU

When we fuck, stars don't peer down: they can't. Housebound. Amy Gerstler. ExTi

When we go out into the fields of learning. Fields of Learning. Josephine Miles. NoAM

When we go to the temple, let's see Aphrodite's. Nossis. SaLy, tr. by Diane Rayor

When we heard of a lady who. Serenades in Virginia. Andrew Hudgins. CBCWP

When we heard the tree hum. Five from Three. Alice Jones. Vesp

When we know we are on the way out. Only with Radiance. Margit Szécsi. IQMS, tr. by Kenneth McRobbie

When we last hugged each other. My Father Is Shrinking. Susan Wicks. BeAl

When we launched life. You Tell Us What to Do. Faiz Ahmad Faiz. PoetW; VCWP, tr. by Agha Shahid Ali

When we left for Kansas with a great herd of cattle. Unknown. NAAPv.1 Fr. Ballad of Kansas, The [El corrido de Kiansis].

When we lit our torches. Augusto Jandolo: On Excavating an Etruscan Tomb. Tom Sleigh. PtR

When We Look Up. Denise Levertov. TaR

When We Meet Again. Giovanna Pollarolo. TANSG, tr. by Marjorie Agosin

When we met first and loved, I did not build. Elizabeth Barrett Browning. CenSon Fr. Sonnets from the Portuguese.

When we pull off ourselves each kind of clothing. Sin. David Gwenallt Jones. BBMWP, tr. by Joseph P. Clancy

When we razed it, we didn't suspect. Wall, The: For october 3, 1990. Reiner Kunze. GTCP, tr. by Reinhold Grimm

When we reach the field. Celebration: Birth of a Colt. Linda Hogan. HATNAP

When we reached the island. Second Island, The. Derick Thomson. EdScPo

When we sat silent. Trilogy of Travel. Abd al-Karim Kassid. IrPoTo, tr. by Chuck Miller and Saadi A. Simawe

When we saw Grandma come running out. Going Back to Ireland. Violette Newton. TiP2

When we saw human dignity. Easter 1984. Les A. Murray. ChIV-2; UpMys

When we saw our leader running, we all started to run. Sound Waves. Fergus Allen. NIrP

When We Say "Hiroshima." Kurihara Sadako. AtGh, tr. by Richard H. Minear

When we say I. Swept. Hayden Carruth. PoDa

When we sleep the deer return. Histories, The. Victoria Edwards Tester. ICANM

When we speak to each other our voices are a little gruff. (LL) Gwendolyn Brooks. CAP-8; ESEAA; OxAAAP Fr. Womanhood, The.

When we spin and shine. (LL) Every Where and Every When. Arthur Sze. FTtHH; OpBo

When we start breaking up in the wet darkness. Consolations of Philosophy. Derek Mahon. HarvBoo

When we stride or stroll across the frozen lake. Gratitude to Old Teachers. Robert Bly. P180

When we took my mother. Remission. Katherine Frost. Prnts

When We Two Parted. Lord Byron. IJHIL; NAEL-6v2; NAEL-7v2; NoP-4; NoP-5; NPBRoP; OBEV; PoPoPo; TFi; UV

When We Two Parted. John C. Desmond. UV

When we watch the spinning of the sky. Nabi. OLP, tr. by Walter Andrews, Najaat Black and Mehmet Kalpakli

When we were boys. Back in the Day. Lorenzo Thomas. AnSo; FuFl

When we were by ourselves. Mewl. Zulaykha Abu-Risha. PoArWo, tr. by Clarissa C. Burt

When we were charming Backfisch. Friendship. Katherine Mansfield. PoBW

When We Were Children. Alexander the Wild. WoPoe, tr. by David Ferry

When we were children old Nurse used to say. Quiet House, The. Charlotte Mew. HarvBoo; NALW; NPeEn

When we were farm-boys, years ago. Recollections of "Lalla Rookh." John Townsend Trowbridge. APN-2

When We Were Good. Leanne O'Sullivan. NIrP

When we were idlers with the loitering rills. To a Friend. Hartley Coleridge. CenSon

When We Were Very Silly. John Bingham Morton.
 Hush, Hush. UV
 Someone Asked the Publisher. UV

When we were young. Thinking of a Friend. Carl Mayfield. ICANM

When we were young and immortal. Communal Living. Alice Jones. BloBone

When we were young we'd lie outside at night. Lunar Eclipse. Tracy Ryan. NeBl

When we would reach the anguish of the dead. Near an Old Prison. Frances Darwin Cornford. OBMV

When weary with the long day's care. To Imagination. Emily Jane Brontë. VWP

When we'd climbed the panting hill. Koprivshtitsa. Ivan Tsanev. CSCBP, tr. by Georgi Belev and Lisa Sapinkopf

When well we speak, & nothing do that's good. Chewing [of] the Cud, The. Robert Herrick. ChIV-1

When We'll Worship Jesus. Imamu Amiri Baraka. APSN

When were done she said it burned. Love can, I said. Allegheny Happiness. Dave Jeddie Smith. CAP-8

When were the stones and trees born? 158. Shih Shu. CSKM, tr. by James H. Sanford

When wert thou born, Desire? Of the Birth and Bringing Up of Desire. Edward, 17th Earl of Oxford De Vere. NoSic

When Westwall Downes [or Westwell Downs] I gan to tread. On Westwall Downes [or On Westwell Downs]. William Strode. NOSC; NPeEn

When, when, and whenever death closes our eyelids. Ezra Pound. APT-1; NPeEn; OBMV; PoA 2002 Fr. Homage to Sextus Propertius.

When whispering strains do softly steal. In Commendation of Music. William Strode. OBEV

When white dew descends on the hundred grasses. Han Yü. CCL1 Fr. Autumn Thoughts.

When, wild and high, the uproar swells. Cornelius Mathews. APN-1 Fr. Poems on Man in His Various Aspects under the American Republic.

When wild disorder gripped the Western Capital. Poem of Seven Sorrows. Wang Ts'an. CCL1, tr. by John Frodsham

When will father return home? Victory Arches. Yosano Tekkan. CAoMJL1, tr. by Leith Morton

When will men again. Leaping Laughers, The. George Barker. OBMV

When will my May come, that I may embrace thee? Richard Barnfield. CAGL Fr. Affectionate Shepherd [or Shephearde], The.

When will the bell ring, and end this weariness? Last Lesson of the Afternoon. D. H. Lawrence. NoAM

When will the flowers grow there? I cannot tell. No Help. Sarah Morgan Bryan Piatt. NCAP

When will the last flower fall, the last moon fade? River Rolling Eastward, The. Li Yu [or Li Hou-Chu]. CCL1, tr. by Cyril Birch

When will they ever learn? When will they ever learn? (LL) Where Have All the Flowers Gone? Pete Seeger. NoP-4; NoP-5

When will ye think of me, my friends? Parting Song, A. Felicia Dorothea Hemans. NPBRoP; VWP

When will you ever finish using words? Job 18, 2. José Emilio Pacheco. TCLAP, tr. by Alastair Reid

When Willie Mae went down to the barber shop. Choosing the Blues. Angela Jackson. ISC

When Wilt Thou Save the People? Ebenezer Elliott. OxAEP-2

When Wilt Thou Teach the People? D. H. Lawrence. OBSV

When wilt thou wake, O Mother, wake and see. Sleep-Worker, The. Thomas Hardy. OxBSo

When winds that move not its calm surface sweep. Ocean, The. Moschus. OBVE, tr. by Percy Bysshe Shelley

When Windsor walls sustain'd my wearied arm. Henry Howard, Earl of Surrey. CABP

When winter snow[e]s upon thy golden [or sable] hair[e]s. (LL) Samuel Daniel. AEP; NAEL-7v1; NAEL-7v1; NoP-4; NoP-5; NoSic; OBEV Fr. Sonnets to Delia.

When winter snow[e]s upon thy golden [or sable] hair[e]s. Samuel Daniel. NoSic; PBRV Fr. Sonnets to Delia.

When wintry tempests agitate the deep. To Melancholy. Susan Evance. CenSon

When wise Ulysses from his native Coast. Argus. Alexander Pope. DiBP

When, with a pain he desires to explain to his servitors, Baby. Rudyard Kipling. NoAM *Fr.* Land and Sea Tales.

When with a serious musing I behold. George Wither. NOSC; SacPr *Fr.* Collection of Emblemes, Ancient and Moderne, A.

When, with his children clad in animal-skins. Conscience. Victor Hugo. SxFrPo, *tr. by* A. M. and E. H. Blackmore

When with much pains this boasted learning's got. Charles Churchill. OBSV *Fr.* Author, The.

When with pale cheek and sunken eye I sang. Henry David Thoreau. AmWaPo

When with the Virgin morning thou dost rise. Matins [*or* Mattens], or Morning Prayer. Robert Herrick. BASC

When within my arms I hold you. Aurelia. Robert Malise Bowyer Nichols. OBMV

When woods are odorous at eve. Wood Carols. Henrietta Cordelia Ray. CBWP-3

When World War II was declared. Can't Tell. Nellie Wong. ItWoWo; LTA; OpBo

When worn and tired with toil and care. She Waits for Me. *Unknown.* ArBi

When worry moved in it clasped itself. Worry. Suzanne Matson. PfS

When, wounded sore, the stricken soul. Touched with a Feeling of Our Infirmities. Cecil Frances Alexander. SacPr

When Yahweh spoke to me, when I saw His name. Battle, The. Abraham Abulafia. WoPoe, *tr. by* Stanley Moss

When Yankies, skill'd in martial rule. John Trumbull. TCAPo *Fr.* M'Fingal.

When years go by, when. Letters to an Unknown Woman. Nicanor Parra. BLPSL, *tr. by* Rene de Costa, Rigas Kappatos and Eleni Paidoussi

When yet a Child, I read great Virgil o'er. Dream, The; An Epistle to Mr. Dryden. Elizabeth Thomas. EMWP

When Yon Full Moon. W. H. Davies. MoBrPo

When you and I go down. Harold Monro. OBMV *Fr.* Midnight Lamentation.

When you and I have play'd the little hour. Reunited. Sir Gilbert Parker. OBEV

When you and I on the Palos Verdes cliff. Shane O'Neill's Cairn. Robinson Jeffers. NoAM

When You and I Were Young, Maggie. George W. Johnson. TCAPo

When you are called on to perform a duty. Do Your Best. Mrs. Henry Linden. CBWP-4

When you are caught breathless in an empty station. Horace Gregory. MoAmPo *Fr.* Passion of M'Phail, The.

When You Are Grown, Amanda Rose. Laura Boss. OPRER

When you are grown, Amanda Rose. When You Are Grown, Amanda Rose. Laura Boss. OPRER

When you are old and grey [*or* gray] and full of sleep. When You Are Old. William Butler Yeats. AmFaPo; BrAP; ClHu; HeIP-4; MoBrPo; NAEL-6v2; NAEL-7v2; NAWM-7v2; NoAM; NoP-4; NoP-5; OBEV; OxBEV; StAl; TFi; WoPoe

When you are old, at evening candle-lit. Pierre de Ronsard. WoPoe *Fr.* Sonnets to Helen.

When you are the hammer, Strike. (LL) Preparedness. Edwin Markham. MoAmPo; NAAPv.1

When you are walking by yourself. Kick a Little Stone. Dorothy Aldis. TLR

When you are wrapped in happy sleep. Stolen Visit, A. Rosa Mulholland. PoBW

When you bared your china. Party Favour. Daniel David Moses. HATNAP

When you bury me. Under the Sod. Colette Ni Ghallchóir. NIrP, *tr. by* the author

When You Call Again. Francine Witte. PfS

When you came and you talked and you read with your. To William Carlos Williams. Galway Kinnell. NoAM

When you came, you were like red wine and honey. Decade, [A]. Amy Lowell. MoAmPo; NAAPv.2; NALW; NAMCP V.1; OxBoAm; PasH; PoBW

When You Can't Leave Me Anymore. Lynn Davies. Coast

When you climb. Water Song, The. Glenna Luschei. GeoHom

When you come and sleep with me. When You Come Sleep with Me. Yona Volach. DTA, *tr. by* Miriyam Glazer

When you come, as you soon must, to the streets of our city. Advice to a Prophet. Richard Wilbur. AtGh; GPTC; HarvBoo; MoAmPo; NoP-4; NoP-5; OBWP; OxBoAm; UpMys; VCAP

When you come back to me. Poems. Ruth Stone. BeAl; PoCho; StAl; TAPaP

When You Come Sleep with Me. Yona Volach. DTA, *tr. by* Miriyam Glazer

When you come to our country. Crown and Country. Jackie Kay. MFPA

When you come to our house, my love, the "little horror" grows angry. *Unknown.* SLW, *tr. by* Marjolijn De Jager, Sayd Bahodin Majrouh and André Velter

When you come to smoke. Cigarette Case. Stephen Kessler. CalPo; GeoHom

When you come to visit. My Native Costume. Martín Espada. TouFir

When you consider the radiance, that it does not withhold. City Limits, The. A. R. Ammons. EMP; GPTC; InGu; NAMCP V.2; NoAM; NoP-4; NoP-5; OxBoAm; PoPoPo; VCAP

When you cut the bread. To a Fisherman with the Present of a Knife. Naomi Mitchison. EdScPo

When you destroy a blade of grass. To Iron-Founders and Others. Gordon Bottomley. OBEV; OBMV

When you did not come for dinner, I ate leftovers for days. Year, The. Janet Bowdan. PoDa

When you die you'll lie dead, no memory of you. Sappho. SaLy, *tr. by* Diane Rayor

When you died, it was time to light the first. Candle in a Glass, A. Marge Piercy. TaR

When you dig into the earth, water springs forth. For a Zen Seeker. Mookam Choinul. BecRai, *tr. by* Kim Daljin, Kim Won-Chung and Christopher Merrill

When you discover. For Those Whom the Gods Love Less. Denise Levertov. BodElec

When you discovered. Dance Lesson, A. A. Van Jordan. SpirFl

When you don't have it. Souvenirs. Jessica Tarahata Hagedorn. ReBoTo

When you fall asleep in transit. Liminal Highway. John K. Samson. PoPra

When you feel like saying something. Most Vital Thing in Life, The. Grenville Kleiser. SoSe-8

When you gain her Affection, take care to preserve it. Mary Barber. IrLP *Fr.* Conclusion of a Letter to the Rev. Mr C———, The.

When you get rid of an adjective on your lips by spitting it at your lover's face. Ignorance. Gerardo Deniz. RMCMP, *tr. by* Mónica de la Torre

When you get the nomination, the award, the promotion. For Those Dead, Our Dead. Ernesto Cardenal. PoetW, *tr. by* Jonathan Cohen

When you get there, do not greet them. Tommorow. Amal Dunqul. NAfrP, *tr. by* Sharif Elmusa and Thomas G. Ezzy

When you go away. Azaleas. Kim Sowŏl. CAMKP, *tr. by* David R. McCann

When you go away the wind clicks around to the north. When You Go Away. W. S. Merwin. CAP-8

When you go to the tyrant. Keep your head on a platter. Paavo Haavikko. WoPoe *Fr.* Fifteen Epigrams in Praise of the Tyrant.

When you got up this morning the sun. Gary Soto. NoAM *Fr.* Elements of San Joaquin, The.

When you ground the lenses and the moons swam free. Emancipators, The. Randall Jarrell. PoA 2002

When You Grow Up. Anadad Eldan. NRoS, *tr. by* Esther Raizen

When you grow up, are no more children. Parent to Children. Robert Graves. OxAEP-2

When you have both. (LL) Toads. Philip Larkin. BeAl; NoAM; OxAEP-2; SoSe-8

When You Have Emptied Our Calabashes. Iyamide Hazeley. NAfrP

When you have forgotten Sunday: the love story. Gwendolyn Brooks. ItP

When you have money, buy me a ring. Whatever You Want. Angel González. VCWP, *tr. by* Steven Ford Brown and Revuelta Gutierrez

When you have nothing more to say, just drive. Peninsula, The. Seamus Heaney. HarvBoo

When you have tidied all things for the night. Solitude. Harold Monro. MoBrPo

When you hear me say "darling" or "dear." Who Besides You. Bart Howard. ReLy

When you hear me singing. Margaret Atwood. NIP-4 *Fr.* Songs of the Transformed.

When you imagine trumpet-faced musicians. Homage to Literature. Muriel Rukeyser. SeSe

When you kiss me, moths flutter in my mouth. Beija-Flor. Diane Ackerman. NIP-4

When You Leave. Juan Delgado. TouFir

When you left home. Seeing Off the Monk Ts'ung-Ch'ih Returning to the Capital. Chia Tao. CSKM, *tr. by* Mike O'Connor

When you lie. Paul Celan. VCWP, *tr. by* Michael Hamburger

When you lie sleeping by my side. Marina. Eugenio Montejo. BLPSL, *tr. by* Rene de Costa, Rigas Kappatos and Eleni Paidoussi

When you live in Jerusalem you begin. Stones. Shirley Kaufman. DTA

When you look at me. Colorstruck. Askhari. InTrad

When you look at me as if to say. Species. Charles Boyle. EmeKit

When you look life in the face. Round About. Ogden Nash. ReLy

When you loved me. Look How Rich We are Together. Micere Githae Mugo. HAWP

When you lunch in a town which has recently known war. Lunch in Nablus City Park. Naomi Shihab Nye. CFP

When you meet a young boy, be direct. Addaeus. CAGL, *tr. by* Daryl Hine

When You Open the Gates. Norman Fischer. WANABP

When you plunged. Otter, The. Seamus Heaney. IrLP; NoAM; PNI

When you said the Shema Yisroel that meant something different each time. Eliahu. Tamara Kamenszain. MirDau, *tr. by* Roberta Gordenstein

When you say no. Merilene M. Murphy. BtF

When you say, "Quick, I'm going to come,." Martial. EroLit, *tr. by* James Michie

When you see. Catalyst. Zoila Ellis. OWABP

When you see millions of the mouthless dead. Sonnet, A. Charles Hamilton Sorley. EdScPo; FaBoWar; NPeEn; OBWP; OxBSo; PoAgWa; PoWW

When you see us swarm—rustle of. Swarm. Nick Flynn. LegDan

When you seek variety. Tan Manhattan. Andy Razaf. ReLy

When you seem to be listening to my words, they seem to be yourwords, with me listening. Voices (an Excerpt). Antonio Porchia. TAPaP, *tr. by* W. S. Merwin

When you send it out of the body to seek. What the Voice Sees. Catherine Hunter. PoPra

When you send out invitations, don't ask me. Palladas. OBVE, *tr. by* Tony Harrison

When you set out for Afrika. To the Diaspora. Gwendolyn Brooks. NAAL-5; NIL-7

When you set out for Ithaka. Ithaka. Constantine P. Cavafy. WoPoe, *tr. by* Edmund Keeley and Philip Sherrard

When you set out on your journey to Ithaca. Ithaca. Constantine P. Cavafy. BLPJKO, *tr. by* Rae Dalven

When you set up a mirror on the western side of Easter Island, it runs backward. Behavior of Mirrors on Easter Island, The. Julio Cortázar. TCLAP, *tr. by* Paul Blackburn

When you shake loose your hair from all controlling. On Lisi's Golden Hair. Francisco de Quevedo y Villegas. WoPoe, *tr. by* Roy Campbell

When you shut your eyes, you find a string. Acanthus. Arthur Sze. AmAlph; BAP-04

When you smoke with both hands all night, both sets of fingers smell. Candy Poem, The. Amy Lingafelter. FreRad

When you speak about ice, do you mean live ice. About Ice. Malcolm Lowry. OxBSo

When you speak to me I feel my blood sliding. Note Folded Thirteen Ways. Richard Garcia. TouFir

When you stir. Understanding *King Lear*. Stephen Corey. IaFF

When you stop to consider. Dog Days. Derek Mahon. OPOU

When you studied the sea it seemed to carry. Langston. Frederick D'Aguiar. Oth

When you suddenly. Godlike. Anselm Hollo. PmAP

When You Talk That Talk. Viki Radden. BtF

When you tell me that you were unpopular as a child. Johann Wolfgang von Goethe. WoPoe *Fr.* Roman Elegies, The.

When you, that at this moment are to me. Edna St. Vincent Millay. AmFaPo

When you think of me. Love Poem. Ziya Osman Saba. NaPG, *tr. by* Talat Sait Halman

When you think of the hosts without no. Cautionary Limerick. *Unknown*. NBLV

When you think of your country. Firewing. Breyten Breytenbach. VCWP, *tr. by* Ernst van Heerden

When you think to call my name. (LL) Briefly It Enters, and Briefly Speaks. Jane Kenyon. AFaM; HW

When you think you've hit the bottom. You Mustn't Feel Discouraged. Betty Comden and Adolph Green. ReLy

When you touch down upon this earth. little reindeers. D. A. Powell. LegDan

When you tried to tell me. Baseball. Linda Pastan. MoASP

When you tug at the rip cord. When the Parachute Does Not Open. Yevgeny Mikhailovich Vinokurov. TCRusP, *tr. by* Daniel Weissbort

When you turn at the road's. Cain the Immortal. Yusuf Al-Khal. PFTM-2, *tr. by* Sargon Boulus and Samuel Hazo

When you turn to me, carrying your weight on your side. Visitor. Ingrid de Kok. TSAP

When you wake at night. Yearning throughout Life, The. Kathleen Spivack. PfS

When you wake up from sleeping with women. Studying Horses. Robert Kelly. APSN

When you walk in the country, she further confided to him. Henri Michaux. GPTC; MotU *Fr.* I Am Writing to You from a Far-Off Country.

When you walk through a storm. You'll Never Walk Alone. Oscar Hammerstein, II. ReLy

When you walked here. Dumbfounding, The. Margaret Avison. BrAP

When you wear a cloudy collar and a shirt that isn't white. When Your Pants Begin to Go. Henry Lawson. NOBAu

When you were a holy priest. Marvellous Grass. Nuala Ni Dhomhnaill. PBCIP, *tr. by* Michael Hartnett

When you were a tadpole and I was a fish. Evolution. Langdon Smith. BRP

When you were alive, at least. Dead Friend, The. Agnes Mary Frances Robinson. VWP

When you were alive, we often dreamed together. Three Dreams in Chiang-ling. Yüan Chěn. CrYelRi, *tr. by* Sam Hamill

When you were born, all the poets I knew. Poem for My Sons. Minnie Bruce Pratt. WiU

When you were drunk you could always whip Joe Louis. My Right Hand Don't Leave Me No More. Carter Revard. HATNAP

When you were here we never knew such a thing as evil. Love. İlhan Berk. NaPG, *tr. by* Talat Sait Halman

When you were king of the mountains. For Fausto Coppi (1916–60) et Tous les Copains de la Bicyclette. Jeff Cloves. ArBi

When you were there, and you, and you. Dining-Room Tea. Rupert Brooke. MoBrPo

When You Wish Upon a Star That Turns into a Plane. James Harms. SwNoth

When young I lived up to my chin. Ram. Ani Ilkov. CSCBP, *tr. by* Georgi Belev and Lisa Sapinkopf

When young I was awed by authority. Italics. Anselm Hollo. PmAP

When Young Melissa Sweeps. Nancy Byrd Turner. NTCP

When your body brushed against me and I. Turn-on (with most of a line by Spicer). Del Ray Cross. FreRad

When your client's hopping mad. Advertising Agency Song, The. *Unknown*. NBLV

When your eyes are tired. Sweet Darkness. David Whyte. TWF

When your father dies, say the Irish. Shifting the Sun. Diana Der Hovanessian. GoPo

When your hair beats over me like gold. Risks. Joan Larkin. FiBr

When your husband finds out he'll be furious but so far we've escaped. David McFadden. NLPA

When your lobster was lifted out of the tank. Something Else. Paul Muldoon. ModIr

When your longing spans the earth. Thirst. Thurayya Al-Urayyid. PoArWo, *tr. by* Farouk Mustafa

When Your Lover Has Gone. E. A. Swan. ReLy

When Your Pants Begin to Go. Henry Lawson. NOBAu

When your water reaches me. Land of Mirrors, The. Amira El-Zein. PoArWo, *tr. by* Husain Haddawy

When you're alive you get to. I Blinked My Eyes, Looked Up and Everyone Was 25 Years Older. Joanne Kyger. WANABP

When you're awake, the things you think. Where or When. Lorenz Hart. ReLy

When you're away I sleep a lot. Method, The. J. D. McClatchy. MakPoe

When you're both alive and dead. Bunan. ZenPo, *tr. by* Takashi Ikemoto and Lucien Stryk

When You're Feeling Kind of Bonkers. Richard Tipping. OBCoV

When you're gone. Love's footprints. *Unknown*. SonAtl, *tr. by* P. Barsten, Billy Saan and Tracey Yuan

When you're gone out of town, the way I get you back is. Done. Minnie Bruce Pratt. BeAl

When you're lying awake with a dismal headache, and repose is taboo'd by anxiety. William Schwenck Gilbert. OBCoV *Fr.* Iolanthe.

When you're sad and down in the dumps. Say "Cheese!" Fran Landesman. ReLy

When youthful faith hath fled. Lines. John Gibson Lockhart. OBEV

When you've got the plan of your life. When You've Got. Helen Dunmore. StAl

When you've laughed out loud and said a friendly. Nossis. SaLy, *tr. by* Diane Rayor

When you've shouted "Rule Britania," when you've sung "God Save the Queen." Absent-Minded Beggar, The. Rudyard Kipling. FaBoWar

When Yuba Plays the Rumba on the Tuba. Herman Hupfeld. ReLy

When Yü-k'o painted bamboo. Su Tung-p'o. ColAnChi, *tr. by* Burton Watson

Whenas in furs my Julia goes. Upon Julia's Clothes. Edmund George Valpy Knox. UV

Whenas in silks my Julia goes. William Cole. AmWit *Fr.* Uncoupled Couplets.

Whenas in silks my Julia goes. Upon Julia's Clothes. Robert Herrick. BASC; BrAP; CABP; CavPo; ClHu; HeIP-4; NAEL-6v1; NAEL-7v1; NBLV; NIL-7; NIP-4; NoP-4; NoP-5; NOSC; OBEV; OxAEP-1; OxBEV; PoPoPo; TFi; TRP; UV; WaAnP; WeW-3; WoPoe

(When as in the silks my Julia goes.) ItP

Whenas [*or* When as] the Rye [*or* Rie] reach to the chin. George Peele. FaBoVe; NoSic; NPeEn; OxBEV; TFi *Fr.* Old Wives' [*or* Wife's] Tale, The.

"Whence are you, learning's son?" End of Clonmacnois, The. *Unknown*. WoPoe, *tr. by* Frank O'Connor

Whence came his feet into my field, and why? Dante Gabriel Rossetti. OxBSo *Fr.* House of Life, The.

Whence come [or came] ye, Cherubs? from the moon? Chanting Cherubs, The [A Group by Greenough]. Richard Henry Dana. APN-1

Whence comes those many-colored birds. Birds of Passage, The. Jones Very. NCAP

Whence did all that fury come? Stick of Incense, A. William Butler Yeats. ChIV-2

Whence have you fallen, have you fallen? Haida Cradle-Song. *Unknown.* TCAPo

Whence that low voice?—A whisper from the heart. William Wordsworth. CenSon *Fr.* River Duddon [A Series of Sonnets], The.

Whenceness of the Which. *Unknown.* UV

Whene'er a noble deed is wrought. Santa Filomena. Henry Wadsworth Longfellow. FaBoWar

Whene'er I recollect the happy time. Frances Anne Kemble. CenSon

Whene'er, in morning airs, I walk abroad. My Shadow's Stature. John James Piatt. APN-2

Whene'er the old exchange of profit rings. Francis Quarles. BASC; NOSC *Fr.* Emblems (Fragments).

Whene'er the waist makes too much haste. Girdle, A. William Strode. NOSC

Whene'er with haggard eyes I view. George Canning, George Ellis *and* John Hookham Frere *and* John Hookham Frere. NPBRoP; OBCoV *Fr.* Rovers, The; or, The Double Arrangement.

Whenever a butterfly. Lesson of Silence, A. Tymoteusz Karpowicz. PoSu, *tr. by* Czeslaw Milosz.

Whenever a good-looking secretary walks down the aisle at. Inspection, The. Fred Voss. BeAl

Whenever all the world declares fair "fair." Lao Tzu. WoPoe *Fr.* Tao Te Ching.

Whenever Auntie moves around. Auntie's Skirts. Robert Louis Stevenson. WHSW

Whenever I go by there nowadays. Tavern, The. Edwin Arlington Robinson. NCAP

Whenever I Have. Furnley Maurice. NOBAu

Whenever I have, in all humility, moved. Whenever I Have. Furnley Maurice. NOBAu

Whenever I have nightmares. Shooshoon. Felix Morisseau-Leroy. OGAHCP, *tr. by* Boadiba and Jack Hirschman

Whenever I hear. Kyozan Joshu. WhBo

Whenever I kissed her. Compromise. Akhtar-ul-Iman. WoPoe, *tr. by* Vinay Dharwadker and C. M. Naim

Whenever I listen to Billie Holliday, I am reminded. 1974: My Story in a Late Style of Fire. Larry Levis. BodElec

Whenever I looked in the mirror. Inna L'vovna Lisnyanskaya. ItGoST, *tr. by* Judith Hemschemeyer

Whenever I love a woman. Beyond. Fazil Hüsnü Daglarca. NaPG, *tr. by* Talat Sait Halman

Whenever I Make a New Poem. Lew Welch. BB; OxBoAm

Whenever I pause. Noise of the Village, The. *Unknown.* OBVE, *tr. by* Frances Densmore

Whenever I plunge my arm, like this. Under the Waterfall. Thomas Hardy. NAEL-6v2; NAEL-7v2; NoP-4; NoP-5

Whenever I see a production. Amazed by Chekhov. David Kirby. SUP

Whenever I think of you. Never Did I See Such Loves Nor Such Separations. İlhan Berk. NaPG, *tr. by* Talat Sait Halman

Whenever I walk to Suffern along the Erie track. House with Nobody in It, The. Joyce Kilmer. ChAP

Whenever Jesus appears at the murky well. French Generals, The. Robert Bly. BAP-01

Whenever Mr. Edwards spake. Theology of Jonathan Edwards, The. Phyllis McGinley. MoAmPo

Whenever my mood. Title of This Poem Was Lost, The. Pedro Juan Pietri. PueRic

Whenever people are driving along and stop. Yuusthiwa. Simon J. Ortiz. ICANM

Whenever Richard Cory went down town [or downtown]. Richard Cory. Edwin Arlington Robinson. APN-2; ChAP; ColAP; CtM; IJHIL; MoAmPo; NAAL-5; NAAPv.1; NAMCP V.1; NCAP; NoP-4; NoP-5; OxBoAm; PoPoPo; PtR; TCAPo; TFi; WaAnP

Whenever skies look gray to me. I Concentrate on You. Cole Porter. ReLy

Whenever sleep comes down on me. (LL) Claudette Colvin Goes to Work. Rita Dove. FuFl; NAMCP V.2

Whenever something dies. Malva Flores. RMCMP *Fr.* Turbid Diction.

Whenever the moon faintly shines. (LL) On Love. Hsü Tsai-ssu. CrYelRi; ErotSp, *tr. by* Sam Hamill

Whenever the prodigal son returns home. Inna Kabysh. CRWP, *tr. by* Alex Marshall and Fay Marshall

Whenever the sunlit rain. Streams. Derek Walcott. ItP

Whenever they come from Kansas. Coming from Kansas. Myra Cohn Livingston. CalPo; NOxBChV

Whenever war is spoken of. Great War, The. Vernon Scannell. OBWP

Whenever we wake. Beautiful Signor. Cyrus Cassells. WiU

Whenever you take a step. Horizon, The. Kevin Hart. NOBAu

Whenver Mother was out at the market. Women Next Door, The. Barbara Tran. AmWaPo

Wher beth they biforn us weren. *Unknown.* OHMEL

Where. William Heyen. AmZen

Where. Issa. EH, *tr. by* Robert Hass

Where? France Preseren. SonAtl, *tr. by* Merica Delic, Ursula Hobday and Ziva Pecavar

Where a fallen farmhouse leaves a scar. John Wheelwright. AmWit

Where a great road has its start. Shaman's Song. *Hungarian Oral Tradition.* IQMS, *tr. by* Adam Makkai

Where a Roman consul once judged a foreign people. Notre Dame. Osip Emilevich Mandelstam. TCRusP, *tr. by* John Glad

Where a Roman judged a foreign people. Notre Dame. Osip Emilevich Mandelstam. OBVE, *tr. by* James Greene

Where all lost jewels are reposited. In the Rubble. Judson Crews. ICANM

Where all Manhattan that I've seen must disappear. (LL) My Sad Self. Allen Ginsberg. BrAP; VCAP

Where All Were Good to Me, God Knows. Glyn Jones. TCAWP

Where am I, or how came I here, hath death. On Lazarus Raised From Death. Henry Colman. ChIV-2

Where ancient music weaves its shapes. Warning. Nikolai Alekseievich Zabolotsky. TCRusP, *tr. by* Daniel Weissbort

Where and What You Are. Robert McDowell. CalPo

Where and when exactly did we first have sex? History. Paul Muldoon. StAl

Where angels turned into honeysuckle & poured nectar into my mouth. Backyard. Diane Di Prima. PmAP; WaAnP

Where antique woods o'erhang the mountain's crest. Contemns Philosophy. Mary Robinson. CenSon; RWP

Where are all the fussy waders. Mud-Flat. Willem Jan Otten. TuT, *tr. by* Seán Lysaght

Where are Elmer, Herman, Bert, Tom and Charley. Edgar Lee Masters. ColAP; IllVoic; NAMCP V.1; NoAM; OxBoAm *Fr.* Spoon River Anthology.

Where are my first-born, said the brown land, sighing;. First-born, The. Jack Davis. BMAP

Where are our horses. Viktor Aleksandrovich Sosnora. TCRusP, *tr. by* Daniel Weissbort

Where are the brass islands? Relics, The. Harry Mathews. NYP2

Where are the braves, the faces like autumn fruit. Indian Reservation: Caughnawaga. Abraham Moses Klein. NoP-4

Where are the cabalists, the insidious committees. Cities of the Plain. Edgar Lee Masters. TCAPo

Where are the future's clawlets? Tatiana Shcherbina. CRWP, *tr. by* Daniel Weissbort

Where are the girls who were beautiful? Julia Alvarez. RA

Where are the horses of the sun? Charioteer of Delphi, The. James Merrill. GS

Where are the Men Chased Away by that Mad Wind? Alda do Espirito Santo. HAWP, *tr. by* Jacques-Noël Gouat

Where are the passions they essayed. Ballade of Dead Actors. W. E. Henley. OBMV

Where are the poems gone, of our first days? Some Time After. Anne Ridler. SacPr

Where are the poems I promised. Search, The. Gabriel Rosenstock. IrLP

Where are the political parties? Political Parties. Fereydun Rafiq Hilmi. IrPoTo, *tr. by* Muhammad Ali

Where are the ribbons I tie my hair with? Ballade of Lost Objects. Phyllis McGinley. NBLV

Where are the Summer Worlds. Summer Worlds: A Mythic Landscape. Askia Muhammad Touré. FuFl

Where are the tearful smiles of youthful Spring. Written in Ill Health at the Close of Spring. Susan Evance. CenSon

Where Are the War Poets? Cecil Day Lewis. NAMCP V.1; NoP-4; NoP-5; OBWP

Where Are the Waters of Childhood? Mark Strand. EmeKit; EMP; VCAP; WeW-3

Where are the women who, *entre deux guerres.* Ballad of Ladies Lost and Found. Marilyn Hacker. FFC; InoFa; VCAP

Where are they? So the World Changes. Kofi Awoonor. VCWP

Where Are They? Yasser Musa. OWABP

Where are they going, the crowds that pass in the street? Returning to the Port of Authority: A Picaresque. Constance Urdang. PBCAP

Where are they gone, the old familiar faces? Charles Lamb. *See* I have had playmates, I have had companions.

Where are they? I have never missed before. Leaves. Michael Field. VWP

Where are those Songs? Micere Githae Mugo. HAWP; PoetW

Where are those songs. Where are those Songs? Micere Githae Mugo. HAWP; PoetW

Where are we going? where are we going. Song of Slaves in the Desert. John Greenleaf Whittier. APN-1

Where Are You? Harold Adamson. ReLy

Where Are You. Benjamin Péret. SurPaPo; YaTCFP, tr. by Rachel Stella

Where Are You? Carole Satyamurti. Prnts

Where are you, boy? Memory of Bathurst Street. Raymond Souster. BrAP

"Where are you coming from, Lomey Carter." Old Christmas Morning. Roy Helton. MoAmPo

Where are you, glory of old? Lost deep in the night of the shadows? Flight of Zalán, The. Mihály Vörösmarty. IQMS, tr. by Watson Kirkconnell

Where Are You Going, Maiden. Félix Lope de Vega Carpio. SpanPo, tr. by W. S. Merwin

Where are you going, maiden. Where Are You Going, Maiden. Félix Lope de Vega Carpio. SpanPo, tr. by W. S. Merwin

Where Are You Going, My Pretty Maid. Unknown. NBLV

Where are you going, soldiers. To Canaan: A Puritan War-Song. Oliver Wendell Holmes. PCW

Where are you going, son of refugees. Gwilym R. Jones. BBMWP Fr. Atomic Factory, The.

Where are you going through the streets of Rome. Roman Evening. Pier Paolo Pasolini. CLPP

Where are you going to, Hywel and Blodwen. Hywel and Blodwen. Idris Davies. AngWePo

Where are you going to-night, to-night. John Evereldown. Edwin Arlington Robinson. APN-2; NAAPv.1; NCAP

(Where are you going tonight, tonight.) ColAP

Where are you in peril? Inscription on a Staff. Unknown. CCL1, tr. by James Legge

Where are you now, little wandering. Questions. William Hurrell Mallock. DiBP

Where are you now? Who lies beneath your spell tonight. Ghazal. Agha Shahid Ali. NAMCP V.2

Where are you, Robert Frost? The First poems. Late December, Where Are You, Robert Frost? Willis Barnstone. VisFro

Where are your monuments, your battles, martyrs? Sea Is History, The. Derek Walcott. BrAP; NAMCP V.2

Where are your woo-trysts and your heart-wreches now, Ghalib? Ghazal 13. Mirza Asadullah Khan Ghalib. SonAtl, tr. by Esfandiar Kiani and Sunil Sidpara

Where Art Is a Midwife. Tom Paulin. ModIr; NPeEn

Where art thou, Muse, that thou forget'st so long. William Shakespeare. TreFP Fr. Sonnets.

Where art thou, my beloved Son. Affliction of Margaret, The. William Wordsworth. RACG

Where, as a lordly dream. Bridge, The. John Banister Tabb. APN-2

Where Babies Come From. James Tate. NAMCP V.2

Where Be You [or Ye] Going, You [or Ye] Devon Maid? John Keats. NPBRoP

Where beth they beforen us weren? Unknown. WeW-3

Where Blind Sorrow Is Taught to See. Suzanne Gardinier. AmPoNex

Where blood is a rock too big to understand. Ball of the foot. Counting the Years. Anne Marie Macari. MotU

Where both he and I are the hunters. (LL) My Father's Wedding. Robert Bly. NAMCP V.2; NoAM; RaBo

Where, but here / would you. Matachines, The. Charles Tomlinson. ICANM

Where can I go. Captive's Song. Unknown. APN-2, tr. by Fannie Reed Giffen

Where Can I Hide in January. Osip Emilevich Mandelstam. TCRusP, tr. by John Glad

Where can you be, Sanoe? Sanoe. Queen Lili'u-o-ka-lani. NAAPv.1

Where can you go / without me. (LL) Poem to my uterus. Lucille Clifton. BeAl; CAP-8; NAMCP V.2; PoCu

Where Carpos wandered and died, I will fall headlong. Nonnus. CAGL Fr. Dionysiaca.

Where convex and concave. To the Creator of My Bones. Anna Hajnal. IQMS, tr. by Jeannette Nichols

Where cool'd by rills and curtain'd round by woods. Erasmus Darwin. NOBRP Fr. Botanic Garden, The.

Where death is waiting, dressed as an admiral. (LL) Only Death. Pablo Neruda. ConPit; PFTM-1, tr. by Clayton Eshleman

"Where did I come from, Mother, and why?" Christmas Lullaby for a New-Born Child. Yvonne Gregory. NOxBChV

Where did I see this region before with its bleak earth. Baffling Picture. Lajos Kassák. IQMS, tr. by Edwin Morgan

Where did it roll in from, that sea of light. In Two Fields. Waldo Williams. OBWVE, tr. by Gwyn Jones

Where did Odysseus go? (LL) Fred Wah. NLPA; OpeFie Fr. This Dendrite Map: Father / Mother Haibun.

Where did the sea of light roll from. In Two Fields. Waldo Williams. BBMWP, tr. by Anthony Conran

Where did these enormous children come from. Parents' Pantoum. Carolyn Kizer. MakPoe

Where did you come from, baby dear? George Macdonald. ITBLP; WHSW Fr. At the Back of the North Wind.

Where did you go, Holy One, after you left my body? Where Did You Go? Mirabai. WED, tr. by Robert Bly

Where did your underwear wander. Sleepwalking Soho. Stuart Dybek. IllVoic

Where dips the rocky highland. Stolen Child, The. William Butler Yeats. NAEL-6v2; NAEL-7v2; NoP-4; NoP-5; WaAnP

Where Do I Come From? Gustavo Adolfo Bécquer. SpanPo, tr. by Edward F. Gahan

Where do I come from? Where Do I Come From? Gustavo Adolfo Bécquer. SpanPo, tr. by Edward F. Gahan

Where do I get this landscape? Two river-roads. Harpers Ferry. Adrienne Rich. BodElec

Where do I sit. Tea at the Magdalene. Clara Silva. TANSG, tr. by Celeste Kostopulos-Cooperman

Where do I stand and where do you? Seems like. Edoardo Cacciatore. ItPo Fr. Full Powers: Five Warning Signs.

Where do people go to when they die? Inside Our Dreams. Jeanne Willis. StAl

Where Do School Days End? Josephine D. Henderson Heard. CBWP-4

Where do these trees come from. Emaciated Teeth. Fatma Kandil. PoArWo, tr. by Khaled Mattawa

Where do we live? Variations for Two Voices. Roberta Hill Whiteman. HATNAP

Where do we see it from is the question. (LL) Adrienne Rich. BeAl; NAAL-5; StAl; WaAnP Fr. Atlas of the Difficult World, An.

Where does it come from, the sound of a flute. Upon Listening to the Flute. Pak P'aengnyŏn, Sin Sukchu, Sŏng [or Sung] Sammun, Yi Kae and Yi Sŏkhyŏng. CATKP, tr. by Peter H. Lee

Where does she go around the corner? There Is an Error at the Heart of Desire. Chard DeNiord. PfSP

Where does Spring return? Tune: "Ch'ing-P'ing Song." Huang T'ing-chien. ChinPo, tr. by Ye Weilian [or Yeh Wei-lien or Wai-lim Yip]

Where does the ark take us, stoics? The gray weather. Barrage. Ruth Garnett. BtF

Where Does the Dance Begin, Where Does it End? Mary Oliver. CAP-8

Where does the note fall among reaching boughs. My Voice Faithful as a Shadow. Tedi López Mills. RMCMP, tr. by Esther Allen

Where does your body enter alleviating the wait of the test I must make of my body. Thus I Find My Legs. Pam Rehm. OnScMo

Where dost [or; do'st] thou careless[e] lie. Ode to Himself, An. Ben Jonson. BASC; CABP; NoP-4; NoP-5; NOSC; NPeEn; OxAEP-1; PBRV; WaAnP

Where dost thou lie, great Nimrod of the West! Richard Henry Wilde. APN-1 Fr. Hesperia.

Where down the blind are driven. (LL) Eros Turannos. Edwin Arlington Robinson. AmFaPo; APT-1; HeIP-4; MoAmPo; NAAPv.1; NAMCP V.1; NoAM; NoP-4; OxBoAm; PoA 2002; PoPoPo; TCAPo; TFi; TRP; WoPoe

Where drowsy sound of college-chimes. Cambridge in the Long. Amy Levy. ViWPN

Where dwell the lovely, wild white women folk [or womenfolk]. White Women, The. Mary Elizabeth Coleridge. NALW; PEW; ViWPN; VWP

Where ends our chancel in a vaulted space. George Crabbe. OBSV Fr. Borough, The.

Where Engels Fears to Tread. Cyril Connolly.
  "Come on Percy, my pillion-proud, be." OBCoV
  "It was late last night when my lord came home." OBCoV
  "M is for Marx." OBCoV
  "Something is going to go, baby." OBCoV

Where England's Damon used [or us'd] to keep. Pastoral on the King's Death, The; [Written in 1648]. Alexander Brome. NOSC

Where Everybody is King. Tanure Ojaide. NAfrP

Where Fancy paints with Nature's simplest hues. Ode on Truth: Addressed to George Dyer. Anne Batten Cristall. RWP

Where Fire Burns. Gladys Cardiff. HATNAP

Where folds the central lotus. William Yeats in Limbo. Sidney Keyes. MoBrPo

Where, from islands in the river. Unknown. CCL1 Fr. Guan-ju.

Where glide my thoughts, rash inclinations stay. Reflection, The. Elizabeth Singer Rowe. EMWP

Where Go the Boats? Robert Louis Stevenson. NOxBChV; NTCP; TLR; WHSW

Where had I heard this wind before. Bereft. Robert Frost. APT-1; MoAmPo; SoSe-8

Where has tenderness gone, he asked the mirror. Malcolm Lowry. NoP-4; NoP-5 Fr. Cantinas, The.

Where has the black flower seed gone. Single Blossom, A. Mun Chônghui. EcSo, *tr. by* Catherine J. Kim

Where has the lustre of your eyes descended? To the Day-Dreamer. Mihály Vörösmarty. IQMS, *tr. by* Hymen H. Hart and Watson Kirkconnell

Where have all the flowers gone?—long time passing. Where Have All the Flowers Gone? Pete Seeger. NoP-4; NoP-5

Where have I wander'd, London, from thy haunts? Charles Lloyd. NOBRP *Fr.* Desultory Thoughts in London.

Where have these hands been. Musician. Louise Bogan. APT-2

Where have you been. Interview from the Belly of a Whale. Konstantin Pavlov. CSCBP, *tr. by* Georgi Belev and Lisa Sapinkopf

Where Have You Been Dear? Karla Kuskin. NTCP

Where have you disappeared to, horses with the trembling top-knots. In Memory of the Funeral Horses. Zoltán Jékely. IQMS, *tr. by* Geroge Gömöri and Adam Makkai

Where have you gone blue middle of a decade? the gates creak. a sigh is so vastly different. Ode. D. A. Powell. NAPBL

Where have you hidden away? Spiritual Canticle. San Juan de la Cruz. SpanPo, *tr. by* John Frederick Nims

Where have you hidden away. Spiritual Canticle, The. San Juan de la Cruz. STV, *tr. by* John Frederick Nims

Where her house stood, she goes on living. Woman, A. Gabriela Mistral. TCLAP, *tr. by* Doris Dana

Where her poor Werter—and his sorrows sleep! (LL) By the Same. Charlotte Smith. CenSon; RWP

Where high-country evergreens grown taller. Morning Snowfield. Reg Saner. PoCoUp

Where his glory forever I'll share. (LL) Old Rugged Cross, The. George Bennard. NAAPv.2; TCAPo

Where Home Was. Augusta Davies Webster. ViWPN

Where Hope Lives. Carol Bell. GeoH

Where I? Robinson Jeffers. OxBSo

Where I cling. (LL) Last Leaf, The. Oliver Wendell Holmes. BRP; ITBLP; NAAL-3; TCAPo

Where I Come From. Elizabeth Brewster. Coast

Where I come from the language is water. World is everything, The. Ann Sansom. NeBl

Where I go are flowers blooming. Les Planches-en-Montagnes. Michael Roberts. OBMV

Where I Grew Up. Jeff Gundy. ACAMVP

Where I Live. Wanda Coleman. GeoHom

Where I Live. Günter Eich. GTCP, *tr. by* David Young

Where I Live. Wesley McNair. TRP

Where I live is like an island. Confession, A. Jenő Dsida. IQMS, *tr. by* Geroge Gömöri and Clive Wilmer

Where I live, there are more. Scarecrows. James Kirkup. NOxBChV

Where I made One—turn down an empty Glass! (LL) Rubáiyát of Omar Khayyám [of Naishápúr], The. Omar Khayyám. NAEL-6v2; NAEL-7v2; NoP-4; NoP-5; TRP, *tr. by* Edward Fitzgerald

Where I made one—turn down an empty Glass. (LL) Rubáiyát of Omar Khayyám [of Naishápúr], The. Omar Khayyám. NPeEn; OxAEP-2; OxBEV; TAL; UV, *tr. by* Edward Fitzgerald

Where I may not remove, nor be removéd. (LL) William Shakespeare. FaBoWar; GoPo; OxAEP-1 *Fr.* Sonnets.

Where I put myself in third person in a bed I know. First person plural is a house. Brian Teare. LegDan

Where I ramble. Era of Easy Meat at Locarno, An. George McWhirter. IFF

Where I Saw the Snake. Mark Van Doren. APT-2

Where I saw the snake. Where I Saw the Snake. Mark Van Doren. APT-2

Where I shall need no glass. (LL) They Are All Gone into the World of Light! Henry Vaughan. BASC; CABP; InoFa; NAEL-6v1; NAEL-7v1; NoP-4; NoP-5; NOSC; NPeEn; PBRV; PoPoPo; RSR; TFi; WaAnP; WoPoe

Where I Stand with Regard to the Game. Joe Wenderoth. LegDan

Where I Was. Dan Brown. P180

Where I work. Small Secrets. John Montague. ModIr

Where icy and bright dungeons lift. Hart Crane. ColAP; MoAmPo *Fr.* Voyages.

Where if you glance behind. James Dean. Rae Desmond Jones. BMAP

Where ignorant armies clash by night. (LL) Dover Beach. Matthew Arnold. AmFaPo; BrAP; BRP; CABP; ClHu; CtM; HeIP-4; ITBLP; MakPoe; NAEL-6v2; NAEL-7v2; NIL-7; NIP-4; NoP-4; NoP-5; NPeEn; OxBEV; PoPoPo; TFi; WaAnP; WoPoe

Where in the world is Helen gone. Gone Ladies. François Villon. WoPoe, *tr. by* Christopher Logue

Where, in what bubbly land, below. Ballade of Dead Gentlemen. Clive Staples Lewis. OBCoV

Where in what ever-blissfully watered gardens, upon what trees. Rainer Maria Rilke. OBVE *Fr.* Sonnets to Orpheus.

Where, Industry, thy daughter fair? Edward Young. STuOW *Fr.* Imperium Pelagi, or, The Merchant.

Where Innocent Bright-Eyed Daisies Are. Christina Georgina Rossetti. Spl

Where is. List, The. Lawson Fusao Inada. WhBo

Where is a foot worthy to walk a garden,. Jelaluddin Rumi. RaBo *Fr.* Four Quatrains.

Where is all the bright company gone. Song. Dame Edith Sitwell. NALW

Where is David?..Oh God's people. In Which Roosevelt Is Compared to Saul. Vachel Lindsay. ChIV-1

Where is dew? Where is sand? Where the moon? Where a star? Judith. Gertrud Kolmar. AF, *tr. by* David Kipp

Where is he now, I wonder? Friendship. Anatoly Steiger. TCRusP, *tr. by* Paul Schmidt

Where is India or even one body. World, The. Donald Revell. BodElec

Where is it, the sad lyre which follows the quick flute? Li Shang-yin. CCL1, *tr. by* A. C. Graham

Where is it, where am I? Yun Sŏndo. CATKP *Fr.* Angler's Calendar, The.

Where is Japanese Poetry? Fujii Sadakazu. *tr. by* Christopher Drake
  Small Dream. PFTM-2, *tr. by* Christopher Drake
  Wolf. PFTM-2, *tr. by* Christopher Drake

Where is my bay? Bring it, Thestylis. Where are my charms? Theocritus. HePo *Fr.* Idylls.

Where is my boy, my boy. Edgar Lee Masters. APT-1 *Fr.* Spoon River Anthology.

Where is my cat, my rake. Bad Times Song. Jean Garrigue. OxBoAm

Where is my Chief, my Master, this bleak night, *mavrone!*. O'Hussey's Ode to the Maguire. James Clarence Mangan. CABP

Where Is My Country? Nellie Wong. UnSA

Where is my country? Where Is My Country? Nellie Wong. UnSA

Where is my husband now? *Unknown.* NAAPv.2

Where is my ruined life, and where the fame. Khwaja Shams-ad-din Muhammad Hafiz. TAL *Fr.* Odes.

Where is neither faith nor wonder. (LL) Song with Words. James Agee. ChIV-1; MoAmPo

Where is poetry for the people? Poetic Voice. Rebecca Seiferle. TAPaP

Where is she, I wondered, when she wasn't there. Where is She? Peter Cherches. P180

Where is Talcott Parsons Now? Sophie Hannah. MFPA

Where is Tangwen now, where Nest, where is Gwenllian. Fragment: Where Is Tangwen Now? Glyn Jones. TCAWP

Where is that baleful maid. Betty Barnes, the Book-Burner. Rosamund Marriott Watson. ViWPN

Where Is That Gate for Grief. Jan Kochanowski. WoPoe *Fr.* Laments, The.

Where is that gate for grief which, long ago. Jan Kochanowski. WoPoe *Fr.* Laments, The.

Where is that holy fire, which verse is said. John Donne. RACG *Fr.* Elegies.

Where is that homeland, on which Árpád's blood. Zrínyi's Song. Ferenc Kölcsey. IQMS, *tr. by* Watson Kirkconnell

Where is that old "feast of reconciliation"? One for the "Ancient Gypsy." Gyula Juhász. IQMS, *tr. by* Adam Makkai

Where is that sugar, Hammond. Early Evening Quarrel. Langston Hughes. SAmP

Where is the beauty. West Texas. Bettye Hammer Givens. TiP2

Where is the dragon's cave? Kanzan-Shigyo. ZenPo, *tr. by* Takashi Ikemoto and Lucien Stryk

Where is the duke my father with his power? William Shakespeare. OxAEP-1 *Fr.* King Richard III.

Where is the eighth bend? Yi I. CATKP *Fr.* Nine Songs of Mount Ko.

Where is the fifth bend? Yi I. CATKP *Fr.* Nine Songs of Mount Ko.

Where is the first bend? Yi I. CATKP *Fr.* Nine Songs of Mount Ko.

Where is the fourth bend? Yi I. CATKP *Fr.* Nine Songs of Mount Ko.

Where is the grave of Sir Arthur O'Kellyn? Knight's Tomb, The. Samuel Taylor Coleridge. NPeEn

Where is the hand to trace. With a Coin from Syracuse. Oliver St. John Gogarty. OBMV

Where is the Jack that built the house. Château Jackson. Louis MacNeice. OxBEV

Where is the Jim Crow section. Merry-Go-Round. Langston Hughes. AmFaPo; BLPJKO; SAmP

Where is the letter? Portrait. Bernard Noël. YaTCFP, *tr. by* Michael Tweed

Where Is the Life That Late I Led? Cole Porter. ReLy

Where is the lumber-room of what was important? Sheila Wingfield. MoWP *Fr.* Beat Drum, Beat Heart.

Where is the man who sold the best jelly donuts and coffee. Old Neighborhood, The. Andrea Carter Brown. PA9/11

Where is the nightingale. "H. D." APT-1; MoAmPo *Fr.* Songs from Cyprus.

Where is the ninth bend? Yi I. CATKP *Fr.* Nine Songs of Mount Ko.

Where is the promise of my years. Infelix. Adah Isaacs Menken. CBWP-1; NAAPv.1; TCAPo

Where is the restaurant cat? Grand Canyon, The. Jean Garrigue. APT-2

Where is the ring. Laments for the Afghan Women. Hettie Jones. PrTe

Where is the second bend? Yi I. CATKP *Fr.* Nine Songs of Mount Ko.

Where is the seventh bend? Yi I. CATKP *Fr.* Nine Songs of Mount Ko.

Where is the sixth bend? Yi I. CATKP *Fr.* Nine Songs of Mount Ko.

Where is the summer with her golden sun? Ancient Greek Song of Exile. Felicia Dorothea Hemans. RWP

Where is the Temple of Teeming Fragrance? Passing the Temple of Teeming Fragrance. Wang Wei. ChinPo, *tr. by* Ye Weilian [*or* Yeh Wei-lien *or* Wai-lim Yip]

Where is the third bend? Yi I. CATKP *Fr.* Nine Songs of Mount Ko.

Where is the time to light a cigarette. Yannis Ritsos. PFTM-2 *Fr.* Second Series.

Where Is the Wagon Going? Meret Oppenheim. SurWo, *tr. by* Catherine Schelbert

Where is the wonder. Wish You Were Here. Harold Rome. ReLy

Where is the wonder to not know? Clark Coolidge. PFTM-2 *Fr.* Crystal Text, The.

Where is the world we roved, Ned Bunn? To Ned. Herman Melville. APN-2; NAAL-3; TCAPo

Where is there an end of it, the soundless wailing. T. S. Eliot. AmFaPo *Fr.* Four Quartets.

Where is this stupendous stranger. Christopher Smart. ChrPo; NPeEn; OxBEV; SacPr *Fr.* Hymns and Spiritual Songs for the Fasts and Festivals of the Church of England.

Where is Tomorrow? Yasser Musa. OWABP

Where is your home, the interviewer asked him. Why Bodhidharma Went to Howard Johnson's. Jane Hirshfield. WANABP

Where Israel's tents do shine so bright. (LL) Mock On, Mock On, Voltaire, Rousseau. William Blake. ChIV-1; NAEL-6v2; NAEL-7v2; NAWM-7v2; NoP-4; NoP-5; NPeEn; TFi

Where It Ends. William Bronk. APSN

Where it goes on Here not anywhere. Prayers, The. Brian Coffey. Oth

Where it says snow. Errata. Charles Simic. CAP-8

Where it should have been there were only memories. House. Laura Mullen. ExTi

Where it will break at last. (LL) Indian Serenade, The. Percy Bysshe Shelley. OBEV; RaBo; TreFP

Where Josh makes faces, grinning at me.. (LL) David Wojahn. AllShUp; PBCAP *Fr.* Mystery Train: A Sequence.

Where laurel hedges hide the coal and coke. Crematorium. Sir John Betjeman. PoA 2002

Where Leftover Misery Goes. Alice Notley. BAP-01

Where let them wend at will, whilest here I do respire. (LL) Edmund Spenser. NAEL-6v1; NAEL-7v1 *Fr.* Faerie Queene, The.

Where lies the city of the Holy Grail. City of the Grail, The. Henry E. G. Rope. SacPr

Where lies the Land to which yon Ship must go? William Wordsworth. CenSon

Where, like a pillow on a bed. Ecstasy, The. John Donne. BASC; CABP; FSCP; NAEL-6v1; NAEL-7v1; NoP-4; NoP-5; OBEV; OxBEV; TFi; WaAnP

Where, like the prophet, thou shalt find thy God. (LL) To the Right Honourable William, Earl of Dartmouth. Phillis Wheatley. NAAL-5; NAAPv.1; NALW; OxBoAm

Where Liver Eatin' Johnson lies. Old Trail Town, Cody, Wyoming.sie. John Garmon. OBEV

Where lives the man that never yet did hear. Orchestra; or, A Poem[e] of Da[u]ncing. Sir John Davies. NoSic

Where lives the Man that never yet did heare. Sir John Davies. OxBEV *Fr.* Orchestra; or, A Poem[e] of Da[u]ncing.

Where London's column, pointing at the skies. Alexander Pope. NPeEn *Fr.* Epistle III, To Allen Lord Bathurst.

Where long the shadows of the wind had rolled. Sheaves, The. Edwin Arlington Robinson. APT-1; ItP; MoAmPo; NAMCP V.1; NoAM; OxBoAm; SoSe-8

Where met our bards of old, the glorious throng. Felicia Dorothea Hemans. RWP *Fr.* Siege of Valencia, The.

Where metalled road invades light thinning air. Sándor Weöres. OBVE *Fr.* Lost Parasol, The.

Where Mountain Lion Lay [*or* Laid] Down with Deer. Leslie Marmon Silko. TRP

Where My Books Go. William Butler Yeats. OBEV

Where my grandfather is in the ground. Mi Abuelo. Alberto A. Ríos. NAMCP V.2; NIL-7; PoPoPo; WaAnP

Where My Mother Cries. Juanita Brunk. ACAMVP

Where my Sun-flower wishes to go. (LL) William Blake. NAEL-6v2; NAEL-7v2; NIP-4; NOBRP; NoP-4; NoP-5; NPBRoP; NPeEn; PoPoPo; TFi; WaAnP; WeW-3 *Fr.* Songs of Experience.

Where nothing grew I set a knot of herbs. Ann Lauinger. IaFF *Fr.* Three Songs for *King Leir*.

Where now is Britain?—where her laurelled names. Henry Kirke White. STuOW *Fr.* Time: A Poem.

Where now is the young Adam, sultry in his Aiden? Nocturne. John Crowe Ransom. APT-1

Where now the vital energy that moved. William Cowper. NPeEn *Fr.* Task, The.

Where, O, Where? Elinor Wylie. NAAPv.2

Where, O! where's the chain to fling. Letitia Elizabeth Landon. NOBRP *Fr.* Golden Violet, The.

Where of old, responsive. Echoes. John Banister Tabb. APN-2

Where often clouds shall lean their swan-white neck. (LL) Pylons, The. Stephen Spender. BrAP; NAMCP V.1; NoAM

Where olive leaves are twinkling in every wind that blew. Damsel of Peru, The. William Cullen Bryant. APN-1

Where on earth. Question of Time, The. William Peskett. PNI

Where once you could win over grasping boys. Glaukos. CAGL, *tr. by* Daryl Hine

Where one needs one's brains all the time. (LL) Lake Isle, The. Ezra Pound. OBCoV; OxBoAm; PoA 2002

Where or When. Lorenz Hart. ReLy

Where others love, and praise my Verses; still. To the Detracter. Robert Herrick. PBRV

Where pomelo hangs down lovely fruit. Pomelo, The. *Unknown.* WoPoe, *tr. by* Anne Birrell

Where praise already is is the only place Grief. Rainer Maria Rilke. RaBo *Fr.* Sonnets to Orpheus.

Where red sun and sand shine. Letter from Kuwait. Lenard D. Moore. BtF

Where rest not England's dead. (LL) England's Dead. Felicia Dorothea Hemans. NAEL-6v2; NAEL-7v2; NoP-4; NoP-5; WaAnP

Where San Juan and Chacabuco intersect. Houses like Angels. Jorge Luis Borges. TCLAP, *tr. by* Robert Fitzgerald

Where Seed Falls. Essex Hemphill. GT

Where seek out Tyranny? One Sentence on Tyranny. Gyula Illyés. IQMS, *tr. by* Adam Makkai, Károly Nagy and Vernon Watkins

Where, selfwrung, selfstrung, sheathe- and shelterless, thóughts agáinst thoughts ín groans grínd. (LL) Spelt from Sibyl's Leaves. Gerard Manley Hopkins. NAMCP V.1; NPeEn; OxBEV; OxBSo

Where shall I find, in all this fleeting earth. Thought from an Italian Poet. Felicia Dorothea Hemans. RWP

Where shall I lead the flocks to-day? Where the Flocks Shall Be Led. Adah Isaacs Menken. CBWP-1

Where shall the eyes a darkness find. Huw Menai. OBWVE *Fr.* Back in the Return.

Where shall we go? where shall we go? June Fugue. Thomas William Shapcott. NOBAu

Where she lived the close remained the best. Way a Ghost Dissolves, The. Richard Hugo. NoAM; NoP-4; NoP-5

Where she, of all the plains of Britain that doth bear. Michael Drayton. NOSC *Fr.* Polyolbion [*or* Poly-Oobion].

Where she sits, there is only a partial view of the courtyard. Museum. Catherine Imbriglio. IAoNAP

Where should this Musick be? I'th'aire, or th'earth? William Shakespeare. NPeEn *Fr.* Tempest, The.

Where silent, unrefractive whiteness lies. (LL) Stories of Snow. Patricia K. Page. BrAP; NoP-4; NoP-5

Where some murdered man must be. (LL) Sea-Side Cave, The. Alice Cary. APN-2; ColAP; NAAPv.1

Where Souls Go. August Kleinzahler. StAl

Where Spring Is. Steve Healey. LegDan

Where stars are concerned, I am as enthusiastic. Star Apocrypha. Christopher Buckley. PoDa

Where tadpoles are never allowed to grow into frogs! (LL) On Being Asked to Write a Poem for 1979. Jack A. Mapanje. AF; NAfrP

Where tender grasses rim the stream. At Chuzhou on the Western Stream. Wei Ying-wu. CCL1, *tr. by* Witter Bynner

Where the bee sucks, there suck I. William Shakespeare. BLPJKO; NBLV; NoSic; OBEV; TFi *Fr.* Tempest, The.

Where the bishop groans to view him. (LL) Rich and Poor; or, Saint and Sinner. Thomas Love Peacock. OBSV; OxBEV

Where the blood pours out the dead come to the feast. (LL) In Memoriam. Martin Johnston. BMAP; NOBAu

Where the Boul' Mich' meets the Rue. Paris. Miklós Radnóti. IQMS, *tr. by* Zsuzsanna Ozsváth and Frederick Turner

Where the bridesmaid waits in the vestibule. Wedding Song. Mary Louise Sullivan. PfS

Where the cars razored past on the blue highway. Pastorale. Michael Hofmann. HarvBoo

Where the city's ceaseless crowd moves on the livelong day. Sparkles from the Wheel. Walt Whitman. NAAL-3; SAmP

Where the Corrib river chops through the Claddagh.   Last Galway Hooker, The.   Richard Murphy.   PBCIP

Where the Deer Go.   Dabney Stuart.   PoCoUp

Where the deer sometimes showed themselves at sundown.   (LL)   Image, The.   Robert Hass.   BLT; CAP-8

Where the dogs bark.   On Visiting a Taoist Master in the Daitian Mountains and Not Finding Him.   Li Po.   CCL1, *tr. by* Arthur Cooper

Where the flat water.   At Toombridge.   Seamus Heaney.   NAMCP V.2

Where the Flocks Shall Be Led.   Adah Isaacs Menken.   CBWP-1

Where the flowers lean to their shadows on the wall.   Shadows of Chrysanthemums.   Edith Jay Scovell.   HarvBoo

Where the forest breaks.   Tune: "Partridge Sky."   Su Tung-p'o.   ColAnChi, *tr. by* Jiaosheng Wang

Where the Great Northern plunged in.   Wreck of the Great Northern, The.   Robert Hedin.   GM

Where the great trees were felled.   Wendell Berry.   PfSP *Fr.* Sabbaths.

Where the Grieved Ones Sat.   Dolores Kendrick.   FuFl

Where the Heart Is.   Ntozake Shange.   GT

Where the Hudson is getting drunk on its oil.   (LL)   New York.   Federico García Lorca.   RaBo; RaW; WED, *tr. by* Robert Bly

Where the language is lost.   (LL)   This Poem.   Barbara Leslie Jordan.   ExTi; PoDa

Where the Light.   Giuseppe Ungaretti.   WoPoe, *tr. by* Denis Devlin

Where the lizard ran to its little prey.   Range in the Desert, The.   Randall Jarrell.   PoWW

Where the long hall ended the living-room.   Second Home.   Julia Copus.   BeAl

Where the mind is without fear and the head is held high.   Rabindranath Tagore.   ItP; PtR; TWF *Fr.* Gitanjali.

Where the Mississippi meets the Amazon.   Ntozake Shange.   ISC

Where the mist has torn.   Niu Hsi-chi.   EaWin, *tr. by* W. S. Merwin

Where the Nightmare Begins.   Tanure Ojaide.   NAfrP

Where the old trees reign with their forward dark.   Provinces.   C. D. Wright.   AmAlph

Where the path opened.   In Duffryn Woods.   John Stuart Williams.   AngWePo

Where the path to the lake twists out of sight.   Bather, The.   Charles Simic.   PoDa

Where the person vanishes the god appears.   Peter Riley.   VaPo *Fr.* Excavations.

Where the pines rise up, the road ends.   Jastrzebia Góra.   Cathal McCabe.   NIrP

Where the pipe ends he had fixed the long trough.   Windmill At Mandanthanunguna.   Pambardu.   NOBAu, *tr. by* George von Brandenstein

Where—the place of concatenations.   Nostoi.   Rodolfo Di Biasio.   NeIt, *tr. by* Stephen Sartarelli

Where the plovers cry.   Lady Otomo no Sakanoé.   ArkPo, *tr. by* Edwin A. Cranston

Where the pools are bright and deep.   Boy's Song, A.   James Hogg.   NOxBChV; OBEV; OxAEP-2

Where the quiet-colo[u]red end of evening smiles.   Love among the Ruins.   Robert Browning.   NAEL-6v2; NAEL-7v2; OBEV

Where the Rainbow Ends.   Robert Lowell.   MoAmPo; PoetW

Where the remote *Bermudas* ride.   Bermudas.   Andrew Marvell.   BASC; NAEL-6v1; NAEL-7v1; NoP-4; NoP-5; NOSC; NPeEn; OBEV; PBRV; TFi; WoPoe

Where the residents are ghosts or images of the dead.   (LL)   Michael Longley.   ModIr; NPeEn *Fr.* Odyssey.

Where the river cleaves.   For the Drunk.   Carole Oles.   OPRER

Where the river gets swift.   Detailed History of the Western World.   Joe Wenderoth.   AmPoNex

Where the road turns to water.   Cross Country.   Rod Moran.   NOBAu

Where the rue de la Verrerie.   St Merri district, The.   Robert Desnos.   MFP, *tr. by* Martin Sorrell

Where the scorched quietness is swathed.   Tortoise.   Nina Gabrielian.   CRWP, *tr. by* Peter France

Where the sea gulls sleep or indeed where they fly.   Ballet of the Fifth Year, The.   Delmore Schwartz.   APT-2

Where the Slow Fig's Purple Sloth.   Robert Penn Warren.   APT-2; NAMCP V.1 *Fr.* Island of Summer.

Where the slow river.   Leda.   "H. D."   BrAP

Where the still sunshine falls.   Moor Girl's Well, The.   Rosamund Marriott Watson.   ViWPN

Where the Stillaguamish River cuts down.   Desire.   Linda Bierds.   AmAlph

Where the stone and the ink meet, there is blackness.   Writing on an Ink-Stone, A.   *Unknown.*   CCL1, *tr. by* James Legge

Where the stone steps.   Calvary Path, A.   Denise Levertov.   UpMys

Where the stream ox-bowed.   Sap.   Robert Minhinnick.   AngWePo

Where the stream winds pine winds linger.   Jade Flower Palace.   Tu Fu [*or* Du Fu].   ColAnChi, *tr. by* David Lattimore

Where the Sun Ends.   Peter Davison.   ChIV-1

Where the sun rises.   *Unknown.*   APN-2 *Fr.* Mountain Chant, The.

Where the sun was always setting on the play.   (LL)   Long Garden, The.   Patrick Kavanagh.   HarvBoo; OBGa

Where the swan drifts upon a darkening flood.   (LL)   Coole Park and Ballylee, 1931.   William Butler Yeats.   NoAM; OBGa; OBMV

Where the tall towers of the city rise.   Junkyard.   Greg Williamson.   LegDan

Where the tennis court once was, enclosed by the small rectangle.   Where the Tennis Court Was.   Eugenio Montale.   MotU, *tr. by* Charles Wright

Where the Tennis Court Was.   Eugenio Montale.   MotU, *tr. by* Charles Wright

Where the thistle lifts a purple crown.   Daisy.   Francis Thompson.   MoBrPo; OBEV

Where the Three Roads Meet.   Palladas.   WoPoe, *tr. by* Anselm Hollo

Where the three roads meet.   Where the Three Roads Meet.   Palladas.   WoPoe, *tr. by* Anselm Hollo

Where the tracks sidewind through.   Summer Nights.   Paul Christensen.   TiP2

Where the weather is not water.   Mexican Fire Breather, A.   Juan Delgado.   TouFir

Where the Weather Suits My Clothes.   John Godfrey.   PmAP

Where the wheel turned the water / gently shirred.   (LL)   Event, The.   Rita Dove.   ESEAA; NoAM

Where the Wicked Cease from Troubling, and the Weary Are at Rest.   Henry Hart Milman.   SacPr

Where the wife is scouring the frying pan.   Land of Little Sticks, 1945.   James Tate.   AtGh; BodElec

Where the wild woods and pathless forests frown.   Charlotte Smith.   CenSon

Where the wind.   Footprints on the Glacier.   W. S. Merwin.   NoAM

Where the wings of a sunny Dome expand.   America.   Herman Melville.   APN-2

Where the Wolf Sings.   Mary Low.   SurWo

Where the wood starts.   Agricola.   Natalia Toledo.   RMCMP, *tr. by* Alberto A. Ríos

Where then shall Hope and Fear their objects find?   Juvenal.   OxBEV *Fr.* Vanity of Human Wishes, The; The Tenth Satire of Juvenal [Imitated].

Where there are humans / you'll find flies.   Issa.   ZenPo, *tr. by* Takashi Ikemoto and Lucien Stryk

Where there is no head.   (LL)   Amaryllis.   Mark Wunderlich.   LegDan; Vesp

Where there is personal liking we go.   Marianne Moore.   PoA 2002 *Fr.* Part of a Novel, Part of a Poem, Part of a Play.

Where there was some hole.   Ruskie's Boy.   Víctor Hernández Cruz.   PueRic

Where they come from.   (LL)   These Days: "Whatever you have to say, leave."   Charles Olson.   APT-2; RaBo; TWF

Where they sell greetings cards for jail.   Report from High School.   Terese Svoboda.   RWB

Where they will bury me.   Temporarily in Oxford.   Anne Stevenson.   NoP-4; NoP-5

Where things began to happen and I knew it.   (LL)   Ground Swell.   Mark Jarman.   GeoHom; MoASP

Where Things of a Kind.   Heather Ramsdell.   IAoNAP

Where this is freedom: free to follow each desire.   Freedom.   Friedrich von Logau.   GePo, *tr. by* George C. Schoolfield

Where time and outward form[e] would show [*or* shew] it dead.   (LL)   Sonnet 108.   William Shakespeare.   PBRV; TreFP *Fr.* Sonnets.

Where To?   Ernesto Lumbreras.   RMCMP, *tr. by* Rebecca Seiferle

Where to get back to the truth.   George Stanley.   NLPA *Fr.* Mountains and Air.

Where, to me, is the loss.   No Newspapers.   Mary Elizabeth Coleridge.   NPeEn

Where to store furs and how to treat the hair.   (LL)   If I should learn, in some quite casual way.   Edna St. Vincent Millay.   APT-1; HeIP-4; NAAPv.2; OxBoAm

Where to? what next?   (LL)   Carl Sandburg.   MoAmPo; NoAM *Fr.* People, Yes, The.

Where tomorrow he will try and fail his license to live.   (LL)   Learning Experience.   Marge Piercy.   NAMCP V.2; NoAM

Where tossing in grey sheets you weep.   Loba as Eve.   Diane Di Prima.   HW

Where trees are actual and take no holiday.   (LL)   Robinson.   Weldon Kees.   NoP-5; OxBoAm; StAl

Where two or three were flung together, or fifty.   March 2, The.   Robert Lowell.   AmWaPo

Where unincarnate spirits purely aspire!   (LL)   To George Sand: A Recognition.   Elizabeth Barrett Browning.   NAEL-6v2; NAEL-7v2; NALW; PEW; PoBW; VWP

Where voices vanish into dream.   Elected Silence.   Siegfried Sassoon.   MoBrPo

Where was I last night? In whose arms?   Morning.   Miryana Basheva.   CSCBP, *tr. by* Georgi Belev and Lisa Sapinkopf

Where was it left—the key for us to open.   Ivan Davidkov.   CSCBP *Fr.* Tune for a Flute.

Where was it one first heard of the truth? The the. (LL) Man on the Dump, The. Wallace Stevens. APT-1; NAMCP V.1; NAWM-7v2; NoAM; OxBoAm

Where We All Went. G. Travis Regier. RWB

Where We Are. Stephen Dobyns. StAl

Where we are. Gerald Locklin. GoPo

Where we are, and at what speed: I know. Steadying, The. William Heyen. AmWaPo

Where we are the flowers in our clocks flare up their feathers ring the. Great Lament of my Obscurity Three, The. Tristan Tzara. PFTM-1

Where We Crashed. Richard Hugo. PWW2

Where we finally move closer, but instead we don't move closer at all. Still Life. Lisa Jarnot. VaPo

Where we had stood. Wilpena Pound. Charles Buckmaster. BMAP

Where we sat, on the flagstone terrace behind the house. And in the Afternoons I Botanized. Elton Glaser. PoDa

Where we stood, saying I. (LL) In Those Years. Adrienne Rich. ExTi; LoL

Where we went. Daphne Marlatt. NLPA Fr. Touch to My Tongue.

Where we went in the boat was a long bay. Mediterranean, The. Allen Tate. APT-2; FuPo; InGu; MoAmPo; NAAPv.2; OxBoAm; WoPoe

Where were the greenhouses going. Big Wind. Theodore Roethke. ColAP; HarvBoo; TRP; WaAnP

Where Were You. Ethan Paquin. LegDan

Where were you in the marriage season? Too Late for a Husband. *Unknown*. WoPoe, tr. by Nguyen Ngoc Bich

Where When Was. Reginald Shepherd. GT

Where, where are my masters? My Masters. Sandor Csoori. VCWP, tr. by Len Roberts

Where, where but here have Pride and Truth. On Hearing That the Students of Our New University Have Joined the Agitation against Immoral Literature. William Butler Yeats. NoAM

Where white clouds rise. Yun Sŏndo. CATKP Fr. Angler's Calendar, The.

Where wil you have your vertuous names safe laid. Samuel Daniel. NPeEn Fr. Musophilus; or, Defence of All Learning.

Where Will I Go? Nezahualcoyotl. WoPoe, tr. by Thelma D. Sullivan

Where will I go? Where Will I Go? Nezahualcoyotl. WoPoe, tr. by Thelma D. Sullivan

Where will the locust, pine and. Twenty Years From Auschwitz, Bergen-Belsen and Other Camps. Luisa Futuransky. MirDau, tr. by Celeste Kostopulos-Cooperman

Where will you and I sleep? *Wintu Oral Tradition*. NAAPv.1 Fr. Six Dream Songs.

Where Will You Be? Patricia Parker. AfrBLW

Where will you drift, Sadie. In Oak. Marianne Bluger. IFF

Where, without bloodshed, can there be. Long Feud. Louis Untermeyer. MoAmPo

Where would you look for blessing who are caught. And No Help Came. Peter Porter. BMAP

Where wrought iron spears. Goodbye, Post Office Square. Fanny Howe. OxBoAm

Where yon proud turrets crown the rock. Bleeding Nun, The. *Unknown*. NOBRP

Where yonder ridgy mountains bound the scene. Anne Grant. RWP Fr. Highlanders, The.

Where you are. Peony Afternoon. Sŏ Chŏngju. VCWP, tr. by David R. McCann

Where you are going. Peter Levitt. WhBo

Where you are it will not be snowing. December 25, 1991. Rose Solari. AmPoNex

Where you are. You must let it find you. (LL) Lost: "Stand still. The trees ahead and bushes beside you." David Wagoner. GoPo; PoA 2002; TWF

Where you have fallen, you stay. On the Wall of a KZ-Lager. János Pilinszky. AF; HP; PoSu

Where your skin / is your passport. (LL) Untitled Blues; After a Photograph by Yevgeni Yevtushenko. Yusef Komunyakaa. ESEAA; GT; UnSA

Whereas galoshed my Julia goes. Upon Julia's Arctics. Bert Leston Taylor. NBLV

Whereas he's bravely judged by the illiterate. Hungarian Writer, The. János Batsányi. IQMS, tr. by Adam Makkai

Whereas, in the opinion of the Government of the United States the coming of bitter labor. Xenophobic Nightmare in a Foreign Language. Harryette Mullen. PrTe; WANABP

Whereas it minds its own business. Emancipation Proclamation. William Heyen. PoCoUp

Where'er you find "the cooling western breeze." Alexander Pope. OBCoV Fr. Essay on Criticism, An.

Wherefore I marvel greatly of myself. The Lady of the Arbour. OBGa Fr. Flower and the Leaf, The.

Wherefore I was among them well I knew. (LL) I Dreamed I Moved among the Elysian Fields. Edna St. Vincent Millay. NoP-4; NoP-5

Wherein I move, a mote. (LL) John Berryman. InoFa; NAMCP V.2; NoAM; TRP Fr. Dream Songs.

Wherein lies happiness? In that which becks. John Keats. NPBRoP Fr. Endymion: A Poetic Romance.

Wherein space is constructed that matter may reside in. Michele Glazer. IAoNAP

Wherein to play your violin with grace. (LL) Gwendolyn Brooks. NIL-7; NIP-4; PtR Fr. Womanhood, The.

Wherelings whenlings / (daughters of if but offspring of hopefear). E. E. Cummings. WeW-3

Where's Brude? Where's Brude? Columba's Song. Edwin Morgan. HarvBoo

Where's my hairbrush? Where's the belt? Sizing. Heather McHugh. ExTi

Where's probity in this. To the High Court of Parliament. Geoffrey Hill. NAMCP V.2

Where's that boy with the bugle? If He Walked into My Life. Jerry Herman. ReLy

Where's that careless chambermaid? Lulu's Back in Town. Al Dubin. ReLy

Where's / the Eyeshop? Eyeshop, The. Okot P'Bitek. SonAtl, tr. by E. M. Dipuo

Whereso'er you are, my heart shall truly love you. (LL) "Were I as Base as Is the Lowly Plain." Joshua Sylvester. GSo; NoSic

Whereto should I express. To His Lady. Henry VIII, King of England. NoSic

Wherever are the lowly, the suffering, and the poor. Najrul Islām. SinGod, tr. by Rachel Fell McDermott

Wherever God erects a house of prayer. Daniel Defoe. OBSV Fr. True-born Englishman, The.

Wherever I am, now, I'm braced. On Being Asked My Opinion About an Autopsy. Robin Behn. AmAlph

Wherever I arrive. When I Arrive. Fazil Hüsnü Daglarca. NaPG, tr. by Talat Sait Halman

Wherever I go (these). Poem Against the State (Of Things): 1975. June Jordan. ISC

Wherever I Hang. Grace Nichols. NAMCP V.2

Wherever in this city, screens flicker. Twenty-one Love Poems. Adrienne Rich. NAMCP V.2

Wherever Kenji Takezo goes. When for Weeks the Sea is Flat. Rick Noguchi. MoASP

Wherever Summer is a country still. Friedrich Hölderlin. WoPoe Fr. Seasons, The.

Wherever that may be? (LL) Questions of Travel. Elizabeth Bishop. ColAP; HarvBoo; OxBoAm

Wherever there's a woman in any Bengali home. Mā Bāsantī Cakrabarttī. SinGod, tr. by Rachel Fell McDermott

Wherever we dug for safety, we dug into corpses. State Executive. Tanure Ojaide. PML

Wherever we go. Together Wherever We Go. Stephen Sondheim. ReLy

Wherever we remove. (LL) God's Residence. Emily Dickinson. SAmP; WPoS

Wherever we turn in the storm of roses. In the Storm of Roses. Ingeborg Bachmann. AF, tr. by Mark Anderson

Wherever you are. Woman with Flaxen Hair in Norfolk Heard, A. Robert Kelly. PmAP

Wherever you are, and how. José Hierro. ConPit, tr. by Clayton Eshleman

Wherever you are, dig deeply! Undiscouraged. Friedrich Wilhelm Nietzsche. WoPoe, tr. by Robert Bly

Wherever you are, or there in heaven. (LL) Prayer: "You are here on earth, our Father." Gloria Fuertes. GPTC; RaW, tr. by John Haines

Wherever you are, you'll know what I'm saying, and why. Poem Without Music. José Hierro. TAPaP, tr. by Stephen Berg

Wherever you go there you are like Patti Smith's shoulders. "Colors" starring Patti, Grandma, & me at twenty-five. Jeni Olin. FreRad

Wherever you sit. For a Texas Beauty. Jerry Bradley. TiP2

Whether Armilla is like this because it is unfinished or because it has been demolished. Italo Calvino. MotU Fr. Invisible Cities.

Whether, as the intensity of seeing increases, one's distance from Them, the people , does not also increase. George Oppen. NAMCP V.1 Fr. Of Being Numerous.

Whether astringent. Chiyojo. NIL-7, tr. by Daniel C. Buchanan

Whether at doomsday tell, ye reverend wise. Quaerè. George Farewell. NPeEn; OBCoV

Whether by sea or river or in mountains. Night Talk in a Dream Chamber. Ikkyu Sojun. ErotSp, tr. by Sam Hamill

Whether eagles or wrens, scattered in sparks or perched like candelabra. Aviary, The. Saint-Pol Roux. YaTCFP, tr. by Robin Magowan

Whether his mouth be open or shut. (LL) T. S. Eliot. NBLV; OBCoV; UV Fr. Five-Finger Exercises.

Whether I live or fail. (LL) V-Letter. Karl Shapiro. IllVoic; NoAM

Whether I see you now. *Unknown*. ErotSp, tr. by Sam Hamill

Whether it be new or old! (LL)   William Stevenson and John Still.   HeIP-4; NAEL-6v1 *Fr.* Gammer Gurton's Needle.

Whether it is fiction or not. (LL)   Synopsis of the Great Welsh Novel.   Harri Webb.   AngWePo; TCAWP

Whether it is from Eden's sacred plan.   Hartwell Gardens.   A. of Aylesbury Merrick.   OBGa

Whether it rose up as a small brown bird.   Questions about Poetry since Auschwitz.   Tadeusz Rózewicz.   AF, *tr.* by Robert A. Maguire

Whether it's sunny or not, it's sure.   Poem about Morning.   William Meredith.   GoPo

Whether of the seven spear-points.. (LL)   "H. D."   NAAPv.2; NALW; NAMCP V.1 *Fr.* Tribute to the Angels.

Whether on Ida's shady brow.   To the Muses.   William Blake.   HeIP-4; NAEL-6v2; NoP-4; NoP-5; OBEV

Whether one is eminent or humble depends on Fate.   Juan Chi.   ColAnChi *Fr.* Songs of My Soul.

Whether one paints five Helens.   Ultimate Antientropy, The.   Theodore Weiss.   NoAM

Whether or Not.   D. H. Lawrence.   MoBrPo

Whether or not he wore spurs.   Words Before a Statue of Champlain.   Raymond Souster.   BrAP

Whether or not I shall fly.   And I Speak of Cosmic Things.   Vsevolod Nekrasov.   TCRusP, *tr.* by Daniel Weissbort

Whether some great, supreme o'er-ruling Power.   Anti-Jacobins, The and George Canning and William Gifford.   NOBRP *Fr.* Progress of Man, The. A Didactic Poem.

Whether that soul which now comes up to you.   Hymn to the Saints, and to Marquis Hamilton, An.   John Donne.   NOSC

Whether the sensitive plant, or that.   Percy Bysshe Shelley.   NPeEn *Fr.* Sensitive Plant, The.

Whether the Turkish new moon minded be.   Sir Philip Sidney.   NoSic *Fr.* Astrophil and Stella.

Whether they are drunk or sober.   Some People Are about Jam.   Sandra Maria Esteves.   PueRic

Whether they work together or apart. (LL)   Tuft of Flowers, The.   Robert Frost.   APT-1; MoAmPo; NAAPv.2

Whether those shores are habitable or no. (LL)   Ararat.   Charles Tomlinson.   NoP-4; NoP-5

Whether thou getst them green, or let[s] them seed. (LL)   Upon Wedlock and Death of Children.   Edward Taylor.   ColAP; NAAL-3; NAAL-5; NAAPv.1; NoP-4; NoP-5; SacPr; TCAPo

Whether thou smile or frown, thou beauteous face.   Charles Lloyd.   CenSon

Whether to approach from the North or South.   Union Square.   Lori Shine.   IIR

Whether to cry or whether to be proud.   Till Evening.   Jakov Steinberg.   FIT, *tr.* by Robert Friend

Whether to drink or not to drink: that was.   Alcohol Question, The.   Thomas Whitbread.   TiP2

Whether upon the garden seat.   To Any Reader.   Robert Louis Stevenson.

Whether what we sense of this world.   Metonymy as an Approach to a Real World.   William Bronk.   APSN

Whether you are here or yonder.   More Than You Know.   Edward Eliscu and Billy Rose.   ReLy

Whether you had been asking or telling. (LL)   Armenonville.   Edna St. Vincent Millay.   NoP-4; NoP-5

Whether you say it, think it, know it.   Ted Hughes.   NoAM *Fr.* Stations.

Whether you sing or scream.   To No One in Particular.   Marvin Bell.   TAPaP

Which blamed the living man. (LL)   Growing Old.   Matthew Arnold.   NAEL-6v2; NPeEn

Which but expressions be of inward evils. (LL)   Fulke, 1st Baron Brooke Greville.   NAEL-7v1; NPeEn *Fr.* Caelica.

Which carries the feathered grass a long way down the upbreathing air. (LL)   Adrienne Rich.   ErotSp; NoAM; TRP *Fr.* Twenty-one Love Poems.

Which caused her thus to send thee out of door. (LL)   Author to Her Book, The.   Anne Bradstreet.   BASC; BrAP; ColAP; EMWP; MakPoe; NAAL-3; NAAL-5; NAAPv.1; NALW; NoP-4; NoP-5; OxBoAm; TCAPo; WaAnP

Which Claus of Innsbruck cast in bronze for me! (LL)   My Last Duchess.   Robert Browning.   AmFaP; BrAP; CABP; ClHu; CtM; HeIP-4; ITBLP; MakPoe; NAEL-7v2; NAWM-7v2; NIL-7; NIP-4; NoP-4; NoP-5; NPeEn; OxBEV; PoPoPo; SoSe-8; TFi; TRP; WaAnP

Which contained some red earth and a few half-rotten bananas. (LL)   Beggar Woman of Naples, The.   Max Jacob.   MotU; PoCho, *tr.* by John Ashbery

Which Contains a Fantasy Satisfied with a Love Befitting It.   Sor Juana Inés de la Cruz.   ErotSp, *tr.* by Alan S. Trueblood

Which cover lightly, gentle earth. (LL)   On My First Daughter.   Ben Jonson.   BASC; NAEL-6v1; NAEL-7v1; NoP-4; NoP-5; NOSC; WaAnP

Which die for goodnes[s], who have lived [*or* liv'd] for crime. (LL)   William Shakespeare.   NoSic; NPeEn; PBRV *Fr.* Sonnets.

Which dies [*or* dyes]. (LL)   Longing.   George Herbert.   FSCP; UV

Which Earth grants all her kind. (LL)   She Hears The Storm.   Thomas Hardy.   NAEL-6v2; NAEL-7v2

Which fails to clarify what it is that distinguishes us from beasts. (LL)   Send New Beasts.   Joe Wenderoth.   BodElec; LegDan

Which for all you know is the life you've chosen. (LL)   God Who Loves You, The.   Carl Dennis.   BeAl; PoDa

Which form of you should I imitate to be called yous?   Shipwreck.   Biancamaria Frabotta.   CItWP, *tr.* by Cinzia Sartini Blum and Lara Trubowitz

Which gods gave birth to which language?   Word Between the World and God, The.   Emily Warn.   TAPaP

Which goes with Bridge, and Women and Champagne. (LL)   On a General Election.   Joseph Hilaire Pierre Belloc.   NPeEn; OBSV; OxBEV

Which He from Heaven doth bring[e]. (LL)   New Prince, New Pomp[e].   Robert Southwell.   ChrPo; NoSic; SacPr; WaAnP

Which he must.   To Help the Monkey Cross the River.   Thomas Lux.   AmAlph

Which heaves but with the heaving deep. (LL)   Alfred Tennyson.   BrAP; HeIP-4; NAEL-6v2; NAEL-7v2; NAWM-7v2; NoP-5; NPeEn; OxBEV; WaAnP *Fr.* In Memoriam A. H. H.

Which I am afraid to put on. (LL)   Empire of Dreams.   Charles Simic.   BLT; VCAP

Which I have loved long since, and lost awhile. (LL)   Pillar of the Cloud, The.   John Henry, Cardinal Newman.   ChIV-1; InvLi; NPeEn; SacPr

Which I was given because.   Lines on Roger Hilton's Watch.   William Sydney Graham.   NPeEn

Which I wish to remark.   Plain Language from Truthful James.   Bret Harte.   APN-2; CalPo; OBCoV; UV

Which I wish to remark.   Heathen Pass-ee, The.   Arthur Clement Hilton.   UV

Which I wish to say is this.   Gertrude Stein.   NoP-4; NoP-5 *Fr.* Stanzas in Meditation.

Which is also the case when our women are crazy. (LL)   When Our Women Go Crazy.   Julia Kasdorf.   NeAmPo; PBCAP; SweBea

Which is bitter. (LL)   Strange Type.   Malcolm Lowry.   NoP-4; NoP-5; NPeEn

Which is called civilization over there. (LL)   Australia.   Alec Derwent Hope.   BMAP; BrAP; NAMCP V.1; NoAM; NoP-4; NoP-5

Which is I stood and loved you while you slept. (LL)   Poem for Emily, A.   Miller Williams.   InGu; WeW-3

Which is in me / like a hill. (LL)   Hill, The.   Robert Creeley.   BrAP; RaBo; TRP

Which is just beginning to close around the butt of a revolver. (LL)   Lines of the Hand, The.   Julio Cortázar.   MotU; TCLAP, *tr.* by Paul Blackburn

Which is like love, which is like everything. (LL)   Wedding.   Alice Oswald.   BeAl; MFPA; MoWP; NeBrP

Which is not thought, but the airless stare.   Light.   Marianne Boruch.   PoSol

Which is real— / This bottle of indigo glass in the grass.   Indigo Glass in the Grass, The.   Wallace Stevens.   PoA 2002

Which is the reason my Damon that although.   Sonnet 12.   Francesco de Aldana.   BLPSL, *tr.* by Rene de Costa, Rigas Kappatos and Eleni Paidoussi

Which is the storehouse rich of Nature sweet. (LL)   Pastime of the Queen of Fairies, The.   Margaret Lucas Cavendish, Duchess of Newcastle.   BASC; NAEL-6v1

Which is, to keep that hid. (LL)   Undertaking, The.   John Donne.   NAEL-6v1; NAEL-7v1

Which is what the first idiot says.   Nothing.   Terrance Hayes.   RD

Which is worse.   *Unknown.*   WoPoe *Fr.* Eiga Monogatari, The.

Which is you, old two-in-one?   Archibald MacLeish.   ChIV-1 *Fr.* Songs for Eve.

Which it is not my style.   Truthful James to the Editor.   Bret Harte.   APN-2

Which I've not only lost, but forgotten how to say. (LL)   Making for Planet Alice.   Deryn Rees-Jones.   MFPA; StAl

Which keep their only threat at bay: of separation. (LL)   King and Queen of Dumfriesshire, The.   W. N. Herbert.   EdScPo; NeBrP

Which makes some evenings harder to enjoy. (LL)   Video Blues.   Mary Jo Salter.   P180; WaAnP

Which mortals dream of, but which angels know. (LL)   John Pierpont.   APN-1; TreFP *Fr.* Airs of Palestine.

Which my God feels as blood [*or* bloud]; but I, as wine. (LL)   Agony [*or* Agonie], The.   George Herbert.   CABP; FSCP

Which now the angels sing! (LL)   It Came upon the Midnight Clear.   Edmund Hamilton Sears.   APN-1; ChrPo; SacPr; TCAPo

Which of the seven deadly sins is worst?   Greed.   Giuseppe Gioacchino Belli.   WoPoe, *tr.* by Anthony Burgess

Which One Is Genuine?   Charles Baudelaire.   RaBo, *tr.* by Robert Bly

Which One Is the Grown-up?   Haiku.   Liz Rosenberg.   InvLad

Which ones are theirs, be gentle to everybody. (LL)   Their Bodies.   David Wagoner.   EMP; PoA 2002

Which otherwise had only venial been. (LL)   To My Young Lover.   Jane Barker.   BASC; LW

Which reaches, sooner or later, the breaker of a taboo. (LL) Bypassing Rue Descartes. Czeslaw Milosz. FaoP; VCWP, *tr.* by Renata Gorczynski and Robert Hass

Which Religion Vouchsafes. Jane Miller. GifTon

Which reminds me of another knock-on-wood. Minor Miracle. Marilyn Nelson. CAP-8

Which the Chicken, Which the Egg? Ogden Nash. APT-2

Which the click of the powerful but well-oiled spring pleasantly confirms. (LL) Delights of the Door, The. Francis Ponge. RaBo; WED, *tr.* by Robert Bly

Which the same I am free to maintain. (LL) Plain Language from Truthful James. Bret Harte. APN-2; CalPo; OBCoV; UV

Which they that know the rest, know more than I. (LL) Answer, The. George Herbert. FaBoVe; NPeEn

Which those who never loved, can never know! (LL) Her Confirmed Despair. Mary Robinson. CenSon; RWP

Which thou in Pearles did'st lend. (LL) On the Wounds of Our Crucified Lord. Richard Crashaw. NAEL-6v1; NAEL-7v1

Which to heare, vouchsafe, O dearest dred a-while, The. (LL) Edmund Spenser. NAEL-7v1; NoP-5 *Fr.* Faerie Queene, The.

Which turns the volume higher? (LL) America. Tony Hoagland. FaoP; StAl

Which used to lead something into somewhere. (LL) Ponder, darling, these busted statues. E. E. Cummings. NIL-7; NIP-4

Which Washington? Eve Merriam. NTCP

Which way are you going? Footprints. Caitlin O'Donnell. WhBo

Which way he went? Rondelet. May Probyn. VWP

Which we prefer to the alternative. (LL) Invocation: "This is for Elsa, also known as Liz." Marilyn Hacker. ExTi; PuP-23; WiU

Whichever one of you throwing a party at home. *Unknown.* PriapPo *Fr.* Priapus Poems, The.

Whichever way you turn her. (LL) Tyranny of Choice. Elizabeth Garrett. NeBl; StAl

Whiffenpoof Song. Ted. B. Galloway, Meade Minnigerode and George S. Pomeroy. TCAPo

Whig's the first letter of his odious name. Acrostic on Wharton, An. *Unknown.* OBSV

While. Bruce Andrews. FTOS

While ago, A. Promise, The. Heberto Padilla. TCLAP, *tr.* by Alexander Coleman and Alastair Reid

While all about us peal the loud, sweet *Te Deums* of the Canterbury bells. (LL) Madonna of the Evening Flowers. Amy Lowell. NAAL-5; NALW

While an intrinsic ardor prompts to write. To the University of Cambridge, in New-England. Phillis Wheatley. NAAL-3; NAAL-5; NAAPv.1; TCAPo

While Andrew sleeps. What effect has your new son had on your writing life? Richard Jones. PoChi

While apparition is the instant of illumination and of being touched. Suicide with Squirtgun. Tom Clark. PmAP

While as I lived no house I had. Upon the Grave of a Beggar. Timothy Kendall. NoSic

While Babylon's managers burn in the rage of the Lamb. (LL) Prophecy. Donald Hall. NoP-5; OxBoAm

While battles rage and cannons roar. Drill's the Thing. *Unknown.* FaBoWar

While boats list in port. Mother and I. Takahashi Shinkichi. ZenPo, *tr.* by Takashi Ikemoto and Lucien Stryk

While briers an' woodbines budding green. Robert Burns. NPBRoP *Fr.* Epistle to J. Lapraik, an Old Scotch Bard.

While Bustopher Jones wears white spats! (LL) Bustopher Jones: The Cat About Town. T. S. Eliot. OBCoV; TriCat

While Butler, needy wretch, was yet alive. On the Setting Up of Mr. Butler's Monument in Westminster Abbey. Samuel Wesley. NBLV

While by the rosebed gay you stood, and revelled in the multitude. One among the Roses. Edmund Charles Blunden. OBGa

While coming to the feast I found. Léonie Adams. *See* In coming to the feast I found.

While Communing with a Tree Near My Home. M. Eliza Hamilton. BtF

While driving, Kukutis exclaims. Kukutis's Trip on the Samogitian Highway. Marcelijus Martinaitis. TWW, *tr.* by Laima Sruoginis

While driving north, lost. I Was Looking for the University. Clarence Major. GT

While drunk, I seek merriment. Tune: "Moon of the Western River." Hsin Ch'i-chi. ChinPo, *tr.* by Ye Weilian [*or* Yeh Wei-lien *or* Wai-lim Yip]

While eating dinner, this dear little child. Julia A. Moore. STuOW *Fr.* Little Libbie.

While Eve waited. Sleep of Adam, The. John Hejduk. ChIV-1

While everything external / dies away in the far off. As the Human Village Prepares for Its Fate. Tom Clark. BodElec

While, [far] above [them], that harp assumes their sighs. (LL) Seascape. Stephen Spender. NoP-4; NoP-5

While from the dizzy precipice I gaze. Her Reflections on the Leucadian Rock Before She Perishes. Mary Robinson. CenSon; RWP

While from the dizzy precipice I gaze. Mary Robinson. NPBRoP *Fr.* Sappho and Phaon.

While gazing round this dear ramshackle one. Other People's Glasshouses. Ruth Pitter. OBGa

While God is marching on. (LL) Battle Hymn [*or* Battle-Hymn] of the Republic, The. Julia Ward Howe. AmWaPo; APN-1; BRP; CBCWP; HHAm; NAAPv.1; NoP-5; OBWP; OxBoAm; SWaP; TCAPo; TFi

While going the road to sweet Athy. Johnny, I Hardly Knew Ye. *Unknown.* FaBoWar; IrV; NPeEn; PoAgWa

While greasy [*or* greasie] Joan[e] doth keel[e] the pot. (LL) William Shakespeare. ClHu; MakPoe; NAEL-6v1; NIL-7; NIP-4; NoP-4; NoP-5; OBEV; OxBEV; TFi; TRP; WaAnP; WeW-3 *Fr.* Love's Labour's Lost.

While half the globe away the highest peak of Everest. Disproportionate. Timothy Geiger. AmPoNex

While he slept, I poured salt in his ears. Judith Recalls Holofernes. Maura Stanton. YaYoPo

While he turned back to an empty room. (LL) Man on a Fire Escape. Edward Hirsch. OxBoAm; UrbNat

While her fond heart against the deed rebels. Widow's Remarriage, The. Mary F. Johnson. CenSon

While her husband spent his afternoons napping. Spirit Papers. Teresa D. Cader. ExTi

While His Body's Vigor Is Whole. Bhartrihari. WoPoe, *tr.* by Barbara Stoler Miller

While his body's vigor is whole. While His Body's Vigor Is Whole. Bhartrihari. WoPoe, *tr.* by Barbara Stoler Miller

While his own silence taught me every secret thing he knew. (LL) Soaking Up Sun. Tom Hennen. GoPo; IPoFL

While his sensible daddy goes straight into town. (LL) To a Friend Whose Work Has Come to Triumph. Anne Sexton. CAP-8; OtW

While Homer and Whitman roared in the pines? (LL) Edgar Lee Masters. ColAP; MoAmPo; NAMCP V.1; NoAM; TCAPo *Fr.* Spoon River Anthology.

While homeward bound I thought about. Plans Gone Up In Smoke. Sándor Petőfi. IQMS, *tr.* by Leslie A. Kery

While I asked myself. *Unknown.* ArkPo, *tr.* by Helen Craig McCullough

While i believe that what im doing depends essentially upon. Real Estate. David Antin. FTOS

While I dread looking into the mirror. Melancholy. Hwang Jiwoo. CAMKP, *tr.* by Young-Jun Lee and Scott Swaner

While I dread looking into the mirror. Hwang Jiwoo. CAMKP *Fr.* Melancholy.

While I droop here. (LL) I Am a Parcel of Vain Strivings Tied. Henry David Thoreau. APN-1; ColAP; NoP-4; NoP-5; OxBoAm; TCAPo

(In a bare cup.) (LL) NoP-4; NoP-5

While I examine my hands. (LL) Leap, The. James Dickey. NIL-7; NIP-4

While I fled. (LL) Intimates. D. H. Lawrence. NBLV; RaBo

While I, not less an-hungered, gaze and sing. (LL) Art and Life. Agnes Mary Frances Robinson. OxBSo; VWP

While I recline / At ease beneath. Cotton Boll, The. Henry Timrod. APN-2

While I savour woodstove-scented sleep. Tonight the Sky Is My Begging Bowl. Sina Queyras. IFF

While I sit at the door. Eve. Christina Georgina Rossetti. ChIV-1; NALW; NIL-7; NIP-4

While I sit down scribbling herring verses. Artist and a Wailing Mother, An. Freddy Macha. NAfrP

While I sit in south light, suspecting nothing. Coming into History. Jeanne Murray Walker. PoA 2002

While I Slept. Robert Francis. APT-2

While I slept it was all over. Pipe, The. Takahashi Shinkichi. ZenPo, *tr.* by Takashi Ikemoto and Lucien Stryk

While I slept, while I slept and the night grew colder. While I Slept. Robert Francis. APT-2

While I stood here, in the open, lost in myself. Milkweed. James Wright. ColAP; RaBo

While I was building neat. It Is Dangerous to Read Newspapers. Margaret Atwood. HeIP-4; ItP; OBWP

While I was musing on my theme. Chiyojo. AWTN, *tr.* by Asatarō Miyamori

While I was studying the copper cistern. Chardin Exhibition, The. Edward Hirsch. RoV

While I watch the Christmas blaze. Reminder, The. Thomas Hardy. ChAP; OBCP

While I watch the moon go down, a crow caws throught the frost. Night-Mooring near Maple Bridge, A. Chang Chi. CCL1, *tr.* by Witter Bynner

While I watch the yellow wheat. Watching the Wheat. John Jones. AngWePo

While in long exile far from you I roam. To Dr Moore, in Answer to a Poetical Epistle Written by Him in Wales. Helen Maria Williams. WoRP

While in my simple gospel creed. Tartarus. Oliver Wendell Holmes. NCAP

While in this garden *Proserpine* was taking hir pastime. Ovid. NPeEn *Fr.* Metamorphoses.

While it breaks, breaks, breaks on the sheltering bars. (LL) Heart of a Woman, The. Georgia Douglas Johnson. ISC; NAAPv.2

While it's still dark. Las Magdalenas. Judith Ortiz Cofer. TouFir

While Jove's planet rises yonder, silent over Africa. (LL) Home-Thoughts, from the Sea. Robert Browning. NAEL-6v2; NAEL-7v2

While joy gave clouds the light of stars. Villain, The. W. H. Davies. AngWePo; MoBrPo

While joy reanimates the fields. Song on Leaving the Country Early in the Spring. Anne Batten Cristall. RWP

While later that night they flurried in, A. Sarah Arvio. KGB *Fr.* Visits from the Seventh.

While Love, his arrows broke, retires forlorn. (LL) Temple of Chastity, The. Mary Robinson. CenSon; RWP

While Love, his arrows broke, retires forlorn. (LL) Mary Robinson. NPBRoP; STuOW *Fr.* Sappho and Phaon.

While, Lydia, I was lov'd of thee. Horace. OBVE *Fr.* Odes.

While lying on the cold hood of her car. Remembering Emily. Rita Mae Reese. PfS

While Many a Merry Tale. Samuel Johnson. UV

While Marquis de Sade had himself buggered. Eastern European Cooking. Charles Simic. NAMCP V.2

While my city gently sleeps. Lament. Harold Carrington. EGAG

While My Father. Giovanna Pollarolo. TANSG, *tr. by* Marjorie Agosin

While my father prospered. While My Father. Giovanna Pollarolo. TANSG, *tr. by* Marjorie Agosin

While my father walked through mud. 1905. David Ignatow. TaR

While my hair was still cut straight across my forehead. River Merchant's Wife, The; A Letter. Li Po. AmFaPo; APT-1; BrAP; ClHu; ColAP; EMP; HarvBoo; HeIP-4; MoAmPo; NAAL-5; NAAPv.2; NAMCP V.1; NDACCP; NIL-7; NIP-4; NoAM; NoP-4; NoP-5; NPeEn; OBMV; OBVE; OxBoAm; PoPoPo; RaBo; RACG; TCAPo; TFi; TRP; WaAnP; WeW-3, *tr. by* Ezra Pound

While my little boat moves on its mooring of mist. Night Mooring on the Jiande River, A. Meng Hao Jan. CCL1, *tr. by* Witter Bynner

While my sad Muse the darkest Covert Sought. Congratulatory Poem to Her Sacred Majesty Queen Mary, Upon Her Arrival in England, A. Aphra Behn. EMWP

While my wife at my side lies slumbering, and the wars are over long. Artilleryman's Vision, The. Walt Whitman. CBCWP; PCW

While one sere leaf, that parting autumn yields. Anna Seward. WoRP *Fr.* Sonnets.

While passing through a. No Deposit Returns. Carlos Cumpian. ReTh

While presumably you. Levitation. Carl Phillips. OxAAAP

While reading. Kagawa Kageki. EMJL, *tr. by* Haruo Shirane

While she pulls herself free, and rows her dull mound along. (LL) Lui et Elle. D. H. Lawrence. NAMCP V.1; NoAM

While shepherds watched their flocks by night. Carol. "Saki." UV

While Shepherds Watched [Their Flocks by Night]. Nahum Tate. ChrPr; NOSC; SacPr; UV

While shines the sun, the storm even then. In Bonds. Alice Cary. SWaP

While Sidney Bechet was. Tuskegee Experiment. Mohammed Sadiq. SeSe

While Sleeping at the Southern Sea. Chunghur Hyujung. BecRai, *tr. by* Kim Daljin, Kim Won-Chung and Christopher Merrill

While smoking her cigarette down to the very end. (LL) Great Palaces of Versailles, The. Rita Dove. ESEAA; NAMCP V.2; NoAM

While snow fell carelessly. Crack, The. Denise Levertov. NALW

While snows the window-panes bedim. December. John Clare. OBCP

While something hummed along the river. From the Sun Itself. Roberta Hill Whiteman. HATNAP

While spoon-feeding him with one hand. Parkinson's Disease. Galway Kinnell. FaoP

While strolling through the hills one day. Tannhauser. Newman Levy. AmWit

While such as he fall. (LL) R.A.F. "H. D." PWW2; WaAnP

While summer roses all their glory yield. To the Poppy. Anna Seward. CenSon; WoRP

While summer-suns o'er the gay prospect played. Thomas, the Younger Warton. CenSon

While sun and sea—and I, and I. Island, The. Randall Jarrell. HarvBoo

While sweet breezes were stroking the young poplars. Requiescat. Leo Ross. TuT, *tr. by* Eamon Grennan

While Tate recites the catalog of ships. (LL) Gambier. Joe Osterhaus. AmPoNex; NAPBL

While that futile old gentleman dozed. (LL) Limerick: "There was an Old Man who supposed." Edward Lear. NAEL-6v2; NAEL-7v2

While that my soul repairs to her devotion. Church Monuments. George Herbert. BASC; NAEL-6v1; NAEL-7v1; NOSC; NPeEn; TRP

While the blue noon above us arches. Annihilation. Conrad Potter Aiken. MoAmPo

While the bombers, southward flocking, set Italian cities rocking. Croaked the Eagle: "Nevermore." "Sagittarius." UV

While the Chinamen was crying on the roof. Federico García Lorca. WED *Fr.* Poet in New York.

While the Choir Sang. Priscilla Jane Thompson. CBWP-2

While the city of Troy gave itself up to lamentation, the Achaeans withdrew to the Hellespont. Homer. CAGL *Fr.* Iliad, The.

While the city sleeps there's this blast of silence that follows the whine of daylight. Slowly I Open My Eyes. Amy Gerstler. MotU; SUP

While the dead. Seminar for Backward Pupils. Günter Eich. AF, *tr. by* David Young

While the earth is still turning, while there is still bright light. François Villon. Bulat Shalvovich Okudzhav. TCRusP, *tr. by* Denis Johnson, Aleksandar Petrov and Shirley Rihner

While the fish of fire curves its arc. Siesta. Antonio Machado Ruiz. SpanPo, *tr. by* Kate Flores

While the hum and the hurry. Under a Hat Rim. Carl Sandburg. APT-1

While the innocents were being massacred who says. Who Says. Julia Hartwig. GI

While the long grain is softening. Early in the Morning. Li-Young Lee. LoL

While the mayor sits with his head in his hands. (LL) Great Society, The. Robert Bly. NAMCP V.2; NoAM

While the MP's wait. Sojin Takei. NAAPv.2

While the people pressed upon him to hear the word of God. Czeslaw Milosz. GI *Fr.* St. Luke.

While the Record Plays. Gyula Illyés. PFTM-1

While the rest of us read the death scene. On First Reading *Romeo and Juliet*. Diane Lockward. IaFF

While the rich idle on their yachts. End of January, The. Cathal McCabe. NIrP

While the river banks are quarreling. Agon. Branko Miljkovic. WoPoe, *tr. by* Charles Simic

While the south rains, the north. Sled Burial, Dream Ceremony. James Dickey. NoP-4; NoP-5

While the sun still spends his fabulous money. Kenneth Patchen. CLPP

While the Tragedy's afoot. Colophon. Oliver St. John Gogarty. OBMV

While the Wolf Walks the Edge of the Woods. Mary Sue Koeppel. AmZen

While the years draw nigh when the clattering typewriter is a burden. Evil Days, The. Dennis Joseph Enright. OBCoV

While There Is Still the Color of a Rose. Baldomero Garcilaso de la Vega. SpanPo, *tr. by* Edwin Morgan

While there is still the color of a rose. While There Is Still the Color of a Rose. Baldomero Garcilaso de la Vega. SpanPo, *tr. by* Edwin Morgan

While they met with the real estate brokers. Beach, The. Douglas Goetsch. AmPoNex

While they sit and walk in alternation, their glance. Retreat toward the Spring. Nathaniel Tarn. WANABP

While this America settles in the mold [*or* mould] of its vulgarity, heavily thickening to empire. Shine, Perishing Republic. Robinson Jeffers. APT-1; CalPo; ColAP; HarvBoo; NAAL-5; NAMCP V.1; NoAM; NoP-4; NoP-5; OxBoAm; PoPoPo; TFi; WaAnP

While this good household thus were living on. William Wordsworth. NPBRoP *Fr.* Michael [A Pastoral Poem].

While this kind of consolation and exhortation. Surplus. Abigail Child. FTOS

While this was singing, Ovid young in love. George Chapman. NoSic *Fr.* Ovid's Banquet of Sense.

While those disintegrated by exocet. Shot of War, A. J. S. Harry. BMAP

While Thracians shal with arrowes war, Iaziges with bowe. Ovid. OBVE *Fr.* Invective against Ibis.

While through our air thy kindling course was run. Cold Meteorite, The. William Reed Huntington. APN-2

While thus Florinda spake, the dog who lay. Robert Southey. DiBP *Fr.* Roderick, The Last of the Goths.

While thus he thought, a monst'rous wave up-bore. Homer. OBVE *Fr.* Odyssey.

While thus I wander'd, step by step led on. William Wordsworth. OxAEP-1 *Fr.* Prelude, The; Growth of a Poet's Mind [1805 version].

While to you we true children of Liberty pray. Humble Petition of the British Jacobins to their Brethren of France, The. *Unknown.* NOBRP

While Traveling. Chia Tao. CSKM, *tr. by* Mike O'Connor

While traveling in a plane coming back from seeing a married lover, place a tennis ball under your left buttock. Remedy for Backache. Judith Taylor. SUP

While unquiet, *Juvenal*, you haunt. Martial. RomPo, *tr. by* Peter Whigham

While venal crowds for worthless men engage. Elegy on the Death of Mr Sterne. Miles Peter Andrews. NOBRP

While Visiting on the South Stream the Taoist Priest Chang. Liu Ch'ang-ch'ing. CCL1, *tr. by* Witter Bynner

While vulgar souls their vulgar love pursue. Cloe to Artimesa. *Unknown.* PoBW

While Waiting for a Friend to Come to Visit a Friend in a Mental Hospital. Russell Atkins. EGAG

While walking down a strange street. Streetcar That Lost Its Way, The. Nikolai Stepanovich Gumilyov. TCRusP, *tr. by* Denis Johnson and Kathy Lewis

While walking toward housewife wheeling baby. Street Instructions at the Crotch. Edward Field. CAGL

While Watching *Cops* I Think of You. Virginia Chase Sutton. MAAN

While Watching Sunset. Ch'oe Sûngja. EcSo, *tr. by* Mickey Hong

While we are all together under burring bulbs we would do well. Planks. C. D. Wright. CAP-8

While we lie tumbling in the hay. (LL) William Shakespeare. NoP-4; NoSic; OxAEP-1; TFi; UV; WaAnP *Fr.* Winter's Tale, The.

While we loved those who never read our poems. Jay Macpherson. IFF *Fr.* Way Down, The.

While we searched for screams. Boeing. Angela Agali. NeNiPo

While we slept, these formal gardens. Snowfall on a College Garden. Cecil Day Lewis. OBGa

While We Spend Our Lives Ironing. Marianne van Hirtum. SurWo, *tr. by* Guy Flandre and Peter Wood

While we spend our lives ironing. While We Spend Our Lives Ironing. Marianne van Hirtum. SurWo, *tr. by* Guy Flandre and Peter Wood

While we were marching through Georgia. (LL) Marching through Georgia. Henry Clay Work. APN-2; CBCWP

While We're Young. William Engvick. ReLy

While with a feeling skill I paint my hell. (LL) Sir Philip Sidney. NAEL-6v1; NAEL-7v1 *Fr.* Astrophil and Stella.

While yet it was the Empire of the Night. On the Birth-Day of Queen Katherine. Anne Killigrew. EMWP

While yet Rolfe's foot in stirrup stood. Herman Melville. APN-2 *Fr.* Clarel: A Poem and Pilgrimage in the Holy Land.

"While yet we wait for spring, and from the dry." GSo

While you acknowledge no wrongheaded wish to lay waste. *Unknown.* PriapPo *Fr.* Priapus Poems, The.

While you are sleeping. Counting. Mark Bibbins. WiU

While you clambered up ahead. Climbing Gannett. Roberta Hill Whiteman. HATNAP

While you / Cultivate the soul and embrace unity. Lao Tzu. ColAnChi *Fr.* Tao Te Ching.

While you that in your sorrow disavow. Christmas Sonnet, A. Edwin Arlington Robinson. ChrPo

While you walk the water's edge. Beach Glass. Amy Clampitt. MoWP; NAMCP V.2; NoAM; NoP-4; NoP-5; VCAP

While you were away. Phyllis Webb. NLPA *Fr.* Naked Poems.

While you would find my two sisters bickering almost whenever you looked. Bickering. Elke Erb. OnScMo, *tr. by* Rosmarie Waldrop

While your love is hotter than a fire that will melt steel, your touch is cold. Your Touch. Han Yong'un [*or* Yongwun]. CAMKP, *tr. by* Sammy Solberg

While you're a white-hot youth, emit the rays. Richard Wilbur. NBLV *Fr.* Flippancies.

While you're alive I'm hopeful, rustic guard. *Unknown.* PriapPo *Fr.* Priapus Poems, The.

Whiles someone did chant this lovely lay, The. Edmund Spenser. OBVE *Fr.* Faerie Queene, The.

Whilom [*or* Whylom] ther was dwellyng[e] [*or* dwelling] at Oxenford[e]. Geoffrey Chaucer. NAEL-6v1; NAEL-7v1 *Fr.* Canterbury Tales, The.

Whil'st Alexis lay prest [*or* press'd]. John Dryden. NPeEn *Fr.* Marriage à la Mode.

Whilst all ages run. (LL) Hymn: "Now the day is over." Sabine Baring-Gould. CaPr; WHSW

Whilst dear Sophia plans some pictured strife. Winter in Wales, A. Hester Lynch Salusbury Thrale [*later* Mrs. Piozzi]. CABP

Whilst happy I Triumphant stood. On a Juniper-Tree, Cut Down to Make Busks. Aphra Behn. BASC

Whilst in this cold and blust'ring clime. To My Dear and Most Worthy Friend, Mr. Isaac Walton. Charles Cotton. NPeEn

Whilst my heart bleeding writes that deadlie wound. Written upon the Death of the Most Noble Prince Henrie. Sir Arthur Gorges. PBRV

Whilst my soul's eye beheld no light. Dialogue betwixt God and the Soul, A. Sir Henry Wotton. SacPr

Whilst on Septimius' panting Breast. Catullus. OBVE

Whilst sitting with my fanny on the desk. For I Have Taught the Japanese. Lucia Maria Perillo. ExTi

Whilst the red spittle of the grape-shot sings. Evil. Arthur Rimbaud. FaBoWar, *tr. by* Norman Cameron

Whilst thine the Victor is, and free. (LL) Song. Love Arm'd [*or* Armed]. Aphra Behn. BASC; LW; NALW; NoP-4; NoP-5; NOSC; NPeEn; OBEV; OxAEP-1; OxBEV; PEW; WeW-3

Whilst thou art far away, I am at peace. Siena. Lily Thicknesse. LW

Whilst what I write I do not see. Abraham Cowley. CABP *Fr.* Mistress, The.

Whilst yet to prove. Farewell to Love. John Donne. BASC

Whilst youth and error led my wandring [*or* wand'ring] mind[e]. Samuel Daniel. AEP *Fr.* Sonnets to Delia.

Whim of Time, A. Stephen Spender. MoBrPo

Whip it on down. Huddie Ledbetter. Paul Foreman. TiP2

Whip, The. Robert Creeley. ICANM; PFTM-2

Whipping fishtails beneath the microscope, The. Night Watch in the Laboratory. Ann Townsend. NAPBL

Whipping, The. Robert Earl Hayden. PoCho; SoSe-8; SSLK

Whipping, The. Samuel F. Reynolds. SpirFl

Whippoorwill Calls, The. Beverly McLoughland. HHAm

Whippoorwill in the Woods, A. Amy Clampitt. OWoS

Whip-the-World. Hugh MacDiarmid. FaBoVe

Whirl and click of sprocket and chain. Song of the Wheel, The. George Lynde Richardson. ArBi

Whirl, snow, on the blackbird's chatter. Eager Spring. Gordon Bottomley. MoBrPo

Whirl up, sea. Oread. "H. D." APT-1; BrAP; ColAP; HeIP-4; MoAmPo; MoWP; NAAL-5; NAAPv.2; NALW; NAMCP V.1; NoAM; NPeEn; OxBoAm; PoPoPo; TCAPo

Whirl Wind Must, The. George Oppen. BodElec

Whirled by the three passions, one's eyes go blind. Ungo Kiyo. ZenPo, *tr. by* Takashi Ikemoto and Lucien Stryk

Whirled ten years beyond all bounds. Tu Mu. CCL1 *Fr.* Recalling Former Travels.

Whirling along its living freight, it came. Christopher Pearse Cranch. APN-1; GM *Fr.* Seven Wonders of the World.

Whirling Round the Sun. Suzanne Noguere. FFC

Whirling Wheel, The. *Unknown.* ArBi

Whirlwinds of hot autumn dust. Dust World. Adrian C. Louis. UnSA

Whiskers Meets Polly. Michael Stillman. TLR

Whisky on your breath, The. Theodore Roethke. *See* Whiskey on your breath, The.

Whiskey on your breath, The. My Papa's Waltz. Theodore Roethke. AmFaPo; APT-2; BeAl; BrAP; CAP-8; ClHu; ColAP; EMP; HeIP-4; NAAL-5; NAMCP V.1; NBLV; NIL-7; NIP-4; NoAM; NoP-4; NoP-5; NOxBChV; OxBoAm; PoPoPo; RaBo; TFi; TRP; WaAnP

(Whisky on your breath, The.) ChAP

Whiskey-Bomb Battle. Mayme Evans. TiP2

Whisky Lovers. *Vietnamese Oral Tradition.* CaDao, *tr. by* John Balaban

Whisper. Mona Fayad. PoArWo

Whisper. John Banister Tabb. APN-2

Whisper, The. Eugene Gloria. OpBo

Whisper flies to the empty sleeve, A. Sequel of Appomattox. Donald Davidson. CBCWP; FuPo

Whisper in the Dark. Sándor Weöres. IQMS, *tr. by* Edwin Morgan

Whisper is a sibilant thing, A. Whisper. Mona Fayad. PoArWo

Whisper it. And, Yes, Those Spiritual Matters. Christopher Gilbert. ESEAA; InoFa

Whisper of the wind in, The. Theocritus. WoPoe *Fr.* Idylls.

Whisper of yellow globes. Her Lips Are Copper Wire. Jean Toomer. APT-2; GT; NAAPv.2; NAMCP V.1; NoAM

Whisper to me some beautiful secret you remember from life. (LL) Invitation to a Ghost. Donald Justice. InGu; PfSP

Whisper Words of Love to Me. Lizelia Augusta Jenkins Moorer. CBWP-3

Whispered. Jiri Orten. AF, *tr. by* Lyn Coffin

Whispered, "Darling, you have saved me! curfew will not ring tonight." (LL) Curfew Must Not Ring Tonight [*or* To-Night]. Rose Hartwick Thorpe. APN-2; BRP; SWaP

Whisperer, The. James Stephens. IrV

Whisperer, The. Mark Van Doren. MoAmPo

Whispering to each handhold, "I'll be back." After Arguing against the Contention That Art Must Come from Discontent. William Stafford. NoAM

Whispering worshipping. (LL) Mice in the Hay. Leslie Norris. NOxBChV; OBCP

Whisperjet swings wildly, The. In Flight. Jennifer Regan. OtW

Whispers antiphonal in azure swing. (LL) Bridge, The. Hart Crane. APT-2; NAMCP V.1

Whispers in a Country Church. Alvin Aubert. OxAAAP

Whispers of Immortality. T. S. Eliot. APT-1; NAMCP V.1; NoAM; OBMV; OxAEP-2

Whispers run and trip down the pebbled. Rain Falls on Utopia Too. Arnold Rattenbury. RSaN

Whispers, Secrets, and Promises. E. Ethelbert Miller. FuFl

Whistle. Janet Holmes. ExTi

Whistle, The. Charles Murray. EdScPo

Whistle, and I'll Come to You, My Lad. Robert Burns. OxAEP-2

Whistle howls, the wheels click along, The. (LL) David Wojahn. GM; PBCAP Fr. Mystery Train: A Sequence.

Whistle into night. Scroll No. 1. Cecil Taylor. EGAG

Whistle of a blackbird, envious of the crackling of a fire, ends by, The. Landscape Heard, A. Filippo Tommaso Marinetti. PFTM-1

Whistlecraft. John Hookham Frere.
    "And certainly they say, for fine behaving." OBCoV
    Irrational Gigantic Anger. NPBRoP

Whistlin' Thief, The. Samuel Lover. IrV

Whistling arrow flies less eagerly, The. Luis de Góngora y Argote. WoPoe, tr. by Robert Lowell

Whistling fury of the frozen northern tempests. Winter's Approach. Ábrahám Barcsay. IQMS, tr. by Thomas Kabdebo

Whistling in January. David J. Rothman. GeoH

Whistling knot of highway, A. Interchange. Ted Kooser. UrbNat

Whistling Woman. Al Zolynas. PML

Whit for Whitman, A. David Mason. ViWalt

Whit Monday. Louis MacNeice. ChIV-1

White. Grace Nichols. Oth

White. Ronaldo V. Wilson. BtF

White against a ruddy cliff you stand, chalcedony on sard. (LL) Cameo, The. Edna St. Vincent Millay. GPTC; MoAmPo

White Album. Jim Behrle. FreRad

White and Black Bones, The. Konrad Bayer. PFTM-2, tr. by Malcolm Green

White angels swim through its waters. Love and the Forest. Gülseli İnal. NaPG, tr. by Talat Sait Halman

White ants, white ants and the little ribs. (LL) Snow. Charles Wright. CAP-8; ColAP; OxBoAm

White Apples. Donald Hall. LoL

White as her hand fair Julia threw. Snow-Ball, The. Soame Jenyns. OBVE

White as I can, though not as thee. (LL) Nymph Complaining for the Death of Her Faun [or Fawn], The. Andrew Marvell. BASC; HeIP-4; NAEL-6v1; NAEL-7v1; RACG

White as the sacrament, in my grandmother's house the mantles. Mantles. Kit Wright. NoP-5

White as the snow on mountaintop. Lament of a Graying Woman. Cho Wen-chun. NDACCP, tr. by William Carlos Williams

White ash amid funereal cypresses. (LL) Helen. "H. D." APT-1; BrAP; ColAP; EMP; FTtHH; MoAmPo; NAAL-5; NAAPv.2; NALW; NAMCP V.1; NIL-7; NoAM; NoP-4; NoP-5; OxBoAm; PoPoPo

White Asparagus. Sujata Bhatt. HarvBoo; StAl

White Banners. Sŏng [or Sung] Sammun. WoPoe, tr. by Jean S. Grigsby

White bark writhed and sputtered like a fish, The. Edna St. Vincent Millay. NALW Fr. Sonnets from an Ungrafted Tree.

White bars from the window. Antonio Porta. ItPo Fr. Essences.

White, bathing moon, The. Hymn for Portia White. George Elliott Clarke. IFF

White Bear. Joy Harjo. NAAL-5

White Bears: Tolstoy at Astapovo. Linda Bierds. AmAlph

White bird. Wakayama Bokusui. CAoMJL1, tr. by Janine Beichman

White bird featherless. Riddle. Unknown. FaBoVe; OxBEV

White Bird, The. Rosamund Marriott Watson. VWP

White birds over the grey river. Another Spring. Tu Fu [or Du Fu]. BLT, tr. by Kenneth Rexroth

White—bloodred. Polish Colours. Maria Pawlikowska-Jasnorzewska. SonAtl, tr. by Sue Eley and Katarzyna Pollonska

White Blossom, A. D. H. Lawrence. MoBrPo

White blossom, white, white shell; the Nazarene. Music of Colours—White Blossom. Vernon Watkins. AngWePo; TCAWP

White blossoms of the pear. Buson. EH, tr. by Robert Hass

White brick steps were steep and off-level, The. My Father at the North Street Boarding House. James Kimbrell. AmPoNex

White butterfly / Darting among pinks. Masaoka Shiki. ZenPo, tr. by Takashi Ikemoto and Lucien Stryk

White butterfly speckled with pollen joined me in my prayer yesterday. Wolf Warrior. Joy Harjo. PfSP

White Cap, The. Unknown. CCL1 Fr. Su-guan [Translations].

White cat splendid in trilliums, A. Poem Upon the Forcible Entry by Cat into a Poem Originally Upon Trilliums. M. Travis Lane. Coast

White Center. Richard Hugo. NAMCP V.2

White chocolate jar full of petals, The. Chez Jane. Frank O'Hara. ColAP; NoAM; PoA 2002

White Christmas. Irving Berlin. ReLy

White Christmas. William Robert Rodgers. MoBrPo

White chrysanthemums. Basho. EMJL, tr. by Haruo Shirane

White circle, white line white X, warm white. White Album. Jim Behrle. FreRad

White circles of conical hats have come out, The. Night Harvest. Lam Thi My Da. PoCho, tr. by Martha Collins and Thuy Dinh

White City, A. James Schuyler. OxBoAm

White City, A: "In the dream, N. is singing "a white city." A teacher he had is wearing a girdle." Michael Burkard. IJHIL

White City, The. Claude McKay. APT-1; NAMCP V.1; NoAM; OxBoAm; RaBo

White Claw, The. Alfonsina Storni. TCLAP, tr. by Andrew Rosing

White cloth spread. Towards Abraham's Bosom. Amelia Blossom Pegram. HAWP

White clouds encircle the waist of the hills like a belt. Written on a Landscape Painting in an Album. Shen Chou. ColAnChi, tr. by Daniel Bryant

White Clover. Marvin Bell. CAP-8; InvLad; VCAP

White coat worn over a violet waistcoat, A. Elegant Things. Unknown. EMJL, tr. by Edward Putzar

White cormorants shaped like houses stare down at you, The. Party at Hydra. Irving Layton. HeIP-4

White Crane. Dean Young. IllVoic

White Crane Hill. Su Tung-p'o. ColAnChi; GifTon, tr. by Burton Watson

White crosses alter whenever I move, The. Flag Memoir. Reg Saner. AmWaPo

White dawn. Stillness. When the rippling began. Tree Telling of Orpheus, A. Denise Levertov. APSN; MiVo

White day, black river. Predicter of Famine, The. William Carlos Williams. APT-1

White Days. Reginald Shepherd. GT

White decorators interested in art. Nights of 1964–66: The Old Reliable. Marilyn Hacker. OxBoAm; VCAP

White Deer, The. Jay Wright. ESEAA

White Devil, The. John Webster.
    Call for the Robin-Redbreast and the Wren. NOSC; NPeEn; OxAEP-1; OxBEV; TFi
    (Dirge, A.) OBEV; WoPoe

White dew. Buson. EH, tr. by Robert Hass

White dove at my window, A. I look at its eye, the world's mystery turns in its arid eye. Visitation. Mónica Nepote. SPV, tr. by Jen Hofer

White doves of Cytherea, by your quest. Pledge, The. Adelaide Crapsey. NAAPv.2

White Dress. Yüan Chĕn. CrYelRi, tr. by Sam Hamill

White Dress, The. Lynn Emanuel. SUP

White Dress, The. Marya Alexandrovna Zaturenska. MoAmPo

White drops of dew, The. Lady Kasa. ArkPo, tr. by Edwin A. Cranston

White Dust, The. Wilfrid Wilson Gibson. MoBrPo

White Dwarf. Gerry LaFemina. AmPoNex

White Earth. Gerald Vizenor. HATNAP

White Echo. A. R. Ammons. PfSP

White egg and a colored pan and a cabbage showing settlement, a constant increase, A. Gertrude Stein. MotU Fr. Tender Buttons.

White Feather Legion, The. T. W. H. Crosland. FaBoWar

White fingers of the sexton sleep heavy upon us. Concert in the Old School Garret. Unknown, fr. Terezin Concentration Camp. INSAB

White fire of winter stars. Sitting Up Late with My Father, 1977. Franz Wright. AmAlph

White Fish in Reeds. Joseph Ceravolo. BodElec; NYP2

White flesh quakes to the negro soul, The. Widow's Jazz, The. Mina Loy. NAMCP V.1

White floating clouds. Clouds like the plains come and water the earth. Rain Song of the Quer'ränna Chai'än, A. Unknown. APN-2, tr. by Matilda Coxe Stevenson

White flour, earth-flesh, a cold fleece on the mountain. Snowfall, The. Gwerfyl Mechain. OBWVE, tr. by Kenneth Hurlstone Jackson

White Flowers. Jocelyn Emerson. IAoNAP

White fog lifting and falling on mountain-brow. Wales Visitation. Allen Ginsberg. APSN; BB; ColAP; VCAP

"White folks is white," says Uncle Jim. Uncle Jim. Countee Cullen. GT

White Foolscap / Book of Cordelia. Susan Howe. PmAP

White founts falling in the courts of the sun. Lepanto. G. K. Chesterton. FaBoWar; MoBrPo; OBMV; OBNV

White foxes howl at mountain wind beneath the moon. Ravine on a Cold Evening. Li Ho. ColAnChi, tr. by Maureen Robertson

White. From the / Under arm of T. George Oppen. APT-2; PFTM-1

White Fury of the Spring, The. Lizette Woodworth Reese. APT-1

White fuzz in the air froze on a screen. Baby danced the cancan. Carla Harryman. BAP-04 Fr. Baby.

White Giant Leper of the Countryside. Tristan Tzara. YaTCFP, tr. by Mary Ann Caws

White girl. Registering the Little One. Derec Llwyd Morgan. BBMWP, *tr.* by Catherine Fisher

White girl smiles, The. McDonald's, Scottsboro, April, 1997. Anthony Walton. RD

White Goddess, The. Robert Graves. HarvBoo; MoBrPo; NAEL-6v2; NAEL-7v2; NoP-4; NoP-5

White goose by palm tree, palm ragged, among stones the. Robert Penn Warren. FuPo

White Great Nimble Cat, A. Sir Philip Sidney. TriCat

White Hair. Ch'i-chi. CSKM, *tr.* by Burton Watson

White hair covers my temples. Putting the Blame on His Sons. T'ao Ch'ien. CCL1, *tr.* by William Acker

White hair shrouds both my temples. Blaming Sons. Ch'ien T'ao. ColAnChi, *tr.* by Burton Watson

White hair tossed, a black cape flecked with snow. (LL) Richard Murphy. ModIr; PBCIP *Fr.* Battle of Aughrim, The.

White hands. Naturalization. Erich Fried. GTCP, *tr.* by Reinhold Grimm

White Heart of God, The. Jack Gilbert. BodElec

White Heliotrope. Arthur Symons. NPeEn

White Hope. Ishmael Reed. ISC

White Horse. Gwyneth Lewis. BBMWP, *tr.* by the author and Richard Poole

White Horses. Ts'ao Chih. CCL1, *tr.* by John Frodsham

White horses, all adorned with golden bridles. White Horses. Ts'ao Chih. CCL1, *tr.* by John Frodsham

White Hotel. Carol Potter. PfS

White House, A. Rossana Ombres. NeIt, *tr.* by Pietro Pedace and Robert McCracken

White House, The. Claude McKay. ISC; NIP-4

White House Blues. *Unknown.* APT-1

White house in front of the park, A. White House, A. Rossana Ombres. NeIt, *tr.* by Pietro Pedace and Robert McCracken

White Hunter, A. Gertrude Stein. PFTM-1

White hunter is nearly crazy, A. White Hunter, A. Gertrude Stein. PFTM-1

White hunter is nearly crazy, A. Gertrude Stein. NAAPv.2; NAMCP V.1 *Fr.* Tender Buttons.

White ignorant hollow of his face, The. (LL) Father and Son. Stanley Kunitz. AF; TaR, *tr.* by Jack Bevan

White in the Woods. Jan Clausen. RWB

White iris sprang up, A. Marina Dolia. CRWP *Fr.* Silence.

White is lying on top of the green, The. Snow. Jorge Guillén. RaW, *tr.* by Robert Bly

White is my favorite color. To John Ashbery. Tom Clark and Lewis Warsh. AHA

White Island, The: or Place of the Blest. Robert Herrick. NoP-4; NoP-5; NOSC; NPeEn

White Knight's Song, The. Lewis Carroll. BrAP; NAEL-6v2; NAEL-7v2; NoAM; NoP-4; NoP-5; TFi; UV *Fr.* Through the Looking-Glass.

White Lady. Lucille Clifton. ESEAA; SUP

White Lady, The. Rosamund Marriott Watson. ViWPN; VWP

White Land, The. Roberta Hill Whiteman. HATNAP

White lather on black soap. Black Soap. Sandra McPherson. VCAP

White Lie, The. Don Paterson. NeBrP

White Lies. Natasha Trethewey. TWW

White light of dawn grows wider, The. *Unknown.* SLW, *tr.* by Marjolijn De Jager, Sayd Bahodin Majrouh and André Velter

White light, receive me your sojourner; O milky way. Elegy of the Wind. Christopher Okigbo. VCWP

White lighthouse in the hard flat, A. Edward Hopper's "Lighthouse at Two Lights." Tony Quagliano. PoSol

White light's wet glaze on asphalt city floor. Studying the Signs. Allen Ginsberg. FTOS

White lights, white noise and white punctuation marks. White Flowers. Jocelyn Emerson. IAoNAP

White Lilies, The. Louise Glück. PoPoPo

White Lines. Fanny Howe. Eno

White lotus. Buson. WoPoe; ZenPo, *tr.* by Takashi Ikemoto and Lucien Stryk

White Low Sun . . . , A. Marina Ivanovna Tsvetayeva. AF, *tr.* by David McDuff

White low sun, low thunderclouds; and back, A. White Low Sun . . . , A. Marina Ivanovna Tsvetayeva. AF, *tr.* by David McDuff

White Man and the Judge, A. Kevin Simmonds. BtF

White man drew a small circle in the sand, The. Circles. Carl Sandburg. HHAm

White Man's Burden, The. Rudyard Kipling. WaAnP

White man's soul, it thirsts for gain, The. Indian's Retort, The. Jones Very. NCAP

White Marble Stone, The. *Unknown.* SSUS

White mares of the moon rush along the sky, The. Night Clouds. Amy Lowell. MoAmPo

White, Mauve, Yellow. Anne Simpson. Coast

White men are behind this night's door. Echoes of the Murder of Emmett Till. Ira B. Jones. InTrad

White men handed papers to my mother. Eviction. Michelle T. Clinton. ISC

White metal tubes contain. Planes Landing. Jamie Grant. NOBAu

White, moist, orange. Slug. Robert Siegel. PfSP

White moon gleams through scudding, The. Sorrow. Chu Shu-chen. NDACCP, *tr.* by Kenneth Rexroth

White moon is rising, The. Moon Is Rising, The. *Unknown.* TAL

White moon, perfect, The. About the Men. Adele Ne Jame. PoArWo

White Moonglow, The. Paul Verlaine. NAWM-7v2, *tr.* by Carlyle Ferren MacIntyre

White Moonglow, The. White Moonglow, The. Paul Verlaine. NAWM-7v2, *tr.* by Carlyle Ferren MacIntyre

White moose, geese in the sky, nibbling ribbons. (LL) Fred Wah. IFF; NLPA *Fr.* This Dendrite Map: Father / Mother Haibun.

White moths in crazy mobs. Snow. M. C. Richards. WhBo

White Mouses Petition to Lamira the Right Honble the Lady Anne Tufton now Countess of Salisbury, The. Anne Finch, Countess of Winchilsea. PoBW

White Night. Mary Oliver. AWTN

White Night. Boris Leonidovich Pasternak. RusPo, *tr.* by Robert Arthur Douglas Ford

White night in which the transparent water. Beside Christ's Lake in Aldehuela de Yeltes, on a Night with a Full Moon. Miguel de Unamuno. RaW, *tr.* by Robert Bly

White Nights. Lewis Warsh. KGB

White Nile Elegy. Khaled Mattawa. NAPBL

White on White. Eugenio de Andrade.
  "Friend is sometimes desert, A." VCWP

White on White. Maria Luisa Spaziani. NeIt, *tr.* by Beverly Allen

White on white's a flatness. Nikolay Novikov. TCRusP, *tr.* by Daniel Weissbort

White one?, The. (LL) Wings, The. Denise Levertov. APSN; NALW

White Oxen. Louis Simpson. NAMCP V.2; NoAM

White Paintings I. Laura Mullen. RoV

White Paintings II (in parenthesis). Laura Mullen. RoV

White Paintings III. Laura Mullen. RoV

White Paintings IV (Independence Day). Laura Mullen. RoV

White Paintings V. Laura Mullen. RoV

White peacock roosting, The. What I Saw. Robert Duncan. NAMCP V.2

White Peacock, The. Dmitry Vasil'evich Bobyshev. ItGoST, *tr.* by Michael Van Walleghen

White Peacock, The. Alice Notley. FTOS

White pearls. Pearls. Léopold Sédar Senghor. VCWP, *tr.* by Melvin Dixon

White pebbles jut from the river-stream. In the Hills. Wang Wei. TAL

White peonies blooming along the porch. Peonies at Dusk. Jane Kenyon. LoL

White petals afloat. Sadakichi. NAAPv.1 *Fr.* Haikai.

White Petticoats. Chana Bloch. MPUn

White Phosphorus. Alice Notley. FTOS

White plum blossoms. Buson. EMJL, *tr.* by Haruo Shirane

White plum blossoms. Buson. EMJL *Fr.* Spring Breeze on the Kema Embankment.

White Porch, The. Cathy Song. BeAl; NAAL-5; YaYoPo

White Port and Lemon Juice. Yusef Komunyakaa. ISC

White receiver, The. Scan at 8 Weeks. Helen Dunmore. BeAl

White reeds grow on chilly sands. Shipboard Song. Yüan Chüeh. ColAnChi, *tr.* by John Timothy Wixted

White reflection retreats to western hills. On and On: An Ancient Song (Yueh-Fu). Li Ho. ChinPo, *tr.* by Ye Weilian [*or* Yeh Wei-lien *or* Wai-lim Yip]

White residence. Collection of White Poems. Kitasono Katsue. CAoMJL1, *tr.* by John Solt

White rhododendron has come into flower, The. Anniversary. Lauris Edmond. BeAl

White room that I eat in and write in, The. Shortest Day, The. William Dickey. InoFa

White Rose, A. John Boyle O'Reilly. OBEV

White rose in red rose-garden. Algernon Charles Swinburne. *See* Glad, but not flush'd with gladness.

White Rose is a quiet horse. Four Horses, The. James Reeves. TLR

White Rose, The. Louise Glück. CAP-8

White Roses. David Biespiel. AmPoNex

White Settlement. William Wenthe. TiP2

White sheep, white sheep, on a blue hill. Riddle. *Unknown.* FaBoVe

White sheet on the tail-gate of a truck, A. Elegy for a Dead Soldier. Karl Shapiro. OBWP

White Ship, The. Dante Gabriel Rossetti. OBNV

White silence on the water pulls me in and under. And I know it. Mute Swan, The. Constance Merritt. AmPoNex

White sky is exactly the same white, The. Before the Beginning: Maybe God and a Silk Flower Concubine Perhaps. Pattiann Rogers. PuP-23

White sky, over the hemlocks bowed with snow. Buck in the Snow, The. Edna St. Vincent Millay. ColAP; MoWP; NALW; NoP-4; NoP-5; WaAnP

White Sleep. Sadiq al-Saygh. IrPoTo, tr. by Saadi A. Simawe

White Soil. Joy Lahey. AnSo

White Solitude. Leopoldo Lugones. TCLAP, tr. by Julie Schumacher

White southern businessman needed, The. New Windows. Claudia Rankine. GT

White Spine. Henri Cole. NAMCP V.2

White Stallion, The. Abu-I-Salt Umayyah. WoPoe, tr. by Cola Franzen

White Star, The. Minnie Bruce Pratt. ExTi

White stone lady on the grass, The. White Lady, The. Rosamund Marriott Watson. ViWPN; VWP

White substitute teacher, A. View of the Library of Congress from Paul Laurence Dunbar High School. Thomas Sayers Ellis. FuFl; GT

White Summer Clothes are Folded Away, The. Cristina Campo. CItWP, tr. by Cinzia Sartini Blum and Lara Trubowitz

White sun. Zebra. Judith Thurman. SSCS

White sun ends with the mountains. Ascend the Heron Tower. Wang Chih-huan. ChinPo, tr. by Ye Weilian [or Yeh Wei-lien or Wai-lim Yip]

White sun is hidden in the mountains, The. View from Heron Tower. Wang Chih-huan. CrYelRi, tr. by Sam Hamill

White sun leaning on the mountain disappears, The. Climbing the Stork Pavilion. Wang Chih-huan. ColAnChi, tr. by Richard W. Bodman

White sun up behind pines. Allen Ginsberg. WhBo

White swan of cities, slumbering in thy nest. Venice. Henry Wadsworth Longfellow. APN-1

White teeth, The. Spring Day. Cho Chihun. CAMKP, tr. by Kevin O'Rourke

White teeth smiling. Tsangyang Gyatso. WoPoe Fr. Love-Poems of the Sixth Dalai Lama.

White the October air, no snow, easy to breathe. How to Get There. Frank O'Hara. NoP-4; NoP-5

White Things. Anne Spencer. InGu; NAAPv.2

White Thought, The. Stevie Smith. Spl

White Tiger Leaps, The. Sarah Gorham. FFC Fr. Notes From a Chinese Love Manual.

White Tiger, The. Ronald Stuart Thomas. AngWePo

White Towels. Richard Jones. P180

White Trace Close. Christine Monhollen. Eno

White Troops Had Their Orders but the Negroes Looked Like Men. Gwendolyn Brooks. NAAL-5

White undervest nestling on black trousers. Walnut and Lily. Douglas Oliver. Oth

White violet, The. Sea Violet. "H. D." APT-1; MoWP; NAMCP V.1; NoP-4; NoP-5

White Was I. Félix Lope de Vega Carpio. SpanPo, tr. by Kate Flores

White was I. White Was I. Félix Lope de Vega Carpio. SpanPo, tr. by Kate Flores

White Wedding. Gordon Rodgers. Coast

White Wedding Slippers. Anna Swirszczynska [or Swir]. AF, tr. by Czeslaw Milosz

White well, A. Incantation. Elinor Wylie. APT-1; NAMCP V.1

White, White. David Morley. NLP

White, white gulls wheel inland, The. Midnight Harvest, A. Rosamund Marriott Watson. ViWPN

White white iris, blue-veined. this stillness is bloodstone, flagstone, the cold stone air winding. Syliva Legris. PoPra Fr. Negative Garden.

White wing brushing the building, A. (LL) Owl and the Lightning, The. Martín Espada. TouFir; UrbNat

White Witch, The. James Weldon Johnson. APT-1

White with the starlight folded in its wings. Shapes of a Soul. Sarah Morgan Bryan Piatt. NAAPv.1

White woman. Circular Fate. Askhari. InTrad

White woman across the aisle from me says, "Look", The. On the Amtrak from Boston to New York City. Sherman Alexie. NAMCP V.2; PoPoPo

White Women, The. Mary Elizabeth Coleridge. NALW; PEW; ViWPN; VWP

White World. "H. D." WPoS
  (Whole White World, The.) APT-1

White world after a urine-yellow sundown. Visiting Hour (Repatriation Hospital). Michael Dransfield. BMAP

White yuppies in santa monica go through their attics. History as Trash. Michelle T. Clinton. SpirFl

Whitebait, The. Basho. EH, tr. by Robert Hass

White-faced, white-suited, as big as the full moon in the tropical sky. Man in the Moon, The. Alvin Greenberg. OPRER

White-habited, the mystic Swan. Swan, The. Jay Macpherson. NoP-4; NoP-5; WaAnP

White-haired, but wanton still. Unknown. CATKP, tr. by Kevin O'Rourke

White-haired woman of winter. Tiva's Tapestry: La Llorona. Linda Hogan. FTtHH

Whitelight, keenair, someone. To John Ashbery on Szymanowski's Birthday. Frank O'Hara. BodElec

White-maned, wide-throated, the heavy-shouldered children of the wind leap at the sea-cliff. Granite and Cypress. Robinson Jeffers. APT-1

Whiteness near and far, The. From a Notebook. James Merrill. MoW

Whiteness, or Chastity. Joseph Beaumont. NOSC

Whiteness! Whiteness! Whiteness. Zishe Vaynper. Prolet, tr. by Amelia Glaser

Whiter than a mountain glacier. White Peacock, The. Dmitry Vasil'evich Bobyshev. ItGoST, tr. by Michael Van Walleghen

Whites alone upon the jury in a number of the states. Injustice of the Courts. Lizelia Augusta Jenkins Moorer. CBWP-3

Whites of the city spill out, The. Go. Betrayed by KC. Jenny Mueller. IAoNAP

White-tipped but dark underneath, racing out of town. (LL) Saturday at the Canal. Gary Soto. P180; TWF

Whitewash of Houston. Vassar Miller. TiP2

Whitewashed pane cheers the road to sand-plugged, A. Isipingo. Douglas Livingstone. TSAP

Whither away good neighbour. Martin Parker. PBRV Fr. Well met Neighbour.

WHITHER away so fast. Unknown. NoSic

Whither, I dread to think—but he is gone. (LL) Manfred. Lord Byron. NAEL-6v2; NAEL-7v2; NOBRP

Whither, 'midst falling dew. To a Waterfowl. William Cullen Bryant. APN-1; ColAP; CtM; ITBLP; NAAL-3; NAAL-5; NAAPv.1; NCAP; NoP-4; NoP-5; OWoS; OxBoAm; SoSe-8; TFi; WaAnP

Whither, O splendid ship, thy white sails crowding. Passer-by, A. Robert Bridges. MoBrPo; OBEV

Whither Thou Goest. Bob Hicok. AmAlph

Whit'll ye dae when the wee Malkies come. Coming of the Wee Malkies, The. Stephen Mulrine. EdScPo

Whitman. Larry Levis. ReTh; ViWalt

Whitman Again. John Judson. ViWalt

Whitman among the wounded, at the bedside. Reading with the Poets. Stanley Plumly. ViWalt

Whitman, Come Again to the Cities. Toi Derricotte. ViWalt

Whitman had no sirens to attend to. Varied Carol, The. David Graham. ViWalt

Whitman in a Corner. Paul Hoover. ViWalt

Whitman in Black. Ted Berrigan. NYP2; ViWalt

Whitman is dead and his thought. Ship of State and Grandpa. Howard Phelps Putnam. OxBoAm

Whitman Leaves the Boardwalk. Edward Hirsch. ViWalt

Whitman on the Beach. Mark Bibbins. WiU

Whitman Pinch Hits, 1861. Floyd Skloot. ViWalt

Whitman Portrait, A. Steve Kowit. ViWalt

Whitman Stock-Taking, Cataloguing. James Schevill. ViWalt

Whitman: The Wall. Philip Dacey. ViWalt

Whitman thought he could live with animals, they were. Small Acts. Thomas Centolella. GifTon; ViWalt

Whitman would have admired Willimantic's. Under the Sign of Walt Whitman. Gray Jacobik. ViWalt

Whitman's Confession: In the Cleft of Eternity. Beckian Fritz Goldberg. ViWalt

Whitman's Grass. Martin Bell. ViWalt

Whitman's walk unchanged after its fashion. (LL) Whitman in Black. Ted Berrigan. NYP2; ViWalt

Whitsun Weddings, The. Philip Larkin. BeAl; HeIP-4; NAMCP V.2; NoAM; NoP-4; NoP-5; OxAEP-2

Whizzing, whizzing down the street-car tracks. (LL) Seventh Street. Jean Toomer. APT-2; NAAPv.2

Who? Abd al-Rahim Salih al-Rahim. IrPoTo, tr. by Saadi A. Simawe and Daniel Weissbort

Who. Mari E. Evans. ISC

Who? Oscar, II Hammerstein and Otto Harbach. ReLy

Who? Czeslaw Milosz. BodElec Fr. Lithuania, After Fifty-two Years.

Who. Tim Seibles. ISC

Who. Frederick Ward. IFF

Who affirms that crystals are alive? Snow. John Davidson. EdScPo; NePenScot; NPeEn

Who alone is Lord and God! (LL) Laus Deo! John Greenleaf Whittier. CBCWP; PCW

Who Am I? Dietrich Bonhoeffer. HP, tr. by Reginald H. Fuller

Who am I? A tramp, I guess. Jack Rhymer. David Brendon Hopes. UpMys

Who am I if not outside, a blizzard and borrowed. Manhattan Valley. Lynn Melnick. IIR

Who Am I in Twilight. Al Young. ASA

Who am I? Only one of the commonest common people. Out of the Darkness. Voltairine de Cleyre. SWaP

Who am I? They often tell me. Who Am I? Dietrich Bonhoeffer. HP, *tr. by* Reginald H. Fuller

Who Among Common Men of Their Time? Angus Martin. EdScPo

Who among us can truly say. Garden. John Engels. PfSP

Who and Each. Ron Padgett. PmAP

Who and what am I then? Whence do I come? György Bessenyei to Himself. György Bessenyei. IQMS, *tr. by* Watson Kirkconnell

Who and Where. Marvin Bell.

"Who I am is a short person with small feet." InvLad

Who are a little wise, the best fools be. (LL) Triple Fool, The. John Donne. FSCP; NOSC; SoSe-8

Who are my friends / the sick / the weak / the poor in spirit. Nicanor Parra. GI *Fr.* New Sermons and Preachings of the Christ of Elqui (1979).

Who Are These Children? William Soutar. EdScPo

Who are these figures in the street? Smiling Through. Reed Whittemore. BodElec

Who are these people at the bridge to meet me? They are the villagers. Bee Meeting, The. Sylvia Plath. HarvBoo; NALW

Who / are these two women, walking. Operations: Desert Shield, Desert Storm. Eleanor Wilner. FiBr

Who are these? Why sit they here in twilight? Mental Cases. Wilfred Owen. NAMCP V.1; NoAM

Who are they? Death and Death's dog, Time. (LL) Two Figures. N. Scott Momaday. NoP-4; NoP-5

Who are they now? since the Bathurst ground. From a Republican Grave: Daniel Henry Deniehy, 1828–1865. Philip Mead. NOBAu

Who are they to be in their skin. Subway Witnesses, The. Lorenzo Thomas. GT

Who are we. Etheridge Knight. BodElec

Who are you? Woman and a Man, A. Adonis. PML, *tr. by* Abdullah Al-Udhari

Who Are You? Abd al-Rahim Salih al-Rahim. IrPoTo, *tr. by* Saadi A. Simawe and Daniel Weissbort

Who are you. Marla Jernigan. AnSo

Who are you? and with whom do you sleep here? (LL) On a cold night I came through the cold rain. James Vincent Cunningham. TRP; VCAP

Who are you? asks my mother. Have We Had Easter Yet? Alison Pryde. BeAl

Who are you, coming without flash and standing high. Bedrooms. Sandra McPherson. ExTi

Who are you, fair-haired lady. Rhinemaiden. D. L. Crockett-Smith. OxAAAP

Who are you,little i. E. E. Cummings. NoP-5

"Who are you, Sea Lady." Santorin. James Elroy Flecker. OBMV

"Who are you that so strangely woke." Princess of Scotland, The. Rachel Annand Taylor. NePenScot

Who are you there that from your icy tower. Astronomers of Mont Blanc, The. Edgar Bowers. PoA 2002

Who art as black as hell, as dark as night. (LL) William Shakespeare. AEP; NAEL-6v1; NAEL-7v1; OxAEP-1 *Fr.* Sonnets.

Who asked the sun to set in the evening? Just Because I Am. Malkia Amala Cyril. InTrad

Who asks forgiveness. Sin. Ben Scammell. NLP

Who Besides You. Bart Howard. ReLy

Who broke these mirrors. Poetry. Sa'di Yusuf. IrPoTo, *tr. by* Khaled Mattawa

Who Burns for the Perfection of Paper. Martín Espada. InvLad

Who by low creatures leads to heights of love. (LL) Flush or Faunus. Elizabeth Barrett Browning. DiBP; VWP

"Who called?" I said, and the words. Echo. Walter De la Mare. OBMV

Who called to us for food. (LL) Last Lie, The. Bruce Weigl. AF; AmWaPo

Who calls? Welcome Eumenides. Eleanor Ross Taylor. InGu; NALW

Who can be a wild deer among deserted mountains. Han-shan Te-ch'ing. CSKM, *tr. by* Red Pine

Who can believe with common sense. Epigram on Fasting. Jonathan Swift. OBVE

Who can describe the waves of Mother Syama's world? Kamalākānta Bhattācārya. SinGod, *tr. by* Rachel Fell McDermott

Who can doubt, Rice, to which eternal place. On Mr. Rice the Manciple of Christ Church in Oxford. Richard Corbet. NOSC

Who can forget the attitude of mothering? Mother Love. Rita Dove. AFaM

Who can hold a fire in his hand? You spread your fingers. Four About Metaphysics. David Young. MotU

Who can I tell? I miss my disguises. Ann Lauinger. IaFF *Fr.* Three Songs for *King Leir.*

Who can I turn to. Who Can I Turn To (When Nobody Needs Me?). Leslie Bricusse and Anthony Newley. ReLy

Who Can I Turn To? William Engvick. ReLy

Who can I turn to. Who Can I Turn To? William Engvick. ReLy

Who Can I Turn To (When Nobody Needs Me?). Leslie Bricusse and Anthony Newley. ReLy

Who can keep a blazing fire tied in a cotton cloth? Lex Hixon. HW

Who can live in heart so glad. Nicholas Breton. NoSic *Fr.* Passionate Shepherd, The.

Who can say for certain that such creatures. Topsell's Beasts. Julia Copus. MoWP

Who can say? It is silent now. (LL) What Were They Like? Denise Levertov. HeIP-4; NIP-4; OBWP; PoAgWa

Who can say what love is? But Beautiful. Johnny Burke. ReLy

Who can show [*or* shew] all his love, doth love but lightly. (LL) Samuel Daniel. NoP-4; NoP-5 *Fr.* Sonnets to Delia.

Who can tell the difference between the state. Grace. Laura Kasischke. NAPBL

Who can understand Kali? Rāmprasād Sen. SinGod, *tr. by* Rachel Fell McDermott

Who Can Understand This? László Mécs. IQMS, *tr. by* Kenneth Thomas

Who Cares? Ira Gershwin. ReLy

Who Cares for the Blind Stork. Blaga Dimitrova. CSCBP, *tr. by* Georgi Belev and Lisa Sapinkopf

Who come in the night whispering. Two Girls. Suzanne Gardinier. KGB; NeAmPo

Who comes? Two Tongue-Pointing (Satirical) Songs. *Unknown.* NOBAu

Who comes is occupied. George Oppen. APT-2; PFTM-1

Who comes to the table fresh. Setting the Table. Don McKay. OpeFie

Who could believe it? A twin-bladed arrow. On the Bird Which Still Flew, Though Its Head Was Severed. Janus Pannonius. IQMS, *tr. by* Anthony Barrett

Who could believe it? O, the fates are fickle. *Unknown.* PriapPo *Fr.* Priapus Poems, The.

Who could declare your death, standing. Facing It. Daniel Berrigan. UpMys

Who could have baked my entire heart's desire. Sylvia Kantaris. NewEx

Who could have guessed, attention glued. Mortal Remains. Kimiko Hahn. PA9/11

Who could make her do anything. (LL) Reunion. Carolyn Forché. NAMCP V.2; NoAM

Who could outbalance poised. To the High Court of Parliament. Geoffrey Hill. OxBEV

Who could tire of the long shadows. February Days. May Sarton. APT-2

Who cried at their tent flap. Dakota dawn. Hamartia Symbolized by the Stray. Joel Brouwer. LegDan

Who crossed cold Lethe, thought it Rubicon. (LL) Fording the River. Seamus Deane. PBCIP; PNI

Who / 'd / of / thought / the / morning / 'd / be / so / late. Ted Greenwald. AHA *Fr.* Makes Sense.

Who dare pull down a crown, tear up a tomb? (LL) Upon the Double Murther of King Charles I. Katherine Philips. BASC; NAEL-7v1

Who dares approach the lion's. Daigu. ZenPo, *tr. by* Takashi Ikemoto and Lucien Stryk

Who dares deny the burning truth of the sun? Virgil. WoPoe *Fr.* Georgics.

Who decrees a great epoch? The meridian of Greenwich. Derek Walcott. NoP-5 *Fr.* Omeros.

Who deem epigrams mere trifles. Martial. RomPo, *tr. by* Peter Whigham

Who did I write last night? leaning. Trust Me. Jean Valentine. LaCa

Who did kill Cock Robbin? Mother Goose. *See* Who killed Cock [*or* poor] Robin? [*or* Here lies Cock Robin].

Who died on the wires, and hung there, one of two. Ivor Gurney. HarvBoo; NAEL-6v2; NAEL-7v2; NAMCP V.1; NoP-4; NoP-5; NPeEn; OBWP; PoWW *Fr.* Silent One, The.

Who does not love the spring deserves no lovers. Georgian Spring. Roy Campbell. OBSV

Who does not love the *Titanic*? Titanic. David R. Slavitt. GoPo

Who does not sit in the seat of the scoffer. Blessed Is the Man. Marianne Moore. ChIV-1

Who doesn't. Who. Tim Seibles. ISC

Who doesn't have the money to buy himself an island. Hôtel Fraternité. Hans Magnus Enzensberger. CLPP, *tr. by* Jerome Rothenberg

Who doesn't love. Hummingbird Pauses at the Trumpet Vine. Mary Oliver. NAAL-5

Who doubts? The laws fell down from heaven's height. Joseph Hall. OBSV *Fr.* Virgidemiarum.

Who Drags the Fiery Artist Down? Clarence Day. NBLV

Who dreamed [*or* dream'd] that beauty passes like a dream? Rose of the World, The. William Butler Yeats. MoBrPo; NAEL-6v2; NAEL-7v2

Who dwelleth in that secret place. Rest. George Macdonald. SacPr

Who Eats Who? Allen Ginsberg. BodElec

Who else / is kneeling. This Gate. Beau Beausoleil. Eno

Who else will care for me. Tune: "Sand of Silk-Washing Brook" In Memoriam. Nara Singde. ColAnChi, *tr. by* Jiaosheng Wang

Who ere she[e] be[e]. Wishes. To His (Supposed) Mistress[e]. Richard Crashaw. BASC; NOSC; OBEV; OxAEP-1

Who even dead, yet hath his mind entire! Ezra Pound. APT-1 *Fr.* Cantos.

Who ever again will be able to say. Patrizia Cavalli. ItPo, *tr. by* Gayle Ridinger

Who ever knew the heavens menace so? William Shakespeare. OxAEP-1 *Fr.* Julius Caesar.

Who ever thought a warm neck would become an armrest, or legs eager. Armchairs. Zbigniew Herbert. MotU, *tr. by* Czeslaw Milosz

Who eye pass who eye. Dreadtalk. Frederick D'Aguiar. WaCA

Who fed me from her gentle breast. My Mother. Jane Taylor. ITBLP

Who fired France for Mary without spot. (LL) Duns Scotus's Oxford. Gerard Manley Hopkins. CABP; NAEL-6v2; NAEL-7v2; NoAM; OBMV; OxAEP-2

Who first of Christian warriors now did chance. Torquato Tasso. FaBoWar *Fr.* Jerusalem Delivered.

Who first said "false as dreams?" Not one who saw. Dreams. Henry Timrod. APN-2

Who flowered broke the shine in on us. Put Together How It Will. Marla Jernigan. AnSo

Who fly with wings shut, then beating, and again shut. (LL) Poetry and Religion. Les A. Murray. UpMys; WaAnP

Who forked me like compost from my country? Who spat. Answers on a Postcard. David Morley. NLP

Who fought for Uncle Sam! (LL) Colored Soldiers, The. Paul Laurence Dunbar. APN-2; CBCWP

Who fought their way from night to day and struggled up to God. (LL) Unsung Heroes, The. Paul Laurence Dunbar. AmWaPo; CBCWP

Who gives him the Bath? New Knighthood, The. Rudyard Kipling. UV

Who gives this woman to this man? Epithalamium for a Niece. Norman Nicholson. NLP

Who goes there? God knows. I'm nobody. How should I answer? Etosion achthos aroures. Robert Bridges. OxBEV

Who goes there? hankering, gross, mystical, nude. Walt Whitman. BrAP; CAGL; ColAP *Fr.* Song of Myself.

Who Goes with Fergus? William Butler Yeats. NAEL-6v2; NAEL-7v2; NAMCP V.1; NoAM; TRP

Who gonna bargain for my soul. Who. Frederick Ward. IFF

Who got off at Edgehill, of course. Revisionism. Gordon Wardman. RSaN

Who grows old in fifty pages of Plutarch. Lament for Crassus. Michael Hofmann. NeBrP

Who gwine to lay dis body, / Member, O, shout glory. Graveyard, The. *Unknown.* SSUS

Who had always been so careful while her mistress lived. (LL) Aunt Helen. T. S. Eliot. FTtHH; NPeEn

Who had the girl turning handsprings. You're Lookin' at Me. Bobby Troup. ReLy

Who has a face sees. Shed the Fear. Anselm Hollo. PmAP

Who has ever stopped to think of the divinity of Lamont Cranston? In Memory of Radio. Imamu Amiri Baraka. BB; NoP-4; NoP-5; RWPCtW

Who has gone farthest? for I would go farther. Excelsior. Walt Whitman. SAmP

Who has made all things well! (LL) Cecil Frances Alexander. *See* He gave us eyes to see them, And lips that we might tell, How great is God Almighty, Who has made all things well.

Who has not been sleeping on an inspired day? The mind of the day sleeps us. That Can Not Be Taken Away From It. Carla Harryman. FTOS

Who has not found the Heaven—below. God's Residence. Emily Dickinson. SAmP; WPoS

Who has not seen their lover. Avenue, The. Frances Darwin Cornford. LW

Who has not waked to list the busy sounds. London's Summer Morning. Mary Robinson. NAEL-7v2; RWP; WoRP

Who has said that the desert is like the sea. Surfaces. Harvena Richter. ICANM

Who Has Seen the Wind? Christina Georgina Rossetti. BLPJKO; ITBLP; NTCP; SacPr; TLR; WHSW

(Wind, The.) ChIV-2

Who has told you what discoveries. Basics. James Dickey. BodElec

Who hath beheld the goddess face to face. Poetry. Madison Cawein. APN-2

Who hath his Maker's nod. (LL) Inspiration ("Whate'er we leave to God, God does.") Henry David Thoreau. APN-1; ColAP; NCAP; OxBoAm

Who hath not knowne or herd. Luke Sheperd. PBRV *Fr.* Upcheringe of the Messe, The.

Who hath not sent out ships to sea? Ship That Went Down, The. Adah Isaacs Menken. CBWP-1

Who hath prophetic vision sees. Prophecy of a Ten Ton Cheese. James McIntyre. VerBaPo

Who have been lonely once. Careless Love. Stanley Kunitz. FaBoWar; PWW2

Who have not yet bruised you. (LL) Advice to a First Cousin. Alberto A. Ríos. NAAL-5; NIL-7

Who have twice come in from the cold? (LL) Dejection [Ode]. Derek Mahon. PBCIP; WoPoe

Who, having lived more than a moment. Forces, The. Michael C. Blumenthal. PML

Who hunts so late 'neath evening skies. Julia Ward Howe. SWaP *Fr.* Lyrics of the Street.

Who I am is a short person with small feet. Marvin Bell. InvLad *Fr.* Who and Where.

Who I Think You Are. Elizabeth Alexander. FFC; RA

Who I Write For. Vicente Aleixandre. TAPaP, *tr. by* Lewis Hyde

Who in One Lifetime. Muriel Rukeyser. NALW

Who, in the garden-pony carrying skeps. Horses. Dorothy, Duchess of Wellington Wellesley. OBMV

Who in them loved [*or* lov'd] and sought thy face! (LL) Book, The. Henry Vaughan. AngWePo; BASC; InvLi; PBRV

Who is. Paul Reps. WhBo

Who is a friend? Who is a foe? Gripe. Lincoln Kirstein. PoWW

Who Is a Poet. Tadeusz Rózewicz. VCWP

Who is, as if he weren't and ne'er had even come. "Angelus Silesius." GePo *Fr.* Cherubical Wanderer, The.

Who Is Awake in the Dead of Night? Bairagi. HotL, *tr. by* V. Narayana Rao

Who is faultless, and doesn't exist. (LL) Eve to Her Daughters. Judith Wright. NALW; NoP-4; NoP-5

Who is he, this regretful man. Days of Rain. Li Ho. CrYelRi, *tr. by* Sam Hamill

Who is here with me? Morning. Ron Padgett. NYP2

Who is it accuses us of safety. Who Is It Accuses Us? Linda Pastan. FaoP

Who is it hides my sandals when I'm trying to get dressed? Late for Breakfast. Mary Dawson. TLR

Who is it sings the gypsies' song to-night. Serenade. Rosamund Marriott Watson. ViWPN

Who Is It Talks of Ebony? Manmohan Ghose. OBMV

Who is it that rides through the forest so fast? Johann Wolfgang von Goethe. *See* O who rides by night thro' the woodland so wild?

Who is it that this dark[e] night. Sir Philip Sidney. NAEL-6v1; NAEL-7v1; NoSic; OxAEP-1 *Fr.* Astrophil and Stella.

Who is it, then, that love deceives? (LL) Juan's Song. Louise Bogan. NoP-4; NoP-5; OxBoAm

Who is James Brown, / God? (LL) In the Funk World. Imamu Amiri Baraka. FuFl; NAMCP V.2

Who is my father in this world, in this house. Irish Cliffs of Moher, The. Wallace Stevens. RaBo

Who Is My Neighbor? Josephine D. Henderson Heard. CBWP-4

Who is on the Lord's side? Frances Ridley Havergal. SacPr

Who Is on the Lord's Side. *Unknown.* SSUS

Who is she that comes, makyng turn every man's eye. Sonnet [*or* Sonetto] 7. Guido Cavalcanti. OBVE, *tr. by* Ezra Pound

Who is she, the poor maniac, whose wildly-fixed eyes. Robert Southey. NPBRoP

Who is Silvia? what is she. William Shakespeare. NoSic; WaAnP *Fr.* Two Gentlemen of Verona, The.

Who is singing of light in the dark. Out of the Depths. Moishe Nadir. Prolet, *tr. by* Amelia Glaser

Who is that blond child laughing as he runs after his colored marbles? Pierre Albert-Birot. CuPo

Who is that BRAHMA? What that Soul of Souls. *Unknown.* TAL *Fr.* Bhagavad-Gita, The.

Who is that in the tall grasses singing. Song for Naomi. Irving Layton. IFF

Who is that running away. C. C. Rider. Lucille Clifton. GT

Who is that Syama woman. Rāmprasād Sen. SinGod, *tr. by* Rachel Fell McDermott

Who is the author of Disaster? John Winthrop, "Reasons to be Considered for...the Intended Plantation in New England," 1629. Nicole Cooley. NeAmPo

Who is the East? Yellow Man, Purple Man. Emily Dickinson. TLR

Who is the man that stands against this bridge. For Danton. Charles Tomlinson. HarvBoo

Who is the man who will spend or will even lend? Harrigan. George M. Cohan. NAAPv.2

Who is the Poet? He who sings. For Adelaide. Bessie Rayner Parkes. VWP

Who is there? Me.   Kenneth Rexroth.   APSN *Fr.* Love Poems of Marichiko, The.

Who is there still remembers.   Bertolt Brecht.   FaBoA *Fr.* Late Lamented Fame of the Giant City of New York.

Who is this.   Kamalākānta Bhattācārya.   SinGod, *tr.* by Rachel Fell McDermott

Who is this.   Raghunāth Rāy.   SinGod, *tr.* by Rachel Fell McDermott

Who is this, all alone? Whose woman is She.   Mahārājādhirāja Māhtābcānd.   SinGod, *tr.* by Rachel Fell McDermott

Who is this? An almoner.   Almoner, An.   Michael Field.   VWP

Who is this black.   Dāśarathi Rāy.   SinGod, *tr.* by Rachel Fell McDermott

Who is this coming towards you.   Ghost, The.   Iain Crichton Smith.   NOxBChV

Who is this enchantress.   Kamalākānta Bhattācārya.   SinGod, *tr.* by Rachel Fell McDermott

Who is this fish, still wearing its wealth.   Wreath to the Fish, A.   Nancy Willard.   P180

Who is this I hear?—Lo, this is I, thine heart.   Dispute of the Heart and Body of François Villon, The.   François Villon.   OBVE, *tr.* by Algernon Charles Swinburne

Who is this Man.   Genesis XXIV.   Arthur Hugh Clough.   ChIV-1

Who is this that comes in splendour, coming from the blazing East?   Airy Christ, The.   Stevie Smith.   ChIV-2

Who is This that Cometh from Edom?   William Herebert.   ChIV-1; SacPr

Who is your lord, more than any other lord.   Give Away the Lie.   Pedro Pérez Conde.   RMCMP, *tr.* by Michael Wiegers

Who isn't happy when it rains during drought?   Rain During Drought.   Master Naong.   BecRai, *tr.* by Kim Daljin, Kim Won-Chung and Christopher Merrill

Who keeps the owl's breath? Whose eyes desire?   Elegy.   David St. John.   AmAlph

Who Killed Cock Robin.   Mother Goose.   UV

Who killed Cock Robin?   Coroner's Inquest.   W. D. Snodgrass.   OxBEV

Who Knew.   Martha Rhodes.   LaCa

"Who knocks at my door, so late in the night?"   Pilgrims in Mexico.   *Unknown.*   OBCP

Who knocks? I, who was beautiful.   Ghost, The.   Walter De la Mare.   InoFa; MoBrPo

Who Knows?   Harold Rome.   ReLy

Who Knows?   José Santos Chocano.   TCLAP, *tr.* by Andrew Rosing

Who knows, but beasts, as they do lie.   Discourse of Beasts, A.   Margaret Lucas Cavendish, Duchess of Newcastle.   BASC; PEW

Who knows how long this small psalm to an old pear tree.   Roy Kiyooka.   NLPA *Fr.* Pear Tree Pomes.

Who knows if i'll be around.   Roy Kiyooka.   NLPA *Fr.* Pear Tree Pomes.

Who knows if they sing in their webs.   Ability to Make a Face Like a Spider While Singing Blues: Junior Wells, The.   Sandra McPherson.   SeSe

Who knows the Hidden Fragrance Temple.   Passing Hidden Fragrance Temple.   Wang Wei.   CCL1, *tr.* by Jerome P. Seaton

Who knows the precise moment when she the stream.   Kenny Fries.   AmPoNex *Fr.* Healing Notebooks, The.

Who knows this or that?   Limits.   Ralph Waldo Emerson.   APN-1

Who knows what is going on on the other side of each hour?   Who Knows What Is Going On.   Juan Ramón Jiménez.   WED, *tr.* by Robert Bly

Who knows what led me there—a twelve-year-old.   First One, The.   Jeffrey McDaniel.   NevBe

Who knows what the moonlight means?   Magic Composer.   Gilbert Sorrentino.   FTOS

Who knows what would happen if you stopped?   By Forced Marches.   Michael Hofmann.   HarvBoo

Who Knows Where the Time Goes?   Michael Brownstein.   AHA

Who knows whether the sea heals or corrodes?   Plague of Dead Sharks.   Alan Dugan.   NoAM; PtR

Who knows why the sea.   Can This Be Love?   Paul James.   ReLy

Who knows why we talk of death.   Drowning of the Facts of a Life, The.   Michael S. Harper.   ESEAA

Who knows why you and I fell off the roster?   Why You and I.   Harryette Mullen.   FaoP

Who lay in a ditch, his mouth full of dying fires. (LL)   Hamnavoe Market.   George Mackay Brown.   EmeKit; NePenScot

Who Learns My Lesson Complete.   Walt Whitman.   APN-1 *Fr.* Leaves of Grass [1855 Version].

Who least, hath some; who most hath never all. (LL)   Times [*or* Tymes] Go[e] By Turn[e]s.   Robert Southwell.   ChIV-1; NoSic

Who left / this wooly caterpillar.   Query.   Kate Knapp Johnson.   NevBe

Who Likes the Idea of Guide Cats?   Gavin Ewart.   NOxBChV

Who list his wealth and ease retain.   Sir Thomas Wyatt.   NAEL-7v1; NoSic

Who list the Romane greatnes forth to figure.   Joachim Du Bellay.   OBVE *Fr.* Ruins of Rome.

Who lists to see, what ever nature, arte.   Edmund Spenser.   PBRV *Fr.* Ruines of Rome: by Bellay.

Who lit the furnace of the mammoth's heart?   Francis Thompson.   MoBrPo *Fr.* Ode to the Setting Sun.

Who live in troubled regions. (LL)   Storm Warnings.   Adrienne Rich.   NAAL-5; NIL-7; NIP-4; PtR; YaYoPo

Who lived in the eternal bastard present all their lives.   Pity the Bastards.   Tom French.   BeAl; NIrP

Who lives where beggars rarely speed.   My Mary.   John Clare.   NOBRP; NPBRoP

Who liveth alone longeth for mercy.   Wanderer, The.   *Unknown.*   WoPoe, *tr.* by Michael Alexander

Who looked upon her awful brow.   Ambrose Bierce.   APN-2 *Fr.* Devil's Dictionary, The.

Who looks after you kids while you work?   Who Looks after Your Kids?   Kirsten Emmott.   BloBone

Who Looks after Your Kids?   Kirsten Emmott.   BloBone

Who lowers the unseen hat from on high.   Mac Wellman.   HeMarv *Fr.* Rat Minaret: Miniaturist-Divan, The.

"Who made God, daddy?"   Question Time.   Jack Lindsay.   NOBAu

Who made honey long ago. (LL)   Forefathers.   Edmund Charles Blunden.   NoP-4; NoP-5; OBEV; OBMV

Who made the world?   Summer Day, The.   Mary Oliver.   AmFaPo; BeAl; CAP-8; TWF

Who made the world, sir?   Ants.   Alfred Kreymborg.   APT-1

Who, maiden, makes this river flow?   Medicine Song of an Indian Lover.   *Unknown.*   APN-2, *tr.* by Charles Fenno Hoffman

Who make up a heaven of our misery. (LL)   William Blake.   BrAP; NAEL-6v2; NAEL-7v2; NAWM-7v2; NPBRoP *Fr.* Songs of Experience.

Who, mid the grasses of the field.   Dante.   William Cullen Bryant.   APN-1

Who Needs Two.   James McManus.   "Commercials exaggerate."   IllVoic

Who never asked.   Let's Hear It for Goliath.   Jon Dressel.   AngWePo; TCAWP

Who never let each other sleep above it. (LL)   I know the truth—give up all other truths!   Marina Ivanovna Tsvetayeva.   OPOU; PLBUT, *tr.* by Elaine Feinstein

Who now / leaves the door open a crack.   Nights with the Star-Ladle Over the House.   Beckian Fritz Goldberg.   AmAlph

Who of little Love—know how to starve. (LL)   Victory comes late.   Emily Dickinson.   APN-2; SWaP

Who of those who step into the stream.   Mikhail Aizenberg.   ItGoST, *tr.* by J. Kates

Who oft as he saunter'd the streets curv'd with his arm the shoulder of his friend, while the arm of his friend rested upon him also. (LL)   Recorders Ages Hence.   Walt Whitman.   HeIP-4; MoAmPo; SAmP

Who often found their way to pleasant meadows.   Elegy for Minor Poets.   Louis MacNeice.   CABP; PNI

Who Owns the Homeland?   Abdul Wahab Al-Bayati.   IrPoTo, *tr.* by Farouk Abdel Wahab

Who Owns the Night and Lease Stars.   Reginald Shepherd.   AmPoNex

Who owns these scrawny little feet?   *Death.* Examination at the Womb-Door.   Ted Hughes.   NAEL-6v2; NAEL-7v2; NoP-4; NoP-5

Who owns this body of mine?   Starved.   Laura Riding Jackson.   FuPo

Who painted magnificent pictures in his old age. (LL)   When I Was Prettiest in My Life.   Ibaragi Noriko.   CFP; WoPoe, *tr.* by Naoshi Koriyama and Edward Lueders

Who peered from the invisible world.   Seven Forbidden Words.   Michael Palmer.   HarvBoo

Who Placed, Amidst the Tracts of Ash.   Antonio Machado Ruiz.   SpanPo, *tr.* by Kate Flores

Who placed, amidst the tracts of ash.   Who Placed, Amidst the Tracts of Ash.   Antonio Machado Ruiz.   SpanPo, *tr.* by Kate Flores

Who plainly say, *My God, My King.* (LL)   Jordan (1).   George Herbert.   BASC; BrAP; FSCP; NAEL-6v1; NAEL-7v1; NoP-4; NoP-5; NOSC; OxBEV; TFi; WoPoe

Who planted banana trees in front of my window?   Banana Trees.   Li Ch'ing-chao.   NDACCP, *tr.* by Kenneth Rexroth

Who planted seeds, musing ahead to their far blossoming. (LL)   Edna St. Vincent Millay.   ColAP; NALW *Fr.* Sonnets from an Ungrafted Tree.

Who prop, thou ask'st, in these bad days, my mind?   To a Friend.   Matthew Arnold.   NAEL-6v2

Who purchases this garment—Sire—buys death. (LL)   Anna Hempstead Branch.   APT-1; NALW *Fr.* Sonnets from a Lock Box.

Who pure as light and chaste as origin has stayed.   "Angelus Silesius."   GePo *Fr.* Cherubical Wanderer, The.

Who really respects the earthworm.   Earthworm, The.   Harry Edmund Martinson.   RaBo, *tr.* by Robert Bly

Who Remains Standing?   Andrée Chedid.   CFP; HAWP; WoPoe, *tr.* by Mirène Ghossein and Samuel Haze

Who rides at night, who rides so late? Invisible King, The. Johann Wolfgang von Goethe. RaBo, *tr.* by Robert Bly

Who rideth through the driving rain. King's Son, The. Thomas Boyd. OBMV

Who Runs America? Allen Ginsberg. FaBoA

Who rustles drily inside my gown? (LL) Nuns of Childhood, The: Two Views. Maxine W. Kumin. FFC; WaAnP

Who said / If you took the name All-Destroyer. Giríscandra Ghos. SinGOd, *tr.* by Rachel Fell McDermott

Who said, "Peacock Pie"? Song of the Mad Prince, The. Walter De la Mare. CtM; MakPoe; NoAM; OxAEP-2

Who said to the trout. Pisces. Ronald Stuart Thomas. CABP

Who saw nothing. (LL) Seated on her bed legs spread open. Joyce Mansour. HAWP; WoPoe, *tr.* by Willis Barnstone

Who Says. Julia Hartwig. GI

Who Says a Painting Must Look Like Life? Su Tung-p'o. ColAnChi, *tr.* by Burton Watson

Who says a woman's work isn't high art? Woman's Work. Julia Alvarez. RA

Who says my poems are poems? Ryokan. EMJL, *tr.* by Burton Watson

Who Says That Drought Was Here? Niyi Osundare. HBAPE; NAfrP

Who say[e]s that fictions on[e]ly and false hair. Jordan (1). George Herbert. BASC; BrAP; FSCP; NAEL-6v1; NAEL-7v1; NoP-4; NoP-5; NOSC; OxBEV; TFi; WoPoe

Who says that Giles and Joan at discord be? On Giles and Joan. Ben Jonson. NAEL-6v1; NAEL-7v1

Who says that they have seen the sky? Shin Tongyŏp. CAMKP *Fr.* Kŭm River.

Who Says Words with My Mouth. Jelaluddin Rumi. AmFaPo, *tr.* by Coleman Barks and John Moyne

Who see no friend in God—in Satan's host no foes. (LL) Doubt. Mary Elizabeth Coleridge. NALW; ViWPN

Who sees, will spew; who smells, be poisoned [or poison'd]. (LL) Beautiful Young Nymph Going to Bed, A. Jonathan Swift. EroLit; NoP-5; NPeEn; OxBEV

Who seh Belize people culture weak? Dis Da Me. Philip Lewis. OWABP

Who / SELF, / The World. Job's Epitaph. Joshua Sylvester. ChIV-1

Who set their captives free. (LL) Song, A: "Strephon, your breach of faith and trust." Laetitia Pilkington. IrLP; LW; PEW

Who sews the split calabash? Who mends. Senegal Sestina. Odetta D. Norton. BtF

Who Sez Thunderbirds Can't Fly. Gary Lilley. BtF

Who Shall Deliver Me? Christina Georgina Rossetti. SacPr

Who shall doubt, Donne, where [or whe'er] I a poet be[e]. To John Donne. Ben Jonson. NoP-4; NoP-5

Who shall invoke when we are gone. Tragic Love. Walter James Turner. OBMV

Who shall open the closed book? Introitus. János Pilinszky. IQMS, *tr.* by Ted Hughes

Who shall tell what did befall. Wealth. Ralph Waldo Emerson. APN-1

Who she was. Back Far Enough, Down Deep Enough. Constance Urdang. PBCAP

Who showed me. To Flossie. William Carlos Williams. SAmP

Who sings the source. Edward Young. STuOW *Fr.* Ocean, an Ode.

Who sleeps at night? No one is sleeping. Marina Ivanovna Tsvetayeva. AWTN *Fr.* Insomnia.

Who sliced the crescent moon so small. Yi Yŏng. CATKP, *tr.* by Kevin O'Rourke

Who so list to hount[e] I know[e] where is an hynde. Sir Thomas Wyatt. *See* Whoso list to hunt, I know where is an hind.

Who speaks of the strong currents. White Asparagus. Sujata Bhatt. HarvBoo; StAl

Who speaks the sound of an echo? Tree-Leaf Woman. WPoS

Who speaks? Who whispers there? A light! A light! Thomas Lovell Beddoes. NPBRoP *Fr.* Bride's Tragedy, The.

Who spurs on the road when the day is done. Erl-King. Johann Wolfgang von Goethe. WoPoe, *tr.* by John Frederick Nims

Who still says that drought was here? (LL) Who Says That Drought Was Here? Niyi Osundare. HBAPE; NAfrP

Who Stops the Dance? "Hsiung Hung." CFP, *tr.* by Chung Ling and Kenneth Rexroth

Who straight, *Your suit is granted,* said, and died. (LL) Redemption. George Herbert. BASC; CABP; FSCP; GSo; NAEL-6v1; NAEL-7v1; NoP-4; NoP-5; NOSC; NPeEn; OxBEV; OxBSo; PBRV; PoPoPo; SoSe-8; TFi; WeW-3

Who strolls so late, for mugs a bait. French Lisette: A Ballad of Maida Vale. William Plomer. OBCoV

Who subdues? And who is subdued? This story is told. Ana Maria Shúa. MirDau *Fr.* Golem and Rabbi.

Who swerve and vanish in the river. (LL) Snowflake Which Is Now and Hence Forever, The. Archibald MacLeish. NoP-4; NoP-5

Who swerves from innocence, who makes divorce. William Wordsworth. CenSon *Fr.* River Duddon [A Series of Sonnets], The.

Who take today and jerk it out of joint. Young Africans. Gwendolyn Brooks. NoAM

Who taught me betimes to love working and reading. (LL) Sluggard, The. Isaac Watts. OxBEV; UV

Who taught thee conflict with the pow'rs of night. On the Death of a Young Gentleman. Phillis Wheatley. SacPr

Who then has strangled the weary voice. Call. Noémia da Sousa. HAWP, *tr.* by Jacques-Noël Gouat

Who think you comes there? *Sioux Oral Tradition.* APN-2 *Fr.* Ghost-Dance Songs.

Who thinks of June's first rose to-day? June, 1915. Charlotte Mew. OxAEP-2

Who told you / you were visible? Plan, The. Rae Armantrout. AWPTFC; BAP-01

Who Translates a Poet Badly. Manuel González Prada. SpanPo, *tr.* by William M. Davis

Who travels [or trauels] by the wearie wandring way. Edmund Spenser. OxAEP-1 *Fr.* Faerie Queene, The.

Who trusteth in hilarity. Marianne Vitale. HeMarv *Fr.* On Justifying Cuckoo La Goose.

Who, trusting his mind, could praise the man of Lindos, Kleoboulos. Simonides. SaLy, *tr.* by Diane Rayor

Who wants to claw my heart. Who? Abd al-Rahim Salih al-Rahim. IrPoTo, *tr.* by Saadi A. Simawe and Daniel Weissbort

Who wants to die at peace in his bed / besides. (LL) William Carlos Williams. NAMCP V.1; NoP-5 *Fr.* Asphodel, That Greeny Flower.

Who wants to think of us as five? Five keen-nosed grey-maned black-. Aleksei Eliseievich Kruchyonykh. PFTM-1 *Fr.* Sahara to America, The.

Who was a man. (LL) Malcolm X. Gwendolyn Brooks. IllVoic; OxAAAP

Who was asking for it. Boys, the Broom Handle, the Retarded Girl, The. Alicia Ostriker. ExTi

Who was born, not of a virgin but a real woman. Jah Son / Another Way. Kendel Hippolyte. WaCA

Who was helpless back in Prague. Man Proposes, God Disposes. Bachner, Miroslav Košek and Hanuš Löwy. INSAB

Who was it who held me on her knee? Mother. Josephine D. Henderson Heard. CBWP-4

Who was it who suggested that the opposite of war. All of These People. Michael Longley. StAl

Who was Mary Shelley? Lorine Niedecker. APSN

Who Was Mary Shelley? Lorine Niedecker. OxBoAm

Who was my grandmother? La Sombra de Who I Am. Michaela Raen. PoArWo

Who was responsible for the very first arms deal. Peace. Tibullus. PBCIP, *tr.* by Michael Longley

Who was St. Vincent. (LL) St. Vincent's. W. S. Merwin. CAP-8; VCAP

3: Who Was That? I Ask. Richard Sanger. IFF

Who was that? I ask. You've been gone for ages. 3: Who Was That? I Ask. Richard Sanger. IFF

Who was that woman sleeping. Courtesan to Her Lover, A. Kshetrayya. WoPoe, *tr.* by V. Narayana Rao, A. K. Ramanujan and David Shulman

Who watches on the mountain with the dead. Vigil of Rizpah, The. Felicia Dorothea Hemans. CenSon

Who weds a sot to get his cot. Proverbial Advice on Marriage. *Unknown.* NBLV

Who Were before Me. John Drinkwater. OBMV

Who were we in our past life? My Love. Nanduri Subbarao. HotL, *tr.* by V. Narayana Rao

Who What. Michel Deguy. YaTCFP, *tr.* by Clayton Eshleman

Who, who had only seen wings. Paired Things. Kay Ryan. CalPo

WHO? WHOOOOOO? in aching heat. (LL) Simple Story, A. Gwen Harwood. BeAl; NOBAu

Who Will Be My Friend Always. Claudio Rodríguez. RaW, *tr.* by W. S. Merwin

Who will believe me later, when I say. Last of the Courtyard, The. Emily Grosholz. FFC

Who Will Buy Me an Orange? José Gorostiza. TCLAP, *tr.* by Rachel Benson

Who will buy me an orange? Who Will Buy Me an Orange? José Gorostiza. TCLAP, *tr.* by Rachel Benson

Who will give me an axe without a handle. Axe without a Handle. Great Master Wonhyo. BecRai, *tr.* by Kim Daljin, Kim Won-Chung and Christopher Merrill

Who will go drive with Fergus now. Who Goes with Fergus? William Butler Yeats. NAEL-6v2; NAEL-7v2; NAMCP V.1; NoAM; TRP

Who will in fairest book of Nature know. Sir Philip Sidney. NAEL-6v1; NAEL-7v1; NoP-4; NoP-5; NoSic *Fr.* Astrophil and Stella.

Who will in fairest booke of Nature know.   Sir Philip Sidney. *See* Who will in fairest book of Nature know.

Who Will Know Us?   Gary Soto.   GM

Who will last? And what? The wind will stay.   Abraham Sutskever.   BBASP *Fr.* Poems from a Diary.

Who will Live in Our Houses When We Die?   Michael C. Blumenthal.   NoAM

Who will remember, now I write? (LL)   William Habington.   ChIV-1; NOSC *Fr.* Castara.

Who will remember, passing through this Gate.   On Passing the New Menin Gate.   Siegfried Sassoon.   NAEL-6v2; NAEL-7v2; NAMCP V.1; NoAM; NoP-4; NoP-5; OBMV; PoWW

Who Will Show Us Any Good?   Lady Jane Francesca Wilde.   VWP

Who Will Throw the First Stone?   Clara Silva.   TANSG, *tr. by* Celeste Kostopulos-Cooperman

Who wisely would for his retreat.   Boethius.   FSCP *Fr.* De Consolatione Philosophiae [Trans. Henry Vaughan].

Who with salt tears this last farewel [*or* farewell] did take. (LL)   Before the Birth of One of Her Children.   Anne Bradstreet.   AmFaPo; ColAP; EMWP; NAAL-3; NAAL-5; NAAPv.1; NoP-4; NoP-5; OxBoAm; PEW; SacPr

(Who with salt tears this last farewell did take.) (LL)   BrAP; ColAP; NoP-4; PEW

Who won: the Babylonian system.   Election.   Oswald de Andrade.   TCLAP, *tr. by* Flavia Vidal

Who won't praise green. Each minute to caress each minute blade of spring.   Green slice us open.   D. A. Powell.   NAPBL; NeAmPo

Who works harder on earth.   Pablo Neruda.   GifTon *Fr.* Book of Questions, The.

Who worshipfully memorize their every sestina. (LL)   My Confessional Sestina.   Dana Gioia.   PoA 2002; RA

Who wot now that is heer / Wher he shal be another yeer?   *Unknown*.   OHMEL

Who would be / A merman bold.   Merman, The.   Alfred Tennyson.   UV

Who would be a turtle who could help it?   Turtle.   Kay Ryan.   CalPo

Who would be able to seduce the willow's powerful arms!   Herbarium.   Laura Solórzano.   SPV, *tr. by* Jen Hofer

Who would be waiting for us.   Shipping Out.   Fadil Azzawi.   IrPoTo, *tr. by* Ralph Saverese and Saadi A. Simawe

Who would carve words must carve himself.   Conrad Potter Aiken.   NAAPv.2

Who would divorce her lover with a phone.   Marilyn Hacker.   NIL-7

Who would have guessed.   Anne Boleyn.   Erica Bernheim.   LegDan

Who would have loved you in a day or two. (LL)   I think I should have loved you presently.   Edna St. Vincent Millay.   APT-1; NAAL-5; NAAPv.2

Who Would Have Thought It.   Marie Luise Kaschnitz.   PFTM-2, *tr. by* Lisel Mueller

Who would have thought it Sir, actually putting ME in a WRITING!   Peter Reading.   FaBoVe

Who would have thought of her as mother small.   Whitewash of Houston.   Vassar Miller.   TiP2

Who would have thought she'd end that way? (LL)   Mourning Poem for the Queen of Sunday.   Robert Earl Hayden.   InoFa; NAMCP V.2; NoAM; NoP-4; NoP-5; PoPoPo

Who would / listen for what goes bump in the.   Zoo.   Bin Ramke.   LiTh

Who would not be.   Laureate, The.   William Edmonstoune Aytoun.   UV

Who would not live long. (LL)   Shield of Achilles, The.   W. H. Auden.   BeAl; NAEL-6v2; NAEL-7v2; NAMCP V.1; NoAM; NoP-4; NoP-5; NPeEn; OxAEP-2; OxBEV; OxBoAm; PoA 2002; WaAnP; WeW-3

Who would not sing in May. (LL)   Crazy Woman, The.   Gwendolyn Brooks.   ItWoWo; NALW

Who would not weep, if Atticus were he? (LL)   Alexander Pope.   OxBEV; TRP *Fr.* Epistle to Dr. Arbuthnot.

Who would perish of excess. (LL)   Promises like Pie-Crust.   Christina Georgina Rossetti.   NAEL-6v2; NAEL-7v2; NPeEn

Who would true Valour see.   John Bunyan.   OxBEV *Fr.* Pilgrim's Progress, The.

Who would want to die defending Firestone Tire.   Firestone.   David Rivard.   PBCAP

Who would want to give it up, the coal.   Smoke.   Dorianne Laux.   RoV

Who writes the words and music.   Dames.   Al Dubin.   ReLy

Who wrote / in the great world.   In Memoriam Charles Reznikoff.   George Oppen.   APT-2

Who wrote *Who wrote Icon Basilike?*.   On ["Who Wrote Icon Basilike" by Dr.] Christopher Wordsworth, Master of Trinity.   Benjamin Hall Kennedy.   OBCoV

Who'd Want to Be a Man?   Gregory Orr.   BodElec

Who'd want to without the trees' consolation!   End of a Summer, The.   Günter Eich.   GTCP, *tr. by* Reinhold Grimm

Whoe'er she be.   Richard Crashaw. *See* Who ere she[e] be[e].

Whoe'er sighs most, is cruellest, and hastes the other's death. (LL)   Valediction, A: of Weeping.   John Donne.   BASC; FSCP; HeIP-4; NAEL-6v1; NAEL-7v1; NoP-4; NoP-5; NOSC; WeW-3

Whoever [*or* Who ever] comes to shroud me, do not harm[e].   Funeral[l], The.   John Donne.   FSCP; HeIP-4; NAEL-6v1; NAEL-7v1; NAWM-5v1; NoP-4; NoP-5; OBEV; TFi

Whoever despises the clitoris despises the penis.   Speed of Darkness, The.   Muriel Rukeyser and Leif Sjoberg.   APSN; APT-2; PFTM-2

Whoever Finds a Horseshoe.   Osip Emilevich Mandelstam.   PFTM-1

Whoever has a mind to abundance of Trouble.   Voyage to Marryland, A; or, The Ladies Dressing Room.   Mary Evelyn.   EMWP

Whoever Has Become All Divine.   "Angelus Silesius."   GePo *Fr.* Cherubical Wanderer, The.

Whoever has Cold Mountain's poems.   Han-shan (Cold Mountain).   ColAnChi, *tr. by* Red Pine

Whoever has never choked on a word.   Verily.   Ingeborg Bachmann.   GTCP, *tr. by* Irmgard Hunt

Whoever has not choked on a word.   Truly.   Ingeborg Bachmann.   PoSu

Whoever [*or* Who ever] hath her wish, thou hast thy Will.   William Shakespeare.   NAEL-6v1; NAEL-7v1; NoP-5; PBRV *Fr.* Sonnets.

Whoever heard of a black cowboy?   Nat Love: Black Cowboy.   Lee Bennett Hopkins.   HHAm

Whoever hurts my favor with my lady.   Heinrich von Veldeke.   GePo

Whoever let language into the house goes.   Roches Moutonnees.   Ralph Adamo.   AnSo

Whoever lives true life, will love true love.   Elizabeth Barrett Browning.   OxAEP-2 *Fr.* Aurora Leigh.

Whoever looks round sees Eternity there. (LL)   Autumn.   John Clare.   BBASP; WeW-3

Whoever loves, if he do not propose.   John Donne.   BASC *Fr.* Elegies.

Whoever passes by my tomb, know.   Callimachus.   HePo, *tr. by* Barbara Hughes Fowler

Whoever reads my poems.   Han-shan (Cold Mountain).   ColAnChi, *tr. by* Red Pine

Whoever said a good man was hard to find.   My Handy Man.   Andy Razaf.   ReLy

Whoever spoke first would lose something.   After the Argument.   Stephen Dunn.   GoPo

Whoever then are you? Whose wretched bones are these.   Leonidas of Tarentum.   HePo, *tr. by* Barbara Hughes Fowler

Whoever trusts power and plays potent lord.   Trojan Women.   Seneca.   RomPo, *tr. by* Anthony James Boyle

Whoever water drinks, writes wretched poetry.   Water and Wine.   Friedrich von Logau.   GePo, *tr. by* George C. Schoolfield

Whoever You Are.   W. S. Merwin.   NoP-5

Whoever You Are.   Matthew Zapruder.   LegDan

Whoever you are, go out into the evening.   Initiation.   Rainer Maria Rilke.   ItP, *tr. by* C. F. MacIntyre

Whoever You Are Holding Me Now in Hand.   Walt Whitman.   APN-1; CAGL; NAAL-3

Whoever you are: in the evening step out.   Entrance.   Rainer Maria Rilke.   AmFaPo, *tr. by* Edward Snow

Whoever you are: step out of doors tonight.   Entrance.   Rainer Maria Rilke.   PoDa, *tr. by* Dana Gioia

Whoever you are, we too lie in drifts at your feet. (LL)   As I Ebb'd with the Ocean of Life.   Walt Whitman.   APN-1; NAAL-3; NAAL-5; NAAPv.1; OxBoAm; TCAPo

Whoever's seen them carries them in marble.   One Hundred Eighty.   Giusi Busceti.   ItPo, *tr. by* Gayle Ridinger

Whole afternoon field inside me from one stem of reed, A.   Answers from the Elements.   Jelaluddin Rumi.   BBASP, *tr. by* Coleman Barks and John Moyne

Whole afternoon glistening, The.   October Observed, Hudson Falls, New York in Bill's Back Yard.   Richard Elman.   PoCoUp

Whole body of the One Thus Come, The.   All of Us So Close to Buddha.   Taigen Dan Leighton.   WhBo

Whole city seductively lit up, The.   Tatiana Shcherbina.   ItGoST, *tr. by* J. Kates

Whole city strains, the tension, The.   Solar Eclipse, St. John's, Newfoundland.   Carmelita McGrath.   Coast

Whole Duty of Children.   Robert Louis Stevenson.   NBLV

Whole Earth Catalogue, The.   Albert Goldbarth.   CAP-8

Whole field of.   Basho.   EMJL, *tr. by* Haruo Shirane

Whole, full, flirtatious span of it, The. (LL)   Black Lace Fan My Mother Gave Me, The.   Eavan Boland.   HarvBoo; ModIr; MoWP; NPeEn

Whole green sky is dying, The. The last tree flares.   On a Line from Valéry.   Carolyn Kizer.   FFC; GifTon

Whole health resides with peace.   Description of Elysium.   James Agee.   YaYoPo

Whole idea of it makes me feel, The.   On Turning Ten.   Billy Collins.   TWF

Whole lot is now dark and out of sorts, The. The corner then finally vanishes. Carla Harryman. BAP-04 *Fr.* Baby.

Whole man flies, The. Death of Saint Marinus, The. *Unknown.* SonAtl, *tr. by* Alessandro Della Balda and Robert Gasparoni

Whole Mess . . . Almost, The . . Almost, The. Gregory Corso. BB

Whole nation, some seven hundred scattered, The. Architect Monk, The. Laurence Lieberman. BodElec

Whole New Scene, A. John Fuller. NOxBChV

Whole night, A. Giuseppe Ungaretti. PLBUT

Whole night through, A. Watch. Giuseppe Ungaretti. FaBoWar, *tr. by* Patrick Creagh

Whole of doghood I've seen in my time, The. Dogs. Rhydwen Williams. BBMWP, *tr. by* Nigel Jenkins

Whole of this last end is to say which of two. Gertrude Stein. PoA 2002 *Fr.* Stanzas in Meditation.

Whole place airier, The. Big summer trees. Seamus Heaney. IrLP; NoP-5 *Fr.* Glanmore Revisited.

Whole populations have been shattered. Black Experience, The. Mwatabu Okantah. BtF

Whole process is a lie, The / unless, / crowned by excess. Ivy Crown, The. William Carlos Williams. ItP; NAAPv.2; NAMCP V.1; NoAM

Whole Question, The. Robert Penn Warren. BodElec; OxBoAm

Whole School of Bourgeois Primitives, A. Christopher Reid. NeBrP

Whole Self, The. Naomi Shihab Nye. PoArWo

Whole Story, The. Margaret Avison. GPPA

Whole town came into my room, The. Horizon. Philippe Soupault. YaTCFP, *tr. by* Mary Ann Caws and Patricia Terry

Whole town, The. Karai Senryū. EMJL, *tr. by* Makoto Ueda

Whole Truth So Help Me God—Also Known as the Gettin' Rid of Nigguz Business. Lorena M. Craighead. InTrad

Whole two weeks after The Million Man March; and still, if you'd ask me, this is all I could say about it, A. Richard Rykard. SpirFl

Whole universe is full of God, The. Yunus Emre. EaWin, *tr. by* Talat Sait Halman and W. S. Merwin

Whole valley has been under for centuries, The. Only the deacon. After the Flood. Maurice Kilwein Guevara. NAPBL

Whole weeping body of the world?, The. (LL) Riding Out at Evening. Linda McCarriston. BBASP; WaAnP

Whole western sky is lemon yellow, The. Tenebrae. Juan Ramón Jiménez. SpanPo, *tr. by* Alice Sternberg

Whole Wheat, Decaf Black, a Morbid Curiosity. David Citino. UpMys

Whole white world is ours, The. White World. "H. D." WPoS

Whole White World, The. "H. D." *See* White World.

Whole Works, The. Federico García Lorca. PFTM-1 *Fr.* Night (Suite for Piano and Poet's Voice).

Whole world, A. Family. Pak Mogwŏl [*or* Mokwŏl]. CAMKP, *tr. by* Edward W. Poitras

Whole world is clear and empty, The. No End Point. Muso Soseki. EaWin, *tr. by* W. S. Merwin

Whole world is coming, The. *Sioux Oral Tradition.* NAAL-5; TCAPo *Fr.* Ghost-Dance Songs.

Whole World Is Coming, The. *Sioux Oral Tradition.* NAAPv.1 *Fr.* Ghost-Dance Songs.

Whole world was there, plucking their linen, The. Walt, the Wounded. W. S. Di Piero. ViWalt

Whole-breasted as billows that break on a bank—unwilling! Cassandra. Elena Chizhova. ARWW, *tr. by* Catriona Kelly

Wholeness. Gwyneth Lewis. *tr. by* the author
    Half. BBMWP, *tr. by* the author
    Llanbadarn Baptism 1843. BBMWP, *tr. by* the author

Wholes. Larry Eigner. PmAP

Who'll Bear Love. László Nagy. SonAtl, *tr. by* Helen Bell, Vasy Geza, Adam Horvath, Nike Koos, Zsuzsanna Rozsafalvi and Zsofia Zachar

Who'll Ferry Love to the Yonder Shore. László Nagy. IQMS, *tr. by* Adam Makkai

Who'll marry me? Cold Saturday. *Will he leave me?* With the. Questions and Answers. Diana O'Hehir. AFaM

Whom God has not visited. (LL) John Berryman. CAP-8; ChIV-2 *Fr.* Dream Songs.

Whom have We next? (His syntax is). Reckoning. Fay Zwicky. NOBAu

Whom having brought, as they are taught. Michael Wigglesworth. NAAPv.1 *Fr.* Day of Doom, The: Or, A Poetical Description of the Great and Last Judgment.

Whom none but Daisies—know. (LL) Aurora. Emily Dickinson. APN-2; NCAP; PCW

Whom the kites of Heaven solicited with sweet cries. (LL) Necrological. John Crowe Ransom. FuPo; NAAPv.2

Whom weave ye in. Rolfe and the Palm. Herman Melville. NCAP

Whomp and moonshiver of salt surf on sand. Whomp and Moonshiver. Thomas Whitbread. TiP2

Whooping Crane. James Cody. TiP2

Whoops! *Unknown.* NTCP

Whoosh of rush hour traffic washes through my head, The. Swifts at Evening. Jeffrey Harrison. UrbNat

Whore and monk, we sleep. Basho. SoOfWa, *tr. by* Sam Hamill

Whores. Margaret Abigail Walker. NALW

Whorl inside my head buzzes, The. Terminus. Peter Rose. BMAP

Who's going to read that? Persius. RomPo *Fr.* Satires.

Who's got the last laugh now? (LL) They All Laughed. Ira Gershwin. APT-2; ReLy

Who's Joking with the Photographer? Anne Stevenson. BeAl; MoWP

Who's on first? Why That Abbott and Costello Vaudeville Mess Never Worked with Black People. Paul Beatty. AmPoNex

Who's on first? The dust descends as. Whose Language. Charles Bernstein. PmAP

Who's Sorry Now? Bert Kalmar *and* Harry Ruby and Harry Ruby. ReLy

Who's that? Epitaph: Tristran Tzara. Philippe Soupault. SurPaPo, *tr. by* Mary Ann Caws and Patricia Terry

Who's that? Yasui. EMJL *Fr.* Mad Verse.

Who's that? Yasui. EMJL

Who's that coming down the street? Yes, Sir! That's My Baby. Gustave Kahn. ReLy

Who's that dark woman. Whispers in a Country Church. Alvin Aubert. OxAAAP

Who's that knocking on my ring, says the chin. Selima Hill. NewEx

Who's that knocking on the window. Innocent's Song. Charles Causley. OBCP

Who's that rowing a black boat. Cry Me a River. Wopko Jensma. TSAP

"Who's that tickling my back?" said the wall. Tickle Rhyme, The. Ian Serraillier. NTCP; Spl

Who's the enemy, year after year? Allen Ginsberg. AmWaPo *Fr.* Iron Horse.

Who's the Jew. David Meltzer. TaR

Who's the jew where is he she it that looms up in your face. Who's the Jew. David Meltzer. TaR

Who's therefore true, because her truth kills me[e]. (LL) Twickenham [*or* Twicknam] Garden. John Donne. BASC; OBGa

Who's Who. W. H. Auden. GoPo; MoBrPo; NAMCP V.1; NoAM

Whose accent no farewell can know. (LL) Hart Crane. ColAP; MoAmPo *Fr.* Voyages.

Whose accent no farewell can know. (LL) Voyages. Hart Crane. APT-2; CAGL; NAAPv.2; NAMCP V.1; NoAM; NoP-5

Whose adoration. Erin Mouré. NLPA *Fr.* Wittgenstein Letters to Mel Gibson's Braveheart, The.

Whose baggage from land to land is despair. Palladas. WoPoe, *tr. by* Frank Kuenstler

Whose brest hath marble beene to me. (LL) William Habington. NOSC; OBEV *Fr.* Castara.

Whose broken window is a cry of art. Boy Breaking Glass. Gwendolyn Brooks. ESEAA; NAMCP V.2; NoAM; NoP-4; NoP-5; PtR

Whose candles light the tulip tree? Tulip Tree. Sacheverell Sitwell. MoBrPo

Whose Children Are These? Gerald William Barrax. OxAAAP

Whose clay courts did he water and roll? First Job Viper. Peter Wood. NevBe

Whose counted smile of hours and days, suppose. Hart Crane. ColAP *Fr.* Voyages.

Whose day shall never die [*or* dy] in Night. (LL) Epitaph Upon Husband and Wife Who Died and Were Buried Together, An. Richard Crashaw. OBEV; OxAEP-1

Whose demon are you. Head of a Doll. Charles Simic. NAMCP V.2

Whose Doom to whom? (LL) Pit—but Heaven over it, A. Emily Dickinson. APN-2; NCAP

Whose fault is it that your tree can't be seen. In Central Park. Moyshe-Leyb Halpern. WoPoe, *tr. by* John Hollander

Whose feet are so deep in the sand. (LL) Yves Tanguy. David Gascoyne. NoP-4; NoP-5

Whose fire from which I came, has now grown cold? (LL) One Flesh. Elizabeth Jennings. LW; NoP-4; NoP-5; OxAEP-2; Prnts

Whose fruitlesse worke is broken with least wynd. (LL) *Penelope* for her *Ulisses* sake. Edmund Spenser. NoP-4; PBRV

Whose green adventure is to run to seed. (LL) Remembering the 'Thirties. Donald Davie. HarvBoo; NAMCP V.2; NoP-4; NoP-5

"Whose heart" "might be lost?" "Whose mask is this?" "Who has a mask." White Phosphorus. Alice Notley. FTOS

Whose home is in the straw. Brave Sparrow. Michael Collier. UrbNat

Whose is that long white box in the grove, what have they accomplished, why am I cold. (LL) Bee Meeting, The. Sylvia Plath. HarvBoo; NALW

Whose is the love that, gleaming through the world. Percy Bysshe Shelley. NPBRoP *Fr.* Queen Mab.

Whose is this horrifying face. David Gascoyne. ChIV-2; NoP-4; NoP-5; OBWP *Fr.* Miserere.

Whose jade-flute is this, notes flying invisibly. Hearing the Flute in the City of Loyang in a Spring Night. Li Po. ChinPo, *tr. by* Ye Weilian [*or* Yeh Wei-lien *or* Wai-lim Yip]

Whose Language. Charles Bernstein. PmAP

Whose laughter plays like summer lightning there. (LL) Cattle Show. Hugh MacDiarmid. MoBrPo; OBMV; OxBEV

Whose longing was to wash away to sea. (LL) Wild Cherry, The. Malcolm Lowry. NoP-4; NoP-5

Whose Lyre throbs only to the touch of Love! (LL) Laments the Volatility of Phaon. Mary Robinson. CenSon; RWP

Whose modest tresses were bound up for thee! (LL) To Spring. William Blake. NAEL-6v2; NAEL-7v2; OBEV

Whose name derives from *vespa*, which has nothing. Flowers and Water. Nancy Vieira Couto. PoDa

Whose [*or* Who's] hat was in his hand. (LL) Ballad: "I put my hat upon my head." Samuel Johnson. OxAEP-1; UV

Whose scales turn aside the sun's sword by their polish. (LL) Egyptian Pulled Glass Bottle in the Shape of a Fish, An. Marianne Moore. APT-1; NALW

Whose senses in so evil consort, their stepdame Nature lays. Sir Philip Sidney. NoP-4; NoP-5

Whose songs shall never be heard. (LL) Spectral Lovers. John Crowe Ransom. APT-1; HeIP-4

Whose sweetheart is very drunk? Chinook Songs. *Unknown.* APN-2, *tr. by* Franz Boas

Whose white head is lost for this province? (LL) South-Folk in Cold Country. Li Po. NDACCP; OBVE, *tr. by* Ezra Pound

Whose wing impersonates a wing or crutch, whose flight. Erin Mouré. NLPA *Fr.* Wittgenstein Letters to Mel Gibson's Braveheart, The.

Whose wood this is I think I know. Now He Knows All There Is to Know: Now He Is Acquainted with the Day and Night. Delmore Schwartz. VisFro

Whose woods these are I think I know. Stopping by Woods on a Snowy Evening. Robert Frost. APT-1; BLPJKO; BrAP; BRP; ChAP; ClHu; ColAP; EMP; HarvBoo; HeIP-4; ITBLP; MoAmPo; NAAL-5; NAAPv.2; NAMCP V.1; NIL-7; NIP-4; NoAM; NoP-4; NoP-5; NTCP; OxBoAm; PoPoPo; SAmP; SoSe-8; StAl; TFi; TRP; WaAnP

Whose wounds are not the end of anything. (LL) We Need a God Who Bleeds Now. Ntozake Shange. FaoP; HW

Whoso answers my questions. Bayard Taylor. APN-2 *Fr.* Echo Club, The.

Whoso Gives Freely, Shall Freely Receive! Josephine D. Henderson Heard. CBWP-4

Whoso list to hunt, I know where is an hind. Whoso List to Hunt. Sir Thomas Wyatt. CABP; ItP; NAEL-6v1; NAEL-7v1; NoP-5; NoSic; OBVE; OxBSo; TFi; WoPoe

   (Who so list to hount[e] I know[e] where is an hynde.) BrAP; NPeEn; OxBEV; PBRV

Whoso saw on rode. *Unknown.* OHMEL

Whosoever steals a rosebud. *Unknown.* PriapPo *Fr.* Priapus Poems, The.

Whuh folks, whuh folks; don' wuk muh brown too hahd! Scotty Has His Say. Sterling Allen Brown. APT-2

Whut do i keer ef de white-folks do 'buse us! Uncle Rube's Defense. Clara Ann Thompson. CBWP-2

Why. Brad Leithauser. RA

Why? Myra Cohn Livingston. CA

Why. Andrey Andreievich Voznesensky. RusPo, *tr. by* Robert Arthur Douglas Ford

Why? Mary Webb. LW

Why . . . do I get riled at the small things. Emerging from the Old Palace One Day. Kim Suyŏng. CAMKP, *tr. by* Ellie Choi

Why a Boy. Justin Chin. WiU

Why a Woman Can't Be Pope. Sandra Kohler. FiBr

Why all these sidelong looks, you shameless tarts? *Unknown.* PriapPo *Fr.* Priapus Poems, The.

Why am I. Contentment. Brian MacGuigan. IrLP

Why am i doing this? Failure. Failures in Infinitives. Bernadette Mayer. NYP2

Why am I if I am uncertain reasons may inclose. Gertrude Stein. NAMCP V.1; PoA 2002 *Fr.* Stanzas in Meditation.

Why am I not as they? (LL) Lineage. Margaret Abigail Walker. ItP; ItWoWo; NALW; OxWW

Why am I so afraid. I Am Afraid of Fire. Anna Swirszczynska [*or* Swir]. AF, *tr. by* Czeslaw Milosz

Why are candles brightly burning. Christmas Tree, The. Lizelia Augusta Jenkins Moorer. CBWP-3

Why are epics. Note on the Iliad. Raymond Garlick. AngWePo; TCAWP

Why are my songs so simple. So Simple. Mark Van Doren. APT-2

Why are people gay. Love Is Sweeping the Country. Ira Gershwin. ReLy

Why Are Seaman Always Miserable? Zahrah Youssri. AnVo, *tr. by* Mohamed Enani

Why Are Those Who Are Loved So Dull and Leaden? Patrizia Valduga. CItWP, *tr. by* Cinzia Sartini Blum and Lara Trubowitz

Why are we[e] by all creatures waited on? John Donne. BASC *Fr.* Holy Sonnets.

Why are you adrift, like a boat, in the midst of a river. Your Thwarts in Pieces, Your Mooring Rope Cut. *Unknown.* WoPoe, *tr. by* Erica Reiner

Why are you not here to overpower me with your tense and urgent love? (LL) Vernal Equinox. Amy Lowell. APT-1; NAAPv.2

Why are you silent, poets of Israel? Public Outcry. Karen Alkalay-Gut. DTA

Why are you taking me this way? Where does this road go? Tell me. Unanswered. Yannis Ritsos. AF, *tr. by* Edmund Keeley

Why are your lilies so tall and pure. Cry of a People. Mary Evelyn Moore Davis. SWaP

Why Arrange the Pillows. Kabir. WED, *tr. by* Robert Bly

Why art thou changed? O Phaon! tell me why? To Phaon. Mary Robinson. CenSon; RWP

Why / as the tips of the petals curl and darken does. Adagio at Twilight. John Carter. PasH

Why blow'st thou not, thou wintry wind. All Saints' Day. John Keble. SacPr

Why boast, O arrogant, imperious man. On Mrs. Montagu. Ann Yearsley. RWP

Why Bodhidharma Went to Howard Johnson's. Jane Hirshfield. WANABP

Why bother with the world? Ryushu Shutaku. ZenPo, *tr. by* Takashi Ikemoto and Lucien Stryk

Why Brownlee left, and where he went. Why Brownlee Left. Paul Muldoon. EmeKit; NAMCP V.2; NoP-4; NoP-5; NPeEn; OxBSo; PBCIP; StAl; WaAnP

Why, by an ingrained habit, deviate. With the Grain. Donald Davie. NoAM

Why, Cambria did I quit thy shore. Edward Williams. AngWePo *Fr.* Stanzas Written in London in 1773.

Why can't I be the girl that I want to be? Femininity. Ray Evans and Jay Livingston. ReLy

Why can't I forget like I should? Memories of You. Andy Razaf. ReLy

Why Can't I Leave You? Ai. CAP-8

Why can't they give these damn mountains. Viewpoint. Tessa Ransford. EdScPo

Why cherish thus the senseless thing? That Glove. Mary E. Tucker. CBWP-1

Why Come Ye Not to Court. John Skelton. "Such a prelate, I trow." OBSV

Why confer on us the piercing vision. To Charlotte von Stein. Johann Wolfgang von Goethe. STV, *tr. by* John Frederick Nims

Why, Corydon, the silence and that frequent frown? Titus Calpurnius Siculus. RomPo *Fr.* Eclogues.

Why could you not come? For what reason. *Unknown.* CATKP, *tr. by* Wen Hsia-min

Why *Damon*, why, why, why so pressing? Song. Mary Lee, Lady Chudleigh. LW

Why did baby die. . .? Christina Georgina Rossetti. InoFa; VWP

Why did Ben Jonson. Mute Swans. Neil Curry. NLP

Why did I bring you to this Hull. Envoi. Douglas Dunn. EdScPo

Why Did I Laugh Tonight? John Keats. CenSon; NAEL-6v2; NAEL-7v2

   ("Why did I laugh to-night? No voice will tell.") GSo

"Why did I laugh to-night? No voice will tell." John Keats. *See* Why Did I Laugh Tonight?

Why did I print upon myself the names. Requiem for the Death of a Boy. Rainer Maria Rilke. ItP, *tr. by* Randall Jarrell

Why did I wander. Isn't It a Pity? Ira Gershwin. ReLy

Why did I wrong my judgement so. Upon His Unconstant Mistress. Sir Robert Aytoun. NOSC

Why did Massenet compose *Thaïs*? Greetings from the Chateau. James Schuyler. FTOS

Why did my parents send me to the schools. Sir John Davies. ChIV-1 *Fr.* Of Human Knowledge.

Why did our blessed Savior please to break. On the Holy Scriptures. Francis Quarles. ChIV-2

Why did she cross the road? Chicken. Kim Addonizio. BAP-04

Why did she not stay where she is. Hans Faverey. WoBe *Fr.* Eighteen Poems.

Why did she seek out the mountains. Heading for the Heights. Merryn Williams. Prnts

Why Did Stingy Thomas. William M. Davis. SpanPo

Why did stingy Thomas. Why Did Stingy Thomas. William M. Davis. SpanPo

Why did the clerk drag his fingertips. Great Helmsman, The. David Woo. OpBo

Why did the maid weep? (LL) Behold, the grave of a wicked man. Stephen Crane. APN-2; NoP-4; NoP-5; OxBoAm

Why did the sun his beams conceal. Crucifixion, The. Mary Weston Fordham. CBWP-2

Why did the wild pink break? Issa. EH, *tr. by* Robert Hass

Why did we waver that day, facing the forest. Premonition. Francisco Segovia. RMCMP, *tr. by* Michael Wiegers

Why did you abandon me? Interior with Faded Colors. Blaga Dimitrova. CSCBP, *tr. by* Georgi Belev and Lisa Sapinkopf

Why did you choose me for your wife, Joseph? Asenath. Diana Hume George. ChIV-1

Why did you come. "H. D." PFTM-2 *Fr.* Hermetic Definition.

Why did you come / to trouble my decline? Red Rose and a Beggar. "H. D." APSN

Why did you come, with your enkindled eyes. Why? Mary Webb. LW

Why did you, feeble as you were, attempt. Cornelius Whur. STuOW *Fr.* Village Musings.

Why did you give no hint that night. Going, The. Thomas Hardy. HarvBoo; InoFa; NAMCP V.1; OxAEP-2

Why did you reproach him. Protest. Amal Al-Juburi. PoArWo, *tr. by* Salih J. Altoma

Why did you stay away. Way the Cards Fall, The. Yusef Komunyakaa. GT

Why Didnt He Tell Me the Whole Truth. Imamu Amiri Baraka. OxAAAP

Why didn't the first philosopher want to go on living. Theory of Tragedy. Joseph Duemer. BodElec

Why Didn't They Apologize. . .? Buland Al-Haidari. IrPoTo, *tr. by* Hussein Kadhim and Christopher Merrill

Why didn't we think of clothes before? Dennis Joseph Enright. OBCoV *Fr.* Paradise Illustrated.

Why didst thou promise such a beauteous day. William Shakespeare. HeIP-4; OxAEP-1 *Fr.* Sonnets.

Why do all his women die. Sadder Man, The. Meelaad Zakaria Youssef. AnVo, *tr. by* Mohamed Enani

Why do boys' dicksies for a soft cunny yearn and the girls *vice versa*? Difficult and Weighty Question, A. Janus Pannonius. IQMS, *tr. by* Adam Makkai

Why do flowers fade so soon. Yun Sŏndo. CATKP *Fr.* Songs of Five Friends.

Why do I allow my heart. Fools Fall in Love. Irving Berlin. ReLy

Why do I carry, she said. Road 1940. Sylvia Townsend Warner. RSaN

Why do I curse the jazz of this hotel? Jazz of This Hotel, The. Vachel Lindsay. SeSe

Why do I do just as you say. It Had to Be You. Gustave Kahn. ReLy

Why do I draw this coole releeving ayer. Barnabe Barnes. PBRV *Fr.* Parthenophil and Parthenophe.

Why do I follow you. Sunset. Joseph Ceravolo. FTOS

Why do I hate that lone green dell? Emily Jane Brontë. VWP

Why do I just wither and forget all resistance. Nearness of You, The. Ned Washington. ReLy

Why do I live to loathe the cheerful day. Laments her Early Misfortunes. Mary Robinson. CenSon; RWP

Why do I love? Go ask the Glorious Sun. To One That Asked Me Why I Loved J.G G. "Ephelia." EMWP; NOSC

"Why do I love" You, Sir? Emily Dickinson. APN-2; LW

Why do I remember the sky. Crab-Boil. Rita Dove. CAP-8

Why do I use my paper, ink, and pen. Verses Made by a Catholic in Praise of Campion That Was Executed at Tyburn for Treason, As Is Made Known by the Proclamation. *Unknown.* NoSic

Why do I weep? to leave the vine. Bride's Farewell, The. Felicia Dorothea Hemans. TreFP

Why do I write today? Apology. William Carlos Williams. NAAPv.2; SAmP

Why do lampreys swim from Riga back. Why. Andrey Andreievich Voznesensky. RusPo, *tr. by* Robert Arthur Douglas Ford

Why do men smile when I speak. Is It Because I Am Black? Joseph Seamon, Jr. Cotter. OxAAAP

Why do people sit in darkness as regards the Negro race? Truth Suppressed, The. Lizelia Augusta Jenkins Moorer. CBWP-3

Why Do Poets Write? TAPaP

Why Do So Few Blacks Study Creative Writing? Cornelius Eady. GT; LTA; OxAAAP

Why do the Gentiles tumult, and the Nations. Bible, *O.T.* OBVE

Why do the houses stand. Song. George Macdonald. NePenScot

Why do these elders always exploit our disbelief? (LL) These Too Are Our Elders. Jack A. Mapanje. HBAPE; NAfrP

Why do these prudes fear Prakrit poetry. *Unknown.* GifTon, *tr. by* David Ray

Why do they come? What do they seek. On a Replica of the Parthenon. Donald Davidson. FuPo

Why do they stare. On Killing a Tax Collector. Murragh O'Daly. WoPoe, *tr. by* Richard O'Connell

Why do they think up stories that link my name with yours? People Will Say We're in Love. Oscar Hammerstein, II. ReLy

Why do we bother with the rest of the day. Morning. Billy Collins. WaAnP

Why do we in worries waste our lives, and torture. Marcus Manilius. RomPo *Fr.* Astronomica, The.

Why do we live, why do we hope. Sadakichi. NAAPv.1 *Fr.* My Rubaiyat.

Why do we love her?—that she gave us birth? This World. Sarah Morgan Bryan Piatt. NCAP

Why do we waste so much time in arguing? Sushi. Paul Muldoon. CABP

Why do women call out. Liliane Giraudon. SCFWP *Fr.* Poem with Incense Paper.

Why do you come to me so seldom? *Unknown.* SLW, *tr. by* Marjolijn De Jager, Sayd Bahodin Majrouh and André Velter

Why do you come, white moths, so oft to me? Why Do You Come, White Moths. Georg Heym. GTCP, *tr. by* Reinhold Grimm

Why do you dig like long-clawed scavengers. Verlaine. Edwin Arlington Robinson. APN-2; NCAP

Why Do You Feel Differently. Gertrude Stein. ItWoWo; PFTM-1

Why do you feel differently about a very little snail and a big one. Why Do You Feel Differently. Gertrude Stein. ItWoWo; PFTM-1

Why do you hide, O dryads! when we seek. Chant for Reapers. Wilfrid Thorley. OBEV

Why do you lie with your legs ungainly huddled. Dug-Out, The. Siegfried Sassoon. MoBrPo

Why do you play such dreary music. Radio. Frank O'Hara. PoA 2002

Why do you rack the ore? The cornerstone alone. "Angelus Silesius." GePo *Fr.* Cherubical Wanderer, The.

Why do you rush through the field in trains. Fat White Woman Speaks, The. G. K. Chesterton. OBCoV; UV

Why do you shrink away, and start and stare? At the Convent Gate. Charlotte Mew. VWP

Why do you stare so stupidly? Kukutis's Sermon to the Pigs. Marcelijus Martinaitis. TWW, *tr. by* Laima Sruoginis

Why do you, Summer Garden, press close to my lips. Summer Garden, The. Elena Ignatova. ItGoST, *tr. by* Sibelan Forrester

Why do you talk so much. For Robert Frost. Galway Kinnell. VisFro

Why do you think of your father so much? Fred Wah. NLPA *Fr.* This Dendrite Map: Father / Mother Haibun.

Why do / You thus devise. Susanna and the Elders. Adelaide Crapsey. APT-1; NAAPv.2; OxBoAm; TCAPo

Why Do You Want to Be English? Peter Finch. Oth

Why do you watch me so sadly and inquisitively. Dog. Stefan Tsanev. CSCBP, *tr. by* Georgi Belev and Lisa Sapinkopf

Why doe I quake my down-fall to reporte? Michael Drayton. CAGL *Fr.* Piers Gaveston [1619].

Why does a cauliflower so much resemble a brain? Binary. Chris Wallace-Crabbe. OBCoV

Why does it feel like I'm dreaming. When I Think About the Past. Hô Sugyông. EcSo, *tr. by* Youngju Ryu

Why does it snow? Why does it snow? Laura Elizabeth Richards. NOxBChV

Why does she lie to me. December. Miriam Van hee. TuT, *tr. by* Joan McBreen

Why does that pine tree stand. Chŏng Ch'ŏl. WoPoe *Fr.* Snow Falling in the Pine Forest: Two Poems.

Why does the sea burn? Why do the hills cry? Zaydee. Philip Levine. TaR

Why does the sea moan evermore? By the Sea. Christina Georgina Rossetti. NPeEn

Why does the spring grab me by the throat? what does it want of me? Lynch 1. Aimé Césaire. ConPit, *tr. by* Clayton Eshleman

Why does the thin grey strand. Sorrow. D. H. Lawrence. InoFa; NAMCP V.1; NPeEn; OBMV

Why [*or* Quhy] does [*or* dois] your brand sae [*or* so] drop wi' blude [*or* drap wi bluid]. Edward [*or* Edward, Edward]. *Unknown.* ClHu; NoP-4; OBEV; OxBEV; SoSe-8; TFi; TRP

Why don't I? O. F. Diaz-Duque. ReTh

Why don't people leave off being lovable. Elemental. D. H. Lawrence. NoP-4; NoP-5

Why don't we rock the casket here in the moonlight? Pale Blue Casket, The. Oliver Pitcher. EGAG

Why don't we say goodbye right now. Early Afterlife, An. Linda Pastan. ExTi

Why don't you drink. Time Break. Everett Hoagland. FuFl

Why don't you / go down Old Hannah. Ol' Hannah. Doc Reese. PFTM-1

Why don't you read? You could listen to music. Pale. Jane Routh. PoCu

Why don't you shock the whole town and ride down. Dear Rosario. Maria Elena Caballero-Robb. ReBoTo

Why dost not speak? William Shakespeare. OxAEP-1 *Fr.* Coriolanus.

Why dost thou beat thy breast and rend thine hair. Robert Southey. CenSon

Why dost thou haste away. Sir Philip Sidney. NoSic *Fr.* Countess of Pembroke's Arcadia, The.

Why dost thou hate return instead of love. Ditty. Edward Herbert, 1st Baron Herbert of Cherbury. NOSC

Why dost thou shade thy lovely face? O why. To His Mistress. John Wilmot, 2d Earl of Rochester. OBEV

Why dost thou shade thy lovely face? O[h] why. Francis Quarles. BASC; NOSC; OxAEP-1; SacPr *Fr.* Emblems (Fragments).

Why dost thou so explore. Homer. OBVE *Fr.* Iliad, The.

Why Fool Around? Stephen Dobyns. PML; PoDa

Why Fortune Is the Empress of the World. Turner Cassity. PoA 2002

Why give signs of life? No Sign of Life. Jorge Teillier. TCLAP, *tr. by* Carolyne Wright

Why go further? One might conceivably rectify the rhythm. William Carlos Williams. TCAPo *Fr.* Kora in Hell.

Why go toward the palaces of description. Painter Asks, The. John Yau. BodElec

Why God Chose Robert Frost Over Elvis. Lynn Veach Sadler. VisFro

Why God Invented the Cold. Catie Rosemurgy. AmPoNex

Why God Permits Evil: For Answers to This Question of Interest to Many Write Bible Answers, Dept. E-7. Miller Williams. InGu

Why has our poetry eschewed. Food and Drink. Louis Untermeyer. MoAmPo

Why has Spring one syllable less. What's in a Name? Christina Georgina Rossetti. FaBoVe

Why hast thou nothing in thy face? Eros. Robert Bridges. CABP

Why have crowds as magnets drawn. Why We Meet. Lizelia Augusta Jenkins Moorer. CBWP-3

Why have such scores of lovely, gifted girls. Slice of Wedding Cake, A. Robert Graves. BrAP; NAEL-6v2; NAEL-7v2

Why Have They Moved Me. Carlos German Belli. TCLAP *Fr.* O Hada Cibernetica.

Why have they moved me. Carlos German Belli. TCLAP *Fr.* O Hada Cibernetica.

Why have you given us this misery. Wales. David Gwenallt Jones. BBMWP, *tr. by* Joseph P. Clancy

Why have you made life so intolerable. To God. Ivor Gurney. OxBEV

Why, having won her, do I woo? Coventry Patmore. OBEV; OxAEP-2; SacPr *Fr.* Angel in the House, The.

Why, he aimed the car right at that girl! Oracular Degeneration. Karl Kirchwey. KGB

Why He Had to Go. Justin Chin. AmPoNex

Why he turned them inside outside. (LL) George A. Strong. OBCoV; UV *Fr.* Song of Milkanwatha, The.

Why He Was There. Edwin Arlington Robinson. APT-1; OxBSo

Why, hermit Marvan, sleepest thou not. King and Hermit. *Unknown.* IrV, *tr. by* Kuno Meyer

Why, Hyllus, do you deny to me today. Martial. RomPo, *tr. by* Mollie Barger

Why I Am a Whore. Donna Brook. PrTe

Why I Am Not a Buddhist. Molly Peacock. ExTi

Why I Am Not a Painter. Frank O'Hara. CAP-8; EMP; NAMCP V.2; NoAM; NoP-4; NoP-5; OxBoAm; PoPoPo; VCAP; WaAnP

Why I Be a Goddess. Rha Goddess. BRtP

Why I Became a Saint. Oliver Cadiot. YaTCFP, *tr. by* Cole Swensen

Why I Believe in Angels. Rick Mulkey. AmPoNex

Why I Choose Black Men for My Lovers. La Loca. CLPP

Why I Choose Red. Hugh MacDiarmid. RSaN

Why I Do It. Luke E. Ramirez. OWABP

Why I Dont Leave the Apartment Until After Ten Some Mornings. Kalamu ya Salaam. BtF

Why I Don't Speak Italian. Arthur L. Clements. UnSA

Why I Forgive My Younger Self Her Transgressions. Ruth L. Schwartz. NeAmPo

Why I Hate Theory. Bruce Weigl. AmAlph

Why I Left the Church. Richard Garcia. SUP

Why I Look at Girls. Christian Langworthy. IIR

Why I Make the Best Barrels. Eliza Garza. IPoFL

Why I Often Allude to Osiris. Ishmael Reed. GT

Why I sit sighing here ask me no more. Upon the Imprisonment of His Sacred Majesties that Unparaleld Prince King Charles the First. Hester Lee Pulter. EMWP

Why I Skip My High School Reunions. Craig Arnold. AmPoNex

Why I Think About Hiroshima and Nagasaki. Edward A. Dougherty. AtGh

Why I tie [*or* tye] about thy wrist. Bracelet to Julia, The. Robert Herrick. BASC; OBEV

Why I Voted the Socialist Ticket. Vachel Lindsay. MoAmPo

Why I Want to Be the Next Poet Laureate. Elliot Fried. SUP

Why I Wont Wear a Tatoo. Tracie Morris. BtF

Why, I'd forgotten these half-human faces. Drugstore Trolls. Maura Stanton. SUP

Why I'm Different in Wyoming. Suellen Wedmore. RWB

Why I'm in Favor of a Nuclear Freeze. Christopher Buckley. AtGh

Why in all the many races of the country where we live. Why Negroes Don't Unite. Lizelia Augusta Jenkins Moorer. CBWP-3

Why in Christ's name. And another thing. Edwin Brock. BeAl

Why interrupt. Foreign Land. Greta Knutson. SurWo, *tr. by* Penelope Rosemont

Why Is God Love, Jack? Allen Ginsberg. FTOS

Why Is It? Lizelia Augusta Jenkins Moorer. CBWP-3

Why is it I can't sleep tonight? Bucket, The. Rose Romano. UnSA

Why is it in my middle-aged dream. Black and White. Shirley Lim. UnSA

Why is it modern books are little read. Martial. RomPo, *tr. by* Olive Pitt-Kethley

Why is it modern poets are ignored. Martial. PoDa *Fr.* Epigrams.

Why is it not enough, to want death's certain peace? Lamentation during His Most Painful Illness. Simon Dach. GePo, *tr. by* Ingrid Waløe-Engel

Why is it so hard to meet a man these days? For the Sake of Man Again. Mun Chônghui. EcSo, *tr. by* Catherine J. Kim

Why is it that women. Pure Pop. Allison Joseph. NeAmPo

Why Is It This Way, Almighty God? Violeta Parra. TANSG, *tr. by* Shaun Griffin and Emma Sepúlveda-Pulvirenti

Why is it this way, Almighty God? Why Is It This Way, Almighty God? Violeta Parra. TANSG, *tr. by* Shaun Griffin and Emma Sepúlveda-Pulvirenti

Why is it, when I am in Rome. On Being a Woman. Dorothy Parker. BrAP

Why is my heart like a flag in the wind. My October Song. Yuri Suhl. Prolet, *tr. by* Amelia Glaser

Why is my verse so barren of new pride? William Shakespeare. NoP-5; NoSic; OxAEP-1 *Fr.* Sonnets.

Why is she sleeping on some steps. Yana Tokareva. CRWP, *tr. by* Daniel Weissbort

Why is that I begin to worship you with tears? (LL) Ishtar. Judith Wright. NALW; NAMCP V.2; NoAM

Why is the cuckoo's melody preferred. Wren, The. John Clare. CenSon

Why is the word pretty so underrated? Pretty. Stevie Smith. NAEL-6v2; NAEL-7v2; NAMCP V.1; NoAM; NoP-4

Why is the world beloved, that fals is and vein. Despise the World. *Unknown.* WaAnP

Why Is This Night Different from All Other Nights? Nadine Brummer. Prnts

Why / is what i ask myself. Hag Riding. Lucille Clifton. ExTi

Why isn't it all. Why Isn't It All More Marked. Kay Ryan. ExTi

Why Isn't It All More Marked. Kay Ryan. ExTi

Why, it's but the motion of eyes and brows! Yuishun. ZenPo, *tr. by* Takashi Ikemoto and Lucien Stryk

Why, let the strucken deer go weep. William Shakespeare. NoSic *Fr.* Hamlet.

Why Life Is Worth Living. Suzanne Lummis. SUP

Why Log Truck Drivers Rise Earlier Than Students of Zen. Gary Snyder. GeoHom; LoL

"Why look at me like that?" Nocturne by Ben Shahn. Ronald Stuart Thomas. OxAEP-2

Why look back at the old roads again? Drugs and buggery flourished. My grief took root. Nostalgia. Stephen Berg. OPRER

Why looks your Grace so heavily today? William Shakespeare. OxAEP-1 *Fr.* King Richard III.

Why 'm i. 4 Or 5 Tadpoles. Kusano Shimpei. PFTM-1

Why make it doubt—it hurts it so. Emily Dickinson. NALW

Why make it so short? Have you lost your old liking. Brevity. Friedrich Hölderlin. NAWM-7v2, *tr. by* Christopher Middleton

Why, Man of Morals, tell me why? (LL) Drinking. Abraham Cowley. NPeEn; OBEV; OBVE; OxAEP-1; OxBEV, *tr. by* Abraham Cowley

Why Mira Can't Go Back to Her Old House. Mirabai. WED; WPoS, *tr. by* Robert Bly

Why must it come just now to trouble me. Cry from Childhood, A. Valeri Petrov. PML, *tr. by* Richard Wilbur

Why must that slight man. Walk, The. Ethan Gilsdorf. OPRER

Why must the noble rose. Seducing the Sparrow. Sam Hamill. WANABP

Why Must the Show Go On? Noël Coward. ReLy

Why Must U Be Unfaithful (4 Women). Tupac Shakur. FTtHH

Why Must You Know? John Wheelwright. APT-2; OxBoAm

Why my legs. In the Gloom on the Left. Joyce Mansour. PFTM-2, *tr. by* Molly Bendall

Why Negroes Don't Unite. Lizelia Augusta Jenkins Moorer. CBWP-3

Why no! I never thought other than. Via Negativa. Ronald Stuart Thomas. InvLi; StAl

Why not merely the despaired of. Cascando. Samuel Beckett. IrLP; ModIr

Why not simply moonlight on a swirling leaf? Death, Dark Agent. Jotie T'Hooft. TuT, *tr. by* Seán Lysaght

Why not violate sense and say. W. S. Di Piero. PoCoUp

Why Nothing Changes for Miss Ngo Thi Thanh. Bruce Weigl. AmAlph

Why of the sheep do you not learn peace? Answer to the Parson, An. William Blake. NBLV; WoPoe

Why oh why can't I? (LL) Over the Rainbow. E. Y. Harburg. NAAPv.2; ReLy

Why, on a Bad Day, I Can Relate to the Manatee. Denise Duhamel. SUP

Why only boulders across the graves? Child Is Born, A. Mailabattula Satish Chandar. HotL, *tr. by* V. Narayana Rao

Why People Murder. Ellen Bass. RaF

Why puts our grand-dame [*or* Grandame] Nature on. On the Unusual Cold and Rainy [*or* Rainie] Weather in the Summer, 1648. Robert Heath. NOSC

Why Ralph Refuses to Dance. C. D. Wright. CAP-8

Why reclining, interrogating? why myself and all drowsing? To the States, To Identify the 16th, 17th, or 18th Presidentiad. Walt Whitman. NAAL-3; RaBo

Why Regret? Galway Kinnell. OxBoAm

Why remember that I am a poet. Protest. Romelia Alarcón de Folgar. TANSG, *tr. by* Alison Ridley

Why ride so fast through the wind and rain. Grey Rider, The. Norah M. Holland. IFF

Why, rustic Pan, sitting in the lone shady wood. Anyte. SaLy, *tr. by* Diane Rayor

Why She Hurries Out, Then Home. Martha Rhodes. OPRER

Why she should trouble her young. I Have Two Sons and the One I Love Best Is Robert. Paula Tatarunis. BloBone

Why She Suffers. Anne Valley Fox. ICANM

Why sholde I noght as wel eek telle yow al. Geoffrey Chaucer. NPeEn *Fr.* Canterbury Tales, The.

Why should a foolish marriage vow. John Dryden. NAEL-6v1; NAEL-7v1; NIL-7; NIP-4 *Fr.* Marriage à la Mode.

Why should a woman who is healthy and strong. Many a New Day. Oscar Hammerstein, II. ReLy

Why should I be ashamed. Letter to a Friend. Marjorie Oludhe Macgoye. HAWP

Why should I blame her that she filled my days. No Second Troy. William Butler Yeats. HarvBoo; NAEL-6v2; NAEL-7v2; NAMCP V.1; NoAM; NoP-5; OxAEP-2; TFi; WaAnP; WeW-3

Why should I call Thee Lord, Who art my God? After Communion. Christina Georgina Rossetti. SacPr; WPoS

Why should I fear in evil days. John Quincy Adams. SacPr

Why should I fear the spirits of the dead? Written at Netley Abbey. Susan Evance. CenSon

Why should I feel discouraged. His Eye Is on the Sparrow. C. D. Martin. TCAPo

Why should I have returned? Noah's Raven. W. S. Merwin. ChIV-1

Why should I keep holiday. Compensation. Ralph Waldo Emerson. APN-1

Why should I let the toad *work*. Toads. Philip Larkin. BeAl; NoAM; OxAEP-2; SoSe-8

Why should I not sing *them*, the dead, the innocent? (LL) Hamish Henderson. EdScPo; PoWW; RSaN *Fr.* Elegies for the Dead in Cyrenaica.

Why should I praise thee, blissful Aphrodite? Michael Field. ViWPN

Why should I seek for love or study it? Ribh Considers Christian Love Insufficient. William Butler Yeats. BBASP; RaBo

Why should I sit alone, eyes closed. Rāmrenu Mukhopādhyāy. SinGod, *tr. by* Rachel Fell McDermott

Why should I speak of motherhood? Pulse. Jane Holland. MFPA

Why should I still pour out my intense desire. Michelangelo Buonarroti. CAGL, *tr. by* James M. Saslow

Why should I tarry here, to be but one. Above the Tree. Elizabeth Stoddard. SWaP

Why should it be *my* loneliness. Tell Me. Langston Hughes. APSN; SAmP

Why should my bells, which chime thy praise, when thou. Edward Taylor. ChIV-2 *Fr.* Preparatory Meditations Before My Approach to the Lord's Supper.

Why Should the American Negro Be Proud? Maggie Pogue Johnson. CBWP-4

Why should the arabs come to my window. Write Off. Breyten Breytenbach. PoetW, *tr. by* Denis Hirson

Why should the scribblers discompose. Scribblers, The. Walter Savage Landor. OBSV

Why should the tiny harp be chained to themes. Powers of the Sonnet. Ebenezer Elliott. CenSon

Why should this Negro insolently stride. August. Elinor Wylie. APT-1; MoAmPo

Why should we two ever want to part? Owl and the Moon, The. Kabir. WED, *tr. by* Robert Bly

Why should you freeze to sleep? Hanu. CATKP, *tr. by* Peter H. Lee

Why should you swear I am forsworn. Richard Lovelace. CavPo

Why should your face so please me. Song. Edwin Muir. EdScPo

Why Shouldn't It Happen to Us? Mann Holiner. ReLy

Why, sir, as to that—I did not know it was time for the. Pique at Parting, A. Sarah Morgan Bryan Piatt. NCAP

Why Snow Is White. Dafydd Iwan. BBMWP, *tr. by* Geriant Løvgreen

Why so desolate? Is Your Town Nineveh? Marianne Moore. APT-1

"Why so droopy?" did I hear you say? Horace. EroLit *Fr.* Epodes.

Why so pale and wan, fond lover? Sir John Suckling. BASC; CavPo; ClHu; HeIP-4; ITBLP; NAEL-6v1; NAEL-7v1; NBLV; NIL-7; NIP-4; NoP-4; NoP-5; NPeEn; OBEV; OxAEP-1; OxBEV; TFi; WaAnP *Fr.* Aglaura.

Why solitary crow? He in his feathers. Solitary crow. Norman Alexander MacCaig. NoP-4

Why, Some of My Best Friends Are Women. Phyllis McGinley. AmWit

Why some people be mad at me sometimes. Lucille Clifton. ESEAA

Why speak of memory and death. Two Views of Two Ghost Towns. Charles Tomlinson. NAMCP V.2; NoAM

Why stand aghast. He Hath Need of Rest. Josephine D. Henderson Heard. CBWP-4

Why such harsh machinery? Sweetness, Always. Pablo Neruda. BeAl, *tr. by* Alastair Reid

Why Tell Me What to Do? Chandidas. WoPoe, *tr. by* Tony Barnstone

Why tell me what to do? Why Tell Me What to Do? Chandidas. WoPoe, *tr. by* Tony Barnstone

Why Ten Men? Rodger Kamenetz. TaR

Why ten men? Why Ten Men? Rodger Kamenetz. TaR

Why That Abbott and Costello Vaudeville Mess Never Worked with Black People. Paul Beatty. AmPoNex

Why That's Bob Hope. William Hathaway. ReTh

Why the blue bruises high up on your thigh. Farm Woman, The: 1942. Naomi Mitchison. EdScPo; RSaN

Why the Elgin Marbles Must be Returned to Elgin. W. N. Herbert. EdScPo

Why the Heart Never Develops Cancer. Bill Mohr. SUP

Why the hell do you grumble and blame tourism. Progressive Man's Indignation, A. Dimitris Tsaloumas. BMAP

Why the laughter, witless female? *Unknown.* PriapPo *Fr.* Priapus Poems, The.

Why the Old Woman Limps. Lupenga Mphande. HBAPE

Why the sea? Pointless Journey. Yolanda Bedregal. TANSG, *tr. by* Carolyne Wright

Why the Stone Remains Silent. William Kloefkorn. GifTon

Why the wooden chair begins. Affair With a Chair, An. Christopher Pilling. NLP

Why There Are Children. Leslie Ullman. YaYoPo

Why, there are maidens of heroic touch. "George Eliot." LW *Fr. from* Felix Holt, The Radical.

Why There Are No Unicorns. Judith Ortiz Cofer. PfSP; PueRic

Why, through each aching vein, with lazy pace. Her Passion Increases. Mary Robinson. CenSon; RWP

Why, through each aching vein, with lazy pace. Mary Robinson. NPBRoP *Fr.* Sappho and Phaon.

Why, tonight. I Ask in Late Evening. Yi Sanghûi. EcSo, *tr. by* Jennifer M. Lee

Why trouble you religion's sacred stream. New Illiterate Lay-Teachers, The. Rowland Watkyns. BASC

Why Try to Change Me Now? Joseph McCarthy, Jr. ReLy

Why try to recontruct with words. In the Body. Ferreira Gullar. TCLAP, *tr. by* Renato Rezende

Why utter the names of gods or stars. Other, The. Rosario Castellanos. TCLAP, *tr. by* Maureen Ahern

Why was Charlie Charlie? Why was Joe Joe? Charlie and Joe. John Redmond. NIrP

Why Was I Born? Oscar Hammerstein, II. ReLy

Why was it that the thunder voice of Fate. Robert Gould Shaw. Paul Laurence Dunbar. CBCWP; PoPoPo

Why was that door locked? I want. Conservation of Energy, The. Chana Bloch. CFP

Why was the airman taking such pains? Airman, The. Aleksandr Semionovich Kushner. TCRusP, *tr. by* Daniel Weissbort

Why We Are Forgiven. Bruce Weigl. BodElec

Why We Are Late. Josephine Miles. NALW

Why we ask you not to touch. Charles Bernstein. NoP-5

Why We Bombed Haiphong. Jonathan Holden. ReTh

Why We Fear the Amish. Robin Becker. BodElec

Why We Meet. Lizelia Augusta Jenkins Moorer. CBWP-3

Why We Play Basketball. Sherman Alexie. MoASP

Why we so worried 'bout 2G. 2G (Another Millennium Poem). C. Leigh McInnis. BRtP

Why weep on the hairless skull of tedium. Desire as Light as a Shuttle. Joyce Mansour. HAWP, *tr. by* Mary Beach

Why weep ye by the tide, ladie? Jock of Hazeldean. Sir Walter Scott. NAEL-6v2; NAEL-7v2; NOBRP

Why were you born when the snow was falling? Dirge, A. Christina Georgina Rossetti. OxBEV

Why were you not like the tree Trung Quan? What Things Are Called. Erich Fried. AF, *tr.* by Georg Rapp

Why, what a particularly pure young man this pure young man must be! (LL) William Schwenck Gilbert. NAEL-6v2; NAEL-7v2; NBLV *Fr.* Patience.

Why, when I gaze on Phaon's beauteous eyes. Sappho Discovers her Passion. Mary Robinson. CenSon; RWP

Why, when I gaze on Phaon's beauteous eyes. Mary Robinson. NPBRoP *Fr.* Sappho and Phaon.

Why, whenever she can spy me. Horace. OBVE *Fr.* Odes.

Why, who makes much of a miracle? Miracles. Walt Whitman. SAmP

Why will Delia thus retire. Receipt to Cure the Vapours, A. Lady Mary Wortley Montagu. NoP-4; NoP-5; NPeEn; OxBEV; PEW

Why will they never speak. Grandfathers, The [*or* After a Line by John Peale Bishop]. Donald Justice. NAMCP V.2

Why will you vex me with. To His Skeleton. Richard Wilbur. UpMys

Why, William, on that old grey [*or* gray] stone. Expostulation and Reply. William Wordsworth. NAEL-6v2; NAEL-7v2; NOBRP; NoP-5

Why Women Become Water. Annette Spaulding-Convy. RWB

Why won't Eve eat of the fruit? Eve Oh Eve. Taslima Nasrin. VCWP

Why worry when skies are gray? Let's Have Another Cup of Coffee. Irving Berlin. ReLy

Why You and I. Harryette Mullen. FaoP

Why, you ask, do painted gonads. *Unknown.* PriapPo *Fr.* Priapus Poems, The.

Why you? Even I didn't think I could write anything at all. Invocation. N. Revathi Devi. HotL, *tr.* by V. Narayana Rao

Why you need to have one. Secret Life, A. Stephen Dunn. GoPo

Why you no rhythm. Stall Me Out. Paul Beatty. AmPoNex

Why Young Men Wore Their Hair Long in the Sixties. Jeff Poniewaz. RWB

Why Your Father Cried. Elaine Terranova. PoChi

Why Your Grandfather Stopped Playing the Viola. Alice Wirth Gray. MiVo

Why'n't you bring me. To Greet a Letter-Carrier. William Carlos Williams. SAmP

Why's / Wise. Imamu Amiri Baraka.
  Wise 1. NAMCP V.2; PFTM-1
  Wise 3. FTOS
  Y The Link Will Not Always Be "Missing" #40. NAMCP V.2

Wi' Jock of Hazeldean. (LL) Jock of Hazeldean. Sir Walter Scott. NAEL-6v2; NAEL-7v2; NOBRP

Wi' Jock the byreman's braith. (LL) Cloudburst and Soaring Moon. Hugh MacDiarmid. NAMCP V.1; NoAM

Wichita Vortex Sutra. Allen Ginsberg.
  "Turn Right Next Corner / *The Biggest Little Town in Kansas.*" FTOS

Wicked and the base do compass round, The. Fear not: for they that are with us are more than they that are with them. 2 Kings 6:16. Jones Very. ChIV-1

Wicked Women. *Vietnamese Oral Tradition.* CaDao, *tr.* by John Balaban

Wicker Basket, A. Robert Creeley. NAMCP V.2; NoAM

Wicker chair / In pinetree's shade. Masaoka Shiki. ZenPo, *tr.* by Takashi Ikemoto and Lucien Stryk

Wickson Plums. William Corbett. PmAP

Widdershins. Ellie McDonald. EdScPo

Wide around. John Dyer. STuOW *Fr.* Fleece, The.

Wide enough for sleep, poems seek. Fine Occupation, A. Ryan Fitzpatrick. PoPra

Wide enough to keep you looking. Earth Verse. Gary Snyder. WhBo

Wide, Ho? / A reed will cross its flow. *Unknown.* NDACCP; OBVE, *tr.* by Ezra Pound

Wide Mind. Joanne Kyger. WANABP

Wide sea—black night—I woke up lovesick. Wind, The. Léon Damas. SonAtl, *tr.* by Kurt Ganzl and Christophe Mirambeau

Wide wide Yangtze, dragons in deep pools, The. Merchant's Joy, The. Lu Yu. ColAnChi, *tr.* by Burton Watson

Wide-Eyed. William D. Barney. TiP2

Wide-eyed child in love with maps and plans, The. Voyaging. Charles Baudelaire. SxFrPo, *tr.* by James McGowan

Widening Spell of the Leaves, The. Larry Levis. PBCAP

Widening, The. Carol Moldaw. NevBe

Wider than winter. Carmen Ancillare. John Hollander. YaYoPo

Widespread Implications. A. R. Ammons. BodElec

Widgeon. Seamus Heaney. NPeEn

Widow. Bryan Martin Davies. BBMWP, *tr.* by Elin ap Hywel

Widow. William Stafford. CAP-8

Widow, A. Ted Kooser. PBCAP

Widow, The. Robert Southey. NOBRP; UV

Widow and the Soldier or: The Measure of a Woman's Inconstancy and Lust, The. Phaedrus. RomPo, *tr.* by Eugene O'Connor

Widow at Windsor, The. Rudyard Kipling. NAEL-6v2; NAEL-7v2; NoAM

Widow Has Buried Her Second Husband, The. William Dunbar. RACG *Fr.* Tretis [*or* Book] of the Tua Mariit Wemen [*or* Two Married Women] and the Wedo[w] [*or* Widow], The.

Widow in her late seventies, A. Amsterdam Chronicle. Rein Bloem. TuT, *tr.* by John Hughes

Widow in Red Shoes. Tess Gallagher. PoCu

Widow in Wintertime, A. Carolyn Kizer. CAP-8

Widow Opening Her Heart, The. Mary McGinnis. ICANM

Widow refuses sleep, for sleep pretends, The. Exile. Ellen Bryant Voigt. AWTN

Widow stands at the door, The. After the Funeral. Meg Bateman. BeAl, *tr.* by the author

Widow Zebach. Charles Behlen. TiP2

Widowed reasons why. Thirteen Propositions against Trivial Love. David Huerta. RMCMP, *tr.* by Mark Schafer

Widower. Julia Copus. NeBl

Widower's Courtship, The. Elizabeth Hands. WoRP

Widows. Edgar Lee Masters. MoAmPo

Widows' House, The. Sarah Orne Jewett. APN-2

Widow's Hymn, A. George Wither. OBEV

Widow's Jazz, The. Mina Loy. NAMCP V.1

Widow's Lament in Springtime, The. William Carlos Williams. APT-1; CtM; FTtHH; NAAL-5; NAMCP V.1; NoAM; SAmP; SoSe-8; TCAPo

Widow's Remarriage, The. Mary F. Johnson. CenSon

Widow's Song, The. Edward Coote Pinkney. APN-1

Widow's Tears [*or* Widdowes Teares]: or, Dirge of Dorcas, The. Robert Herrick. ChIV-2

Widow's Winter. Marilyn Bowering. IFF

Width of a cube spans defensive rapture. Defensive Rapture. Barbara Guest. AWPTFC; FTOS

Wiederkehr. Rita Dove. BodElec

Wife a-Lost, The. William Barnes. OBEV

Wife and servant are the same. To the Ladies. Mary Lee, Lady Chudleigh. BrAP; CABP; NALW; NIL-7; PEW

Wife—at Daybreak I shall be, A. Emily Dickinson. TCAPo

Wife Hits Moose. Thomas Lux. StAl

Wife in London, A. Thomas Hardy. OBWP

Wife Of. Vicki L. Reitenauer. FiBr

Wife of All Ages, The. Edith Nesbit. VWP

Wife of Asdrubal, The. Felicia Dorothea Hemans. ViWPN

Wife of Bath Speaks in Brixton Market. Jean Binta Breeze. MoWP

Wife of Bath, The. Geoffrey Chaucer. *Fr.* Canterbury Tales, The.

Wife of Bath's Prologue, The. Geoffrey Chaucer. NAEL-6v1; NAEL-7v1; NoP-5 *Fr.* Canterbury Tales, The.

Wife of Bath's Tale, The. Geoffrey Chaucer. NAEL-6v1; NAEL-7v1; NoP-5 *Fr.* Canterbury Tales, The.

Wife of Carcassone, The. A. G. Prys-Jones. TCAWP

Wife of Crowle, The. James Hogg. NPBRoP

Wife of Llew, The. Francis Ledwidge. MakPoe

Wife of Master Mason Clement, The. *Hungarian Oral Tradition.* IQMS, *tr.* by Adam Makkai

Wife of the Husband. Micere Githae Mugo. HAWP

Wife of Usher's Well, The. *Unknown.* MakPoe; NAEL-6v1; NAEL-7v1; NePenScot; NoP-4; NoP-5; NPeEn; OBEV; OxAEP-1; TFi

Wife Speaks, The. Elizabeth Stoddard. SWaP

Wife to a Friend, A. Kshetrayya. WoPoe, *tr.* by V. Narayana Rao, A. K. Ramanujan and David Shulman

Wife to Husband. Fleur Adcock. BrAP

Wife to Husband. John Harington. NoSic

Wife Who Smashed Television Gets Jail. Paul Durcan. CABP

Wife's Lament, The. *Unknown.* NoP-4; NoP-5, *tr.* by Richard Hamer

Wife's Thoughts, The. Hsü Kan. CCL1, *tr.* by Burton Watson

Wight. Stanley Plumly. PoA 2002

Wiglaf. Marisa De Los Santos. NAPBL

Wilberforce. Josephine D. Henderson Heard. CBWP-4

Wild and windy was the day. Zhong-feng: Wild and Windy. *Unknown.* CCL1, *tr.* by Arthur Waley

Wild Ass. Padraic Colum. MoBrPo

Wild Bees. James Keir Baxter. NoP-4; NoP-5

Wild bird 'bode in the tame bird's tether, The. White Bird, The. Rosamund Marriott Watson. VWP

Wild bird, whose warble, liquid sweet. Alfred Tennyson. NAEL-6v2; NAEL-7v2; NoP-5 *Fr.* In Memoriam A. H. H.

Wild Birds. E. A. Mares. ICANM

Wild birds on the roof are bitterly complaining to man, The. Seeking Spring Beyond the city. Su Tung-p'o. TAL

Wild Boar and the Ram, The. John Gay. NPeEn *Fr.* Fables.

Wild Carthage held her, Rome. Puritan Lady, A. Lizette Woodworth Reese. MoAmPo

Wild Cherry. Nigel Jenkins. TCAWP

Wild Cherry, The. Malcolm Lowry. NoP-4; NoP-5

Wild Common, The. D. H. Lawrence. NAMCP V.1; NoAM

Wild creeper noses up, The. Wild Creeper. Geōrgios Drosinēs. SonAtl, *tr. by* Maria Henson and Con Wilde

Wild Dog Rose, The. John Montague. PBCIP *Fr.* Rough Field, The.

Wild Dreams, The. *Unknown.* NAWM-7v1, *tr. by* Ned Dubin

Wild-eared, / singing. (LL) Sunday Greens. Rita Dove. AmAlph; GT

Wild Edge, The. Gary Snyder. NAMCP V.2

Wild fields of Ocean, piling heap on heap. Mid-Ocean. Emily Jane Pfeiffer. ViWPN

Wild Flower. Maurice Kenny. PoCoUp

Wild Flower Man, The. Lu Yu. NDACCP, *tr. by* Kenneth Rexroth

Wild for Love. Delmira Agustini. TANSG, *tr. by* Mark McCaffrey

Wild gander leads his flock through the cool night, The. Walt Whitman. ColAP *Fr.* Song of Myself.

Wild Gardens Overlooked by Night Lights. Barbara Guest. FTOS; PmAP

Wild geese / Fellow travelers. Chine-Jo, Lady. ZenPo, *tr. by* Takashi Ikemoto and Lucien Stryk

Wild Geese: "You do not have to be good." Mary Oliver. BLT; GoPo; PoCu; TWF

Wild Geese. Mary Oliver. StAl

Wild Geese, The. Wendell Berry. TRP

Wild Geese, The. Gareth Alban Davies. BBMWP, *tr. by* the author

Wild Geese Flying. Barbara Howes. OWoS

Wild geese go north of the passes. Variant on the Songs of the East and West Gates. Ts'ao Ts'ao. WoPoe, *tr. by* David Lattimore

Wild geese have all flown away. Cho Myŏngni [*or* Myŏnghŭi]. CATKP, *tr. by* Peter H. Lee

Wild geese waking in the March wind. Withdrawal Letter. Jim Carroll. PmAP

Wild Glee from Elsewhere. Joyce Mansour. SurWo

Wild Goat, The. Claude McKay. RACG

Wild Grapes. Jean Janzen. ACAMVP

Wild Grapes. Kenneth Slessor. BrAP

Wild grass, miles on end. Bearers' Song. T'ao Ch'ien. ChinPo, *tr. by* Ye Weilian [*or* Yeh Wei-lien *or* Wai-lim Yip]

Wild Gratitude. Edward Hirsch. IllVoic; WaAnP

Wild heart grew white in the forest, The. Heart, The. Georg Trakl. WED, *tr. by* Robert Bly

Wild Honey. Francis Webb. NOBAu

Wild Honey Suckle, The. Philip Freneau. ColAP; ITBLP; NAAL-3; NAAPv.1; OxBoAm; TCAPo

Wild Hooves. Gary Rosenthal. WhBo

Wild horses running in the hills. Tsangyang Gyatso. WoPoe *Fr.* Love-Poems of the Sixth Dalai Lama.

Wild Hyacinth. Joan I. Siegel. PoCoUp

Wild Iris. Patricia Y. Ikeda. WhBo

Wild Iris, The. Louise Glück. ColAP; MoWP; NAMCP V.2; StAl

Wild is the foaming sea! The surges roar! Phaon Forsakes Her. Mary Robinson. CenSon; RWP

Wild is the Wind. Travis Nichols. IIR

Wild Man Comes to the Monastery, The. *Unknown.* RaBo

Wild midst the teeming buds of opening May. Morning. Rosamonde. Anne Batten Cristall. RWP

Wild mists veil the emerald stairs. Parting by Moonlight in a River Pavilion. Wang Po. CCL1, *tr. by* Stephen Owen

Wild Night, A. Katie Donovan. NIrP

Wild Night, A. Julia Ward Howe. ColAP

Wild Night at Treweithan. Gwyn Williams. AngWePo; TCAWP

Wild Nights—Wild Nights! Emily Dickinson. APN-2; EroLit; ErotSp; HeIP-4; NAAL-3; NAAL-5; NAAPv.1; NALW; NAMCP V.1; NCAP; NIL-7; NIP-4; NoAM; NoP-4; NoP-5; OxBoAm; PoBW; PoPoPo; PtR; RaBo; TCAPo; WaAnP; WPoS

Wild Oats. Norman Alexander MacCaig. NePenScot; NPeEn

Wild Old Wicked Man, The. William Butler Yeats. RaBo

Wild Orchard. William Carlos Williams. PoA 2002

Wild Party, The. Joseph Moncure March.
  "Gang was there when midnight came, The." APT-2
  "Queenie was a blonde, and her age stood still." OBCoV

Wild patience has taken me this far, A. Integrity. Adrienne Rich. ColAP; StAl

Wild Peaches. Elinor Wylie. APT-1; ColAP; NAAPv.2; NALW; NAMCP V.1; OxBoAm; TCAPo

  Puritan Sonnet. MoAmPo

Wild Pigs of Kalimantan, The. Kazuko Shiraishi. WoBe, *tr. by* Samuel Grolmes and Yumiko Tsumura

Wild Plum. John Orrick. APT-1

Wild Provoke of the Endurance Sky. Joseph Ceravolo. BodElec; NYP2

Wild Radishes. John Kinsella. NeBl

Wild Raspberries. John Fuller. NPeEn

Wild raspberries gathered in a silent valley. Wild Raspberries. John Fuller. NPeEn

Wild Ride, The [*abr.*]. Louise Imogen Guiney. ColAP; RACG; TCAPo

Wild roadside flowers, blooming in boundless numbers. Su Tung-p'o. WoPoe *Fr.* Roadside Flowers, Three Poems with Introduction.

Wild Root. Juana de Ibarbourou. TCLAP, *tr. by* Sophie Cabot Black and Maria Negroni

Wild root turns through the chives, The. Call and Response. Ken Harris. AnSo

Wild Rose. Vitalina Tkhorzhevskaya. CRWP, *tr. by* Daniel Weissbort

Wild Rose of Plymouth, The. Jones Very. APN-1

Wild Rose, The. Wendell Berry. UpMys

Wild rove the flocks, no burdening fleece they bear. John Dyer. STuOW *Fr.* Fleece, The.

Wild Salmon: Stillaguamish Tribal Hatchery. Joan Swift. PoCoUp

Wild sea, A. Basho. EH, *tr. by* Robert Hass

Wild sea, A. Basho. EMJL, *tr. by* Haruo Shirane

Wild Sleeve. Marjorie Welish. FTOS

Wild Sports of the West. John Montague. CABP

Wild stinking fire, love and death. John Tranter. VaPo *Fr.* Blackout.

Wild Strawberries. Helen Dunmore. BeAl

Wild Strawberry. Maurice Kenny. HATNAP

Wild sun, an architecture of souls descending. Dead Mouth, High Weather, Mixture. Jon Gill Bentley. ICANM

Wild Sunflower. Yvor Winters. APT-2

Wild Swans. Edna St. Vincent Millay. HarvBoo; MoAmPo; MoWP; OWoS

Wild Swans at Coole, The. William Butler Yeats. HeIP-4; MoBrPo; NAEL-6v2; NAEL-7v2; NAMCP V.1; NoAM; NoP-4; NoP-5; NPeEn; OWoS; PoPoPo; SoSe-8; TFi

Wild to be wreckage forever. (LL) Cherrylog Road. James Dickey. ColAP; NIL-7; NIP-4; WaAnP; WeW-3

Wild Turkeys; The Dignity of the Damned. Brigit Pegeen Kelly. ExTi; IllVoic

Wild warblers are warbling in the jungle, The. Meditation Celestial & Terrestrial. Wallace Stevens. APT-1

Wild West Workshop Poem. Anselm Hollo. PmAP

Wild white dress. Clothes. *Unknown.* SonAtl, *tr. by* P. Nbe Ondo

Wild White Horses. Laurie Anderson. WhBo

Wild, wild the storm, and the sea high running. Patrolling Barnegat. Walt Whitman. APN-1

Wild winds weep, The. Mad Song. William Blake. IJHIL; NAEL-6v2

Wild wing my notes, fierce passions urge the strain. Anne Batten Cristall. RWP *Fr.* Enthusiast, The. Songs of Arla.

Wild winter wind, A. Richard Wright. APT-2

Wild With It. Aliki Barnstone. ViWalt

Wild woman of the forests, The. Mirabai. WoPoe; WPoS, *tr. by* Jane Hirshfield

Wild World. Cat Stevens. UV

Wild-cat come-upon. First English Wildcat, The. Colin Simms. Oth

"Wilde is the easiest", said my master, one. Lőrinc Szabó. IQMS *Fr.* Cricket Music.

Wilderness. Faye George. PoCoUp

Wilderness. Lorine Niedecker. OxBoAm

Wilderness. Vern Rutsala. UrbNat

Wilderness. Carl Sandburg. RaBo

Wilderness, A. Tu Mu. CCL1, *tr. by* H. A. Giles

Wilderness, The. Sidney Keyes.
  "Red rock wilderness, The." OBWP; PoWW

Wilderness alone remains, A. Wilderness, A. Tu Mu. CCL1, *tr. by* H. A. Giles

Wilderness Gothic. Alfred Wellington Purdy. BrAP; HeIP-4; NoP-4

Wilderness and the solitarie place shall be glad for them, The. Bible, *O.T.* OBVE *Fr.* Isaiah.

Wilderspin. Mary Elizabeth Coleridge. ViWPN; VWP

Wildest idea!!!, The / Of Frankie Avalon. (LL) Double Trouble. David Trinidad. PmAP; SUP

Wildflowers. Richard Howard. NoAM

Wildlife. Tracy Philpot. AmPoNex

Wildlife. Karen Williams. BRtP

Wildling Peace. Yehuda Amichai. NRoS, *tr. by* Esther Raizen

Wildly and mournfully the Indian drum. American Forest Girl, The. Felicia Dorothea Hemans. RWP

Wildsisters Bar. Judith Vollmer. SwNoth

Wildwest. Archibald MacLeish. AmWaPo

Wilful, credulous, obstinate, old man, A. Munich. Sir Alec Cairncross. EdScPo

Will. L. S. Asekoff. KGB

Will, The. John Donne. NoSic

Will a god trust in the world. (LL) Hedgehog. Paul Muldoon. NAMCP V.2; NoAM; PBCIP; WaAnP

Will a man come for me? Song of a Marriageable Girl. *Unknown*. WoPoe, *tr. by* Willard Trask

Will a mouth that's muttered its goodbyes. Joseph Brodsky. TCRusP *Fr.* Sonnets on the Statue of Mary, Queen of Scots, in the Luxembourg Gardens, Paris.

Will and Testament. Isabella Whitney. *See* Aucthour Maketh Her Wyll and Testament, The.

Will anyone tell me what Minne is? Walther von der Vogelweide. GePo

Will appear as short as one. (LL) On a Fly Drinking out of [*or* from] His Cup. William Oldys. OBEV; OxAEP-1; OxBEV

Will be remembered by a random few. Night before the last day of January, The. Kona Macphee. BeAl

Will betray the company I keep. (LL) Disquieting Muses, The. Sylvia Plath. NALW; NAMCP V.2

Will bury their own, don't worry. (LL) Journey, The. James Wright. CAP-8; GPTC; NAAL-5; NoAM

Will Campbell Displays His Craniotribe. H. J. Van Peenen. BloBone

Will cave in on him by and by. (LL) Renascence. Edna St. Vincent Millay. BRP; ColAP; MoAmPo

Will cease to translate silence. One Day I Know the Page. Amina Saïd. PoArWo, *tr. by* Lucy McNair

Will commit that indiscretion. (LL) Garden, The: "Like a skein of loose silk blown against a wall." Ezra Pound. APT-1; BrAP; HeIP-4; MoAmPo; NIL-7; NIP-4; NoP-4; NoP-5; OxBoAm; PoPoPo

Will drown the silence. (LL) Boundaries. José Emilio Pacheco. PoetW; STV; TCLAP, *tr. by* John Frederick Nims

Will find its symbol, the woman thinks. (LL) History: "Everything's a metaphor, some wise." Rita Dove. ExTi; FFC; WaAnP

Will flash along the chords and go. (LL) Alfred Tennyson. NAEL-6v2; NAEL-7v2; NoP-5 *Fr.* In Memoriam A. H. H.

Will go on prancing, proud and unafraid. (LL) Aunt Jennifer's Tigers. Adrienne Rich. BrAP; ColAP; HeIP-4; NALW; NAMCP V.2; NIL-7; NIP-4; NoAM; NoP-4; NoP-5; OPOU; OxBoAm; TRP

Will He No Come Back Again? *Unknown*. OBEV

Will hear of as a god. (LL) How We Heard the Name. Alan Dugan. NoAM; PtR; YaYoPo

Will I! Will You Write Me a Christmas Poem? Lorine Niedecker. FTOS

Will I die? you ask. And so I enter on. For Andrew. Fleur Adcock. BeAl

Will i hate mirrors? Rebecca. E. Ethelbert Miller. ISC

Will it ever be finished, this house. Oeuvre. Lucien Stryk. IllVoic

Will it last? he says. Snowflake Which Is Now and Hence Forever, The. Archibald MacLeish. NoP-4; NoP-5

Will it snow, or will it rain? Chŏngsŏn Arirang. *Korean Oral Tradition*. CATKP, *tr. by* David R. McCann

Will know where they are by the absence. Emigrants. Jane Griffiths. NeBl; StAl

Will lead my steps aright. (LL) To a Waterfowl. William Cullen Bryant. APN-1; ColAP; CtM; ITBLP; NAAL-3; NAAL-5; NAAPv.1; NCAP; NoP-4; NoP-5; OWoS; OxBoAm; SoSe-8; TFi; WaAnP

Will linger, though enjoyed, like joy in memory yet. (LL) Stanzas Written in Dejection, Near Naples [*or* —December 1818, near Naples]. Percy Bysshe Shelley. ItP; NAEL-6v2; NAEL-7v2; NAWM-7v2; NoP-4; NoP-5; NPBRoP

Will, lost in a sea of trouble. Archilochus. AmFaPo, *tr. by* Kenneth Rexroth

Will Love again awake. Muse and Poet. Robert Bridges. OBMV

Will make the Gods of humane crimes partake. (LL) I am that Dido which thou here do'st see. Ausonius. NoSic; OBVE

Will make the whole read human and exact. (LL) Devil's Advice to Story-Tellers, The. Robert Graves. NAEL-6v2; NoAM

Will make their answer to the shuttered heart. (LL) Poet's Obligation. Pablo Neruda. PoetW; VCWP, *tr. by* Alastair Reid

Will make your glistering [*or* glist'ring] gold but more to shine. (LL) Prologue, The: "To sing of wars, of captain[e]s, and of kings." Anne Bradstreet. BASC; BrAP; EMWP; NAAL-3; NAAL-5; NAAPv.1; NALW; NoP-4; NoP-5; OxBoAm; PEW; TCAPo

Will mean the resurrection of her eyes. (LL) Her Eyes. Helen Hunt Jackson. PoBW; TCAPo

Will never come back to me. (LL) Break, Break, Break. Alfred Tennyson. BrAP; BRP; ClHu; HeIP-4; NAEL-6v2; NAEL-7v2; NIL-7; NIP-4; NoP-4; NoP-5; SoSe-8; TFi; TreFP; WaAnP; WeW-3

Will no young British bard, on rhyme intent. Edward Davies. AngWePo *Fr.* Chepstow: A Poem.

Will not be there. (LL) That the Science of Cartography Is Limited. Eavan Boland. EMP; HarvBoo; NAEL-7v2; NoP-4; NoP-5

Will not respond, choked off by tears of joy. (LL) Flowers, and tall-stalked grasses, and a bee. Ivan Alekseievich Bunin. GI; WoPoe, *tr. by* David Curzon and Vladislav L. Gucrassev

Will not tolerate will expend offer known facts armed with knives. Tactics. Jen Hofer. Eno

Will one of you go. Asking Favors. Wilma Elizabeth McDaniel. GeoHom

Will people accept them? Ezra Pound. PoA 2002 *Fr.* Contemporania.

Will press the life-drops from the heart. (LL) Slave Auction, The. Frances Ellen Watkins Harper. APN-2; ColAP; ISC; NAAPv.1; PCW

Will pronounce the latter tribe / as your type. (LL) Joseph Brodsky. AmWaPo; FaBoWar

Will remain when there is no heart to break for it. (LL) Credo: "My friend from Asia has powers and magic, he plucks a blue leaf from the young blue-gum." Robinson Jeffers. MoAmPo; OxBoAm

Will Run Like Rabbits for Food. Chris O. Cook. FreRad

Will shed some light, but never keep us warm. (LL) Love-Letter-Burning. Daniel Hall. NoP-4; NoP-5

Will snarl—and man can never be alone. (LL) Wolves, The. Allen Tate. APT-2; NAAPv.2; OxBoAm

Will soon learn to hunt. (LL) Why There Are No Unicorns. Judith Ortiz Cofer. PfSP; PueRic

'Will sprawl, now that the heat of day is best. Caliban upon Setebos; or, Natural Theology in the Island. Robert Browning. NAEL-6v2; NAEL-7v2; OxAEP-2

Will Spring Return to Stolen Fields? Yi Sanghwa. CAMKP, *tr. by* David R. McCann

Will tear through you with his tangled. One Night America: A Boy and His Blowtorch. M. Loncar. NAPBL

Will, The. Buland Al-Haidari. IrPoTo, *tr. by* Hussein Kadhim and Christopher Merrill

Will the machinegunners please step forward? (LL) Poem Some People Will Have to Understand, A. Imamu Amiri Baraka. GT; RaBo

Will the Real Me Please Stand Up? A. L. Hendriks. PML

Will the wise Elephant desert the wood. Nature Queries [*or* Epistle to Mr. Fox, from Hampton Court]. Lord John Hervey. STuOW

Will there be snowfall on lofty Soracte. Winter in Brighton. Mortimer Collins. NPeEn

Will there be time for eggnogs and eclogues. What the Spider Heard. Weldon Kees. NoP-5

Will there never come a season. To R. K. James Kenneth Stephen. NBLV; UV

Will They Always Remember. Tracy Clarke. InTrad

Will they never fade or pass! Farmer Remembers the Somme, The. Vance Palmer. NOBAu

Will those dreams. What the Deal, Son? Kevin Powell. BRtP

Will to Will. Keith Waldrop. PmAP

Will wake from sleep and perhaps bark back. (LL) Cemetery Nights. Stephen Dobyns. CAP-8; StAl

Will waste, as this flea's death took life from thee. (LL) Flea, The. John Donne. AmFaPo; BASC; BrAP; FSCP; NAEL-6v1; NAEL-7v1; NBLV; NIL-7; NIP-4; NoP-4; NoP-5; NoSic; OxAEP-1; TFi; WaAnP

We will tell the bees be bees tell us it's no sadder—another fall whose ever fall it is? Telling the Bees. Carol Frost. CAP-8

Will Ye Na Can Ye Na Let Me Be. *Unknown*. FaBoVe

Will Ye No Come Back Again? Carolina Oliphant, Baroness Nairne. NePenScot

Will You Be as Hard? Douglas Hyde. IrLP; OBMV, *tr. by* Augusta, Lady Gregory

Will you be back on New Year's Day? (LL) Emmanuel Hocquard. OnScMo; YaTCFP *Fr.* At Christmas.

Will You Crucify Your King? Michael Field. ViWPN

Will you find out the secret. Secret, The. Fanny Carrión de Fierro. TANSG, *tr. by* Sally Cheney Bell

Will you glimmer on the sea? Moonrise. "H. D." PoA 2002

Will you go away? Will You Go? *Unknown*. CATKP, *tr. by* Peter H. Lee

Will you heare the Mode of france. Mode of France, The. *Unknown*. PBRV

Will you leave the hills of Scotland? Highland Mary. Mary Weston Fordham. CBWP-2

Will you lend me your eyes to look at you? Myopia. Biancamaria Frabotta. CItWP, *tr. by* Cinzia Sartini Blum and Lara Trubowitz

Will You Love Me When I'm Old? *Unknown*. ITBLP

Will you marry it, marry it, marry it. (LL) Applicant, The. Sylvia Plath. BeAl; EmeKit; NAMCP V.2; OxBoAm; PoPoPo

Will You Marry Me? Taeko Tomioka. CFP, *tr. by* Aoyami Miyuki and Leza Lowitz

Will you permit me. Virgo Poem, The: Ouspensky Addresses a Congress of Virgoes. Charles Stein. AHA

Will you please rush down and see. To Close. William Carlos Williams. SAmP

Will you seek afar off? you surely come back at last. Walt Whitman. ChIV-1 *Fr.* Song for Occupations, A.

Will you speak before I am gone? will you prove already too late? (LL) Walt Whitman. CAGL; ColAP; NAWM-7v2 *Fr.* Song of Myself.

Will You Still Be Mine? Tom Adair. ReLy

Will you stop for a while, stop trying to pull yourself. Moderation Is Not a Negation of Intensity, But Helps Avoid Monotony. John Tagliabue. GoPo

Will you take care? Farewell. Adriaan Morriën. TuT, *tr. by* Peter van de Kamp

Will you turn a deaf ear. Questioner Who Sits So Sly, The. W. H. Auden. OxAEP-2

"Will you walk a little faster?" said a [*or* the] whiting to a [*or* the] snail. Lewis Carroll. NoAM; OxAEP-2; UV *Fr.* Alice's Adventures in Wonderland.

"Will you walk into my parlor?" said the Spider to the Fly. Spider and the Fly, The. Mary Howitt. ITBLP; UV

Will you, won't you, will you, won't you, won't you join the dance? (LL) Lewis Carroll. NoAM; OxAEP-2; UV *Fr.* Alice's Adventures in Wonderland.

Will You Write Me a Christmas Poem? Lorine Niedecker. FTOS

Willa Mae's battered foot locker holds. Queen Ijo's Blues. Carole Boston Weatherford. FuFl

Willed down, waited for, in place at last and for good. Settle Bed, The. Seamus Heaney. NoP-5

Willesden Gree. Jimmy Pearse. UV

William. Lesley Dauer. AmPoNex

William and Margaret. David Mallet. OxAEP-1

William Bailey. George Crabbe. *Fr.* Tales of the Hall.

William Blake. James Thomson. CABP

William Carlos Williams. Cornelius Eady. GT

William / Carlos / Williams / alive! Louis Zukofsky. PFTM-1 *Fr.* Songs of Degrees.

William Dewy, Tranter Reuben, Farmer Ledlow late at plough. Friends Beyond. Thomas Hardy. FaBoVe; OBEV

William has whole buildings inside him. William. Lesley Dauer. AmPoNex

William / Holden as. Bridge. Bill Berkson. Eno

William House and Family. Julia A. Moore. STuOW

     Hic Finis Rapto 2. STuOW

William Lamb's Return from Paris, Asking Me My Wish. Lady Caroline Lamb. RWP *Fr.* Fugitive Pieces and Reminiscences of Lord Byron with Some Original Poetry, Letters and Recollections of Lady Caroline Lamb, ed. I. Nathan.

William Lloyd Garrison. Henrietta Cordelia Ray. CBWP-3

William Oliver maker. Ancestors. Raymond Garlick. AngWePo

William Shakespeare. William Cole. AmWit *Fr.* Uncoupled Couplets.

William Street. Kenneth Slessor. BMAP

William Stukeley made his own Stonehenge. Ronald Johnson. OBGa

William Wordsworth (1770-1850). Gavin Ewart. NoAM

William Yeats in Limbo. Sidney Keyes. MoBrPo

William Zanzinger killed poor Hattie Carroll. Lonesome Death of Hattie Carroll, The. Bob Dylan. WaAnP

Williams: An Essay. Denise Levertov. PmAP

Williams Was Wrong. Greg Delanty. WaAnP

Williamsbridge. Jana Beranová. TuT, *tr. by* Aidan Sharkey

Willie. Max Adeler. OBCoV

Willie Baird. Robert Williams Buchanan.

     Schoolmaster's Story, The. DiBP

Willie got born somewhere near Austin. Ballad for Bill Pickett, A. William D. Barney. TiP2

Willie Metcalf. Edgar Lee Masters. APT-1 *Fr.* Spoon River Anthology.

Willie poisoned Auntie's tea. Willie the Poisoner. *Unknown.* NTCP

Willie the Poisoner. *Unknown.* NTCP

Willie Winkie. William Miller. OxBEV

Willing. Paula McLain. AmPoNex

Willing it, my ailment. (LL) No Road. Philip Larkin. MoBrPo; OxAEP-2

Willing Mistress, The. Aphra Behn. NALW

Willing Mistress, The. Aphra Behn. LW

Willing to give thy Essence. Vow 2. Pam Rehm. IIR

Willingness. Chairil Anwar. PoetW, *tr. by* Burton Raffel

Will-o'-Wisp. Nancy Morejón. TANSG, *tr. by* Joy Renjilian-Burgy

Willow. Elizabeth Delmore. NLP

Willow. Richard Watson Dixon. OBEV

Willow. Wang Chien. CCL1, *tr. by* Marsha Wagner

Willow. Willow. Wang Chien. CCL1, *tr. by* Marsha Wagner

Willow, The. Buson. EMJL *Fr.* Spring Breeze on the Kema Embankment.

Willow Eyebrows. Chao Luan-luan. CCL1; NDACCP, *tr. by* Chung Ling and Kenneth Rexroth

Willow herb, The. Rose Bay Willow Herb. Judy Ray. AtGh

Willow in Spring Wind: A Showing. Jorie Graham. ExTi

Willow Jar. Gu Cheng. WoBe *Fr.* Liquid Mercury.

Willow leans into the water, The. Serenade for Ilonka. Jenő Dsida. IQMS, *tr. by* Joseph Leftwich

Willow leaves fallen. EMJL, *tr. by* Haruo Shirane

Willow leaves fallen, The. Buson. EH, *tr. by* Robert Hass

Willow Poem. William Carlos Williams. WaAnP

Willow Song. Anne Stevenson. NoP-4

Willowherb. Peter Rafferty. NLP

Willows bend to the sea breeze. Late Spring. Tzu Yeh. CrYelRi, *tr. by* Sam Hamill

Willows carried a slow sound, The. Repose of Rivers. Hart Crane. APT-2; ColAP; MoAmPo; NAMCP V.1; OxBoAm

Willows droop, The. Winter and Spring Scene, A. Henry David Thoreau. NCAP

Willow's knotty threads, The. White Echo. A. R. Ammons. PfSP

Willows shadows hang straight. Tune: "Prince Lan-Ling." Chou Pang-yen. ChinPo, *tr. by* Ye Weilian [*or* Yeh Wei-lien *or* Wai-lim Yip]

Willows tangle like silk threads. Spring. Shen Yüeh. CCL1, *tr. by* Anne Birrell

Willows trail such glory that the birds are struck dumb, The. Spring View. Tran Nhan-tong. WoPoe, *tr. by* Nguyen Ngoc Bich

Willows whisper very, very low, The. Noonday Rest. Mathilde Blind. ViWPN

Willow-tassels grow in tremors of the spring wind. Lines to Do with Youth. Witter Bynner. PoA 2002

Willowware Cup. James Merrill. VCAP

50: Willowwood ("And now Love sang: but his was such a song"). Dante Gabriel Rossetti. CABP; NAEL-6v2; OxBSo *Fr.* House of Life, The.

49: Willowwood ("I sat with Love upon a woodside well"). Dante Gabriel Rossetti. NAEL-6v2; OxBSo *Fr.* House of Life, The.

51: Willowwood ("O ye, all ye that walk in Willowwood"). Dante Gabriel Rossetti. NAEL-6v2; OxBSo *Fr.* House of Life, The.

52: Willowwood ("So sang he: and as meeting rose and rose"). Dante Gabriel Rossetti. NAEL-6v2; OxBSo *Fr.* House of Life, The.

Wilpena Pound. Charles Buckmaster. BMAP

Wilson and Pilcer and Snack stood before the zoo elephant. Elephants Are Different to Different People. Carl Sandburg. MoAmPo

Wilson County Farmer, A. James Applewhite. LPSFW

Wilt thou follow me into the wild? Mistress to the Spirit of Her Lover, The. Charlotte Dacre. RWP

Wilt thou forgive that sin[ne] where I begun[ne]. Hymn[e] to God the Father, A. John Donne. BASC; FSCP; NAEL-6v1; NAEL-7v1; NoP-5; NOSC; NPeEn; OxBEV; SacPr; SoSe-8; TFi

Wilt thou go with me sweet maid. Invite to Eternity, An. John Clare. NAEL-6v2; NAEL-7v2

Wilt Thou not visit me? Prayer, The. Jones Very. APN-1

Wilt thou seal up the avenues of ill? Ralph Waldo Emerson. APN-1 *Fr.* Quatrains.

Wilt thou use turners craft still? ye by my trouth. John Heywood. PBRV *Fr.* Epygrams.

Wily Fox, The. Edward Davies. OBWVE, *tr. by* Joseph P. Clancy

Wind. Dionne Brand. NOxBChV

Wind: "This is the wind, the wind in a field of corn." James Fenton. BeAl; NAEL-6v2; NAEL-7v2; NeBrP

Wind. Hsüeh T'ao [*or* Xue Tao]. ColAnChi, *tr. by* Jeanne Larsen

Wind. Ted Hughes. HarvBoo; NAEL-6v2; NAEL-7v2; NoP-4; NoP-5

Wind: "Like a well-trained soldier." Ok-Ku Kang. WhBo

Wind. Improvisation. Alfred Kreymborg. APT-1

Wind. Dana Levin. AmPoNex

Wind: "Wind: what is it? You don't see it but you hear it, and you feel its force." Eliot Weinberger. WANABP

Wind, The. Thomas Holley Chivers. APN-1

Wind, The. Dafydd ap Gwilym. WoPoe, *tr. by* Daniel Huws

Wind, The. Dafydd ap Gwilym. OBWVE, *tr. by* Joseph P. Clancy

Wind, The: "Wide sea—black night—I woke up lovesick." Léon Damas. SonAtl, *tr. by* Kurt Ganzl and Christophe Mirambeau

Wind, The. Emily Dickinson. APN-2

Wind, The. Boris Leonidovich Pasternak. RusPo, *tr. by* Robert Arthur Douglas Ford

Wind, The. Christina Georgina Rossetti. *See* Who Has Seen the Wind?

Wind, The. Space. Verneda Sagay-Lights. BtF

Wind, The. Vladimir Alekseievich Soloukhin. TCRusP, *tr. by* Daniel Weissbort

Wind, The. James Stephens. NoAM

Wind, The. Sung Yu. ColAnChi, *tr. by* Burton Watson

Wind. Lizette Woodworth Reese. APT-1

Wind. Gary Soto. NoAM *Fr.* Elements of San Joaquin, The.

Wind, a rustle of leaves, The. Edge of Autumn, The. Michael Anania. NoAM

Wind and clouds are storming angrily, The. Running Into Snow While Journeying Through the Suburbs. Yu Hsin. CCL1, *tr. by* John Frodsham

Wind and frost on ordinary silk. On a Portrait of a Falcon. Tu Fu [*or* Du Fu]. CrYelRi, *tr. by* Sam Hamill

Wind and Glacier Voices. Simon J. Ortiz. HATNAP

Wind and Hardscrabble. Walter McDonald. TiP2

Wind and Silver. Amy Lowell. HeIP-4; MoAmPo; Spl; TCAPo

Wind and the Moon, The. George Macdonald. NOxBChV

Wind / and the sound. Long Beach Suite. Tom Wayman. BrAP

Wind and Tree. Paul Muldoon. NPeEn

Wind and Water and Stone. Octavio Paz. ItP; TCLAP, *tr. by* Mark Strand

Wind and waves rising on Lake Tung-t'ing. Stopping at Night at Hsiang-yin. Ch'i-chi. CSKM, *tr. by* Burton Watson

Wind and Window Flower. Robert Frost. MoW

Wind animates the weathervane. (LL) Riddle: "Invisible, chimerical." Daryl Hine. NoP-4; NoP-5

Wind, Ant, History. Özdemir İnce. WoPoe, *tr. by* Talat Sait Halman

Wind appears, The. Barnyard, The. Yvor Winters. APT-2

Wind at the Door, The. William Barnes. OxAEP-2

Wind at the ear says *June*. June. Bei Dao. WoBe, *tr. by* Iona Man-Cheong and Eliot Weinberger

Wind at war with wind. Warlike Angels, The. Rafael Alberti. AF, *tr. by* Geoffrey Connell

Wind at Your Door, The. Robert David Fitzgerald. NOBAu

Wind away, The. (LL) Small Song. A. R. Ammons. NAMCP V.2; NoAM

Wind begun to knead the Grass, The [First Version]. Emily Dickinson. NIL-7; WeW-3

(This wind begun to knead the Grass.) NAAL-3

(Wind begun to rock the Grass, The.) NAAL-3

Wind begun to rock the Grass, The. Emily Dickinson. *See* Wind begun to knead the Grass, The.

Wind begun to rock the Grass, The. Thunder-Storm, A. Emily Dickinson. APN-2; NCAP; WeW-3

Wind billowing out the seat of my britches, The. Child on Top of a Greenhouse. Theodore Roethke. NoP-4; NoP-5; NOxBChV; PtR

Wind, bird, and tree. Words, The. David Wagoner. OxBoAm; PoA 2002

Wind Blew like Water. Alice Sadongei. HATNAP

Wind Bloweth Where It Listeth, The. Countee Cullen. GT

Wind blows, The. Wind God Sends Forth, The. Pak Sôwôn. EcSo, *tr. by* Julie C. Park

Wind blows a piece of paper to my feet, The. At the Crossroads. Bill Knott. PBCAP

Wind blows along the trails, The. My Mother Tongue. Gary Daniel. OGAHCP, *tr. by* Boadiba and Jack Hirschman

Wind blows and makes the light tremble, The. Inna L'vovna Lisnyanskaya. ItGoST, *tr. by* Judith Hemschemeyer

Wind blows, and with a little broom, The. Cathleen Sweeping. George Johnston. IFF

Wind blows hard across the polder, The. North of Amsterdam. Larry Rubin. ArBi

Wind blows high above the people's heads. North Wind, The. Frederick van Eeden. TuT, *tr. by* Michael Longley

Wind Blows High, The. *Unknown.* FaBoVe

Wind blows lilacs out of the east, The. Santa Fe. Joy Harjo. ICANM

Wind blows the line out from his fishing pole, The. Fisherman. Ou-yang Hsiu. BLT, *tr. by* Kenneth Rexroth

Wind blows up the tent like a balloon, The. Crimson Tent. John Dos Passos. PoA 2002

Wind Burial. Hwang Tonggyu. CAMKP, *tr. by* Kevin O'Rourke

Wind Burial 1. Hwang Tonggyu. CAMKP, *tr. by* Anthony, Brother of Taizé

Wind Burial 3. Hwang Tonggyu. CAMKP, *tr. by* Anthony, Brother of Taizé

Wind came in for several thousand miles all night, The. On an East Wind from the Wars. Alan Dugan. AF; GPTC

Wind came up out of the sea, A. Daybreak. Henry Wadsworth Longfellow. ITBLP

Wind, Clouds, and the Delicate Curve of the World. Louis Simpson. ASA

Wind, cold, rain. History of France. Kenward Elmslie. NYP2

Wind comes from opposite poles, The. Marriage, The. Mark Strand. NoAM

Wind comes from the north, The. Suspense. D. H. Lawrence. MoBrPo

Wind comes rushing from the sea, The. One Night at Victoria Beach. Gabriel Okara. PoetW

Wind Debates Asian Immigration, The. Peter Rose. BMAP

Wind disturbing the eave-chimes again. Tune: "San-fan Yü-lou Jen." *Unknown.* ColAnChi, *tr. by* James I. Crump

Wind Domes, The. Joyelle McSweeney. LegDan

Wind doth blow to-day, my love, The. Unquiet Grave, The. *Unknown.* CABP; HeIP-4; NoP-4; NoP-5; TFi; WeW-3; WoPoe

Wind dying, I find a city deserted, except for crowds of, The. Poet. Keith Waldrop. OnScMo

Wind finds the northwest gap, fall comes. Heart of Autumn. Robert Penn Warren. APT-2; ColAP; FuPo; InGu; WaAnP

Wind flapped loose, the wind was still, The. Woodspurge, The. Dante Gabriel Rossetti. CABP; CtM; HeIP-4; NAEL-6v2; NAEL-7v2; NoP-4; NoP-5; NPeEn; OBEV; OxBEV; TFi

Wind / Flies above the sea, The. Wind, The. Vladimir Alekseievich Soloukhin. TCRusP, *tr. by* Daniel Weissbort

Wind frightens my dog, but I bathe in it, The. April Gale. Ivor Gurney. Spl

Wind from a Wing, A. William Stafford. CAP-8

Wind from the east, oh Lapwing of the day. Khwaja Shams-ad-din Muhammad Hafiz. TAL *Fr.* Odes.

Wind from the northwestern quarter is lifting him high above. Hawk's Cry in Autumn, The. Joseph Brodsky. WaAnP, *tr. by* Alan Myers and the author

Wind frustrates itself held, The. Song to the Banyan. Virgil Suárez. AmPoNex

Wind gathers the lake. Teaching My Husband to Swim. Lesley-Anne Bourne. Coast

Wind, gigantic, wrestles the April leaves;. April Wind. Frederick Turner. RA

Wind giving presence to fragments. (LL) Sonnet 1. Ted Berrigan. FTOS; NYP2 *Fr.* Sonnets, The.

Wind God Sends Forth, The. Pak Sôwôn. EcSo, *tr. by* Julie C. Park

Wind grinds bones to dust, The. Wind Grinds, The. Eytan Eytan. PoCho, *tr. by* Moshe Dor

Wind Grinds, The. Eytan Eytan. PoCho, *tr. by* Moshe Dor

Wind had hanged itself on the plane tree, The. Wind, Ant, History. Özdemir İnce. WoPoe, *tr. by* Talat Sait Halman

Wind has all its answers, The. Night Things. Greg Kuzma. InvLad

Wind has at last got into the clock, The. Wind, the Clock, the We, The. Laura Riding Jackson. APT-2; FaBoVe

Wind has blown a corner of your shawl, The. Bright Sunlight. Amy Lowell. APT-1

Wind has blown the rain away and blown, A. E. E. Cummings. HarvBoo; MoAmPo

Wind has died, The. To the Tune: Happiness Approaches. Li Ch'ing-chao. CrYelRi, *tr. by* Sam Hamill

Wind has subsided, The. Tune: Spring at Wu Ling. Li Ch'ing-chao. ColAnChi, *tr. by* Jiaosheng Wang

Wind Has Such a Rainy Sound, The. Christina Georgina Rossetti. TLR

Wind has such a rainy sound, The. Wind Has Such a Rainy Sound, The. Christina Georgina Rossetti. TLR

Wind in a Box. Terrance Hayes. LegDan

Wind in bare vines. Emily Wilson. LegDan

Wind in the fur of living buffalo dead. Words. William Heyen. AmZen

Wind / In the house of the heart. Four Beats of the Heart. Sajidah al-Musawi. IrPoTo, *tr. by* Basima Qattan Bezirgan and Elizabeth Fernea

Wind in the park. Envoi: Washington Square Park. Myra Cohn Livingston. SSCS

Wind in the pines cleans man's ears, The. At Daedun Temple. Jungkwan Ilson. BecRai, *tr. by* Kim Daljin, Kim Won-Chung and Christopher Merrill

Wind in the Room, The. Karl Krolow. GTCP, *tr. by* Reinhold Grimm

Wind in the Trees, The. Cathy Song. OpBo

Wind in the west / Fallen leaves. Buson. ZenPo, *tr. by* Takashi Ikemoto and Lucien Stryk

Wind in the Willow. Jack Segal. ReLy

Wind in the willow, why do you weep? Wind in the Willow. Jack Segal. ReLy

Wind in the Willows, The. Kenneth Grahame.

Carol. RSR

Duck"s Ditty. NOxBChV; NTCP; WHSM

Song of Mr Toad, The. NOxBChV

Wind Invites Wind. Chimako Tada. VCWP, *tr. by* Naoshi Koriyama and Edward Lueders

Wind Is Blind, The. Alice Thompson Meynell. MoBrPo

Wind is blowing, The. Pak Mogwöl [*or* Mokwöl]. CAMKP *Fr.* Nature of Gravel, The.

Wind is blowing, A. The book being written. Novel, The. Denise Levertov. BrAP

Wind is blowing from side to side, The. Old Trees with Hands Sawing the Air. Margit Szécsi. IQMS, *tr. by* Agnes Arany-Makkai

Wind Is Blowing West, The. Joseph Ceravolo. NYP2; OxBoAm

Wind is born from the land, The. Wind, The. Sung Yu. ColAnChi, *tr. by* Burton Watson

Wind is cold, forbidding, The.   Truth.   Kim Chiha.   CAMKP, tr. by Kevin O'Rourke

Wind Is Coming and I Love You, The.   Binyo Ivanov.   CSCBP, tr. by Georgi Belev and Lisa Sapinkopf

Wind is not nigh.   Zone of Death.   William Everson.   SacPr

Wind is not right today, The.   Bodega, Goodbye.   Edwin Honig.   NoAM

Wind is passing by, The. (LL)   Who Has Seen the Wind?   Christina Georgina Rossetti.   BLPJKO; ITBLP; NTCP; SacPr; TLR; WHSW

Wind is piercing chill, The.   Battlefield.   Richard Aldington.   OBWP

Wind is ruffling the tawny pelt, A.   Far Cry from Africa, A.   Derek Walcott.   AmFaPo; BrAP; ESEAA; HeIP-4; NAEL-6v2; NAEL-7v2; NAMCP V.2; NIL-7; NoAM; NoP-4; NoP-5

Wind keen, the sky high, the gibbons wailing, The.   On Climbing the Heights on the Ninth Day of the Ninth Moon.   Tu Fu [or Du Fu].   TAL

Wind Last Night Blew Down.   Unknown.   WoPoe, tr. by Virginia Olsen Baron and Chung Seuk Park

Wind last night blew down.   Wind Last Night Blew Down.   Unknown.   WoPoe, tr. by Virginia Olsen Baron and Chung Seuk Park

Wind led me here, The.   Wind Thoughts.   Pinkie Gordon Lane.   GT

Wind, like the dodo's. (LL)   Bedtime Story.   George MacBeth.   EmeKit; SoSe-8

Wind may blow the snow about, The.   Country Boy in Winter, A.   Sarah Orne Jewett.   APN-2; ColAP

Wind of autumn sends leaves fluttering down, The.   Singing-Girls in the Brazen Bird.   Ho Hsun.   CCL1, tr. by John Frodsham

Wind of Liberty.   Amélia Veiga.   HAWP, tr. by Julia Kirst

Wind of old cocoa farms, The.   Africa Sky.   Kojo Laing.   HBAPE

Wind of Our Going: Adagio Ma Non Troppo.   Patricia Goedicke.   MiVo

Wind, one brilliant day, called, The.   Wind, One Brilliant Day, The.   Antonio Machado Ruiz.   RaBo; WED, tr. by Robert Bly

Wind one morning sprung up from sleep, The.   William Howitt.   NOxBChV

Wind / only, The.   Song of the Trees.   Unknown.   OBVE, tr. by Frances Densmore

Wind. / Outside my suite, wind screams.   Stillborn Night.   Beth Brant.   ReEnLa

Wind paces on the lower branch, The.   Olga Sulchinskaya.   CRWP, tr. by Richard McKane

Wind piercing, hill bare, hard to find shelter.   Unknown.   OBWVE Fr. Winter.

Wind plays with the moon; the moon, with the wind, The.   Linked Verses.   Vietnamese Oral Tradition.   CaDao, tr. by John Balaban

Wind pushed the sun, The.   On The Day They Buried My Mother.   Miguel Piñero.   PueRic

Wind rips through the.   David Kherdian.   UrbNat Fr. Taking the Soundings on Third Avenue.

Wind rises among the water chestnut, A.   Yun Sŏndo.   CATKP Fr. Angler's Calendar, The.

Wind rocks our tent.   The storm.   Thunder Storm.   George Keithley.   PasH

Wind rose cold under our robes, and straw blew loose.   Boy Shepherds' Simile, The.   David Bottoms.   PoA 2002

Wind runs free across our plains, The.   For Adolf Eichmann.   Primo Levi.   AF, tr. by Ruth Feldman and Brian Swann

Wind sal[l] blaw for evermair, The. (LL)   Twa Corbies, The.   Unknown.   NePenScot; NoP-5; NPeEn; OBEV; OWoS; OxBEV

Wind shoves my New Year's Day sun in my face, The.   Edoardo Sanguineti.   ItPo Fr. Scartabello.

Wind Sickness Strikes.   Po Chü-i.   NDACCP, tr. by David Hinton

Wind sighs through the Flame tree, The [or A].   Homesick Bride, The.   Vietnamese Oral Tradition.   CaDao, tr. by John Balaban

Wind skips in from the sea, The.   Poetry Reading at the Varna Ruins.   John Balaban.   TAPaP

Wind Song.   Carl Sandburg.   MoAmPo

Wind Speaks, The.   Alfred Austin.

"Flocks of the wandering waves I hold, The."   VerBaPo

Wind sprays pale dirt into my mouth, The.   Elements of San Joaquin, The.   Gary Soto.   GeoHom; PBCAP

Wind stirs lightly as the sun's, The.   Unknown.   WoPoe Fr. Cambridge Songs.

Wind stood up, and gave a shout.   Wind, The.   James Stephens.   NoAM

Wind stretches fields, The.   Train.   Georgi Belev.   CSCBP, tr. by the author and Lisa Sapinkopf

Wind strokes the posters, The.   Movie-house.   Philippe Soupault.   YaTCFP, tr. by Mary Ann Caws

Wind suffers of blowing, The.   Wind Suffers [of Blowing], The.   Laura Riding Jackson.   NAAPv.2; NoP-4; NoP-5; NPeEn

Wind, surf, rock-cliff, sunlight.   Power Quest, Sooke Park.   Jarold Ramsey.   PoCoUp

Wind sways over my face, The.   Stroll to Parfondeval, A.   Remco Campert.   TuT, tr. by Theo Dorgan

Wind sways the pines, A.   Dirge in Woods.   George Meredith.   NAEL-6v2; OBEV

Wind—tapped like a tired Man, The.   Wind's Visit, The.   Emily Dickinson.   APN-2

Wind—tapped like a tired man, The.   Emily Dickinson.   FaBoVe; MoAmPo

Wind that melted the spring hills, The.   U T'ak.   CATKP, tr. by Peter H. Lee

Wind that rolls a heart on the pavement of courtyards, The.   Man Condemned to Death, The.   Jean Genet.   CAGL, tr. by David Fisher and Guy Wernham

Wind that scatters, The.   Ki no Tsurayuki.   WoPoe, tr. by Helen Craig McCullough

Wind that went through the head left it plural, The.   Reading Reverdy.   Ron Padgett.   OxBoAm

Wind, the Clock, the We, The.   Laura Riding Jackson.   APT-2; FaBoVe

Wind, the season-climate mixer.   Clear and Colder.   Robert Frost.   OBCoV

Wind the wind the wind blows high, The.   Wind Blows High, The.   Unknown.   FaBoVe

Wind Thoughts.   Pinkie Gordon Lane.   GT

Wind thrashes the maple seed-pods, The.   John Ashbery.   APSN Fr. Skaters, The.

Wind to the Stones, The.   Pak Nohae.   CAMKP, tr. by Scott Swaner

Wind today is full of fish, The.   Rising Asleep.   Penelope Rosemont.   SurWo

Wind Turns, The.   Nicole Espagnol.   SurWo, tr. by Myrna Bell Rochester

Wind vast and slow, A.   Tomas Tranströmer.   WoBe Fr. Haiku.

Wind visions are honest.   Vision Shadows.   Simon J. Ortiz.   NAAL-5

Wind was a torrent of darkness among the gusty trees, The.   Highwayman, The.   Alfred Noyes.   BRP; ChAP; ITBLP; NOxBChV; OBNV; OBSP

Wind was in another country, and, The.   Mirage.   R. P. Blackmur.   APT-2

Wind was not, flat was, but was imminent.   Seas Incarnadine.   R. P. Blackmur.   APT-2

Wind waves the lotuses in the scented palace by the water, The.   For the Dancer of the King of Wu, When She Is Half Drunk.   Li Po.   CCL1; TAL, tr. by Robert Payne

Wind: what is it? You don't see it but you hear it, and you feel its force.   Wind.   Eliot Weinberger.   WANABP

Wind whines and whines the shingle.   On the Beach at Fontana.   James Joyce.   MoBrPo; OBMV; RaBo

Wind whines the wine-colored telephone lines.   Andy Hasselgard.   Dave Etter.   IllVoic

Wind whistles past, The.   Spanish Lullaby.   Aaron Kurtz.   Prolet, tr. by Amelia Glaser

Wind will call me—and some day I'll depart, The.   Some Day.   Ivan Davidkov.   CSCBP, tr. by Georgi Belev and Lisa Sapinkopf

Wind, wind, give me back my feather.   Child on the Shore, The.   Ursula K. Le Guin.   ASA

Wind won't come to draw smiles in the sand of dreams, The.   Elegy.   Yehuda Amichai.   PFTM-2, tr. by Stephen Mitchell

"Wind-blown clamour of the barnacle-geese, The." (LL)   Beggar to Beggar Cried.   William Butler Yeats.   NoAM; OxAEP-2

Windblown forest: the slender moon has fallen.   Night feast at the Tsos.   Tu Fu [or Du Fu].   ChinPo, tr. by Ye Weilian [or Yeh Wei-lien or Wai-lim Yip]

Windbreaker is white with a world map, The.   Self-Portrait in Tyvek(TM) Windbreaker.   James Merrill.   NAMCP V.2; OxBoAm

Wind-Clouds and Star-Drifts.   Oliver Wendell Holmes.
   9. Rights.
   Questions.   DiBP
   3. Sympathies.   APN-1

Windfall.   William Heyen.   PoCoUp

Windharp.   John Montague.   PNI

Windhover, The.   Gerard Manley Hopkins.   AmFaPo; BrAP; CABP; ClHu; MoBrPo; NAEL-6v2; NAEL-7v2; NAMCP V.1; NIL-7; NoAM; NoP-4; NoP-5; NPeEn; OWoS; OxAEP-2; OxBEV; OxBSo; PoPoPo; SacPr; TFi; TRP; WaAnP

Windigo.   Louise Erdrich.   NAMCP V.2; NoAM; PoPoPo

Winding around the waters of the world. (LL)   Theodore Roethke.   ColAP; NAMCP V.1; NoAM Fr. North American Sequence.

Winding Banks of Erne, The[: Or, The Emigrant's Adieu to His Birthplace].   William Allingham.   IrV

Winding Up.   Derek Walcott.   NoAM

Winding-up Time.   Jean Ingelow.   VWP

Windmill.   Gillian Clarke.   TCAWP

Windmill At Mandanthanunguna.   Pambardu.   NOBAu, tr. by George von Brandenstein

Windmills of Your Mind, The.   Alan Bergman and Marilyn Bergman.   ReLy

Window.   Meirion MacIntyre Huws.   BBMWP, tr. by Geriant Løvgreen

Window.   Carl Sandburg.   APT-1

Window, The.   Marianne Boruch.   AmAlph

Window, The.   Dino Campana.   STV, tr. by John Frederick Nims

Window, The.   Raymond Carver.   BLT

Window, The.   Robert Creeley.   FTOS; NoAM; PmAP

Window, The.   Enrique Gonzáles Martínez.   TCLAP, tr. by Elizabeth Gordon

Window, The. Lynda Hull. ExTi

Window, The. Derek Mahon. NoP-5

Window, The. Kay Sage. SurWo

Window, The: "I stand on tiptoe to reach the window that's open a crack." Boris Hristov. CSCBP, *tr. by* Georgi Belev and Lisa Sapinkopf

Window at Key West, A. Honor Moore. KGB; WiU

Window, at the Moment of Flame, The. Alicia Ostriker. PA9/11

Window Box. Thomas Scott Fisken. IJHIL

Window Dressing. William Peskett. PNI

Window into the ground, A. Skara Brae. Michael Longley. PBCIP

Window is nailed and boarded, The. Hallaig. Sorley MacLean. EdScPo; HarvBoo; NePenScot; NPeEn; WoPoe

Window Just Over the Street, The. Alice Cary. PoBW; SWaP

Window Ledge in the Atom Age. Elwyn Brooks White. NBLV

Window makes a frame for the sky, The. Collection, The. Zhao Zhenkai. VCWP, *tr. by* Chen Maiping and Bonnie S. McDougall

Window of Our Soul. Len Roberts. NevBe

Window of the little inn shows light, The. Hungarian Winter. Gyula Juhász. IQMS, *tr. by* Jess Perlman

Window open, The. Hearing. Tree Falling in a Vacant Forest, The. Linda Gregg. ExTi

Window Poems. Wendell Berry.
 "Peace. Let men, who cannot be brothers." UpMys

Window remained as before, The. The cold. Telegram. Milo De Angelis. NeIt, *tr. by* Lawrence Venuti

Window Seat at the Paradise. Lee Upton. AmAlph

Window Shopping. Lamont B. Steptoe. SpirFl

Window was made of ice with bears lumbering across it, The. Bad Dream. Louis MacNeice. NoAM

Window Washing. Phyllis Thompson. ICANM

Window window window pane. Summer Shower. David McCord. TLR

Windowpane I. Chŏng Chiyong. CAMKP, *tr. by* Anthony, Brother of Taizé

Windows. Guillaume Apollinaire. CuPo

Windows. Guillaume Apollinaire. YaTCFP, *tr. by* Roger Shattuck

Windows. Frank O'Hara. BodElec

Windows, The. George Herbert. BASC; NAEL-6v1; NAEL-7v1; NoP-4; NoP-5

Windows, The. Chris Wallace-Crabbe. BMAP

Windows, The: "Here is a child who presses his head to the ground." W. S. Merwin. PoChi

Windows are black tonight, The. The lamp. Prayer. Elaine Feinstein. HarvBoo

Windows bang, The. Nuit Blanche, Une. Emily Warn. FiBr

Window's length beyond the Pleiades, A. First Snow on an Airfield. John Ciardi. PoA 2002

Windows of my poetry are wide open on the boulevards and in the shop windows, The. Contrasts. Blaise Cendrars. CuPo

Windows of Sarajevo, The. David Grubb. RSaN

Windows of the Castle, The. Russell Edson. MotU

Windows wide through day and night, The. Last Days at Teddington. Thom Gunn. OBGa

Windowseat. Sandra Meek. OtW

Winds moving clouds. Winds. Jeannette Armstrong. OpeFie

Winds are bleak, stars are bright. Victoria Markets Recollected in Tranquility, The. Furnley Maurice. NOBAu

Winds are dark passages among the stars, The. Turtle. Peter Blue Cloud. HATNAP

Winds come blowing leaves astir. Peach. Shen Yüeh. CCL1, *tr. by* Anne Birrell

Winds' enclosure, Atlantic's premises, The. Hebrides, The. Michael Longley. PBCIP

Wind's hand, The. Federico García Lorca. PFTM-1 *Fr.* Night (Suite for Piano and Poet's Voice).

Winds here, and sleet, and frost that bites like steel. Winter Fields, The. Sir Charles G. D. Roberts. BrAP

Wind's in the heart of me, a fire's in my heels, A. Wanderer's Song, A. John Masefield. MoBrPo

Wind's Lament, The. John Morris-Jones. OBWVE, *tr. by* Anthony Conran

Wind's mane, The. Elena Lazutkina. CRWP, *tr. by* Robert Reid

Winds of Fate, The. Ella Wheeler Wilcox. BRP

Wind's on the wold, The. Inscription for an Old Bed. William Morris. OBEV

Wind's Visit, The. Emily Dickinson. APN-2

Winds whistle. Tune: "Vast Virtue." Kuan Han-ch'ing. ChinPo, *tr. by* Ye Weilian [*or* Yeh Wei-lien *or* Wai-lim Yip]

Winds: "Winds moving clouds." Jeannette Armstrong. OpeFie

Winds, Winds, Winds. Sergey Aleksandrovich Yesenin. TCRusP, *tr. by* Nigel Stott

Winds, winds, winds. Winds, Winds, Winds. Sergey Aleksandrovich Yesenin. TCRusP, *tr. by* Nigel Stott

Windsor Castle. Henry Howard, Earl of Surrey.
 Prisoned in Windsor, He Recounteth His Pleasure There Passed. CABP; NAEL-6v1; NAEL-7v1

Windsor-Forest [*or* Windsor Forest]. Alexander Pope.
 "Here too, 'tis sung, of old Diana stray'd." OxAEP-1
 "Thy forests, Windsor! and thy green retreats." OxAEP-1

Wind-swung, pine-shaded gate and moonlit court. To the Monk Dúc Son at Thanh-phong Monastery. King Trăn Thái-Tông. AWTN, *tr. by* Huỳnh Sanh Thông

Wind-walkers. Elegy for *Challenger*. Diane Ackerman. OtW

Windward, never leeward, always windward. Invisibles. Joanne M. Braxton. BtF

Windy City. Stuart Dybek. IllVoic; PoCho

Windy clear day, A. Keith Abbott. WhBo

Windy Day. No Hyangnim. EcSo, *tr. by* Aimee N. Kwon

Windy Day/Slayton, Texas. Charles Behlen. TiP2

Windy fall. Issa. EH, *tr. by* Robert Hass

Windy windows! looking out of you. Windy Windows. Hilmi Yavuz. NaPG, *tr. by* Talat Sait Halman

Windy woods thin moon going down. Night Feast, Zuo Family Village. Tu Fu [*or* Du Fu]. CCL1, *tr. by* David Lattimore

Wine. Li Po. NDACCP, *tr. by* Ezra Pound

Wine and Water. G. K. Chesterton. ChIV-1; MoBrPo

Wine and woman and song. Villanelle of the Poet's Road. Ernest Dowson. OBMV

Wine and Wooing. Donny O'Rourke. EdScPo

Wine Bowl. "H. D." NoP-4; NoP-5

Wine from Bordeaux. Sujata Bhatt. AtGh

Wine, I Say! I'll Drink to Madness! Mary Tighe. RWP

Wine Is Drunk, The. Gwen Harwood. LW

Wine is gone, The. Geological Hymn. Joseph Ceravolo. PmAP

Wine Menagerie, The. Hart Crane. APT-2; NoAM

Wine of Love is music, The. James Thomson. OBEV *Fr.* Sunday up the River.

Wine of Love, The. James Thomson. OBEV *Fr.* Sunday up the River.

Wine, the red coals, the flaring gas. At the Cavour. Arthur Symons. NPeEn

Wine, water. Young Monk (Denver). David Craig. UpMys

Winegrower, The. Milán Füst. IQMS, *tr. by* Jess Perlman

Winemaking. Gwyn Williams. BBMWP, *tr. by* Christopher Meredith

Wine's a sov'reign cure for sorrow. Wine, I Say! I'll Drink to Madness! Mary Tighe. RWP

Wing and Prayer. Jack Marshall. GeoHom

Wing and thorn remain, etched into my mind. Rewind. Ger Killeen. AmPoNex

Wing dip studded braille dots flap or dip. Plane song. Dana Lisa Lustig. AnSo

Wing of the ostrich rejoiceth, The. Bible, *O.T.* OWoS *Fr.* Job.

Wing Road. Eamon Grennan. PBCIP

Wing thy race when the night comes down. By the Sea-Wall. Vincent O'Sullivan. IrLP

Wingaersheek Beach. Marsden Hartley. APT-1

Winged Abyss. Nathaniel Mackey. ESEAA

Winged bulletins issued from frontier outposts. Going Out Through the North Gate of Chi. Pao Chao. ColAnChi, *tr. by* Daniel Bryant

Winged Horse, The. Louise Glück. BodElec

Winged in Gold. Euros Bowen. OBWVE, *tr. by* the author

Winged Man. Stephen Vincent Benét. MoAmPo

Winged mimic of the woods! thou motley fool[!]. To the Mocking-Bird. Richard Henry Wilde. APN-1

Winged Snake Found on a Path. Matthew Rohrer. NevBe; PoDa

Winged Sphinx. Margaret Fuller. TCAPo

Winged Torso of Eros. Daniel Hall. PoA 2002

Winged women was saying. Mary's Dream. Lucille Clifton. NALW

Winged Words. Rachel Hadas. FFC

Wingfoot Lake [Independence Day, 1964]. Rita Dove. CAP-8; NAMCP V.2; PoPoPo

Wingless. Sándor Weöres. IQMS, *tr. by* Adam Makkai and Donald E. Morse

Wingless Victory, The. Hervey Allen. YaYoPo

Wings. John Godfrey. PmAP

Wings. Michael Haslam. Oth *Fr.* Continual Song.

Wings. Miroslav Holub. PoSu, *tr. by* Ian Milner and George Theiner

Wings. Brendan Kennelly. IrLP

Wings. Ku Sang. CAMKP, *tr. by* Kevin O'Rourke

Wings. Mary Oliver. PoCoUp

Wings. Maureen Seaton. FFC

Wings. Susan Stewart. AmAlph

Wings. *Unknown.* HePo, *tr. by* Barbara Hughes Fowler

Wings. Judith Wright. NOBAu

Wings, The. Delmira Agustini. TCLAP, *tr. by* Elizabeth Gordon

Wings, The. Denise Levertov. APSN; NALW

Wings and Seeds: For My Birth Mother. Sandra McPherson. LoL; PoA 2002

Wings blur, a bird hovers. Hovering. Jessica Lowenthal. OnScMo

Wings filmed, the threads of knowledge thicken. Jam Trap, The. Charles Tomlinson. MoBrPo

Wings of a Dove. Edward Kamau Brathwaite. BrAP; NAMCP V.2 *Fr.* Arrivants: A New World Trilogy, The.

Wings of Time are black and white, The. Compensation. Ralph Waldo Emerson. APN-1

Wings suffer most, The. They stop shining. Biological Imperative. Joan Houlihan. IAoNAP

Wings tremble, it is the red admiral, The. Red Admiral, The. Charles Hubert Sisson. HarvBoo

Wing-set lone seagull, The. David Kherdian. UrbNat *Fr.* Taking the Soundings on Third Avenue.

Winifreda. *Unknown.* OBEV

Wink. Roger Gilbert-Lecomte. PFTM-1

Wink. Benjamin Péret. YaTCFP, *tr. by* Mary Ann Caws and Jean-Pierre Cauvin

Wink as they will. Wink most when widows wince. (LL) High-Toned Old Christian Woman, A. Wallace Stevens. NAAL-5; NAAPv.2; NoAM; OxBoAm

Wink at it only with thine eyes. To the Wine Treasurer of the Circuit Mess. UV

Winked too much and were afraid of snakes. Monkeys, The. Marianne Moore. APT-1

Winners. Katherine Frost. Prnts

Winnetou Old. Pierre Joris.

   "Vier Takte vor K time then before." PFTM-2

Winnie. Gwendolyn Brooks.

   Song of Winnie. ESEAA

   "Winnie Mandela, she." FuFl

Winnie Mandela got fired from the revolution. Fired Up!! Everett Hoagland. OxAAAP

Winnie Mandela, she. Gwendolyn Brooks. FuFl *Fr.* Winnie.

Winnings. Garrett Kaoru Hongo. FTtHH; GeoHom; OpBo

Wino, always stumbling. Homyo. ZenPo, *tr. by* Takashi Ikemoto and Lucien Stryk

Wino Rhino. Harryette Mullen. AWPTFC

Winslow Homer. Winfield Townley Scott. APT-2

Winston Churchill. David Scott. NLP

Wintah Styles, De. Maggie Pogue Johnson. CBWP-4

Winter. Rae Armantrout. FTOS

Winter. Alexander Barclay. PBRV *Fr.* Eclogues.

Winter: "Cold, moist, young phlegmy Winter now doth lie." Anne Bradstreet. MoW

Winter. John Clare. CenSon

Winter. John Davies. AngWePo

Winter ("Green Mistletoe! / Oh, I remember now.") Walter De la Mare. OBMV

Winter ("Clouded with snow / The cold winds blow.") Walter De la Mare. OBMV

Winter. Hesiod. NOSC *Fr.* Georgics of Heisod, The.

Winter. Friedrich Hölderlin. WoPoe *Fr.* Seasons, The.

Winter. Richard Hughes. OBMV; OBWVE

Winter. Anne Hunter. CenSon

Winter. Judy Jordan. AmPoNex

Winter / morning. / Snowflakes. Snow Poem. Roger McGough. Spl

Winter. Pascalle Monnier. YaTCFP, *tr. by* Serge Gavronsky

Winter. Ngo Chi Lan. EaWin, *tr. by* W. S. Merwin and Nguyen Ngoc Bich

Winter. Marie Ponsot. ExTi

Winter. Ryokan. *tr. by* John Stevens

   "Late at night, listening to the winter rain." AWTN, *tr. by* John Stevens

Winter. Philip Salom. NOBAu

Winter: "When icicles hang by the wall." William Shakespeare. ClHu; MakPoe; NAEL-6v1; NIL-7; NIP-4; NoP-5; OBEV; OxBEV; TFi; TRP; WaAnP; WeW-3 *Fr.* Love's Labour's Lost.

Winter. Robert Southey. CenSon; GSo

Winter: "Ten o'clock train to New York, The." Ruth Stone. InoFa; OxBoAm

Winter: "Now winter's standing at the door." Yuri Suhl. Prolet, *tr. by* Amelia Glaser

Winter. John Millington Synge. OBMV

Winter. *Unknown.* CCL1 *Fr.* Tzu Yeh Songs.

Winter. *Unknown.*

   "Wind piercing, hill bare, hard to find shelter." OBWVE

Winter. Sheila Wingfield. LW; MoWP

Winter. Judith Wright. HarvBoo *Fr.* Shadow of Fire: Ghazals, The.

Winter. Yun Sŏndo. CATKP *Fr.* Angler's Calendar, The.

Winter, The. Morgan Llwyd. AngWePo *Fr.* 1648.

Winter, The. *Unknown.* SSUS

Winter 6: "Guests have arrived at last, The. The old." Patrick Lane. BrAP

Winter 9: "Each day the time grows less, the hours." Patrick Lane. BrAP

Winter 40: "She is a northern woman, barely more." Patrick Lane. BrAP

Winter, 1963. David Mason. VisFro

Winter 1967. Lenard D. Moore. ISC

Winter afternoon. Stanford M. Forrester. AmZen

Winter alleys are warm. Daddy's Friends. Esther Iverem. GT

Winter and Spring have come and gone. In Mourning for His Dead Wife. P'an Yüeh. CCL1, *tr. by* Kenneth Rexroth

Winter and Spring Scene, A. Henry David Thoreau. NCAP

Winter and Summer. Stephen Spender. MoBrPo

Winter Angel. Ágnes Nemes Nagy. PoSu, *tr. by* Hugh Maxton

Winter Answer. Ilse Aichinger. GTCP, *tr. by* Michael Hamburger

Winter at Gurnard's Head. David Wright. NLP

Winter at the Intersection. Chris Willerton. TiP2

Winter, Austin, 1964. October 31, 1981. Albert Huffstickler. TiP2

Winter Ball. August Kleinzahler. MoASP

Winter Beauty. William Soutar. EdScPo

Winter, Before the War. Waclaw Potocki. WoPoe, *tr. by* Jerzy Peterkiewicz and Burns Singer

Winter began with. Lake of the Woods, The. Richard Ryan. PBCIP

Winter being over, The. Anne Collins. PEW *Fr.* Another Song Exciting to Spirituall Mirth.

Winter Billet. Peter Huchel. PoSu, *tr. by* Michael Hamburger

Winter Birds. David Brendon Hopes.

   "Don't think the stars and moon are all." UpMys

Winter blooms, turns. Shuffles. Brian Bartlett. IFF

Winter burn. Miriam Sagan. WhBo

Winter by Breughel, the hill with hunters. Breughel's Winter. Rutger Kopland. VCWP, *tr. by* James Brockway

Winter Campaign, A. Eochaidh Ó Heóghusa. CABP

Winter can't have changed much for us. Note for Robert Henryson, A. Robin Fulton. EdScPo

Winter comes to rivers and lakes. Maeng Sasŏng. CATKP *Fr.* Four Seasons by the Rivers and Lakes.

Winter Coming On. Martin Bell. OBVE

Winter Cricket. John Heath-Stubbs. OBCP

Winter crisp and the brittleness of snow. Words for Love. Ted Berrigan. NYP2; PmAP

Winter Dawn. Tu Fu [*or* Du Fu]. BLT, *tr. by* Kenneth Rexroth

Winter Dawn. Xiao Zihui. CCL1, *tr. by* John Frodsham

Winter Day, A. Joanna Baillie.

   Morning.

   "Fam'ly cares call next upon the wife, The." NePenScot

Winter Day, A. Philip Lamantia. CLPP

Winter day after days, The. Looking Way Off. A. R. Ammons. PfSP

Winter Daybreak above Vence, A. James Wright. VCAP

Winter Days. Gareth Owen. OBCP

Winter deepening, the hay all in, The. Sonnet. Richard Wilbur. OxBSo

Winter Drive. James Philip McAuley. BMAP; PoA 2002

Winter: *eat the little, talk a lot.* Excellence in the Small. Tears Frozen on Your Face. Lorna Crozier. IFF

Winter Epigrams. Dionne Brand.

   21. IFF

Winter Evening. Archibald Lampman. BrAP; NIL-7

Winter evening, A. Grating Parmesan. Barbara Crooker. SweBea

Winter Evening, Berlin. Oskar Loerke. GTCP *Fr.* At the Edge of the Great City.

Winter evening settles down, The. Preludes. T. S. Eliot. APT-1; BrAP; HeIP-4; NAAPv.2; NAMCP V.1; OBMV; OxBoAm; PtR; TCAPo; WeW-3

Winter Evening, The: A Brown Study. William Cowper. NAEL-6v1; NAEL-7v1 *Fr.* Task, The.

Winter Fairyland in Vermont. Francis P. Osgood. WeW-3

Winter Fields, The. Sir Charles G. D. Roberts. BrAP

Winter Fires. David St. John. AmAlph

Winter fly, The. Issa. SoOfWa, *tr. by* Sam Hamill

Winter for a moment takes the mind; the snow. Conrad Potter Aiken. APT-1; NAAPv.2; OxBoAm *Fr.* Preludes for Memnon; or, Preludes to Attitude.

Winter Fruit. Juan Delgado. TouFir

Winter garden. Basho. EH, *tr. by* Robert Hass

Winter Garden. Janet Lewis. APT-2

Winter goes out in a humid March wind, The. By the River. Martin Birnbaum. Prolet, *tr.* by Amelia Glaser

Winter Grieving Poem. Kate Horsley. ICANM

Winter had arrived. Lonely Journey, A. Kim Suyŏng. CAMKP, *tr.* by Anthony, Brother of Taizé

Winter hanging over the dark well, A. Well, The. Jay Macpherson. BrAP; NoP-4

Winter has moved off. Rhododendrons. Larry Levis. GeoHom

Winter has reached thee once again at last. To Hampstead. Leigh Hunt. CenSon

Winter Holding off the Coast of North America. N. Scott Momaday. ColAP

Winter in America. Gil Scott-Heron. ISC

Winter in Brighton. Mortimer Collins. NPeEn

Winter in Durnover Field. Thomas Hardy. MoBrPo

Winter in Minneapolis. Richard Ryan. PBCIP

Winter in their cry. (LL) Something Told the Wild Geese. Rachel Lyman Field. ChAP; NTCP

Winter in Wales, A. Hester Lynch Salusbury Thrale [*later* Mrs. Piozzi]. CABP

Winter is come again. The sweet south west. January 1, 1829. Nathaniel Parker Willis. APN-1

Winter is icumen [*or* icummen] in. Ancient Music. Ezra Pound. AmWit; HeIP-4; NBLV; OBCoV; TCAPo; UV

Winter is settling on the place; the sedge. Virginia Portrait. Sterling Allen Brown. GT; OxAAAP

Winter is the king of showmen. Winter Morning. Ogden Nash. TLR

Winter (January / February 1978). Larry Eigner. PFTM-2

Winter Landscape. John Berryman. GS; HarvBoo; MoAmPo; OxBoAm

Winter Landscape. Luciana Notari. CItWP, *tr.* by Cinzia Sartini Blum and Lara Trubowitz

Winter Landscape. Alfonsas Nyka-Niliunas. MotU, *tr.* by Jonas Zdanys

Winter Landscape. Stephen Spender. MoBrPo

Winter Landscape, A. Mathilde Blind. ViWPN

Winter Lanscape—Halifax. Douglas Lochhead. NIP-4

Winter leeks,The. Basho. EH, *tr.* by Robert Hass

Winter lull / No talents. Issa. ZenPo, *tr.* by Takashi Ikemoto and Lucien Stryk

Winter makes a last stand. Skull. Douglas Burnet Smith. Coast

Winter Marsh. Andrew Steeves. Coast

Winter Mirror. Judith Mok. TuT, *tr.* by Michael O'Loughlin

Winter Mirror II. Judith Mok. TuT, *tr.* by Michael O'Loughlin

Winter Moon. Langston Hughes. SAmP

Winter moon. Issa. IllVoic *Fr.* Issa: A Suite of Haiku.

Winter Moon Haiku. Thomas Rain Crowe. AmZen

Winter morning. Getting Up in Winter. Emperor Ch'ien-wen of Liang. BLT, *tr.* by Kenneth Rexroth

Winter Morning. Ogden Nash. TLR

Winter mornings I see. Freight, The. Richard Jones. PoChi

Winter: My Secret. Christina Georgina Rossetti. NAEL-6v2; NAEL-7v2; NPeEn; VWP

Winter, Never Mind Where. Hyam Plutzik. APT-2

Winter Night. Cecil Day Lewis. PoA 2002

Winter Night. Chandra Mayor. PoPra

Winter Night. Edna St. Vincent Millay. APT-1

Winter Night. Stanislav Kostka Neumann. SonAtl, *tr.* by Dorli Meek, Ziva Pecavar and Josef Pettersen

Winter Night. Boris Leonidovich Pasternak. WoPoe, *tr.* by Edwin Morgan

Winter Night: "Snow, snow over the whole land." Boris Leonidovich Pasternak. GPTC, *tr.* by Richard McKane

Winter Night ("Those I love scattered away, poor.") Po Chü-i. NDACCP, *tr.* by David Hinton

Winter Night. Po Chü-i. CCL1, *tr.* by Arthur Waley

Winter Night. Charles Simic. MoW

Winter Night. John Greenleaf Whittier. CtM *Fr.* Snow-Bound [*or* Snow-Bound] [A Winter Idyl].

Winter Night, A. William Barnes. WoPoe

Winter Night, A. Priscilla Jane Thompson. CBWP-2

Winter Night, A. Georg Trakl. MotU, *tr.* by Robert Bly

Winter Night Farewell. Chia Tao. CSKM, *tr.* by Mike O'Connor

Winter Night, Glencoe. Anne B. Murray. CFP

Winter Night: Mount Royal. Abraham Moses Klein. NoAM

Winter Nightfall. Robert Bridges. MoBrPo; OBEV

Winter Nights. Thomas Campion. *See* Now Winter Nights Enlarge.

Winter Nocturne: The Hospital. Alter Brody. APT-2

Winter Noon. Umberto Saba. STV, *tr.* by John Frederick Nims

Winter Ode to the Old Men of Lummus Park, Miami, Florida, A. Donald Justice. WeW-3

Winter of Thirty-Eight, The. Robert Ivanovich Rozhdestvensky. TCRusP, *tr.* by Daniel Weissbort

Winter of thirty-eight, The. Winter of Thirty-Eight, The. Robert Ivanovich Rozhdestvensky. TCRusP, *tr.* by Daniel Weissbort

Winter Offerings. Frank Ormsby. PNI

Winter owl banked just in time to pass, The. Questioning Faces. Robert Frost. APT-1

Winter Palace, The. Paavo Haavikko. *tr.* by Anselm Hollo

"Bastard Son is born with a tooth in his mouth and hair on his." WoPoe, *tr.* by Anselm Hollo

First Poem, The. PFTM-2, *tr.* by Anselm Hollo

Second Poem, The. PFTM-2, *tr.* by Anselm Hollo

Winter Piece, A. William Cullen Bryant. APN-1; ColAP

Winter Ploughing. William Everson. ASA

Winter Poem. Frederick Morgan. GoPo

Winter pushes into my room. I waken. What We Leave Behind. Elmaz Abinader. PoArWo

Winter rain. Basho. EH, *tr.* by Robert Hass

Winter rain. Almost Midwinter. Kitasono Katsue. CAoMJL1, *tr.* by John Solt

Winter rain on moss. Buson. SoOfWa, *tr.* by Sam Hamill

Winter Rain, The. Jones Very. NCAP

Winter Regrets. Bill Knott. BodElec

Winter report. Lionel Abrahams. TSAP

Winter Resolve. Peter Grant. ArBi

Winter Rose, The. Gillian Ferguson. NeBl

Winter seclusion—. Basho. SoOfWa, *tr.* by Sam Hamill

Winter shall not find me withered. Stocking Up. Sylvia Kantaris. LW

Winter showers. Basho. SoOfWa, *tr.* by Sam Hamill

[Winter Sketches I]. Charles Reznikoff. PoA 2002

[Winter Sketches II: Subway]. Charles Reznikoff. PoA 2002; WoPoe

[Winter Sketches III]. Charles Reznikoff. PoA 2002

[Winter Sketches IV]. Charles Reznikoff. PoA 2002

[Winter Sketches V]. Charles Reznikoff. PoA 2002

Winter skies are cold and low. Song. Tzu Yeh. CrYelRi; ErotSp, *tr.* by Sam Hamill

Winter Sky. John Cope. GeoH

Winter Sky. Sŏ Chŏngju. CAMKP; VCWP, *tr.* by David R. McCann

Winter sky past the feeder, The. In the Kitchen before Dinner. Jane Rohrer. ACAMVP; BodElec

Winter snowes, all covered is the grounde, The. Alexander Barclay. PBRV *Fr.* Eclogues.

Winter solitude. Basho. EH, *tr.* by Robert Hass

Winter Solstice. Jean Bleakney. NIrP

Winter solstice. Pentti Saarikoski. VCWP *Fr.* Dance Floor on the Mountain, The.

Winter Song. Elizabeth Tollet. WaAnP

Winter Sonnet. Linda Beatrice Brown. GT

Winter Sonnets, The. Vyacheslav Ivanovich Ivanov. TCRusP, *tr.* by Mary Jane White

Winter? Spring! Who knows! Tanka. Sadakichi. NAAPv.1

Winter? Spring! Who knows. Sadakichi. NAAPv.1 *Fr.* Tanka.

Winter Stars. Larry Levis. GeoHom

Winter Storm. Lucien Stryk. UrbNat

Winter storm, The. Basho. EH, *tr.* by Robert Hass

Winter Storms, The. Sir William Davenant. NOSC

Winter sun, The. Basho. EH, *tr.* by Makoto Ueda

Winter Sunflowers. Gillian Ferguson. NeBl

Winter Sunrise. Laurence Binyon. NPeEn

Winter Swan. Louise Bogan. APT-2; ColAP; OWoS; OxBoAm

Winter Swim. Pimone Triplett. NAPBL

Winter Tenement. Malcolm Cowley. APT-2

Winter, the empty air, outside. Time with Stevie Wonder in It. Christopher Gilbert. SwNoth

Winter, the old drover, has brought. Ponies, Twynyrodyn. Meic Stephens. AngWePo

Winter Time [*or* Winter-Time]. Robert Louis Stevenson. MoBrPo

Winter to Spring: the west wind melts the frozen rancour. Horace. WoPoe *Fr.* Three Odes of Horace.

Winter Traveler, The. Henry Kirke White. CenSon

Winter Tree. Im Yŏngjo. CAMKP, *tr.* by Edward W. Poitras

Winter Trees. Ágnes Nemes Nagy. IQMS, *tr.* by Adam Makkai

Winter Trees. Ágnes Nemes Nagy. IQMS, *tr.* by Ila Egon

Winter Trees. Ágnes Nemes Nagy. IQMS, *tr.* by Hugh Maxton

Winter Tuesday, the city pouring fire, A. Coming Home, *Detroit*, 1968. Philip Levine. UrbNat

Winter Twilight. Anne Porter. APT-2

Winter Twilight, A. Angelina Weld Grimké. MoW
Winter Twilight, A. John Banister Tabb. APN-2
Winter Twilight, Glowing Black and Gold, The. Delmore Schwartz. NoAM
Winter uncovers distances, I find. Wintry Mind, The. Witter Bynner. NoP-4; NoP-5
Winter Views Serene. George Crabbe. WoPoe Fr. Borough, The.
Winter Visit, A. Dannie Abse. NoAM
Winter Voyage. Anne-Marie Albiach. PFTM-2, tr. by Joseph Simas
Winter, Voyeurism. William Olsen. MAAN
Winter Walk at Noon, The. William Cowper. NPeEn Fr. Task, The.
Winter Walking. Alfred Wellington Purdy. NoAM
Winter warbler. Buson. EH, tr. by Robert Hass
Winter Warfare. Edgell Rickword. FaBoWar; OBWP; PoWW
Winter was a vestibule, storing brooms. Standard Time. Ira Sadoff. BodElec
Winter wears blue sky on its shoulders. Winter Grieving Poem. Kate Horsley. ICANM
Winter Wedding, The. Paul Henry. TCAWP
Winter Wheat. Paul Muldoon. GPPA
Winter will bar the swimmer soon. Swimming Chenango Lake. Charles Tomlinson. NAMCP V.2; NoAM
Winter wind. Stanford M. Forrester. AmZen
Winter Winds Cold and Blea. John Clare. GoPo
Winter Wise. Unknown. Spl
Winter with the Gulf Stream. Gerard Manley Hopkins. NoAM
Winter withering. Tan Taigi. OxBEV, tr. by Anthony Thwaite
Winter Work. Peter Fallon. PBCIP
Winter-burning in the fields. (LL) Crows, The. Louise Bogan. ItP; NAAPv.2; NALW
Winterdirge. Charles S. Taylor. TiP2
Wintering. Alicia Ostriker. ExTi Fr. Mastectomy Poems, The.
Wintering. Sylvia Plath. MoW; NALW
Wintering. Jane Satterfield. SweBea
Wintering Over at the End of the Century. Alvin Greenberg. UrbNat
Winterlong, off La Manche, wind leaning. Gray stones of the gray. Flaubert in Egypt. Robert Penn Warren. NoAM
Wintermelon. Alan Chong Lau. WhBo
Winter-Piece, A. Ambrose Philips. NPeEn
Winter's affection, A; radiomimetic. Matt Robinson. Coast
Winter's Approach. Ábrahám Barcsay. IQMS, tr. by Thomas Kabdebo
Winter's asperity mollifes under the assault of April. Winter's asperity mollifies. Donald Hall. PfSP
Winters at home brought wind. Once in a Lifetime, Snow. Les A. Murray. NoP-4; NoP-5
Winters close, Springs open, no child stirs, The. John Berryman. NAAL-5; NoP-4; NoP-5 Fr. Homage to Mistress Bradstreet.
Winter's Day, A. Joanna Baillie. NAEL-7v2; WoRP
Winter's End. Dan Pagis. FIT, tr. by Robert Friend
Winter's hobbles break. Polite Debate, A. Princess Nukada. SonAtl, tr. by Mitsuko Ishino, Hiroko Ohara, Phoebe Ravenhall and Wakiko Tsujimoto
Winter's last rain and a light I don't recognize. Impossible, The. Bruce Weigl. BodElec
Winter's Tale, A. D. H. Lawrence. MoBrPo
Winter's Tale, A. Sylvia Plath. FaBoA
Winter's Tale, A. Wyatt Prunty. RA
Winter's Tale, The. William Shakespeare.
 "As she liv'd peerless." OxAEP-1
 Autolycus as Peddler. NoSic; NPeEn
 Autolycus's Song ("Jog on, jog on, the footpath way"). NoSic
 "Give me those flowers there, Dorcas. Reverend sirs." OxAEP-1
 "I have said / She 's adulteress; I have said with whom." OxAEP-1
 "If you would seek us." OxAEP-1
 (Pedlar's Song, The.) NBLV
 "To your owne bents dispose you: you'le be found." FaBoVe
 When Daffodils Begin to Peer. NoP-4; NoSic; OxAEP-1; TFi; UV; WaAnP
Winter's thunder. Unknown. FaBoVe
Winterspring, nightfall, thawing. March Evening. Harry Edmund Martinson. WED, tr. by Robert Bly
Winter-Worship. Charles Wright. PfSP
Wintery Music. Sarah Kirsch. GTCP, tr. by Reinhold Grimm
Wintry chill is in the atmosphere, A. Winter Resolve. Peter Grant. ArBi
Wintry day / On my horse. Basho. ZenPo, tr. by Takashi Ikemoto and Lucien Stryk
Wintry haw is burning out of season, The. Haw Lantern, The. Seamus Heaney. HarvBoo; MakPoe; NoAM; PNI
Wintry Mind, The. Witter Bynner. NoP-4; NoP-5
Wintry night, the hearth inhales, A. Remembering Carrigskeewaun. Michael Longley. PBCIP

Wintry wind. Basho. EH, tr. by Robert Hass
Wintry winds have ceased to blow, The. Resurrection. George Crabbe. SacPr
Wipe off my tear[e]s with handkerchief[e]s of praise. (LL) Poet[r]ess's Hasty Resolution, The. Margaret Lucas Cavendish, Duchess of Newcastle. BASC; NAEL-7v1
Wiped out by the hugeness of the big electric crane. On All Fours. Benjamin Péret. PFTM-1
Wipp Protest. Carol Merrill. ICANM
Wire. Rod Moran. NOBAu
Wire Song. Mark Todd. GeoH
Wire Tap. Miguel Algarin. PueRic
Wire, The. Robert Garioch. NePenScot
Wire, the ghetto, an eastern landscape, The. Solo. Anna Glazova. CRWP, tr. by Max Nemtsov
Wired In. Lamont B. Steptoe. UnSA
Wireless. Michael Symmons Roberts. RWPCtW
Wireless, The. Desmond Graham. RWPCtW
Wireless Aerial, The. Edward Storey. RWPCtW
Wireless at Night. Unknown. RWPCtW
Wiring appears to be five years old, The. Richard II. Veronica Forrest-Thomson. Oth
Wiry and headstrong in life, so in death. Winter Solstice. Jean Bleakney. NIrP
Wisconsin Horse hears the geese, The. Simon J. Ortiz. NAAL-5 Fr. Poems from the Veterans Hospital.
Wisconsin Horse, The. Simon J. Ortiz. PFTM-2
Wisdom. William Cowper. ChIV-1 Fr. Olney Hymns.
Wisdom. Sara Teasdale. MoAmPo
Wisdom and learning I abhor. Song of Disillusionment, A. Hsi K'ang. CCL1, tr. by John Turner
Wisdom and Spirit of the universe! William Wordsworth. OxBEV Fr. Prelude, The; Growth of a Poet's Mind [1850 version].
Wisdom, Aspasia, by thy gentle muse. To Aspasia. Susanna Highmore Duncombe. PoBW
Wisdom Is. Quo Vadis Gex-Breaux. FuFl
Wisdom is / sweeter than honey. Makeda (Queen of Sheba). HW; WPoS
Wisdom is vain, and prophesy. (LL) Conflict of Convictions, The. Herman Melville. APN-2; CBCWP
Wisdom of AE, The. Thomas McCarthy. PBCIP
Wisdom of Geese, The. Nancy Willard. PfSP
Wisdom of Merlyn, The. Wilfrid Scawen Blunt.
 "Wouldst thou be wise, O Man? At the knees of a woman begin." OBMV
Wisdom of Shelley, The. George Elliott Clarke. OpeFie
Wisdom of the, The. b. Charles Bukowski. BodElec
Wisdom of the World, The. Siegfried Sassoon. MoBrPo
Wise 1. Imamu Amiri Baraka. NAMCP V.2; PFTM-1 Fr. Why's / Wise.
Wise 3. Imamu Amiri Baraka. FTOS Fr. Why's / Wise.
Wise 5. Imamu Amiri Baraka. BB Fr. Wise/Whys.
Wise emblem of our politic[k] world. Snail [or Snayl], The. Richard Lovelace. NPeEn
 (Wise Emblem of our Politick World.) PBRV
Wise guys, The. Kid Stuff. Frank Horne. NOxBChV
Wise in the ways of county fair judges. Parents They Would Be, The. Joe-Anne McLaughlin-Carruth. PoA 2002
Wise man does not fear the world, The. A E Housman. R. Williams Parry. BBMWP, tr. by Joseph P. Clancy
Wise men all have come to this conclusion. There's Magic in the Air. Ira Gershwin. NAAPv.2
Wise Men Ask the Children the Way, The. Heinrich Heine. OBCP, tr. by Geoffrey Grigson
Wise men have shown. To Each His Own. Ray Evans and Jay Livingston. ReLy
Wise men in long white togas come forward during the. Inventions. Miroslav Holub. PoSu, tr. by George Theiner
Wise men of yesterday, like the shrimp, The. Shrimp and Her Daughter, The. Jean de La Fontaine. WoPoe, tr. by Bruce Boone and Robert Glück
Wise Rejoice with Ganymede, The. Unknown. CAGL Fr. Leiden Manuscript, The.
Wise teacher tell me. Jelaluddin Rumi. EaWin, tr. by Talat Sait Halman and W. S. Merwin
Wise Triangle, A. Vasco [or Vasko] Popa. PoSu Fr. Yawn of Yawns, The.
Wise/Whys. Imamu Amiri Baraka.
 Wise 5. BB
Wisely and well was it said of him, "Hang it all, he's a." Addition to Kipling's "The Dead King (Edward VII), 1910." Max Beerbohm. OBCoV
Wisely the Hebrews admit no Present tense in their language. Elegiac Verse 12. Henry Wadsworth Longfellow. TCAPo

Wisest men that Nature e'er could boast, The. Francis Quarles. ChIV-1 *Fr.* Job Militant.

Wisest of all men lies buried on this spot, The. Daniel Casper von Lohenstein. GePo *Fr.* Arminius.

Wisest scholar of the wight most wise, The. Sir Philip Sidney. NoP-4; NoP-5 *Fr.* Astrophil and Stella.

Wise-Unto-Hell Ecclesiast. Past Thinking of Solomon. Francis Thompson. ChIV-1

Wise-Woman, The. Agnes Mary Frances Robinson. VWP

Wish. William Heyen. PfSP

Wish. Maggie Nelson. AmPoNex

Wish, A. Olga Fiodorovna Berggolts. TCRusP, *tr.* by Daniel Weissbort

Wish, A. Samuel Rogers. OBEV; OxAEP-2

Wish, A. Gertrude Stein. OxBoAm *Fr.* Book Concluding with As A Wife Has a Cow a Love Story, A.

Wish, A ("Be where I may when death brings in his bill.") John Clare. NPBRoP

Wish, A: "May one sorrow every day." John Millington Synge. IrLP

Wish, The. Mary Lee, Lady Chudleigh. LW

Wish, The. John Clare. OBGa *Fr.* Wish, The.

Wish, The. John Clare.
     Wish, The. OBGa

Wish, The. Abraham Cowley. BASC; NoP-4; NoP-5; NOSC; OBEV; OxAEP-1; PBRV *Fr.* Mistress, The.

Wish a greater knowledge, then t'attaine. Christ and Our Selves. Francis Quarles. SacPr

Wish, By a Young Lady, The. Laetitia Pilkington. PEW

Wish for a Young Wife. Theodore Roethke. NAAL-5; NAMCP V.1; NoAM; NoP-4; NoP-5; WaAnP

Wish for something better, A. (LL) Domestic Work, 1937. Natasha Trethewey. PoDa; SpirFl; SweBea

Wish Foundation, The. Carol Muske-Dukes. PBCAP

Wish Fulfillment. Maggie Nelson. HeMarv

Wish I had a place to walk to. It's Kind of Lonesome Out Tonight. Don George. ReLy

Wish of my Amala, The. Ngodup Paljor. WhBo

Wish, that of the living whole, The. Alfred Tennyson. BrAP; NAEL-6v2; NAEL-7v2; NAWM-7v2; NoP-5; SacPr; WaAnP *Fr.* In Memoriam A. H. H.

Wish to Be Believed, The. Mona Van Duyn. PoA 2002

Wish You Were Here. Harold Rome. ReLy

Wishbone. Frank X. Walker. SpirFl

Wishbone, The. Paul Muldoon. PBCIP

Wishbone USA. Joyce Sutphen. RWB

Wished-For Song, A. Jelaluddin Rumi. LoL, *tr.* by Coleman Barks

Wishes. Philippe Jaccottet. MFP, *tr.* by Martin Sorrell

Wishes. Ger Killeen. AmPoNex

Wishes. Carlos Pellicer. TCLAP, *tr.* by Donald Justice

Wishes. Robert Louis Stevenson. OBEV
     (Go Little Book.) MoBrPo

Wishes for Her. Denis Devlin. IrLP

Wishes for Sons. Lucille Clifton. CAP-8; SUP

Wishes of an Elderly Man[, Wished at a Garden Party, June 1914]. Sir Walter Alexander Raleigh. NBLV; OBCoV

Wishes. To His (Supposed) Mistress[e]. Richard Crashaw. BASC; NOSC; OBEV; OxAEP-1

Wishful Fall. Michael Thorpe. Coast

Wishful Thinking Is the Master of Reality. Duo Duo. AF, *tr.* by Gregory Lee and John Cayley

Wishful to add to my mental power. Ballade of Schopenhauer's Philosophy. Franklin Pierce Adams. AmWit

Wishin' Well, The. Helen B. Cruickshank. EdScPo

Wishing Bone Cycle, The. Jacob Nibenegenesabe. *tr.* by Howard Norman
     "I try to make wishes right." WoPoe, *tr.* by Howard Norman

Wishing is good time wasted. Carolina in the Morning. Gustave Kahn. ReLy

Wishing not to have. Foreward. Yun Tongju. CAMKP, *tr.* by Kay Richards and Steffen Richards

Wishing Poem. *Unknown.* NTCP

Wishing to entrust him with a great task. *Various authors.* CATKP *Fr.* Songs of Flying Dragons.

Wishing to praise. Simplicity. Sandra M. Gilbert. WaAnP

Wishing to take her son. Korinna [*or* Corinna]. SaLy, *tr.* by Diane Rayor

Wishing You. C. D. Grant. BRtP

Wishon Line, The. Sherley Anne Williams. GeoHom

Wisselton, wasselton, who lives here? Wassailing Song. *Unknown.* OBCP

Wistaria. Witter Bynner. APT-1

Wistaria-faced Visigoth, The. Ivano Fermini. ItPo, *tr.* by Gayle Ridinger

Wisteria. Eloise Klein Healy. GeoHom

Wistful vistas are living in objects, The. Sonnet for the Season. Art Lange. PmAP

Wistfulness covers the windows like drapes. Ten men armed with hankies. Dead Letter Office, The. Maxine Chernoff. SUP

Wiston Vault. Katherine Philips. BASC; NOSC

Wit and Learning. James Cawthorn.
     "Wit was a strange unlucky child." OBCoV

Wit and Wisdom. Ambrose Philips. OxAEP-1

Wit that can creep, and pride that licks the dust. (LL) Alexander Pope. OBSV; OxBEV *Fr.* Epistle to Dr. Arbuthnot.

Wit was a strange unlucky child. James Cawthorn. OBCoV *Fr.* Wit and Learning.

Wit was his nakede brest and red of blod his side. *Unknown.* SacPr

Witch! Leonora Speyer. APT-1

Witch, The. Mary Elizabeth Coleridge. CABP; NAEL-7v2; NALW; PoBW; ViWPN; VWP

Witch, The. Adelaide Crapsey. APT-1; NAAPv.2

Witch, The. Santal. RaBo

Witch Doctor. Robert Earl Hayden. GPTC; NAMCP V.2; NoAM

Witch Doctor's Magic Flight, The. Smiler Narautjarri. NOBAu, *tr.* by George von Brandenstein

Witch in the Glass, The. Sarah Morgan Bryan Piatt. NAAPv.1

Witch o' Fife, The. James Hogg. NePenScot

Witch of Coös, The. Robert Frost. APT-1; NoAM; PoA 2002 *Fr.* Two Witches.

Witch of Willowby Wood, The. Rowena Bastin Bennett.
     Witch of Willowby Wood, The. ChAP

Witch pours out a libation of wine, The. Magic Strings. Li Ho. CCL1, *tr.* by John Frodsham

Witch that came (the withered hag), The. Provide, Provide. Robert Frost. APT-1; ChIV-1; HarvBoo; NAMCP V.1; NoAM; NoP-4; NoP-5; OxBoAm; TFi; WeW-3; WoPoe

Witch the lakemen call her, this wind. David Brendon Hopes. UpMys *Fr.* Julian.

Witchcraft. Carolyn Leigh. ReLy

Witchcraft: New Style. Lascelles Abercrombie. MoBrPo

Witch-elms that counterchange the floor. Alfred Tennyson. NAEL-7v2; OBGa *Fr.* In Memoriam A. H. H.

Witches' Ride, The. Karla Kuskin. NOxBChV; TLR

Witches' Spells. Madeleine Edmondson. NTCP

Witches' Wood, The. Mary Elizabeth Coleridge. VWP

Witch-Hazel Wood, The. Emily Hiestand. UrbNat

Witching Time, The. John Keats. NPBRoP

Witch's Ballad, The. William Bell Scott. OBEV; RACG

Witch's Chant, A. James Hogg. NOBRP

Witch's Last Ride, The. Emily Jane Pfeiffer. ViWPN

Witch-Wife. Edna St. Vincent Millay. APT-1

With a broken hoe. (LL) Justice Denied in Massachusetts. Edna St. Vincent Millay. MoAmPo; NAAPv.2

With a calm and very clear eye. (LL) Pebble, The. Zbigniew Herbert. AmFaPo; PoetW, *tr.* by Czeslaw Milosz and Peter Dale Scott

With a candle, searching for survivors. (LL) Survivors, The. Tracey Herd. BeAl; NeBl

With a chaste heart. Ode to a Beautiful Nude. Pablo Neruda. WaAnP, *tr.* by Nathaniel Tarn

With a clover in her hand. (LL) Question, The. Frederick Goddard Tuckerman. APN-2; ColAP

With a Coin from Syracuse. Oliver St. John Gogarty. OBMV

With a copy of Nagatsuka's *I Was a Kamikaze* on my lap. David McFadden. NLPA

With a decent happiness. (LL) Rain, The: "All night the sound had." Robert Creeley. AmFaPo; BeAl; BrAP; ColAP; ErotSp; ICANM; InvLad; PmAP; RaBo; TRP; WaAnP

With a Fa, la, la, la, la. (LL) Song Written at Sea in the First Dutch War (1665), the Night before an Engagement. Charles, 6th Earl of Dorset Sackville. OBEV; OBWP; OxAEP-1

With a fixed stare. In the Steam Bath. Manuel Ulacia. RMCMP, *tr.* by Indran Amirthanayagam

With a flurry of sidestrokes, the March wind. Seconds, The. Linda Bierds. RoV

With a garlande of thornes kene. Seven Sins, The. *Unknown.* SacPr
     (Wyth a gerlond of thornes kene.) OHMEL

With a gay lady. (LL) London Bridge. Mother Goose. FaBoVe; NPeEn

With a Green Scarf. Martin Sorescu. VCWP, *tr.* by Michael Hamburger

With a heavy paw he guards the frontier. Stone Dog, The. King Lě Thánh–tông. WoPoe, *tr.* by Nguyen Ngoc Bich

With a Heigho, maybe Begorrah, and certainly Fiddlededee. (LL) Irish Song [Rosie O'Grady]. Noël Coward. NBLV; OBCoV

With a lantern that wouldn't burn. Draft Horse, The. Robert Frost. APT-1; EmeKit; HeIP-4; SAmP; TRP; WoPoe

With a Lifting of the Head. Hugh MacDiarmid. MoBrPo

With a light frost, crouched an outrageous bird. (LL) Birdwatchers of America. Anthony Hecht. NAMCP V.2; NoAM

With a line and hook. Boy's Summer, A. Paul Laurence Dunbar. CA

With a long stirrup under fern. Craswall. Roland Mathias. OBWVE

With a lurch, an earthquake visits. Diana Hartog. NLPA *Fr.* Oasis.

With a mere glance at the fur coat. *Unknown.* NAAPv.2

With a mermaid crucified to the wheel while she was still beautiful. (LL) Mathios Paskalis among the Roses. George Seferis. PFTM-1; PoetW, *tr. by* Edmund Keeley and Philip Sherrard

With a metal paring knife. How to Build a Prayer. S. Pearl Sharp. BtF

With a muff and a cloak and a tippet—poor Anne. (LL) On Lady Anne Hamilton. Richard Brinsley Sheridan. NPeEn; OBCoV

With a nose for small. Stem of the Tree of Orestes. Jennifer Moxley. VaPo

With a pair of tweezers he picks up a teardrop. My room is lifted, and my face with it. Teardrop, A. Kim Hyesun. EcSo, *tr. by* Youngju Ryu

With a pint of flour and a sheet of bark. Limejuice Tub, The. *Unknown.* NOBAu

With a pull-through and the .22. Premeditations. Geoff Page. NOBAu

With a radish. (LL) Man pulling radishes, The. Issa. EH; IPoFL; PtR, *tr. by* Robert Hass

With a rattle we are walking. Between Scylla and Charybdis. Yunna Petrovna Moritz. ItGoST, *tr. by* Daniel Weissbort

With a runny nose. Buson. SoOfWa, *tr. by* Sam Hamill

With a scribble like yours. Shorthand. Theodore Weiss. BodElec

With a simple, truly unrebellious pen. Joseph Brodsky. TCRusP *Fr.* Sonnets on the Statue of Mary, Queen of Scots, in the Luxembourg Gardens, Paris.

With a single indecorous groan. Penguin Jane Austen, The. Debora Greger. OWoS

With a small bumping sound. Gu Cheng. WoBe *Fr.* Liquid Mercury.

With a Song in My Heart. Lorenz Hart. ReLy

With a *stake* in his inside! (LL) Faithless Nelly Gray. Thomas Hood. NOBRP; UV

With a terrible stare. But not feel it. And not know it. (LL) Dolls Museum in Dublin, The. Eavan Boland. NAEL-7v2; NoP-4; NoP-5

With a thousand night's dream. Winter Sky. Sŏ Chŏngju. CAMKP; VCWP, *tr. by* David R. McCann

With a thud. (LL) Let's Hear It for Goliath. Jon Dressel. AngWePo; TCAWP

With a warbler for. Basho. SoOfWa, *tr. by* Sam Hamill

With a whirl of thought oppressed. Day of Judgement, The. Jonathan Swift. ChIV-1; NPeEn; OBSV; OxBEV

With a woman friend. Buson. SoOfWa, *tr. by* Sam Hamill

With a world where credos don't wear out. (LL) History. Carl Dennis. BAP-97; OxBoAm

With a Yo, Ho, Ho. Edward Young. STuOW *Fr.* Foreign Address, The.

With afternoon tea-cakes and scones. (LL) How to Get On in Society. Sir John Betjeman. OBSV; UV

With alacrity. How to Leave an Island. Carmelita McGrath. Coast

With all a woman's virtues but the pox. Alexander Pope. OBSV *Fr.* First Satire of the Second Book of Horace [Imitated], The.

With all a woman's virtues but the pox. Alexander Pope. OBSV *Fr.* Second Satire of the Second Book of Horace Imitated, The.

With all my faults. Famous Flames. Ron Padgett. NYP2

With all my possessions. Love Burned Out the Light. Hala Mohammad. PoArWo, *tr. by* Cornelia Al-Khaled

With all my will, but much against my heart. Coventry Patmore. OBEV *Fr.* Unknown Eros, The.

With all of us there, our anonymities. (LL) Seamus Heaney. IPoFL; PNI *Fr.* Mossbawn.

With all respect and humble duty. White Mouses Petition to Lamira the Right Honble the Lady Anne Tufton now Countess of Salisbury, The. Anne Finch, Countess of Winchilsea. PoBW

With all that soft old curd. (LL) Elegy on an X-ray Photo of My Skull. Yelena Shwarts. ItGoST; VCWP, *tr. by* Catriona Kelly and Michael Molnar

With all the power rushing past. Conductor, The. Adam Sol. IFF

With all the subtle paints of Fragonard. Flamingos, The. Rainer Maria Rilke. OWoS, *tr. by* Stephen Mitchell

With all their eyes, all creatures see. Rainer Maria Rilke. BeAl *Fr.* Duino Elegies, The [Robert Kelly Translation].

With angry brow and stately tread. Earthquake of 1886, The. Josephine D. Henderson Heard. CBWP-4

With banners furled, and clarions mute. Herman Melville. NCAP

With blackest moss the flower-pots [*or* flowerpots]. Mariana. Alfred Tennyson. NAEL-6v2; NAEL-7v2; NOBRP; OBEV; OxAEP-2; TFi
(With blackest moss the flower-plots.) NoP-4; NoP-5

With bleeding back, from tyrant's lash. Fugitive, The. Priscilla Jane Thompson. CBWP-2

With Bolts of Melody! (LL) I would not paint—a picture. Emily Dickinson. APN-2; NAAL-3; NAAL-5; NoP-4; NoP-5; OxBoAm; TCAPo; TRP

With both knees pressed down on the sill. Through a Window-Light. Sofiya Parnok. ARWW, *tr. by* Catriona Kelly

With Bridget and with Nell. (LL) Ballad[e] [upon a Wedding], A. Sir John Suckling. BASC; NAEL-7v1; NoP-4; NoP-5; WaAnP

With bridles in the evening come. (LL) At Grass. Philip Larkin. HarvBoo; NPeEn; OxBEV; WeW-3

With broken wing they limped across the sky. Reported Missing. John Clifford Bayliss. PoWW

With bruise of lash or stone. (LL) Simon the Cyrenian Speaks. Countee Cullen. ChIV-2; MoAmPo; OxAAAP

With burning fervour. Crystal, The. George Barker. OBMV

With burning horns, two twisted candles under a radiant yellow halo. Death of an Ox, The. Abraham Sutskever. MotU, *tr. by* Ruth R. Wisse

With butterflies in my stomach, flowers in my hair. Thoughts from a Bar Stool. Deirdre May. BRtP

With camel's hair I clothed my skin. Dream. Richard Watson Dixon. OxBEV

With cast–off rags of the past. Crazy Mother, The. Margherita Guidacci. CItWP, *tr. by* Cinzia Sartini Blum and Lara Trubowitz

With Chang Hung-lüeh, Court Attendant, Discussing Literature. Yüan Hao-wen. ColAnChi, *tr. by* John Timothy Wixted

With cheerful mind we yield to men. Frances Gray. FaBoVe

With Cheerful Speed. Tanya Larkin. FreRad

With Child. Genevieve Taggard. MoAmPo; NAAPv.2

With 'Chuck, chuck, chuck, chuck!'. (LL) John Skelton. NoSic; NPeEn; OBEV *Fr.* Garland [*or* Garlande *or* Garlands] of Laurel[l], The.

With Circes let them dwell that think[e] not so. (LL) Homage to Diana. Sir Walter Ralegh. NoSic; NPeEn

With clinical eye and mind alert. Poet, The. Dale R. Carver. FaBoWar

With closed eyes, full of intimate voices. Poem of My Sleeping Sorrow. Julia de Burgos. TANSG, *tr. by* Heather Rosario Sievert

With clothes shaken out at Pure Sound Pavilion. Pure Sound Pavilion. Wang Shih-chieng. ColAnChi, *tr. by* Richard John Lynn

With coat like any mole's, as soft and black. Mole Catcher. Edmund Charles Blunden. OBMV

With company coming. Thanksgiving Dinner. Aileen Fisher. CA

With compassionate hands. Muso Soseki. EaWin, *tr. by* W. S. Merwin

With cords of love God often strove. Michael Wigglesworth. NAAL-3 *Fr.* Day of Doom, The [First Section].

With courage to endure! (LL) Old Stoic, The. Emily Jane Brontë. BrAP; NALW; OBEV; OxAEP-2

With Dad gone, Mom and I worked. Adolescence—3. Rita Dove. ISC; NAAL-5; NoAM

With darkest thoughts my mind is overcast. Another for Miss Pardo's Album. Mihály Vörösmarty. IQMS, *tr. by* Paul Tabori

With darkness and the death-hour rounding it. (LL) Elizabeth Barrett Browning. BrAP; CenSon; LW; NAEL-6v2; NAEL-7v2; NALW; OBEV *Fr.* Sonnets from the Portuguese.

With dead shapes of heroes. Evening, The. Georg Trakl. PFTM-1, *tr. by* Robert Firmage

With deep affection / And recollection. Bells of Shandon, The. Francis Sylvester Mahony. OBEV

With delicate, mad hands, behind his sordid bars. To One in Bedlam. Ernest Dowson. GSo; MoBrPo; OBMV

With deportment learnt from samurai films. Glasnevin Cemetery. Michael O'Loughlin. PBCIP

With dewdrops dripping. Basho. SoOfWa, *tr. by* Sam Hamill

With difficulty persist here and there on earth. (LL) Another Epitaph on an Army of Mercenaries. Hugh MacDiarmid. FaBoWar; NAEL-6v2; NAEL-7v2; NAMCP V.1; NoAM; NoP-4; NoP-5; OBWP; WaAnP

With divine rhythm the ocean. Rocking. Gabriela Mistral. SpanPo, *tr. by* Muriel Kittel

With Donne, whose muse on dromedary trots. On Donne's Poetry. Samuel Taylor Coleridge. NAEL-6v2; NAEL-7v2; UV

With double portion of his father's art. (LL) Mac Flecknoe [or, A Satire upon the True-Blue Protestant Poet T. S.]. John Dryden. BASC; CABP; NAEL-6v1; NAEL-7v1; NoP-4; NoP-5; OBSV; OxAEP-1; TFi

With dull, sea-spent eyes. (LL) Meeting-House Hill. Amy Lowell. APT-1; ColAP; MoAmPo; TCAPo

With each flowing pastel note, crowds swooned to the unmistakable. Waxing Poetic on Marvin. Gordon Chambers. InTrad

With each recurrence of this glorious morn. Composed in One of the Valleys of Westmoreland, on Easter Sunday. William Wordsworth. ChIV-2

With each subway rereading. New York Newsday: Truth, Justice and Vomit. Paul Beatty. InTrad

With Earth's first Clay They did the Last Man knead. Omar Khayyám. CABP *Fr.* Rubáiyát of Omar Khayyám [of Naishápúr], The.

With easy hands upon the rein. Who Are These Children? William Soutar. EdScPo

With echoing step the worshippers. Give Me Thy Heart. Adelaide Anne Procter. SacPr

With Effort, I Sit up and Look Outside. Philippe Jaccottet. YaTCFP, *tr. by* Hoyt Rogers

With elegies, sad songs, and mourning lays. Sextain. William Drummond of Hawthornden. NOSC

With endless life are crowned [*or* crown'd]. (LL) To Live Merrily, and To Trust to Good Verses. Robert Herrick. BASC; CavPo; NOSC

With energy to burn. (LL) One of the Boys. James Simmons. ModIr; PNI

With Esther. Wilfrid Scawen Blunt. OBEV; OBMV *Fr.* Esther [a Young Man's Tragedy].

With evening. Patio. Jorge Luis Borges. TCLAP, *tr. by* Robert Fitzgerald

With everybody's initials on it. (LL) Man Lying on a Wall. Michael Longley. ModIr; NPeEn; PNI

With eye and with gesture. Stephen Crane. IJHIL

With eye unpraised his master's look to scan. Friend of Man, The. *Unknown.* DiBP

With eyes filled with tears. *Unknown.* NAAPv.2

With eyes happy. Grief. Francisco Brines. RaW, *tr. by* David Ignatow

With falling Oars they kept the time. (LL) Bermudas. Andrew Marvell. BASC; NAEL-6v1; NAEL-7v1; NoP-4; NoP-5; NOSC; NPeEn; OBEV; PBRV; TFi; WoPoe

With faults and all, not nobler, just there. (LL) Sea Canes. Derek Walcott. HeIP-4; InoFa

With favour and fortune fastidiously blessed [*or* blest]. Character of Sir Robert Walpole, The. Jonathan Swift. WaAnP

With feeble frame, by ling'ring sickness worn. Visit, The. Mary Bryan.

With fifteen-ninety or sixteen-sixteen. On an Anniversary. John Millington Synge. OBMV

With fifty years not lived but gone, we find. Cloak, The. James McAuley. BMAP

With fingers weary and worn. Song of the Shirt, The. Thomas Hood. BRP

With FitzRoy's twenty-two chronometers. Galapagos. Neil Curry. NLP

With Flute, with Violin. Lőrinc Szabó. IQMS *Fr.* Cricket Music.

With focus sharp as Flemish-painted face. Dome of Sunday, The [*or* A]. Karl Shapiro. MoAmPo; NoAM

With fond embrace she clasped her long lost son. Mary Tighe. NOBRP *Fr.* Psyche.

With footstep slow, in furry pall yclad. On Christmas. John Codrington Bampfylde. CenSon

With forbearance. (LL) To Those Born Later. Bertolt Brecht. AF; GTCP, *tr. by* Erich Fried, Ralph Manheim and John Willett

With frantic pain. (LL) Mad Song. William Blake. IJHIL; NAEL-6v2

With fruit and flowers the board is decked. At a Dinner Party. Amy Levy. PoBW

With gentle fingers. David Vogel. FIT, *tr. by* Robert Friend

With gently smiling jaws! (LL) Lewis Carroll. BLPJKO; ChAP; NBLV; OxBEV; TFi; UV *Fr.* Alice's Adventures in Wonderland.

With glad reception our Commander meets. Luis de Camões [*or* Camõens *or* Camoëns]. FaBoWar *Fr.* Lusiads, The.

With glittering fingers, diamond brooch. Heiress, The. Raymond Garlick. TCAWP

With gold unfading, WASHINGTON! be thine. (LL) To His Excellency General Washington. Phillis Wheatley. AmWaPo; NAAL-3; NAAL-5; NAAPv.1

With gory Death companioned and at play. (LL) Blood, blood! The lines of every printed sheet. George Henry Boker. APN-2; PCW

With grace she granted. Visit to the Palace of Venus. Irene Young. HW

With green stagnant eyes. Idiot, The. Charles Reznikoff. APT-2

With grown-up clever hands. Galina Zelenina. CRWP, *tr. by* Daniel Weissbort

With guilt and grief by half and half. Gegard. Fazil Abdulovich Iskander. ItGoST, *tr. by* Avril Pyman

With hands all reddened and sore. Washerwoman, The. Mary Weston Fordham. CBWP-2

With hands grown learned as cotton stalks have grown fibrous. Picking Cotton. Mary Loving Blanchard. TiP2

With hanging gardens. Tomas Tranströmer. WoBe *Fr.* Haiku.

With head hung, to the dormitory. (LL) Haskell. Witter Bynner. NoP-4; NoP-5

With heavenward-look, and Phoenix-plumes upsoaring! (LL) Meditations. Margaret Fuller. NAAPv.1; SWaP

With Her. Czeslaw Milosz. GI, *tr. by* the author and Robert Hass

With her buskins tipped with dew. May's Invocation after a Tardy Spring. Henrietta Cordelia Ray. CBWP-3

With her evil yellow eyes. Marin Georgiev. CSCBP *Fr.* Memory.

With her forehead always bandaged. Na Victórica Litru. Natalia Toledo. RMCMP, *tr. by* Alberto A. Ríos

With her hair unbound, and he his own skiffsman! (LL) Poem by the Bridge at Ten-shin. Li Po. InoFa; NDACCP; OBVE, *tr. by* Ezra Pound

With her hands cupped. (LL) Hill-track, The. Kathleen Jamie. MoWP; NeBrP

With her, her sister went, a warlike maid. Phineas Fletcher. NOSC *Fr.* Purple Island, The.

With her nylon veil. Plastic Virgin. Gloria Fuertes. RaW, *tr. by* Philip Levine

With her pure nails offering their onyx high. Stéphane Mallarmé. SxFrPo, *tr. by* A. M. and E. H. Blackmore

With her shiny black-patent sandals. Juneteenth. Marilyn Nelson. ExTi

With him there often walked in friendly wise. William Wordsworth. NPBRoP *Fr.* Castle of Indolence Stanzas, The.

With Him who sets the lily on the stem. Prayer. Hildegarde Flanner. CalPo

With hindsight, of course, I can see that the hedge. Hedge, The. Gwyneth Lewis. MFPA

With his beard long like war. Santa Claus. Dunya Mikhail. IrPoTo, *tr. by* Salaam Yousif

With His Book, Of Gardening. Walafrid Strabo. WoPoe, *tr. by* Tim Reynolds

With his fiftieth birthday behind him, a man sees with fair clarity. Dead, The. David Gwenallt Jones. BBMWP, *tr. by* Anthony Conran

With his head he says no. Dunce, The. Jacques Prévert. MFP, *tr. by* Martin Sorrell

With his heart. Who'd Want to Be a Man? Gregory Orr. BodElec

With his own hand he has given himself away. Reading the Writing. John N. Morris. PoA 2002

With his pale Trophees *Death* hath hung his Armes. (LL) Sonnet: "As in a duskie [*or* dusky] and tempestuous night." William Drummond of Hawthornden. NOSC; OxAEP-1

With his toe he traces the arabesques from the walls onto the bottom of the bath. Matthea Harvey. IAoNAP *Fr.* Thermae.

With his trowel point, letter by strange letter. (LL) Alphabets. Seamus Heaney. NAMCP V.2; NoAM

With his venom. Sappho. ItP, *tr. by* Mary Barnard

With his waterman fountain pen poised wallace stevens. Roy Kiyooka. NLPA *Fr.* Pear Tree Pomes.

With his white and tousled godly beard. At the Foot of Mount Zion. Endre Ady. IQMS, *tr. by* Leslie A. Kery

With honeysuckle, over-sweet, festooned [*or* festoon'd]. Coventry Patmore. OxBEV *Fr.* Unknown Eros, The.

With houses hung that slanted and remote. Montesano Unvisited. Richard Hugo. OxBoAm

With how sad steps, O Moon[e], thou climb'st the skies. Sir Philip Sidney. AEP; CABP; GSo; HeIP-4; NAEL-6v1; NAEL-7v1; NoP-4; NoP-5; NoSic; NPeEn; OxAEP-1; OxBEV; OxBSo; TFi; TRP; WaAnP *Fr.* Astrophil and Stella.

"With how sad steps, O Moon, thou climb'st the sky." William Wordsworth. CenSon

With huge impatience, he inly swelt. Edmund Spenser. NoSic *Fr.* Faerie Queene, The.

With huge, with strangers' eyes. Battle, The. Dan Pagis. FIT, *tr. by* Robert Friend

With human love. (LL) Prayer for My Son, A. William Butler Yeats. OxAEP-2; RaBo

With hunched-up shoulders, eyes shut tight. Idiot in the Bath, The. M. Vasalis. TuT, *tr. by* Peter van de Kamp

With huntis vp, with huntis vp. *Unknown.* NePenScot *Fr.* Gude and Godlie Ballatis, The.

With implements to fly away, / Passing Pomposity? (LL) Bring me the sunset in a cup. Emily Dickinson. APN-2; MoAmPo

With innocent wide penguin eyes, three. Bird-witted. Marianne Moore. APT-1

With intolerant repose. Pathological Beings. David Huerta. RMCMP, *tr. by* Mark Schafer

With its baby rivers and little towns, each with its abbey or its cathedral. England. Marianne Moore. MoAmPo

With its cloud of skirmishers in advance. Army Corps on the March, An. Walt Whitman. CBCWP

With its five fingers spread. (LL) Delta. Adrienne Rich. HarvBoo; LoL; NIL-7; NIP-4

With its great dead ship. (LL) Shipwreck: "Watching, watching from the shore." Rosalie Moore. CalPo; YaYoPo

With its great length of stay. (LL) Within This Book, Called Marguerite. Marjorie Welish. FTOS; PmAP

With its rat's tooth the clock. Alarum, The. Sylvia Townsend Warner. MoBrPo

With its rifle butt. (LL) Anne Carson. BodElec; OxBoAm; WoBe *Fr.* Truth About God, The.

With its storks and pagoda. (LL) Tête-à-Tête. May Probyn. NPeEn; VWP

With its tender flakes, snow flutters about. KaracaoĞlan. NaPG, *tr. by* Talat Sait Halman

With Janice. Kenneth Koch. PmAP

With joy Britannia sees her fav'rite goose. To the Marquis of Graham on His Marriage. *Unknown.* OBSV

With joy the guardian Angel sees. Samuel's Prayer. John Keble. ChIV-1

With Kit, Age 7, at the Beach. William Stafford. CAP-8; PoCho; RaBo

With leaden foot Time creeps along. Absence. Richard Jago. OBEV

With leering looks, bullfac'd, and freckled fair. On Jacob Tonson, His Publisher. John Dryden. OBSV

With lifted feet, hands still. Going Down Hill on a Bicycle. Henry Charles Beeching. ArBi; NOxBChV; OBEV

With Light and With Death. Odysseus Elytis. *tr. by* Olga Broumas
  "Even when they destroy you it will still be beautiful." GifTon, *tr. by* Olga Broumas

With lightly closed fists and arms partially rais'd. (LL) Runner, The. Walt Whitman. BLT; ItP; SAmP

With limb-loosening desire; and her glances are more melting than sleep or death. Alcman. EroLit, *tr. by* David A. Campbell

With lions, tigers, leopards, and their kind. (LL) Greater Cats, The. Victoria Mary Sackville-West. OBMV; Spl

With lips of flame and heart of stone. (LL) Impression du Matin. Oscar Wilde. MoBrPo; NAEL-6v2; NAEL-7v2; NoAM

With long sobs. Autumn Song. Paul Verlaine. NAWM-7v2, *tr. by* Carlyle Ferren MacIntyre

With lovers 'twas of old the fashion. To a Young Lady, with Some Lampreys. John Gay. CABP; OBCoV

With luck I'll help her make beneath it. (LL) Design for a Quilt. John Ormond. AngWePo; TCAWP

With Lullay, Lullay, Like a Child. John Skelton. NoSic *Fr.* Garland [*or* Garlande *or* Garlands] of Laurel[l], The.

With many a weary step, and many a groan. Homer. UV *Fr.* Odyssey.

With marjoram [*or* margerain] gentle [*or* jentyll]. John Skelton. OBEV *Fr.* Garland [*or* Garlande *or* Garlands] of Laurel[l], The.

With me. (LL) Woman. Hira Bansode. CFP; ItWoWo; WoPoe, *tr. by* Vinay Dharwadker

With Me. Yvonne Cullen. NIrP

With Me. Oscar Williams. YaYoPo

With Me My Lover Makes. Cecil Day Lewis. OBMV

With me, the young daughter, Vietnam. Interview with a Combat Photographer. Chivas Sandage. MAAN

With me you have done all you ever wanted. *Unknown.* SLW, *tr. by* Marjolijn De Jager, Sayd Bahodin Majrouh and André Velter

With Meaning. John Weiners. BB

With meek eyes. Mohab Nasr. AnVo, *tr. by* Mohamed Enani

With Mercy for the Greedy. Anne Sexton. CAP-8; MoWP; NIL-7; VCAP

With monkeys whimpering on the shadowy mountain. From a Mooring on the Tonglu to a Friend in Yangzhou. Meng Hao Jan. CCL1, *tr. by* Witter Bynner

With moons of dark / Indian blood. (LL) Indian Blood. Mary Tallmountain. FiBr; UnSA

With morning tears thy mournful twilight blesses. (LL) Letter from a Girl to Her Own Old Age, A. Alice Thompson Meynell. MoBrPo; VWP

With most of the bronzes. Charioteer, The. Faye George. PoA 2002

With much effort, I glimpse in the darkness and rubbish. Svetlana Kekova. CRWP, *tr. by* Ruth Fainlight

With much noise. Act. Gerardo Deniz. RMCMP, *tr. by* Mónica de la Torre

With my back to the wall. Hard Drive. Paul Muldoon. KGB

With my fair love far away. Waiting. Cho Chihun. CAMKP, *tr. by* Kyung-Ja Chun

With my father. Issa. EH, *tr. by* Robert Hass

With my feet braced. Examination. StacyLynn. BtF

With my feet clothed and covered. (LL) To My Little Girl. Shakuntala Hawoldar. CFP; HAWP

With my forked branch of Lebanese cedar. Dowser, The. Edwin Morgan. NoP-4; NoP-5; NPeEn

With my girl. Phooie! Robert Garioch. FaBoWar

With my heart spiked and bleeding in its branches. (LL) Book Full of Pictures, A. Charles Simic. NoP-4; NoP-5

With my high starched collar. Trolley Song, The. Ralph Blane and Hugh Martin. ReLy

With My Little Red Knife. Patrick Galvin. IrLP

With my looks I am bound to look simple or fast I would rather look simple. Magna Est Veritas. Stevie Smith. NPeEn; OxBEV

With My Mother, Missing the Train. Helena Nelson. Prnts

With my old man's wrinkled hand. I Guard Your Eyes. Endre Ady. IQMS, *tr. by* Adam Makkai

With my own hands I have sent you off to die. *Unknown.* SLW, *tr. by* Marjolijn De Jager, Sayd Bahodin Majrouh and André Velter

With my sick body I climb a mountain. Certain Sickness, Deep Love. Yi Kyŏngnim. EcSo, *tr. by* Peter H. Lee

With my teeth. No. Not this pig. (LL) Animals Are Passing from Our Lives. Philip Levine. CalPo; CAP-8; ColAP; RaBo; WaAnP

With Names we summon Cosmos out of Chaos. Ode of Signs. Muhammad 'Abd al-Hayy. NAfrP, *tr. by* Alistair Elliot and Matthew Sorenson

With night full of spring and stars we stand. Young Girls. Raymond Souster. BrAP; HeIP-4

With no clock running down, and mirrors. (LL) Cheap Seats, the Cincinnati Gardens, Professional Basketball, 1959. William Matthews. MoASP; PML

With No Experience in Such Matters. Stephen Dunn. ItP

With no help. Dragon-Gate House. Muso Soseki. EaWin, *tr. by* W. S. Merwin

With no star in its crown. (LL) Tadeusz Rózewicz. AF; HP

With no tear-marks between the shoulders. Coat, The. Dewi Stephen Jones. BBMWP, *tr. by* the author

With no underrobes. Buson. SoOfWa, *tr. by* Sam Hamill

With not a thought. Tangled Hair. Lady Izumi. WoPoe, *tr. by* Steven D. Carter

With oh such peculiar branching and over-reaching of wire. St. Saviour's, Aberdeen Park, Highbury, London, N. Sir John Betjeman. SacPr

With old hours all belfry heads. Ding-Donging. Laura Riding Jackson. NAMCP V.1; NoP-4; NoP-5

With one bold stoke. Corporal Who Killed Archimedes, The. Miroslav Holub. PoSu, *tr. by* Ian Milner and Jarmila Milner

With One Long Kiss. John Millington Synge. IrLP

With one thumb extended he could eclipse the whole. Masaccio's *Expulsion from Paradise.* Julia Copus. MFPA

With one who safeguards Gwynedd. Stallion, The. Tudur Aled. OBWVE, *tr. by* Joseph P. Clancy

With One Woven Basket. *Hawaiian Oral Tradition.* NAAPv.2

With only his dim [*or* feeble] lantern. Charon's Cosmology. Charles Simic. PoPoPo; WaAnP

With only two or three stamens, masculine flowers burst. They rise from their own depths, glistening and moist. Loosely turning over, they bring themselves up under the sky midway between light and shadow. Voiceless they wilt. Sluggish they die. María Baranda. RMCMP, *tr. by* Mónica de la Torre

With open shells in seas, on heauenly due. Comparison of His Thoughts to Pearls. William Drummond of Hawthornden. NePenScot

With our monocles, our frayed pants. Another Planet. Boris Iulianovich Poplavsky. TCRusP, *tr. by* Emmett Jarrett, Dick Lourie and Richard Lourie

With our own brown hands. (LL) What the Gypsy Said to Her Children. Judith Ortiz Cofer. OxWW; UnSA

With outward signs, as well as inward life. First Atlantic Telegraph, The. Jones Very. NCAP

With Pantheist energy of will. Venice. Herman Melville. APN-2

With Passion without Compassion. Oscar Hahn. BLPSL, *tr. by* Rene de Costa, Rigas Kappatos and Eleni Paidoussi

With paste of Almonds, *Syb* her hands doth scoure;. Robert Herrick. PBRV

With peace, let tares and acorns be my food. (LL) Country-Mouse, The. Abraham Cowley. NPeEn; OBVE

With peace on earth, good will to men. (LL) Christmas Bells. Henry Wadsworth Longfellow. ChrPo; OBCP

With pinched cheeks hollow and wan. Outcast, The. Josephine D. Henderson Heard. CBWP-4

With plain face and wrinkled forehead. Just an Ordinary Joe. John Wieners. AHA

With Plain Words. José Ángel Valente. RaW, *tr. by* Robert Mezey and Hardie St. Martin

With plum blossom scent. Basho. SoOfWa, *tr. by* Sam Hamill

With pointed head she rises above the roofs. With Pointed Head She Rises. Georg Heym. GTCP, *tr. by* Reinhold Grimm

With pointer in hand Mr. Dheeb al-Rifa'i ordered me to hold my arms out to the fullest extent. Mr. Dheeb Al-Rifa'i. Nasri Hajjaj. Eno, *tr. by* Ibrahim Muhawi

With powerful Saint Cyprian. Raising the Mediating Center and the Field of Evil with the Twenty-Five Thousand Accounts and the Chant of the Ancients. Eduardo Calderón. PFTM-2, *tr. by* F. Kaye Sharon

With proud thanksgiving, a mother for her children. For the Fallen. Laurence Binyon. NPeEn; OBEV; OBWP

With respect to the understanding of what is symbolized. (LL) Money. Howard Nemerov. VCAP; WeW-3

With reverence and submission due. Petition from the Chain Gang at Newcastle to Captain Furlong the Superintendent, A. Francis MacNamara. NOBAu

With rhetoric, promising nothing under the sun. (LL)   Ecclesiastes.   Derek Mahon.   BeAl; ChIV-1; ModIr; PNI

With roars of laughter and banging of doors.   Wind in the Room, The.   Karl Krolow.   GTCP, *tr. by* Reinhold Grimm

With rocks, and stones, and trees. (LL)   William Wordsworth.   BrAP; CtM; HeIP-4; InoFa; NAEL-6v2; NAEL-7v2; NOBRP; NoP-4; NoP-5; NPBRoP; NPeEn; OxBEV; PoPoPo; WeW-3 *Fr.* Lucy.

With ruder pomp, in more barbaric taste.   William Gilmore Simms.   APN-1 *Fr.* City of the Silent, The.

With rue my heart is laden.   Samuel Hoffenstein.   NBLV *Fr.* Mimic Muse, The.

With rue my heart is laden.   A. E. Housman.   HeIP-4; InoFa; MoBrPo; NAEL-6v2; NAEL-7v2; NAMCP V.1; NoAM; NoP-4; NoP-5; PoPoPo; TFi *Fr.* Shropshire Lad, A.

With sails full set, the ship her anchor weighs.   Emigravit.   Helen Hunt Jackson.   SWaP

With sedative voices we joke and spar.   Millie's Date.   Dannie Abse.   BloBone

With serving still.   His Reward.   Sir Thomas Wyatt.   NoSic

With Ships the sea was sprinkled far and nigh.   William Wordsworth.   CenSon; WoPoe

With *Sibells* I cannot Devine.   Song Composed in Time of the Civill Warr, when the Wicked Did Much Insult over the Godly, A.   Anne Collins.   EMWP

With sick and famished [*or* famisht] eyes.   Longing.   George Herbert.   FSCP; UV

With silence and tears. (LL)   When We Two Parted.   Lord Byron.   IJHIL; NAEL-6v2; NAEL-7v2; NoP-4; NoP-5; NPBRoP; OBEV; PoPoPo; TFi; UV

With Silence My Companion.   Shuntaro Tanikawa. *tr. by* William I. Elliott and Kazuo Kawamura

"I know how worthless this poem will be."   PFTM-2, *tr. by* William I. Elliott and Kazuo Kawamura

With Singing Angels hence she posts away.   Parthenea, an Elegy.   Elizabeth Singer Rowe.   PoBW

With sleep-drunken birds.   Safe-Conduct.   Ingeborg Bachmann.   PoSu, *tr. by* Daniel Huws

With snowy coats, snowy crests, and sapphire bills.   Egrets.   Tu Mu.   CCL1, *tr. by* R. F. Burton

With snowy light of moon I cannot you compare.   Martin Opitz.   GePo

With so much on my mind.   While Traveling.   Chia Tao.   CSKM, *tr. by* Mike O'Connor

With so much winter in my head and hand. (LL)   Paperweight, The.   Gjertrud Schnackenberg.   MoW; VCAP

With solitude what sorts, that here's not wondrous rife?   Michael Drayton.   NOSC *Fr.* Polyolbion [*or* Poly-Oobion].

With some surprise, I balance my small female skull in my hands.   Small Female Skull.   Carol Ann Duffy.   EmeKit; HarvBoo; MoWP

With someone who is not in love with.   Being in Love.   Marvin Bell.   InvLad; StAl

With something of angelic [*or* an angel] light. (LL)   She Was a Phantom of Delight.   William Wordsworth.   HeIP-4; NoP-5; NPBRoP; OBEV; TFi

With songs of Liberty! (LL)   On Liberty and Slavery.   George Moses Horton.   APN-1; NAAPv.1

With speed the prior body.   Bright Receding.   Heather Ramsdell.   AmPoNex; IAoNAP

With stones, then drive away. (LL)   Paul Laurence Dunbar.   Robert Earl Hayden.   ESEAA; GT; InoFa; NoP-4; NoP-5

With strange motives, barbarous splendors! (LL)   Triple Feature.   Denise Levertov.   NoP-4; NoP-5

With studied ease they take their places, withdrawn.   Practice.   Meg Schoerke.   PoDa

With subtle poise he grips his tray.   Atlantic City Waiter.   Countee Cullen.   APT-2; NAMCP V.1

With such a Pulse, with such disorder'd Veins.   Epistle from Alexander to Hephaestion in His Sickness, An.   Anne Finch, Countess of Winchilsea.   EMWP

With such a sound of gently pitying laughter. (LL)   My Grandmother's Love Letters.   Hart Crane.   BeAl; GPTC; NAAPv.2; NoAM; NoP-4; NoP-5; OxBoAm; PtR; WaAnP

With such compelling cause to grieve.   Alfred Tennyson.   NAEL-6v2; NAEL-7v2 *Fr.* In Memoriam A. H. H.

With such faint brightness. (LL)   With the Face.   Laura Riding Jackson.   APT-2; NAMCP V.1

With swift.   Release.   Adelaide Crapsey.   APT-1; NAAPv.2; OxBoAm

With Tears A-Flowing.   *Unknown.*   IQMS, *tr. by* John P. Sadler

With tears a-flowing I sign.   With Tears A-Flowing.   *Unknown.*   IQMS, *tr. by* John P. Sadler

With tears, his mother stayed him in the door.   Albery Allson Whitman.   NAAPv.1 *Fr.* Octoroon, The.

With tears I cling to your sleeves.   Yi Myŏnghan.   CATKP, *tr. by* Peter H. Lee

With teats distended with their milky store.   Bible, *O.T.*   STuOW *Fr.* Paraphrase on the Book of Job, A.

With Thanks to Eddie Shaw.   Janet Lowe.   PasH

With that delight the royal captive's brought.   Richard Lovelace.   CavPo

With that he stripped him to the ivory skin.   Christopher Marlowe.   WaAnP *Fr.* Hero and Leander.

With that I saw two swans of goodly hue [*or* hew].   Edmund Spenser.   OWoS *Fr.* Prothalamion.

With that mine hand in his he took anon.   Geoffrey Chaucer.   OBGa *Fr.* Parlement of Foules, The.

With that prodigious tongue.   Great Spotted Woodpecker, The.   Gordon Meade.   EdScPo

With that same unsettling instinct for how.   Romeo and Juliet.   Sherod Santos.   IaFF

With that the Wretched Child expires. (LL)   Henry King, Who Chewed Bits of String, and Was Early Cut Off in Dreadful Agonies.   Joseph Hilaire Pierre Belloc.   NBLV; OBCoV; OxAEP-2

With the All-Highest's Son, inseparable from Him. (LL)   Patmos.   Friedrich Hölderlin.   OBVE; WoPoe, *tr. by* David Gascoyne

With the awareness of a creature awaiting some kind of collapse.   I Usually Look Around Me.   Iman Mirsal.   NAfrP, *tr. by* Clarissa C. Burt

With the blaring Texas sun beating down against my bent back.   Good-bye Summer.   Jas. Mardis.   TiP2

With the blue-dark dome old-starred at night, green boat-lights purring over water,.   Galilee Shore.   Allen Ginsberg.   ChIV-2; FTOS

With the bulge and nuzzle of the sea. (LL)   When God Lets My Body Be.   E. E. Cummings.   MoAmPo; WaAnP

With the china and tea-leaves. (LL)   Modern Secrets.   Shirley Lim.   OPOU; StAl; UnSA

With the clear.   Olga Broumas.   WiU *Fr.* Caritas.

With the door closed. (LL)   Hanging Fire.   Audre Lorde.   BrAP; NAMCP V.2; NIL-7; NIP-4; NoAM; NoP-4; PoPoPo; TRP

With the exact security of the hoisting crane.   Monument to Birds (Max Ernst).   Luiza Neto Jorge.   SurWo, *tr. by* Jean R. Longland

With the eye of an anarchist? (LL)   To Carry the Child.   Stevie Smith.   NAMCP V.1; NoAM

With the face goes a mirror.   With the Face.   Laura Riding Jackson.   APT-2; NAMCP V.1

With the first light of the early morning dawning.   *Unknown.*   WoPoe *Fr.* Epic of Gilgamesh, The.

With the fragrance of twenty-five bodies burning with desire.   Birth, A.   N. Revathi Devi.   HotL, *tr. by* V. Narayana Rao

With the ghostly shapes of dead heroes.   Evening, The.   Georg Trakl.   WED, *tr. by* Robert Bly

With the gods overthrown like that, nobody knew which way to turn.   End of Dodona II, The.   Yannis Ritsos.   VCWP; WoPoe, *tr. by* Edmund Keeley

With the Grain.   Donald Davie.   NoAM

With the grave's narrowness, though not its peace. (LL)   Sick Love.   Robert Graves.   HarvBoo; NPeEn; OxAEP-2

With the head of a drum for my desk, I sit on a southern slope.   Soldier's Letter, A.   Fitz-James O'Brien.   PCW

With the heart of a child. (LL)   I Found Her Out There.   Thomas Hardy.   NAMCP V.1; NoAM; OxAEP-2

With the Herring Fishers.   Hugh MacDiarmid.   CABP

With the hot sand engraving a symbol of light upon time.   There Are No Doors.   Olga Orozco.   BLPSL, *tr. by* Rene de Costa, Rigas Kappatos and Eleni Paidoussi

With the last garden the road.   If.   Daria Menicanti.   CItWP, *tr. by* Cinzia Sartini Blum and Lara Trubowitz

With the last kindness of a foe or friend? (LL)   Jungle, The.   Alun Lewis.   AngWePo; OBWVE

With the map of the winter sky you drew for me.   Map of the Winter Sky, The.   Margherita Guidacci.   CItWP, *tr. by* Cinzia Sartini Blum and Lara Trubowitz

With the men of that old time? (LL)   Sequel of Appomattox.   Donald Davidson.   CBCWP; FuPo

With the mistake your life goes in reverse.   Mistake, The.   James Fenton.   BeAl

With the moon so bright.   After a Winter of Grieving.   Sam Hamill.   AmZen

With the night, my demon appears.   Magdalene (I).   Boris Leonidovich Pasternak.   GI, *tr. by* Nina Kossman

With the noon conch blown.   Buson.   SoOfWa, *tr. by* Sam Hamill

With the other husks of summer. (LL)   Dragonfly, The.   Louise Bogan.   APT-2; HeIP-4

With the others. (LL)   "H. D."   NAAPv.2; NALW *Fr.* Tribute to the Angels.

With the pear perhaps they are.   Josée Lapeyrère.   SCFWP *Fr.* Apples.

With the raw hungers of thy solitude. (LL)   Eros.   Michael Field.   NAEL-7v2; VWP

With the same heart, I said, I'll answer thee.   Elizabeth Barrett Browning.   CenSon *Fr.* Sonnets from the Portuguese.

With the satin stitch. Little Girl. Vivian Lamarque. CItWP, *tr.* by Cinzia Sartini Blum and Lara Trubowitz

With [*or* Wi'] the Scotch lords at his feet. (LL) Sir Patrick Spens [*or* Spence]. *Unknown.* BrAP; ClHu; GoPo; MakPoe; NAEL-6v1; NAEL-7v1; NePenScot; NIL-7; NIP-4; NoP-4; NoP-5; NPeEn; OBEV; OBSP; OxBEV; PoPoPo; TFi; WaAnP; WeW-3

With the second drink, at the restaurant. Promise, The. Sharon Olds. ExTi

With the Ships of Passage. Georg Heym. WoPoe, *tr.* by Peter Viereck

With the ships of passage. With the Ships of Passage. Georg Heym. WoPoe, *tr.* by Peter Viereck

With the slow smokeless burning of decay. (LL) Wood-Pile, The. Robert Frost. APT-1; ColAP; MoW; NAAL-5; NAAPv.2; NAMCP V.1; NoAM; NoP-4; NoP-5; OxBoAm; SAmP

With the storm moved on the next town. Centipede. Rita Dove. InvLad

With the Tide: A Cry of Weakness. Louisa Sarah Bevington. PEW *Fr.* Two songs.

With the tongue of Priapus and hands manifest and courteous. Inventory. Pedro Serrano. RMCMP, *tr.* by Geoff Hargreaves

With the wasp at the innermost heart of a peach. Scherzo, A. Dora Greenwell. NPeEn

With the window sliced open. Thirteenth Ode. Sekeena Shaben. PoArWo

With the world that will pass in a twinkling. (LL) On Pilgrimage. Czeslaw Milosz. AmFaPo; BeAl, *tr.* by the author and Robert Hass

With Thee a moment! Then what dreams have play! Desire. George Russell. OBMV

With thee conversing I forget all time. John Milton. UV; WoPoe *Fr.* Paradise Lost.

With their own personality. (LL) Willow Eyebrows. Chao Luan-luan. CCL1; NDACCP, *tr.* by Chung Ling and Kenneth Rexroth

With their poor frozen life and shallow banishment. (LL) Scotland's Winter. Edwin Muir. EdScPo; NePenScot

With their respective lions. Sea Unicorns and Land Unicorns. Marianne Moore. NALW; PFTM-1

With these green guests around. Who Says That Drought Was Here? Niyi Osundare. HBAPE; NAfrP

With these heaven-assailing spires. New York. George Russell. OBMV

With this ambiguous earth. Christ in the Universe. Alice Thompson Meynell. MoBrPo; OxAEP-2; VWP

With this change to indoor lighting. Sarah Messer. LegDan

With this gift of dirty pictures. *Unknown.* PriapPo *Fr.* Priapus Poems, The.

With this new Zoloft prescription, your eyes have become pools. With this change to indoor lighting. Sarah Messer. LegDan

With this rising bath-mist. Issa. SoOfWa, *tr.* by Sam Hamill

With throbbings of noontide. (LL) I Look into My Glass. Thomas Hardy. HarvBoo; NAEL-6v2; NAEL-7v2; NAMCP V.1; NoP-4; NoP-5; OxAEP-2; WeW-3

With thy rugged, ice-girt shore. Alaska. Mary Weston Fordham. CBWP-2

With tongs I trim the lamp. Kyunyŏ, Great Master. CATKP *Fr.* Eleven Poems on the Ten Vows of the Universally Worthy Bodhisattva.

With too much hope. Life at the Capital. Li Ho. CrYelRi, *tr.* by Sam Hamill

With tossed-aside, bruised fruit. (LL) Adrienne Rich. AmFaPo; BeAl; LoL *Fr.* Not Somewhere Else, But Here.

With trembling fingers did we weave. Alfred Tennyson. NAEL-6v2; NAEL-7v2 *Fr.* In Memoriam A. H. H.

With troubled heart and trembling hand I write. In Memory of My Dear Grandchild Anne Bradstreet Who Deceased June 20, 1669, Being Three Years and Seven Months Old. Anne Bradstreet. InoFa; NAAL-3

With two white roses on her breasts. Brown Girl Dead, A. Countee Cullen. GT; InoFa

With ŭ, with i, the overture begins. Lőrinc Szabó. IQMS *Fr.* Cricket Music.

With us, come home. (LL) Illumination. R. T. Smith. PoDa; Vesp

With *Usura*. Ezra Pound. APT-1; ColAP; HarvBoo; NAAL-5; NAAPv.2; NAMCP V.1; NoP-5; OxBoAm *Fr.* Cantos.

With visionary care. Summer Noon: 1941. Yvor Winters. ColAP

With voices as rich and husky as Nina's, with eyes that flirt like Yati's? (LL) Heaven. Chairil Anwar. PML; PoetW, *tr.* by Burton Raffel

With Walt Whitman at Fredericksburg. Dave Jeddie Smith. ViWalt

With Walter and Amati. Gabriel Preil. FIT, *tr.* by Robert Friend

With water warm enough to make me. Black and White Galaxie, The. Afaa Michael Weaver. UnSA

With what a childish and short-sighted sense. Danger. Helen Hunt Jackson. NAAPv.1

With what a gentle sound. September. Henrietta Cordelia Ray. CBWP-3

With what attentive courtesy he bent. Guitarist Tunes Up, The. Frances Darwin Cornford. SoSe-8

With what can I string this antique lyre. Unstrung Lyre, The. Eric Pankey. PoDa

With what Concern I sat and heard your Play. To My Much Esteemed Friend on Her Play Call'd Fatal-Friendship. Lady Sarah Piers. EMWP

With What Courage. Alessandro Ceni. ItPo, *tr.* by Gayle Ridinger

With what, dear bridegroom, can I fairly compare you? Sappho. SaLy, *tr.* by Diane Rayor

With what deep murmurs through time's silent stealth. Waterfall [*or* Waterfall], The. Henry Vaughan. AngWePo; NAEL-6v1; NAEL-7v1; NoP-4; NoP-5; NOSC; OBWVE; OxAEP-1; SacPr; WaAnP

With what sense is it that the chicken shuns the ravenous hawk? William Blake. OxBEV *Fr.* Visions of the Daughters of Albion.

With what sharp checks I in myself am shent. Sir Philip Sidney. NAEL-6v1; NAEL-7v1; NoSic *Fr.* Astrophil and Stella.

With what you know now about a garden by the sea. Tide Line Garden. W. S. Merwin. BodElec

With which to search for light. (LL) Generation, A. Gu Cheng. PFTM-2; VCWP, *tr.* by Sam Hamill

With Whitman at the Friendship Hotel. Anthony Piccione. ViWalt

With whom / do you leave yourself. Articulation. Rae Armantrout. OxBoAm

With Whom Is No Variableness, Neither Shadow of Turning. Arthur Hugh Clough. SacPr

With Whom, then, should I Sleep? George Ives. CAGL

With whom, then, should i sleep? perhaps with thee. With Whom, then, should I Sleep? George Ives. CAGL

With wings, I'll fly in the sky. On Reading Namwha Sutra. Jungkwan Haean. BecRai, *tr.* by Kim Daljin, Kim Won-Chung and Christopher Merrill

With wings that will not ever. Fumi Saito. WoPoe, *tr.* by Edith Marcombe Shiffert and Yuki Sawa

With words: "The whole point seems to be the idea of giving away the giver." (LL) Charnel Ground, The. Allen Ginsberg. BB; BodElec

With worms eternally. (LL) To the Oaks of Glencree. John Millington Synge. InoFa; MoBrPo

With yellow pears leans over. Half of Life. Friedrich Hölderlin. OBVE

With yellow pears the country. Half of Life, The. Friedrich Hölderlin. NAWM-7v2, *tr.* by Christopher Middleton

With you an immediacy stalls. Wittgenstein Letters to Mel Gibson's Braveheart, The. Erin Mouré. NLPA

With you I begin. David Steinberg. PasH

With you, I sip one *mojito* after another. Hemingway. Cyril Dabydeen. PML

With you I will roam to the river's nine channels. Yellow River's Earl, The. Ch'u Yüan. WoPoe, *tr.* by Stephen Owen

With you on my mind I walked away. You on My Mind. Kavikondala Venkatarao. HotL, *tr.* by V. Narayana Rao

With your Death full of Flowers. (LL) Allen Ginsberg. BB; CLPP *Fr.* Kaddish.

With your enemies, the swift departing years. (LL) Elegy: "April again, and it is a year again." Sidney Keyes. NoP-4; NoP-5

With your hands you freed. Boy with the Empty Cage, The. José Hierro. RaW, *tr.* by Rachel Benson

With Your Mother in a Café. Shaun Levin. PML

With your one wild and precious life? (LL) Summer Day, The. Mary Oliver. AmFaPo; BeAl; CAP-8; TWF

With Your Permission. Mario Benedetti. TCLAP, *tr.* by David Arthur McMurray

With your tall. Tengan Osho's Visit to Erin-ji. Muso Soseki. EaWin, *tr.* by W. S. Merwin

With your teepee and Lucky Strike. And Where Were You. Len Roberts. BodElec

With your tiny, timorous toes. (LL) Grass Fingers. Angelina Weld Grimké. APT-1; NAAPv.2

Withal a meagre [*or* meager] man was Aaron Stark. Aaron Stark. Edwin Arlington Robinson. APN-2; MoAmPo

(Withal a meagre man was Aaron Stark.) NCAP

Withdrawal Letter. Jim Carroll. PmAP

Withdrawing all his postal savings. Two Tokyos. Shuntaro Tanikawa. PoetW, *tr.* by Harold Wright

Withdrawing from the amorous grasses. Snake, The. Kenneth Mackenzie. BrAP

Wither excursive fancy tends thy flight? Newspaper, The. Penina Moise and Edward N. Calisch. SWaP

Withered fields, The. Issa. EH, *tr.* by Robert Hass

Withered Fish, A. *Unknown.* CCL1, *tr.* by Anne Birrell

Withered fish by a river wept, A. Withered Fish, A. *Unknown.* CCL1, *tr.* by Anne Birrell

Withered grass on ground. Shonan Suzuki. NAAPv.2

Withered grass / Under piling. Basho. ZenPo, *tr.* by Takashi Ikemoto and Lucien Stryk

Withered leaves that drift in Russell Square, The. Drilling in Russell Square. Edward Richard Burton Shanks. OBMV

Withered Lotus. Yosano Tekkan. CAoMJL1, *tr.* by Leith Morton

Withered Tree, A. Han Yü. CCL1, *tr.* by A. C. Graham

Withered tree doesn't blossom, The. Kamalākānta Bhattācārya. SinGod, *tr.* by Rachel Fell McDermott

Withered vines cling to the old tree. In Autumn. Ma Chih-yüan. CrYelRi, *tr. by* Sam Hamill

Withered wisteria, old tree, darkling crows. Tune: "Heaven-Cleansed Sands." Ma Chih-yüan. ColAnChi, *tr. by* Victor H. Mair

Withered, withered, by the wind's omen. *Unknown.* NDACCP, *tr. by* Ezra Pound

Withered Zen. Muso Soseki. EaWin, *tr. by* W. S. Merwin

Withering winds. Basho. EMJL, *tr. by* Haruo Shirane

Withers benumbed in a world his joy might have helped to illume. (LL) On a Forsaken Lark's Nest. Mathilde Blind. ViWPN; VWP

Within. Philip Booth. PoCoUp

Within a churchyard, on a recent grave. Caged Goldfinch, The. Thomas Hardy. OWoS

Within a dark and cheerless hut. Old Saint's Prayer, The. Priscilla Jane Thompson. CBWP-2

Within a ditch beyond my wall. Wounded Falcon, The. Han Yü. CCL1, *tr. by* H. A. Giles

Within a dream. (LL) Vitae Summa Brevis Spem Nos Vetat Incohare Longam. Ernest Dowson. CABP; NoP-4; NoP-5; NPeEn; OBEV; OxBEV; TFi

Within a fog that enfolds the trees, their leaves are spirited away. Trees That Come Undone within a Sphere of Fog. Francis Ponge. YaTCFP, *tr. by* Lee Fahnestock

Within a frame, more glorious than the gem. Frances Sargent Osgood. ColAP

Within a London hospital there lies. His Mother Drinks. Edwin Emanuel Bradford. VerBaPo

Within an avalanche of glory hallelujah skybreaks. Avalanche. Quincy Troupe. PFTM-2; SpirFl

Within and Without. Elizabeth Jessup Blake. YaYoPo

Within each petal. Peter Levitt. WhBo

Within five weeks. My Son's Wedding, My Daughter's. Barbara Hurd. NevBe

Within four walls and one window. Excavation, The. Carl Hancock Rux. HeMarv

Within her someone perpares a banquet. Cycle of Months (Menstruation). Shuntaro Tanikawa. PFTM-2, *tr. by* Harold Wright

Within herself. Uma Worshipping Shiva (On a Kangra miniature). Elsa Cross. TANSG, *tr. by* Patricia Dubrava

Within his office, smiling. Dove, The. Victor James Daley. NOBAu

Within his tent of pain and oxygen. Last Rites. Francis Reginald Scott. BrAP

Within its boundaries—no people, only birds. Yo Hermitage. Pou Kuksa. BecRai, *tr. by* Kim Daljin, Kim Won-Chung and Christopher Merrill

Within just ten days. Keiho Soga. NAAPv.2

Within me a half-veined magnolia. Women Within Me. Na Hûidôk. EcSo, *tr. by* Peter H. Lee

Within my bosom a man has lived for nearly three million years. Nearly Three Million Years Ago. Mohamed Lasheen. AnVo, *tr. by* Mohamed Enani

Within my casement came one night. Dawn of Love, The. Henrietta Cordelia Ray. CBWP-3

Within my head, aches the perpetual winter. Winter and Summer. Stephen Spender. MoBrPo

Within my heart Love himself made Heliodora. Meleager. HePo, *tr. by* Barbara Hughes Fowler

Within My Life. J. Slauerhoff. TuT, *tr. by* Desmond Egan

Within my life, which is continually torn. Within My Life. J. Slauerhoff. TuT, *tr. by* Desmond Egan

Within— / The beaten pride. Uncle Tom. Langston Hughes. SAmP

Within the day a seventh time. Gift from Kenya. May Miller. OxAAAP

Within the Dome. Ron Padgett and James Schuyler. AHA

Within the edges of sense, indifferent. Eye Occupation, The. Jennifer Timoner. ICANM

Within the flower there lies a seed. Spell of Creation. Kathleen Jessie Raine. PoCho

Within the gentle heart Love shelters him. Canzone: Of the Gentle Heart. Guido Guinicelli. OBVE, *tr. by* Dante Gabriel Rossetti

Within the Gorges there is no lack of men. Invitation to Hsiao Ch'u-shih. Po Chü-i. OBVE, *tr. by* Arthur Waley

Within the great grey flapping tent. Auction Sale, The. Henry Reed. MoBrPo

Within the groves of Grongar Hill. (LL) Grongar Hill. John Dyer. CABP; NoP-4; OxAEP-1

Within the lamplight's radius. Needlework. Mimi Khalvati. MFPA

Within the pain of words. (LL) Heartsong. Khaled Mattawa. BAP-97; NAPBL; NeAmPo

Within the Seasons. Peter Blue Cloud. HATNAP
    Spring Equinox. ChAP

Within the soul's courts is a temple fair. Soul's Courts, The. Henrietta Cordelia Ray. CBWP-3

Within the sum of words, there are words. Foreign Relations. Fergus Allen. NIrP

Within the town of Buffalo. Vachel Lindsay. AmWit *Fr.* Niagara.

Within the wires of the post, unloading the cans of garbage. Prisoners. Randall Jarrell. AmWaPo

Within this black hive to-night. Beehive. Jean Toomer. GT; OxBoAm

Within This Book, Called Marguerite. Marjorie Welish. FTOS; PmAP

Within this mindless vault. James Vincent Cunningham. WoPoe *Fr.* Epigrams: A Journal.

Within this pleasant wood, beside the lane. Woodland Seat, A. John Clare. CenSo

Within this sober frame expect. Upon Appleton House [To My Lord Fairfax]. Andrew Marvell. BASC; NAEL-7v1

Within this vale. Burma-Shave Roadside Signs. *Unknown.* OBCoV

WITHIN THIS VALE. *Unknown.* OBCoV *Fr.* Advertising Rhymes.

Within those halls where student zeal. Alfred Denis Godley. TriCat

Within two equal days. (LL) Lisp in Numbers, A. Edward Edwin Foot. STuOW; VerBaPo

Without. Bruce Berger. OPRER

Without. Donald Hall. PoA 2002

Without. Gary Snyder. WhBo

Without a hillock stretched the plain. In Louisiana. John William DeForest. AmWaPo

Without a jot of ambition left. Ryokan. ZenPo, *tr. by* Takashi Ikemoto and Lucien Stryk

Without a king, to see the end of time. (LL) On Mr. Paine's Rights of Man. Philip Freneau. NAAL-3; NAAL-5; NAAPv.1

Without a label. It's for you. (LL) Guide to the Other Gallery. Dana Gioia. RA; WaAnP

Without a net, eh? Orpheus then is. For the Late R. F. Thom Gunn. VisFro

Without a pass. (LL) Child Who Was Shot Dead by Soldiers at Nyanga, The. Ingrid Jonker. HAWP; WoPoe, *tr. by* Jack Cope, Uys Krige and William Plomer

Without a single sun. Under the Ninth Sky. Georg Nikolic. IllVoic

Without a Song. Edward Eliscu and Billy Rose. ReLy

Without a song. Without a Song. Edward Eliscu and Billy Rose. ReLy

Without a sound. Ransetsu. SoOfWa, *tr. by* Sam Hamill

Without a stone to mark the spot. To Thyrza. Lord Byron. CAGL

Without a word writ down. Sikong Tu. CCL1 *Fr.* Twenty-Four Modes of Poetry.

Without an audience or a history. Being an Immigrant. Matilde Salganicoff. MirDau, *tr. by* Celeste Kostopulos-Cooperman

Without any travelers, and lonely for no one. (LL) Eating Together. Li-Young Lee. CAP-8; IllVoic; InvLad; NAAL-5; NAMCP V.2

Without breaking anything. (LL) Spring is like a perhaps hand. E. E. Cummings. NoP-4; NoP-5

Without Ceremony. Vassar Miller. MoAmPo

Without doubt man in nature. Natus de Muliere, Brevi Vivens. Emilio Villa. ItPo, *tr. by* Gayle Ridinger

Without doubt there should be an armed uprising of the gums. Hostility. Gerardo Diego. RaW, *tr. by* Ralph Nelson and Hardie St. Martin

Without dressmakers to connect. Because of Clothes. Laura Riding Jackson. APT-2; OxBoAm

Without external reference. Two Horses and a Dog. James Galvin. GifTon

Without fail runaways go to the Monument. Skills. Celia de Fréine. NIrP, *tr. by the author*

Without fear. Vulnerability. Fedya Filkova. CSCBP, *tr. by* Georgi Belev and Lisa Sapinkopf

Without fear or fault, the green. Morningside Park. Stephen Burt. LegDan

Without friends, longing to be there. Sikong Tu. CCL1 *Fr.* Twenty-Four Modes of Poetry.

Without God's blessing, the world goes on for now. Without God's Blessing. Herschel Miller. Prolet, *tr. by* Amelia Glaser

Without going out-of-doors. Lao Tzu. ColAnChi *Fr.* Tao Te Ching.

Without Guile. Paul Verlaine. SxFrPo, *tr. by* Martin Sorrell

Without haste! without rest! Haste Not! Rest Not! Johann Wolfgang von Goethe. TreFP, *tr. by Unknown*

Without Heat. Alexei Remizov. MotU, *tr. by* Nancy Condee

Without Histories. Blanca Wiethüchter. TANSG, *tr. by* Shaun Griffin and Emma Sepúlveda-Pulvirenti

Without kings and warriors occasional verse fails. On Being Asked to Write a Poem for 1979. Jack A. Mapanje. AF; NAfrP

Without lights, now totally dark, fierce. Without Lights. Jorge Guillén. RaW, *tr. by* Charles Guenther

Without Me. Leontia Flynn. NIrP

Without me and without you, what's the point. Without Me. Leontia Flynn. NIrP

Without me anyway without way I came near without bread. Without Me Anyway. Meret Oppenheim. SurPaPo, *tr. by* Catherine Schelbert

Without me you can only. Kenneth Rexroth. APSN; APT-2 *Fr.* Love Poems of Marichiko, The.

Without muscles without slipping. Silvana Colonna. ItPo, *tr. by* Gayle Ridinger

Without my having known. Boy Died in My Alley, The. Gwendolyn Brooks. NAMCP V.2; NoAM

Without my knowing it you are the bottom of my mind. You Are at the Bottom of My Mind. Iain Crichton Smith. WoPoe

Without my lyrical wizardry. Kill the dj. Reg E. Gaines. BRtP

Without my mother tongue and my country. Identity. Margit Mikes. IQMS, *tr. by* Susanne K. Walther

Without my own. (LL) All the World Moved. June Jordan. EGAG; GT

Without obsessions. Obsession. Angelina Muñiz Huberman. MirDau, *tr. by* Aurora Camacho

Without Pity. Elizabeth Willis. IIR

Without pleasure. Simonides. SaLy, *tr. by* Diane Rayor

Without Presumptions. Chris Forhan. NAPBL

Without question, / Without kiss. (LL) Lethe. "H. D." APT-1; MoAmPo; TCAPo

Without seemliness / without love. (LL) Mutes, The. Denise Levertov. BeAl; CAP-8; ErotSp; NALW; OxBoAm

Without Shadow. Rudy Bee Graham. EGAG

Without stating them. / Buildings. (LL) Lights, paving—, The. George Oppen. APT-2; PFTM-1

Without the Boy. Nathan Yonathan. NRoS, *tr. by* Esther Raizen

Without the damn god of love? (LL) Nine Sentiments, The. Michael Ondaatje. NLPA; OpeFie

Without the decency of shells. Slugs. Gillian Ferguson. MFPA

Without the hall, and close upon the gate. Homer. OBVE *Fr.* Odyssey.

Without—the power to die. (LL) My Life had stood—a Loaded Gun. Emily Dickinson. APN-2; HeIP-4; NAAL-3; NAAL-5; NAAPv.1; NALW; NAMCP V.1; NAWM-7v2; NCAP; NIL-7; NIP-4; NoP-4; NoP-5; OxBoAm; OxWW; PoPoPo; SAmP; SWaP; TCAPo; TRP; WaAnP; WeW-3

Without thinking you were alive again. (LL) Embrace, The. Mark Doty. AmAlph; AmFaPo; BeAl; NAMCP V.2

Without thought. (LL) At the Ball Game. William Carlos Williams. BrAP; MoASP; NoAM

Without Title. Li Shang-yin. CCL1, *tr. by* James J. Y. Liu

Without Title (1). Li Shang-yin. ChinPo, *tr. by* Ye Weilian [*or* Yeh Wei-lien *or* Wai-lim Yip]

Without Title (2). Li Shang-yin. ChinPo, *tr. by* Ye Weilian [*or* Yeh Wei-lien *or* Wai-lim Yip]

Without touch he seems to hold on. Therapist, The. Leanne O'Sullivan. NIrP

Without us you would have no life. (LL) Seder Night with My Ancestors. Joanne Limburg. BeAl; NeBl

Without Villages. Ray Gonzalez. TouFir

Without Warning. Angel González. RaW, *tr. by* Robert Mezey and Hardie St. Martin

Without warning, the idea of the poem. Carpet. Nancy Morejón. TANSG, *tr. by* Joy Renjilian-Burgy

Without wine I stop singing. Sung Impromptu. Yi Kyubo. CATKP, *tr. by* Kevin O'Rourke

Without words or plans I was arriving. Humus. Karen Press. TSAP

Without you I am like the Portuguese in Mergui. Portuguese in Mergui, The. George Green. P180

Without you, I prefer the nights. Vicki Feaver. NewEx

Witless of my grief was I. Lament of Mary, The. *Unknown.* IQMS, *tr. by* Watson Kirkconnell

Witness. Bruce Beasley. AmAlph

Witness. William Heyen. CAP-8

Witness. David Ignatow. PoA 2002

Witness. Denise Levertov. BLT; TWF

Witness. Ráchel Wetzsteon. AmPoNex

Witness, The. Jorge Luis Borges. MotU, *tr. by* Mildred Boyer

Witness, The. Rose Drachler. TaR

Witness, The. Ken Mikolowski. PrTe

Witness, The. Eve Triem. PWW2

Witness Remains, The. Thich Nhat Hanh and Jane Hirshfield. WhBo

Witness, Susanna Dickinson, The. Violette Newton. TiP2

Witness the sarcophagus of non-Raphael. Earthworker's God is Healed, The. Bernadette Mayer. FTOS

Witnesses, The. Henry Wadsworth Longfellow. PCW

Witnessing the Launch of the Shuttle *Atlantis.* Howard Nemerov. OtW

Wit's [*or* Thought's] forge and fire-blast [*or* furnace], meaning's press [*or* mangle-press] and screw. (LL) On Donne's Poetry. Samuel Taylor Coleridge. NAEL-6v2; NAEL-7v2; UV

Wit's Pilgrimage. John Davies of Hereford.
  9. OxBSo
  31. OxBSo
  69. OxBSo
  78. OxBSo

Wits, The; A Session[s] of the Poets. Sir John Suckling. BASC; CABP

Wittgenstein held a sweaty mother once too. Like Beatrix Potter. Jeni Olin. FreRad

Wittgenstein Letters to Mel Gibson's Braveheart, The. Erin Mouré. NLPA
  Archaic Torso of Kim. NLPA
  Bestows profound benefits on her practitioner. NLPA
  Girl Profligacy, A. NLPA
  Her glad hand. NLPA
  My will. NLPA
  Socially-constituted objects include ourselves. NLPA
  Their tautology. NLPA
  Tremendous assertion. NLPA
  Whose adoration. NLPA
  You place. NLPA

Wittler, Hittler, or something like that. (LL) Portrait of a House Detective. Hans Magnus Enzensberger. HP; PoSu, *tr. by* Michael Hamburger

Wives of my friends, The. At the Cookout. Charles Simic. PML

Wizard. Thomas Campbell. NePenScot *Fr.* Lochiel's Warning.

Wizard snuck into his hometown, A. Deathbed Song. Hueung Powoo. BecRai, *tr. by* Kim Daljin, Kim Won-Chung and Christopher Merrill

Wizard's Chant, The. *Unknown.* APN-2, *tr. by* Charles Godfrey Leland

Wizened, spoiling for a fight, Frost is here. Frost. Floyd Skloot. VisFro

Wlk'n down regent street i see. Blkfern-jungal. Aileen Corpus. BMAP

Wo/man's Voice Must Be Heard, A. Lorena M. Craighead. InTrad

Wo/men. Chiqui Vicioso. TANSG, *tr. by* Daisy Cocco De Filippis

Wo/men draped in black. Wo/men. Chiqui Vicioso. TANSG, *tr. by* Daisy Cocco De Filippis

Wodwo. Ted Hughes. BrAP; HarvBoo; NAMCP V.2; NoAM; WoPoe

Woe. Ethan Paquin. IIR

Woe Indeed! Ts'ao Chih. ChinPo, *tr. by* Ye Weilian [*or* Yeh Wei-lien *or* Wai-lim Yip]

Woe indeed, this tumbleweed! Woe Indeed! Ts'ao Chih. ChinPo, *tr. by* Ye Weilian [*or* Yeh Wei-lien *or* Wai-lim Yip]

Woe: lightly to part with one's soul as the sea with its foam! Tarpeia. Louise Imogen Guiney. NAAPv.1

Woe Then to the Gossips. Meinloh von Sevelingen. GePo, *tr. by* J. W. Thomas

Woe then to the gossips! They show their evil will. Woe Then to the Gossips. Meinloh von Sevelingen. GePo, *tr. by* J. W. Thomas

Woe to England, when the Kings Life is gone! Revelation 5, October 8. Anne Wentworth. EMWP

Woe to Him Who Slanders Women. Gerald Fitzgerald, 4th Earl of Desmond. IrLP

Woe to us who know the words without knowing the Word that is there. Adrift. David Gwenallt Jones. BBMWP, *tr. by* Joseph P. Clancy

Woe! Woe! / Hearken ye! Chant from the Iroquois Book of Rites. *Unknown.* APN-2, *tr. by* Horatio Hale

Woe, woe to them, who (by a ball of strife). To the King and Queen[e], upon Their Unhappy Distances. Robert Herrick. BASC

Woeful mankind, born to a woeful earth! Voltaire. WoPoe *Fr.* Poem Upon the Lisbon Disaster; or, An Inquiry into the Adage, "All Is for the Best."

Woful Words of the Hart, The. George Turberville. DiBP

Woke up this mornin'. I'm Gonna Go Fishin'. Peggy Lee. ReLy

Woke up this mornin' when chickens was crowin' for days. Young Woman's Blues. Bessie Smith. NAAPv.2

Woke up this morning with a / limp. Poem With a Limp. Roger McGough. OBCoV

Woke up to one of those cold. Barrio Beateo. Jesse F. García. UnSA

Woke up to the finches crowing. Contentment. Miriam Sagan. WANABP

Wold Clock, The. William Barnes. FaBoVe

Wold clock's feäce is still in pleäce, The. Wold Clock, The. William Barnes. FaBoVe

Wolde God that hyt were so. *Unknown.* EMWP

Wolf. Peter Blue Cloud. HATNAP

Wolf. Fujii Sadakazu. PFTM-2 *Fr.* Where is Japanese Poetry?

Wolf, The. Georgia Roberts Durston. TLR

Wolf, The. Jennifer Grotz. LegDan

Wolf and a lamb had come to the same little brook, A. Wolf and the Lamb, The. Phaedrus. RomPo, *tr. by* Eugene O'Connor

Wolf and Hound. Adam Lindsay Gordon.
  Fight in the Cave, The. STuOW

Wolf and the Dog, The. Jean de La Fontaine. OBVE, *tr. by* Elizur Wright

Wolf and the Lamb, The. Marie de France. NAEL-7v1, *tr. by* Harriet Spiegel

Wolf and the Lamb, The. Phaedrus. RomPo, *tr.* by Eugene O'Connor

Wolf and the Sow, The. Marie de France. NAEL-7v1, *tr.* by Harriet Spiegel

Wolf and the Stork, The. Jean de La Fontaine. OBVE, *tr.* by Marianne Moore

Wolf at the door, The. Early Instruments. Don McKay. OpeFie

Wolf "Aunt." Maurice Kenny. HATNAP

Wolf God, The. Anne Carson. WoBe *Fr.* Truth About God, The.

Wolf is still under the blanket, The. Sounds That Arrived, The. Milo De Angelis. NeIt, *tr.* by Lawrence Venuti

Wolf met a spring, A. Aesop Revised by Archy. Don Marquis. APT-1

Wolf of Gubbio, The. William Matthews. P180

Wolf Packet and Rural America. Matthew Wascovich. BeDoSh

Wolf Ridge. John Ashbery. BAP-04; VaPo

Wolf Soup. Vijay Seshadri. LiTh

Wolf Speaks, The. Paul Klee. PFTM-1

Wolf speaks, while chewing, The. Wolf Speaks, The. Paul Klee. PFTM-1

Wolf that follows, the fawn that flies, The. (LL) Algernon Charles Swinburne. NAEL-6v2; NAEL-7v2; OBEV; OxBEV; TFi; WeW-3 *Fr.* Atalanta in Calydon.

Wolf wails or wild-wind screeches. Yelling-alive. Ianka Kupala. SonAtl, *tr.* by Rashed Chowdhury and Maria Tchoudkhouri

Wolf Warrior. Joy Harjo. PfSP

Wolf-bait on the bush beside the spring, The. (LL) Frederick Goddard Tuckerman. APN-2; TCAPo *Fr.* Sonnets.

Wolfram's Dirge. Thomas Lovell Beddoes. OBEV; OxAEP-2

Wolf's Road, The. Stanley Noyes. ICANM

Wolves. Louis MacNeice. NoAM

Wolves. Peter Mortimer. RSaN

Wolves. Y. A. Rontsh. Prolet, *tr.* by Amelia Glaser

Wolves, The. Allen Tate. APT-2; NAAPv.2; OxBoAm

Wolves are coming back to Germany, The. Immigrants. Lotte Kramer. RSaN

Wolves can outeat anyone. Wolf and the Stork, The. Jean de La Fontaine. OBVE, *tr.* by Marianne Moore

Wolves in the Zoo. Howard Nemerov. NoAM

Woman. Hira Bansode. CFP; ItWoWo; WoPoe, *tr.* by Vinay Dharwadker

Woman: "Weeds loom." Georgi Belev. CSCBP, *tr.* by the author and Lisa Sapinkopf

Woman. Ina Coolbrith. FTtHH; NAAPv.1

Woman. Alaide Foppa. TANSG, *tr.* by Celeste Kostopulos-Cooperman

Woman. Oliver Goldsmith. *See* When Lovely Woman Stoops to Folly.

Woman: "Women carry life." Michel-Ange Hyppolite. OGAHCP, *tr.* by Boadiba and Jack Hirschman

Woman. Juana de Ibarbourou. TCLAP, *tr.* by Sophie Cabot Black

Woman. Kang Ŭn'gyo. CAMKP, *tr.* by Kevin O'Rourke

Woman. Sute-Jo, Lady. ZenPo, *tr.* by Takashi Ikemoto and Lucien Stryk

Woman. Ella Wheeler Wilcox. SWaP

Woman, A. Gabriela Mistral. TCLAP, *tr.* by Doris Dana

Woman, A. Robert Pinsky. WeW-3

Woman, A / makes the sign of the cross. Ana Belén López Pulido. SPV, *tr.* by Jen Hofer

Woman, A. Sa'di Yusuf. PML, *tr.* by Lena Jayyusi and W. S. Merwin and Naomi Shihab Nye

Woman, The. Shakuntala Hawoldar. HAWP

Woman, The. Kristina Rungano. HAWP

Woman, a pleasing but a short-lived flow'r [*or* flower]. Essay on Woman, An. Mary Leapor. BrAP; NAEL-7v1

Woman Alone, A. Denise Levertov. BodElec; MoWP

Woman alone, living. From the Garden of the Women Once Fallen. Lorna Goodison. VCWP

Woman and a Man, A. Adonis. PML, *tr.* by Abdullah Al-Udhari

Woman and a man carried along by life, A. Man and a Woman, A. Juan Gelman. BLPSL, *tr.* by Rene de Costa, Rigas Kappatos and Eleni Paidoussi

Woman and Beauty. Goran. IrPoTo, *tr.* by Abdul Kadir Said Ferhadi

Woman and Cat. Paul Verlaine. WoPoe, *tr.* by Felicity Bast

Woman and falcons—they are easily tamed. Der von Kürenberg. GePo

Woman and Fame. Felicia Dorothea Hemans. ViWPN; VWP

Woman and the Angel, The. Robert W. Service. ChIV-1

Woman as Artist. Eleanor Ross Taylor. InGu

Woman as Market. Muriel Rukeyser. NoAM

Woman asleep. Marie-Claire Bancquart. MFP, *tr.* by Martin Sorrell

Woman at Lit Window. Eamon Grennan. BLT

Woman at the lecture waves her hand, A. Everyone Who Wants to Work Can. Brooke Wiese. OPRER

Woman at the Piano. Marya Alexandrovna Zaturenska. MoAmPo

Woman at the table beside mine is crying, The. At the Frenchman's. Kendra Hamilton. BRtP

Woman at the Washington Zoo, The. Randall Jarrell. BrAP; InGu; ItP; OxBoAm; VCAP

Woman at the Washtub, The. Victor James Daley. NOBAu

Woman Bathing. Raymond Carver. PasH

Woman begins to hide her age, A. Elderly Woman, An. Mun Chônghui. EcSo, *tr.* by Catherine J. Kim

Woman begins to weep, A. (LL) Afterimages. Audre Lorde. LTA; VCAP

Woman beside me on the Jitney weeps, The. Free Mercy. Philip Schultz. PA9/11

Woman bore me, I will rise. (LL) A. E. Housman. FaBoWar; MoBrPo; OBWP *Fr.* Shropshire Lad, A.

Woman / breathing. (LL) Death of Marilyn Monroe, The. Sharon Olds. HeIP-4; InoFa; ReTh

Woman came into "a car I rode" "about thirty-seven" "maybe", A. Alice Notley. OxBoAm

Woman came toward me through the woods with a hatchet, The. Walk, The. Oni Buchanan. BAP-04

Woman, caught in a homeland-trap of the Chosen People: you, A. National Thoughts. Yehuda Amichai. PFTM-2, *tr.* by Stephen Mitchell

Woman Cleaning Lentils, The. Zehrd [*or* Zahrad]. PML, *tr.* by Diana Der Hovanessian and Marzbed Margossian

Woman coming down the snowy road, A. Grey Woman. Gladys Cardiff. GifTon

Woman crossed the park and laughed, A. Enveloping Echo, The. Ion Caraion. AF, *tr.* by Marguerite Dorian and Elliott B. Urdang

Woman Death. Hazel Hall. APT-1

Woman Dragged by Welsh Corgis. Joan Retallack. FTOS

Woman drest by Age, A. Margaret Lucas Cavendish, Duchess of Newcastle. BrAP; PEW

Woman eternal my muse, lean toward me. Paul Goodman. BodElec

Woman fears for man, he goes. Abel's Bride. Denise Levertov. NALW; OxBoAm

Woman fresh off the train, A. There Goes the Bride. M. Loncar. AmPoNex

Woman from Ch'ang-kan, The. Li Po. CrYelRi *Fr.* Women of Yueh.

Woman from the Book of Genesis, A. Dovid Knut. TCRusP, *tr.* by John Glad

Woman Gave Me a Red Star to Wear on My Headband, A. Jimmie Durham. HATNAP

Woman gets all the blame, A. Trouble Is a Man. Alec Wilder. ReLy

Woman Going Blind. Rainer Maria Rilke. GTCP, *tr.* by Felix Pollak

Woman grows hard and skinny, A. Ride the Turtle's Back. Beth Brant. ItWoWo

Woman had the boy by the hand, The. Advice Like That. Eloise Klein Healy. SUP

Woman Hanging from Lightpole, Illinois Route 136. Lucia Cordell Getsi. IllVoic

Woman Hanging from the Thirteenth Floor Window, The. Joy Harjo. HATNAP

Woman Hanging Laundry. Kang Ŭn'gyo. EcSo, *tr.* by Ann Y. Choi

Woman "heard angels", A. The paper says angels. Talk Show, The. Albert Goldbarth. CAP-8; IllVoic; ReTh

Woman Holding a Fox. David Yezzi. PoDa

Woman I am, The. Unquiet Bed, The. Dorothy Livesay. BrAP

Woman I Carelessly Killed, The. Kim Chôngnan. EcSo, *tr.* by Peter H. Lee

Woman I have never seen before, A. Transit. Richard Wilbur. NIL-7

Woman I Know, The. Jeannette Miller. TANSG, *tr.* by Paula Vega

Woman I know, The. Woman I Know, The. Jeannette Miller. TANSG, *tr.* by Paula Vega

Woman I used to know well died, A. Memory. Hayden Carruth. GoPo

Woman in exile never stops dying, The. *Unknown.* SLW, *tr.* by Marjolijn De Jager, Sayd Bahodin Majrouh and André Velter

Woman in front of you's black hair blowing over itself. Rodeo Tangent. Kendra Borgmann. MoASP

Woman in Heat Wiping Herself, A. Sharon Olds. CAP-8

Woman in Kitchen. Eavan Boland. WaAnP

Woman In Love. Paul Éluard. NAWM-7v2, *tr.* by Lloyd Alexander

Woman in middle-life. Lorine Niedecker. APT-2

Woman in my building who skips, The. Alms. Stanley Plumly. BodElec

Woman in my shower now, A. What Goes Around Comes Around, or The Proof is in the Pudding. Cheryl Clarke. FFC

Woman in the Film, The. Lesley Dauer. NAPBL

Woman in the Moon, The. Nadya Aisenberg. PfS

Woman in the pointed hood, The. Village Mystery. Elinor Wylie. APT-1

Woman in the Red House. Michael Burkard. LaCa

Woman in the shape of a monster, A. Planetarium. Adrienne Rich. BrAP; CAP-8; EMP; NALW; NAMCP V.2; NIL-7; NIP-4; NoAM; VCAP

Woman inside every woman, The. Why There Are Children. Leslie Ullman. YaYoPo

Woman inside turns flour to dumplings, The. What Lies Beneath. Shara McCallum. SweBea

Woman is by aptitude. *Unknown.* OBWVE *Fr.* Against Women.

Woman is perfected, The. Edge. Sylvia Plath. BrAP; InoFa; NALW; NAMCP V.2; NPeEn; OxBoAm; PoPoPo; VCAP

Woman is reading a poem on the street, A. Hug, The. Tess Gallagher. StAl

Woman Is Running for Her Life, A. Sheila Demetre. FiBr

Woman is singing in the valley. The shadows falling blot her out, A. Song. Gabriela Mistral. WPoS, *tr. by* Langston Hughes

Woman is sitting reading a prayer, A. For the Far-Out Experimental Writer. Víctor Hernández Cruz. PueRic

Woman is using a handkerchief, The. At the Hammersmith Palais. Alan Riddell. NOBAu

Woman is Waiting for a Bus, A. Maura Eichner. UpMys

Woman is wild, The. Still life. Ingrid de Kok. TSAP

Woman Kneeling in the Sorry Jelly, A. Joyce Mansour. HAWP, *tr. by* Albert Herzing

Woman kneeling in the sorry jelly, A. Woman Kneeling in the Sorry Jelly, A. Joyce Mansour. HAWP, *tr. by* Albert Herzing

Woman lay dying on a pallet in a gateway, A. Good Lord Saved Her, The. Anna Swirszczynska [*or* Swir]. PoSu

Woman living in the Northern Hemisphere sets the dripping-clean bowl, A. Coriolis Effect, The. Chuck Wachtel. PrTe

Woman Me. Maya Angelou. OxWW

Woman Measures, A. Jean Daive. MFP, *tr. by* Julie Kalendek and Martin Sorrell

(Eden.) OnScMo

Woman Measures, A. Woman measures, A. Jean Daive. MFP, *tr. by* Julie Kalendek and Martin Sorrell

Woman Meets an Old Lover, A. Denise Levertov. BLT

Woman Mopping With a Rag Mop. Yi Chinmyông. EcSo, *tr. by* Carolyn U. So

Woman Mourned by Daughters, A. Adrienne Rich. InoFa

Woman much missed, how you call to me, call to me. Voice, The. Thomas Hardy. HarvBoo; InoFa; NAEL-6v2; NAEL-7v2; NAMCP V.1; NoAM; NoP-4; NoP-5; NPeEn; OxAEP-2; OxBEV; TFi

Woman named Tomorrow, The. Four Preludes on Playthings of the Wind. Carl Sandburg. MoAmPo

Woman of Color. Constance Merritt. AmPoNex

Woman of mine with woodfire hair. Free Union. André Breton. NAWM-7v2, *tr. by* Mary Ann Caws and Jean-Pierre Cauvin

Woman of rich aroma approaches, A. Kiss. Kitahara Hakushū. CAoMJL1, *tr. by* Leith Morton

Woman of Three Cows, The. *Unknown.* OBCoV, *tr. by* James Clarence Mangan

Woman of Three Minds, The. Thomas Centolella. GifTon

Woman on the Dump, The. Elizabeth Spires. EmeKit

Woman on the subway touches my hand by mistake, and in that. Recognition. Eve Wood. BAP-97

Woman, parents, brothers, even God, A. Those Who Love. Cyprian Norwid. WoPoe, *tr. by* Jerzy Peterkiewicz, Burns Singer and Jon Stallworthy

Woman precedes me up the long rope, A. Climbing. Lucille Clifton. GT; LoL

Woman raises her garment, rain, wind, darkness rise, The. Paavo Haavikko. WoPoe, *tr. by* Anselm Hollo

Woman refugee arms herself with pride and faith. Her Heart Is a Rose Petal and Her Skin Is Granite. Lorene Zarou-Zouzounis. PoArWo

Woman Resting on a Bundle of Kindling. Margaret Gibson. AmZen

Woman sat on the mountain, A. Spring. Adelaida Gertsyk. ARWW, *tr. by* Catriona Kelly

Woman scolds him, The. Marriage. Friederike Roth. GTCP, *tr. by* Irmgard Hunt

Woman Seed Player. Roberta Hill Whiteman. HATNAP

Woman Singing. Tsujii Takashi. PML, *tr. by* Robert Brady and Susanne Akemi Wegmüller

Woman sits back on her heels, A. Size of a Bed Sheet, The. Amy Dryansky. SweBea

Woman sits on her porch. Song. Earle Thompson. HATNAP

Woman stood up in front of the table, The. Her sad hands. Miniature. Yannis Ritsos. GPTC; VCWP, *tr. by* Edmund Keeley

Woman strangles her fourteen-year-old daughter, A. Woman Strangles, A. Robert Hershon. PrTe

Woman sweeping a floor, darkness growing. (LL) Sheep Fair Day. Kerry Hardie. BeAl; MoWP; NIrP

Woman tells me, A. Story, A. Jane Hirshfield. BLT

Woman that kissed him and—pinched his poke—was the lady that's known as Lou, The. (LL) Shooting of Dan McGrew, The. Robert W. Service. BrAP; BRP; EdScPo; UV

Woman: The Eternal. Rafiq Azad. PML, *tr. by* Afia Dil

Woman the world is furnished by your eyes. Vincente Huidobro. BLPSL *Fr.* Altazor.

Woman there was balancing her baby, A. Past All Understanding. Heather McHugh. ExTi

Woman throws her children, A. Topography. Maureen Owen. PrTe

Woman to Child. Judith Wright. BrAP

Woman to Man. Ai. NoAM

Woman to Man. Judith Wright. BMAP; BrAP; NoP-4; NoP-5; StAl

Woman travels to Brazil for plastic, A. Tomatoes. Stephen Dobyns. CAP-8

Woman Turns Herself into a Fish, The. Eavan Boland. WaAnP

Woman 12, A. Hugo Claus. TuT, *tr. by* Peter van de Kamp

Woman Waits for Me, A. Walt Whitman. ErotSp; HeIP-4

Woman Walking. William Carlos Williams. ColAP

Woman walking in a walker on the cliffs, A. One Life. Adrienne Rich. CAP-8; OxBoAm

Woman walking out of the water. Flow. Marcel Gerard. SonAtl, *tr. by* Gregory Beaven, Kurt Ganzl, Germaine Goetzinger, Christophe Mirambeau and Pascal Nicolay

Woman walking turns her head, The. Through a Slit in the Tent. Carole Glasser Langille. Coast

Woman wandered, A. Celebration. Gzar Hantoosh. IrPoTo, *tr. by* Saadi A. Simawe and Ellen Doré Watson

Woman wants monogamy. General Review of the Sex Situation. Dorothy Parker. NAAPv.2

Woman was cooking a mouse for her husband's dinner, A. Russell Edson. SoSe-8

Woman was old, and ragged, and gray, The. Somebody's Mother. *Unknown.* ChAP

Woman Washing. Patricia Bishop. Prnts

Woman washing her hair at sunrise, The. Taklamakan. Kim Hyesun. EcSo, *tr. by* Youngju Ryu

Woman went into the same resturant every Tuesday night, A. Sandwiches. David Donnell. NoAM

Woman Who Allowed Light to Have Its Way with Her, The. Dannye Romine Powell. PoDa

Woman Who Died in Line, The. Patricia Smith. SpirFl

Woman Who Drank Us Up, The. Lesley Quayle. Prnts

Woman Who Fell from the Sky, The. Joy Harjo. BodElec

Woman who has grown old, The. Crows, The. Louise Bogan. ItP; NAAPv.2; NALW

Woman Who Jumped, The. M. Eliza Hamilton. BtF

Woman who kicked out the back window, The. Stephen Dobyns. BodElec *Fr.* 0   Great Doubters of History, The.

Woman who looks like my mother sees a man who looks like / me, A. Four Resurrections in the Valley of the Ghosts. Yehuda Amichai. VCWP, *tr. by* Benjamin Harshav and Barbara Harshav

Woman Who Married a Caterpillar, The. *Unknown.* WoPoe, *tr. by* Armand Schwerner

Woman Who Mistook her Father for an Irishman, The. Nicki Jackowska. Prnts

Woman Who Raised Dogs, The. Lisa D. Chavez. AmPoNex

Woman Who Weeps. Ellen Bryant Voigt. CAP-8; OPRER

Woman who writes feels too much, A. Black Art, The. Anne Sexton. PoA 2002

Woman Who Wrote Too Much, The. Kay Ryan. ExTi

Woman who's making jam in July, A. Making Jam in July. Inna Kabysh. CRWP, *tr. by* Alex Marshall and Fay Marshall

Woman wired in memories, A. Adrienne Rich. NoP-4

Woman wired in memories, A. Adrienne Rich. NoP-5 *Fr.* Eastern War Time.

Woman with Chrysler. Jeremy Countryman. PoDa

Woman with Flaxen Hair in Norfolk Heard, A. Robert Kelly. PmAP

Woman with Flower. Naomi Long Madgett. GT; OxAAAP

Woman with no face walked into the light, A. Homage to Hieronymus Bosch. Thomas MacGreevy. ModIr

Woman with no feet sits on the porch, The. Interruption of Flight. Lisa Williams. AmPoNex

Woman with the caught fox. Plea for a Captive. W. S. Merwin. NoAM

Woman with the Screw in Her Mouth Speaks, The. Sheri Hostetler. ACAMVP

Woman with Whom I Share My Husband, The. Okot P'Bitek. NAMCP V.2; PoetW *Fr.* Song of Lawino.

Woman wore a floral apron around her neck, The. Floral Apron, The. Marilyn Chin. LoL; SweBea

Woman Writer Does Laundry, A. Anna Swirszczynska [*or* Swir]. TAPaP, *tr. by* Czeslaw Milosz and Leonard Nathan

Woman, you are afraid of the forest. Maria Wine. ItWoWo, *tr. by* Nadia Christensen

Woman, you'll never credit what. Shepherd's Tale, The. James Kirkup. OBCP

Womanhood, The. Gwendolyn Brooks.
    Beverly Hills, Chicago. CAP-8; ESEAA; OxAAAP
    Children of the Poor, The. PoA 2002
        First Fight. Then Fiddle. NIL-7; NIP-4; PtR
    Rites for Cousin Vit, The. InoFa; NAMCP V.2; NoP-4; NoP-5; OxAAAP; WeW-3
    "Stand off, daughter of the dusk,." NALW
Womanhood, The. Elizabeth Garrett. MFPA
Woman's Answer, A. Adelaide Anne Procter. VWP
Woman's Beauty. Lascelles Abercrombie. MoBrPo Fr. Emblems of Love.
Woman's Cause Is Man's, The. Alfred Tennyson. NAEL-6v2; NAEL-7v2 Fr. Princess, The.
Woman's Constancy. John Donne. NBLV; NOSC
Woman's Constancy. Sir John Suckling. CavPo
Woman's face with nature's own[e] hand painted, A. William Shakespeare. CAGL; HeIP-4; NAEL-6v1; NAEL-7v1; NoP-4; NoP-5; NoSic; OxAEP-1; PBRV; WaAnP Fr. Sonnets.
Woman's Future. May Kendall. ViWPN; VWP
Woman's Heart, A. Vietnamese Oral Tradition. CaDao, tr. by John Balaban
Woman's Intuition, A. Ned Washington. ReLy
Womans Labour, an epistle, The. Mary Collier. PEW
Woman's Last Word, A. Robert Browning. NAEL-6v2; RACG
Woman's Last Word, A. Adelaide Anne Procter. VWP
Woman's Love. Unknown. TreFP
Woman's Love Song. Somali Oral Tradition. ErotSp, tr. by Sam Hamill
Woman's Mourning Song, The. Bell Hooks. ISC
Woman's Portrait, The. Wisława Szymborska. FiBr, tr. by Grazyna Drabik and Sharon Olds
Woman's Question, A. Lena Lathrop. ITBLP
Woman's Rights. Rebekah Gumpert Hyneman. SWaP
Woman's Ritornelle. Theodor Storm. WoPoe, tr. by James Wright
Woman's Song. Chippewa Oral Tradition. See My Love Has Departed.
Woman's Sorrow, A. Im Che. CATKP, tr. by Peter H. Lee
Woman's voice is reading out, A. Forecast. Duncan Forbes. RWPCtW
Woman's white body is a song. Song of Songs, The. Heinrich Heine. EroLit, tr. by Louis Untermeyer
Woman's Work. Julia Alvarez. RA
Woman's worth to the world can never be told. Oh Woman, Blessed Woman! Mrs. Henry Linden. CBWP-4
Womanskin. Maxine Tynes. BrAP
Womb. Sonia Sekula. SurWo
Womb refused, The. Miscarriage. Jane Duran. PoCu; StAl
Women: "They stand there and chat near the breakwater." İlhan Berk. NaPG, tr. by Talat Sait Halman
Women. Louise Bogan. APT-2; MoAmPo; NAAPv.2; NALW; NAMCP V.1; NoAM; WoPoe
Women. Larry Fagin. AHA Fr. Parade of the Caterpillars, The.
Women. Heath. NoSic
Women. Frances Horovitz. LW
Women: "Did I write that I'll endure this." Kim Hyesun. EcSo, tr. by Youngju Ryu
Women. Kim Hyesun. CAMKP, tr. by Jiwon Shin
Women. Zakiyya Malallah. PoArWo, tr. by Wen Chin Ouyang
Women. Adrienne Rich. TRP
Women. May Swenson. NALW
Women. Trần Tê Xu'o'ng. EaWin; WoPoe, tr. by W. S. Merwin and Nguyen Ngoc Bich
Women. Alice Walker. CFP Fr. In These Dissenting Times.
Women, The. Eavan Boland. MoWP; NAMCP V.2
Women, The. Cyrus Cassells. UnSA
Women, The. Joseph Ceravolo. FTOS
Women all / cause rue. Palladas. WoPoe, tr. by Tony Harrison
Women and Roses. Robert Browning. NAEL-6v2
Women! / Announce a debauch in honor of Bacchos. Lystrata. Aristophanes. NAWM-7v1, tr. by Douglass Parker
Women Are Different. Marsha Prescod. LW
Women Are Not Gentlemen. Harley Matthews. NOBAu
Women Are Not Roses. Ana Castillo. IllVoic
Women are on their way. Fugue. Robyn Sarah. IFF
Women are returning, The. No Need to Discourage Dreams. Ihab Khalifa. AnVo, tr. by Mohamed Enani
Women are walking to town, The. Rainy Season, The. Linda Hogan. HATNAP; TRP
Women, as some men say, unconstant be. Epigram. George Wither. NOSC
Women as women, me had never charmed. Unknown. CAGL Fr. Don Leon.
Women at the Crossroad / (May Elegba Forever Guard the Right Doors). Opal Palmer Adisa. GT

Women at the Pit-head, The. Bobi Jones. BBMWP, tr. by Joseph P. Clancy
Women at the Temple. Herodas. HePo, tr. by Barbara Hughes Fowler
Women behind us, The. Certain women. Women with light and deep, dark memory. Women's Words—Yellow-Green Leaves and Low Sun. Kim Chôngnan. EcSo, tr. by Peter H. Lee
Women ben full of ragerie [in imitation of Chaucer]. Imitation of Chaucer. Alexander Pope. OBCoV
Women carry life. Woman. Michel-Ange Hyppolite. OGAHCP, tr. by Boadiba and Jack Hirschman
Women, Children, Babies, Cows, Cats. Robert Lowell. PoAgWa
Women come to sing are singing, The. Song of Quavering, A. Jerome Rothenberg. FTOS
Women Don't Die on the Front Lines. Belkis Cuza Malé. CFP; TANSG, tr. by Pamela Carmell
Women don't fantasize about a leathery toad. Miss Gee Meets W. H. Auden in Heaven. Vanessa Haley. PfS
Women Fell like Beautiful Horses, The. Gloria Bird. FiBr
Women Gather, The. Nikki Giovanni. ISC
Women gather, The. Women Gather, The. Nikki Giovanni. ISC
Women gather, their dreams, The. Dream of the Hair Burning Smell. Jana Harris. AtGh
Women have loved before as I love now. Sonnet. Edna St. Vincent Millay. HeIP-4; NALW; NIL-7; PoA 2002
Women have no. Women Are Not Roses. Ana Castillo. IllVoic
Women have no wilderness in them. Women. Louise Bogan. APT-2; MoAmPo; NAAPv.2; NALW; NAMCP V.1; NoAM; WoPoe
Women He Liked. Edward Thomas. TCAWP
Women in Dutch Painting. Eunice De Souza. NAMCP V.2
Women in the Cold War. Alison Fell. RSaN
Women Laughing. U. A. Fanthorpe. ItWoWo; MoWP
Women loving each other. Bad Girl Blues. Wille ("Memphis Willie B.") Borum. FTtHH
Women murmur for, The. (LL) Ripeness Is Rapid. Rosalie Moore. CalPo; YaYoPo
Women Must Put Off Their Rich Apparel. Joy Katz. NeAmPo
Women must put off their rich apparel. Women Must Put Off Their Rich Apparel. Joy Katz. NeAmPo
Women Next Door, The. Barbara Tran. AmWaPo
Women of Dan Dance with Swords in Their Hands to Mark the Time When They Were Warriors, The. Audre Lorde. MoWP; NALW; NoAM
Women of Jericho, The. Phyllis McGinley. ChIV-1
Women of Lockerbie, The. Richard Robbins. OtW
Women of My Country. Jean-Marie Willer Denis. OGAHCP, tr. by Boadiba and Jack Hirschman
Women of Nigeria. Night in Nigeria. Ellease Southerland. GT
Women of Rubens, The. Wisława Szymborska. PoSu; VCWP
Women of Trachis. Sophocles. tr. by Ezra Pound
    "Torn between griefs, which grief shall I lament." APT-1; OBVE, tr. by Ezra Pound
Women of Yueh. Li Po. tr. by Sam Hamill
    "Gathering lotuses by Yeh River." CrYelRi; ErotSp, tr. by Sam Hamill
    "Mirror Lake's waters are moon-clear." CrYelRi; ErotSp, tr. by Sam Hamill
    "Southern women have alabaster skin." CrYelRi; ErotSp, tr. by Sam Hamill
    "Woman from Ch'ang-kan, The." CrYelRi, tr. by Sam Hamill
Women over fifty, The. At the Party. Ursula K. Le Guin. FiBr
Women Pleased. John Fletcher.
    (To His Sleeping Mistress.) NOSC
Women reminded him of lilies and roses. Thoughts After Ruskin. Elma Mitchell. EdSoCy; MoWP; NPeEn; StAl
Women resemble the clouds. Lightening, The. Gabriella Sica. CItWP, tr. by Cinzia Sartini Blum and Lara Trubowitz
Women say: "it looks like rain", The. The clouds burst, they all go inside. Women Say, The: 'It Looks Like Rain'. Jean Follain. MotU, tr. by Mary Feeney and William Matthews
Women Sing, The. Luvuyo Mkangelwa. NAfrP
Women sing, The. Women Sing, The. Luvuyo Mkangelwa. NAfrP
Women spend the afternoon squatting on the porch. Another Life. Taslima Nasrin. VCWP, tr. by Carolyne Wright
Women spin and dance in skirts, sleep and wake. Skirts. Gray Jacobik. PoDa
Women stripped to the waist. Out-Patients. Carole Satyamurti. PoCu; StAl
Women Watching Basketball. Marisa De Los Santos. NAPBL
Women / we keepers and sharers of ancient secrets. Womanskin. Maxine Tynes. BrAP
Women were making clay bowls, The. What the Women Told Me. E. Ethelbert Miller. GT
Women who fan, The. Another Century. David Keplinger. AmPoNex
Women Who Love Angels. Judith Ortiz Cofer. TouFir

Women Who Love Elvis All Their Lives, The. Fleda Brown Jackson.
  AllShUp
Women who sing themselves to sleep. Light Sleep. Hazel Hall. APT-1;
  NAAPv.2
Women who Speak with Steak Knives. Susan Hampton. BMAP
Women who were mothers told us about it. Portrait of Auntie Blodwen.
  Elwyn Davies. AngWePo
Women who would gather in the vale, The. Cherry Laurel, The. Russell
  Thornton. IFF
Women with hats like the rear ends of pink ducks. To a Waterfowl. Donald
  Hall. BodElec
Women Within Me. Na Hûidôk. EcSo, tr. by Peter H. Lee
Women without hesitancy began to descend, The. Farewell Stairway, The.
  Barbara Guest. AWPTFC; NYP2
Women! Women! Zuveliskes's Women Mourn Over Kukutis. Marcelijus
  Martinaitis. TWW, tr. by Laima Sruoginis
Women women call, The. Blues Variations. Lorenzo Thomas. AnSo
Women You Are Accustomed To, The. Lucille Clifton. ErotSp; GT
Women's Blood. Vicki Feaver. MoWP
Women's Labors. Lee Upton. PoCho
Women's Language. Kim Chôngnan. EcSo, tr. by Peter H. Lee
Women's Locker Room. Marilyn Nelson Waniek. LTA
Women's Rondo. Unknown. NOBAu
Women's Room in Pennsylvania Station, The. Kate Daniels. GM
Women's Rule [epigram]. Friedrich von Logau. GePo, tr. by George C.
  Schoolfield
Women's Words—Yellow-Green Leaves and Low Sun. Kim Chôngnan.
  EcSo, tr. by Peter H. Lee
Women's Work. Gillian Clarke. MoWP
Wonder. Thomas Traherne. BASC; NAEL-6v1; NAEL-7v1; NoP-4; NoP-5;
  NPeEn; OxBEV; WaAnP
Wonder, The. John Banks. STuOW Fr. Albion Queens, The.
Wonder, The. Thylias Moss. ChAP
WONDER BAR / WISHING WELL. Neon Signs. Langston Hughes.
  APSN; PFTM-1
Wonder Bread. Alice Fulton. ExTi
Wonder—is not precisely Knowing. Emily Dickinson. NCAP
Wonder of these! glory of other times! To the Right Honorable, the Lady Mary,
  Countess of Pembroke. Samuel Daniel. NAEL-6v1
Wonder Stings Me More than the Bee. Alice Fulton.
  Elvis from the Waist Up. AllShUp
Wonder / why illness. Daniel Berrigan. UpMys Fr. Astonishment.
Wonderful. Ania Walwicz. BMAP
Wonderful grace of Jesus, Greater than all my sin. Haldor Lillenas. SacPr
Wonderful Guy, A. Oscar Hammerstein, II. ReLy
Wonderful in Poetry, or a Victim of Goldfish, The. Konstantin Pavlov.
  CSCBP, tr. by Georgi Belev and Lisa Sapinkopf
Wonderful! / Oh, it's wonderful. Louise. Leo Robin. ReLy
Wonderful Things. Ron Padgett. AHA; PmAP
Wonderful— / under cherry blossoms. Issa. IllVoic Fr. Issa: A Suite of Haiku.
Wonderful was the long secret night you gave me, my Lover. Terminus. Edith
  Wharton. APT-1
Wonderful Whale, The. Eve Merriam. YaYoPo
Wonderful workings of the world: wonderful, Title. Cut the Grass. A. R.
  Ammons. WeW-3
Wondering how a good woman can murder. Judith. Vicki Feaver. MoWP
Wondering which of all the saints. In a Calendar of Saints. Neil Curry. NLP
Wonders. Unknown. NPeEn
Wonders of the Peak, The. Charles Cotton.
  Chatsworth. OBGa
Wonder-Teacher, The. Cynthia Ozick. TaR
Wond'rous crowd then 'gan aloud, A. Michael Wigglesworth. NAAL-3 Fr.
  Day of Doom, The [First Section].
Wondrous, I grant, and caught from heaven the flame. Literature and Action.
  Goronva Camlan. AngWePo
Wondrous life! cried Marvell at Appleton House. Round. Weldon Kees.
  OxBoAm
Wondrous light is filling the air, A. Spirit of the Age, The. Christopher Pearse
  Cranch. APN-1
Wongòl Poem. Emmanuel Eugene. OGAHCP, tr. by Boadiba and Jack
  Hirschman
Won't It Be Fine? Robert Creeley. BAP-97
Won't let wanting anything. Sesshin Poem. Norman Fischer. WhBo
Won't you become too tired, and quit smiling at me when I languish. For
  Laura. Mihály Vörösmarty. IQMS, tr. by Adam Makkai
Won't you celebrate with me. Lucille Clifton. BodElec
"Won't you look out of your window, Mrs. Gill?" Mocking Fairy, The.
  Walter De la Mare. MoBrPo

Wood. Patricia Y. Ikeda. MotU; WhBo
Wood, The. Geraint Jarman. BBMWP, tr. by Peter Finch
Wood and Fire. Kuong Viet. WoPoe, tr. by Huynh Sanh Thong
Wood Carols. Henrietta Cordelia Ray. CBWP-3
Wood Dove, The. Ernest Francisco Fenollosa. NAAPv.1
Wood Garden. Dana Gelinas. SPV, tr. by Jen Hofer
Wood in Sound, A. Takahashi Shinkichi. ZenPo, tr. by Takashi Ikemoto and
  Lucien Stryk
Wood is not the past tense of fire. Prayer Flag. Miriam Sagan. WANABP
Wood merchant's parlour, The. Pierre McOrlan. MFP, tr. by Martin Sorrell
Wood of my thoughts is on fire, The. Valerio Magrelli. ItPo, tr. by Gayle
  Ridinger
Wood of the madrone burns with a flame at once / lavender and mossy green,
  The. He Thanks His Woodpile. Lew Welch. BB
Wood Road, The. Edna St. Vincent Millay. APT-1
Wood smoke smudges the sea. Menelaus. Derek Walcott. BrAP
Wood Song. Sara Teasdale. APT-1
Wood Stove Sunday. Tammy Armstrong. Coast
Wood with bushes broad there was, begrown with bigtree boughs, A. Virgil.
  NoSic Fr. Aeneid [or Eneados or Aeneis], The.
Woodcarver of Stendal, The. Sheenagh Pugh. TCAWP
Wood-chuck. Unknown. TLR
Woodchucks. Maxine W. Kumin. CAP-8; NIL-7; NIP-4
Woodcock Feather. Peter Sanger. Coast
Woodcut on the Cover of Robert Frost's Complete Poems, The. Hayden
  Carruth. VisFro
Woodcutter. Song of the Barren Orange Tree. Federico García Lorca.
  AmFaPo; RaW, tr. by W. S. Merwin
Woodcutter on His Way Home, A. Unknown. EaWin, tr. by W. S. Merwin
  and Nguyen Ngoc Bich
Wood-Cutter, The. Lupenga Mphande. HBAPE
Woodcutter wakes up: mountain moon is low. Tune: "Song of Clear River."
  Ma Chih-yüan. ChinPo, tr. by Ye Weilian [or Yeh Wei-lien or Wai-lim
  Yip]
Wood-doves are singing along the Perkiomen, The. Thinking of a Relation
  between the Images of Metaphors. Wallace Stevens. SAmP
Wooded area has wed itself. Eohippus. Larissa Szporluk. LegDan
Wooden alveoli erect and fragile. Cenozoic Asylum, The [2002 Version].
  Christopher Dewdney. OpeFie
Wooden belly iron back. Riddle. Unknown. FaBoVe
Wooden box rattled, A. Moon Shatters on Alabama Avenue, The. Martín
  Espada. PueRic
Wooden Dog. Christopher Middleton. OnScMo
Wooden Handle, The. Gojko Djogo. AF, tr. by Michael March and Dušan
  Puvaić
Wooden Horse. Nagnamuni. HotL, tr. by V. Narayana Rao
Wooden Horse Is Brought into Troy, The. Virgil. OBVE Fr. Aeneid [or
  Eneados or Aeneis], The.
Wooden Horse, The. Mary Mapes Dodge. SWaP
Wooden Horses. Paul Verlaine. NAWM-7v2, tr. by Carlyle Ferren MacIntyre
Wooden Leg. James McIntyre. VerBaPo
Wooden rocking-horse in Reyes Cardenas' yard, The. At the Very Last Battle.
  Carmen Tafolla. TiP2
Wooden saint, A. Railway Station, The. Jejuri Arun Kolatkar. EmeKit
Wooden spoon, A. Sorting Things Out. Wanda Barford. Prnts
Woodland Cross, The. Endre Ady. IQMS, tr. by Anton N. Nyerges
Woodland flowers lose their vernal color. Tune: "Joy of Encounter." Li Yü.
  ColAnChi, tr. by Jiaosheng Wang
Woodland God. Johannes Bobrowski. WoPoe, tr. by Rich Ives
Woodland heather is blue in springtime. In Memory of John Keats. Yury
  Mikhailovich Kublanovich. TCRusP
Woodland Mass, The. Dafydd ap Gwilym. OBWVE, tr. by Gwyn Williams
Woodland rivulet,—a Poet's death, A. (LL) After Dark Vapours Have
  Oppressed Our Plains. John Keats. CenSon; NPeEn
Woodland Seat, A. John Clare. CenSon
Woodlands clothe the slender shoots. Song of Summer. Unknown. NAWM-
  7v1, tr. by Jan Ziolkowski
Woodman, Spare That Tree. George Pope Morris. BRP; TCAPo
  (Oak, The.) APN-1
Woodmanship. George Gascoigne. See Gascoigne's Woodmanship.
Woodnotes II ("As sunbeams stream through liberal space"). Ralph Waldo
  Emerson.
  "Once again the pine-tree sung." APN-1
Woodpecker. Sandra Alcosser. PfSP
Woodpecker. Gerald Bullett. OWoS
Woodpecker, The. Issa. EH, tr. by Robert Hass
Woodpecker, The. Elizabeth Madox Roberts. TLR
Woodpecker Finch. Robyn Schiff. LegDan

Woodpecker on. Issa. IllVoic *Fr.* Issa: A Suite of Haiku.

Woodpecker pecked out a little round hole, The. Woodpecker, The. Elizabeth Madox Roberts. TLR

Wood-Pile, The. Robert Frost. APT-1; ColAP; MoW; NAAL-5; NAAPv.2; NAMCP V.1; NoAM; NoP-4; NoP-5; OxBoAm; SAmP

Woods: "Tree trembles, A." Kang Ŭn'gyo. EcSo, *tr. by* Ann Y. Choi

Woods: "Midwinter and this beech wood's mind." Gwyneth Lewis. NeBrP

Woods. David Waltner-Toews. IFF *Fr.* Coming Up for Air.

Woods, The. Louise Erdrich. WaAnP

Woods, The. Derek Mahon. PBCIP

Woods Are Wild and Were Not Made for Man, The. Petrarch. WoPoe, *tr. by* Edwin Morgan

Woods are wild and were not made for man, The. Woods Are Wild and Were Not Made for Man, The. Petrarch. WoPoe, *tr. by* Edwin Morgan

Woods Burial. John Peck. PoCoUp

Woods decay, the woods decay and fall, The. Tithonus. Alfred Tennyson. CABP; NAEL-6v2; NAEL-7v2; NAWM-7v2; NoP-4; NoP-5; NPeEn; OxBEV

Woods devoid of beasts, roads that please the foot. (LL) Against Romanticism. Kingsley Amis. NAMCP V.2; NoAM

Woods of Arcady are dead, The. Song of the Happy Shepherd, The. William Butler Yeats. NoAM

Woods of Kylinoe, The: Song of the Irish Emigrant in North America. Ellen Fitz-Simon. IrV

Woods—oh! solemn are the boundless woods, The. Edith; a Tale of the Woods. Felicia Dorothea Hemans. RWP

Woods reached water and there was immense silence, The. House in Krasnogruda. Czeslaw Milosz. BodElec, *tr. by* the author and Robert Hass

Woods sleep bathed in shadow, The. Evensong. Paul Gerhardt. GePo, *tr. by* Ingrid Waløe-Engel

Woods were dark, The. Into the Woods. Ko Ŭn. CAMKP, *tr. by* David R. McCann

Woodspurge has a cup of three, The. (LL) Woodspurge, The. Dante Gabriel Rossetti. CABP; CtM; HeIP-4; NAEL-6v2; NAEL-7v2; NoP-4; NoP-5; NPeEn; OBEV; OxBEV; TFi

Woodspurge, The. Dante Gabriel Rossetti. CABP; CtM; HeIP-4; NAEL-6v2; NAEL-7v2; NoP-4; NoP-5; NPeEn; OBEV; OxBEV; TFi

Woodstock. Iwan Llwyd. "El Buen Samaritano keeps reappearing." ATSWP, *tr. by* Robert Minhinnick

Woodstock. Jan-Mitchell Sherrill. ReTh

Woodtown Manor. John Montague. PBCIP

Woodwoodwoodwoodwoodwoodwoodwood. Window, The. Derek Mahon. NoP-5

Woodworker's Ballad. Herbert Edward Palmer. OBEV

Woody Guthrie Visited by Bob Dylan: Brooklyn State Hospital, New York, 1961. David Wojahn. PBCAP; SwNoth *Fr.* Mystery Train: A Sequence.

Woof of the sun, ethereal gauze. Henry David Thoreau. NAAPv.1; NCAP

Woof reversed the fatal shuttles weave, A. Strikers in Hyde Park. Louise Imogen Guiney. APN-2

Woofers stacked to pillars made a disco of a city-block. Block Party. Major L. Jackson. FuFl

Wooing Song. Giles, the Younger Fletcher. OBEV *Fr.* Christ's Victory and Triumph.

Wooing the Bicycle. Grace Duffie Boylan. ArBi

Wool-chafed and wet-shoed I went forth after. William Langland. NAEL-6v1; NAEL-7v1 *Fr.* Vision of Piers Plowman, The.

Woolly Words. Robert N. Feinstein. NBLV

Woolworth's. Donald Hall. ItP; OBCoV

Woolworth's. Mark Irwin. GoPo

Woolworth's Poem, The. Quraysh Ali Lansana. IllVoic

Woo's People. Harold Carrington. EGAG

Wooyeo Ball, The. *Unknown.* NOBAu

Wops came down to the port, The. City of Beggars, The. Alfred Hayes. FaBoWar; PWW2

Word: "So many bright words covered." Zishe Vaynper. Prolet, *tr. by* Amelia Glaser

Word, A. Gottfried Benn. GTCP, *tr. by* Richard Exner

Word, A. Overflow. Nada El-Hage. PoArWo, *tr. by* Nathalie El-Hani

Word, A. Alvaro Mutis. TCLAP, *tr. by* Sophie Cabot Black and Maria Negroni

Word, The. Colette Bryce. MoWP

Word, The: "Though I have the gift of tongues." Alden Nowlan. BrAP

Word, The. Stevie Smith. MoWP

Word, The ("Word! it cannot fail; it ever speaks, The.") Jones Very. NCAP

Word, a phrase—from ciphers rise, A. Word, A. Gottfried Benn. GTCP, *tr. by* Richard Exner

Word arrives from far P'ing-yin. Word from My Brothers. Tu Fu [*or* Du Fu]. CrYelRi, *tr. by* Sam Hamill

Word at last, The. Emperor Kōkō. ZenPo, *tr. by* Takashi Ikemoto and Lucien Stryk

Word before the Last about Loss, A. Linda Zisquit. DTA

Word Between the World and God, The. Emily Warn. TAPaP

Word comes in this afternoon. Big Fort Island Buddha. Mac Lojowski. AmZen

Word Drunk. James Harrison. TAPaP

Word eats a road, The. Nursery Rhyme in Eight Strophes. Rossana Ombres. CItWP, *tr. by* Cinzia Sartini Blum and Lara Trubowitz

Word Faith means when someone sees, The. Faith. Czeslaw Milosz. RaBo, *tr. by* Robert Hass, Robert Pinsky and Renata Gorcynski

Word for everybody, myself nobody, A. In Flood. Charles Hubert Sisson. HarvBoo

Word for Summer, A. George Seferis. AF

Word for the Hour, A. John Greenleaf Whittier. NCAP; PCW

Word from a Petitioner. John Pierpont. Ballot, The. APN-1

Word from My Brothers. Tu Fu [*or* Du Fu]. CrYelRi, *tr. by* Sam Hamill

Word from the Gray Soldiers. Hillel Omer. NRoS, *tr. by* Esther Raizen

Word from the "great house" came—a master's call. Albery Allson Whitman. NAAPv.1 *Fr.* Octoroon, The.

Word from the Loki, A. Maurice Riordan. ModIr; NIrP

Word Gifts for an Australian Critic. Merlinda Bobis. ReBoTo

Word goes round Repins, The. Absolutely Ordinary Rainbow, An. Les A. Murray. HarvBoo; StAl

Word I had no one left but God. (LL) Bereft. Robert Frost. APT-1; MoAmPo; SoSe-8

Word I spoke in anger, The. Quarrel, The. Stanley Kunitz. APT-2; TaR

Word in Edgeways, A. Charles Tomlinson. CABP

Word is an Egg, The. Niyi Osundare. NAfrP

Word is coming up on the screen, give me a moment, A. Michael Palmer. MotU

Word is dead, A. Emily Dickinson. PtR; SAmP; TCAPo

Word is identical with a word & nothing else in the world, A. Morphine, Or The Cutting Stone. Erin Mouré. OpeFie

Word is imitative, The. Mummer. Jack Spicer. APSN

Word is my sword, The. Logos. Erich Fried. GTCP, *tr. by* Reinhold Grimm

Word is the father of the saints, The. Macumba Word. Aimé Césaire. PFTM-1

Word! it cannot fail; it ever speaks, The. Word, The. Jones Very. NCAP

Word iz. Poem for Trish, A. Gavin Moses. InTrad

Word Knows How to Seduce the Flesh, The. Patrizia Valduga. CItWP, *tr. by* Cinzia Sartini Blum and Lara Trubowitz

Word/Life. Charlie R. Braxton. BtF

Word life / vs. verses where words urge murder/ curses / criminal cultjams. Rep/resent. Douglas Kearney. BRtP

Word made Flesh is seldom, A. Emily Dickinson. APN-2; ChIV-2; NAAL-3; NALW; TCAPo

Word Made Flesh, The. Walter James Turner. OBMV

Word: Man, A. Washington Allston. APN-1

Word of Encouragement, A. J. R. Pope. NBLV

Word of endless adoration. Christopher Smart. ChrPo *Fr.* Hymns and Spiritual Songs for the Fasts and Festivals of the Church of England.

Word of God came unto me, The. In the Garden of the Lord. Helen Keller. SacPr

Word of Mouth. Ted Greenwald. "Open mouth open through." FTOS

Word of the Lord by night, The. Boston Hymn. Ralph Waldo Emerson. CBCWP; InvLi; PCW; TCAPo

Word of this prodigy might well have stirred. Ovid. NAWM-7v1 *Fr.* Metamorphoses.

Word of Water, The. Edward Leslie Mayo. PoA 2002

Word outleaps the world, and light is all, The. (LL) Four for Sir John Davies. Theodore Roethke. APT-2; MoAmPo; NoAM

Word over all, beautiful as the sky. Reconciliation. Walt Whitman. AmWaPo; APN-1; FaBoWar; MoAmPo; NAAL-3; NAAL-5; NAAPv.1; NoP-4; NoP-5; OBWP; OxBoAm; PCW; WeW-3; WoPoe

Word *Plum,* The. Helen Chasin. NIL-7; NIP-4

Word Problems. Kate Rushin. PfS

Word Sonnets. Seymour Mayne. Hail. IFF

Word that ascended the summer:/flower (graft moon a thin incision, look at her sli-), The. Syliva Legris. PoPra *Fr.* Negative Garden.

Word that sings out of the ground, and the sound of mourning, The. Peter Riley. VaPo *Fr.* Excavations.

Word they had spoken, The. *Ancient Sumerian Oral Tradition* and *Unknown, fr. Sumerian cuneiform.* EroLit *Fr.* Courtship of Inanna and Dumuzi, The.

Word to come lies in a little night, A. Little Night, A. Douglas Oliver. Oth

Word to Husbands, A.   Ogden Nash.   OBCoV

Word to the Wise, A.   Octavio Armand.   TCLAP, *tr. by* Carol Maier

WORD was/is/will BE, The.   Genesis 2.   Etheridge Knight.   BodElec

Wordless, alone I ascend the West Tower.   Tune: "Joy of Encounter."   Li Yü.   ColAnChi, *tr. by* Jiaosheng Wang

Words.   Carlos A. Angeles.   ReBoTo

Words.   Samuel Alfred Beadle.   TCAPo

Words.   Elsa Cross.   RMCMP, *tr. by* Margaret Sayers Peden

Words.   Mahmoud Darwish.   VCWP, *tr. by* Rana Kabbani

Words.   Catherine Fisher.   TCAWP

Words: "Simple contact with a wooden spoon and the word, The."   Barbara Guest.   AWPTFC; FTOS; OxBoAm

Words: "Wind in the fur of living buffalo dead."   William Heyen.   AmZen

Words: "Words are shadows."   Eugen Gomringer.   GTCP, *tr. by* Michael Hamburger and Charlotte Melin

Words.   Kitasono Katsue.   CAoMJL1, *tr. by* John Solt

Words.   Sylvia Plath.   NALW; OxBoAm; VCAP

Words.   Adelaide Anne Procter.   SacPr

Words.   William Robert Rodgers.   PNI

Words.   Vern Rutsala.   WeW-3

Words.   Tomaz Salamun.   PoCho, *tr. by* the author and Christopher Merrill

Words: "I don't take your words."   Takahashi Shinkichi.   WhBo

Words ("La Pologne? La Pologne? It's awfully cold there, isn't it? she asked.")   Wisława Szymborska.   MotU, *tr. by* Krystyna Piorkowski

Words ("La Pologne? La Pologne? It's very cold over there, isn't it? the lady.")   Wisława Szymborska.   PoSu, *tr. by* Krystof Zarzecki

Words: "My dream won't last long."   Gu Cheng.   WoBe, *tr. by* Joseph R. Allen

Words.   Emilio Villa.   *tr. by* Gayle Ridinger

"It is world of the back hune wone it is."   ItPo

"Lend me a battle of unavoidable suggestions."   ItPo, *tr. by* Gayle Ridinger

"Trees were moving."   ItPo, *tr. by* Gayle Ridinger

"Ugly season of putrifying buzzards, An."   ItPo, *tr. by* Gayle Ridinger

Words, The.   Michael Palmer.   WoBe

Words, The.   David Wagoner.   OxBoAm; PoA 2002

Words and Music.   Samuel Beckett.

Song.   ModIr

Words are a monstrous excrescence.   Phrase-Book.   Veronica Forrest-Thomson.   HarvBoo

Words are but leaves to the tree of mind.   Words.   Samuel Alfred Beadle.   TCAPo

Words are for those with promises to keep. (LL)   Their Lonely Betters.   W. H. Auden.   NAEL-6v2; NAEL-7v2; NoAM; NoP-5; OBGa

Words are hoops.   Horses.   Witter Bynner.   APT-1

Words are lighter than the cloud-foam.   Words.   Adelaide Anne Procter.   SacPr

Words are sand.   Kim Namjo.   CAMKP Fr. Love's Cursive.

Words are shadows.   Words.   Eugen Gomringer.   GTCP, *tr. by* Michael Hamburger and Charlotte Melin

Words Before a Statue of Champlain.   Raymond Souster.   BrAP

Words cage heart and breath.   Cancer Diagnosis.   Marjorie Maddox.   IaFF

Words can't do.   Four Sonnets About Food.   Adrienne Su.   NAPBL

Words can't ignite them nor.   Song of Diamond Eyes, The.   Franco Buffoni.   ItPo, *tr. by* Gayle Ridinger

Words, dear companions! In my curtained cot.   Words.   Mary Elizabeth Coleridge.   ViWPN

Words escape through gaps.   Man Escaped, A.   Lewis Warsh.   BodElec

Words for Jazz Perhaps.   Michael Longley.   SeSe

Words for Love.   Ted Berrigan.   NYP2; PmAP

Words for My Daughter.   John Balaban.   PoChi; RaBo; SUP

Words for Worry.   Li-Young Lee.   P180

Words from Confinement.   Cesare Pavese.   AF, *tr. by* William Arrowsmith

Words from Robert W. Service.   Charles North.   NYP2

Word's gane to the kitchen.   Mary Hamilton.   *Unknown.*   NePenScot; NoP-4; NoP-5

Word's gone out, and now they spread the main, The.   Daniel Defoe.   OBWP Fr. Spanish Descent, The.

Words grow shoots in the bin.   Throwing Out My Father's Dictionary.   Moniza Alvi.   MoWP; Prnts

Words gush out of his wrung soul's roots.   Poet's Poem, The.   Kama Kamanda.   SonAtl, *tr. by* Gregory Beaven and Christophe Mirambeau

Words have been said, The.   Wings.   Brendan Kennelly.   IrLP

Words "I love you," The.   *Unknown.*   ArkPo, *tr. by* Helen Craig McCullough

Words in the Shadow.   Victor Hugo.   WoPoe, *tr. by* Louis Simpson

Words Is Not Enough.   Bob Stewart.   WaCA

Words, korean mums, The. (LL)   Korean Mums.   James Schuyler.   OxBoAm; PmAP; VCAP

Words no longer inflect.   Iteration.   Piera Oppezzo.   CItWP, *tr. by* Cinzia Sartini Blum and Lara Trubowitz

Words no longer need.   Expect Nothing Else from Me.   Rita Joe.   ReEnLa

Words of a Toast, The.   Denis Johnson.   LaCa

Words of an Old Woman.   Howard Phelps Putnam.   APT-2

Words of Comfort to Be Scratched on a Mirror.   Dorothy Parker.   AmWit

Words of Departure.   Jorge de Lima.   TCLAP, *tr. by* Luiz Fernández García

Words of Evening, The.   Yves Bonnefoy.   VCWP, *tr. by* Richard Pevear

Words of Love.   Carl Phillips.   AmAlph

Words of Oblivion and Peace.   Gabriel Preil.   FIT, *tr. by* Robert Friend

Words of our day, The.   Same Side of the Canoe, The.   Alda do Espirito Santo.   HAWP, *tr. by* Allan Francovich and Kathleen Weaver

Words of Tayko-mol.   William Oandasan.   HATNAP Fr. Past, The.

Words of the All-Wise, The.   *Unknown.*   WoPoe Fr. Elder Edda, The.

Words of the Poem, The.   André Frénaud.   YaTCFP, *tr. by* Michael Sheringham

Words, one by one.   Freedom.   Wimal Dissanayake.   ChAP

Words. Or find some words that make the Truth come true. (LL)   Whole Question, The.   Robert Penn Warren.   BodElec; OxBoAm

Words repeated a thousand times.   Mechanical Heart.   Josué Ramírez.   RMCMP, *tr. by* Mónica de la Torre

Words scored upon a bone.   Meditation on a Bone.   Alec Derwent Hope.   BrAP; NoAM; WoPoe

Words she cannot bear to sing. (LL)   To the Tune: The Wine Spring: "Rain falls on fallen flowers."   Li Hsun.   CrYelRi; ErotSp, *tr. by* Sam Hamill

Words shipwreck upon ecstasy, yet are.   At the Coast.   Ray Ragosta.   OnScMo

Words suggest illegal, The.   Improper Disposal.   John Bradley.   LiTh

Words that come in smoke and go.   Notes for Echo Lake 3.   Michael Palmer.   PmAP; WaAnP

Words to My Mother.   Alfonsina Storni.   TANSG, *tr. by* Mark McCaffrey

Words unto Adam, His Own Scriveyn.   Geoffrey Chaucer. *See* Chaucer's Wordes unto Adam, his Owne Scriveyn.

Words we use have been handed down to me and I use them, The.   Pounding and Gism.   Antonin Artaud.   ConPit, *tr. by* Albert James Arnold and Clayton Eshleman

Words were made to prevent us near. (LL)   Sonnet: "My love, if I write a song for you."   Veronica Forrest-Thomson.   EdScPo; HarvBoo; MoWP

Words which are flowers become fruits which are deeds. (LL)   Hymn Among the Ruins.   Octavio Paz.   PFTM-1; TCLAP, *tr. by* William Carlos Williams

Words, Wide Night.   Carol Ann Duffy.   NePenScot

Words with no connection. (LL)   Kenneth Rexroth.   APSN; APT-2; NAAPv.2 Fr. Love Poems of Marichiko, The.

Words won't change again, The. Sad friend, you cannot change. (LL)   North Haven.   Elizabeth Bishop.   InoFa; NAMCP V.2

Words! Words!   Jessie Redmond Fauset.   NAAPv.2

Words, Words, Words, and Nothing Doing.   Heinrich Heine.   WoPoe, *tr. by* W. D. Jackson

Words, words, words, and nothing doing!   Words, Words, Words, and Nothing Doing.   Heinrich Heine.   WoPoe, *tr. by* W. D. Jackson

Wordsworth.   Charlotte L. Forten Grimke.   TCAPo

Wordsworth on Lloyd George.   Mary Visick.   UV

Wordsworth upon Helvellyn! Let the cloud.   On a Portrait of Wordsworth by B. R. Haydon.   Elizabeth Barrett Browning.   HeIP-4

Wordsworth's Socks.   Elliot Fried.   SUP

Wordsworths: William and Dorothy, The.   Thomas Lux.   BodElec

Work.   Andrei Codrescu.   PmAP

Work.   Luciana Frezza.   CItWP, *tr. by* Cinzia Sartini Blum and Lara Trubowitz

Work.   David Huddle.   AmWaPo

Work.   Gyula Illyés.   RaBo, *tr. by* William Jay Smith

Work.   Yusef Komunyakaa.   CAP-8; LPSFW

Work.   D. H. Lawrence.   OBMV

Work.   Henry Van Dyke.   SacPr

Work, The.   Armand Schwerner.   BodElec

Work, The.   Tom Sleigh.

6. The Current.   InoFa

Work Channel.   George Stanley.   NLPA Fr. Mountains and Air.

Work goes on, The.   Creation Continues.   Carol Fonesca Galvez.   OWABP

Work? / I don't have to work.   Necessity.   Langston Hughes.   APSN; RaBo

Work is a blessing, / I tell you that, I—professional sluggard!   Aleksander Wat.   AF

Work is heavy, The. I see.   To the Shade of Po Chü-I.   William Carlos Williams.   HarvBoo

Work is the health of love.   Occam's Razor.   Thomas Rain Crowe.   AmZen

Work, No Light.   Reed Bye.   AHA

Work of pain on earth, The. (LL)   On Parting.   Edward Coote Pinkney.   APN-1; TCAPo

Work of the woman, The.   Work.   Luciana Frezza.   CItWP, *tr. by* Cinzia Sartini Blum and Lara Trubowitz

Work on the impossible. Tanka. Toki Zenmaro. CAoMJL1, *tr. by* Makoto Ueda

Work out a perfect will.. (LL) By the Statue of King Charles [*or* I] at Charing Cross. Lionel Pigot Johnson. MoBrPo; OBEV; OBMV

Work out. Ten laps. Heartbeats. Melvin Dixon. ESEAA

Work Song. Mark Levine. AmPoNex

Work Song. Robyn Selman. TaR

Work to Be Done. Sam Cornish. BtF

Work We Hate and Dreams We Love. Jimmy Santiago Baca. LoL

Work without Hope. Samuel Taylor Coleridge. CenSon; GSo; NAEL-6v2; NAEL-7v2; NPBRoP; OBEV; OxAEP-2; OxBSo; WoPoe

Workaholic. Nadia Hazboun Reimer. PoArWo

Workbox, The. Thomas Hardy. NAEL-6v2; NAEL-7v2

Workday. Linda Hogan. HATNAP

Worked its filthy way out like a tongue. (LL) Welcome to Hiroshima. Mary Jo Salter. AmWaPo; AtGh; NIL-7; NIP-4; RA

Worked Late on a Tuesday Night. Deborah Garrison. GoPo

Worker Bee, The. Allan Cooper. Coast

Worker Dies, A. Clementina Suárez. TANSG, *tr. by* Janet N. Gold

Worker, The ("Grizzly squab comrade, A.") Nikolai Stepanovich Gumilyov. SonAtl, *tr. by* Tamara Romanyk

Workers. David Hernandez. IllVoic

Workers (attendants). Nick Flynn. IIR

Workers earn it. Money. Richard Armour. NBLV

Worker's Hall could do with some work, The. DIY. Grahame Davies. BBMWP, *tr. by* the author

Workers in Love. Kavikondala Venkatarao. HotL, *tr. by* V. Narayana Rao

Workers in Metal. Edith Jay Scovell. RSaN

Workin girl, I wake up every day. Self-Sufficient Blues. Maureen Hynes. IFF

Working. Maxine Scates. PBCAP

Working and Waiting. Adah Isaacs Menken. CBWP-1

Working at the Wholesale Curtain Showroom. Ed Ochester. SUP

Working class clouds are living together. Clouds. Stanley Moss. BodElec

Working Construction. Eric Chock. OpBo

Working for British Telecom. Ben Scammell. NLP

Working for school clothes. My Room at Aunt Eura's, 1937. Wilma Elizabeth McDaniel. GeoHom

Working for the Government. Wang An-shih. CrYelRi, *tr. by* Sam Hamill

Working Girl. David Marlatt. AmPoNex

Working Habits. George Starbuck. AmWit

Working in Darkness. Thomas McGrath. BodElec

Working in the Rain. Robert Morgan. GoPo

Working late. Louis Simpson. CAP-8

Working Man, The. Ellen Johnston. VWP

Working Mother. Kathleen Aguero. PfS

Working on the '58 Willys Pickup. Gary Snyder. WANABP

Working on the Railway. *Unknown.* APN-2

Working Party, A. Siegfried Sassoon. AF

Working surely overtime, the scaffolders. Workers in Metal. Edith Jay Scovell. RSaN

Working the strawberry fields. (LL) How I See Things. Yusef Komunyakaa. ESEAA; OxAAAP

Working Tobacco. Janet Kauffman. ACAMVP

Working Together. David Whyte. TWF

Working up the slopes. Tomas Tranströmer. WoBe *Fr.* Haiku.

Working week comes to an end, The. Vladimir Uflyand. TCRusP, *tr. by* Daniel Weissbort

Working with Mother. Myra Cohn Livingston. TLR

Working with my back to the window for more natural light. dog. Fred Wah. NLPA *Fr.* This Dendrite Map: Father / Mother Haibun.

Working with one eye closed or heads buried. War Photographers, The. Frank Ormsby. PNI

Working with Tools. A. R. Ammons. TRP

Workingman's Wife: *Who She Is, Who She Is Not, What She Buys—And Why.* Chuck Wachtel. PrTe

Work-in-Progress. Lawrence Ferlinghetti. "And Pablo Neruda / that Chilean omnivore of poetry." BB

Workmen Photographed inside the Reactor. David Wojahn. IllVoic

Workmen shall not always work; who builds, The. Laborers, The. Jones Very. SacPr

Works and Days. David Baker. PoDa

Works and Days. Hesiod. *tr. by* Richmond Lattimore "Beware of the month Lenaion, bad days." WoPoe, *tr. by* Richmond Lattimore

Work's end. *Unknown.* SonAtl, *tr. by* Lester Browne, Cleveland Thompson and Janet Williams

Work's finished. Silk Cotton Tree. *Unknown.* SonAtl, *tr. by* Cheryl Borde and Emma Gonzalez

Workshop. Billy Collins. OxBoAm

Work-table, litter, books and standing lamp. Night Sweat. Robert Lowell. HarvBoo; OxBoAm

Work-week's end and there's enough. Secular. Natasha Trethewey. SpirFl

Workwoman's Death, A. Clementina Suárez. SonAtl, *tr. by* Carole Gibson, Anne Swann and Lee Weingast

World Above Suffering, A. Albert Goldbarth. TaR

World and I, The. Laura Riding Jackson. APT-2; ColAP; HarvBoo; NAAPv.2; OxBoAm

World and the Child, The. James Merrill. MakPoe

World as I Found It, The. Lawrence L. White. IAoNAP

World as Meditation, The. Wallace Stevens. HeIP-4

World as Will and Representation, The. Robert Hass. RoV

World at Night, The. Matthew Rohrer. "I went out one night with people from work." LegDan

World, because I loved you. Selfwriting. Moishe Nadir. Prolet, *tr. by* Amelia Glaser

World begins at a kitchen table, The. No matter what, we must eat to live. Perhaps the World Ends Here. Joy Harjo. IPoFL; MakPoe; ReEnLa; SweBea

World below the Brine, The. Walt Whitman. APN-1; NoP-4

World broods with warm breast and with ah! Bright wings. (LL) God's Grandeur. Gerard Manley Hopkins. AmFaPo; BBASP; BrAP; CABP; ChAP; ClHu; GSo; ITBLP; ItP; MoBrPo; NAEL-6v2; NAEL-7v2; NAMCP V.1; NIL-7; NIP-4; NoAM; NoP-4; NoP-5; OxBEV; OxBSo; PoCho; PoPoPo; RaBo; SacPr; SoSe-8; TFi; WaAnP; WeW-3

World Contracted to a Recognizable Image, The. William Carlos Williams. APT-1

World currently expended figuratively. Ready-Made World. Piera Oppezzo. CItWP, *tr. by* Cinzia Sartini Blum and Lara Trubowitz

World dances with hate, The. Lamenting the Inevitable. Alicia Ostriker. UnSA

World, Do Not Ask Those Snatched from Death. Nelly Sachs. BBASP, *tr. by* Matthew Mead and Ruth Mead

World, do not ask those snatched from death. World, Do Not Ask Those Snatched from Death. Nelly Sachs. BBASP, *tr. by* Matthew Mead and Ruth Mead

World does not close in your eyes; there, The. Braille for Left Hand. Octavio Armand. TCLAP, *tr. by* Carol Maier

World exists again, The. The roses drop their petals. Echoes. Timothy Liu. ReTh

World—feels Dusty, The. Flags Vex a Dying Face. Emily Dickinson. MoAmPo

World for some years, The. Why Must the Show Go On? Noël Coward. ReLy

World gives and the white doves praise all of it. (LL) Dark Thing Inside the Day, A. Linda Gregg. BLT; OxBoAm

World Goes Black, The. Enid Shomer. Dive from 45,000 Feet. OtW

World / has become divided, The. Charles Olson. APSN; ColAP *Fr.* Maximus Poems, The.

World has become, The. Radiant Inventory. Christopher Dewdney. OpeFie

World has held great Heroes, The. Kenneth Grahame. NOxBChV *Fr.* Wind in the Willows, The.

World History. Carl Dennis. OxBoAm

World I see looks to me like a game of children, The. Some Exaggerations. Mirza Asadullah Khan Ghalib. WED, *tr. by* Robert Bly

World I See, The. Mari E. Evans. OxAAAP

World in My Mother's Hair, The. Lisa Glatt. SUP

World in Yellow, A. Marcel Duchamp. PFTM-1

World is a beautiful place, The. 25. Lawrence Ferlinghetti. CLPP; HHAm

World is a garden, The. A light bathes the world. Grace. Adelia Prado. TCLAP, *tr. by* Marcia Kirinus

World Is a Wedding, The. Adele Ne Jame. PoArWo

World is all orange-round, The. Walking Road, The. Richard Hughes. OBMV

World is an invention of the spirit the spirit, The. Revisionist Poem—Octavio Paz. Thomas McGrath. TAPaP

World is Bitter, The. Alfonsina Storni. TANSG, *tr. by* Mark McCaffrey

World is bitter, The. World is Bitter, The. Alfonsina Storni. TANSG, *tr. by* Mark McCaffrey

World is but a sorry scene, The. Christopher Smart. ChIV-2 *Fr.* Hymns and Spiritual Songs for the Fasts and Festivals of the Church of England.

World is charged with the grandeur of God, The. God's Grandeur. Gerard Manley Hopkins. AmFaPo; BBASP; BrAP; CABP; ChAP; ClHu; GSo; ITBLP; ItP; MoBrPo; NAEL-6v2; NAEL-7v2; NAMCP V.1; NIL-7; NIP-4; NoAM; NoP-5; OxBEV; OxBSo; PoCho; PoPoPo; RaBo; SacPr; SoSe-8; TFi; WaAnP; WeW-3

World is complete, The.   Complete Thought I - XXV.   Barrett Watten.
    PFTM-2

World is everything that is the case, The.   Poem Beginning With a Line of
    Wittgenstein.   Donald Hall.   PoA 2002

World is everything that is the case, The.   Tractatus.   Derek Mahon.   ModIr

World is everything, The.   Ann Sansom.   NeBl

World is full of cats, The.   For My Sister Shura.   Sergey Aleksandrovich
    Yesenin.   TCRusP, tr. by Nigel Stott

World Is Full of Remarkable Things, The.   Imamu Amiri Baraka.   SSLK

World is heated seven times, The.   Night in June, A.   Duncan Campbell Scott.
    IFF

World is large and wide and long, The.   Song of an Old Gray Wolf.   Unknown.
    APN-2, tr. by Alfred Kroeber

World is lyrical, The.   Dancing on the Ceiling.   Lorenz Hart.   ReLy

World is made of his voice, The. (LL)   Armand Schwerner.   PFTM-2; WoPoe
    Fr. Tablets, The.

World is my dream, says the wise child, ever so wise, The.   Karl Shapiro.
    BodElec Fr. Bourgeois Poet, The.

World Is Not a Pleasant Place to Be, The.   Nikki Giovanni.   InvLad

World is only air / shining, granular, transparent things, The.   World is Only
    Air, The.   Jan Polkowski.   AF, tr. by Michael March and Jaroslaw Anders

World is Only Air, The.   Jan Polkowski.   AF, tr. by Michael March and
    Jaroslaw Anders

World is right, The.   Fit As a Fiddle.   Arthur Freed.   ReLy

World is so full of a number of things, The.   Happy Thought.   Robert Louis
    Stevenson.   BRP; Spl

World is somewhere visibly round, The.   You Finish It: I Can't.   Daniel
    Berrigan.   PLBUT

World is, The / not with us enough.   O Taste and See.   Denise Levertov.
    AFaM; BeAl; ChIV-1; IPoFL; NoP-4; NoP-5; PoPoPo

World is the stuff, The.   Winter Answer.   Ilse Aichinger.   GTCP, tr. by
    Michael Hamburger

World is to run from, my child, The.   In the Bedroom of Fear.   David Citino.
    LiTh

World is too much with us; late and soon, The.   World Is Too Much with Us,
    The.   William Wordsworth.   BRP; CABP; CenSon; ClHu; GSo; HeIP-4;
    IJHIL; ItP; NAWM-7v2; NOBRP; NoP-4; NoP-5; NPBRoP; OBEV;
    PoPoPo; RaBo; SacPr; SoSe-8; TFi; TRP; WeW-3

World is Turned Upside Down, The.   Unknown.   NOSC

World, its hopes, and fears, have passed away, The.   To the Memory of John
    Keats.   John Clare.   CenSon

World laid low, and the wind blew like a dust, The.   Epigram.   Unknown.
    FaBoWar, tr. by Thomas Kinsella

World last summer didn't yet exist, last summer still was universal darkness,
    chaos, pain, The. (LL)   Question, The.   C. K. Williams.   NoP-4; NoP-5

World like a mutilated tree, A.   Eternal, The.   Blas de Otero.   RaW, tr. by
    Hardie St. Martin

World map, The.   Home.   Pauline Kaldas.   PoArWo

World might end in crispness, The.   Prediction.   Michael Lieberman.
    BloBone

World of books amid a world of green, A.   Library in a Garden, A.   Richard
    Le Gallienne.   OBGa

World of dew, A.   Issa.   SoOfWa, tr. by Sam Hamill

World of dew, The.   On the Death of the Poet's Daughter Sato.   Issa.   WoPoe,
    tr. by Conrad Totman

World of dew, The.   Issa.   EH, tr. by Robert Hass

World of Dreams, The.   Philip Salom.   NOBAu

World of Lightning, A.   Mahmoud al-Braikan.   IrPoTo, tr. by Saadi A. Simawe
    and Ellen Doré Watson

World of money, promise and disease, A. (LL)   Man from Washington, The.
    James Welch.   HATNAP; NoAM; PoPoPo; RaBo; WaAnP

World of trials, A.   Issa.   SoOfWa, tr. by Sam Hamill

World of Words, The.   Hugh MacDiarmid.
    In Memoriam Dylan Thomas.   BrAP

World of worlds as pendents in each ear, A. (LL)   Of Many Worlds in This
    World.   Margaret Lucas Cavendish, Duchess of Newcastle.   NOSC;
    NPeEn

World on Sunday.   James McAuley.   BMAP

World Outside, The.   Denise Levertov.   TRP

World Poetry Circuit.   Alfred A. Yuson.   ReBoTo

World pursues the very track, The.   Chaunts of the Brazen Head, The. II.
    Winthrop Mackworth Praed.   NOBRP

World put back on its.   Voice.   Jacqueline Risset.   OnScMo, tr. by Jennifer
    Moxley

World seems glad after its hearty drink, The.   Leigh Hunt.   STuOW Fr. Legend
    of Florence, A.

World should listen then—as I am listening now, The. (LL)   To a Skylark.
    Percy Bysshe Shelley.   BrAP; BRP; NAEL-6v2; NAEL-7v2; NOBRP;
    NoP-4; NoP-5; NPBRoP; OBEV; OWoS; OxAEP-2; TFi; WaAnP

World sleeps in me, The.   Bardo of Sleep and Dream.   Janet Rodney.
    ICANM

World. Some monuments move. (LL)   Ancient Monuments.   John Ormond.
    AngWePo; OBWVE

World State, The.   G. K. Chesterton.   SacPr

World stops in the middle of its course, The.   Quiet Spaces.   Vicente
    Huidobro.   TCLAP, tr. by Stephen Fredman

World, that all containes, is ever moving, The.   Fulke, 1st Baron Brooke
    Greville.   NoSic Fr. Caelica.

World, The.   William Bronk.   APSN

World, The.   Robert Creeley.   NoP-4; NoP-5; PmAP; VCAP

World, The.   George Herbert.   CtM; NOSC

World, The.   Alice Jones.   ASA

World, The.   Czeslaw Milosz. tr. by the author
    Love.   BeAl, tr. by the author
    Sun, The.   ChAP, tr. by the author

World, The.   William Brighty Rands.   NOxBChV

World, The.   Donald Revell.   BodElec

World, The.   Christina Georgina Rossetti.   NALW; PEW; ViWPN

World, The / is going upstairs.   Homage.   Barbara Guest.   AHA

World, The: "It was just a gas station. It was not spectacular carnage."   Gillian
    Conoley.   BodElec; RoV

World, The (1).   Henry Vaughan.   ChIV-2; FSCP; NAEL-6v1; NAEL-7v1;
    NoP-5; NOSC; NPeEn; OxAEP-1; OxBEV; PBRV; SacPr; TFi; WaAnP
    (Eternity, The.)   OBEV

World this morning is wide as this sea, The.   Darwin's Unfinished Notes to
    Emma.   Amy Newman.   IAoNAP

World to be stuttered after.   Paul Celan.   PoetW, tr. by John Felstiner

World Trade Center, The.   David Lehman.   PA9/11

World Truffle.   Sarah Lindsay.   BeAl; PoDa

World Voice, The.   Bliss Carman.   BrAP

World War II.   Edward Field.   PWW2

World War II.   Langston Hughes.   APT-2; PoPoPo

World was first a private park, The.   Fisherman, The.   Jay Macpherson.   BrAP

World was full of peaceful sounds, The.   Last Letter, The.   Bertus Aafjes.
    TuT, tr. by Tony Curtis

World was quiet then, The.   My Childhood in Another Part of the World.
    Rafael Campo.   NeAmPo

World was very large, The. Then.   Aubade.   Louise Glück.   BodElec

World we found was not something, The.   Discovering America Again.
    Lorenzo Thomas.   RD

World Well Lost 18, The.   Marc André Raffalovich.   CAGL

World Well Lost 4, The.   Marc André Raffalovich.   CAGL

World Where News Travelled Slowly, A.   Lavinia Greenlaw.   MFPA; MoWP;
    NoP-5

World! why do you hound me like this?   World! why do you hound me?   Sor
    Juana Inés de la Cruz.   SonAtl, tr. by Lisa Martin, Lisandro Pena and Lee
    Weingast

World with all of its thought and action, The.   God's Electric Power.   Mrs.
    Henry Linden.   CBWP-4

World Without End.   Kevin Stein.   SwNoth

World Without Objects Is a Sensible Emptiness, A.   Richard Wilbur.
    MoAmPo; NoAM; PoA 2002; UpMys

World world world world.   Enueg 2.   Samuel Beckett.   ItP; NoAM

Worldling.   Elizabeth Spires.   ExTi

Worldly Failure.   Richard Eberhart.   VisFro

Worldly sky / From now on.   Issa.   ZenPo, tr. by Takashi Ikemoto and Lucien
    Stryk

Worldman, A.   Knocking Donkey Fleas off a Poet from the Southside of Chi.
    Haki R. Madhubuti.   SeSe

World-Mother's police chief, The.   Rāmprasād Sen.   SinGod, tr. by Rachel Fell
    McDermott

World's a bubble, and the life of man, The.   Life of Man, The.   Francis Bacon.
    NoSic

World's a floor, whose swelling heaps retain, The.   Deuteronomy 30.19.
    Francis Quarles.   ChIV-1

World's a garden; pleasures are the flowers, The.   Garden, The.   Joshua
    Sylvester.   OBGa

World's a popular disease, that reigns, The.   Luke 6.25.   Francis Quarles.
    ChIV-2

World's a shoreless ocean, The.   Rāmprasād Sen.   SinGod, tr. by Rachel Fell
    McDermott

World's a Stage, The.   Joseph Hilaire Pierre Belloc.   OBCoV

World's a stage. The trifling entrance fee, The.   World's a Stage, The.   Joseph
    Hilaire Pierre Belloc.   OBCoV

World's a stranger's room, we meet to part, The.   You Gave Me Hyacinths First
    a Year Ago.   Dorothy Hewett.   BMAP

World's a theater, the earth a stage, The.   Thomas Heywood.   NOSC; WaAnP
    Fr. Apology for Actors, An.

Worlds are breaking in my head, The. Yves Tanguy. David Gascoyne. NoP-4; NoP-5

Worlds are drunk and drinking, The. Quaternary. Gottfried Benn. WoPoe, *tr. by* Teresa Iverson

Worlds are reconciled, The. (LL) Christmas Hymn, A. Richard Wilbur. ChIV-2; ChrPo; OBCP

World's birds gathered for their conference, The. Farid-uddin Attar. WoPoe *Fr.* Conference of the Birds, The.

World's deceitful, and man's life at best, The. On Mortality. Henry Colman. ChIV-1

World's First Face, The. W. S. Rendra. WoPoe, *tr. by* Burton Raffel

World's gone forward to its latest fair, The. Moor, The. Ralph Hodgson. MoBrPo

World's great age begins anew, The. Percy Bysshe Shelley. HeIP-4; NoP-4; NoP-5 *Fr.* Hellas.

World's Greatest Tricycle-Rider, The. C. K. Williams. ArBi

World's infection, to be none of it, The. (LL) John Donne. NAEL-6v1; NAEL-7v1 *Fr.* Anatomy [*or* Anatomie] of the World, An: The First Anniversary.

Worlds light shines; shine as it will, The. Bible, *N.T.* ChIV-2 *Fr.* St. John.

World's light shines; shine as it will, The. But Men loved Darkness[e] Rather Than [*or* Then] Light. Richard Crashaw. ChIV-2

World's, The / not wanton. Implosions. Adrienne Rich. PoA 2002

World's Oldest Comedian Is Dead. Iain Sinclair. Oth *Fr.* Ebbing of Kraft, The.

Worlds on worlds are rolling ever. Percy Bysshe Shelley. HeIP-4; NAEL-6v2; NAEL-7v2 *Fr.* Hellas.

World's One Hope, The. Bertolt Brecht. AF

World's pottage, the rat's star, The. (LL) With Mercy for the Greedy. Anne Sexton. CAP-8; MoWP; NIL-7; VCAP

World's too beautiful for human blood, The. Wound seen from afar. Philippe Jaccottet. MFP, *tr. by* Martin Sorrell

World's Wanderers, The. Percy Bysshe Shelley. TreFP

World's wonder, I liven wenches, The. *Unknown.* WoPoe *Fr.* Riddles (Exeter Book).

World's wrong, mother, The. Wyndmere, Windemere. Carol Muske-Dukes. PBCAP

World-Soul, The. Ralph Waldo Emerson. APN-1; NCAP

Worm Either Way. D. H. Lawrence. NoAM

Worm Fed on the Heart of Corinth, A. Isaac Rosenberg. NPeEn; PoWW

Worm tranquil and slobbering, A. Epigram for a Worm. Daria Menicanti. CItWP, *tr. by* Cinzia Sartini Blum and Lara Trubowitz

Worm unto his love, The: lo, here's fresh store. Coffin Worm, The. Ruth Pitter. MoBrPo; MoWP

Worms and leaves. (LL) Geoffrey Hill. NAMCP V.2; NoAM *Fr.* Mercian Hymns.

Worms at Heaven's Gate, The. Wallace Stevens. NAMCP V.1; NoAM

Worm's Life Not Everything, A. William Wordsworth. STuOW

Wormwood. Thomas Kinsella. PBCIP

Wormwood has enchanted me completely. Hayim Lenski. FIT, *tr. by* Robert Friend

Worn and torn by many fingers. Family Album, A. Alter Brody. TaR

Worn like a hand-me-down. Growing into my name. Harriet Jacobs. SpirFl

"Worn out of virtue, as the time of year,." David and Bathsheba in the Public Garden. Robert Lowell. ChIV-1

Worn out slightly by carelessness. (LL) Far from kingdoms. Patrizia Cavalli. NeIt; VCWP, *tr. by* Judith Baumel

Worn out were the buildings, I. Death of a Farmyard. Geoffrey Grigson. EmeKit

Worn with life's care, love yet was love. (LL) Marriage Ring, The. George Crabbe. OBEV; OxBEV

Worn-Out Pop Song, A. Jotie T'Hooft. TuT, *tr. by* Pat Boran

Worn-out pop song, a tattered blues, A. Worn-Out Pop Song, A. Jotie T'Hooft. TuT, *tr. by* Pat Boran

Worn-out voice of the clock breaks on the hour, The. Prize for Good Conduct. Kenneth Allott. OBWP

Worried. Nguyen Binh Khiem. WoPoe, *tr. by* Nguyen Ngoc Bich

Worries creep like insects. At Night. Stephanie Goldstein. PfS

Worry. Aaron Anstett. AmPoNex

Worry. Suzanne Matson. PfS

Worry All the Time. Alison Morris. BtF

Worry Yr Logos: Conversant You Speak to the Dead. Anne Waldman. "Death is all things we see awake." Eno

Worrying the carcase of an old song. (LL) Welsh Landscape. Ronald Stuart Thomas. NoP-4; NoP-5; TCAWP

Worschippe ye that loveris bene this May. Spring Song of the Birds. James I, King of Scotland. OBEV

Worse. J. R. Solonche. VisFro

Worse days are coming. Time Allotted, The. Ingeborg Bachmann. PFTM-2, *tr. by* Jerome Rothenberg

Worse goddam job of all, The. Tuesday Morning, Loading Pigs. David Lee. P180

Worship. Ralph Waldo Emerson. APN-1

Worship. John Greenleaf Whittier. ChIV-2

Worst Fate Bookes have, when they are once read, The. Common Fate of Books, The. Margaret Lucas Cavendish, Duchess of Newcastle. PBRV

Worst Fear, The. George MacBeth. OxBSo

Worst is yet to come, The. (LL) Testimony of Light,The. Carolyn Forché. AFaM; ExTi

Worst of it, The. Craig Reynolds. CAGL

13. The Worst of People. David McFadden. NLPA

Worst was this;—my love was my decay, The. (LL) William Shakespeare. CAGL; OxAEP-1 *Fr.* Sonnets.

Worst winter in ages—pipes freeze, nerves fizzle, The. Wintering. Jane Satterfield. SweBea

Worsted Heather. Jody Gladding. YaYoPo

Worstest beast that swims in the sea, The. Worstest Beast, The. Alan Jackson. EdScPo

Worth Dying For. Christina Georgina Rossetti. LW

Worth keeping your foot in the door. Respectable House. Anne Stevenson. NALW

Worthless as was her itinerary to fame. Amelia Rosselli. ItPo, *tr. by* Gayle Ridinger

Worthy object: our lord's Feet, A. (LL) Saint Mary Magdalene or The Weeper. Richard Crashaw. BASC; ChIV-2

Worthy of a lover have I loved. White Peacock, The. Alice Notley. FTOS

Would but indulgent Fortune send. Wish, The. Mary Lee, Lady Chudleigh. LW

Would congregate endlessly. (LL) Water. Philip Larkin. EmeKit; NAMCP V.2

Would drop Him—Bone by Bone. (LL) There is a pain—so utter. Emily Dickinson. APN-2; NCAP

Would equal, if alive. (LL) Braly Street. Gary Soto. GeoHom; UnSA

Would god that deth with cruell darte. Ellin Thorne Songe. Ellin Thorne. EMWP

Would I could cast a sail on the water. Collarbone [*or* Collar-Bone] of a Hare, The. William Butler Yeats. OxAEP-2

Would I go back? The childhood bike. Cycles. Alison Brackenbury. ArBi

Would I have marched with you Martin. Time for Guns, A. Darryl Holmes. InTrad

Would I write it if I could? Last Poem in the World, The. Hayden Carruth. TAPaP

Would it please you if I strung my tears. Race Question, The. Naomi Long Madgett. LTA

Would it wake the drowned out of their anviled sleep. Ars Poetica (the idea). Dana Levin. LegDan

Would pause with his needle in the air. (LL) Illustrious Ancestors. Denise Levertov. OxBoAm; PmAP; TaR

Would pulse with all the life there was within. (LL) Battle, The. Louis Simpson. AmWaPo; NAMCP V.2; OBWP; PoWW

Would say: / "writing to be used in the body". With a Little Notebook at the Met. Cecilia Vicuña. WANABP, *tr. by* Rosa Alcalá

Would scarcely know that we were gone. (LL) There Will Come Soft Rains. Sara Teasdale. AmWaPo; APT-1; WaAnP

Would she have been a person. My Mother, If She Had Won Free Dance Lessons. Cornelius Eady. ISC

Would that all my good deeds. Kyunyŏ, Great Master. CATKP *Fr.* Eleven Poems on the Ten Vows of the Universally Worthy Bodhisattva.

Would that by Hindu magic we became. Buddha. Vachel Lindsay. NAAPv.2

Would that the structure brave, the manifold music I build. Abt Vogler. Robert Browning. NAEL-6v2; NAEL-7v2

Would that there had never been swift ships! Callimachus. HePo, *tr. by* Barbara Hughes Fowler

Would this help: a grocery list with color codes. One Quick Quiz. Paula Sergi. SweBea

Would 'twere underground! (LL) Bereft. Thomas Hardy. NAMCP V.1; NoAM

Would wake and weary and fall asleep. (LL) From the Antique. Christina Georgina Rossetti. OxBEV; PEW

Would [*or* Wo'd] ye[e] have fresh cheese and cream? Fresh Cheese and Cream. Robert Herrick. BASC

Would ye, with faultless judgement, learn to plan. Richard Jago. OBGa *Fr.* Edge-Hill.

Would you adopt a strong logical attitude. Synchoresis. Godfrey Turner. OBCoV

Would you be a man in fashion? *Unknown.* NOSC

Would you be an angel. Something of a Departure. Paul Muldoon. IrLP; PBCIP

Would You Believe It? Bart Howard. ReLy

Would you believe, when you this Monsieur see. On English Monsieur. Ben Jonson. AEP; NBLV; NoP-4; NoP-5

Would you but soon return, and speak it here. (LL) Letter to Daphnis, A. Anne Finch, Countess of Winchilsea. EMWP; LW; MakPoe; NALW; PEW

Would you care for a smoke or a sherry? Mopev. UV

Would you care to hear the strangest story. Polka Dots and Moonbeams. Johnny Burke. ReLy

Would you compare me to some kind of clown. Goodsonnet. J. D. Smith. IaFF

Would You Have a Young Virgin? John Gay. NAEL-6v1 *Fr.* Beggar's Opera, The.

Would you have freedom from wage slavery? There Is Power in a Union. Joe Hill. HHAm

Would you hear of an old-time [*or* old-fashioned] sea fight? Walt Whitman. SAmP *Fr.* Song of Myself.

Would you kindly direct me to hell? (LL) Coda: "There's little in taking or giving." Dorothy Parker. AmWit; APT-1

Would you like a very Scottish servant all your own. Advertisement for a Scottish Servant. Ron Butlin. EdScPo

Would You Like to Play? Dezső Kosztolányi. IQMS, *tr. by* Thomas Kabdebo

Would you like to swing on a star. Swinging on a Star. Johnny Burke. ReLy

Would You Like to Take a Walk? Mort Dixon and Billy Rose. ReLy

Would you, my friend, in little room express. Martial. OBVE

Would you prefer the examples? The pancakes? Or the words? Male, The. Carla Harryman. PmAP

Would You Think? John Wheelwright. APT-2; OxBoAm

Would You Wear My Eyes? Bob Kaufman. GT

Would you your son should be a sot or dunce. William Cowper. OBSV *Fr.* Tirocinium; or, A Review of Schools.

Would-be Critic, The. Mrs. Henry Linden. CBWP-4

Wouldn't it be a change for you and me. Sleepy Time Gal. Joseph Reed Alden and Raymond B. Egan. ReLy

Wouldn't it be great to get away? Melbourne or the Bush. Philip Mead. BMAP

Wouldn't It Be Luverly? Alan Jay Lerner. ReLy

Wouldst know the lark? Listener's Guide to the Birds, A. Elwyn Brooks White. OWoS

Wouldst thou be wise, O Man? At the knees of a woman begin. Wilfrid Scawen Blunt. OBMV *Fr.* Wisdom of Merlyn, The.

Wouldst Thou but gild my should with ty bright ray. (LL) Edward Taylor. NAAL-3; NAAL-5; NAAPv.1; TCAPo *Fr.* Preparatory Meditations Before My Approach to the Lord's Supper.

Wouldst thou hear what man can say. Epitaph on Elizabeth, L. H. Ben Jonson. NAEL-6v1; NIL-7; NIP-4; NoP-4; NoP-5; NOSC; OBEV

Wouldst thou love long? The only means are these. He Lives Long Who Lives Well. Thomas Randolph. TreFP

Would'st thou then have *me* tempt the comic scene. To Miss C—on Being Desired To Attempt Writing a Comedy. Charlotte Smith. RWP

Wound. Alaide Foppa. TANSG, *tr. by* Celeste Kostopulos-Cooperman

Wound, The. Louise Glück. NoAM

Wound, The. Thom Gunn. NPeEn

Wound Man, The. D. A. Feinfeld. BloBone

Wound Man, The. Sinéad Morrissey. BeAl; NIrP

Wound of Love, The. Heinrich von Morungen. NAWM-7v1, *tr. by* Peter Dronke

Wound seen from afar. Philippe Jaccottet. MFP, *tr. by* Martin Sorrell

Wound-Dresser, The. Walt Whitman. AmWaPo; APN-1; CBCWP; ColAP; NAAL-3; NAAL-5; NAAPv.1; OBWP; PCW; TCAPo

"Bearing the bandages, water and sponge." FaBoWar

Wound-dresser's Dream, The. Pauline Stainer. NeBl

Wounded Angel, The. Robert Phillips. Vesp

Wounded Breakfast, The. Russell Edson. MotU

Wounded Cupid, The. Robert Herrick. OBVE

Wounded Deer Leaps Highest, A. Emily Dickinson. APN-2

Wounded Falcon, The. Han Yü. CCL1, *tr. by* H. A. Giles

Wounded hands, the weary human face, The. (LL) E Tenebris. Oscar Wilde. ChIV-2; GSo; MoBrPo; NAEL-6v2; NAEL-7v2; OxAEP-2

Wounded, he'd have. Arrow, The. Martin Sorescu. StAl, *tr. by* Hilde Ottschofski and John Hartley Williams

Wounded horse dies without a whinny. Horse, The. Marie Laurencin. CuPo

Wounded I sing, tormented I indite. Joseph's Coat. George Herbert. ChI-1

Wounded Man, The. Miguel Hernández. RaW, *tr. by* James Wright

Wounded Otter, The. Michael Hartnett. PBCIP

Wounded Self-Portrait, A. Homero Aridjis. WoBe, *tr. by* George McWhirter

Wounded stretch out across the battlefields, The. Wounded Man, The. Miguel Hernández. RaW, *tr. by* James Wright

Wounding us, making us whole. (LL) Love, Like Water. Julia Copus. BeAl; MoWP

Wounding words, whetted on flesh. Nightspell. Jon Furberg. IFF

Wounds. Michael Longley. ModIr; NAMCP V.2; NPeEn; PBCIP; PNI; PoAgWa

Wounds are terrible, The. The paint is old. Dolls Museum in Dublin, The. Eavan Boland. NAEL-7v2; NoP-4; NoP-5

Wounds, as Wells of Life, The. *Unknown.* SacPr

Woven you are of the spring, lovers. Rose of Fire. Antonio Machado Ruiz. SpanPo, *tr. by* Kate Flores

Wow, I said I'd love a Big Mac. Federal Case. Julie O'Callaghan. StAl

Wow man I said / when you tipped my chin. Short Note on the Sparseness of the Language. Diane Di Prima. BB

Wow! wow! wow! (LL) Lewis Carroll. NBLV; UV *Fr.* Alice's Adventures in Wonderland.

Wraith of the Rose, The. Frances Sargent Osgood. NAAPv.1

Wraith-Friend, The. George Barker. OBMV

Wrap a live microphone with a very large. Micro 1. Takehisa Kosugi. WhBo

Wrap it up wrap it up in a mat. (LL) Harvest of War. Catherine Obianuju Acholonu. HAWP; NAfrP

Wrap the light in tendrons and no one. E Questa Vita Un Lampo. Peter Riley. Oth

Wrap the steamed rice in lotus leaves. Yun Söndo. CATKP *Fr.* Angler's Calendar, The.

Wrap their babies in the American flag. Immigrants. Pat Mora. UnSA

Wrap Your Troubles in Dreams. Ted Koehler. ReLy

Wrapped, surrounded by ten thousand mountains. On the Road to T'ien-t'ai. Yuan Mei. GifTon, *tr. by* Jerome P. Seaton

Wrapping dumplings in. Basho. SoOfWa, *tr. by* Sam Hamill

Wrapping presents, I look up. Smoke We Make Pictures Of, The. Cortney Davis. FiBr

Wrapping the rice cakes. Basho. EH, *tr. by* Robert Hass

Wrapt in the old miasmal mist. (LL) Hippopotamus, The. T. S. Eliot. NAEL-6v2; OBMV; SacPr; TCAPo

Wrapt up, O Lord, in mans degeneration. Fulke, 1st Baron Brooke Greville. NoSic *Fr.* Caelica.

Wrath, as I bigan yow for to seye, The. Geoffrey Chaucer. OxBEV *Fr.* Troilus and Criseyde [*or* Criseide].

Wrath of *Peleus* Son, O Muse, resound, The. Homer. OBVE *Fr.* Iliad, The.

Wrath to Sadness. Robert Grenier. PmAP

Wrathful winter, proaching on apace, The. Thomas, 1st Earl of Dorset Sackville. NoSic *Fr.* Mirror for Magistrates.

Wreath, A. George Herbert. NOSC; NPeEn

Wreath, A. Gyula Illyés. IQMS, *tr. by* William Jay Smith

Wreath for Emmett Till, A. Marilyn Nelson. CAP-8

Wreath to the Fish, A. Nancy Willard. P180

Wreathèd garland of deservèd praise, A. Wreath, A. George Herbert. NOSC; NPeEn

Wreath-heavy, a child's body. Raising the Dead. Fatima Lim-Wilson. ReBoTo

Wreathing themselves in the living fire. (LL) Wild Gratitude. Edward Hirsch. IllVoic; WaAnP

Wreaths. Geoffrey Hill. PoA 2002

Wreaths. Michael Longley.

  Civil Servant, The. ModIr

  Greengrocer, The. ModIr

  Linen Workers, The. ModIr; NPeEn

Wreck, The. Felicia Dorothea Hemans. TreFP

Wreck, The. Don Paterson. PoDa

Wreck in the Woods. Dave Jeddie Smith. NAMCP V.2; RoV

Wreck of the Circus Train, The. Hayden Carruth. GM

Wreck of the Deutschland, The. Gerard Manley Hopkins. NAMCP V.1; NoAM; OxAEP-2; OxBEV; WaAnP

  "On Saturday sailed from Bremen."

  "Sister, a sister calling." FaBoVe

  "Thou mastering me." NPeEn

Wreck of the Edmund Fitzgerald, The. Gordon Lightfoot. NoP-4

Wreck of the Great Northern, The. Robert Hedin. GM

Wreck of the Hesperus, The. Henry Wadsworth Longfellow. APN-1; BRP; NAAPv.1; OBNV; TCAPo; TreFP

Wreck of the Old 97. David Graves George. GM

Wreck of the *Platonic*,The. B. J. Atwood-Fukuda. FreRad

Wreck the shroud, don't move. (LL) Fission. Jorie Graham. NAMCP V.2; OxBoAm

Wreckage along the River, The. Jeff Knorr. LiTh

Wreckage is the only Answer. Barry MacSweeney. VaPo

Wrecked castaway. Robinson Crusoe Daniel Defoe. Maurice Sagoff. NBLV

Wrecked Creeves.   Katrina Porteous.   NeBl

Wrecked Town, The.   Han-shan (Cold Mountain).   CCL1, *tr.* by Gary Snyder

Wrecked World.   Marilyn Annucci.   PoDa

Wreckers, The.   Rafael Zepeda.   SUP

Wren.   Beckian Fritz Goldberg.   AmAlph

Wren, A.   Denise Levertov.   PoCoUp

Wren dropped down on my window sill, A.   Little Wren, A.   Priscilla Jane Thompson.   CBWP-2

Wren, The.   John Clare.   CenSon

Wren, The.   Issa.   NTCP, *tr.* by R. H. Blyth

Wrested long since from tyranny's black heel.   To General Pershing.   Hilton Ross Greer.   TiP2

Wrestle for this. (LL)   Wrestling.   Louisa Sarah Bevington.   LW; PEW

Wrestle on, Jacob.   *Unknown.*   SSUS

Wrestling.   Louisa Sarah Bevington.   LW; PEW

Wrestling.   "Rachel."   FIT, *tr.* by Robert Friend

Wrestling Jacob.   Charles Wesley.   OBEV; OxAEP-1

Wretched are the poor in spirit: for what they were on earth.   Jorge Luis Borges.   GI *Fr.* Apocryphal Gospel, An.

Wretched Catullus! You have to stop this nonsense.   Catullus.   NAWM-7v1 *Fr.* Carmina [Charles Martin Translation].

Wretched estate of men, by fortune blest.   George Chapman.   NOSC *Fr.* Tears of Peace, The or Euthymia Raptus.

Wretched Flavia, on her couch reclined, The.   Lady Mary Wortley Montagu.   BrAP; NoP-5 *Fr.* Six Town Eclogues.

Wretched Ierne! with what grief I see.   Jonathan Swift.   OBSV *Fr.* Verses Occasioned by the Sudden Drying Up of St. Patrick's Well.

Wretched Married Life (Folk Song from Koch'ang).   *Korean Oral Tradition.*   CATKP, *tr.* by Peter H. Lee

Wretched me / I live a rustic live.   Alcaeus.   SaLy, *tr.* by Diane Rayor

Wretten by Me at the Death of My 4th Sonne and 5th Child Perigrene Payler.   Mary Carey.   EMWP

Wrights' Biplane, The.   Robert Frost.   AmWit; WeW-3 *Fr.* Ten Mills.

Wring the Swan's Neck.   Enrique Gonzáles Martínez.   TCLAP, *tr.* by Samuel Beckett

Wrinkled, callow, calloused fingers.   Major, The.   Bernard Keller.   BtF

Wrinkled, crabbèd man they picture thee, A.   Robert Southey.   OxBSo

Wrinkles: like / valleys etched by glaciers.   Riding the North Point Ferry.   Wing Tek Lum.   OpBo

Wrinkles on the brown face, The.   Militance of a Photograph in the Passbook of a Bantu under Detention, The.   Michael S. Harper.   VCAP

Wrinkling Together.   Leo Vroman.   TuT, *tr.* by Anne Kennedy

Wrist-wrestling father.   Orval Lund.   GoPo

Writ in my psalter. (LL)   His Prayer to Ben Jonson.   Robert Herrick.   BASC; NAEL-6v1; NAEL-7v1; NoP-4; NoP-5; NOSC

Write before other people get up.   Dress.   Maxine Hong Kingston.   WhBo

Write each of your poems.   Ars Poetica.   Blaga Dimitrova.   PoCho, *tr.* by Ludmilla G. Popova

Write it. Write. In ordinary ink.   Wisława Szymborska.   AF

Write like one walks.   Juliana Spahr.   IIR

"Write me a sonnet. On the spot," said she.   Sonnet Right off the Bat.   Félix Lope de Vega Carpio.   STV, *tr.* by John Frederick Nims

Write Off.   Breyten Breytenbach.   PoetW, *tr.* by Denis Hirson

Write poems when I'm sober, and sing when I'm drunk.   Lazy Cloud's Nest 1.   Ali Hsiying.   ColAnChi, *tr.* by Jerome P. Seaton

Write the last rules first: that each specific.   Found Missing.   Jasper Bernes.   IAoNAP

Write the poem.   Pyramids, The.   Nick Piombino.   FTOS

Write this. We have burned all their villages.   Sun.   Michael Palmer.   APSN; CAP-8; FTOS; NAMCP V.2; PFTM-2

Write to Sardis, saith the Lord.   William Cowper.   ChIV-2 *Fr.* Olney Hymns.

Write to thine eyes? Why, my poor pen.   To Fannie.   Mary E. Tucker.   CBWP-1

Write with color.   Be a Painter.   Joe Lothamer.   GeoH

Write write yow Croniclers of Tyme and Fame.   George Peele.   PBRV *Fr.* Anglorum Feriae.

Writer.   Joe Wenderoth.   BodElec

Writer, The.   Richard Wilbur.   CAP-8; NAMCP V.2; NoAM; PoPoPo; SoSe-8

Writer depersonalises his dreamwork, The.   Chris Wallace-Crabbe.   BMAP *Fr.* Sonnets to the Left.

Writer in sand, The.   Lionel Abrahams.   TSAP

Writers.   Robert Lowell.

   Robert Frost.   NoAM

Writhes and wallows till death. (LL)   Calvary: "My eye is not on Calvary."   Sorley MacLean.   EdScPo; NePenScot

Writhing.   Stroke.   Hugh Seidman.   BodElec

Writing.   Howard Nemerov.   VCAP

Writing.   Octavio Paz.   PoCho, *tr.* by Eliot Weinberger

Writing a Curriculum Vitae.   Wisława Szymborska.   PoSu, *tr.* by Grazyna Drabik

Writing a haiku.   Stanford M. Forrester.   AmZen

Writing a poem.   Believing in the Absurd.   Harold Norse.   CLPP

Writing about the mysteries.   Mysteries, The.   Brenda Hillman.   ExTi

Writing Brush.   Gu Cheng.   WoBe *Fr.* Liquid Mercury.

Writing Class.   Stephen Berg.   TAPaP

Writing for a young man on the redline train: "to his boy mistress."   D. A. Powell.   LegDan

Writing in a nearly lightless loft.   Michael Haslam.   Oth *Fr.* Continual Song.

Writing in Prison.   Ken Smith.   NPeEn

Writing in the Afterlife.   Billy Collins.   CAP-8

Writing is a room, a method of dilating the pupils. Horace speaks: "Listen."   Room.   Bob Perelman.   ASA

Writing Is an Aid to Memory.   Lyn Hejinian.

   1.   AWPTFC

   2.   AWPTFC

   9.   AWPTFC

Writing is inhibiting. Sighing, I sit, scribbling in ink.   Christian Bök.   OpeFie *Fr.* Chapter I.

Writing issues from pained reflection.   With Chang Hung-lüeh, Court Attendant, Discussing Literature.   Yüan Hao-wen.   ColAnChi, *tr.* by John Timothy Wixted

Writing of poems, The.   First Drift.   Ron Padgett.   FTOS

Writing on a Door, A.   *Unknown.*   CCL1, *tr.* by James Legge

Writing on a gradual tuning scale.   Green Hill, a Green Hill, A.   Ernesto Lumbreras.   RMCMP, *tr.* by Rebecca Seiferle

Writing on a Tombstone.   J. C. Bloem.   TuT, *tr.* by Desmond Egan

Writing on Aisha's Tomb.   Abdul Wahab Al-Bayati.   IrPoTo, *tr.* by Farouk Abdel Wahab

Writing on an Ink-Stone, A.   *Unknown.*   CCL1, *tr.* by James Legge

Writing poems about writing poems.   Always on the Train.   Ruth Stone.   TAPaP

Writing poetry is a consummate art.   On Poetry.   Yi Kyubo.   CATKP, *tr.* by Kevin O'Rourke

Writing / Rubbing it out—.   Hokushi.   ZenPo, *tr.* by Takashi Ikemoto and Lucien Stryk

Writing shit about new snow.   Issa.   EH, *tr.* by Robert Hass

Writing the Poem.   Gary H. Holthaus.   TAPaP

Writing themselves. (LL)   Construction of the Museum.   Michael Palmer.   BodElec; WoBe

Writing these poems!/ Imagine! (LL)   Autobiographia Literaria.   Frank O'Hara.   OxBoAm; PtR

Writing through the Cantos.   John Cage.   PmAP

Writing verse is cycling up Mont Ventoux.   Mont Ventoux.   Jan Kal.   ArBi, *tr.* by John Irons

Writing What I've Seen.   Yuan Mei.   GifTon, *tr.* by Jerome P. Seaton

Writing with the sun on my hand.   Sun On My Hand, The.   Bert Voeten.   TuT, *tr.* by Tony Curtis

Written After Climbing Kaguyama to Survey the Land.   Emperor Jomei.   WoPoe, *tr.* by Helen Craig McCullough

Written After Hearing About the Soviet Invasion of Afghanistan.   Sujata Bhatt.   FiBr

Written After Swimming from Sestos to Abydos.   Lord Byron.   NAEL-6v2; NAEL-7v2; NBLV; NoP-4; NoP-5

Written Answer, A.   Tom Paulin.   ModIr

Written at a Farm.   John Codrington Bampfylde.   CenSon

Written at [or in] an Inn at Henley.   William Shenstone.   OBEV; OxAEP-1; OxBEV

Written at Bamborough Castle.   William Lisle Bowles.   CenSon

Written at Bignor Park in Sussex, in August, 1799.   Charlotte Smith.   CenSon

Written at Jumble-Rock Mountain by the South Sea.   Du Shenyan.   CCL1, *tr.* by Stephen Owen

Written at Killarney. July 29, 1800.   Mary Tighe.   CenSon

Written at Netley Abbey.   Susan Evance.   CenSon

Written at Rossana. November 18, 1799.   Mary Tighe.   CenSon

Written at Scarborough.   Mary Tighe.   CenSon; NPBRoP; WaAnP

Written at Sea, in the First Dutch War.   Charles, 6th Earl of Dorset Sackville.   *See* Song Written at Sea in the First Dutch War (1665), the Night before an Engagement.

Written at the Close of Spring.   Charlotte Smith. *See* Sonnet Written at the Close of Spring [or Elegiac Sonnet].

Written at the Couch of a Dying Parent.   Eliza Cook.   CenSon

Written at the Dwelling of a Recluse.   Chia Tao.   CSKM, *tr.* by Mike O'Connor

Written at the Eagle's Nest, Killarney. July 26, 1800.   Mary Tighe.   CenSon; OxBSo

Written at the Hotwells, near Bristol.   Charles Lloyd.   CenSon

Written at Tinemouth, Northumberland, after a Tempestuous Voyage.   William Lisle Bowles.   CenSon

Written Between Dover and Calais, July 1792.   Martha Robinson.   NPBRoP

Written by Chance.   Li Ch'ing-chao.   NDACCP, tr. by Kenneth Rexroth

Written December 1790.   Anna Seward.   CenSon

Written, Directed by and Starring.   James Simmons.   PBCIP

Written During the Author's Imprisonment, November 1814.   Leigh Hunt. See To Hampstead.

Written for Love of an Ascension—Coltrane.   Carolyn M. Rodgers.   SeSe

Written for My Son, and Spoken by Him at His First Putting on Breeches.   Mary Barber.   CABP

Written for Old Friends in Yang-Jou City While Spending the Night on the Tung-Lu River.   Meng Hao Jan.   WoPoe, tr. by Greg Whincup

Written Impromptu upon Returning to My Hometown.   Ho Ch'e Ch'ang.   ColAnChi, tr. by Victor H. Mair

Written in a Blank-Paper Book Given to the Author by a Friend.   Mary Russell Mitford.   PoBW

Written in a Carefree Mood.   Lu Yu.   ColAnChi, tr. by Burton Watson

Written in a Ruinous Abbey.   Susan Evance.   CenSon

Written in a Shrubbery Towards the Decline of Autumn.   Mrs. B. Finch.   CenSon

Written in a Sick Chamber.   Samuel Rogers.   NOBRP

Written in a Winter's Morning.   Mrs. B. Finch.   CenSon

Written in an Album.   William Wordsworth. See To a Child [Written in Her Album].

Written in an Ovid.   Matthew Prior.   OBCoV

Written in Autumn.   Mary Tighe.   CenSon; OxBSo

Written in Blood.   Tiffany Midge.   ReEnLa

Written in Blood.   Sue Owen.   PoA 2002

Written in Bracing, Gray L.A. Rainlight.   Al Young.   SpirFl

Written in Butler's Sermons.   Matthew Arnold.   OxBSo

Written in Devonshire, Near the Dart.   Anne Batten Cristall.   RWP

Written in Farm Wood, South Downs, in May 1784.   Charlotte Smith.   RWP

Written in Ill Health.   Anna Maria Smallpiece.   CenSon

Written in Ill Health at the Close of Spring.   Susan Evance.   CenSon

Written in Juice of Lem[m]on.   Abraham Cowley.   CABP Fr. Mistress, The.

Written in London, September, 1802.   William Wordsworth.   SacPr
(England, 1802, I.)   OBEV

Written in March [While Resting on the Bridge at the Foot of Brother's Water].   William Wordsworth.   ChAP; NAEL-6v2; NTCP
(Cock is Crowing, The.)   NPBRoP

Written in My Dream by W. C. Williams.   Allen Ginsberg.   PoA 2002

Written in Northampton County Asylum.   John Clare. See I Am.

Written in October.   Charlotte Smith.   NoP-4; NoP-5

Written in pencil.   In Pencil.   Moishe Nadir.   Prolet, tr. by Amelia Glaser

Written in Pencil in the Sealed Railway-Car.   Dan Pagis.   AF, tr. by Stephen Mitchell

Written in Rain.   Blas de Otero.   RaW, tr. by Hardie St. Martin

Written in the Church-yard at Middleton in Sussex.   Charlotte Smith. See Pressed by the Moon, Mute Arbitress of Tides.

Written in the Mountains.   Kuan Hsiu.   WoPoe, tr. by Jerome P. Seaton

Written in the Spring that Succeeded Imprisonment, May 1815.   Leigh Hunt.   NPBRoP

Written in the Workhouse.   Thomas Hood.   CenSon

Written in Tintern Abbey, Monmouthshire.   CenSon

Written near a Port on a Dark Evening.   Charlotte Smith.   CenSon; NoP-4; NoP-5

Written on a Cold Evening.   Yang Wan-li.   ColAnChi, tr. by Jonathan Chaves

Written on a Landscape Painting in an Album.   Shen Chou.   ColAnChi, tr. by Daniel Bryant

Written on a Summer Day in the City.   Ch'i-chi.   CSKM, tr. by Burton Watson

Written on a Wall at Hsiu-Ching Monastery in Wu-Ch'ang.   Li Po.   NDACCP, tr. by David Hinton

Written on Seeing the Flowers, and Remembering My Daughter.   Kao Ch'i.   ColAnChi, tr. by F. W. Mote

Written on the Day That Mr. Leigh Hunt Left Prison.   John Keats.   CenSon

Written on the First Day of the Fifth Month.   T'ao Ch'ien.   CCL1, tr. by William Acker

Written on the Lake on My Way Back to the Retreat at Stone Cliff.   Hsieh Ling-yün.   CCL1, tr. by John Frodsham

Written on the Lake While Returning to Stone Cliff Hermitage.   Hsieh Ling-yün.   CrYelRi, tr. by Sam Hamill

Written on the Ninth Day of the Ninth Month of the Year Yi-you.   T'ao Ch'ien.   CCL1, tr. by William Acker

Written on the Painting "Cold River Snow."   Ching An.   CSKM, tr. by Jerome P. Seaton

Written on the Sea Shore.—October, 1784.   Charlotte Smith.   CenSon; RWP

Written on the Sea-Shore.   Felicia Dorothea Hemans.   RWP

Written on the Seventh Day of the Seventh Month.   Li Ch'ing-chao.   NDACCP, tr. by Kenneth Rexroth

Written on the Tavern Wall.   Wang Ji.   CCL1, tr. by Stephen Owen

Written on the Wall at Chang's Hermitage.   Tu Fu [or Du Fu]. See Written on the Wall at Zhang's Hermitage.

Written on the Wall at Chang's Recluse Home.   Tu Fu [or Du Fu].   NDACCP, tr. by David Hinton

Written on the Wall at Master Wei Feng's.   Pao Hsien.   CSKM, tr. by Paul Hansen

Written on the Wall at Zhang's Hermitage.   Tu Fu [or Du Fu].   CCL1, tr. by Kenneth Rexroth
(Written on the Wall at Chang's Hermitage.)   NDACCP

Written on the Wall of Ch'önsu Monastery.   Yi Illo.   CATKP, tr. by Peter H. Lee

Written September 1791, During a Remarkable Thunder Storm, in which the Moon Was Perfectly Clear, While the Tempest Gathered in Various Directions Near the Earth.   Charlotte Smith.   CenSon

Written so long ago, I didn't even.   Verses.   Marina Ivanovna Tsvetayeva.   MoWP, tr. by Elaine Feinstein

Written structure.   George Oppen.   APT-2; PFTM-1

Written to the Tune "The Fisherman's Honor."   Li Ch'ing-chao. See "Fisherman's Honor," The.

Written upon the Death of the Most Noble Prince Henrie.   Sir Arthur Gorges.   PBRV

Written When the Mind Was Oppressed.   Anne Batten Cristall.   RWP

Written While Drunk.   Ch'ien T'ao.   WoPoe, tr. by William Acker and Cyril Birch

Written While Riding the Long Island Rail Road.   May Swenson.   GM

Written with a Diamond On Her Window at Woodstock.   Queen of England Elizabeth I.   PEW

Wrong #.   Lee Ranaldo.   HeMarv

Wrong? are they wrong? Of course they are.   England's Alfred Abroad.   Sir Owen Seaman.   UV

Wrong Color.   Christopher Stanard.   SpirFl

Wrong! Is it wrong? Well, may be.   Alfred Austin.   UV Fr. Jameson's Ride.

Wrong Kitchen, The.   Nikki Giovanni.   FuFl

Wrong Room, The.   Anna Mendelssohn.   VaPo

Wrong Side of the Door, The.   Ray DiPalma.   FTOS

Wrong somehow, they would rather be trees. (LL)   Margaret Atwood.   NAMCP V.2; NoAM Fr. Circe / Mud Poems.

Wrong Street, The.   Cornelius Eady.   OxAAAP

Wrong Way Will Haunt You, The.   Sydney Lea.   RA

Wrongly called Fidelity. (LL)   Punctilio.   Mary Elizabeth Coleridge.   OBEV; PoBW

Wrote about this: all misunderstanding. (LL)   One You Wanted to Be Is the One You Are, The.   Jean Valentine.   BodElec; ExTi

Wrote Great.   Ishikawa Takuboku.   CAoMJL1, tr. by Carl Sesar

Wrought Figure.   Linda McCarriston.   FaoP

Wryneck's Nest, The.   John Clare.   CenSon

Wu.   Po Chü-i.   CCL1, tr. by Marsha Wagner

Wu Gambinos.   Jeni Olin.   FreRad

Wu-Chueh.   Tu Fu [or Du Fu].   ChinPo, tr. by Ye Weilian [or Yeh Wei-lien or Wai-lim Yip]

Wuddup.   Gription.   Paul Beatty.   InTrad

Wu-jiang da-ju: don't Walk Beside the Big Carriage.   Unknown.   CCL1, tr. by Burton Watson

Wulf and Eadwacer: A Woman's Lament.   Unknown.   WoPoe, tr. by Jonathan McKeage

Wurlitzer stirs, all girl, all groan, The.   Small Pleasures.   Angela Shaw.   NeAmPo

Wyatt resteth here, that quick could never rest.   Wyatt Resteth Here.   Henry Howard, Earl of Surrey.   NoP-4; NoP-5

Wye Below Bredwardine, The.   John Powell Ward.   TCAWP

Wyll and Testament.   Isabella Whitney. See Aucthour Maketh Her Wyll and Testament, The.

Wyndham! 'tis not thy blood, tho' pure it runs.   To the Earl of Egremont.   Charlotte Smith.   RWP
(Wyndham! 'tis not thy blood, though pure it runs.)   NPBRoP

Wyndham! 'tis not thy blood, though pure it runs.   Charlotte Smith. See Wyndham! 'tis not thy blood, tho' pure it runs.

Wyndmere, Windemere.   Carol Muske-Dukes.   PBCAP

Wynken, Blynken, and Nod one night.   Wynken, Blynken, and Nod.   Eugene Field.   ChAP; ITBLP; NBLV; NOxBChV; NTCP; TFi

Wynkyn de Worde.   Edmund Clerihew Bentley.   OBCoV Fr. Clerihews.

Wynter Wakeneth Al My Care.   Unknown.   OHMEL

Wynter wakeneth al my care.   Wynter Wakeneth Al My Care.   Unknown.   OHMEL

Wystan.   Paul Muldoon.   NAMCP V.2 Fr. 7, Middagh Street.

Wystan, you got off to a wrong start. Memo to Auden. Anne Rouse. MFPA; NeBrP

Wyth a gerlond of thornes kene. *Unknown. See* With a garlande of thornes kene.

Wythop Mill. Annie Foster. NLP

X

X. Amina Baraka. BRtP

X. Daniel Hall. YaYoPo

X. Jean Valentine. ExTi

X and O. Arthur Sze. AmAlph

X = your zenith. (LL) ABC. Robert Pinsky. BeAl; FaoP; NAMCP V.2; NoP-5

X Files, The. Rafael Campo. PoDa

X Files, The: Bonnybridge, October '95. Hugh McMillan. EdScPo

X in My Name, The. Francisco X. Alarcón. CalPo

X L E B. Jack Hirschman. CLPP

X Minus X. Kenneth Fearing. OxBoAm

Xana ti yaga duga naca xandu. Bertha Beninu. Natalia Toledo. RMCMP

Xanthippe, singing at her lyre. Philodemus. ErotSp, *tr. by* Sam Hamill

Xanthippe's strumming, her chatter, her speaking eye, her song. Philodemus. HePo *Fr.* Epigrams.

Xena, Warrior Princess. Campbell McGrath. MAAN

Xenia: Stranger/Guest. David Gewanter. NAPBL

Xenophanes. Ralph Waldo Emerson. APN-1

Xenophanes. Louis Zukofsky. APT-2

Xenophobic Nightmare in a Foreign Language. Harryette Mullen. PrTe; WANABP

Xenophon's Song. István Vas. IQMS, *tr. by* Geroge Gömöri and Clive Wilmer

Xhoopa' diidxa' rui' xiinga guendaranaxhii. Víctor Terán. RMCMP

Xi Shi dreaming at dawn. Song: A Lovely Girl Combing Her Hair. Li Ho. CCL1, *tr. by* John Frodsham

Xiangyang Song. Li Po. CCL1, *tr. by* Elling O. Eide

Xishi always lives in golden houses. *Unknown.* NAAPv.2

Xmas for the Boys. Gavin Ewart. OBSV

Xnich k'anal tak'in. Pedro Pérez Conde. RMCMP

Xochiquetzal. Pauline Stainer. NeBl

X-Ray. Dannie Abse. AngWePo; BloBone; PoA 2002

X-Ray. Else Von Freytag-Loringhoven. SurPaPo

X-Ray, The. Andrew Elliott. PNI

X-Rays. I. K. Bonset. TuT, *tr. by* Desmond Egan

Xtale doo rié ne reeda. Liidxi na Olga. Natalia Toledo. RMCMP

XX. Craig Arnold. NAPBL

XX. P. Inman. FTOS

XXX. Dulce Maria Loynaz. TANSG, *tr. by* Alan West

XYZ. Robert Pinsky. OxBoAm

Y

Y, The. Brenda Hillman. MoASP

Y ahora me voy sin haber recibido mi legado. Y Ahora Me Voy. León Felipe. RaW

Y alguien dirá mañana. Yo No Soy el Gran Buzo. León Felipe. RaW

Y Ddraig Goch. Henry Treece. TCAWP

Y de fondo: llamaradas la sinfonía del lubricán, rojos. Angélica Tornero. SPV

Y era el demonio de mi sueño, el ángel. Antonio Machado Ruiz. RaW

Y. M. C. A, The. Mrs. Henry Linden. CBWP-4

Y nada importa ya que el vino de oro. Antonio Machado Ruiz. RaW

Y nunca quise. Tedi López Mills. RMCMP

Y Sé Muy Clara y Tristemente Bien. Luis Rosales. RaW

Y Si No Fueran las Sombras. Pedro Salinas. RaW

Y si yo en vez de ir esta noche al teatro me fuese a Viet-Nam. Especie de, Una. Blas de Otero. RaW

Y sin embargo. Ana Belén López Pulido. SPV

Y The Link Will Not Always Be "Missing" #40. Imamu Amiri Baraka. NAMCP V.2 *Fr.* Why's / Wise.

Ya Got Trouble. Meredith Willson. ReLy

Ya que no somos nada, por ejemplo. Eduardo Milán. RMCMP

Ya sabemos lo que cuesta. Verano y Humo. Manuel Vázquez Montalbán. RaW

Ya say something botherin you. Grandma Talk. Sonya Brooks. InTrad

Ya Se Van Los Pastores. Dudley Fitts. APT-2

Yacht, The. Catullus. OBVE

Yachts on the Nile. Bernard Spencer. NoAM

Yachts, The. William Carlos Williams. APT-1; BrAP; HeIP-4; MoAmPo; NAAPv.2; NAMCP V.1; NoAM; NoP-4; NoP-5; SAmP; TFi

Yagul. John Brandi. ICANM

Yahrtzeit Light, The. Lyn Lifshin. UnSA

Yahrzeit. Susan Fromberg Schaeffer. TaR

Yak, The. Joseph Hilaire Pierre Belloc. MoBrPo; NBLV; NoAM

Yak, The. Theodore Roethke. BLPJKO

Yala, this song's for you, Yala. Smalltown Yala. *Unknown.* SonAtl, *tr. by* Alan Brierly, Brenda Ginever and Malcolm Ginever

Yalding, 1912. My father. On Finding an Old Photograph. Wendy Cope. HarvBoo

Y'all carry weapons up here. Philly in the Light. Honorée Fanonne Jeffers. RD

Y'all listen to me. Self Defense. Ai. ESEAA

Yamadera. Charles Tomlinson. WoBe *Fr.* Zipangu.

Yammering, squabbling—all of it. Playful Poem. Chiao-jan. CCL1, *tr. by* Stephen Owen

Yankee Doodle. *Unknown.* TCAPo
  (Yankee's Return from Camp, The.) NAAPv.1

Yankee Doodle Boy, The. George M. Cohan. ReLy

Yankee Man-of-War, The. *Unknown.* TCAPo

Yankee ship came [or comes] down the river, A. Blow, Boys, Blow [or Blow, Bullies, Blow]. *Unknown.* FaBoVe

Yankees in East Texas. Joe Benevento. RWB

Yankee's Return from Camp, The. *Unknown. See* Yankee Doodle.

Yao's Warning. *Unknown.* CCL1, *tr. by* James Legge

Yard. No Hyangnim. EcSo, *tr. by* Aimee N. Kwon

Yard, The. David Baker. PfSP

Yard, littered, The. Cleaning. Rick Alley. AmPoNex

Yard, one's got to cross it, The. Total nostalgia. Leslie Kaplan. SCFWP *Fr.* L'Excès-L'usine.

Yard Work. Charles Wright. WaAnP

Yards of Sarajevo, The. Richard Hugo. AF

Yarn of the *Nancy Bell*, The. William Schwenck Gilbert. TFi; UV
  (Yarn of the "Nancy Bell," The.) CABP

Yarrow. Leonard Neufeldt. ACAMVP

Yasnaya Polyana. R. Gerallt Jones. BBMWP, *tr. by* Robert Minhinnick

Yawil yawal sts'unu/b te kajwal. Xnich k'anal tak'in. Pedro Pérez Conde. RMCMP

Yawn, The. Paul Blackburn. P180

Yawn of Yawns, The. Vasco [or Vasko] Popa. PoSu *Fr.* Yawn of Yawns, The.

Yawn of Yawns, The. Vasco [or Vasko] Popa. *tr. by* Anne Pennington
  Petrified Echoes. PoSu
  Wise Triangle, A. PoSu
  Yawn of Yawns, The. PoSu

Yay! a Visitor! Day one. Ten-Day Visitor, The. *Unknown.* SonAtl, *tr. by* Brenda Ginever, Malcolm Ginever, Badisa Macasi and Kgosi Puleng

Ye Alps audacious, thro' the Heavens that rise. Joel Barlow. NAAL-3; NAAPv.1; OxBoAm; ReLy *Fr.* Hasty Pudding, The [complete text].

Ye angells bright, pluck from your wings a quill. Edward Taylor. ChIV-2 *Fr.* Preparatory Meditations Before My Approach to the Lord's Supper.

Ye are hamburgers. (LL) That Dada Strain. Jerome Rothenberg. FTOS; PFTM-2

Ye are many—they are few. (LL) Mask [or Masque] of Anarchy, The. Percy Bysshe Shelley. NPBRoP; OBSV; OxAEP-2

Ye aspiring ones, listen to the story of the unknown. Edgar Lee Masters. NAAPv.1 *Fr.* Spoon River Anthology.

Ye aye sall be my dearie! (LL) Robert Burns. OBEV; OxAEP-1

Ye ayres and windes, ye elves of hilles. Ovid. OBVE *Fr.* Metamorphoses.

Ye banks and braes and streams around. Highland Mary. Robert Burns. NPBRoP; OBEV

Ye banks and braes o' bonie [or bonnie] Doon [see also "Ye flowery banks o' bonie Doon"]. Banks o' Doon, The. Robert Burns. BrAP; OxBEV

Ye beauties! O how great the sum. Christopher Smart. *See* Ye beauties! O how great the sum.

Ye beauties! O how great the sum. On a Bed of Guernsey Lilies. Christopher Smart. BBASP
  (Ye beauties! O how great the sum.) CABP; PoPoPo

Ye[e] blushing virgins happy are. William Habington. NOSC; OBEV *Fr.* Castara.

Ye Bruthers Dogg. Jon Anderson. NBLV

Ye buds of Brutus' land, courageous youths, now play your parts! For Soldiers. Humphrey Gifford. FaBoWar; NoSic

Ye captive soules of blindefold Cyprians boate. Thomas Watson. *See* Ye captive souls of blindfold Cyprian's boat.

Ye captive souls of blindfold Cyprian's boat. My Love is Past. Thomas Watson. NoSic

(Ye captive soules of blindefold Cyprians boate.) NPeEn

Ye cats that at midnight spit love at each other. Appeal to Cats in the Business of Love, An. Thomas Flatman. OBCoV

Ye clouds and darkness, hosts of night. Prudentius. SacPr, *tr.* by R. M. Pope

Ye companies of governor-spirits grave. Crystal, The. Sidney Lanier. TCAPo

Ye congregation of the tribes. Bible, *O.T.* NoP-4; NoP-5 *Fr.* Translation of the Psalms of David, A.

Ye daffodilian days, whose fallen towers. Atoning Yesterday, The. Louise Imogen Guiney. SWaP

Ye distant spires, ye antique towers. Ode on a Distant Prospect of Eton College. Thomas Gray. NAEL-6v1; NAEL-7v1; NoP-4; NoP-5; OxAEP-1

Ye dogg, O'Toole. Ye Bruthers Dogg. Jon Anderson. NBLV

Ye elms that wave on Malvern Hill. Malvern Hill. Herman Melville. APN-2; CBCWP; ColAP; PCW

Ye elves of hill(s), brooks, standing lakes, and groves. William Shakespeare. OxAEP-1; WaAnP *Fr.* Tempest, The.

Ye elves of hills, brooks, standing lakes, and groves. Ovid. *Fr.* Metamorphoses.

Ye fair, for whom the hands of Hymen weave. Latte, Il. Edward Jerningham. STuOW

Ye flaming Powers, and winged Warrio[u]rs bright. Upon the Circumcision. John Milton. ChIV-2

Ye flowery banks o' bon[n]ie Doon [*see also* "Ye banks and braes o' bonie Doon"]. Banks o' Doon, The. Robert Burns. NAEL-6v2; NoP-5; NPBRoP

Ye glorious Jove-born imps how you rejoice. On the Three Children in the Fiery Furnace. Henry Colman. ChIV-1

Yee Gote-heard Gods, that love the grassie mountaines. Sir Philip Sidney. *See* Ye [*or* you] goat-herd gods, that love the grassy mountains.

Ye [*or* you] goat-herd gods, that love the grassy mountains. Sir Philip Sidney. NAEL-6v1; NoSic *Fr.* Countesse of Pembroke's Arcadia, The.

Ye Goat-herd Gods. Sir Philip Sidney. NAEL-6v1; NoSic *Fr.* Countesse of Pembroke's Arcadia, The.

Ye golden lamps of heaven, farewell. Hymn. Philip Doddridge. SacPr

Ye grateful Britons, bless the year. Colley Cibber. STuOW *Fr.* New Year's Ode, 1731.

Ye haue heard this yarn afore. Peter Reading. EmeKit

Ye have been fresh and green. To Meadows [*or* Meddowes]. Robert Herrick. BASC; NOSC; NPeEn; OBEV; PBRV

"Ye have robbed," said he, "ye have slaughtered and made an end." He Fell among Thieves. Sir Henry John Newbolt. OBEV; OBWP

Ye Highlands [*or* hielands] and ye Lawlands [*or* lowlands]. Bonny Earl of Murray, The [Version from Tea-Table Miscellany]. *Unknown.* NAEL-6v1; NAEL-7v1; NOSC; OBEV

Ye holy towers that shade the wave-worn steep. Written at Bamborough Castle. William Lisle Bowles. CenSon

Ye jovial boys who love the joys. Fornicator. A New Song, The. Robert Burns. NPeEn

Ye learned sisters which have oftentimes. Epithalamion. Edmund Spenser. NAEL-6v1; NAEL-7v1; NoP-5; NoSic; OBEV; OxAEP-1; WaAnP

Ye living Lamps, by whose dear light. Mower to the Glowworms [*or* Glow-Worms *or* Glo-Worms], The. Andrew Marvell. BASC; FSCP; NAEL-6v1; NAEL-7v1; NoP-4; NoP-5; NPeEn; PBRV; TFi

Ye Mariners of England. Thomas Campbell. OBEV; OBWP; OxAEP-2; WaAnP

Ye may pass me by with pitying eye. Song of the Imprisoned Bird. Eliza Cook. VWP

Ye Mongers Aye Need Masks for Cheatrie. Sydney Goodsir Smith. EdScPo

Ye Nations, Tremble! Parliament has Met. Edward Young. STuOW *Fr.* Foreign Address, The.

Ye Nymphs of Solyma! begin the song. Messiah [a Sacred Eclogue, in Imitation of Virgil's Pollio]. Alexander Pope. ChIV-1

Ye nymphs who cultivate the highest mountains of Fife. Midden-Battle between Lady Scotstarvit and the Mistress of Newbarns, The. William Drummond of Hawthornden. NePenScot, *tr.* by Allan H. MacLaine

Ye paltry [*or* paultry] underlings of state. On the Irish Club. Jonathan Swift. OBSV

Ye people all in one accord. John Hopkins. SacPr

Ye plains, where threefold harvests press the ground. Passage of the Mountain of St. Gothard, The. Georgiana Cavendish, Duchess of Devonshire. RWP

Ye praise the humble: of the meek ye say. Sonnet. Sir Aubrey De Vere. SacPr

Ye prone to sleep (whom sleeping most annoys). John Armstrong. STuOW *Fr.* Art of Preserving Health, The.

Ye remember the gentylman ryghte nowe. John Skelton. OxBEV *Fr.* Bouge of Court, The.

Ye sailors bold both great and small. Fishing Lass of Hakin, The. Lewis Morris. AngWePo

Ye say they all have passed away. Indian Names. Lydia Huntley Sigourney. APN-1; ColAP; SWaP

Ye [*or* You] should stay longer if we durst. Francis Beaumont. NOSC *Fr.* Masque of the Inner Temple and Gray's Inne, The.

Ye sinful wights, and cursed sprights. Michael Wigglesworth. *Fr.* Day of Doom, The: Or, A Poetical Description of the Great and Last Judgment.

Ye sons of Columbia, who bravely have fought. Adams and Liberty. Robert Treat Paine. NAAPv.1

Ye sons of earth prepare the plough. William Cowper. ChIV-2 *Fr.* Olney Hymns.

Ye sylvan Muses, loftier strains recite. Birth of the Squire; an Eclogue, The. John Gay. NAEL-6v1

Ye tender young virgins attend to my lay. Perplexity: A Poem. Elizabeth Hands. WoRP

Ye That Pasen by the Weye. *Unknown.* NAEL-7v1

Ye tradeful merchants that, with weary toil. Edmund Spenser. HeIP-4; NIP-4; NoP-5 *Fr.* Amoretti.

Ye tradeful Merchants that with weary toyle. Edmund Spenser. *See* Ye tradeful merchants that, with weary toil.

Ye vales and woods! fair scenes of happier hours. Petrarch. RWP *Fr.* Sonnets to Laura.

Ye virgins that from Cupid's tents. Isabella Whitney. PEW *Fr.* Admonition by the Auctor to all yong Gentilwomen: And to al other Maids being in Love, The.

Ye wastefull woodes bear witness of my woe. Edmund Spenser. MakPoe *Fr.* Shepherd's Calender, The.

Ye Wearie Wayfarer. Adam Lindsay Gordon. Warning, A. STuOW

Ye wha are fain to hae your name. Braid Claith. Robert Fergusson. OxBEV

Ye white antarctic birds of upper 57th street. Ye White Antarctic Birds. Lisa Jarnot. P180

Ye, who in alleys green and leafy bowers. Laments the Volatility of Phaon. Mary Robinson. CenSon; RWP

Ye, who in alleys green and leafy bowers. Mary Robinson. NPBRoP *Fr.* Sappho and Phaon.

Ye who intelligent the Third Heaven move. First Canzone of the Convito, The. Dante Alighieri. OBVE, *tr.* by Percy Bysshe Shelley

Ye whose hearts are beating high. Address to Poets. John Keble. SacPr

Ye Yankees who, mole-like, still throw up the earth. Burrowing Yankees. *Unknown.* AmWaPo; NAAPv.1

Yea, and a good cause why thus should I plain. Nicholas Grimald. NoP-4 *Fr.* Funeral Song, Upon the Decease of Annes His Mother, A.

Yea, beds for all who come. (LL) Uphill [*or* Up-Hill]. Christina Georgina Rossetti. BrAP; CABP; CtM; NAEL-6v2; NAEL-7v2; NALW; NoP-4; NoP-5; OBEV; PEW; PoPoPo; SacPr; TFi; WaAnP; WeW-3

Yea, gold is son of Zeus: no rust. Gold Is the Son of Zeus: Neither Moth nor Worm May Gnaw It. Michael Field. OBMV

Yea: how dignified, and worthy, full of privilege and happiness. Portrait of a Victorian Author. Martin Farquhar Tupper. STuOW

Yea, though I'm sorry for thee. (LL) Youth Mowing, A. D. H. Lawrence. MoBrPo; NAMCP V.1; NoAM

Yeah, I been to juvee, what about it? Rhonda, Age 15, Emergency Room. Letta Neely. WiU

Yeah, it will double cross you [/] and leave you with them empty bed blues. (LL) Empty Bed Blues. Bessie Smith. APT-2; OxBoAm

Yeah, man, / I'll help out / with the / memorial for / Trane. Memorial for Trane. Sam Greenlee. SeSe

Yeah Yeah Yeah. Roddy Lumsden. EdScPo; NeBl

Year. Milo De Angelis. NeIt, *tr.* by Lawrence Venuti

Year. Jenny Mueller. IAoNAP

Year, The. Janet Bowdan. PoDa

Year after year. Basho. EH, *tr.* by Robert Hass

Year after year. Discourse on an Ornament. Hong Yunsuk. CAMKP, *tr.* by Genell Y. Poitras

Year after Year. Bart Howard. ReLy

Year after year. Toki-no-Ge (Satori Poem). Muso Soseki. EaWin, *tr.* by W. S. Merwin

Year after year in the snow, intoxicated. To the Tune "Clear Peace Happiness." Li Ch'ing-chao. NDACCP, *tr.* by Kenneth Rexroth

Year after year, not a sign of spring. (LL) Rough and Dark. Han-shan (Cold Mountain). CCL1; NDACCP, *tr.* by Gary Snyder

Year after year the princess lies asleep. Parabola. Alec Derwent Hope. BrAP; NOBAu; PoA 2002

Year ago I fell in love with the functional ward, A. Hospital, The. Patrick Kavanagh. CABP; EmeKit; ModIr; NPeEn

Year ago the weather was better, A. Topiary. Maurice Riordan. NIrP

Year ago we walked the wood, A. Vies Manquées. Edith Nesbit. VWP

Year ago you came, A. Pietá. James McAuley. BMAP

Year before, this desert, A. Protesting at the Nuclear Test Site. Denise Levertov. PoCoUp

Year began with baleful auguries, The. Ancient History. Jamie McKendrick. NeBrP

Year dead-ends here, The. Clumsy December. Bird Nests. Angela Shaw. NeAmPo

Year dies fiercely: out of the north the beating storms, The. Year's End. William Everson. NoAM

Year does not matter, The. On Reading Virgil. Tedi López Mills. RMCMP, *tr. by* C. M. Mayo

Year Draws to Its End, The. *Unknown.* CCL1

Year 1812, The. Adam Mickiewicz. OBVE; OBWP; WoPoe, *tr. by* Donald Davie

Year from Monday, A. Tom Clark and Lewis Warsh. AHA

Year grows late beneath the eastern cliff, The. On Old Zhang's Pine Tree. Sung Chih-Wen. CCL1, *tr. by* Stephen Owen

Year I Found, The. Dieter Weslowski. IJHIL

Year I returned to my village, the papers, The. Two Variations on a Theme by Kobayashi. Larry Levis. BodElec

Year I Was Diagnosed with a Sacrilegious Heart, The. Martín Espada. RWB; TouFir

Year I was sick, The / and you took care of me. Disfortune. Joe Wenderoth. AmPoNex

Year in Hawaii. Marianne Boruch. AmAlph

Year is 1938, The. Martyrdom and Triumph of Sergei Korolev. Andrew Duncan. VaPo

Year is sullen, sullen is the day, The. Sullenness. Michael Field. VWP

Year Jimmy had four pearls, the. Torture Boy at the Easter Confest, Repentance Creek. Beckian Fritz Goldberg. MAAN

Year Keng-Wu, Night of the Fifteenth, Facing the Moon, The. Ch'i-chi. CSKM, *tr. by* Burton Watson

Year Nixon showed up in Moscow, The. Kitchens: 1959. Juliana Baggott. SweBea

Year of griefs being through, they had to merge, The. Blank, A. Thom Gunn. NAMCP V.2

Year of the Foxes, The. David Malouf. NOBAu

Year of the monkey, year of the human wave. Way of Tet, The. Bruce Weigl. AF; AmAlph

Year of the Olive Oil, The. Charles North. FTOS; NYP2

Year of their ultimate squalor, The. Bio 7. David Moolten. BloBone

Year Passes in My Morning Teacup, The. Marilyn Chin. GeoHom

Year revolves, and I again explore, The. Parish Register, The. George Crabbe.

Year That Trembled and Reel'd beneath Me. Walt Whitman. ItP

Year the institutions would not hold, The. Becoming of Age. Simon Armitage. HarvBoo

Year the Space Age Was Born, The. Floyd Skloot. SwNoth

Year the white women came like the plague, The. Feel Free. Natasha Tarpley. ISC

Year this truck was made, The. Working on the '58 Willys Pickup. Gary Snyder. WANABP

Year 2120, The. No reason why it should be remembered by a nation. Body as What Is Remembered. Tsering Wangno Dhompa. WANABP

Year was as long and dark as a bed, The. Potato Thief. Pentti Saarikoski. VCWP, *tr. by* Herbert Lomas

Year was tan-wo, it was the fourth month, summer's first, The. Owl, The. Chia Yi. ColAnChi, *tr. by* James Robert Hightower

Year was tan-wo, it was the fourth month, summer's first, The. Chia Yi. WoPoe *Fr.* Rhymeprose on an Owl.

Year well remembered! Happy who beheld thee! Year 1812, The. Adam Mickiewicz. OBVE; OBWP; WoPoe, *tr. by* Donald Davie

Yearbook. Milo De Angelis. NeIt, *tr. by* Lawrence Venuti

Yearling in a drained dike, A. Missing. John McAuliffe. NIrP

Yearn On. Katie Donovan. NIrP

Yearning for Death. "Novalis." NAWM-7v2, *tr. by* Charles E. Passage

Yearning for Winter. Karl Wilhelm Ramler. GePo, *tr. by* George C. Schoolfield

Yearning of Karakashian, The. Chava Pinchas-Cohen. DTA, *tr. by* Miriyam Glazer

Yearning stars ask, The. When the Moon Isn't Shining. L. Miller. Prolet, *tr. by* Amelia Glaser

Yearning throughout Life, The. Kathleen Spivack. PfS

Years. Walter Savage Landor. OBEV

Years, The. Catherine Davis. FFC

Years, The: "Sometimes to get their own back." Tom Pow. EdScPo

Years, The: "What do I owe the years, that I should bring." Ina Coolbrith. CalPo

Years ago, alone in her room, my mother cut. Cartoon Physics, Part 2. Nick Flynn. NAPBL

Years ago, at a private school. Ever-Fixed Mark, An. Kingsley Amis. NAMCP V.2; NoAM

Years ago I came here. Bonanza Creek. John E. Smelcer. PoCoUp

Years ago I was a gardener. Writing in Prison. Ken Smith. NPeEn

Years and years ago, these sounds took sides. Casting and Gathering. Seamus Heaney. NoP-4; NoP-5

Year's at the spring, The. Robert Browning. BRP; ITBLP; NTCP; OBEV *Fr.* Pippa Passes.

Year's "Casualties", A. Ambrose Bierce. PCW

Years circling the same circle. Yield Everything, Force Nothing. Jean Valentine. ExTi

Year's End. Chang K'o-chiu. CrYelRi, *tr. by* Sam Hamill

Year's End. William Everson. NoAM

Year's End. Marilyn Hacker. NAMCP V.2; WiU

Year's End. Ted Kooser. PBCAP

Year's End. Frank Lima. BodElec

Year's End. Ellen Bryant Voigt. NoAM

Year's End. Richard Wilbur. GoPo; HeIP-4; MoW

Year's end / All corners. Basho. ZenPo, *tr. by* Takashi Ikemoto and Lucien Stryk

Year's end / Still in straw hat. Basho. ZenPo, *tr. by* Takashi Ikemoto and Lucien Stryk

Years from Now. Kim Sowŏl. WoPoe, *tr. by* Kevin O'Rourke

Years had rubbed out his youth, The. Sootie Joe. Melvin B. Tolson. OxBoAm

Years have gone, The. It is spring. Andrée Rexroth. Kenneth Rexroth. APSN

Years have gone, The. It is spring. Kenneth Rexroth. CalPo *Fr.* Andrée Rexroth.

Years have made up my face, The. Toward Myself. Leah Goldberg. FIT, *tr. by* Robert Friend

Years have taken from me, The. Softly I go now, pad pad. (LL) Pad, Pad. Stevie Smith. NPeEn; OxBEM

Years in the blood keep us naked to the bone, The. Art of Clay, The. Duane Niatum. HATNAP

Years keeping that in mind. Anbun. ZenPo, *tr. by* Takashi Ikemoto and Lucien Stryk

Years later, it was, after everything / got hazy in my head. Mary. Philip Appleman. GI

Years, many parti-coloured years. Years. Walter Savage Landor. OBEV

Years of a lifetime do not reach a hundred, The. *Unknown.* CCL1,

Years of manhood had not tinged, The. Charley du Bignon. Mary E. Tucker. CBWP-1

Years of Solitude. Dionisio D. Martinez. PtR

Years of the Modern. Walt Whitman. NCAP

Years of the modern! years of the unperform'd! Years of the Modern. Walt Whitman. NCAP

Years pass like donkeys, The. Ultimate Argument. Ion Caraion. AF, *tr. by* Marguerite Dorian and Elliott B. Urdang

Years ride out from the world like couriers gone to a throne, The. Stephen Vincent Benét. MoAmPo *Fr.* John Brown's Body.

Years saw me still Acasto's mansion grace. Old Cat's Dying Soliloquy, An. Anna Seward. OxBEV

Year's Spinning, A. Elizabeth Barrett Browning. NAEL-6v2

Years—years ago,—ere yet my dreams. Winthrop Mackworth Praed. NOBRP *Fr.* Every Day Characters.

Yeats at Athenry Perhaps. Padraic Fallon. ModIr

Yeats. Yeats. Yeats. Yeats. Yeats. Yeats. John Thompson. IFF *Fr.* Stilt Jack.

Ye'd wonder foo the seasons rin. Neep-Fields by the Sea, The. Violet Jacob. EdScPo

Yeerd she hadde, enclosed al aboute, A. Geoffrey Chaucer. OWoS *Fr.* Canterbury Tales, The.

Yell / You won't scatter the scree's flock. Crib Goch. T. Rowland Hughes. BBMWP, *tr. by* Catherine Fisher

Yellah. Lisa Pegram. BRtP

Yelled on the view the opening pack. Sir Walter Scott. DiBP *Fr.* Lady of the Lake, The.

Yelling. For. Fun. Carla Harryman. BAP-04 *Fr.* Baby.

Yelling never works, but I'm told. Serenade. Angie Estes. GeoHom

Yelling-alive. Ianka Kupala. SonAtl, *tr. by* Rashed Chowdhury and Maria Tchooudkhouri

Yellow. De Leon Harrison. EGAG

Yellow. Josephine Jacobsen. APT-2

Yellow became alive. Yellow. Josephine Jacobsen. APT-2

Yellow Bell Coda. Kuan Han-ch'ing. ColAnChi, *tr. by* Wayne Schlepp

Yellow Bike, The. John Lancaster. ArBi

Yellow Bittern, The. Tom MacIntyre. PBCIP

Yellow Blight. Cemal Süreya. NaPG, *tr. by* Talat Sait Halman

Yellow Book, The. Derek Mahon.
Bonn´n Buí, An. NAMCP V.2
Yellow Book, The. Muriel Spark. EdScPo
Yellow coverlet, A. Song. Rosanna Warren. ExTi; MakPoe; PfSP
Yellow Crane Tower. Ts'ui Hao. CCL1, *tr.* by Stephen Owen
Yellow Dog Blues. William Christopher Handy. NAAPv.2
Yellow Dog Café. Yusef Komunyakaa. LPSFW
Yellow Dot, The. Robert Bly. CAP-8
Yellow dusk: messenger fails to appear. *Unknown.* OBVE; OxBEV, *tr.* by Arthur Waley
Yellow dust drifts down the road to Ch'ang-an. Song. *Unknown.* CrYelRi, *tr.* by Sam Hamill
Yellow ears are crammed in Mr. Cromartie's bin, The. Master and Man. Sterling Allen Brown. OxBoAm
Yellow ear's rustle of praise. Reaping. Dic Jones. BBMWP, *tr.* by Joseph P. Clancy
Yellow Eyes, look at me and look for me. Let me see. *Unknown.* APN-2 *Fr.* Minnetare Songs.
Yellow fades from red to green, The. Windows. Guillaume Apollinaire. YaTCFP, *tr.* by Roger Shattuck
Yellow feather, A. Good Morning. Carl Rakosi. FTOS
Yellow feathers. Entertaining the Canary. Charles Simic. CAP-8
Yellow Flower, The. William Carlos Williams. HarvBoo
Yellow freesia arc like twining arms;. Letter: Blues. Elizabeth Alexander. RA
Yellow ghost. Ghost. Cathy Song. NAMCP V.2
Yellow Glove. Naomi Shihab Nye. LoL; PoArWo
Yellow House Writes a Story for the Boy, The. Robin Behn. AmAlph
Yellow Is Me, But All the Same Are We. Joan Adams. BtF
Yellow Its Color. Jafar ibn Uthman al-Mushafi. WoPoe, *tr.* by Leticia Garza-Falcón and Christopher Middleton
Yellow its color. Yellow Its Color. Jafar ibn Uthman al-Mushafi. WoPoe, *tr.* by Leticia Garza-Falcón and Christopher Middleton
Yellow leaves swirl. Indian Summer. Karen Chamberlain. GeoH
Yellow Light. Garrett Kaoru Hongo. GeoHom; OpBo; WaAnP
Yellow, Loveliest, enters my city. Poem. İlhan Berk. NaPG, *tr.* by Talat Sait Halman
Yellow Man, Purple Man. Emily Dickinson. TLR
Yellow Orioles. Tu Fu [*or* Du Fu]. CCL1, *tr.* by Florence Ayscough and Amy Lowell
Yellow orioles, two, call from willows, kingfisher-green. Yellow Orioles. Tu Fu [*or* Du Fu]. CCL1, *tr.* by Florence Ayscough *and* Amy Lowell
Yellow pears slope down. Halflife. Friedrich Hölderlin. WoPoe, *tr.* by Vyt Bakaitis
Yellow River's Earl, The. Ch'u Yüan. WoPoe, *tr.* by Stephen Owen
Yellow Room, The. Juan Felipe Herrera. TouFir
Yellow Rose of Texas, The. *Unknown.* TCAPo
Yellow Season, The. William Carlos Williams. MoAmPo
Yellow silk and wildflower garlands lie on dark sandaloiled skin. Jayadeva. WoPoe *Fr.* Gita Govinda, The.
Yellow Slicker, The. Stuart Dischell. GoPo
Yellow Spring. Juan Ramón Jiménez. SpanPo, *tr.* by Angel Flores
Yellow Star Again, The. Max Jacob. PoCho, *tr.* by William Kulik
Yellow Violet, The. William Cullen Bryant. NAAL-3
Yellow wood, A. Anascesis and Wreckage. Phillip Foss. ICANM
Yellow/brown woman. Lorna Goodison. *See* Yellow/brown woman / fingers smelling always of onions.
Yellow/brown woman / fingers smelling always of onions. I Am Becoming My Mother. Lorna Goodison. OPOU (Yellow/brown woman.) GT
Yellowish-grey, friable at the top, firm below, creaking sand. Sphinx, The. Ivan Turgeniev. MotU, *tr.* by Isabel Florence Hapgood
Yellowjacket. Peter Blue Cloud. HATNAP
Yellowjackets. William Heyen. CAP-8
Yellow-legs ekes lower at nightfall to a stick nest. Thrasher. Karen Solie. OpeFie
Yellow-oatmeal flowers of the windmill palms. Eden. David Woo. OpBo
Yellows and creams, The. Symbols of Transformation. Ron Padgett. FTOS
Yellows cast their spells: the evening primrose. Crepuscule. Angela Shaw. NeAmPo
Yellowstone, 1989. Solid Ground. Mary Beath. ICANM
Yelping Nuisance of the Way, The. John Gay. DiBP *Fr.* Fables: First Series.
Yemoja. Baba Ifa Karade. HW
Yemoja, mother of the fishes. Yemoja. Baba Ifa Karade. HW
Yen-chou City Wall Tower. Tu Fu [*or* Du Fu]. CrYelRi, *tr.* by Sam Hamill
Yeoman of the Guard. William Schwenck Gilbert. Family Fool, The. NBLV
Yerba Buena, Nick & Jerry. Reed Bye. AHA

Yes. E. E. Cummings. *See* I Thank You God.
Yes. Denise Duhamel. AmPoNex
Yes. Tess Gallagher. StAl
Yes. Daphne Marlatt. NLPA *Fr.* Touch to My Tongue.
Yes. Muriel Rukeyser. MakPoe; StAl
Yes. (LL) What Do I See. Gertrude Stein. ItWoWo; PFTM-1
Yes, a walking cabbage just went by. Somewhere in the middle, Sunday. Wopko Jensma. TSAP
Yes, All-Highest, to God, be sure. (LL) Death-Bed, A. Rudyard Kipling. OxBEV; PoWW
Yes, and chilled with fear and despair. (LL) Judith of Bethulia. John Crowe Ransom. APT-1; NoAM
"Yes, and continue," said Conscience, and I came to the church. (LL) William Langland. NAEL-6v1; NAEL-7v1 *Fr.* Vision of Piers Plowman, The.
Yes, artwork is better. Art. Théophile Gautier. WoPoe, *tr.* by Louis Simpson
Yes! Beauty still rebels! Art, I. Alfred Noyes. OBEV
Yes Bees! JA ZZ : (The "Say What?") IS IS JA LIVES. Imamu Amiri Baraka. SpirFl
Yes, Breisach, your decrease is profit yet and prize. To Breisach, Taken by That Supremely Celebrated Hero, Bernhard, Duke of Saxony. Georg Rudolph Weckherlin. GePo, *tr.* by George C. Schoolfield
Yes, but the body is made of water. That's. Bodies of Water. Greg Williamson. NAPBL; NeAmPo
Yes, but we must be sure of verities. Spring Poem, The. Dave Jeddie Smith. PoPoPo
Yes, call me by my pet-name! let me hear. Elizabeth Barrett Browning. CenSon *Fr.* Sonnets from the Portuguese.
Yes, come to my arms, little doves of iron. Martyrdom of Saint Sebastian, The. Eugenio Florit. TCLAP, *tr.* by Peter Fortunato
Yes, crazy to suppose one could describe them. Robert Pinsky. NoP-4; NoP-5 *Fr.* Essay on Psychiatrists.
Yes! e'en in Sleep th'impressions all remain. George Crabbe. NPeEn *Fr.* Borough, The.
Yes, even the Devil should have his due. To an Anthologist. Theodore Roethke. PoA 2002
Yes, faint was my applause and cold my praise. To a Friend. Joseph Rodman Drake. APN-1
Yes feminine and fat and scarlet. More and More Woman. Pierre Jean Jouve. YaTCFP, *tr.* by Mary Ann Caws
"Yes, go on! This is plain talk of plainer feelings now,." John Hollander. VCAP *Fr.* Powers of Thirteen.
Yes, God has made me a woman. My Rights. Susan Coolidge. SWaP
Yes God the desire hangs there unfilled turns into smoke!! Small Secret Book, A. Michael McClure. PFTM-2
Yes, his face really is so terrible. Sudden Appearance of a Monster at a Window. Lawrence Raab. BLT; SUP
Yes! hope may with my strong desire keep pace. Love's Justification. Michelangelo Buonarroti. OBVE, *tr.* by William Wordsworth
Yes I admit a degree of unease about my. Anne Carson. WaAnP *Fr.* TV Men.
Yes I am a border crosser. Love letter sent south. Pat LittleDog. TiP2
Yes, I am not emitting articulate sound. Barry MacSweeney. Oth *Fr.* Pearl.
"Yes," I answered you last night. Lady's "Yes," The. Elizabeth Barrett Browning. ViWPN
Yes, I can hear you, father. Soup and Slavery. Myra Schneider. Prnts
Yes, I did write in my letter. Non-Military Statements. Dunya Mikhail. WoBe, *tr.* by Liz Winslow
Yes, I do feel like a visitor. Postcards from God (1). Imtiaz Dharker. NeBl
Yes, I do see many of us afraid of scraps. Quilt of Rights. Sandra McPherson. LoL
Yes I have dreams where I am rescued by men. Feminist Poem Number One. Elizabeth Alexander. FaoP; NAPBL
Yes, I have lied, and so must walk my way. Arthur Hugh Clough. CenSon *Fr.* Blank Misgivings of a Creature Moving About in Worlds Not Realized.
Yes, I have lov'd: yet often have I said. Sappho; or, The Resolve. Charlotte Dacre. NOBRP
Yes, I know: only the happy man. Bad Time for Poetry. Bertolt Brecht. PoSu, *tr.* by Ralph Manheim and John Willett
Yes, I know that you once were my lover. First Love. Caroline Elizabeth Norton. NPBRoP
Yes, I only got here on my own. On My Own. Philip Levine. PtR
Yes, I remember Adlestrop. Adlestrop. Edward Thomas. CtM; HarvBoo; NAEL-6v2; NAEL-7v2; NAMCP V.1; NoP-4; NoP-5; OBEV; UV; WaAnP
Yes, I remember Willesden Gree. Willesden Gree. Jimmy Pearse. UV
Yes I saw your look. Epitaph: André Breton. Philippe Soupault. SurPaPo, *tr.* by Mary Ann Caws and Patricia Terry
Yes, I say, I know. Cante Jondo. Yusef Komunyakaa. BodElec
Yes, I wanted them to levitate. At the School for the Gifted. Carol Muske-Dukes. ExTi
Yes I was a cowgirl. Cowgirl. Pat LittleDog. TiP2

Yes, I will go, where circling whirlwinds rise. Resolves to Take the Leap of Leucata. Mary Robinson. CenSon; RWP

Yes, I will go, where circling whirlwinds rise. Mary Robinson. NPBRoP *Fr.* Sappho and Phaon.

Yes, I'd rather hear Heliodora's voice. Meleager. HePo, *tr.* by Barbara Hughes Fowler

Yes, If I Could Only Smash. Juan Ramón Jiménez. RaW, *tr.* by Ralph Nelson and Rita García Nelson

Yes, in the end they are much of a pair. Heinrich Heine. WoPoe *Fr.* Dying in Paris.

Yes! in the sea of life enisled. Matthew Arnold. BrAP; NAEL-6v2; NAEL-7v2; NoP-5; NPeEn; OxBEV; SoSe-8; WaAnP *Fr.* Switzerland.

Yes, indeed. (LL) Slim Greer. Sterling Allen Brown. NAAPv.2; NAMCP V.1

Yes, injured Woman—rise, assert thy right! Rights of Woman, The. Anna Laetitia Barbauld. BrAP; CABP; NAEL-6v2; NAEL-7v2; NoP-4; NoP-5; PEW; WaAnP; WoRP

Yes it can be done just like. Library. Pierre Alféri. YaTCFP, *tr.* by Cole Swensen

Yes, it looked dark and dreary. Three Evenings in a Life. Adelaide Anne Procter. VWP

Yes, it seems like something out there. No Moment Past This One. Stephen Dobyns. IJHIL

Yes, it would be good to have boxes. Poet's Insurance Risk, The. Myrddin ap Dafydd. BBMWP, *tr.* by Gillian Clarke

Yes! let the rich deride, the proud disdain. Oliver Goldsmith. OBSV *Fr.* Deserted Village, The.

Yes, let us speak, with lips confirming. William Larminie. IrLP *Fr.* Fand.

Yes, Lizbie Browne! (LL) To Lizbie Browne. Thomas Hardy. FaBoVe; OxAEP-2

Yes, long shadows go out. Twilight: After Haying. Jane Kenyon. GoPo

Yes, / Longfellow wrote about me. Paul Revere Speaks. Myra Cohn Livingston. HHAm

Yes, love, that's why the warning light comes on. don't. Very Simply Topping Up the Brake Fluid. Simon Armitage. NeBrP

Yes, me bredren. Champion Chant. Rohan B. Preston. WaCA

Yes, my Captain, I was there. Driving Past My Exit. Alan Michael Parker. LegDan

Yes, my darling, when life's shadows. In Memoriam. Alphonse Campbell Fordham. Mary Weston Fordham. CBWP-2

Yes! my Lesbia! let us prove. Catullus. *See* Lesbia / live with me.

Yes, nonsense is a treasure! Lines on Nonsense. Eliza Lee Cabot Follen. SWaP

Yes, oblivion will come. Oblivion. Fanny Carrión de Fierro. TANSG, *tr.* by Sally Cheney Bell

Yes, our faces are ten blanks. Hands, The. Daniel David Moses. IFF

Yes! pause and think, within one fleeting hour. Robert Montgomery. STuOW *Fr.* Omnipresence of the Deity, The.

Yes, rub some soap upon your feet! Hike on the Downs, A. Sir John Betjeman. OBCoV

"Yes," said the boy, "first come the gum-tree crowds." Boy who Dreamed the Country Night, The. Christopher Koch. NOBAu

Yes, she's a good dog. Dog Parted from Her Master. Hsüeh T'ao [*or* Xue Tao]. CCL1; WoPoe, *tr.* by Jeanne Larsen

Yes! Sir! That's My Baby. Gustave Kahn. ReLy

Yes, somehow and somewhere and always. White Feather Legion, The. T. W. H. Crosland. FaBoWar

Yes, that is the door and behind it tey live. Door, The. David Constantine. StAl

Yes, that was me you saw shaking with bravery, with a government issued rifle on my back. No. Joy Harjo. PrTe

Yes, That's the Way Things Are. Bachner, Miroslav Košek and Hanuš Löwy. INSAB

Yes, the Agency Can Handle That. Kenneth Fearing. WeW-3

Yes the bottle comes wrapped in bladderwrack. Christmas Present for My Mother. Sue MacIntyre. Prnts

Yes, the circus has finally come to town! Monkey Blues. Michael Brownstein. AHA

Yes, the porpoises of course, it could. Mayan Glyphs Unread, The. William Bronk. APSN

Yes, the time / yes. Lighthouse of Alexandria, The. Mercedes Roffé. TANSG, *tr.* by Kathryn Kopple

Yes, there is a vault in the ruined castle. Broceliande. Marilyn Hacker. ExTi

Yes there was a visitor again last night. Analysis, The. David Citino. UpMys

Yes, they are alive and can have those colors. Blessing in Disguise, A. John Ashbery. ColAP; ItP

Yes, they begin out in a willow, I think. Crucifix in a Deathhand. Charles Bukowski. PmAP

Yes, theyll let you play. Poem for Players, A. Al Young. LTA; OxAAAP

Yes, this is my voice. Voices. Nesta Wyn Jones. BBMWP, *tr.* by Anthony Conran

Yes; / This is the silence of our speedy uncurling youth-tangles. Three mothers, The. Mongane Wally Serote. TSAP

Yes, this is where I stood that day. Ballad of Hector in Hades. Edwin Muir. HarvBoo; NAMCP V.1; NoAM

Yes to the dark, uneven body of each tree. Falling in Love after Forty. Ruth L. Schwartz. NeAmPo

Yes, we are fighting at last, it appears. This morning, as usual. Arthur Hugh Clough. NPeEn; OxAEP-2 *Fr.* Amours de Voyage.

Yes, we are going to suffer, now; the sky. W. H. Auden. NAMCP V.1

Yes, we'll rally round the flag, boys, we'll rally once again. Battle-Cry of Freedom, The. George Frederick Root. CBCWP

Yes we'll rally round the flag boys, we'll rally once again. Battle Cry of Freedom, The. *Unknown.* NAAPv.1

Yes, we'll walk up the Avenue 'till we're there. (LL) Couple of Swells, A. Irving Berlin. OBCoV; ReLy

Yes. Whý do we áll, séeing of a soldier, bless him? bléss. Soldier, The. Gerard Manley Hopkins. FaBoWar

Yes, yes, dear love! I am dead! Resurgam. Adah Isaacs Menken. CBWP-1

Yes yes / yeah. Brown Skin Girl. Tommy McClennan. FaBoVe

Yes Yes Yes. (LL) God Says Yes to Me. Kaylin Haught. BeAl; P180

Yes Yoko Ono. Shin Yu Pai. WANABP

Yes, you must have had the camera. Forest. Priscilla Borthwick. Prnts

Yes, Your Honor, there are rodents. Tires Stacked in the Hallways of Civilization. Martín Espada. InvLad

Yesterday. Angel González. VCWP, *tr.* by Steven Ford Brown and Revuelta Gutierrez

Yesterday: "My friend says I was not a good son." W. S. Merwin. GoPo; OxBoAm; PML; PoChi; RaBo

Yesterday. Mary Weems. SpirFl

Yesterday a cloud burst. Respite. Tatamkulu Afrika. TSAP

Yesterday a little girl got slapped to death by her daddy. Patriotics. David Baker. LiTh

Yesterday, against admonishment. Father's Song. Gregory Orr. PoChi

Yesterday all the past. The language of size. Spain [1937]. W. H. Auden. AF; NAEL-6v2; NAEL-7v2; NAMCP V.1; NoP-4; NoP-5; OBWP

Yesterday, all winter. Flemish Beauty. Ansel Talvikki. AmPoNev

Yesterday at ten below. First Winter: Joy. Peggy Shumaker. PBCAP

Yesterday, at the Sessions held in Buckingham. Case at Sessions, A. Walter Savage Landor. OBSV

Yesterday, dreamed He was near me. Antonio Machado Ruiz. STV

Yesterday explorers found. Clarence Day. OBCoV *Fr.* Scenes from the Mesozoic.

Yesterday has flown, leaving only its sorrows. Seeing Off a Friend. Li Po. CrYelRi, *tr.* by Sam Hamill

Yesterday He Was Nowhere to Be Found. Ted Hughes. NOxBChV

Yesterday his eyes stared into mine. Ancient Song, An. Marina Ivanovna Tsvetayeva. TCRusP, *tr.* by John Glad

Yesterday, I discovered my wife. Living with Others. Al Zolynas. SUP

Yesterday, I exposed myself on the train. Indecent Exposure (A True Story). Linwood M. Ross. InTrad

Yesterday I felt this ode. Ode to Laziness. Pablo Neruda. TCLAP, *tr.* by William Carlos Williams

Yesterday, I have always seen him. I followed him into Paris: here was the entrance. His Promise. Aaron Shurin. FTOS

Yesterday I heard a lover sigh. Toot, Toot, Tootsie! (Good-bye). Gustave Kahn. ReLy

Yesterday, I lay awake in the palm of the night. Names, The. Billy Collins. FTtHH

Yesterday I met a new. Afternoon of the Sheep, The. Kazuko Shiraishi. WoBe, *tr.* by Samuel Grolmes and Yumiko Tsumura

Yesterday I remembered a clear winter day. I remembered. Bridge in the South. Jorge Teillier. TCLAP, *tr.* by Carolyne Wright

Yesterday I saw that sun-faced beauty. Lami'i Çelebi. OLP, *tr.* by Walter Andrews, Najaat Black and Mehmet Kalpakli

Yesterday I saw the sun. Lyn Hejinian. NAMCP V.2 *Fr.* Cell, The.

Yesterday / I saw them dragging you. Song of Freedom, A. Roland A. Parks. OWABP

Yesterday I wanted to. For Love. Robert Creeley. NAMCP V.2; PmAP; VCAP

Yesterday I was observing the animals and it made me think of you. Jaime Sabines. MotU *Fr.* Adam and Eve.

Yesterday / i was runnin. Runnin. Jamila Z. Wade. BRtP

Yesterday I went to a cloud observatory. Han-shan (Cold Mountain). ColAnChi, *tr.* by Red Pine

Yesterday, in a big market, I made seven thousand dollars. Back through the Looking Glass to This Side. John Ciardi. NBLV

Yesterday in São Paulo they buried. Oswald Dead. Ferreira Gullar. TCLAP, *tr. by* Renato Rezende

Yesterday in the bath Diodes' penis. Strato. CAGL, *tr. by* Daryl Hine

Yesterday Morning. *Unknown.* CCL1, *tr. by* Marsha Wagner

Yesterday morning I went early to bid farewell to the traveling man. Yesterday Morning. *Unknown.* CCL1, *tr. by* Marsha Wagner

Yesterday Mrs. Friar phoned. "Mr. Ciardi." Suburban. John Ciardi. NBLV

Yesterday Reflecting Upon Death. Nikolai Alekseievich Zabolotsky. TCRusP, *tr. by* Daniel Weissbort

Yesterday she claimed adherence to the mirror. Self-Portrait in the Third Person. Biancamaria Frabotta. CItWP, *tr. by* Cinzia Sartini Blum and Lara Trubowitz

Yesterday, / snow lay thick on our town. Snow in Wrexham. Bryan Martin Davies. BBMWP, *tr. by* Elin ap Hywel

Yesterday the fields were only grey with scattered snow. Winter's Tale, A. D. H. Lawrence. MoBrPo

Yesterday the gentle. St. Stephen's Day. Patric Dickinson. OBCP

Yesterday the sky filled with petroleum. On-the ground. Lisa Gill. ICANM *Fr.* Letters to a Dead Trappist.

Yesterday the tulip shoots, considering. March Again. Philip Booth. PfSP

Yesterday the UN report on weapons inspections was released. January 28, 2003. Juliana Spahr. LegDan

YESTERDAY *This* Day's Madness did prepare. Omar Khayyám. CABP *Fr.* Rubáiyát of Omar Khayyám [of Naishápúr], The.

Yesterday was I, sure of purpose. Fox, The. Dafydd ap Gwilym. NAWM-7v1, *tr. by* Richard Morgan Loomis

Yesterday was Wednesday all morning. Yesterday. Angel González. VCWP, *tr. by* Steven Ford Brown and Revuelta Gutierrez

Yesterday we root-picked up the new ground. Rock Pickers. Cyd Adams. TiP2

Yesterday / When I found. Reticence. May Muzaffar. PoArWo, *tr. by* Tahia Abdel Nasser

Yesterday, while dreaming about a long evening's labor. Pipe, The. Stéphane Mallarmé. MotU, *tr. by* Michael Benedikt

Yesterday you came my way. I Can't Believe That You're in Love with Me. Clarence Gaskill. ReLy

Yesterdays. Otto Harbach. ReLy

Yesterdays. Yesterdays. Otto Harbach. ReLy

Yesterday's conversation. That Which Hovers. Lara Ramsey. RWB

Yesterday's conversation has been on my mind all day. Consolation. Dimitris Tsaloumas. BMAP

Yesterday's Illusion *or* Remembering the Thirties. Alun Llywelyn-Williams. OBWVE, *tr. by* R. Gerallt Jones

Yesterday's rain. Sergey Aleksandrovich Yesenin. CAGL, *tr. by* Simon Karlinsky

Yesterday's rain is still on the ground. Yesterday's rain. Sergey Aleksandrovich Yesenin. CAGL, *tr. by* Simon Karlinsky

Yesterday's sorrows defrost. Springs. Nike Adesuyi. NeNiPo

Yesterday's sundown was very beautiful—I know it is out of fashion to say so, I think we are fools. Ocean's Tribute, The. Robinson Jeffers. NAAPv.2

Yet. Mary Dalton. OpeFie

Yet a Little While Is the Light With You. Francis Quarles. ChIV-2

Yet another epiphany. Lisa Pegram. BtF

Yet another great truth I record in my verse. Viper, The. Joseph Hilaire Pierre Belloc. NoAM

Yet Another Home. Yun Tongju. CAMKP, *tr. by* Kay Richards and Steffen Richards

Yet art hath less of instinct than of thought. Criticism. Ebenezer Elliott. CenSon

Yet burnished by its passage, and still warm. (LL) Harvest Bow, The. Seamus Heaney. HarvBoo; ModIr; NoAM; PBCIP; PNI

Yet C[h]loe sure was form'd without a Spot—. Alexander Pope. OBSV *Fr.* Epistle [II,] to a Lady[: Of the Characters of Women].

Yet count this quest the holiest of thy days. (LL) Quest of the Ideal, The. Henrietta Cordelia Ray. CBWP-3; SWaP

Yet Dish. Gertrude Stein.
"Put a sun in Sunday, Sunday." TCAPo

Yet Do I Marvel. Countee Cullen. AmFaPo; APT-2; BrAP; InvLi; NAAL-5; NAAPv.2; NAMCP V.1; NIL-7; NoAM; NoP-5; SSLK; WaAnP

Yet do not be afraid, yet give no post forlorn. To Himself. Paul Fleming. GePo, *tr. by* George C. Schoolfield

Yet each man kills the thing he loves. Oscar Wilde. OxBEV *Fr.* Ballad of Reading Gaol, The.

Yet / Ere the season died a-cold. Ezra Pound. NAAPv.2 *Fr.* Cantos.

Yet, even 'mid merry boyhood's tricks and scapes. Frederick Goddard Tuckerman. APN-2 *Fr.* Sonnets.

Yet[t] faith still cries, Love will not[t] falsify [*or* falsefy]. (LL) Mary Sidney Wroth, Countess of Montgomery. NAEL-6v1; NAEL-7v1; NOSC; PEW *Fr.* Pamphilia to Amphilanthus.

Yet find not much more anguish? Be content. (LL) Pessimist's Vision, The. Constance Naden. ViWPN; VWP

Yet for one rounded moment I will be. Mortal Lease, The: V. Edith Wharton. LW

Yet Ha'e I Silence Left. Hugh MacDiarmid. NAEL-6v2; NAEL-7v2 *Fr.* Drunk Man Looks at the Thistle, A.

Yet ha'e I Silence left, the croon o' a'. Hugh MacDiarmid. NAEL-6v2; NAEL-7v2 *Fr.* Drunk Man Looks at the Thistle, A.

Yet he was there, and all my thirst. And If He Had Been Wrong for Me. Robert Duncan. RaBo

Yet heed thou wisely this; give seldom to thy better. Art of Giving, The (1850). Martin Farquhar Tupper. STuOW

Yet here, tho' amusing the Sight. River Dove: a Lyric Pastoral, The. Samuel Bently. VerBaPo

Yet how the solitude of man torments. Journey into Misery. Iwan Goll. GTCP, *tr. by* Christopher Middleton

Yet I know I will enter again and again. (LL) Kenneth Rexroth. APSN; APT-2 *Fr.* Love Poems of Marichiko, The.

Yet I would bear its darkest woes to dream that dream again. (LL) Corinne's Last Love-Song. Lady Jane Francesca Wilde. IrLP; VWP

Yet if for sylvan sports thy bosom glow. Rural Sports. John Gay. DiBP

Yet If His Majesty, Our Sovereign Lord. *Unknown. See* Guest, The.

Yet if his majesty, our sovereign [*or* soveraign] Lord. Guest, The. *Unknown.* SacPr

(Yet if his Majestie our Sovareigne lord.) PBRV

(Yet if his majesty, our sovereign lord.) NoP-4

Yet if some voice that man could trust. Alfred Tennyson. NAEL-6v2; NAEL-7v2 *Fr.* In Memoriam A. H. H.

Yet ignobler band is guarded round, A. Bull-Baiting. Edward Lovibond. DiBP

Ye[t]t is ther hope: Then Love but[t] play thy part. Mary Sidney Wroth, Countess of Montgomery. NoP-5 *Fr.* Pamphilia to Amphilanthus.

Yet like grandfather. Extended Family. A. K. Ramanujan. NAMCP V.2

Yet Listen Now. Amy Carmichael. SacPr

Yet London, empress of the northern clime. John Dryden. NAEL-6v1; NAEL-7v1 *Fr.* Annus Mirabilis.

Yet, love, mere love, is beautiful indeed. Elizabeth Barrett Browning. CenSon; OxAEP-2 *Fr.* Sonnets from the Portuguese.

Yet often I think the king of that country. Gospel of Labor, The. Henry Van Dyke. SacPr

Yet on the other side, faine would he start. Giovanni Giambattista. OBVE *Fr.* Massacre of the Innocents, The.

Yet once again heaven's king, and Earth's great lord. Abraham's Sacrifice of Isaac. Sir John Stradling. NOSC

Yet once more, O ye Laurels and once more. Lycidas. John Milton. AmFaPo; BASC; BrAP; CABP; ClHu; InoFa; MakPoe; NAEL-6v1; NAEL-7v1; NIL-7; NoP-4; NoP-5; NOSC; NPeEn; OBEV; OxAEP-1; OxBEV; PBRV; PoPoPo; TFi; WaAnP

Yet one smile more, departing, distant sun! November. William Cullen Bryant. APN-1; GSo; TreFP

Yet Ostia boasts of her regeneration. Daniel Defoe. OBSV *Fr.* Reformation of Manners.

Yet our hymn is *For the Beauty of the Earth.* Still dark when we file like children out on the turf. Sydney Lea. Vesp

Yet out of that I have written these songs. (LL) Sometimes with One I Love. Walt Whitman. APN-1; SAmP

Yet, paying, is not paid until I die. (LL) To Her Father, with Some Verses. Anne Bradstreet. NAAL-3; NAAL-5; NAAPv.1; NALW

Yet, Percy, not for this, should he whose eye. To the Same. Leigh Hunt. CenSon

Yet resurrection is a sense of direction. "H. D." APT-1 *Fr.* Flowering of the Rod, The.

Yet[t] since: O me[e]: a lover I have been [*or* binn]. (LL) Mary Sidney Wroth, Countess of Montgomery. BASC; CABP; MakPoe; NAEL-6v1; NAEL-7v1; NoP-5 *Fr.* Pamphilia to Amphilanthus.

Yet Still. Rashidah Ismaili. HAWP; ItWoWo

Yet the language so lovely! like the dyes from gas-tar. (LL) When I Read Shakespeare. D. H. Lawrence. NoAM; OBCoV

Yet there belongs a Sweetnesse, softnesse too. On Sanazar's being honoured with six hundred Duckets by the Clarissimi of Venice, for composing an Elegiack Hexastick of The City. A Satyre. Richard Lovelace. PBRV

Yet there is no great problem in the world today. Hugh MacDiarmid. NoP-5 *Fr.* Lament for the Great Music.

Yet there is no joy. (LL) Fill and Illumined. Joseph Ceravolo. ChIV-1; OxBoAm

Yet they never persuaded your heart. Praxilla. SaLy, *tr. by* Diane Rayor

Yet this is you. (LL) Ezra Pound. APT-1; BrAP; MoAmPo; NAAL-5; NAMCP V.1; NoAM; NoP-4; NoP-5; OxBoAm; TCAPo *Fr.* Ripostes of Ezra Pound.

Yet to Come. Luke E. Ramirez. OWABP

Yet we, the latter-day twice-born. "H. D." APT-1 *Fr.* Walls Do Not Fall, The.

Yet we were looking away! (LL) Self-Unseeing, The. Thomas Hardy. MoBrPo; NAMCP V.1; OxAEP-2; OxBEV; PtR; WeW-3

Yet will I fear no evil: not even here. Château, The. Henry Reed. NoP-4

Yet will I love her till I die. (LL) There Is a Lady Sweet and Kind. Thomas Ford. HeIP-4; NoP-4; NoP-5; NOSC; OBEV

Yet will I sing "any food, any feeding." (LL) Tom o' Bedlam's Song. *Unknown.* BASC; NoP-4; NoP-5; NPeEn; TFi

Yet, yet a moment, one dim ray of light. Alexander Pope. NAEL-6v1; NAEL-7v1 *Fr.* Dunciad, The.

Yet you (great lady) mistress of that place. Emilia Lanier and Aemilia Bassano Lanyer. OBGa *Fr.* Description of Cooke-ham [*or* Cookham], The.

Yeti. John Haines. PoCoUp

Yet-to-be-dismantled elms, the geese, The. (LL) Poem: "About the size of an old-style dollar bill." Elizabeth Bishop. Coast; NAMCP V.2; NoAM; PoetW; PoPoPo; VCAP

Yeux Glauques. Ezra Pound. MoAmPo; NAAPv.2 *Fr.* Hugh Selwyn Mauberley (Life and Contacts).

Yew. Elizabeth Delmore. NLP

Yew Berries. Ruth Padel. MFPA

Yew of Llanddeiniolen, The. W. J. Gruffydd. BBMWP, *tr.* by Joseph P. Clancy

Ye-you man-cao: Mid the Bind-Grass. *Unknown.* CCL1, *tr.* by Ezra Pound

Ye-you si-jun: Lies a Dead Deer. *Unknown.* APSN; CCL1; NDACCP, *tr.* by Ezra Pound

Yf I had as faire a face as John Williams. Anne Wrigglesworth. EMWP

Yf there be any man that can tell me quicklye. Honor Strangman *et al..* EMWP

Yggdrasill. Paul Muldoon. PBCIP

Yi surta. Song. Tom Leonard. Oth

Yiddish Muses, The. Jacqueline Osherow. TaR

Yiddish Poets in America. Richard Chess. TaR

Yiddishe Kopf. Allen Ginsberg. BodElec; TaR

Yield Everything, Force Nothing. Jean Valentine. ExTi

Yielding cell from celluloid, a script for two. Lucky Smile. Michele Wolf. LiTh

Yielding to a love. Ono no Komachi. WoPoe, *tr.* by Helen Craig McCullough

Ying clan disrupted Heaven's ordinance, The. Peach Blossom Spring, The. T'ao Ch'ien. CCL1, *tr.* by James Robert Hightower

Ying from "The Nine Declarations." Ch'u Yüan. ChinPo, *tr.* by Ye Weilian [*or* Yeh Wei-lien *or* Wai-lim Yip]

Yin-yo laps in the reeds, my guest departs. Po Chü-i. NDACCP, *tr.* by Ezra Pound

Yippee! she is shooting in the harbor! he is jumping. Blocks. Frank O'Hara. OxBoAm

"Yis, dame," quod he, "tel forth, and I wol heere." (LL) Geoffrey Chaucer. NAEL-6v1; NAEL-7v1; NoP-5 *Fr.* Canterbury Tales, The.

Yiskor. Gloria Gervitz. *tr.* by Stephen Tapscott
    "And what were you searching for, in that dream?" MirDau, *tr.* by Stephen Tapscott
    "Can you hear me? Under my name I am." MirDau, *tr.* by Stephen Tapscott
    "I listen through underground walls like prisoners signaling." MirDau, *tr.* by Stephen Tapscott
    "Maybe we are the same darkness the same words." MirDau, *tr.* by Stephen Tapscott
    "Nothing you tell me nothing." MirDau, *tr.* by Stephen Tapscott
    "She detaches herself from her shadow. She is an old woman and still beautiful." MirDau, *tr.* by Stephen Tapscott
    "She is crying." MirDau, *tr.* by Stephen Tapscott
    "Silence is a task that will last all her life. It continues." MirDau, *tr.* by Stephen Tapscott
    "We docked at noon in the port of Veracruz. We wore our Russian furs." MirDau, *tr.* by Stephen Tapscott

Yi-xi: Halloa! *Unknown.* CCL1, *tr.* by Man Wong

Yo black. I Know You Are, But What Am I? Paul Beatty. InTrad

Yo bust it: a lost generation. Don't Feel No Way. Kevin Powell. InTrad

Yo Hermitage. Pou Kuksa. BecRai, *tr.* by Kim Daljin, Kim Won-Chung and Christopher Merrill

Yo, José Hierro, un hombre. Tarde Cualquiera, Una. José Hierro. RaW

Yo nací provinciano en los domingos. Lugar Vacío en la Celebración. José Ángel Valente. RaW

Yo no creo nada, yo colaboro, ayudo. Eduardo Milán. RMCMP

Yo No Soy el Gran Buzo. León Felipe. RaW

Yo no soy nadie: un hombre. León Felipe. RaW *Fr.* Perro Negro Duerme Sobre la Luz, Un.

Yo No Soy Yo. Juan Ramón Jiménez. RaW

Yo, pecador, artista del pecado. Juicio Final. Blas de Otero. RaW

Yo que he olvidado las palabras. Fabio Morabito. RMCMP

Yo soy india / pero no soy. Tribal Chant. Carol Lee Sanchez. ReEnLa

YOhoheyheyeyheyahyeyeyhahhehyohoheyheyeyHEY. Richard Johnny John, Jerome Rothenberg and Ian Tyson. PFTM-1 *Fr.* Songs from the Society of the Mystic Animals.

Yojimbo. Miriam Sagan. WANABP

Yoke, The. Frank Bidart. OxBoAm

Yoking the cow, saint Mary, yoking her. Another. Holley Blackwell. AnSo

Yoko. Thom Gunn. NoAM; PtR

Yolanda Meets the Wild Boys. Jessica Tarahata Hagedorn. OpBo

Yollim Kut Song. Shin Kyong-Nim. PML, *tr.* by Anthony, Brother of Taizé

Yom HaShoah in Florida. Rick Hilles. RWB

Yom Kippur, 5726. Cynthia Ozick. TaR

Yom Kippur 1984. Adrienne Rich. NoAM; PfS; TaR

Yom Kippur Sonnet, with a Line from Lamentations. Jacqueline Osherow. PoCho

Yom Kippur, Taos, New Mexico. Robin Becker. TaR

Yom Kippur: wearing a bride's dress bought in Jerusalem. Prayer. Grace Schulman. PuP-23

Yon black man-of-war hawk that wheels in the light. Man-of-War Hawk, The. Herman Melville. APN-2; OWoS

Yon Far Country. A. E. Housman. HarvBoo; MoBrPo; NoAM; NPeEn; OPOU; OxAEP-2; OxBEV; TFi; WaAnP *Fr.* Shropshire Lad, A.

Yon rising Moon that looks for us again. Omar Khayyám. TRP *Fr.* Rubáiyát of Omar Khayyám [of Naishápúr], The.

Yon silvery billows breaking on the beach. Sonnet's Voice, The. Theodore Watts-Dunton. GSo

Yon strange blue city crowns a scarpèd steep. Mona Lisa. Edith Wharton. GS

Yonder are spirits laughing and talking as though drunk. Tohono O'odham. NAAPv.1 *Fr.* Songs for Treating Sickness, Sung during the Four Parts of the Night.

Yonder, calm as a cloud, Alcott stalks in a dream. James Russell Lowell. TCAPo *Fr.* Fable for Critics, A.

Yonder lies the spirit land. Tohono O'odham. NAAPv.1 *Fr.* Songs for Treating Sickness, Sung during the Four Parts of the Night.

Yonder on the linden tree there sang a merry little bird. Dietmar von Aist [*or* Eist]. GePo

Yonder Tree, The. Joshua Weiner. PtR

Yonder, yonder, / Yonder. (LL) Leaden Echo and the Golden Echo, The. Gerard Manley Hopkins. MoBrPo; OBMV

Yonnondio. Walt Whitman. NAAL-3

Yorkshire Wife's Saga. Ruth Pitter. NALW

Yorkshiremen in Pub Gardens. Gavin Ewart. GoPo

Yorkville. James Schuyler. AHA

Yoruba Love. Molara Ogundipe-Leslie. HAWP

Yoshiwara. Karai Senryū. EMJL, *tr.* by Makoto Ueda

You: "When afternoon." Lucile Adler. ICANM

You. Tom Clark.
    You (III). PmAP
    You (I). PmAP

You. Gillian Coote. WhBo

You. Shakuntala Hawoldar. HAWP

You. D. H. Lawrence. NAMCP V.1; NoAM

You: "You're mine." Ismail. HotL, *tr.* by V. Narayana Rao

You. Dennis O'Driscoll. StAl

You. Nelly Sachs. AF, *tr.* by Matthew Mead and Ruth Mead

You: "Back from being." *Unknown.* SonAtl, *tr.* by Rowena Astill, Alan Brierly and Abigail Herzen

You / catch my breath with your waking. Blues 1. Barry Wallenstein. SeSe

You / come from my village. You Come from My Village. Wang Wei. CCL1, *tr.* by C. H. Kwock and Vincent McHugh

You (III). Tom Clark. PmAP *Fr.* You.

You abandon your intent. (LL) Jellyfish, A. Marianne Moore. ItP; NAAPv.2

You all by yourself fulfilled. *Unknown.* WoPoe *Fr.* Elegy for the Great Inca Atawallpa, The.

You all caboose. Ride the High Country. Joel Dailey. AnSo

You All Know the Story of the Two Lovers. Carlota Caulfield. TANSG, *tr.* by Chris Allen

You, all-accomplishing. Song to the Creator. Hildegard von Bingen. WPoS, *tr.* by Barbara Newman

You almost home boy. Go on cross that sea! (LL) My Father's Geography. Afaa Michael Weaver. GT; OxAAAP; PBCAP

You almost trip as you hear. Rufous Hummingbird. Duane Niatum. PoCoUp

You already know. Kim Namjo. CAMKP *Fr.* Love's Cursive.

You Also, Gaius Valerius Catullus. Archibald MacLeish. NoAM

You also, our first great. To Whistler, American. Ezra Pound. FaBoA; PoA 2002

You always belonged here. Here. Jane Kenyon. LoL

You always did like your men well hung. Thin-Legged Lover. Kate Mullen. PfS

You always knew you wrote for him, you said. Retrun of the Muse, The. Sandra M. Gilbert. WaAnP

You always read about it. Cinderella. Anne Sexton. BrAP; HeIP-4

You always sang at break of day. Wolfram von Eschenbach. GePo

You always seem to get it all wrong about me. Seeing Red. Al Young. FTtHH

You and baby you know me and I am. Incidentals in the Day World. Alice Notley. AHA

You and I. Henry Alford. ITBLP

You and I. Dinah Elena Consuegra. RWB

You and I. *Unknown.* WoPoe, *tr.* by Stanley Moss

You and I and a fat lady. At the Party. Mikhail Alekseievich Kuzmin. CAGL, *tr.* by Simon Karlinsky

You and I and Amyas. William Cornish. NoSic

You and I Are Disappearing. Yusef Komunyakaa. AmAlph; PoCho

You and I, are we in the same story? Battle of Wills Disguised, A. Marge Piercy. HeIP-4

You and I / Have so much love. Married Love. Kuan Tao Shěng. PasH; WoPoe, *tr.* by Chung Ling and Kenneth Rexroth

You and I Saw Hawks Exchanging the Prey. James Wright. NoAM

You and I Shall Go. *Wintu Oral Tradition.* NAAPv.1 *Fr.* Six Dream Songs.

You and I will fold the sheets. Rosemary Dobson. ItWoWo; NOBAu *Fr.* Daily Living.

You and the Night and the Music. Howard Dietz. ReLy

You and the Tijuana Mule. Rigoberto González. GeoHom

You and Them. Patty Seyburn. AmPoNex

You and You, In the Pink. Christopher Pilling. NLP

You and your client continue to walk. Fiona Templeton. FTOS *Fr.* You: The City.

You and your naked sleep. You don't know it. Sleeplessness. Gerardo Diego. BLPSL, *tr.* by Rene de Costa, Rigas Kappatos and Eleni Paidoussi

You, Andrew Marvell. Archibald MacLeish. APT-1; BeAl; BrAP; ColAP; HeIP-4; MoAmPo; NAMCP V.1; NoAM; NoP-4; SoSe-8; TFi; TRP

You answered, when I held you. Look at Me. Kim Ly Bui-Burton. PasH

You appear in a tinny, nickel-and-dime light. The light of turned milk and gloved insults. Bitter Angel. Amy Gerstler. MotU; PmAP

You, apple. Ode to the Apple. Pablo Neruda. IPoFL, *tr.* by Ken Krabbenhoft

You approach. Tango'd Love. J. B. Bernstein. PasH

You Are. Mimi Goese. HeMarv

You Are a Daughter of the Lagides. Alvaro Mutis. BLPSL, *tr.* by Rene de Costa, Rigas Kappatos and Eleni Paidoussi

You are a daughter of the Lagides. You Are a Daughter of the Lagides. Alvaro Mutis. BLPSL, *tr.* by Rene de Costa, Rigas Kappatos and Eleni Paidoussi

You are a friend then, as I make it out. Ben Jonson Entertains a Man from Stratford. Edwin Arlington Robinson. MoAmPo

You are a man, tonight! Kassacks. Annette M'Baye d'Erneville. HAWP, *tr.* by Brian Baer

You are a picture no artist could paint. I've Got a Feelin' You're Foolin'. Arthur Freed. ReLy

You are a riddle I would not unravel. Riddle. Josephine Miles. CalPo

You are a search party traveling back for your great. Voices Are Coming Up, The. Frances Payne Adler. FiBr

You are a stool pigeon and. Martial. WoPoe, *tr.* by Kenneth Rexroth

You are a sunrise. To a Golden-Haired Girl in a Louisiana Town. Vachel Lindsay. MoAmPo

You are a tulip seen today. Meditation for His Mistress[e], A. Robert Herrick. NOSC; OBEV

You are a wild look—out of an egg. Ted Hughes. NoAM *Fr.* Stations.

You are adapted to speeches of silence, speak he said, speak. How Thubten Sang His Songs. Tsering Wangno Dhompa. WANABP

You are alone and you are easy. You see. I Love How Your Eyes Close Every Time You Kiss Me. Erica Bernheim. LegDan

You are already. Touch. Thom Gunn. HarvBoo

You are already dead when I am told. Dead Stepfather, The. Terry Wolverton. WiU

You are an extended branch of me. You. Shakuntala Hawoldar. HAWP

You are an island in a very old atlas. İlhan Berk. NaPG *Fr.* History of a Face, The.

You are as gold. Song. "H. D." APT-1; MoAmPo; TCAPo

You Are at the Bottom of My Mind. Iain Crichton Smith. WoPoe

You are beautiful and faded. Lady, A. Amy Lowell. MoAmPo; TCAPo

You are beautiful as a stone. Waltz, The. Vicente Aleixandre. RaW, *tr.* by Robert Bly

You are blind like us. Your hurt no man designed. To Germany. Charles Hamilton Sorley. MoBrPo

You are born into an aptitude for original patterns. Soleil Cou Coupé. Jennifer Moxley. VaPo

You are carrying me, full consciousness, god that has desires. Full Consciousness. Juan Ramón Jiménez. RaW, *tr.* by Robert Bly

You are caught pulling the brake. Desert Run Scenario. Kathleen Norris. UpMys

You are clear / O rose, cut in rock. Garden. "H. D." APT-1; NAMCP V.1; NoAM

You are coming to woo me, but not as of yore. Lips That Touch Liquor. George W. Young. NBLV

You are coming toward us. Aunt Laura Moves toward the Open Grave of Her Father. Joseph De Roche. HeIP-4

You are disdainful and magnificent. Sonnet to a Negro in Harlem. Helene Johnson. APT-2; NIL-7; NIP-4; OxAAAP; SSLK

You Are Distant, You Are Already Leaving. David Constantine. HarvBoo

You are downtrodden. Wheels of Jagannatha, The. Sri Sri. HotL, *tr.* by V. Narayana Rao

You are driving to the airport. Kenneth Rexroth. GoPo *Fr.* Air and Angels.

You are facing the harbor and the open sea. North Star. L. S. Asekoff. BodElec

You are far away, blocked by passes and mountains. Sent to My Fourth Son, Shao-Wu (to the Tune "Southern Countryside"). Liang Te-sheng. WoPoe, *tr.* by Nancy Hodes and Tung Yuan-fang

You are for dreams and slumbers, brother priest. William Shakespeare. OxAEP-1 *Fr.* Troilus and Cressida.

You are going to ask: and where are the lilacs? I'm Explaining a Few Things. Pablo Neruda. TCLAP, *tr.* by Nathaniel Tarn

You are gorgeous and I am not getting to know you any better I feel. You Are Not Gorgeous and I Am Coming Anyway. Lee Ann Brown. VaPo

You are handsome, aren't you. Courtesan to a Young Customer, A. Kshetrayya. WoPoe, *tr.* by V. Narayana Rao, A. K. Ramanujan and David Shulman

You Are Happy. Margaret Atwood. TRP

You Are Here. Carl Phillips. GT

You are here in my little room. My Mother, in memoriam. Fadhil Assultani. IrPoTo, *tr.* by Melissa Brown and Saadi A. Simawe

You are here now. Sleeping Fury, The. Louise Bogan. NAAPv.2; NALW

You are here on earth, our Father. Prayer. Gloria Fuertes. GPTC; RaW, *tr.* by John Haines

You are holding my sister in your arms. Father and Daughter. Cathy Song. OpBo

You are holding up a ceiling. Marriage, A. Michael C. Blumenthal. PoPoPo

You are horizontal. Footpaths Cross in the Rice Field. "Lin Ling." CFP, *tr.* by Chung Ling and Kenneth Rexroth

You are ice and fire. Opal. Amy Lowell. NALW

You are ideal. Amulet. Carl Rakosi. APT-2

You are impatient, says the oracle. Reading, A. Virginia Hooper. KGB

You are in Camagüey when we arrive. Primos. Sandra M. Castillo. TouFir

You are Jehova, and I am a wanderer. You and I. *Unknown.* WoPoe, *tr.* by Stanley Moss

You are leaving me. Something to Remember You By. Howard Dietz. ReLy

You are like a sun of the tropics. Luxury. Donald Justice. HeIP-4

You are like dust along the road. To an Ancient Tune. Yao K'uan. CrYelRi, *tr.* by Sam Hamill

You are lying on the carpet of your bedroom dead. Acts of Love. Edgar Silex. NAPBL

You are Mad: and I Mean It! Phumzile Zulu. HAWP

You are made of almost nothing. Dragonfly, The. Louise Bogan. APT-2; HeIP-4

You are Mine said she. (LL) May i feel said he. E. E. Cummings. HeIP-4; NAMCP V.1; NBLV; NoP-5; OBCoV; OxBoAm; PoPoPo

You are mistaken confuse everything stop then. Liliane Giraudon. SCFWP *Fr.* Poem with Incense Paper.

You are my companion. Companion, The. Mary Low. SurWo

You are my effendi, if I have any respect in the world. Şeyh Galib. OLP, *tr.* by Walter Andrews, Najaat Black and Mehmet Kalpakli

You are my finest hour. You Are. Mimi Goese. HeMarv

You are my secret coat. You're never dry. Cousin Coat. Sean O'Brien. NeBrP; NoP-5

You are nearly as old as the number of years it has been since I came to America. Dainin Katagiri. WhBo

You are not a drill or a mole or at a film. Below the Cellar of the Yellow House There Is Another Set of Stairs. Robin Behn. AmAlph

You are not a tree. Yun Söndo. CATKP *Fr.* Songs of Five Friends.

You are not beautiful, exactly. To Dorothy. Marvin Bell. CAP-8; InvLad; VCAP

You are not dead, no. Love. Juan Ramón Jiménez. SpanPo, *tr.* by Angel Flores

You are not even here. (LL) This Room. John Ashbery. ItP; OxBoAm

You Are Not Gorgeous and I Am Coming Anyway. Lee Ann Brown. VaPo

You are not looked for through the smog, you turn blindly. To the Moon, 1969. Babette Deutsch. OtW

You are not merry, brother. Why not laugh. Prodigal Son, The. Edwin Arlington Robinson. GI; MoAmPo

You are not nearer God than we. Annunciation. Rainer Maria Rilke. OBVE, *tr.* by James Blair Leishman

You are not not. (LL) November 26, 1992: Thanksgiving at the Sea Ranch, Contemplating Metempsychosis. Sandra M. Gilbert. InoFa; PoDa

You are not outside this film (or movie). Fables of Critique. Peter Gizzi. VaPo

You Are Not Poetry. Rosario Castellanos. TCLAP, *tr.* by Maureen Ahern

You are not wanted. Periphery. Ruth Stone. NALW

You are not with me in fleeting moments. Spiritual Wedding. Manuel Bandeira. TCLAP, *tr.* by Candace Slater

You are now traversing. Bardo of Leaving. Janet Rodney. WANABP

You are often hunched over in an armchair to confide sweet nothings to the side of a face. 13. Linh Dinh. BAP-04

You are old enough. Push-Pull of This Love, The. Susan Spady. FiBr

"You are old, Father William," the young man cried. Old Man's Comforts and How He Gained Them, The. Robert Southey. UV

You are old, Father William, the young man said. Lewis Carroll. IJHIL *Fr.* Alice's Adventures in Wonderland.

You are one of those clear cold creeks. Creek, The. Roland Robinson. NOBAu

You are parceled out over the post office. De Carlo Lots, The. Anne Waldman. AHA

You are perched on a padded board. First Haircut. Richard Frost. NevBe

You are pretty Solange. Solange. Rashidah Ismaili. HAWP

You are probably dreaming. Where the Nightmare Begins. Tanure Ojaide. NAfrP

You are punctual. (LL) Lightly stepped a yellow star. Emily Dickinson. MoAmPo; SAmP

You Are Right. Cathryn Essinger. PoA 2002; PoDa

You are running away from everyone. Opposite of Nostalgia, The. Eric Gamalinda. PoDa

You are sad. It is the same with me. (LL) Nocturne at Bethesda. Arna Bontemps. ChIV-2; NAAPv.2; OxAAAP

You are safe / You are lying in a hammock. Lullaby. Alpay Ulku. AmPoNex

You are saying good-bye to your last. Good-Bye. Joan Larkin. LaCa; WiU

You are small and intense. To a Child Running with Outstretched Arms in Canyon de Chelly. N. Scott Momaday. HATNAP

You are so beautiful and I am a fool. Nightclub. Billy Collins. FaoP; GoPo; SUP

You are so elegant in your robes. Woman's Love Song. *Somali Oral Tradition.* ErotSp, *tr.* by Sam Hamill

You are so small, I. Miss Cho Composes in the Cafeteria. James Tate. WeW-3

You are somewhat slighter. Angela Dominguez, Ever Present. Nancy Morejón. TANSG, *tr.* by Joy Renjilian-Burgy

You are still the one with stone and sling. Salvatore Quasimodo. AF

You are Sucha Fool. Ntozake Shange. ISC

You are sucha fool / i haveta love you. You are Sucha Fool. Ntozake Shange. ISC

You are the baby in the barn. (LL) Nick and the Candlestick. Sylvia Plath. ItP; NALW

You are the Brave. Raymond R. Patterson. NIP-4

You are the bread and the knife. Litany. Billy Collins. BeAl; CAP-8; NoP-5; OxBoAm; SUP

You are the companion I talk with. Poetry. Xavier Villaurrutia. TCLAP, *tr.* by Dana Stangel

You are the daughter who is sleep's beauty. Victory, Victoria, My Beautiful Whisper. Luis J. Rodriguez. FaoP

You are the faintest freckles on the hide. Sonnet. Elinor Wylie. APT-1

You are the fish that hides. Legendary. James McAuley. BMAP

You are the golden eternity because there is. Jack Kerouac. WhBo *Fr.* Scripture of the Golden Eternity, The.

You are the kind of beauty. New World, The. Valerie Martínez. TouFir

You are the man. Wilderness. Lorine Niedecker. OxBoAm

You are the one. Other One, The. André Velter. YaTCFP, *tr.* by Mary McCaws

You are the owner of one complete thought. Voice and Address. Michael Palmer. FTOS; PmAP

You are the plainest moon. Forget all others. Diary Moon. Paul Farley. NeBrP

You are the salt of the earth. Gail Holst-Warhaft. GI *Fr.* St. Matthew.

You are the sandstorm beneath my skin. Song. Odia Ofeimun. NAfrP

You are the scorpion whose affinities reveal past lives. Tonal Embryology. Folade Mondisa Speaks. BRtP

You are the song that lies beyond the ear. On Sparrows. Suji Kwock Kim. LegDan

You are the stilled. To God. Tatamkulu Afrika. TSAP

You are tired. Midnight Tennis Match, The. Thomas Lux. MoASP

You are tired at last this old world. Zone. Guillaume Apollinaire. YaTCFP, *tr.* by Roger Shattuck

You are to me the secret of my soul. World Well Lost 18, The. Marc André Raffalovich. CAGL

You Are Too Beautiful. Lorenz Hart. ReLy

You are too naked for touching. Morning. Jeni Couzyn. HAWP

You are too splendid for this city street! (LL) Sonnet to a Negro in Harlem. Helene Johnson. APT-2; NIL-7; NIP-4; OxAAAP; SSLK

You are traveling within the boundaries of your time together. Seizing the Day. Judith Ortiz Cofer. PueRic; SwNoth

You are / walking up the stairs. Trans-Relational Love Poem. Caroline Crumpacker. IIR

You are welcome to our country, dear Antonio. Duchess of Malfi, The. John Webster. NAEL-7v1

You are with me Oregon. Oregon. Bob Kaufman. EGAG; GT

You arrived that bad winter. Solstice. Gerald Dawe. PNI

You Art A Scholar, Horatio, Speak to It. Olena Kalytiak Davis. BAP-04

You ask. Rachel Tzvia Back. DTA

You ask how I spend my time. To Tu Fu from Shantung. Li Po. CrYelRi, *tr.* by Sam Hamill

You ask how it is. I will tell you. Blaen Cwrt. Gillian Clarke. AngWePo

You ask how old am I. Twice Times Then Is Now. Ibn Hazm al-Andalusi. OBVE; WoPoe, *tr.* by Omar S. Pound

You ask me how Contempt who claims to sleep. Epigram. James Vincent Cunningham. VCAP

You ask me how I became a madman. It happened thus. Madman (Prologue), The. Kahlil Gibran. TCAPo

You ask me how it is living in exile, friend. Eavesdropper. Breyten Breytenbach. PML; PoetW, *tr.* by Ernst van Heerden

You ask me my name? They got lotsa names. Madarika. Vince Gotera. OpBo; ReBoTo

You ask me, Queen, time after time. Kamalākānta Bhattācārya. SinGod, *tr.* by Rachel Fell McDermott

You ask me what I do, and how I live? Robert Herrick. CavPo

You ask me what I mean. Sujata Bhatt. PFTM-2 *Fr.* Search for My Tongue.

You ask me what I thought about. Kenneth Rexroth. APSN; APT-2; NAMCP V.1 *Fr.* Love Poems of Marichiko, The.

You ask me what since we must part. Gifts. Juliana Horatia Ewing. LW

You ask me why I'm always teasing you. Pretty Baby. Gustave Kahn. ReLy

You ask my wish—the boon I crave. Lady Caroline Lamb. RWP *Fr.* Fugitive Pieces and Reminiscences of Lord Byron with Some Original Poetry, Letters and Recollections of Lady Caroline Lamb, ed. I. Nathan.

You ask what I think of your new acquisition. Bitcherel. Eleanor Brown. MFPA; NeBl; StAl

You ask what our son's profession should be. Our Son's Profession. Ha Thi Thao. WoPoe, *tr.* by Nguyen Ngoc Bich

You ask: when to return? don't know when. Night Rains: A Letter to Go North. Li Shang-yin. ChinPo, *tr.* by Ye Weilian [or Yeh Wei-lien or Wai-lim Yip]

You ask which is better, whether a king or a senate rules. Neither, if, as. Quis Optimus Reipublicae Status. Sir Thomas More. PBRV

You ask why I don't hide my filthy charms? *Unknown.* PriapPo *Fr.* Priapus Poems, The.

You ask why I live. Questions Answered. Li Po. CrYelRi, *tr.* by Sam Hamill

You ask why I live. Conversation among the Mountains. Li Po. CCL1, *tr.* by David Young

You ask why I've settled in these emerald mountains. Mountain Dialogue. Li Po. NDACCP, *tr.* by David Hinton

You asked me once for something really Native. Connuche. Catron Grieves. ReEnLa

You asked me to sing. Song. Lorenzo Thomas. EGAG

You asked me what is the good of reading the Gospels in Greek. Readings. Czeslaw Milosz. GI, *tr.* by the author and Lillian Vallee

You asked neither for glory nor tears. Stanzas Against Forgetting. Guillaume Apollinaire. AF, *tr.* by Carolyn Forché

You asked us to hear the softest vocable of wind. Lines for Roethke Twenty Years after His Death. Duane Niatum. HATNAP

You at the Pump. Frank O'Hara. FTOS

You attribute my recovery. Therapy. John Wright. BloBone

You awoke. Day Within a Day. Fazil Hüsnü Daglarca. NaPG, *tr.* by Talat Sait Halman

You awoke at midnight. Beyond the window. Storm, A. Nikolai Nikolaevich Morshen. TCRusP, *tr.* by John Glad

You balanced her within a cyclone. Woman Seed Player. Roberta Hill Whiteman. HATNAP

You be like you, ever. Paul Celan. GTCP, *tr. by* John Felstiner

You be tellin' me You Be Black. Open Letter to All Black Poets, An. Samuel F. Reynolds. SpirFl

You beastly child, I wish you had miscarried. Lightly Bound. Stevie Smith. NALW

You Beauteous Dames. Jane Colman Turell. TCAPo

You beauteous dames, if that my love you see. You Beauteous Dames. Jane Colman Turell. TCAPo

You became / In many acts and quiet observances. My Company. Sir Herbert Read. PoWW

You began with the heavens. Heaven and Earth. Vera Pavlova. CRWP, *tr. by* Maura Dooley and Terence Dooley

You Begin. Margaret Atwood. NoP-4; NoP-5

You believed in your own story. Fairy Tales. "Shu Ting." VCWP

You belong to the tired, modern kind. Kind of Culture, A. Mihály Babits. IQMS, *tr. by* Peter Zollman

You, Benjamin Jones. Jon Dressel. AngWePo

You, Benjamin Jones, dead seventeen. You, Benjamin Jones. Jon Dressel. AngWePo

You bent to whisper to a small granddaughter. Hybrid Magnolias in Late April. Gibbons Ruark. PoDa

You bet I would! (LL) Rich Man, The. Franklin Pierce Adams. AmWit; NBLV

You Bet Your Life. Nancy Vieira Couto. PBCAP

You better check yourself, don't know what you're doing. Check Yourself. Lowell Fulson. ASA

You better sure shall live, not evermore. Horace. OBVE,

You Black Bright Stars. Thomas Morley. NoSic

You black bright stars, that shine while daylight lasteth. You Black Bright Stars. Thomas Morley. NoSic

You black-maned, horse-haired, long-faced creature. To the Gentlewoman of Llanarth Hall. Evan Thomas. OBWVE, *tr. by* Gwyn Jones

You blame me that I do not write. Letter to a Friend. Jon Stallworthy. NoAM

You blessed Soules, who stand before. Dame Clementia Cary. EMWP

You blockheads who ask what Buddha is. Asking the Way. Ko Un. WhBo

You bound strong sandals on my feet. Song. Sara Teasdale. PoBW

You Brandenburg's support and Prussia's guarantee. On the Entrance of the Castle Bridge. Simon Dach. GePo, *tr. by* George C. Schoolfield

You brave heroic [*or* heroique] minds. To the Virginian Voyage. Michael Drayton. BASC; NOSC; OBEV

(You brave heroic minds.) CABP

(You brave Heroique Minds.) PBRV

You brave Heroique Minds. Michael Drayton. *See* You brave heroic [*or* heroique] minds.

You breathe by words ten thousand times a day. And to Be Born Is Here an Unnameable Feast. Gonzalo Rojas. TCLAP, *tr. by* Christopher Maurer

You bright star of the space. Bright Star. Békes. IrPoTo

You Bring Me Back. Patti Tana. PasH

You bring me good news from the clinic. Face Lift. Sylvia Plath. BrAP

You bring me (neighbourly). Gifts. Thelma Tyfield. PoBW

You Bring Out the Mexican in Me. Sandra Cisneros. IllVoic; WaAnP

You bring the child back to its mother. (LL) Evening Star who gathers everything. Sappho. SaLy; WPoS, *tr. by* Diane Rayor

You brought sweetfish. EMJL, *tr. by* Haruo Shirane

You burned the dawn / with the flame of your guitar. Wake for Papa Montero. Nicolás Guillén. PFTM-1

You but unlock[e], so we each other bless[e]. (LL) To a Lady That Desired I Would Love Her. Thomas Carew. BASC; CavPo

You buy some flowers for your table. Samuel Hoffenstein. OBCoV *Fr.* Poems in Praise of Practically Nothing.

You buy yourself a new suit of clothes. Samuel Hoffenstein. OBCoV *Fr.* Poems in Praise of Practically Nothing.

You by my side subtracting miles traveled from miles to go. (LL) Indian Song. Major L. Jackson. FuFl; WaAnP

You call. Midnight. Terrance Hayes. BtF

You call yourself a church member. O Daniel. *Unknown.* SSUS

You called me a name on such and such a day—. For T.S.E. Only. Hyam Plutzik. APT-2; TaR

You Called Me *Corazón.* Sandra Cisneros. AmFaPo; RaF

You called me from lakes and hills. Reply to Prefect Liu. T'ao Ch'ien. CrYelRi, *tr. by* Sam Hamill

You Called to Me, Prison Windows. Danièle Amrane. HAWP, *tr. by* Eric Sellin

You Came a Long Way from St. Louis. Bob Russell. ReLy

You came a long way from St. Louis. You Came a Long Way from St. Louis. Bob Russell. ReLy

You came and did (well); I felt for you. Sappho. SaLy, *tr. by* Diane Rayor

You Came Down from the Mountains. Marcelle Ferry. SurWo, *tr. by* Myrna Bell Rochester

You came down from the mountains. You Came Down from the Mountains. Marcelle Ferry. SurWo, *tr. by* Myrna Bell Rochester

You came down to the earth when no one was listening. You Came Down. José Luis Hidalgo. RaW, *tr. by* Hardie St. Martin

You came into my life. First Night. Julia H. Ackerman. PasH

You came like a sweet bird to teach us. To My First Teacher. Tenshin Reb Anderson. WhBo

You came / to be / in the Month of Malcolm. Circling the Daughter. Etheridge Knight. OxAAAP

You came to it through wild country, there the sea's voice. House in the Green Well, The. John Hall Wheelock. MoAmPo

You came to me a little while before. Visit, The. Ibn Hazm al-Andalusi. WoPoe, *tr. by* Leticia Garza-Falcón and Christopher Middleton

You Came to Rest. Emilio Adolfo Westphalen. BLPSL, *tr. by* Rene de Costa, Rigas Kappatos and Eleni Paidoussi

You came to rest on a leaf of my body. You Came to Rest. Emilio Adolfo Westphalen. BLPSL, *tr. by* Rene de Costa, Rigas Kappatos and Eleni Paidoussi

You Came with Shells. June Jordan. NoAM

You can actually hear it in his voice. Leadbelly. Cornelius Eady. ESEAA

You can almost see him, looking as if well. Spell, The. William Burford. TiP2

You can always spot them, even from high up. From Altitude, the Diamonds. Richard Hugo. MoASP

You can become a shaman. New Indian Medicine. Emma Lee Warrior. HATNAP

You can come to terms with anyone. At the Cave. Artur Miedzyrzecki. PoSu

You Can Discover. Barbara Guest. BodElec

You can discover for yourself. You Can Discover. Barbara Guest. BodElec

You can find. As Dancers. Lisa Teasley. BtF

You can get lost in America. You Meet Yourself. Katie Donovan. NIrP

You can go back. Hope for refugees. Karen Press. TSAP

You can go now yes go now. Go east or west, go north or. Carl Sandburg. HHAm *Fr.* People, Yes, The.

You can go on holiday now, you can dabble in verse. Olesya Nikolayeva. CRWP, *tr. by* Catriona Kelly

You can hang or drown at last. (LL) Short Song of Congratulation, A [*or* To a Young Heir]. Samuel Johnson. NAEL-6v1; NPeEn; OBCoV; OBSV; OxAEP-1; OxBEV; TFi; WoPoe

You can hardly see him. Night Toad. Susan Wicks. MoWP; StAl

You can hate the sea as it floods. New Year's Eve, in Hospital. Philip Levine. MAAN

You Can Have It. Philip Levine. AmFaPo; CAP-8; EMP; NAMCP V.2; NoP-4; NoP-5; OxBoAm; VCAP

You can hear it but never see it. Spring Wind. Ho Hsun. CCL1, *tr. by* John Frodsham

You can hear the silence of it. David Jones. FaBoWar *Fr.* In Parenthesis.

You can imagine the gestures appropriate to this tale of injury. Concession to Perpetuity No. 166. Rod Mengham. VaPo

You can lead a horse to water but you can't make it hold. Symposium. Paul Muldoon. BeAl

You can make this swooped transition on your lips. Ted Berrigan. FTOS *Fr.* Sonnets, The.

You can move on in it. Labyrinth. Walter Helmut Fritz. GTCP, *tr. by* Reinhold Grimm

You can never choose away from. (LL) In the Orchard. Anne Stevenson. ColAP; WaAnP

You can never paint the same stroke. Crazy Jane Goes to Painting Class. Jane Hilberry. FiBr

You can no longer. Wreath, A. Gyula Illyés. IQMS, *tr. by* William Jay Smith

You can ride your hangover out. Mobile City. Machine Wilkins. ArBi

You Can Say That the Bird as the Saying Goes. Nicholás Maré. PML, *tr. by* Gilbert Wesley Purdy

You can say the broken word but cannot speak. Wheel. Michael Palmer. BodElec

You can say what you want about the evils of technology. Over Ohio. Michael C. Blumenthal. OtW

You can see all the way to heaven. (LL) Heaven. Cathy Song. NAAL-5; NIL-7; NoAM

You can see from their faces. Photographs of Pioneer Women. Ruth Dallas. BeAl

You can see her, hair down, sipping a Coke. What a Little Moonlight Can Do. Joe Heithaus. SeSe

You can see it in the faces of the valley rats. Los Angeles. Nick Van Brunt. FTtHH

You can see the face of everything, and it is white. Dawn Outside the City Walls. Juan Ramón Jiménez. RaW, *tr.* by Robert Bly

You can see them everywhere in Cuba. Landscapes. Heberto Padilla. VCWP

You can see why men are such monsters. St. Clare's Underwear. Barbara Hamby. ReTh

You can sense, after a slow apprenticeship. Sex. Ricardo Feierstein. PML, *tr.* by J. Kates and Stephen A. Sadow

You Can Start the Poetry Now, Or: News from Crazy Horse. Thomas McGrath. TAPaP

You can stroll home after sunset. (LL) Tea. Ch'u Ch'uang I. CCL1; NDACCP, *tr.* by Kenneth Rexroth

You can talk about. Visitors to the Black Belt. Langston Hughes. NAAL-5

You can talk to me of sin and related matters. (LL) Welshman in Exile Speaks, The. T. Harri Jones. AngWePo; OBWVE

You can tell by the angle. Londonderry Air, The. Nicolas Bentley. OBCoV

You cannot build bridges between the wandering islands. Wandering Islands, The. Alec Derwent Hope. HarvBoo

You cannot call it love, for at your age. Mark Antony's Valentine. Steven Marx. IaFF

You cannot fall. 13. Jennifer Murphy. BRtP

You cannot hope. British Journalist, The. Humbert Wolfe. OBCoV; OxBEV

You cannot light a match on a crumbling wall. (LL) British Leftish Poetry, 1930–40. Hugh MacDiarmid. NAMCP V.1; NoAM

You cannot recognise me now. Streams in the Desert. Christine de Luca. EdScPo

You can't be serIous she said. John Cage. APT-2 *Fr.* Composition in Retrospect.

You can't beat English lawns. Our final hope. Rolling the Lawn. William Empson. HarvBoo; MoBrPo; OBGa

You can't blow up the buddha. Mark S. Kuhar. AmZen

You can't catch the thief, Mind. Mahendranāth Bhattācārya. SinGod, *tr.* by Rachel Fell McDermott

You can't do English much. Why Do You Want to Be English? Peter Finch. Oth

You can't drive through a rainbow I said hills to myself in the mountains. Fred Wah. IFF; NLPA *Fr.* This Dendrite Map: Father / Mother Haibun.

You can't escape chickens. Chickens are all the rage. Alone in. Chickens Everywhere. Richard Garcia. SUP

You Can't Escape Your Life Record. Manila Koordada. WoPoe

You Can't Get a Man with a Gun. Irving Berlin. ReLy

You can't get rid of it. Hope. Dolores de Iruretagoyena de Humphrey. ReBoTo

You Can't Go Back to Sleep. T. Cole Rachel. BeDoSh

You can't hang a heavy mirror. June. Monica Raymond. PfS

You can't just call it a pig. James Dean and the Pig. Joseph Like. ReTh

You can't just go into the shoestore and say. Shoes, The. Nina Nyhart. PfS

You Can't Kill a Baby Twice. Dahlia Ravikovitch. VCWP

You can't leave your home. Side 20. Víctor Hernández Cruz. PueRic

You can't look at yourself. Federico García Lorca. PFTM-1 *Fr.* Night (Suite for Piano and Poet's Voice).

You Can't Make Love by Wireless. George Grossmith and P. G. Wodehouse. ReLy

You can't negate negation. 93. Shih Shu. CSKM, *tr.* by James H. Sanford

You can't say it that way any more. And "Ut Pictura Poesis" Is Her Name. John Ashbery. EMP; VCAP

You can't spend all day staring into the sea, however. War. Michael Brownstein. FTOS

You can't step out of your tragedy, it wouldn't be a tragedy. Good Night, Star. Michael Earl Craig. IIR

You Can't Stop Me from Lovin' You. Mann Holiner. ReLy

You can't stop people from talking. Say It Isn't So. Irving Berlin. ReLy

You can't take her out for a night on the town. Cathleen. Nuala Ni Dhomhnaill. ModIr, *tr.* by Paul Muldoon

You can't take with you. Paavo Haavikko. WoPoe, *tr.* by Anselm Hollo

You can't talk about it, but you live it. Root, The. Luis Rosales. RaW, *tr.* by Ralph Nelson and Rita García Nelson

You can't walk barefoot in the city. Barefoot in the City. Lisa Buscani. AmPoNex

You can't write. You can't open a magazine. Two in a Room. Viktor Krivulin. TCRusP, *tr.* by Anna Barker and Daniel Weissbort

You cared whether I died or not. Martha Anthony. InTrad

You cathedral, you! Pure astonishment! To Freedom. Ágnes Nemes Nagy. PoSu, *tr.* by Bruce Berlind

You change a life. To Judgement: An Assay. Jane Hirshfield. AmZen

You chinchilla in the marketplace in france. Song of the Chinchilla. Lisa Jarnot. LegDan

You chose the taste of dust. Footnotes. Arkadii Dragomoschenko. ItGoST, *tr.* by Elena Balashova and Lyn Hejinian

You clambered into the glass of whisky. Glass. Anne Rouse. NeBl

You climb. Reply to Gen'no Osho's Poem. Muso Soseki. EaWin, *tr.* by W. S. Merwin

You closed the door. Poem for My Father. Toi Derricotte. LiTh

You coax the blues right out of the horn. Mame. Jerry Herman. ReLy

You come down, after. Wisdom of Shelley, The. George Elliott Clarke. OpeFie

You come from a line of. Power. Alma Villanueva. ItWoWo

You Come from My Village. Wang Wei. CCL1, *tr.* by C. H. Kwock and Vincent McHugh

You come from poets, kings, bankrupts, preachers. For My Son. Muriel Rukeyser. TaR

You come from the ages' origin. Going Forth. Andrée Chedid. PoArWo, *tr.* by Lucy McNair

You come late. "H. D." GifTon *Fr.* Priest.

You come to a place in winter woods. Another Place. Paul Zimmer. PfSP

You come to fetch me from my work tonight. Putting in the Seed. Robert Frost. APT-1; IPoFL; NAMCP V.1; NoAM; OxBoAm

You come to in the past, dark, where the fires still burn. Train Wreck, 1890: My Grandmother Lies Down with the Dead. T. R. Hummer. GM

You come to me at night. Bitch, A. Anna Swirszczynska [*or* Swir]. GifTon, *tr.* by Czeslaw Milosz and Leonard Nathan

You come to me from the oldest wound of wind. Breath. Deema K. Shehabi. PoArWo

You come to Paris, you come to play. You don't Know Paree. Cole Porter. ReLy

You come with the light on your face. Wave, The. Witter Bynner. APT-1

You conclude by saying. Ending by Pound, An. Tedi López Mills. RMCMP, *tr.* by C. M. Mayo

You could be sitting now in a carrel. Late Aubade, A. Richard Wilbur. BrAP; SoSe-8

You could call it abandon, but never leisure. Life of the Body, The. Diane Bonds. PoSol

You could draw a straight line from the heels. Man Lying on a Wall. Michael Longley. ModIr; NPeEn; PNI

You could have been just another maggot. Modern Sorcery. Charles Simic. StAl

You Could Have Been Me. Belle Waring. PoDa

You could live in a world so solidly blue. (LL) Falling. Lesley Dauer. AmPoNex; NAPBL

You could love here, not the lovely goat. Milltown Union Bar, The. Richard Hugo. NoAM

You could mount him like a park bench. Steel Horse. Dana Gelinas. SPV, *tr.* by Jen Hofer

You could play that woman thing all the way. Madam President. Boadiba. OGAHCP, *tr.* by the author and Jack Hirschman

You could say that the streets flow softly in the night. Los Angeles Nocturne. Xavier Villaurrutia. TCLAP, *tr.* by Rachel Benson

You could see him, walking between the rifles. Crime Was in Granada, The. Antonio Machado Ruiz. SpanPo, *tr.* by Kate Flores

You could turn this way. Basho. EH, *tr.* by Robert Hass

You Couldn't Be Cuter. Dorothy Fields. ReLy

You couldn't find a better time to meet me, Marcus. Pacifico Massimi. CAGL *Fr.* Hecateleguim.

You count the fingers first: it's traditional. Counting. Fleur Adcock. BeAl

You cradle mouthless smiling flowers. Winter Sunflowers. Gillian Ferguson. NeBl

You crash over the trees. Storm. "H. D." APT-1

You crown me king and queen. There is a name. Dedicace. Aleister Crowley. CAGL

You cry, *She's bred in the Old Way*. To Novella, on Her Saying Deridingly, that a Lady of Great Merit, and Fine Address, Was Bred in the Old Way. An Epigram. Mary Barber. NIL-7

You Cry, Whine, Peer Strangely at Me. Philodemus. WoPoe, *tr.* by George Economou

You cry, whine, peer strangely at me. You Cry, Whine, Peer Strangely at Me. Philodemus. WoPoe, *tr.* by George Economou

You cut off your feelings for your parents to enter the priesthood. Haesunja Asks for an Enlightenment Song. Master Naong. BecRai, *tr.* by Kim Daljin, Kim Won-Chung and Christopher Merrill

You dance anger chanting. Ballerina. Rosario Ferré. TANSG, *tr.* by Nancy Diaz

You danced a magnetic dance. So Many Feathers. Jayne Cortez. ISC

You dare not let your eyes meet theirs. Women Are Different. Marsha Prescod. LW

You dark mouth inside me. Mood of Depression, The. Georg Trakl. WED, *tr.* by Robert Bly

You, dead in '92 and '93. Arthur Rimbaud. OBWP *Fr.* Eighteen-Seventy.

You decline to write poetry, won't listen to sutras. Admonishing a Younger Teacher. Ch'i-chi. CSKM, *tr.* by Burton Watson

You deserve and.　Alex Rawls.　AnSo *Fr.* What's Your Sign?

You did it, didn't you?　Passacaglia.　Don Hymans.　BAP-97

You did not bend.　Elegy for Joan.　Anthony Walton.　RD

You did not come.　Broken Appointment, A.　Thomas Hardy.　HarvBoo; NAEL-6v2; NAEL-7v2; NAMCP V.1; NoAM; NoP-4; NoP-5; PtR

You did not come to the Paris exposition of 1937 on the opening night when I asked you.　Kay Boyle.　SurPaPo *Fr.* Complaint for Mary and Marcel, A.

You Did Not Find Me.　Rabindranath Tagore.　WoPoe, *tr. by* Pratimer Bowes

You did not find me, you did not.　You Did Not Find Me.　Rabindranath Tagore.　WoPoe, *tr. by* Pratimer Bowes

You did not know we loved you. (LL)　We Assume: On the Death of Our Son, Reuben Masai Harper.　Michael S. Harper.　CAP-8; GT; NAMCP V.2; OxAAAP

You did not open the door.　In the Night.　Carmela Raàm-Lachish.　NRoS, *tr. by* Esther Raizen

You did not see Him on the mountain of Transfiguration.　To the Good Thief.　Saunders Lewis.　OBWVE, *tr. by* Gwyn Morgan

You did not walk with me.　Walk, The.　Thomas Hardy.　NAEL-6v2; NAEL-7v2; NPeEn; OxBEV

You did not want to remember.　Late Words for My Sister.　Robin Becker.　ExTi

You Didn't Fit.　Susan Musgrave.　NIL-7

You didn't show.　Little Magic, A.　Steve Jonas.　EGAG

You died in spring, father, and now the autumn dies.　American Sonnets for My Father.　Daniela Gioseffi.　UnSA

You died of a bomb blast in Nagasaki, and there were parades. (LL)　To World War Two.　Kenneth Koch.　BAP-01; OxBoAm; PWW2

You died without my knowing.　Elegy for My Friend E. Galo.　Raymond Mazisi Kunene.　PoetW

You died young, uncle, only fifty-two.　Profaning the Dead.　Carole Bernstein.　AmPoNex

You dive in, head for the other side, sure.　Pregnant Poets Swim Lake Tarleton, New Hampshire.　Barbara Ras.　NAPBL

You do look a little ill[, now].　Alcohol.　Franz Wright.　AmAlph

You do not always know what I am feeling.　For Grace, after a Party.　Frank O'Hara.　CAP-8

You do not do, you do not do.　Daddy.　Sylvia Plath.　BeAl; BrAP; CAP-8; ColAP; HeIP-4; HP; MakPoe; MoWP; NAAL-5; NALW; NAMCP V.2; NIL-7; NIP-4; NoAM; NoP-4; NoP-5; OxBoAm; PoPoPo; TFi; VCAP; WaAnP

You do not have to be good.　Wild Geese.　Mary Oliver.　BLT; GoPo; PoCu; TWF

You do not have to be good.　Wild Geese.　Mary Oliver.　StAl

You do not hear me, Dad. (LL)　Child to His Sick Grandfather, A.　Joanna Baillie.　CABP; RACG; WoRP

You do not know how hard it is.　Intimations of Anxiety.　Laila Al-Saih.　PoArWo, *tr. by* May Jayyusi and Naomi Shihab Nye

You do not know / I die? (LL)　Minstrel Man.　Langston Hughes.　AmFaPo; ItP

You do not move about, but try.　Getting Lost in Nazi Germany.　Marvin Bell.　TaR

You do peruse the rest? (LL)　I. W. To her unconstant Lover.　Isabella Whitney.　EMWP; PBRV

You do understand I've waited long enough.　Complaint: To the Muse.　Philip Whalen.　BB

You, Doctor Martin, walk.　You, Doctor Martin.　Anne Sexton.　MoAmPo

You doe looke (my son) in a mov'd sort.　William Shakespeare.　OxBEV

You don't even have any sins!　Géza Páskándi.　IQMS *Fr.* Language Memory.

You don't find so many of them on regular days, in normal months.　New Year's Season and Its Poetasters, The.　Trần Tế Xu'o'ng.　WoPoe, *tr. by* Nguyen Ngoc Bich

You don't have "bad" days and "good" days.　Jelaluddin Rumi.　IJHIL, *tr. by* Coleman Barks

You don't have syphilis. the doctor says.　D. A. Powell.　FaoP

You don't have to be awake.　New Year's Morning.　Elmaz Abinader.　PoArWo

You don't have to give me your seat, lady.　Don't, Don't.　Huan Fu.　PML, *tr. by* Zhang Cuo

You don't have to go very far.　Some Sights Sometimes Seen and Seldom Seen.　William Cole.　TLR

You don't have to know a person. Out this far.　Customs of the Country.　Del Marie Rogers.　TiP2

You don't have to listen to folk stories.　I Saw It!　Ilya L'vovich Selvinsky.　TCRusP, *tr. by* Denis Johnson

You don't have to understand a nightingale's song.　Speech.　Leopold Staff.　PoSu, *tr. by* Adam Czerniawski

You don't Kill Babies Twice.　Dahlia Ravikovitch.　NRoS, *tr. by* Esther Raizen

You don't know I pretend my dumb.　Plea to Those Who Matter.　James Welch.　WaAnP

You don't Know Paree.　Cole Porter.　ReLy

You don't know that I felt good.　Lorenz Hart.　*See* Sleepless nights, The.

You don't Know What Happened When You Froze.　Ansel Talvikki.　NeAmPo

You don't know what it was like.　Ugly Step Sister, The.　Denise Duhamel.　SweBea

You don't Know What Love Is.　Ken Harris.　AnSo

You don't Know What Love Is.　Don Raye.　ReLy

You don't know what love is.　You don't Know What Love Is.　Don Raye.　ReLy

You don't remember what you did.　Intermission from Friday.　Pedro Juan Pietri.　PueRic

You don't see buffalo skulls very much any more.　Something Starting Over.　Thomas Hornsby Ferril.　APT-2

You don't see it.　Poverty.　Julia Darling.　RSaN

You, don't sing.　Song.　Nakano Shigeharu.　CAoMJL1, *tr. by* Miriam Silverberg

You Don't Understand Me.　Marge Piercy.　NALW

You don't want madhouse and the whole thing there. (LL)　Let It Go.　William Empson.　HarvBoo; NPeEn; OxBEV

You don't Want to Hear a Poem, Do You?　Don Weinstock.　SUP

You don't want to know how quiet my life's become.　Tracy and Joe.　Lisa Lewis.　SUP

You draw me skating on the sky through a black mirror.　Britain 1967.　Anna Mendelssohn.　VaPo

You dream someone is leaving you, though he says kindly, *It's not that you're cold.*　Estrangement.　Jane Cooper.　ExTi

You dreamed of drowning there, but couldn't read.　Another Version of an Ocean.　Reginald Shepherd.　NeAmPo

You dreamed the sound of your own name.　Whatever Light.　Stephen Corey.　IaFF

You dreamt of being a dancer, but frightened.　Abused Child.　Michael O'Reilly.　BloBone

You drift from youth into manhood.　Unnoticed.　Miklós Radnóti.　PoChi, *tr. by* Stephen Berg, S. J. Marks and Steven Polgar

You drifted from across the sea.　*Bui Doi*, Dust of Life.　Yusef Komunyakaa.　AmWaPo

You drifted lazily from the sky.　Looking Back.　Joanna Kadi.　PoArWo

You drink from crystal.　Laurie Duggan.　BMAP *Fr.* Epigrams of Martial, The.

You drink to piss it all away.　Anacreontic.　R. S. Gwynn.　RA

You drink wind to empty yourself.　Cicada.　Yi Illo.　CATKP, *tr. by* Peter H. Lee

You drive in across this bridge they've built.　Welcome to Wales.　John Tripp.　AngWePo

You drive, the road aims for a mountain.　View, A.　Mona Van Duyn.　VCAP

You each guardian Fay shall bless. (LL)　Inscription in a Beautiful Retreat Called Fairy Bower.　Hannah More.　NoP-4; NoP-5

You eat me, your.　Mother Love.　Elaine Feinstein.　HarvBoo

You endless torments that my rest opress.　Mary Sidney Wroth, Countess of Montgomery.　NoP-5 *Fr.* Pamphilia to Amphilanthus.

You enter the door.　Temporary Insanity.　Tanai Sanders.　BRtP

You envied the flying birds and stones.　Bakhyt Kenjeev.　ItGoST, *tr. by* Nina Kossman

You excellent women, you valiant men.　Walther von der Vogelweide.　GePo

You excommunicate the Spleen. (LL)　Matthew Green.　NoP-4; NoP-5 *Fr.* Spleen, The.

You exquisite girl, dressed absurdly deliciously artifically.　Sweet Disorder in the Dress, A.　Harry Hooton.　NOBAu

You, Failed Pronoun.　Eleanor Wilner.　ExTi

You Fascinate Me So.　Carolyn Leigh.　ReLy

You fear.　Qaus-e Qazah.　Shajahana Begum.　HotL, *tr. by* V. Narayana Rao

You feed us milkfish stew.　Milkfish.　Eugene Gloria.　OpBo

You feel adequate to the demands of this position?　You Will Be Hearing from Us Shortly.　U. A. Fanthorpe.　OBCoV

You Figure It Out.　Betsy Sholl.　PfS

You fill me up so much.　Where the Mississippi meets the Amazon.　Ntozake Shange.　ISC

You find a box beneath the bed.　Emma and the Radio.　James Priory.　RWPCtW

You find them in the darker woods.　Persistence of Nature in Our Lives, The.　Andrew Hudgins.　WeW-3

You Finish It: I Can't.　Daniel Berrigan.　PLBUT

You first, shift your attention (that is, if you withdraw).　Angelo Lumelli.　ItPo, *tr. by* Gayle Ridinger

You fit into me.　You Fit into Me.　Margaret Atwood.　IFF; NALW; NAMCP V.2; NoAM

You fix a Dagger in my Heart.　To the Same; Enquiring Why I Wept.　Mary Masters.　PoBW

You fled this island in a bark.　Verdict of Stone, A.　Tanure Ojaide.　NAfrP

You float inside your water.　Fanny Howe.　FTOS *Fr.* O'Clock.

You fold your clipped wings in your father's house. Departure. Edgar Silex. NAPBL

You follow me as I come and go. Song for My Shadow, A. Kim Pyŏngyŏn. CATKP; WoPoe, *tr.* by Richard John Lynn

You for eternity, and have no other choice? (LL) Obit. Robert Lowell. PoetW; VCAP

You, for My Meditation. Sara de Ibáñez. TCLAP, *tr.* by Andrew Rosing

You force me to touch. Finished. Ai. CAP-8

You forgot where you lived at. Intermission from Saturday. Pedro Juan Pietri. PueRic

You found it difficult to woo. Daphnis and Chloe. Haniel Long. APT-1

You gather them in the shade of pine trees. Eating Roasted *Matsutake* Mushrooms. Ishikawa Jōzan. WoPoe, *tr.* by Jonathan Chaves

You gave and gave. After the End of It. Anne Stevenson. StAl

You gave Bithynicus thousands yearly; still. Martial. RomPo, *tr.* by J. P. Sullivan

You gave me a love bite the week. From *Rice*. Joan Logghe. ICANM

You Gave Me Hyacinths First a Year Ago. Dorothy Hewett. BMAP

You get a wife, you get a house. Cat, The. Ogden Nash. WHSW

You get comfortable beneath the snow. Constellations of Self, The. Tracy Philpot. IAoNAP

You get money. Alex Rawls. AnSo *Fr.* What's Your Sign?

You get these thoughts in melancholy Autumn. Together Again. Victor Vroomkoning. TuT, *tr.* by James Simmons

You Get What You Pay For. Allen Curnow. HarvBoo

You gets no bread with. One Meat Ball. Thomas Lux. ReTh

You girls. At the Makeshift Aid Station. Tōge Sankichi. AtGh, *tr.* by Richard H. Minear

You give the appearance of listening. Evening Walk. Charles Simic. PoA 2002

You glow in my heart. Bungler, The. Amy Lowell. LW

You glutton up my stairs. Interruption. Sarah Fox. PfS

You go between wet hands. Fish. José Luis Hidalgo. RaW, *tr.* by Ralph Nelson

You go by the local line. Charles Tomlinson. WoBe *Fr.* Zipangu.

You go down the hall. Annie Dillard. UpMys *Fr.* Tickets for a Prayer Wheel.

You go down to go up. Booster. Bill Berkson. NYP2

You go home one evening tired from work. Turtle Soup. Marilyn Chin. LoL

You go into the shy hills. Stability. Tim Lilburn. OpeFie

You go into your parents' house. Self-Portrait in the Doorway. Homero Aridjis. WoBe, *tr.* by George McWhirter

You go--it seems to me--with a hint. Disconnections. Silvana Colonna. ItPo, *tr.* by Gayle Ridinger

You go to high school, even college. Samuel Hoffenstein. AmWit *Fr.* Poems in Praise of Practically Nothing.

You Go to My Head. Haven Gillespie. ReLy

You go to my head. You Go to My Head. Haven Gillespie. ReLy

You go to my head, the song says: I wouldn't take. Three A.M. Eternal. Reginald Shepherd. WiU

You go up there cocked. Swinging on the First Pitch. Dabney Stuart. MoASP

You gods of sea and sky—what's left me now but prayer? Ovid. RomPo *Fr.* Tristia.

You golden freedom, both my wish and my desire. Martin Opitz. GePo

You gon find out. (LL) Super High. Evan X. Hyde. OWABP; PML

You got to walk that lonesome valley. Lonesome Valley. *Unknown.* APN-2

You Gotta Have Your Tips on Fire. Víctor Hernández Cruz. PueRic, *tr.* by Julio Marzán and Carmen Valle

You gotta watch / out for the "Ol Liver." (LL) Welcome Back, Mr. Knight: Love of My Life. Etheridge Knight. LaCa; PBCAP; RaBo

You grow impatient while I focus, fiddle. You Have Shown Me a Strange Image, and We Are Strange Prisoners. Jeni Couzyn. PBCAP

You grow less agile, more compliant. Exile, Representative. Breyten Breytenbach. AF, *tr.* by Denis Hirson

You gulp, a frog suddenly on my dinner. You Don't Understand Me. Marge Piercy. NALW

You had a country touch, a Yankee air. Frost. Laurence Snydal. VisFro

You had a skirt with flounces. Another Kind of Skin. Frances Sackett. Prnts

You had no independence. To My Old Poems. Kenneth Koch. PoA 2002

You had to stop giving blood. On the Road to Denver in a Coat and Tie, I Think of My Old Friend Master Red Pine and the Example He Inspires. Mike O'Connor. WANABP

You had wanted to go back, to step. Positions of the Body, 8. Carol Snow. ASA

You hang back, call me. Bathing My Mother. Frances Wilson. Prnts

You happened to me. I was happened to. Nearly a Valediction. Marilyn Hacker. PoDa

You Hated Spain. Ted Hughes. EmeKit

You have a good vagina. It makes me crazy. Sex. Viki Radden. BtF

You have a lovely and familiar gravity. From a Distance I Can See. Jennifer Moxley. IIR

You have all read the beautiful story. Beautiful Texas. Wilbert Lee O'Daniel. TiP2

You have an idea of yourself. Only Fortunate Thing, The. Joe Wenderoth. BodElec

You have anti-freeze in the car, yes. Christmas Card. Ted Hughes. OBCP

You have as many defects as a pig has lice and you will rub against me in vain to get. To My Love. Kjell Hjern. PML, *tr.* by Leif Sjöberg and William Jay Smith

You have been declining the land's. Hod Carrier, The. John Ashbery. AHA

You have been gone for years. Hotel. Jane Rohrer. ACAMVP

You have begun to wonder, a glass world. Noah. Ricardo Pau-Llosa. Vesp

You have bicycled off a cliff. Your Wife, a Widow, Waits for You. Jesse Lee Kercheval. SUP

You have called at the gate of the True Vehicle. Saying Good-bye to a Singing Girl Who Has Decided to Become a Nun. Mo Shih-lung. ColAnChi; WoPoe, *tr.* by Jonathan Chaves

You have come back to me older and sadder in the drowsy. Coming Back of an Assassinated Poet, The. Rafael Alberti. RaW, *tr.* by Mark Strand

You have confessed, and by a recent Act. Samuel Carter. STuOW *Fr.* Arthur Mervyn; A Tale of Social Grievances.

You have considered the lilies of the field. Consider. Andrew Hudgins. UpMys

You have consumed my mouth but are not satisfied. *Unknown.* SLW, *tr.* by Marjolijn De Jager, Sayd Bahodin Majrouh and André Velter

You have decided to live. This is your fifth. Recovery. Marie Howe. LaCa

You have edited a thousand pages of palm-leaf manuscripts. To the Monk Wu-hsia on the Occasion of His Editing the Lotus Sutra. Mo Shih-lung. ColAnChi, *tr.* by Jonathan Chaves

You have forty-nine days between. In the Park. Maxine W. Kumin. CAP-8

You have gone. Ah, you have gone. Your Silence. Han Yong'un [or Yongwun]. CAMKP, *tr.* by Sammy Solberg

You have gone, old tooth. My Last Tooth. *Unknown.* VerBaPo

You have heard it said before. Handle for the Flutist, A. Odia Ofeimun. HBAPE

You have heard the story of Jesse James. Story of Bonnie and Clyde, The. Bonnie Parker. TiP2

You have here no otherness. James Vincent Cunningham. APT-2

You have left the train too early. Meeting Place. Pauline Hawkesworth. Prnts

You have lips like a drop of water. Courtesy. Alexander Gerov. CSCBP, *tr.* by Georgi Belev and Lisa Sapinkopf

You have lived a long time. Farewell to Monk Chih-Hsing. Chia Tao. CSKM, *tr.* by Mike O'Connor

You Have Lost, They Tell Me, Your Reason. Rosario Ferré. TANSG, *tr.* by Patricia Santoro

You have lost, they tell me, your reason. You Have Lost, They Tell Me, Your Reason. Rosario Ferré. TANSG, *tr.* by Patricia Santoro

You have made God small. Raptor. Ronald Stuart Thomas. EmeKit

You Have No Horses. *Teton Sioux Oral Tradition.* NAAPv.2

You have no right to trouble me. Magic Formula. *Unknown.* CA

You have nothing to do with me, alas. Lőrinc Szabó. IQMS *Fr.* Cricket Music.

You have now come with me, I have now come with you. Poet: A Lying Word. Laura Riding Jackson. HarvBoo

You have obviously been here. Stopping by Fields on a Snowy Afternoon. Jane Rohrer. ACAMVP

You have oh haven't we every tenacious moment wet revolve trying. You Oh Even. Marianne Vitale. HeMarv

You have only to wait, they will find you. Messengers. Louise Glück. ColAP; VCAP; WaAnP

You have power politics, Paul. Lorine Niedecker. FTOS

You have rented an apartment. Cabbage, The. Ruth Stone. PoChi

You have said; but whether wisely or no, let the forest judge. Enter Celia, with a Writing. Bin Ramke. RoV

You have seen / somewhere so lush. Somewhere So Lush. Lee Upton. AmAlph

You Have Shown Me a Strange Image, and We Are Strange Prisoners. Jeni Couzyn. PBCAP

You have stolen their souls with your eyes. (LL) Seizing the Day. Judith Ortiz Cofer. PueRic; SwNoth

You have stopped beating the drums. Anno Domini MCMXLVII. Salvatore Quasimodo. GI, *tr.* by Jack Bevan

You have taken our love and turned it into coins of silver. Poet's Wife, A. Cho Wen-chun. NAAPv.2, *tr.* by Amy Lowell

You have ten seconds. Ten Seconds. Rohan B. Preston. WaCA

You have the cool clear eyes. I Believe in You. Frank Loesser. ReLy

You have the emergence in human society. Police State. M-1 and Sticman. FTtHH

You have the light of my life, in your clear and pleasing face, and don't see me. Cecco Nuccoli. CAGL, *tr.* by Jill Claretta Robbins

You Have the Lovers. Leonard Cohen. BrAP

You have the right to remain silent. Body Cavity. Martin Ross. IIR

You have to be able to hear past the pain, the obvious. Dissidence. Anthony Walton. NAPBL; RD

You have to be healthy to stretch a cord. Saint Vitus's Dance in October 10. Leonard Nolens. TuT, *tr.* by Michael O'Loughlin

You have to begin somewhere. Lonely Tylenol. Peter Gizzi. ReTh; VaPo

You have to believe children of the Olmecs once dreamed too. Tulum Saw the Coming. Alan Napier. AtGh

You have to go down without fear. You Have to Go Down. José Luis Hidalgo. RaW, *tr.* by Herbert Baird and William Stafford

You have to inhabit poetry. Making Poetry. Anne Stevenson. MoWP

You have to learn. The trees in winter. Winter Trees. Ágnes Nemes Nagy. IQMS, *tr.* by Adam Makkai

You have to leave this space to its own fruition. Speak. Pierre Albert Jourdan. YaTCFP, *tr.* by Mary Ann Caws

You have to quit talking. You have to. Quilts. Kathleen Peirce. PBCAP

You Have to Strike Back. Kate Lilley. BMAP

You Have Touched My Skin. Shakuntala Hawoldar. HAWP

You have touched my skin. You Have Touched My Skin. Shakuntala Hawoldar. HAWP

You have turned our land into a desolate place. Desolation. Jack Davis. BMAP

You Have Your Calamity And I Have Mine. Murad Mikha'il. IrPoTo, *tr.* by Christina Coyle and Sadok Masliyah

You have your calamity, with its shower of evils. You Have Your Calamity And I Have Mine. Murad Mikha'il. IrPoTo, *tr.* by Christina Coyle and Sadok Masliyah

You have your hat and coat on and she says she will be right down. Evening Out, The. Ogden Nash. MoAmPo

You have your language too. Wellfleet Whale, The. Stanley Kunitz. CAP-8; NoAM

You haven't finished your ape, said mother to father, who had. Ape. Russell Edson. PmAP; RaBo; SUP

You hear him cry in the. Four O'Clock, New Year's Morning, New River Beach. Elisabeth Harvor. Coast

You hear that heroic big land music? Poem. Alice Notley. PmAP

You hear the chain striking the wall. Well, The. Yves Bonnefoy. VCWP, *tr.* by John Naughton

You hear the hollow hoofbeats of. Lost Horseman, The. Endre Ady. IQMS, *tr.* by Anton N. Nyerges

You hear the scraping of my bicycle. Moving Out. Martha Ramsey. PfS

You hear them kids over there laugh this old woman? Lament for the Drowned Country. Mary Durack. NOBAu

You hear? Tomorrow, they say? No Dream. Maria Mikhailovna Shkapskaya. ARWW, *tr.* by Catriona Kelly

You heard it for the first time. Unaccompanied Suite. Barbara Winder. MiVo

You heard the gentleman, with automatic percision, speak the truth. 1933. Kenneth Fearing. APT-2; FTtHH

You Hebrews are too snug in Ur. Joshua at Shechem. Charles Reznikoff. ChIV-1

You held my lotus blossom. To the tune "Soaring Clouds." Huang O. EroLit

You hike along the tops of cliffs above the sea, over miles of green meadows dotted with buttercups and ramshackle fences. Ballybunion. B. J. Atwood-Fukuda. FreRad

You hire a cook, but she can't cook yet. Samuel Hoffenstein. OBCoV *Fr.* Poems in Praise of Practically Nothing.

You Hit the Spot. Mack Gordon. ReLy

You hitch a ride with a cyclist. You sit in back. In Your Racing Dream. Richard Hugo. BodElec

You hold a thousand miles. August on Sourdough, a Visit from Dick Brewer. Gary Snyder. LoL; NAAL-5

You hold it like a lit bulb. Jar of Honey, A. Jacob Polley. BeAl

You hold out to each prisoner like a cup of light? (LL) Heat. Denis Johnson. MakPoe; SwNoth

You holding me. (LL) Hawk's Shadow. Louise Glück. HarvBoo; StAl

You hover above the page staring. Like God. Lynn Emanuel. PuP-23

You hungry You thirsty Turn. (LL) Two Girls. Suzanne Gardinier. KGB; NeAmPo

You hurried through my twenties as if there were nowhere to look. To Old Age. Kenneth Koch. PoCho

You, hypocrite lecteur! mon semblable! mon frère! (LL) For T.S.E. Only. Hyam Plutzik. APT-2; TaR

You (I). Tom Clark. PmAP *Fr.* You.

You I give no name to / The mysterious things within you / are an untrodden bower. Ahmad al-Mushari al-'Udwani. BBASP *Fr.* Signs.

You I give no name to / The mysterious things within you / are fragrance, light and melody. Ahmad al-Mushari Al-'Udwani. BBASP *Fr.* Signs.

You I know is losing you, The. Ivano Fermini. ItPo, *tr.* by Gayle Ridinger

You, I, Love, Beauty, Earth. Rita Joe. Coast

You, I presume, could adroitly and gingerly. Aristophanes. FaBoWar *Fr.* Lysistrata.

You idiot! What makes you think decay will. Basil Bunting. StAl

You in despair, take heart! Life shall renew. Seer, The. János Batsányi. IQMS, *tr.* by John Fuller

You in My Dream. Nanduri Subbarao. HotL, *tr.* by V. Narayana Rao

You / in the night. You. Nelly Sachs. AF, *tr.* by Matthew Mead *and* Ruth Mead

You, in the old photographs, are always. U. A. Fanthorpe. MoWP; Prnts *Fr.* Stations Underground.

You! Inez! Alice Moore Dunbar-Nelson. NAAPv.2

You intend, it seems. *Unknown.* ArkPo, *tr.* by Helen Craig McCullough

You introduced me to my first goddess. In memoriam Akbar Babool. Wopko Jensma. TSAP

You jerk me. Ringmaster's Wife. Fatima Lim-Wilson. ReBoTo

You jerk you didn't call me up. Sonnet. Bernadette Mayer. OxBoAm

You Keep Coming upon Your Breath at the Altar. George Kalamaras. Vesp

You keep me waiting in a truck. Twenty-Year Marriage. Ai. CAP-8; GT; NAMCP V.2; NoAM; WaAnP

You keep watch from this room. Existing. Alejandra Pizarnik. MirDau, *tr.* by Roberta Gordenstein

You kept your hats, a fine assortment. Nest of Hats, A. Annie Foster. NLP

You kept your tools sequestered. Spirit Level, The. David Barber. AmPoNex

You killed the Dalmatian puppy. Dogs, The. Afaa Michael Weaver. PBCAP

You kissed me once and now I wait for more. Zodiac. Elizabeth Alexander. FFC

You kissed me once by mistake. Make the Man Love Me. Dorothy Fields. ReLy

You kissed my mouth as if it were my sex. Rubyfruit. Jenny Factor. CalPo

You knew he. Lying in Small Pieces. Carol Bell. GeoH

You knew I was coming for you, little one. Windigo. Louise Erdrich. NAMCP V.2; NoAM; PoPoPo

You Know. Valerie Graham. PfS

You know all those sonnets the ones where I said, I love you, well. Sonnet. Tom Devaney. AmPoNex

You know, dear, that this vicious world. Mrs. Myrick's Lecture. Mary E. Tucker. CBWP-1

You know every fruit grows more handsome in the light of the sun. (LL) That Journeys Are Good. Jelaluddin Rumi. RaBo; WED, *tr.* by Robert Bly

You know his destination by the hardness of his sleeve (right). His sleeve. Dinogon. Michael Portnoy. HeMarv

You know how in the zoo most of the polar bears. One Polar Bear, The. Peter Sears. OPRER

You know how the mad come into a room. Beanstalk Country, The. Tennessee Williams. APT-2

You Know I Like to Be. Chrystos. WiU

You know, I must leave you again and I can't. Eugenio Montale. PoetW, *tr.* by William Arrowsmith

You know I'm thinking about China again. Man and a Woman Standing in the Rain in Front of a Candy Store, A. Jennifer Bartlett. ICANM

You know it might happen to you. (LL) House Without Walls. Han-shan (Cold Mountain). BB; CCL1; NDACCP; WoPoe, *tr.* by Gary Snyder

You know I've seen a lot of what the world can do. Vile World. Simon Rae. UV

You know I've seen a lot of what the world can do. Wild World. Cat Stevens. UV

You know our office on the 18th. Above the City. James Laughlin. OtW

You know, she said, they made you. Dress of Fire, A. Dahlia Ravikovitch. VCWP

You know, she said, 'you were at'. Sexpot. Charles Bukowski. BeAl

You know that I know, my lord, that you know. Michelangelo Buonarroti. CAGL, *tr.* by James M. Saslow

You know that, if you ever come back. (LL) To My Twenties. Kenneth Koch. EMP; NoP-5

You know that land, her lemon groves in bloom? Johann Wolfgang von Goethe. STV

You know that portrait of him that caused such a ruckus? Whitman Portrait, A. Steve Kowit. ViWalt

You know that something's not quite right. Riding Westward. John Balaban. GifTon

You know that they burned her horse. Coursier de Jeanne d'Arc, Le. Linda McCarriston. FaoP

You know the cadence of my footsteps now. My Old Friend Hospital. Julia Darling. PoCu

You know the feeling. Laura. Johnny Mercer. ReLy

You know the hay's in. Hay-Making. Gillian Clarke. AngWePo

You know the old woman. Old Woman, The. Beatrix Potter. NTCP

You know the parlor trick. Embrace. Billy Collins. SUP

You know the school; you call it old. Country School. Allen Curnow. HarvBoo

You know the signs: the sweet flower's. Ghosts in the Stacks. Richard H. W. Dillard. PoDa

You know, there's a Venture. Christmas Shopping. Carter Revard. UrbNat

You know this: I must lose you again and cannot. Eugenio Montale. WoPoe *Fr.* Motets [Mottetti].

You know, Tut, they were wrong. Next to Tut. Jon Veinberg. GeoHom

You know we French stormed [*or* storm'd] Ratisbon. Incident of the French Camp. Robert Browning. OBWP

You know, we looked at, touched carefully, and studied a copy of. Marginalia. Stephanie Brown. AmPoNex

You know what I'm. This Is What I Wanted to Sign Off With. Alden Nowlan. PoCu; StAl

You Know What I'm Saying? Irving Feldman. BAP-97

You know what there is in your voice? 8:10 Ferry, The. Cemal Süreya. NaPG, *tr. by* Talat Sait Halman

You Know Where You Did Despise. Vincent Voiture. WoPoe, *tr. by* Alexander Pope

You know where you did despise. You Know Where You Did Despise. Vincent Voiture. WoPoe, *tr. by* Alexander Pope

You know you are old when you are fifty lines long. Poem Looking in a Mirror, A. Awwad Nasir. IrPoTo, *tr. by* Ralph Saverese and Saadi A. Simawe

You ladies all of merry England. Signior Dildo. John Wilmot, 2d Earl of Rochester. BASC

You laugh / Because I'm poor and black and funny. Black Clown, The. Langston Hughes. WaAnP

You lay down in your bed. Dark Existence. Brenda Hillman. BodElec

You lay in the nest of your real death. Elizabeth Gone. Anne Sexton. WaAnP

You lean against me. Dancing in Paradise. Achy Obejas. WiU

You leap out of bed; you start to get ready. Samuel Hoffenstein. AmWit *Fr.* Poems in Praise of Practically Nothing.

You learn to accommodate yourself to others, to fit into the space left by their. Avila. John Yau. BodElec

You learned Lear's *Nonsense Rhymes* by heart, not rote. Plea to Boys and Girls, A. Robert Graves. NAEL-6v2

You leave, I write what happened, type it—onionskin. A romance. Poem for the End. Honor Moore. WiU

You Leave Me Breathless. Ralph Freed. ReLy

You leave without a trace! (LL) Song for My Shadow, A. Kim Pyŏngyŏn. CATKP; WoPoe, *tr. by* Richard John Lynn

You led me to sling my rifle. To Carelessness. Kenneth Koch. PWW2

You left a message on the board. Visit, The. NLP

You left, but don't forget, my heart. Esrâr Dede. OLP, *tr. by* Walter Andrews, Najaat Black and Mehmet Kalpakli

You left in the morning. In the evening, my heart in a thousand shards. Buson. EMJL, *tr. by* Haruo Shirane

You left in the morning. Tonight my heart is in a thousand pieces. Mourning for Hokuju Rosen. Buson. EH, *tr. by* Robert Hass

You left me my lips, and they shape words, even in silence. (LL) You Took Away All the Oceans and All the Room. Osip Emilevich Mandelstam. OPOU; Spl, *tr. by* Clarence Brown and W. S. Merwin

You left me sad and lonely. You're Driving Me Crazy (What Did I Do?). Walter Donaldson. ReLy

You left me with this empty house. After You Left. Mark Ivey. ICANM

You let down, from arched. Family Affairs. Maya Angelou. OxAAAP

You licked the dust that covered their antiques. In Front of the House. Aliyah Abdul-Salaam. AnVo, *tr. by* Mohamed Enani

You lie and I concur. You "give." Martial. WoPoe *Fr.* Epigrams.

You lie down in the deer's bed. Contemplation Is Mourning. Tim Lilburn. OpeFie

You lie now in many coffins. For Malcolm: After Mecca. Gerald William Barrax. OxAAAP

You lie with me nightly. In bathrooms I'm there. Pamela Gillilan. NewEx

You lights, for which on earth my sight's thirst ne'er is stilled. To the Stars. Andreas Gryphius. GePo, *tr. by* George C. Schoolfield

You like. Family Romance. Paul Hoover. IllVoic

You like it under the trees in autumn. Motive for Metaphor, The. Wallace Stevens. APT-1; BrAP; MoAmPo; NAMCP V.1; OxBoAm

You like peaches and cream. Peaches and Cream. Mudrooroo Narogin. BMAP

You little box I carried on that trip. To My Little Radio. Bertolt Brecht. RWPCtW, *tr. by* John Willett

You little stars that live in skies. Fulke, 1st Baron Brooke Greville. NoP-4; NoP-5 *Fr.* Caelica.

You live in dishonor grave, Dukes and Mighty Princes. András Szkhárosi Horvát. IQMS *Fr.* About the Princes.

You live in the thousand rooms. In My Dream. A. V. Christie. AmPoNex

You live in this, and dwell in lovers' eyes [*or* eies]. (LL) William Shakespeare. AEP; CABP; CtM; GSo; HeIP-4; NAEL-6v1; NAEL-7v1; NIL-7; NIP-4; NoP-4; NoP-5; NoSic; NPeEn; OxAEP-1; OxBSo; PBRV; WaAnP *Fr.* Sonnets.

You live secure. Primo Levi. *See* You who live secure.

You live under the microscope. Under the Microscope. Slavko Mihalic. PoSu, *tr. by* Charles Simic

You live where green mountains reach almost. Looking for Master Yung Ts'un near His Hermitage. Li Po. CrYelRi, *tr. by* Sam Hamill

You lived and moved among the best society. W. H. Auden. OBSV *Fr.* Letter to Lord Byron.

You lived in hardy commonness: the feel. Oppa. Jim Linebarger. TiP2

You load, focus, aim. Shooting Back. Thomas Sayers Ellis. GT

You look as though. James Dickey. OtW *Fr.* Apollo.

You look for Rome in Rome, O traveler! To Rome Entombed in Her Ruins. Francisco de Quevedo y Villegas. SpanPo, *tr. by* Kate Flores

You look / like two doves. Shir Asheydim Ansher. Yosl Cutler. Prolet, *tr. by* Amelia Glaser

You look sleazy tonight. don't Cheapen Yourself. Jana Harris. SUP

You looked like him. Thank you anyway. (LL) I Thought It Was Harry. William Bronk. APSN; OxBoAm

You lose and I lose. (LL) Relationship. János Pilinszky. IQMS; StAl, *tr. by* Peter Jay

You love a woman and you wonder where she goes all night in some tricked. You Love, You Wonder. Brenda Shaughnessy. LegDan

You, love, and I. Counting the Beats. Robert Graves. HarvBoo; OxAEP-2; WeW-3; WoPoe

You Love Her. *Unknown.* WoPoe *Fr.* Gathasaptasati, The.

You love her, while I love you. *Unknown.* WoPoe *Fr.* Gathasaptasati, The.

You love not me? (LL) Broken Appointment, A. Thomas Hardy. HarvBoo; NAEL-6v2; NAEL-7v2; NAMCP V.1; NoAM; NoP-4; NoP-5; PtR

You love the hum of well-oiled engine about to turn 200,000. Because You're American. Kevin Stein. ReTh

You love us when we're heroes, home on leave. Glory of Women. Siegfried Sassoon. FaBoWar; NAEL-6v2; NAEL-7v2; NoP-4; NoP-5; OBWP; OxAEP-2; OxBSo

You Love, You Wonder. Brenda Shaughnessy. LegDan

You love your dog and carve his steaks. So You Put the Dog to Sleep. Thomas Lux. SUP

You loved when all was young. (LL) Charles Kingsley. GoPo; OxAEP-2 *Fr.* Water Babies, The.

You lower my emotions, sealed in their casket. Parting, The. Sara Berkeley. PBCIP

You lumbered along the stadium. My Father's First Baseball Game. Afaa Michael Weaver. PBCAP

You lunged. Epitaph for Etheridge Knight. Melba Joyce Boyd. BRtP

You 'made a virtue of necessity'. To Conscripts. Alice Thompson Meynell. SacPr

You Made Me Love You (I Didn't Want to Do It). Joseph McCarthy. ReLy

You made the home where I go home in dream. To My Mother. Anna Adams. Prnts

You made the silence of lilacs swaying. Recognition. Alejandra Pizarnik. TANSG, *tr. by* Susan Bassnett

You made the stormy days seem sunny. (LL) Love Song: "I shaved my legs a second time." Frederick Seidel. BAP-04; OxBoAm

You make it in your mess-tin by the brazier's rosy gleam. Pot of Tea, A. Robert W. Service. PoWW

You Make Me Feel So Young. Mack Gordon. ReLy

You make me think of many men. To an Intra-Mural Rat. Marianne Moore. APT-1

You manage to fall in love. Of course. Short Hand. Lawrence Goeckel. ICANM

You, Marc Chagall, should be able to tell us. Ascensions, The. William Pillen. RaBo

You marched away and left this town. They're Either Too Young or Too Old. Frank Loesser. ReLy

You marched off southward with the fire of twenty. Danny. Malcolm Cowley. PoA 2002

You, Mascolo, came and went, a half hour in all. Redefining "Orthodoxy." Pier Paolo Pasolini. ItPo, *tr. by* Gayle Ridinger

You, master of delays. Killing No Murder. Sylvia Townsend Warner. MoBrPo

You may also look absurd with a miserable face. (LL) Dear Female Heart. Stevie Smith. ItWoWo; NALW

You may appear in a tinny, nickel-and-dime light. Bitter Angel. Amy Gerstler. CalPo

You may ask the world. Memories of Mudland-Meadow. István Sinka. IQMS, *tr. by* Adam Makkai

You may be right: 'How can I dare to feel?'. Rejoinder to a Critic. Donald Davie. CABP; NoP-4

You may catch / a butterfly. Ars Poetica. Linda Pastan. NIP-4

You may catch all the others, but you wo———. (LL) Slithergadee, The. Shel Silverstein. NBLV; OBCoV

You may confidently. Breathcrystal. Paul Celan. PFTM-2, *tr. by* Pierre Joris

You may for ever [*or* forever] tarry. (LL) To the Virgins, to Make Much of Time. Robert Herrick. BASC; BrAP; CavPo; ClHu; CtM; HeIP-4; ITBLP; NAEL-6v1; NAEL-7v1; NBLV; NIL-7; NIP-4; NoP-4; NoP-5; NOSC; NPeEn; OBEV; OxAEP-1; OxBEV; PoPoPo; PtR; SoSe-8; TFi; UV; WaAnP

You may have grain, but nobody to eat it. Laughing at Myself. Chŏng Yagyong. CATKP, *tr. by* Chi-gyu Kim [*or* Kim Chonggil]

You may have heard. Sed Non Frustra. Anton Korteweg. TuT, *tr. by* Seamus Deane

You may "have" sex. Disown. Rae Armantrout. FTOS

You may not get a chance. Ploughman. John Tripp. TCAWP

You May Not Love Me. Johnny Burke. ReLy

You may speak of a grave in a distant land. Reverie, A. Mary Weston Fordham. CBWP-2

You may talk as you please of the joys of Jamaica. Song of the Transportationist, The. *Unknown.* NOBAu

You may talk o' gin and [*or* an'] beer. Gunga Din. Rudyard Kipling. BRP; MoBrPo

You may then live in joy perdurably . . .. (LL) Stephen Hawes. NoSic; OBEV *Fr.* Pastime of Pleasure, The.

You may want to cut them down. You may want to use a knife. Chrysanthemums. Irene McKinney. PBCAP

You may write me down in history. Still I Rise. Maya Angelou. BeAl

"You mean," he said, "a crocodile." (LL) Purist, The. Ogden Nash. MoAmPo; NBLV

You mean Josie with the small eyes? New Verses for June 7, 1951. Jan Hanlo. TuT, *tr. by* Eamon Grennan

You meaner beauties of the night. On His Mistress [*or* Mistris], the Queen of Bohemia. Sir Henry Wotton. BASC; NOSC; NPeEn; OxBEV; TFi

You meet them at mid-afternoon receptions. Justin Quinn. NIrP

You Meet Yourself. Katie Donovan. NIrP

You merit more; nor could [*or* cou'd] my Love do less. (LL) To My Dear Friend Mr Congreve [on His Comedy Called "The Double-Dealer"]. John Dryden. NPeEn; OxAEP-1

You might as well live. (LL) Résumé. Dorothy Parker. AmWit; APT-1; EMP; HeIP-4; IJHIL; NALW; NAMCP V.1; NBLV; NoP-4; NoP-5; OxBoAm; PtR; UV

You might as well think one thing or another. Amelia Rosselli. ItPo, *tr. by* Gayle Ridinger

You might be sleeping next to me. Your head. 152 Into 5,*El Centro Palabra de Fe.* M. L. Williams. GeoHom

You might come here Sunday on a whim. Degrees of Gray in Philipsburg. Richard Hugo. CAP-8; ItP; NAMCP V.2; NoAM; OxBoAm; TRP; VCAP; WaAnP

You might easy know a doffer. *Unknown.* FaBoVe

You might have been a meadowlark making. Standing Between Two Ideas. Maurya Simon. InvLad

You might imagine the desert as a rectangle without angles, as a. Desert, II, The. Edmond Jabès. AF, *tr. by* Rosmarie Waldrop

You might not think Toulouse-Lautrec and Mother Teresa. Controlling Factors. Mary Ruefle. ExTi

You might suppose it easy. Boatman, The. Jay Macpherson. BrAP

You might want to be amused at the work. Women's Labors. Lee Upton. PoCho

You, mine, my love. *Unknown.* WoPoe *Fr.* Conversations in Courtship.

You missed it by a day—the shuttle Atlantis. Bad Alchemy. Dionisio D. Martinez. FaoP

You Missed the Earthquake, Bill. Charles Harper Webb. GeoHom

You Mock Me Now in Your Youth. Shmuel HaNagid. WoPoe, *tr. by* Peter Cole

You modern wits, who call this world a star. To the Same [My Dear Sister, Mrs S.]: The Tears. William Hammond. NOSC

You, Morningtide Star, now are steady-eyed, over the east. Lying Awake. Thomas Hardy. FaBoVe; NPeEn

You move between the soldiers' cots. Nurse Whitman. Sharon Olds. ViWalt

You muses nine, with me combine; assist me with your aid. John McGoldrick's Trial for the Quaker's Daughter. *Irish Oral Tradition.* IrV

You must. Marionette. Maher Sabry. AnVo, *tr. by* Mohamed Enani

You must admit it's natural. Clyde Peeling's Reptiland in Allenwood, Pennsylvania. Kevin Young. NeAmPo

You must always be high. Everything depends on it: it is the only question. Get High. Charles Baudelaire. MotU, *tr. by* Edward K. Kaplan

You must answer softly. Answer. Mildred Bowers. YaYoPo

You must be endless in your loving touch of each other, continuance the answers. (LL) Union of Two, The. Haki R. Madhubuti. ISC; SpirFl

You must be proud, if you'll be wise. (LL) To the Ladies. Mary Lee, Lady Chudleigh. BrAP; CABP; NALW; NIL-7; PEW

You Must Be Pure and Holy. *Unknown.* SSUS

You Must Believe in Spring. Jacques Demy. ReLy, *tr. by* Alan Bergman, Marilyn Bergman and Michel Legrand

You Must Believe in Spring. Jan Zwicky. OpeFie

You must change your life fourteen times. Archaic Torsos. David Shapiro. BodElec

You must come back, as your grandmother did. Dandelion Greens. Jane Flanders. AFaM; IPoFL

You must come to them sideways. Mirrors at 4 A.M. Charles Simic. AWTN

You must develop a feeling for these symbols. Introduction to Methods of Mathematical Physics. Lisa Rosenberg. PoA 2002

You must dig in black ashes a long time. Pavel Grigoryevich Antokolsky. TCRusP *Fr.* Son.

You must exist. Writing this book depends on it. It has occurred to. Lydia Kwa. OpeFie *Fr.* Roadbook: Suite of Hands.

You must feel loved when you read this. In These Dark Times. Julia Vinograd. ASA

You must find out, for I don't know.. (LL) Three Wise Old Women. Elizabeth T. Corbett. NOxBChV; OBSP

You must have. House Call to a Man with Parkinson's Disease, A. Michael O'Reilly. BloBone

You Must Have Been a Beautiful Baby. Johnny Mercer. ReLy

You must have made your entry from the rear. Ballad of the Gasfitter. Gerrit Achterberg. LWR, *tr. by* John M. Coetzee

You must have missed the signpost, took. At the Poem. Clark Coolidge. AHA; NYP2

You must have music first of all. Art of Poetry, The. Paul Verlaine. NAWM-7v2, *tr. by* Carlyle Ferren MacIntyre

You Must Help Me Gather. Shakuntala Hawoldar. HAWP

You must help me gather. You Must Help Me Gather. Shakuntala Hawoldar. HAWP

You must hide yourself. To Live in This World Again. Joanne Kyger. WANABP

You must learn about wolves. Wolves. Peter Mortimer. RSaN

You must not hope to arrive. (LL) Tourist from Syracuse, The. Donald Justice. NAMCP V.2; NoAM; OxBoAm; VCAP

You must not, said the owl to the capercailzie. End of ARt, The. Reiner Kunze. PoSu, *tr. by* Michael Hamburger

You must not wonder, though you think it strange. George Gascoigne. *See* For That He Looked Not upon Her.

You must remember this when I am gone. Sanctuary. Donald Davidson. APT-1; FuPo

You Must Sing. Li-Young Lee. CAP-8; PLBUT

You must sing to be found; when found, you must sing. (LL) You Must Sing. Li-Young Lee. CAP-8; PLBUT

You must stand erect but at your ease, a posture. Singing Lesson, The. David Wagoner. NoAM

You must understand how pinched she's been. Fisherman's Wife, The. Jody Gladding. YaYoPo

You musta' got me switched. I Think You Got Me Confused. Timothy Anderson. BeDoSh

You Mustn't Feel Discouraged. Betty Comden and Adolph Green. ReLy

You, my friend, fallen among thieves. Thief and Samaritan. James Keir Baxter. HarvBoo

You, my Lord, were dressed in astonishing disguises. Disguises, The. Patricia K. Page. PoCho

You, my love, encourage me. Return to Avondale. Eithne Cavanagh. IrLP

You, my photographer, you, most aware. Poem. Delmore Schwartz. PoA 2002

You nature poets think you've got it, hostaged. Smell and Envy. Douglas Goetsch. P180

You need me for sitting. Michael Rosen. NewEx

You need no door with me, never the manifold tints. Ian Patterson. VaPo *Fr.* Hardihood.

You need some help. Hired Hand. David Lee. GifTon

You need to know, son. Mississippi: Bell Zone 1. Jerry W., Jr. Ward. BtF

You Never Ask. *Unknown.* SonAtl, *tr. by* Gris Klamas and Tina Ritson

You never asked for sunshine. Tubman Strong. Darryl Holmes. InTrad

You never claimed to be someone special. She Mends an Ancient Wireless. Paul Durcan. IrLP; PBCIP

You never could tell what my dead Uncle Arthur heard. And Don't Be Deaf to the Singing Beyond. Carter Revard. HATNAP

You never hear me, your letter said. Drinker's Wife Writes Back, The. Jean Valentine. LaCa

You never hear 'the People' now. People, No, The. Vicki Raymond. NOBAu

You Never Knew About Me. P. G. Wodehouse. ReLy

You never know the sky. Late Winter in West Texas. Robert Burlingame. TiP2

You never know who has your memory. You Gotta Have Your Tips on Fire. Víctor Hernández Cruz. PueRic, tr. by Julio Marzán and Carmen Valle

You never know who you're gonna meet. (LL) In Line at the Supermarket. Greg Pape. PBCAP; SUP

You never think it will happen to you. Alicia Ostriker. ExTi Fr. Mastectomy Poems, The.

You never thought it would come to this. Playing Basketball with the Viet Cong. Kevin Bowen. MoASP

You, no doubt, have heard the story told of Charleston by the sea? Crum Appointment, The. Lizelia Augusta Jenkins Moorer. CBWP-3

You no give me one wacky you can't pass. Dry River. Unknown. FaBoVe

You no sooner attain the great void. Hakuin. ZenPo, tr. by Takashi Ikemoto and Lucien Stryk

You no sooner got out of prison. Evening Walk, The. Nazim Hikmet. AF

You noble diggers all stand up now. Diggers' Song, The. Unknown. PBRV

You noble Diggers all, stand up now, stand up now. Digger's Song, The. Gerrard Winstanley. BASC; NOSC

You noble fountain set in peace and joy's design. Concerning the Wolffsbrunnen near Heidelberg. Martin Opitz. GePo, tr. by George C. Schoolfield

You not alone, when you are still alone. Michael Drayton. OxBSo Fr. Idea.

You nurtured grief until that leap. Waiting for Robinson. Roberta Hill Whiteman. HATNAP

You, Odysseus trainer of the wooden horse of pleasure. Odyssey or "On Absence," The. Chimako Tada. VCWP, tr. by Naoshi Koriyama and Edward Lueders

You of the same mind, moor-wandering near one. Largo. Paul Celan. PoSu, tr. by Michael Hamburger

You often say my work is coarse. It's true. Martial. CAGL Fr. Epigrams.

You Oh Even. Marianne Vitale. HeMarv

You: on candy cameo. Me: ate dumb flash. Stage Duo. Kenward Elmslie. FTOS

You on my Mind. Kavikondala Venkatarao. HotL, tr. by V. Narayana Rao

You, once a belle in Shreveport. Snapshots of a Daughter-in-Law. Adrienne Rich. MoWP; NAAL-5; NALW; NAMCP V.2; NIL-7; NIP-4; NoAM; NoP-4; NoP-5; PoPoPo; VCAP; WaAnP

You once asked, it's said. Wales '99. Donald Evans. BBMWP, tr. by Gillian Clarke

You open P-K4, it thinks, or blinks. Playing the Machine. Howard Nemerov. BodElec

You open the door after a long ride home in the dark. (LL) Refuge at the One Step Down. Belle Waring. PBCAP; SeSe

You or You. Laura Riding Jackson. MoWP

You ought to know Mr Mistoffelees! Mr Mistoffelees. T. S. Eliot. NOxBChV

You pass it on. (LL) What Have I Learned. Gary Snyder. LoL; TWF

You pass the tomb of Battus' son, well skilled. Callimachus. HePo, tr. by Barbara Hughes Fowler

You pass through me. Yarrow. Leonard Neufeldt. ACAMVP

You pay for it, for sure, dont let nobody tell you you don. You pay. Minute of Consciousness, The. Imamu Amiri Baraka. APSN

You pedal furiously. Stationary Bicycle. Linda Pastan. ArBi

You people / of the future. Screaming My Head Off. Vladimir Vladimirovich Mayakovsky. PFTM-1

You perpetuate! Roll on, reels of celluloid, as the great earth rolls on! (LL) To the Film Industry in Crisis. Frank O'Hara. GPTC; OxBoAm

You phone to say birds have gouged. Apples. Patricia Pogson. NLP

You place. Erin Mouré. NLPA Fr. Wittgenstein Letters to Mel Gibson's Braveheart, The.

You planted life, protecting. Discords. Fabio Doplicher. NeIt, tr. by Dana Gioia

You play the flute well; I love your swing curls and your earlocks. His Hair. Mirabai. WED, tr. by Robert Bly

You played and she sang at my wedding. Winter Wedding, The. Paul Henry. TCAWP

You praise my self-sacrifice, Spoon River. Edgar Lee Masters. APT-1 Fr. Spoon River Anthology.

You praise the firm restraint with which they write. On Some South African Novelists. Roy Campbell. MoBrPo; OBCoV; OxAEP-2; OxBEV

You pray. You forgive your enemies. Flt #4372. Jeanne Murray Walker. OtW

You prayer—, you blasphemy, you. Plashes the Fountain. Paul Celan. OBVE, tr. by Michael Hamburger

You prisoners of New South Wales. Convict's Tour to Hell, A. Francis MacNamara. NOBAu

You promise heavens free from strife. Mimnermus in Church. William Johnson Cory. OBEV

You promised you would never keep. Green Corn Season. Diana García. TouFir

You, proud curve-lipped youth, with brown sensitive face. Edward Carpenter. CAGL Fr. Towards Democracy.

You pursue my figure. Dies Merini. Alda Merini. CItWP, tr. by Cinzia Sartini Blum and Lara Trubowitz

You / Put success in the mouth. Sappho. SaLy, tr. by Diane Rayor

You put this pen. Shall become as. Evie Shockley. RD

You raise the axe. Anniversary, The. Ai. BodElec

You raise the creases. Earth, The. Christopher Pilling. NLP

You read about the wreckage. Lear Drives His Rambler across Laurel Mountain. Charles Clifton. IaFF

You read with Auden. In Memorium: Robert Hayden. Norman J. Loftis. SpirFl

You, reading over my shoulder, peering beneath. Reader over My Shoulder, The. Robert Graves. NAEL-6v2; NAEL-7v2

You Reading This, Be Ready. William Stafford. TWF

You really got thru to me. Allen. Joe Lothamer. GeoH

You really know your art you. Anne Portugal. SCFWP, tr. by Serge Gavronsky

You recommend that the motive, in Chapter 8, should be changed. Yes, the Agency Can Handle That. Kenneth Fearing. WeW-3

You refuse to become a deer or tree. Textile 9. Marjorie Welish. VaPo

You remember being bathed. Accessible Heaven. Thylias Moss. OxAAAP

You remember the joke, right? Letter to Ibrahim. Khaled Mattawa. AmPoNex

You remember the sun of Auschwitz. Sun of Auschwitz, The. Tadeusz Borowski. AF, tr. by Larry Rafferty

You remember the sun of Auschwitz. Sun of Auschwitz, The. Tadeusz Borowski. HP, tr. by Tadeuszt Pióro

You return on currents and tides. Return of the Banished. Li Po. CrYelRi, tr. by Sam Hamill

You rise in my dreams. Venus of Laussel. Patricia Monaghan. HW

You roar over the meadow and roar. Last Days. Richard Hugo. PoA 2002

You rocked my cradle, Charidemus, once. Martial. RomPo, tr. by J. P. Sullivan

You rose from our embrace and the small light spread. Hayden Carruth. ErotSp Fr. Sonnets.

You run alone, burdened. Three Bridges. Sa'di Yusuf. IrPoTo, tr. by Khaled Mattawa

You run round the back to be in it again. Good Teachers, The. Carol Ann Duffy. ItWoWo; NAMCP V.2

You rush into the shopping arcade. Second Person. Sam Gardiner. NIrP

You said, "Come in to the light." Painter of Destinies, A. Molly Bendall. NAPBL

You said good-bye at Yellow Crane Pavilion. Saying Good-bye to Meng Hao-jan at Yellow Crane Pavilion. Li Po. CrYelRi, tr. by Sam Hamill

You said I could talk. Leaking Roof. Gahlia Gwangwa'a. NAfrP

You said, "I will go to another land, I will go to another sea." City, The. Constantine P. Cavafy. PLBUT; WoPoe, tr. by Rae Dalven

You said: "I'll go to another country, go to another shore." City, The. Constantine P. Cavafy. AmFaPo; BeAl, tr. by Edmund Keeley and Philip Sherrard

You said: it's hot tonight. Maurizio Cucchi. ItPo, tr. by Gayle Ridinger

You said may God go with you, son. May God Go with You, Son. C. Wright. FaBoWar

You, said the Lionwoman. Flask of Brandy, A. Padraic Fallon. ModIr

You said the sun would rise. Song to Fidel. Ernesto "Che" Guevara. TCLAP, tr. by Gordon Brotherston and Edward Dorn

You said to me if you write me. Letter. Blaise Cendrars. YaTCFP, tr. by Ron Padgett

You said you would no more forget me. Regret. Sinch'ung. CATKP, tr. by Peter H. Lee

You sang a race from wood and stone to Christ. (LL) O Black and Unknown Bards. James Weldon Johnson. APT-1; ColAP; HeIP-4; NAAPv.1; NAMCP V.1; OxBoAm; TCAPo; WaAnP

You sang, you sang! you mountain brook. Reason for Silence, A. Louise Imogen Guiney. SWaP

You saved me, you should remember me. Vita Nova. Louise Glück. NAMCP V.2; NoP-5

You saw Big Mama Thornton. Bumblebee, You Saw Big Mama. Jayne Cortez. SurWo

You saw the wind as the breath of God. After the Hurricane. Sinéad Morrissey. MFPA

You say, but with no touch of scorn. Alfred Tennyson. NAEL-6v2; NAEL-7v2 Fr. In Memoriam A. H. H.

You say, Columbus with his argosies. Trumbull Stickney. APN-2

You say eating is pointless.   Existentially Speaking.   Joe-Anne McLaughlin-Carruth.   AFaM

You say: I am sitting in a room.   At a Sunlit Window.   Ondra Lysohorsky.   AF, *tr. by* Ewald Osers

You say, I love.   Lesson in Natural History, A.   Vyacheslav Kupriyanov.   TCRusP, *tr. by* Pamela Davidson

You say it's nothing.   Vedantist, The.   Sri Sri.   HotL, *tr. by* V. Narayana Rao

You say nothing is created new?   Antonio Machado Ruiz.   WED *Fr.* Moral Proverbs and Folk Songs.

You say—one shouldn't weep.   Recollections of Siberia.   Bella Akhatovna Akhmadulina.   RusPo, *tr. by* Robert Arthur Douglas Ford

You say, *Postumus*, you'll live tomorrow.   Martial.   RomPo, *tr. by* Peter Whigham

You say sir that yor-life depends.   Gentlewomans Answer to One, that Sayd He Should Dye, if Shee Refuse His Desires, A.   *Unknown.*   EMWP

You say / Stars.   Fazil Hüsnü Daglarca.   NaPG *Fr.* Poems of the Mediterranean.

You say that you would live in Newfound-land.   To a Worthy Friend, Who Often Objects the Coldnesse of the Winter in Newfound-Land.   Robert Hayman.   IFF

You say: Today!   Ernst Mirville.   OGAHCP, *tr. by* Boadiba and Jack Hirschman

You say wind is only wind.   Credo.   Andrew Zawacki.   IAoNAP; LegDan

You say you had a letter from.   First Letter From Tamara A.   Reiner Kunze.   PoSu, *tr. by* Ewald Osers

You say you walk and sew alone?   You Art A Scholar, Horatio, Speak to It.   Olena Kalytiak Davis.   BAP-04

You say you want to go home.   Minding You.   Catherine Byron.   Prnts

You say you're glad I write—oh, say not so!   Impromptu.   Frances Anne Kemble.   APN-1

You scarcely move your foot when out of nowhere spring.   Voices.   Wisława Szymborska.   PoSu, *tr. by* Magnus F. Krynski

You scramble eggs with chorizo.   Tortillas.   Margie Norris.   AFaM

You sea! I resign myself to you also—I guess what you mean.   Walt Whitman.   CAGL *Fr.* Song of Myself.

You see a man / trying to think.   Ghost of a Chance.   Adrienne Rich.   OxBoAm

You see a pair of laughing eyes.   (Love Is) The Tender Trap.   Sammy Cahn.   ReLy

You see an actor as if through crystal.   Nerve Meter, The.   Antonin Artaud.   YaTCFP, *tr. by* Mary Ann Caws and Patricia Terry

You see birds, hundreds of them.   George Stanley.   NLPA *Fr.* Mountains and Air.

You see how far Mans wisedom here extends.   John Wilmot, 2d Earl of Rochester.   OxBEV *Fr.* Satire [*or* Satyre *or* Satyr] against [Reason and] Mankind, A.

You see how, white with snows to the north of us.   Horace.   STV *Fr.* Odes.

You see I went out for a minute.   Man in a Semi-Detached House.   John Thorpe.   AHA

You see it happen.   Descent in Broad Daylight.   Rutger Kopland.   LWR, *tr. by* John M. Coetzee

You see me dying trial, gun inna the dance.   Dance Hall: Version.   Geoffrey Philp.   WaCA

You see that forest on the height?   Pastoral.   John Stuart Williams.   TCAWP

You see that high crag.   Archilochus.   SaLy, *tr. by* Diane Rayor

You see the fellow with the scarlet sash?   Imre Madách.   IQMS *Fr.* Tragedy of Man.

You see the slender spire that peers.   Days of Yore, The.   Douglas Thompson.   TreFP

You see the smoke at Kapunda.   Song: The Railway Train.   *Unknown.*   NOBAu, *tr. by* George Taplin

You see them.   Asking for it.   Carmel Gahan.   BBMWP, *tr. by* Robert Minhinnick

You see, they have no judgment.   Drowned Children, The.   Louise Glück.   NAMCP V.2; OxBoAm; VCAP

You See This Body.   Marcie Rendon.   ReEnLa

You see this body.   You See This Body.   Marcie Rendon.   ReEnLa

You see this dog? It was but yesterday.   Flush or Faunus.   Elizabeth Barrett Browning.   DiBP; VWP

You see us in this picture.   Mrs. Biswas Goes Through a Photo Album.   Reetika Vazirani.   AmPoNex

You see, we have to be forgiven things.   Paul Verlaine.   SxFrPo, *tr. by* Martin Sorrell

You see what I am: change me, change me! (LL)   Woman at the Washington Zoo, The.   Randall Jarrell.   BrAP; InGu; ItP; OxBoAm; VCAP

You see, where'er you look, on earth but vainness' hour.   All Is Vanity.   Andreas Gryphius.   GePo, *tr. by* George C. Schoolfield

You seemed a guileless youth enough.   Meng: To a Man.   *Unknown.*   CCL1, *tr. by* H. A. Giles

You seemed to know the most about the dark.   Robert Frost.   Kim Bridgford.   VisFro

You seldom talked about the Indian side.   Reservation, The.   Susan Clements.   UnSA

You Send Me: Bertha Franklin, December 11, 1964.   E. Ethelbert Miller.   SpirFl

You send me your first book. a text.   Fundoscopy.   Maura Dooley.   MoWP

You serve the best wines always, my dear sir.   Martial.   RomPo, *tr. by* James Vincent Cunningham

You set the olives down beside the *feta*.   Red.   Grahame Davies.   BBMWP, *tr. by* the author

You Shall Above All Things Be Glad and Young.   E. E. Cummings.   ColAP; NoAM; TWF

You shall be free to wander in the woods.   First Amendment.   Aliki Barnstone.   RWB

You shall be true to them, who are false to you. (LL)   Indifferent, The.   John Donne.   BASC; NAEL-6v1; NAEL-7v1; NAWM-5v1; NOSC; SoSe-8

You shall have, for survival.   For Survival.   Andrée Chedid.   HAWP, *tr. by* Marie Ponsot

You shall hear how Hiawatha.   Henry Wadsworth Longfellow.   NAAPv.1 *Fr.* Song of Hiawatha, The.

You shall listen to all sides and filter them from yourself. (LL)   Walt Whitman.   CAGL; ColAP *Fr.* Song of Myself.

You shall love beauty, which is the shadow of God over the Universe.   Decalogue of the Artist.   Gabriela Mistral.   TCLAP, *tr. by* Doris Dana

You shall not despair.   Dylan Thomas.   ItP

You shall say that I am your sister. I don't know what became of them. (LL)   William Langland.   NAEL-6v1; NAEL-7v1 *Fr.* Vision of Piers Plowman, The.

You shanghaied me to this oak.   Kosmos [2003].   Yusef Komunyakaa.   ViWalt

You share your mourning with all Moscow. There.   Pavel Grigoryevich Antokolsky.   TCRusP *Fr.* Son.

You shine, my love, like a sugar maple in October.   Raisin Pumpernickel.   Marge Piercy.   StAl

You should at times go out.   Elizabeth Daryush.   MoWP

You should be done with blossoming by now.   To a Vine-clad Telegraph Pole.   Louis Untermeyer.   MoAmPo

You should bid me welcome.   Walther von der Vogelweide.   GePo

You should enjoy your suffering.   New Sentience, The.   Alan Davies.   FTOS

You should have asked me in the cradle: oh yes, then.   Fourth Eclogue, The.   Miklós Radnóti.   IQMS, *tr. by* John Wain

You should have disappeared years ago.   On Third Avenue.   Mina Loy.   APT-1; HarvBoo

"You should have many lovers."   Very Sad Conversation at Night, A.   Anna Swirszczynska [*or* Swir].   PoSu

You should have married Seymour Brilkin.   Adventure.   Betty Comden and Adolph Green.   ReLy

You should know the kind.   After Estrangement.   Molly Bendall.   AmPoNex

You should lie down now and remember the forest.   Forest, The.   Susan Stewart.   AmAlph

You should slice the lying tongue of your love.   Wasted.   June Jordan.   IJHIL

You shout and hurry through.   Scaffold, The.   Amal Dunqul.   NAfrP, *tr. by* Sharif Elmusa and Thomas G. Ezzy

You show me the poems of some woman.   Translations.   Adrienne Rich.   OxBoAm

You showed your dirty face first in Detroit.   To the Eminent Scholar and Meddler.   Kofi Awoonor.   HBAPE

You shriek, 'Alas, *but I have failed*!'. (LL)   Failures.   May Kendall.   ViWPN; VWP

You sing a hard blues.   Bulosan Listens to a Recording of Robert Johson.   Alfred Encarnacion.   OpBo

You sir have bought yourself a shiny train. (LL)   Wedding Day.   Mark Levine.   AmPoNex; BAP-01

You sit in a chair, touched by nothing, feeling.   In Celebration.   Mark Strand.   NAMCP V.2; NoAM

You sit in the back.   Sorrow Since Sitting Bull, A.   Christopher Gilbert.   ESEAA

You sit to have waves rush to your open hands.   To a Poetess.   Jim Carroll.   AHA

You slapped me.   For My Torturer, Lieutenant D.   Leila Djabali.   CFP; HAWP, *tr. by* Anita Barrows

You slapped my face.   Short Poem.   William Carlos Williams.   SAmP

You sleep little and light.   Airy Hall Nightmare.   Fred D'Aguiar.   NeBrP

You sleep on one side, your spine.   Enough.   Tracy Ryan.   NeBl

You smiled when we parted.   Who's Sorry Now?   Bert Kalmar and Harry Ruby.   ReLy

You so sleepy baby Who you been.   At Work.   Suzanne Gardinier.   AmPoNex

You So Woman.   Ruth Forman.   SpirFl

You sold a slave just yesterday.   Martial.   WoPoe *Fr.* Epigrams.

You, sons of Adam. Down with Love. E. Y. Harburg. ReLy

You Sort Old Letters. Robert Penn Warren. BodElec

You speak of back home. Scissortails. Teresa Whitman. TWW

You spoke all evening hatred and contempt. In the Last Circle. Edgar Bowers. CalPo

You spotted snakes [with double tongue]. William Shakespeare. NoSic *Fr.* Midsummer Night's Dream, A.

You Stand. Ben Cami. TuT, *tr. by* Pat Boran

You stand behind the old black mare. Why Can't I Leave You? Ai. CAP-8

You stand hoping that reticence will pass. To a Shy Girl at a Party. Ken Morrice. EdScPo

You stand, leaning on your spade, and rest. You Stand. Ben Cami. TuT, *tr. by* Pat Boran

You stand near the window as lights wink. 23rd Street Runs into Heaven. Kenneth Patchen. APT-2

You stand on a chair with a wrinkled nose. Making for Planet Alice. Deryn Rees-Jones. MFPA; StAl

You Stand There Fishing. Angie Estes. GeoHom

You stand waist-high in snakes. Alice. Michael S. Harper. ISC

You start here—Cozumel—it's an island, some people. You Are Here. Carl Phillips. GT

You start it all. You are lovely. To Women. Richard Hugo. NIP-4

You start to fall upward. (LL) Sun Underfoot Among the Sundews, The. Amy Clampitt. NoP-4; NoP-5; OxBoAm; StAl

You stay far far away. Union, The. Ifi Amadiume. HAWP

You steal into my room. Sleeping Beauty. Ai. NAMCP V.2

You stepped off the wrong train they made you flit through the city's mirror. First. Sezai Karakoç. NaPG, *tr. by* Talat Sait Halman

You Stepped Out of a Dream. Gustave Kahn. ReLy

You stepped through. Archangel. Ai. SeSe

You stood with your back to me. Sundial, The. Douglas Dunn. NPeEn

You stop to watch the Mandarin ducks. Urban Love Songs. Wing Tek Lum. OpBo

You strange, astonished-looking, angle-faced. Fish, the Man, and the Spirit, The. Leigh Hunt. OBEV; OxBSo

You strange, astonished-looking, angle-faced. Leigh Hunt. NBLV; NPeEn *Fr.* Fish, the Man, and the Spirit, The.

You, stranger, soul-mate. Grief. Siamanto. AF, *tr. by* Peter Balakian and Nevart Yaghlian

You stretched out your hungry voice. Madonna for the Damned—a 1980s Heroine. Corie Rosen. FTtHH

You, student, whistling those elusive bits. Carnal Knowledge. Dannie Abse. BloBone

You stupid men, who do accuse. Verses Against the Inconsequence of Men's Taste and Strictures. Sor Juana Inés de la Cruz. SpanPo, *tr. by* Muriel Kittel

You survive the surreal. Journey 55. Jerry W., Jr. Ward. FuFl

You sway like a crane to the tunes of tossed stones. Fierce Girl Playing Hopscotch. Alice Fulton. PoA 2002

You sweet soft murderess. *Unknown.* GePo

You swim afro cuban cadences. Conversations in the struggle. Pamela Plummer. BRtP

You take a piece of clay and mold it, shaping it into a human being. Ana Maria Shúa. MirDau *Fr.* Golem and Rabbi.

You take a woman. Trampling. Miguel Algarin. PueRic

You take me to the room of clocks. Visit to the British Museum. Frances Horovitz. MoWP

You take my hand; then we're alone. Quiet Evening. Louise Glück. NAMCP V.2

You take off, he takes off, we take off. Clothes. Wisława Szymborska. PoSu, *tr. by* Grazyna Drabik and Sharon Olds

You take the rest. (LL) Crossed Apple, The. Louise Bogan. HeIP-4; NALW

You take the stairs one at a time, squinting after the dark green of the woods. Home. David Walker. MotU

You talk about disappointment. Being a Monster. Lawrence Raab. OPRER

You talk like. Langston Hughes. APSN; APT-2; OxBoAm *Fr.* Lenox Avenue Mural.

You talk of art, of work, of books. You Talk of Art. Joan Murray. OxBoAm

You talk to me, I listen. I. Civilization. Bill Kushner. PA9/11

You tap on my window with a gun. Jacked. Lola Haskins. LiTh

You taste what has fallen. (LL) Starfish. Eric Ormsby. NoP-4; NoP-5

You Taught Me. Thomas McGrath. PoChi

You taught me the land so well. Trees. Cheryl Savageau. TWW

You tell me about the rickety truck. Jamaica, October 18, 1972. Shara McCallum. AmPoNex; BtF

You tell me then Christ was born nearly twenty centuries ago in a little horse town called Bethlehem. Christ is a Dixie Nigger. Frank Marshall Davis. APT-2

You tell me, fair one, that you ne'er can love. Female Philosopher, The. Charlotte Dacre. NOBRP; RWP

You tell me you loved fishing. Fish Daughter, The. Pascale Petit. MoWP

You tell the stars. For Sister Gwen Brooks. Sonia Sanchez. FuFl

You tell us how to heal these wounds. (LL) You Tell Us What to Do. Faiz Ahmad Faiz. PoetW; VCWP, *tr. by* Agha Shahid Ali

You Tell Us What to Do. Faiz Ahmad Faiz. PoetW; VCWP, *tr. by* Agha Shahid Ali

You tense up like a bow. Silver Clasps. Paul Dermée. CuPo

You that a stranger in mid-Rome seek Rome. Rome. "Panormitanus." OBVE, *tr. by* James Vincent Cunningham

You that are sprung of northern stock. To a Calvinist in Bali. Edna St. Vincent Millay. NoAM

You that do search for every purling spring. Sir Philip Sidney. NoSic; OxAEP-1 *Fr.* Astrophil and Stella.

You that have spent the silent night. Gascoigne's Good-Morrow. George Gascoigne. NoSic

You that Jehovah's servants are. Bible, *O.T.* NoSic

You that love England, who have an ear for her music. You That Love England. Cecil Day Lewis. RSaN

You that love lovers. Music Master. Jelaluddin Rumi. ErotSp, *tr. by* Coleman Barks

You that seeke what Life is in Death. Fulke, 1st Baron Brooke Greville. PtR *Fr.* Caelica.

You that through all the dying summer. Late Wasp, The. Edwin Muir. HarvBoo

You that unto your mistress' eyes. Love Deposed. Thomas Stanley. NOSC

You that will a wonder know. In Praise of His Mistress. Thomas Carew. BASC

You that with allegory's curious frame. Sir Philip Sidney. NAEL-7v1; NoSic *Fr.* Astrophil and Stella.

You: The City. Fiona Templeton.

Act II - Crossing At the Tracks. FTOS

You, the woman; I, the man; this, the world. Character of Love Seen as a Search for the Lost, The. Kenneth Patchen. CLPP

You There. Judith Barrington. FiBr

You there! / Listen, please, to my sorrowful words. Song of an Old Maid. *Unknown.* CATKP, *tr. by* Carolyn So

You there with the sticky fingers. *Unknown.* PriapPo *Fr.* Priapus Poems, The.

You think. (LL) Myth. Muriel Rukeyser. APT-2; NAAL-5; NALW; NIL-7; OxBoAm

You think gasoline extinguishes fires. Laughin at cha. Kenneth Carroll. BRtP

You think I give myself to you? Giving. Nora B. Cunningham. LW

You think I have a merry heart. I'm Saddest When I Sing. Thomas Haynes Bayly. STuOW

You think it horrible that lust and rage. Spur, The. William Butler Yeats. NAMCP V.1; OxAEP-2; WeW-3

You think the coldest girls in the world are Eskimos. Turn On the Heat. Lew Brown, B. G. DeSylva and Ray Henderson. ReLy

You think this cruel? take it for a rule. Alexander Pope. NPeEn *Fr.* Epistle to Dr. Arbuthnot.

You think this is going to be about death. Feeding the Worms. Tania Rochelle. NevBe

You think you can leave the matter to your lips. Kiss. Emanuel Carnevali. APT-2

You think you did not nurse because you did not. Great with Child. Judith Arcana. FiBr

You think yourself, perhaps, more than a speck. Another Voice. Victor Hugo. SxFrPo, *tr. by* A. M. and E. H. Blackmore

You though! Die and you'll lie dumb in the dirt; nobody care, and none. On a Lady Indifferent to Poetry. Sappho. STV, *tr. by* John Frederick Nims

You thought I had the strength of men. Clever Woman, A. Mary Elizabeth Coleridge. ViWPN; VWP

You threw me a lemon, oh it was sour. You Threw Me a Lemon. Miguel Hernández. WED, *tr. by* Robert Bly

You tire of it, this. Self-analysis. Michael Dransfield. BMAP

You told me, if something is not used it is meaningless, and took my temperature. Rosmarie Waldrop. FTOS; PFTM-2 *Fr.* Reproduction of Profiles, The.

You told me it was / because of me. Lady Izumi. WoPoe, *tr. by* Willis Barnstone

You told me, Rose, of this river, how the Susquehanna. Drowned River, The. Dolores Kendrick. FuFl

You Too Lie down. Dennis Lee. TLR

You Too? Me Too—Why Not? Soda Pop. Robert Hollander. NIL-7; NIP-4

You, too, perished by a bush with tangled roots. Anyte. SaLy, *tr. by* Diane Rayor

You too, you realize, began your days as a conveyance. Ode to the Bicycle. Cees Buddingh'. ArBi, *tr. by* John Irons

You Took Advantage of Me.　Lorenz Hart.　ReLy

You Took Away All the Oceans and All the Room.　Osip Emilevich Mandelstam.　OPOU; Spl, *tr. by* Clarence Brown and W. S. Merwin

You took my cake and you walked.　No Jive.　Raymond R. Patterson.　BRtP

You took my kisses and you took my love.　All of Me.　Gerald Marks and Seymour Simons.　ReLy

You took your father.　Spanish of Our Out-Loud Dreams, The.　Martín Espada.　PueRic

You toss now to the left; you toss now to the right.　Crinagoras.　HePo *Fr.* Epigrams.

You Touch Me.　Andrena Zawinski.　PasH

You trick your thorny rope with little joys.　Geometry of the Soul.　Fawziyya Abu Khalid.　PoArWo, *tr. by* Farouk Mustafa

You tried coming back as a spider.　November 26, 1992: Thanksgiving at the Sea Ranch, Contemplating Metempsychosis.　Sandra M. Gilbert.　InoFa; PoDa

You try to hush me, and hearten me.　Refuge.　Gyula Illyés.　IQMS, *tr. by* Peter Zollman

You Turn Around.　Jordan Davis.　HeMarv

You turn around.　You Turn Around.　Jordan Davis.　HeMarv

You turn towards meteor showers in August.　That Falling.　Jane Hirshfield.　BodElec

You turned down the wrong street.　On the Murder of an Ice Cream Man.　Hayan Charara.　AmPoNex

You Twist Your Death in Nooses.　Nikolai Alekseievich Klyuyev.　TCRusP, *tr. by* John Glad

You twist your death in nooses.　You Twist Your Death in Nooses.　Nikolai Alekseievich Klyuyev.　TCRusP, *tr. by* John Glad

You two gardeners.　New Jersey Boys.　Robert Coles.　BloBone

You two sit at the table late, each, now and then.　After the Dinner Party.　Robert Penn Warren.　NAAL-5; PoCho

You understand him not. Christ does not claim.　Understanding.　István Vas.　IQMS, *tr. by* Godfrey Turton

You understand the colors on the hillside have faded.　Crucifixion.　Hayden Carruth.　BodElec; PLBUT

You unseen lightning flash, you darkly radiant light.　On the Ineffable Inspiration of the Holy Spirit.　Catharina Regina von Greiffenberg.　WoPoe; WPoS, *tr. by* Michael Hamburger

You use your mind.　To Military Progress.　Marianne Moore.　NAAPv.2

You used to let me watch to time the eggs. (LL)　Tony Harrison.　EmeKit; HarvBoo; NAMCP V.2 *Fr.* School of Eloquence, The.

You used to say that you wished to know only Catullus.　Catullus.　NAWM-7v1 *Fr.* Carmina [Charles Martin Translation].

You uterus / you have been patient.　Poem to my uterus.　Lucille Clifton.　BeAl; CAP-8; NAMCP V.2; PoCu

You vanish with early tears. (LL)　Tear.　Thomas Kinsella.　ModIr; NoP-4; NoP-5; OxBEV

You visit me inside the apple.　Inside the Apple.　Yehuda Amichai.　ItP, *tr. by* Chana Bloch

You visit our colony each year.　Mannyelanong.　Huw Jones.　BBMWP, *tr. by* the author

You wait for a right moment.　Sea Without Poets.　Branko Miljkovic.　WoPoe, *tr. by* Charles Simic

You waited with impatience.　Still.　Ronald Stuart Thomas.　TCAWP

You wake at the end of night.　Situation No. 9: The Corposant.　David Citino.　UpMys

You wake in a Córdoba.　Don José Gorostiza Encounters El Cordobés.　Jay Wright.　ESEAA

You wake me.　Kenneth Rexroth.　APSN; NAMCP V.1 *Fr.* Love Poems of Marichiko, The.

You wake to birdcalls.　Letter to Myself as a Child.　Juanita Brunk.　ACAMVP

You wake up and you don't know who it is there breathing.　Region of Unlikeness, The.　Jorie Graham.　HarvBoo

You wake up filled with dread.　Up.　Margaret Atwood.　NoP-4; NoP-5

You walk for miles beside me.　Walk in the Rain.　Polly Clark.　NeBl

You walk into an ordinary room.　Laburnum.　Paula Meehan.　ModIr

You walk on air.　Glance.　Dhabya Khamees.　PoArWo, *tr. by* Clarissa C. Burt

You walk up there in the light.　Hyperion's Song of Fate.　Friedrich Hölderlin.　NAWM-7v2, *tr. by* Christopher Middleton

You walked, all of a sudden, through.　In Memory of Gerard Dillon.　Michael Longley.　PBCIP

You walked dusty dry roads;.　Southern Road.　Mwatabu Okantah.　SeSe

You, Walking Past Me.　Marina Ivanovna Tsvetayeva.　AF, *tr. by* Mary Maddock

You, walking past me.　You, Walking Past Me.　Marina Ivanovna Tsvetayeva.　AF, *tr. by* Mary Maddock

You wander down in brightness.　Friedrich Hölderlin.　WoPoe *Fr.* Hyperion.

You wandered in the desert waste, athirst.　Oasis, An.　Agnes Mary Frances Robinson.　VWP

You want biographical news, you want.　Biographical News.　Daria Menicanti.　CItWP, *tr. by* Cinzia Sartini Blum and Lara Trubowitz

You want corporate woman I get her for you.　Lilies of the Field.　Anne Rouse.　MFPA; NeBl

You want love but not to give up anything.　Emergency Response.　Karen Solie.　OpeFie

You want me pure.　You Want Me White.　Alfonsina Storni.　FiBr, *tr. by* Almitra David

You want me to call you generous.　Martial.　RomPo, *tr. by* Dorothea Wender

You Want Me White ("You want me pure.")　Alfonsina Storni.　FiBr, *tr. by* Almitra David

You want more? You want some more of this shit?　Pulp Fiction.　David Baker.　MAAN

You want this world, smudge of oil on the feather.　Ruth.　Mary Crockett Hill.　AmPoNex

You want to be alone, when you feed us to the tigers and kiss. (LL)　Cho-Fu-Sa.　Tanya Larkin.　FreRad; IIR

You want to be entertained.　Enter(f*#@ckin)tained.　Nzinga Regtuinah Chavis.　BRtP

You want to change your name. You're looking.　Riddle of Noah, The.　Maxine W. Kumin.　OPRER

You want to climb the steps.　Daigan Lueck.　WhBo

You want to make some honey?　Bee.　X. J. Kennedy.　Spl

You want us to believe.　To Our Cosmeticians.　Dzvinia Orlowsky.　PfS

You want? You're in my way. (LL)　Not My Best Side.　U. A. Fanthorpe.　EmeKit; MoWP

You wanted to compare, and there.　Amazon Twins.　Olga Broumas.　FiBr

You wanted to hear angels sing—to render audible.　You Wanted to Hear.　John Smith.　Coast

You wanted to up-end the boat.　On Waitakere Dam.　Sinéad Morrissey.　NIrP

You wanton, quiet memory that haunts me all the while.　Forgotten.　*Unknown, fr. Terezin Concentration Camp.*　INSAB

You wear, and the star running down his cheek. (LL)　Swimming By Night.　James Merrill.　ColAP; HarvBoo

You wear the morning like your dress.　Song.　Joseph Hilaire Pierre Belloc.　OBEV

You well-compacted groves, whose light and shade.　Edward Herbert, 1st Baron Herbert of Cherbury.　OxBSo

You well[-]compacted groves, whose light and shade.　Sonnet Made upon the Groves near Merlou [or Merlow] Castle.　Edward Herbert, 1st Baron Herbert of Cherbury.　NOSC; NPeEn

You went away, I let you.　Lover, Come Back to Me!　Oscar Hammerstein, II.　ReLy

You went away to die, like an ailing pet.　To a Late Local Environmentalist.　Jane Epton Seale.　TiP2

You went by my house.　Magic.　Glenna Luschei.　ICANM

You went downstairs.　Poet to Tiger.　May Swenson.　PoBW

You went out with the turning tide.　Exit Amor.　Virginia Hamilton Adair.　APT-2

You went to the front like sheep.　First World War Poets.　Edward Bond.　FaBoWar

You were.　Praise Song for My Mother.　Grace Nichols.　Prnts

You were a child, and liked me, yesterday.　Arthur Symons.　OxBSo *Fr.* Violet.

You were a fool, Old Man of the Moon.　Nguyễn Gia Thiều.　WoPoe *Fr.* Sorrows of an Abandoned Queen.

You were a girl of satin and gauze.　Wheel Revolves, The.　Kenneth Rexroth.　NAMCP V.1; NoAM

You were a haughty beauty, Polly.　Private Theatricals.　Louise Imogen Guiney.　PoBW

You were a swan, you're now a crow.　Martial.　RomPo, *tr. by* Olive Pitt-Kethley

You were a tender desire, an insinuating cloud.　Luis Cernuda.　CAGL, *tr. by* Rick Lipinski

You were a victim of semiromantic anarchism.　Devils, The.　Charles Simic.　OxBoAm

You were born.　Child of Wonder.　Bill Pearlman.　ICANM

You were born; must die; were loved; must love.　Sonnet: "You were born; must die; were loved; must love."　Stephen Spender.　MoBrPo

You Were Broken.　Giuseppe Ungaretti.　STV, *tr. by* John Frederick Nims

You were caught for ever.　Dylan Iorwerth.　BBMWP *Fr.* Sand.

You were dead, but how sleek and darkly calm you were!　Dream of William Carlos Williams, A.　Robert Bly.　BodElec

You were drawn in the voice of my mother.　Line.　Colette Bryce.　NIrP

You were framed by your dark chestnut hair.　Working for British Telecom.　Ben Scammell.　NLP

You were half-right, I let lie.　On Apologies.　Jean Valerie.　SpirFl

You were hiding behind the door.　*Unknown.*　SLW, *tr. by* Marjolijn De Jager, Sayd Bahodin Majrouh and André Velter

You were invited there.　Death of Poetry, The.　Bob Holman.　BRtP

You were lying here. Dream of the White-headed Boy, A. Colette Ni Ghallchóir. NIrP, *tr.* by the author

You were made. Creation. Jeni Couzyn. HAWP

You Were Meant for Me. Arthur Freed. ReLy

You were my adored one. Blame It on My Youth. Edward Heyman. ReLy

You were my beginning and again I am with you, here, where I learned the four quarters of the globe. In Szetejnie. Czeslaw Milosz. BodElec, *tr.* by the author and Robert Hass

You were my death. Paul Celan. PoetW, *tr.* by John Felstiner

You were my home. Smike. Lucile Adler. ICANM

You were my mother, thorn apple bush. Graves, The. Lorine Niedecker. APT-2

You Were Never Lovelier. Johnny Mercer. ReLy

You Were Never Miss Brown to Me. Sherley Anne Williams. GT

You were never told, Mother, how old Illya was drunk. Czar's Last Christmas Letter, The: A Barn in the Urals. Norman Dubie. NoAM; PoChi

You were not gone. Loved One. Sam White. IIR

You were / nothing. Flower. Kim Ch'unsu [*or* Chun-soo]. CAMKP, *tr.* by Kevin O'Rourke

You were on your way out of the Monopoly game when all of a sudden zap! Going to Jail. Tom Clark and Lewis Warsh. AHA

You were reading. I was dreaming. Reading, Dreaming, Hiding. Kelly Cherry. FFC

You were ready to die, embarrassed that your four. Gangrene. Vanessa Haley. PfS

You were right, your cat knows his own name. He's asleep right now. David McFadden. NLPA

You were so beautiful. I held my breath. You fell asleep and reached the land of winds. Sea at Twenty-Four, The. Kim Chôngnan. EcSo, *tr.* by Peter H. Lee

You were still waving, beloved. *Unknown.* NAAPv.2

You were the light that brightened my life. It's a Blue World. George Forrest and Robert Wright. ReLy

You were the morning star among the living. Aster. Plato. WoPoe, *tr.* by Peter Jay

You were the one for skylights. I opposed. Seamus Heaney. NoP-5; OxBSo *Fr.* Glanmore Revisited.

You were the reason for staying. Notes to my Daughters. Shirley Kaufman. PoChi

You were upstairs in Helana's, less. Paula Cunningham. NIrP *Fr.* Dog Called Chance, A.

You were with us all along. Runaway. Nancy Mitchell. LaCa

You were your own and not mine and I had not lost you. (LL) Epitaph for a Poet. Homero Aridjis. PoetW; STV; TCLAP, *tr.* by John Frederick Nims

You weren't going to go insane, you said. Frost Song. William Heyen. VisFro

You weren't well or really ill yet either. Embrace, The. Mark Doty. AmAlph; AmFaPo; BeAl; NAMCP V.2

You who. Maram Masri. PoArWo, *tr.* by Amal Amireh

You who are born in decay. Firefly. Tu Fu [*or* Du Fu]. CrYelRi, *tr.* by Sam Hamill

You, who are lieutenants in the army. Sebestyén Tinódi. IQMS *Fr.* Call to Lieutenants.

You who are reading this work without malice, may you. Ovid. RomPo *Fr.* Tristia.

You who are still and white. Slain. T. W. H. Crosland. OBWP

You, who behold in wonder Rome and all. Rome. Joachim Du Bellay. WoPoe, *tr.* by Yvor Winters

You who can see the future. Oracle. Fanny Carrión de Fierro. TANSG, *tr.* by Sally Cheney Bell

You who come from my village. Poem. Wang Wei. NDACCP, *tr.* by Gary Snyder

You who come from the old village. Verses. Wang Wei. TAL

You who come home do not tell me. Returning Exile. Iain Crichton Smith. EdScPo

You who desired so much—in vain to ask. To Emily Dickinson. Hart Crane. ColAP; NIL-7; NIP-4; NoAM; NoP-5; OxBoAm

You who draw into yourself each depth. Merciful Shore, The. Maria Luisa Spaziani. NeIt, *tr.* by Beverly Allen

You who dump the beer cans in the lake. Malediction. Barry Spacks. RaF

You, who gave colour to the dawn. Hymn. T. Rowland Hughes. BBMWP, *tr.* by Sally Roberts Jones

You who have forgotten yourself in this moving tomb. Short Revelation Concerning Death and Chaos. René Daumal. PFTM-1

You who hear in scattered rhymes the sound of those sighs with. Petrarch. NAWM-7v1 *Fr.* Sonnets to Laura.

You who in evenings by the fire. These Poems. John Jarmain. FaBoWar

You, who inconstancy so constantly can squander. To the Moon. Paul Fleming. GePo, *tr.* by George C. Schoolfield

You who knew nothing, understood everything. Now That I Have Grown Up, Mother. Clementina Suárez. TANSG, *tr.* by Janet N. Gold

You who live secure. Shemà. Primo Levi. AF; BeAl; FaBoWar; HP; PLBUT; PoAgWa, *tr.* by Ruth Feldman and Brian Swann

(You live secure.) PoCho

You who look lovely from the windows. Praxilla. SaLy, *tr.* by Diane Rayor

You Who Occupy Our Land. Maria Manuela Margarido. HAWP, *tr.* by Allan Francovich

You who pull the oars, who meet the dead. Charon. Zonas. PoDa, *tr.* by Brooks Haxton

You who rest your belly on a pair of fat pilings. Trumpet, Shout, Carry! Velemir Khlebnikov. TCRusP, *tr.* by Kathy Lewis and Bob Perelman

You Who Sleep. Philippe Soupault. AF, *tr.* by Eden Paul

You who smile from the disarmed. Possibility. Tiziano Rossi. ItPo, *tr.* by Gayle Ridinger

You who snore with your sleeping wife so near. Tristan Corbière. OBVE *Fr.* Litany of Sleep.

You, who thought that my heart would be full of anguish. Song of Reproach. Ferenc Apáti. IQMS, *tr.* by Adam Makkai

You, who to avoid my manhood. *Unknown.* PriapPo *Fr.* Priapus Poems, The.

You who want. Hadewijch II. HW; WPoS

You who were darkness warmed my flesh. Woman to Child. Judith Wright. BrAP

You who will emerge from the flood. Bertolt Brecht. AF *Fr.* To Those Born Later.

You who wronged a simple man. You Who Wronged. Czeslaw Milosz. ItP, *tr.* by Richard Lourie

You whom I could not protect. Fragments of the Forgotten War. Suji Kwock Kim. AmWaPo

You whom I could not save. Dedication. Czeslaw Milosz. AF; BeAl; PoAgWa; WoPoe, *tr.* by the author

You, whose day it is, make it beautiful. Song to Bring Fair Weather. *Unknown.* WoPoe, *tr.* by Frances Densmore

You, whose head once gazed at a sky so lofty. To a Fallen Walnut Tree. Dávid Baróti Szabó. IQMS, *tr.* by Watson Kirkconnell

You, wild hawk. *Unknown.* CATKP, *tr.* by Peter H. Lee

You will always be an some border. We All Conspire. Mario Benedetti. TCLAP, *tr.* by Sophie Cabot Black and Maria Negroni

You will ask: And where are the lilacs? I Explain a Few Things. Pablo Neruda. PoetW, *tr.* by Nathaniel Tarn

You will be able to see me. (LL) This Is a Photograph of Me. Margaret Atwood. BrAP; NALW; NAMCP V.2; NoAM; NoP-4; NoP-5

You Will Be Astonished. Michel Deguy. PFTM-2, *tr.* by Clayton Eshleman

You will be astonished to hear the freedom of Paul. You Will Be Astonished. Michel Deguy. PFTM-2, *tr.* by Clayton Eshleman

You Will Be Hearing from Us Shortly. U. A. Fanthorpe. OBCoV

You will be obscured by a cloud of postures. Nadar. Richard Howard. GS

You will come into an antique town. Where I Live. Wesley McNair. TRP

You will come to a well on the left side of hell's house. Petelia Tablet, The. *Unknown.* WoPoe, *tr.* by Robert Bringhurst

You Will Come to Me. Celâl Sılay. NaPG, *tr.* by Talat Sait Halman

You will find here a new representation of the universe. Horse Calligram. Guillaume Apollinaire. PFTM-1

You will find my past not spotless. My Future Just Passed. George Marion, Jr. ReLy

You will find your voices as I found mine. To a Poet (the Pearl). Gus Blaisdell. ICANM

You Will Forget. Chenjerai Hove. HBAPE; NAfrP; PLBUT

You will have smiled, I shall have tossed your hair. (LL) À Quoi Bon Dire. Charlotte Mew. MakPoe; NPeEn; OxBEV; VWP

You will know that boy on sight. Man and Boy. John N. Morris. PoA 2002

You Will Know When You Get There. Allen Curnow. EmeKit; NoP-4

You will leave your home. What the Oracle Said. Shara McCallum. BRtP

You will marry that mouth in your mind. (LL) Mission Poem. Tarin Towers. AmPoNex; PuP-23

You will need. Truganinny. Wendy Rose. HATNAP

You will never change, your life. Winged Torso of Eros. Daniel Hall. PoA 2002

You will not always have me here to say. Storm, The. George Scarbrough. LPSFW

You will not be able to buy. Child Bride. Garnett Kilberg Cohen. MPUn

You will not tame this sea. Sea and the Man, The. Anna Swirszczynska [*or* Swir]. BLT

You will remember that strange precipice. Sonnet 4. Pablo Neruda. BLPSL, *tr.* by Rene de Costa, Rigas Kappatos and Eleni Paidoussi

You will remember, when the bombs. Paris—Christmas 1938. Edwin Rolfe. APT-2

You will say that I am stupid for telling this. I am stupid and no one is interested. When I Got My First Tattoo I Was. Jennifer Bartlett. ICANM

You will see me in the wolf's footstep. Signs. Silvia Grénier. SurWo, *tr. by* Myrna Bell Rochester

You will speak of our days in whispers. Eclipse. John Haines. PoCoUp

You will stop suffering now and you will sleep. Bedtime Story. Lee Upton. AmAlph

You wished for a love-letter, Doctor. Love-letter, A. Mary E. Tucker. CBWP-1

You with the beard as red as Barbarossa's. For My Great-Grandfather: A Message Long Overdue. Maxine W. Kumin. UnSA

You with your back to the wall. (LL) Orion. Adrienne Rich. BrAP; NAMCP V.2; NIP-4; NoAM; NoP-4; NoP-5

You with Your Beautiful Swaying Walk. Amaru. WoPoe, *tr. by* Henry Heifetz

You with your beautiful swaying walk, where. You with Your Beautiful Swaying Walk. Amaru. WoPoe, *tr. by* Henry Heifetz

You, with your rainbow-brows woven of light. Hymn for All Seasons. László Nagy. IQMS, *tr. by* Adam Makkai

You wonder at that Georgian terrace. Lychees. Medbh McGuckian. PBCIP

You wonder, since I'm wooden front to rear. *Unknown.* PriapPo *Fr.* Priapus Poems, The.

You wonder who this is! And, why I name. On the Town's Honest Man. Ben Jonson. NOSC

You wonder why Drab sells her love for gold? Epigram. James Vincent Cunningham. APT-2

You wonder why I sail along in uncertainty. Bird-Shooting. Eugenio Montale. ItPo, *tr. by* Gayle Ridinger

You wonder why it is they write of it, sing of it. Up on the Roof. Maura Dooley. NeBl

You wonder why it never changes. Thousand Cranes, A. Dale Ritterbusch. AmWaPo

You won't be the one to turn away when death. Clay Pipes, The. Cathal Ó Searcaigh. ModIr, *tr. by* Seamus Heaney

You won't find them in places where society goes. Dandelions. Will D. Stanton. SoSe-8

You won't hear a world of chair after that. (LL) Conversation. Mihangel Morgan. BBMWP; BeAl, *tr. by* Martin Davis

You won't know me. Any resemblance. Cardio Room, Young Women's Christian Association. Karen Solie. OpeFie

You won't let me be ostrich, armadillo. Zoology Is Destiny. Linda France. StAl

You Words. Ingeborg Bachmann. PoSu, *tr. by* Mark Anderson

You words, come, after me! You Words. Ingeborg Bachmann. PoSu, *tr. by* Mark Anderson

You wore blue peddle pushers and polka dot tops. Girl. Kelly Norman Ellis. SpirFl

You worked me well, Mr Thomas. Master, The. Bryn Griffiths. TCAWP

You worry me whoever you are. Badman of the Guest Professor. Ishmael Reed. EGAG; SSLK

You Worthless. *Unknown.* FaBoVe

You would always offer me a mug. Big John's Tears Fall to the River. Siobhan Campbell. MFPA

You would be a heap of ashes instantly. *Unknown.* SLW, *tr. by* Marjolijn De Jager, Sayd Bahodin Majrouh and André Velter

You would have scoffed if we had told you yesterday. To a Child in Death. Charlotte Mew. ChIV-2; MoBrPo

You Would Have Understood Me [*lyric*]. Paul Verlaine. MoBrPo

You would not believe it; I sat. Giving Thanks. Anne K. Smith. PasH

You would not believe, would you. Edgar Lee Masters. APT-1 *Fr.* Spoon River Anthology.

You would not guess it is the voice. Frog Song. Hildegarde Flanner. APT-2

You would not recognize me. Tourist from Syracuse, The. Donald Justice. NAMCP V.2; NoAM; OxBoAm; VCAP

You would shrink back / jump up. July 4, 1984: For Buck. June Jordan. NAMCP V.2; NoAM

You would think that night could lift. Testament of Loss. Gloria C. Oden. ESEAA

You would think the fury of aerial bombardment. Fury of Aerial Bombardment, The. Richard Eberhart. AmWaPo; APT-2; BrAP; HeIP-4; InoFa; NAAPv.2; NAMCP V.1; NIL-7; NIP-4; NoAM; NoP-4; NoP-5; OBWP; OtW; PoAgWa; PoWW; PWW2; WaAnP

You wouldn't be so depressed. Jane Kenyon. LoL *Fr.* Having It Out with Melancholy.

You wouldn't believe all this house has cost me. Flitting, The. Medbh McGuckian. PBCIP; PNI

You wouldn't fit in your coffin. You Didn't Fit. Susan Musgrave. NIL-7

You wretch who did not come last evening! *Unknown.* SLW, *tr. by* Marjolijn De Jager, Sayd Bahodin Majrouh and André Velter

You write: "I am here, faithful to the echo of your voice: silent, unexpressed." Faithful Betrayal. Victor Segalen. YaTCFP, *tr. by* Timothy Billings and Christopher Bush

You wrong me, Strephon, when you say. Song. "Ephelia." EMWP

You wrong that lovely time to smile and say. Hundred Years Ago, A. Sarah Morgan Bryan Piatt. NAAPv.1

You wrote such a love poem that I was. Seaside, The. Lee Harwood. AHA

You wrote this from Beirut, two years before. Homage to Faiz Ahmed Faiz. Agha Shahid Ali. OpBo

You / You're like a crocus, like a sugar maple. Spring Fever. Rosario Morales. PueRic

You yourself must be the seventh. (LL) Seventh, The. Attila József. AF; PtR, *tr. by* John Batki

You'd Be Surprised. Irving Berlin. ReLy

You'd better abandon all idea of feelings altogether. (LL) To Women, as Far as I'm Concerned. D. H. Lawrence. NPeEn; RaBo

You'd dozed in front of the TV. Old Days, The. Raymond Carver. LaCa

You'd get it and be right here. (LL) Way to Cold Mountain, The. Han-shan (Cold Mountain). CCL1; NDACCP, *tr. by* Gary Snyder

You'd have men's hearts up from the dust. Near Perigord. Ezra Pound. APT-1

You'd know the folly of being comforted. (LL) Folly of Being Comforted, The. William Butler Yeats. HeIP-4; IJHIL; IrLP; NAEL-6v2; NAEL-7v2

You'd like to kiss your little boy but he doesn't want to. Lady on Streetcar. Sandro Penna. STV, *tr. by* John Frederick Nims

You'd never set foot in this part of town before. Failure. Katha Pollitt. OxBoAm

You'd think all these mandarins, big shots. Mandarins Got Their Raise, The. Tu Mo. WoPoe, *tr. by* Nguyen Ngoc Bich

You'd think they discovered injustice and achieved. Gulls at Cannon Beach. William Stafford. PoCoUp

You'd think they'd be with family. Christmas Eve. Sascha Feinstein. SeSe

You'd think this piece of road. How the Elderly Drive. Erin Belieu. AmPoNex

You'd think we'd know by now (Aren't these the days). Be Careful of the Lilies! Jean Bleakney. NIrP

You-hu: There's Fox. *Unknown.* CCL1, *tr. by* Arthur Cooper

You'll get fucked, thief, for the first time. *Unknown.* PriapPo *Fr.* Priapus Poems, The.

You'll have to be a little more standoffish. All er Nothin'. Oscar Hammerstein, II. ReLy

You'll have to rethink the whole question. This. Whole Question, The. Robert Penn Warren. BodElec; OxBoAm

You'll have understood by then what these Ithakas mean. (LL) Ithaka. Constantine P. Cavafy. BeAl; PtR, *tr. by* Edmund Keeley and Philip Sherrard

You'll hear her all the time on the street, talking quite sociably. Portrait of an Overpopulated Woman. Bobi Jones. BBMWP, *tr. by* Joseph P. Clancy

You'll learn, should you steal apples in my care. *Unknown.* PriapPo *Fr.* Priapus Poems, The.

You'll need a tiller's hand to steer this through. To Smithereens. Vona Groarke. MoWP; NIrP

You'll never know. (LL) Certain Lady, A. Dorothy Parker. NIL-7; NIP-4

You'll never sleep tonight. Insomnia. Cornelius Eady. AWTN; ESEAA

You'll never understand *No Road This Way*. Past Time. Edith Jay Scovell. HarvBoo

You'll Never Walk Alone. Oscar Hammerstein, II. ReLy

You'll ruin your eyesight, lad. As Old As Then. Jan Eijkelboom. TuT, *tr. by* Michael O'Loughlin

You'll see me park my car upon. Red Light District Nurse, The. James Fenton and John Fuller. OBCoV

You'll show a hat that's white, or a feather! (LL) John Burns of Gettysburg. Bret Harte. CBCWP; PCW

You'll stand waiting in the rain your eyelashes will grow long. I Love You So. Ahmet Ada. NaPG, *tr. by* Talat Sait Halman

Young, The. David Alpaugh. CalPo

Young Africans. Gwendolyn Brooks. NoAM

Young and Healthy. Al Dubin. ReLy

Young and Old. Charles Kingsley. GoPo; OxAEP-2 *Fr.* Water Babies, The.

"Young and old, rejoice." Neidhart von Reuental. GePo

Young and willing to learn (but what?) he was the boy. Razzmatazz. Gilbert Sorrentino. FTOS

Young are quick of speech, The. On Teaching the Young. Yvor Winters. APT-2; MakPoe; NoAM

Young are walking on the riverbank, The. Kissing. Fleur Adcock. StAl

Young at Heart. Carolyn Leigh. ReLy

Young attendants wrapped him in a red, The. Inpatient. Dolores Kendrick. FFC

Young Ben he was a nice young man. Faithless Sally Brown. Thomas Hood. OBNV

Young Birch, A. Robert Frost. SAmP

Young black girl stopped by the woods, A. Interpretation of a Poem by Frost. Thylias Moss. NAMCP V.2; VisFro

Young Boys, The. Linda Hogan. ArBi

Young British Soldier, The. Rudyard Kipling. "When first under fire an' you're wishful to duck." FaBoWar

Young but not youthful he thou lovest not. Rose Leaves When the Rose Is Dead. Marc André Raffalovich. CAGL

Young children do not yet know worry, The. *Unknown.* NAAPv.2

Young Chinese gets down!, The. Midnight Rocker, Tiananmen Square, May 27, 1989. Edith Rylander. MiVo

Young clerk peruses the court's files, A. Corruption. Freddy Macha. NAfrP

Young Clovis by a happy chance. On a Bashful Shepherd. "Ephelia." PEW

Young, coat still downy. Pamela Alexander. AmAlph *Fr.* Foxlight.

Young composer, working that summer at an artist's colony, had watched her for a week, The. Story about the Body, A. Robert Hass. CAP-8; FaoP; OxBoAm; RaBo

Young Coridon and Phillis. Sir Charles Sedley. BASC

Young dead soldiers do not speak, nevertheless they are heard, The. Young Dead Soldiers, The. Hayim Hefer. NRoS, *tr. by* Esther Raizen

Young Don't Want to Be Born. James Wright. BodElec

Young Elvis. Cornelius Eady. AllShUp

Young engineer receives a wooden crate marked: *unusual cargo*, A. In the Interest of Possibility. Thom Ward. AmPoNex

Young finch asked the old one why he wept, The. Caged Birds. Ignacy Krasicki. WoPoe, *tr. by* Jerzy Peterkiewicz and Burns Singer

Young Fools, The. Paul Verlaine. WoPoe, *tr. by* Louis Simpson

Young, gifted, and black. To be Young, Gifted, and Black. Weldon J., Jr. Irvine. ISC

Young Girl. Carl Rakosi. APT-2

Young Girl, A. Waldo Williams. BBMWP, *tr. by* Anthony Conran

Young girl dancing lifts her face, The. Dancer, The. Walter James Turner. NOBAu; OBMV

Young Girl Peeling Apples. Mary Jo Salter. FFC

Young Girl Sleeping. Jean Cocteau. YaTCFP, *tr. by* Alfred Corn

Young girl to marry. Lorine Niedecker. NAAPv.2

Young Girl with a Pitcher Full of Water, A. David Wagoner. NAMCP V.2; NoAM

Young Girls. Patricia K. Page. BrAP; StAl

Young Girls. Raymond Souster. BrAP; HeIP-4

Young girls walk by looking like wedding, The. Peonies. Susan Firer. SweBea

Young good man walked out savoring, The. Young Good Man, The. James Wright. CAP-8

Young grass and shriveled. Hakuro Wada. NAAPv.2

Young, having risen early, had gone, The. Guardians, The. Geoffrey Hill. NoP-4; NoP-5

Young homosexuals and the horny girls, The. Single Gentleman. Pablo Neruda. ConPit, *tr. by* Clayton Eshleman

Young Horseman. Lajos Kassák. IQMS, *tr. by* Edwin Morgan

Young Housewife, The. William Carlos Williams. APT-1; ColAP; HeIP-4; NAAL-5; NAAPv.2; NAMCP V.1; OxBoAm; WaAnP

Young I am, and yet unskill'd. Song for a Girl. John Dryden. ErotSp

Young Ionia, The. John Frederick Nims. IllVoic

Young Johnnie Jones, he had a cute little boat. Row, Row, Row. William Jerome. ReLy

Young Juan now was sixteen years of age. Lord Byron. NPBRoP *Fr.* Don Juan.

Young Juan wandered by the glassy brooks. Lord Byron. OBCoV *Fr.* Don Juan.

Young king must have been terrible to behold, The. Alexander at Thebes. Anna Andreyevna Akhmatova. FaBoWar, *tr. by* Max Hayward and Stanley Kunitz

Young lass, A. Spring Song. Li Po. NDACCP, *tr. by* William Carlos Williams

Young Laundryman, The. William Carlos Williams. SAmP

Young Lochinvar. Sir Walter Scott. *See* Lochinvar.

Young Love. Andrew Marvell. OxAEP-1

Young Love. William Carlos Williams. APT-1

Young maiden, young maiden, where do you go? Spider Lilies. Kitahara Hakushū. CAoMJL1, *tr. by* Leith Morton

Young man and I face each other, The. On The Subway. Sharon Olds. LTA

Young man, before time flies further away. Advice to a Young Man. *Unknown.* CAGL, *tr. by* James J. Wilhelm

Young man came to me with a message from his brother, A. Walt Whitman. APN-1 *Fr.* Leaves of Grass [1855 Version].

Young man, do not hurl yourself. Crone, The. Karolina Pavlova. ARWW, *tr. by* Catriona Kelly

Young man, hardly more, The. Gettysburg, July 1, 1863. Jane Kenyon. CBCWP

Young man / I love you and life is wonderful, The. Spurt of Blood, The. Antonin Artaud. PFTM-1

Young man in his prime, let's call him M., goes out to pick flowers in the meadow, A. In the Picture. Elke Erb. MotU, *tr. by* Craig Federhen

Young Man Loves a Maiden, A. Heinrich Heine. NAWM-7v2, *tr. by* Hal Draper

Young man loves a maiden, A. Young Man Loves a Maiden, A. Heinrich Heine. NAWM-7v2, *tr. by* Hal Draper

Young Man Naughty's Adventure. Charlotte Brontë. VWP

Young Man of Galway's Lament, The. James Harpur. IrLP

Young man of twenty-five, a paper and a pen, and an attempt to put the last five years into language, A. Declining Sun. Bahaa Awwad. AnVo, *tr. by* Mohamed Enani

Young man with desires so bad, he needs to save the world. This I Whisper. Horehound Stillpoint. BeDoSh

Young man with long thick eyelashes is, The. Next Bend in the Road, The. Michael Fried. PoCho

Young Mary, loitering once her garden way. Mary and Gabriel. Rupert Brooke. ChIV-2

Young master, The. Karai Senryū. EMJL, *tr. by* Makoto Ueda

Young Maury loved his slave—she was his own. Albery Allson Whitman. NAAPv.1 *Fr.* Octoroon, The.

Young May Moon, The. Thomas Moore. OBEV

Young men always expose themselves to me on Amtrak. Tea Dance. Wayne Koestenbaum. WiU

Young Men Come Less Often, The—Isn't It So? Horace. WoPoe, *tr. by* Robert Fitzgerald

Young Men Dead. John Peale Bishop. APT-1

Young men, defend me, defend your very honor! *Unknown.* SLW, *tr. by* Marjolijn De Jager, Sayd Bahodin Majrouh and André Velter

Young men give ear to me a while. Maid's Complaint for Want of a Dil Doul, The. *Unknown.* EroLit

Young Men of Blackburn, The. Dennis O'Donnell. EdScPo

Young men should not write sonnets, if they dream. Sonnet-writing. To F. W. F. Frederick William Faber. CenSon

Young Miracle Stag, The. László Nagy. IQMS, *tr. by* Adam Makkai

Young model undressed before the poet, The. Evening Wind. William Carpenter. PoSol

Young Monk (Denver). David Craig. UpMys

Young Mothers 1. Sharon Olds. EMP

Young mouse, poor, no experience, A. Jean de La Fontaine. WoPoe, *tr. by* Bruce Boone and Robert Glück

Young Oaks, The. Andrew Hudgins. LPSFW

Young once / and dreaming. *Unknown.* SonAtl, *tr. by* Billy Galdes, Estelle Norden and P. Wynne

Young persons, it is true, admire. True Friend, The. Ann Plato. SWaP

Young Pete. Mihály Vörösmarty. IQMS, *tr. by* Yakov Hornstein

Young poet comes to me, A. Blind Solo. Afaa Michael Weaver. UnSA

Young priest, dead suddenly, A. In Memoriam (2). Daniel Berrigan. UpMys

Young Prince of Tyre ['Thy ear is liable, thy food is such As hath been belch'd on by infected lungs' Pericles]. "Ern Malley." BMAP

Young rhymester, don't try to gag the old muse. Mortality. R. Williams Parry. BBMWP, *tr. by* Martin Davis

Young rice plants are just being. Heart's Garden, the Garden's Heart, The. Kenneth Rexroth.

Young schizophrenic named Struther, A. Limerick. *Unknown.* OBCoV

Young skull which the wind scrapes, which the sand. On the Relative Merit of Friend and Foe, Being Dead. Donald Thompson. FaBoWar

Young skunk. Shu Swamp, Spring. May Swenson. APT-2

Young Sleep, most gentle of gods, by what misdeed. Publius Papinius Statius. RomPo *Fr.* Sylvae [*or* Silvae].

Young Son, The. John Ashbery. YaYoPo

Young Soul. Imamu Amiri Baraka. OxAAAP

Young Spain, A. Antonio Machado Ruiz. RaW, *tr. by* Charles Guenther

Young sparrows. Issa. SoOfWa, *tr. by* Sam Hamill

Young Sun's Greeting, The. Léopold Sédar Senghor. YaTCFP, *tr. by* Hoyt Rogers

Young Sycamore. William Carlos Williams. APT-1

Young then, / we were bored already. Epitaph. Eleanor Wilner. ChIV-1

Young Timothy Timid is cautious and wealthy. By Proxy. Amos Russel Wells. ArBi

Young trees the bright green of a moonless night. August Zero. Jane Miller. BodElec

Young Wife, A. D. H. Lawrence. MoBrPo

Young Wife's Lament. Brigit Pegeen Kelly. CFP; IllVoic

Young Woman at a Window. William Carlos Williams. HHAm

Young woman is just sitting on the bed, The. Edward Hopper, "Hotel Room," 1931. Larry Levis. PoSol

Young Woman of Beare, The. Austin Clarke. NAMCP V.1; NoAM "Through lane or black archway." ModIr

Young Woman Stands on the Edge of Her Life, The. Kerry Hardie. NIrP

Young Woman Who Becomes a Bear set fire in the mountains. *Unknown.* APN-2 *Fr.* Mountain Chant, The.

Young Woman's Blues. Bessie Smith. NAAPv.2

Young Woman's Complaint about Her Sweetheart, A. Elen Gwdman. EMWP

Younger, / I felt the dead. Roots. Seamus Deane. PNI

Younger Poet, A. Peter Schjeldahl. PoA 2002

Younger Than Springtime. Oscar Hammerstein, II. ReLy

Youngest Daughter, The. Cathy Song. NoAM; WaAnP

Your Absence. Roy Fuller. OxBSo *Fr.* Cancer Hospital, The.

Your Absence. Arthur Nortje. TSAP

Your absence has gone through me. Separation. W. S. Merwin. NoP-4; NoP-5

Your alms are my salary. Torture Chamber. Enrique Lihn. PoetW; VCWP, *tr. by* Mary Crow

Your ambitions ran short. Last Word, The. Gaylord Brewer. RWB

Your ancient tiers climb among the stars. Old City, The. Ivan Teofilov. CSCBP, *tr. by* Georgi Belev and Lisa Sapinkopf

Your Anger. Paz Molina. TANSG, *tr. by* Steven F. White

Your Appearance is Pleasing. Baudri of Bourgueil. CAGL, *tr. by* Thomas Stehling

Your appearance is pleasing because it is proper and handsome. Your Appearance is Pleasing. Baudri of Bourgueil. CAGL, *tr. by* Thomas Stehling

Your are cordially invited. Testimonial. Harry Newman, Jr. GoPo

Your arm is gone. D-Day, 1994. Jack Coulehan. BloBone

Your Arms. Dora Teitelboim. Prolet, *tr. by* Amelia Glaser

Your arms have drawn me in. Your Arms. Dora Teitelboim. Prolet, *tr. by* Amelia Glaser

Your ashen hair Shulamite. (LL) Death Fugue, A. Paul Celan. CLPP; GifTon; PFTM-2, *tr. by* Jerome Rothenberg

Your ashen hair Shulamith. (LL) Fugue of Death. Paul Celan. OBVE; PoetW, *tr. by* Christopher Middleton

Your ashen hair Shulamith. (LL) Death Fugue. Paul Celan. GPTC; HP; VCWP; WoPoe, *tr. by* Michael Hamburger

Your ashes will not stir, even on this high ground. In Carrowdore Churchyard. Derek Mahon. NoP-4; NoP-5; PBCIP; PNI

Your attention, ladies and gentlemen, your attention for one moment. Pilgrim, The. Nicanor Parra. VCWP

Your Attention Please. Peter Porter. OBWP

Your average tourist: Fifty. 2.3. James Merrill. BeAl; NIP-4 *Fr.* Topics.

Your baby grows a tooth, then two. Little Tooth, A. Thomas Lux. BodElec; GoPo

Your Beauty and My Reason. *Unknown.* NoSic

Your beauty is one thing in the mirror. People Will Talk. Orban Veli Kanik. NaPG, *tr. by* Talat Sait Halman

Your Beauty, ripe and calm, and fresh. Lover and Philosopher. Sir William Davenant. OBEV

Your beauty, ripe, and calm, and fresh. Sir William Davenant. OxBEV

Your beauty, which I lost sight of once. Love Song. Denise Levertov. PtR

Your bed's got two wrong sides. Your life's all grouse. Tony Harrison. NAEL-6v2; NAEL-7v2 *Fr.* School of Eloquence, The.

Your behavior proves how stingy You are, Ma. Mahendranāth Bhattācārya. SinGod, *tr. by* Rachel Fell McDermott

Your birth to a mule-trader in 1884. Harry S Truman Library, Independence, Missouri. Diane Glancy. AtGh

Your body derns. Scunner. Hugh MacDiarmid. NePenScot

Your Body Glistens From the Bath. Charles Rossiter. PasH

Your body is a garden, a bush of flowers. Jorge Carrera Andrade. BLPSL *Fr.* Body of the Beloved, The.

Your body is a golden temple. Jorge Carrera Andrade. BLPSL *Fr.* Body of the Beloved, The.

Your body is bathed eternally. Jorge Carrera Andrade. BLPSL *Fr.* Body of the Beloved, The.

Your body is night. Form. Elsa Cross. RMCMP, *tr. by* Margaret Sayers Peden

Your body this humid afternoon is another. Parfum Exotique. Padraic Fallon. IrLP

Your body tolls the hour. Glass, The. Carolyn Kizer. ErotSp

Your body's a small word with many meanings. Canadian Love Song. Alden Nowlan. StAl

Your bones have crumbled and turned into stones. Yollim Kut Song. Shin Kyong-Nim. PML, *tr. by* Anthony, Brother of Taizé

Your bones refused to burn. Cremation. Agha Shahid Ali. InoFa

Your book surprised me on the bookstore shelf. On Not Shoplifting Louise Bogan's *The Blue Estuaries*. Julia Alvarez. WaAnP

Your breasts will not fall. Se Praj. ErotSp, *tr. by* Sam Hamill

Your brother has leukemia? Carve ivory. The elections were rigged? Write a villanelle. Aesthetics. Joel Brouwer. LegDan

Your burning blood, your dancing tongue. (LL) Women You Are Accustomed To, The. Lucille Clifton. ErotSp; GT

Your camera / has caught it all, the lit. Snapshot. Charles Tomlinson. NAMCP V.2

Your chance of death. (LL) Fragment 68: "I envy you your chance of death." "H. D." NAAPv.2; NAMCP V.1

Your Character is Your Destiny. Erin Belieu. ExTi

Your Chariot. Viswanatha Satyanarayana. HotL, *tr. by* V. Narayana Rao

Your chest, hospital gown. My Father's Neck. Robert Bly. BodElec

Your childhood. My Pain. Yu Wang. CFP, *tr. by* Tang Chao

Your children's new names in the tombstone of thin air. (LL) On an East Wind from the Wars. Alan Dugan. AF; GPTC

Your clear eye is the one absolutely beautiful thing. Child. Sylvia Plath. NAAL-5

Your clear hands call my name. Dead of Winter. Salvatore Quasimodo. WoPoe, *tr. by* George Garrett

Your coat, beer-and-milk, with crowns on velvet. Brenin Gwalia. John Roderick Rees. BBMWP, *tr. by* the author

Your coffin looked unreal. Child Burial. Paula Meehan. EmeKit; InoFa; MakPoe; ModIr

Your comedy I've read, my friend. To a Living Author. *Unknown.* NBLV

Your compassionate mind. Lover of Mountains. Muso Soseki. EaWin, *tr. by* W. S. Merwin

YOUR coulter cuts the soil that erst was sown. Poor Ploughman to a Gentleman for Whom He Had Taken a Little Pains, A. George Turberville. NoSic

Your daffodils rose up. Letter with No Address. Donald Hall. InoFa

Your dance is age- / less; it transcends. Prince of the Dance. Cecil Rajendra. PML

Your daughter, fifteen, has drunk half a bottle. Father of the Man. David Graham. SwNoth

Your daughter is dead. Violence. Wendy Bishop. LiTh

Your Death and Mine. János Pilinszky. IQMS, *tr. by* Adam Makkai

Your dishpan is quiet as a pond. Wrecked World. Marilyn Annucci. PoDa

Your door is shut against my tightened face. White House, The. Claude McKay. ISC; NIP-4

Your dream: / The letters HIV appear. Hayden Carruth. GifTon *Fr.* Sleeping Beauty, The.

Your dream (you tell me). Polestar. Christopher Stahl. BeDoSh

Your dresses never kept you warm. Jean Rhys. William Scammell. NLP

Your dry voice from the centre of the bed. Safe period. Helen Dunmore. StAl

Your dying was a difficult enterprise. Lament. Thom Gunn. CAGL; GPTC; InoFa

Your earlier life? images & thots just like now, but fewer words—a. Barry McKinnon. NLPA *Fr.* Arrhythmia.

Your energies are. Alex Rawls. AnSo *Fr.* What's Your Sign?

Your every day is a pilgrimage. To An Old Black Woman, Homeless and Indistinct. Gwendolyn Brooks. ESEAA

Your eyen two will slay me suddenly. Geoffrey Chaucer. NAEL-6v1 *Fr.* Merciles[s] Beaute [*or* Beautée *or* Beauty].

Your Eyes Are Always Open. Gerardo Diego. RaW, *tr. by* Ralph Nelson

Your eyes are just. Four-Word Lines. May Swenson. OxBoAm

Your eyes are like. Sextet. C. Yaphet Brinson. BtF

Your eyes are so beautiful. I could live in them. (LL) Small Acts. Thomas Centolella. GifTon; ViWalt

Your eyes are the eyes of a man in love. For Two Voices. Luis Cernuda. CAGL, *tr. by* Rick Lipinski

Your eyes are the grey of fields of dew. Walk toward Love, The. Gaston Miron. YaTCFP, *tr. by* Mary Ann Caws

Your eyes don't shine like they used to shine. (I'm Afraid) The Masquerade Is Over. Herb Magidson. ReLy

Your eyes drink of me. Mystery, The. Sara Teasdale. PasH

Your eyes lit up with that gleam. Come So Far as You Can Feel. Gültekin SamanoĞlu. NaPG, *tr. by* Talat Sait Halman

Your Eyes, O My Beloved. Nelly Sachs. WPoS, *tr. by* Matthew Mead and Ruth Mead

Your eyes, O my beloved. Your Eyes, O My Beloved. Nelly Sachs. WPoS, *tr. by* Matthew Mead and Ruth Mead

Your eyes stolen. Lello Voce. ItPo *Fr.* Variation 3 (On Love and More).

Your eyes were ever brown, the colour. On Not Being Your Lover. Medbh McGuckian. IrLP; PBCIP; PNI

Your eyes were not there. Lonely Night. P. C. Boutens. TuT, *tr. by* Tony Curtis

Your face broods from my table, Suicide. John Berryman. CAP-8 *Fr.* Dream Songs.

Your face did not rot. Lost Pilot, The. James Tate. AmWaPo; EmeKit; InoFa; NAMCP V.2; NoAM; OBWP; OtW; OxBoAm; PWW2; WaAnP

Your Face Has No Name. Dacia Maraini. CItWP, *tr. by* Cinzia Sartini Blum and Lara Trubowitz

Your Face Here. Robin S. Chapman. PoCoUp

Your face is the face of all the others. Face of Love, The. Ingrid Jonker. HAWP, *tr. by* Jack Cope

Your face is the unexplored earth. Flash, A. May Muzaffar. PoArWo, *tr. by* Tahia Abdel Nasser

Your Face Is Written in My Soul. Baldomero Garcilaso de la Vega. SpanPo, *tr. by* Edwin Morgan

Your face is written in my soul, and when. Your Face Is Written in My Soul. Baldomero Garcilaso de la Vega. SpanPo, *tr. by* Edwin Morgan

Your faith is in what you hold. Chicago. Lola Ridge. PoA 2002

Your Family. Black and Divided or Chittlins and Caviar. Nicole Breedlove. InTrad

"Your father walks like you." Family Stories. Dacia Maraini. CItWP, *tr. by* Cinzia Sartini Blum and Lara Trubowitz

Your father's mustache. Possessive Case, The. Lisel Mueller. GoPo

Your Figure or the War Against Fat. Joyce Mansour. SurPaPo, *tr. by* Mary Ann Caws

Your final bed was not adorned with roses. Requiem. Annette M'Baye d'Erneville. HAWP, *tr. by* Brian Baer

Your fingers circle. Adria Klinger. PasH

Your fingers fully awake, it. Alan Brownjohn. NewEx

Your fingers touch me like a bird's wing. Bird of Endless Time, The. James Laughlin. WeW-3

Your first question. Birds Love the Net. Kondepudi Nirmala. HotL, *tr. by* V. Narayana Rao

Your foot would lift, as if levitating. Middle Path. Galway Kinnell. PoA 2002

Your footprints of light on sensitive paper. Modotti. Adrienne Rich. NoP-5

Your foot's on my gown. After. May Probyn. VWP

Your foundations are strong. Lewis. Derick Thomson. EdScPo

Your four ancestors never enjoyed peace. *Various authors.* CATKP *Fr.* Songs of Flying Dragons.

Your friend, the end, comes every day. Apprentice Eats Glass, The. David Craig. UpMys

Your friend's arriving on the bus. Craig Arnold. BAP-04

Your fury explodes. Kali. Elsa Cross. TANSG, *tr. by* Patricia Dubrava

Your gaze stays awake in the night. Leaf. Fazil Hüsnü Daglarca. NaPG, *tr. by* Talat Sait Halman

Your Glance Will Trip on My Shadow. Lyubov Sirota. FiBr, *tr. by* Leonid Levin and Elisavietta Ritchie

Your gloves. Small Ode to a Black Cuban Boxer. Nicolás Guillén. TCLAP, *tr. by* Robert Marquez and David Arthur McMurray

Your Going. Carol Baker. PfS

Your grace, and falter on the stony path! (LL) Last Days of Alice. Allen Tate. APT-2; FuPo

Your Grace is welcome from the Queen of Scotland. John Banks. STuOW *Fr.* Albion Queens, The.

Your Grave Disfigures Me. Eibhlin Dubh O'Connell. WoPoe *Fr.* Death of Art O'Leary, The.

Your gravity. Force of Gravity, The. Luiza Neto Jorge. SurWo, *tr. by* Jean R. Longland

Your great hooves sunk. Horse. John Thompson. Coast

Your hair. I Have Touched. Patti Tana. PasH

Your hair is dragging a wall your eyes have a beast's glare. Tigerish. Cahit Zarifoğlu. NaPG, *tr. by* Talat Sait Halman

Your hair is drunk again. Descriptive Passages. William Matthews. BodElec

Your hair is like a panther's shadow. *Unknown.* NAAPv.2

Your hair is tied back in a puritan bunch. Phoenician Statuette, A. Nina Gabrielian. CRWP, *tr. by* Peter France

Your Hand Full of Hours. Paul Celan. OBVE; PoetW, *tr. by* Michael Hamburger

Your hand. I wouldn't swim. I wouldn't fly. (LL) American River Sky Alcohol Father. Jean Valentine. CAP-8; ExTi; LaCa

Your Hand in Mine. Alaide Foppa. TANSG, *tr. by* Celeste Kostopulos-Cooperman

Your hand in mine, we walk out. Kenneth Rexroth. StAl *Fr.* Lights in the Sky are Stars, The.

Your hand is heavy, Night, upon my brow. Wole Soyinka. WaAnP; WoPoe *Fr.* Idanre and Other Poems (1967).

Your hand on her hand—you've never been. Translation. Gillian Clarke. MoWP

Your Hands. Marjorie Agosin. PoDa, *tr. by* Mary C. Berg

Your hands cracked and calloused in summer, bled. Sonnets for Stan Gage (1945–1992). Sascha Feinstein. SeSe

Your hand's fraught interpretation calls forth deep affect. Erin Mouré. NLPA *Fr.* Wittgenstein Letters to Mel Gibson's Braveheart, The.

Your hands have work in them like the weather. Poems to My Father. Mick North. NLP

Your hands lie open in the long fresh grass. Dante Gabriel Rossetti. BrAP; GSo; NAEL-6v2; NAEL-7v2; NoP-4; NoP-5 *Fr.* House of Life, The.

Your hands, my dear, adorable. Chilterns, The. Rupert Brooke. MoBrPo

Your Hands, My Love. Elena Clementelli. CItWP, *tr. by* Cinzia Sartini Blum and Lara Trubowitz

Your hat blows off. Breezy Delicious Day. Edwin Torres. HeMarv

Your hat smelt of dead moths. Your flabby fingers. About Love. Evgeniya Lavut. CRWP, *tr. by* Yury Drobyshev and Carol Rumens

Your head is still. Prayer for My Father. Robert Bly. PoA 2002

Your head it waves outside. Poem. Víctor Hernández Cruz. PueRic

Your hearse pulled by deep summer twilight. Watching the Hearse. Charles Simic. BodElec

Your heart is all you need. To Make a Talisman. Olga Orozco. TCLAP, *tr. by* Stephen Tapscott

Your Heart?—It Is a Frozen Orange. Miguel Hernández. WED, *tr. by* Robert Bly

Your heart, like an old milk tooth. Heart. Maura Dooley. NeBl

Your hidden loneliness, Lord. Psalm. Lucian Blaga. PFTM-1

Your hip replacement mended. Orchestration. Jane Mayes. PasH

Your honor. White Man and the Judge, A. Kevin Simmonds. BtF

Your Honor, when my mother stood. To Judge Faolain, Dead Long Enough: A Summons. Linda McCarriston. FaoP; LoL

Your horse is black your cloak is black. Yscolan. Myrddyn (Merlin). WoPoe, *tr. by* W. S. Merwin

Your house like the upper deck of a ship. Pot. Tiziano Rossi. ItPo, *tr. by* Gayle Ridinger

Your husband gave you a Ring. Lady T-rc----l's Ring. *Unknown.* NOBRP

Your husband, your daughters, your son. (LL) Dream, The. Irving Feldman. TaR; VCAP

"Your husband's lying here in the next bed." They Lay Dying Side by Side. Anna Swirszczynska [*or* Swir]. PoSu

Your ideas of home life. I don't Know Exactly. Eva Svankmajerová. SurWo, *tr. by* Katerina Pinosová

Your image, tormenting and elusive. Osip Emilevich Mandelstam. BBASP, *tr. by* David McDuff

Your job's to work the surface. don't. Michele Roberts. NewEx

Your kind of night, David, your kind of night. Night Thoughts. Henri Coulette. CalPo

Your kindness has painted the singing of the birds. Poem of the Sea and of Her. Carlos Oquendo de Amat. BLPSL, *tr. by* Rene de Costa, Rigas Kappatos and Eleni Paidoussi

Your kiss does not satisfy the heart. Figani Ramazan Çelebi. OLP, *tr. by* Walter Andrews, Najaat Black and Mehmet Kalpakli

Your Last Drive. Thomas Hardy. NAMCP V.1

Your last night in the darkness of the Bronx—I phonecalled—thru hospital to secret police. Allen Ginsberg. NAMCP V.2 *Fr.* Kaddish.

Your laugh, your scarves, the gloss of your makeup. Maxine W. Kumin. NAMCP V.2 *Fr.* Letters.

Your leaves bound up compact and fair. To an Author. Philip Freneau. ColAP

Your leaving brought an end to spring. End to Spring, An. Tzu Yeh. CrYelRi, *tr. by* Sam Hamill

Your legs would be pretty, if you had legs. Portrait of a Nun. Bobi Jones. OBWVE, *tr. by* Joseph P. Clancy

Your letter unfolds and unfolds forever. Letter Smuggled in a Fish. Yüan Chên. CrYelRi, *tr. by* Sam Hamill

Your letters are like folded moons on onionskin. Postman's Knock. Dorothy Molloy. NIrP

Your letters flinging their good seed. Old Letters. Edward Dowden. IrLP

Your life for the privilege, / all your life. (LL) Catch, The. Stanley Kunitz. APT-2; NAMCP V.1; PtR

Your life has a simple pattern. Dung Beetle, The. Pennar Davies. BBMWP, *tr. by* Joseph P. Clancy

Your life hurts me, son. Wound. Alaide Foppa. TANSG, *tr. by* Celeste Kostopulos-Cooperman

Your life is a baby not yet born. Maria Luisa Spaziani. NeIt

Your Lily Eyes Said Yes. Manuel González Prada. SpanPo, *tr. by* Kate Flores

Your lily eyes said yes. Your Lily Eyes Said Yes. Manuel González Prada. SpanPo, *tr. by* Kate Flores

Your lips were like a red and ruby chalice. Midnight Sun. Johnny Mercer. APT-2; ReLy

Your lips were so laughing. Langston Blues. Dudley Randall. SeSe

Your little dog that barked as I came by. To His Wife, for Striking Her Dog. Sir John Harington. WaAnP

Your little hands. Samuel Hoffenstein. AmWit; NBLV; OBCoV *Fr.* Love-songs, at Once Tender and Informative.

Your little mind! (LL) Samuel Hoffenstein. AmWit; NBLV; OBCoV *Fr.* Love-songs, at Once Tender and Informative.

Your look to me. Emblem. David Chaloner. VaPo

Your lot, O Ovid, the prince of your art. On the Second Tristia of Ovid. Elizabeth Jane Leon. EMWP

Your Love fond fugitive to gain. (LL) Song: "Nothing ades to Loves fond fire." Elizabeth Wilmot, Countess of Rochester. EMWP; LW

Your love has wrested me away from me. Yunus Emre. NaPG, *tr. by* Talat Sait Halman

Your love is water and it is fire. *Unknown.* SLW, *tr. by* Marjolijn De Jager, Sayd Bahodin Majrouh and André Velter

Your love never deserted me. Your Love Never Left. Ahmed Arif. NaPG, *tr. by* Talat Sait Halman

Your Love Never Left. Ahmed Arif. NaPG, *tr. by* Talat Sait Halman

Your lover held you. Ophelia. Michael Stillman. IaFF

Your loving Cousin / *Deborah Dough*. (LL) Epistle of Deborah Dough, The. Mary Leapor. BrAP; NoP-4

Your machete slices through my jungle. Machete. Rikki Ducornet. SurWo

Your Magnificent Lord. Concerning the Islands Newly Discovered. Joy Katz. NeAmPo

Your mainland split. Elegy to Atlantis. Tatyana Retivova. CRWP, *tr. by* Tatyana Retivova

Your man, says the Man, *will walk into the bar like this*—here his. Bloody Hand. Ciaran Carson. PBCIP

Your master died from drinking too much. Taoist Huang Has Died of Alcoholism, The. Shen Chou. ColAnChi, *tr. by* Jonathan Chaves

Your matronly face is. Summer Fires of Mulanje Mountain. Edison Mpina. NAfrP

Your messenger came to bring me a jewelled mirror. Maid's Thanks for a Mirror, A. HSü Ling. CCL1, *tr. by* Anne Birrell

Your milk was already poisoned. Childhood. Edith Bruck. AF

Your mind and you are our Sargasso Sea. Ezra Pound. APT-1; BrAP; MoAmPo; NAAL-5; NAMCP V.1; NoAM; NoP-4; NoP-5; OxBoAm; TCAPo *Fr.* Ripostes of Ezra Pound.

Your mission, in any disputed area, is to find. Diplomacy: The Father. W. D. Snodgrass. BrAP

Your mother and I were young and the war. . .Never a brouhaha about the water then. Back When. Nance Van Winckel. RWB

Your mother is not your mother. When the Kingdom Comes. Jill Alexander Essbaum. NAPBL

Your mother slept through it all. Early Morning Test Light over Nevada, 1955. Robert Vasquez. AtGh; GeoHom

Your mother, tall as a flower. In the Shakespeare Garden at Northwestern University. Paul Carroll. IllVoic

Your Mozart is not my Mozart anymore. Valediction. Clare Rossini. BAP-97

Your name? (LL) Notes on the Peanut. June Jordan. NAMCP V.2; NoAM

Your name—a bird on my hand. Marina Ivanovna Tsvetayeva. TCRusP *Fr.* Poems to Blok.

Your name doesn't matter. I Am on My Way to Oklahoma to Bury the Man I Nearly Left My Husband For. Sandra Cisneros. TiP2

Your name, *Esther,* in your mother's shy *campesino* voice. Estel. Julia Alvarez. ExTi

Your Name is Gift. Stella P. Chipasula. HAWP

"Your name is Rumplestiltskin!" cried. Rumplestiltskin. Glyn Maxwell. OBCoV

Your name is the Wheel of Progress—a pleasant name indeed. To the Wheel of Progress. Mrs. Henry Linden. CBWP-4

Your Name on It. Brenda Shaughnessy. LegDan

Your nurse could only speak Italian. Sailing Home from Rapallo. Robert Lowell. InoFa; PoetW; PoPoPo

Your offspring avert their faces from you. (LL) Shemà. Primo Levi. AF; BeAl; FaBoWar; HP; PLBUT; PoAgWa, *tr. by* Ruth Feldman and Brian Swann

Your old hat hurts me, and those black. Dad. Elaine Feinstein. InoFa; Prnts

Your old house in Davis Square looks the same. Letters to the Dead: Denise Levertov. Dick Lourie. PrTe

Your old words lean tips of flames towards me. Kabuki. Yvonne Cullen. NIrP

Your One Good Dress. Brenda Shaughnessy. AmPoNex

Your open spaces. Graffito in Meknès. Murilo Mendes. Eno, *tr. by* Chris Daniels

Your Ostrich Nature. Elin Llwyd Morgan. BBMWP, *tr. by* the author and Richard Poole

Your own greyhounds bark at your side. Midnight Diner by Edward Hopper, A. David Ray. PoSol

Your own hands are lying. (LL) Taking Off My Clothes. Carolyn Forché. NAMCP V.2; NIL-7; NoAM

Your Own Image. Michael Ryan. YaYoPo

Your parents look at you. Parents. Marta Kornblith. MirDau, *tr. by* Roberta Gordenstein

Your past was bereft of pleasure. Sighing. József Bajza. IQMS, *tr. by* Watson Kirkconnell

Your pen wrote Chinese and your name in a smooth swoop with. Fred Wah. NLPA; OpeFie *Fr.* This Dendrite Map: Father / Mother Haibun.

Your penis rolls to the dream. Ana Istarú. TANSG, *tr. by* Shaun Griffin and Emma Sepúlveda-Pulvirenti

Your perch is the branch. To a Sparrow. William Carlos Williams. OWoS

Your photograph won't do you justice. Letters to a Young Poet. Adrienne Rich. ExTi

Your pinking, winter-white shoulders bent. Augury. Sherod Santos. PfSP

Your place is the land of fire under water. Geography Lesson. Robin Morgan. FiBr

Your poise! / Your pose! You Couldn't Be Cuter. Dorothy Fields. ReLy

Your poore estates, alone. (LL) To Meadows [*or* Meddowes]. Robert Herrick. BASC; NOSC; NPeEn; OBEV; PBRV

Your presence is requested. don't Bring Lulu. Lew Brown and Billy Rose. ReLy

Your promises come to me always together with your betrayals, which you have more of than the fox. Cecco Nuccoli. CAGL, *tr. by* Jill Claretta Robbins

Your protagonist is not at home just now. Message on the Machine. Ken Smith. BeAl

Your Radiola recording of the Amos 'n Andy Show. Only Now I Realize. Luis Lopez. GeoH

Your rebellious glance lines up the cavalry. Baqi. OLP, *tr. by* Walter Andrews, Najaat Black and Mehmet Kalpakli

Your residence, Meng. Meng Jung, Gainfully Unemployed. Chia Tao. CSKM, *tr. by* Mike O'Connor

Your retreat hardly prompted. Recollection of Gabriela Mistral. Claudia Lars. TCLAP, *tr. by* Nancy Christoph

Your rhythmic nursing slows. I feel. Anne Winters. BeAl *Fr.* Elizabeth Near and Far.

Your Rose is Dead. Michael Field. VWP

Your *rose is dead,*. Your Rose is Dead. Michael Field. VWP

Your rosy-fingered prick that used to charm. Strato. CAGL, *tr. by* Daryl Hine

Your rusty Chrysler was advertised in the *K. C. Star.* For Harry S Truman in Hell. David Ray. AtGh

Your scent is in the room. Jasmine. Claude McKay. APT-1; GT

Your selfe the Sonne, and I the meltinge froste. Sonnet. Sir Arthur Gorges. OxBSo

Your shameful parts are the white man's gramophone. After a Native Poem from the Solomon Islands that Begins: "Your Shameful Parts Are the White Man's Gramophone." Gabriel Celaya. RaW, *tr. by* Robert Mezey

Your shaved head on my thigh. Three. Lavinia Greenlaw. NeBrP

Your Shoulders Hold Up the World. Carlos Drummond de Andrade. PoetW, *tr. by* Mark Strand

Your Silence. Han Yong'un [*or* Yongwun]. CAMKP, *tr. by* Sammy Solberg

Your silence is leaning toward judgement. Unanswered Letter. Tess Gallagher. NIP-4

Your silver hair, a galaxy. Love Poem. Carol Merrill. ICANM

Your sins have brought my mind so low. Catullus. ErotSp, *tr. by* Sam Hamill

Your Sister. Michael Dennis Browne. ViWalt

Your sister is telling the story. It was. Why Your Father Cried. Elaine Terranova. PoChi

Your Sister Life. Michael Burkard. LaCa

Your sky is a hard and a dazzling blue. In Spain. Emily Lawless. IrV

Your slave boy's cock is aching, Naevolus. Martial. CAGL *Fr.* Epigrams.

Your Sleep. Iwan Goll. AF, *tr. by* Paul Zweig

Your sleep is a closed almond. Your Sleep. Iwan Goll. AF, *tr. by* Paul Zweig

Your sleep will be. Caterpillar's Lullaby. Jane Yolen. Spl

Your small hands, precisely equal to my own. Adrienne Rich. TRP *Fr.* Twenty-one Love Poems.

Your smile, delicate. Woman Me. Maya Angelou. OxWW

Your smile, the only thing that glimmered through. Pictures of Maurice Among Funeral Flowers. Amittai F. Aviram. WaAnP

Your smiles are not, as other womens be [*or* bee]. To the Lady May. Aurelian Townshend. OxBEV

Your Socks. Raiah Harnik. NRoS, *tr. by* Esther Raizen

Your socks are in the drawer. Your Socks. Raiah Harnik. NRoS, *tr. by* Esther Raizen

Your song caresses. Basho. SoOfWa, *tr. by* Sam Hamill

Your song is welcome, Melissus, a most welcome gift. Queen's Answer, The. Queen of England Elizabeth I. EMWP

Your soul is like a painter's landscape where. Moonlight. Paul Verlaine. NAWM-7v2, *tr. by* Carlyle Ferren MacIntyre

Your spouse not laboured-at nor spun. (LL)　Habit of Perfection, The.　Gerard Manley Hopkins.　ChIV-2; MoBrPo; NAMCP V.1; NoAM; OBEV; OBMV; OxAEP-2; SacPr; TFi

Your stars are muscled like the lion. (LL)　Baseball and Writing.　Marianne Moore.　FaBoA; MoASP

Your step at once.　In the Forest.　Heather Allen.　GifTon

Your Street Again.　Sophie Hannah.　MFPA

Your street at sundown.　Look.　Belle Waring.　ExTi

Your sun-face is a mirror of the soul.　Sheykhi.　OLP, tr. by Walter Andrews, Najaat Black and Mehmet Kalpakli

Your Sweaters.　Herman De Coninck.　TuT, tr. by Eamon Grennan

Your sweaters.　Your Sweaters.　Herman De Coninck.　TuT, tr. by Eamon Grennan

Your sweet black eyes, heavy with shade.　Silence of Eyes, A.　Fabio Fiallo.　SonAtl, tr. by Eleanor Davidson

Your sweet voice is trapped in the drum.　Singing Drum, The.　Frank Mkalawile Chipasula.　NAfrP

Your swim bladder vibrates like a drum—.　Toadfish.　Stephen Perry.　MiVo

Your tears. You are not worth their merriment. (LL)　Apologia Pro Poemate Meo.　Wilfred Owen.　MoBrPo; NAEL-6v2; NAEL-7v2; NAMCP V.1

Your teeth are loose, your head is bald.　Admonition to Myself, An.　Chao Meng-fu.　WoPoe, tr. by Jonathan Chaves

Your thighs are appletrees.　Portrait of a Lady.　William Carlos Williams.　HarvBoo; NAAL-5; NAAPv.2; NAMCP V.1; NoAM; NoP-5; OxBoAm; WaAnP

Your thought.　Cloud in Trousers, A.　Vladimir Vladimirovich Mayakovsky.　TCRusP, tr. by Kathy Lewis and Bob Perelman

Your Thwarts in Pieces, Your Mooring Rope Cut.　Unknown.　WoPoe, tr. by Erica Reiner

Your tongue has spent the night.　Dream-Language of Fergus, The.　Medbh McGuckian.　MoWP; NAMCP V.2

Your tongue like a barefoot walk.　Language.　Marjorie Agosin.　TANSG, tr. by Cola Franzen

Your tongue thrums and moves.　Kenneth Rexroth.　APSN; APT-2; NAAPv.2; NAMCP V.1 Fr. Love Poems of Marichiko, The.

Your torch flames.　Lady of Largest Heart.　Enheduanna.　HW, tr. by Betty De Shong Meador

Your Touch.　Han Yong'un [or Yongwun].　CAMKP, tr. by Sammy Solberg

Your tune is a tempest of heat.　July.　Daniel Gray-Kontar.　SpirFl

Your tune trickles on as it has always done.　Cricket.　Ivan Tsanev.　CSCBP, tr. by Georgi Belev and Lisa Sapinkopf

Your turn you are next. (LL)　Eddie Priest's Barbershop and Notary.　Kevin Young.　AmPoNex; ISC; SpirFl

Your ugly token.　Upon a Dead Man's Head.　John Skelton.　WoPoe (Youre ugly tokyn.)　CABP; OxBEV

Your unmistakable breasts, plain, finely wrinkled.　Changing.　Jason Shinder.　NevBe

Your upset / or mine? (LL)　Bible Study.　Gloria C. Oden.　ESEAA; GT

Your vividness grants color where.　To Sallie, Walking.　Sterling Allen Brown.　GT

Your voice is the color of a robin's breast.　To O. E. A.　Claude McKay.　GT

Your voice unwrapping.　Haiku.　Sonia Sanchez.　FFC

Your voice watered the doubt of my breast in the sweet wooden booth.　Federico García Lorca.　CAGL Fr. Sonetos del Amor Oscuro [Sonnets of Dark Love].

Your volume proves that 'Nothing is worth while'.　To a Pessimist.　Ronald Arbuthnott Knox.　OBCoV

Your walls do not fall, he said.　"H. D."　NALW Fr. Tribute to the Angels.

Your walls fold gently.　Jerusalem Song.　Lisa Suhair Majaj.　PoArWo

Your way of loving is too slow for me.　Difference, The.　Dorothy Livesay.　BrAP

Your wedding poem. (LL)　Sacrament of Poverty, The.　Marilyn Nelson Waniek.　ExTi; GT

Your weight sweetly upon me.　Made Out of Links.　Hilda Morley.　PmAP

Your wheel sings, Potter.　Song of the Wheel.　Adam David Miller.　FuFl

Your white robes are made of white clouds.　In Praise of the Portrait of My Former Master.　Sŏsan, Great Master.　CATKP, tr. by Peter H. Lee

Your whole life is a parallelogram.　Triptych of Reflection.　Inna L'ovna Lisnyanskaya.　CRWP, tr. by Ruth Fainlight

Your whole life you've hailed police cars.　Bewilderment Is Love.　Lesley Dauer.　PoDa

Your wicked minds requite. (LL)　Babes in the Wood, The.　Unknown.　OBNV; OxAEP-1

Your Wife, a Widow, Waits for You.　Jesse Lee Kercheval.　SUP

Your wife's forty-five.　Gift Horse.　Yusef Komunyakaa.　GT

Your womb is smarter than your head.　Madrigal.　Nicolás Guillén.　CLPP, tr. by Kenneth Rexroth

Your words are mine, at the end. (LL)　Net of Place, The.　Paul Blackburn.　PFTM-2; PmAP

Your words blaze.　Wands.　Veronica Volkow.　RMCMP, tr. by Margaret Sayers Peden

Your Words, My Answers.　Burns Singer.　HarvBoo

Your words my friend (right healthful caustics) blame.　Sir Philip Sidney.　NAEL-7v1; NoP-5; NoSic Fr. Astrophil and Stella.

Your work, that was done, to be done to be done to be done. (LL)　To the Diaspora.　Gwendolyn Brooks.　NAAL-5; NIL-7

Your young breasts were gleaming.　River, The.　Jacques Prévert.　MFP, tr. by Martin Sorrell

You're a better man than I am, Gunga Din! (LL)　Gunga Din.　Rudyard Kipling.　BRP; MoBrPo

You're a flake of frost on the deck.　Zen Frost.　John Gilgun.　AmZen

You're a girl.　Character.　Taslima Nasrin.　VCWP

You're a good girl; you're gray with virtue.　Samuel Hoffenstein.　AmWit Fr. Poems in Praise of Practically Nothing.

You're a Grand Old Flag.　George M. Cohan.　NAAPv.2; ReLy

You're a teeming truce today, my ladybug, red elytra.　Unfinished Exile.　Fabio Doplicher.　NeIt, tr. by Stephen Sartarelli

You're all the hurt geography I own. (LL)　Geography Lesson.　Carol Rumens.　BeAl; MoWP

You're always giving, my therapist said.　Lending Out Books.　Hal Sirowitz.　GoPo

You're an Old Smoothie.　B. G. DeSylva.　ReLy

You're as thrilling as a college cheer.　You Hit the Spot.　Mack Gordon.　ReLy

You're better than ever.　Comments upon my last book of poesy.　Charles Bukowski.　OxBoAm

You're clean shaven in this country.　Vegetable Air, The.　Cathy Song.　NoAM

You're clear out of this world.　Out of This World.　Johnny Mercer.　ReLy

You're Driving Me Crazy (What Did I Do?).　Walter Donaldson.　ReLy

You're excused, my father would say.　As We Forgive Those.　Eric Pankey.　GI

You're fiddling with something in the barn.　My Love about his Business in the Barn.　Paula Meehan.　MoWP

You're Getting to Be a Habit with Me.　Al Dubin.　ReLy

You're going by, west of the sun.　Marina Ivanovna Tsvetayeva.　TCRusP Fr. Poems to Blok.

You're gone so long / so long. (LL)　So Long.　Langston Hughes.　APSN; APT-2

You're gone—I'm alone in the company.　Neshâtî.　OLP, tr. by Walter Andrews, Najaat Black and Mehmet Kalpakli

You're Gonna Lose Your Gal.　Joe Young.　ReLy

You're / good.　Ice Cube.　Kit Robinson.　ASA

You're home, Uma! Stay here.　Gíríscandra Ghos.　SinGod, tr. by Rachel Fell McDermott

You're in Love.　Bobby Troup.　ReLy

You're in the city, somewhere. I suppose if I stood.　Lost Love.　Dick Allen.　NIP-4

You're in the prime.　Karai Senryū.　EMJL, tr. by Makoto Ueda

You're in this dream of cotton plants.　Red Palm, A.　Gary Soto.　CalPo

You're jealous if I kiss this girl and that.　Constancy.　Elsa Gidlow.　PoBW

You're just a lonely little river.　River, Stay 'Way from My Door.　Mort Dixon.　ReLy

You're Just in Love.　Irving Berlin.　ReLy

You're Laughing at Me.　Irving Berlin.　ReLy

You're like a bough, so silky-whispery.　Images.　Miklós Radnóti.　IQMS, tr. by Peter Zollman

You're Lookin' at Me.　Bobby Troup.　ReLy

You're Lucky to Me.　Andy Razaf.　ReLy

You're mine.　You.　Ismail.　HotL, tr. by V. Narayana Rao

You're Mine, You!　Edward Heyman.　ReLy

You're more beautiful than a silvery ball.　Sweet Talk.　Ferreira Gullar.　TCLAP, tr. by Renato Rezende

You're No Exception.　Yüan Chên.　CCL1, tr. by John A. Scott

You're Not a Man If You don't Die.　Husein Tahmiscic.　PML, tr. by John Hartley Williams

You're Not a Man If You don't Die.　Ülkü Tamer.　PML, tr. by Talat Sait Halman

You're not going back out, as mad as you are?　Night of Terror.　Giuseppe Gioacchino Belli.　PoCho, tr. by Miller Williams

You're not mine.　Visitor, A.　Idea Vilariño.　TANSG, tr. by Louise B. Popkin

You're not so sure about this world?　Talking to God on the Seventh Day.　Ruth L. Schwartz.　BeAl

You're only a baby.　Poor Little Rich Girl.　Noël Coward.　ReLy

You're pregnant, he says, looking at me over the stack.　Roof over far away.　Ana Doina.　RWB

You're pressing your fingers against the sky.　Falling.　Lesley Dauer.　AmPoNex; NAPBL

You're right. In the Library. Michael Patrick Hearn. NTCP

You're right—"the way is narrow." Emily Dickinson. TCAPo

You're sad because you're sad. Sad Child, A. Margaret Atwood. IJHIL

You're searching for some [blue bird] thing in the living room. God Gave Safe Passage to the Animals through His Forest of Bright Spectrums. Jennifer L. Knox. FreRad

You're shivering my memory. Immortal, The. Charles Simic. PoA 2002

You're sleeping, Zenophila, my tender bloom. I wish. Meleager. HePo, *tr. by* Barbara Hughes Fowler

You're so late getting home from the office. Guess Who I Saw Today. Elisse Boyd. ReLy

You're so yourself sometimes I'm sure it's you. History of the Human Body, The. Edmund Berrigan. IIR

You're song, / a wished-for song. Wished-For Song, A. Jelaluddin Rumi. LoL, *tr. by* Coleman Barks

You're the Cream in My Coffee. Lew Brown, B. G. DeSylva and Ray Henderson. ReLy

You're the smoothest so and so. You're an Old Smoothie. B. G. DeSylva. ReLy

You're the Top. Cole Porter. NBLV *Fr.* You're the Top.

You're the Top. Cole Porter. ReLy

You're The Top. NBLV

You're the Top [*parody*]. *Unknown.* NBLV

You're the type of guy. Enemy. Beau Sia. HeMarv

You're the woman I love best and forget fastest, my love. Tall Weeds. W. S. Rendra. WoPoe, *tr. by* Burton Raffel

You're thin again handsome. in our last. D. A. Powell. WiU

You're thinking, aren't you, that this is no right. Bertolt Brecht. ASA *Fr.* Good Woman of Szechwan, The.

You're Thinking of Children. Vladimir Holan. PoSu, *tr. by* Ian Milner and Jarmila Milner

You're thinking of children, of their. You're Thinking of Children. Vladimir Holan. PoSu, *tr. by* Ian Milner and Jarmila Milner

You're tired of this old world at last. Zone. Guillaume Apollinaire. PFTM-1

You're told the ingredients. Situation No. 33: The Feast. David Citino. UpMys

You're too late, Lycidas. Nyctilus and boy Alcon. Titus Calpurnius Siculus. RomPo *Fr.* Eclogues.

You're too wild. Understanding Each Other. Linda Noel. ReEnLa

Youre ugly tokyn. John Skelton. *See* Your ugly token.

You're undressing as though for the doctor. Dénouement. Lyubomir Levchev. CSCBP, *tr. by* Georgi Belev and Lisa Sapinkopf

You're upright, standing on two feet in the usual way, and then suddenly you have a different point of view. Fainting. Margaret Atwood. MotU

You're walking down the street alone. Self-Portrait in the New World Order. Reginald Shepherd. RD

You're with your mother now. (LL) What I Heard at the Discount Department Store. David Budbill. RaBo; TRP

Yours is a journey everlasting. Beloved Ones, The. Eunice Juaquina Watkins-Cothran. BtF

Yours is not (I regret to say) the story they tell. Anne Carson. WoBe *Fr.* Truth About God, The.

Yours is the face that the earth turns to me. Love-Poem. Kathleen Jessie Raine. LW; MoBrPo

Yours is the only body. And This Is So. Joseph H. Ball. PasH

Yourself. Jones Very. APN-1; OxBoAm

Yourself and Myself. *Unknown.* IrLP, *tr. by* Thomas Kinsella

Yourself walked in the room tonight. Away. Robert Creeley. ICANM

Youth. Aneirin. WoPoe *Fr.* Gododdin, The.

Youth. "Odor like an acid sword made, An." Pablo Neruda. WED, *tr. by* Robert Bly

Youth. David J. Rothman. GeoH

Youth. Vernon Rowe. BloBone

Youth. *Unknown.* WeW-3, *tr. by* Laurence Hope

Youth. James Wright. OxBoAm

Youth and Age. Samuel Taylor Coleridge. OBEV

Youth and Age. *Unknown.* IrV, *tr. by* Eleanor Hull

Youth and Art. Robert Browning. NAEL-6v2; NPeEn

Youth and Maidenhood. Sarah Williams. LW

Youth at night would have himself, The. Short Talk on the Youth at Night. Anne Carson. OpeFie

Youth buried you, Captain; as sons for their mother, The. Anyte. SaLy, *tr. by* Diane Rayor

Youth gone, and beauty gone if ever there. Christina Georgina Rossetti. GSo; OxBSo *Fr.* Monna Innominata.

Youth, I offer you this silver cup. Fount, The. Rubén Darío. SpanPo, *tr. by* William M. Davis

Youth in apparel that glittered, A. Stephen Crane. APN-2; MoAmPo; NAAPv.1

Youth Mowing, A. D. H. Lawrence. MoBrPo; NAMCP V.1; NoAM

Youth of the Language, The. Euros Bowen. BBMWP, *tr. by* Joseph P. Clancy

Youth, That Pursuest. Richard Monckton, 1st Baron Houghton Milnes. TreFP

Youth, that pursuest, with such eager page. Youth, That Pursuest. Richard Monckton, 1st Baron Houghton Milnes. TreFP

Youth there was, Elpenor was he nam'd, A. Homer. OBVE *Fr.* Odyssey.

Youth who is one's personal servant, The. Things the Smaller the Better. *Unknown.* EMJL, *tr. by* Edward Putzar

Youth, with proud heart, pure and strong, A. After-Glow of Pain, The. Clara Ann Thompson. CBWP-2

Youthful, caressing, boisterous, tender. I Love Old Whitman So. Allen Ginsberg. ViWalt

Youthful poet, pen in hand, The. Joanna Baillie. NPBRoP *Fr.* Address to the Muses, An.

Youth's a stuff[e] will not endure. (LL) William Shakespeare. AEP; ClHu; NAEL-6v1; NBLV; NoP-4; NoP-5; NoSic; TFi; WoPoe *Fr.* Twelfth Night.

Youth's the season made for joys. John Gay. NoP-4; NoP-5 *Fr.* Beggar's Opera, The.

You've aroused the lilacs and they brew violets. Hoopla. Star Black. KGB

You've asked me what the lobster is weaving there with his golden feet? Enigmas. Pablo Neruda. WED, *tr. by* Robert Bly

You've been a long time making up your mind. Psalm. Charles Simic. StAl

You've been asking me that question. Blue Clay. Ellease Southerland. GT

You've been away on this journey too long. Suspended Elegy, A. M. S. C. Okolo. NeNiPo

You've been blackberrying again. Spin-Cycle. Jane Holland. MFPA

You've been Englished but you won't forget it, never. (LL) England Nil. Anne Rouse. MFPA; NeBl

You've been given keys. Prospero. Michael Stillman. IaFF

You've been in Rome a long time, Corydon. It must. Titus Calpurnius Siculus. RomPo *Fr.* Eclogues.

You've been walking through. Marrying. Charles Harper Webb. SUP

You've come. Ulysses Embroidered. Miriam Waddington. NIL-7

You've come a long way (they said). En Route. Alan Ross. FaBoWar

You've destroyed it everywhere in the world. (LL) City, The. Constantine P. Cavafy. AmFaPo; BeAl, *tr. by* Edmund Keeley and Philip Sherrard

You've died so many times; we've said good bye. Return. Rosario Castellanos. FiBr, *tr. by* Carolyne Wright

You've done taken my blues and gone—. Langston Hughes. *See* You've taken my blues and gone.

You've drawn 3 rings around me. Complaint for a Sorcerer. Susy Hare. SurWo

You've enchanted the world. Mahārāja Nandakumār Rāy. SinGod, *tr. by* Rachel Fell McDermott

You've forgotten that village lost in the rows and rows. Joseph Brodsky. StAl *Fr.* Part of Speech, A.

You've found a place in time—no permanent shade. Making Camp. David Wagoner. PoCoUp

You've got no time for me. I've Got Your Number. Carolyn Leigh. ReLy

You've got to give. Glory of Love, The. Billy Hill. ReLy

You've got to hand it to the fairer sex. Are You Makin' Any Money? Herman Hupfeld. ReLy

You've gotta have heart. Richard Adler and Jerry Ross. ReLy *Fr.* Damn Yankees.

You've gotta throw yourself at the other baby because you've been abandonned and forsaken. Carla Harryman. BAP-04 *Fr.* Baby.

You've gotten in through the transom. To a Child Trapped in a Barber Shop. Philip Levine. NoAM

You've heard monkeys crying. Basho. EH, *tr. by* Robert Hass

You've hooked up fish line and a sinker. On Building a Nest: St. Peter's, Saskatchewan. Susan Goyette. Coast

You've left no door or I'd knock. Kind of Wakefulness, A. Robert J. Gibbs. Coast

You've lived there long, away from the trappings of office. To a Hermit in the Mountains. Hsü Pen. ColAnChi, *tr. by* Jonathan Chaves

You've lost your religion, the Rabbi said. Debate with the Rabbi. Howard Nemerov. TaR

You've maced me and attacked me. Transferred me from private prison. Trouble I've Seen, The. Fred Hampton Jr. BRtP

You've never been a pal of mine. Front Line. Lyubomir Levchev. PML, *tr. by* Theodore Weiss

You've never known. Jeep Cherokee. Bruce A. Jacobs. PoDa

You've not been to the local bathhouse. Bathhouse, The. Boris Abramovich Slutsky. TCRusP, *tr. by* Daniel Weissbort

You've only just heard? Paid on Both Sides. W. H. Auden.

You've planted seven wealthy husbands. Agriculture. Martial. WoPoe, *tr. by* Fred Chappell

You've pluck'd [or plucked] a curlew, drawn a hen. On an Island. John Millington Synge. FaBoVe; MoBrPo; NPeEn; OxBEV

You've pulled back, like. Grass Crust, The. Christiania Whitehead. NeBl

You've rocked at many passage rites, at drums. On African Writing. Jack A. Mapanje. HBAPE

You've seen a cat consume a hummingbird, seen. Amaryllis. Mark Wunderlich. LegDan; Vesp

You've seen a herd of goats. Lame Goat, The. Jelaluddin Rumi. TWF, *tr. by* Coleman Barks

You've seen a strawberry. Nevertheless. Marianne Moore. HarvBoo; NAAPv.2; NoP-4; NoP-5; SoSe-8

You've taken my blues and gone. Note on Commercial Theatre. Langston Hughes. NAAL-5

   (You've done taken my blues and gone—.) SSLK

You've thrown a life still hungry. Sergei Yesenin. Sergey Aleksandrovich Yesenin. Prolet, *tr. by* Amelia Glaser

You've told me, Maro. Martial. NIL-7; NIP-4, *tr. by* F. Lewis

You've tried the rest. Rest, The. Lawrence Raab. PoA 2002

Yow that take pleasure in yowr cruelty. Sonnet 25. Robert Sidney. PBRV

Yow! Yow! Night gibbons cry. Listening to Gibbons at Rock-Pool Creek. Shen Yüeh. ColAnChi, *tr. by* Richard W. Bodman

Yr Iaith. Nigel Jenkins. AngWePo

Yramín and the Sea. Manuel Vázquez Montalbán. RaW, *tr. by* Robert Mezey

Yramín y el Mar. Manuel Vázquez Montalbán. RaW

Yscolan. Myrddyn (Merlin). WoPoe, *tr. by* W. S. Merwin

Yu Chieh Yuan (Jade Steps Grievance, Yueh-fu). Li Po. ChinPo, *tr. by* Ye Weilian [*or* Yeh Wei-lien *or* Wai-lim Yip]

Yu No Send. Me No Come. Shara McCallum. BtF

Yu teach me. Speak. Benjamin Zephaniah. Oth

Yuan Zhen to Bo Juyi. Yüan Chĕn. CCL1, *tr. by* Arthur Waley

Yuba City School. Chitra Divakaruni. GeoHom; LTA; OpBo

Yudu. Natalia Toledo. RMCMP

Yue-chu [Translations]. *Unknown.* CCL1

   Moon Rising, A. CCL1, *tr. by* Arthur Waley

   Moonrise. CCL1, *tr. by* John Cayley

Yugoslav Story. Susan Hampton. BMAP

Yuki. Mary Fenollosa. NAAPv.1

Yu-li: Fine Fish to Net. *Unknown.* CCL1; OBVE, *tr. by* Ezra Pound

Yum Yab. Anne Waldman. WhBo

Yun'er's Bell. Yun'er. WoPoe, *tr. by* Constance A. Cook

Yung Wind. *Unknown. tr. by* Ezra Pound

   Sans Equity and sans Poise. WoPoe, *tr. by* Ezra Pound

Yuusthiwa. Simon J. Ortiz. ICANM

Yuying, you have more spontaneous sting in you. Jiang Yuying, Famous Professor at Beijing University, Who Daringly Rendered into Chinese the First Complete Walt Whitman. Willis Barnstone. ViWalt

Yves Tanguy. David Gascoyne. NoP-4; NoP-5

Yvette Mimieux in *Hit Lady*. David Trinidad. SUP

Z

Z is the Zenith from which we decline. Zewhyexary. Thomas M. Disch. OBCoV

Zacoalco o paisaje. Laura Solórzano. SPV

Zacoalco or Landscape. Laura Solórzano. SPV, *tr. by* Jen Hofer

Zai-shan: Weed Grass. *Unknown.* CCL1, *tr. by* Man Wong

Zang Tumb Tuuum. Filippo Tommaso Marinetti.

   Correction of proofs + desires in speed. PFTM-1

Zangezi. Velemir Khlebnikov.

   Plane Four. PFTM-1

Zangezi: R, K, L, G—. Velemir Khlebnikov. PFTM-1

Zapato, El. Richard Garcia. TouFir

Zapolya. Samuel Taylor Coleridge.

   Song. OBEV

Zapruder. Thomas Sayers Ellis. LegDan

Zaps of Zombifying Powder. Denizé Lauture. OGAHCP, *tr. by* Boadiba and Jack Hirschman

Zarathustra. Friedrich Wilhelm Nietzsche. *tr. by* Ivor Armstrong Richards

   Notes. WoPoe, *tr. by* Ivor Armstrong Richards

Zarian was saying: Florence is youth. Water-Colour of Venice, A. Lawrence Durrell. MoBrPo

Zaydee. Philip Levine. TaR

Zaynab complained against me. Throbbings. Jamil B. Holway. NAAPv.2, *tr. by* George Dimitri Selim

Zazen / Fat mosquitoes. Tan Taigi. ZenPo, *tr. by* Takashi Ikemoto and Lucien Stryk

Zazen on Ching-t'ing Mountain. Li Po. CrYelRi, *tr. by* Sam Hamill

Zea. Richard Wilbur. NoP-5

Zealous. Joshua Clover. PuP-23

Zealous Admonition to Praise. Catharina Regina von Greiffenberg. GePo, *tr. by* George C. Schoolfield

Zealous flea. Issa. EH, *tr. by* Robert Hass

Zealous Puritan, The. *Unknown.* NOSC

Zealous to deliver the suffering people. *Various authors.* CATKP *Fr.* Songs of Flying Dragons.

Ze-bi: By That Swamp's Shore. *Unknown.* CCL1, *tr. by* Arthur Waley

Zebra. Judith Thurman. SSCS

Zebra. Natasha Trethewey. TWW

Zebra Goes Wild Where the Sidewalk Ends, The. Henry Dumas. GT

Zebra, The. Marie Laurencin. CuPo

Zebras, The. Roy Campbell. MoBrPo; OxBSo

Zeitgehoft. Paul Celan. AmFaPo *Fr.* Zeitgehoft.

Zeitgehoft. Paul Celan. *tr. by* Michael Hamburger

   Zeitgehoft. AmFaPo, *tr. by* Michael Hamburger

Zeke. Leonard Alfred George Strong. MoBrPo

Zelfrepeterend gedicht. Sybren Polet. LWR

Zella Wheeler! did I evah? Interrupted Reproof, The. Priscilla Jane Thompson. CBWP-2

Zen 101. Nin Andrews. AmZen

Zen Acorn. Harryette Mullen. WANABP

Zen Americana. Paula Gunn Allen. PoPoPo

Zen Baker. Jordan Jones. WhBo

Zen Corners. Michael Wenger. WhBo

Zen Frost. John Gilgun. AmZen

Zen Living. Dick Allen. PoA 2002

Zen meditation should be done in good faith. Hyunsonja Asks for an Enlightenment Song. Master Naong. BecRai, *tr. by* Kim Daljin, Kim Won-Chung and Christopher Merrill

Zen Mountain Center. David Tokuyu Reid-Marr. WhBo

Zen of Housework, The. Al Zolynas. BLT

Zen Sermon. Xuanjian. CCL1, *tr. by* Graeme Wilson

Zen Sky. John Gilgun. AmZen

Zenaida. Natalia Toledo. RMCMP

Zenaida. Natalia Toledo. RMCMP

Zenaida. Natalia Toledo. RMCMP, *tr. by* Alberto A. Ríos

Zenith. Sonia Delaunay. CuPo

Zenith. Juan Ramón Jiménez. SpanPo, *tr. by* Kate Flores

Zenith / noon beats out / on its solar anvil / the rays of light. Zenith. Sonia Delaunay. CuPo

Zeno's Progress. Thomas Centolella. ArBi

Zephyr's Sigh, The. *Unknown.* CCL1 *Fr.* Gu-feng [Translations].

Zero. Susan Stewart. AmAlph

.05. Ishmael Reed. ESEAA

Zero hour. Waiting yet again. James Merrill. NAMCP V.2 *Fr.* Book of Ephraim, The.

Zero, this spume—a virgin verse. Toast. Stéphane Mallarmé. WoPoe, *tr. by* Frederick Morgan

Zero Tolerance. Bruce Andrews. PFTM-2

Zero tolerance is too wet for me. Zero Tolerance. Bruce Andrews. PFTM-2

Zettel, 592. See how it flushes like the cheeks of a small bird. I cannot observe myself unobserved. Skip Fox. AnSo

Zeus and Ganymede. Ovid. CAGL *Fr.* Metamorphoses.

Zeus as an eagle came to Ganymede. *Unknown.* CAGL, *tr. by* Daryl Hine

Zeus, / Brazen-thunder-hurler. Faun Sees Snow for the First Time, The. Richard Aldington. MoBrPo

Zeus, Father Zeus, you've power over heaven. Archilochus. SaLy, *tr. by* Diane Rayor

Zeus lies in Ceres' bosom. Ezra Pound. APT-1; HarvBoo; NAMCP V.1; NoAM; RaBo *Fr.* Cantos.

Zeus was once overheard to shout at Hera. Weather of Olympus, The. Robert Graves. OBCoV

Zeus, Zeus himself could not undo these nets. Labyrinth, The. Jorge Luis Borges. PoetW; WoPoe, *tr. by* John Updike

Zewhyexary. Thomas M. Disch. OBCoV

Zhi-hu: Young Soldier Thinks of Home. *Unknown.* CCL1, *tr. by* Rewi Alley

Zhong-feng: Wild and Windy. *Unknown.* CCL1, *tr. by* Arthur Waley

Zhongnan, The Great One, so near the Celestial City. Mount Zhongnan. Wang Wei. CCL1, *tr. by* Jerome P. Seaton

Zhu-gan: This Rod. *Unknown.* CCL1, *tr. by* V. W. X.

Zig zag mothers of the gods, The. That Dada Strain. Jerome Rothenberg. FTOS; PFTM-2

Zi-jin: The Student's Blue Collar or Lapel. *Unknown.* CCL1, *tr. by* Ezra Pound

Zijn lichaam strandde op het zand. Tien manieren om P.B. Shelley te zien. Hugo Claus. LWR

Zilch Movement. Georges Castera. OGAHCP, *tr. by* Boadiba and Jack Hirschman

Zimmer Drunk and Alone, Dreaming of Old Football Games. Paul Zimmer. PBCAP

Zimmer Imagines Heaven. Paul Zimmer. PBCAP

Zimmer in Fall. Paul Zimmer. CA

Zimmer in Grade School. Paul Zimmer. PBCAP

Zimmer's Head Thudding against the Blackboard. Paul Zimmer. PBCAP

Zimri: The Duke of Buckingham. John Dryden. OBSV *Fr.* Absalom and Achitophel.

Zinc. Yasser Musa. OWABP

Zinc music of traffic on the boulevards and paisley dahlias catching fire. Sext. Jeanne Shannon. ICANM

Zing! Went the Strings of My Heart. James F. Hanley. ReLy

Zing—Boom—Snap. Still-Life. Tatiana Shcherbina. ItGoST, *tr. by* J. Kates

Zinnias. Valerie Worth. NTCP

Zinnias, stout and stiff. Zinnias. Valerie Worth. NTCP

Zion me wan go home. *Unknown.* FaBoVe

Zip. Lorenz Hart. ReLy

Zip, zip the valley wind. Gu-feng: The Valley Wind. *Unknown.* CCL1, *tr. by* Arthur Waley

Zip, zip the valley wind! *Unknown.* CCL1 *Fr.* Gu-feng [Translations].

Zipangu. Charles Tomlinson. WoBe
   Epilogue. WoBe
   Heron. WoBe
   Pines at Hakone, The. WoBe
   Shugakuin Garden. WoBe
   Yamadera. WoBe

Zippo lighter, A. Off the Back of a Lorry. Tom Paulin. ModIr; PBCIP

Zirma. Italo Calvino. MotU,

Zizi's Lament. Gregory Corso. BB

Zizwe. Tanya Tyler. BRtP

Zodiac. Elizabeth Alexander. FFC

Zodiac, The. Guillaume de Salluste Du Bartas. NOSC *Fr.* Divine Weeks and Works, The.

Zoe and the Ghosts. Dieter Weslowski. InvLad

Zohar. Tom Carey. KGB

Zombie. Jean-Marie Willer Denis. OGAHCP, *tr. by* Boadiba and Jack Hirschman

Zombie. Thomas Heise. LegDan

Zombie Jet. Connie Deanovich. AmPoNex

Zombie Sunday (Had We but World Enough and Time). Josh Bell. LegDan

Zombies. Lavinia Greenlaw. BeAl; NeBrP

Zombies. Felix Morisseau-Leroy. OGAHCP, *tr. by* Boadiba and Jack Hirschman

Zombies Arise. Alexander Akao. OGAHCP, *tr. by* Boadiba and Jack Hirschman

Zone. Guillaume Apollinaire. CuPo

Zone. Guillaume Apollinaire. WoPoe, *tr. by* Samuel Beckett

Zone. Guillaume Apollinaire. PFTM-1

Zone. Guillaume Apollinaire. YaTCFP

Zone. Guillaume Apollinaire. YaTCFP, *tr. by* Roger Shattuck

Zone. Louise Bogan. APT-2

Zone of Death. William Everson. SacPr

Zoning. Joanne M. Braxton. BtF

Zonnebeke Road, The. Edmund Charles Blunden. OBWP

Zoo. Georgi Belev. CSCBP, *tr. by* the author and Lisa Sapinkopf

Zoo. Polly Clark. NeBl

Zoo. Bin Ramke. LiTh

Zoo. Shuntaro Tanikawa. PoetW, *tr. by* Harold Wright

Zoo raccoon lifts its food pellet, The. Because the Eye Is a Flower Whose Root is the Hand. Dennis Schmitz. TAPaP

Zoo, The. Jordan Davis. HeMarv

Zoology Is Destiny. Linda France. StAl

Zoom! Simon Armitage. HarvBoo; StAl

Zoom (The Commodores). Thulani Davis. ISC

Zoot Sims, Joshua Redman. Fantastic Names of Jazz, The. Hayden Carruth. GoPo

Zophiël or, the Bride of Seven. Maria Gowen Brooks.
   Palace of the Gnomes. APN-1

Zounds, gramercy, and rootity-toot! Phyllis McGinley. OBSV *Fr.* Speaking of Television.

Zrínyi, who knew well that his life's end was nearing. Sortie, The. Miklós Zrínyi. IQMS, *tr. by* Thomas Kabdebo

Zrinyiad, The. Miklós Zrínyi. *tr. by* Thomas Kabdebo
   Invocation. IQMS, *tr. by* Thomas Kabdebo

Zrínyi's Second Song. Ferenc Kölcsey. IQMS, *tr. by* Adam Makkai

Zrínyi's Song. Ferenc Kölcsey. IQMS, *tr. by* Watson Kirkconnell

Zuleika mute and motionless. Lord Byron. NPBRoP *Fr.* Bride of Abydos, The.

Zulu Girl, The. Roy Campbell. NoP-4; NoP-5; OBMV; OxAEP-2

Zun-da-lu: If Along the Highroad. *Unknown.* CCL1, *tr. by* Arthur Waley

Zuni Dancers. Eric Mottram. Oth

Zuni Ring. David St. John. RoV

Zurich, at the Stork. Paul Celan. PoetW, *tr. by* John Felstiner

Zurich Chronicle February 1916. Tristan Tzara. PFTM-1

Zürich, the Stork Inn [*For Nelly Sachs*]. Paul Celan. BBASP; HP, *tr. by* Michael Hamburger

Zuveliskes's Women Mourn Over Kukutis. Marcelijus Martinaitis. TWW, *tr. by* Laima Sruoginis

ZZZZZ. Carl Rakosi. NAAPv.2

AUTHOR INDEX

Pseudonymous names are enclosed in quotation marks.

A

"A., F. P." *See* Adams, Franklin Pierce
Aafjes, Bertus (1914–92)
Last Letter, The.
Aal, Katharyn Machan
Leda's Sister and the Geese.
Aalfs, Janet E.
Sewing the Torn Sleeve.
Ab Edmwnd, Dafydd (*fl.* 1450–80)
Girl's Hair, A.
Abad, Gemino H.
Holy Order.
Jeepney.
Light in One's Blood, The.
Toys.
Abayomi-Paul, Atinuke *See* Empress [*or* Atinuke Abayomi-Paul]
Abbey, Louis M.
Broken Silence.
Abbot, Elizabeth
Awakening.
Abbott, Deborah
All Day at Work.
Abbott, Keith (b. 1944)
Billygoat watches me work.
Drop my new pen.
Grief counselor, The.
Illusion Collector, Age 37, The.
Our honest neighbor's rolled.
What she thought was.
Windy clear day, A.
Abbott, Ward
Aspen Meadows.
First Rain.
Funeral, The: "I see, under the canopy of death."
Quite Mercenary He Stalked Her.
'Abd al-Hayy, Muhammad (b. 1944)
Ode of Signs.
'Abd Rabbihi, Ahmad ibn Muhammad
Praise be to Him who is not contained in any region nor reached by any vision.
Abdal, Pir Sultan (*fl.* c.1550)
Ilahi.
Abdul Karim, Abdul Maqsoud (b. 1956)
Nightmare 1.
Nightmare 3.
Abdul-Salaam, Aliyah
Bird Close to Old Houses, A.
In Front of the House.
Mermaid, The.
Village Near a Church, A.
Abdullah, Fathi
On the Declaration of Joy.
Small Bodies That Cannot Be Healed.
Abdullatif, Yasser
Archeology.
Abelard, Peter (1079–1142)
David's Lament for Jonathan.
More than a brother to me, Jonathan.
Abercrombie, Lascelles (1881–1938)
Emblems of Love, *sels.*
Epitaph: "Sir, you should notice me: I am the Man."
Fear, The.
Hope and Despair.
Judith, *sels.*
Mary and the Bramble.

Stream's Song, The.
Witchcraft: New Style.
Abinader, Elmaz (b. 1954)
Although the Sky.
Letters from Home.
New Year's Morning.
On a Summer Night.
What We Leave Behind.
Abish, Walter (b. 1931)
What Else (*Part 2*).
Abiyah
Fatherless Townships.
Ablan, Huda (b. 1971)
Strangers.
Abley, Mark (b. 1955)
Down.
Abner, Patricia A. Holt
Lest We Forget.
Aborigine Oral Tradition
Captain Cook.
Mapooram.
Platypus, The.
Star-Tribes, The.
Two Sisters, The.
Abrahams, Lionel (b. 1928)
After winter '76.
Agnostic's funeral prayer.
At revolution's end.
Don't say it.
Dry self-portrait.
Family man.
Flesh.
Our way of life.
Out of illness.
Privacy.
Song for the new order.
Spring report.
Stone stood in her house, A.
Thoughts on Johannesburg's centenary.
Thresholds of tolerance.
To Halley's Comet.
To the idealistic killers.
Winter report.
Writer in sand, The.
Abse, Dannie (b. 1923)
Brueghel in Naples.
Carnal Knowledge.
Case History.
Cousin Sidney.
Doctor, The.
Epithalamion: "Singing, today I married my white girl."
Footnote Extended, A.
Hunt the Thimble.
In the Theatre.
Lunch and Afterwards.
Millie's Date.
New Diary, A.
Not Adlestrop.
Origin of Music, The.
Pathology of Colours.
Peachstone.
Photograph and White Tulips.
Return to Cardiff.
Snake.
Souls.
Stethoscope, The.
Thankyou Note.
Welsh Valley Cinema, 1930s.
Winter Visit, A.
X-Ray.

Abu Dhu'ayb al-Hudhali (d. 649?)
Lament for Five Sons Lost in a Plague.
Abu-I-Salt Umayyah (1067–1134)
White Stallion, The.
Abu Ishaq al-Ilbin (d. 1067)
O say to all of the inhāja, the full moons of the time, and the lions of the thicket.
Abu Khalid, Fawziyya (b. 1955)
Country, A.
Geometry of the Soul.
Mother's Inheritance.
Tattoo Writing.
To Enjoy the Horror.
Two Little Girls.
Abu-l-Hasan Ibn Al-Qabturnuh (*fl.* 12th cent.)
In Battle.
Abu Madi, Ilya (1890–1957)
Holiday Present.
Abu Nuwas
Party's Over, The.
Abu-Risha, Zulaykha
Khobayza.
Marble.
Mewl.
Tree.
Abu Sa'id (978–1066)
I Asked My Love.
Abulafia, Abraham (*fl.* c.1250)
Battle, The.
Acam-Oturu, Assumpta (b. 1953)
Agony . . . A Resurrection, An.
Arise to the Day's Toil.
Acconci, Hannibal Vito
Placable Caps, The.
Achebe, Chinua (b. 1930)
Bull and Egret.
Christmas in Biafra (1969).
Love Cycle.
We Laughed at Him.
Acholonu, Catherine Obianuju
Dissidents, The.
Going Home.
Harvest of War.
Nigeria in the Year 1999.
Other Forms of Slaughter.
Spring's Last Drop, The.
Water Woman.
Way, The.
Achterberg, Gerrit (1905–62)
Across the Jarbok.
Ballad of the Gasfitter.
Ballade van de gasfitter.
Departure.
Instrument.
Pentecost.
Trinity.
Ackerman, Diane (b. 1948)
Beija-Flor.
Climbing Out.
Elegy for *Challenger*.
Pumping Iron.
San Francisco Sunrise.
Sweep Me through Your Many-Chambered Heart.
We Are Listening.
Ackerman, Julia H.
First Night.
Ackland, Valentine (1906–69)
Clock Plods On, The.
Communist Poem, 1935.

Eyes of [or the] body, being blindfold by night,
The.
Since the first toss of gale that blew.
Acorn, Milton (b. 1923)
Ballad of the Pink-Brown Fence, The.
Charlottetown Harbour.
Completion of the Fiddle, The.
Island, The.
I've Tasted My Blood.
Squall, The.
That Corrugated Look To Water.
Acosta, Teresa Palma
Apparition (ca. 1896).
Dangereux avril.
For Maximino Palomo.
Fragile soy.
Museum Piece (ca. Now).
Acquah, Kobena Eyi (b. 1952)
I Want to Go to Keta.
They're Tearing Up the Old Graveyard.
"Ada" (Sarah Louisa Forten) (1814–98?)
Appeal to Women, An.
Scroll is open, The.
Slave Girl's Farewell, The.
Slave, The.
Ada, Ahmet (b. 1947)
I Love You So.
Adair, Tom (1913–88)
Everything Happens to Me.
Let's Get Away from It All.
Night We Called It a Day, The.
Violets for Your Furs.
Will You Still Be Mine?
Adair, Virginia Hamilton (b. 1913)
Ants on the Melon.
Blueberry City.
Buckroe, After the Season, 1942.
Cutting the Cake.
Exit Amor.
Last Marriage, A.
Adam, Helen (b. 1909)
Huntsman, The.
I Love My Love.
Mune Rune.
Pre-Teen Trot.
Shallow-Water Warning.
Song for a Sea Tower.
Adamo, Ralph (b. 1948)
Bicameralization, The, *sels*.
New Orleans.
Roches Moutonnees.
Adams, Anna (b. 1926)
To My Mother.
Adams, Ayin
Cooking.
Adams, Cyd (1949–2005)
Azaleas and Dogwoods.
Longview, Texas.
Omens.
Pete's Poem.
River Road.
Rock Pickers.
Adams, Francis Lauderdale (1862–93)
To the Christians: "Take, then, your paltry
Christ."
Adams, Franklin Pierce ("F. P. A.") (1881–1960)
Ballade of Schopenhauer's Philosophy.
Composed in the Composing Room.
If.
Lines Where Beauty Lingers.
Rich Man, The.
Those Two Boys.
To a Thesaurus.
Us Poets.
Adams, Henry
Buddha and Brahma.
Prayer to the Virgin of Chartres.
Adams, Jean (1710–65)
There's Nae Luck about the House.
Adams, Joan
Yellow Is Me, But All the Same Are We.
Adams, John Quincy (1767–1848)
Lord of all worlds, let thanks and praise.
To a Bereaved Mother.

To Sally.
To the Sun-Dial.
Wants of Man, The.
Why should I fear in evil days.
Adams, Lee (b. 1924)
But Alive.
Kids!
Once Upon a Time.
Put on a Happy Face.
Those Were the Days.
Adams, Léonie (1899–1988)
April Mortality.
Bell Tower.
Country Summer.
Death and the Lady.
Figurehead, The.
Fragmentary Stars.
Ghostly Tree.
Grapes Making.
Gull Goes Up, A.
Home-coming.
Horn, The.
Kingdom of Heaven.
Light at Equinox.
Lullaby: "Hush, lullay."
Magnificat in Little.
Moon and Spectator, The.
Mount, The.
Night-Piece.
River in the Meadows, The.
Rounds and Garlands Done, The.
Sundown.
This Measure.
Thought's End.
Twilit Revelation.
Adams, Mary (fl. 1676)
Oh London I once more to thee do speak.
Adams, Sam (b. 1934)
Gwbert: Mackerel Fishing.
Hill Fort, Caerleon.
Rough Boys.
Sliding.
Adams, Sarah Flower (1805–48)
Nearer, My God, to Thee.
Adams, Sylvia (b. 1934)
Shakespeare's Eyebrows.
Adamson, Harold (1906–80)
Everything I Have Is Yours.
I Just Found Out About Love.
It's a Most Unusual Day.
It's Been So Long.
Make with the Feet.
Time on My Hands.
Where Are You?
Adamson, Robert (b. 1944)
Action Would Kill It / A Gamble.
Dead Horse Bay.
Dreaming Up Mother.
Edinburgh.
Elm Tree in Paddington, An.
Gutting the Salmon.
Home, The Spare Room, The.
My House.
My Tenth Birthday.
Passing Through Experiences.
Private, The.
Rimbaud Having a Bath.
Sibyl.
Sonnets to be Written from Prison, *sel*.
Southern skua, The.
Stone Curlew, The.
Adcock, Betty (b. 1938)
Kaiser's Burnout.
Photograph of the Courthouse Square, 1950s.
Poem for Dizzy.
Adcock, Fleur (b. 1934)
Advice to a Discarded Lover.
Against Coupling.
Below Loughrigg.
Bogyman.
Counting.
Dreaming.
Ex-Queen Among the Astronomers, The.
For a Five-Year-Old.
For Andrew.

Halfway Street, Sidcup.
Happy Ending.
Immigrant.
Kissing.
Leaving the Tate.
Poem Ended by a Death.
Prelude: "Is it the long dry grass that is so
erotic."
Soho Hospital for Women, The.
Surprise in the Peninsula, A.
Things: "There are worse things than having
behaved foolishly in public."
Three-Toed Sloth, The.
Trees.
Unexpected Visit.
Video, The.
Way Out, A.
Weathering.
Wife to Husband.
Addaeus
When you meet a young boy, be direct.
Addison, Joseph (1672–1719)
Campaign, The, *sels*.
Cato, *sels*.
Ode: "Spacious firmament on high, The."
Rosamond, *sels*.
When All Thy Mercies.
Addison, Lloyd (b. 1931)
After MLK: the marksman marked leftover
kill.
All the things of which there are none.
I by you put on.
Umbra.
**Addison, Medora C. (Mrs. Charles Read Nutter)
(b. 1890)**
Names.
Addonizio, Kim (b. 1954)
Alone in Your House.
At Moss Beach.
Beer. Milk. The Dog. My Old Man.
Bird.
Broken Sonnets.
Chicken.
China Camp, California.
Conversation in Woodside.
Event.
First Kiss: "Afterwards you had that drunk,
drugged look."
First Poem for You.
For Desire.
From Then to Now.
Gravity.
Late Round.
Night of the Living, Night of the Dead.
Prayer: "Sometimes, when we're lying after
love."
Stolen Moments.
Them.
Theodicy.
What Do Women Want?
What the Dead Fear.
Ade, George (1866–1944)
R-E-M-O-R-S-E.
Adebajo, Kunle
Moonlight on the Lake.
Adelman, Patricia
My Exorcist Mother.
Adesuyi, Nike
New Testament, The.
Rains.
Springs.
Adewale, Toyin
Explorer of Aromas.
Olayimika.
Adisa, Opal Palmer
Count Ossie.
Cultural Trip, A.
Discover Me.
Ethiopia Unda a Jamaican Mango Tree.
Fennel.
No, Women Don't Cry.
Rainbow, The.
Things No One Told Me.
Women at the Crossroad / (May Elegba
Forever Guard the Right Doors).

Adkins, Geoffrey
Arthur.
Children in Armour.

Adler, Frances Payne (b. 1942)
Riding the Eye.
Voices Are Coming Up, The.

Adler, Lucile
Geranium Flame.
Last Day, The.
On the Night of the Day the Worlds Ends.
Plaisir.
Smike.
Traveling Out, The.
You: "When afternoon."

Adler, Richard (b. 1921)
Damn Yankees, sels.
Hernando's Hideaway.
Hey There.
There Once Was a Man.
Whatever Lola Wants (Lola Gets).

Adnan, Etel (b. 1925)
Indian Never Had a Horse, The, sel.
Maïakovsky.
Spring Flowers Own, The, sel.
There, sel.

Adonis [or Adunis] ('Ali Ahmad Sa'id) (b. 1929)
Beginning Speech.
Desert, The, sels.
Desire Moving Through the Maps of the
  Material, sels.
Elegy for the Time at Hand.
Mirror for the Twentieth Century, A.
New Noah, The.
Passage, The.
Song of a Man in the Dark.
Tree of Fire.
Woman and a Man, A.

Ady, Endre (1877–1919)
Adam, Where Art Thou?
Ancient "Kayán", The.
At the Foot of Mount Zion.
Autumn Slipped Into Paris.
Behold My Treasures, Darling.
Black Piano, The.
Blood and Gold.
Grandson of György Dózsa, The.
Hackney Coach, The.
I Guard Your Eyes.
I Want to Be Loved.
In Front of Good Prince Silence.
Judas and Jesus.
Kinsman of Death, The.
Lady of the White Castle, The.
Lord's Arrival, The.
Lost Horseman, The.
Magyar Fallow, The.
Magyar Messiahs, The.
Matthias' Demented Scholar.
Memories of a Summer Night.
On Elijah's Chariot.
On New Waters.
On the Tisza.
Peacock Takes Its Perch, A.
Poet of the Hortobágy, The.
Prayer After War.
Saint Margaret's Legend.
Song of a Hungarian Jacobin.
Tethered Souls, The.
Two Kinds of Welsh Bards.
Woodland Cross, The.

AE See Russell [or AE], George

Aeschylus (525–456 B.C.)
Agamemnon.
Eumenides, The.
Libation Bearers, The.

Aesop (6th cent. B.C.)
Dog and the Shadow, The.
Dog in the Manger, The.

Africa-Bolasco, Karina
Sauna 2.

Afrika, Tatamkulu (1920–2002)
Accident, The.
Dancing in My City.
Fist, The.
Funeral of Anton Fransch, The.

Funeral, The: "Her smile drains."
Glimpse of God.
Hit squad.
Maqabane.
Nightrider.
Queue.
Respite.
Sleepless.
To God.

Afsar (b. 1964)
Prayer: "We praise only you. We cringe with
  shame like crumbs."

Afterman, Allen (b. 1941)
Pietà.
Their Thoughts Cling to Everything They See
  on the Way.
Van Diemen's Land.

Agali, Angela
Boeing.
Sister: "House, A. A car. Sweet things. Gold."

Agard, John (b. 1949)
English Girl Eats Her First Mango.
For Bob Marley.
Half-caste.
Listen Mr Oxford Don.
Palm Tree King.
Poetry Jump-Up.

Agathias (Agathias Scholasticus) (536–82)
Beautiful Melite, in the throes of middle age.

Agee, James (1909–55)
Description of Elysium.
In Heavy Mind.
Lyrics, sel.
Permit Me Voyage.
Rapid Transit.
Song with Words.
Sonnets, sels.
This little time the breath and bulk of being.
To Walker Evans.
Two Songs on the Economy of Abundance.

Ager, Milton
Louisville Lou (The Vampin' Lady).

Agodon, Kelli Russell
What Comes after Because.

Agoos, Julie
Portinaio.
To Atlas in the Attic.

Agosin, Marjorie
Dance, The.
Disappeared Woman V.
Fear.
Fear 2.
Language.
Memorial.
Mi Estomago / My Belly.
Miriam.
Most Unbelievable Part, The.
Night.
Obedient Girl, The.
Questions.
Seven Stones.
Traveling Valise.
When she showed me her photograph.
Your Hands.

Agran, Rick (b. 1960)
Cakes Continue to Rise.
Door Thrown Open to Daisies.
Swimming with Seiger.
Wearing Dad's White Shirt Backwards.

Ågren, Gösta (b. 1936)
Death's Secret.

Aguero, Kathleen
Looking for Another Version.
Working Mother.

Agüeros, Jack
Psalm for Amadou Diallo.
Psalm for Distribution.
Psalm for the Damnation of Pig Pino Oink
  Ochet, Who Unlike His Victims Will Neither
  Die nor Disappear, Because He Was Never
  Human.
Psalm for the Next Millennium.

Aguilar-Cariño, Maria Luisa B.
Dinakdakan.

Familiar.
For the Lover.
Gabi.

Aguilar, Luis Miguel (b. 1956)
Memo, Who Loved Motorcycles.

Aguilar, Macel
Sunshine.

Aguilar, Mila D.
Pall Hanging over Manila.
Poem from Sierra Madre.

Aguilera Díaz, Gaspar (b. 1947)
Does Anyone Know Where Roque Dalton
  Spent His Final Night?

Agustini, Delmira (1886–1914)
Another Race.
Break, The.
In Fields of Sleepdreaming.
Ineffable, The.
Ineffable, The.
Intruder, The.
Life.
Marble Beads.
Miraculous Ship, The.
Night Came in the Drowsy Living Room, The.
Public Prayer.
Shadow Beds.
Swan, The.
Sweet Reliquaries, The.
To Death, from the Genie of My Poetry.
Vision.
Wild for Love.
Wings, The.

**"Agyeya" (Sachidananda Hirananda Vatsyayan)
(1911–86)**
Hiroshima.

Ahern, Tom (b. 1947)
Popeye in the 19th Century.
Popeye's Last Words.
Rubber Knight, The.
Titled.
Unbruised.

Ahl, Liz
Ammo.
Defining Moment.

Ahmed Arif (1927–91)
Your Love Never Left.

Ahmed Dâi (1387–1421)
Torture of the beloved is no punishment, The.

Ahmed Pasha (d. 1496)
Ask about my wailing from the prayers.
Is there any heart not bleeding.

Ahmet Hasim (1883–1933)
Moonstruck Storks.

Ahti, Risto (b. 1943)
Beloved's Face, The.

Ai (Florence Anthony) (b. 1947)
Anniversary, The.
Archangel.
Back in the World.
Before You Leave.
Blue Suede Shoes.
Calling, The.
Chance.
Charisma.
Cockfighter's Daughter, The.
Country Midwife, The: A Day.
Cuba, 1962.
Deserter, The.
Disregard.
Endangered Species.
Everything: Eloy, Arizona, 1956.
Family.
Finished.
German Army, Russia, 1943, The.
Good Shepherd, The: Atlanta, 1981.
I Can't Get Started.
I Have Got to Stop Loving You. So I Have
  Killed My Black Goat.
Kid, The.
Killing Floor.
Man with the Saxophone, The.
More.
Mortician's Twelve-year-old Son, The.
Mother's Tale, The.

Ai Ch'ing

New Crops for a Free Man.
Paparazzi, The.
Resurrection of Elvis Presley, The.
Riot Act, April 29, 1992.
Rwanda.
Salome.
Self Defense.
Sleeping Beauty.
Starvation.
Testimony of J. Robert Oppenheimer, The.
Twenty-Year Marriage.
Why Can't I Leave You?
Woman to Man.

Ai Ch'ing (b. 1910)
Chilean Cigarette Pack, The.

Aichinger, Ilse (b. 1921)
Correspondence.
Enumeration.
Glimpse from the Past.
Hemlin.
In Which Names.
Winter Answer.

Aig-Imoukhuede, Frank (b. 1935)
One Wife for One Man.

Aiken, Conrad Potter (1889–1973)
All Death, All Love.
All the Radios.
And in the Hanging Gardens.
Animula Vagula Blandula.
Annihilation.
At a Concert of Music.
But How It Came from Earth.
Chance Meetings.
Dear Uncle Stranger.
Discordants, sels.
Hatteras Calling.
Herman Melville.
Letter from the Grass, A.
Limerick: "It's time to make love. Douse the glim."
Miracles.
North Infinity Street.
Preludes for Memnon; or, Preludes to Attitude, sels.
Priapus and the Pool, sels.
Punch, the Immortal Liar, sel.
Quarrel, The.
Road, The.
Room, The.
Sea Holly.
Senlin; a Biography, sels.
Seven Twilights, sel.
Solitaire.
Summer.
Tetélestai.
Things, The.
Three Star Final.
When the Tree Bares.

Aiken, Joan (b. 1924)
Do It Yourself.
John's Song.
Palace Cook's Tale.
Rhyme for Night.

Aimone, Joe
Second-Grade Incident from Robert Frost's Childhood, A.

Aini, Leah
Empress of Imagined Fertility, The.
In Their House.
Liquidation.
One Girl's Dance.
Shower.

Ainsworth, Henry (1571–c.1623)
Fire in My Meditation Burned.
Give Ear, O Heavens, to That Which I Declare.

Aird, Thomas (1802–76)
Fellowship in Grief.

Aisenberg, Nadya
Leaving Eden.
Woman in the Moon, The.

Aist [or Eist], Dietmar, von (fl. 12th cent.)
Gay Summer's Bliss, Good-bye.
How can I hope a wise heart to attain.
Lady Stood Alone, A.
Yonder on the linden tree there sang a merry little bird.

Aitchison, James
Dipper Territory.
Inheritance, The.

Aitken, E.
Elaine, pretending it was salt.

Aitken, Robert
Gathas.

Aiyejina, Funso
Dialogue, The.
May Ours Not Be.
When the Monuments.

Aizenberg, Mikhail (b. 1948)
Look what's come to light.
Not in the chimney, but in the gas-pipes.
So where is that guy who left us piles.
Who of those who step into the stream.

Aizenberg, Susan
Art.
Kiss.
Meeting the Angel.

Ajada, Raphika See Azad, Rafiq

Ajanta (1929–98)
Dateline Hyderabad.
Me on the Wall.
Sleep: "Nobody nowhere they've all gone home."

Akahito, Yamabé no See Yamabe no Akahito

Akao, Alexander
Zombies Arise.

Akenside, Mark (1721–70)
Amoret.
Complaint, The.
Inscriptions, sels.

Akera Kanko (1740–1800)
Chased round and round.
Under a ragged loincloth.

Akers, Elizabeth
Bringing Our Sheaves with Us.

Akers, Elizabeth Chase See Allen, Elizabeth Akers

Akers, Ellery
Dead, The: "Dead come, looking for their shoes, The."

Akhenaton [or Akhnaton] (Amenhotep IV) (d. c.1354 B.C.)
Hymn to the Sun.

Akhmadulina, Bella [or Izabella] Akhatovna (b. 1937)
Bride, The.
Chill, A.
Chills.
Coffee Imp, The.
God.
I was so buoyant.
In the Botkin Hospital.
Lines Written During a Sleepless Night in Tbilisi.
Lunatics.
Queen, A.
Recollections of Siberia.
Snow Maiden, The.
To Await Arrival.

Akhmatova, Anna Andreyevna (Anna Andreyevna Gorenko) (1889–1966)
Alexander at Thebes.
Alone.
As if with a straw.
Cleopatra.
Dante.
Death of Sophocles, The.
Dedication.
Don't Frighten Me.
Dream, A.
Fear turns objects over in the darkness.
Guest, The.
Guest, The.
I taught myself to live simply and wisely.
I wrung my hands under my dark veil.
In 1940, sels.
In Memory of M. B.
In the Evening ("Music rang out in the garden, The.")
Instead of a Preface.
Introduction.

Land not mine, still, A.
Muse, The.
Muse, The.
1915.
Northern Elegies.
Our Own Land.
Pavlovsk.
Poem: "Twenty-first, The. Night. Monday."
Poem without a Hero, sels.
Reading Hamlet.
Requiem.
Requiem 1935-1940, sels.
Requiem: "No foreign sky protected me."
Requiem: "No, not under the vault of alien skies."
Sentence, The.
Sister, I have come to take your place.
So, I Remained Alone.
Solitude.
Such Days as These.
There Is A Boundary.
Twenty-First. Night. Monday.
Visitor, The.
We Do Not Know How to Say Goodbye.
When in the throes of suicide.

Akhtar-ul-Iman (b. 1915)
Compromise.

Akimine (Ki no Akimine) (fl. 9th cent.)
Kokin Shu, sel.

Akimine, Ki no See Akimine

Akinlolu, Segun
Can't You See?

Akiwumi, Viki
Different Ones #6—Future Possibilities (An Aids Soliloquy).
Unconditionals #3.

Aksal, Sabahattin Kudret (1920–93)
Love Poem: "First line of this poem, The."

Akst, Harry
Straw Hat in the Rain.

Aktan, Feriha (1924–83)
Letter, The: "Few broken things linger in my palm, A."
Pia.

Akutagawa Ryunosuke (1892–1927)
Sick and feverish.
Slime on the stones.
Unable to stand.

Al-Abyad, Abū Bakr ibn Muhammad ibn Ahmad al-Anṣārī al-Ishbīlī (d. c.1133)
Drinking of wine is not pleasing to me, The.

Al-A'mā at-Tuṭīlī, Abū l-'Abbās (d. 1126)
Laughing out of pearls, / A full moon appears.
Tears that are shed and a breast that is burned Water and fire! / Things never joined save for matters of moment!

Al-Aziz, Malak' Abd (b. 1935)
Fall, The.
We Asked.

Al-Bayati, Abdul Wahab (1926–99)
Dragon, The.
Elegy to Aisha, An.
I am Born and I Burn in My Love.
Love Under the Rain.
Nightmare, The.
Nine Ruba'iyat.
Secret of Fire.
Shiraz Moon.
Three Ruba'iyat.
To Naguib Mahfouz.
To TS Eliot.
Transformations of Aisha: Aisha's Birth and Death in the Magical Rituals Inscribed in Cuneiform on the Nineveh Tablets.
Two Poems for My Son, Ali.
Who Owns the Homeland?
Writing on Aisha's Tomb.

al-Braikan, Mahmoud (1932–2002)
Empty City, An.
Face, The.
Meditations on a World of Stones.
Monkey's Journey, The.
Possessed, The.
World of Lightning, A.

Al-Ghanim, Nujoum
Sand in Flames.
Trespasses, *sel.*
Al-Ghuzzi, Muhammad (b. 1949)
Female.
Pen, The.
Quatrains for Joy.
Al-Haidari, Buland (1926–96)
City Ravaged by Silence, The.
Death in Four Voices.
Dialogue of the Colours.
From Behind the Closed Door.
Old Age: "Another winter."
Premature Elegy.
So That We Do Not Forget.
Why Didn't They Apologize. . .?
Will, The.
Al-Haj [*or* Hajj], Unsi (b. 1937)
Charlatan, The.
Al-Harizi, Judah (*fl.* early 13th cent.)
Lightning, The.
Lute, The.
Sun, The.
Al-Jawahiri, Muhammad Mahdi (b. 1900)
Lullaby for the Hungry, A.
Al-Juburi, Amal (b. 1967)
Enheduanna and Goethe.
Protest.
Al-Khal, Yusuf (1917–87)
Cain the Immortal.
Wayfarers, The.
Al-Maghut, Muhammad (b. 1934)
Executioner of Flowers.
al-Mala'ika, Nazik (b. 1923)
Cholera.
Elegy for a Woman of No Importance.
Five Hymns to Pain.
Hijrah [Migration] to God, The.
Jamilah and Us.
Lover River, The.
Myths.
Song for the Moon.
To Poetry.
Al-Mansouri, Al-Zahra
Abandonment.
Secrecy of Mirrors, The.
Al-Muntafil
Mole, The.
al-Musawi, Sajidah
Four Beats of the Heart.
Al-Mushafi, Jafar ibn Uthman (d. 982)
Yellow Its Color.
Al-Na'mani, Houda (b. 1930)
Purple Thought, The.
Stone Will Talk, The.
Al-Neimi, Salwa
Dracula.
Paranoia.
Temptation.
Al-Qasim, Samih (b. 1939)
General's Property, The.
Sons of War.
Al-Qasimi, Maysoun Saqr (b. 1958)
Cusp of Desire, The.
Dream Recalling a Temptation, A.
Morning of Every Sin, The, *sels.*
al-Rahim, Abd al-Rahim Salih (b. 1950)
Everyday.
My Heart.
Poisonous Illusions.
Road, The.
Shadow, A.
Wailing.
Who?
Who Are You?
Al-Rihani, Amin (1876–1940)
It Was All for Him.
Lilatu Laili.
Al-Sabah, Su'ad al-Mubarak (b. 1942)
Mad Woman.
al-Sa'igh, Yousif (b. 1932)
Final Question, The.
Habitude.

Intermittent.
Iraqi Evening, An.
Supper.
Thread.
Tune, The.
Turtle.
Wake Up, Yousif.
Al-Saih, Laila
Intimations of Anxiety.
al-Samawi, Aziz *See* Samawi, Aziz
Al-Samman, Ghada (b. 1942)
Lover of Blue Writing above the Sea, The.
Lover of Rain in an Inkwell, The.
al-Saygh, Sadiq (b. 1936)
Dread.
Mysterious.
Sanctions.
Schwartzkopf's Copters.
White Sleep.
al-Sayyab, Badr Shakir (1926–64)
Love Me.
River and Death, The.
Singer Has Aged, The.
Al-Sindi, Fawziyya
Awakening.
Banners of the Heart.
al-Tajir, Salman (c.1875–1925)
Poet to a Poet.
Al-'Udwani, Ahmad al-Mushari (b. 1923)
Signs, *sels.*
Al-Udwany, Najaat (b. 1956)
Boat on the Pacific, A.
Butterflies of Anxiety.
Carthage.
Al-Urayyid, Thurayya
In the Stealth of Stillness.
Thirst.
Al-Wahaybi, Al-Munsif (b. 1929)
Desert, The.
Alabaster, William (1568–1640)
AWAY, fear, with thy projects, no false fire.
Dear, and so worthy both by your desert.
Divine Meditations, *sels.*
Divine Sonnet, A.
Exaltatio Humanae Naturae.
Incarnatio Est Maximum Dei Donum [*or*
   Donum Dei].
Of the Reed That the Jews Set in Our
   Saviour's Hand.
To Christ.
To the Blessed Virgin.
Upon the Crucifix.
Upon the Ensigns of Christ's Crucifying.
What should there be in Christ to give offense?
Alabaú, Magali (b. 1945)
Sister.
Alakoye, Adesanya (1943–80)
Eshu.
Alarcón, Francisco X. (b. 1954)
Blues del SIDA / AIDS Blues.
Border.
Frontera.
Frontera / Border.
Las calles lloran / Streets Are Crying.
Los árboles son poetas / Trees Are Poets.
Prayer: "I want a god."
Viernes Santo / Good Friday.
X in My Name, The.
Alasdair, Alasdair Mac MacMhaighstir *See*
   MacDonald, Alexander
Albanez, Franciso
One Who Is at Home, The.
Albert, Heinrich (1604–51)
Musical Pumpkin-Hut.
Albert-Birot, Pierre (1876–1967)
Balalaïka.
Bluesky.
City is free of sin, The.
In the Paul Guillaume Gallery.
Who is that blond child laughing as he runs
   after his colored marbles?
Alberti, Rafael (b. 1902)
Al Sol de la Guerra.

Amparo.
Amparo.
Ángel Bueno, El.
Ángel de Arena, El.
Angel of Sand, The.
Angels of the Ruins, The.
Aparecido, El.
Blue.
Bosch.
Buster Keaton Looks in the Woods for His
   Love Who is a Real Cow.
Canción: "Quisiera cantar: ser flor."
Coming Back of an Assassinated Poet, The.
Desahucio.
Eviction.
Ghost, The.
Giotto.
Going Back Through Color.
Going Up the Rivers.
Good Angel, The.
Homecoming of Love Amongst Illustrious
   Ruins.
If My Voice Dies While on Land.
Millares 1965.
Millares 1965.
Punishments.
Remontando los Ríos.
Retornos a Través de los Colores.
Retornos de un Poeta Asesinado.
Si Mi Voz Muriera en Tierra.
Soldados se Duermen, Los.
Soldiers Sleep, The.
Song: "I want to sing: to be a flower."
To the Sun of the War.
Warlike Angels, The.
Albiach, Anne-Marie (b. 1937)
Chemin de l'ermitage, Le, *sel.*
Hermitage Road, The.
Incantation: "She / impregnates my face. Her
   hair taken, and in the veins addicted blood."
"Theatre."
Winter Voyage.
Albizzi, Niccolò degli (*fl.* 13th cent.)
Prolonged Sonnet: When the Troops were
   Returning from Milan.
Albrecht, Abigail
Anacapa.
Below White Cliffs.
Elkhorn Slough.
Passing Piedras Blancas.
Alcaeus [*or* Alkaios] (b. c.620 B.C.–c. 580 B.C.)
And excited the heart of Argive.
Come! Put by Pelops' Isle.
Come tip a few with me.
Come to me, leaving the Peloponnesos.
Drink...with me, Melanippos. Why (think that).
Having done most shameful, unjust things.
Her heart so stricken, Helen.
I don't understand the conflict of the winds.
I long for the call to council.
Story goes, from evil, The.
Wet your lungs with wine—the dogstar rises.
Wretched me / I live a rustic live.
Alcayaga, Lucila Godoy *See* Mistral, Gabriela
Alcman (*fl.* 7th cent. B.C.)
All asleep: mountain peaks and chasms.
But often on the mountain peaks when.
Desire Loosening.
Fragment 58: Night and Sleep.
It isn't Aphrodite, but wild Eros.
Love, again sweetly streaming down.
No longer, O honeytongued, holyvoiced
   maidens.
Olympian [Muses], round my mind.
Polydeukes.
With limb-loosening desire; and her glances
   are more melting than sleep or death.
Alcosser, Sandra
Approaching August.
By the Nape.
Dancing the Tarantella at the County Farm.
Glory Monster.
Golden-Mantled Ground Squirrel.
My Number.
Pole Boat at Honey Island.

Warrior's Tale, A.
Woodpecker.

Alcott, Amos Bronson (1799–1888)
Sonnet 14: "Not Wordsworth's genius,
  Pestalozzi's love."
Sonnet 18: "Adventurous mariner! in whose
  gray skiff."

Alcott, Louisa May (1832–88)
Lay of a Golden Goose, The.

Alcox, Anna (b. c.1645)
All you that are to mirth Inclin'd.

Alcuin (c.735–804)
Lament for the Cuckoo.
Love has pierced my heart with its flame.

Aldana, Francesco de
Sonnet 12: "Which is the reason my Damon
  that although."

Alden, Joseph Reed
Sleepy Time Gal.

Aldington, Richard (1892–1962)
After Two Years.
At the British Museum.
Battlefield.
Choricos.
Evening.
Faun Sees Snow for the First Time, The.
Images.
Possession.
Vicarious Atonement.

Aldis, Dorothy (1896–1966)
Hiding.
Kick a Little Stone.
Little.
No One Heard Him Call.

Aldrich, Henry (1647–1710)
Catch, A.

Aldrich, Thomas Bailey (1836–1907)
By the Potomac.
Fredericksburg.
Identity.
Lycidas.
Memory.
Song: "Chestnuts shine through the cloven
  rind, The."

Alechinsky, Pierre
Ad Miró.

Aled, Sion (b. 1957)
Sunset Over Llŷn.
Tracks of Longing.
Weather Forecast.

Alegría, Claribel (b. 1924)
Accounting.
Ars Poetica.
Desire.
Documentary.
Erosion.
From the Bridge.
Grandmother, The.
Have Pity.
I Am Root.
Letter to an Exile.
Nocturnal Visits.
Savoir Faire.
Silence.
Summing Up.
Toward the Jurassic Age.
We Were Three.

Aleixandre, Vicente (1898–1984)
Ante el Espejo.
Body and the Soul, The.
Cerrada.
Closed.
Como Moisés Es el Viejo.
Cuerpo y el Alma, El.
In Front of the Mirror.
It's Raining.
Life: "Paper bird I have in my chest, A."
Llueve.
Man Doesn't Exist.
No Existe el Hombre.
Old Man and the Sun, The.
Old Man Is Like Moses, The.
Vals, El.
Vida.

Viejo y el Sol, El.
Waltz, The.
Who I Write For.

Alepoudelis, Odysseus *See* Elytis, Odysseus

Aleshire, Joan (b. 1938)
Double, The.
Fingers in the Bread.

Alexander, Alan (b. 1941)
For Raftery.
Gathering Place, The.

Alexander, Cecil Frances (1818–95)
All Things Bright and Beautiful.
Dreams.
Hymn: "Eternal gates lift up their heads, The."
Jesus calls us! O'er the tumult.
Reason and Faith.
Touched with a Feeling of Our Infirmities.

Alexander, Elizabeth (b. 1962)
Affirmative Action Blues (1993).
Apollo.
Aspirin.
At the Beach.
Boston Year.
Compass.
Deadwood Dick.
Equinox.
Farewell to You.
Female seer will burn upon this pyre, The.
Feminist Poem Number One.
Josephine Baker Museum, The.
Kevin of the N.E. Crew.
Ladders.
Letter: Blues.
Minnesota Fats Describes His Youth.
Narrative: Ali.
Neonatology, *sel.*
Nineteen.
Ode.
Overture: Watermelon City.
Painting / (Frida Kahlo).
Passage.
Robeson at Rutgers.
Stravinsky in L.A.
Today's News.
Venus Hottentot, The.
Washington Etude.
West Indian Primer.
Who I Think You Are.
Zodiac.

Alexander, Lewis (1900–45)
Dream Song.

Alexander, Margaret Walker
Chicago.
Iowa Farmer.
Memory.
October Journey.
People of Unrest.

Alexander, Meena
News of the World.
River and Bridge.

Alexander, Pamela
Antichromatic.
Bicycle Sprint.
Comma a Portrait, The.
Crossing.
First Relations.
Flight: "Series of white squares, each, A."
Foxlight, *sels.*
Inventory. Journal.
Lightfall.
Look Here.
Manners.
Marriage of Sorts, A.
Mt. Auburn Owl.
Northeast Suite.
Person of.
Reprise.
Scherzo.
Sight.
Soon.
Understory.
Vines.
Well-Known Elizabethan Double Entendre, A.

Alexander, Robert
For Years My Father.

Alexander, Will (b. 1948)
Albania and the Death of Enver Hoxha.
Asia, *sel.*
Concerning the Henbane Bird, *sel.*
Solea of the Simooms, *sel.*

**Alexander, William, Archbishop of Armagh
(1824–1911)**
Birthday Crown, The.

Alexander the Wild (*fl.* 13th cent.)
Strawberry Picking.
When We Were Children.

Alexandru, Ioan
End of the War, The.

Alexie, Sherman (b. 1966)
After the Trial of Hamlet, Chicago.
Airplane.
At Navajo Monument Valley Tribal School
  (from the Photograph by Skeet Mcauley).
Capital Punishment.
Crazy Horse Speaks.
Crow Testament.
Defending Walt Whitman.
Evolution.
Exaggeration of Despair, The.
Father and Farther.
How to Write the Great American Indian
  Novel.
I Would Steal Horses.
Indian Boy Love Song (#2).
November 22, 1983.
On the Amtrak from Boston to New York City.
One Stick Song.
Penance.
Powwow at the End of the World, The.
Powwow Polaroid.
Reservation Love Song.
Sonnet: Tattoo Tears.
Texas Chainsaw Massacre.
Theology.
Tourists.
Translated from the American.
Vision (2).
Why We Play Basketball.

Alexopoulos, Marion (b. 1948)
Night Flight.

Alféri, Pierre (b. 1963)
Bibliothèque.
Choirist.
Choriste.
Library.
Quand rien n'entraîne rien.
When Nothing Entices Nothing.

Alfonso X (1221–84)
Scorpions, The.

Alford, Henry (1810–71)
Harvest Home.
You and I.

Algarin, Miguel
Always Throw the First Punch.
And in the U.S.A.
Angelitos Negros: A Salsa Ballet, *sels.*
At the Electronic Frontier.
Broadway Opening.
Christmas Eve: Nuyorican Café.
Dante Park.
El Jibarito Moderno.
Happy New Year.
Infections.
Meeting Gaylen's 5th Grade Class.
Nudo de Claridad.
Rosa.
San Fransisco.
Talking.
Taos Pueblo Indians: 700 strong according to
  Bobby's last census.
Tato—Reading at the Nuyorican Poets' Cafe.
Tiger Lady.
Trampling.
Wire Tap.

Ali, Agha Shahid (b. 1949)
Country Without a Post Office, The, *sel.*
Cracked Portraits.
Cremation.
Dacca Gauzes, The.
Dream of Glass Bangles, A.

Farewell: "At a certain point I lost track of you."
Ghazal: "Only language of loss left in the world is Arabic, The."
Ghazal: "What will suffice for a true-love knot? Even the rain?"
Ghazal: "Where are you now? Who lies beneath your spell tonight."
Homage to Faiz Ahmed Faiz.
Houses.
I See Chile in My Rearview Mirror.
In Arabic.
Jogger on Riverside Drive, 5:00 A.M., The.
Land.
Leaving Sonora.
Lenox Hill.
Lost Memory of Delhi, A.
Of Fire.
Postcard from Kashmir.
Purse-Seiner *Atlantis*, The.
Return to Harmony 3.
Rooms Are Never Finished.
Snow on the Desert.
Stars.
Stationery.

Ali, Mahdi Muhammad
Condition.
Expatriation.
Flight.
Heritage.
Homeland.
Upside Down Picture, An.

Ali, Taha Muhammad (b. 1931)
Abd El-Hadi Fights a Superpower.

Ali Hsiying
Lazy Cloud's Nest 1.
Lazy Cloud's Nest 2.

Aliesan, Jody
There is no real edge to anything.

Aliger, Margarita Iosifovna (1918–92)
I live / with a bullet in my heart.

Alipiev, Petar (b. 1930)
Old Man: "On his tired memory a splendid."
Warmth, The.

Alkaios *See* Alcaeus

Alkalay-Gut, Karen (b. 1945)
Between Bombardments: A Journal, *sels.*
Kitzbuhl Church.
Public Outcry.
Transportation.

Allah, Fareedah *See* Saunders, Ruby C.

Allan, Lewis (fl. 1939)
Strange Fruit.

Allbery, Debra
Assembler.
Carnies.
Offering.
Produce.

Allen, Alfred (b. 1925)
Love and the Years.

Allen, Alma Stacey
Road Trip.

Allen, Annette
This River.

Allen, Dick (b. 1939)
Coming of the First Aeroplanes, The.
Lost Love.
Poet at Eighteen, The.
Time to Hear Ourselves Think.
Zen Living.

Allen, Elizabeth Akers (Elizabeth Chase Akers) (1832–1911)
In the Defences.
Rock Me to Sleep[, Mother].
Street Music.

Allen, Fergus (b. 1921)
Elegy for Faustina.
Fall, The.
First-born.
Foreign Relations.
Glenasmole.
Modern Times.
Sodium Light.
Sound Waves.

Surveyor's Story, The.
Time for Blushing, A.
Two-day-old Grandchild.
Visitant, The.
Way Back Then.
When the Car Gave Up the Ghost.

Allen, Gilbert (b. 1951)
Good Duke Speaks, The.

Allen, Graham (b. 1938)
Poem For My Father.

Allen, Heather
In the Forest.

Allen, Hervey (1889–1949)
Dragon's Breath.
Wingless Victory, The.

Allen, Jeffery Renard (b. 1963)
Deep Rock.
For Michael Griffith, Murdered Dec. 21, 1986, Howard Beach, NY.
Hunger.
Mud Wit.
Prayer to Eshbu-Elegba.

Allen, Lillian (b. 1951)
Riddim an' Hardtimes.
Rub a Dub Style inna Regent Park.

Allen, Marie Louise (b. 1911)
Mitten Song, The.

Allen, Paul
Judy.
Pickup.
Tattoo #47, "Happy Dragon."

Allen, Paula Gunn (b. 1939)
Dear World.
He Na Tye Woman.
Kopis'taya.
Meditations on the Moon.
Soundings.
Taku Skanskan.
Teaching Poetry at Votech High, Santa Fe, the Week John Lennon Was Shot.
Weed.
Zen Americana.

Allen, Richard (1760–1831)
Epitaph for the Western Intelligentsia.

Allen, Richard (b. 1960)
See! How the Nations Rage Together.

Allen, Samuel ("Paul Vesey") (b. 1917)
Apple Trees in Sussex, The.
Harriet Tubman aka Moses.
I Say, Mr. A.
In My Father's House.
Lingering Doubt, The.
Moment Please, A.
To Satch.
View from the Corner.

Allen, William S. (1803–79)
Erie Canal, The.

Allen, Willis Boyd
Away from the Office.

Allestry, Jacob (1653–86)
What art thou, love? Whence are those charms.

Alley, Rick (b. 1963)
Canary Man and You, The.
Cleaning.
Dissecting Uncle Sorrow.
Growing Days, The.

Allingham, William (1824–89)
Dream, A [*or* The].
Everything passes and vanishes.
Fairies, The.
Four Ducks on a Pond.
In a Spring Grove.
In Snow.
Lovely Mary Donnelly.
No funeral gloom, my dears, when I am gone.
Swing Song, A.
Winding Banks of Erne, The[: Or, The Emigrant's Adieu to His Birthplace].

Allison, Drummond (1921–43)
Funeral Oration, A.

Allison, Oktavi
Billy.

Allnutt, Gillian (b. 1949)
About Benwell.
Bringing the Geranium in for Winter.
Held To.
Notes on Living inside the Lightbulb.
Road Home, The.
Sarah's Laughter.
Scheherazade.
Silk Light of Advent, The.

Allott, Kenneth (b. 1912)
Prize for Good Conduct.

Allston, Washington (1779–1843)
America to Great Britain.
Art.
On a Falling Group in the Last Judgement of Michael Angelo, in the Cappella Sistina.
On Kean's Hamlet.
On Michael Angelo.
On Rembrant; Occasioned by His Picture of Jacob's Dream.
On Seeing the Picture of Æolus by Pelegrino Tibalbi, in the Institute at Bologna.
On the Group of the Three Angels Before the Tent of Abraham, by Raffaelle, in the Vatican.
On the Luxembourg Gallery.
On the Statue of an Angel, by Bienaimé, in the Possession of J.S. Copley Greene, Esq.
Rubens.
Sylphs of the Seasons, The, *sel.*
To My Venerable Friend, the President of the Royal Academy.
Word: Man, A.

'Allush, Laila
Path of Affection, The.

Alon, Eli (b. 1935)
Always in Anguish.
Coffins.
If There is a God.
In the Mount of Final Repose.
Leave-Taking ("Death in a war.").
Missing Out.

Alpaugh, David
Herbie.
Young, The.

"Alta" (b. 1942)
Judy Comes to Visit.

Alterman, Nathan (1910–70)
Around the Campfire.
First Smile.
Householder Departs from the City, The.
Mole, The.
Moon.
Shadow, The.
Silver Platter, The.
Spinner, The.
Summer Night.
Time and the Response, The.

Althaus, Keith
Little Elegy.

Altizer, Nell
("Love Letters to Her Who Lives [Alas!] Away"), *sels.*
Sonnet 5: "No, I'll not, carrion, comfort you. Comfort."

Alun Cilie (1897–1975)
Old Chapel, The.

Alvarez, Julia (b. 1950)
Against Cinderella.
Bilingual Sestina.
Cows.
Estel.
How I Learned to Sweep.
Naming the Fabrics.
On a Hill Above Your House.
On Not Shoplifting Louise Bogan's *The Blue Estuaries*.
Papi Working.
Redwing Sonnets.
33, *sels.*
Wallpaper.
Woman's Work.

Alves, Rubin
Tomorrow's Child.

Alvi, Moniza (b. 1954)
Arrival 1946.
Backgrounds.
Bed, The.
Carrying My Wife.
Country at My Shoulder, The.
Fish.
Houdini.
I Would Like to be a Dot in a Painting by
    Miró.
Laughing Moon, The.
Man Impregnated.
Missing.
Presents from My Aunts in Pakistan.
Sari, The.
Throwing Out My Father's Dictionary.
Alviso, Madeline
Barbies, Las.
Ama Ata Aidoo, Christine (b. 1942)
For Kinna 2.
Gynae One.
Issues.
Totems.
Amadiume, Ifi (b. 1947?)
Be Brothers.
Bitter.
Bloody Masculinity.
Creation.
4th Witness—The Petty Thieves.
Mistress of My Own Being.
Nok Lady in Terracotta.
Oya Now.
Union, The.
We Have Even Lost our Tongues!
Amaker, Arthur Ade
Roots.
Amalrik, Andrey Alekseievich (1938–80)
Lake Baskunchak.
Amara, Lamea Abbas (b. 1927)
Commandments, The.
San Diego (On a rainy day).
Amaru (fl. 7th cent.)
Lying in Bed.
Much Too Close.
You with Your Beautiful Swaying Walk.
Ambrose, Saint (c.340–97)
O splendour of God's glory bright.
Amenhotep IV See Akhenaton [or Akhnaton]
Amichai, Yehuda (b. 1924)
All the Generations Before Me.
All the Generations Before Me.
Almost a Love Poem.
And That Is Your Glory.
Anniversaries of War.
Appendix to the Vision of Peace, An.
Biblical Meditations.
Couplets.
Course of a Life, The.
Death of My Father, The.
Diameter of the Bomb, The.
Don't prepare for tomorrow, enter the narrow
    lane.
Elegy: "Wind won't come to draw smiles in
    the sand of dreams, The."
Flock of Sheep Near the Airport, A.
Four Resurrections in the Valley of the Ghosts.
From the Songs of the Land of Zion and
    Jerusalem.
God Has Mercy on Kindergarten Children.
God Has Pity on Kindergarten Children.
Half of the people in the world.
Ibn Gabirol.
Ideal Woman, An.
Ideal Woman, An.
Inside the Apple.
Instructions for a Waitress.
Jerusalem.
Jewish Time Bomb, The.
Jews in the Land of Israel.
King Saul and I.
Laments on the War Dead, sel.
Letter.
Letter of Recommendation.
Like Our Bodies' Imprint.
Lips of the dead once thoughtlessly.

Little Ruth.
Luxury.
Man in His Life, A.
Mayor.
My Child Blossoms Sadly.
My Child Smells of Peace.
My Father.
My father fought their war four years or so.
My Father's Memorial Day.
My Mother Once Told Me.
My Son.
National Thoughts.
Near the Wall of a House.
Not like the cypress.
Patriotic Songs, sels.
Pity, A. We Were Such a Good Invention.
Psalm: "Psalm on the day, A."
Quick And Bitter.
Radius of the bomb was twelve inches, The.
Rain on the Battlefield.
Rustle of History's Wings, as They Used to
    Say Then, The.
Savage Memories.
Seven Laments for the War-Dead.
Since Then.
Song of Lies on Sabbath Eve, A.
Summer or Its Ending.
Thoughts came to him like long lines of
    freight, The.
To My Love, Combing Her Hair.
Tourists.
Travels of a Latter-Day Benjamin of Tudela,
    sel.
Two of Us Together, Each of Us Alone, The.
Two Poems about the First Battles.
Two Songs of Peace.
Two Songs of Peace.
We Have Done Our Duty.
We Have Done Our Duty.
We Have No Unknown Soldiers.
What drove young Joseph to interpret dreams.
What is it? An airplane at dawn. No.
Wildling Peace.
Amiel, Barry
Death Is a Matter of Mathematics.
**Aminado, Don (Aminado Petrovich Shpolyansky)
(1888–1957)**
Our Sunday Rest.
Amir, Devorah (b. 1948)
After Fall, 1956.
I Have Longings for My Dead.
Nightingale of Uncle Yair, The.
Thoughts about Sari's Jump.
What Seeps In.
Amirthanayagam, Indran (b. 1960)
Elephants Are in the Yard, The.
So Beautiful.
There Are Many Things I Want to Tell You.
Amis, Kingsley (1922–95)
Against Romanticism.
Autobiographical Fragment.
Dream of Fair Women, A.
Evans Country, The, sels.
Ever-Fixed Mark, An.
Last War, The.
Mightier than the Pen.
New Approach Needed.
Note on Wyatt, A.
Science Fiction.
Sight Unseen.
Ammianus (fl. 2d cent.)
Epitaph of Nearchos.
Ammons, A. R. (Archie Randolph) (1926–2001)
Above the Fray Is Only Thin Air.
Alligator Holes Down Along About Old Dock.
All's All.
Anxiety's Prosody.
Arc Inside and Out, The.
Ballad: "I want to know the unity in all things
    and the difference."
Cascadilla Falls.
City Limits, The.
Close-up.
Coming Right Up.
Conserving the Magnitude of Uselessness.

Constant, The.
Corsons Inlet.
Cut the Grass.
Easter Morning.
Enfield Falls.
First Cold.
Foot-Washing, The.
Garbage, sels.
Grassy Sound.
Gravelly Run.
He Held Radical Light.
Hymn: "I know if I find you I will have to
    leave the earth."
I Went Back.
Improvisation for Jerald Bullis, An.
Improvisation for the Stately Dwelling, An.
In Memoriam Mae Noblitt.
In View of the Fact.
Laser.
Looking Way Off.
Love Song: "Like the hills under dusk you."
Mansion.
Motion's Holdings.
Mountain Talk.
Needs.
Parting.
Pet Panther.
Play.
Reflective.
Silver.
Singing & Doubling Together.
Small Song.
So I Said I Am Ezra.
Somers Point.
Sphere, sels.
Spit.
Spring Coming.
Standing Light Up.
Still.
Strip, sels.
Strolls.
Terrain.
Their Sex Life.
This Black Rich Country.
Tombstones, sels.
Triphammer Bridge.
White Echo.
Widespread Implications.
Working with Tools.
Ammuvanar
They Shout Out the Price of Salt.
Amor, Pita (b. 1920)
CXLII.
CXXX.
CXXXIV.
CXXXIX.
Amorosi, Ray
Good Teacher, The.
Amrane, Danièle (b. 1931)
You Called to Me, Prison Windows.
An Jung-Sŏp
Drinking Alone on a Spring Night.
An Minyŏng (fl. 1870–80)
Speak, chrysanthemum, why do you you shun.
Anacreon Anacreontea (582–485 B.C.)
Again Love struck me like a smith with a
    giant.
Already my temples are grey.
Come, boy, bring us.
Count, if you can, every leaf on every tree.
Dice of Love are, The.
Elegy 2.
Epicure, The.
Fragment 17.
Fragment 360.
Grasshopper, The.
I implore you, deer-shooter.
Lad, glancing like a virgin.
Not / But near another you have a timid.
O Lord, with whom subduer Love.
Odes, sels.
Soaring again from the Leukadian Rock.
Thracian filly, why do you.
Tossing a crimson ball.
Weaving a garland long ago.

Anacreontea *See* Anacreon

Anania, Michael (b. 1939)
Edge of Autumn, The.
Fall, The.
Interstate 80.
Judy Travaillo Variations, The.
Memorial Day.
On the Conditions of Place.
Riversongs of Arion, The.

Anatolius (*fl.* 7th cent.)
Fierce was the wild billow, Dark was the night.

Anawrok, Edgar
Each Time.

Anaya, Rudolfo
Isis in the Heart.

Anbun
Years keeping that in mind.

Ancient Sumerian Oral Tradition
Bridegroom, dear to my heart.
Courtship of Inanna and Dumuzi, The, *sel.*

Andal (*fl.* 10th cent.)
Tiruppavai, The, *sels.*

Anday, Melih Cevdet (b. 1915)
Horses Before Troy, *sels.*

Anderson, Alice (b. 1966)
Licking Wounds.
Suicide Year, The.

Anderson, Curt
Platonic Love.

Anderson, Daniel (b. 1964)
Executive Geochrone.
Nightly News, The.

Anderson, Doug
Infantry Assault.
Itinerary.
Papasan.
Purification.

Anderson, Ethel Louisa Mason (1883–1958)
Afternoon in the Garden.

Anderson, Jack (b. 1935)
American Flag.
Going to Norway.
Ode to Pornography.
Waking Up Twice.

Anderson, Jolivette
13th Letter, The.

Anderson, Jon (b. 1940)
Ye Bruthers Dogg.

Anderson, Judith
Re-member Us.

Anderson, Laurie
Dog Show.
Red Hot.
Wild White Horses.

Anderson, Louis *See* Lukata, Baba

Anderson, Maggie
Closed Mill.
Country Wisdoms.
Invention of Pittsburgh, The.
Sleep Writer, The.
Spitting in the Leaves.

Anderson, Maxwell (1888–1959)
It Never Was You.
Lost in the Stars.
September Song.

Anderson, Patrick (1915–79)
Sestina in Time of Winter.

Anderson, Sherwood (1876–1941)
American Spring Song.
Evening Song.
Evening Song.
Song of the Soul of Chicago.

Anderson, Tenshin Reb
To Bodhidharma.
To My First Teacher.

Anderson, Timothy
I Think You Got Me Confused.

Anderson, William (1762–1790)
I'm Naebody Noo.

Anderson, William
There's Not a Friend like the Lowly Jesus.

Anderson-Thompkins, Sibby (b. 1966)
Brken Promises.
Epitaph for Willie or Little Black Poet with No Future.
Interlude.
To Love a Stranger.

Anderton, Anne
Marking of Folders.

Andrade, Eugenio de (1923–2005)
Fable.
Music.
Penniless Lovers.
Silence.
Walt Whitman and the Birds.
White on White, *sel.*

Andrade, Mário de (1893–1945)
Inspiration.
Nocturne.
Ode to the Bourgeois Gentleman.
Processions, The.
Sunday.

Andrade, Oswald de (1890–1953)
Babbling.
Election.
Frontier.
Good Luck.
Hierofant.
Portuguese Mistake.

Andreus, Hans (Johan van der Zant) (1926–77)
Empty Room, The.
Empty Room, The.
For Some Future Day.
Song: "All roocoogirls."

Andrew, Ginger (b. 1956)
Down on My Knees.
Evidently, She Says.
Housewife, The.
Hurricane Sisters Work Regardless, The.
O That Summer.
Prayer: "God bless the chick in Alaska."
Rolls-Royce Dreams.

Andrews, Bruce (b. 1948)
AKA.
Bomb Then, Bomb Now.
Dang Me, *sels.*
DDD.
Gestalt Me Out!
Impatient Heart, The.
Methodology.
Rich little circle south.
Species Means Guilt.
Stalin's Genius.
Tizzy Boost, *sel.*
West West.
While.
Zero Tolerance.

Andrews, Clement
Morn's Recompense.

Andrews, Linda
Time Signature.

Andrews, Miles Peter ("Arley") (d. 1814)
Elegy on the Death of Mr Sterne.

Andrews, Nin (b. 1958)
Crossing.
Nirvana: "After you left me, I was so lonely and sad, I became but an apparition, a ghost of who I had been."
Notes for a Sermon on the Mount.
Philosophical Inquiry into the Nature of the Human Cock, A.
Poets on Poets.
Satori.
That Cold Summer.
Zen 101.

Andrews, Tom
Cinema Vérité: Jacques Derrida and God's *Tsimtsum.*
Cinema Vérité: The Death of Alfred, Lord Tennyson.
Cinema Vérité: William Makepeace Thackeray Follows His Bliss.
Six One-Line Film Scripts.

Andriescu, Radu (b. 1962)
Apple, The.

Aneirin (*fl.* 6th cent.)
Gododdin, The, *sels.*
Gorcheau: The Three Laments.

Anene, Lawrence Okezie Chibueze (b. 1948)
Democracy.
D-Hour.

Angel, Ralph (b. 1951)
And the Grass Did Grow.
Breaking the Rock Down.
Evolving Similarities.
Nothing That Is, The.
Twilight.
Veils of Prayer.
Vigil, The.

Angela, Frances
Old Stone Age.

Angeles, Carlos A.
Light Invested.
Words.

Angelou, Maya (b. 1928)
Africa.
Caged Bird.
Come, and Be My Baby.
Family Affairs.
Life Doesn't Frighten Me.
Many and More.
Miss Scarlet, Mr. Rhett and other Latter-Day Saints.
Our Grandmothers.
Pickin Em Up and Layin Em Down.
Still I Rise.
Woman Me.

"Angelus Silesius" (Johannes Scheffler) (1624–77)
Cherubical Wanderer, The, *sels.*

Angguish, Dallas
Arrythmia (1–10).

Angira, Jared (b. 1936)
Dialogue.
Newscast.
Obbligato from a Public Gallery.
Old Wharf Canto.
Symphony from the Balcony.

Anguita, Eduardo (1914–92)
Real Moment, The.

Angus, Marion (1870–1946)
Alas! Poor Queen.
Anemones.
Blue Jacket, The.
Doors of Sleep, The.
Fiddler, The.
Invitation.
Mary's Song.

Angwin, Roselle
I offer you four things.

Anhalt, Diana
That Jewish Crusader.

Anna, Glory
Bicycle Glee Song, A.

Annand, James King (b. 1908)
Arctic Convoy.
Fur Coats.
Heron.
I Winna Let On.
Mavis.
Mountain Pule.

Annensky, Innokenty Fiodorovich (1856–1909)
Capitol, The.
One Second.

Annucci, Marilyn
Wrecked World.

Ansari, Kwaja Abdullah (1006–89)
I came out of the unmade.
Intimate Conversations with God, *sel.*

Ansen, Alan (b. 1922)
Fatness.

Anstett, Aaron (b. 1968)
Man Saves Own Life.
Pharmacy.
Shift.
Worry.

Antar [or Antara] (*fl.* 6th cent.)
Black Night, The.

Anthony, Florence *See* Ai

Anthony, Martha (b. 1967)
So suddenly.
Ugly Heart, The.
You cared whether I died or not.

Anti-Jacobins, The
Progress of Man, The. A Didactic Poem, *sels*.
Rovers, The; or, The Double Arrangement.

Antin, David (b. 1932)
David ross called up from syracuse and wanted to know if.
Definitions for Mendy.
Endangered Nouns.
List of the Delusions of the Insane / What They Are Afraid Of, A.
Private Occasion in a Public Place, A.
Real Estate.

Antipater of Sidon (*fl.* 2d cent. B.C.)
Amyntor.
Artemeias, surely when you from the nether world's bark.
Here beside the threshing floor, O hardworking ant.
I, who used to ward off the starlings and that snatcher.
Let the four-clustered ivy flourish about you, Anacreon.
Myriad times, Ptolemy, your father, myriad times.
Never again, Orpheus.
Priapos of the Harbor.
Tell me, woman, your parents, your name, your land. B. Calliteles.
This is Anacreon's grave. Here lie.
This is the barrow of grizzled Maronis, on which you see.
To Pallas, three girls, all of an age, skilled as the spider.
To Pan three brothers hung up these tools of the trade.

Antipater of Thessalonica (*fl.* 1st cent b.c.e.)
I've Never Feared.
Priapus, seeing Cimon's rigid rod.

Antiphanes (c.388–c.311 B.C.)
Strange race of critics, A.

Antiphilus (*fl.* 1st cent b.c.e.)
On the Death of the Ferryman, Glaucus.

"Antler" (b. 1946)
American History in Context.
Bringing Zeus to His Knees.
Factory, *sel*.
Factory, *sel*.
One Breath.
Raising My Hand.
Star-Struck Utopias of 2000.
Thoughts Breathing in a Blizzard.
Trees Seen Now.

Antoine, Pierre *See* Motteux, Peter Anthony

Antokolsky, Pavel Grigoryevich (1896–1978)
Son, *sels*.

Anton, Sinan
Milky Way, The.
Phantasmagoria.
Prism, A: Wet With Wars.
Prisoner's Song, A.
Wars 1.

Antoninus, Brother *See* Everson, William

"Anvari" (Awhad ad-Din 'Ali ibn Vahid ad-Din Muhammad Khavarani) (1126?–1190?)
Composing.
Drunkenness.
Take What He Gives You.

Anwar, Chairil (1922–49)
At the Mosque.
Heaven.
Light Leaving a Small Harbour.
Me.
Ordinary Song, An.
Tuti's Ice Cream.
Twilight at a Little Harbor.
Willingness.

Anyidoho, Kofi (b. 1947)
Desert Storm.
Elegy for the Revolution.
Murmuring.

Our Birth-Cord.
They Hunt the Night.
Tsitsa.

Anyte (*fl.* 290 B.C.E.)
Behold the horned goat of Bacchos, how lordly.
Damis erected this mound for his dead steadfast.
Epigrams, *sels*.
For the cricket (nightingale of the field) and oak.
I, Hermes, have been set up.
I, Hermes, stand here by the windy tree-lined.
I mourn maiden Antibia: desiring her, many.
Instead of bridal bed and holy wedding songs.
Lone Theudotos placed this gift beneath the mountain.
No longer, as before, plying with whirring wings.
No longer will I fling up my neck, exulting.
Often keening on her daughter's tomb, Kleina.
Ox-sized cauldron, Kleubotos gave, An.
Putting red reins on you, goat, with a noseband.
Sit, everyone, under the luxuriant laurel.
Stand there, manslaying spear; no longer drip.
Stranger, below the boulder rest your spent limbs.
This is Kypris' place; it ever pleases her.
This Lydian earth covers Amyntor, Philip's son.
This Manes alive once was a slave; now dead.
Throwing her arms around her dear father.
We go, Miletos, dear fatherland, spurning.
Why, rustic Pan, sitting in the lone shady wood.
You, too, perished by a bush with tangled roots.
Youth buried you, Captain; as sons for their mother, The.

Anzai Hitoshi (b. 1919)
New Blade.

Anzaldúa, Gloria (b. 1946)
Cultures.
Horse.

Ap Glyn, Ifor (b. 1961)
Cucumbers of Wolverhampton, The.
Englyns.
I'm the Guy with the Gut.

Ap Gwilym, Gwynn (b. 1950)
Badger, The.
Penyberth.

Ap Hywel, Elin (b. 1962)
Blue.
Blue.
Disarmed.
Goddesses.
Goddesses.
History.
In My Mother's House.
In My Mother's House.
Song about Soup, A.
Stitching.
Thing.
Treasure.
Understanding Light.
Understanding the Light.
Useful.

Apache Oral Tradition
Corn Ceremony.

Apáti, Ferenc (*fl.* early 16th cent.)
Song of Reproach.

Apollinaire, Guillaume (1880–1918)
Adieu, L'
Always.
Bonds.
Calligram, 15 May 1915.
Cantor.
Cavalier's Farewell, The.
Farewell, The.
Fenêtres, Les.
Fete.
Heart, Crown, and Mirror, *sels*.
Horse Calligram.
Little Car, The.

Meadow Saffron.
Mirabeau Bridge.
Mirabeau Bridge, The.
Miroir.
Monday rue Christine.
Petite Auto, La.
Poems for Lou, *sel*.
Post Card.
Pretty Redhead, The.
Stanzas Against Forgetting.
To Linda.
Toujours.
Traveller, The.
Victoire, *sels*.
Voyager, The.
Windows.
Windows.
Zone.
Zone.
Zone.
Zone.
Zone.

Apollonius Rhodius (*fl.* 3rd cent. B.C.)
Argonautica, The.

Apotheker, Alison
Burning Bush.

Apparao, Gurajada (1862–1915)
Comet, The.
Gold.

Appel, Karel (b. 1921)
Mad Talk.

Appleman, Philip (b. 1926)
Birthday Card to My Mother.
Landing Pattern.
Mary.
O Karma, Dharma, pudding and pie.
Peace with Honor.
St. Matthew, *sels*.

Applewhite, James (b. 1935)
Flight Instructor.
Home Team.
Map of Simplicities, A.
On the Mississippi.
Prayer for My Son.
Road Down Home.
Southland Drive-In.
Village After Sunset, The.
Water from the Lamp Bottle.
Wilson County Farmer, A.

Áprily, Lajos (1887–1967)
Antigone.
March in Transylvania.
Night in Kolozsvár.
Night Song.
Nostalgia.
On the Wall of My Age.
Plea to Old Age.
Stag of Irisoda, The.
Victor, The.

Aprin Çor Tigin (*fl.* 6th? cent.)
My darling, / Best of all.

Apuleius, Lucius
I who am Nature, mother of all.

'Aql, Sa'id (b. 1912)
More Beautiful Than Your Eyes.

Aragon, Francisco
Century, The.
Doubletalk.
Earplugs.
Tricycles.

Aragon, Louis (1897–1982)
Big Spectacular Play.
Embrace, The.
Étreinte, L'
Lilacs and the Roses, The.
Little Suite for Loudspeaker, *sel*.
Night at Dunkirk.
Parti Pris.
Partial.
Pièce à grand spectacle.
Poem to Shout in the Ruins.
Richard II Forty.
Waltz of the Twenty-Year-Olds, The.

Araidi, Na'im (b. 1950)
Return to the Village.
Arakida Moritaké (Moritaké) (1473–1549)
Falling flower, The.
Haiku: "Fallen flowers rise."
Haiku: "Falling flower, The."
Arana, Milton
Birth of a Nation.
Arany, János (1817–82)
Bards of Wales, The.
Civilisation.
Cosmopolitan Poetry.
Family Circle.
Imprisoned Souls.
Mistress Agnes.
Mother of King Matthias, The.
Nighingale, The.
Reply to Petőfi.
Scholar's Cat, The.
Toldi, sels.
Two Pages of Szondi, The.
Arany, László (1844–98)
Elfrida.
Hero of the Mirages, The, sel.
Arapaho Oral Tradition
Ghost-Dance Songs, sels.
He'Yoho'Ho! He'Yoho'Ho!
My Son, Let Me Grasp Your Hand.
Spirit Host Is Advancing, They Say, The.
When I Met Him Approaching.
Aratus (fl. 3d cent. B.C.)
Phaenomena, sels.
Arber, Carol
Sketching in Barnstable.
Arbiter, Caius Petronius See Petronius Arbiter
Arcana, Judith (b. 1943)
Great with Child.
Archilochus (c.680?–c.640? B.C.)
Attribute all to the gods: often they raise.
Be Bold! That's One Way.
Buffeted by the waves.
Decks awash, / Mast-top dipping.
Fireworks on the Grass.
Fox knows many things, The.
Glaukos, look: already the deep sea is troubled.
Heart, my heart churning with fathomless
   cares.
Here is a fable men tell.
Hold back completely.
I am a servant of the War Lord.
I don't give a damn if some Thracian ape strut.
I don't like a tall general, swaggering.
Ideal General, The.
If only I might touch Neobule's hand.
Like Odysseus under the ram.
May he lose his way on the cold sea.
Miserable I lie in desire.
My friend, limb-loosening.
No townsman, Perikles, will blame us for
   groaning.
Nothing is unexpected or sworn impossible.
Seduction, The, sel.
She delighted to hold a slip of myrtle.
Some Saian sports my splendid shield.
Some Thracian exults in an excellent shield.
Strategy.
Such passion for love coiled in my heart.
This island, garlanded with wild woods.
What Gyges so golden has doesn't matter to
   me.
Will, lost in a sea of trouble.
You see that high crag.
Zeus, Father Zeus, you've power over heaven.
Archpoet, The (c.1130–c.65)
Confession, The, sel.
His Confession.
Arcos, René
Dead, The.
Arends, Jan (1925–74)
I.
I Have.
Arensberg, Walter Conrad
Arithmetical Progression of the Verb "To Be"
Axiom.

Ing.
Theorem.
Voyage à l'Infini.
Aretino, Pietro (1492–1556)
If famous Apelles with his hand of art.
Argensola, de, Lupercio Leonardo
Damon's Lament for His Clorenda, Yorkshire,
   1654.
Argentarius (Marcus Argentarius) (fl. c.60 B.C.)
Her perfect naked breast.
I can't bear to watch your hips.
Argentarius, Marcus See Argentarius
Arghezi, Tudor
Flowers of Mildew.
Last Hour, The.
Psalm.
Testament.
Arguelles, Ivan (b. 1939)
I Danced with You Once Only Onliest One.
Aridjis, Homero [or Umberto] (b. 1940)
Borders, Cages and Walls.
Decomposition with Laughter.
Epitaph for a Poet.
Letter from Mexico.
Poem, The.
Rain is Falling, The.
Rivers.
Self-Portrait at Age Sixteen.
Self-Portrait at Age Ten.
Self-Portrait at Eleven on a Train.
Self-Portrait at Fifty-Four Years Old.
Self-Portrait at Six Years of Age.
Self-Portrait at Thirteen Years of Age.
Self-Portrait in the Doorway.
To Emerge from a Woman Is to Become
   Separate.
Wounded Self-Portrait, A.
Arif, Ahmed See Ahmed Arif
Arif, Iftiqar (b. 1943)
Twelfth Man, The.
Ariosto, Ludovico (1474–1533)
Orlando Furioso, sels.
Aristophanes (c.450–c.385 B.C.)
Lysistrata, sels.
Lysistrata.
Aristophanes of Byzantium
On the advice of Praxilla.
Arkell, Reginald (1882–1959)
What is a Garden?
Arlen, Harold
One for My Baby (And One More for the
   Road).
"Arley" See Andrews, Miles Peter
Armand, Octavio
Another Poetics.
Braille for Left Hand.
Poem with Skin.
Sonnet: "I am an honest man."
Word to the Wise, A.
Armantrout, Rae (b. 1947)
Almost.
Articulation.
As We're Told.
Attention.
Disown.
Garden, The.
Generation.
Getting Warm.
Incidence.
Language of Love.
Leaving.
Manufacturing.
Native.
Necromance.
Plan, The.
Sense.
Single Most.
Traveling Through the Yard.
Up to Speed.
View.
Winter.
Armitage, Simon (b. 1963)
Becoming of Age.
Before You Cut Loose.

Book of Matches, sel.
Dead Sea Poems, The.
Hitcher.
In Our Tenth Year.
Kid.
Killing Time, sel.
Killing Time #2.
Not the Furniture Game.
Poem: "And if it snowed and snow covered the
   drive."
Robinson's Resignation.
Shout, The.
Tyre, The.
Very Simply Topping Up the Brake Fluid.
Zoom!
Armour, Richard (b. 1906)
Hiding Place.
Money.
Pachycephalosaurus.
Armstrong, Jeannette
Blood.
Green: "Green silence softly."
I Study Rocks.
Winds: "Winds moving clouds."
Armstrong, John (1709–79)
Art of Preserving Health, The, sels.
Armstrong, Keith
Cuba, Crocodiles, Rain.
Armstrong, Peter
Sunderland Nights.
Armstrong, Tammy (b. 1974)
Boat Builder.
Horse Girls.
Mother's Winter Guests.
Presque Isle, Maine.
Wood Stove Sunday.
Armstrong, Tim
Knowledge.
Arnaout, 'Aisha (b. 1946)
Orbits.
Spinal Cord.
Arnett, Carroll ("Gogisgi") (b. 1927)
Powwow.
Arnold, Bob
No Tool or Rope or Pail.
Arnold, Craig (b. 1967)
Disembodied Voices of Women, The.
Extravagance of Zoos, The.
Locker Room Etiquette.
My Love Is Sick.
Party She Outdid Herself, The.
Why I Skip My High School Reunions.
XX.
Your Friend's Arriving on the Bus.
Arnold, Denise Y.
Song to the Alpaca.
Arnold, Matthew (1822–88)
Atossa.
Below the Surface-Stream.
Buried Life, The.
Dover Beach.
Empedocles on Etna, sels.
Forsaken Merman, The.
Growing Old.
In Harmony with Nature.
Kaiser Dead.
Lines Written in Kensington Gardens, sel.
Longing.
Memorial Verses.
Philomela.
Progress.
Requiescat.
Resignation, sels.
Scholar Gypsy, The, sels.
Shakespeare: "Others abide our question. Thou
   art free."
Sohrab and Rustum, sels.
Stanzas from the Grande Chartreuse.
Strayed Reveller, The, sels.
Switzerland, sels.
Thyrsis.
To a Friend.
To the Hungarian Nation.
Written in Butler's Sermons.

Arodin, Sidney
Lazy River.
Aroniawenrate *See* Blue Cloud, Peter
Aronsten, Joan (b. 1914)
Ad Infinitum.
Arouet, François Marie *See* Voltaire
Arp, Hans [or Jean] (1887–1966)
Around the Star's Throne.
Cities Have Been Cut Off at the Feet, The.
Domesticated Egg, A.
Dragon Carries the Inscription "Kunigundula" and Is Led on a Leash, The.
For that Reason We Are Also Not Obliged to Polish the Claws, Horns, and Weather Vanes.
Great Unrestrained Sadist, The.
Kaspar Is Dead.
Kaspar Is Dead.
Man, The. The Woman.
Monomaniacal Possessor of the Firmament.
People.
Snakebread.
Arreola, Juan José (b. 1918)
Deer.
Toad, The.
Arrillaga, Maria
Dream.
Like Raquel.
Mariana II.
Rosa/Filí.
Arrington, Lauren Anita
Untitled: "Tomorrow night."
Arroyo, Rane (b. 1954)
Longing: "It wasn't just about sex, but about."
My Mysterious Body.
Arsone, Sarah
Father's Poem, A.
Artaud, Antonin (1896–1948)
All Writing Is Garbage.
Amour sans trêve, L'
Civil Status.
I Spit on the Innate Christ.
Letter to André Breton.
Love with No Letup.
Nerve Meter, The.
Pèse-nerfs, Le, *sel*.
Pounding and Gism.
Revolt Against Poetry.
Spurt of Blood, The.
Ten years that the language is gone.
To be Christ is not to be Jesus Christ.
To Have Done with the Judgment of God, *sel*.
Arteaga, Alfred (b. 1950)
Corrido Blanco.
Artmann, H. C. (b. 1921)
Ah rosie.
Blacksmith's Shop, The.
Optician has a Glass Heart, An.
Tea Merchant, The.
Arturo, Aurelio (1906–74)
Madrigal 3.
Song of the Silent Night.
"Arudra" (Bhagavatula Sankara Sastri)
Death of Man.
Arundel, Honor (b. 1919)
Adam.
Arvio, Sarah
Love: "It was not to them I wanted to speak."
Visits from the Seventh, *sels*.
As-Sabah, Sabah (b. 1966)
I'll Never Know No Sunday in This Weekday Room.
Jubilee.
Transition #2.
Asaf, Özdemir (1923–81)
Lavinia.
Aşar, M. Sami (b. 1932)
Weekly Agenda of Love.
Asbaje, Juana Rumirez de *See* Juana Inés de la Cruz, Sor
Asch, Frank (b. 1946)
Leaves.
Play.

Summer.
Sunflakes.
Asclepiades (*fl.* 270 B.C.)
Didyme waved an olive branch at me.
Dorkion, sweet little tomboy.
Here Lies Archeanassa.
I am not yet twenty-two and I am tired of living.
Lysidice dedicated to you, Cypris.
Think how unspeakably sweet.
This is the sweet work of Erinna, not much, of course.
We were having fun, that devil Hermione and I.
Asekoff, L. S.
Crowdoll.
Invisible Hand.
North Star.
Rounding the Horn.
Starwork.
Will.
Ash, John (b. 1948)
Desert Song.
Ferns and the Night.
Following a Man.
Memories of Italy (Broken Sestina).
Monuments, The.
Poor Boy: Portrait of a Painting.
Sky My Husband, The.
Them/There.
Ungrateful Citizens, The.
ash-Sharīf aṭ-Ṭalīq *See* At Taliq
Ashanti, Baron James (*fl.* 20th cent.)
Just Another Gig.
Ashbery, John (b. 1927)
All Messages Have Been Played.
And "Ut Pictura Poesis" Is Her Name.
Archipelago, The.
As One Put Drunk into the Packet-Boat.
At North Farm.
Blessing in Disguise, A.
Brute Image.
Business Personals.
Cæsura.
Chapter 2, Book 35.
City Afternoon.
Couple in the Next Room, The.
Crazy Weather.
Crossroads in the Past.
Decoy.
Evening in the Country.
Farm Implements and Rutabagas in a Landscape.
Flow Chart, *sels*.
For John Clare.
Forgotten Song.
Forties Flick.
Franchises in Flux.
Glazunoviana.
Hard Times.
History of My Life, The.
Hod Carrier, The.
Holding Mode, A.
Hotel Lautréamont.
How Much Longer Will I Be Able to Inhabit the Divine Sepulcher.
How to Continue.
Ice-Cream Wars, The.
If the Birds Knew.
Illustration.
Improvement, The.
Instruction Manual, The.
Interesting People of Newfoundland.
Into the Dusk-Charged Air.
Just Walking Around.
Knocking Around.
Late Echo.
Leaving the Atocha Station.
Life As a Book That Has Been Put Down.
Limited Liability.
Lost and Found and Lost Again.
Meaningful Love.
Melodic Trains.
Mixed Feelings.
Morning Jitters.

My Erotic Double.
My Name Is Dimitri.
My Philosophy of Life.
Myrtle.
New Constructions.
Nut Castle.
Ode to Bill.
Of the Light.
Old Complex, The.
On The Empress's Mind.
One Coat of Paint.
One Thing That Can Save America, The.
Operators Are Standing By.
Other Tradition, The.
Painter, The.
Pantoum.
Paradoxes and Oxymorons.
Path to the White Moon, The.
Picture of Little J. A. in a Prospect of Flowers, The.
Pied Piper, The.
Poem of Unrest, A.
Problem of Anxiety, The.
Pyrography.
Rain.
Rain Moving In.
Rivers and Mountains.
Scheherazade.
Self-Portrait in a Convex Mirror.
Skaters, The, *sels*.
Some Trees.
Song: "Song tells us of our old way of living, The."
Soonest Mended.
Spring Day.
Statuary.
Street Musicians.
Syringa.
Template, The.
Tennis Court Oath, The.
These Lacustrine Cities.
This Room.
Thoughts of a Young Girl.
Three Madrigals.
Train Rising Out of the Sea.
Variant.
Walkways, The.
Wet Casements.
What Is Poetry.
Wolf Ridge.
Young Son, The.
Ashur-Nasir-Pal, King of Assyria (*fl.* 1000 B.C.)
Hymn to Ishtar.
Asim, Jabari
Baby's Breath.
Dumas.
1st Lt. John R. Fox: Rain of Fire.
1st Lt. Vernon J. Baker: Hero on the Hill.
Harlem Haiku: A Scrapbook.
Hip Hop Bop.
Let's Just Tell It.
Memory of Wings.
Staff Sgt. Edward A. Carter, Jr.: There and Back.
Askew, Anne (1520–46)
Ballad Which Anne Askew[e] Made and Sang When She Was in Newgate, The.
Voyce of Anne Askewe out of the 54. Psalme of David, Called, Deus in Nomine Tuo, The.
Askhari
Circular Fate.
Colorstruck.
Isalutu.
REcreation.
Aspden, Bryan (b. 1933)
News of the Changes.
Asquith, Herbert (1881–1947)
Volunteer, The.
Asservero, Vicki-Ann
Lock and Key, The.
Assiba d'Almeida, Irène
Sister, You Cannot Think a Baby Out!
Assultani, Fadhil
Incomplete Anthem.
Morning.

My Mother, in memoriam.
RS Thomas.
That Thing.
Tree, A.
Van Gogh.

Astell, Mary (1666–1731)
In Emulation of Mr Cowleys Poem Call'd The
Motto.

Astley, Neil (b. 1953)
East of Easter.

Aston, Alasdair (b. 1930)
Everything in the Garden Is Lovely.

Aston, Katherine Thimelby (c.1620s–1650s)
To My Daughter Catherine on Ashwednesday
1645, Finding Her Weeping at Prayers,
Because I Would Not Consent to Her
Fasting.
Upon the LD Saying KT Could Be Sad in Her
Company.

At Taliq (c.961–1009)
Branch which sways on a rounded sand dune,
and from which my heart gathers [a harvest
of] fire, A.

Atabay, Cyrus
Pallas.

Atalla, S. V.
Diaspora.
Visiting the West Bank.

Atkins, Russell (b. 1926)
At Night Keep Still.
Christophe.
Dark Area.
Furious'd Garb.
Imaginary Crimes in a Real Garden.
Irritable Songs.
L L L.
Lakefront, Cleveland.
Late Bus (After a Series of Hold-Ups).
Lines in Recollection.
Lisbon.
Narrative.
New Storefront.
Night and a Distant Church.
Spyrytual.
While Waiting for a Friend to Come to Visit a
Friend in a Mental Hospital.

Ato Tobira (fl. 8th cent.)
Only one fleeting.

Attlee, Clement (1883–1967)
Few thought he was even a starter.

Atwood, Margaret (b. 1939)
Animals in That Country, The.
At the Tourist Centre in Boston.
Autobiography: "First thing I can remember is
a blue line, The. This was on the left."
Before the War.
Circe / Mud Poems, sels.
Daguerreotype Taken in Old Age.
Daphne and Laura and So Forth.
Death of a Young Son by Drowning.
Dream 1: the Bush Garden.
Fainting.
Flowers: "Right now I am the flower girl."
Footnote to the Amnesty Report on Torture.
Four Small Elegies, sels.
Further Arrivals.
Habitation.
Is / Not.
It Is Dangerous to Read Newspapers.
Journey to the Interior.
Landcrab I.
Landcrab II.
Landlady, The.
Loneliness of the Military Historian, The.
Making Poison.
Manet's Olympia.
Miss July Grows Older.
Moment, The.
More and More.
Morning in the Burned House.
Postcard.
Procedures for Underground.
Progressive Insanities of a Pioneer.
Puppet of the Wolf, The.
Romantic.

Sad Child, A.
Songs of the Transformed, sels.
Spelling.
Strawberries: "Strawberries when I first
remember them are not red but blue, The."
They Eat Out.
This Is a Photograph of Me.
Thoughts from Underground.
Tricks With Mirrors.
Up.
Variation on the Word Sleep.
Variations on the Word Love.
Victory Burlesk, The.
Vultures.
You Are Happy.
You Begin.
You Fit into Me.

Atwood-Fukuda, B.J.
Ballybunion.
Wreck of the Platonic,The.

Aua
Magic Words, sels.

Aubert, Alvin (b. 1930)
Baobab.
Bessie.
Bessie Smith's Funeral.
Blood to Blood.
December 1982/Detroit.
James Baldwin, 1924–1987.
Nat Turner in the Clearing.
Opposite of Green, The.
Whispers in a Country Church.

Auchterlonie, Dorothy (b. 1915)
Tree, The.

Audelay, John (fl. c.1425)
Seven Gifts of the Holy Ghost, The.

Auden, W. H. (Wystan Hugh) (1907–73)
A. E. Housman.
Academic Graffiti, sels.
Adolescence.
Always the Following Wind.
As I Walked Out One Evening.
Ascent of F6, The, sels.
At Last the Secret Is Out.
Atlantis.
Bird-Language.
Capital, The.
Cave of Making, The.
Consider.
Death's Echo.
Dog beneath the Skin, The, sel.
Doggerel by a Senior Citizen.
Edward Lear.
Epitaph on a Tyrant.
Fall of Rome, The.
Five Songs, sels.
For Christopher Isherwood and Chester
Kallman.
For the Time Being; a Christmas Oratorio, sels.
Gare du Midi.
Happy New Year, A.
Healthy Spot, A.
Hell.
Horae Canonicae, sels.
If I Could Tell You.
In Memory of Sigmund Freud.
In Memory of W. B. Yeats.
In Praise of Limestone.
It's No Use Raising a Shout.
Journey to Iceland.
Jumbled in the Common Box.
Law like Love.
Leap Before You Look.
Legend.
Letter, The.
Letter to Lord Byron, sels.
Love Feast, The.
Lullaby, A: "Din of work is subdued, The."
Lullaby: "Lay your sleeping head, my love."
Memorial for the City, sel.
Miss Gee.
Moon Landing.
More Loving One, The.
Mundus et Infans.
Musée des Beaux Arts.

New Year Greeting, A.
New Year Letter, sel.
1929.
O What Is That Sound [Which So Thrills the
Ear].
Ode to the Diencephalon.
Ode to the Medieval Poets.
On This Island.
Our Hunting Fathers.
Oxford.
Paid on Both Sides, sel.
Passenger Shanty.
Paysage Moralisé.
Petition.
Platonic Blow, The, sel.
"Prolific and the Devourer," The, sels.
Prologue at Sixty.
Question, The.
Questioner Who Sits So Sly, The.
Sea and the Mirror, The, sels.
Secret Agent, The.
September 1, 1939.
Shield of Achilles, The.
Shorts [1939–1947], sels.
Shorts [1948–1957], sels.
Shorts I, sels.
Six Commissioned Texts, sels.
Spain [1937].
St. Luke, sel.
Strings' Excitement, The.
Summer Night, A.
Taller To-day.
Ten Songs, sels.
Their Lonely Betters.
This Lunar Beauty.
Three Posthumous Poems, sels.
Truest Poetry Is the Most Feigning, The [or,
Ars Poetica for Hard Times].
Twelve Songs, sels.
Under Which Lyre: A Reactionary Tract for
the Times.
Unknown Citizen, The.
Villanelle: "Time can [or will] say nothing but
I told you so."
Voyage, A, sels.
Wanderer, The.
Who's Who.

Aue, Hartmann von (1170–1215)
I go, with your good grace, lords and kinsmen.
I said I would always live for her.
Often a friend will greet me thus.

Ausländer, Rose (b. 1918)
In the Color of Sleep.
Motherland.
My Nightingale.
So That No Light Would Remain to Love Us.
Well, The.

Ausonius (Decimus Magnus Ausonius) (c.310–95)
Echo.
Fields of Sorrow, The.
I am that Dido which thou here do'st see.
I used to tell you, "Frances, we grow old"
On the Sicilian strand a hare well wrought.

Ausonius, Decimus Magnus See Ausonius

Austen, Katherine (1628–83)
Dec. 5th 1644 Upon Robin Austins Recovery
of the Smal Pox and General Popams Son
John Diing of Them.
On the Situation of Highbury.

Austin, Alfred (1835–1913)
Go Away, Death!, sel.
Human Tragedy, The, sels.
Jameson's Ride, sel.
Wind Speaks, The, sel.

Austin, John
Love of Christ, The.

Austin, Louie See Hunter, Albert

Austin, Mary (1868–1934)
Grizzly Bear.

Austin, William
Sepulchrum Domus Mea Est.

Automedon (fl. c.6th cent. B.C.)
Turkish. Belly-dancer. Sexy tricks.

Autumn Maid Tu (Tu Ch'iu-niang) (*fl.* 807)
  Robe of Golden Thread, The.
Avellán, Hector (b. 1973)
  Declaration of Love to Kurt Cobain.
Averill, Diane
  Shoplifter Hands.
Avianus
  Calf and the Ox, The.
Avidan, David (1934–95)
  Life of a Dead Dog.
  Settlement.
  Six Local Poems.
Aviram, Amittai F. (b. 1957)
  Pictures of Maurice Among Funeral Flowers.
Avison, Margaret (b. 1918)
  Balancing Out.
  Butterfly Bones; or, Sonnet against Sonnets.
  Butterfly, The.
  Cycle of Community.
  Dumbfounding, The.
  Nameless One, A.
  New Year's Poem.
  Party, The.
  Present From Ted.
  Prospecting.
  Ramsden.
  Rondeau Redoublé.
  Swimmer's Moment, The.
  Tennis.
  Voluptuaries and Others.
  Whole Story, The.
'Avnî, Yenishehirli (1827–84)
  Don't think we came to ask for wealth.
Awoonor, Kofi (George Williams) (b. 1935)
  Agosu if you go tell them.
  America.
  American Memory of Africa, An.
  First Circle, The.
  I Rejoice.
  Night of My Blood (1971), *sels.*
  On Having Been an Experimental Sacred Cow
    for Four Years, and a Token African on
    Faculty.
  On the Way to Durham, N.C.
  Sea Eats the Land at Home, The.
  So the World Changes.
  Something has happened to me.
  Song of War.
  Songs of Abuse: To Stanislaus the Renegade.
  Songs of Sorrow.
  They Shall Know.
  This Earth, My Brother.
  To Dennis Brutus.
  To the Eminent Scholar and Meddler.
  Weaver Bird, The.
Aworinde, Awotunde
  If a Suite in Praise of the Yoruba Oracle, *sels.*
Awwad, Bahaa
  Declining Sun.
'Awwad, Thérèse (b. 1933)
  I found one word.
  I Undressed Myself.
  My Loneliness.
Axelrod, David B. (b. 1943)
  Guide to Urban Birds, A.
Ayewanu, Sunday
  God's Voice.
  Man with a Hat, A.
Aygi, Gennady (b. 1934)
  Again: Air in the Tops—Of Birches.
  Beginning from the Field.
  Day—Towards Evening.
  Dream: Flight of a Dragonfly.
  Dream: Queue for Paraffin.
  During a Friend's Illness.
  Fields of this Summer.
  From Lines in a Dream.
  Going to Sleep in Childhood.
  House in the Field.
  House—In the Grove of the World.
  People Are a Temple, The.
  Poppies of This Year.
  Quietness with a Happening.
  Rose of Silence.

  Rustle of Birches.
  Supper: House Outside Town.
  This August's Phloxes.
  Two Epilogues: "Cleanness of the path."
Ayhan, Ece
  Epitafio.
  Geranium and the Child.
  Nigger in a Photograph, The.
  To Trace from Hebrew.
Ayres, Philip (1638–1712)
  Cynthia on Horseback.
  Death of Adonis, The.
  Fly, The.
Ayres, Robert
  Corporeal.
  Neighbor's Elm, The.
Aytoun [or Ayton], Sir Robert (1570–1638)
  Answer, The.
  On the Prince's Death, to the King.
  Posy, A: "Dear love, I am resolved with thee to
    live."
  Rejection, The.
  Song, A: On His Mistress.
  Song: "What means this strangeness now of
    late."
  Sonnet: On The Loss Of His Mistress.
  Sonnet: On the River Tweed.
  There is none, no none but I.
  To His Coy Mistress.
  To His Forsaken Mistress.
  Upon His Unconstant Mistress.
  Upon Mr Thomas Murrays Fall.
  Upon Platonic Love: To Mistress Cicely
    Crofts, Maid of Honour.
  Upone Tabacco.
  Valediction.
**Aytoun, William Edmonstoune [*or*
  Edmondstoune] (1813–65)**
  American's Apostrophe to Boz, The.
  Edinburgh after Flodden, *sel.*
  Execution of Montrose, The, *sel.*
  Laureate, The.
  Royal Banquet, The.
  Sonnet to Britain.
Ayukawa Nobuo (1920–86)
  Last I Heard, The.
  Love: "I'm Japanese."
  Sister, I'm Sorry.
Azad, Rafiq
  Woman: The Eternal.
Azevedo, Kathleen de
  Famous Women—Claudette Colbert.
Azuah, Unoma Nguemo
  Forbidden.
  Frame of Fear.
Azzawi, Fadil (b. 1940)
  Crossing the Valley.
  Every Morning the War Gets Up from Sleep.
  Film in a Railway Station, A.
  For Everyone His Own Tree.
  In a Magic Land.
  Last Iraq, The.
  Leave the Earth behind You!
  Lion and the Apostle, The.
  Night with the Vampire, The.
  On a Dying Planet.
  Poet, The.
  Political Prisoner.
  Self-Defeating Poem, The.
  Shipping Out.
  Song of the Slave Girl, The.
  Unknown man, The.

B

B., L.
  After School Commute with My Girl.
"B. V." *See* Thomson (1834–82) [*or* Bysshe
  Vanolis], James
Ba, Oumar (b. 1900?)
  Seen to be Done.
Babb, Stanley E.
  Galveston.

  Portrait of a Pirate.
Babcock, H.
  Leaf from a Log Book, A.
Babcock, Maltbie Davenport (1858–1901)
  Be Strong.
Babits, Mihály (1883–1941)
  Against Horace.
  Before Easter.
  Book of Jonah, The.
  Danaïds, The.
  Gypsy in the Condemned Cell, A.
  Jonah's Prayer.
  Kind of Culture, A.
  Like a Dog.
  Lyric Poet's Epilogue, The.
  Memorial.
  Psychologia Christiana.
  Question at Night.
  Tomb of Hegeso, The.
Babstock, Ken (b. 1970)
  First Lesson in Unpopular Mechanics.
  Palindromic.
  Pragmatist.
  What We Didn't Tell the Medic.
Babu, Srirangam Narayana (1906–62)
  Blade of Grass, A.
  Let's Go to Hell.
  Sex Everywhere.
  Sound of Silence, The.
Baca, Jimmy Santiago (b. 1952)
  Bells.
  Cloudy Day.
  Green Chile.
  Healing Earthquakes, *sels.*
  How We Carry Ourselves.
  I Applied for the Board.
  Immigrants in Our Own Land.
  It Started.
  Like an Animal.
  Mantanza to Welcome Spring.
  Mi Tío Baca el Poeta de Socorro.
  Oppression.
  Perfecto Flores.
  So Mexicans Are Taking Jobs from Americans.
  Thirteen.
  Voz de la Gente.
  Work We Hate and Dreams We Love.
Bacchylides (b. 450 B.C.)
  Ode 6: "Lachon has brought home the bacon."
Bach ap Madog Wladaidd, Dafydd (*fl.* 1340–90)
  Christmas Revel, A.
Bacharach, Deborah
  New Joke, The.
Bacharach, Naftali
  Poem for the Sefirot as a Wheel of Light, A.
Bachhuber, David
  Mozart in a Classroom of Children.
Bachinsky, Elizabeth (b. 1976)
  ATM.
Bächler, Wolfgang (b. 1925)
  Revolt in the Mirror, A.
Bachmann, Ingeborg (1926–73)
  Curriculum Vitae.
  Early Noon.
  Every Day.
  Every Day.
  Every Day.
  Exile.
  Firstborn Land, The.
  Fog Land.
  Go, My Thought.
  In the Storm of Roses.
  Invocation of the Great Bear.
  Kind of Loss, A.
  Land of Fog.
  No Delicacies.
  Paean to the Sun, A.
  Paris.
  Safe-Conduct.
  Settlement.
  Songs from an Island.
  Time Allotted, The.
  To the Sun.
  Truly.

Verily.
You Words.

Bachner
Little Mouse, The.
Man Proposes, God Disposes.
Yes, That's the Way Things Are.

Bachri, Sutardji Calzoum (b. 1942)
Soldiers.

Back, Rachel Tzvia (b. 1960)
Abu Salim, Healer.
After Eden.
Gaza, Undated.
Notes: From the Wait.
You ask.

Bacmeister, Rhoda Warner (b. 1893)
Galoshes.

Bacon, Anne Cooke (1528?–1610)
A—B—on the Learned Bartholo Sylva.

Bacon, Crystal
Outlook.

Bacon, Francis (1561–1626)
Life of Man, The.

Bador, Bernard
Birth: "Camels pregnant."
Cape of Wild Flies, A.
Curdled Skulls.
Essence.
Evil Port.
Hand, The.
Journey to the End of Night.
Odyssey.
Progress: "Jacaranda blindings."
Transparent Man, The.

Baehr, Anna Ruth Ediger (1916–98)
Christina.
Cleaning the Cistern.
I Am Dancing with My Mennonite Father.
I Will Not Pretend.
Ritual.

Baekoon Kyunghan (1299–1375)
Mountain Life.
Twelve More Songs for Master Jikong.
Untitled: "I've traveled eight thousand miles."

Baer, William
Prosecutor.

Baffo, Giorgio (1694–1768)
Sonnet: "My meditation turns to thinking."

Baggett, Rebecca
Art of the Amish: A Quilt Exhibition, sels.
Barely Eight.

Baggok Choneung (1617–80)
Leaving the Mountain.
Sending off My Fellow Monk Hae.

Baggott, Julianna (b. 1969)
Kitchens: 1959.
Mary Rockwell, 1950.
Poetry Despises Your Attempts at Domesticity.

Bahâyî, Sheyhülislâm (1601–53)
Oh cry, what are you doing, disturbing.

Bahdal, Maisun bint (d. 700 A.D.)
Give me. . .I'll give you.

Baiho (1633–1707)
On Entering His Coffin.

Bailey, Alfred Goldsworthy (b. 1905)
Isosceles Lighthouse, The.
La Route Jackman.
Rivière du Loup.
Unreturning, The: "Blue is my sky peter."

Bailey, Jane
Ceasefire.

Bailey, Peter
Don't be saddish.
Practice.

Bailey, Philip James (1816–1902)
Country Town, A, sel.

Bailey, R. V.
Father's Things.

Bailey, Scott
Hide-n-Seek.

Baillie, Lady Grisel (1665–1746)
Were Ne My Hearts Light I Wad Dye.

Baillie, Joanna (1762–1857)
Address to the Muses, An, sel.
Blackcock, The [or The Black Cock].
Child to His Sick Grandfather, A.
Disappointment, A.
Ghost of Fadon, The.
Hay making.
Hooly and Fairly.
Mother to Her Waking Infant, A.
Outlaw's Song, The.
Reverie, A.
Song (Poverty Parts Good Company, For an
    Old Scotch Air).
Song: "What voice is this, thou evening gale!"
Song: Woo'd and Married and A'
Storm-Beat Maid, The.
Summer's Day, A.
Tam O' the Lin.
To Cupid.
Winter Day, A, sels.
Winter's Day, A.

Baingana, Doreen
More Than Anything.
Song to Come, The.

Bairagi (1925–78)
Give Me Confidence.
Who Is Awake in the Dead of Night?

Baird, Martha (1921–81)
Do Not Make Things Too Easy.

Bajza, József (1804–58)
Autumn Song.
Prophecy, The.
Sighing.

Baker, Carol
Your Going.

Baker, David (b. 1954)
Deer, The.
8-Ball at the Twilite.
Envoi: Waking After Snow.
Heavenly.
Mercy.
More Rain.
Patriotics.
Pulp Fiction.
Puritan Way of Death, The.
Sex.
Works and Days.
Yard, The.

Baker, Houston A., Jr. (b. 1943)
Of Walter White's Father in the Rain.
Set Piece.
Tobacco Warehouse Blues.
Toward Guinea: For Larry Neal, 1937–1981.

Baker, Howard (b. 1905)
Advice to a Man Who Lost a Dog.
Sappho's Leap.

**Baker, Karle Wilson ("Charlotte Wilson") (b.
1878)**
Eagle Youth.
Nacogdoches Speaks.
Some Towns of Texas, sels.
Texas Cowboy.

Baker, Kathleen Leland (b. 1951)
Baby Hilary, Sir Edmund, The.
Honey Moon.

Baker, Thomas (b. 1871)
Steam Engine; or, The Power of the Flame,
    The, sels.

Baker, Tony (b. 1954)
Armillaria mellea.
Le passage (Morbihan).
Pavane on Mr Wray's Locations, A.

Baker, Winona (b. 1924)
Spring, sel.

Baki See Baqi [or Baki]

Bakusui (1720–83)
Returning / By an unused path—violets.

Bal, Willy (b. 1916)
Fire!

Balaban, John (b. 1943)
After Our War.
Anna Akhmatova Spends the Night on Miami
    Beach.
April 30, 1975.

At 4:00 A.M. Asleep.
Atomic Ghost.
Daddy Out Hitch-Hiking at 3:30 A.M.
For the Missing in Action.
Georgi Borisov in Paris.
Guard at the Binh Thuy Bridge, The.
Heading Out West.
Hurricane.
News Update.
Poetry Reading at the Varna Ruins.
Riding Westward.
Thoughts Before Dawn.
Words for My Daughter.

Balakian, Peter (b. 1951)
After the Survivors Are Gone.
Back Yard, The.
End of the Reagan Era, The.
Idyll: "I lived behind a window."
Ocean.
Rock 'n Roll.

Balamani Amma, N. (b. 1909)
To My Daughter.

Balassi, Bálint (1554–94)
For Wine Drinkers.
Having to Part From His Mistress at Dawn.
He Pleads for Forgiveness Before His Intended
    Marriage.
In Which He Rejoices Over Having Discarded
    Love.
Soldier's Song.
When He Met Julia, He Greeted Her Thus.

Balbulus, Notker (c.840–912)
Hymn to Holy Women, A.

Balce, Nerissa S.
Pizza and Pretense.

Balderston, Jean (b. 1936)
Anne Steele.

Baldwin, Andrew J.
Glass Box Puzzle No. 1.
Moons. . .tides.

Baldwin, Barbara
Field of Poppies, A.
Relics.

Baldwin, James (1924–87)
Guilt, Desire and Love.

Baldwin, Sandy
Artificial Terra-cotta Skin Mutagen Mask of
    Humbaba/Humwawa.
[Basic system code].
Heralds of the hurricane.

Balestrini, Nanni (b. 1935)
Instinct of Self-Preservation, The, sel.
Tape Mark.

Balingit, Joann
Quiet Evening, Home Away.

Ball, Angela (b. 1952)
Attempt, An.
Dance Pianist, The.
Jazz.
Kiss, The.
Man in a Shell, The.
Premature Burial Gazette.

Ball, Caroline Augusta (b. 1825)
Jacket of Gray, The.

Ball, Hugo (1886–1927)
Complete Sound-Poems of Hugo Ball, The.
Flight out of Time, sels.
Sun, The.

Ball, Joseph H.
And This Is So.

Ballagas, Emilio (1908–54)
Nocturne and Elegy.
Of Another Fashion.

Ballantine, James
Castles in the Air.

Ballard, Barry
Hate Crime.

Ballav, Iswar (b. 1937)
Stride On.

Ballowe, James (b. 1933)
Coal Miners, The.
Starved Rock.

Bamber, Jill
  Broken Necklace.
Bamford, Samuel (1788–1872)
  Touch Him!
Bampfylde, John Codrington (1754–96)
  As when, to one who long hath watched, the
    morn.
  On a Frightful Dream.
  On a Wet Summer.
  On Christmas.
  Written at a Farm.
Banchs, Enrique (1888–1968)
  Mumbling.
Banckes, Elizabeth (fl. 1616)
  Roysters give Roome, for here comes a Lass.
Bancks, John (1709–51)
  Description of London, A.
Bancquart, Marie-Claire (b. 1932)
  Baroque.
  Contrefable d'Orphée.
  Counterfable of Orpheus.
  Curriculum vitae.
  Epitaph.
  I Walk in the Solitude of Books.
  Je marche dans la solitude des livres.
  Portrait of Jonah with woman.
  Retour d'Ulysse.
  Return of Ulysses.
  Sea.
  Town.
  Vanished, The.
  Woman asleep.
Bandeira, Manuel (1886–1968)
  Evocation of Recife.
  Interview.
  Mozart in Heaven.
  Off to Pasárgada.
  Poetics.
  Portrait.
  Rondeau of the Little Horses.
  Spiritual Wedding.
Bandele, Asha (b. 1966)
  After Diana Died.
  1980–1990: A Poet's Personal Review.
  Prayer for the Living, A.
  Subtle Art of Breathing, The.
Bang, Mary Jo
  Constant Bride, The.
  Crossed-Over, Fiend-Snitched, X-ed Out.
  Dog Bark, The.
  Eye Like a Strange Balloon Mounts Toward
    Infinity, The.
  It Says, I Did So.
  Like a Fire in a Fire.
  Louise in Love.
  Night Falling Fast.
  Star's Whole Secret, The.
Bangaramma, Chavali (1897–1978)
  Hibiscus on the Lake.
  My Brother.
Bangs, Carol Jane (b. 1949)
  Touching Each Other's Surfaces.
Bangs, John Kendrick (1862–1922)
  Little Elf, The.
  My Dog.
Banks, John (fl. 1677–96)
  Albion Queens, The, sels.
  Anna Bullen, sels.
Banks, Theodore H., Jr.
  Tempest.
Bannerman, Frances
  Upper Chamber, An.
Banning, Lex (b. 1921)
  And No Regrets.
  Epitaph for a Scientist.
  Romancero.
Bansode, Hira (b. 1939)
  Woman.
Banzon, Krissi
  Here's a Match.
Bapiraju, Adivi (1895–1952)
  Steps.

Baqi (1526–1600)
  Fountain of my spirit thirsts for your ruby,
    The.
  If only the bud would open like the beloved's
    ruby lips.
  Oh Beloved, Since the Origin We Have Been.
  Sparks from my heart rise.
  That tyrant, is she not persuaded by the tears.
  Your rebellious glance lines up the cavalry.
Baraka, Amina
  To Aretha Franklin from Sparkle.
  X.
Baraka, Imamu Amiri (b. 1934)
  A, B, C's, The.
  Agony, An. As Now.
  Alba.
  All is One for Monk.
  Am/Trak.
  Babylon Revisited.
  Balboa, the Entertainer.
  Biography.
  Black Art.
  Black Bourgeoisie.
  Black Dada Nihilismus.
  Careers.
  Clay.
  Contract. (For The Destruction and Rebuilding
    of Paterson), A.
  Courageousness.
  Cuba Libre.
  Das Kapital.
  Dope.
  Duke's World.
  For Hettie.
  For Maulana Karenga & Pharoah Sanders.
  Funk Lore.
  Heavy, The.
  How People Do.
  Hymn for Lanie Poo, sels.
  I Am.
  I Investigate the Sun.
  I Substitute For The Dead Lecturer.
  In Memory of Radio.
  In the Funk World.
  Incident.
  Invention of Comics, The.
  JA ZZ : (The "Say What?") IS IS JA LIVES
  John Coltrane (1926–1967).
  Ka 'Ba.
  Kenyatta Listening to Mozart.
  Last Word, The.
  Leadbelly Gives an Autograph.
  Lefty.
  Legacy.
  Leroy.
  Like Rousseau.
  Look for You Yesterday, Here You Come
    Today.
  Minute of Consciousness, The.
  Monk's World.
  Nation Is Like Ouselves, The.
  New Reality Is Better Than a New Movie!, A.
  New World, The.
  Node.
  Numbers, Letters.
  Ostriches & Grandmothers!
  Pause of Joe, The.
  Poem for Black Hearts, A.
  Poem for Deep Thinkers, A.
  Poem for Speculative Hipsters, A.
  Poem for Willie Best, A.
  Poem of Destiny, A, sel.
  Poem Some People Will Have to Understand,
    A.
  Political Poem.
  Preface to a Twenty Volume Suicide Note.
  Return of the Native.
  Short Speech to My Friends.
  Song Form.
  State/meant.
  Study Peace.
  Three Modes of History and Culture.
  Violence of the mind is the violence of god,
    The.
  W. W.
  When We'll Worship Jesus.

  Why Didnt He Tell Me the Whole Truth.
  Why's / Wise, sels.
  Wise/Whys, sels.
  World Is Full of Remarkable Things, The.
  Young Soul.
Baraka, Ras (b. 1969)
  After-Word.
  American Poetry.
  Five-O.
  For the Brothers Who Aint Here.
  I Remember Malcolm.
  In the Tradition Too.
Baranczak, Stanislaw (b. 1946)
  December 14, 1979: A Poetry Reading.
  February 8, 1980: And No One Has Warned
    Me.
  N. N. Tries to Remember the Words of a
    Prayer.
  Three Magi, The.
Baranda, María (b. 1962)
  Bodas de las Flores se Dan Sobre el Estigma,
    Las.
  Con sólo dos o tres estambres revientan las
    flores masculinas.
  Ecstasy.
  Epistle of the Shipwreck.
  Epístola del náufrago.
  Éxtasis.
  Weddings of flowers take place upon the
    stigma, The.
  With only two or three stamens, masculine
    flowers burst.
Baratier, David (b. 1970)
  American Standard.
  Estrella's Prophecies #47.
  Estrella's Prophecies #18.
  Fall of Because, The.
  She Wants.
Baraza, David
  Place Without Shame, A.
Barba-Jacob, Porfirio (Miguel Angel Osorio
  Benitez) (1883–1942)
  Song of an Impossible Blue, sels.
Barbauld, Anna Laetitia (1743–1825)
  Call, The.
  Eighteen Hundred and Eleven, a Poem.
  Hymn 2.
  Life.
  Life, sels.
  Ode to Spring.
  On a Lady's Writing.
  Rights of Woman, The.
  Sonnet to France On Her Present Exertions.
  Summer Evening's Meditation, A, sel.
  To a Little Invisible Being Who Is Expected
    Soon to Become Visible.
  To Mr. S. T. Coleridge.
  To the Poor.
  Tomorrow.
  Washing-Day.
Barber, David (b. 1960)
  Little Overture.
  Nocturne.
  Small Hours.
  Spirit Level, The.
Barber, Mary (1690?–1757)
  Conclusion of a Letter to the Rev. Mr. C——,
    The.
  Conclusion of a Letter to the Rev. Mr C——,
    The, sels.
  To Novella, on Her Saying Deridingly, that a
    Lady of Great Merit, and Fine Address, Was
    Bred in the Old Way. An Epigram.
  Written for My Son, and Spoken by Him at
    His First Putting on Breeches.
Barber, William (b. 1947)
  Explanation.
  Gay Poet, The.
Barbir, Ahmad ibn Abd al-Latif (1747–1812)
  Ah, Mr Businessman!
Barbour, Dave
  It's a Good Day.
  Mañana (Is Soon Enough for Me).

Barbour, Douglas (b. 1940)
Flame on the Spanish Stairs, A: John Keats in Rome, *sel.*

Barbour, John (1316?–1395)
Bruce, The, *sels.*

Barclay, Alexander (1475–1552)
Eclogues, *sels.*

Barcsay, Ábrahám (1742–1806)
On Sweet Coffee.
On Sweet Coffee.
To Pál Ányos.
To the Poets.
Winter's Approach.

Bard, W. E.
Seventh Seal, The.

Bardoloi, Nirmalprabha (b. 1933)
Dawn.

Bardwell, Leland (b. 1928)
How my true love and I lay without touching.

Barer, Marshall (1923–98)
Beyond Compare.
Here Come the Dreamers.
On Such a Night As This.
Shall We Join the Ladies?
Very Soft Shoes.

Barford, Wanda
Sorting Things Out.

Barham, Richard (1788–1845)
Cynotaph, The.

Barham, Richard Harris *See* Ingoldsby, Thomas

Baring, Anne
Song, The: "Beehive source."

Baring-Gould, Sabine (1834–1924)
Hymn: "Now the day is over."
Onward, Christian Soldiers.

Barkan, Sarah (1889–1957)
Bring Me Your Woes.
I Have not Woven My Poems.
Italian Masons.
Negro Song.

Barkan, Stanley H.
Two Grandmas.

Barker, David
Make Your Mark.

Barker, George (1913–91)
Crystal, The.
Cycle of Six Lyrics, *sel.*
First Cycle of Love Poems, *sel.*
Gardens of Ravished Psyche, The.
He Comes Among.
How many apples grow on the tree?
Leaping Laughers, The.
Morning in Norfolk.
Not in the poet is the poem or.
O Hero Akimbo on the Mountains of To-morrow.
Second Cycle of Love Poems, *sel.*
Secular Elegies, *sels.*
Sonnet to My Mother.
Street Ballad.
Summer Song I.
Third Cycle of Love Poems, *sel.*
To Whom Else.
Turn on Your Side and Bear the Day to Me.
Verses for a First Birthday.
Wraith-Friend, The.

Barker, Jane (1652–1727?)
Invitation to my Friends at Cambridge, An.
Necessity of Fate, The.
On the Death of My Dear Friend and Play-Fellow Mrs. E. D. Having Dream'd the Night Before I Heard Thereof that I Had Lost a Pearl.
Prospect of a Landscape, Beginning with a Grove, The.
To Dame—Augustin nun on her curious gum-work.
To Her Lover's Complaint.
To My Friends Against Poetry.
To My Young Lover.

Barker, Shirley
There was not loveliness nor fortune there.

Barker, Wendy
Trying To.

Barkova, Anna (1901–76)
Few Autobiographical Facts, A.
Tatar Anguish.

Barks, Coleman (b. 1937)
Becoming Milton.

Barlow, George (b. 1948)
Dream of the Ring: The Great Jack Johnson, A.
4½ Months: Halfway Song.
In My Father's House.
Mingus Speaks: Found Poems.
Nook.
Painting Drunken Twilight.
Place Where He Arose, The.
Salt.

Barlow, Jane (1857–1917)
Christmas Rede.

Barlow, Joel (1754–1812)
Advice to a Raven in Russia [December, 1812].
Columbiad, The, *sels.*
Hasty Pudding, The [complete text], *sels.*
Vision of Columbus, The, *sel.*

Barnard, Lady Anne (*née Lindsay*) (**1750–1825**)
Auld Robin Gray.

Barnard, Mary (b. 1909)
Fable of the Ant and the Word.
Field, The.
Lethe.
Logging Trestle.
Pleiades, The.
Shoreline.
Solitary, The.
Static.

Barnes, Barnabe (1569–1609)
Parthenophil and Parthenophe, *sels.*

Barnes, Billy (*fl.* 1957)
Something Cool.

Barnes, Dick
Chuang Tzu and Hui Tzu*.
Every Man His Own Cross.
Few and Far Between.

Barnes, Djuna (1892–1982)
Portrait of a Lady Walking.
Walking-Mort, The.

Barnes, F. J (*fl.* 1909)
I've Got Rings on My Fingers.

Barnes, Jane (b. 1943)
Passion at Forty.

Barnes, Jim (b. 1933)
Autobiography, Chapter XLII: Three Days in Louisville.
Autobiography, Chapter XVII: Floating the Big Piney.
Ex-Deputy Sheriff Remembers the Eastern Oklahoma Murderers, An, *sels.*
For Roland, Presumed Taken.
Four Things Choctaw.
Halcyon Days.
Heartland.
La Plata, Missouri: Clear November Night.
Return to La Plata, Missouri.
Season of Loss, A.
Skipping.
Sunday Dreamer's Guide to Yarrow, Missouri, A.
Tracking the Siuslaw Man.

Barnes, Kate
Night Light.

Barnes, S. Brandi (b. 1947)
Back to the Blues.
Gentleman in the Barber Shop.

Barnes, William (1801–86)
Clote, The.
False Friends-like.
Heäre, The.
Hill-Shade, The.
Leaves a-Vallen.
Lwonesomeness.
Mater Dolorosa.
My Orcha'd in Lindèn Lea.
Shellbrook.

Sister Gone.
Turnstile, The.
Wife a-Lost, The.
Wind at the Door, The.
Winter Night, A.
Wold Clock, The.

Barnett, Anthony (b. 1941)
Critique.
Extraction.
Forest Utilization.
Music of the Spheres.
Turbulence and Tongue.

Barnett, Catherine (b. 1960)
Into Perfect Spheres Such Holes Are Pierced.
Return, 2, The.

Barnett, Ruth Anderson
Anorexic, The.
Taxidermist at the Zoo, The.

Barney, Natalie Clifford (1877–1972)
Habit.

Barney, William D.
Ballad for Bill Pickett, A.
Long Gone to Texas.
Mr. Bloomer's Birds.
Mr. Watts and the Whirlwind.
Rufous-Crowned Sparrow Seen Loitering below Possum Kingdom Dam.
Wide-Eyed.

Barnfield [or Barnefield], Richard (1574–1629)
Affectionate Shepherd [or Shephearde], The, *sels.*
Comparison of the Life of Man, A.
Cynthia, with Certain[e] Sonnets, *sels.*
Passionate Pilgrim, The, *sels.*

Barnie, John (b. 1941)
I Had Climbed the Long Slope.
Town Where I Was Born, The.

Barnstone, Aliki (b. 1956)
First Amendment.
Wild With It.

Barnstone, Tony, Willis Barnstone (b. 1927) *and* **Haixin Xu**
Hair of the Field.
Trying to Sleep on My Father's Couch and Staring at the Fractured Plaster, I Recall.

Barnstone, Willis (b. 1927)
Jiang Yuying, Famous Professor at Beijing University, Who Daringly Rendered into Chinese the First Complete Walt Whitman.
Late December, Where Are You, Robert Frost?

Barolini, Helen (*fl.* 20th cent.)
Having the Wrong Name for Mr. Wright.

Baron, RoByn
Diner.

Baron, Suze
Tenebrae.
They Say.
Tom-Tom Talk.

Baron Supervielle, Silvia (b. 1934)
Here Time.
Ici l'heure.

Barot, Rick (b. 1969)
Eight Elegies.
Many Are Called.
Portishead Suite.
Reading Plato.
Riffing.
Three Amoretti.

Barras, Jonetta (b. 1950)
Peace.

Barrax, Gerald William (b. 1933)
Adagio.
Domestic Tranquility.
For Malcolm: After Mecca.
In the Restaurant.
King: April 4, 1968.
Last Letter.
Pittsburgh, 1948, the Music Teacher.
Scuba Diver Recovers the Body of a Drowned Child, The.
Singer, The.
Strangers Like Us: Pittsburgh, Raleigh, 1945–1985.
There Was A Song.

Visit.
Whose Children Are These?

Barresi, Dorothy (*fl.* 20th cent.)
Back-Up Singer, The.
Bad Joke.
Called Up: Tinker to Evers to Chance.
Class Dress.
How It Comes.
In Waking Words.
Late Summer News.
Lifting.
Nine of Clubs, Cleveland, Ohio.
Prodigal Daughter, The.
Vacation, 1969.
Venice Beach: Brief Song.
When I Think About America Sometimes (I Think of Ralph Kramden).

Barrington, Judith
Blood.
Villanelle VI.
You There.

Barrington, Patrick (b. 1908)
I Had a Duck-billed Platypus.
I Had a Hippopotamus.
Take Me in Your Arms, Miss Moneypenny-Wilson.

Barrow, Raymond
Dawn is a Fisherman.
There is a Mystic Splendour.

Barrows, Anita (b. 1947)
How many million years before wood turns to stone?

Barrows, Anne
Pleasures of the Flesh.

Barry, Celia
Finding.

Barry, Michael J. (1817–89)
Hymn of Freedom.

Barry, Quan
Asylum.

Barskova, Polina (b. 1976)
Evening at Tsarskoe Selo.
Poet has passed away, The. Or rather, snuffed.

Bart, Lionel (1930–98)
As Long As He Needs Me.
Fings Ain't Wot They Used t'Be.
Reviewing the Situation.

Bartee, Richard
Beginning at the End: Capital/Capitol Punishment.

Bartlett, Brian (b. 1954)
Afterlife of Trees, The.
Always.
Basement Tale, A.
Shuffles.
Talking to the Birds, *sels.*

Bartlett, Elizabeth (b. 1913)
Birth.
God Is Dead—Nietzche.
Neurosis.
Smile for Daddy.
Stretchmarks.
Themes for Women.

Bartlett, Jennifer
From a Paris Hotel Room.
Man and a Woman Standing in the Rain in Front of a Candy Store, A.
When I Got My First Tattoo I Was.

Bartlett, Lee (b. 1950)
Letters for a Document.
Successions, The.
What It Means to be Avant-Garde.

Bartlett, Mary Dougherty
Burning of Margaret Moone, The.
Only Death.
Spring in Placitas.
What We Say in New Mexico.

Bartók-Baratta, Edward
Men Who Killed My Brother, The.

Bartolomé, Efraín (b. 1950)
Agua desdichada, El.
Ill-fated Water, The.
Intermedio con cinco cocodrilos.

Intermezzo with Five Crocodiles.
Tattoos in the Water.
Tatuajes en el Agua.

Başcıllar, Seyfettin (1930–2002)
Sea, the Memory, and the Woman, The.

Basheva, Miryana (b. 1947)
Fast train, The? The express?
Fifth Floor.
It Was War.
Morning: "Where was I last night? In whose arms?"
N. N.
Not long ago a whole sun.

Bashir, Samiya Adelle (b. 1970)
Her Scream Has Been Stolen.

Basho (Matsuo Basho) (1644–94)
All along this road.
All the field hands.
All this foolishness.
Along my journey.
Along the shore.
Among moon gazers.
Ancient silent pond.
Another year gone.
Around existence twine.
As for the hibiscus.
As the sound fades.
At the ancient pond.
Autumn approaches.
Autumn deepening.
Autumn / Even the birds.
Autumn going.
Autumn moon / Tide foams.
Autumn moonlight.
Autumn wind / Blasting the stones.
Autumnal full moon.
Awake at night.
Awake at night.
Awakened at midnight.
Awe inspiring!
Banana tree, The.
Bee, A.
Beginning of art, The.
Beginnings of poetry.
Behind Ise Shrine.
Between the waves.
Blowing stones.
Breakfast enjoyed.
Bucket of azaleas, A.
Buddha's death-day / Old hands.
Bush warbler.
But for a woodpecker.
By the old temple.
Calm moon, A.
Caterpillar, A.
Cats making love.
Cat's wife, A.
Cedar umbrella / Off to Mount Yoshino.
Chestnut by the eaves.
Chilling autumn rains.
Chrysanthemum scent.
Cicada shell, A.
Clear water.
Clouds, The.
Cloud peaks.
Clouds come and go, The.
Clouds now and then.
Clouds of blossoms.
Clouds of cherry blossoms!
Cold night: the wild duck.
Cold rain starting, A.
Come, let's go / snow-viewing.
Come out to view.
Come, see / real flowers.
Cool fall night, A.
Cool it is, and still.
Coolness.
Coolness.
Coolness of melons.
Cormorant fishing / How stirring.
Crane's legs, The.
Crossing half the sky.
Crow, A.
Crow's / Abandoned nest.
Crows resting.
Cuckoo, A.

Cuckoo, The.
Cuckoo cries, A.
Culture's beginnings.
Culture's beginnings.
Deep autumn.
Delight, then sorrow.
Don't imitate me.
Dozing on horseback / smoke from tea-fires.
Dragonfly, The.
Dried salmon.
Dried salmon.
Dusk.
Early dawn.
Early fall.
Even in Kyoto.
Even in Kyoto.
Even these long days.
Exciting at first.
Exhausted, I sought.
Exhausted, / time to find a lodging.
Fall going.
Fall of night.
Farewell! Like a bee.
Farmer's roadside, The.
Felling a tree.
Field of cotton, A.
First day of spring.
First snow.
First winter rain.
Fish shop.
Fishy smell, A.
Fleas, lice.
Fleas, lice.
Forbidden to speak.
From all these trees.
From deep within.
From every direction.
From Hot Springs Mountain.
Gathering.
Gathering the rains.
Girl cat / So thin.
Give your longing to wound.
Good house.
Gray hairs being plucked.
Group of them, A.
Haiku: "Lightning flashes, The!"
Haiku: "Lightning gleam, A."
Hailstones.
Harvest moon.
Have the summer rains.
Having planted a banana tree.
Heard, not seen.
Heat waves shimmering.
Hollyhocks, The.
Holy mirror, The.
How admirable!
How marvelous the man is.
How pitiful!
How reluctantly.
How rough a sea.
How very noble!
How wild the sea is.
Hut of the Phantom Dwelling, The.
I don't know.
I would like to use.
I'm a wanderer.
In the fish shop.
In the mountain village.
In the shallows.
In the withering gusts.
It would melt.
It's fall and a full moon.
It's fall and dusk.
It's late fall.
It's not like anything.
It's quiet, all right.
It's spring, all right.
Jars of octopus, The.
Journey's end / Still alive.
June rain / hollyhocks turning.
Kannon's tiled temple.
Kisagata.
Lead my pony.
Let's go.
Life in this world.
Lightning.

Lightning flash.
Lightning in the clouds!
Lightning-gleam, A.
Linked-Verse Sequence Throughout the Town, The, *sel.*
Loneliness.
Lonely silence.
Long conversations.
Long rains, The.
Longing for the plum blossoms.
Lovely spring night, A.
Mad Verse, *sels.*
Many, many things.
Many nights on the road.
Melon / In morning dew.
Midfield.
Midnight frost.
Misty rain.
Monk sips morning tea, A.
Moonlight slanting.
Moor / Point my horse.
More than ever I want to see.
Morning glories, The.
Morning glory also, The.
My summer robes.
No rice—In that hour.
Not this human sadness.
Nothing in the cry.
Now I see her face.
Oak tree, The.
Octopus traps.
Octopuses caught in floating pots.
Old pond, The.
Old pond, The.
Old pond—a frog jumps in, kerplunk!, The.
Old Pond, An.
Old pond:/ frog-jump-in.
Old pond—frogs jumped in—sound of water.
Old pond / Leap-splash.
Old silent pont, An.
Old-time pond, from off whose shadowed depth, An.
On a withered branch.
On Buddha's birthday.
On Buddha's deathday.
On New Year's Day.
On the cow shed.
On the way to the outhouse.
Peasant's child, The.
Petal shower, A.
Pine mushroom.
Planting rice seedlings.
Plates and bowls.
Ploughing the land.
Plum Blossom Scent, *sels.*
Polished and polished.
Pouring the hot day.
Sad beauty?
Sad nodes.
Sea darkening, The.
Sea darkening, The.
Sea grows dark, The.
Sea grows rough, The.
Searching storehouse eaves.
Seas slowly darken.
Secluded for a while.
Seeing people off.
Seen in plain daylight.
Seventh Month, The.
She cat, The.
Shrieking plovers / Calling darkness.
Sick on a journey.
Sick on a journey.
Sick on a journey / Over parched fields.
Sick on my journey.
Sickly.
Singing, flying, singing.
Singing, planting rice.
Skylark.
Smell of autumn / Heart longs.
Snowy morning, A.
Solitary, A.
Some of them with staves.
Southern Kyoto.
Spider, if you had a voice.
Spring!

Spring going.
Spring going.
Spring / gradually taking form.
Spring moon—.
Spring rain.
Spring we don't see, The.
Squid seller's call, The.
Staying at an inn.
Still alive.
Still old pond, The.
Stillness.
Stillness.
Storm on Mount Asama!
Such stillness.
Summer grass.
Summer grasses.
Summer grasses.
Summer grasses.
Summer grasses / All that remains.
Summer grasses grow, The.
Summer mountains.
Taking a midday nap.
Taking a nap.
Taking coolness.
Teeth sensitive to the sand.
Temple bell / A cloud of cherry flowers.
Temple bell stops, The.
That great blue oak.
There is the old pond!
They don't live long.
This autumn.
This bright harvest moon.
This dark autumn.
This first fallen snow.
This hot day swept away.
This old village.
This road.
This road.
This ruined temple.
Through frozen rice fields.
Time even for the grass hut.
Tired.
To the capital / Snow-clouds forming.
To the willow.
Tomb, bend / To autum wind—.
Traveling this high.
Tremble, oh my gravemound.
Under the same roof.
Ungraciously, under.
Very brief.
Village where they ring, A.
Village without bells, A.
Visting the graves.
Warbler sings, The.
Warmly wrapped.
Water-drawing rites.
Weathered bones.
Weathered skeleton, A.
Wet with morning dew.
What fish feel.
What voice.
When I looked under the hedge.
When the winter chrysanthemums go.
White chrysanthemums.
Whitebait, The.
Whole field of.
Whore and monk, we sleep.
Wild sea, A.
Wild sea, A.
Winter garden.
Winter leeks,The.
Winter rain.
Winter seclusion—.
Winter showers.
Winter solitude.
Winter storm, The.
Winter sun, The.
Wintry day / On my horse.
Wintry wind.
With a warbler for.
With dewdrops dripping.
With plum blossom scent.
Withered grass / Under piling.
Withering winds.
Wrapping dumplings in.
Wrapping the rice cakes.

Year after year.
Year's end / All corners.
Year's end / Still in straw hat.
You could turn this way.
Your song caresses.
You've heard monkeys crying.

Bass, Ellen (b. 1947)
All the Trees.
Bearing Witness.
God and the G-Spot.
They're Family Men.
To Praise.
Why People Murder.

Bass, Franta (1930–44)
Garden, The.
Home.
I am a Jew.
Illness.
Old House, The.

Basse [*or* Bas], William (1602–53)
Anglers Song, The, *sels.*

Bassus [*or* Bassos] (Lollius Bassus) (*fl.* A.D. 1st cent.)
Epigrams, *sel.*

Bassus, Lollius *See* Bassus [*or* Bassos]

Basu, Rām (1738–1812)
How are you faring, Uma.
I had a good dream last night.

Basu Rāy, Śyāmāpad
Three Kalis appeared in Daksinesvar.

Basualto, Neftalí Ricardo Reyes *See* Neruda, Pablo

Bat-Miriam, Yocheved (b. 1901)
Monasteries Lift Gold Domes, The.
Precious stones that my mother.
Sound of the waves in the silence, The.

Bat-Tzion, Ellla
Peace.

Bataille, Georges (1897–1962)
I Dreamed of Touching.
Je rêvais de toucher.
Night Is My Nudity.
Nuit est ma nudité, La.

Bateman, Claire
Bicycle Slow Race, The.

Bateman, Edgar (1860–1946)
Cockney's Garden, The.
It's a Great Big Shame.

Bateman, Meg
After the Funeral.
Aotromachd.
Decline of Gaelic, The.
Fhir luraich's fhir àlainn.
Lightness.
O Bonnie Man, Lovely Man.
Picture of My Mother.
Thank You, My Little Son.

Bates, Charles
Hard-Hearted Hannah (The Vamp of Savannah).

Bates, Katharine Lee (1859–1929)
America the Beautiful.
Even as this Globe Shall Gleam and Disappear.

Bathurst, Bill
To Marthe.

Batista Felix, Hilario
Coumbite.

Batizi, András (c.1510–50)
Remembrance of Death.

Baton, Maisha
Childhood in the Country, A.
Flight of the Daughter, The.
Unspeakable Wounds of War, The.

Batraville, Dominique (b. 1962)
Paper 8.
Paper 18.
Paper 33.
Paper 43.

Batsányi, János (1763–1845)
Encouragement.
Hungarian Writer, The.
On the Changes in France.
Rhythm Is Only a Servant.

Seer, The.
Battin, Wendy
Mondrian's Forest.
Baudelaire, Charles (1821–67)
Albatross, The.
Albatross, The.
Autumn Lament.
Autumn Song.
Blind, The.
Carcass, A.
Carcass, A.
Cats.
Clock, The.
Clock, The.
Correspondences.
Correspondences.
Cracked Bell, The.
Fuses I and II.
Get High.
Giantess, The.
Giantess, The.
Gypsies on the Move.
Harmony of Evening, The.
Head of Hair.
Her Hair.
Intimate Associations.
Invitation au Voyage, L'
Invitation to the Voyage.
Joker, A.
Owls.
Possessed.
Sed non satiata.
Seven Old Men, The.
Seven Old Men, The.
Snake that Dances, The.
Song of Autumn I.
Soup and the Clouds, The.
Spleen LXXV.
Spleen LXXVI.
Spleen LXXVII.
Spleen LXXVIII.
Stranger, The.
Swan, The.
Swan, The.
To the Reader.
To the Reader.
To the Reader.
Voyage, The.
Voyage to Cythera, A.
Voyage to Cythera, A.
Voyaging.
Way her silky garments undulate, The.
Which One Is Genuine?
Baudri of Bourgueil (1046–1130)
Your Appearance is Pleasing.
Bauer, Grace
Oldies But Goodies.
On Seeing a '57 Chevy Cruising 16th and O.
She Calms the Savage Beast with Her Aubade.
So You Want to Hear the Blues.
Baugh, Edward (b. 1939)
Carpenter's Complaint, The.
Nigger Sweat.
Baumel, Judith (b. 1956)
Let Me In.
Samuel.
Snow-Day.
To the Parents of a Childhood Friend, a
Suicide.
Bausch, Victor H. (b. 1945)
What They Wanted.
Bawer, Bruce (b. 1956)
Grand Central Station, 20 December 1987.
On Leaving the Artists' Colony.
View from an Airplane at Night, over
California, The.
Bawon, Siz See Baron, Suze
Baxter, Charles (b. 1947)
Diptych: Jesus and the Stone.
Purest Rage, The.
Baxter, James Keir (1926–72)
Autumn Testament, sel.
Bay, The.
Buried Stream, The.
East Coast Journey.

Elegy for an Unknown Soldier.
Firemen, The.
Homecoming, The.
Ikons, The.
Jerusalem Sonnets, sels.
Lazarus.
Morning and Evening Calm.
My Love Late Walking.
New Zealand.
Thief and Samaritan.
Tomcat.
Twenty Little Engines.
Wild Bees.
Baxter, Richard (1615–91)
Good Shepherd, The.
Now it belongs not to my care.
Resolution, The.
Bayer, Konrad (1932–64)
Philosopher's Stone, The, sels.
White and Black Bones, The.
Bayliss, John Clifford (1919–78)
Reported Missing.
Bayly, Thomas Haynes (1797–1839)
I'd Be a Butterfly.
I'm Saddest When I Sing.
Novel of High Life, A.
Oh, No! We Never Mention Her.
Out, John.
Soldier's Tear, The.
Something to Love.
We Met.
Baytelman, Shlomit
My Name is Shlomit.
Beach, Joseph Warren (b. 1880)
Horatian Ode.
Beach, Luci
2 Months Rent Due and 1 Bag of Rice.
"Beachcomber" See Morton, John Bingham
Beachy-Quick, Dan (b. 1973)
Afterword.
Botany.
Echo and A.
Flag-Tree.
Halt (Naïve).
Nightbook.
Prologue: "Editor, / Here are the lines my mind
fathomed."
Psalm (Traherne).
Stellar Elements.
Unworn.
Beadle, Samuel Alfred (1857–1932)
Words.
Beasley, Bruce
Hermetic Diary.
Lord Brain.
Red Reed.
Spiritual Alphabet in Midsummer, sel.
What Did You Come to See.
Witness.
Beath, Mary (b. 1950)
Oregon Inlet.
Put a Stone in Your Mouth.
Solid Ground.
**Beatrice [or Beatritz or Beatriz], Countess de Die
[or Dia] (fl. late 12th cent.)**
Lover's Prize, A.
Beattie, James (1735–1803)
Edwin, The Minstrel.
Epitaph, An: "Like thee I once have stemm'd
the sea of life."
Beatty, Adisa Vera
Distance.
Geography.
Memorization.
Beatty, Jan
Modern Love: "Early evening, five minutes
before."
Pittsburgh Poem.
Beatty, Paul (b. 1962)
Doggin the Rockman.
Gription.
I Know You Are, But What Am I?
Independent Study.
New York Newsday: Truth, Justice and Vomit.

Stall Me Out.
That's Not in My Job Description.
Why That Abbott and Costello Vaudeville
Mess Never Worked with Black People.
Beaulieu, Derek
Pronoun Woven.
Summer Triangle.
Beaumont, Francis (1584–1616)
Masque of the Inner Temple and Gray's Inne,
The, sels.
On the Tombs in Westminster Abbey, sels.
**Beaumont, Francis (1584–1616) and John
Fletcher**
Captain, The, sel.
Love's Cure, sels.
Maid's Tragedy, The, sels.
Beaumont, Isobel (b. 1589, d. after 1607)
Poor Bess Turpin, I pytty thy case as farr as I
can.
Beaumont, Jeanne Marie
After: "All long labors, whether for hunger, for
duty, for."
Beaumont, Sir John (1583–1627)
Description of Love, A.
In Desolation.
Of My Dear Son, Gervase Beaumont, sels.
Of the Epiphany.
Upon a Funeral.
Beaumont, Joseph (1616–99)
Cheat, The.
Garden, The.
Gentle Check, The.
Gnat, The.
Hourglass, The.
Love's Mystery.
Morning Hymn.
Whiteness, or Chastity.
Beausoleil, Beau (b. 1941)
This Gate.
Traces.
Wearing.
Beaver, Bruce (b. 1928)
Angels' Weather.
Déjeuner Sur l'Herbe.
Drummer, The.
Entertainer, The.
Folk Song: "O I'm off to Hullaboola where the
climate's never cooler."
Letters to Live Poets, sel.
More than 9 Lives.
Odes and Days, sels.
Silo Treading.
Beccadelli, Antonio See "Panormitanus"
Beck, Art (b. 1940)
Castro Street.
Nicotine.
Beck, Julian (1925–85)
State Will Be Served Even By Poets, The.
Beck, Rachel
Epilogue for Emilia.
Interlude: "Sing together."
Beck, Thomas (fl. 1780–1820)
Sonnet to Nothing.
Becker, Jürgen (b. 1932)
In the Proximity of Andy Warhol.
Becker, Robin
Bath, The.
Bicycle Days.
Crypto-Jews, The.
Dog-God.
Dreaming at the Rexall Drug.
Grief.
History of Sexual Preference, A.
In Pompano Beach, Florida.
Incarnate.
Late Words for My Sister.
Life Forms.
Medical Science.
Midlife.
Monarchs of Parque Tranquilidad.
Near Sheridan.
On the Eve of the Warsaw Uprising.
Peter Pan in North America.
Riding Lesson.

Sad Sestina.
Selective Memory.
Sonnet to the Imagination.
Spiritual Morning.
Story I Like to Tell, The.
Subject / Matter.
Subject of Our Lives, The.
Why We Fear the Amish.
Yom Kippur, Taos, New Mexico.

Beckett, Samuel (1906–89)
Cascando.
Dieppe.
Dieppe.
Echo's Bones.
Enueg 1.
Enueg 2.
Imagination Dead Imagine.
Je suis ce cours de sable qui glisse.
Music of Indifference.
Musique de l'indifférence.
My way is in the sand flowing.
Ooftish.
Que ferais-je sans ce monde sans visage sans questions.
Roundelay: "On all that strand."
Saint-Lô.
Something There.
What is the Word.
What would I do without this world faceless incurious.
Words and Music, *sels.*

Beckford, William (1759–1844)
Elegiac Sonnet to a Mopstick.

Beckman, Joshua (b. 1971)
Canals, The. The liquor coming through.
Don't be mad.
Final poem for the gently sifting public begins on the streets.
I like your handsome drugs. Your pleasant.
Lament for the Death of a Bullfighter.
Ode to the Air Traffic Controller.
Thirst of the crowd, The. We laid the surfer down.

Bécquer, Gustavo Adolfo (1836–70)
Arrow Flying Past, An.
As the Breeze that Cools the Blood.
Black Swallows Will Return, The.
Dark in a Corner of the Room.
Darkling Swallows Will Come Again, The.
Gentle Breeze with a Whispered Cry, The.
Great Waves Breaking with a Roar.
I Am Ardent, I Am Brunette.
I Know a Strange, Gigantic Hymn.
I Lay Awake, Wandering in that Limbo.
Into Her Eyes a Tear Crept.
Invisible Atoms of the Air, The.
It Goes Against My Interest to Confess It.
Nameless Spirit.
Sighs Are Air, and Go to the Air.
They Closed Her Eyes.
To See the Hours of Fever.
When They Told Me I Felt the Cold.
Where Do I Come From?

Beddoes, Thomas Lovell (1803–49)
Bride's Tragedy, The, *sel.*
Death's Jest Book, *sels.*
Dream-Pedlary.
Last Man, The, *sels.*
Phantom-Wooer, The.
Sonnet: To Tartar, a Terrier Beauty.
To Night.
Torrismond, *sels.*

Bede, The Venerable (c.672–c.735)
Hymn: "Hymn of glory let us sing, A."

Bedell, Jack (b. 1966)
Mains du Bon Dieu, Les.

Bedford, Madeline Ida
Munition Wages.

Bedient, Cal (b. 1935)
Leonardo's Bicycle.
When the Gods Put on Meter.

Bedregal, Yolanda (b. 1916)
Gestures From My Window.
Intact Pitcher.
Martyrdom.

Night, I Know All About You.
Nocturne of Hope.
Pointless Journey.
Poppies.

Beecher, John (1904–80)
Altogether Singing.
Appalachian Landscape.
One More River to Cross.
Report to the Stockholders.
We Want More Say.

Beeching, Henry Charles (1859–1919)
Going Down Hill on a Bicycle.
Knowledge after Death.
Prayers.

Beeching, Jack (b. 1922)
Gaudy Camp Follower, The.

Beedome, Thomas (d. 1641?)
Petition, The.
Question and Answer, The.

Beer, Patricia (1924–99)
Ballad of the Underpass.
Christmas Eve.
Christmas Tree, The.
Dream of Hanging, A.
Faithful Wife, The.
Flood, The.
Footbinding.
Grave Doubts.
In Memory of Stevie Smith.
Jane Austen.
John Milton and My Father.
Lemmings.
Lost Woman, The.
Middle Age.
Millennium.
Ninny's Tomb.

Beerbohm, Max (1872–1956)
Addition to Kipling's "The Dead King (Edward VII), 1910"
After Hilaire Belloc.
After Hilaire Belloc.
Ballade Tragique à Double Refrain.
Brave Rover.
Chorus of a Song That Might Have Been Written by Albert Chevalier.
In a Copy of More's (or Shaw's or Wells's or Plato's or Anybody's) Utopia.
Luncheon, A.
On the Imprint of the First English Edition of "The Works of Max Beerbohm"
Prayer, A: "If I popped in at Downing Street."
Same Cottage—But Another Song, of Another Season.
Thomas Hardy and A. E. Housman.
Time, you thief, who love to get.

Beers, Ethel Lynn (1827–79)
All Quiet Along the Potomac.

Beeson, Colleen
Minnie Henderson.

Beeson, Jane
Bald head with the fringe, The.

Beeson, Miranda
Flight.

Beg, Abdula Sulaiman Abdula *See* Goran

Beg, Faiq Abdulla *See* Bêkes

Begay, Shonto (b. 1954)
Mother's Lace.

Begley, T.
Photovoltaic.
Sappho's Gymnasium ("For healthy cells please remember.").
Sappho's Gymnasium ("Outside memory worship never dies.").

Begum, Shajahana (b. 1974)
Qaus-e Qazah.

Behar, Ruth
Jewish Cemetery in Guanabacoa, The.
Survivals.

Behlen, Charles
My Grandfather's Hammer.
Two Ice Storms.
Widow Zebach.
Windy Day/Slayton, Texas.

Behn, Aphra (1640–89)
Angellica's Lament.
Cabal at Nickey Nackeys, The.
Congratulatory Poem to Her Sacred Majesty Queen Mary, Upon Her Arrival in England, A.
Disappointment, The.
Dutch Lover, The, *sels.*
Epitaph on the Tombstone of a Child, the Last of Seven that Died Before.
In a cottage by the mountain.
In Imitation of Horace.
Love's Witness.
Lucky Chance, The, *sel.*
Oh, How the Hand the Lover Ought to Prize.
On a Juniper-Tree, Cut Down to Make Busks.
On Desire. A Pindarick.
On Her Loving Two Equally.
On the Death of the Late Earl of Rochester.
Paraphrase on Oenone to Paris, A.
Pindaric on the Death of our Late Sovereign: with an Ancient Prophecy on His Present Majority, A.
Silvio's Complaint: A Song, to a Fine Scotch Tune.
Song: "I led my Silvia to a grove."
Song. Love Arm'd [*or* Armed].
Song: On Her Loving Two Equally.
Thousand Martyrs I Have Made, A.
To Alexis in Answer to His Poem Against Fruition.
To Alexis in Answer to His Poem Against Fruition. Ode.
To Damon. To Inquire of Him if He Cou'd Tell Me by the Style, Who Writ Me a Copy of Verses that Came to Me in an Unknown Hand.
To Lysander, on Some Verses Be Writ, and Asking More for His Heart.
To Mrs. W. on Her Excellent Verses.
To My Lady Morland at Tunbrige [*or* Tunbridge].
To the Fair Clarinda [*or* Clorinda], Who Made Love to Me, Imagin'd [*or* Imagined] More than Woman.
Verses Design'd by Mrs. A. Behn to be Sent to a Fair Lady.
Voyage to the Isle of Love, A, *sels.*

Behn, Harry (1898–1973)
Circles.
New Little Boy, The.

Behn, Robin
Ancient New Parents.
Aubade: "After the sadness of apples in August."
Below the Cellar of the Yellow House There Is Another Set of Stairs.
Drownproofing Lesson.
Green Field, The.
Like a Horse.
On Being Asked My Opinion About an Autopsy.
On Giving My Father a Book About Roses.
Origin.
Still Life: "There is a train, no, there are train."
Vigil: Dwindle.
Yellow House Writes a Story for the Boy, The.

BehramoǦlu, Ataol (b. 1942)
All Over Again.

Behrle, Jim
Beacon Arms.
Charm of the Highway Strip, The.
Good Night, All You Ships at Sea, You.
White Album.

Bei Dao (b. 1949)
Accomplices.
Answer.
Answer, The.
August Sleepwalker, The.
Bouquet, A.
Collection.
Discovery.
End or a Beginning, An.
Evening Scene, An.
He Opens Wide a Third Eye.

In Memory.
June: "Wind at the ear says *June*."
Landscape Over Zero.
Leaving Home.
Mission.
Moon Festival.
Night Sky.
Postwar.
Ramallah.
Reading: "Taste the unnecessary tears."
Résumé.
Rose of Time, The.
Smells.
Stretch out your hands to me.
Untitled: "Trumpet like a sharp plow, A."

Beissel, Henry (b. 1929)
Tanka: "Ice rain coats berries."

Bejerano, Maya
Hymns of Job, *sels.*
I Made a New Memory for You.
States of War.

Bek, Tatiana (b. 1949)
Beneath the flakes of Russian snow.
I breathed my fill—and then breathed out.
If a song flies to me from the garden.
Oh life, long as an epic.
We've all got history on our hands.

Bêkes (1905–48)
Bright Star.
I Who Have Nothing.
Oh, Moon.

Bekes Jr.
Love: "There is many a country."
Picture.
Separation.

Bekri, Tahar (b. 1951)
Retour en Tunisie, *sels.*
Return to Tunisia.

Bektaş, Cengiz (b. 1934)
Now: "I long for my voice that found you."

Belchenko, Natalya (b. 1973)
Chameleons are fine.
I'd happily survey the world.
It's boring looking at the same old contents.

Belev, Georgi (b. 1945)
Dream: "When the trees began to calcify, and
the birds to coalesce with the branches."
Lake.
Love: "What do you scrawl."
Tale: "Children's poet's own child is dying,
A."
Train.
Woman: "Weeds loom."
Zoo.

Belieu, Erin
Against Writing about Children.
Another Poem for Mothers.
At St. Sulpice.
Choose Your Garden.
Erections.
How the Elderly Drive.
I Can't Write a Poem about Class Rage.
Legend of the Albino Farm.
Love Poem: "There are too many similes for
bed."
Lovely.
Man Who Tried to Rape You, The.
My Field Guide.
Nocturne: My Sister Life.
Part of the Effect of the Public Scene Is to
Importune the Passing Viewer.
Radio Nebraska.
Rondeau at the Train Stop.
Sleeping Man Must Be Awakened to Be
Killed, A.
Your Character is Your Destiny.

Belitt, Ben (b. 1911)
Kites: Ars Poetica.
Orange Tree, The.
Spool, The.

"Bell, Acton" *See* Brontë, Anne

Bell, Ann
This is my work so.

Bell, Carol
Lying in Small Pieces.
Where Hope Lives.

"Bell, Currer" *See* Brontë, Charlotte

Bell, Eddie
Help is a Discotheque.

"Bell, Ellis" *See* Brontë, Emily Jane

Bell, James Madison (1826–1902)
Poem Entitled the Day and the War, A, *sels.*

Bell, Josh (b. 1971)
Beautiful American Poem, The.
Meditation on *The Consolation of Philosophy*.
Poem to Line My Casket with, Ramona.
Sleeping with Artemis.
Zombie Sunday (Had We but World Enough
and Time).

Bell, Julian (1908–37)
Redshanks, The.

Bell, Martin (1918–78)
David Guest.
Reason for Refusal.
Senilio Passes, Singing.
Whitman's Grass.
Winter Coming On.

Bell, Marvin (b. 1937)
Ars Poetica at the Window.
Being in Love.
Book of the Dead Man #1, The.
Book of the Dead Man (#13), The.
Book of the Dead Man #33, The.
Book of the Dead Man #43, The.
Book of the Dead Man #58, The.
Book of the Dead Man #87, The.
Dew at the Edge of a Leaf.
Drawn by Stones, by Earth, by Things That
Have Been in the Fire.
Eastern Long Island.
Ending With a Line From *Lear*.
Extermination of the Jews, The.
First Poem: "Bulletin board flutters with a flair,
The."
Further Pulsations.
Getting Lost in Nazi Germany.
Hole in the Sea, The.
How I Got the Word.
Instructions to Be Left Behind.
Introduction to My Anthology, An.
Israeli Navy, The.
Last Thing I Say, The.
Man May Change, A.
Marco Polo.
Mystery of Emily Dickinson, The.
Nature: "Hand that tries to shake a hand, A."
Old Trembling, An.
Primer about the Flag, A.
Pulsations.
Self and the Mulberry, The.
Sevens (Version 3): In the Closed Iris of
Creation.
Shakespeare's Wages.
Slow.
Someone Is Probably Dead.
Sounds of the Resurrected Dead Man's
Footsteps (#1).
Sound of the Resurrected Dead Man's
Footsteps (#2).
Sounds of the Resurrected Dead Man's
Footsteps (#3).
Street Fair: The Quartet.
These Green-Going-to-Yellow.
Things We Dreamt We Died For.
To an Adolescent Weeping Willow.
To Be.
To Dorothy.
To No One in Particular.
True Story, A.
Unable to Sleep in Frost's Bed in Franconia.
Uniform, The.
We Have Known.
Wednesday.
What They Do to You in Distant Places.
White Clover.
Who and Where, *sel.*

Belle, Felice
Exceptions.

Bellen, Martine
Cucina.

Bellerby, Frances (1899–1975)
Night.
Voices.

Bellerose, Sally
Bye Bye Barbara.

Belli, Carlos German (b. 1928)
Down with the Money-Exchange.
Father, Mother.
My Parents, Know It Well.
O Hada Cibernetica, *sels.*
Poem: "Our love is not found in our
respective."
Segregation #1.
Unknown Voice, An.

Belli, Gioconda (b. 1948)
Birth.
Blood of Others, The.
Brief Lessons in Eroticism 1.
Nicaragua Water Fire.

Belli, Giuseppe Gioacchino (1791–1863)
Bosses of Rome, The.
Greed.
Night of Terror.
Revenge 1.
What Might Have Been.

Bellinger, Alfred Raymond
Bright as a single poppy in a field.

Bellman, Carl Michael (1740–95?)
Fredman's Epistlar, 1790, *sels.*

Belloc, Joseph Hilaire Pierre (1870–1953)
Almighty God, Whose Justice Like a Sun.
Ballade of Hell and of Mrs. Roebeck.
Big Baboon, The.
Bison, The.
But how much more unfortunate are those.
Charles Augustus Fortescue.
Child, Do Not Throw This Book About.
Early Morning, The.
Elephant, The.
Epitaph on the Favourite Dog of a Politician.
Epitaph on the Politician Himself.
Evenlode, The.
Fatigue.
Franklin Hyde.
Frog, The.
Ha'nacker Mill.
Henry King, Who Chewed Bits of String, and
Was Early Cut Off in Dreadful Agonies.
Her Faith.
Imitation.
Is there any reward?
Jim Who Ran Away from His Nurse, and Was
Eaten by a Lion.
Justice of the Peace, The.
Lines to a Don.
Lion, The.
Lord Finchley.
Lord Heygate.
Lord Hippo.
Lord Lucky.
Lord Lundy.
Love and Honour.
Modern Traveller, The, *sels.*
Moral Alphabet, A, *sels.*
Night, The.
Noël.
Obiter Dicta.
On a Dead Hostess.
On a General Election.
On His Books.
On Hygiene.
On Jam.
On Lady Poltagrue, A Public Peril.
On Mundane Acquaintances.
Pacifist, The.
Prophet Lost in the Hills at Evening, The.
Song: "You wear the morning like your dress."
Sonnet: "We will not whisper, we have found
the place."
South Country, The.
Statue, The.
Tarantella.
This, the last ornament among the peers.

Tiger, The.
To Dives.
Viper, The.
Vulture, The.
West Sussex Drinking Song.
World's a Stage, The.
Yak, The.

Beltrán, Carmen Celia (1905–2002)
Dried Flowers.

Bely [*or* Belyi], Andrey [*or* Andrei] (Boris Nikolaevich Bugayev) (1880–1934)
Dramatic Symphony, The, *sel.*

Ben-Lev, Dina (b. 1964)
Broken Helix.
Sensualist Speaks on Faith, A.

Ben Yitzhak, Avraham (1883–1950)
Blessed Are They That Sow.
Blessed Are They Who Sow and Do Not Reap.

ben Yoseph, Reuven (b. 1937)
On the Readiness for Sacrifice.

Benbow, Margaret
Larson Arson.

Bendall, F. W. D. (1882–1953)
Outposts.

Bendall, Molly (*fl.* 20th cent.)
After Estrangement.
Book of Sharp Silhouettes, The.
Book of Style, The.
Conversation with Isadora Duncan.
Fete on the Lake.
Matinée Idylls.
Need for Shoes, The.
Painter of Destinies, A.

Benedetti, Mario (b. 1920)
Magnet, The.
We All Conspire.
With Your Permission.

Benedict, Elinor (b. 1931)
At Ease.

Benedikt, Michael (b. 1937)
Editing *The Gazette of the Infinite.*
Meat Epitaph, The.
Moralist of Bananas, The.

Benét, Rosemary *and* Stephen Vincent Benét
Cotton Mather.
Daniel Boone.
Hernando De Soto.
Nancy Hanks.
U. S. A, *sel.*
Western Wagons.

Benét, Stephen Vincent (1898–1943)
American Names.
Ballad of William Sycamore, The.
Cotton Mather.
Daniel Boone.
For City Spring.
John Brown's Body, *sels.*
John Brown's Body, *sels.*
King David.
Metropolitan Nightmare.
Nightmare Number Three.
1935.
Rain after a Vaudeville Show.
U. S. A, *sel.*
Western Wagons.
Winged Man.

Benét, Stephen Vincent *See Also* Benét, Rosemary
Benét, William Rose (1886–1950)
Brazen Tongue.
Eternal Masculine.
Fawn in the Snow, The.
Horse Thief, The.
Inscription for a Mirror in a Deserted Dwelling.
Jesse James.
Merchants from Cathay.
Night.
Sagacity.
Whale.

Benevento, Joe (b. 1955)
May 31, 1989.
Yankees in East Texas.

Benjamin, Bennie
Oh! What It Seemed to Be.

Benjamin, Park (1809–64)
Press On.

Benlowes, Edward (1603?–1676)
Theophia, *sels.*

Benn, Gottfried
Before a Cornfield.
Bunch of Drifter Sons Hollered, A.
Cycle.
Fragments.
Little Aster.
Man and Woman Go Through the Cancer Ward.
Monologue.
Night Café.
Quaternary.
Subway Train.
This Is Bad.
Word, A.

Bennard, George (1873–1958)
Old Rugged Cross, The.

Bennett, Alan (b. 1934)
Place-Names of China.

Bennett, Alberto A.
My Wheel and I.

Bennett, Bruce (b. 1940)
True Story of Snow White, The.

Bennett, Charles
Drowned Radio, The.
I live alone where echoes roost.

Bennett, Gwendolyn B. (1902–81)
Hatred.
Heritage.
Street Lamps in Early Spring.
To a Dark Girl.

Bennett, J. Alexander
Tribute to a Mohogany Cutter.

Bennett, John (1865–1956)
Her Answer.
In a Rose Garden.

Bennett, Keith (b. 1954)
99.9 FM Radio Nostalgia.

Bennett, Louise (b. 1919)
Colonization in Reverse.
Dry-Foot Bwoy.
Independance.
Independence Dignity.
Jamaica Oman.
No Lickle Twang.
Pass fi White.
South Parade Peddler.

Bennett, Nancy (b. 1962)
Ghost of His Hand, The.

Bennett, Rowena Bastin (b. 1896)
Gingerbread Man, The.
Smoke Animals.
Witch of Willowby Wood, The.
Witch of Willowby Wood, The, *sels.*

Bennis, Mohammad (b. 1948)
Belonging to a New Family.

Benserade, Isaac de (*fl.* c.1650)
Translation of Lines by Benserade.

Bensko, John (b. 1949)
Bones of Lazarus.
Butterfly Net, The.
Last Look in the Sambre Canal, A.

Bensley, Connie (b. 1929)
Bloomsbury Snapshot.
One's Correspondence.
Single Parent.
War Games.

Benson, Arthur Christopher (1862–1925)
Phoenix, The.

Benson, Gerard
Ben Barley.
Cat and the Pig, The.
Limerick: "There once was a bard of Hong Kong."
Play No Ball.
Probatioun Officeres Tale, The.

Benson, Judi
Columbarium.

Benson, Leticia R. (b. 1963)
Asante.

P Word Poem, The.

Benson, Steve
Beaten Track, The.
Beethoven's Sixth Symphony.
Blue Book 18 Pages 1–4.
Reverse Order, *sel.*

Benson, Tish
Enemies.

Bentley, Edmund Clerihew (1875–1956)
Clerihews, *sels.*

Bentley, Elizabeth (1767–1839)
On Education, December 1789.

Bentley, Jon Gill
Dead Mouth, High Weather, Mixture.
First Bird.
Half-Done, Half-Turn.

Bentley, Nelson (d. 1990)
Iron Man of the Hoh.

Bentley, Nicolas (1907–78)
Cecil B. De Mille.
Londonderry Air, The.
On Lady A———.

Bently, Samuel (*fl.* 1760s)
River Dove: a Lyric Pastoral, The.

Benton, Suzanne
Lilith.
Second Coming, The.

Benttinen, Ted
Maritime Pastoral.

Beranová, Jana
Mother's Mark.
Williamsbridge.

Berberova, Nina Nikolaevna (b. 1901)
To Shakespeare.

Berenguer, Amanda
Signs on the Table, The.

Beresford, Ann (b. 1919)
Courtship, The.

Berezan, Jennifer
Hail Mother full of grace power is with thee.

Berezovchuk, Larisa (b. 1948)
Calm rocks to sleep in your usual place.

Berg, Stephen (b. 1934)
Desnos Reading the Palms of Men on Their Way to the Gas Chambers.
Don't Forget.
Nostalgia.
On This Side of the River.
Orpingalik's My Breath: Eskimo Song.
Prayer: "Nobody understands so let the Rabbi."
Ritual.
Ten fussy days running this temple all red tape.
Writing Class.

Berger, Bruce (b. 1938)
Ambition.
Ballad of the Bright Angel.
Haunts of the Mirage.
Misconstrued, The.
Photo Safari.
Plagiarist, The.
Salad Days.
Silver-Paced.
Stout Brahms.
To Answer Your Question.
Transmigration.
Trophy Homes.
Waterfall: "Creek's easy purr, The."
Without.

Berger, Donald
Dinner in the Sun.
Language Pile, The.
Lincoln Bedroom, The.

Berger, Jacqueline (b. 1960)
Between Worlds.
Getting to Know Her.
Gun, The.

Berger, Maxianne (b. 1949)
Constrained Response.
Empty Chairs.

Berggolts [*or* Bergholts], Olga Fiodorovna (1910–75)
Blockade Swallow, The.
Don't turn around, don't look back.

Indian Summer.
My insatiable memory is like.
To My Sister.
Wish, A.

Bergland, Brita (b. 1954)
Up Yonder in the Meadow of Children.

Bergman, Alan (b. 1925)
Summer Me, Winter Me.
Way We Were, The.
Windmills of Your Mind, The.

Bergman, Alexander (1921–41)
To Eugene P. Loveman.

Bergman, Mara
Sore Thumb.

Bergman, Marilyn (b. 1929)
Summer Me, Winter Me.
Way We Were, The.
Windmills of Your Mind, The.

Bergner, Zekharye Khone See Ravitch, Melech

Bergvall, Caroline (b. 1962)
Hungry Form.

Berk, İlhan (b. 1916)
History of a Face, The, *sels.*
I Woke, This Meant a Love in the World.
Love: "When we were here we never knew such a thing as evil."
Never Did I See Such Loves Nor Such Separations.
Poem: "Yellow, Loveliest, enters my city."
Sonnet: "Suns, she is all in all, I stood on a sea, The."
Women: "They stand there and chat near the breakwater."

Berke, Judith
Dancing to the Track Singers at the Nightclub.
Fifties Rock Party, 1985.

Berkeley, George (1685–1753)
On the Prospect of Planting Arts and Learning in America.

Berkeley, Sara (b. 1967)
Mass is Over, The.
Parting, The.

Berkson, Bill (b. 1939)
All You Want.
Bicycle Thief, The.
Blue Is the Hero.
Booster.
Breath.
Bridge.
By Halves.
Fixture, A.
Fourth Street, San Rafael.
Gloria.
Head at the Covers, A.
In a Hand Not My Own.
Instinct.
Melting Milk.
Non Dimenticar.
Obvious Tradition, The.
October: "It's odd to have a separate month. It."
Out There.
Perfect Work.
Rebecca Cutlet.
Roots.
Russian New Year.
Sheer Strips.
Stains of Stalin.
Strawberry Blond.
Traveler's Companion.
Variation.
Vibration Society.
Wake Up (Call).

Berland, Dinah
Blazon.

Berlin, Eric
Sea World.

Berlin, Irving
Alexander's Ragtime Band.
Always.
Blue Skies.
Change Partners.
Cheek to Cheek.
Couple of Swells, A.

Easter Parade.
Fools Fall in Love.
Heat Wave.
How Deep Is the Ocean? (How High Is the Sky?).
I Got Lost in His Arms.
I Got the Sun in the Morning.
Isn't This a Lovely Day (To Be Caught in the Rain?).
It's a Lovely Day Today.
I've Got My Love to Keep Me Warm.
Let Me Sing and I'm Happy.
Let's Face the Music and Dance.
Let's Have Another Cup of Coffee.
Little Things in Life, The.
Manhattan Madness.
Oh! How I Hate to Get Up in the Morning.
Pack Up Your Sins and Go to the Devil.
Pretty Girl Is Like a Melody, A.
Puttin' on the Ritz (Original Version).
Puttin' on the Ritz (Revised Version).
Remember.
Say It Isn't So.
Slumming on Park Avenue.
Song Is Ended (But the Melody Lingers On), The.
Supper Time.
There's No Business Like Show Business.
They Say It's Wonderful.
This Is the Army, Mr. Jones.
Top Hat, White Tie, and Tails.
What'll I Do?
When the Midnight Choo-Choo Leaves for Alabam'
White Christmas.
You Can't Get a Man with a Gun.
You'd Be Surprised.
You're Just in Love.
You're Laughing at Me.

Berlin, Monica
Fungus Considered.

Berman, Cassia
Deep inside me at my core is where my mother lives, *sel.*
Mother Lakshmi's Poem.
Poem for the Shechina.

Berman, David (b. 1967)
April 13, 1865.
Classic Water.
Community College in the Rain.
Democratic Vistas.
From His Bed in the Capital City.
Snow: "Walking through a field with my little brother Seth."

Bermeo, Oscar (b. 1969)
Oda para Leticia.

Bernard, April
Praise Psalm of the City-Dweller.
See It Does Rise.

Bernard, Artis
Snowfall.

Bernard [or Bernart] de Ventadour [or Ventadorn] (c. 1145–80)
Can Vei La Lauzeta Mover.
Chantars No Pot Gaire Valer.
Good time of the year, The.
Joy! a heart so overflowing.
Men, a word of wisdom. Give.
To see the lark, delighted, dare.
When—presto—turf and trees are green.

Bernard of Clairvaux (1091–1153)
Jesus, Thou Joy of Loving Hearts.

Berners, Dame Juliana (b. 1388?)
Properties of a Good Greyhound, The.

Bernes, Jasper (b. 1974)
Desiderata on a Desert Island.
Found Missing.
Outside You Cannot Breathe.
Rave.
Sonnet with Lock and Key.
South Central: Notes toward a Shooting Script.

Bernheim, Erica (b. 1974)
Anne Boleyn.
I Love How Your Eyes Close Every Time You Kiss Me.

Like a Face.
Pavese Said Death Will Come Bearing Your Eyes.

Bernheimer, Alan (b. 1948)
20 Questions.

Bernick, Julian (b. 1970)
Iago.

Bernie, Ben (fl. 1925)
Sweet Georgia Brown.

Bernlef, J. (b. 1937)
Beatrice.
Disconcerting Object.
Uncle Charles: A Home Movie.

Bernstein, Carole (b. 1960)
Caught.
Cup of Coffee, The.
Profaning the Dead.
When My Grandmother Said "Pussy"

Bernstein, Charles (Henk Marsman) (b. 1950)
Age of Correggio and the Carracci, The.
Artifice of Absorption, *sels.*
Autonomy Is Jeopardy.
Dysraphism.
Frequently unasked questions.
Freud's Butcher.
From Lines of Swinburne.
Gradation.
Have Pen, Will Travel.
Kiwi Bird in the Kiwi Tree, The.
Klupzy Girl, The.
Let's Just Say.
Lives of the Toll Takers, The, *sel.*
Loose Shoes.
Matters of Policy.
Memories.
Of Time and the Line.
Outrigger.
Poem: "Here. Forget."
Sign Under Test.
Solidarity Is the Name We Give to What We Cannot Hold.
Take Then, These.
This poem intentionally left blank.
Virtual Reality.
Wait.
Whose Language.
Why we ask you not to touch.

Bernstein, J. B.
Tango'd Love.

Bernstein, Marion (fl 1876)
Manly Sports.

Berrigan, Anselm
Advice to a Young Philosopher.
Anti-Preening Poem.
Bloodletting.
Drugged and Hooded into a Prose Poem.
Four Minute History of Getting It Together in Order to Be Fabulous, Briefly, A.
Looking Up My Balance.
Mercy Flight.
Ode to Election Day.
Sabotage.
Selected Poses.
Short History of Autumn, A.
Token Enabler.
Various multitudes contained by the loves of my love, The.

Berrigan, Daniel (b. 1921)
Astonishment, *sel.*
Crucifix, The.
Facing It.
Funeral Oration as Pronounced by the Compassionate Buddha, The, *sel.*
In Memoriam (2): "Young priest, dead suddenly, A."
My Name.
Prague: Old Woman in the Street.
Prayer: "I left Cornell / with half a wit; six mismated socks."
Rehabilitative Report: We Can Still Laugh.
We Will Now Hear the Word of God from Each of Our Beloved Chaplains.
You Finish It: I Can't.

Berrigan, Edmund (b. 1974)
History of the Human Body, The.

Berrigan, Ted (1934–83)
American Express.
Anti-Memoirs, *sel.*
Bean Spasms.
For You.
Go fly a kite he writes.
Great Stories of the Chair.
I Remember.
In Bed with Joan & Alex.
Last Poem.
Living with Chris.
London Air.
Many Happy Returns.
Mud on the first day (night, rather).
My Autobiography.
Now she guards her chalice in a temple of fear.
Other Contexts.
Où sont les neiges des neiges?
People of the Future.
Personal Poem # 7.
Personal Poem # 8.
Sonnets, The, *sels.*
To gentle, pleasant strains.
Waterloo Sunset.
We remove a hand.
Whitman in Black.
Words for Love.

Berry, Betsy
Afternoon in Austin.

Berry, Ciaran (b. 1971)
Uascán.

Berry, David Chapman (b. 1947)
After Finding a One Hundred Dollar Bill.
Hambone Two Tongue.
Hamlet Off-stage: Laertes Cool.
On Reading Poems to a Senior Class at South
    High.

Berry, Jake
Brambu Drezi, *sels.*

Berry, James (b. 1924)
Benediction.
Fantasy of an African Boy.
Girls Can We Educate We Dads?
I am cuddle-shaped and freckled.
Lucy's Letter.
One.
Sounds of a Dreamer.

Berry, Wendell (b. 1934)
Against the War in Vietnam.
Air and Fire.
Anniversary, An.
At a Country Funeral.
Country of Marriage, The.
Dark with power.
Dust.
Enemies.
Enriching the Earth.
First time I remember waking up.
Getting Away: Verses and Choruses for
    Various Voices.
Guest, The.
Handing Down, The, *sels.*
Her First Calf.
History.
In Rain.
Independence Day.
Let Us Pledge.
Mad Farmer, Flying the Flag of Rough Branch,
    Secedes from the Union, The.
Mad Farmer Revolution, The.
Man Born to Farming, The.
Manifesto: The Mad Farmer Liberation Front.
Manifesto: The Mad Farmer Liberation Front,
    sel.
Marriage.
Meditation in the Spring Rain.
Morning's News, The.
Old Man Climbs a Tree, The.
Our Christmas Tree.
Peace of Wild Things, The.
Prayers and Sayings of the Mad Farmer, *sels.*
Purification, A.
Ripening.
Sabbaths, *sels.*
Slip, The.

Sparrow.
Stay Home.
Sycamore, The.
Testament, *sels.*
Third Possibility, A.
Three Elegiac Poems, *sels.*
To My Mother.
To Tanya at Christmas.
To the Unseeable Animal.
Vacation, The.
Way of Pain, The.
Wheel, The.
Wild Geese, The.
Wild Rose, The.
Window Poems, *sel.*

Berryman, John (1914–72)
Alcoholic.
Alcoholic in the 3rd Week of the 3rd
    Treatment, The.
American Lights, Seen from Off Abroad.
Ball Poem, The.
Boston Common.
Cage, The.
Canto Amor.
Carpenter's Son, The.
Desires of Men and Women.
Despair: "It seems to be DARK all the time."
Dream Songs, *sels.*
Dry Eleven Months.
Eleven Addresses to the Lord, *sels.*
5th Tuesday.
Four Dream Songs, *sels.*
4th Weekend.
Group.
He Resigns.
Henry by Night.
Henry's Fate.
Henry's Understanding.
Homage to Mistress Bradstreet, *sels.*
King David Dances.
Moon and the Night and the Men, The.
Of Suicide.
Parting as Descent.
Phase Four.
Professor's Song, A.
Recognition, The.
Scholars at the Orchid Pavilion.
Snow Line.
Sonnets to Chris, *sels.*
Soviet Union, The.
Sympathy, A Welcome, A.
To My Father.
Traveller [*or* Traveler], The.
Winter Landscape.

Bersohn, Robert
Dignity of Labor, The.

Berssenbrugge, Mei-Mei (b. 1947)
Alakanak Break-Up.
Chronicle.
Constellation Quilt, The.
Fog: "Hundreds of millions of years ago, days
    were many hours shorter."
Four Year Old Girl, *sels.*
Heat Bird, The.
Jealousy.
Kali, *sels.*
Retired Architect, The, *sels.*
Safety, *sels.*
Swan, The.
Tan Tien.
Texas.

Bertolino, James
Baying, The.
See Willow.
Snail River.

Bertrand, Aloysius (1807–1841)
Five Fingers of the Hand, The.
Lepers.
Mason, The.
Mason, The.
Moonlight.
Tulip Merchant, The.

Bertrans de Born (c.1140–1215)
In Praise of War.
Planh for the Young English King.

Protestation.
Sirventes.

Berzsenyi, Dániel (1776–1836)
Approaching Winter, The.
Horace.
Hungary.
My Portion.
Philosophy of Life.
Prayer: "Oh, God, beyond the wit of the
    genius."
Solitude.
To Napoleon.
To the Hungarians: "Oh you, once mighty
    Hungary, gone to seed."
To the Hungarians: "Seas of Sorrow boil with
    a rage, Magyar, The."
Unfinished Letter to My Lady.

Beskin, Lisa
On the Sixth Day the Word Is Taken from Me.

Bessenyei, György (1747?–1811)
György Bessenyei to Himself.
Morning Splendour of the Tisza, The.

Betham-Edwards, Matilda Barbara
In a Letter to A.R.C. on Her Wishing to Be
    Called Anna.
To a Llangollen Rose, the Day after It Had
    Been Given by Miss Ponsonby.
Urge me no more! nor think, because I seem.

Bethel, Marion (b. 1953)
Reggae Prophecy.

**Bethell, Mary Ursula ("Evelyn Hayes") (1874–
1945)**
Discipline.
Fortune.
Time.

Bethune, Lebert (b. 1937)
For Singing In Good Mood.
Harlem Freeze Frame.
Today Tutu Is Beating the Same Burru As Me.

Betjeman, Sir John (1906–84)
Advent 1955.
Arrest of Oscar Wilde at the Cadogan Hotel,
    The.
Ballad of George R. Sims, The.
Before the Anæsthetic; or, A Real Fright.
Blame the Vicar.
Business Girls.
Christmas.
City.
Cottage Hospital, The.
Crematorium.
Death in Leamington.
Death of King George V.
Devonshire Street W.1.
East Anglian Bathe.
False Security.
Hike on the Downs, A.
House of Rest, *sels.*
How to Get On in Society.
Hunter Trials.
Huxley Hall.
In Memory of Basil, Marquess of Dufferin and
    Ava.
In Westminster Abbey.
Incident in the Early Life of Ebenezer Jones,
    Poet, 1828, An.
Inevitable.
Late-Flowering Lust.
Licorice Fields at Pontefract, The.
Longfellow's Visit to Venice.
Metropolitan Railway, The.
Old Land Dog, The.
On Seeing an Old Poet in the Café Royal.
Potpourri from a Surrey Garden.
Remorse.
Reproof Deserved; or After the Lecture.
St. Saviour's, Aberdeen Park, Highbury,
    London, N.
Shropshire Lad, A.
Slough.
Subaltern's Love-Song, A.
Undenominational.

Betsugen (1294–1364)
All night long I think of life's labyrinth.

Bettarini, Mariella (b. 1942)
Biography.
Epilogue (At the Proper Distance).
Fragment for the Mother.
Holm Oak, The.
I Say That the Cricket the Scorpion the
  Grasshopper.
If Nature Bellows.
In That Moment When the Body Drowns.
Let Us Love As We Choose: Water.
Name, The.
Poet's Home, The, *sel.*
There Is Only One Almighty.

Betts, Tara
Dreadlocks.

Bevan, Maggie
Confrontation with a Bouquet.

Beveridge, Judith (b. 1956)
Catching Webs.
Dining Out.
Domesticity of Giraffes, The.
In the Park.

Bevington, Helen Smith (b. 1906)
Ballade of Poetic Material.
Mr. Rockefeller's Hat.
Mrs. Trollope in America.
Princess and the Pea, The.
To Helen.

Bevington, Louisa Sarah (1847–95)
Afternoon.
Am I to Lose You?
Dreamers?
'Egoisme à Deux'
Measurements.
Midnight.
Morning.
One More Bruised Heart!
Twilight.
Two songs, *sels.*
Wrestling.

Bewe (*fl.* c.1576)
I Would I Were Actaeon.

Bewick, Elizabeth
Black my beginning.

Bey, Râsih (d. 1731)
Don't lower your languid eyes, don't aim.

Beznos, Fanny (1907–194?)
I Go, the Wind Pushing Me Along.
PURITY! PURITY! PURITY!

Bhairavayya (b. 1942)
Raped Poem.

Bhāndārī, Śāradā
Ma, You are Brahmani in the world of Brahma.
Menaka says, Hey listen, Mountain King.

Bhartrihari (*fl.* c.500)
Apathy Is Ascribed to the Modest Man.
Bald-Headed Man, A.
Bearing the lustre of a full moon.
Man May Tear a Jewel, A.
Sweet Maid.
While His Body's Vigor Is Whole.

Bhatt, Sujata (b. 1956)
Different History, A.
Fischerhude, 2001.
Looking Through a French Photographer's
  Portrayal of Rajasthan with Extensive Use of
  Orange Filters.
Looking Up.
Muliebrity.
Parvati.
Search for My Tongue, *sel.*
Shérdi.
Stinking Rose, The.
Understanding the *Ramayana.*
What Does One Write When the World Starts
  to Disappear?
What Is Worth Knowing?
White Asparagus.
Wine from Bordeaux.
Written After Hearing About the Soviet
  Invasion of Afghanistan.

Bhattācārya, Āśutos
Get up, get up, Mountain: no more sleep for
  you!

Bhattācārya, Kamalākānta (c.1769–1821)
Bee of my mind, The.
Consulting the omens.
Crazy Mind.
Ever-blissful Kali.
External rituals mean nothing.
From her autumn-lotus mouth.
From now on.
Go, my Lord of the Mountains.
Hara came and made off with my Gauri.
Here, Queen of the Mountains.
Hey, Hara, Ganges-Holder.
Hey, Mountain King, Gauri is sulking.
How can that black woman be so beautiful?
How could you have forgotten her.
How will You rescue me, Tara?
I know, I know, Mother.
Is my black Mother Syama really black?
Jaya, tell him that Uma will not be sent.
Kali / Is everything You do misleading?
Kali! / Today in the dark grove.
Kali, what family are You from?
Kali, you have removed all my difficulties.
King of the Mountains is on his way to Hara's
  abode, The.
Mother / You're always finding ways to amuse
  Yourself.
My Gauri / You've come home!
My Uma has come!
Other than Your two red feet, Syama.
Queen asks, The.
So, forgetful Mahadeva.
Stay within yourself, Mind.
Tara, Mother / Lift me out by the hair.
Tell me, Syama.
Tell me / What can I do?
Turn back, Uma.
Unperturbed at the battle.
What a dream I had last night!
What happened? / The ninth night is over.
What's the fault of the poor mind?
Who can describe the waves of Mother
  Syama's world?
Who is this.
Who is this enchantress.
Withered tree doesn't blossom, The.
You ask me, Queen, time after time.

Bhattācārya, Mahendranāth (1843–1908)
Come, brothers, everyone together.
Everyone's flocking to Gajan.
I've gone mad drinking nectar.
Look at all these waves.
Ma, are you really dead?
Oh Ma Kali, for a long time now.
Screening its face amongst lotus stalks.
Tell me, what are you doing now, Mind.
There's a huge hullabaloo in my lotus heart.
What shall I say to You, Sankari?
You can't catch the thief, Mind.
Your behavior proves how stingy You are, Ma.

Bhattacharya, Kashyap (b. 1979)
Cricketer, The.

**Bialik, Hayyim Nahman [*or* Khayim Nakhman
  or Chaim Nachman] (1873–1934)**
At Twilight.
Do not.
If you found my heart's scroll in the dust.
My Soul Sinks.
Only a single ray, but suddenly.
Orphanhood.
Stars shine and go out.
Summer is dying in the purple and gold and
  russet.
Summer Night.

Bialosky, Jill (b. 1957)
Adolescent Suicide, The.
Fathers in the Snow, *sel.*
Silver.

Bialoszewski, Miron (b. 1922)
Ballad of Going Down to the Store, A.

Bibb, Eloise (Eloise Bibb Thompson) (1878–1927)
Anne Boleyn.
Belshazzer's Feast.
Capt. Smith and Pocahontas.
Catharine of Arragon.

Charmion's Lament.
Class Song of '91.
Destiny.
Early Spring.
Eliza in Uncle Tom's Cabin.
Expulsion of Hagar, The.
Gerarda.
Hermit, The.
Imogene.
In Memoriam Frederick Douglass.
In Memory of Arthur Clement Williams.
Judith.
Leona, dear, twelve months ago.
Lines to Mrs. M. C. Turner.
Lines to the Hon. George L. Knox.
Ode to the Sun.
Offering, An.
Sonnet: "O thou who never harbored fear."
Tale of Italy, A.
Tribute.
Vestal Virgin, The.
Wandering Jew, The.

Bibbins, Mark
All but Lost.
Blasted Fields of Clover Bring Harrowing and
  Regretful Sighs, *sels.*
Bluebeard.
By the Skin of Our Luck.
Counting.
Geometry Class.
Groupie.
Just Yesterday.
Mud.
Pathology of Proximity, The.
Sinking.
Slutty.
Whitman on the Beach.

Bible, Apocrypha
Ecclesiasticus, *sels.*
Jeremie 17.
Steel Usurps the Forests; Silence Dethrones
  Dialogue.

Bible, *N.T.*
First Corinthians, *sel.*
Revelation of St. John the Divine, The, *sel.*
St. John, *sels.*
St. Luke, *sels.*
St. Mark, *sels.*
St. Matthew, *sels.*

Bible, *O.T.*
Bay Psalm Book, The.
But God is Silent / Psalm 114.
Deuteronomy, *sel.*
Ecclesiastes, *sels.*
Exodus, *sels.*
Ezekiel.
Genesis, *sels.*
Glory Glory / Psalm 19.
Inscription on the Liberty Bell.
Isaiah, *sels.*
Jeremiah, *sel.*
Job, *sels.*
Lamentations.
Micah, *sel.*
New Version of the Psalms of David, Fitted to
  the Tunes Used in Churches, A, *sels.*
Numbers, *sels.*
Paraphrase on the Book of Job, A, *sels.*
Paraphrase on the Psalms of David, *sel.*
Paraphrase Upon Job, A, *sels.*
Proverbs, *sels.*
Psalm 58: "Do ye, o congregation."
Psalm 58: "Judges, who rule the world by
  laws."
Psalm 114.
Psalm 114: "When Isr'el, freed from Pharoh's
  hand."
Psalm 137: "Along the banks where Babel's
  current flows."
Psalme 91.
Psalms, *sels.*
Psalms, *sels.*
Psalms, *sels.*
Psalms [David Rosenberg Adaption], *sels.*
Psalms, *sels.*
Second Samuel, *sels.*

Song: "I was asleep but my heart stayed awake."
Song of Solomon, *sels.*
Song of Solomon, The, *sels.*
Song of Solomon, The, *sels.*
Song of Solomon, The, *sels.*
Song of Solomon, The, *sel.*
Song of Solomon, The [*or* The Song of Songs], *sels.*
Stanzas Imitated From Psalm 119.
Translation of the Psalms of David, A, *sels.*

Bickerstaffe, Isaac (c.1735–c.1812)
Expostulation, An.
Recruiting Serjeant, The, *sel.*

Bidart, Frank (b. 1939)
Another Life.
Coin for Joe, with the Image of a Horse, A; c. 350-325 BC.
Curse.
Ellen West.
For the Twentieth Century.
Golden State.
Happy Birthday.
If I Could Mourn Like a Mourning Dove.
Lament for the Makers.
Sacrifice, The.
Self-Portrait [1969].
To the Dead.
Yoke, The.

Bidgood, Ruth (b. 1922)
All Souls'
Banquet.
Burial Path.
Chimneys.
Dragon.
Hawthorn at Digiff.
Little of Distinction.
Old Pump-house, Llanwrtyd Wells.
Safaddan.
Standing Stone.

Bielski, Alison (b. 1925)
Intruder.
Token.

Bienek, Horst (b. 1930)
Exodus.
Our Ashes.
Resistance.
Vorkuta.

Bierce, Ambrose (1842–c.1914)
Confederate Flags, The.
Death of Grant, The.
Devil's Dictionary, The, *sels.*
Don't steal. Thou'lt never thus compete.
For those this mausoleum is erected.
General B. F. Butler.
Here Stanford lies, who thought it odd.
Hesitating Veteran, The.
Passing Show, The.
Rational Anthem, A.
Statesmen, The.
To E. S. Salomon.
To the Bartholdi Statue.
Year's "Casualties", A.

Bierds, Linda (b. 1945)
After-Image.
Altamira: What She Remembered.
Depth of Field.
Desire.
Hunter.
In the Beeyard.
It.
Lawrence and Edison in New Jersey: 1923.
Memento of the Hours.
Muybridge.
Pasteur on the Rue Vauquelin.
Phantom Pain.
Quickly and Fully.
Ritual for the Dead, Lake Sakami, Quebec, 1980.
Safe.
Seconds, The.
Stillness, the Dancing, The.
Thinking of Red.
Van Leeuwenhoek: 1675.
Vespertilio.

White Bears: Tolstoy at Astapovo.

Biespiel, David (b. 1964)
After the Wedding.
Heat Sours, The.
Lilacs.
There Were No Deer in the Thicket.
Tower.
Under a Blossoming Plum Tree.
White Roses.

Big Boy, Marla
I Will Bring You Twin Grays.

Bigelow, Bob
Hard-Hearted Hannah (The Vamp of Savannah).

Bigelow, Marion Albina (*fl.* 1850)
Children Disinterred, *sel.*
Two Smothered Children.

Bihari
All day she studies her new.
As if to lift my babe-in-arms.
Loveliness beyond words.
Satasai, The, *sel.*
When I found her in the bathing pool.

Bilgere, George (b. 1951)
At the Vietnam Memorial.
Catch.
Like Riding a Bicycle.
Madeleine, A.

Bilhana (*fl.* 11th cent.)
Fantasies of a Love-Thief, *sel.*

Billings, William (1746–1800)
Let Tyrants Shake Their Iron Rod.

Bin Hassan, Umar
Grace.

Bingen, Hildegard von (1098–1197)
Alleluia-verse for the Virgin.
Antiphon for Divine Wisdom.
Antiphon for the Angels.
Antiphon for the Holy Spirit.
Earth is at the same time mother, The.
Hymn to St. Maximinus.
I am the one whose praise.
Song to the Creator.

Bingxin (b. 1900)
Myriad Stars, Part 132.
Paper Boat—Sent to Mother.
Springwater, Part 105.

Binyon, Laurence (1869–1943)
Beauty.
Burning of the Leaves, The, *sel.*
For Mercy, Courage, Kindness, Mirth.
For the Fallen.
For the Fallen, *sel.*
Harebell and Pansy.
House That Was, The.
Invocation to Youth.
Little Dancers, The.
Nothing Is Enough.
Statues, The.
Tristram's End.
Unreturning Spring, The.
Winter Sunrise.

Bion (c.315–255 B.C.)
Lament for Adonis.
Lament for Adonis.

Birche, William
Songe betwene the Quenes majestie and Englande, A.

Bird, Gloria
Women Fell like Beautiful Horses, The.

Birkelbach, Alan
Coronado Points.

Birken, Sigmund von (1626–81)
Shepherd-Song.
Shepherd-Song.

Birnbaum, Martin
By the River.
Man Who Hanged Himself, The.
Visiting Jesus.

Birney, Earle (b. 1904)
Anglo Saxon Street.
Bear on the Delhi Road, The.
Bushed.

El Greco: Espolio.
From the Hazel Bough.
Gray Woods Exploding, The.
Irapuato.
Slug in Woods.
Twenty-third Flight.
Vancouver Lights.

Bishop, Elizabeth (1911–79)
Armadillo, The.
At the Fishhouses.
Behind Stowe.
Bight, The.
Brazil, January 1, 1502.
Cape Breton.
Casabianca.
Chemin de Fer.
Cold Spring, A.
Crusoe in England.
End of March, The.
Exchanging Hats.
Filling Station.
First Death in Nova Scotia.
Fish, The.
Five Flights Up.
For C.W.B.
Four Poems, *sels.*
From the Country to the City.
From Trollope's Journal.
Imaginary Iceberg, The.
In the Waiting Room.
Insomnia.
Invitation to Miss Marianne Moore.
Letter to N.Y.
Little Exercise.
Man-Moth, The.
Manners.
Map, The.
Miracle for Breakfast, A.
Monument, The.
Moose, The.
North Haven.
One Art.
Over 2000 Illustrations and a Complete Concordance.
Paris, 7 A.M.
Pink Dog.
Poem: "About the size of an old-style dollar bill."
Prodigal, The.
Questions of Travel.
Rainy Season; Sub-Tropics, *sels.*
Roosters.
Sandpiper.
Seascape.
Sestina: "September rain falls on the house."
Shampoo, The.
Sleeping on the Ceiling.
Some Dreams They Forgot.
Song for the Rainy Season.
Song: "Summer is over upon the sea."
Songs for a Colored Singer.
Sonnet: "Caught—the bubble."
Sonnet: "I am in need of music that would flow."
Twelfth Morning; or What You Will.
Unbeliever, The.
Under the Window: Ouro Prêto.
Vague Poem.

Bishop, John Peale (1892–1944)
Aliens.
Dream, The: "And once again I was within that house."
In the Dordogne.
Metamorphoses of M.
Past and Present.
Recollection, A.
Return, The.
Speaking of Poetry.
Young Men Dead.

Bishop, Morris Gilbert (1893–1973)
Adventures of Id, The.
Ah, To Be In.
Anatomy of Humor, The.
Dark Christmas on Wildwood Road, The.
Diogenes.
Eschatology.

Flowers of Rhetoric.
Fragment from "The Maladjusted: A Tragedy"
Joker who haunts Monticello, A.
Limerick: "Limerick Is Furtive and Mean,
    The."
My Friend the Cuckold.
Naughty Preposition, The.
Ozymandias Revisited.
Public Aid for Niagara Falls.
Sales Talk for Annie.
We Have Been Here Before.

Bishop, Patricia
Like the tides I rise and fall.
Woman Washing.

Bishop, Wendy
Evidence of Death's Voodoo—Inside and
    Outside the "Gun As Art Exhibit"
Violence.

Bitar, Walid
Happy Hour.

Bitsui, Sherwin (b. 1975)
Apparition: "I haven't."
Chrysalis.
Northern Sun, The.

Black, D. M. (b. 1941)
Educators, The.
For and Against the Environment.
Red Judge, The.
Water-Lily, The.

Black, Johnny S.
Paper Doll.

Black, Sophie Cabot
Hunt, The: "To be in the way, belonging. To
    wait."

Black, Star
Asylum.
Blank Abandon of Beds, The.
Hoopla.
Lust.
Personals.
Rilke's Letter from Rome.
Skyscrapers.
To a War Correspondent.

Black Elk (1863–1950)
Everything the Power of the World Does is
    Done in a Circle.

Blackburn, John (fl. 1944)
Moonlight in Vermont.

Blackburn, Michael
Before That.

Blackburn, Paul (1926–71)
At the Well.
Brooklyn Narcissus.
El Camino Verde.
Net of Place, The.
Park Poem.
Phone Call to Rutherford.
Selection of Heaven, The, sel.
Yawn, The.

Blackburn, Thomas (1916–77)
Now Light Congeals.

Blackhall, Sheena (b. 1947)
Doric's No Dodo.
Spik o' the Lan, The.
Walk On.

Blackhawk, Terry
Dawn of the Navajo Woman, The.

Blacklock, Thomas (1721–91)
To a Young Lady's Dog.

Blackman, Peter
My Song is for All Men, sel.

Blackmore, Sir Richard (1653–1729)
Creation, sels.
Prince Arthur, sels.

Blackmore, Richard Doddridge (1825–1900)
Dominus Illuminatio Mea.

Blackmur, R. P. (Richard Palmer) (1904–65)
Communiqués from Yalta, The.
Mirage.
One grey and foaming day.
Redwing.
Seas Incarnadine.
Since There's No Help . . .

Sunt Lacrimae Rerum et Mentem Mortalia
    Tangunt.

Blackwell, Holley
Another.
August 2000.
Law of Trichotomy.
Message No. 57.
Message No. 44.
Message No. 69.
Message No. 32.
New Poem.
SEEing yu.

Blaeser, Kimberly M. (fl. 20th cent.)
Certificate of Live Birth.
Dictionary for the New Century.
Rituals, Yours—and Mine.
What They Did by Lamplight.

Blaga, Lucian (1895–1961)
I Will Not Crush the World's Corolla of
    Wonders.
Psalm.

Blagden, Isa (?1816–73)
Alice.
To George Sand on her Interview with
    Elizabeth Barrett Browning.

Blagg, Teresa
In Bed this Morning.

Blair, Eric See Orwell, George

Blair, Hamish (b. 1872–1935)
Bloody Orkneys, The.

Blair, Robert (1699–1746)
Grave, The, sels.

Blaisdell, Gus
After the Symbols.
Occassional Loquats.
Omoide no Tsukimi.
To a Poet (the Pearl).

Blake, Elizabeth Jessup
Within and Without.

Blake, James W. (1862–1935)
Sidewalks of New York, The.

Blake, William (1757–1827)
All Religions Are One.
America: A Prophecy, sel.
Answer to the Parson, An.
Auguries of Innocence, sels.
Book of Thel, The, sel.
Book of Urizen [or First Book of Urizen], The.
Cradle Song, A: "Sleep, sleep, beauty bright."
Crystal Cabinet, The.
Epitaph, An: "I was buried near this dyke [or
    Dike]."
Europe; A Prophecy, sel.
Everlasting Gospel, The, sels.
Fair Elenor.
Gates of Paradise, The, sels.
Ghost of Abel, The.
Gnomic Verses, sel.
Grey Monk, The.
How Sweet I Roamed [or Roam'd] from Field
    to Field.
I told my love I told my love.
In a Myrtle [or Mirtle] Shade.
Island in the Moon, An, sels.
Jerusalem, sels.
Lacedemonian Instruction.
Love's Secret.
Mad Song.
Marriage of Heaven and Hell, The.
Marriage of Heaven and Hell, The, sels.
Mental Traveller, The.
Merlins Prophecy.
Milton, sels.
Mock On, Mock On, Voltaire, Rousseau.
Morning.
Orator Prigg.
Several Questions Answered, sels.
Smile, The.
Soft Snow.
Song: "Memory, hither come."
Song: "My silks and fine array."
Songs of Experience, sels.
Songs of Innocence, sels.
There Is No Natural Religion.

To Autumn.
To Flaxman.
To Morning.
To Spring.
To the Evening Star.
To the Muses.
Vala; or The Four Zoas, sel.
Visions of the Daughters of Albion, sels.

Blaker, Margaret
Pippa Passes, But I Can't Get Around This
    Truck.

Blamire, Susanna (1747–94)
North Country Village, A.
O Bid Me Not to Wander.
O Donald! Ye Are Just the Man.
Siller Croun, The.

Blanchard, Mary Loving
Bloodlines.
East Texas Blues.
Picking Cotton.

Blanchfield, Brian (b. 1973)
Endowment Becoming Less An Institution,
    The.

Blanco, Alberto (b. 1951)
Accuracy of the Scale, The.
Fiel de la balanza, El.
Mapas.
Maps.
Metamorfosis de la silla.
Metamorphosis of a Chair.
Music in the Age of Iron.
Poem Seen in a Motel Fan.
Quantum Theory.
Set Theory.
Teorí de Fractales.
Teoría cuántica.
Teoría de conjuntos.
Teoría de la luz.
Theory of Light.
Three States and Three Kingdoms.
Tres estados y los tres reinos, Los.

Blanco, Patricia
Mango's Core, The.
Soldiers.

Blanco, Richard (b. 1968)
El Malibú.
Elegant Endings.
How It Begins / How It Ends.
Last Night in Havana.
Letter to El Flaco on His Birthday.
Perfect City Code.
Shaving.
Silver Sands, The.
Tía Olivia Serves Wallace Stevens a Cuban
    Egg.
We're Not Going to Malta.

Bland, Edith Nesbit See Nesbit, Edith

Bland, James A. (1854–1911)
Carry Me Back to Old Virginny.
Oh, Dem Golden Slippers!

Bland, Peter (b. 1934)
Notes for the Park Keeper.

Blandiana, Ana (b. 1942)
Covered with Dew.

Blanding Henriette de Saussure (b. 1890)
Aftermath (1945).

Blane, Ralph (1914–95)
Ev'ry Time.
Have Yourself a Merry Little Christmas.
I Never Felt Better.
Love: "Love can be a moment's madness."
Occasional Man, An.
Spring Isn't Everything.
That Face.
Trolley Song, The.

Blankenburg, Gary
Mouse, The.

Blanvillain, Jean-Marie
(All of a Sudden) My Heart Sings.

Blaser, Robin (b. 1925)
Ah.
Cups #5.
Even on Sunday.
Finder, The.

Image-Nation, *sels*.
Ruler, The.
Suddenly.
Universe is Part of Ourselves, The.

Blasing, Randy
Refuge.

Blaustein, Noah
Water and Light.

Bleakney, Jean (b. 1956)
Be Careful of the Lilies!
Black and White.
By Starlight on Narin Strand.
Depending on the Angle.
Fairytale Land of Um, The.
In Memoriam: "If it's over, *let it be over.*"
On Going Without Saying.
Summer love was ever thus.
Winter Solstice.

Blessing, Richard
Elegy for Elvis.

Bletsoe, Elizabeth
Weird stuff this.

Blevins, Steven (d. 1994)
New York.

Blicher, Steen Steensen (1782–1848)
My birthplace is the brown heather-land.

Blickstein, J. J.
Vision of Salt & Water: Elijah's Horn.

Blight, John (b. 1913)
Anchor, The.
Coral Reef, The.
Death of a Whale.
Down from the Country.
Garfish.
Into the Ark.
Landfall, The.
Mangrove.
Oyster-Eaters, The.
Sun.

Blind, Mathilde (1841–96)
Ascent of Man, The, *sels*.
Beautiful Beeshareen Boy, The.
Dead, The.
Entangled.
Fantasy, A.
Haunted Streets.
Love in Exile, *sels*.
Manchester by Night.
Many Will Love You.
Message, The.
Mourning Women.
Noonday Rest.
On a Forsaken Lark's Nest.
Once We Played.
Red Sunsets, 1883, The.
Russian Student's Tale, The.
Scarabaeus Sisyphus.
Winter Landscape, A.

"Blind Harry" *See* Henry the Minstrel

Bliss, Daniel (1740–1806)
Epitaph of John Jack.

Bliss, Philip Paul (1838–76)
Last Hymn.

Bloch, Chana (b. 1940)
Act One.
Conservation of Energy, The.
Discipline of Marriage, The.
How the Last Act Begins.
Kiss, The.
Natural History.
Puzzle Pieces.
Visiting Hours Are Over.
What a Poet Does.
White Petticoats.

Bloem, J. C. (1887–1966)
After Liberation.
Dapper Street.
Honeysuckle.
Sunday.
Writing on a Tombstone.

Bloem, Rein (b. 1932)
Amsterdam Chronicle.

Blok, Aleksandr Aleksandrovich (1880–1921)
Dances of Death, *sels*.

Dances of Death, *sel*.
Kite, The.
On the Plain of Kulikovo.
Red Glow in the Sky, A.
Twelve, The, *sel*.
Visitor.

Blomer, Yvonne (b. 1970)
Landscapes and Home / Ghazal 22.

Blood, Benjamin Paul (1832–1919)
Bride of the Iconoclasts, The, *sel*.
Late.

Bloom, Valerie (b. 1956)
Sun-a-shine, Rain-a-fall.
Wha Fe Call I'

Bloomfield, Robert (1766–1823)
Farmer's Boy, The, *sels*.

Blount, Roy, Jr. (b. 1941)
Against Broccoli.
Song to Onions.

Bloze, Vytautas
Beneath the Stars.

Blue Cloud, Peter (b. 1933)
Bear: A Totem Dance As Seen by Raven.
Coyote Makes the First People.
Crazy Horse Monument.
Deeper Than a Dream.
Ochre Iron.
Old man's lazy, The.
Rattle.
To-ta Ti-om.
Turtle.
Within the Seasons, *sels*.
Wolf.
Yellowjacket.

Bluger, Marianne (b. 1945)
In Oak.
Leafsmoke.

Blumenthal, Michael C. (b. 1949)
Abandoning Your Car in a Snowstorm:
   Rosslyn, Virginia.
Accountant, The.
Back from the Word-Processing Course, I Say
   to My Old Typewriter.
Cherries.
Deep Ecology.
Disappointments of Childhood, The.
Elephants Dying, The.
Forces, The.
Geologist, The.
Inventors.
Litrajure of Everyday Life, The.
Man Lost by a River, A.
Marriage, A.
Meditation on Politics at the Quabbin
   Reservoir.
Over Ohio.
Squid.
What I Believe.
Who Will Live in Our Houses When We Die?

Blumstein [or Blaustein or Bluwstein], Rahel *See*
   "Rachel [or "Rahel"]

Blundell, G. J.
Squire Squint, shooting at a pheasant.

Blunden, Edmund Charles (1896–1974)
Almswomen.
Barn, The.
Behind the Line.
Concert Party: Busseboom.
Country God, A.
Eastern Tempest.
Forefathers.
In Festubert.
Midnight Skaters, The.
Mole Catcher.
1916 Seen from 1921.
One among the Roses.
Poor Man's Pig, The.
Recovery, The.
Report on Experience.
Survival, The.
Two Voices.
Vlamertinghe.
Zonnebeke Road, The.

Blunt, Wilfrid Scawen (1840–1922)
Esther [a Young Man's Tragedy], *sels*.
Farewell, then. It is finished. I forego.
Gibraltar.
Honour Dishonoured.
Love Sonnets of Proteus, The, *sels*.
Nocturne: "Moon has gone to her rest, The."
Old Squire, The.
On Her Vanity.
To One Who Would Make a Confession.
Wisdom of Merlyn, The, *sel*.

Bly, Robert (b. 1926)
After Long Busyness.
After the Industrial Revolution, All Things
   Happen at Once.
Afternoon Sleep.
Anger Against Children, *sels*.
As a Child.
August Rain.
Come with Me.
Counting Small-Boned Bodies.
Day We Visited New Orleans, The.
Dead Seal [near McClure's Beach], The.
Defeated.
Dream of Retarded Children, A.
Dream of William Carlos Williams, A.
Driving through Minnesota during the Hanoi
   Bombings.
Driving to Town Late to Mail a Letter.
Driving West in 1970.
Eel in the Cave, The.
Empty Place, An.
Evolution from the Fish.
Exhausted Bug, The.
For My Son Noah, Ten Years Old.
French Generals, The.
Frost and His Enemies.
Gaiety of Form, The.
Gratitude to Old Teachers.
Great Society, The.
Hunting Pheasants in a Cornfield.
In a Train.
Johnson's Cabinet Watched by Ants.
Kneeling Down to Look [or Peer] into a
   Culvert.
Listening to a Cricket in the Wainscoting.
Listening to the Köln Concert.
Looking at New-Fallen Snow from a Train.
Looking into a Tide Pool.
Man Who Didn't Know What Was His, The.
My Father at 85.
My Father's Neck.
My Father's Wedding.
Night Abraham Called to the Stars, The.
Old Boards.
On the Oregon Coast.
Pitzeem and the Mare.
Potato, A.
Prayer for My Father.
Prodigal Son, The.
Resemblance Between Your Life and a Dog,
   The.
Romans Angry about the Inner World.
Russian, The.
Scandal, The.
Seeing the Eclipse in Maine.
Six Winter Privacy Poems.
Snowbanks North of the House.
Taking the Hands of Someone You Love.
Things My Brother and I Could Do.
Things to Think.
This Night: For Walt Whitman.
To President Bush at the Start of the Gulf War.
Turtle, A.
Two Ramages for Old Masters.
Visiting Emily Dickinson's Grave with Robert
   Francis.
Waking from Sleep.
Warning to the Reader.
Watering the Horse.
Week after Your Death, A.
When My Dead Father Called.
Yellow Dot, The.

Boadiba
Autozobop.
Madam President.

We Pass through a Foreigner's House.
Boake, Barcroft Henry (1866–92)
Digger's Song, The.
Boas, Guy (1896–1966)
Beard and Bicycle.
Bobis, Merlinda
Driving to Katoomba.
Word Gifts for an Australian Critic.
Bobrowski, Johannes (1917–65)
Dead Language.
Deserted Village.
East.
Elderblossom.
In the Torrent.
Invocation: "High on, above the lake, the mute Nowgorod."
Kaunas 1941.
Latvian Autumn, The.
Latvian Songs.
Novgorod: Coming of the Saints.
Place of Fire.
Pruzzian Elegy.
Report.
Trakl.
Volga Towns, The.
When the Rooms.
Woodland God.
Bobyshev, Dmitry [or Dmitrii] Vasil'evich (b. 1936)
Indifference.
Other World, The.
Return.
Trotsky in Mexico.
White Peacock, The.
Boccaccio, Giovanni (1313–75)
Two Dreams, The.
Bock, Jerry
Little Tin Box.
Too Close for Comfort.
Bodecker, N. M. (b. 1922)
Cats and Dogs.
First Snowflake.
Garden Calendar.
Hurry, Hurry, Mary Dear!
Miss Bitter.
Mr. 'Gator.
Mr. Slatter.
One Year.
Radish.
Small Rains.
Snowman Sniffles.
Bodel, Jean (fl. c.1200)
Les Congés du Lépreux.
Boden, Carrie
Sombreo Beach, Vancouver Island, BC.
Boden, F. C.
As I Came Home from Labour.
Bodenheim, Maxwell (1893–1954)
Death.
Interlude.
Old Age.
Poem to Gentiles.
Rear Porches of an Apartment Building, The.
Upper Family.
Bodman, Manoah (1765–1850)
Oration on Death, An, sel.
Bödvarsson, Gudmundur (1904–74)
Brother.
Boe, Deborah
Jigsaw Puzzle.
Boece [or Boethius], Hector (1465?–1536?)
Buik of the Cronicles of Scotland, sels.
Boethius (Anicius Manlius Severinus Boethius) (480–524)
Consolation of Philosophy, The ("De Consolacione Philosophie"), sels.
De Consolatione Philosophiae [Trans. Henry Vaughan], sels.
Boethius, Anicius Manlius Severinus See Boethius
Bogan, Louise (1897–1970)
After the Persian.
Alchemist, The.
Baroque Comment.

Cartography.
Cassandra.
Come, Break with Time.
Crossed Apple, The.
Crows, The.
Dark Summer.
Decoration.
Didactic Piece.
Dragonfly, The.
Dream, The.
Evening in the Sanitarium.
Evening-Star.
Heard by a Girl.
Henceforth, from the Mind.
Hypocrite Swift.
Juan's Song.
July Dawn.
Kept.
Knowledge.
Last Hill in a Vista.
Late.
M., Singing.
Man Alone.
Medusa.
Meeting, The.
Men Loved Wholly Beyond Wisdom.
Morning.
Musician.
My Voice Not Being Proud.
Night: "Cold remote islands, The."
Psychiatrist's Song.
Roman Fountain.
Several Voices Out of a Cloud.
Short Summary.
Simple Autumnal.
Sleeping Fury, The.
Song for the Last Act.
Song: "It is not now I learn."
Statue and Birds.
Sub Contra.
Tale, A.
Tears in Sleep.
To an Artist, to Take Heart.
To My Brother: Killed: Hammont Wood: October, 1918.
Train Tune.
Winter Swan.
Women.
Zone.
Bogardus, Edgar
Narcissus to Echo.
Bogen, Don
All Shook Up.
Bogen, Laurel Ann
Havana.
I Eat Lunch with a Schizophrenic.
Pygmy Headhunters and Killer Apes, My Lover and Me.
Boiardo, Matteo Maria (1441–94)
Canto de li Augei di Frunda in Frunda, Il.
Boileau-Despéaux, Nicolas (1636–1711)
Epistle to My Gardener, sels.
Boisseau, Michelle
Cassiopeia at Noon.
Fog.
Sleeplessness.
Bök, Christian (b. 1966)
Chapter A, sel.
Chapter E, sels.
Chapter I, sel.
Chapter O, sel.
Chapter U, sel.
Boker, George Henry (1823–90)
Blood, blood! The lines of every printed sheet.
Brave comrade, answer! When you joined the war.
Dirge for a Soldier.
Oh! craven, craven! while my brothers fall.
Sonnets: A Sequence on Profane Love, sels.
Bokuo (1384–1455)
For seventy-two years / I've kept the ox well under.
Boland, Eavan (b. 1944)
Achill Woman, The.
Anna Liffey.

Anorexic.
Black Lace Fan My Mother Gave Me, The.
Blossom, The.
Daphne with Her Thighs in Bark.
Distances.
Dolls Museum in Dublin, The.
Domestic Interior, sel.
Emigrant Irish, The.
Famine Road, The.
Fever.
Fond Memory.
From the Painting "Back from Market" by Chardin.
Game, The.
How We Made a New Art on Old Ground.
Huguenot Graveyard at the Heart of the City, The.
I Remember.
In Her Own Image.
Irish Poetry.
It's a Woman's World.
Latin Lesson, The.
Listen. This is the Noise of Myth.
Lost Land, The.
Love: "Dark falls on this mid-western town."
Midnight Flowers.
Mise Eire.
Mother Ireland.
My Country in Darkness.
Ode to Suburbia.
Oral Tradition, The.
Other Woman, The.
Pomegranate, The.
Ready for Flight.
Self-Portrait on a Summer Evening.
Story.
That the Science of Cartography Is Limited.
War Horse, The.
What We Lost.
Woman in Kitchen.
Woman Turns Herself into a Fish, The.
Women, The.
Bold, Alan (b. 1943)
Edinburgh Castle, sel.
Engima, The.
Malfeasance, The.
Shore.
Bold, Henry (1627–83)
Song: "Chloris, forbear a while."
Bolger, Dermot (b. 1959)
Lament for Arthur Cleary, The, sel.
Bolt, Thomas
Glimpse of Terrain.
Meditation in Loudoun County.
Way Out of the Wood, The, sel.
Bolton, Deric (1908–93)
Schiehallion.
Bolton, Edmund (1575?–1633?)
Palinode, A.
To Favonius.
Bolton, Gillie
Little Red Riding Hood and the Wolf.
Bolton, Joe (1961–90)
American Tragedy.
Fin de Siècle.
In Memory of the Boys of Dexter, Kentucky.
Lights at Newport Beach, The.
Parthenon at Nashville, The.
Bolton, Ken (b. 1949)
In Ferrara.
Nonplussed.
Bolton, Ken See Also Jenkins, John
Bomani, Mawiyah Kai el-Jamah
Roots.
Voudou Mama.
Bomani, Nadir Lasana
1/Vacant.
Bona, Mary Jo (fl. 20th cent.)
Amazone.
Dream Poem.
Bonar, Horatius (1808–90)
Fill thou my life, O Lord my God.
My Old Letters, sel.
Not what my hands have done.

Precedence.
This Do in Remembrance of Me, *sel.*
Thy Way, Not Mine.

Bonazzi, Robert
Changing Borders.
Houston's Adolescence.

Boncho (Nozawa Boncho) (d. 1714)
Linked-Verse Sequence Throughout the Town,
    The, *sel.*
Nightingale / My clogs.
Piled for burning/ Brushwood.

Boncho, Nozawa *See* Boncho

Bond, Alec
After Snow-Mobiling.

Bond, Bruce (b. 1954)
Aim.
Host.
Transparencies.

Bond, Edward
First World War Poets.
How We See.
If.

Bond, Sandra Turner (b. 1951)
Tuesday Night Affair.

Bonds, Diane
Life of the Body, The.

Bone, Kate Y. A. (1896–1985)
Catlike.
Corners.
What Might Have Been.

Bonhoeffer, Dietrich
Who Am I?

Bonitaz Nuño, Rubén (b. 1923)
Smoke.

Bonitto-Burwell, Toneka Nathene
Going Home.
Leaving Winston-Salem.

Bonnefoy, Yves (b. 1923)
À la voix de Kathleen Ferrier.
All, the Nothing, The.
Book, for Growing Old, The.
Book, for Growing Old, The.
De Natura Rerum.
Livre, pour vieillir, Le.
Neige, La.
Passer-by, these are words.
Remember the Island Where They Build the
    Fire.
Snow, The.
Stone, A.
Summer Again.
Tâche d'espérance, La.
Task of Hope, The.
To the Voice of Kathleen Ferrier.
Top of the World, The.
Voice, A.
Voix, Une.
Well, The.
What House Would You Build For Me.
Words of Evening, The.

Bonset, I. K. (1883–1931)
Remembering the Night Fountains.
X-Rays.

Bontemps, Arna (1902–73)
Black Man Talks of Reaping, A.
Blight.
Dark Girl.
God Give to Men.
My Heart has Known its Winter.
Nocturne at Bethesda.
Nocturne of the Wharves.
Reconnaissance.
Return, The.
Southern Mansion.
To a Young Girl Leaving the Hill Country.

Booth, Hilary (b. 1956)
Our Skin Is Paper.
Poem for Central America.
Preface to I Am Rain.

Booth, Kwan
Untitled One.

Booth, Philip (b. 1925)
Bee.
First Lesson.

Fog-Talk.
Heading Out.
How to See Deer.
March Again.
Navigation.
Original Sequence.
Public Broadcast.
Relations: Old Light / New Sun / Postmistress /
    Earth / 04421.
Seasons.
Seeing Auden Off.
Sixty-Six.
Stations.
Stefansson Island.
Within.

Boothby, Frances (*fl.* c.1669)
To My Most Honord Cosen, Mrs Somerset on
    the Unjust Censure Past Upon My Poore
    Marcelia.

Bopp, Raul (1898–1984)
Black Snake, *sels.*

Borawski, Walta (b. 1947)
Power of One.
Some of Us Wear Pink Triangles.
Talking to Jim.

Borden, William
Morning Chamber Orchestra Near Piney Crick,
    Wyoming, 7 A.M., The.

Borges, Jorge Luis (1899–1986)
Apocryphal Gospel, An, *sels.*
Ars Poetica: "To look at the river made of time
    and water."
Baruch Spinoza.
Borges and I.
Borges and Myself.
Camden, 1892.
Chess.
Compass.
Conjectural Poem.
Dreamtigers.
Enigmas, The.
Everness.
Everything and Nothing.
Ewigkeit.
Golem, The.
Houses like Angels.
In Praise of Darkness.
Inferno 1, 32.
John 1:14 (1964).
John 1:14 (1969).
Juan Lopez and John Ward.
Labyrinth, The.
Limits.
Limits (or Good-byes).
Limits (or Good-byes).
Manuscript Found in a Book of Joseph Conrad.
Matthew XXV:30.
Mythical Founding of Buenos Aires, The.
Oedipus and the Riddle.
Other Tiger, The.
Other Tiger, The.
Page to Commemorate Colonel Suárez, Victor
    at Junín, A.
Patio.
Poem of the Gifts.
Poem Written in a Copy of *Beowulf.*
Possession of Yesterday.
Sea, The.
Soldier of Urbina, A.
Spinoza.
St. John, *sels.*
St. Luke, *sels.*
St. Matthew, *sels.*
To the Nightingale.
Toenails.
Witness, The.

Borgmann, Kendra
Bed.
Rodeo Tangent.

Borisov, Georgi (b. 1950)
And when the winter wind rushed straight into
    my heart.
Gates.
Horse, The: "Up the moss-grown."
Ravens.

What Freedom Said.

Borisova, Maya
Dry birch tree stood, The.
It's not when they leave.

Born, Anne
End of the Row.
I chuck their chins.

Bornemisza, Péter (1535–84)
How Woeful It Is For Me.

Bornholdt, Jenny
Instructions for How to Get Ahead of Yourself
    While the Light Still Shines.

Boroditskaya, Marina (b. 1954)
Christmas Eve.
Now I am a fan of silence.
Poor composer.
So much gentleness from unknown men.
Sound Letter.

Borowski, Tadeusz (1922–51)
Farewell to Maria.
Green of the distant meadows, lightly.
Night over Birkenau.
Project: Flag.
Sun of Auschwitz, The.
Sun of Auschwitz, The.
Two Countries.

Borregaard, Ebbe (b. 1933)
Sketches for 13 Sonnets.

Borson, Roo (b. 1952)
After a Death.
City Lights.
Rain.
Save Us From.
Talk.

Borthwick, Pat
Scan.
Ward Mouth.

Borthwick, Priscilla
Forest.
Out of Bounds.

Boruch, Marianne (b. 1950)
All Those People.
Book of Hand Shadows, The.
Camouflage.
Elegy: "Before the basil blackened. Before
    plates."
Hammer Falls, Is Falling, The.
Interior with a Violin.
Light.
Moss Burning.
Omens.
Perennial Garden.
Piano Tuning.
Sewing.
Simple Machines.
Think of the Words.
Way the Dying Hear Things, The.
Window, The.
Year in Hawaii.

Borum, Wille ("Memphis Willie B.")
Bad Girl Blues.

Boryu (*fl* 18th cent.)
Cloud above lotus / It too.

Bosley, Keith
Bird Sips Water.

Bosnick, Eli
Larger Loneliness, A.

Bosquet, Alain (1919–98)
Celebrities.
Lovers, The: "I said: 'Your Christian name?'."
Old Gentleman, An.

Boss, Laura (b. 1938)
At the Nuclear Rally.
Candy Lady, The.
My Ringless Fingers on the Steering Wheel
    Tell the Story.
Sitting in the Doctor's Office the Next Day.
When You Are Grown, Amanda Rose.

Bosselaar, Laure-Anne (b. 1943)
English Flavors.
Listener of Bats.

Bossidy, John Collins (1860–1928)
Boston.

Boston, B. H.
Apiary.
By All Lights: 1959.
Savage, Our Fathers, The.

Boswell, Margie B. (1875–1952)
Girls of the Rodeo.

Bottke, Amy
How to Approach Your Lover's Wife.

Bottomley, Gordon (b. 1874)
Dawn.
Eager Spring.
End of the World, The.
Suilven and the Eagle, sels.
To Iron-Founders and Others.

Bottoms, David (b. 1949)
Armored Hearts.
Boy Shepherds' Simile, The.
Bronchitis.
Chinese Dragons.
Daughter's Fever, A.
Desk, The.
Homage to Lester Flatt.
Horseshoes.
In a U-Haul North of Damascus.
In the Black Camaro.
Night Strategies.
Recording the Spirit Voices.
Sierra Bear.
Sunday Dinner, A.
Under the Vulture-Tree.

Boucicault, Dion (1820–1890)
I'm Very Happy Where I Am: A Peasant
  Woman's Song, 1864.
Wearing of the Green, The.

Boughton, Mrs. (b. c.1600, d. after 1650)
Epitaph: "When Oxford gave thee two degrees
  in art."

Boullosa, Carmen (b. 1954)
Elysian Garden.
Jardín Elíseo.

Boulus, Sargon (b. 1944)
Entries for a Possible Poem.

Bourdillon, Francis William (1852–1921)
Night Has a Thousand Eyes, The.

Bourne, Lesley-Anne (b. 1964)
Boy I Never Met, The.
Out of the Blizzard.
She Sends Him a Postcard of the Sea.
Teaching My Husband to Swim.

Bourne, Vincent (1695–1747)
Snail, The.

Bourne, W. O.
Heart's Fine Gold, The.

Bourque, Darrell
Durer's Apollo.
Old Women Fishing from Bridges.

Bousoño, Carlos (b. 1923)
Cost of Truth, The.
Door, The.
En la Ceniza Hay un Milagro.
How Am I To Tell You.
Pero Cómo Decírtelo.
Precio de la Verdad.
Puerta, La.
There's a Miracle Going On in the Ashes.
Three Poems on Death.
Tres Poemas Sobre la Muerte.

Boutens, P. C. (1870–1943)
Lonely Night.

Bouvard, Marguerite
Landscape: "Dimensions are dizzying; peaks,
  The."

Bouwers, Lenze L. (b. 1940)
Final Signs, The.

Bowdan, Janet
Year, The.

**Bowen, Charles Synge Christopher Bowen,
  Baron (1835–96)**
Rain It Raineth, The.

Bowen, Euros (b. 1904)
Blackthorn.
In Chartres.
Nettles in May.

Nettles in May.
Nightingale, The.
Power of Song, The.
Winged in Gold.
Youth of the Language, The.

Bowen, Geraint (b. 1915)
Ode in Praise of the Farmer, sels.

Bowen, Kevin
Playing Basketball with the Viet Cong.

Bowering, George (b. 1938)
Dancing Bones.
Do Sink.
Grandfather.
Kerrisdale Elegies, sel.
Kingdome 1974, The.
Leaves Flipping.
My Father in New Zealand.
Swing, The.

Bowering, Marilyn (b. 1949)
Autobiography, sels.
Madrigal, a Lullaby for Xan.
Widow's Winter.

Bowers, Edgar (b. 1924)
Afternoon at the Beach, An.
Aix-La-Chappelle, 1945.
Amor Vincit Omnia.
Astronomers of Mont Blanc, The.
Autumn Shade, sels.
Elegy, An: December, 1970.
From William Tyndale to John Frith.
In the Last Circle.
Living Together.
Prince, The.
Stoic, The: For Laura Von Courten.

Bowers, Mildred
Answer.

Bowers, Neal
Conversions.
Dead Man Interview.
Flight: "River slops under the bridge, The."
On the Elvis Mailing List.
Tenth-Year Elegy.

Bowes-Lyon, Lilian (1895–1949)
Feather, The.

Bowles, Paul (1910–86)
Extract.

Bowles, William Lisle (1762–1854)
At a Village in Scotland.
Coombe Ellen, sel.
Grown Old Together.
Languid, and sad, and slow.
On the Death of William Linley, esq.
Sonnet 5: "Evening, as slow thy placid shades
  descend."
Time and Grief.
To a Friend.
To the River Cherwell.
To the River Itchin, near Winton.
To the River Wenbeck.
Written at Bamborough Castle.

Bowling, Tim (b. 1964)
Morenz.

Bowman, Catherine (b. 1957)
Demographics.
Dove at Sundown.
El Paso Times "World of Women," The, sel.
Heart.
Jackie in Cambodia.
My Knicks Are Going to Beat Your Spurs—
  NBA Souvenir Bracelet 1999 for My Long
  Distance Love.
No Sorry.
1-800-HOT-RIBS

Bowman, Peter (b. 1952)
Beach Red, sel.

Bowring, Sir John (1510–55)
In the Cross of Christ I Glory.

Boyarskikh, Ekaterina (b. 1976)
Person is reflected by the whirlpool, not the
  face, A.

Boychuk, Bogdan
Fairy Tale, A.

Boyd, Elisse (fl. 1952)
Guess Who I Saw Today.

Boyd, Marion Margaret
Sea Spray.

Boyd, Mark Alexander (1563–1601)
Fra Bank to Bank, Fra Wood to Wood I Rin.

Boyd, Melba Joyce (b. 1950)
Epitaph for Etheridge Knight.

"Boyd, Nancy" See Millay, Edna St. Vincent

Boyd, Thomas (1898–1935)
King's Son, The.

Boyden, Polly Chase
Mud.

Boye, Karin (1900–41)
That profound waiting time.

Boylan, Grace Duffie (1861–1935)
Dames of Washington.
Wooing the Bicycle.

Boyle, Charles (b. 1951)
Species.

Boyle, Darl Macleod
Curtain, The.

Boyle, Frances (b. 1954)
Hand Game.

Boyle, Kay (b. 1903)
Complaint for Mary and Marcel, A, sels.
Monody to the Sound of Zithers.
Mothers: "In the still of night."
Ode to a Maintenance Man and His Family.
Poets.
Summer: "Flying curved to the wind shear-
  waters turn their bodies in the wave."
To a Seaman Dead on Land.
What Parents Do Not Yet Know.

Boyle, Maxwell
Silver Creature.

Boyse, Samuel (1708–49)
Triumphs of Nature, The, sels.

Brabazon, Francis
Victoria Market.

Bracho, Coral (b. 1951)
Allure of Forms, The.
Deleite de las formas, El.
Desde esta luz.
En esta oscura mezquita tibia.
Fish of Fleeting Skin.
From Their Eyes Adorned With Vitreous
  Sands.
From This Light.
Hipotético espectador, El.
Hypothetical Spectator, The.
In This Warm Dark Mosque.
Misterios del tacto, Los.
Mysteries of Touch, The.
On Contact Opens Its Indigo Pit.
On the Facets: The Flashing.
Peces de piel fugaz.
Piedra en el agua de la cordura, Una.
Piedra en la arena.
Sediment of Lukewarm and Radiant Rain.
Sobre él discurren con suavidad.
Stone in the Sand.
Stone in the Water of Sanity, A.
Upon It They Gently Reflect.

Brackenbury, Alison (b. 1953)
Cycles.
Produce of Cyprus.

Bradbury, Ray
Byzantium I Come Not From.
Switch on the Night.

Bradford, Edwin Emanuel (1860–1944)
His Mother Drinks.
Tree of Knowledge, The, sels.

Bradford, Elizabeth (1663?–1731)
To the Reader, in Vindication of This Book.

Bradford, Perry (1893–1970)
Crazy Blues.

Brading, Tilla
Punt gliding under a chain of smiles, A.

Bradley, Dickie
Sista.
Souls of Poets, The.

Bradley, George (b. 1953)
At the Other End of the Telescope.
E Pur Si Muove.

Electrocuting an Elephant.

Bradley, Jerry
  For a Texas Beauty.
  How the Big Thicket Got Smaller.

Bradley, John (b. 1950)
  Improper Disposal.
  Sailors Shielding Their Eyes During Atomic
    Bomb Test, Bikini, 1947.

Bradley, Leo
  Sub Umbra.

Bradstreet, Anne (c.1612–72)
  Another ("Anne Bradstreate.").
  Another.
  Another.
  As Weary Pilgrim, Now at Rest.
  Author to Her Book, The.
  Before the Birth of One of Her Children.
  Contemplations, sels.
  Dialogue between Old England and New, A.
  Epitaph on my Dear and Ever Honored Mother
    Mrs. Dorothy Dudley.
  Flesh and the Spirit, The.
  For Deliverance from a Fever.
  Four Ages of Man, The, sels.
  [Here Follows Some] Verses upon the Burning
    of Our House [July 10th, 1666. Copied Out
    of a Loose Paper].
  In Honour of that High and Mighty Princess
    Queen Elizabeth of Happy Memory, sels.
  In Memory of My Dear Grandchild Anne
    Bradstreet Who Deceased June 20, 1669,
    Being Three Years and Seven Months Old.
  In Memory of My Dear Grandchild Elizabeth
    Bradstreet Who Deceased August, 1665,
    Being a Year and Half Old.
  In Reference to Her Children, 23 June, 1659
    [or 1659].
  Letter to Her Husband, Absent upon Public[k]
    Employment, A.
  On My Dear Grandchild Simon Bradstreet,
    [Who Died on 16TH November, 1669,
    Being But A Month And One Day Old].
  Prologue, The: "To sing of wars, of
    captain[e]s, and of kings.", sel.
  To Her Father, with Some Verses.
  To My Dear and Loving Husband.
  To My Dear Children.
  To the Memory of My Dear and Ever Honored
    Father Thomas Dudley Esq. Who Deceased
    July 31, 1653, and of His Age 77.
  Vanity of All Worldly Things, The.
  Vanity of All Worldly Things, The, sel.
  Winter: "Cold, moist, young phlegmy Winter
    now doth lie."

Brady, Edwin James (1869–1925)
  Whaler's Pig, The.

Braid, Kate (b. 1947)
  Glenn Gould Poems, sels.

Brainard, Joe (b. 1942)
  Aug. 29, 1967.
  I Remember.
  I Remember, sel.
  I Remember More, sel.
  More I Remember More, sel.

Braithwaite, William Stanley (1878–1962)
  City Garden, A.
  House of Falling Leaves, The.
  Rhapsody.
  Rye Bread.

Brammer, Julius
  Just a Gigolo.

Branch, Anna Hempstead (1875–1937)
  Connecticut Road Song.
  Ere the Golden Bowl Is Broken.
  In the Beginning Was the Word.
  Monk in the Kitchen, The.
  Sonnets from a Lock Box, sels.

Branch, John Watusi
  Farewell Queen Mother Moore.

Brand, Dionne (b. 1953)
  Blues Spiritual for Mammy Prater.
  Canto 1: "Ashes head to toes."
  Canto 2: "Ancestor dirt."
  Every Chapter of the World, sel.

Hard Against the Soul, sel.
  No Language Is Neutral.
  Thirsty.
  Wind.
  Winter Epigrams, sels.

Brandi, John
  After Li Ch'ing-Chao.
  In What Disappears.
  Perhaps.
  Preparing the Nets at New Stuyahok.
  Yagul.

Brandt, Diana (b. 1952)
  Great dark rush of mothering, The.
  Little one, black angel.
  My mother found herself one late summer.
  Nonresistance, or love Mennonite style.
  There are no words in me for Gaza, for what i
    saw.
  When i was five i thought heaven was located.

Brannan, Jay
  Texas Sunrise, A.

Brannon, Jack
  Evolution on 38th Street.

Brant, Beth (b. 1941)
  Ride the Turtle's Back.
  Stillborn Night.

Braschi, Giannina (b. 1954)
  Final Manuscript.

Brasfield, James
  Celan.

Brass, Perry (b. 1947)
  I Have This Vision of Madness.
  Only Silly Faggots Know.
  There Isn't Any Death.

Brathwaite, Edward Kamau (b. 1930)
  Ancestors.
  Arrivants: A New World Trilogy, The, sels.
  Blues.
  Caliban.
  Calypso.
  Citadel.
  Colombe.
  How Europe Underdeveloped Africa.
  Irae.
  Journeys, The.
  Making of the Drum, The.
  Mmenson.
  Naima.
  New Year Letter.
  Ogun.
  Prelude: "Drum skin whip."
  Rites, sel.
  Stone: "When the stone fall that morning out
    of the johncrow sky."
  Trane.
  Visibility Trigger, The.

**Brathwaite [or Brathwait], Richard (1588?–
1673)**
  Vandunk's Four Humours, in Quality and
    Quantity.

Braun, Henry
  To Fat Boy, the Bomb.

Braun, Richard Emil (b. 1934)
  Goose.
  Lilies, The.
  Seeking an Explanation.

Braun, Volker
  Desert Storm.

Braunstein, Evan
  Newark.

Brautigan, Richard (1935–c.1990)
  All Watched Over by Machines of Loving
    Grace.
  It's Raining in Love.

Braxton, Charlie R. (b. 1961)
  Apocalypse.
  Arts Are Black, The.
  Bluesman.
  Word/Life.

Braxton, Joanne M. (b. 1950)
  Invisibles.
  Zoning.

Braxton, Jodi (b. 1950)
  Conversion.

Bray, J. J. (b. 1912)
  Execution of Madame du Barry, The.

Brebner, Diana (1956–2001)
  Golden Lotus, The, sels.

Brecht, Bertolt (1898–1956)
  Alabama Song.
  Bad Time for Poetry.
  Burning of the Books, The.
  Changing the Wheel.
  Concerning the Infanticide, Marie Farrar.
  Contemplating Hell.
  Epistle on Suicide.
  First Psalm (Posthumous).
  Fishing-Tackle, The.
  Friends, The.
  From a German War Primer.
  German War Primer, A, sel.
  God of War, The.
  Good Woman of Szechwan, The, sels.
  I, the Survivor.
  In Dark Times.
  Late Lamented Fame of the Giant City of New
    York, sels.
  Letter to the Actor Charles Laughton
    concerning the Work on the Play "The Life
    of Galileo"
  Mary.
  Mask of Evil, The.
  1940.
  Of Poor B.B.
  On Reading a Recent Greek Poet.
  One-Armed Man in the Undergrowth, The.
  Solution, The.
  St. Luke, sels.
  There is no greater crime than leaving.
  This Summer's Sky.
  Three Fragments.
  To My Little Radio.
  To Those Born Later, sels.
  War Has Been Given a Bad Name.
  What a bankruptcy! How.
  What Did the Nazi Send His Wife?
  What people they were! Their boxers the
    strongest!
  When Evil-Doing Comes Like Falling Rain.
  World's One Hope, The.

Brecht, Stefan (b. 1924)
  Sex, sel.
  Silence.
  Silence, 2.
  Thanksgiving (1974).

Breckenridge, Jill
  Civil Blood, sels.
  Cooking Catalogue.
  General John Cabell Breckinridge.

Breedlove, Nicole (b. 1971)
  Black and Divided or Chittlins and Caviar.
  New Miz Praise de Lawd, The.

Breeze, Jean Binta (b. 1957)
  Dubbed Out.
  Eena Mi Corner.
  Mother. . .Sister. . .Daughter.
  Natural High.
  Playing the Messiah.
  Red Rebel Song.
  Riddym Ravings (The Mad Woman's Poem).
  Wife of Bath Speaks in Brixton Market.

Brehm, John (b. 1955)
  At the Poetry Reading.
  Sea of Faith.
  When My Car Broke Down.

Breidenbach, Tom
  Confessional.

"Breitman, Hans" See Leland, Charles Godfrey

Bremer, Carla Faesler (b. 1967)
  Butcher Shop.
  Carnicería.
  Cena de un 10 de Abríl.
  Crack, The.
  Dinner on an April 10th.
  En la ventana.
  Festival of Izcalli or Eighteenth Month.
  Festival of Xócotl Huetzi or Tenth Month.
  Fiesta de izcalli o décimo octavo mes.
  Fiesta de xócotl huetzi o décimo mes.

Grieta, La.
In the Window.
Metro Taxqueña.
Metro Taxqueña.
No hay centros pero el círculo existe.
There are no centers but the circle exists.

Brendan-Brown, Sean
Dark Side of Dazzle, The.

Brennan, Christopher John (1870–1932)
Quest of Silence, The, *sels.*
Sweet Silence after Bells!

Brent, Earl (*fl.* 1946)
Angel Eyes.

Brent, Hally Carrington (b. 1943?)
I Think I Know No Finer Things than Dogs.

Brereton, John Le Gay (1871–1933)
Unborn.

Breton, André (1896–1966)
Always for the First Time.
Corset Mystère, Le.
Dreaming I See You.
Free Union.
Free Union.
Free Union.
Go For Broke.
In the Eyes of the Gods.
Magnetic Fields, The, *sels.*
Man and a Woman Absolutely White, A.
Man and Woman Absolutely White, A.
Manifesto of Surrealism (1924), *sels.*
Marquis de Sade, The.
More than Suspect.
Mystery Corset, The.
Mystery Corset, The.
Ode to Charles Fourier, *sel.*
On me dit que là-bas.
On the Road to San Romano.
On the Road to San Romano.
Poem-Object.
Sur la route de san romano.
They Tell Me That Over There.
Toujours pour la première fois.
Union libre, L'
Vigilance.
Vigilance.
War.

Breton, Andre *See Also* Eluard, Paul

Breton, Nicholas (1542–1626)
Arbor of Amorous Devises, The, *sels.*
Chess Play, The.
Honourable Entertainment Given to the
 Queen's Majesty in Progress at Elvetham,
 1591, The, *sels.*
Oh That My Heart Could Hit Upon a Strain.
Olden Love-making.
Passionate Shepherd, The, *sels.*
Report Song [in a Dream], A.
Service Is No Heritage.
Solemne Long Enduring Passion, A, *sels.*

Brett, Doris (b. 1953)
For My Mother.

Brett, Lily
I Keep Forgetting.
La Pathétique.
Leaving You.
My Mother's Friend.

Brew, Kwesi (b. 1928)
Plea for Mercy, A.

Brewer, Gaylord (b. 1965)
Christ, the End.
Essays on Excess and Escape.
Journals, The.
Last Word, The.
Mountains.
Penance and the Work Week.
Teen Drowns in Rehabilitation Camp Days
 Before 17th Birthday, Questions Persist.
Transport of the Dead.

Brewka, N. M.
Elinor White Frost Speaks.

Brewster, Elizabeth (b. 1922)
Moving Image, The.
Return of the Native: "This is the true land of
 fairy tales."

Where I Come From.

Breytenbach, Breyten (b. 1939)
Asylum.
Black City, The.
Breyten Prays for Himself.
Constipation.
Dar es-Salaam: Harbour of Peace.
Dreams Are Also Wounds.
Dung-beetle.
Eavesdropper.
Exile, Representative.
Firewing.
First Prayer for the Hottentotsgod.
Journey.
Lullaby.
Out There.
Padmapani.
Struggle for the Taal, The.
There Is Life.
Threat of the Sick.
Write Off.

Bricusse, Leslie (b. 1931)
Candy Man, The.
Goldfinger.
What Kind of Fool Am I?
Who Can I Turn To (When Nobody Needs
 Me?).

Bridgeman, Pam (b. 1950)
Cockatoo.

Bridges, Constance Quarterman
Gordian Knot.

Bridges, Robert (1844–1930)
Awake, My Heart, to Be Loved.
Elegy on a Lady, Whom Grief for the Death of
 Her Betrothed Killed.
Eros.
Etosion achthos aroures.
Evening Darkens Over, The.
Garden in September, The.
Ghosts.
Growth of Love, The, *sels.*
I Have Loved Flowers.
I Heard a Linnet Courting.
I Love All Beauteous Things.
In Autumn Moonlight, When the White Air
 Wan.
London Snow.
Low Barometer.
Muse and Poet.
My Delight and Thy Delight.
Nightingales.
Noel; Christmas Eve, 1913.
On a Dead Child.
Passer-by, A.
Pater Filio.
Snow Lies Sprinkled on the Beach, The.
Storm is over, the land hushes to rest, The.
Testament of Beauty, The, *sels.*
Thee will I love, my God and King.
Thou Didst Delight My Eyes.
To Francis Jammes.
Weep Not To-Day.
When Death to Either Shall Come.
Winter Nightfall.

Bridges, Thomas
Homer Travestie, *sel.*

Bridgford, Kim (b. 1959)
Robert Frost.

Bridgwater, Emmy (b. 1906)
Back to the First Bar.
Journey, The.
On the Line.

Bridie, James (1888–1951)
West End Perk, The.

Briggs, G.W. (1875–1959)
Lord, who hast made me free.

Bright, Susan
Makes Them Wild.
Riding the Currents.

Brines, Francisco (b. 1932)
Ashes in Oxford.
Beggar, The.
Ceniza en Oxford.
Dolor, El.

Grief: "With eyes happy."
Having Sunk His Chin in His Hand.
Hay una Luz que Cubre Todo el Campo.
Mendigo, El.
Mirándose.
There Is a Light That Shrouds the Whole Field.

Bringhurst, Robert (b. 1946)
Conversations with a Toad, *sel.*
Dogen, *sel.*
For the Bones of Josef Mengele, Disinterred
 June 1985.
Parable of the Voices.
Parśvanatha.
Song of Ptahhotep, The.
These Poems, She Said.

Brinkmann, Rolf Dieter (1940–75)
Self-Portrait in the Supermarket.

Brinks, Dave
Any Blue Movie.
Halo Factory, The.
Please the Carrots.
Proscenium Moon.
Secret Brain, The.
Story Pillow, The.
Tao Sequence, The.

Brinson, C. Yaphet (d. 1999)
Haiku: "Black, brother, nigga."
Sextet.

Brion, Rofel G.
Good Friday.
If Fortune Smiles.
Love Song: "One long and humid afternoon."
One Morning Beside a Pond.

Brissenden, Robert Francis (b. 1928)
Verandahs.

Bristol, Augusta Cooper (b. 1835)
Crime of the Ages, The.
Night.

Brittain, I. J. (*fl.* 1918)
Tragedy of Ida Ball Warren and Samuel
 Christie, The, *sel.*

Brock, Edwin (b. 1917)
And another thing.
Five Ways to Kill a Man.

Brock, Van K. (b. 1932)
All the Stars Are Foxfire.
I Stopped in Tupelo, Elvis.
Mary's Dream.
Remembering Dresden.
Sphinx.

Brock-Broido, Lucie
Am Moor.
Carrowmore.
Domestic Mysticism.
Her Habit.
Housekeeping.
Of the Finished World.
One Thousand Days, The.
Periodic Table of Ethereal Elements.
Prescient.
Radiating Naïveté.
Soul Keeping Company.

Broda, Martine (b. 1947)
I Wanted to Tell You.
I Wash.
Je lave.
Je voulais te l'avouer.

Brodey, Jim (b. 1942)
Identikit, *sel.*
Stone Free.

Brodsky, Joseph
Belfast Tune.
Berlin Wall Tune, The.
Elegy: "About a year has passed. I've returned
 to the place of battle."
Hawk's Cry in Autumn, The.
I Sit by the Window.
In the Lake District.
Lagoon.
Letters from the Ming Dynasty.
Love Song: "If you were drowning, I'd come
 to the rescue."
May 24, 1980.
New Stanzas to Augusta, *sel.*

October Tune.
Odysseus to Telemachus.
Part of Speech, A, *sels.*
Polar Explorer, A.
Roman Elegies.
Six Years Later.
Sonnets on the Statue of Mary, Queen of Scots, in the Luxembourg Gardens, Paris, *sels.*
To Urania.

Brody, Alter (b. 1895)
Family Album, A.
Ghetto Twilight.
Kartúshkiya-Beróza.
Lamentations.
Times Square.
Winter Nocturne: The Hospital.

Brome, Alexander (1620–66)
Epithalamy.
Leveller's Rant, The.
New-Courtier, The.
On Sir G. B. his defeat.
Pastoral on the King's Death, The; [Written in 1648].
Plain Dealing.
Prisoners, The, *sel.*
Resolve, The.
Riddle, The: "No more, no more."
Saints' Encouragement, The.
Satire on the Rebellion, A.

Bromige, David (b. 1933)
Choice.
Eastward Ho! A Succession.
Edible World, The.
Lines: "Repressive desublimation."
Log.
Logical Positivist, The.
Point, The.
Tight Corners, *sel.*

Bronk, William (1918–99)
At Tikal.
Corals and Shells.
I Thought It Was Harry.
Ignorant Lust After Knowledge, The.
Life Supports.
Mayan Glyphs Unread, The.
Memorial: "If we do not lift quickly the dead bodies from the beaches."
Metonymy as an Approach to a Real World.
Plainest Narrative, The.
Soldiers in Death.
Strong Room of the House, The.
Way, The.
Where It Ends.
World, The.

Brontë, Anne ("Acton Bell") (1820–49)
Captive Dove, The.
Doubter's Prayer, The.
Fragment, A: "Maiden, thou wert thoughtless once."
He Doeth All Things Well.
Home.
Night.
Penitent, The.
Song.

Brontë, Charlotte ("Currer Bell") (1816–55)
Again I find myself alone.
Diving.
Is this my tomb, this humble stone.
Like wolf—and black bull or goblin hound.
Lonely Lady, The.
Obscure and little seen my way.
On the Death of Anne Brontë.
On the Death of Emily Jane Brontë.
Orphan Child, The.
Pilate's Wife's Dream.
Reason.
Retrospection, *sel.*
'What does she dream of'
Young Man Naughty's Adventure.

Brontë, Emily Jane ("Ellis Bell") (1818–48)
All hushed and still within the house.
Alone I sat; the summer day.
Aye there it is! It wakes tonight.
Come, walk with me.
Day Dream, A.

Death Scene, A.
F. de Samara to A. G. A.
Hope.
I am the only being whose doom.
I'm happiest when most away.
Little while, a little while, A.
Long Neglect Has Worn Away.
Love and Friendship.
Night Wind, The.
No Coward Soul is Mine.
Old Stoic, The.
Prisoner, The. A Fragment, *sels.*
Remembrance: "Cold in the earth—and the deep snow piled above thee!"
Shall Earth no more inspire thee.
Song: "Fall, leaves, fall; die, flowers, away;."
Song: "Linnet in the rocky dells, The."
Spellbound.
Stanzas: "Often rebuked, yet always back returning."
Stars.
Tell me, tell me, smiling child.
To Imagination.
Visionary, The.
What winter floods, what showers of spring.
Why do I hate that lone green dell?

Brook, Donna
April 27, 1994.
Message to Mary Ferrari in Jo'Burg.
Pink Diapers.
Poem Wrapped Around Quotation from Samantha Power.
Why I Am a Whore.

Brooke, Henry (1703?–1783)
Fox Hunt, The.

Brooke, L. Leslie (1862–1940)
Johnny Crow's Garden.

Brooke, Rupert (1887–1915)
Busy Heart, The.
Chilterns, The.
Clouds.
Dining-Room Tea.
Dust.
Great Lover, The.
Heaven.
Hill, The.
Mary and Gabriel.
Now, God be thanked Who has matched us with His hour, *sels.*
Old Vicarage, Grantchester, The.
Second Best.
Sonnet: In Time of Revolt.
Sonnet: "Oh! Death will find me, long before I tire."
Sonnet Reversed.

Brookes, John
Officers and Gentlemen Down Under.

Brooks, Adrian (b. 1947)
Here is the queen.

Brooks, Brenda (b. 1952)
Anything.
Life, Having Become Still.
Moon in the Mirror.

Brooks, Charles Timothy (1813–88)
Lines: Composed at the Old Temples of Maralipoor.
Our Island Home.

Brooks, Fred Emerson (1850–1923)
New Baby, The.
Old Eagle, *sel.*
Stuttering Lover, The.

Brooks, Gwendolyn (1917–2000)
Battle, The.
Bean Eaters, The.
Birth in a narrow room, The.
Blackstone Rangers, The.
Blackstone Rangers, The, *sels.*
Boy Breaking Glass.
Boy Died in My Alley, The.
Bronzeville Mother Loiters in Mississippi, A. Meanwhile, a Mississippi Mother Burns Bacon.
Bronzeville Woman in a Red Hat.
Building.
Children Going Home, *sels.*

Coora Flower, The.
Crazy Woman, The.
Cynthia in the Snow.
Egg Boiler, The.
Gay Chaps at the Bar, *sels.*
In Honor of David Anderson Brooks, My Father.
Jessie Mitchell's Mother.
Langston Hughes.
Last Quatrain of the Ballad of Emmett Till, The.
Life of Lincoln West, The.
Lovely Love, A.
Lovers of the Poor, The.
Malcolm X.
Marie Lucille.
Medgar Evers.
Mentors.
Michael Is Afraid of the Storm.
Mrs. Small.
Music for Martyrs.
My dreams, my works must wait till after hell.
Narcissa.
Near-Johannesburg Boy, The.
Negro Hero.
Notes from the Childhood and the Girlhood, *sels.*
Of Robert Frost.
Penitent Considers Another Coming of Mary, A.
Pete at the Zoo.
Piano after War.
Primer for Blacks.
Queen of the Blues.
Riot.
Second Sermon on the Warpland, The.
Speech to the Young Speech to the Progress-Toward (Among Them Nora and Henry III).
Still Do I Keep My Look, My Identity.
Street in Bronzeville, A, *sels.*
Sundays of Satin-Legs Smith, The.
Third Sermon on the Warpland, The.
To An Old Black Woman, Homeless and Indistinct.
To Be in Love.
To Black Women.
To the Diaspora.
Ulysses, *sels.*
We Real Cool.
When you have forgotten Sunday: the love story.
White Troops Had Their Orders but the Negroes Looked Like Men.
Winnie, *sels.*
Womanhood, The, *sels.*
Young Africans.

Brooks, Jonathan Henderson (1904–45)
Muse in Late November.

Brooks, Maria Gowen (1795–1845)
Zophiël or, the Bride of Seven, *sels.*

Brooks, Phillips (1835–93)
O Little Town of Bethlehem.

Brooks, Shelton (1886–1975)
Darktown Strutter's Ball, The.
Some of These Days.
(That's the Way) Dixieland Started Jazz.
Walkin' the Dog.

Brooks, Shirley (1816–74)
For A' That and A' That.

Brooks, Sonya (b. 1968)
Grandma Talk.
Middle Passage.
Sweet molasses.

Brooks, William E.
Pilate Remembers.

Broome, William (1689–1745)
Rose-Bud, The.

Broonzy, Big Bill
Southern Blues, The.

Brosman, Catharine Savage
Olives.

Brossa, Joan (1919–99)
Note.

Brossard, Nicole (b. 1943)
Barbizon, The, *sels.*
I Want to Revise This Sequence.
Je veux revoir cette séquence.
Typhoon Thrum.

Brother Yao
Born.
Passing Through This House.
Science of Forgetting, The.
Soledad.

Brougham and Vaux, Henry Peter Brougham, 1st Baron (1778–1868)
Orator's Epitaph, The.

Broughton, James
Twin Flames.

Broughton, James Richard (b. 1913)
Aglow in Nowhere.

Broughton, T. Alan (b. 1936)
Shall I Compare Thee?

Broumas, Olga (b. 1949)
After *The Little Mariner.*
Amazon Twins.
Artemis.
Beauty and the Beast.
Calypso.
Caritas, *sel.*
Choir, The.
Etymology.
For Every Heart.
If I Yes.
Landscape with Next of Kin.
Lumens.
Masseuse, The.
Next to the *Café Chaos.*
Old Wives' Tale.
On Earth.
Oregon Landscape with Lost Lover.
Pealing, The.
Perpetua.
Photo Genic.
Photovoltaic.
Privacy.
Rapunzel.
Sappho's Gymnasium ("For healthy cells please remember.").
Sappho's Gymnasium ("Outside memory worship never dies.").
Sometimes, as a Child.
Song / for Sanna.
Touched.
Tryst.
Way a Child Might Believe, The.

Brouwer, Joel (b. 1968)
Aesthetics.
Conjurer's Honor.
Conservatory Pond, Central Park, New York, New York.
Development: "I learned to fuck one summer in a burgeoning subdivision."
Divorce.
Hamartia Symbolized by the Stray.
History: "In Boston, a tongue of red paint traces the city's history, from Massacre to Tea Party to Faneuil Hall."
Kelly, Ringling Bros. Oldest Elephant, Goes On Rampage.
Space Memorabilia Auction, Superior Stamp and Coin, Beverly Hills, California.
Spots, The.
Steve's Commando Paintball, San Adriano, California.

Brown, Andrea Carter (b. 1949)
Ash Wednesday, 2002.
Old Neighborhood, The.

Brown, Arthur (1947–82)
Assassination of Charlie Parker, The.

Brown, Cecil (b. 1943)
Integrating the Strawberry Swimming Pool in 1998.

Brown, Christy (1932–81)
What Her Absence Means.

Brown, D. F.
When I Am 19 I Was a Medic.

Brown, Dan (*fl.* 1996)
Where I Was.

Brown, Dorothy (Diorbhail nic a Bhriuthainn) (c.1620s–late 17th cent.)
Song to Alasdair Mac Colla, A.

Brown, Eleanor (b. 1969)
Beauty and the Prince Formerly Known as Beast.
Bitcherel.
Jezebel to the Eunuchs.
Out.
Probably the most human thing I do.
Sonnet 43.
Sonnet: "Not if you crawled from there to here, you hear?"
Tell me I'm beautiful, and bring me flowers.
Tragic Hero.
What do I have, when I contemplate this.
What Song the Syrens Sang.
When I recall you—as I often do.

Brown, Fleda
Elvis Decides to Become a Monk.

Brown, Ford Madox (1821–93)
Last of England, The.

Brown, George Mackay (b. 1921)
Ballad of John Barleycorn, the Ploughman, and the Furrow, The.
Haddock Fishermen.
Hamnavoe.
Hamnavoe Market.
Hawk, The.
Ikey: His Will in Winter Written.
Kirkyard.
Lodging, The.
Mother, The: "On Monday she stood at the wooden wash-tub."
Net, The.
Old Women, The.
Shroud.
Taxman.

Brown, Hamish
Counting Sheep.
Dogs: "We humans talk."
Salting of Snow, A.

Brown, J. Lorraine
Sonnet at Three-Speed.

Brown, James (b. 1966)
Bicycle, The.
Lesson, The: "Cleaned, lubed and wiped."

Brown, James (b. 1928) *and* Alfred Ellis
Say It Loud—I'm Black and I'm Proud.

Brown, Judy
Fire: "What makes a fire burn."

Brown, Kurt
First Time at the Wheel.
'49 Merc, A.
Good Devil, The.
Money As Water.
Return of the Prodigals.

Brown, Kysha N. (b. 1978)
Lonely Women.
Song for Serpents, A.

Brown, Laura Soul
Oh! Mercy Mercy Me! A Family Gathers to Marvin Gaye.

Brown, Lee Ann (b. 1963)
After Sappho.
Call for Vertical Integration in the Eye of the Storm, A.
Encyclopedia Botanica.
Impulse to Call & Spring Upon, The.
My epithalamion.
My Uncruel April, My Totally Equal Unfortold April Unfolded.
Respond to Me.
Shiny jewel eye.
Sonnet Around Stephanie.
You Are Not Gorgeous and I Am Coming Anyway.

Brown, Lew (1893–1958)
Best Things in Life Are Free, The.
Birth of the Blues, The.
Button Up Your Overcoat.
Don't Bring Lulu.

(Here Am I) Broken Hearted.
I Want to Be Bad.
If I Had a Talking Picture of You.
It All Depends on You.
Life Is Just a Bowl of Cherries.
Magnolia.
Maybe This Is Love.
Never Swat a Fly.
Straw Hat in the Rain.
Sunny Side Up.
Thank Your Father.
That Old Feeling.
Turn On the Heat.
Varsity Drag, The.
You're the Cream in My Coffee.

Brown, Linda Beatrice
Green Arbor, A.
Winter Sonnet.

Brown, Margaret Gillies (1921–96)
Calgary Bay.
Village Woman.

Brown, Margaret Wise (1910–52)
Little Black Bug.

Brown, Melvin E. (b. 1950)
Survival Motion: Notice.

Brown, Nathan (1807–86)
My soul is not at rest. There comes a strange.

Brown, Pamela (b. 1948)
I Remember Dexedrine. 1970.
Leaving.

Brown, Polly
This Is for Megan.

Brown, Rita Mae (b. 1944)
Sappho's Reply.

Brown Rosellen
Fry says a word.
I have a neighbor.
I want to understand light years.
Storm high.
This is no baby skin—.

Brown, Solyman (1790–1865?)
Dentologia; a Poem on the Diseases of the Teeth and Their Proper Remedies, *sel.*

Brown, Stephanie (b. 1961)
Agapé.
Allegory of the Supermarket.
Chapter One.
Feminine Intuition.
I Was a Phony Baloney!
Interview with an Alchemist in the New Age.
It Took a Village.
Marginalia.
Marriage.
No, No Nostalgia!
Schadenfreude.

Brown, Sterling Allen (1901–89)
After Winter.
Bitter Fruit of the Tree.
Cabaret.
Call Boy.
Children's Children.
Chillen Get Shoes.
Conjured.
Harlem Happiness.
He Was a Man.
Legend: "Old black man was stood on the block, The."
Long Gone.
Long Track Blues.
Ma Rainey.
Master and Man.
Memo: For the Race Orators.
Memphis Blues.
Odyssey of Big Boy.
Old King Cotton.
Old Lem.
Old Woman Remembers, An.
Riverbank Blues.
Scotty Has His Say.
Sister Lou.
Slim Greer.
Slim in Atlanta.
Slim Lands a Job?
Southern Cop.

Southern Road.
Sporting Beasley.
Strong Men.
Thoughts of Death.
To Sallie, Walking.
Virginia Portrait.
When de Saints Go Ma'chin' Home.

Brown, Stewart (b. 1951)
Let Them Call It Jazz.

Browne, Sir Thomas (1605–82)
Religio Medici, sels.
Signs of Spring.

Brown, Thomas [or "Tom"] (1663–1704)
Epitaph upon That Profound and Learned
    Casuist, the Late Ordinary of Newgate, An.
Oaths.

Brown, Thomas Edward (1830–97)
Between Our Folding Lips.
Disguises.
I Bended unto Me.
Indwelling.
Land, Ho!
My Garden.
Pain.
Preparation.
Salve!

Browne, Emma Alice
When I Am Dead.

Browne, Francis Fisher (b. 1843)
Australian Emigrant, The, sels.

Browne, Isaac Hawkins (1705–60)
Pipe of Tobacco, A, sel.

"Browne, Matthew" See Rands, William Brighty

Browne, Michael Dennis (b. 1940)
His Toys.
Knock Knock.
Lamb.
Your Sister.

Browne, Susan (b. 1952)
First Drink.

Browne, William (1591–1643)
Britannia's Pastorals, sels.
Brittania's Pastorals Book 2, sel.
[Epitaph] In Obitum M.S., X° Maij [or Maii],
    1614.
Inner Temple Masque, The, sels.
Love Who Will, for I'll Love None.
On the Countess Dowager of Pembroke.
Praise of Spenser.
Shepherd's Pipe, The, sels.
Song: "For her gait, if she be walking."
Visions, sels.

Browne, Sir William (1692–1774)
Epigram: "King to Oxford sent a troop of
    horse, The."

Brownell, Henry Howard (1820–72)
Bay Fight, The.
John Brown's Body.
Suspiria Noctis.

Browning, Elizabeth Barrett (1806–61)
Aurora Leigh, sels.
Bereavement.
Bertha in the Lane.
Best, The.
Best Thing in the World, The.
Casa Guidi Windows, sels.
Child's Thought of God, A.
Comfort.
Cowper's Grave.
Cry of the Children, The.
Cry of the Human, The, sels.
Curse for a Nation, A.
Farewells from Paradise.
Fifth Book.
Flush or Faunus.
Forced Recruit, The.
Grief.
Hiram Powers' "Greek Slave"
L.E.L.'s Last Question.
Lady Geraldine's Courtship, sels.
Lady's "Yes," The.
Lord Walter's Wife.
Loved Once.
Man's Requirements, A.

Mask, The.
Meaning of the Look, The.
Mother and Poet.
Musical Instrument, A.
My Heart and I.
On a Portrait of Wordsworth by B. R. Haydon.
Only a Curl.
Out in the Fields [with God].
Romance of the Swan's Nest, The.
Runaway Slave at Pilgrim's Point, The.
Sleep, The.
Sonnets from the Portuguese, sels.
Substitution.
Thought for a Lonely Death-Bed, A.
To Flush, My Dog.
To George Sand: A Desire.
To George Sand: A Recognition.
True Dream, A.
Year's Spinning, A.

Browning, Robert (1812–89)
Abt Vogler.
Andrea del Sarto.
Any Wife to Any Husband.
Apparent Failure.
Bishop Orders His Tomb at Saint Praxed's
    Church, The.
Blot in the 'Scutcheon, A, sels.
Caliban upon Setebos; or, Natural Theology in
    the Island.
Childe Roland to the Dark Tower Came.
Dialogue between Father and Daughter.
Dîs Aliter Visum; or, Le Byron de Nos Jours.
Epilogue: "At the midnight in the silence of
    the sleep-time."
Epilogue: "On the first of the Feast of Feasts."
Epistle Containing the Strange Medical
    Experience of Karshish, the Arab Physician,
    An.
Eternity Affirms the Hour.
Evelyn Hope.
Flight of the Duchess, The, sel.
Fra Lippo Lippi.
Garden Fancies, sels.
Grammarian's Funeral, A.
Home-Thoughts, from Abroad.
Home-Thoughts, from the Sea.
House.
How It Strikes a Contemporary.
How They Brought the Good News from
    Ghent to Aix.
In a Gondola, sels.
Incident of the French Camp.
Italian in England, The.
Johannes Agricola in Meditation.
Laboratory, The (Ancien Régime).
Last Ride Together, The.
Lost Leader, The.
Lost Mistress, The.
Love among the Ruins.
Love in a Life.
Meeting at Night.
Memorabilia.
Misconceptions.
"Moses" of Michael Angelo, The.
My Last Duchess.
Names, The.
Now.
Paracelsus, sels.
Parting at Morning.
Pauline [or Pauline; A Fragment of a
    Confession], sel.
Pied Piper of Hamelin, The, sel.
Pippa Passes, sels.
Pisgah-Sights. I.
Pisgah-Sights. II.
Porphyria's Lover.
Prospice.
Rabbi Ben Ezra.
Rhyme for a Child Viewing a Naked Venus in
    a Painting [of "The Judgement of Paris"].
Ring and the Book, The, sel.
Saul, sel.
Soliloquy of the Spanish Cloister.
Solomon and Balkis.
Sordello, sels.
Through the Metidja to Abd-el-Kadr.

To Edward FitzGerald.
Toccata of Galuppi's, A.
Twins, The.
Two in the Campagna.
Waring.
Woman's Last Word, A.
Women and Roses.
Youth and Art.

Brownjohn, Alan (b. 1931)
In a Convent Garden.
Looking at Her.
Pitman's Common Sense Arithmetic, 1917,
    sels.
September 1939.
Sonnet of a Gentleman.
Your fingers fully awake, it.

Brownlow, Timothy (b. 1941)
James Clarence Mangan in Trinity College
    Library.

Brownstein, Michael (b. 1943)
Against the Grain.
Glass Enclosure, The.
Jet Set Melodrama.
Last Spell Cast, The.
Monkey Blues.
Ninth Symphony.
Oracle Night, sel.
Paris Visitation.
Pounds and Ounces.
Stepping Out.
War.
Who Knows Where the Time Goes?

Bruce, Charles (1906–71)
Early Morning Landing.
Eastern Shore.
Nova Scotia Fish Hut.
Orchard in the Woods.

Bruce, Debra
"The Light They Make", sels.
Plunder.
Prognosis.
Two Couples.

Bruce, George (b. 1909)
Departure and Departure and.
Gateway to the Sea—St. Andrews.
Inheritance.
Kinnaird Head.
Love in Age.
Soup and Sherry.

Bruce, Michael (1740–67)
To the Cuckoo.

Bruce, Wallace (b. 1844)
Holland Brick, A.

Bruchac, Joseph (b. 1942)
Birdfoot's Grampa.
Canticle: "Let others speak."
Let the Midnight Special.
Prayer: "Let my words."
Spring Peepers.
Wahsah Zeh (War Dance)—As Long as the
    Grass.

Bruck, Edith (b. 1932)
Childhood.
Pretty Soon.

Brummer, Nadine
That Rank Bed.
Why Is This Night Different from All Other
    Nights?

Brün, Frederike
Chamouni at Sunrise.

Bruna, Carmen (b. 1928)
Moi-Même.

Brunk, Juanita (b. 1955)
All Sweet Things, Like Forgiveness, Are a
    Falling.
Letter to Myself as a Child.
My Father's Tongue.
On This Earth.
Papaya: Lancaster County.
Where My Mother Cries.

Brunt, Nick Van
Los Angeles.

Bruschetto, Lodovico See Bryskett, Lodowick [or
Lewis]

Brutus, Dennis (b. 1924)
At Night.
Endurance.
I Am Alien in Africa and Everywhere.
Let not this plunder be misconstrued.
Nightsong: City.
Off to Philadelphia in the Morning.
On the Island.
Postscripts 2.
Prayer: "O let me soar on steadfast wing."
Robben Island Sequence.
Sand Wet and Cool, The.
Simple lust is all my woe, A.
Somehow We Survive.
Sometimes a mesh of ideas.
Sounds Begin Again, The.
Their Behaviour.
There Was a Time When the Only Worth.
They Hanged Him, I Said Dismissively.
Under House Arrest.

Bryan, Alfred
Peg O' My Heart.

Bryan, J. B.
Bindweed.
Contentment: "Strung along back elm."
I've Looked Everywhere.
Rich Ink, Still Slightly Moist.

Bryan, Mary (fl. 1815)
Maniac, The (2).
To My Brother ("O, thou art far away from me—dear boy!").
To My Brother ("Oh transient sorrows, light as morning dews.").
To My Brother ("Once in our customed walk a wounded bird.").
To———: "O thou unknown disturber of my rest."
To———: "O timeless guest!—so soon returned art thou."
Visit, The, sel.

Bryan, Sharon (b. 1943)
BE-.
Beyond Recall.
Lunch with Girl Scouts.
Sweater Weather: A Love Song to Language.

Bryan, Tom (b. 1950)
Planting Potatoes during Chernobyl.

Bryant, Tisa
Stranger.

Bryant, William Cullen (1794–1878)
African Chief, The.
After a Tempest.
Ages, The.
Autumn Woods.
Conjunction of Jupiter and Venus, The.
Constellations, The.
Crowded Street, The.
Damsel of Peru, The.
Dante.
Death of Lincoln, The.
Death of Slavery, The.
Death of the Flowers, The.
Disinterred Warrior, The.
Forest Hymn, A, sels.
Fountain, The.
Green River, sel.
Hymn of the City.
Hymn to the North Star.
I Cannot Forget with What Fervid Devotion.
Indian at the Burial-Place [or Burying-Place] of His Fathers, An.
Indian Story, An.
Inscription for the Entrance to a Wood.
June.
Midsummer.
Mutation.
Night Journey of a River, The.
Not Yet.
November.
October.
Oh [or O] Fairest of the Rural Maids.
Painted Cup, The.
Poet, The.
Prairies, The, sel.
Return of Youth, The.

Rivulet, The.
Scene on the Banks of the Hudson, A.
Song of the Stars.
Summer Wind.
Thanatopsis, sel.
To a Waterfowl.
To Cole, the Painter, Departing for Europe.
To the Fringed Gentian.
Winter Piece, A.
Yellow Violet, The.

Bryce, Colette (b. 1970)
Break.
Day: "That was the day that went too far."
Deposition, The.
Epilogue: "Journey back was a nightmare, The."
Every Winged Fowl of the Air.
Form.
Full Indian Rope Trick, The.
Heel of Bernadette, The.
Line: "You were drawn in the voice of my mother."
Lines: "I have given birth to a see-through child."
Word, The.

Bryden, Diana Fitzgerald
Age and the Secretary.
Always, Not Always.
Clinic Day.
Fertility Test.
Sleepers Awake.

Brydges, Sir Samuel Egerton (1762–1837)
No more by cold philosophy confined.
On Dreams, October 15, 1782.

Bryher, Winifred (b. 1894)
Thessalian.

Bryll, Ernest (b. 1935)
Ballad of the Bayonet, A.
Nike.

Bryner, Jeanne
Desert Flowers.
Part of a Larger Country.

Bryskett, Lodowick [or Lewis] (Lodovico Bruschetto) (1546–1612)
Pastoral Eclogue upon the Death of Sir Philip Sidney Knight, A.

Bu-er, Sun (b. 1124)
Cut brambles long enough.
Late Indian summer's.

Buchan, John, 1st Baron Tweedsmuir (1875–1940)
Alastair Buchan (1917).
Fisher Jamie.

Buchan, Tom
Everlasting Astronauts, The.
Scotland the Wee.

Buchanan, George (1506–82)
May Morning.
Pope from penance purgatorial, The.
To Henry Darnley, King of Scots.

Buchanan, George (1904–89)
Conversations with Strangers.
I Suddenly.
Jill's Death.
Lewis Mumford.
Lyle Donaghy, Poet, 1902-1949.
Neaera when I'm there is adamant.
Song for Straphangers.
Speaker in the Square, A.
Theatrical Venus.
War-and-Peace.

Buchanan, Oni (b. 1975)
Girls, The.
Only Yak in Batesville, Virginia, The.
Room 40.
Term, The.
Transporter.
Walk, The.

Buchanan, Robert Williams (1841–1901)
Bicycle Song (For Women).
Wanderers, The.
Willie Baird, sels.

Buchanan, Shonda
Alone in Belize.

Buchman, Ruth
Short Story.

Buchsbaum, Julianne (b. 1970)
In Squire Park with M., Esquire.
Phantoms of Utopia.
Power Plant, The.
Slowly, Slowly, Horses.
Thrillsville.

Buchwald, Emilie
As Soon As It's Here It's Gone But So What.

Buck, Howard
Mort, Le.

Buckholts, Claudia
Old Woman Reclining.

Buckley, Christopher (b. 1948)
Autumn's End.
Catechism of the Sea.
Concerning Paradise.
Early Morning—Ucross, Wyoming.
Father, 1952.
Inverse Square Law of the Propagation of Light, The.
Leaving the West Coast.
Nostalgia.
Playing for Time.
Presocratic, Surfing, Breathing Cosmology Blues, The.
Rain/Light.
Sleep Walk.
Sparrows: "Like the poor, they are with us always."
Star Apocrypha.
Sycamore Canyon Nocturne.
Train in the Desert—1916.
20 Years of Grant Applications and State College Jobs.
Why I'm in Favor of a Nuclear Freeze.

Buckley, Vincent (1925–88)
Child is Revenant to the Man, The.
Ghosts, Places, Stories, Questions.
Man, a Woman, A.
Origins.
Stroke, sel.
Teaching German Literature.

Buckmaster, Charles (1951–72)
End to Myth, An.
Seed.
Wilpena Pound.

Budapest, Z
Medea Speaks, sel.

Budbill, David
Dilemma.
First Green of Spring, The.
Irrelevant and Useless.
Like Smoke from Our Campfire.
Sixth of January, The.
Thirty-Five Miles to a Traffic Light.
This Shining Moment in the Now.
Three Goals, The.
Tomorrow: "Tomorrow / we are."
What I Heard at the Discount Department Store.
What Issa Heard.

Budde, Robert (b. 1966)
Anorexia.
Bodiless.
Bruise.
Gag.
Lesion.
Stitch.
Tattoo.

Buddingh', Cees (b. 1918)
Hyena, The.
Ode to the Bicycle.
Some Biographical Data.

Buddy, Callin
Callin Buddy / Bolden.

Budenz, Julia
Poeta Fui.

Budy, Andrea Hollander
Ellis Island, September 1907.
First Books.
First Night in the New House.
On High Street.

Buffoni, Franco (b. 1950)
And in the end, the entire earth may answer to a single name.
And those level fingernails of theirs.
De Pisis--Piacenza Papers.
On Poetry.
Partitions.
Song of Diamond Eyes, The.
To be soldiers together and allies.
When he was far away from those evenings.

Bugayev, Boris Nikolaevich See Bely [orBelyi], Andrey [or Andrei]

Bugeja, Michael
Conifer King, The.
Littleton.
Shooter Rules.

Buhyu Sunsoo (1543–1615)
Biding Farewell to My Cousin, Haeil, on His Return Home.
Deathbed Song.
On Hearing a Pipe.
Reply to a Poem by Songgyedang.
To a Monk.
To an Outstanding Elder.

Bui-Burton, Kim Ly
Look at Me.
My Love is Like a Lily.
Poem for R.

Bukowski, Charles (1920–94)
b.
Black Poets, The.
Comments upon my last book of poesy.
Crucifix in a Deathhand.
Dostoevsky.
Drooling Madness at St. Liz.
Elvis Lives.
Eulogy to a hell of a dame.
Freaky time.
I Am Dead But I Know the Dead Are Not Like This.
Last song, The.
Me against the world.
Mockingbird, The.
My old man.
Nobody but you.
Not Much Singing.
Not So Good Night in the San Pedro of the World, A.
No. 6.
Poetry readings.
Secret, The.
Sexpot.
So you want to be a writer?
Startled into Life Like Fire.
3 Old Men at Separate Tables.
Tragedy of the leaves, The.
Trouble with spain.
Way it is now, The.

Bulich, Vera (1898–1954)
From My Diary, 3.
Omnibus, The.

Bullett, Gerald (b. 1893)
Footnote to Tennyson.
Woodpecker.

Bullock, Michael (b. 1918)
Garden.

Bun-Etsu, Unpo
Sixty-five years.

Bunan (1602–76)
Moon's the same old moon, The.
When you're both alive and dead.

Bunimovich, Yevgeny [or Evgenii] (b. 1954)
Excuse and Explanation.

Bunin, Ivan Alekseievich (1870–1953)
Flowers, and tall-stalked grasses, and a bee.

Bunina, Anna Petrovna (1774–1829)
Conversation between Me and the Women.
From the Seashore.
Though poverty's no stain.

Bunner, Henry Cuyler (1855–96)
Behold the Deeds!
In School House, sels.
Their Wedding Journey, sel.

Bunno [Wen Wang or King Wen] (ca. 1100 BCE)
Song of the Bowmen of Shu [1915].
Song of the Bowmen of Shu [1954].

Bunting, Basil (1900–85)
Briggflatts [An Autobiography], sels.
Chomei at Toyama, sel.
Fearful Symmetry.
I am agog for foam. Tumultuous come.
Now that sea's over that island.
On the Fly-Leaf of Pound's Cantos.
Orotava Road, The.
Personal Column.
Thrush in the syringa sings, A.
To Violet.
Vestiges, sel.
Villon, sels.
What the Chairman Told Tom.
You idiot! What makes you think decay will.

Bunyan, John (1628–88)
Author's Apology for His Book, The, sel.
Pilgrim's Progress, The, sels.

Burdick, Brad See Antler

Burford, William (b. 1927)
Christmas Tree, A.
South, Southwest.
Spell, The: "You can almost see him, looking as if well."

Bürger, Gottfried August (1748–94)
Lass of Fair Wone, The.
Lenora.

Burgess, Frank Gelett (1866–1951)
Cinq Ans Après.
On Digital Extremities.
Purple Cow, The.
Purple Cow, The: Suite.
Table Manners: "Goops they lick their fingers, The."
Trapping Fairies.

Burgess, Helen Chalakee
Rational.

Burgess, Leslie
Prostitute's Notebook, The.

Burgon, John William (1813–88)
Petra, sel.

Burgoyne, John (1722–92)
Dashing White Sergeant, The.

Burich, Vladimir (b. 1932)
Precepts for City Living.

Burkard, Michael (b. 1947)
Breathless Storm.
But Beautiful.
Cloud of Dusk, A.
Dogs on the Cliffs, The.
Foolish Thing.
How I Shaded the Book.
I have a silence in the rain.
Meditation Brought About by George Bogin's Translation of Jules Supervielle's Poem "The Sea"
My Aunt and the Sun.
Notes About My Face.
Personal Histories, The.
Sober Ghost.
Summer after Last, The.
2 Poems on the Same Theme.
Weather.
White City, A: "In the dream, N. is singing "a white city." A teacher he had is wearing a girdle."
Woman in the Red House.
Your Sister Life.

Burke, Cheryl
Lizzie.
Motor Oil Queen.

Burke, Johnny (1908–64)
Ain't It a Shame About Mame.
But Beautiful.
Good Time Charlie.
Here's That Rainy Day.
Imagination.
It Could Happen to You.
I've Got a Pocketful of Dreams.
Like Someone in Love.
Misty.

Moonlight Becomes You.
My Heart Is a Hobo.
Pennies from Heaven.
Personality.
Polka Dots and Moonbeams.
Road to Morocco, The.
Sleigh Ride in July.
Swinging on a Star.
Welcome to My Dream.
You May Not Love Me.

Burke, Marianne
Former WWII Paratrooper Dreams of Suicide, 1977, A.

Burke, Sonny
Black Coffee.

Burleson, Derick
Democracy.

Burlingame, Robert
After Bird Watching near the Mexican Border.
Desert, Not Wasteland.
Late Winter in West Texas.
Walking Past the Dugout of Felix McKittrick.

Burliuk, D., Aleksandr Kruchenykh, V. Mayakovsky and Viktor Khlebnikov
Slap in the Face of Public Taste, A, sels.

Burn, Michael
For the Common Market.
In Japan.
Welsh Love Letter.

Burnett, W. Hodgson (fl. c.1920)
My Shadow.

Burnham, Deborah
Maintaining the Species.

Burns, Elizabeth (b. 1957)
Jesus Speaks to the Church at Eastertime.
Ophelia: "Always the daughter."

Burns, Jim (b. 1936)
Confessions of an Old Believer.

Burns, Joanne (b. 1945)
How.
Marble surfaces.
Reading.
Revisionism.

Burns, Ralph
Fishing in Winter.

Burns, Robert (1759–96)
Address to the Deil.
Address to the Unco Guid, or the Rigidly Righteous.
Address to the Woodlark.
Ae Fond Kiss.
Auld Lang Syne.
Banks o' Doon, The ("Ye banks and braes o' bonie [or bonnie] Doon.").
Banks o' Doon, The ("Ye flowery banks o' bon[n]ie Doon.").
Bonnie Lesley.
Comin' thro' the Rye.
Comin[g] thro' [or through] the Rye.
Cotter's Saturday Night [Inscribed to Robert Aiken [or R. A****], Esq.], The.
Dedication to G**** H******* Esq, A, sel.
De'il's [or Deil's] Awa wi' th' [or the] Exciseman, The.
Despondency, an Ode.
Epistle to J. Lapraik, an Old Scotch Bard, sel.
First Six Verses of the Ninetieth Psalm, The.
For A' That and A' That ["Is there, for honest poverty"].
Fornicator. A New Song, The.
Grace at Kirkudbright.
Green Grow the Rashes [A Fragment].
Green Sleeves [and Tartan Ties].
Halloween.
Highland Mary.
Holy Fair, The.
Holy Willie's Prayer.
John Anderson, My Jo ("John Anderson, my jo, John, / I wonder what ye mean.").
John Anderson, My Jo ("John Anderson my jo, John / When we were first acquent.").
Man Was Made to Mourn, a Dirge.
Mary Morison.
Memory.

My Heart's in the Highlands.
O Were My Love Yon Lilac[k] Fair.
Of A' the Airts [the Wind Can Blaw].
O[h] Wert Thou in the Cauld Blast.
Patriarch, The.
Prayer, in the Prospect of Death, A.
Rantin' Dog, the Daddie o't, The.
Red, Red Rose, A.
Scotch Drink.
Scots Wha Hae.
Second Epistle to Davie.
Silver Tassie, The.
Sonnet upon Sonnets, A.
Such a Parcel of Rogues in a Nation.
Tam o' Shanter; A Tale.
To a Haggis.
To a Louse [On Seeing One on a Lady's
   Bonnet at Church].
To a Mountain Daisy [On Turning One Down,
   with the Plough, in April—1786].
To a Mouse; On Turning Her up in Her Nest,
   with the Plough, November, 1785.
Twa Dogs, The.
Up in the Morning Early.
Wat Ye What My Minnie Did.
Whistle, and I'll Come to You, My Lad.
Burnshaw, Stanley (b. 1906)
Bread.
End of the Flower World (A.D. 2300).
House in St. Petersburg.
Burnside, John (b. 1955)
Anstruther.
Autobiography.
Dundee.
History.
Home Farm.
Lost: "Fog walks down the hill and finds our
   yard, The."
Men's Harbour, The.
Old Gods, The.
Out of Exile.
Parousia.
Penitence.
Swimming in the Flood.
Tundra's Edge.
Unwittingly.
Variation on a Theme of Wallace Stevens.
Burr, Amelia Josephine (b. 1878)
Lynmouth Widow, A.
Burrell, Lady Sophia (1750?–1802)
Chloe and Myra, *sels.*
Burrington, E. H. (*fl.* 1830–80)
Beautiful, The.
Burris, Jim (*fl.* 1913)
Ballin' the Jack.
Burris, Sidney (b. 1953)
On Living with a Fat Woman in Heaven.
Very True Confessions.
"Burroughs, Ellen" *See* Jewett, Sophie
Burroughs, William S. (1914–97)
Cold Lost Marbles.
Fear and the Monkey.
My Legs Señor.
Burrows, Suzanne
Time of Cherries, A.
Bursk, Christopher (b. 1943)
Does Poetry Matter?
Tearing Up the Tracks.
What a Boy Does Not Say.
Bursky, Rick
Decisions, The.
Burt, Lucile
Melissa Quits School.
Burt, Stephen (b. 1971)
Morningside Park.
Ocean State.
Paysage Moralisé.
Persephone (Unplugged).
Sudden Rain in the Green Mountains, A.
Burton, Robert (1577–1640)
Anatomy of Melancholy, The, *sels.*
Buscani, Lisa (b. 1964)
Barefoot in the City.
Downtime.

Miss Mary Mack.
Busceti, Giusi (b. 1955)
Dissonances.
Eight Phases of Contemplation.
Exhausted Inconsistency Floats Here, An.
One Hundred Eighty.
Suddenly on a day in July.
Busch, Trent (b. 1937)
Heartland.
Bush, Barney (b. 1945)
Autumn Warrior.
Directions in Our Blood.
Her Voice.
Memory Sire, The.
Taking a Captive / 1984.
Voyeur's Dream.
Bush, Duncan (b. 1946)
Aquarium du Trocadéro.
Drainlayer.
Hook, The.
Living in Real Times.
Pneumoconiosis.
Summer 1984.
Sunday the Power Went Off, The.
Bush, Narda
Noodling.
Busia, Abena (b. 1953)
Exiles.
Illicit Passion.
Liberation.
Mawu of the Waters.
Buson (Yosa Buson) (1716–83)
Along the roadside.
Amid white plum blossoms.
Apprentice's day off.
Around the small house.
At a roadside shrine.
At the ancient well.
At the old pond.
Autumn breezes.
Autumn evening.
Avoiding fishnet.
Bamboo hat, straw coat—.
Bat flits, A.
Bats flitting here and there.
Before the white chrysanthemum.
Behavior of the pigeon, The.
Blossoms on the pear.
Blow of an ax.
Blown from the west.
Brushing flies.
Butterfly.
Buying leeks.
By flowering pear.
By moonlight.
Calligraphy of geese.
Camellia, The.
Camellia tips, The.
Cherry blossoms fallen.
Chrysanthemum growers.
Clinging to the bell.
Coming back.
Conversation.
Coolness.
Cover my head.
Crossing.
Crossing the autumn moor.
Cut the peony.
Darting here and there.
Dawn.
Day slow in going, A.
Deer in rain / Three cries.
Dew on the bramble / Thorns.
Dewy morn / These saucepans.
Dog barking, A.
Early summer rain.
End of spring, The.
End of spring, The.
Escaped the nets.
Evening cloudburst—, An.
Evening primrose.
Evening wind.
Fallen petals of red plum.
Fallen red blossoms.
Ferry departs, The.

Field of bright mustard.
Field of bright mustard.
Field of mustard, A.
Flash of lightning.
Flowers offered to the Buddha.
Flying squirrel, A.
Flying squirrel, A.
Fox disguised, The.
Gleaning the rice field.
Going home.
Goodbye. I willgo.
Green leaves.
Green plum.
Gust of wind, A.
Happy traveler / Mosquito wick.
Harvest moon.
Having reddened the plum blossoms.
Head pillowed on arm.
Heavy cart rumbles by, A.
He's on the porch.
How awkward it looks.
I go.
I go.
I go.
I go out alone.
In a bitter wind.
In pale moonlight.
In seasonal rain.
In sudden flare / Of the mosquito wick.
In the drained fields.
In the summer rain.
In the white plum blossoms.
Iris, An.
It cried three times.
It pierces through me.
Korean ship, The.
Late evening cow, The.
Leaves seem trout.
Light of the moon.
Light winter rain.
Lighting one candle.
Lighting the lantern.
Lightning flash—,A.
Lights are going out, The.
Listening to the moon.
Listening to the moon.
Listening to the plovers.
Long hard journey, A.
Long, slow days of spring, The.
Mad girl, The.
Makes the eye happy.
Mason's finger, The.
May rains.
Miles of frost / On the lake.
Misty grasses.
Moon in midsky, high.
Moored boat, A.
Morning breeze.
Mountain cuckoo, The.
Mountain cuckoo, The.
Mountains of Yoshino / Shedding petals.
Mourning for Hokuju Rosen.
My arm for a pillow.
My ax sinks in.
My old man's ears.
My village / Dragonflies.
New Year's first poem.
Night deepens.
No bridge.
No poem you send.
Nobly, the great priest.
Not a leaf stirring.
Not cherry blossoms.
Not quite dark yet.
Oh, how cool.
Old calendar, The.
Old cormorant keeper, The.
Old man, The.
Old well.
On the iris / Kite's.
On these southern roads.
Only Mount Fuji.
Only the shoots.
Over water / Sharp sickles.
Owner of the field, The.
Paper kite, A.

Passing spring, The.
Peonies scattering.
Peony petals scatter, The.
People visiting all day.
Petals fall, The.
Piercing chill.
Plum blossoms here and there.
Plum blossoms in bloom.
Plum blossoms scent.
Plum scent / Haloing.
Plums in blossom.
Plum-viewing.
Priestly poverty—.
Pure white plum blossoms.
Raftsmen on their floats.
Rain falls on the grass.
Rainy season, The.
Remembering how.
Riding.
Roots of the camphor tree.
Scattering bloom, The.
Short nap / Waking.
Short night, The / 2 broom thrown away.
Short night, The / broken, in the shallows.
Short night, The / bubbles of crab froth.
Short night, The / near the pillow.
Short night, The / on the hairy caterpillar.
Short night, The / on the outskirts of the
  village.
Short night, The / patrolmen.
Short night, The / shallow footprints.
Short night, The / the Oi River.
Short night, The / the peony.
Short night, The / waves beating in.
Shortcut, A.
Sick man passing.
Sleeping late.
Slung over a screen.
Song of the Yodo River.
Sound of a bell.
Sound of a saw.
Sparrow singing.
Spring Breeze on the Kema Embankment, sels.
Spring passing.
Spring rain! And as yet.
Spring sea rising, The.
Spring Wind on the Riverbank at Kema.
Straw sandal half sunk.
Such a moon.
Sudden chill, A / In our room my dead wife's.
Sudden shower.
Swallows / In eaves of mansions.
Sweet springtime showers.
Tea flowers.
Tears.
Ten holy nights / Even tea.
Tethered horse, A.
That axe that I hear.
That handsaw marks time.
That snail.
These lazy spring days.
They end their flight.
They swallow clouds.
This cold winter night.
Through snow / Lights of homes.
Thwack of an ax, The.
Tilling the field.
Toward Toba Palace.
Tub with no bottom, A.
Two plum trees, The.
Urine-stained quilt, A.
Utter aloneness—.
Village with a thousand eaves.
Wading through it.
Walking on dishes.
Washing the hoe.
When a heavy cart.
White blossoms of the pear.
White dew.
White lotus.
White plum blossoms.
Willow leaves fallen, The.
Wind in the west / Fallen leaves.
Winter rain on moss.
Winter warbler.
With a runny nose.

With a woman friend.
With no underrobes.
With the noon conch blown.
You left in the morning. In the evening, my
  heart in a thousand shards.
Buson, Yosa *See* Buson
Butcher, Grace (b. 1934)
  Crow Is Walking.
Butler, Charles E. (1909–81)
  Darkness, The.
  Letter to the Survivors.
  Other Places, The.
  Rifle Range: Louisiana.
Butler, Samuel (1612–80)
  Hudibras, sels.
  Law, The.
  Love.
Butler, Samuel (1835–1902)
  O God! O Montreal!
  Righteous Man, The.
  She was too kind, wooed too persistently.
Butlin, Ron (b. 1949)
  Advertisement for a Scottish Servant.
  Bath, The.
Butson, Denver (b. 1965)
  Tuesday 9:00 AM.
Butterfield, F. G.
  For Services Rendered.
Butts, Anthony (b. 1969)
  Belle Isle Men, The.
  Nature of Braille, The.
  Poe Story, A.
  Skin.
Butts, Antony
  Massenet.
Buuck, David
  Stanzas in Mediation, sel.
Buxton, Esther W. (fl. c.1910)
  Putting the World to Bed.
Buzbee, Lewis
  Sunday, Tarzan in His Hammock.
Buzzi, Paolo (1874–1956)
  Finger-nails.
Byard, Olivia
  In Intensive Care.
Bye, Reed (b. 1948)
  Blessing.
  Captain Oaks.
  Car Music.
  Dear Mozart.
  Effendi.
  Frank's Song.
  Indiana.
  Not Tyrants.
  On the Rails.
  Prescott Slur, The.
  Work, No Light.
  Yerba Buena, Nick & Jerry.
Bykova, Zinaida
  At the Stop.
  Close of day.
  Potatoes in flower.
**Bynner, Witter ("Emanuel Morgan") (1881–
  1968)**
  All tempest.
  And that was the jolly part of it.
  Any other time would have done.
  But for these apertures.
  Chinese Drawings, sels.
  Defeat.
  Donald Evans.
  Driftwood.
  Foreigner, A.
  Haskell.
  Highest Bidder, The.
  Horses.
  Idols.
  Lightning.
  Lines to Do with Youth.
  Lovers: "From somewhere over the houses,
    through the silence."
  Moon, The.
  More Lovely than Antiquity.
  Opus 17.

  Opus 2.
  Sigh, A.
  Snake Dance.
  Spectra, sel.
  Tiles.
  Titanic, The.
  Wall, The.
  Wave, The.
  Wintry Mind, The.
  Wistaria.
Byok Namkung (fl. 20th cent.)
  Grass.
Byrd, Bobby
  Breaking and Entering: A Very Short Novel in
    Verse.
  Gabachos in the Photograph, The.
  Good Life, The.
  On Karma at 9.11.85.
  Steak and Eggs.
  Things You Can't Do in Albuquerque or Santa
    Fe, #11.
Byrd, Brigitte
  Top Stories.
Byrd, William (1543–1623)
  Lulla Lullaby.
  Quiet Life, The.
  Song: "Let not the sluggish sleep."
Byrne, Edward
  Early Evening.
  Envying the Art of the Cartographer.
Byrne, Elena Karina
  In Particular.
Byrne, William A.
  Song of a Turf-sod.
Byrom, John (1692–1763)
  Careless Content.
  Hymn: "Christians, awake, salute the happy
    morn", sel.
  My Spirit Longeth for Thee.
  Nimmers, The.
  On the Origin of Evil.
Byron, Catherine (b. 1947)
  Minding You.
  Shipping the Pictures from Belfast.
**Byron, George Gordon Noel Byron, 6th Baron
  (1788–1824)**
  Abdiel.
  Age of Bronze, The, sel.
  'All Is Vanity, Saith the Preacher.'
  Aristomenes.
  Beppo; a Venetian Story, sel.
  Bride of Abydos, The, sel.
  By the Rivers of Babylon We Sat Down and
    Wept.
  Cain: A Mystery, sels.
  Childe Harold's Pilgrimage, sels.
  Cornelian, The.
  Corsair, The, sels.
  Darkness, sels.
  Deformed Transformed, The, sels.
  Destruction of Sennacherib, The.
  Don Juan, sels.
  English Bards and Scotch Reviewers [1810
    version], sels.
  English Bards and Scotch Reviewers [1812
    version], sels.
  Epistle to Augusta.
  Fare Thee Well.
  Giaour, The.
  Harp the Monarch Minstrel Swept, The.
  If Sometimes in the Haunts of Men.
  Jephtha's Daughter.
  Lachin y Gair.
  Lara, sels.
  Last Words on Greece.
  Lines on Hearing That Lady Byron Was Ill.
  Lines to Mr Hodgson.
  Love and Death.
  Manfred, sels.
  Mazeppa, sel.
  Napoleon's Farewell.
  Nurse's Dole in the Medea, The.
  Oh! Weep for Those.
  On a Carrier Who Died of Drunkenness.
  On Jordan's Bank.

On This Day I Complete My Thirty-sixth Year.
One Struggle More, and I Am Free.
Prayer of Nature, The.
Prisoner of Chillon, The, *sels.*
Prometheus.
Remember Thee! Remember Thee!
She Walks In Beauty.
Siege of Corinth, The, *sels.*
So We'll Go No More A-Roving.
Song of Saul before His Last Battle.
Sonnet on Chillon.
Sonnet to Lake Leman.
Sonnet, to the Same.
Spirit Pass'd Before Me, A.
Stanzas for Music ("There be none of Beauty's daughters.").
Stanzas for Music ("There's not a joy the world can give like that it takes away.").
Stanzas to Augusta ("Though the day of my destiny's over.").
Stanzas: "When a man hath no freedom to fight for at home."
Stanzas Written on the Road between Florence and Pisa.
Tear, The.
To Belshazzar.
To Mr. Murray.
To Thyrza.
Vision of Judgment, The, *sels.*
Waltz, The.
When We Two Parted.
Written After Swimming from Sestos to Abydos.

Byron, Henry James (1834–84)
Adage: "Gardener's rule applies to youth and age, The."

C

Caballero-Robb, Maria Elena
Dear Rosario.
Memoranda for Rosario.

Cabalquinto, Luis
Depths of Fields.
Ordinance, The.
Value Added in Smashing a German Roach on the Bathroom Door, The.

Cabañas, Suzana
It's Called Kings.

Cabico, Regie
Afternoon in Pangasinan with No Electricity, An.
Antonio Banderas in His Underwear.
Art in Architecture.
Check One.
Gameboy.
In Bed with James Tate.
Mango Poem.

Cable, George Washington (1844–1925)
Belle Layotte.
Criole Candjo.
Dirge of St. Malo, The.
English muskets went bim! bim!, The.
Song of Cayetano's Circus, The.

Cabral de Melo Neto, João (b. 1920)
Canefield and the Sea, The.
Cemetery in Pernambuco: Our Lady of Light.
Daily Space.
Education by Stone.
Emptiness of Being a Man, The.
Emptiness of Man, The.
End of the World, The.
Knife All Blade, A.
Knife That Is All Blade, The, *sel.*
Landscape of the Capibaribe River.
Sea and the Canefield, The.
Tecendo a manhã.
To Carlos Drummond de Andrade.
Two of the Festivals of Death.
Weaving the Morning.

Cabri, Louis (b. 1960)
Salon, Salon.

Cacciatore, Edoardo (b. 1912)
Full Powers: Five Warning Signs, *sels.*

Caddel, Richard
Against Numerology.
For Tom.

Caddy, Caroline (b. 1944)
Three-Inch Reflector.

Cader, Teresa D.
Empress Shōtoku Invents Printing in 1770.
Promise, A.
Season for Hunting, A.
Spirit Papers.

Cadiot, Oliver (b. 1956)
Hep!
Pourquoi je deviens un saint.
Psst!
Why I Became a Saint.

Cadwallender, Kevin
Baz and the Freedom of the Press.

Cady, Joseph
After Hearing Heterosexual Poets in October 1974: What It Seems Like To Write a Male Homosexual Love Poem Now.

Caedmon (fl. c.675)
Caedmon's Hymn.
Caedmon's Hymn.
Cædmon's Hymn, West Saxon Version.

Caeiro, Alberto
Sheep's Vigil for a Fervent Person, *sel.*

Caesar, Irving
Animal Crackers in My Soup.
Crazy Rhythm.
I Want to Be Happy.
Is It True What They Say About Dixie?
Sometimes I'm Happy.
Spanish Jake.
Tea for Two.
Too Many Rings Around Rosie.
What a Perfect Combination.

Caesar, Valerie
In 5th Grade.

Cafagña, Marcus
Hawthorne Metal, Detroit, 1939.
Lithium.

Cage, John (1912–92)
Composition in Retrospect, *sel.*
Diary: How to Improve the World (You Will Only Make Matters Worse), *sels.*
Lecture on Nothing.
Song Books, *sels.*
There is no.
25 Mesostics Re and Not Re Mark Tobey.
Two Mesostics Re Merce Cunningham.
2 Pages, 122 Words on Music and Dance.
Writing through the Cantos.

Cager, Chezia Thompson
Callaloo.

Cagnone, Nanni (b. 1939)
General names, no other.
It isn't any of this.
It lies—when urged to, it lies.
No place is extreme.
Vaticinio, *sels.*

Cahn, Sammy (1913–93)
All the Way.
Call Me Irresponsible.
Come Fly with Me.
Day by Day.
Guess I'll Hang My Tears Out to Dry.
I Fall in Love Too Easily.
I Should Care.
I'll Walk Alone.
It's Magic.
Let It Snow! Let It Snow! Let It Snow!
Love and Marriage.
(Love Is) The Tender Trap.
Put 'Em in a Box, Tie 'Em with a Ribbon (And Throw 'Em in the Deep Blue Sea).
Second Time Around, The.
Teach Me Tonight.
Things We Did Last Summer, The.
Time After Time.
Until the Real Thing Comes.

Cahun, Claude (Lucy Schwob) (1894–1954)
Sadique Judith, La.
Sadistic Judith.

Caie, John M. (1878–1949)
Puddock, The.

Cain, Edney
Sunset Reverie.

Cain, Justin
My Required Tool.

Caird, Janet (1913–92)
Emigrants.
John Donne, You Were Wrong.

Cairncross, Sir Alec (1911–98)
Covenanting Country.
Munich.

Cairns, Scott
Adulterer, The.
After the Last Words.
And Also from the Son.
Another Song.
Coming Forth.
Exile: "Here *exactly*—a little elbow room. Here, in this margin of poor housing."
Glass Man, The.
Imperative.
In Praise of Darkness.
In the General Area of North Texas.
Lucifer's Epistle to the Fallen.
Martyr, The.
More Earnest Prayer of Christ, The.
On Slow Learning.
Our Lost Angels.
Prospect of the Interior.
Recuperation of Sin, A.
Regarding the Monument.
Salvation.
Surprise.
Theology of Doubt, The.
Translation of Raimundo Luz, The: My Amusing Despair.
Translation of Raimundo Luz, The: My Farewell.
Translation of Raimundo Luz, The: My Good Luck.
Translation of Raimundo Luz, The: My Imitation.
Translation of Raimundo Luz, The: My Incredulity.
Waking Here.

Cakrabartī, Nabīncandra
Can you claim to win.

Cakrabarttī, Mā Bāsantī
Ma, if You wore a Benarasi sari.
Wherever there's a woman in any Bengali home.

Calbert, Cathleen
Like.

Calder, Angus (b. 1942)
Curling: Old Murrayfield Ice Rink.
Greeting, Not Greeting.
October Opera for Kate.

Calder, Robert R. (b. 1950)
Love in the Abstract.

Calderón, Eduardo
Raising the Mediating Center and the Field of Evil with the Twenty-Five Thousand Accounts and the Chant of the Ancients.

Calderón, Teresa (b. 1955)
Affairs of Memory.
Domestic Blues.
Exile.
"From Your Depths and Kneeling . . ."
State of Seige.

Calderón de la Barca, Pedro (1600–81)
Life Is a Dream.
Those Which Were Pomp and Delight.

Caldwell, Anne
I Know That You Know.
Left All Alone Again Blues.
Raggedy Ann.

Caldwell, E. K.
Love Poem: "Olfactory paradise."

Caldwell, Kim
Moonlight.

Caldwell, Rozell (b. 1948)
Bible Buckle, The.
Caleshu, Anthony (b. 1970)
After the Word Love Was Spoken.
Church Full of Objections.
Collaboration: A Day at the Beach.
Collaboration: Between Countries.
Collaboration: Migration Patterns.
Collaboration: Storming the Beaches.
Homecoming.
Calil, Amina (b. 1970)
Blouse of Felt.
Calisch, Edward N. *See* Moise, Penina
Callanan, Jeremiah Joseph
Outlaw of Loch Lene, The.
Callimachus (c.300–240 B.C.)
At dawn we buried Melanippus. At sunset.
Do not say "Godspeed" to me, wicked heart.
Epigram.
Galataea, *sel.*
"Goodbye, O sun," said Cleombrotus of
  Ambracia.
Hecale, *sels.*
Here Philip the father buried.
Hesiod's is the theme and his the style.
Hymns, *sels.*
I hate the cyclic poem, nor do I rejoice.
Mousetrap, The.
News of Your Death.
On the mountain, Epicydes the hunter seeks.
Prologue to the Aetia.
Someone told me, Heracleitus.
These gifts to Aphrodite.
Timon, for you exist no more.
Whoever passes by my tomb, know.
Would that there had never been swift ships!
You pass the tomb of Battus' son, well
  skilled.
Calloway, Cab
Minnie, the Moocher.
Calpurnius Siculus, Titus, (*fl.* 1st cent. A.D.)
Eclogues, *sels.*
Calverley, Charles Stuart (1831–84)
Ballad: "Auld wife sat at her ivied door, The."
Disaster.
Flight.
In the Gloaming.
Calvino, Italo (1923–85)
Invisible Cities, *sels.*
Cambridge, Ada (1844–1926)
Desire.
Fashion.
Future Verdict, The.
Virgin Martyr, The.
Cambridge, Gerry (b. 1959)
Drunken Lyricist, The.
Fallen Maple Leaves.
Foxgloves.
Shore Crab.
Camerarius, Philipp (1537–1624)
Faithfullest Beast, The.
**Cameron, Mary (Mairi Chamaran, Nighean
Fream Challaird) (b. c.1625)**
Song of Sorrow, A.
Cameron, Nigel
I have no substance and no form.
Cameron, Norman (b. 1905)
Fight with a Water-Spirit.
Forgive Me, Sire.
Green, Green Is El Aghir.
Meeting My Former Self.
Naked among the Trees.
Unfinished Race, The.
Cami, Ben (b. 1920)
You Stand.
Camlan, Goronva (*fl.* c.1846)
Education in Wales.
Lady Charlotte Guest.
Literature and Action.
**Camões [*or* Camõens *or* Camoëns], Luis de
(1524–80)**
Do This Favour For Me.
Lusiads, The, *sels.*
On a Shipmate, Pero Moniz, Dying at Sea.

Sonnet: My Errors My Loves My Unlucky
  Star.
Sonnet: That Sad and Joyful Dawn.
Campana, Dino (1885–1932)
Autumn Garden.
Faenza.
Florence.
Genoa.
Toscanità.
Window, The.
Campbell, Calder
When midst the summer-roses the warm bees.
Campbell, David (1915–79)
Anguish of Ants, The.
Duchesses.
Hear the Bird of Day.
Here, under Pear-trees.
Hotel Marine.
Ku-ring-gai Rock Carvings, *sels.*
Man in the Honeysuckle, The.
Mothers and Daughters.
Small-town Gladys.
Song for the Cattle.
Starting from Central Station, *sels.*
Campbell, Dorothea Primrose
To Miss Sophia Headle.
Campbell, James Edwin (1867–96)
Mors et Vita.
Campbell, Janet (Seònaid Chaimbeul) (*fl.* c.1645)
This night tonight is cold.
Campbell, Jimmy
Good Night, Sweetheart.
If I Had You.
Try a Little Tenderness.
**Campbell, Joseph (Seosamh MacCathmhaoil)
(1881–1944)**
Blind Man at the Fair, The.
Dancer, The.
Hills of Cualann, The.
I Am the Mountainy Singer.
Old Woman, The.
Sighle of the Lovespot.
Campbell, Rick
In a Motel in Louisiana I Watch the Pirates
  And the OJ Simpson Freeway Chase at the
  Same Time.
Campbell, Roy (1902–57)
Autumn.
Choosing a Mast.
Flaming Terrapin, The, *sel.*
Georgiad, The, *sel.*
Georgian Spring.
Good Resolution, A.
Luis de Camões.
Mass at Dawn.
On Some South African Novelists.
On the Same.
Palm, The.
Serf, The.
Sisters, The.
Toledo.
Tristan da Cunha.
Veld Eclogue, A: The Pioneers.
Volunteer's Reply to the Poet, The.
Wayzgoose, The, *sel.*
Zebras, The.
Zulu Girl, The.
Campbell, Siobhan (b. 1962)
Big John's Tears Fall to the River.
Chairmaker, The.
Constant Welcome, The.
Legacy.
Campbell, Thomas (1774–1844)
Battle of the Baltic.
Gertrude of Wyoming, *sels.*
Hohenlinden.
Last Man, The.
Lines Written on Visiting a Scene in
  Argyleshire.
Lochiel's Warning, *sels.*
Lord Ullin's Daughter.
Pleasures of Hope, The, *sels.*
Soldier's Dream, The.
To the Evening Star.
Ye Mariners of England.

Campert, Jan (1902–43)
Eighteen Dead, The.
Campert, Remco (b. 1929)
Avignon.
Futile Poem, A.
Message About the Times.
Sign of the Times.
Silver Talk.
Stroll to Parfondeval, A.
Theatre.
Theatre, The.
Campion, Thomas (1567–1620)
As by the stream[e]s of Babylon [*or* Babilon].
Author of light, revive my dying spright.
Awake, Awake! [Thou Heavy Sprite].
Fain Would I Wed.
Fire, fire, fire, fire!
Follow Thy Fair Sun[ne] [Unhappy Shadow].
Heart's Music.
Hymn in Praise of Neptune, A.
I Care Not for These Ladies.
Man of Life Upright, The.
Now Winter Nights Enlarge.
O Come Quickly!
Observations in the Art of English Poesie, *sels.*
Seek the Lord.
Shall I Come, Sweet Love.
Sweet, exclude me[e] not, nor be divided.
Think'st thou to seduce me then.
Thrice Toss[e] These Oaken Ashes in the Air
  [*or* Ayre].
View Mee, Lord.
What Fair[e] Pomp[e].
When to Her Lute Corinna [*or* Corrina] Sings.
Campo, Cristina (1923–77)
At Times I Say: Let's Try to Be Joyous.
Devout like a Branch.
Indian Summer.
Love, Today My Lip.
Now I Want All My Letters White Again.
Tiger's Absence, *sels.*
White Summer Clothes are Folded Away, The.
Campo, Rafael (b. 1964)
Allegory.
Asylum.
Aunt Toni's Heart.
Battle Hymn of the Republic, The.
Begging for Change in Winter.
Belonging.
El Curandero.
El Día de los Muertos.
For J. W.
Her Final Show.
Lost in the Hospital.
Lost Plaza Is Everywhere, The.
My Childhood in Another Part of the World.
My Voice.
S. W.
Song for My Lover, *sels.*
Superman Is Dead.
Ten Patients, and Another, *sels.*
Towards Curing AIDS.
What the Body Told.
X Files, The.
Campos, Álvaro de [Fernando Pessoa]
Tobacco Shop, The.
Campos Cervera, Hérib
Sent.
Canan, Janine (b. 1942)
Goddesses, The.
Inanna's Chant.
Mother Dawning.
Oh Kali.
Radioactive.
Candelaria, Cordelia
Killers.
Candī, Andha
Bring Tara quickly, Mountain.
Cane, Melville (b. 1879)
Dawn Has Yet to Ripple In.
Hymn to Night.
Tree in December.
Cangiullo, Francesco (1884–1977)
Detonation.

Cankoçak, Gülten Akın (b. 1933)
Not the Fear of Shivering.
Cannan, May Wedderburn (1893–1973)
Rouen.
Cannell, Skipwith (1887–1957)
King, The.
Canning, George (1770–1827) and John Hookham Frere
Friend of Humanity and the Knife Grinder, The.
Canning, George (1770–1827) and William Gifford (1756–1826)
Progress of Man, The. A Didactic Poem, *sels.*
Canning, George (1770–1827), George Ellis and John Hookham Frere
Rovers, The; or, The Double Arrangement, *sels.*
Canning, Josiah D. (1816–92)
Indian Gone!, The.
Cannon, Hughie
Bill Bailey, Won't You Please Come Home.
Cannon, Melissa
Sisters, The.
Cano, Luis
I Light My Lamp.
Cansever, Edip (1928–86)
Eyes: "It seems nothing can provoke."
Cantor, Michael
Tour de France.
Cao Bá Quát (1809–53)
On Reading *The Book of Odes*.
Caples, Garrett (b. 1972)
Targets and Flowers (Begun with Lines from Breton).
Capone, Giovanna (Janet)
In Answer to Their Questions.
Caraion, Ion (1923–86)
Enveloping Echo, The.
Remember.
Song from the Occupation Time.
Tomorrow the Past Comes.
Ultimate Argument.
Carberry, H. D.
It takes a mighty fire.
Carbó, Nick
Civilizing the Filipino.
I Found Orpheus Levitating.
In Tagalog Ibon Means Bird.
Little Brown Brother.
Robo.
Verso Libre.
Votive Candles.
When the Grain Is Golden and the Wind Is Chilly, Then It Is the Time to Harvest.
Carbone, Lisa M.
Flight from the Marriage Bed.
Cardenal, Ernesto (b. 1925)
For me to lose you and for you to lose me, we both lose.
For Those Dead, Our Dead.
From those theaters, Claudia, from those feasts.
Gethsemani, KY, *sels.*
I offer these verses to you, Claudia, because you are their mistress.
In Xóchitl in Cuícatl.
León.
Lights.
Mosquito Kingdom.
Prayer for Marilyn Monroe.
Psalm 5: "Give ear to my words, O Lord."
Room 5600.
St. Luke, *sel.*
Unrighteous Mammon (Luke 16:9).
Cárdenas, Brenda
Sonido Ink(quieto).
Cardiff, Gladys (b. 1942)
Candelaria and the Sea Turtle.
Combing.
For His Ring and Watch on the Night Stand.
Grey Woman.
Hunting the Dugong.
It has something to do with final words.

Making Lists.
Tsa'lagi Council Tree.
Where Fire Burns.
Cardona-Hine, Alvaro
Acquaintances.
Enough Horses.
Listen Galaxea.
Trumpet Voluntary in Praise of My Four Children.
Carew, Thomas (1594?–1640?)
Another [On the Duke of Buckingham].
Ask Me No More.
Beautiful Mistress, A.
Deposition from Love, A.
Disdain Returned.
Divine Mistress, A.
Elegy upon the Death of the Dean of [St.] Paul's, Dr. John Donne, An.
Epitaph on the Lady Mary Villiers ("Lady Mary Villiers lies, The.").
Fancy, A.
In Praise of His Mistress.
Ingrateful[l] Beauty Threatened.
Lips and Eyes.
Maria Wentworth.
Mediocrity in Love Rejected.
Prayer to the Wind, A.
Rapture, A, *sels.*
Second Rapture, The.
Song[, A]: "Ask[e] me no more where Jove bestow[e]s."
Spring, The: "Now that the Winter's gone, the earth hath lost."
To a Lady That Desired I Would Love Her.
To Ben Jonson.
To Celia, upon Love's Ubiquity.
To My Inconstant Mistress [*or* Mistris].
To My Mistress[e] in My Absence.
To My Rival.
To Saxham.
Upon a Ribbon [*or* Ribband].
Carey, Henry (1693?–1743)
Author's Quietus, The.
Drinking-Song, A.
Lilliputian Ode on Their Majesties' Accession, A.
Namby-Pamby. A Panegyric on the New Versification, Address'd to A——— P———, Esq. ("All ye poets of the age.").
Namby-Pamby; or, A Panegyric on the New Versification ("Naughty Paughty Jack-a-Dandy.").
Sally in Our Alley.
Carey, Mary (d. after 1680)
Wretten by Me at the Death of My 4th Sonne and 5th Child Perigrene Payler.
Carey [*or* Cary], Patrick (c.1623–57)
Fig for the Lower House, A.
Carey, Steve (b. 1945)
Fames Away.
Carey, Tom (b. 1951)
Zohar.
Cariaga, Catalina (b. 1958)
Family Tree, The.
Plantings.
Carifi, Roberto (b. 1948)
Things don't forget.
Carkesse, James (fl. 1678)
His Rule of Behaviour: If You Are Civil, I Am Sober.
On the Doctors' Telling Him that till He Left off Making Verses He Was Not Fit to be Discharged.
Carle, Frankie
Oh! What It Seemed to Be.
Carleton, Bob (1896–1956)
Ja Da.
Carleton, Will M. (1845–1912)
Centurion, A.
Wheelmen's Song.
Carlson, Douglas
Russ Joy Little League.
Carlson, Sir Edward
Scribbled at a Cabinet Meeting.

Carlson, Elizabeth (1943–2000)
Imperfection.
Carman, Bliss (William Bliss Carman) (1861–1929)
Buie Annajohn.
Eavesdropper, The.
Low Tide on Grand Pré.
Northern Vigil, A.
Vagabond Song, A.
Vestigia.
World Voice, The.
Carman, William Bliss *See* Carman, Bliss
Carmi, T. (1925–94)
Memorial Day, 1969.
Military Funeral in the Heat of Day.
Short Song.
Carmichael, Amy
Do We Not Hear Thy Footfall?
Yet Listen Now.
Carmichael, Hoagy (1899–1981)
Don't Forget to Say No, Baby.
Hong Kong Blues.
I Get Along Without You Very Well.
Lazy River.
Rockin' Chair.
Carmona, Belinda Zubicueta (b. 1955)
Another Day.
Between the Lines.
Daily Task.
Storing Memories.
Stretched Out in Solitude.
Tenderness.
Carnevale, Robert
Walking by the Cliffside Dyeworks.
Carnevali, Emanuel (b. 1898)
Almost a God.
Kiss.
Serenade.
Sermon.
Walt Whitman.
Carolan [*or* O'Carolan], Turlough (1670–1738)
Gracey Nugent.
Mabel Kelly.
Peggy Browne.
Carpenter, Edward (1844–1929)
Towards Democracy, *sels.*
Carpenter, Maurice (b. 1911)
Ballad of John Nameless, The, *sel.*
Carpenter, William (b. 1940)
Evening Wind.
Ghosts.
Night Shadows.
Carper, Thomas (b. 1936)
Aerial Photograph, An.
Oh Keep the Poet Hence.
Carr, Mary Jane
Castle in the Fire, The.
Carr, Sally
Easter Outing.
Carranza, Eduardo (1913–85)
Azure Because of You.
Carrara, Carli
On Weekends.
Carrera Andrade, Jorge (d. 1903)
Body of the Beloved, The, *sels.*
Clock, The.
Perfect Life, The.
Second Life of My Mother.
Sunday.
Transfiguration of the Rain.
Carrier, Constance (b. 1908)
Clause for a Covenant.
Elegy.
Helianthus.
Laudare.
Point of View, A.
Carrington, Harold (d. 1964)
Lament: "While my city gently sleeps."
Sting—a South Carolina Ave. Folk Tale.
Woo's People.
Carroll, Jim (b. 1951)
Blue Poles.
Burning of Bustin's Island, The.

Heroin.
Love Rockets.
Maybe I'm Amazed.
Paregoric Babies.
Poem on My Son's Birthday.
Styro.
To a Poetess.
Withdrawal Letter.

Carroll, Kenneth (b. 1959)
DC Nocturne.
Domino Theory (or Snoop Dogg rules the world), The.
For Brothas That Like to Holla.
Laughin at cha.
Short Poem.
Something easy for Ultra Black nationalists.
Theory on Extinction or what happened to the dinosaurs?
Truth About Karen, The.
Upper Marlboro.

Carroll, Lewis (Charles Lutwidge Dodgson) (1832–98)
Alice's Adventures in Wonderland, *sels.*
Brother and Sister.
Hunting of the Snark, The, *sels.*
Little Birds Are Playing.
Long Tale, A.
Poeta Fit, Non Nascitur.
Sum, A.
Sylvie and Bruno, *sels.*
Through the Looking-Glass, *sels.*
Visitor, A.

Carroll, Paul (b. 1927)
In the Shakespeare Garden at Northwestern University.
Ode on a Bicycle on Halsted Street in a Sudden Summer Thunderstorm.
Ode to the Angels Who Move Perpetually toward the Dayspring of Their Youth.

Carruth, Hayden (b. 1921)
Alive.
At Seventy-Five: Rereading an Old Book.
Bearer, The.
California: "To come again into the place of revolutionary."
Camps, The.
Capper Kaplinski at the North Side Cue Club.
Cows at Night, The.
Crucifixion.
Essay on Death.
Fantastic Names of Jazz, The.
Forty-Five.
Impossible Indispensability of the Ars Poetica, The.
Last Poem in the World, The.
Little Citizen, Little Survivor.
Memory.
No Matter What, After All, and That Beautiful Word So.
Of Distress Being Humiliated by the Classical Chinese Poets.
On a Certain Engagement South of Seoul.
On Being Asked to Write a Poem Against the War in Vietnam.
Paragraph 36.
Paragraphs, *sels.*
Pittsburgh.
Quality of Wine.
Saturday at the Border.
Scrambled Eggs and Whiskey.
Sleeping Beauty, The, *sels.*
Soft Time of the Year, The.
Sonnet: "Well, she told me I had an aura. 'What?' I said."
Sonnets, *sels.*
Swept.
Testament.
Time, Place, and Parenthood.
Vermont, *sel.*
Woodcut on the Cover of Robert Frost's *Complete Poems*, The.
Wreck of the Circus Train, The.

Carryl, Charles Edward (1841–1920)
Admiral's Caravan, The, *sel.*
Davy and the Goblin, *sels.*

Sleepy Giant, The.

Carryl, Guy Wetmore (1873–1904)
Ballad: "As I was walkin' the jungle round, a-killin' of tigers an' time."
Embarrassing Episode of Little Miss Muffet, The.
Harmonious Heedlessness of Little Boy Blue, The.
Patrician Peacocks and the Overweening Jay, The.
Sycophantic Fox and the Gullible Raven, The.

Carson, Anne
Beauty of the Husband, The, *sels.*
Epitaph: Zion.
Essay on What I Think about Most.
Father's Old Blue Cardigan.
Glass Essay, The, *sels.*
Gnosticism.
Kitchen.
Lazarus (1st draft).
Lazarus Standup: Shooting Script.
Life of Towns, The, *sels.*
Longing, a Documentary.
New Rule.
Short Talk on Gertrude Stein About 9:30.
Short Talk on Orchids.
Short Talk on Reading.
Short Talk on the Sensation of Aeroplane Takeoff.
Short Talk on the Truth to Be Had From Dreams.
Short Talk on the Youth at Night.
Short Talk on Trout.
Short Talk on Walking Backwards.
Stanzas, Sexes, Seductions.
Sumptuous Destitution.
Truth About God, The, *sels.*
TV Men, *sels.*

Carson, Ciaran (b. 1948)
Army.
Asylum.
Bagpipe Music.
Belfast Confetti.
Bloody Hand.
Calvin Klein's Obsession.
Campaign.
Céilí.
Clearance.
Cocktails.
Dresden.
Hamlet.
Irish for No, The.
Judgement.
Knee, The.
Mouth, The.
Slate Street School.
Turn Again.

Carson, Jo
I Am Asking You to Come Back Home.

Cărtărescu, Mircea (b. 1956)
Happy Day in My Life, A.

Cartelli, Mary Anne (b. 1952)
Water.

Carter, Anne Babson
Cobb's Barns.

Carter, Charlotte Osgood
Parts of a Mystery.

Carter, John
Adagio at Twilight.

Carter, Martin (b. 1927)
Bitter Wood.

Carter, Samuel (*fl.* 1848–51)
Arthur Mervyn; A Tale of Social Grievances, *sels.*
Avenger, The, *sels.*
London, *sels.*

Cartwright, Keith (b. 1960)
ALL-YOU-CAN-EAT / catfish houses.
Delta, The / Itch of cayenne.
In / dreams / diving deeper / than my disbelief.

Cartwright, William (1611–43)
Dream Broke, A.
Falsehood.
No Platonic [*or* Platonique] Love.

On a Virtuous Young Gentlewoman That Died Suddenly.
On the Great Frost (1634).
On the Queen's Return from the Low Countries.
Song of Dalliance, A.
To Chloe, Who Wished Herself Young Enough for Me.

Carus, Titus Lucretius *See* Lucretius

Carver, Dale R.
Poet, The.

Carver, Raymond (1938–88)
Alcohol.
At Least.
Bonnard's Nudes.
Catch, The.
Cobweb, The.
Drinking While Driving.
Gravy.
Happiness.
Late Fragment.
Luck.
My Dad's Wallet.
NyQuil.
Old Days, The.
Quiet Nights.
River, The: "I waded, deepening, into the dark water."
This Morning.
Waiting.
Walk, A.
What the Doctor Said.
Window, The.
Woman Bathing.

Cary, Alice (1820–71)
Autumn.
Bridal Veil, The.
Contradiction.
In Bonds.
Katrina on the Porch.
My Creed.
Sea-Side Cave, The.
Telling Fortunes.
To Solitude.
West Country, The.
Window Just Over the Street, The.

Cary, Dame Clementia (1615–71)
You blessed Soules, who stand before.

Cary, Elizabeth *See* Falkland, Elizabeth Cary, Countess of

Cary, Phoebe (1824–71)
Advice Gratis to Certain Women.
Day Is Done, The.
Dorothy's Dower.
Granny's House.
Harvest Gathering.
Homes for All.
Human and Divine.
Hymn: "How dare I in thy courts appear."
Jacob.
Leak in the Dike, The.
Legend of the Northland, A.
Nearer Home.
Prodigals.
Samuel Brown.
Shakespearian Readings.
Unbelief.
When Lovely Woman.

Casal, Julián de (1863–93)
My Loves.

Cascella, Anna (b. 1941)
Difficult with You.
Even Your Escape Is a Bit Special.
Forgetfulness Is Not.
In the Deposits of the Heart.
Nomad of the Sky, The.
To One Afflicted with Adolescence.

Case, David
Fear No More.

Casey, Kenneth (*fl.* 1925)
Sweet Georgia Brown.

Casey, Michael (b. 1947)
Bummer, A.
Learning.

LZ Gator Body Collector, The.
On What the Army Does with Heads.

Cashdan, Liz
Laughing All the Way.

Casiano, Americo
Puente.

Casper, Robert N. (b. 1970)
Untitled: "Remember our ecstatic parade."

Cassells, Cyrus (b. 1957)
Beautiful Signor.
Courtesy, Trenchant Grace, A.
From the Theater of Wine.
Magician-Made Tree, The, *sels.*
Marathon.
New Song of Solomon.
Soul Make a Path Through Shouting.
These Are Not Brushstrokes.
Women, The.

Cassian, Nina (b. 1924)
Bread and Wine.
Capital Punishment.
Ghost.
I Left Those Walls.
Lady of Miracles.
Like Ana.
Morning Exercises.
Orbits.
Other Life, the.
Part of a Bird.
Rabbit, The.
Sacrilege.
Sand.
Temptation.
Us Two.

Cassity, Turner (b. 1929)
Meaner Than a Junkyard Dog; or, Turner's
Evil Twin.
Other-Directed.
Why Fortune Is the Empress of the World.

Casson, Christine
To the South: "Journey to Italy began in your
youth, The."

Castellanos, Rosario (1925–74)
Destiny.
Farewell, The.
Hecuba's Testament.
Love: "Only the voice, the skin, the polished."
Meditation on the Threshold.
Nazareth.
Origin.
Other, The.
Palm Tree, A.
Parable of the Unfaithful Wife.
Poetry Is Not You.
Return.
Return, The.
Silence Around an Ancient Stone.
Speaking of Gabriel.
Two Meditations.
Two Poems.
You Are Not Poetry.

Castera, Georges (b. 1936)
Blood.
Both Yesterday and Today.
Cemetery Gate.
I Have a Comrade.
Zilch Movement.

Casterton, Julia
One Flesh.

Castillero, Silvia Eugenia (b. 1963)
Astilla.
Chimera.
Diminuto Anfibio.
Entraña.
Hare, The.
Innard.
Jeopard, The.
Jeopardo, El.
Liebre, La.
Madeja.
Minute Amphibian.
Quimera.
Skein.
Splinter.

Castillo, Ana (b. 1953)
Me and Baby.
Nani Worries about Her Father's Happiness in
the Afterlife.
Toltec, The.
Women Are Not Roses.

Castillo, Otto René (1936–67)
Apolitical Intellectuals.
Before the Scales, Tomorrow.
Distances.

Castillo, Ricardo (b. 1954)
Ode to the Urge.

Castillo, Sandra M.
Almendares.
Apagón, El.
At the Havana Hilton.
Contra, The.
Cuba.
En el Sol de Mi Barrio.
Letter to Yeni on Peering into Her Life.
Monday Night at Pedro's.
Primos.
Rincón.
Voyeur.

Casto, Robert Clayton (b. 1932)
Salt Pork, The.

Caston, Anne
Blowing Eggs.
Burden, The.
Gathering at the River.

Castro, Adrian (b. 1967)
Hoodoo Whisper.

Castro, Michael (b. 1945)
Blew It.
New York City.

Castro, Rosalía de (1837–85)
Ailing Woman Felt Her Forces Ebb, The.
As I Composed This Little Book.
Atmosphere Is Incandescent, The.
Bells, The.
Black Mood.
Black Mood.
Candescent Lies the Air.
Feeling Her End Would Come with Summer's
End.
Feet of Spring Are on the Stair, The.
Glowworm Scatters Flashes, A.
He Who Weeps Goes Not Alone.
Hour After Hour, Day After Day.
I in My Bed of Thistles.
I Know Not What I Seek Eternally.
I Love You... Why Do You Hate Me?
I Was Born at Birth of Blossoms.
Justice of Men! I Go in Search of You.
Mild Was the Air.
Now all that sound of laughter, sound of
singing.
Now that the Sunset of Hope.
Spring Does Not Flow Now, The.
They Say that the Plants Do Not Speak.
When the Frosts Cover Them.

Catacalos, Rosemary
Casa, La.
Homesteaders.
Katakalos.
Letter to a Brother in Exile.
One Man's Family.
Swallow Wings.

Catalano, Gary (b. 1947)
Australia.
Jews Speak in Heaven, The.

Cataldi, Lee (b. 1942)
Advice.
It's Easy.
13 November 1983.
We Could Have Met.

Cather, Willa Sibert (1876–1947)
Grandmither, Think Not I Forget.
Macon Prairie.
Prairie Spring.

Catherine of Siena (Saint Catherine) (1347–1380)
Prayer 20, *sel.*

Ćatić, Musa Ćatim (1878–1915)
Nostalgia: "Way. . .way back. . .nine hills
away."

Catling, Brian (b. 1948)
Pittancer, The.

**Catullus (Gaius [*or* Caius] Valerius Catullus)
(87–c.54 B.C.)**
Accept, O Priapus, the moister.
By strangers' coasts and waters, many days at
sea.
Carmen: 11.
Carmina, *sels.*
Carmina [Charles Martin Translation], *sels.*
De Amore Suo.
He is like a god.
He Seems to Me Almost a God.
Ipsithilla, my pet, my favorite dish.
Just now I found a young boy.
Lesbia.
Lesbia's sparrow!
My lovely, sweet Ipsithilla.
My Sweetest Lesbia.
My woman says she'd rather have me.
Odi et Amo.
Sweet sparrow, my lover's pet.
31.
To Aurelius.
To Aurelius and Furius.
To Juventius.
Unto no body my woman saith she had rather
a wife be [*or* bee].
What for?
Your sins have brought my mind so low.

Catulus, Quintus (*fl.* 102 B.C.)
Waking Intuitively.

Caulfield, Carlota (b. 1953)
For Albert, the Terrible.
In My Labyrinth (The Minotaur's Game).
Merci Bien, Monsieur.
You All Know the Story of the Two
Lovers.

Causley, Charles (b. 1917)
Angel's Song.
Apple-Tree Man, The.
Armistice Day.
At Candlemas.
At the British War Cemetery, Bayeux.
Betjeman, 1984.
By St. Thomas Water.
Conversation in Gibraltar 1943.
Death of a Poet.
Eden Rock.
Figgie Hobbin.
Forest of Tangle, The.
HMS *Glory.*
I Am the Great Sun.
I Am the Song.
I Saw a Jolly Hunter.
Infant Song.
Innocent's Song.
Mary's Song.
Nursery Rhyme of Innocence and Experience.
On Being Asked to Write a School Hymn.
On the Thirteenth Day of Christmas.
Sailor's Carol.
Song of Samuel Sweet, The.
Song of the Dying Gunner A.A.1.
What Has Happened to Lulu?

Cavafy, Constantine P. (1863–1933)
At the Cafe Door.
Bandaged Shoulder, The.
Candles.
Che Fece . . . Il Gran Rifiuto.
City, The.
City, The.
Comes to Rest.
Days of 1908.
Days of 1908.
In Despair.
In the Street.
Ithaca.
Ithaka.
Ithaka.
One Night.
Passing Through.
Return.
Supplication.
Their Beginning.

Waiting for the Barbarians.
Waiting for the Barbarians.
Waiting for the Barbarians.
When They Come Alive.

Cavalcanti, Guido (1250–1301)
Ballata II: Last Song: from Exile.
Encounter, An.
Sonnet [or Sonetto] 7: "Who is she that comes, makyng turn every man's eye."
To Dante [or Sonnet: Guido Cavalcanti to Dante Alighieri].

Cavalieri, Grace
First, The.
Grandmother.

Cavalli, Patrizia (b. 1949)
Across My Face the Nights Fall.
Ah, yes, to your misfortune.
And to see the city again and to see it again.
Before when you left you would always forget.
But first one must free oneself.
Far from kingdoms.
Far from the Kingdoms.
How pointless this straining.
I don't have any seed to cast about the world.
I Go, but Where? Oh Gods!
I Have No Seed to Scatter through the World.
I pretend to wait for you to enlarge the minutes.
I remember little of myself.
If Now You Knocked on My Door.
In that small dark fever of every reawakening.
In the Just Dampened Park.
In the shade of a metaphor.
Inside Your Sea My Boat Was Sailing.
It Will Not Apprehend the Object.
Little of myself do I remember.
Moroccans with the carpets, The.
Now that the time seems all mine.
Of All Distances the Best Possible One.
Of all the huntresses.
Outside, in fact, there wasn't any change.
Outside nothing's really changed.
Rain brings me back, The.
Someone told me.
Stunned I Was Looking for Reasons.
That white cloud in its contrast.
This time I won't permit the blue.
To simulate the burning of the heart.
To Simulate the Burning of the Heart, the Humiliation.
Together eternity and death threaten me.
When I listen for the sound of.
When suddenly, you're hit with good health.
Who ever again will be able to say.

Cavanagh, Eithne
Return to Avondale.

Cave, Jane (c.1754–1813)
Elegy on a Maiden Name, An.

Cavé, Syto (b. 1944)
Permit.

Cavendish, George (1499?–1561?)
Epitaph of Our Late Queen Mary, An.

Cavendish, Lady Jane (1621–1669)
Answeare to my Lady Alice Edgertons Songe, Of I prethy send mee back my Hart, An.
On my honorable Grandmother, Elizabeth Countess of Shrewbury.
On the 30th of June to God.

Cavendish, William, Duke of Newcastle (1592–1676)
Love's Matrimony.
Love's Sun.

Cavendish, Margaret Lucas, Duchess of Newcastle (1623?–73)
Body, The: A Fancy.
Claspe, The.
Common Fate of Books, The.
Courting the Faerie Queen.
Dialogue betwixt Man, and Nature, A.
Dialogue betwixt the Body and the Mind, A.
Discourse of Beasts, A.
Discourse of Melancholy, A.
Dissert, A, sel.
Fort or Castle of Hope, The, sel.
Her Descending Down.

Hunting of a Stag, The.
Hunting of the Hare, The.
Imagination.
Landscape, A.
Of Cold Worlds.
Of Many Worlds in This World.
Of Stars.
Of the Animal Spirits.
Pastime of the Queen of Fairies, The.
Poetresses Petition, The.
Poet[r]ess's Hasty Resolution, The.
Posset for Nature's Breakfast, A.
Ruine of this Island, The.
Sea Similized to Meadows and Pastures, The: the Mariners, to Shepherds: the Mast, to a May-Pole: the Fish, to Beasts.
Woman drest by Age, A.

Cawein, Madison (1865–1914)
Beauty.
Caverns.
Dead Cities.
Deserted.
Echo.
Mnemosyne.
Music.
On Reading the Life of Haroun Er Reshid.
Orgie.
Poetry.
Purple Valleys, The.
Rome.
Stars, The.
Three Elements, The.
Uncalled.
Unimaginative, The.

Cawthorn, James (1719–61)
Wit and Learning, sel.

Cayetano, E. Roy
Drums of My Fathers.

Caylely, John (b. 1956)
Reveal Code: Indra's Net 8, sels.

Ceccoli, Marino (fl. 14th cent.)
Oh, and yet I see that I will return to you anyway, and throw myself at your feet and cry a lot over my sins, until my crime will be pardoned.
Sir, I have remained so overcome, that I can no longer suffer your attacks.

Cecil, Mildred, Lady Burleigh (1526–89)
As when at first primitive men were dwelling on the fruitful earth.

Cecil, Richard
Apology.
Richard's Blues.
Some Terms in Real Estate Defined.
Threnody for Sunrise ("Please, when you ask me in this dream.").
Threnody for Sunset ("It's five o'clock. Someone's taped my name out.").

Cedering, Siv
Regarding Music.
Variations for the Piano.

"Ceiriog" See Hughes, John Ceiriog

Celan, Paul (1920–70)
Alchemical.
All those sleep shapes.
Aspen Tree.
Aspen Tree . .
Breathcrystal.
Corona.
Death Fugue.
Death Fugue, A.
Deathfugue.
Etched Away From.
Fugue of Death.
I am the first.
I HEAR THAT THE AXE HAS FLOWERED.
In Prague.
Into the Foghorn.
Irish.
Jugs, The.
Language Mesh.
Largo.
Leaf, treeless, A.
Leaf, Treeless for Bertolt Brecht, A.
Leap-Centuries.

Little night.
Mandorla.
Matière de Bretagne.
Matière de Bretagne.
Near, in the aorta's arch.
Night Ray.
Nothingness, for the, The.
Once, / I heard him.
Plashes the Fountain.
Poles / are within us, The.
Profuse announcement.
Psalm.
Psalm: "No one kneads us again out of earth and clay."
Psalm: "No one moulds us again out of earth and clay."
Shibboleth.
Shot Forth.
Speak You Too.
Tenebrae.
Tenebrae.
There was earth inside them, and.
There was earth inside them, and.
Thread suns.
Threadsuns / over the grayblack wasteness.
When you lie.
World to be stuttered after.
You be like you, ever.
You were my death.
Your Hand Full of Hours.
Zeitgehoft, sels.
Zurich, at the Stork.
Zürich, the Stork Inn.

Celaya, Gabriel (1911–91)
After a Native Poem from the Solomon Islands that Begins: "Your Shameful Parts Are the White Man's Gramophone."
Great Moments.
Life One Leads, The.
Meaning of Soup, The.
Momentos Felices.
Poesía Es un Arma Cargada de Futuro, La.
Poetry Is a Weapon Loaded with the Future.
Sentido de la Sopa, El.
Sobre un Poema Nativo de las Islas Salomón que Comienza: "Tu Vergüenza Genital Es el Gramófono del Hombre Blanco."
Teoría de Silencios.
Theory of Silences.
Vida que Uno Lleva, La.

Çelebi, Asaf Halet (1907–58)
Maria 1.
Maria 2.
My Little Woman.

Célestin-Mégie, Emile (b. 1922)
I'm Writing a Poem.

Cemal Süreya (1931–90)
Butt Cast in the Sea, A.
8:10 Ferry, The.
Kiss Me, Then Give Birth to Me.
Rose: "Seated at the core of the rose I weep."
Yellow Blight.

Cempulappeyanirar
What He Said.

Cendrars, Blaise (Frédéric-Louis Sauser-Hall) (1887–1961)
Aleutian Islands.
Contrasts.
Fish Cove.
Frisco-City.
Great Fetishes, The.
Hammock.
Harvest.
Head, The.
Journal.
Letter.
Lettre.
Ma Danse.
Medrano Academy.
Menus.
My Dance.
My Dance.
Newspaper.
Prose du Transsibérien et de la Petite Jeanne de France, sels.

Prose of the Trans-Siberian and Little Jean of
   France.
Prose of the Trans-Siberian and of Little
   Jeanne of France, The.
Prose of the Trans-Siberian and of Little
   Jeanne of France, The, *sel.*
South.

Ceni, Alessandro (b. 1957)
Atrium.
Fragment.
Key and the Tree, The.
Reconciled Flame.
With What Courage.

Centamputan, Maturai Eruttalan
What She Said.

Centolella, Thomas (b. 1952)
Joy.
Small Acts.
Woman of Three Minds, The.
Zeno's Progress.

Cepollaro, Biagio (b. 1959)
Requiem in C.

Ceraman Kottampalattut
Great It May Be.

Ceravolo, Joseph (1934–88)
After the Rain.
Autumn-Time, Wind and the Planet Pluto.
Caught in the Swamp.
Celebration.
Conception.
Dangers of the Journey to the Happy Land.
Data.
Drunken Winter.
Dusk: "Before the dusk grows deeper."
Fill and Illumined.
Geological Hymn.
Grow.
Happiness in the Trees.
Heart Feels the Water.
Ho Ho Ho Caribou.
I Like to Collapse.
Indian Suffering.
Invisible Autumn.
Lighthouse.
May: "I am lost. / I had swum before."
New Realism.
Pregnant, I Come.
Rain: "Rain is not surrounded by sleep like a
   drum."
Sculpture.
Song of Autumn, A.
Spring in This World of Poor Mutts.
Spring of Work Storm.
Stolen Away.
Sunset.
Warmth.
White Fish in Reeds.
Wild Provoke of the Endurance Sky.
Wind Is Blowing West, The.
Women, The.

Cerenio, Virginia
My Mother.
13 June 1994.
20 July 1994.
23 October 1992.

Cernuda, Luis (1903–63)
A Larra con Unas Violetas.
Boy Behind a Window.
Cementerio en la Ciudad.
Cemetery in the City.
De Qué País.
For Two Voices.
From What Country.
I don't want to return a sad spirit.
If Man Could Name.
I'll Tell You How You Were Born.
Impresión de Destierro.
Impression of Exile.
Invisible wall, The.
Lover Digresses, The.
Niño Tras un Cristal.
No Decía Palabras.
Nocturnal, you sword-fight.
Remordimiento en Traje de Noche.
Remorse Dressed Up as Night.

Shadow, The.
Speaking Other Than with Words.
That Which Is Enough for Love.
To Larra with Some Violets.
You were a tender desire, an insinuating cloud.

Cerruto, Oscar (1912–81)
Love: "Afternoon is offered to us, The."

Cervantes, Lorna Dee (b. 1954)
A un Desconocido.
Archeology.
Beneath the Shadow of the Freeway.
Body as Braille, The.
Cannery Town in August.
Como lo Siento.
Emplumada.
First Beating.
Freeway 280.
Interpretation of Dinner by the Uninvited
   Guest, An.
Isla Mujeres.
Levee: Letter to No One, The.
Meeting Mescalito at Oak Hill Cemetery.
On the Poet Coming of Age.
Poem for the Young White Man Who Asked
   Me How I, An Intelligent, Well-Read Person
   Could Believe in the War Between Races.
Poema para los Californios Muertos.
Poet Is Served Her Papers, The.
Refugee Ship.
Starfish.
To We Who Were Saved by the Stars.
Uncle's First Rabbit.
Visions of Mexico While at a Writing
   Symposium in Port Townsend, Washington.

Césaire, Aimé (b. 1912)
An neuf.
Automatic Crystal, The.
Automatic Crystal, The.
Batouque.
Blank to Fill in on the Visa of Pollen.
Bucolic.
Configurations, *sel.*
Cristal Automatique.
Day and Night.
Different Horizon.
Do Not Have Pity.
In Memory of a Black Union Leader.
In Order to Speak.
Lagoonal Calendar.
Laughable.
Lay of the Rover.
Lynch 1.
Macumba Word.
Miraculous Weapons, The.
New Year.
Notebook of a Return to the Native Land, *sel.*
On the Islands of All Winds.
Since Akkad, Since Elam, Since Sumer.
Sun Serpent.
Three for Bear.
Virgin Forest, The.

Cesaire, Aime *and* **Rene Depestre**
Discourse on Colonialism, *sel.*

Cetina, Gutierre de (c.1520–c.1557)
Happy Hours that Hurry Away.
In What Region, in What Part of the World.
Madrigal 1.
Madrigal: Eyes of Clear Serenity.

Ch'en Meng-chia (1911–66)
Old White Russian, An.

Ch'en Yün (1886–1910)
Twilight.

Cha, Theresa Hak Kyung (1951–82)
Dictée, *sels.*
Morcels: Between the Lines.

Chabbi, Fadhila (b. 1946)
Blind Goddess, The.
Engraving Twenty-Nine.

Chadwick, Jerah
Eight-Legged Colt, Chernobyl.

Chagy, John (1912–90)
Haggai.

Chaikin, Miriam (b. 1928)
Light Another Candle.

One-Upmanship.

Chajang, Great Master (590–658)
Hymn to Sarira.

Chalfi, Raquel
Night Hair.
Reading the I Ching.

Chalkhill, John (fl. c.1600)
Coridon's Song.

Chaloner, David
Emblem.
Spring and Other Places.
Thicket of Time.
Unnamed.
Vista Vert.
Waste.

Chamberlain, Brenda (1912–71)
Dead Ponies.
Islandman.
Seal Cave.

Chamberlain, Karen
Airlift.
Indian Summer.
Riding the Lion, Riding the Lamb.
Stepping in the Same River.

Chamberlayne, William (1619–89)
Pharonnida, *sels.*

Chambers, Gordon
If Only for One Night.
Meditations on Stevie.
Waxing Poetic on Marvin.

Chambers, Jane (1937–83)
To Beth On Her Forty-Second Birthday.

Chambers, Stephen
Her.

Champ, Amy
Buddha is neither asian nor male. she could be
   an african woman.

Chan Fang-sheng (fl. c.400)
Poem About My Study at the Back of the
   House.
Sailing Back to the Capital.
Sailing into the South Lake.

Chandar, Mailabattula Satish (b. 1958)
Birth Postponed, A.
Child Is Born, A.

Chandidas (fl. 1375–1450)
Why Tell Me What to Do?

Chandra, G. S. Sharat
Peasants Waiting for Rain.

Chang Chi (768–830)
Coming at Night to a Fisherman's Hut.
Elegy: "We carved our names."
Maple Bridge Night Mooring.
Night at Anchor by Maple Bridge.
Night-Mooring at Maple Bridge.
Night-Mooring near Maple Bridge, A.

Ch'ang Chien (fl. c.749)
Buddhist Retreat Behind Broken-Mountain
   Temple, A.

Chang Chiu-ling (673–740)
Climbing a Tall Building on an Autumn
   Evening: I Gaze to Where the South River
   Touches the Shixing Road.
Poems of Reflection on the Vicissitudes of
   Life, *sel.*

Chang, Diana (b. 1934)
Foreign Ways.
On Being in the Midwest.

Chang, Edmond Yi-teh (b. 1965)
After the Storm.
Bamboo Elegy: Two.
Near-Sightedness.

Chang Heng (A.D. 78–139)
Bones of Zhuangzi, The.

Chang Jo-Hsü *See* Zhang Ruoxu

Chang K'o-chiu (1265?–1345?)
At Waterfall Temple.
Tune: "Merriment Before the Palace Hall"
Tune: "Traveler Welcoming the Immortal"
Tune: "Unbroken"
Year's End.

Chang Pi
Butterfly.

Chang, Victoria
Five-Year Plan.
Chang Wu-chien
Vase of Perfume, The.
Chang Yang-hao (1269–1329)
Ch'ü Yüan's "sorrow."
Tune: "Sheep on the Mountain Slope."
T'ung Pass.
Chang Yen (1248–c.1320)
Tune: "Pure Serene Music"
Chang Yü (1333–85)
Merchant's Joy, The.
Pavilion for Listening to Fragrance, The.
Chang Yüeh (667–730)
Composition in Drunkenness.
Hearing Bells at Night in the Mountains.
Chang-soo Koh *See* Ko Changsu
Channing, William Ellery (1818–1901)
Barren Moors, The.
Chant to the Fire-fly.
Earth Spirit, The, *sel.*
Harbor, The.
Hymn of the Earth.
Murillo's Magdalen.
Walden.
Chao Luan-luan (*fl.* 8th? cent.)
Cloud Hairdress.
Creamy Breasts.
Red Sandalwood Mouth.
Slender Fingers.
Willow Eyebrows.
Chao Meng-fu (1254–1322)
Admonition to Myself, An.
To a Pyrotechnist.
Chao Shan-ch'ing (*fl.* c.1320)
Autumn on the Riverbank.
Chapman, Arthur (1873–1935)
Out Where the West Begins.
Chapman, George (1559?–1634)
Coronet for His Mistress Philosophy, A, *sels.*
Eugenia, *sels.*
Euthymia Raptus, *sels.*
Hero and Leander, *sels.*
Homer and the Brazen Head of Rumour.
Homer's Iliad, To the Reader, *sel.*
Ovid's Banquet of Sense, *sels.*
Chapman, J. Wilbur (1859–1918)
Jesus! What a friend for sinners!
One Day!
Chapman, John Alexander (b. 1875)
Gipsy Queen.
Chapman, Lyn'elle Patrice
Stevie Wonder.
Chapman, Robin S.
Your Face Here.
Chappell, Fred (b. 1936)
Attending, The.
Cleaning the Well.
Guess Who.
My Father's Hurricane.
My Mother's Hard Row to Hoe.
Narcissus and Echo.
Remembering Wind Mountain at Sunset.
Truth at Last, The.
Char, René (b. 1907)
Alberto Giacometti.
Argument.
At the Gates of Aerea.
Chambre dans l'espace, La.
Disdained Apparitions.
Dowry of Maubergeonne, The.
Dyne.
Every Life.
Faction Du Muet.
Fighters.
Leaves of Hypnos, *sel.*
Leaves of Hypnos No. 128.
Lied du figuier.
Lied of the Fig Tree.
Lutteurs.
Man flees suffocation.
Martinet, Le.
Mortal Partner, The.
Mortel Partenaire, Le.

On the Bell Frieze of a Roman Church.
Redonnez-leur.
Restore to Them.
Room in Space.
Swift, The.
To Friend-Tree of Counted Days.
Toute Vie.
Tree Frog, The.
Unbending Prayer.
Vers l'arbre-frère aux jours comptés.
Charach, Ron
Evidence on Film, The.
Labour and Delivery.
MRI.
Question of Vitamins, A.
Charara, Hayan (b. 1972)
Hamza Aweiwi, a Shoemaker in Hebron.
Here It Is.
Holy Water.
More Than We Dared.
My Father Breaks the Neighbor's Nose.
On the Murder of an Ice Cream Man.
Thinking American.
Charbonel, Monique (1941–71)
It's a Wonder.
Charlemagne (742?–814)
Veni Creator Spiritus.
Charles, Dorthi (b. 1963)
Getting Dirty.
Charles, J. B. (1910–83)
Polish Girl Standing on a Chair, A.
Charles, Tony
I saw a great building with many storeys piled
high.
Charlton, John *See* Afrika, Tatamkulu
Charry Lara, Fernando (b. 1920)
I Would Have Loved You.
Chase, Karen
Before She Died.
Venison.
What You Can't See.
Chase, Naomi Feigelson
He Comes to Lie Down.
Music Mother.
My Mother, Listening to Flowers.
Plenty.
Chasin, Helen (b. 1938)
City Pigeons.
Getting the News.
In Communication with a UFO.
Joy Sonnet in a Random Universe.
Strength.
Word *Plum*, The.
Chatterton, Thomas (1752–70)
Aella; a Tragycal Enterlude, *sels.*
Elegy on Mr. William Smith, *sel.*
Excelente Balade of Charitie, An.
Ode to Miss Hoyland.
Chaucer, Geoffrey (1340?–1400)
Book of the Duchesse, The, *sels.*
Canterbury Tales, The, *sels.*
Chaucer's Wordes unto Adam, his Owne
Scriveyn.
Legend of Good Women, The, *sels.*
Love Unfeigned, The.
Merciles[s] Beaute [*or* Beautée *or* Beauty],
sels.
Parlement of Foules, The, *sels.*
Troilus and Criseyde [*or* Criseide], *sels.*
Chavarría, Lismaco (1878–1913)
Lone Tree.
Chavez, Lisa D. (b. 1961)
After the Prom.
Clean Sheets.
In the Season of Suicides.
Woman Who Raised Dogs, The.
Chavis, Nzinga Regtuinah
Enter(f*#@ckin)tained.
Chazal, Malcolm de
It was / so hot.
Logic.
Logique, La.
Plastic Sense (1947 version).
Plastic Sense (1948 version).

Sens Plastique, *sel.*
Sens plastique (1947), *sel.*
Sens plastique (1948), *sel.*
Chedid, Andrée (b. 1920)
Épreuves du poète.
For Survival.
Full face.
Future and the Ancestor, The.
Going Forth.
Imagine.
Looking at Childhood.
Man-today.
Movement.
Naked Face, The.
Regarder l'enfance.
Renegade.
Stepping Aside.
Trials of the Poet.
Turn.
What are We Playing at?
Who Remains Standing?
Cheek, Cris
Rollercoaster.
Cheke, Lady Mary (c.1527–1616)
Erat Quaedam Mulier.
Chen Huan (776–839)
Presented to the Taoist Paragon Mao.
Ch'en Lin (d. 217)
Horses at a Breach in the Great Wall.
Song: "I watered my horse at the Long Wall
caves."
Chen Shubao, Emperor (553–604)
Jade Tree Blossoms in the Back Garden, A.
Ch'en Tao (779–843)
Turkestan.
Ch'en Tzu-ang (661–702)
Poems of Reflection on the Vicissitudes of
Life, *sels.*
Ch'en Yü-yi (1090–1138)
Tune: "Immortal at the Riverbank"
Chen Zi'ang (661–702)
Entering Quiao Gorge and Anju Creek.
Meditation on the Past at White Emperor City.
Song on Youzhou Terrace.
Staying in Luoxiang County for the Evening.
Chenette, Sue (b. 1942)
Ritual.
Cheney-Coker, Syl
Analysis.
Childhood.
Dead Eyes.
Letter to a Tormented Playwright.
On Being a Poet in Sierra Leone.
Outsider, The.
Peasants.
Poet Among Those Who Are Also Poets.
Cheng Hsieh (1693–1765)
Song of Surfing on the Bore.
Ch'eng-kung Sui (231–273)
Rhapsody on Whistling.
Chénier, André Marie de (1762–94)
Elegies, *sel.*
Hermes, *sel.*
We live; we live in squalor. And so? It had to
be.
Chenkó, Jag
Di Brook Di Dry.
Cherches, Peter
Where is She?
Chernoff, Maxine (b. 1952)
Breasts.
Dead Letter Office, The.
God: "God is in the high notes."
How Lies Grow.
Japan, *sels.*
Lost and Found.
Man Struck Twenty Times by Lightning, The.
Miss Congeniality.
News, The.
Tenderitis.
Toothache.
Vanity, Wisconsin.

Cherokee Oral Tradition
Formula to Cause Death.
Formula to Secure Love.

Cherry, Andrew
Green Little Shamrock of Ireland, The.

Cherry, James E.
Amadou.
Bird.
Pretty White Girls.

Cherry, Kelly (b. 1940)
Bride of Quietness, The.
For Teen-Age Boys Murdered in Texas: The
    Refusal to Dramatize Bloodlust.
Forecast.
History.
How to Wait.
In the Garden By the Sea: Easter.
Late Afternoon at the Arboretum.
On Watching a Young Man Play Tennis.
Pines Without Peer, The.
Prayer for a Future Beyond Ideology and War.
Raiment We Put On, The.
Reading, Dreaming, Hiding.
Rose, The.
Waiting for the End of Time.

Chesimard, JoAnne See Shakur, Assata

Chess, Richard (b. 1953)
Growing Up in a Jewish Neighborhood.
No Music.
Two and One.
Yiddish Poets in America.

Chester, Anson G. (1824–1911)
Tapestry Weaver, The.

Chester, Laura (b. 1949)
Free Rein, sel.

Chester, Tessa Rose (b. 1950)
Buttons.
Candle at Canterbury, A.
Running Hares.

**Chesterfield, Philip Dormer Stanhope, 4th Earl
of (1694–1773)**
On Lord Ila's Improvements, near Hounslow
    Heath.

Chesterton, G. K. (Gilbert Keith) (1874–1936)
Antichrist, or the Reunion of Christendom; an
    Ode.
Aristocrat, The.
Ballade of Suicide, A.
Certain Evening, A.
Christmas Carol, A: "God rest you merry
    gentlemen."
Christmas Carol: "Christ child lay on Mary's
    lap, The."
Convert, The.
Donkey, The.
Donkey, The [1920 version].
Ecclesiastes.
Elegy in a Country Churchyard.
English Graves, The.
Fantasia.
Fat White Woman Speaks, The.
Femina Contra Mundum.
For a War Memorial.
From a Spanish Cloister.
Holy of Holies, The.
House of Christmas, The.
Joseph.
Lepanto.
Lucasta Replies to Lovelace.
On Reading "God."
Post-Recessional.
Praise of Dust, The.
Prayer in Darkness, A.
Rolling English Road, The.
Sea Replies to Byron, The.
Song against Grocers, The.
Songs of Education, sels.
Sword of Surprise, The.
Ultimate.
Variations on an Air Composed on Having to
    Appear in a Pageant as Old King Cole, sels.
Wine and Water.
World State, The.

Chevalier, Albert (1860–1923)
Sich a Nice Man Too!, sel.

Chevremont, Evaristo Ribera (1896–1975)
Symphony of the Hammers.

Cheyne, Jane See Cavendish, Lady Jane

Ch'i-chi
Admonishing a Younger Teacher.
After the Rebellion, Visiting West Mountain
    Temple.
Autumn Evening: To Send to my Nieces and
    Nephews.
Delighted That the Monk Ch'ien-chou Has
    Come a Long Way to Visit Me.
Don't Ask, sels.
Early Plum Blossoms.
Little Pines.
Not Sleeping.
Old Farmer, The.
On an Autumn Evening Listening to Reverend
    Yeh Play the Ch'in.
Quietly Discussing My Thoughts with the
    Collator of Texts Ts'ui.
Sent to a Poetry Friend.
Song of the Insolent Air.
Song of the Old Sword.
Song of the Spring Wind.
Speaking My Mind.
Start of Autumn: Hearing a Cicada While Sick
    in Bed.
Stopping at Night at Hsiang-yin.
Thinking of a Monk of Flower Summit on
    Mount T'ien-t'ai.
Up after Illness, I Watch the Idle Clouds.
White Hair.
Written on a Summer Day in the City.
Year Keng-Wu, Night of the Fifteenth, Facing
    the Moon, The.

Chia Tao (779–843)
Abode of the Unplanned Effect.
At I-Chou, Climbing the Tower of Lung-Hsing
    Temple to View the High Northern
    Mountains.
At Ni-Yang Inn.
Auspicious Arrival of Yung T'ao.
Evening View as the Snow Clears.
Farewell to Master Tan Returning to Min.
Farewell to Monk Chih-Hsing.
Farewell to T'ien Cho on Retreat on Hua
    Mountain.
Late in the Day, Gazing Out from a River
    Pavilion.
Looking for a Recluse but Failing to Find Him.
Looking for the Recluse and Not Finding Him.
Memento on the Departure of a Friend, from
    Yeh, Last Day of the Second Moon.
Meng Jung, Gainfully Unemployed.
Morning Travel.
Passing by a Mountain Village at Dusk.
Seeing Off the Monk Ts'ung-Ch'ih Returning
    to the Capital.
Seeing Off the Mountain Monk Ch'u,
    Returning to Japan.
Seeking but Not Finding the Recluse.
Sick Cicada, A.
Spending the Night at a Mountain Temple.
Spring Travel.
Thinking of Retired Scholar Wu on the River.
Watching the Late Day Clear after Snowfall.
Weeping for the Zen Master Boyan.
While Traveling.
Winter Night Farewell.
Written at the Dwelling of a Recluse.

Chia Yi (201–196 B.C.)
Owl, The.
Owl, The.
Rhymeprose on an Owl, sel.

Chiang Chieh (fl. 13th cent.)
To the Tune "The Fair Maid of Yu."

Ch'iao Chi (1280–1345)
Love Song: "Orioles and orioles."

Chiao-jan (730–99)
Cold Mountain.
I don't like foreign languages; I won't study
    them.
I hide my heart and not my deeds.
Playful Poem.

Ch'iao Lai (1640–94)
Tune: "Partridge Sky" I Rejoice to Meet a
    Friend Visting at My Rustic Study.

Chiasson, Dan
Elephant, The.
My Ravine.
Poem Beginning with a Line from Frost.
Purple Blouse.
Song for a Play.
Spade.
Stealing from Your Mother.
Vermont.

Chiasson, Herménégilde
And the Season Advances.
Apollo at Aberdeen.

Chichester, Sir Richard of (c.1197–1253)
Day by Day.

Chien Chang (fl. 10th cent. A.D.)
Given to Master Ch'ing-lun of Hsia Mountain.
Sent to Zen Master Yun-Shui.

Ch'ien Ch'i (fl. 8th cent.)
Dedicated to the Hermit Cui.
From My Study at the Mouth of the Valley: A
    Message to Censor Yang.
Kingfisher with Fish in Beak.
Visit to the Hermit Ts'ui.

Ch'ien T'ao (fl. early 11th cent.)
Blaming Sons.
In Praise of Ching K'o.
On Reading the Seas and Mountains Classic.
Poems After Drinking Wine.
Written While Drunk.

Ch'ien-wu, Ch'en See Fu, Huan

Chifu
No mind, no Buddhas, no live beings.

Chih-Wen, Sung
On Old Zhang's Pine Tree.

Chih Yuan See Zhiyuan [or Chih Yuan], Shi

Chikako (Jusammi Chikako) (fl. c.1290–1316)
On this summer night.

Chikako, Jusammi See Chikako

Chikamatsu Monzaemon (1653–1725)
Love Suicides at Sonezaki, The, sels.

Chikusen (1292–1348)
He's part of all, yet all's transcended.

Chilam Balam
Flight of the Itzás.

Child, Abigail (b. 1950)
Motive for Mayhem, A.
Squeeze.
Surplus.

Child, Lydia Maria (1802–80)
Thanksgiving Day.

Childress, William (b. 1933)
Trying to Remember People I Never Really
    Knew.

Chimi Sucho (1590–1668)
Mountain Life.
Returning to Dongrae.
Returning to My Hometown.
To a Monk Asking About Zen.

Chimombo, Steve (b. 1945)
Death Song, A.
Derailment: A Delirium.
Four Ways of Dying.
Messengers, The.
Obituary.
Of Promises and Prophecy.

Chimsoro, Samuel (b. 1949)
Change, The.
Curfew Breakers, The.

Chin, David
Sleeping Father.
Sterling Williams' Nosebleed.

Chin Ho (1819–85)
Ballad of the Maiden of Lan-ling.

Chin, Justin
Bergamot.
Cocksucker's Blues.
Ex-Boyfriends Named Michael.
Night.
Undetectable.
Why a Boy.

Why He Had to Go.

Ch'in Kuan (1049–1100)
Along the Grand Canal.
Farewell Song.
From a Dream.
Sleepless.
Song: "Pleading eyebrows, intoxicating eyes!"
Tune: "Happiness Approaches."
Tune: "Perfumed Garden."
Tune: "Rouged Lips."
Tune: "Sand of Silk-Washing Brook."
Tune: "Spring in the Painted Hall."

Chin, Marilyn
Altar.
American Rain.
Aubade: "Waking is this easy."
Autumn Leaves.
Barbarian Suite.
Beijing Spring.
Chinese Quatrains (The Woman in Tomb 44).
Composed Near the Bay Bridge (after a wild party).
Disorder, The.
Elegy for Chloe Nguyen.
Exile's Letter (Or: An Essay on Assimilation).
Floral Apron, The.
How I Got That Name.
Is It Snowing in Guangzhou?
Leaving San Francisco.
Prelude.
Repulse Bay.
Turtle Soup.
Urban Love Poem.
We Are Americans Now, We Live in the Tundra.
Year Passes in My Morning Teacup, The.

Chine-Jo, Lady (*fl.* late 17th cent.)
Wild geese / Fellow travelers.

Chinese Oral Tradition
Ballad of the Hidden Dragon, *sels.*
Expository Tale on King Wu's Expedition Against Chow, *sels.*
Song of the Wife of a Gold Mountain Man.
Transformation Text on Mahāmaudgalyāyana Rescuing His Mother from the Underworld.
Transformation Text on the Boy Shun's Extreme Filial Piety.

Ching An (1851–1912)
At Hu-k'ou, Mourning for Kao Po-tsu.
At Lushan Temple.
Beating the Heat at Jade Lake.
Crossing the Yang-Chia Bridge Once More.
Dusk of Autumn: Writing What My Heart Embraces.
Facing Snow and Writing What My Heart Embraces.
Laughing at Myself 1.
Laughing at Myself 2.
Moored at Maple Bridge.
Night Sitting.
On a Painting.
On the Road: A Spring Day at Ling-Feng.
On the Spot Where Shih-chia Tzu Sits in Meditation.
Over King Yu Mountain with a Friend.
Passing by Where Hsu, "The Wine-Flushed Immortal," Used to Live.
Returning Clouds.
Third Time Wandering to Cloud Sluice Peak.
To Show You All, on the First Morning of the Year.
Written on the Painting "Cold River Snow."

Chinn, Daryl Ngee
Not Translation, Not Poetry.
Skin Color from the Sun.

Chinnov, Igor Vladimirovich (b. 1909)
Black bird on a black and snowy branch, A.
Do you think we might go to hell too?
Gust of memory stirs faded letters, A.
In the land of Schlaraffenland.
Instance of fore-ordained harmony, An.

Chinook Oral Tradition
I won't care / if you desert me.

Chipasula, Frank Mkalawile (b. 1949)
Because the Wind Remembers.

Double Song.
Everything to Declare.
Friend, Ah You Have Changed!
Going Back Patiently.
Love Poem for My Country, A.
Manifesto on Ars Poetica.
My Blood Brother.
My Friendly People.
Nightsong, *sels.*
Ritual Girl.
Singing Drum, The.
Talking of Sharp Things.
Those Rainy Mornings.
Tramp.

Chipasula, Stella P.
I'm My Own Mother, Now.
Your Name is Gift.

Chippewa Oral Tradition
Approach of the Storm, The.
Arrow Song.
Chippewa Music, *sels.*
Love-Charm Song.
My Love Has Departed.
Sioux Woman Defends Her Children, The.
Sioux Women Gather Up Their Wounded, The.
Song of the Captive Sioux Woman.
Song of the Crows.

Chirikure, Chirikure (b. 1962)
This Is Where We Laid Him to Rest.

Chisholm, Alison
Contact.

Chisholm, Thomas O.
Great Is Thy Faithfulness.

Chitre, Dilip (b. 1938)
My Father Travels.

Chitsu
No more head shaving.

Chittenden, William Lawrence
Cowboys' Christmas Ball, The.
Old Mackenzie Trail, The.

Chittendon, Larry
Ennui.
Old Fort Phantom Hill.

Chitwood, Michael (b. 1958)
After the Missionaries.
Division.
Hard Surface Road.
Hardened Arm, The.

Ch'iu Chin (1879–1907)
To the Tune "The River Is Red."

Chiu Tsz-yung (*fl.* 1820–30)
Cantonese Love-Songs, *sels.*

Ch'iu Wei (694–789?)
Seeking a Hermit on West Mountain and Not Finding Him.

Chiun (*fl.* 15th cent.)
Nameless / Weed quickening.

Chivers, Thomas Holley (1809–58)
Apollo.
Avalon.
Call, A.
Lily Adair.
Miss Adair.
Miss Lee [*or* Rosalie Lee].
Shell, The.
To Isa Sleeping.
Vigil of Aiden, The, *sel.*
Wind, The.

Chiyojo [*or* Chiyo *or* Chiyo-Ni *or* Kaga no Chiyo *or* Fukuda Chiyo-Ni] (1703–75)
Bearing no flowers.
From the mind.
Grazing.
In the well-bucket / A morning glory.
Morning glory!, The.
Since morning glories.
Were it not for / Cries in snow.
Whether astringent.
While I was musing on my theme.

Chizhova, Elena (b. 1957)
Cassandra.

Chmielarz, Sharon
They Come Humming.

Cho, Pyong-hwa (b. 1921)
One Wintry Day.

Cho Chihun (1920–68)
Ancient Temple.
Apparition.
As I Play the Flute.
At Toriwpn.
Falling Petals.
Nun's Dance, The.
Spring Day.
Waiting.

Cho Chonsŏng (1553–1627)
Four Songs Calling a Boy, *sels.*

Cho Hŏn (1544–92)
Rain sprinkles on the pond.

Cho Hwi (*fl.* 1568–1608)
In Peking to a Woman with a Veil.

Cho Myŏngni [*or* Myŏnghŭi] (1697–1756)
Sky-geese have gone, The.
Wild geese have all flown away.

Cho Sik (1501–72)
Wearing hemp clothes in the coldest winter.

Cho Wen-chun (*fl.* 2nd cent.)
Lament: "Hills are white with snow, The."
Lament of a Graying Woman.
Poet's Wife, A.

Cho-yong (c.1050–1100)
Song: "I carouse all night."

Chock, Eric (b. 1950)
Bait, The.
Poem for George Helm: Aloha Week 1980.
Working Construction.

Ch'oe Ch'iwŏn (b. 857)
On a Rainy Autumn Night.

Ch'oe Ch'ung (984–1068)
In the Night.

Ch'oe Kinam (*fl.* 17th cent.)
Elegy to Myself.

Ch'oe Sŭngja (b. 1952)
About Women.
Do You Remember Ch'ôongp'a Street?
For the Second Time in Thirty-Three Years.
From Early On I Was.
House of Memories.
Instead of a Dream.
My Phone Rings Endlessly.
Night Owl.
Portrait of the Marginalized.
Untitled 2.
Voice, A: "Voice hidden in midair, The."
While Watching Sunset.

Choeui Eusoon (1786–1866)
Arriving at Yongmun Temple.
Autumn Thought.
On the Bank of a Stream by Taedun Temple.

Ch'ŏn Kŭm
Night draws near in a mountain village.

Ch'ŏn Yanghŭi (b. 1942)
At Moments Like This, I Always Blush.
Black Cove.
Crescent Moon.
Entering Chikso Falls.
Every Morning in the Mirror.
Millet Field in My Mind.
Mountain Stroll.
One Day.
Thoughts on a Bird.
To Single Women.

Chonaill, Eibhlin Dubh Ni *See* O'Connell, Eibhlin Dubh

Chŏng Chisang (d. 1135)
Parting.

Chŏng Chiyong (1902–?)
Home.
Homesickness.
Paengnokdam: White Deer Lake.
Rain.
Sea 6.
Spring Snow.
Star.
Windowpane I.

Chŏng Ch'ŏl (1537–94)
Boys have gone out to gather bracken.

Continued Song of Longing.
Dash of rain upon, A.
Juice of bitter herbs has, The.
Let forty thousand pecks of pearls.
Let's drink a cup of wine; let's drink another!
Little Odes on Mount Star.
Magistrate.
Milky rain on the green hills.
Snow Falling in the Pine Forest: Two Poems, *sels*.
Song of Longing.

Chông Hwajin (b. 1959)
Bowl of Mul Kimch'i, A.
Dance: "Billions of maggots are being sucked into a whirlpool."
Hidden Path, The.
I'm a Dragonfly Caught in a Net.
Knife Gets Bigger, A.
Monsoon Season Opens Children's Eyes.
Sewing Box, The.
South Yard, The.
Suddenly, the Yard Where Rice and Yeast Brew.
Sunlight Showers Down in Sheets.
Water in a Gourd.

Chông Hyônjong (b. 1939)
Are You a Star?
Blood of Daybreak, The.
Country Bus at Night.
Greenly the Earth.
Like Leaving an Umbrella Somewhere.

Chông Kŭgin (1401–81)
In Praise of Spring.

Chông Mongju (1337–92)
Though this frame should die and die.

Chông Sŏ (c.1151–70)
Regret.

Chong Xiong
Because I am it's a race thing trip.

Chông Yagyong (1762–1836)
Laughing at Myself.

Chŏnggam, Great Master (1533–1609)
At the Moment of My Death.

Chou Pang-yen (1056–1121)
Peach Blossom Stream.
Tune: "Prince Lan-Ling."

Choudhury, Malay Roy (b. 1939)
Stark Electric Jesus.

Ch'ŏyong (c.879)
Song of Ch'ŏyong.

Searle, Chris
Balthazar's Poem.

Christensen, Inger (b. 1935)
Alphabet, *sels*.
Poem on Death.

Christensen, Paul
Driving Towards Houston.
Going Postal.
Houston: An Ode, *sels*.
Summer Nights.
What the Citizens of Corpus, Rockport, Palacios, or Bryan Need.

Christie, A. V. (b. 1963)
Belongings.
Coming Off a Depression, She Prepares for Venice.
Dusk and the Wife.
Hollywood Finch, The.
In My Dream.
Overture.
Possible Man, The.

Christie, Jason
Neutrino (means little one).
Solvent.
Vernal Conifer Seance.

Christine de Pisan (1364–c.1430)
Alone in Martyrdom.

Christopher, Nicholas (b. 1951)
Far from Home.
Midsummer.
Palm Reader, The.
Through the Window of the All-Night Restaurant.
Trópico.

Walt Whitman at the Reburial of Poe.

Chrystos (b. 1946)
As I Leave You.
I Bought a New Red.
I Bring You Greetings: How.
I Have Not Signed a Treaty with the United States Government.
I Suck.
I Walk in the History of My People.
Okeydoekey Tribe, The.
Old Indian Granny, The.
Portrait of Assimilation.
Real Indian Leans Against, The.
Soap Bubbles.
Today Was a Bad Day Like TB.
You Know I Like to Be.

Chu, Bao-Long (b. 1965?)
Mother's Pearls.

Ch'u Ch'uang I (*fl.* 8th cent.)
Evening in the Garden, Clear after Rain.
Mountain Spring, A.
Tea.

Chu Hsiang (1904–33)
Pawnshop, The.

Ch'u Kuang-hsi (707–59)
Streets of Ch'ang-an.

Chu Shu-chen (*fl.* early 12th cent.)
Plaint.
Sorrow: "White moon gleams through scudding, The."
Spring Joy.
Spring Night.

Chu Tun-ju (1081?–1159?)
To an Ancient Tune.
Tune: "Nien-nu Is Charming"

Chu Ûisik (1675–1720)
Boy stops outside my window, A.
What is life, I ponder.

Chu Yohan (1900–80)
Fireworks.
Life, Death.
Sound of Rain, The.
To Catch the Moon.

Ch'u Yüan (*fl.* 4th cent. B.C.)
After Ch'u Yuan.
Heaven Questions, The, *sel*.
Heavenly Questions.
Nine Songs, The.
On Encountering Trouble.
Summons of the Soul, The.
Yellow River's Earl, The.
Ying from "The Nine Declarations."

Chu Yün-ming (1461–1527)
Fan from Korea, A.

Chuang Tzu
Breath of Nature, The.
Man: "Consider: if we measured the Four Oceans."
Man Is Born in Tao.
Need to Win, The.

Chubb, Ralph (1892–1960)
Song of My Soul.
Transfiguration.

Chubb, Thomas Caldecot (b. 1899)
Merlin.

Chudakov, Sergey [*or* Sergei] (b. 1936)
Suicide is a duel with yourself.
When the cry goes up.

Chudleigh, Mary Lee, Lady (1656–1710)
Ladies Defence, The: Or, The Bride-Woman's Counsellor Answer'd: A Poem in Dialogue Between Sir John Brute, Sir William Loveall, Melissa, and a Parson, *sel*.
Resolve, The.
Song: "Why *Damon*, why, why, why so pressing?"
To Almystrea.
To the Ladies.
Wish, The.

Chuilleanáin, Eiléan Ní (b. 1942)
Horses of Meaning, The.
Rose Geranium, The, *sels*.

Chula, Margaret (b. 1947)
This Winter's Night.

Chung-ch'ang T'ung (179–220)
Speaking My Mind.

Chunbong Manwoo (b. 1357)
On the Mountain.

Ch'ungdam, Master (c.742–65)
Ode to Knight Kip'a.
Statesmanship.

Chunggwan, Great Master (*fl.* 1590)
Upon Reading Chuang Tzu.

Chunghur Hyujung (1520–1604)
Deathbed Song.
Looking Back at My Shadow.
On Hearing the Sound of a Komunko While Passing a Mansion.
Pulil Hermitage.
Reply to King Sunjo's Poem on Bamboo.
Seeing Wonsunja Off to Kwandong Province.
Song for Three Dreams.
Thought on My Sickness, A.
To My Old Friend Lee.
While Sleeping at the Southern Sea.

Chungji (1226–92)
Casual Line, A.
Hermit's Life, A.
In My Leisure.
Instructing Fellow Buddhists after Picking Brackens.
Leisurely Enjoyment.
Mountain Life.
On Autumn.
Parody.
Waking from a Nap.
Watching the Rain at Hoeduk Inn.

Chuo Wen-chün (179?–117? B.C.)
Song of White Hair, A.

Church, Richard (1893–1972)
Earphones.
On Hearing the First Cuckoo.

Churchill, Charles (1731–64)
Author, The, *sels*.
Dedication: "Health to great Gloucester—from a man unknown."
Duellist, The, *sel*.
Ghost, The, *sel*.
Night; an Epistle to Robert Lloyd, *sel*.
Prophecy of Famine, The, *sels*.
Times, The, *sel*.

Churchyard, Thomas (c.1520–1604)
Musicall Consort, A, *sel*.
Tale of a Friar and A Shoemaker's Wife, A.

Chute, Marchette (1909–94)
Day before Christmas.
My Dog.
My Plan.

Ciardi, John (1916–86)
All about Boys and Girls.
Back through the Looking Glass to This Side.
Box Comes Home, A.
Censorship.
Death's the Classic Look.
Elegy for a Cave Full of Bones.
Elegy Just in Case.
Faces.
First Snow on an Airfield.
I Wouldn't.
Journal.
Sometimes Even Parents Win.
Song: "Bells of Sunday rang us down, The."
Stranger in the Pumpkin, The.
Suburban.
V-J Day.
What Johnny Told Me.

Cibber, Colley (1671–1757)
Another [Birthday Ode], 1743, *sel*.
Birthday Ode, 1732, *sel*.
New Year's Ode, 1731, *sel*.

Cisneros, Antonio (b. 1942)
Dedicatory (to My Wife).
Karl Marx Died 1883 Aged 65.
Loneliness, *sels*.
Spider Hangs Too Far from the Ground, The.
To a Dead Lady.

Cisneros, Sandra
Bienvenido Poem for Sophie.

Black Lace Bra Kind of Woman.
14 de julio.
Good Hot Dogs.
Heart, My Lovely Hobo.
I Am on My Way to Oklahoma to Bury the Man I Nearly Left My Husband For.
I Am So in Love I Grow a New Hymen.
Las Girlfriends.
Loose Women.
Man in My Bed Like Cracker Crumbs, A.
Muddy Kid Comes Home.
My Wicked Wicked Ways.
Poet Reflects On Her Solitary Fate, The.
Rafaela Who Drinks Coconut & Papaya Juice on Tuesdays.
You Bring Out the Mexican in Me.
You Called Me *Corazón*.

Cistulli, Carson
Twenty-Six Friends, That's the Same as Your Age, *sels.*

Citino, David (b. 1947)
Agatha.
Analysis, The.
Christina the Astonishing: Virgin.
Cleveland, Angels, Ogres, Trolls.
Francis Meets a Leper.
Ignatius, Bishop and Martyr.
In the Bedroom of Fear.
Invention of Secrecy, The.
Last Rites.
Letter from the Shaman: The Tribe with No Myth.
Man Who Couldn't Believe, The.
Neanderthal, with Help from Cave and Bear, Invents the Flute.
Newborn Found Alive in Shallow Grave.
Principles of Scarcity, Doctrines of Growth.
Sea of Kansas, Ohio Tundra, Time Still Running Out, The.
Sister Mary Appassionata Lectures the Bible Study Class: Homage to Onan.
Sister Mary Appassionata Lectures the Eighth Grade Boys and Girls on the Nature of the Candle.
Sister Mary Appassionata Lectures the Eighth Grade Boys and Girls: The Family Jewels.
Sister Mary Appassionata Lectures the Folklore Class: Doctrines of the Strawberry.
Sister Mary Appassionata Lectures the Home Ec Class: The Feast.
Sister Mary Appassionata Lectures the Pre-Med Class, *sels.*
Sister Mary Appassionata Lectures the Science Class: Fossils, Physics, Apple, Heart.
Sister Mary Appassionata Proves to the Entomology Class That Woman and Man Descended from the Cricket.
Sitting in the Sixth Grade at Ascension of Our Lord School in Cleveland, Ohio, Reading a Pamphlet Entitled "Possession in Iowa"
Situation No. 7: The Poison Lover.
Situation No. 9: The Corposant.
Situation No. 13: City Hall.
Situation No. 33: The Feast.
Walt Whitman in New Orleans, 1848.
Whole Wheat, Decaf Black, a Morbid Curiosity.

Cixous, Hélène (b. 1937)
Vivre L'Orange, *sel.*

Claman, Elizabeth
Show Biz Parties.

Clampitt, Amy (1920–94)
Athena.
Baroque Sunburst, A.
Beach Glass.
Beethoven, Opus 111.
Cormorant in Its Element, The.
Cure at Porlock, A.
Dancers Exercising.
Dodona: Asked of the Oracle.
Easter Morning.
Fog.
From a Clinic Waiting Room.
Gooseberry Fool.
Green.

Hairline Fracture, A.
Hispaniola.
Imago.
Kingfisher, The.
Marine Surface, Low Overcast.
Medusa.
Meridian.
Palm Sunday.
Procession at Candlemas, A.
Silence, A.
Stacking the Straw.
Sun Underfoot Among the Sundews, The.
Syrinx.
Times Square Water Music.
Whippoorwill in the Woods, A.

Clanchy, Kate (b. 1965)
Deadman's Shoes.
Driving to the Hospital.
For a Wedding.
Foreign.
I had my eyes shut the whole time.
Love.
Men From the Boys.
Miscarriage, Midwinter.
Mitigation.
One Night When We Paused Half-way.
Recognition.
Slattern.
Spell.
Stance.
Timetable.
War Poetry.
We Have Some Urgent Messages.

Clancy, Joseph P. (b. 1928)
Miscarriage.

Clapp, Jeffrey
Kaczynski.

Clare, Eli
Learning to Speak.
This Familiarity.

Clare, John (1793–1864)
After Reading in a Letter Proposals for Building a Cottage.
Ants, The.
Autumn.
Badger.
Badger, The.
Ballad: "Mary, fate lent me a moment of pleasure."
Birds' Nest.
Clock-A-Clay.
December.
December, *sel.*
Fallen Elm, The.
Farewell: "Farewell to the bushy clump close to the river."
First Love.
Flitting, The.
Gipsies [*or* The Gipsy Camp]: "Snow falls deep; the forest lies alone, The."
Give Me the Gloomy Walk.
God Looks on Nature With a Glorious Eye.
Green Woodpecker's Nest, The.
Gypsy's Evening Blaze, The.
Hares at Play.
Helpstone, *sel.*
I Am.
I Am.
I Feel I Am.
Invite to Eternity, An.
Lament of Swordy Well, The.
Lamentations of Round-Oak Waters, *sel.*
Last of April, The.
Little Trotty Wagtail.
Lord, Hear My Prayer.
Love's Emblem.
Maple Tree, The.
Mist in the Meadows.
Mouse's Nest.
My Mary.
Nightingale's Nest, The.
Noon.
Nutting.
Old pond full of flags and fenced around, The.
Old Year, The.

Pastoral Poesy.
Peasant Poet, The.
Pewits Nest.
Primrose, The.
Remember Dear Mary.
Returned Soldier, The.
Rural Scenes.
Sand Martin, The.
Shadows.
Shepherd Boy, The.
Shepherd's [*or* Shepheards] Calendar, The, *sels.*
Shepherd's Tree, The.
Sky Lark, The.
Soldier, The.
Song: "I peeled bits of straw and I got switches too."
Song: "Mary leave thy lowly cot."
Song: "Sad was the day when my Willie did leave me."
Sudden Shower.
Superstition's Dream, *sel.*
Thunder mutters louder and more loud, The.
To an Angry Bee.
To an Hour-Glass.
To the Memory of John Keats.
Turkeys, *sel.*
Vision, A.
Water-Lilies.
Winter.
Winter Winds Cold and Blea.
Wish, A ("Be where I may when death brings in his bill.").
Wish, The, *sels.*
Woodland Seat, A.
Wren, The.
Wryneck's Nest, The.

Clare of Assisi (1193–1253)
Blessing Attributed to Saint Clare, The.

Clare, Sidney (fl. 1934)
On the Good Ship Lollipop.

Clark, Badger See Clark, Charles Badger, Jr.

Clark Bekederemo, John Pepper (b. 1935)
Abiku.
Casualties, The.
Death of a Lady.
Epilogue to Casualties.
Family Procession, A.
New from Ethiopia and the Sudan, The.
Order of the Dead, The.

Clark, Charles Badger, Jr. (Badger Clark) (1883–1957)
Border Affair, A.

Clark, Leonard (1905–88)
Ground Elder.
Singing in the Streets.

Clark, Moira
Mushrooms.

Clark, Polly (b. 1968)
Elvis the Performing Octopus.
Excitement.
Kleptomaniac.
My Life with Horses.
Walk in the Rain.
Zoo.

Clark, T. J. (b. 1943)
Landscape with a Calm.

Clark, Thomas A. (b. 1944)
Blessing on the house, A.
Shadow extends the tree.
Sit for a while on a stone.
Sixteen Sonnets, *sels.*
Some Details of Hebridean House Construction.

Clark, Tom (b. 1941)
As the Human Village Prepares for Its Fate.
Baseball and Classicism.
Before Dawn.
Bun.
Dover Beach.
Elegy: "It's a pity we have to suffer."
Free Speech.
Going to Jail.
Lake, The.
"Like Musical Instruments.."

Neil Young, *sel.*
On the Beach.
Prophet.
Society.
Sonnet: "Five a.m. on East Fourteenth I'm out
    to eat."
Suicide with Squirtgun.
Time.
To John Ashbery.
What I've Learned in My Travels.
Year from Monday, A.
You, *sels.*

Clarke, Austin (1896–1974)
Celibacy.
Early Unfinished Sketch.
Envy of Poor Lovers, The.
Lost Heifer, The.
Martha Blake.
Martha Blake at Fifty-one.
Miss Marnell.
Penal Law.
Planter's Daughter, The.
St Christopher.
Straying Student, The.
Tiresias, *sel.*
Vengeance of Fionn, The, *sels.*
Young Woman of Beare, The.
Young Woman of Beare, The, *sel.*

Clarke, Cheryl (b. 1947)
14th Street Was Gutted in 1968.
Make-Up.
Nothing.
Palm Leaf of Mary Magdalene.
Passing.
Poet's Death, A.
Rondeau: "They are bodies left unburied."
Stuck.
Tortoise and Badger.
Vicki and Daphne.
What Goes Around Comes Around, or The
    Proof is in the Pudding.

Clarke, George Elliott (b. 1960)
April 19, 19—: A Sonnet.
Blank Sonnet.
Blue Elegies, *sels.*
Haligonian Market Cry.
Hymn for Portia White.
King Bee Blues.
Lear Of Whylah Falls.
Love Poem / Song Regarding Weymouth Falls.
Monologue for Selah Bringing Spring to
    Whylah Falls.
Prelude: "Shelley's a garden."
Quilt.
Student's Tale, The.
To Selah.
Wisdom of Shelley, The.

Clarke, Gillian (b. 1937)
All afternoon I hope.
Baby-Sitting.
Blaen Cwrt.
Border.
Field-Mouse, The.
Foghorns.
Glass, *sels.*
Hare, The.
Hay-Making.
Lament: "For the green turtle with her pulsing
    burden."
Les Grottes.
Marged.
Neighbours.
No Hands.
On Air.
Overheard in County Sligo.
Ram.
St. Thomas's Day.
Suicide on Pentwyn Bridge.
Taid's Grave.
Translation.
Windmill.
Women's Work.

Clarke, Grant
Am I Blue?
Everything Is Peaches Down in Georgia.

Rag Time Cowboy Joe.
Second Hand Rose.

Clarke, John
Accounting Cat, The.
Jenny Hit Me.
Story So Far, The.
There was an old man with a beard.

Clarke, Marcus (1846–81)
Wail of the Waiter, The.

Clarke, Tracy
For Babies Unborn.
Will They Always Remember.

Clarkson, Laurence (1615–67)
Single Eye All Light, No Darkness, A, *sel.*

Clary, Killarney (b. 1953)
Another hot afternoon upstairs after school.
Camellia, It's that Moist and Sensitive.
In this wind, the sharp blue cut of the San
    Gabriels flattens against the neon east.
Lightning. And the Mile Between.
Mr. Dooms would meet us across the Bay
    Bridge at a restaurant that featured "Dancing
    Waters."
Restless before the canary, wave of traffic on
    an inhale, I can just barely see on a dark
    blue ground black arabesques.
When my heart asked for a way free, it was led
    into this lightless room.

Claudel, Paul
October.
Octobre.
Sadness of Water, The.
Tristesse de l'Eau.

Claudian (Claudius Claudianus) (c.370–404)
Old Man of Verona, The.

Claudianus, Claudius *See* Claudian

Claus, Hugo (b. 1929)
Ten Ways of Looking at P.B. Shelley.
Tien manieren om P.B. Shelley te zien.
Tollund Man.
Tollund Man, The.
Woman 12, A.

Clausen, Jan (b. 1950)
White in the Woods.

Clawson, Jim
Fearless Rider.

Clay, Clairesa
Blue Black Pearl, A.

Clay, Willy
On Me, the Imported Skies.

Cleage, Pearl (b. 1948)
Confession.

Cleary, Brendan (b. 1958)
Boys' Own.
Chicken & Sex.
New Rock n Roll, The.
Sealink.
Slouch.

Cleary, Suzanne
Acting: "I most remember the class where we
    lie."

Clegg, Denise
Five Senses.

Cleghorn, Sarah Norcliffe (1876–1959)
Comrade Jesus.

Clemens, Prudentius Aurelius *See* Prudentius

Clemens, Samuel Langhorne *See* Twain, Mark

Clementelli, Elena
Circle and Obsession of Walls.
Etruscan Notebook, *sels.*
I'd Like to Try Telling You of Spring.
Moviola.
Your Hands, My Love.

Clements, Arthur L.
Elegy.
Why I Don't Speak Italian.

Clements, Brian
Historia.

Clements, Susan
Deer Cloud.
Matinee.
Reservation, The.
Susans.

Clephane, Elizabeth Cecilia (1830–69)
Beneath the cross of Jesus.

Clerk, Sir John, of Penicuik (1676–1755)
Country Seat, The, *sels.*

Clerq, J. G. Clemenceau Le *See* Tanaquil, Paul

Cleveland, John (1613–58)
Antiplatonic[k], The.
Epitaph on the Earl of Strafford.
General Eclipse, The.
King's Disguise, The.
Rebel Scot, The, *sels.*

Cleveland, Philip Jerome (b. 1903)
By Night.
I Yield Thee Praise.
There is a love that tumbles like a stream.

Cleveland, Ta'Lease Niche (b. 1976)
Our Fathers.

Clewell, David
Accomplice, The.
Going Wrong in the House of Neptune.
Poem for the Man Who Said Shit.
Vegetarian Physics.

Cleyre, Voltairine de (1866–1912)
Love's Compensation.
Out of the Darkness.

Cliff, Michelle (b. 1946)
History of Costume, A.

Clifton, Charles
Lear Drives His Rambler across Laurel
    Mountain.

Clifton, Harry (b. 1952)
Death of Thomas Merton.
Distaff Side, The.
Eccles Street, Bloomsday, 1982.
Euclid Avenue.
Id.
Monsoon Girl.

Clifton, Lucille (b. 1936)
Admonitions.
Anna Speaks of the Childhood of Mary Her
    Daughter.
Astrologer Predicts at Mary's Birth, The.
At last we killed the roaches.
1. at nagasaki.
At the cemetery, walnut grove plantation, south
    carolina, 1989.
Atlantic is a sea of bones.
Blake.
Blessing the boats.
C. C. Rider.
Cain.
Calming Kali.
Cigarettes.
Climbing.
Cruelty. Don't talk to me about cruelty.
Cutting greens.
Dear Jesse Helms.
Death of Crazy Horse, The.
Death of thelma sayles, The.
December.
Dialysis.
Donor.
Driving through new england.
Earth Is a Living Thing, The.
11/10 Again.
Eviction.
4/30/92 for Rodney King.
Fury.
Gift, The.
Good Friday.
Good Times.
Hag Riding.
Harriet.
Here is another bone to pick with you.
Holy Night.
Homage to my hips.
How Is He Coming Then.
I am accused of tending to the past.
I was born with twelve fingers.
In Salem.
In the Inner City.
In White America.
Island Mary.
June 20.
Kali.

Leda 3.
Let There Be New Flowering.
Light / on my mother's tongue.
Listen Children.
Lorena.
Lost baby poem, The.
Lost Women, The.
Love the Human.
Lumpectomy Eve.
Malcolm.
Mary.
Mary's Dream.
Miss Rosie.
Mississippi river empties into the gulf.
Move.
My Dream About the Cows.
My Dream About the Poet.
My Mama Moved among the Days.
Night Vision.
1994.
Note, Passed to Superman.
Photograph.
Poem to my uterus.
Powell (officer charged with the beating of
   rodney king).
Praise song.
Quilting.
Sam.
Scar.
Shapeshifter Poems.
She Lived.
Slave Cabin, Sotterly Plantation, Maryland,
   1989.
Slaveship[s].
Song at Midnight.
Song of Mary, A.
Sorrow Song.
Spring Song.
Still.
Them and Us.
Thirty-Eighth Year, The.
Those boys that ran together.
To Michal.
To Ms. Ann.
To my Friend, Jerina.
To my last period.
We are running.
When did she know, when did she know it.
When i stand around among poets.
White Lady.
Why some people be mad at me sometimes.
Wishes for Sons.
Women You Are Accustomed To, The.
Won't you celebrate with me.

Clinton, Michelle T. (b. 1954)
Black Rape.
Eviction.
History as Trash.
I Wanna Be Black.
Plan of the Klan.
Traditional Post-Modern Neo-HooDoo Afra-
   Centric Sister in a Purple Head Rag
   Mourning Death and Cooking.
Warning to Young Bright Sisters / White AM.
   Culture 101A.

Clinton, Robert (b. 1946)
Modulation.

Clive, Caroline
Mosel, The.
Mother, The.
Old Age.

Close, John (d. 1964)
Beelah Viaduct, The.
Haloes, Not Hats [or A Vision of the Gods].
In Respectful Memory of Mr. Yarker, sels.

Clough, Arthur Hugh (1819–61)
Across the Sea, Along the Shore.
Amours de Voyage, sels.
Blank Misgivings of a Creature Moving About
   in Worlds Not Realized, sels.
Bothie of Tober-na-Vuolich, The [A Long-
   Vacation Pastoral], sels.
Dipsychus [and the Spirit], sels.
Epi-strauss-ium.
Genesis XXIV.

Latest Decalogue, The.
Qua Cursum Ventus.
Questioning Spirit, The.
Revival.
Say Not the Struggle Nought Availeth.
Spectator ab Extra, sels.
What we, when face to face we see.
With Whom Is No Variableness, Neither
   Shadow of Turning.

"Clout, Colin" See Spenser, Edmund
Clover, Joshua
Alas, That Is the Name of Our Town; I Have
   Been Concealing It All This Time.
Archive of Confessions, a Genealogy of
   Confessions, An.
Bathtub Panopticon.
Ceriserie.
El periférico, or Sleep.
Family Romance.
Feral Floats the Form in Heaven and of Light.
Institute for Social Change, The.
Map Room, The.
There Is the Body Lying in State.
Zealous.

Cloves, Jeff
For Fausto Coppi (1916–60) et Tous les
   Copains de la Bicyclette.

Clurman, Dan
Berkeley Marina at Dusk, The.
To David.

Clutesi, George (b. 1905)
Beast in Man, The.
Ko-Ishin-Mit Goes Fishing.
Song of the Yellow Cedar Face, A.
West Coast Indian.

Cluysenaar, Anne (b. 1936)
Poems of Memory, sel.

Coates, Florence Earle (1850–1927)
Unconquered Air, The.

Coates, Ta-Nehisi
Gale Sayers.

Coatsworth, Elizabeth Jane (b. 1893)
Barn, The.
Circus-Postered Barn, The.
Daniel Webster's Horses.
Lady Comes to an Inn, A.
March.
Mouse, The.
Old Mare, The.
On a Night of Snow.
Open Door, The.
Song of the Rabbits Outside the Tavern, The.
Swallows, The.
Swift Things Are Beautiful.
Violets, Daffodils.

Cobbe, Eliza See Tuite, Eliza Cobbe, Lady
Cobbett, William
Elegy in Newgate.

Cobbing, Bob (1920–2002)
Bird Bee.
Hymn to the Sacred Mushroom.

Cobbold, Elizabeth (1767–1824)
On Some Violets Planted in My Garden by a
   Friend.
Sonnets of Laura, sels.

Coccia, Miek
We Are Not Vegetarians.

Coccimiglio, Vic
Night Beach.
St. Francis Speaks to Me at a Young Age.

Cochran, Jo Whitehorse (b. 1958)
To Keep the Spirits.

Cockburn, Catherine (1679–1749)
Caution, A.
To Mrs. Manley. By the Author of Agnes de
   Castro.
Vain Advice, The.
Verses Sent to Mr Bevil Higgons, on His
   Sickness and Recovery from the Small-pox,
   in the Year 1693.

Cocker, William Dixon (1882–1970)
Deluge, The.

Cocteau, Jean (1891–1963)
Cape of Good Hope, The.
Fairy Scene.
Jeune Fille Endormie.
Young Girl Sleeping.

Codling, Caroline
Assist me while I wander here.

Codrescu, Andrei (b. 1946)
Against Meaning.
Circle Jerk.
Paper on Humor.
Telyric.
Work.

Cody, James
Big Thicket Words.
Heart of Texas, The.
Whooping Crane.

Coe, Charles
Possibility.

Coelho, Art
Drifter's Brand, A.

Cofer, Judith Ortiz (b. 1952)
Anniversary.
Campesino's Lament, The.
Chameleon, The.
Changeling, The.
Correspondence.
Counting.
Cultivator.
Dream of Birth, The.
Drowned Sailor, The.
Fever.
Hour of the Siesta, The.
How to Get a Baby.
Idea of Islands, The.
Las Magdalenas.
Learning to Walk Alone.
Lesson of the Sugarcane, The.
Lesson of the Teeth, The.
Letter from Home in Spanish.
Life of an Echo, The.
My Grandfather's Hat.
Old Women.
Photographs of My Father.
Purpose of Nuns, The.
Saint Rose of Lima.
Seizing the Day.
Spring.
They Never Grew Old.
Three Poems in Memory of Mamá
   (Grandmother), sels.
Unspoken.
What the Gypsy Said to Her Children.
What We Feared.
Why There Are No Unicorns.
Women Who Love Angels.

Coffey, Brian (1905–95)
Death of Hektor, The, sel.
For What For Whom Unwanted, sels.
Prayers, The.

Coffin, Charles (1676–1749)
Advent of our God With eager hearts we greet,
   The.

Coffman, Lisa (b. 1963)
Cheerleaders.
Courage, or One of Gene Horner's Fiddles.
Girl/Spit.
Likely.

Cogswell, Fred (b. 1917)
Beach at Noon, The.
Edge, The.
George Burroughs.
Valley-Folk.
Water and the Rock, The.

Cohan, George M. (1878–1942)
Down by the Erie Canal.
Forty-five Minutes from Broadway.
Give My Regards to Broadway.
Harrigan.
I Want to Hear a Yankee Doodle Tune.
If I'm Going to Die I'm going to Have Some
   Fun.
If Washington Should Come to Life.
I'm Mighty Glad I'm Living and That's All.
Life's a Funny Proposition after All.

Mary's a Grand Old Name.
Nothing New Beneath the Sun.
Over There.
So Long, Mary.
Twentieth-Century Love.
When a Fellow's on the Level with a Girl
    That's on the Square.
Yankee Doodle Boy, The.
You're a Grand Old Flag.

Cohen, Bruce
Ghosts of Luxury, The.
Cohen, Garnett Kilberg
Child Bride.
Cohen, Jonathan
Walt Whitman in Ohio.
Cohen, Leonard (b. 1934)
Bus, The.
Elegy: "Do not look for him."
I Have Not Lingered in European Monasteries.
Kite Is a Victim, A.
Suzanne [Takes You Down].
Twelve O'Clock Chant.
You Have the Lovers.
Cohen, Lynne
Body Doubled.
Cohen, Marc (b. 1951)
Evensong.
Cohen, Nan (b. 1968)
Horatio.
Cohn, Jim (b. 1953)
Jemez Mountains Meditation.
On Non-Violence & Observation.
Coiffait, Carol
Last Apple, The.
Coke, A. A. Hedge
Change, The.
Cokinos, Christopher
Earth Movers, The.
Colby, Todd
Boy and the Girl, The.
Captain's Log.
Dear, I Love.
Labor Day Picnic Poem.
Think Eight.
Cold Mountain *See* Han-shan (Cold Mountain)
Cole, Forrest
America™.
Cole, Henri (b. 1956)
Buddha and the Seven Tiger Cubs.
Cabbage Butterfly, The.
Childlessness.
Cleaning the Elephant.
Folly.
40 Days and 40 Nights.
Harvard Classics.
Horses: "Setting out on my bicycle alone."
Original Face.
Roman Baths at Nîmes, The.
White Spine.
Cole, Joanna (b. 1944)
Happy New Year, Anyway.
Hippopotamus.
Cole, Maude E.
Over Texas Hills.
Prairie Friend.
Cole, Peter
Isaac: a Poise.
Cole, Thomas (1801–48)
Dial, The.
I Saw a Cave of Sable Depth Profound.
Lago Maggiore.
Lament of the Forest, The.
Lines Suggested by Hearing Music on the
    Boston Common at Night.
Painter, A.
To Her Modest Mirth-Making Friend, Mr
    Robert Dover.
Voyage of Life, The, *sel.*
Cole, William (b. 1919)
Mutual Problem.
Oh, Noa, Noa!
Some Sights Sometimes Seen and Seldom
    Seen.

Uncoupled Couplets, *sels.*
Colebatch, Hal (b. 1947)
On the Death of Ludwig Erhard.
One Tourist's Cologne.
Coleman, Anita Scott (b. 1906)
Portraiture.
Coleman, Edison
Esta Es Mi Tierra.
Coleman, Horace
OK Corral East: Brothers in the Nam.
Poem for a "Divorced" Daughter.
Coleman, James
Black Women with Jewish Names.
Vipers, Flies, and Women of the Cloth.
Coleman, Jane
Soap.
Coleman, John (*fl.* **early 17th cent.**)
Poor Bess Turpin, I pytty thy case as farr as I
    can.
Coleman, Taiyon J.
Chicago on the Day Brother Increases His
    Chances of Reaching Age 21.
Coleman, Wanda (b. 1946)
African Beneath the American, The.
African Sleeping Sickness.
American Sonnet (10).
American Sonnet (46).
April in Hollywood.
Aunt Jessie.
Breast Examination.
Brute Strength.
Chuck Man.
Coffee.
Cousin Mary.
Dog Suicide.
Essay on Language.
Having Lost My Son, I Confront the
    Wreckage.
I Live for My Car.
ISM, The.
Metaphysically Niggerish.
Notes on a Departure.
Prisoner of Los Angeles (2).
Three Trees.
Three-Headed Womon Song.
Wanda Why Aren't You Dead.
Where I Live.
Coleridge, Hartley (1796–1849)
All nature ministers to Hope. The snow.
Dedicatory Sonnet to S. T. Coleridge.
Early Death.
First Birthday, The.
He Lived amidst th' Untrodden Ways.
Is love a fancy, or a feeling? No.
Jesus Praying.
Long Time a Child.
"Multum Dilexit."
Night.
Prayer.
She Is Not Fair to Outward View.
She Was a Queen.
Sonnet 27.
Sonnets to the Seasons, *sels.*
To a Friend.
To a Lofty Beauty, from Her Poor Kinsman.
Coleridge, Mary Elizabeth (1861–1907)
Alcestis to Admetus.
Awake.
Blue and White.
Broken Friendship.
But in That Sleep of Death What Dreams May
    Come?
Clever Woman, A.
Contents of an Ink-bottle, The.
Day-dream, A.
Death, *sel.*
Devil's Funeral, The.
Doubt.
Fire, the lamp, and I, were alone together, The.
Friends—With a Difference.
Gifts.
Gone.
He Came unto His Own, and His Own
    Received Him Not.
Huguenot, A.

Hush.
I envy not the dead that rest.
I saw a stable, low and very bare.
Impromptu.
In Dispraise of the Moon.
In London Town.
Insincere Wish Addressed to a Beggar, An.
Jealousy.
Lady of Trees, The.
Lord of the winds, I cry to Thee.
Marriage.
Master and Guest.
Mistaken.
Moment, A.
Mortal Combat.
No Newspapers.
Not Yet.
On a Bas-relief of Pelops and Hippodameia.
Only a little shall we speak of thee.
Other Side of a Mirror, The.
Our Lady.
Poison Flower, The.
Pride.
Punctilio.
Regina.
Sadness.
September.
Shadow.
Solo.
Some in a child would live, some in a book.
To a Piano.
To Memory.
True to myself am I, and false to all.
Unwelcome.
Wasted.
White Women, The.
Wilderspin.
Witch, The.
Witches' Wood, The.
Words.
Coleridge, Samuel Taylor (1772–1834)
Answer to a Child's Question.
Christabel.
Christmas Carol, A: "Shepherds went their
    hasty way, The."
Cologne.
Constancy to an Ideal Object.
Dejection: An Ode.
Devil's Thoughts, The.
Duty Surviving Self-Love.
Effusions, *sels.*
Epitaph: "Stop, Christian passer-by!—Stop,
    child of God."
Fancy in Nubibus.
Fears in Solitude [Written in April, 1798,
    during the Alarm of an Invasion], *sels.*
Fire, Famine, and Slaughter.
Forbearance.
Frost at Midnight [1798 version].
Frost at Midnight [1829 version], *sel.*
Hexameters[; Paraphrase of Psalm XLVI].
Homeric Hexameter, The.
Hymn before Sunrise, in the Vale of
    Chamouni.
Keepsake, The.
Knight's Tomb, The.
Kubla Khan: or, A Vision in a Dream.
Letter to Sara Hutchinson.
Love: "All thoughts, all passions, all delights."
Metrical Feet.
My Baptismal Birthday [*or* Birth-Day].
Ne Plus Ultra.
Old Man's Sigh, The. A Sonnet.
On an Infant Which Died before Baptism.
On Donne's Poetry.
Pains of Sleep, The.
Pantisocracy.
Phantom.
Raven, The.
Recollections of Love.
Religious Musings, *sel.*
Rime of the Ancient Mariner (1817 version).
Rime of the Ancient Mariner, The (1798
    version), *sels.*
Sonnet Composed on a Journey Homeward;
    the Author Having Received Intelligence of

the Birth of a Son, 20 September 1796.
Sonnet to a Friend Who Asked How I Felt
When the Nurse First Presented My Infant
to Me.
Sonnet to the River Otter.
Sonnets Attempted in the Manner of
Contemporary Writers, *sels*.
This Lime-Tree Bower My Prison.
Time, Real and Imaginary.
To Nature.
To William Wordsworth [1817 version].
Visit of the Gods, The.
What Is an Epigram?
Work without Hope.
Youth and Age.
Zapolya, *sels*.

Coleridge, Sara (1802–52)
Blest is the tarn which towering cliffs
o'ershade.
Father! no amaranths e'er shall wreathe my
brow.
Garden Year, The.
Storm, The.

Coles, Gladys Mary (b. 1942)
Dornier, The.
Heron in the Alyn.
Ithaca-Liverpool.

Coles, Robert
Christmas, Belfast.
Goddam Street, The.
New Jersey Boys.
On Dutch's Death.

Collier, Mary (1690?–c.1762)
Womans Labour, an epistle, The.

Collier, Michael
Argos.
Brave Sparrow.
Consider the Garden.
Landscape: "Stupid. But each of us took
turns."
North Corridor.
Real-Life Drama, A.
Robert Wilson.
Seneca Street.
Snake, The.
2212 West Flower Street.

Collin, Bernard (b. 1927)
Perpetual *Look* Physics: 17/5.
Perpétuel *voyez* physique, 17/5.

Collin, Judyth
Layman's Lament, The.

Collins, Andrea
Hiroshima Day at the Riviera Coffeeshop.

Collins, Anne (fl. c.1653)
Another Song Exciting to Spirituall Mirth, *sels*.
Song Composed in Time of the Civill Warr,
when the Wicked Did Much Insult over the
Godly, A.

Collins, Billy (b. 1941)
Another Reason Why I Don't Keep a Gun in
the House.
By a Swimming Pool Outside Siracusa.
Centrifuge, The.
Dead, The.
Death of Allegory, The.
Dharma.
Dog.
Embrace.
First Reader.
Forgetfulness.
Going Out for Cigarettes.
History Teacher, The.
Introduction to Poetry.
Japan.
Lines Composed Over Three Thousand Miles
From Tintern Abbey.
Lines Lost among Trees.
Litany: "You are the bread and the knife."
Man in Space.
Man Listening to Disc.
Marginalia.
Memento Mori.
Morning: "Why do we bother with the rest of
the day."
Names, The.

Nightclub.
No Time.
Nostalgia.
On Turning Ten.
Osso Buco.
Passengers.
Putting Down the Cat.
Shoveling Snow with Buddha.
Snow Day.
Sonnet: "All we need is fourteen lines, well,
thirteen now."
Taking Off Emily Dickinson's Clothes.
Tomes.
Tuesday, June 4, 1991.
Workshop.
Writing in the Afterlife.

Collins, Jeneanne
Big World Look Out.

Collins, Kimberly Ann (b. 1964)
I Am Africa.
Sisters.
Trio.

Collins, Martha (b. 1940)
Border, The.
Epiphany.
Lies.
Like Her Body The World.
Lines: "Draw a line. Write a line. There."
Out of My Own Pocket.
Pentecost.
Re:composition.
Rights.
Warmer.

Collins, Mortimer (1827–76)
If.
Tory, a Puppy.
Winter in Brighton.

Collins, William (1721–59)
How Sleep the Brave.
Ode on the Poetical Character.
Ode on the Popular Superstitions of the
Highlands of Scotland, An.
Ode to Evening.
Ode to Simplicity.

Collobert, Danielle (1940–78)
Dont le soleil.
For Which the Sun.
I Time of What.
Je temps de quoi.
III: "As if dead the buried text."

Collom, Jack (b. 1932)
3-4-00.

Collop, John (1625–62?)
Praise of a Yellow Skin, The; or, An Elizabeth
in Gold.

Collymore, Frank A. (1893–1980)
Ballad of an Old Woman.

Collyn, Marie (b. 1555 or 1556, d. after 1600)
Thursday Before New Yeares Day (Being on
the Satterdy) the Maide, by Councell of On,
She Trustid Well, Excussid Herself on This
Wise to Milord, The.

Colman, Benjamin (1673–1747)
Another to Urania.

Colman, George, the Younger (1762–1836)
London Rurality, *sels*.

Colman, Henry (fl. 1640)
On Lazarus Raised From Death.
On Mortality.
On the Inscription Over the Head of Christ on
the Cross.
On the Strange Apparitions at Christ's Death.
On the Three Children in the Fiery Furnace.

Colonna, Silvana (b. 1942)
But what an idea she'd gotten into her head.
But your imagining was wrong.
Disconnections.
He spins about (laughing) then shows.
Orientation from Afar.
So it tries to reach her inside her mind.
Without muscles without slipping.

**Colonna, Vittoria da, Marchesa di Pescara
(1490–1547)**
I see in my mind, surrounding God.

Colosi, David
Sun with Issues.

Colquitt, Betsy
Duet.
Honor Card.
Man in the VA Hospital, The.
Poetry and Post, Texas.

Colum, Padraic (1881–1972)
Drover, A.
Interior.
No Child.
Old Soldier.
Old Woman of the Roads, The.
Plower, The.
She Moved through the Fair.
Wild Ass.

Columba, Saint (fl. c.543–615)
Maker on High, The.

Comden, Betty (b. 1917)
Adventure.
All of My Life.
Conga.
I Can Cook, Too.
If You Hadn't—But You Did.
Just in Time.
Little Bit in Love, A.
Lonely Town.
Lucky to Be Me.
Make Someone Happy.
New York, New York.
Not Mine.
Party's Over, The.
Some Other Time.
Thanks a Lot, but No Thanks.
You Mustn't Feel Discouraged.

Comer, Carrie St. George (b. 1971)
Arbor.
Long Goodbye.
Shelburne Falls.

Cometas (fl. c.950)
Phyllis, loving Demophoon.

Comfort, Alex (b. 1920)
Epitaph: "One whom I knew, a student and a
poet."
Fear of the Earth.
Letter to an American Visitor.
Song for the Heroes.
Song of Lazarus, The, *sels*.

Compton, Wayde (b. 1972)
Alley Blues.
Jump Rope Rhyme of the 49er Daughters.

Condee, Nancy
Mrs. Charles Sanders Peirce, or The Solution
to the Universe.

Confucius (551–479 B.C.)
Great Digest, The, *sels*.

Congreve, William (1670–1729)
Aisle of a Temple, The.
Doris.
False Though She Be.
Hue and Cry after Fair Amoret, A.
Mourning Bride, The, *sels*.
Song: "I tell thee, Charmion, could I time
retrieve."
Pious Selinda [*or* Celinda].
Way of the World, The.

Conkling, Grace Hazard (b. 1878)
I Will Not Give Thee All My Heart.

Conley, Larry (fl. 1930)
Cottage for Sale, A.

Conn, Stewart (b. 1936)
First Light: "Near Nunnerie, where Daer and
Potrail meet."
Stolen Light.
Todd.
Tremors.
Under the Ice.
Visiting Hour.

Connelly, Reginald
Good Night, Sweetheart.
If I Had You.
Try a Little Tenderness.

Connolly, Cyril (1903–74)
On Geoffrey Grigson.

Connolly _(continued)_

On Himself.
To Osbert Sitwell.
Where Engels Fears to Tread, *sels*.

Connolly, David (b. 1949)
Little Man, The.

Connolly, Geraldine (b. 1947)
Mother, a Young Wife Leans to Sew.
New House.
Summer I Was Sixteen, The.

Connor, T. W. (b. 1936)
She Was One of the Early Birds.

Conoley, Gillian (b. 1955)
After: "Composition was shy, The."
As in the Small Gaps Between Minutes.
Beauty and the Beast.
Beckon.
Masters, The.
New.
Sky Drank In, The.
Violence, The.
Walt Whitman in the Car Lot, Repo or Used.
World, The: "It was just a gas station. It was
    not spectacular carnage."

Conquest, Robert (b. 1917)
Bagpipes at the Biltmore.
Progress.
Rokeby Venus, The.

Conran, Anthony (b. 1931)
Death of a Species.
Elegy for Sir Ifor Williams.
Elegy for the Welsh Dead, in the Falkland
    Islands, 1982.
Fledgling.
Spirit Level.
Thirteen Ways of Looking at a Hoover.

Constable, Henry (1562–1613)
Diana, *sels*.
On the Death of Sir Philip Sidney.
To God the Holy Ghost.
To Our Blessed Lady.
To Saint Margaret.
To Saint Mary Magdalen.
To St. Michael the Archangel.
To St. Peter and St. Paul.
To St John Baptist.
To St Mary Magdalen.
To the Blessed Sacrament.
To the Marquess of Piscat's Soul.

Constantine, David (b. 1944)
As our bloods separate.
Common and Particular.
Door, The.
He arrived, towing a crowd, and slept.
Hoist, The.
Lasithi.
New Year Behind the Asylum.
Pity the Drunks.
Pleasure.
Wasps, The.
Watching for Dolphins.
What we reminded you of you are already
    forgetting.
You Are Distant, You Are Already Leaving.

Consuegra, Dinah Elena
You and I.

Converse, Florence (b. 1871)
Friendship.

Conway, Jack (1887–1952)
Clothes Make the Man.

Conway, Jack
This Is What Happens When You Let Hamlet
    Play Quarterback.

Conway, Jeffery
Hangover.
Marlo Thomas in Seven Parts and Epilogue.
Modern English.
Odd Years, The.
Weight Belt.

Conyus (b. 1942)
Day in the Life of . . . , A.
Six Ten Sixty-Nine.
Upon Leaving the Parole Board Hearing.

Coogler, J. Gordon (1865–1901)
Alas! Carolina!

Byron.
God Correctly Understood.
How Strange Are Dreams, *sel*.
Lover's Return on a Bicycle, The, *sel*.
More Care for the Neck Than for the Intellect.
O that the lilies and roses were mine.

Cook, Chris O.
Anthelmintic.
8 O'Clock Defeat, Approximately.
It's Just As Well About Heather.
Will Run Like Rabbits for Food.

Cook, Christopher
For being unfaithful though ever true.

Cook, Ebenezer (c.1670–c.1732)
Sot-Weed Factor, The.

Cook, Eliza (1818–89)
Building upon the Sand.
Carrion Crow, The, *sel*.
Entry of the Marines [*or* The Red Cross of
    England].
Idiot-Born, The.
Lines Among the Leaves, *sel*.
Lines / Suggested by the Song of a
    Nightingale.
Live and Let Live.
Mouse and the Cake, The.
Old Arm-Chair, The.
On Seeing a Bird-Catcher.
Our Father.
Pathetic Lament, A.
Song for the Workers, A.
Song of the Imprisoned Bird.
Song of the Modern Time.
Song of the Rushlight.
Song of the Seaweed, *sels*.
Song of the Ugly Maiden.
Surgeon's Knife, The, *sel*.
There is Nothing in Vain, *sels*.
Thought, A [*or* Sunshine].
'Tis Well to Wake the Theme of Love.
To Charlotte Cushman.
To My Lyre.
To the Late William Jerdan.
Written at the Couch of a Dying Parent.

Cook, Geoffrey (b. 1963)
Chopping Wood.
Lorne, Nova Scotia.
Watermarks.

Cook-Lynn, Elizabeth (b. 1830)
Grandfather at the Indian Health Clinic.
Journey.
My Grandmother's Burial Ground.

Cook, Stanley (b. 1922)
Christmas Tree.

Cook, William
Endangered Species.

Cook, William W.
Indian Corn, *sel*.
Seth Bingham.
Spiritual: "How did you feel when you come
    out the wilderness?"
Still-Life with Woodstove.

Cooke, Angela
I Stand at the Window and Wave My Arms
    About.

Cooke, Captain Henry (d. 1672)
Song: "Goe turne away those Cruell Eyes."

Cooke, Philip Pendleton (1816–50)
Florence Vane.
Orthone.

Cooke, Rose Terry (1827–92)
Arachne.
Bluebeard's Closet.
Captive.
Che Sara Sara.
Hospital Soliloquy, A.
R. W. Emerson.
Schemhammphorasch.
Semele.

Cookshaw, Marlene (b. 1953)
In the Spring of No Letters.

Coolbrith, Ina (1841–1948)
Captive of the White City, The.
Copa de Oro (The California Poppy).

Lines.
Longing.
Mariposa Lily, The.
My Cloth of Gold.
Ownership.
Retrospect: "Breath of balm—of orange
    bloom!, A."
Sailed.
Sea-Shell, The.
Woman.
Years, The: "What do I owe the years, that I
    should bring."

Cooley, Nicole (b. 1966)
Arson.
Diane Arbus, New York.
Family History, The.
Good Friday, Alice Liddell.
John Winthrop, "Reasons to be Considered
    for...the Intended Plantation in New
    England," 1629.
Mary Warren's Sampler.
Mother: Dorcas Good, The.
Publick Fast on Account of the Afflicted:
    March 31, 1692.
Resurrection.
Undine.

Cooley, Peter (b. 1940)
Brother Body.
Fathers and Sons.
For Hamlet.
For Jude the Obscure.
History of Poetry, The.
Incantation.
Language of Departure.
Poem on My Birthday.
Poem on the First Day of School.
Poem on the First Day of Spring.
Psalm before Sleep.
Secret, The.
Sleep of Beasts, The.
Vespers: "Now it is evening, the light rushes to
    fall."

Coolidge, Clark (b. 1939)
Album—A Runthru.
Ashbery Explains.
At Egypt, *sels*.
At the Poem.
Bee Elk.
Brill.
By a I.
Country Autumns, The.
Crack, The.
Crystal Text, The, *sel*.
Dalliance with Salt Sides, A.
Darkling Thrums.
Disturbing the Sallies Forth.
Fall Returns, The.
Glance in White Space.
Hand Further, The.
He walked around and couldn't think of
    anything.
Ing, *sels*.
Jerome in His Study.
Leaving Rattle Bar.
Listene / secting.
Ments of a rift in a crusted so as Fairy.
Miss ship.
Noon Point.
Note, A.
On Induction of the Hand.
On the Road.
One of Essence's Entrances.
Ounce code orange.
Peru Eye, the Heart of the Lamp.
Saturday Night.
Soda Gong.
Some Glow on the Sill.
Styro.
Tab, The.
There Is a Caterpillar That Makes a Very
    Complicated Hammock.
This Garden Being: The Hanging of Books.
Though in should flags.
What Is Thought but Won't Hold Still.

Coolidge, Susan (Sarah Chauncey Woolsey) (1835–1905)
  Home, A.
  My Rights.
Coon, Miles A.
  Trade Show.
Cooper, Afua (b. 1957)
  Stepping to da Muse/Sic.
Cooper, Allan (b. 1954)
  After Rain.
  To an Unborn Child.
  Worker Bee, The.
Cooper, Dennis (b. 1958)
  After School, Street Football, Eighth Grade.
  Being Aware.
  David Cassidy Then.
  Dreamt Up.
  Drugs.
  No God.
  Poem for George Miles.
  Some Adventures of John Kennedy Jr, *sels*.
  Teen Idols.
  10 Dead Friends.
Cooper, Jane (b. 1924)
  After the Bomb Tests, *sel*.
  Childhood in Jacksonville, Florida.
  Estrangement.
  Faithful, The.
  Hotel de Dream.
  Long, Disconsolate Lines.
  My Mother in Three Acts.
  Rent.
  Wanda's Blues.
Cooper, Katherine Bradley *and* **Edith** *See* Field, Michael
Cooper, Wyn
  Leaving the Country.
  Pollen.
  Postcard from Robert Frost's Grave.
Cooperman, Robert
  Good-by and Keep Cold.
Coote, Gillian
  Tenzo's Song.
  You.
Cope, David
  Labor Day.
Cope, John (b. 1934)
  Copula.
  Dementia.
  Solstice for John.
  Sunset.
  Winter Sky.
Cope, Wendy (b. 1945)
  At 3 A.M.
  Bloody Men.
  Budgie Finds His Voice.
  Cherry blossom, The.
  Emily Dickinson.
  Engineers' Corner.
  Exchange of Letters.
  Flowers: "Some men never think of it."
  I Worry.
  Lavatory Attendant, The.
  Lonely Hearts.
  Mr. Strugnell.
  My Lover.
  Names: "She was Eliza for a few weeks."
  Not only marble, but the plastic toys.
  On Finding an Old Photograph.
  Orange, The.
  Reading Scheme.
  Rondeau Redoublé.
  Serious Concerns.
  Sisters.
  Strugnell's Bargain.
  Strugnell's Rubáiyát.
  Strugnell's Sonnets, *sels*.
  Triolet.
  Two Cures for Love.
  Uncertainty of the Poet, The.
  Usquebaugh.
  Valentine.
  Variation on Belloc's "Fatigue"
  Waste Land Limericks.

Copeland, James (1918–2002)
  Bayonet, The.
  Ed.
Copioli, Rosita (b. 1948)
  Eurydice.
  Heart and the Severed Head, The.
  Make Your Body a Heart.
  Sea Dreams.
Copland, Robert (*fl.* 1508–47)
  High Way to the Spital House, The (Hye Way to the Spyttell Hous, The), *sel*.
Coppard, Alfred Edgar (1878–1957)
  Apostate, The.
  Epitaph: "Like silver dew are the tears of love."
  Mendacity.
Copus, Julia (b. 1969)
  Art of Interpretation, The.
  Back Seat of My Mother's Car, The.
  Breast.
  Clothes, The.
  Cricketer's Retirement Day, The.
  Forgiveness.
  In Defence of Adultery.
  Love, Like Water.
  Making of Eve, The.
  Masaccio's *Expulsion from Paradise*.
  Miss Havisham's Letter.
  Pulling the Ivy.
  Sea-Polyp, The.
  Second Home.
  Topsell's Beasts.
  Widower.
Coralin, Jane Alberdeston
  Rosa's Beauty.
Corben, John
  Harlech Castle.
  In the eggs.
  On the Beach.
Corbet [*or* Corbett], Richard (1582–1635)
  Distracted Puritan, The.
  Elegy upon the Death of His Own Father, An.
  On Mr. Rice the Manciple of Christ Church in Oxford.
  On the Lady Arabella.
  Proper New Ballad Entitled [*or* Intituled] The Fairies' [*or* Faeryes] Farewell, or God-a-Mercy Will, A.
  To His Son [*or* Sonne], Vincent Corbet[t].
  Upon an Unhandsome Gentlewoman, who made Love unto him.
  Upon Fairford Windows.
Corbett, Elizabeth T. (*fl.* c.1880)
  Three Wise Old Women.
Corbett, William (b. 1942)
  Cold Lunch.
  Columbus Square Journal, *sel*.
  Vermont Apollinaire.
  Wickson Plums.
Corbière, Edouard Joachim *See* Corbière, Tristan
Corbière, Tristan (Edouard Joachim Corbière) (1845–75)
  Afterwards, *sel*.
  Blindman's Cries, The.
  Insomnia.
  Litany of Sleep, *sel*.
  Old Roscoff.
Corbin, Alice (Alice Corbin Henderson) (1881–1949)
  Love Me At Last.
Corcadail, Aithbhreac Inghean (*fl.* 1460)
  O rosary that recalled my tear.
Corcoran, Kelvin (b. 1956)
  In the Red Book.
  Music of the Altai Mountains.
  When Suzy Was.
Cordeiro, James
  Monsoon Song.
Cording, Robert
  Elegy for John, My Student Dead of AIDS
  Peregrine Falcon, New York City.
Corey, Stephen (b. 1948)
  Complicated Shadows.
  Preparing to Live Among the Old.

  Tempest, The.
  Understanding *King Lear*.
  Whatever Light.
Corfield, Joy
  Morse Lesson.
Corinna *See* Korinna [*or* Corinna]
Corman, Cid (b. 1924)
  Learn to live.
Corn, Alfred (b. 1943)
  Billie's Blues.
  Call in the Midst of the Crowd, A, *sels*.
  Conch from Sicily, A.
  Contemporary Culture and the Letter "K."
  Darkening Hotel Room.
  Grass.
  Kimchee in Worcester (Mass.).
  Long-Distance Call to Gregg, Who Lived with AIDS as Long as He Could.
  Marriage in the Nineties, A.
  Naskeag.
  Navidad, St. Nicholas Ave.
  Photographs of Old New York.
  Reading *Pericles* in New London.
  To Hermes.
  Walrus Tusk from Alaska, A.
  Water: City Wildlife and Greenery.
Cornett, Sheryl
  Lear Expands His Last Words to Cordelia.
Cornford, Adam (b. 1950)
  Rapture, The, *sel*.
Cornford, Frances Darwin (1886–1960)
  At Night.
  Avenue, The.
  Childhood.
  Child's Dream, A.
  Country Bedroom, The.
  Glimpse, A.
  Guitarist Tunes Up, The.
  Hills, The.
  London Despair.
  Near an Old Prison.
  New-Born Baby's Song, The.
  Ode on the Whole Duty Of Parents.
  Parting in Wartime.
  Sick Queen, The.
  To a Fat Lady Seen from the Train.
  Unbeseechable, The.
  Wasted Day, A.
  Watch, The.
Cornford, John (1915–36)
  Full Moon at Tierz: Before the Storming of Huesca.
  Letter from Aragon, A.
Cornish, Mary
  Numbers: "I like the generosity of numbers."
Cornish, Sam (b. 1935)
  Brother of the Streets.
  Brown Bomber.
  Death of Dr. King.
  Elvis.
  Generations 1.
  Generations 2.
  Harriet Tubman.
  His Fingers Seem to Sing.
  In Mr. Turner's Fields.
  Love Song of a Red Cap.
  Mississippi on the Doorstep.
  My Father's House.
  Something Terrible Something.
  We Have Never Loved.
  Work to Be Done.
Cornish, William (c.1465–c.1523)
  Pleasure It Is.
Cornwall, Barry (Bryan Waller Proctor) (1787–1874)
  Address to the Ocean.
  For a Fountain.
  Leveller, The.
  Sonnet; A Still Place.
  To My Child.
Corob, Tricia
  Either Way.
Corpi, Lucha (b. 1945)
  Premonition.

Corpus, Aileen (b. 1950)
Blkfern-jungal.
Corrie, Joe (b. 1894)
Image o' God, The.
Rebel Tam.
Corso, Gregory (1930–2001)
Bomb.
Dream of a Baseball Star.
I Held a Shelley Manuscript.
Love Poem for Three for Kaye & Me.
Mad Yak, The.
Marriage.
Ode to Coit Tower.
Poets Hitchhiking on the Highway.
Rembrandt—Self Portrait.
Sea Chanty.
Song: "Oh, dear! Oh, me! Oh, my!"
30th Year Dream.
Transformation and Escape.
Whole Mess . . . Almost, The . . Almost, The.
Zizi's Lament.
Cortázar, Julio (1914–84)
Behavior of Mirrors on Easter Island, The.
Clocks.
Instructions on How to Cry.
Lines of the Hand, The.
Loss and Recovery of the Hair, The.
Normal Behavior of the Famas.
Therapies.
Travel.
Very Real Story, A.
Cortes, Alfonso
Great Prayer.
Space Song.
Cortes, Fidelito
Dolce Far Niente.
Fish 2.
Palace of Fine Arts in San Francisco, The.
Poem Composed During a Brownout.
Cortez, Jayne (b. 1936)
Adupe.
Bumblebee, You Saw Big Mama.
Consultation.
Drying Spit Blues.
Feathers.
Flame.
For the Poets.
Give me the Red on the Black of the Bullet
(for Claude Reece Jr.).
Global Inequalities.
Grinding Vibrato.
Guitars I Used to Know, The.
Heavy Headed Dance, The.
How Long Has Trane Been Gone.
I Am New York City 2.
I See Chano Pozo.
In the Line of Duty.
Indelible.
Into This Time.
Jazz Fan Looks Back.
Make Ifa.
Nighttrains.
No Simple Explanations.
Ogun's Friend.
Opening Act.
Phraseology.
Pray for the Lovers.
Rape.
Sacred Trees.
Say It.
So Long.
So Many Feathers.
There It Is.
Under the Edge of February.
What's Happening.
What's Your Take.
When I Look at Wifredo Lam's Paintings.
Cortéz, Lydia
I Remember: "I remember kindergarten."
Cortez, Sarah
Attempt to Locate.
Interlude: "I watch a handsome young female."
Reunion.
Corwin, Nina
Grandmother Living in Fear of Free Verse.

Cory, David (1872–1966)
Miss You.
Cory, William Johnson (1823–92)
Desiderato.
Deteriora.
Heraclitus.
Mimnermus in Church.
Parting.
Preparation.
Coslett, Coslett (1834–1910)
Pole Star, The.
Coslow, Sam (1902–83)
Cocktails for Two.
(I'm In Love With) The Honorable Mr. So and
So.
It's Love Again.
My Old Flame.
True Blue Lou.
(Up on Top of a Rainbow) Sweepin' the
Clouds Away.
Costanzo, Gerald (b. 1945)
Everything You Own.
In the Aviary.
Jeane Dixon's America.
Old Neighborhood, The.
Washington Park.
Costello, Michael (b. 1976)
Ode to My Flint and Boom Bolivia.
Costello, Rita D.
Battle Hymn.
Uncertain Geometry.
When My Sister Was Fifteen.
Cothi, Lewis Glyn (fl. 1447–86)
Lament for Siôn y Glyn.
On the Death of His Son.
Cott, Jonathan
Elective Affinities.
Enjoyment Body.
He Dreams What Is Going On Inside His
Head.
Isis (Lady of Petals).
Natural Functions.
Cotter, Joseph Seamon, Jr.
Is It Because I Am Black?
Cottle, Joseph (1770–1853)
Affectionate Heart, The.
Expostulatory Epistle to Lord Byron, An, sels.
Malvern Hills, sels.
Cottle, Katherine
My Poetess' Eyes.
Cotton, Charles (1630–87)
Burlesque upon the Great Frost, sel.
Epitaph on M. H., An.
Litany: "From a ruler that's a curse."
Morning Quatrains, The.
On Tobacco.
Resolution in Four Sonnets, of a Poetical
Question Put to Me by a Friend, Concerning
Four Rural Sisters.
Song: Montrose.
To Coelia.
To My Dear and Most Worthy Friend, Mr.
Isaac Walton.
Wonders of the Peak, The, sels.
Cotton, John (1584–1652)
We are a crystal zoo.
Cotton, John (1640–99)
Bacon's Epitaph, Made by His Man.
Cotton, Nathaniel (1705–80)
On Lord Cobham's Garden.
Couani, Anna (b. 1948)
Map of the World, The.
Never-Dead, The.
Obvious, The.
What a Man, What a Moon.
Coulehan, Jack
Anatomy Lesson.
Azalea Poem, The.
D-Day, 1994.
Dynamizer and the Oscilloclast, The.
I'm Gonna Slap Those Doctors.
Lovesickness: A Medieval Text.
Man with a Hole in His Face, The.
Rule of Thirds, The.

Coulette, Henri (b. 1927)
Correspondence.
Night Thoughts: "Your kind of night, David,
your kind of night."
Postscript: "There are some questions one
should know by heart."
Coultas, Brenda
Capitalist Projections.
Dr. Wasserman.
Human Museum, The.
Lecture #1.
Third Farming Poem.
Weather Report.
Country Joe McDonald See McDonald, Joe
Countryman, Jeremy
Woman with Chrysler.
Countryman, L. William (b. 1941)
Going to God with the Shepherds.
Cousin, Anne R.
In Emmanuel's Land.
Cousins, Linda
Ms. Cousins' Rap.
Couto, Nancy Vieira
Flowers and Water.
Living in the La Brea Tar Pits.
Lizzie.
Tea Party.
You Bet Your Life.
Couzyn, Jeni (b. 1942)
Christmas in Africa, sel.
Creation.
Heartsong.
House of Changes.
Morning.
Mystery, The.
Pain, The.
Spell for Birth.
Spell for Jealousy.
Spell to Cure Barrenness.
Spell to Protect Our Love.
Spell to Soften the Hard Heart of a Woman.
Transformation.
Way Out, The.
You Have Shown Me a Strange Image, and We
Are Strange Prisoners.
Coverdale, Miles (1488–1569)
Let Go the Whore of Babylon.
Of the Resurrection.
Song of the Virgin Mary, The.
Coviello, Michelangelo (b. 1950)
Caravaggio, sels.
Well of Clouds, The, sel.
Coward, Noël (1899–1973)
Any Part of Piggy.
Bar on the Piccola Marina, A.
Contours.
Don't Let's Be Beastly to the Germans.
He Never Did That to Me.
I Wonder What Happened to Him.
I'll See You Again.
(I'm So) Weary of It All.
Irish Song [Rosie O'Grady].
I've Been to a Marvelous Party.
Let's Do It.
Little Ones' A. B. C., The, sel.
London Pride.
Mad About the Boy.
Mad Dogs and Englishmen.
Mrs Worthington, sels.
Never Again.
Nina.
Poor Little Rich Girl.
Sail Away.
Stately Homes of England, The.
Stately Homes of England, The, sel.
What's Going to Happen to the Tots?
Why Must the Show Go On?
Cowley, Abraham (1618–67)
Brutus.
Cheer Up, My Mates.
Christ's Passion.
Chronicle, The; a Ballad.
Country-Mouse, The.
Davideis, sels.

Drinking.
Epicure, The, *sel.*
Garden, The, *sels.*
Grasshopper, The.
In Praise of Hope.
Innocent Ill, The.
London Subverted by the Furies.
Mistress, The, *sels.*
Motto, The.
Ode: Of Wit.
Ode upon Doctor Harvey, *sel.*
Of Myself [*or* My Self].
Of Solitude.
On the Death of Mr. Crashaw.
On the Death of Mr. William Hervey [*or* Harvey], *sel.*
Pindarique Odes, *sels.*
Powers of Darkness.
Reason.
Swallow, The.
Sylva, *sels.*
34. Chapter of the Prophet Isaiah, The.
Tree of Knowledge, The.

Cowley, Hannah ("Anna Matilda") (1743–1809)
Departed Youth.
Invocation. To Horror.
Ode to Della Crusca.
Off Duty [*or* To Della Cruscà].
To Della Crusca. The Pen.
Well-Aimed Tear, The [*or* To Della Crusca].

Cowley, Malcolm (1898–1989)
Blue Juniata, *sels.*
Chateau de Soupir, 1917.
Danny.
Ernest.
Long Voyage, The.
Winter Tenement.

Cowper, Maria Frances Cecelia (1726–97)
Task, The, *sel.*

Cowper, William (1731–1800)
Beau's Reply.
Castaway, The.
Epitaph on a Hare.
Lines Written During a Period of Insanity.
Negro's Complaint, The.
Olney Hymns, *sels.*
On the Receipt of My Mother's Picture out of Norfolk, the Gift of My Cousin Ann Bodham.
Poplar Field, The.
Shrubbery, The.
Sweet Meat Has Sour Sauce.
Task, The, *sels.*
Tirocinium; or, A Review of Schools, *sels.*
To a Young Lady.
To George Romney, Esq.
To Mary.
To Mary Unwin.

Cox, Jimmie
Nobody Knows You When You're Down and Out.

Cox, Mark
At the Crematorium, My Son Asks Why We're All Wearing Black.
Barbells of the Gods, The.
Garglers, The.
Moles, The.
Sonata.
Style.
Things My Grandfather Must Have Said.
Treasure: "Ax heads and sledges, musket balls and elixir bottles."

Cox, Nancy
Singing Alone.

Cox, Palmer (1840–1924)
Mouse's Lullaby, The.

Coxon, William W.
Flash Colonial Barman, The.

Coyote, Peter
Do you think.

Crabbe, George (1754–1832)
Borough, The, *sels.*
Dealer and the Clerk, The, *sels.*
Delay Has Danger.
Lover's Journey, The, *sel.*

Marriage Ring, The.
Meeting.
Parish Register, The.
Reflections, *sels.*
Resurrection.
Tales, *sels.*
Tales of the Hall, *sels.*
Village, The, *sels.*

Craig, David (b. 1932)
Latest News.

Craig, David (b. 1951)
Apple Fools.
Apprentice Eats Glass, The.
Apprentice Is Amazed, The.
Apprentice Prophecies, The.
Apprentice Sees Himself in the Sunset, The.
Christ Bearing the Cross by El Greco.
Francis Helps a Brother Who Is in Sin.
Gethsemane: "Damp wind, the innocent."
Gospel Poem #1.
Gospel Poem #2.
Gospel Poem #3.
Hewn Hands.
Hyperbole.
John Says Mass on All Souls' Day.
Litany: "Mother of Sorrow."
Marian Sector, *sel.*
Nursing Home, 3rd Shift.
Our Father.
Pentecost.
Peter Maurin (1877–1949), *sel.*
Presence of God, The.
Prothalamion, *sel.*
Young Monk (Denver).

Craig, Maurice James (b. 1919)
Love Poem: "Flowers upon your lips and hands."

Craig, Michael Earl (b. 1970)
Good Night, Star.

Craighead, Lorena M. (b. 1968)
Dancin' Our Lives Away.
Whole Truth So Help Me God—Also Known as the Gettin' Rid of Nigguz Business.
Wo/man's Voice Must Be Heard, A.

Craik, Dinah Maria Mulock (1826–87)
Douglas, Douglas, Tender and True.
Friendship.

Cramer, Steven
For the Bullies of West Morris High.

Cranch, Christopher Pearse (1818–92)
Autumn Rain, The.
Bird and the Bell, The.
Bird Language.
Cataract Isle, The.
Cornucopia.
Correspondences.
December.
Evening Primrose, The.
In the Palais Royal Garden.
Music.
My Old Palette.
Old Cat's Confessions, An.
Pines and the Sea, The.
Seven Wonders of the World, *sels.*
Spirit of the Age, The.

Crane, Hart (1899–1932)
Air Plant, The.
And Bees of Paradise.
At Melville's Tomb.
Black Tambourine.
Bridge, The, *sels.*
Broken Tower, The.
C33.
Chaplinesque.
Circumstance, The.
Emblems of Conduct.
Enrich My Resignation.
Episode of Hands.
Eternity.
For the Marriage of Faustus and Helen, *sel.*
Forgetfulness.
Garden Abstract.
Hurricane, The.
In Shadow.
Modern Craft.

My Grandmother's Love Letters.
O Carib Isle!
Praise for an Urn.
Purgatorio.
Repose of Rivers.
Royal Palm.
Sad Indian, The.
Stark Major.
Sunday Morning Apples.
To Emily Dickinson.
To the Cloud Juggler.
Voyages, *sels.*
Wine Menagerie, The.

Crane, Stephen (1871–1900)
Ah, God, the way your little finger moved.
Battle Hymn, The.
Behold, the grave of a wicked man.
Black riders came from the sea.
Each small gleam was a voice.
God in wrath, A.
God lay dead in Heaven.
I explain the silvered passing of a ship at night.
I met a seer.
I saw a man pursuing the horizon.
I stood upon a high place.
I walked in a desert.
If I should cast off this tattered coat.
Impact of a dollar upon the heart, The.
In Heaven, / Some little blades of grass.
In the desert.
Learned man came to me once, A.
Little birds of the night.
Little ink more or less!, A.
Livid lightnings flashed in the clouds, The.
Man adrift on a slim spar, A.
Man feared that he might find an assassin, A.
Man said to the universe, A.
Man saw a ball of gold in the sky, A.
Many red devils ran from my heart.
Mystic shadow, bending near me.
Naked woman and a dead dwarf, A.
Newspaper is a collection of half-injustices, A.
Once, I knew a fine song.
Once there came a man.
Should the wide world roll away.
There is a grey thing that lives in the tree-tops.
There was a man with tongue of wood.
There was set before me a mighty hill.
Think as I think, said a man.
Unwind my riddle.
War Is Kind.
Wayfarer / Perceiving the pathway to truth, The.
With eye and with gesture.
Youth in apparel that glittered, A.

Crapsey, Adelaide (1878–1914)
Amaze.
Anguish.
Arbutus.
Fragment.
Guarded Wound, The.
Languor After Pain.
Laurel in the Berkshires.
Lonely Death, The.
Madness.
Moon-Shadows.
Niagara.
Night Winds.
November Night.
Pledge, The.
Release.
Snow.
Song: "I make my shroud but no one knows."
Sun-Dial, The.
Susanna and the Elders.
To a Hermit Thrush.
Trapped.
Triad.
Warning, The.
Witch, The.

Crase, Douglas (b. 1944)
Astropastoral.
Continent as the Letter M, The.
Covenant.
Elegy for New York, The.
There Is No Real Peace in the World.

Crashaw, Richard (1613?–1649)
And He Answered Them Nothing.
Bulla, *sels.*
But Men Loved Darkness[e] Rather Than [*or* Then] Light.
C[h]aritas Nimia; or, The Dear[e] Bargain.
Christ Crucified.
Christ's Victory.
Come See the Place Where the Lord Lay.
Epitaph Upon Husband and Wife Who Died and Were Buried Together, An.
Flaming Heart, The, *sels.*
Hymn to the Name and Hono[u]r of the Admirable Saint[e] Teresa, A, *sels.*
I Am the Door [*or* Doore].
In Memory of the Vertuous and Learned Lady Madre de Teresa that Sought an Early Martyrdome, *sel.*
In the Holy Nativity of Our Lord God, *sel.*
Luke 10.
Luke 11: Blessed Be the Paps Which Thou Hast Sucked.
Music[k]'s Duel[l].
Neither Durst Any Man From That Day Ask Him Any More Questions.
On the Baptized Ethiopian.
On the Wounds of Our Crucified Lord.
Saint Mary Magdalene or The Weeper.
Samson to His Delilah.
Song: "Lord, when the sense of Thy sweet grace."
Strage degli innocenti, La, *sels.*
Tear[e], The.
To Our Blessed Lord upon the Choice of His Sepulchre.
To the Infant Martyrs.
To the Noblest and Best of Ladies, the Countess of Denbigh.
Two Went Up into the Temple To Pray.
Upon Bishop Andrewes's [*or* Andrewes His] Picture before His Sermons.
Upon the Asse That Bore Our Saviour.
Upon the Body of Our Blessed Lord, Naked and Bloody.
Upon the Infant Martyrs.
Weeper, The.
Wishes. To His (Supposed) Mistress[e].

Craveirinha, José (b. 1922)
3D.

Craven, Jerry
Last Running, The.
Midsummer Farewell.
Spring in Palo Duro Canyon.

Craven, Sherry
Chalk Draw Ranch.
Garden City Diner: Loving Back.

Crawford, Isabella Valancy (1850–87)
Camp of Souls, The.
City Tree, The.
Dark Stag, The.

Crawford, Robert (b. 1959)
Alba Einstein.
Downtown Sunday.
Fiat Lux.
Handshakes, The.
Masculinity.
Result, The.
Saltcoats Structuralists, The.
Scotch Broth.
Sobieski-Stuarts.

Crawford, Roger
Love Song of Tommo Frogley.

Crawley III, William T. (b. 1966)
Bud.
Poetry for the Goddess.

Creamer, Henry (1879–1930)
After You've Gone.
If I Could Be with You.
Way Down Yonder in New Orleans.

Creedon, Carolyn (b. 1969)
Litany.

Creeley, Robert (1926–2005)
Act of Love, The.
After Lorca.
Again.
Age ("Most explicit— / the sense of trap.").
Air: "The Love of a Woman"
All That Is Lovely in Men.
America.
Anger.
Away.
Ballad of the Despairing Husband.
Be of Good Cheer.
Body.
Bresson's Movies.
Buffalo Evening.
Company, The.
Dishonest Mailmen, The.
Door, The: "It is hard going to the door."
Echo ("Brutish recall.").
Edge, The ("Long over whatever edge.").
Edges.
En Famille.
Faces, The.
Fathers.
Feeling, A.
Figures, The.
First Love.
Flower, The: "I think I grow tensions."
For Friendship.
For Love.
For My Mother: Genevieve Jules Creeley.
For W. C. W ("Rhyme is after, The.").
Form of Women, A.
Heroes.
Hill, The.
House, The ("Mas-Soñer / Restaurat—Any.").
I Keep to Myself Such Measures.
I Know a Man.
If You.
In a Boat Shed.
In London.
Invitation, The.
Kitchen.
Kore.
Language, The.
Life and Death, *sels.*
Like They Say.
Marriage, A.
Mazatlan: Sea.
Memory Gardens.
Messengers, The.
Mother's Voice.
Naughty Boy.
Oh No.
Other.
Parade.
Place, The ("Afternoon it changes.").
Rain, The: "All night the sound had."
Rescue, The.
River wandering down, *sel.*
Road, The.
Self-Portrait.
Something.
Something for Easter.
Somewhere.
Song: "What I took in my hand."
Song: "What's in the body you've forgotten."
Stairway to Heaven.
This House.
Time: "How long for the small yellow flowers."
To And.
Turn, The.
Warning, The.
Way, The.
Whip, The.
Wicker Basket, A.
Window, The.
Won't It Be Fine?
World, The.

Crenner, Jim
Out-of-Body Experience.

Crevel, René (1900–35)
Nighttime.

Crews, Judson
Declaration at Forty.
Essence.
In the Rubble.
It Is Not Golgotha—It Is.
Mullhaven.
Rejoice.
Tone, The.

Crinagoras (b. c.70 B.C.)
Epigrams, *sel.*

Crist-Evans, Craig (1954–2005)
No Guarantee.

Cristall, Anne Batten (b. c.1798)
Before Twilight. Eyezion.
Elegy on a Young Lady.
Elegy: "Wander, my troubled soul, sigh mid the night thy pain."
Enthusiast, The. Arla.
Enthusiast, The. Songs of Arla, *sels.*
Evening. Gertrude.
Holbein.
Morning. Rosamonde.
Noon. Lysander.
Ode, An: "Almighty Power! who rul'st this world of storms!"
Ode on Truth: Addressed to George Dyer.
Snow-Fiend, The.
Song: "Both gloomy and dark was the shadowy night."
Song: "Come, let us dance and sing."
Song: "Eve descends with radiant streaks, The."
Song of Arla, Written During Her Enthusiasm, A.
Song on Leaving the Country Early in the Spring.
Song: "Through springtime walks, with flowers perfumed."
Song: "Tossed midst life's terrific storms."
Song. Tune, The Heavy Hours: "Balmy comforts that are fled, The."
Song: "Wandering in the still of eve."
Thelmon and Carmel; An Irregular Poem, *sels.*
To a Lady on the Rise of Morn.
Triumph of Superstition, The. Raphael and Ianthe.
Verses Written in the Spring.
Written in Devonshire, Near the Dart.
Written When the Mind Was Oppressed.

Crockett-Smith, D. L. (b. 1954)
Hell Hound Blues.
Homestead, USA.
Rhinemaiden.

Croft, Andy (b. 1956)
Beasts of England, The.

Croft, Julian
D-Zug.
Graffiti.
Greenhalgh's Pub.

Croft, Roy (1919–77)
Love.

Croly, George (1780?–1860)
Aestuary, An.
Domestic Love.
Supplication, A.

Crompton, Hugh (*fl.* 1657)
Epigram VII: Winifred.
Epigram LXVII: Time, the Interpreter.

Cromwell, Ann *See* Williams, Ann

Cromwell, Baptina Palavicino (c.1595–1618)
Eternal power from whose allseeing eye.

Cromwell, Elizabeth (*fl.* late 1630s?)
Sisters Newyearsgift from Elizabeth to Mary a Happie Mother of Good Children, The.

Cronin, Anthony (b. 1925)
Elegy for the Nightbound.
Lines for a Painter.
R.M.S. *Titanic, sel.*
Responsibilities.
Surprise.

Cronin, Jeremy (b. 1949)
Motho Ke Motho Ka Batho Babang (A Person Is a Person Because of Other People).
Naval Base (Part III), The.

Crooker, Barbara (b. 1945)
Barbie and Ken Maximize Their Options.
Grating Parmesan.

Crosby, Ernest (1856–1907)
Military Creed, The.
War and Hell, *sels.*

Crosby, Fanny (Frances Jane Crosby) (1820–1915)
Blessed Assurance.
I Am Thine, O Lord.
Let Me Die on the Prairie.
Mandan Chief, The.
On Hearing a Description of a Prairie.
Thoughts in Midnight Hours.
To God be the glory, great things he hath done!
We Are Going.

Crosby, Frances Jane *See* Crosby, Fanny

Crosby, Harry (1898–1929)
Photoheliograph (For Lady A.).
Vision.

Crosland, T. W. H. (1865–1924)
Slain.
White Feather Legion, The.

Cross, Del Ray
All the flutterlings gone.
Big words.
Bus poems, The.
Can't Oh.
Ceci n'est pas une pipe.
Cinema Yosemite.
Let's try something.
Massimo del Panino, Il.
Office Depot parking lot.
Painted Ladies, The.
Rothko.
Sterling Park.
Trilogy.
Turn-on (with most of a line by Spicer).
Vote, The.

Cross, Elsa (b. 1946)
Balancing Act.
Baniano.
Banyan.
Banyan.
Epifanía.
Epiphany: "Sometimes you show yourself."
Equilibrismo.
Fabulación.
Fabulation.
Form.
Forma.
Hiedra.
Ivy.
Kali.
Mandap.
Mandap.
Monsoon.
Monzón.
Pabellón.
Palabras.
Pavilion.
Seva.
Seva.
Shakti.
Shakti.
Sri Nityananda Mandir (The Temple of Nityananda).
Uma Worshipping Shiva (On a Kangra miniature).
Visions.
Words.

Cross, Mary Ann [or Marian] Evans Lewes *See* Eliot, George

Cross, Teri Ellen
Complected.

Crossley-Holland, Kevin (b. 1941)
They're marked men. Their park is like an open prison.

Crouch, A. L.
Mirabeau B. Lamar.

Crouch, Stanley (b. 1945)
Blackie Thinks of His Brothers.
Chops Are Flyin.
Like a Blessing.
Revelation, The.
Riding Across John Lee's Finger.
Up on the Spoon.

Crow, Christine
City Park.

Crow, Mary
Cityscape.

Crow, Steve (b. 1949)
El Alamein.
Louisiana.
Revival.
Songs, *sel.*
Water Song.

Crowe, Thomas Rain (b. 1949)
After Reading Han-Shan.
Occam's Razor.
Pond in the Woods, A.
Saw-Mill Shack, The.
Tools.
Winter Moon Haiku.

Crowe, William (1745–1829)
In evil hour, and with unhallow'd voice.

Crowell, Elizabeth
Portraits of the Ladies.

Crowell, Grace Noll (b. 1877)
Prayer for Texas, A.
Summer Nights in Texas.
Texas Autumn.

Crowell, Norman H.
Texas Trails.

Crowley, Aleister (1875–1947)
Ballad of Passive Paederasty, A.
Dedicace.
Go into the Highways and Hedges, and Compel Them to Come In.
Rondels.

Crowley, Robert
Of Unsaciable Purchasers.
Sunday Bear-Baiting.

Crown, Kathleen
Holy Ghost Flies into Second Baptist on Airline Highway in Baton Rouge, The.
Necklace: Rich Pink Corona Round a Flashing Yellow Heart.

Crozier, Andrew (b. 1943)
Blank Misgivings.
Driftwood and Seacoal.
Heifer, The.
Humiliation in Its Disguises.
Loopy Dupes.

Crozier, Lorna (b. 1948)
Carrots.
Cucumbers.
Dirty Thirties, The.
Excellence in the Small. Tears Frozen on Your Face.
Fear Of Snakes.
Inventing the Hawk.
Last Testaments, *sels.*
Onions.
Packing for the Future: Instructions.
Poem for Sigmund.
So This Is Love.

Crucefix, Martyn
Air-Waves.
Pietá.
There is a whole world involved in me.

Cruickshank, Helen B.
Comfort in Puirtith.
Fate: "Fate fell upon a man."
Ponnage Pool, The.
Sae Lang Has Sorrow.
Shy Geordie.
Wishin' Well, The.

Crummey, Michael (b. 1965)
Capelin Scull.
Loom: Burnt Woods Cemetery, Western Bay, Newfoundland.
Naked Man, The.
Painting the Islands.
What's Lost.

Crumpacker, Caroline (b. 1964)
Trans-Relational Love Poem.

Crunk, T.
Leaving.
Reunion.
Visiting the Site of One of the First Churches My Grandfather Pastored.

"Crusca, Della" *See* Merry, Robert

Cruz, Cynthia (b. 1968)
Ariadne, Waiting.
Briar Rose Waltz.
How to Catch a Ghost in a Jar.
Persephone.
Persephone 2.
Praying ("I was kneeling in the willow when.").
Praying ("In the middle of the night.").
Praying ("Into the ice ravaged rag-weed and phlox.").
Praying ("When I was set in that field.").
Self Portrait in Froehlichia.
Self Portrait in Horse Hair Wig.
Traveling Gospel.

Cruz e Sousa, João da (1861–98)
Acrobat of Pain.
Antiphony.
Good Friday.
Sacred Hatred.

Cruz, San Juan de la (1542–91)
Christmas Ballad.
Coplas about the Soul Which Suffers with Impatience to See God, *sel.*
Dark Night.
Dark Night, The.
I Entered Where I Did Not Know.
I Know Full Well the Water's Flowing Power.
I Live and Do Not Live in Myself.
Not Without Hope Pulsing My Breast.
O Living Flame of Love.
Obscure Night of the Soul, The.
One Dismal Night.
Shepherd, Young and Mournful, Grieves Alone, A.
Spiritual Canticle.
Spiritual Canticle, The.

Cruz Varela, Maria Elena (b. 1953)
Invocation.
Kaleidoscope.
Love Song for Difficult Times.

Csoori, Sandor (b. 1930)
For the Seventh Day.
My Masters.
Postponed Nightmare.
Somebody Consoles Me with a Poem.
Thin, Black Band, A.
Visitor's Memories, The.
We Were Good, Good and Obedient.

Cuadra, Angel (b. 1931)
Brief Letter to Donald Walsh (in memoriam).
In Brief.

Cuadra, Pablo Antonio
Birth of the Sun, The.
Evening Star, The.
Horses in the Lake.
Manuscript in a Bottle.
Manuscript in a Bottle.

Cucchi, Maurizio (b. 1945)
Every season has its dead.
Hibernation.
I wouldn't know what it's like to be a pawn.
It's over now, the time for observation, for.
Like the Chinese, I too am going to.
You said: it's hot tonight.

Cuddihy, Michael
Solitude.
This Body.

Cuetzpaltzin, Ayocuan (*fl.* late 15th cent.)
Let the earth last.

Culbert, Steven Tye
Hoodoo Scott Cooley Scalps John Wohrle.
Van Horn.

Cullar, Carol
Heat.
He's Crossed the River.
12,000 Years Is Not Too Long.

Cullen, Countee (1903–46)
Atlantic City Waiter.
Brown Girl Dead, A.
Christus Natus Est.
Colored Blues Singer.
For a Mouthy Woman.
For a Poet.

Cullen

For a Virgin Lady.
For Daughters of Magdalen.
For Hazel Hall, American Poet.
For One Who Gayly Sowed His Oats.
Four Epitaphs, *sels.*
From Life to Love.
From the Dark Tower.
Heritage.
In Memory of Colonel Charles Young.
Incident.
Leaves.
Litany of the Dark People, The.
Night Rain.
Nothing Endures.
Sacrament.
Simon the Cyrenian Speaks.
Song in Spite of Myself.
Tableau.
Timid Lover.
To John Keats, Poet, at Springtime [*or* Spring Time].
Uncle Jim.
Wind Bloweth Where It Listeth, The.
Yet Do I Marvel.

Cullen, Lisa

Reasons to Meditate.

Cullen, Yvonne (b. 1966)

For Letters.
Kabuki.
Memorial: "There had to be a way of making a building talk."
Not a Letter.
Signals.
This.
To the Lighthouse.
With Me.

Cumalı, Necati (1921–2001)

Güler's Hours of Love.

Cumberbatch, Lawrence S.

Again the Summoning.
I Swear to You, That Ship Never Sunk in Middle-Passage!
In the Early Morning Breeze.

Cumberland, Margaret Russell Clifford, Countess of (1560–1616)

Epitaph for Richard Cavendish, Engraved on His Monument in Hornsey Church.

Cumbie, Richard

New Jersey Turnpike.

Cummings, E. E. (1894–1962)

All in green went my love riding.
All nearness pauses,while a star can grow.
Always before your voice my soul.
Anyone lived in a pretty how town.
Bigness of cannon, The.
Boys i mean are not refined, The.
Buffalo Bill's Lament.
Cambridge ladies who live in furnished souls, The.
Come,gaze with me upon this dome.
God pity me whom (god distinctly has).
Goodby Betty,don't remember me.
Greedy the people, The.
Hist whist / little ghostthings.
Hours rise up putting off stars and it is, The.
How many moments must(amazing each).
I carry your heart with me(i carry it in).
I like my body when it is with your.
I Thank You God.
I was sitting in mcsoreley's. outside it was New York and beauti- / fully snowing.
If everything happens that can't be done.
If there are any heavens my mother will (all by herself) have.
If(touched by love's own secret)we,like homing.
In heavenly realms of hellas dwelt.
In Just.
Item.
L(a.
Little joe gould has lost his teeth and doesn't know where.
Little tree / little silent Christmas tree.
Maggie and milly and molly and may.
Man who had fallen among thieves, A.

May i feel said he.
Me Up at Does.
Mr U.
My father moved through dooms of love.
My sweet old etcetera.
Next to of course god america i.
No Thanks, No. 70.
Nobody loses all the time.
Noster, The.
Now comes the good rain farmers pray for(and).
Now is a ship / which captain am.
O pr / gress verily thou art m.
O sweet spontaneous.
Out of midsummer's blazing most not night.
Picasso / you give us Things.
Pity This Busy Monster,Manunkind.
Plato told.
Plato Told Him.
Poem, or Beauty Hurts Mr. Vinal.
Politician, A.
Ponder, darling, these busted statues.
Right here the other night something.
R-P-O-P-H-E-S-S-A-G-R.
Salesman, A.
She being Brand.
Since feeling is first.
Sonnet IV.
Space being(don't forget to remember)Curved.
Spring is like a perhaps hand.
Spring omnipotent goddess thou dost.
Sunset ("Stinging / gold swarms.").
Thy fingers make early flowers of.
Way to hump a cow is not, The.
What If a Much of a Which of a Wind.
When God Lets My Body Be.
Wherelings whenlings / (daughters of if but offspring of hopefear).
Who are you,little i.
Wind has blown the rain away and blown, A.
You Shall Above All Things Be Glad and Young.

Cummings, Peter

Hamlet to Ophelia.

Cummins, Deborah

To the Days Lost in August.

Cummins, James

Sestina: "He wanted to tell her the weekend idea was "neat"."

Cumpian, Carlos (b. 1953)

Armadillo Charm.
Estrellitas.
No Deposit Returns.

Cunard, Nancy

To Eat To-day.

Cuney, Waring (1906–76)

Conception.
Death Bed, The.
No Images.

Cunningham, Allan (1784–1842)

Hame, Hame, Hame.
Sea-Song, A.
Thistle's Grown aboon the Rose, The.

Cunningham, James Vincent (1911–85)

Absence, my angel, presence at my side.
Aged Lover Discourses in the Flat Style, The.
All in Due Time.
Ars Amoris.
Coffee.
Epigram: "Good Fortune, when I hailed her recently."
Epigram: "Here lies my wife. Eternal peace."
Epigram: "Here lies New Critic who would fox us."
Epigram: "I had gone broke, and got set to come back."
Epigram: "You ask me how Contempt who claims to sleep."
Epigram: "You wonder why Drab sells her love for gold?"
Epigrams: A Journal, *sels.*
Epigrams, *sels.*
Fear.
Five Epigrams, *sels.*
For a Woman with Child.

For My Contemporaries.
Half hour for coffee, and at night, A.
I drive Eastward. The ethics of return.
I drive Westward. Tumble and loco weed.
I married in my youth a wife.
I write only to say this.
In a few days now when two memories meet.
Innocent to innocent.
Interview with Doctor Drink.
Jack and Jill.
Life flows to death as rivers to the sea.
Love's Progress.
Montana Pastoral.
Moral Poem, A.
Nescit Vox Missa Reverti.
Night is still, The. The unfailing surf.
On a cold night I came through the cold rain.
On either side of the white line.
Soft lights, the companionship, the beers, The.
To My Wife.
Traveller, the highway my guide, A.
You have here no otherness.

Cunningham, Nora B.

Giving.

Cunningham, Paula (b. 1963)

Aubade: "Man is squeezing oranges in my kitchen, A."
Cats—A Retrospective.
Dog Called Chance, A, *sels.*
On Being the Least Feminist Woman You've Ever Met.

Cunninghame-Graham, Robert *See* Graham, Robert

Curbelo, Silvia (b. 1955)

Among Strangers.
Bedtime Stories.
Between Language and Desire.
Dreaming Horse.
Drinking Song.
Fall: "It was a wing, it was a kiss."
If You Need a Reason.
Lake Has Swallowed the Whole Sky, The.
Last Call.
Listening to a White Man Play the Blues.
Photograph from Berlin.
Photograph of My Parents.
Tonight I Can Almost Hear the Singing.
Tourism in the Late 20th Century.
Tourist Weather.

Curdy, Averill

On a Painting by a Member of the Northwest Visionary School.

Curnow, Allen (b. 1911)

Continuum.
Country School.
House and Land.
Landfall in Unknown Seas.
On the Road to Erewhon.
Out of Sleep.
Pacific 1945-1995.
Skeleton of the Great Moa in the Canterbury Museum, Christchurch, The.
This Beach Can Be Dangerous.
Unhistoric Story, The.
You Get What You Pay For.
You Will Know When You Get There.

Currey, Ralph Nixon (b. 1907)

Burial Flags.
Unseen Fire.

Currie, Mary Montgomerie Currie, Baroness *See* Fane, Violet

Curry, Neil (b. 1937)

Anne Hathaway Composes Her 18th Sonnet.
Dandelion.
Galapagos.
Gardens.
In a Calendar of Saints.
Mute Swans.
Poppy Heads.
St Kilda.
Swallows and Tortoises.

Curtis, Lillian E. (fl. 1870)

Only One Eye.
Potato, The.
Two Bears, The.

Curtis, Tony (b. 1946)
Brigitte Bardot in Grangetown.
Eighth Dream, The.
Gambit.
Games with My Daughter.
Land Army Photographs.
Neighbour's Pear Tree.
Pembrokeshire Buzzards.
Portrait of the Painter Hans Theo Richter and
His Wife Gisela in Dresden, 1933.
Preparations.
Queen's Tears.
Soup.
Spirit of the Place, The.
To My Father.
We Can Say That.
Curzon, David (b. 1941)
Instructions to a Seed.
Proverbs 6:6.
Tour of Ein Kerem, A.
Cushing, James (fl. 20th cent.)
Autumn Leaves.
Every Time We Say Goodbye.
Lover Man.
Cushman, Stephen (b. 1956)
Make the Bed.
Cussrooee, Biddy
My Grief on the Sea.
Cust, Henry (1861–1917)
Non Nobis.
Cuthand, Beth
Dancing with Rex.
She Ties Her Bandanna.
Cuthbert, John Rozel
Memories of St. George's Caye.
Cutler, Bruce
February 12, 1865.
Cutler, Yosl (1896–1935)
Neckst.
Not-a.
Shir Asheydim Ansher.
Cutts, John, Baron Cutts (1661–1707)
To a Lady, Who Desired Me Not To Be in
Love with Her.
Cutts, Simon
Pianostool Footnotes, sel.
Cynan (1895–1970)
Monastîr.
Prodigal Son, The, sel.
Cynddelw Brydydd Mawr (fl. 1155–1200)
In Praise of Owain Gwynedd.
Petition for Reconciliation.
Poem on His Death-Bed.
Cynewulf (fl. late 7th cent.)
Ascension, The, sels.
Nature of the Siren, The.
Phoenix, The, sel.
Riddles (Exeter Book), sels.
Cyril, Malkia Amala (b. 1974)
Children's Games.
Jump Black Honey Jump Black.
Just Because I Am.
What Has Yet to Be Sung.
Czerkawska, Catherine Lucy (b. 1950)
Thread.

D

da Silva, Adelina (b. 1958)
Along the Banks of the Charles.
Return to the Homeland.
da Todi, Jacopone (1228–1306)
Praise of Diseases.
Dabney, Betty Page (b. 1911)
Earth's Bondman.
Dabydeen, Cyril (b. 1945)
Hemingway.
Dacey, Philip (b. 1939)
Coke.
Drummer, The.
Form Rejection Letter.
Four Men in a Car.

Jack, Afterwards.
Last Picture, The.
Musica.
Musician, The.
Rules, The.
Squeak.
Whitman: The Wall.
Dach, Simon (1605–59)
Bonds of Friendship, The.
Lamentation During His Most Painful Illness.
On the Entrance of the Castle Bridge.
To Be Read above the Castle-Gate, When His
Princely Highness Rode in to His Marriage
Bed.
Dacre, Charlotte ("Rosa Matilda") (1782–c.1841)
Female Philosopher, The.
Kiss, The: "Greatest bliss, The."
Mistress to the Spirit of Her Lover, The.
Poor Negro Sadi, The.
Power of Love, The.
Sappho; or, The Resolve.
Similie.
Unfaithful Lover, The.
We Can Love But Once.
Dadié, Bernard (b. 1916)
I Give You Thanks My God.
Daegak Euchon (1050–1101)
At Chonymyung Temple.
At Hongbub Temple.
For Sanje, a Hermit.
Reply to Sir Kukwon's "Sleeping in the
Temple in Autumn"
Retreat at Haein Temple.
Riding a Horse in the Rain.
Studying in the Temple.
Daegam Tanyon (1070–1179)
At Munsoo Temple.
Dafydd [or David] ap Gwilym (fl. 1340–70)
Fox, The.
Girls of Llanbadarn, The.
In Morfudd's Arms.
May.
Mirror, The.
Mis Mai, sel.
Penis, The.
Rattle Bag, The.
Ruin, The.
Seagull, The.
Wind, The.
Wind, The.
Woodland Mass, The.
Dafydd [or David] Benfras (d. 1257)
From Exile.
Daglarca, Fazil Hüsnü (b. 1914)
Beauty and Mind.
Beyond: "Whenever I love a woman."
Day Within a Day.
Is.
Leaf: "Your gaze stays awake in the night."
Poems of the Mediterranean, sel.
Shadow: "Person we love, The."
Sultan of the Animals Is the Night, The.
Unity.
When I Arrive.
D'Aguiar, Frederick (b. 1960)
Airy Hall Iconography.
Airy Hall Nightmare.
Cow Perseverance, The.
Dread.
Dreadtalk.
English Sampler, An.
GDR, sels.
Home: "These days whenever I stay away too
long."
Langston.
Mama Dot.
Mama Dot Warns Against an Easter Rising.
Obeah Mama Dot.
Sound Bite.
Dahlberg, Edward (1900–77)
February Ground.
Kansas City West Bottoms.
Walt Whitman.
Daiches, David (b. 1912)
Notes for a History of Poetry.

Daiches, Jenni (b. 1941)
Geometry.
Horse in Glasgow.
Jewish Cemetery, Frankfurt.
Daichi (1290–1366)
Thoughts arise endlessly.
Daichu
Fiery unicorn snapped, The.
Daie-Soko (1089–1163)
Life's as we / Find it—death too.
Daigu (1584–1669)
Here none think of wealth or fame.
Who dares approach the lion's.
Dailey, Joel (b. 1953)
Call Me 'Shortchange.'
Dear Bubble.
Poetry fro Dummies.
Ride the High Country.
Right Away.
Rio.
S'what Up.
Thong.
Daio (1235–1308)
I have had a companion on the road.
Daisen (fl. 13th cent.)
All things come apart.
Daito (1282–1337)
At last I've broken Unmon's barrier!
To slice through Buddhas, Patriarchs.
Daive, Jean (b. 1941)
I rise from the depths.
Lost in contemplation.
Nomad, A.
She does not move.
Space instead.
Under the wind.
Woman measures, A.
Dalby, Lacey A.
MacArthur High School.
Dalchev, Atanas (1904–78)
Snow: "Over strip-raked iron rooves."
Dale, Peter (b. 1938)
I start with a straight back and two points.
Daley, Victor James (1858–1905)
Dove, The.
Mother Doorstep.
Vision of Sunday in Heaven, A.
Woman at the Washtub, The.
Dali, Salvador (1904–89)
Great Masturbator, The.
Dallas, Ruth (b. 1919)
Photographs of Pioneer Women.
Dallerès, Josep-Enric (b. 1949)
Museum.
D'Almeida, Fernando (b. 1955)
By Forty-Sixth.
Dalton, Amanda (b. 1957)
Dad-Baby, The.
How to Disappear.
Kitchen Beast.
Room of Leaves, sels.
Dalton, Annie Charlotte (1865–1938)
Praying-Mantis, The.
Dalton, Mary
Burn.
Conkerbells.
Doctor, The.
Down the Bay.
Flirrup.
Mad Moll And Crazy Betty.
Marriage, The.
My One Brother.
She.
Sterricky.
Water Man, The.
Yet.
Dalton, Roque
Ars Poetica.
From a Revolutionary to J. L. Borges.
Looking for Trouble.
Memory.
My Neighbor.
Petty Bourgeoisie, The.

Soldier's Rest.
Daly, Thomas Augustin (1871–1948)
Mia Carlotta.
Damacion, Kenneth Zamora
Canciones.
Damas, Léon (b. 1912)
Hiccups.
Just Like the Legend.
No One Remembers.
On Sale.
Par la fenêtre ouverte à demi.
Solde.
S.O.S
Through the Half-Opened Window.
Wind, The: "Wide sea—black night—I woke
up lovesick."
Dame, Enid
On the Road to Damascus, Maryland.
Seder, The.
Dameron, Chip
Banding near the South Texas Coast, Late
April.
South Texas Boxcar Blues.
Dana, Mary Stanley Bunce (1810–83)
Real Comfort.
Dana, Richard Henry (1787–1879)
Chanting Cherubs, The [A Group by
Greenough].
Daybreak.
Dying Raven, The.
Husband's and Wife's Grave, The.
Pleasure Boat, The [or Pleasure-Boat, The].
Dana, Robert Patrick (b. 1929)
A Capella.
Elegy for the Duke.
Figures, The.
Here and Now.
In Heaven.
Mark, The.
Radiance.
Dancer, John (fl. 1660–1707)
Variety, The.
Dancing Bear, J. P.
Caliban.
Heart-Shaped Island, A.
Iago, the Poet.
Making Fire.
Dangai
Earth, river, mountain.
Dangel, Leo
After Forty Years of Marriage, She Tries a
New Recipe for Hamburger Hot Dish.
Daniel, Arnaut (fl. c.1180–1210)
Art of Love, The.
Firm desire which enters, The.
Resolute Desire That Enters, The.
Daniel, Gary (b. 1958)
It Makes Me Sad.
My Mother Tongue.
What Have We Done.
Daniel, George (1616–57)
After a Storm, Going a Hawking.
Landscape, The.
Robin, The.
Daniel, Samuel (1562–1619)
Civil Wars, The, sels.
Sonnets to Delia, sels.
Epistle. To Prince Henrie, sel.
Hymen's Triumph, sel.
Musophilus; or, Defence of All Learning, sels.
Ode: "Now each creature joys the other."
Tethy's Festival, sels.
To the Lady Margaret, Countess [or Countesse]
of Cumberland.
To the Right Honorable, the Lady Mary,
Countess of Pembroke.
Ulysses and the Siren [or Syren].
Daniells, Roy (b. 1902)
Noah.
Daniels, Jim
Blessing the House.
Falling Bricks.
Hard-Boiled Egg.
Hoagie Scam, The.

911.
Short-Order Cook.
Ted's Bar and Grill.
Time, Temperature.
Wheels: "My brother kept."
Daniels, Kate (b. 1953)
After Reading Reznikoff.
Bus Ride.
Ethiopia.
Not Singing.
Prayer for My Children.
Prayer to the Muse of Ordinary Life.
War Photograph.
Women's Room in Pennsylvania Station, The.
Dankyo-Myorin (fl. 13th cent.)
Coming, I clench my hands.
D'Annunzio, Gabriele (1863–1938)
I pastori (The Shepherds).
Dante Alighieri (1265–1321)
Convito, sel.
Divina Commedia, sels.
Divine Comedy, The (Mandelbaum
Translation), sels.
First Canzone of the Convito, The.
Great Canzon, The.
Love and Poetry.
New Love and the Gentle Heart.
Sestina: "I have reached, alas, the long
shadow."
Sestina: Of the Lady Pietra degli Scrovigni.
To Waning Day, To the Wide Round of
Shadow.
Vita Nuova, La, sel.
D'Anvers, Alicia (1688?–1725)
Academia; or The Humours of the University
of Oxford, sels.
Oxford-Act, The, sels.
Da'oud, Siham
I Love in White Ink.
D'Aquino, Alfonso (b. 1959)
Amoroso.
Amorous.
Boda, La.
Brief Viper.
Hotel.
Hotel.
Metempsicosis del perro.
Metempsychosis of the Dog.
Naranja de luz abierta, La.
Opened Orange of Light, The.
Sol abre los labios y nos dice, El.
Sun opens its lips and says to us, The.
Vibora breve.
Wedding, The.
**Darío, Rubén (Né: Fé Rubén García Sarmiento)
(1867–1916)**
Autumn Verses.
Autumn Verses.
Autumnal.
Doom.
Eheu!
Far Away and Long Ago.
Fatality.
Fount, The.
I Love, You Love.
I Pursue a Form.
I Seek a Form.
It Was a Gentle Air.
Leda.
Marguerite.
Melancholy.
Nicaraguan Triptych.
Nocturne.
Nocturne.
Philosophy.
Seashell.
Seashell, The.
Sonatina.
Sonatina.
Spring.
Springtime.
Story for Margarita.
Swan, The.
Swans, The.
Symphony in Gray Major.

To Roosevelt.
Triumphal March.
Tropic Afternoon.
Tropical Afternoon.
Unhappy He.
Victory of Samothrace, The.
Dark, Eileen See O'Connell [or Dark], Eileen
Darley, George (1795–1846)
Fallen Star, The.
Free-booter, The.
It Is Not Beauty I Demand.
Nepenthe, sels.
Pass of Death, The.
Rebellion of the Waters, The.
Song: "Sweet in her green dell the flower of
beauty slumbers."
Sylvia; or, The May Queen, sels.
Syren Songs, sels.
To Helene.
Darling, Julia (B. 1956)
Chemotherapy.
How to Behave with the Ill.
My Old Friend Hospital.
Nurses.
Poverty.
Too Heavy.
Waiting Room in August, A.
Darlington, Tenaya (b. 1971)
Field Guide to Western Intimacy.
Darr, Ann (b. 1920)
At Sixteen.
Flight as a Way of Life.
Darragh, Tina (b. 1950)
Footnote at "Figure of Speech."
Lattice at/of (Com)pare (Dis)pair.
Lattice at "Split."
"Legion" to "Lent" for "R."
"Luteous" to "Lymph" for "F."
Numb to Number.
Pie in the Sky: Part 2.
Sis Boom Ba.
Throwing Out at / of (Com)pare (Dis)pair, A.
Volcanic tuff.
Darwin, Erasmus (1731–1802)
Botanic Garden, The, sels.
Economy of Vegetation, The, sels.
Temple of Nature; or, The Origin of Society,
The, sels.
Darwish, Mahmoud (b. 1942)
August, Beirut, 1982.
Earth Poem.
Eleven Stars over Andalusia, sels.
Give Birth to Me Again That I May Know.
Guests on the Sea.
He Embraces His Murderer.
Identity Card.
In This Land.
On a Canaanite Stone in the Dead Sea.
On Wishes.
Poem for the Land, sel.
Poems after Beirut, sels.
Prison.
Psalm 2.
Ramallah—January, 2002.
Sirhan Drinks His Coffee in the Cafeteria.
Steps in the Night.
We Walk Towards a Land.
Words.
Daryush, Elizabeth (1887–1976)
Children of Wealth.
Forbidden Love.
I saw the daughter of the sun.
Still-Life.
Subalterns.
You should at times go out.
Dās, Raghunāth (fl. late 18th cent.)
Now I'll see whether Siva.
Dāsdatta, Rāmlāl
Because You love cremation grounds.
Datcher, Michael (b. 1967)
I am open.
Joseph speaks to gericault in the studio.
Soul gestures in spring.

Dater, Tony
Thunderbirds.
Dauenhauer, Nora (b. 1927)
Grandmother Eliza.
How To Make Good Baked Salmon from the
River.
Kelp.
Skiing on Russian Christmas.
Tlingit Concrete Poem.
Tlingit Concrete Poem.
Voices.
Dauenhauer, Richard
Driving in a Snowstorm, King Salmon to
Naknek.
Dauer, Lesley (b. 1965)
Bewilderment is Love.
Falling.
Lois at the Hair Salon.
Mammals.
Philip the Store Policeman.
20th Century, The.
William.
Woman in the Film, The.
Daugherty, Brad
Lilac.
Nightfire.
Daugherty, James Henry (1889–1974)
Trail Breakers, sel.
Daumal, René (1908–44)
Clavicles for a Great Poetic Game, sels.
I Speak in All Ages.
Je parle dans tous les âges.
Jesus Before Pilate.
Mot et la mouche, Le.
Persephone That Is to Say Double Issue.
Poetry and Thought.
Short Revelation Concerning Death and Chaos.
St. Matthew, sels.
Dauthendey, Max
Inside the Bouquet.
Davenant [or D'Avenant], Sir William (1606–68)
Countess of Anglesey Lead Captive by the
Rebels, at the Disforresting of Pewsam, The.
For the Lady Olivia Porter; a Present upon a
New Year's Day.
Gondibert, sels.
Gondibert Book 2, sel.
Lark Now Leaves His Watery [or Wat'ry]
Nest.
Law against Lovers, The, sel.
Lover and Philosopher.
O Thou That Sleep'st Like Pig in Straw.
Soldier Going to the Field, The.
'Tis, in good truth, a most wonderful thing.
To the Queen[e], Entertain[e]d at Night by the
Countess[e] of Anglesey.
Davenport, Robert (fl. 1624–40)
Sacrifice, A.
Davenport, Steven
Up from the Wreck Conjuring Montana
Sonnet.
Davico, Oskar (1909–89)
Cell, The.
David, Mack (1912–93)
Candy.
I'm Just a Lucky So-and-So.
Sinner Kissed an Angel, A.
Sunflower.
Davidkov, Ivan (1926–90)
Clay and Star, sels.
Meteor.
Monastery.
Returning from the Fair.
Some Day.
Tune for a Flute, sels.
Villages Like Ghosts.
Davidman, Joy (b. 1915)
And Pilate Said.
Lament for Evolution.
Night-Piece.
Davidson, Chad (b. 1970)
I Took by the Throat the Circumcised Dog.
Davidson, Donald (1893–1968)
Hermitage, sels.

Immigrant, The.
In Blue-Stocking Hollow.
Lee in the Mountains.
Lines for a Tomb.
Lines Written for Allen Tate on His Sixtieth
Anniversary.
On a Replica of the Parthenon.
Randall, My Son.
Redivivus.
Refugees.
Sanctuary.
Sequel of Appomattox.
Twilight on Union Street.
Utterance.
Davidson, John (1857–1909)
Ballad of a Nun, A.
Ballad of Hell, A.
Battle.
Crystal Palace, The, sel.
New Year's Eve, sels.
Northern Suburb, A.
Runnable Stag, A.
Snow: "Who affirms that crystals are alive?"
Song: "Boat is chafing at our long delay, The."
Testament of John Davidson, The, sel.
Thirty Bob a Week.
Unknown, The.
Davidson, Lucretia (1808–25)
America.
Charnel Ship, The.
Fear of Madness, The.
Davidson, Michael (b. 1944?)
Bad Modernism.
Century of Hands.
Dream Dream, The.
Et in Leucadia Ego.
Feeling Type and His Friends, The.
Form of Chiasmus; The Chiasmus of Forms,
The.
Framing.
Landing of Rochambeau, The.
Sensation Type and His Friends, The.
Thinking the Alps.
Troth.
Davidson, R. R.
Gravy Train, The.
Davie, Donald (1922–95)
Across the Bay.
Barnsley and District.
Devil on Ice.
Epistle to Enrique Caracciolo Trejo.
Fountain of Cyanë, The.
Fountain, The.
Garden Party, The.
Gardens No Emblems.
Hill Field, The.
In California.
In the Stopping Train, sel.
Jacob's Ladder.
Ordinary God.
Pilate.
Prose for Des Esseintes.
Rejoinder to a Critic.
Remembering the 'Thirties.
Rodez.
Their Rectitude Their Beauty.
Time Passing, Beloved.
Tunstall Forest.
With the Grain.
Davies, Alan (b. 1951)
Name, sel.
New Sentience, The.
Outer Layers of Nervousness, The.
Pain, sel.
Thirty East Forty-Second Street.
Davies, Aneirin Talfan
Books.
I Looked You in the Face Last Night.
Davies, Arthur
West Paddocks.
Davies, Bryan Martin
Berne.
Blue.
Consideration.
Snow in Wrexham.

Widow.
Davies, Dudley G. (1891–1981)
At Branwen's Grave.
Carmarthenshire.
Davies, Edward (1718–89)
Chepstow: A Poem, sel.
Wily Fox, The.
Davies, Eleanor Touchet (1590–1652)
Gatehouse Salutation, The.
When Hee Was Come to the Other Side of the
Contrye, of the Gergesenes, There Mett Him
Two: Possessed with Devils Coming Out of
the Tombes.
Davies, Elwyn (b. 1912)
Portrait of Auntie Blodwen.
Davies, Gareth Alban (b. 1926)
Chilean People, The.
Christmas Card to a Friend Who Might Be
Dead.
Dance, The.
Death in Venice.
Incomers.
Ruins, sels.
Time's Muteness.
Wild Geese, The.
Davies, Gloria Evans (b. 1932)
Her Name like the Hours.
Holly Gone.
Davies, Grahame
DIY.
Liverpool.
Red.
Rough Guide.
Waste.
Davies, Hilary
Beachy Head.
Davies, Idris (1905–53)
Angry Summer 20, The.
Angry Summer 28, The.
Angry Summer, The ("From Abertillery and
Aberdare.").
Angry Summer, The ("Mrs. Evans fach, you
want butter again.").
Capel Calvin.
Consider Famous Men, Dai Bach.
Do You Remember 1926?
Gwalia Deserta, sels.
Hywel and Blodwen.
In Gardens in the Rhondda.
What will you do with your shovel, Dai.
Davies, J. Eirian (1918–98)
Bafflement.
Black Thorn, The.
Hard Song.
Davies, J. Kitchener (1902–52)
Sound of the Wind That Is Blowing, The, sel.
Davies, Sir John (1569–1626)
Epigrams, sels.
Faith (wench) I cannot court thy sprightly eyes.
Gulling[e] Sonnets, The, sels.
Nosce Teipsum, sels.
Of Human Knowledge, sel.
Orchestra; or, A Poem[e] of Da[u]ncing, sels.
Davies, John (b. 1944)
Acclamation, An.
At the Zoo.
How to Write Anglo-Welsh Poetry.
In Port Talbot.
Intellectual Powers of the Soul, The.
Port Talbot.
Sunny Prestatyn.
Three Kinds of Life Answerable to the Three
Powers of the Soul.
Visitor's Book, 8, The.
Visitor's Book, 9, The.
Winter.
Davies, John, of Hereford (c.1565–1618)
Cambria, sel.
Scourge of Folly, The, sels.
Wit's Pilgrimage, sels.
Davies, Lynn (b. 1954)
Cape Enrage.
In the Beginning.
On the Train.

When Ships Sail Too Close.
When You Can't Leave Me Anymore.
Davies, Mary Carolyn
Love Song: "There is a strong wall about me
   to protect me."
Davies, Mererid Puw (b. 1970)
Computers Are Poets Too.
Over a Drink.
Poet on 'Poets on Poets', A: And Other Poems.
Davies, Oliver (1881–1960)
Urban.
Davies, Pennar (1911–96)
Ave Atque Vale.
Dung Beetle, The.
I Was with Ulysses.
When I Was a Boy.
Davies, Samuel (1723–61)
One Thing Needful Generally Neglected, The.
Science.
Thou only Good! Eternal All!
Davies, T. Glynne (b. 1926)
Bailiff, The.
Caernarfon, 2 July [or July 2] 1969.
Old Man in a Moon Loft.
Ruins, sels.
Sentences While Remembering Hiraethog.
Davies, Walter (1761–1849)
Nightfall.
To W.S.—On his Wonderful Toys.
Davies, W. H. (William Henry) (1871–1940)
Ambition.
Bed-Sitting Room, The.
Best Friend, The.
Bright Day, A.
Days That Have Been.
Days Too Short.
Dog, The.
Dumb World, The.
Elements, The.
Example, The.
Great Time, A.
Greeting, A.
Hermit, The.
Hill-Side Park, The.
Hour of Magic, The.
Inquest, The.
J is for Jealousy.
Jenny Wren.
Joy and Pleasure.
Kingfisher, The.
Leaves.
Leisure.
Mind's Liberty, The.
Money.
Moon, The.
No Man's Wood.
Rat, The.
School's Out.
Sheep.
Sluggard, The.
Songs of Joy.
To a Lady Friend.
Truly Great.
Tugged Hand, The.
Two Stars, The.
Villain, The.
Visitor, The.
When Yon Full Moon.
Dávila Andrade, César
Abandoned House, The.
Davis, Benny (fl. 1921)
I'm Nobody's Baby.
Davis, Catherine (1924–2002)
Belongings.
Out of Work, Out of Touch, Out of Sorts.
Years, The.
Davis, Christopher (b. 1960)
Any Nest I Can't Sleep in Should Be Burned.
Displaced Person.
God's Cut-Off TV Screen's Vanishing Mirror
   Seems an Unshared Point.
How Can I Turn Off This Engine Now?
Jojo's.
Little Crisis Framed in My Window.

Murderer, The.
Nod.
Pietà.
Davis, Cortney (b. 1945)
It Is August 24th.
Smoke We Make Pictures Of, The.
What Man Might Kill.
Davis, Dick (b. 1945)
Christmas Poem, A.
Davis, Frank Marshall (b. 1905)
Christ is a Dixie Nigger.
Giles Johnson, Ph.D.
Jazz Band.
Sam Jackson.
Davis, Glover (b. 1939)
August Fires.
Children in the Arbor.
Orphan, The.
Davis, Harold Lenoir (1896–1960)
Proud Riders.
Davis, Hayes
Ali, Bomaye.
Davis, Jack (b. 1917)
Desolation.
First-born, The.
One Hundred and Fifty Years.
Warru.
Davis, Jordan (b. 1970)
Boat, A.
Fire Barns.
He Is Lightning.
Kids on Television Imagine Me, The.
Time Bum.
You Turn Around.
Zoo, The.
Davis, Kathe
Animal Zen.
Green Noise of Ohio Hardwoods, The.
Miracle.
Searching for Mooncakes.
Davis, Lydia
Mown Lawn, A.
Davis, Mary [or Mollie] Evelyn Moore
Cry of a People.
Going Out and Coming In.
Davis, Olena Kalytiak
All the Natural Movements of the Soul.
If You Are Asked.
In the Clear Long After.
Moorer Denies Holyfield in Twelve.
New Philosophy of Composition, or, How to
   Ignore the Non-Reasoning Creature Capable
   of Speeech Perched Outside Your Bathroom
   Window, A.
Panic of Birds, The.
Six Apologies, Lord.
Small Number, A.
Sweet Reader, Flanneled and Tulled.
Thirty Years Rising.
Unbosoming, The.
You Art A Scholar, Horatio, Speak to It.
Davis, Robert H. (b. 1954)
At the Door of the Native Studies Director.
Black Buoy.
Raven is Two-Faced.
Raven Tells Stories.
Davis, Stella (b. 1948)
Friends Beyond.
Davis, Thulani
Aria from X.
Boppin' is Safer than Grindin'
C. T. at the Five Spot.
Desire 1.
Playing Solitaire.
Rogue and Jar: 4/27/77.
Skin of Clouds.
Susannah.
Zoom (The Commodores).
Davis, Todd
Building Walls.
Elkhart, Indiana.
Letter to My Mother, Sixteen Years after the
   Fact.
Loving the Flesh.

Ripe.
Davis, William M.
Why Did Stingy Thomas.
Davis, William Virgil
In a Room.
I-35, South of Waco.
On Lookout: Guadalupe River Ranch.
Overnight Winder: Texas.
Sleep of the Insomniac, The.
Snow.
Spider.
Texas: Sesquicentennial.
Davison, Edward (b. 1898)
In This Dark House.
Davison, Peter (b. 1928)
Breaking of the Day, The, sels.
Cross Cut.
Equinox 1980.
From the Outland.
Frozen Drought.
Getting over Robert Frost.
Motley.
Star Watcher, The.
Under the Roof of Memory.
Where the Sun Ends.
Davitt, Michael (b. 1950)
Counterfeiter, The.
Mirror, The.
Old People.
Shortening the Road.
Dawe, Bruce (b. 1930)
At Shagger's Funeral.
Beatitudes.
Copy-writer's Dream, The.
Dogs in the Morning Light.
Drifters.
Elegy for Drowned Children.
Family Man, The.
First Corinthians at the Crossroads.
Going.
Gorilla Gorilla.
Happiness Is the Art of Being Broken.
Homecoming.
Homo Suburbiensis.
Morning Becomes Electric.
On the Death of Ronald Ryan.
Only the Beards Are Different.
Renewal Notice.
Suburban Lovers.
Victorian Hangman Tells His Love, A.
Weapons Training.
Dawe, Gerald (b. 1952)
Likelihood of Snow, The/The Danger of Fire.
Names.
Question of Covenants, A.
Seamen's Mission.
Sheltering Places.
Solstice.
Dawe, Tom (b. 1940)
Abandoned Outpost.
Daedalus.
If Sonnets Were in Fashion.
Riddle: "I see them in summer."
Dawes, Kwame (b. 1962)
Black Heart.
Some Tentative Definitions 1.
Some Tentative Definitions 11.
Some Tentative Definitions 4.
Some Tentative Definitions 4.
Trickster 1 (for Winston Rodney).
Trickster 2 (for Lee "Scratch" Perry).
Trickster 4 (for Sister Patra).
Dawson, Joy
Locks.
Dawson, Mary
Late for Breakfast.
Day, Clarence (1874–1935)
Egg, The.
Might and Right.
Scenes over the Mesozoic, sel.
Who Drags the Fiery Artist Down?
Day, Cort (b. 1961)
Once As Thoth Beside The Sea.

Day, Jean
From Momentary Work, A Wrench.
Moving Object.
Prose of the World Order.
Reservation.
Day, Jeffery (1896–1918)
North Sea.
Day, John (1574–1640)
Man's Natural Infirmity.
Picket before Bull Run, The.
Prayer: "Grant that no Hobgoblins fright me."
Day Lewis, Cecil (1904–72)
Almost Human.
Can the Mole Take.
Carol, A.
Chiefly to Mind Appears.
Christmas Tree, The.
Come Up, Methuselah.
Conflict, The.
Consider These, for We Have Condemned
   Them.
Do Not Expect Again a Phoenix Hour.
Few Things Can More Inflame.
From Feathers to Iron, *sel.*
Jig.
Magnetic Mountain, The, *sels.*
Nabara, The.
Newsreel.
Poem for an Anniversary.
Reconciliation.
Rest from Loving and Be Living.
Sheepdog Trials in Hyde Park.
Snowfall on a College Garden.
Stand-To, The.
Two Songs.
Two Songs, *sels.*
Walking Away.
When They Have Lost.
Where Are the War Poets?
Winter Night.
With Me My Lover Makes.
You That Love England.
Day, Lucille (b. 1947)
Reject Jell-O.
Self-Portrait at the Health Museum, *sels.*
Ddu, Ieuan *See* Thomas, John L.
de Aerenlund, Consuelo
Cuando el tecolote canta, el Indio muere.
De Angelis, Milo (b. 1951)
And Then the Water.
Continuous Time.
Every Metaphor.
Finite Intuition.
Hilbert's Program.
In the Lungs.
July Has Come for the Dead.
Line.
Main Idea, The.
Narrator, The.
Now She Is Unadorned.
On the Way to Mind.
Protect Me, My Talisman.
Reasons for the Beginning.
Rowing in Familiar January.
Sounds That Arrived, The.
Telegram.
There's a Hand that Nails Down.
Towards the Mind.
Year.
Yearbook.
de Burgos, Julia (1914–53)
Ay, Ay, Ay of the Kinky-Haired Negress.
I Have Lost A Verse.
Poem Arrested at Daybreak.
Poem of My Sleeping Sorrow.
Poem to My Death.
Sea and You, The.
Seawall.
To Julia de Burgos.
Transmutation.
De Burine, Claude (b. 1931)
But When I Have.
Greet You.
Mais quand j'aurai.
Te Saluer.

de Campos, Haroldo
Transient Servitude, *sel.*
De Coninck, Herman (b. 1944)
Ballad of Indolence.
If Only.
Your Sweaters.
De Cristoforo, Violet Kazue (b. 1940)
Dooshi Sorou Soshite Matsu No Me Futori
   Shoka No Sora.
Konchu Kazu Aru Yube Ako Iyo-Iyo Seicho
   Shitari.
Orokashisa Tada Ni Natsu No Hi O Kurashi
   Mukou Castle Rock.
Stockade Prisoners on Hunger Strike: Nani Mo
   Mite Inai Kokoro No Hi Ga Tsuzuki Kogen
   Natsu Takenawa.
Tenth Wedding Anniversary (July 3, 1994):
   Tsuki Oboro Totsugishi Yoru No Sora Datta.
de Fierro, Fanny Carrión (b. 1939)
Grain of Sand.
Heart of Time.
Hidden Pleasure.
If Time Waits.
Oblivion.
Only You.
Oracle.
Secret, The.
Speak to Me.
de Folgar, Romelia Alarcón (b. 1920)
Irreverent Epistle to Jesus Christ.
Monday.
Nocturnal.
Panorama.
Panorama 2.
Protest.
De Forest, John William (1826–1906)
Campaigning, *sel.*
In Louisiana.
Storming Column, The.
de Fréine, Celia (b. 1950)
Bubbles.
Chattels.
Mother Tongue.
Price on My Head, A, *sels.*
Skills.
de Gillies, Giles
De Puerorum osculis.
de Gonz'les, Merced J.
Mexico Will Be Free.
De [or Du] Guillet, Pernette (c.1520–45)
Élegie, *sel.*
de Jesús, Teresa
Curfew.
Flag of Chile, The.
Proverbs.
De Kok, Ingrid (b. 1951)
Al Wat Kind Is.
At the Commission.
At this resort.
Dream of a trophy.
Ecotone.
Ground wave.
Inner note.
Leavetaking.
Mending.
My father would not show us.
My mother's house hold.
Our Sharpeville.
Salamander.
Shadows behind, Before.
Small passing.
Stay here.
Still life: "Woman is wild, The."
Talking cure, The.
Text of necessity.
This thing we learn from others.
To drink its water.
Transfer.
Visitor.
**De la Mare, Walter ("Walter Ramal") (1873–
1956)**
Alas, Alack!
All but Blind.
All That's Past.

Antiques.
As Lucy Went A-Walking.
At the Keyhole.
Autumn.
Ballad of Christmas, A.
Berries.
Birthnight: To F, The.
Christmas Eve.
Cupboard, The.
Dear Sir.
Dove, The.
Echo.
Epitaph, An: "Here lies a most beautiful lady."
Fare Well.
Ghost, The ("Peace in thy hands / Peace in
   thine eyes.").
Ghost, The ("Who knocks? I, who was
   beautiful.").
Hi!
Immanent.
Jenny Wren.
Last Chapter, The.
Listeners, The.
Martha.
Miss T.
Mocking Fairy, The.
Moonshine.
Motley.
Napoleon.
Nod.
Old Men, The.
Old Susan.
Owl, The.
Pooh!
Portrait, A.
Ride-by-Nights, The.
Sam.
Scarecrow, The.
Scholars.
Scribe, The.
Shubble, The.
Silver.
Silver Penny, The.
Sleeper, The ("As Ann came in one summer's
   day.").
Slim Cunning Hands.
Snow.
Some One.
Someone [or Some One].
Song of Finis, The.
Song of the Mad Prince, The.
Song of the Shadows, The.
Stone, The.
Storm, The.
Summer Evening.
There Blooms No Bud in May.
Things: "Things are the mind's mute looking-
   glass."
Thomas Hardy.
Three Cherry Trees, The.
Tired Tim.
Truants, The.
Two Gardens.
Winter ("Clouded with snow / The cold winds
   blow.").
Winter ("Green Mistletoe! / Oh, I remember
   now.").
de la Parra Jr., John G.
Awakening.
Courage!
De la Selva, Salomon
Deliverance.
Tropical Childhood.
Tropical Town.
De la Tierra, Tatiana (b. 1961)
Butterflying.
De la Torre, Monica *See* Torre, Mónica de la
De León, Luís (1528–91)
At the Ascension.
Life Withdrawn, The.
O Courtesy, O Harborage Most Sweet.
Ode to Francisco Salinas.
On Leaving Prison.
Tranquil Night.

de Lille, Abbé Jacques
Gardens, The, *sels.*
de Lorris, Guillaume (c.1215–c.1278)
Romance [*or* Romaunt] of the Rose, The, *sel.*
De Los Santos, Marisa
Milagros Mourns the Queen of Scat.
Wiglaf.
Women Watching Basketball.
De Luca, Christine (b. 1947)
Dancing with Demons.
Streams in the Desert.
Telling the Time.
De' Medici, Maria (1573–1642)
(To the Virgin).
De Mello Breyner, Sophia (b. 1919)
Beach.
Day of Sea.
Flute, The.
I Feel the Dead.
Inscription.
Muse.
Night and the House.
Small Square, The.
de Portalatin, Aida Cartagena
Black Autumn.
Humble Litany.
Second Elegy.
De Roche, Joseph (b. 1938)
Aunt Laura Moves toward the Open Grave of
Her Father.
Blond.
De Roux, Paul (b. 1937)
Cold Again, The.
Day's Labor, The.
Encore le froid.
Labeur du jour.
De Tabley, John Byrne Leicester Warren, 3d
Baron (1835–95)
Sonnet: "Record is nothing, and the hero
great."
Two Old Kings, The.
De Trejo, Angela
Farewell San Miguel, splendid with your
harvested fields.
De Vere, Sir Aubrey (1788–1846)
Children Band, The.
Reality.
Right Use of Prayer, The.
Sonnet: "Ye praise the humble: of the meek ye
say."
De Vere, Aubrey Thomas (1814–1902)
Implicit Faith.
New Race, The.
Serenade: "Softly, O midnight Hours!"
Song: "Slanting both hands against her
forehead."
Sorrow.
De Vere, Edward, 17th Earl of Oxford (1550–
1604)
Court lady Addresses Her Lover, A.
If Women Could Be Fair.
Lively lark stretched forth her wing, The.
Of the Birth and Bringing Up of Desire.
Pains and Gains.
Poem: "Were I a king, I could command
content."
SITTING alone upon my thought, in melancholy
mood.
De Viau, Theophile (1591–1626)
Ode: "Raven croaks before me, A."
De Villagrá, Gaspar Pérez
History of New Mexico, *sels.*
de Vries, Hendrik (1896–1989)
My Brother.
De Vries, Peter (b. 1910)
Bacchanal.
Christmas Family Reunion.
Conscript, *sels.*
Poets Have Their Ear to the Ground.
Sacred and Profane Love, or, There's Nothing
New under the Moon Either.
To His Importunate Mistress.
De Vries, Rachel
On Alabama Ave., Paterson, NJ, 1954.

Dean, Debra Kang (b. 1955)
Arrival.
Back to Back.
Hail.
Immigrants.
In the Way Back.
Stitches.
Taproot.
Deane, John F. (b. 1943)
On a Dark Night.
Deane, Seamus (b. 1940)
Brethren, The.
Burial, A.
Fording the River.
History Lessons.
Osip Mandelstam.
Power Cut.
Reading *Paradise Lost* in Protestant Ulster
1984.
Return.
Roots.
Schooling, A.
Deanovich, Connie
American Avalon.
Ephemera Today on "All My Children", *sel.*
Frankenstein.
My Favorite Monk Is.
Requirements for Suggesting Fats Waller.
Zombie Jet.
Deb, Āśutos (1805–56)
I started a fire with Kali's name.
DeBerry, Jarvis Q. (b. 1975)
Plain Ole Brother Blues.
Debī, Tārinī
Tara, this is why I call upon You.
Debravo, Jorge (1938–67)
Beds of Purification.
DeCarteret, Mark (b. 1960)
Coloring.
Town Clerk, The.
DeCormier-Shekejian, Regina
Grandmother.
Left Eye of Odin, The.
Snow.
Dede, Esrâr (1748–96)
In the ruins, in the tavern.
You left, but don't forget, my heart.
Dede, Jean Dorcely (b. 1941)
Bits.
Deerchild, Rosanna
Snag.
This is a small northern town.
Defoe, Daniel (1660–1731)
More Reformation, *sel.*
Reformation of Manners, *sels.*
Spanish Descent, The, *sel.*
True-born Englishman, The, *sels.*
DeFoe, Mark
Aviary.
Dream Lover.
Forgetting the Sixties.
Red Salamander—Video Store Parking Lot.
DeFrees, Madeline (b. 1919)
Beetle Light.
Blueprints.
Census of Animal Bodies: Driving Home.
Family Group, The.
Figures for a Carrousel, *sels.*
Going Back to the Convent.
In the Locker Room.
In the middle of Priest Lake.
Letter to an Absent Son.
Still Life: "After your letter arrived I left the
oven on."
deFreese, Allison A.
Cycles in Flight: The Racing Bike.
Degenaar, Job (b. 1952)
Irish Sheep, The.
Phenomenon, A.
Degentesh, Katie
5-Year-Old Girls Encountered.
Seeds.

Deguy, Michel (b. 1930)
Ballad, The: "In those days, wasy of feinting
and of tenderness."
Ballade, La: "En ce temps-là, façons de feinte
et de tendresse, la peste ayant figure d'ennui
dans les villes."
Grey Pier.
Here Often I Am.
Ici souvent je suis.
Mur, Le.
O Great Apposition of the World.
O la grande apposition du monde.
Quai gris.
Qui quoi.
This Lady and Her Beautiful Window.
To Forget the Image.
Wall, The.
When the Wind.
Who What.
You Will Be Astonished.
Deharme, Lise (d. 1979)
Empty Cage, The.
Little Girl of the Black Forest.
Dehmel, Richard (1863–1920)
Quiet Town, The.
Dehn, Paul (1912–76)
Alternative Endings to an Unwritten Ballad.
Potted Swan, *sel.*
St. Aubin d'Aubigne.
Dekker, Thomas
Art thou poore yet hast thou golden Slumbers.
Dekker, Thomas (1572?–1632?)
Folly's Song.
Old Fortunatus, *sels.*
Pleasant Comedy of Patient Grissell [*or* Grissel
or Grissill], The, *sels.*
Portrait, A.
Shoemaker's Holiday, The, *sels.*
Sun's Darling, The, *sel.*
Del Valle, Sandra (b. 1963)
Political Life of Palm Trees, The.
DeLange, Eddie (1904–49)
Darn That Dream.
Shake Down the Stars.
Solitude.
Delano, P. L.
Sonnet for an SR-71.
Delanty, Greg (b. 1958)
Alien, The.
Compositor, The.
Goat, the.
Williams Was Wrong.
Delaunay, Sonia (1885–1979)
Greetings, Blaise Cendrars.
Zenith.
Delgado, Alvin
When I Was a Kid in Nueva York.
Delgado, Juan (b. 1960)
Awakened in a Field.
Campesinos.
Chuparosa.
Con Los Pájaros.
Dandelion.
Flora's Plea to Mary.
I-5 Incident.
La Llorona.
Lame Boy Returns, The.
Letters from School, The.
Mexican Fire Breather, A.
Phone Booth at the Corner, The.
Recommitted.
Two Timer.
Visiting Father.
When You Leave.
Winter Fruit.
Della Cruscans (*fl.* **1785–92)**
Moods 1.
Moods 2.
Notice to Tourists.
Delmore, Alton (1908–64)
Girl by the River, The.
Delmore Brothers
Wabash Cannonball, The.

Delmore, Elizabeth (b. 1916)
Difference, The.
Is It Not Strange?
Marmalade.
Such Sweet Sorrow.
Willow.
Yew.

Deloney, Thomas (1543–1600)
Destruction of Jerusalem, The, *sels*.
Long have I lov'd this bonny Lasse.
Weavers Song, The.

Delp, Mike
Fishing the Dream.

Deltoro, Antonio (b. 1947)
Almohadas.
Anestesia.
Anesthesia.
Cartografía.
Cartography.
Contemporáneos.
Contemporaries.
Domingo.
Eggs Laid by a Tiger.
Huevos puestos por un tigre.
Libro de Segunda Mano.
Neighbors.
Pillows.
Secondhand Book.
Shy Ones, The.
Submarine.
Sunday.
Tímidos, Los.
Vecinos.
Viaje.
Voyage.

Demetre, Sheila
Woman Is Running for Her Life, A.

Demetriadis, Mary
When Lovely Woman.

Deming, Alison
Arboretum.
Tilden Park.

Demy, Jacques
You Must Believe in Spring.

Denby, Edwin (b. 1903)
Aaron.
Alex Katz Paints His North Window.
Ciampino: Envoi.
City Without Smoke.
Climate, The.
Delos.
Domestic Cat, A.
Mykonos.
New York Face, A.
Northern Boulevard.
Old age, lookit, it's stupid, a big fart.
On the Home Front—1942.
Out of Bronx subway June forest.
People on Sunday.
Sant' Angelo d'Ischia.
Silence at Night, The.
Snoring in New York, *sels*.
Subway, The.
Summer: "I stroll on Madison in expensive
 clothes, sour."
Trastevere: A Dedication.
Villa d'Este.

Dengina, Svetlana (b. 1968)
Autumnal Equinox.
Russia.

Denham, Joe
Breakfast.
Fo'c'sle Dreams.
Gutting.
Mending.
Morning Set.
Night Haul.
Scotchman Salvage.
Setting.
Shoreline, The.

Denham, Sir John (1615–69)
Cooper's Hill, *sels*.
Preface to *The Progress of Learning*.
Song, A: "Morpheus, the humble god, that
 dwells."

Deni, Jan-Mari Wilè *See* Denis [*or* Deni *or* Jan
 Mapou], Jean-Marie Willer [*or* Jan-Mari Wilè]

DeNicola, Deborah (b. 1947)
My Father's First Fight.

DeNiord, Chard
I Stand Beneath the Mountain with an Illiterate
 Heart.
Soul as a Body, The.
There Is an Error at the Heart of Desire.
This Is a Blessing, This Is a Curse.

Denis, Jean-Marie Willer (b. 1941)
Women of My Country.
Zombie.

Deniz, Gerardo (b. 1934)
Act.
Acto.
Arca.
Ark.
Auditor.
Authoritarian School and How a Respectable
 Literary Genre Was Born, The.
Childish.
Christmas.
Classified Ads.
Edipo al cubo.
Escuela autoritaria y cómo nació un respetable
 género de literatura, La.
Ignorance.
Ignorancia.
Map.
Mapa.
Meditar.
Meditate.
Merlin.
Merlín.
Musa.
Muse.
Navidades.
Oedipus to the Third Power.
Ofertas.
Oyente.
Pueril.
Superior.
Superior.

Denney, Reuel (b. 1915)
Building the Dam.
Elegy on the Pilot, *sel*.
Mathematician's Dream, The.
Song: "No use to aim that sextant now."

Dennis, C. J. (1876–1938)
Traveller, The.

Dennis, Carl
Defining Time.
God Who Loves You, The.
History.
Spring: "All the truth you'll ever be able to
 cull."
St. Francis and the Nun.
To Reason.
Tune-Up.
World History.

Densmore, Frances
Chippewa Music, *sels*.
Songs for Treating Sickness, Sung durring the
 Four Parts of the Night, *sels*.

Dent, Alan (b. 1951)
Restricting Gate, The.

Dent, Tom (b. 1932)
For Cool Papa Bell.

Denwood, Jonathan (1869–1933)
For Whom.

Depero, Fortunato (1892–1960)
Colors.

Depestre, René (b. 1926)
Ballad of a Little Lamp.
Rainbow for the Christian West, A, *sels*.
Romancero d'une petite lampe.
Season of Anger.

Depestre, Rene *See Also* Cesaire, Aime

Der Hovanessian, Diana
Shifting the Sun.

Dèr Mouw, J. Adwaita (1863–1919)
Audible Still.
Does Anyone Know This Feeling.

I Am Brahman.

Derieva, Regina (b. 1949)
Beyond Siberia again Siberia.
I don't feel at home where I am.
On the sea-shore, smell of iodine.
Theory of Recruiting.

Derksen, Jeff (b. 1958)
Interface.

Dermée, Paul (Camille Janssen) (1886–1951)
Coffee grinder.
Poem.
Poem: "I play tennis with the shells."
Poem: "Is it a plane in the sky."
Silver Clasps.
These apples.

Derricotte, Toi (b. 1941)
After a Reading at a Black College.
Allen Ginsberg.
Black Boys Play the Classics.
Blackbottom.
Bookstore.
Boy at the Paterson Falls.
Christmas Eve: My Mother Dressing.
Exits from Elmina Castle: Cape Coast, Ghana.
Family Secrets.
Fears of the Eighth Grade.
For Black Women Who Are Afraid.
For Sister Sue Ellen and Her Special
 Messenger.
Friendship, The.
From a Letter: About Snow.
Furious Boy, The.
High School.
In an Urban School.
Invisible Dreams.
Minks, The.
1994 Inventory.
Note on My Son's Face, A.
On Stopping Late in the Afternoon for
 Steamed Dumplings.
On the Turning Up of Unidentified Black
 Female Corpses.
Passing.
Poem for My Father.
Promise, The.
St. Peter Claver.
Struggle, The.
Weakness, The.
Whitman, Come Again to the Cities.

Derry, Alice
Anne.

des Forëts Louis-René (1918–2000)
Il n'est que temps.
It Is High Time.

Des Rochers, Alfred (1901–78)
City-Hotel.

Desbordes-Valmore, Marceline (1786–1859)
Intermittent Dream of a Sad Night.
Memory, A.
My Room.

Deschamps, Eustache (1346–1410)
Ballade 1.
Ballade 2.
Rondeau: "Fleas, stink, pigs, mold."

Désiré, Jean R. (b. 1959)
Dream: "Last night in sleep."
Philosophy, A.

Desmond, John C.
When We Two Parted.

Desnos, Robert (1900–45)
Ars Poetica.
Comme.
Cuckoo.
Epitaph: "I lived in those times. For a thousand
 years."
Hour Farther.
I Have So Often Dreamed of You.
If, like winds.
If You Knew.
I've Dreamed of You So Much.
I've dreamed such dreams of you.
I've Dreamt of You So Often.
J'ai tant rêvé de toi.
Jamais d'autre que toi.

Language Event Two.
Last Poem.
Letter to Youki.
Like.
Like.
Midway.
Mid-way.
Never Anyone but You.
Night Watchman of Pont-au-Change, The.
No, Love Is Not Dead.
No, Love Is Not Dead.
Non l'amour n'est pas mort.
Notre Paire.
Obsession.
Oh Pangs of Love!
Si Tu Savais.
Sleep Spaces.
St Merri district, The.
There once was a leaf.
Three Stars.
Trance Event.
When children slap their father's face.

Desportes, Philippe (1545–1606)
Conquest [or His Lady's Might].

Desprez, Frank
Lasca.

DeSylva, B. G. (1895–1950)
April Showers.
Best Things in Life Are Free, The.
Birth of the Blues, The.
Button Up Your Overcoat.
California, Here I Come.
Do It Again.
I Want to Be Bad.
If I Had a Talking Picture of you.
If You Knew Susie (Like I Know Susie).
I'll Say She Does.
It All Depends on You.
Look for the Silver Lining.
Magnolia.
Maybe This Is Love.
Never Swat a Fly.
Somebody Loves Me.
Stairway to Paradise.
Sunny Side Up.
Thank Your Father.
Turn On the Heat.
Varsity Drag, The.
You're an Old Smoothie.
You're the Cream in My Coffee.

Detsinyi, Ludwig *See* Martin, David

Dett, Robert Nathaniel (1882–1943)
Conjured.

Deutsch, Babette (1895–1982)
Creatures in the Zoo.
Flight, The: "Earthen shadow lay on men's
   endeavor, An."
Memory.
Poem, The: "Painter of Dante's awful ferry-
   ride, The."
Solitude.
"To an Amiable Child"
To the Moon, 1969.
Urban Pastoral.

Devaney, James (b. 1890)
Vision.

Devaney, Tom (b. 1969)
American Pragmatist Fell in Love, The.
Sonnet: "You know all those sonnets the ones
   where I said, I love you, well."

Devara Dasimayya (fl. 1008–1050)
Tattered Sack, The.

Devi, N. Revathi
Birth, A.
Cold Meat.
Distance.
Going Out of Town.
Invocation.
No Break.
This World, Poor Thing.

Devlin, Denis (1908–59)
Ank'hor Vat.
Ascension.
Little Elegy.
Memoirs of a Turcoman Diplomat, *sels.*

Renewal by Her Element.
Wishes for Her.

**Devonshire, Georgiana Cavendish, Duchess of
(1757–1806)**
Passage of the Mountain of St. Gothard, The.
To Lady Elizabeth Foster, from Georgiana,
   Duchess of Devonshire, When She Was
   Apprehensive of Losing Her Eyesight–1796.

Dewdney, Christopher (b. 1951)
Cenozoic Asylum, The [1982 Version].
Cenozoic Asylum, The [2002 Version].
Concordat Proviso Ascendant, *sel.*
Depth Sounding, Lake Windermere.
Grid Erectile.
Immaculate Perception, The.
Memory Table 1, The.
Radiant Inventory.
Spring Trances in the Control Emerald Night,
   sel.

Dey, Atanu
Buddha and I, The.

D'Haen, Christine (b. 1923)
Epiphany.
Mole, The.

Dharker, Imtiaz (b. 1954)
Another Woman.
Blessing.
Grace.
Honour Killing.
Living Space.
Minority.
Name of God, The.
Namesake.
Postcards from God (1).
Purdah, 1.
They'll Say, "She Must Be from Another
   Country."
This Room.

Dhompa, Tsering Wangno (b. 1969)
Autonomy of the Mind.
Bardo.
Body as What Is Remembered.
How Thubten Sang His Songs.
Sun Storm.

"Dhoomil" (Sudama Pandeya) (1935–75)
City, Evening, and an Old Man: Me, The.

Di Biasio, Rodolfo (b. 1937)
Cuncta Semper.
Nostoi.
Poem of the Dawn and the Night.
Snow Poem.

Di Cicco, Pier Giorgio (b. 1949)
Male Rage Poem.

Di Michele, A.
About the Extinction Of.
Archipelago (Interra Diocesan).
Solstice / Surgery.
Unica Zurn's Loam Bowl.

Di Piero, W. S. (b. 1945)
Near Damascus.
Walt, the Wounded.
Why not violate sense and say.

Di Prima, Diane (b. 1934)
Abyss.
After months of sitting.
American Indian Art: Form and Tradition.
April Fool Birthday Poem for Grandpa.
Backyard.
Black and white cat.
Brief Wyoming Meditation.
Death Poems in September.
Death Sunyata Chant: A Rite for Passing Over.
Dokusan: Visit to Katagiri Roshi.
For H.D.
For Suzuki Roshi.
For the Dead Lecturer.
Fragmented Address to the FBI.
Hebron.
I Ching.
I Fail as a Dharma Teacher.
In This Landscape.
Les Americains.
Letter to Jeanne (at Tassajara).
Loba, *sels.*

Loba Addresses the Goddess, The / or The
   Poet as Priestess Addresses the Loba-
   Goddess.
Loba as Eve.
Montezuma.
Notes on the Art of Memory.
Notes Toward a Poem of Revolution.
On Sitting Down to Write, I Decide Instead to
   Go to Fred Herko's Concert.
Pine shadow falls on the tent wall, The.
Poem in Praise of My Husband (Taos).
Poem on the Limits for My Writing Group:
   Atlantic Center for the Arts, New Smyrna
   Beach, Florida.
Practice of Magical Evocation, The.
Prophetissa.
Rant, *sel.*
Revolutionary Letter #1.
Short Note on the Sparseness of the Language.
Studies in Light.
Summer Retreat: Pema Osel Ling.
Tassajara, 1969.
Tassajara, Early 1970's.
Three "Dharma Poems."
To Philip Whalen, 1999.
To the Unnamed Buddhist Nun Who Burned
   Herself to Death on the Night of June 3,
   1966.
Travel Poem.

Diaper, William (1686?–1717)
Brent; a Poem to Thomas Palmer Esq, *sels.*
Halieutica, *sels.*

Dias, Robert Vas (b. 1931)
At the Controls.

Diaz-Duque, O. F.
Why Don't I?

Dib, Mohammed
A un voyageur.
Formulaires, *sel.*
To a Voyager.

Dibdin, Charles (1745–1814)
Jolly Young Waterman, The.

Dibdin, Thomas (1771–1841)
Origins of Naval Artillery.

Dickens, Charles (1812–90)
Fine Old English Gentleman, The; New
   Version.
Great Expectations, *sels.*

Dickey, James (b. 1923)
Adultery.
Apollo, *sels.*
At Darien Bridge.
Basics.
Bee, The.
Buckdancer's Choice.
Cherrylog Road.
Dusk of Horses, The.
Eagles.
Falling.
Firebombing, The.
For the Death of Vince Lombardi.
Heaven of Animals, The.
Hospital Window, The.
Hunting Civil War Relics at Nimblewill Creek.
In the Marble Quarry.
Inside the River.
Leap, The.
Lifeguard, The.
Magus, The.
One, The.
Performance, The.
Poisoned Man, The.
Sheep Child, The.
Sled Burial, Dream Ceremony.
Snow on a Southern State.
Strength of Fields, The.
Walking on Water.
Weeds.

Dickey, Ralph (1945–72)
Father.
Leaving Eden.
Mulatto Lullaby.

Dickey, William (b. 1928)
Armageddon.
Arrival of the Titanic, The.

Cassandra.
Death of John Berryman,The.
For Easter Island or Another Island.
Memoranda.
Plot, The.
Poet's Farewell to His Teeth, The.
Shortest Day, The.

Dickinson, Adam
Contributors to Geometry: Cold Hands.
Cryo.

Dickinson, Emily (1830–86)
Abraham to kill him.
Admirations—and Contempts—of time, The.
After a hundred years.
After great pain a formal feeling comes.
All Circumstances are the Frame.
Alter! When the Hills do—.
Altered look about the hills, An.
Although I put away his life.
Ample make this Bed.
Apparently with no surprise.
Art thou the thing I wanted?
As if some little Arctic flower.
As imperceptibly as Grief.
At Half past Three, a single Bird.
At least—to pray—is left—is left.
Aurora.
Baffled for just a day or two.
Bat, The.
Bee is not afraid of me, The.
Bee, The.
Bees.
Before I got my eye put out.
Before you thought of Spring.
Behind Me—dips Eternity.
Belshazzar had a Letter.
Bereavement in their death to feel.
Better—than Music! For I—who heard it.
Between the form of Life and Life.
Bible is an antique Volume, The.
Bird came down the Walk, A.
Bone that has no Marrow, The.
Brain, within its Groove, The.
Bring me the sunset in a cup.
Bustle in a House, The.
Butterfly upon the Sky, The.
By a departing light.
By the Sea.
Called Back.
Cat.
Caterpillar ("How soft a Caterpillar steps—.").
Cemetery, A.
Choice.
Civilization—spurns—the Leopard!
Clock stopped, A.
Clock strikes one that just struck two, The.
Clover's simple Flame, The.
Color, Caste, Denomination.
Come show thy Durham Breast.
Come slowly—Eden!
Consulting summer's clock.
Could I but ride indefinite.
Crumbling is not an instant's Act.
Daisy follows soft the Sun, The.
Dare you see a Soul *at the White Heat?*
Day that I was crowned, The.
Dear March, Come in.
Death is a Dialogue between.
Death is the supple Suitor.
Did the Harebell loose her girdle.
Difference between Despair, The.
Do People moulder equally.
Dropped into the Ether Acre.
Drowning is not so pitiful.
Dust is the only Secret.
Each Life Converges to some Centre.
Earth has many keys, The.
Eden is that Old-Fashioned House.
Elijah's Wagon knew no thill.
Ended, ere it begun.
Escape is such a thankful Word.
Essential oils—are wrung.
Everywhere of Silver, An.
Except the Heaven had come so near.
Experiment escorts us last.
Exultation is the going.

Faith is a fine invention.
Faith—is the Pierless Bridge.
Fame is a bee.
Fame is a fickle food.
Far from Love the Heavenly Father.
Farthest Thunder that I heard, The.
Final Inch, The.
Finding is the first Act.
Finite—to fail, but infinite to Venture.
First Day's Night had come, The.
Flags Vex a Dying Face.
For each ecstatic instant.
For largest Woman's Heart I knew.
Four Trees—upon a solitary Acre.
Further in Summer than the Birds.
Glee—The great storm is over.
Go not too near a House of Rose.
Go slow, my soul, to feed thyself.
Go tell it—What a Message.
God is a distant—stately Lover.
God's Residence.
Good Morning—Midnight.
Grass, The.
Great Streets of silence led away.
He ate and drank the precious Words.
He fought like those Who've nought to lose.
He fumbles at your Soul.
He preached upon "Breadth" till it argued him
   narrow.
He Put the Belt Around My Life.
He touched me, so I live to know.
Heart asks Pleasure—first, The.
Heart! We [*or* Heart, we] will forget him!
Heaven has different Signs—to me.
"Heaven"—is what I cannot reach!
"Heavenly Father"—take to thee.
Her breast is fit for pearls.
Her face was in a bed of hair.
Her—"last Poems"
Her Losses make our Gains ashamed.
Her Sweet turn to leave the Homestead.
Her sweet Weight on my Heart at Night.
His Feet are shod with Gauze.
Hope is the thing with feathers.
How brittle are the Piers.
How happy is the little Stone.
How many times these low feet staggered.
Hummingbird, A.
I am afraid to own a Body.
I am alive—I guess.
I asked no other thing.
I Can Wade Grief.
I cannot be ashamed.
I cannot dance upon my Toes.
I cannot live with You.
I died for Beauty—but was scarce.
I dreaded that first Robin, so.
I dwell in Possibility.
I felt a Cleaving in my Mind.
I Felt a Funeral in My Brain.
I found the words to every thought.
I gave myself to Him—.
I got so I could take his name.
I had been hungry, all the Years.
I had no time to Hate.
I have no Life but this.
I heard a Fly buzz—when I died.
I know some lonely Houses off the Road.
I know that He exists.
I like a look of Agony.
I many times thought Peace had come.
I measure every Grief I meet.
I met a King this afternoon!
I never hear the word "escape"
I never lost as much but twice.
I never saw a Moor.
I reason, Earth is short.
I reckon—when I count at all.
I saw no Way. The Heavens were stitched.
I shall keep singing!
I shall know why—when Time is over.
I should have been too glad, I see.
I showed her Heights she never saw.
I stepped from Plank to Plank.
I suppose the time will come.
I Taste a Liquor Never Brewed.

I think I was enchanted.
I think the Hemlock likes to stand.
I think to Live—may be a Bliss.
I took my Power in my Hand.
I took one Draught of Life.
I was the slightest in the House.
I watched the Moon around the House.
I would not paint—a picture.
I Years had been from Home.
If any sink, assure that this, now standing.
If I can stop one Heart from breaking.
If I may have it, when it's dead.
If What we could—were what we would.
If you were coming in the Fall.
I'll tell you how the Sun rose.
I'm ceded—I've stopped being Theirs.
I'm Nobody! Who are you?
I'm sorry for the Dead—Today.
In this short Life.
In Winter in my Room.
Indian Summer.
Infinite a sudden Guest, The.
It always felt to me—a wrong.
It ceased to hurt me, though so slow.
It Dropped So Low in My Regard.
It feels a shame to be Alive.
It might be lonelier.
It was a quiet way—.
It was not Death, for I stood up.
It was too late for Man.
It would have starved a Gnat.
It would never be Common—more—I said.
It's easy to invent a Life.
It's like the Light.
I've known a Heaven, like a Tent.
I've seen a Dying Eye.
Just as He spoke it from his Hands.
Last Night that She Lived, The.
Let me not thirst with this Hock at my Lip.
Let my first Knowing be of thee.
Letter to Bee.
Life's Trades.
Light exists in Spring, A.
Lightly stepped a yellow star.
Lightning is a yellow Fork, The.
Like Rain it sounded till it curved.
Little Dog that wags his tail, A.
Little East of Jordan, A.
Little Madness in the Spring, A.
Little Road—not made of Man, A.
Loneliness One dare not sound, The.
Look of thee, what is it like, The.
Loss of something ever felt I, A.
Man may make a Remark, A.
Martyr Poets—did not tell, The.
Me from Myself—to banish.
Me—come! My dazzled face.
Mine Enemy is growing old.
Mine—by the Right of the White Election!
Missing All—prevented Me, The.
Moon is distant from the Sea, The.
Moon upon her fluent Route, The.
More than the Grave is closed to me.
Morning after Woe, The.
Morns are meeker than they were, The.
Mountains grow—unnoticed, The.
Much Madness is divinest Sense.
Murmur of a Bee, The.
Murmuring of Bees, has ceased, The.
Musicians wrestle everywhere.
My Cocoon tightens—Colors tease.
My life closed twice before its close.
My nosegays are for Captives.
My period had come for Prayer.
My Portion is Defeat—today.
My Triumph lasted till the Drums.
Name—of it—is "Autumn," The.
Nature—sometimes sears a Sapling.
Nearest Dream recedes—unrealized, The.
Nearness to Tremendousness, A.
No Bobolink—reverse His Singing.
No Brigadier throughout the Year.
No Passenger was known to flee.
No Rack can torture me.
None can experience stint.
Not any higher stands the Grave.

Not probable—The barest Chance.
Of Course—I prayed.
Of Paul and Silas it is said.
Oh give it Motion—deck it sweet.
Oh Sumptuous moment.
On a Columnar Self.
On such a night, or such a night.
One Blessing had I than the rest.
One crown that no one seeks.
One Crucifixion is recorded—only.
One need not be a Chamber—to be Haunted.
One of the ones that Midas touched.
One who could repeat the Summer day, The.
Only News I know, The.
Opinion is a flitting thing.
Our journey had advanced.
Our lives are Swiss.
Ourselves we do inter with sweet derision.
Outer—from the Inner, The.
Over and over, like a Tune.
Over the fence.
Pain Has an Element of Blank.
Pain—expands the Time.
Partake as doth the Bee.
Pass to thy Rendezvous of Light.
Pedigree of Honey, The.
Perception of an object costs.
Perhaps I asked too large.
Pit—but Heaven over it, A.
Poets light but Lamps, The.
Popular Heart is a Cannon first, The.
Prayer is the little implement.
Precious—moldering pleasure—'tis, A.
Presentiment—is that long Shadow—on the
    lawn.
Prison gets to be a friend, A.
Promise This, When You be Dying.
Props assist the House, The.
Province of the Saved, The.
Publication—is the Auction.
Purple Clover.
Rearrange a "Wife's" affection!
"Remember me" implored the Thief!
Remorse—is Memory—awake.
Renunciation.
Renunciation—is a piercing Virtue.
Return, The.
Riddle we can guess, The.
Saddest noise, the sweetest noise, The.
Satisfaction—is the Agent.
Savior must have been, The.
Severer Service of Myself.
Shade upon the mind there passes, A.
She dealt her pretty words like Blades.
She Rose to His Requirement—Dropt.
Single Screw of Flesh, A.
Sky is low—the Clouds are mean, The.
Snake, The.
Snow flakes / I counted till they danced so.
Snow, The.
So much Summer.
So well that I can live without.
Soft Sea washed around the House, A.
Solemn thing—it was—I said, A.
Some keep the Sabbath going to Church.
Some one prepared this mighty show.
Some things that fly there be.
Somehow myself survived the Night.
Soul has Bandaged moments, The.
Soul selects her own Society, The.
Soul that hath a Guest, The.
Soul's distinct connection, The.
Soul's Superior instants, The.
Sown in dishonor!
Spider sewed at Night, A.
Spirit lasts, but in what mode, The.
Split the Lark—and you'll find the Music.
Still—Volcano—Life, A.
Storm.
Strong Draughts of Their Refreshing Minds.
Struck, was I, not yet by Lightning.
Success is counted sweetest.
Sun and Fog Contested, The.
Sun kept setting—setting—still, The.
Sunrise runs for Both, The.
Surgeons must be very careful.

Suspense.
Sweet Mountains—Ye tell Me no lie.
That after horror that was us.
That I did always love.
That it will never come again.
That Love is all there is.
Their Height in Heaven comforts not.
There came a Wind like a Bugle.
There comes an hour when begging stops.
There is a morn by men unseen.
There is a pain—so utter.
There is a Zone whose even Years.
There is another Loneliness.
There is No Frigate Like a Book.
There's a certain Slant of light.
There's been a Death, in the Opposite House.
These are the Nights that Beetles love.
These Strangers, In a Foreign World.
These—saw Visions.
They have a little Odor—that to me.
They might not need me—yet they might.
They put Us far apart.
They Say That Time Assuages.
They shut me up in Prose.
This Consciousness that is aware.
This dirty—little—Heart.
This docile one inter.
This Is My Letter to the World.
This was a Poet—It is That.
This World Is Not Conclusion.
Those—dying then.
Thought beneath so slight a film, The.
Thought went up my mind today, A.
Throe upon the features, A.
Through the Dark Sod—as Education.
Thunder-Storm, A.
Tie the Strings to my Life, My Lord.
Tint I cannot take—is best, The.
'Tis customary as we part.
'Tis little I— could care for Pearls.
'Tis not that Dying hurts us so.
'Tis Opposites—entice.
Title divine—is mine!
To fight aloud, is very brave.
To know just how He suffered—would be
    dear.
To lose one's faith—surpass.
To make a prairie it takes a clover and one bee.
To make One's Toilette—after Death.
To pile like Thunder to its close.
Too happy Time dissolves itself.
Tree in Winter.
Trees like Tassels—hit—and swung, The.
Triumph—may be of several kinds.
Truth—is as old as God.
'Twas Crisis—All the length had passed.
'Twas here my summer paused.
'Twas warm—at first—like Us.
Two swimmers wrestled on the spar.
Under the Light, yet under.
Union.
Victory comes late.
Visitor in Marl, A.
Volcanoes in Sicily.
Water, is taught by thirst.
We do not play on Graves.
We don't [or dont] cry—Tim and I.
We grow accustomed to the Dark.
We learned the Whole of Love.
We lose—because we win.
We miss Her, not because We see.
We outgrow love like other things.
We Play at Paste.
Went up a year this evening!
What care the Dead, for Chanticleer.
What mystery pervades a well!
What Soft—Cherubic Creatures.
When Bells stop ringing—Church—begins.
When Night is almost done.
"Why do I love" You, Sir?
Why make it doubt—it hurts it so.
Wife—at Daybreak I shall be, A.
Wild Nights—Wild Nights!
Wind begun to knead the Grass, The.
Wind, The.
Wind's Visit, The.

Wind—tapped like a tired man, The.
Wonder—is not precisely Knowing.
Word is dead, A.
Word made Flesh is seldom, A.
Wounded Deer Leaps Highest, A.
Yellow Man, Purple Man.
You're right—"the way is narrow."

Dickinson, John
    Liberty Song, The.
Dickinson, Patric (b. 1914)
    Advent; a Carol.
    St. Stephen's Day.
Dickinson, Peter (b. 1927)
    Moses and the Princess.
Dickson, John
    Aragon Ballroom, The.
    Fossil Fuel.
    Poemectomy.
Dickson, Samuel Henry (1798–1872)
    Song—Written at the North.
Didsbury, Peter (b. 1946)
    Bee, A.
    Chandlery.
    Drainage, The.
    Hailstone, The.
    In Britain.
    Malediction, A.
    Part of the Bridge.
    Priest in the Sabbath Dawn Addresses His
        Somnolent Mistress, A.
    Shorter Life, The.
    That Old-Time Religion.
Diego, Gerardo (1896–1987)
    Al Zarpar.
    Biografía Incompleta.
    Condicional.
    Hostilidad.
    Hostility.
    I Stripped Your Soul Down.
    Julio Campal.
    Julio Campal ("We were walking to your
        funeral, eleven friends.").
    Movimiento Perpetuo.
    On These Conditions.
    Perpetual Motion.
    Setting Sail.
    Siempre Abiertos Tus Ojos.
    Sleeplessness.
    Una a Una Desmonté las Piezas de Tu Alma.
    Unfinished Life Story.
    Your Eyes Are Always Open.
Dienstfrey, Patricia (b. 1939)
    Arrival.
    Let the Raspberry Jam in the Crystal Jar Stand
        for It.
Dierking, Kirsten (b. 1962)
    Delacroix's Version.
Dietz, Howard (1896–1983)
    Alone Together.
    Blue Grass.
    Dancing in the Dark.
    Haunted Heart.
    I Guess I'll Have to Change My Plan.
    I See Your Face Before Me.
    If There Is Someone Lovelier Than You.
    Rhode Island Is Famous for You.
    Something to Remember You By.
    That's Entertainment.
    Triplets.
    You and the Night and the Music.
Digby, John (1580–1655)
    Grieve Not, Dear Love.
Digges, Deborah
    Akhmatova.
    Broom.
    Five Smooth Stones.
    Rough Music.
    Seersucker Suit.
Diggs, Latasha Natasha
    Fullness.
Dillard, Annie
    Dash It.
    Deathbeds, sel.
    Feast Days, sels.

God: "Numbers from one to ten, however, are
   called."
Man Who Wishes to Feed on Mahogany, The.
Observations and Experiments.
Sign of Your Father, The.
Teaching a Stone to Talk, *sel.*
Tickets for a Prayer Wheel, *sel.*

Dillard, Richard H. W. (b. 1937)
Ghosts in the Stacks.

Diller, John Irving
Lullaby Town.

Dillon, George (b. 1906)
Hours of the Day, The.
Marching Song.
Snow.

Dimitrova, Blaga (b. 1922)
Ars Poetica.
Ars Poetica: "Write each of your poems."
Blind woman was more intimate with it, The.
Forbidden Sea, *sels.*
Grass.
Hotel Room.
Interior with Faded Colors.
Sunstroke.
Units of Measurement.
Who Cares for the Blind Stork.

Dine, Carol (b. 1943)
Fugue, *sels.*

Dings, Fred
Redwing Blackbirds.

Dinh, Linh (b. 1963)
13.

Dīnrām
Being the child of a Mad Mother.
From the time of the womb.
I've given up wanting.
Ma, I've drunk Your poisoned nectar.
O Baba! Look at this Cadak tree.
Out of love for You.
Renunciation's agonies.

Diodes
Somebody said when snubbed, "Is Damon so."

Diop, Birago (b. 1906)
Vanity.

Diop, David (1927–60)
Vultures, The.

Diophanes of Myrina
On Love.

Dioscorides (*fl.* 1st cent. B.C.)
Epigrams, *sels.*

Diotimus (*fl.* c.250 B.C.)
Epigrams, *sels.*

DiPalma, Ray (b. 1943)
Annotations Tropes and Lacunae of the Itoku
   Master.
Bed, The.
Each Moment is Surrounded.
Empire Smoke, Forgeries, Salient and the Ritz.
Fragment.
Hadrian's Lane.
Memory's Wedge.
Motion of the Cypher.
Pink Maniac, A.
Poem for Claude.
Poem: "In danger of which."
Prerogative of Lieder, The.
Rebus Tact.
Rumor's Rooster.
Sheaf Mark.
Table, The.
We Forego Mimicry.
When Torrid Rhymes with Forehead.
Wrong Side of the Door, The.

DiPrima, Chani
Her Eyes a Thousand Times Over.

Dıranas, Ahmet Muhip (1908–80)
Oblivion: "Twilight hours are always gruff and
   gory."

Disch, Thomas M. [*or* "Tom"] (b.1940)
Abecedary.
Agreement of Predicate Pronouns, The.
Ballade of the New God.
Bookmark, A.
Clouds, The.

Concise History of Music, A.
Convalescing in London.
Crumbling Infrastructure, The.
Entropic Villanelle.
Garage Sale as a Spiritual Exercise, The.
Hooray for Hollywood.
La, La, La!
Poems: "I think that I shall never read."
Rapist's Villanelle, The.
Vowels of Another Language, The.
Zewhyexary.

Dischell, Stuart (*fl.* 20th cent.)
Tenant at Will, A.
Yellow Slicker, The.

Dissanayake, Wimal (b. 1939)
Freedom.

Ditlevsen, Tove (1918–76)
Eternal Three, The.

Dittberner-Jax, Norita
Blues for Aunt Ruth.

Ditzanny, Ramy
Brand Plucked from the Anti-tank Fire, A.
Complicated and Innovative Orthopedic
   Surgery.
Legging Behind.
My Hand is Extended for the Peace of the
   Galilee.
Piggy-back.

Divakaruni, Chitra (b. 1956)
Alley of Flowers, The.
Brides Come to Yuba City, The.
Childhood.
Founding of Yuba City, The.
Indian Movie, New Jersey.
Indigo.
Leaving Yuba City.
Outside Pisa.
Quilt, The.
Restroom.
Yuba City School.

Dixon, Bob
Remembering the Invasion of Grenada by the
   USA.

Dixon, Melvin
Getting Your Rocks Off.
Grandmother: Crossing Jordan.
Heartbeats.
Place, Places.
Tour Guide: La Maison des Esclaves.

Dixon, Mort (1892–1956)
Bye Bye Blackbird.
Great Big Bunch of You, A.
I Found a Million Dollar Baby (In a Five and
   Ten Cent Store).
Lady in Red, The.
Nagasaki.
River, Stay 'Way from My Door.
Would You Like to Take a Walk?

Dixon, Richard Watson (1833–1900)
Dream.
To Peace.

Dixon, Sarah (*fl.* 1716–45)
Request of Alexis, The.

Dixon, Zuhur (b. 1933)
Season of Beginning and End.

Dizhur, Bella Abramovna (b. 1903)
Eve's Monologue.
Here is an island. Here is a house on stilts.
Silence.

DJ Renegade
Adventures of Grandmaster Flash, The.
Call and Response.
Father and Son.
Fireflies in a Jar.
Subterranean Night-Colored Magus.
Thursday Poem.

Djabali, Leila (b. 1933)
For My Torturer, Lieutenant D.

Djanikian, Gregory (b. 1949)
How I Learned English.
Immigrant Picnic.
In the Elementary School Choir.
When I First Saw Snow.

Djogo, Gojko (b. 1940)
Black Sheep, The.
National Hero, The.
Wooden Handle, The.

Djoko Damono, Sapardi (b. 1940)
Mask.

Djurberaui
All You Others, Eat.

Dlugos, Tim (d. 1991)
Gilligan's Island.

Đỗ Tấn Xuân
Twenty Years.

Doan Van Kham (*fl.* 1090)
Remembering Priest Quang Tri.

Dobell, Sydney Thompson (1824–74)
Balder, *sels.*
Liberty to M. le Diplomate.
Nuptial Eve, A, *sels.*
Roman, The, *sels.*

Dobie, James Frank (1888–1964)
Vanitas.

Dobie, Kirkpatrick (1909–99)
Aberfan.
King Claudius.

**Dobson, Austin (Henry Austin Dobson) (1840–
1921)**
Ballad of 'Beau Brocade', The.
Fame and Friendship.
Garden Song, A.
In After Days.
In Town.
Rose-Leaves, *sels.*
Sundial, The.

Dobson, Henry Austin See Dobson, Austin

Dobson, Rosemary (b. 1920)
Being Called For.
Country Press.
Daily Living, *sels.*
Edge, The.
Eutychus.
Three Fates, The.

Dobyns, Stephen (b. 1941)
Allegorical Matters.
Bowlers Anonymous.
Cemetery Nights.
Confession.
Counterparts.
Dancing in Vacationland.
Exile.
Fragments: "Now there is a slit in the blue
   fabric of air."
Freight Cars.
Frenchie.
Great Doubters of History, The, *sel.*
His life was the practice of forming a single.
How To Like It.
Long Story.
Loud Music.
Music One Looks Back On, The.
No Map.
No Moment Past This One.
Nouns of Assemblage.
Pony Express.
Seeing Off a Friend.
Spiritual Chickens.
Tenderly.
Tomatoes.
Utopian Melodies.
When a Friend.
Where We Are.
Why Fool Around?

Docwra, Anne (1624–1710)
Mystery of Profession great, The.

Dodd, Elizabeth (b. 1962)
Dieback.
Like Memory, Caverns.
Lyric: "It doesn't matter / whether / a tree
   falls."
Touched.

Dodd, Wayne (b. 1930)
Of His Life.
Of Rain and Air.

Doddridge, Philip (1702–51)
Hark! the glad sound! the Savior comes.

Hymn: "Ye golden lamps of heaven, farewell."
Live While You Live.
Meditations on the Sepulchre in the Garden.

Dodge, Charles Richards (1847–1918)
Wheel Ethics.

Dodge, Mary Abigail (Gail Hamilton) (1833–96)
Note.

Dodge, Mary Mapes (1831–1905)
Early to Bed.
Fire in the window.
Mayor of Scuttleton, The.
Moon Came Late, The.
Poor Crow!
Shepherd John.
Someone in the Garden.
Taking Time to Grow.
Tinker, Come Bring Your Solder.
Way To Do It, The.
Wooden Horse, The.

Dodgson, Charles Lutwidge *See* Carroll, Lewis

Dodson, Owen (1914–83)
Black Mother Praying.
Open Letter.
Sorrow Is the Only Faithful One.

d'Oettingen, Hélène (d. 1950)
Kilimanjaro.
Outcries.
To Il y a.

Dogen (1200–53)
Coming, going, the waterfowl.
Western Patriarch's doctrine is transplanted!,
    The.

Doherty, Tyler (b. 1973)
Bodhidharma Never Came to Hatboro.
Raven's Revenge.

Doina, Ana
Roof over far away.

Dolben, Digby Mackworth (1848–67)
One night I dreamt that in a gleaming hall, *sel.*

Dolia, Marina (b. 1951)
Silence, *sels.*

Dolin, Sharon
My Soul's Wardrobe.

Domanski, Don (b. 1950)
Banns.
Child of the Earth.
Drowning Water.

Domin, Hilde (b. 1912)
Exile.
Remigration.

Domina, Lynn
Pharoah's Army Got Drowned.

Donaghy, Michael (b. 1954)
Bacchae, The.
Caliban's Books.
Inheritance.
Machines.
My Flu.
Present, The.
Repertoire, A.
Shibboleth.

Donaldson, Walter
Because My Baby Don't Mean Maybe Now.
Little White Lies.
You're Driving Me Crazy (What Did I Do?).

Donegan, Patricia (b. 1945)
Check Up.
Half-Open.
Something Happened.
Tonight / while shampooing my hair.

Donhauser, Michael (b. 1956)
Quince, The.

Donne, John (1572–1631)
Air[e] and Angels.
Anatomy [*or* Anatomie] of the World, An: The
    First Anniversary, *sels.*
Anniversary [*or* Anniversarie], The.
Antiquary.
Apparition, The.
Bait[e], The.
Blossom[e], The.
Bracelet, The.
Break of Day.

Broken Heart, The.
Burnt Ship, A.
Calm[e], The.
Canonization, The.
Computation, The.
Confined Love.
Damp[e], The.
Dream[e], The.
Ecstasy, The.
Elegies, *sels.*
Epithalamion, or Marriage Song on the Lady
    Elizabeth and Count Palatine Being Married
    on St. Valentine's Day, An.
Farewell to Love.
Flea, The.
Funeral[l], The.
God grant thee thine own wish, and grant thee
    mine.
Good Friday [*or* Goodfriday], 1613. Riding
    Westward.
Good-Morrow, The.
Hero and Leander.
Holy Sonnets, *sels.*
Hymn[e] to God My God, In My Sickness[e],
    A.
Hymn to the Saints, and to Marquis Hamilton,
    An.
Hymn[e] to Christ, at the Author's Last Going
    into Germany, A.
Hymn[e] to God the Father, A.
Indifferent, The.
Lame Beggar, A.
Lamentations of Jeremy, for the Most Part
    According to Tremeullius.
Lecture upon the Shadow, A.
Lovers' Infiniteness[e].
Love's Alchemy [*or* Alchemie].
Love's Deity [*or* Deitie].
Love's Growth.
Nocturnal[l] upon Saint Lucy's [*or* S. Lucy's
    or S. Lucies] Day, Being the Shortest Day,
    A.
Ode: "Vengeance will sit above our faults; but
    till."
Of the Progress of the Soul: The Second
    Anniversary, *sels.*
Paradox, The.
Prohibition, The.
Relic, The.
Resurrection, Imperfect.
Satire 4, *sel.*
Satires, *sels.*
Song: "Go and catch a falling star."
Song: "Sweetest love, I do not go[e]."
Storm[e], The.
Sun Rising, The.
To Mr. George Herbert.
To Sir Henry Wotton ("Here's no more news,
    than virtue, I may as well.").
To Sir Henry Wotton ("Sir, more than kisses,
    letters mingle souls.").
To the Countess of Bedford ("Madam, /
    Reason is our soul's left hand, Faith her
    right.").
Triple Fool, The.
Twickenham [*or* Twicknam] Garden.
Undertaking, The.
Valediction, A: Forbidding Mourning.
Valediction, A: Forbidding Mourning, *sel.*
Valediction, A: of Weeping.
Will, The.
Woman's Constancy.

Donnell, David (b. 1939)
Lakes.
Potatoes.
Sandwiches.

Donnelly, Susan (b. 1939)
Eve Names the Animals.

Donnelly, Timothy (b. 1969)
Birdsong from Inside the Egg.
Isn't It Romantic?
New Intelligence, The.
Purgatory Chasm.
Three Panels Depending on the Heart.
Twenty-seven Props for a Production of *Eine
    Lebenszeit.*

Donovan, Katie (b. 1962)
Coral.
Entering the Mare.
Grooming.
Moon.
Old Women's Summer.
Potter's House, The.
Prayer of the Wanderer.
Stitching.
These Last Days.
Underneath Our Skirts.
Watermelon Man.
Wild Night, A.
Yearn On.
You Meet Yourself.

Donze, Richard
Vermont Has a High Suicide Rate.

Dooley, David (b. 1947)
How I Wrote It.

Dooley, Maura (b. 1957)
At Les Deux Magots.
Dancing at Oakmead Road.
Does It Go Like this?
Explaining Magnetism.
Freight.
Fundoscopy.
Heart.
Heat.
History.
Letters from Yorkshire.
Mansize.
Mind the Gap.
No, Go On.
Up on the Roof.
What Every Woman Should Carry.

Dooley, Twain
Kitchen: "Everywhere I go it's the same old
    thing."

Doolittle, Hilda (Doolittle, H.) (1886–1961)
Antistrophe.
Archer.
At Baia.
At Ithaca.
Birds in Snow.
Egypt.
Epigram: "Golden one is gone from the
    banquets, The."
Epitaph: "So I may say."
Epode.
Eurydice, *sel.*
Evadne.
Evening.
Flowering of the Rod, The, *sels.*
Fragment 36 [*or* Thirty-Six]: "I know not what
    to do."
Fragment 40: "Keep love and he wings."
Fragment 113: "Not honey, / not the plunder of
    the bee."
Fragment 68: "I envy you your chance of
    death."
Garden.
Garden, The, *sels.*
Halcyon, *sel.*
Helen.
Helen in Egypt, *sels.*
Helmsman, The.
Hermes of the Ways.
Hermetic Definition, *sels.*
Hippolytus Temporizes.
Holy Satyr.
In Time of Gold.
Islands, The.
Lais.
Leda.
Let Zeus Record, *sels.*
Lethe.
Mid-day.
Moonrise.
Mysteries, The.
Orchard.
Oread.
Pear Tree.
Pool, The.
Priest, *sel.*
R.A.F.

Red Rose and a Beggar.
Sagesse, *sel.*
Sea Iris.
Sea Poppies.
Sea Rose.
Sea Violet.
Sheltered Garden.
Shrine, The.
Sigil, *sels.*
Song: "You are as gold."
Songs from Cyprus, *sels.*
Storm.
Strophe.
Trance.
Tribute to the Angels, *sels.*
Walls Do Not Fall, The, *sels.*
White World.
Wine Bowl.

Doplicher, Fabio (b. 1938)
Asymmetry of the Universe.
Discords.
Interludes.
Unfinished Exile.

Dorantes, Dolores (b. 1973)
Approach the enigma.
Arena en blanco.
Asómate al enigma.
Black sand.
Dark shards, The.
En coma.
En la profunda cueva.
Es un batimiento.
Fencewalled / circundressed.
Fosfórico / el sitio que hiela.
Iguana láctea.
In a comma.
In the deep cave.
Irradia / la coraza de ceniza.
Irradiates / the ash carapace.
It's a beating.
Lacteal iguana.
Lou cierra el párpado.
Lou's eyelid closing.
Meter todas las manos en el agua.
Murocercados / circodesnudos.
Oscuros cristales, Los.
Palpitar / que nos fuiste.
Palpitate / that you left us.
Perfil / Filoso perfil.
Phosphoric / the site that freezes.
Profile / knife-filed profile.
Redonda suerte.
Round fortune.
Tilde impar, La.
To put all hands into the water.
Uneven tilde, The.

Dorcey, Mary (b. 1950)
Night.

Dorchester, Katherine Colyear, Countess of (1657–1717)
As Frazier one night at her Post in the Drawing Room stood.

Dorfman, Ariel (b. 1942)
I Just Missed the Bus and I'll Be Late for Work.
Last Waltz in Santiago.
Vocabulary.

Dorgan, Theo (b. 1953)
Choice, The: "I watched Odysseus go on board the flagship."
Death Will Come.
Up All Night.

D'Orleans, Charles
Oft in My Thought.

Dormer, Anne, Lady Hungerford (d. 1603)
Lady Hungerford's Meditacions upon the Beades, The.

Dorn, Edward (b. 1929)
From Gloucester Out.
Geranium.
Gunslinger, *sels.*
Morning to Remember, A; or, E Pluribus Unum.
On the Debt My Mother Owed to Sears Roebuck.

Rick of Green Wood, The.

Dorris, Michael (1945–97)
Prey.

Dorsett, Thomas
Survivor, The.

Dorsey, Thomas A. (1899–1993)
Take My Hand, Precious Lord.

Dos Passos, John (1896–1970)
Crimson Tent.

Dotremont, Christian (1922–79)
Some Lapland Views.

Doty, Mark (b. 1953)
Almost Blue.
Atlantis, *sels.*
Aubade: Opal and Silver.
Brilliance.
Coastal.
Crêpe de Chine.
Days of 1981.
Death of Antinoüs.
Display of Mackerel, A.
Elizabeth Bishop, *Croton.*
Embrace, The.
Fish R Us.
Flit.
Fog.
Fog Argument, *sels.*
Green Crab's Shell, A.
Homo Will Not Inherit.
Letter from the Coast, A.
Letter to Walt Whitman.
Lilacs in NYC.
Migratory.
My Tattoo.
No.
Parable of a Marriage (Chi Gong).
Retrievers in Translation.
Tiara.
Ware Collection of Glass Flowers and Fruit, Harvard Museum, The.

Doubiago, Sharon (b. 1941)
Ground Zero.
How to Make Love to a Man.
South America Mi Hija, *sel.*

Doubleday, Thomas (1790–1870)
Friends, when my latest bed of rest is made.
No walk today;—November's breathings toss.
Poppies, that scattered o'er this arid plain.

Dougherty, Edward A.
Why I Think About Hiroshima and Nagasaki.

Dougherty, Sean Thomas (b. 1965)
Cocoons.
Double Helix.
Long Coats with Deep Pockets.
Pantoum of the Working Classes.
Puerto Rican Girls of French Hill, The.

Douglas, Keith (1920–44)
Aristocrats.
Cairo Jag.
Desert Flowers.
Egypt.
Enfidaville.
Gallantry.
How to Kill.
Knife, The.
Offensive, The.
On a Return from Egypt.
Prisoner, The.
Simplify Me When I'm Dead.
Soissons.
Vergissmeinnicht.

Douglas, Lord Alfred Bruce (1870–1945)
Dead Poet, The.
Green River, The.
Impression de Nuit; London.
To Olive.
To Sleep.
Two Loves.

Douglass, Frederick (c.1817–95)
Narrative of the Life of Frederick Douglass, an American Slave, *sels.*

Douskey, Franz (b. 1941)
Dog Days and Delta Nights.
Wet Bodies.

Dovaston, John F. M. (1782–1852)
Streamlet! methinks thy lot resembles mine.
There are who say the sonnet's meted maze.

Dove, Angela
Crab.

Dove, Rita (b. 1952)
Adolescence—1.
Adolescence—2.
Adolescence—3.
After Reading *Mickey in the Night Kitchen* for the Third Time Before Bed.
Agosta the Winged Man and Rasha the Black Dove.
Alfonzo Prepares to Go Over the Top.
All Souls'
American Smooth.
Banneker.
Beauty and the Beast.
Belinda's Petition.
Bistro Styx, The.
"Blown Apart By Loss . . . "
Blue Days.
Breathing, the Endless News, The.
Canary.
Centipede.
Charm, The.
Claudette Colvin Goes to Work.
Crab-Boil.
David Walker (1785–1830).
Daystar.
Demeter, Waiting.
Desert Backyard.
Dissolve.
Dog Days, Jerusalem.
Dusting.
Enactment, The.
Event, The.
Exit.
Fifth Grade Autobiography.
First Book, The.
Fish in the Stone, The.
Flash Cards.
Flirtation.
Freedom Ride.
Genie's Prayer Under the Kitchen Sink.
Geometry.
Götterdämmerung.
Great Palaces of Versailles, The.
Great Piece of Turf, The.
History: "Everything's a metaphor, some wise."
Horse and Tree.
House Slave, The.
Hully Gully.
In the Old Neighborhood.
Island Women of Paris, The.
La Chapelle. 92nd Division. Ted.
Lady Freedom Among Us.
Lint.
Listen to the Sound of My Horn.
Mississippi.
Mother Love.
Musician Talks about "Process," The.
Nexus.
Nigger Song: An Odyssey.
Ö.
On Veronica.
Other Side of the House, The.
Parsley.
Passage, The.
Persephone Underground.
Poem in Which I Refuse Contemplation.
Political.
Quaker Oats.
Revenant.
Rosa.
Rusks.
Secret Garden, The.
Sightseeing.
Small Town.
Sonnet in Primary Colors.
Suite for Augustus, A, *sels.*
Sunday Greens.
Ta Ta Cha Cha.
Taking in Wash.
Teach Us to Number Our Days.

Testimonial.
This Life.
Thomas and Beulah, *sels.*
Tou Wan Speaks to Her Husband Liu Sheng.
Turning Thirty, I Contemplate Students
    Bicycling Home.
Vacation.
Weathering Out.
Wiederkehr.
Wingfoot Lake.

Dover, Sibella Cole (*fl.* 1630)
To Her Modest Mirth-Making Friend, Mr
    Robert Dover.

Dow, Robert
How Should I Say This?

Dowden, Edward (1843–1913)
In the Garden, *sels.*
Leonardo's "Mona Lisa"
Love's Chord.
Old Letters.
Plummet, The.
Two Infinities.

Dowe, Katherine (*fl.* before 1588)
Arise earelie.

Dowland, John (1562–1626)
Come Away, Come, Sweet Love.
Fine Knacks for Ladies.

Downie, Freda
For Wilfred Owen.
Italians Are Excited, The.
O Mary.
Some Poetry.

Dowriche, Anne (*fl.* 1589–96)
Admiralls Being Slaine, They Likewise . . . ,
    The.
French Historie, The, *sels.*
Verses Written by a Gentlewoman upon the
    Jaylors Conversion.

Dowson, Ernest (1867–1900)
Carthusians.
Dregs.
Exchanges.
Extreme Unction.
Flos Lunae.
Last Word, A.
Non Sum Qualis Eram Bonae sub Regno
    Cynarae.
O Mors! Quam Amara Est Memoria Tua
    Homini Pacem Habenti In Substantiis Suis.
Spleen.
To One in Bedlam.
Vesperal.
Villanelle of His Lady's Treasures.
Villanelle of Marguerites.
Villanelle of the Poet's Road.
Vitae Summa Brevis Spem Nos Vetat Incohare
    Longam.

Dōyaku Sensei, Master Artery (1752–1801)
Housemaid's Ballad, The.
Kyoto Minor Retainer.
To Master Groggy, From Afar.

Doyle, Sir Arthur Conan
To An Undiscerning Critic.

Doyle, Ben (b. 1973)
Error of the Hydrographers, An.
Forensics.
Our Man.
War Is Over, The.

Doyle, Sir Francis Hastings (1810–88)
Private of the Buffs; or, The British Soldier in
    China.
Spark Divine, A.

Doyle, R. Erica (b. 1968)
Ma Ramon.
Susu.

Doyle, Susanne
Hell to Pay.
Some Girls.
This Shade.

Drachler, Rose (b. 1911)
As I Am My Father's.
Athens and Jerusalem.
Evening of the Sixth Day, The.
Prophet, The.

Witness, The.

Dragomoschenko, Arkadii (b. 1946)
Footnotes.
Instructing Clarity in a Confusion.
March Elegy.
Sentimental Elegy, A.

Drake, Ervin (b. 1919)
Friendliest Thing (Two People Can Do), The.
It Was a Very Good Year.
Just for Today.

Drake, Joseph Rodman (1795–1820)
American Flag, The.
Bronx.
Mocking-Bird, The.
National Painting, The.
Niagara.
To a Friend.

Drake, Joseph Rodman *See Also* Halleck, Fitz-
    Greene

Drake, Nick (b. 1961)
Foley Artist, The.
Man in the White Suit, The.
Very Rich Hours, The.

Dransfield, Michael (1948–73)
Day at a Time.
Endsight.
Epiderm.
Fix.
Flying.
Memoirs of a Velvet Urinal.
Minstrel.
Pioneer Lane.
Portrait of the Artist as an Old Man.
Self-analysis.
Strange Bird, A.
That Which We Call a Rose.
Visiting Hour (Repatriation Hospital).
War of the Roses, The.

Draycott, Jane
Night Driving.
Night Tree, The.
Prince Rupert's Drop, The.

Drayton, Michael (1563–1631)
Crier, The.
Dancing Dog, The.
David and Goliath, *sel.*
England's Heroical Epistles, *sels.*
Heart, The.
His Defence Against the Idle Critic.
Idea, *sels.*
Idea's Mirrour, *sel.*
Moses His Birth and Miracles, *sel.*
Most Excellent Song Which Was Solomon's,
    The, *sel.*
Muses' Elysium [*or* Elizium], *sels.*
Muses' Elysium X, The, *sel.*
Noah's Flood, *sels.*
Nymphidia, *sel.*
Ode Written in the Peak[e], An.
Other Song of the Faithful, for the Mercies of
    God, An.
Piers Gaveston [1619], *sels.*
Polyolbion [*or* Poly-Oobion], *sels.*
Roundelay Between Two Shepherds, A.
Sacrifice to Apollo, The.
Shepherd's Garland, The, *sels.*
Shepherd's Sirena, The, *sel.*
Song of Jonah in the Whale's Belly, The.
Song of the Faithful, A.
To His Coy Love, A Canzonet.
To My Noble Friend Master William Browne:
    Of the Evil Time.
To the New Year.
To the Virginian Voyage.

Drennan, John Swanwick [*or* **Swanick] (1809–
93)**
Not Gone Yet.

Drennan, William (1754–1820)
Eire.

Dressel, Jon (b. 1931)
Dai, Live.
Drouth, The.
Intercity, Swansea-London.
Let's Hear It for Goliath.
You, Benjamin Jones.

Drew, George
Apparently Someone in the Department.

Drieu la Rochelle, Pierre (1893–1945)
Roundness.
Tennis.

Drinan, Adam
Florence: Sleeping in Fog.
Measures.
Men on the Rocks, The.

Drinkwater, John (1882–1937)
Cottage Song.
Moonlit Apples.
Reciprocity.
Sun, The.
Who Were before Me.

Driscoll, Frances
Real Life.

Driscoll, Louise (b. 1875)
Hold Fast Your Dreams.

Driskell, Maudelle
Talismans.

Dromgoole, Will Allen (1865–1943)
Building the Bridge.
Old Ladies.

Drosinēs, Geōrgios (1859–1951)
Wild Creeper.

Drown, D.A.
Rose by the Wayside, The.

Druce, Robert (b. 1929)
Apropos of Garden Statuary: A Disquisition
    upon a Minor Genre.

Drummond, Ron
As Zeus.

Drummond, William Henry (1854–1907)
To spread the azure canopy of heaven.

**Drummond, William, of Hawthornden (1585–
1649)**
Against the King.
All Changeth.
Blessedness of Faithfull Soules by Death,
    The.
Book, The.
Change Should Breed Change.
Comparison of His Thoughts to Pearls.
Content and Resolute.
Dog Star, The.
Faith Above Reason.
For a Lady's Summons of Non-Entry.
For the Baptiste.
For the Magdalene.
Forth Feasting, *sel.*
Hymn of the Fairest Fair, The, *sel.*
Hymn to the Fairest Fair, A, *sel.*
If of the dead save good nought should be said.
Invocation: "Pheobus, arise! / And paint the
    sable skies."
Madrigal: "Ah! silly soul, what wilt thou say."
Madrigal: "Daedal of my death, A."
Madrigal: "Like the Idalian Queen[e]."
Madrigal: "My thoughts hold mortal[l] strife."
Madrigal: "This life, which seems so fair."
Madrigal: "Unhappie [*or* Unhappy] Light."
Mans Knowledge, Ignorance in the Misteries
    of God.
Melampus' Epitaph.
Midden-Battle between Lady Scotstarvit and
    the Mistress of Newbarns, The.
Miserable Estate of the World Before the
    Incarnation of God.
On Pym.
Saint John Baptist.
Sextain: "Sith gone is my delight and only
    pleasure."
Sextain: "With elegies, sad songs, and
    mourning lays."
Sleep, Silence' Child.
Sonnet: "Alexis, here she stayed; among these
    pines."
Sonnet: "As in a duskie [*or* dusky] and
    tempestuous night."
Sonnet: "How many times night's silent queene
    her face."
Sonnet: "Slide soft, fair forth, and make a
    crystal plain."

Spring Bereaved.
Spring Bereaved 2.
To a Nightingale.
To His Lute.
Urania, or Spiritual Poems, *sels.*

Drummond de Andrade, Carlos (1902–87)
Ballad of Love through the Ages.
Boi Vě os Homens, Um.
Boy Crying in the Night.
Dead in Frock Coats, The.
Diminutive.
Don't Kill Yourself.
Don't Kill Yourself.
Elegy: "I've won (lost) my day."
Elephant, The.
In the Middle of the Road.
In the Middle of the Road.
Infancy.
Looking for Poetry.
Motionless Faces.
Ox Looks at Man, An.
Portrait of a Family.
Residue.
Residue.
Seven-Sided Poem.
Traveling as a Family.
Your Shoulders Hold Up the World.

Dryansky, Amy (b. 1960)
Size of a Bed Sheet, The.

Dryden, Charles (1860–1931)
Scorcher's Farewell to His Steed, The.

Dryden, John (1631–1700)
Absalom and Achitophel, *sels.*
Absalom and Achitophel, Part 2, *sel.*
Alexander's Feast; or, The Power of Music [*or* Musique].
Amboyna; or, The Cruelties of the Dutch to the English Merchants, *sels.*
Amphitryon, *sel.*
Annus Mirabilis, *sels.*
Astraea Redux, *sels.*
Cleomenes, *sel.*
Conquest of Granada, The, *sel.*
Cymon and Iphigenia, *sels.*
Don Sebastian, *sel.*
Hind and the Panther, The, *sels.*
Indian Emperor, The, *sel.*
Lines Printed under the Engraved Portrait of Milton [In Tonson's Folio of the "Paradise Lost"].
Love Triumphant, *sel.*
Mac Flecknoe [or, A Satire upon the True-Blue Protestant Poet T. S.], *sels.*
Marriage à la Mode, *sels.*
Oedipus, *sel.*
On Jacob Tonson, His Publisher.
Religio Laici, *sels.*
Secret Love; or, The Maiden Queen, *sel.*
Secular Masque, The, *sel.*
Silent Woman to the University of Oxford, The, *sel.*
Song for a Girl.
Song for St Cecilia's Day, 1687, A, *sel.*
Song to a Fair Young Lady, Going Out of the Town in the Spring.
Spanish Friar [*or* Fryar], The, *sels.*
Theodore and Honoria, From [Fables Ancient and Modern from] Boccace, *sels.*
Threnodia Augustalis, *sels.*
To My Dear Friend Mr Congreve [on His Comedy Called "The Double-Dealer"].
To the Memory of Mr Oldham.
To the Pious Memory of the Accomplished [*or* Accomplisht] Young Lady, Mrs. Anne Killigrew, [Excellent in the Two Sister-Arts of Poesie and Painting. An Ode].
Troilus and Cressida, *sel.*
Tyrannic Love, *sels.*

Drysdale, Ann (b. 1942)
Lament of the White Queen.
Language Difficulty.

Dsida, Jenő (1907–38)
Confession, A.
Maundy Thursday.
Poet's Resurrection, The.

Serenade for Ilonka.
Verse of Darkness, The.
What Will Come of This?

Du Bartas, Guillaume de Salluste (1544–90)
Divine Weeks and Works, The, *sels.*

Du Bellay, Joachim (1522–60)
Epitaph on a Pet Cat.
Heureux Qui, Comme Ulysse, A Fait un Beau Voyage.
Las, Où Est Maintenant Ce Mespris de Fortune.
Regrets, *sels.*
Rome.
Rome.
Ruins of Rome, *sels.*

Du Bois, Dorothea (1728–74)
Song: "Scholar first my Love implor'd, A."

Du Bouchet, André (b. 1924)
Fraction.
Fraction.
Light of the Blade, The.
Lumière de la lame, La.
Pierre ou eau.
Stone or Water.

Du Maurier, George (1834–96)
Music.

du Perron, E. (1899–1940)
Sick Man, The.

Du Shenyan (648?–708)
Lodging in Annam.
Written at Jumble-Rock Mountain by the South Sea.

Du Tử' Lě Lě Cu' Phách
What I Leave to My Son.

Dubie, Norman (b. 1945)
Anagram Born of Madness at Czernowitz, 12 November 1920.
Annual of the Dark Physics, An.
Apocrypha of Jacques Derrida, The.
Ars Poetica: A Stone Soup.
Ars Poetica: "It is almost polio season. The girls."
At Midsummer.
Aubade of the Singer and Saboteur, Marie Triste: 1941.
Buffalo Clouds over the Maestro Hoon.
Coleridge Crossing the Plain of Jars [1833].
Czar's Last Christmas Letter, The: A Barn in the Urals.
Death of the Race Car Driver, The.
Dementia.
Elegy for Wright & Hugo.
Elizabeth's War with the Christmas Bear.
February: The Boy Breughel.
Funeral, The.
Genesis Text for Larry Levis, Who Died Alone, A.
Grandfather's Last Letter, A.
Hummingbirds.
Lamentations.
Last Poem, Snow Tree.
New England, Springtime.
Obscure, The.
Of Art & Memory.
Of Politics, & Art.
Parish.
Peace of Lodi, The.
Pendulum, The.
Poem: "Mule kicked out in the trees, A. An Early."
Sanctuary.
Sky Harbor.
Thomas Hardy.
Trakl.

Dubin, Al (1891–1945)
Cup of Coffee, a Sandwich, and You.
Dames.
Forty-second Street.
I Only Have Eyes for You.
I'll String Along with You.
Lullaby of Broadway.
Lulu's Back in Town.
Remember Me?
September in the Rain.
She's a Latin from Manhattan.

Shuffle Off to Buffalo.
Young and Healthy.
You're Getting to Be a Habit with Me.

DuBois, William Edward Burghardt (1868–1963)
Litany of [*or* at] Atlanta, A.
My Country 'Tis of Thee.
Quadroon, The.
Song of the Smoke, The.

Dubrava, Patricia
Miraculous Marriage of Zarife Dominquez.

Ducal, Charles (b. 1952)
Duke and I 2, The.

Duchamp, Marcel (1887–1968)
Cast Shadows.
Deferment.
Electricity Breadthwise.
1914 Box, The.
Speculations.
SURcenSURE.
World in Yellow, A.

Duck, Stephen (1705–56)
On Richmond Park, *sels.*

Duclaux, Mme *See* Robinson, Agnes Mary Frances

Ducornet, Rikki
Dark Star, Black Star.
Machete.
My Special Madness.
Necromancy.

Dudek, Louis (b. 1918)
At Lac en Coeur.

Dudis, Ellen Kirvin
Riding Their Bikes.

Dudley, Anne Seymour (b. after 1535, d. 1587)
Hecatodistichon, *sel.*

Dudley, Ellen
Pathologist.

Dudley, Lady Jane Grey (1537–54)
Certaine verses written by the said ladie Jane with a pinne.

Duemer, Joseph
Theory of Tragedy.

Dufault, Peter Kane (b. 1923)
Burden.
First Night, A.
Mud Dauber Wasp, The.

Duff, Valerie
Letters from an Exile.

Dufferin and Clandeboye, [*née* Sheridan] Helen Selina Blackwood, Baroness (1807–67)
Charming Woman, The.
Lament of the Irish Emigrant.
Mother's Lament, The.

Duffield, George, Jr. (1818–88)
Stand Up! Stand Up for Jesus.

Dufflar, Carlos Raul
Amadou Diallo from Guinea to the Bronx Dead on Arrival.

Duffy, Carol Ann (b. 1955)
Adultery.
Anne Hathaway.
Circe.
Close.
Comprehensive.
Foreign.
Funeral.
Girlfriends.
Good Teachers, The.
Grammar of Light, The.
Havisham.
In Your Mind.
Little Red-Cap.
Making Money.
Medusa.
Mrs Lazarus.
Mrs Midas.
Oppenheim's Cup and Saucer.
Plainsong.
Prayer: "Some days, although we cannot pray, a prayer."
Queen Herod.
Small Female Skull.
Stealing.
Valentine: "Not a red rose or a satin heart."

War Photographer.
Warming Her Pearls.
Words, Wide Night.

Duffy, Maureen (b. 1933)
Eureka.
I Am Beset with a Dream of Fair Woman.
Semi-Skilled Lover.

Dugan, Alan (1923–2003)
Actual Vision of Morning's Extrusion.
Against a Sickness: To the Female Double
    Principle God.
American Variation on How Rilke Loved a
    Princess and Got to Stay in Her Castle.
Barefoot Homiletics, after Wittgenstein and
    Boswell.
Drunken Memories of Anne Sexton.
Elegy: "I know but will not tell."
Fabrication of Ancestors.
For Euthanasia and Pain-Killing Drugs.
From Heraclitus.
Glad at the Cold (1955).
How We Heard the Name.
Internal Migration: On Being on Tour.
Last Statement for a Last Oracle.
Let Heroes Account to Love.
Letter to Eve.
Love Song: I and Thou.
Memorial Service for the Invasion Beach
    Where the Vacation in the Flesh Is Over.
Niagara Falls.
Nomenclature.
On an East Wind from the Wars.
On Being a Householder.
On Hurricane Jackson.
On the Elk, Unwitnessed.
On Trees.
Plague of Dead Sharks.
Poem for Elliot Carter on His 90th Birthday.
Portrait from the Infantry.
Prayer: "God, I need a job because I need
    money."
Prison Song.
Self-Exhortation on Military Themes.
Stentor and Mourning.
Swing Shift Blues.
Weeds as Partial Survivors.

Dugan, Maurice
Coolun, The.

Duggan, Laurie (b. 1949)
Ash Range, The, *sels*.
Dogs, *sels*.
Eight xx.
Epigrams of Martial, The, *sels*.
Qantas Bags.
Ten ii.
Three Found Poems, *sels*.
Three xlvii.
Town on the Ten Dollar Note, The.

Duhamel, Denise (b. 1961)
Art.
Barbie's Molester.
Bicentennial Barbie.
Buddhist Barbie.
Crater Face.
Ego.
Four Hours.
How Much Is This Poem Going to Cost Me?
I'm Dealing with My Pain.
Kinky.
Sex with a Famous Poet.
Ugly Step Sister, The.
Why, on a Bad Day, I Can Relate to the
    Manatee.
Yes.

Duhig, Ian (b. 1954)
Chocolate Soldier.
First Second, The.
Fred.
From the Irish.
Fundamentals.
I prayed to the ghost of Carrie.
I'r Hen Iaith a'i Chaneuon.
Lammas Hireling, The.
Margin Prayer from an Ancient Psalter.
No Derry slubberdegullion with college airs.

Reforma Agraria.

Duke, Richard (1658–1711)
To Caelia.

Duke, Vernon
Autumn in New York.

Dumas, Henry (1935–68)
Afro-American.
America.
Concentration Camp Blues.
If I Were Earth.
Island within Island.
Knees of a Natural Man.
Root Song.
Saba.
Son of Msippi.
Zebra Goes Wild Where the Sidewalk Ends,
    The.

Dumdum, Simeon
Li Pos of the Polis.
Some Die of Light.
To My Mother.

Dunbar-Nelson, Alice Moore (1875–1935)
I Sit and Sew.
Snow in October.
Sonnet: "I had no thought of violets of late."
You! Inez!

Dunbar, Paul Laurence (1872–1906)
Accountability.
Ante-Bellum Sermon, An.
Black Samson of Brandywine.
Boy's Summer, A.
Choice, A.
Colored Soldiers, The.
Common Things.
Companion's Progress, A.
Compensation.
Conquerors, The: The Black Troops in Cuba.
Dawn: "Angel, robed in spotless white, An."
Death Song, A.
Debt, The.
Distinction.
Douglass.
Ere Sleep Comes Down to Soothe the Weary
    Eyes.
Frederick Douglass.
Harriet Beecher Stowe.
Haunted Oak, The.
He Had His Dream.
Hymn, A: "Lead gently, Lord, and slow."
Hymn: "When storms arise."
Little Brown Baby.
Longing.
Made to Order Smile, The.
Mystery, The.
Negro Love Song, A.
Night.
Paradox, The.
Passion and Love.
Place Where the Rainbow Ends, The.
Poet, The.
Prayer, A: "O Lord, the hard-won miles."
Resignation.
Robert Gould Shaw.
Ships That Pass in the Night.
Signs of the Times.
Slow Through the Dark.
Song of Summer.
Spiritual, A.
Summer in the South.
Summer's Night, A.
Sympathy: "I know what the caged bird feels,
    alas!"
Theology.
To Alice Dunbar.
Unsung Heroes, The.
We Wear the Mask.
When All Is Done.
When Dey 'Listed Colored Soldiers.
When Malindy Sings.

Dunbar, William (c.1465–c.1530)
Amendis [*or* Amends] to the Telyouris [*or*
    Tailors] and Sowtaris [*or* Soutaris *or* Soutars
    or Shoemakers].
Ballat [*or* Ballad] of Our Lady, [Ane].
Done is a battell [*or* battle] on the dragon blak

[*or* black].
Flyting of Dumbar [*or* Dunbar] and Kennedie
    [*or* Kennedy], The, *sels*.
In Prais[e] of Women [*or* Wemen].
In to thir dirk and drublie day[i]s.
Lament for the Makaris [*or* Makars *or*
    Makers].
Magryme, The.
Now cumis aige quhair yewth hes bene.
O wreche [*or* wretch], be war [*or* beware], this
    warld [*or* world] will wend the[e] fro.
Off Februar the fyiftene nycht, *sels*.
Of[f] Lentren in the first mornyng [*or*
    morning].
To a Lady[e].
To [*or* In Honour of] the City of London, *sel*.
Tretis [*or* Book] of the Tua Mariit Wemen [*or*
    Two Married Women] and the Wedo[w] [*or*
    Widow], The, *sels*.

Duncan, Andrew (b. 1956)
Andy-the-German Servant of Two Masters.
Ghost of Fusion, The.
Martyrdom and Triumph of Sergei Korolev.
Shield of Perseus, The.

Duncan, Eric (1858–1944)
Drought.

Duncan, Lesley
Festive Tolls.
Visit, The: "Mary, more than quite contrary,
    bars the door."

Duncan, Robert (1919–88)
Achilles' Song.
African Elegy, An.
After a Long Illness.
Among My Friends.
And If He Had Been Wrong for Me.
Ark for Lawrence Durrell, An.
At the Poetry Conference: Berkeley After the
    New York Style.
Ballad of Mrs. Noah, The.
Bending the Bow.
Childhood's Retreat.
Chords Passages 14.
Close.
Dancing Concerning a Form of Women, A.
Dante, *sel*.
Drinking Fountain, The.
For the Assignment of the Spirit.
Glimpse, A.
I Am a Most Fleshly Man.
I have.
Letting the Beat Go.
Morning Letter, A.
My Mother Would Be a Falconress.
Often I Am Permitted to Return to a Meadow.
Passage over Water.
Passages, *sels*.
Passages 37.
Poem Beginning with a Line by Pindar, A.
Poems from the Margins of Thom Gunn's
    Moly, *sels*.
Poetry, a Natural Thing.
Presence of the Dance / The Resolution of the
    Music, The.
Returning to Roots of First Feeling.
Rites of Participation, *sels*.
Rites of Passage, *sel*.
Roots and Branches.
Sentinels, The.
Sleep is a Deep and Many Voiced Flood.
Songs of an Other.
Spring Memorandum, A: Fort Knox.
Structure of Rime XVIII.
Structure of Rime XXIII.
Structure of Rime, The, *sel*.
Styx.
Temple of the Animals, The.
This Place Rumord to Have Been Sodom.
Torso, The / Passages 18.
What I Saw.

**Duncan [Too-qua-stee], DeWitt Clinton (1829–
1909)**
Dead Nation, The.

Duncombe, John (1729–89)
Feminead, or Female Genius, The, *sels*.

Duncombe, Susanna Highmore (1725–1812)
To Aspasia.
Dunkerley, William Arthur See Oxenham, John
Dunmore, Helen (b. 1952)
Blessing, The.
Candle Poem.
Domestic Poem.
Glad of These Times.
Safe period.
Scan at 8 Weeks.
Three Ways of Recovering a Body.
To Virgil.
When You've Got.
Wild Strawberries.
Dunn, Antony (b. 1973)
Radio.
Dunn, Carolyn Marie
Margaret/Haskell Indian School.
Dunn, Douglas (b. 1942)
Ballad of the Two Left Hands.
Dining.
Elegies, *sels.*
Envoi: "Why did I bring you to this Hull."
France: "Dozen sparrows scuttled on the frost,
A."
From the Night-Window.
Gardeners.
Glasgow Schoolboys, Running Backwards.
I Am a Cameraman.
In the Grounds.
Kaleidoscope, The.
Land Love.
Landscape with One Figure.
Men of Terry Street.
Modern Love.
On Roofs of Terry Street.
Ratatouille.
Removal from Terry Street, A.
Ships.
St Kilda's Parliament: 1879–1979.
Sundial, The.
War Blinded.
Dunn, Gwen
Journey Back to Christmas.
Dunn, J. P. (fl. 1917)
Kansas.
Ode to Governor Capper, An.
Dunn, Max (b. 1895)
O, Where Were We Before Time Was.
Dunn, Rhoda Hero
Aeronauts, The.
Dunn, Stephen (b. 1939)
After Making Love.
After the Argument.
At the Smithville Methodist Church.
Because You Mentioned the Spiritual Life.
Blind Date with the Muse.
Cocked Finger, The.
Cohabiting.
Competition.
Corners.
Criminal.
Dancing with God.
Day and Night Handball.
Each from Different Heights.
Father, Mother, Robert Henley, who hanged
himself in the ninth grade, et al.
From the Manifesto of the Selfish.
Grudges.
Guardian Angel, The.
Happiness.
Impediment.
In the House.
Insistence of Beauty, The.
Instead of You.
Landscape at the End of the Century.
Little Essay on Communication.
Man Who Closed Shop, The.
Odysseus's Secret.
On Hearing the Airlines Will Use a
Psychological Profile to Catch Potential
Skyjackers.
On the Death of a Colleague.
Religion.
Routine Things Around the House, The.

Sadness.
Secret Life, A.
Shame Place, The.
Stairway, The.
Sweetness.
Tenderness.
That Saturday Without a Car.
To a Terrorist.
What They Wanted.
With No Experience in Such Matters.
Dunn, Stephen P. (b. 1928)
Men Talk.
Dunne, Sean (1956–95)
Sydney Place, *sels.*
Dunqul, Amal (1940–82)
City a Wrecked Ship, The.
Corner.
Scaffold, The.
Tommorow.
Duo Duo (Li Shizheng) (b. 1951)
At Parting.
Handicraft—After Marina Tsvetaeva.
In England.
Looking Out from Death.
Morning.
Night.
No More Than One Allowed.
None.
North Sea.
Thoughts and Recollections, *sels.*
Thousands of images have suddenly brightened
in the emptiness.
When People Rise from Cheese, Statement #1.
Wishful Thinking Is the Master of Reality.
Dupin, Jacques (b. 1927)
At Instants I Thought.
Begin Like Tearing.
Commencer.
Even If the Mountain.
He Breathes before Writing.
I Am Forbidden.
Il m'est interdit.
Il respire avant d'écrire.
Il y a.
J'ai cru rejoindre.
Let Us Salute.
Même si la montagne.
Mineral Kingdom.
Quand il est impossible.
Songs of Rescue, *sel.*
There Exists.
When It Is Impossible.
DuPlessis, Rachel Blau
Draft 55: Quiptych.
Dupree, Edison
At Present I Am Working as a Security Guard.
Durack, Mary (b. 1913)
Lament for the Drowned Country.
Duran, Jane
Conversations with Louis.
For the Woman Who Dressed Up to Listen to
Gigli on the Radio.
Great Grandfathers.
Mere Pleasure of Flying, The.
Miscarriage.
Mr Teller the Piano Teacher.
Silences from the Spanish Civil War, *sels.*
Stillborn.
Time Zones.
When I lean down to stir the bathwater.
Durand, Marcella (b. 1967)
Reading Postures 3.
Durant, Mrs. Kenneth See Taggard, Genevieve.
Durcan, Paul (b. 1944)
Around the Corner from Francis Bacon.
Backside to the Wind.
Birth of a Coachman.
Bloomsday Murders, 16 June 1997, The.
Death by Heroin of Sid Vicious, The.
Difficulty That Is Marriage, The.
Divorce Referendum, Ireland, 1986, The.
Going Home to Mayo, Winter, 1949.
Hat Factory, The.
Haulier's Wife Meets Jesus on the Road Near
Moone, The.

Honeymoon Postcard.
In Memory: The Miami Showband—
Massacred 31 July 1975.
Ireland 1972.
Irish Hierarchy Bans Colour Photography.
Kilfenora Teaboy, The.
Late Mr Charles Lynch Digresses, The.
Levite and His Concubine at Gibeah, The.
Martha's Wall.
Micheál Mac Liammóir.
My Belovèd Compares Herself to a Pint of
Stout.
Nessa.
Pietà's Over, The.
Raymond of the Rooftops.
Sally.
She Mends an Ancient Wireless.
Sister Agnes Writes to Her Beloved Mother.
Six Nuns Die in Convent Inferno, *sel.*
Tullynoe: Tête-à-Tête in the Parish Priest's
Parlour.
Weeping Headstones of the Isaac Becketts,
The.
Wife Who Smashed Television Gets Jail.
D'Urfey [or Durfey], Thomas (1653–1723)
Chloe Divine.
Fisherman's Song, The.
Durham, Jimmie (b. 1940)
Columbus Day.
Justiniano Lamé Has Been Killed.
Middle.
Woman Gave Me a Red Star to Wear on My
Headband, A.
Durkin, Kevin
American Pylons.
Durrell, Lawrence (b. 1912)
Acropolis.
Ballad of the Oedipus Complex.
Delos.
Eight Aspects of Melissa, *sels.*
In Arcadia.
In the Garden: Villa Cleobolus.
Strip-tease.
Swans.
Vega.
Water-Colour of Venice, A.
Durston, Georgia Roberts
Wolf, The.
Dutton, Anne See King, Anne
Dutton, Geoffrey (b. 1922)
Burning Off.
Finished Gentleman, A.
Fish Shop Windows.
Dutton, Paul (b. 1943)
So'net 3.
Dwight, Timothy (1752–1817)
Country Pastor, The.
I Love Thy Kingdom, Lord.
Dybek, Stuart (b. 1942)
Benediction.
Brass Knuckles.
Cherry.
Daredevil.
Gradually.
Mowing.
My Father's Fights.
My Neighborhood.
Sleepwalking Soho.
Stain.
Summer Afternoon in Solon, Iowa.
Windy City.
Dye, Jeffrey
Copyright Renewal Under the Texaco Star.
**Dyer, Lady Catherine [or Katherine]
(fl. c.1641)**
M. S. Sir Will: Dyer, Kt: Who Put on
Immortality Aprill the 29th Anno Domini
1621.
Sir William Dyer, Knight, *sels.*
Dyer, Sir Edward (c.1540–1607)
Lowest trees have top[p]s, the ant[e] her gall,
The.
My Mind to Me a Kingdom Is.
PROMETHEUS, when first from heaven high.

Dyer

Dyer, Eric
Painting the Nude.
'Round Killar.
Dyer, John (1699–1758)
Fleece, The, *sels.*
Grongar Hill, *sel.*
My Ox Duke.
Ruins of Rome, The.
Dylan, Bob (Robert Zimmerman) (b. 1941)
Boots of Spanish Leather.
Desolation Row.
Lonesome Death of Hattie Carroll, The.
Quinn the Eskimo.
Three Angels.
Dyment, Clifford (1914–70)
As a Boy With a Richness of Needs I
Wandered.
Derbyshire Born, Monmouth Is My Home.
Swans, The.
Dyson, Will (1880–1938)
Trucker, The.

E

"E." *See* Fullerton, Mary Elizabeth
"E. D." *(fl. 1587)*
E. D. in Commendation of the Author and His
Choise.
E. D. in Prayse of Mr. W. Fouler Her Friend.
Eady, Cornelius (b. 1954)
April.
Birthing.
Chittlin's.
Chuck Berry.
Composite.
Crows in a Strong Wind.
Dance, The.
Drizzle.
False Arrest.
Hank Mobley's.
How I Got Born.
How to Do.
I'm a Fool to Love You.
Insomnia.
Jack Johnson Does the Eagle Rock.
Jazz Dancer.
Johnny Laces Up His Red Shoes.
Leadbelly.
Muddy Waters and the Chicago Blues.
My Mother, If She Had Won Free Dance
Lessons.
My Mother is a God Fearing Woman.
Nature Poem.
Paradiso.
Photo of Ron Carter, Playing His Bass.
Radio.
Running Man.
Seduction.
Sherbet.
Song: *"Nigger-Lover* is a song, spat out."
Success.
Thrift.
Too Young to Know.
View from the Roof, Waverly Place.
Why Do So Few Blacks Study Creative
Writing?
William Carlos Williams.
Wrong Street, The.
Young Elvis.
"Eagle, Solomon" *See* Squire, John Collings, Sir
Earhart, Amelia (1898–1937)
Courage: "Courage is the price that life exacts
for granting peace."
Earle, Jean (b. 1909)
At the South Pole.
Backgrounds Observed.
Blondie.
Exits.
Jugged Hare.
May Tree, The.
Old Tips.
Saturday in the '20s, A.
Tea Party, The.

Village.
Visiting Light.
Earley, Tom (b. 1911)
Lark.
Rebel's Progress.
Early, Gerald
Country or Western Music.
Innocency or Not Song X.
"Eastaway, Edward" *See* Thomas, Edward
Eastman, Max (1883–1969)
To Genevieve Taggard Who Called Me Traitor
in a Poem.
To John Reed.
Ebb, Fred (b. 1932)
And All That Jazz.
Cabaret.
Class.
Happy Time, The.
My Coloring Book.
Nowadays.
Quiet Thing, A.
Eberhart, Richard (1904–2005)
Aesthetics after War, *sel.*
Blunting, The.
Brotherhood of Men.
Centennial For Whitman.
Ceremony by the Sea, A.
Chart Indent.
Dam Neck, Virginia.
For a Lamb.
Fury of Aerial Bombardment, The.
Garden God, The.
Gnat on My Paper.
Groundhog, The.
Hard Structure of the World, The.
Horse Chestnut Tree, The.
I Walked over the Grave of Henry James.
Immortal Picture, The.
La Crosse at Ninety Miles an Hour.
Loon Call, A.
New England Bachelor, A.
On a Squirrel Crossing the Road in Autumn, in
New England.
Rainscapes, Hydrangeas, Roses, and Singing
Birds.
Seals, Terns, Time.
Spider, The.
This Fevers Me.
Under the Hill.
Worldly Failure.
Eclipse
Cicada.
Edelman, Bart (b. 1951)
Buffalo Dreams.
Edelman, Marian Wright (b. 1939)
I Care and I'm Willing to Serve.
E'der, Elsa Rediva
La Puente.
Once We Were Farmers.
Edgar, Christopher (b. 1961)
Cloud of Unknowing, The.
Edgar, Marriott (1880–1951)
Lion and Albert, The.
Edmond, Lauris (b. 1924)
Anniversary.
Bicycle Dream.
Girls.
Jardin des Colombières.
Presences.
Tempo.
3 A.M.
Edmondson, Madeleine
Witches' Spells.
Edson, Russell (b. 1935)
Antimatter.
Ape.
Automobile, The.
Bringing a Dead Man Back into Life.
Canoeing, The.
Categories, The.
Conjugal.
Cottage in the Wood, A.
Counting Sheep.
Crumble-Knees, The.

Dr. Nigel Bruce Watson Counting.
Elephant Tears.
Fall, The: "There was a man who found two
leaves and came indoors holding them out
saying to his parents that he was a tree."
Feeding the Dog.
Good Son Jim.
Neighborhood Dog, The.
Optical Prodigal, The.
Ox, The.
Performance at Hog Theater, A.
Retirement of the Elephant, The.
Rule and Its Exception, The.
Toy-Maker, The.
Windows of the Castle, The.
Wounded Breakfast, The.
Edwards, Dianne Edenfield (b. 1945)
Birthday: "I have fallen to the ground."
Not Having.
Things, As They Are.
Edwards, J. M. (1903–78)
Christmas in Europe: 1945.
Few, The.
Edwards, Kari (b. 1954)
Short Sorry.
Edwards, Ken (b. 1950)
Five Nocturnes, after Derek Jarman, *sels.*
Good Science.
Provisionally.
3600 Weekends, *sels.*
Unconsciously.
Edwards [or Edwardes], Richard (1523–66)
Blue Room, The.
Recollections of an Old Spook.
When I Was Three.
Edwards, Sonia (b. 1961)
Between Two Lovers.
Empty Place, An.
Edwards, Thomas (1699–1757)
On the Edition of Mr. Pope's Works with a
Commentary and Notes.
Sonnet on a Family Picture.
Egan, Raymond B. (fl. 1925)
Ain't We Got Fun.
Sleepy Time Gal.
Egan, Ted
Drover's Boy, The.
Egatz, Ron
Into First.
Egemo, Constance
Silver Poplar at Sunrise.
Egerton, Elizabeth, Lady Brackley (1626–63)
On My Boy Henry.
Egerton, Sarah Fyge (1670–1723)
Emulation, The.
Female Advocate Or, An Answer to a Late
Satyr, The, *sel.*
Liberty, The.
On My Wedding Day.
To Orabella, Marry'd to an Old Man.
Eggen, Arnljot (b. 1923)
He Called Her His Willow.
Eggleton, David (b. 1953)
Bouquet of Dead Flowers.
Eglinton, Edna
Alive, I flourish.
Eguren, José María (1882–1942)
Dead, The.
Girls of the Light, The.
Peregrin, Wandering Hunter of Faces.
Towers, The.
**Ehrenburg [or Erenburg], Ilya Grigoryevich
(1891–1967)**
Our Grandsons Will Be Astonished.
Ehret, Terry
Lost Body.
Ehrhart, William Daniel
Beautiful Wreckage.
Cycling the Rosental.
Finding My Old Battalion Command Post.
How It All Comes Back.
Way Light Bends, The.

Eian
Joshu's "Oak in the Courtyard."

Eich, Günter (1907–72)
End of a Summer, The.
Geometrical Place.
Huge Person, The.
Inventory.
Inventory.
Lauras.
Man in the Blue Smock, The.
Marketplace.
Old Postcards.
Salt.
Seminar for Backward Pupils.
Viareggio.
Where I Live.

Eichendorff, Joseph, Freiherr von (1788–1857)
On My Child's Death.

Eichner, Maura (b. 1921?)
Back Porch Fundamentalist.
Dream Songs Concluded.
Eclogue and Elegy.
Father, The.
From a Woman's Life.
Imagist at Coney Island.
Letter from Santa Cruz.
Litany for the Living.
Message from Inland.
Out of Cana, sel.
Summer: "Fills the white enamel bucket, overflows."
What My Teachers Taught Me I Try to Teach My Students.
Woman is Waiting for a Bus, A.

Eichu (1340–1416)
My eyes eavesdrop on their lashes!

Eidenier, Elon G.
Failure of Language, The.

Eigner, Larry (b. 1927)
Ah, so, yes.
Back to it.
Environs.
Explanation / tangent things.
For Sleep.
How It Comes About.
If You Weep, I Think That.
In Imitation.
It Sounded.
Letter for Duncan.
Live /, Bird Which.
Noise absorbed.
Open Air Where.
Side by side.
Temporary Language, A.
Three Poems 1989.
Trees Green the Quiet Sun.
Wholes.
Winter (January / February 1978).

Eijkelboom, Jan (b. 1926)
A Nos Glorieux Morts.
As Old As Then.
Sometimes.
Town a Bird Sanctuary, The.

Eimers, Nancy
Another Kimono.
Morbid.
Night Without Stars, A.
No Moon.

Einzig, Barbara and Jerome Rothenberg
Reading for Pleasure.
Slide Show, The.

Eirian, Siôn (b. 1954)
Adolescent Experiences, sels.
My Dad Versus Ginsberg.
Pain, The.

Eiseley, Loren C. (1907–77)
And as for Man.
Prairie Spring.

Ejèn, Emanyèl See Eugene [or Ejèn or Manno Ejèn], Emmanuel [or Emanyèl]

Ekelof, Gunnar
Absentia Animi.
Ayásma.
Études, sels.

Greece.
Guide to the Underworld, sel.
Hangman.
If You Ask Me.
If You Ask Me Where I Live.
Like Ankle-Rings, This Music.
Mölna Elegy, sels.
Monologue with Its Wife.
Moon, The.
Questionnaire.
Swan, The, sels.
Variations, sels.

Ekevall, Kay (b. 1911)
Telling Myself.

Ekpe, Komi
Abuse Poems: For Kodzo and Others.

El-Dinasouri, Osama
If I Were a God.

El-Gabry, Magdy
Child Hunting Tales, A.

El-Hadi, Suliaman
Drama, The.
Tired Man, The.

El-Hage, Nada (b. 1958)
Follow Me.
Journey of the Shadow, The.
Land Stretching Up to the Sky, A.
Overflow.

El-Iryaan, Shehata
Thermometer of Happiness.

El Janabi, Abdel Kader (b. 1940)
Against Ibn Arabi.
If Only the Horse Was Left to Its Solitude.
Ink.

El-Shafa'i, Ghada
Interlaced Lines for the Same Moment.
Scene for the Mornings Preceding the Fire, A.

El-Shawwaf, Haytham
Devil's Symbol, The.
Half a Lemon, Half a Cigarette, and Half a Desire to Have It Off.

El-Sousy, Sumaiya (b. 1974)
Voices.

El-Zein, Amira
Land of Mirrors, The.

Elagin, Ivan Venediktovich (Ivan Venediktovich Matveyev) (1918–87)
Amnesty.
My murderer is no thief.

Elam, Patricia
Mother's Day at McDonald's.

Elbe, Susan
Practicing Eternity.

Elburg, Jan G. (b. 1919)
Nothing of All That.
Wanting To.

Eldan, Anadad (b. 1924)
When You Grow Up.

Elfyn, Menna (b. 1951)
Belly Button Song.
Broadway Morning.
Burning Multitude, The.
Cell Angel.
Couplings.
Driver.
Handkerchief Kiss.
May in My Lai.
Nothing but Curves.
Passing On.
Pins.
Rice Papers.
Sardines.
Some Kind of Thanks.
Theology of Hair, The.
Welsh Ice.

Elhami, Hussein (fl. 20th cent.)
Lyric in Exile, A.

Eli, A. See Alon, Eli

Elijio, Catharino James
Hummingbird at Dawn.

"Eliot, George" (Mary Ann [or Marian] Evans Lewes Cross) (1818–90)
Armgart, sel.

Brother and Sister.
Death of Moses, The.
Felix Holt, The Radical, sels.
How Lisa Loved the King, sels.
In a London Drawingroom.

Eliot, T. S. (Thomas Stearns) (1888–1965)
Ash Wednesday [or Ash-Wednesday], sels.
Aunt Helen.
Boston Evening Transcript, The.
Bustopher Jones: The Cat About Town.
Choruses from "The Rock", sels.
Conversation Galante.
Coriolan, sels.
Five-Finger Exercises, sels.
Four Quartets, sels.
Gerontion, sel.
Hippopotamus, The.
Hollow Men, The.
Hysteria.
Journey of the Magi.
La Figlia Che Piange.
Landscapes, sels.
Lines for an Old Man.
Love Song of J. Alfred Prufrock, The.
Macavity: The Mystery Cat.
Marina.
Mr. Apollinax.
Mr Mistoffelees.
Morning at the Window.
Naming of Cats, The.
Portrait of a Lady.
Preludes: "Winter evening settles down, The."
Rhapsody on a Windy Night.
Rock, The, sels.
Rum Tum Tugger, The.
Song for Simeon, A.
St. Luke, sel.
St. Matthew, sel.
Sweeney Agonistes, sel.
Sweeney among the Nightingales.
There shall always be the Church and the World.
Waste Land, The, sels.
Whispers of Immortality.

Eliscu, Edward (1901–98)
Flying Down to Rio.
Great Day.
More Than You Know.
Without a Song.

"Eliza" (fl. 18th cent.)
To Generall Cromwell.
To My Husband.

Elizabeth I, Queen of England (1533–1603)
Ah silly pug wert thou so sore afraid.
Doubt of Future Foes.
Dread of future foes exyle my present Joy, The.
Genus Infoelix Vitae.
On Monsieur's Departure.
Queen's Answer, The.
Songe Made by Her Majestie and Songe before Her at Her Cominge from White Hall to Powles through Fleete Streete in Anno Domini 1588, A.
When I Was Fair and Young.
Written with a Diamond On Her Window at Woodstock.

Elizabeth, Martha
Manon Reassures Her Lover.
On the Porch—Denton, Texas.
She Teaches Him to Reach Out.
Way of Words, The.

Elizabeth, Queen of Bohemia (1596–1660)
Verses by the Princess Elizabeth, Given to Lord Harington, of Exton, Her Preceptor.

Elledge, Jim
Duckling, Swan.
14 Reasons Why I Mention Mario Lanza to the Man I Love Every Chance I Get Tonight.
Household Gods.
Man I Love and I Have a Typical Evening the Night Richard M. Nixon Dies, The.
Man I Love and I Shop at Jewel, The.
Strangers: An Essay.
Their Hats Is Always White.

Triptych.

Ellingham, Lewis (b. 1933)
Tompkins Sq. Branches With Snowy Arms.

Ellington, Duke
It Don't Mean a Thing (If It Ain't Got That Swing).

Elliot, Alistair (b. 1932)
Latitudes of Home, The.
Northern Morning, A.

Elliot, Jane [or Jean] (1727–1805)
Flowers of the Forest, The.

Elliott, Andrew (b. 1961)
Angel.
Here Today.
Love Poem, The.
Stay Behind, The.
X-Ray, The.

Elliott, Charlotte
Just as I Am.

Elliott, Ebenezer (1781–1849)
Battle Song.
Child, Is Thy Father Dead?
Criticism.
Drone v. Worker.
Fatal Birth, The.
My Only Friends.
Plaint.
Powers of the Sonnet.
Splendid Village, The, sel.
Spring.
Three Marys at Castle Howard, in 1812 and 1837, The.
Village Patriarch, The, sel.
War.

Elliott, Emily E. S.
O Come to My Heart, Lord Jesus.

Elliott, George P. (b. 1918)
Poem About Myself.

Ellis, Alfred See Brown, James

Ellis, Edwin John
Himself, sel.

Ellis, Kelly Norman
Girl.
Tougaloo Blues.

Ellis, R.H.
Ode to St Crispin's Day, sel.

Ellis, Robert (1812–75)
Hour of Sleep, The.

Ellis, Thomas Sayers
Atomic Bride.
Being There.
Break of Dawn, The.
Hush Yo Mouf.
Kiss in the Dark, A.
Making Ends Meet.
On Display.
Practice.
Practice: For Derek Walcott.
Psychoalphadiscobetabioaquadoloop, A.
Shooting Back.
Sir Nose D'VoidofFunk.
Slow Fade to Black.
Star Child.
Sticks.
T.A.P.O.A.F.O.M.
Tambourine Tommy.
Tapes.
View of the Library of Congress from Paul Laurence Dunbar High School.
Zapruder.

Ellis, Zoila
Catalyst.
Luwani Dangriga.

Elman, Richard (d. 1997)
October Observed, Hudson Falls, New York in Bill's Back Yard.

Elmslie, Kenward
Amazon Club.
Bare Bones.
Big Bar.
Circus Nerves and Worries.
Diddly Squat From Cyberspace.
Duo-Tang.
Easter for Joe.

Experts at Veneers.
Feathered Dancers.
Fruit.
Girl Machine.
History of France.
Island Celebration.
Japanese City.
Marbled Chuckle in the Savannahs.
One Night Stand.
Picnic.
Shirley Temple Surrounded by Lions.
Sibling Rivalry.
Squatter in the Foreground.
Stage Duo.
Venus Preserved.

Elmslie, Susan (b. 1968)
Forecast: Nadja.

Elon, Florence
In the New World.

Elsschot, Willem (1882–1960)
Mother.

Elton, W.R.
Hopper: In the Cafe.

Éluard, Paul (Eugène Grindel) (1895–1952)
Amoureuse, L'
Dawn Dissolves the Monsters.
Deaf and Blind, The.
Diamant qu'il ne t'a pas donné, Le.
D'un et de deux, de tous.
Elle est.
Je te l'ai dit.
Lady Love.
Meetings.
Mirror of a Moment, The.
Nature Was Caught in the Nets of Your Life.
Nazi Song.
November 1936.
Nuits partagées, sel.
She Is Always Unwilling to Understand.
Terre est bleue comme une orange, La.
To Her of Whom They Dream.
Unknown, She Was My Favorite Shape.
Woman in Love.

Eluard, Paul and Andre Breton
Diamond He Didn't Give You, The.
Earth Is Blue like an Orange, The.
Identities.
Immaculate Conception, The, sels.
I've Told You.
Loving.
Of One and Two, of All.
152 Proverbs Mis au Goût du Jour, sel.
Second Nature.
Shared Nights.
She Exists.
Victory at Guernica, The.

Elvey, George J.
Come, Ye Thankful People, Come.

Elytis, Odysseus (Odysseus Alepoudelis) (1911–91)
Aegean Melancholy.
Anniversary.
Anoint the Ariston, sels.
As Endymion.
Autopsy, The.
Axion Esti, sel.
Mad Pomegranate Tree, The.
March toward the Front, The.
Origin of Landscape or the End of Mercy, The.
Sun the First.
This Wind That Loiters.
With Light and With Death, sel.

Ema Saikō (1787–1861)
Evening Stroll.

Emans, Elaine V.
Crew of Apollo 8, The.

Emanuel, James A.
Emmett Till.
Fourteen.

Emanuel, Lynn
At the Ritz.
Blond Bombshell.
Corpses, The.
Elsewhere.

Halfway Through the Book I'm Writing.
Homage to Sharon Stone.
In English in a Poem.
Like God.
Of Your Father's Indiscretions and the Train to California.
Outside Room Six.
Politics of Narrative, The: Why I Am a Poet.
She.
Technology of Spring, The.
Walt, I Salute You!
White Dress, The.

Emerson, Claudia
Flood: "This had happened before: rain that began."

Emerson, Jocelyn (b. 1964)
Apophatic.
Architecture.
Architecture (2).
Lighthouse, The.
Night Blindness.
Vigil.
White Flowers.

Emerson, Ralph Waldo (1803–82)
Alphonso of Castile, sels.
Art.
Astræa.
Awed I behold once more.
Bacchus.
Blight.
Boston Hymn.
Brahma.
Chartist's Complaint, The.
Circles.
Compensation ("Why should I keep holiday.").
Compensation ("Wings of Time are black and white, The.").
Concord Hymn.
Days.
Day's Ration, The.
Dear Brother, Would You Know the Life.
Dirge: "I reached the middle of the mount."
Each and All.
Eros.
Experience.
Fable: "Mountain and the squirrel, The."
Forerunners.
Freedom.
Friendship.
Give All to Love.
Grace.
Hamatreya.
Hamatreya.
Harp, The.
History.
Humble-Bee, The.
I have an arrow that will find its mark.
Illusions.
Initial, Dæmonic, and Celestial Love, sels.
Intellect.
Life, sel.
Limits.
Maia.
Merlin, sels.
Merops.
Mithridates.
Monadnoc, sel.
Motto to "The Poet"
Musketaquid.
Nature [1836].
Nature [1844].
Nominalist and Realist.
Ode, Inscribed to W. H. Channing.
Past, The.
Patient Pan, The.
Problem, The.
Quatrains, sels.
Rhodora, The [On Being Asked Whence Is the Flower].
Saadi.
Sea-Shore.
Snow-Storm [or Snowstorm], The.
Song of Nature.
Sphinx, The.
Spiritual Laws.
Sursum Corda.

Terminus ("It is time to be old.").
Thine Eyes Still Shined.
Threnody: "South-wind brings, The."
To Rhea.
Two Rivers.
Unity.
Uriel.
Visit, The.
Voluntaries, sel.
Waldeinsamkeit.
Water: "Water understands / Civilization well, The."
Wealth.
Woodnotes II ("As sunbeams stream through liberal space"), sel.
World-Soul, The.
Worship.
Xenophanes.

Eminescu, Mihai (1850–89)
Goodbye: "From now till never, goodbye."

Emmens, Jan (b. 1924)
Lion of Judah, The.

Emmett, Daniel Decatur (1815–1904)
Blue Tail Fly or Jimmy Cracked Corn, The.
Boatman's Dance.
Dixie [or Dixie's Land].

Emmott, Kirsten
Labour Pantoum.
Who Looks after Your Kids?

Emperor Ch'ien-wen of Liang
Getting Up in Winter.

Emperor Kōkō
Word at last, The.

Empress [or Atinuke Abayomi Paul]
Creation Is a Cycle.

Empson, William (1906–84)
Ants, The.
Arachne.
Aubade: "Hours before dawn we were woken by the quake."
Bacchus.
Beautiful Train, The.
Death of the King's Canary, The, sel.
Homage to the British Museum.
Ignorance of Death.
Just a Smack at Auden.
Legal Fiction.
Let It Go.
Missing Dates.
Note on Local Flora.
Rolling the Lawn.
Teasers, The.
This Last Pain.
To an Old Lady.
Villanelle: "It is the pain, it is the pain, endures."

Emre, Yunus
Burning, burning, I drift and tread.
Dear Friend, let me plunge into the sea of love.
Go and let it be known to all lovers.
Hear me out, my dear friends.
I love you beyond the depths of my own soul.
Love is minister to us, our flock is the inmost soul.
My Lord granted me such a heart.
Now hear this, lovers, my friends.
Whole universe is full of God, The.
Your love has wrested me away from me.

Emrys James, Dewi (1881–1952)
Pwllderi.

Encarnacion, Alfred (b. 1958)
Bulosan Listens to a Recording of Robert Johson.
Seattle, Autumn, 1933.
Threading the Miles.

Endrezze, Anita (b. 1952)
Birdwatching at Fan Lake.
Girl Who Loved the Sky, The.
Hansel, Gretel and Ruby Redlips.
Language of Fossils, The.
Meditating on Star Light While Traveling Highway.
November Harvest.
Return of the Wolves.

Reviewing Past Lives while Leaf-Burning.
Song-Maker.
Stripper, The.
Sunset at Twin Lake.

Engels, John (b. 1931)
Bullhead.
Fish Dream, The.
Garden.
In March.
Landslide.
Meadow.
Walking to Cootehill.

England, Amy (b. 1962)
Art of the Snake Story, The.

Engle, Paul (b. 1908)
Hart Crane.
Images of China, sels.
Look! The air shudders when you breathe it in.

English, Mary (1652?–94)
May I with Mary choose the better part.

English, Thomas Dunn (1819–1902)
Ben Bolt.

English, William (1710?–78)
Cashel of Munster.

Engman, John
Mushroom Clouds.

Engvick, William (b. 1914)
Crazy in the Heart.
While We're Young.
Who Can I Turn To?

Enheduanna (fl. c.2300 B.C.)
From The Hymn to Inanna.
Lady of Largest Heart.

Ennis, John (b. 1944)
Alice of Daphne, 1799.
Coyne's.
Drink of Spring, A.
Road to Patmos, The.

Enquist, Anna (b. 1945)
December Offensive.
Invasion.

Enright, Dennis Joseph (1920–2002)
Apocalypse.
As You Say.
Dreaming in the Shanghai Restaurant.
Evil Days, The.
Flowers.
Kyoto Garden, A.
Paradise Illustrated, sels.
Posterity.
Remembrance Sunday.
Since Then.

Enzensberger, Hans Magnus (b. 1929)
At Thirty-Three.
Divorce, The.
End of the Owls, The.
Explaining the Declaration.
Finnish Tango.
For a Senior College Textbook.
For the Grave of a Peace-Loving Man.
For the Primer of Senior High.
Holiday, The.
Hôtel Fraternité.
In Memory of Sir Hiram Maxim (1840–1916).
In Memory of William Carlos Williams.
Last Will and Testament.
Middle Class Blues.
Old Revolution.
Poem about the Future.
Poison, The.
Portrait of a House Detective.
Reprieve, The.
Rich, The.
Short History of the Bourgeoisie.
Sinking of the Titanic, The, sels.
Song for Those Who Know.
Vanished Work.
Vending Machine.
War, Like.

Eochaidh, Eibhlín Nic
How to kill a living thing.

"Ephelia" (Joan Philips) (fl. c.1679)
Advice to His Grace.
First Farewell to J.G.

In the Person of a Lady, to Bajazet, Her Unconstant Gallant.
On a Bashful Shepherd.
Song: "You wrong me, Strephon, when you say."
To a Proud Beauty.
To J. G.
To J.G. on the News of His Marriage.
To Madam Bhen.
To My Rival.
To One That Asked Me Why I Loved J.G.
To Phylocles, Inviting Him to Friendship.

Ephraim ben Jacob, Rabbi (1132–1200)
Sacrifice of Isaac, The.

Epictetus
Pleasd with thy Place.

Epstein, Daniel Mark (b. 1948)
Mannequins.

Equi, Elaine (b. 1953)
Autobiographical Poem.
Being Sick Together.
Bouquet of Objects, A.
Date With Robbe-Grillet, A.
In a Monotonous Dream.
Lesbian Corn.
Puritans.
Things to Do in the Bible.

Erb, Elke (b. 1938)
Banat Museum.
Bickering.
Diary Entry, January Seven.
In the Picture.
Inedible.
Stove Problem, The.
Text and Commentary.
This and That.
Well, Is it Going to Budge, the Beast?

Ercilla, Maria
Oysters and Zarzuelas.

Erdélyi, József (1896–1978)
Black Kőrös.
Cherry-Tree.
Sons Changed Into Stags, The.
Splendid Stags, The.

Erdrich, Heid E. (b. 1963)
Fat in America.
Future Debris.
Good Woman.
Hopi Prophet Chooses a Pop.
Quiet Earth, The.
Sweeping Heaven.

Erdrich, Louise (b. 1954)
Angels.
Birth.
Butcher's Wife, The.
Captivity.
Christ's Twin.
Dear John Wayne.
Family Reunion.
Fence, The.
Fooling God.
Francine's Room.
I Was Sleeping Where the Black Oaks Move.
Immaculate Conception.
Indian Boarding School: The Runaways.
Jacklight.
King of Owls, The.
Lady in the Pink Mustang, The.
Leonard Commits Redeeming Adulteries with All the Women in Town.
Leonard Refuses to Atone.
Love Medicine, A.
Mary Kröger.
Mary Magdalene.
New Vows.
Night Sky.
Old Man Potchikoo.
Owls.
Portrait of the Town Leonard.
Sacraments, The.
Saint Clare.
Savior, The.
Strange People, The.
That Pull from the Left.
Windigo.

Woods, The.
Eriksen, Mariane Baggers
  I dropped something. I picked it up.
Erín Moure *See* Mouré, Erin
Erinna (*fl.* **3d cent. B.C.**)
  Delicate hands fashioned this portrait: good
    Prometheus.
  Epigrams, *sels.*
  Escort fish, Pompilos, sending sailors a fair
    sailing.
  From here an empty echo penetrates to Hades.
  Girls / Brides / Tortoise.
  I'm the tomb of Baukis, a bride; passing the
    deeply lamented.
  Stele and my sirens and mournful urn.
Erlich, Sara Riwka
  Garden of Shanah.
  Jerusalem.
Ermakova, Irina (b. 1951)
  Gethsemane: "Moon swims to the fore in the
    pale heavens, The."
  Lullaby for Odysseus.
  Toward morning around seven.
Ermoshina, Galina (b. 1962)
  And also—the Minotaur, farmer, owner,
    respondent.
  Autumn your bellringing, the apple of bright
    weeping.
"Ern Malley" (1918–43)
  Baroque Exterior.
  Boult to Marina.
  Coda: "We have lived as ectoplasm."
  Colloquy with John Keats.
  Culture as Exhibit.
  Documentary Film.
  Dürer: Innsbruck, 1495.
  Egyptian Register.
  Night Piece.
  Night-piece.
  Palinode.
  Perspective Lovesong.
  Petit Testament.
  Sonnets for the Novachord.
  Sweet William.
  Sybilline.
  Young Prince of Tyre.
Ernst, Max (1891–1976)
  Hundred Headless Woman, The, *sels.*
Erskine, Ralph (1685–1752)
  Believer's Riddle, The, *sels.*
  Fourfold Exercise for the Believer in His
    Lodging on Earth, A.
**Erskine, Thomas Erskine, 1st Baron
  (1750–1823)**
  Deserted Died.
  On Scott's Poem "The Field of Waterloo."
Escandor, Virginia E.
  Summer Nostalgia.
Eschenbach, Wolfram von (1170?–1220?)
  "Its claws have struck through the clouds."
  You always sang at break of day.
Eshleman, Clayton (b. 1935)
  Deeds Done and Suffered by Light.
  Hades in Manganese.
  Lich Gate, The.
  Notes on a Visit to Le Tuc d'Audoubert.
  Our Lady of the Three-Pronged Devil.
  Placements I.
Eskimo Oral Tradition
  Love Song: "I cannot bear it, I cannot bear it at
    all."
  Magic Words.
  Magic Words to Cure a Sick Child.
  Song: "And I thought over again."
Espada, Martín (b. 1955)
  Alabanza: In Praise of Local 100.
  All the People Who Are Now Red Trees.
  Another Nameless Prostitute Says the Man is
    Innocent.
  Beloved Spic.
  Bully.
  Cada Puerco Tiene Su Sábado.
  Coca-Cola and Coco Frío.
  Cockroaches of Liberation.

Community College Revises Its Curriculum in
    Response to Changing Demographics, The.
  Courthouse Graffiti for Two Voices.
  Dándole la mano a Mongo.
  David Leaves the Saints for Paterson.
  Do Not Put Dead Monkeys in the Freezer.
  Ezequiel.
  Fidel in Ohio.
  For the Jim Crow Mexican Restaurant in
    Cambridge, Massachusetts, Where My
    Cousin Esteban was Forbidden to Wait
    Tables Because He Wears Dreadlocks.
  Ghazal for Open Hands.
  Green and Red, Verde y Rojo.
  Imagine the Angels of Bread.
  Jeep Driver, The.
  La tormenta.
  Latin Night at the Pawnshop.
  Majeski Plays the Saxophone.
  Man Who Beat Hemingway, The.
  Mayan Astronomer in Hell's Kitchen, A.
  Moon Shatters on Alabama Avenue, The.
  My Cockroach Lover.
  My Native Costume.
  Other Alamo, The.
  Owl and the Lightning, The.
  Prisoners of Saint Lawrence, The.
  Savior Is Abducted in Puerto Rico, The.
  Shaking Hands with Mongo.
  Shiny Aluminum of God, The.
  Spanish of Our Out-Loud Dreams, The.
  Thanksgiving.
  Tires Stacked in the Hallways of Civilization.
  Tony Went to the Bodega but He Didn't Buy
    Anything.
  Toque de queda: Curfew in Lawrence.
  Transient Hotel Sky at the Hour of Sleep.
  Water, White Cotton, and the Rich Man.
  When the Leather Is a Whip.
  Who Burns for the Perfection of Paper.
  Year I Was Diagnosed with a Sacrilegious
    Heart, The.
Espagnol, Nicole (b. 1937)
  Conclusion Is Not Drawn, The.
  Female Socket.
  Heartstopping.
  Wind Turns, The.
Espaillat, Rhina P. (b. 1932)
  Find Work.
  For Robert Frost.
  Metrics.
  Psyche Revised.
Espinet, Ramabai (b. 1948)
  Merchant of Death.
Espino, Alfredo (1900–28)
  Sweet Pale Girl.
Espirito Santo, Alda do (b. 1926)
  Far from the Beach.
  Grandma Mariana.
  Same Side of the Canoe, The.
  To Tania.
  Where are the Men Chased Away by that Mad
    Wind?
Esposito, Nancy
  Doing Good.
Espy, Willard R. (b. 1910)
  My TV Came down with a Chill.
Esquinca, Jorge (b. 1957)
  Fable of the Hunter.
Eşrefoğlu (d. 1469)
  O My God Do Not Part Me from Thee.
Essbaum, Jill Alexander
  In the Beginning.
  Paradise.
  Post-Communion Striptease.
  When the Kingdom Comes.
Essex, Robert Devereux, 2d Earl of (1567–1601)
  Happy Were He.
Essinger, Cathryn (b. 1947)
  You Are Right.
**Esson, Louis (Thomas Louis Buvelot Esson)
  (1879–1943)**
  Shearer's Wife, The.
Esson, Thomas Louis Buvelot *See* Esson, Louis

Esteban, Claude (b. 1935)
  Once Evening's Fallen.
  Soir venu, Le.
Estep, Maggie
  I Have to Go Now.
Estes, Angie
  Annunciation in an Initial R.
  Nocturne.
  Now and Again: An Autobiography of
    Basket.
  Serenade.
  You Stand There Fishing.
Estess, Sybil Pittman (b. 1942)
  Mack Charles Parker Lynching, The.
  Mastodon Teeth.
  Sunset on the Bayou.
Esteves, Sandra Maria
  Ahora.
  Celebration of Home Birth: November 15th,
    1981, A.
  1st Poem for Cuba.
  For Fidel Castro.
  For Lolita Lebron.
  For South Bronx.
  From Fanon.
  Here.
  In the Beginning.
  It Is Raining Today.
  Lil' Pito.
  Motherseed.
  One Woman.
  Some People Are about Jam.
  South Bronx Testimonial.
  Take the Hearts of Children.
  Weaver.
Etherege, Sir George (1653–91)
  Song: "If she be not as kind as fair."
  To a Lady Asking Him How Long He Would
    Love Her.
Etherege, Sir George *See Also* Walsh, William
Etheridge, Ken (1911–81)
  Annunciation.
Ethuin, Anne (b. 1921)
  Legend.
Etienne, Frank (b. 1936)
  Cockfight Marathon, *sel.*
Étienne, Marie
  Cauchemars.
  Nightmares.
Etsujin (1656–1739)
  First snow / Head clear.
Etter, Dave (b. 1928)
  Andy Hasselgard.
  Drink and Agriculture.
  Elwood Collins: Summer of 1932.
  Farm in the Green Mountains, A.
  Great Northern.
  Green-Eyed Boy after Reading Whitman and
    Sandburg.
  Monk's Dream.
  Riding the Rock Island through Kansas.
  Roma Higgins.
  Romp.
  Singing in the Toyota.
  Stuffy Turkey.
  Well You Needn't.
Ettinger, Esther
  Believe Me.
  Excerpts from the Sabbath Dream Book.
  Glass, The.
  Micrographic Manuscript, Miniature (1).
  Micrographic Manuscript, Miniature (2).
"Ettrick Shepherd, The" *See* Hogg, James
Eubulus (*fl.* **4th cent.**)
  Benefits and Abuse of Alcohol, The.
**Euenus (Euenus the Grammarian, Euenus of
  Askelon, Euenus of Paros)** (*fl.* **5th cent. B.C.**)
  To a Swallow.
  To the Swallow.
Eugene, Emmanuel
  Wongòl Poem.
Eugenius Vulgarius (*fl.* **c.1900 B.C.**)
  Metrum Parhemiacum Tragicum.

Euripides (485–406 B.C.)
Fragment 652.
Iphigenia [*or* Iphigeneia] in Aulis, *sel.*
Medea, *sels.*
Evance, Susan (*fl.* 1808–18)
To a Violet.
To Melancholy.
To the Clouds.
Written at Netley Abbey.
Written in a Ruinous Abbey.
Written in Ill Health at the Close of Spring.
Evans, Abbie Huston (b. 1881)
Fringed Gentians.
Juniper.
Martian Landscape.
Old Yellow Shop, The.
Under Cover.
Evans, Abel (1679–1737)
On Sir John Vanbrugh [Architect].
Evans, Aled Lewis (b. 1961)
Alone.
Evans, Amanda R.
Playing for Love.
Something More Obvious.
Evans, Brett
K-Doe Codas.
Evans, Christine
Callers.
Enlli.
Lucy's Bones.
Evans, David Allan (b. 1940)
Pole Vaulter.
Song of Racquetball.
Evans, Donald (1884–1921)
Creation.
Dinner at the Hotel de la Tigresse Verte.
En Monocle.
In the Vices.
People, The.
Pig Killing Day.
Rubbish Tip, The.
Wales '99.
Evans, Einion (b. 1926)
Gadafi's Little Daughter.
Evans, Ellis Humphrey *See* Hedd Wyn [*or* Ellis Humphrey Evans]
Evans, Evan (1731–88)
Hall of Ifor Hael, The.
Love of Our Country, The, *sel.*
Evans, George (b. 1948)
Eye Blade.
Horse on a Fence.
Renaissance Drunk, A.
Revelation in the Mother Lode.
Evans, Margiad (1909–58)
Rain.
Resurrection.
Snowdrops.
Evans, Mari E. (b. 1923)
And the Old Women Gathered.
Black Queen Blues.
Boss Communication.
Speak the Truth to the People.
When in Rome.
World I See, The.
Evans, Mayme
Song for a Baby on Padre Island.
Whiskey-Bomb Battle.
Evans, Ray (b. 1915)
Buttons and Bows.
Femininity.
Haven't Got a Worry.
Keep It Simple.
Mona Lisa.
Never Let Me Go.
To Each His Own.
Whatever Will Be, Will Be (Que Sera, Sera).
Evans, Redd (*fl.* 1947)
No Moon at All.
Evans, William *See* Ifan, Wil
Evans-Jones, Albert *See* Cynan
Evasco, Marjorie M.
Baked Oysters Rockefeller.

Dancing a Spell.
Elemental.
Heron-Woman.
Eveleigh, George
Science Revealed, *sels.*
Evelyn, Mary (1665–85)
Mundus Muliebris.
Voyage to Marryland, A; or, The Ladies Dressing Room.
Everaerts, Jan Nicolai *See* Secundus, Johannes
"Everage, Edna" *See* Humphries, Barry
Everhard, Jim (b. 1946)
Curing Homosexuality.
Everson, William (Brother Antoninus) (1912–94)
Canticle to the Waterbirds, A.
Falling of the Grain, The, *sels.*
Flight in the Desert, The.
Gale at Dawn.
High Embrace, The.
Making of the Cross, The.
Man-Fate, The.
Muscat Pruning.
Passion Week.
Poet Is Dead, The.
Raid, The.
Rainy Easter.
Runoff.
Stone Face Falls.
Tendril in the Mesh, *sel.*
These Are the Ravens.
Tor House.
What Birds Were There.
Winter Ploughing.
Year's End.
Zone of Death.
Everwine, Peter (b. 1930)
Distance.
From the Meadow.
Gray Poem.
Just Before Sleep.
Perhaps It's as You Say.
"Evoe" *See* Knox, Edmund George Valpy
Ewart, Gavin (b. 1916)
Black Box, The.
Bofors A. A. Gun, The.
Dream of a Slave.
Ella Mi Fu Rapita!
Ending.
14-Year-Old Convalescent Cat in the Winter, A.
Great Women Composers, The.
It's Hard to Dislike Ewart.
Jubilate Matteo.
Larkin Automatic Car Wash, The.
Not Wavell but Browning.
Nursery Rhyme.
Officers' Mess.
Old Husband Suspects Adultery, An.
One for the Anthologies.
Owl Writes a Detective Story, The.
Personal Footnote, A.
Radio Cricket.
Robert Graves.
Semantic Limerick According to Dr. Johnson's Dictionary (Edition of 1765), The.
Semantic Limerick According to the Shorter Oxford English Dictionary (1933), The.
Short Time.
Sonnet: How Life Too Is Sentimental.
Sonnet: The Last Things.
To the Virgins, to Make the Most of Time.
Warm to the Cuddly-toy Charm of a Koala Bear.
When a Beau Goes In.
Who Likes the Idea of Guide Cats?
William Wordsworth (1770-1850).
Xmas for the Boys.
Yorkshiremen in Pub Gardens.
Ewer, W. N. (1885–1977)
Chosen People, The.
Gentlemen.
May Day, 1917.
Only Way, The.
Ewing, Blair
Stealth-pirates of Cyberia.

Ewing, Juliana Horatia (1841–85)
Gifts.
Eyen, Jennifer Pierce
New Dream, A (Wuski A-Baw-Tan).
Eytan Eytan
Wind Grinds, The.
Eyton, Frank
Body and Soul.
Eyuboğlu, Bedri Rahmi (1913–75)
Black Mulberries.
Ezeanah, Chiedu
Song of Songs, *sels.*
Ezekiel, Nissim (b. 1924)
Case Study.
Company I Keep, The.
Goodbye Party for Miss Pushpa T. S.
Hymns in Darkness, *sel.*
In India.
In the Garden: "It seemed to me so much like you."
Night of the Scorpion.
Patriot, The.
Poems in the Greek Anthology Mode, *sel.*
Poet, Lover, Birdwatcher.
Songs for Nandu Bhende, *sels.*
Ezenwa-Ohaeto
I Wan Bi President.
Ezrokhi, Zoya (b. 1946)
Day at Home, A.
Repetition.

F

Faber, Frederick William (1814–63)
After-State.
Confessional, The.
Dream of Blue Eyes, A.
Eternity of God, The.
My God, how wonderful Thou art.
Shadow of the Rock, The.
Sonnet-writing. To F. W. F.
Faber, Reginal
Forward to Nationhood.
Fabian, Cosi
Liturgy for Lilith.
On reading the new physics—Creation and Cosmology.
Prayer of Dedication.
Qadesha (Sacred Whore).
Fabio, Sarah Webster (1928–79)
For Louis Armstrong, A Ju-Ju.
Tribute to Duke.
Facos, James (b. 1924)
Fable.
Factor, Jenny
Mother to Son.
On Nursing.
Rubyfruit.
Scotch and Soda.
Song Beside a Sippy Cup.
Fagan, Kathy
California, *She Replied.*
Charm for What Looks Like.
Desire.
In California.
Little Bad Dream Charm.
Moving and St Rage.
Revisionary Instruments 1.
She Attempts to Tell The Truth About True Romance.
Weather They Were Written In, The.
Fage, Mary (*fl.* 1637)
To Their Most Excellent Majesty of Great Brittaines Monarchy.
Fagg, Martin
Elegy on Thomas Hood.
Golden Road to Barcelona: 1992, The.
Mrs Nightingale.
Fagin, Larry (b. 1937)
Landscape.
Little Hand.
Parade of the Caterpillars, The, *sels.*

Twelve Poems.

Fahy, Francis A. (1854–1935)
Little Mary Cassidy.

Faigao, Bataan
Balitaw.
Kundiman.

Fainlight, Ruth (b. 1931)
Archive Film Material.
Handbag.
Sheba and Solomon, *sels.*

Faiq, Sherko *See* Bekes Jr.

Fairchild, B. H.
Body and Soul.
Dumka, The.
Flight.
Machinist, Teaching His Daughter to Play the Piano, The.
Old Men Playing Basketball.

Fairfax, James Griffyth (1886–1976)
Forest of the Dead, The.

Fairfax, John
My emblem is an arrow.

Fairfax of Cameron, Thomas Fairfax, Baron (1612–71)
On the Fatal Day January 30, 1648.
Shortness of Life.
Upon the New Building at Appleton.

Fairley, Barker (1887–1986)
Bach Fugue.

Faiz, Faiz Ahmad (1911–84)
Any Lover to Any Beloved.
Before You Came.
Before You Came.
Day Death Comes, The.
Don't Ask Me for That Love Again.
Fragrant Hands.
Love I Gave You Once, The.
No Sign of Blood.
Once Again the Mind.
Prison Daybreak, A.
Prison Evening, A.
So Bring the Order for My Execution.
Tyrant, The.
Vista.
We Who Were Executed.
When Autumn Came.
You Tell Us What to Do.

Falcón, Jessica Smucker (b. 1977)
Burial Clothes.
Hemispheres.
Indian Locks.
Sycamore.

Falconer, William (1732–69)
Shipwreck, The, *sels.*

Falk, Marcia (b. 1946)
Home for Winter.
Morning *Minyan.*
Sabbath Morning.
Shulamit in Her Dreams.

Falkland, Elizabeth Cary, Countess of (c.1585–1639)
Chorus: "Tis not enough for one that is a wife."

Falkner, John Meade (1858–1922)
Christmas Day; the Family Sitting.

Fall, Malick (1920–78)
Nightstart.

Faller, Kevin (b. 1920)
Like Seals from Sleep.

Fallon, Padraic (1905–74)
Bit of Brass, A.
Flask of Brandy, A.
Holy Well.
Kiltartan Legend.
Parfum Exotique.
Poems of Love, The.
Three Houses, *sels.*
Yeats at Athenry Perhaps.

Fallon, Peter (b. 1951)
Airs and Graces.
Herd, The.
Himself.
Meadow, The.

Spring Song.
Winter Work.

Faludi, Ferenc (1704–79)
Fickle Fortune.
Spring.
Unspeakable.

Fan Chung-yen (989–1052)
Tune: "Sumuche Dancers."
Tune: "Trimming the Silver Lamp."
Tune: "Walk on the Imperial Street."

Fanailova, Elena (b. 1962)
Better this way: it's you with nothing to hold on to.
Frida's Album (*Frida Kahlo's Album*).

Fane, Violet (Mary Montgomerie Currie, Baroness Currie) (1843–1905)
At Her Feet.
In an Irish Churchyard.
Siren, The.

Fanning, Micheál
Consolation: "I wend to the sea."

Fanning, Roger (b. 1962)
Baudelaire's Ablutions.
In the Barn.
Middle Age, The: "Between TV and computer screens."
Oink as Taunt.
Parable of the Boy and the Polar Bear.
Space Needle, The.

Fanshawe, Catherine Maria (1765–1834)
Enigma.
Riddle, A: "'Twas in heaven pronounced, and 'twas muttered in hell."
When Last We Parted.

Fanshawe, Sir Richard (1608–66)
Il Pastor Fido, *sels.*

Fanthorpe, U. A. (b. 1929)
After Visiting Hours.
Atlas.
BC:AD.
Children Imagining a Hospital.
Door, A.
Nativities.
Not My Best Side.
Only Here for the Bier, *sels.*
Our Dog Chasing Swifts.
Person's Tale, The.
Portraits of Tudor Statesmen.
Reindeer Report.
Relief of Myopia, The.
Stations Underground, *sels.*
Unprofessionals, The.
Waiting Room.
What the Donkey Saw.
Women Laughing.
You Will Be Hearing from Us Shortly.

Farawell, Martin Jude
Everything I Need to Know I Learned in Kindergarten.

Farber, Norma (1909–84)
Manhattan Lullaby.
Taking Turns.

Farewell, George (*fl.* c.1733)
Privy-Love for My Landlady.
Quaerè.

Fargas, Laura
If There Is a.
Out of Time.

Fargnoli, Patricia
Lightning Spreads Out across the Water.

Fargue, Léon-Paul (1876–1947)
Boulevard, The.
Fragrance of Night, A.
In Yellow Towns.
Odeur nocturne, indéfinissable et qui m'apporte un doute obscur, Une.

Farid-uddin Attar (1119–1202)
Conference of the Birds, The, *sel.*
Invocation to the Conference of the Birds.

Farish, Helen
Look at These.
Newly Born Twins.

Farjeon, Eleanor (1881–1965)
Cats.

Down! Down!
F is for Forecast.
Good Night.
Keeping Christmas.
Mrs. Peck-Pigeon.
Night Will Never Stay, The.
Over the Garden Wall.
Tide in the River, The.

Farley, Estelle E.
Grand Canyon.
Home Cookin.

Farley, Henry (*fl.* c.1621)
Bounty of Our Age, The.

Farley, Paul (b. 1965)
Diary Moon.
Interior, An.
Lamp, The.
Laws of Gravity.
Peter and the Dyke.
Treacle.

Farquhar, George (1678–1707)
Recruiting Officer, The, *sels.*
Song, A.
Trifles.

Farr, Robert
At General Electric, where They Eat Their/ Young.

Farrar, John Chipman (1896–1976)
Comparison, A.
Song for a Forgotten Shrine to Pan.

Farrell, Fiona
Credo.

Farrow, Stephanie
Civil War, The.

Faruqi, Moeen
Return, The: "After washing Paddington loos."

Fatchen, Max (b. 1920)
Hullo, Inside.

"Father Prout" *See* Mahony, Francis Sylvester

Fathy, Safaa (b. 1958)
Don Quixote and the Flour Mills.
For Heiner Muller: Poem 1.
For Heiner Muller: Poem 2.
For Heiner Muller: Poem 3.
Sailor, The.
Seasons.

Faugeres, Margaretta (1771–1801)
Friendship.

Faulkner, D. W.
Phoebe on a Bicycle.

Fauset, Jessie Redmond (1888–1961)
La Vie C'est la Vie.
Oriflamme.
Touché.
Words! Words!

Faust, Henri
After the Storm.
Six Cranes at Dusk.

Faverey, Hans (b. 1933)
Aan de vaas.
Aarde; uit aardewerk bestaande, De.
Bit by Bit.
Chrysanten, roeiers.
Earth; consisting of earthenware, The.
Eighteen Poems, *sels.*
From the vase.
In the Service of the Wheel.

Favilla, Candice
Red Clay.
West Texas Rain Journal.

Fay, Julie
Estuary.
Flowers.
Mother of Andromeda, The.
Santorini Daughter.
Stereograph: 1903.

Fay, Steve (b. 1952)
Back in My Day.

Fayad, Mona
Salma in Wonderland.
Whisper.

Fazekas, Mihály (1776–1828)
Matt the Gooseherd, *sel.*

To Spring.

Fearing, Kenneth (1902–61)
AD.
American Rhapsody.
Any Man's Advice to His Son.
Aphrodite Metropolis (3).
Art Review.
Ballad of the Salvation Army.
Beware.
Bryce & Tomlins.
Death and Transfiguration of Fourteenth Street.
Dirge: "1-2-3 was the number he played but
   today the number came 3-2-1."
Escape.
4 A.M.
Green Light.
How Do I Feel?
Literary.
Love, 20c the First Quarter Mile.
1933.
Obituary.
Old Story.
People vs. the People, The.
Portrait.
Readings, Forecasts, Personal Guidance.
Reception Good.
Twentieth-Century Blues.
X Minus X.
Yes, the Agency Can Handle That.

Feaver, Vicki
Coat.
Crab Apple Jelly.
Glow Worm.
Hemingway's Hat.
Judith.
Lily Pond.
River God, The.
Way We Live, The.
Without you, I prefer the nights.
Women's Blood.

Feela, David J.
Cut.

Fei Ma (b. 1936)
Drunkard, A.

Feierstein, Ricardo (b. 1944)
Sex: "You can sense, after a slow
   apprenticeship."

Feilding, Frances (1650?–1709)
One the Morening the King was Taken Ill my
   Dreame of Him.

Fein, Richard
To Walt Whitman.

Feinfeld, D. A.
Carmelita.
Wound Man, The.

Feinstein, Elaine (b. 1930)
Annus Mirabilis 1989.
At Seven a Son.
Aviation.
Bathroom.
Dad.
Getting Older.
Infidelities.
Lazarus' Sister.
Magic Apple Tree, The.
Mother Love.
Patience.
Prayer.

Feinstein, Penny
Health Check.

Feinstein, Robert N. (b. 1915)
Woolly Words.

Feinstein, Sandy
Catch, The.
Tendered.

Feinstein, Sascha
Blues for Zoot.
Blues Villanelle for Sonny Criss.
Christmas Eve.
Singapore, July 4th.
Sonnets for Stan Gage (1945–1992).
Summerhouse Piano.

Feirstein, Frederick (b. 1940)
Mark Stern.

Mark Stern Wakes Up.
Rune-Maker, The.

Fel-Yelin, Sarah (1895–1962)
Breath of Spring.

Feld, Andrew (b. 1961)
Boxers, The.
Intermission.
On Fire.

Feldman, Alan (b. 1945)
Contemporary American Poetry.
This Fog.

Feldman, Berl *See* Gilboa, Amir

Feldman, Irving (b. 1928)
All of Us Here, *sels*.
Dream, The.
Family History.
Handball Players at Brighton Beach, The.
Pripet Marshes, The.
Se Aprovechan.
To the Six Million.
You Know What I'm Saying?

Felipe, León (1884–1968)
Biografía, Poesía y Destino.
Biography, Poetry, Destiny.
Black Dog is Sleeping on Top of the Light, A,
   sel.
Caption for "The Child from Vallecas" by
   Velázquez.
Farm Is Yours, The.
I Am Going Because the Ear of Wheat and the
   Dawn Are Not Mine.
I Am Not the Great Diver.
I Have Not Come to Sing.
Let the Poet Come.
Me Voy Porque la Espiga y la Aurora No Son
   Mías.
No He Venido a Cantar.
Now I Am Going.
Perro Negro Duerme Sobre la Luz, Un, *sel*.
Pie Para el Niño de Vallecas de Velázquez.
Que Venga el Poeta.
Tuya Es la Hacienda.
Y Ahora Me Voy.
Yo No Soy el Gran Buzo.

Fell, Alison (b. 1944)
And Again.
August 6, 1945.
Pigeons: "Pigeons / Are tossing."
Pushing Forty.
Rannoch Moor.
Women in the Cold War.

Fell, Frank
Gifted with vision the snowman would see.

Felltham [*or* Feltham], Owen (c.1602–68)
On a Hopeful Youth.
On the Duke of Buckingham, Slain by Felton,
   the 23rd August, 1628.
To Phryne.
Upon a Rare Voice.

Feng Chih (b. c.1905)
Sonnet: "We often pass a night warm and
   intimate."

Fĕng Mĕng-lung (c. 1590–1646)
Mountain Songs, *sels*.

Feng Yen-ssu (903–60)
Cloud That Drifted, The.

Fennelly, Beth Ann (b. 1971)
Asked for a Happy Memory of Her Father, She
   Recalls Wrigley Field.
Latching On, Falling Off.

Fenollosa, Ernest Francisco (1853–1900)
East and West, *sels*.
Fuji at Sunrise.
Ode on Reincarnation, *sels*.
Wood Dove, The.

Fenollosa, Mary (1865–1954)
Miyoko San.
Yuki.

Fenton, James (b. 1949)
Ballad of the Shrieking Man, The.
Born Too Soon.
Cambodia.
Dead Soldiers.
For Andrew Wood.

German Requiem, A, *sel*.
God, A Poem.
Ideal, The.
In a Notebook.
In Paris with You.
Jerusalem.
Kingfisher's Boxing Gloves, The.
Let's Go Over It All Again.
Lines for Translation into Any Language.
Mistake, The.
Poem against Catholics.
Possibility, The.
Red Light District Nurse, The.
Skip, The.
Staffordshire Murderer, A.
This Octopus Exploits Women.
Tiananmen.
Wind: "This is the wind, the wind in a field of
   corn."

**Ferch Gruffyd ab Ieuan ap Llewelyn Fychan,
Alis (*fl.* 1540–70)**
Verses Written by Alis Daughter of Gryffydd
   Son of Iefan When Her Father Asked Her
   What Sort of Husband She Would Like.
When Her Father a Widower Asked What She
   Would Say to His Intention of Marrying a
   Young Girl.

**Ferch Gruffydd ab Ieuan ap Llywelyn Fychan,
Catrin (*fl.* 1555)**
Praise Poem to Christ, A.

Ferdowsi, Abulqâsem (941–1021)
I've worked, I've worked so hard; reading,
   reading.

Ferebee, Gideon
Fallen Bodies.
For My Mother Magnetic Poetry Series.
Refugee.

Ferguson, Gillian (b. 1965)
Fear of the Future.
Grey Kirk in the Mearns.
In Hospital-land.
Inhaling His Hair.
Scan.
Silent as Roses.
Slugs.
Swimming Pool Ghost, The.
Winter Rose, The.
Winter Sunflowers.

Ferguson, Gus (b. 1940)
Bhakti Yogi Buys a Bike, The.
Puncture Near Wittedrif.
Puritan against the Wind.

Ferguson, Sir Samuel (1810–86)
Lament for the Death of Thomas Davis.
Lark in the Clear Air, The.

Fergusson, Robert (1750–74)
Auld Reikie, a Poem, *sels*.
Braid Claith.
Daft Days, The.
Drinking Song.
To the Principal and Professors of the
   University of St Andrews, on their Superb
   Treat to Dr Samuel Johnson.

Ferlinghetti, Lawrence (b. 1919)
Adieu à Charlot.
At Kenneth Rexroth's.
Baseball Canto.
Buddha in the Woodpile, A.
Constantly Risking Absurdity.
Cro-Magnons.
Dark Portrait, A.
Dog.
Ecolog.
Extasis.
Green Street Mortuary Marching Band, The.
History of the Airplane.
In Golden Gate Park that day.
In Goya's greatest scenes we seem to see.
Lost Parents.
Millennium Cities.
Monet's Lilies Shuddering.
Old Italians Dying, The.
Oral Messages, *sel*.
Pennycandystore beyond the El, The.
People Getting Divorced.

Poem for Old Walt.
Retired Ballerinas, Central Park West.
River Still To Be Found, A.
Sometime During Eternity.
Starting from San Francisco.
Third World Calling.
21.
25.
#2.
Underwear.
Work-in-Progress, sel.
World is a beautiful place, The, sel.

Fermini, Ivano (b. 1948)
Detouring through the rooms were men and
    fumes.
First unexpected pain is beautiful, The.
It descends rapidly under the twistable vine in
    the sky.
Moments that hands without a vine...laughter.
Statue, The.
That bound and tied they fled.
Waiting for sleep at the air roots.
Wistaria-faced Visigoth, The.
You I know is losing you, The.

Fernandez, Maria
Broken Ends Broken Promises.

Fernández Retamar, Roberto
Man and a Woman, A.

Ferrari, Mary (b. 1928)
Eternity!
Ristorante San Marco, The.

Ferraz, Leila (b. 1944)
My Love, I Speak to You of a Love.

Ferré, Rosario (b. 1940)
Ballerina.
Message.
Opprobium.
You Have Lost, They Tell Me, Your Reason.

Ferrell, Monica (b. 1975)
Geburt des Monicakinds.
King with His Queen, The.
Myths of the Disappearance.
Stories from the Tower.

Ferril, Thomas Hornsby (b. 1896)
Jupiter at Beer Springs.
Noon.
Something Starting Over.
Waltz against the Mountains.

Ferry, David (b. 1924)
Anasazi drink from underground rivers, The.
Cythera.
Embarkation for Cythera, The.
Guest Ellen at the Supper for Street People,
    The.
He stands against what looks like the other
    side.
Photographs from a Book: Six Poems, sels.
Picture of Eakins and a couple of other people,
    A.
Plate 134. By Eakins. 'A cowboy in the West.'
Seen through a Window.
There is a strange, solemn, silent, graceless.

Ferry, Marcelle (d. 1992)
Frenzy, Sweet Little Child, You Sleep.
One Seated on the Stones of Cheops, The.
When He Went Away.
You Came Down from the Mountains.

Fetherston, Kate
Hating.

Fetter, Ted
Taking a Chance on Love.

Fevrî (d. 1570)
Arrow of your glance pierces my wounded,
    The.

Fiacc, Padraic (b. 1924)
British Connection, The.
Enemy Encounter.
First Movement.
Gloss.
Intimate Letter 1973.
Saint Coleman's Song for Flight/ An Ite Missa
    Est.
Soldiers.

Fiallo, Fabio (b. 1865)
Silence of Eyes, A.

Fichman, Jacob (1881–1958)
Eve.
Jerusalem.
Secrets of the Landscape, The.

Ficke, Arthur Davison (1883–1945)
Four Japanese Paintings, sels.
Opus 118.
Opus 131.
Sonnet: "There are strange shadows fostered of
    the moon."
Three Sisters, The.

Fickert, Kurt J.
Bad Weather at the Airport.

Ficowski, Jerzy
Assumption of Miriam from the Street in the
    Winter of 1942, The, sels.
Both Your Mothers.
Cogito Ergo.
Execution of Memory, The.
5.8.1942 / In Memory of Janusz Korczak.
Girl of Six from the Ghetto Begging in Smolna
    Street in 1942, A.
I Did Not Manage To Save.
I would like just to be silent.
Ovid Twice Exiled.
Pawiak 1943.
Seven Words, The.

Field, Anne Vavasour (b. c.1560, d. after 1622)
Thoughe I seem straunge sweete freende be
    thou not so.

Field, Barron (1786–1846)
Kangaroo, The.

Field, Edward (b. 1924)
Both My Grandmothers.
Bride of Frankenstein, The.
Callas.
Curse of the Cat Woman.
Farewell, The: "They say the ice will hold."
Graffiti.
Icarus.
Journey, A.
Lower East Side: The George Bernstein Story.
Mae West.
New Cycle, A.
New Yorkers.
Oh, the Gingkos.
Open Sesame.
Street Instructions at the Crotch.
Whatever Became Of: Freud?
World War II.

Field, Eugene (1850–95)
Duel, The.
Jest 'fore Christmas.
Little Boy Blue.
Mr. Billings of Louisville.
Piazza Tragedy, A.
Red.
Sugar-Plum Tree, The.
Wynken, Blynken, and Nod.

Field, Michael (Katherine Bradley and Edith
Cooper)
After Soufrière.
Ah, Eros doth not always smite.
Almoner, An.
Already to mine eyelids' shore.
And on My Eyes Dark Sleep by Night.
Aridity.
As two fair vessels side by side.
Atthis, my darling, thou did'st stray.
Beloved, My Glory in Thee is Not Ceased.
Beloved, Now I Love God First.
Bury Her at Even.
Climbing the hill a coil of snakes.
Come, Gorgo, put the rug in place.
Constancy.
Cyclamens.
Dying Viper, A.
Ebbtide at Sundown.
Elsewhere.
Embalmment.
Eros.
Fellowship.
Fifty Quatrains.

Flaw, A.
Girl, A.
Goad, The.
Gold Is the Son of Zeus: Neither Moth nor
    Worm May Gnaw It.
I Am thy Charge, thy Care!
I love you with my life.
I sing thee with the stock-dove's throat.
If They Honoured Me, Giving Me Their Gifts.
Irises.
It was deep April, and the morn.
La Gioconda; Leonardo Da Vinci, The Louvre.
Leaves.
Life Plastic.
L'indifférent.
Lo, my loved is dying, and the call.
Love rises up some days.
Loved, on a sudden thou didst come to me.
Lovers.
Maidenhair.
Maids, not to you my mind doth change.
Mummy Invokes His Soul, The.
Nests in Elms.
Nightfall.
Nought to me! So I choose to say.
O Wind, thou hast thy kingdom in the trees.
Onycha.
Palimpsest, A.
Penetration.
Picture, A.
Portrait, A.
Prometheus fashioned man.
Renewal.
Second Thoughts.
She is Singing to Thee, Domine!
'Sing to us Sappho!' cried the crowd.
So jealous of your beauty.
Sometimes I do despatch my heart.
Sullenness.
Sweet-Briar in Rose.
Sweeter Far than the Harp, More Gold than
    Gold.
Thanatos, Thy Praise I Sing.
They Shall Look on Him.
Tiger-Lilies.
To Christina Rossetti.
To the Lord Love.
To the Winter Aphrodite.
Tragic Mary Queen of Scots, The.
Tragic Mary Queen of Scots, II, The.
Trinity.
Unbosoming.
Wheat-miners.
Why should I praise thee, blissful Aphrodite?
Will You Crucify Your King?
Your Rose is Dead.

Field, Miranda (b. 1962)
Childhood's House.
Housefire.
Miraculous Image.
Scold's Mask.
Subway.

Field, Rachel Lyman (1894–1942)
Dancing Bear, The.
General Store.
Manhattan Lullaby.
Skyscrapers.
Some People.
Something Told the Wild Geese.
Summer Morning, A.

Field, Thalia (b. 1966)
Compass Room, The: East.

Fielding, Henry (1707–54)
Tom Thumb the Great, sels.

Fields, Annie (1834–1915)
Ephemeron.

Fields, Dorothy
Blue Again.
Bojangles of Harlem.
Don't Blame Me.
Fine Romance, A.
Have Feet, Will Dance.
I Can't Give You Anything but Love.
I Won't Dance.
I'm in the Mood for Love.

I'm Livin' in a Great Big Way.
It's All Yours.
Lovely to Look At.
Make the Man Love Me.
Never Gonna Dance.
On the Sunny Side of the Street.
Pick Yourself Up.
Remind Me.
There Must Be Somethin' Better Than Love.
Way You Look Tonight, The.
You Couldn't Be Cuter.

Fields, James Thomas (1817–81)
Alarmed Skipper, The.
Ballad of the Tempest.

Fields, Julia (b. 1938)
Citizen.
Jolly Fat Widows, The.

Fields, Rick
Very Short Sutra on the Meeting of the Buddha
and the Goddess, The.

Fife, Connie
Dear Webster.

Figani Ramazan Çelebi (1505–32)
My sad heart is burnt black in the fire.
Your kiss does not satisfy the heart.

Figueroa, Jose Angel (b. 1946)
Boricua.
Confessions from the Last Cloud.
Cowboynomics.
Felipa, La Filosofa de Rincon que Nació a los
98 Años.
Homemade Smiles.
Jelly Bean Policy, The.
Murdered Luggage.
Pablo Neruda.
Poet Pedro Pietri.
Puerto Rico Made in Japan.
Taino.

Fiksman, David Mironovich See Knut, Dovid

Filkova, Fedya (b. 1950)
Arrival: "Did you hear."
Buchenwald.
Friendship: "Death gives way sometimes."
Frost: "Hospital garden on Sunday, A."
Under a Wing.
Vulnerability.

Filliou, Robert
14 Songs and 1 Riddle, sel.

Filoktèt, Rene See Philoctete [or Filoktèt], René

Finch, Anne (b. 1908)
Dickinson.
For Grizzel McNaught (1709–1792).
Reply From His Coy Mistress, A.
Sapphics for Patience.

Finch, Annie (b. 1956)
Intellect of Woman, The.
Landing under Water, I See Roots.
Native American Birds, The.
Night Call.
Perdita's Song.

Finch, Mrs. B. (fl. 1805)
Written in a Shrubbery Towards the Decline of
Autumn.
Written in a Winter's Morning.

Finch, Eleanora Wyatt (late 1590s–1623)
Lady weare those bayes, you may.
'Tis true I weepe, I sigh, I wring my hands.
When I first was brought to light.

Finch, Francis Miles (1827–1907)
Blue and the Gray, The.

Finch, Peter (b. 1947)
Acer.
Fists.
How Callum Innes Paints.
Marks the English Left on the Map.
Reds in the Bed.
Scaring Hens.
Tattoo, The.
We Are in the Fields.
Welsh Wordscape, A.
Why Do You Want to Be English?

Finch, Robert (b. 1900)
Crib, The.
Egg-and-Dart.

Epitaph: "Here lies a man who was so bright."

Fincke, Gary
Class A, Salem, the Rookie League.

Fingueret, Manuela
86 Pasteur Corner.
Eve in Eden.
Games at the Hour of the Desert.
Genesis (Chapter 7, Verse 5).
Jerusalem.
Leviticus (Chapter 7, Verse 2-5).
My Father.
Psalms (Chapter 137, Verse 5-6).
Second Portrait.
Tovu-Vavohu.

Fink, Robert A.
Abilene, TX: We Pull Out For New England.
At Our Backs.
Atmosphere for Poetry in Abilene, The.
Aunt May.
Certified Public Accountant Recalls the Early
1950s, The.
Drought: Sure Signs in Merkle, Texas.
For Micha's Mother, Who Signs.
Mesquite.

Finkel, Donald (b. 1929)
Hound Song.
Metaphysic of Snow.
Party, The.

Finkelstein, Caroline (b. 1941)
Afterthought.
Casus Belli.
Not Responsible.
Persephone's Notes.

Finlay, Ian Hamilton (b. 1925)
Bedtime.
Boat's Blueprint, The.
Cloud's Anchor, The.
Evening—Sail.
Finlay's House (in Rousay).
Garden Poem.
Gift: "How silly and how dear, how very
dear."
Images from the Arcadian Dream Garden, sel.
Lackblockblackb.
O.H.M.S.

Finnell, Dennis
Over Voice of America.

Finney, Janice
Lightning and Thunder.

Finney, Nikky (b. 1957)
Fishing Among the Learned.
Lobengula: Having a son at 38.
Uncles.

Finnin, Olive Mary (b. 1906)
Man from Strathbogie, The.

Fiorentino, Jon Paul
Mission Street Song.
Prairie Long Poem.

Firdowsi (Abul Kasim Mansur) (940–1020)
Shahnamah, The, sels.
When the sword of sixty comes nigh his head.

Firer, Susan
Mrs. Post's 6th-Hour English Class.
1956, The Year My Sister, Using Her Ill Health
Once Again, Blackmailed My Parents into
an Accordion.
Peonies: "Young girls walk by looking like
wedding, The."
Saxophone Julie.

Fischer, Norman (b. 1946)
Favorable Prospects.
How the Mighty Have Fallen.
I've Changed.
Lotus Sutra.
Model of the Universe, A.
Poetry's a Way Not a Subject.
Sesshin Poem.
Slipped Away.
Success, sels.
Violence of Oneness, The.
When You Open the Gates.

Fisher, Aileen (b. 1906)
Cat in the Snow.
Caterpillars.

Fair Exchange.
Houses.
Listening.
Mouse Dinner.
On Mother's Day.
Thanksgiving Dinner.

Fisher, Aileen and Olive Rabe
Martin Luther King.
Pioneers.

Fisher, Allen (b. 1944)
African Boog.
Birdland.
Conga.
Continental Walk.
Emergent Manner, sels.
Stepping Out, sels.

Fisher, Catherine (b. 1957)
Frozen Tarn.
Severn Bore.
Those Who Make Paths.
Words.

Fisher, Diane Gilliam (b. 1957)
After the Miscarriage.
Sweet Hour.

Fisher, Doris (b. 1915)
Put the Blame on Mame.
That Old Devil Called Love.
Tired.

Fisher, Janet (b. 1943)
Camp.
Gooseflesh.
It's February But.
Life, A.
Pearls.
There are only so many words.

Fisher, John G. (fl. 19th cent.)
Back on the Job.

Fisher, Jonathan (b. 1970)
Six Part Lust Story.

Fisher, Lillian M.
Child of the Sun.
Pioneers.

Fisher, Mahlon Leonard (b. 1874)
In Cool, Green Haunts.

Fisher, Roy (b. 1930)
As He Came Near Death.
Burning Graves at Netherton, The.
City, sels.
Cut Pages, The, sels.
Entertainment of War, The.
Least, The.
Memorial Fountain, The.
Occasional Poem 7.1.72.
Rules and Ranges for Ian Tyson.
Sign Illuminated, A.
Supposed Dancer, The.
Thing About Joe Sullivan, The.
Toyland.

Fisher, Salih Michael (b. 1956)
Hometown.

Fishman, Charles
Blue Bicycles.
Whapmagoostui.

Fishman, Lisa (b. 1966)
Diagnosis: My Mother's Breast.
Promiscuity.
V's Farmhouse.

Fisk, Molly
Late Afternoon.
Red River.

Fisken, Thomas Scott
Window Box.

Fiskin, Jeffrey
Magi, The.

Fitnet Khanim (d. 1780)
In a heart that bears the image.

Fitts, Dudley (1903–68)
Ya Se Van Los Pastores.

Fitts, Susan Love
Anonymous: "To the Department of Motor
Vehicles."
Clearly Through My Tears.

Fitz-Simon, Ellen (1805–83)
Woods of Kylinoe, The: Song of the Irish
Emigrant in North America.

Fitzgerald, Edward (1809–83)
Old Song.
War begets Poverty.

Fitzgerald, F. Scott (Francis Scott Key Fitzgerald) (1896–1940)
Obit on Parnassus.

Fitzgerald, Francis Scott Key See Fitzgerald, F. Scott

Fitzgerald, John (b. 1927)
Being (Human).
God in Hiding, God of Faith.
Great Little One.
House Beyond, The.
There Is But One True Friend.

Fitzgerald, Robert (1910–85)
Amphibians.
Epiphany: "Unearthly lightning of presage."
Et Quidquid Aspiciebam Mors Erat.
Farewell.
Figlio Maggiore.
History.
Horae.
Manuscript with Illumination.
Metaphysical.
Mutations.
Pacific.
Souls Lake.
South Side.
Spring Shade.

Fitzgerald, Robert David (1902–87)
Copernicus.
Grace before Meat.
Wind at Your Door, The.

Fitzhardinge, Maurice Frederick Fitzhardinge Berkeley, 1st Baron (1788–1867)
Louis.

Fitzmaurice, Gabriel (b. 1952)
In the Midst of Possibility.

Fitzpatrick, Conal (b. 1951)
Discovering Lasseter.

Fitzpatrick, Kevin (b. 1949)
Highland, 1955.

Fitzpatrick, Ryan
Fine Occupation, A.

Flaccus, Aulus Persius See Persius

Flaccus, Gaius Valerius (d. c. 93–5)
Argonautica, The, sels.

Flaccus, Quintus Horatius See Horace

Flanagan, Dorothy Belle
Three Years from Sorrento.

Flanders, Jane (b. 1940)
Big Cars.
Cloud Painter.
Dandelion Greens.
Handbell Choir, The.
House That Fear Built: Warsaw, 1943, The.
Other Lives of the Romantics.
Planting Onions.
Twirling.

Flanders, Michael (1922–75)
Have Some Madeira, M'dear?

Flanner, Hildegarde (1899–1987)
Dumb.
Fern Song.
Frog Song.
Moment: "I saw a young deer standing."
Noon on Alameda Street.
Prayer: "With Him who sets the lily on the stem."
True Western Summer.

Flatman, Thomas (1637–88)
Appeal to Cats in the Business of Love, An.
Sad Day, The.
Thought of Death, A.

Flavell [or Lavell], Thomas (b. 1906)
County of Mayo, The.

Fleckenstein, Mark
Getting Even.

Flecker, James Elroy (1884–1915)
Ballad of Hampstead Heath, The.

Golden Journey to Samarkand, The, sels.
Hassan, sels.
Old Ships, The.
Rioupéroux.
Santorin.
Stillness.
Tenebris Interlucentem.
To a Poet a Thousand Years Hence.
Town without a Market, The.

Flecknoe, Richard (1600–78)
Ant, The.

Fleischman, Paul (b. 1952)
Fireflies.

Fleming, Marjory (1803–11)
Melancholy Lay, A.

Fleming, Paul (1609–40)
Concerning Himself.
Devotion.
How He Should Like to Be Kissed.
It Is in Vain, the Sorrow.
To Himself.
To the Great City of Moscow, as He Was Leaving June 25, 1636.
To the Moon.

Fleming, Robert (b. 1950)
For All Unwed Mothers.
Long Walk Home, The.
This Mortal Coil.

Fletcher, Giles, the Elder (c.1549–1611)
Crucify Him!
Licia, sel.

Fletcher, Giles, the Younger (1585–1623)
Christs Victorie, and Triumph in Heaven, and Earth, Over, and After Death, sel.
Christ's Victory and Triumph, sels.
To Whom Else Can We Fly?

Fletcher, John (1579–1625)
Beggar's Bush, sels.
Elder Brother, The, sels.
Faithful Shepherdess, The, sels.
Little French Lawyer, The, sels.
Lover's Progress, The, sels.
Nice Valor, The, sels.
Queen of Corinth, sel.
Take, Oh, Take Those Lips Away.
Tragedy of Valentinian, The, sels.
Women Pleased, sel.

Fletcher, John See Also Beaumont, Francis

Fletcher, John (1564–1616) and William Shakespeare
King Henry VIII, sels.
Two Noble Kinsmen, The, sels.

Fletcher, John Gould (1886–1950)
Before Olympus.
Blue Symphony.
Clipper-Ships.
Green Symphony.
Irradiations, sels.
Lincoln.
London Nightfall.
Rebel, A.
Skaters, The.

Fletcher, Louisa
Land of Beginning Again, The.

Fletcher, Phineas (1580–1650)
Against a Rich Man Despising Poverty.
Divine Wooer, The, sel.
Dying Husband's Farewell, The.
Hymn, An: "Wake, O my soul; awake, and raise."
Hymn: "Drop, drop, slow tears, and bathe those beauteous feet."
Locusts, or Appolyonists, The, sels.
Ocean of Light.
Purple Island, The, sels.
To Thomalin.

Flexner, Hortense King (b. 1885)
Contemporary.

Flint, James (1779–1885)
Metropolitan Metaphysics.

Flint, Roland
August from My Desk.
2-26-91.
Seasonal, 1991.

Flores, Jaime Shaggy
Last Visit to Chestnut Middle School.

Flores, Malva (b. 1961)
Casa nómada, sel.
Nomad House, sel.
Turbia dicción, sel.
Turbid Diction, sel.

Florian, Douglas (b. 1950)
First.
Send My Spinach.

Florián, Mario (b. 1917)
Pastora.

Florit, Eugenio (b. 1903)
Elegy for Your Absence.
Martyrdom of Saint Sebastian, The.
Present Evening, The.

Florsheim, Stewart (b. 1952)
Jewish Singles Event, The.

Flower, Robin Ernest William (1881–1946)
At Parting: "False love, since thou and I must sever."
Proud Lady, The.

Floyd-Miller, Cherryl "Blue"
Roots 1: big momma speaks to jimmy's wife.
Roots 2: the conjure woman replies.
She kneels at the wailing wall.
Taboo.

Flynn, Elizabeth (1890–1964)
After Grave Deliberation.

Flynn, Leontia
Brinkwomanship.
By My Skin.
Come Live with Me.
Furthest Distances I've Travelled, The.
Miracle of F6/18, The.
My Dream Mentor.
Myth of Tea Boy, The.
Naming It.
Perl Poem.
What You Get.
Without Me.

Flynn, Nick (b. 1960)
Bag of Mice.
Cartoon Physics, Part 1.
Cartoon Physics, Part 2.
Emptying Town.
Fragment (Found Inside My Mother).
God Forgotten.
Hive.
Swarm.
Workers (attendants).

Fodeba, Keita (1921–69)
And it's morning.

Foerster, Richard
Bronx Park.
Clearing, The: "Always in that clearing."
Failure of Similes, The.
Mozart's Death.
Petit Mal.
Playland.
Tantum Ergo.

Fogarty, Lionel (b. 1958)
Am I.
Biral Biral.
By Accident, Blinked.
Fuck All Departments.
Kath Walker.
Memo to Us (story).
No Grudge.
Remember Something Like This.

Fogdall, Kristin
Demas, in Love with This Present World.

Fogel, Aaron (b. 1947)
Printer's Error, The.
337,000, December, 2000.

Fogel, Alice B. (b. 1954)
Now and Then.

Fogel, Ephim G. (1920–92)
Shipment to Maidanek.

Foix, J. V. (1893–1987)
I Arrived in that Town, Everyone Greeted Me and I Recognized No One. When I Was Going to Read My Verses, the Devil, Hidden Behind a Tree, Called Out to Me

Sarcastically and Filled My Hands with
    Newspaper Clippings.
Sonnet: "Alone, in mourning, wearing an
    archaic black gown."
When I Sleep, Then I See Clearly.

Folade Mondisa Speaks
Tonal Embryology.

Foley, Helen (1896–1937)
Touch Wood.

Foley, Jack (b. 1940)
Eli, Eli.
Poet's Tango, The.
Prose for Two Voices.
Skeleton's Defense of Carnality, The.

Foley, Kate
Matching Flowers.
My Father, Counting Sheep.

Foley, Michael (b. 1947)
Brothers and Sisters.
Lucky Eugene.
Middle Manager in Paradise, The.
On the Waterfront.
Provincial Adolescence, A.
True Life Love Stories, *sels.*

Folger, Peleg (1734–89)
Praise Ye the Lord, O Celebrate His Fame.

Follain, Jean (1903–71)
Black Meat.
Bliss.
Buying.
Églogue: "Dans la maison refermée."
Eclogue: "In the closed house."
Face the Animal.
Félicité.
First Grade.
Hardware Store.
Landscapes They Walk Through, The.
Marshmallow Man, The.
Mirror, A.
Music of Spheres.
One Day I Suddenly Notice.
Pomme Rouge, La.
Quincaillerie.
Red Apple, The.
School and Nature.
She Stops Short.
Shops.
Should the Schoolboy Pull.
Speech Alone.
Taxidermist, A.
This Plant, So Exceptional.
Useful, The.
Women Say, The: 'It Looks Like Rain.'

Follen, Eliza Lee Cabot (1787–1860)
Children in Slavery.
For the Fourth of July.
Lines on Nonsense.

Follon, Cheryl (b. 1978)
Love Rats.

Fong, Herman (b. 1963)
Asylum.

Fontana, Jennie
Ask many women and they'll claim no
    knowledge, but some.

Fontanella, Luigi (b. 1943)
After the Party.
Father-Sequence.
For Emma.
I'm on a straight path with the sun gone down.
Image of the frozen lake, The.
In The Nighttime Someone.
It's a slow warmth I find once more.
Mimikòs.
Sleeplessness.
Transparent Life, The.
Turning of the car.
Victoria Station.

Foot, Edward Edwin (b. 1828)
Christening the Prince, *sels.*
Homeward-Bound Passenger Ship, The, *sels.*
Jane Hollybrand; or, Virtue Rewarded, *sels.*
Lisp in Numbers, A.

Foppa, Alaide (b. 1932)
First Portrait of My Son.

Nocturne.
Woman.
Wound.
Your Hand in Mine.

Forbes, Calvin (b. 1945)
Blue Monday.
Dark Mirror.
Gone.
Hand Me Down Blues.
Home.
Killer Blues.
My Father's House.
Picture of a Man.
Plea, The.
Poet's Shuffle, The.
Potlicker Blues.
Potter's Wheel, The.
Reading Walt Whitman.

Forbes, Duncan (b. 1947)
Forecast.
Recension Day.

Forbes, Jack
Something Nice.

Forbes, John (b. 1950)
Age of Plastic, The.
Angel.
Death, an Ode.
Love Poem.
Malta.
Monkey's Pride.
Speed, a Pastoral.
Up, Up, Home & Away.

Forbes, Lillias Scott (b. 1918)
Half-Inch Tweeddale, The.
Turning a Fresh Eye.

Forché, Carolyn (b. 1950)
Ancapagari.
As Children Together.
Colonel, The.
Elegy.
Garden Shukkei-en, The.
Kalaloch.
Memory of Elena, The.
Morning Baking, The.
Ourselves or Nothing.
Return.
Reunion.
Selective Service.
Skin Canoes.
Taking Off My Clothes.
Testimony of Light,The.
Visitor, The.

**Ford, Ford Madox (Ford Madox Hueffer) (1873–
1939)**
Antwerp, *sels.*
That Exploit of Yours.

Ford, John (1586–1640?)
Broken Heart, The, *sels.*
Lover's Melancholy, The, *sels.*

Ford, Katie (b. 1975)
Colosseum.
Flesh.
Hands of the Body Without the Body, and
    Nothing to Hold, The.
Nocturne: "I can see the whole city, lights
    edging the harbor like yellow pins in
    uneven."

Ford, Mark (b. 1962)
Early to Bed, Early to Rise.
Long Man, The.
Looping the Loop.

Ford, Simon (1619?–99)
London's Resurrection, *sel.*

Ford, Terri
Panty Raid.

Ford, Thomas (1580–1648)
There Is a Lady Sweet and Kind.

Ford, William (fl. 20th cent.)
Of Miles Davis.

Ford Lena, Guilbert (1870–1916)
Keep the Home Fires Burning (Till the Boys
    Come Home).

Fordham, Mary Weston (fl. c.1897)
Alaska.

Atlanta Exposition Ode.
Bells of St. Michael.
By the Rivers of Babylon.
Cherokee, The.
Chicago Exposition Ode.
Christ Child, The.
Coming Woman, The.
Creation.
Crucifixion, The.
Death of a Grandparent. Mrs. Jennette
    Bonneau.
Dedicated to the Right Rev'd D. A. Payne.
Dying Girl, The.
Exile's Reverie, The.
For Who?
Grafted Bud, The.
Highland Mary.
In Memoriam. Alphonse Campbell Fordham.
In Memoriam. Susan Eugenia Bennett.
June.
Lines to———.
Lines to Florence.
Lines to Mrs. Isabel Peace.
Magnolia.
Maiden and River.
Marriage.
Mother's Recall.
Mr. Edward Fordham.
Mrs. E. Cohrs Brown.
Mrs. Louise B. Weston.
Mrs. Mary Furman Weston Byrd.
Mrs. Rebecca Weston.
Nativity, The.
Nestle-down Cottage.
October.
Ode to Peace.
On Parting with a Friend.
Passing of the Old Year.
Past, The.
Pen, The.
Queenie.
Rally Song.
Requiem: "O, insatiable monster! Could'st thou
    not."
Rev. Samuel Weston.
Reverie, A.
Saxon Legend of Language, The.
Serenade: "Sleep, love sleep."
Shipwreck.
Snow Storm, The.
Snowdrop, The.
Song to Erin.
Sonnet to My First Born.
Stars and Stripes.
Sunset.
To a Loved One.
To an Infant.
To My Mother.
To Rev. Thaddeus Saltus.
To the Eagle.
To the Mock-Bird.
Tribute to a Lost Steamer.
Tribute to Capt. F. W. Dawson.
Twilight Musings.
Uranne.
Valentine, The.
Washerwoman, The.

Fore, Brian
They Told Me, Heraclitus.

Foreman, Paul (1919–2002)
Brazos de Dios.
Huddie Ledbetter.
Impressionist.
Pecans.

Forhan, Chris
Big Jigsaw.
Gouge, Adze, Rasp, Hammer.
My Gospel Is.
Taste of Wild Cherry, The.
Without Presumptions.

Forman, Ruth (b. 1968)
Abraham Got All the Stars n the Sand.
Green Boots n Lil Honeys.
Kin.
Someone.
This Poem.

Waitin on Summer.
We Are the Young Magicians.
Wedding.
You So Woman.

Forrest, George (1915–99)
And This Is My Beloved.
Baubles, Bangles, and Beads.
It's a Blue World.
Strange Music.
Stranger in Paradise.

Forrest-Thomson, Veronica (1947–75)
Garden of Proserpine, The.
In This House.
Lemon and Rosemary.
Michaelmas.
Not Pastoral Enough.
Pfarr-Schmerz (Village-Anguish).
Phrase-Book.
Richard II.
Sonnet: "My love, if I write a song for you."

Forrester, Stanford M. (b. 1963)
Autumn wind.
Backyard sun shower.
Daylight. . . / no one notices.
Dog shit.
End of summer.
Gray autumn sky.
How quickly.
Just within my reach the lightning bug turns
    off.
Meditation hall.
Melting into pure water the snow buddha.
Monk's bowl.
Morning light.
Only one flower.
Plum blossom breeze.
Stone, A / i saved.
Summer afternoon.
Sun on the windowsill.
Temple bell ringing.
Temple ruin.
Winter afternoon.
Winter wind.
Writing a haiku.

Forster, Edward Morgan (1879–1970)
I Strove with None.

Forsyth, Sarah
My Christmas; Mum's Christmas.

Fort, Charles
For Martin Luther King.

Fort, Paul (1872–1960)
Sailor and the Shark, The.

Forten, Sarah L. *See* "Ada" (Sarah Louisa Forten)

Fortes, Corsino (b. 1933)
Island.

Fortini, Franco (b. 1917)
Italy 1942.
Perhaps the Time of Blood.
Poetry of Roses, The.
Seed, The.

Foss, Phillip
Anascesis and Wreckage.
Overfire: Andante.

Foss, Sam Walter (1858–1911)
House by the Side of the Road, The.
"Hullo!"

Foster, Annie (b. 1955)
Ashes.
Caterpillar.
Field.
Gap, The.
God and the Holy Stones.
Nest of Hats, A.
No Dice.
Starting School.
Union.
Wythop Mill.

Foster, David (b. 1944)
Fleeing Atalanta, The, *sels.*

Foster, Jeanne
Seder.

Foster, Michael
Recruiting Song.

Foster, S. Conant (*fl.* 1880–84)
Boycycle, The.
From Out the Heated City.
To Flight.
Toasting Song.

Foster, Stephen Collins (1826–84)
Jeanie with the Light Brown Hair.
My Old Kentucky Home.
Oh! Susanna.
Old Folks at Home.

Foster, Tonya
Folktale, A: "Father stands on a walkway
    talking, A."
Grammar of Waking, A.

Fouad, Imad
Truth: I Have Five Fingers on Each Hand!

Fouché, Frank (1915–78)
What Did They Think They Did?

Fouilloux, Jacques du (1521?–80)
Blazon Pronounced by the Huntsman, The.

Foulcher, John (b. 1952)
After the Flood.
Wars of Imperialism.

Fourcade, Dominique (b. 1938)
Ensembles.
Ensembles.
Moral.
Mural.

Fournier, Rick
Encounter.

Foust, Graham (b. 1970)
On the Evening of a Wedding.

Fowler, William (1560–1612)
Ship-broken Men Whom Stormy Seas Sore
    Toss.
Tarantula of Love, The, *sel.*

Fox, Anne Valley (b. 1946)
After Seven Years.
Why She Suffers.

Fox, Sarah
Interruption.

Fox, Siv Cedering (b. 1939)
Almagest, Last Letter to Zakarias.
Grandmother.
In the Evening.
Miss Pimberton Of.
Peaches.

Fox, Skip
Another.
Economics of Metonymy ("Balancing as metal,
    its sound, the metal in its sound.").
Economics of Metonymy: sic transit.
I cannot observe myself unobserved.
In Referring to What Does Not Exist.
Most Notoriously Absent North American Bird
    in Her Face, The.
Perhaps the rain on the roof is some hyper-
    phrenetic code from Shadowland.
Sic transit gloria mundi.
Sic transit ("Kingfisher in highest cypress
    green.").
Sic transit ("Neither does the world answer
    but.").
Sic transit ("Thus does the sun.").
Sic Transit ("We who were alive, held you in
    arms, welcomed you to table, to.").

Foxe, Emma (d. 1570)
To you that lyfe possess grete troubles do
    befall.

Foy, James L.
Autopsy.

Frabotta, Biancamaria (b. 1946)
Dianae Sumus in Fide.
Dim Light Splits the Woods in Two Distinct
    Lines, The.
Erosion of Utopia or Rigor of Patience?
Heloise, *sel.*
It Is True. I Am Not a Poet the Way You Are.
Myopia.
Self-Portrait in the Third Person.
Shipwreck.

Fraire, Isabel (b. 1936)
Minute the sun comes out, The.

France, Linda (b. 1958)
Blues for Bird.
Body Language.
Chip City.
Eater of Wives, The.
Gentleness of the Very Tall, The.
If Love Was Jazz.
In Kind.
In the Waiting Room: "Consult your tongue
    like a weather forecast."
Mess With It.
Meteorology.
My Muse, the Whore.
New York Spring.
North and South.
On the Game, *sels.*
Stateless.
Zoology Is Destiny.

France, Peter
Death.

France de Bravo, Brandel
Unrepentant.

Francia, Luis H.
In Gurgle Veritas.
Is there There in dying.
Secret in the Roar, The.
Video Victim.

Francis, Arthur (fl. 1922)
Stairway to Paradise.

Francis, Marvin (1955–2005)
Sitting with My Uncle.
West Nile Crow.

Francis, Robert (b. 1901)
As Easily As Trees.
Base Stealer, The.
Bouquets.
Broken View, A.
Buzz Plane, The.
By Night.
Catch.
Coming and Going.
Curse, The.
Cypresses.
Earthworm.
Farm Boy after Summer.
Hogwash.
Hound, The.
Mouse Whose Name Is Time, The.
Museum Vase.
Night Train.
On a Theme by Frost.
Onion Fields.
Part for the Whole.
Pitcher, The.
Rock Climbers, The.
Slow.
Sound I Listened For, The.
Swimmer.
Three Woodchoppers.
Two Wrestlers.
Waxwings.
While I Slept.

Francis, Samuel Trevor (1834–1925)
O the deep, deep love of Jesus!

Francis, Vievee
First Stone, The.

Francis of Assisi, Saint (1181–1226)
Cantica: Our Lord Christ: Of Order.
Canticle of the Brother Sun, The.
Canticle of the Creatures.
Prayer of St. Francis of Assisi for Peace.

Francisco, Nia (b. 1952)
Kayenta Times Yet Dreaming On.
Modern on the Surface.
Roots of Blue Bells.
To a Man Who is Rob Southland.

Frankau, Gilbert (1884–1952)
Deserter, The.

Frankau, Ronald (1894–1951)
Thoughts While Broadcasting.

Frankétienne *See* Etienne, Frank

Franklin, Benjamin (1706–90)
Epitaph: "Body / of / Benjamin Franklin, The."

Franklin, Krista
  Tattooing the Motherline.
Fraser, George Sutherland (1915–80)
  Home Town Elegy.
  Lament: "In a dismal air; a light of breaking
    summer."
  Lean Street.
  Rostov.
  Traveller Has Regrets, The.
Fraser, Kathleen (b. 1937)
  Change of Address.
  History of My Feeling, The.
  One is whole. One is not.
  Re:searches (Fragments, after Anakreon, for
    Emily Dickinson).
Fraser, Sanford
  Elevator: "Passing my floor."
  Looking Out to Sea Again on the Uptown
    Express.
Frater, Hugh (1915–80)
  Wee Cock Sparra, The.
Frazier, John Alexander, Jr.
  Audre's Son.
  Deposed.
  Guard, A.
  Sorrow Song.
  Visiting Hours.
Freed, Arthur (1894–1973)
  All I Do Is Dream of You.
  Broadway Melody.
  Fit As a Fiddle.
  Good Morning.
  I Cried for You.
  I've Got a Feelin' You're Foolin.'
  Singin' in the Rain.
  This Heart of Mine.
  You Were Meant for Me.
Freed, Ralph (1907–73)
  Babes on Broadway.
  How About You.
  You Leave Me Breathless.
Freeman, Jan
  Autumn Sequence, sels.
Freeman, Jessica
  Bayou Arabic Argot.
  Customer #!
  Ewe's Candy Canes Red Sea Outerbank.
  Garden District Soubrette.
  Houseboat Ferry.
  Mourning dove ragpicks bargemen.
  November 1st.
  Part Evil.
  Slate Roof Blues.
  Up Tchoupitoulas Nom de Guerre.
Freeman, John (1880–1929)
  Asylum.
  Hounds, The.
  To End Her Fear.
Freer, Ulli (b. 1947)
  Dents, sel.
  Fragmento.
  TM.
Freisinger, Randall R.
  Walt Whitman at Timber Creek.
Frémon, Jean (b. 1946)
  Automne, L.'
  Autumn: "Shogun, always on the lookout for
    ways to increase his glory, The."
Frénaud, André (b. 1907)
  Création de soi, La.
  Paroles du poème, Les.
  Self-Creation.
  Toast en réponse.
  Toast in Response.
  Words of the Poem, The.
French, Nora May (1881–1907)
  Ave Atque Vale: "It gathers where the moody
    sky is bending."
  Mourner, The: "Because my love has wave and
    foam for speech."
French, Tom (b. 1966)
  Asperger Child.
  Ghost Ship.
  Holding the Line.

  No Man's Land.
  Pity the Bastards.
  Striking Distance.
  Touching the River.
French, William Percy (1854–1920)
  Mountains of Mourne, The.
  Queen's After-Dinner Speech, The.
Freneau, Philip (1752–1832)
  American Soldier, The.
  British Prison Ship, The, sel.
  Epitaph for Jonathan Robbins.
  George the Third's Soliloquy, sel.
  House of Night, The, sels.
  Hurricane, The.
  Indian Burying Ground, The.
  Jeffery, or, the Soldier's Progress.
  Libera nos, Domine—Deliver Us, O Lord.
  New York Tory, to His Friend in Philadelphia,
    A.
  On Mr. Paine's Rights of Man.
  On Observing a Large Red-Streak Apple.
  On the Civilization of the Western Aboriginal
    Country.
  On the Conflagrations at Washington.
  On the Emigration to America [and Peopling
    the Western Country].
  On the Great Western Canal of the State of
    New York.
  On the Religion of Nature.
  On the Uniformity and Perfection of Nature.
  To a New England Poet.
  To an Author.
  To Mr. Blanchard, the Celebrated Aeronaut in
    America.
  To Sir Toby.
  Vanity of Existence, The.
  Wild Honey Suckle, The.
Frere, John Hookham (1769–1846)
  Fable, A.
  Prospectus and Specimen of an Intended
    National Work by William and Robert
    Whistlecraft...Relating to King Arthur and
    His Round Table, sel.
  Rovers, The; or, The Double Arrangement,
    sels.
  Whistlecraft, sels.
Frere, John Hookham See Also Canning [with
  George Ellis and John Hookham Frere],
  George
Frere, John Hookham See Also Canning [with
  John Hookham Frere], George
Frezza, Luciana (b. 1926)
  Against the Current.
  Eurydice.
  Old Dedication.
  Places.
  Smile, The.
  Summer.
  To Allen Ginsberg & Co.
  Work.
Fried, Barbara (b. 1924)
  Good Old Days, The.
Fried, Daisy
  She Didn't Mean to Do It.
  Story Having to Do with Walt Whitman, A.
Fried, Elliot (b. 1944)
  Chain Mail.
  Marvel Mystery Oil.
  Why I Want to Be the Next Poet Laureate.
  Wordsworth's Socks.
Fried, Erich (b. 1921)
  Conversation with a Survivor.
  Exile.
  Invitation to Forget.
  Logos.
  Measures Taken, The.
  My Girlfriends.
  Naturalization.
  One Kind of Freedom Speaks.
  Retrospect.
  What Happens.
  What Things Are Called.
Fried, Michael (b. 1939)
  Next Bend in the Road, The.
  Send-Off, The.

Fried, Philip (b. 1945)
  Early, Late.
Friedlaender, Violet Helen
  Progress: "There was a time when peace at
    evening."
Friedlander, Ben
  Dick Cheney's Heart.
  L. B. J. Tapes, The.
  State of the Union.
Friedman, Betsalel (1897–1941)
  Scottsboro.
Friedman, Ed
  Cultivation.
  Heading for Manhattan by Train.
  Isolated Bourgeoisie.
  Mao & Matisse.
Friedmann, Pavel (1921–44)
  Butterfly, The.
  Butterfly, The.
Fries, Kenny (b. 1960)
  Healing Notebooks, The, sels.
Friesen, Patrick (b. 1946)
  Anna, sels.
  Clearing Poems, sels.
  Moon in the streets, The.
  Pa Poem 1: Firstborn.
  Pa Poem 4: Naked and Nailed.
Friman, Alice (b. 1933)
  Diapers for My Father.
  Honeymoon.
  Ophelia.
  Trip to Delphi.
Frishberg, Dave (b. 1933)
  Another Song About Paris.
  I'm Hip.
  Peel Me a Grape.
  Van Lingle Mungo.
Fritz, Walter Helmut
  Almost Bashfully.
  Atlantis.
  Columbus.
  Fiasco, The.
  Labyrinth.
  Love Poem (2): "Because you turn."
Frost, Carol
  Being.
  Chimera.
  Consent.
  Custom.
  Fury.
  Homo Sapiens.
  Laws.
  Papilio.
  Part of the Bee's Body Embedded in the Flesh,
    The.
  Refusal.
  St. Louis Zoo, The.
  Scorn.
  Sexual Jealousy.
  Sin: "Tree bore the efflorescence of October
    apples, The."
  Telling the Bees.
  To Kill a Deer.
  Undressing, The.
Frost, Frances Mary (1905–59)
  Deserted Orchard.
Frost, Katherine
  Remission.
  Winners.
Frost, Richard (b. 1929)
  Fifteen: "Late that summer my girlfriend's
    boyfriend."
  First Haircut.
  Marriage: "First, it was the common magic."
  Night Person, The.
Frost, Robert (1874–1963)
  Acceptance.
  Acquainted with the Night.
  After Apple-Picking.
  Aim Was Song, The.
  All Revelation.
  America Is Hard to See.
  Answer, An.
  At Woodward's Gardens.

Bear, The.
Bearer of Evil Tidings, The.
Bereft.
Beyond Words.
Birches.
Black Cottage, The.
Bond and Free.
Brown's Descent; or, The Willy-Nilly.
Cabin in the Clearing, A.
Canis Major.
Choose Something like a Star.
Clear and Colder.
Cliff Dwelling, A.
Code, The.
Come In.
Considerable Speck, A.
Cow in Apple Time, The.
Death of the Hired Man, The.
Departmental.
Desert Places.
Design.
Directive.
Draft Horse, The.
Drumlin Woodchuck, A.
Dust of Snow.
Egg and the Machine, The.
Ends.
Fire and Ice.
Fireflies in the Garden.
Flower-Boat, The.
For John F. Kennedy; His Inauguration.
For Once, Then, Something.
Forgive, O Lord, my little jokes on Thee.
Freedom of the Moon, The.
From Plane to Plane.
Gift Outright, The.
Good Hours.
Happiness Makes Up in Height for What It
   Lacks in Length.
Hill Wife, The, *sels.*
Hillside Thaw, A.
Home Burial.
Hyla Brook.
Immigrants.
In a Poem.
In White.
In winter in the woods alone.
Investment, The.
It takes all sorts of in- and outdoor schooling.
Last Word of a Bluebird, The.
Leaf-Treader, A.
Lockless Door, The.
Lost in Heaven.
Lovely Shall Be Choosers, The.
Lucretius versus the Lake Poets.
Master Speed, The.
Meeting and Passing.
Mending Wall.
Minor Bird, A.
Moon Compasses.
Most of It, The.
Mowing.
My November Guest.
Need of Being Versed in Country Things, The.
Neither Out Far Nor In Deep.
Never Again Would Birds' Song Be The Same.
Not to Keep.
Nothing Gold Can Stay.
Objection to Being Stepped On, The.
Old Man's Winter Night, An.
On a Bird Singing in its Sleep.
On a Tree Fallen Across the Road (To Hear Us
   Talk).
On the Heart's Beginning to Cloud the Mind.
Once by the Pacific.
One More Brevity.
Onset, The.
Out, Out—.
Oven Bird, The.
Pasture, The.
Patch of Old Snow, A.
Peaceful Shepherd, The.
Prayer in Spring, A.
Provide, Provide.
Putting in the Seed.
Questioning Faces.

Range-finding.
Reluctance.
Revelation.
Road Not Taken, The.
Rose Family, The.
Runaway, The.
Sand Dunes.
Semi-Revolution, A.
Silken Tent, The.
Sitting by a Bush in Broad Daylight.
Sound of Trees, The.
Spring Pools.
St. Luke, *sel.*
Star in a Stoneboat, A.
Stopping by Woods on a Snowy Evening.
Storm Fear.
Strong Are Saying Nothing, The.
Subverted Flower, The.
Ten Mills, *sels.*
To Earthward.
Tree at My Window.
Tuft of Flowers, The.
Two Look at Two.
Two Tramps in Mud Time.
Two Witches, *sels.*
U. S. 1946 King's X.
Unharvested.
West-Running Brook.
Wind and Window Flower.
Wood-Pile, The.
Young Birch, A.

Fructuoso, Eric
   Astig.

Frumkin, Gene
   Bad Dream and the Friend.
   Escalator.
   Falling into Meditation.
   Life of Eternity, The.
   Surreal Love Life.

Fry, Caroline (1787–1846)
   Dog of St. Bernard's, The.

Frydman, Anne *See* Valentine, Jean

Frym, Gloria (b. 1947)
   Mind Over Matter, *sel.*

Fu Hsüan (d. 278)
   Pity Me!

Fu, Huan (Ch'en Ch'ien-wu) (b. 1922)
   Don't, Don't.
   Flower.

Fuertes, Gloria (b. 1920)
   Amor Te Convierte, El.
   Birds Nest.
   Climbing.
   Cosas, Las.
   Desconocido Atrae También a los Cobardes,
      Lo.
   Escalando.
   Flacas Mujeres, Las.
   Love Turns You into a Rosebush.
   Oración: "Que estás en la tierra, Padre
      nuestro."
   Pájaros Anidan, Los.
   Painted Windows.
   Plastic Virgin.
   Prayer: "You are here on earth, our Father."
   Scrawny Women, The.
   Things.
   Unknown Also Attracts Cowards, The.
   Ventanas Pintadas.
   Virgen de Plástico.

Fugai (*fl.* 17th cent.)
   Only the Zen-man knows tranquillity.

Fuhaku (1714–1807)
   So very still, even.

Fuhrman, Joanna (b. 1972)
   Atlantis.
   Evidence.
   Here, I Say.
   How Many More Minutes Until We Can
      Devour Our Breached Contract?
   Personal Ad.
   Return to Normalcy.
   Watching Trains.

Fujii Sadakazu (b. 1942)
   Where is Japanese Poetry?, *sels.*

Fujita, Jun (1888–1963)
   Chicago River.
   Michigan Boulevard.

Fujiwara no Teika (1162–1241)
   After his tryst.
   Those long black tresses.
   Weary wild geese who came.

Fujiwara no Yasusue
   Nothing Whatsoever.

Fuller, Cynthia (b. 1948)
   Guests.
   My Father's Dreams.

Fuller, Heather
   Comic.
   Day Labor.
   Multiple-Theater.

Fuller, Hugh
   To a Tropic Reef.

Fuller, John (b. 1937)
   Born Too Soon.
   Butterfly, The.
   De Sade.
   God Bless America.
   Poem against Catholics.
   Red Light District Nurse, The.
   Whole New Scene, A.
   Wild Raspberries.

Fuller, Margaret (1810–50)
   Flaxman.
   Let Me Gather from the Earth.
   Lines Written in Boston on a Beautiful
      Autumnal Day.
   Meditations.
   One in All, The.
   Sistrum.
   Winged Sphinx.

Fuller, Margaret Witter (1872–1954)
   To A.H.B.

Fuller, Roy (b. 1912)
   Autobiography of a Lungworm.
   Autumn 1942.
   Cancer Hospital, The, *sels.*
   Christmas Day.
   Coptic Socks.
   Crustaceans.
   Death.
   In Africa.
   Middle of a War, The.
   Sonnet: "Crumbled rock of London is dripping
      under, The."
   What Is Terrible.

Fullerton, Mary Elizabeth ("E.") (1868–1946)
   Man's [a] Sliding Mood, A.
   Poetry.
   St. John, *sels.*
   Unit.

Fulson, Lowell (1921–99)
   Check Yourself.

Fulton, Alice (b. 1952)
   About Face.
   A.M.: The Hopeful Monster.
   Doing the Evolution Shuffle.
   Fierce Girl Playing Hopscotch.
   Fix.
   Give: A Sequence Reimagining Daphne &
      Apollo, *sels.*
   It might mean immersion, that sign.
   Little Heart to Heart with the Horizon, A.
   My Second Marriage to My First Husband.
   New Release, A.
   News of the Occluded Cyclone.
   Some Cool.
   Supernal.
   Take: A Roman Wedding.
   What I Like.
   Wonder Bread.
   Wonder Stings Me More than the Bee, *sels.*

Fulton, Robin (b. 1937)
   End of an Age, The.
   Forecast for a Quiet Night.
   Note for Robert Henryson, A.

Fumi Saito (b. 1909)
As a landscape in the far distance.
Lit up.
Palm of the hand, The / Is not aware of dying as.
With wings that will not ever.
Fumon (1302–69)
Magnificent! Magnificent!
Funkhouser, Erica
Lilies.
Furber, Douglas
Lambeth Walk.
Me and My Girl.
Furberg, Jon (1944–92)
Blōdmōnath.
Nightspell.
Furey, Tseverin
Verse for First.
Furnival, Christine (b. 1931)
Rhiannon.
Fusselman, Amy
Journal.
Mother Nature.
Puffy Jacket.
Sleeper.
Ticker.
Füst, Milán (1888–1967)
Death of Sagittarius.
Drunken Merchant, The.
Ghost Street.
If I Have to Yield My Bones.
Letter about Horror, A.
Mississippi.
Old Age.
Self-Portrait.
Winegrower, The.
Futuransky, Luisa
Israel Revisited.
Jerusalem, a Whirling Glass.
Jerusalem, Timeless.
More Chagall than Chagall.
Twenty Years From Auschwitz, Bergen-Belsen and Other Camps.
Fuyo-Dokai (1042–1117)
Seventy-six: done.
Fuzuli (1495–1556)
For long years we have been haunting the quarter.
I reap no gains but trouble at your place when I come near.
If my heart were a wild bird, it would nest.
Oh God, don't let anyone be like me.
Pointed reproach of the enemy, The.
Fychan, Anne (fl. 1688)
On the Seven Bishops.
Fyfe, Anne-Marie
Upturn.
Fyleman, Rose (1877–1957)
Cat, The.
Goblin, The.
(Mice).
Punch and Judy.
Solo with Chorus.

G

Gabrielian, Nina (b. 1953)
Erebuni, sels.
Phoenician Statuette, A.
Tortoise.
Gach, Gary
Inflight.
Gaffarel, Jacques
Celestial Alphabet Event.
Gahagan, Judy
Colour of the Old Man's Eyes, The.
Gahan, Carmel (b. 1950)
Asking for It.
Gaines, Reg E. (b. 1954)
Kill the Dj.
Gaitán Durán, Jorge (1924–62)
They Unite Naked.

Gaius Valerius Catullus See Catullus
Galanskov, Yury [or Iurii] Timofeievich (1939–72)
Bird-cherry was my wife, The.
I am in pain.
Intellectual, The.
It shames one to look.
Last Platform, The.
Murder.
Galassi, Jonathan (b. 1949)
Argument.
Siren.
Gale, Norman (b. 1862)
Country Faith, The.
Galeano, Juan Carlos (b. 1958)
Eraser.
Tree: "Man in love with a tree goes to live with him awhile before getting married, A."
Galef, David (b. 1929)
Bicycle Race in *Beowulf*, The.
Galemire, Julia
Inventing Fables about the Stone.
Galich, Aleksandr Arkadevich (1919–77)
Goldminers' Waltz, The.
Hospital Gypsy Song.
Galina, Mariya (b. 1958)
Ghazal: "For the sake of a Turkish woman from Shiraz, consumed in the deadly fumes."
I said to him—Just don't throw me into that briar patch.
What, in July's honey heat, do you weep for, poor goy.
Galindo, David Escobar (b. 1943)
Short Story, A.
Gallagher, Katherine (b. 1935)
Distances.
Girl's Head, A.
Gallagher, Tess (b. 1943)
Black Silk.
Choices.
Coming Home.
Crazy Menu.
Even Now You Are Leaving.
Fresh Stain.
Heart-Mirror.
Hug, The.
I Stop Writing the Poem.
Kidnap[p]er.
Little Invitation in a Hushed Voice.
Mixed.
Monologue at the Chinook Bar and Grill.
Not a Sparrow.
Not There.
On Your Own.
Sah Sin.
Sea Inside the Sea.
Sudden Journey.
3 A.M. Kitchen: My Father Talking.
Trace, In Unison.
Un Extraño.
Unanswered Letter.
Unsteady Yellow.
Valentine Delivered by a Raven.
Wake.
Widow in Red Shoes.
Yes.
Gallaher, Cynthia
Deb at the Ham Slicer.
Gallico, Paul (1897–1976)
Application.
Confession.
Galloway, Ted B.
Whiffenpoof Song.
Gallup, Dick (b. 1941)
Backing into the Future.
Guard Duty.
Pretty Beads.
Struggle for the Border, The.
Galvez, Carol Fonesca
Creation Continues.
Galvin, Brendan (b. 1938)
Bullfrog.
Cougar.

For a Daughter Gone Away.
Inside Job, An.
Knot Hole Gang, The.
Mail from Right Here, The.
Returning a Lawn to the Field It Was.
Running.
Galvin, James (b. 1951)
Art Class.
Dear Nobody's Business.
Independence Day, 1956: A Fairy Tale.
Indirective.
Little Dantesque.
Nature, Beside Herself.
On Exploration.
Post-Modernism.
Shadow-Casting.
Station (1).
Station (2).
Station (4).
Stories Are Made of Mistakes.
Story of the End of the Story, The.
Two Horses and a Dog.
Galvin, Patrick (b. 1927)
With My Little Red Knife.
Gamalinda, Eric
Denials.
La Naval De Manila: Selim Sot as a Modern Political Observer.
Lament Beginning w/a Line after Cavafy.
Light Falls Obliquely.
Opposite of Nostalgia, The.
Gambino, Erica Lynn
This Is Just to Say.
Gan Bao (fl. 315)
Grave Wedding of Lu Chong.
Gander, Forrest (b. 1956)
Deflection Toward the Relative Minor.
Macula of Light, A.
Mission Thief.
Sinister.
Gandlevsky, Sergey (b. 1952)
Dear God, allow me to recall my works.
Is it time to change the record? But I'm dreaming again.
Oh, how the lilacs are this May! Bulging-large bunches fell.
There's our street, let's say.
Ganev, Nedelcho (b. 1944)
Further.
Height.
Matter.
Soul, The: "Flame is full, The."
Verb, The.
Gangemi, Kenneth
Notes on a Moonwatcher.
Gangopadhyay, Sunil (b. 1934)
Blindfold.
From Athens to Cairo.
Gannon, Kim (1900–74)
Dreamer's Holiday, A.
Moonlight Cocktail.
Reciprocity.
Gannon, Thomas
Meeting the Master.
Garay, János (1812–53)
King Matthias in Gömör.
Old Veteran and Napoleon, The.
Garboushian, Kristi (b. 1968)
Ribbon on Hell's Tree, The, sels.
García, Diana
Clog of Her Body, The.
Curandera, La.
Green Corn Season.
Matter of Control, A.
Orchard of Figs in the Fall, An.
Other Marías.
Serpentine Voices.
Squaring the Names.
Tísica.
Turns at the Dance.
Garcia, Edward H.
Chicana.
García, Jesse F.
Barrio Beateo.

I Ain't Going to Hurry No More.

Garcia, Richard
Book of Dreams, The.
Brief Entanglements.
Chickens Everywhere.
Dangerous Hats.
Death in Larkspur Canyon, A.
Diver for the NYPD Talks to His
    Girlfriend, A.
Elite Syncopations.
Los Amantes.
Mi Mamá, the Playgirl.
Nobody Here But Us.
Note Folded Thirteen Ways.
Story of Keys, The.
Vernon.
Why I Left the Church.
Zapato, El.

Garcia-Camarillo, Cecilio
Chivo.
Dream 8.
Family Photographs.
Rancho.

García Lorca, Federico (1895–1936)
Amparo.
Arrest of Antoñito el Camborio.
August: "August. / The opposing."
Ballad of Black Grief.
Ballad of One Doomed to Die.
Boy Unable to Speak, The.
Canciones para Terminar, *sels.*
Casida of Sobbing.
Casida of the Dark Doves.
Casida of the Rose.
City That Does Not Sleep.
Ciudad sin Sueño. Nocturno del Brooklyn
    Bridge.
Death of Antoñito el Camborio.
Elegy for Joan the Mad One.
Faithless Wife, The.
Gacela of Unforeseen Love.
Gacelas, *sel.*
Ghazal of the Dark Death.
Ghazal of the Terrifying Presence.
Gráfico de la Petenera, *sels.*
Guitar, The.
Lament for Ignacio Sánchez Mejías.
Lament for Ignacio Sánchez Mejías.
Lament for Ignacio Sanchez Mejias, *sels.*
Lament for Ignacio Sánchez Mejias, *sel.*
Little Ballad of the Three Rivers.
Little Infinite Poem.
Little Mute Boy, The.
Llanto por Ignacio Sánchez Mejías, *sels.*
Malaguena.
Moon Sails Out, The.
My Little Girl Went to the Sea.
New York.
Night (Suite for Piano and Poet's Voice), *sels.*
1910.
Niño Mudo, El.
Nueva York. Oficina y Denuncia.
Ode to Walt Whitman ("Along the East River
    and the Bronx.").
Poet in New York, *sel.*
Portrait of Silverio Franconetti.
Preciosa and the Wind.
Quarrel.
Quarrel, The.
Questions: "Parliament of grasshoppers is in
    the field, A."
Reyerta.
Romance Somnambulo by Garcia Lorca.
Rundown Church (Ballad of the First World
    War).
Second Anniversary.
Six Strings, The.
Sleepwalkers' Ballad.
Sleepwalkers' Ballad.
Sleepwalking Ballad, The.
Somnambulist Ballad.
Sonetos del Amor Oscuro [Sonnets of Dark
    Love], *sels.*
Song of the Barren Orange Tree.
Song of the Cuban Blacks.
Song of the Rider.

Song of the Rider ("Córdoba. / Distant and
    alone.").
Song of the Sterile Orange Tree.
Song Wants to Be Light, The.
Sonnet of Sweet Complaint.
Spring Song.
Teorías, *sel.*
Thamar and Amnon ("Moon turns in the sky,
    The.").
Tres Ciudades, *sels.*
Unfaithful Married Woman, The.
Unfaithful Wife, The.
Unfaithful Wife, The.
Unfaithful Wife, The.

Garcilaso de la Vega, Baldomero (1503?–36)
Eclogue 1, *sel.*
First Eclogue, *sel.*
I Came to a Valley in the Wilderness.
Nemoroso.
One Moment My Hope Rises Up On Wings.
Rough Are the Roads.
Song 3: "Surrounded by the gentle sound."
Sonnet 5.
Sonnet 10: "Oh, sweet gifts brought forth for
    my misfortune."
Sweet Gifts.
While There Is Still the Color of a Rose.
Your Face Is Written in My Soul.

Gardelle, Charlotte (b. 1879)
Air.
Peaceful Sunday.
Rain.

Gardiner, Sam (b. 1936)
Brought Up.
Cactus.
Colorado Desert Night.
Door Shed, The.
Flight.
Identity Crisis.
No Title.
Second Person.

Gardinet, Carlos Omar
Wet Dream.

Gardinier, Suzanne (b. 1961)
Admirals (Columbus).
At Work.
Blues.
Democracy.
Ghost of Santo Domingo, The.
Letter to My Mother.
Memorials: "Walt Whitman I lay on the grass
    today."
To Peace.
Two Girls.
Where Blind Sorrow Is Taught to See.

Gardner, Isabella (1915–81)
In the Museum.
Milkman, The.

Gardner, John (1933–82)
Feat of Gardening, The, *sels.*

"Gardons, S. S." *See* Snodgrass, W. D. (William
    DeWitt)

Garelli, Jacques (b. 1931)
Démesure de la Poésie.
Excess of Poetry.

Garfitt, Roger
Rarest of the esculents, its distribution.

Gargulinski, Ryn
We.

Garioch, Robert (Robert Sutherland) (1909–81)
Campidoglio.
Did Ye See Me?
Elegy: "They are lang deid, folk that I used to
    ken."
Fair Cop, A.
I Was Fair Beat.
Judgment Day.
Maple and the Pine, The.
Nemo Canem Impune Lacessit.
1941.
Phooie!
Property.
Sanct Christopher II.
Wire, The.

Garland, Hamlin (1860–1940)
Boyish sleep.
Do You Fear the Wind?
Fighting Fire.
In August.
Indian Summer.
Mountains Are a Lonely Folk, The.
On the Mississippi.
Plowing: A Memory.

Garlick, Raymond (b. 1926)
Ancestors.
Anthem for Doomed Youth.
Behind the Headlines.
Capitals.
Consider Kyffin.
Dylan Thomas at Tenby.
Heiress, The.
Map Reading.
Note on the Iliad.
Poetry of Motion, The.
Still Life.

Garman, Douglas (*fl.* 1920–30)
Ode on the Death of Haig's Horse, *sel.*

Garner, Alan (b. 1934)
Summer Solstice.

Garner, Peter (b. 1965)
Lucy, *Lucie.*

Garnett, Ruth (b. 1954)
Barrage.
Concerning Violence.
Dealing Scraps.

Garren, Christine
Figure and Ground.

Garrett, Edward Cortez
Bachelors, The.
Grandfather's Mint.

Garrett, Elizabeth (b. 1958)
Airborne.
Anatomy of Departure.
Contrary Motion.
Double.
History Goes to Work.
I am the difficult silk that slides from your
    grasp.
Lost Property.
Love's Parallel.
Mimesis.
Miser.
Moules à la Marinière.
Reprieve, The.
Ribes rubrum.
Tyranny of Choice.
Unguentarium.
Vista.
Womanhood, The.

Garrett, George (b. 1929)
Crows at Paestum.
Envoy: "Little poem, the two of us know too
    much."
For a Bitter Season.
Luck's Shining Child.
Old Slavemarket: St. Augustine, Fla.
Pastoral: "Ghosts of summer learn, The."
Rugby Road.

Garrick, David (1716–79)
Heart of Oak.
On Oliver Goldsmith.
On Sir John Hill, M. D., Playwright.

Garrigue, Jean (1914–72)
After Reading "The Country of the Pointed
    Firs"
Amsterdam Letter.
Bad Times Song.
Cracked Looking Glass.
Dialog.
Grand Canyon, The.
Grenoble Café.
Movie Actors Scribbling Letters Very Fast in
    Crucial Scenes.
Song in Sligo.
To Speak of My Influences.

Garrison, Deborah (b. 1965)
Fight Song.
I Saw You Walking.

Worked Late on a Tuesday Night.

Garry, Flora (1900–2000)
Professor's Wife, The.
Rostov-on-Don.

Garshman, Barbara J.
Keys.

Garth, Sir Samuel (1661–1719)
Dispensary, The.
What Frenzy Has of Late Possess'd the Brain.

Garza, Danusha Laméris de
Act One.

Garza, Eliza
Why I Make the Best Barrels.

Gasan (1275–1365)
Invaluable is the Soto Way.

Gascoigne, George (1539–77)
Adventures of Master F. I, The, *sel.*
De Profundis, *sels.*
For That He Looked Not upon Her.
Fruits of War, The, *sels.*
Gascoigne's Good-Morrow.
Gascoigne's Memories, *sels.*
Gascoigne's [or Gascoygnes] Good-Night.
Gascoigne's Woodmanship.
Gloze Upon This Text, *Dominus iis opus habet,* A.
Green Knight's Farewell to Fancy, The.
Lullaby [or Lullabie] of a Lover, The.
Magnum Vectigal Parsimonia.
Steele Glas, The, *sel.*

Gascoyne, David
De Profundis.
Miserere, *sels.*
Night Thoughts, *sels.*
Rex Mundi.
Snow in Europe.
Uncertain Battle, The.
Wartime Dawn, A.
Yves Tanguy.

Gashe, Marina
Village, The.

Gaskill, Clarence (1892–1948)
I Can't Believe That You're in Love with Me.
Minnie, the Moocher.
Prisoner of Love.

Gaspar, Frank (b. 1946)
Part of What I Mean.
Tree, The.

Gaspar, Lorand (b. 1925)
Flute Player.
Joueur de flûte.
Late Minoan I: (Ewers of Hagia Triada).
Minoen récent 1 (Aiguières d'Hagia Triada).

Gaspar de Alba, Alicia
Elemental Journey: Anniversary Gift, *sels.*
Making Tortillas.

Gassner, Herbert (b. 1955)
Fear: "Fear of the icy moon."

Gates, Beatrix (b. 1949)
Triptych, *sels.*

Gates, Ellen M. Huntington (1835–1920)
My Mother's Hands.

Gatina, Dina (b. 1981)
I'm being stalked by a bird.
My eyes are.

Gautier, Théophile (1811–72)
Art.
Carmen.
Unknown Shores.

Gay, Garry (b. 1951)
Bald tire.
Family reunion.
Hole in the ozone.
New snow.
Slowly. . . / The Scarecrow.

Gay, John (1685–1732)
Acis and Galatea: An English Pastoral Opera, *sels.*
Beggar's Opera, The, *sels.*
Birth of the Squire; an Eclogue, The.
Fable XXI: The Rat-catcher and Cats.
Fables, *sels.*
Fables: First Series, *sels.*

Fables: Second Series, *sels.*
Molly Mog [or The Fair Maid of the Inn].
Mr. Pope's Welcome from Greece.
My Own Epitaph.
Rural Sports.
To a Lady.
To a Young Lady, with Some Lampreys.
To My Ingenious and Worthy Friend William Lowndes, Esq.
Trivia; or, The Art of Walking the Streets of London, *sels.*
Two Monkeys, The.

Gay, Noel (1898–1954)
Lambeth Walk.
Leaning on a Lamppost.
Me and My Girl.

Gbadamosi, Gabriel (b. 1961)
Death of the Polar Explorers.
Reading, The.
Sango, *sel.*

Gebeyli, Claire (b. 1930)
Beirut.
Man Is Dead, A.

Geddes, Alexander (1737–1802)
Infallible Doussiekie.

Gefen, Jonathan (b. 1947)
Setting-Up Camp.

Gehrke, Steve (b. 1971)
Mouth to Mouth.
Near the Mississippi.
Walking Fields at Night South of Hampton, Iowa.

Geier, Joan Austin
On Your Twenty-First Birthday.

Geiger, Timothy
Disproportionate.
Dry Spell of Faith, A.
Soundtracks.

Gekko-Sojo
How Zenists carry on.

Gekkutsu-Sei
I set down the emerald lamp.

Gelbtrunk, Aida (d. 1999)
All Illusion Is a Form of Hope.
Coincidence.
Empty House, The.
God said to Abraham.

Gelinas, Dana (b. 1962)
Arca del día, El.
Ark of Day, The.
Caballo de acero, El.
Dream of the Just, The.
Jardín de madera.
Miracle Country.
País de los milagros, El.
Steel Horse.
Sueño de los justos, El.
Wood Garden.

Gellert, Leon (b. 1892)
House-Mates.

Gellis, Willard
City of No Reprieve.

Gelman, Juan (b. 1930)
Epochs.
Eyes.
History.
Man and a Woman, A.

Gemin, Pamela (b. 1954)
Upper Peninsula Landscape with Aunts.

Genet, Jean (1910–86)
Man Condemned to Death, The.

Geng Wei (*fl.* late 8th cent. A.D.)
Autumn Day.

Genko (d. 1505)
Unaware of illusion or enlightenment.

Genoways, Ted
Under the Big Top.

Gensei (1623–68)
Distant View from a Grass Hill.
Evening View from Grass Hill.

Gensler, Kinereth
Bowl with Pine Cones.

Gensui
Birds.

Geoghegan, Arthur G. (1810–89)
Mountain Fern, The.

George, Bruce
In this day and age.

George, David Graves
Wreck of the Old 97.

George, Diana Hume (b. 1948)
Asenath.

George, Don (1909–85)
I Ain't Got Nothin' But the Blues.
I'm Beginning to See the Light.
It Shouldn't Happen to a Dream.
It's Kind of Lonesome Out Tonight.
Tulip or Turnip.

George, Eirwyn (b. 1936)
Family.

George, Faye
Charioteer, The.
Shagbark.
Sudden Tug of the Familiar, The.
Wilderness.

George, Kadija
Six Minutes Writing.

George, Phillip [or "Phil"] William
Battle Won Is Lost.

George, Stefan (1868–1933)
Antichrist, The.
Come to the park they say is dead and see.
Do Not Ponder Too Much.
Have you his lovely image still in mind.
What marvels smiles the morning-earth.

George, William Richard Philip (b. 1912)
Armstrong and Aldrin on the Moon.

Georges, Danielle Legros (b. 1964)
Anacona.
Another Ode to Salt.
Grasshopper.

Georges, Esther Valck
Alley Cat.

Georgiev, Marin (b. 1946)
Memory, *sels.*
Native Soil.
Riverbend.
Silence: "In the afternoon hours of autumn heading home."

Georgiou, Elena
From Where I Stand.
Intimate Mixture.
Space Between, The.
Talkin' Trash.
Week in the Life of the Ethnically Indeterminate, A.

Gerard, Marcel (b. 1917)
Flow.

Gerbasi, Vicente
Hallucinatory Sunset, with Sons.

Gerber, Dan (b. 1940)
Afterwords.
Bear on Main Street, The.

Gerhardt, Ida G. M. (b. 1905)
Buried Birds, The.
Expectation.
Rejected Gift, The.
Rejected Gift, The.
Remembrance Day.
Remembrance Day.

Gerhardt, Paul (1607–76)
Commit thy way unto the Lord.
Evensong.
Go out in this dear summertime.
O Sacred Head Now Wounded.
O sacred head, now wounded.

Gerlach, Eva (b. 1948)
Turn and Turn About.

Germain, Carmen (b. 1951)
Literature 100.

Gerner, Ken
House of Breath.
Prey.

Gerov, Alexander (b. 1919)
Accra.

Birds: "They don't plow, nor do they sow."
Courtesy.
Dandelion.
Eternity: "She's neither ugly nor fearful."
Eye to Eye.
Matter.
Mice.
Problem, A.
Urban Tree.

Gershon, Karen (b. 1923)
At a Reception.
Experiments with God.
I Was Not There.
Race.
To My Children.
Uphold Me.

Gershwin, George (1898–1937)
Summertime.

Gershwin, Ira (1896–1983)
Babbitt and the Bromide, The.
Bidin' My Time.
Blah, Blah, Blah.
But Not for Me.
Do, Do, Do.
Embraceable You.
Fascinating Rhythm.
Foggy Day (in London Town), A.
Fun to be Fooled.
How Long Has This Been Going On?
I Can't Get Started.
I Got Plenty o' Nuthin'
I Got Rhythm.
Isn't It a Pity?
It Ain't Necessarily So.
Let's Call the Whole Thing Off.
Let's Take a Walk Around the Block.
Long Ago (And Far Away).
Love Is Here to Stay.
Love Is Sweeping the Country.
Man I Love, The.
Man That Got Away, The.
My Ship.
Nice Work If You Can Get It.
Of Thee I Sing.
Oh, Lady, Be Good!
One Life to Live.
'S Wonderful.
Saga of Jenny, The.
Someone to Watch over Me.
'Strike Up the Band.
Sunny Disposish.
Tchaikowsky (And Other Russians).
There's Magic in the Air.
They All Laughed.
They Can't Take That Away from Me.
Things Are Looking Up.
Who Cares?

Gerstler, Amy (b. 1956)
Bitter Angel.
Bitter Angel.
BZZZZZZZ.
Dear Boy George.
Fan Letter, A.
Housebound.
Marriage.
Nature of Suffering, The.
Saints.
Seesaw.
Sinking Feeling, A.
Siren.
Slowly I Open My Eyes.
True Bride, The.
Unexpected Adventure, An.
Unforeseen, The.

Gertler, Pesha
Right Thing, The.
Standing with Chiyo-Ni.

Gertsyk, Adelaida (1874–1925)
Silent, draped in the garments of sacrifice.
Spring.

Gervitz, Gloria (b. 1943)
Life is nothing but time.
Migraciones, sel.
Migrations, sel.
Yiskor, sels.

Gesshu Soko (1618–96)
Seven seas sucked up together, The.

Getsi, Lucia Cordell
Washing Your Hair.
Woman Hanging from Lightpole, Illinois Route
136.

Getsudo (1285–1361)
I moved across the Dharma-nature.

Gevirtz, Susan (b. 1955)
Hyphen's Hyphen.

Gewanter, David
Divorce and Mr. Circe.
One-Page Novel.
Xenia: Stranger/Guest.

Gex-Breaux, Quo Vadis
Jazz Rain.
Memory Waves.
Padded Steps/Sister Song (a litany).
Wisdom Is.

Gezelle, Guido (1830–99)
Ego Flos.
Little Mother.

Ghalib, Mirza Asadullah Khan (1797–1869)
Clay Cup, The.
Don't Skimp with Me Today.
Freely in Hidden Fire.
Ghazal.
Ghazal 5.
Ghazal 12.
Ghazal 13: "Where are your woo-trysts and
your heart-wrenches now, Ghalib?"
Ghazal 15.
Ghazal 21.
Ghazal 25.
Ghazal 34.
I'm Neither the Loosening of Song nor the
Close-Drawn Tent of Music.
Leftovers in the Cup.
My Destiny.
My Head and My Knees.
My Spiritual State.
Not All, Only a Few, Return As the Rose or
the Tulip.
Questions: "Since nothing actually exists
except You."
Some Exaggerations.
When the Day Comes.

Ghazoul, Ferial J. (b. 1939)
Abel's Brothers.

Gheraducci, Vera (b. 1928)
April 5th.
December 15th.
June 30th.
October 27th.
September 22nd.

Ghigna, Charles (b. 1946)
Lesson of Night, A.
Park Elms.

Ghiselin, Brewster (b. 1903)
Bath of Aphrodite.
Food of Birds, The.
Learning the Language.
Net Breaker, The.
Rattler, Alert.
Shore Bird.

Ghos, Giríscandra (1844–1912)
I plaster myself with ashes.
Who said / If you took the name All-
Destroyer.
You're home, Uma! Stay here.

Ghose, Manmohan (1869–1924)
Who Is It Talks of Ebony?

Giacometti, Alberto
Brown Curtain, The.

Gibb, Blair
Vigil.

Gibb, Robert
Letter to Russel Barron.
Paul Butterfield, Dead at 44.

Gibbens, John
To the Bicycle.

Gibbons, Orlando (1583–1625)
Silver Swan, The.

Gibbons, Reginald (b. 1947)
Affect of Elms, The.
American Trains.
Breath.
Cash or Turtle or Heaven.
For My Daughter.
Life Everlasting, The.
Luckies.
Pine Island.
Ruined Motel, The.
Sparrow.
We Say.

Gibbons, Stella (b. 1902)
Truce, The.

Gibbs, Robert J. (b. 1930)
All this night long.
Death of My Father, The.
Kind of Wakefulness, A.
Manes P. Aground Off Fort Dufferin, The.
This Catching of Breath at the Top.

Gibran, Kahlil (1883–1931)
Fox, The.
Madman (Prologue), The.
Seven Stages, The.

Gibson, Colin (b. 1933)
There's a straw in the manger and babies in
danger.

Gibson, Douglas
January.

Gibson, Magi (b. 1953)
Goldilocks.
Just Like Eve.
Reading in Bed.

Gibson, Margaret (b. 1944)
One Body.
Radiation.
Strange Altars.
Summer Birds and Flowers (2).
Woman Resting on a Bundle of Kindling.

Gibson, Walker (b. 1919)
Advice to Travelers.

Gibson, Wilfrid Wilson (1878–1962)
Breakfast.
Golden Room, The.
In the Ambulance.
Luck.
Music Stole In.
Old Skinflint.
Parrot, The.
Prelude: "As one, at midnight wakened by the
call."
Sight.
Stone, The.
White Dust, The.

Gidlow, Elsa (b. 1898)
Constancy.
Creed for Free Women, A.
Let Wisdom Wear the Crown: Hymn for
Gaia.
Philosophy.
Relinquishment.

Gido (1325–88)
Inscription over His Door.

Gier, Jean V.
California Coast.
Examining the I.
First View of the Islands, A.
Going Baroque.

Giffard, Martha, Lady (1638–1722)
Of Sleep.
To Mother Luddwels Cave and Spring.

Gifford, Fannie Stearns (b. 1884)
Songs of Conn the Fool, The, sels.

Gifford, Humphrey [or Humfrey] (fl. c.1580)
For Soldiers.
In the Praise of Music.

Gifford, William (1756–1826)
Baviad, The, sel.

Gifford, William See Also Canning, George

Gil de Biedma, Jaime (1929–90)
Art of Poetry, The.
Arte Poética.
De los Años Cuarenta.
Elegía y Recuerdo de la Canción Francesa.

In Mournful Praise and Memory of the French
    Song.
In the Forties.
Noche Triste de Octubre, 1959.
Prince of Aquitania, in His Torn-down Tower,
    The.
Príncipe de Aquitania, En Su Torre Abolida.
Sad Night of October 1959.

Gilbart, Thomas (fl. c.1583)
Declaration of the Death of John Lewes, A.

Gilberg, Gail Hosking (b. 1950)
Poetry's Beginning.

Gilbert, Alan
Relative Heat Index.

Gilbert, Celia (b. 1932)
Midwives, The.
Questions about the Sphinx.

Gilbert, Christopher (b. 1950)
African Sculpture.
And, Yes, Those Spiritual Matters.
Beginning by Value.
Chosen to Be Water.
Directions, The.
Enclosure.
Glimpses.
Kite-Flying.
Now.
Pushing.
Resonance.
She.
Sorrow Since Sitting Bull, A.
Theory of Curve.
This Bridge Across.
Time with Stevie Wonder in It.

Gilbert, Jack (b. 1925)
Abnormal Is Not Courage, The.
Elephant Hunt in Guadalajara.
Explicating the Twilight.
Getting Ready.
Great Fires, The.
Haunted Importantly.
Hunger.
It Is Clear Why the Angels Come No More.
Malvolio in San Francisco.
Measuring the Tyger.
Perspective He Would Mutter Going to Bed.
Pewter.
Prospero Listens to the Night.
Revolution, The.
Searching for Pittsburgh.
To See if Something Comes Next.
White Heart of God, The.

Gilbert, Lady See Mulholland, Rosa

Gilbert, Mercedes
Friendless Blues.

Gilbert, Samuel (d. 1692?)
Florist's Vade-Mecum, The, sels.

Gilbert, Sandra M. (b. 1936)
Afternoon Walk: The Sea Ranch.
Against Poetry.
Elegy: "Pages of history open, The. The dead
    enter."
June 15, 1992: Widow's Walk, Harpswell,
    Maine.
Ladies' Home Journal, The.
Mafioso.
November 26, 1992: Thanksgiving at the Sea
    Ranch, Contemplating Metempsychosis.
Return of the Muse, The.
Simplicity.

Gilbert, Sky (b. 1952)
Island of Lost Tears, The.

Gilbert, William Schwenck (1836–1911)
Captain Reece.
Ferdinando and Elvira; or, The Gentle Pieman.
Gilbertian Cats.
Gondoliers, The, sel.
Iolanthe, sels.
Mikado, The, sel.
Patience, sels.
Pirates of Penzance, The, sels.
Ruddigore, sels.
To the Terrestrial Globe.
Trial by Jury, sels.
Utopia Limited, sels.

Yarn of the *Nancy Bell*, The.
Yeoman of the Guard, sels.

Gilbert-Lecomte, Roger (1907–43)
Preface or The Drama of Absence in an
    Eternal Heart.
Son of the Bone Speaks, The.
Wink.

Gilboa, Amir (1917–84)
And My Brother Was Silent.

Gilder, Richard Watson (1844–1909)
Hour in a Studio, An.
On the Bay.
Sonnet, The.
Two Worlds.

Gildner, Gary (b. 1938)
Digging for Indians.
4th Base.
High-Class Bananas, The.
Nails.
They Have Turned the Church Where I Ate
    God.

Giles, Joseph (fl. late 18th cent.)
Leasowes: Or, A Poetical Description of the
    Late Mr. Shenstone's Rural Retirement, The,
    sels.

Gilfillan, Merrill (b. 1945)
Horseshoe.
Proposed Elegy for Hart Crane.

Gilfillan, Robert
Exile's Song, The.

Gilgun, John
Ars Poetica: "About writing a poem. It occurs
    to me."
Buddha Is Lord of Our Town.
Lights Out.
Zen Frost.
Zen Sky.

Gilkes, Dana
Rain Making.
Thoughts from a 747.

Gill, Charmaine A.
Memorial: "Burnt sugar skeletons."

Gill, Kuldip (b. 1934)
Ghazal 5: "My white mare on the Punjabi
    plains, the stamp of her hooves."

Gill, Lisa (b. 1970)
Letters to a Dead Trappist, sels.

Gillan, Maria
Arturo.
Growing Up Italian.
In Memory We Are Walking.
In New Jersey Once.
Public School No. 18: Paterson, New Jersey.
Waiting for the Results of a Pregnancy Test.

Gillespie, Abraham Lincoln (1895–1950)
Purplexicon of Dissynthegrations, A.
Readie-Soundpiece (For Bob Brown's Reading
    Machine), sel.

Gillespie, Haven (1888–1975)
Breezin' Along with the Breeze.
Santa Claus Is Comin' to Town.
That Lucky Old Sun.
You Go to My Head.

Gillespie, Netta
Blessing of Snow, The.
Bus Driver, The.
Road Kill.
Seated in a Chinese Painting, He Speaks.

Gilliams, Maurice (1900–82)
Autumn.
Tristitia Ante.

Gillies, Valerie (b. 1948)
Look-Alike, The.
Summer Bull.
We Meet Again.

Gillilan, Pamela
Four Years.
Looking North.
Mistress, The.
You lie with me nightly. In bathrooms I'm
    there.

Gillilan, Strickland W. (1869–1954)
On the Antiquity of Microbes.

Gilman, Caroline (1794–1888)
Oracles for Youth, sels.

Gilman, Charlotte Perkins Stetson (1860–1935)
Anti-Suffragists, The.
California Colors: A Song.
Christian Virtues.
Homes.
Matriatism.
Mother's Charge, The.

Gilmore, Brian G. (b. 1962)
Bow to Allah.
Coming to the Net (for Arthur Ashe).
Elvis.
Gas Station Attendant.
Georgia avenue, washington d.c.
Hazing (for tony new and albee).
Revolution.
To be or not to be.

Gilmore, Joseph Henry (1834–1918)
He Leadeth Me.

Gilmore, Mary (1865–1902)
Eve-Song.
Harvesters, The.
Little Shoes That Died, The.
Saturday Tub, The.

**Gilmore, Patrick Sarsfield ("Louis Lambert")
(1829–92)**
When Johnny Comes Marching Home.

Gilonis, Harry (b. 1956)
Answer to Herrick, An.
Forty Fungi, sels.
Song 9.
Song for Annie.

Gilsdorf, Ethan
Away from Us.
Walk, The.

Gilyard, Keith (b. 1952)
Daughter, That Picture of You.
Letter.
On Top of It All.
Portraits of a Moment.

Ginsberg, Allen (1926–97)
After Lalon.
After Yeats.
Against red bark trunk.
America: "America I've given you all and now
    I'm nothing."
At Apollinaire's Grave.
At 4:00 a.m. the two.
Back on Times Square, Dreaming of Times
    Square.
Blue Angel, The.
Bricklayer's Lunch Hour, The.
Caw caw caw crows shriek in the white sun
    over grave stones.
Chances "R."
Change, The: *Kyoto-Tokyo Express*.
Charnel Ground, The.
City Midnight Junk Strains.
Death News.
Describe: The Rain on Dasaswamedh Ghat.
Don't Grow Old, sels.
Easter Sunday.
Elegy for Neal Cassady.
First Party at Ken Kesey's with Hell's Angels.
Footnote to Howl.
Four skinheads stand.
Fourth Floor, Dawn, Up All Night Writing
    Letters.
Further Proposal, A.
Galilee Shore.
Gray-haired man, The.
Green Automobile, The.
Grim Skeleton.
Homeless Compleynt.
Homework.
Howl, sels.
I Am a Victim of Telephone.
I Love Old Whitman So.
In back of the real.
Iron Horse, sel.
Is About.
Kaddish, sels.
Kral Majales.

Land O'Lakes, Wisconsin: Vajrayana
  Seminary.
Last Night in Calcutta.
Lion for Real, The.
Looking over my shoulder.
Malest Cornifici Tuo Catullo.
Manhattan May Day Midnight.
Mescaline.
Moon in the dewdrop is the real moon, The.
Mugging.
My Alba.
My Sad Self.
New Stanzas for *Amazing Grace*.
No Way Back to the Past.
Not a word! Not a word!
Not Dead Yet.
Ode to Failure.
On Neal's Ashes.
Personals Ad.
Please Master.
Plutonian Ode, *sel.*
Psalm III: "To God: to illuminate all men.
  Beginning with Skid Road."
Reflections at Lake Louise.
Siesta in Xbalba, *sel.*
Sitting crosslegged on a wooden floor.
Sphincter.
Stood on the porch in.
Strange New Cottage in Berkeley, A.
Studying the Signs.
Sunflower Sutra.
Supermarket in California, A.
Sweet Levinsky.
Terms in Which I Think of Reality, The.
Thief Stole This Poem, A.
This Form of Life Needs Sex.
To Aunt Rose.
Transcription of Organ Music.
Velocity of Money.
Visiting Father and Friends.
Vow, A.
Wales Visitation.
Walking into King Sooper after Two-Week
  Retreat.
We Rise on Sun Beams and Fall in the Night.
White sun up behind pines.
Who Eats Who?
Who Runs America?
Why Is God Love, Jack?
Wichita Vortex Sutra, *sel.*
Written in My Dream by W. C. Williams.
Yiddishe Kopf.

Ginsberg, Arthur
Chief of Medicine, The.
Line Drive.
Stroke.

Gioia, Dana (b. 1950)
All Souls'.
Alley Cat Love Song.
Archbishop, The.
Becoming a Redwood.
California Hills in August.
Counting the Children.
Country Wife, The.
Cruising with the Beach Boys.
Failure.
Guide to the Other Gallery.
In Chandler Country.
In Cheever Country.
Insomnia.
Litany, The.
Lives of the Great Composers.
Los Angeles after the Rain.
Maze Without a Minotaur.
My Confessional Sestina.
Next Poem, The.
Pentecost: "Neither the sorrows of afternoon,
  waiting in the silent house."
Planting a Sequoia.
Prayer: "Echo of the clocktower, footstep."
Rough Country.
Summer Storm.
Sunday News, The.
Unsaid.
Voyeur, The.

Giorno, John (b. 1936)
Birds, *sel.*

Capsule.
Life Is a Killer.
Pornographic Poem.
Scum & Slime.

Gioseffi, Daniela
American Sonnets for My Father.
Bicentennial Anti-Poem for Italian-American
  Women.
Last Fire Feast, The, *sel.*

Giovanna
Therapy.
What Do I Know.

Giovanni, Nikki (b. 1943)
Alabama Poem.
Always There Are the Children.
Basketball.
Beautiful Black Men.
Crutches.
December of My Springs, The.
Drum, The.
Ego Tripping (There May Be a Reason Why).
Forced Retirement.
Genie in the Jar, The.
Knoxville, Tennessee.
Legacies.
Life I Led, The.
Monday.
Mothers.
Nikki-Rosa.
Poem (for Langston Hughes), A.
Poem For My Nephew.
Poetry: "Poetry is motion graceful."
Springtime.
Three/Quarters Time.
Train Rides.
Trips.
Walking Down Park.
Women Gather, The.
World Is Not a Pleasant Place to Be, The.
Wrong Kitchen, The.

Giovannitti, Arturo (1884–1959)
Walker, The.

**Gippius, Zinaida Nikolayevna [*or* Nikolaevna]
  (1869–1945)**
Incantation.
Seamstress, The.
Wedding Ring, The.

Giraudon, Liliane (b. 1946)
Poem with Incense Paper, *sels.*
Quand il n'y a plus rien à attendre, *sel.*

Giscombe, C. S. (b. 1950)
Ballad Values (2).
Black River, The.
from the "In" Sequence, *sels.*
Home Avenue.
Light, Bright, Etc.
Negromania, Negrophilia, Negrophobia.
1980.
1978, Remembering 1962.
1962 At the Edge of Town.
Recent Past, The.

Gittins, Chrissie
There Are Things I Must Realise You Can No
  Longer Do.

Gittins, Diana
I flash for megabucks.

Giussani, Silvio (b. 1951)
Abel and Abel.
Aridness of Air, The.
Body Politic.
Clothes Without the Monk, The.
Hot and Cold.
In the Distance.
Towards a Beginning.
Vegetable Calendar.

Given, Thomas
Poetical Epistle tae Cullybackey Auld
  Nummer.
Song for February, A.

Givens, Bettye Hammer
Lonesome Texas.
West Texas.

Giya, Mèsedès F. *See* Guignard, Mercedès F

Gizzi, Michael (b. 1949)
Baghdad.
Versailles.

Gizzi, Peter
Another Day on the Pilgrimage.
Ding Repair.
Fables of Critique.
It Was Raining in Delft.
Last Cigar.
Lonely Tylenol.
New Picnic Time.
Tout les Matins du Monde.

Gladding, Jody
Blue Willow.
Fisherman's Wife, The.
Locust Shell.
Worsted Heather.

Gladstone, William Ewart (1809–98)
To a Rejected Sonnet.

Glancy, Diane
Battery.
First Reader Santee Training School, 1873,
  The.
Great Indian Father in the Subway.
Harry S Truman Library, Independence,
  Missouri.
Hides.
Kemo Sabe.
Landscape Painting.

Glaser, Elton
And in the Afternoons I Botanized.
Blues for the Nightowl.
Cheap Replicas of the Eiffel Tower.
Confluences at San Francisco.
Coroner.
Revelation: The Movie.
Smoking.

Glaser, Isabel Joshlin
Depression.
Last Good War—and Afterward, The.

Glaser, Michael S.
Changing Address Books.
English-Speaking Persons Will Find
  Translations.
Magnificat!
Preparations for Seder.
Quarreling with Robert Frost.

Glass, Jesse
Lecturing on Walt Whitman and Emily
  Dickinson in China.

Glassman, Bernard Tetsugen
Ascending the Mountain.

Glatstein, Jacob (1896–1971)
St. Matthew, *sel.*
To a Friend Who Wouldn't Bother to Strain
  His Noodleboard Because Even So It Is
  Hard to Go Hunting When Your Rifle Is
  Blunt and Love Is Soft as an Old Blanket.

Glatt, Lisa
Amanda.
Leash.
One Night With a Stranger at 30.
Talking About Boys.
What We Did After My Mother's Mastectomy.
World in My Mother's Hair, The.

Glaukos
Where once you could win over grasping boys.

Glazer, Jane
Final Disposition.
Point of No Return.

Glazer, Michele
All That in the Voice I Have Adopted for This
  Lie.
Box.
Early Romance, Japanese Garden (*In the Heart
  of the City*).
Echo to Narcissus.
Map.
Matter.
Purpose of Design Is to Make the Whole
  Greater Than the Sum of Its Parts, The.
Science.
Sonnet: "Invisible in vernal pools."
Star-Spangled.

2 Blinds & a Bittern.
Wherein Space Is Constructed that Matter May Reside in.

Glazier, Lyle
On TV.

Glazova, Anna (b. 1973)
Cities, *sels.*
Grant of Death, The.
Solo.

Gleashure, James
Mary Hogan's Quatrains, *sel.*

Gleason, Kate
After Fighting for Hours.

Gleason, Madeline (b. 1913)
We Are Like These Things.

Gleim, Johann Wilhelm Ludwig (1719–1803)
Anacreon.
To Death.

Glen, Duncan (b. 1933)
Bell Barrow.
My Father: "Staunin noo aside his braw bress-haunled coffin."
Twa Warlds.

Glenday, John (b. 1952)
Concerning the Atoms of the Soul.
Day at the Seaside, A.
Empire of Lights, The.
Garden, The: "Just for a quarter of a day, I'd have you."
Hydrodamalis Gigas.

Glickman, Susan
But till that morning, ain't no one gonna harm you.

Glissant, Édouard (b. 1928)
For Mycea.
Pour Mycéa.

Gloeggler, Tony
Foreplay.
Fowler Street.

Gloria, Eugene (b. 1957)
Aleng Maria.
Assimilation.
In Language.
Milkfish.
Rizal's Ghost.
Touch.
Whisper, The.

Glover, Denis (1912–80)
Magpies, The.

Glover III, Hoke S. *See* Brother Yao

Glover, Sheilah
Power of the Soul.

Glück, Louise (b. 1943)
All Hallows.
Aubade: "World was very large, The. Then."
Balcony, The.
Baskets.
Brown Circle.
Celestial Music.
Circe's Power.
Condo.
Cottonmouth Country.
Day Without Night.
Dedication to Hunger, *sels.*
Departure.
Descending Figure.
Drowned Children, The.
Earthly Love.
Edge, The.
Elms.
Eurydice.
Fantasy, A.
First Memory.
Firstborn.
Garden, The: "I couldn't do it again."
Garden, The: "One sound. Then the hiss and whir."
Gift, The.
Gratitude.
Gretel in Darkness.
Happiness.
Hawk's Shadow.
Hesitate to Call.
Horse.

Hyacinth.
Illuminations.
Labor Day.
Lamentations.
Lamium.
Legend.
Letters, The.
Lullaby: "My mother's an expert at one thing."
Magi, The.
Marathon, *sels.*
Matins: "Sun shines; by the mailbox, leaves, The."
Matins: "Unreachable father, when we were first."
Messengers.
Midnight.
Mirror Image.
Mirror, The.
Mock Orange.
Moonless Night.
Mount Ararat.
Mountain, The.
Mutable Earth.
Mythic Fragment.
Nativity Poem.
New Life, The.
Nostos.
Palais des Arts.
Parable of Flight.
Penelope's Song.
Poem: "In the early evening, as now, a man is bending."
Pond, The.
Queen of Carthage, The.
Quiet Evening.
Racer's Widow, The.
Red Poppy, The.
Retreating Wind.
Roman Study.
St. Luke, *sel.*
School Children, The.
Scilla.
Seven Ages, The.
Siren.
Terminal Resemblance.
Time: "There was too much, always, then too little."
Trillium.
Triumph of Achilles, The.
Unwritten Law.
Vespers: "I don't wonder where you are anymore."
Vespers: "In your extended absence, you permit me."
Vita Nova.
White Lilies, The.
White Rose, The.
Wild Iris, The.
Winged Horse, The.
Wound, The.

Glück, Robert
Burroughs.
Invaders from Mars.
Pasolini.
Visit, The, *sels.*

Godden, James
Lost.

Goddess, Rha
Why I Be a Goddess.

Godfrey, Glenn
New Spirit, The.

Godfrey, John (b. 1945)
Air.
Bath.
In Front of a Large Number of People.
My Mother, Life.
One or More Together.
Our Lady.
Radiant Dog.
Show Me a Rose.
So Let's Look at It Another Way.
Unholy Spring.
What It Takes.
What Say.
Where the Weather Suits My Clothes.

Wings.

Godley, Elizabeth
Ninety-Nine.

Godolphin, Margaret, Lady (1652–78)
Song: "As F—at her Toilet sat."

Godolphin, Sidney (1610–43)
Constancy[e].
Faire Friend, 'tis true, your beauties move.
Hymn: "Lord, when the wise men came from far[r]."
Song: "Or love me less, or love me more."
Thou Joy of my Life.

Goeckel, Lawrence
Message from the Photo-Mat.
Short Hand.
Wave Falling on the Beach, A.

Goedicke, Patricia (b. 1931)
American Exercises.
And Yet.
At the Center.
For Walt Whitman.
From the Boat.
Ground Beneath Us, The.
Imprint of Microscopic Life Found in Arctic Stones.
Interior Music, The.
Lacrimae Rerum.
Meaning of Life, The.
My Brother's Anger.
Shadow.
Wind of Our Going: Adagio Ma Non Troppo.

Goese, Mimi
Dive, The.
I slowly crack my joints to ready and steady myself. Sharpen my mind on.
Love Ghost.
You Are.

Goethe, Johann Wolfgang von (1749–1832)
Anacreon's Grave.
Death of a Fly.
Diary, The.
Ecstatic Longing.
Erl-King.
Erl-King, The.
Faust, *sels.*
Fisherman, The.
Found.
Haste Not! Rest Not!
Holy Longing, The.
Hunter's Song at Nightfall, The.
Ill Humor.
Invisible King, The.
Journey in Winter, *sels.*
King in Thule, The.
May Song.
Meeting, the Departure, The.
Mignon.
Mignon Aspiring to Heaven.
Nature and Art.
Permanence in Change.
Roman Elegies, The, *sels.*
Rosebud in the Heather.
Song from the Coptic, A.
Song of the Traveler at Evening.
Sonnet: "To work away in art's traditional measure."
To Belinda.
To Charlotte von Stein.
To the Moon.
Trilogy of Passion.
United States, The.
Violet, The.
Wanderer's Night Song.
Whatever You Can Do.
Wilhelm Meister's Apprenticeship, *sel.*

Goetsch, Douglas (b. 1963)
Bachelor Song.
Beach, The.
First Time Reading Freud.
Nobody's Hell.
Smell and Envy.
Urban Poem.
Walls, The.
What Keeps Animals Sane?

Goetz, E. Ray
For Me and My Gal.

Goetz, Greta
Construction Papers, *sel.*

Goff, Cindy
Addiction.
Drinking Beer with Sir.
First Sober Morning, The.
I Feel Unattractive during Mating Season.
Turning into an Oak Tree.

Goffette, Guy (b. 1947)
Max Jacob.
Max Jacob.
Raising of Icarus, The: Envoi.
Relèvement d'Icare, L': Envoi.

Goffstein, M. B. (b. 1940)
On This Day.

Gogarty, Oliver St. John (1878–1957)
After Galen.
Colophon.
Conquest, The.
Dedication: "Tall unpopular men."
Good Luck.
Image-Maker, The.
Leda and the Swan.
Marcus Curtius.
Non Dolet.
On First Looking into Krafft-Ebing's
  Psychopathosexualis [or Psychopathia
  Sexualis].
Palinode.
Per Iter Tenebricosum.
Perfection.
Plum Tree by the House, The.
Portrait with Background.
Ringsend.
Tell Me Now.
To a Boon Companion.
To Death.
To Petronius Arbiter.
Verse: "What should we know."
With a Coin from Syracuse.

"Gogisgi" *See* Arnett, Carroll

Gojusan
Seamless.

Goldbarth, Albert (b. 1948)
Ancestored-Back Is the Overpresiding Spirit of
  This Poem.
Arguing Bartusiak.
Book of Human Anomalies, The.
Closer.
Columbine High School / Littleton, CO.
Complete with Starry Night and Bourbon
  Shots.
Counterfeit Earth!, The.
Edgewater Hospital.
Gallery.
Letter to Friends East and West.
Life Is Happy.
Meop.
People Are Dropping Out of Our Lives.
Poem of the Praises, The.
Reality Organization.
Recipe.
Sciences Sing a Lullabye, The.
Seriema Song.
Shoyn Fergéssin: "I've Forgotten" in Yiddish.
Steerage.
Talk Show, The.
Whole Earth Catalogue, The.
World Above Suffering, A.

Goldberg, Beckian Fritz
Bedtime Story.
Blossom at the End of the Body.
Eros in His Striped Shirt.
Fetish.
God Body.
He Said Discipline Is the Highest Form of
  Love.
Hound and Leper.
Lilies at Night.
Money.
My Bomb.
My Husband's Bride.
Nights in the Constellation of the Tree

Stepping from its Robe.
Nights with the Star-Ladle Over the House.
Once a Shoot of Heaven.
Passing House, The.
Rebirth.
Retro Lullaby.
Say.
Since I Have Lived.
Swallower.
Third Body.
Torture Boy at the Easter Confest, Repentance
  Creek.
Twentieth Century Children.
Twentieth Century Children (2).
Twentieth Century Children (5): Blood-
  Kissing.
Whitman's Confession: In the Cleft of Eternity.
Wren.

Goldberg, Jacqueline (b. 1966)
Luba, *sels.*

Goldberg, Leah (1911–70)
From My Mother's Home.
God Once Commanded Us, A.
Heavenly Jerusalem, Jerusalem of the Earth.
In the Jerusalem Hills.
Not for a long time now has anyone waited for
  me.
Prodigal Son, The.
Song of the Strange Woman.
Tel Aviv 1935.
That poem I didn't write.
Toward Myself.

Goldberg, Natalie
Two Iowa Farmers.

Goldensohn, Barry (b. 1937)
Arch of Titus.
Mountain Lion.

Golding, Arthur
Ovid's Metamorphoses Book 6, *sel.*

Golding, Nicolette
My Father Makes a Lightbox for Vivienne
  Westwood.
Wardrobes.

Goldman, Judith
Real Devotion of Events, The.

Goldsmith, Kenneth
Punk, *sel.*

Goldsmith, Oliver (1730?–74)
Captivity, The, *sels.*
Deserted Village, The, *sels.*
Double Transformation, The.
Epilogue to "The Sister", *sel.*
Gift, The. To Iris, in Bow Street, Covent
  Garden.
Retaliation, *sels.*
Traveller, The; or, A Prospect of Society, *sels.*
Vicar of Wakefield, The, *sels.*

Goldstein, Laurence
Firmament on High.

Goldstein, Stephanie
At Night: "Worries creep like insects."

Goldsworthy, Peter (b. 1951)
Act Six.
After Babel.

Golffing, Francis C. (b. 1910)
Higher Empiricism, The.

Goll, Iwan [or Yvan] (1891–1950)
Ferry of Lead, The.
I'd like to be nothing.
In Age-Old Lakes.
Journey into Misery.
Lackawanna Elegy.
Last River, The.
On the five thousandth evening of our love.
Salt Lake, The.
Your Sleep.

Gomes, Alberto Ferreira (b. 1957)
Martyred Tamarind, The.

Gomez, Cynthia
San José: A Poem.

Gomez de Avellaneda, Gertrudis (1814–73)
Imitating an Ode by Sapho.

Gomez, Jewelle (b. 1948)
My Chakabuku Mama: A Comic Tale.

Gomez, Magdalena (b. 1954)
Chocolate Confessions.
Desert Cry, A.
Looking Deep.
Lost Daughter.
Making It.
Solo Palabras.
To the Latin Lover I Left at the Candy Store.
Troubled Awakening.

Gomringer, Eugen
Hang and swinging hang and swinging.
Mist.
[Untitled Concrete Poem].
Words: "Words are shadows."

Góngora y Argote, Luis de (1561–1627)
Capture of Larache, The.
Deceiver Time.
Fable of Polyphemus and Galatea, *sels.*
First Solitude, The.
O Noble and Most High in Beauty, Thou.
On the Armada That Battled Against England.
Pride of the Fourth and Liquid Element.
Roistering I'll Chaff.
Ruins of Time, The.
Solitudes, The, *sels.*
Sonnet 103.
Sonnet 82.
Spectre of the Rose, The, *sels.*
Whistling arrow flies less eagerly, The.

González, Angel
Battlesfield, The.
Before I Could Call Myself Ángel González.
Cadáver Ínfimo.
Campo de Batalla, El.
City.
Death in the Afternoon.
Diatribe Against the Dead.
Estío en Bidonville.
Future, The.
Inventory of Places Propitious for Love.
Least Corpse, The.
Muerte en la Tarde.
Mundo Asombroso.
Summer in Slumville.
Whatever You Want.
Without Warning.
Yesterday.

Gonzales, Jacinta (d. 1916 or 17)
Hey, fog, go home.

Gonzalez, N. V. M. (b. 1915)
Deepest Well in Madras, The.
How the Heart Aches.
I Made Myself a Path.
Wanderer in the Night of the World, A.

González, Rafael Jesús
Grace.

Gonzalez, Ray
Angels of Juárez, Mexico, The.
At the Rio Grande Near the End of the
  Century.
Beyond Having.
Brown Pot.
Cabato.
Calling the White Donkey.
For the Other World.
José's Japanese Sword.
Prayer to the Boys of San Antonio.
San Jacinto Plaza.
Savior.
Some Sixties.
Still Life with Endings.
There.
Without Villages.

Gonzales, Ray
Aztec Father.
Head of Pancho Villa, The.
Paso del Norte.
Praise the Tortilla, Praise the Menudo, Praise
  the Chorizo.
Prison, San Elizario, Texas, The.
Roberto Meets Cabeza de Vaca in the Desert.
Three Snakes, Strawberry Canyon, Berkeley.

González, Rigoberto (b. 1970)
Crush.
Day of the Dead.

Death of the Farm Workers' Cat.
Marías, Old Indian Mothers.
Mariposa.
Penny Men.
Perla at the Mexican Border Assembly Line of
   Dolls.
Rapist: A Romance.
You and the Tijuana Mule.

Gonzáles Martínez, Enrique (1871–1952)
Last Journey.
Like Sister and Brother.
Nectar of Ápan, The.
Pain.
Window, The.
Wring the Swan's Neck.

González Prada, Manuel (1848–1918)
Cosmos Shows His Power, The.
Forced Labour.
How Old Is Pilar?
If the Tomb Is Not Oblivion.
Inca's Arrows, The.
Into the Hearth They Are Tossing Logs.
Living and Dying.
Mitayo, The.
Pope.
To Be with the Dead.
Treasures and Glories of Life, The.
Very Strong Stomach Has Mr. Luke, A.
Who Translates a Poet Badly.
Your Lily Eyes Said Yes.

Goode, Starr
Lady of Pazardzik.

Goodell, Larry (b. 1935)
History of Myself.
Human Non-Sequitur.
I Was Going to Be.
Our Red Wheelbarrow.
Sarcophagus.

Goodge, W. T. (1862–1909)
Bad Break!, A.
Federation.
How We Drove the Trotter.
Smithville Tandem Bike, The.

Goodhue, Sarah (1641–81)
My first, as thy name is Joseph, labour so in
   knowledge to increase.

Goodison, Lorna (b. 1947)
Always Homing Now Soul Toward Light.
Annie Pengelly.
Bam Chi Chi Lala.
Birth Stone.
For Don Drummond.
From the Garden of the Women Once Fallen.
Guinea Woman.
Heartease 3.
Hungry Belly Kill Daley.
I Am Becoming My Mother.
In the Mountains of the Moon, Uganda.
Jah Music.
Jamaica 1980.
Kenscoff.
Nanny.
On Becoming a Mermaid.
On Becoming a Tiger.
Quartet of Daffodils, A.
Road of the Dread, The.
Songs of the Fruits and Sweets of Childhood.
Turn Thanks to Miss Mirry.
Upon a Quarter Million.
Wedding in Hanover.

Goodland, Giles
More powerful than the government.

Goodman, Melinda (b. 1957)
Cobwebs.
February Ice Years.
Lullabye for a Butch.
New Comers.
Open Poem.

Goodman, Miriam
Poems from a Country House.
Upkeep.

Goodman, Paul (1911–72)
Ballade of the Moment After.
Birthday Cake.
Chess Game, A.

Connary, Blodgett, Day, Hapgood.
Dreams Are the Royal Road to the
   Unconscious.
Gravestone, August 8, 1968, A.
I planned to have a border of lavender.
In the Jury Room, in Pain.
It was good when you were here.
Little Ode.
Little Prayers.
Lordly Hudson, The.
Sentences After *Defence of Poetry*.
Sentences for Matthew Ready, Series 2, *sel.*
Woman eternal my muse, lean toward me.

**Goodrich, Samuel Griswold ("Peter Parley")
(1783?–1860)**
Higglety, Pigglety, Pop!

Goodtimes, Art
Art of Getting Lost, The.
Jojopan.
Learning to Smile.
Roadkill Coyote.
Sartor Resartus.

Goodwin, Eli
After an All Day Skirmish with the Clouds.
Confession: "I held your sins against you for
   so long."
Untitled: "Number 1 bus jerks to a stop at
   Mass. Ave., The."

Goodwin, Everett
John Birks Gillespie: An Appreciation and
   Reflection.
Mom Used to Listen to Erroll Garner.

Goodwin, Sister Elizabeth Hope
Centennial Year for the Spirits.

Goodyear, Dana
Umbra.

Googe, Barnabe (1540–94)
Coming Homeward out of Spain.
Of Money.
To Doctor Bale.

Goralik, Linor (b. 1975)
Every few weeks I see there is an empty chair
   in our nursery.
Here I am, looking at you, my orphan. Your
   thick scarf. Your cold cigarette.

Goran (1904–62)
Lover's Song, A.
Woman and Beauty.

Göransson, Johannes
Last Instrument, The.

**Gorbanevskaya [or Gorbanyevskaya or
Gorbanevskaia], Natalya [or Natal'ia] (b.
1936)**
And, having started singing this melody.
Curse! Joy! Writing!, A.
Drought, malevolent stepmother.
Epiphanies, / and commas, commas.
Hold out a handful of snow.
Hurry, take pleasure in the oblique caress of
   rain while the sun shines.
I will not be able to explain why.
It is time to think.
Notes of a Cold War Veteran.
Rhymes picked me in a ditch, The.
Savage years of Russian winters, The.
Square of the Holy Passion, gaze on the
   demonstrators.
Sukhanovo.
That time I did not save Warsaw, nor Prague
   later.
This is sung at dawn.
We live—sometimes.
What I drink is not hot, not sweet.

Gordon, Adam Lindsay (1833–70)
Ashtaroth: A Dramatic Lyric, *sels.*
Wolf and Hound, *sels.*
Ye Wearie Wayfarer, *sels.*

Gordon, Carol
Calling Out the Names.

Gordon, G. Timothy
At Jhong-Jhou Train Station.

Gordon, Gerry
Gas.
Tercios del Muerte.

Gordon, Irving (1915–96)
Be Anything (But Be Mine).
Prelude to a Kiss.
Unforgettable.

Gordon, Joan
Love.

Gordon, Mack (1904–59)
Chattanooga Choo-Choo.
Head Over Heels in Love.
I, Yi, Yi, Yi, Yi (I Like You Very Much).
I've Got a Gal in Kalamazoo.
Love Thy Neighbor.
Mam'selle.
Meet the Beat of My Heart.
Serenade in Blue.
There Will Never Be Another You.
There's a Lull in My Life.
Time on My Hands.
You Hit the Spot.
You Make Me Feel So Young.

Gordon, Rebecca
Adolescence.
Nights in Siuna.

Gordon, Roxy
Living Life as a Living Target.
West Texas Mid-Century.

Gore-Booth, Eva (1872–1926)
Travellers, The.
Vision of Niamh, The.

Gorenko, Anna (1972–99)
Death covers up nakedness.
Flowers live faster than rotting of cherries.
Houses like piles of children's books.
There the folk museum alone lies in its embers.
Translated from the European.

Gorenko, Anna Andreyevna *See* Akhmatova,
Anna Andreyevna

Gorey, Edward (1925–2000)
Limerick: "From Number Nine, Penwiper
   Mews."
Limerick: "From the bathing machine came a
   din."
Limerick: "Some Harvard men, stalwart and
   hairy."
Limerick: "To his club-footed child said Lord
   Stipple."
Proctor buys a pupil ices, The.

Gorges, Sir Arthur (1577–1625)
Her Face, Her Tongue, Her Wit.
Sonnet: "Your selfe the Sonne, and I the
   meltinge froste."
Tell me my harte how wilte thow doe.
Written upon the Death of the Most Noble
   Prince Henrie.

Gorham, Sarah
Empress Receives the Head of a Taiping
   Rebel, The.
Notes From a Chinese Love Manual, *sels*.
Princess Parade.

Gorlanova, Nina (b. 1947)
Three-Liners.

Gorostiza, José (1901–73)
Death Without End, *sel.*
Elegy: "Alone, with harsh marine aloneness."
Fireflies.
Who Will Buy Me an Orange?

Gorrell, Stuart (*fl.* 1930)
Georgia on My Mind.

Gosse, Sir Edmund William (1849–1928)
Revelation.
Sestina: "In fair Provence, the land of lute and
   rose."

Gotera, Vince (b. 1952)
Dance of the Letters.
First Mango.
Gambling.
Madarika.
Manong Chito Tells Manong Ben about His
   Dream over Breakfast at the Manilatown
   Cafe.
Pacific Crossing.

Gotlieb, Phyllis (b. 1926)
Death's Head.

Gotoba, Emperor (1180–1239)
There Were Those I Loved.
Gottlieb, Ann (b. 1946)
Meditation on the Feminine Nature of
Shekinah, A.
Gottlieb, Lynn
Greeting Shekinah.
Göttner-Abendroth, Heide
Thou Gaia Art I.
Götz, Johann Nikolaus (1721–81)
First Rondeau: After a French Poet of the
Fourteenth Century.
Second Rondeau.
Gould, Alan (b. 1949)
Demolisher.
Galaxies.
Ice.
Observed Observer, The.
Pearls.
Gould, Hannah Flagg (1789–1865)
Apprehension.
Butterfly's Dream, The.
Child's Address to the Kentucky Mummy, The.
Gould, Janice (b. 1949)
Coyotismo.
Earthquake Weather.
Easter Sunday.
Going Home.
I Learn a Lesson About Our Society.
Tanana Valley.
Gould, Roberta
Amateur Drummer.
Gowar, Mick (b. 1951)
Annabell and the Witches.
Christmas Thank You's.
Rat Trap.
Gowdie, Isabel (fl. 1662)
Charm to Destroy the Male Child of the Laird
of Parkis.
For Cadging Fish.
Shapeshifting.
Gower, John (1325–1408)
Address to the King, An, sels.
Confessio Amantis, sels.
This World Fares as a Fantasy, sel.
Goyette, Susan
In This January.
Moon on Friday Night, The.
Mythology of Cures, The.
On Building a Nest: St. Peter's, Saskatchewan.
Peonies, The.
This Contradiction of Passion.
True Names of Birds, The.
Gōzō, Yoshimasu
Pulling in the Reins.
Grabill, James ("Jim")
Dream of the Closeness of Venus, A.
Lightning, The.
Grace, Patricia
Butterflies.
Grade, Chaim (b. 1910)
Refugees.
Graham, Allan
Flowers', The.
Hands and feet.
Is life.
Languish.
Life and death.
No reason given.
Singularity.
Graham, David (1808–52)
Dogs in Dutch Paintings, The.
Father of the Man.
Jesus Never Sleeps.
Robert Frost's Writing Desk.
Varied Carol, The.
Graham, Desmond (b. 1940)
Wireless, The.
Graham, Harry ("Col. D. Streamer") (1874–1936)
Battue of Berlin, The, sel.
Cockney of the North, The.
Gourmand, The.

Grandpapa.
Indifference.
L'Enfant Glacé.
Mr. Jones.
Opportunity.
Some Ruthless Rhymes, sels.
Waste.
Graham, Jorie (b. 1951)
At Luca Signorelli's Resurrection of the Body.
Breakdancing.
Complex Mechanism of the Break, The.
Covenant.
Dream of the Unified Field, The.
Erosion.
Exit Wound.
Fission.
For One Must Want / To Shut the Other's
Gaze.
Geese, The.
Guardian Angel of Not Feeling, The.
Guardian Angel of Self-Knowledge, The.
Gulls.
Hiding Place, The.
History.
In/Silence.
Mind.
My Garden, My Daylight.
Of Forced Sightes and Trusty Ferefulness.
Of the Ever-Changing Agitation in the Air.
Opulence.
Orpheus and Eurydice.
Over and Over Stitch.
Philosopher's Stone.
Prayer: "Over a dock railing, I watch the
minnows, thousands, swirl."
Region of Unlikeness, The.
Salmon.
San Sepolcro.
Scirocco.
Soul Says.
Surface, The.
Swarm, The.
Tennessee June.
Thinking.
Underneath (1).
Underneath (2).
Underneath (3).
Underneath (7).
What the End Is For.
Willow in Spring Wind: A Showing.
Graham, Joyce Anstruther Maxtone See Struther,
Jan
Graham, Matthew (fl. 20th cent.)
After the War; When Coltrane Only Wanted to
Play Dance Tunes.
Matthew Brady Speaks of Whitman.
Graham, Robert (Robert Cunninghame-Graham) (1735–99)
If doughty [or daughty] deeds my lady
please[s].
Graham, Rudy Bee (b. 1947)
Lynching for Skip James, A.
Without Shadow.
Graham, Taylor (b. 1944)
Chances.
Pieces of Henry.
Graham, Valerie
You Know.
Graham, Virginia (b. 1912)
Disillusionment.
Ein Complaint.
Graham, William Sydney (1918–86)
Beast in the Space, The.
Conscript Goes, The.
Greenock at Night I Find You.
Imagine a Forest.
Johann Joachim Quantz's Five Lessons.
Letter VI.
Lines on Roger Hilton's Watch.
Loch Thom.
Malcolm Mooney's Land.
Night's Fall.
Thermal Stair, The.
What's the News?

Graham-Pole, John
Candor.
Leaving Mother, 1954.
Pain, The.
Venipuncture.
Grahame, Kenneth (1859–1932)
Wind in the Willows, The, sels.
Grahn, Judy (b. 1940)
Ah, Love, You Smell of Petroleum.
Common Woman, The, sels.
Edward the Dyke and Other Poems, sel.
Fortunately the skins.
Grand Grand Mother is returning.
I Have Come to Claim Marilyn Monroe's
Body.
They Say She Is Veiled.
Grainger, James (1724–67)
Bryan and Pereene.
Sugar Cane, The, sels.
Granados, Jorge Fernández (b. 1965)
Account of the Marvels Whispered in a
Mannequin's Ear.
Espectros.
Minimal Ulysses.
Mínimos Ulises.
Perfumist, The.
Perfumista, La.
Promised Land, The.
Relación de maravillas susurradas al oído de
un maniquí.
Specters.
Tierra prometida, La.
Grandmont, Dominique
Down Here, sels.
Grangaud, Michelle (b. 1941)
Isidore Ducasse comte de Lautréamont.
Isidore Ducasse Comte de Lautréamont.
Waiting room, The.
Grano, Paul (b. 1894)
Headlined in Heaven.
In a Chain-Store Cafeteria.
Grant, Anne (1755–1838)
Highlanders, The, sels.
Metrical Translation of the Song of Macgregor
Na Ruara.
Nymph of the Fountain to Charlotte, The.
Grant, C. D.
Wishing You.
Grant, Jamie (b.1949)
Auditor Thinks about Female Nature, An.
Planes Landing.
Skywriting.
Grant, Peter (fl. 1897)
Winter Resolve.
Grant, Sir Robert (1779–1838)
O worship the King all glorious above.
**Granville [or Grenville], George, Baron
Lansdowne (1666–1735)**
Cloe.
To Cloe.
Grapes, Jack
I Like My Own Poems.
Listen.
My Rodeo.
Grass, Günter (b. 1927)
Afterwards.
Gasco.
In the Egg.
Music for Brass.
Saturn.
Transformation.
Grattan, Paul (b. 1971)
Little Night Music, A.
Signs of an Organised Hand.
Grattius, Faliscus
Cynegeticon Liber, sels.
Graves, Alfred Perceval
Irish Spinning-Wheel, The.
Song of the Ghost, The.
Graves, Jackie
What the Dead Do.
Graves, Robert (1895–1985)
All Except Hannibal.

Angry Samson.
Apple Island.
Beauty in Trouble.
Blue-Fly, The.
Carol of Patience.
Christmas Robin, The.
Cloak, The.
Cool Web, The.
Corporal Stare.
Counting the Beats.
Cry Faugh!
Dead Cow Farm.
Devil's Advice to Story-Tellers, The.
Down.
Down, Wanton, Down!
1805.
Epitaph on an Unfortunate Artist.
Escape.
Face in the Mirror, The.
Fallen Tower of Siloam, The.
False Report, A.
Forced Music, A.
Foreboding, The.
Frosty Night, A.
Gardener.
Goliath and David.
Grotesques.
Henry and Mary.
Hide and Seek.
I Wonder What It Feels Like to Be Drowned?
I'd Love to Be a Fairy's Child.
In Broken Images.
In the Beginning Was a Word.
In the Wilderness.
It Was All Very Tidy.
It's a Queer Time.
Laureate, The.
Leveller, The.
Lost Acres.
Lost Love.
Love Story, A.
Love Without Hope.
My Name and I.
Naked and the Nude, The.
Neglectful Edward.
Nobody.
Not at Home.
Ogres and Pygmies.
On Portents.
One Hard Look.
Parent to Children.
Persian Version, The.
Pier-Glass, The.
Pinch of Salt, A.
Plea to Boys and Girls, A.
Queen Mother to New Queen.
Reader over My Shoulder, The.
Recalling War.
Return of the Goddess [Artemis].
Rocky Acres.
Sergeant-Major Money.
She Tells Her Love While Half Asleep.
Sick Love.
Slice of Wedding Cake, A.
Song: Lift-Boy.
Spoils.
Star-Talk.
Tilth.
To Bring the Dead to Life.
To Evoke Posterity.
To Juan at the Winter Solstice.
Travel[l]er's Curse after Misdirection[, The].
Troll's Nosegay, The.
Twins.
Ulysses.
Vain and Careless.
Valentine, A.
Warning to Children.
Weather of Olympus, The.
Wellcome, to the Caves of Artá!
Welsh Incident.
When I'm Killed.
White Goddess, The.

Gray, Sir Alexander (1882–1968)
Fine Fechtin Mouse, The.
On a Cat Aging.

Scotland.
Gray, Alice Wirth
Music in the Meadow.
Why Your Grandfather Stopped Playing the
    Viola.
Gray, David (1838–61)
Sonnet: "October's gold is dim—the forests
    rot."
Gray, Frances
With cheerful mind we yield to men.
Gray, Robert (b. 1945)
Curriculum Vitae.
Dusk, The.
Flames and Dangling Wire.
Journey: the North Coast.
Gray, Thomas (1716–71)
Bard, The [A Pindaric Ode].
Curse upon Edward, The.
Descent of Odin, The.
Elegy Written in a Country Churchyard, sel.
Ode on a Distant Prospect of Eton College.
Ode on the Death of a Favo[u]rite Cat,
    Drowned in a Tub [or Bowl] of Gold Fishes.
On Lord Holland's Seat near Margate, Kent.
Progress of Poesy, The, sel.
Sonnet [on the Death of Mr. Richard West].
Tophet.
Gray, Victor (b. 1926)
All the World's a Stage.
Gray-Kontar, Daniel
Breath.
Cuz' mama played jazz.
July.
Not no socialism/communism classical, but
    some power to the people jazz.
Greacen, Robert (b. 1920)
Bird, The.
Captain Fox.
Carnival at the River.
Father and Son.
St. Andrew's Day.
Summer Day, A.
Grealy, Lucy
Murder.
Green, Adolph (b. 1915)
Adventure.
All of My Life.
Conga.
I Can Cook, Too.
If You Hadn't—But You Did.
Just in Time.
Little Bit in Love, A.
Lonely Town.
Lucky to Be Me.
Make Someone Happy.
New York, New York.
Not Mine.
Party's Over, The.
Some Other Time.
Thanks a Lot, but No Thanks.
You Mustn't Feel Discouraged.
Green, Bud (fl. 1928)
Sentimental Journey.
That's My Weakness Now.
Green, D. Rubin
Names and Sorrows.
Green, George
Portuguese in Mergui, The.
Green, Matthew (1696–1737)
Spleen, The [Complete], sels.
Spleen, The, sels.
Green, Michelle Calhoun
Finished Poem.
For My D.C. Girlfriends.
Green, Rayna
Coosaponakeesa (Mary Mathews Musgrove
    Bosomsworth), Leader of the Creeks, 1700–
    1783.
Greenaway, Kate (1846–1901)
Three Little Girls.
Greenberg, Alvin
City Life.
Freight Train, Freight Train.
Man in the Moon, The.

Wintering Over at the End of the Century.
Greenberg, Arielle (b. 1972)
Afterward, There Will Be a Hallway.
Analogies.
Berlin Series.
Letters from Camp.
Nostalgia, Cheryl, Is the Best Heroin.
Saints.
Greenberg, Samuel (1893–1917)
African Desert.
Conduct.
East River's Charm.
Etching.
Glass Bubbles, The.
God.
Secrecy.
To Dear Daniel.
Greenberg, Uri Zvi (1896–1981)
Hour is tired as if it were time for bed, The.
I have never been at the top of wind-played
    Olympus.
I thirst for water; wine is my need no longer.
Memorial: "He who knew to serve as one of
    the oridnary soldiers."
Ones Living by Their Virtue Say, The.
Poem of Blessing.
Song of Earth.
Song of My People-Forest, People-Sea.
Song of the Great Mind.
Song to Heaven.
Splendor from the Splendid.
Greene, A. C. (1924–2002)
Hawk Over Inwood Road, A.
Greene, Jonathan (b. 1943)
Hut Poem #1.
Ruts.
Greene, Richard (b. 1961)
Crossing the Straits.
Utopia.
Greene, Robert (1558?–92)
Description of the Shepherd and His Wife,
    The.
Greene's Groatsworth of Wit, sel.
Greene's Mourning Garment, sels.
Greene's Vision, sels.
Menaphon, sels.
Never Too Late, sels.
Night Visitor, A.
Palmer, The.
Pandosto: The Triumph of Time, sel.
Perimedes [or Perimedes, the Blacksmith], sel.
Greenfield, Eloise (b. 1929)
Moochie.
Greenhalgh, Chris
Big No-No, The.
Man in the Valley of Women, A.
My Funny Valentine.
Night I Met Marilyn, The.
Of Love, Death and the Sea-Squirt.
Greening, Michael
Missing — Believed Drowned.
Greening, Tom (b. 1930)
My Children Visit the Zendo.
Greenlaw, Lavinia (b. 1962)
Clownfish.
Earliest Known Representation of a Storm in
    Western Art, The.
Electricity.
Five O'Clock Opera.
Galileo's Wife.
Iron Lung.
Love from a Foreign City.
Millefiori.
New Year's Eve.
Reading Akhmatova in Midwinter.
Shape of Things, The.
Skin Full.
Spirit of the Staircase, The.
Three: "Your shaved head on my thigh."
Tryst.
What's Going On.
World Where News Travelled Slowly, A.
Zombies.

Greenlee, Sam (*fl.* 20th cent.)
Memorial for Trane.
Greenwald, Roger
Half-Life of Sorrow, The.
Greenwald, Ted (b. 1942)
And, Hinges.
Anyway.
I Hear a Step.
Licorice Chronicles, *sel.*
Makes Sense, *sel.*
Privets Come into Season at High Tide.
Word of Mouth, *sel.*
Greenway, William (b. 1947)
Anniversary.
Atom Bum, The.
Ophelia Writes Home.
Vines, The.
Greenwell, Anne (1630s–80)
Some Account of Anne Whitehead's Early
Experience, as Written by Her Near Thirty
Years Ago.
Greenwell, Bill
Christopher Robin Changes Guard with Dylan
Thomas.
When my stomach bulges, I hurl wild whoops.
Greenwell, Dora (1812–82)
Broken Chain, The.
Christina.
Demeter and Cora.
Fidelity Rewarded.
Man with Three Friends, The.
Reconciliation.
Scherzo, A.
Sun-Flower, The.
To Christina Rossetti.
To Elizabeth Barrett Browning, in 1851.
To Elizabeth Barrett Browning, in 1861.
Greer, Hilton Ross (1879–1949)
To General Pershing.
Greer, Jane
Rodin's "Gates of Hell."
Greger, Debora (b. 1949)
Frog in the Swimming Pool, The.
Lives of the Saints, *sel.*
Man on the Bed, The.
Penguin Jane Austen, The.
Prince of the Powers of the Air.
Psyche and Eros in Florida.
Gregerman, Debra (b. 1962)
High Speed.
Lullaby.
Silent Globe.
Strictly Speaking.
Gregerson, Linda (b. 1950)
Bicameral.
Cranes on the Seashore.
Elegant.
For the Taking.
Line Drive Caught by the Grace of God.
Mother Ruin.
Norway.
Safe.
Saint's Logic.
Waterborne.
Gregg, Linda (b. 1942)
Adult.
Clapping, The.
Dark Thing Inside the Day, A.
Edge of Something, The.
Fish Tea Rice.
Fishing in the Keep of Silence.
Flower No More Than Itself, A.
Lamb, The.
Limits of Desire, The.
Marriage and Midsummer's Night.
Night Music.
Official Love Story.
Past Perfect.
Poet Goes about Her Business, The.
Precision, The.
Singers Change, the Music Goes On, The.
Skylord.
Stuff.
Tree Falling in a Vacant Forest, The.

Unknowing, The.
What Is Kept.
Gregorio, Renée (b. 1955)
Clown, The.
Long Hill of Garrapata, The.
Marginal Way.
Solitude Dinner.
Gregory, Augusta, Lady (1852–1932)
Day Draws Near, The.
Donal[l] Oge [*or* Og]: Grief of a Girl's Heart.
What Have I Gained?
Gregory, Horace (1898–1982)
Cage of Voices, The.
Chinese Garden, The.
Chorus for Survival, *sels.*
Death and Empedocles 444 B.C.
For You, My Son.
Passion of M'Phail, The, *sels.*
Poems for My Daughter.
Postman's Bell Is Answered Everywhere, The.
They Found Him Sitting in a Chair.
Valediction to My Contemporaries.
Gregory, Mrs. Horace *See* Zaturenska, Marya
Alexandrovna
Gregory, Yvonne (b. 1919)
Christmas Lullaby for a New-Born Child.
Greiffenberg, Catharina Regina von (1633–94)
Concerning the Fruit-bringing Autumn Season.
On the Fruit-Providing Autumn Season.
On the Ineffable Inspiration of the Holy Spirit.
On the Sweet Comfort Brought by Grace, *sel.*
Spring Joy Praising God.
Zealous Admonition to Praise.
Greig, Andrew
Interlude on Mustagh Tower.
Orkeny / This Life.
Pre-Breakfast Rant, A.
Ruth Says.
Still.
Gréki, Anna (1931–67)
Before Your Waking.
Future is for Tomorrow, The.
Grenfell, Joyce (1910–79)
Stately as a Galleon.
Grenfell, Julian (1888–1915)
Into Battle.
Grenier, Robert (b. 1941)
Autumn Moon Rising.
Crow.
Has Faded in Part But Magnificent Also Late
for RC / Mirrors.
Oakland, *sel.*
Phantom Anthems, *sels.*
Sunday Morning.
Wrath to Sadness.
Grénier, Silvia
Salomé.
Signs.
Grennan, Eamon (b. 1941)
Breaking Points.
Conjunctions.
Detail.
Facts of Life, Ballymoney.
Few Last Lines of Laundry, A.
Four Deer.
Journey: "Get the word and go."
Lizards in Sardinia.
Men Roofing.
On a 3 1/2 Oz. Lesser Yellowlegs, Departed
Boston August 28, Shot Martinique
September 3.
One Morning: "Looking for distinctive stones,
I found the dead otter."
Pause.
Shoreline After Storm.
Soul Music: The Derry Air.
Sunday Morning Through Binoculars.
Totem.
Wing Road.
Woman at Lit Window.
Greppi, Cesare (b. 1936)
Boy's Afraid of the Live Tiger, The.
If it had been possible.
If you dropped me on the table.

Like a handful of leaves.
Rain of hollow malice, A.
Subtle erratic vocation, A.
Those quiet little feet in the reflected room.
What words must rush in.
Greshoff, J. (1888–1971)
Friendship for a Woman of Grace.
I Greet You.
Greville, Fanny [*or* Frances] Macartney (c. 1727–
89)
Prayer for Indifference, A, *sels.*
Greville, Fulke, 1st Baron Brooke (1554–1628)
Caelica, *sels.*
Caelica, *sels.*
Mustapha, *sels.*
Treatise of Monarchy, A, *sels.*
Treatise of Religion, A, *sel.*
Treaty of Human Learning, A, *sel.*
What is the cause, why states, that war and
win.
Grey, Clifford (1887–1941)
Hallelujah!
If You Were the Only Girl in the World.
Spread a Little Happiness.
Grieve, Christopher Murray *See* MacDiarmid,
Hugh
Grieves, Catron
Connuche.
Indian Car.
Griffin, Bartholomew (d. 1602)
Fidessa, More Chaste than Kind[e], *sels.*
Venus and Adonis.
Griffin, Gerald (1803–40)
Eileen Aroon, *sel.*
Gille Machree.
Song: "Place in thy memory, dearest, A."
Griffin, Jonathan
Emperor, The.
Night Sky Hiss.
One's Country.
Venerating Senses Save Us.
Griffin, Paul
New Tarantella.
To His Importunate Mistress.
Griffin, Shaun
This Is Not Love's Offering.
Griffin, Susan (b. 1943)
Born into a World Knowing.
Daughter.
Holy Body.
I Like to Think of Harriet Tubman.
I Sit.
Ordinary, as Love.
Our Mother.
Our Mother Talks about Metaphor.
Prayer for Continuation.
Summer Night.
To the Far Corners of Fractured Worlds.
Two, Hers and Mine.
Griffin, Tim
Closed Discussion about the Future.
I Have Folded This Letter in Ten Places.
Imitation.
Observation.
Griffith, Kevin (b. 1964)
Hamlet Meets Frankenstein.
Griffith, Llewelyn Wyn (1890–1977)
Barren Tree, The, *sel.*
Exile: Welsh Service from Daventry.
Office Window.
Silver Jubilee.
Griffiths, Ann (1776–1805)
His left hand, in heat of noonday.
Lo, between the Myrtles Standing.
Griffiths, Bill (b. 1948)
Building: The New London Hospital, *sels.*
For P—Celtic: found text from Machen.
Griffiths, Bryn (b. 1935)
Dolphins.
Master, The.
Griffiths, Jane (b. 1970)
Emigrants.
Errata.

Lost and Found.
Migration.
Griffiths, John Gwyn (b. 1911)
Parasites.
Rosa Mystica.
There Are Limits to Brotherly Love.
Two Are Embracing.
Griffiths, Steve (b. 1949)
Getting It Wrong, Again.
Just a Product of a Certain Situation.
Mines in Sepia Tint, The.
Grigson, Geoffrey (b. 1905)
Death of a Farmyard.
In the Spring Garden.
Landscape Gardeners, The.
Grimald, Nicholas (1519–62)
Funeral Song, Upon the Decease of Annes His
    Mother, A, sels.
True Love, A.
Grimberg, Faina (b. 1951)
Reflection of a wet finger that slipped over the
    faded oil-cloth, The.
Grimes, Anne
Alice's Cat, New Year's Eve 1990.
Grimké, Angelina Weld (1880–1958)
At April.
Beso, El.
Black Finger, The.
Black Runner, The.
Butterflies.
Caprichosa.
Dawn.
Dusk.
Epitaph on a Living Woman.
Eyes of My Regret, The.
Fragment.
Grass Fingers.
Little Grey Dreams.
Mona Lisa, A.
Rosabel.
Tenebris.
Want of You, The.
Winter Twilight, A.
Grimke, Charlotte L. Forten (1837–1914)
Gathering of the Grand Army, The.
Wordsworth.
Grimm, Reinhold (b. 1931)
Assault.
**Grimmelshausen, Hans Jakob Christoffel von
(1621–76)**
Come, balm of night, oh nightingale.
Grin, Ber (1901–89)
Dead Chrysanthemums.
Man Falls at Work, A.
Morris Winchevsky.
My Shtetl on the Dnestr.
On Roads.
Rain: "Little ears of corn are parched, The."
Sacco and Vanzetti.
Strike of the Coal Miners.
Grindel, Eugène See Éluard, Paul
Grindrod, Cathy
Searching.
Grinshpan, Yosl
Grand Central by Night.
In Any Case.
Miner's Family, The.
To My Shtetl Years.
Vanzetti's Ghost.
Griswold, Jay
Origami.
Groarke, Vona
Family.
Family Photograph, The.
Flight.
Folderol.
Glasshouse, The.
History of My Father's House, The.
Imperial Measure.
Indoors.
Islands.
Lighthouse, The.
Pop.
Rainbearers.

Riverbed, The.
Shale.
Thistle.
To Smithereens.
Tonight of Yesterday.
Trousseau.
Veneer.
Way It Goes, The.
Grobman, Mikhail
In mass graves the bodies of plants.
Grosholz, Emily
Back Trouble.
Eden.
Last of the Courtyard, The.
Legacies.
Life of a Salesman.
Old Fisherman, The.
On the Ferry, Toward Patras.
Outer Banks, The.
Remembering the Ardèche.
Grosjean, Jean (b. 1912)
Aïeul, L'
Ancestor, The.
Désert à l'essai.
Trial Desert.
Gross, Philip (b. 1952)
Mappa Mundi.
Two spiral stairs we climb to bed together.
Wasting Game, The, sel.
Grossberg, Benjamin Scott (b. 1971)
Advice to a Coming Child.
Grossman, Allen (b. 1932)
Enough Rain for Agnes Walquist.
Runner, The.
Grossmith, George
You Can't Make Love by Wireless.
Grotz, Jennifer
First Glasses.
Kiss of Judas.
Last Living Castrato, The.
Not Body.
Self-Portrait as a Drowned Man.
Wolf, The.
Grover, Dorys Crow (b. 1921)
Ranch on the Limpia, The.
Groves, Paul
Anniversary Soak.
Back End of the Horse, The.
Heroine.
Turvy-Topsy.
Grubb, David
Windows of Sarajevo, The.
Grue, Lee Meitzen
Dogs of New York, The.
Gruffudd ab yr Ynad Coch (fl. c.1280)
Lament for Llywelyn ap Gruffudd.
Gruffydd, Owen (1643–1730)
Men That Once Were, The, sel.
Gruffydd, Peter (b. 1935)
Digging Soil.
Slate Quay: Felinheli.
Gruffydd, W. J. (1881–1954)
Gwladys Rhys.
Gwladys Rhys.
In Memoriam.
1914–1918 The Young to the Old.
This Poor Man.
This Poor Man.
Yew of Llanddeiniolen, The.
Grumman, Bob
Cryptographiku for Jim L5ftwich.
Cryptographiku for Wallace Stevens.
Cryptographiku No. 1.
Mathemaku for Beethoven.
Mathemaku No. 16.
Mathemaku No. 17.
Reality.
Summer Rain.
Grünbein, Durs
Alba.
Bad Luck with the Second Throw.
Grunberger, Aimée (1954–98)
Old Road, The.

Swimming Upstream.
Grunke, Ann Lundberg
Learning to Live with the Piano.
Gryphius, Andreas (1616–64)
All Is Vanity.
Epitaph for Mariana Gryphius, His Brother
    Paul's Little Daughter.
Evening.
Hell.
Human Misery.
Midnight.
Misery.
My Country Weeps.
Not Mine the Years Time Took Away.
On the Birth of Jesus.
Solitude.
Tears of the Fatherland, Anno Domini 1636.
To Himself.
To the Stars.
To the Virgin Mary.
Gu Cheng (1956–93)
Ark.
Bulin File, The, sels.
Crossing the Border.
Days Gone By.
Forever Parted: Graveyard.
Gaze, The.
Generation, A.
Holy Child Descends, The.
Liquid Mercury, sels.
Oman.
Seven Days.
Words: "My dream won't last long."
Guarini, Giovanni Battista (1537–1612)
Shepherd Thirsis longed to die, The.
Guchu (1334–1409)
Men without rank, excrement spatulas.
Gudding, Gabriel
One Petition Lofted into the Ginkgos.
Gudo (1579–1661)
It's not nature that upholds utility.
**Gudzenko, Semyon [or Semion] Petrovich (1922–
53)**
Before the Attack.
Guernsey, Bruce (b. 1944)
Apple, The.
Maps.
Guerra, Tonino (b. 1920)
Canto Three.
Canto Twenty-Four: "Cunt is a spiderweb,
    The."
Guest, Barbara (1920–2006)
Advance of the Grizzly, The.
Bleat.
Blurred Edge.
Confession of My Images.
Defensive Rapture.
Dissonance Royal Traveller.
Eating Chocolate Ice Cream: Reading
    Mayakovsky.
Emphasis Falls on Reality, An.
Farewell Stairway, The.
Fit Für Gaing Farth.
Geese Blood.
Heavy Violets.
Homage.
Hungry Knight, The.
If So, Tell Me [1999].
Motion Pictures: 15.
Motion Pictures: 4.
Nebraska.
Nostalgia of the Infinite.
On the Verge of the Path.
Otranto.
Outside of This, That Is.
Parachutes, My Love, Could Carry Us Higher.
Prairie Houses.
Red Dye.
Red Lilies.
River Road Studio.
Roses.
Santa Fe Trail.
Sassafras.
Twilight Polka Dots.
Valorous Vine.

Walking Buddha.
Way of Being, A.
Wild Gardens Overlooked by Night Lights.
Words: "Simple contact with a wooden spoon
    and the word, The."
You Can Discover.

Guest, Edgar Albert (1881–1959)
Don't Quit.
Home.
It Couldn't Be Done.
Just Folks.
Let's Be Brave.
Sittin' on the Porch.
Things that Make a Soldier Great, The.

Guest, Harry (b. 1932)
No fragrance yet the fold.
Wales Re-visited.

Guest, Paul
Intrusion of Ovid, The.

Guevara, Ernesto "Che" (1928–67)
Song to Fidel.

Guevara, Maurice Kilwein (b. 1961)
Abuelo, Answers and Questions.
After the Colombian Earthquake.
After the Flood.
Buddy Holly Poem, The.
Doña Josefina Counsels Doña Concepción
    Before Entering Sears.
Easter Revolt Painted on a Tablespoon, The.
Hands of the Old Métis, The.
Long Distance.
Long Woman Bathing, The.
Magic Carpet, The.
Make-Up.
Miniaturist, The.
Once When I Was in the Eighth Grade.
Postmortem.
Reader of This Page.
Rhyme for Halloween, A.
Tuesday Shaman.

Guevara, Miguel de (c.1585–c.1646)
To Christ Crucified.

Guglielmoni, Linda M. Rodriguez
Hurakán: A Two Way Poem.

Guidacci, Margherita (b. 1921)
Anniversary with Agave Plants.
Before Our Encounter.
Crazy Mother, The.
It Is like a Shortness of Breath.
Madame X.
Map of the Winter Sky, The.
Meditations and Maxims, sels.
Spring.

Guiducci, Armanda (b. 1923)
Brevity of Embraces.
Delivery.
I Look at You So Old.
In Emily's Manner.
Perhaps One Day There Will Be Ways.
Readings.
Under an Impure Star.
Upon Closing the Book.

Guignard, Lilace Mellin
Homing In.

Guignard, Mercedès F. (b. 1935)
They're Leaving with a Bridle Round the
    Neck, sel.

Guillén, Jorge (1893–1984)
Anulación de lo Peor.
Beato Sillón.
City Life.
Death of a Pair of Shoes.
Flight.
Happy Armchair.
I Want to Sleep.
Last Land of Exile.
Muerte de Unos Zapatos.
Naturaleza Viva.
Nature Alive.
Nieve, La.
Quiero Dormir.
Riachuelo con Lavanderas.
Río.
River.

Shadows, The.
Snow: "White is lying on top of the green,
    The."
Sombras, Las.
Stream with Washerwomen.
Última Tierra en el Destierro.
Vida Urbana.
Without Lights.

Guillén, Nicolás (b. 1904)
Bars.
Daily Daily, The, sels.
Don't Know No English.
Madrigal.
Moon.
My Last Name.
Sensemayá.
Small Ode to a Black Cuban Boxer.
Usurers, The.
Wake for Papa Montero.

Guillevic, Eugène (b. 1907)
I Don't Speak.
Je ne parle pas.
Quand il eut regardé.
When He'd Looked Hard.

Guillory, Dan (b. 1944)
Snowpoems, sel.

Guilpin, Everard (b. 1572?)
Skialetheia Satire 5, sel.

Guiney, Louise Imogen (1861–1920)
At a Symphony.
Atoning Yesterday, The.
Borderlands.
Deo Optimo Maximo.
Down Stream.
Fog.
Garden Chidings.
In the Reading-Room of the Brtish Museum.
Kings, The.
Knight Errant, The, sels.
Lights of London, The.
Open, Time.
Planting the Poplar.
Private Theatricals.
Reason for Silence, A.
Salutation, A.
Strikers in Hyde Park.
Sunday Chimes in the City.
Tarpeia.
W. H.
When on the Marge of Evening.
Wild Ride, The.

Guinicelli, Guido (fl. 13th cent.)
Canzone: Of the Gentle Heart.
Love and Nobility.

Guinness, Bryan
Forlorn Queen, The.

Guiterman, Arthur (1871–1943)
Anthologistics.
Elegy: "Jackals prowl, the serpents hiss, The."
Everything in Its Place.
Little Lost Pup.
Local Note.
Lyric Baedeker, The, sels.
Of Courtesy.
On the Vanity of Earthly Greatness.
Routine.
Sea-Chill.
Three Ponies.

Gullar, Ferreira (b. 1930)
In the Body.
Noise.
Oswald Dead.
Poster.
Sweet Talk.
There Are Many Traps in the World.

**Gumilyov [or Gumiliov or Gumilev], Nikolai
Stepanovich (1886–1921)**
Baby Elephant, A.
Childhood.
First Canzone.
Fragments 1920–1921.
Moon at Sea.
Porcelain Pavilion, The.
Pre-Memory.
Streetcar That Lost Its Way, The.

Worker, The ("Grizzly squab comrade, A.").

Gundy, Jeff (b. 1952)
Ancient Themes: The Night.
Cookie Poem, The.
For the New York City Poet Who Informed Me
    that Few People Live This Way.
How to Write the New Mennonite Poem.
Inquiry into Gifts, or the Indigo Bunting.
Old Water.
Rain.
Where I Grew Up.

Gunn, Thom (b. 1929)
All Do Not All Things Well.
Allegory of the Wolf Boy, The.
Autobiography.
Black Jackets.
Blank, A.
Breaking Ground, sel.
Byrnies, The.
Claus von Stauffenberg.
Considering the Snail.
Death's Door.
Discovery of the Pacific, The.
Donahue's Sister.
Elegy on the Dust.
Elvis Presley.
Feel of Hands, The.
Flying Above California.
For the Late R. F.
From the Wave.
Gas-poker, The.
High Fidelity.
Hug, The.
Idea of Trust, The.
In Santa Maria del Popolo.
In the Post Office.
In the Tank.
Innocence.
J Car, The.
Lament: "Your dying was a difficult
    enterprise."
Last Days at Teddington.
Last Man, The.
Lines for a Book.
Man With Night Sweats, The.
Map of the City, A.
Martial.
Messenger, The.
Misanthropos, sels.
Missing, The.
Moly.
My Sad Captains.
Night Piece, The: "Fog drifts slowly down the
    hill, The."
Night Taxi.
On the Move.
Painkillers.
Pope's Carnations Knew Him.
Problem, The.
Reassurance, The.
San Francisco Streets.
Skateboard.
Small Plane in Kansas.
Still Life: "I shall not soon forget."
Street Song.
Tamer and Hawk.
Terminal.
Three for Children, sels.
Three Songs, sels.
Touch.
Unsettled Motorcyclist's Vision of His Death,
    The.
Victim, The.
Wound, The.
Yoko.

Günther, Johann Christian (1695–1723)
Consolation Aria.
Departure Aria.

Gupta, Īśvarcandra (1818–59)
I got some news from Kailasa!

Gurevitch, Zali (b. 1949)
Everyone's dancing where I live.
Line of a Poem.

Guri, Haim (b. 1923)
Behold, Our Bodies are Laid Out.

Current Account.
Death of the Man in the Field, The.
Heritage.
Like Beirut.
On a Stone Pillow.
Ones Forgotten, The.
Prayer: "Bestow a blessing on the young men, because the time has come."

Gurney, Ivor (1890–1937)
After War.
April Gale.
Bach and the Sentry.
Ballad of the Three Spectres.
Behind the Line.
Bohemians, The.
December 30th.
Felling a Tree.
First March.
First Time In.
High Hills, The.
If I Walked Straight Slap.
La Gorgue.
Laventie.
Mangel-Bury, The.
Not-Returning, The.
Old Dreams.
Possessions.
Silent One, The, *sels.*
Soaking, The.
Song: "Only the wanderer."
Strange Hells.
To God.
To His Love.
To the Prussians of England.
Towards Lillers.

Gurnis, Peter
Body of Liberties, The.

Gürpınar, Melisa (b. 1941)
Like a Stranger.

Gurr, Robin
Creation.

Gustafson, Jim (b. 1949)
Idea of Detroit, The.

Gustafson, Ralph (b. 1909)
In the Yukon.
Of Green Steps and Laundry.

Gustafsson, Lars
Ballad of the Dogs.

Guthrie, Ramon (1896–1973)
Elegy for Mélusine from the Intensive Care Ward.
Magi, The.
Red-Headed Intern, Taking Notes.
Scene: A Bedside in the Witches' Kitchen.

Guthrie, Woody (1912–67)
Blinding of Isaac Woodard, The.
Dust Storm Disaster.
Talking Dust Bowl.
Vigilante Man.

Gutiérrez Nájera, Manuel (1859–95)
Non Omnis Moriar.

Gutteridge, Bernard (b. 1916)
Enemy Dead, The.
In September 1939.
Shillong.

Gvadányi, József (1725–1801)
Village Notary's Journey to Buda, A, *sels.*

Gwala, Mafika Pascal (b. 1946)
Attempt at communication, An.
Beyond fences.
Bonk'abajahile.
Children of Nonti, The.
Election pincers.
From the Outside.
Getting off the ride.
Gumba, gumba, gumba.
Jive, The.
One small boy longs for summer.
Promise!

Gwangwa'a, Gahlia
Leaking Roof.

Gwdman, Elen (*fl.* 1609)
Young Woman's Complaint about Her Sweetheart, A.

"Gwenallt" *See* Jones, David Gwenallt

Gwyer, Joseph
Ode on the Visit of the Shah of Persia, *sel.*
On a Procession with the Prince of Wales, *sel.*
On the Death of the Duke of Clarence, *sel.*
On the Funeral of Dr. Livingston, *sel.*
To Alfred Gwyer.

Gwynn, Harri (d. 1985)
Creature, The, *sel.*

Gwynn, R. S. (b. 1948)
Among Philistines.
Anacreontic.
Approaching a Significant Birthday, He Peruses The Norton Anthology of Poetry.
Body Bags.
Classroom at the Mall, The.
Drive-In, The.
Horatio's Philosophy.
Iago to His Torturers.
Oprah Out of Control.
Randolph Field, 1938.
Release.
Shakespearean Sonnet.
Snow White and the Seven Deadly Sins.

Gyatso, Tsangyang (1683–1706)
Love-Poems of the Sixth Dalai Lama, *sels.*

Gylys, Beth (b. 1964)
Balloon Heart.
Family Reunion—Aunt Vern's Two Cents.
Fat Chance.

Gyodai (Kato Gyodai) (1732–92)
Inching / From dark to dark—.
Slowly / Over cedars.
Whales / Bellowing dawn.

Gyodai, Kato *See* Gyodai

Gyöngyösi, István (1629–1704)
Beauty of Ilona Zrínyi, The.
János Kemény, *sel.*

Gywnn, R. S.
At Rose's Range.

H

"H. D." *See* Doolittle, Hilda
"H., H." *See* Jackson, Helen Hunt
Ha Jin
Past, The.
Ways of Talking.

Ha-Levi, Judah (1085–1140)
Distant Dove.
On the Sea, *sel.*
On the Voyage to Jerusalem, *sels.*
Poem in Parts.
Summer.

Ha Thi Thao (*fl.* 1940 B.C.)
Our Son's Profession.

Haavikko, Paavo (b. 1931)
Bowmen, The.
Darkness, *sel.*
Fifteen Epigrams in Praise of the Tyrant, *sels.*
Short Year, The, *sel.*
Soul against the state, The.
Winter Palace, The, *sels.*
Woman raises her garment, rain, wind, darkness rise, The.
You can't take with you.

Habila, Helon (b. 1967)
After the Obsession.
Birds in the Graveyard.

Habington, William (1605–54)
Castara, *sels.*

Hachenburg, Hanuš (1929–43)
Terezin.

Hacker, Marilyn (b. 1942)
Almost Aubade.
Aubade 1: "Five-thirty, little one, already light."
Autumn 1980.
Ballad of Ladies Lost and Found.
Boy, The.
Broceliande.
Cancer Winter.

Canzone: "Consider the three functions of the tongue."
Canzone: "No better lost than any other woman."
Coda, *sels.*
Coming Downtown.
Crepuscule with Muriel.
Dusk: July.
Eight Days in April.
Elegy for a Soldier.
Elysian Fields.
Feeling and Form.
Going Back to the River.
Graffiti from the Gare Saint-Manqué.
Invocation: "This is for Elsa, also known as Liz."
Love, Death and the Changing of the Seasons, *sel.*
Mythology.
Nearly a Valediction.
Nights of 1964–66: The Old Reliable.
O little one, this longing is the pits.
Paragraphs from a Day-Book, *sel.*
Rondeau after a Transatlantic Telephone Call.
Runaways Café II.
Rune of the Finland Woman.
Separations Sequence, *sels.*
Squares and Courtyards.
Taking Notice, *sels.*
Twelfth Floor West.
Verlaine.
Villanelle: "Every day our bodies separate."
Villanelle: Late Summer.
Wagers.
Who would divorce her lover with a phone.
Year's End.

Hackett, J. W.
Up close, at the place.

Hadas, Pamela White (b. 1946)
Curious Experiments.
Lion of God in Vermont in May.

Hadas, Rachel (b. 1948)
Easter Afternoon.
Falcon.
House Beside the Sea, The.
Humble Herb is Rival to Prozac.
In the Grove.
Journey Out.
Lair, The.
Mars and Venus.
Moments of Summer.
Mutability.
On That Mountain.
Red Hat, The.
Riverside Park.
Sentimental Education.
Shells.
Still Life in Garden.
Sunday Afternoon.
Tangerine Orchids.
Three Silences.
Twelfth Birthday.
Winged Words.

Hadewijch (*fl.* 13th cent.)
All things.
Cult of Love, The.
If I desire something, I know it not.
Knowing Love in Herself.
Love has seven names.
Love has subjugated me.
Love's Constancy.
Love's Maturity.
Madness of Love, The.
Tighten.
You who want.

Hadfield, Charles
My skin shimmers with all the colours.

Hadfield, Jen
Staple Island Swing.

Hadrian, Emperor (Publius Aelius Hadrianus) (A.D. 76–138)
Adriani Morientis ad Animam Suam.
Emperor Hadrian on his Soul.
Hadrian's Address to His Soul When Dying.

Hadrianus, Publius Aelius *See* Hadrian, Emperor

Haewŏn (1691–1770)
On Hearing the Song of the Geese.
Regarding the Heart.
Song for My Own Shadow.

Hafiz, Khwaja Shams-ad-din Muhammad [or Hafez] (1320–89)
As Rich as Solomon (21).
Come pass me the cup quickly and hand it on.
Cries We Make, The (64).
Deciding Not to Go to India (147).
Fish in Deep Water, The (144).
Five Days Remaining, The (75).
Gabriel's News (37).
Ghazal 24: For Years My Heart Asked Me for Jamshid's Cup.
Ghazal: Half-Way Through the Night.
Light of my eyes, there *is* something to be said.
Lost Daughter, The (19).
Night and Dawn.
Night Visit, The (22).
Odes, *sels.*
On the Way to the Garden (77).
Sitting in the Grief House (250).
Stain of the Sea, The (414).
Three Poems on Friendship, *sels.*

Hagedorn, Friedrich von (1708–54)
Anacreon.

Hagedorn, Jessica Tarahata (b. 1949)
Filipino Boogie.
Latin Music in New York.
Smokey's Getting Old.
Something about You.
Song of Bullets, The.
Souvenirs.
Vulva Operetta.
Yolanda Meets the Wild Boys.

Hagiwara Sakutaro (1886–1942)
Army, The.
Bamboo.
Chair.
Corpse of a Cat, The.
On a Trip.
One Who's in Love with Love, The.
Sickly Face at the Bottom of the Ground.
So Terrifyingly Melancholy.
Spring Night.

Hahn, Kimiko (b. 1955)
Annotation in Her Last Court Diary.
Artist's Daughter, The.
Bath, The: August 6, 1945.
Boat Down the River of Yellow Silt, A.
Boerum Hill Tanka.
Clippings.
Everest.
Firsts in No Particular Order.
Glass Bracelets, The.
Hula Skirt, 1959, The.
Izu Dancer, The.
Mortal Remains.
Older Child, The.
Open Kitchen, The.
Pine.
Radiator.
Reckless Sonnet.
Rockhopper, The.
Sewing Without Mother: A Zuihitsu.
Shower, The.
These Current Events.

Hahn, Oscar
Candlelight Dinner.
Death Is Sitting at the Foot of My Bed.
Gladioli by the Sea.
Good Night Dear.
Little Phantoms.
Man.
No Place Is Here or There.
Vision of Hiroshima.
With Passion without Compassion.

Hahn, Susan
Baobab Tree 1996, The.
Confession.
Fifth Amendment, The.
For Beauty.
Her Purse, at the Winter Solstice.

Holiday, *sels.*
Incontinence.
January Ovaries.
Nijinksy's Dog.
Perennial.

Hahne, Marj
Lies We Tell Ourselves.

Hai-Jew, Shalin
Kinged.
Three Gypsies.

Haida
Song for Smooth Waters.

Haines, Anne
Catching the Scent.

Haines, John (b. 1924)
Eclipse.
Evening Change.
If the Owl Calls Again.
Mothball Fleet: Benicia, California.
Nocturnal.
On a Certain Field in Auvers.
Roadside Weeds.
Sun on Your Shoulder, The.
To Turn Back.
Train Stops at Healy Fork, The.
Yeti.

Hairston, William [or Will] (b. 1928)
Alabama Bus.

Hajjaj, Nasri
Hebron (Al-Khalil).
Honey Fig.
Hungry Orange, A.
In the Burning Wood.
Laila's Face.
Man Who Devoured Himself, The.
Mr. Dheeb Al-Rifa'i.
Psychotherapy.
Three Cows in Hamra Street.

Hajnal, Anna (1907–77)
After Life.
April in the Old Park.
Cyclones.
Deserted Angel, The.
In Praise of the Body.
Makpelah.
To the Creator of My Bones.

Hakkaku
Days when I laughed, The.

Hakugai (1343–1414)
Last year in a lovely temple in Hirosawa.

Hakuin (1685–1768)
How lacking in permanence the minds of the sentient.
Past, present, future: unattainable.
Priceless is one's incantation.
Tea-kettle / Hooked in mid-air.
You no sooner attain the great void.

Hakutsu (*fl.* c.704)
Manyo Shu, Part 3 of 4, *sel.*

Hakuyo
Over the peak spreading clouds.

Halaby, Laila
Handfuls of Wind.
Long Distance.
Refugee.

Halbur, Adam
4-H.

Hale, Sarah Josepha Buell (1788–1879)
Mary's Lamb [or Mary and Her Lamb].
Three Hours; or, The Vigil of Love, *sels.*

Haley, Margaret
Tropicalia.

Haley, Vanessa
Gangrene.
Miss Gee Meets W. H. Auden in Heaven.

Halfe, Louise Bernice
Pähkahkos.

Hall, Daniel (b. 1952)
Dusting.
Hardy's "Shelley's Skylark."
Hermit with Landscape.
Love-Letter-Burning.
Mangosteens.

Short Circuit.
Winged Torso of Eros.
X.

Hall, Donald (b. 1928)
Ardor.
Carol, A.
Digging.
Eating the Pig.
Eighth Inning, The.
Eleanor's Letters.
Exile.
Fifth Inning, The.
For an Early Retirement.
Goggles and Helmet.
Grace, A.
Her Garden.
Her Long Illness.
Impossible Marriage, The.
Independence Day Letter.
Last Days.
Letter after a Year.
Letter with No Address.
Man in the Dead Machine, The.
Maple Syrup.
Mount Kearsarge.
Mount Kearsarge Shines.
My mother said, "Of course."
My Son, My Executioner.
Names of Horses.
Old Pilot, The.
Ox Cart Man.
Peaches.
Pluvia.
Poem Beginning With a Line of Wittgenstein.
Poem, The: "It discovers by night."
Porcelain Couple, The.
Prophecy.
St. Matthew, *sels.*
Sister on the Tracks, A.
Small Fig Tree, A.
Snow, The: "Snow is in the oak."
Surface.
T. R.
To a Waterfowl.
Valentine.
When the Young Husband.
White Apples.
Winter's asperity mollifies.
Without.
Woolworth's.

Hall, Douglas Kent (b. 1938)
Footnote.
New Mexico.

Hall, H. Palmer (b. 1942)
Death on Village Creek, A.
Ghost Lights.
Requiem for James Byrd, Jr.
Romeo Is Dead.

Hall, Hazel (1886–1924)
Baby's Dress, A.
Instruction.
Light Sleep.
Listening Macaws, The.
Made of Crêpe de Chine.
Maker of Songs.
Seams.
Things That Grow.
Woman Death.

Hall, J. C. (b. 1920)
Twelve Minutes.

Hall, John (1529–66)
Job. I.
Numeri XIII.
Praise of Faith, The.
Praise of Godly Love Out of 1 John. 4, The.
Proverb, XXX.
Song of Esechia, The.

Hall, John (1627–56)
Call, The.
Epicurean Ode, An.
Even as the Wandering Traveler.

Hall, Joseph (1574–1656)
Anthem for the Cathedral of Exeter.
Coxcomb, The.
For Christmas Day.

Satire VIII.
Virgidemiarum Book 5, *sel.*
Virgidemiarum, *sels.*

Hall, Leilani R.
Ophelia's Rant before She's Heavy with Drink.

Hall, Richard (1817–66)
Crickhowel.
Pontypool.
Venni-Vach Revisited, *sel.*

Hall, Rodney (b. 1935)
Journey.

Hallam, Arthur Henry (1811–33)
Scott's Dogs at Melrose Abbey.

Halleck, Fitz-Greene (1790–1867)
Alnwick Castle.
Connecticut.
Fanny.
Marco Bozzaris, *sel.*
On the Death of Joseph Rodman Drake.
Red Jacket.

Halleck, Fitz-Greene and **Joseph Rodman Drake**
Croaker Papers, The, *sels.*

Halliday, Mark
Case Against Mist, The.
Credentials.
First: "For me it was Robin Hentz."
Get It Again.
My Moral Life.
Ode: The Capris.
Pink Car, The.
Population.
Questmale.
Reality U.S.A.
Sax's and Selves.

Halman, Talat Sait
Love Tomorrow.

Halperin, Mark (b. 1950)
Tulips.
Two Lines from Paul Celan.

Halpern, Daniel (b. 1945)
Annuals.
Approach, The.
Bravura Lament.
Dance, The.
Her Body.

Halpern, Leivick *See* Leivick [*or* Leyvick], H.

Halpern, Moyshe-Leyb (1886–1932)
Bird, The.
In Central Park.
Long for Home.

Halpine, Charles Graham (1829–68)
Quakerdom (The Formal Call).

Halsey, Alan (b. 1949)
Robin Hood Book, A, *sels.*

Halswell, Henry (fl. 1656)
Upon Mr. Hopton's Death.

Hamadani, Ayn Al-Qozat (1098—1132)
Quatrain.

Hamburger, Michael (b. 1924)
Between the Lines.
Garden, Wilderness.
Treblinka.
Weeding.

Hamby, Barbara
Beriberi.
Invention.
Mr. Pillow.
Six, Sex, Say.
St. Clare's Underwear.

Hamer, Forrest
Allegiance.
Because We Need Good Maps.
Berkeley, Late Spring.
Charlene-N-Booker 4Ever.
Crossroads.
Different Strokes Bar, San Francisco, The.
Lesson.
Line Up.
Origins.

Hamhur Kiwha (1376–1433)
Because of Certain Things.
Higher Living Away from the World.
Lament: "I heard that many temples were
destroyed."

My Hobby on the Mountain.
Pine Bark Bread.

Hamill, Gerry (b. 1919)
Limerick: ""If you're aristocratic," said
Nietzsche."

Hamill, Sam (b. 1942)
Abstract.
After a Winter of Grieving.
Another Duffer.
Gift of Tongues, The.
Midsummer: "Two yearling deer."
Natural History: "Late afternoon, autumn
equinox."
New York Poem, The.
Orchid Flower, The.
Reading Seferis.
Reply to T'ao Ch'ien.
Rising.
Seducing the Sparrow.
Tao of Poetry, A, *sel.*
Ten Thousand Sutras.
To Hayden Carruth on His Eightieth Birthday.
True Illumination Is Habitude.
What the Water Knows.

Hamilton, David Osborne
Ajax.

**Hamilton, George Rostrevor ("George
Rostrevor") (1888–1967)**
Don's Holiday.

Hamilton, Ian ("Edward Pygge") (b. 1938)
Newscast, The.
Visit, The.

Hamilton, Janet (1795–1873)
Oor Location.

Hamilton, Kendra
At the Frenchman's.

Hamilton, Lucy
My Father's Words.

Hamilton, M. Eliza
Midnight in Mississippi.
While Communing with a Tree Near My
Home.
Woman Who Jumped, The.

Hamilton, Nancy (fl. 1940)
How High the Moon.

Hamilton, Sarah (c.1769–1843)
Farewell to France.
Poppy, The.

Hamilton, Saskia (b. 1967)
Species of Audibles.

Hamilton, William (1704–54)
Bonny Heck.

Hamlett, Jenny
Therapist's Comment, The.

Hammad, Suheir (b. 1973)
Broken and Beirut.
Manifest Destiny.
Of Woman Torn.
On the state-sanctioned murder of shaka
sankofa.

Hammerstein II, Oscar (1895–1960)
All er Nothin.'
All the Things You Are.
Can't Help Lovin' Dat Man.
Dat's Love (Habanera).
Don't Ever Leave Me.
Folks Who Live on the Hill, The.
Gentleman Is a Dope, The.
Happy Talk.
Hello, Young Lovers.
I Cain't Say No.
If I Loved You.
I'll Take Romance.
It Might As Well Be Spring.
I've Told Ev'ry Little Star.
June Is Bustin' Out All Over.
Last Time I Saw Paris, The.
Lover, Come Back to Me!
Make Believe.
Many a New Day.
Mister Snow.
My Favorite Things.
Oh, What a Beautiful Mornin'!

Ol' Man River.
People Will Say We're in Love.
Shall We Dance?
Soliloquy.
Some Enchanted Evening.
Song Is You, The.
Sound of Music, The.
Surrey with the Fringe on Top, The.
There Is Nothin' like a Dame.
Who?
Why Was I Born?
Wonderful Guy, A.
You'll Never Walk Alone.
Younger Than Springtime.

Hammial, Philip (b. 1937)
Automobiles of the Asylum.
Jane.
Petit Guignol.
Russians Breathing.
Sadie.
Treason's Choice.

Hammond, Amy (d. 1693)
Verses by My Mother in Her Own Hand.

Hammond, Mac (b. 1926)
Thanksgiving.

Hammond, Mary Stewart
Blessings, *sels.*
GWB in the Rain, The.

Hammond, William (b. 1614?)
On the Same [Death of My Dear Brother, Mr.
H.S., Drowned]: The Boat.
To the Same [My Dear Sister, Mrs S.]: The
Tears.

Hamod, Sam (b. 1936)
After the Funeral of Assam Hamady.
Dying with the Wrong Name.
Joe Williams at the Blue Note/Chicago, 1955;
March 30 1999.
Leaves.
Libyan Airliner/Egyptian Acrobats/Israeli Air
Circus [2004 version].
Moving, *sel.*

Hamoir, Irène
Aria.
Pearl.

Hampton, Jr, Fred (b. 1970)
Trouble I've Seen, The.

Hampton, Susan (b. 1949)
Crafty Butcher, The.
Fire Station's Delight, The.
In Andrea's Garden.
Women who Speak with Steak Knives.
Yugoslav Story.

Han-ch'ing *See* Kuan Han-ch'ing

Han Kwak (fl. 16th cent.)
Don't Bring Out the Straw Mat.

Han-shan (Cold Mountain) (c.730–c.850)
Back at Cold Mountain.
Body Asking Shadow.
Cold Mountain.
Cold Mountain has many hidden wonders.
Cold Mountain Path, The.
Cold Mountain Poem No. 158.
Ever since I left home.
Graceful handsome youth, A.
Happy Among These Cliffs.
His mind is as high as a mountain.
House Without Walls.
I can't stand these bird-songs.
I live in a little country village.
If you're still and never speak.
In a Tangle of Cliffs.
In the Mountains.
I've lived at Cold Mountain—how many
autumns.
Like a Drifting Boat.
My home was at Cold Mountain from the start.
My place is on Cold Mountain.
One Budding-Talent Wang.
People ask about Cold Mountain Way.
People ask the way to Cold Mountain.
Pole your three winged galleons.
Raise girls but not too many.
Reading won't save us from death.

Han-shan
Rough and Dark.
Settled at Cold Mountain.
Some critic tried to put me down.
Someone sits in a mountain gorge.
Storied cliffs were the fortune I cast.
There's a naked bug at Cold Mountain.
They laugh at me hey farm boy.
Try and Make It.
Unfortunate human disorder, The.
Way to Cold Mountain, The.
Whoever has Cold Mountain's poems.
Whoever reads my poems.
Wrecked Town, The.
Yesterday I went to a cloud observatory.

Han-shan Te-ch'ing (1546–1623)
After late spring rain the falling petals swirl.
Bone-chilling snow on a thousand peaks.
Clouds release the hillsides and wake the
    scenes of spring.
Deep among ten thousand peaks I sit alone
    cross-legged.
Fire pit is cold the stone bed like ice, The.
Flat Lake cold penetrates water-lily clothes.
Flat Lake's autumn water merges with the
    winter sky.
Hard cold rain a forest of wind, A.
Hundred thousand worlds are flowers in the
    sky, A.
I follow my impulsive feet wherever they
    might go.
I let mind and body go and gained a life of
    freedom.
I wake up a novice and ask him to make tea.
In Jetavana Park I found a place to rest.
Late at night I sit alone and work on deadwood
    zen.
Moonlight and the sound of pines are things
    we all know.
Mountain Living, sel.
Mountains stand unmoving just the way they
    are, The.
My body is like deadwood my thoughts are
    like ashes.
My long white hair is framed by green
    mountains.
Resting at my open window I gaze out at
    mountains.
Shade of noble trees spreads in all directions,
    The.
Single cloud envelops ten-thousand streamside
    pines, A.
Snow besieges my plank door I crowd the
    stove at night.
Snow covers earth and sky everything is new.
Snow obstructs my brushwood door with me
    inside alone.
Solitary winter lantern casts a feeble shadow,
    A.
Spring has come again the snow has finally
    stopped.
Tiny hut in a world of plants, A.
Who can be a wild deer among deserted
    mountains.

Han Wo (fl. c.902)
Letter to a Zen Master.

Han Yong'un [or Yongwun] (1879–1944)
Artist, The.
Artist, The.
Come to Me.
Embroidery's Secret, The.
Ferryboat and the Traveler.
I Cannot Know.
Inverse Proportion.
Love's Reasons.
Master's Sermon, The.
Preface.
To the Readers.
Upon Reading Tagore's "The Gardener"
Your Silence.
Your Touch.

Han Yü (786–824)
Autumn Thoughts, sels.
Discontent.
Girl of Mount Hua, The.
Humanity.
Losing a Tooth.

Poem on Losing One's Teeth.
Song of the Stone Drums.
To Hou Xi.
Withered Tree, A.
Wounded Falcon, The.

HaNagid, Shmuel (993–1056)
First War.
Gazelle, The.
I'd sell my soul for that fawn.
One Who Works and Buys Himself Books.
Prison, The.
That's it—I love that fawn.
You Mock Me Now in Your Youth.

Hancock, Butch
Circumstance.
My Mind's Got a Mind of Its Own.

Hancock, Leigh
Rain on Snow.

Hand, Monica A.
She-Ghost of Tiresias.
Tattooed Girl.

Handal, Nathalie
Forgetting, Love.
Goran's Whispers.
Sigh, The.

Hands, Elizabeth (fl. c.1789)
Epistle, An.
Favourite Swain, The.
On an Unsociable Family.
Perplexity: A Poem.
Poem on the Supposition of the Book Having
    Been Published and Read, A.
Widower's Courtship, The.

Handy, Jewell M.
Mata Hari Blues or Why I Will Never Be a
    Spy.

Handy, William Christopher (1873–1958)
Beale Street Blues.
Yellow Dog Blues.

Hanh, Thich Nhat and Jane Hirshfield
Reverence is the nature of my love.
Witness Remains, The.

Hanighen, Bernie (fl. 1944)
'Round Midnight.

Hanim, Leylâ (d. 1847)
Drink all you want in the rose-garden. Who
    cares what they say!
Get on with the festivities—let them say what
    they will.

Hanim, Nigâr (1862–1918)
Tell Me Again.

Hankey, Katherine
I love to tell the story, sel.

Hanley, James F.
Zing! Went the Strings of My Heart.

Hanlo, Jan (1912–69)
New Verses for June 7, 1951.

Hanlon, Guy
They Told Me, Heraclitus.

Hannah, Sophie (b. 1971)
End of Love, The.
Good Loser, The.
My Enemies.
Narrow for love that must be fitted in.
Norbert Dentressangle Van, The.
Postcard from a Travel Snob.
Symptoms.
Two Hundred and Sixty-Five Words.
Where is Talcott Parsons Now?
Your Street Again.

Hannaham, Dawn L.
I Love You, Though You're Unemployed.
If There's No Sugar.
To a Flasher.

Hannan, Maggie
Bone Die, The.
Coming Down from Derry Hill.
Drive.
Inmates.
Lamper, The.
Life Model.
Making Conversation.
Seq.

Tap.
Tom Passey's Child.

Hannon, Michael (b. 1939)
Beneath Cold Mountain.
Beyond Freedom.
Homeless.
Real Estate.
Subterranean.
Temporary Heart.

Hans, Marcie
Fueled.
Hurt.

Hanscombe, Gillian Eve
Well, Then Let Slip the Masks.

Hanscombe, Gillian See Also Namjoshi, Suniti

Hanson, Martha (fl. 1809)
How proudly Man usurps the power to reign.
Occasioned by Reading Mrs. M. Robinson's
    Poems.
To Fancy.
To Mrs. Charlotte Smith.

Hantoosh, Gzar
Celebration.
Glass of Ancient Wine, A.
Happiest Man in the World, The.
Love in the Time of Cholera.
Poems for Rasmia.
Take Me, Loneliness.

Hanu
Four Songs Calling a Boy.
Some said the northern window was bright.
Why should you freeze to sleep?

Hanzlicek, C. G.
Egg.
Feeding Frenzies.
Last Trains, The.
Moment.
On the Road Home.
Sierra Noon.
What I Want Is.

Hanzlik, Josef (b. 1938)
Clap Your Hands for Herod.

Haraway, Fran
Midnight Vigil.

Harbach, Otto (1873–1963)
Let's Begin.
Love Nest, The.
Poor Pierrot.
She Didn't Say "Yes."
Smoke Gets in Your Eyes.
Who?
Yesterdays.

Harburg, E. Y. [or "Yip"] (1898–1981)
April in Paris.
Brother, Can You Spare a Dime?
Down with Love.
Eagle and Me, The.
Fun to be Fooled.
Happiness Is Just a Thing Called Joe.
How Are Things in Glocca Morra?
I Like the Likes of You.
If I Only Had a Brain (If I Only Had a Heart)
    (If I Only Had the Nerve).
If This Isn't Love.
It's Only a Paper Moon.
Last Night When We Were Young.
Let's Take a Walk Around the Block.
Lydia, the Tattooed Lady.
Moon About Town.
Necessity.
Old Devil Moon.
Over the Rainbow.
Springtime Cometh, The.
Then I'll Be Tired of You.
We're Off to See the Wizard (The Wonderful
    Wizard of Oz).
What Is There to Say?
When I'm Not Near the Girl I Love.

Hardenberg, Friedrich von See "Novalis"

Hardi, Choman
Escape Journey, 1988.

Hardie, Kerry (b. 1951)
Autumn Cancer.
Avatar, The.

Daniel's Duck.
Hunter Home from the Hill, The.
On Derry's Walls.
Rain in April.
She Goes with Her Brother to the Place of
    Their Forebears.
She Replies to Carmel's Letter.
Sheep Fair Day.
Signals.
Stranger.
Things That Are Lost.
We Change the Map.
What's Left.
Young Woman Stands on the Edge of Her Life,
    The.

Harding, Deborah
Intelligence Quotient, The.

Harding, Rachel E. (b. 1962)
Brother is a Star.
Ezili Impending.

Harding, Samuel (fl. 1640)
Noblest bodies are but gilded clay.

Hardy, Jackie (b. 1946)
Computer Aided Design: Creation.
Difference, The.
Objection Overruled.
Wet Feet.

Hardy, Thomas (1840–1928)
After a Journey.
Afterwards.
Agnosto Theo [To an Unknown God].
Ah, Are You Digging on My Grave?
At Casterbridge Fair, sels.
At Castle Boterel.
At the Railway Station, Upway.
Bedridden Peasant, The.
Beeny Cliff.
Bereft.
Birds at Winter Nightfall.
Bride-Night Fire, The, sel.
Broken Appointment, A.
Caged Goldfinch, The.
Channel Firing.
Christmas Ghost-Story, A.
Christmas: 1924.
Church Romance, A.
Circus-Rider to Ringmaster.
Colonel's Soliloquy, The.
Convergence of the Twain, The.
Dark-Eyed Gentleman, The.
Darkling Thrush, The.
Domicilium.
Dream Question, A.
Drummer Hodge.
During Wind and Rain.
Dynasts, Part 2, The, sel.
Dynasts, The, sels.
Embarcation.
Epitaph on a Pessimist.
Exeunt Omnes.
First Sight of Her and After.
For Life I Had Never Cared Greatly.
Friends Beyond.
Frozen Greenhouse, The.
God-Forgotten.
Going and Staying.
Going, The.
Hap.
Harbour Bridge, The.
He Never Expected Much.
Heredity.
His Visitor.
I Found Her Out There.
I Look into My Glass.
I Looked Up from My Writing.
I Need Not Go.
Impercipient, The.
In Tenebris, sels.
In the Servants' Quarters.
In Time of "The Breaking of Nations."
Let Me Enjoy.
Liddell and Scott.
Light Snow-Fall after Frost, A.
Lines to a Movement in Mozart's E-Flat
    Symphony.

Lying Awake.
Man He Killed, The.
Men Who March Away.
Midnight on the Great Western.
Minute before Meeting, The.
My Spirit Will Not Haunt the Mound.
Nature's Questioning.
Near Lanivet, 1872.
Neutral Tones.
New Toy, The.
New Year's Eve.
Nobody Comes.
Often When Warring.
On a Midsummer Eve.
On an Invitation to the United States.
One We Knew.
Oxen, The.
Pine Planters, The.
Places.
Placid Man's Epitaph, A.
Poet, A.
Rain on a Grave.
Reminder, The.
Respectable Burgher, The.
Roman Road, The.
Ruined Maid, The.
Satires of Circumstance in Fifteen Glimpses,
    sels.
Self-Unseeing, The.
She Hears The Storm.
Shelley's Skylark.
Shut Out That Moon.
Sleep-Worker, The.
Snow in the Suburbs.
Subalterns, The.
Tess's Lament.
Thoughts of Phena.
To Lizbie Browne.
Trampwoman's Tragedy, A.
Transformations.
Tree and the Lady, The.
Under the Waterfall.
Unkept Good Fridays.
Voice of Things, The.
Voice, The.
Voices from Things Growing in a Churchyard.
Waiting Both.
Walk, The.
Weathers [or Weather].
When I Set Out for Lyonnesse.
Wife in London, A.
Winter in Durnover Field.
Workbox, The.
Your Last Drive.

Hare, Maurice Evan (1886–1967)
Alfred de Musset.
Determinism.

Hare, Patrick (b. 1936)
Deceit in the Park.

Hare, Susy
Complaint for a Sorcerer.

Harechavi, Hedva
Already Night, Already Day.
And It Is Still That Way.
1 x 2.

Harer, Katharine
Lucky 7.

Harford, Lesbia (1891–1927)
I can't feel the sunshine.
I Count the Days Until I See You, Dear.
Poem: "I'm like all lovers, wanting love to
    be."
Poem: "Sometimes I wish that I were Helen-
    fair."
Poem: "When I was still a child."

Hargreaves, William (1881–1941)
Burlington Bertie from Bow.

Harington, John (d. 1582)
Husband to Wife.
Sonnet Written upon My Lord Admiral
    Seymour, A.
To His Mother.
Wife to Husband.

Harington [or Harrington], Sir John (1561–1612)
Ariosto's Orlando Furioso Book 34, sel.

Epigrams, sels.
Fair, Rich, and Young.
Groome of the Chambers religion in King
    Henry the eights time, A.
Of honest Theft. To my good friend Master
    Samuel Daniel.
Of the Wars in Ireland.
Of Treason.
Orlando Furioso, sels.
Sir John Raynsford's Confession.
To His Wife, for Striking Her Dog.
Tragicall Epigram, A.

Harington, Lucy, Countess of Bedford (d. 1627)
Elegy: "Death be not proud, thy hand gave not
    this blow."

Harjo, Joy (b. 1951)
Anchorage.
Anniversary: "When the world was created
    wasn't it like this?"
Autobiography.
Bird.
Call It Fear.
Creation Story, The.
Deer Dancer.
Eagle Poem.
For Alva Benson, and for Those Who Have
    Learned to Speak.
He Told Me His Name Was Sitting Bull.
Healing Animal.
I Give You Back.
Insomnia and the Seven Steps to Grace.
Mourning Song.
My House Is the Red Earth.
New Orleans.
No.
Path to the Milky Way Leads Through Los
    Angeles, The.
Perhaps the World Ends Here.
Post-colonial Tale, A.
Rainy Dawn.
Remember.
Resurrection.
Returning from the Enemy, Part 6.
Santa Fe.
She Had Some Horses.
She Had Some Horses, sels.
Skeleton of Winter.
Strange Fruit.
Transformations.
We Encounter Nat King Cole as We Invent the
    Future.
White Bear.
Wolf Warrior.
Woman Hanging from the Thirteenth Floor
    Window, The.
Woman Who Fell from the Sky, The.

Harland-Watts, Joette (b. 1968)
For a Woman's Rights.
Let It Be Known.
Resist Confinement.

Harlow, Michael (b. 1937)
No Problem, But Not Easy.

Harmon, Beatrice E.
Chanson Delice.

Harmon, William (b. 1938)
Concrete Seascape.

Harms, James
After West.
After Yes.
As Always.
Dogtown.
Elegy as Evening, as Exodus.
From Now On.
Joy Addict, The.
Los Angeles.
Los Angeles, The Angels.
My Androgynous Years.
My Own Little Piece of Hollywood.
Reel Around the Shadow.
Sky.
Soon.
Tomorrow, We'll Dance in America.
When You Wish Upon a Star That Turns into a
    Plane.

Harmsen van Beek, Fritzi (b. 1927)
Introduction to a Prayer.
Harney, W. E. (1895–1903)
West of Alice.
Harnick, Sheldon
Ballad of the Shape of Things, The.
Boston Beguine, The.
If I Were a Rich Man.
(I'll Marry) the Very Next Man.
Matchmaker.
She Loves Me.
Someone's Been Sending Me Flowers.
Sunrise, Sunset.
Tonight at Eight.
Harnik, Raiah (b. 1933)
And at Night.
Your Socks.
Harper, Cynthia
Día de Los Muerto.
Water Birds.
Harper, Frances Ellen Watkins (1825–1911)
Aunt Chloe, *sels.*
Bible Defence of Slavery.
Bury Me in a Free Land.
Double Standard, A.
Eliza Harris.
Lines: "At the Portals of the Future."
Moses: A Story of the Nile, *sels.*
Slave Auction, The.
Slave Mother, The.
Slave Mother, The: A Tale of the Ohio.
Vashti.
Harper, Michael S. (b. 1938)
Alice.
Alone.
American History.
Archives.
Bandstand.
Black Cryptogram.
Breaded Meat, Breaded Hands.
Brother John.
Camp Story.
Clan Meeting: Births and Nations: A Blood
    Song.
Dear John, Dear Coltrane.
Deathwatch.
Debridement.
Double Elegy.
Drowning of the Facts of a Life, The.
Elvin's Blues.
Eve (Rachel).
Fireplace, The.
For Bud.
Grandfather.
Here Where Coltrane Is.
High Modes: Vision as Ritual: Confirmation.
Homage to the Brown Bomber.
Homage to the New World.
If You Don't Force It.
In Hayden's Collage.
Jazz Station.
Kin.
Last Affair: Bessie's Blues Song.
Loon, The.
Love Medley: Patrice Cuchulain.
Makin' Jump Shots.
Martin's Blues.
Militance of a Photograph in the Passbook of a
    Bantu under Detention, The.
Narrative of the Life and Times of John
    Coltrane, A: Played by Himself.
Nightmare Begins Responsibility.
Peace Plan: Meditation on the 9 Stages of
    "Peacemaking" as Tribute to Senator
    Claiborne Pell: 1997.
Reuben, Reuben.
Sandra: At the Beaver Trap.
Song: I Want a Witness.
Studs.
This Is My Son's Song: *"Ungie, Hi Ungie."*
Three O'Clock Love Song.
Tongue-tied in Black and White.
We Assume: On the Death of Our Son, Reuben
    Masai Harper.

Harpur, Charles (1813–68)
Basket Of Summer Fruit, A.
Flight of Wild Ducks, A.
Wellington.
Harpur, James
I stretch my arms.
I work in the evening, alone and in silence.
Young Man of Galway's Lament, The.
Harries, E. Howard (1876–1961)
Bone Prison, The.
Harrigan, Stephen
Papalote Creek.
Pecos Bill in Decline.
Poem Of Adulthood, A.
Harrington, James (1611–77)
Inconstancy.
Harrington, Jonathan
Rain of Bicycles, A.
Harris, Allison
Nothing Much.
Harris, Duriel (b. 1969)
For My Father.
For My Mother.
Landscapes.
Meditations 1: "For the beginning and the
    end."
On the Uptown Lexington Avenue Express:
    Martin Luther King Day 1995.
Water from the Well.
What We Have lost.
Harris, James
Balance.
Harris, Jana (b. 1947)
Beneath the Pole of Proud Raven.
Don't Cheapen Yourself.
Dream of the Hair Burning Smell.
Fever.
Sending the Mare to Auction.
Harris, Ken
A in *I* as was Blackening Read (Mandala).
Bough Well Bounds The Vowel Bounds Well,
    A.
Call and Response.
Directions to the Maze.
Fire After Fire, The.
Old Poetess Makes a Child, The.
Poem In Progress.
Vigil.
You Don't Know What Love Is.
Harris, Marie
Trial Separation.
Harris, Max (b. 1921)
Martin Buber in the Pub.
Message from a Cross.
Harris, Peter (b. 1955)
I Know I Aint Hip No More.
Next Malcolm Poem, The.
Some Songs Women Sing.
Harris, Reginald
Usual Suspects, The.
Harris, Robert (b. 1951)
Ambition, The.
Call, The.
Isaiah by Kerosene Lantern Light.
Literary Excellence.
Riding Over Belmore Park.
Sydney.
Harris, Theodore A.
For Lady and Prez.
Harris, Venus
Dare to Be Different.
Harris, William J. (b. 1942)
Grandfather Poem, A.
Practical Concerns.
Rib Sandwich.
Samantha Is My Negro Cat.
We Live in a Cage.
Harrison, De Leon (b. 1941)
Collage for Richard Davis—Two Short Forms,
    A.
Formula for Blue Blues Babies.
Yellow.

Harrison, Gregory (b. 1928)
Playground, The.
Harrison, James [*or* Jim] (b. 1937)
Braided Creek, *sel.*
Geo-Bestiary #X.
Ghazal 39: "If you laid out all the limbs from
    the Civil War hospital."
Helen.
Leda's Version.
Letters to Yesenin, *sels.*
Not here and now but now and here.
Penelope.
Word Drunk.
Harrison, Jeffrey
Adirondack Moosehead.
Arrival: "I will consider my son William."
Birds That Woke Us: An Urban Pastoral, The.
God's Penis.
Hitting Golfballs off the Bluff.
Our Other Sister.
Swifts at Evening.
Harrison, Susan Frances (*Seranus*) (1859–1935)
Catharine Plouffe.
Harrison, Tony (b. 1937)
Art and Extinction.
Breaking the Chain.
Bright Lights of Sarajevo, The.
Call of Nature, The.
Continuous.
Cycles of Donji Vakuf.
Durham.
Earthen Lot, The.
Flood.
Heartless Art, The.
I've done my bits of mindless aggro too.
Kumquat for John Keats, A.
Long Distance II.
Red Lights of Plenty, The.
Remains.
School of Eloquence, The, *sels.*
Study.
Them & [uz].
V.
Harry, J. S. (b. 1939)
Honesty-Stones.
Poem Films Itself, The.
Shot of War, A.
Walking, When the Lake of the Air Is Blue
    with Spring.
Harryman, Carla
Allegory.
Baby, *sels.*
Magic (or Rousseau).
Male, The.
Master Mind, The.
Matter.
Mothering.
My Story.
Not-France.
Privacy.
Realism.
Rowboat was caught in the mudflats, The. A
    few gulls padded around it.
That Can Not Be Taken Away From It.
Hart, David
Hair on your body, The.
Hart, Henry (b. 1954)
Riddle: "Rooted in fresh earth, I am a bush of
    flies."
Hart, Joanne
Only Applebaum Can Make a Tree.
Hart, Kevin (b. 1954)
Dark Angel.
Flemington Racecourse.
Gift, The.
Horizon, The.
Last Day, The.
Members of the Orchestra, The.
Room, The.
Story, The.
Hart, Lorenz (1895–1943)
Bewitched, Bothered and Bewildered.
Blue Moon.
Blue Room, The.
Dancing on the Ceiling.

Falling in Love with Love.
Glad to Be Unhappy.
Have You Met Miss Jones?
He Was Too Good to Me.
I Didn't Know What Time It Was.
I Wish I Were in Love Again.
It Never Entered My Mind.
It's Got to Be Love.
I've Got Five Dollars.
Johnny One-Note.
Lady Is a Tramp, The.
Little Girl Blue.
Manhattan.
Most Beautiful Girl in the World, The.
Mountain Greenery.
My Funny Valentine.
My Heart Stood Still.
My Romance.
Nobody's Heart.
Ship Without a Sail, A.
Spring Is Here.
Ten Cents a Dance.
There's a Small Hotel.
This Can't Be Love.
Thou Swell.
To Keep My Love Alive.
Wait Till You See Her.
Where or When.
With a Song in My Heart.
You Are Too Beautiful.
You Took Advantage of Me.
Zip.

Hart, Seitu J.
Sundays.

Hart-Smith, William (b. 1911)
Boomerang.
Golden Pheasant.
Inca Tupac Upanqui, The.
Nullarbor.

Harte, Bret (Francis Bret Harte) (1836–1902)
Ballad of the Emeu, The.
California Madrigal.
Chicago.
John Burns of Gettysburg.
Miss Edith's Modest Request.
Mrs. Judge Jenkins[; Being the Only Genuine
    Sequel to "Maud Muller"].
Plain Language from Truthful James.
Relieving Guard.
Second Review of the Grand Army, A.
Society upon the Stanislaus, The.
Tale of a Pony, The.
Truthful James to the Editor.
What the Bullet Sang.

Harte, Francis Bret *See* Harte, Bret

Harteis, Richard (b. 1946)
Tempus Fugit.

Harter, Penny
Sister Death.
Tulip.
Turtle Blessing.

**Hartigan, Patrick Joseph ("John O'Brien")
    (1879–1952)**
Field of the Cloth of Gold, The.

Hartley, Marsden (1877–1943)
As the Buck Lay Dead.
Fishmonger.
Lapping of waters / thick, upon razorblade.
This Crusty Fragment.
West Pitch at the Falls.
What Have We All—a Soliloquy of Essences.
Wingaersheek Beach.

Hartman, Jill (b. 1974)
Baroque Excess of Pig Latin and.
J Unsubtle Serif H or Gemini a Fish or
    Eternity In(terrupt)completed, A.
Lost. Children Have Been Known to.
Petition Hecate at the Seal.
[She Unties the Straps of Her Corselette Fire].
Shy Breathing of the Radiator, The. Night
    Sighs.
So Harmless and Regal in the Hieratic Dark.

Hartmann, Sadakichi (1867–1944)
Cyanogen Seas Are Surging.
Haikai, *sels*.

My Rubaiyat, *sels*.
Tanka, *sels*.

Hartnett, Michael (b. 1941)
Death of an Irishwoman.
Farewell to English, A, *sel*.
For My Grandmother, Bridget Halpin.
I Have Exhausted the Delighted Range.
Last Vision of Eoghan Rua Ó Súilleabháin,
    The.
Man Who Wrote Yeats, the Man Who Wrote
    Mozart, The.
Moonsnow '77.
Notes on My Contemporaries, *sels*.
Pity the Man Who English Lacks.
Prayer for Sleep, A.
Quicksand.
Retreat of Ita Cagney, The.
Small Farm, A.
There Will Be a Talking.
Thirteen Sonnets, *sels*.
Visit to Castletown House, A.
Wounded Otter, The.

Hartog, Diana
Oasis, *sels*.

Hartwig, Julia (b. 1921)
Above Us.
St. Matthew, *sels*.
Who Says.

Harvey, Andrew
Prayer to the Divine Mother, A.

Harvey, Christopher (1597–1663)
Church Festivals.

Harvey, James Clarence (1859–1917)
At Eventide.
Swiftly We Fly.
Versicle, A.

Harvey, Matthea (b. 1973)
Abandoned Conversation with the Senses.
By Bicycle.
Crowds Cheered as Gloom Galloped Away,
    The.
Definition of Weather.
Festival of Giovedo Grasso, The.
Ideas Go Only So Far.
Image Cast by a Body Intercepting Light.
In Defense of Our Overgrown Garden.
Introduction to Eden.
Nude on a Horsehair Sofa by the Sea.
One Filament against the Firmament.
Our Square of Lawn.
Pity the Bathtub Its Forced Embrace of the
    Human Form.
Thermae, *sels*.
Translation.

Harvey, Sean
Mighty Tropicale Orchestra, The.

Harvey, Yona
Museum Cashier, The.
Sex.

Harvor, Elisabeth (b. 1936)
Damp Hips of the Women, The.
Four O'Clock, New Year's Morning, New
    River Beach.

Harwood, Gwen (1920–95)
Andante.
At Mornington.
Bone Scan.
Carnal Knowledge 2.
Clair de Lune.
Cups.
Death Has No Features of His Own.
Game of Chess, A.
Homage to Ferd. Holthausen.
Hospital Evening.
In the Park.
Long After Heine.
Mid-Channel.
Naked Vision.
Nightfall.
Sea Anemones, The.
Simple Story, A.
Wine Is Drunk, The.

Harwood, Lee (b. 1939)
As Your Eyes Are Blue.

Czech Dream.
Landscape with 3 People.
Poem for Writers, A.
Rain Journal: London: June '65.
Seaside, The.
Summer: "These hot afternoons "it's quite
    absurd" she whispered."
That Evening Pierre Insisted That I Had Two
    Roast Pigeons at Dinner.

Hashimoto, Sharon (b. 1953)
Eleven A.M. on My Day Off, My Sister
    Phones Desperate for a Babysitter.
Mirror of Matsuyama, The.
Standing in the Doorway, I Watch the Young
    Child Sleep.

Hashin
No sky and no earth at all.

Hashmi, Alamgir
Pro Bono Publico.

Haskell, Dennis (b. 1947)
Call, The.

Haskins, Lola
Dearborn North Apartments Chicago, Illinois.
Jacked.
Message.
Prayer for the Everglades.
Prodigy, The.
Shoes, The.
Times.
To Play Pianissimo.

Haslam, Michael (b. 1947)
Continual Song, *sels*.

Hasluck, Nicholas (b. 1942)
Islands.
Rottnest Island, *sels*.

Hass, Robert (b. 1941)
After I Seized the Pentagon.
Against Botticelli.
Bashō, A Departure.
Between the Wars.
Bookbuying in the Tenderloin.
Churchyard.
Concerning the Afterlife, the Indians of Central
    California Had Only the Dimmest Notions.
Elegy Residence on Earth.
Elm.
Envy of Other People's Poems.
Faint Music.
Feast, The.
Forty Something.
Futures in Lilacs.
Happiness: "Because yesterday morning from
    the steamy window."
Heroic Simile.
House.
Image, The.
Interrupted Meditation.
Late Spring.
Letter to a Poet.
Measure.
Meditation at Lagunitas.
Misery and Splendor.
Now Winter Nights.
On the Coast near Sausalito.
Our Lady of the Snows.
Pact, A.
Palo Alto: the Marshes.
Pornographer, The.
Privilege of Being.
Return of Robinson Jeffers, The.
San Pedro Road.
Song: "Afternoon cooking in the fall sun."
Sonnet: "Man talking to his ex-wife on the
    phone, A."
Spring Drawing 2.
Spring Rain.
Story about the Body, A.
Supple Wreath of Myrtle, A.
Tahoe in August.
Time and Materials.
To Phil Dow, in Oregon.
World as Will and Representation, The.

Hassaan, Youssri
I Considered Myself.

Hathaway, William (b. 1944)
Why That's Bob Hope.

Hātim Ibn Sa'īd
Sun drew near to a full moon: wine and a drinking companion!, A.

HatipoĞlu, Aydın (b. 1940)
Am I the Only One.

Hatshepsut, Queen (d. 1468 B.C.)
Obelisk Inscriptions, *sel.*

Hattersley, Geoff (b. 1956)
Death's Boots.
Frank O'Hara Five, Geoffrey Chaucer Nil.
New Mr Barnsley Something, The.
On the Buses with Dostoyevsky.
Remembering Dennis's Eyes.
Singing.

Hatton, Joseph (1840–1907?)
Christmas Bills.

Hatton, Julia Ann (1764–1838)
Swansea Bay.

Hatton, R. (*fl.* 1631)
Epithalamium: "Hymen hath together tied."

Hatubou, Salim (b. 1972)
Night 1.
Night 9.

Hatun, Mihri (d. 1504)
At one glance.
At times, my longing for the beloved slays me.
I opened my eyes from sleep, and suddenly.
My heart burns in flames of sorrow.

Haug, James
Pool is a Godless Sport.
Tennessee Waltz, The.

Hauge, Olav H.
Across the Swamp.
Big Scales, The.
Carpet, The.
Don't Come to Me with the Entire Truth.
Dream, The: "Let us slip into."
Evening Clouds.
Harvest Time.
I Stand Here, Do You Understand.
It Is That Dream.
Leaf Huts and Snow Houses.
Looking at an Old Mirror.
Midwinter. Snow.

Haught, Kaylin (b. 1947)
God Says Yes to Me.

Hausen, Friedrich von (d. 1190)
Help! How Minne has deserted me.
I think sometimes about.
My heart and my body want to separate.
She may not accuse me.
When I parted from my Good.

Hausman, Gerald
Appaloosa Hail Storm.
September City.

Havel, Vaclav (b. 1936)
It Is I Who Must Begin.

Havergal, Frances Ridley (1836–79)
Afterwards.
Just When Thou Wilt.
One Reality, The.
Perfect Peace.
Take My Life and Let It Be.
Thoughts of God, The, *sel.*
True-hearted, whole-hearted, faithful and loyal.
Trusting Jesus.
Under the Surface.
Vessels of mercy, prepared unto glory!
Who is on the Lord's side?

Havey, Elianour (*fl.* 1658)
Acrostick Eligie on the Death of the No Less Prudent than Victorious Prince Oliver Lord Protector, An.

"Havhesp, Dewi" *See* Roberts, David

Haviaras, Stratis (b. 1935)
Checkmark.
Easter Feast.
Still Life.
Stone-Throw.
Tree.

Hawaiian Oral Tradition
Contract is over and yet, The.
Five O'Clock Whistle, The.
Hana-Hana: Working.
I hate hole hole work.
If we can get married.
In the rush at pau hana.
Laborers keep on coming, The.
My Mother Dear.
Should I return to Japan?
Stripping Leaves from Sugarcane.
With one woven basket.

Hawes, Stephen (1474–1523)
Pastime of Pleasure, The, *sels.*

Hawker, Robert Stephen (1804–75)
Are They Not All Ministering Spirits?
King Arthur's Waes-hael.
Mystic Magi, The.

Hawkesworth, Pauline
Meeting Place.
Two Statues.

Hawkey, Christian (b. 1969)
Fräulein, can you.

Hawkhead, John
I am a glider on time's thermals.

Hawkhead, Patricia
I am the swift scribble.

Hawkins, Desmond
Night Raid.

Hawkins, Jane (*fl.* 1629)
O lett it be for ever told.

Hawoldar, Shakuntala (b. 1944)
Beyond Poetry.
Destruction.
I Am Not Just a Body for You.
I Have Gone into My Prison Cell.
In the Fist of Your Hatred.
It Is Not Just.
To Be a Woman.
To My Little Girl.
Woman, The.
You.
You Have Touched My Skin.
You Must Help Me Gather.

"Hawthorne, Alice" *See* Winner, Septimus

Hawthorne, Nathaniel (1804–64)
I Left My Low amd Humble Home.
Ocean, The.
Oh Could I Raise the Darken'd Veil.

Haxton, Brooks (b. 1950)
Gloss.
Interval of Five Tones Being the Dominant, An.

"Hay, Elijah" *See* Seiffert, Marjorie Allen

Hay, George Campbell (1915–84)
Bizerta.
Hind of Morning, The.
Homer.
Old Fisherman, The.
Still Gyte, Man?

Hay, John Milton (1838–1905)
Jim Bludso of the Prairie Belle.

Hayâlî (d. 1557)
They do not know how to search for the World-Adorner.
We are among those who came to be moths.
When dawn hennas her hands with the blood.

Hayati, Bibi (d. 1853)
Before there was a trace of this world of men.
Is this darkness the night of Power, or the black falling of your hair?

Hayden, Robert Earl (1913–80)
[American Journal].
Astronauts.
Ballad of Remembrance, A.
Ballad of Sue Ellen Westerfield, The.
Beginnings.
Bone-Flower Elegy.
Broken Dark, The.
Crispus Attucks.
Diver, The.
Double Feature.
Dream, The.
Elegies for Paradise Valley.

El-Hajj Malik El-Shabazz.
For a Young Artist.
Frederick Douglass.
Free Fantasia: Tiger Flowers.
Full Moon.
Homage to the Empress of the Blues.
Ice Storm.
Islands, The.
Letter from Phillis Wheatley, A.
Middle Passage.
Monet's "Waterlilies."
Mourning Poem for the Queen of Sunday.
Mystery Boy Looks for Kin in Nashville.
Names.
Night, Death, Mississippi.
Night-Blooming Cereus, The.
October.
Paul Laurence Dunbar.
Perseus.
Plague of Starlings, A.
Point, The.
Road in Kentucky, A.
Runagate Runagate.
Soledad.
Sphinx.
Tattooed Man, The.
Those Winter Sundays.
Whipping, The.
Witch Doctor.

Hayes, Alfred (1911–85)
City of Beggars, The.

"Hayes, Evelyn" *See* Bethell, Mary Ursula

Hayes, Terrance (b. 1971)
At Pegasus.
Blue Terrance, The.
Boxcar.
Clarinet.
Elegant Tongue, The.
Goliath Poem.
Harryette Mullen Lecture on the American Dream.
Midnight: "You call."
Mute Trout.
Nothing.
Ohio River Region.
Postcard from Okemah, A.
Talk.
What I Am.
Wind in a Box.

Hayford, Gladys May Casely (Aquah Laluah) (1904–50)
Shadow of Darkness.

Hayley, William (1745–1820)
To Mrs. Hayley, On Her Voyage to America. 1784.

Hayman, Robert (1579?–1631?)
Owen's Epigrams, *sels.*
To a Worthy Friend, Who Often Objects the Coldnesse of the Winter in Newfound-Land.
To All Those Worthy Women, Who Have Any Desire to Live in Newfound-Land.

Hayne, Paul Hamilton (1830–86)
Charlotte Brontë.
October.
On the Occurrence of a Spell of Arctic Weather in May, 1858.
Vicksburg.

Haynes, Carol (b. 1897)
Any Wife or Husband.

Hayretî (d. 1534)
We are not slaves of Süleymân, nor the captives.

Hays, Mary (1760–1843)
Ah! let not hope fallacious, airy, wild.

Hayward, Amey (*fl.* 1699)
Spiritual Meditation upon a Bee, A.

Hayward, Charles W. (1866–1950)
King George V.

Hayward, David
To the Man Saying "Come on Seis" at Hollywood Park.

Hayzler, Kalman (1899–1966)
At the Machine.
Machine, The.

Hazeley, Iyamide
Beloved.
Lungi Crossing.
When You Have Emptied Our Calabashes.
Hāzim al-Qarṭājannī (1211–85)
Dawn for you is night and darkness is
light;[now] the girls of enjoyable company
shy away, contrary to the days of youth.
Healey, Steve (b. 1966)
As Western Culture Declined Without Its
Knowing.
Interview with a Piece of Smoke.
My Wrist Split Open.
Where Spring Is.
Healey, Trebor (b. 1962)
Bubble.
Ode to DJ.
Healy, Eloise Klein
Advice Like That.
Artemis in Echo Park.
Changing the Oil.
Changing What We Mean.
City Beneath the City, The.
From Los Angeles Looking South.
Louganis.
Moon on the Porch.
Moroni on the Mormon Temple / Angel on the
Wall.
Pope at 7:00 P.M., The.
Toltecs.
Two Centuries in One Day.
What It Was Like the Night Cary Grant Died.
Wisteria.
Healy, Randolph (b. 1956)
Mutability Checkers.
Primula veris.
Size of This Universe, The.
Heaney, Seamus (b. 1939)
Alphabets.
Anahorish.
At Toomebridge.
Badgers, The.
Birthplace, The.
Blackberry-Picking.
Bog Queen.
Bogland.
Broagh.
Casting and Gathering.
Casualty.
Churning Day.
Clearances, *sels.*
Cure at Troy, The, *sels.*
Death of a Naturalist.
Digging.
Disappearing Island, The.
Docker.
Dog Was Crying Tonight in Wicklow Also, A.
Dream of Jealousy, A.
Drink of Water, A.
Electric Light.
Follower.
Forge, The.
Fosterling.
From the Canton of Expectation.
From the Frontier of Writing.
From the Republic of Conscience.
Funeral Rites.
Glanmore Revisited, *sels.*
Glanmore Sonnets, *sel.*
Grauballe Man, The.
Guttural Muse, The.
Harvest Bow, The.
Haw Lantern, The.
Hazel Stick for Catherine Ann, A.
His Dawn Vision.
In Memoriam Francis Ledwidge.
Iron Spike.
Keeping Going.
Limbo.
Mid-Term Break.
Mossbawn, *sels.*
Mud Vision, The.
New Song, A.
Other Side, The.
Otter, The.

Outlaw, The.
Oysters.
Peninsula, The.
Personal Helicon.
Pitchfork, The.
Poor Women in a City Church.
Postcard from North Antrim, A.
Postscript.
Punishment.
Railway Children, The.
Requiem for the Croppies.
Scaffolding.
Seeing Things, *sels.*
Settle Bed, The.
Sharping Stone, The.
Ship of Death, A.
Shooting Script, A.
Singing School, *sels.*
Skunk, The.
Sloe Gin.
Sofa in the Forties, A.
Song: "Rowan like a lip-sticked girl, A."
Sophoclean.
Squarings, *sels.*
Station Island, *sels.*
Stone Verdict, The.
Strand at Lough Beg, The.
Suit, The.
Summer Home.
Summer of Lost Rachel, The.
Sweeney Redivivus, *sels.*
Terminus.
Testimony.
Tinder.
Tollund Man, The.
Toome Road, The.
Turkeys Observed.
Two Lorries.
Ulster Twilight, An.
Waterfall.
Wedding Day.
Westering.
Whatever You Say Say Nothing.
Wheels within Wheels.
Widgeon.
Heard, Josephine D. Henderson (b. 1861)
Admiration.
Advance of Education, The.
Assurance.
Bereft.
Birth of Jesus, The.
Birth of Time, The.
Bishop James A. Shorter.
Black Sampson, The.
City by the Sea, The.
Day after Conference, The.
December.
Deception.
Decoration Day.
Do You Think?
Doxology.
Earthquake of 1886, The.
Easter Morn.
Epitaph, An: "When I am gone."
Eternity.
Fame.
Farewell to Allen University.
Forgetfulness!
General Robert Smalls.
Happy Heart, A.
He Comes Not To-night.
He Hath Need of Rest.
Heart-Hungry.
Hope.
Hope Thou in God.
I Love Thee.
I Will Look Up.
In Memory of James M. Rathel.
Judge Not.
Love Letters.
Matin Hymn.
Message to a Loved One Dead, A.
Morn.
Mother.
Mother's Love, A.
Music.

My Canary.
My Grace Is Sufficient.
My Husband's Birthday.
My Mocking Bird.
National Cemetery, Beaufort, South Carolina,
The.
New Organ, The.
Night.
On Genessarett.
Out in the Desert.
Outcast, The.
Parting Kiss, The.
Parting, The.
Quarrel, The.
Quarto Centennial, The.
Question, The.
Resting.
Retrospect.
Rev. Andrew Brown, over the Hill to Rest.
Rt. Rev. Richard Allen.
Sabbath Bells.
Slumbering Passion.
Solace.
Sunshine after Cloud.
Tennyson's Poems.
They Are Coming?
Thine Own.
Thou Lovest Me.
To Clements' Ferry.
To Whittier.
To Youth.
Truth.
Unuttered Prayer.
Welcome Home.
Welcome to Hon. Frederick Douglass.
When I Would Die.
Where Do School Days End?
Who Is My Neighbor?
Whoso Gives Freely, Shall Freely Receive!
Wilberforce.
Hearle, Kevin (b. 1958)
Lesson, The.
Politics of Memory, The.
Hearn, Michael Patrick
At Dawn.
In the Library.
Hearne, Betsy
Commuters.
Hearne, Vicki (b. 1946)
Gauguin's White Horse.
Hearson, Harry (fl. c.1940)
Nomenclaturik.
Heath (fl. c.1500)
Women.
Heath, Robert (b. 1931)
On Clarastella Walking in Her Garden.
On the Unusual Cold and Rainy [*or* Rainie]
Weather in the Summer, 1648.
Seeing Her Dancing.
Heath-Stubbs, John (b. 1918)
December: Prayer to St. Nicholas.
February.
Footnote to Belloc's "Tarantella"
For the Nativity.
History of the Flood, The.
January.
Jays, The.
Kingfisher, The.
Not Being Oedipus.
One.
Simcox.
Starling, The.
Vision of Beasts, A.
Watching Tennis.
Winter Cricket.
Heber, Reginald (1783–1826)
Brightest and Best of the Sons of the Morning.
From Greenland's Icy Mountains.
Holy, Holy, Holy.
Hébert, Anne (b. 1916)
Earth at Its Origin.
I Am Earth and Water.
Je suis la terre et l'eau.
Terre originelle.
Tomb of the Kings, The.

Hecht, Anthony (1923–2004)
Adam.
Alceste in the Wilderness.
Anthem.
At the Frick.
Behold the Lilies of the Field.
Birdwatchers of America.
Book of Yolek, The.
Christmas Is Coming.
Death the Painter.
Deodand, The.
Dover Bitch, The.
Down There on a Visit.
End of the Weekend, The.
Exile.
Feast of Stephen, The.
Firmness.
From the Grove Press.
Gardens of the Villa D'Este, The.
Ghost in the Martini, The.
Goliardic Song.
Handicap.
Hill, A.
House Sparrows.
Illumination.
It Never Rains.
It Out-Herods Herod. Pray You, Avoid It.
Jason.
Man Who Married Magdalene, The.
More Light! More Light!
Mysteries of Caesar, The.
Naming the Animals.
Paradise Lost, Book V: An Epitome.
Peripeteia.
Prospects.
Rites and Ceremonies, *sels*.
Samuel Sewall.
Sarabande on Attaining the Age of Seventy-
   Seven.
Sestina d'Inverno.
Still Life.
Third Avenue in Sunlight.
To Fortuna Parvulorum.
Venetian Vespers, The, *sels*.
Vow, The.
Hecht, Jennifer Michael
History.
On the Strength of All Conviction and the
   Stamina of Love.
September.
Hedd Wyn (1887–1917)
Black Blot, The.
War.
Hedderman, Richard
First Player's Monologue, The.
Ophelia.
Hedge, Frederic Henry (1805–90)
Mighty Fortress Is Our God, A.
Hedin, Robert
At Betharram.
At the Olive Grove of the Resistance.
Old Liberators, The.
Transcanadian.
Wreck of the Great Northern, The.
Hedrington, William (1947–71)
Bicycling Away from the Library.
Hedyla (*fl.* 3rd cent. A.D.)
Either cockleshells from the Erythraian reef as
   gifts.
Heermann, F. (1585–1647)
Ah, holy Jesus, how hast thou offended.
Hefer, Hayim (b. 1925)
Other Days, The.
Parade of the Fallen.
Paratroopers are Weeping, The.
Sappers, The.
We Left Slowly.
Young Dead Soldiers, The.
Heffernan, Michael (b. 1942)
Africa: "I looked out toward the pasture at the
   cows."
Message, The.
Presidents.
Reading Aquinas.

Heford, Will
That God Made.
Hegland, Jean (b. 1956)
Crone I Will Become, The.
Hegley, John (b. 1953)
Dreaming My Dad.
I'm skulking by the scandal and the handle on
   the door.
Heide, Florence Parry (b. 1919)
Rocks.
Heidsieck, Bernard (b. 1928)
Canal Street, *sels*.
Heifetz-Tussman, Malka (b. 1896)
Keep Me.
Heighton, Steven (b. 1961)
Blackjack.
Heikel, Karen Alice *See* Vala, Katri
Hein, Piet
Noble Funerals Arranged.
Heine, Heinrich (1797–1856)
Ah, Death is Like the Long Cool Night.
Anno 1829.
Dying in Paris, *sels*.
Envenomed are my songs.
Good Luck and Bad.
Grenadiers, The.
Mein Kind, wir waren Kinder.
Memory, A.
Night Thoughts.
Pine Is Standing Lonely, A.
Revenge—?
Sea-Sickness.
Silesian Weavers, The.
Song of Songs, The.
To the World We Must Appear.
Wise Men Ask the Children the Way, The.
Words, Words, Words, and Nothing Doing.
Young Man Loves a Maiden, A.
Heinemann, Margot (1913–92)
For R. J. C. (Summer, 1936).
Ringstead Mill.
Heinowitz, Cole
Five Men.
Heise, Thomas (b. 1971)
Corrections.
My Pietà.
Zombie.
Heissenbüttel, Helmut
Combination II.
Didactic Poem on the Nature of History, A.D.
   1954.
Fragment 3: "All horizons are round."
Homesick.
Simple sentences.
Textbook 10, *sels*.
Heithaus, Joe (*fl.* 20th cent.)
What a Little Moonlight Can Do.
Hejduk, John
Sleep of Adam, The.
Hejinian, Lyn (b. 1941)
Beginner, The.
Book of a Thousand Eyes, The, *sel*.
Cell, The, *sels*.
Erosion of rocks blooms, The. The world.
Fatalist, The, *sels*.
Guard, The, *sel*.
Happily, *sels*.
It Was Only a Coincidence.
Mask of Anger, A.
My Life, *sels*.
Nights.
Oxota: A Short Russian Novel, *sels*.
Person, The, *sel*.
Redo, *sel*.
Sight, *sels*.
Writing Is an Aid to Memory, *sels*.
Held, George
Learning to Ride My Bike.
Split.
Helfand, Jody
Boy Girl Game, The.
Girl in the Boy's Dressing Room, The.

Helfgott, Sarina (b. 1928)
Trains, The.
Helfrich, Karen
Influencing Factors.
Helle, Anita
Poem for Natalia Ginzburg.
Heller, Richard
Minister has all his notes in place, The.
Helton, Roy (b. 1886)
Lonesome Water.
Old Christmas Morning.
Helwig, David (b. 1938)
Cape Breton in Autumn.
Departures.
Lot.
On the Island, *sel*.
Hemans, Felicia Dorothea (1793–1835)
American Forest Girl, The.
Ancient Greek Song of Exile.
Arabella Stuart.
Beings of the Mind, The.
Bride of the Greek Isle, The.
Bride's Farewell, The.
Bring Flowers.
Casabianca.
Chamois Hunter's Love, The.
Corinna at the Capitol.
Costanza.
Despondency and Aspiration.
Diver, The.
Dreaming Child, The.
Edith; a Tale of the Woods.
Effigies, The.
England's Dead.
Epitaph on Mr W—.
Evening Prayer, at a Girls' School.
Gertrude; or, Fidelity till Death.
Grave of a Poetess, The.
Graves of a Household, The.
Homes of England, The.
Hour of Death, The.
Illuminated City, The.
Image in Lava, The.
Imelda.
Indian City, The.
Indian Woman's Death-Song, The.
Joan of Arc, in Rheims.
Juana.
Landing of the Pilgrim Fathers [in New
   England], The.
Last Banquet of Antony and Cleopatra, The.
Last Song of Sappho, The.
Lost Pleiad, The.
Madeline, A Domestic Tale.
Magic Glass, The.
Mary at the Feet of Christ.
Memorial of Mary, The.
Memorial Pillar, The.
Mirror in the Deserted Hall, The.
Night-Blooming Flowers.
Palm Tree, The.
Parting Song, A.
Pauline.
Peasant Girl of the Rhone, The.
Properzia Rossi.
Queen of Prussia's Tomb, The.
Records of the Spring of 1834, *sels*.
Return, The.
Revellers, The.
Rock of Cader Idris, The.
Second Sight.
Siege of Valencia, The, *sels*.
Song of Emigration.
Sonnets, Devotional and Memorial, *sels*.
Spirit's Mysteries, The.
Spirit's Return, A.
Stanzas to the Memory of the Late King.
Statue of the Dying Gladiator, The.
Stranger in Louisiana, The.
Stranger's Heart, The.
Switzer's Wife, The.
Thought from an Italian Poet.
Thoughts during Sickness, *sels*.
To a Departed Spirit.
To a Wandering Female Singer.

To My Eldest Brother, With the British Army
    in Portugal.
To [or the Poet] Wordsworth.
Trumpet, The.
Vigil of Rizpah, The.
Voice of Spring, The.
Wife of Asdrubal, The.
Woman and Fame.
Wreck, The.
Written on the Sea-Shore.

Hemensley, Kris (b. 1946)
Mile from Poetry, A, *sels.*
Sulking in the Seventies.

Hemingway, Ernest (1899–1961)
Age Demanded, The.
Champs d'Honneur.
Chapter Heading.
Earnest Liberal's Lament, The.
Lady Poets With Foot Notes, The.
Riparto d'Assalto.
Valentine.

Hemphill, Essex (1957–95)
Better Days.
Cordon Negro.
Family Jewels.
Homocide.
Soft Targets.
Where Seed Falls.

Hemschemeyer, Judith (b. 1935)
Commandments.
O Mother My Giant Redwood.

Henderson, Alice Corbin *See* Corbin, Alice

Henderson, David (b. 1943)
African Burial Ground called Tribeca, The.
Alvin Cash/Keep on Dancin.'
Blackman in the Desecrated Synagogue—
    Living in the Last Days.
Downtown-Boy Uptown.
Elvin Jones Gretsch Freak.
Horizon Blues.
In Williams.
Lee Morgan.
Lock City.
Sketches of Harlem.
Song of Devotion to the Forest.

Henderson, Donna
Transparent Woman.

Henderson, Hamish (b. 1919)
Ballad of the D-Day Dodgers.
Ballad of the Taxi Driver's Cap.
Elegies for the Dead in Cyrenaica, *sels.*
51st Highland Division's Farewell to Sicily,
    The.
Flyting o' Life and Daith, The.
Opening of an Offensive.
We Show You That Death as a Dancer.

Henderson, Ray (1896–1970)
Best Things in Life Are Free, The.
Birth of the Blues, The.
Button Up Your Overcoat.
I Want to Be Bad.
If I Had a Talking Picture of You.
It All Depends on You.
Magnolia.
Maybe This Is Love.
Never Swat a Fly.
Sunny Side Up.
Thank Your Father.
Turn On the Heat.
Varsity Drag, The.
You're the Cream in My Coffee.

Henderson-Holmes, Safiya (b. 1952)
Battle, Over and Over Again, The.
"C" ing in Colors: Blue.
"C" ing in Colors: Red.
Failure of an Invention.
Friendly Town #1.
Friendly Town #3.
Goodhousekeeping #17.
My First Riot: Bronx, NYC.
To Hell and Back, with Cake.

Hendriks, A. L. (b. 1922)
Will the Real Me Please Stand Up?

Hendry, J. F. (b. 1912)
Constant North, The.
Ship, The.

Henein, Georges
Healthy Remedies.

Heng Chao (*fl.* 10th cent. A.D.)
Farewell to Vinaya Master Ts'ung, Traveling in
    the West.
Listening to Master Yu Chao Play the Lute.

Henley, William Ernest (1849–1903)
At Queensferry.
Ballade Made in the Hot Weather.
Ballade of Dead Actors.
Echoes, *sels.*
For England's Sake, *sel.*
Hawthorn and Lavender, *sels.*
In Hospital, *sels.*
Madam Life's A Piece in Bloom.
Moral, The.
Out of Tune.
Song of the Sword, *sel.*
To Robert Louis Stevenson.
Villon's Straight Tip to All Cross Coves.

Hennen, Tom
Life of a Day, The.
Soaking Up Sun.

Henniker-Heaton, Peter J.
Post Early for Space.

Henry VIII, King of England (1491–1547)
Pastime.
To His Lady.

Henry, Brian (b. 1972)
Across the River.
Break It on Down.
Discovery.
Garage Sale.
Look Around.
Moraine Lake.
Pyramid, The.
Rooms.
Skin: "Never mind the fantasy about the
    tweezers and the tongue."
Submarine.

Henry, James (1798–1876)
Another and another and another.
Son's a poor, wretched, unfortunate creature,
    The.
Two hundred men and eighteen killed.
Very Old Man.

Henry, Michael
Though starlings imitate me.

Henry, Paul (b. 1959)
Love Birds.
Winter Wedding, The.

Henry the Minstrel ("Blind Harry") (1440–92)
Actis and Deidis of the Illustere and Vailyeand
    Campioun Schir William Wallace, Knicht of
    Ellerslie, The, *sels.*
Sir William Wallace, *sels.*

Henryson, Robert (c.1425–c.1506)
Morall Fabillis of Esope the Phrygian, The,
    sels.
Orpheus and Eurydice, *sel.*
Robin [or Robene] and Makyne.
Testament of Cresseid, The, *sels.*

Henson, Lance (b. 1944)
At Chadwicks Bar and Grill.
Coyote Fragments.
Day Song.
Grandfather.
I Am Singing the Cold Rain.
Near Twelve Mile Point.
North.
Solitary.
Splitting Wood Near Morris, Oklahoma on
    Robbie and Lesa McMurtry's Farm.

Henson, Stuart
Grab the beast by the horns.
Heron, The.

Heóghusa, Eochaidh Ó
On Maguire's Winter Campaign.
Winter Campaign, A.

Hepburn, Mrs. Patrick *See* Wickham, Anna

Heraclitus of Halicarnassus (*fl.* c.240 B.C.)
Soil is freshly dug, the half-faded wreaths of
    leaves, The.

Herarty, Toeti (b. 1935)
Cyclus.

Herbert, Sir Alan Patrick (1890–1971)
General inspecting the trenches, The.
I Like Them Fluffy.
Saturday Night.
Triangular Legs.

Herbert, Bill
I do not have a body.

Herbert, Cicely (b. 1937)
Everything Changes.

**Herbert, Edward, 1st Baron Herbert of
Cherbury (1583–1648)**
Another Sonnet to Black It Self [or Itself].
Breaking from under that thy cloudy veil.
Ditty: "If you refuse me once, and think
    again."
Ditty: "Why dost thou hate return instead of
    love."
Elegy over a Tomb.
Epitaph on Sir Philip Sidney Lying in St Paul's
    without a Monument, to be Fastned upon the
    Church Door.
Kissing.
La Gialletta Gallante, or the Sunburned Exotic
    Beauty.
Ode, upon a Question Moved, Whether Love
    Should Continue Forever?, An.
Platonic Love.
Sonnet Made upon the Groves near Merlou [or
    Merlow] Castle.
Sonnet of Black Beauty.
Thought, The.
To One Black, and Not Very Handsome, Who
    Expected Commendation.
You well-compacted groves, whose light and
    shade.

Herbert, George (1593–1633)
Aaron.
Affliction (1).
Affliction (2).
Affliction (3).
Affliction (4).
Agony [or Agonie], The.
Altar, The.
Anagram.
Answer, The.
Artillery [or Artillerie].
British Church, The.
Bunch of Grapes, The.
Call, The.
Christmas.
Church Militant, The, *sel.*
Church Monuments.
Church-Floor[e], The.
Church-Music[k].
Collar, The.
Complaining.
Dawning, The.
Death: "Death, thou wast once an uncouth
    hideous thing."
Denial[l].
Dialogue, A.
Discipline.
Divinity.
Dotage.
Easter ("I got me flowers to straw [or strew or
    strow] Thy [or the] way.").
Easter ("Rise heart; thy Lord is risen. Sing his
    praise.").
Easter Wings.
Elixir [or Elixer], The.
Employment.
Flower, The.
Forerunners, The.
Grace.
Heaven.
Holdfast, The.
Holy Baptism (2).
Holy [or H.] Communion, The ("Not in rich
    furniture, or fine array.").
Hope.

Humility.
Iesu.
Invitation, The.
Jesu.
Jordan (1).
Jordan (2).
Joseph's Coat.
Judge Not the Preacher; for He is Thy Judge.
L'Envoy.
Life.
Longing.
Love (3): "Love bade me welcome: yet my soul drew back."
Love Unknown.
Man.
Mary [or Marie] Magdalene.
Memoriae Matris Sacrum, sel.
Mortification.
Paradise.
Paradise.
Peace.
Pearl, The. Matth. 13:45.
Pilgrimage, The.
Posy [or Posie], The.
Praise (2).
Prayer (1): "Prayer the Church's banquet, Angels' age."
Providence, sel.
Pulley, The.
Quidditie [or Quiddity], The.
Quip, The.
Redemption.
Sin (1).
Sin's Round.
Sion.
Son[ne], The.
Sonnet: "My God, where is that ancient heat towards Thee."
Sonnet: "Sure, Lord, there is enough in Thee to dry."
Superliminare.
Temper (1), The.
Time.
Unkindness.
Vanity [or Vanitie] (1).
Virtue [or Vertue].
Windows, The.
World, The.
Wreath, A.

Herbert, Joyce (b. 1923)
Dossers at the Imperial War Museum.
Irish Scullery Maid, The.

Herbert, W. N. (b. 1961)
Baby Poem Industry Poem, The.
Black Wet, The.
Cabaret McGonagall.
Coco-de-Mer.
Harvest in March, The.
King and Queen of Dumfriesshire, The.
Looking Up from Aeroplanes.
Praise of Italian Chip-Shops.
Slow Animals Crossing.
Smirr.
Socialist Manifesto for East Balgillo, The.
Three Year Ode, A.
To a Mousse.
Why the Elgin Marbles Must be Returned to Elgin.

Herbert, Zbigniew (b. 1924)
Abandoned, The.
Apollo and Marsyas.
Armchairs.
At the Gate of the Valley.
Biology Teacher.
Conch.
Damastes (Also Known As Procrustes) Speaks.
Devil, A.
Drawer.
Elegy of Fortinbras.
Emperor's Dream, The.
Envoy of Mr. Cogito, The.
Five Men.
From the Technology of Tears.
Georg Heym—The Almost Metaphysical Adventure.
Hakeldama.

Hen.
Hygiene of the Soul, The.
I Would Like to Describe.
In a City.
Knocker, A.
Longobards, The.
Meditations of Mr. Cogito on Redemption.
Mr. Cogito and the Imagination.
Mr. Cogito Meditates on Suffering.
Mr. Cogito Tells about the Temptation of Spinoza.
Our Fear.
Painter.
Pan Cogito on Virtue.
Passion of Our Lord Painted by an Anonymous Hand from the Circle of Rhenish Masters, The.
Pebble, The.
Power of Taste, The.
Rain, The.
Remembering My Father.
Report from the Besieged City.
Return of the Proconsul, The.
Rosy Ear.
Silk of a Soul.
Speculations on the Subject of Barabbas.
St. Matthew, sels.
To Marcus Aurelius.
Tongue, The.
Transformations of Livy.
Trial, The.
Voice.
Wall, The.
What I Saw.
What Mr. Cogito Thinks About Hell.
What Mr. Cogito Thinks About Hell.

Herd, Tracey (b. 1968)
Bathing Girls, The.
Big Girls.
Bombshell.
Coronach.
Exhibits, The.
Gia.
Hyperion's Bones.
Marilyn Climbs Out of the Pool.
Missing.
Mystery of the Missing Century, The, sels.
On the Glittering Beaches.
Ophelia's Confession.
Pat Taffe and Arkle.
Pink Rose Rings, The.
Some Mangled Dream Songs for Henry Who is Twenty-eight Years Dead and Past Caring, sel.
Survivors, The.

Herdi, Ahmed (b. c.1933)
God's Freedom Lovers.

Herebert, William (c.1270–c.1333)
My Folk, What Have I Done Thee?
Steddefast cross, inmong alle other.
Who is This that Cometh from Edom?

Herford, Oliver (1863–1935)
I Heard a Bird Sing.
Smile of the Goat, The.
Smile of the Walrus, The.

Herlin, Louise (b. 1925)
Echo of fireplace, An.
Gull inch-perfect over water, The.
Light brush of dawn, A.
Morning space.
Red round sun, The.
Sky has recovered, The.
So many traces.
Warmth of the wind-break wall, The.

Herman, Grace
Clinic, The.

Herman, Jerry (b. 1931)
Before the Parade Passes By.
Hello, Dolly!
I Won't Send Roses.
If He Walked into My Life.
Mame.
Tap Your Troubles Away.
Time Heals Everything.

Hernandez, David (fl. 20th cent.)
Armitage Street.
Martin and My Father.
Pigeons.
Rooftop Piper.
Welcome.
Workers.

Hernandez, Francisco (b. 1946)
Autograph.
De Cómo Robert Schumann Fue Vencido por los Demonios.
On How Robert Schumann Was Defeated by Demons.

Hernández, Miguel (1910–42)
Cada Vez Que Paso.
Cementerio Está Cerca, El.
Cemetery Lies Near, The.
Each Time I Pass.
Final Sonnet.
For Pulling the Feathers from Icy Archangels.
Herido, El.
Humming Eyelashes.
I Go on in the Dark, Lit from Within.
I Have Plenty of Heart.
July 18, 1936–July 18, 1938.
Letter: "Pigeon-house of letters, The."
Lullabies of the Onion.
Lullaby of the Onion.
Me Sobra el Corazón.
My heart can't go on any longer.
Nanas de la Cebolla.
Rumorosas Pestañas.
Sitting on Top of Corpses.
Sonreír con la Alegre Tristeza del Olivo.
To Smile with the Joyful Sadness of the Olive Tree.
Tomb of the Imagination.
Tu Corazón, una Naranja Helada.
Waltz Poem of Those in Love and Inseparable Forever.
War.
Wounded Man, The.
You Threw Me a Lemon.
Your Heart?—It Is a Frozen Orange.

Hernández-Ávila, Inés
Presente.

Hernández Cruz, Víctor (b. 1949)
Anonymous.
Areyto.
Art of Hurricanes, The.
Borinkins in Hawaii.
Caminando.
Discovery.
Energy.
Entering Detroit.
Essay on William Carlos Williams, An.
For the Far-Out Experimental Writer.
Going Uptown to Visit Miriam.
If Chickens Could Talk.
Ironing Goatskin.
Islandis.
It's Miller Time.
Keeping Track of the Serpents.
Latin and Soul for Joe Bataan.
Loíza Aldea.
Man Who Came to the Last Floor, The.
Mesa Blanca.
Milagrosa, La.
Mountain Building.
New/Aguas Buenas/Jersey.
Perlas.
Physics of Ochun, The.
Poem: "Greater cities are, The."
Poem: "Think with your body."
Poem: "Your head it waves outside."
Problems With Hurricanes.
Puerta Rica.
Ruskie's Boy.
Scarlet Skirt.
Side 4.
Side 12.
Side 18.
Side 20.
Side 21.
Side 22.
Side 26.

Side 32.
Slick.
Snaps of Immigration.
Song 1 from "Three Songs from the 50's"
Spirits.
Swans' Book, The.
Tale of Bananas, A.
Three Days/out of Franklin.
Thursday.
Today Is a Day of Great Joy.
Two Guitars.
You Gotta Have Your Tips on Fire.

Hernández de Valle-Arizpe, Claudia (b. 1963)
Hemicránea, *sel.*
Hemicránea, *sel.*

Hernton, Calvin C. (b. 1932)
Ballad of the Life and Times of Joe Louis, A.
Being Exit in the World.
Distant Drum, The.
Long Blues, The.
Medicine Man.
Mob, The.
Poem: "And I went up to that chandeliered place."
Wall, The.

Herodas (*fl.* 3d cent. B.C.)
Friends in Private.
Procuress, The.
Schoolmaster, The.
Women at the Temple.

Hérold, Vera
Big L, The.

Herrera, Fernando de (1534–97)
Sonnet 32.

Herrera, Juan Felipe
After All.
Atavistic: Traces after the Rain.
Cherry Bowl with Blue Revolver: Neo-American Landscape.
Crack Inside My Breast, A.
Dream of Christopher Columbus, The.
Earth Chorus.
Exiles: "At the greyhound bus stations, at airports, at silent wharfs."
Fuselage Installation.
Future Martyr of Supersonic Waves.
Hallucinogenic Bullfighter.
House Is Empty Now.
Iowa Blues Bar Spiritual.
Mexican World Mural / 5 x 25.
Poetry of America, The.
Portrait of Woman in Long Black Dress / Aurelia.
Resurrection of the Flesh, The.
Ten Still Lives.
We Are Made.
Weaning of Furniture-Nutrition.
When He Believed Himself to Be a Young Girl Lifting the Skin of the Water.
Yellow Room, The.

Herrera y Reissig, Julio (1875–1910)
Grey Dawn.
Heraldic Decoration.
Heraldic Decoration.
July.
Return, The.
Sadistic Love.
Siesta.
Sorrowful Shadow, The.

Herrick, Robert (1591–1674)
Argument of His Book, The.
Art above Nature, to Julia.
Ass[e], The.
Bad Season Makes the Poet Sad, The.
Bracelet to Julia, The.
Casualties.
Ceremonies for Christmas[se].
Ceremony upon Candlemas Eve.
Cheat of Cupid; or, The Ungentle Guest, The.
Cherry-ripe [*or* Cherrie-ripe].
Chewing [of] the Cud, The.
Clothes Do But Cheat and Cozen [*or* Cousen] Us.
Comfort to a Youth That Had Lost His Love.
Coming of Good Luck, The.

Corinna's Going a-Maying.
Cross-tree, The.
Cruelties.
Delight in Disorder.
Departure of the Good Daemon, The.
Difference Betwixt King and Subjects, The.
Dirge of Jephthah's Daughter, The.
Dream[e]s.
Duty to Tyrants.
Evensong.
Four[e] Things Make Us Happy Here.
Fresh Cheese and Cream.
Funeral[l] Rites of the Rose, The.
Gods Anger without Affection.
Gods Keyes.
Gods Presence ("God's evident, and may be said to be.").
Gods Providence.
Good Friday: Rex Tragicus, or, Christ Going to His Cross[e].
Grace for a Child.
Hell ("Hell is no other, but a soundlesse pit.").
Her Bed.
Her Legs.
His Content in the Country.
His Farewell [*or* Fare-well] to Sack.
His Grange, or Private Wealth.
His Litany to the Holy Spirit.
His Offering, with the Rest, at the Sepulcher.
His Poetry His Pillar.
His Prayer for Absolution.
His Prayer to Ben Jonson.
His Request to Julia.
His Return to London.
His Saviour['] s Words, Going to the Cross[e].
His Tears to Thamesis [*or* Thamasis].
His Winding-Sheet.
Hock-Cart, or Harvest Home, The.
How Roses Came Red ("Roses at first were white.").
How Roses Came Red ("'Tis said, as Cupid danced [*or* danc't] among.").
Hymn to the Graces, A.
Hymne to Love, An.
Ill Government.
King and No King, A.
Mad Maid's Song, The.
Matins [*or* Mattens], or Morning Prayer.
May-Pole, The.
Meditation for His Mistress[e], A.
My Ben.
Neutrality Loathsome.
Night-Piece, to Julia, The.
No Coming to God without Christ.
Oberon's Feast.
Observation ("Virgin-Mother stood at distance (there), The.").
Ode for Him [*or* Ben Jonson], An.
Ode on the Birth of Our Saviour, An.
On Himself[e] ("Here down my wearied [*or* wearyed] limbs I'll [*or* Ile] lay.").
On Himself[e] ("I fear[e] no Earthly Powers.").
On Himself[e] ("I will no longer kiss.").
On Himself[e] ("Lost to the world; lost to my selfe [*or* myself]; alone.").
On Himselfe ("Weepe for the dead, for they have lost this light.").
Persecutions Purifie.
Pillar of Fame, The.
Power in the People, The.
Predestination.
Primrose, The.
Rainbow; or Curious Covenant, The.
Request to the Graces, An.
Revenge.
Right Hand, The.
Sabbaths.
Salutation.
Seest thou those diamonds which she wears.
Shame, No Statist.
Silken Snake, The.
Temporall Goods.
Temptation.
Thanksgiving to God for His House, A.
To Anthea, Who May Command Him Anything.

To Blossoms.
To Daffodils.
To Daffodils [*or* Daffadills].
To Daisies, Not to Shut So Soon[e].
To Dean-bourn, a Rude River in Devon, by Which Sometimes He Lived.
To Dianeme ("Show [*or* Shew] me thy feet; show [*or* shew] me thy legs, thy thighs.").
To Dianeme ("Sweet, be not proud of those two eyes.").
To Electra ("I dare not ask a kiss[e].").
To Find[e] God.
To Fortune.
To God: an Anthem, Sung in the Chapel at White-Hall, Before the King.
To God ("Come to me God; but do not come.").
To God ("Do with me, God! as Thou didst deal with John.").
To God ("God's undivided, One in Persons Three.").
To God ("If any thing delight me for to print.").
To Heaven.
To His Book[e] ("Have I not blessed [*or* blest] thee? Then go forth; nor fear.").
To His Book[e] ("Make haste away, and let one be.").
To His Conscience.
To His Dying Brother, Master William Herrick.
To His Ever-Loving God.
To His Honoured and Most Ingenious Friend Mr. Charles Cotton.
To His Mistress[es] ("Help[e] me! help[e] me! now I call.").
To His Peculiar Friend Master Thomas Shapcott, Lawyer.
To His Savior [*or* Saviour]. The New Years [*or* yeers] Gift.
To His Saviour.
To His Saviour, a Child; a Present, by a Child.
To Julia ("Julia, when thy Herrick dies.").
To Keep a True Lent.
To Live Merrily, and To Trust to Good Verses.
To Meadows [*or* Meddowes].
To Music, to Becalm His Fever.
To Oenone ("What conscience, say, is it in thee.").
To Perilla.
To the Detracter.
To the King and Queen[e], upon Their Unhappy Distances.
To the King; Upon His Com[m]ing with His Army into the West.
To the King; Upon His Taking of Leicester.
To the Most Fair and Lovely Mistress Anne Soame, Now Lady Abdie.
To the Most Illustrious and Most Hopeful[l] Prince, Charles, Prince of Wales.
To the Sour[e] Reader.
To the Virgins, to Make Much of Time.
To the Water Nymphs, Drinking at the Fountain.
To the Western Wind.
To the Willow-Tree.
To Violets.
Upon a Child.
Upon a Child That Died [*or* Dyed].
Upon Ben Jo[h]nson.
Upon Himselfe Being Buried.
Upon His Spaniel[l] Tracie [*or* Tracy].
Upon His Verses.
Upon Jack and Jill: Epigram.
Upon Julia's Breasts.
Upon Julia's Clothes.
Upon Julia's Voice.
Upon Prudence Baldwin Her Sickness[e].
Upon Prue [*or* Prew], His Maid.
Upon the Loss[e] of His Mistresses.
Upon the Nipples of Julia's Breast.
Upon the Troublesome Times.
Vine, The.
Vision, The ("Methought I saw (as I did dream[e] in bed).").
Vision, The ("Sitting alone (as one forsook).").
Wassaile, The.

What God Is.
When He Would Have His Verses Read.
White Island, The: or Place of the Blest.
Widow's Tears [or Widdowes Teares]: or, Dirge of Dorcas, The.
Wounded Cupid, The.

Herschberger, Ruth (b. 1917)
Huron, The.
Page Torn from a Notebook.
Virgin, The.

Hershenson, Miriam
Husbands and Wives.

Hershon, Robert (b. 1936)
Calls from the Outside World.
Cowboy and the Farmer Should Be Friends, The.
Light and Dark, East and West.
Minnesota Farmers Blame Bad Crop on Jews.
Sentimental Moment or Why Did the Baguette Cross the Road?
Unless You Are a Horse.
Woman Strangles, A.

Hertz, Dalia
Return, The.

Hertzler, Terry (b. 1949)
Just squeeze.

Hervey, Christopher (fl. mid–18th cent.)
Confusion.

Hervey, Lord John (1696–1743)
Nature Queries [or Epistle to Mr. Fox, from Hampton Court].

Herzberg, Judith (b. 1934)
Loss.
Morning.
Seagulls.

Herzog, Arthur, Jr. (fl. 1941)
God Bless the Child.

Hesiod (fl. c.700 B.C.)
Georgics of Heisod, The, sels.
Theogony, sels.
Works and Days, sel.

Hesketh, Phoebe (1909–2005)
Death of a Gardener.
Dilemma.
Love's Advocate.

Hesse, Hermann (1877–1962)
Evil Time.
How Heavy the Days.

Hetherington, Graeme (b. 1937)
Man from Changi, The.

Hewett, Dorothy (b. 1923)
Anniversary.
In Moncur Street.
Summer Solstice, sel.
This Version of Love.
You Gave Me Hyacinths First a Year Ago.

Hewison, R. J. P.
Limerick: "Said an erudite sinologue: "How"."

Hewitt, Geof (b. 1943)
Sailor, The.

Hewitt, John (1907–87)
Because I Paced My Thought.
Colony, The.
Father's Death, A.
Freehold, sels.
From the Tibetan.
I Write For.
Irishman in Coventry, An.
Local Poet, A.
Once Alien Here.
Ram's Horn, The.
Scar, The.
Search, The.
Sonnets for Roberta (1954), sels.
Substance and Shadow.

Heyen, William (b. 1940)
Blackbird Spring.
Blue.
Bread: "I'm standing in elm shadow."
Canary.
Crane in Reeds.
Derailment.
Emancipation Proclamation.
Frost Song.

Fur.
Grace.
King's Men, The.
Mantle.
N.
Passover: the Injections.
Pigeons, The.
Poison.
Return, The.
Riddle: "From Belsen a crate of gold teeth."
Sake Gold.
Simple Truths.
Stadium, The.
Steadying, The.
Tie, The.
Where.
Windfall.
Wish.
Witness.
Words: "Wind in the fur of living buffalo dead."
Yellowjackets.

Heym, Georg
Clearer Now the Days Are Passing.
Demons of the Cities, The.
Final Vigil.
Seafarers.
Umbra Vitae.
Why Do You Come, White Moths.
With Pointed Head She Rises.
With the Ships of Passage.

Heyman, Edward (1907–81)
Blame It on My Youth.
Body and Soul.
Easy Come, Easy Go.
Ho Hum.
I Cover the Waterfront.
I Wanna Be Loved.
When I Fall in Love.
You're Mine, You!

Heynen, Jim
Bloating and Its Remedies.
Boys Go to Ask a Neighbor for Some Apples, The.
Clean People, The.
I Think That I Shall Never See.

Heyrick, Thomas (1649–94)
On a Peacock.
On a Sunbeam.
On an Indian Tomineois, the Least of Birds.

Heyward, DuBose (1885–1940)
Jasbo Brown.

Heywood, John (c.1497–1580)
Ballad on the Marriage of Philip and Mary, A, sel.
Epygrams, sel.
Praise of His Lady, A.
Quiet Neighbour, A.

Heywood, Thomas (1575?–1650)
Apology for Actors, An, sels.
Rape of Lucrece, The, sel.

Hezutsu Tosaku (1726–89)
Affluence—define it as.
On the crest of the hills.

Hickey, Emily (1845–1924)
For Richer, For Poorer.
I Think of You as of a Good Life-boat.
Song: "Beloved, it is morn!"

Hicok, Bob (b. 1960)
Absence: "There are men and women huddled in rooms tonight."
Active Reader, The.
Alzheimer's.
Angels of Mercy.
Arch of Sanctification, The.
Bald Truth, The.
Bond, The.
Busy Days of My Nights, The.
Dropping the Euphemism.
Goodbye in the Shape of a Knot.
Heroin.
Man of the House.
Memory: "I hated the Road Runner."
Once a Green Sky.
Over Coffee.

Radical Neck.
Small Purchase.
Sudden Movements.
Team Effort.
Whither Thou Goest.

Hidalgo, José Luis (1919–1947)
Espera Siempre.
Fish.
Flores Bajo los Muertos.
Flowers Under the Dead.
Has Bajado.
Hay que Bajar.
It's Always Waiting.
Orilla de la Noche.
Pez.
Shore of Night.
Sol de la Muerte.
Sun of Death.
You Came Down.
You Have to Go Down.

Hiebert, Paul Gerhardt (b. 1892)
Farmer and the Farmer's Wife, The.

Hierro, José
Accelerando.
Acelerando.
Any Afternoon.
Boy with the Empty Cage, The.
Encuentro, El.
Fe de vida.
Meeting, The.
Niño de la Jaula Vacía, El.
Poem Without Music.
Requiem ("Manuel de Río, natural.").
Requiem ("Manuel del Río, born.").
Tarde Cualquiera, Una.
Wherever you are, and how.

Hiestand, Emily
Day Lily and the Fox, The.
Moon Winx Motel.
Witch-Hazel Wood, The.

Higgerson, Rick
Utah Jazz, The.

Higgins, Beda (b. 1960)
Strange Beasts.

Higgins, Frank
Tennis in the City.

Higgins, Frederick Robert (1896–1941)
Ballad of O'Bruadir, The.
By the Field of the Crab-Trees.
Father and Son.
Little Clan, The.
Old Jockey, The.
Padraic O'Conaire—Gaelic Storyteller.
Roving Lover, The.
Song for the Clatter-Bones.

Higgins, Larkin
Re: Robert.

Higgins, Mary Rising See Rising-Higgins, Mary

Higgins, Rita Ann (b. 1955)
Almost Communication.
Did-You-Come-Yets of the Western World, The.
Middle-aged Irish Mothers.
Power of Prayer, The.
Some People.

Higginson, Ella (1862–1940)
Dawn.
Dawn on the Willamette.
Dream of Sappho, A.
Eve.
Four-Leaf Clover.
Moonrise in the Rockies.
Opal Sea, The.
Statue, The.

Highfill, Mitch
Marginalization of Poetry, The.
Rebis.
Sea Breeze.

Hightower, James Robert
On Reading the Seas and Mountains Classic.

Hightower, Scott (b. 1952)
Cruising a Hungry World.
Spending the Night.
Tontine.

Hikmet, Nazim (1902–63)
About Mount Uludağ.
All the things I've written about us are untrue.
Angina Pectoris.
Cucumber, The.
Evening Walk, The.
I Shut My Eyes Tight.
Kneeling, I'm staring at the soil.
Letters from a Man in Solitary.
Letters from Chankiri Prison.
Letters to Taranta Babu, *sels.*
My Lady's Eyes Are Hazel.
On Living.
Poems from Prison.
Poems of Nine to Ten P.M.
Prison to Prison.
Rubai.
Since I Was Thrown Inside.
Snow closed the road.
Things I Didn't Know I Loved.
Three Storks Restaurant.

Hilal, Dima
Bedouin Eyes.
Different Morning Altogether, A.
Ghaflah—the Sin of Forgetfulness.

Hilary (*fl.* c.1125)
To an English Boy: "Beautiful boy, flower fair."
To an English Boy: "Hail, fair youth, who seeks no bribe."

Hilberry, Conrad (b. 1928)
Body and Mind.

Hilberry, Jane
Crazy Jane Goes to Painting Class.

Hildebrandt, Rosemary C.
O Eve.

Hildebrandt, Ziporah
In Hecate's Garden.
Kali.
Persephone.

Hill, Aaron (1685–1750)
Garden Window, The.

Hill, Adam
Between Worlds.

Hill, Billy (*fl.* 1936)
Glory of Love, The.

Hill, Clyde Walton
Little Towns of Texas, The.

Hill, Geoffrey (b. 1932)
Apology for the Revival of Christian Architecture in England, An, *sels.*
Bibliographers, The.
Canticle for Good Friday.
Christmas Trees.
Distant Fury of Battle, The.
Funeral Music, *sels.*
Genesis.
Genesis, *sel.*
Guardians, The.
Holy Thursday.
Humanist, The.
Hymns to Our Lady of Chartres, *sels.*
Imaginative Life, The.
In Memory of Jane Fraser [*or* Frazer].
Lachrimae; or Seven Tears Figured in Seven Passionate Pavans, *sels.*
Locust Songs, *sels.*
Mercian Hymns, *sels.*
Merlin.
Metamorphoses, *sels.*
Mystery of the Charity of Charles Péguy, The, *sels.*
Of Commerce and Society: Variations on a Theme, *sel.*
Orpheus and Eurydice.
Ovid in the Third Reich.
Pastoral, A: "Mobile, immaculate and austere."
Picture of a Nativity.
Pre-Raphaelite Notebook, A.
Requiem for the Plantagenet Kings.
Scenes with Harlequins, *sel.*
September Song.
Speech! Speech!, *sel.*
Tenebrae.
To the High Court of Parliament ("Where's probity in this.").

To the High Court of Parliament ("Who could outbalance poised.").
Triumph of Love, The, *sel.*
Turtle Dove, The.
Two Formal Elegies.
Veni Coronaberis.
Vergine bella.
Wreaths.

Hill, Joe (1879–1914)
Preacher and the Slave, The.
There Is Power in a Union.

Hill, Judyth
Dream of Frida, A.
Economics of Gererosity, The.
Grist for Grace.
Season with Angels.
That's Good, That's Enough.

Hill, Mary Crockett (b. 1969)
Abomination.
Bad Karma.
Ruth.
Sleep.

Hill, Michael
City in You.

Hill, Norah (b. 1945)
Dürer's 'Young Hare.'

Hill, Roberta
To Rose.
Waning August Moon.

Hill, Roberta *See* Whiteman, Roberta Hill

Hill, Selima (b. 1945)
Accumulation of Small Acts of Kindness, The, *sels.*
Being a Wife.
Cow.
Desire's a Desire.
Don't Let's Talk About Being in Love.
Elegy for the Bee-god.
Hairbrush.
House.
I Know I Ought to Love You.
I Will Be Arriving Next Thursday in My Wedding-Dress.
My Sister's Jeans.
Parrots.
Please Can I Have a Man.
Prawns de Jo.
Questioning Mr Bonnet.
Small Hotel, A.
Who's that knocking on my ring, says the chin.

Hillard, Jeffrey
Message, The.

Hillel, Ayin *See* Omer, Hillel

Hilles, Rick
Yom HaShoah in Florida.

Hilliard, Bob (1918–71)
Civilization (Bongo, Bongo, Bongo).
Coffee Song (They've Got an Awful Lot of Coffee in Brazil), The.
In the Wee Small Hours of the Morning.

Hillman, Brenda (b. 1951)
Adult Joy.
Arroyo, The.
Black Series.
Cheap Gas.
Dark Existence.
Every Life.
Foghorn, A.
Formation of Soils, The.
Geology, A.
Left Eye.
Little Furnace.
Male Nipples.
Mysteries, The.
On the Pier.
Pre-Uplift of the Sierra.
Recycling Center.
Shared Custody.
Spark, The.
Unbeginning, The.
Y, The.

Hillyer, Robert Silliman (1895–1961)
As One Who Bears beneath His Neighbor's Roof.

Assassination, The.
Dead Man's Corner.
Letter to Robert Frost, A.
Pastoral: "So soft in the hemlock wood."
Prothalamion, *sel.*

Hilmi, Fereydun Rafiq (b. 1942)
Political Parties.

Hilton, Arthur Clement (1851–77)
Heathen Pass-ee, The.
Octopus.

Hilton, David (b. 1938)
I Try to Turn in My Jock.
In Praise of Bic Pens.

Hinckley, Priscilla Baird
New Our Father, The.

Hincks, Elizabeth (*fl.* 1671)
Some More Scruples Clear'd.
Something about Silence.

Hindle, Annie (b. c.1847, d. after 1897)
Her Gift.

Hine, Daryl (b. 1936)
After the Solstice.
Apart from You.
Côte de Liesse.
Destruction of Sodom, The.
Here is another poem in a picture.
Letting Go.
Lines on a Platonic Friendship.
Man's Country.
Northwest Passages.
Point Grey.
Riddle: "Invisible, chimerical."
Sapphics.
Tabula Rasa?
Under the Hill.

Hines, P. R.
My Garden.

Hinkson, Katharine Tynan *See* Tynan Hinkson, Katharine

Hinojosa, Rolando (b. 1929)
Eighth Army at the Chongchon, The.
Jacob Mosqueda Wrestles with the Angels.
January-May 1951 Slaughter, The.
Rest Due and Taken.
Vale.

Hinsey, Ellen
Approach of War, The.
Art of Measuring Light, The.
Body in Youth, The.
On the Uncountable Nature of Things.
Planisféria, Map of the World, Lisbon, 1554.
Roman Arbor, The.
Update on the Last Judgment.

Hinz-Penner, Raylene (b. 1949)
Crossing Over.
Flowers: "I have not missed the irony of this magnetism, my being."
Once, in Santa Fe.
Opening in Santa Fe, The.
Prayer for the End of the World.

Hippolyte, Kendel (b. 1952)
Antonette's Boogie.
Jah Son / Another Way.
Reggae Cat (for Boston Jack).
Revo Lyric.
So Jah Sey.

Hipponax (*fl.* 6th cent. B.C.)
Still Waiting for My Winter Coat: A Sequence of Fragments.

Hirsch, Edward (b. 1950)
American Apocalypse.
Ancient Signs.
And So It Begins Again.
Art Pepper.
Boy With a Headset.
Chardin Exhibition, The.
Days of 1968.
Edward Hopper and the House by the Railroad.
Evening Star.
Fast Break.
First Snowfall: Intimations.
For the Sleepwalkers.
History of My Stupidity, The: Volume 3, Chapter 5.

Husband and Wife.
In Memoriam Paul Celan.
In Spite of Everything, the Stars.
In the Midwest.
Lectures on Love, The.
Magic Mirror, The.
Man on a Fire Escape.
Milena Jesenká.
My Father's Back.
My Grandfather's Poems.
Paul Celan: A Grave and Mysterious
    Sentence.
Poor Angels.
Second Story Warehouse.
Self-Portrait.
Short Lexicon of Torture in the Eighties, A.
Simone Weil: In Assisi.
Song Against Natural Selection.
Song: "This is a song for the speechless."
Summer Surprised Us.
Tristan Tzara.
Whitman Leaves the Boardwalk.
Wild Gratitude.

Hirsch, Eugene
Two Suffering Men.

Hirschhorn, Norbert
Number Our Days.

Hirschman, Jack (b. 1933)
Headlands.
Painting, The.
Transfiguration.
Tremor, The.
Weeping, The.
X L E B.

Hirshfield, Jane
Adamantine Perfection of Desire, The.
After Long Silence.
Against Certainty.
Ars Poetica.
At Night.
Cedary Fragrance, A.
Dead Do Not Want Us Dead, The.
Each Happiness Ringed by Lions.
Each Moment a White Bull Steps Shining into
    the World.
Each Step.
Earthly Beauty, An.
Half-sleeping, / my body pulls toward yours.
Heart's Counting Knows Only One, The.
In Praise of Coldness.
Inspiration: "Think of those Chinese monks'
    tales."
Invocation: "This August night, raccoons."
It Was Like This : You Were Happy.
Knowing Nothing.
Leaving the October Palace.
Letter to Hugo from Later.
Lighthouse.
Lives of the Heart,The.
Man Walks through His Life, A.
Monk Stood Beside a Wheelbarrow, The.
Music Like Water, The.
Not-Yet.
Of Gravity and Angels.
On the Beach.
Osiris.
Painting.
Picnic.
Poe: An Assay (1).
Pomegranates.
Rain in May.
Reading Chinese Poetry before Dawn.
Recalling a Sung Dynasty Landscape.
Red Onion, Cherries, Boiling Potatoes, Milk.
Room, A.
Spell to Be Said After Illness.
Story, A.
Stream of It, The.
Studying Wu Wei, Muir Beach.
That Falling.
Theology.
To Drink.
To Judgement: An Assay.
Tree.
Why Bodhidharma Went to Howard Johnson's.

Hirshfield, Jane *See Also* Hanh, Thich Nhat
Hisle, Janeya K.
And All the Sisters Said.
For Fatma and Her Co-Wives.
We.

Hitchcock, George
Solitaire.

Hitchman-Britton, Oneca
Road to the Presidency.

Hitomaro, Kakinomoto no *See* Kakinomoto no
    Hitomaro

Hixon, Lex
My blissful Mother exists fully through every
    creature!
Who can keep a blazing fire tied in a cotton
    cloth?

Hjern, Kjell (1916–84)
On the Growth of Hair in Middle Age.
To My Love.

Ho Ch'e Ch'ang (659–744)
Homecoming: "I was a boy when I left home."
Return, The.
Returning after I left my home in childhood.
Written Impromptu upon Returning to My
    Hometown.

Ho Ch'i-fang
Get Drunk.

Ho Chi Minh (1890–1969)
Two Prison Poems.

Ho Ching-ming (1483–1521)
Ballad of the Government Granary Clerk.

Ho Hsun (d. 527)
Singing-Girls in the Brazen Bird.
Spring Wind.
Watching the New Moon, I Compose These
    Verses to Show to My Fellow-Travelers,
    Stranded with Me.

Hŏ Nansŏrhŏn (1563–89)
For My Brother Hagok.
Poor Woman.

Hô Sugyông (b. 1964)
Butterfly, The.
Love in an Empty Lot.
No Return.
One at Rest, The.
One White Dream.
Poem: "Slash my back with a sickle."
Sober, Remaining.
Train Leaving.
Weeping Singer, A.
When I Think About the Past.

Ho Thien
Green Beret.

Hô Xuân Huong (*fl.* 18th–19th cent.)
Condition of Women, The.
Country Scene.
General's Plaque, The.
On a Portrait of Two Beauties.

Hoagland, Everett (b. 1942)
Anti-Semanticist, The.
Big Zeb Johnson.
Fired Up!!
From Ground Zero.
Gorée.
How Could All That Have Happened Here?
Kinda Blue Miles Davis Died Today.
Love Jam.
Puttin' on the Dog.
Time Break.

Hoagland, Tony
America.
Benevolence.
Candlelight.
Change, The.
Collaboration, The.
Dickhead.
Ecology.
Grammar.
Kind of Shadow That Calls Out Fate, The.
Lawrence.
Lucky.
Medicine: "Black hair of my Chinese doctor,
    The."
Migration.

My Country.
Oh Mercy.
Reading *Moby-Dick* at 30,000 Feet.
Sweet Ruin.

Hoban, Russell (b. 1925)
Egg Thoughts.
Jigsaw Puzzle.
Old Man Ocean.
Pedalling Man, The.
Tin Frog, The.

Hobday, Charles (b. 1917)
Thirty Years On.

Hoberman, Mary Ann (b. 1930)
Bugs, *sels*.
Let's Dress Up.

Hobson, Geary (b. 1941)
Buffalo Poem #1.

Hoby, Elizabeth Cooke (1540–1609)
Elizabeth Hoby, Wife, to Thomas Hoby,
    Knight, Her Husband.
Epicedium by Elizabeth Hoby, Their Mother,
    on the Death of Her Two Daughters
    Elizabeth and Anne, An.

Hoccleve [*or* Occleve], Thomas (1370?–1450?)
De Regimine Principum, *sel*.
Description of His Ugly Lady, A.
My Compleinte, *sels*.

Hoch, James
Riding Backwards on a Train.

Hochman, Sandra (b. 1936)
Cannon Hill.
Hairbrush, The.
Manhattan Pastures.
Sphinxes.

Hocquard, Emmanuel (b. 1940)
À Noël, *sels*.
At Christmas, *sels*.
Three Moral Tales.
Trois leçons de morale.

Hodgeon, Gordon (b. 1941)
In Conference.

Hodges, Cyril (1915–74)
Naturalised.

Hodges, Janice W.
Annuals and Perennials.
Bruised Children.
Control.

Hodgins, Philip (b. 1959)
Death Who.
Making Hay.
Self-Pity.
Shooting the Dogs.

Hodgson, Ralph (1871–1962)
After.
Bells of Heaven, The.
Birdcatcher, The.
Bull, The.
Eve.
Ghoul Care.
Gipsy Girl, The.
Hammers, The.
Late, Last Rook, The.
Moor, The.
Mystery, The.
Song of Honor [*or* Honour], The.
Stupidity Street.
Time, You Old Gypsy Man.

Hoekstra, Han G. (1906–88)
Cedar, The.

Hofer, Jen
Of Deaths, Days, Futures, Nations ("Do i need
    to (need to).").
Of Deaths, Days, Futures, Nations ("On the
    corner of plato and national army a man
    early.").
Of Deaths, Days, Futures, Nations ("Question,
    the action, the speech, the taxi, the proof, the
    reference, forgotten, The.").
Tactics ("Licit tremendous unjust oxidized
    fancified notions tremulously.").
Tactics ("Will not tolerate will expend offer
    known facts armed with knives.").
Three ("Once upon a time there would be the
    bluest bitch of the pack.").

Hoffenstein, Samuel (1890–1947)
As the Crow Flies, Let Him Fly, *sel.*
Babies Haven't Any Hair.
Birdie McReynolds.
Couplets, Rare, Medium, and Well-Done, *sels.*
I'm Fond of Doctors.
Invocation, *sel.*
Love-songs, at Once Tender and Informative, *sels.*
Mimic Muse, The, *sel.*
Miss Millay Says Something Too.
Notebook of a Schnook, The, *sels.*
Poems in Praise of Practically Nothing, *sels.*
Progress.
Songs about Life and Brighter Things Yet, *sels.*
Songs of Fairly Utter Despair, *sel.*

Hoffman, Daniel
Riddle, A.

Hoffman, Daniel Gerard (b. 1923)
Armada of Thirty Whales, An.
At Provincetown.
Crossing Walt Whitman Bridge.
Ephemeridae.
First Flight.
In the Days of Rin-Tin-Tin.
Lobsterpot Labyrinths.
Seals in Penobscot Bay, The.

Hoffmann, Heinrich (1809–94)
Story of Augustus Who Would Not Have Any Soup, The.

Hoffmann, Roald
Bering Bridge, The.

Hofmann, Michael (b. 1957)
Ancient Evenings.
By Forced Marches.
Eclogue: "Industry undressing in front of Agriculture."
Lament for Crassus.
Late Richard Dadd, 1817–1886, The.
Machine That Cried, The.
Pastorale.
Postcard from Cuernavaca.

Hofmannsthal, Hugo von (1874–1929)
Do You See the Town?
Evanescence.
On the Transitory.
Traveller's Song.
Twilight of the Outward Life.
Two of Them, The.
Two, The.

Hofmannswaldau, Christian Hofmann von
Beauty's Transitoriness.
Description of Perfect Beauty.
He Loves in Vain.
So sweet, so golden.

Hogan, Linda (b. 1947)
Bear Fat.
Celebration: Birth of a Colt.
Chambered Nautilus.
Crossings.
Eclipse II.
Gamble.
Heartland.
Heritage.
Man in the Moon.
Map.
New Apartment.
Nothing.
Potatoes.
Potholes.
Prayer for Men and Children.
Rainy Season, The.
Return: Buffalo.
Seeing through the Sun.
Skin.
Tear.
Tiva's Tapestry: La Llorona.
To Light.
Truth Is, The.
Workday.
Young Boys, The.

Hoge
How long the tree's been barren.

Hogg, James ("The Ettrick Shepherd") (1770–1835)
Boy's Song, A.
Charlie is My Darling.
Deep-Toned Jowler, The.
Isabelle.
James Rigg.
Lock the Door, Lariston.
Mador of the Moor, *sels.*
Queen's Wake, The, *sels.*
When Maggy Gangs Away.
When the Kye Comes Hame.
Wife of Crowle, The.
Witch o' Fife, The.
Witch's Chant, A.

Hoggard, James
Anniversary Trip.
Dove Hunting Each Labor Day.
Eye of the Tornado.
My Auld Hector.
November: "Shimmering spreads of golden fire."
Oil Field Road off Clyte Escarpment.

Hogue, Cynthia
Monique.

Hoilette, Andre O.
Blooming Death. . .Blossoms.

Hoin
On the rocky slope, blossoming.

Hoitsu (1760–1828)
Buddha / Cherry flowers.

Hokko
Hay spread for.
Sprinkling.

Hokushi (1655–1718)
My house gutted.
Sailboats in line.
Writing / Rubbing it out—.

Holan, Vladimir (1905–80)
Between.
But.
Chicken, The.
Children at Christmas in 1945.
During an Illness.
Epoch.
Glimpsed.
How?
In the Yard of the Policlinic.
Meeting in a Lift.
Mother.
Night with Hamlet, A, *sel.*
Old Priest, The.
Reminiscence.
Resurrection.
She Asked You.
Snow.
To the Enemies.
You're Thinking of Children.

Holcroft, Thomas (1745–1809)
Gaffer Gray.

Holden, Clive (b. 1959)
Antarctica.
Biblical Winnipeg.
Train Phone Sext.

Holden, Jonathan (b. 1941)
Face Up.
How to Play Night Baseball.
Liberace.
Men in the Hoboken Bar, the.
Poem for Ed "Whitey" Ford, A.
Saturday Afternoon, October.
September: Nederland, Colorado.
Why We Bombed Haiphong.

Holden, Molly (b. 1927)
Seaman, 1941.

Hölderlin, Friedrich (1770–1843)
All the fruit is ripe, plunged in fire, cooked.
Bread and Wine, *sel.*
Brevity.
Descriptive Poetry.
Half of Life.
Half of Life, The.
Halflife.
Hymns and Fragments, *sel.*

Hyperion, *sels.*
Hyperion's Song of Fate.
In the Days of Socrates.
No Pardon.
Patmos.
Ripe, Being Plunged into Fire.
Seasons, The, *sels.*
Tinian, *sel.*
To the Fates.
To the German People.

Holdsworth, Ethel Carnie
Freedom.

Holiday, Billie (1915–59)
God Bless the Child.

Holiner, Mann (1897–1958)
Until the Real Thing Comes.
Why Shouldn't It Happen to Us?
You Can't Stop Me from Lovin' You.

Holland, Henry Scott (1847–1918)
Judge eternal, throned in splendours.

Holland, Hugh (1569–1635)
Owen Tudor.
Upon the Lines and Life of the Famous Scenic Poet, Master William Shakespeare.

Holland, Jane (b. 1966)
Baize Queens.
Having Read Up on the Subject.
Loco.
Pulse.
Sleep.
Spin-Cycle.
Three Tests for Darwin Duke.
Wavelength.

Holland, Josiah Gilbert (1819–81)
Christmas Carol, A: "There's a song in the air!"
Marble Prophecy, The, *sel.*
Wanted.

Holland, Norah M. (1876–1925)
Grey Rider, The.

Holland, Walter
Black Water Creek.
Christopher Street 1979.
Journal of the Plague Years, A.

Hollander, John (b. 1929)
Adam's Task.
At the New Year.
Back to Town.
By Heart.
By the Sound.
Carmen Ancillae.
Coordinating Conjunction.
Danish Wit.
Edward Hopper's Seven A.M.
Effet de Neige.
For Both of You, the Divorce Being Final.
For "Fiddle-De-De."
Forget How to Remember How to Forget.
Great Bear, The.
Heliogabalus.
Historical Reflections.
Lady at the Castle, The.
Lady's-Maid's Song, The.
Late August on the Lido.
Letter to Jorge Luis Borges: Apropos of the Golem.
Lion Named Passion, A.
Mad Potter, The.
Morning in the Islands.
Night Mirror, The.
No Foundation.
Old-Fashioned Song, An.
Owl.
Powers of Thirteen, *sels.*
Russian Soul II, The.
Science and Human Behavior.
Some Walks With You.
Song at the End of a Meal.
State of Nature, A.
Sunday A.M. Not in Manhattan.
Swan and Shadow.
Under Cancer.
Variations on a Fragment by Trumbull Stickney.
What the Lovers in the Old Songs Thought.

Hollander, Robert (b. 1933)
You Too? Me Too—Why Not? Soda Pop.

Hollander, Vicki
Rosh Chodesh Tisheri.

Höllerer, Walter
Held Back, Like a Bow Drawn Tight.
Particularly Effortless He Lay.
Tarry Awhile, Restless Bird.

Holley, Margaret
Dancer, The.
Tree of Life, The.

Holley, Mary Austin (1784–1846)
Plea of Texas, The.

Hollis, Mark (b. 1908)
Careless Talk.
'Twixt Cup and Lip.

Hollis, Matthew (b. 1971)
And Let Us Say.

Hollo, Anselm (b. 1934)
Dream of Instant Total Representation, The.
Godlike.
Guests of Space, *sel.*
Italics.
Journey, 1966.
Le Jazz Hot.
Shed the Fear.
Wild West Workshop Poem.

Holloway, Geoffrey
Bash on Basho: Six of the Best.
Ford Castle: The Borders.
Hand for Some Others, A.
Hypochondriac.
Indian Rope Trick.
Lovers, The.
Monitors.
Non-Accidental Injury Slides.
Old Man.
Things.
Virtue of Slovenliness, The.

Holloway, John (b. 1920)
London, Greater London (After *Satire III*).

Holloway, Stanley (1890–1982)
Old Sam.

Holm, Bill
Advice.
Blizzard.
Icelandic Language, The.
Playing the Goldberg Variations on Sunday
Morning.
Scott Joplin.
Whale Breathing: Bartlett Cove, Alaska.

Holman, Bob (b. 1948)
Death of Poetry, The.
1990.
Performance Poem.

Holman, Felice (b. 1919)
I Can Fly.

Holman, M. Carl (b. 1919)
Mr. Z.

Holmes, Darryl (b. 1958)
Nostalgia.
Time for Guns, A.
Tubman Strong.
We Have Never Seen the Sky Light Up.

Holmes, Elizabeth
Fathers, The: "Something's familiar about that
villain."

Holmes, Janet
Depressive Episode.
Fantasie Metropolitan.
Green Tuxedo, The.
Mediterranean Cooking for Two.
Whistle.

Holmes, John (1904–62)
Four and a Half.
Map of My Country.
Old Professor, The.

Holmes, John (*fl.* 1600)
Thus Bonny-boots the birthday celebrated.

Holmes, Oliver Wendell (1809–94)
After-Dinner Poem (Terpsichore), An.
At the "Atlantic" Dinner, December 15, 1874.
Autocrat of the Breakfast Table, The, *sels.*
Ballad of the Oysterman, The.
Cacoëthes Scribendi.
Flaneur [*or Flâneur*], The.
Illustration of a Picture.
International Ode.
Iris, Her Book.
Last Leaf, The.
Latter-Day Warnings.
Nearing the Snow-Line.
Old Ironsides.
On Lending a Punch-Bowl.
Our Limitations.
Peau de Chagrin of State Street, The.
Ploughman, The.
Poesy.
Poet Grows Old, The.
Prelude to a Volume Printed in Raised Letters
for the Blind.
Prologue.
Tartarus.
To Canaan: A Puritan War-Song.
Two Streams, The.
Welcoming the Dawn.
Wind-Clouds and Star-Drifts, *sels.*

Holofcener, Larry
Too Close for Comfort.

Holst-Warhaft, Gail
In the End Is the Body.
Old Men of Athens, The.
St. John, *sels.*
St. Matthew, *sels.*

Holt, Rochelle Lynn
Pleasure of Feeling Inside Your Body, The.

Holtby, Mary
Answer to a Kind Enquiry.
Dawn Chorus.
Sister Swallow to Swinburne.

Holtby, Winifred (1898–1935)
Man Who Hated the Spring, The.

Holthaus, Gary H.
Unexpected Manna.
Writing the Poem.

Hölty, Ludwig Heinrich Christoph (1748–76)
Legacy.

Holub, Miroslav (b. 1923)
Achilles and the Tortoise.
Brief Reflection on Accuracy.
Brief Reflection on Brief Reflections.
Brief Thoughts on Cats Growing on Trees.
Brief Thoughts on Cracks.
Brief Thoughts on Floods.
Corporal Who Killed Archimedes, The.
Dead, The.
Death in the Evening.
Distant Howling.
Door, The.
End of the World, The.
Five Minutes after the Air Raid.
Fly, The.
Forest, The.
Funeral, The.
Helping Hand, A.
History Lesson, A.
How to Paint a Perfect Christmas.
Immanuel Kant.
In the Miscroscope.
Inventions.
Žito the Magician.
Jewish Cemetery at Olsany, Kafka's Grave,
April, Sunny Weather, The.
Lesson, THe.
Meeting Ezra Pound.
Napoleon.
On the Origin of the Contrary.
Polonius.
Silence.
Special Performance for Statues, A.
Suffering.
Teaching About Disease.
Teeth.
Vanishing Lung Syndrome.
Wings.

Holway, Jamil B. (1883–1946)
Throbbings.

Holz, Arno (1863–1929)
Phantasus, *sel.*

Holzer, Remy
Current "Now, Voyager" Fantasy.

"Home, Cecil" *See* Webster, Augusta Davies

Homer (*fl.* before 700 B.C.)
Iliad, The, *sels.*
Odyssey, The, *sels.*
Odyssey, *sels.*

Homfray, Francis (*fl.* c.1817)
Thoughts on Happiness.

Homyo
Wino, always stumbling.

Hone, William (1780–1838)
Political House that Jack Built, The, *sel.*

Hong Yunsuk (b. 1925)
Discourse on an Ornament.
My Sea Has One Island.
That I Can Do This Autumn.

Hongnang (*fl.* 1567–1608)
I send you, my love.

Hongo, Garrett Kaoru (b. 1951)
Cruising 99, *sels.*
Eruption: Pu'u Ō'ō.
Hilo: First Night Back.
Hongo Store 29 Miles Volcano Hilo, Hawaii,
The.
Legend, The.
Mendocino Rose.
O-Bon: Dance for the Dead.
Off from Swing Shift.
Pier, The.
Redness: Thinking it Through.
Something Whispered in the *Shakuhachi*.
Stomping with Pettit on the Battenkill.
Unreal Dwelling: My Years in Volcano, The.
Winnings.
Yellow Light.

Honig, Edwin (b. 1919)
Bodega, Goodbye.
November through a Giant Copper Beech.
Now, My Usefullness Over.
Tête-à-Tête.
To Restore a Dead Child, *sels.*
[Walt Whitman]: "W / A / L / WHITMAN."

Hood, Thomas (1799–1845)
Autumn: "I saw old Autumn in the misty
morn."
Bridge of Sighs, The.
Choosing Their Names.
Death in the Kitchen.
Death-Bed, The.
Domestic Poems, *sels.*
Dream of Eugene Aram [the Murderer], The.
Dust to Dust.
Fair Ines.
Faithless Nelly Gray.
Faithless Sally Brown.
False Poets and True.
First Attempt in Rhyme, A.
Good Night.
I Remember, I Remember.
Jack Hall.
Last Man, The.
Literary Reminiscences.
Mary's Ghost.
Miss Kilmansegg and Her Precious Leg, *sels.*
No!
Our Village—by a Villager.
Parental Ode to My Son, Aged Three Years
and Five Months, A.
Public Dinner, A.
Ruth.
Silence.
Song of the Shirt, The.
Sonnet to a Sonnet.
Sonnet to Vauxhall.
Time, Hope, and Memory.
To Minerva.
To the Ocean.
Written in the Workhouse.

Hoofdakker, Rudi van den *See* Kopland, Rutger

Hoogerhuis, Inge
Search, The.

Hoogs, Rebecca
Lion's Teeth.

Hooker, Eva
Ariel.
What Bottom Said When He Came Home.

Hooker, Jeremy (b. 1941)
Gull on a Post.
Take a long view from Mynydd Bach.

Hookes, N. (1628–1712)
To Amanda Walking in the Garden.

Hooks, Bell (b. 1952)
As they bury the dead.
Body Inside the Soul, The.
Woman's Mourning Song, The.

Hooper, Patricia
At the Terminal.
Listening to Mozart at Meadow Brook.

Hooper, Virginia (b. 1955)
Reading, A.

Hoornik, Ed. (1910–70)
Pogrom.
To Love a Woman.

Hooson, I. D. (1880–1948)
Flame, The.
Red Poppy, The.

Hooton, Harry (1908–61)
Sweet Disorder in the Dress, A.

Hoover, Paul (b. 1946)
American Heaven.
Baseball.
California.
Desire.
Family Romance.
Heart's Ease.
Kiss, The: "She had imagined the kiss."
Letter to Einstein Beginning Dear Albert.
Night of the Hunter.
Poems We Can Understand.
Theoretical People.
Whitman in a Corner.

Hope, Alec Derwent (b. 1907)
Advice to Young Ladies.
Australia.
Bed, The.
Beware of Ruins.
Beyond Phigalia.
Blason, A.
Commination, A.
Death of the Bird, The.
Easter Hymn.
Fafnir.
Faustus.
Flower Poem.
Gloss to Matthew V 27–28.
Hay Fever.
Imperial Adam.
Inscription for a War.
Lingam and the Yoni, The.
Lot and His Daughters I.
Lot and His Daughters II.
Massacre of the Innocents.
Meditation on a Bone.
Möbius Strip-Tease.
Observation Car.
On an Engraving by Casserius.
Parabola.
Paradise Saved.
Pleasure of Princes, The.
Return of Persephone, The.
St. Luke, sels.
Under Sedation.
Wandering Islands, The.

Hope, Andrew, III
Shagoon 1–4.

Hope, Christopher (b. 1944)
In the Country of the Black Pig.

Hope, Laurence (Adela Florence "Violet" Nicolson) (1865–1904)
I Shall Forget.

Hope, Melanie
Bare Floors.
INRI.
Only Days.
Our Mothers.

Praise the Daughter.
Sacrifice.
Sixth Grade.

Hopes, David Brendon (b. 1953)
Advent Sequence, sel.
Birdbones.
Five Neo-Platonic Commentaries, sels.
Glacier's Daughters, The.
Holy Innocents.
Invalid of Park Street, The.
Jack Rhymer.
Job from His Mountain, sel.
Julian, sel.
October: "It's nuthatch on the box elder outside the window."
On the Feast of Saint John the Evangelist.
Planxty Irwin.
Something of the Flowers, sel.
Song of Mercies, A, sel.
Swimmers, The.
Under the Drumlin.
Winter Birds, sel.

Hopkins, Gerard Manley (1844–89)
Andromeda.
As Kingfishers Catch Fire.
Binsey Poplars (Felled 1879).
Bugler's First Communion, The.
Caged Skylark, The.
Candle Indoors, The.
Carrion Comfort.
Cuckoo, The.
Duns Scotus's Oxford.
Epithalamion: "Hark, hearer, hear what I do; lend a thought now, make believe."
Felix Randal.
God's Grandeur.
Habit of Perfection, The.
Hailstorm in May.
Handsome Heart, The.
Harry Ploughman.
He hath abolished the old drouth, sel.
Heaven-Haven.
Hurrahing in Harvest.
I Wake and Feel the Fell of Dark, Not Day.
In the Valley of the Elwy.
Inversnaid.
Lantern Out of Doors, The.
Leaden Echo and the Golden Echo, The.
Let me be to Thee as the circling bird.
Moonless darkness stands between.
Moonrise.
My Own Heart Let Me More Have Pity On.
Myself unholy, from myself unholy.
No Worst, There Is None. Pitched Past Pitch of Grief.
Peacock's Eye, The.
Pied Beauty.
Sea and the Skylark, The.
Soldier, The.
Spelt from Sibyl's Leaves.
Spring and Fall [To a Young Child].
Spring: "Nothing is so beautiful as Spring."
Starlight Night, The.
That Nature Is a Heraclitean Fire and of the Comfort of the Resurrection.
Thee, God, I come from, to Thee go, sel.
Thou Art Indeed Just, Lord.
To His Watch.
To R. B.
To Seem the Stranger.
Windhover, The.
Winter with the Gulf Stream.
Wreck of the Deutschland, The, sels.

Hopkins, John (c.1520–70)
Ye people all in one accord.

Hopkins, John Henry, Jr. (1810–91)
We Three Kings of Orient Are.

Hopkins, Lee Bennett (b. 1938)
En-vi-RON-ment.
Flash.
John Hancock.
Nat Love: Black Cowboy.
Subways Are People.
This Tooth.

Hopkins, Lightnin' (1912–82)
Death Bells.

Hopkinson, Francis (1737–91)
O'er the Hills.
Toast to Washington, A.

Hopwood, Mereid (b. 1964)
Rebirth.

Horace (Quintus Horatius Flaccus) (65–8 B.C.)
Anger Poem, The (1.16).
Art of Poetry, The, sels.
Bring Roses and Cardamom (2.3).
Epodes, sels.
Good bailiff of my farm, that snug domain.
Grieving Too Long (2.9).
If, O Maecenas, versed in lore antique.
Late Night Ode.
Let's Do This Poem (1.26).
Ne'er fash your thumb what gods decree.
Odes, sels.
Odes, sels.
Old Malediction, An.
Poem for Artemis (3.22).
Satires, sels.
Three Odes of Horace, sels.
What young Raw Muisted Beau Bred at his Glass.
Young Men Come Less Often—Isn't It So, The?

Horan, Robert (b. 1922)
Little City.
Prometheus.
Soft Swimmer, Winter Swan.

Horder, John (b. 1936)
Sick Image of My Father Fades, The.

Horgan, Paul (b. 1903)
Tintype of a Private in the Fifteenth Georgia Infantry.

Horne, Frank (b. 1899)
Kid Stuff.

Horne, Nanna Banyiwa (b. 1949)
Messages.
Note to My Liberal Feminist Sister, A.

Horne, Richard Henry [or Hengist] (1803–84)
Beth Gelert.
Plough, The.

Horovitz, Frances (1938–83)
Brigomaglos, a Christian, Speaks.
Do You Not Know that I Need to Touch You.
Loving You.
Night-Piece.
Rain—Birdoswald.
Visit to the British Museum.
Women.

Horsfield, Knight (b. 1856)
Old Rocket.

Horsley, Kate (b. 1952)
Poem to Ophelia.
Winter Grieving Poem.

Horst, Carmen (b. 1971)
Everything I Know.
Interpreter.
Siesta.
Swimming.
Ugly Poem.

Horton, George Moses (1797?–1883?)
Early Affection.
General Grant—the Hero of the War.
On Hearing of the Intention of a Gentleman to Purchase the Poet's Freedom.
On Liberty and Slavery.

Horvát, András Szkhárosi (fl. early 16th cent.)
About the Princes, sel.
About Two Kinds of Faith: That of Christ and That of the Pope's Ragged Patchwork, sel.
Curse, The, sel.

Horváth, Ádám Pálóczi (1760–1820)
Dance of the Magyars, The.
Lover Under Suspicion.

Hoshi, Saigyo See Saigyō

Hoskyns [or Hoskins], John (1566–1638)
Epitaph, An: On a Man for Doing Nothing.

Hostetler, Ann Elizabeth (b. 1954)
Female Ancestor.

Iconoclast.
Painting with My Daughter.
Priestess of Love.
Resisting Geometry.
Hostetler, Sheri (b. 1962)
Instructions.
Not of This World.
Say Yes Quickly.
Woman with the Screw in Her Mouth Speaks,
The.
Hottel, Jodi L.
Shikata ga nai.
Houellebecq, Michel (b. 1958)
Dans l'air limpide.
In the Limpid Air.
Houghton, Firman
Mr. Frost Goes South to Boston.
Houghton, Liz
Caustic Soda.
Saturday with Dad.
Houle, Adam
I Learned about Being Tough from a Stetson
Ad.
Houlihan, Joan
All the Cold Mechanicals.
And Everywhere Offering Human Sound.
Ardor.
Biological Imperative.
H. Antecessor.
Hydrangeas.
Incarnation.
Infant Spouse, The.
Matter.
Squall Line.
House, Boyce (1896–1961)
Beauty is Elsewhere.
Justice in Old Ranger.
Mocking-bird, A.
Housman, A. E. (Alfred Edward) (1859–1936)
African Lion, The.
As into the Garden Elizabeth Ran.
Astronomy.
Because I liked you better.
Could man be drunk for ever.
Crossing Alone the Nighted Ferry.
Deserter, The.
Diffugere Nives.
Easter Hymn.
Eight O'Clock.
Epitaph: "Here dead lie we because we did not
choose."
Epitaph on an Army of Mercenaries.
Fragment of a Greek Tragedy.
Fragment of an English Opera.
G. K. Chesterton on His Birth.
Grenadier.
He would not stay for me; and who can
wonder?
Hell Gate.
Her Strong Enchantments Failing.
Ho, everyone that thirsteth.
I Counsel You Beware.
Infant Innocence.
Inhuman Henry.
Jack and Jill.
Lancer.
Laws of God, the Laws of Man, The.
Mark 16:19–20; So then the Lord Jesus, after.
Night Is Freezing Fast, The.
Oh stay at home, my lad, and plough.
Oh who is that young sinner with the
handcuffs on his wrists?
Olive, The.
Pope, The.
Purple William or The Liar's Doom.
Shades of Night, The.
Shake hands, we shall never be friends, all's
over.
Shropshire Lad, A, sels.
Soldier from the Wars Returning.
Some can gaze and not be sick.
Tell Me Not Here [It Needs Not Saying].
They Say My Verse Is Sad: No Wonder.
Wake Not for the World-heard Thunder.
When Adam walked in Eden young.

When the bells justle in the tower.
When the Eye of Day Is Shut.
Yon Far Country.
Houston, Douglas (b. 1947)
Lines on a Van's Dereliction.
Night Out, A.
Houston, Libby (b. 1941)
I can lift gravity's stern glower.
Old Woman and the Sandwiches, The.
Story of Canobie Dick, The.
Houston, Margaret Bell (1877–1966)
Old Oak Speaks, The.
Song from the Traffic.
Houston, Margaret Moffette Lea (1819–67)
To My Husband—December 1844.
Houston, Sam (1793–1863)
Texian Call to Arms.
Hovald, Isabelle
Stele for Lenz.
Hovanessian, Diana Der
Exiles.
Inside Green Eyes, Black Eyes.
Mixed Marriage.
On Commonwealth Avenue and Brattle Street.
Two Voices.
Hove, Chenjerai
Child's Parliment.
Country Life.
Lost Bird.
Migratory Bird.
Other Syllabus, The.
Red Hills of Home.
You Will Forget.
**Hovell-Thurlow, Edward, 2d Baron Thurlow
(1781–1829)**
May.
Hovey, Richard (1864–1900)
Accident in Art.
At Sea.
Evening on the Potomac.
Mocking-Bird, The.
Sea Gypsy, The.
Song by the Shore, A.
Verlaine.
Howard, Anne, Duchess of Arundel (1557–1630)
Good Shepherd's Sorrow for the Death of His
Beloved Son, The, sels.
Howard, Bart (b. 1915)
Fly Me to the Moon (In Other Words).
Who Besides You.
Would You Believe It?
Year After Year.
Howard, Ben (b. 1944)
Break.
For the Calvinists.
River Song.
River's Answer, The.
Howard, Hannah
Soulgroovin Ditty #7.
Howard, Joseph E.
Hello! My Baby.
Howard Jr., Willie Abraham
Cross Burning Black.
Memorial Drive.
Paralyzed.
Howard, Margaret, Lady (1515–78)
Now that ye be assemblld heer.
Sueden chance ded mak me mues, The.
Howard, Richard (b. 1929)
After 65.
Among the Missing.
At the Monument to Pierre Louÿs.
Giovanni da Fiesole on the Sublime.
Job Interview, The.
Keeping.
Landed: A Valentine.
Like Most Revelations.
Man Who Beat Up Homosexuals Reported to
Have AIDS Virus.
Mrs. Eden in Town for the Day.
My Last Hustler.
Nadar.
Nikolaus Mardruz to his Master Ferdinand,
Count of Tyrol, 1565.

1915: A Pre-Raphaelite Ending, London.
Oystering.
Stanzas in Bloomsbury.
209 Canal.
Venetian Interior, 1889.
Vocational Guidance, with Special Reference
to the Annunciation of Simone Martini.
Wildflowers.
Howe, Fanny (b. 1940)
As Like As Not.
Basic Science.
Bathroom.
Catholic.
Crossing Out.
Doubt.
First Chance Twice.
From a donkey, excuse me, one lesson is
given.
Goodbye, Post Office Square.
Little Wrongs.
My Broken Heart.
O'Clock, sels.
Passion, The, sels.
Scattered Light.
Seeking Out His Face in a Cup.
9-11-01.
Splinter, The, sels.
Starlet.
Veteran.
What We Learned.
White Lines.
Howe, Julia Ward (1819–1910)
Battle Hymn [or Battle-Hymn] of the Republic,
The.
House of Rest, The.
Kosmos.
Lyrics of the Street, sels.
My Last Dance.
Robert E. Lee.
Wild Night, A.
Howe, Marie (b. 1950)
Attic, The.
Certain Light, A.
Dream, The.
How Many Times.
How Some of It Happened.
Kiss, The.
Mother, The.
Part of Eve's Discussion.
Practicing.
Promise, The: "In the dream I had when he
came back, not sick."
Recovery.
Sixth Grade.
What the Living Do.
Howe, Susan (b. 1937)
Bed Hangings, sel.
Bride's Day.
Chair, sel.
He plodded away through drifts of ice.
Pythagorean Silence, sel.
Rückenfigur.
Scattering as Behavior Toward Risk.
Secret History of the Dividing Line, sel.
Silence Wager Stories.
Speeches at the Barriers, sels.
Thorow.
Thorow, sels.
WHITE FOOLSCAP / Book of Cordelia.
Howe, William Walsham (1823–97)
Funeral Hymn.
Howell, Christopher (b. 1945)
Blessing's Precision.
Bride of Long Division, The.
Christian Science Minotaur, The.
He Writes to the Soul.
In the Spring of Hjalmar Calrson: The Real
Story.
New Orpheus, The.
Howell, James (1594–1666)
Elegy upon His Tomb in Herndon-Hill Church,
Erected by His Wife, Who Speaks, An.
Upon Dr. Davies's British Grammar.
Upon the Poet of His Time, Ben Jonson: His
Honoured Friend and Father.

Howell IV, Thomas C.
Ginsburg.

Howells, William Dean (1837–1920)
Earliest Spring.
Empty House, The.
Forlorn.
November.
Royal Portraits, The.

Howes, Barbara (b. 1914)
Death of a Vermont Farm Woman.
On a Bougainvillaea Vine at the Summer
Palace [or in Haiti].
On Galveston Beach.
Portrait of the Boy as Artist.
Wild Geese Flying.

Howitt, Mary (1799–1888)
Cry of the Animals, The.
Dying Child, The.
Sketches of Natural History, sels.
Spider and the Fly, The.

Hristic, Jovan (b. 1933)
That Night They All Gathered on the Highest
Tower.

Hristov, Boris (b. 1945)
At Night: "Our tree's shadow is green at
night."
Dandelion Bone.
Evening Trumpet.
My Mother's Wedding.
Sign from Heaven, A.
Solitary Man.
Window, The: "I stand on tiptoe to reach the
window that's open a crack."

Hsi Chou (fl. 10th cent. A.D.)
Broken Tablets.
Early Spring at the Capital, Sent to the
Honorable Kuan.
Farewell to Wei Feng, Going to Far-South
Mountain.
Sent to Huai Ku.

Hsi-chün (fl. c.105 B.C.)
Lost Horizon.

Hsi K'ang (c.223–262)
Lute, The: A Rhapsody, sels.
Song of Disillusionment, A.

Hsi-tseng Tsiang
Shantung.

Hsiang Chi (232–202 B.C.) (Hsiang Yü)
Hegemon's Lament, The.

Hsiang Yu See Xiang Xiu [or Hsiang Yu]

Hsiao Kang
I Can Sigh.
I Play My Zither.
Pheasant on His Morning Flight, A.
Soft Echoes.
Spiders' Spun Threads.
Watching a Lonely Wild Goose at Nightfall.

Hsiao Tzu-hui See Xiao Zihui

Hsiao Yen [or Emperor Wu of Liang] (464–549)
Border Guard, A.
Candle, The.
Flute, The.
Morning Sun.

Hsiao-yün-shih-hai-ya See Kuan Yün-shih

Hsieh Chin (1369–1415)
Song of Cursive Calligraphy.

Hsieh Ling-yün (385–433)
All Around My New House at Stone Gate.
Climbing Stone Drum Mountain.
Crossing the Mountain, I Follow the Chin-chu
River.
Dwelling in the Mountains, sel.
From Chin-Chu Creek, Past the Ridge, Along
the Stream.
I Follow the Jinzhu Torrent.
Last Poem.
Night: Setting out from Shih-Kuan Pavilion.
On Cimbing Mount Green Crag in Yongjia.
On Climbing Stone Drum Mountain, Near
Shangshu.
On Climbing the Highest Peak of Stone Gate.
On Climbing the Highest Peak of Stone Gate
Mountain.
On My Way from South Mountain to North

Mountain, I Glance at the Scenery from the
Lake.
On Spending Some Time at the Bai'an
Pavilion.
Poem on Stone House Mountain, A.
Replying to a Poem from My Cousin Huilian.
Scene from South Hill to North Hill Passing
the Lake.
Visiting Pai-an Pavilion.
What I Saw When I Had Crossed the Lake.
Written on the Lake on My Way Back to the
Retreat at Stone Cliff.
Written on the Lake While Returning to Stone
Cliff Hermitage.

Hsieh T'iao (464–99)
Ascend the Three Mountains Toward the
Evening: Looking Back at the Capital.
Autumn Night, An.
Complaint Near the Jade Stairs.
Complaint of the Jade Staircase.
I Sit in My Lofty Study.
In a Provincial Capital Sick in Bed.
Looking at the Morning Rain.
Prince Went Wandering, A.
Roaming the East Field.
To Hsuan-Ch'eng, Past Hsin-Lin-P'u, Toward
Pan-Ch'iao.
Viewing the Three Lakes.

Hsin Ch'i-chi (1140–1207)
To an Old Tune.
Tune: "Moon of the Western River."
Tune: "Partridge Sky" At Po-shan Monastery.
Tune: "Partridge Sky" For a Friend.
Tune: "Picking Mulberry Seeds" Written on a
Wall en Route to Po-shan.
Tune: "Pure Serene Music" en Route to Po-
shan.
Tune: "Pure Serene Music" Rural Life.
Tune: "Spring in the Ch'in Garden"
Tune: "The Bodhisattva's Golden Headdress."
Tune: "The Dark Clouds of Ch'u" Visiting the
Rainy Crag Alone.

"Hsiung Hung" (Hu Mei-tzu) (b. 1940)
If You Think With Fire.
Thinking of Someone.
Who Stops the Dance?

Hsu Hsuan (916–91)
Lu-lung Village, Autumn.

Hsü Kan (171–217)
Wife's Thoughts, The.

Hsü Ling (507–83)
Bagatelle.
Dance, The.
Maid's Thanks for a Mirror, A.

Hsü Pen (1335–80)
To a Hermit in the Mountains.

Hsü Tsai-ssu (fl. c.1300)
On Love.

Hsü Wei (1521–93)
Buddhist Monk Cut and Burned His Own
Flesh to Make The Rains Stop—A Man
From His Native Place Asked Me to Write a
Poem to Send to Him, A.

Hsüan-yeh (1654–1722)
Lines in Praise of a Self-Chiming Clock.

Hsüan-ying See Su Man-shu

Hsueh Chao-yun (900–32)
Oriole Song.
To the Tune: In the Hills.

Hsüeh T'ao [or Xue Tao] (768–831)
Cicadas.
Crabapple Brook.
Dog Parted from Her Master.
Gazing at Spring.
Listening to a Monk Play the Reed Pipes.
Lotus-Gathering Boat.
Parrot Parted from Her Cage.
Trying on New-Made Clothes: Three Poems,
sels.
Wind.

Hu Chih-yu (1227–93)
Love Song: "Lazy flowers brew honey for the
bees."

Hu Shih (fl. c.1927)
Dream and Poetry.

Huai Ku (fl. 10th cent. A.D.)
Living at a Monastery, Sent to Chien Chang.
Living on the Plain in Early Autumn.
Rotten Axe-Handle Mountain.

Huang E (1498–1569)
Pearl-teardrops roll and gather.

Huang O [or Huang Ho] (1498–1569)
Farewell to a Southern Melody, A.
To the Tune "A Floating Cloud Crosses
Enchanted Mountain."
To the tune "Soaring Clouds."

Huang T'ing-chien (1045–1105)
To Go with Shih K'o's Painting of an Old Man
Tasting Vinegar.
Tune: "A Thousand Autumns."
Tune: "Ch'ing-P'ing Song."
Tune: "Courtyard Full of Fragrance, The."
Tune: "Joy of Returning to the Fields."
("Evening rain drips on the steps.").
Tune: "Joy of Returning to the Fields."
("Spring scene finds me thinner still, The.").

Hubbard, Sue
Letter.

Hubbell, Lindley Williams
Beer Bottles.
Birth-Hour.
Ordovician Fossil Algae.
Sounds.
Student Who Sat Facing Me on the Osaka
Express, A.
Waka.

Hubbell, Patricia (b. 1928)
Shadows.
Streetcleaner's Lament, The.

Hubert, Sir Francis (1568 or 1569–1629)
Egypt's Favorite, sels.
Life and Death of Edward II, The, sel.

Huchel, Peter (1903–81)
Aristeas 2.
Garden of Theophrastus, The.
In the rush odour of Danish meadows.
King Lear.
Landscape Beyond Warsaw.
Psalm: "That from the seed of men."
Roads.
Roads.
Rome.
Under the naked hoe of the moon.
Winter Billet.

Hucks, Joseph (d. 1800)
To Freedom.

Huddle, David (b. 1942)
Almost Going.
Delivering the Times, 1952–1955.
Gregory's House.
Haircut.
Holes Commence Falling.
Inside the Hummingbird Aviary.
Miss Florence Jackson.
Mouth of Him, The.
Music.
My Daddy, Whenever He Went Some Place.
Ooly Pop a Cow.
Perspective.
Snow Monkey Argues with God, The.
Town History, 1917.
Vermont.
Visit of the Hawk.
Work.

Hudgins, Andrew (b. 1951)
Adoration of the Magi, The.
After the Wilderness.
Air, The.
Around the Campfire.
As a Child in the Temple.
Ashes.
At Chancellorsville.
At the Piano.
Beneath Searchlights.
Burial Detail.
Cestello Annunciation, The.
Childhood of the Ancients.

Hudspith *(continued)*
Chinaberry, The.
Chinaberry Trees, The.
Christ as a Gardener.
Colonel.
Consider.
Crucifixion (Montgomery, Alabama).
Dead Christ.
Ecce Homo.
Elegy for My Father, Who Is Not Dead.
Fire and St. Francis.
Flag of Honeysuckle, A.
Flamingos Have Arrived in Ashtabula.
Gift, The: "They hung the lambs and cut their white throats. Blood."
Gospel.
Grandmother's Spit.
Hawk above the House, The.
Heat Lightning in a Time of Drought.
Hereafter, The.
How Shall We Sing the Lord's Song in a Strange Land?
In.
In Alesia.
In the Well.
Late Spring in the Nuclear Age.
Liar's Psalm, The, *sels.*
Loose Change.
Mary Magdalene's Left Foot.
Mostly My Nightmares Are Dull.
One Threw a Dirt Clod and It Ran.
Persistence of Nature in Our Lives, The.
Praying Drunk.
Psalm Against Psalms, *sel.*
Road Home, The.
Serenades in Virginia.
Soldier on the Marsh, A.
Southern Crescent Was on time, The.
Southern Literature.
Supper.
Telling, The.
Tools: An Ode.
Tree.
Two Ember Days in Alabama.
Versification of a Passage from Penthouse.
What Light Destroys.
Young Oaks, The.

Hudspith, Vicki
Nodding Cranes.

Hueffer, Ford Madox *See* Ford (Hueffer), Ford Madox

Huelsenbeck, Richard (1892–1974)
"We Hardly."

Huelsenbeck, Richard (1892–1974), Marcel Janko *and* **Tristan Tzara**
L'amiral cherche une maison à louer.

Hueng Guobin *(fl.* c.1978)
Mountain Life.

Huerta, David (b. 1949)
Baraja.
Baroque Cell, A.
Bolero at Armageddon.
Bolero en Aramgedón.
Cancellation of a Construction Project.
Cauldron, The.
Celda barroca, Una.
Deck of Cards.
Descender.
Descent.
Light from Parallel Worlds.
Luz de los mundos paralelos.
Machinery.
Maquinarias.
Neblina veraniega.
Olla, La.
Oración del 21 de agosto.
Pathological Beings.
Prayer for August 21.
Seres patológicos.
Summer Mist.
Suspensión de una obra.
Thirteen Propositions against Trivial Love.
Trece intenciones contra el amor trivial.

Huerta, Efraín (1914–82)
Declaration of Hate.
Men of Dawn, The.

This Is a Love.

Huerta, Javier Omar
Toward a Portrait of the Undocumented.

Hueung Powoo (d. 1565)
Climbing Enlightenment Mountain.
Deathbed Song.
Deciding to Live in an Empty Cave on Kumgang Mountain.
Spring on the Mountain.
Taking Pleasure in Myself.

Hufana, Alejandrino
Contemporary.
Floating Epitaphs, Their Possible Explanations in Poro Point.
From the Raw.
Insides of Alfred Hitchcock, The.

Huff, Steven
First Time I Heard Elvis, The.
Sperm Count.

Huffstickler, Albert
In the Compound.
Johnson City, Texas.
October 31, 1981.
Passing of the Old Man, The.
Travel Note.

Hughes, Audrey (b. 1934)
Logocyclegram.

Hughes, Daniel (1929–2003)
Too Noble.

Hughes, Frieda (b. 1960)
Bird.
Birds.
Different Voice, The.
Foxes.
In the Shadow of Fire.
Kookaburra.
Laszlo.
Stonepicker.

Hughes, Holly
At the Teahouse, 7 am.
At the Teahouse, 6 am.
Invitation to the Cricket.
Mind Wanting More.

Hughes, John (b. 1962)
Dog Day Lesson.
Knowingness.
Respect for Law and Order, A.

Hughes, John Ceiriog ("Ceiriog") (1832–87)
Epilogue to Alun Mabon.
Mountain Stream, The.

Hughes, Langston (1902–67)
Advertisement for the Waldorf-Astoria.
Advice.
Aesthete [*or* Esthete] in Harlem.
Afro-American Fragment.
American Heartbreak.
April Rain Song.
As Befits a Man.
Aunt Sue's Stories.
Bad Luck Card.
Bad Man.
Ballad of the Girl Whose Name Is Mud.
Ballad of the Landlord.
Ballad of the Man Who's Gone.
Bar.
Beaumont to Detroit: 1943.
Be-Bop Boys.
Bitter River, The.
Black Clown, The.
Blue Bayou.
Blue Monday.
Blues at Dawn.
Blues, The.
Boogie: 1 a.m.
Bound No'th Blues.
Brass Spittoons.
Casualty.
Catch.
Children's Rhymes ("By what sends.").
Chord.
Christ in Alabama.
College Formal: Renaissance Casino.
Come to the Waldorf-Astoria.
Croon.

Cross.
Cubes.
Curious.
Danse Africaine.
Daybreak in Alabama.
Dead in There.
Deferred.
Desire.
Dinner Guest: Me.
Dive.
Dream Boogie.
Dream Boogie: Variation.
Dream Dust.
Dream Keeper, The.
Dream Variation[s].
Dreams.
Drum.
Early Evening Quarrel.
Easy Boogie.
Evil.
Fact.
Feet o' Jesus.
50–50.
Florida Road Workers.
For Russell and Rowena Jelliffe.
Frederick Douglass: 1817–1895.
Freedom Train.
Gal's Cry for a Dying Lover.
Gauge.
Genius Child.
Goodbye Christ.
Hard Daddy.
Harlem Sweeties.
High to Low.
Homecoming.
Homesick Blues.
Hope ("He rose up on his dying bed.").
Hope ("Sometimes when I'm lonely.").
House in Taos, A.
I Dream a World.
I, Too.
In Time of Silver Rain.
Jam Session.
Jazz Band in a Parisian Cabaret.
Jazzonia.
Jim Crow Car.
Juke Box Love Song.
Justice.
Lady's Boogie.
Lament over Love.
Lenox Avenue Mural, *sels.*
Let America Be America Again.
Letter from Spain.
Letter to the Academy.
Life Is Fine.
Lincoln Monument: Washington.
Little Lyric (*Of Great Importance*).
Little Old Letter.
Little Song ("Carmencita loves Patrick.").
Lover's Return.
Low to High.
Luck ("Sometimes a crumb falls.").
Madam and Her Madam.
Madam and the Census Man.
Madam and the Minister.
Madam and the Rent Man.
Madam and the Wrong Visitor.
Madam's Calling Cards.
Madam's Past History.
Madrid [—1937].
Merry-Go-Round.
Minstrel Man.
Miss Blues'es Child.
Morning After.
Mother to Son.
Motto.
Mulatto.
My People.
Mystery.
Necessity.
Negro.
Negro Speaks of Rivers, The.
Neighbor.
Neon Signs.
Night Funeral in Harlem.
Nightmare Boogie.

Note on Commercial Theatre.
Old Walt.
125th Street.
Passing.
Pennsylvania Station.
Piggy-back.
Po' Boy Blues.
Poem [2]: "I loved my friend."
Preference.
Projection.
Question ("Said the lady, *Can you do*.").
Railroad Avenue.
Request.
Sailor.
Saturday Night.
Sea Calm.
Shame on You.
Share-Croppers.
Shepherd's Song at Christmas.
Sister.
Situation.
Sliver of Sermon.
So Long.
Song for a Dark Girl.
Song for a Suicide.
Song to a Negro Wash-woman, A.
Songs.
Still Here.
Stony Lonesome.
Strange Hurt.
Street Song.
Subway Face.
Suicide's Note.
Summer Night.
Sunday by the Combination.
Sweet Words on Race.
Sylvester's Dying Bed.
Tag.
Tambourines.
Tell Me.
Testimonial.
Theme for English B.
Three Songs about Lynching, *sels*.
To Midnight Nan at Leroy's.
Tomorrow.
Trumpet Player.
Ultimatum: Kid to Kid.
Un-American Investigators.
Uncle Tom ("Within— / The beaten pride.").
Up-Beat.
Vagabonds.
Visitors to the Black Belt.
Wake.
Warning: Augmented.
Warning ("Daddy, / don't let your dog.").
Water-Front Streets.
Weary Blues, The.
What?
When Sue Wears Red.
Winter Moon.
World War II.

Hughes, Richard (1900–76)
Burial of the Spirit of a Young Poet.
Felo de Se.
Gipsy-Night.
Glaucopis.
Image, The.
Invocation to the Muse.
Lover's Reply to Good Advice.
Old Cat Care.
On Time.
Ruin, The.
Sermon, The.
Tramp.
Walking Road, The.
Winter.

Hughes, T. Rowland (1903–49)
Crib Goch.
Hymn: "You, who gave colour to the dawn."
Salem.

Hughes, Ted (1930–98)
After Lorca.
Amulet.
Bones.
Bride and Groom Lie Hidden for Three Days.
Buzz in the Window.

Childish Prank, A.
Christmas Card.
Cleopatra to the Asp.
Crow, *sels*.
Crow and the Birds.
Crow's First Lesson.
Crow's Last Stand.
Crow's Theology.
Curlews [Lift], *sel*.
Daffodils.
Day He Died, The.
Esther's Tomcat.
Examination at the Womb-Door.
February 17th.
Full Moon and Little Frieda.
God, A.
Gog.
Grin, A.
Hawk in the Rain, The.
Hawk Roosting.
Heptonstall.
Her Husband.
Horses, The.
I See a Bear.
Jaguar, The.
Man Seeking Experience Enquires His Way of
     a Drop of Water, The.
Minstrel's Song.
Modest Proposal, A.
Moon-Hops.
New Year's [or Year] Song.
October Robin, An.
October Salmon[, An].
Old Age Gets Up.
Orf.
Other, The.
Otter, An.
Out.
Pike.
Platform One.
Relic.
Revenge Fable.
River.
Roe-Deer.
Roger the Dog.
Rooks Love Excitement.
St. Matthew, *sel*.
Second Glance at a Jaguar.
Seven Sorrows, The.
Six Young Men.
Snowdrop.
Stations, *sels*.
Swifts.
Telegraph Wires.
That Morning.
Theology.
Thistles.
Thought-Fox, The.
Thrushes.
To Paint a Water Lily.
Tractor.
View of a Pig.
Walt.
Wind.
Wodwo.
Yesterday He Was Nowhere to Be Found.
You Hated Spain.

Hughes, Thomas (*fl.* 1818–65)
Cheese for the Archdeacon, A.

Hugo, Lynne
Small Power.

Hugo, Richard (1923–82)
Death in the Aquarium.
Degrees of Gray in Philipsburg.
Driving Montana.
Elegy: "I expected him to look dead in the
     casket."
Ferniehirst Castle.
Flying, Reflying, Farming.
Freaks at Spurgin Road Field, The.
From Altitude, the Diamonds.
Graves at Elkhorn.
In Your Dream after Falling in Love.
In Your Racing Dream.
Lady in Kicking Horse Reservoir, The.
Langaig.

Last Days.
Letter to Birch from Deer Lodge.
Letter to Blessing from Missoula.
Letter to Gale from Ovando.
Letter to Goldbarth from Big Fork.
Letter to Haislip from Hot Springs.
Letter to Hill from St. Ignatius.
Letter to Libbey from St. Regis.
Letter to Mantsch from Havre.
Letter to Oberg from Pony.
Living Alone.
Map of Montana in Italy, A.
Milltown Union Bar, The.
Missoula Softball Tournament.
Montesano Unvisited.
My Buddy.
Napoli Again.
Neighbor.
Note from Capri to Richard Ryan on the
     Adriatic Floor.
On Hearing a New Escalation.
Places and Ways to Live.
River Now, The.
Salt Water Story.
Skykomish River Running.
Spinazzola: *Quella Cantina Là*.
To Women.
View from Cortona, A.
Way a Ghost Dissolves, The.
Where We Crashed.
White Center.
Yards of Sarajevo, The.

Hugo, Victor (1802–85)
After the Battle.
After the Voices.
Another Voice.
Another Voice.
At the Window in the Dark.
At Villequier.
Be Like the Bird.
Boaz Asleep.
Bridge, The.
Broken Vase, The.
Conscience.
Djinns, The.
Et Nox Facta Est.
Expiation, *sels*.
Grandmother, The.
I could see, far above my head, a black speck.
Inquisition, The.
Jeanne was holed up (pitch darkness; bread
     and water).
More about God (But with Some
     Reservations).
Night of the Fourth: A Recollection, The.
Open Windows.
Russia 1812.
Set Him Apart!
Shepherds and Flocks.
Sound, sound forever, trumpet-calls of thought!
That Night.
Tomorrow, when the meadows grow.
Trumpet of Judgement, The.
Words in the Shadow.

Hui Ch'ung (*fl.* 10th cent. A.D.)
Given to Wen Chao.

Huidobro, Vicente (1893–1948)
Altazor, *sels*.
Ars Poetica.
Blind.
Cow Boy.
Eiffel Tower.
Express.
Midnight.
Morning.
New Song.
Poetry Is a Heavenly Crime.
Quiet Spaces.
Sailor.

Hüimyŏng (c.762–65)
Hymn to the Thousand-Eyed Sound Observer.

Huiyin, Lin (1904–55)
Do Not Throw Away.

Hull, Akasha (Gloria) (b. 1944)
Another Rhythm.

Hull, Coral
Flying Kangaroos.
Hull, Eleanor
Flower of Nut-Brown Maids, The.
Sleep-Song of Grainne over Dermuid, The.
What Is Love?
Hull, Lynda
Adagio.
Lost Fugue for Chet.
Midnight Reports.
Night Waitress.
Ornithology.
Red Velvet Jacket.
Visiting Hour.
Window, The.
Hulme, Doris
In grandfather's house I ran up and down.
Hulme, Thomas Ernest (1883–1917)
Autumn.
Embankment, The (The Fantasia of a Fallen
Gentleman on a Cold, Bitter Night).
Image.
Hulse, Michael (b. 1955)
Concentrating.
Hulü Chin (fl. 6th cent.)
Song of the Tölös.
Hume, Alexander (c.1556–1609)
Of the Day Estivall, sel.
Hume, Christine (b. 1968)
Animal House Shape of God.
Arctic Sun.
Birthday.
Comprehension Questions.
Dialogue of Thunder.
Dirty Money.
Explanation.
Helicopter Wrecked on a Hill.
Hume's Suicide of the External World.
Lies Concerning Speed.
Log Written by an Unkown Hand in the.
Million Futures of Late, A.
Miraculous Panoptic Precipitations.
Night Sentence.
Sampler City.
Sickness & the Magnet, The.
True and Obscure Definitions of *Fly*, Domestic
and Otherwise.
Truth about Northern Lights, The.
Various Readings of an Illegible Postcard.
Humes, Harry
Butterfly Effect, The.
Hummell, Austin (b. 1963)
I Never Saw a Goddess Go.
Panic.
Salt Longing.
Saraband.
Sculpture Garden.
Hummer, T. R. (b. 1950)
Antichrist in Arkansas, The.
Courtly Love.
Ideal, The.
Mechanics.
Plate Glass.
Poem in the Shape of a Saxophone.
Train Wreck, 1890: My Grandmother Lies
Down with the Dead.
Walt Whitman in Hell.
Humphrey, Dolores de Iruretagoyena de
April in Houston.
Hope.
No Immunity.
Humphreys, Emyr (b. 1919)
Ancestor Worship.
Apple Tree and a Pig, An.
From Father to Son.
On the Guincho.
Poughkeepsie.
Humphries, Barry ("Edna Everage") (b. 1934)
Edna's Alphabet.
Edna's Hymn.
Humphries, Rolfe (1894–1969)
Dafydd ap Gwilym Resents the Winter.
Europa.
From the Green Book of Yfan.

Test Paper.
Hung, Eva
I Never Dream of My Father.
Hung Hung
Helas!
Hymn to Hualien, A.
Hungarian Oral Tradition
Blessed Pentecost.
By Three Kinds of Flowers I'm Challenged.
Dead Brother, The.
Dear Child, My Darling Daughter.
Fire Is Laid, The.
Fisherman, Hey!
Hey There, Peacock.
I Chant of the Miracle Stag (Christian
Version).
I Chant of the "Miracle Stag" (Shamanistic
Version).
I Left My Home.
Ilona Budai, The Cruel Mother.
Katie Kádár.
King's Courtyard, The.
Mallard Nests, The.
Rare Is the Wheat-Field in Which There's No
Blemish.
Shaman's Song.
There Was a Prince.
Wife of Master Mason Clement, The.
Hunt, G. W.
McDermott's War Song, sel.
Hunt, Irmgard
Midday.
Hunt, Leigh (1784–1859)
Abou Ben Adhem.
Blue-Stocking Revels; or, The Feast of the
Violets, sels.
Christmas.
Faith, Hope, and Charity Are the Prospects of
Manhood.
Feast of the Poets, The, sel.
Fish, the Man, and the Spirit, The, sels.
Iterating Sonnet.
Legend of Florence, A, sels.
Nile, The.
Rondeau: "Jenny kissed [*or* kiss'd] me when
we met."
St James's Phenomenon, The, sel.
Story of Rimini, The, sels.
To Hampstead ("Sweet upland, to whose
walks, with fond repair.").
To Hampstead ("Winter has reached thee once
again at last.").
To John Keats.
To Percy Shelley.
To the Grasshopper and the Cricket.
To the Same.
Hunter, Albert (1897–1984) *and* **Louie Austin
(1897–1972)**
Down-Hearted Blues.
Hunter, Anne (1742–1841)
Winter.
Hunter, Catherine (b. 1959)
Two Thousand and Two.
What the Voice Sees.
Hunter, Kim (b. 1955)
Accident in a naked place.
I worked on race at the factory.
No like place.
Hunter, Terra
Wanting You.
**Huntingdon, Lucy Hastings, Countess of (1613–
79)**
Bowells of the Earth my bowells hide, The.
Huntington, Cynthia
Hot Wind, Provincetown Harbor.
Virtue: "All the houses are white."
Huntington, William Reed (1838–1909)
Cold Meteorite, The.
From Green Mountain.
Lowlands.
Hupfeld, Herman (1894–1951)
Are You Makin' Any Money?
As Time Goes By.
Let's Put Out the Lights and Go to Sleep.

When Yuba Plays the Rumba on the Tuba.
Hurbak Myungjo (1593–1661)
Dream of a Butterfly, The.
Sitting Alone.
Hurd, Barbara (b. 1949)
My Son's Wedding, My Daughter's.
Hurley, Maureen
Country of Origin.
Hurreh, Ismael
Pardon Me.
Hurvits, Ya'ir (1941–88) *See Also* Hurvitz, Yair
Autobiographical Moment, An.
Hurvitz, Yair (1941–88)
Around the Water Near the Birds.
Hussein, Hoda (b. 1972)
Childhood.
I Can Talk to Them.
Male Grownups.
Room of One's Own, A.
Hussein, Nadir (1939–79)
Wedding, A.
Hutchinson, Lucy (b. 1620, d. after 1675)
Another on the Sun Shine.
Argument of the Third Booke, The.
On my Visitt to WS Which I Dreamt of That
Night.
To the Gardin att O: [Owthorpe] 7:th.
Verses Written by Mrs. Hutchinson.
Hutchinson, Pearse (b. 1927)
Amhrán na mBréag.
Be Born a Saint.
Bright after Dark.
Flames.
Fleadh Cheoil.
Frost is All Over, The.
Gaeltacht.
Into Their True Gentleness.
Look, No Hands.
Málaga.
Sometimes Feel.
True Story Ending in False Hope, A.
Hutchison, Joseph
Joni Mitchell.
Hutten, Ulrich von (1488–1523)
Ulrich von Hutten's Song.
Huws, Meirion MacIntyre (b. 1963)
City, The.
Coat.
Conscience.
Window.
Huxley, Aldous Leonard (1894–1963)
Antic Hay, sel.
Armour.
Burning Wheel, The.
Fifth Philosopher's Song.
Second Philosopher's Song.
Hwang Chini (c.1506–44)
Ah, what have I done?
Blue mountains speak of my desire.
Do not boast of your speed.
I will break the back.
I Will Cut Out the Middle Watch.
Mountains are steadfast.
Taking Leave of Minister So Seyang.
When was I unfaithful to you?
Hwang, Cynthia
Potato Manifesto, The.
Hwang Hŭi (1363–1452)
Are chestnuts falling.
Hwang Hyŏn (1855–1910)
On Killing Myself.
Hwang Insuk (b. 1958)
All Dreams Are Sexual.
Beneath Her Ribs.
Dance of Death.
Huge Mouth.
I'm Surplus.
New Year's Card, A.
Sorrow Wakes Me.
Two Doors.
Walk, A.
When He Said "Soul."

Hwang Jiwoo (b. 1952)
527.
Melancholy, *sels.*
Memo on Composition.
Out of the Winter-Tree Into the Spring-Tree.
Variety Show, 1984.

Hwang O
Swing, The.

Hwang Tonggyu (b. 1938)
Cricket, The.
Happy Letter, A.
One Flower and Another Flower.
Port of Call.
When I See a Wheel.
Wind Burial.
Wind Burial 1.
Wind Burial 3.

Hwansung Jian (1664–1729)
Enjoying Spring.
Silly Song, A.

Hyde, Douglas (1860–1949)
Cold, Sharp Lamentation.
He Meditates on the Life of a Rich Man.
Will You Be as Hard?

Hyde, Evan X.
About Poems.
Explaining.
Super High.

Hyde, Lewis
Goldfish in the Charles River.

Hyecho, Great Master (*fl.* 8th cent. A.D.)
Elegy: "Lamp lost its master at home, The."
Loneliness of a Wayfarer, The.

Hyegŭn *See* Naong, Master

Hyman, Amitiyah Elayne
Surrender.

Hymans, Don (b. 1970)
Passacaglia.

Hyneman, Rebekah Gumpert (1812–75)
Female Scriptural Characters, *sels.*
Woman's Rights.

Hynes, Maureen (b. 1948)
Self-Sufficient Blues.

Hyppolite, Michel-Ange
Caribbean Islands.
Speech.
Woman: "Women carry life."

Hywel ab Owain Gwynedd (d. 1170)
Exultation.
Poet's Loves, The.

I

Ibáñez, Sara de (1910–71)
Empty Page, The.
I Cannot.
Island in the Earth.
Island in the Light.
You, for My Meditation.

Ibaragi Noriko (b. 1926)
What a Little Girl Had on Her Mind.
When I Was at My Most Beautiful.
When I Was Prettiest in My Life.

Ibarbourou, Juana de (1897–1979)
Hour, The.
Life-Hook.
Rainy Night.
Strong Bond, The.
Wild Root.
Woman.

Ibarra, Filomena
In Ancient Rome There Stood.

Ibn Abdūn, Abd al-Majīd ibn Abd Allāh (d. 1134)
It is Fate [alone] that causes us distress, first by the blow itself and then by the traces it leaves; so what is the use of weeping over illusions and vain imagings?

Ibn al-Arabi (1165–1240)
O doves of the *arāk* and the *bān* trees; take pity; to not redouble my sorrows with [your] mourning.

Ibn al-Hammarah, Abu Amir (*fl.* 12th cent.)
Insomnia.

Ibn al-Khatīb (d. 1374)
May the rain cloud be bountiful to you when the rain cloud pours, O time of love union in al-Andalus!

Ibn al-Labbānah, Muhammad ibn Īsá (d. 1113)
Heavens weep with their morning and evening rain clouds over those excellent lords, the Banū 'Abbād, The.

Ibn 'Ammār, Abu Bakr (1031–84)
Pass round the glass for the breeze has arisen and the stars have slackened the reins of night travel.

Ibn Arfa' Ra'suh (*fl.* 11th cent.)
Singing Lute, The.

Ibn az-Zaqqāq, 'Alī ibn 'Aṭiyya Abū l-Hasan al-Bulughghīnī al-Mursī (1096–1134)
My two friends, the love of one's two sons is not heresy, so surely you will both establish my innocence concerning the matter.

Ibn Bājja (d. 1138)
Trail the edge of your robe wherever it pleases, and add more drunkenness to your intoxication.

Ibn Baqī, Abū Bakr Yahya ibn Muhammad ibn 'Abd ar-Rahmān al-Qaisī (d. 1145)
I have no wine other than sorrows mixed in the cup with flowing tears.

Ibn Billita, Abu'l Qasim As'ad (*fl.* c.1050)
Rooster, The.

Ibn Darrāj al-Qastallī, Ahmad ibn Muhammad
May [God's] mercy and power be bestowed plentifully upon this kingship, and may safety and piety be granted to both the religious and the secular [branches].

Ibn Ezra, Abraham (1092–1167)
My Stars.

Ibn Ezra, Moses (c.1070–1138)
And Where Are the Graves.

Ibn Hamdīs, Abd al-Jabbār ibn Abī Bakr (1055–1133)
Fortune that is wont to stumble often brought you honor, and a time in which you succored us has done you wrong, A.
I remember a certain brook that offered the impiety of drunkenness to the topers [sitting] along its course, with [its] cups of golden [wine].

Ibn Hānī' Abū al-Qāsim Muhammad (937?–973)
Sons of al-'Abbās say, The: "Has Egypt been conquered?" Therefore reply to the sons of al-'Abbās: "The matter has already been accomplished"

Ibn Hariq, Ali (d. 1225)
Galley Oars.

Ibn Hazm al-Andalusi (994–1064)
I love you with a love that knows no waning, whereas some of men's loves are midday mirages.
Separation by Death.
Twice Times Then Is Now.
Visit, The.

Ibn 'Iyad (1083–1149)
Grainfield.

Ibn Kamal (d. 1573)
How an Old Man Can Regain His Youth Through Sexual Potency.

Ibn Khafāja, Ibrāhīm ibn Abī al-Fath (1058–1139)
By your life, do you know whether it is the violence of the south winds dashing against my saddle, or the backs of excellent camels?

Ibn Quzman, Abu Bakr ibn Abd al-Malik (c.1086–1160)
I am madly in love despite the angry behavior of one who finds fault [with me]!
My life is spent in dissipation and wantonness!
To a Beauty, White, Pure, and Constant.

Ibn Sahl al-Isrāīlī, Ibrāhīm (d. 1251)
Does the fawn of al-imā know that he has kindled the heart of a lover in which he dwelt.

Ibn Sara (d. 1123)
Eggplant.

Ibn Sharaf (d. 1068)
Satire.

Ibn Shuhayd, Abū Āmir Ahmad (992–1035)
I observe certain eyes gazing steadily at me as if speckled snakes [issuing from them] were attacking me from both sides.
There is no one in the abandoned encampment to inform us of the beloved ones, so from whom will we seek information about their condition?
When I observed that life had turned away its head and I became assured beyond doubt that death would seize me.

Ibn 'Ubāda al-Qazzāz, Abū 'Abdillāh Muhammad
I would give my father in ransom for a gazelle of imā guarded by a lion of the thicket.
I would give my father in ransom for a precious possession that clings to [my] soul!

Ibn Zaydūn, Ahmad ibn 'Abd Allāh (1003–71)
Morning hour of mutual separation has replaced that of mutual proximity and the moment of our mutual separation from the sweetness of our proximity has come, The.

Ibn Zuhr, Muhammad ibn Abd al-Malik (1113–1199)
O cupbearer, our complaints are addressed to you; we have called upon you even though you do not listen!

Ibn Zumruk, Muhammad ibn Yūsuf (*fl.* 14th cent. A.D.)
Question the horizon adorned by the bright stars, for I have entrusted a description of my condition to it.

Ibycus (*fl.* 564 B.C.–561 B.C.)
Again Love, glancing meltingly.
And I killed the Molione boys.
In Spring.
In the Spring the quince and the.
On its highest leaves.
They destroyed the famous and wealthy.

Iché, Laurence
I Prefer Your Uneasiness Like a Dark Lantern.
Scissors Strokes by the Clock.

Ichigen
Joshu exclaimed, "Dog's no Buddha."
Seventy-eight awkward years.

Ieuan ap Hywel Swrdwal (*fl.* 1430–80)
Hymn to the Virgin, The, *sel.*

Ifan, Wil (1882–1968)
In Porthcawl.
Nant yr Eira.
Vale of My Youth, The.

Ifowodo, Ogaga
Abundance of Grey, An.
Homeland.

Iglesias, Holly (b. 1949)
Feeding Frenzy.
Thursday Afternoon: Life Is Sweet.

Igloria, Luisa (b. 1961)
Lost Photograph.

Ignatova, Elena (b. 1947)
I have encountered a valley, in ragged bast matting.
Summer Garden, The.
Then there was the rose I fell in love with.
To Ovid.
To sob, pressing oneself against the officer's greatcoat.
Verses about Music, *sel.*

Ignatow, David (1914–97)
All Quiet.
Bagel, The.
Boxing Match, The.
Cloud Creates, A.
Crystal Chandeliers.
Each Day.
First on TV, A.
For Medgar Evers.
Harold.
Kaddish.
1905.

No Theory.
Pit, The.
Rescue the Dead.
Rightful One, The.
Simultaneously.
Suburbia.
Sunday at the State Hospital.
Time Comes When You Are Facing Him, The.
Walt Whitman in the Civil War Hospitals.
Witness.

Iijima Koichi
Imperfect Poetry and Meaningless Poetry.

Iio Sogi (Sogi) (1421–1502)
Life in this world.
Night frost / Pulsing wings.
Spring.

Ikeda, Patricia Y.
Salt.
Three Churches.
Wild Iris.
Wood.

Ikkyu Sojun (1394–1481)
After ten years in the red-light district.
Elegy: "We first lay down among flowers."
Face to Face with My Lover on Daito's
    Anniversary.
Form in Void.
Four Poems, sels.
I like my anger my grouchy furious love.
My Hand is Lady Mori's Hand.
My Love's Dark Place Is Fragrant Like
    Narcissus.
My Real Dwelling.
Night Talk in a Dream Chamber.
Song of the Dream Garden.
Void in Form.

Ikuo-Joun
This fellow, perfect in men's eyes.

Ikuo-Myotan
Seventy-two years I've hung.

Ilagha, Nengi (b. 1963)
Adam's Cry.
Nike.
Nora.

Ilhami, Sultan Selim III
Coy like a lovebird, she flirts with hundreds,
    she with that lovely face.

Ilio, Dominador I. (b. 1913)
Children of the Atomic Age.
Marikudo in Kalibo, 1979.
Prokosch in Tehran, 1978.
Site of My Grandfather's House, The.

Ilkov, Ani (b. 1957)
Dreamsters.
Evaporations.
Green and Gold.
Muses.
Orbis Tertius, sels.
Peony and a Lion, A.
Ram.
Scene, A.

Illyés, Gyula (1902–83)
Apricot Tree, The.
Bartók.
Bondage.
Faithful Mirror.
Fatherland in the Heights.
Horror.
Logbook of a Lost Caravan.
Marked Ones, The.
On Seeing the Reformation Memorial in
    Geneva.
One Sentence on Tyranny.
Piece of Advice, A.
Refuge.
Sacrifice.
While the Record Plays.
Work.
Wreath, A.

Ilton, Phil
No Goalies.

Im Che (1549–97)
Deep among the green valley grasses.
In a mound where the grass grows long.

Woman's Sorrow, A.

Im Hwa (1908–53)
Again at the Crossroads.
My Brother and the Brazier.
Pier of Yokohama under the Umbrella, The.

Im Ŏngnyŏng (1469–1568)
To a Friend.

Im Yŏngjo (b. 1943)
Carpenter's Song, A.
Matches.
Soap.
Textbook.
Winter Tree.

Image, Selwyn (1849–1930)
Meditation for Christmas, A.

Iman, Yusef
Love Your Enemy.

Imara, Lamiah Abbas
Diogenes.

Imbriglio, Catherine
Aubade: "Dead woodchuck in the dog's mouth
    drooped, The."
Block Island Ferry.
Emily.
Gospel According to How We Throw Stones.
Gospel According to One Who Always Needs
    an Audience.
Gospel According to the Middle.
I Loved Ophelia.
In Nomine.
Motive.
Museum.
Psalm: "Each now dropped / Lay your hands
    upon me, you in the black bent grass, the
    body in motion."
Rumor.

Imoja, Nailah Folami See Gill, Charmaine A.

Imr el [or ul] Kais [or Qais](520–65)
Mu'allaqat, The, sels.
Ode of Imr El-Qais, The.

Inada, Lawson Fusao (b. 1938)
Chinks.
Clearing.
Concentration Constellation.
Father of My Father.
Filling the Gap.
Forest Family.
Fresno Truth, The.
Great Bassist, The.
High-Five for I-5, A.
In So Doing.
In/Vocation.
Japs.
Just Made It.
Keep Quiet.
Legends from Camp, sels.
List, The.
Making It Stick.
Ness.
Nice Place, A.
Picking Up Stones.
Pledge.
Projected Scenario of a Performance to Be
    Given Before the UN.

Inagaki Chikai (fl. 1881–82)
Butterflies.

Inahata Teiko (b. 1931)
As if happiness.

İnal, Gülseli (b. 1947)
Love and the Forest.

Inber, Vera (1890?–1972)
Pulkovo Meridian, The, sel.

İnce, Özdemir (b. 1938)
Wind, Ant, History.

Inez, Colette (b. 1931)
Courtyard Noises from the North, Twenty-
    fourth Precinct.
Lake Song.
Listening to Dvorak's Serenade in E.
Monologue of the Falconer's Wife.
September Morning.
Skeptic, The.
Taking Calls in Freeport, NY.

Ingalls, Jeremy (b. 1911)
Apprehension.
For the Intellectuals.
Gun Emplacement: Sundown.
Vision of St. Michael and St. John, The.

Ingamells, Rex (1913–55)
Great South Land, The, sel.
Unknown Land, sel.

Ingebretsen, Edward J. (b. 1950)
Unlettered.

Ingelow, Jean (1820–97)
And didst thou love the race that loved not
    thee?
Brothers, and a Sermon, sels.
Divided, sel.
For Exmoor.
High Tide on the Coast of Lincolnshire, 1571,
    The.
Little babe, while burns the west.
Long White Seam, The.
Songs of Seven, sels.
Story, A.
Winding-up Time.

**Ìnghean Uí Domhnaill Bhriain (O'Brien),
Fionnghuala (fl. c.1617)**
May your journey, Uaithne, be in the name of
    the Holy Spirit.

**Ingoldsby, Thomas (Richard Harris Barham)
(1788–1845)**
Ingoldsby Legends, The, sels.
Jackdaw of Rheims, The.
Lines Left at Mr Theodore Hook's House in
    June, 1834.
Not a Sous Had He Got.

Ingolosby See Barham, Richard

Ingram, Anne, Viscountess Irwin (c.1696–1764)
Castle Howard, the Seat of the Rt. Hon.
    Charles, Earl of Carlisle, sels.
Epistle to Mr. Pope Occasioned by His
    Characters of Women, An.

Ingram-Roberts, Audrey
Poem 2 (for Duckie Simpson of Black Uhuru).

Inman, P.
Centered.
Colloam.
Dust Bowl, sel.
Numb to Number.
Subtracted Words.
XX.

Innocent, Claude
Poor Man's Life, The.

Inosan, Klod See Innocent, Claude

Inp'yŏng, Prince (1622–58)
Don't mock a pine.

Insana, Jolanda (b. 1937)
Colic Passion, The, sel.
Parabola of the Heart, The, sel.
Rooting, The, sels.
Scream of Abû Nuwàs, The, sel.
Tapestry of the Heart, The.
To Know Me?

Inuit Oral Tradition
Oxaitoq's Song.
Utitia'q's Song.

Iofe, Yury
Olsanski Cemetery, The.
Thing or Two about Childhood, A.

Iolo Goch (c.1320–c.1398)
Labourer, The.

Iorwerth, Dylan (b. 1957)
Sand, sels.

Iosifova, Ekaterina (b. 1941)
At My Doorstep.
Beneath Winter's Roof.
Cloud, The: "It's darker and cooler."
If the Silence Should Suddenly Return.
March: "I'm going to your fair."
Nightfall: "Shadows dart, the wind has risen."

Iozia, John
Fag Art.
Last Night at the Flamingo.

Ipadeola, Tade
August.

Companions.

Ipolit, Mikèlanj *See* Hyppolite, Michel-Ange

Iqbal, Mohammed (1876–1938)
Make Your Radiant Twining Curls.
Poem: "Are you Alive, Dead or DeadAlive?"

Irby, Kenneth (b. 1936)
Heredom.
I met the Angel Sus on the Skin Bridge.
January 1965, Looking on.
[Record].
Sequence.
Slowly the old stone building walls downtown dissolve.
Three Sets of Three, *sel.*
Trash.

Iremonger, Valentin (1918–91)
Clear View in Summer.
Hector.
Icarus.
This Houre Her Vigill.

Irish Oral Tradition
Convict of Clonmel, The.
I Shall Not Die for Thee.
Irish Sailor, The.
John McGoldrick's Trial for the Quaker's Daughter.
O Donall Oge : The Grief of a Girl's Heart.
Pearl of the White Breast.

Ironbiter, Suzanne
Song to the Mother of the World.

Iroquois Oral Tradition
Dancing Speech of O-No'-Sa, The.
Tree of the Great Peace, The.

Irtenev, Igor Moiseievich (b. 1947)
At the Pavelets radial-line station.

Irvine, Weldon J., Jr. (b. 1943)
To be Young, Gifted, and Black.

Irving, Minna (b. 1872)
Marching Still.

Irwin, Mark
Autumnal.
Five Panels.
Give.
My Father's Hats.
Tree, A.
Woolworth's.

Irwin, Thomas Caulfield (1823–83)
Potato-Digger's Song, The.

Isaacs, Anasuya
Mi Negrito.

Isfoel (1881–1968)
Tractor, The.

Isharaza, Grace Birabwa
Grand Get Together, The.

Isherwood, Christopher (1904–86)
Ascent of F6, The, *sels.*
Common Cormorant [*or* Shag], The.

Ishigaki, Rin (b. 1920)
Hands.

Ishihara Yoshiro (1915–77)
Wheat.

Ishikawa Jōzan (1583–1672)
Eating Roasted *Matsutake* Mushrooms.
Gardening Chrysanthemums, I Think of [T'ao] Yüan-Ming.

Ishikawa, Lady (*fl.* c.7th–8th cent.)
For Her Lover.

Ishikawa Takuboku (1885–1920)
After Endless Discussions.
At my words, "Christ was a man."
Better Than Crying.
Do Not Get Up.
Give me / the creeps.
He sees me.
Like being.
Never forget.
Old newspaper!, An.
Once in a while.
Spoonful of Cocoa, A.
Suddenly forgetting my illness one day.
Tanka: "Accidentally / having broken a teacup."
Tanka: "As if in water."

Tanka: "I work."
Tanka: "Just for fun."
Tanka: "Like a white lotus."
Tanka: "On the roadside."
Tanka: "Sorrow / its outlines blurred."
What prompted her.
Wrote Great.

Ishkhan, Moushegh (b. 1913)
Armenian Language Is the Home of the Armenian, The.

Iskander, Fazil Abdulovich (b. 1929)
Blind Man, The.
Gegard.
Once a girl, all April-fresh.

Iskrenko, Nina (b. 1951)
Another Woman.
Hair.
How To Live Through This Night (A Dream).
Isn't She Not a Bird.
Polystylistics.
Sex—A Five-Minute Briefing.

Islām, Najrul (1899–1976)
Don't go back, Ma, don't go back, Mother.
He who has seen my Mother.
Let's be girls, Ma.
Now there'll be a new mantra, Mother.
Oh hey, All-Destroyer.
Syama Mother's lap a-climbing.
Syama wakes on the cremation grounds.
Talk to me, *javas*, talk to me.
Wake up, Syama, wake up, Syama!
Wherever are the lowly, the suffering, and the poor.

Ismail (b. 1928)
Buried Poem, The.
Donkeys in Anantapur.
Poetry: "Beautiful woman, A."
Seen from an Island in Godavari.
Suggestion, A.
Van Gogh's Ear.
You: "You're mine."

Ismail, Donia, El-Amal (b. 1971)
Moment of Mourning, A.

Ismaili, Rashidah (b. 1941)
Bajji.
Lagos.
Queue.
Solange.
Yet Still.

Israeli, Amichai
Eulogy: "This should be a eulogy without words."

Israeli, Henry (b. 1967)
Bicycle Ride, The.
Sway.

Issa (Kobayashi Issa) (1763–1827)
About the field / Crow moves.
After a long nap.
All the time I pray to Buddha.
As I grow older.
As the great old trees.
As we grow old / What triumph.
Asked how old he was.
At prayer / Bead-swinging.
Autumn evening.
Autumn evening / Knees in arms.
Autumn moon.
Autumn wind / Mountain's shadow.
Autumn wind / The beggar looks.
Bath when you're born.
Bats flying.
Be respectful / Sparrows.
Bedbugs, The.
Before I arrived.
Before this autumn wind.
Blossoming plum!
Blossoms at night.
Borrowing my house / From insects.
Brilliant moon.
Buddha Law / Shining.
Buddha's Nirvana / Beyond flowers.
Changing clothes / But not.
Cherry blossoms? / In these parts.
Children / Don't harm the flea.
Children imitating cormorants.

Climb Mount Fuji.
Closer, closer / to paradise—.
Clouds of mosquitoes / It would be bare.
Come and.
Come what may.
Cool breeze.
Counting.
Crescent moon.
Cricket.
Cricket, be.
Cries of wild geese.
Crow, The.
Cuckoo singing.
Cuckoo sings, The.
Cuckoo sings / To me, to the mountain.
Cuckoo's crying / Nothing special to do.
Deer licking.
Delicious Looking!
Dew spread / The seeds of hell.
Distant mountains, The.
Don't fly off, nightingale.
Don't kill that fly!
Don't kill that poor fly!
Don't know about the people.
Don't weep, insects / Lovers, stars, themselves.
Don't worry, spiders.
Dragonfly, The.
Dry riverbed, A.
Ducks bobbing on the water.
Even a fleabite.
Even considered.
Even on the smallest islands.
Even with insects.
Evening clears, The.
Evening moon.
Face of the spring moon.
Faint yellow rose, A.
Farmer / Pointing the way.
Fat priest, The.
Fireflies / Entering my house.
First cicada / Life is.
First firefly / Why turn away.
Five yen each / A cup of tea.
Fleas in my hut.
Flies in the temple, The.
Flies swarming / What do they want of.
Flopped on the fan.
Flowering plum, A.
For you too, my fleas.
For your fleas too.
Frog.
From burweed / Such a butterfly.
From now on.
From that woman.
From the bough.
From the end of the nose.
From the Great Buddha's.
Full moon.
Garden butterfly.
Geese, fresh greens / Wait for you.
Give me a homeland.
Goes out.
Going to Tend Our Family Graves.
Good world, A.
Gratitude for gifts.
Having slept, the cat gets up.
Her row veering off.
Here.
Here in Shinano.
Hey, don't swat the fly!
Hey, sparrow!
His sleeping form.
Holes in the wall, The.
How *much*.
Huge frog and I, A.
I envy.
I wish she were here.
If the times were good.
I'm going out.
I'm going to roll over.
I'm leaving / Now you can make love.
In a dream.
In my hidden house.
In my house / Mice and fireflies.
In spring rain.
In the beggar's tin.

In the midst of this world.
In the thicket's shade.
In this mountain village.
In this world.
In this world / Even butterflies.
Insects.
Insects on a bough.
Issa: A Suite of Haiku, *sels.*
It once happened.
Its mother on guard.
January.
Just beyond the gate.
Just by being / I'm here.
Just to say the word.
Kites shriek / Together—.
Lanky frog, hold.
Last time, I think.
Leaping for the river, the frog.
Let's take / The duckweed way.
Like misty moonlight.
Line of ants, The.
Listen / All creeping things.
Little sparrows.
Lost in bamboo.
Man pulling radishes, The.
Melting snow.
Mokuboji Temple.
Moon and the flowers, The.
Moon, plum blossoms.
Moon tonight, The.
Morning glories, yes.
Mosquito at my ear.
Mother I never knew.
Mother, I weep.
Mountain cuckoo, The.
My cat.
My dear old village.
My hut / Thatched.
My noontime nap.
My old home.
My old village lies.
My spring is just this.
Naked.
Napped half the day.
Napping at midday.
Never forget / We walk on hell.
New foal, The.
New year arrived, The.
New Year's Day.
New Year's morning.
Night is so long, The.
Nightingale's song / this morning.
No doubt about it.
No talent.
Noon.
Not knowing.
Not very anxious.
Not yet become a Buddha.
Now listen, you watermelons.
Now we are leaving.
Nursing her child.
O autumn winds.
O flea! whatever you do.
O owl!
O summer snail.
Old dog bends his head listening, The.
Old dog listens, The.
Old dog, The.
On the Death of the Poet's Daughter Sato.
One bath / After another.
One human being.
Outliving / Them all, all.
Over paddies / At its foot.
Owls are calling / "Come, come."
People working fields.
Pheasant cries, The.
Pigeon Makes His Request, The.
Pissing in the snow.
Plumes of pampas grass.
Poor box, A.
Poor quarter, A.
Prostitute's shack, The.
Red morning sky.
Reflected / In the dragonfly's eye—.
Seen.
Sheet of rain, A.

She's put the child to sleep.
Shinano.
Short night / Scarlet flower.
Shush, cicada / Old Whiskers.
Six Ways, The.
Skinny frog.
Skylarks singing / The farmer.
Snail gets up.
Snail gets up, The.
Snow is melting, The.
So many flea bites.
Spring day, The.
Spring rain.
Summer night.
That gorgeous kite.
That pretty girl.
That wren.
These sea slugs.
They don't notice.
This, I guess, is.
This line of black ants.
This moth saw brightness.
This stupid world.
This world of dew.
This world of dew's.
This year on, forever.
Thus spring begins: old.
Toad! It looks like, The.
Tonight you too / Are rushed.
Treated shabbily / by fleas, by flies.
Under cherry trees / There are.
Under my house.
Under the evening moon.
Under the image of Buddha.
Under this bright moon.
Vanity of men, The.
Village named Little-Plum-Tree, A.
Visiting the graves.
Washing the saucepans.
Watch it—you'll bump / Your heads.
Were it sweet.
What a strange thing!
What a world / Where lotus flowers.
What good luck!
What's the lord's vast wealth.
When I go / Guard my tomb well.
When plum / Blooms—.
When the wild turnip.
Where.
Where there are humans / you'll find flies.
Why did the wild pink break?
Windy fall.
Winter fly, The.
Winter lull / No talents.
With my father.
With this rising bath-mist.
Withered fields, The.
Woodpecker, The.
World of dew, A.
World of dew, The.
World of trials, A.
Worldly sky / From now on.
Wren, The.
Writing shit about new snow.
Young sparrows.
Zealous flea.

Istarú, Ana (b. 1954)
Bodies / tidal waves.
Crescent moon, A.
From where you have come.
Moon became mired on our bed, The.
Then / an awakened citron.
To the cove of my breasts your forehead will
    return.
Your penis rolls to the dream.

Itaikkunrurkilar
His Legs Strong and Lithe.

**Italicus, Catius As Conius Silius (c. 25–c. 101
    A.D.)**
Punica, The, *sels.*

Itō Hiromi (b. 1955)
Near Kitami Station on the Odakyū Line.

Ivanov, Binyo (b. 1939)
Bulletin.
Crickets, Green-faced.

Man, A.
One Can Rest.
Summer: "On this long farm facing Rila
    Mountain."
Tale That's Not a Tale, A.
Wind Is Coming and I Love You, The.

**Ivanov, Georgy [or Georgii] Vladimirovich
    (1894–1958)**
Not so long ago, the world was complete.
Oh, how fastidious you once were.
Old man shuffles to the fish market, The.
On the boundary of snow and melting.
Quarter century of exile has passed, A.
Should I tell of all the absolute fools.
Unharnessed, the white horse ambles along.

Ivanov, Vyacheslav Ivanovich (1866–1949)
Winter Sonnets, The.

Ivanova, Olga (b. 1965)
Do I hold the past in my hands.
I meet myself each and every day.
Time turned inside out.
To Russian Women.

Ivanova, Svetlana
Bird, start up your moan, your whine.
O caterpillar, daughter of the butterfly.
Subterranean River Poem.

Ivask, Yury [or Iurii] (1907–86)
Emily Dickinson.
Ode for the Dancing Khlysty.
Shall we forget the shiver.

Iverem, Esther (b. 1960)
Daddy's Friends.
Earth Screaming.
Faith #1.
Journalist's Convention 1987.
Keeper.
Murmur.
Peace Be Still.

Ives, George (1867–1950)
With Whom, then, Should I Sleep?

Ivey, Mark
After You Left.
Golden, New Mexico.
Preparing for Snow.
Subterranean Business.

Ivory, Helen (b. 1969)
Note to the reader: this is not a poem.
Sleeping with the Fishes.

Ivsic Radovan (b. 1921)
Mavena.
Mavena.

Iwan, Dafydd (b. 1943)
Why Snow Is White.

Izumi, Lady (Izumi Shikibu) (c.974–c.1030)
Although the wind.
Being a person.
From one darkness.
I cannot say.
If Someone Would Come.
If you love me.
In My Idleness.
In the Autumn, on Retreat at a Mountain
    Temple.
Lying down alone.
Lying here alone.
My black hair tangled.
On nights when hail / falls noisily.
So forlorn am I.
Tangled Hair.
Watching the moon.
Watching the moon.
Way I must enter, The.
When I think of you.
You told me it was / because of me.

İzzet Molla (1785–1829)
Everyone knows this world will not be ruined.
I am a nightingale in the garden of grief.

J

Jabeen, Mahe (b. 1961)
Act of Caution, An.
Author's Consent.

Fall: "He always did that."
Ideal Wife.
Live Walls.
Physical Geography.
Relationships.

Jaber, 'Enayat
Circle.
Clarity.
Smell.
Solitude.

Jabès, Edmond (b. 1912)
Beginning of the Book, The.
Book of Questions, The, *sels.*
Book, The.
Desert, II, The.
Desert, The.
Miroir et le mouchoir, Le.
Mirror and Scarf.
Notebook, Two.
Soleilland.
Sunland.

Jaccottet, Philippe (b. 1925)
Clouded Skies.
Dawn.
Daybreak.
Distances.
Don't worry.
Fruit.
Glimpses.
I Rise with an Effort.
In the Steps of the Moon.
Je me redresse avec effort.
Lessons, *sel.*
Letter of the 26th June.
Pensées sous les nuages.
Reason.
Right at the end of night.
Sérénité.
Serenity.
Songs from Below, *sel.*
Sur les pas de la lune.
Swifts.
These wood-shadows.
Wishes.
With Effort, I Sit up and Look Outside.
Wound seen from afar.

Jacinto, Antonio (b. 1924)
Letter from a Contract Worker.
Monangamba Estate.

Jacinto, Jaime
Absence.
Heaven Is Just Another Country.
Tongue Tied.
Visitation.

Jacir, Annemarie
Pistachio Ice Cream.

Jackowska, Nicki (b. 1942)
Proud Shore For Legends, A.
Woman Who Mistook her Father for an
    Irishman, The.

Jackson, Alan (b. 1938)
Confessio.
Hitch-Haiku.
Proddy Heebie Jeebies, The.
Worstest Beast, The.

Jackson, Angela (b. 1951)
Billie in Silk.
Cayenne.
Choosing the Blues.
Fitting Room, The.
Love of Travellers, The.
Loving.
Make/n My Music.
Miz Rosa Rides the Bus.
Moment.
Ohnedaruth.
Spinster Song: African-American Woman
    Guild.
Transformable Prophecy.

Jackson, Anna (b. 1967)
Peacock of Motherhood, The.

Jackson, Bessie (Lucille Bogan) (1897–1948)
Tired as I Can Be.

Jackson, Bruce (b. 1963)
Another Impostor.
In Exchange for Forty Acres.
Riot at Winchell's.
Shooting, Killing, Drug Busts, Cover-Ups,
    Fuck-Ups, Lighter Sides, Weather, and
    Sports.

Jackson, David (b. 1931)
Grandmother Jackson.

Jackson, David Earl (1950–2001)
Nice Sister-Scholars Need Loving, Too.

Jackson, Fleda Brown (b. 1944)
Death of Gladys Presley, The.
Elvis Acts as His Own Pallbearer.
Elvis at the End of History.
Elvis Goes to the Army.
Elvis Reads The Wild Swans at Coole.
Elvis Sings Gospel.
Highway 5.
I Visit the Twenty-four Coin-op Church of
    Elvis.
Industrial Teflon Comes Into Domestic Use.
Women Who Love Elvis All Their Lives, The.

Jackson, Gale (b. 1958)
Alice.
Fugitive Slaves.
1619. Virginia.
1691. Tituba of Salem.
Some of Betty's Story Round 1850.

Jackson, Helen Hunt ("H. H."; "Saxe Holm")
(1830–85)
Cheyenne Mountain.
Crossed Threads.
Danger.
Distance.
Dreams.
Emigravit.
Found Frozen.
Friends.
Her Eyes.
My House Not Made with Hands.
My Lighthouses.
My Strawberry.
October.
October's Bright Blue Weather.
Opportunity.
September [Days Are Here].
Solitude.
Tides.
Two Truths.

Jackson, Laura Riding (1901–91)
All Things.
Ancient Revisits, An.
As Well As Any Other.
Because of Clothes.
Chloe or.
City Seems, A.
Death as Death.
Dimensions.
Ding-Donging.
Divestment of Beauty.
Elegy in a Spider's Web.
Faith Upon the Waters.
Footfalling.
Helen's Burning.
Lucrece and Nara.
Map of Places, The.
Mask, The.
Nothing So Far.
O Vocables of Love.
One Self.
Only Daughter, The.
Opening of Eyes.
Poet: A Lying Word.
Poet's Corner, The.
Postponement of Self.
Prisms.
Reasons of Each, The.
Sea, False Philosophy.
Starved.
Summary for Alastor.
Take Hands.
There Is No Land Yet.
Tiger, The.
Toward the Corner.

Troubles of a Book, The.
Unthronged Oracle, The.
Virgin, The.
Wind Suffers [of Blowing], The.
Wind, the Clock, the We, The.
With the Face.
World and I, The.
You or You.

Jackson, Major L.
Block Party.
Blunts.
Don Pullen at the Zanzibar Blue Jazz Cafe,
    1994 [1997].
Don Pullen at the Zanzibar Blue Jazz Café
    [2006].
Euphoria.
How to Listen.
Indian Song.
Pest.
Some Kind of Crazy.
To Afaa Michael S. Weaver.
Urban Renewal, *sels.*
Urban Renewal 12.

Jackson, Murray (b. 1926)
Detroit Addendum.
Gifts.
Old Mongoose, The—*for Mac.*
San Diego Goodbye—*1944, Jacksaw Arena.*

Jackson, Reuben (b. 1956)
After the Dance.
Albert James.
Big Chill Variations.
For Duke Ellington.
For Thurman Thomas.
Jamal's Lamentation.
Lady's Way.
Lonely Affair, A.
Love # 49: "This is how I felt."
1973.
One More Once.
63rd and Broadway.
Smile.
Sunday Brunch.
Tee.
Thelonious.

Jackson, Richard
Eight Ball.
For a Long Time I Have Wanted to Write a
    Happy Poem.
Other Day, The.
Poem That Was Once Called "Desperate" But
    Is Now Striving to Become the Perfect Love
    Poem.
Shadows.
Sonata of Love's History.
Sprites.

Jackson, Yvonne
How to Make It.

Jacob, Max (1876–1944)
Beggar Woman of Naples, The.
Cock and the Pearl, The, *sel.*
Egg, An.
Horrible Today, The.
In Honor of the Sardana and the Tenora.
In Search of the Traitor.
In the Hill Country.
Invitation to a Voyage.
Little Poem.
Mauvais caractère.
Meeting.
Moon Poem.
1914.
Oeuf, Un.
Réunion.
Révélation, La.
Revelation, The.
Rooster and the Pearl, The.
Rue Ravignan, La.
Rue Ravignan, The.
Shady Soul.
Spanish Generosity.
Translated from the German or the Bosnian.
Visitation.
Visitation.
Wallpaper of Mr. R. K., The.

War.
Yellow Star Again, The.
Jacob, Violet (1863–1946)
Neep-Fields by the Sea, The.
Tam i' the Kirk.
Water-Hen, The.
Jacobik, Gray (b. 1944)
Dust Storm.
From the Porch of the Frost Place.
Skirts.
Sphere, The: "Their first time, they were
wonderfully tender."
Turkeys in August.
Under the Sign of Walt Whitman.
Jacobs, Bruce A.
After the 200th White Person Locks Her Car
Door at Me.
Black on Black.
Friendly Skies.
It's a Dog's Life.
Jeep Cherokee.
Lost.
Jacobs, Harriet (b. 1951)
About Our Hips.
And Sometimes I Hear This Song in My Head.
Goree.
Growing into My Name.
Imagination in Flight: an Improvisational Duet.
It Is not Just.
On Extending the Olive Branch to My Own
Self.
On Growing Up the Darker Berry.
Jacobs, J. L. (b. 1967)
Nearing Long Moons.
Snakeroot.
Two Varieties of the Bitter Orange.
Jacobs, Leland B. (b. 1907)
Subway Train, The.
Jacobsen, Josephine (b. 1908)
Birthday Party, The.
Blue-Eyed Exterminator, The.
Bush.
Hourglass.
Limbo Dancer, The.
Monosyllable, The.
Only Alice.
Poems for My Cousin.
Primer, The.
Yellow.
Jacobsen, Rolf (b. 1907)
Age of the Great Symphonies, The.
Catacombs in San Callisto, The.
Cobalt.
Country Roads.
Crust on Fresh Snow.
Express Train.
Gaslight.
Green Light.
Guardian Angel.
Light Pole.
Meadowsweet.
Memories of Horses.
Moon and Apple.
Old Age.
Old Women, The.
Road's End.
Silence Afterwards, The.
Some People.
Sunflower.
Sunflower.
Jacobson, Dale (b. 1950)
Night Vision of the Gulf War.
Jaewol Kyunghun (1542–1632)
Longing for a Man Faraway.
Sleeping in Pulil Hermitage.
Strangeness of Mountains after Rain, The.
To a Fellow Monk.
Jaffee, Marc (b. 1984)
King of Repetition.
Jagger, Barbara
Anyway.
Jago, Richard (1715–81)
Absence.
Edge-Hill, *sels.*

Jaimes Freyre, Ricardo (1870?–1933)
Dawn, The.
Eternal Farewell.
Night-time.
Sad Voices, The.
Jakiela, Lori
Personal History of Hands, A.
Jakushitsu (1290–1367)
Refreshing, the wind against the waterfall.
Jamal, Paul
Edge, The.
"James" *See* James, Alice Archer Sewall
**James, Alice Archer Sewall ("James") (b.
c.1870?)**
Graffiti.
James, Cliff (b. 1943)
Welsh Homer.
James, Clive (b. 1939)
Book of My Enemy Has Been Remaindered,
The.
Bring Me the Sweat of Gabriela Sabatini.
Johnny Weissmuller Dead in Acapulco.
To Pete Atkin: A Letter from Paris, *sel.*
James, David Emrys (1891–1952)
Horizon.
James, Elinor (*fl.* late 17th cent.)
Injured Prince Vindicated, or, A Scurrilous and
Detracting Pamphlet Answered, An.
James, George (*fl.* 1616)
Roysters give Roome, for here comes a Lass.
James, John (b. 1939)
Bye Bye Blackbird.
Idyl: "Tiny fish."
Shakin All Over.
Sister Midnight.
**James, John (1633–1729) *and* Robert
Wedderburn**
Balulalow.
James, Noberto
I Had No Books.
James, Paul
Can This Be Love?
Can't We Be Friends?
Fine and Dandy.
James, Sibyl
How I'll Live Then.
Sisters of Saida Manoubia, The.
James, Thomas (1593?–1635?)
Lines on His Companions Who Died in the
Northern Seas.
James, Thomas (1946–73)
Reasons.
James I, King of England (1566–1625)
Lady Cicely Wemyss.
James I, King of Scotland (1394–1437)
Kingis Quair, The, *sels.*
Spring Song of the Birds.
Jamie, Kathleen (b. 1962)
Arraheids.
Bogey-Wife, The.
Bosegran.
Child with Pillar Box and Bin Bags.
Crossing the Loch.
Den of the Old Men.
Flower-sellers, Budapest.
God Almighty the First Garden Made.
Hill-track, The.
Inhumation.
Meadowsweet.
Mother-May-I.
Mr and Mrs Scotland Are Dead.
Mrs McKellar, Her Martyrdom.
One of Us.
Pipistrelles.
Queen of Sheba, The.
Rooms.
Skeins o Geese.
St Bride's.
Ultrasound.
Way we live, The.
Jamieson, Robert Alan
De.

Jamme, Franck André (b. 1947)
Life of a Beetle, The.
Often You Come.
Récitation de l'oubli, La.
Recitation of Forgetting, The.
Tu viens souvent.
Vie du scarabée, Le, *sel.*
Jammes, Francis (1868–1938)
Five Sorrowful Mysteries, The.
Prayer to Go to Paradise with the Donkeys, A.
Jana Bai (*fl.* 14th cent.)
Cast off all shame.
Jandl, Ernst (b. 1925)
At the Delicatessen Shop.
Big e, The.
Calypso.
Canzone: "Ganz."
Chanson.
Ch[i/o]mp.
Count.
Dilection.
Fr[o/i]sch.
Gestures: A Game Anglican.
Medieval.
My : T.
Pockets.
Preliminary Studies for the Frankfurt Readings
1984.
Romance, A.
Summer Song, A.
Janeczko, Paul B. (b. 1945)
Blanket Hog.
Mail King.
Janess, Danielle (b. 1978)
Night, Hornby Island.
Janevski, Slavko
Silence.
Jang-hi Lee *See* Yi Jang'hi
Jankovich, Ferenc (1907–71)
In the Courtyard of the Servants.
On the Shores of Szántód.
Janosco, Beatrice
Garden Hose, The.
Jansma, Esther (b. 1958)
Descent.
Janssen, Camille *See* Dermée, Paul
Janzen, Jean
At Summer's End.
August Nights.
Chicken Guts.
Claiming the Dust.
How They Loved.
Learning to Sing in Parts.
Pomegranate.
These Words Are for You, Grandmother.
Wild Grapes.
Japicx, Gysbert (b. 1603)
Lovelight.
Jaques, Florence Page (1890–1972)
There Once Was a Puffin.
Jara, Víctor (1935–73)
Estadio Chile.
Jaramillo Agudelo, Darío (b. 1947)
Some Day.
Jarmain, John
El Alamein.
Embarkation, 1942.
Prisoners of War.
Sand.
These Poems.
Jarman, Geraint (b. 1950)
Dad and Me.
Wood, The.
Jarman, Joseph
Non-cognitive aspects of the City.
What we all.
Jarman, Mark (b. 1955)
Astragaloi.
Black Riviera, The.
Butterflies under Persimmon.
Cavafy in Redondo.
Chimney Swifts.
Desire of Water, The.

Ground Swell.
Psalm: The New Day.
Supremes, The.
Unholy Sonnets, *sels*.
Wave.

Jarnot, Lisa (b. 1967)
Brooklyn Anchorage.
Diary of a Rough Trade Angel.
Girl Who Couldn't Be Loved, The.
My Terrorist Notebook.
New Life, The.
Poem Beginning with a Line by Frank Lima.
Song of the Chinchilla.
Specific Incendiaries of Springtime, The.
Still Life.
Swamp Formalism.
They Loved These Things Too.
United States of America, The.
Valley of the Shadow of the Dogs.
What In Fire Did I, Firelover, Starter of Fires, Love?
Ye White Antarctic Birds.

Jarrell, Randall (1914–65)
Aging.
Bats.
Bronze David of Donatello, The.
Burning the Letters.
Camp in the Prussian Forest, A.
Cinderella.
Country Life, A.
Dead Wingman, The.
Death of the Ball Turret Gunner, The.
Description of Some Confederate Soldiers, A.
Eighth Air Force.
Emancipators, The.
Face, The.
Field Hospital, A.
Front, A.
Game at Salzburg, A.
Girl in a Library, A.
Hope ("Week is dealt out like a hand, The.").
In a Hospital Garden.
In the Camp There Was One Alive.
Island, The.
Islands, The.
Jews at Haifa.
Jonah.
Knight, Death, and the Devil, The.
Losses.
Lost Children, The.
Lost World, The, *sels*.
Man Meets a Woman in the Street, A.
Märchen, The.
Mockingbird, The.
Nestus Gurley.
Next Day.
90 North.
O My Name It Is Sam Hall.
On the Railway Platform.
Orient Express, The.
Pilot from the Carrier, A.
Pilots, Man Your Planes.
Player Piano, The.
Prisoners.
Protocols.
Range in the Desert, The.
Refugees, The.
Say Good-bye to Big Daddy.
Second Air Force.
Sick Child, A.
Sleeping Beauty, The: Variation of the Prince.
Thinking of the Lost World.
Transient Barracks (1944).
Truth, The.
Variations.
Well Water.
Woman at the Washington Zoo, The.

Jarry, Alfred (1873–1907)
Passion of Jesus Considered as an Uphill Race, The.

Jarvenpa, Diane
Polka.

Jarwood, Su
I am a winged creature, flightless.

Jashuva, Gurram (1895–1971)
Bat Messenger, The.
I Was One of Them.

Jastrun, Tomasz (b. 1950)
Hat.
Polish Knot, The.
Scrap.
Seed, The.

Jastrzebska, Maria
Cracking Walnuts.

Jaufré Rudel (*fl.* mid–12th cent.)
Love Song.

Jauss, David (b. 1951)
After the End of the World.
Black Orchid.
Last Solo: Charlie Parker, Hotel Stanhope, March 12, 1955.
Quotations for a Winter Evening.

Jay, T.E.
Fir.

Jayadeva (*fl.* 12th cent.)
Gita Govinda, The, *sels*.

Jayyusi, Salma Khadra (b. 1926)
Dearest Love.
In the Casbah.
Sunken Ship, The.

Jean de Meun *See* de Lorris, Guillaume

Jean-Gilles, Mirlande
Circumcising Pandora.

Jeffers, Honorée Fanonne (b. 1967)
Another Easter Poem.
Eatonton Tableaux.
Ellen Craft.
Eyes of Soon Children.
Ezekiel Saw de Wheel.
Five Note Range of Sorrow.
Hold it Steady.
I Am Your Courtier.
Instructions for Academic Poets Who Talk to God.
Mary, Don't You Weep.
Philly in the Light.
To Keep from Shouting Something.
Tuscaloosa: Riversong.

Jeffers, Lance (1919–85)
How High the Moon.
My Blackness Is the Beauty of This Land.
My Children.
Nina Simone.
O Africa, Where I Baked My Bread.
When I Know the Power of my Black Hand.

Jeffers, Robinson (1887–1962)
Advice to Pilgrims.
Age in Prospect.
Animals.
Ante Mortem.
Apology for Bad Dreams.
Artist, An.
Autumn Evening.
Ave Caesar.
Beaks of Eagles, The.
Beauty of Things, The.
Bed by the Window, The.
Birds.
Birds and Fishes.
Birth-Dues.
Bloody Sire, The.
Boats in a Fog.
But I Am Growing Old and Indolent.
Carmel Point.
Cassandra.
Clouds of Evening.
Compensation.
Continent's End.
Credo: "My friend from Asia has powers and magic, he plucks a blue leaf from the young blue-gum."
Cremation.
Deer Lay Down Their Bones, The.
Divinely Superfluous Beauty.
Evening Ebb.
Eye, The.
Fawn's Foster-Mother.
Fire on the Hills.

For Una.
Gale in April.
Granite and Cypress.
Hands.
Haunted Country.
Home.
Hurt Hawks.
Inquisitors, The.
Love the Wild Swan.
May-June, 1940.
New Mexican Mountain.
Night.
Noon.
November Surf.
Ocean's Tribute, The.
Original Sin.
Pearl Harbor.
Pelicans.
Place for No Story, The.
Post Mortem.
Prescription of Painful Ends.
Promise of Peace.
Purse-Seine, The.
Return.
Roan Stallion.
Rock and Hawk.
Salmon Fishing.
Shane O'Neill's Cairn.
Shine, Perishing Republic.
Shiva.
Sinverguenza.
Stars Go Over the Lonely Ocean, The.
Summer Holiday.
To the Stone-Cutters.
Tor House.
Vulture.
Where I?

Jefferson, Blind Lemon
Easy Rider Blues.
Long Distance Moan.

Jefferson, Thomas
Passage from a Letter to William Charles Jarvis, September 28, 1820.

Jefferys [*or* Jeffries], Charles
We Have Lived and Loved Together.

Jeffrey, Francis, Lord Jeffrey (1773–1850)
In Christ Church, Bristol, on Thomas Turner, Twice Master of the Company of Bakers.
On Peter Robinson.

Jékely, Zoltán (1913–82)
Dragon Slaying.
Footballers.
In Memory of the Funeral Horses.
In the Church of Marosszentimre.
Ode to Chaplin.
To My Bones.
Towards the New Millennium.

Jellicoe, S. Charles
Advice to a Lover.

Jelus, Susan
Factory Town on the 4th of July.

Jemeni
America Eats Its Young.

Jĕn Jui (d. 1949)
Midnight.

Jenkins, Alan (b. 1955)
Barcelona.
Chopsticks.
Inheritance.
Murphy's Law.
Portrait of a Lady.
Road Less Travelled, The.
Street Life.
Visiting.

Jenkins, John (b. 1949) *and* **Ken Bolton (b. 1949)**
In Ferrara.

Jenkins, Joyce (b. 1952)
Piano Man.

Jenkins, Louis (b. 1942)
Appointed Rounds.
Basketball.
Confessional Poem.
Flight.
Football: "I take the snap from center, fake to the right, fade back."

In a Tavern.
Library.
Place for Everything, A.
Walking through a Wall.
Jenkins, Mike (b. 1953)
Chartist Meeting.
Diver-Bird.
Martins.
Survivor.
Truant, A.
Jenkins, Nigel (b. 1949)
Ainadamar.
Castration.
Land of Song.
Shirts.
Wild Cherry.
Yr Iaith.
Jenkins, Paul
Six Small Fires.
Jenkinson, Biddy (b. 1929)
Spray.
Jennings, Elizabeth (b. 1926)
About These Things.
After a Time.
Afterthought.
Annuciation, The.
Child's Story, The.
Christ Seen by Flemish Painters.
Delay.
Fear, A.
First Love.
Identity.
Letter to Peter Levi, A.
Lord's Prayer, The.
Mental Hospital Sitting-Room, A.
My Grandmother.
Not at Home.
One Flesh.
Resurrection, The.
Second World War, The.
Song for a Birth or a Death.
Thinking of Love.
Ugly Child, The.
Unknown Child, The.
Jennings, Kate
Couples.
Just the Two of Us.
Jensen, Laura (b. 1948)
To a Stranger (At the End of a Caboose).
Jensma, Wopko (b. 1939)
Black bottom stomp.
Blue 2.
Chant of praise for the idi amin dada.
Confidentially Yours.
Cry Me a River.
Fear freedom.
I come.
In memoriam Akbar Babool.
In memoriam Ben Zwane.
In solitary.
Lemmy knows two.
Letter to Thelonius.
No dreams.
Pointless objects riddle, The.
Portrait of the artist.
Ring da till.
Somewhere in the middle, Sunday.
Spanner in the what? works.
Suspect under section a1 special.
Till no one.
Jenyns, Soame (1704–87)
Doctor Johnson.
Epistle Written in the Country to the Right
  Honourable the Lord Lovelace, An, sel.
Modern Fine Gentleman, The, sel.
Modern Fine Lady, The, sel.
Snow-Ball, The.
Jernigan, Marla
Glorious.
Kind of Ransom.
Palm at the Entrance to the Arm, A.
Past Qualm of Hours.
Put Together How it Will.
This is Still Life.

Who Are You.
Jerningham, Edward (1737–1812)
Latte, Il.
Jerome, William
Row, Row, Row.
Jerrold, Sydney E.
Beggar Maid, The.
Christopher.
Earthly Joy.
Hope.
John in Prison.
Non Te Rapiet Quisquam de Manua Mea.
Jerry, Bongo (Robin Small) (b. 1948)
Mabrak.
Jess, Tyehimba
Father Country.
Father's Shoes.
Letter to an Unconceived Son.
What Does a Man Do.
Jevon, Rachel (b. 1627, d. after 1662)
Exultationis Carmen To the Kings Most
  Excellent Majesty upon His Most Desired
  Return.
Jewell, Terri L. (b. 1954)
Felled Shadows.
Sistah Flo.
Jewett, Sarah Orne (1849–1909)
At Home from Church.
Caged Bird, A.
Country Boy in Winter, A.
Widows' House, The.
Jewett, Sophie ("Ellen Burroughs") (1849–1909)
For a Birthday.
Letter, A.
Jewsbury, Maria Jane (1800–33)
Farewell to the Muse, A.
My Heart's in the Kitchen, My Heart Is Not
  Here.
Summer Eve's Vision, A.
To My Own Heart.
Verses: "I am monarch of troubles a host."
Jex, Zelma
What Colour's a Man.
Jian, Yu (b. 1954)
Thank You Father.
Jiang Zong (518–90)
Melancholy in the Women's Apartments.
Jien (Former Chief Priest) (1155–1225)
Too Much to Ask.
Jigerkhwen (1903–84)
I Am the Voice.
Jiji, Dobashi
My Bicycle Bell.
Jiles, Paulette (b. 1933)
Paper Matches.
Jiménez, Juan Ramón (1881–1958)
Adolescence: "We were alone together."
At First She Came to Me Pure.
Aurora.
Aurora de Trasmuros.
Author's Club.
Barco Entra, Opaco y Negro, El.
Black Thought, A.
Canción: "Me colmó el sol del poniente."
Cobré la Rienda.
Conciencia Plena.
Countryside Sleeps, Trembling, The.
Dawn Outside the City Walls.
Daybreak.
Definitve Journey, The.
Dejad las Puertas Abiertas.
Faster, Earth, Faster.
Fleeting Return.
Full Consciousness.
Full Moon.
I Am Not I.
I Pulled on the Reins.
I Shall Run through the Shadow.
I Took Off Petal After Petal.
I wish that all my poems.
Immense Hour.
Inteligencia, Dame.
Intelligence, Give Me.
Lamb Was Bleating Softly, The.

Lavender Windowpanes and White Curtains.
Leave the Doors Standing Open.
Love.
Lumber Wagons, The.
Mares.
Mariner's Ideal Epitaph.
Mis Pies ¡Qué Hondos en la Tierra!
Moguer ("Anochecido, grandes nubes ahogan
  el pueblo.").
Moguer ("Dusk. Enormous clouds press down
  on the town.").
Moon, The.
Moon Was Gliding the River, The.
Music: "Music— / a naked woman."
My Feet, So Deep in the Earth.
Name Drawn from the Names, The.
Night Piece.
Nightfall. The Coolness of My Watered
  Garden.
Nombre Conseguido de los Nombres, El.
Oceans.
Oh, Sí; Romper la Copa.
¡Oh Tiempo, Dame Tu Secreto.
Oxcarts Are Now on Their Way, The.
Poe's House.
Recuerdo Se Va, El.
Remembrance Is Moving, A.
Road: "They are all asleep, below."
Ruta.
Se Entró en Mi Frente el Pensamiento Negro.
Sea Is Enormous, The.
Ship, Solid and Black, The.
Song: "Setting sun left my heart, The."
Street Is Waiting for the Night, The.
Sunset.
Ten Short Poems, sels.
Tenebrae.
Time, Give Me the Secret.
Vigil.
Vino, Primero, Pura.
Voy a Correr por la Sombra.
Walt Whitman: "But do you really want to see
  Whitman's house instead of Roosevelt's?"
Who Knows What Is Going On.
Yellow Spring.
Yes, If I Could Only Smash.
Yo No Soy Yo.
Zenith.
Jin, Meiling (b. 1956)
Judgement.
Jinkag Haesim (1178–1234)
At the Zendo.
Bamboo Tree.
Because of the Rain.
By the Water.
Facing the Shadow.
Fan.
Fisherman's Song, A.
For the Great Zen Master Sagum.
Maxim for a Man of Virtue.
May Day.
Mountain Excursion.
On Arriving at Oeo Temple.
On the Death of the Most Reverend Priest.
Sitting and Teaching at Night.
Upon Entering the Priesthood: A Warning.
Jinzu
In serving, serve.
Joans, Ted (b. 1928)
Overloaded Horse, The.
Skip The Byuppie.
.38, The.
Jobim, Antonio Carlos
Quiet Nights of Quiet Stars (Corcovado).
Joe, Rita
Expect Nothing Else from Me.
Old Stories.
Passamaquoddy Song of the Stars.
Plawej ans L'nui'site'w (Partridge and Indian-
  Speaking Priest).
You, I, Love, Beauty, Earth.
Johannsdorf, Albrecht von (fl. 1185–1209)
God's Gifts.
I discovered the sweet lovely lady.
This I know, how love begins to be.

John Paul II, Pope *See* Wojtyla, Karol
John, Richard Johnny, Jerome Rothenberg *and*
Ian Tyson
Songs from the Society of the Mystic Animals,
sels.
Johns, Larry Wayne
Pink Triangles.
Johns, Orrick (1887–1946)
Invitation.
Salon de Vers.
Johnson, A. R.
Joint is Jumpin', The.
Johnson, Amryl (b. 1939)
Rainbow Dragon Trilogy, *sels.*
Johnson, Ben
Advice to a Reckless Youth.
Johnson, Brandon D.
Artifice of War, The.
Storm: "Edges of slave ships are narrow and
difficult for footing, The."
Johnson, Dan (b. 1952)
Maybe Desdemona.
Johnson, David
Bilingual Means Having Two Tongues.
Dust of Mexico, The.
Migration.
Road-Kill.
Johnson, Denis (b. 1949)
Heat.
Heavens, The.
Honor, The.
Incognito Lounge, The.
Poem: "There was something I can't bring
myself."
Words of a Toast, The.
Johnson, Emily Pauline [or Tekahionwake]
(1886–1913)
Joe.
Marshlands.
Train Dogs, The.
Wave-Won.
Johnson, Eric
Chelsea.
Johnson, Fenton (1886–1958)
Aunt Hannah Jackson.
Aunt Jane Allen.
Children of the Sun.
Minister, The.
Song of the Whirlwind.
Tired.
Johnson, George W.
When You and I Were Young, Maggie.
Johnson, Georgia Douglas (1886–1966)
Common Dust.
Escape.
Heart of a Woman, The.
I Want to Die While You Love Me.
Motherhood.
Prejudice.
Suppliant, The.
Johnson, Halvard (b. 1936)
Berlioz in the Madhouse.
Fringe-Area Reception.
Johnson, Harold L.
At the Jackson Pollock Retrospective in L.A.
Names of Summer, The: A War Memory.
Johnson, Helene (1907–95)
Bottled [New York].
Magalu.
Sonnet to a Negro in Harlem.
Johnson, J. C.
Joint is Jumpin', The.
Johnson, Jacqueline (b. 1957)
Phyllis.
Saudades.
What Is There For Us?
Johnson, James Weldon (1871–1938)
Before a Painting.
Brer Rabbit, You's de Cutes' of 'Em All.
Color Sergeant, The.
Creation, The.
Down by the Carib Sea, *sels.*

Envoy: "If homely virtues draw from me a
tune."
Fifty Years.
Girl of Fifteen.
Go Down Death (A Funeral Sermon).
Judgment Day, The.
Lift Every [or Ev'ry] Voice and Sing.
My City.
O Black and Unknown Bards.
O Southland!
Sence You Went Away.
We To America.
White Witch, The.
Johnson, Jay Emerson (b. 1961)
Silent Promise, A.
Johnson, Jenna
Inside Out.
Johnson, Jim
Music for the Cows.
Johnson, Jonathan (b. 1967)
Eclipse.
Midnight Run.
Unmarked Stop in Front of Westmond General
Store, Westmond, Idaho.
View Café, The.
Johnson, Joyce
Bat that blocks at close of play, The.
Johnson, Kate Knapp
Meadow, The.
Query: "Who left / this wooly caterpillar."
Johnson, Kent (b. 1955)
High Altitude Photo of Hiroshima (Circa
1944).
Trilobytes.
Johnson, Leslie
Paradise Lost, Book IV, lines 639—654.
Johnson, Linton Kwesi (b. 1952)
Five Nights of Bleeding.
Mi Revalueshanary Fren.
Reggae Sounds.
Sonny's Lettah.
Johnson, Lionel Pigot (1867–1902)
Age of a Dream, The.
Burden of Easter Vigil, A.
By the Statue of King Charles [I] at Charing
Cross.
Cadgwith.
Church of a Dream, The.
Collins.
Dark Angel, The.
My Own Fate.
Mystic and Cavalier.
Precept of Silence, The.
Red Wind, The.
Te Martyrum Candidatus.
To a Traveler.
To Morfydd.
Johnson, Lisa Elaine
Spirit of the Dancer.
Johnson, Lynne d
Flow, The.
Johnson, Maggie Pogue (b. 1949)
Ambition.
As We Sow We Shall Reap.
Christmas Times.
Dat Mule ob Brudder Wright's.
Day befo' Thanksgibin', De.
Dedicated to Dr. W. H. Sheppard.
Dedication Day.
Dream, A.
I Wish I Was a Grown Up Man.
James Hugo Johnston.
Krismas Dinnah.
Leap Yeah Party, De.
Lost Teddy Bear, The.
Meal Time.
Men Folks ob Today, De.
Negro Has a Chance, The.
Old Maid's Soliloquy.
People's Literary, De.
Poet of Our Race.
Sister Johnson's Speech.
Sometimes.
Story of Lovers Leap, The.
Strawberry, The.

Superstitions.
Thoughts.
To Professor Byrd Prillerman.
To See Ol' Booker T.
V. N. and C. I, The.
What's de Use ob Wukin in de Summer Time
at All.
What's Mo' Temptin' to de Palate?
When Daddy Cums from Wuk.
Why Should the American Negro Be Proud?
Wintah Styles, De.
Johnson, Margaret (b. 1926)
Visit to the Cities of Cheese, A.
Johnson, Markham
All-Night Diner, The.
Johnson, Mary F. (d. 1863)
Idiot Girl, The.
Invocation to the Spirit Said to Haunt Wroxall
Down.
Second Evening.
Thunder Storm.
Village Maid, The.
Widow's Remarriage, The.
Johnson, Michael L.
Old Dog.
Johnson, Peter
Accomplice.
Enigma of the Stigma, or Vice Versa.
Genesis: A Retrospective.
Hell.
Tattoo.
Travels with Oedipus, *sels.*
Johnson, Pyke, Jr. (1889–1969?)
Toucan, The.
Johnson, Robert (1911–38)
Hellhound on My Trail.
Me and the Devil Blues.
Reverse Engineering.
Stones in my Passway.
Johnson, Ronald (b. 1935)
Ark, *sels.*
William Stukeley made his own Stonehenge.
Johnson, Samuel (1709–84)
Ballad: "I put my hat upon my head."
Ballad: "If the man who turnips cries."
Ballad: "Tender infant, meek and mild, The."
Hermit Hoar.
Lines Contributed to Goldsmith's "The
Traveller."
Lines Contributed to Hawkesworth's "The
Rival."
London: A Poem in Imitation of the Third
Satire of Juvenal, *sels.*
On the Death of Dr [or Mr] Robert Levet [a
Practiser in Physic].
Paraphrase.
Prologue Spoken by Mr[.] Garrick at the
Opening of the Theatre in Drury Lane, 1747.
Prologue to Hugh Kelly's *A Word to the Wise.*
Short Song of Congratulation, A [or To a
Young Heir].
Verses in Baretti's Commonplace Book.
While Many a Merry Tale.
Johnson, Trasi (b. 1967)
Matisse, Cut Outs.
12 second poem.
Until He Comes.
Johnson, Wendy
River Meditation.
Johnston, Arthur (1587–1641)
To Robert Baron.
Johnston, Bertha
Did You Ever Hear an English Sparrow Sing?
Johnston, Charles (d. 1823)
I know thee not, bright creature, ne'er shall
know.
Spirit of evil, with which the earth is rife.
Johnston, Devin (b. 1970)
Pyramus & Thisbe.
Johnston, Ellen (1835–73)
Address to Nature on its Cruelty, An.
Last Sark, The.
Lines: To a Young Gentleman of Surpassing
Beauty.

Lines to Ellen, the Factory Girl.
Mother's Love, A.
Nelly's Lament for the Pirnhouse Cat.
Working Man, The.

Johnston, Gary
Blood Is the Argument.

Johnston, George (b. 1913)
Cathleen Sweeping.

Johnston, Martin (b. 1947)
Gorey at the Biennale.
In Memoriam.
In Transit: A Sonnet Square, *sels*.
Sea-Cucumber, The.

Johnston, Patricia
I'll Remember April.

Johnston, Percy (b. 1930)
Blaupunkt (Choruses Pepper Adams Never
Took).
Dewey Square, 1956.
Lexington Avenue Express.
Round About Midnight, Opus #6.
To Paul Robeson, Opus No. 3.

Johnstone, Philip
High Wood.

Johnstone, Robert (b. 1951)
Eden Says No.
Every Cache, *sels*.
Fruit of Knowledge, The.
New Incidents in the Life of Shelley, *sel*.
Robot Camera.
Undertakers.

Jolas, Eugene (1894–1952)
Mater Dolorosa.

Jolson, Al
California, Here I Come.
I'll Say She Does.

Jomei, Emperor (593–641)
Written After Climbing Kaguyama to Survey
the Land.

Jonas, Steve (1927–70)
IV.
Book V.
Ear Injured by Hearing Things, An.
For LeRoi Jones.
Lens.
Little Magic, A.
Muddle, A.
Orgasm 0.
What you can see.

Jones, Alice
Anorexia.
Communal Living.
Five from Three.
Tap.
World, The.

Jones, Anna Maria (1748–1829)
To Echo.
To the Moon.

Jones, Bobi (b. 1929)
Beethoven's Ears.
Bilbao Churchyard.
Chestnut Tree Deciding to Fly in May, The.
Conversation of the Deaf, The.
Engine Driver.
Having Our Tea.
Landscape without a Hat.
March Lambs.
Portrait of a Nun.
Portrait of a Pregnant Woman.
Portrait of an Engine Driver.
Portrait of an Overpopulated Woman.
Pregnant Woman.
South Shore (Aberystwyth), The.
Spring at Nant Dywelan.
Vermeer's Paint.
Wasp.
Women at the Pit-head, The.

Jones, Ceri Wyn (b. 1967)
Honour.
Influence.
Legacy.

Jones, D. Cyril (b. 1947)
Letters to a Kenyan Friend.

Jones, Dafydd *See* Isfoel

Jones, Daryl E.
Going On.
Triangulation.

Jones, David (1895–1974)
A, A, A, Domine Deus.
Anathemata, The, *sels*.
In Parenthesis, *sels*.
Mabinog's Liturgy, *sel*.
Sleeping Lord, The, *sels*.
Tribune's Visitation, The, *sel*.
Tutelar of the Place, The, *sel*.

Jones, David Gwenallt ("Gwenallt") (1899–1968)
Adrift.
Cymru.
Dartmoor.
Dead, The.
Depression, The.
Earth, The.
Hedgehog, The.
Old Woman, An.
Rhydcymerau.
Sin.
Wales.

Jones, Dewi Stephen (b. 1940)
Coat, The.
Diptych.
House, The.
In a Beautiful Glass.
Last Window.

Jones, Dic (b. 1934)
Harvest and Spring.
Lamentation.
On Seeing a Dead Lamb.
Reaping.

Jones, Douglas G. (b. 1929)
Summer Is a Poem by Ovid.

Jones, Ebenezer (1820–60)
When the World Is Burning.

Jones, Einir (b. 1950)
Cockles.
Ffynnon Grandis.
Grey.
Picture, The.
Shadows of Trees on the Lawn, January.

Jones, Ellis (1884–1948?)
Eaves.

Jones, Ernest Charles (*fl.* c.1852)
Song of the Lower Classes, The.

Jones, Evan (b. 1927)
Dream, A.
Genesis.
Lament of the Banana Man, The.
Point, The.
Song of the Banana Man, The.
Study in Blue.

Jones, Glyn (1905–95)
Again.
Common Path, The.
Dafydd's Seagull and the West Wind.
Esyllt.
Fragment: Where Is Tangwen Now?
Merthyr.
Morning.
Profile of Rose.
Swifts.
Where All Were Good to Me, God Knows.

Jones, Gwilym R. (b. 1903)
Atomic Factory, The, *sels*.
Psalm to the Creatures.

Jones, Gwyn (b. 1951)
Blue Day Journey, The.

Jones, Henry (1721–70)
On a Fine Crop of Peas Being Spoiled by a
Storm.

Jones, Hettie (b. 1934)
Caught, April 2002—A Prayer for Peace.
Emine and Hamide.
Genuflection to Petty Officer First Class
Leonette Masters.
Laments for the Afghan Women.
New Southern Exposure.
Weather.

Jones, Huw (b. 1955)
Man Lying in a Hallway.

Mannyelanong.

Jones, Ira B.
Alley Games 6/The Ascension.
Echoes of the Murder of Emmett Till.
Haiku for My Brothers.
Revolutionary Vision, The.

Jones, Jacquie (b. 1965)
Drugs.

Jones, John (1788–1858)
Holywell, *sel*.

Jones, John ("Talhaiarn") (1810–69)
Glyndwr's War Song.
Watching the Wheat.

Jones, Jordan
Zen Baker.

Jones, LeRoi *See* Baraka, Imamu Amiri

Jones, Llion (b. 1964)
Illusions.

Jones, M. Keel
Election Reflection.

Jones, Mary (1707–78)
After the Small Pox.

Jones, Moses Glyn (b. 1913)
Candle's Fly, The.
Living Spring, The.
Old Light, The.
Sand-time Measuring.

Jones, Nesta Wyn (b. 1947)
Beaches.
Poppies.
Scream!
Shadows.
Voices: "Yes, this is my voice."

Jones, Patricia (b. 1951)
Billie Holiday Chronicles, The, *sels*.
If I Were Rita Hayworth.
Song: "I have so little sorrow."

Jones, Patricia Spears (b. 1955)
All Saints Day, 2001.
Glad All Over.

Jones, Peter (b. 1929)
In the Formal Garden.
In the Park.

Jones, Peter Thabit (b. 1951)
Modris.

Jones, R. Gerallt
For Ewan McLachlan.
Geese at Gregynog.
Nurse, The.
To Derek Walcott.
Yasnaya Polyana.

Jones, Rae Desmond (b. 1941)
Front Window, The.
James Dean.
Shakti.

Jones, Richard
After Work.
Apology to Andrew.
Beginning, A.
Bell, The.
Comment on This: in the Real Scheme of
Things, Poetry Is Marginal.
Freight, The.
Key, The.
Loft, The.
Novel, The.
Poet's Heart, The.
Portrait of My Father and His Grandson.
Son.
Song of the Old Man.
Storm, The.
Times Like This.
What Effect Has Your New Son Had on Your
Writing Life?
White Towels.

Jones, Rodney (b. 1950)
Blasphemy, A.
Carpe Diem: "Though pretty, it rarely worked,
lining seduction."
Elegy for a Bad Example.
End of Communism, The.
Failed Memory Exercise.
Letters from the Earth.

My Manhood.
Nell.
News of the Cranes.
Nudes.
Obsolescence of *Thou*, The.
On the Bearing of Waitresses.
One of the Citizens.
Remembering Fire.
Small Lower-Middle-Class White Southern
  Male.
Sweep.
TV.
Jones, Roger
Photo of a Rotary Crew, Sour Lake Oilfield,
  1904.
Strata.
Uncle Fenster's Grave.
Jones, Roland
Foam.
Jones, Sally Roberts (b. 1935)
Ann Griffiths.
Another Lazarus.
Community.
Household Cavalry, Llanstephan.
Illusions.
New World.
Jones, Samuel (d. 1732)
Force of Love, The.
Jones, T. Gwynn (1871–1944)
Argoed.
Humanity.
Meal, The.
Pro Patria, *sel*.
Jones, T. Harri (1921–65)
Back?
Bird on a Jaunt.
Cwmchwefri.
Difference.
Llanafan Unrevisited.
Mr Jones as the Transported Poet.
My Grandmother Died in the Early Hours of
  the Morning.
Rhiannon.
Welshman in Exile Speaks, The.
Jones, Thomas James (b. 1934)
Dyfed Devastated?
Dylan.
Face to Face.
Thursday.
Jones, Tudur Dylan (b. 1965)
Gardening.
Great Glasshouse at the National Botanic
  Garden of Wales.
Jones, Sir William (1746–94)
Epigram: "On parent knees, a naked new-born
  child."
Hymn to Indra, A.
Hymn to Na'a'yena, A.
Hymn to Su'rya, A.
Jones, William Basil Tickell
Match Me Such Marvel.
Jong, Erica (b. 1941)
Alcestis on the Poetry Circuit.
Castration of the Pen.
Climbing You.
Colder.
Jubilate Canis.
Parable of the Four-Poster.
Testamant (Or, Homage to Walt Whitman).
Jonker, Ingrid (1933–65)
Child Who Was Shot Dead by Soldiers at
  Nyanga, The.
Dog.
Face of Love, The.
I Am with Those.
I Don't Want Any More Visitors.
I Drift in the Wind.
Pregnant Woman.
Jonson, Ben (1572–1637)
Alchemist, The, *sel*.
Carol.
Celebration of Charis in Ten Lyric[k] Pieces
  [*or* Peeces], A, *sels*.
Cynthia's Revels, *sels*.

Dream, The.
Elegy, An: "Though beauty be the mark of
  praise."
Epicoene; or, The Silent Woman, *sels*.
Epigram, An. To the Small-Pox.
Epistle Answering to One That Asked to Be
  Sealed of the Tribe of Ben, An.
Epistle to a Friend, to Persuade Him to the
  Wars, An, *sel*.
Epistle to Master John Selden, An.
Epitaph on Elizabeth, L. H.
Epitaph on S. P. [*or* Salomon Pavy], a Child of
  Queen Elizabeth's Chapel.
Eupheme, *sels*.
Fair friend, 'tis true, your beauties move.
Fit of Rhyme against Rhyme, A.
Gypsies Metamorphosed, The, *sels*.
Hour-Glass, The.
Hymn[e] on the Nativity [*or* Nativitie] of My
  Saviour, A.
Hymn[e] to God the Father, A.
Inviting a Friend to Supper.
Key Keeper, The, *sels*.
Martial. Epigram XLVII, Book X.
Masque of Christmas, The.
Masque of Queens, The, *sel*.
My Picture Left in Scotland.
New Inn, The, *sels*.
Ode to Himself, An ("Where dost [*or*; do'st]
  thou careless[e] lie.").
Of Life and Death.
On Don Surly.
On English Monsieur.
On Giles and Joan.
On Groin.
On Gut.
On Lieutenant Shift.
On Lucy, Countess of Bedford.
On My First Daughter.
On My First Son.
On Playwright ("Playwright convict of public
  wrongs to men.").
On Something, that Walks Somewhere.
On Spies.
On the Famous Voyage, *sel*.
On the Town's Honest Man.
Pleasure Reconciled to Virtue, *sels*.
Pleasures of Heaven, The.
Sad Shepherd, The, *sel*.
Song. To Celia ("Drink to me only with thine
  eyes.").
Sonnet to the Noble Lady, the Lady Mary
  Wroth, A.
To Alchemists.
To Captain Hungry.
To Censorious Courtling.
To Clement Edmonds, on His *Caesar's
  Commentaries* Observed, and Translated.
To Doctor Empiric[k].
To Edward Alleyn.
To Elizabeth, Countess of Rutland.
To Fine Lady Would-Be.
To Fool or Knave.
To Heaven.
To John Donne ("Donne, the delight of
  Phoebus, and each Muse.").
To John Donne ("Who shall doubt, Donne,
  where [*or* whe'er] I a poet be[e].").
To Lucy, Countess of Bedford, with Mr.
  Donne's Satires.
To Mary, Lady Wroth ("Madam[e], had all
  antiquity [*or* antiquitie] been lost.").
To My Book.
To Penshurst.
To Sir Henry Cary.
To Sir Henry Goodyere.
To Sir Henry Savile [upon His Translation of
  Tacitus].
To Sir Thomas Roe.
To the Immortal Memory and Friendship of
  That Noble Pair, Sir Lucius Cary and Sir H.
  [*or* Henry] Morison, *sels*.
To the Memory of My Beloved, the Author Mr
  [*or* Master] William Shakespeare: And What
  He Hath Left Us, *sel*.

To the Reader ("Pray thee, take care, that tak'st
  my book[e] in hand.").
To the Same [Robert, Earl of Salisbury] [Upon
  the Accension of the Treasurership to Him].
To the Same [Sir Thomas Roe].
To Thomas Palmer [on His Book *The Sprite of
  Trees and Herbs*].
To William Camden.
To William Roe ("When Nature bids us leave
  to live, 'tis late.").
Volpone, *sels*.
Volpone, *sels*.
Jooris, Roland (b. 1936)
Village, A.
What Does One Do.
Jordan, A. Van
Beggar's Song.
Black Drag Queen.
Debt is Paid, A.
Kind of Blue.
N-e-m-e-s-i-s Blues.
Orientation: Wittenberg University, 1983.
Public Radio Plays Eddie Harris.
Jordan, Barbara Leslie (b. 1915)
Peaceable Kingdom.
This Poem.
Viper Light.
Jordan, Judy (b. 1961)
Sandbar at Moore's Creek.
Through These Halls.
Winter.
Jordan, June (1936–2002)
All the World Moved.
Bus Window.
DeLiza Spend the Day in the City.
Directions for Carrying Explosive Nuclear
  Wastes through Metropolitan New York.
For Beautiful Mary Brown: Chicago Rent
  Strike Leader.
Grand Army Plaza.
If You Saw a Negro Lady.
July 4, 1984: For Buck.
Mendocino Memory.
Mid-Year Report: For Haruko.
Nobody Riding the Roads Today.
Notes on the Peanut.
October 23, 1983.
Onesided Dialog.
Owed to Eminem.
Poem about heartbreak that go on and on.
Poem About My Rights.
Poem Against the State (Of Things): 1975.
Reception, The.
Roman Poem Number Nine.
San Juan.
Second Poem from Nicaragua Libre: War
  Zone.
Something Like a Sonnet for Phillis Miracle
  Wheatley.
Speculations on the Present through the Prism
  of the Past.
Test of Atlanta 1979, The.
Toward a Personal Semantics.
Wasted.
What Would I Do White?
You Came with Shells.
Jordan, Norman (b. 1938)
When A Woman Gets Blue.
Jordan, Thomas (1612?–35)
Double Acrostich on Mrs Svsanna Blvnt, A.
Jorge, Luiza Neto (1939–89)
Another Genealogy.
Fable: "Animal understands itself, The."
Force of Gravity, The.
Monument to Birds (Max Ernst).
Joris, Pierre (b. 1946)
Fin-de-Siècle Identikit.
9/11/01.
Winnetou Old, *sel*.
Josefowitz, Natasha
Foreplay.
Music.
Joselow, Beth Baruch
We Startle Things.

Joseph, Allison (b. 1967)
Adolescence.
Chalazion.
Domestic Humiliation.
Fourth Supreme, The.
Good Humor.
In the Bookstore.
Junior High Dance.
Kitchen.
Learning to Drive at 32.
Learning to Laugh.
My Father's Heroes ("He gloried in the
    feats.").
My Father's Heroes ("Not JFK, not MLK.").
Noon Talk at Georgia's Coffee Shop.
Not Ophelia.
Numbers: "My father taught me to measure."
On Being Told I Don't Speak Like a Black
    Person.
On Sidewalks, on Streetcorners, as Girls.
On Viewing Two Different Date Rape Movies.
Pleasure.
Plenty.
Poem for the Purchase of a First Bra.
Pure Pop.
Reading Room.
Searching for *Melinda's Magic Moment*.
Shame of the Writers' Conference.
Soul Train.
Teenage Interplanetary Vixens Run Wild on
    Bikini Beach.
Traitor.
Wedding Party.
Joseph, Jenny (b. 1932)
Ant nest.
Inland sea, The.
Warning.
Joseph, Lawrence (b. 1948)
Curriculum Vitae.
Do What You Can.
Here.
In the Age of Postcapitalism.
Sand Nigger.
Some Sort of Chronicler I Am.
That's All.
Then.
When One Is Feeling One's Way.
Joseph, M. K. (1914–81)
Riddle, A: Of the Soul.
Joshu, Kyozan
Whenever I hear.
Joso See Naito Joso
Joubert, Jean ((b. 1928)
Brilliant Sky.
Jourdan, Pierre-Albert (1924–89)
Parle.
Prayer: "Let innocence remain."
Prière.
Speak.
Jouve, Pierre Jean (1887–1976)
After the Deluge.
Après le déluge.
De plus en plus femme.
Lament for the Stag.
Lamentations au cerf.
More and More Woman.
Joyce, James (1882–1941)
Bahnhofstrasse.
Blurb for *Anna Livia Plurabelle*, A.
Ecce Puer.
Finnegans Wake, *sel.*
Flood.
Flower Given to My Daughter, A.
Holy Office, The.
I hear an army charging upon the land.
My dove, my beautiful one.
On the Beach at Fontana.
Post Ulixem Scriptum.
Though I thy Mithridates were.
Tutto è Sciolto.
Ulysses, *sel.*
Joyner, Carolyn
They Do Not Have to Nest in Your Hair: A
    Tribute to Ron Brown.

József, Attila (1905–37)
Ars Poetica.
Attila József.
Belated Lament.
By the Danube.
City Limits, The.
Dead Landscape.
Dog, The.
Encouraging.
For My Birthday.
For My Birthday.
For My Birthday.
For My Birthday.
Freight Trains.
How Long the Lord.
Humans.
Hunger.
I Have Done My Reckoning.
Lullaby: "Sky is letting its blue eyes close,
    The."
Mother.
Ode: "Here I'm perched on a sheer cliff."
On Mankind.
Seventh, The.
Songs of Innocence.
They Who Are Poor.
Three Kings of Bethlehem, The.
To Sit, to Stand, to Kill, to Die.
True Man, A.
Welcome to Thomas Mann.
Juan Chi (210–63)
As Dew-Drops Freeze.
Day and Night.
In My Youth.
In the Shadow of Death.
Inscribe on Your Heart.
Last Rays of the Sun.
Learning.
Mujin Flowers Blossom on the Rolling Graves,
    The.
Sleepless at Midnight.
Songs of My Soul, *sels.*
Ten Suns Rise in the East, The.
Weird Dances.
**Juana Inés de la Cruz, Sor (Juana Rumirez de
Asbaje) (1651–95)**
Describes Rationally the Irrational Effects of
    Love.
Elusive Shadow of My Substance, Stay.
Fifth Villancico, in Alternating Voices, Written
    for the Feast of the Nativity in Puebla, 1689,
    The, *sels.*
First Villancico, Written for the Nativity of Our
    Lord, Puebla, 1689, The, *sel.*
Hope.
I Can Neither Hold You Nor Let You Go.
In Acknowledgment of the Praises of European
    Writers.
In Containing a Thought Satisfied with Chaste
    Love.
Oh World, Why Do You Thus Pursue Me?
On Her Portrait.
On Her Portrait.
Perpetual Infirmity of Hope.
Pleaure Given by Suspicion with the Rhetoric
    of Crying, The.
This Evening When I Spoke to You.
Verses Against the Inconsequence of Men's
    Taste and Strictures.
Verses Expressing the Feelings of a Lover.
Which Contains a Fantasy Satisfied with a
    Love Befitting It.
World! Why Do You Hound Me?
Juarroz, Roberto (b. 1925)
Any movement kills something.
Eleventh Vertical Poetry, *sel.*
Fifth Vertical Poetry, *sel.*
Life Draws a Tree.
Look First at the Air and Its Black Element
    Which Never Stops.
Ninth Vertical Poetry, *sel.*
Seventh Vertical Poetry, *sel.*
Sixth Vertical Poetry, *sel.*
Somewhere There's a Man.
Tenth.9.
There Are Points of Silence Circling the Heart.

Third Vertical Poetry, *sel.*
Vertical Poetry, *sel.*
Judson, John
Whitman Again.
Jūgo
Mad Verse.
Juhász, Ferenc (b. 1928)
Biography of a Woman, The.
Birth of the Foal.
Boy Changed into a Stag Clamours at the Gate
    of Secrets, The.
Rainbow-Colored Whale, The.
Juhász, Gyula (1883–1937)
Death of Shakespeare, The.
Hungarian Summer [1918].
Hungarian Winter.
Lost Behind the Back of God.
Magyar Scene Through Magyar Eyes, A.
One for the "Ancient Gypsy"
Song about Kőrösi Csoma.
To Lord Byron.
Village Night.
What Was Her Blondness Like.
Juma'h, Jamal (b. 1956)
Letters to My Brother, *sel.*
Jünger, Friedrich Georg (b. 1898)
Ultima Ratio.
Jungkwan Haean (b. 1567)
Deathbed Song.
On Reading Namwha Sutra.
Ridiculing the Monk Who Builds a Stupa.
Various Songs of Leisure.
Jungkwan Ilson (1533–1608)
At Daedun Temple.
On My Way Back to Kojokdae.
Returning to Dupawon.
Revisiting Kumkang Pavilion.
To an Old, Deaf, and Blind Monk.
Juntoku, Emperor
Royal Dwellings.
Juo
Beyond the snatch of time, my daily life.
Jussawalla, Feroza F. (b. 1953)
Indian.
Justice, Donald (b. 1925)
About My Poems.
Absences.
After a Phrase Abandoned by Wallace Stevens.
American Sketches (for William Carlos
    Williams), *sels.*
Anonymous Drawing.
Assassination, The.
But That Is Another Story.
Children Walking Home from School through
    Good Neighborhood.
Counting the Mad.
Evening of the Mind, The.
First Death.
Grandfathers, The [*or* After a Line by John
    Peale Bishop].
Here in Katmandu.
In Memory of My Friend the Bassoonist John
    Lenox.
In Memory of the Unknown Poet, Robert
    Boardman Vaughn.
In the Attic.
Insomnia of Tremayne, The.
Invitation to a Ghost.
Luxury.
Man of 1794, A.
Men at Forty.
Mrs. Snow.
Mule Team and Poster.
Nostalgia of the Lakefronts.
Ode to a Dressmaker's Dummy.
On a Painting by Patient B of the
    Independence State Hospital for the Insane.
On the Death of Friends in Childhood.
Pantoum of the Great Depression.
Poet at Seven, The.
Psalm and Lament.
Pupil, The.
Self-Portrait as Still Life.
Sonatina in Yellow.

Tourist from Syracuse, The.
Train.
Variations for Two Pianos.
Variations on a Text by Vallejo.
Villanelle at Sundown.
Voice of Col. Von Stauffenberg Rising from
    Purgatory.
Winter Ode to the Old Men of Lummus Park,
    Miami, Florida, A.
Juvenal (c.50–c.130 A.D.)
Satires, *sels.*
Vanity of Human Wishes, The; The Tenth
    Satire of Juvenal [Imitated], *sels.*

K

"K."
How Firm a Foundation.
Jungle Night.
Ka, R. G.
To My Beloved.
Kabir (c.1488–1512)
Ascetic Dyes His Robes, The.
Clay Jug, The.
Eternity.
Give up erotic games, Kabir.
Guest Is Inside, The.
Hopeful Spiritual Athlete, The.
How Much Is Not True.
I Cherish That Love.
Knowing Nothing Shuts the Iron Gates.
Lamp without Oil, The.
Meeting, The: "When my friend is away from
    me, I am depressed."
Music without Strings, The.
My First Marriage.
Only Woman Awake, The.
Owl and the Moon, The.
Simple Purification, The.
Sometimes, everywhere I look.
Thirsty Fish, The.
To Be a Slave of Intensity.
What Made Kabir a Servant.
Why Arrange the Pillows.
Kabysh, Inna (b. 1963)
Making Jam in July.
Whenever the prodigal son returns home.
Kaddour, Hédi (b. 1945)
Bus Driver, The.
Chauffeur, Le.
Variations.
Variations.
Kadi, Joanna
ArabInnocents.
Looking Back.
Kadima-Nzuji, Mukula
Incantations of the Sea: Moando Coast.
Kadir, A. (1916–79)
On Bald Mountain.
Kaffka, Margit (1880–1918)
Dawn Rhythms.
Litany: "My sweet, beloved companion."
Kafka, Franz (1883–1924)
Before the Law.
In the Evening's Gentle Sunshine.
Leopards in the Temple.
Robinson Crusoe.
Sirens, The.
Kagami Shiko (1665–1731)
Arid fields / The only life—.
Night snow / Neighbor's cock.
Small fish-boats / After what.
Kagawa Kageki (1768–1843)
Buy it! But it!
Looking back upon.
While reading.
Kageyama, Claire
Mama.
Kahal, Irving (1903–42)
I Can Dream, Can't I?
I'll Be Seeing You.
Night Is Young and You're So Beautiful,
    The.

Wedding Bells Are Breaking Up That Old
    Gang of Mine.
When I Take My Sugar to Tea.
Kahf, Mohja
First Thing, The.
On the Death of Nizar Qabbani.
Roc, The.
Kahn, Gustave (1886–1941)
Ain't We Got Fun.
All God's Chillun Got Rhythm.
Carolina in the Morning.
Flying Down to Rio.
Guilty.
I'll Say She Does.
I'll See You in My Dreams.
I'm Through with Love.
It Had to Be You.
Love Me or Leave Me.
Makin' Whoopee.
My Baby Just Cares for Me.
No, No, Nora.
Okay, Toots.
One I Love (Belongs to Someone Else), The.
Pretty Baby.
Tomorrow Is Another Day.
Toot, Toot, Tootsie! (Good-bye).
When My Ship Comes In.
Yes, Sir! That's My Baby.
You Stepped Out of a Dream.
Kahn, Mandy
Untitled: "Goddamn you, sliding around
    under."
Kai, Nwenna
Beauty Rituals 2000.
Kaigen
Old master held up fluff, The.
Kain, Gylan
Cocaine Mad-Scream Article #33 LoveSong.
Kakei (1648–1716)
At the break of dawn.
In the withering gusts.
Mad Verse, *sels.*
Morning glory / So pure.
Kakinomoto no Hitomaro (fl. 7th–8th cent.)
Manyo Shu, Part 2 of 4, *sel.*
Mourning Princess Asuka.
My thoughts are with a boat.
Kakkai Patiniyar Naccellaiyar
Many Said.
Kal, Jan
Mont Ventoux.
Kalagoe, Celo (d. 2001)
This johnny / is Mr Strong from Strongtown.
Kalamaras, George (b. 1956)
Banaras Is Another Name for the World.
Lamps Are Brought In, The.
Mud.
You Keep Coming upon Your Breath at the
    Altar.
Kalar, Joseph (1906–72)
Papermill.
Kaldas, Pauline
Home.
Landscapes.
Morning.
Kalendek, Julie
No Part of the Hand Was Hungry.
Take Five of These.
Kalia, Mamta
After Eight Years of Marriage.
Kaliba, Layding Lumumba (b. 1947)
Bebop Trumpet.
Kalidasa (fl. c.500)
Cloud Messenger, The, *sel.*
Even the man who is happy.
Kalina, Rosita (b. 1932)
Cabalistic Rabbis, The.
Dayeinu—they said.
I Am of the Tribe of Yehuda.
Ritual.
Testimonies.
Testimonies.
To Anne Frank.

Kalinski, Eitan
1936–1986.
Teacher of Defeated Hebrew Language.
Kallatanar
What She Said.
Kalmar, Bert (b. 1895) *and* **Harry Ruby**
Nevertheless (I'm in Love with You).
Three Little Words.
What a Perfect Combination.
Who's Sorry Now?
Kálnoky, László (1912–1985)
De Profundis.
Hamlet's Lost Monologue.
Heart Escaping.
Meeting.
Remembering.
Svidrigailov's Last Night.
Swept Away.
Wanderings on a Heavenly Body.
What Man Can Do on This Planet.
Kalu, Uduma
Extended Relations (1).
Kamakaeha, Lydia *See* Lili'u-o-ka-lani, Queen
Kamala Das (b. 1934)
Introduction: "I don't know politics but I know
    the names."
Kamanda, Kama (b. 1952)
Poet's Poem, The.
Kambala
KYE HO! Wonderful!
Kamenetz, Rodger (b. 1950)
History of the Invisible.
Lighter Fluid.
Missing Jew, The.
This Is the Map.
Why Ten Men?
Kamenszain, Tamara
Eliahu.
Mea Shearim.
Return 2.
Torah Braids.
Kamienska, Anna (1920–86)
Annunciation.
On the Cross.
Prayer That Will Be Answered, A.
Saint Martha.
St. Luke, *sel.*
St. Luke, *sels.*
St. Matthew, *sel.*
Things of This World.
Those Who Carry.
Kaminsky, Ilya (b. 1977)
Author's Prayer.
Dancing in Odessa.
Maestro.
Kaminsky, Marc (b. 1943)
Questions: "If I shriek."
Kan, Toni
And He Whispered Stolen Words.
Prayer for a Good Death, A.
Kan Chazan (1748–1828)
Reading a Book on a Winter Night.
Kana-jo, Lady
Quivering together / Ears of barley.
Kanastoga, Wasabi
El Elvis.
Kanchev, Nikolai (b. 1936)
Birthplace.
Church: "I've come to kneel before you, while
    you're falling down."
Feeling.
Glory: "Sky with reddened eyelids foretells
    windy weather, The."
Miracle.
Seventh Heaven Can Be Seen at First Glance.
Smile, A.
Kandel, Lenore (b. 1932)
First They Slaughtered the Angels.
Spring 61.
Kandil, Fatma (b. 1958)
Emaciated Teeth.
Thorny Gaps Suddenly Moving.
Veins All Dried Up.

Kandinsky [or Kandinskii], Wassily (1866–1944)
Chalk and Soot.
Sounds.
Kando (1825–1904)
It's as if our heads were on fire, the way.
Kane, Julie
Reasons for Loving the Harmonica.
Kane, Paul
Disciples Asleep at Gethsemane.
Kaneko, Lonny
Bailey Gatzert: The First Grade, 1945.
Kaneko Mitsuharu (1895–1975)
Mount Fuji.
Kanemitsu-Kogun (fl. 19th cent.)
My hands released at last, the cliff soars.
Kang [Grossjean], Ok-Ku [or Ok-Koo] (b. 1940)
Garden: "Space, The."
Iris.
Were I a Flower.
Wind: "Like a well-trained soldier."
Kang Ŭn'gyo (b. 1945)
Azalea.
Becoming Water.
In the Fog.
It Speaks.
Leaves of Grass.
Love's Way.
Poem's Visit, A.
Rise, Grass.
Rotation 1.
Sleet.
Sleet.
Sound 8.
Spider: "What I throw out to the world."
Twilight Song.
Woman.
Woman Hanging Laundry.
Woods: "Tree trembles, A."
Kanik, Orban Veli (1914–50)
Did I Fall in Love?
Erol Güney's Cat.
I Am Listening to Istanbul.
People Will Talk.
Kannan
What Her Girl Friend Said to Him.
Kantaris, Sylvia (b. 1936)
Airing the Chapel.
Body Language.
Not-loving.
Stocking Up.
Who could have baked my entire heart's
desire.
Kanzan-Shigyo
Where is the dragon's cave?
Kao Ch'i (1336–74)
Silkworm Song of Torchlit Fields.
Song of the Man of Green Hill, The.
Written on Seeing the Flowers, and
Remembering My Daughter.
Kao Shih (702?–65)
Ji Gate.
North Tower of Golden Fort, The.
Ruined Terrace, The.
Song of the Fisherman, The.
Kaplan, Allan (b. 1932)
Hey.
Kaplan, Leslie (b. 1943)
L'Excès-L'usine, sels.
Livre des ciels, Le, sels.
Règne, sels.
Kaplinski, Jaan (b. 1941)
Death does not come from outside.
East-West border, The.
My Wife and Children.
Night comes and extinguishes the numbers and
the year.
Once I got a postcard from the Fiji Islands.
Poetry is Verdant.
Shunryu Suzuki.
To Eat a Pie and to Have it.
To Write More.
We started home, my son and I.
Kapos, Martha
Pulse, The.

Kapovich, Katia
Green One over There, The.
Parting makes simple sense.
Something from an untidy Russian life.
Kaprow, Allan (b. 1927)
Suppose you telephone your own answering.
Kaputikyan, Silva (b. 1919)
In the Sevan Mountains.
KaracaoḠlan (fl. 17th cent.)
With its tender flakes, snow flutters about.
Karade, Baba Ifa
Yemoja.
Karakoç, Sezai (b. 1933)
First: "You stepped off the wrong train they
made you flit through the city's mirror."
Hobbyhorse, The.
Karasumaru-Mitsuhiro (1579–1638)
Beware of gnawing the ideogram of
nothingness.
Kariara, Jonathan (b. 1935)
Leopard Lives in a Muu Tree, A.
Karim, Fawzi (b. 1945)
Crumbled Paper for Future Poems.
Malice.
Robin (The bird that was devoured by the cat
in the garden of the house).
What Was My Choice?
Karinthy, Frigyes (1887–1938)
Dandelion.
Mene Tekel.
Message in the Bottle,The.
Struggle for Life.
Karm, Dun See Psaila, K.
Karp, Vickie
Harm.
Karpowicz, Tymoteusz (b. 1921)
Dog Which Barked Itself Out, The.
Hunting.
Lesson of Silence, A.
Rifle, The.
Silence.
Karr, Mary
Diogenes Tries to Forget.
History of Photography, A.
Hubris.
Patient, The.
Kasa, Lady (fl. mid–8th cent.)
As one hears the cry.
Have I let my love.
I love and fear him.
I shall think of you.
Look at this keepsake.
White drops of dew, The.
Kaschnitz, Marie Luise (1901–74)
Genazzano.
Hiroshima.
My Ground.
Not Courageous.
Outside the Door.
Poem: A "Poem made of words, A."
Return to Frankfurt, sel.
Who Would Have Thought It.
Kaschock, Kirsten
As Birds in Rain.
Kasdorf, Julia
Body Remembers, The.
Dying with Amish Uncles.
Eve's Striptease.
First TV in a Mennonite Family.
Green Market, New York.
Grossdaadi's Funeral.
Leftover Blessings.
Mennonites.
Poetry in America.
Riding Bike with No Hands.
Streak, The.
Uncle.
Vesta's Father.
What I Learned from My Mother.
When Our Women Go Crazy.
Kasischke, Laura
Bike Ride with Older Boys.
Dinner.
Fatima.

Grace.
Hostess.
Housekeeping in a Dream.
My Heart.
Oven.
Pall.
Please.
Sad Song.
Visibility of Spirits, The.
Kassabova, Kapka (b. 1973)
And they were both right.
Door, The: anticipation of wisdom.
Mirages.
Preparation for the Big Emptiness.
Someone else's life.
Kassák, Lajos (1887–1967)
Baffling Picture.
Dictator, The.
Factory, The.
I Am With You.
Like This.
My Poetry.
Snapshot.
To a Hooligan Girl.
Young Horseman.
Kassiane (b. 804?)
Troparion.
Kassid, Abd al-Karim (b. 1945)
Leaves.
Seer, The.
Trilogy of Travel.
What the Shadow Said in the Presence of the
Poem.
Kastra, Jòj See Castera, Georges
Katagiri, Dainin (1928–1990)
Peaceful Life.
You are nearly as old as the number of years it
has been since I came to America.
Katay, Taro
Shouldering.
Kateb Yacine (1929–89)
Hello.
Kates, J.
No Altarpiece.
Nothing in Art.
Katona, József (1791–1830)
Bánk the Palatine, sel.
Katrovas, Richard (b. 1953)
Black English.
Doggerel for the Great Czech Phallometer.
Rehab.
Sky.
Katz, Eliot (b. 1957)
In Praise of the Seattle Coalition.
Weather Seems Different, The.
When the Skyline Crumbles.
Katz, Joy (b. 1963)
Concerning the Islands Newly Discovered.
Falling.
Imperfect Is Our Paradise, The.
Taxonomy.
Women Must Put Off Their Rich Apparel.
Katz, Leandro (b. 1938)
Spread.
Katz, Mati (1944–64)
Into a Dead Zone.
Katz, Menke
Brave Coward, The.
Her Three Unborn Baby Boys.
Hungerdance, The.
Suicide: "As if a wood of oaks gave."
To a Butterfly.
Katzin, Olga See "Sagittarius"
Kaucher, Jennifer Hill
Reading Othello and Watching a Girl Skip
Rope.
Kauffman, Janet (b. 1945)
Hunting.
Mennonite Farm Wife.
Round Lake.
Working Tobacco.
Kaufman, Bob (b. 1925)
African Dream.

All those ships that never sailed.
Awe.
Battle Report.
Celebrated White-Cap Spelling Bee, The.
Crootey Songo.
East Fifth Street (N.Y.).
I am a Camera.
I Have Folded My Sorrows.
January 30, 1976: Message to Myself.
Late Lamented Wind, Burned in Indignation, The.
Lorca.
"Michaelangelo" the Elder.
No More Jazz at Alcatraz.
Novels from a Fragment in Progress.
Oregon.
Picasso's Balcony.
Private Sadness.
Round About Midnight.
Solitary thoughts on death and other illegal mysteries carried off.
SUN IS A NEGRO, THE.
Terror Is More Certain, A.
There is a silent beat in between the drums.
Trip, Dharma Trip, Sangha Trip, The.
Unhistorical Events.
Walking Parker Home.
Would You Wear My Eyes?

Kaufman, Shirley (b. 1923)
Above Vitebsk.
Accuser, The.
After.
Apples.
Bread and Water.
Buddha of Sŏkkuram, The.
By the Rivers.
Daily Ritual.
Déjà Vu.
Emperor of China, The.
Job's Wife.
Mothers, Daughters.
Mount of Olives, The.
Next Year, in Jerusalem.
Notes to My Daughters.
Poem in November.
Roots in the Air.
Security.
Stones.
Vows.
Waiting: "After the fervor."
Western Wall, The.

Kavanagh, P. J. (b. 1931)
Goldie Sapiens.

Kavanagh, Patrick (1904–67)
Bluebells for Love.
Canal Bank Walk.
Christmas Childhood, A.
Come Dance with Kitty Stobling.
Consider the Grass Growing.
Elegy for Jim Larkin.
Epic.
Father Mat.
Great Hunger, The, sels.
Hospital, The.
I Had a Future.
In Memory of My Mother.
Inniskeen Road: July Evening.
Innocence.
Intimate Parnassus.
Kerr's Ass.
Long Garden, The.
Memory of Brother Michael.
On Raglan Road.
One, The.
Question to Life.
Sanctity.
Self-slaved, The.
Shancoduff.
Spraying the Potatoes.
Stony Grey Soil.
Tarry Flynn.
Tinker's Wife.
To the Man after the Harrow.
Twelfth of July, The.
Wet Evening in April.

Kave, Sito See Cavé, Syto

Kavulu, Nirasana
Forces of Production.
Me?

Kawai Chigetsu [or Chigetsu-Ni] **(1634?–1718)**
Chirping / Grasshopper.

Kawai Suimei (1874–1965)
Living Voice.
Snowflame.

Kawamura Yoichi
On the Sand Dune.

Kawano, Yuko (b. 1946)
Climbing the mountain pass.

Kay, Elizabeth
Phoenix.

Kay, Jackie (b. 1961)
Adoption Papers, The, sels.
Birth and Death of Bette Davis, The.
Close Shave.
Crown and Country.
Dance of the Cherry Blossom.
Dressing Up.
English Cousin Comes to Scotland.
Even the Trees.
Finger.
In My country.
Maw Broon Visits a Therapist.
Old Tongue.
Other Lovers, sel.
Pounding Rain.
Pride.
Shoes of Dead Comrades, The.
Somebody Else.
Stincher, The.
Teeth.
Telling Part, The.
Twelve Bar Bessie.
Virus.
Waiting Lists, The.
What Jenny Knows.

Kaya Shirao (Shiroa) (1738?–91)
Forty years / How sharp.
Moonlit night / By melon flowers.
Mountain mist / Torches dropped.

Kayacan, Feyyaz (b. 1919)
Division of Labor.

Kazantzis, Judith
Midwife.
My Dada.
Thatcher, A.

Kazinczy Ferenc (b.1759–1831)
Boat, The.
Hard and Easy.
Merits of Writers.
Our Tongue.
Soul of a Man, The.
Vajdahunyad.

Kearney, Douglas
Rep/resent.

Kearney, Larry (b. 1943)
Man with His Kids on a Table, The.

Kearney, Matthew
After Barranquillo, before Belize.

Kearney, Meg
First Blow-Job.
Goodnight, Goodbye.
Nature Poetry.

Kearney, Tapa
Cuba, sel.

Kearns, Josie (b. 1954)
Moving Furniture.

Keary, Eliza (fl. 1857–88)
Old Age: "Such a wizened creature."

Keats, John (1795–1821)
Addressed to Haydon.
After Dark Vapours Have Oppressed Our Plains.
Belle Dame sans Merci, La [A Ballad].
Blue! 'Tis the Life of Heaven, the Domain.
Bright Star.
Day Is Gone and All Its Sweets Are Gone, The.
Endymion: A Poetic Romance, sels.
Eve of St. Agnes, The.
Eve of St. Agnes, The, sels.

Fall of Hyperion, The; A Dream, sel.
Fancy.
Fragment of an Ode to Maia Written on May Day, 1818.
Great Spirits Now on Earth.
Happy Is England! I Could Be Content.
How Many Bards Gild the Lapses of Time!
Hyperion, sel.
I Cry Your Mercy, Pity, Love—Ay, Love!
If by Dull Rhymes Our English Must Be Chained.
In [a] Drear-nighted December.
Isabella, or The Pot of Basil, sel.
Lamia, sel.
Meg Merrilies [or Merrilees].
O Solitude! If I Must With Thee Dwell.
O Thou Whose Face Hath Felt the Winter's Wind.
Ode: "Bards of passion and of mirth."
Ode on a Grecian Urn.
Ode on Indolence.
Ode on Melancholy.
Ode to a Nightingale.
Ode to Psyche.
On a Leander Gem which Miss Reynolds, My Kind Friend, Gave Me.
On First Looking into Chapman's Homer.
On Leaving Some Friends at an Early Hour.
On Seeing the Elgin Marbles.
On Sitting Down to Read *King Lear* Once Again.
On the Grasshopper and [the] Cricket.
On the Sea.
Sleep and Poetry, sels.
Song about Myself, A, sel.
This Living Hand, Now Warm and Capable.
Three Undated Fragments, sel.
To ———: "Had I a man's fair form, then might my sighs."
To a Cat.
To a Friend Who Sent Me Some Roses.
To Ailsa Rock.
To Autumn: "Season of mists and mellow fruitfulness!"
To B.R. Haydon, with a Sonnet Written on Seeing the Elgin Marbles.
To Chatterton.
To Homer.
To J. H. Reynolds, Esq, sels.
To Kosciusko.
To One Who Has Been Long in City Pent.
To Sleep.
To Some Ladies.
Two Sonnets on Fame, sels.
When I Have Fears [That I May Cease to Be].
Where Be You [or Ye] Going, You [or Ye] Devon Maid?
Why Did I Laugh Tonight?
Written on the Day That Mr. Leigh Hunt Left Prison.

Keble, John (1792–1866)
Address to Poets.
All Saints' Day.
Christmas Day: "What sudden blaze of song."
Flowers of the Field.
Forest Leaves in Autumn, sels.
Happiness.
Hezekiah's Display.
Lyra Apostolica, sels.
Malvern at a Distance.
Rainbow, The.
Samuel's Prayer.
See Lucifer Like Lightning Fall.
Sun of my soul, thou Saviour dear.
Waterfall, The, sels.

Keçecizade İzzet Molla See İzzet Molla

Keckler, W. B. (b. 1966)
Wedding, A.

Keelan, Claudia (b. 1959)
Blue Diamond.
Embers.
End is an Animal, The.
Gravity and Grace.
Instead of Reading Marcus Aurelius.
My Twentieth Century.
Romanticism.

Secularist, The.
To the New World.
Keeler, Charles Augustus
Drouth, The.
Keenan, Terrance (b. 1947)
After the Neutron.
Keene, Jarret (b. 1973)
Black Revolver.
Captain America at Home.
Exodus.
God Lovingly Counterattacks.
Keene, John (b. 1965)
After C (3): Tayloriana.
Haymarket, The.
Keener, LuAnn (b. 1954)
Dehorning the Yearlings.
Kees, Weldon (1914–55)
After the Trial.
Aspects of Robinson.
City as Hero, The.
Coming of the Plague, The.
Crime Club.
Five Villanelles, *sels*.
For H. V. (1901–1927).
For My Daughter.
Henry James at Newport.
If this Room is Our World.
June 1940.
1926.
River Song.
Robinson.
Round: "Wondrous life! cried Marvell at
    Appleton House."
Small Prayer.
What the Spider Heard.
When the Lease Is Up.
Keeshig-Tobias, Lenore
I Grew Up.
Mother with Child.
Keesing, Nancy (b. 1923)
Queer Thing, A.
Reverie of a Mum.
Kefala, Antigone
Freedom Fighter.
Industrial City.
Party, The.
Sunday Visit.
Keineg, Paol (b. 1944)
Boudica.
Keita, Nzadi Z.
Back road.
Black Tax.
Cycles.
Dedicated to the domestics.
Lessons in lying.
My Sleeping Husband.
Rapid Transit.
Rising.
What is left.
Keith, Sally (b. 1973)
Gallery, The.
Mechanics.
Orphean Song.
Subtraction Song.
Keithley, George (b. 1935)
First Morning.
Small Moon on the Shoulder of New York.
Thunder Storm.
Kekova, Svetlana (b. 1951)
Already, no more suffering, no.
Ants, The.
Everything has come true. The punishment fits
    the crime.
Having submitted your petition for dismissal.
Look, a man is flying and.
Running water is cold, the river from Eden
    flows east.
Sky is covered with stars, like a body with
    sores, The.
Space is arched like a sail.
Tsar sits on his throne as if he sat on bones,
    The.
With much effort, I glimpse in the darkness
    and rubbish.

Kelber, Mim
Pledge of Allegiance to the Family of Earth, A.
Kelen, S. K. (b. 1956)
First Circle, The.
Gods Ash Their Cigarettes, The.
Rabbit Shoeshine.
Kell, Richard (b. 1927)
Spring Night.
Kelleher, Daniel Lawrence (1883–1948)
For C. K. at His Christening.
Keller, Bernard
Keep a Good Thought.
Major, The.
One Million Men Marching 2.
Keller, David
After Supper.
After the First Snow.
Joining the Circus.
Man Who Knew the Words to "Louie, Louie",
    The.
Melancholy.
Keller, Gottfried (1819–90)
Now Have I Fed and Eaten Up the Rose.
Venus de Milo.
Keller, Helen (1880–1968)
In the Garden of the Lord.
Kelley, Eliza
At the Center, Creator Hourglass.
Kello, Esther (1571–1624)
Prayer to God.
Kelly, Aileen
Given Flesh Returns Nothing but Bread, The.
Kelly, Brigit Pegeen
Arguments of Everlasting.
Botticelli's St. Sebastian.
Imagining Their Own Hymns.
Leaving, The.
Orchard, The.
Petition.
Southern Review, The, *sels*.
Those Who Wrestle with the Angel for Us.
To the Lost Child.
Visitation, The.
Wild Turkeys; The Dignity of the Damned.
Young Wife's Lament.
Kelly, Erren Geraud
7-30-96.
Kelly, Maeve (b. 1930)
Half Century.
Kelly, Robert (b. 1934)
Bittersweet Growing Up the Red Wall.
Coming.
Flowers of Unceasing Coincidence, The, *sels*.
Holy Sonnet.
In June.
Life of Intimate Fleeing, A.
Looking.
Man Who Loved White Chocolate, The.
Ode to Language.
Poem for Easter.
Rainmakers, The.
Recessional.
Sermon on Language.
Studying Horses.
Those who are beautiful.
Threads, *sels*.
Tune.
Woman with Flaxen Hair in Norfolk Heard, A.
Kelly, Thomas
Head That Once Was Crowned with Thorns,
    The.
Second Advent, The.
We sing praise of him who died.
Kelly, Timothy (b. 1954)
Babe Ruth Pointing.
Kemal [Beyatlı], Yahya (1884–1958)
Tryst: "My eyes transfixed on the road, I
    strained in their light to see."
Kemble, Frances Anne [*or* "Fanny"] (1809–93)
Cover me with your everlasting arms.
Faith.
Farewell to Italy.
Impromptu.
Lines.

Noonday Vision, A.
On an Irish Retriever.
Parting.
Petition, A.
Sonnet: "If there were any power in human
    love."
Sonnet: "Thou poisonous laurel leaf, that in the
    soil."
Sonnet: "What is my lady like? thou fain
    would'st know."
To Mrs. Norton.
To Shakspeare.
To the Wissahiccon.
Whene'er I recollect the happy time.
Kemp, Anne (*fl.* 1650s)
Contemplation on Bassets Down-Hill by the
    Most Sacred Adorer of the Muses Mrs. A.
    K., A.
Kemp, Arnold J.
100 Times.
Kemp, Penn (b. 1944)
Bidding Spell.
Ken, Thomas (1637–1711)
Morning Hymn.
Now.
Priest of Christ, The.
Kendall, Henry Clarence (1839–82)
Bell-Birds.
Beyond Kerguelen.
Mooni.
Kendall, May (1861–1943)
Ballad of the Cadger.
Ballad of the Ichthyosaurus.
Church Echoes.
Education's Martyr.
Envoy.
Ether Insatiable.
Failures.
Fossil, A.
In the Toy Shop.
Last Performance, The.
Lay of the Trilobite.
Legend of the Crossing-Sweeper.
Lower Life, The.
Philanthropist and the Jelly-fish, The.
Pure Hypothesis, A.
Sandblast Girl and the Acid Man, The.
Underground.
Vision of Noah, The.
Woman's Future.
Kendall, Timothy (*fl.* 1577)
Desire of Dominion.
Difference Between a King and a Tyrant, The.
Of a Good Prince and an Evil.
Tyrant in Sleep, Naught Differeth from a
    Common Man, A.
Upon the Grave of a Beggar.
Kendall, Walter G.
Men Who Ride for Fun, The.
Kendrick, Dolores (b. 1927)
Alone for a Week.
Drowned River, The.
For Gwendolyn Brooks: As I Civilize a Space.
Gethsemane A. D.
Inpatient.
Jenny in Love.
Jenny in Sleep.
Note to the Ophthalmologist.
Sadie Snuffs a Candle.
Sidney, Looking for Her Mother.
Solo: The Good Blues.
Sophie, Climbing the Stairs.
Three Observations on the Zombie Culture,
    sels.
We are the Writing on the Wall.
Where the Grieved Ones Sat.
Kenjeev, Bakhyt (b. 1950)
And a fool, and a smart one, a miser.
Gone is the sound of my favorite misfortune,
    which even yesterday.
You envied the flying birds and stones.
Kenneally, Brendan
Reconciliation: "Do not torment me, woman."

Kennedy, Benjamin Hall (1804–89)
Bad Luck to This Marching.
On ["Who Wrote Icon Basilike" by Dr.]
  Christopher Wordsworth, Master of Trinity.
Kennedy, Imogene Elizabeth
One day.
Kennedy, Jimmy (1902–84)
Teddy Bear's Picnic.
Kennedy, Laura H.
I am in the most exquisite distress.
Moonburn.
Kennedy, Sarah (b. 1960)
How My Mother-in-Law Instructed Me in
  Slaughter.
Maid.
Kennedy, X. J. (b. 1929)
Bee.
Brats.
Close Call.
Curse on a Thief, A.
Emily Dickinson in Southern California.
Epitaph for a Postal Clerk.
For Allen Ginsberg.
Help!
Hummingbird.
In a Prominent Bar in Secaucus [One Day].
Japanese Beetles [2003].
Joshua.
Keep a Hand on Your Dream.
Landscapes with Set-Screws.
Lighting a Fire.
Little Elegy.
Loneliness of Lincoln, The.
Loose Woman.
Mother's Nerves.
Nude Descending a Staircase.
One Winter Night in August.
Poets.
Robert Frost Discovers Another Road Not
  Taken.
To Someone Who Insisted I Look up Someone.
Vulture.
Kennelly, Brendan (b. 1936)
Begin.
Big Words, The.
Bread.
Clearing a Space.
Cromwell, *sels.*
Dream of a Black Fox.
Glimpse of Starlings, A.
I See You Dancing, Father.
Island, The.
Limerick Train, The.
Love-Cry.
My Dark Fathers.
Poem from a Three Year Old.
Proof.
Raglan Lane.
Restoration, A.
Scarf, The.
Story, The.
Swimmer, The.
We Are Living.
Wings.
Kenney, Richard (b. 1948)
Apples on Champlain.
Aubade: "Cold snap. Five o'clock."
Battle of Valcour Island, The.
Concrete Delivery Delayed by Goose and
  Gosling Crossing, Late March, Mallett's
  Bay.
In April.
Lens.
Millenary.
Plume.
Sailing.
Sawmill.
Kenny, Maurice (b. 1929)
December.
First Rule.
Joshua Clark.
Legacy.
O Wendy, Arthur.
Reverberation.
Still-Life.

Strawberrying.
Sweetgrass.
They Tell Me I Am Lost.
Wild Flower.
Wild Strawberry.
Wolf "Aunt."
Kenny, Melanie
Hungry as the Sea.
Kenyon, James Benjamin (1858–1924)
Noiseless Wheel, The.
Kenyon, Jane (1947–95)
At a Motel near O'Hare Airport.
August Rain, after Haying.
Back: "We try a new drug, a new
  combination."
Bat, The.
Briefly It Enters, and Briefly Speaks.
Depression in Winter.
Dutch Interiors.
Eating the Cookies.
February: Thinking of Flowers.
Finding a Long Gray Hair.
From Room to Room.
Gettysburg, July 1, 1863.
Happiness.
Having It Out with Melancholy, *sels.*
Here.
In the Nursing Home.
Insomnia at the Solstice.
Let Evening Come.
Man Eating.
Otherwise: "I got out of bed."
Peonies at Dusk.
Pharaoh.
Travel: After a Death.
Twilight: After Haying.
Walking Alone in Late WInter.
Kenyon, John (1784–1856)
Champagne Rosée.
Keplinger, David (b. 1968)
Another Century.
Distance Between Zero and One, The.
Inside: George Gaines at Graterford Prison,
  1981.
Robert Frost.
Keppo
Searching Him took.
Kercheval, Jesse Lee (b. 1956)
Children's Book of Knowledge, The.
Ham and the Moon.
Things That Have Escaped Me.
Your Wife, a Widow, Waits for You.
Kerim, Ussin
Mother.
Kerlikowske, Elizabeth
Acceptance Speech.
Kerman, Judith (b. 1945)
In Tornado Weather.
Kerouac, Jack (John Kerouac) (1922–69)
And What Do I Owe You, God.
Bath Tub Thought.
Birds singing.
Bottoms of my shoes, The.
Buddha.
Flies.
How to Meditate.
Hymn.
In my medicine cabinet.
Mexican Loneliness.
Mexico City Blues, *sels.*
Missing a kick.
Moon had, The.
Orizaba Blues: 64th Chorus.
Orlanda Blues: 24th Chorus.
Poem: "Anyway the time has come to
  explain."
Poem: "I could become a great grinning host."
Poem: "I demand that the human race."
Scripture of the Golden Eternity, The, *sels.*
Thrashing Doves, The.
To Edward Dahlberg.
Kerouac, John *See* Kerouac, Jack
Kerrigan, T.S.
Elvis Kissed Me.

Kersch, Gerald
Soldier, A: His Prayer.
Kessler, Milton (b. 1930)
Secret Love.
Waxwings.
Kessler, Rod
Elm Tree on Lafayette Street, The.
Kessler, Stephen (b. 1947)
Cigarette Case.
Jack's Last Words.
Marty's Mother.
Key, Francis Scott (1779–1843)
Lord with glowing heart I'd praise thee.
Star-Spangled Banner, The.
Keyes, Sidney (1922–43)
Advice for a Journey.
Dunbar, 1650.
Early Spring.
Elegy: "April again, and it is a year again."
Europe's Prisoners.
Expected Guest, The.
Foreign Gate, The, *sels.*
Gardener, The.
Greenwich Observatory.
Neutrality.
Timoshenko.
War Poet.
Wilderness, The, *sel.*
William Yeats in Limbo.
Kgositsile, Keorapetse (b. 1938)
Acknowledgement.
For Art Blakey and the Jazz Messengers.
Gods Wrote, The.
To Mother.
To My Daughter.
Khagen, Marina (b. 1974)
In the branches' shade.
Khaïr-Eddine, Mohammed
Barbarian.
Refusal to Inter.
Khali, Saddi
Walking On: A Declaration of Wholeness.
Khalid, Alaa
Aïda.
Morning Window, A.
Relic, A.
Khalifa, Ihab
No Need to Discourage Dreams.
Khalique, Harris
In London.
Khalvati, Mimi (b. 1944)
Amanuensis.
Baba Mostafa.
Blue Moon.
Coma.
Entries on Light, *sel.*
Needlework.
On Reading Rumi.
One eye crystal, one eye flame, it arrives.
Persian Miniature, A.
Rubaiyat.
Stone of Patience.
Khamees, Dhabya (b. 1958)
Glance.
Gulf.
Letter.
Loneliness.
Standing Worship.
Khamees, Hamda (b. 1946)
Time for Dejection.
Time to Shine.
What Is Not Mine.
Kharabarov, Ivan (1935–70)
Taiga, The.
Kharms, Daniil (1905–42)
Beginning of a Beautiful Day (A Symphony),
  The.
Death of the Wild Warrior.
Event on the Street, An.
Incidents.
Optical Illusion, An.
Symphony No. 2.
**Khavarani, Awhad ad-Din 'Ali ibn Vahid ad-Din
  Muhammad** *See* "Anvari"

Khayr, Abu Sa'id Abul (967–1048)
Four Poems on Death, *sels.*

Khayyám, Omar (d. 1123)
Rubáiyát of Omar Khayyám [of Naishápúr], The, *sels.*
Rubáiyát of Omar Khayyám [of Naishápúr], The, *sels.*
Rubáiyát of Omar Khayyám [of Naishápúr], The.

Khazak, Yekhi'el (b. 1936)
Dead in a Bereft Horah.
I saw you. / You were like scarred stones scattered on the green.
Wake.

Kherdian, David (b. 1931)
Taking the Soundings on Third Avenue, *sels.*

Khlebnikov, Velemir [or Viktor Vladimirovich] (1885–1922)
Four Poems.
Hey . . . y! Uh . . . hm!, covered with sweat.
I Went Out.
Incantation by Laughter.
Iranian Song.
It Has the Unassuming Face of a Burnt-out Candle.
Laundress, The, *sels.*
Lonely Masquerader.
Me and Russia.
Once More, Once More.
One Book, The.
Russia, I give you my divine.
Suppose I Make a Timepiece of Humanity.
To Everyone.
Trumpet, Shout, Carry!
Zangezi, *sels.*
Zangezi: R, K, L, G—.

Khlebnikov, Viktor *See* Burliuk, D.

Khodasevich, Vladislav Felitsianovich (1886–1939)
Automobile, The.
Bride, The.
Dactyls.
Monkey.
Monument, A.
Music.
On the Death of My Tomcat Murr.

Khomin, Igor
Dike, a flower bed, a bare linden tree, A.
They drank. They ate. They smoked.
They met at the Tagansky subway station.

Khong Lo
Ideal Retreat, The.

Khoury-Gata, Venus (b. 1937)
Automne précéda l'été, L'.
Autumn Preceded Summer.
Because They Hesitated Between Roses and Darkness.
Elle lançait sa vieille vaisselle.
Here there was once a country.
Humbly, He Speaks to His Tools.
It Was a Season Tattooed on the Forehead of the Earth.
She Used to Throw Her Old Crockery.
They.

Khoury, Nidaa (b. 1959)
Death Is Your Salvation.
Last Bullet, The.
People of Figs.
People of Fire.
People of Fire.
People of Grapes.
People of Olives.
People of Pomegranates.

Khurshid-Banu
To My Son, Abbas.

Khvostova, Olga (b. 1965)
Flood Songs.

Ki Joon
Elegy for Myself.

Ki no Tsurayuki (868–946)
Hue is as rich, The.
On a spring hillside.
Out in the marsh reeds.
Wind that scatters, The.

Kickham, Charles Joseph (1826–82)
Irish Peasant Girl, The.
Slievenamon.

Kikaku (1661–1707)
Above the boat.
Cicada chirp / Fan peddler.
Evening bridge / A thousand hands.
Full autumn moon / On the straw mat.
Her mate devoured.
I begin each day.
In the Emperor's bed.
Leaf / Of the yam.
May he who brings / Flowers tonight.
O Great Buddha.
On Buddha's birthday.
Over the long road.
Riding the wide leaf.
Sacred night / Through masks.
Scratching.
Shrine gate / Through morning mist.
Single yam leaf, A.
Sprinkle water wide / For the sparrow.
Summer airing / Trying on a quilt.

Kiko
Mount Sumeru—my fist!

Kil Chae (1353–1419)
I return on horseback.

Kilbride, Jerry
Cool surface, The.
Firecrackers.
Harpist, The.
Jumping rope.
Nurse speaks of christmas, The.
Still in the taste.
Wheelchair child, The.

Kildibekova, Mariya (b. 1976)
Everybody was going on talking the same talk.
Pizza's a populous island.

Killeen, Ger (b. 1960)
At the Black Edge.
My Father's Angels.
Rewind.
Tristia.
Wishes.

Killigrew, Anne (1660–85)
Alexandreis.
Cloris' Charms Dissolved by Eudora.
Complaint of a Lover, The.
Discontent, The.
Farewell to Worldly Joys, A.
On a Picture Painted by Herself [or Her self], Representing Two Nymphs [or Nimphs] of Diana's, One in a Posture to Hunt, the Other Bath[e]ing.
On Death.
On the Birth-Day of Queen Katherine.
On the Soft and Gentle Motions of Eudora.
Pastoral Dialogue.
Upon the Saying That My Verses Were Made by Another.

Killigrew, Katherine (1542?–83)
Lady Katherine Killigrew Wrote This Poem about Her Own Death, The.
Mildred, if you take the trouble to send me what I want.

Killigrew, Thomas (1612–83)
Epilogue to "The Parson's Wedding."

Kilmer, Joyce (1886–1918)
House with Nobody in It, The.
Trees.

Kim, Kalehua Parrilla
Ka Hale / The Nurturing Place.

Kim, Myung Mi (b. 1957)
Under Flag.

Kim, Suji Kwock (b. 1968)
Chasm, The.
Flight.
Fragments of the Forgotten War.
Monologue for an Onion.
Occupation.
On Sparrows.

Kim Ch'anghyŏp (1651–1708)
Mountain Folk.

Kim Chiha (b. 1941)
Core.
In Burning Thirst.
No One.
Road to Seoul, The.
Story of a Sound, The.
Truth.
Well.

Kim Chôngnan (b. 1953)
Between May and June.
Images: "Scene 1. Front angle, dark sky, or the middle of the universe."
In the Subway—Getting Used to Ugliness 3.
Leafy Plant of Wisdom, A.
Phone Call From Immortality—From Agnes to Mr. Kundera, A.
Poetry: "Many entrances. Open. Everywhere. But reaching nowhere. Wandering."
Rain: "From which heaven did you return."
Sea at Twenty-Four, The.
Veronica, a Double Life.
Woman I Carelessly Killed, The.
Women's Language.
Women's Words—Yellow-Green Leaves and Low Sun.

Kim Ch'ŏnt'aek (c.1725–76)
Having given my clothes to a boy.

Kim Ch'unsu [or Chun-soo] (b. 1922)
Flower.
Lilac Petals.
Masks.
Prelude to a Poem.
Riding a Mule.
Snow over Chagall's Village.

Kim Hyesun (b. 1955)
Bloody Clock, A.
Daybreak in Seoul.
Driving During a Shower.
In the Night.
Inside the Iris.
Memories of the Day I Gave Birth to a Daughter.
Mice.
National Museum Hallway.
Not Knowing He's Dead.
Old Hotel, The.
Remembering the Day I Gave Birth to a Daughter.
Ripe Apple.
Saturday Night, Arriving in Seoul.
Taklamakan.
Teardrop, A.
Titanic, Reincarnate, The.
Very Old Hotel, A.
Women.
Women: "Did I write that I'll endure this."

Kim Koengp'il (1454–1504)
My Way.

Kim Ku (1488–1534)
I Spy the Three-Colored Peach Blossom.
Until the duck's short legs.

Kim Kwang-kyu (b. 1941)
Sketch of a Fetish.

Kim Kwangsŏp (1905–77)
Having Died.

Kim Kwanguk (1580–1656)
Bamboo stick, the sight of you.
Bundle the piles of verbose missives.
Have you seen a person.

Kim Namjo (b. 1927)
Evening Primrose.
For Baby.
Love's Cursive, *sels.*
Moonlit Night.

Kim Pyŏngyŏn [Kim Sakkat] (1807–63)
Song for My Shadow, A.

Kim Sangyong (1561–1637)
Listlessly I hear the rain.
Love is a deceit.
Love Is False.

Kim Sisŭp (1435–93)
Now Shine, Now Rain.

Kim Sŏnggi (c.1725–76)
Shaking off the red dust.

Kim Sowŏl (1902–34)
Azaleas.
Cigarette.
Cuckoo, The.
Day Long After, A.
Forsaken.
Golden Meadow, The.
Mountain Flowers.
Road Away, The.
Road, The.
Years from Now.
Kim Sujang (b. 1690)
Deception.
In my quiet grass hut.
Moonlight shines on the lotus pond.
Of all the dogs around me, spotted, black, and
   hairy.
Standing in your lofty tower.
Kim Sŭnghŭi (b. 1952)
Between Saint and Witch.
Female Buddha.
Floating Metonymy 2.
Floating Metonymy 5.
Growing Pearl 1.
Horror Movie.
Institutions.
Life in the Egg 3.
Life Within an Egg.
Love Song for the Belly Button 1.
Mother's Feet.
Na Hyesŏk's Complex.
Roses and Thorns.
Soaring.
Song of Children in the Land of Ice Who Love
   the Sun.
Sun Mass.
Wailer.
Kim Suyŏng (1921–68)
Beauty, A.
Emerging from the Old Palace One Day.
Grass.
Ha . . . No Shadows.
Journal *Encounter*, The.
Lonely Journey, A.
Sex.
Snow.
Vinegar of Cruelty.
Kim Yŏng (fl. 1776–1800)
Snowflakes flutter—butterflies chase flowers.
Kim Yŏngnang (1903–50)
At the Sight of Water.
Endless River Flows, An.
Intoxicating Moonlight.
Selections from "Quatrains"
Someone Who Knows My Heart.
Until Peonies Bloom.
Kim Yuk (1580–1658)
Be sure to invite me.
Kimball, Harriet McEwen (1834–1912)
Angel of the Rain.
In Reverie.
Kimbrell, James (b. 1967)
Empty House.
Letters to a Vanishing Fiancée.
Mt. Pisgah.
My Father at the North Street Boarding House.
My Psychic.
Rooftop.
Salvation.
Self-Portrait, Jackson.
Slow Night on Texas Street, A.
True Descenders.
Kincaid, Jamaica
Letter from Home, The.
Kindman, Sarah (1901–74)
Fight and Play.
King, Anne (b. 1621, d. after 1671)
Essay upon Good-Friday, An.
King, Ben (Benjamin Franklin King) (1857–99)
Pessimist, The.
King, Benjamin Franklin *See* King, Ben
King, Harriet Hamilton (1840–1920)
Dream Maiden, A.
Moonlight Ride, A.

King, Henry, Bishop of Chichester (1592–1669)
Boy's Answer to the Blackmoor, The.
Change, The.
Contemplation upon Flowers, A.
Double Rock, The.
Exequy, The.
Forfeiture, The.
Renunciation, A.
Sic Vita.
Silence: A Sonnet.
Sonnet: "Tell me[e] no more how fair[e] she[e]
   is."
Surrender, The.
Upon the Death of My Ever Desired Friend
   Doctor [*or* Dr] Donne Dean of Paul's.
King, I. W. (b. 1955)
If Ye Hivni.
King James Version
Psalms, *sels.*
King, Jane (b. 1952)
Intercity Dub.
King, Julie
Giving the House Away.
King, Rosamond S.
Another day.
H E L P.
King, Stoddard (1889–1933)
Crime at Its Best.
Idyll: "He was a selfish shellfish"
Trombone Solo.
Kingsley, Charles (1819–75)
Airly Beacon.
Ode to the Northeast Wind.
Sands of Dee, The.
Water Babies, The, *sels.*
Kingsley, Henry (1830–76)
Magdalene at Michael's gate.
Kingsmill, Hugh (1889–1949)
Poem, after A. E. Housman.
Summer Time on Bredon.
Kingsolver, Barbara
Beating Time.
Middle Daughter, The.
Remember the Moon Survives.
Waiting for the Invasion.
Kingston, Maxine Hong
Absorption of Rock.
Birds: "I'm living in one place so long."
Idea!: Four-word poems!
Restaurant.
Saturday April 8 Swansea, where Dylan
   Thomas was born on October 27th, the same
   day I was born.
Spring Harvest of Snow Peas.
Write before other people get up. Dress.
Kinnell, Galway (b. 1927)
After Making Love We Hear Footsteps.
Angel, The.
Angling, a Day.
Another Night in the Ruins.
Bear, The.
Blackberry Eating.
Correspondence School Instructor Says
   Goodbye to His Poetry Students, The.
Crying.
Daybreak: "On the tidal mud, just before
   sunset."
First Song.
Flower Herding on Mount Monadnock.
Flower of Five Blossoms.
For Robert Frost.
Fundamental Project of Technology, The.
Gray Heron, The.
Hitchhiker.
How Many Nights.
In a Parlor Containing a Table.
Lackawanna.
Last Gods.
Last Songs.
Lastness, *sel.*
Man on the Hotel Room Bed, The.
Man Splitting Wood in the Daybreak, The.
Memories of My Father, *sel.*

Memory of Wilmington.
Middle of the Way, *sel.*
Middle Path.
Oatmeal.
On the Oregon Coast.
On the Tennis Court at Night.
Parkinson's Disease.
Pen, The.
Perch, The.
Porcupine, The.
Quick and the Dead, The.
Rapture.
Saint Francis and the Sow.
Seekonk Woods, The.
Sheffield Ghazal 4: Driving West.
That Silent Evening.
To Christ Our Lord.
To William Carlos Williams.
Under the Williamsburg Bridge.
Vapor Trail Reflected in the Frog Pond.
Vow, The.
Waking, The.
When One Has Lived a Long Time Alone,
   sels.
When the Towers Fell.
Why Regret?
Kino Sadamaru (1760–1841)
Though this body, I know.
Kinoshita Mokutarō (1885–1945)
Gold Leaf Brandy.
Nagasaki Style.
Kinsella, John (b. 1963)
Akbar.
Archetypal Chillies.
Bluff Knoll Sublimity.
Bright Cigar-Shaped Object Hovers Over
   Mount Pleasant, A.
Chess Piece Cornered.
Cormorants.
Drowning in Wheat.
Fall, The.
Orpheus.
Pig Melons.
Plumburst.
Rabbiters: A Pastoral, The.
Radnoti Quarantine: Razglednicas.
Rust Eclogues, The: Radnoti, Poetry, and the
   Strains of Appropriation.
Sick Woman.
Visitant Eclogue.
Warhol at Wetlands.
Wild Radishes.
Kinsella, Thomas (b. 1929)
All is Emptiness, And I Must Spin.
Ancestor.
Anniversaries, *sels.*
Another September.
At the Crossroads.
Baggot Street Deserta.
Chrysalides.
Death Bed.
Downstream ("Drifting to meet us on the
   darkening stage.").
Endymion.
Harmonies.
Hen Woman.
In the Ringwood.
Je t'adore.
Lady of Quality, A.
Laundress, The.
Messenger, The, *sel.*
Mirror in February.
Monk, The.
Nightwalker, *sel.*
Notes, *sels.*
Nuchal, a Fragment.
One, *sels.*
One Fond Embrace, *sel.*
Portrait of the Artist, A.
Route of the Táin, The.
Soft, To Your Places.
Songs of the Psyche, *sel.*
Tao and Unfitness at Inistiogue on the River
   Nore.
Tear.
Thinking of Mr D.

Wormwood.

Kinsley, Robert
Those Mornings.
Walk Along the Old Tracks, A.

Kinzie, Mary
Among mosquitoes.
Beautiful Days.
Bolt, The.
Boy.
But her arm—damp, small.
Canicula.
Engraving of Blake, An.
Glinting like water.
Heat-heavy creatures.
In air hard as sand.
Lunar Frost.
Muse of Satire, The.
Orchard dying, The.
Ringing Words.
Sound Waves.
Summers of Vietnam.
Sun and Moon.
Want, predation, sleep.

Kipling, Rudyard (1865–1936)
Absent-Minded Beggar, The.
American, An.
Arithmetic on the Frontier.
Astrologer's Song, An.
At His Execution.
Ballad of East and West, The.
Bonfires, The.
Boots.
Bridge-Guard in the Karroo.
Broken Men, The.
Brown Bess.
Cells.
Cholera Camp.
Christmas in India.
Conundrum of the Workshops, The.
Danny Deever.
Death-Bed, A.
Debits and Credits, sels.
Derelict, The.
Dykes, The.
Eddi's Service.
Envoi: "There's a whisper down the field
    where the year has shot her yield."
Epitaphs of the War [1914–1918], sels.
Evarra and His Gods.
Fabulists, The.
For to Admire.
Fuzzy-Wuzzy.
Gallio's Song.
Gentlemen-Rankers.
Gethsemane.
Glory of the Garden, The.
Gods of the Copybook Headings, The.
Gunga Din.
Half-Ballad of Waterval.
Hyaenas [or Hyenas], The.
Hymn before Action.
If.
Jungle Book, The, sels.
Just-So Stories, sels.
Kim, sels.
King, The.
Ladies, The.
Land and Sea Tales, sels.
Land, The.
Last Chantey, The.
L'Envoi.
Looking Glass, The.
Loot, sel.
Mandalay.
Mesopotamia.
Naaman's Song.
Nativity, A.
New Knighthood, The.
Nuit Blanche, La.
Old Men, The.
Puck of Pook's Hill, sels.
Rabbi's Song, The.
Recessional.
Return, The.
St. Helena Lullaby, A.
Screw-Guns.

Second Jungle Book, The, sels.
Sergeant's Weddin', The.
Servant When He Reigneth, A.
Sestina of the Tramp-Royal.
Shillin' a Day.
Sons of Martha, The.
Spies' March, The.
Storm Cone, The.
Story of the Gadsbys, The, sel.
Story of Uriah, The.
Tommy.
Vampire, The.
Way Through The Woods, The.
White Man's Burden, The.
Widow at Windsor, The.
Young British Soldier, The, sel.

Kipp, Karen
Ditches.
I'm Sending You Saint Francis Preaching to
    the Birds.
Rat, The.

Kirby, David (b. 1944)
Amazed by Chekhov.
Dance of Husbands in Bathrobes, The.
Dear Derrida.
Half-Dead.
I Think I Am Going to Call My Wife
    Paraguay.
Moderation Kills (Excusez-Moi, je Suis Sick as
    a Dog).
Nosebleed, Gold Digger, KGB, Henry James,
    Handshake.
Search for Baby Combover, The.
To a French Structuralist.

Kirchner, Frederic William
In Cold February Twilight.
Reasons to Commute by Bicycle.

Kirchwey, Karl (b. 1956)
He Considers the Birds of the Air.
Maculate Beauty.
Nocturne, Morningside Heights.
Oracular Degeneration.
St. Matthew, sels.

Kirilenko-Voloshin, Maksimilian See Voloshin,
    Maksimilian Aleksandrovich

Kirk, Kathleen
Exit, Pursued by a Bear.
Lavinia.
Miranda.
Portia.

Kirkpatrick, Patricia (b. 1949)
Class.

Kirkup, James (b. 1923)
Baby's Drinking Song.
No More Hiroshimas.
Scarecrows.
Shepherd's Tale, The.

**Kirsanov, Semyon [or Semion] Isaakovich (1906–
72)**
I Am White, Darling.
New Heart, The.
Suddenly.

Kirsch, Melissa (b. 1974)
Sleep's Underside.

Kirsch, Sarah (b. 1935)
Already the Air Smells of Snow.
I Am Very Gentle.
I Wanted to Kill My King.
In an Airplane I'm Supposed To.
Kite-Flying, sels.
Legend of Lilja.
Mail.
Mail.
Pandora's Box.
Pictures.
Thank-You Note.
Wels a Fish that Lives on the Bottom, The.
Wintery Music.

Kirstein, Lincoln (b. 1907)
DP's.
Foresight.
Gloria.
Gripe.
P.O.E.

Patton.
Rank.
Snatch.

Kisfaludy, Károly (1788–1830)
Mohács, sel.
Plowman of Rákos Under the Turks.

Kisfaludy, Sándor (1772–1844)
Song: "I have heard the silvery note."
Unhappy Love, sel.

Kishkan, Theresa (b. 1955)
Spell for a Daughter.

Kishu
Once the goal's reached.

Kisielewsky, Sergio
Cough Drops.

Kiss, József (1843–1921)
About My Grandfather, sel.
Fires.
Oh, Why So Late.
Rhyme Is Running Out, The.

Kistler, William
Kyoto 1—Kinkaku-ji.
Kyoto 2—Ryoanji.
Standing Near the Ghats Along the Ganges.

Kitahara Hakushū (1885–1942)
Ailing child, An.
Anesthesia of Red Flowers.
Birds of spring.
Completely blind.
Kiss.
Moon god's light, The.
My senses are stirred.
Secret Song of the Heretics.
Spider Lilies.
Summer Mist, A.

Kitasono Katsue (b. 1902)
Almost Midwinter.
Collection of White Poems.
In leaden slippers I laugh at the fountain of
    night, and scorn a solitary swan.
Under the umbrella of concrete, yesterday, we
    laughed at tomato for its carelessness.
Vin du Masque.
Words.

Kitchener, Lord (b. 1922)
Miss Tourist.

Kitson, Helen (b. 1965)
Post-operative.

Kittredge, Walter
Tenting on the Old Camp Ground.

Kiyohi Hama See Yoneda, Karl

Kiyooka, Roy (b. 1926)
Pear Tree Pomes, sels.

Kizer, Carolyn (b. 1925)
Afternoon Happiness.
American Beauty, An.
Amusing Our Daughters.
Ashes, The.
Bitch.
Children.
Copulating Gods, The.
Dangerous Games.
Dixit Insipiens.
Election Day, 1984.
Fearful Women.
Food of Love.
For Jan as the End Draws Near.
For Sappho/After Sappho.
Glass, The.
Great Blue Heron, The.
Horseback.
Ingathering.
Intruder, The.
Muse of Water, A.
Not Writing Poems about Children.
On a Line from Valéry.
Oration, The.
Parents' Pantoum.
Pro Femina, sels.
Promising Author.
Race Relations.
Reunion.
Semele Recycled.
Singing Aloud.

Thrall.
To an Unknown Poet.
Twelve O'Clock.
Ungrateful Garden, The.
Widow in Wintertime, A.

Klaj, Johann (1616–56)
Oh golden life, waken! Fortunate night!
Stroll-Joy.

Klappert, Peter (b. 1942)
For the Poet Who Said Poets Are Struck by
Lightning Only Two or Three Times.
In Memory of H. F.
Pieces of the One and a Half Legged Man,
sels.
To Whom.

Klassen, Sarah (b. 1932)
Act of Mercy.
Artist and Medium.
Making the Rate (factory journals).
Repenting.
Russian Fables.

Klauber, Edgar
On Buying a Dog.

Kleban, Edward (fl. 1975)
One.

Klee, Paul (1879–1940)
Friend, A.
Happy One, The.
Poem: "Big animals: despondent / at table:
unsated, The."
Poem: "I stand in full armor."
Wolf Speaks, The.

Klein, Abraham Moses (1909–72)
Autobiographical.
For the Sisters of the Hôtel Dieu.
Heirloom.
Indian Reservation: Caughnawaga.
Lone Bather.
Montreal.
Political Meeting.
Portrait of the Poet as Landscape.
Psalter of Avram Haktani, The, sels.
Rocking Chair, The.
Still Small Voice, The.
Winter Night: Mount Royal.

Klein, Michael
Guardian Life.
Letters from the Front.
Range of It, The.
Scenes for an Elegy.
Tides, The.

Kleinschmidt, Edward (b. 1951)
Cooking to Music.
Giorni.
Orchestrion.

Kleinzahler, August (b. 1949)
Autumnal Sketch, An.
Case in Point, A.
Ebenezer Californicus.
Green Sees Things in Waves.
Hamburger.
Lunatic of Lindley Meadow, The.
Poetics.
Snow in North Jersey.
Spleen.
Watching Dogwood Blossoms Fall in a Parking
Lot Off Route 46.
Where Souls Go.
Winter Ball.

Kleiser, Grenville (1868–1953)
Most Vital Thing in Life, The.

Kleist, Ewald von (1715–59)
Song at Graveside.

Klepfisz, Irena (b. 1941)
Bashert, sels.
Death Camp.
Fradel Schtok.
My Mother's Sabbath Days.
Perspectives on the Second World War.

Kletke, Glenn (b. 1942)
O Grandfather Dust.

Klinger, Adria
Transformation.
Your fingers circle.

Klink, Joanna (b. 1969)
And Having Lost Track.
Apology: "Lately, too much disturbed, you stay
breathing in me."
Circadian.
Lodestar.
Mariana Trench.
Orpheus. Eurydice. Hermes.
Porch in Snow.
River in Dusk.
Scarcity.
Sea by Dusk.
Shooting Star.

Klipschutz
Funicello at 50.

Kloefkorn, William
News.
Why the Stone Remains Silent.

Kloos, Willem (1859–1938)
Evening.
Self-Transformation.
Sonnet.
Trees, Late in the Season.

Klopstock, Friedrich Gottlieb (1724–1803)
Early Graves, The.
Fredensborg.
Lake of Zurich, The.
Rose Wreaths, The.
Summer Night, The.

Klugman, Elana
She Who Listens.

Klugman, Sara
God's Body.

**Klyuyev [or Kliuev or Klyuev], Nikolai
Alekseievich (1884–1937)**
Can I Tell You My Love with a Portrait.
Conversational Melody, A Good Verse, A.
Fourth Rome, The.
Mother Sabbath.
October, A Copper-Crawed Cock.
Sky Lies Blue—Like a Sea, The.
You Twist Your Death in Nooses.

Knevet, Ralph (1600–71)
Bottle, The.
Contrition.
Habitation, The.
Harp, The.
Navigation.
Vote, The.

Knibbe, Hester (b. 1946)
Skater, The.

Knight, Etheridge (1933–91)
Another Poem for Me (after Recovering from
an O.D.).
As You Leave Me.
Black Poet Leaps to His Death, A.
Bones of My Father, The.
Circling the Daughter.
Dark Prophecy: I Sing of Shine.
Feeling Fucked/Up Up.
For Black Poets Who Think of Suicide.
For Freckle-Faced Gerald.
Genesis 2.
Green Grass and Yellow Balloons.
Haiku: "Eastern guard tower."
Haiku, sel.
Hard Rock Returns to Prison from the Hospital
for the Criminal Insane.
He Sees Through Stone.
Idea of Ancestry, The.
My Uncle Is My Honor and a Guest in My
House.
On the Removal of the Fascist American Right
from Power.
On the Yard.
Once on a Night in the Delta: A Report From
Hell.
Poem for Myself (Or Blues for a Mississippi
Black Boy), A.
Poem of Attrition, A.
Poem to Galway Kinnell, A.
To Make a Poem in Prison.
Two Poems for Black Relocation Centers, sels.
Warden Said to Me the Other Day, The.

WASP Woman Visits a Black Junkie in Prison,
A.
Welcome Back, Mr. Knight: Love of My Life.

Knight, Richard Payne (1750–1824)
Landscape, The, sels.

Knight, Stephen
Big Parade, The.
Daedalus.
Double Writing.
Eyeball Works, The.
In Case of Monsters.
Mermaid Tank, The.
Surf Motel, The.

Knighton, Ryan (b. 1972)
Ballad of Echolocation, The.

Knoepfle, John (b. 1923)
Bath.
Confluence.
Dark Spaces: Thoughts on All Souls Day.
Harpe's Head.
Late Winter in Menard County.

Knorr, Jeff (b. 1966)
Wreckage along the River, The.

Knott, Bill
Advice from the Experts.
Ant Dodger.
At the Crossroads.
Christmas at the Orphanage.
Comic Look at Damocles, A.
Crux.
Death: "Going to sleep, I cross my hands on
my chest."
Feeding the Sun.
Funny Poem.
Monodrama.
Mrs. Frye and the Pencilsharpener.
Save As: Salvation.
Shorts / Excerpts.
Sonnet: "Way the world is not, The."
Two Vietnam Poems: (1966).
Unsubscriber, The.
Winter Regrets.

Knowles, Herbert (1798–1817)
Lines Written in the Church Yard of
Richmond, Yorkshire.

**Knox, Edmund George Valpy ("Evoe") (1881–
1971)**
Director, The.
Upon Julia's Clothes.

Knox, Janet Norman
Daycare in a Doublewide.

Knox, Jennifer L. (b. 1968)
Bright Light of Responsibility, The.
Chicken Bucket.
Cruising for Prostitutes.
God Gave Safe Passage to the Animals
through His Forest of Bright Spectrums.
My Big German Bra.
Pastoral with Internet Porn.
Son of The House of a Thousand Chandeliers.

Knox, Ronald Arbuthnott (1888–1957)
Anglican curate in want, An.
Idealism.
To a Pessimist.

**Knut, Dovid (David Mironovich Fiksman) (1900–
55)**
Walking along the Sea of Galilee.
Woman from the Book of Genesis, A.

Knutson, Greta (b. 1899)
Foreign Land.
Moon Fishing.
Pêche Lunaire.

Ko Changsu (Chang-soo Koh) (b. 1934)
Ocean Liner.

Ko Chônghûi
It Will Be a New World.
Let's Open the Dam.
Letter Written With the Left Hand, A.
On the Way to Ch'ôngju.
Our Baby is a Living Prayer.
People of the Earth 8.
Prague Spring 6.
Prague Spring 8.
Sisters, Now We Are the Path and the Light.
Study of Women's History 4, A.

Study of Women's History 6, A.
What Is History? 1.

K'o Chun (961–1023)
Springtime South of the Yangtze.

Ko Ŭn (b. 1933)
Beside the Evening River.
Chrysanthemums.
Crossing Rice Fields at Nightfall.
For an Island.
Great Springtime.
Impermanence.
Into the Woods.
Memory of the Graves.
No-More-Daughters's.
Slice of Moon, A.

Ko Un (b. 1933)
Annihilation.
Asking the Way.
Baby.
Headmaster Abe.
Ripples.
Walking Down a Mountain.

Ko Won
Jack in the Box.

Kobayashi Issa *See* Issa

Kocan, Peter (b. 1947)
AIDS, Among Other Things.
Cows.
Inmate, An.
Mutineer's Ballad, The.

Kocbek, Edvard (1904–81)
Dialectics.
Earth, I Get Everything From You.
Game, The.
Hands.
I Haven't Done Playing With Words.
Longing for Jail, A.

Koch, Christopher (b. 1932)
Boy who Dreamed the Country Night, The.
Shelly Beach.

Koch, Kenneth (1925–2002)
Airplane Betty in Holland.
Alive for an Instant.
Boiling Water, The.
Circus, The ("I remember when I wrote The
    Circus.").
Circus, The ("We will have to go away, said
    the girls in the circus.").
Cycle of Six Lyrics.
Days and Nights, *sels.*
Energy in Sweden.
Fresh Air, *sel.*
Geography.
Girl and Baby Florist Sidewalk Pram Nineteen
    Seventy Something.
In Love with You.
Irresistible.
Man, The.
Mending Sump.
New Guide, A.
One Train May Hide Another.
Permanently.
Poem for My Twentieth Birthday.
Proverb.
Railway Stationery, The.
Schoolyard in April.
To Carelessness.
To Marina.
To My Old Poems.
To My Twenties.
To Old Age.
To the Roman Forum.
To World War Two.
To You: "I love you as a sheriff searches for a
    walnut."
Variations on a Theme by William Carlos
    Williams.
Ville de Nice, La.
With Janice.
You Were Wearing.

Kochanowski, Jan (1530–84)
In Defence of Drunkards.
Laments, The, *sels.*
To a Mathematician.

Kocot, Noelle (b. 1969)
Bad Aliens.
Bicycle Poem.
Civilization Day.
Consolations Before an Affair, Upper West
    Side.
Gypsy Summer.
I Am Like a Desert Owl, an Owl Among the
    Ruins.
Ordinary Evening, An.

Kodama Kagai (1874–1943)
Setting Sun, The.
Suicide of an Unemployed Person, The.

Kodo (1370–1433)
Serving the Shogun in the capital.

Koehler, Ted (1894–1973)
Animal Crackers in My Soup.
As Long As I Live.
Between the Devil and the Deep Blue Sea.
Don't Worry 'Bout Me.
Good for Nothin' Joe.
Happy As the Day Is Long.
I Gotta Right to Sing the Blues.
Ill Wind.
I've Got the World on a String.
Let's Fall in Love.
Sing, My Heart.
Spreadin' Rhythm Around.
Stop! You're Breakin' My Heart.
Stormy Weather (Keeps Rainin' All the Time).
Tess's Torch Song (I Had a Man).
Truckin'
When the Sun Comes Out.
Wrap Your Troubles in Dreams.

Koeppel, Mary Sue
Begin with the Heron and the Bat.
Meditation: "Sorrow is to be discarded."
9 PM Summer.
While the Wolf Walks the Edge of the Woods.

Koertge, Ron (b. 1940)
All Suffering Comes from Attachment.
Coloring.
Dear Superman.
Even Ornaments of Speech Are Forms of
    Deceit.
Foolish Earthlings.
Lazarus.
Lilith.
My Students.
Redondo.
Seven Dwarfs, Each on His Deathbed,
    Remember Snow White, The.
Sidekicks.
What She Wanted.

Koestenbaum, Phyllis (b. 1930)
Sonnet 37: "I'd decided I initiate most."

Koestenbaum, Wayne
Erotic Collectibles, *sels.*
Gaudy Slave Trader.
Tea Dance.

Koethe, John (b. 1945)
From the Porch.
Moore's Paradox.
Morning in America.
North Point North.
Songs of the Valley.
Sorrento Valley.
To an Audience.

Kogawa, Joy (b. 1935)
Bread to Stone.

Kohler, Sandra
Ars Poetica Feminae, *sels.*
Why a Woman Can't Be Pope.

Kojijū (1121–1201)
On the Spirit of the Heart as Moon-Disk.

Kokai (1403–69)
Taking hold, one's astray in nothingness.

Kolatkar, Jejuri Arun (b. 1932)
Low Temple, A.
Railway Station, The.

Kölcsey, Ferenc (1797–1838)
Huszt.
Köcsey.
Libations.

National Anthem.
One For a Keepsake Album.
One For Balassi.
Szondi.
Vanitatum Vanitas.
Zrínyi's Second Song.
Zrínyi's Song.

Kollan Alici
What Her Friend Said.

Kollar, Sybil
Late Arrivals.
Sunday Matinee.

Koller, James (b. 1936)
Sitting Alone One Cold June Night Before an
    Empty Whiskey Bottle a Coffee Pot & an
    Oil Stove with a Window through which I
    Watched the Flames.

Kolmar, Gertrud (1894–1943?)
Judith.
Sacrifice, The.
Unicorn, The.

Kolodinsky, Alison
Midnight.

Kolodny, Susan
Tsuneko—Psychiatric Medications Clinic.

Kolsson, Kali (d. 1158)
For five loathsome weeks.
I have nine principal talents.

Kombem, Sim (b. 1962)
Another Moment.

Komrij, Gerrit (b. 1944)
Park of the Dead.
Poet, The.

Komunyakaa, Yusef (b. 1947)
After the Fall [of Saigon].
Ambush.
Anodyne.
April Fools' Day.
Audacity of the Lower Gods.
Back Then.
Banking Potatoes.
Between Days.
Blackberries.
Boat People.
Boxing Day.
Boys in Dresses.
Bui Doi, Dust of Life.
Buried Light.
Camouflaging the Chimera.
Cante Jondo.
Captain Amasa Delano's Dilemma.
Chastity Belt.
Copacetic Mingus.
Devil's Workshop, The.
Elegy for Thelonious.
Euphony.
Facing It.
Family Tree.
February in Sydney.
Forgive and Live.
Fragging.
Gift Horse.
Gristmill.
Hanoi Market, The.
Heart's Graveyard Shift, The.
Homage to a Bellhop.
Homo Erectus.
How I See Things.
Ignis Fatuus.
In the Background of Silence.
Instructions for Building Straw Huts.
Jeanne Duval's Confession.
Knights of the White Camellia and Deacons of
    Defense.
Kosmos [2003].
Let's Say.
Little Man around the House.
Looking for Choctaw.
Losses.
Missing in Action.
Monoon Season.
My Father's Love Letters [or Loveletters].
Never Land.
No-Good Blues.
Ode to the Maggot.

Once the Dream Begins.
Please.
Poetics.
Pride.
Prisoners.
Reed Boat, A.
Report from the Skull's Diorama.
Salt.
Sappers.
Seven Deadly Sins.
Slam, Dunk, & Hook.
Smokehouse, The.
Songs for My Father.
Songs for My Father, sels.
Speed Ball.
Starlight Scope Myopia.
Sunday Afternoons.
Thanks.
Thorn Merchant's Mistress, The.
Toys in a Field.
Troubling the Water.
Tu Do Street.
Tunnels.
Twilight Seduction.
2527th Birthday of the Buddha.
Untitled Blues; After a Photograph by Yevgeni
   Yevtushenko.
Urban Renewal.
Venus's-flytraps.
Villon/Leadbelly.
Water Buffalo.
Way the Cards Fall, The.
We Never Know.
When Loneliness Is a Man.
White Port and Lemon Juice.
Work.
Yellow Dog Café.
You and I Are Disappearing.

Komuro, Kyotaro
Passed guard tower.
Want to be with children.

Koncel, Mary A.
Come Back, Elvis, Come Back to Holyoke.

Kong Rong (153–208)
First-Born, A.

Konie, Gwendoline C.
In the Fist of Your Hatred.
We Are Equals.

Konishi Raizan (Raizan) (1654–1716)
For rice-planting women.
Girls planting paddy.
Green, green, green / Herbs splash.

Kool, Marga (b. 1949)
Different.

Koontz, Tom
Bending the Light.

Koordada, Manila
You Can't Escape Your Life Record.

Kooser, Ted (b. 1939)
Abandoned Farmhouse.
At the End of the Weekend.
At the Office Early.
Braided Creek, sel.
City Limits.
Dishwater.
Dog's Grave, A.
Flying at Night.
Hands in the Wind.
Happy Birthday, A.
How to Make Rhubarb Wine.
In the Basement of the Goodwill Store.
Interchange.
Late Lights in Minnesota.
Myrtle.
Selecting a Reader.
Self-Portrait at Thirty-Nine.
Shooting a Farmhouse.
Very Old, The.
Widow, A.
Year's End.

Kopland, Rutger (Rudi van den Hoofdakker) (b. 1934)
Afdaling op Klaarlichte Dag.
Breughel's Winter.
Descent in Broad Daylight.

Johnson Brothers Ltd.
Natzweiler.
Ontology.
Thanks to the Things.
Ulumbo, a Cat.

Korean Oral Tradition
Abandoned Princess, The.
Chŏngsŏn Arirang.
Song of Entertaining the Holy One.
Transplanting Song.
Wretched Married Life (Folk Song from
   Koch'ang).

Korican, Leah
City Goddess.
Her Story.

Korinna [or Corinna] (fl. c.500? B.C.)
Are you, happy man, grandson of Kronos.
Are you sleeping endlessly? You never did
   before, Korinna.
But I sing the excellence of heroes.
But let one of you hear this.
Daughter of Hyria, land of lovely dances.
I blame even clear-voiced.
Kouretes hid the goddess's, The.
Leaving the [streams] of Ocean.
Mighty Orion conquered.
Of your daughters: Zeus, Father.
Over you, Hermes fights.
Terpsichore [told] me.
That grudging man [can't hurt] you.
Thespia, bearing a beautiful race, stranger-
   loving, Muse-beloved.
Wishing to take her son.

Korman, N. D. (1901–81)
Eviction Fight.

Kornblith, Marta (1959–97)
Books of the Dead, The.
Mirrors.
Parents.

Koroneu
Funeral Eva.

Kort, Ellen (b. 1936)
Gardener, The.
Letter from McCarty's Farm.

Korteweg, Anton (b. 1944)
Entirely You.
Sed Non Frustra.

Korzhavin, Naum (Naum Moiseievich Mandel) (b. 1925)
We can string words on a line.

Košek, Miroslav (1932–44)
It All Depends on How You Look at It.
Little Mouse, The.
Man Proposes, God Disposes.
Yes, That's the Way Things Are.

Kosen (1808–93)
Blind horse trotting up an icy ledge, A.

Kosman, Admiel (b. 1957)
Games.
Something Hurt.

Kossman, Nina
Backward Sound.
Bomb said to a city, A.
Cassandra to Agamemnon.
Judas' Reproach.
Pilate's Wife.
St. John, sel.

Kostelanetz, Richard (b. 1940)
A / ABA.

Koster, Edward B. (1861–1937)
Shoal of Silver Angelfish, A.

Kostyleva, Elena (b. 1977)
Vacancy instead of you, A.

Kosugi, Takehisa (b. 1938)
Anima 1.
Chironomy.
Manodharma with Mr. Y.
Micro 1.
Organic Music.
Theater Music.

Kosztolányi, Dezső (1885–1936)
Conductor, The.
Dark Fates, The.
Deep Are the Wells.

Eminent Public Figure.
Funeral Oration.
Laments of a Poor Little Child, sels.
Laments of a Sad Man, sel.
Marcus Aurelius.
Revolutionary,The.
Society Woman, The.
Song About Benedek Virág.
Song of "Kornél Esti", The.
To My Dog, Swan.
Would You Like to Play?

Kouchag, Nahabed (d. 1592)
I Was Suffering Exile.

Koufman, Stefanie
Violins tickling.

Kouwenaar, Gerrit (b. 1923)
Elba.
4 Variations On.

Kovacic, Kristin (b. 1963)
Brick.
Covered Dish.

Kovaleva, Irina
And there was beauty.
I can still make you out.

Kovner, Abba (1918–87)
I sat upon the ground, and the ground was fire.
My comrades / Inasmuch as they are comrades
   do not need to study the map.
My Little Sister, sels.
To Myself.
What's Not in the Heart.

Kovur Kilar
We Hope For Patrons.

Kowit, Steve (b. 1938)
Cosmetics Do No Good.
Grammar Lesson, The.
Hell: "I died & went to Hell & it was nothing
   like L.A."
I Attend a Poetry Reading.
In the Morning.
Lurid Confessions.
Notice.
Snapshot.
Trick, A.
What Chord Did She Pluck.
Whitman Portrait, A.

Kozameh, Alicia
Saltos Sobre El Exilio, sels.

Kramer, Aaron (b. 1921)
Kennedy Airport.

Kramer, Alex
Candy.

Kramer, Larry
Brilliant Windows.
Images of the San Francisco Disaster.
Night Bird, The.
Strong Winds Below the Canyons.

Kramer, Lotte
I am chained.
Immigrants.
Love Letters.
Non-Emigrant, The.
On Shutting the Door.
Red Cross Telegram, The.
Shoemaker's Wife, The.

Krapf, Norbert (b. 1943)
Civil War Veteran from Indiana Recalls
   Visiting with Walt Whitman in a Washington
   Hospital, A.
Dark and Deep.

Krasicki, Ignacy (1735–1801)
Caged Birds.
Lamb and the Wolves, The.
Master and the Dog, The.

Kraus, Sharon (b. 1961)
(We) Promenade.

Krause, Kerry
Eid Al-Fitr.

Kraushaar, Mark
Dear Mr. Whitman.
Free Throw.

Krayer, Stevie
My Mother Dressed for the Wedding.

Krechel, Ursula (b. 1947)
Early November.
To Mainz!
Kreitman, Norman (b. 1927)
Bonfire in April.
Glossy Mail.
In Torrett, Minorca.
Lizard.
Kremer, Pem
Choice, Inanna and the Galla.
Epiphany.
Kresh, David
Musical Saw.
Kress, Leonard
Backyards of America.
Kreymborg, Alfred (1883–1966)
Ants.
Culture.
Improvisation.
Tiger Lily.
To W. C. W. M. D.
Tree, The.
Kreyter, Shmuel (1899–1978)
Vengeance: "Once on a night of sparkling sin."
Kriapur (Kristianto Agus Purnomo) (1959–87)
Men on Fire.
Krige, Uys (b. 1910)
Taking of the Koppie, The.
Krivulin, Viktor (b. 1944)
And the silver age, unattainable.
Crossing the keyboards of the palace.
Glory to caesar! and glory to God in the
highest!
Guard.
Idea of Russia, The.
Southwest.
Two in a Room.
Kroetsch, Robert (b. 1927)
Ledger, The.
Sounding the Name.
Krohn, Lita Hunter
Recollections.
Krolow, Karl
Fear.
Free Fall.
In the Rearview Mirror.
Robinson.
Wind in the Room, The.
Kronenfeld, Judy
Peaceful Sentiment.
Kruchyonykh, Aleksei Eliseievich (1886–1968)
Declaration of the Word as Such.
Pomade, sels.
Sahara to America, The, sels.
Krúdy, Gyula (1878–1933)
This city, Budapest, smells of violets in the
spring as do mesdames along the
promenade.
To breakfast on a light-blue tablecloth,
smelling of milk.
What somehow echo through the clanging of
the town bells.
Kruit, Johanna (b. 1940)
Birds Leaving.
Giving Way.
House By the Sea.
Landscape.
Post Heads.
Way of the Water, The.
Krukowski, Damon
Intellectual Life, The.
Minor Poets, The.
Krylova, Ella (b. 1967)
Cornflowers.
Pilgrims, The.
Krynicki, Ryszard (b. 1943)
I Can't Help You.
Krysl, Marilyn
Carpe Diem: Time Piece.
Persephone, to Demeter.
Warscape, with Lovers.
Kshemendra (fl. 1150)
Kavikanthabharana, sels.

Kshetrayya (fl. 17th cent.)
Courtesan to a Young Customer, A.
Courtesan to Her Lover, A.
Wife to a Friend, A.
Ku K'uang (725?–c.814)
Hard Traveling.
Ku Sang (b. 1919)
Shame.
Spring Chrysanthemums.
Wings.
Kuan Chung (d. 645 B.C.)
Kuan Tzu, sels.
Kuan Han-ch'ing (Han-ch'ing) (c.1220–c.1300)
In the Southern Mode, to the Tune "A Sprig of
Flowers" The Refusal to Get Old.
To the Tune "A Spray of Flowers" (Not Giving
In to Old Age).
Tune: "Four Pieces of Jade."
Tune: "Vast Virtue."
Yellow Bell Coda.
Kuan Hsiu (832–912)
Bad Government.
I came in a dream to a mountain in the sea.
Nacreous land had no dust, The.
Palace halls loomed high, encaged in purple
vapor.
Song of the Palace of Ch'en.
Three or four young sylph women.
Written in the Mountains.
Kuan Kuan (b. 1930)
Autobiography of a Sloppy Sluggard.
Kuan P'an-p'an (fl. 8th or 9th cent.)
Mourning.
Kuan Tao Shěng (1262–1319)
Married Love.
**Kuan Yün-shih (Hsiao-yün-shih-hai-ya) (1286–
1324)**
Love Song: "Fondling and snuggling."
Tune: "Rapt with Wine, Loudly Singing; Joy in
Spring's Coming."
Kublanovsky, Yury Mikhailovich (b. 1947)
In Memory of John Keats.
In Petrograd, sel.
Kuchu
Joshu's word—Nothingness.
Kudimova, Marina (b. 1953)
Pleated strata of air, The.
Prison, zona, the camps, Taldái-Kustanái, and
the low road.
Kuhar, Mark S. (b. 1958)
All holyroadz home.
On the death of philip whalen.
On the galloping cusp of the new now.
Suburban buddha, coffeehouse christ.
You can't blow up the buddha.
Kuhlmann, Quirinus (1651–89)
15th Kühl-Psalm, The.
From Deepest Need.
Kukoku (1328–1407)
Riding backwards this wooden horse.
Külebi, Cahit (1917–97)
Lost Love: "She keeps singing a song."
Once Upon a Time: "Every morning you used
to play hooky."
Kulik, William
Fictions.
Flexible.
Hi.
Old House Blues.
Kulishova, Inna (b. 1969)
Till now / I've not been able to imagine.
Total darkness / The light's off in the kitchen.
Kulman, Elisaveta (1808–25)
To Diana.
Kumar, Amitava (b. 1963)
Primary Lessons in Political Economy.
Kumin, Maxine W. (b. 1925)
Almost Spring, Driving Home, Reciting
Hopkins.
Bangkok Gang, The.
Calling, A.
Chain, The.
Chores.

Credo.
Despair.
Early Thoughts of Winter.
Envelope, The.
Excrement Poem, The.
Family Reunion.
Final Poem, The.
For My Great-Grandfather: A Message Long
Overdue.
400-Meter Freestyle.
Getting the Message.
Grace of Geldings in Ripe Pastures, The.
Hay.
Heaven as Anus.
Height of the Season, The.
Highwaymen, The.
How It Is.
How to Survive Nuclear War.
In the Absence of Bliss.
In the Park.
In the Pea Patch.
Insider's View of the Garden, The.
Junior Life Saving.
Letters, sel.
Living Alone with Jesus.
Long Marriage, The.
Magellan Street, 1974.
Making the Jam without You.
Morning Swim.
Notes on a Blizzard.
Nuns of Childhood, The: Two Views.
Nurture.
October, Yellowstone Park.
Our Ground Time Here Will Be Brief.
Plans.
Poet Visits Egypt and Israel, The.
Requiem on I-89.
Retrieval System, The.
Riddle of Noah, The.
Seeing the Bones.
Sound of Night, The.
Spree.
Thinking of Death and Dogfood.
To Swim, to Believe.
Video Cuisine.
Woodchucks.
Kunene, Raymond Mazisi (b. 1930)
Elegy for My Friend E. Galo.
Kunert, Günter (B. 1929)
Jewish Cemetery at Berlin-Weissensee, The.
Sestri Levante / Liguria 2.
Theatrum Mundi.
Venice Lost.
K'ung Chih-kuei (448–501)
Proclamation on North Mountain.
Trip on Mount T'ai-p'ing.
Wandering Round Mount Taiping.
Kunin, Aaron (b. 1973)
Sore Throat, The.
Kunina, Yuliya (b. 1966)
I'm trying to fit my destiny into.
Inconsistent Self-Portrait.
Kunitz, Stanley (1905–2006)
Abduction, The.
After the Last Dynasty.
Approach to Thebes, The.
Careless Love.
Catch, The.
Day of Foreboding.
Dragonfly, The.
End of Summer.
Father and Son.
Flight of Apollo, The.
Game, The.
He.
Hornworm: Autumn Lamentation.
Hornworm: Summer Reverie.
Intimations of Mortality.
King of the River.
Last Picnic, The.
Layers, The.
Long Boat, The.
Magic Curtain, The.
Night Letter.
Old Cracked Tune, An.

Passing Through.
Portrait, The.
Quarrel, The.
Quinnapoxet.
Reflection by a Mailbox.
River Road.
Robin Redbreast.
Round, The.
Route Six.
Science of the Night, The.
Snakes of September, The.
Testing-Tree, The.
Thief, The.
Three Floors.
Three Small Parables for My Poet Friends.
Touch Me.
War against the Trees, The.
Wellfleet Whale, The.
When the Light Falls.

Kunze, Reiner (b. 1933)
Aerial, The.
Brief Curriculum.
Bringers of Beethoven, The.
End of Art, The.
First Letter From Tamara A.
Hymn To a Woman Under Interrogation.
Low Volume.
Need for Censorship, The.
Reply.
Wall, The: For October 3, 1990.

Kuo, Alex (b. 1939)
Lives in Dreadful Wanting, sel.

Kuo Mo-jo (1892–1978)
Earthquake.

Kuo P'o (276–324)
First Poem of Wandering Immortals.
Kingfishers sport among orchids and begonias.
Poem on the Wandering Immortal.
Vision: Second Poem of Wandering Immortals.

Kuong Viet (fl. 1050)
Wood and Fire.

Kupala, Ianka (1882–1942)
Yelling-alive.

Kuppner, Frank (b. 1952)
Old Guidebook to Prague, An, sels.

Kupriyanov [or Kuprianov], Vyacheslav (b. 1939)
Everything gets forgotten.
For a long time he tried to survive.
Lesson in Natural History, A.

Kürenberg, Der von (1150–75)
Late at night I stood on a battlement.
Morning star goes under cover, The.
Woman and falcons—they are easily tamed.

Kurihara Sadako
Let Us Be Midwives!
When We Say "Hiroshima."

Kurt, Kemal (1947–2002)
GYN-astics.

Kurtz, Aaron (1891–1964)
Andalusian Landscape.
Call, The.
No Pasarán.
Spanish Lullaby.
Two Songs of a Blacksmith.

Kusano Shimpei (b. 1903)
Birthday Party.
4 or 5 Tadpoles.
Mount Fuji [Selections, 1943].
Skylarks and Fuji.

Kushner, Aleksandr Semionovich (b. 1936)
Airman, The.
As Catullus wrote, a man's voice deserts him.
Cypress.
Don't bother about the news!
Memoirs.
Oak, The.
Picture, A.
Rooster, The.
Star burns out over the tree tops, The.
To B. P.

Kushner, Bill (b. 1931)
Civilization.
Friends.

In the Hairy Arms of Whitman.
Up.

Kushner, Dale M.
Grandma in the Shower.

Kushner, Tony (b. 1956)
Hydriotaphia, sel.

Kuskin, Karla (b. 1932)
Catherine.
I Woke Up This Morning.
Question, The.
Rose on My Cake, The.
When I Went Out.
Where Have You Been Dear?
Witches' Ride, The.

Kutchins, Laurie
Clothesline.

Kuusisto, Stephen
Erasing Stars.
Night Seasons.
Summer at North Farm.

Kuzma, Greg (b. 1944)
Ice Skating.
Night Things.
Peace, So That.
Poetry: "Old forms are like birdhouses that, The."

Kuzmin, Dmitry (b. 1968)
Our hairdresser friend.

Kuzmin, Mikhail Alekseievich (1875–1936)
Ah, those lips, kissed by so many.
Antinous.
At noon I must have been conceived.
At the Party.
Leaving my house in the morning.
Nine delightful birthmarks.
Not for nothing did we read the theologians.
People see gardens and houses.
Were I a general of olden times.
Were you apprenticed to a fortune teller?
When it was I first encountered you.

Kuzmina-Karavayeva, Elizaveta (Mother Maria [or Mat' Mariia]) (1891–1945)
Long-Barrow Princess 2.
Ruth.

Kuznetsova, Inga (b. 1974)
Breadcrumbs falling from the table.
For a centenary.
Repairs are like the fall of Pompeii.
Seagull shrilly in my head, A.
Speech is a stream.
Wand, A.

Kuzwayo, Ellen K. (b. 1914)
Choice, The.

Kwa, Lydia
Roadbook: Suite of Hands, sel.

Kwabena, Atiba
Doin.'

Kwakiutl Oral Tradition
Fires run through my body—the pain of loving you.

Kwangdŏk
Prayer to Amitāyus.

Kwŏn Homun (1532–87)
Nature makes clear the windy air.
Nights After Rain When the Moon.

Kwŏn P'il (1569–1612)
Alone at Night.
Leaves fall with rain in these vacant mountains.
Upon Reading Tu Fu's Poetry.

Kydios
Beware. There are fawns.

Kyei, Kojo Gyinaye (b. c.1930)
Tough Guy of London, The.

Kyerang [Yi Hyanggŭm] (1513–50)
Under a shower of pear blossoms.

Kyffin, Morris (c.1555–98)
Blessednes of Brytaine, The, sel.

Kyger, Joanne (b. 1934)
And with March a Decade in Bolinas.
Bird family.
Caption for a Miniature.
Deeply Immoral Arrogant and Ignorant.

Descartes and the Splendor of a Real Drama of Everyday Life. In Six Parts.
Destruction.
Dew Sweet Law, The.
Dream: "I'm doing this poetry reading with Simone."
Duncan's class met last night and more talk.
Empty Shrine Buddha, The.
Every day I burn a stick of incense.
For Your Birthday, Philip: And upon the Occasion of Becoming Abbot of the Hartford Street Zen Center.
I Blinked My Eyes, Looked Up and Everyone Was 25 Years Older.
It Certainly Was Divine Running into You.
It's a great day. Last night I visited my old.
It's been a long time.
Joanne.
Maze, The.
Never talk ahead.
News bulletin from Keith Lampe.
Oh Man is the highest type of animal existing.
On the Other Side.
Once Again Another Century Ahead.
Pan as the Son of Penelope.
Philip Whalen's Hat.
Replacement Buddhas.
Retirement: "Unfamiliar warble 9 times more, An."
Snow fall on green leaves.
To Live in This World Again.
Unexpectedly, from the outside.
Watching TV.
Wide Mind.

Kyle, Christiane Jacox
Argument, The.
Fire in Early Morning.
Season of Locking-In, The.

Kyme, Anne See Askew, Anne

Kynaston, Sir Francis (1587–1642)
To Cynthia.

Kyokusui
Thorns of the iron fence.

Kyong-Nim, Shin (b. 1935)
Yollim Kut Song.

Kyoriku (fl. 1692)
Next to even.
Scent of plum blossoms.

Kyunyŏ, Great Master (923–73)
Eleven Poems on the Ten Vows of the Universally Worthy Bodhisattva, sels.

Kyurin-Eki
Eighty-three years—at last.

L

"L., L. E." See Landon, Letitia [or Laetitia] Elizabeth

La Fontaine, Jean de (1621–95)
Aesop's Fable of the Frogs.
Donkey and the Lapdog, The.
Eagle and the Beetle, The.
Fox and the Crow, The.
Hag and the Slavies, The.
Man and His Image, The.
Phoebus and Boreas.
Pig, Goat, Sheep.
Rat and the Elephant, The.
Saddled Ass, The.
Shrimp and Her Daughter, The.
Wolf and the Dog, The.
Wolf and the Stork, The.
Young mouse, poor, no experience, A.

La Loca
Why I Choose Black Men for My Lovers.

La Morticella, Barbara
Liturgy for Trinity, A.

Laâbi Abdellatif (b. 1942)
Demain sera le même jour.
Portrait du Père, Le.
Portrait of the Father, The.
Tomorrow Will Be the Same Day.

LaBarre, Michelle
For Gloucester on Being Newly Blind.
L'Abbé, Sonnet
Dumb Animal, *sel.*
Freestyle (Why They Don't Like Rap).
Reaction To What You Said.
Theory My Natural Brown Ass.
Labé, Louise (1524–66)
Bright Venus, Who Across the Heavens

Stray.
Kiss me again, and kiss me still, and kiss.
Long-Felt Desires.
Sonnet 17: "I flee the city, temples, and each place."
Labid (Labid Ibn Rabia)
Mu'allaqat, The, *sel.*
Labrador, Sean Manzano (b. 1972)
Dark Continent, The.
Labrunie, Gérard *See* Nerval, Gérard de
Lacavaro, Anthony
Advantages of Being a World Class Athlete, The.
Ladd, Michael C.
Tragic Mulatto is Neither, The.
Lady Ise (d. 939)
Because we suspected / the pillow would say "I know."
Flower of waves, A.
If it is you, there / in the light boat on the pond.
Pillows know, they say.
Seeing the Returning Geese.
Lady of the Arbour, The (*fl.* c.1450)
Flower and the Leaf, The, *sels.*
Lady of the Assembly, The (*fl.* late 15th cent.)
Assembly of Ladies, The, *sels.*
LaFemina, Gerry (b. 1968)
Her Rose Tattoo.
White Dwarf.
Lafleur, William R. (b. 1936)
Wedding Party.
Laforgue, Jules (1860–87)
Clair de Lune.
Complaint on the Oblivion of the Dead.
Mystery of the Three Horns, The.
Pierrot Says.
Sunday Piece.
Lagier, Jennifer
Second Class Citizen.
Lagrone, Oliver (1906–95)
I Heard the Byrd.
Lahey, Anita (b. 1972)
Post-War Procession.
Lahey, Joy
Buckles.
Cattails Along Red River.
Cotton and Gladiolas.
Habitat Photo.
.22.
U-turn.
White Soil.
Lai, Larissa (b. 1967)
All the exposure.
Left the opium and myopia outside.
Laine, Frankie (*fl.* 1945)
We'll Be Together Again.
Laing, Allan M. (b. 1887)
Grace for Ice-Cream, A.
New Jerusalem, The.
This Railway Station.
Laing, Kojo
Africa Sky.
Godhorse.
Huge Car with the Sad Voice, The.
I Am the Freshly Dead Husband.
Many Worlds Are Walked Once.
One Hundred Lines for the Coast.
Race on Gathering Bites.
Same Corpse, The.
Senior Lady Sells Garden Eggs.
Steps.
Tatale Swine.
Laing, Ronald David (b. 1927)

Sonnet 4: "When I consider what you mean to me."
Sonnet 16: "Now all our guests have come and gone away."
Laird, Nick (b. 1975)
Bearhug, The.
Cuttings.
Evening Forecast for the Region, The.
Layered, The.
Length of a Wave, The.
Poetry: "It's a bit like looking through the big window."
Lake, Paul
Blue Jay.
Crime and Punishment.
In Rough Weather.
Introduction to Poetry.
Pieces.
Lakhish, Karmela *See* Raàm-Lachish, Carmela
Lakshminkara (fl. 8th cent.)
Lay your head on a block of butter and chop.
Lal Ded [or Lalla] (*fl.* 14th cent.)
At the end of a crazy-moon night.
Coursing in emptiness.
I drag a boat over the ocean.
I searched for my Self.
I was passionate.
On the way to God the difficulties.
Soul, like the moon, The.
This world.
To learn the scriptures is easy.
Laleau, Léon (b. 1892)
Hot Ports.
Lalic, Ivan V. (b. 1931)
Places We Love.
Laluah, Aquah *See* Hayford, Gladys May Casely
Lam, Fiona Tinwei (b. 1964)
Loop.
Lam Thi My Da (b. 1949)
Garden Fragrance.
Night Harvest.
Lamantia, Philip (b. 1927)
High.
Romantic Movement, The.
There Are Many Pathways to the Garden.
Time Traveler's Potlatch.
Voice of Earth Mediums.
Winter Day, A.
Lamar, Mirabeau Buonaparte (1798–1859)
Carmelita.
San Jacinto.
Lamarque, Vivian (b. 1946)
Gentleman and the Lady, The.
Gentleman in Front, The.
Gentleman in the Heart, The.
I Wanted to Dream the Mailman.
Illegitimate Poem.
Lady of the Last Time, The.
Lady of the Snow, The.
Little Girl.
Looking at the Moon.
Newborn Lover.
Prayer of Mothers Who Unintentionally Failed Their Children.
There Was a Castle.
Lamartine, Alphonse Marie Louis de (1790–1869)
Autumn.
Infinite in the Skies, The.
Isolation.
Lake, The.
Lake, The.
Lizard, The.
Valley, The.
West, The.
Lamb, Arthur J.
Bird in a Gilded Cage, A.
Lamb, Charles (1775–1834)
Anger.
Childhood Fled.
David in the Cave of Adullam.
Envy.
Family Name, The.
First Tooth, The.
Gipsy's Malison, The.

Hester.
If From My Lips Some Angry Accents Fell.
In My Own Album.
Nonsense Verses.
O! I Could Laugh to Hear the Midnight Wind.
Old Familiar Faces, The.
On an Infant Dying as Soon as Born.
Salome.
Timid grace sits trembling in her eye, A.
To Dora W[ordsworth]; *On Being Asked By Her Father to Write in Her Album.*
To Louisa M[artin], Whom I Used to Call "Monkey."
Triumph of the Whale, The, *sel.*
Was it Some Sweet Device of Faery Land.
Lamb, Helen (1899–1976)
Evidence: "He brought her presents."
Intensive Care.
She Said / He Said.
Lamb, Joe
Cherries.
Lamb, Lady Caroline (1785–1828)
By Those Eyes Where Sweet Expression.
Duet.
Fugitive Pieces and Reminiscences of Lord Byron with Some Original Poetry, Letters and Recollections of Lady Caroline Lamb, ed. I. Nathan, *sels.*
If Thou Couldst Know What 'Tis to Weep.
Sing Not for Others, But for Me.
Lamb, Mary (1764–1847)
Anger.
Envy.
First Tooth, The.
Helen.
Parental Recollections.
Salome.
Two Boys, The.
"Lambert, Louis" *See* Gilmore, Patrick Sarsfield
Lambert, Richard (b. 1947)
Prayer: "Bones in your foot that were shattered, The."
Lami'i Çelebi (1472–1532)
Yesterday I saw that sun-faced beauty.
LaMon, Jacqueline Jones
Sammy Davis, Jr.
Lamothe, Ferdinand Joseph *See* Morton, "Jelly Roll."
Lampadius, Sabina (*fl.* 377)
As a symbol.
Lampman, Archibald (1861–99)
City of the End of Things, The.
Frogs, The.
Heat.
In November: "Hills and leafless forests slowly yield, The."
King's Sabbath, The.
Morning on the Lièvre.
Winter Evening.
Lamport, Felicia (b. 1916)
Eggomania.
Mother, Mother, Are You All There?
Poll Star.
Lamrani, Wafaa' (b. 1960)
I Am Consecrated to the Coming One.
Wail of Heights, The.
Lancaster, John (b. 1946)
Yellow Bike, The.
Landesman, Fran (b. 1927)
Ballad of the Sad Young Men, The.
Say "Cheese!"
Spring Can Really Hang You Up the Most.
Landon, Letitia [or Laetitia] Elizabeth ("L. E. L.") (1802–38)
Airey Force.
Banquet, The.
Bonds of Affection.
Castle of Chillon, The.
Child Screening a Dove from a Hawk, A.
Dancing Girl, The.
Death in the Flower.
Dying Child, The.
Enchanted Island, The.
Experience Too Late.

Factory, The.
Farewell, The.
Felicia Hemans.
Fountain's Abbey.
Fragments, *sels.*
Gifts Misused.
Girl at Her Devotions, A.
Golden Violet, The, *sels.*
History of the Lyre, A.
Improvisatrice, The, *sels.*
Lady, thy face is very beautiful.
Lines of Life.
Lines Written Under a Picture of a Girl
   Burning a Love-Letter.
Little Shroud, The.
Love's Last Lesson.
Marriage Vow, The.
Mask of Gaiety, The.
New Monthly Magazine, 44 286–8, *sels.*
Poet's Lot, The.
Poor, The.
Power of Words, The.
Princess Victoria, The.
Proud Ladye, The.
Revenge.
Scale Force, Cumberland.
Scenes in London, *sels.*
She Sat Alone beside Her Hearth.
Small Miseries.
Song: "Farewell!—and never think of me."
Stern Truth.
To My Brother: "Do you recall the fancies of
   many years ago."

Landor, Walter Savage (1775–1864)
Age.
Alas! 'Tis Very Sad to Hear.
Alciphron and Leucippe.
Bourbons.
Case at Sessions, A.
Citation and Examination of William
   Shakespeare, The, *sels.*
Crimean Heroes, The.
Death of the Day.
Dragon-Fly, The.
Foreign Ruler, A.
Gebir, *sels.*
Georges, The.
God Scatters Beauty.
Heart's Abysses, The.
Hearts-Ease.
Ianthe, *sels.*
Idle Words.
Last Fruit Off an Old Tree, The, *sels.*
Memory.
Mother, I Cannot Mind My Wheel.
On Catullus.
On Seeing a Hair of Lucretia Borgia.
Pericles and Aspasia, *sels.*
Plays.
Rose Aylmer.
Scribblers, The.
Separation.
Tears of the Dying.
Three Roses, The.
To a Spaniel.
To Arthur de Noé Walker.
To Robert Browning.
Twenty Years Hence.
Years.

Lane, M. Travis (b. 1934)
Codicil: Including the cost of a monument and
   inscription.
For Brigid.
Poem Upon the Forcible Entry by Cat into a
   Poem Originally Upon Trilliums.
Portobello.

Lane, Patrick (b. 1939)
Garden Temple, The.
Linen Crow, a Caftan Magpie, A, *sel.*
Pissaro's Tomb.
Winter 6: "Guests have arrived at last, The.
   The old."
Winter 9: "Each day the time grows less, the
   hours."
Winter 40: "She is a northern woman, barely
   more."

Lane, Pinkie Gordon (b. 1937)
Children.
Girl at the Window.
Lake Murry.
Lyric: I Am Looking at Music.
Midnight Song.
Nuclear Peril.
On Being Head of the English Department.
Port Townsend Poems.
Rain Ditch.
Spring.
Wind Thoughts.

Lang, Andrew (1844–1912)
Brahma.
Odyssey, The.
Romance.

Lang, John Dunmore (1799–1878)
Colonial Nomenclature.

Lange, Art (b. 1952)
Perugia.
Sonnet for the Season.

Langford, G. W.
Speak Gently.

Langgässer, Elisabeth (1899–1950)
Daphne.

Langhorne, John (1735–79)
Studley Park.

Langille, Carole Glasser
Crows.
Prayer: "Every hour I am disappearing."
Sadness of Windows, The.
Scanning an Afternoon in Winter.
Through a Slit in the Tent.

Langland, William (1330–1400)
Vision of Piers Plowman, The, *sels.*

Langley, Eve (b. 1908)
This Year, before It Ends.

Langley, R. F.
Jack's Pigeon.
Mariana.

Langworthy, Christian (b. 1967)
Why I Look at Girls.

Lanier, Emilia (1569–1645)
Author's Dream to the Lady Mary, the
   Countess Dowager of Pembroke, The.
Description of Cooke-ham [*or* Cookham], The,
   sels.
Salve Deus Rex Judaeorum, *sels.*
To All Virtuous Ladies in General.
To the Lady Anne, Countess of Dorset, *sel.*
To the Lady Arabella.

Lanier, Sidney (1842–81)
Ballad of Trees and the Master, A.
Clover, *sel.*
Crystal, The.
Dying Words of Stonewall Jackson, The.
From the Flats.
Hymns of the Marshes, *sels.*
Laughter in the Senate.
Mocking Bird, The.
Nirvâna.
Raven Days, The.
Revenge of Hamish, The.
Song for "The Jacquerie"
Song of the Chattahoochee.
Street Cries, *sels.*
To Bayard Taylor.
To Beethoven.
Waving of the Corn, The.

Lanigan, George Thomas (1845–86)
Threnody: "What, what, what / What's the
   news from Swat?"

Lansana, Quraysh Ali (b. 1964)
For Gwendolyn Brooks.
Woolworth's Poem, The.

Lansdown, Andrew (b. 1954)
Behind the Veil.
Golgotha.
Mercy.
Two Men.

Lansky, Bruce (b. 1941)
Oh, Woe Ith Me!

"Lantos" *See* Tinódi, Sebestyén

Lanyer, Aemelia [*or* Aemilia Bassano Lanyer]
See Lanier, Emilia

Lanzilloti, Das
In the Boobiehatch.
Ornate Iron Gates.

Lao Tzu (c.604–531 B.C.)
Tao Te Ching, *sels.*
Valley Spirit Never Dies, The.
Way and Its Power, The, *sels.*
Weapons are the tools of violence.

Lapeyrère, Josée
Apples, *sels.*
Dishes, The, *sels.*
Skirt, The, *sels.*

Lapierre, Bob
Tomorrow's Hope.

Lapyè, Bob *See* Lapierre, Bob

Lara, Alda (b. 1930)
Nights.

Larak, Pòl *See* Laraque, Paul

Laraque, Paul (b. 1920)
Exile Is Stale Bread.
Mardi Gras.
My Broad Back.
Poem for You, A.
Rainbow.

Larbaud, Valery (1881–1957)
Don de soi-même, Le.
Gift of Oneself, The.
Images.
Ode: "Lend me your great sound, your fine
   smooth speed."
Ode: "Prête-moi ton grand bruit, ta grande
   allure si douce."

Larcom, Lucy (1824–93)
Little Cavalier, A.
November, *sel.*
They Said.
What the Train Ran Over.

Large, Josaphat Robert (b. 1942)
Snowcone Vendor.
Text XXX.

Larkin, Joan (b. 1939)
Beatings.
Co-alcoholic.
Cold River.
Genealogy.
Good-Bye.
Housework.
How the Healing Takes Place.
Inventory.
Legacy.
My Body.
Origins.
Risks.
Self-Love.

Larkin, Philip (1922–85)
Absences.
Afternoons.
Age.
Ambulances.
Annus Mirabilis.
Arrivals, Departures.
Arundel Tomb, An.
As Bad as a Mile.
At Grass.
Aubade: "I work all day, and get half-drunk at
   night."
Born Yesterday.
Broadcast.
Card-Players, The.
Church Going.
Coming.
Counting.
Cut Grass.
Days.
Deceptions.
Dockery and Son.
Dublinesque.
Explosion, The.
Faith Healing.
Fiction and the Reading Public.
First Sight.
For Sidney Bechet.

Forget What Did.
Going.
Going, Going.
Here.
High Windows.
Homage to a Government.
Home Is So Sad.
I Remember, I Remember.
Limerick: "There was an old fellow of Kaber."
Lines on a Young Lady's Photograph Album.
Livings, *sels*.
Love Again.
Love Songs in Age.
Money.
Mr Bleaney.
Myxomatosis.
New Year.
Next, Please.
MCMXIV.
No Road.
Old Fools, The.
Poetry of Departures.
Reasons for Attendance.
Sad Steps.
St. Matthew, *sels*.
So through that unripe day you bore your head.
Solar.
Spring.
Study of Reading Habits, A.
Sunny Prestatyn.
Talking in Bed.
This Be The Verse.
Toads.
Toads Revisited.
Trees, The: "Trees are coming into leaf, The."
Waiting For Breakfast, While She Brushed Her Hair.
Water.
Whatever Happened?
Whitsun Weddings, The.
Larkin, Tanya
Cho-Fu-Sa.
With Cheerful Speed.
Larminie, William (1885–1930)
Fand, *sels*.
Lars, Claudia (1899–1974)
Recollection of Gabriela Mistral.
Sketch of the Frontier Woman.
Larsen, Lance (b. 1961)
Lips.
Peach.
Red.
Larsen, Wendy Wilder
After: "Once upon a time."
Bluebird in Cutleaf Beech.
Learning the War.
Larsen, William
Surrender.
Lasheen, Mohamed
Nearly Three Million Years Ago.
Nightmares Fit to Arouse Misgivings.
Lasker-Schüler, Else (1876–1945)
And Look for God.
Chronica.
Georg Trakl.
George Grosz.
My Blue Piano.
My Blue Piano.
My People.
O God.
Only for You.
To The Barbarian.
Laskey, Michael (b. 1944)
Tightrope Wedding, The.
Tray of Eggs, A.
Lasoen, Patricia (b. 1948)
That April Morning.
Lassaw-Paljor, Denise
Counting Breaths.
For a Moose.
Lassell, Michael (b. 1947)
Brady Street, San Francisco.
Going to Europe.
How to Watch Your Brother Die.

Kissing Ramén.
Sunset Stripping: Visiting L.A.
Three Poems.
Lathbury, Mary Artemisia ("Aunt Mary") (1841–1913)
Day Is Dying in the West.
Lathrop, Lena
Woman's Question, A.
Latouche, John (1917–56)
Cabin in the Sky.
Honey in the Honeycomb.
Lazy Afternoon.
Love Turned the Light Out.
Maybe I Should Change My Ways.
Not a Care in the World.
Summer Is a-Comin' In.
Taking a Chance on Love.
Lattany, Kristin (b. 1931)
Question of Identity, The.
Lattimore, Richmond (1906–84)
Flesh Tones.
North Philadelphia, Trenton, and New York.
Note on the L and N.
Lau, Alan Chong
Bittermelon.
Eating habits of the old man.
Morning reflections over the miso soup.
My Ship Does Not Need a Helmsman.
Sun Yat Sen Comes to Lodi.
Upside Down Basket, The.
Wintermelon.
Lauder, Marie Maitland (*fl.* 16th cent.)
As phoebus in his spheris hicht.
Laughlin, James (1914–97)
Above the City.
Bird of Endless Time, The.
Deep Pool, the.
I Know How Every Poet.
Inn at Kirchstetten, The.
My Ambition.
O Best of All Nights, Return and Return Again.
Our Bicycles.
Poets.
Rhyme.
Then and Now.
What Is Hoped For.
Lauinger, Ann (b. 1948)
Three Songs for *King Leir*, *sels*.
Laurencin, Marie (1885–1956)
Horse, The.
Present, The.
Tiger, The.
Zebra, The.
Lauter, Estella (b. 1940)
Spots.
Lauterbach, Ann (b. 1942)
After Mahler.
Boy Sleeping.
Clamor.
Gesture and Flight.
Here and There ("Some days start already swung from rafters.").
Here and There ("Today I wake having swung, naked, in London.").
How Things Bear Their Telling.
Hum.
In the Museum of the Word (Henri Matisse).
Invocation.
Meanwhile the Turtle.
Mimetic.
Novelist Speaks, The.
Platonic Subject.
Procedure.
Revelry in Black-and-White.
Santa Fe Sky.
Stones (Istanbul, Robert Smithson).
Untoward.
Werner Herzog 68 / Iowa City 88.
Lautréamont, Comte de
Maldoror, *sel*.
Lauture, Denizé (b. 1946)
Our Destiny.
Strokes of an Adult's Pencil.

Zaps of Zombifying Powder.
Laux, Dorianne (b. 1952)
Children's Train, The.
China.
Dust.
Each Sound.
Fast Gas.
Finding What's Lost.
Firestarter.
Garden, The.
Homecoming.
Idea of Housework, The.
If This Is Paradise.
Laundromat, The.
Lovers, The.
Nurse, The.
Prayer: "Sweet Jesus, let her save you, let her take."
Reetika Arranges My Closet.
Singing Back the World.
Smoke.
Thief, The.
This Close.
Trying to Raise the Dead.
2 am.
What Could Happen.
What I Wouldn't Do.
Lavater, Louis (1867–1953)
Barrier, The.
Lavender, Bill
Note to Skip on Max and Maxine, A.
Pentacl, *sels*.
Lavieri, Jon
Autobiography of John Doe, The.
Lavut, Evgeniya (b. 1972)
About Love.
In the body of the town I'm a pupil.
Lawless, Emily (1845–1913)
After Aughrim.
In Spain.
Lawrence, Anthony (b. 1957)
Cro-Kill.
Fencing.
Goanna.
Robert Penn Warren's Book.
Lawrence, Arthur H. (*fl.* 1897)
Song of the Wheel, A.
Lawrence, D. H. (David Herbert) (1885–1930)
After the Opera.
Andraitx—Pomegranate Flowers.
Argonauts, The.
Aware.
Bare Almond-Trees.
Bare Fig-trees.
Bavarian Gentians.
Blue Jay, The.
Body of God, The.
Bombardment.
Bride, The.
Broadcasting to the G.B.P.
Butterfly.
Cherry Robbers.
Collier's Wife, The.
Cypresses.
Discord in Childhood.
Drained Cup, The.
Elemental.
Eloi, Eloi, Lama Sabachthani?
End of Another Home Holiday.
English Are So Nice!, The.
Enkindled Spring, The.
Evening Land, The.
Fight! O My Young Men.
Figs.
Gloire de Dijon.
Grasshopper Is a Burden.
Green.
Hands of God, The.
Healing.
Hills, The.
History.
How Beastly the Bourgeois Is.
Humming-Bird.
Hymn to Priapus.
I Am in a Novel.

In Trouble and Shame.
Innocent England.
Intimates.
Kisses in the Train.
Last Lesson of the Afternoon.
Let There Be Light!
Lightning.
Little Fish.
Living Quetzalcoatl, The.
Love On the Farm.
Love Thy Neighbour.
Lui et Elle.
Maximus.
Medlars and Sorb-Apples.
Middle of the World.
Morning Work.
Mosquito Knows, The.
Mosquito, The.
Mountain Lion.
Mystic.
O! Start a Revolution.
Paradise Re-entered.
Pax.
Piano.
Piano, The.
Race and Battle.
Red Geranium and Godly Mignonette.
Root of Our Evil, The.
St. Matthew, sel.
Self-Protection.
Ship of Death, The ("Now it is autumn and the
    falling fruit.").
Sicilian Cyclamens.
Snake.
Song of a Man Who Has Come Through.
Song of a Man Who Has Come Through, sels.
Sorrow.
Southern Night.
Spring Morning.
Storm in the Black Forest.
Suburbs on a Hazy Day.
Suspense.
Tabernacle.
Things Made by Iron.
Thought.
To Women, as Far as I'm Concerned.
Tommies in the Train.
Tortoise Shout.
Tortoise-Shell.
Trees in the Garden.
Twilight.
Wedding Morn.
Whales Weep Not!
When I Read Shakespeare.
When Wilt Thou Teach the People?
Whether or Not.
White Blossom, A.
Wild Common, The.
Winter's Tale, A.
Work.
Worm Either Way.
You.
Young Wife, A.
Youth Mowing, A.

Lawrence, Jack (b. 1912)
All or Nothing at All.
Foolin' Myself.
Linda.
Other Half of Me, The.
Sleepy Lagoon.
Tenderly.
What's Your Story, Morning Glory.

Lawrence, Philippa
Hit Men, The.

Lawson, Henry (1867–1922)
English Queen, The.
Men Who Come Behind, The.
When Your Pants Begin to Go.

Lawson, Mrs. David See Ridge, Lola

Lax, Robert (b. 1915)
Alley Violinist.

Layamon (fl. c.1200)
Brut, The, sels.

Layton, Irving (b. 1912)
Aubade, An.

Berry Picking.
Birth of Tragedy, The.
Black Huntsmen, The.
Bull Calf, The.
Butterfly on Rock.
Cain.
Cold Green Element, The.
Fertile Muck, The.
From Colony to Nation.
Keine Lazarovitch, 1870-1959.
Party at Hydra.
Song for Naomi.
Street Funeral.
Tall Man Executes a Jig, A.

Layzer, Robert (b. 1931)
Lawn Roller, The.

Lazar, David
My Gun Has So Many Places to Hide.

Lazard, Naomi
In Answer to Your Query.
Ordinance on Arrival.

Lazarus, Emma (1849–87)
City Visions.
Cranes of Ibycus, The.
Crowing of the Red Cock, The.
Echoes.
1492.
How Long?
In Exile.
In the Jewish Synagogue at Newport.
Long Island Sound.
New Colossus, The.
Phantasies (After Robert Schumann), sels.
South, The.
Success.
Venus of the Louvre.

Lazer, Hank
Days, sels.
New Spirit, The, sels.

Lazić, Radmila (b. 1949)
I'll Be a Wicked Old Woman.
Pleasures.

Lazutkina, Elena (b. 1975)
I stand and inspect the phenomena drawn up.
Ruined so many romances.
Wind's mane, The.

Le Brun, Annie (b. 1942)
Des fêtes.
Des rites.
Festivals.
Rituals.

Le Fanu, Joseph Sheridan (1814–73)
Drunkard's Address to a Bottle of Whiskey, A.

Le Gallienne, Richard (1866–1947)
Beauty Accurst.
Library in a Garden, A.
Song: "She's somewhere in the sunlight
    strong."

Le Guin, Ursula K. (b. 1929)
At the Party.
Child on the Shore, The.
Coming of Age, sels.
For CALYX.
His Daughter.
Riding on the Coast Starlight.

Le Ngoc Hiep (1944–70)
I Am Sad.

Lễ, Nguyễn Thú' See Thế Lữ'

Le Pan, Douglas (b. 1914)
Country without a Mythology, A.
Coureurs de Bois.
Incident, An.

Le Roy, Jean
Instant of Clearness.

Le Sueur, Meridel (b. 1900)
Behold This and Always Love It.

Lễ Thánh–tông, (King) (1442–97)
Stick and Hat.
Stone Dog, The.

Lea, Sydney
At the Flyfisher's Shack.
Clouded Evening, Late September.
Do not trust in these deceptive words.
Feud, The.

Fish Pond, The [1993] ("Not full of fish—
    that's imprecise—but full.").
Green Room, The.
Hundred Himalayas, A.
Insomnia: The Distances.
Late Season.
One White Face in the Place, The.
Paternity.
Prospect.
Still dark when we file like children out on the
    turf.
Telescope.
Tempted by the Classical on Returning from
    the Store at Twenty Below Zero.
Wrong Way Will Haunt You, The.

"Leadbelly" (Huddie Ledbetter)
Take this Hammer.

Leader, Mary
Her Door.
Impetus.
Madrigal: "How the tenor warbles in April!"
Portrait.
Skin.

Leahy, Anna (b. 1965)
History of Air Travel, A.

Leapor, Mary (1722–46)
Epistle of Deborah Dough, The.
Epistle to a Lady, An.
Essay on Friendship, sel.
Essay on Woman, An.
Headache, The.
Mira's Will.
On Winter.
Sacrifice: An Epistle to Celia, The.
Strephon to Celia. A Modern Love-Letter.

Lear, Edward (1812–88)
Calico Pie.
Children of the Owl and the Pussy-Cat, The.
Cold Are the Crabs.
Dong with a Luminous Nose, The.
How Pleasant to Know Mr. Lear.
Incidents in the Life of My Uncle Arly.
Jumblies, The.
Limerick: "There was a Young Lady of
    Parma."
Limerick: "There was a young lady of
    Portugal."
Limerick: "There was a young person whose
    history."
Limerick: "There was an old lady of Chertsey."
Limerick: "There was an old Lady of
    Winchelsea."
Limerick: "There was an old man of
    Thermopylae."
Limerick: "There was an old man of
    Toulouse."
Limerick: "There was an Old Man of
    Whitehaven."
Limerick: "There was an Old Man on some
    rocks."
Limerick: "There was an old man who
    screamed out."
Limerick: "There was an Old Man who
    supposed."
Limerick: "There was an old man whose
    despair."
Limerick: "There was an Old Person of
    Basing."
Limerick: "There was an old person of Bow."
O dear! How disgusting is life!
Owl and the Pussy-Cat [or Pussycat], The.
Pelican Chorus, The.
Table and the Chair, The.
There Was an Old Man who Forgot.
There Was an Old Man With a Beard.

Lechlitner, Ruth (b. 1901)
Kansas Boy.

Lecky, William E. H. (1838–1903)
Decline of Love, The.

Leconte de Lisle, Charles Marie René (1818–94)
Jaguar's Dream, The.
Venus de Milo.

Ledbetter, Huddie See Leadbelly

Lederer, Katherine (b. 1972)
Dream of Mimesis, A.

In Las Vegas.
Sympathy and Envy.
Ledwidge, Francis (1891–1917)
Meeting, The: "She'll meet me with the gate
   thrown wide."
Spring Love.
Wife of Llew, The.
Lee, Alice
Confession.
Lee, Ann (*fl.* 1660s)
On the Returne of King Charles 2nd.
Lee, Bert *See* Weston, R. P.
Lee, Charles (1870–1956)
Proem: "Bad Verse I sing, and since 'twere
   best, I deem."
Lee, David
Benediction.
Driving and Drinking, *sel.*
First Turtle.
For Jan, with Love.
Hired Hand.
Jan's Birthday.
Lazy.
Loading a Boar.
Tuesday Morning, Loading Pigs.
Lee, Dennis (b. 1939)
Billy Batter.
Civil Elegies, *sels.*
Coat, The.
Coming of Teddy Bears, The.
Dickery Dean.
1838.
I Eat Kids Yum Yum!
Last Cry of the Damp Fly, The.
On a Kazoo.
Un, *sel.*
You Too Lie down.
Lee, Don L. *See* Madhubuti, Haki R.
Lee, Eleanor Percy (1820–49)
Forests and Caverns.
Sun-Struck Eagle, The.
Lee-Hamilton, Eugene (1845–1907)
Sunken Gold.
What the Sonnet Is.
Lee, James R.
Stranger at Home.
Lee, Joseph (1862–1937?)
German Prisoners.
Lee, Joyce (b. 1913)
Firebell for Peace.
My Father's Country.
Lee, Kim C. (b. 1967)
Haiku #3.
On South Africa.
Lee, Laurie (1914–97)
Christmas Landscape.
Moment of War, A.
Lee, Li-Young (b. 1957)
Become Becoming.
Between Seasons.
City in Which I Love You, The.
Cleaving, The, *sel.*
Dreaming of Hair.
Early in the Morning.
Eating Alone.
Eating Together.
Eternal Son, The.
From Blossoms.
Gift, The: "To pull the metal splinter from my
   palm."
I Ask My Mother to Sing.
Interrogation, The.
Irises.
Little Father.
Little Round.
Mnemonic.
My Indigo.
Nativity.
Night Mirror.
Out of Hiding.
Persimmons.
Pillow.
Story, A.
Table in the Wilderness, A.

Tearing the Page.
This Hour and What Is Dead.
This Room and Everything in It.
Visions and Interpetations.
Weight of Sweetness, The.
Words for Worry.
You Must Sing.
Lee, Malka (1904–76)
Child, You New Man.
Kiss, A.
Negro on the Subway.
Lee, Nathaniel (1653?–92)
Rival Queens; or, Alexander the Great, The,
   sel.
Lee, Peggy (b. 1920)
I Don't Know Enough About You.
I Love Being Here with You.
I'm Gonna Go Fishin.'
It's a Good Day.
Mañana (Is Soon Enough for Me).
That's My Style.
Lee, Wendy
Lovers' Duet.
Sex Has a Way.
Lee, Wil'um
Aunt Martha.
Simple Like That.
Leeflang, Ed (b. 1929)
1945.
Leeke, Kiamsha Madelyn
October Death.
Lees, Gene (b. 1928)
Right to Love, The.
Waltz for Debby.
Lees, Joseph (1748–1824)
Jone o' Grinfilt.
Lefevre, Adam
Halftime.
LeFlore, Shirley Bradley
Dream/Eaters.
Rayboy Blk & Bluz.
This Poem.
Lefroy, Edward Cracroft (1855–91)
Idler Listening to Socrates Discussing
   Philosophy with His Boy-Friends, An.
Palaestral Study, A.
Leftwich, Jim
Eleusis.
Legaré, James Matthew (1823–59)
Tallulah.
To a Lily.
Léger, Alexis Saint-Léger *See* Perse, St.-John
Leggott, Michele
Dark Torch.
Omphalos.
Songs of Good Hope, The.
Thoroughfares Await Them.
Legiardi-Laura, Roland
Trickster Rabbit.
Legris, Sylvia
Negative Garden, *sels.*
Lehman, David (b. 1948)
Alternative to Speech, An.
Difference Between Pepsi and Coke, The.
Drowning, The.
First Offense.
Greenhouses and Gardens.
January 20.
June 11.
November 19.
On the Nature of Desire.
One Size Fits All: a Critical Essay.
Prophet's Lantern, The.
9/14/01.
9/15/01.
Towards the Vanishing Point.
World Trade Center, The.
Lehmann, Geoffrey (b. 1940)
Harold's Walk.
Night Flower.
Poem for Maurice O'Shea, A.
Pope Alexander VI.
Roses, *sels.*

Ross's Poems, *sel.*
Lehrer, Tom (b. 1928)
Alma.
Elements, The.
Wernher von Braun.
Leiber, Jerry *and* **Michael E. Stoller**
Searchin.'
Leifso, Brenda (b. 1977)
What Do You Want?
Leigh, Carolyn (1926–83)
Best Is Yet to Come, The.
Hey, Look Me Over.
How Little We Know (How Little It Matters).
I Walk a Little Faster.
It Amazes Me!
I've Got Your Number.
Real Live Girl.
Rules of the Road, The.
When in Rome (I Do As the Romans Do).
Witchcraft.
You Fascinate Me So.
Young at Heart.
Leigh, Helen (*fl.* 1788, d. c.1795)
Lady and the Doctor, The.
Natural Child, The.
Leigh, Richard (1649?–1728)
Greatness in Little.
On a Fair Lady, Looking in the Glass.
Leighton, Taigen Dan
All of Us So Close to Buddha.
Giving Buddha to all beings is giving to
   oneself.
Leiris, Michel (1901–90)
Avare.
Maldonne.
Misdeal.
Miserly.
Vertical.
Vertical.
Leiter, Deborah
Midsummer's Eve.
Leithauser, Brad (b. 1953)
At an Island Farm.
Buried Graves, The.
Ghost of a Ghost, The.
Haunted, The.
In a Japanese Moss Garden.
In Minako Wada's House.
Mosquito, A.
Old Bachelor Brother.
Leivaditis, Tasos (b. 1922)
Eternal Dialogue.
Leivick, H. (Leivick Halpern) (1888–1962)
Lament at Night.
Lejeune, Claire (b. 1926)
Death, I Speak of It.
Illettrée.
Illiterate.
Mort, j'en parle, La.
Où donc.
So Where.
**Leland, Charles Godfrey ("Hans Breitman")
   (1824–1903)**
Ballad by Hans Breitmann.
Breitmann in Paris.
Hans Breitmann as a Politician, *sel.*
Hans Breitmann's Party [*or* Barty].
Wein Geist.
Lem, Carol
California Dreaming.
Office Hour.
So Now You're Chicana.
Temple City Blvd. and Ellis Ln.
Lemm, Richard (b. 1946)
Metamorphosis.
My Class Draws a Blank on Robbie Burns.
Perfect Circle.
Spark.
Lenfestey, James P.
Landing.
L'Engle, Madeleine (b. 1918)
Lines Scribbled on an Envelope.
Risk of Birth, The.
Three Songs of Mary, *sels.*

Lenier, Sue (b. 1957)
Finale.

Lenk, Elisabeth
Automatic Text for Anne Ethuin.

Lennon, John (1940–80)
Fat Budgie, The.

Lennox, Charlotte (1729?–1804)
Ardelia to Flavia, an Epistle.
Art of Coquetry, The, *sels.*

Lenski, Hayim (1905–41)
Day turns to evening on the lake.
Incredible splendour—ethereal, delicate!
Light, my light, who commanded, 'Disappear!
Lightly a slight shadow floats on the March
  snows.
Moon's brightness turns a freezing blue, The.
Near the Mill.
There broke into my cell last night.
Wormwood has enchanted me completely.

Lenski, Lois (1893–1974)
Sing a Song of People.

Lenton, Mrs. Babington *See* Pope, Jessie

Leon, Elizabeth Jane (1582–1612)
On the Death of the Noble and Gentle Woman,
  Lady Joanna Kelley.
On the Flooding of Prague, which Arose from
  Continuous Rain in the Year 1596.
On the Second Tristia of Ovid.
To the Reader.

Leon, Raphael de (*fl.* 1920s–1930s)
Have you not heard the gossip and the rumour
  going around.

Leonard, Henry Charles (b. 1836)
Lost Friend, A.

Leonard, Tom (b. 1944)
Before the 1820 rising in the West of Scotland
  a network of.
Evidence, The.
Fathers and Sons.
Feed Ma Lamz.
Four of the Belt.
Good Thief, The.
Jist Ti Let Yi No.
100 Differences Between Poetry and Prose.
Opting for Early Retirement.
Song: "Yi surta."
Unrelated Incidents, *sels.*

Leonard, William Ellery (1876–1944)
Two Lives, *sels.*

Leong, Russell (b. 1950)
Aerogrammes, *sels.*
Threads.
What Does the Body Dream at Rest?

Leonidas of Tarentum (c.290–c.220 B.C.)
Forever brigands and pirates, the Cretans are
  never just.
Get out of my hut, you stealthy vermin!
  Leonidas.'
Gloomy minister of Hades who sail this
  stream.
His ball, beautiful leaved, and his noisy
  boxwood rattle.
If the tombstone placed over me is small to see
  and close.
Old Platthis often thrust away her morning's
  sleep.
Theris, the old man who lived by his fish traps.
Theris, thrice-old, who got his living from.
Thundering sea, why in savage storm did you
  plunge.
To Gluttony and Guzzling, that fastidious
  gourmet.
To Pallas, Theris, cunning of hand, dedicated.
Wallet, the hide of a goat, tough and untanned,
  a stick, A.
Whoever then are you? Whose wretched bones
  are these.

Leonidov, Rumen (b. 1953)
Another Stone in the Swamp.
Misery.
Mouths of the people eating their lunch, The.
Stone in the Swamp, A.

Leopardi, Giacomo (1798–1837)
Antistrophe.

Broom, The; or, The Flower of the Desert, *sel.*
Infinite, The.
Remembering Leopardi's Moon.
Saturday Night in the Village.
To Himself.
To Sylvia.
Village Saturday, The.

Lepson, Ruth
October 7, 1994.
They Were Gliding.

Lermontov, Mikhail Yuryevich (1814–41)
Borodino.
Dream.

Lerner, Alan Jay (1918–86)
Almost Like Being in Love.
Camelot.
Come Back to Me.
Heather on the Hill, The.
Hymn to Him, A.
I Could Have Danced All Night.
I Left My Hat in Haiti.
I Remember It Well.
If Ever I Would Leave You.
I'm Glad I'm Not Young Any More.
I've Grown Accustomed to Her Face.
On a Clear Day You Can See Forever.
On the Street Where You Live.
Paris Is Paris Again.
Rain in Spain, The.
Wouldn't It Be Luverly?

Lerner, Sammy
Is It True What They Say About Dixie?
Spanish Jake.

Lersch, Heinrich (1889–1936)
Brothers.

Lesley [or Leslie or Lesly], George (d. 1701)
Fire and Brimstone; or, The Destruction of
  Sodom, *sel.*

Leslie, Edgar
Among My Souvenirs.
For Me and My Gal.
Kansas City Kitty.
Little Bit Independent, A.
T'ain't No Sin to Dance Around in Your
  Bones.

Leslie, Kenneth (1892–1974)
By Stubborn Stars, *sels.*

Leslie, Sir Shane (1886–1971)
Muckish Mountain (The Pig's Back).

Lesser, Rika (b. 1953)
Translation.

Leto, Denise Nico
Anna Magnani at the Castro.
For Talking.
Mary Morelle Show, The.

Leto, Gabriella (b. 1930)
Among Myths and Specters of the Future.
Here Where the Path.
If a Privileged Light.
Indeed You Came Home Too Late.
It Wasn't the Love of Others or Mine.
Love Dream Verse.
Ship Waits in the Harbor, The.
Steep Acquisitions Motionless Fears.
There Is Not and There Will Never Be So
  Much.
What is Left and by Now Reduced to Little.

Letters, Francis (1897–1964)
Inglorious Milton, The.

Levchev, Lyubomir
Cronies.
Dénouement.
Front Line.
Rooftops.
Weasel.

Levchev, Vladimir (b. 1960)
Athens.
Beacon.
Blue Pond at Berkovitsa.
Four Seekers of the Great Metaphor.

Levertov, Denise (1923–97)
Abel's Bride.
About Marriage.
Ache of Marriage, The.

Acolyte, The.
Advent 1966.
After "Mindwalk"
Age of Terror.
Another Revenant.
Arctic Spring.
Aware.
Caedmon.
Calvary Path, A.
Cancion: "When I am the sky."
Celebration.
Change, The.
Christmas 1944.
Closed World, The.
Clouds.
Come into Animal Presence.
Contraband.
Crack, The.
Day the Audience Walked Out on Me, and
  Why, The.
Dead Butterfly, The.
Death in Mexico.
Divorcing.
Dog of Art, The.
Don't You Hear that Whistle Blowin.'
Embracing the Multipede, *sel.*
Eros.
Eros at Temple Stream.
Everything That Acts Is Actual.
Eye Mask.
February Evening in Boston, 1971.
February Evening in New York.
Flickering Mind.
For Those Whom the Gods Love Less.
Fragrance of Life, Odor of Death.
Gathered at the River.
Goddess, The.
Goodbye to Tolerance.
Gypsy's Window, The.
Hymn, The.
Hymn to Eros.
Hypocrite Women.
I Learned That Her Name Was Proverb.
Ikon: The Harrowing of Hell.
Illustration, The [—a Footnote].
Illustrious Ancestors.
In California During the Gulf War.
In Mind.
In Thai Binh (Peace) Province.
Intrusion.
Invocation: "Silent, about-to-be-parted-from
  house."
Jacob's Ladder, The.
Last Night's Dream.
Laying the Dust.
Life at War.
Life of Art, The.
Living.
Losing Track.
Love Poem: "What you give me is."
Love Song: "Your beauty, which I lost sight of
  once."
Malice of Innocence, The.
Man Wearing Bird.
Matins.
Métier of Blossoming, The.
Midnight Gladness.
Mutes, The.
Note to Olga (1966), A.
Novel, The.
O Taste and See.
Oblique Prayer.
October.
Olga Poems, *sel.*
On a Theme from Julian's Chapter 20.
One December Night.
Our Bodies.
Overland to the Islands.
People at Night.
Perhaps No Poem at All But All I Can Say and
  I Cannot Be Silent.
Pleasures.
Poem Unwritten, The.
Poet and Person.
Prisoners.
Protesting at the Nuclear Test Site.

Quest, The.
Reminder, The.
Re-Rooting.
St. Peter and the Angel.
Salvator Mundi: Via Crucis.
Scenes from the Life of the Peppertrees.
Scraps of moon.
Sea's Wash in the Hollow of the Heart, The.
Secret, The.
Seeing for a Moment.
September 1961.
Showings, The: Lady Julian of Norwich, 1342-
  1416, sels.
Six Variations, sel.
Son, The.
Song for Ishtar.
Staying Alive, sels.
Stele (1-2 c. B.C.).
Stepping Westward.
Task, The.
Tenebrae.
Terror.
This Day.
Time Past, A.
To Rilke.
To the Muse.
To the Snake.
Tree Telling of Orpheus, A.
Triple Feature.
Uncertain Oneiromancy.
Variation and Reflection on a Theme by Rilke
  (The Book of Hours, Book 1, Poem 7).
Variation on a Theme by Rilke.
Watching "Dark Circle."
Wavering.
Wedding-Ring.
Weeping Woman.
What Were They Like?
Where Is the Angel?
Williams: An Essay.
Wings, The.
Witness.
Woman Alone, A.
Woman Meets an Old Lover, A.
World Outside, The.
Wren, A.

Levi, Jan Heller (b. 1954)
Not Bad, Dad, Not Bad.
Tuscarora.

Levi, Peter (b. 1931)
New Year's Eve Poem 1965.

Levi, Primo (1919–87)
Annunciation.
Buna.
Delilah.
For Adolf Eichmann.
Reveille.
Samson.
Shemà.
Survivor, The.
Voices.

Levin, Dana (b. 1965)
Ars Poetica: "Six monarch butterfly cocoons."
Ars Poetica (the idea).
Ars Poetica: "This hush, my pollen—the
  ordinary grace in the buds."
Chill Core.
Cinema Verité.
Field.
Glass Heart.
Marvelous Father.
Red Water.
Wind.

Levin, Phillis (b. 1954)
Blizzard, The: "Now that the worst is over,
  they predict."
Citizens and Sky.
Dark Horse.
Lost Bee, The.
Meeting of Friends, A.
Night Coach.
Planting Roses.
Shadow Returns, The.
Third Day, The.

Levin, Shaun
With Your Mother in a Café.

Levine, Anne-Marie
Four November 9ths.

Levine, Jeffrey
Dawn, with Cardinals.

Levine, Mark (b. 1965)
Everybody.
Wedding Day.
Work Song.

Levine, Philip (b. 1928)
And the Trains Go On.
Angel Butcher.
Animals Are Passing from Our Lives.
Baby Villon.
Belief.
Belle Isle, 1949.
Clouds above the Sea.
Coming Home, Detroit, 1968.
Death of Saul, The.
Detroit, Tomorrow.
Drum: Leo's Tool & Die, 1950.
Every Blessed Day.
Fear and Fame.
Fox, The.
Genius: "Two old dancing shoes my
  grandfather."
Horse, The: "They spoke of the horse alive."
I Caught a Glimpse.
I Sing the Body Electric.
I Was Born in Lucerne.
Keep Talking.
Later Still.
Life Ahead, The.
Listen Carefully.
My Father with Cigarette Twelve Years Before
  the Nazis Could Break His Heart.
Never Before.
New Days for Old, Old Days for New.
New Year's Eve, in Hospital.
Old Testament, The.
On a Drawing by Flavio.
On My Own.
On the Birth of Good and Evil During the
  Long Winter of '28.
On the Murder of Lieutenant José del Castillo
  by the Falangist Bravo Martinez, July 12,
  1936.
Poem of Chalk, The.
Poem of Flight, The.
Rain Downriver.
Red Dust.
Red Shirt, The.
Return, The: "All afternoon my father drove
  the country roads."
Right Cross, The.
Salami.
Sea We Read About, The.
Sierra Kid.
Simple Truth, The.
Sleepless Night, A.
Smoke.
Snow: "Today the snow is drifting."
Soloing.
Starlight.
Sweet Will.
They Feed They Lion.
To a Child Trapped in a Barber Shop.
Travelling Music.
28.
Two, The.
Waking in March.
Water's Chant, The.
What Work Is.
You Can Have It.
Zaydee.

Levis, Larry (b. 1946)
Anastasia and Sandman.
At the Grave of My Guardian Angel: St. Louis
  Cemetery, New Orleans.
Caravaggio: Swirl and Vortex.
Cry, The: "Then, everything slept."
Decrescendo.
Edward Hopper, "Hotel Room," 1931.
Elegy with a Bridle in Its Hand.

Elegy with a Chimneysweep Falling Inside It.
Elegy with a Thimbleful of Water in the Cage.
Family Romance.
Morning After My Death, The.
1974: My Story in a Late Style of Fire.
Oldest Living Thing in L.A., The.
Photograph: Migrant Worker, Parlier,
  California, 1967.
Picking Grapes in an Abandoned Vineyard.
Poem You Asked For, The.
Poet at Seventeen, The.
Rhododendrons.
Sensationalism.
There Are Two Worlds.
Those Graves in Rome.
Two Variations on a Theme by Kobayashi.
Whitman.
Widening Spell of the Leaves, The.
Winter Stars.

Levison, Brian (b. 1941)
Eighth Symphony Interruptus.

Levitt, Peter (b. 1946)
Before falling to the scythe.
Bell, The.
Four hundred hairs of a brush.
It's easy to die.
Measure, The.
Mother, you were born.
My robe hangs in the garden.
No life but this one.
On my altar.
Though she is deaf.
Walking the path.
Watermelon and Zen students.
Where you are going.
Within each petal.

Levy, Amy (1861–89)
At a Dinner Party.
Ballad of Religion and Marriage, A.
Ballade of an Omnibus.
Cambridge in the Long.
Captivity.
Christopher Found.
Cross-Road Epitaph, A.
Epitaph: "This is the end of him, here he lies."
Felo de Se.
First Extra, The.
In the Mile End Road.
London in July.
London Plane-Tree, A.
London Poets.
Magdalen.
March Day in London, A.
Minor Poet, A.
Oh, Is It Love?
Old House, The.
On the Threshold.
Philosophy.
Reminiscence, A.
Run to Death.
Sequel to "A Reminiscence," The.
Sinfonia Eroica.
Straw in the Street.
To Lallie.
To Vernon Lee.
Twilight.

Levy, Diane
Honey.

Levy, Elvira
Gradually.
It Is Still Early.

Levy, Newman (1888–1966)
Carmen.
Pelleas and Melisande.
Rigoletto.
Tannhauser.

Lewis, Alun (1915–44)
All Day It Has Rained.
Autumn, 1939.
Christmas Holiday.
Dawn on the East Coast.
Easter at Christmas.
Goodbye.
In Hospital: Poona (1).
Infantry.

Jungle, The, *sel.*
Karanje Village.
Mahratta Ghats, The.
Mountain over Aberdare, The.
Peasants, The.
Post-Script: for Gweno.
Raiders' Dawn.
Sentry, The.
Song (On Seeing Dead Bodies Floating Off the Cape).
To a Comrade in Arms.
To Edward Thomas.
Unknown Soldier, The.

Lewis, Clive Staples (1898–1963)
After Prayers, Lie Cold.
Apologist's Evening Prayer, The.
Ballade of Dead Gentlemen.
Epitaph, An: "Erected by her sorrowing brothers."
Late Passenger, The.
Nativity, The.
On a Theme from Nicolas of Cusa.
Prayer: "Master, they say that when I seem."
Reason.
Stephen to Lazarus.

Lewis, Dominic Bevan Wyndham ("Timothy Shy") (1891–1969)
Downland Crisis, A, *sel.*
If So the Man You Are.
Lost Chord, The.
Pastoral: "The Lumpish trollop!."
Shot at Random, A.

Lewis, Eiluned (1900–79)
We Who Were Born.

Lewis, Emyr (b. 1957)
Dawn, *sels.*
Drivel.
Freedom, *sels.*
Hayes, The.
London, 1792.
M4.
Once-in-a-Lifetime, Never-to-Be-Repeated, A.
Revolution, *sel.*
Taliesin.

Lewis, Gwyneth (b. 1959)
Beginning to Forget.
Drew trips over his shadow by the pool.
Farmer's Evidence, The.
Flaggy Shore, The.
Flyover Elegies.
Hedge, The.
Her End.
Herod's Palace.
In the Open Air.
Interview with the Poet.
It looks like she's drowning.
Language Murderer, The, *sels.*
Language's Will and Testament, The.
Last Minutes, The.
Last suppers, I fancy, are always wide-screen.
Mapmaker's Song, The.
Ménage à Trois.
'No' Madonnas, The.
One day, feeling hungry.
Parables & Faxes, *sels.*
Pentecost.
Poet Fishing, The.
Poet's Confession, A.
Ritual.
Second time the comet swung by, The.
Six Poems on Nothing.
Strip-Tease.
Sunday Park.
There are great advantages to having been dead.
Thousands arrive when a bird's about to fly.
Walking with the God.
Watch, The.
Welsh Espionage, *sels.*
What is her vanishing point?
White Horse.
Wholeness, *sels.*
Woods: "Midwinter and this beech wood's mind."

Lewis, Howell Elvet [*or* Elfed] (1860–1953)
Life's Morning.

Lewis, J. Patrick (b. 1942)
Holding the Holy Card.
How to Tell a Camel.
Stories.

Lewis, Janet (b. 1889)
Ancient Ones, The: Betátakin.
At Carmel Highlands.
For the Father of Sandro Gulotta.
Garden Note I, Los Altos.
Garden Note II, March.
Girl Help.
Grandmother Remembers, A.
Helen Grown Old.
Indians in the Woods, The.
Reader, The.
Remembered Morning.
Time and Music.
Winter Garden.

Lewis, Jenny
I'm not in court to be judged.

Lewis, Lisa (b. 1956)
February.
May Mowing Clover.
Responsibility.
Tracy and Joe.

Lewis, Marcela (b. 1920)
Beiguga Luma Inaruni.

Lewis, Matthew Gregory ("Monk" Lewis) (1775–1818)
Alonzo the Brave and the Fair Imogine.

Lewis, Melvin E.
Gullah Women.
Hearts.
My Mother.

Lewis, Naomi
Footprint on the Air, A.

Lewis, Philip
A Si Wha New Belize.
Dis Da Me.

Lewis, Sam M. (1885–1959)
Dinah.
Five Foot Two, Eyes of Blue (Has Anybody Seen My Girl?).
For All We Know.
How 'Ya Gonna Keep 'Em Down on the Farm? (After They've Seen Paree).
I Wonder Why She Kept on Saying "Si-Si-Si-Si-Senor."
I'm Sitting on Top of the World.
Just Friends.
Rock-a-Bye Your Baby with a Dixie Melody.
Street of Dreams.

Lewis, Saunders (1893–1985)
Ascension Thursday.
Ascension Thursday.
Chance Child.
Deluge, 1939, The.
Deluge 1939, The.
Et Homo Factus Est. Crucifixus.
Mary Magdalen.
Mary Magdalene.
Pine, The.
Prayer at the End.
Scene in a Café.
To the Good Thief.
Vineyard Place in My Care, A.

Lewis, William Henry
Some Solace, Some Yearning.
To the People of a Small Town in Ohio, Who As I Approach Them on the Street, Are Afraid That This Black Man Is Going to Do Them Harm.

Ley, Anna Norman (b. before 1620, d. 1641)
Upon a Booke Written at the Beginning of the Parliament 1640.
Upon the Necessity and Benefite of Learning Written in the Beginning of a Common Place Booke Belonging to W. B. a Young Scholler.

Lezama Lima, José (1910–76)
Ah, That You Escape.
Call of the Desirous.

Dark Meadow Invites Me, A.
Fragments of the Night, The.
Portrait of José Cemí.
Rhapsody for the Mule.

Li Chih-yi (*fl.* 1071)
Tune: "The Diviner."

Li Ching (916–61)
Sorrow for Spring.
West Wind Ferries Grief, The.

Li Ch'ing-chao (1084–1151)
Banana Trees.
Boat of Stars.
Butterflies Love Flowers.
End to Spring, An.
Fading Plum Blossoms.
"Fisherman's Honor," The.
Hopelessness.
Long Melancholy Tune, A.
Lyric to the Tune "Immortal by the River."
On Spring.
Plum Blossoms.
Sorrow of Departure.
Spring at Wu Ling.
Spring Fades.
To the Tune: Bodhisattva's Headdress.
To the Tune "Clear Peace Happiness."
To the Tune: Drunk in Flower Shadows.
To the Tune: Eternal Joy.
To the Tune: Happiness Approaches.
To the Tune: Lips Painted Red.
To the Tune: Magnolia Blossoms.
To the Tune: Partridge Sky.
To the Tune: Partridge Sky.
To the Tune: Sands of the Washing Stream.
To the Tune "The Bodhisattva's Headdress."
To the Tune "You Move in Fragrance."
Tune: "Airing Inmost Feelings."
Tune: "Dream Song."
Tune: "Fisherman's Pride."
Tune: "Joy of Eternal Union."
Tune: "Magnolia Flowers."
Tune: "On the Trail of Sweet Incense."
Tune: "Partridge Sky."
Tune: "Rouged Lips."
Tune: Spring at Wu Ling.
Tune: "The Charm of a Maiden Singer;" Spring Thoughts.
Washing Stream, The.
Written by Chance.
Written on the Seventh Day of the Seventh Month.

Li Cunxu, Emperor (885–926)
Deep Peach Glades.

Li Ho (791–817)
Arrowhead from the Ancient Battlefield of Ch'ang-p'ing, An.
At Ch'ang-ku, Reading: To Show to My Man Pa.
Chang'gu: A Poem Written on the Twenty-Seventh Day of the Fifth Month.
Cold in the North (After Yueh-Fu).
Country Road, A.
Days of Rain.
Drinking All Night, Sleeping All Day.
Farewell Song of Magic Strings.
Flying Light.
Grave of Little Su, The.
High the Mount of Wu.
King Ch'in Drinks Wine.
King of Ch'in Drinks Wine, The.
Lament for a Courtesan.
Life at the Capital.
Lute Player, The.
Magic Strings.
Melancholic.
My Man Pa Replies.
On and On: An Ancient Song (Yueh-Fu).
Ravine on a Cold Evening.
Song: A Lovely Girl Combing Her Hair.
Song: Dragons at Midnight.
Song: Green Water, Singing Girl.
Song of an Arrowhead from Changping.
Song of the Magic Strings.
Under the Walls of Ping City.

Li Hsun (855–930)
To the Tune: The Wine Spring: "Eternal autumn rain—evening sounds."
To the Tune: The Wine Spring: "Rain falls on fallen flowers."

Li K'ai-hsien (1502–68)
Earthquake, *sel.*
On the Cold Food Festival, Entertaining at the Southern Estate—the Guests Were Li Chiu-ho, Ma Nan-yeh, Wei Tung-kao, Li Hu-ch'uan, Huang K'ung-ts'un, Li Lung-t'ang, and Hu Hu-shan.
Parable, A.
Sent to the Master Physician, "Almond Orchard" Shih.
Thanking Doctor Jen.
Watching the Swinging, *sel.*

Li Kuang-t'ien (1906–68)
Dead Turk, A.

Li Mi-an (*fl.* 16th cent.?)
Half-and-Half Song, The.

Li Po (701–62)
Abandon.
About Tu Fu.
Ancient Air.
Ancient Airs.
Ascend the Phoenix Terrace.
At Ch'ang-men Palace.
Autumn Cove.
Autumn Lines.
Awakening from Drunkenness on a Spring Day.
Ballad of Long Bank, The.
Barbarian pass is filled with windblown sand, The.
Best of Life Is But, The.
Birds have Vanished, The.
Blue Water.
Boating Song.
Bring On the Wine.
Calm Night Thought.
Ch'ang-Kan Village Song.
City of Choan, The.
Climbing Xie Tiao's North Tower at Xuan in Autumn.
Conversation among the Mountains.
Conversations in the Mountains.
Crossing Ching-Men to See a Friend Off.
Crows at Dusk.
Drinking Alone in Moonlight.
Drinking Alone in the Moonlight.
Drinking Alone in the Moonlight.
Drinking Alone under Moonlight.
Drinking Alone with the Moon.
Drinking Alone with the Moon.
Drinking in the Mountains with a Recluse.
Drinking Together.
Drinking Wine with a Mountain Hermit.
Drinking with a Friend, Among the Mountains.
Early Departure from White Emperor Fortress.
En Bateau.
Exile's Letter.
Fall River Song.
Fall River Song.
Farewell Dinner for My Uncle Li Yun, the Collator, at Xie Tiao's Tower in Xuan Prefecture.
Farewell to Yin Shu.
Fighting on the South Frontier.
Fighting South of the Wall.
Flûte Mystérieuse, La.
For Du Fu.
For Meng Hao-Jan.
For the Dancer of the King of Wu, When She Is Half Drunk.
Girl of Yueh, The.
Girls of Yueh, The.
Going to Visit a Taoist Recluse on Heaven's Mountain Only to Find Him Gone.
Great Bird, The.
Hard Is the Journey.
Hearing the Flute in the City of Loyang in a Spring Night.
Her Presence Was a Roomful of Flowers.
In a Village by the River.
In Memory of Ho Chi-chen.

In Praise of a Gold and Silver Painted Scene of the Buddha Manifestation in the Pure Land of the West, with a Preface.
In the Mountains on a Summer Day.
Inscribed at Summit Temple.
Inscribed on the Wall of Hsü Hsüan-Ping's Retreat.
Inscription on an Old Tomb at Guangling.
Intoxication of Love.
Ivresse d'Amour.
Jade-Staircase Grievance.
Jewel Stairs' Grievance, The.
Jour de Printemps Le Poète Exprime Ses Sentiments au Sortir de l'Ivresse, Un.
Ku Feng (After the Style of Ancient Poems).
Lament of the Frontier Guard.
Late Bloomer at the Front of My Garden.
Leave-taking Near Shoku.
Letter, A: "My love, / When you were here there was."
Listening to a Flute in Yellow Crane Pavilion.
Listening to a Flute on a Spring Night in Lo-yang.
Listening to a Monk from Shu Playing the Lute.
Listening to the Lute Played by Monk Chun from Shu.
Lonely Wife, The.
Long Banister Lane.
Longing.
Longing for Someone.
Looking for Master Yung Ts'un near His Hermitage.
Lu Mountain Song For the Palace Censor Empty-Boat Lu, A.
Moon over the Mountain Pass, The.
Mountain Dialogue.
Mountain Drinking Song.
My Trip in a Dream to the Lady of Heaven Mountain A Farewell to Several Gentlemen of Eastern Lu.
Night Morring at Cow's Creek: I Think of the Old Man.
Night Thoughts.
Night with a Friend, A.
Old Dust.
Old Style Poem.
Old Tai's Wine Shop.
O-mei Mountain Moon.
On Climbing the Phoenix Tower at Chinling.
On Dragon Hill.
On Hsin-P'ing Tower.
On Phoenix Tower in Chin-Ling.
On Visiting a Taoist Master in the Daitian Mountains and Not Finding Him.
On Visiting Taoist Recluse of Tai-Tien-Shan and Not Finding Him.
On Yellow-Crane Tower, Farewell to Meng Hao-Jan Who's Leaving for Yang-Chou.
Parting.
Poem by the Bridge at Ten-shin.
Poem Composed at the Command of the Emperor.
Poems in an Old Style, *sels.*
Questions Answered.
Quiet Night Thought.
Quiet Night Thoughts.
Quiet Night Thoughts.
Red sun comes out of the Eastern corner, The.
Remembering Ancient Days in Yueh.
Remembering East Mountain.
Remembering Our Excursion in the Past.
Resentment Near the Jade Steps.
Retreat of Hsieh Kung, The.
Return of the Banished.
Rhymeprose on the Sword Gallery.
Rising Drunk on a Spring Day.
River Merchant's Wife, The; A Letter.
River Song.
Road to Shu Is Hard, The.
Saying Farewell to a Friend.
Saying Good-bye in a Ch'i-ling Wineshop.
Saying Good-bye to Meng Hao-jan at Yellow Crane Pavilion.
Seeing Off a Friend.
Separation on the River Kiang.

Snapshot, A.
Solitary Carouse on a Day in Spring, A.
Song for the Falling Kingdom.
Song of Ch'ang-kan.
Song of Ch'ang-Kan (Yueh-Fu), The.
Song of the Heavenly Horse.
Song of War, A.
South-Folk in Cold Country.
Spring Night in Luoyang—Hearing a Flute.
Spring Song: "Young lass, A."
Spring Thoughts.
Springtime South of the Yangtze.
Still Night Thoughts.
Suite in the Ch'ing-p'ing Mode, A.
Summer Days in the Mountains.
Summer Song ("Mirror Lake, The.").
Summit Temple, The.
Sy-che and the King.
Take Wine.
Taking Leave of a Friend.
Taking Leave of a Friend.
Taking Leave of a Friend ("Blue mountains to the north of the walls.").
Thinking of East Mountain ("It's forever since I faced East Mountain.").
Third month in T'ientsin, The.
Thoughts in Night Quiet.
To a Friend.
To Meng Hao-jan.
To See a Friend Off to Shu.
To See Meng Hao-Jan Off to Yang-Chou.
To See Secretary Shu-Yun Off at the Hsieh T'iao Tower at Hsuan-Ch'eng.
To Send Far Away.
To Send to Tu Fu as a Joke.
To Tan Ch'iu.
To the Tune: Beautiful Barbarian.
To Tu Fu.
To Tu Fu from Shantung.
To Wang Lun.
Trinker im Frühling, Der.
Tune: "Beautiful Barbarians"
Up into the Clouds Music.
Verses: "Clean is the autumn wind."
Viewing the Waterfall at Mount Lu.
Wandering Ch'ing-Ling Strea in Nan-Yang.
War South of the Great Wall.
Waterfall at Lu-shan.
Wine.
Women of Yueh, *sels.*
Written on a Wall at Hsiu-Ching Monastery in Wu-Ch'ang.
Xiangyang Song.
Yu Chieh Yuan (Jade Steps Grievance, Yueh-fu).
Zazen on Ching-t'ing Mountain.

Li Qi (*fl.* 725 A.D.)
To Zhang Xu.

Li Shang-yin (812–58)
Alone by the Autumn River.
Bite back passion. Spring now sets.
Boasting of My Son.
Chamber Music.
Chance to Meet Is Difficult, The.
Ch'ang-O.
Coming was an empty promise, you have gone, and left no footprint.
East wind sighs, the fine rains come, The.
For ever hard to meet, and as hard to part.
From the Heights.
Hearing a Startled Bird During Stayover at Chin-Ch'ang Pavilion.
High Noon.
Inlaid Lute, The.
Master Chia.
Night Rains: A Letter to Go North.
Patterned Lute, The.
Phoenix tail on scented silk, flimsy layer on layer.
Spring Rain.
Walls of Emerald, The.
Where is it, the sad lyre which follows the quick flute?
Without Title.
Without Title (1).
Without Title (2).

Li Shen (772–846)
Pitying the Farmer.

Li Te-yü (787–849)
To Patriarch Sun at Hua-yang Grotto.

Li Tung-yang (1447–1511)
On a Painting of Fish Being Caught, A Song.

Li Yeh (*fl.* **8th cent.)**
Greeting to Lu Yu, A.

Li Yen-nien (c.140–87 B.C.)
Song, A: "In the north there is a lovely
  woman."
Song: "There's a beautiful woman in the
  north."

Li Yi (c.749–c.829)
Listening to a Flute at Night near the City
  Wall.
On Hearing a Flute at Night from the Wall of
  Shouxiang.

Li Yu [*or* **Li Hou-Chu] (937–78)**
Bella Donna Iu.
Flowered Woods, The.
Immeasurable Pain.
My Idlest Dreams.
Nightlong I Wander.
One Dream.
Past, The.
River Rolling Eastward, The.
Shaken, They Cling Again.
Silent and Alone.
Silently I ascend the western pavilion.
To the Tune: Beautiful Lady Yu.
To the Tune "Meeting Happiness."
Tune: "Beating Silk Floss."
Tune: "Beauty Yu."
Tune: "Joy of Encounter."
Tune: "Joy of Encounter."
Tune: "Memories of the South."
Tune: "New Bounty of Royalty."
Tune: "Pure Serene Music."
Tune: "Sand Washed by Waves."
Tune: "Sand Washed by Waves."
Tune: "The Beauty of Yü."
Tune: "The Crow's Nocturnal Cry."

Li'aibi, Shakir (b. 1940)
Butterfly frozen in stone, A.
My days pass with the beads of the rosary.
Soul of a pebble on top of the mountain, The.
Stone of the Arabian woman, The.

Liang Te-sheng (1886–1910)
Sent to My Fourth Son, Shao-Wu (to the Tune
  "Southern Countryside").

Liang Xiaobin (b. 1956)
China, I've Lost My Key.

Liban, Alex (b. 1942)
At a Time Like This.

Lichtenstein, Alfred (1889–1914)
Morning.

Lichtman, Risa
Bicycle, The.

Lickbarrow, Isabella
On Esthwaite Water.
On Sensibility: A Fragment.
On the Slave-Trade.
Patterdale.

Lieberman, Laurence (b. 1935)
Architect Monk, The.
Compass of the Dying.
Ether.
God's Measurements.
Lobsters in the Brain Coral.
Organist's Black Carnation, The.

Lieberman, Michael
Olivos, Los.
On the Anniversary of My Father's Death.
Prediction.
Regret.

Lifshin, Lyn (b. 1944)
After the Anti-Semitic Calls on a Local Talk
  Station.
Being Jewish in a Small Town.
Child We Won't Have Is Crowding Us in the
  Front, The.
Curling on the Bottom of My Mother's Bed.
I Remember Haifa Being Lovely But.

Night Robert Frost Died, The.
Yahrtzeit Light, The.

Light, Kate (b. 1960)
Because.
Five Urban Love Songs, *sels.*
Idea of Love Between Us, The.
My Worst Nightmare.

Lightburn, Staci
Dancing after Sanchez.

Lightfoot, Gordon (b. 1938)
Wreck of the Edmund Fitzgerald, The.

Lightfoot, Toni Asante
In Oklahoma.

Lihn, Enrique (1929–88)
Cemetery in Punta Arenas.
Dark Room, The.
Farewell.
Favorite Little Shrine, A.
Goodnight, Achilles.
Memories of Marriage.
Mud.
Of All Despondencies.
Old Man's Monologue with Death, The.
Revolution.
Six Poems of Loneliness.
Torture Chamber.

Like, Joseph
James Dean and the Pig.
Postmodern: A Definition.

Lilburn, Tim
Contemplation Is Mourning.
How To Be Here?
Pumpkins.
Stability.
Sunflowers at Prime.

Lili'u-o-ka-lani, Queen (1838–1917)
Aloha'oe.
Ka Waiapo Lani.
Ku'u Pua I Paoakalani.
Lawn Sprinkler, The.
Sanoe.
Sanoe ("Where can you be, Sanoe?").

Lillenas, Haldor
Wonderful grace of Jesus, Greater than all my
  sin.

Lilley, Gary
Funeral: "Naked in eastern mournin sun."
Meetin the Conjure Woman.
Who Sez Thunderbirds Can't Fly.

Lilley, Kate (b. 1960)
Sewing Lesson, The.
You Have to Strike Back.

Lim, Genny (b. 1946)
Animal Liberation.

Lim, Shirley (b. 1944)
Black and White.
Father from Asia.
I Defy You.
In California with Neruda.
Learning to Love America.
Lost Name Woman.
Modern Secrets.
Monarchs Steering.
Pantoun for Chinese Women.
Riding into California.
Starlight Haven.

Lim-Wilson, Fatima (b. 1961)
Alphabet Soup.
Beginning of Things, The.
Explaining the Origin of My Name.
Raising the Dead.
Ringmaster's Wife.
Upon Overhearing Tagalog.
Wave, The.

Lima, Frank (b. 1938)
Cuauhtemoc.
Good Morning America.
Hand, The.
Harbour.
Lime.
Year's End.

Lima, Jorge de (1893–1953)
Big Mystical Circus, The.
Distribution of Poetry.

Enormous Hand, The.
Poem of any Virgin.
Stranger, Stranger.
That Black Girl Fulô.
Trumpets, The.
Words of Departure.

Lima, Maria Eugénia (b. 1935)
Madalena.
Marketwoman of Luanda.
Shoeshine Boy.

Limburg, Joanne (b. 1970)
Barton in the Beans.
Inner Bloke.
Queen of Swords, The.
Return, The.
Seder Night with My Ancestors.

**Limonov, Eduard Veniaminovich (Eduard
Veniaminovich Savenko) (b. 1943)**
As if a quiet branch drew a line.
Secret Notebook, *sels.*

Lin, Dolores, B. (b. 1926)
Nostalgia: "O, fruitful district Corozal!"

"Lin Ling" (Hu Yün-shang) (b. 1935)
Footpaths Cross in the Rice Field.

Lin Pu (967–1028)
Locust Wood Mallet for Papermaking, A.

Lincoln, Abraham (1809–65)
Gettysburg Address, The.
My Childhood-Home I See Again.

Lind, Michael
Alamo, The: An Epic, *sel.*

Lindamichellebaron
I'm the Man.

Lindbergh, Anne Morrow (b. 1906)
Ascent.

Linden, Mrs. Henry (b. 1859)
All We Ask Is Justice.
As Women of Our Race.
Bird Song, The.
Brave Man and Brave Woman.
Church Bells, The.
Count Your Blessings.
Cultivation.
Do Your Best.
Encouragement.
Fall Is Here, The.
For the Good of the Pythian Order.
God's Electric Power.
Golden Jubilee of Wilberforce.
Gossip.
Household of Ruth, The.
I Am as Happy as a Queen on Her Throne.
Last Day of the Year; or, New Year's Eve, The.
Let Us Strive to Do Something.
Life's Golden Sunset.
Lonely World.
Man Is What He Wills to Be.
Marriage Vow.
May.
Missionary, The.
New Year's Morning; or, the First Day of the
  Year.
October Is Here.
Oh Woman, Blessed Woman!
Orphan Girl, An.
Our Club Work.
Our Noble Booker T. Washington.
Parting Lovers, The.
Paul Laurence Dunbar.
Pay Your Debts.
Prospect of the Future, The.
Riot, A.
Scraps of Time.
Silent Night, The.
Sun of Our Existence, The.
Tell Her So.
This Country's Needs.
To the Conference.
To the Queen of the British Government.
To the Wheel of Progress.
Wayward Son, The.
What Is Woman?
Would-be Critic, The.
Y. M. C. A, The.

Linder, April
First Kiss.
Lindley, David (b. 1946)
By Fire or Flood.
Cromwell: The Last Portrait.
Cryptogram, The.
Curly Kale.
Fennel.
Marxist to Liberals, A.
Nearness.
Potato Blight.
Lindsay, Caroline (1844–1912)
Love or Fame.
To My Own Face.
Lindsay, Christian (fl. 1580s)
Christen Lyndesay to Ro. Hudsone.
Lindsay, Jack (b. 1900)
Angry Dusk.
It Has Happened.
Question Time.
Sudden Discords in the Trumpets of
Overdelayed Last Judgement, 1956.
To My Father Norman Alone in the Blue
Mountains.
Voice of the Wheat, The.
Lindsay, Maurice (b. 1918)
At Hans Christian Andersen's Birthplace,
Odense, Denmark.
Hurlygush.
'Tis Sixty Years Since.
Lindsay, Ruth Temple
Hunters, The.
Lindsay, Sarah
World Truffle.
Lindsay, Vachel (1879–1931)
Abraham Lincoln Walks at Midnight.
Booker Washington Trilogy, The, sels.
Bryan, Bryan, Bryan, Bryan.
Buddha.
Chinese Nightingale, The.
Colloquial Reply, A: To Any Newsboy.
Congo, The.
Dove of New Snow, The.
Eagle That Is Forgotten, The.
Factory Windows Are Always Broken.
Flower-fed Buffaloes, The.
General William Booth Enters into Heaven.
Ghosts of the Buffaloes, The.
Horrid Voice of Science, The.
In Which Roosevelt Is Compared to Saul.
Indian Summer Day on the Prairie, An.
Jazz of This Hotel, The.
Kalamazoo.
Leaden-eyed, The.
Little Turtle, The.
Mae Marsh, Motion Picture Actress, sels.
Niagara, sels.
Rain.
To a Golden-Haired Girl in a Louisiana Town.
To Mary Pickford—Moving Picture Actress.
Traveler, The.
Unpardonable Sin, The.
Why I Voted the Socialist Ticket.
Lindsey, Kay
Stringbeans.
Lindtová, Anna (1930–44)
Campfire.
Linebarger, Jim
Coyote.
Oppa.
Linett, Deena
Cathedral: "For hours I held one of my son's
infant twins."
Lingafelter, Amy
Candy Poem, The.
Grandmothers, The.
Lingche (746–816)
In Reply to Wei Dan.
Spending the Night at East Forest Temple.
Link, Lenore M.
Holding Hands.
Lion-Face, Dakini
KYE HO! Wonderful!

Lippman, Matthew (b. 1965)
Hallelujah Terrible.
Lipton, James (b. 1946)
Misericordia!
Lipton, Lenny (b. 1940)
Puff the Magic Dragon.
Liptsin, Sam (1893–1980)
Going Up.
Lisboa, Henriqueta
Beyond the Image.
Camellia.
Echo.
Elegy: "At first the dead."
Idyll: "Lord, forgive me if I do not look for
you."
Lisella, Julia
Song of the Third Generation.
Lisick, Beth (b. 1968)
Empress of Sighs ("Mom and Dad have
abandoned the family home and retired to
Palm.").
Empress of Sighs ("Mom says getting to the
new home is a snap.").
Pantoumstone for a Dying Breed.
**Lisnyanskaya [or Lisnianskaia], Inna L'vovna (b.
1928)**
Between hope and failure.
Jealousy: "I look out of the window at the
retreating back."
Like the earth turning, I creak, and dream.
Ode to the Computer.
Quiet days and quiet evenings.
To be thought an outcast in my beloved
country.
Triptych of Reflection.
Two carousing hawk moths, their wings like
nervous silk.
Whenever I looked in the mirror.
Wind blows and makes the light tremble, The.
Lister, Richard Percival (b. 1914)
Mind Reborn in Streatham Common, A.
Toast to 2,000, A.
Little, Lessie Jones
My Yellow Straw Hat.
LittleCoon See Oliver, Louis
Littledale, Freya
When My Dog Died.
LittleDog, Pat (b. 1941)
Cowgirl.
Crossing the river to juárez.
In austin reigns a bald-headed queen.
Love letter sent south.
Litvak, Sveta (b. 1959)
I catch the smell of beans.
Shadows of the plane-tree leaves.
Liu, Timothy
Against Nature.
Ariel Singing.
Brooklyn Botanic Garden, The.
Echoes.
Highway 6.
Ikon.
Kindertotenlieder.
Mama.
Poem.
Poem: "Late butterflies gliding through the
air."
Reading Whitman in a Toilet Stall.
Size of It, The.
Strange Fruit.
Sunday.
Thoreau.
Vox Angelica.
Wellfleet.
Liu Ch'ang-ch'ing (710?–785?)
Climbing in Autumn for a View from the
Temple on the Terrace of General Wu.
On Parting with the Buddhist Pilgrim Ling-
Ch'ě.
On Seeing Wang Leave for the South.
Rejoicing that the Zen Master Pao Has Arrived
from Dragon Mountain.
Sent to the Taoist of Dragon Mountain, Hsu
Fa-leng.

Snow on Lotus Mountain.
While Visiting on the South Stream the Taoist
Priest Chang.
Liu Cheng (d. 217)
Cockfight.
Poem without a Category.
Liu Chi-hsün (fl. c.100 B.C.)
Lament.
Liu Chih (c.1280–c.1335)
Tune: "Sheep on the Mountain Slope."
Liu Kexiang See Liu K'o-hsiang
Liu K'o-hsiang (b. 1957)
Choice.
Liu Ling (225–80 A.D.)
Hymn to the Virtue of Wine.
Liu Pang (256–195 B.C.)
Song of the Great Wind.
Song of the Great Wind.
Liu Shih (1618–64)
Tune: "Dreaming of Southland" Thinking of
Someone.
Liu Tsung-yüan (773–819)
Dwelling by a Stream.
From the City-Tower of Liuzhou To My Four
Fellow-Officials at Zhang, Ding, Feng, and
Lian Districts.
Morning Walk in Autumn to South Valley
Passing an Abandoned Village.
Old Fisherman, The.
On Covering the Bones of Chang Chin, the
Hired Man.
Reading Buddhist Classics with Chao at His
Temple in the Early Morning.
River Snow.
River Snow ("These thousand peaks cut off the
flight of birds.").
River Snow ("Thousand peaks: no more birds
in flight, A.").
River-Snow.
Snowy River.
Thousand mountains without a bird, A.
Liu Yin (1249–82)
Miscellaneous Poem on Rural Life.
Liu Yu Hsi (772–842)
Blacktail Row.
Gazing on Lake Dongting.
Looking at My Knife-Hilt, a Song.
Parrot Island.
Raven Robe Lane.
Red Blossoms.
Tune: "Memories of the South."
Liu Yung (fl. c.1034)
Cicada Song.
Lament: "Late autumn, a brief shower."
Song: "After the eating, the drinking, the
singing."
Song: "Because spring brings miserable green
and painful red."
Song: "It's the wine, this ache, this longing."
Song: "She lowers her fragrant curtain."
Song to the Tune "Ting Feng Po."
Tune: "Bells in the Rain."
Tune: "Bells Ringing in the Rain."
Tune: "Eight Beats of a Kan-chou Song."
Livesay, Dorothy (b. 1909)
Arms and the Woman.
Bartok and the Geranium.
Children's Letters, The.
Difference, The.
Eve.
Going to Sleep.
Green Rain.
Lament: "What moved me, was the way your
hand."
On Looking into Henry Moore.
Other.
Three Emily's, The.
Uninvited, The.
Unquiet Bed, The.
Livingston, Jay (b. 1915)
Buttons and Bows.
Femininity.
Haven't Got a Worry.
Keep It Simple.

Mona Lisa.
Never Let Me Go.
To Each His Own.
Whatever Will Be, Will Be (Que Sera, Sera).

Livingston, Myra Cohn (b. 1926)
Angry Valentine, An.
Arthur Thinks on Kennedy.
Birds Know.
Car Wash.
Coming from Kansas.
Dark, The.
Doll.
Envoi: Washington Square Park.
Father.
First Thanksgiving.
Invitation.
Lazy Witch.
Lemonade Stand.
Night, The.
Paul Revere Speaks.
74th Street.
Swimming Pool.
Tape, The.
12 October.
Why?
Working with Mother.

Livingstone, Dinah
May Day.
Stepmother.

Livingstone, Douglas (b. 1932)
Darwinian preface, A.
Dust: "Bundle in the gutter had its skull, The."
Giovanni Jacopo meditates.
Isipingo.
Lake Morning in Autumn.
Morning, A.
Mpondo's smithy, Transkei.
One Golgotha.
One Time.
Recondite war on women, The.
Sleep of my lions, The.
Sonatina of Peter Govender, beached.
Traffic interlude: Descent from the Tower.
Vanderdecken.
Waste land at Station 14, The.
Wheels.

Liyong, Taban lo
55.
60.

Llawdden (fl. c.1460)
No Place Like Home.

Lleshanaku, Luljeta (b. 1968)
Absence.
Awakening of the Eremite, The.
Betrayed.
Chronic Appendicitis.
Electrolytes.
Half Past Three.
Out of Boredom.
Self-Defense.
Still Life: "Here in a summer full of dust."

Llewellyn, Kate (b. 1940)
Colonel.
Finished.

Llewellyn-Williams, Hilary (b. 1951)
Feeding the Bat.
Little Cloth, The.
Making Babies.
Short Wave.
Two Rivers.

Lloréns [or Lorens] Torres, Luis (1876–1944)
Ugly Duckling, The.

Lloyd, C. Robert
Gate Gate Paragate Parasmgate Bodhi Svaha.
Looking at a Portrait Sculpture of the Indian
    Holy Man, Asanga, (Japanese, Mujaku,
    Flowered about 350 C.E.—Stands in the
    Kofukuji Treasure Hall of Nara Japan.
Nightfall.

Lloyd, Charles (1775–1839)
Desultory Thoughts in London, sel.
Erst when I wandered far from those I loved.
Metaphysical Sonnet.
My pleasant home! where erst when sad and
    faint.

Oh, I have told thee every secret care.
Oh, she was almost speechless! nor could hold.
On the Death of Priscilla Farmer.
Whether thou smile or frown, thou beauteous
    face.
Written at the Hotwells, near Bristol.

Lloyd, David (1597–1633)
Legend of Captain Jones, The, sel.

Lloyd, Evan (1734–76)
Methodist, The, sel.
Portrait of a Bishop.
Powers of the Pen, The, sels.

Lloyd, John (1797–1875)
Kingfisher, The.
Thoughts of Boyhood.

Lloyd, Ludovic (fl. 1573–1610)
Sidanen, sel.

Lloyd, Margaret
Simplest and the Hardest, The.

Lloyd, Paul
Michelle Granguad Creating Anagrams.

Lloyd, Robert (1733–64)
Familiar Epistle to J. B. Esq, A, sel.

Lloyd, Rosemary
Michelle Granguad Creating Anagrams.

Lluellyn [or Lluelyn], Martin (1616–82)
Epithalamium: To Mistress M. A.

Llwyd, Alan (b. 1948)
Bull of Bryncelyn, The.
Chaplin and Others.
Hawk Above Felindre, The.
Moons of Llŷn, The.
Our Godless Days.
Scream, The: Edvard Munch (1893).
Welsh Language, The.

Llwyd, Catherin Owen (d. 1602)
To Siôn Lloyd: the Mother's Advice to Her
    Heir.

Llwyd, Huw (c.1568–1630)
Fox's Counsel, The.

Llwyd, Iwan (b. 1957)
Automobiles.
Disappeared, The.
Dust Truck Blues.
Far Rockaway.
Fingerprints.
Harley Davidson.
Meet me at the St Francis.
No Man's Land.
Old Photograph, An.
Spider.
Sure, You Can Ask Me a Personal Question.
Woodstock, sel.

Llwyd, Morgan (1619–59)
Awake, O Lord, Awake Thy Saints.
Charles, the Last King of Britain, sel.
Come Wisdome Sweet.
1648, sels.
Summer, The, sel.

Llwyd, Richard (1752–1835)
Beaumaris Bay, sels.

Llywelyn ab y Moel (d. 1440)
Battle of Waun Gaseg, The.

Llywelyn Goch ap Meurig Hen (fl. 1360–90)
Lament for Lleucu Llwyd.

Llywelyn-Williams, Alun (b. 1913)
In Berlin, August 1945: Lehrte Bahnhof.
On a Visit.
Pont y Caniedydd.
When I Was a Boy.
When I Was Young.
Yesterday's Illusion or Remembering the
    Thirties.

Lo Pin-Wang (640?–84?)
Mooring by Jiangzhen in the Evening.
On the Cicada: In Prison.

Lochhead, Douglas (b. 1922)
Cemetery at Loch End, Catalone, Cape Breton,
    The.
John Thompson.
Nothing: "Now, this beginning."
Winter Lanscape—Halifax.

Lochhead, Liz (b. 1947)
Dreaming Frankenstein.
Empty Song, The.
Grim Sisters, The.
Hickie, The.
I Wouldn't Thank You for a Valentine.
Interference Song.
My Rival's House.
My Way.
Neckties.
Noises in the Dark.
Poem for My Sister.
Promises.
Rapunzstiltskin.
Riddle-Me-Ree.
Something I'm Not.
Sorting Through.

Locke, Anne Vaughan (c.1530–c.1590)
Sin and Despair Have So Possess'd My Heart.
So Foul Is Sin and Loathsome in Thy Sight.

Locke, Mary (fl. 1786–1816)
Sonnet: "I hate the Spring in parti-coloured
    vest."

Locker-Lampson, Frederick (1821–95)
My Life Is a———.
Old Oak Tree at Hatfield Broadoak, The.
Our Photograph[s].
Terrible Infant, A.

Lockett, Reginald (b. 1933)
Oaktown CA.

Lockhart, John Gibson (1794–1854)
Lines: "When youthful faith hath fled."

Locklin, Gerald (b. 1941)
Beer.
California: "What the hell am i doing
    anyway?"
Do You Remember the Scene in The
    Godfather.
Iceberg Theory, The.
Leader of the Pack, The.
Learning to See Crooked.
Stranger, The.
Tap Dancing Lessons.
Where we are.

Lockward, Diane
My Husband Discovers Poetry.
On First Reading Romeo and Juliet.
Vegetable Love.

Lockwood, Margo (b. 1939)
Bookshop in Winter.

Lodeizen, Hans (1924–50)
Its Pliancy.
Ode: In a Few Hours.

Loden, Rachel
Far In.
Gospel According to Clairol, The.
Miss October.
My Test Market.
Reconstructed Face.
Revenge, Like Habanero Peppers.
Tumbling Dice.

Lodge, George Cabot
Fall.
Lower New York.
On an Æolian Harp.
Pastoral: "Slopes of the sun and vine, and thou
    dark stream."
Strong saturation of sea! O widely flown.
Tuckanuck.

Lodge, Thomas (1558?–1625)
Animal Weather-Forecasting.
Phyllis, sels.
Robert, Second Duke of Normandy, sels.
Rosalynde; or Euphues' Golden Legacy, sels.
Scillaes Metamorphosis, sel.
Shepherd's Sorrow, Being Disdained in Love,
    The.

Loerke, Oskar
At the Edge of the Great City, sels.

Loesser, Frank (1910–69)
Adelaide's Lament.
Baby, It's Cold Outside.
Boys in the Backroom, The.
Fugue for Tinhorns.

I Believe in You.
I Don't Want to Walk Without You.
I Hear Music.
I Wish I Didn't Love You So.
If I Were a Bell.
Lady's in Love with You, The.
Luck, Be a Lady.
Make a Miracle.
Murder, He Says.
My Darling, My Darling.
Once in Love with Amy.
Sand in My Shoes.
Sit Down, You're Rockin' the Boat.
Somebody, Somewhere.
Spring Will Be a Little Late This Year.
Take Back Your Mink.
They're Either Too Young or Too Old.
Two Sleepy People.

Loewinsohn, Ron (b. 1937)
Siv, With Ocean (Pacific).

Loftin, Elouise (b. 1950)
April '68.
Barefoot Necklace.
Bkln.
Black Lady, A.
Scabible.
Weeksville Women.
What Sunni Say.

Loftis, Norman J. (b. 1943)
Big John.
Brief Encounter.
Changes—Eight.
Changes—Five.
Changes—One.
Delirium.
Fights After School.
In Memorium: Robert Hayden.
Ruth.

Logan, John (1923–71?)
Picnic, The: "It is the picnic with Ruth in the spring."

Logan, William (b. 1950)
Song: "Her nose is like a satellite."
Valentine for Matthew Arnold, A.

Logau, Friedrich von (1604–55)
Best Medecines, The.
Birth is Death, Death is Birth.
Booty from the German War.
Divine Revenge.
Drunkenness.
Faith.
Fools and Wise Men.
Freedom.
French Dress.
Frog, A.
German Language, The.
Old Nobility, The.
One Faith and No Faith.
Our Naughty Time.
Physicians' Fortune, The.
Powerful Servants.
Soul and Body.
Water and Wine.
Women's Rule.

Logghe, Joan
Española Pantoum.
From *Rice*.
Her First Jew.
Insomnia Litany.
Madonna of the Peaches.
Marriage of Heaven and Hell in Española.
Mixed Marriage.
Something Like Marriage.

Logue, Christopher (b. 1926)
Good Taste.
I Shall Vote Labour.
Know Thy Enemy.
Rat, O Rat.
Song of the Dead Soldier, The.
To My Fellow Artists.
War Music, *sels*.

Lohenstein, Daniel Casper von (1635–83)
Arminius, *sels*.
Her Eyes.
Night Thoughts Concerning a Dream.

Lojowski, Mac (b. 1977)
Big Fort Island Buddha.
Horizon.
In the Cage of Doves.
On the Sixth Day of the War.

Lok [or Locke], Anne (b. c.1535, d. after 1590)
Anna Dering on Bartolomeo Silva, Doctor of Turin.
Necessitie and Benefit of Affliction, The.

Lom, Iain (John MacDonald) (1620?–1716?)
Lament for the State of the Country, A.

Lomas, Herbert
I quake like Satan.

Lomax, Marion (b. 1953)
Amor Diving.
Gruoch.
Gulf.
July.
Kith.
Other Woman, The.

Lombardy, Anthony (b. 1954)
Shall I Compare Thee. . .?

Loncar, M. (b. 1968)
As My Cat Eats the Head of a Field Mouse He Has Caught.
Insomniac.
Kentucky.
One Night America: A Boy and His Blowtorch.
Peoria.
Picasso Shag.
There Goes the Bride.

London, Jack (1876–1916)
Triolet: "He came in."

London, Rick
Coming Down.
Folk Form.
Performance Sequence.

London, Sara
Cold War.

"Long, Doc" *See* Long, Doughtry

Long, Doughtry ("Doc Long")
Black Love Black Hope.

Long, Haniel (b. 1888)
Cobweb.
Daphnis and Chloe.
Day and Night.
For Tony, Embarking in Spring.
In the Dark World.
Lightning.
New Music, A.
Our Spring Needs Shoveling.

Long, Joel (b. 1964)
Bermuda Triangle.
Music's Wife.

Long, Norman (b. 1893)
We Can't Let You Broadcast That, *sel*.

Long, Robert (b. 1954)
Muse Is Gone, The.
What's So Funny 'bout Peace, Love and Understanding.

Long, Robert Hill
Conspiracy, The.

Longchamps, Guy W.
O Luxury.

Longenbach, James
Learning Window.
Orphic Night.
Undiscovered Country.
What You Find in the Woods.

Longfellow, Henry Wadsworth (1807–82)
Aftermath.
Afternoon in February.
Arrow and the Song, The.
Arsenal at Springfield, The.
Autumn.
Belisarius.
Bells of San Blas, The.
Bridge, The.
Broken Oar, The.
Building of the Ship, The.
Building of the Ship, The, *sels*.
Chaucer.

Children's Hour, The.
Christmas Bells.
Couplet: February 24, 1847.
Cross of Snow, The.
Cumberland, The.
Curfew.
Dante.
Day Is Done, The.
Daybreak.
Dedication.
Delia.
Disasters.
Divina Commedia.
Elegiac Verse, *sel*.
Elegiac Verse 12.
Evangeline: A Tale of Acadie, *sels*.
Evening Star, The.
Excelsior.
Fire of Drift-Wood, The.
Fragment: August 4, 1856.
Fragment: December 18, 1847.
From the Anglo-Saxon.
Galaxy, The.
Galley of Count Arnaldos, The.
Golden Mile-Stone, The.
Harvest Moon, The.
Haunted Houses.
Hymn to the Night.
In the Churchyard at Cambridge.
Jewish Cemetery at Newport, The.
Judas Maccabaeus, *sels*.
Jugurtha.
Kéramos.
Killed at the Ford.
Mezzo Cammin.
Michael Angelo: A Fragment, *sels*.
Milton.
My Lost Youth.
Nature.
Night.
Old Clock on the Stairs, The.
Poet's Calendar, The.
Poets, The.
Psalm of Life, A.
Rain in Summer.
Rhyme of Sir Christopher, The.
Ropewalk, The.
Sand of the Desert in an Hour-Glass.
Sandalphon.
Santa Filomena.
Seaweed.
Skeleton in Armor [*or* Armour], The.
Slave in the Dismal Swamp, The.
Slave's Dream, The.
Snow-Flakes.
Song of Hiawatha, The, *sels*.
Sound of the Sea, The.
Spirit of Poetry, The.
Tales of a Wayside Inn, *sels*.
There Was a Little Girl.
Three Kings, The.
Tide Rises, the Tide Falls, The.
Venice.
Village Blacksmith, The.
Warning, The.
Witnesses, The.
Wreck of the Hesperus, The.

Longinovic, Tomislav (b. 1955)
Glorious Ruins.

Longley, Michael (b. 1939)
All of These People.
Amish Rug, An.
Ash Keys.
Beech Tree, The.
Between Hovers.
Björn Olinder's Pictures.
Caravan.
Casualty.
Ceasefire.
Comber, The.
Death of a Horse.
Detour.
Echoes.
Fleance.
Flowering, A.
Freeze-Up.

Frozen Rain.
Ghetto.
Ghost Town.
Gorse Fires.
Hebrides, The.
Horses, The.
I flourish between pleasure and pain.
In Mayo.
In Memoriam.
In Memory of Gerard Dillon.
Linen Industry, The.
Man Lying on a Wall.
Mayo Monologues, *sels.*
No Continuing City.
Odyssey, *sels.*
Pattern, The.
Persephone.
Remembering Carrigskeewaun.
River and Fountain.
Scissors Ceremony, The.
Self-Portrait.
Skara Brae.
Sulpicia.
Swans Mating.
Third Light, The.
Touch, A.
Water-burn.
Waterfall, The.
West, The.
Words for Jazz Perhaps.
Wounds.
Wreaths, *sels.*

Lönnrot, Elias (1802–84)
Kalevala, The, *sel.*

Loomis, Charles Battell (1861–1911)
O-U-G-H.

Lope de Vega Carpio, Félix (1562–1635)
At Dawn the Virgin Is Born.
Ice and Fires Contend with My Child.
If You Leave at Daybreak.
In Santiago.
Judith.
Lachrimae; or Seven Tears Figured in Seven
    Passionate Pavans, *sels.*
Little Carol of the Virgin, A.
May Song.
Pentecost Castle, The, *sels.*
Seguidillas of the Guadalquivir River.
Shepherd Who With Your Tender Calls.
Sonnet 188.
Sonnet 61.
Sonnet All of a Sudden, A.
Sonnet Right off the Bat.
Strange Shepherd, Set My Bellwether Free.
Stranger to Love, Whoever Loves Not Thee.
Today Delight's Fair Ship.
What Do I Have, That You Seek Out My
    Friendship?
Where Are You Going, Maiden.
White Was I.

Lopez, Barry
Desert Reservation.

Lopez, Luis
Abiquiu.
Images of San Luis.
NEHI Strawberry Down-and-Away.
Only Now I Realize.
To a Coal Miner in Madrid, New Mexico.
Tomás.

Lopez, Tony (b. 1956)
Assembly Point D, *sel.*
Dint.
In Memory.
No Transport.
Path Marked with Breadcrumbs, A.
Studies in Classic American Literature.

López-Adorno, Pedro (b. 1954)
Throbs for the Instructress.

López Colomé, Pura (b. 1952)
Cachorros, Los.
Cubs, The.
Death of the Kiss.
Dolor de corazón.
Dramatis Personae.
Dramatis personae.

Heartache.
Muerte del beso, La.

López Mills, Tedi (b. 1959)
Advertisement.
And Never Did.
Anuncio.
Carta.
Dead Weight of the Land, The.
Ending by Pound, An.
Final de Pound, Un.
Letter: "Endings always erase the traces of
    their plot."
Leyendo a Virgilio.
Mi voz fiel como la sombra.
My Voice Faithful as a Shadow.
On Reading Virgil.
Peso muerto de la tierra, El.
Y nunca quise.

López Velarde, Ramón (1888–1921)
Ants.
Baleful Return.
In the Dying Afternoon.
Malefic Return, The.
My Cousin Agueda [*or* Agatha].
My Heart, Faithful.
Provincial Sundays.
Purple Spot, The.
Wet Earth.

Loran, Gila *See* Zelenina, Galina

Lorde, Audre (1934–92)
Afterimages.
Art of Response, The.
Ballad from Childhood.
Beams.
Between Ourselves.
Black Mother Woman.
Black Unicorn, The.
Burning the Water Hyacinth.
Coal.
Coniagui Women.
Dahomey.
Day They Eulogized Mahalia, The.
Echo.
Echoes.
Ethiopia.
Father Son and Holy Ghost.
Fishing the White Water.
For the Record.
From the House of Yemanjá.
Hanging Fire.
Harriet.
Learning to Write.
Love Poem: "Speak earth and bless me with
    what is richest."
Memorial 1: "If you come as softly."
Movement Song.
Naturally.
Night-Blooming Jasmine, The.
Now That I Am Forever with Child.
On a Night of the Full Moon.
125th Street and Abomey.
Outside.
Power.
Prologue.
Question of Climate, A.
Recreation.
Song for a Thin Sister.
Stations.
Story Books on a Kitchen Table.
Today Is Not the Day.
What My Child Learns of the Sea.
Women of Dan Dance with Swords in Their
    Hands to Mark the Time When They Were
    Warriors, The.

Loseff [*or* Losev], Lev Vladimir (b. 1937)
Conversation with a New York Poet.
I know—the Mongol yoke, the years of
    famine.
Petrograd Side, The.

Lothamer, Joe
Allen.
Be a Painter.
October Falls in Black and White.

Lott, Bret
Post Script.

Lotu, Denize *See* Lauture, Denizé

Louis, Adrian C. (b. 1946)
At the House of Ghosts.
Dust World.
Nevada Red Blues.
Something About Being an Indian.
Sonny's Purple Heart.
That Great Wingless Bird.

Louise, Esther
Footprints.
Jesus' Song.
Swinging doors of knocking-wood cowards: 8
    for us.

Lourie, Dick (b. 1931)
Jewish.
Letters to the Dead: Denise Levertov.
Portrait in Rhythm and Blues.
Song Embodying What I've Learned in Thirty-
    Five Years.
Theological.
Three Recent Trips to the Golden Past: East
    Village, Clarksdale Mississippi, Athens.

Love, B.D.
Bryan Ferry.

Love, Candice Nicole
Modern Love Poem, A.

Love, Monifa Atungaye (b. 1955)
Initiation.
Objects of Desire.
Shall We Gather at the River?
Trying to Sleep After Studying Color Photos of
    Goma.

Love, Rowena M.
Puncture Wounds: A Baiku.

Lovecraft, Howard Phillips (1890–1937)
Alienation.
Well, The.

Lovelace, Richard (1618–58)
Another.
Ant, The.
Elinda's [*or* Ellinda's] Glove.
Grasshopper, The [To My Noble Friend Mr
    Charles Cotton: Ode].
Gratiana Dancing [*or* Dauncing] and [*or* &]
    Singing.
Her Muffe.
La Bella Bona-Roba.
Love Made in the First Age[: To Chloris].
On Sanazar's being honoured with six hundred
    Duckets by the Clarissimi of Venice, for
    composing an Elegiack Hexastick of The
    City. A Satyre.
Snail [*or* Snayl], The.
Song: "Strive not, vain Lover, to be fine."
To a Lady with Child that Asked [*or* Ask'd] an
    Old Shirt.
To Althea, from Prison.
To Amarantha, That She Would Dishevel[l]
    Her Hair[e].
To Lucasta.
To Lucasta, from Prison.
To Lucasta, [on] Going beyond the Seas.
To Lucasta, [on] Going to the War[re]s.
To My Worthy Friend Mr. Peter Lely [*or*
    Lilly].

Lover, Samuel (1797–1868)
I'm Not Myself at All!
What Will You Do, Love?
Whistlin' Thief, The.

Løvgreen, Geraint (b. 1955)
First Day, The.
Life's Dovey Junctions.

Lovibond, Edward (1724–75)
Bull-Baiting.

Low, Mary
Companion, The.
Encounter.
Perchance to Dream.
Q.E.D.
Where the Wolf Sings.

Lowbury, Edward (b. 1913)
Huntsman, The.

Lowe, Janet
With Thanks to Eddie Shaw.

Lowe, Janice (b. 1963)
Between Acts.
Club House.
Lowe, Lorna
Sea Shells.
Lowe, Robert, Viscount Sherbrooke (1811–92)
Songs of the Squatters, *sels.*
Lowell, Amy (1874–1925)
Afterglow.
April.
Aubade: "As I would free the white almond
from the green husk."
Bright Sunlight.
Bungler, The.
Captured Goddess, The.
Carrefour.
Decade, [A].
Dissonance.
Falling Snow.
Free Fantasia on Japanese Themes.
Guns as Keys: And the Great Gate Swings, *sel.*
Hoar-Frost.
In Time of War.
Katydids.
Lady, A.
Letter, The.
Lilacs.
Lover, A.
Madonna of the Evening Flowers.
Meeting-House Hill.
Moon Haze.
Music.
New Heavens for Old.
Night Clouds.
Nuance.
Opal.
Patterns.
Pike, The.
St. Louis.
September, 1918.
Shore Grass.
Shower, A.
Sisters, The.
Solitaire.
Spring Longing.
Taxi, The.
Towns in Colour, *sels.*
Venus Transiens.
Vernal Equinox.
Vespers.
Vicarious.
Weather-Cock Points South, The.
Wind and Silver.
Lowell, James Russell (1819–91)
Aladdin.
Bibliolaters, *sels.*
Biglow Papers, The, *sels.*
Boss, The.
Contrast, A.
Darkened Mind, The.
Fable for Critics, A, *sels.*
First Snowfall [*or* Snow-Fall], The.
First Snow-fall, The.
Fountain, The.
In a Copy of Omar Khayyám.
Memoriae Positum R. G. Shaw.
Ode Recited at the Harvard Commemoration
(July 21, 1865).
Our Own—Progression F, *sel.*
Present Crisis, The.
Remembered Music.
Science and Poetry.
Sonnet: "Amid these fragments of heroic
days."
Street, The.
To the Dandelion.
Under the Willows, *sel.*
Vision of Sir Launfal, The, *sels.*
Lowell, Maria White (1821–53)
Africa.
Opium Fantasy, An.
Rouen, Place de la Pucelle.
Sick-Room, The.
Lowell, Robert (1917–77)
After the Convention.

After the Surprising Conversions.
As a Plane Tree by the Water.
Bomber, The.
Book of Wisdom, The.
Colloquy in Black Rock.
Commander Lowell.
David and Bathsheba in the Public Garden.
Dead in Europe, The.
Death of the Sheriff, The.
Dolphin.
Drunken Fisherman, The.
Epilogue: "Those blessèd structures, plot and
rhyme."
Eye and Tooth.
Ezra Pound.
Fall 1961.
Falling Asleep over the Aeneid.
Fishnet.
Flaw, The.
For Sheridan.
For the Union Dead.
Grandparents.
Harriet ("Repeating fly, blueback,
thumbthick—so gross, A.").
History.
Holy Innocents, The.
Home After Three Months Away.
Inauguration Day: January 1953.
It Did.
Man And Wife.
March 1, The.
March 2, The.
Memories of West Street and Lepke.
Mouth of the Hudson, The.
Mr. Edwards and the Spider.
My Last Afternoon with Uncle Devereux
Winslow.
New Year's Day.
Night Sweat.
Nihilist as Hero, The.
Notice.
Obit.
Old Flame, The.
On the Eve of the Feast of the Immaculate
Conception: 1942.
Public Garden, The.
Quaker Graveyard in Nantucket, The.
Reading Myself.
Robert Frost.
Sailing Home from Rapallo.
Shifting Colors.
Skunk Hour.
T. S. Eliot.
To Speak of Woe That Is in Marriage.
Violence.
Waking Early Sunday Morning.
Waking in the Blue.
Watchmaker God.
Water.
Where the Rainbow Ends.
Women, Children, Babies, Cows, Cats.
Writers, *sel.*
Lowenfels, Walter (1897–1976)
Elegy in the Manner of a Requiem in Memory
of D.H. Lawrence, *sels.*
Execution, The.
Lowenthal, Jessica
Hovering.
Lowery, Janet
Houston Heights.
Texas Splendor.
Lowery, Joanne (b. 1945)
Hate Crimes.
Lowry, Brigid
In the World.
Lowry, Malcolm (1909–57)
About Ice.
Cantinas, The, *sels.*
Epitaph: "Malcolm Lowry."
Eye-Opener.
Strange Type.
Volcano is Dark, The.
Wild Cherry, The.
Lowry, Robert (1862–99)
Beautiful River.

Up from the Grave He Arose.
Lowther, John
Asleeping: a Kind of Rendezvous.
Löwy, Hanuš (1931–44)
Little Mouse, The.
Man Proposes, God Disposes.
Yes, That's the Way Things Are.
Loy, Mina (1882–1966)
Anglo-Mongrels and the Rose, *sels.*
Apology of Genius.
Brancusi's Golden Bird.
Der Blinde Junge.
Effectual Marriage, The.
Gertrude Stein.
Jules Pascin.
Love Songs to Joannes, *sels.*
Lunar Baedeker.
On Third Avenue.
One O'Clock at Night.
Poe.
There is no Life or Death.
Three Moments in Paris.
Widow's Jazz, The.
Loydell, Rupert M. (b. 1960)
Flesh and Fluids.
Loynaz, Dulce Maria
Calm, The.
Cloud, The.
Embrace.
Futile Flight, Futile Fugue.
Last Days of Home, *sel.*
Sea Surrounded.
Snow.
Time.
XXX.
Lu Chao-lin (c.641–80)
Chang'an.
Old Idea of Choan by Rosoriu.
Lu Chi (261–303)
Art of Writing, The, *sels.*
Rhymeprose on Literature.
She Thinks of Her Beloved.
Song of Mount T'ai.
Summoning the Recluse.
Lu Chih (1246?–1309?)
Seventy Years Are Few.
Tune: "Drunk in the East Wind."
"Lu Hsün" (Chou Shu-jen) (1881–1936)
Call to Arms.
Hesitation.
Lu Lun (*fl.* c.770)
Black moon geese fly high.
Grass rustle through dim woods.
Lu Mei-Po
Snow and the Plum, The—1.
Snow and the Plum, The—2.
Lu Yu (1125–1210)
At Ta-an I Got Sick from Wine and Had to
Lay Over for Half a Day. Governor Wang
Invited Me to His Place Again.
Blue Rapids.
I Had Occasion to Tell a Visitor about an Old
Trip I Took.
Idleness.
Insomnia: "Even when I fall asleep early."
Lazy.
Merchant's Joy, The.
Mural, Ch'ien-ming Temple.
Night Thoughts.
Night Thoughts.
Rain on the River [1956].
Rain on the River [1970].
Stone on the Hilltop, The.
To Show to My Sons.
Tune: "Hairpin Phoenix"
Wild Flower Man, The.
Written in a Carefree Mood.
Lubasch, Lisa (b. 1973)
Enough to Say.
Lubomirski, Karl (b. 1939)
Mother.
Luca, Gherasim (1913–94)
End of the World, The: To Embody.
Fin du monde, La: Prendre corps.

Ma déraison d'être.
My Folly of Being.

Lucan (Marcus Annaeus Lucanus) (A.D. 39–65)
Civil War [Bellum Civile] or Pharsalia, sels.

Lucanus, Marcus Annaeus See Lucan

Lucas, John
Good Sunday.
Nes From Nowhere.

Lucas, Tony (b. 1941)
Town Garden, A.

Lucca, Carmen D.
Conversation with Duke Ellington and Louis (Pops) Armstrong.

Luce, Nancy (fl. 1860)
Poor Little Hearts, sel.

"Lucebert" (L. J. Swaanswijk) (b. 1924)
Fishermen from Ma Yuan.
I Reel Off.
9000 Jackals Swimming to Boston.
Rousseau Le Douanier.

Lucilius (d. c.102 B.C.)
Lean Gaius, who was thinner than a straw.

Lucretius (Titus Lucretius Carus) (94–55 B.C.)
De Rerum Natura (On the Nature of Things), sels.

Ludvigson, Susan Bartels (b. 1942)
Inventing My Parents.
Not Swans.

Lueck, Daigan
You want to climb the steps.

Lugones, Leopoldo (1874–1938)
Gray Waves.
Indulgence.
Rain Psalm.
Slow Delight.
White Solitude.

Lukata, Baba
Ashy Gal.
Interpretations.
Rehearsal.

Lum, Wing Tek
Chinese Hot Pot.
Going Home.
Picture of my Mother's Family, A.
Riding the North Point Ferry.
Urban Love Songs.

Lumbreras, Ernesto (b. 1966)
Arde el horizonte.
Cielo, El.
Cielo, El / puede venirse abajo esta mañana.
Colina verde, una colina verde, Una.
Good-for-nothings on a White Corner.
Green Hill, a Green Hill, A.
¿Hacia Donde?
Horizon Burns, The.
Keys of the Saint.
Llaves de santo.
Overflowing Willow.
Regresión del sauce.
Regression of the Willow.
Reunión de violonchelos.
Reunion of Cellos.
Sauce desbordado.
Sky, The.
Sky, The / could collapse this morning.
Vagos en una esquina blanca.
Where To?

Lumelli, Angelo (b. 1944)
Candid Camera.
There are no pacts.
They could be reservoirs for water.
You first, shift your attention (that is, if you withdraw).

Lummis, Suzanne (b. 1951)
Femme Fatale.
Fish I Remember.
Letter to My Assailant.
Sea Chanty.
Shangri-la.
Why Life Is Worth Living.

Lumsden, Roddy (b. 1966)
Always.
Beginning of the End, The.
Incident in a Filing Cupboard.

ITMA.
Man I Could Have Been, The.
Mercy.
Older Woman, An.
Piquant.
Prayer to Be with Mercurial Women.
Show and Tell.
Then.
Tricks for the Barmaid.
Vanishing.
Yeah Yeah Yeah.

Lund, Orval
Wrist-wrestling Father.

Lundberg, John
Chivalry.

Luschei, Glenna
Arrangement.
Here.
Highway.
Magic: "You went by my house."
Pozo Basket, The.
Water Song, The.

Lustig, Dana Lisa
And I am lonely and small in all this, goodnight.
Barefoot/extinguish at will.
Big guns go boom! (for Mark Prejsnar).
Plane song.

Luterman, Alison
Another Vigil at San Quentin.
Justice of the Peace, The.
On Not Flying to Hawaii.

Luther, Martin (1483–1546)
From Depths of Woe I Cry to You.
From Heaven Above to Earth I Come.
In the Very Midst of Life.
Mighty Fortress Is Our God, A.

Luttrell, Henry (1765?–1851)
Letter to Julia, in Rhyme, sels.

Luu Trong Lu
Autumn End.

Lux, Thomas (b. 1946)
Amiel's Leg.
Black Road Over Which Green Trees Grow.
Bodo.
Can Tie Shoes but Won't.
Commercial Leech Farming Today.
Creature Has a Purpose, The.
Dark Comes On in Blocks, in Cubes, The.
Ecstasy Notebook.
Fisherman's Pants, The.
From the High Ground.
Gorgeous Surfaces.
Grain Burning Far Away.
Grim Town in a Steep Valley.
Hungry Gap-Time, The.
I Love You Sweetheart.
Language Animal, The.
Large Branch Splintering Off a Tree in a Storm, A.
Little Tooth, A.
Loudmouth Soup.
Man Gets Off Work Early, A.
Man into Whose Yard You Should Not Hit Your Ball, The.
Marine Snow at Mid-Depths and Down.
Men with Small Heads.
Midnight Tennis Match, The.
My Grandmother's Funeral.
Neighborhood of Make-Believe, The.
Night above the Town.
One Meat Ball.
People of the Other Village, The.
Perfect God, The.
Plague Victims Catapulted Over Walls Into Besieged City.
Poem in Thanks.
So You Put the Dog to Sleep.
Solo Native.
Swimming Pool, The.
Tarantulas on the Lifebuoy.
There Were Some Summers.
Thirst of Turtles, The.
Thrombosis Trombone.
To Help the Monkey Cross the River.

Ultima Thule.
Unlike, for Example, the Sound of a Riptooth Saw.
Upon Seeing an Ultrasound Photo of an Unborn Child.
View From a Porch.
Walt Whitman's Brain Dropped on Laboratory Floor.
Wife Hits Moose.
Wordsworths: William and Dorothy, The.

Luzi, Mario (b. 1914)
In the Dark Body of Metamorphosis, sels.
Pieces from a Mortal Duet, sels.

Ly Ngoc Kieu (Dieu Nhan) (1041–1113)
Birth, old age.

Lydgate, John (1370?–1451?)
Complaint of the Black Knight, The, sels.
Daunce of Death, The, sel.
Duplicity of Women, The.
Like a Midsummer Rose.
Thank God for All.
Vox Ultima Crucis.

Lyly, John (1553–1606)
Alexander and Campaspe, sels.
Endimion, sels.
Midas, sels.
Sapho and Phao, sels.

Lyman Jr., Dean B.
Eternal Controversy, The.

Lynch, Charles (b. 1943)
Ancestral Echoes/Rap Music.

Lynch, Kathleen
Ophelia in Utah.

Lynch, Peggy Zuleika
True Texan, A.

Lynch, Thomas (b. 1948)
At the Opening of Oak Grove Cemetary Bridge.
Custody.
Death, A: "In the end you want the clean dimensions of it mentioned."
Grimalkin.
Maura.
Skating with Heather Grace.

Lyndsay [or Lindsay], Sir David (c.1486–1555)
Ane Satire [or Satyre] of the Three [or Thrie] Estaitis, sel.
Bagsche's Complaint.
Dreme, The, sels.
Monarche, The, sels.

Lynes, Jeanette (b. 1956)
Brave.
Fern Kidnappings, The.
Muskoxen.
Valley, After Blossoms, The.
What We Learned on the Highway Near St. John's.

Lyon, George Ella (b. 1949)
Foot-Washing, The.

Lyons, Stephen J.
Loving Along Western Rivers.
Remembering.
Touching You Underwater.

Lysaght, Edward (1763–1810)
Garnyvillo.
Kitty of Coleraine.
Our Dear Native Island.

Lysohorsky, Ondra (1909–89)
At a Sunlit Window.
Ballad of Jan Palach, Student and Heretic.
22.6.1941.

Lyte, Henry Francis (1793–1847)
Abide With Me.

Lytton, Edward Robert Bulwer (1831–91)
Arthur, sels.
Count Rinaldo Rinaldi, sels.
Going Back Again.
Midges, sel.
Misery, sels.
Vampyre, The, sel.

Lytton, Edward Robert Bulwer-Lytton, 1st Earl of See Lytton, Edward Robert Bulwer [Owen Meredith]

M

M-1
Police State.

M–rt–n, B–ll (*fl.* c.1726)
Humble Wish, The.

"Ma" *See* Rainey, Gertrude "Ma"

Ma Chih-yüan (1260?–1334?)
Evening Bells near a Temple.
In Autumn.
Love Song: "Clouds circle the moon."
Tune: "Heaven-Cleansed Sands."
Tune: "Sky-Pure Sand."
Tune: "Song of Clear River."
Tune: "Winds of Falling Plums."

Maar, Dora (1907–97)
Grandes Constructions, Les.
If the Touching Memory.
Si l'attendrissant souvenir.
These Tall Constructions.

Maassen, Ruth
Confessions of a Pisciphobe.

Mabuza, Lindiwe
Death to the Gold Mine!
Dream Cloud.
Love Song, A: "It was good."
Tired Lizi Tired.

mac Lenini, Colman
In Praise of a Sword Given Him by His Prince.

Mac Lochlainn, Gearóid (b. 1967)
Artists, The.
Irish-speaking Mynah, The.
Rite of Passage.
Second Tongue.

Mac Low, Jackson (1922–2004)
Almost Casanova Electricity.
Antic Quatrains.
Asymmetry 205.
Central America.
59th Light Poem: for La Monte Young and
  Marian Zazeela—6 November 1982.
Galactic anachronisms enslave assessments.
Giant Otters.
Giant Philosophical Otters.
Lack of Balance but not Fatal, A.
Mani-Mani Gatha.
Pieces O'six—XVIII.
Pieces O'six—XXIV.
Presidents of the United States of America,
  The, *sels.*
Pronouns, The—A Collection of 40 Dances—
  For the Dancers, *sels.*
7th Light Poem: For John Cage—17 June
  1962.
3rd Light Poem: For Spencer, Beate, &
  Sebastian Holst—12 June 1962.
34th Merzgedicht in Memoriam Kurt
  Schwitters.
Trope Market.
Twenties 3.
Twenties 27.
Twenties 26.
Waves Broke on the Shore, The.

MacAdams, Lewis (b. 1944)
Pockets of Haze.

Mac-An-T-Saoir, Donnchadh Bàn Mac *See*
MacIntyre, Duncan Ban

Macaoidh, Rob Donn *See* MacKay, Robert

Macari, Anne Marie
After the Rain.
Burial Mound.
Counting the Years.
Even Love.
New York, 1927.

**Macartney, Frederick Thomas Bennett (1887–
1980)**
Kyrielle: Party Politics.

**Macaulay, Thomas Babington Macaulay, 1st
Baron (1800–59)**
Battle of Naseby, The.
Country Clergyman's Trip to Cambridge, The.
Dies IrÆ.
Jacobite's Epitaph, A.

Lays of Ancient Rome, *sels.*
Radical War Song, A.

MacBeth [*or* Macbeth], George (1932–92)
Alsatian.
Bedtime Story.
Crab-Apple Crisis, The.
God of Love, The.
Land-Mine, The.
Orange Poem, The.
Owl.
Rumanian of Maria Banus, The, *sels.*
Shotts.
Snowdrops.
Ward, The.
Worst Fear, The.

MacCaig, Norman (1910–96)
Basking Shark.
Blue Tit on a String of Peanuts.
Byre.
Chauvinist.
Climbing Suilven.
Crossing the Border.
Double Life.
Feeding Ducks.
Fetching Cows.
Frogs.
Golden Calf.
Gone Are the Days.
Heron.
Instrument and Agent.
Intruder in a Set Scene.
Kingfisher.
Likenesses.
No Choice.
No Consolation.
Notations of Ten Summer Minutes.
Of You.
Praise of a Collie.
Red and the Black, The.
Return to Scalpay.
Ringed Plover by a Water's Edge.
Sleeping Compartment.
Sleet.
Small Lochs.
So Many Summers.
Solitary Crow.
Stars and Planets.
Summer Farm.
Toad.
Wild Oats.

MacCarthy, Catherine Phil (b. 1954)
Island of Miracles.

MacCarthy, Charlotte
Contentment, to a Friend.
To the Same.

MacCathmhaoil, Seosamh *See* Campbell, Joseph

MacConglinne (*fl.* 12th cent.)
Vision of MacConglinne, The.

MacDermott, Martin
Girl of the Red Mouth.

**MacDiarmid, Hugh (Christopher Murray
Grieve) (1892–1978)**
Another Epitaph on an Army of Mercenaries.
At My Father's Grave.
Ballad of the General Strike.
Bonnie Broukit Bairn, The.
British Leftish Poetry, 1930–40.
By Wauchopeside.
Caledonian Antisyzygy, The.
Cattle Show.
Cloudburst and Soaring Moon.
Crystals like Blood.
Dead Liebknecht, The.
Drunk Man Looks at the Thistle, A, *sels.*
Eemis-Stane, The.
Empty Vessel.
Ex Vermibus.
Glass of Pure Water, The.
I Heard Christ Sing.
In Memoriam James Joyce, *sels.*
In the Children's Hospital.
In the Pantry.
Innumerable Christ, The.
Lament for the Great Music, *sel.*
Light and Shadow.

Little White Rose, The.
Lo! A Child Is Born.
Milk-Wort and Bog Cotton.
Moonstruck.
O Jesu Parvule.
O Wha's the Bride?
Of John Davidson.
On a Raised Beach, *sel.*
On the Oxford Book of Victorian Verse.
Parley of Beasts.
Perfect.
Poetry and Science.
Robber, The.
Sauchs in the Reuch Heuch Hauch, The.
Scotland Small?
Scunner.
Second Hymn to Lenin.
Skeleton of the Future, The.
Spur of Love, The.
Sunny Gale.
To a Friend and Fellow Poet.
To a Sea Eagle.
Two Memories.
Under the Greenwood Tree.
Vision of Myself, A.
Watergaw, The.
Wheesht, Wheesht.
Whip-the-World.
Why I Choose Red.
With a Lifting of the Head.
With the Herring Fishers.
World of Words, The, *sels.*

Macdonagh, Thomas (1878–1916)
John-John.

**MacDonald, Alexander (Alasdair MacMhaighstir
Alasdair) (1700–70)**
Clanranald's Galley, *sels.*
Song of Summer, *sel.*

MacDonald, Ballard
Somebody Loves Me.

Macdonald, Cicely *See* Na Ceapaich, Sileas

MacDonald, Cynthia (b. 1932)
And Cause His Countenance to Shine upon
  You: *Corpus Christi, Texas.*
Dangers of Looking Back, The.
Kilgore Rangerette Whose Life Was Ruined,
  The.
Lobster, The.
Two Brothers in a Field of Absence.

Macdonald, George (1824–1905)
At the Back of the North Wind, *sels.*
Baby-Sermon, A.
Christmas Carol, A.
Dorcas.
Father's Hymn for the Mother to Sing.
Lost and Found.
Mammon Marriage.
O Thou of Little Faith!
Paul Faber, Surgeon, *sels.*
Prayer, A: "When I look back upon my life
  nigh spent."
Rest ("When round the earth the Father's
  hands.").
Rest ("Who dwelleth in that secret place.").
Sheep and the Goat, The.
Song.
Sonnet: "This infant world has taken long to
  make."
Sweet Peril.
This, this is what I love, and what is this?
What love I when I love Thee, O my God?
Wind and the Moon, The.

MacDonald, Hugh (b. 1945)
Digging of Deep Wells, The.
Shingle Flies.

MacDonald, John *See* Lom, Iain

MacDonogh, Patrick (1902–61)
She Walked Unaware.

MacEwen, Gwendolyn (b. 1941)
Child Dancing, The.
Children Are Laughing, The.
Dark Pines under Water.
Death of the Loch Ness Monster, The.
Discovery, The.
Eden, Eden.

Inside the Great Pyramid.
Letter to a Future Generation.
Open Secrets.
T. E. Lawrence Poems, The, *sels.*

MacGabhrain, Aodh *See* MacGowran, Hugh
MacGill, Patrick (b. 1890)
Matey.
MacGill-Eain, Somhairle *See* MacLean, Sorley
Macgillivray, Pittendrigh (1856–1938)
Mercy o' Gode.
MacGowran, Hugh (Aodh MacGabhrain) (*fl. c.1720*)
Description of an Irish Feast, The.
Macgoye, Marjorie Oludhe
August the First; Court Martial. The Mother Speaks.
August the First: The Shadow. Patel Speaks.
August the First: The Watchman Speaks.
For Miriam.
Freedom Song, A.
Letter to a Friend.
Mathenge.
Muffled Cry, A.
Omera.
MacGreevy [*or* McGreevy], Thomas (1894–1967)
Aodh Ruadh O'Domhnaill.
Dechtire.
Homage to Hieronymus Bosch.
Homage to Jack Yeats.
Recessional.
MacGregor, Mrs., of Glenstrae (*fl. 1570*)
Lament for MacGregor of Glenstrae.
MacGuigan, Brian
Contentment: "Why am I."
Macha, Freddy
Artist and a Wailing Mother, An.
Corruption.
Machado Ruiz, Antonio (1875–1939)
A Don Francisco Giner de los Ríos.
Allá, en las tierras altas.
Amancer de Otoño.
And He Was the Evil Spirit of My Dreams.
Autumn Sunrise.
Breeze Tells Me, Loved One, The.
Campo.
Clock Struck Twelve Times, The.
Close to the Road.
Clouds Ripped Open.
Come sing with me in chorus: it's nothing, all we know.
Crime Was in Granada, The.
Daydreams Have Endlessly Turning Paths.
Deep Song.
Del Camino, *sels.*
Denuded Is the Earth.
Desde el umbral de un sueño me llamaron.
Desgarrada la nube; el arco iris.
España Joven, Una.
Eye You See Isn't, The.
Eyes, The.
For Don Francisco Giner de Los Ríos.
From the Doorsill of a Dream.
Good Thing Is, We Know, The.
He andado muchos caminos.
Her Street Is Dark.
Here's another Spaniard! Welcome!
House of Alvargonzález, The.
I go on dreaming.
I Have Never Wanted Fame.
I Have Walked Down Many Roads.
If I were a poet / of love, I would make.
In the Fields.
Is My Soul Asleep?
It Doesn't Matter Now.
It's Possible That While We Were Dreaming.
Lament of the Virtues and Verses on Account of the Death of Don Guido.
Last Night.
Last night while I was sleeping.
Look, our Spaniard's yawning.
Lord, You Have Ripped Away.
Meditation for this Day.
Memory from Childhood.
Moldering Hulk, The.
Moral Proverbs and Folk Songs, *sels.*

On the Banks of the Duero.
On the Bare Roadway.
Parables, I.
People Possess Four Things.
Plaza and the Flaming Orange Trees, The.
Plaza Has a Tower, The.
Poem: "Figures in the fields against the sky!"
Poem: "Frail sound of a tunic trailing, A."
Poem: "Naked is the earth."
Poem: "We think to create festivals."
Portrait.
Portrait.
Portrait ("My childhood is memories of a patio in Seville.").
Primavera.
Rainbow at Night.
Recuerdo Infantil.
Rose of Fire.
Siesta.
Song: "Now the moon is rising."
Spring Has Come.
Summer Night.
Summer's Night, A.
Tavern Guitar Playing a *Jota* Today.
Tell Me If You Remember, Love.
There, in the High Part.
Today's Meditation.
Walker, It Is Your Footsteps.
Water Wheel, The.
Water Wheel, The ("Afternoon arrived, The.").
Who Placed, Amidst the Tracts of Ash.
Wind, One Brilliant Day, The.
Y era el demonio de mi sueño, el ángel.
Y nada importa ya que el vino de oro.
Yesterday, dreamed He was near me.
Young Spain, A.
Machan, Katharyn Howd
Hazel Tells LaVerne.
In 1969.
No, Superman Was Not the Only One.
Machej, Zbigniew (b. 1958)
Orchards in July.
MacInnes, Mairi (b. 1925)
I Object, said the Object.
Mass.
MacIntyre, Duncan Ban (1724–1812)
Last Farewell to the Hills, *sels.*
MacIntyre, Sue
Christmas Present for My Mother.
Letters from the Concertina File 1939–1940.
MacIntyre, Tom (b. 1933)
On Sweet Killen Hill.
Yellow Bittern, The.
Mack, Cecil
Charleston.
Charleston.
He's a Cousin of Mine.
That's Why They Call Me "Shine."
MacKay, Charles (1814–89)
Clear the Way.
Man's Heart, A, *sels.*
Only a Thought.
Volunteers, The, *sels.*
MacKay, Isabel Ecclestone (1875–1928)
Meeting, The.
Mackay, Jessie (1864–1938)
In Galilee.
Mackay, John Henry (1864–1933)
Nameless Love, The.
Tomorrow.
MacKay, Robert (Macaoidh, Rob Donn) (1714–78)
Rispond Miser, The.
Mackay-Warna, Gordon
Cattle Loading.
MacKellar, Dorothea (b. 1885)
Arms and the Woman.
Fancy Dress.
Heritage.
MacKenzie, John (b. 1968)
Hearthouse.
Me as an Archaeologist.
My love is strung with the ancient.
Sledgehammer.

Mackenzie, Kenneth (1913–55)
Caesura.
Children Go, The.
Door swung open . . . , The.
Fool, The.
Ginger-flowers.
Heat.
Searchlights.
Shall Then Another.
Sick Men Sleeping.
Snake, The.
Table-Birds.
Two Trinities.
MacKenzie, Rob (b. 1964)
Blue Sky in Morning.
Category Mistakes in Biochemistry.
Like Pornography.
Square.
Mackey, Nathaniel (b. 1947)
Alphabet of Ahtt.
Degree Four.
Dream Thief.
Ghede Poem.
Glenn on Monk's Mountain.
Go Left Out of Shantiville.
Kiche Manitou.
Phantom Light of All Our Day, The.
Shower of Secret Things, The.
Song of the Andoumboulou, *sels.*
Song of the Andoumboulou: 15.
Sound and Cerement.
Winged Abyss.
MacKie, Alastair (b. 1925)
Pieta.
Primary Teachers.
Schoolquine.
Mackie, Albert D. (b. 1904)
Molecatcher.
Newsboy.
Mackinnon, Rayne (1937–2002)
After the Snow.
Bruckner.
Cuillin, The.
Scotland: "Green-coated elms stand placidly around."
Mackintosh, Ewart Alan (1893–1917)
Cha Till Maccruimein (Departure of the 4th Camerons).
In Memoriam, Private D. Sutherland.
Macklin, Elizabeth (b. 1952)
House Style, The.
Mackowski, Joanie
Self-Portrait, Double Exposed.
MacLaine, Brent (b. 1952)
Making the Middle Be.
North Shore Park.
Story of My Land, The, *sels.*
Maclaren, Hamish
Island Rose.
Maclean, Alasdair (b. 1926)
After Culloden.
Question and Answer.
Rams.
MacLean, Sorley (Somhairle MacGill-Eain) (b. 1911)
Calbharaigh.
Calvary: "My eye is not on Calvary."
Coin is madaidhean-allaidh.
Death Valley.
Dogs and Wolves.
Ebb.
Hallaig.
Hallaig.
Heroes.
Highland Woman, A.
Kinloch Ainort.
Lìonmhorachd anns na speuran.
My Een Are Nae on Calvary.
Shores.
Tràighean.
Tumultuous Plenty in the Heavens.
Turmoil, The.
MacLeish, Archibald (1892–1982)
Ars Poetica: "Poem should be palpable and mute, A."

Autumn.
Burying Ground by the Ties.
Conquistador, *sels*.
Cook County.
Dover Beach—a Note to That Poem.
Eleven.
End of the World, The.
Epistle to Be Left in the Earth.
Epistle to the Rapalloan.
Immortal Autumn.
Invocation to the Social Muse.
Memorial Rain.
Old Men in the Leaf Smoke, The.
Panic.
Pastoral.
Reconciliation, The.
Return.
Sentiments for a Dedication.
Snowflake Which Is Now and Hence Forever,
   The.
Songs for Eve, *sels*.
Speech to a Crowd.
Too-Late Born, The.
Voyage to the Moon ("Wanderer in our
   skies.").
Voyage West.
What Any Lover Learns.
Wildwest.
You Also, Gaius Valerius Catullus.
You, Andrew Marvell.
MacLellan, Robert (b. 1907)
   Sang.
MacLeod, Anne (b. 1951)
   Persephone's Daughter.
   Shakespeare No More.
Macleod, Mary (Màiri Nighean Alasdair Ruaidh)
   (b. c.1615, d. after 1705)
   Blue Song.
   Dirge: "It is harm to me and anguish."
   Tricky Margaret.
Macleod, Norman (1812–72)
   Waggin' O' Our Dog's Tail, The.
MacLeod, Sue (b. 1955)
   Especially after rain, the gulls.
   This is the body, consoling itself.
   When night meets thread and needle and lies
      down among the bedclothes.
MacMuireadach, Niall Mor (c.1550–c.1615)
   Farewell for ever to last night.
   Farewell to Last Night.
MacNamara, Francis (b. 1811?)
   Convict's Tour to Hell, A.
   For the Company Underground.
   Petition from the Chain Gang at Newcastle to
      Captain Furlong the Superintendent, A.
MacNaughton, Anne (b. 1945)
   Cassin's Finch.
   Feast Day Dog.
   New Mex Hip.
   Season, The.
MacNeacail, Aonghas (b. 1942)
   Anoch is tu bhuam.
   Gaelic is alive.
   Oideachadh Ceart.
   Proper Schooling, A.
   Tonight You Being From Me.
MacNeice, Louis (1907–63)
   Autobiography.
   Autumn Journal, *sels*.
   Autumn Sequel, *sels*.
   Bad Dream.
   Bagpipe Music.
   Birmingham.
   British Museum Reading Room, The.
   Brother Fire.
   Carrickfergus.
   Charon.
   Château Jackson.
   Christmas Shopping.
   Circe.
   Cradle Song: "Clock's untiring fingers wind
      the wool of darkness, The."
   Cradle Song: "Sleep, my darling, sleep."
   Eclogue for Christmas, An.

Elegy for Minor Poets.
Entirely.
Evening in Connecticut.
Hand of Snapshots, A, *sels*.
House on a Cliff.
Individualist Speaks, The.
Introduction, The: "They were introduced in a
   grave glade."
Libertine, The.
London Rain.
Mayfly.
Meeting Point.
Morning Sun.
Museums.
Nature Morte.
Nostalgia.
Nuts in May.
Perdita.
Prayer Before Birth.
Selva Oscura.
Snow.
Soap Suds.
Springboard, The.
Star-Gazer.
Streets of Laredo, The.
Suicide, The.
Sunday Morning: "Down the road someone is
   practising scales."
Sunlight on the Garden, The.
Taxis, The.
Thalassa.
This Is the Life.
Trilogy for X, *sels*.
Trolls, The, *sel*.
Truisms, The.
Variation on Heraclitus.
Western Landscape.
What is Truth? Says Pilate.
Whit Monday.
Wolves.
MacNutt, F. B. (1873–1949)
   Let all the multitudes of light.
Macphee, Kona (b. 1969)
   IVF.
   My People.
   Night before the last day of January, The.
   No fairy story.
   Ultrasound at 13 Weeks.
Macpherson, Hugh (d. 2001)
   Looking for 78's in the 40's.
Macpherson, James ("Ossian") (1736–96)
   Fragments of Ancient Poetry, Collected in the
      Highlands of Scotland, *sels*.
Macpherson, Jay (b. 1931)
   Beauty of Job's Daughters, The.
   Boatman, The.
   Fisherman, The: "World was first a private
      park, The."
   Lost Soul, A.
   Swan, The.
   Third Eye, The.
   Way Down, The, *sels*.
   Well, The.
Macrae, Duncan (1905–67)
   Wee Cock Sparra, The.
Macrae, John (d. 1780)
   Sleep Softly.
MacSweeney, Barry (1948–2000)
   Cute Petite.
   Far Cliff Babylon.
   Flame Ode.
   I Looked Down on a Child Today.
   Ode Long Kesh.
   Ode: "Urals post-master, this is your."
   Pearl, *sels*.
   Seared to the echo.
   Totem Banking.
   Wreckage is the only Answer.
MacThomais, Ruaraidh *See* Thomson, Derick
MacWard, Owen Roe (d. 1849) *and* **Hugh**
   O'Donnell
   Dark Rosaleen.
Madách, Imre (1823–64)
   Tragedy of Man, *sels*.

Madan, Judith (1702–81)
   Abelard to Eloisa.
Madani, Rachida (b. 1953)
   Here I am Once More.
Madden, Edward (1898–1952)
   By the Light of the Silvery Moon.
Maddox, Marjorie (b. 1959)
   Cancer Diagnosis.
Madeira, Paul (*fl.* 1942)
   I'm Glad There Is You (In This World of
      Ordinary People).
Madge, Charles (1912–96)
   Solar Creation.
   Times, The.
Madgett, Naomi Long (Naomi Long
   Witherspoon) (b. 1923)
   Black Woman.
   Echoes.
   Images.
   Last Happy Day, The.
   Offspring.
   Old Women, The.
   Packrat.
   Plea for My Heart's Sake.
   Race Question, The.
   Reluctant Light.
   Simple.
   Woman with Flower.
Madhubuti, Haki R. (Don. L. Lee) (b. 1942)
   After Her Man Had Left Her for the Sixth
      Time That Year (An Uncommon
      Occurrence).
   Assassination.
   B Network, The.
   Big Momma.
   Books as Answer.
   Don't Cry, Scream.
   Empty Warriors.
   Gwendolyn Brooks.
   Killing Memory.
   Knocking Donkey Fleas off a Poet from the
      Southside of Chi.
   Loneliness, A.
   Magnificent Tomorrows.
   Malcolm Spoke / Who Listened?
   Men and Birth: the Unexplainable.
   Mothers.
   My Brothers.
   Poem Looking for a Reader, A.
   Poet: What Ever Happened to Luther?
   Possibiliites: Remembering Malcolm X.
   Self-Hatred of Don L. Lee, The.
   So Many Books, So Little Time.
   Sun House.
   Union of Two, The.
   We Walk the Way of the New World.
Madigan, Rick
   Curtis Fuller.
   Stereo Time with Booker Little.
Madonick, Michael David (b. 1950)
   Settled In.
Maeng Sasŏng (1360–1438)
   Four Seasons by the Rivers and Lakes, *sels*.
Maezumi, Taizan (1931–95)
   Untransmittable and moving eastward.
Magdeburg, Mechthild von (1210–94)
   Desert Has Many Teachings, The.
   Fish cannot drown in water, A.
   God Speaks to the Soul.
   God's Absence.
   How God Answers the Soul.
   How God Comes to the Soul.
   How the Soul Speaks to God.
   I cannot dance, O Lord.
   Of all that God has shown me.
   True love in every moment praises God.
Magee, John Gillespie, Jr. (1922–41)
   High Flight.
Magee, Thomas D'Arcy (*fl.* c.1848)
   Home Thoughts.
Magee, Wes (b. 1939)
   British Garden, A.
   Giant Rocket.
   How to Reach the Sun . . . on a Piece of Paper.

Maggs, Randall (b. 1944)
Night Crossing in Ice.
Signal Hill.
Tropical Toads.

Magidson, Herb (1906–86)
Continental (You Kiss While You're Dancing),
    The.
Gone with the Wind.
(I'm Afraid) The Masquerade Is Over.
Music, Maestro, Please!
T'Ain't No Use.

Maginn, William (1793–1842)
Rime of the Auncient Waggonere, The.

Magrelli, Valerio (b. 1957)
Before the last curve of the day.
Each photographed face.
Especially in weeping.
Every evening, bent over the bright.
I have a brain populated by women.
I have finally learned.
I have from you this red.
I have often imagined that glances.
I look for a way of writing.
I love uncertain gestures.
I prefer to come from silence to talk.
I sit, in treatment, at the movies, devoted.
If I must dial a number to call you.
If you melt some lead.
I'm what is missing.
In summer, like the theaters, I close up.
In the evening when the light is dim.
Like ground that's been walked over, it echoes.
Pen slides, The.
Side by side after the meal.
Ten poems written in one month.
There are words that coast alongside thought.
There's silence between one page and another.
Things have an admirable life.
This handwriting wears itself away.
Tomorrow morning I will take a shower.
We go through life this way.
Wood of my thoughts is on fire, The.

Maguire, Sarah (b. 1957)
Communion.
Divorce Referendum, The.
Fall, The.
Invisible Mender, The.
Liminal.
Perfect Timing.
Spilt Milk.

Mahadevi (Mahadeviyakka) (fl. 12th cent.)
I do not call it his sign.
It was like a stream.
Like an elephant.
On Her Decision to Stop Wearing Clothes.
So long as this breath fills your nostrils.
Vein of sapphires, A.
When I am hungry.
When the body becomes Your mirror.

Mahadeviyakka See Mahadevi

Mahapatra, Anuradha (b. 1956)
Tamburā.

Mahapatra, Jayanta (b. 1928)
Ash.
Main Temple Street, Puri.
Monsoon Day Fable, A.
Sanskrit.
Shadows: "Shadows can never open their
    mouths."
Summer Poem, A.
Taste for Tomorrow.

Mahdi, Sami (b. 1940)
War Diaries.

Maher, Mary
Not like a sock. The one.

Mahmoud, Fatima
What Was Not Conceivable.

Mahon, Derek (b. 1941)
Achill.
Afterlives.
Antarctica.
As It Should Be.
Consolations of Philosophy.
Courtyards in Delft.

Dejection [Ode].
Disused Shed in Co. Wexford, A.
Dog Days.
Dying Art, A.
Ecclesiastes.
Everything Is Going to Be All Right.
Ford Manor.
Garage in Co. Cork, A.
Girls on the Bridge.
Globe in [North] Carolina, The.
Going Home.
Grandfather.
Hunt by Night, The.
Image from Beckett, An.
In Carrowdore Churchyard.
Last of the Fire Kings, The.
Lives.
Mayo Tao, The.
Morning Radio.
Old Snaps, The.
Poem Beginning with a Line by Cavafy.
Rathlin.
Refusal to Mourn, A.
Snow Party, The.
Spring Vacation, The.
Swim in Co. Wicklow, A.
Tractatus.
Unborn Child, An.
Window, The.
Woods, The.
Yellow Book, The, sels.

**Mahony, Francis Sylvester ("Father Prout")
(1804–66)**
Bells of Shandon, The.

Māhtābcānd, Mahārājādhirāja (1825–79)
Who is this, all alone? Whose woman is She.

Maiden, Jennifer (b. 1949)
Air.
Anorexia.
Climbing.
Foundations, The.
Green Side, The.
In the Gloaming.
Language.
Mother-in-Law of the Marquis de Sade, The.
New.
Taste.

Maier, Julia
Timbalero.

Maihiot, Michelle M.
Playing Fields.

Maio, Samuel (b. 1955)
In Memoriam: "On this coast where they once
    arrived destined."
Love Song: "New pier is concrete, the streets
    are paved, The."

Maitland, Sir Thomas
Sir Thomas Maitland's Satyr upon Sir Niel
    Laing.

Majaj, Lisa Suhair
Arguments.
First Light.
In Season.
Jerusalem Song.
Recognized Futures.

Majer, Hugo
On my winter walk.
Spring.

Major, Clarence (b. 1936)
All the Same.
Apple Core.
Balance and Beauty.
Beaulieu.
Bruce and Nina.
Doll Believers, The.
Edge Guide for Impression.
Education by Degrees.
Funeral.
Giant Red Woman.
I Was Looking for the University.
Inside Diameter.
Isolate.
Jefferson Company, The.
Large Room with Wood Floor.
Little Girls Posing All Dressed Up.

Lost in the Desert.
Media on War: or, the Square Root of Vietnam.
Mortal Roundness.
News Story.
1915 Interior.
Not This—This Here!
On Trying to Imagine the Kiwi Pregnant.
Paragraph from English Speaking World.
Petition for Langston Hughes, A.
Pictures.
Poem Americans Are Going to Have to
    Memorize Soon, A.
Purchase, The.
Swallow the Lake.
Vietnam.
Water USA.

Major, Devorah (b. 1952)
Nommo: how we come to speak.

Majorino, Giancarlo (b. 1928)
Doing.
Hints.
Kisses.
Mirrored.
My Flesh in its Sweat.
Say--So I'll Say.
Scene-Script.

Majumdār, Harināth (1833–96)
Jaya / Don't wake up Hara's wife.

Mak, Lev (b. 1939)
Farewell to Russia.

Makah Oral Tradition
Song of Repulse to a Vain Lover.

Makeda (Queen of Sheba) (fl. 1000 B.C.)
I fell.
Wisdom is / sweeter than honey.

Makin, Bathsua Pell (fl. 17th cent.)
To Frederick V, by the Grace of God . . .
Upon the Much Lamented Death of the Right
    Honourable, the Lady Elizabeth Langham.

Makofske, Mary
Viola, to Olivia.

Maksimovic, Desanka (1898–1993)
For the Barren Woman.
St. Matthew, sels.

Makuck, Peter
Jet Lag.
Prey.
Story of Sound.

Makusho, Layman
Loving old priceless things.

Malachi
Psalm of Silk.

Malallah, Zakiyya (b. 1959)
Little Tales.
Women.

Malam, Charles (b. 1906)
Steam Shovel.

Malancioui, Ileana (b. 1940)
My Sister, the Empress.

Malanga, Gerard (b. 1943)
Apprentice, The.
3 Poems for Benedetta Barzini.

Malanova, Mara (b. 1970)
Among the men some carved-bone dice are
    thrown.
Like a faded painting.
Many films begin with a funeral.
Morning: "Main thing is not to oversleep, so as
    later not to have to run for dear life, The."

Malczewski, Anton (1793–1826)
After the Battle.

Malé, Belkis Cuza (b. 1942)
And Here are the Poets in Their Sad Portraits.
Creed.
For the Moment.
Glance.
Greek Metamorphosis.
Poet's Biography.
Women Don't Die on the Front Lines.

Malenis, Leonidas (b. 1937)
Hopeless Eveningsong.

Mallarmé, Stéphane (1842–98)
Afternoon of a Faun, The.

Afternoon of a Faun, The.
Album Leaf.
Favn in the Afternoon, A.
Fine suicide fled victoriously, The.
Gift of the Poem.
Glazier, The.
Le Livre, *sel.*
Pipe, The.
Saint.
Saint.
Sea Breeze.
Sea Breeze.
This virginal long-living lovely day.
Toast.
Toast.
Tomb.
Tomb of Charles Baudelaire, The.
Tomb of Edgar Allan Poe, The.
Tomb of Edgar Poe, The.
Virginal, vibrant, and beautiful dawn, The.
Virginal, Vivid, Beautiful, Will This Be.
When the shade threatened with the fatal
    decree.
With her pure nails offering their onyx high.

Mallet, David (1705–65)
Alfred: A Masque, *sels.*
On an Amorous Old Man.
William and Margaret.

Malloch, Donald (1877–1938)
Manly Love.

Malloch, Douglas (1877–1938)
Up and Doing.

Mallock, William Hurrell (1849–1923)
Questions: "Where are you now, little
    wandering."

Maloney, Frank R.
Grandmothers in Green and Orange.

Malouf, David (b. 1934)
Bicycle.
For Two Children.
Guide to the Perplexed.
Judas Touch, the.
Year of the Foxes, The.

Malroux, Claire (b. 1935)
Appointment in June.
Every Breath.
Every morning.
Fingers probe.
Il y a la Guerre ou la Paix.
In October.
Octet Before Winter.
Rendez-vous en juin.
There's War or There's Peace.
Toutes les haleines.

Maltby, Richard, Jr. (b. 1937)
I Don't Remember Christmas.
Little Bit Off, A.
Today Is the First Day of the Rest of My Life.

Malveisin, William (d. 1238)
Fergus of Galloway: Knight of King Arthur,
    sels.

Mamalatan
What She Said.

Man Giac (1051–1096)
Rebirth.

Manan (1591–1654)
Unfettered at last, a traveling monk.

Mandal, Bhadreśvar
I'm not a child any more, Syama.

Mandel, Eli W. (b. 1922)
City Park Merry-Go-Round.
Houdini.

Mandel, Naum Moiseievich *See* Korzhavin, Naum

Mandel, Tom (b. 1942)
Actor, The.
Jews in Hell.
Of Birds.
Realism.
Say Ja.

Mandela, Zindzi (b. 1959)
I Have Tried Hard.
I Saw as a Child.
I Waited for You Last Night.
Lock the Place in Your Heart.

Saviour.
There's an Unknown River in Soweto.

Mandell, Arlene L.
Middle Age.

Mandelstam [*or* Mandelshtam], Osip Emilevich
(1892–1938)
Ariosto.
Batyushkov.
Because I Let Go Your Hands.
Charlie Chaplin Poem, The.
Eyesight of Wasps.
Finding a Horseshoe.
I Am Deaf.
I Drink to the Asters of War.
I Hate the Light.
I Was Washing Outside in the Darkness.
In This Cool Transparent Spring.
Insomnia.
Insomnia. Homer. Taut Sails.
Lamarck.
[Last Poems].
Leningrad.
Leningrad.
Lightheartedly Take from the Palms of My
    Hands.
Like Grumbling Roman Plebs.
Mounds of Human Heads.
Mounds of Human Heads Are Wandering into
    the Distance.
Not yet dead, not yet alone.
Notre Dame.
Notre Dame.
O how much I would like—.
O Lord, Help Me to Live Through This Night.
Ode on Slate, The.
On Stony Pierian Spurs.
Phaedra.
Shy speechless sound, The.
Sleeplessness. Homer. The sails tight.
Stalin Epigram, The.
Three Octets.
Tristia.
Tristia, *sels.*
Valley Bleeds with Roman Rust, The.
When Psyche, Who Is Life, Descends Among
    the Shades.
Where Can I Hide in January.
Whoever Finds a Horseshoe.
You Took Away All the Oceans and All the
    Room.
Your image, tormenting and elusive.

Mandiela, Ahdri Zhina
Mih Feel It.
Speshal Rikwes.

"Mang Ke" (Jiang Shi-wei) (b. 1951)
Apeherd, *sels.*

Mangan, Gerald (b. 1951)
Ailsa Craig.
Glasgow 1956.
Kirkintilloch Revisited.

Mangan, James Clarence (1803–49)
Lover's Farewell, The.
Nameless One, The.
O'Hussey's Ode to the Maguire.
Siberia.
St. Patrick's Hymn Before Tara, *sel.*
To Amine.
Twenty Golden Years Ago.

Manguso, Sarah (b. 1974)
Piano, The: "I try to imagine the lid closing
    but it won't."
Rider, The.

Manhire, Bill (b. 1946)
Brazil.
Distance between Bodies, The.
On Originality.
Out West.

Manifold, John Streeter (1915–85)
Defensive Position.
Fife Tune.
Griesly Wife, The.
Makhno's Philosophers.
Night Piece.
Sirens, The.

Manigat, Max (b. 1931)
Morisseau-Leroy.

Manilius, Marcus (*fl.* c.1st cent. A.D.)
Astronomica, The, *sel.*

Manley, Delariviere (1670–1724)
Lost Lover, The, *sels.*
Song and Musick, Set by Mr. Eccles, and Sung
    by Mrs. Leveridge.
To the Author of Agnes de Castro.

Manley, Rachel
Bob Marley's Dead.

Mann, David
No Moon at All.

Mann, Randall
Elegy for the Hurdler.
Fiduciary.

Manning, Frederic (1882–1935)
Leaves.
Trenches, The.

Manning, Maurice (b. 1966)
Condensed History of Beauty, A.
First.
O boss of ashes boss of dust.
On Death.
On God.

Mannyng [*or* Manning], Robert (1288–1338)
Praise of Women.

Manrique, Jaime
Barcelona Days.
Baudelaire's Spleen.
My Night with Frederico García Lorca (As
    Told by Edouard Roditi).
Tarzan.

Mansei *See* Mansei, Sami

Mansei, Sami (*fl.* 8th cent.)
Our Life in This World.

Mansfield, Katherine (Kathleen Beauchamp
Murry) (1888–1923)
Friendship.
Man with the Wooden Leg, The.
Meeting, The.
Secret Flowers.
To L. H. B.

Mansour, Ali
There Is Music Going Down the Stairs.
We Must Be Assured That a Fine Poet Will Be
    Born, Even after Fifteen Years.

Mansour, Joyce (b. 1928)
Anti-mnemonic self-vaccination.
Auditory Hallucinations.
Beyond the breakers.
Desire as Light as a Shuttle.
Embrace the Blade.
Empty Black Haunted House.
From an ass to an analyst and back.
Gently stroke a wound.
Going and Coming of Sequins.
I Opened Your Head.
I Saw the Red Electric.
I Saw You through My Closed Eye.
I Want to Sleep with You.
In the Gloom on the Left.
Into the Red Velvet.
Je veux dormir avec toi.
Last night I saw your corpse.
Lovely Monster.
Mango, A.
Men's Vices.
Night in the Shape of a Bison.
Of Sweet Rest.
Orage tire une marge argentée, L'
Papier d'argent.
Pericoloso Sporgersi, *sel.*
Rappelle-toi.
Regulation equipment.
Remember.
Seated on her bed legs spread open.
Storm Sketches a Silver Margin, The.
Sun is in Capricorn, The.
Ten to One to No.
They Have Weighed.
Tinfoil.
Vices of Men, The.
Wild Glee from Elsewhere.

Woman Kneeling in the Sorry Jelly, A.
Your Figure or the War Against Fat.
Mansour [or Mansur], Monica (b. 1946)
Desert 1.
My Memory.
Mansur, Abul Kasim See Firdowsi
Mant, Bishop Richard (1776–1848)
Church Bells, The.
House of God, The.
Social Worship.
True Knowledge.
Manyarrows, Victoria Lena (fl. 20th cent.)
Lakota Sister/Cherokee Mother.
See No Indian, Hear No Indian.
Today We Will Not Be Invisible Nor Silent.
Manzan (1635–1714)
One minute of sitting, one inch of Buddha.
Mao Tse-tung [or Mao Zedong] (1893–1976)
Chinese Ballad.
Glitter of a northern kingdom.
I stand alone in the cold autumn.
Return to Shaoshan.
Mao Wen-hsi (fl. c.930)
Drunk Among the Flowers.
I Mustn't Ask.
Mapanje, Jack A.
After Wiriyamu Village Massacre by
Portuguese.
Another Fools' Day Touches Down: Shush.
Cheerful Girls at Smiller's Bar, 1971, The.
From Florrie Abraham Witness, December
1972.
Glory Be to Chingwe's Hole.
Making Our Clowns Martyrs.
Messages.
On African Writing.
On Being Asked to Write a Poem for 1979.
On His Royal Blindness Paramount Chief
Kwangala.
These Too Are Our Elders.
Visiting Zomba Plateau.
We Wondered about the Mellow Peaches.
Mapun, Dus
O Myland Woman.
Mar, Yekhi'el (1921–69)
Anonymous Squad, An.
Between Sickle and Sword.
Maraini, Dacia (b. 1936)
Family Stories.
I Am Two.
I Dreamt a Pig.
I Spent the Night.
Lemon, Hot Water and a Blood Clot.
Little Woman with Medusa Eyes, A.
Love If This Is Love.
Man with Long Legs, The.
Plaza de Mayo.
Your Face Has No Name.
Marais, Eugène (1871–1936)
Dance of Sister Rain.
Marbod of Rennes (1035–1123)
Unyielding Youth, The, sels.
March, Ausiàs (1397?–1459)
As someone on his back for months of illness.
Day's in dread of losing her bright features,
The.
Know what I'm like? Some captain moors his
ship.
Let others hail the holidays with laughter.
Much as a man who takes delight in dreaming.
Not so with me as with the little page.
Out scouting for sound counsels? How to
prosper?
March, Joseph Moncure (1899–1977)
Wild Party, The, sels.
March, Sydney
Knockout, The.
Legacy.
Monk's Misterioso.
Thousand Marionettes, A.
Marchant, Frederick
Screen Porch.
Marchenko, Nikolai Nikolaevich See Morshen,
Nikolai Nikolaevich

Marcinkevičius, Justinas
Prelude to 'Blood and Ash.'
Marckant, John (fl. 16th cent.)
Lamentation, The.
Marcus, Adrianne (b. 1935)
Cleopatra.
Marcus, Ben
Battle at Horizon.
Delaying Relevance.
Justice.
Plagiarism.
Marcus, Morton (b. 1936)
Forgiveness.
I Think of Those Mornings.
Letter, The.
My Father's Hobby.
Picnic on the Bay Bridge.
Poem for Gonzales, California, The.
Whales.
Mardis, Jas. (b. 1961)
Good-bye Summer.
Perseverance.
Maré, Nicholás (1968–93)
You Can Say That the Bird as the Saying
Goes.
Marechera, Dambudzo (1954–87)
Cemetery in the Mind, The.
Desert Crossing.
Neither Innocence or Experience.
Old Man Inside Me, The.
When Love's Perished.
Marennikova, Kseniya (b. 1981)
Don't let me leave you, I may die.
I, Mariya, burn your fingers.
Mother, squatting hurts.
My head is spinning to the right.
Mares, E. A. (b. 1938)
Canyon, Texas Sestina.
Liberación.
Millennium.
Wild Birds.
Margarido, Maria Manuela (b. 1926)
Landscape.
Roça.
Socope.
You Who Occupy Our Land.
Margolis, Gary (b. 1945)
Autumn Bees on Broccoli Blossoms Gone-by.
Kicking and Breathing.
Lacrosse.
On the Way to the Sitter's.
Town Meeting.
**Marguerite Antoinette Jeanne Marie Ghislaine
Cleenwerke de Crayencour** See Yourcenar,
Marguerite
Margulies, Stephen (b. 1951)
Relentlessly Lovelorn, the Non-Sleeper
Whispers and Re-Whispers a Magic Charm
Against His Wound's Roar.
"Maria, Laura" See Robinson, Mary
Mariani, Paul (b. 1940)
Betty.
Landscape with Dog.
Moonrise as Abstraction.
Mountain View with Figures.
Shadow Portrait.
Variations on a Theme by Justice.
Marie de France (c.1155–89)
Lanval.
Wolf and the Lamb, The.
Wolf and the Sow, The.
Marinetti, Filippo Tommaso (1876–1944)
Landscape Heard, A.
Manifesto of Futurism, The, sel.
They are Coming.
Variety Theater Manifesto, The, sels.
Zang Tumb Tuuum, sels.
Marinho, Tony
Colour.
Ear of a Goat, The.
**Marino, Giambattista [or Giovanni Battista]
(1569–1625)**
Massacre of the Innocents, The, sel.

Out of the Italian.
Strage degli innocenti, La, sels.
Marion, George, Jr. (1909–68)
Ladies Who Sing with a Band, The.
Love Is a Random Thing.
My Future Just Passed.
There's a Man in My Life.
Marion, Paul (b. 1954)
Found Poem, North of Boston.
Mariposa See Fernandez, Maria
Mark, Diane Mei Lin
Suzie Wong Doesn't Live Here.
Mark, Sabrina Orah (b. 1975)
Babies, The.
Experiments Lasted Through the Winter, The.
Hello: "I am one anatomy and take turns.
Sometimes after dinner I wrap them in a
newspaper."
Mustache, The.
Transylvania, 1919.
Markell, Jennifer
Veterinary Student, The.
Markham, E. A. (b. 1939)
Sea, The.
Markham, Edwin (1852–1940)
After Reading Shakspere.
Avengers, The.
In Death Valley.
Leaf from the Devil's Jest-Book, A.
Lincoln, the Man of the People.
Man with the Hoe, The.
Outwitted.
Preparedness.
Markham, Malinda
After Aesop.
Compendium Notes.
Having Cut the Sparrow's Heart.
Obedience / Intention to Hunt.
Of Children on Wood.
Orange Tree Glistens, The.
Petition.
Rock in the Garden Allows People In, The.
To Understand Flight.
We Folded the Hours and Set Them in the
Rain.
Markotić, Nicole (b. 1962)
No such thing as a prose poem.
Repeat the capitalism of narrative.
Seven blind curves.
Try book-ending punctuation vouchers.
Verbatim begins with this decade's hit and
miss.
Markovitch, Henriette Theodora See Maar, Dora
Marks, Corey (b. 1970)
After the Shipwreck.
Portrait of a Child.
Three Bridges.
Marks, Gerald
All of Me.
Marks, S. J. (b. 1939)
Losing Myself.
November Woods.
Poem in Three Parts.
Poem With Two Seasons Right Now.
Returning in Wind and Drizzle to My Home.
To Go Through Life Is to Walk Across a Field.
To the Ocean.
Markus, Peter (b. 1966)
Black Light.
Light.
Shooting Crows.
Marlatt, Daphne (b. 1942)
Coming to You.
Small print.
Steveston, sels.
Touch to My Tongue, sels.
Marlatt, David (b. 1963)
Bruce and the Bluegills.
Katherine's Hair.
Summer of the New Well.
Working Girl.
Marlis, Stefanie (b. 1951)
Risible.
Snack.

Marlowe, Alex
He Does Not Give the Reader One Line of
Information.
Marlowe, Christopher (1564–93)
Dido, Queen of Carthage, *sel*.
Doctor Faustus, *sels*.
Edward the Second, *sels*.
Hero and Leander, *sels*.
Lucan's Pharsalia Book 1, *sel*.
Ovids Elegies Book 1, *sel*.
Passionate Shepherd to His Love, The.
Tamburlaine the Great, *sels*.
Tamburlaine the Great, Part 2, *sels*.
Tragedy of Dido, The, *sel*.
'Marnia (1968–92)
Accoutrement.
I Must be Able to Protect You.
I Want to Love You Very Much.
Maro, Publius Vergilius *See* Virgil [*or* Vergil]
Maroon, Bahiyyih (b. 1973)
Fire Keeper.
Neighbor.
Nude Womon Spotted in Cappuccino Cup.
**Marquis, Don (Donald Robert Perry Marquis)
(1878–1937)**
Aesop Revised by Archy.
Archy and Mehitabel, *sels*.
Archys Life of Mehitabel, *sels*.
Certain Maxims of Archy, *sel*.
Coming of Archy, The, *sel*.
Mehitabel S Extensive Past.
Mehitabel's Extensive Past, *sel*.
Mehitabel's Song.
Song of Mehitabel, The.
When One Loves Tensely.
Marquis, Donald Robert Perry *See* Marquis, Don
Marsh, Barbara
Papa.
Marshak, Samuel (1887–1904)
Immortality.
Marshall, Jack (b. 1937)
Air Dagger.
Gift, A.
In the Shadow of the Poisoned Wind.
Wing and Prayer.
Marshall, Susan
Chicago.
Marshall-Stoneking, Billy (b. 1947)
On the Death of Muriel Rukeyser.
Passage.
Picture Postcard.
Seasons of Fire, The.
Marsman, Hendrik (1899–1940)
Holland.
Landscape.
Memory of Holland.
Paradise Regained.
Polderland.
Polderland.
Marsman, Henk *See* Bernstein, Charles
Marson, Una (1905–65)
Gettin[g] de Spirit.
Kinky Hair Blues.
Marston, John (1575–1634)
Metamorphosis of Pigmalions Image, The, *sel*.
Satires, *sels*.
Scourge of Villainy [*or* Villanie], The, *sels*.
Scourge of Villanie, The, *sel*.
Marston, Philip Bourke (1850–87)
Love's Music.
Speechless: Upon the Marriage of Two Deaf
and Dumb Persons.
Vain Wish, A.
Marteau, Robert (b. 1925)
I Consent That Everything Vanishes.
Je consens que tout s'efface.
Martelli, Jennifer
Mal'Occhio.
Martí, José (1853–95)
I Dream Awake.
I grow a white rose.
I want, in the shade of a wing.
Opposite of Ornate and Rhetorical Poetry, The.

Simple Verses, *sels*.
Two Countries.
Martial (Marcus Valerius Martialis) (c.40–c.104)
Ad Quintilianum.
After her wedding-night, the nymph.
Agriculture.
Aulus, my girlfriend's in a dreadful plight.
Believe me, sir, I'd like to spend whole days.
Breath of balm from foreign branches pressed,
The.
Cornelius sighs . . . the lines I write.
Cure of my unquietness.
Dasius, chucker-out / at the Turkish Baths.
De Cœnatione Micae.
Did he have eyes and, if so, did he look.
Doctor Fell.
Epigram: Likeness, The.
Epigram: "Milo's from home; and, Milo being
gone."
Epigrams, *sels*.
Epitaph on Erotion.
For rank, descent and title famed.
Fronto, Father, Flaccilla, Mother, extend.
Gaurus, you have a fault for which.
Happy Life, A.
Happy Life, The.
He scanned me closely, Rufus, just as.
How to Do It.
Irresolute the down upon your cheek.
Just half our three score years and ten.
Lentinus! thou dost nought but fume, and fret.
Let every prudish reader use his feet.
Ligurra's fearful I'll contrive.
Lydia is as wide and slack.
My carefree Namesake, this the art.
My taste in women, Flaccus? Give me one.
Near the Vipsanian columns where the
aqueduct.
Oh If the Gods Would Make Me Rich.
Out of an Epigram of Martial.
Out of the house or be the wife I want.
People have the oddest kinks.
Post-Obits and the Poets.
Pre-eminent among scholars.
Procrastination.
Read of *Thyestes, Oedipus,* dark suns.
Roman Presents.
Roman Thank-You Letter, A.
Rome, I am Scorpus, foremost in the race.
Since you, Charmenion, come from Corinth.
Slipshod writing, premature publication.
They smell of *Corycian* saffron, of a.
This was the young Camonus; this his face.
To Cloe.
To His Book[e].
Traveller on the Flaminian Way.
Were lives of ease, dear Namesake, ours.
What a host you are, Mancinus.
When you say, "Quick, I'm going to come."
While unquiet, *Juvenal,* you haunt.
Who deem epigrams mere trifles.
Why, Hyllus, do you deny to me today.
Why is it modern books are little read.
Would you, my friend, in little room express.
You are a stool pigeon and.
You gave Bithynicus thousands yearly; still.
You rocked my cradle, Charidemus, once.
You say, *Postumus,* you'll live tomorrow.
You serve the best wines always, my dear sir.
You want me to call you generous.
You were a swan, you're now a crow.
You've told me, Maro.
Martialis, Marcus Valerius *See* Martial
Martien, Jerry
In Wild Iris Time.
Late 20th Century: Spring.
Rocks Along the Coast, The.
Martin, Angela
Viewing Mona Lisa.
Martin, Angus (b. 1952)
Passchendaele.
Who Among Common Men of Their Time?
Martin, C. D. (b. 1943)
His Eye Is on the Sparrow.

Martin, Camille
Learning to talk over and over.
No truck, *sels*.
Solfège parasite.
To abcs and from rimbaud.
Martin, Charles (b. 1942)
E. S. L.
Easter Sunday, 1985.
Metaphor of Grass in California.
Reflections after a Dry Spell.
Satyr, Cunnilinguent: To Herman Melville.
Speech Against Stone.
Terminal Colloquy.
Victoria's Secret.
What the Dark Proposes.
Martin, David (Ludwig Detsinyi) (b. 1915)
Dreams in German.
Martin, Douglas A.
Clock.
If We Were in a Gregg Araki Movie.
Martin, Gail
God Packs Lunches.
God Scrubs the Tub.
God Vacuums the Pool.
Lemons.
Martin, Herbert (b. 1933)
Miss Rosie Mae Watches Elvis Presley on The
Ed Sullivan Show.
Martin, Hugh (b. 1914)
Ev'ry Time.
Have Yourself a Merry Little Christmas.
I Never Felt Better.
Love: "Love can be a moment's madness."
Occasional Man, An.
That Face.
Trolley Song, The.
Martin, Philip (b. 1931)
Tongues.
Martin, Steve (b. 1945)
Cows in Trouble.
Demolition of the Cathedral at Chartres.
Martinaitis, Marcelijus
Forbid!
Kukutis Describes His Hut.
Kukutis in the Reich's Guard House.
Kukutis's Consciousness Becomes Alienated.
Kukutis's Fruitless Bread.
Kukutis's Lament under the Heavens.
Kukutis's Sermon to the Pigs.
Kukutis's Sinful Spirit.
Kukutis's Song.
Kukutis's Swallow's Hymn.
Kukutis's Trip on the Samogitian Highway.
Last Farewell to Kukutis.
Pony in Kukutis's Ear, A.
Silly Spring.
Unhappy Kukutis in the Potato Patch.
Zuveliskes's Women Mourn Over Kukutis.
Martineau, James (1805–1900)
Life's Success.
Martineau, Jean-Claude
Haiti Tomorrow.
Hooker.
Viejo.
Martinez, Demetria
Blessing Poem.
Remedios.
Song: "I dreamed my voice was an Anasazi
pot."
Martinez, Dionisio D.
Altruism.
Bad Alchemy.
Carp.
Cole Porter.
Cultivation of Orchids, The.
Death of Isadora Duncan, The.
Discreet Prayer, A.
Hysteria.
In a Duplex Near the San Andreas Fault.
Kinescope.
Matisse: Blue Nude, 1952.
Moto Perpetuo.
Need.
Nocturnes: "He closed the deal on the night. A
real."

Pain.
Prodigal Son Considers a Diplomatic Career,
  The.
Prodigal Son in His Own Words, The: Bees.
Standard Time: Novena for My Father.
Temporary Losses.
What the Men Talk About When the Women
  Leave the Room, *sels*.
Years of Solitude.

Martínez, Valerie (b. 1961)
Absence, Luminescent.
Camera Obscura.
Children of the Disappeared.
Coastal.
Ever So, Between.
Human Universe, The.
Into the Next One.
It Is Not.
New World, The.
Night of Fathers.
Nocturne: "To the interior, limbs folded."
Reliquaries, The.
Tesoro.
Traveler.

Martínez de Navarrete, José Manuel (1768–1809)
Separation from Clorila, The.

Martins, Maria (1900–73)
I Am the Tropical Night's High Noon.

Martinson, Harry Edmund (1904–78)
Cable Ship, The.
Cotton.
Creation Night.
Dusk in the Country.
Earthworm, The.
Hades and Euclid (first version).
Henhouse.
Letter from a Cattleboat.
Lighthouse Keeper.
Makers of Perpetuum Mobile, The.
March Evening.
No Name for It.
On the Congo.
Once I Came to Paradise.
Peonies.
Santa Claus: "Each year when the trees turn
  white."
Sea Wind, The.

Martory, Pierre (d. 1998)
Blues.

Martos, Marco (b. 1942)
Casti Connubi.

Martynova, Olga (b. 1962)
Night unwraps the true stuff of the world.
What does the river know of its own bed.

Marvell, Andrew (1621–78)
Bermudas.
Character of Holland, The.
Coronet, The.
Damon the Mower.
Definition of Love, The.
Dialogue Between The Resolved Soul and
  Created Pleasure, A.
Dialogue between the Soul and [the] Body, A.
Eyes and Tears.
Fair Singer, The.
First Anniversary of the Government under His
  Highness the Lord Protector, 1655, The.
First Anniversary of the Government under
  O.C, The, *sel*.
Flecknoe, an English Priest at Rome.
Gallery, The.
Garden, The.
Garden, The ("How vainly men themselves
  amaze").
Horatian Ode upon Cromwell's Return from
  Ireland, An.
Last Instructions to a Painter, The, *sels*.
Mower Against Gardens, The.
Mower to the Glowworms [*or* Glow-Worms *or*
  Glo-Worms], The.
Mower's Song, The.
Nymph Complaining for the Death of Her
  Faun [*or* Fawn], The.
On a Drop of Dew.

On Mr Milton's "Paradise Lost."
Picture of Little T. C. in a Prospect of Flowers,
  The.
To His Coy Mistress.
Upon Appleton House [To My Lord Fairfax],
  sels.
Upon the Hill and Grove at Bilbrough.
Victory Obtained by Blake over the Spaniards,
  in the Bay of Santa Cruz in the Island of
  Teneriffe, 1657, *sel*.
Young Love.

Marvin, Cate
Alba: Aberdeen.
House, Garden, Madness.

Marx, Steven (b. 1942)
Mark Antony's Valentine.

"Mary, Aunt" *See* Lathbury, Mary Artemisia

Mary, Queen of Scots *See* Mary Stuart, Queen of
Scots

Mary Stuart, Queen of Scots (1542–87)
He is, in truth, lacking in civility.
In my sweet and sad song.
My lord and my God, I have hoped in Thee.
Sonnets to Bothwell, *sel*.
Verses in Italian and French, Written by the
  Queen of Scots to the Queen of England.

Marzán, Julio (b. 1946)
Emergency.
Eve.
In the Backyard.
Sunday Morning in Old San Juan.

Marzials, Théophile Julius Henry
Tragedy, A.

Masahide (1657–1723)
Barn's burnt down.
When bird passes on.

Masalha, Salman (b. 1953)
Cage.
On Artistic Freedom in the Nationalist Era.

Masaoka Shiki (1867–1902)
Aged nightingale / How sweet.
Amid a jumble of.
Among Saga's / Tall weeds.
Autumn come / Cicada husk.
Autumn wind / Gods, Buddha.
Buddha too.
Chilly nights.
Dew, clinging / To potato field.
Evening bell / Persimmons pelt.
Fifteen Haiku, *sels*.
Glass door.
Hands so cold.
Heath grass / Sandals.
I eat a persimmon.
I keep asking.
Imagine / The monk took off.
Indian summer / Dragonfly shadows seldom.
Little knife, The.
Midnight sound / Leap up.
No one to busy.
Pine needles.
Stone / On summer plain.
Storm—chestnuts / Race along.
Such silence / Snow tracing wings.
Sudden rain / Rows of horses.
Summer sky / Clear after rain.
Swatting mosquitoes.
Tenement house.
Thing long forgotten.
Thirty-nine Haiku, *sels*.
White butterfly / Darting among pinks.
Wicker chair / In pinetree's shade.

Maschwitz, Eric (1901–69)
Nightingale Sang in Berkeley Square, A.
Paris Is Not the Same.
These Foolish Things (Remind Me of You).

Masefield, John (1878–1967)
Autumn Ploughing.
C. L. M.
Captain Stratton's Fancy.
Cargoes.
Consecration, A.
Dauber, *sels*.
Epilogue: "I have seen flowers come in stony
  places."

Everlasting Mercy, The, *sel*.
Fellow Mortal, A.
Laugh and Be Merry.
Lollingdon Downs, *sels*.
Night on the Downland.
No man takes the farm.
On Growing Old.
Passing Strange, The.
Port of Holy Peter.
Port of Many Ships.
Reynard the Fox, *sels*.
Sea Change.
Sea Fever.
Sonnets, *sel*.
Sorrow of Mydath.
To-morrow.
Trade Winds.
Valediction, A (Liverpool Docks).
Wanderer's Song, A.
West Wind, The.

Masham, Damaris, Lady (1659–1708)
Irreconcilable, The.
On Damons Loveing of Clora.

Mashinskaya, Irina (b. 1958)
Newspapers on the Plateau.
So I stood by and watched.

Masini, Donna
Two Men, Two Grapefruits.

Mason, David
Spooning.
Whit for Whitman, A.
Winter, 1963.

Mason, Francis Claiborne
Sunken Sailor.

Mason, Keith Antar
I Am a Creature of the Obvious.

Mason, Ronald Allison Kells (1905–71)
Judas Iscariot.
On the Swag.

Mason, William (1725–97)
English Garden, The, *sels*.
Heroic Epistle to Sir William Chambers, An,
  sels.
To a Gravel Walk.

Masri, Maram
Small Sins.
You who.

Mass, Rochelle (b. 1943)
No Surprises.

Massey, Gerald (1828–1907)
Babe Christabel, *sel*.
Dead Boy's Portrait and His Dog, The.

Massimi, Pacifico (fl. 15th cent.)
Hecateleguim, *sels*.

Massinger, Philip (1583–1640)
Emperor of the East, The, *sel*.
Men May Talk of Country-Christmasses.

Massoni, Marie-Dominique (b. 1947)
How Old Is the Old Mole?
Two Seconds.

Masters, Edgar Lee (1869–1950)
Battle of Gettysburg, The.
Business Reverses.
Chicago, *sel*.
Cities of the Plain.
Gettysburg.
In Memory of Bryan Lathrop.
Jennie McGrew.
Lost Orchard, The.
Many Soldiers.
Margaret Fuller Slack.
New Spoon River, The, *sels*.
Silence.
Spoon River Anthology, *sels*.
Veterans of the Wars.
Wedding Feast, The.
Week-End by the Sea.
Widows.

Masters, Mary (c.1694–1771)
To the Same; Enquiring Why I Wept.

Masterson, Robert
Bunch of Pictures Back from the Drugstore, A:
  The Four Good Ones.

Chinese Stripper.
Making Love in the Meat Locker.
She Called Them Stones.
Mastin, Florence Ripley (b. 1896)
Flying.
From the Telephone.
Masuri, S. N.
Day's End.
Mataka, Laini (b. 1949)
Can We Talk?
Licorice.
Next Door.
Ornithology.
Matanov, Ivan (b. 1952)
Still I See in Front of Me.
Mateo, Noel
Jeepneyfying.
There Is No Word for Sex in Taglog.
Mather, Cotton (1663–1728)
Epitaph: "Dummer the Shepherd Sacrific'd.",
sel.
Excellent Wigglesworth, Remembered by
Some Good Tokens, The.
Mather, Tinker
If you're looking for water.
Matherne, Beverly
La Fabrique de Tabac (Tobacco Harvest).
Les Fils (Sons).
Matheson, George (1842–1906)
Christian Freedom.
O Love That Wilt Not Let Me Go.
Mathew, Ray (b. 1929)
One Day.
Poem in Time of Winter.
Seeing St. James's.
Mathews, Aidan Carl (b. 1956)
Caedmon.
Death of Irish, The.
Letter Following.
Minding Ruth.
Spectrum.
Two Months Married.
Mathews, Cornelius (1817–89)
Poems on Man in His Various Aspects under
the American Republic, sels.
Mathews, Eliza Kirkham (1772–1802)
Indian, The.
Mathews, Harry (b. 1930)
Cassation on a Theme by Jacques Dupin.
Comatas.
Dream-Work, The.
Histoire.
Invitation to a Sabbath.
Lateral Disregard.
Ledge, The.
Out of Bounds.
Relics, The.
Ring, The.
Sad Birds, The.
Sense of Responsibility, The.
Spell.
Mathias, John (b. 1941)
Bogomil in Languedoc.
Mathias, Roland (b. 1915)
Brechfa Chapel.
Cae Iago: May Day.
Craswall.
Departure in Middle Age.
Flooded Valley, The.
Grasshoppers.
Memling.
Porth Cwyfan.
Sanderlings.
Sir Gelli to R.S.
Testament.
Tide-Reach, sels.
Mathis, Cleopatra (b. 1942)
Angels, The.
Blues: Late August.
Getting Out.
Lessons, sels.
"Matilda, Anna" See Cowley, Hannah
"Matilda, Rosa" See Dacre, Charlotte

Matino, Jan-Klod See Martineau, Jean-Claude
Matos-Teixera, Narlan (b. 1975)
My Father's House.
Matson, Clive
Bedside.
Matson, Suzanne
Beach, The.
Worry.
Mattawa, Khaled
Before.
Bus Driver Poem, The.
Cricket Mountain.
Echo and Elixir 1.
Echo and Elixir 2.
Growing Up with a Sears Catalog in Benghazi,
Libya.
Heartsong.
History of My Face.
I Was Buried in Janzoor.
Ismailia Eclipse.
Letter to Ibrahim.
Road from Biloxi, The.
White Nile Elegy.
Mattes, L. (1904–86)
On the Street Corner.
Matthews, Geoffrey (b. 1920)
For Edward Thomas Killed at Arras.
Matthews, Harley (b. 1889)
Women Are Not Gentlemen.
Matthews, Jack (b. 1889)
Inverse Proportions.
Matthews, Marc (b. 1937)
By a Ways.
Language.
Matthews, Tom (b. 1945)
Cowboy Film.
Even the Whales.
Happy Arabia.
Private But Sulphurous.
Robert Sat.
Matthews, William (1942–97)
Accompanist, The.
Bear at the Dump, The.
Black Box.
Bud Powell, Paris, 1959.
Buddy Bolden Cylinder, The.
Cheap Seats, the Cincinnati Gardens,
Professional Basketball, 1959.
Cloister, The.
Descriptive Passages.
Dire Cure.
Dogs of Montone, The.
Elegy for Bob Marley, An.
Foul Shots: A Clinic.
Good Company.
Grandmother, Dead at 99 Years and 10
Months.
Grief.
Housework.
In Memory of the Utah Stars.
Inspiration: "Rumpled, torpid, bored, too
tasteful to rhyme."
Last Words.
Mail Order Catalogs.
Men at My Father's Funeral.
Mingus at The Showplace.
Misgivings.
Mood Indigo.
Moving Again.
Names.
No Return.
Old Folsom Prison.
On the Porch at the Frost Place, Franconia,
NH.
Onions.
Penalty for Bigamy Is Two Wives, The.
Photo of the Author with a Favorite Pig.
Pissing off the Back of the Boat into the
Nivernais Canal.
Poetry Reading at West Point, A.
Psychopathology of Everyday Life, The.
Rented House in Maine, The.
Sentence: "Bloated and mesmerized by
rasberries."
Story Often Told in Bars, A: The Reader's
Digest Version.

Telegram from the Muse, A.
Unrelenting Flood.
Vermin.
Wolf of Gubbio, The.
Mattson, Nancy (b. 1947)
Her Other Language.
Maturaikkataiayattar Makan Vennakan
What She Said to Her Girl-Friend.
Matveyev, Ivan Venediktovich See Elagin, Ivan
Venediktovich
**Matveyeva [or Matveieva], Novella Nikolaevna
(b. 1934)**
Eggplants Have Pins and Needles, The.
Ginger-Haired Girl, The.
I'm no fighting man, he says.
Re-Conversion.
Maude, Caitlin (1941–82)
Entanglement.
Maule, Thomas (c.1645–1724)
To Cotton Mather, from a Quaker.
Maulpoix, Jean-Michel (b. 1952)
Giving Birth, The.
Mise au monde, La.
Maunick, Edouard J. (b. 1931)
Les Manèges de la Mer (1964).
Seven Sides and Seven Syllables.
Maurice, Furnley (Frank Wilmot) (1881–1942)
Echoes of Wheels.
Victoria Markets Recollected in Tranquility,
The.
Whenever I Have.
Maurice, Thomas (1754–1824)
Richmond Hill, sels.
Maurus, Hrabanus (776–856)
To Grimold, Abbot of St. Gall.
Maurus, Hrabanus See Also Charlemagne
Max, Lin
Equal Temperament.
Pedagogy.
Stone Fruit.
When the Tules Are Peppered with Red-
winged Blackbirds.
Maxted, Eleanor
Slow train, A. Few travellers. If.
Maxton, Hugh (b. 1947)
Deutschland.
Dialectique.
Elegies.
Ode.
On Failing to Translate.
Urgent Letter, An.
Maxwell, Derrin
All Up in There.
Maxwell, Glyn (b. 1962)
Helene and Heloise.
Letters to Edward Thomas, sel.
Mild Citizen.
My Turn.
Nerve, The.
Poem Recalls the Poet, The.
Poisonfield.
Rumplestiltskin.
We Billion Cheered.
Maxwell, James Clerk (1831–79)
Rigid Body Sings.
Maxwell-Hall, Agnes (b. 1894)
Jamaica Market.
May, Deirdre
Thoughts from a Bar Stool.
May, Julian (b. 1955)
On the Air.
May, Kenneth (fl. 20th cent.)
Valentine's Day.
**Mayakovsky [or Maiakovskii], Vladimir
Vladimirovich (1893–1930)**
At the Top of My Voice, sel.
Cloud in Trousers, A.
Crimea.
Good Attitude to Horses, A.
Last Page of the Civil War.
Last Statement.
Listen.

Listen!
Past One O'Clock . . . .
Screaming My Head Off.

Maybe, Ellyn (b. 1964)
Umbilical Cord.

Mayer, Bernadette (b. 1945)
Aeschyleans, The.
America: "As for me, when I saw you."
Birthday Sonnet for Grace.
Boats.
Booze Turns Men into Women.
Corn.
Earthworker's God is Healed, The.
Easy Puddings.
End of Human Reign on Bashan Hill, The.
Failures in Infinitives.
First Turn to Me.
Garden, The.
Gay Full Story.
Generic Elbows.
Holding the Thought of Love.
House Cap.
Incorporation of Sophia's Cereal, The.
Index.
Inventing Stasis.
Laura Cashdollars.
Maple Syrup Sonnet ("For over ten years now.").
Maple Syrup Sonnet ("Syrup's up again.").
Max Carries the One.
Moving, *sel.*
Palm Sunday Maple Syrup Poem.
Poem: "I am beginning to alter."
Port, The.
Sea: "It's he, it's sea. the sea is continuous; a continuous body."
Sonnet: "Beauty of songs your absence I should not show."
Sonnet: Kamikaze: "Dawn and night of fighting, lovers like actual wars."
Sonnet: "Love is a babe as you know and when you."
Sonnet: "So long honey, don't ever come around again, I'm sick of you."
Sonnet: "Thousand apples you might put in your theories."
Sonnet: "You jerk you didn't call me up."
Spring House.
Steps.
Turning Prose into Poetry.
We've Solved the Problem.

Mayer, Gerda (b. 1927)
Ballad: "Knight went down to the river's rim, A."
Bilberries.
Count Carrots.
Crunch, The.
Dandelions.
529 1983.
Make Believe.
Narcissus.

Mayer, Hansjörg (b. 1943)
Oil.

Mayes, Frances
Sister Cat.

Mayes, Jane
Descant.
Orchestration.
Pedaling Paranoia.

Mayfield, Carl
In a Glazed-Over World.
Oh, It's You Again.
Thinking of a Friend.
When I Moved into the Neighborhood.

Mayhall, Jane (b. 1921)
Painkiller.

Mayne, Jasper (1604–72)
Time.

Mayne, Seymour (b. 1944)
Word Sonnets, *sels.*

Mayo, C. M.
Meteor.

Mayo, Edward Leslie (b. 1904)
Word of Water, The.

Mayor, Chandra (b. 1973)
Driving Away.
Winter Night.

Mayr, Suzette
Watching a Dance Rehearsal in a Calgary Theatre with a Concrete Floor.
Watching a Dance Rehearsal in a Calgary Theatre with a Concrete Floor 2.

Mayröcker, Friederike (b. 1924)
Ostia Will Receive You.
Ostia Will Receive You.
Schubert, or: Notes on the Weather, Vienna.
Spirit of '76, The.

Mays, Mariiane
(HERO)neck: attempts at a portrait, *sels.*

Mazur, Gail (b. 1937)
Acorn, The.
After the Storm, August.
Bluebonnets.
Common, The.
In Houston.
Keep Going.
Then.

"Mbala" (Michael Bailey)
History of Dub Poetry, The.
New Dub, A.

M'Baye d'Erneville, Annette (b. 1927)
Kassacks.
Labane.
Requiem.

McAdams, Janet
Leaving the Old Gods.

McAlmon, Robert (1896–1956)
For Instance.

McAuley, James (b. 1935)
Blue Horses, The.
Cloak, The.
Dialogue.
Envoi.
Gnostic Prelude.
Hero and the Hydra, The, *sels.*
In a Late Hour.
Keep the Season.
Late Winter.
Legendary.
Nocturne.
One Tuesday in Summer.
Pietá.
Released on Parole.
Seven Days of Creation, The, *sels.*
Wet Day.
World on Sunday.

McAuley, James Philip (1917–76)
Because.
Family of Love, The, *sels.*
In the Twentieth Century.
Jesus.
Liberal, or Innocent by Definition.
Terra Australis.
Winter Drive.

McAuliffe, John (b. 1973)
Calm, The.
Effects.
Flood.
Missing.
Nightjar.
North Brunswick Street Lullaby.
Vision of Rahoon, A.

McBride, Mekeel (b. 1950)
Knife-Thrower's Wife, The.

McCabe, Brian (b. 1951)
Kite.
Seagull.

McCabe, Cathal (b. 1963)
Ancutsa, Ancutsa.
End of January, The.
In Memory of My Mother.
Jastrzebia Góra.
Light & Love.
Postcard from London, A.
Summer in Killowen.

McCabe, Victoria (b. 1948)
People at the Pay Telephone, The.

McCaffery, Steve (b. 1947)
Evoba, *sel.*
Little Hans.
Panopticon, *sel.*
Some Versions of Pastoral.
Teachable Texts.

McCallum, Shara (b. 1972)
Calypso.
Collage.
Deer, The.
Fugue.
In My Other Life.
In the Beginning.
Jamaica, October 18, 1972.
Perfect Heart, The.
What Lies Beneath.
What My Mother Taught Me.
What the Oracle Said.
Yu No Send. Me No Come.

McCann, Anthony (b. 1973)
Confessions: "Before money and California."

Mccann, Sarah Katherine
Robert Frost as Father.

McCarriston, Linda
Billy.
Castle in Lynn, A.
Coursier de Jeanne d'Arc, Le.
Healing the Mare.
Hotel Nights with My Mother.
January, Anchorage.
Kitchen Terrarium.
Riding Out at Evening.
To Judge Faolain, Dead Long Enough: A Summons.
Wrought Figure.

McCarthy, Eugene (1916–70?)
Dulles Airport.
Page of Short Poems, A, *sel.*

McCarthy, Gerald
Hooded Legion, The.

McCarthy, Joseph (1885–1943)
Alice Blue Gown.
I'm Always Chasing Rainbows.
You Made Me Love You (I Didn't Want to Do It).

McCarthy, Joseph, Jr. (1922–75)
Cloudy Morning.
I'm Gonna Laugh You Right Out of My Life.
Riviera, The.
Why Try to Change Me Now?

McCarthy, Lee (b. 1938)
Running Loose around the Castle.

McCarthy, Thomas (b. 1954)
Claud Cockburn.
Emigration Trains, The.
Mr. Nabokov's Memory.
Persephone, 1978.
Phenomenology of Stones, The.
Quatrain without Sparrows, Helpful Bells or Hope.
Standing Trains, The.
State Funeral.
Toast.
Wisdom of AE, The.

McCaslin, Susan (b. 1947)
Triolet for the Amphetamine Afflicted.

McClanahan, Rebecca
Bridal Rites.
Burial: "Like a sister who borrows."

McClatchy, J. D. (b. 1945)
Aden.
Bishop Reading.
Capriccio of Roman Ruins and Sculpture with Figures, A.
Chott.
Essay on Friendship, An, *sels.*
First Steps, *sels.*
Jihad.
Landing, The.
Method, The.
My Mammogram.
Old Song Ended, An.
Pibroch.
Pleasure of Ruins, The.

Tattoos.
What They Left Behind.
McClellan, George Marion (b. 1860)
September Night, A.
McClennan, Tommy
Brown Skin Girl.
McClure, Dave
Hampton Lock.
McClure, Michael (b. 1932)
Black Dahlia.
Canticle: "Sharks tooth is perfect for biting, The. The Intent."
Flowers of Politics, I, The.
For Monk.
Ghost Tantras, *sels.*
Haiku Rows, *sels.*
Hymn to Saint Geryon.
Jazz at the Intergalactic Nightclub.
Mad Sonnet: Fame.
Mad Sonnet: Grace.
Madame Secretary.
Ode to Jackson Pollock.
Peyote Poem, *sel.*
Plum Stones, *sels.*
Reading Frank O'Hara in a Mexican Rainstorm.
Senate Hearings.
Small Secret Book, A.
Song: "I work with the shape."
Song: "Platinum fur and brass revolver shine."
Souls.
Thoreau's Eyes: Two Poems for Kazuaki Tanahashi.
Touching the Edge: Dharma Devotions, *sels.*
Unchanged.
McCollough, Aaron (b. 1969)
Eros, Ethos, Economuos.
McCombs, Judith (b. 1939)
Epithet.
Love Poem, Later.
McCord, David (b. 1897)
Ascot Waistcoat.
Baccalaureate.
Blessed Lord, What It Is to Be Young.
Convalescence.
Crickets.
Crows.
Crows, The.
Epitaph on a Waiter.
Every Time I Climb A Tree.
Five Chants.
Glowworm.
History of Education.
Perambulator Poems, I-VII, *sel.*
Pickety fence, The.
Song of the Train.
Summer Shower.
This Is My Rock.
McCorkle, James (b. 1954)
Infidelities.
McCosker, Karen (b. 1948)
Tinnitus.
McCrae, Hugh Raymond (1876–1958)
Mimshi Maiden, The.
McCrae, John (1872–1918)
In Flanders Fields.
McCree, Junie (fl. 1910)
Put Your Arms Around Me, Honey.
McCuaig, Ronald (b. 1908)
Au Tombeau de Mon Père.
Betty by the Sea.
Recitative: "Farmer's son is good and mad," The.
McCullagh, James C.
Mermaid's Song.
McDaniel, Jeffrey
Archipelago of Kisses, The.
Bad Pilgrim Room, The.
D.
Dear America.
Disasterology.
First One, The.
First Person Omniscient.
Following Her to Sleep.

Friends and High Places.
Hunting for Cherubs.
Leonard.
Lineage.
Logic in the House of Sawed-Off Telescopes.
Modern Day Sisphus.
Multiple Floor, The.
1977.
Obvious, The.
Opposites Attack.
Play It Again, Salmonella.
Quiet World, The.
Uncle Eggplant.
McDaniel, Wilma Elizabeth
Asking Favors.
Burned in the Test.
California Entertainment, 1936.
First Spring in California, 1936.
My Room at Aunt Eura's, 1937.
Realist of 1939–40, A.
Ruby Red's Migrant Camp.
McDonald, Charles (b. 1957)
Asdrubral Jiménez.
At the Gwen John Exhibition.
Cheers.
Fresh Mussels.
Nightfishing.
Oxford Gardens.
McDonald, Ellie (b. 1937)
Itherness.
Uncle: "Sam was a family embarrassment."
Widdershins.
McDonald, Joe (b. 1942)
I-Feel-Like-I'm Fixin'-To-Die Rag.
McDonald, Nan (1921–73)
Burragorang.
Hatters, The.
McDonald, Peter (b. 1962)
Cash Positive.
Christmas.
Peacetime.
Pleasures of the Imagination.
Sunday in Great Tew.
Totalled.
McDonald, Roger (b. 1941)
Apis Mellifica.
Blizzard, The.
Hollow Thesaurus, The.
Incident in Transylvania.
1915.
McDonald, Walter (b. 1934)
After the Noise of Saigon ("If where we hunt defines us.").
After the Rains of Saigon ("I put back the rifle on a steel rack.").
After the Random Tornado.
All the Old Songs.
Children of Saigon, The.
Christmas Bells, Saigon.
Crossing the Road.
Digs in Escondido Canyon, The.
Flying Dutchman, The.
Hauling Over Wolf Creek Pass in Winter.
Hawks in a Bitter Blizzard.
Heirlooms.
Honky-Tonk Blues.
I Still Can't Say the Word.
In Fields of Buffalo.
Last Still Days in a Bunker, The.
Losing a Boat on the Brazos.
Middle Years, The.
Songs We Fought For, The.
Starting a Pasture.
War in Bosnia, The.
Wind and Hardscrabble.
McDowell, Garrett
Blooming in the Valley, A.
Child in the New Delhi Sun.
Lights of the Bigtop.
McDowell, Robert (b. 1953)
Elegy in August.
Origin of Fear, The.
Where and What You Are.
McDuffie, Carrington
Finally the Rain.

McElroy, Colleen J. (b. 1935)
At 102, Romance Comes Once a Year.
Circus of the City, The.
End of Civilization as We Know It, The.
Foul Line—1987.
From Homegrown: An Asian-American Anthology of Writers.
Ghost-Who-Walks, The.
Griots Who Know Brer Fox, The.
Horoscope.
Illusion.
In My Mother's Room.
Learning to Swim at Forty-Five.
Mae West Chats It Up with Bessie Smith.
Ruth.
This Is the Poem I Never Meant to Write.
To Welcome a Changeling.
Under the Oak Table.
McElroy, David (b. 1941)
Present Moments.
McFadden, David (b. 1940)
Shouting Your Name Down the Well.
McFadden, Roy (b. 1921)
Contemplations of Mary.
Epithalamium: "So you are married, girl. It makes me sad."
First Letter to an Irish Novelist.
For the Record.
Grand Central Hotel, The.
Memories of Chinatown, *sels.*
My Mother's Young Sister.
Stringer's Field.
McFall, Gardner
Missing.
McFarland, Ron
Memoir of the Cosmopolite Who Stayed Home.
McFayden, Stazja
Not My Knees.
McFee, Michael (b. 1954)
Cold Quilt.
First Radio.
McFerren, Martha
Metaphor Crosses the Road, A.
McFerrin, Bobby
23rd Psalm, The: "Lord is my Shepherd, I have all I need, The."
McGinley, Phyllis (1905–78)
Adversary, The.
All around the Town, *sel.*
Ballade of Lost Objects.
Blues for a Melodeon.
City Christmas.
Daniel at Breakfast.
Day After Sunday, The.
Evening Musicale.
Garland of Precepts, A.
How to Start a War.
I Know a Village, *sels.*
Lady Selecting Her Christmas Cards.
Midcentury Love Letter.
New England Pilgrimage.
Notes for a Southern Road Map.
Ode to the End of Summer.
Office Party.
Portrait of a Girl with Comic Book.
Public Journal.
Reflections at Dawn.
Speaking of Television, *sels.*
Spectator's Guide to Contemporary Art, *sels.*
Spring Comes to the Suburbs.
Theology of Jonathan Edwards, The.
Trinity Place.
Twelfth Night.
Velvet Hand, The.
View from a Suburban Window.
Village Spa.
Why, Some of My Best Friends Are Women.
Women of Jericho, The.
McGinn, Matt (1928–77)
Big Orange Whale, The.
Coorie Doon.
McGinnis, Mary (b. 1946)
Letter to My Mother.

New Mexico Time.
Sending Men Back to the Sea.
Widow Opening Her Heart, The.

McGlashan, June
Island of Women, The.

McGonagall, William (1825–1902)
Address to the New Tay Bridge, An, *sel.*
Calamity in London; Family of Ten Burned to Death.
Clepington Catastrophe, The, *sel.*
Death of Lord and Lady Dalhousie, The, *sel.*
Famous Tay Whale, The, *sel.*
Funeral of the German Emperor, The, *sel.*
Hen It Is a Noble Beast, The.
Late Sir John Ogilvy, The.
Railway Bridge of the Silvery Tay, The, *sel.*
Royal Review, The, *sel.*
Sprig of Moss, The, *sel.*
Tale of the Sea, A, *sel.*
Tay Bridge Disaster, The.
Tay Bridge Disaster, The, *sel.*

McGough, Robert
Fight of the Year, The.

McGough, Roger (b. 1937)
Cinders.
Defying Gravity.
40— Love.
Health Forecast, The.
Italic.
Kleptomaniac, The.
Leader, The.
Mother the Wardrobe Is Full of Infantrymen.
Noah's Ark.
P.C. Plod versus the Dale St. Dog Strangler.
Poem With a Limp.
Prayer to Saint Grobianus.
Snipers.
Snow Poem.
Snowman in a field.
Summer with Monika, *sel.*
Survivor.
Though giving pleasure to many.

McGrath, Beth
Concert Choir.

McGrath, Campbell
At the Freud Hilton.
Capitalist Poem #36.
Delphos, Ohio.
First Trimester, The.
Florida.
Florida Anasazi, The.
Jack Gilbert.
Jeffrey Lee Pierce.
Prose Poem, The.
Shrimp Boats, Biloxi.
Smokestacks, Chicago.
Spring Comes to Chicago.
Wheatfield Under Clouded Sky.
Xena, Warrior Princess.

McGrath, Carmelita (b. 1960)
Booman.
How to Leave an Island.
Let Us Go and Find a Place of Worship.
Solar Eclipse, St. John's, Newfoundland.

McGrath, Gerry
Noticing a man unable.

McGrath, Thomas (1916–90)
Advertisements.
After Tomasito's Departure.
Black Train, The.
Blues for Warren.
Bread of this World; Praises III, The.
Celebration: "How wonderful, Tomasito!"
Coal Fire in Winter, A.
End of a Season.
End of the Line, The.
End of the World, The.
Epitaph: "Again, traveller, you have come a long way led by that star."
Fresco: Departure for an Imperialist War.
Go Ask the Dead.
Guiffre's Nightmusic.
Half Measures.
Homecoming: "After the cries of gulls and the fogbound island."

Language of the Dead, The.
Last Will and Testament.
Letter to an Imaginary Friend, *sels.*
Longing.
Night Meeting.
Nocturne Militaire.
Nuclear Winter.
Ode for the American Dead in Korea.
Offering.
On the Head of a Pin.
Ordonnance.
Poem: "My little son comes running with open arms!"
Poem: "My little son, laughing, singing...."
Poem: "When I carry my little son in the cold."
Probable Cause.
Reading by Mechanic Light.
Remembering That Island.
Return, The.
Revisionist Poem—Octavio Paz.
Skull of the Horse.
Song: Miss Penelope Burgess, Balling the Jack.
Visit to the House of the Poet—Nicaragua, 1987—Homage to Rubén Darío on His Birthday, A.
War Resisters' Song.
Working in Darkness.
You Can Start the Poetry Now, Or: News from Crazy Horse.
You Taught Me.

McGuckian, Medbh (b. 1950)
Aphrodisiac, The.
Aviary.
Captain Lavender.
Coleridge.
Dream-Language of Fergus, The.
Flitting, The.
Flower Master, The.
From the Dressing-room.
Gateposts.
Little House, Big House.
Lychees.
Mantilla.
Mr. McGregor's Garden.
On Ballycastle Beach.
On Not Being Your Lover.
Orchid House, The.
Porcelain Bells, *sels.*
Presence, The.
Sea or Sky?
Seed-Picture, The.
Sitting, The.
Slips.
Sofa, The.
To a Cuckoo at Coolanlough.
Tulips.
Vanessa's Bower.
War Ending, The.

McGuire, Jack
Streets of Forbes, The.

McGuire, Jerry
Cages, The.
Feeling Rosemary.
Gongula.
Not A Ton Notation.
Plate Pieces.

McGuire, Virginia
Leaning into the Tilt.

McHugh, Heather (b. 1948)
After You Left.
Animal Song.
Coming.
Etymological Dirge.
Fence, The.
Form.
Ghazal of the Better-Unbegun.
I Knew I'd Sing.
ID.
Language Lesson 1976.
My One.
Night in a World, A.
Or Else.
Past All Understanding.

Sizing.
Three To's and an Oi.
20-200 on 737.
What Could Hold Us.
What He Thought.

McHugh, Jimmy
Lovely to Look At.

McIlroy, Leslie Anne (b. 1965)
Good-Bye, Valentine.
How to Change a Flat.
Siesta.

McInnis, C. Leigh
2G (Another Millennium Poem).

McIntyre, James (1827–1906)
Disaster to Steamer Victoria at London.
English Poets, *sel.*
Oxford Cheese Ode, *sel.*
Potato Bug Exterminators, *sel.*
Prophecy of a Ten Ton Cheese.
Wooden Leg.

McKain, David
Opening Day.

McKay, Claude (1889–1948)
Africa.
America: "Although she feeds me bread of bitterness."
Baptism.
Birds of Prey.
Castaways, The.
Dawn in New York.
Harlem Dancer, The.
Harlem Shadows.
If We Must Die.
Jasmine.
Lynching, The.
Midnight Woman to the Bobby, A.
My Mother.
My Mother.
Negro Spiritual.
Outcast.
Spring in New Hampshire.
Subway Wind.
To O. E. A.
Tropics in New York, The.
White City, The.
White House, The.
Wild Goat, The.

McKay, Don (b. 1942)
Chickadee Encounter.
Close-up on a Sharp-shinned Hawk.
Early Instruments.
Kinds of Blue #41 Far Hills.
Laugh, The.
Matériel, *sels.*
Setting the Table.
Sometimes a Voice 1.
Waking At The Mouth Of The Willow River.

McKean, James (b. 1946)
After Listening to Jack Teagarden . . . .
Good "D."

McKendrick, Jamie (b. 1955)
Ancient History.
Beyond.
One-Star, The.
Shortened History in Pictures, A.
Six Characters in Search of Something.
Sky Nails.

McKinney, Irene
Chrysanthemums.
Dance, The.
Deep Mining.
Rapt.
Sunday Morning, 1950.
Twilight in West Virginia: Six O'Clock Mine Report.
Visiting My Gravesite: Talbott Churchyard, West Virginia.

McKinney, Laurence (b. 1944)
Oboe.

McKinnon, Barry (b. 1944)
Arrhythmia, *sels.*

McKinnon, Karen
Crossing: "Have we always been close to."
Moving My Mother.

Vintage.

McLagan, Elizabeth (b. 1947)
At Twelve.
Reading the Names.

McLain, Paula (b. 1965)
Beauty, That Lying Bitch.
Connor in the Wind and Rain with His Coat
on.
Fishing.
Home Remedy.
Residue.
Willing.

McLaughlin, Damon
Battle of Johnny Freedom, The.

McLaughlin-Carruth, Joe-Anne
Black Irish Blues.
Existentially Speaking.
Introducing New Year's SOLUTIONS, from
Saint Terri's Inc.
Parents They Would Be, The.

McLeod, Irene (b. 1891)
Lone Dog.

McLoughland, Beverly
Crazy Boys.
Whippoorwill Calls, The.

McLucas, Leroy
Graph.
Negotiation.

McMahon, Lynne
All Quail to the Wallowing.
Barbie's Ferrari.
Elvis for the Ages, An.
Not Falling.
Peace Studies.

McManus, James (b. 1951)
Two Songs for Hendrix.
Who Needs Two, sel.

McManus, Ken
450 Years of Selective Memory (Smile).

McMaster, Rhyll (b. 1947)
Back Steps Lookout.
Clockface.
Mutton Bird Man.
Tanks.

McMichael, James (b. 1939)
Each in a Place Apart, sel.
Four Good Things, sel.
Lutra, the Fisher.
Posited.
Pretty Blue Apron.

McMillan, Hugh (b. 1955)
Leaving Scotland by Train.
X Files, The: Bonnybridge, October '95.

McMorris, Mark (b. 1960)
Aphrodite of Economy.
Au Café Noir.
Evening.
Geometry of the Figure.
More Than Once in Caves.
Near Speech, The.
Prayer to Shadows on My Wall.
Some Days in the City.
Tell me again, Love, what is a wedding?
Time Once Again.

McMurtry, Larry (b. 1936)
For Erwin Smith, Cowboy Photographer.

McNair, Wesley (b. 1941)
Big Cars.
Goodbye to the Old Life.
Killing the Animals.
Mina Bell's Cows.
Visit, The: "We were at the camp, it must have
been."
What Became.
Where I Live.

McNally, Leonard
Lass of Richmond Hill, The.

McNaughtan, Adam (b. 1939)
Jeelie Piece Song, The.
Oor Hamlet.

McNaughton, Anne
Balls.

McNeil, Rodney M. (b. 1966)
Angel in the Temple of Luxor, An.
It Just Doesn't Matter.
Mirrors in the Room.

McNeill, Anthony (fl. c.1941)
Bob Marley New King of the Music.
For the D.
Ode to Brother Joe.
Saint Ras.

McNiece, Ray
After its caw.
Bare birch mountainside.
Blowing out the candle.
Driving the Midwest.
Kerouac, we knock.
Kudzu has crossed.
Letter Left On the Porch of the Kerouac
House.
Low gray skies over.
Memorizing your face.
My shadow in waves.
Old Joe the stray dog.
Ordinary, The.
Skinny-Dipping the Ganges.
Wet sand raven tracks.

McNulty, Tim
Bodhidharma Crossing the Graywolf River on
a Ry-Krisp.

McOrlan, Pierre (1882–1970)
Accessories shop, The.
Battery woman.
Hairdresser's, The.
Horse butcher, The.
Modern circus, The.
Produce from the colonies.
Weighing-machine, The.
Wood merchant's parlour, The.

McPherson, Sandra (b. 1943)
Ability to Make a Face Like a Spider While
Singing Blues: Junior Wells, The.
Bedrooms.
Black Soap.
Genius of Fog at Ecola Creek Mouth.
Helen Todd: My Birthname.
His Body.
Michael.
Microscope in Winter, The.
Morning Glory Pool.
Outsider: Minnie Evans.
Pornography, Nebraska.
Pregnancy.
Quilt of Rights.
Six Movements for Portraits of Erzulie.
Sock, A.
Some Metaphysics of Junior Wells.
Streamers.
Suspension: Junior Wells on a Small Stage in a
Converted Barn.
Three from the Market, sel.
Wings and Seeds: For My Birth Mother.

McQuade, Molly
Bees Stumble.

McQuilkin, Rennie
Learning the Angels.

McRay, Paul
Performance.

McSweeney, Joyelle (b. 1976)
Persuasion.
Still Life w/Influences.
Wind Domes, The.

McVeigh, Jane
Eve Falling.

McWhirter, George (b. 1939)
Era of Easy Meat at Locarno, An.

Mead, Jane (b. 1958)
Concerning That Prayer I Cannot Make.
Delphi, Coming Around the Corner.
Fall: "This morning I found."
However.
Incomplete Scenario Involving What the Voice
Said.
La Guardia, the Story.
Memory, The.
On the Lawn at the Drug Rehab Center.

Paradise Consists of Forty-Nine Rotating
Spheres.
Point and Counter-Point in All Things.
Sometimes the Mind.
Third Stair, Seventh Stair, Landing.

Mead, Philip (b. 1953)
Cinema Point.
From a Republican Grave: Daniel Henry
Deniehy, 1828–1865.
Man and the Tree, The.
Melbourne or the Bush.
There.

Meade, Gordon (b. 1957)
Great Spotted Woodpecker, The.
In Eyemouth Harbour.
Schrimshaw Sailor, The.

Meador, Betty De Shong
Fields Belong to Woman, The.

Meads, Kate (b. 1951)
Dogs.

Mearns, Hughes (1875–1965)
Perfect Reactionary, The.

Mechain, Gwerfyl (c.1460–1500)
Female Genitals, The.
Hostess of the Ferry Inn, The.
Snowfall, The.

Meckel, Christoph (b. 1935)
Speaking of the Poem.

Mécs, László (1895–1978)
Going Down, Please.
My Dear Little Fellow.
On the Tomb of the Unknown Soldier.
Prayer for the Great Lunatic.
Who Can Understand This?

Meda, Bobi See Medard, Bobby

Medard, Bobby (b. 1939)
Tonton Macoutes Steal Dreams.

Meddeb, Abdelwahab (b. 1946)
I Take the Path.
Je prends le chemin.
On Forgotten Tracks.
Sur des traces oubliées.

Meddemmen, J. G.
L.R.D.G.

Medina, Pablo
Exile, The.
Nocturno de Washington.

Medina, Tony (b. 1966)
After the Verdict.
Big House Revisited, The.
Don't Say Goodnight to Etheridge Knight.
Poem for Teacup Mantlepiece Poets Palpitating
Poot Booty Plagiarists Imprisoned in Ivy
League White Supremacist Mental
Biological Warfare Labs.
Rhudine Rhudine.
Way We Move, The.

Medrano, Francisco de (1570–1607)
Sonnet 41.

Meehan, Paula (b. 1955)
Autobiography.
Child Burial.
Laburnum.
My Love about his Business in the Barn.
Pattern, The.

Meek, Sandra
Windowseat.

Meeks, Brian (b. 1953)
Is Culcha Weapon?
March 9 1976.
Twin Barrel Bucky: A Kingston 12 Dub, The.

Meenakshi, R. (b. 1944)
If Hot Flowers Come to the Street.

Megnen, Jeanne
Noise Will Start Tomorrow, The.

Mehmedinović, Semezdin
Essay, An.
Hero.
Only Dream, The.

Mehren, Stein (b. 1935)
Mother, We Were a Heavy Burden.

Mei Ch'eng (d. 140 B.C.)
Seven Stimuli.

Mei Sheng (1st cent. B.C.)
Beautiful Toilet, The.
Seven Exhortations to Rise, The.
Mei-tzu, Hu See "Hsiung Hung"
Mei Yao Ch'en (1002–60)
Crescent Moon, The.
Dappled Horse, The.
Dream at Night, A.
Excuse for Not Returning the Visit of a Friend,
An.
I Remember the Blue River.
Lice, The.
Marrying Again.
Melon Girl.
Necessities.
Next Door.
Offering for the Cat, An.
On the Death of a New Born Child.
Sad Remembrance.
Sharing Lodging with Hsieh Shih-hou.
Shih-hou Pointed Out to Me That from Ancient
Times There Had Never Been a Poem on the
Subject of Lice.
Solitary Falcon above the Buddha Hall of the
Monastery of Universal Purity, A.
Sorrow.
Meidhre, Brian MacGiolla See Merriman, Brian
Meier, Richard (b. 1966)
Eclipsed.
**Meigs, Mildred Plew (Mildred Plew Merryman)
(d. 1944)**
Abraham Lincoln.
Pirate Don Durk of Dowdee, The.
Meilyr Brydydd (fl. 1100–1137)
Poem on His Death-Bed.
Meinke, Peter
Anthills.
Atomic Pantoum.
Blow, Blow, Thou Winter Wind.
Death of the Pilot Whales, The.
Helen.
Love Poem 1990.
Noreen.
Poet, Trying to Surprise God, The.
Rage.
Robert Frost in Warsaw.
Sonnet on the Death of the Man Who Invented
Plastic Roses.
Supermarket.
This is a Poem to My Son Peter.
Unnatural Light.
Vincent.
Meireles, Cecília (1901–64)
Ballad of the Ten Casino Dancers.
Dead Horse, The.
Portrait.
Sketch.
Vigil.
Meister, Ernst
In That Place Was Another House.
Meitner, Erika (b. 1975)
All the Pools in Queens.
Gentrification.
Job: "My mother sold life insurance."
Mejía Godoy, Luis Enrique (b. 1945)
Revenge.
Melançon, Robert (b. 1947)
Beginning of Summer.
Début de l'été, Le.
Éveil.
Wakening.
Meleager (fl. 1st cent. B.C.)
Cup takes its sweet joy and tells how it
touches, The.
Did I not tell you, my soul, "By Cypris, you
will be caught."
Epigram: "At 12 o'clock in the afternoon."
Flower-feasting bee, why do you touch upon.
Hot day. Dying of thirst. Slake myself.
I say that my sweetly prattling Heliodora will
someday.
I was a quick-footed, long-eared hare, just
snatched from my mother's.
If you burn my scorched soul too often, Love,
she'll fly.

I'll weave in the white violet. I'll weave in.
I'm down. Step on my neck, you savage god,
with your heel.
Love fed Heliodora's fingernail and made.
Love-prone Asclepias with eyes like a
summer's day.
Love's night and a lamp.
Mosquito, may you fly, a swift courier for me.
Mosquitoes, shameless and shrill of voice,
sucking the blood.
Night Alone, The.
Now the white violet blooms and narcissus that
loves.
Pour and say again and again and yet again.
Pour for Heliodora Persuasion and pour for
Cypris.
Sell it, though it sleeps still at its mother's
breast!
Shrilling cicada, drunk on drops of dew, you
sing.
Still in his mother's lap the baby Love played.
Tears beneath the earth, Heliodora, I give.
To Aristogoras.
To Diodorus, Dorotheus, Callicrates et al.
Upon a Maid That Died [or Dyed] the Day She
Was Married [or Marryed].
Within my heart Love himself made Heliodora.
Yes, I'd rather hear Heliodora's voice.
You're sleeping, Zenophila, my tender bloom. I
wish.
Meléndez, Jesús Papoleto
¡Hey Yo / Yo Soy!
Oye Mundo/Sometimes.
Melhem, Diana Helen (b. 1926)
Boy in a Hospital.
Country, sels.
Rest in Love, sel.
Melinno (fl. 2nd cent. A.D.)
Hail, Roma, daughter of Ares.
Melnick, Lynn (b. 1973)
Manhattan Valley.
Melnyczuk, Askold
Usual Immigrant Uncle Poem, The.
Melo, Michael
Red Lipstick on a Straw.
Scrambled Eggs and Garlic Pork.
Unlearning English.
Meltzer, David (b. 1937)
For Jack Spicer.
Hero/Lil, sels.
17:II:82.
Tell Them I'm Struggling to Sing with Angels.
Tishah B'Ov / 1952.
What Do I Know of Journey.
Who's the Jew.
Melville, Elizabeth, Lady Culross (fl. c.1603)
Ane Godly Dream, sels.
Sonnet sent to Blackness to Mr. John Welsch,
by the Lady Culross, A.
Melville, Herman (1819–91)
Aeolian Harp, The.
After the Pleasure Party [Lines Traced under
an Image of Amor Threatening].
America.
Apparition, The—A Retrospect.
Arch, The.
Archipelago, The.
Armies of the Wilderness, The.
Art: "In placid hours well-pleased we dream."
Attic Landscape, The.
Ball's Bluff.
Battle Summers, The.
Bench of Boors, The.
Berg, The.
Billy Budd, Foretopman, sels.
By the Jordan.
Chipmunk, The.
Clarel: A Poem and Pilgrimage in the Holy
Land, sels.
College Colonel, The.
Coming Storm, The.
Conflict of Convictions, The.
Dirge for McPherson, A.
Enthusiast, The.

Enviable Isles, The.
Formerly a Slave.
Fragments of a Lost Gnostic Poem of the
Twelfth [or 12th] Century.
Fruit and Flower Painter.
Greek Architecture.
Guide and Guard.
Haglets, The.
Herba Santa.
House-Top, The.
Immolated.
In a Bye-Canal.
In a Church of Padua.
In the Desert.
Inscription: "To them who crossed the flood."
Iris.
Island, The.
John Marr.
Little Good Fellows, The.
Maldive Shark, The.
Malvern Hill.
Man-of-War Hawk, The.
March into Virginia, The.
Martyr, The.
Meditation, A.
Memorial on the Slain at Chickamauga.
Misgivings.
Moby Dick, sels.
Monody: "To have known him, to have loved
him."
My Jacket Old.
Parthenon, The.
Pebbles.
Pontoosuce.
Portent, The.
Ravaged Villa, The.
Requiem[:] for Soldiers Lost in Ocean
Transports, A: "When, after storms that
woodlands rue."
Rolfe and the Palm.
Rosary Beads.
Rose Farmer, The.
Rose Window.
Rusty Man, The.
Shelley's Vision.
Sheridan at Cedar Creek.
Shiloh (A Requiem).
Song from Mardi.
Spirit Appeared to Me, A.
Stonewall Jackson.
Swamp Angel, The.
Temeraire, The.
Time's Betrayal.
Timoleon.
To———: "Ah, wherefore, lonely, to and fro."
To Ned.
Tom Deadlight.
Tuft of Kelp, The.
Uninscribed Monument on One of the
Battlefields of the Wilderness, An.
Utilitarian View of the Monitor's Fight, A.
Venice.
We Fish.
Memmi, Albert (b. 1920)
Shot of sunlight, A.
Menai, Huw (1887–1961)
Back in the Return, sels.
Rooks: December.
To One Who Died in a Garret in Cardiff.
Menashe, Samuel (b. 1925)
Annunciation, The.
Beachhead.
49th Birthday Trip (What Are You On?).
Mendelssohn, Anna (b. 1948)
Britain 1967.
Footsteps climb whereas they descend.
Franked.
On being reproached by saintly mediators for
bad budgeting.
Photrum.
Strictly personal.
Wrong Room, The.
Mendes, Murilo (b. 1902)
Chaos's Window, sel.
Christmas 1961.

Graffito in Meknès.
Menefee, Sarah (b. 1946)
September 30.
Menes, Orlando Ricardo
Raspa.
Sodomy.
Meng Chiao (751–814)
Apricots Die Young, *sels.*
Despair.
Lament for Lu Yin.
Laments of the Gorges, *sels.*
Laments of the Gorges ("Long ago, everyone
laughed together.").
Mourning Lu Yin, *sel.*
On Failing the Examination.
Risks.
Stones Where the Haft Rotted, The.
Meng Hao Jan (689–740)
At the Mountain-Lodge of the Buddhist Priest
Ye Waiting in Vain for My Friend Ding.
From a Mooring on the Tonglu to a Friend in
Yangzhou.
In Passing an Old Friend's Farm.
In spring you sleep and never know when the
morn comes.
In Summer at the South Pavilion Thinking of
Xing.
Lake of the Ten Thousand Mountains, The.
Late Spring.
Mooring on Chien-Te River.
Night Mooring on the Jiande River, A.
Night on the Great River.
Passing Seven-League Rapids.
Returning at Night to Lumen Mountain.
Returning by Night to Lu-Men.
Returning Home to Deer-Gate Mountain at
Night.
Returning Late to Lu-men Shan.
Seeking out Master Chan on Incense
Mountain.
Spring Dawn.
Spring Dawn ("Spring sleep, not yet awake to
dawn.").
Spring Dreams.
Spring Morning, A.
Springtime Sleep.
Stayover at Chien-Teh River.
Steering my little boat towards a misty islet.
Taking Leave of Wang Wei.
Written for Old Friends in Yang-Jou City
While Spending the Night on the Tung-Lu
River.
Mengham, Rod
Allegory of Good Government.
Another Name for the Cassiterides.
Concession to Perpetuity No. 166.
Names in the Bark.
Smitten.
To the Soviet Embalmers.
Menicanti, Daria (b. 1914)
Biographical News.
Chameleon.
Epigram for a Worm.
Felines.
I Don't Know.
If.
Love Says.
Seagulls.
To the Readers Who Write to Me.
What's Left of You.
Menken, Adah Isaacs (1839?–68)
Adelina Patti.
Answer Me.
Aspiration.
Autograph on the Soul, The.
Battle of the Stars.
Dreams of Beauty.
Drifts That Bar My Door.
Dying.
Fragment: "Cold chain of life presseth heavily
on me tonight, The."
Genius.
Hear, O Israel!
Hemlock in the Furrows.
In Vain.

Infelix.
Into the Depths.
Judith.
Karazah to Karl.
Memory, A.
Miserimus.
My Heritage.
Myself.
One Year Ago.
Pro Patria.
Release, The.
Resurgam.
Sale of Souls.
Saved.
Ship That Went Down, The.
To———, Sleeping.
Venetia.
Where the Flocks Shall Be Led.
Working and Waiting.
Meogo, Pero (fl. c.1250)
Cantiga de Amigo.
Cossante.
Mercado, Nancy (b. 1959)
Going to Work.
Milla.
Somalia.
Mercer, Johnny (1909–76)
Accentuate the Positive.
Arthur Murray Taught Me Dancing in a Hurry.
Blues in the Night.
Come Rain or Come Shine.
Day In—Day Out.
Early Autumn.
Glow-Worm, The.
Hooray for Hollywood.
How Little We Know.
I Remember You.
I Thought About You.
I Wonder What Became of Me.
I'm Old-Fashioned.
Jeepers Creepers.
Jubilation T. Cornpone.
Laura.
Midnight Sun.
Moon River.
My Shining Hour.
On the Atchison, Topeka and the Santa Fe.
One for My Baby (And One More for the
Road).
Out of This World.
P.S. I Love You.
Satin Doll.
Skylark.
Something's Gotta Give.
Tangerine.
That Old Black Magic.
Too Marvelous for Words.
You Must Have Been a Beautiful Baby.
You Were Never Lovelier.
Mercredi, Duncan (b. 1951)
Coffee Table Blues.
Meredith, Christopher (b. 1954)
Christening Pot Boiler.
Jets.
Plasnewydd Square.
Meredith, George (1828–1909)
Camelus Saltat.
Camelus Saltat: Continued.
Dirge in Woods.
Empty Purse, The, *sel.*
Islet the Dachs.
Love in the Valley.
Lucifer in Starlight.
Modern Love, *sels.*
Phoebus with Admetus.
Meredith, Louisa (1812–95)
Tasmanian Scenes.
Meredith, William (b. 1919)
Airman's Virtue.
American Living Room, The: A Tract.
Bachelor.
Consequences.
Country Stars.
Crossing Over.
Dying Away.

Effort at Speech.
For His Father.
Illiterate, The.
In Memory of Robert Frost.
Jain Bird Hospital in Delhi, The.
John and Anne.
June: Dutch Harbor.
Korean Woman Seated by a Wall, A.
Last Things.
Love Letter from an Impossible Land.
Myself, Rousseau, a Few Others.
Navy Field.
On Falling Asleep by Firelight.
Parents.
Poem about Morning.
Rhode Island.
Simile: "As when a heavy bomber in the
cloud."
Thoughts on One's Head.
To the Thoughtful Reader.
Traveling Boy.
Two Masks Unearthed in Bulgaria.
What I Remember the Writers Telling Me
When I Was Young.
Meredith, William Tuckey (b. 1839)
Farragut, Farragut.
Merini, Alda (b. 1931)
Ah If at Least I Could.
Bird of Fire, The.
Dies Merini.
Genesis.
Hymn: "If in my womb and mind You placed."
I Leave You These Imprints on the Earth.
I Open the Cigarette.
I Was Born on the Twenty-First in Spring.
Overcoat, The.
Song of Reply.
Merkureva, Vera (1876–1943)
Grandmother of Russian Poetry: A Self-
Portrait, The.
Merriam, Eve (b. 1916)
Esther.
How to Eat a Poem.
Lazy Thought, A.
Lullaby "Purple."
Of Dogs and Ostriches.
One, Two, Three—Gough!
Spell of Weather, A.
Summer's End.
Tube Time.
Wall, The.
Weather.
Which Washington?
Wonderful Whale, The.
Merrick, A. of Aylesbury
Hartwell Gardens.
Merrill, Bob (1920–98)
Don't Rain on My Parade.
Music That Makes Me Dance.
People.
Staying Young.
Merrill, Carol
Love Poem: "Your silver hair, a galaxy."
Wipp Protest.
Merrill, Christopher
Bees, The.
Boy Juggling a Soccer Ball, A.
Day Lilies: Instructions and an Elegy.
Diver, The.
Erosion.
Merrill, James (1926–95)
About the Phoenix.
Above All That?
After Greece.
Angel.
Annie Hill's Grave.
Arabian Night.
Body [*or* B o d y].
Book of Ephraim, The, *sels.*
Broken Bowl, The.
Broken Home, The.
Charioteer of Delphi, The.
Charles on Fire.
Childlessness.
Clearing the Title.

Coda: The Higher Keys, *sel.*
Country of a Thousand Years of Peace, The.
David's Night in Veliès.
Days of 1994.
Days of 1964.
Days of 1935.
Dedication: "Hans, there are moments when the whole mind."
Downward Look, A.
Five Old Favorites, *sels.*
From a Notebook.
Graffito.
Grass.
Green Eye, The.
Hôtel de l'Univers et Portugal.
Kimono, The.
Laboratory Poem.
Mad Scene, The.
Maisie.
Mirabell: Books of Number, *sel.*
Mirror.
My Father's Irish Setters.
Neo-Classic.
Octopus, The.
Peacock, The.
Pier: Under Pisces, The.
Processional.
Renewal, A.
Self-Portrait in Tyvek(TM) Windbreaker.
Swimming By Night.
Syrinx.
Tomorrows.
Topics, *sels.*
Upward Look, An.
Urban Convalescence, An.
Victor Dog, The.
Voices from the Other World.
Watching the Dance.
Willowware Cup.
World and the Child, The.

Merrill, Stuart (1863–1915)
Ballade of the Chinese Lover.
Ballade of the Outcasts.

Merriman [*or* Merryman], Brian [*or* Bryan] (1747–1805)
Midnight Court, The, *sels.*

Merritt, Constance (b. 1966)
Lullaby: "Say to me: out there are only streets, and cars."
Mute Swan, The.
Woman of Color.

Merry, Robert ("Della Crusca") (1755–98)
Adieu and Recall to Love, The.
Elegy Written after Reading the "Sorrows of Werter."
Laurel of Liberty. A Poem, The, *sel.*
Madness.
Poet is Piqued, The [*or* Anna Matilda].
Rush to the Lakes, The [*or* Anna Matilda].
Some Terrify Lions [*or* Anna Matilda].
Tiff, The [*or* The Interview].
To Anna Matilda.

Merryman, Mildred Plew *See* Meigs, Mildred Plew

Merryweather, Anne (d. after 1702)
Prince who said an English Senate can, The.

Mersaal, Eman
Neutrality.
Portrait, A.
Repetition.
Too Many Times.

Mersal, Iman
Solitude Exercises.

Merson, Billy (1881–1947)
Spaniard That Blighted My Life, The.

Merton, Thomas (1915–68)
Cables to the Ace, *sel.*
Cana.
Dark Morning, The.
Evening Prayer.
Geography of Lograire, The, *sels.*
St. Paul.

Merwin, W. S. (William Stanley) (b. 1927)
After the Alphabets.
Air: "Naturally it is night."

Airport.
Animals, The.
Asians Dying, The.
Avoiding News by the River.
Ballad of John Cable and Three Gentlemen.
Before a Departure in Spring.
Berryman.
Bread.
Broken, The.
Burning the Cat.
Burnt Child, The.
Calling, A.
Carol of the Three Kings.
Carol: "On vague hills the prophet bird."
Chaff, The.
Dachau Shoe, The.
Dead Hand.
Departure's Girl-Friend.
Dictum: For a Masque of Deluge.
Drunk in the Furnace, The.
Dusk in Winter.
Encampment at Morning, An.
Feast Day.
Field Mushrooms.
Fly.
Fog-Horn.
Footprints on the Glacier.
For a Coming Extinction.
For the Anniversary of My Death.
Gardens of Zuñi, The.
Given Day, A.
Glassy Sea.
Good-Bye Shirts, The.
Hearing.
Home for Thanksgiving.
Hope for Her.
How We Are Spared.
Hydra, The.
Lament for the Makers.
Last One, The.
Learning a Dead Language.
Leviathan.
Losing a Language.
Marfa Lights, The.
Migrants by Night.
Moths, The.
Night of the Shirts, The.
Noah's Raven.
Odysseus.
On the Subject of Poetry.
One of the Lives.
Plea for a Captive.
Poem, The: "Coming late, as always."
Postcards from the Maginot Line.
"Prodigal Son," The, *sels.*
Rain Travel.
River of Bees, The.
Rose Beetle, The.
St. Vincent's.
Search Party.
Second Psalm: The Signals.
Separation.
Shore, The.
Some Last Questions.
Spiders I Have Known.
Stranger, The.
Strawberries.
Thing of Beauty, A.
Tide Line Garden.
To Luck.
Unknown Forebear.
Utterance.
Vixen.
Waves in August.
Weight of Sleep, The.
West Wall.
Wheels of the Trains, The.
When You Go Away.
Whoever You Are.
Windows, The: "Here is a child who presses his head to the ground."
Yesterday: "My friend says I was not a good son."

Mesmer, Sharon
Lonely Tylenol.
My Life in Yonago.

What Becomes Us.
Messer, Sarah (b. 1966)
Look.
Marriage Proposal.
Rendered Dog.
Some Women Marry Houses.
With this Change to Indoor Lighting.

Messerli, Douglas (b. 1947)
Actually Swallowed.
Along Without: A Fiction in Film for Poetry, *sel.*
Angry with China.
Annunciation, The.
Closure.
Essay on Concrete, An.
From Hear to Air.
Going to Sea.
Harrowing.
Scared Cows.
This That and Then.

Metastasio, Pietro (1698–1782)
On thy grey bark, in witness of my flame.

Metodiev, Ivan (b. 1947)
Songs for Orphans Big and Small, *sels.*

Metras, Gary
Anniversary.
Robert Frost's Chair.
Utilities Advertisement in the Wake of Three Mile Island.
Vanishing Point.

Metwalli, Mohamed (b. 1970)
This Is How the Magician Produces a Dove out of the Hat.
Untitled: "We are two straw dolls."

Metz, Robin
Father of the Bride.

Mew, Charlotte (1869–1928)
À Quoi Bon Dire.
Absence.
Again.
At the Convent Gate.
Beside the Bed.
Call, The.
Cenotaph, The.
Fame.
Farmer's Bride, The.
Forest Road, The.
Here Lies a Prisoner.
I Have Been through the Gates.
I so liked Spring last year.
In Nunhead Cemetery.
In the Fields.
June, 1915.
Ken.
Madeleine in Church.
Madeleine in Church, *sels.*
May, 1915.
Ne Me Tangito.
Not for That City.
Old Shepherd's Prayer.
On the Asylum Road.
On the Road to the Sea.
Pedlar, The.
Quiet House, The.
Rooms.
Sea Love.
Song: "Love, love today, my dear."
To a Child in Death.
Trees Are Down, The.

Meyer, Bruce
Diet, The.
Ferry to South Baymouth, The.
Lovers' Sestina, The.

Meyer, Conrad Ferdinand (1825–98)
Blackshadow Chestnut.

Meyer, Kuno
Liadan and Curithir.

Meyer, Thomas
Dancing There.
Merchant's Daughter.
Uranium Ore.

Meyerhoff, Jamie
On Impermanence.
Three Ravens.

Meyerhoff, Jessemyn
　Million times, A.
　Resounding echo of the buddha's words, The.
　Snow.
Meyers, Bert (1928–79)
　Arc de Triomphe.
　Garlic, The.
Meynell, Alice (1847–1922)
　Advent Meditation.
　At Night.
　Beyond Knowledge.
　Chimes.
　Christ in the Universe.
　Cradle-Song at Twilight.
　Crucifixion, The.
　Easter Night.
　Father of Women, A [Ad Sororem E. B.].
　Girl on the Land, The.
　I Am the Way.
　Lady Poverty, The.
　Letter from a Girl to Her Own Old Age, A.
　Maternity.
　Messina, 1908.
　Modern Mother, The.
　November Blue.
　October Redbreast, The.
　Parentage.
　Renouncement.
　Shepherdess, The.
　Song of Derivations, A.
　Study, A.
　Summer in England, 1914.
　Sunderland Children, The.
　Thoughts in Separation.
　Thrush before Dawn, A.
　To 'A Certain Rich Man.'
　To a Daisy.
　To Conscripts.
　To Silence.
　To the Beloved.
　Unto Us a Son Is Given.
　Watershed, The.
　Wind Is Blind, The.
Meynell, Mrs. Wilfrid See Meynell, Alice
Meynell, Viola (1886–1956)
　Sympathy.
Meyrelles, Isabel (b. 1929)
　I Will Tell You During the Walk.
　Night Words.
　Once again.
　To forget.
　Tyger, Tyger.
Mezey, Robert (b. 1935)
　At the Point.
　Couplets, sel.
　Evening, An.
　Evening Wind.
　How Much Longer?
　My Mother.
　Owl.
　Reaching the Horizon.
　Silence, The.
　Thousand Chinese Dinners, A, sel.
　To Levine on the Day of Atonement.
　Touch It.
　Twilight Under Pine Ridge.
　Wandering Jew, The.
Mhac an tSaoi, Máire (b. 1922)
　Finit.
　Jack.
　Lament.
　Mary Hogan's Quatrains.
　No Second Deirdre.
Mhlophe, Gcina (b. 1958)
　Sometimes When It Rains.
Mhurchaidh, Ian Mac See Macrae, John
Michaelis, Hanny (b. 1922)
　Brilliantly Philosophising.
　I Was About Three Years of Age.
Michaels, Anne (b. 1958)
　Passionate World, The.
　Sublimation, sel.
　What the Light Teaches, sel.

Michaels, Denise Calvetti
　Returning from Italy.
Michaels, Jesse
　Knowledge.
Michaux, Henri (1899–1984)
　Avenir.
　Future.
　I Am Writing to You from a Far-Off Country,
　　sels.
　Jetty, The.
　Mes statues.
　My Statues.
　Saisir, sel.
　Simplicity.
　Slices of Knowledge, sels.
　Tranches de savoir, sel.
Michelangelo Buonarroti (1474–1564)
　Flee, lovers, from Love, flee from his fire.
　From sweet weeping to a painful smile.
　I live in sin, and dying to myself I live.
　I see in your beautiful face, my lord.
　It was over here that my love, in his mercy.
　Like dry wood in a burning fire.
　Love's Justification.
　My lady, how comes it about—what all can
　　see.
　"Night" in the Medici Chapel.
　Soul tries a thousand remedies in vain, The.
　Very dear though it was I have bought you.
　Violent burning for prodigious beauty, A.
　Why should I still pour out my intense desire.
　You know that I know, my lord, that you
　　know.
Michelson, Joan
　Departures, sels.
Michelson, Peter
　Enduring Witness, the Mosques of Kattankudi.
Michie, James (b. 1927)
　Arizona Nature Myth.
Michie, Susan
　Connecting Light.
Michiura, Motoko (b. 1947)
　Suddenly.
Mickiewicz, Adam (1798–1855)
　Ackermann Steppe, The.
　Mushroom Gatherers, The.
　Storm, The.
　Year 1812, The.
Middleton, Christopher (b. 1926)
　Anasphere: Le torse antique.
　Saloon with Birds.
　Wooden Dog.
Middleton, David (b. 1949)
　Embertide in Advent.
Middleton, Richard (1882–1911)
　Carol of the Poor Children, The.
Middleton, Thomas (1580–1627)
　Melancholy.
Midge, Tiffany
　Written in Blood.
Miedzyrzecki, Artur (b. 1922)
　At the Cave.
　At Work.
　Can You Imagine.
　End of the Game.
　Golden Age, The.
　Penguins.
　29-77-02.
　What Does the Political Scientist Know?
Mif
　Terezin.
Mignon, Auguste
　One Heart's Enough for Me.
Mihaiu, Virgil (b. 1951)
　Ultimate Luxury Woman, The.
Mihalic, Slavko (b. 1928)
　Atlantis.
　Drinking Spree Beneath the Open Sky.
　Elegy: "From the old settlements only the
　　writings."
　Exile's Return, The.
　I Cannot Say the Name of the City.
　Large Grieving Women.

　Morning Roar of the City, The.
　On the Carpet, Staring at Myself.
　Screams in the Dark.
　Second-Class Citizen.
　Under the Microscope.
Miidhu
　War Dance.
Mikes, Margit (1897–1976)
　Glassworks.
　Identity.
　Poet in the Kitchen.
　To My Daughter.
Mikhail, Dunya (b. 1965)
　America: "Please don't ask me, America."
　Chaldean Ruins, The.
　Christmas.
　Dawn Fairy, The.
　Jewel, The.
　Non-Military Statements.
　Prisoner, The.
　Rain.
　Santa Claus.
　Snow Storm.
　Urgent Call, An.
　War Works Hard, The.
Mikha'il, Hanan
　Demonstration.
Mikha'il, Murad (1906–89)
　Beggar, The.
　Crazy Satan.
　Don't Despair.
　Imprisoned God, The.
　Talk.
　Three Flags.
　Voice of Conscience, The.
　You Have Your Calamity And I Have Mine.
Miko, Chelle
　Mississippi Girls, Plaited.
Mikolowski, Ken
　Witness, The.
Milán, Eduardo (b. 1952)
　Cinco, sel.
　¿Cuál coro?
　Do you care to remedy the faces of the gods?
　　Make white.
　Eficaz la pata de conejo, el no estar.
　Esto no puede seguir así: sé sincero, uno.
　Five, sel.
　He sends word for them not to be in His place.
　I believe in nothing, I collaborate, I assist.
　I let myself be led because I let loose.
　I mean you as though referring to two furies
　　because.
　Manda decir que no estén en Su lugar.
　Marionetas son metáforas perfectas, Las.
　Me dejo guiar porque he dejado ir.
　Me refiero a ti como a dos fieras porque.
　No hay porqué, hay órdenes de canto.
　Now that we're nothing, for example.
　One's alone in this: making masks.
　¿Quieres curar las caras de los dioses? Haz
　　máscaras.
　Rabbit-foot effectiveness, nonentity of.
　Riddle me what marionettes are.
　There is no wherefore, there is a command of
　　song.
　Uno está solo frente a esto: haciendo máscaras.
　We can't go on like this: be truthful, empty.
　What chorus?
　Ya que no somos nada, por ejemplo.
　Yo no creo nada, yo colaboro, ayudo.
Milè, Woudòf See Muller, Rudolph
Miles, Josephine (1911–85)
　After noon I lie down.
　Album: "This is a hard life you are living."
　All Hallow.
　As Difference Blends into Identity.
　Belief.
　Bounty.
　Bureau 2.
　Center.
　Conception: "Death did not come to my
　　mother."
　Concert.
　Conservancies.

Dear Frank, Here is a poem.
Dec. 7, 1941.
Doctor Who Sits at the Bedside of a Rat, The.
Doll.
Dream: "I see you displaced, condensed, within my dream."
Entrepreneur chicken shed his tail feathers, surplus, The.
Fields of Learning.
Forecast.
Government Injunction [Restraining Harlem Cosmetic Co.].
Gypsy.
Housewife.
In the town where every man is king.
Made Shine.
Oedipus.
On Inhabiting an Orange.
Parent.
Preliminary to Classroom Lecture.
Reason: "Said, Pull her up a bit will you, Mac, I want to unload there."
Riddle: "You are a riddle I would not unravel."
Ride.
Sale.
So Graven.
Tally.
Why We Are Late.

Miles, Susan (Ursula Roberts) (b. 1887)
Hares, The.
Plumbers.

Miliauskaite, Nijole (b. 1950)
In the Damp Places.
On Winter Nights.
Temporary City.
These are Lilacs.

Miljkovic, Branko (1934–60)
Agon.
Miners.
Sea Without Poets.
Sleepers.

Millar, Joseph
Fiber Optics.
Midlife.
Poem for a New Girlfriend.
Telephone Repairman.

Millay, Edna St. Vincent ("Nancy Boyd") (1892–1950)
Afternoon on a Hill.
Ancient Gesture, An.
And must I then, indeed, Pain, live with you.
Apostrophe to Man.
Armenonville.
Bean-Stalk, The.
Bluebeard.
Buck in the Snow, The.
Burial.
Cameo, The.
Childhood Is the Kingdom Where Nobody Dies.
Conscientious Objector.
Counting-out Rhyme.
Courage that my mother had, The.
Departure.
Dirge Without Music.
Eel-Grass.
Elegy before Death.
Epitaph for the Race of Man, sels.
Euclid Alone Has Looked on Beauty Bare.
Evening on Lesbos.
First Fig.
Fitting, The.
From a Train Window.
From a Very Little Sphinx.
God's World.
Grow not too high, grow not too far from home.
Grown-up.
Hearing Your Words, and Not a Word Among Them.
I, Being Born A Woman [And Distressed].
I Dreamed I Moved among the Elysian Fields.
I Forgot for a Moment.
I know I am but summer to your heart.
I shall forget you presently, my dear.

I shall go back.
I think I should have loved you presently.
I too beneath your moon, almighty Sex.
If I should learn, in some quite casual way.
If in the years to come you should recall.
In the Grave No Flower.
Inland.
It is the fashion now to wave aside.
Journey: "Ah, could I lay me down in this long grass."
Justice Denied in Massachusetts.
Little Ghost, The.
Love is not all: it is not meat nor drink.
Love is not blind. I see with single eye.
Love me no more, now let the god depart.
Make Bright the Arrows.
Memorial to D. C., sels.
Menses.
My Heart, Being Hungry.
Never May the Fruit Be Plucked.
Night is my sister, and how deep in love.
Not to Be Spattered by His Blood.
Oh, my belovèd, have you thought of this.
Oh, Oh, you will be sorry for that word!
Oh, think not I am faithful to a vow!
On Hearing a Symphony of Beethoven.
Only until this cigarette is ended.
Passer Mortuus Est.
Pear Tree, The.
Pity me not because the light of day.
Poet and His Book, The.
Portrait by a Neighbor.
Ragged Island.
Recuerdo.
Renascence, sel.
Rendezvous.
Return, The.
Say that We Saw Spain Die.
Scrub.
Second Fig.
Siege.
Since of no creature living the last breath.
Sonnet 2: "Time does not bring relief; you all have lied."
Sonnet 11: "Not in a silver casket cool with pearls."
Sonnet 43: "What lips my lips have kissed, and where, and why."
Sonnet to Gath.
Sonnet: "Women have loved before as I love now."
Sonnets from an Ungrafted Tree, sels.
Sorrow.
Spring: "To what purpose, April, do you return again?"
Thursday.
To a Calvinist in Bali.
To Elinor Wylie ("Oh, she was beautiful in every part!").
To Inez Milholland.
To Jesus on His Birthday.
When I too long have looked upon your face.
When you, that at this moment are to me.
Wild Swans.
Winter Night.
Witch-Wife.
Wood Road, The.

Miller, Adam David (b. 1922)
Eye Behind the I, The.
Forever Afternoon.
My Trip.
Song of the Wheel.

Miller, Carolyn
Night in San Francisco.

Miller, Chuck
In Celebration of Surviving.

Miller, Cincinnatus Heine [or Hiner] See Miller, Joaquin

Miller, David
In the Field.

Miller, E. Ethelbert (b. 1950)
Another Love Affair/Another Poem.
Boys of Summer, The.
Bringing Back the Draft.
Father's Day.

Incantation: "Let all poems speak and address themselves."
Jasmine.
Mississippi.
Morning Buddhism.
My Father's Girlfriend.
Night Before the First Day of School, The.
Players.
Rebecca.
Roy Campanella: January, 1958.
She Is Flat on Her Back.
Tomorrow.
What the Women Told Me.
Whispers, Secrets, and Promises.
You Send Me: Bertha Franklin, December 11, 1964.

Miller, Herschel
Kaddish.
Without God's Blessing.

Miller, Jane (b. 1925)
American Odalisque.
Any Two Wheels.
August Zero.
Foundered Star.
Giants.
Impossible, The.
O Pioneers!
Poetry: "Invited onto the grounds of the god."
Sonnet Against Nuclear Weapons.
Topos.
Which Religion Vouchsafes.

Miller, Jeannette (b. 1944)
Bird dressed as solitude and tears.
Crazed Woman, The.
Four times during the night.
I remember the long corridors.
Rise of the Afternoon is a Wide Glory, The.
These Green Paths.
This sense of space.
Woman I Know, The.

Miller, Joaquin (Cincinnatus Heine [or Hiner] Miller) (1841–1913)
Africa.
At Our Golden Gate.
Bravest Battle, The, sel.
By the Pacific Ocean.
California Christmas, A.
Columbus: "Behind him lay the gray Azores."
Dead in the Sierras.
Defense of the Alamo, The.
In Père La Chaise.
Sierras.

Miller, L.
Man Who Is Out of Work Talks to His Son about the Sunset, The.
Triangle.
When the Moon Isn't Shining.

Miller, Larisa (b. 1940)
Heavens are playing with the earth, The.
Let's fill in the form: date of birth.
Light cross of lonely strolls, The.

Miller, Leslie Adrienne
Convolvulus Tricolor.

Miller, Mary Britton (1883–1975)
Cat.

Miller, May (b. 1918)
Calvary Way.
Closing, A.
Gift from Kenya.

Miller, Nyere-Gibran
My Family.

Miller, Ruth (b. 1919)
Aspects of Love, sels.

Miller, Thomas (1807–74)
Evening.

Miller, Vassar (b. 1924)
Bout with Burning.
Christmas Mourning.
Defense Rests.
Dirge in Jazz Time.
How Far?
Judas.
Light Reading.
Morning Person.

On a Weekend in September.
Whitewash of Houston.
Without Ceremony.

Miller, William (1810–72)
Willie Winkie.

Milligan, Bryce (b. 1953)
Copano, 1834.
San Antonio Nights.
Trusting Steel.

Milligan, James (fl. 1800)
Science of Geology, The, sel.

Milligan, Spike (1918–2002)
Bad Report—Good Manners.
Christmas 1970.
My Sister Laura.
Teeth.
Thousand Hairy Savages, A.

Million, Dian
Housing Poem, The.

Mills, Billy (b. 1954)
Ballad: Of Motion.

Mills, David S. (b. 1965)
And Now Yu.
Chembank Card.

Mills, Irving
Minnie, the Moocher.
Prelude to a Kiss.
Solitude.
Sophisticated Lady.

Mills, Laurel
Days of My Mother, The.

Mills Jr., Ralph J.
Evening Song.
For Lorine Niedecker in Heaven.
Water Lilies.

Milman, Henry Hart
Crucifixion, The.
Holy Field, The.
Hymn: "When our heads are bowed with woe."
Martyr of Antioch, The, sel.
O help us, Lord! Each hour of need.
Where the Wicked Cease from Troubling, and
the Weary Are at Rest.

Milne, Alan Alexander (1882–1956)
Bad Sir Brian Botany.
Disobedience.
Happiness.
Hoppity.
King's Breakfast, The.
More It Snows, The.
Vespers, sel.

Milne, Drew (b. 1964)
As It Were, sel.
Bench Marks, sel.

**Milnes, Richard Monckton, 1st Baron Houghton
(1809–85)**
Lady Moon.
Men of Old, The.
Youth, That Pursuest.

Milosz, Czeslaw (1911–2004)
Abundant Catch (Luke 5:4–10).
After Paradise.
And Yet the Books.
Bypassing Rue Descartes.
Cafe.
Child of Europe.
Dedication: "You whom I could not save."
Elegy for N. N.
Encounter.
Esse.
Faith.
Felicitous Life, A.
Gift: "Day so happy, A."
House in Krasnogruda.
In Szetejnie.
Incantation.
Lithuania, After Fifty-two Years, sels.
Mistake, A.
My Faithful Mother Tongue.
On Angels.
On Pilgrimage.
On the Other Side.
Poetic State, A.
Preparation.

Reading the Japanese Poet Issa (1762–1826).
Readings.
Report.
Six Lectures in Verse, sels.
Slow River.
St. Luke, sels.
St. Mark, sel.
St. Matthew, sels.
St. Matthew, sels.
Task, A.
Temptation.
Tidings.
Veni Creator.
Voices of Poor People, sels.
With Her.
World, The, sels.
You Who Wronged.

Milosz, O. V. de L. (1877–1939)
Bridge, The.
King Don Luis.
La Berline Arrêtée Dans la Nuit.

Milova, Tatyana (b. 1965)
Erotic Fruit, sels.
I've overslept my stop. . .the train will spit me
out.
Sometimes, not often, it's true.

Milton, John (1608–74)
Arcades, sels.
At a Solemn Music[k].
Comus; a Masque Presented at Ludlow Castle,
sels.
How soon hath Time the subtle [or suttle] thief
[or theef] of youth.
Il Penseroso.
L'Allegro.
Lycidas.
On His Blindness.
On His Deceased Wife.
On Shakespear[e].
On the Detraction Which Followed upon My
Writing Certain Treatises ("Book was writ[t]
of late called [or call'd] Tetrachordon, A.").
On the Detraction Which Followed upon My
Writing Certain Treatises ("I did but prompt
the age to quit their [or thir] clogs.").
On the Late Massacre [or Massacher] in
Piedmont [or Piemont].
On the Lord Gen[eral] Fairfax at the Siege of
Colchester.
On the Morning of Christ's Nativity, sels.
On the New Forcers of Conscience Under the
Long Parliament.
On the University Carrier Who Sick'n'd [or
Sickened] in the Time of His Vacancy [,
Being Forbid to go to London, by Reason of
the Plague].
On Time.
Paradise Lost, sels.
Paradise Regained [or Regain'd], sels.
Samson Agonistes, sels.
Sonnet 9: "Ladie [or Lady], that in the prime
of earliest youth."
Sonnet: On the Religious Memorie of Mrs.
Catherine Thomason My Christian Friend
Deceas'd Decem. 1646.
To Charles Diodati.
To Cyriack Skinner.
To Mr. Cyriack Skinner upon His Blindness.
To Mr. H. Lawes On His Airs.
To Mr. Lawrence.
To Sir Henry Vane the Younger.
To the Lady Margaret Ley.
To the Lord General Cromwell.
Upon the Circumcision.
When the Assault Was Intended to the City.

Min, Neeltje Maria (b. 1944)
Deep in the Pit.
My Mother Has Forgotten My Name.

Ming, T'ao T'ung See T'ao Hung Ching

Minhinnick, Robert (b. 1952)
Aerial, The.
After a Friendship.
Boathouse, The.
Catching My Breath.
Children, The.

Drinking Art, The.
Grandfather in the Garden.
House, The.
Looters, The.
Sap.
Sax.
She Drove a 'Seventies Plymouth.
Sunday Morning.
Surfers.
Twenty-Five Laments for Iraq.

Minnema, Sybe See Polet, Sybren

Minnigerode, Meade (1887–1967)
Whiffenpoof Song.

Minnis, Chelsey (b. 1970)
Skull Ring, The.

Minton, Helena
Building the Compost.
Day Surgery Pre-Op.

Minulescu, Ion (1881–1944)
Mechanical-landscape-poem.

Mipham, Sakyong (b. 1962)
Snow Fell Twice, the Sun Always Shone.

Mirabai [or Mira Bai] (1498–1547)
All I Was Doing Was Breathing.
Ankle Bells.
Clouds, The.
Coffer with the Poisonous Snake, The.
Dark One, / all I request is a portion of love.
Dark one, / how can I sleep?
Don't block my way, friend.
Don't Go, Don't Go.
Faithfulness.
Glimpse of your body, A.
Having wet me with love.
Heat of Midnight Tears, The.
His Hair.
I was going to the river for water.
It's True I Went to the Market.
Music, The.
O friend, understand: the body.
O friends, I am mad.
O friends on this Path.
Song of the flute, O sister, is madness, The.
Where Did You Go?
Why Mira Can't Go Back to Her Old House.
Wild woman of the forests, The.

Miranda, Deborah A.
Stories I Tell My Daughter.

Miranda, Gary (b. 1938)
Second-Born Son: Lines for Walt Whitman
Composed on Nantucket Island.

Miri, Angela (b. 1959)
Do Not Stop Me!

Miriana Basheva See Basheva, Miryana

Mirikitani, Janice
Doreen.
Fisherman, The.
Shadow in Stone.
Soul Food.
Suicide Note.

Miron, Gaston (1928–96)
Marche à l'amour, La, sel.
Walk toward Love, The.

Mirosevich, Toni (b. 1952)
Hygiene.

Mirsal, Iman (b. 1966)
Abortion.
Confessions.
I Usually Look Around Me.

Mirville, Ernst (b. 1940)
All the tongues are wagging.
Don't give me food.
In the land of Haiti.
Liberty.
Nine months in the belly.
Pretty little dress,. . .stockings full of holes.
Talk, talk, talk. . .talk, talk, talk.
You say: Today!

Mishol, Agi (b. 1947)
Estate.
Gravity, Death.
Sacred Cow of Hardship, The.
Shopping.

Miss Queenie See Kennedy, Imogene Elizabeth

Mistral, Gabriela (Lucila Godoy Alcayaga) (1889–1957)
Absence.
Autumn.
Ballad: "He passed by with another."
Ballad: "He was strolling with another woman."
Ballad: "He went by with another."
Caribbean Sea.
Close to Me.
Close to Me.
Dawn.
Decalogue of the Artist.
Dusk.
Earthen Jugs.
Empty Walnut, The.
Final Tree.
Flower of Air, The.
House, The.
House, The.
I Love, Love.
Intimate.
Lady Spring.
Let Him Not Grow Up.
Liana, The.
Little Box from Olinalá, The.
Martha and Mary.
Morning.
My Mother.
Night.
Night.
One Word.
Piececitos.
Pious One, The.
Prayer, *sel*.
Rocking.
Rocking.
Rocking.
Rose, The.
Rose, The.
Serene Words.
Song.
Stranger, The.
Those Who Do Not Dance.
To the Children.
Woman, A.
Mitcham, Judson
On the Otis Redding Bridge.
Mitchell, Adrian (b. 1932)
Celia Celia.
Dog Called Elderly, A.
Dumb Insolence.
Fifteen Million Plastic Bags.
From Rich Uneasy America to My Friend Christopher Logue.
Giving Potatoes.
Goodbye.
Icarus Schmicarus.
Nature Poem.
Nothingmas Day.
Puppy Called Puberty, A.
Quite Apart from the Holy Ghost.
Speck Speaks, A.
To Whom It May Concern (Tell Me Lies about Vietnam).
Victor Jara of Chile.
Mitchell, C. T.
Roll On, Shining Wheel!
Mitchell, Elma (b. 1919)
Alice Uglier.
Crucifixion Will Not Take Place, The.
Death of Adam, The.
I wear bright colours.
Mother, Dear Mother.
Passenger Opposite, The.
This Poem.
Thoughts After Ruskin.
Mitchell, Frank (b. 1912)
12th Horse Song of Frank Mitchell (Blue), The.
Mitchell, Karen L. (b. 1955)
Monster, The.
Night Rain.
On the Anniversary Of Your Death.
Tree Stillness.

Mitchell, Lucy Sprague (1878–1967)
House of the Mouse, The.
Mitchell, Mrs. James Herbert *See* Strobel, Marion
Mitchell, Nancy
Incognito.
Leaving, The.
Love Story in Subtitles.
Runaway.
Mitchell, Roger
It.
North.
Out Here.
To Walt Whitman on America's Birthday.
Mitchell, Sam
Thunderstorm.
Mitchell, Silas Weir (1829–1914)
How the Cumberland Went Down.
Mitchell, Stephen (b. 1943)
Annunciation, The.
Bamboo.
Good Samaritan et Al, The.
Orchid and Rock.
Parable of the Sower, The.
Sense of Proportion, The.
St. Luke, *sel*.
St. Matthew, *sel*.
Vermeer.
Mitchell, Susan (b. 1944)
Dead, The: "At night the dead come down to the river to drink."
From the Journals of the Frog Prince.
Golden Bough: The Feather Palm.
Grove at Nemi, The.
Havana Birth.
Smoke.
Mitchell, Susan Langstaff (1866–1926)
Amergin.
Mitchell, Susanna Valentine
Of Earthly Love.
Mitchelson, Tom
Circa.
Mitchison, Naomi (b. 1897)
Dick and Colin at the Salmon Nets.
Farm Woman, The: 1942.
Hartmanswillerkopf.
House of the Hare, The.
My True Love Hath My Heart.
Nettlebed Road.
Scottish Renaissance in Glasgow, The: 1935.
To a Fisherman with the Present of a Knife.
To Some Young Communists from an Older Socialist.
Mitford, Mary Russell (1787–1855)
Fleet Marmion.
Forget-Me-Not, The.
Manx.
On a Beautiful Woman.
Song: "Fairest things are those which live, The."
To Tray—Stolen.
Written in a Blank-Paper Book Given to the Author by a Friend.
Mitsui, James Masao (b. 1940)
At Bon Odori.
Because of My Father's Job.
Destination: Tule Lake Relocation Center, May 20, 1942.
Katori Maru, October 1920.
Nisei: Second Generation Japanese-American.
Photograph of a Child, Japanese-American Evacuation, Bainbridge Island, Washington, March 30, 1942.
Picture of a Japanese Farmer, Woodland, California, May 20, 1942.
Mivil, Ens *See* Mirville, Ernst
Miyazawa Kenji (1896–1933)
Dawn: "Rolling snow turned peach-color."
Daydreaming on the Trail.
Morning of the Last Farewell, The.
November 3rd.
Pictures of the Floating World.
Politicians, The.
Snow on Saddle Mountain, The.

Some Views Concerning the Proposed Site of a National Park.
Spring & Asura.
Spring and the Ashura.
Miyoshi Toyoichiro
Shadow 1.
Mkangelwa, Luvuyo (b. 1977)
Observations.
Women Sing, The.
Mlinko, Ange (b. 1969)
Just Dump Me on the Palace Steps.
Mnasalces (*fl.* 3d cent. B.C.)
Epigrams, *sel*.
Mnookin, Wendy
Signs.
Mo Shih-lung (c.1539–87)
Saying Good-bye to a Singing Girl Who Has Decided to Become a Nun.
To the Monk Wu-hsia on the Occasion of His Editing the Lotus Sutra.
Moan
Clear, clear—clearest!
Moat, John
Twilight by the plantation.
Mock, Jeff
Epithalamion for Sarah and Tony.
Mocoancoeng, J.G.
Drought.
Moerman, Ernst (*fl.* 20th cent.)
Louis Armstrong.
Moffat, Mrs. Curtis *See* Tree, Iris
Moffett, Judith (b. 1942)
Reaching Around.
Moffitt, John (b. 1908)
To Look at Any Thing.
Mohammad, Hala (b. 1959)
At the Door of Anticipation.
Love Burned Out the Light.
Man Who Offers Me His Chest, The.
What Am I Chasing!
Mohammad, K. Silem (b. 1962)
Mars Needs Terrorists.
Mohar, Yehiel *See* Mar, Yekhi'el
Mohiuddin, Khadar (b. 1955)
Birthmark.
Mohr, Bill
In Line at Pancho's Tacos.
Why the Heart Never Develops Cancer.
Mohr, Joseph (1792–1848)
Silent Night.
Silent Night! Holy Night!
Moir, David Macbeth (1798–1851)
Dying Oscar.
Moir, Lyn (b. 1934)
Handnotes.
Moiro
Beneath Aphrodite's golden portico you now lie.
Great Zeus was reared in Krete and no one.
Tree nymphs, daughters of River, ambrosial.
Moise, Penina (1797–1880) and Edward N. Calisch
Newspaper, The.
To Persecuted Foreigners.
Mok, Judith (b. 1958)
Winter Mirror.
Winter Mirror II.
Mokusen (1847–1920)
On Climbing the Mountain Where Buddha Trained.
Mokusetsu (*fl.* 17th cent.)
Long summer rains / Barley's tasteless.
Moldaw, Carol (b. 1956)
Anastylosis.
Nest, The.
Widening, The.
Mole, John
Jack-in-the-Box.
Mine is the ungloved.
Penny Toys, *sels*.
Taking the Plunge.
Trick, The.

Molina, Enrique (b. 1910)
As the Great Days Flow.
To Vahine (Painted by Gaugin).
Way It Must Be, The.

Molina, Paz (b. 1945)
Events Like Palaces.
Scream is a Kind of Coffin, The.
Things of the Blind.
Your Anger.

Molinari, Ricardo (b. 1898)
Little Ode to Melancholy.
Ode to a Long Sorrow.
Poem of the Girl from Velázquez.

Moll, Ernest G. (b. 1900)
Beware the Cuckoo.
Bush Speaks, The.
Clearing for the Plough.

Moller, Vera
Faithfullest Beast, The.

Mollineux, Mary (1651–95)
Another Letter to a Friend.
Even what the hungry Wolf in Field would do.
Lord of them that hurt his Saints, doth say, The.
Meditations on Persecution.
Solitude.

Molloy, Dorothy (1942–2004)
Chacun à son goût.
Conversation Class.
Envelope of Skin.
First Blood.
Grandma's Zoo.
Grands Seigneurs, Les.
Looking for Mother.
Pascual the Shepherd.
Postman's Knock.

Molodovsky [or Molodowsky], Kadya (1894–1975)
Merciful God.
Mother, A: "Mother in the green sweater walks and walks along the street, The."
Prayers: I.

Molony, Linda (b. 1960)
Cat Washing.

Momaday, N. Scott (b. 1934)
Angle of Geese.
Bear, The.
Burning, The.
Carriers of the Dream Wheel.
Colors of Night, The.
Eagle-Feather Fan, The.
Earth and I Gave You Turquoise.
Four Notions of Love and Marriage.
Gift, The: "Older, more generous."
Headwaters.
North Dakota, North Light.
Pit Viper.
Rainy Mountain Cemetery.
Story of a Well-made Shield, The.
To a Child Running with Outstretched Arms in Canyon de Chelly.
Two Figures.
Walk on the Moon.
Winter Holding off the Coast of North America.

Monaghan, Patricia
Persephone's Journey.
Venus of Laussel.

Monck, Mary (1678–1715)
On A Romantic Lady.
Verses Written on Her Death-bed at Bath to Her Husband in London.

Monette, Paul (1945–95)
Half Life.
No Goodbyes.

Monhollen, Christine
White Trace Close.

Monju-Shindo
Joshu's "Oak in the courtyard"

"Monk" See Lewis, Matthew Gregory

Monk, Geraldine (b. 1952)
AC.
CS
La Tormenta.

South Bound: Facing North.

Monk, Mary (?1677–1715)
Fire Us with Ice, Burn Us with Snow.

Monkhouse, Cosmo (1840–1901)
Any Soul to Any Body.
Limerick: "There was a young lady of Riga."
There Was a Young Lady of Niger.

Monks, Arthur W.
Twilight's Last Gleaming.

Monnier, Pascalle (b. 1958)
Été, L' ("Bon, c'est la chaleur.").
Été, L' ("Ce sont les premiers beaux jours.").
Hiver, L'
Summer ("Good, it's hot.").
Summer ("These are the first fine days.").
Winter.

Monro, Harold (1879–1932)
Bird at Dawn, The.
Bitter Sanctuary.
Cat's Meat.
Children of Love.
City-Storm.
Dog.
Every Thing.
Hearthstone.
Hurrier, The.
Man Carrying Bale.
Midnight Lamentation, sel.
Milk for the Cat.
Natural History, sel.
Nightingale near the House, The.
Solitude.
Strange Meetings, sels.
Week-End, sel.

Monroe, Arthur W.
To W. S. M.

Monroe, Bill
In the Pines.

Monroe, Harriet (1861–1936)
Bicyclers, The.
Farewell, A: "Good-bye!—no [or nay] do not grieve that it is over."
Garden, The.
In High Places.
Meeting, The.
Radio.
Rubens.
These Two.

Monsour, Leslie
Dream of Dying, A.
Emily's Words.
Nimis Compos Mentis.
Parking Lot.
Sweeping.

Montag, Tom
Ben Zen Poems, sel.
Plain Poems: A Fairwater Daybook, sels.

Montagu, Lady Mary Wortley (1689–1762)
Between Your Sheets.
Epistle from Mrs. Yonge to Her Husband.
Epitaph: "Here lies John Hughes and Sarah Drew."
Lover, The; a Ballad.
Man in Love, A.
On the Death of Mrs. Bowes.
Reasons That Induced Dr. Swift to Write a Poem Called "The Lady's Dressing-Room", The.
Receipt to Cure the Vapours, A.
Six Town Eclogues, sels.
Summary of Lord Lyttleton's 'Advice to a Lady', A.
To a Lady Making Love.
Verses Addressed to the Imitator of the First Satire of the Second Book of Horace, sel.

Montague, John (b. 1929)
All Legendary Obstacles, sels.
Cave of Night, The, sels.
Chosen Light, A, sels.
Dead Kingdom, The, sels.
Deer Park.
Dowager.
Drink of Milk, A.
Footnote on Monasticism, A: Dingle Peninsula.

Great Cloak, The, sels.
Hearth Song.
King & Queen.
Old Mythologies.
Rough Field, The, sels.
Small Secrets.
Time in Armagh, sels.
Wild Sports of the West.
Windharp.
Woodtown Manor.

Montale, Eugenio (1896–1981)
Bird-Shooting.
Bring Me the Sunflower.
Bring me the sunflower, I'll plant it here.
Buffalo.
Day and Night.
Don't ask us for the word to frame.
Dora Markus.
Ecologue.
Eel, The.
Eel, The.
Eel, The.
Eel, The.
Elegy of Our Times.
Fan, The.
Haul Your Paper Boats.
I repeat I'm ready, but ready for what?
In the Greenhouse.
Lemon Trees, The.
Lemon Trees, The.
Little Testament.
Motets [Mottetti], sels.
Murder's not my forte.
My Muse.
Ours is group solitude.
Personae Separatae.
Prisoner's Dream, The.
Sit the noon out, pale and lost in thought.
Soliloquy.
Storm, The.
Story of Every Day, The.
Visit to Fadin.
What you knew of me.
Where the Tennis Court Was.
You know, I must leave you again and I can't.

Montalvan, Juan Perez de (1602–38)
Self-Deceaver, The.

Montejo, Eugenio (b. 1938)
Marina.

Montemayor, Carlos (b. 1947)
Cytherea.

Montes de Oca, Marco Antonio (b. 1932)
Fusion of Shadows, A.
Hands, The.

Montgomerie, Alexander (1556?–1610?)
Description of Tyme, A.
Dreame, Ane.
Night Is Near [or Neir] Gone, The.
Remembers thou in Æsope of a taill.
Royall Palice of the Heichest Hewin, The.
Sonet: "Thocht Polibus, pisander, and with them."

Montgomerie, William (b. 1904)
Epitaph: "My brother is skull and skeleton now."
Flodden.

Montgomery, James F. (1771–1854)
Brahmin, The, sel.
Come to Calvary's holy mountain.
On the Loss of Friends.
Stranger and His Friend, The.

Montgomery, Judith H.
Ophelia, in Winter.

Montgomery, Robert (1807–55)
Omnipresence of the Deity, The, sels.

Montgomery, Vaida Stewart (1888–1959)
Cattle Brands.
Funeral.
To the Rattlesnake.

Montgomery, Whitney
Death Rode a Pinto Pony.
Outlaws.

Montrose, James Graham, Marquess of (1612–50)
My Dear and Only Love.
On Himself, upon Hearing What Was His Sentence.

Montrose, Percy
My Darling Clementine.

"Monty Python"
All Things Dull and Ugly.

Monzón, Roberto Guillermo
Opaque Copper.

Moody, Elizabeth (d. 1814)
To a Friend, Who Gave the Author a Reading Glass.
To a Lady, Who Was a Great Talker.

Moody, William Vaughn (1869–1910)
Bracelet of Grass, The.
Departure, The.
Faded Pictures.
Gloucester Moors.
Harmonics.
Ode in the Time of Hesitation, sels.
Ode in Time of Hesitation, An.
On a Soldier Fallen in the Philippines.

Mookam Choinul (1722–95)
Bath, A.
For a Zen Seeker.
Living at Eunjok Hermitage.
Sitting Alone.

Moolten, David (b. 1961)
Bio 7.
Brandy Station, Virginia.
Madame Butterfly.
Motorcycle Ward.
Ode for Orville and Wilbur Wright.
Voyeur.

Moon, Kamilah Aisha
Daughter-to-Father Talk.

Moon, Susan
Unintended.

Mooney, Martin (b. 1964)
Anna Akhmatova's Funeral.
Footballers in the Snow.
For Thoth.
Gone for Some Time.
In the Parlour.
Neanderthal Funeral.
Painting the Angel.
Salting the Brae.

Moore, Bertha
Child's Thought, A.

Moore, Clement Clarke (1779–1863)
Visit from St Nicholas, A.

Moore, Dinty
What Surprises Him.

Moore, Edward (1712–57)
To the Right Hon. Henry Pelham.

Moore, Frances
For a Working Woman.

Moore, George (1852–1933)
Rondo: "Did I love thee? I only did desire."

Moore, Honor (b. 1945)
Blues: "I meet you again in public. I."
Edward.
First Time: 1950.
Girl in a Fur-Trimmed Dress.
Green Place, A.
Poem for the End.
Spuyten Duyvil.
To Janet, on Galileo.
Window at Key West, A.

Moore, Janice Townley (b. 1939)
To Love That Well.

Moore, Jessica Care
I'm a Hip Hop Cheerleader.

Moore, Julia A. (1847–1920)
Ashtabula Disaster, The.
Author's Early Life, The, sel.
Brave Page Boys, The, sel.
Carrie Monro, sels.
Centennial Celebration, The, sels.
Croquet by Moonlight, sel.
Grand Rapids Cricket Club, The, sel.

Hattie House, sel.
Hiram Helsel.
Hurrah for Cooper and Cary, sels.
John Robinson, sels.
Little Henry, sels.
Little Libbie, sels.
Maryette Myers, sels.
Roll On, Time, Roll On, sel.
Temperance Army, The, sels.
Temperance Reform Clubs, sels.
To My Friends and Critics, sels.
William House and Family, sels.

Moore, Lenard D. (b. 1958)
Again.
Airport.
Bad Times.
Black Girl Tap Dancing.
Black Soldier, A.
Bluesman's Blues, A.
Eternal Landscape, The.
From the Field.
Gifts.
Haiku.
Haiku.
Haiku.
Homeplace, The.
Indian Girl.
Letter from Kuwait.
Praisesong: From Son to Mother.
Song Poem, The.
Tanka.
Tanka.
Winter 1967.

Moore, Lilian (b. 1909)
Bedtime Story.
In the Fog.
Listen!
No One.
Pigeons.
Sometimes.
Until I Saw the Sea.

Moore, Malkia M'Buzi
Another Scream.

Moore, Marianne (1887–1972)
At Rest in the Blast.
Baseball and Writing.
Bird-witted.
Black Earth.
Blessed Is the Man.
Bowls.
Camellia Sabina.
Charity Overcoming Envy.
Critics and Connoisseurs.
Egyptian Pulled Glass Bottle in the Shape of a Fish, An.
England.
Fish, The: "Wade / through black jade."
Grave, A.
He "Digesteth Harde Yron."
He Wrote the History Book.
His Shield.
I May, I Might, I Must.
In Distrust of Merits.
In the Days of Prismatic Color.
Is Your Town Nineveh?
Jellyfish, A.
Jerboa, The.
Keeping Their World Large.
Like a Bulrush.
Love in America.
Marriage.
Mind Is an Enchanting Thing, The.
Monkeys, The.
Nevertheless.
No Swan So Fine.
O To Be A Dragon.
Octopus, An.
Pangolin, The.
Paper Nautilus, The.
Part of a Novel, Part of a Poem, Part of a Play, sels.
Past Is the Present, The.
Peter.
Poetry [1921 version]: "I, too, dislike it: there are things that are important beyond all this fiddle."

Poetry [1925 Version].
Poetry [1967 Version].
Sea Unicorns and Land Unicorns.
Silence.
Smooth Gnarled Crape Myrtle.
Sojourn in the Whale.
Spenser's Ireland.
Student, The.
Talisman, A.
That Harp You Play So Well.
Then the Ermine.
Those Various Scalpels.
To a Chameleon.
To a Snail.
To a Steam Roller.
To an Intra-Mural Rat.
To Military Progress.
Tom Fool at Jamaica.
What Are Years?
When I Buy Pictures.

Moore, Merrill (1903–57)
Americans in 1933–4–5–6–7–8–, Etc.
And to the Young Men.
Book of How, The.
Cumae.
How She Resolved to Act.
It Is Winter, I Know.
Literature: The God, Its Ritual.
Noise That Time Makes, The.
Odor of a Metal Is Not Strong, The.
Old Men and Old Women Going Home on the Street Car.
Pandora and the Moon.
Shot Who? Jim Lane!
Unknown Man in the Morgue.
Village Noon; Mid-Day Bells.
Warning to One.

Moore, Opal (b. 1953)
Eulogy for Sister.
Taste of Life Going On, The.

Moore, Richard (b. 1927)
On Coming to Nothing.

Moore, Robert John (b. 1950)
Golden Book of Bovinities, The, sel.
Room with a View.
Skin You Wore, The.

Moore, Rosalie (b. 1910)
Catalogue, sels.
Dirge for the Living.
Doors.
Height.
Memory of Quiet.
Mind's Disguise, The.
Personal Atlas.
Ripeness Is Rapid.
Shipwreck: "Watching, watching from the shore."
Still without Life.

Moore, Thomas (1779–1852)
Announcement of a New Grand Acceleration Company for the Promotion of the Speed of Literature.
Away with this Pouting.
Believe Me, If All Those Endearing Young Charms.
Canadian Boat Song, A.
Cherries; a Parable, The.
Comforter, The.
Copy of an Intercepted Despatch from His Excellency Don Strepitoso Diabolo.
Did Not.
Duke Is the Lad [to Frighten a Lass], The.
Echo ("At the mid hour of night, when stars are weeping, I fly.").
Echo ("How sweet the answer Echo makes.").
Fancy.
Fudge Family in Paris, The, sels.
Fum and Hum, the Two Birds of Royalty.
Harp That Once through Tara's Halls, The.
Journey Onwards, The.
Kiss, The.
Lalla Rookh, sels.
Love Thee, Dearest? Love Thee?
Meeting of the Waters, The.
Minstrel Boy, The.

No—Leave My Heart to Rest.
Odes to Nea, *sel.*
Oft in the Stilly Night.
Oh! blame not the bard, if he fly to the bowers.
Pastoral Ballad by John Bull, A.
Pro Patria Mori.
Rhymes on the Road, *sels.*
Scene from a Play, Acted at Oxford, Called "Matriculation."
She Is Far from the Land.
Sound the Loud Timbrel.
Thee, Thee, Only Thee.
This World Is All a Fleeting Show.
Time I've Lost in Wooing, The.
To Sir Hudson Lowe.
Tory Pledges.
Venetian Air.
Weep, Children of Israel.
Young May Moon, The.

Moore, Thomas Sturge (1870–1944)
Duet, A.
Dying Swan, The.
Event, The.
Gazelles, The.
Kindness.
Response to Rimbaud's Later Manner.
Sent from Egypt with a Fair Robe of Tissue to a Sicilian Vinedresser.
Variation on Ronsard.

Moorer, Lizelia Augusta Jenkins
Accompanying a Gift.
Accompanying a Gift.
Africa.
Benefits of Sorrow.
Bible, The.
Birthday Wishes to a Husband.
Birthday Wishes to a Minister of the Gospel.
Birthday Wishes to a Physician.
Christmas Eve.
Christmas Tree, The.
Circle, The.
Claflin's Alumni.
Crum Appointment, The.
Dedication Day Poem.
Dialogue, A.
Door of Hope, The.
Duty, or Truth at Work.
Easter; or, Spring-Time.
Emancipation Day.
Eutawville Lynching, The.
Hallowe'en.
Immortality.
In Memoriam of E. B. Clark.
Injustice of the Courts.
Jim Crow Cars.
Legal Mouse, A.
Lela's Charms.
Lines to a Graduate.
Loyalty to the Flag.
Lynching.
Misunderstood.
Mountain Tops.
Must Be Freed.
Negro Ballot, The.
Negro Heroines.
Negro Schools, The.
Notable Dinner, A.
Peonage System, The.
Pharaohs of Today, The.
Prejudice.
Presidents, The.
Price of Disrespect, The.
Refining Fire.
Retribution.
Russia's Resentment.
Social Glass, The.
Social Life, The.
Song of the Angels.
Southern Press, The.
Southern Pulpit, The.
Southern Work of Dr. and Mrs. L. M. Dunton.
Sympathy.
Thanksgiving.
Tree of Knowledge, The.
Truth Suppressed, The.
Voice of the Negro, The.

What We Teach at Claflin.
Whisper Words of Love to Me.
Why Is It?
Why Negroes Don't Unite.
Why We Meet.

Moossy, Brenda J.
I Can No Longer Care for the Dying.
Notion of Grace, A.
When Fat Women Fear Famine.

Mopev
Would you care for a smoke or a sherry?

Mor, Amus
Coming of John, The.

Mora, Pat (b. 1942)
Bruja: Witch.
Cortez's Horse.
Depression Days.
Elena.
Gentle Communion.
Immigrants.
La Migra.
Loss of Control.
Sonrisas.

Morabito, Fabio (b. 1955)
Compared to the condos of the living.
Elefantes nacen viejos, Los.
Elephants are born old.
Esponja, La.
I do not wish, in spite of all.
I've forgotten the words.
I've never been in love enough.
Junto a los condominios de los vivos.
Mapas, Los / se hacen los domingos.
Maps are drawn / on Sundays.
Master of an Expanse.
No he amado bastante.
No quiero, pese a todo.
Piazza Gimma.
Piazza Gimma.
Scissors.
Sponge.
Tijeras, Las.
Yo que he olvidado las palabras.

Moraes, Dom (b. 1938)
Gardener.
Kanheri Caves.
Santa Claus.
1668.
Snow on a Mountain.
Two from Israel, *sels.*

Moraes, Vinícius de (b. 1913)
Song: "Never take her away."

Moraga, Cherríe (b. 1952)
For the Color of My Mother.
Half-Breed.
La Dulce Culpa.

Morales, Aurora Levins (b. 1954)
Child's Christmas in Puerto Rico, A.
Ending Poem.
Immigrants.
Kitchens.
1930.
Old Countries.
Other Heritage, The.
Puertoricanness.
South.
Sugar Poem.
Tita's Poem.

Morales, Rosario
Africa.
Dinner, The.
Ending Poem.
Getting Out Alive.
I Am the Reasonable One.
I Recognize You.
My Revolution.
Old.
Spring Fever.

Moramarco, Fred (b. 1928)
Clark Kent, Naked.
Fortune Cookies.
Novel.
Volunteer's Fairy Tale, A.

Moran, Michael ("Zozimus")
Pharao's Daughter.

Moran, Rod (b. 1952)
Cross Country.
Wire.

Morant, Harry (1864–1902)
Last Rhyme and Testament of Tony Lumpkin.

Morcott, Anne (fl. 1692)
Loyal English Man's Wish for the Preservation of the King and Queen, The.

Mordaunt, Charles, Earl of Peterborough (1658–1735)
I Said to My Heart.

Mordaunt, Elizabeth, Viscountess (d. 1678)
Sepr. ye 6th 1666 Thursday A Thanks Geving for the Stoping of the Fire in London.

Mordaunt, Thomas Osbert (1730–1809)
Verses Written during the War, 1756–1763, *sel.*

Mordecai, Pamela (b. 1942)
Jesus Is Condemned to Death.

More, Dame Gertrude (1604–33)
Dittie to the Same Subject, A.
Short Oblation of This Smal Work by the Writer Gatherer Thereof to Our Most Sweet and Merciful God, A.

More, Hannah (1745–1833)
Bas Bleu; Or, Conversation, The, *sel.*
Cheap Repository: The Story of Sinful Sally. Told by Herself.
Florio: A Tale, and The Bas-bleu; or, Conversation.
Hackney Coachman, The; Or, The Way to Get a Good Fare.
Inscription in a Beautiful Retreat Called Fairy Bower.
Patient Joe; or, The Newcastle Collier.
Sensibility: A Poetical Epistle to the Hon. Mrs. Boscawen.
Slave Trade, The, *sels.*
Slavery, *sel.*

More, Henry (1614–87)
Charity and Humility.
Psychozoia, or, the Life of the Soul, *sels.*

More, Saint Thomas *See* More, Sir Thomas

More, Sir Thomas (Saint Thomas More) (1478–1535)
Astrologer, The.
Child's Song.
Consider Well.
De Principe Bono et Malo.
Fortune.
Good Princes and Bad.
Mine high estate, power and auctority.
Prayer, A.
Quis Optimus Reipublicae Status.

Morejón, Nancy (b. 1944)
Angela Dominguez, Ever Present.
Carpet.
Disillusion for Rubén Darío.
Havana Harbor.
I Never Saw Great Lakes.
Love, Attributed City.
Mother.
Mother.
Poem Fifty.
Requiem for the Left Hand.
Richard Brought His Flute.
Tame and Ferocious Animal, A.
To a Boy.
Tree of Earthly Delights.
Will-o'-Wisp.

Morgan, Bill
Among Goldfinches.

Morgan, Derec Llwyd
Bow and Arrow.
Registering the Little One.

Morgan, Dyfnallt
Curtain, The.

Morgan, Edwin (b. 1920)
At Eighty.
Cinquevalli.
Columba's Song.
Computer's First Christmas Card, The.
Dowser, The.

First Men on Mercury, The.
From the Domain of Arnheim.
Glasgow Green.
Glasgow Sonnets.
Glass, The.
Itinerary.
King Billy.
Loch Ness Monster's Song, The.
Message Clear.
My Greenhouse.
Opening the Cage.
Shilpit dog fucks grimly by the close, A.
Siesta of a Hungarian Snake.
Sir James Murray.
Sonnets from Scotland, *sels*.
Strawberries.
Video Box: 25, The.
View of Things, A.

Morgan, Elin Llwyd (b. 1966)
Contemporary Jezebel, The.
Schizo de Picasso.
Your Ostrich Nature.

Morgan, Elizabeth (b. 1947)
Birthday, The: "I'm driving tonight into
   November."
Euripides' Cave.

"Morgan, Emanuel" *See* Bynner, Witter

Morgan, Esther (b. 1970)
Sea, The.

Morgan, Frederick (b. 1922)
Busses, The.
1904.
Winter Poem.

Morgan, John (1827–1903)
My Welsh Home.

Morgan, John (b. 1943)
Cyclist, The, *sel*.

Morgan, Mihangel
Conversation.
Legend of the Baker and Her Daughter, The.
Red High-heeled Shoes.
Unidentified Flying Object on an Errand of
   Love.

Morgan, Robert (b. 1920)
Blood Donor.
Shadow Valley.

Morgan, Robert (b. 1944)
Bellrope.
Code, The.
Grain of Sound, The.
Grandma's Bureau.
Honey.
Horace Kephart.
Jutaculla Rock.
Man and Machine.
Mica Country.
Music of the Spheres.
Rearview Mirror.
Road from Elmira, The.
Stretching.
Uranium.
Working in the Rain.

Morgan, Robin (b. 1941)
Add-Water Instant Blues.
Battery.
Damn You, Lady.
Geography Lesson.
Network of the Imaginary Mother, The, *sel*.

Morganwg, Iolo *See* Williams, Edward

Morgenstern, Christian (1871–1914)
Anxiety for the Future.
Blueprint for Disaster.
Fish's Nightsong.
Summons.

Morgenstern, Felicia L.
Hues of Electric Blue.
Ride Me Baby, Ride Me.
Soul Roots.
Temple of Your Familiar.

Mori, Kyoko
At Thirty.
Barbie Says Math is Hard.
Speaking Through White: For My Mother.

Moriarty, Laura (b. 1952)
Beautiful House, The.

Morikawa Kyoroku (1656–1715)
Even the dumplings / Are smaller.
Summer airing / On one pole.

**Mörike [*or* Möricke], Eduard Friedrich (1804–
75)**
Beauty Rohtraut.
Forest Murmurs.
Forsaken Girl, The.
Remember It, My Soul.

Moriso-Lewa, Feliks *See* Morisseau-Leroy, Felix

Morisseau-Leroy, Felix (1913–1998)
Down with All Candidates.
Shooshoon.
Sometimes I'm Not Myself.
Testament.
Zombies.

Moritake (d. 1549)
Those falling blossoms.

Moritaké *See* Arakida Moritaké

**Moritz [*or* Morits], Yunna Petrovna [*or* Iunna
Pinkhusovna] (b. 1937)**
Between Scylla and Charybdis.
Crow.
Eternally to be waiting for bloody news.
Fisherman, The.
Leader, The.
Memorandum.
My apple-tree, my willow.
Parting the curtains on the other world.

Morley, Christopher Darlington (1890–1957)
Dial Call.
Elegy Written in a Country Coal-Bin.
Gospel of Mr. Pepys, The.
In Honour of Taffy Topaz.
Pennsylvania Deutsch.
Plumpuppets, The.
Public Beach (Long Island Sound).

Morley, David (b. 1964)
Air Street.
Answers on a Postcard.
Enniskillen.
Errand.
Exact Fares.
Jerusalem.
Metal-work.
On Fire.
Politicisation of the North Wind, The.
White, White.

Morley, Hilda (b. 1916)
Curve of the Water.
For Elaine de Kooning.
Lizard, The.
Made Out of Links.
Parents.

Morley, Thomas (1557–1602)
Sing We and Chant It.
You Black Bright Stars.

Mörling, Malena (b. 1965)
Ashes.
For F. M. Who Did Not Get Killed Yesterday
   on 57th Street.
For the Woman with the Radio.
In a Motel Room at Dawn.
Three-Card Monte.

Morninghouse, Sundaira *See* Wilson, Carletta
Carrington

Moro, César (1903–56)
Balcony.
Battle at the Edge of the Falls.

Moronelli da Fiorenza, Pier (*fl.* 13th cent.)
Canzonetta: A Bitter Song to His Lady.

Morotskaya, Stella
Erotic Fruit.
Morning sleep / it's sweeter than your palms.
Screams and hair come out.

Moroz, Raisa (b. 1937)
There's a cinnamon tree that grows on the
   Moon.

Morozov, Sergey
Poem about the Blue Horse.

Morra, Rawia (b. 1966)
Ghurba, *sel*.

Morrice, Ken (1924–2002)
Crossing the Alps.
To a Shy Girl at a Party.
Voyager.

Morriën, Adriaan (b. 1912)
Farewell.

Morrill, Donald (b. 1955)
Man who melts a plastic garbage bag, The.

Morris, Alison
Imani's Song.
Worry All the Time.

Morris, Brian (b. 1930)
Dinas Emrys.

Morris, George Pope (1802–64)
Woodman, Spare That Tree.

Morris, Herbert (b. 1928)
Duesenberg, 1929.

Morris, John N. (b. 1931)
Life Beside This One, The.
Man and Boy.
Reading the Writing.
Schedule of Benefits, A.
Untrimming the Tree.

Morris, Joseph
One Step at a Time.

Morris, Lewis (1701–65)
Fishing Lass of Hakin, The.
Miner's Ballad, The.
Poem of the Frost and Snow.
To the Tormentors.

Morris, Sir Lewis (1833–1907)
Lydstep Caverns, *sel*.
St. David's Head, *sel*.

Morris, Matt
Sham Jew.

Morris, Mervyn (b. 1937)
For Consciousness.
Pond, The.
Rasta Reggae.
Valley Prince.

Morris, Tracie
Apology to Pangea.
Just Say No Blues.
Lovers Total Recall.
Myomectomy Cycle, The, *sels*.
Prelude to a Kiss.
Why I Wont Wear a Tatoo.

Morris, William (1834–96)
Another for the Briar Rose.
Death Song, A.
Defense of Guenevere, The.
Earthly Paradise, The, *sels*.
French Noel.
Haystack in the Floods, The.
In Prison.
Inscription for an Old Bed.
Life and Death of Jason, The, *sel*.
Love Is Enough, *sels*.
No Master, High or Low!
Pomona.
Summer Dawn.
Two Red Roses across the Moon.

Morris-Jones, John (1864–1929)
North Star, The.
Old Age.
Wind's Lament, The.

Morrison, Blake
Ballad of the Yorkshire Ripper, The, *sel*.

Morrison, Lillian (b. 1917)
Sidewalk Racer Or, On the Skateboard, The.
Surf.

Morrissey, Sinéad (b. 1972)
After the Hurricane.
And Forgive Us Our Traspasses.
Clocks.
February: "There is no kindness in me here. I
   ache to be kind, but the weather."
Genetics.
Goldfish.
Hazel Goodwin Morrissey Brown.
If Words.

Jo Gravis in His Metal Garden.
My New Angels.
On Waitakere Dam.
Post Mortem.
Sea Stone.
Stitches.
There was Fire in Vancouver.
Thoughts in a Black Taxi.
To Look Out Once from High Windows.
Wound Man, The.

Morse, Brian
Day on the Planet, A.

Morse, Gail
He kneels on the rumpled bed.

Morshen, Nikolai Nikolaevich (Nikolai Nikolaevich Marchenko) (b. 1917)
Andreyevsky Church, The.
At the Lighthouse.
In superstitious panic.
Storm, A.

Morsztyn, Zbigniew (1620–90)
Emblem 51.

Morter-Lewis, Corinth
Belizean Dawn, A.
Lost: "African drumbeat."
Sunset on the River.

Mortimer, Peter
Wolves.

Morton, Arthur Leslie (b. 1903)
Cokaigne Fantasy.
Shortest Day.

Morton, Colin (b. 1948)
Hortus Urbanus / Urban Garden, sel.
Three Small Rooms, sel.

Morton, "Jelly Roll" (1890–1941)
Mamie's Blues.

Morton, John Bingham ("Beachcomber") (1893–1979)
Another Canto.
John Percy.
On Sir Henry Ferrett, M.P.
Spring in London.
To Hilda Dancing.
When We Were Very Silly, sels.

Morton, Thomas (1764–1838)
Epitaph: "Time that brings [or bringes] all things to light."
Poem, The: "Rise Oedipus, and if thou canst unfold."
Song, The: "Drink and be merry, merry, merry boys."

Morungen, Heinrich von (d. 1222)
Alas, shall I not see again.
I believe there is no one alive who weeps for my sorrow.
I heard on the meadow.
It has gone with me as with a child.
Legacy, The.
Many a man gets bewitched by the elves.
Wound of Love, The.

Morus, Huw (1622–1709)
In Praise of a Girl.

Mosby, George, Jr.
To Josh Gibson (Legendary Slugger of the Old Negro Baseball League).

Moschus (fl. 3d cent. B.C.)
Europa.
Lament for Bion.
Ocean, The.
Pan, Echo, and the Satyr.

Moscona, Myriam (b. 1955)
Naturalization Papers.

Moses, Daniel David (b. 1952)
Corn, The.
Fall, The.
Hands, The.
Party Favour.
Report on Her Remains.
Some Grand River Blues.

Moses, Gavin
Black Banana House.
Poem for Trish, A.

Moskowitz, Faye
Bird Lives.

Mosquera, Alison
Tamoxifen.

Moss, Howard (b. 1922)
Einstein's Bathrobe.
Elegy for My Sister.
Geography: a Song.
King Midas.
King Midas, sels.
Long Island Night, The.
Making a Bed.
Ménage à Trois.
Miami Beach.
New Hampshire.
New York Notebooks, The.
Persistence of Song, The.
Pruned Tree, The.
Rules of Sleep.
Shorelines.
Summer Thunder, The.
Tourists.
Wars, The.
Water Island.

Moss, Jeff
On the Other Side of the Door.

Moss, Stanley (b. 1935)
Clouds.
Dog, The.
Exchange of Hats, An.
Lace Makers, The.
Postcard to Walt Whitman from Siena.

Moss, Thylias (b. 1954)
Accessible Heaven.
Anointing, An.
Ant Farm.
Botanical Fanaticism.
Crystals.
Fisher Street.
Goodness and the Salt of the Earth.
Interpretation of a Poem by Frost.
Landscape with Saxophonist.
Last Chance for the Tarzan Holler.
Lessons from a Mirror.
Lynching, The.
November and Aunt Jemima.
One for All Newborns.
Owl In Daytime, The.
Raising a Humid Flag.
Rapture of Dry Ice Burning off Skin as the Moment of the Soul's Apotheosis, The.
Reconsideration of the Blackbird, A.
Sunrise Comes to Second Avenue.
Tornados.
Undertaker's Daughter Feels Neglect, The.
Wonder, The.

Mother Goose (fl. 17th–18th cent.)
As I was going to St. Ives.
Baa, baa, black sheep, have you any wool?
Birthdays.
Boys and girls come out to play.
Bye, baby bunting.
Daffadowndilly.
Dance to your [or thee] daddy.
Ding, dong, bell.
Dingty diddlety.
Flying-Man.
Forehead, Eyes, Cheeks, Nose, Mouth, and Chin.
God made the bees.
House That Jack Built, The.
Humpty Dumpty sat on a wall.
Hush-a-bye, baby, on the tree-top.
I saw a ship a-sailing.
Intery, mintery, cutery corn.
Ladybird, Ladybird fly away home.
Little Bo-Peep.
Little Jack Horner/ Sat in a corner.
Little Jumping Joan.
London Bridge.
Man In the Wilderness Asked [of] Me [or said to me], The [or A].
Old Mother Twitchett had [or has] but one eye.
Rain, rain, go to Spain.
Sing a song of sixpence.

Solomon Grundy.
Teeth and Gums.
They That Wash on Monday.
This is the House that Jack Built.
This Little Pig Went to Market.
Three blind mice, see how they run!
Three wise men of Gotham.
Two Legs Sat Upon Three Legs.
What Are Folks Made Of.
When the wind is in the east.
Who Killed Cock Robin.

Mother Maria [or Mat' Mariia] See Kuzmina-Karavayeva, Elizaveta

Motherwell, William (1797–1835)
Jeanie Morrison.

Motion, Andrew (b. 1952)
Anne Frank Huis.
Close.
Glass of Wine, A.
Letter, The: "If I remember right, his first letter."
Lines, The: "November, and the Sunday twilight fallen."
Mythology.
One Life.
Reading the Elephant.
Wall, A.

Motsapi, Seitlhamo (b. 1966)
Aambl.
Andif.
Brotha saul.
Brotha saul (furtha meditashuns).
Djeni.
Enia.
Ityopia phase-in.
Kulu.
Missa joe.
Roses for the folks we know, A.
Samaki.
Shak-shak.
Sol/o.

Motteux, Peter Anthony (Pierre Antoine) (1660–1718)
Song, A: "Slaves to London, I'll deceive you."

Mottram, Eric (1924–95)
Elegy 11: Ford.
Zuni Dancers.

Moulds, Julie (b. 1962)
Late Summer Litany.
Renoir's Bathers.
When Bad Angels Love Women.

Moulsworth, Martha
Memorandum of Martha Moulsworth, Widow, The.

Moultrie, John (1799–1874)
Fairy Maimounè, The.
Forget Thee?

Mouré, Erin (b. 1955)
8 Little Theatres of the Cornices.
Morphine, Or The Cutting Stone.
Thirteen Years.
Toxicity.
Wittgenstein Letters to Mel Gibson's Braveheart, The, sels.

Moussa, Amal (b. 1971)
Autumn Rose.
Formal Poem, A.
Love Me.

Moustaki, Nikki (b. 1970)
How to Write a Poem after September 11th.

Moxley, Jennifer (b. 1964)
Easter Lesson, The.
From a Distance I Can See.
Soleil Cou Coupé.
Stem of the Tree of Orestes.
Transom Over Death's Door, A.

Moxon, Edward
Loud midnight-soothing melancholy bird.

Mphahlele, Ezekiel (b. 1919)
Homeward Bound.
Poem, A: "What is there that we can do or say."

Mphande, Lupenga (b. 1947)
I Was Sent For.

Pain.
Walking the Plateau.
Why the Old Woman Limps.
Wood-Cutter, The.

Mpina, Edison
Reborn.
Summer Fires of Mulanje Mountain.

Mr. Social Control
History Never Happened.

Mririda n'Ait Attik
Praise to the Tattoo Mistress.

Msham, Mwana Kupona (c.1810–60)
Poem to Her Daughter, *sel.*

Mtshali, Mbuyiseni Oswald (b. 1940)
Boy on a Swing.
Voice from the Dead, A.

Mu Hua (*fl.* c.300)
Sea, The.

Mu, King of Paekche (*fl.* 600–14)
Song of Sŏdong.

Mudie, Ian (1911–76)
This Land.

Mudrooroo Narogin (b. 1938)
Hide and Seek.
Peaches and Cream.
Song Cycle of Jacky, The, *sels.*

Mueller, Ilze
Night Shift at the Fruit Cannery.

Mueller, Jenny
Betrayed by KC.
Bonneville.
Diorama.
Fisher Towers.
Life in the Comics.
Peninsula.
Portrait of My Father as the Boy of Winander.
Year.

Mueller, John
Rubber Eraser.

Mueller, Lisel (b. 1924)
Alive Together.
American Literature.
Animals Are Entering Our Lives.
Another Version.
Commuter.
Concert, The.
Curriculum Vitae.
Deaf Dancing to Rock, The.
Farewell, a Welcome, A.
Happy and Unhappy Families 1.
Happy and Unhappy Families 2.
Highway Poems.
Hope.
Late Hours.
Late-Born Daughters, The.
Losing My Sight.
Love Like Salt.
Monet Refuses the Operation.
Naming the Animals.
Not Only the Eskimos.
Nude by Edward Hopper, A.
Palindrome.
Possessive Case, The.
Romantics: Johannes Brahms and Clara
  Schumann.
Statues.
Triage.
What Is Left to Say.
What the Dog Perhaps Hears.
When I Am Asked.

Muench, Simone
Elegy for the Unsaid.

Muffareh, Sa'adyya
Spell of Blazing Trees, The.

Mugo, Micere Githae
I Want You to Know.
Look How Rich We are Together.
Where are those Songs?
Wife of the Husband.

Mugrón, Abbot of Iona (d. 980)
Christ's Cross.

Muhamad, Sheikh Mus Hasan *See* Jigerkhwen [*or*
  Sheikh Mus Hasan Muhamad]

Muhammad, Mursalata
Last Days of a Slow Cooker.

Muhammad, Sakinah Carol
Rain Lover.

Muhammad, Tufara Waller
Extremes Ain't My Thing As Salaam Alaikum.

Muhammad ibn Ghalib al-Rusafi (d. 1177)
Blue River.
Were you to go to the fire of the Guidance on
  the side of Mount Sinai, you could take all
  the knowledge and light you wish.

Muhammadi, Habiba
In the Forests of Sleep.

Muhawi, Ibrahim
Bad Moon Rising.

Muhibbi (1494–1566)
My very own queen, my everything.
No end to this separation, no limit to this cruel
  pain.
Till the day I die, I shall never leave her
  beauty's sun.

Muir, Edwin (1887–1959)
Abraham.
Absent, The.
Adam's Dream.
Animals, The.
Annunciation, The.
Ballad of Hector in Hades.
Brothers, The.
Child Dying, The.
Childhood.
Combat, The.
Good Man in Hell, The.
Horses, The.
In Love For Long.
Interrogation, The.
Killing, The.
Labyrinth, The.
Late Wasp, The.
Mary Stuart.
Merlin.
Milton.
Myth, The.
Mythical Journey, The.
One Foot in Eden.
Refugees, The.
Scotland 1941.
Scotland's Winter.
Song: "Why should your face so please me."
Then.
Three Mirrors, The.
Transfiguration, The.
Troy.
Wheel, The.

Muirhead, Eric
Closing Time.
Reflection on the Paintings of Mark Rothko's
  Chapel, A.

Mukai Kyorai (1651–1704)
After the green storm / True color.
Even in my town / Now, I sleep.
Even while chopping.
Linked-Verse Sequence Throughout the Town,
  The, *sel.*
On a veranda.
Returning from a funeral.

Mukand, Jon
First Payment.
Lullaby.

Mukhopādhyāy, Kalyānkumār
Am I afraid of the tenth day?
Is there any treasure like the Mother's name?
Ma, the mail train is leaving now.

Mukhopādhyāy, Nīlkantha (1841–1912)
Use your mental eye.

Mukhopādhyāy, Rāmrenu
Why should I sit alone, eyes closed.

Muktibodh, G. M. (1917–64)
Void, The.

Muldoon, Paul (b. 1951)
Aftermath.
Aisling.
All I Did For Him.
Ancestor, The.

Anseo.
Avenue, The.
Beagles.
Birth, The.
Briefcase, The.
Brock.
Cauliflowers.
Cuba.
Electric Orchard, The.
Eugenio Montale: The Eel.
Field Hospital, The.
Gathering Mushrooms.
Glad Eye, The.
Grand Conversation, The.
Hard Drive.
Hats.
Hedgehog.
History.
Homesickness.
Hydrangea.
Inkspot, The.
Ireland.
Lass of Aughrim, The.
Last Time I Saw Chris, The.
Loaf, The.
Long Finish.
Lunch with Pancho Villa.
Ma.
Making the Move.
Meeting the British.
Milkweed and Monarch.
Mimi.
Misfits, The.
Mixed Marriage, The.
More a Man Has the More a Man Wants, The.
Mules.
Narrow Road to the Deep North, The.
On.
Our Lady of Ardboe.
Peaches.
Quoof.
Right Arm, The.
Rune.
7, Middagh Street, *sels.*
Sightseers, The.
Soap-Pig, The.
Something Else.
Something of a Departure.
Sonogram, The.
Spider: "How you like these threads, said
  white spider."
Stoic, The.
Sushi.
Symposium.
They That Wash on Thursday.
Third Epistle to Timothy.
Throwback, The.
Truce.
Weepies, The.
Why Brownlee Left.
Wind and Tree.
Winter Wheat.
Wishbone, The.
Yggdrasill.

Mulford, Wendy
Nevrazumitelny.

Mulholland, Rosa (Lady Gilbert) (1841–1921)
Stolen Visit, A.

Mulkey, Rick (b. 1963)
Blind-Sided.
Why I Believe in Angels.

Mullen, F.
I took him by the arm and said.
Let Observation, Shuddering the While.

Mullen, Harryette (b. 1953)
Anatomy.
Anthropic Principle, The.
Bilingual Instructions.
Blah-Blah.
Bumper to Bumper.
Dance She Does, The.
Denigration.
Dim Lady.
Drinking Mojitos in Cuba Libre.
Exploring the Dark Content.

Eyes in the Back of Her Head.
Fancy Cortex.
Father (Part 1).
Headlines.
Joy, The.
Kamasutra Sutra.
Kirstenography.
Land of the Discount Price, Home of the Brand Name.
Malecón, El.
Mantra for a Classless Society, or Mr. Roget's Neighborhood.
Mermaid of Palmares.
Momma Sayings.
Muse and Drudge, *sel.*
Music for Homemade Instruments.
#6 Sepulveda.
Omnivore.
Present Tense.
Pretty Piece of Tail.
Roadmap.
Saturday Afternoon, When Chores Are Done.
Sleeping with the Dictionary.
Souvenir from Anywhere.
Unacknowledged Legislator.
Viejas Locas.
We Are Not Responsible.
Why You and I.
Wino Rhino.
Xenophobic Nightmare in a Foreign Language.
Zen Acorn.

Mullen, Kate
Thin-Legged Lover.

Mullen, Laura (b. 1958)
After I Was Dead.
Alba.
Applications of.
Catch, The.
For the Reader (Blank Book).
Frames.
House.
Sandbox. 1952.—*Homage to Joseph Cornell.*
Self-Portrait as Somebody Else.
Series of Failures So That I'm Sick of the Word, A.
Stopping By.
White Paintings I.
White Paintings II (in parenthesis).
White Paintings III.
White Paintings IV (Independence Day).
White Paintings V.

Müller, Heiner
Brecht.

Muller, Rudolph (b. 1950)
16 Year-Old Girl Who's Standing, A.

Mulligan, J. B.
Shylock.

Mulock, Dinah Maria
Labor and Rest.

Mulrine, Stephen (b. 1937)
Coming of the Wee Malkies, The.

Mumon Gensen (1323–90)
Life: a cloud crossing the peak.

Mumon-Ekai (1183–1260)
Thunderbolt—eyes wide, A.

Mun Chônghui (b. 1947)
Elderly Woman, An.
For the Sake of Man.
For the Sake of Man Again.
Letter, The.
Little Kitchen Song, A.
Seeing Snow.
Single Blossom, A.
Song of a Middle-Aged Woman.
Stare, The.
Storm, The: "Isn't there a man."
To My Son.
To You, My Beloved Ssuma Ch'ien.

Munda, Constantia (*fl.* 1617)
To the Right Worshipful Lady Her Most Dear Mother, the Lady Prudentia Munda, the True Pattern of Piety and Virtue, C. M. Wisheth Increase of Happiness.

Munday, Anthony (1553–1633)
Primaleon of Greece, *sels.*

Muñiz Huberman, Angelina
Ablution.
Cabalists, The.
Cascades of Death.
Circle of the Golem, The.
Eye of Creation, The.
Manuscript.
Obsession.
Prodigal Daughter.
Sanctuary.

Muñoz, Charles (b. 1926)
Lockerbie.

Munro, Hector Hugh *See* "Saki"

Munro, Neil (1864–1930)
Heather, The.
Hey, Jock, Are Ye Glad Ye 'Listed?

Mura, David
Argument: on 1942, An.
Blueness of the Day, The.
Colors of Desire, The.
Gardens We Have Left.
Grandfather and Grandmother in Love.
Grandfather-in-law.
Hibakusha's Letter (1955), The.
Letters from Poston Relocation Camp (1942–45).
Natives, The.
Nisei Picnic: From an Album, A.
Once near the Border.
To H.N.

Murasaki Shikibu (974–1031)
Tale of Genji, The, *sel.*

Muratori, Fred
Re-Emergence of the Trombone, The.

Mure, Sir William (1594–1657)
Cry of Blood, and of a Broken Covenant, The, *sel.*

Murford, Nicholas (*fl.* 1647–52)
Storm and Calm: Sent from Embden to M. Edw. Ma. and M. Tho. Ly, The.

Murillo, Rosario
Angel in the Deluge.
Conversation in Front of a Helicopter.

Murphey, John Collin
First Birthday After Death, The.
Lake Austin Diorama.
Re-stringing 100 Year Old Wire.
Texas Boomer.

Murphy, E. G. (1867–1939)
Smiths, The.
Thank you, Mr Rason, for the Apples.

Murphy, Jack E.
Heave Me a Mountain, Lord! (Prayer from the Plainview Rest Home).
I Dreamt of Lasca.

Murphy, Jennifer
13.

Murphy, Kay
Eighties Meditation.
Girl with the Bad Rep, The.
Meditation on the Great Blue Heron.

Murphy, Merilene M. (b. 1955)
Park mole.
When you say no.

Murphy, Michael (b. 1965)
Al-Khamasin.
Common Ground.
Contact Sheet.
47° 28' N, 19° 1' E.
Occasions.
Vertigo.
Villa Fidelia.

Murphy, Peter E.
Learning to Swim at Poverty Beach.
Manifesto.
New Boy, The.
Sequence: "Standing in her basement."

Murphy, Richard (b. 1927)
Battle of Aughrim, The, *sels.*
Beehive Cell.
Gate Lodge.

Last Galway Hooker, The.
Moonshine.
Morning Call.
Price of Stone, The, *sels.*
Reading Lesson, The.
Sailing to an Island.
Seals at High Island.
Stormpetrel.

Murphy, Timothy
Mentor.

Murray, Anne B.
Under the Stars.
Winter Night, Glencoe.

Murray, Charles (1864–1941)
Charon's Song.
Dockens afore His Peers.
Gin I Was God.
Whistle, The.

Murray, Christopher
I Got Beat Up A Lot in High School.
Mickey Mouse.

Murray, Donald S. (b. 1956)
Incomplete History of Rock Music in the Hebrides, An.

Murray, G. E. (b. 1920)
American Cheese.
Art of a Cold Sun.
On Being Disabled by Light at Dawn in the Wilderness.
Rounds, The.
Shopping for Midnight.

Murray, George (*fl.* 1891)
Statue, The.

Murray, Joan (1917–42)
And As I Came Out from the Temples.
Epithalamium, An.
Even the Gulls of the Cool Atlantic.
Here We Stand Before the Temporal World.
Lullaby: "Sleep, little architect. It is your mother's wish."
Men and Women Have Meaning Only as Man and Woman.
Survivors—Found.
There Has Been More Than Beginning and End to Face.
You Talk of Art.

Murray, Les A. (b. 1938)
Absolutely Ordinary Rainbow, An.
Animal Nativity.
Broad Bean Sermon, The.
Buladelah-Taree Holiday Song Cycle, The, *sels.*
Bulahdelah—Taree Holiday Song Cycle, The, *sel.*
Burning Want.
Chimes of Neverwhere, The.
Corniche.
Cotton Flannelette.
Craze Field, The.
Dog Fox Field.
Dream of Wearing Shorts Forever, The.
Drugs of War, The.
Easter 1984.
Equanimity.
Folklore.
Gaelic Long Tunes, The.
Gods, The.
Greenhouse Vanity, The.
Hearing Impairment.
Immortal, An.
It Allows a Portrait in Line Scan at Fifteen.
Lament for the Country Soldiers.
Last Hellos, The.
Louvres.
Man with the Hoe, The.
Milk Lorry, The.
Misery Cord (In Memory of F. S. Murray), The.
Mitchells, The.
Mollusc.
Morse.
Noonday Axeman.
On Removing Spiderweb.
Once in a Lifetime, Snow.
Performance.

Pigs.
Poetry and Religion.
Powerline Incarnation, The.
Quality of Sprawl, The.
Quality of Sprawl, The, *sel.*
Satis Passio.
Say-but-the-Word Centurion Attempts a
  Summary, The.
Smell of Coal Smoke, The.
Sydney Highrise Variations, The, *sels.*
Tall Wood twins, The.
Tin Wash Dish, The.
Transposition of Clermont, The.
Walking to the Cattle Place, *sels.*

Murray, Paul (b. 1947)
  Canticle of the Void, The.
  Introit.

Murray, Pauli (b. 1910)
  Conquest.
  For Mack C. Parker.
  Redemption.
  Returning Spring.

Murry, Kathleen Beauchamp *See* Mansfield,
  Katherine

Murthy, Janaki Srinivas *See* "Vaidehi"

Musa, Yasser
  Imagine a Revolution.
  There Is a Dead Poet Alive.
  Where Are They?
  Where is Tomorrow?
  Zinc.

Musgrave, Susan (b. 1951)
  At Nootka Sound.
  Burial of the Dog.
  Equinox.
  Hidden Meaning.
  I Am Not a Conspiracy Everything Is Not
    Paranoid The Drug Enforcement
    Administration Is Not Everywhere.
  Lure.
  Salad Days.
  You Didn't Fit.

Muske-Dukes, Carol (b. 1945)
  Applause.
  At the School for the Gifted.
  August, Los Angeles, Lullaby.
  Blue Kashmir, '74.
  Blue Rose.
  Call, The: "When I heard the voice on the
    telephone."
  Coming Over Coldwater.
  Crack the Whip.
  Dulce Lignum, Dulces Clavos.
  Epith.
  Eulogy, The.
  Fault, The.
  Field Trip.
  Former Love, a Lover of Form, A.
  Heroine.
  Ideal.
  Intensive Care.
  Jacaranda.
  Last Take.
  Like This.
  Love Song: "Love comes hungry to anyone's
    hand."
  Miracles.
  Our Kitty.
  Ovation.
  Pediatrics.
  Red Trousseau.
  Request Radio.
  Stage and Screen, 1989.
  Wish Foundation, The.
  Wyndmere, Windemere.

Muslih-Din [or Musliud-Din] *See* Sadi

Muso Soseki (1275–1351)
  Abiding Mountain.
  All on my own I'm happy.
  All worries and troubles.
  Among rocks and valleys.
  Ancient Origin.
  Another Summit.
  Ashikaga Tadayoshi's Palace.
  At Gen's Embarkation for Yuan China.

At Iku's Embarkation for Yuan China.
At Kan's Embarkation for Yuan China.
At the Nachi Kannon Hall.
At Whole-World-In-View-Hut.
Bamboo Garden.
Beyond Light.
Beyond the World.
Bridge Where the Moon Crosses, The.
Buddha's Satori.
By the sea.
Cave of the Thousand Pines.
Chick feed is what I eat.
Clear Valley.
Climbing Down the Snowy Mountain.
Cloud Mountain.
Curtain of cloud hangs, A.
Digging Out the Buddha Relic.
Don't ask suspiciously.
Dragon-Gate House.
Dry Tree.
East of the strait.
East Peak.
Flat Mountain.
For a Monk Going West.
For Gen the New Head Priest of Erin-ji.
For Ko Who Has Come Back from China.
For Myo's Departure for Anzen-ji.
For Myo's Departure for Shofuku-ji.
For Sho the New Head Priest of Erin-ji.
For Taihei Osho.
For Tetsu the New Head Priest of Erin-ji.
For the Death of a Monk.
For years I dug in the earth.
Fragrance of the Udumbara, The.
Free Old Man.
From My Hut in Miura.
From the beginning.
Garden at the General's Residence, The.
Gate of Universal Light, The.
Gem Creek.
Gem Forest.
Gem Mountain.
Green mountains.
Hall of the Guardian God.
Heaven Peak.
House of Spring.
Hui-neng's Pond.
Hut in Harmony.
I wake from my noon nap.
I'm not so deep in it.
In these mountain villages and harbor towns.
In this small hut.
Inauguration of Fukusan Dormitory.
Incomparable-Verse Valley.
It.
Jewel Cliff.
Jewel Field.
Joy Mountain.
Lamenting the Civil War.
Laughing Mountain.
Lodging House in Town, A.
Loud thunder.
Lover of Mountains.
Magnificent Peak.
Many times the mountains have turned from
  green to yellow.
Moon Mountain.
Moon Tree Cliff.
Mourning for the Layman Named Cloud Peak.
Mugoku Osho's Snow Poem.
My thatched hut.
No End Point.
No Gain.
No Precedent.
No-Word Hut.
Old Creek.
Old Hut.
Old Man Advancing.
Old Man at Leisure.
Old Man in Retirement.
Old Man of Few Words.
Old Man To-The-Point.
Old Mountain.
On the blue waves.
On the Wall of Cloud-Friend Hut.
One Hut.

Ox Turned Loose.
Patriarch Peaks.
Peak of the Held-Up Flower, The.
People's abuse.
Pine Shade.
Plum Window.
Poem on Dry Mountain (A Zen Garden).
Pure Sound Pavilion of the Riverside Temple,
  The.
Reizan Osho Visits Me.
Reply to a Friend's Poem.
Reply to Bukko Zenji's Poem at Seiken-ji.
Reply to Gen'no Osho's Poem.
Reply to Reizan Osho.
Reply to Suzan Osho's Snow Poem.
Snow.
Snow at Rohatsu Sesshin.
Snow Garden.
Snow Valley.
Spring Cliff.
Strange Peak.
Suzan Osho's Visit.
Suzan Oshos's Visit to My West Mountain
  Hut.
Temple of Eternal Light.
Tengan Osho's Visit to Erin-ji.
Thanks for Daisen Osho's Visit.
Thanks Sent to Taihei Osho.
Three-Step Waterfall.
Tiger Valley.
Time for a walk.
To Kengai Osho of Engaku-ji.
To the Emperor's Messenger.
Toki-no-Ge (Satori Poem).
Truth Hall.
Turtle Head Stupa.
Vainly I dug for a perfect sky.
Very high this mountain.
Visiting My Old Hut in Late Spring.
Wandering.
With compassionate hands.
Withered Zen.

Musset, Alfred de (1810–57)
  Night in May, A, *sels.*

Mu'tamid, King of Seville (1040–95)
  Rest your heart; let your cares not overcome
    you. What good will grief and apprehension
    do you?
  Stranger, captive in the lands of the West, will
    be mourned by a certain pulpit and throne,
    A.

Mutén, Burleigh
  Demeter's Blessing.
  Hesperides, The.
  Queen Hera.
  Queen Medusa.
  Urania.

Mutis, Alvaro
  Amen.
  East Song.
  Sonata.
  Word, A.
  You Are a Daughter of the Lagides.

Muyassar, Orkhan (1914–65)
  Lost.

Muyong Sooyon (1651–1719)
  Fisherman at Byolam.
  To the Reverend Bagam.

Muzaffar, May
  Absent, The.
  Flash, A.
  Friends.
  Reticence.
  Spinning.
  Voice, The.

Myer, Michael
  Cool Cat.

Myers, Barbara
  Dream Prison.

Myers, Frederic William Henry (1843–1901)
  Hymn: "Hark what a sound, and too divine for
    hearing."
  Surrender to Christ.

Myers, Jack (b. 1941)
  Experts, The.

Gift, The.
Instinct, The.
Jake Addresses the World from the Garden.
Lightweight.
Mom Did Marilyn, Dad Did Fred.
Perfect Recall.
Training Horses.
Visitation Rites.
We Go Away at Home.
What's Left.

Myles, Eileen (b. 1949)
American Poem, An.
December 9th.
Eileen's Vision.
Flowers.
Maxfield Parrish.
Merk.
Milk.
New England Wind.
No Rewriting.
Rotting Symbols.
Sadness of Leaving, The.
School of Fish.
Sleepless.
Sweet Pain of It, The.
Taxing.

Myöngok (fl. late 16th cent.)
Dreams.
Snow falls on the mountain village.
They say dream visits.

Myoyu (1333–93)
Defying the power of speech, the Law
    Commission on Mount Vulture!

Myrddin ap Dafydd (b. 1954)
Gwenllian.
Language Is Only Words, A.
Poet's Insurance Risk, The.
War Cabinet, The.

Myrddyn (Merlin)
Yscolan.

Mystic, Rabi'a the *See* Rabi'a al-Adawiyya

N

Na Ceapaich, Sileas (c.1660–c.1729)
Alasdair of Glengarry, *sel.*
Conversation with Death, A.

Na Hûidôk (b. 1966)
Cold Rain Comes, A.
Dirty Nylons.
Five A.M.
For Five Minutes.
Like the Vineyard.
Sleeping on the Nail.
Song of Grass.
That Place Isn't Far.
There's Such an Evening.
Women Within Me.

Nabbes, Thomas (1605?–41)
Song, The: "Beauty no more the subject be."
Song: "What a dainty life the milkmaid leads!"

Nabhan, Gary Paul
Coming Out on Solid Ground After the Ice
    Age.

Nâbî (c. 1642–1712)
At the gathering of joy, the wine cup.
In the Garden of Time and Destiny.
When we watch the spinning of the sky.

**Nabokov, Vladimir Vladimirovich (Vladimir
Sirin) (1899–1977)**
Lolita, *sels.*
On Translating "Eugene Onegin."
When he was small, when he would fall.

Na'car, Pancho (1909–63)
Foreigner Who Died in Juchitán, The.

Nadal, Lenina
Warrior Womb.

Naden, Constance (1858–89)
Evolutional Erotics, *sels.*
Love Versus Learning.
Love's Mirror.
Moonlight and Gas.
Pantheist's Song of Immortality, The.

Pessimist's Vision, The.
Poet and Botanist.
Sister of Mercy, The.
Two Artists, The.

Nadir, Moishe (1885–1943)
Afterwards: "Earth will flame and glow, The."
In Pencil.
My Bas-Sheva.
My Heart.
Old Woman, The.
Out of the Depths.
Selfwriting.
Third, A.

Nadja (1902–40)
Blue Wind, The.

Nádvorníková, Alena (b. 1942)
Art History (Sandro Botticelli).
Determination of Time.

Nag Hammadi Library
Thunder, The: Perfect Mind, *sels.*

Nagai, Mariko
Histories of Bodies.

Nagase, Kiyoko (b. 1906)
Surf.

Nageshbabu, Madduri (b. 1964)
What Do I Want?

Nagnamuni (b. 1931)
Wooden Horse.

Nagy, László (1925–78)
Bartók.
City's Coat of Arms, The.
Coalmen, The.
Csontváry.
Frosts are Coming.
Grasshoppers on the Bell.
Hymn for All Seasons.
Who'll Bear Love.
Who'll Ferry Love to the Yonder Shore.
Young Miracle Stag, The.

**Nahman [or Nachman] of Bratzlav, Rabbi (1770–
1811)**
From "The Torah of the Void."

Na'ili [or Yeni-Zada Mustafa Efendi] (d. 1666)
My tears became desire that illuminates.
Since the thunderbolt of disaster set our.
We are the snake hidden in the staff.
What witch are you, that entangles our hearts.

Naimy, Mikhail (1889–1988)
Chord [or Cord] of Hope, The, *sel.*
Hunger.
My Brother.

Nairne, Carolina Oliphant, Baroness (1766–1845)
Caller Herrin.'
Heiress, The.
Laird o' Cockpen, The.
Land o' the Leal, The.
Will Ye No Come Back Again?

Naisby, T. H. (1931–89)
Reflections on Hillsborough in Memoriam.

Naito Joso (Joso) (1662–1704)
About the grave / Waves of spring mist.
Gruel heaped / In a perfect bowl.
How green— / Flowering slopes.
No need to cling.
These branches.

Nakano Shigeharu (1902–79)
Imperial Hotel.
Paul Claudel.
Rate of Exchange, The.
Song: "You, Don't sing."

Nakasuk
Invisible Men, The.

Na'mani, Huda (b. 1930)
Love Poem: "In your quest or request God is
    remote."

Nameroff, Rochelle
California Dreaming.
Elvis Presley.

Namjoshi, Suniti (b. 1941)
Caliban's Journal.
Not loved enough, nor yet quite lost.

Namjoshi, Suniti and Gillian Hanscombe
Well, Then Let Slip the Masks.

Nan-o-myo
Not falling, not ignoring.

Nance, Berta Hart (b. 1883)
Cattle.
Frontier Mystery.
Moonlight.
Old Fort Griffin.
Rio Grande Hills.
State Song.

Nandī Majumdār, Rāmkumār
Mind, I'm talking to you.

Nandī, Rāmdulāl (d. 1851)
I understand now, Tara, I understand.
Mind, let's go to an estate that's decent.

Nanei (1363–1438)
Splitting the void in half.

Nanmor, Dafydd (fl. 1450–80)
Ode to Rhys ap Maredudd of Tywyn.

Nantembo (1839–1925)
On New Year's Day.

Naong, Master (1320–76)
Auspicious Cloud.
Bamboo Forest.
Haesunja Asks for an Enlightenment Song.
Hyunsonja Asks for an Enlightenment Song.
Illusory Hermitage.
Lonely Hermitage.
Mosquito.
Playing at Jeoksun Pond on a Moonlit Night.
Rain During Drought.
Song for Late Autumn.
Song of the Pure Land.
Western Peak.

Napier, Alan
Tulum Saw the Coming.

Napier, Felicity
I Do Not Want the Ceiling of the Sistine
    Chapel.
I Have Taken the Suits and Shoes to Oxfam.

Nara Singde (1655–85)
Tune: "As If in a Dream."
Tune: "Butterflies Lingering over Flowers."
Tune: "Sand of Silk-Washing Brook" In
    Memoriam.

Naranjo, Carmen (b. 1930)
Part One: The Orders Begin.

Naranjo-Morse, Nora
Gia's Song.
Tradition and Change.

Narautjarri, Smiler
Witch Doctor's Magic Flight, The.

Narcisse, Pierre-Richard
Singing Queen, Where Are You?

Narihira (Ariwara no Narihira) (825–80)
Is that the same moon.
Ise Monogatari, The, *sels.*

Narihira, Ariwara no *See* Narihira (Ariwara no
Narihira)

**Narovchatov, Sergey [or Sergei] Sergeievich
(1919–81)**
In Those Years.

Nartsissov, Boris (b. 1906)
Marated Bastilled age, A.

Nash, Ogden (1902–71)
Adventures of Isabel.
Arthur.
Beginner's Guide to the Ocean, A.
Cat, The.
Columbus.
Cow, The.
Curl Up and Diet.
Dog, The.
Eel, The.
Emmet, The.
Evening Out, The.
Experiment Degustatory.
Germ, The.
Golly, How Truth Will Out.
Grackle, The.
Grandpa Is Ashamed.
Ha! Original Sin!
Here Usually Comes the Bride.
I'm a Stranger Here Myself.

Inter-Office Memorandum.
Introspective Reflection.
Just How Low Can a Highbrow Go When a
   Highbrow Lowers His Brow?
Kind of an Ode to Duty.
Lion, The.
Long Time No See, 'Bye Now.
Man Can Complain, Can't He?, A.
Mermaid, The.
Mr. Artesian's Conscientiousness.
Necessary Dirge, A.
No Wonder Our Fathers Died.
One from One Leaves Two, *sel.*
Panther, The.
Parent, The.
Parsnip, The.
Please Pass the Biscuit.
Portrait of the Artist as a Prematurely Old
   Man.
Private Dining Room, The.
Purist, The.
Reflection on Babies.
Reflections on Ice-breaking.
Requiem: "There was a young belle of old
   Natchez."
Rhinoceros, The.
Round About.
Samson Agonistes.
Sea-Gull and the Ea-Gull, The.
Sea-Gull, The.
Seven Spiritual Ages of Mrs. Marmaduke
   Moore, The.
Song of Songs, The.
Song of the Open Road.
Song to Be Sung by the Father of Infant
   Female Children.
Speak Low.
Spring Comes to Murray Hill.
Sweet Bye and Bye.
Tale of Custard the Dragon, The.
Termite, The.
Terrible People, The.
Turtle, The.
Tweedledee and Tweedledoom.
Unwinged Ones, The.
Very Like a Whale.
Wapiti, The.
Watchman, What of the First First Lady?
What Do You Want: A Meaningful Dialogue,
   or a Satisfactory Talk?
What's in a Name? Some Letter I Always
   Forget.
Which the Chicken, Which the Egg?
Winter Morning.
Word to Husbands, A.

Nashe [*or* Nash], Thomas (1567–1601)
Choise of Valentines, The.
Summer's Last Will and Testament, *sels.*

Nasir, Amjad (b. 1955)
Loneliness.
Parade.

Nasir, Awwad (b. 1950)
Moment of Love, A.
Poem Looking in a Mirror, A.
Poet's Fate, A.
Trilogy of the Man in Black.

Nasis, Pyè-Richa *See* Narcisse, Pierre-Richard

Naso, Publius Ovidius *See* Ovid

Nasr, Mohab
With meek eyes.

Nasrallah, Ibrahim
Mirrors, *sel.*
Salvos of Mercy, *sel.*

Nasrin, Taslima (b. 1962)
Another Life.
At the Back of Progress . . . .
Border.
Character.
Eve Oh Eve.
Happy Marriage.

Nathan, Leonard (b. 1924)
At the Well.
Bladder Song.
Body Count.
Breathing Exercises.

Circlings.
Coup.
Election, The.
Hole.
Letter: "Dear Antigone."
Making a Love Poem.
Quartet.
Ragged Sonnet: So Shall I Live.
Ragged Sonnet: When in a Deep Depression.
So?
Toast.
United Flight 608.

Nathaniel, Isabel
Coast of Texas, The.
Elegy at Mustang Island.
Galveston.
Weepers, The.

Natsagdorzh, D. (1906–37)
My Country.

Natsume Soseki (1867–1916)
Is it showering?
It comes to my shoulder.
Not a Christian, not a Buddhist, not a
   Confucian either.
Once I was a poor man's son.
Onto a charcoal kiln.
True path is shadowy and still, far away and
   hard to find, The.

Natzler, Caroline
There.

Navajo Oral Tradition
Coyote, Skunk, and the Prairie Dogs.
Creation of the Earth, The.
Night Chant, The, *sels.*
Song of the Earth.

Navies, Kelly Elaine
Birth.

Nawaz, Gharib (1143–1236)
Riddle.

Nawaz, Shuja
Initiation, The.

Nawwab, Muzaffar (b. 1932)
Bridge of Old Wonders.

Naylor, James Ball (1860–1945)
Authorship.

Nazareno, Clovis L.
Bohol's Tarsier Population.
Cortes Swamp, The.

Nazario, Amanda
Kevin and Nicole.
Melt me.

Ne Jame, Adele
About the Men.
Somnambulist.
Song of a Thousand Empty Hands.
World Is a Wedding, The.

Neal, Gaston
Monk.

Neal, John (1793–1876)
Battle of Niagara, The, *sels.*

Neal, Larry (b. 1937)
Holy Days.
Lady's Days.

Neale, John Mason (1818–66)
Guide from St. Stephen the Sabaite, The.

Nealon, Mary Jane
Moon Landing, 1969.

Neander, Joachim (fl. 1680)
Praise to the Lord the Almighty.

Necatigil, Behçet (1916–79)
Secret Love: "It was seven or eight years ago."

Neckar, Ninon (*fl.* 1883)
On the Road.

Nedim (d. c.1733)
As the morning wind blows, you are
   disheveled.
At the gathering of desire you made me a
   wine-cup.
Delicacy was drawn out like the finest wire.
Song: "Come, let's grant joy to this heart of
   ours that founders in distress."
Take Yourself to the Rose-Garden.
When the east wind leaves that curl.

Needell, Claire (b. 1965)
Not a Balancing Act.

Needham, Frederick B.
Round of the Clock, The, *sel.*

Neely, Letta
Eight Ways of Looking at Pussy.
Multiple Assaults.
Rhonda, Age 15, Emergency Room.

Nef'i (d. 1635)
Heart is both the cup and the wine, The.
That black drunken eye has become a tavern.
Those who painted my portrait painted me.

Negar (b. 1975)
Dust: "Dead ringing of distant steps, The."
Forgive me that I opened your door silently.

Negroni, Maria
Theory of a Good Death.

Neiburg, A. J. (*fl.* 1933)
It's the Talk of the Town.

Neidhardt, Frances E. (b. 1928)
Street Flower in Big D.

Neidjie, Bill (1913–2002)
This earth.

Neihardt, John Gneisenau (1881–1973)
Song of the Indian Wars, The, *sel.*
Song of the Messiah, The, *sel.*

Neill, William (b. 1922)
Are You There, Mr Punch?
Celtic History, A.
Lark.

Neilson, John Shaw (1872–1942)
May.
Schoolgirls Hastening.
To the Red Lory.

Neilson, Shane (b. 1975)
Rural Gothic.

Nejati (d. 1508)
Heart is pleased when black down covers, The.
Spiraling, the sparks.
Those glances rain down arrows on the
   country.
Those tulip-cheeked ones—what they dared do
   in the garden!

Nekrasov, Vsevolod (b. 1934)
And I Speak of Cosmic Things.
I repeat.
So who of us.
Somehow I really want to go.
What kind of Pushkin am I.

Nelligan, Emile (1879–1941)
Roundel to My Pipe.
Watteau, a Dream.

Nelson, Gale
I am too.
Shelving Fixtures.
Stare Decisis.

Nelson, Helena
No Hands.
With My Mother, Missing the Train.

Nelson, Howard
Journey, The: "I am wearing my gray wool
   pants, and my brown boots."
My Father Went to Funerals.
Peepers.
Reading "Crossing Brooklyn Ferry" on a
   Summer Morning.

Nelson, Jo
Our Love.

Nelson, John
For Whom the Bells Toll and Toll and Toll.
If a Fish Fell in a Forest.
If You Knew September.
Just Word Wranglin.'
Never Eat Oranges!
Teed Off.

Nelson, Lynn *See* Waniek, Marilyn Nelson

Nelson, Maggie (b. 1973)
Brightness.
56 Westervelt.
Misunderstanding, A.
Molino.
Motel Story.
Proposal.

Shiner.
Subway in March, 5:45 P.M.
Vallejo.
Wish.
Wish Fulfillment.

Nelson, Marilyn (b. 1946)
Balance.
Ballad of Aunt Geneva, The.
Chopin.
Chosen.
Cover Photograph.
Drifter.
How I Discovered Poetry.
I Decide Not to Have Children.
Juneteenth.
Love Song.
Minor Miracle.
Prayer of Miss Budd, The.
Washboard Wizard.
Wreath for Emmett Till, A.

Nelson, Sandra
Anti-Foucault Poem, The.

Nemerov, Howard (b. 1920)
Amateurs of Heaven, The.
At the Airport.
Author to His Body on Their Fifteenth
    Birthday, 29.ii.80, The.
Because You Asked about the Line between
    Prose and Poetry.
Blue Suburban.
Blue Swallows, The.
Bluejay and the Mockingbird, The.
Boom!
Boy with Book of Knowledge.
Brainstorm.
Brief Journey West, The.
Cabinet of Seeds Displayed, A.
Celestial Emperor, The.
Creation Myth on a Moebius Band.
Debate with the Rabbi.
Dependencies, The.
Easter: "Even this suburb has overcome
    Death."
Einstein & Freud & Jack.
Epigrams, *sel.*
Fable of the War, A.
For Robert Frost, in the Autumn, in Vermont.
Gnomes, *sels.*
"Good-bye," said the river, "I'm going
    downstream."
Goose Fish, The.
Grace to Be Said at the Supermarket.
Grand Central, with Soldiers, in Early
    Morning.
Gyroscope.
Historical Judas, The.
Holding the Mirror Up to Nature.
I Only Am Escaped Alone to Tell Thee.
Icehouse in Summer, The.
IFF.
In the Beginning.
Intimations.
Learning by Doing.
Learning the Trees.
Life, A.
Life Cycle of Common Man.
Low-Level Cross-Country.
Manners.
Memory of the War, A.
Models.
Modern Poet, A.
Money.
More Joy in Heaven.
Mystery Story.
Nicodemus.
Night Operations, Coastal Command RAF.
Painter Dreaming in the Scholar's House, The.
Playing the Machine.
Primer of the Daily Round, A.
Reading Pornography in Old Age.
Redeployment.
Reflexions on the Seizure of the Suez, and on a
    Proposal to Line the Banks of That Canal
    with Billboard Advertisements.
St. John, *sels.*
Salt Garden, The.

September, the First Day of School.
Sigmund Freud.
Snow Globe, The.
Snowflakes.
Song of Degrees, A.
Storm Windows.
Strange Metamorphosis of Poets.
Style.
To D———, Dead by Her Own Hand.
To My Least Favorite Reviewer.
Town Dump, The.
Ultima Ratio Reagan.
Vacuum, The.
Vermeer.
Waiting Rooms.
Walking the Dog.
War in the Air, The.
Way of Life, A.
Western Approaches, The.
Witnessing the Launch of the Shuttle *Atlantis*.
Wolves in the Zoo.
Writing.

Nemes Nagy, Ágnes (1922–91)
Between.
Between.
Bird.
Carbon Dioxide.
Comparison, A.
Conciousness.
Conversation.
Defend It.
Earth Remembers, The.
Four-Light Window, A.
Garden of Eden, The.
Geyser, The.
Ghost, The.
I Carried Statues.
Ice.
Lake Balaton.
Lazarus.
Lazarus.
Lazarus.
Lazarus.
Like One Who.
Pinetree.
Proportions of the Street, The.
Scene, The.
Shapelessness, The.
Simile.
Sincerity.
Storm.
Terraced Landscape.
To a Poet.
To Freedom.
To Liberty.
To My Craft.
Towards Springtime.
Trees.
Walk at the Museum, A.
Winter Angel.
Winter Trees.
Winter Trees.
Winter Trees.

Nensho (1409–82)
Only genuine awakening results in that.

Nepote, Mónica (b. 1970)
A esta mujer la sangre se le fuga.
Blood leaks from this woman, The.
Hielo.
Ice.
Image of the Fish.
Imagen del Pez.
Lugar, El.
Piensa en esa estatua abierta en el corazón de
    la ciudad.
Place, The.
Think of that statue open in the heart of the
    city.
To take up the word again.
Tomar de nuevo la palabra.
Visitación.
Visitation.

Neri, Giampiero (b. 1927)
Case of the Same Name, A.
Inn of Angels, The.
Natural History.

Seasons.

**Neruda, Pablo (Neftalí Ricardo Reyes Basualto)
(1904–73)**
Absence of Joaquín.
Almería.
Ambassador, The.
America, I Do Not Call Your Name Without
    Hope.
Amor America (1400).
Autumn Returns.
Births.
Body of a Woman.
Body of a Woman.
Book of Questions, The, *sels.*
Broken Glish.
Burial in the East.
Burial in the East.
Dead Gallop.
Dead Woman.
Dictators, The.
Different Ship, A.
Enigmas: "You've asked me what the lobster is
    weaving there with his golden feet?"
Every Day, Matilde.
Fable of the Mermaid and the Drunks.
Final.
Flag, The.
Forgive me if my eyes see.
From My Notebook.
From the explosion to the iron split.
Funeral in the East.
Heights of Macchu Picchu, The, *sels.*
Hero, The.
Homecomings.
Horses.
I did not touch your night, or your air, or
    dawn.
I Explain a Few Things.
I love the handful of the earth you are.
I remember you as you were that ultimate
    autumn.
If Each Day Falls.
I'm Explaining a Few Things.
Introduction: My Themes.
Keeping Quiet.
Leaning into the Afternoons.
Letter to Miguel Otero Silva, in Caracas, *sel.*
Love Song: "I love you, I love you, is my
    song."
Melancholy in the Families.
Melancholy inside Families.
Men grow with all that grows.
My love, if I die and you don't.
Nothing but Death.
Nuptial Material.
Oda a la Cebolla.
Oda a la Manzana.
Ode to a Beautiful Nude.
Ode to Bicycles.
Ode to César Vallejo.
Ode to Federico García Lorca.
Ode to Laziness.
Ode to My Socks.
Ode to My Socks.
Ode to Salt.
Ode to Salt.
Ode to the Apple.
Ode to the Cat.
Ode to the Lemon.
Ode to the Onion.
Ode to the Onion.
Ode to the Seagull.
Ode to Walt Whitman.
Ode with a Lament.
100 Love Sonnets, *sels.*
Only Death.
Pardon me, if when I want.
Past.
Poem.
Poem 15.
Poem 20.
Poetry.
Poet's Obligation.
Poet's Obligation, The.
Red Bird, *sels.*
Ritual of My Legs.

Sexual Water.
Single Gentleman.
Some Beasts.
Sonnet 4.
Still Another Day, *sels*.
Still, I am here.
Sweetness, Always.
Taste.
There Is No Forgetting (Sonata).
They Receive Instructions Against Chile.
Tonight I Can Write the Saddest Lines.
Too Many Names.
United Fruit Co.
United Fruit Co., The.
Unity.
Walkin' Around.
Walking Around.
Walking Around.
Walking Around.
Walking Around ("It happens that I am tired of
     being a man.").
We Are Many.
Youth: "Odor like an acid sword made, An."

Nerval, Gérard de (Gérard Labrunie) (1808–55)
El Desdichado.
Fantasy.
Golden Sayings.
To J—Y Colonna.

Nervo, Amado (1870–1919)
Cowardice.
Ecstasy.
Gift, The.
Revenge.
Sorrow Vanquished.

Nesbit, Edith (Edith Nesbit Bland) (1858–1924)
Appeal.
At Parting.
Child's Song in Spring.
Dead to the Living, The.
Goose-Girl, The.
Gray Folk, The.
Great Industrial Centre, A.
Haunted.
Husband of To-Day, The.
Kiss, The.
Song: "Oh, baby, baby, baby dear."
Things That Matter, The.
To Vera, Who Asked a Song.
Vies Manquées.
Villeggiature.
Wife of All Ages, The.

Neshâtî (d. 1674)
Sky's face has turned dark, don't believe, The.
We are desire hidden in the love-crazed call.
You're gone—I'm alone in the company.

Nesimi (c.1369–c.1418)
Oh my idol of the temple, in the dark of night.

Nester, Daniel (b. 1969)
Third Maisie Poem.

Neto, Agostinho (1922–79)
African Poem.
Grieved Lands, The.
Kinaxixi.
Saturday in the Sand-Slums.

Neufeldt, Leonard (b. 1937)
Dyke View Berry Farm.
Man with the glass eye, The.
Tree with a hole in our front yard, The.
Yarrow.

Neumann, Stanislav Kostka (1875–1947)
Winter Night.

Neumark, Georg (fl. 1641)
If thou but suffer God to guide thee.

Nev'î (1533–99)
Help me, oh sapling of the tulip cheek.
We don't need the cup of pleasure.

**Nevill, Frances Manners, Lady Abergavenny (b.
after 1527, d. 1576)**
Necessarie Praier in Meeter Against Vices, A.

New, William H. (b. 1938)
Acoustics.

Newbolt, Sir Henry John (1862–1938)
Clifton Chapel.
Drake's Drum.

He Fell among Thieves.
Non-Combatant, The.
Vitaï Lampada.

Newburn, Laura
Office Geraniums.

Newell, Elizabeth (fl. 1655–68)
Dialogue, A.

Newley, Anthony
What Kind of Fool Am I?
Who Can I Turn To (When Nobody Needs
     Me?).

Newman, Amy (b. 1957)
Architecture of the Wings, The.
Darwin's Unfinished Notes to Emma.
Fall back. To give ground; recede; retreat.
Fall for. *Informal.* 1. To become infatuated
     with; fall suddenly in love with. 2. To be
     tricked or deceived by; be taken in by.
Fall under. To succumb to; come under an
     influence or power.

Newman, Edward (fl. 1840)
Earwigs.

Newman, Harry, Jr.
Testimonial.

Newman, John Henry, Cardinal (1801–90)
Angel.
Desolation.
Elements, The.
Melchizedek.
Path of the Just, The.
Pillar of the Cloud, The.
Taormini.

Newman, Richard
Salem, Indiana, 1983.
Theology.

Newton, Byron Rufus (1861–1938)
Owed to New York.

Newton, John (1725–1807)
Amazing Grace.
"In Evil Long I Took Delight."
Name of Jesus, The.

Newton, Violette
Caddo Mounds, The.
Going Back to Ireland.
Mythology of Snow, A.
Texas Poetry.
Witness, Susanna Dickinson, The.

Nezahualcoyotl (1402–72)
Be Indomitable, O My Heart.
Can It Be True That One Lives on Earth?
Flowers of Red and Blue.
I, Nezahualcóyotl ask it.
Our Lord.
Where Will I Go?

Nezhukumatathil, Aimee
Tallahassee.

Nezval, Vitězslau (1900–58)
City With Towers.
Lilac by the Museum on St. Wenceslas Square,
     The.
Moon over Prague.
Prague in the Midday Sun.
Trap Door.
Walker in Prague.

Ngafua, Zizwe
Nommo.

Ngai, Sianne
Discredit.

Ngo Chi Lan (fl. 15th cent.)
Autumn.
Winter.

Ngoma
Demockery.

Ngunaitponi (David Unaipon) (1873–1967)
Song of Hungarrda, The.

Nguyen, Hoa (b. 1967)
Buddha's ears are droopy touch his shoulders.
Calm in the Vegetable Beard of Time.
Calmly grass becomes a wave.
Captive and Able.
Crows and grackles grackles.
Dark.
House on fire my mom's.

Kerouac Creek Work Tune.
Lozenge.
Mission Dolores.
Roll in your skull gone green.
Shred.
Sitting there nearly translucent You'll end up.
Unorthodox and impractical one not led.

Nguyen Binh Khiem (1491–1585)
Hated Rats, The.
Worried.

Nguyễn Chí Thiện (b. 1933)
Jungle Night, A.
Model Children of the Regime, The.
Sundry Notes, *sel*.
This Land's No Joy.
Travel with Grief—Goodbye to Joy.

Nguyễn Gia Thiều (1741–98)
Sorrows of an Abandoned Queen, *sel*.

Nguyễn Khuyến (1835–1909)
Man Who Feigns Deafness, The.
To the Singing Girl Named Luu.

Nguyễn Trãi (1380–1442)
Bamboo Hut, The.
Plough and a Spade, A.

Nguyễn Văn Lạc (1842–1915)
Shrimps.

Nhan, Dieu *See* Ly Ngoc Kieu

Nhat Hanh, Thich (b. 1926)
Existence.
Journey: "Here are words written down."
Please Call Me by My True Names.

Ní Chuilleanáin, Eiléan (b. 1942)
Deaths and Engines.
House Remembered, The.
Informant, The.
Pygmalion's Image.
Real Thing, The.
Saint Margaret of Cortona.
Second Voyage, The.
Secret, The.
Street.
Studying the Language.
Swineherd.
Swineherd.
Tale of Me, The.

Ni Dhomhnaill, Nuala (b. 1952)
Annunciations.
As for the Quince.
As for the Quince.
Aubade: "It's all the same to morning what it
     dawns on."
Bond, The.
Broken Doll, The.
Cathleen.
Celebration.
Deep-Freeze.
I Cannot Lie Here Anymore.
Labasheedy (The Silken Bed).
Language Issue, The.
Language Issue, The.
Leaba Shíoda.
Marvellous Grass.
Miraculous Grass.
Race, The.
Shannon Estuary 1988.
Shannon Estuary Welcomes the Fish, The.
Unfaithful Wife, The.

Ni Ghallchóir, Colette (b. 1950)
Big Glen, The.
Divorce 19th-century Style.
Dream of the White-headed Boy, A.
Escape.
In the Garden of Apples.
Refusal.
Spark of Joy, The.
Under the Sod.

Ni Tsan (1301–74)
Inscribed on a Painting by Myself.

Niatum, Duane (b. 1938)
Apology.
Art of Clay, The.
Drawings of the Song Animals.
First Spring.
In the Labyrinth of Elements.

Lines for Roethke Twenty Years after His
    Death.
Maggie.
Novelty Shop, The.
Pieces.
Reality of Autumn, The.
Rufous Hummingbird.
Salmon, The.
Snowy Owl near Ocean Shores.
Stones Speak of an Earthless Sky.
Traveler, The.
Tribute to Chief Joseph, A.

Nibenegenesabe, Jacob
Quiet Until the Thaw.
Wishing Bone Cycle, The, *sel.*

Nicarchus of Alexandria (*fl.* **1st cent. A.D.**)
Variations of Greek Themes, *sels.*

Niccolai, Giulia (b. 1934)
Clear Form Clashes, The.
Frisbees, *sel.*
Frisbees '88, *sel.*
Frisbees on Light.
From the Novissimi.
Geographical History, The.
Harry's Bar Ballad.
Only Indirectly.
So Inferred.
Syntactic and Verbal.

Nichol, B. P. (b. 1944)
Blues.
Cycle #22.
Easter Pome.
Ferry Me Across.
From Catullus Poem LI.
Inchoate Road, *sels.*
Landscape: 1.
Little song, A.
Love song 2.
Martyrology 7, The, *sels.*
Monotones.
Scraptures: 7th Sequence.
Some Nets.
Song for Saint Ein.
St. Anzas VI.
St. Anzas IX.
Turnips Are.

Nicholas, A. X. (b. 1943)
Strange / that we wake.

Nicholas, James (b. 1928)
Bush, The.

Nicholas, T. E. (1879–1971)
Caernarfon Circus, 1969.
To a Sparrow.

Nicholl, Theodore (1902–73)
His Friend's Last Battle.

Nicholls, Judith
Journey.
Mary Celeste.
Polar Cub.
Season Song.
Storytime.

Nichols, Grace (b. 1950)
Beverley's Saga.
Black.
Configurations.
Epilogue: "I have crossed an ocean."
Fat Black Woman Versus Politics, The.
Holding My Beads.
Invitation.
Invitation, *sel.*
Like a Beacon.
Long-Man.
Out of Africa.
Praise Song for My Mother.
Sugar Cane.
Thoughts drifting through the fat black
    woman's head while having a full bubble
    bath.
Tropical Death.
Waterpot.
Wha Me Mudder Do.
Wherever I Hang.
White.

Nichols, Kevin
Feast of Stephen, The.

Nichols, Robert Malise Bowyer (1893–1944)
Aurelia.
Don Juan's Address to the Sunset.
Fisbo, *sel.*
Flower of Flame, The, *sel.*
Get-Away, *sel.*
Moon behind High Tranquil Leaves, The.
Sonnets to Aurelia.
To D'Annunzio: Lines from the Sea.

Nichols, Travis (b. 1979)
Wild is the Wind.

Nicholson, Norman (1914–87)
Blackberry, The.
Carol for the Last Christmas Eve.
Carol: "Mary laid her Child among."
Comet Come.
Epithalamium for a Niece.
Five Minutes.
For Hokey and Henrietta.
From a Boat at Coniston.
Halley's Comet.
Michaelmas.
On the Closing of Millom Ironworks.
Rockferns.
Sea to the West.
Shepherds' Carol.
Stalingrad: 1942.
To the River Duddon.
Tune the Old Cow Died Of, The.

Nickel, Barbara (b. 1966)
For Peter, My Cousin.
Lines: "Empty foolscap, The."
Three Poems for Violin.

Nickelson, Christopher
Angry sisters.
Charleston, South Carolina.
Three men.
Untitled: "I don't get."

Nickerson, Sheila
At Auke Bay the whales dance.
Seal's cry has lain against my leg, A.

NicNèill, Siùsaidh (b. 1955)
For Eric Blair.
Steel Yourself.

Nicolson, Adela Florence Cory *See* Hope,
Laurence

Niedecker, Lorine (1903–70)
Clothesline post is set, The.
Cricket-song.
Darwin.
Death of my poor father, The.
Dusk— / He's spearing from a boat.
Element Mother, The.
Element Mother, The.
Fancy Another Day Gone.
Far reach.
Frog noise / suddenly stops.
Get a load.
Graves, The.
He lived—childhood summers.
I married.
I rose from marsh mud.
If I Were a Bird.
Lake Superior, *sels.*
Men leave the car, The.
Monster owl, A.
Museum man!, The.
My friend tree.
My Life by Water.
My life is hung up.
New-sawed.
Paean to Place.
Paul / when the leaves.
Poems at the Porthole.
Poet's Work.
Popcorn-can cover.
Radio talk this morning, The.
Remember my little granite pail?
River-marsh-drowse.
Sewing a Dress.
Something in the water.
Stone / and that hard.
Subliminal.
Swept snow, Li Po.
There's a better shine.

Thomas Jefferson.
War.
Well, spring overflows the land.
What horror to awake at night.
Who Was Mary Shelley?
Who was Mary Shelley?
Wilderness.
Will You Write Me a Christmas Poem?
Woman in middle-life.
You have power politics, Paul.
Young girl to marry.

Nielsen, Dan
My Philosophy.
Paranoid Egotist, A.
Saturday Morning Ultimatum.

Nielsen, Kristy
Self Portrait as Nancy Drew, Girl Sleuth.

Niemoller, Pastor (1892–1984)
First They Came for the Jews.

Nienhauser, William H.
Sent to the Taoist of Dragon Mountain, Hsu
    Fa-leng.

Nietzsche, Friedrich Wilhelm (1844–1900)
Against the Laws.
Undiscouraged.
Zarathustra, *sels.*

**Nighean Dhonnchadh (The Daughter of Duncan
    Campbell of Glenlyon)** (*fl.* **1570**)
Early on Lammas Morning.

Nighean Uisdein, Mor (*fl.* **c.1615**)
Ay, Bashful Thou!

Nijhoff, Martinus
At a Grave.
Dancer.
Last Day.
Light.
Light, The.
Musician, The.
New Stars, The.
Soldier Who Crucified Jesus, The.

**Nikolayeva [*or* Nikolaeva], Olesya [*or* Olesia] (b.
    1955)**
Daughter.
Here, everything gets eaten: drippings,
    marinade.
Once I used to study languages dead for
    millenia.
Party on Women's Day, A.
Seven Beginnings.
You can go on holiday now, you can dabble in
    verse.

Nikolic, Georg (b. 1949)
Key to Dreams.
Under the Ninth Sky.

Nikonova, Rea (b. 1942)
Along the thread of veins.
Earth is burning, The.
I sit over grief.
Six charred leaves drift.

Nilsson, HeidiLynn (b. 1974)
How Came What Came Alas.
My Least Skirtable Deficiency.
On Inheriting Departure.
We Are Easily Reduced.

Nimmo, Dorothy
Exorcism.
Good Gifts.
Ill-Wishing Him.
My Father's Shadow.

Nims, Bonnie
On a Cold Autumn Day.

Nims, John Frederick (b. 1913)
Christmas.
Evergreen, The.
Freight.
Knowledge of God.
Love Poem: "My clumsiest dear, whose hands
    shipwreck vases."
Mouse, The.
New Year's Eve, 1938.
Shot Down at Night.
Six-Cornered Snowflake, The, *sel.*
Tennis Trophy.
Tide Turning.

Trainwrecked Soldiers.
Trick or Treat.
Understanding the Universe.
Verse Translator.
Watching the Planes Come in at La Guardia.
Young Ionia, The.

Nirmala, Kondepudi (b. 1957)
Birds Love the Net.

Nisâyî (d. c.1555)
We are the Mejnûn of our age, we dwell in the wilderness.

Nisbet, Hume (1849–1921?)
Isandula.

Nishikawa, Etsudo
Round, round, more round than the moon.

Nishiwaki Junzaburo (b. 1894)
Ceylon.
Eye.
Hand.
January in Kyoto.
Man Reading Homer, A.
Man Who Reads Homer, A.
Primitiveness of a Cup, The.
Rain.
Shepherd in Capri.

Nishiyama Soin (1605–82)
Cherry blossoms / dizzying.
Settling, white dew.

Nisker, Wes "Scoop"
I sit in wonder.
No tears and no fears.
Whatever.

Niu Hsi-chi (fl. c.930)
Spring Mountains.
Where the mist has torn.

Nixon-Roulet, Mary F.
Highroller.

Niyazi, Salah (b. 1935)
Thinker Between the Bronze Shield and the Human Flesh, The.

Nizami Arudi (1141–1203)
Calling the Doctor (1000 A.D.).

No Ch'ŏnmyŏng (1912–57)
Deer.
Lemon for Me, A.
Nameless Woman.
Nameless Woman, A.
Nostalgia.
Performer, Male.
Road.
Spring of the Steel Bar Window.

No Hyangnim (b. 1942)
Ap'ae Island 1—Diving Women.
Ap'ae Island 45—Once Upon a Time.
Autumn Letter.
Black Hole.
Country Where Snow Has Not Yet Fallen, A.
Dream: "Sea was in front of me, The."
Nature: "In a corn field."
Nursery.
Rooftop Violin.
Windy Day.
Yard.

No Hyegyông (b. 1958)
Children on Top of the Hill.
Disease That Arrives at Death.
Face: "Suddenly below my ankles."
Fish and Sauce.
Happy Walk.
Memory of Underdevelopment.
Miscellaneous Bouquet.
Peace on Earth.
Song of Mary.
Triangle, Comb.
Triangle, Mirror.
Wedding: "Inside the womb-like darkness."

Noble, Ray (1903–78)
Good Night, Sweetheart.
I Hadn't Anyone Till You.
Touch of Your Lips, The.
Very Thought of You, The.

Nobleman, Blythe
Tabloid News.

Nobles, Edward
Nuclear Winter.

Noël, Bernard (b. 1930)
Angers.
Angers.
Portrait.
Portrait.

Noel, Linda
Understanding Each Other.

Noel-Scott, Barbara
Hansel and Gretel.

Noguchi, Rick (b. 1967)
Breath He Holds, The.
From Rooftops, Kenji Takezo Throws Himself.
His Waves.
I, the Neighbor Mr. Uskovich, Watch Every Morning Kenji Takezo Hold His Breath.
Japanese Hokkus, sels.
Kenji Takezo Becomes Water.
Not Surfing Some Days.
Really Long Ride, The.
Turn of Privacy, The.
When for Weeks the Sea is Flat.

Noguchi, Yonejiro (Yone) (1875–1947)
Are the fallen stars.
I Hear You Call, Pine Tree.
In Japan Beyond.
It's too late to hear a nightingale.
Japanese Hokkus, sels.
Leaves blown.
Like a cobweb hung upon the tree.
Lines: "Sun I worship, The."
Suppose the stars.

Nogueras, Luis Rogelio (1944–85)
Poem, A.

Noguere, Suzanne (b. 1947)
Barney Bigard.
Scribes, The.
Secret, The.
Soma.
Whirling Round the Sun.

Noin (988?–1050)
Spring in a Mountain Village.

Nokhem, Y. (1888–1966)
Fly, The.
Hounds Howl at the Moon.

Nolens, Leonard (b. 1947)
Address.
Origins.
Paranoia.
Place and Date.
Poetic License.
Saint Vitus's Dance in October 10.
Tributary.

Noll, Bink (b. 1927)
Abraham's Madness.

Nolla, Olga (b. 1938)
Erotic Suite.
Greek History.
Manifest, The.
Reencounter with the Goddess.
Thoughts on Innocence.
Troubadour Love.

Nomura Akitari (fl. 1882)
Butterflies.

Nonnus (fl. 5th cent.)
Dionysiaca, sels.

Nooteboom, Cees (b. 1933)
Basho 1.
Basho 2.
Basho 3.
Basho 4.
Basho ("Old man among the reeds mistrust of the poet.").
Basho ("Oude man tussen het riet achterdocht van de dichter.").
Midday.

Nordbrandt, Henrik
China Observed Through Greek Rain in Turkish Coffee.
No Matter Where We Go.
Old Man in Meditation.
Our Love Is Like Byzantium.
Sailing.

Streets.

Nordhaus, Jean
Adirondack Return.
Aunt Lily and Frederick the Great.
Bluegrass.
Protecting the Children from Hurricanes.

Norgate, Stephanie
Perfect example of a paralysed larynx, A.
Water on the Moon.

Norman, Lissette
SpaNglisH.

Norman, Peter
I could have been Lord Dacre or a balalaika-maker.

Norman, Pierre
When I Take My Sugar to Tea.

Norris, John (1657–1711)
Meditation, The.
My Estate.

Norris, Kathleen (b. 1947)
Blue Light, The.
Desert Run Scenario.
Emperor Has No Clothes!, The.
Hester Prynne Recalls a Sunday in June.
Inheritance.
Lilith and the Doctor.
Luke 14: A Commentary.
Monastery Orchard in Early Spring, The.
Mrs. Adam.
Mysteries of The Incarnation: "She Said Yeah."
Naming the Living God.
New Year's Eve in Bismarck, North Dakota.
Persephone.
Prayer to Eve, A.
Throne of Grace, The.
True Love.
Washing Dishes Late at Night.
Wedding in the Courthouse, The.

Norris, Leslie (b. 1921)
Ballad of Billy Rose, The.
Barn Owl.
Belonging.
Bridges.
Early Frost.
Elegy for David Beynon.
Elegy for Lyn James.
His Father, Singing.
Hudson's Geese.
Hyperion.
Merlin and the Snake's Egg.
Mice in the Hay.
Pit Ponies, The.
Ravenna Bridge.
Shepherd's Dog, The.
Small War, A, sels.
Stone and Fern.
Water.

Norris, Margie
Tortillas.

Norse, Harold (b. 1926)
Believing in the Absurd.
Business of Poetry, The.
I Would Not Recommend Love.
I'm Not a Man.
Picasso Visits Braque.

Norte, Marisela (b. 1955)
Angel.
Peeping Tom Tom Girl.

North, Charles (b. 1941)
Air and Angels.
Dawn, The: "TO BE / Immortal."
Detail.
Elizabethan and Nova Scotian Music.
Eye Reflecting the Gold of Fall.
Few Facts about Me, A.
For a Cowper Paperweight.
For Dorothy Wordsworth.
From the French.
Hospital.
Landscape and Chardin.
Leap Year.
Little Cape Cod Landscape.
Note to Tony Towle (After WS), A.

Pastoral, The: "Now the body is the body's flower."
Philosophical Songs.
Postcard Element in Winter, The.
Sunrise with Sea Monster.
Words from Robert W. Service.
Year of the Olive Oil, The.

North, Dudley, 3d Baron North (1581–1666)
Platonic.

North, Mick (b. 1958)
Account, An.
Ordnance Survey in the Northern Counties.
Pheasant Plucker's Son, The.
Pinder.
Poems to My Father.
Portrait in a Brass Gong.
Red Desiré.
Shap.

NorthSun, Nila
Moving Camp Too Far.

Nortje, Arthur (1942–73)
All hungers pass away.
Asseverations.
At Lansdowne Bridge.
Autopsy.
Cosmos in London.
Episodes with unusables.
Hangover.
Immigrant.
Letter from Pretoria Central Prison.
Nasser is dead.
Native's letter.
Newcombe at the Croydon Gallery.
Night ferry.
Reflections in a passing mirror.
Soliloquy: South Africa.
Sonnet one: "Supremely individual, flamboyant, proud."
Sonnet two: "I have drunk up nights and spent the days."
Waiting: "Isolation of exile is a gutted, The."
Your Absence.

Norton, Caroline Elizabeth (1808–77)
Bingen on the Rhine.
Dreams: "Surely I heard a voice—surely my name."
Faithless Knight, The.
First Love.
I Do Not Love Thee.
In the cold change, which time hath wrought on love.
Marriage and Love, sel.
Mother's Heart, The.
Obscurity of Woman's Worth.
Picture of Sappho, The.
Recollections: "Do you remember all the sunny places."
Sonnet 7: "Like an enfranchised bird, who wildly springs."
To My Books.
Undying One, The, sel.
Voice from the Factories, A, sels.

Norton, George (fl. 1912)
My Melancholy Baby.

Norton, Odetta D.
Bound.
Senegal Sestina.
Tattoo, or Henna.

Norton, Thomas
O all ye nations of the Lord.

Norwid, Cyprian (1821–83)
But Just to See.
Recipe for a Warsaw Novel.
Those Who Love.

Norwood, Nick
For the Drowned.

Norworth, Jack (1879–1959)
Shine On, Harvest Moon.
Take Me Out to the Ball Game.

Nossis (fl. c.290 B.C.)
Even from a distance, this picture is known.
It seems that Aphrodite took with joy.
Kallo dedicated her portrait in the house of golden.

Melinna herself is re-created: notice the face.
Nothing is sweeter than love, all other riches.
O Artemis of Delos and lovely Ortygia.
O Honored Hera, who often descending from heaven.
Shields Bruttians threw from their doomed shoulders.
Stranger, if you sail to the land of lovely dances, Mitylene.
This portrait captures Thaumareta's form—it renders.
When we go to the temple, let's see Aphrodite's.
When you've laughed out loud and said a friendly.

Notari, Louis (1879–1961)
Wee bird sang in the wasteland, A.

Notari, Luciana (b. 1944)
Body and Soul.
Brief Ectasy.
Distance.
Harsh Metropolitan Season.
If One Always Denies.
Winter Landscape.

Notley, Alice (b. 1945)
April Not an Inventory but a Blizzard.
Baby Is Born Out of a White Owl's Forehead—1972, A.
Back.
Beginning with a Stain.
California Girlhood, A.
Désamère, sel.
Destroy.
How Spring Comes.
How the Dead Women May Operate from Negative Space.
Incidentals in the Day World.
I—Towards a Definition.
Jack Would Speak Through the Imperfect Medium of Alice.
Latticed Culotte and Starry Blouse.
Mysteries of Small Houses.
Poem: "You hear that heroic big land music?"
State of the Union.
Three Strolls.
Where Leftover Misery Goes.
White Peacock, The.
White Phosphorus.
Woman came into "a car I rode" "about thirty-seven" "maybe", A.

Novak, Helga (b. 1935)
Freezing Pan, The.
Letter to Medea.
Packing Herring.

Novakovich, Josip (b. 1956)
Shadow.

"Novalis" (Friedrich von Hardenberg) (1772–1801)
Hymns to the Night, sels.
When geometric diagrams and digits.
Yearning for Death.

Novello, Ivor
We'll Gather Lilacs.

November, Deena
Always Secondary.
Clean that god damned room already.
Melba Street.

November, Yehoshua
Brotherhood: "First boy to fall in, The."
How a Place Becomes Holy.

Novikov, Nikolay (b. 1933)
Stone and Sky, sel.
White on white's a flatness.

Nowlan, Alden (1933–83)
And He Wept Aloud, So That the Egyptians Heard It.
Aunt Jane.
Britain Street: Saint John, New Brunswick.
Bull Moose, The.
Canadian Love Song.
Daughter of Zion.
Day's End.
Exchange of Gifts, An.
Execution, The.
Great Things Have Happened.

He Sits Down on the Floor of a School for the Retarded.
I, Icarus.
In Praise of the Great Bull Walrus.
In Those Old Wars.
It's Good To Be Here.
Mother and Son.
Only When My Heart Freezes.
Red Wool Shirt, The.
Rites of Manhood, The.
Sacrament.
Thief, The.
This Is What I Wanted to Sign Off With.
Warren Pryor.
Weakness.
Word, The: "Though I have the gift of tongues."

Noyes, Alfred (1880–1958)
Anvil, The.
Art, I.
Art, II.
Barrel-Organ, The.
Barrel-Organ, The.
Butterfly Garden, The.
Dane Tree, The.
Double Fortress, The.
Flower of Old Japan, The, sels.
Highwayman, The.
Night Journey.
Resurrection.

Noyes, Stanley
Beach House.
Dream Painter, The.
Seascape.
Wolf's Road, The.

Ntiru, Richard (b. 1946)
Rhythm of the Pestle, sel.

Nuccoli, Cecco (fl. 14th cent.)
Since I abandoned and tied my soul to your sweet appearance and manners oh Sir, guide and light of my life, will I ever see you before I die?
You have the light of my life, in your clear and pleasing face, and don't see me.
Your promises come to me always together with your betrayals, which you have more of than the fox.

Nukada, Princess (fl. late 7th cent.)
Polite Debate, A.

Nŭngun
Waiting for My Love.

Nuriddin, Jalauddin Mansur (b. 1944)
Children of the Future.

Nurkse, Dennis
August Horizon.
Birth Room, The.
Letter to Ko.
Liberators.
October Marriage.
Olmos.
Swiftness With Which Those Cities Fell, The.

Nurske, D.
Involuntary Music.

Nutter, Geoffrey (b. 1968)
Air War, The.
Boy Leading a Horse.
Definition of Swan, The.
Pastoral: "We're passing the whole summer, all of us."
Pond and Peace.
Summer Evening, A, sel.
Train Station Zoetrope.
II:II.

Nutter, Mrs. Charles Read See Addison, Medora C.

Nwankwo, Chimalum (b. 1945)
Asphalt.
Poem: "In sand."

Nwosu, Maik
Ballad of the Rainmaker.

Nye, Jim (b. 1939)
Dead Weight.

Nye, Naomi Shihab (b. 1952)
Across the Bay.

Arabic.
Arabic Coffee.
Art of Disappearing, The.
At Mother Teresa's.
Boy Removes All Traces from His Room, The.
Catalogue Army.
Endurance of Poth, Texas, The.
Famous.
For Mohammed Zeid, Age 15.
Fuel.
I Still Have Everything You Gave Me.
Jerusalem.
Kindness: "Before you know what kindness
  really is."
Last Day of August, The.
Little Brother Poem, The.
Lost Parrot, The.
Lunch in Nablus City Park.
Man Who Makes Brooms, The.
Mind of Squash, The.
Morning Paper, Society Page.
My Father and the Fig Tree.
New Year.
Ongoing.
Rain: "Teacher asked Paul, A."
Rebellion against the North Side.
Rider, The.
Shapes of Mouths at Parties, The.
Shoulders.
Site of the Indian Fights of 1871, Abilene.
Small Vases from Hebron, The.
So Much Happiness.
Steps.
Thinking About Cows at Ten O'Clock in the
  Morning, Abilene.
Traveling Onion, The.
Vocabulary of Dearness.
What Brings Us Out.
Whole Self, The.
Yellow Glove.
Nyhart, Nina
Playing the Part.
Shoes, The.
Vow.
Nyka-Niliunas, Alfonsas
Winter Landscape.
Nystrom, Debra (b. 1954)
Homesteaders.
Insomnia.
Regardless of the Final Score.
Nyunai, Jean-Paul (b. 1951)
Hour of Life, An.

O

O Cham (fl. 1274–1308)
Turkish Bakery, The.
Ó Dálaigh, Muireadhach Albanach (fl. 1200–24)
Elegy on Mael Mhedha, his Wife.
O Direain, Mairtin (1910–88)
Era's End.
Memory of Sunday.
Strong Beams.
O Riordain, Sean (1917–77)
Claustrophobia.
Fever.
Frozen Stiff.
Mount Melleray.
My Mother's Burial.
Switch.
Syllabling.
Ó Searcaigh, Cathal (b. 1956)
Clay Pipes, The.
Lament: "I cried on my mother's breast, cried
  sore."
Runaway Cow, A.
Oakes-Smith, Elizabeth (1806–93)
Atheism, sels.
Ode to Sappho.
Sinless Child, The, sels.
Unattained, The.
Oandasan, William (b. 1947)
Acoma.

Grandmothers Land.
Past, The, sels.
Song of Ancient Ways, The.
Oates, Joyce Carol (b. 1938)
Edward Hopper's Nighthawks, 1942.
Insomnia.
Waiting on Elvis, 1956.
Obadike, Mendi Lewis (b. 1973)
Fifteen.
Protest Poem.
Tradition/Abstraction.
Obejas, Achy
Dancing in Paradise.
Lifes.
Public Place (After Olga Broumas), The.
Sunday.
Obenzinger, Hilton
This Passover or the Next I Will Never Be in
  Jerusalem.
Obradović, Biljana Dragoslav
Intrusion, The.
O'Brien, Charlotte Grace (1845–1901)
River, The: "Poor Mick was trotting on to the
  town."
O'Brien, Fitz-James (1828–62)
Ghost, The.
Soldier's Letter, A.
O'Brien, Geoffrey (b. 1948)
Aubade 2.
Bed in the Wilderness, The.
Lake, The.
Techniques of Mass Persuasion.
O'Brien, John
Revelation on a Summer Walk.
"O'Brien, John" See Hartigan, Patrick Joseph
O'Brien, Lawrence F.
Diabolus in Musica.
O'Brien, Michael
Poem: "Little bones of."
O'Brien, Sean (b. 1952)
After Laforgue.
Amateur God, The.
Before.
Cousin Coat.
HMS Glasshouse.
In Residence: A Worst Case View.
Welcome, Major Poet!
O'Callaghan, Conor (b. 1968)
Anon.
Bypass, The.
Coventry.
East.
Fall.
Green Baize Couplets.
History of Rain, The.
Loose Change, sels.
On Re-entering the Lavender City.
Pigeons.
River at Night.
O'Callaghan, Julie (b. 1954)
Federal Case.
Managing the Common Herd: Two Approaches
  for Senior Management.
Ocampo, Silvina
Report on Heaven and Hell.
Occom, Samson (1723–92)
Waked [or Wak'd] by the Gospel's Powerful
  Sound.
Ochiai Naobumi (1861–1903)
Song of the Faithful Daughter Shiragiku.
Ochester, Ed (b. 1939)
Mary Mihalik.
Pocahontas.
Thanksgiving.
Working at the Wholesale Curtain Showroom.
**O'Connell, Eibhlin Dubh (Eibhlin Dubh Ni
Chonaill) (b. 1743)**
Death of Art O'Leary, The, sels.
O'Connell, Eileen (b. c.1743)
Dirge on the Death of Art O'Leary.
**O'Connor, Frank (Michael Francis O'Donovan)
(1903–66)**
Exile: "What happier fortune can one find."

Learned Mistress, A.
O'Connor, Mark (b. 1945)
Fire.
Sun-Hunters, The.
Turtles Hatching.
O'Connor, Mike
Kuan-Yin Shan: Mother-of-Mercy Mountain.
On the Road to Denver in a Coat and Tie, I
  Think of My Old Friend Master Red Pine
  and the Example He Inspires.
Overnight at a Buddhist Mountain Temple.
Sakura.
Soliloquy of the Danish Cloister.
O'Connor, Ulick (b. 1928)
Oscar Wilde.
O'Curry, Eugene
Litany to Our Lady.
O'Daly, Bill
Whale in the Web, The.
O'Daly, Murdoch (1180–1225)
Consecration.
Shaving of Murdoch, The.
O'Daly, Murragh (fl. c.1250)
On Killing a Tax Collector.
O'Daly, William
Naturalist, A.
O'Daniel, Wilbert Lee (1890–1969)
Beautiful Texas.
Odarchenko, Yury [or Iurii] Pavlovich (1903–60)
Claudia Petrovna.
Only for you my tea roses.
Path I'm following, The.
Odell, Jonathan (1737–1818)
Song for a Fishing Party.
Oden, Gloria C. (b. 1923)
Bible Study.
Private Letter to Brazil, A.
Review from Staten Island.
Riven Quarry, The.
Testament of Loss.
Odio, Eunice (b. 1947)
Creation.
Creation, sel.
In the Life and Death of Rosamel Del Valle,
  sels.
Letter to Carlos Pellicer.
Memory of My Private Childhood.
Prologue to a Time That Is Not Itself.
**O'Donnell, Brigid (Bríd Inían Iarla Chille Dara)
(b. c.1590, d. after 1607)**
O young man who composes the poem.
O'Donnell, Caitlin (b. 1989)
Footprints.
O'Donnell, Charles Leo (1884–1934)
Process.
Resolution.
Security.
O'Donnell, Dennis (b. 1951)
Crab, The.
Even Solomon.
Young Men of Blackburn, The.
O'Donnell, Hugh See MacWard, Owen Roe
O'Donoghue, Bernard (b. 1945)
Apparition, The.
Concordiam in Populo.
Going Without Saying.
Nun Takes the Veil, A.
Weakness, The.
O'Donoghue, Mary (b. 1975)
Bova.
Go-Summer.
Harmony in Blue.
She-Machines, The.
Stylist, The.
Textures, The.
This is Sunday.
O'Donovan, Michael Francis See O'Connor, Frank
O'Dowd, Bernard (1866–1953)
Cupid.
O'Driscoll, Dennis (b. 1954)
Experimental Animals.
Home.
Lads, The.

Life.
Lighting Up Time.
Missing God.
Someone.
Tomorrow: "Tomorrow I will start to be happy."
You.

O'Dwyer, Caley
Texas.

Oeur, U Sam *See* U Sam Oeur

Ofeimun, Odia
Beyond Fear.
Handle for the Flutist, A.
How Can I Sing.
Judgement Day.
Landing on the Moon.
Let Them Choose Paths.
Naming Day, A.
New Brooms, The.
Poet Lied, The.
Prologue: "I have come down."
Song: "You are the sandstorm beneath my skin."

Ofek, Uriel (1926–87)
Hagomel.

Ogata Kenzon (1663–1743)
Retrospective.

O'Gillan, Angus (*fl.* 14th cent.)
Dead at Clonmacnois [*or* Clonmacnoise], The.

Ogilvy, Eliza (1822–1912)
Grannie's Birthday.
Natal Address to My Child, March 19th 1844, A.
Newly Dead and Newly Born.

Ogiwara Seisensui (1885–1976)
I suck at.
It walks the sky, cloudless.
Morning with a baby crying with all its might.

O'Gnive [*or* O'Gnimh], Fearflatha (*fl.* c.1562)
Downfall of the Gael, The.
Lament of O'Gnive, The.

O'Grady, Desmond (b. 1935)
Dark Edge of Europe, The, *sel.*
Dying Gaul, The.
Great Horse Fair, The.
Hellas, *sel.*
In the Greenwood.
Lines in a Roman Schoolbook, *sels.*
Love War, The.
Page from a Diary.
Professor Kelleher and the Charles River.
Purpose.
Reading the Unpublished Manuscripts of Louis MacNeice at Kinsale Harbour.

O'Grady, Jennifer (b. 1963)
Anonymous Wedding Photo.
Buster's Last Hand.
Poem for the Womb.

O'Grady, Thomas (b. 1956)
Cormorants.
Dark Horses.
Prayer for My Daughters, A.
Some Days, Paradise.

Oguma Hideo (1901–40)
Long, Long Autumn Nights.

Ogundipe-Leslie, Molara
Nigeria of the Seventies.
On Reading an Archeological Article.
Rain at Noon-time.
Song at the African Middle Class.
Tendril Love of Africa.
Yoruba Love.

O'Hara, Frank (1926–66)
Abortion, An.
Animals.
Aus Einem April.
Autobiographia Literaria.
Ave Maria.
Blocks.
Captains Courageous.
Chez Jane.
Cornkind.
Critic, The.
Day Lady Died, The.

Elegy: "Ecstatic and in anguish over lost days."
Elegy: "Salt water. and faces dying."
Female Torso.
For Grace, after a Party.
Forest Divers.
Getting Up Ahead of Someone (Sun).
Greek Girl at Riis Beach, A.
Having a Coke with You.
Homosexuality.
How to Get There.
Ideal Bar, The.
In Favor of One's Time.
In Memory of My Feelings.
Lebanon.
Les Luths.
Lines to a Depressed Friend.
Litany, A.
Madrid.
Mary Desti's Ass.
Meditations in an Emergency.
Memorial Day 1950.
Military Ball, A.
My Heart.
Ode: Salute to the French Negro Poets.
Ode to Joy.
On Rachmaninoff's Birthday #158.
Oranges.
Painter's Son, The.
Personal Poem.
Poem: "And tomorrow morning at 8 o'clock in Springfield, Massachusetts."
Poem: "At night Chinamen jump."
Poem: "Eager note on my door said "Call me", The."
Poem: "Green things are flowers too."
Poem: "I don't know as I get what D.H. Lawrence is driving at."
Poem: "Lana Turner has collapsed!"
Poem: "Light clarity avocado salad in the morning."
Poetry.
Radio.
Raspberry Sweater, A.
Rhapsody.
Rogers in Italy.
Short History of Bill Berkson, A.
Sonnet: "Blueness of the hour, The."
Step Away from Them, A.
Steps.
To John Ashbery.
To John Ashbery on Szymanowski's Birthday.
To the Film Industry in Crisis.
To the Harbormaster.
Trout Quintet, The.
True Account of Talking to the Sun at Fire Island, A.
War, The.
Why I Am Not a Painter.
Windows.
You at the Pump.

O'Hara, Geoffrey (*fl.* 1918)
K-K-K-Katy.

O'Hehir, Diana (b. 1902)
Bedside.
Home Free.
Questions and Answers.
Wedding Banquet.

Ohnishi, Takajiro
Blossoms in the Wind.

Ojaide, Tanure
Consolation.
Daydream of Ants, The.
Emergency Kit.
Fate of Vultures, The.
Launching Our Community Development Fund.
State Executive.
Verdict of Stone, A.
Ward 6.
What They Said.
When Tomorrow Is Too Long.
Where Everybody is King.
Where the Nightmare Begins.

Ojibwa Oral Tradition
Loon upon the Lake, The.

Okamoto, Kanoko (1889–1939)
Tanka: "As I gaze upon."
Tanka: "Flower blooms, A."
Tanka: "Having let flow."
Tanka: "Innately reserved."
Tanka: "Stark naked."
Tanka: "Ten years ago."

Okantah, Mwatabu
Afreeka Brass.
African Morning.
Black Experience, The.
Market Day.
Southern Road.

Okara, Gabriel (b. 1921)
One Night at Victoria Beach.
Piano and Drums.

O'Keefe, Eamer
Chords.

O'Keefe [*or* O'Keeffe], John (1747–1833)
Amo, Amas, I Love a Lass.

O'Keeffe, Adelaide (1776–1855)
Kite, The.

Okekwe, Promise Ogochukwu
Two Beautiful Creatures.

Okereke, Chioma
Starlette.

Okigbo, Christopher (1932–67)
Come Thunder.
Elegy for Alto.
Elegy for Slit-Drum.
Elegy of the Wind.
Heavensgate, *sels.*
Hurrah for Thunder.
On the New Year.
Thunder Can Break.

Okita, Dwight
Nice Thing About Counting Stars, The.
Notes for a Poem on Being Asian American.

Okolo, M. S. C.
Still Burn.
Suspended Elegy, A.

Okpala, Jude Chudi
When Africa Speaks.

Oktavi
At Five.

Oktenberg, Adrian (b. 1947)
It was an open-air market.

Okudzhava, Bulat Shalvovich (b. 1924)
Ah, Nadya, Nadyenka.
Departure.
François Villon.
How the young flutist smiles.
I never soared, and never did I soar.
Not About Death.
Once there was a soldier boy.
Ruispiri—A Comic Ballad.
Save us, the poets, save us, we have but.
To me, Muscovites are sweethearts out of old stories.

Ōkuma Kotomichi (1798–1868)
Kite, The.
Pinwheel, A.
Vespers.

Okura *See* Yamanoé [*or* Yamanoué] no Okura

O'Lahsen, Malika (b. 1930)
Dead Erect, The.
It Took One Hundred Years.

Older, Julia (b. 1941)
Two Worlds.

Oldham, John (1653–83)
Quiet Soul, A.
Satire, A, *sel.*
Satires, *sel.*
Satyr, A, *sels.*
Satyr Address'd to a Friend That Is About to Leave the University, and Come Abroad in the World, A, *sels.*
Upon a Bookseller.

Olds, Sharon (b. 1942)
April, New Hampshire.
Beyond Harm.

Bread: "When my daughter makes bread, a cloud of flour."
Clasp, The.
Connoisseuse of Slugs, The.
Death of Marilyn Monroe, The.
Early Images of Heaven.
Ecstasy.
Eggs.
Elder Sister, The.
Exact Moment of His Death, The.
First.
First Birth.
Forty-one, Alone, No Gerbil.
Glass, The.
Good Will.
Greed and Aggression.
Guild, The.
Her First Week.
Her List.
His Ashes.
His Costume.
His Smell.
I Go Back to May 1937.
In the Hospital Near the End.
Indictment of Senior Officers.
It.
Knowing, The.
Language of the Brag, The.
Last Acts.
Last Night.
Leningrad Cemetery, Winter of 1941.
Lifelong.
Lifting, The.
May 1968.
Moment of My Father's Death, The.
Moment the Two Worlds Meet, The.
Monarchs.
Mother, The.
My Father Speaks to Me from the Dead.
My First Weeks.
Necking.
New Mother.
Nurse Whitman.
On The Subway.
Once.
One Girl at the Boys Party, The.
Photograph of the Girl.
Pope's Penis, The.
Promise, The.
Quake Theory.
Quest, The.
Race, The.
Request, The.
Satan Says.
Saturn.
Seventh Birthday of the First Child.
Sex without Love.
Sisters of Sexual Treasure, The.
Space Heater, The.
Station.
Summer Solstice, New York City.
Summer-Camp Bus Pulls Away from the Curb, The.
This Hour.
Topography.
True Love.
Try-Outs, The.
Unjustly Punished Child.
Unswept, The.
Victims, The.
Waste Sonata.
Wedding Vow, The.
Wellspring, The.
When.
Woman in Heat Wiping Herself, A.
Young Mothers 1.

Oldys, William (1687–1761)
On a Fly Drinking out of [or from] His Cup.

Olebara, Nnamdi
Warrior's Lament, A.

Oles, Carole (b. 1939)
Cedar Waxwing, The.
For the Drunk.
One Page in *The American Heritage Dictionary*.
Radioactive Ball, The.

To a Daughter at Fourteen Forsaking the Violin.

Olin, Jeni
Blue Collar Holiday.
"Colors" starring Patti, Grandma, & me at twenty-five.
Don't Let Me Eat Dinner.
Larry Kept Saying Primo Levi Was an Accident.
Like Beatrix Potter.
My Boyfriend, the Infidel.
No Matter What Sign You Are.
Para-Olympic Legacy, The.
Shark Wrangler Goes to Church, The.
Stick-up.
Tom Brokaw.
Vanishing Point.
Warner Bros. Newest Thriller *Valentine*.
Wu Gambinos.

Olinka, Sharon
Bird of Death.
Chinese Man in Smyrna, A.

Oliphant, Dave
Beaumont: Class Reunion, *sel*.
Dallas.
Denton.
Eugene Wukasch, Texas Architect.

Oliveira, David
Laurence Olivier's Hamlet.
Little Travel Story, A.
Paso Robles, San Luis Obispo, San Luis Obispo.
San Joaquin.
Summer.

Oliver, Douglas (1937–2000)
Little Night, A.
Oracle of the Drowned, The.
"u", "je", "r", "r", "im", "a", "finally."
Walnut and Lily.

Oliver, Louis (LittleCoon) (b. 1904)
Empty Kettle.
Horned Snake, The.
Wagon Full of Thunder.

Oliver, Mary (b. 1935)
At the Shore.
August: "When the blackberries hang."
Bats.
Black Snake, The.
Black Walnut Tree, The.
Crows.
Design.
Fox, The.
Foxes in Winter.
Going to Walden.
Goldenrod.
Hawk.
Hermit Crab, The.
House, The.
How Everything Adores Being Alive.
Hummingbird Pauses at the Trumpet Vine.
In Blackwater Woods.
Journey, The.
Kingfisher, The.
Landscape.
Lilies.
Little Owl Who Lives in the Orchard.
Look and See.
Morning.
Morning Poem.
Picking Blueberries, Austerlitz, New York, 1957.
Rain: "All afternoon it rained, then."
Rice.
Roses, Late Summer.
Singapore.
Skunk Cabbage.
Sleeping in the Forest.
Snapshots.
Some Questions You Might Ask.
Spring Azures.
Summer Day, The.
Swans on the River Ayr.
Through Ruddy Orchards.
University Hospital, Boston.
Waking on a Summer Morning.

West Wind, *sels*.
When Death Comes.
Where Does the Dance Begin, Where Does it End?
White Night.
Wild Geese.
Wild Geese: "You do not have to be good."
Wings.

Olivers, Thomas (1725–99)
God of Abraham praise, The.

O'Loughlin, Michael (b. 1958)
Cuchulainn.
Elegy for the Unknown Soldier.
Glasnevin Cemetery.
Irish Requiem, An.
Posthumous.
Shards, The, *sels*.

Olsen, William
Blood.
Frost's Last Lecture: A Tape: His Audience—1963.
Winter, Voyeurism.

Olson, Charles (1910–70)
Anecdotes of the Late War.
As Cabeza de Vaca was.
As the Dead Prey upon Us.
At Yorktown.
Chain of memory is resurrection I am a vain man, The.
In Cold Hell, in Thicket.
Kingfishers, The.
La Préface.
Librarian, The.
Maximus Poems, The, *sels*.
Merce of Egypt.
Moon Is the Number 18, The.
My memory is.
Newly Discovered "Homeric" Hymn, A.
O Quadriga.
Pacific Lament.
Peloria the dog's upper lip kept curling.
Perfume / of flowers! A haw, The.
Plan for a Curriculum of the Soul, A.
Sun / right in my eye.
These Days: "Whatever you have to say, leave."
Thing Was Moving, The.
Variations Done for Gerald Van De Wiele.

Olson, Elder (1909–92)
Ballad of the Scarecrow Christ.
Four Black Bogmen, The.
Presence, The.

Olson, Ted (b. 1899)
Hypothesis.

Olstein, Lisa
We Still Have Basketball, Sara.

O'Malley, Mary (b. 1954)
Shoeing the Currach.

Omar, Ibrahim al-Osta (1908–1950)
Not Quiet.

Ombres, Rossana (b. 1931)
Angel Who Separated Us with the Flame, The.
Ballad of Noah's Daughter.
Bella and the Golem.
Embalmer.
Ensnaring Flower of Psalms.
Excursion to Ravenna of A Young Girl with Her Parents, *sels*.
Meadow Bug.
Nursery Rhyme in Eight Strophes.
Rondeau Tempo.
Sentimental Suffering of the Oyster of Smoke.
Strange Adventure.
Talin of the Pasta Factory.
Twelve.
White House, A.

Ome Shushiki (1668–1725)
After dream / How real.
Frost of separation / Father, child.

O'Meally, Bob (b. 1948)
Make Music with Your Life.

Omer, Hillel (1926–90)
Squad in the Land, A.
To the Memory of a Comrade.

Word from the Gray Soldiers.

Onassis, Jacqueline Kennedy (1929–94)
Meanwhile in Massachusetts.
Sea Joy.
Thoughts.

Ondaatje, Michael (b. 1943)
Agatha Christie Books By The Window, The.
Bearhug.
Bessie Smith at Roy Thomson Hall.
Biography: "Dog scatters her body in sleep, The."
Buried, sel.
Buried 2, sel.
Burning Hills.
Cinnamon Peeler, The.
Dates.
Driving with Dominic in the Southern Province We See Hints of the Circus.
Elizabeth.
Gentleman Compares His Virtue to a Piece of Jade, A.
Henri Rousseau and Friends.
House on a Red Cliff.
Inner Tube.
King Kong Meets Wallace Stevens.
Letters & Other Worlds.
Light.
Nine Sentiments, The.
Notes for the Legend of Salad Woman.
Rat Jelly.
Rock Bottom, sel.
7 or 8 Things I Know About Her—A Stolen Biography.
Strange Case, The.
Tin Roof, sel.
To a Sad Daughter.

O'Neill, Ann
Dr Hanagan.

O'Neill, Eugene (1888–1953)
Lament of a Subwayite.
To a Bull Moose.

O'Neill, Mary
Sound of Water.
What Is Black?

O'Neill, Moira (Nesta Higginson Skrine) (1870–1955)
Grand Match, The.

O'Neill, Rose Cecil (1874–1944)
I Made a House of Houselessness.

Oness, C. Mikal
August 1990.
Climbing.
Of All There Is.
Pulling in the Nets.

Onitsura (Uejima Onitsura) (1661–1738)
Autumn wind / Across the fields.
Cherry blossoms, The.
Come! Come! Though I call.
Leaping trout sees, The.
Plum blossoms / One's nose.
To finally know.
True obedience.

Onitsura, Uejima See Onitsura

Ono, Yoko (b. 1933)
Mother of the Universe.
Painting to be Constructed in Your Head.
Painting To Hammer a Nail.
Smoke Painting.

Ono no Komachi (834–80)
Although my feet.
Autumn nights, it seems.
Diver does not abandon, A.
Doesn't he realize / that I am not / like the swaying kelp.
I long for him most.
Thinking about him.
Though I go to you.
When longing for you.
Yielding to a love.

Ono no Yoshiki (d. 902)
Kokin Shu, sel.

Ontjes, Linden
Kepler Considers the Dimensions of a Sheep.

Oodgeroo of the tribe Noonuccal (Kath Walker) (1920–93)
Dawn Wail for the Dead.
Last of His Tribe.
No More Boomerang.
We Are Going.

O'odham, Tohono [Owl Woman] [Juana Manwell]
Songs for the Four Parts of the Night.
Songs for Treating Sickness, Sung during the Four Parts of the Night, sels.

Ōoka Mokoto (b. 1931)
Marilyn.

Oomen, Anne-Marie
Peaches: "In the only moment of ecstasy I have."

Oommen, George
Private Sorrow, A.

Opie, Amelia Alderson (1769–1853)
Negro Boy's Tale, The.
Ode to Borrowdale in Cumberland.
On the Approach of Autumn.
Stanzas Written Under Aeolus' Harp.
To a Maniac.
To Mr. Opie, On His Having Painted for Me the Picture of Mrs Twis.
To Winter.

Opitz, Martin (1597–1639)
Ah Dearest, let us haste us.
Concerning the Wolffsbrunnen near Heidelberg.
I'll lay this halfway me, which we the body name.
To This Book.
With snowy light of moon I cannot you compare.
You golden freedom, both my wish and my desire.

Opoku-Agyemang, Kwadwo (b. 1951?)
King Tut in America.

Oppen, George (b. 1908)
Animula.
As I saw.
Bad times: / The cars pass.
Bicycles and the Apex, The.
Bolt / In the frame.
Boy's Room.
Building of the Skyscraper, The.
Chartres.
Civil war photo.
Closed car—closed in glass.
Confession.
Daedalus: The Dirge.
Deaths everywhere.
Disasters.
Drawing.
Eclogue: "Men talking, The."
Edge of the ocean, The.
Evening, water in a glass, The.
Exodus.
Five Poems about Poetry, sel.
Flight: "Outside the porthole life, or what is."
Forms of Love, The.
Fragonard, / Your spiral women.
From a Photograph.
From Disaster.
From this distance thinking toward you.
Gold on Oak Leaves.
Gold on Oak Leaves Said Young.
Her ankles are watches.
Image of the Engine.
In Memoriam Charles Reznikoff.
It brightens up into the branches.
Knowledge not of sorrow, you were, The.
Lights, paving—, The.
Mast / Inaudibly soars; bole-like, tapering, The.
Myself I Sing.
Myth of the Blaze.
Near your eyes.
No interval of manner.
O city ladies.
Occurrences, The ("Simplest / Words say the grass blade, The.").
Of Being Numerous, sels.

On the water, solid.
Party on Shipboard.
Pedestrian.
Penobscot.
Population.
Power, the Enchanted World.
Product.
Psalm: "In the small beauty of the forest."
Resort.
Route.
Semaphoring chorus.
She lies, hip high.
Solution.
Some San Francisco Poems, sels.
Survival: Infantry.
This land: / The hills, round under straw.
Three wide, The / Funnels raked aft, and the masts slanted.
Thus / Hides the.
To the Poets: To Make Much of the World.
Town, a town.
Tug against the river.
Undertaking in New Jersey, The.
Whirl Wind Must, The.
White. From the / Under arm of T.
Who comes is occupied.
Written structure.

Oppenheim, Meret (1913–85)
Dream in Barcelona.
Finally.
If You Say the Right Word, I Can Sing.
My Friend's Dog.
Rêve à Barcelone.
Round the World with the Rumpus God.
Where Is the Wagon Going?
Without Me Anyway.

Oppezzo, Piera (b. 1934)
Demand.
Iteration.
Now Melanctha Had neither Home, nor Regular Occupation. Life Was Just Beginning for Her.
Project.
Ready-Made World.

Oppian of Apamea [or Pella] (fl. 3rd century)
Cynegetica, sels.

Oppian [of Corycus] (fl. 2nd cent)
Halieutica, sels.

Oquendo de Amat, Carlos (1905–36)
Poem of the Sea and of Her.

O'Rahilly [or O'Reilly or Ó Rathaille], Egan [or Aodhagán] (1670–1726)
Enchanted Mistress, The.
Grey Eye Weeping, A.
Inis Fal.
Lament for Tadhg Cronin's Children.

Orban, Otto (b. 1936)
Blade of Grass, A.
Chile.
Letter, The.

O'Reilly, Caitríona
Augury.
Brief History of Light, A.
Duets.
Envoi: "And although it will be."
Flames and Leaves.
Hide.
Lecture Upon the Bat, A.
Octopus.
Possession.
Proserpine.
Qing Dish, A.
Six.
Thin.
To the Muse.
Weekend in Bodega Bay, A.

O'Reilly, John Boyle (1844–90)
White Rose, A.

O'Reilly, Michael (d. 1988)
Abused Child.
House Call to a Man with Parkinson's Disease, A.
Potter.
Small Girl Brings an Injured Bird into the Surgery, A.

Orerulavanar
What He Said.
Oresick, Peter
American Peace, An, *sel.*
Orientius (c.450)
Poem on Divine Providence, *sel.*
"Orinda" *See* Philips, Katherine
Orléans, Charles, Duc d' (1391–1465)
Balade.
Ballade: "I was in blossom when I was a child."
Go forth myn hert wyth my lady.
Las! Mort Qui T'a Fait Si Hardie.
Lost.
Quant Souvenir Me Ramentoit.
Roundel: "Take, take this cosse, atonys, atonys, my hert!"
Smiling Mouth [and Laughing Eyen Grey], The.
Temps a Laissié, Le.
Orlen, Steve [or Stephen] (b. 1942)
Androgyny.
Happy As I Am.
Onomastics and the Falling Snow.
Orlovsky, Peter (b. 1933)
Collaboration: Letter to Charlie Chaplin.
Dick Tracy's Yellow Hat.
Dream May 18, 1958.
I Dream of St. Francis.
Poems from Subway to Work.
Snail Poem.
Orlowsky, Dzvinia
Losing My Hair.
To Our Cosmeticians.
Ormond, John (1923–90)
Ancient Monuments.
At His Father's Grave.
Cathedral Builders.
Certain Questions for Monsieur Renoir.
Definition of a Waterfall.
Design for a Quilt.
Design for a Tomb.
Gift, The.
In September.
Key, The.
Lament for a Leg.
My Dusty Kinsfolk.
My Grandfather and His Apple-Tree.
To a Nun.
Ormsby, Eric (b. 1941)
Jaham Sings of the Fear of the Moon.
My Mother in Old Age.
Origins.
Skunk Cabbage.
Starfish.
Ormsby, Frank (b. 1947)
Day in August, A.
Home.
Landscape with Figures.
My Careful Life.
Northern Spring, A, *sels.*
Paris Honeymoon, A, *sels.*
Passing the Crematorium.
Spot the Ball.
Under the Stairs.
War Photographers, The.
Winter Offerings.
O'Rourke, Donny (b. 1959)
Algren.
Clockwork.
Letter From My Father, A.
Wine and Wooing.
Orozco, Olga (b. 1920)
Miss Havisham.
Olga Orozco.
Reality and Desire.
There Are No Doors.
To Make a Talisman.
Twilight (Between Dog and Wolf).
Orpingalik
Alcheringa Definitions.
Songs Are Thoughts, Sung Out with the Breath.

Orr, Gregory (b. 1947)
All Morning.
Available Now: Archaic Torsos of Both Sexes.
Best.
City of Salt, The.
Cliff, The.
Dark Prayer.
Father's Song.
Gathering the Bones Together.
Gray Fox, The.
Hand, The: "Brightness Falls from the Air."
Insomnia Song.
Lament: "I thought of you."
Meadow in Spring.
Some Part of the Lyric.
Sweater, The.
We Must Make a Kingdom of It.
Who'd Want to Be a Man?
Orr, Thomas Alan
Soybeans.
Orrick, John
Wild Plum.
Orten, Jiri
Last Poem, The.
Whispered.
Ortiz, Deanna
Again.
Ladders.
Ortiz, Simon J. (b. 1941)
Bend in the River.
Creation.
Dry Root in a Wash.
Earth and Rain, the Plants & Sun.
Final Solution: Jobs, Leaving.
Four Bird Songs.
From Sand Creek, *sel.*
Juanita, Wife of Manuelito.
Look to the Mountain.
My Father's Song.
My Mother and My Sisters.
On late-night television, two U.S. scientists talk about why the U.S.
Poems from the Veterans Hospital, *sels.*
Returned from California.
San Diego Poem, A: January–February 1973.
Serenity in Stones, The.
Speaking.
Spreading Wings on Wind.
State's Claim That It Seeks in No Way to Deprive Indians of Their Rightful Share of Water, The.
Story of How a Wall Stands, A.
Telling About Coyote.
Travels in the South.
Upstate.
Vision Shadows.
Watching You.
What I Tell Him.
Wind and Glacier Voices.
Wisconsin Horse, The.
Yuusthiwa.
Orton, Barbara J. (b. 1969)
Bacchanal.
Beekeeper.
Love Poem.
Sea Monkeys, The.
Orwell, George (Eric Blair) (1903–50)
Italian soldier shook my hand, The.
Ory, Carlos Edmundo de (b. 1923)
Silence: "No one's here I'm alone with the violin of silence."
Osbey, Brenda Marie (b. 1951)
Everything Happens to (Monk and) Me.
Geography.
Osborn, John
Whaling Song, A.
Osborne, Jennie
Naming of Flowers, The.
Osgood, Frances Sargent (1811–50)
Ah! Woman Still.
Ellen Learning to Walk.
Garden of Friendship, The.
He Bade Me Be Happy.
Lines: "Oh, ye who in those Houses hold."

Maiden's Mistake, The.
Wraith of the Rose, The.
Osgood, Francis P. (b. 1910)
Winter Fairyland in Vermont.
Osgood, Kate Putnam (1841–1910)
Driving Home the Cows.
O'Shaughnessy, Arthur William Edgar (1844–81)
Ode: "We are the music-makers."
Song: "I made another garden, yea."
Osherow, Jacqueline
Dust on the Mantel: Sonnet.
Ghazal: Comet.
My Cousin Abe, Paul Antschel and Paul Celan.
Phantom Haiku/Silent Film.
Scattered Psalms, *sels.*
Song for the Music in the Warsaw Ghetto.
To Eva.
Villanelle for the Middle of the Night.
Villanelle from a Sentence in a Poet's Brief Biography.
Yiddish Muses, The.
Yom Kippur Sonnet, with a Line from Lamentations.
Ōshima Ryōta (1718–87)
On rainy leaves / Glow.
Pure brush-clover / Basket of flowers.
Oshio
Stepping through snow.
O'Siadhail, Micheal
Between.
Welcome.
Osman, Jena
Dropping Leaflets.
Twelve Parts of Her, *sels.*
Osofisan, Femi (b. 1946)
Longing.
Paris Latin Quarter.
Release.
She Thinks in Song.
Osorio Benitez, Miguel Angel *See* Barba-Jacob, Porfirio
"Ossian" *See* Macpherson, James
Ossip, Kathleen (b. 1959)
Nature of Things, The.
Nursling.
Osterhaus, Joe (b. 1960)
Gambier.
New York Minute.
Pepper.
Shall We Dance.
Ostriker, Alicia (b. 1937)
After the Shipwreck.
Army of Lovers, An.
Boys, the Broom Handle, the Retarded Girl, The.
Bride, The.
Eighth and the Thirteenth, The.
I Brood about Some Concepts, for Example.
I Can't Speak.
Idea of Making Love, The.
In the Twenty-Fifth Year of Marriage, It Goes On.
Lamenting the Inevitable.
Mastectomy Poems, The, *sels.*
Meditation in Seven Days, A.
Meditation in Seven Days, A, *sel.*
Millennial Polka.
Minor Van Gogh (He Speaks), A.
Opinion of Hagar, The.
Shekhinah as mute, The.
Story of Abraham, The.
Story of Joshua.
Studio, The (Homeage to Alice Neel).
To Love Is, *sel.*
Window, at the Moment of Flame, The.
Ostroff, Anthony
Sparrows at the Airport, The.
O'Sullivan, Leanne
Being Free.
Cord, The.
Earth.
Getaway Car.
Journey, The.

Prayer, The.
Therapist, The.
When We Were Good.

O'Sullivan, Maggie (b. 1951)
Doubtless, *sel.*
Giant Yellow.
Hill Figures.
Lesson from the Cockerel.
Narrative Charm for Ibbotroyd.
2nd Lesson from the Cockerel.

O'Sullivan, Vincent (b. 1937)
By the Sea-Wall.

Osundare, Niyi (b. 1947)
Excursion.
Eyeful Glances.
Goree.
I Sing of Change.
Moonsongs, *sels.*
Our Earth Will Not Die.
Waiting Laughters, *sel.*
Who Says That Drought Was Here?
Word is an Egg, The.

Oswald, Alice (b. 1966)
April: "Sheer grip and the push of it—growth
    gets, The."
Ballad of a Shadow.
Bike Ride on a Roman Road.
Excursion to the Planet Mercury.
Melon Grower, The.
Mountains.
Owl Village.
Pilchard-Curing Song, The.
Prayer: "Here I work in the hollow of God's
    hand."
Sea Sonnet.
Wedding.

Oswald, H. S. (1751–1834)
O let him whose sorrow.

Otero, Blas de (1916–79)
A Punto de Caer.
About to Fall.
Cap. 10 Lib. 2.
Censored.
Censoria.
Chap. 10 Book 2.
Children of the Planet.
Claustro de las Sombras, El.
Cloister of the Shades, The.
Escrito con Lluvia.
Especie de, Una.
Eternal, The.
Eterno, Lo.
Far Away.
Hijos de la Tierra.
Juicio Final.
Last Judgement.
Muy Lejos.
Something Like A.
Written in Rain.

Othman, Abubakar
Dual Call, The.
This Year.

Otiono, Tony Nduka (b. 1964)
Moon Dance (Listen Sylvia).
Rainsong.

Otogami
In the blackberry.

Otomo no Sakanoé, Lady (c.728–46)
Don't you cut the brush.
It is other people who have separated.
Though in my heart.
Till the rough-gem moon.
Where the plovers cry.

Otomo no Sakanoé, *the elder daughter of* Lady
(*fl.* 8th cent.)
Were you a string of beads.
When we could have met.

Otomo no Tabito (Tabito) (665–731)
To sit silent.

Otsu, Prince (663–86)
For You.

Otsuyu (1674–1739)
Cry of the deer / Where at its depths.

Otten, Willem Jan (b. 1951)
All Soul's Day.
Mud-Flat.
Mud-Flat.
Poet Dives, The.

Otway, Thomas (1652–85)
Enchantment, The.

Ou-yang Chiung (896–971)
Offering Congratulations to the Enlightened
    Reign.

Ou-yang Hsiu (1007–72)
Cutting, A.
Deep, Deep in the Shade of the Court.
East Wind.
Faint Thunder Drifts beneath the Willow.
Fisherman.
Green Jade Plum Trees in Spring.
Old Age.
Old Fisherman.
Pear Leaves Redden, Cicada's Song is Done,
    The.
Pool is Full of Autumn Sky, Rippled by Gentle
    Breezes, The.
Reading the Poems of an Absent Friend.
Tune: "Drunk in Fairyland."
Tune: "Gathering Mulberry Leaves."
Tune: "Magnolia Flower."

Outram, Richard (1930–2005)
Round of Life.
Tourist Stricken at the Uffizi.

Ouwens, Kees (b. 1944)
Farmer, The.
New Sweater.
Some Tears.

Overbury, E. J.
Springtime It Brings On the Shearing, The.

Overton, Ron
Blues in "C."
Fire and Ice by Robert Frost: an early draft.
Psychic Killed by Train.
Re: The Tobacco Institute.
Two Stories.

Ovid (Publius Ovidius Naso) (43 B.C.–A.D. 17)
Amores, *sels.*
Amores (after Ovid).
Confessio Amantis, *sels.*
De Ponto.
Elegies, *sels.*
Heroides, *sel.*
Invective against Ibis, *sel.*
Metamorphoses [Hughes Translation], *sels.*
Metamorphoses, *sels.*
Tristia, *sels.*
Tristium, *sels.*

Owen, Catherin *See* Llwyd, Catherin Owen

Owen, Ellis (1789–1868)
Epitaph: On the Near-Death Experience.

Owen, Gareth (b. 1922)
Gathering in the Days.
Jonah and the Whale.
Uncle Alfred's Long Jump.
Waterfall.
Winter Days.

Owen, Gerallt Lloyd (b. 1944)
Cilmeri.
Inheritance: "We had a country to keep."
Man on the Horizon, The.
Shame of Llanfaes, The.
To the Death.

Owen, Gilberto (1905–52)
Interior.

Owen, Goronwy (1723–69)
Elegy for His Daughter Ellen.
Invitation, The.

Owen, J. Dyfnallt (1873–1956)
Hour of Fear.

Owen, Jan
Visitation, The.

Owen, Louise
Chart Showing Rain, Winds, Isothermal Lines
    and Ocean Currents.

Owen, Maureen (b. 1943)
African Sunday.
All That Glitters.

For Emily (Dickinson).
Topography.

Owen, Sue
Written in Blood.

Owen, Wilfred (1893–1918)
A Terre.
Anthem for Doomed Youth.
Apologia Pro Poemate Meo.
Arms and the Boy.
At a Calvary near the Ancre.
Conscious.
Disabled.
Dulce et Decorum Est.
End, The.
Exposure.
From My Diary, July 1914.
Futility.
Greater Love.
Hospital Barge at Cérisy.
Insensibility.
Maundy Thursday.
Mental Cases.
Miners.
Music.
Parable of the Old Men and the Young, The.
S.I.W.
Send-Off, The.
Sentry, The, *sel.*
Show, The.
Sonnet, to a Child.
Strange Meeting.
To Eros.
To My Friend (With an Identity Disc).
To ———: "Three rompers run together, hand
    in hand."
Unreturning, The.

Owens, Philip (b. 1947)
Croeso i Gymru.

Owens, Rochelle (b. 1936)
Dedication.
I Am the Babe of Joseph Stalin's Daughter.
W.C. Fields in French Light, *sel.*

Owenson, Sydney, Lady Morgan (1783?–1859)
Fragment 3.
Joy.
Lay of an Irish Harp, or Metrical Fragments,
    The, *sels.*

Owl Woman *See* O'odham (Juana Manwell),
    Tohono

Oxenham, John (William Arthur Dunkerley)
(1861–1941)
All One in Christ.
Dies Ire-Dies Pacis.
Fair Raiment.
Hammer and Anvil.
My Treasure.
Profit and Loss.
Pruner, The.
So Little and So Much.
Vimy Ridge.
Watchman! What of the night?

Oxley, William
Men stare at me more than at women.

Oxlie, Mary, of Morpeth (*fl.* c.1656)
To William Drummond of Hawthornden.

Oyake
Hidden in the clouds.

Oyewole, Abiodun
We're Not Well Here.

Ozaki Hosai (1885–1926)
All day long.
I have no bowl.
In coughing too.
Splendid breasts.
When I wash the soles of my feet.

Ozawa Roan (1723–1801)
By the Ōi River.

Özer, Adnan (b. 1957)
Unknown Love.

Ozer, Kemal (b. 1935)
For Many Years.

Ozick, Cynthia (b. 1928)
In the Synagogue.
Origins, Divergences.

When That with Tragic Rapture Moses Stood.
Wonder-Teacher, The.
Yom Kippur, 5726.

P

P, Koven L. *See* Paul, Cauvin L.
Pacheco, José Emilio (b. 1939)
Boundaries.
Enquiry Concerning the Bat, An.
From Some Time to This Place.
High Treason.
Job 18, 2.
On the Fragile Labyrinth.
Song to Be Written on a Wave.
Pack, Robert (b. 1929)
Black Hole, The.
Bounty.
Elk in Winter.
Fathering the Map.
Her Black Hair.
It Would Have Been Enough.
Mountain Ash without Cedar Waxwings.
Proton Decay.
Thrasher in the Willow by the Lake, The.
Watchers.
Padel, Ruth (b. 1946)
Angel.
Icicles Round a Tree in Dumfriesshire.
On the Line.
On the Venom Farm.
Scotch.
Skin.
Starling, The.
Tell Me About It.
Tinderbox.
Trial.
Yew Berries.
Padgett, Ron (b. 1942)
Big Bluejay Composition.
Blue Bananas.
Bun.
Detach, Invading.
Early Triangles.
Fairy Tale: "Little elf is dressed in a floppy cap, The."
Famous Flames.
First Drift.
Flower's Escape.
High Heels.
Joe Brainard's Painting "Bingo."
Ladies and Gentlemen in Outer Space.
Light as Air.
Louisiana Perch.
Love Poem: "We have plenty of matches in our house."
Lucky Strikes.
Morning.
Nothing in That Drawer.
Ode to Bohemians.
Poem for El Lissitzky.
Poetic License.
Prose Poem: "Morning coffee, The. I'm not sure why I drink it."
Reading Reverdy.
Second Why.
Something or Other.
Statue of a Libertine, The.
Symbols of Transformation.
Talking to Vladimir Mayakovsky.
Tell Us, Josephine.
Voice.
Waterloo Sunset.
Who and Each.
Within the Dome.
Wonderful Things.
Padilla, Heberto (b. 1932)
Daily Habits.
Discourse on Method, The.
Fountain, a House of Stone, A.
History.
In Trying Times.
Landscapes.
Legacies.

Man on the Edge.
Nuclear Umbrella.
Prayer for the End of the Century, A.
Promise, The.
Question for the Frankfurt School, A.
Self-Portrait of the Other.
Sometimes I Plunge into the Ocean.
Song of the Juggler.
Paek Sŏk (1912–?)
Mountain Rain.
Natasha, the White Donkey, and I.
On the White Wall.
Samch'ŏnp'o.
Sound of the Mountain Bird.
Pafunda, Danielle (b. 1977)
RSVP.
Saltbox Brothel.
Page, Ebony
To Become Unconscious.
Page, G. K.
Kaleidoscope.
Page, Geoff (b. 1940)
Elegist, The.
Grit.
In Dante's Hell.
Inscription at Villers-Bretonneux.
Jerry's Plains, 1848.
Late Night Radio.
Premeditations.
Road Show.
Smalltown Memorials.
Page, Patricia K. (b. 1916)
About Death.
After Rain.
Alphabetical, *sel.*
Castle, The.
Cross.
Deaf-Mute in the Pear Tree.
Disguises, The.
Funeral Mass.
Images of Angels.
Landlady, The.
Metal and the Flower, The.
Permanent Tourists, The.
Photos of a Salt Mine.
Planet Earth.
Schizophrenic.
Selves, The.
Stenographers, The.
Stories of Snow.
Suffering.
T-Bar.
Typists.
War Lord in the Early Evening.
Water and Marble.
Young Girls.
Pagis, Dan (1930–1986)
Art of Reduction, The.
Autobiography.
Autobiography.
Autobiography.
Balloons.
Battle, The.
Conversation.
Devotion.
Draft of a Reparations Agreement.
Ein Leben.
Ein Leben.
End of the Questionnaire.
Europe, Late.
Evidence.
Footprints.
Homily.
In the Laboratory.
Instructions for Crossing the Border.
Last Ones, The.
Late Author: Snapshot in the Rain, The.
Lesson in Observation, A.
Mosquito, The.
Picture Postcard from Our Youth.
Ready.
Roll Call, The.
Roll-Call in the Concentration Camp.
Scrawled in Pencil in a Sealed Car.
Snake.

Sominex.
Souvenir, The.
Story, The.
Testimony.
Twelve Faces of the Emerald.
Twenty Years in the Wadi.
Wall Calendar.
Winter's End.
Written in Pencil in the Sealed Railway-Car.
Pahmeier, Gailmarie (b. 1957)
Grief Comes in Smallest Ways.
Sunday Baking.
Pai, Shin Yu (b. 1975)
Circle, triangle, square.
Fall aster with firefly.
Fruit They Had in Common.
Gathering at the Orchid Pavilion, The.
Milkstone.
Office Feng Shui.
Poem: "Life, A / of collecting pollen."
Yes Yoko Ono.
Pain, Philip (d. 1668?)
Meditation 8.
Paine, Robert Treat (1773–1811)
Adams and Liberty.
Paine, Thomas (1737–1809)
Liberty Tree.
Paino, Frankie
Each Bone of the Body.
Matter of Division, A.
1965.
Truth, The.
Painter, F. V. N. (Franklin Verzelius Newton) (1852–1931)
Pastoral, A: "Sun looks o'er the mountain fair, The."
Paisley, Janet (b. 1948)
Feminist.
Intellectual, The.
Turning, The.
Paiute Oral Tradition
Like always / like forever.
Pak Chaesam (1933–97)
Autumn River in Burning Tears.
Immortals' Paduk Game.
In sunlight suffused.
Looking at Winter Trees.
Night at Tongbak Temple.
Nothing.
Road Back, The.
Sound of the Taffy-Seller's Shears.
Spring's Path.
Pak Hyogwan (c.1850–80)
If my lovesick dream.
She came to my dream.
Pak Illo (1561–1643)
Lament on the Water.
Song of Peace.
Pak Inhwan (1926–56)
Fortnight.
Rocking Horse and the Lady, The.
Sleepless Night, A.
Towards a New Resolve.
When Seasons Pass.
Pak Mogwŏl [*or* Mokwŏl] (1916–78)
April.
Bare Wind, A.
Blue Deer.
Family.
Hanbok.
Nature of Gravel, The, *sels.*
Prayer in Four Verses.
Wayfarer, The.
Pak Nohae (b. 1957)
How Much Is This One?
Road to Corruption, The.
Wind to the Stones, The.
Pak P'aengnyŏn
Upon Listening to the Flute.
Pak Sôwôn (b. 1960)
Highway, The.
Lies: "Little bitch!"
Menstrual Irregularities.
Midnight Caller, The.

Obsession: "Knife on the fruit dish, The."
Plantain.
Recurring Nightmare, A: My Amputation.
Small Wooden Vessel, A.
To the Man Holding a Sickle.
Wind God Sends Forth, The.

Pak Tujin (1916–98)
Book of Poems.
Inscription Etched by Water.
Song in a Graveyard.
Sun.
Tobong Mountain.

Palasovszky, Ödön (1899–1980)
Humiliating the Laser-Beam.
Lapiade, Opus 3.
Susannah Bathing.

Palazzeschi, Aldo (1885–1974)
Nuns Go Walking.
Stranger, The.

Palés Matos, Luis (1898–1959)
Calling, The.
Elegy for the Duke of Marmalade.
Pueblo.

Paley, Grace (b. 1922)
Here.
People in My Family.
Sad Children's Song, The.
Some days I am lonesome I want to talk to my
mother.
Two Villages.
Warning, A.

Palgrave, Francis Turner (1824–97)
Eutopia.

Palis, Yolanda
Floor, The.
Waking Up.

Paljor, Ngodup (1947–88)
Cars stuck in the snow.
Exhausted by jogging.
I woke up early.
Robert Frost and I.
Way, The.
Wish of my Amala, The.

Palladas [or Pallades] (360–430)
Grammar commences with a 5-line curse.
Having Slept with a Man.
Loving the rituals that keep men close.
Murderer and Sarapis, The.
Poor devil that I am, being so attacked.
Racing, reckoning fingers flick.
This Life a Theater.
When you send out invitations, don't ask me.
Where the Three Roads Meet.
Whose baggage from land to land is despair.
Women all / cause rue.

Palma, Michael (b. 1945)
Coming of Age.

Palmer, Debbra
Wade's Hoggers.

Palmer, Herbert Edward (b. 1880)
Ishmael.
Woodworker's Ballad.

Palmer, John Williamson (1825–1906)
Stonewall Jackson's Way.

Palmer, Julea (fl. 1671–3)
Fruit of Sin, or a Lamentation for England,
The.

Palmer, Michael (b. 1943)
All those words we once used for things but
have now discarded in order to come to
know things.
Autobiography 2 (hellogoodby).
Autobiography: "All clocks are clouds."
Barely anything to say, everything said.
Construction of the Museum.
Dearest Reader.
Desire was a quotation from someone.
Dream of a Language that Speaks.
Eighth Sky.
Erolog.
Fifth Prose.
Flower of Capital, The.
H.
Here the image of a child on a hill.

I am an architect in Vienna.
I Do Not.
I killed a bee on the Street of Scissors.
Letters to Zanzotto, sels.
Man Undergoes Pain Sitting at a Piana, A.
Ninth Symmetrical Poem.
Noche, Una.
Notes for Echo Lake 3.
Nowness and nowness sings the crow.
O you in that little bark.
Of This Cloth Doll Which.
Or Anything Resembling It.
Painted Cup, The.
Project of Linear Inquiry, The.
Recursus.
Said the speaker.
Series, sels.
Seven Forbidden Words.
Six Hermetic Songs, sel.
Song of the Round Man.
Sonnet: "Now I see them sitting me before a
mirror."
Sun ("Headless man walks, lives, A."), sel.
Sun ("Write this. We have burned all their
villages.").
Theory of the Flower, The.
This Time.
Thought, The.
Twenty-four Logics in Memory of Lee
Hickman.
Untitled (April '91).
Untitled (February 2000).
Village of Reason, The.
Voice and Address.
We will call today.
Wheel.
Word is coming up on the screen, give me a
moment, A.
Words, The.

Palmer, Opal (b. 1954)
Wasting Time.

Palmer, R. F.
Conchie, The.

Palmer, Ray (1808–87)
Hymn: "Jesus these eyes have never seen."
My Faith Looks Up to Thee.

Palmer, Ron
Logic of Queerness, The: (Releasing Your Ivy
Evening Within).

Palmer, Ronald D.
Sterling Brown.

Palmer, T. H. (1782–1861)
Try, Try Again.

Palmer, Vance (1885–1959)
Farmer Remembers the Somme, The.
Snake, The.

Paloff, Benjamin
My Corpses.
On Transportation.

Paman, Clement (fl. c.1660)
On Christmas Day to My Heart.

Pambardu
Windmill At Mandanthanunguna.

Pan Chao (A.D. 48–117?)
Needle and Thread.
Needle and Thread, The.

Pan Chieh-yû (fl. c.48–46 B.C.)
Fan-Piece, for Her Imperial Lord.
Present from the Emperor's New Concubine,
A.
Song of Regret.

P'an Yüeh (d. 300)
Homeward.
In Mourning for His Dead Wife.

Pande, Mrinal (b. 1946)
Two Women Knitting.

Pandeya, Sudama See "Dhoomil"

Pankey, Eric (b. 1959)
As We Forgive Those.
Confession of Cleopas, The.
Reason, The.
Resurrection of the Body, The.
St. Luke, sel.
Unstrung Lyre, The.

**Panmure, Margaret Maule, Countess of (c.1667–
1731)**
Now let us unto some fair Medow goe.

Pannonius, Janus (1434–72)
About a Transdanurban Almond Tree.
About the Shipwrecked Frandus.
Difficult and Weighty Question, A.
Farewell to Várad.
On the Bird Which Still Flew, Though Its Head
Was Severed.
One for Pope Paul.
To Mars, a Prayer for Peace.

"Panormitanus" (Antonio Beccadelli)
Rome.

Pantani, Marco (1970–2004)
Sometimes We Close Our Eyes.

"Pantycelyn" See Williams, William

Pao Chao (414–66)
Ascend Lu-Shan.
Ballad: A Song in the Night.
Ballad in Imitation of "The Prince of
Huainan."
Ballad: The Boatman's Song.
Dalei Riverbank.
Desolate City, The: A Rhapsody.
Folded Wings.
Goblet of Wine, A.
Going Out Through the North Gate of Chi.
Grass by the River, The.
Imitating the Old Poems.
Magic Cinnabar.
Rough Road, A.
Ruined City, The.
Scholar Recruit, The.
This Bronze Censer.
Water Spilt.
Weary Road, The, sels.

Pao Hsien (fl. 10th cent. A.D.)
Autumn Path.
Sent to Yuan Chen at White Cabin Peak.
Written on the Wall at Master Wei Feng's.

Pao Ling-hui (fl. 5th cent.)
Added to a Letter Sent to a Traveler.
In the Key of Farewell.
Poem Sent to a Traveler.

Papago
There was a mountain, over its black roots [the
deer].

Papaionnou, Yannis (1913–72)
Nights Without Hope (Rebetiko Song).

Papaleo, Joseph (d. 2004)
American Dream: First Report.

Pape, Gertrude (1907–88)
Lake, The.

Pape, Greg (b. 1947)
Birds of Detroit.
Dinner on the Miami River.
In Line at the Supermarket.
In the Bluemist Motel.
Indian Ruins Along Rio de Flag.
Minotaur Next Door, The.
Storm Pattern.
Storm Surf.
Street Music.

Paquet, Basil T.
Basket Case.
It Is Monsoon at Last.

Paquin, Ethan (b. 1975)
Capstone.
Hearing Music Through Dark Trees.
Where Were You.
Woe.

Paramore, Edward E., Jr. (1895–1956)
Ballad of Yukon Jake, The.

Pardlo, Gregory
Harvest: A Line Drawing.

Pardo, Patrick (b. 1969)
I was on the couch when the jehova's
witnesses came.

Paredes, Emilia
Gathering the Wild Figs—Vizcaina, Gomera.

Parfi, Rauf (b. 1943)
Today I dreamed all day. I dreamed.

Parham, Mary Gomez
Belize Cemetery, The.
Chasm.
Other People's Pain.
Tarde de Sol.

Parini, Jay (b. 1948)
After the Terror.
Belonging.
Bliss.
Coal Train.
Function of Winter, The.
Mizzle.
Ruined House, The.
Some Compensation.
Stars Falling.
To His Dear Friend, Bones.

Paris, Traci
First Proof.
Memory Span of a Goldfish Is Three Seconds, The.
Reception.

Parish, Mitchell
Deep Purple.
Sophisticated Lady.
Star Dust.
Stars Fell on Alabama.
Sweet Lorraine.

Parke, Walter (b. 1845)
Buying a Cycle.

Parker, Alan Michael
Abandoing All Pretense, the Vandals.
Above the Timberline.
After the Poem Who Knows.
Alchemy.
Another Poem about the Vandals.
Cruelty, the Vandals Say.
Days like Prose.
Driving Past My Exit.
Eclipse, The: "Having never been to a drive-in movie."
God of Pepper, The.
Lullaby: "Sleep and rain, two gangsters."
Magpie.
No Fool, the God of Salt.
Practicing Their Diffidence, the Vandals.
Sears Catalogue, The.
Vandals Dying, The.
Vandals, Horses.
Vandals in the Garden.
Vandals, The.

Parker, Bonnie (1910–33)
Story of Bonnie and Clyde, The.

Parker, Dominique (b. 1964)
Art of the Nickname, The.
Foxfire.
Sand.
When Mark Deloach Ruled the World.

Parker, Dorothy (1893–1967)
Anecdote: "So silent I when Love was by."
Autumn Valentine.
Ballade at Thirty-Five.
Bohemia.
Bric-à-Brac.
Certain Lady, A.
Chant for Dark Hours.
Coda: "There's little in taking or giving."
Comment.
Danger of Writing Defiant Verse, The.
Experience.
Fighting Words.
Flaw in Paganism, The.
Frustration.
General Review of the Sex Situation.
Healed.
Indian Summer.
Inscription for the Ceiling of a Bedroom.
Inventory.
Little Old Lady in Lavender Silk, The.
Maid-Servant at the Inn, The.
Men.
Neither Blood Nor Bowed.
News Item.
Observation.
On Being a Woman.
One Perfect Rose.

Penelope.
Pictures in the Smoke.
Pig's-Eye View of Literature, A, *sels.*
Portrait of the Artist.
Pour Prendre Congé.
Prophetic Soul.
Red Dress, The.
Résumé.
Sanctuary.
Social Note.
Song of One of the Girls.
Sonnet for the End of a Sequence.
Story.
Symptom Recital.
Tombstones in the Starlight, *sels.*
Unfortunate Coincidence.
Words of Comfort to Be Scratched on a Mirror.

Parker, Sir Gilbert (1862–1932)
Reunited.

Parker, Martin (c.1600–c.1656)
Cupid's Wrongs Vindicated, *sel.*
Maunding Soldier; or, The Fruits of Warre Is Beggery, The.
Well Met Neighbour, *sel.*

Parker, Patricia (b. 1944)
For Willyce.
I Have a Dream.
Where Will You Be?

Parkerson, Michelle (b. 1953)
Statistic.

Parkes, Bessie Rayner (1829–1925)
Dream Fears.
For Adelaide.
Summer Sketches, *sels.*
To an Author who Loved Truth More than Fame.
To Elizabeth Barrett Browning.

Parkinson, Thomas (1920–92)
Homage to a Tom-Cat.

Parks, Roland A. (b. 1955)
Dawn of Freedom.
Song of Freedom, A.

"Parley, Peter" *See* Goodrich, Samuel Griswold

Parnell, Pat
Apotheosis of Medusa.
Medusa and Perseus III: Lilith.
Sheila the Hat.
Sile Na gCioch.

Parnell, Thomas (1679–1718)
Hezekiah, *sel.*
Night Piece on Death, *sel.*
Song: "When thy beauty appears."

Parnok, Sofiya (1885–1933)
Childhood memory: those pears, A.
I shall not lie to find a lurid rhyme.
Through a Window-Light.

Paros, Euenus the Grammarian, Euenus of Askelon, Euenus of *See* Euenus

Parr, Catherine, Lady Borough (1512–48)
In Contemplation of My Wretched Life, *sel.*

Parra, Nicanor (b. 1914)
Anti-Lazarus, The.
Discourse of the Good Thief, The.
I Move the Meeting Be Adjourned.
I Take Back Everything I've Said.
Individual's Soliloquy, The.
Inflation.
Journey Through Hell.
Letters from the Poet Who Sleeps in a Chair.
Letters to an Unknown Woman.
Litany of the Little Bourgeois.
Lord's Prayer.
Man, A.
Modern Times.
Mummies.
New Sermons and Preachings of the Christ of Elqui (1979), *sel.*
Note on the Lessons of Antipoetry.
Piano Solo.
Pilgrim, The.
Poems of the Pope, The.
Resounding Zero, A.
Roller Coaster.

Roller Coaster.
Sentences.
Seven Voluntary Labors and One Seditious Act.
Something Like That.
Test.
To Make a Long Story Short.
Tunnel, The.
Vices of the Modern World.
Viper, The.
Warnings.

Parra, Violeta (1917–62)
At the Center of Injustice.
Attention Young Bachelors.
Because the Poor Have Nothing.
Here's to Life.
I Curse in the Highest Sky.
I Thank Life for So Many Gifts.
Song for a Seed.
To Be Seventeen Again.
Why Is It This Way, Almighty God?

Parrington, Georgia Bailey (*fl.* 1907)
Elegy to a Dissected Puppy, An, *sel.*

Parrott, E. O.
More Bagpipe Music.

Parry, David Fisher (b. 1908?)
Miniver Cheevy, Jr.

Parry, Edward Abbott (1803–1943)
I Would Like You for a Comrade.

Parry, Joseph (1841–1903)
New Friends and Old Friends.

Parry, R. Williams (1884–1956)
A E Housman.
Branwen's Starling.
Fox, The.
Geese, The.
Hedd Wyn.
J S L.
Miraculous Dawn.
Mortality.
Old Boatman of Death's River, The.
Old Boatman, The.
On a Soldier Killed in the Great War.
Pagan.
Propaganda of the Poet, The.
Spring: "After the bitter weather."
Strangeness of Dawn, The.
Two Hearts Divided.
Wales 1937.

Parry-Williams, T. H. (1887–1975)
Barrenness.
Christmas Carol, A: "It is close to a quarter of a century since then."
Christmas Carol: "Close to a quarter of a century since then."
Conviction.
From a Travel Diary.
Girl on the Quay at Rio, The.
Life: "O the blessedness of life! It's lucky, no doubt."
Llyn y Gadair.
Return.
These Bones.
This One.
Tŷ'r Ysgol.
Two Poems.

Parson-Nesbitt, Julie
Strange Country.

Parsons, William (1758?–1828)
Moods 3.

Partlow, Lucy
Overworked.

Partnoy, Alicia (b. 1955)
To *El Mingo* (with Whom I Share Eva Victoria and Anahi Paz).

Partridge, Dixie (b. 1943)
Hostage.

Partridge, Elise
Vuillard Interior.

Pascal, Paul (b. 1925)
Tact.

Paschen, Elise
Angling.
Between the Acts.

Birth Day.
Confederacy.
Litany.
12 East Scott Street.
Two Standards.
Voir Dire.

Pasha, Koja Râgıb (1699–1763)
Dark thought is revealed in the twists and
    curves.

Páskándi, Géza (1933–95)
First Resurrection.
Language Memory, *sels.*
Last Will and Testament.

Pasman, Heinz
Black Hairs, The.

Pasolini, Pier Paolo (1922–75)
Civil Song.
Day of My Death, The.
Desperate Vitality, A, *sel.*
Lines from the Testament.
Part of a Letter to the Codignola Boy.
Prayer to My Mother.
Presence, The.
Redefining "Orthodoxy."
Roman Evening.
St. John, *sel.*
Sex, Consolation for Misery.
Southern Dawn.

Pasos, Joaquín (1914–47)
This Is Not Her.

Passerat, Jean (1534–1602)
Song: "Shephard loveth thow me vell?"
Sonnet Addressed to Henry III on the Death of
    Thulène, the King's Fool.
Villanelle: "I've lost her now, my turtle-dove."

Pastan, Linda (b. 1932)
After Minor Surgery.
Agoraphobia.
Apple Shrine, The.
Ars Poetica.
At Gettysburg.
At the Jewish Museum.
At the Train Museum.
Baseball.
Beall Mountain Seasonal.
Bess.
Birds, The.
Death's Blue-Eyed Girl.
Departures.
Early Afterlife, An.
Egg.
Erosion.
Ethics.
Five Stages of Grief, The.
Hardwood.
Hat Lady, The.
I Am Learning to Abandon the World.
Imperfect Paradise, The, *sels.*
Last Train, The.
Love Poem.
Marks.
Muse.
Name, A.
Obligation to Be Happy, The.
Old Photograph Album.
Orpheus.
Overture.
Passover.
Remembering Frost at Kennedy's Inauguration.
Returning.
Self-Portrait.
September.
Shadblow.
Short History of Judaic Thought in the
    Twentieth Century, A.
Stationary Bicycle.
To a Daughter Leaving Home.
Turnabout.
25th Anniversary.
Weather.
What We Want.
Who Is It Accuses Us?

Pasternak, Boris Leonidovich (1890–1960)
As With Them.
Christmas Star, The.

Courage.
Don't Touch.
Evil Days, The.
Fresco Come to Life.
Garden of Gethsemane, The.
Hamlet.
Illness, *sel.*
Indian Summer.
Let the Words.
Magdalene (I).
Mary Magdalene (I).
Miracle, The.
Mirror, The.
Moochkap.
St. Mark, *sels.*
St. Matthew, *sels.*
St. Matthew, *sel.*
Snow Is Falling.
Storm, an Endless Instant.
Sultry Night, A.
To Be Famous Isn't Decent.
To Love.
White Night.
Wind, The.
Winter Night.
Winter Night: "Snow, snow over the whole
    land."

Pastior, Oskar (b. 1927)
Abracadabra.
Ble.
Irreversible? Is time—were it as itself—
    reading underneath the influence of
    palindromitis.
O Magdalen!
What, However, is the discretion of left to
    your?

Pastnor, Paul
Silent Steed, The.

Pastorius, Francis Daniel (1651–1720)
Delight in books from evening.
Penance, A.

Pat Ellis Taylor See LittleDog, Pat

Patacara (*fl.* 6th cent. B.C.)
When they plow their fields.

Patchen, Kenneth (1911–72)
Body Beside the Ties, The.
Character of Love Seen as a Search for the
    Lost, The.
Deer and the Snake, The.
Do the Dead Know What Time It Is?
Eight Early Poems, *sels.*
Empty Dwelling Places.
Figure Motioned with Its Mangled Hand
    Toward the Wall Behind It, The.
From My High Love.
Great-Sledmakers, The.
Horses of Yilderin, The.
In Memory of Kathleen.
Like a Mourningless Child.
Lions of fire, The.
Lonesome Boy Blues.
Moon, Sun, Sleep, Birds, Live.
O All Down within the Pretty Meadow.
'O Now the Drenched Land Wakes.'
Only Cherries?
Origin of Baseball, The.
Pastoral: "Dove walks with sticky feet, The."
Religion Is That I Love You.
State of the Nation, The.
Street Corner College.
23rd Street Runs into Heaven.
We Go Out Together.

Pater, Walter (1839–94)
Mona Lisa.

Paterson, Andrew Barton (1864–1941)
Father Riley's Horse.
Mulga Bill's Bicycle.
Old Australian Ways.
Travelling Post Office, The.

Paterson, Don (b. 1963)
Chartres of Gowrie, The.
Eyes, The.
Imperial.
Poetry: "In the same way that the mindless
    diamond keeps."

Private Bottling, A.
St Brides: Sea-Mail.
Trans-Siberian Express, The.
White Lie, The.
Wreck, The.

Paterson, Evangeline
Griselda.
History Teacher in the Warsaw Ghetto Rising.

Pathabhi (b. 1919)
Moon in China Bazaar.
Sita.

Pāthak, Ganapti
I'll worship You with tears, Ma.

Patmore, Coventry Kersey Dighton (1823–96)
Angel in the House, The, *sels.*
Fool and Wise.
Rods and Kisses.
Unknown Eros, The, *sels.*
Vesica Piscis.
Victories of Love, The, *sels.*

Patrick, Saint (*fl.* c.5th cent.)
St Patrick's Breastplate.
Saint Patrick's Breastplate; or, The Deer's Cry.

Patten, Brian (b. 1946)
Complacent Tortoise, The.
How the New Teacher Got Her Nickname.
Job Hunting.
Lion and the Echo, The.
Squeezes.
Through frost and snow and sunlight.
What Happened to Miss Frugle.

Patterson, G. E. (b. 1960)
Autobiographia.
Autobiography of a Black Man.
BLS
I Used to Go to Church.
Lament.
Letter from Home.
Saint's First Wife Said, The.

Patterson, Ian (b. 1948)
Hardihood, *sels.*

Patterson, Raymond R. (b. 1929)
Black Power.
Forerunner.
Harlem Suite.
Hopping Toad Blues.
Lumumba Blues.
No Jive.
Sundown Blues.
Twenty-Six Ways of Looking at a Blackman.
You Are the Brave.

Patton, Charlie (1887–1934)
High Water Everywhere.

Patton, Lee
When Everything Is Goneril.

Patumanār
What She Said.

Pātunī, Nīlmani (d. 1825)
Ma, Hara's Beloved, Tara.

Pau-Llosa, Ricardo
Frutas: "Growing up in Miami any tropical
    fruit I ate."
Hollow, The.
Kendall Gulls.
Noah.
Paredón.
Quilt Complex.
Segovia.

Pauker, John (1921–91)
Jethro Somes' Apostrophe to His Former
    Comrades.

Paul, Cauvin L.
Flame.
Georgina.

"Paul, John" See Webb, Charles Henry

Paul, Louis (1901–70)
Cynical Portraits.

Paulding, James Kirke (1779–1860)
Backwoodsman, The, *sels.*

Paulin, Tom (b. 1949)
Anastasia McLaughlin.
Cadaver Politic.
Desertmartin.

Impossible Pictures, The.
In the Lost Province.
Lonely Tower, The.
Lyric Afterwards, A.
Manichean Geography I.
Off the Back of a Lorry.
Other Voice, The.
Peacetime.
Personal Column.
Pot Burial.
Presbyterian Study.
Settlers.
Sting, The.
Surveillances.
Ulster Unionist Walks the Streets of London,
    An.
Under the Eyes.
Where Art Is a Midwife.
Written Answer, A.

Paulinus of Nola (353–431)
To Ausonius.

Paulus [or Paulos] Silentiarius (fl. c.560)
And there lay the lovers, lip-locked.
Come, give me kisses, Rhodope.
Even clothed in wrinkles, dear Philinna.
Take off your clothes, my love!
Tantalos.

Pavese, Cesare (1908–50)
August Moon.
Goat God, The.
Grappa in September.
Morning Star.
Poetics.
Words from Confinement.

Pavlich, Walter
Black Flower.

Pavlov, Konstantin (b. 1933)
Adaptation.
End of Mythology, The.
Interview from the Belly of a Whale.
Wonderful in Poetry, or a Victim of Goldfish,
    The.

Pavlova, Karolina (1807–93)
Crone, The.
Life calls us, and we go, massing our courage.

Pavlova, Vera (b. 1963)
And God saw.
Armpits smell of linden blossom.
Grass: "Oh praise the lowly stalk."
Heaven and Earth.
Letter from Memory, sels.
On the way to you.
Signs of Life, sels.
This is the way a row of official tulips.

Pawlak, Mark
Ace.
After Burying Her Son, A Mother Speaks.
All the News—September 23, 2001.
East-West Dialog 2002.
Official Versions.
Protective and Defensive Devices.

Pawlikowska-Jasnorzewska, Maria (1845–1945)
Polish Colours.

Pawnee Oral Tradition
Song of the Pleiades.

Payn, James (1830–98)
Our Dog Jock.

Payne, Fredrica Africa
Conjugation of the verb: to blow.

Payne, John Howard (1791–1852)
Clari, the Maid of Milan, sels.

Paz, Octavio (b. 1914)
After: "After chopping off all the arms that
    reached out to me."
Along Galeana Street.
As One Listens to the Rain.
Between Going and Staying.
Between What I See and What I Say.
Blanco, sel.
Brotherhood.
Certainty.
Dawn.
Exclamation.
Girl.

Grove, The.
Here.
Here.
Hymn Among the Ruins.
I Speak of the City.
Key of Water, The.
Lake.
Landscape.
Mystery.
Native Stone.
Pause.
Reliefs.
Relieves.
Response and Reconciliation.
Shrine.
Small Variation.
Solo for Two Voices.
Stanzas for an Imaginary Garden.
Sunstone, sels.
Sunstone, sels.
Tree Within, A.
Village.
Wind and Water and Stone.
Writing.

P'Bitek, Okot (1931–82)
Eyeshop, The.
Song of Lawino, sels.

Peabody, Josephine Preston (1874–1922)
After Music.
Far-Off Rose, A.
House and the Road, The.

Peacock, Molly (b. 1947)
Anger Sweetened.
Breakfast with Cats.
Buffalo.
ChrisEaster.
Desire.
Devolution.
Dogged Persistence.
Dream Come True.
Fare, The.
Good Girl.
Have You Ever Faked an Orgasm?
How I Come to You.
How I Had to Act.
Land of the Shí, The.
Little Miracle.
Lull, The.
Lullaby: "Big as a down duvet the night."
Matins.
My God, Why Are You Crying?
Next Afternoon.
Of Night.
Purr, The.
Raptor, The.
Return, The.
Say You Love Me.
Spell, The.
Surge, The.
Sweet Time.
Those Paperweights with Snow Inside.
Veil of If, The.
Wheel, The.
Why I Am Not a Buddhist.

Peacock, Thomas Love (1785–1866)
Crotchet Castle, sels.
Ghosts, The.
Grave of Love, The.
Gryll Grange, sels.
In the days of old.
Legend of Manor Hall, The.
Maid Marian, sels.
Misfortunes of Elphin, The, sels.
Nightmare Abbey, sel.
Rhododaphne, sel.
Rich and Poor; or, Saint and Sinner.

Peacocke, M. R. (b. 1930)
At the Entrance.
Final reductions.
Goddess, The.
In Memoriam.
Late Snow.
Railway Allotments.
Remembrance.
Soap.

We're Staying at the Castlemount, Western
    Esplanade.

Peake, Mervyn Laurence (1911–68)
Conceit.
I cannot give the reasons.
O here it is! And there it is!
Rhyme of the Flying Bomb, The, sel.

Pearlberg, Gerry Gomez
Dog Star.
Loop-the-Loop in Prospect Park (1905).
Marianne Faithfull's Cigarette.
Sailor.
Think Back.

Pearlman, Bill
Child of Wonder.
Endings.
Staying in Touch.

Pearse, Jimmy
Willesden Gree.

Pearse, Padraic (1880–1916)
I Am Ireland.
Naked I Saw You.
Wayfarer, The.

Pearson, Ted
Sound Check.

Peate, Iorwerth Cyfeilog (1901–82)
Airstrip St Athan.
Museum Piece.
Roncesvalles.

Peaux, Augusta (1859–1944)
Cold Landscape.
Old Houses on the Quays.
Spring Landscape.

Peck, John (b. 1941)
Anti-dithyrambics.
Archeus Terrae.
Campagna.
End of July.
From the Viking Museum.
Metal Denser Than, and Liquid, A.
Monologue of the Magdalene.
Mount Bromley Hymn.
Vega over the rim of the Val Verzasca.
Woods Burial.

Peck, Robert Newton
Four of July.

Pecor, Amanda
Product of Evolution, I Invest in a Mutual
    Fund, A.

Pedernal See Feierstein, Ricardo

Pederson, Cynthia S.
Summer Recital.

Pedretti, Erica
Dogs Are Supposed.
Heimgarten.
Here.
It's Snowing in Plouda.
No, That Can't Be.
What Difference Does it Make.

Pedro, Joao (b.1948)
Homecoming.

Peele, George (1559–96)
Anglorum Feriae, sel.
Arraignment of Paris, The, sels.
Old Wives' [or Wife's] Tale, The, sels.
Polyhymnia, sels.

Peeradina, Saleem (b. 1944)
Song of Surrender.
Testament.

Pegram, Amelia Blossom
Burials.
Deliverance.
I Will Still Sing.
Mr. White Discoverer.
Towards Abraham's Bosom.

Pegram, Lisa
Perspective.
Yellah.
Yet another epiphany.

Pei Di
Wheel River, sels.

Peirce, Kathleen
Alcoholic's Son at Ten, The.

Farmers.
Near Burning.
Need Increasing Itself by Rounds.
Quilts.
Riddles: "He opens her. She can't have him."
Peire Cardenal (c.1225–72?)
Clerks pretend to be shepherds, and under,
The.
Peiyu, Gong *See* "Shu Ting"
Pelegrin, Alison
Trailer Trash.
Pelham, Sarah
When i was young.
Pelizzon, V. Penelope (b. 1967)
Clever and Poor.
Feast of San Silvestro, The.
Late Apostasy, A.
Wedding Day, The.
Pelletiere, Marcia
Under Her Crib.
Pellicer, Carlos (1899–1977)
Flocks of Doves.
Studies.
To Poetry.
Wishes.
Pembroke, Mary Sidney Herbert, Countess of (1561–1621)
Dialogue between two shepherds, Thenot and Piers, in praise of ASTRÆA.
If Ever Hapless Woman Had a Cause.
Our Saviour's Passion, *sel.*
Psalms, *sels.*
To the Thrice-Sacred Queen Elizabeth.
Pendell, Dale (b. 1947)
Amra: The Neuropharmacology of Nirvana.
Pender, Lydia
Lizard, The.
Peniarth Poet, The (*fl.* **after 1484)**
Drinking Song, A, *sel.*
Penn, Maggie
Calling Up the Spirit of the Lost Child.
Penn, Peggy (b. 1931)
Soup, The: "On the day of your scan, I make a soup."
Penn, Robert E.
Hand.
Morning Songs.
Penna, Sandro (1906–77)
Always boys in my poems!
Found—my little angel.
Lady on Streetcar.
Life...is remembering waking up.
My poetry will not be.
Pitiless war of love I fought, A.
Shadowless sun on male bodies.
When I don't feel well, I wander among.
Pennar, Meirion (b. 1944)
Branches of a Mabinogi.
Ecce Homo: "On the threshold of the black cave."
Lovers: "As a blind man."
Reading Croce.
Penoyer, Ron
Countdown.
Penrose, Valentine
À mes carreaux.
At My Windows.
Beautiful or Ugly It Doesn't Matter.
Datura the Serpent, The.
I Dream.
May—1941.
Pluie retrouvant, La.
Rain Finding Once More, The.
There Is the Fire.
To a Woman to a Path.
Pepler, H. D. C. (1878–1951)
Concerning Dragons.
Peppermint, Heidi (b. 1971)
Real Toads.
Peralta Family Oral Tradition
O Blanca Virgen.
Percival, James Gates (1795–1856)
Coral Grove, The.

Morning among the Hills.
Perdomo, Willie
New Boogaloo.
Nigger-Reecan Blues.
Revolutionary.
Unemployed Mami.
Pere, Vernice Wineera
At the Wall.
Pereira, Peter (b. 1959)
Pot of Red Lentils, A.
Pereira, Sam
Entity of Its Word, An.
Perelman, Bob (b. 1947)
Broken Mirror, The.
China.
Chronic Meanings.
Cliff Notes.
Here 2.
Let's Say.
Marginalization of Poetry, The.
Money.
Room.
Seduced by Analogy.
Things.
Péret, Benjamin (1899–1959)
Allo.
Clin d'oeil.
Fountain.
Hello.
Hymn of the Patriotic War Veterans.
Joan of Arc.
Listen.
Little Song of the Maimed.
My Final Agonies.
Nungesser und Coli Sind Verreckt.
On All Fours.
152 Proverbs Mis au Goût du Jour, *sel.*
Où Es-Tu.
Source.
Where Are You.
Wink.
Pérez Conde, Pedro
Ak'a ta majtanal te lotil.
Flor de oro.
Flower of Gold.
Give Away the Lie.
Regala la mentira.
Ta te/ak'etik yorail ya x-ajk'otajik.
Tiempo de bailar los árboles.
Time for Trees to Dance.
Xnich k'anal tak'in.
Pérez Estrada, Rafael (1934–2000)
My Uncle the Levitator.
Unpublished Man, The.
Peri Rossi, Cristina (b. 1941)
Evohé, *sel.*
Perillo, Lucia Maria (b. 1958)
Body Mutinies, The.
Dangerous Life.
Destruction of the Mir, The.
Deuxieme Sexe, La.
Floating Rib, The.
For Edward Hopper, from the Floor.
For I Have Taught the Japanese.
For the Pileated Woodpecker and Its Cousin, the Ivory-Billed, Who May or May Not Be Extinct.
Ghost Shirt, The.
Lament in Good Weather.
Needles.
Shrike Tree.
Skin: "Back then it seemed that wherever a girl took off her clothes the police would find her."
Sweaters, The.
Urban Legend.
Perk, Jacques (1859–1881)
Iris.
Perkins, Silas H.
Common Road, The.
Perrie, Walter (b. 1949)
Exilics: Leaving Lochboisdale, 1919.
Perrier, Anne (b. 1922)
All Earth's Things.

Toutes les choses de la terre.
Perrine, Laurence (b. 1915)
Janus.
Limerick: "Sex-life her husband dreamed of, The."
Perronet, Edward (1725–92)
All Hail the Power of Jesus' Name.
Perry, Grace (b. 1927)
Time of Turtles.
Perry, Lilla Cabot (1848–1933)
Quatrain: Forgive Me Not.
Perry, Stephen
Fugue.
Orpheus.
Toadfish.
"Perse, St.-John" (Alexis Saint-Léger Léger) (1887–1975)
Anabasis, *sels.*
Bird, The.
Chanson: "Il naissait un poulain sous les feuilles de bronze."
Chanson: "Mon cheval arrêté sous l'arbre plein de tourterelles."
Exile, *sel.*
Nocturne: "Now! they are ripe, these fruits of a jealous fate."
Nocturne: "Voici mûrs, ces fruits d'un ombrageux destin, Les."
Song: "I have halted my horse by the tree of the doves."
Song: "Under the bronze leaves a colt was foaled."
Persius (Aulus Persius Flaccus) (A.D. 34–62)
Satires, *sels.*
Pertillar, Tammy Lynn
Generation Gap.
Peruñcattan
What Her Girl-Friend Said.
Peseroff, Joyce
After the Argument.
Hardness Scale, The.
Raptor in the Kitchen.
Stray Moth, Asleep.
Peshew, Abdula
Fratricide.
Peskett, William (b. 1952)
Bottles in the Zoological Museum.
From Belfast to Suffolk.
Inheritors, The.
Question of Time, The.
Star and Sea.
Window Dressing.
Pessoa, Fernando (1888–1935)
Autopsychography.
I the roses love in the gardens of Adonis.
Maritime Ode, *sel.*
My smalltown bell.
No One in the Wide Wilderness of the Wood.
Oblique Rain, *sel.*
Rather the Bird Flying By and Leaving No Trace.
Segue O Teu Destino.
"Startling Reality of Things," The.
35 Sonnets, *sel.*
Pestel [*or* **Pestell], Thomas (1585–1667)**
Psalm for Christmas Day.
Peter, Robert (*fl.* **1800)**
On Time, Death, and Eternity.
Peters, Lenrie (b. 1932)
Home Coming.
I am asking about the way ahead.
Isatou Died.
Peters, Nancy Joyce (b. 1936)
General Strike.
To the Death of Mirrors.
Petersen, Marc
What I Would Do.
Petersen, Paulann
Groom of the Animal-Bride.
I Listen to Alice Walker on a Pocket Radio.
Peterson, J. Cody
La Jolla. In 3 Acts.

Peterson, Jim
  As If.
  Stand Still.
Peterson, Liza Jessie
  Wake Up, My Little Pretties.
Peterson, Mattie J.
  I Kissed Pa Twice after His Death.
  Old Homestead, The, *sel.*
Peterson, Robert (b. 1924)
  Autumn.
  Brief History of the City.
  Now and Then.
  San Quentin 1968.
  September 5.
Peterson, Ruth Delong (b. 1606)
  Midwest Town.
Petit, Pascale (b. 1953)
  During the Eclipse.
  Embrace of the Electric Eel.
  Fish Daughter, The.
  My Father's Clothes.
  My Mother's Clothes.
  My Mother's Skin.
  Self-Portrait as a Warao Violin.
  Snake Dress, The.
  Strait-Jackets, The.
Petőfi, Sándor (1823–49)
  At the End of September.
  Autumn Again.
  Cart With Four Oxen,The.
  Clouds, The, *sels.*
  Fate Give Me Space.
  Hungary.
  I'll Be a Tree.
  I'm Troubled By One Thought.
  Like Clouds.
  National Song.
  Okato-Otaia.
  On Hope.
  Plans Gone Up In Smoke.
  Puszta in Winter,The.
  Shepherd Rides on Donkey-Back, The.
  Sir John, The Hero, *sel.*
  Some Old How.
  Song of the Dogs, The.
  Song of the Wolves,The.
  Time of Fear, A.
  Tisza, The.
  To János Arany.
Petrarca, Francesco *See* Petrarch, Francesco
Petrarch (Francesco Petrarca) (1304–74)
  Bicause I have the still kept fro lyes and
    blame.
  Ever mine [*or* myn] hap[pe] is slack and
    slo[w] in coming [*or* commyng].
  For Whatever Animals Dwell On Earth.
  If constancy in love, if a brave heart.
  Love delivers to me its sweetest thoughts.
  Sonnet: "When she walks by here."
  Sonnets to Laura, *sels.*
  Soote Season, The.
  Woods Are Wild and Were Not Made for Man,
    The.
Petri, György (b. 1913)
  By an Unknown Poet from Eastern Europe,
    1955.
  Christmas 1956.
  Electra.
  Gratitude.
  Morning Coffee.
  Night Song of the Personal Shadow.
  To Be Said Over and Over Again.
  To S.V.
Petrie, Paul (b. 1936)
  Indoor Cat, The.
Petröczy [*or* Petröczi], Kata Szidónia (1662–1708)
  Light of Our Souls.
  Rapid Floods.
Petronius Arbiter (Caius Petronius Arbiter) (d. A.D. 66)
  Beauty is not enough; who wishes to be fair.
  Coition's brief, a nasty cheat.
  Doing, a filthy pleasure is, and short.
  Good God, What a Night That Was.
  Long may our hearts, Nealce, guard that night.
  Man in the Middle of the Street.
  My bed was soft, the early night was bliss.
  Satyricon, *sel.*
Petrov, Valeri (b. 1920)
  Cry from Childhood, A.
Petrova, Aleksandra (b. 1964)
  Again sick. / Just now somehow paler.
  In Juda desert.
  Tarantino's languor and dreaming back.
Petrovykh, Maria (b. 1908)
  Air Is Motionless with Heat, The.
Petrushevskaya, Liudmila (b. 1938)
  Poor Ruth.
Pettit, Michael
  Self-Portrait Approaching Promontory, Utah.
  Vanna White's Bread Pudding.
Petty, Noel
  Great Poll-Tax Victory of '88, The.
  It was in the Spring of 1825.
  There's a Breathless Hush.
Peynetsa, Andrew
  Shumeekuli, The.
Pezoa Velíz, Carlos (1879–1908)
  Country Funeral.
Pfeiffer, Emily Jane (1827–90)
  Among the Hebrides.
  Any Husband to Many a Wife.
  Aspiration.
  Bower among the Beans, The.
  Chrysalis, A.
  Cruse of Tears, The. A Russian Legend.
  Fight at Rorke's Drift, The.
  Klytemnestra.
  Lost Light, The.
  Mid-Ocean.
  Nathaniel to Ruth.
  Out of the Night, *sel.*
  Peace to the odalisque, the facile slave, *sel.*
  Song of Winter, A.
  Sonsy Milkmaid, The.
  Studies from the Antique.
  To a Moth that Drinketh of the Ripe October.
  To Nature, *sels.*
  Witch's Last Ride, The.
Phách, Lê Cu' *See* Du Tü' Lê
Phaedrus (*fl.* c. 8 A.D.)
  Widow and the Soldier or: The Measure of a
    Woman's Inconstancy and Lust, The.
  Wolf and the Lamb, The.
Phaire, Dorothy
  Irresistible Light, An.
Pham Tien Duat (b. 1941)
  To Return to the Urges Unconscious of their
    Beginnings.
Phelp, J. A.
  Duke Of Buccleuch, The.
Phelps, Dean (b. 1929)
  Ordinary Country Girl, An.
Phi, Thien-bao Thuc
  Asian Am Anthem, An.
Philip, John (b. 1927)
  Manly Ferry.
Philipott, Thomas (c.1616–82)
  To Sir Henry Newton, upon His Re-edifying
    the Church of Charleton in Kent.
Philips, Ambrose (1675–1749)
  Ode: To Miss Margaret Pulteney [Daughter of
    Daniel Pulteney, Esq., in the Nursery].
  To the Right Honorable Robert Walpole, Esq.
  To the Right Honourable Charles Lord Halifax
    [one of the Lords Justices appointed by his
    Majesty], *sels.*
  Winter-Piece, A.
  Wit and Wisdom.
Philips, Joan *See* "Ephelia"
Philips (*or* Phillips], John (1676–1709)
  Cyder, *sels.*
Philips, Katherine ("Orinda") (1631–64)
  Advice to Virgins.
  Answer to Another Persuading a Lady to
    Marriage, An.
  Corneille's Pompey, *sels.*
  Country Life, A.
  Enquiry, The.
  Epitaph on her Son H. P. at St. Syth's Church
    [where her body also lies Interred].
  Friendship in Emblem[e], or the Seal[e], to my
    dearest Lucasia.
  Friendship's Mystery[s], to my dearest Lucasia.
  Irish Greyhound, The.
  L'Amitié: To Mrs M Awbrey.
  Lucasia, Rosania and Orinda Parting at a
    Fountain, July 1663.
  Married State, A.
  On the 3 of September, 1651.
  On the Death of My First and Dearest Child,
    Hector Philips.
  On the Welsh Language.
  Orinda to Lucasia.
  Orinda to Lucasia Parting, October, 1661, at
    London.
  Retired Friendship, To Ardelia, A.
  To Antenor.
  To Mrs M. A. at Parting.
  To Mr. Henry Lawes.
  To My Excellent Lucasia, On Our Friendship.
  To Rosania (now Mrs Montague) Being With
    Her, 25th September 1652.
  To the Queen of Inconstancy, Regina Collier,
    in Antwerp.
  Upon the Double Murther of King Charles I.
  Upon the Graving of her Name upon a Tree in
    Barnelmes Walks.
  Wiston Vault.
Phillimore, John Swinnerton (1873–1926)
  In a Meadow.
Phillips, Carl (b. 1959)
  Abundance.
  Africa Says.
  As a Blow, from the West.
  As from a Quiver of Arrows.
  Aubade: Some Peaches, After Storm.
  Blue: "As through marble or the lining of."
  Chamber Music.
  Clearing, The.
  Cotillion.
  Custom.
  Erasure.
  Glads.
  Going Under.
  In the blood, Winnowing.
  Kill, The.
  Late Apollo.
  Levitation.
  Little Dance Outside the Ruins of Unreason.
  Loose Hinge.
  Luck.
  Luna Moth.
  Luncheon on the Grass.
  Minotaur.
  One sees pictures of Dante.
  Our Lady.
  Parable: "There was a saint once."
  Passing.
  Pleasure.
  Reach, The.
  Recumbent.
  Regalia Figure.
  Rest of Love, The.
  Singing.
  Somewhere Holy.
  Summer, A.
  Sunday.
  To Break, to Ride.
  Toys.
  Undressing for Li Po.
  Words of Love.
  You Are Here.
Phillips, Dennis (b. 1951)
  Etudes, *sels.*
  Exile, *sels.*
  I Held the Vein, But Death.
  Means, *sel.*
  On Entries Emptiness.
  Twenty Questions, *sels.*
Phillips, Douglas (b. 1929)
  Maridunum.

Phillips, Eluned (b. 1915?)
Ties.

Phillips, Jayne Anne (b. 1952)
Night in Gracie's Face.
Pretty.

Phillips, Louis (b. 1942)
My Son Shows Me a Photograph of Michael
   Jordan Performing a Slam Dunk.

Phillips, Patrick (b. 1970)
Doe, The.

Phillips, Robert (b. 1938)
After the Fact: To Ted Bundy.
At the Summit.
Changed Man, The.
Death of Janis Joplin, The.
Drive Friendly.
Houston Haiku.
Instrument of Choice.
Panic Bird, The.
Persistence of Memory, the Failure of Poetry,
   The.
Wounded Angel, The.

Phillips, Stephen (1864–1915)
Apparition, The.

Phillpotts, Eden (b. 1862)
Man's Days.

Philoctete, René (b. 1932)
I'm Rooted.

Philodemus (c.110–c.130)
Demo and Thermion Both Slay Me.
Epigrams, sels.
I Loved—Who Hasn't?
Make the Bedlamp Tipsy with Oil.
Xanthippe, singing at her lyre.
You Cry, Whine, Peer Strangely at Me.

"Philo-Philippa" (fl. c.1667)
To the Excellent Orinda.

Philp, Geoffrey
Dance Hall.
Dance Hall: Version.
Heirlooms.
One Song.

Philpot, Tracy (b. 1961)
Clump of Gods, The.
Constellations of Self, The.
Descriptions (of Living Elsewhere).
How to Live in the Elegy.
It Was a Boy.
Louisa's Wedding.
On the Eve of Aphrodite.
Rain My Wife, The.
Road Trip as Clues, A.
Thanksgiving.
What There Is, Today.
Wildlife.

Philpot, William (1823–89)
Maritae Suae.

Phylip, Siôn (d. 1620)
Seagull, The.

Phylip, William (d. 1670)
Farewell to Hendre Fechan.

P'i Jih-hsiu (c.833–83)
Impromptu on a Hangover.

Piatt, John James (1835–1917)
Farther.
Fires in Illinois.
My Shadow's Stature.
Taking the Night-Train.
To the Statue on the Capitol.

Piatt, Sarah Morgan Bryan (1836–1919)
Answering A Child.
Army of Occupation.
Child's Party, A.
Doubt, A.
Giving Back the Flower.
Her Blindness in Grief.
Her Word of Reproach.
Hundred Years Ago, A.
If I Had Made the World.
In A Queen's Domain.
In Her Prison.
Lesson in a Picture, A.
No Help.
Palace-Burner, The.

Pique at Parting, A.
Sad Spring-Song.
Shapes of a Soul.
Stone For A Statue.
This World.
We Two.
Witch in the Glass, The.

Picabia, Francis (1879–1953)
Aphorisms.
Eunuch Unique, sels.
Spermal Chimney.

Picasso, Pablo (1881–1973)
Bottle of Suze, A.
Her Great Thighs.
9.1.59: II.
9.1.59: VI.
Ses Grosses Cuisses.

Piccione, Anthony
Watching Ants Play Soccer in Central Park.
With Whitman at the Friendship Hotel.

Piccolo, Lucio (1903–69)
Veneris Venefica Agrestis.

Pickard, Tom (b. 1946)
Bush Telegram.
Devil's Destroying Angel Exploded, The.
My Pen.
What Maks Makems.

Pickering [or Pikerying], John (b. 1567)
Horestes, sels.

Pickering, Robin
Untitled: "First thought in my head waking up
   was, oh no."

Picková, Eva (1929–43)
Fear.

Pickthall, Marjorie Lowry Christie (1883–1922)
Ebb Tide.
Lost Friend, The.
Quiet.
Resurgam.

Pierce, Todd James
Twenty-First Century, Farewell.

Piercy, Marge (b. 1936)
Air Like Stained Glass Cuts Me, The.
At the New Moon: Rosh Hodesh.
Attack of the Squash People.
Barbie Doll.
Battle of Wills Disguised, A.
Bite into the Onion.
Candle in a Glass, A.
Cast Off, The.
Cat's Song, The.
Crabs.
Cyclist, The.
Friend, The.
Growing Up Haunted.
Hello Up There.
I Will Not Be Your Sickness.
Implications of One Plus One.
In the Men's Room(s).
It Arrives Suddenly and Carries Us Off As
   Usual.
Kneeling Here, I Feel Good.
Last Scene in the First Act.
Laying Down the Tower, sels.
Learning Experience.
Low Road, The.
Maggid.
Moon Is Always Female, The.
Moonburn.
Morning Athletes.
Morning Love Song.
My Rich Uncle, Whom I Only Met Three
   Times.
On Guard.
On New Year's Day.
Postcard from the Garden.
Raisin Pumpernickel.
Sand Roads, sels.
Secretary Chant, The.
September Afternoon at Four O'Clock.
Snow, Snow.
To Be of Use.
To Have without Holding.
Token Woman, The.
Watch, The.

What's That Smell in the Kitchen?
When a Friend Dies.
You Don't Understand Me.

Pierman, Carol J.
Apparition, The.

Pierpoint, F. S. (1835–1917)
For the beauty of the earth.

Pierpoint, Katherine (b. 1961)
Combustion Engine.
Cuckoo-spit.
Dreaming Bean, The.
Going Swimmingly.
In the Outhouse.
Steeplejack.
Swim Right Up to Me.
This Dead Relationship.

Pierpont, James S.
Jingle Bells.

Pierpont, John (1785–1866)
Airs of Palestine, sels.
Fugitive Slave's Apostrophe to the North Star,
   The.
O Thou, to Whom in Ancient Time.
Warren's Address at Bunker Hill [or to the
   American Soldiers].
Word from a Petitioner, sels.

Piers, Lady Sarah (d. 1720)
To My Much Esteemed Friend on Her Play
   Call'd Fatal-Friendship.

Piersanti, Umberto (b. 1941)
In Times and Places.
Second Image Sequence.
When Slow October Changes Color.

Pierson, Ernest De Lancey (fl. 1897–1917)
Flying Wheel, The.

Pierson, Jennifer M.
Thrift Shop Ladies.

Pietri, Pedro (b. 1944)
January Hangover.

Pietri, Pedro Juan (b. 1940)
First Day of Spring, The.
First Rock and Roll Song of 1970, The.
1st Untitled Poem.
How Do Your Eggs Want You (?).
Intermission from Friday.
Intermission from Monday.
Intermission from Saturday.
Intermission from Sunday.
Intermission from Thursday.
Intermission from Wednesday.
Night Is out of Sight, The.
9th Untitled Poem.
Old Buildings, The.
7th Untitled Poem.
10th Untitled Poem.
3rd Untitled Poem.
Title of This Poem Was Lost, The.
Traffic Misdirector.

Pigott, Jean Sophia
Jesus I am resting, resting.

Pike, Manley H.
When Gerty Goes A-Wheeling.

Pilinszky, János (1921–81)
Agonia Christiana.
Apocrypha.
Auschwitz.
Crime and Punishment.
Definition of Your Attraction.
Depression.
Desert of Love, The.
Difference.
Extract from a Diary.
Fable: "Once upon a time / there was a lonely
   wolf."
Fish in the Net.
Frankfurt.
French Prisoner, The.
French Prisoner, The.
Hangman's Room, The.
Harbach 1944.
Homage to Issac Newton.
Introitus.
Life Sentence.
Monstrance.

On the Back of a Photograph.
On the Third Day.
On the Wall of a KZ-Lager.
One Fine Day.
Oratorio for a Concentration Camp.
Passion of Ravensbrück.
Passion of Ravensbrück, The.
Relationship.
Rest Is Grace, The.
Scaffold in Winter.
Stone Wall and Celebration.
Stone Wall and Fiesta.
Three-Coloured Banner.
Veil.
Your Death and Mine.

Pilkington, Laetitia (1712?–50)
Dol and Roger.
Fair and Softly Goes Far or, The Wary
    Physician.
Song, A: "Lying is an occupation."
Song, A: "Strephon, your breach of faith and
    trust."
Wish, By a Young Lady, The.

Pillen [or Pillin], William (1910–85)
Ascensions, The.

Pilling, Christopher (b. 1936)
Adoration of the Magi, The.
Affair With a Chair, An.
Cast Away.
Dear Ez.
Earth, The.
Encounter at the Post Office Counter.
Field, The.
Fran.
Nostrum.
Ophelia.
She Lies Silent.
Specimen.
Triptych.
Webern.
You and You, In the Pink.

Pinchas-Cohen, Chava (b. 1955)
Her, Me, and Yochanan.
Journey of a Doe.
My English Teacher.
Remembering Our Fathers.
Yearning of Karakashian, The.

Pindar (c.518–c.438 B.C.)
Ode on Theoxenos.
Olympian Odes, The, sels.
Pythian Odes, sels.

"Pindar, Peter" (John Wolcot) (1738–1819)
Apple Dumplings and a King, The.
Bozzy and Piozzi, sels.
Epigram: "Midas, they say, possessed the art of
    old."
Hymn to the Guilotine.
Old Friends.
On a Stone Thrown at a Very Great Man, But
    Which Missed Him.
Pups and the Alligator, The.

Piñero, Miguel
La Bodega Sold Dreams.
Lower East Side Poem, A.
On The Day They Buried My Mother.
Running Scared.
This Is Not the Place Where I was Born.

Ping, Wang (b. 1957)
Rain, Clouds, Eight Thousand Miles of Roads,
    sel.
Syntax.

Pinkard, Maceo (fl. 1925)
Sweet Georgia Brown.

Pinkerton, Helen
For an End.
Nature Note: The California Poison Oak.
On Dorothea Lange's Photograph "Migrant
    Mother" (1936).
On Vermeer's Young Woman with a Water Jug
    (1658) in the Metropolitan Museum.

Pinkney, Edward Coote [or Coate] (1802–28)
Health, A.
Italy.
On Parting.
Serenade: "Look out upon the stars, my love."

To ———: "'Twas eve; the broadly shining
    sun."
Voyager's Song, The.

Pino, José Manuel del (b. 1958)
Doré V.

Pinosová, Katerina
Piece of Bone, The.

Pinsky, Robert (b. 1940)
ABC.
At Pleasure Bay.
Avenue.
Book: "Its leaves flutter, they thrive or wither,
    its outspread."
Braveries.
City Dark, The.
City Elegies, sels.
Doctor Frolic.
Dying.
Essay on Psychiatrists, sels.
Explanation of America, An, sels.
Figured Wheel, The.
First Early Mornings Together.
From the Childhood of Jesus.
Haunted Ruin, The.
Hearts, The.
If You Could Write One Great Poem, What
    Would You Want It to Be About?
Impossible to Tell.
In Berkeley.
Jar of Pens.
Jersey Rain.
Living, The.
Long Branch Song, A.
Night Game, The.
Ode to Meaning.
Physical Comparison With Professors And
    Others.
Poem about People.
Poem with Refrains.
Questions, The: "What about the people who
    came to my father's office."
Ralegh's Prizes.
Round.
Samba.
Samurai Song.
Shirt.
Street, The.
Uncreation, The.
Want Bone, The.
Woman, A.
XYZ.

Pinter, Harold (b. 1930)
American Football (A Reflection upon the Gulf
    War).

Pinto, Vivian de Sola (1895–1969)
At Piccadilly Circus.

Piombino, Nick (b. 1942)
Frozen Witness, The.
My Lady Carries Stones.
Pyramids, The.
Time Travel.

Piontek, Heinz
In the Woods.

Piper, Edwin Ford (1871–1939)
Big Swimming.
Indian Counsel.

Piper, Paul S. (b. 1951)
Bowing.
Christmas Eve, 2003.
Morning Star, The.
There is no ripple on the world.

Pitcher, Oliver (b. 1923)
Dust of Silence.
Formula for tragedy.
Harlem: Sidewalk Icons, sel.
Iconoclast's Closet, The.
Infant, The.
Pale Blue Casket, The.
Remark, The.
Tango.
Washington Square: August Afternoon.

Pitchford, Kenneth (b. 1930)
Surgery.

Pitt-Kethley, Fiona
God made the sex-shop keeper.

Pitter, Ruth (1897–1992)
Bat, The.
But for Lust.
Coffin Worm, The.
Diehards, The.
Eternal Image, The.
If You Came.
Irish Patriarch, The.
Love and the Child.
Military Harpist, The.
Old, Childless, Husbandless.
Old Nelly's Birthday.
Other People's Glasshouses.
Swan Bathing, The.
Task, The.
Time's Fool.
Unicorn, The.
Victory Bonfire.
Yorkshire Wife's Saga.

Pittman, Al (1940–2001)
Another Night in Crawley's Cove.
Echo of the Ax, The.
Lupines.

Pix, Mary (1666–c.1709)
To Mrs. Manley, upon Her Tragedy Call'd The
    Royal Mischief.
To Mrs S. F. on Her Poems.

Pizarnik, Alejandra (1936–72)
Ashes.
Awakening, The.
Caroline von Günderode.
Deaf Lantern.
Exile.
Existing.
Foundation Stone.
Fragments to Overcome Silence.
Paths of the Mirror.
Poem for My Father.
Poem for the Father.
Recognition.
Shadow of Days to Come.
Silences.
Speaking Your Name.
Suspicion.
Tree of Diana, sel.

Planché, James Robinson (1796–1880)
Self-Evident.

Plarr, Victor Gustave (1863–1929)
Epitaphium Citharistriae.

Plath, Sylvia (1932–63)
Admonitions.
Alicante Lullaby.
Applicant, The.
Ariel.
Arrival of the Bee Box, The.
Bed Book, The, sel.
Bee Meeting, The.
Black Pine Tree in an Orange Light.
Black Rook in Rainy Weather.
Blackberrying.
Child.
Colossus, The.
Crossing the Water.
Cut.
Daddy.
Death and Co.
Death of Myth-making, The.
Disquieting Muses, The.
Edge.
Elm.
Face Lift.
Fever 103°.
Getting There.
Hanging Man, The.
In Plaster.
Incommunicado.
Insomniac.
Kindness.
Lady Lazarus.
Last Words: "I do not want a plain box, I want
    a sarcophagus."
Love Letter.
Magi.

Manor Garden, The.
Mary's Song.
Medallion.
Medusa.
Metaphors.
Mirror.
Moon and the Yew Tree, The.
Morning in the Hospital Solarium.
Morning Song: "Love set you going like a fat
    gold watch."
Mushrooms.
Nick and the Candlestick.
Night Dances, The.
Owl.
Parliament Hill Fields.
Point Shirley.
Polly's Tree.
Poppies in October.
Rhyme.
Sheep in Fog.
Soliloquy of the Solipsist.
Spinster.
Stars over the Dordogne.
Stillborn.
Stings.
Street Song.
Swarm, The.
Tulips.
Wintering.
Winter's Tale, A.
Words.

Plath, Zarina Mullan
Cooking Lesson.

Platke, Stan
Gut Catcher.

Platner, Isaac (1885–1961)
We Are the Heirs.

Plato (fl. 492–347 B.C.)
Apple, The.
Aster.
Epitaph, An: "I am a drowned man's tomb.
    There is a farmer's."
Kiss, The.
Kissing Helena.
Lover to His Lady, The.
To Stella.

Plato, Ann (b. 1920)
Advice to Young Ladies.
Natives of America, The.
True Friend, The.

Platt, Frederic W.
Coincidentally.

Plazewska, Irene (b. 1949)
Newton's Descent.

Pleynet, Marcelin (b. 1933)
Dans la lumière du jour.
In the Daylight.

Plomer, William (1903–73)
Atheling Grange; or, The Apotheosis of Lotte
    Nussbaum.
French Lisette: A Ballad of Maida Vale.
Headline History.
Levantine, A.
Playboy of the Demi-World[: 1938], The.
Scorpion, The.
To the Moon and Back.

Plotkin, Chaim (1910–96)
Greetings from My Shtetl (A Letter from
    Poland).

Plotnick, Harvey M.
Jewish.

Plowman, Max (1883–1941)
Dead Soldiers, The.

Plumly, Stanley (b. 1939)
Alms.
Altitude.
Blossom.
Cardinals in a Shower at Union Square.
Constable's Clouds for Keats.
Dove.
Dusk Coming on Outside ———, New York.
For Esther.
Giraffe.
Human Excrement.

In Answer to Amy's Question What's a
    Pickerel.
Karate.
Nobody Sleeps.
Reading with the Poets.
Wight.

Plummer, Pamela
Conversations in the Struggle.

Plumpp, Sterling (b. 1940)
Another Mule.
Be-Bop.
Billie Holiday.
Daybreak.
History, Hollers, and Horn.
Mary, *sels.*
Ornate with Smoke.
Poem: "Poems are not places."
Remembered.
Saturday Night Decades.
Survivors.
Turf Song.

Plutzik, Hyam (1912–62)
Airman Who Flew over Shakespeare's
    England, The.
As the Great Horse Rots on the Hill.
Cancer and Nova.
Commentary.
For T.S.E. Only.
Portrait.
Winter, Never Mind Where.

Po Chü-i (772–846)
After Collecting the Autumn Taxes.
After Getting Drunk, Becoming Sober in the
    Night.
After Reading Lao Tzu.
At Flowering-Brightness Monastery in Yung-
    Ch'ung District.
At the End of Spring.
Autumn Pool.
Autumn Thoughts, Sent Far Away.
Bamboo by Li Ch'e Yun's Window, The.
Buying Flowers.
Chancelor's Gravel-Drive, The.
Chrysanthemums in the Eastern Garden, The.
Climbing the Ling-ying Terrace and Looking
    North.
Cold Night.
Cranes, The.
Dream of Mountaineering, A.
Dreaming of Long Ago.
Dreaming of Yuan Zhen.
Dreaming that I Went with Li and Yu to Visit
    Yuan Zhen.
Ease.
Eating Bamboo-Shoots.
Evening Rain.
Everlasting Wrong, The.
Flower, A.
Flower Market, The.
Flower No Flower.
For the Beach Gulls.
Golden Bells.
Hangzhou.
Harp, The.
Idle Song.
Inscription Written by Me in My Small
    Garden.
Invitation to Hsiao Ch'u-shih.
Iranian Whirling Girls.
Jiangnan.
Laozi.
Last Poem.
Lazy Man's Song.
Lazy Man's Song.
Letter, The.
Lodging with the Old Man of the Stream.
Lonely Night in Early Autumn.
Long Lines Sent to Ling Hu-Ch'u before He
    Comes to Visit My Tumbledown Home.
Looking in the Lake.
Madly Singing in the Mountains.
Night Duty in the Palace, Dreaming of a
    Hsien-yu Temple.
Night in the Palace with Ch'ien Hui.
Old, and a Fever.
On a Portrait of the Poet.

On an Ancient Tomb East of the Village.
On Hearing Someone Sing a Poem by Yuan
    Zhen.
On His Baldness.
Palace Song.
Passing Tianmen Street in Chang'an and
    Seeing a Distant View of Zhongnan
    Mountains.
Philosophers: Lao-Tzu, The.
Planting Bamboos.
Planting Flowers on the Eastern Embankment.
Poem for Yuan Zhen.
Rain.
Reading Yuan Chen on a Boat.
Realizing the Futility of Life.
Red Cuckatoo, The.
Remembering Golden Bells.
River Flute.
Seeing Hsia Chan off by River.
Sick and Old, Same as Ever: A Poem to Figure
    It All Out.
Sitting at Night.
Sitting Quietly: Written During My Illness.
Sleeping on Horseback.
Song of Everlasting Sorrow.
Song of Lasting Regret, The.
Song of the Pines.
Song of the P'i-P'a.
Starting Early from the Ch'u-ch'ĕng Inn.
To a Talkative Guest.
To a Young Widow.
To the Distant One.
To Yuan Chen.
Tune: "Memories of the South."
Village Snow, Sitting at Night.
Visiting the Hermit Cheng.
Visiting the Recluse Cheng.
Waves Sifting Sand, *sel.*
Wind Sickness Strikes.
Winter Night.
Winter Night ("Those I love scattered away,
    poor.").
Wu.
Yin-yo laps in the reeds, my guest departs.

Pobo, Ken (b. 1954)
Grand Canyon.
Stormy Lear.

Poe, Edgar Allan (1809–49)
Al Aaraaf.
Alone.
Annabel Lee.
Bells, The.
Bridal Ballad.
City in the Sea, The.
Coliseum, The.
Conqueror Worm, The.
Dream within a Dream, A.
Dream-Land [*or* Dreamland].
Dreams: "Oh! That my young life were a
    lasting dream!"
Eldorado.
Eulalie—A Song.
Fairyland [*or* Fairy-Land].
For Annie.
For Annie, *sels.*
Haunted Palace, The.
Israfel.
Lake: To———, The.
Lenore.
Monody on Doctor Olmsted.
Raven, The.
Romance.
Sleeper, The.
Sonnet—Silence.
Sonnet—To Science.
Stanzas.
Stanzas: "How often we forget all time, when
    lone."
To F——.
To Helen ("Helen, thy beauty is to me.").
To Helen ("I saw thee once—once only—years
    ago.").
To My Mother.
To One in Paradise.
Ulalume [*or* Ulalume—a Ballad].
Valley of Unrest, The.

Poetker-Thiessen, Audrey (b. 1962)
Fallen Women.
My kingdom is of this world.
She tries to tell him.
Symbols of Fertility.
Poets of the Tixall Circle (fl. 1630s–50s)
Confession, A.
From a Sick Poetesse to Mrs St George on Her
Feeding the Swans.
To a Gentleman that Courted Several Ladys.
Pogson, Patricia (b. 1944)
Amaryllis Belladonna.
Apples.
Bee.
Bo Tree.
Deep.
Exits.
Face Mask.
Fifteen.
Going Home.
Hairdressing.
In Dreams.
Resin.
Sleeper.
Polak, Jirka (b. 1925)
Storm, The.
Polet, Sybren (Sybe Minnema) (b. 1924)
Self-Repeating Poem.
Zelfrepeterend gedicht.
Politian *See* Poliziano, Angelo
Polito, Robert
Overheard in the Love Hotel.
Poliziano, Angelo [*or* Andrea] (Politian) (1454–94)
Favola di Orfeo, *sel.*
Greek Epigrams, *sels.*
Tournament, The, *sel.*
Polkowski, Jan (b. 1953)
I Don't Know That Man.
Noli Me Tangere.
World is Only Air, The.
Pollak, Felix (b. 1909)
Dream, The.
Pollard, Adelaide A.
Have thine own way, Lord! Have thine own way!
Pollard, Clare (b.1978)
And Another Bloody Thing.
Breakfast Poem.
Friday Night at the End of a Millennium, A, *sels.*
Heavy-Petting Zoo, The.
Pollard, Velma (b. 1937)
Heavens Cherubim High Horsed or The Meeting of the Two Sevens (May 1977).
Pollarolo, Giovanna (b. 1955)
At Breakfast.
During Recess.
Foretold Futures.
Good Marriage, A.
Grocer's Dream, The.
In My Days.
Man Went to See the Doltons, A.
S.L.A.M.
Sunny Afternoon Dream, The.
They All Think.
When We Meet Again.
While My Father.
Polley, Jacob (b. 1975)
Jar of Honey, A.
Moving House.
Smoke.
Pollitt, Katha (b. 1949)
Failure.
Mind-Body Problem.
Onion.
Poet of Our Climate, A.
Small Comfort.
Two Fish.
Pollock, Thomas Benson
We have not known thee as we ought.
Pollok, Robert (1798–1827)
Course of Time, The, *sels.*
Happiness.

Poloskey, Marianne
Encounter.
Polwhele, Elizabeth (b. before 1648, d. after 1672)
On His Royal Highness His Expedition Against the Dutch.
Song: "If I were tortur'd with greensickness."
Polwhele, Richard (1760–1838)
Unsex'd Females, The, *sels.*
Pomerantz, Alexander (1901–65)
Chandeliers.
My Father the Foundryman.
New York.
Sonnet and Duet for Flapper and Poet.
Pomeroy, George S. (fl. 1911)
Whiffenpoof Song.
Pomeroy, Ralph (b. 1926)
Gay Love and the Movies.
Pommy-Vega, Janine (b. 1942)
Ah certainty of love in the hand.
For Boats Only.
Here before the sunrise blue and in this solitude.
Ponge, Francis (1899–1988)
Arbres se défont à l'intérieur d'une sphère de brouillard, Les.
Ardoise, L'
Assiette, The (The Plate).
Blackberries.
Blackberries.
Boat, The.
Candle, The.
Candle, The.
Crate, The.
Delights of the Door, The.
End of Fall, The.
Frog, The.
Frog, The.
Huître, L'
Last Simplicity, The.
Mûres, Les.
Oyster, The.
Oyster, The.
Plaisirs de la Porte, Les.
Pleasures of a Door.
Pleasures of the Door, The.
Pleasures of the Door, The.
Prairie, The.
Rain.
Rain: "Rain falling in the courtyard where I watch adopts three manners, each distinct, The."
Rhetoric.
Sage's Family, The.
Silent World Is Our Only Homeland, The.
Slate.
Sun as a Spinning Top (I), The.
Three Shops, The.
Trees That Come Undone within a Sphere of Fog.
Water.
Water of Tears, The.
Pongnim, Prince [Hyojong] (1619–59)
What amuses you in the sound.
Poniewaz, Jeff
Why Young Men Wore Their Hair Long in the Sixties.
Ponsonby, Sarah (1755–1831)
Song: "By vulgar Eros long misled."
Ponsot, Marie (b. 1922)
A La Une.
Analogue.
I've Been Around: It Gets Me Nowhere.
Matins and Lauds.
Multipara: Gravida 5.
One is One.
Rockefeller the Center.
Story After the Story, The.
Trois Petits Tours et Puis.
Winter.
Pook, John (b. 1942)
In Chapel.
Weekend at Home.

Poole, Richard (b. 1945)
Dark, The.
Popa, Vasco [*or* Vasko] (b. 1922)
Besieged Serenity, *sels.*
Blackbird's Field, The, *sels.*
Burning Shewolf.
Far Within Us, *sels.*
Games, *sels.*
Heaven's Ring.
In the Ashtray.
Little Box, The.
Quartz Pebble, The, *sels.*
Raw Flesh, *sels.*
St Sava's Spring, *sels.*
Song of the Tower of Skulls.
Story of a story, The.
Yawn of Yawns, The, *sels.*
Pope, Aarian
Father's Day.
Pope, Aaron (b. 1975)
Revelation.
Pope, Alexander (1688–1744)
Argus.
Bounce to Fop.
Dunciad, The, *sels.*
Elegy to the Memory of an Unfortunate Lady.
Eloisa to Abelard.
Epigram Engraved on the Collar of a Dog Given [*or* Which I Gave] to His Royal Highness.
Epilogue to the Satires, in Two Dialogues, *sels.*
Epistle IV to Richard Boyle, Earl of Burlington, *sels.*
Epistle III, to Allen Lord Bathurst, *sels.*
Epistle to Dr. Arbuthnot, *sels.*
Epistle to Lord Burlington, *sels.*
Epistle to Miss [*or* Miss Teresa] Blount, on Her Leaving the Town after the Coronation.
Epistle [II,] to a Lady[: Of the Characters of Women].
Epistle [II,] to a Lady[: Of the Characters of Women], *sels.*
Epitaph for One Who Would Not Be Buried in Westminster Abbey.
Essay on Criticism, An, *sels.*
Essay on Man, An, *sels.*
Farewell to London in the Year 1715, A.
First Epistle of the First Book of Horace Imitated, The, *sels.*
First Satire of the Second Book of Horace [Imitated], The, *sel.*
Garden, The.
Happy Life of a Country Parson, The.
Hymn: "What conscience dictates to be done."
Imitation of Chaucer.
Impromptu: To Lady Winchelsea Occasioned by four Satirical Verses on Women Wits, In *The Rape of the Lock.*
Intended for Sir Isaac Newton.
Messiah [a Sacred Eclogue, in Imitation of Virgil's Pollio], *sels.*
Ode on Solitude.
Ode: The Dying Christian to His Soul.
On a Certain Lady at Court.
On Queen Caroline's Deathbed.
Rape of the Lock, The: An Heroi-Comical Poem in Five Cantos, *sels.*
Second Satire of the Second Book of Horace Imitated, The, *sel.*
Three Epitaphs on John Hewet and Sarah Drew.
Universal Prayer, The [Deo Opt. Max.].
Windsor-Forest [*or* Windsor Forest], *sels.*
Pope, Deborah
Getting Through.
Pope, J. R. (1909–91)
Word of Encouragement, A.
Pope, Jessie (Mrs. Babington Lenton) (d. 1941)
Beau Ideal, The.
Pope, Walter (c.1636–1714)
Old Man's Wish, The.
Poplavsky [*or* Poplavskii], Boris Iulianovich (1903–35)
Another Planet.

Popova, Olga (b. 1960)
Among black trees.
Curve of your lips, The.
Lay your head in my lap.
What's left for me to say? God.

Porchia, Antonio (1886–1968)
Voices (an Excerpt).

Pordage, Samuel (1633–c.1691)
To Lucia Playing on Her Lute, Another.

Porete, Marguerite
Beloved, what do you want of me?

Porson, Richard (1759–1808)
Mutual Congratulations of the Poets Anna
Seward and Hayley, The.

Porta, Antonio (b. 1935)
Age of unhappiness has arrived, or is it, The.
Dialogue with Herz.
Essences, *sels.*
I'm walking out on Rome.
To Open.
Traveler.

Portal, Magda (b. 1901)
Attitude.
Thirst for the Sea.
Watch of Time.

Porteous, Katrina (b. 1960)
Calf.
Charlie Douglas.
Decommissioning.
I Envy the Cracked, Black Basalt.
Wrecked Creeves.

Porter, Adrian
Perfect Child, The.

Porter, Anne (b. 1911)
Consider the Lillies of the Sea.
Five Wishes.
For My Son Johnny.
Four Poems in One.
Oaks and Squirrels.
Winter Twilight.

Porter, Browning
First Time Going to School All by Myself.

Porter, Charles
Land of the Lost.

Porter, Cole (1891–1964)
All of You.
Always True to You in My Fashion, *sel.*
Anything Goes.
At Long Last Love.
Begin the Beguine.
Brush Up Your Shakespeare.
Down in the Depths.
Ev'ry Time We Say Good-bye.
Friendship.
From This Moment On.
Get Out of Town.
I Concentrate on You.
I Get a Kick Out of You.
I'm a Gigolo.
In the Still of the Night.
It's All Right with Me.
It's De-Lovely.
I've a Shooting Box in Scotland.
I've Got You Under My Skin.
Just One of Those Things.
Katie Went to Haiti.
Laziest Gal in Town, The.
Let's Do It, Let's Fall in Love.
Let's Not Talk About Love.
Love for Sale.
Miss Otis Regrets.
My Heart Belongs to Daddy.
Night and Day.
Old-Fashioned Garden.
Red, Hot and Blue.
Ridin' High.
So in Love.
Tale of the Oyster, The.
They Couldn't Compare to You.
Too Darn Hot.
What Is This Thing Called Love?
Where Is the Life That Late I Led?
You Don't Know Paree.
You're the Top, *sel.*

Porter, Dorothy (b. 1954)
Lollies Noir.
P. M. T.

Porter, Fairfield (1907–75)
Island in the Evening, The.

Porter, Hal (b. 1917)
Four Winds.
Hobart Town, Van Diemen's Land (11th June,
1837).
In a Bed-Sitter.

Porter, Peter (b. 1929)
Affair of the Heart.
And No Help Came.
Angel in Blythburgh Church, An.
Annotations of Auschwitz.
Australian Garden, An.
Consumer's Report, A.
Cost of Seriousness, The.
Exequy, An.
Happening at Sordid Creek.
In the New World Happiness is Allowed.
Japanese Jokes.
King of the Cats is Dead, The.
Last of England, The.
May, 1945.
On First Looking into Chapman's Hesiod.
On This Day I Complete My Fortieth Year.
Radio Caliban.
Sanitized Sonnets, The, *sels.*
Sex and the Over Forties.
Soliloquy at Potsdam.
Sun King Sulking.
Sydney Cove, 1788.
Talking to You Afterwards.
What I Have Written I Have Written.
Your Attention Please.

Portnoy, Michael
Dinogon.
Evolution of Lather, The.
Hints at Distance.
Instant Control.
Of of Titmouse.
Roget, Papier, Schism!
Voucher.

Ports, Kim
Desire.

Portugal, Anne (b. 1949)
Bath, The, *sels.*
Chaque case.
Every Shack.
Seen from Over Here ("From the horizon
there.").
Seen from Over Here ("Seen from over
here.").
That actual day.
Vu de ce côté-ci ("De l'horizon il se.").
Vu de ce côté-ci ("Vu de ce côté-ci.").
You really know your art you.

Porzecanski, Teresa
Every Month.
What Matters.

Posey, Alexander L.
Autumn.
Hotgun on the Death of Yadeka Harjo.
July.
Midsummer.
Nightfall.
Ode to Sequoyah.
Song of the Oktahutchee.

Postell, Tom
Gertrude Stein Rides the Town Down El.
Harmony.
I Want a Solid Piece of Sunlight and a
Yardstick to Measure it With.

Postnikova, Olga (b. 1943)
Archangel Cathedral.

Potocki, Waclaw (1625–96)
Winter, Before the War.

Potos, Andrea
One Red-haired Summer, The.
Twenty Years Later, to a Friend.

Potter, Beatrix (1866–1943)
Old Woman, The.

Potter, Carol
In the Upstairs Window.
White Hotel.

Potts, Paul (b. 1911)
Comrade Laugher.

Pou Kuksa (1301–1382)
Bamboo Hermitage.
Cloudy Mountain.
Deathbed Song.
Stone Stream.
Untitled: "Unmoving, it presents itself in a
thousand shapes."
Yo Hermitage.

Poulin, A., Jr. (b. 1938)
Red Clock.

Pound, Ezra (1885–1972)
Alba.
Ancient Music.
And the Days Are Not Full Enough.
Ballad for Gloom.
Ballad of the Goodly Fere.
Bathtub [*or* Bath Tub], The.
Cantos, *sels.*
Coming of War, The; Actaeon.
Commission.
Contemporania, *sels.*
Dance Figure.
De Aegypto.
Erat Hora.
For an officer / in the old Capital, fox fur.
For deep deer-copse beneath Mount Han.
Fragmenti.
Full be the year, abundant be the grain.
Garden, The: "Like a skein of loose silk blown
against a wall."
Great Digest of Confucius, The.
Greek Epigram.
Gypsy, The.
"Hid! Hid!" the fish-hawk saith.
Homage to Sextus Propertius, *sels.*
Homme Moyen Sensuel, L', *sels.*
Hugh Selwyn Mauberley (Life and Contacts),
sels.
In a Station of the Metro.
Ité.
Know then: / Toward summer when the sun is
in Hyades.
Lake Isle, The.
L'Art, 1910.
Les Millwin.
Long Wind, the Dawn Wind.
Lustra, *sels.*
Meditatio.
Near Perigord.
Night Litany.
Pact, A.
Papyrus.
Reflection and Advice.
Ripostes of Ezra Pound, *sels.*
Salutation.
Sandalphon.
Sestina: Altaforte.
Soirée.
Song of the Degrees, A.
Speech for Psyche in the Golden Book of
Apuleius.
Study in Aesthetics, The.
Tame Cat.
Tea Shop, The.
Temperaments, The.
Three Cantos of a Poem of Some Length, *sels.*
To Kalon.
To Whistler, American.
Toujours la Politesse.
Tree, The.
Ts'ai Chi'h.
Vitex in swamp ground.

Pow, Tom (b. 1950)
Ascending Strathbraan.
Favourite Stretch of Disused Railway, A.
Years, The: "Sometimes to get their own
back."

Powell, Craig (b. 1941)
Nativity.

Powell, D. A. (b. 1963)
Always Returning: Holidays and Burials. Not
    Every Week.
Coda & discography.
Darling can you kill me: with your
    mickeymouse pillows.
First Fugue.
House Face.
How his body stood against a thicket. rich in
    hardwood gentry: ponderous and gloomy.
Ice Hadn't Cracked, The. Stingy Ground:
    Frozen with its Hoard of Bulbs.
In the course of travel: strychnine every few
    hours. some italian art.
Long line of bohunks and hunyaks, A: we
    settled in podunk. thirteen consonants.
Minotaur at Supper, The: Spare the Noritake
    and the Spode.
Mule-drawn Scraper Packed this Earth, A:
    Levees.
My Father and Me Making Dresses: Together.
My Lot to Spin the Purple: that the Tabernacle
    Should Be Made.
My neck a toothsome feeding ground. vespered
    swarms had drunk of me before this new
    batman.
My Riches I Have Squandered. Spread with
    Honey.
Nicholas the ridiculous: you will always be 27
    and impossible. No more expectations.
Ode: "Where have you gone blue middle of a
    decade? the gates creak. a sigh is so vastly
    different."
Sleek mechanical dart: the syringe noses into
    the blue vein marking the target of me.
Sonnet: "Morsels of my lifework: the story of
    a professional party hostess."
Studs and Rings: Favors of the Piercing Party.
Tall and thin *and young and lovely the* michael
    with kaposi's sarcoma *goes walking.*
Thicknesses of victor decreased: blanket-
    >sheet->floss. Until no material would do,
    The.
Triptych.
What direction will you take when the universe
    collapses. you who when you go must go
    someplace.
When He Comes He Is Neither Sun Nor
    Shade: a China Doll.
When you touch down upon this earth. little
    reindeers.
Who won't praise green. Each minute to caress
    each minute blade of spring. Green slice us
    open.
Writing for a young man on the redline train:
    "to his boy mistress."
You don't have syphilis. the doctor says.
You're thin again handsome. in our last.
Powell, Dannye Romine
Woman Who Allowed Light to Have Its Way
    with Her, The.
Powell, James Henry (*fl.* 1850)
Lines Written for a Friend on the Death of His
    Brother, Caused by a Railway Train
    Running Over Him Whilst He Was in a
    State of Inebriation.
Powell, Jim (b. 1951)
Doxology.
First Light.
It Was Fever That Made the World.
Time and Light, *sel.*
Powell, Kevin (b. 1966)
Don't Feel No Way.
For Aunt Cathy.
Genius Child.
Harlem: Neo-Image.
Love/a Many Splintered Thing.
Mental Terrorism.
Southern Birth.
What the Deal, Son?
Powell, Neil (b. 1948)
Coda: Thelonius Monk, d. 17 February 1982.
Powell, Robat (b. 1948)
For Jurij Koch.
Heysel.

Powers, Arthur
Bag Lady's Body in the Financial District, A.
Historical Site.
Iago.
Powers, Jessica Agnes
Garments of God, The.
Powers, Stephen
Eagles at Dollywood.
Powys, John Cowper (1872–1963)
Ridge, The, *sel.*
Pozzi, Catherine (1882–1934)
Nyx.
Nyx.
Prabhu, Allama
For the Lord of Caves.
Prado, Adelia (b. 1936)
Easter.
Fluency.
Grace.
Heart's Desire.
In Portuguese.
Murmur.
Pelican, The.
Serenade.
Siesta.
Stained Glass Window.
Successive Deaths.
Time.
Prados, Emilio (1899–1962)
Canción de Despedida.
Canción: "Puente de mi soledad."
Cerré Mi Puerta al Mundo.
Cuando Era Primavera.
I Locked the World Out.
I Look into the Sky.
Like a Naked Light.
Recuerdo.
Silencio, Desnudo, El.
Something Remembered.
Song: "Bridge of my solitude."
Song of Taking Leave.
Vuelvo al Cielo Mis Ojos.
When It Was Spring.
Praed, Winthrop Mackworth (1802–39)
Arrivals at a Watering-Place.
Beauty and Her Visitors.
Chancery Morals.
Chaunt of the Brazen Head, The, *sel.*
Chaunts of the Brazen Head, The. II.
Dogs' Welcome, The.
Every Day Characters, *sels.*
Good Night to the Season.
Royal Education.
School and Schoolfellows.
Talented Man, The.
Praitis, Irena
Anthems.
Pranses, Tony
Shovelin' Coal.
Prasad, Vegunta Mohana (b. 1942)
Empty.
First Blood.
Hades.
Liberation.
Stupidity.
Prassinos, Gisèle (b. 1920)
Apostle Qualities.
Conversation, A.
Hair Tonic.
Loving Poem.
Poème Amoureux.
Qualités d'Apôtre.
Pratt, Charles E. (1845–98)
To the Wheel.
Pratt, Edwin John (1882–1964)
Come Not the Seasons Here.
From Stone to Steel.
Highway, The.
Lee-Shore, The.
Prize Cat, The.
Shark, The.
Towards the Last Spike, *sel.*
Pratt, Minnie Bruce (b. 1946)
Bury and Dig.

Crime Against Nature.
Done.
Eating Clay.
Elbows.
Other Side, The.
Poem for My Sons.
Red String.
Shades.
White Star, The.
Pratt, Samuel Jackson (1749–1814)
Cottage Pictures, *sels.*
Lower World, The, *sels.*
Praxilla (*fl.* c.450 B.C.)
Fairest thing I leave behind is sunlight, The.
Learning from the tale of Admetos, my friend,
    love the brave.
Peeking in through.
Watch for a scorpion, my friend, under every
    stone.
Yet they never persuaded your heart.
You who look lovely from the windows.
Preece, Peter (b. 1936)
Cormorant.
Preil, Gabriel (b. 1910)
Brief Note from Jerusalem, A.
Eternal Present, The.
From a Late Diary.
Lesson in Translation, A.
Little Research in Snow, A.
Night. And I am drinking smoky black tea
    from China.
Rain Poem.
Tired Hunter, The.
With Walter and Amati.
Words of Oblivion and Peace.
Prejsnar, Mark
Abusive! that's the word!
Assuage Bane.
Composition with Wire.
Government and Binding.
Ode to Toge.
Prelutsky, Jack (b. 1940)
First Thanksgiving, The.
Goblin, The.
Harvey Always Wins.
Homework! Oh, Homework!
It's Halloween.
Mother Goblin's Lullaby.
Skeleton Parade.
Prescod, Marsha
Vicious Circle.
Women Are Different.
Preseren, France (1800–49)
Where?
Press, John (b. 1920)
African Christmas.
Press, Karen (b. 1956)
Ancestors.
Bird.
Causality and Chance in Love.
Dispossessed words.
First thirty-seven years, The.
Heart's Hunger.
Hope for refugees.
Humus.
I who live here, it is I.
Man with incomplete words on his roof, The.
Reclaiming Our Land.
Rotten Fish.
She Brought Home Poppies.
Statues.
This Is Not a Riot Policeman.
This, Too.
Tiresias in the City of Heroes, *sels.*
Welcome.
Preston, Keith (1884–1927)
Complete Cynic, The.
Lapsus Linguae.
Parental Critic, The.
Probably.
Preston, Margaret Junkin (1820–77)
Erinna's Spinning.
Grave in Hollywood Cemetery, Richmond, A.
Hymn to the National Flag.

Preston, Rohan B. (b. 1966)
Champion Chant.
Chicago Blues.
Deep-Sea Bathing (Inna Reggae Dancehall).
Dream of Mango.
Italist Chant.
Lift Every Fist and Swing.
Mama.
Music.
Ten Seconds.
When I Leave My Body.
Prestwich, Edmond (*fl.* 1651)
How to Choose a Mistress.
Prévert, Jacques (1900–77)
At the Florist's.
August Bank Holiday.
Barbara.
Barbara.
Barbara.
Breakfast.
Discourse on Peace, The.
Dunce, The.
Familial.
I'm the Way I Am.
Inventory.
Last Supper, The.
Message, The.
Quartier Libre.
River, The.
Song in the Blood.
Song of the snails on their way to a funeral.
Whale hunt, The.
Previn, Dory Langdon (*fl.* 1962)
Morning After, The.
Prewett, Frank (1893–1962)
I Shall Take You in Rough Weather.
If I Love You.
Pack, The.
Plea for Peace.
Red-Man, The.
Price, Caroline
Night Fishing.
Price, George Cadle (b. 1919)
Belizeans: Unite to Build our Nation.
Price, Laurence (*fl.* 1625–1680?)
Maidens of London's Brave Adventures, Or, a
Boon Voyage Intended for the Sea, The.
Price, Reynolds (b. 1933)
Good Places, *sels.*
Price, Richard (b. 1966)
Horsehoe Crab in Flagrante Delicto.
On, Off, Over.
Price, V. B. (b. 1940)
Artemis: "Bear mother, supple."
Balancing Zero.
Pride: "It becomes your soul: that sucking, itch
that."
Sloth.
Three Hymns for Aphrodite.
Prichard, Caradog (1904–80)
Bargain, The.
Earthly Turmoil, *sel.*
Prichard, Thomas Jeffrey Llewelyn (*fl.* 1824–61)
Land Beneath the Sea, The, *sel.*
**Prigov, Dmitry [or Dmitrii] Aleksandrovich (b.
1940)**
Dialogue No. 5.
Entry into Jerusalem.
Imagine this: a mighty giant asleep.
In the Desert.
It's better not to live in Moscow.
Primrose, Lady Diana (*fl.* c.1630)
Chain of Pearl, A, *sels.*
Prince, Frank Templeton (1912–2003)
Babiaantje, The.
Epistle to a Patron, An.
False Bay.
For Fugitives.
Not a *Paris Review* Interview, *sel.*
Soldiers Bathing.
Prince, Hughie
Boogie Woogie Bugle Boy.
Prince, Lucy Terry *See* Terry, Lucy

Prior, Edwyna
I am first mouth, then hand.
Prior, Matthew (1664–1721)
Answer to Cloe [*or* Chloe] Jealous.
Chameleon, The.
Dutch Proverb, A.
Earning a Dinner.
Epigram, An: "To John I ow'd great
obligation."
Epitaph, An: "Interr'd [*or* Interred] beneath
this marble stone."
Fable, A: "In Æsop's tales an honest wretch
we find."
Fatal Love.
For My Own Monument.
Human Life.
In Imitation of Anacreon.
Jinny the Just.
Lady Who Offers Her Looking-Glass to Venus,
The.
Letter to the Honourable Lady Margaret
Cavendish Holles-Harley, A.
Ode, An: "Merchant, to secure his treasure,
The."
On Exodus 3: 14: "I am that I am"
On My Birthday, July 21.
Pleasure: The Second Book of Solomon on the
Vanity of the World, *sel.*
Question, to Lisetta, The.
Solomon on the Vanity of the World, *sels.*
To a Child of Quality, Five Years Old, the
Author Suppos'd Forty.
To a Lady: She Refusing to Continue a Dispute
with Me.
True Maid, A.
Written in an Ovid.
Prior-Pitt, Pauline
Fitting.
Priory, James (b. 1973)
Emma and the Radio.
Prismanova, Anna Semionovna (1898–1960)
Brontë Sisters, The.
Lomonosov.
Pritchard, Angharad (1677–1749)
Conversation between Two Sisters, One
Choosing an Aged Man, and the Other
Choosing Youth, A.
Pritchard II, Norman Henry (b. 1939)
Asalteris.
Burnt Sienna.
Cassandra and Friend.
Cloak, The.
From Where the Blues?
Gyre's Galax.
Junt.
Landscape with Nymphs and Satyrs.
Love Poem.
Magma.
Metagnomy.
Narrow Path, The.
Paysagesque.
Springtime.
WE NEED—please read this and see if you.
Probyn, May
After.
Anniversaries.
As the Flower of the Grass.
Ballade of Lovers.
Barcarolle.
Before.
Blossom.
Changes.
China Maniacs.
End of the Journey, The.
Frustrated.
Is It Nothing to You?
Kyrielle.
Lai.
Love in Mayfair.
Masquerading.
Mésalliance, A.
Model, The.
More than They that Watch for the Morning.
Rondelet: "Say what you please."
Rondelet: "Which way he went?"

Song Out of Season, A.
Tête-à-Tête.
Procter, Adelaide Anne (1825–64)
Address to the Ocean.
Dark Side, The.
Divine Presence, The.
Envy.
Give Me Thy Heart.
Homeless.
Incompleteness.
Judge not; the workings of his brain.
Legend, A.
Legend of Provence, A.
Lost Chord, A.
My Journal.
Philip and Mildred.
Pilgrims, The.
Present, The.
Strive, Wait, and Pray.
Thankfulness.
Three Evenings in a Life.
Unexpressed.
Woman's Answer, A.
Woman's Last Word, A.
Words.
Proctor, Bryan Waller *See* Cornwall, Barry
Proctor, Thomas (*fl.* c.1578)
Respice Finem.
Prodromos, Theodore (1098–1150)
To the Emperor.
Propertius (Sextus Propertius) (c.54 B.C.–A.D. c.2)
Ariadne Lay, Theseus' Ship Sailing Away.
Elegies, *sel.*
Ghost, The.
When Thou Must Home.
Propertius, Sextus *See* Propertius
Prospere, Susan (b. 1946)
Heart of the Matter.
**Prudentius (Prudentius Aurelius Clemens) (348–
c.410)**
Of the Father's love begotten Ere the worlds
began to be.
Ye clouds and darkness, hosts of night.
Prufer, Kevin (b. 1969)
Ars Poetica: "I've written love notes all my
life."
Babysitter's Devotion, The.
Car Has Fallen from a Bridge, A.
End of the City, The.
For the Dead.
For the Unfortunates.
Man in Miami, The.
My Father Recounts a Story from His Youth.
On Finding a Swastika Carved on a Tree in the
Hills above Heidelberg.
Pause, Pause.
Rise of Rome, The.
Prunty, Randy
Trigger d'evolution.
Prunty, Wyatt
Ballad of the Several Past.
Downtown Bus, The.
Elbow Tree, The.
Elderly Lady Crossing on Green.
Ferris Wheel, The.
Haying.
Insomnia.
Learning the Bicycle.
Note of Thanks, A.
Offset, The.
Pyromaniac, The.
Reading Before We Read, Horoscope and
Weather.
To be Sung on the Fourth of July.
Vegetable Garden, The.
Winter's Tale, A.
Pryde, Alison
Have We Had Easter Yet?
I'll See You Down the Lane.
Prynne, J. H.
Chromatin.
Evening Walk, An.
Landing Area.
Melanin.

Of Movement towards a Natural Place.
Red D Gypsum, *sel.*

Prynne, Martha Dorsett (b. 1577, d. after 1632)
Memorandum of Martha Moulsworth
Widdowe, The.

Pryputniewicz, Tania
Dragonfly.

Prys, Edmwnd (1544–1623)
Welsh Ballad, A.

Prys, Thomas (c.1564–1639)
Poem to Show the Trouble That Befell Him
When He Was at Sea, A.

Prys-Jones, A. G. (b. 1888)
Cors-y-Gwaed: Fenland of Blood.
Day Which Endures Not, A.
Henry Morgan's March on Panama.
Ploughman: In Welsh Uplands, The.
St. Govan.
Unfortunate Occurrence at Cwm-Cadno.
Wife of Carcassone, The.

Psaila, K. (1871–1961)
Polestar.

Public Enemy
Party for Your Right to Fight.

Pudjipangu
Aeroplane.

Pudney, John (1909–77)
For Johnny.

Pugh, Christina
Rotary.

Pugh, Sheenagh (b. 1950)
Allegiance.
Coming into Their Own.
Do you think we'll ever get to see Earth, sir?
Frozen Field, The.
Guest, The.
Guys.
King Billy on the Walls.
Railway Signals.
Shoni Onions.
Sometimes.
What If This Road.
Woodcarver of Stendal, The.

Pulido, Ana Belén López (b. 1961)
And regardless / the heat.
De la ventana.
Dibuja una letra.
Gets in / the damp.
Girl, A / leans on the railing.
Historia / debe tener.
History / the cathedral.
It is not known.
Meanwhile / a young man.
Mientras / un hombre joven.
Muchacha, Una / se recarga en el barandal.
Mujer, Una / se persigna.
No se sabe.
Out of the window.
Se mete / la humedad.
Traces a letter.
Woman, A / makes the sign of the cross.
Y sin embargo.

Pulter, Hester Lee (1596–1678)
Complaint of Thames 1647 When the Best of
Kings Was Imprisoned by the Worst of
Rebels at Holmbie, The.
On Those Two Unparalleld Friends, Sr: G:
Lisle and Sr: C: Lucas, Who Were Shott to
Death at Colechester.
Upon the Death of My Deare and Lovely
Daughter J. P. Jane Pulter, Baptized May 1
1625 and Died Oct 8 1646 Aet. 20.
Upon the Imprisonment of His Sacred
Majesties that Unparaleld Prince King
Charles the First.

Purdy, Alfred Wellington (b. 1919)
Alive or Not.
Blue City, The.
Cariboo Horses, The.
Country North of Belleville, The.
Lament for the Dorsets.
Madwoman on the Train, The.
On the Decipherment of "Linear B."
Remains of an Indian Village.

Spinning.
Wilderness Gothic.
Winter Walking.

Purdy, James
Do You Wonder Why I Am Sleepy.
From rivers, and from the earth itself.

Purohit, Swami (1882–1936?)
I Know That I Am a Great Sinner.
Miracle Indeed, A.
Shall I Do This.

Purser, John (b. 1942)
Love Poem: "No nightfall in June."
Organist Confesses to His Mirror, The.

Purves, David (b. 1924)
Cleikit.
Crabbit Angels.

Pushkin, Alexander Sergeyevich (1799–1837)
Autumn (A Fragment).
Bronze Horseman, The, *sels.*
Demons.
I Loved You.
Imitation of the Arabic.
Lines Written at Night During Insomnia.
Ode on the Hills of Georgia.
On the Statue of a Player at Svaika.

Püsküllüoğlu, Ali (b. 1935)
Old Pirate in These Waters, An.

**Putnam, Howard Phelps (Phelps Putnam) (1874–
1948)**
Bill Gets Burned.
Hasbrouck and the Rose.
Romeo and Juliet.
Ship of State and Grandpa.
Sonnets to Some Sexual Organs.
Words of an Old Woman.

Putnam, Phelps *See* Putnam, Howard Phelps

Puttenham, George (1529–90)
Her Majestie Resembled to the Crowned Piller.
Ye Must Read Upward.
Partheniades, *sel.*

Pygge, Edward (b. 1938)
Notes for a Revised Sonnet.
Notes for a Sonnet.
Revised Notes for a Sonnet.
Robert Lowell's Notebook.

"Pygge, Edward" *See* Hamilton, Ian

Pyle, Katharine (1863–1938)
Toys Talk of the World, The.

Pyŏn Wŏngyu (fl. 1881–84)
To a Friend.

Pyungyang Ungee (1581–1644)
Flowers in the Garden.
Mountain Life.
On a Cuckoo's Song.
Reply to a Poem by Donglim.

Pzaki, Muin
Prisoner.

Q

"Q" *See* Quiller-Couch, Sir Arthur Thomas

Qabbani, Nizar (b. 1923)
Fortune Teller, The.

Qasmi, Ahmad Nadeem (b. 1916)
Thought.

Quade, Mary
Air Show: F-16s above Cleveland.

Quagliano, Tony
Edward Hopper Retrospective, The.
Edward Hopper's "Lighthouse at Two Lights."

Quarles, Francis (1592–1644)
Argalus and Parthenia, *sels.*
Be Sad, My Heart.
Born in Winter.
Christ and Our Selves.
Crucified.
David's Epitaph on Jonathan.
Deuteronomy 30.19.
Divine Fancies, *sels.*
Eclogue 8.
Emblems (Fragments), *sels.*
Galatians 6.14.

Isaiah 66.11.
Job Militant, *sels.*
Luke 6.25.
Matthew 9.12.
Meditatio Septima.
Mercy Tempering Justice.
Nahum 2.10.
Of St Stephen.
On a Feast.
On Balaam's Ass.
On Dinah.
On God's Law.
On Jacob's Purchase.
On Saul and David.
On the Babel-Builders.
On the Gospel.
On the Holy Scriptures.
On the Life of Man.
On the Ploughman [*or* Plough-Man].
On the Two Great Floods.
On Those That Deserve It.
On Zacheus [*or* Zacchaeus].
Pentelogia, *sel.*
Philippians 1.23.
They Gave Him Vinegar and Gall (Matt. 27)
and Wine Mingled with Myrrh (Mark 15).
Upon the Day of Our Saviour's Nativity.
Yet a Little While Is the Light With You.

Quarles, John (1624–65)
At Home.

Quasimodo, Salvatore (1901–68)
And Suddenly It Is Evening.
Anno Domini MCMXLVII.
Auschwitz.
Dead of Winter.
From the Willow Branches.
Insomnia.
Milan, August 1943.
19 January 1944.
O My Dear Animals.
Only if Love Should Pierce You.
Street in Agrigento.
To the Fifteen of Piazzale Loreto.

Quayle, Lesley
Woman Who Drank Us Up, The.

Queneau, Raymond (1903–76)
If You Imagine.
Je crains pas ça tellment.
Nourishment of Little Birds, The.
Pour nourrir les petits oiseaux.
Reinforcements [1].
Reinforcements [2].
Renfort [1] ("Je vous dis adieu monsieur mon
sergent.").
Renfort [2] ("Je suis vieux et je suis lourd.").
That Don't Scare Me.

Quennell, Peter (b. 1905)
Divers, The.
Leviathan, *sel.*
Procne.

Quevedo y Villegas, Francisco de (1580–1645)
Ah, What of Life! Does No One Answer Me?
Amorous Sonnet Defining Love.
Birds Are in the Air at Ease.
Continues in the Same State of Feeling.
Everything Is Swept Away by the Brief Year.
From the White Day to Take Me.
Happy and Contented in Your Hut.
He Points Out the Brevity of Life, Unthinking
and Suffering, Surprised by Death.
I Gaze Upon My Country's Walls.
Love Beyond Death.
Love Constant Beyond Death.
Love Constant Beyond Death.
Mighty Lord Is Money, A.
Now Great and Awesome in My Heart.
On a Chaplain's Nose.
On Lisi's Golden Hair.
Rosebush, Less Presumption.
Satiric and Censorious Epistle, *sel.*
Sonnet: Death Warnings.
To a Nose.
To Rome Entombed in Her Ruins.
Toothpuller Who Wanted to Turn a Mouth into
a Grinding Machine, The.

Queyras, Sina (b. 1963)
Tonight the Sky Is My Begging Bowl.
Quigless, Helen G. (b. 1944)
Concert.
Quiller-Couch, Sir Arthur Thomas ("Q") (1863–1944)
Harbour of Fowey, The.
Sage Counsel.
Quillinan, Edward (1791–1851)
Hour Glass, The.
Quinn, Justin (b. 1968)
Backgrounds.
Days of the New Republic, *sels.*
Go through and down the steps.
High and Dry.
I wake early into.
Insomnia.
Linger, tag, let go.
Six Household Appliances, *sels.*
Strand of Hair, A.
They stand around. They reach into the offing.
You meet them at mid-afternoon receptions.
Quinonez, Naomi
My Shattered Sister.
Quintana, Leroy V.
187.
At the New Mexico Viet Nam Veterans
Memorial.
Good Nigger.
Poem for Harry Houdini.
Poem for Pancho Gonzales.
Poem for Salt.
Teddy.
Quintane, Nathalie (b. 1964)
Mon Pouchkine.
My Pushkin.
Qunanbaev, Aba (1845–1904)
Summer: "Summer climbs the mountains."
Qunta, Christine (b. 1952)
Know, The.

R

Raab, Esther (b. 1899)
Folk Tune.
Serenade for Two Poplars, A.
Today I am modest like an animal.
Raab, Lawrence (b. 1946)
After Edward Hopper.
Bad Muse, The.
Being a Monster.
My Life Before I Knew It.
Rest, The.
Revised Versions, The.
Sudden Appearance of a Monster at a Window.
Raàm-Lachish, Carmela (b. 1935)
In the Night.
Rabbitt, Thomas (b. 1943)
Dancing Sunshine Lounge, The.
Rabe, Olive *See* Fisher, Aileen
Rabéarivelo [or Rebéarivelo], Jean-Joseph (1901–37)
Cactuses.
Rabi'a al-Adawiyya (Rabi'a the Mystic) (712–801)
I am fully qualified to work as a doorkeeper,
and for this reason.
O my Lord.
O my Lord.
Rabinowitz, Anna
Bricolage: Versicolor.
Ecosystem.
Of Joy Illimited: Polyphonic Soundings: Shore
to Ship.
Rabkin, Sarah (b. 1957)
Wheels.
Raboni, Giovanni (b. 1932)
Alibi of a Dead Man.
For C., Who Died of Childbirth at the Age of
One Year and Eleven Months.
Hospital Interiors.
Madrigal.

Moon.
"Rachel" [or "Rahel"] (1890–1931)
At the Window.
Barn, The.
He too will soon go away.
In my great loneliness.
Love was late in coming, and coming.
Messenger came in the night, The.
My Dead.
Surrender.
Tiny joys, joys like a lizard's tail.
Wrestling.
Rachel, T. Cole
You Can't Go Back to Sleep.
Racin, Kočo (1909–43)
Tobacco Pickers.
Radcliffe, Alexander (*fl.* 1669–96)
As Concerning Man.
Radcliffe, Ann (1764–1823)
Mysteries of Udolpho, The, *sels.*
Night ("Now Ev'ning fades! her pensive step
retires.").
Night ("O'er the dim breast of ocean's
wave.").
Scene on the Northern Shore of Sicily.
Sea-View, A.
Song of a Spirit.
Sonnet: "Now the bat circles on the breeze of
eve."
Storied Sonnet.
Sun-Rise: Sonnet, A.
To the Bat.
To the Visions of Fancy.
To the Winds.
Radden, Viki
Blood.
Our Second Night.
Sex.
When You Talk That Talk.
Radford, Dollie (Mrs. Ernest Radford) (b. 1858)
Soliloquy of a Maiden Aunt.
Radford, Mrs. Ernest *See* Radford, Dollie
Radiguet, Raymond (1903–23)
Handless Clock.
Map.
Poem: "Horizon line."
Poem: "Red eiderdown at the window, A."
Radner, Rebecca
I Want to Write like a Postcard.
Like That.
Radnóti, Miklós (1909–44)
A La Recherche.
Angel of Dread, The.
Anxiously Autumn Arrives.
Clouded Sky.
Eighth Eclogue.
Forced March.
Forced March.
Forced March ("He is a fool who, collapsed on
the ground, gets up and walks on.").
Fourth Eclogue, The.
Fragment: "I lived on this earth in an age."
Il Faut Laisser.
Images.
In Hiding.
Just Walk On, Condemned to Die.
Letter to My Spouse.
Letter to My Wife.
Paris.
Peace, Horror.
Picture Postcards.
Portrait.
Postcard (Found on His body after He Was
Killed by the Nazis).
Razglednica (1).
Razglednica (2).
Razglednica (3).
Razglednica (4).
Razglednica (4) ("I dropped beside him. Taut
as is the cord.").
Razglednica (4) ("I fell beside him and his
corpse turned over.").
Razglednica (4) ("I fell beside him. His
body—which was taut.").
Root.

Root ("Through the root power flashes
unseen.").
Serbian Postcard 1.
Seventh Eclogue.
Seventh Eclogue ("Do you see? Evening falls,
fringed with barbed-wire.").
Thursday.
Unnoticed.
Radoev, Ivan (b. 1927)
Ballad for Dialectical Materialism.
Ballad for the Future.
Parable of the Poet's Reward.
Sweater, The.
Tiny Man, The.
Rae, Simon (b. 1952)
Pulling the Chain.
Vile World.
Raen, Michaela
La Sombra of Who I Am.
Rafat, Tawfiq (b. 1927)
Circumcision.
Raffalovich, Marc André (1864–1934)
Rose Leaves When the Rose Is Dead.
Sonnet 120.
World Well Lost 4, The.
World Well Lost 18, The.
Rafferty, Charles (b. 1965)
Arsonist Tells His Story to the Attorney, The.
Man on the Tower, The.
Story of the Man Whose Tastes Were Too
Refined.
Rafferty, Peter
After Carnival.
Back End.
In the Madonna Dell' Orto.
Off the Beaten Track.
Passage.
Personal.
66°7' N/22°17' W.
View from the Bathysphere.
Willowherb.
Raftery [or Raifteiri], Anthony [or Antoine] (1784–1835)
I Am Raftery [or Raferty].
Mary Hynes.
Shining Posy, The.
Ragain, Maj
Don't Expect Anything.
Hungry Ghost Surrenders His Tackle Box, A.
If You Cannot Find the Truth Right Where You
Are, Where Do You Expect to Find It?
String of Ordinary Words, A.
Ragan, James
Birth of God (from an Early Photograph), The.
Child Christ at the Top of the Stairs.
Huckster at Noontime.
St. Jacob's Church of the Hanging Hand.
Standing at Pasternak's Table, Peredelkino.
Rago, Henry (1915–69)
Childhood Painting Lesson.
Child's Birthday, A.
Distances, The.
Metaphor, The, *sels.*
Ragosta, Ray (b. 1949)
At the Coast.
Capitalization of "Clue", The.
Excursions.
Rahim, Jennifer (b. 1963)
Felling of a Tree, The.
Rahman, Shamsur (b. 1929)
Strike, The.
Rahon, Alice (1904–87)
Appellants, The.
Cave of bronze amplifier of the storms.
Ferns in a Hollow of Absence.
For those parallel destinies.
Glances changed their source.
Hourglass Lying Down.
In the night of the beginning.
Pointed Out Like the Stars.
Sublimated Mercury.
Rai San'yo (1781–1832)
Escorting My Mother Home: A Short Song for
the Road.

On a Painting of Kenshin Attacking Shingen.
Stopping at Amakusa Sea.
Raine, Craig (b. 1944)
Attempt at Jealousy, An.
City Gent.
Dandelions.
For Hans Keller.
Gardener, The.
In Modern Dress.
Man Who Invented Pain, The.
Martian Sends a Postcard Home, A.
Nature Study.
Onion, Memory, The.
Raine, Kathleen Jessie (1908–2003)
Air.
Angelus.
Eileann Chanaidh, sels.
Good Friday.
Heirloom.
Heroes.
Instrument, The.
Isis Wanderer.
Kore in Hades.
Love-Poem: "Yours is the face that the earth
turns to me."
Maire Macrae's Song.
Moment, The.
On its way I see.
Prayer.
Pythoness, The.
Question and Answer.
Spell Against Sorrow.
Spell of Creation.
Star, The.
To My Mountain.
What substance had Euridice.
Rainey, Gertrude "Ma" ("Ma" Rainey) (1886–1939)
Prove It on Me Blues.
See, See Rider.
Rainger, Ralph
Thanks for the Memory.
Raizan See Konishi Raizan
Rajendra, Cecil
My Message.
Prince of the Dance.
Raji Oyelade, Remi (b. 1961)
Cyclone.
Rakan-Keinan
Today Rakan, riding an iron horse.
Rakha, Yusuf
Dust Storm, The.
Rakosi, Carl (b. 1903)
Americana 3.
Amulet.
Avocado Pit, The.
Discoveries, Trade Names, Genitals, and
Ancient Instruments.
Domination of Wallace Stevens (1925), sel.
Exercises in Scriptural Writing (1925–1939),
sel.
Figures in an Ancient Ink.
Fluteplayers from Finmarken.
Founding of New Hampshire, The.
Good Morning.
In the First Circle of Limbo.
Instructions to the Player.
Israel.
January of a Gnat, The.
Journey Away, A.
L'Chayim.
Lobster, The.
Lord, What is Man?
Lying in Bed on a Summer Morning.
Menage, The.
Objectivist Lamp.
Ode on Arrival.
Old Country, The.
Old Lovers.
Origins.
Services.
Song: "There never was."
To an Anti-Semite.
To the Man Inside.
Two Variations on a Theme.

Unswerving Marine.
Young Girl.
ZZZZZ.
Ralegh, Sir Walter (1552?–1618)
Authours Epitaph, Made by Himself, The.
Commendatory Verses to Edmund Spenser's
Fairy Queen, sels.
Even Such Is Time.
Farewell to False Love, A.
Farewell to the Court.
Fortune Hath Taken Away.
Fortune Hath Taken the Away My Love, sel.
Homage to Diana.
Lie, The.
Nature, That Washed [or Washt] Her Hands in
Milk[e].
Nymph's [or Nimphs] Reply to the
[Passionate] Shepherd [or Sheepheard], The.
Ocean's Love to Cynthia, The, sels.
On the Card[e]s, and Dice.
Passionate Man[']s Pilgrimage, The.
Silent Lover, The.
Sir Walter Ralegh to the Queen.
Sir Walter Ra[u]le[i]gh to His Son[ne].
To His Love When He Had Obtained Her.
What Is Our Life?
Raleigh, Sir Walter Alexander (1861–1922)
Lines Suggested by an Edition of Blake's
Poems.
Wishes of an Elderly Man[, Wished at a
Garden Party, June 1914].
Ralin, Radoi (b. 1923)
Home-Study Course in Freedom.
Ideological Tango.
Man Who Didn't Sign, The.
Safety Pins (excerpts).
Seduced and Abandoned.
"Ramal, Walter" See De la Mare, Walter
Ramanujan, A. K. (b. 1929)
Alien.
At Forty.
Breaded Fish.
Chicago Zen.
Death and the Good Citizen.
Drafts.
Elements of Composition.
Extended Family.
Foundlings in the Yukon.
Hindu to His Body, A.
In the Zoo.
Love Poem for a Wife, 2.
Pleasure.
Routine Day Sonnet.
Salamanders.
Self-Portrait.
Snakes.
Some People.
Rambsy II, Howard
Trash Talker, The.
Ramireddy, Duvvuri (1895–1947)
Tryst.
Ramírez, Josué (b. 1963)
Corazón Mecánico.
Ficción y las Cosas, La.
Mechanical Heart.
Of Fiction and Things.
Tepozán.
Tepozán.
Topografía.
Topography.
Ramirez, Luke E.
Why I Do It.
Yet to Come.
Ramke, Bin (b. 1947)
According to Ovid.
Art, Love, Geology.
Astronomer Works Nights: A Parable of
Science, The.
Difference Between Night and Day, The.
Enter Celia, with a Writing.
Famous Poems of the Past Explained.
Like Ulysses.
Paul Verlaine at the Grave of Lucien Létinois.
Revealing Oneself to a Woman.
Thou Hast Blessed the Work of His Hands.

Zoo.
Ramler, Karl Wilhelm (1725–98)
Yearning for Winter.
Rampolekeng, Leseko (b. 1965)
Welcome to the New Consciousness.
Wet Pain . . . Tread with Care.
Ramsay, Allan (1686–1758)
Gentle Shepherd, The, sels.
Jenny Nettles.
Lass of Patie's Mill, The.
Lass with a Lump of Land.
Lucky Spence's Last Advice.
Ode to Mr. F— [or Mr. Forbes].
Poet's Wish, The; an Ode.
Polwart on the Green.
Thou Were My Ain Thing, An.
Up in the Air.
Ramsdell, Heather (b. 1968)
Bright Receding.
Good Sheep.
If It Is True What Is Said of the Work.
In Spite of How.
Moveable Figures.
Nearly Circle.
Vague Swimmers, sels.
Where Things of a Kind.
Ramsey, Jarold (b. 1937)
Comet and Treefrog.
Hand-Shadows.
Ontogeny.
Power Quest, Sooke Park.
Tally Stick, The.
Ramsey, Lara (b. 1974)
That Which Hovers.
Ramsey, Martha (b. 1954)
Moving Out.
Ranaldo, Lee
Five Weeks.
Flash me.
HIS:STORY.
Killed.
No Deal.
Refugee, A.
Steel.
Time Presses Me.
Ttest.
Wrong #.
Randall, Belle (b. 1940)
Be He Ezra Pound, Kennedy, or King.
Randall, Deborah (b. 1957)
Ballygrand Widow.
Blue Dome, The.
Finney's Bar.
Haymakers.
His Favourite Seat.
Nightwatchman.
Randall, Dudley (b. 1914)
Bag Woman.
Ballad of Birmingham.
Blackberry Sweet.
Booker T. and W. E. B.
George.
Idiot, The.
Langston Blues.
Memorial Wreath.
Old Witherington.
Poet Is Not a Jukebox, A.
Southern Road, The.
To the Mercy Killers.
Vacant Lot.
Randall, James A., Jr. (b. 1938)
When Something Happens.
Randall, James Ryder (1839–1908)
My Maryland.
Randall, Margaret (b. 1936)
Borders.
I Want the Words Back.
Nushu.
Past Is, The.
Poetry Became.
Randell, Elaine (b. 1951)
Digging up weeds by the little hedge.
Hard to Place.
Snoad Hill Poems, The, sels.

Songs for the Sleepless, *sel.*
Randolph, Innes (1837–87)
　Rebel, The.
Randolph, Thomas (1605–35)
　Answer to Master [*or* Mr.] Ben Jonson's Ode,
　　to Persuade Him Not to Leave the Stage,
　　An.
　Devout Lover, A.
　Elegy, An: "Love, give me leave to serve thee,
　　and be wise"
　Elegy upon the Lady Venetia Digby, An.
　Epitaph: "Beauty itself lies here, in whom
　　alone."
　Gratulatory to Mr. Ben Johnson for His
　　Adopting of Him to Be His Son, A.
　He Lives Long Who Lives Well.
　In Praise of Women in General.
　Ode to Master [*or* Mr.] Anthony Stafford to
　　Hasten Him into the Country, An.
　On Sir Robert Cotton the Antiquary.
　On the Death of a Nightingale.
　Pastoral Courtship, A.
　Second Epode of Horace Translated, The.
　Upon His Picture.
　Upon the Loss[e] of His Little Finger.
Rands, William Brighty (1823–82)
　Cat of Cats, The.
　Thought, The.
Rankin, Jennifer (1941–79)
　Forever the Snake.
　Love Affair 36.
　Man is following me, A.
　Old Circles.
　Old Currawong.
　Sea and Other Stories, The.
　Sea-bundle.
　Tale.
Rankine, Claudia
　Eden.
　Elsewhere, Things Tend.
　Man. His Bowl. His Raspberries, The.
　New Windows.
　Quotidian, The.
　Short Narrative of Breasts and Wombs in
　　Service of Plot Entitled, A.
　Short Narrative of Hand and Face in Service of
　　Plot, Entitled, A.
　Testimonial.
Rankins, William (*fl.* 1588–1601)
　Satyrus Peregrinans, *sel.*
Ransetsu (Hattori Ransetsu) (1653–1708)
　All by itself.
　Each morn / From the straw raincoat.
　Five rice dumplings.
　Fly, dare take / The rice grain.
　Large slug slides, A.
　Melon / How well.
　On the old plum tree.
　Single leaf falls, A.
　Traveling / old armor.
　Without a sound.
Ransetsu, Hattori *See* Ransetsu
Ransford, Tessa
　First Thaw.
　Stable Relationship, A.
　Viewpoint.
Ransom, Jane R. (b. 1958)
　This Is Just a Fairy Tale.
Ransom, John Crowe (1888–1974)
　Amphibious Crocodile.
　Antique Harvesters.
　Armageddon.
　Bells for John Whiteside's Daughter.
　Blackberry Winter.
　Blue Girls.
　Captain Carpenter.
　Dead Boy.
　Equilibrists, The.
　Good Ships.
　Jack's Letter.
　Janet Waking.
　Judith of Bethulia.
　Lady Lost.
　Necrological.
　Nocturne.

Old Man Pondered.
Old Mansion.
Painted Head.
Painting: A Head.
Parting, without a Sequel.
Philomela.
Piazza Piece.
Sixteen Poems in Eight Pairings, *sels.*
Spectral Lovers.
Spiel of [the] Three Mountebanks.
Survey of Literature.
Tall Girl, The.
Vision by Sweetwater.
Ransom, W. M. (b. 1945)
　Message from Ohanapecosh Glacier.
　Pastime Café.
Ransome-Davies, Basil
　Raymond Chandler: The Big Sleep.
Rao, Abburi Ramakrishna (1896–1979)
　Farmer's Song, The.
　Longing, A.
Rao, Kaloji Narayana (1914–2002)
　We Should Remember.
Rao, Sishtla Uma-Maheswara (1909–53)
　Memories: "My name is Lila."
Rapin, Rene (1621–87)
　Of Gardens, *sels.*
Rapoport, Aaron (1895–1964)
　Strike.
Rapp, Elizabeth
　I hang from a thin green rope.
Ras, Barbara
　Childhood.
　In the New Country.
　My Train.
　Pregnant Poets Swim Lake Tarleton, New
　　Hampshire.
　Sadness of Couples, The.
　Sadness of Memory, The.
Rash, Ron (b. 1953)
　Devil Beating His Wife.
　July, 1949.
Rashad, Johari M.
　Morning After, The.
　Place Setting.
Raskin, Willie
　Wedding Bells Are Breaking Up That Old
　　Gang of Mine.
Ratcliff, Carter
　Big Bad Art Thing, The.
　So Gallantly Streaming: To the Poet.
Ratcliffe, Stephen
　Diagonal plane of low grey white cloud
　　moving.
Rattenbury, Arnold
　Rain Falls on Utopia Too.
　War Memoir, A.
Rattray, David
　They Don't Have to Have That Look.
Ratushinskaya [*or* Ratushinskaia], Irina (b. 1954)
　But Only Not to think.
　For the cry from the well of "mama!"
　I Had a Strange Dream.
　I Will Live and Survive.
　Like Mandelstam's swallow.
　Penelope, the screaming is all over.
　Thus you lived your life without regret.
　Try to Cover Your Shivering Shoulders.
Ratzlaff, Keith (b. 1953)
　Dill.
　Gospel.
　Group Portrait with Ukuleles.
　My Students against the Cemetery Pines.
　Necessity.
　Rough-Cut Head.
Ravenscroft, Edward (c.1643–1707)
　In Derision of a Country Life.
Ravenscroft, Thomas (c.1592–c.1635)
　Belmans Song, A.
　Sing we now merily.
Ravikovitch, Dahlia (b. 1936)
　Blood Heifer.
　Clockwork Doll.

Dress of Fire, A.
Real Love Isn't What It Seems.
Sound of Birds at Noon, The.
Surely You Remember.
Trying Again.
Unusual Autumn, An.
You Can't Kill a Baby Twice.
You Don't Kill Babies Twice.
Ravitch, Melech (Zekharye Khone Bergner)
(1893–1976)
　Twelve Lines about the Burning Bush.
Rawling, Tom
　Gas Drill.
Rawlins, C. L.
　Living in at Least Two Worlds.
Rawls, Alex
　H. S. Mauberley (Life and Contacts) Part 1 by
　　Ezra Pound.
　Marriage of Heaven and Hell by William
　　Blake, The.
　Song of Myself by Walt Whitman.
　What's Your Sign?, *sels.*
Raworth, Tom (b. 1938)
　Bolivia: Another End of Ace.
　Dark Senses.
　Future Models May Have Infra-Red Sensors.
　Jungle Book.
　Lion Lion.
　Out of a Sudden.
　Ozymandias.
　That More Simple Natural Time Tone
　　Distortion.
Rawson, Joanna (b. 1964)
　Border, The ("Leaping from the eucalyptus
　　branch, the wild desert pigs.").
　Border, The ("Sliding from half-up the
　　eucalyptus trees, the wild desert pigs
　　practice flight.").
　Map Burnt Through.
　Self-portraits by Frida Kahlo.
Rāy, Dāśarathi (1807–57)
　It's no one else's fault, Syama Ma.
　Wake up, wake up, Mother!
　Who is this black.
Ray, David (b. 1932)
　At the Washing of My Son.
　Automat.
　Brides of Elvis, The.
　Doing Without.
　Eskimo Girl, The.
　For Harry S Truman in Hell.
　In the Third Month.
　Journey with Basho, A.
　Midnight Diner by Edward Hopper, A.
　Sunday Morning.
　Thanks, Robert Frost.
Ray, Henrietta Cordelia (1861?–1916)
　After the Storm.
　Afterglow, The.
　Ambition.
　Among the Berkshire Hills.
　Anita and Giovanni.
　Antigone and Oedipus.
　April.
　Aspiration.
　At Christmas-Tide.
　At Nature's Shrine.
　At Sunset.
　At the Cascade.
　August.
　Awakening.
　Beethoven.
　Boat Song.
　Broken Heart.
　Charity.
　Charles Sumner.
　Chateaux en Espagne.
　Cloud Fantasy.
　Cloud Song.
　Coming of Spring, The.
　Compensation.
　Cuckoo Song.
　Dante.
　Dawn of Love, The.
　Dawn's Carol.

December.
Dream of Elfland, A.
Dream within a Song, A.
Easter Carol.
Echo Reverie.
Echo's Complaint.
Emerson.
Enchanted Shell, The.
Evening Prayer.
Fading Skiff, The.
Failure.
Fancy and Imagination.
February.
Fisherman's Story, The.
Fragment, A: "Our fancies are but joys all
    unexprest."
Full Vision.
God's Ways, Not Our Ways.
Greeting.
Group of Musings, A.
Hermit and the Soul, The.
Hidden Essence.
Hour's Glory, The.
Hymn to the Thousand Islands.
Ideal, An.
Idyl.
Idyl of Spring, An.
In Memoriam Frederick Douglass.
In Memoriam Paul Laurence Dunbar.
Incompleteness.
Instability.
Invocation to the Muse.
January.
July.
June.
Life.
Life's Boundary.
Limitations.
Lincoln.
Lines Written on a Farewell View of the
    Franconia Mountains at Twilight.
Listening Nydia.
Little Fay's Thanksgiving.
Longfellow.
Lost Opportunities.
Love's Vista.
Maid of Ehrenthal, The.
March.
May.
May's Invocation after a Tardy Spring.
Messengers, The.
Mignon.
Mildred's Doves.
Milton.
Mist Maiden, The.
Musidora's Vision.
My Easter Dove.
My Spirit's Complement.
Nature's Minor Chords.
Nature's Uplifting.
Niobe.
November.
O Restless Heart, Be Still!
Ocean Musing, An.
October.
Ode on the Twentieth Century.
On a Nook Called Fairyland.
On the Concord River.
On the Picture of a Child.
On the Rapids of the St. Lawrence.
Our Task.
Pastoral: "Annette came through the
    meadows."
Perfect Orchestra, The.
Picture, A.
Poet's Ideal, The.
Poet's Ministrants, The.
Prayer: "O Christ, who in Gethsemane."
Quebec.
Quest of the Ideal, The.
Questioning.
Raphael.
Recompensed?
Repose.
Retrospection.
Reunited.

Reverie.
Rhyme of the Antique Forest.
Robert G. Shaw.
Sculptor's Vision, The.
Sea Cadences.
Self-Mastery.
September.
Shadow and Sunrise.
Shakespeare.
Siren Bird, The.
Sky Picture.
Snow Song.
Song: "O sweet, sad, singing river."
Soul Incense.
Soul's Courts, The.
Star Song.
Sunset Picture.
Thought at Walden, A.
Thought of Lake Ontario, A.
Tireless Sculptor, The.
To Laura.
To My Father.
To My Mother.
Toussaint l'Ouverture.
Triple Benison, The.
Two Musicians, The.
Venus of Milo, The.
Verses to My Heart's-Sister.
Vision of Eve, The.
Vision of Moonlight, A.
Voices of the Rain.
Wendell Phillips.
William Lloyd Garrison.
Wood Carols.

Ray, Judy
    Rose Bay Willow Herb.
Rāy, Kumār Śambhucandra (*fl.* **early 19th cent.**)
    Tara, You are Cintamayi, Full of Thought.
Rāy, Mahārāja Nandakumār (d. 1775)
    You've enchanted the world.
Rāy, Mahārāja Rāmkrsna (d. 1795)
    Give me food.
    Moon flashes in Her blessed face, The.
Rāy, Naracandra (*fl.* **early 19th cent.**)
    Everything is Your wish, Tara.
Ray, Nova
    Last Flower, The.
Rāy, Raghunāth (d. 1836)
    Who is this.
Rāy, Rasikcandra (1820–93)
    Mountain / Whose woman have you brought
      home to our mountain city?
Rāy, Tāpas
    Wait a moment, Death.
Rayburn, Mary Kathleen
    Hurdler Explains Her Reasons, A.
Raye, Don (1909–85)
    Boogie Woogie Bugle Boy.
    I'll Remember April.
    Milkman, Keep Those Bottles Quiet!
    Mister Five by Five.
    You Don't Know What Love Is.
Rayes, Mitch (b. 1958)
    Stigmata.
Rayl, Johanna
    Spring Storm.
Raymond, Monica
    Crossing the River.
    First Harvest.
    June: "You can't hang a heavy mirror."
Raymond, Vicki (b. 1949)
    Extinguish, One by One.
    People, No, The.
    Reculver Bay.
Raymund, Bernard
    Well, The.
Raymund, Joan
    Ordeal of Love, The.
Raz, Hilda
    Before John and Maria's Wedding.
    Fast Car On Nebraska I-80: Visting Teacher.
    For Barbara, Who Brings a Green Stone in the
      Shape of a Triangle.
    Teaching, Hurt.

    Volunteers.
Razaf, Andy (1895–1973)
    Ain't Misbehavin.'
    Guess Who's in Town? (Nobody but That Gal
      of Mine).
    Honeysuckle Rose.
    I'd Give a Dollar for a Dime.
    Joint is Jumpin', The.
    Keepin' Out of Mischief Now.
    Memories of You.
    My Handy Man.
    My Handy Man Ain't Handy No More.
    My Man o' War.
    My Special Friend (Is Back in Town).
    Porter's Love Song to a Chambermaid, A.
    S'posin.'
    Stompin' at the Savoy.
    Tan Manhattan.
    You're Lucky to Me.
Razran, Gregory
    Jade's Iguanas Are Dead.
Rea, Tom
    Lugs Benedict on the Coast, 1934.
Read, Sir Herbert (1893–1968)
    End of a War, The.
    Garden Party.
    Happy Warrior, The.
    My Company.
    To a Conscript of 1940.
Read, Thomas Buchanan (1822–72)
    Sheridan's Ride.
    Summer Shower, The.
Reading, Peter (b. 1946)
    Evagatory, *sel.*
    Fates of Men.
    Going On, *sels.*
    Salopian.
    Soon and silently.
    Stet, *sel.*
    Ukulele Music, *sel.*
    Who would have thought it Sir, actually
      putting ME in a WRITING!
    Ye haue heard this yarn afore.
Reagon, Bernice
    Greed.
    They Are All Falling around Me.
Realuyo, Bino A.
    La Querida.
    Sojourners, The.
Reaney, James (b. 1926)
    Bicycle, The.
Rebelo, Jorge
    Poem of a Militant.
Rebolledo, Efrén (1877–1927)
    Sapho's Kiss.
Receveur, Don
    Cobra Pilot.
Rector, Liam (b. 1949)
    David's Rumor.
    First Grade.
    Him, His Place.
    My Grandfather Always Promised Us.
    Showing.
Red Elk, Lois
    For Thieves Only.
Red Hawk
    2 Ways of Crossing the Creek.
Réda, Jacques (b. 1929)
    Amen.
    Amen.
    Autumn Distance.
    Distance de l'automne.
Redcloud, Prince
    Farmer.
Redding, Edward C. (*fl.* **1950**)
    End of a Love Affair, The.
Reddy, Siva (b. 1943)
    Generations.
    We Write.
Reddy, Srikanth (b. 1973)
    Burial Practice.
    Corruption.
    Evening with Stars.

Hotel Lullaby.
Scarecrow Eclogue.
Second Circle.

Redel, Victoria
Bedecked.
Ninth Month.
Singing to Tony Bennett's Cock.

Reder, Claudia M. (b. 1952)
Lesson, The: "Stand next to your bike, like that."

Redgrove, Peter (1932–2003)
My Father's Trapdoors.
Negotium Perambulans.
Song: "I chuck my Bible in the parlour fire."
Visible Baby, The.

Redhill, Michael (b. 1966)
Haiku Monument for Washington, D.C.

Redi, Francesco (1626–98)
Bacchus in Tuscany, *sels.*

Redmond, Eugene B. (b. 1937)
Aerolingual Poet of Prey.
Ballad of Black/Essence.
Dance Bodies #1.
Distance.
11-Haiku-Poem for a Magnificent Million.
Epigrams for My Father.
Gwensways.
Highflown: Love.
Love Is Not a Word.
Love Necessitates.
Milestone: The Birth of an Ancestor.
My Tongue Paints a Path.
New York Seizures.
Poetic Reflections Enroute To, and During, The Funeral and Burial of Henry Dumas, Poet.
River of Bones and Flesh and Blood.
Tune for a Teenage Niece.

Redmond, Glenis
Mama's Magic.

Redmond, John (b. 1965)
Bead.
Bemidji.
Charlie and Joe.
Daumenbreite.
Let's Not Get Ahead of Ourselves.
Role.

Reece, Spencer (b. 1963)
Autumn Song.
Clerk's Tale, The.
Portofino.

Reed, Henry (1914–86)
Auction Sale, The.
Chard Whitlow.
Château, The.
Door and the Window, The.
Dull Sonnet.
Lessons of the War, *sels.*
Map of Verona, A.
Philoctetes.
Sailor's Harbor.

Reed, Ishmael (b. 1938)
Badman of the Guest Professor.
Beware: Do Not Read This Poem.
Black Cock, The.
Dualism in Ralph Ellison's Invisible Man.
Earthquake Blues.
El Paso Monologue.
Going East.
I Am a Cowboy in the Boat of Ra.
I am not the walrus.
Jacket Notes.
Loup Garou Means Change Into.
Nov 22, 1988.
Oakland Blues.
On the Fourth of July in Sitka, 1982.
Paul Laurence Dunbar in The Tenderloin.
Poetry Makes Rhythm in Philosophy.
Railroad Bill, A Conjure Man.
Reactionary Poet, The.
Sky Diving.
Turning Pro.
White Hope.
Why I Often Allude to Osiris.
.05.

Reed, John (1887–1920)
America in 1918, *sel.*

Reed, Pat (b. 1956)
Container of Stars.
September 11.
September 18.

Reed, Tennessee
Disney's Cinderella.

Reedy, Carlyle (b. 1938)
Doll Museum, The.

Rees, Elizabeth
Rockstar Poet.

Rees, John Machreth
Merioneth.

Rees, John Roderick (b. 1920)
Brenin Gwalia.

Rees-Jones, Deryn (b. 1968)
And Please Do Not Presume.
Great Mutando, The.
I Know Exactly the Sort of Woman I'd Like to Fall in Love With.
It Will Not Do.
Largo.
Making for Planet Alice.
Service Wash.
What It's Like To Be Alive.

Reese, Doc
Ol' Hannah.

Reese, Lizette Woodworth (1856–1935)
April in Town.
At Cockcrow.
Crows.
Day Before Spring, The.
Death's Guerdon.
Flower of Mullein, A.
Fog.
In Time of Grief.
Indian Summer.
Lavender Woman, The.
Love, Weeping, Laid This Song.
Lyric on the Lyric, A.
Mid-March.
Mystery.
Nocturne: "Topple the house down, wind."
Old Belle, An.
One Night.
Ownership.
Prayer of an Unbeliever.
Puritan Lady, A.
Rachel.
Renunciation.
Reserve.
Spicewood.
Spring Ecstasy.
Tears.
Telling the Bees.
To Life.
Trust.
War Memory, A.
White Fury of the Spring, The.
Wind.

Reese, Rita Mae
Remembering Emily.

Reeve, F. D. (b. 1928)
Hope.
Illusion, The.
Voices: "When I hear my lover singing, I sing, too."

Reeves, James (1909–78)
Cows.
Four Horses, The.
Mr. Tom Narrow.
Others.
Sea, The.
Slowly.
W.

Regan, Jennifer
In Flight.

Rege, Sadanand (1923–82)
Old Leaves from the Chinese Earth.

Regier, G. Travis
Of Violence.
Where We All Went.

Regino, Juan Gregorio (b. 1962)
Cantares.
Cantares.
Nijmi en Nima.

Rehm, Pam (b. 1967)
Thus I Find My Legs.
Vow 2.

Reibetanz, David (b. 1982)
Norgberto Hernandez—Photographed Falling September Eleventh.

Reibetanz, John (b. 1944)
Head and Torso of the Minotaur.

Reich, Asher (b. 1937)
Siren of Love, A.

Reichard, William (b. 1963)
Cloud Game, The.
Monster's Dream, The.

Reid, Alastair (b. 1926)
Curiosity.
Daedalus.
Figures on the Frieze, The.
Lesson in Music, A.
Manse, The.
Propinquity.
Scotland: "It was a day peculiar to this piece of the planet."
Spell for Sleeping, A.
Weathering.

Reid, Christopher (b. 1949)
Baldanders.
Fetish.
Howl, Howl.
In the Echoey Tunnel.
Memres of Alfred Stoker, *sel.*
Mermaids Explained.
Perversion, A.
Stones and Bones.
What the Uneducated Old Woman Told Me.
Whole School of Bourgeois Primitives, A.

Reid, Dorothy E.
Between Aphorisms.

Reid-Marr, David Tokuyu
Cedar.
Condor.
Live Oak.
Zen Mountain Center.

Reilly, Patricia Lynn
Imagine a Woman, *sel.*

Reimer, Nadia Hazboun
Middle East, The.
To an Old Friend.
Workaholic.

Rein, Yevgeny [or Evgenii] Borisovich (b. 1935)
Breakfast on the Balcony.
Monastery.
Moscow Station, The.
Nanny Tanya.
Return, The.
Secret Agent, A.

Reinmar der Alte (fl. 1185–1205)
Messenger, hear what I say.
No one needs to ask.

Reis, Patricia
Ancient Ones, The.

Reis, Yitzhok *See* Nadir, Moishe

Reisen, Abraham (1876–1953)
Household of Eight.

Reitenauer, Vicki L. (b. 1964)
Wife Of.

Reiter, Thomas
Class Bully.
Rights of Way.

Reito
Ox bridle tossed, vows taken.

Reizan (d. 1411)
Myriad differences resolved by sitting, all doors opened, The.

Rekdal, Paisley (b. 1970)
Americana.
Crash of Rhinos, A.
Strawberry.
Stupid.
What Was There to Bring Me to Delight But to

Love and Be Loved?

Remizov, Alexei (1877–1957)
Eaten by the Wolf.
Mouse, The.
Without Heat.

Remoto, Danton R.
Black Silk Pajamas.
Exile.
Images of John (1967–92).
Rain.

Rendall, Robert (1898–1967)
Angle of Vision.
Horse-Mill, The.

Rendon, Marcie
You See This Body.

Rendra, W. S.
Baby at the Bottom of the River.
Moon's Bed, the Bride's Bed, The.
Tall Weeds.
World's First Face, The.

Renk, Charlotte
Mistletoe Kills.
Past Perm and Glitz.

Renshaw, Edyth
Pantoum: In a Texas Farm-House Kitchen.

Repetto, Vittoria
6th Grade—Our Lady of Pompeii.

Replansky, Naomi (b. 1918)
Dangerous World, The.
Six Million, The.

Reposa, Carol Coffee
Alamo Plaza at Night.
At Fort Clark.
Dawn in El Paso.
Hempstead, 1923.
Hill County Rest Home.

Reps, Paul
Open here.
Pine needling.
Well silently overflowing.
Who is.

Résil, Carlo
Walls of Bois-de-Chene Shacks, The.

Resnikoff, Alexander
Bad and Good.

Restifo, Elaine
Jealousy: "I've watched a young woman
   fondling three strands of her own hair."

Retallack, Joan (b. 1941)
Biographia Literaria.
Here's Looking at You Francis Bacon.
Japanese Presentation I and II.
Not a Cage.
Secret Life of Gilbert Bond, The.
Western CIV, 4 and 5.
Woman Dragged by Welsh Corgis.

Retivova, Tatyana (b. 1969)
Elegy to Atlantis.

Reuental, Neidhart von (fl. 13th cent.)
Sing, my golden cock, I'll give thee grain!
Summer, now we must live without your sweet
   weather.
There is pain in my heart.
Young and old, rejoice.

Reuther, Linda
Homecoming, sel.

Revâni (d. 1524)
What do you say about that cypress body that
   hunts the heart?

Revard, Carter (b. 1931)
And Don't Be Deaf to the Singing Beyond.
Birch Canoe.
Christmas Shopping.
Discovery of the New World.
Dragon-Watching in St. Louis.
Driving in Oklahoma.
In Kansas.
Looking Before and After.
My Right Hand Don't Leave Me No More.
October, Isle of Skye.
Parading with the Veterans of Foreign Wars.
Swinging Low.

Revell, Donald (b. 1954)
At the Exhibition of Parables.
Fauviste.
Fewer Than Music.
How Passion Comes to Matter.
Last.
Lyre.
Memory of New England, The.
1919.
Tooms 4.
What Can Stop This.
World, The.

Reverdy, Pierre (1889–1960)
Adieu.
Air: "Forgetting."
Behind Eyelids.
Breath.
Ça.
Dans les champs ou sur la colline.
Departure.
Endless Journeys.
Fires Smoulderning Under Winter.
Head Filled with Beauty, The.
Heavier.
In the Fields or on the Hill.
Internal Travels.
Is Ajar.
Nocturne: "Street is pure black and there are
   no seasonal traces, The."
On the Threshold.
Plus Lourd.
Post.
Road.
Secret.
S'entre-bâille.
Souffle.
Spirit Escapes, The.
Squares.
Tête Pleine de Beauté, La.
That.
Trame, La.
Web, The.

Revett, Eldred (b. c.1635)
Ode: Hastening His Friend into the Country.

Reviczky, Gyula (1855–89)
Death of Pan, The.
I Am the Son of King Gog of Magog.
To János Arany in Answer to His Poem
   "Cosmopolitan Poetry."

Rexford, Eben Eugene (1848–1916)
Joy: "It's joy to be up in the morning when the
   dew's on the grass and clover."

Rexroth, Kenneth (1905–82)
Air and Angels, sels.
American Century, The.
Andrée Rexroth ("Now once more gray
   mottled buckeye branches.").
Andrée Rexroth ("Years have gone, The. It is
   spring."), sels.
Another Spring.
Asagumori.
August 22, 1939.
Bad Old Days, The.
Blues: "Tops of the higher peaks, The."
City of the Moon, The, sel.
Delia Rexroth ("California rolls into.").
Delia Rexroth ("Under your illkempt yellow
   roses.").
Earth Sky Sea Trees Birds House Beasts
   Flowers, sel.
Empty Mirror.
Floating.
For Eli Jacobson.
Heart's Garden, the Garden's Heart, The, sel.
Homer in Basic.
It Is a German Honeymoon.
Lights in the Sky are Stars, The, sels.
Love Poems of Marichiko, The, sels.
Lyell's Hypothesis Again.
On Flower Wreath Hill.
Poem: "As the full moon rises."
Prolegomenon to a Theodicy, A, sels.
Proust's Madeleine.
Quietly.
Requiem for the Spanish Dead.

Signature of All Things, The.
Silver Swan, The, sels.
Sottoportico San Zaccaria.
Toward an Organic Philosophy, sels.
Vitamins and Roughage.
Wednesday of Holy Week, 1940.
Wheel Revolves, The.

Reyes, Alfonso (1889–1959)
Menace of the Flower, The.
Monterrey Sun.
Scarcely.
Tarahumara Herbs.
To-and-Fro of Saint Theresa.

Reyes, Carlos
Arizona Nocturne.
Bridges: "My first bridge was a log—a
   slippery one across a muddy creek."

Reynolds, A. Wanjiku H.
Rock Candy.

Reynolds, Craig (b. 1952)
Worst of it, The.

Reynolds, Elinor Wyn (b. 1970)
I Had a Really Good Idea for a Poem in
   Cynwil Elfed.
Night I Won the Crown in the National
   Eisteddfod of My Dreams, The.

Reynolds, Henry (fl. 1628)
Black Maid to the Fair Boy, The.

Reynolds, John (fl. 17th cent.)
Nosegay, A.

Reynolds, Malvina
This World.

Reynolds, Oliver (b. 1957)
Hazel.
Spanish Dancer.
Tone Poem, sels.

Reynolds, Rebecca (b. 1962)
Object of Burial Is Intent, The.
Peridot.
Surplus.

Reynolds, Samuel F. (b. 1967)
Moon/light Quarter/back Sack.
Open Letter to All Black Poets, An.
Whipping, The.

Reynolds, Tim (b. 1936)
To a Bad Heart.

Rezil, Kalo See Résil, Carlo

Reznikoff, Charles (1894–1976)
Among the heaps of brick and plaster lies.
Aphrodite Vrania.
April.
As I Was Wandering with My Unhappy
   Thoughts.
Babylon: 539 B.C.E.
Beggar Woman.
Bridge, The.
By the Well of Living and Seeing, sels.
Children.
David.
Day of Atonement.
Dead gull in the road, A.
Deserter, A.
Early History of a Writer, sels.
Epidemic.
Epilogue: "Blessed / in the light of the sun at
   the sight of the world."
Epitaph: "Not the five feet of water to your
   chin."
Epitaphs: "Drowning / I felt for a moment
   reaching towards me."
Exodus.
Four sailors on the bus, dressed in blue denim
   shirts.
Free Verse.
Girls outshout the machines, The.
Grove of small trees, branches thick with
   berries, A.
Heart and Clock.
Her work was to count linings.
Holocaust, sels.
House-wreckers, The.
How difficult for me is Hebrew.
I Do Not Believe That David Killed
   Goliath.

I have learnt the Hebrew blessing before eating bread.
I have not even been in the fields.
I like this secret walking.
I met in a merchant's place.
I walked through the lonely marsh.
I will write songs against you, *sel.*
Idiot, The.
If the ship you are traveling on is wrecked.
If there is a scheme.
If you cannot look at the sun.
In the shop, she, her mother, and grandmother.
Israel, *sel.*
Israel II.
It had long been dark, though still an hour before supper-time.
Jews in Babylonia, *sels.*
Joshua at Shechem.
Kaddish.
Kaddish.
Luzzato.
Mass Graves, *sel.*
Massacres.
Millinery District ("Clouds, piled in rows like merchandise, The.").
Millinery District ("Many fair hours have been buried here.").
My grandfather, dead long before I was born.
My work done, I lean on the window-sill.
New Year's.
Of course, we must die.
On Brooklyn Bridge I saw a man drop dead.
Out of the hills the trees bulge.
Permit me to warn you.
Rainy Season.
Romance.
She sat by the window opening into the airshaft.
She who worked patiently.
Shopgirls leave their work, The.
Showing a torn sleeve, with stiff and shaking fingers the old man.
Similes.
Still much to read, but too late.
Te Deum.
Testimony, *sels.*
Testimony: The United States (1901–1910) Recitative/The South.
They have built red factories along Lake Michigan.
Though our thoughts often, we ourselves.
What are you doing in our street among the automobiles, horse?
[Winter Sketches I].
[Winter Sketches II: Subway].
[Winter Sketches III].
[Winter Sketches IV].
[Winter Sketches V].

Rhianos
To Theodorus et al.

Rhodenbaugh, Suzanne
Civil War, The.

Rhodes, Martha
All the Soups.
Bare Windows.
Behind Me.
Disguised.
For Her Children.
His.
How Fast.
Inside Father's Pockets.
It Being Forbidden.
Robe, The.
Small Pain, A.
Sweeping the Floor.
Through Clouds, Their Whispers.
Who Knew.
Why She Hurries Out, Then Home.

Rhys, Edward Prosser (1901–45)
Memory, *sel.*

Rhys, Ernest (1859–1946)
Ballad of the Homing Man, The.

Rhys, Keidrych (b. 1915)
Interlude.

Riach, Alan
Antenor.

Sankey Hymns.

Ribemont-Dessaignes, Georges (b. 1884)
Artichokes.

Ricard, René (b. 1946)
Oh.
Party Crash.
Visions of Arthur.

Ricardo, Cassiano (1895–1974)
Orchid.

Rice, Dorothy Marie (b. 1948)
Ambrosia.
Remains.
Taproots.

Rice, Nicky
Mother's Room.

Rice, Stan (b. 1942)
Bicycle, The.
Monkey Hill.

Rich, Adrienne (b. 1929)
After Twenty Years.
Architect.
Art of Translation, The.
At a Bach Concert.
At the Jewish New Year.
Atlas of the Difficult World, An, *sels.*
Aunt Jennifer's Tigers.
Burning of Paper instead of Children, The.
Burning Oneself Out.
Camino Real.
Cartographies of Silence.
Children Playing Checkers at the Edge of the Forest.
Clock in the Square, A.
Contradictions: Tracking Poems, *sels.*
Culture and Anarchy.
Delta.
Dialogue.
Diamond Cutters, The.
Diving into the Wreck.
Dreamwood.
Eastern War Time, *sels.*
Eye, The.
Face to Face.
Final Notations.
Food Packages: 1947.
For a Friend in Travail.
For an Album.
For Ethel Rosenberg.
For the Record.
Fox.
From a Survivor.
From an Old House in America.
Ghazal.
Ghost of a Chance.
Grandmothers.
Harpers Ferry.
I Am in Danger—Sir.
I Dream I'm the Death of Orpheus.
Implosions.
In a Classroom.
In the Evening.
In Those Years.
Inscriptions, *sels.*
Insusceptibles, The.
Integrity.
Jerusalem.
Late Ghazal.
Letters in the Family.
Letters to a Young Poet.
Living in Sin.
Living Memory.
Loser, The.
Lucifer in the Train.
Mark of Resistance, A.
Marriage in the Sixties, A.
Mathilde in Normandy.
Middle-Aged, The.
Modotti.
1948: Jews.
Ninth Symphony of Beethoven Understood at Last as a Sexual Message, The.
North American Time, *sel.*
Not Like That.
Not Somewhere Else, But Here, *sels.*
Novel, The.

One Life.
Origins and History of Consciousness.
Orion.
Paula Becker to Clara Westhoff.
Phantasia for Elvira Shatayev.
Phenomenology of Anger, The.
Planetarium.
Power.
Prospective Immigrants Please Note.
Rusted Legacy.
School Among the Ruins, The.
Seven Skins.
Snapshots of a Daughter-in-Law.
Splittings.
Storm Warnings.
Tattered Kaddish.
Translations.
Trees, The.
Trying to Talk with a Man.
Twenty-one Love Poems, *sels.*
Two Songs, *sels.*
Upper Broadway.
Usonian Journals 2000.
Valediction Forbidding Mourning, A.
Versailles.
Walking Down the Road.
Woman Mourned by Daughters, A.
Woman wired in memories, A.
Women.
Yom Kippur 1984.

Richard, Brad
My Sixth Grade Sex Life: Milne Elementary, New Orleans.

Richard, M. C.
Snow: "White moths in crazy mobs."

Richard I, Coeur de Lion (1157–99)
Ja Nul Homs Pris Ne Ira a Raison.

Richardowlands *See* Verstegan [*or* Verstegen], Richard

Richards, Laura Elizabeth (1850–1943)
Eletelephony.
Kindness to Animals.
Molly Pitcher.
Nicholas Ned.
Old Joe Jones.

Richards, Michael (b. 1915)
After Christmas.
Christmas Spider, The.

Richards, Peter (b. 1967)
Away from you the seafloor's longitudinal.

Richards, Tad
Challenge to the Reader, A.

Richardson, Anthony
Song to Hymen: 1942.

Richardson, George Lynde (b. 1867)
Song of the Wheel, The.

Richardson, James
First Lady Challenges a Loa-as-Poem.
J-O-Y.
My Man Caliban!
Parnassus Rising.
Vectors: Aphorisms and Ten-Second Essays, *sel.*
Vectors: Forty-five Aphorisms and Ten-second Essays.

Richardson, Justin (b. 1889)
O To Scuttle From the Battle.
Retort Perfect, The.

Richardson, Kate C.
Aubade: "Geese flew by as you entered me, The."

Richardson, Lloyd
Poet Sings His Painting, The.

Richardson, Mamie A. (*fl.* 1920s)
Sonnet: "I still shall smile and go my careless way."

Richez, Valérie-Catherine (b. 1947)
Little Soul.
Petite âme, *sel.*

Richie, Eugene
Airports of the World.

Richman, Liliane
Rue de Rosiers: To My Brother Fred.
To Valenton: Impressions circa 1947.

Richter, Harvena (b. 1919)
Beginning.
Round Room, The.
Self in Variation, The: Scenes From
    Meditation.
Surfaces.
Richter, Jennifer
Everywhere the Earth Is Opening.
Madonna del Parto: Our Lady of Birth-Giving.
Nothing but Bad News.
Ricketts, Wendell (b. 1958)
Scout.
Ricks, David
Variation on a Theme of Baudelaire.
Rickword, Edgell (1898–1982)
Contemporary Muse, The.
Handmaid of Religion, The.
Luxury.
Moonrise Over Battlefield.
Moon-talk.
Soldier Addresses his Body, The.
To the Wife of a Non-interventionist Statesman
    (March 1938).
Trench Poets.
Winter Warfare.
Riddell, Alan (1927–77)
At the Hammersmith Palais.
Riddell, Elizabeth (b. 1909)
Letter, The.
News of a Baby.
Suburban Song.
Wakeful in the Township.
Ridge, John Rollin (1827–67)
California, *sels.*
Cherokee Love Song, A.
Mount Shasta: "Behold the dread Mt. Shasta,
    where it stands."
Rainy Season in California, The.
Stolen White Girl, The.
Ridge, Lola (Mrs. David Lawson) (1873–1941)
Alley, The, *sel.*
Chicago.
Fifth-Floor Window, The.
Ghetto, The, *sels.*
Kerensky.
Morning Ride.
Phyllis.
Stone Face.
Ridl, Jack (b. 1944)
Coach in Effigy.
Video Mama.
Ridland, John (b. 1931)
Blue Plate Tea Room: Sestina, The.
Lazy Man's Haiku, The.
New Person, A.
Ridler, Anne (1912–2001)
At Parting.
Before Sleep.
Corneal Graft.
Cranmer and the Bread of Heaven.
Edlesborough.
For a Child Expected.
Making Love, Killing Time.
Modern Love.
Some Time After.
Ridley, George
Cushie Butterfield.
Ridlon, Marci (b. 1942)
Fernando.
That Was Summer.
Riesco, Laura (b. 1939)
Burdens.
So You Would Listen to Me.
When I Passed in the Afternoon.
Rieu, Emile Victor (1887–1972)
Unicorn, The.
Rifat, Oktay
Flute, The.
To My Wife: "Anterooms keep nice and cool
    with you."
Rifqa [*or* Rifka], Fu'ad [*or* Fuad] (b. 1930)
Fortune Teller, The.
Riggs, Lynn
Santo Domingo Corn Dance.

Rihaku *See* Li Po
Rihani, Ameen *See* Al-Rihani, Amin
Riley, Denise (b. 1948)
Affections Must Not.
Cruelty Without Beauty.
Lure, 1963.
Lyric: "Stammering it fights to get."
Misremembered Lyric, A.
Seven Strangely Exciting Lies, *sels.*
Shantung.
Riley, James Whitcomb (1849–1916)
Country Pathway, A, *sel.*
Days Gone By, The.
Dubious "Old Kriss," A.
Eternity.
Few of the Bird-Family, A.
Happy Little Cripple, The, *sel.*
Jack the Giant-Killer.
King of Oo-Rinktum-Jing, The.
Little Orphant Annie.
Nine Little Goblins, The.
Nonsense Rhyme, A.
Old Sweetheart of Mine, An, *sel.*
Old Swimmin'-Hole, The.
Raggedy Man, The.
Silence.
Smitten Purist, The.
When the Frost Is on the Punkin.
Riley, John (1937–78)
At the Stanley Spencer Exhibition.
Summer Seeming.
Travel Notes.
Riley, Peter
Alstonefield V, *sel.*
E Questa Vita Un Lampo.
Elf Shots.
Excavations, *sels.*
Riley, Tomás
Low End, The.
Rilke, Rainer Maria (1875–1926)
Annunciation.
Archaic Torso of Apollo.
Archaic Torso of Apollo.
Autumn Day.
Before Summer Rain.
Birth of the Smile, The.
Buddha Inside the Light.
Childhood.
Day in October.
Death.
Departure of the Prodigal Son, The.
Duino Elegies, The [David Young Translation],
    sels.
Duino Elegies, The [Robert Kelly Translation],
    sels.
Duino Elegies, The [Stephen Mitchell
    Translation], *sels.*
Entrance.
Entrance.
Flamingos, The.
Gazelle, The.
Going Blind.
I Am Too Alone in the World.
I Believe in All That Has Never Yet Been
    Spoken.
I Find You.
I Find You, Lord, All Things and In All.
I Have Faith.
Imaginary Career.
Initiation.
Just as The Watchman.
Just as the Winged Energy of Delight.
Last Evening.
Last Evening, The.
Leda.
Life of the Virgin Mary, The, *sels.*
Man Watching, The.
Mary at Peace with the Risen Lord.
Mary's Visitation.
Merry-go-round, The.
Olive Garden, The.
On Music.
On the Marriage at Cana.
Orpheus, Eurydice, Hermes.
Panther, The.

Panther, The.
Panther, The.
Panther, The.
Pietà.
Requiem for the Death of a Boy.
Roman Fountain.
Self-Portrait.
Sometimes a Man Stands Up During Supper.
Sonnets to Orpheus, *sels.*
Spanish Dancer.
Spring Has Returned.
St. John, *sels.*
St. Luke, *sels.*
St. Matthew, *sels.*
Swan, The.
Swan, The ("This clumsy living that moves
    lumbering.").
Three Holy Kings, The.
Tombs of the Hetaerae.
Tombs of the Hetaerae.
Walk, A.
We Must Die Because We Have Known Them.
We Must Die Because We Have Known Them.
Woman Going Blind.
Rimbaud, Arthur (1854–91)
After the Flood.
Bad Blood.
Being Beauteous.
Blackcurrant River.
Bottom.
Cheated Heart.
Cities.
City.
Common Nocturne.
Dawn.
Departure.
Drunken Boat.
Drunken Boat, The.
Drunken Boat, The.
Drunken Boat [*or* Barge], The, *sel.*
Eighteen-Seventy, *sels.*
Evil.
Farewell.
Illuminations.
Lice-Seekers.
Lovely Morning Thought.
Morning.
Morning of Drunkenness.
My Bohemia (Fantasy).
Night Chant, The, *sel.*
Night in Hell.
Night of Hell, *sel.*
O saisons, O châteaux.
O seasons, o châteaux.
Obscur et froncé.
Our Assholes Are Different.
Promontory.
Romance.
Rooks, The.
Royalty.
Runt of a Dream, A.
Ruts.
Sales.
Seascape.
Sleeper in the Valley, The.
Thirst.
Vowels.
Voyelles.
Rimington, John
God of the Flies.
Rinckhart [*or* Rinkhart], Martin (1586–1649)
Now Thank We All Our God.
Riordan, Maurice (b. 1953)
Apples.
Caisson.
Comet, The.
England, His Love.
Holy Land, The.
Lines to His New Instructress.
Milk.
Some Sporting Motifs.
Southpaw.
Time Out.
Topiary.
Word from the Loki, A.

Ríos, Alberto A. (b. 1952)
Advice to a First Cousin.
Anselmo's Moment with God.
At Kino Viejo, Mexico.
Chance Meeting of Two Men, A.
Coffee in the Afternoon.
Death of Anselmo Luna, The.
Domingo Limón.
Dream of Husbands, A.
I Held His Name.
If I Leave You.
Incident at Imuris.
Island of the Three Marias.
Language of Great-Aunts, The.
Madre Sofía.
Man She Called Honey, and Married, The.
Man Then Suddenly Stops Moving, A.
Man Who Became Old, The.
Mi Abuelo.
Nani.
Physics of Sudden Light, A.
Purpose of Altar Boys, The.
Teodoro Luna's Two Kisses.
They Said I Was a Crying Bride.
Wet Camp.

Rising-Higgins, Mary
Black Top River Fires / A Corona.

Risset, Jacqueline (b. 1936)
Instants 1.
Love of Poetry.
M. S. 1544.
M. S. 1544 [Maurice Scève].
Voice: "World put back on its."

Rist, Johann (1607–67)
Eternity, Thou Thunderous Word, sel.
She Boasts of Her Constancy.

Ristovic, Aleksandar (b. 1933)
Essential, The.
Untitled.

Ritch, Olive M.
When I Woke, Everything Was the Same but
Different.

Ritchie, Elisavietta (b. 1932)
How to Write a Villanelle.
Sorting Laundry.

Ritchie, Elspeth Cameron
Electroconvulsive Therapy.

Ritsos, Yannis (b. 1909)
After the Defeat.
Afternoon.
Audible and Inaudible.
Distant, The.
End of Dodona II, The.
Erotica 12.
Evening Walk.
His Lamp Near Daybreak.
Marpessa's Choice.
Meaning of Simplicity, The.
Miniature.
Missing, The.
Morning.
Myopic Child, A.
Naked Face.
Not Even Mythology.
One Skit, Then Another.
Our Land.
Requiem on Poros.
Second Series, sels.
Unanswered.
Underneath Oblivion.

**Rittenhouse, Jessie Belle (Mrs. Clinton Scollard)
(1869–1948)**
Debts.

Ritterbusch, Dale
Choppers.
Thousand Cranes, A.

Rivard, David
Baby Vallejo.
Consolation.
Cures.
Fall River.
Firestone.
For Michaela.
How It Will Always Seem.
1966.

One Too Many Mornings.
Summons.
Torque.

Rivas, José Luis (b. 1950)
Don de resbalar.
Knack for Slipping Away, A.
Marea roja.
Red Tide.
Río 1.
River 1.
Season of Paradise, A.
Temporada de Paraíso, Una.
Thalassa.
Thalassa.

Rivera, Diana
Dinner Together.
Under the Apple Tree.

Rivera, Louis Reyes
Disdirected, The.

Rivera, María (b. 1971)
Transfer of Title.
Traslación de dominio.

Rivera-Garza, Christina (b. 1964)
Tercer Mundo.
Third World.

Rivers, Conrad Kent (1933–68)
Underground.
Watts.

Rivers, James W.
Illinois: At Night, Black Hawk's Statue
Broods.

Rizal, José (1861–96)
Water and Fire.

Rizdvenko, Tatyana (b. 1969)
Frost and sun, as needed.
It was such a pearly, pink season.

Roach, Eric (1915–74)
At Guaracara Park.

Robbins, Mary Susannah
Eclipse of the Moon.

Robbins, Richard
Women of Lockerbie, The.

Robbins, Zachary Scott
Beaches.
December 12th.
October 7th.

Roberson, Ed (b. 1939)
American culture is the pot.
Any Moment (12/4/69 4:30 A.M. Chicago).
Blue Horses.
Eclipse.
Four Lines of a Black Love Letter between
Teachers.
Ideas Gray Suits Bowler Hats Baal.
It must be that in the midst.
News Continued Release.
On the Calligraphy of Black Chant.
Poll.
Poor Houses, The.
Sonnet.
True We Are Two Grown Men.

Roberts, Allan (1905–66)
Put the Blame on Mame.
That Old Devil Called Love.
Tired.

Roberts, Andrea
Epistle to the Revolutionary Bible, An.

Roberts, Sir Charles G. D. (1860–1943)
Autochthon.
Marsyas.
Potato Harvest, The.
Skater, The.
Solitary Woodsman, The.
Sower, The.
Tantramar Revisited, The.
Winter Fields, The.

Roberts, Cindy Day
Enough: "Moon the color of an empty movie
screen, A."
Leopard, The.
Let Go of It.
Poor Zelda.

Roberts, David ("Dewi Havhesp") (1831–84)
Beloved, The.

Roberts, David Thomas
I Mandate Ridges Raving.
Little Pilot Knob.
Rodeo.
Tiff Belt Parley.
Toward Mena.

Roberts, Elizabeth Madox (1886–1941)
Christmas Morning.
Disconsolate Morning.
Evening Song.
Firefly.
Old Love in Song, An.
Orpheus.
People, The.
Sky, The.
Stranger.
Woodpecker, The.

Roberts, Emrys (b. 1926)
Primo Levi.

Roberts, John (b. 1945)
One.

Roberts, Katrina
Cantata, 8: "Early March, trickle and rush of
ice melt in mountains."
How Late Desire Looks.
Postcard from the Coast.

Roberts, Kim (b. 1961)
Constellation Frigidaire, The, sels.
Night Tumbles into Town by Rail.
Plastic Cup, The.

Roberts, Len
Acupuncture and Cleansing at 48.
And Where Were You.
Another Spring on Olmstead Street.
Assignment, The.
God's Blessing.
I Blame It On Him.
Men's Talk.
My Father's Whistle.
Problem, The.
Sister Ann Zita Shows Us the Foolishness of
the Forbidden Books.
Window of Our Soul.

Roberts, Lynnette (1909–95)
Gods with Stainless Ears, sels.
Poem from Llanybri.

Roberts, Michael (1902–48)
Les Planches-en-Montagnes.
Midnight.

Roberts, Michael Symmons
Wireless.

Roberts, Michele (b. 1949)
Magnificat.
Your job's to work the surface. Don't.

Roberts, Nigel (b. 1941)
After / the Moratorium Reading.
Gull's Flight, The.
Max Factor Pink.
Mona Lisa Tea Towel, The.
Nigger and Some Poofters, A.

Roberts, Sybil J.
Poem # 3: "Today, I'm wearing new love."

Roberts, Teresa Noelle
Apotheosis of the Kitchen Goddess 2.

Roberts, Ursula See Miles, Susan

Robertson, Alexander (d. 1916)
Song of the Dove, The.

Robertson, Eliza (1771–1805)
Poetical Epistle to an Absent Friend, A, sel.

Robertson, James Logie (1846–1922)
Discovery of America, The.
George Buchanan in Old Age.
Melt Twa.
Royalty.

Robertson, Lexie Dean (1893–1954)
Aunt Gilly.
Memorabilia.
Pioneer: The Vignette of an Oil-Field.
Texas Memoranda.

Robertson, Lisa
Debbie: An Epic.

Residence at C——— ("Give me hackneyed words because.").
Residence at C——— ("My purpose here is to advance into.").
Tuesday.
Wednesday.

Robertson, Robin (b. 1955)
Aberdeen.
Affair of Kites.
Artichoke.
Camera Obscura, *sels.*
Fall: "Leaves are falling, falling from trees, The."
Flags of Autumn from Camera Obscura.
Fugue for Phantoms.
Immoralist, The.
New Gravity.
Three Ways of Looking at God.
Waves: "I have swum too far."
Wedding the Locksmith's Daughter.

Robeson, Ed
Answers, The.
Counsel of Birds, The.
Memorium.

Robin, Leo (1895–1984)
Beyond the Blue Horizon.
Diamonds Are a Girl's Best Friend.
Easy Living.
For Every Man There's a Woman.
Hallelujah!
Hooray for Love.
In Love In Vain.
Little Girl from Little Rock.
Louise.
Love Is Just Around the Corner.
My Cutey's Due at Two-to-Two Today.
My Ideal.
No Love, No Nothin.'
Prisoner of Love.
Thanks for the Memory.
True Blue Lou.

Robinson, Agnes Mary Frances (Mme Duclaux) (1857–1944)
Art and Life.
Celia's Home-Coming.
Darwinism.
Dead Friend, The.
Idea, The.
Love, Death, and Art.
Neurasthenia.
Oasis, An.
Pallor.
Personality.
Posies.
Rosa Rosarum.
Scape-Goat, The.
Search for Apollo, A.
Sibyl, The.
Song: "Oh for the wings of a dove."
Stornelli and Strambotti.
To a Dead Friend.
To My Muse.
Tuscan Olives.
Unum est Necessarium.
Valley, The.
Venetian Nocturne.
Wise-Woman, The.

Robinson, Corinne Roosevelt (1861–1933)
Path that Leads to Nowhere, The.
We Who Have Loved.

Robinson, Edwin Arlington (1869–1935)
Aaron Stark.
Ballade of Broken Flutes.
Ben Jonson Entertains a Man from Stratford.
Bewick Finzer.
Boston.
Calvary.
Calverly's.
Cassandra.
Children of the Night, The.
Christmas Sonnet, A.
Clerks, The.
Cliff Klingenhagen.
Companion, The.
Credo: "I cannot find my way."

Dark Hills, The.
Eros Turannos.
Exit.
Field of Glory, The.
Firelight.
Flammonde.
Fleming Helphenstine.
For a Dead Lady.
George Crabbe.
Gift of God, The.
Hillcrest.
House on the Hill, The.
How Annandale Went Out.
Isaac and Archibald.
James Wetherell.
John Evereldown.
John Gorham.
Karma.
L'Envoi.
Lingard and the Stars.
Luke Havergal.
Man against the Sky, The.
Many Are Called.
Master, The.
Mill, The.
Miniver Cheevy.
Mr Flood's Party.
New England.
New Tenants, The.
Octaves, *sel.*
Old Story, An.
Pity of the Leaves, The.
Poem for Max Nordau, A.
Poor Relation, The.
Prodigal Son, The.
Reuben Bright.
Richard Cory.
St. Luke, *sel.*
St. Matthew, *sels.*
Shadrach O'Leary.
Sheaves, The.
Sonnet: "Master and the slave go hand in hand, The."
Sonnet: "Oh for a poet—for a beacon bright."
Souvenir.
Supremacy.
Tact.
Tavern, The.
Three Quatrains.
Too Much Coffee.
Torrent, The.
Two Men.
Uncle Ananias.
Unforgiven, The.
Verlaine.
Vickery's Mountain.
Villanelle of Change.
Walt Whitman: "Master-songs are ended, and the man, The."
Why He Was There.

Robinson, Elizabeth (b. 1961)
For Karen.
Fountain.
Meshes.
New Language, The.
Salisbury Plain.
Shatter.
Snow: "Purpose of the blanket, The."
Temple of the Mariposa.
Undoing, The.

Robinson, Kit (b. 1949)
First Thing.
Ice Cube.
Nesting of Layer Protocols.
Nursery Rhyme.
On the Corner.
Pontoon.
Severance.
3D Matchmove Artist, The.
Up Early, *sel.*

Robinson, Mark (b. 1964)
After Eighteen Years of This Sort of Thing.

Robinson, Mary ("Laura Maria") (1758–1800)
Bids Farewell to Lesbos.
Birth-Day, The.
Bower of Pleasure, The.

Camp, The.
Canzonet.
Contemns its Power.
Contemns Philosophy.
Describes Her Bark.
Describes Phaon.
Describes the Characteristics of Love.
Describes the Fascinations of Love.
Determines to Follow Phaon.
Dreams of a Rival.
Foresees Her Death.
Haunted Beach, The.
Her Address to the Moon.
Her Confirmed Despair.
Her Last Appeal to Phaon.
Her Passion Increases.
Her Reflections on the Leucadian Rock Before She Perishes.
Invokes Reason.
January, 1795.
Laments Her Early Misfortunes.
Laments the Volatility of Phaon.
Laura to Petrarch.
London's Summer Morning.
Modern Female Fashions.
Modern Male Fashions.
Negro Girl, The.
Ode Inscribed to the Infant Son of S.T. Coleridge, Esq, *sel.*
Phaon Awakes.
Phaon Forsakes Her.
Poet's Garret, The.
Poor Singing Dame, The.
Previous to Her Interview with Phaon.
Progress of Liberty, The, *sels.*
Reaches Sicily.
Rejects the Influence of Reason.
Reproaches Phaon.
Resolves to Take the Leap of Leucata.
Sappho and Phaon, *sels.*
Sappho Discovers Her Passion.
Sappho Rejects Hope.
Sappho's Address to the Stars.
Sappho's Conjectures.
Sappho's Prayer to Venus.
Savage of Aveyron, The.
She Endeavors to Fascinate Him.
[Sonnet] Conclusive.
Sonnet Introductory.
Stanzas: "In this vain, busy world, where the good and the gay."
Suspects his Constancy.
Temple of Chastity, The.
Thousand Torments, A.
To a Sigh.
To Liberty.
To Phaon ("Can'st thou forget, O! Idol of my soul!").
To Phaon ("Oh! I could toil for thee o'er burning plains.").
To Phaon ("Why art thou changed? O Phaon! tell me why?").
To the Eolian Harp.
To the Muses.
Tyranny of Love, The.
Visions Appear to her in a Dream.
Walsingham; or, the Pupil of Nature.

Robinson, Matt (b. 1974)
Body as dictionary, as bible, The.
Move to liquid, A.
Snow; a fear of dying.
Winter's affection, A; radiomimetic.

Robinson, Robert
Come, thou Fount of ev'ry blessing.

Robinson, Roland (b. 1912)
Cradle, The.
Creek, The.
Deep Well, *sel.*
Jarrangulli.

Robles, Al
Cutting Back the Ifugao Past.
Feasting with Etang a Hundred Times Around.
Manong with a Thousand Tribal Visions, The.
Remembering the Past.
Ryokan the Crazy Snow Poet.

Robson, Jeremy (b. 1939)
Blues for the Lonely.

Rocha, Jofre (b. 1941)
Guerilla Fighter.
Poem of Return.

Rochelle, Tania
Feeding the Worms.

Rochester, Elizabeth Wilmot, Countess of (d. 1681)
Song: "Nothing ades to Loves fond fire."

Rochester, John Wilmot, 2d Earl of (1647–80)
Against Constancy.
Constancy.
Disabled Debauchee, The.
Epitaph on Charles II.
Fall, The.
Imperfect Enjoyment, The.
Impromptu on Charles II.
Letter from Artemisa in the Town, to Chloe [or Cloe], in the Country, A.
Love And Life.
Mistress, The: A Song.
Mock Song, The.
Platonic Lady, The.
Ramble in St. James's Park, A.
Rochester Extempore.
Satire on Charles II, A.
Satire on Charles II, A, sel.
Satire [or Satyre or Satyr] against [Reason and] Mankind, A, sels.
Signior Dildo.
Sodom; or The Quintessence of Debauchery, sels.
Song: "Absent from thee, I languish still."
Song: "By all love's soft, yet mighty powers."
Song: "Give me leave to rail at you."
Song: "Love a woman? You're [or Y'are] an ass."
Song of a Young Lady to Her Ancient Lover, A.
Song: "Quoth the Duchess of Cleveland to counselor Knight."
To His Mistress.
Tunbridge Wells.
Upon [His] Leaving His Mistress.
Upon Nothing.

Rock, Daphne
Changing.
Mother.

Rodas, Ana María (b. 1937)
Poems from the Erotic Left.

Rodefer, Stephen (b. 1940)
Brief To Butterick.
Codex.
Inscription.
Plane Debris, sel.
Pretext.
Stewed and Fraught with Birds.

Rodenko, Paul (1920–76)
Bombing.
February Sun.

Roderick, David
Curlers at Dusk.

Rodgers, Carolyn M. (b. 1942)
Black Heart as Ever Green, The.
Feminism.
Group Therapy.
It Is Deep.
Mama's God.
Not About Poems.
Poem No. 1.
Slave Ritual.
Walk Like Freedom.
Written for Love of an Ascension—Coltrane.

Rodgers, Gordon (b. 1952)
Drowned.
Laboratory, The.
On the Ice.
White Wedding.

Rodgers, William Robert (1909–69)
Carol: "Deep in the fading leaves of night."
Field Day.
Home Thoughts from Abroad.
Lent.

Lovers, The.
Neither Here nor There.
Net, The.
Party, The.
Raider, The.
Resurrection: An Easter Sequence, sel.
Sing, Brothers, Sing!
Snow.
Stormy Night.
Swan, The.
White Christmas.
Words.

Rodney, Janet (b. 1941)
Bardo of Leaving.
Bardo of Perception.
Bardo of Sleep and Dream.
Bardo of the Threshold.
Bardo of War and Peace.
Bardo of Writing.

Rodrigues, Julia Park
Half-.

Rodriguez, Aidé
Sonido Ink(quieto).

Rodríguez, Aleida (b. 1953)
Apple.
Extracted.
Lexicon of Exile.
Torch.

Rodríguez, Claudio (1934–99)
Espuma.
Eugenio de Luelmo.
Eugenio de Luelmo.
Foam.
Gorrión.
Petty Time.
Siempre Será Mi Amigo.
Sparrow.
Tiempo Mezquino.
Who Will Be My Friend Always.

Rodriguez, John
How to Be a Street Poet.

Rodriguez, Judith (b. 1936)
About this Woman.
Eskimo Occasion.
In-flight Note.
Lifetime Devoted to Literature, A.
Mahogany Ship, The.
Nasturtium Scanned.
New York Sonnet.
Nu-plastik Fanfare Red.
Rebeca in a mirror.

Rodriguez, Luis J.
Always Running.
Fire.
Heavy Blue Veins.
Hungry.
Meeting the Animal in Washington Square Park.
My Name's Not Rodriguez.
Rainfall Piano.
Rant, Rave and Ricochet.
Reflection on El Train Glass.
Speaking with Hands.
To the Police Officer Who Refused to Sit in the Same Room as My Son because He's a "Gang Banger"
Victory, Victoria, My Beautiful Whisper.
We Never Stopped Crossing Borders.

Roe, Barbara
Into Concrete Mixer Throw.

Roeske, Paulette (b. 1945)
After the Funeral.
In the Theatre.
Preparing the Dead.

Roethke, Theodore (1908–63)
All the Earth, All the Air.
Bat, The.
Big Wind.
Carnations.
Child on Top of a Greenhouse.
Coming of the Cold, The.
Cuttings.
Cuttings (later) ("This urge, wrestle, resurrection of dry sticks.").
Dolor.

Dream, The.
Duet.
Elegy for Jane.
Field of Light, A.
Follies of Adam, The.
For An Amorous Lady.
Four for Sir John Davies.
Frau Bauman, Frau Schmidt, and Frau Schwartze.
Geranium, The.
Her Reticence.
Heron, The.
I Knew a Woman.
In a Dark Time.
Journey to the Interior.
Judge Not.
Lady and the Bear, The.
Light Listened.
Lizard, The ("Time to Tickle a Lizard, The.").
Long Live the Weeds.
Lost Son, The.
Meadow Mouse, The.
Meditation at Oyster River.
Mid-Country Blow.
Minimal, The.
Monotony Song, The.
Moss-Gathering.
My Papa's Waltz.
Night Crow.
Night Journey.
North American Sequence, sels.
Old Florist.
On the Road to Woodlawn.
Open House.
Orchids.
Otto.
Pike, The.
Praise to the End!, sel.
Premonition, The.
Return, The.
Root Cellar.
Rose, The.
St. Matthew, sels.
Saginaw Song, The.
Serpent, The.
Shape of the Fire, The.
She.
Sloth, The.
Song for the Squeeze-Box.
Thing, The.
Three Epigrams, sels.
To an Anthologist.
To Have the Whole Air!
Visitant, The.
Waking, The.
Waking, The ("I wake to sleep, and take my waking slow.").
Walk in Late Summer, A.
Weed Puller.
Wish for a Young Wife.
Yak, The.

Roffé, Mercedes (b. 1954)
Landscape of return is drawn, A.
Lighthouse of Alexandria, The.
Scene of Return is Sketched, A.
Wanted.

Rogers, Del Marie
Customs of the Country.
Great Blue Heron.
Near the Rio Grand.
Some Nights I Love Everybody in Texas.

Rogers, Elymas Payson (1815–61)
Poem on the Fugitive Slave Law, A, sel.

Rogers, Pattiann (b. 1940)
Before the Beginning: Maybe God and a Silk Flower Concubine Perhaps.
Dead Never Fight against Anything, The.
Elinor Frost's Marble-Topped Kneading Table.
Family Is All There Is, The.
Geocentric.
Infanticide.
Into the Light.
Justification of the Horned Lizard.
Kingdom of Heaven, The.
Moving God.
Opus from Space.

Origin of Order, The.
Rogers, Samuel (1763–1855)
 Boy of Egremond, The.
 Italy, *sels*.
 Italy, *sels*.
 Sleeping Beauty, The.
 To the Fragment of a Statue of Hercules,
  Commonly Called the Torso.
 Wish, A.
 Written in a Sick Chamber.
Roggeman, Willem M. (b. 1935)
 African Queen.
 Archaeological Find.
 Fata Morgana in Flanders.
Rogow, Jack (b. 1952)
 Symmetron: You and Brother Will.
Rohrer, Jane
 Bad Truth.
 Gearshift Poem, The.
 Hotel.
 In the Kitchen before Dinner.
 Mennonite Funeral in the Shenandoah Valley.
 Orchard in the Spring.
 Room 703.
 Stopping by Fields on a Snowy Afternoon.
Rohrer, Matthew (b. 1970)
 After the Wedding Party.
 Brooklyn Bridge.
 Childhood Stories.
 Comet.
 Credo: "I believe there is something else."
 Gliding Toward the Lamps.
 Hotel de L'Etoile.
 Hummock in the Malookas, A.
 Hunger of the Lemur, The.
 Last Look at the Mutineers, A.
 My Government.
 Precision German Craftsmanship.
 Quick Sell the Pig.
 Short History of Illumination, A.
 Starfish Waving to Me from the Sand.
 We Never Should Have Stopped at Pussy
  Island.
 Winged Snake Found on a Path.
 World at Night, The, *sel*.
Rojas, Gonzalo (b. 1917)
 And to Be Born Is Here an Unnameable Feast.
 Beautiful Ones, The.
 Bed with Mirrors.
 Chapter and Verse.
 Coast, The.
 What Do We Love When We Love?
Rojas, Steven Bonafide
 Creed of a Graffiti Writer, The.
Rokaku
 Is this to be?
Roland Holst, Adriann (1888–1976)
 Autumn Wind.
 Beggar Love.
 Being.
 I Who Was Born.
 Night Visit.
 Outside in the Open.
 Quatrain: "We're snug as a bug in a heated
  house."
 Time Now Please.
 Time, Please.
 Visitation.
Rolfe, Edwin (1909–54)
 About Eyes.
 Casualty.
 City of Anguish.
 First Love.
 Paris—Christmas 1938.
Rolle, Sojourner Kincaid
 Birds' Refuge, The.
 Blue Rock, The.
 Hands in the Motion of Prayer.
 Keeping Watch.
Rolle of Hampole, Richard (1300–49)
 Cantus Amoris 2.
 Love Is Life.
 Prayer to Jesus 1.
 Song of the Passion, A.

Rolleston, Thomas William Hazen (1857–1920)
 Grave of Rury, The.
Rollings, Alane (b. 1950)
 Dirty Dreams and God Smiling.
 For Dear Life.
 In Your Own Sweet Time.
 Light Years and the Love Lost in the
  Oleanders.
Rollinson, Neil (b. 1960)
 Ecstasy of St Saviour's Avenue, The.
Rolls, Eric (b. 1923)
 Bamboo.
 Dog Fight.
 Rain Forest.
Romano, Rose (*fl.* 20th cent.)
 Bucket, The.
 But My Blood.
 So I Lost My Temper.
Rome, Harold (1908–93)
 (All of a Sudden) My Heart Sings.
 Call Me Mister.
 Chain Store Daisy.
 Doing the Reactionary.
 Don't Wanna Write About the South.
 F.D.R. Jones.
 Military Life, The.
 Money Song, The.
 Nobody Makes a Pass at Me.
 Ring on the Finger.
 South America, Take It Away!
 Who Knows?
 Wish You Were Here.
Romero, Elaine
 Nuestro Marine.
Romero, Leo
 If Marilyn Monroe.
 Marilyn Monroe Indian.
 My Mother Didn't Learn.
 When She Opens the Door.
Romero, Nidia Sanabria de (b. 1928)
 New Suit, The.
Romo-Carmona, Mariana
 Crows.
 Daylight.
 Fish.
 Signs.
Romond, Edwin
 Lady Macbeth, Afterward.
Romtvedt, David
 Black Beauty, A Praise.
 Eating Dinner at My Sister's.
 Glass Canyons.
 Kiev, the Ukraine, Nuclear Accident.
Ronald of Orkney, Saint
 Attributes of a Gentleman, The.
Ronan, Richard
 Love Among Lepers.
Ronci, Seido Ray
 Becoming a Buddha.
 Cricket.
 Diamond Cutter.
 Old Monks Drinking.
Rondin, Leslie (b. 1954)
 Heraclitus.
Rong Zi
 Flowers No Longer Fly in Our City.
Ronsard, Pierre de (1524–85)
 Corinna In Vendome.
 Fragment of a Sonnet.
 Génèvres Hérissez, et Vous, Houx Espineux.
 Invective Against Denise, a Witch.
 Roses.
 Sonnets to Helen, *sels*.
 Time To Be Up, Marie, Young Sleepyhead.
Rontsh, Y. A. (1899–1985)
 Ballad of the Night.
 Done a Good Job.
 Rosa Luxemburg.
 Scottsboro.
 Wolves.
Rooney-Céspedes, Aidan (b. 1965)
 Cure, The.
 Nativity.

Rainbarrel.
 Retro Creation.
 Twice the Man.
Root, George Frederick (1820–95)
 Battle-Cry of Freedom, The.
Root, William Pitt (b. 1941)
 Sonnet 20: Remembering, from a Nazi Prison,
  a Teacher Years Before.
Rope, Henry E. G. (1880–1978)
 City of the Grail, The.
 Wasted years, the wasted years, The.
Roripaugh, Lee Ann (b. 1965)
 Heart Mountain, 1943, *sels*.
 Hiroshima Maiden.
 Pearls.
 Peony Lover.
Ros, Amanda (1860–1939)
 End of "Pain", The.
 I Love to See a Lady Nice and Natural at Any
  Price.
 Little Belgian Orphan, A.
 Old Home, The.
 On a Girl Who Took Action for Breach of
  Promise.
 On Visiting Westminster Abbey.
 Thoughts.
Rosales, Luis (d. 1992)
 Abrazada a una Lágrima.
 Agua Desatándose.
 Creciendo Hacia la Tierra.
 Evocación Para Grabarla en una Caja de
  Música.
 Evocation to Record a Music Box.
 Growing Toward the Earth.
 He Llegado al Final de la Casa Donde Están la
  Cocina y el Baño.
 I Know Too Well and Sadly Enough.
 I've Come to the Back of the House.
 Locked with a Tear.
 Loosening Water.
 Raíz, La.
 Root, The.
 Y Sé Muy Clara y Tristemente Bien.
Rosario, Maria del
 Latter-day Mother Courage.
Rosario, Marlynn
 Curing.
Roscoe, William Caldwell (1823–59)
 Butterfly's Ball [and the Grasshopper's Feast],
  The.
Roscoe, William Stanley (1782–1843)
 Camellia, The.
 On Being Forced to Part with his Library for
  the Benefit of his Creditors.
 To the Harvest Moon.
Rose, Billy (1899–1966)
 Cup of Coffee, a Sandwich, and You.
 Don't Bring Lulu.
 Great Day.
 I Found a Million Dollar Baby (In a Five and
  Ten Cent Store).
 I Wanna Be Loved.
 It's Only a Paper Moon.
 More Than You Know.
 Night Is Young and You're So Beautiful, The.
 Without a Song.
 Would You Like to Take a Walk?
Rose, Dilya (b. 1954)
 Queen Bee.
Rose, Dilys (b. 1954)
 Figurehead.
Rose, Jennifer (b. 1959)
 Suicide, The.
Rose, Juan Gonzalo (b. 1929)
 Marisel.
Rose, Peter (b. 1955)
 Anglo-Saxon Comedy.
 Terminus.
 Wind Debates Asian Immigration, The.
Rose, Rachel (b. 1970)
 Sestina of the Geographic Tongue.
 What the Japanese Perhaps Heard.
 What We Heard About the Japanese.

Rose, Wendy (b. 1948)
Alaskan Fragments June 1981—Summer Solstice.
Comparison of Hands One Day Late Summer El Sobrante.
Day They Cleaned Up the Border, The: El Salvador, February, 1981.
Endangered Roots of a Person.
For the Angry White Student Who Wanted to Know.
For the White Poets Who Would Be Indian.
If I Am Too Brown or Too White for You.
Leaving Port Authority for the St. Regis Rezz.
Long Division; a Tribal History.
Loo-wit.
Naayawva Taawi.
Naming Power.
Poet Haunted, The.
Robert.
Six Nations Museum Onchiota, New York—January.
Story Keeper.
Ta Tiopa Maza Win / Iron Door Woman.
Throat Song: The Whirling Earth.
Truganinny.

Roseliep, Raymond (1917–83)
EVA Psalm.

Rosemont, Penelope
Bad Days Will End, The.
Candle.
Passage.
Rising Asleep.

Rosemurgy, Catie (b. 1969)
Angel Finally Admits What She Knows to Lou Binkler of Bethany, Missouri, An.
Hard Put.
Love, with Trees and Lightning.
Mostly Mick Jagger.
Why God Invented the Cold.

Rosen, Corie
Madonna for the Damned—a 1980s Heroine.

Rosen, Ellen A.
Out in the Cold.

Rosen, Kenneth (b. 1940)
Along the Charles.
Kildan Women, The.
Of Marilyn, and Marijuana.

Rosen, Michael (b. 1946)
Christmas Dinner.
Eddie and the Birthday.
Fighters For Life.
From the winter wind.
Here is the News.
Humpty Dumpty.
This Morning.
You need me for sitting.

Rosenberg, David (b. 1943)
Isaiah: Chapter 66.
Psalms [David Rosenberg Adaption], sels.

Rosenberg, Isaac (1890–1918)
August 1914.
Break of Day in the Trenches.
Chagrin.
Dawn Behind Night.
Dead Heroes, The.
Dead Man's Dump.
Expression.
God.
I Am the Blood.
Jew, The.
Louse Hunting.
Mirror, The.
On Receiving News of the War.
One Lost, The.
Returning, We Hear the Larks.
Soldier: Twentieth Century.
Troop Ship, The.
Worm Fed on the Heart of Corinth, A.

Rosenberg, Lisa
Big White Dress, The.
Introduction to Methods of Mathematical Physics.

Rosenberg, Liz (b. 1955)
Accident, The.
City Baseball.

End of Winter.
Lesson in Anatomy, A.
Longing for Eternal Life, The.
Married Love.
No Boundaries.
Offspring, The.
Poems of Delight.
Prose Poems, sel.
Silence of Women, The.
Story of My Life, The.
Suburban Childhood, A.
Susquehanna.
Thanksgiving.
They Are Planning to Cancel the School Milk Program to Fund a Tax Cut for the Middle Class.
Which One Is the Grown-up? Haiku.

Rosenblatt, Sarah (b. 1962)
Leaving Home.
Mom and Dad Getting Older.
Procession, The.
Second Half of Our Lives, The.
Should I Stay or Should I Go?
Visiting New York.

Rosenfeld, Morris Jacob (1862–1923)
Memorial to Triangle Fire Victims.

Rosenstock, Gabriel (b.1949)
Search, The: "Where are the poems I promised."

Rosenthal, Gary
Ghetto Dokusan.
Wild Hooves.

Rosenthal, Gideon (1950–73)
Only 20 Years Old.

Rosidi, Ajip (b. 1938)
Only in Poetry.

Rosnay, Jean-Pierre (b. 1926)
Piazza San Marco.

Rospigliosi, Veronica
Leavetaking.

Ross, Abram Bunn (b. 1866)
Two in Bed.

Ross, Alan (1922–2001)
Destroyers in the Arctic.
En Route.
Mess Deck.
Off Brighton Pier.

Ross, Charles Henry (c.1842–97)
Jack.
John, Tom, and James.

Ross, Claire Ottenstein
Judge, The.

Ross, Gigi Maria
At the Threshold of the Moon.

Ross, Grace
Oil Well Fire.

Ross, Jerry (1926–55)
Damn Yankees, sels.
Hernando's Hideaway.
Hey There.
There Once Was a Man.
Whatever Lola Wants (Lola Gets).

Ross, Jerry See Adler, Richard

Ross, Leo (b. 1934)
Requiescat.
Requiescat.

Ross, Linwood M. (b. 1959)
Indecent Exposure (A True Story).
James Brown.

Ross, Martin (b. 1973)
Body Cavity.
This Message Will Self-Destruct in Sixty Seconds.

Ross, William [or Villeam] (1762–90)
Another Song.

Rosselli, Amelia (b. 1930)
Actions in my brain: these verbs, whose celerity.
Around This Body of Mine.
Blue That Isn't Even Blue or in Any Case, A.
Dawn Presented Itself Bare-Armed and Immodest.
Dialogue with the Dead.

Feeble Little Voice: All It Takes Is Barely Opening the Shutter, A.
From relief to relief, the white lines, the white paper.
How many fields which like a sponge.
I Dreamt of Visiting Relatives.
If the Soul Loses Its Gift Then It Loses Ground, If Hell.
In the Evening the Sky Roams, a Meaager.
Infinite We Count the Dead! The Dance is Almost Finished! Death.
Letter to Her Brother.
Martial Variations, sel.
Mirrors, The! The.
Negro blood flowing on his brown.
Sex violent as an object (whitened quarry of marble).
Tonight with Bold Desire.
Worthless as was her itinerary to fame.
You might as well think one thing or another.

Rosser, J. Allyn
First Empathy.
Lover Release Agreement.
Message: Bottle #32.
Parable of the Cheek.

Rossetti, Christina Georgina (1830–94)
Advent.
Advent: "Come, thou dost say to Angels."
Advent ("This Advent moon shines cold and clear.").
After Communion.
After Death.
Amen.
Amor Mundi.
Apple Gathering, An.
At Home.
Autumn ("I dwell alone—I dwell alone, alone.").
Autumn Violets.
Bed of Forget-Me-Nots, A.
Before the Beginning.
Behold a Shaking, sel.
Better Resurrection, A.
Birthday, A.
Bruised Reed Shall He Not Break, A.
By the Sea.
Cardinal Newman.
Caterpillar, The.
Chilly Night, A.
Christ Our All in All, sel.
Christmas Carol, A: "In the bleak mid-winter."
Christmas Eve.
City Mouse and the Garden Mouse, The.
City plum is not a plum, A.
Cobwebs.
Convent Threshold, The.
Cousin Kate.
Dead before Death.
Dirge, A: "Why were you born when the snow was falling?"
Echo.
Enrica, 1865.
Eve.
Ferry Me across the Water.
First Spring Day, The.
Flint.
Fly Away, Fly Away.
Frisky Lamb, A.
From Sunset to Star Rise.
From the Antique.
Goblin Market, sel.
Gone Before.
Good Friday ("Am I a stone and not a sheep.").
Handy Mole who plied no shovel, A.
Hark! the Alleluias of the great salvation.
Heaviness May Endure for a Night, But Joy Cometh in the Morning.
Hopping frog, hop here and be seen.
Horses of the Sea, The.
I caught a little ladybird.
If a pig wore a wig.
If Only.
In An Artist's Studio.
In Progress.
Iniquity of the Fathers upon the Children, The.

Introspective.
Italia, Io Ti Saluto!
"Kookoorookoo! kookoorookoo!" / Crows the
cock before the morn.
Last Rites.
Later Life: A Double Sonnet of Sonnets, sels.
L. E. L.
Let's Be Merry.
Life's Parallels, A.
Long Barren.
Lord, Grant Us Calm.
Maude Clare.
May: "I cannot tell you how it was."
Mix a Pancake.
Monna Innominata, sels.
My Dream.
My Friend.
No, Thank You, John.
Noble Sisters.
Old and New Year Ditties, sels.
Old-World Thicket, An.
On the Wing.
Pain or Joy.
Pause, A.
Prince's Progress, The, sels.
Promises like Pie-Crust.
Queen of Hearts, The.
Reflection.
Remember [Me].
Rest.
St. Michael and all Angels.
St. Peter ("St. Peter once: "Lord, dost Thou
wash my feet?").
Sappho.
Shut Out.
Sing-Song, sels.
Sketch, A.
Sleeping at Last.
Somewhere Or Other.
Song: "Oh roses for the flush of youth."
Song: "She sat and sang alway."
Song: "When I am dead, my dearest."
Soul, A.
Study (A Soul), A.
Summer Is Ended.
Symbols.
Thread of Life, The, sels.
Three Enemies, The.
Triad, A.
Twice.
Two Thoughts of Death.
Under Willows.
Uphill [or Up-Hill].
Venus's Looking-Glass.
What Are Heavy?
What are these that glow from afar.
What Would I Give?
What's in a Name?
Where Innocent Bright-Eyed Daisies Are.
Who Has Seen the Wind?
Who Shall Deliver Me?
Why did baby die. . .?
Wind Has Such a Rainy Sound, The.
Winter: My Secret.
World, The.

Rossetti, Dante Gabriel (1828–82)
Blessed Damozel, The.
Card-Dealer, The.
For "An Allegorical Dance of Women" by
Andrea Mantegna.
For Spring, by Sandro Botticelli, in the
Accademia of Florence.
For The Holy Family, by Michelangelo, in the
National Gallery.
For 'The Wine of Circe' by Edward Burne
Jones.
House of Life, The, sels.
Insomnia.
Marriage of St Katharine, by the same, A; in
the Hospital of St John at Bruges.
Match with the Moon, A.
My Sister's Sleep.
On Refusal of Aid between Nations.
On the Poet, Arthur O'Shaughnessy—.
Orchard-Pit, The.
Sea-Limits, The.

Sudden Light.
Trip to Paris and Belgium, A, sels.
Venetian Pastoral, by Giorgone, in the Louvre,
A ("Water, for anguish of the solstice:—
nay.").
Virgin and Child, by Hans Memmeling, A; in
the Academy of Bruges.
White Ship, The.
Woodspurge, The.

Rossetti, William Michael (1829–1919)
Jesus Wept.

Rossi, Tiziano (b. 1935)
Beach.
Insomnia.
Law.
Leaving.
Possibility.
Pot.
System.

Rossini, Clare (b. 1954)
Cupid.
Valediction.

Rossiter, Charles
Nostalgia.
Your Body Glistens From the Bath.

Rossman, Ed
Double Features.

Rosten, Norman (1914–95)
I am immortal in Cheyenne!
We came during those years.

Roston, Ruth
Program Notes.

Rostopchina, Evdokiya (1812–1858)
Unfinished Sewing, The.

"Rostrevor, George" See Hamilton, George
Rostrevor

Roth, Friederike (b. 1948)
Marriage.
Meadow and Might, sel.

Rothenberg, Jerome (b. 1931)
Aleph Poem.
At the Castle.
At Tsukiji Market Tokyo.
Cokboy.
Connoisseur of Jews, The.
Crazy Dog Events.
Hunger.
In the Dark Word, Khurbn.
Khurbn, sels.
Lorca Variations (XXVIII), The.
Nokh Aushvits (After Auschwitz).
Numerology.
Portrait of Myself with Arshile Gorky and
Gertrude Stein.
Praises of the Bantu Kings (1–10).
Prologomena to a Poetics.
Realtheater Piece Two.
Seneca Journal 1: "A Poem of Beavers"
Song of Quavering, A.
Structural Study of Myth, The.
That Dada Strain.
Visions of Jesus.
Water of the Flowery Mill (II), The.

Rothenberg, Jerome See Also Einzig, Barbara

Rothenberg, Michael (b. 1951)
Apocalyptic Yearnings.

Rothman, David J. (b. 1959)
Let It Snow.
One of the Lords of Life.
Resurrection of a Mouse.
Shape of Water Most Like Love, The.
When the Wind and Dark Waves Come.
Whistling in January.
Youth.

Rottman, Larry
Porter on the Trail, A.

Roubaud, Jacques (b. 1932)
Certaine manière je.
Dans cet arbre.
Everywhere the.
Glace de, Une.
Ice In.
Il pleut.
In This Tree.

It Is Raining.
Light, for Example.
Lumière, par exemple.
Méditation du 8/5/85.
Meditation of 8/5/85.
Partout les.
Passé, Le.
Past, The.
Some Thing Black, sels.
Way I, A.

Rouse, Anne (b. 1954)
Anaesthetist, The.
Birthday, A.
England Nil.
Faith Healers.
Glass.
Her Retirement.
Lilies of the Field.
Memo to Auden.
Narrows, The.
Queynt.
Sacrificial Wolf.
Springfield, Virginia.
Spunk Talking.
Sunday Morning.
Testament: "To my last technician."
Timing.
Uni-Gym, The.
Virginian Arcady.

Routh, Jane
Pale.

Rouweler, Hannie (b. 1951)
Landscape.
Silent Time.

Roux, Saint-Pol (1861–1940)
Aviary.
Lever de Soleil.
Sunrise.
Volière, La.

Rowbotham, David (b. 1934)
Bus-Stop on the Somme, The.
Cliff, The.
Nebuchadnezzar's Kingdom-Come.

Rowe, Elizabeth Singer (1674–1737)
Athenians' Answer, The.
Chapter IV.
Chapter V.
Expostulation, The.
Paraphrase on the Canticles, A, sels.
Parthenea, an Elegy.
Pindaric, to the Athenian Society, A.
Platonic Love.
Poetical Question Concerning the Jacobites,
Sent to the Athenians, A.
Reflection, The.
Reply to Mr.———, The.
To a Very Young Gentleman at a Dancing-
School.
To Celinda.
To Cleone.
To One That Persuades Me to Leave the
Muses, sel.
To Orestes.

Rowe, Henry (1754–1819)
Moon.
Sun.

Rowe, Vernon
MRI of a Poet's Brain.
Time Heals All Wounds—But One.
Youth.

Rowland, J. R. (b. 1925)
Canberra in April.

Rowlands, Dafydd (1931–2001)
Archipelago.
Cricket.
Little Boots, The.
Sawing His Wife in Half.
Schutzstaffeln 45326.
Village, The.

Rowlands, Samuel (1570?–1630?)
Boreas.
Epigram 29: "Gentlewoman of the dealing
trade, A."
Prologue: "Under the shadow of the gloomy
night."

Sir Revel.
Thraso.
Roy, Lucinda
Bread Man, The.
Ride, The.
Suffering The Sea Change: All My Pretty
Ones.
Triple Overtime.
Roy, Tushar (b. 1938)
Nowadays.
Royet-Journoud, Claude (b. 1941)
I.E.
Localité.
Locality.
Rózewicz, Tadeusz (b. 1921)
Busy with Many Jobs.
Fight With An Angel.
Homework Assignment on the Subject of
Angels.
I See Madmen.
In the Middle of Life.
Lament: "I turn to you high priests."
Larva, The.
Memory of a Dream From the Year 1963.
Pigtail.
Posthumous Rehabilitation.
Proofs.
Questions about Poetry since Auschwitz.
Return, The.
She Looked At the Sun.
Survivor, The.
To the Heart.
Transformations.
Voice, A.
Warning.
What Happens.
What Luck.
Who Is a Poet.
Rozga, Margaret
To California Where Rhymes Fail.
**Rozhdestvensky [or Rozhdestvenskii], Robert
Ivanovich (b. 1932)**
In the Night.
Nostalgia.
They Killed the Lad.
Winter of Thirty-Eight, The.
Ruan Yu (d. 212)
Driving My Chariot Through the Northern
Suburbs Gate.
Ruark, Gibbons (b. 1941)
Hybrid Magnolias in Late April.
Postscript to an Elegy.
Robert Frost to Ezra Pound's Daughter from
His Deathbed.
Rubin, Larry (b. 1930)
Houses of Emily Dickinson, The.
North of Amsterdam.
Ruby, Harry (1895–1974)
Give Me the Simple Life.
Nevertheless (I'm in Love with You).
Three Little Words.
What a Perfect Combination.
Who's Sorry Now?
Ruby, Harry See Kalmar, Bert
Rudaki (870?–c.940)
All the teeth ever I had are worn down and
fallen out.
Came to me— / Who?
Prayer.
Spring.
Ruddock, Gilbert (1938–98)
Double-decker.
To a Blind Mother.
Ruddock, Margot
Autumn, Crystal Eye.
Child Compassion, The.
I Take Thee Life.
Love Song: "Though to think / Rejoiceth me."
O Holy Water.
Spirit, Silken Thread.
Take Away.
Ruden, Sarah (b. 1962)
Beggar Outside Cape Town Station, A.
Letter.

Stubble Burning, The.
Rudman, Mark (b. 1948)
Rider, *sels.*
Rudolf, Anthony (b. 1942)
Edward Hopper.
Ruefle, Mary
American Dream, An.
Before Bed.
Controlling Factors.
Evangelical.
Execution Poster, The.
Feast, The.
From Here to Eternity.
Furtherness.
Hand, The: "Teacher asks a question, The."
In the Bitter Country.
Intended, The.
Jewel, The.
Kiss of the Sun.
Letter, The.
March, The.
Melancholiacs, The.
Merengue.
Minor Figure.
National Depression Awareness Week.
Out of a Hundred.
Peeling the Orange.
Perfect Reader.
Perpetually Attempting to Soar.
Public Garden with a Weeping Tree.
Rain Effect.
Rising Bodies.
School of Denial.
Search Party.
Seven Postcards from Dover.
Stopwatch.
Suburb of Long Suffering.
Topophilia.
Wasps' Nest.
Ruffilli, Paolo (b. 1949)
Malaria.
Ruffin, Paul (b. 1941)
Burying.
Female Cousins at Thanksgiving.
Redneck with Hair on His Back.
Storm Cellar, The.
Rufinus (*fl.* 2nd cent. B.C.?)
Dear God, I didn't know that Cytherea was
bathing.
Her foot sparkled like silver.
How could I have known.
Kiss from Her, A.
Lamplighter, if you can't set two equally.
Melissias denies her love, but her body
screams.
Rhodoclea, I send you this wreath which I
wove with my own hands.
Silver-footed girl was bathing, letting the
water, The.
Time has not quenched your beauty. Much of
your bygone prime.
When Pallas and golden-sandaled Hera saw
Maeonis.
Rugo, Mariève
Pietà: "What she holds is the unimaginable."
Ruhani, Ghulam-Rezi
Gaffer Speaks.
Rûhî (1548–1605)
Curse the Thorns of Fate.
Rühm, Gerhard
Few Things, A.
Flower Piece.
Rühmkorf, Peter (b. 1929)
Formerly, When We Still Parted the Big
Rivers.
Ruiz, Juan, Archpriest of Hita (*fl.* c.1343)
Charms of Small Women.
Rukeyser, Muriel (1913–80)
Absalom.
Ajanta.
Akiba.
Alloy.
Along History.
Ballad of Orange and Grape.

Birth of Venus, The.
Blood is Justified, The.
Book of the Dead, The.
Boy with His Hair Cut Short.
Bubble of Air.
Bunk Johnson Blowing.
Burning the Dreams.
Ceiling Unlimited.
Columbus.
Conjugation of the Paramecium, The.
Death and the Dancer.
Desdichada.
Double Dialogue: *Homage to Robert Frost.*
Effort at Speech between Two People.
For My Son.
Gates, The.
George Robinson: Blues.
Gyroscope, The.
Holy Family.
Homage to Literature.
Hostages, The.
In the Underworld.
Iris.
Käthe Kollwitz.
Leg in a Plaster Cast, A.
Letter to the Front, *sels.*
Long Enough. Long Enough.
Madboy's Song.
Meeting, The.
More of a Corpse Than a Woman.
Myth.
Nevertheless the Moon.
Night Feeding.
Night-Music, *sels.*
Outer Banks, The.
Painters.
Paper Anniversary.
Poem as Mask, The.
Poem: "I lived in the first century of world
wars."
Poem out of Childhood, *sel.*
Power of Suicide, The.
Rational Man.
Reading Time : 1 Minute 26 Seconds.
Rondel: "Now that I am fifty-six."
St. Roach.
Sand-Quarry with Moving Figures.
Seventh Avenue.
Sixth Night: Waking, The.
Soul and Body of John Brown, The.
Summer, the Sacramento.
Then I Saw What the Calling Was.
Traditional Tune.
Tunnel, The, *sels.*
Waiting for Icarus.
Who in One Lifetime.
Woman as Market.
Yes.
Rukeyser, Muriel and Leif Sjoberg
Night Flight : New York, *sel.*
Speed of Darkness, The, *sel.*
Rumaker, Michael (b. 1932)
Fairies Are Dancing All Over the World, The.
Rumann, Son of Colman
Storm at Sea.
Rumens, Carol (b. 1944)
Before these Wars.
Double Bed.
Emigrée, The.
From a Conversation During Divorce.
Geography Lesson.
Jarrow.
Like cancer cells, ivy, arthritis.
Marriage.
Memo About the Green Oranges, A.
Star Whisper.
Stealing the Genre.
Two Women.
Rumi, Jalal al-Din See Rumi, Jelaluddin
Rumi, Jelaluddin (1207–73)
Answers from the Elements.
At one time when life was real, your soul was
one with my soul.
Captain Who Walks on His Deck, The.
Caring for My Lover.

Come, come, for the rosebower has blossomed; come, come, for the beloved has arrived.
Come, come, you will never find a friend like me.
Daylight, full of small dancing particles.
Deliberation.
Dīvāni Shamsi Tabrīz, *sel.*
Do you think I know what I'm doing?
Drunkards, The.
Ecstatic Love Is an Ocean.
Edge of the Roof, The.
For years, copying other people, I tried to know myself.
Four Quatrains, *sels.*
Great Wagon, A.
Has Anyone Seen the Boy?
Hawk, The.
Human shape is a ghost, The.
I am your mother, your mother's mother.
I, you, he, she, we.
If you're not going to sleep.
In this river the heart is like a ruined waterwheel; in whichever direction it turns, there is water before it.
Inside water, a waterwheel turns.
Keep walking, though there's no place to get to.
Lame Goat, The.
Light You Give Off, The.
Like the rose I am laughing with all my body, not only with.
Like This.
Listen to the reed-flute telling its tales.
Little by little, wean yourself.
Love and Silence.
Love is the water of eternal life, cures every woe.
Love you alone have been with us.
Mill, the Stone, and the Water, The.
Minute I heard my first love story, The.
Music Master.
New Rule, The.
Night and Sleep.
Night comes so people can sleep like fish.
Out beyond ideas of wrongdoing and rightdoing.
Quietness.
Say Yes Quickly.
So long as I am alive, love enlivens each day.
Someone Digging in the Ground.
Strange Business.
Tell Me, What Have I Lost?
That Journeys Are Good.
That moon which the sky never saw.
There is a light seed grain inside.
Thief in the Night, A.
This is such a day: the sun is dazzling twice as before.
This night there are no limits to what may be given.
Three Quatrains, *sels.*
Twelve Lies, The.
Two Kinds of Intelligence.
Two Kinds of Miracles.
Walking with Others.
We can't help being thirsty.
We take long trips.
What I want is to see your face.
When I am with you, we stay up all night.
When I have you, the passions of love make me stay awake.
When the heart bursts into flame.
Who Says Words with My Mouth.
Wise teacher tell me.
Wished-For Song, A.
You don't have "bad" days and "good" days.

Rumsey, Tessa (b. 1970)
Assembling My Shepherd.
Big Rig the Baroque Sky.
Man-Torpedo-Boat.
More Important Than the Design of Cities Will Be the Design of Their Decay.
Never Mororcco.

Runciman, Lex (b. 1951)
Robert Frost.

Rundī, Abū al-Baqā Sālih ibn Alī (1204–86)
Everything declines after reaching perfection, therefore let no man be beguiled by the sweetness of a pleasant life.

Rungano, Kristina (b. 1963)
After the Rain.
Labour.
Mother.
This Morning.
Woman, The.

Runyan, Tania
Teaching Shakespeare.

Rupchev, Georgi (b. 1957)
Attraction.
Bewilderment.
Ceremony.
Reversal of Worlds.
Still Life: "Cello on the bed, A."

Rupp, Joyce
Sophia.

Rushin, Kate (b. 1951)
Black Back-Ups, The.
Bridge Poem, The.
Coward, The.
In Answer to the Question: Have You Ever Considered Suicide.
Looking for W.E.B.
Word Problems.

Ruskhan (fl. 1550)
In Praise of Krishna.

Ruskin, Harry (fl. 1929)
I May Be Wrong (But I Think You're Wonderful).

Ruskin, John (1817–1900)
Trust Thou Thy Love.

Russell, Bob (1915–70)
Ballerina.
Crazy She Calls Me.
Don't Get Around Much Anymore.
I Didn't Know About You.
You Came a Long Way from St. Louis.

Russell, David Riley (1902–1964)
State Fair.

Russell, George (1867–1935)
By the Margin of the Great Deep.
Cities, The.
Continuity.
Desire.
Epilogue: "Well, when all is said and done."
Exiles.
Forgiveness.
Frolic.
Gay, The.
Germinal.
Great Breath, The.
Illusion.
Immortality.
New York.
Pain.
Reconciliation.
Secret, The.
Self-Discipline.
Tragedy.
Truth.
Unknown God, The.

Russell, Norman H. (b. 1921)
Message of the Rain, The.

Russell, Pat
Be Careful When You Go Looking for a Madonna Cuz You Just Might Find a Woman.

Russell, Thomas (1762–88)
Dear Babe, whose meaning by fond looks expressed.
Sonnet: Suppos'd to Be Written at Lemnos.
Sonnet to Valclusa.
To Boccaccio.
To Oxford.
To the Owl.
To the Spider.

Russell, Timothy
In Simili Materia.

Rutherford, Brett
Viking.

Rutsala, Vern (b. 1934)
House of Cards, The.
Reunion: A Scenario.
Shame.
Summer: "There is no breeze, sounds travel far in the dead air."
Sunday Morning Walk.
Wilderness.
Words.

Rutter, Joseph (fl. 1635)
Epithalamium: "Hymen, god of marriage bed."

Rux, Carl Hancock (b. 1967)
Asphalt Musings.
Asylum of Gestures.
Excavation, The.
Just Asking.
Pledge of Allegiance.
Shunning an Imperative.
Suite Repose.

Ryan, Abram Joseph (Father Ryan) (1839–86)
Lines: "Gather the sacred dust."
Sword of Robert Lee, The.

Ryan, Father See Ryan, Abram Joseph

Ryan, Gig (b. 1956)
Achilleus to Odysseus.
Cruising.
Elegy for 6 So Far.
Epilogue: "His money-making properties come back like a beach."
Global Rewards Redemption Centre, The.
If I Had a Gun.
In the Purple Bar.
Ode to My Car.
Orbit.
Penserosa, La.
Pure and Applied.
Too Bad.

Ryan, Kay
Bad Time for the Sublime, A.
Blandeur.
Chemise.
Death by Fruit.
Elephant Rocks.
Failure.
Home to Roost.
If She Only Had One Minute.
Masterworks of Ming.
Paired Things.
Patience.
Poetry Is a Kind of Money.
Surfaces.
Test.
Turtle: "Who would be a turtle who could help it?"
Why Isn't It All More Marked.
Woman Who Wrote Too Much, The.

Ryan, Michael (b. 1946)
Complete Semen Study.
First Exercise.
God Hunger.
Moonlight.
Passion.
Pure Loneliness, The.
Reminder.
Shape for It, A.
Speaking.
Talking About Things.
This Is a Poem for the Dead.
Use of Poetry, The.
When I Was Conceived.
Your Own Image.

Ryan, Richard (b. 1949)
At the End.
Deafness.
Father of Famine.
Lake of the Woods, The.
Winter in Minneapolis.

Ryan, Tracy
Bite.
Eclipse, Kenwick, 1974.
Enough.
Lunar Eclipse.
Spin.
Trompe l'oeil.

Rybicki, John
Brother Ben.
For Daniel Beels, Third Generation Bricklayer.
In Directions.
This Sun.
Rye, Anthony
Redbreast, The.
Rye, Lisa
Scatological History.
Rykard, Richard (b. 1964)
Whole two weeks after The Million Man March; and still, if you'd ask me, this is all I could say about it, A.
Rylander, Edith
Dancing on Beethoven's Birthday.
Midnight Rocker, Tiananmen Square, May 27, 1989.
Rylant, Cynthia
Soda Jerk, sel.
Ryman, James (fl. late 15th cent.)
Have mynde how I mankynde have take.
Nunc Puer Nobis Natus Est.
Sancta Maria, ora pro nobis.
Song of the Eucharist, A.
Street Scenes: Houston, sel.
Ther is a chielde, a heuenly childe.
Ryman, Sunshine Dickinson
Street Scenes: Houston.
Ryokan (1758–1831)
All my life I've had no interest in worldly success.
Breeze is fresh, The.
Done with a long day's begging.
Faint trickle of.
First Days of Spring.
How admirable—the fine gentleman.
I lie alone in my grass hut.
In my begging bowl.
In my sleeve the colored ball worth a thousand in gold.
I've forgotten.
On a long misty.
Picking violets.
Too Lazy to Be Ambitious.
Wait for the moonlight.
Who says my poems are poems?
Winter, sel.
Without a jot of ambition left.
Ryuichi, Tamura (b. 1923)
Invisible Tree.
My Imperialism.
October Poem.
Standing Coffin.
Ryushu Shutaku (1308–88)
For all these years, my certain Zen.
Mind set free in the Dharma-realm.
Why bother with the world?
Ryuzan (1274–1358)
Clear in the blue, the moon!

S

Saari, Rami (b. 1963)
Only Democracy (in the Middle East), The.
Saarikoski, Pentti (b. 1937)
Dance Floor on the Mountain, The, sel.
I lived in a ruin called The Lion.
Invitation to the Dance, sel.
Potato Thief.
Saba, Umberto (1883–57)
Goat, The.
Insomnia on a Summer Night.
Ulysses.
Winter Noon.
Saba, Ziya Osman (1910–57)
Love Poem: "When you think of me."
Sabgir, Genrikh
Radio Gibberish.
Sabina, María (b. 1894)
Midnight Velada, The, sels.
13th Horse Song of Frank Mitchell, The.

Sabines, Jaime
Adam and Eve, sels.
Capriccios.
Entresol.
I Do Not Know It for Sure.
I Love You at Ten in the Morning.
If Someone Tells You It's Not for Sure.
Lovers, The.
Sabok
At My Mother's Funeral.
Sabry, Maher
Harem, The.
Marionette.
Troy.
Sachdev, Padma (b. 1940)
Well, The.
Sachs, Carly (b. 1979)
Story, The.
Sachs, Hans (1494–1576)
Fair Melody, A: To Be Sung by Good Christians.
Sachs, Nelly (1891–1969)
Already Embraced by the Arm of Heavenly Solace.
Butterfly.
Chorus of the Dead.
Chorus of the Rescued.
Chorus of the Stars.
Dead Child Speaks, A.
How Long Have We Forgotten How to Listen!
If I Only Knew.
If the Prophets Broke in.
In the Blue Distance.
In the Evening Your Vision Widens.
Mouth Sucking in Death.
O Sister.
O the Chimneys.
Oh Those Smokestacks.
Rushing at Times Like Flames.
Sleepwalker, The.
Someone.
Someone Will Take The Ball.
What Secret Cravings of the Blood.
World, Do Not Ask Those Snatched from Death.
You.
Your Eyes, O My Beloved.
Sackett, Frances (b. 1948)
Another Kind of Skin.
Sackville, Charles, 6th Earl of Dorset (1643–1706)
My Opinion.
On Mr. Edward Howard, upon His British Princes.
On the Countess of Dorchester.
Song Written at Sea in the First Dutch War (1665), the Night before an Engagement.
Sackville, Thomas, 1st Earl of Dorset (1536–1608)
Mirror for Magistrates, sels.
Sackville-West, Victoria Mary (1892–1962)
Garden, The.
Greater Cats, The.
Land, The.
No Obligation.
On the Lake.
Sacré, James (b. 1938)
Little Boy, I'm Not Sure Anymore, A.
Sadeh, Pinhas (1929–94)
At Nightfall, 1/27/91.
Sadhu Binning
Revenge: "Hands on the steering wheel."
Sadi [or Saadi or Sa'di] (1184–1291)
He glanced at me one day—but then his mean.
If you should say to me Don't mention love.
Last night without sight of you my brain was ablaze.
O I repented, wore my pious cloak.
Prayers: "My shoes are mulberry with dew."
This I write, mix ink with tears.
Until you can correct and heal yourself.
When once the soul is ready to depart, sir.
Sadiq, Mohammed
Tuskegee Experiment.

Sadler, Lynn Veach
Why God Chose Robert Frost Over Elvis.
Sadoff, Ira (b. 1945)
Against Whitman.
Birches, Revisited: October.
Civil Rights.
Depression, The.
February: Pemaquid Point.
Grazing.
Hopper's "Nighthawks" (1942).
I Join the Sparrows.
In the Bog behind My House.
Izzy.
Nazis.
On the Job.
Red Tail Sonnet.
Soul, The.
Standard Time.
There's No Rigor Like the Old Rigor 2.
Sadoleto, Jacopo (1477–1547)
Poem of Jacobus Sadoletus on the Statue of Laocoon, The.
Sadongei, Alice (b. 1959)
After Seeing Paintings in a Small Book by T. C. Cannon (1946-1978).
Don't Forget.
For Carlos Charles Bucillio.
Poems Come to Me in the Night.
Wind Blew like Water.
Sáenz, Benjamin Alire
Angel.
Benjamín.
Between Worlds.
Creation. Trinity Site, New Mexico. 5:30 A.M. July 16th, 1945.
I Wouldn't Even Bleed.
Saenz, Jaime (1921–86)
Let your permanency under the brilliance of the stars be long.
Safford, June Billings
Very Floor of Our Existence, The.
Saffoti, Carol Lee
Espresso.
Safie, Doris (b. 1940)
Danger, Men in Trees.
Meditation by the Xerox Machine.
Sagan, Miriam
Contentment: "Woke up to the finches crowing."
Gypsy Hand.
Mountain Peak Grave.
Open the Door.
Prayer Flag.
Reading Chiyo-Ni, 1703-1775, Japanese Woman Haikuist.
South Ridge Zendo.
Winter burn.
Yojimbo.
Sagay-Lights, Verneda
If Harriet Tubman Were Alive Today.
Savannah Brass.
Space.
Sage, C. J.
Retired Postman Recalls the Old Route, A.
Sage, Kay (1898–1963)
Chinoiserie.
Fragrance.
Observation, An.
Window, The.
"Sagittarius" (Olga Katzin) (b. 1896)
Come into the Army, Maud.
Croaked the Eagle: "Nevermore."
Freedom in Peril.
Passionate Profiteer to His Love, The.
Servant of the House.
Stalin Moy Golubchik.
Sagoff, Maurice
Preface Shrink Lit: Elements of Style.
Robinson Crusoe Daniel Defoe.
Sahagún, Carlos (b. 1938)
Aquí Empieza la Historia.
De la Vida en Provincias.
En el Principio, el Agua.
Fotografía de Niño.

In the Beginning.
Life in the Provinces.
Photograph of a Boy.
Río.
River: "They named this stretch of river Postwar."
Story Begins Here, The.
Säheb, Anthony
Victory to Yogendra's Wife, Great Illusion!
Sahl, Hans (b. 1902)
Charter Flight into the Past, A.
Sahn, Seung (b. 1927)
Good and Bad are eminent teachers.
Mountain sinks into the sea, The.
Sa'id, 'Ali Ahmad See Adonis [or Adunis]
Saïd, Amina (b. 1953)
Africa of the Statue, The.
And We Were Born.
Bird is Meditation, The.
Earth, The.
I Present Myself to the World.
My Woman's Transparence.
On the Fringe.
On the Tattered Edges.
One Day I Know the Page.
Paths of Light.
Sentiers de lumière, sel.
Terre, La.
Vultures Grow Impatient, The.
Saigyō (Saigyo Hoshi) (1118–90)
I don't even know.
In a tree standing.
Out in the high waves.
Saijo, Albert (b. 1926)
Bodhisattva Vows.
Sail, Lawrence (b. 1942)
Christmas Night.
Up and down I go, my stock.
Saimaro (1656–1737)
Mirrored by stream / Swallow darts—.
Saint, Assotto (b. 1957)
Heart and Soul.
Saint Catherine See Catherine of Siena
St. Germain, Sheryl
Addiction.
Cajun.
St. John, David (b. 1949)
After Esenin.
Black Poppy (At the Temple).
California.
Coffee.
Desire: "There is a small wrought-iron balcony."
Dolls.
Elegy: "It's true such reckless grace should never die."
Elegy: "Who keeps the owl's breath? Whose eyes desire?"
Essay on Liberation, An.
From the Lake.
Gin.
Grandfather's Cap, My.
Guitar.
Homage to Robert Johnson.
Hush.
I Know.
In the Sulphur Garden.
Iris.
Last Night with Rafaella.
Lucifer in Starlight.
Meditation: "Quiet now, sorrow; relax. Calm down, fear."
My Friend.
No Heaven.
Of the Remembered, sels.
Opal Trees, The.
Portrait: "There is in his daughter's gaze."
Quote Me Wrong Again and I'll Slit the Throat of Your Pet Iguana.
Saffron.
Six/Nine/Forty-Four.
Slow Dance.
Swan at Sheffield Park, The.
Temporary Situation, A.

Wedding Preparations in the Country.
Winter Fires.
Zuni Ring.
St. John, Primus (b. 1939)
All the Way Home.
Ars Poetica: "At the edge of the forest."
Benign Neglect / [West Point,] Mississippi, 1970.
Biological Light.
Carnival.
Lynching and Burning.
Obessions Are Important.
Ocean of the Streams of Story.
Pearle's Poem.
Reading a Story to My Child.
Song.
Studying.
Sunday.
Violence of Pronoun, The.
We Are Going to Be Here Now.
Saint-Natus, Clotaire
Poet, The: "Voice of the drum slowly unravels, The."
Saiokuken Socho (Socho) (1448–1532)
Moon this evening, The.
Saisho (d. 1506)
On Joshu's Nothingness.
Sait Faik (1906–54)
Now's the Time for Love.
Saito, Brynn Noelle
Turkey People.
Saitō Mokichi (1882–1953)
As I lie beside my mother.
At daybreak.
Crimson / the crape-myrtle.
I was standing there.
In my calling.
Is this what.
Mother Dies, sel.
No words are left.
To see the charcoal.
Saitō Sanki (1900–62)
Machine gun, A.
Machine gun, A.
Machine gun, A.
Machine gun soars, A.
Photographed / face by face.
Photographed— / prisoners of war shout commands.
Sajé, Natasha (b. 1955)
I am peeling four pink grapefruit.
Male in the Women's Locker Room, A.
Song of the Cook.
What I Want to Make for You.
Sakaki, Nanao
If you have time to chatter.
Let's Eat Stars.
Memorandum.
North America.
Sugar Loaf Hill.
Top Ten of American Poetry.
Sakhltkhutsishvili, Ucha (b. 1946)
Soldiers: "Crossing the mountains."
"Saki" (Hector Hugh Munro) (1870–1916)
Carol: "While shepherds watched their flocks by night."
Salaam, Kalamu ya (b. 1947)
Always Know.
Call of the Wild, The.
Directions for Understanding Modern Jazz Criticism.
5 Minutes, Mr. Salaam.
Flying over America.
Haiku # 135: "My butterfly breaths."
I Just Heard John Buffington Died.
I Live in the Mouth of History.
Moment of the First Day, The.
Name the Oldest Member of Your Family.
New Orleans Haiku, sels.
Our World Is Less Full Now That Mr. Fuller Is Gone.
Sharing is Hereditary.
SOUND is ProFound Sense.

Threnody: "What's your story Atlanta/America?"
Why I Dont Leave the Apartment Until After Ten Some Mornings.
Salaam, Kiini Ibura
N.
Salamun, Tomaz (b. 1941)
Words.
Salazar, Dixie
Cricket at Central California Women's Facility.
E is in Heaven.
Hotel Fresno.
Meteor Showers—Yosemite.
Moulton Transformations.
Piñon Nuts.
Taking It Back.
Sale, Richard
Delayed Love Poem to Odem, Texas.
Farm-to-Market #4.
Stilts and Other Vehicles.
Saleh, Dennis (b. 1942)
Beach, Later.
Crabs.
December Nap.
Sentry.
Summer.
Saleh, Saniyya
Tears: "There is a scream that binds my heart to."
Salerno, Joe
Poetry is the Art of Not Succeeding.
Salganicoff, Matilde
Being an Immigrant.
Girl Refugee, The.
Nightmare.
Shame.
Salih, Saniyya (1939–89)
Choking.
Exile.
Salihoǧlu, Mehmet (b. 1922)
Smoke upon Smoke.
Salinas, Luis Omar (b. 1937)
For Larry Levis in Memory.
Middle Age.
My Fifty-Plus Years Celebrate Spring.
Nights in Fresno.
Sea Song.
Sometimes Mysteriously.
Salinas, Pedro (1892–1951)
Alma Tenías, El.
And if the Shadows Weren't.
Deaths ("First thing I forgot was your voice, The.").
Distánciamela, Espejo.
Do You Hear How They Beg for Realities?
En la Tierra Seca.
I Don't See You, Yet I Know.
¿Las Oyes Cómo Piden Realidades. . .?
Luz lo Malo que Tiene, La.
No en Palacios de Mármol.
No Te Veo, Bien Sé.
Not in Marble Palaces.
On Dry Land.
Set Her Far from Me, Mirror.
So Transparent Your Soul.
Trouble with the Light, The.
Y Si No Fueran las Sombras.
Salinas, Raul
Trip Through the Mind Jail, A.
Salisbury, Ralph (b. 1926)
After Heart-Bypass Surgery, Another Ritual for Continuing Struggle.
Salkeld, Blanaid (1880–1959)
That Corner.
Salkey, Andrew (b. 1943)
Clearsightedness.
Dry River Bed.
Remember Haiti, Cuba, Vietnam.
Sall, Amadou Lamine (b. 1951)
Cloak of Dawn.
Letter to a Roving Poet.
Sallah, Tijan M. (b. 1958)
Elders Are Gods, The.
Mr. Agama.
No Argument Tonight.

Television as God.

Sallaska, Stephanie
To Raise the Blind on Purpose.

Salmon, André (1881–1957)
Painting.
Prikaz.

Salom, Philip (b. 1950)
Ghazal on Signs of Love and Occupation.
Walking at Night.
Well, The.
Winter.
World of Dreams, The.

Saloy, Mona Lisa (b. 1950)
"N" Word, The.
This Poem Is for You, My Sister.
We've Come This Far.

Salsbury, Nate (b. 1888)
Apex.

Salter, Mary Jo (b. 1954)
Absolute September.
Chernobyl.
Distance.
Frost at Midnight.
Half a Double Sonnet.
Home Movies: A Sort of Ode.
Kangaroo.
Liam.
Rainbow Over the Seine, A.
Rebirth of Venus, The.
Robin's Nest, A.
Summer 1983.
Sunday Skaters.
Video Blues.
Welcome to Hiroshima.
What Do Women Want?
Young Girl Peeling Apples.

Saltman, Benjamin
Hunger, A.

Saltus, Francis Saltus (1847–89)
In a Book-store, *sel.*
Kiss, The.
Masters, The, *sel.*
Mothers.
Posthumous Revenge.
Two Loves Found Refuge, *sel.*

Salzman, Eric
Double Dactyls.

Salzman, Eva (b. 1960)
Alex, Tiffany, Meg.
Bargain with the Watchman.
Conch.
Double Crossing.
English Earthquake, The.
Grandmother.
Homesteading.
Physics.
Sexual Love.
Spells.

Sama, Balakrishna
Song, The.

SamanoGlu, Gültekin (1927–2003)
Come So Far as You Can Feel.

Samara, Munia (b. 1955)
Door of Roses.
Door of the Cities.

Samaras, Nicholas
After the Children Have Gone to Bed.
Aubade: Macedonia.
Crossing the Strait.
Elegy for a Professor.
Farasa.
First Nightmare Waking.
Mute Prophets.
Notes in Jerusalem.
Nuclear Winter.
Translation.

Samawi, Aziz (b. 1941)
Iraqi Sorrows.
Mountain of Dreams.
Neighing of the Fingers.
Suns in the Night of the Massacre.

Samawi, Shakir
Dream of a Snow Flower, The.
Quartets of Inner Whispering.

Solo for the Lone Intuition, A.

Sampley, Arthur M. (1903–75)
Coronado at Rio Grande Del Norte.
South Rim: Big Bend National Park.

Sampu (Sugiyama Sampu) (1647–1732)
Moving / Deep into mist.

Sampu, Sugiyama See Sampu

Samson, John K.
Hypothetical.
Liminal Highway.

Samuels, Ian (b. 1975)
Escapology.

Samwell, David (1751–98)
Negro Boy, The.

Samyn, Mary Ann (b. 1970)
Art of Kissing, The.
Poem with Light on Its Shoulder.
Trompe L'Oeil in Winter.

San Juan, Jr., E.
End of the Affair, The.
Entelechy on the Libidinal Fringe.
Owl of Minerva Takes Flight in the Evening,
　The.
Three for the Road.

Sana'i (d. 1131)
Invocation.

Sanchez, Carol Lee (b. 1934)
Corn Children.
Tribal Chant.

Sánchez, Katherine
Porcelain Childhood.

Sanchez, Sonia (b. 1935)
Answer to yo / question / of am I not yo /
　woman / even if you went on shit again.
Anthem, An.
Ballad: "Forgive me if i laugh."
Blues.
Depression.
Earth Mother.
Elegy (for MOVE and Philadelphia).
Father and Daughter.
For Sister Gwen Brooks.
For Sweet Honey in the Rock.
Haiku.
Haiku: "Was it yesterday."
Haiku: "Your voice unwrapping."
July.
Letter to Ezekiel Mphahlele.
Morning Song and Evening Walk.
Norma.
Part Four: Rebirth.
Personal Letter No. 3.
Philadelphia: Spring, 1985.
Poem for July 4, 1994.
Poem for My Father, A.
Prelude to Nothing.
Reflections After the June 12th March for
　Disarmament.
Right On: White America.
Song No. 2: "I say. all you young girls waiting
　to live."
Song No. 3: "Cain't nobody tell me any
　different."
Summer Words of [*or* for] a Sistuh [*or* Sister]
　Addict.
This is Not a Small Voice.
To Anita.
To P. J. (2 Yrs Old Who Sed Write a Poem for
　Me in Portland, Oregon).
Under a Soprano Sky.

Sánchez Peláez, Juan (b. 1922)
Portrait of the Beautiful Unknown Woman.

Sandage, Chivas
Interview with a Combat Photographer.

Sandburg, Carl (1878–1967)
A. E. F.
Adelaide Crapsey.
Among the Red Guns.
Auctioneer.
Bas-Relief.
Be Ready.
Bilbea.
Blue Island Intersection.
Bones.

Broken-Face Gargoyles.
Buffalo Dusk.
Bundles.
Buttons.
Cahoots.
Chicago.
Choose.
Circles.
Cool Tombs.
Early Copper.
Early Lynching.
Elephants Are Different to Different People.
Flash Crimson.
Fog: "Fog comes, The."
For You.
Four Preludes on Playthings of the Wind.
Galoots.
Gargoyle.
Grass.
Halsted Street Car.
Happiness.
Harbor, The.
Harrison Street Court.
Haze.
Hits and Runs.
I Am the People, the Mob.
Illinois Farmer.
In Tall Grass.
Jazz Fantasia.
Languages.
Limited.
Little Girl, Be Careful What You Say.
Long Shadow of Lincoln: A Litany, The.
Losers.
Mag.
Mamie.
Manual System.
Moist Moon People.
Murmurings in a Field Hospital.
Nocturne in a Deserted Brickyard.
Old Timers.
On a Flimmering Floom You Shall Ride.
Onion Days.
People, Yes, The, *sels.*
Portrait of a Motorcar.
Prayers of Steel.
Precious Moments.
Primer Lesson.
Right to Grief, The.
Shirt ("My shirt is a token and symbol.").
Skyscraper.
Smoke and Steel, *sel.*
Soup.
Southern Pacific.
Splinter.
Stars.
Sunset from Omaha Hotel Window.
Sunsets.
Teamster's Farewell, A.
To Beachey, 1912.
Under a Hat Rim.
Upstream.
Washerwoman.
Wilderness.
Wind Song.
Window.

Sandeen, Ernest (b. 1908)
Late Twentieth-Century Prayer, A.
My Two Lives.

Sanders, Benjamin Theolonius
For What It's Worth.

Sanders, Edward (b. 1939)
Cutting Prow, The.
Flower from Robert Kennedy's Grave, A.
Investigative Poetry, *sel.*
Leaves of Heaven, The.

Sanders, James
From the Mark Prejsnar Playbook.
Poem with Referees.

Sanders, Mark (b. 1943)
Vigil at a Missile Silo, A.

Sanders, Peter A.
Tripoli.

Sanders, Tanai
Temporary Insanity.

Sandy, Stephen (b. 1934)
Survivor, Walking.

Sandys, Edwin (1561–1629)
In Pilgrim Life Our Rest.

Sandys, George (c.1577–1644)
Hymn Written at the Holy Sepulchre in
  Jerusalem.
Judah in Exile Wanders.

Sanelli, Mary Lou (b. 1956)
Swansonville.

Saner, Reg (b. 1931)
Autumn Aspens: Cumbres Pass.
Camping Clean.
Desert Wisdom.
Flag Memoir.
Indian Peaks, Colorado.
Morning Snowfield.
Rain Near Heart Lake.
Report to the Stockholders.
Sierra Cup.
They Said.
This Grizzly.
Waking at the Middle of Nowhere.

Sanfield, Steve
Alone in the house.
Birthday Poem.
Concern.
Hills of buttercups.
I like my poems short.
Poem for Those of You Who Are Sometimes
  Troubled by Barking Dogs and Low Flying
  Jets, A.
Walking in the rain.

Sanford, Christy Sheffield
Rachel's Recovery (Fucking with the
  Angels).

Sanger, Peter (b. 1943)
Crabapple Blossoms.
Escalade (Paul-Émile Borduas, 1905-1960).
Heron.
Kestrel.
Woodcock Feather.

Sanger, Richard (b. 1960)
Lines in the Sand.
3: Who Was That? I Ask.

Sangster, Margaret Elizabeth (b. 1894)
Queen of Girlhood, The.

Sanguineti, Edoardo (b. 1930)
Last Stroll, The: Homage to Pascoli.
Reisebilder, *sels.*
Scartabello, *sels.*

Sankichi, Tōge (1917–53)
At the Makeshift Aid Station.
August 6, 1950.
Flames.
Poems of the Atomic Bomb, *sels.*
Shadow, The: "Cheap movie theaters, saloons,
  fly-by-night markets."

Sanpu (1647–1732)
First cherry blossoms.

Sansom, Ann
Confinement.
Cross Country.
From the Moment I Picked Up Your Book.
Prince.
Romance.
Voice.
World is Everything, The.

Sansom, Clive (1910–81)
Innkeeper's Wife, The.
Snowflakes.

Sansom, Martha (1690–1736)
Clio, *sel.*
To My Heavenly Charmer.

Sant, Andrew (b. 1950)
Homage to the Canal People.
Soundwaves.

Santal
Witch, The.

Santayana, George (1863–1952)
Before a Statue of Achilles.
Cape Cod.
Echo.
Normal Madness, *sel.*

Ode 5: "Of thee the Northman by his beachèd
  galley."
On a Piece of Tapestry.
On an Unfinished Statue.
Sonnets, *sels.*
To W. P.

Santly, Lester (fl. 1921)
I'm Nobody's Baby.

Santos Chocano, José (1875–1934)
Dream of the Caiman, The.
Dream of the Condor, The.
Indignation.
Manifesto, A.
Volcanoes, The.
Who Knows?

Santos, Sherod (b. 1949)
Augury.
Dairy Cows of Maria Cristina Cortes.
Jeffers Country.
Midsummer.
Near the Desert Test Sites.
Of Haloes & Saintly Aspects.
On the Last Day of the World.
Romeo and Juliet.
Still Life with Minnows.
Tahoe Nocturne.
Talking Cure, The.

Sapgir, Genrik Veniaminovich (b. 1928)
Dionysus.
From an Album.
Psalm 1.
Psalm 137.

Sapia, Yvonne (b. 1946)
Grandmother, a Caribbean Indian, Described
  by My Father.
Valentino's Hair.

"Sapphire"
American Dreams.

Sappho (fl. c.612 B.C.)
About the Cool Water.
Anaktoria.
And you, Dika, put lovely garlands round your
  hair.
Arbor, The.
Atthis, for you the thought of me has become
  hateful.
Beneath its wings.
Black Dream, you come.
Bride: Virginity, virginity, where have you
  gone leaving me behind?
But as my friend, take to a younger bed.
But I am not someone of spiteful.
Come, divine lyre, speak to me.
Come to me from Krete to this holy.
Delicate Adonis is dying, Kytheria—what
  should we do?
Do I still desire virginity?
Doorkeeper has feet seven fathoms long, The.
Equal to the Gods.
[Eros] came from heaven wearing a purple
  cloak.
Eros seizes and shakes my very soul.
Evening Star who gathers everything.
For me neither honey nor bee.
For you beautiful ones my mind.
Full moon was rising, The.
Gongyla.
Handsome man is good to look at, A.
Happy bridegroom, the marriage that you
  prayed for.
He is almost a god, a man beside you.
Herald came, The.
Herdsmen crush under their feet.
Honestly I'd as soon be dead!
Horses in Flowers.
I don't expect to touch heaven.
I don't know what I should do—I'm of two
  minds.
I have a beautiful child, her form.
I love / love's delicacy.
I loved you Atthis once long ago.
I say someone in another time will remember
  us.
I simply wish to die.
I think no woman of such skill.
I urge you.

I will now sing this beautifully.
I wish to say something to you, but shame.
In my eyes he matches the gods, that man
  who.
In the house of those who serve the Muses, a
  dirge.
In the young spring evening.
It's no use.
Kypris and Nereids, let that brother.
Kypris, / May she find you very bitter.
Leaving Crete, come visit again our temple.
Like the sweet-apple.
Like the very gods in my sight is he who.
Love shook my senses.
Many-colored sandal, A.
Marriage of Hector and Andromache, The.
May I, goldencrowned Aphrodite.
May winds and sorrows.
May you sleep on the breast of a tender
  companion.
Mika / But I will not allow you.
Moon and the Pleiades have set, The.
Moon Has Set, The.
Moon has set, The.
My Atthis, although our dear Anaktoria.
My mother / In her youth it was a great.
Night / Virgins.
Of love.
On a Lady Indifferent to Poetry.
On the throne of many hues, Immortal
  Aphrodite.
On your throne, a marvel of art, immortal.
Once again Love [Eros], the looser of limbs,
  shakes me.
Once again that loosener of limbs, Love.
Percussion, salt and honey, *sel.*
Pleiades disappear, The.
Prayer to Aphrodite.
Prayer to my lady of Paphos.
Queen Hera, may your [graceful form].
Raise high the roof.
Sapphic Fragment.
Sapphics.
Sardis.
Since yes you [were] once a child.
Some prefer a glory of horsemen; warships.
Some say an army of horsemen, others.
Some there are who say that the fairest thing
  seen.
Some think a fleet, a troop of horse.
Star of Evening.
Stars around the fair moon, The.
Stars around the luminous moon—how soon
  they.
Superior, as a singer from Lesbos to those of
  other lands.
Sweet apple reddens on a high branch, The.
Sweet mother, I cannot weave.
That labor / a face to remember in wonder.
That one seems to me to be like the gods, the
  man whosoever sits facing you and listens
  nearby to your sweet speech an desirable
  laughter.
Their souls became cold.
There a bowl of ambrosia.
There is no other girl, bridegroom, like this.
There's a man, I really believe, compares with.
There's a man I really believe's in heaven.
They say that once Leda found.
Throned in splendor, deathless, O Aphrodite.
To goldenhaired Phoibos whom Leto bore.
To me it seems.
Tonight I've watched.
Verses Made by Sappho, Done from the Greek
  by Boyleau, and from the French by a Lady
  of Quality.
What country woman bewitches your mind.
When anger spreads in the breast.
When you die you'll lie dead, no memory of
  you.
With his venom.
With what, dear bridegroom, can I fairly
  compare you?
You came and did (well); I felt for you.
You / Put success in the mouth.

Saraç, Tahsin (1930–89)
To an Immortal Solitude Where We Now Pitch
Our Stately Tent.

Sarah, Robyn (b. 1949)
Courtney, Mentioned in Passing, Years After.
Fugue: "Women are on their way."
Relics.

Sarajlić, Izet (b. 1930)
If I had died that Friday in Paris.
Luck in Sarajevo.

Sarangapani (fl. c.1720)
Madam to a Young Courtesan, The.

Sargant, Jane Alice (fl. 1817–21)
How gladly would I lay my aching head.
'Lo, on her dying couch, the sufferer lies.

Sargent, Epes (1813–80)
Planet Jupiter, The.
Rockall.
Sea-Breeze at Matanzas, The.

Sargent, Robert (b. 1912)
Things of the World, The.

Sarig, Yoseph (1944–73)
Return: "Not thirsting for battle."

Sárközi, György (1899–1945)
Cursed is a Man.
Fog.
Hope for a Miracle.
Hymn of Love, The.
Like Gulliver.
Raindrops.
Unknown World, The.

Sarmiento, Félix Rubén García See Darío, Rubén

"Sarnicol" See Thomas, Thomas Jacob

Saroyan, Aram (b. 1943)
Blod.
Ex- / track.
Film Noir.
Leaf, A / left.
Lobstee.

Sarson, H. M.
Shell, The.

Sarton, May (1914–95)
After a Train Journey.
After All These Years.
August Third.
Autumn Sonnets, The, sel.
Death and the Turtle.
December Moon.
Eine Kleine Snailmusik.
February Days.
Fruit of Loneliness.
Glass of Water, A: "Here is a glass of water
from my well."
Invocation to Kali, The, sel.
Letter from Chicago.
Light Left On, A.
Love: "Fragile as a spider's web."
Moving In.
Muse as Medusa, The.
My Sisters, O My Sisters.
Navigator: "This lazy prince of tennis balls and
lutes."
Now I Become Myself.
Nursery Rhyme.
On a Winter Night.
Silence Now, The.
Small Joys.
Snow Light, The.
Tortured, The.
When a Woman Feels Alone.

Sasabune
Dimples.
Since the day of internment.

Sassoon, Siegfried (1886–1967)
Aftermath.
Ancient History.
Attack.
Babylon.
Base Details.
Blighters.
Case for the Miners, The.
Christ and the Soldier.
Conclusion: "Image dance of change, An."
Conscripts.

Counter-Attack.
Counter-Attack, sel.
Death-Bed, The.
Does It Matter?
Dreamers.
Dug-Out, The.
Elected Silence.
Everyman.
Everyone Sang.
Falling Asleep.
Fight to a Finish.
General, The.
Glory of Women.
Grandeur of Ghosts.
Hero, The.
In Heytesbury Wood.
In Me, Past, Present, Future Meet.
Invocation: "Come down from heaven to meet
me when my breath."
Lamentations.
Limitations.
Memorial Tablet.
On Passing the New Menin Gate.
Power and the Glory, The.
Prehistoric Burials.
Presences Perfected.
Rear-Guard, The.
Repression of War Experience.
Sporting Acquaintances.
Suicide in the Trenches.
"They."
To His Dead Body.
Wisdom of the World, The.
Working Party, A.

Sastri, Bhagavatula Sankara See "Arudra"

Sastri, Chellapilla Venkata (1870–1950)
Born for Poetry.

Sastri, Devulapalli Krishna (1897–1980)
Her Eyes.
In Search of Krishna.
Palanquin, The.

Satchell, Marlon D. (b. 1977)
Grandfather Grandfather.
Velvet Blanket.

Satir, Virginia
Making Contact.

Satterfield, Jane (b. 1964)
Duties and Vocations.
Wintering.

Satyamurti, Carole (b. 1939)
Broken Moon.
Day Trip.
Diagnosis.
Erdywurble.
Ghost Stations.
How Are You?
I Shall Paint My Nails Red.
In-Patient.
Knowing Our Place.
Ourstory.
Out-Patients.
Striking Distance.
Where Are You?

Satyanarayana, Viswanatha (1895–1976)
Blind Beggar, The.
Ramayana, sels.
Song of Krishna.
Your Chariot.

Saudi, Mona (b. 1945)
Blind City.
So Drunk Am I with the Night, the Air, and
the Trees.

Saunders, R. Crombie (b. 1914)
Empty Glen, The.

Saunders, Ruby C. (Fareedah Allah)
Lawd, Dese Colored Chillum.

Sauser-Hall, Frédéric-Louis See Cendrars, Blaise

Savage, Mary (fl. 1763–77)
Letter to Miss E.B. on Marriage, sels.

Savage, Richard (1698–c.1743)
Authors of the Town, The, sel.
Bastard, The, sel.
Progress of a Divine, The, sel.

Savage-Armstrong, George Francis (1845–1906)
Wee Lassie's First Luve, The.

Savageau, Cheryl
All Night She Dreams.
At the Powwow.
Heart.
Henri Toussaints.
Like the Trails of Ndakinna.
Looking for Indians.
To Human Skin.
Trees.

Savenko, Eduard Veniaminovich See Limonov,
Eduard Veniaminovich

Savithri, Machiraju (b. 1951)
Black and White.

Savitz, Michael
Bird, The.
Massive Stoner.
Stations of the Crux.
Sweetness.
To the Horizon.

Savoie, Terry
Reading Whitman's Democratic Vistas.

Sawadsri, Suchart
If You Come Close to Me.

Sawyer, Anna (fl. 1794–1801)
Lines, Written on Seeing My Husband's
Picture, Painted When He Was Young.

Sawyer, Ruth (b. 1880)
Feast o' Saint [or St.] Stephen, The.

Saxe, John Godfrey (1816–87)
Blind Men and the Elephant, The.
News, The.

Sayers, Dorothy Leigh (1893–1957)
War Cat.

Sayigh, Mai (b. 1940)
Departure.
Lament: "Those we love die like birds."

Sayles, James M. (b. 1948)
Star of the Evening.

Scafidi, Steve
Prayer for a Marriage.

Scalapino, Leslie (b. 1948)
Considering How Exaggerated Music Is.
Crowd and Not Evening Or Light, sels.
Flower, Pal Mal Comic Book.
Flush / a Play.
Instead of an Animal.
It's Go In / Quiet Illumined Grass / Land, sel.
Man getting on a bus carrying a huge sack of
crushed cans, A.
New Time, sel.
Or a Play.
Pal Mal Comic, Or.
Picasso and Anarchism.
Sight, sels.
Silver half freezing in day.
Slaves' Outside Evening or Evening, Pal Mal
Comic.
That They Were at the Beach—Aeolotropic
Series, sel.

Scalise, Gregorio (b. 1939)
Amiti´ Amoureuse.
Days pass on that face, The.
Dora Markus and Her Actors.
Man comes last: he's got to.
Passion circles round our body, A.
Testing out the door-posts.
There have never been men crazier than these.

Scamell, Ben (b. 1966)
Actor Speaks, An.
Diaries.
For a Six Year Old.
From the Provinces.
More Rain.
My Lost Brother.
Party, The.
Sin.
Stranger to a Small Child.
Working for British Telecom.

Scammell, Michael See Taufer, Veno

Scammell, William
Act, The.
Christmas at Bristol.

Eclogue: Clerk of the Weather.
Inventions.
Jean Rhys.
Men rigged my chamfered oak.
Nicola.
One Man.
Poem for a Younger Son.
Retrospective.
St Bees in Winter.
Screes, The.
Trains.
Walk, The.

Scannell, Vernon (b. 1922)
Apple-raid, The.
Bayonet Training.
Great War, The.
Hide and Seek.
Poem on Bread.
Popular Mythologies.
Protest Poem.
Walking Wounded.

Scappettone, Jennifer
III.
Consensus Series, *sels*.

Scarbrough, George (b. 1915)
Cutting Sod-Land.
Eastward in Eastanalle.
Field Beyond the Ridge.
Han-Shan Fashions a Myth.
Hymn for the Sound of Hymns.
Letter to Spencer.
Storm, The.
Sunday Shopping.

Scarfe, Francis (1911–86)
Grenade.

Scarlatti, Filippo (c.1442–c.1487)
Lanza 51.

Scates, Maxine
Angel.
Angel's Flight.
Floor Plans.
Going to Mass after Fifteen Years.
1956.
Working.

Scève, Maurice (1500–64)
Dizains, Les.
Every Wide and Long Expanse of Sea.

Schaeffer, Susan Fromberg (b. 1941)
Dog, The.
May Levine.
Yahrzeit.

Scharpenberg, Margot
Field of Red Tulips.

Schechter, Ruth Lisa (1927–89)
What Were You Patching?

Scheele, Roy (b. 1942)
Prose Poem, The.
Thistle.
Wake of Plenty, The.

Scheffler, Johannes *See* "Angelus Silesius"

Schein, Michael
Autumn: "On the first day of Autumn."

Schelling, Andrew (b. 1953)
Below Fourth of July Mine.
Commentary.
Haibun.
Haibun Flycatcher.
Haibun the Migration of Haibun.
High Up the Thunder Gods, Downstairs the Hunger.
Huerfano Valley Seed Songs.
March Crescent Moon Song.
Perfection of Wisdom Suite, A: Hymns for the Perfection of Wisdom in Paradise.
Run My Hand Under.
Tyger Tyger.

Schevill, James (b. 1920)
Love Song in Summer's Furnace Heat.
Whitman Stock-Taking, Cataloguing.

Schevill, Margaret Erwin (1887–1962)
Desert Center.

Schick, Eleanor
Last summer.

Schierbeek, Bert (b. 1918)
Animal Has Drawn a Human, The.
Sun, The: Day.

Schiff, Harris
Eye Poem.
I Should Run for Cover But I'm Right Here.

Schiff, Hilda
Discovery.
German Frontier at Basel: 1942 and 1992, The.
When It Happened.

Schiff, Robyn (b. 1973)
At Shedd Aquarium.
Chanel N° 5.
House of Dior.
Vampire Finch.
Woodpecker Finch.

Schilpp, Margot (b. 1962)
Devotions in Confidence.
Non Sequitur.
Triage.
Under the Scorpion's Heart.

Schippers, K. (Gerard Stigter) (b. 1936)
No, No, Nanette.

Schirmer, David (1623–83)
He Loves.

Schjeldahl, Peter (b. 1942)
Adventures with Nick & Cindy.
David's Sister.
Drugstore.
Dynamite.
Ocean Liner.
Reading, The.
Release.
Talking to Arlene.
Younger Poet, A.

Schlegel, Katharina von
Be Still, My Soul.

Schley, Jim (b. 1956)
Cradle Song: "Reapers and sowers, gleaners and drovers."
Inquest, By Hand.

Schloss, David
Figures in the Carpets, *sels*.

Schmitt, Kate
Fall on Me.
Fallen.
I Told Them I Should Be Here.
Prelude to the Fall.

Schmitt, Peter
Frost in Miami.

Schmitz, Dennis (b. 1937)
Abbott's Lagoon.
Because the Eye Is a Flower Whose Root is the Hand.
Carmel.
Climbing Sears Tower.
Making Chicago.
Monstrous Pictures of Whales.

Schnackenberg, Gjertrud (b. 1953)
Accident, An.
Advent Calendar.
Darwin in 1881.
Gilded Lapse of Time, A, *sel.*
Heavenly Feast, The.
Nightfishing.
Paperweight, The.
Returning North.
Signs.
Supernatural Love.
Two Tales of Clumsy, *sel.*
Walking Home.

Schneeman, George
Landscape.

Schneemann, Carolee
Interior Scroll.

Schneider, Isidor (1896–1977)
History of the Caesars, A.
Insects.

Schneider, Myra (b. 1936)
Bath: "Kindness, an Irish lilt in her voice."
Photograph, The.
Release: "I'm going to slap my anger onto a wet slab."
Soup and Slavery.

When It's All Over.

Schneiderman, Jason
Last Ditch.

Schneiders, Jay
Weight.

Schneurson [*or* Mishkovsky], Zelda *See* "Zelda"

Schockley, Evie
Ballplayer.

Schoenberger, Nancy (b. 1950)
Epithalamion.

Schoerke, Meg
Practice.

Scholasticus, Agathias *See* Agathias

Scholl, J. W.
Light-Bearer of Liberty, The, *sel.*

Schonborg, Virginia (b. 1913)
Rumble, A.

Schoolcraft, Jane Johnston (1800–41)
Forsaken Brother, a Chippewa Tale, The, *sel.*
Otagamiad.
To Sisters on a Walk in the Garden, after a Shower.

Schorn, Brian (b. 1961)
Entering Poetic Blindspots.

Schreiber, Ron (b. 1934)
Chant.
Gay Life.
Public Stammer, The.
Somerville Saturday Night.
They Kill Us.
To Be Held.

Schubert, David (1913–46)
It Is Sticky in the Subway.
Kind Valentine.
Midston House.
Monterey.
No Title.
Peter and Mother.
Prospect Park.
Successful Summer, A.
Victor Record Catalog.

Schulman, Grace
American Solitude.
Crossing the Square.
False Move.
First Nights.
Home Movie.
New Netherland, 1654.
Notes from Underground: W. H. Auden on the Lexington Avenue IRT.
Prayer.
Psalm for an Anniversary.
Two Trees.

Schultz, Philip (b. 1945)
Bar Mitzvah, The.
Dark Between, The.
Eight-Mile Bike Ride, The.
For My Father.
For the Wandering Jews.
Free Mercy.
I'm Not Complaining.
My Friend Is Making Himself.
Stories.

Schultz, Robert (b.1951)
She Speaks to Her Husband, Asleep.

Schulz, Bruno (1892–1942)
Constellation: Prose Poem.

Schulzová, Eva (1931–43)
Evening in Terezin, An.

Schuyler, James (1923–91)
Along Overgrown Paths.
Can I Tempt You to a Pond Walk?
Crystal Lithium, The.
Dec. 28, 1974.
Dining Out with Doug and Frank.
Father or Son.
Freely Espousing.
Greetings from the Chateau.
Haze.
Korean Mums.
Letter to a Friend: Who Is Nancy Daum?
Man in Blue, A.
Master of the Golden Glow, The.

May, 1972.
Noon Office.
Our Father.
Red Brick and Brown Stone.
Reserved Sacrament.
Roof Garden.
Royals.
Self-Pity Is a Kind of Lying, Too.
Shimmer.
Things to Do.
Verge.
View, A.
White City, A.
Within the Dome.
Yorkville.

Schwartz, Chaim (1903–94)
Hands: "Hands were purified in fire."

Schwartz, Delmore (1913–66)
Abraham.
Ballet of the Fifth Year, The.
Darkling Summer, Ominous Dusk, Rumorous
   Rain.
Do the Others Speak of Me Mockingly,
   Maliciously?
Dogs Are Shakespearean, Children Are
   Strangers.
Far Rockaway.
For the One Who Would Take Man's Life in
   His Hands.
I Am Cherry Alive.
In the Naked Bed, in Plato's Cave.
In the Slight Ripple, the Mind Perceives the
   Heart.
Jacob.
Lincoln.
Mind Is an Ancient and Famous Capital, The.
Now He Knows All There Is to Know: Now
   He Is Acquainted with the Day and Night.
O Child, Do Not Fear the Dark and Sleep's
   Dark Possession.
Pleasure.
Poem: "You, my photographer, you, most
   aware."
Repetitive Heart, The, *sels.*
Sarah.
Self Unsatisfied Runs Everywhere, The.
Shenandoah, *sel.*
Sonnet on Famous and Familiar Sonnets and
   Experiences.
Starlight like Intuition Pierced the Twelve.
Tired and Unhappy, You Think of Houses.
Winter Twilight, Glowing Black and Gold,
   The.

Schwartz, Hillel
Recruiting Poster.

Schwartz, Lloyd (b. 1941)
Leaves.
Proverbs from Purgatory.

Schwartz, Perla (b. 1955)
Snapshots of the Chameleon Woman.

Schwartz, Ruth L.
AIDS Education, Seventh Grade.
Can Pigeons Be Heroes?
Edgewater Park.
Falling in Love after Forty.
Flamenco Guitar.
Grief.
Late Summer.
Midnight Supper.
Oh God, Fuck Me.
Possible.
Swan at Edgewater Park, The.
Talking to God on the Seventh Day.
When They Know.
Why I Forgive My Younger Self Her
   Transgressions.

Schwarz, Sibylla (1621–38)
Sonnet: "If love is chaste, what bears
   adultery?"

Schwerner, Armand
Next Two Tablets, The.
Tablet V.
Tablets, The, *sels.*
Work, The.

Schwitters, Kurt (1887–1948)
Anna Blossom Has Wheels.
Anna Blume.
Desire.
Murder Machine 43.
Ur Sonata, *sel.*

Scliar-Cabral, Leonor
Deceiving Words.
Fire and Embers.
Sephirot.

Scobie, Stephen (b. 1943)
Queen Mary, She's My Friend.

Scofield, Gregory (b. 1966)
His Flute, My Ears.

Scollard, Clinton (1860–1932)
As I Came Down from Lebanon.
Ballads of the Wheel.
Bit of Marble, A.

Scollard, Mrs. Clinton *See* Rittenhouse, Jessie
   Belle

Scott, Alexander (1525?–84)
Continent o Venus.
Hence, heart, with her that must depart.
My Heart Is High Above.
New Yeir Gift to the Quene Mary, quhen scho
   come first Hame, 1562, Ane, *sel.*
Return thee, heart.
Rondel of Luve [*or* Love], A.
Sodgers, The.

Scott, Alexander (b. 1920)
Calvinist Sang.
Scotched.
Scotched, *sel.*

Scott, David (b. 1947)
Church Boiler, The.
Churchyard under Snow.
Flanking Sheep in Mosedale.
For Norman Nicholson.
Heart.
Hopkins Enters the Roman Catholic Church.
Illness.
Kirkwall Auction Mart.
Letters from Baron Von Hügel to a Niece.
Locking the Church.
Playing for England.
Scattering Ashes.
Skiddaw House.
Surplice, The.
Winston Churchill.

Scott, David G. W.
Delaware.

Scott, Dennis (1939–91)
Apocalypse Dub.
Dreadwalk.
More Poem.
Uncle Time.

Scott, Duncan Campbell (1862–1947)
At Gull Lake; August, 1810.
Forsaken, The.
Night in June, A.
On the Way to the Mission.
Onondaga Madonna, The.
Watkwenies.

Scott, Francis Reginald (1899–1985)
Brébeuf and His Brethren.
Canadian Authors Meet, The.
Lakeshore.
Last Rites.
Laurentian Shield.
Metric Blues.
Trans Canada.
W. L. M. K.

Scott, Frederick George (1861–1944)
Sting of Death, The.

Scott, Geoffrey (1884–1924)
All Our Joy Is Enough.
Frutta di Mare.
Skaian Gate, The, *sel.*
What Was Solomon's Mind?

Scott, Jacqueline
Hatching Thunder.

Scott, John A. (b. 1948)
Changing Room.
Helen Paints a Room (1984).

Man in Petersham.
Plato's Dog.
Typing the Letters.

Scott, Lady John (1810–1900)
Ettrick.

Scott, Margaret (b. 1934)
Portrait of a Married Couple.

Scott, Mark
Cave of AIDS, The.

Scott, Mary (1752?–93)
On Anna Laetitia Aikin.
On Elizabeth Montagu.

Scott, Mary
At the Crossroads.

Scott of Amwell, John (1730–83)
Ode: "I hate that drum's discordant sound."

Scott, Peter Dale (b. 1929)
Dying In.

Scott, Tom (b. 1918)
Auld Sanct-Aundirans—Brand the Builder.

Scott, W. N. (b. 1923)
Bundaberg Rum.

Scott, Sir Walter (1771–1832)
Bride of Lammermoor, The, *sels.*
Charge at Waterloo.
Doom of Devorgoil, The, *sels.*
Dreary Change, The.
Fire, The.
Heart of Midlothian, The, *sels.*
Hellvellyn.
Ivanhoe, *sel.*
Jock of Hazeldean.
Lady of the Lake, The, *sels.*
Lay of the Last Minstrel, The, *sels.*
Maida.
Marmion, *sels.*
Monastery, The, *sel.*
Old Mortality, *sels.*
Rokeby, *sel.*
Wanderer's Dog, The.
Waverley, *sel.*

Scott, William Bell (1812–90)
Continuity of Life.
Early Aspirations.
Garland for Advancing Years, A.
My Mother.
Witch's Ballad, The.

Scott, Winfield Townley (1910–68)
Come Green Again.
Crocus Air.
Flowering Quince.
Three American Women and a German
   Bayonet.
U.S. Sailor with the Japanese Skull, The.
Uses of Poetry.
We Are So Fond of One Another, Because Our
   Ailments Are the Same.
Winslow Homer.

Scott-Heron, Gil (b. 1949)
I Think I'll Call It Morning.
Winter in America.

Scovell, Edith Jay (1907–99)
Child Waking.
Ghosts, The.
Light the Fire.
Listening to Collared Doves.
Past Time.
River Steamer, The.
Sandy Yard, The.
Shadows of Chrysanthemums.
Space Between, The.
Water Images, *sels.*
Workers in Metal.

Scrimgeour, James R.
Lines Started Outside Filene's Basement.

Scriven, Joseph
Unfailing Friend, The.

Scruton, James (b. 1959)
In the Age of the Radio Telescope.

Scudder, Antoinette (b. 1898, d. after 1949)
Tea Making.

Scully, Maurice (b. 1952)
Variations.

Scupham, Peter (b. 1933)
After Ovid, Tristia.
Although you never asked to come with me.
Beach, The.
Birthday Triptych.
First Things, Last Things.
Guard-Room.
Key, The.
Lesssons in Survival.
Nondescript, The.
Pompeii: Plaster Casts.
Service.
Twelfth Night.

Scurfield, George
Bitter Mangoes, The.

Scythinus
Calamity and conflagration! Strife!
Five Epigrams, sel.

Se Praj (fl. 17th cent.)
Your breasts will not fall.

Seager, Jane (fl. 1589)
Lybica.
To Queen Elizabeth.

Seale, Jane Epton
Big Bend: Lion Warning.
Playing the Flute for the TMR Class.
Subtropical.
To a Late Local Environmentalist.
Travel North: The Rules.

Seaman, E. William (b. 1927)
Double Dactyls.

Seaman, Sir Owen (1861–1936)
Ballad of a Bun, A.
England's Alfred Abroad.
Nocturne at Danieli's, A.

Searle, John
Matthew the Bayman.

Sears, Edmund Hamilton (1810–76)
It Came upon the Midnight Clear.

Sears, Peter
Good Morning Coffee Makes Vivid of the
Vague; Suddenly You Have Hands and Eyes
and Legs!
One Polar Bear, The.
Place for Four-Letter Words.
Volcanic Ash.

Seaton, Maureen
Blonde Ambition.
Cannibal Women in the Avocado Jungle of
Death.
Fear of Shoplifting.
Fear of Subways.
Fiddleheads.
Furious Cooking.
Ice.
Jubilee for the Bomb.
Malleus Maleficarum 4.
Man Who Killed Himself to Avoid August,
The.
Nostradamus Predicts the Destruction of
Chicago.
Story of Stonewall, A.
Tagging.
Wings.

Seay, James (b. 1939)
Audubon Drive, Memphis.
Johnny B. Goode.

**Secundus, Johannes (Jan Nicolai Everaerts)
(1511–36)**
Basia, sels.

Sedakova, Olga
Female Figure.
Fifth Stanzas. De Arte Poetica.
Grasshopper and the Cricket, The.
In Memory of a Poet.
Rain: "It's raining, / and still people say there's
no God!"
Sant'Alessio, Roma.

Sedley, Sir Charles (1639–1701)
Happy Pair, The, sels.
Mulberry Garden, The, sel.
On a Cock at Rochester.
On Fruition.
See! Hymen comes; how his torch blazes!

Song: "Love still has something of the sea."
Song: "Phillis, let's shun the common fate."
Song to Celia.
To Nysus.

Sedulius Scottus (d. 858)
Defeat of the Norsemen, The, sel.
Nunc Viridant Segetes.

See, Patti
Shotgun.

Seed, John
During War, the Timeless Air.
'From Escomb, County Durham': July 1990.
Sofia.
This Curious Involvement, a Dominant
Species.

Seeger, Alan (1888–1916)
Aisne, The (1914–15).
I Have a Rendezvous with Death.

Seeger, Pete
Where Have All the Flowers Gone?

Seely, Shane
Walt Whitman at the Irish Festival, Syracuse,
New York: Four Snapshots.

Seferis, George (1900–71)
Argonautica.
Days of April '43.
Epiphany, 1937.
Euripides the Athenian.
Interlude of Joy.
It's Time for Me to Go.
Last Day, The, sel.
Last Stop.
Mathios Paskalis among the Roses.
Memory 1.
Memory 2.
Mythistorima, sels.
Narration.
Nijinski.
Old Man on the River Bank, An.
Our Sun.
Poplar Leaf, The.
Stratis the Sailor by the Dead Sea.
Word for Summer, A.

Segade, Gustavo Valentin (b. 1936)
Theory of Fractals.

Segal, Jack (b. 1918)
I Keep Going Back to Joe's.
Nothing Ever Changes My Love for You.
When Sunny Gets Blue.
Wind in the Willow.

Segalen, Victor (1878–1919)
Édit Funéraire.
Éloge du Jade.
Faithful Betrayal.
Funerary Edict.
Hidden Name.
In Praise of Jade.
Out of Respect.
Par Respect.
Trahison fidèle.

Segovia, Francisco (b. 1958)
Ahí Donde Duermes.
Ánimo vegetal.
Chrysalis.
Claridad del silencio.
Clarity of Silence.
Crisálida.
Evening Star.
It Isn't Gentleness.
Lucero de la Tarde.
No acabamos nunca.
No es la suavidad.
Premonición.
Premonition.
Promesa.
Promise.
There Where You Sleep.
Vegetal Animus.
We Never Come.

Seibert, T. Lawrence
Casey Jones.

Seibles, Tim (b. 1955)
Douglass, a Last Letter.
First Kiss: "Her mouth."

4AM.
Friend and Beloved.
Manic: A Conversation with Jimi Hendrix.
What It Comes Down To.
Who.

Seidel, Frederick (b. 1936)
Dune Road, Southampton.
Fucking.
Love Song: "I shaved my legs a second time."
Men and Women.
Racine.
Scotland.
To Robert Lowell and Osip Mandelstam.

Seidman, Hugh (b. 1946)
Bleecker Street.
Composition.
Demonstration.
Dirt to Dirt.
End.
Gail.
Laureate.
Making of Color, The.
New York: "I read over my lines."
Photos.
Poem: "War and greed stop food."
Stroke ("He would get the gold.").
Stroke ("Writhing.").
Tale of Genji.

Seiferle, Rebecca (b. 1951)
Catch, The.
Face in the Depths of the Desert, The.
Foundling, The.
Gift, The: "I was wrong when I compared the
mask of my own face."
Mother Tongue.
Muse.
Music We Dance To, The.
Mythology of Heavenly Messengers, The.
Poetic Voice.
Welcome to Ithaca.
What We Need Words For.

Seifert, Jaroslav (1901–86)
Bombing of the Town of Kralupy, The, sels.

Seiffert, Marjorie Allen ("Elijah Hay")
Cubist Portrait.

Seifū (1650–1721)
Faces of dolls, The.

Seigen-yuiin
How vast karma.

Seiho
Sky's not high, earth not solid.

Seiken-Chiju
Twenty years a pilgrim.

Seiler, Barry (b. 1946)
Digging in the Streets of Gold.

Sekioku-Seikyo
This body won't pollute.

Sekishitsu-Soei
Fifty-three years / This clumsy ox has
managed.

Sekula, Sonia (1918–63)
Womb.

Selerie, Gavin
Roxy, sels.

Selesten-Meji, Emile See Célestin-Mégie, Emile

Self, Joan
Quill Holler Waller.

Sellar, W. C. See Yeatman, R. J.

Sellers, Heather (b. 1964)
In the Kitchen Dancing to Kitty Wells.
Some Poems Aren't For You.

Selman, Robyn
Descent.
Exodus.
For the Field.
21 East 10th, 2BR, WBF, EIK.
Work Song.

Selman, Sheikh (b. 1890)
Community School.

Seltzer, Dovid (b. 1904)
Blessing Over Bread, A.

Selvinsky [*or* **Sel'vinskii**]**, Ilya** [*or* **Karl**] **L'vovich (1899–1968)**
I Saw It!

Seminole Oral Tradition
Song for Bringing a Child into the World.
Song for the Dying.

Semonides
Genealogy of Women, The, *sel.*

Sempill, Francis (1616–82)
Banishment of Poverty by His Royal Highness James Duke of Albany, The, *sel.*
Maggie Lauder.

Sempill, Robert (c.1595–c.1665)
Life and Death of [Habbie Simson] the Piper of Kilbarchan, The.

Sen, Rāmprasād (c.1718–75)
At last I have a way to understand.
Black clouds have risen in my sky.
Brother / This world.
Can someone / Called Daughter of a Stone.
Death, get out of here!
Her face / Is a spotless moon.
Hey, it's not wine I drink.
Hey! Who is She, dark as clouds.
How wonderful! Look what.
I came to this world.
I have learned.
I'll die of mental anguish.
It's not Siva.
It's silly to hope for Father's wealth.
Kali, Ma.
Kulakundalini, Goddess Full of Brahman, Tara.
Let me tell You a thing or two, Tara.
Look here.
Love Her, Mind.
Ma, You're inside me.
Managing the house is a big problem.
Meditate on Kali! Why be anxious?
Mind, don't be duped by others' sneers.
Mind, how do you think you'll find Her?
Mind, why this separation from the Mother's feet?
Mind, you're still not rid of your illusions.
Mother, make *me* Your treasurer.
My Mind.
My Mind, my helmsman.
Oh Kali Full of Brahman!
Oh Mind, you don't know how to farm.
Oh my Mind, worship Kali.
Oh my Mind! You're just spinning.
So, Mind / You've decided to go on pilgrimage?
Supreme Savior of Sinners.
Tara, what more are You planning?
Tell me.
This is a fine mess.
This time I've realized the essence.
This time, Kali.
Tongue, call out.
Wait a minute, Death.
What a joke!
What's the fault of the poor mind?
Who can understand Kali?
Who is that Syama woman.
World-Mother's police chief, The.
World's a shoreless ocean, The.

Sen, Samar (b. 1916)
Love.
Solitary.

Sen-Natis, Klotè *See* Saint-Natus, Clotaire

Senard, Jacqueline
Polar.

Seneca (4 B.C.–A.D. 65)
Apocolocyntosis, *sel.*
Britannia, free from foes and foreign kings.
Flee every friendship and live: a greater truth.
Hercules Furens, *sels.*
Hercules Oetaeus [*or* Hercules Oetæus], *sel.*
Medea, *sels.*
O barbarous Corsica, locked in by crags.
Thyestes, *sels.*
Troades, *sels.*
Trojan Women.
Voracious Time, uprooting all, consumes it.

Seng-ts'an (d. 606)
Believing Mind, The.

Sengai Gibon (1750–1837)
On Basho's "Frog."

Senghor, Léopold Sédar (b. 1906)
African Image Is Not An Image by Equation, The.
All Day Long.
Before Night Comes.
Camp 1940.
I Am Alone.
In Memoriam.
Kaya-Magan, The.
Man and Beast.
Nocturne (I Accompanied You).
Nocturne (She Flies She Flies).
Pearls.
Porte Dorée.
Prayer to the Masks.
Prière aux Masques.
Salut du jeune soleil, Le.
Song of the Initiate.
Speech and Image: An African Tradition of the Surreal.
Suddenly Startled.
Taga for Mbaye Dyôb.
To New York.
Totem.
Young Sun's Greeting, The.

Senior, Olive (b. 1943)
Brief Lives.
Meditation on Yellow.
Stowaway.
Together, babe, we could have had the world sewn up.
Tropic Love.

Sennur, Sezer (b. 1943)
Ailing.

Senryū, Karai (1718–90)
All he does at work.
Another letter?
As he smiles.
Baby at her breast.
Doctor disrobed, The.
Doctor has prepared, The.
Each time footsteps.
Even her smile.
Even in the time of gods.
For a housemaid.
Guy, The.
His wife away from home.
How long it seems.
Judging by the pictures.
Laundryman, The.
Laying a fart.
Learning and a ladder.
Now that he has a child.
Off to work.
Official's little son, The.
Priest in charge, The.
Sitting Idly.
Sumo wrestler, The.
Tattoo of, A.
That Tsugunobu.
There'll soon be.
What a miracle.
Whatever he says.
When the night falls.
Whole town, The.
Yoshiwara.
Young master, The.
You're in the prime.

Sepamla, Sipho (b. 1932)
I Remember Sharpeville.
Law That Says, The.
Measure for Measure.
Odyssey, The.
Silence: 2.

Sepúlveda, Ofelia Perez (b. 1970)
Cuatro.
Cuatro ("Pero luego, en el trayecto imaginario de un automóvil blanco.").
Four.
Four ("But then, in the imaginary trajectory of a white automobile.").
Three ("Once upon a time there would be the bluest bitch of the pack.").
Three ("She is of the continent, around her everything is light and I observe her atop the slab in the image of her body.").
Tres ("Es del continente, alrededor de ella todo es luz y yo la observo sobre la plancha en la imagen de su cuerpo.").
Tres ("Habría una vez la perra más azul de la manada.").

Sepúlveda-Pulvirenti, Emma (b. 1950)
From Now Until Chile.
September 11, 1973.
To the Child That Never Was.

"Seranus" *See* Harrison, Susan Frances

Serchuk, Peter
My Other Life.

Sereni, Vittorio (1913–83)
Each Time That Almost.
First Year.

Serge, Victor (1890–1947)
Asphyxiated Man, The.
Constellation of Dead Brothers.
Dialectic.
Hands.

Sergi, Paula (b. 1952)
One Quick Quiz.

Serote, Mongane Wally (b. 1944)
Alexandria.
City Johannesburg.
Hell, well, heaven.
Her name Is 'Dooti.'
Introit.
Long road, The.
Night-time.
No Baby Must Weep, *sels.*
Ofay-watcher looks back.
This Old Woman.
Three mothers, The.

Serpas, Martha
As If There Were Only One.
Faith in Florida.
Finishing Touch.

Serraillier, Ian (b. 1912)
After Ever Happily [*or* The Princess and the Woodcutter].
Anne and the Field-Mouse.
Old Sussex Road, The.
Tickle Rhyme, The.

Serrano, Pedro (b. 1957)
Acotamiento.
Beacon.
Boundary.
Bullfight.
Corrida.
Flying.
Hacho.
Inventario.
Inventory.
Noria, La.
Pool.
Poza.
Prurito.
Rosario.
Rosary.
Ticklish Moments.
Treadmill.
Vértigo.
Vertigo.
Vuelo.

Serros, Michele (b. 1966)
Mr. BOOM BOOM Man.

Servasius, Sulpicius Lupercus (4th cent. A.D.)
Rivers level granite mountains.

Service, Robert W. (1874–1958)
Cremation of Sam McGee, The.
Fulmars.
Inspiration.
Only a Boche.
Pot of Tea, A.
Shooting of Dan McGrew, The.
Woman and the Angel, The.

Sesay, Kadija *See* George, Kadija

Seshadri, Vijay
Disappearances, The.
Lifeline.
Scholar, The.
Sketch from the Campaign in the North, A.
Wolf Soup.

Seth, Vikram (b. 1952)
God's Love.
Golden Gate, The, *sels.*
Pigeons.
Soon.
Unclaimed.

Seto, Thelma
Blood Ties.
Jihad.

Seuss, Diane
Purpose.

Sevelingen, Meinloh von (*fl.* c.1170)
My Eyes Have Seen and Chosen.
Woe Then to the Gossips.

Sewall, Samuel (1652–1730)
Once More, Our God, Vouchsafe to Shine!

Seward, Anna (1742–1809)
By Derwent's Rapid Stream.
Colebrook Dale, *sel.*
December Morning.
Eyam.
Farewell, false Friend!—our scenes of kindness
    close!
In every breast affection fires, there dwells.
Invocation, To the Genius of Slumber Written
    Oct. 1787.
Lake, The; Or, Modern Improvement in
    Landscape.
Llangollen Vale, *sels.*
Old Cat's Dying Soliloquy, An.
On a Lock of Miss Sarah Seward's Hair Who
    Died in her Twentieth Year.
On the damp margin of the sea-beat shore.
Seek not, my Lesbia, the sequestered dale.
Sonnet 31.
Sonnet: Ingratitude.
Sonnet: "Stranger, when o'er yon slant, warm
    field no cloud."
Sonnet Written from an Eastern Apartment in
    the Bishop's Palace at Lichfield, Which
    Commands a View of Stowe Valley.
Sonnets, *sels.*
Speech of the Nymph.
To a Friend, Who Thinks Sensibility a
    Misfortune.
To a Young Lady, Purposing to Marry a Man
    of Immoral Character in the Hope of his
    Reformation.
To Honora Sneyd.
To Mr. Henry Cary, On the Publication of his
    Sonnets.
To the Poppy.
When Life's realities the Soul perceives.
Written December 1790.

Sewell, Elizabeth (b. 1919)
Job.

Sewell, Lisa (b. 1960)
Denied, The.
Expulsion.
Release.

Sexauer, Ted
Ambivalent Nature of Healing, The.
Poem for Têt.
Well, The.

Sexton, Anne (1928–74)
Abortion, The.
All My Pretty Ones.
And One for My Dame.
Author of the Jesus Papers Speaks, The.
Ballad of the Lonely Masturbator, The.
Black Art, The.
Briar Rose (Sleeping Beauty).
Cinderella.
Consorting with Angels.
Courage.
Crossing the Atlantic.
Death Baby, The, *sels.*
Death of the Fathers, The, *sels.*
Elizabeth Gone.

From the Garden.
Funnel.
Furies, The, *sels.*
Fury of Overshoes.
Her Kind.
Housewife.
I Remember.
In Celebration of My Uterus.
In the Deep Museum.
Jesus Asleep.
Jesus Dies.
Jesus Suckles.
Jesus Unborn.
Landscape Winter.
Little Girl, My String Bean, My Lovely
    Woman.
Lobster.
Man and Wife.
Moss of His Skin, The.
Music Swims Back to Me.
Noon Walk on the Asylum Lawn.
O Ye Tongues, *sels.*
Red Roses.
Room of My Life, The.
Small Wire.
Snow White and the Seven Dwarfs.
Some Foreign Letters.
Somewhere in Africa.
Starry Night, The.
Sylvia's Death.
To a Friend Whose Work Has Come to
    Triumph.
Truth the Dead Know, The.
Unknown Girl in the Maternity Ward.
Us.
Wanting to Die.
Welcome Morning.
With Mercy for the Greedy.
You, Doctor Martin.

Sexton, Megan
Marriage Patois.

Sexton, Tom
Seal Island.
Skimming the Ice.

Seyburn, Patty (b. 1962)
Alphabetizer Speaks, The.
First Bookshelf.
Good Water.
Persuasion.
What I Disliked About the Pleistocene Era.
You and Them.

Şeyh Galib
I won't abandon you, though you cause me.
My darling with the rosy face—at one glance.
To me, love is the flame.
You are my effendi, if I have any respect in the
    world.

Seymour, Jane (1541–61)
Hecatodistichon, *sel.*

Seymour, Margaret (*fl.* 1551)
Hecatodistichon, *sel.*

**Seymour, Sir Thomas (Baron Seymour of
Sudeley) (1508?–49)**
Forgetting God.

Shaben, Sekeena
Fourteenth Ode.
Tempest.
Thirteenth Ode.

Shabtai, Aharon (b. 1939)
As We Were Marching.
Basel Square.
Hebrew Culture.
Hope: "It's hopeless, you told me."
I Love Passover.
Nostalgia.
Our Land.
Rosh HaShanah.
Sharon Resembles a Person.
War.

Shafer, Audrey
Gurney Tears.
Monday Morning.

Shafiq, Hashim (b. 1950)
Destinies.
Mirage.

Mountain, The.
Picture of a Tyrant.

Shakan, Jennifer L.
Soft.

Shakespeare, William (1564–1616)
All's Well That Ends Well, *sel.*
Antony and Cleopatra, *sels.*
As You Like It, *sels.*
Comedy of Errors, The, *sel.*
Coriolanus, *sels.*
Cymbeline, *sels.*
Hamlet, *sels.*
Julius Caesar, *sels.*
King Henry V, *sels.*
King Henry IV, Pt. I, *sels.*
King Henry IV, Pt. II, *sels.*
King Henry VI, Pt. I, *sels.*
King Henry VI, Pt. II, *sels.*
King Henry VI, Pt. III, *sels.*
King John, *sels.*
King Lear, *sels.*
King Richard II, *sels.*
King Richard III, *sels.*
Love's Labour's Lost, *sels.*
Macbeth, *sels.*
Measure for Measure, *sels.*
Merchant of Venice, The, *sels.*
Midsummer Night's Dream, A, *sels.*
Much Ado about Nothing, *sels.*
Othello, *sels.*
Passionate Pilgrim, The, *sel.*
Pericles, *sel.*
Phoenix and the Turtle, The.
Rape of Lucrece, The, *sels.*
Romeo and Juliet, *sels.*
Songs for the Seasons: A Distant
    Collaboration.
Sonnets, *sels.*
Taming of the Shrew, The, *sels.*
Tempest, The, *sels.*
Timon of Athens, *sels.*
Titus Andronicus, *sels.*
Troilus and Cressida, *sels.*
Twelfth Night, *sels.*
Two Gentlemen of Verona, The, *sels.*
Venus and Adonis [Complete Text *and*
    Selections from Anthologies], *sels.*
Winter's Tale, The, *sels.*

Shakespeare, William *See Also* Fletcher, John

Shakhova, Elizaveta (1821–99)
Autobiographical Response from a Provincial
    Wasteland (in Reply to a New Year's
    Greeting Sent with a Bouquet).

Shaku Chōkū (1887–1954)
Tanka: "Imagining / the grassy ground not
    shown."
Tanka: "Somewhere around."
Vultures—in the Midst of War.

Shaku, Soyen (1860–1919)
En Route to America.

Shakur, Assata
Tradition, The.

Shakur, Tupac
Why Must U Be Unfaithful (4 Women).

Shaler, Nathaniel Southgate
Marksman's Work, The.
Merry Truce, The.
Near the Front.

Shamaqmaq, Abu (*fl.* 770)
Hungry Master and Hungry Cat.

Shamlu, Almad (1925–2000)
Poetry That Is Life.
Somber Song.

Shanahan, Deirdre (b. 1955)
Morning Radio.

Shange, Ntozake (b. 1948)
About Atlanta.
Ancestral Messengers / Composition 13.
Bocas: A Daughter's Geography.
Dream of Pairing.
Elegance in the Extreme.
For Colored Girls Who Have Considered
    Suicide When the Rainbow Is Enuf, *sels.*
I Live in Music.

If I Go All the Way Without You Where
Would I Go!
It's Not so Good to be Born a Girl/ Sometimes.
Oh, I'm 10 Months Pregnant.
Okra to Greens /, *sels*.
Tango.
We Need a God Who Bleeds Now.
Where the Heart Is.
Where the Mississippi meets the Amazon.
You are Sucha Fool.

Shanks, Edward Richard Burton (1892–1953)
Drilling in Russell Square.
Going In to Dinner.
High Germany.
Sleeping Heroes.

Shannon, Angela
Hands.
Integration.
JoNelle.
Returning the Water.
Sunday: "It could have been the way the
Southern."
Wet Oak.

Shannon, Jeanne
Imbolc.
Lilac.
Sext.

Shaoxuan, Cui
Black hair and red cheeks: for how long?

Shapcott, Jo (b. 1953)
Elizabeth Looks at Robert.
Goat.
Hairless.
I am always behind.
In the Bath.
Lies.
Life.
Lovebirds.
Mad Cow in Love, The.
Mad Cow Tries to Write the Good Poem, The.
Motherland.
Muse.
My Life Asleep.
Phrase Book.
Robert Watches Elizabeth Knitting.
Roses, The, *sels*.
When I Died.

Shapcott, Thomas William (b. 1935)
Blue Paisley Shirt, The.
City of Home, The.
June Fugue.
Litanies of Julia Pastrana (1832-1860), The.
Post Operative.
Shadow of War, 1941.
Turning Fifty.

Shapiro, Alan (b. 1952)
Basement, The.
Christmas Story, A.
Cold Wood.
Familiar Story.
Mezuzah.
Natural Selection.
Old Joke.
Soul.

Shapiro, David (b. 1947)
Archaic Torsos.
Book of Glass, A.
Burning Interior, A.
Canticle.
Commentary Text Commentary Text
Commentary Text.
Counter-Example, The.
Father Knows Best.
For the Princess Hello.
Giants.
House (Blown Apart).
In a Blind Garden.
Lord I Sleep and I Sleep.
Old Poems.
Pin's Fee, or Painting with Star, A.
Realistic Bar and Grill, A.
Song of the Eiffel Tower.
To My Son.
Tracing of an Evening.
Traumerei.

Weak Poet, The.

Shapiro, Harvey (b. 1924)
Bad Days.
Battle Report.
Bible Lesson.
Bus Ride.
Death of a Grandmother.
For Paul Celan and Primo Levi.
Loyalty.
National Cold Storage Company.
News, The.
Nights: "Drunk and weeping. It's another."
6/20/97.
War Stories.

Shapiro, Karl (1913–2000)
Adam and Eve, *sels*.
Alphabet, The.
Auto Wreck.
Bourgeois Poet, The, *sels*.
Buick.
Confirmation, The.
Conscientious Objector, The.
Crossing Lincoln Park.
Cut Flower, A.
Dirty Word, The.
Dome of Sunday, The [*or* A].
Editing *Poetry*.
Elegy for a Dead Soldier.
First Time, The.
Fly, The.
Full Moon: New Guinea.
Funeral of Poetry, The.
Girls Working in Banks.
Homecoming: "Lost in the vastness of the void
Pacific."
I Am an Atheist Who Says His Prayers.
Leg, The.
Lord, I Have Seen Too Much.
Lower the Standard: That's My Motto.
Manhole Covers.
My Father's Funeral.
My Grandmother.
October 1.
151st Psalm, The.
Piano Tuner's Wife, The.
Poet.
Puritan, The.
Recapitulations.
Scyros.
Terminal.
Travelogue for Exiles.
Troop Train.
Twins, The.
Two-Year-Old Has Had a Motherless Week,
The.
University.
V-Letter.

Shapiro, Myra
To Jerusalem, 1990.

Sharaf, Mahmoud
Behind the House.
Dali.

Sharah, Jemal (b. 1969)
Package for Another World.
Parting Roundel.

Share, Don
Divorced.

Sharkey, Michael (b. 1946)
Greenwood's.
Hots, The.

Sharma, Prageeta
Action-Packed Sonnet.
Dear ———.
Performance Test.
Poorly Matched.
Potter's Field.
Principles, When I Felt Them.
Transit.

Sharman, Ruth
By Heart.

Sharp, S. Pearl
How to Build a Prayer.

Sharp, Saundra (b. 1942)
Good Nights.
In the Tradition of Bobbitt.

Tribal Marks.

Sharpless, Stanley J. (b. 1910)
Chaucer: The Wogan's Tale.
Hamlet.
In Praise of Cocoa, Cupid's Nightcap.
Low Church.
Paradise Lost as a Haiku.
Pied Beauty.
Sonnet: "How do I hate you? Let me count the
ways."
There's a Breathless Hush on the Centre Court.

Sharshar, Sadiq
Charlie Chaplin.
Singer, The.

Shatalov, Aleksandr (b. 1957)
Age of aquarius mineral water taking a bath,
The.

Shats, Evelina
Rose, A / a / shameless.
Sleep soundly, dear poet.

Shaughnessy, Brenda (b. 1970)
Epithalament.
Me in Paradise.
Panopticon.
Postfeminism.
Rise.
You Love, You Wonder.
Your Name on It.
Your One Good Dress.

Shauqi, Ahmad (1869–1932)
Andalusian Exile, An.

Shaw, Angela (b. 1967)
April.
Bird Nests.
Crepuscule.
Pornography.
Rear Window.
Small Pleasures.

Shaw, Charles (b. 1892)
Search, The.

Shaw, Dunstan
Retrospection.

Shaw, Jodi A. (b. 1982)
Revelation.

Shaw, Luci (b. 1928)
It is as if infancy were the whole of
incarnation.
Onlookers.
Reluctant prophet.

Shaw, Robert B. (b. 1947)
Chronometrics, *sels*.
Last Days in Camden.
Shut In.
To His Pulse.

Shaw, Stanley
Christopher Smart.

Shcherbina, Tatiana (b. 1954)
About Limits.
Eros Poesis.
Except for love everything.
Stepmother, The.
Still-Life.
Tell me, Comrade God, how can life, over this
stretch.
They cut off my hot water.
What's it you're howling, siren-telephone.
Where are the future's clawlets?
Whole city seductively lit up, The.

Shea, James (b. 1976)
Haiku: "Upon Kissing You after You
Vomited."

Shearin, Faith
Entropy.
Sinking, The.

Sheehan, Marc J.
My Father's Singing.

Sheeler, Jackie
This Old Man.

**Sheffield, John, Duke of Buckingham and
Normandy (1648–1721)**
Ode on the Death of Mr. Henry Purcell, *sels*.
On Brutus, an Ode, *sels*.
On One Who Died Discovering Her Kindness.

Reconcilement, The.

Shehabi, Deema K.
Breath.
Cemetery at Petit Saconnex, The.
Glistening, The.

Shehadeh, Mohammed
Letters to Childhood.

Sheinfeld, Ilan (b. 1960)
War Night 6.

Sheldon, Glenn
Blames, for Rane and Diane.

Shelley, Mary Wollstonecraft (1797–1851)
Stanzas: "Oh, come to me in dreams, my
love!"

Shelley, Percy Bysshe (1792–1822)
Adonais; An Elegy on the Death of John
Keats, *sels.*
Alastor; or, The Spirit of Solitude, *sel.*
Autumn: A Dirge.
Cenci, The, *sels.*
Cloud, The.
Dirge, A: "Rough wind, that moanest loud."
England in 1819.
Epipsychidion.
Feelings of a Republican on the Fall of
Bonaparte.
From the Arabic: An Imitation.
Hellas, *sels.*
Hymn of Pan.
Hymn to Intellectual Beauty.
Indian Serenade, The.
Julian and Maddalo; A Conversation, *sel.*
Laon and Cythna [Earlier version of The
Revolt of Islam], *sel.*
Lines: "When the lamp is shattered [*or*
shatter'd]."
Lines Written in the Bay of Lerici.
Love's Philosophy.
Mask [*or* Masque] of Anarchy, The, *sel.*
Mont Blanc.
Mutability ("Flower that smiles today, The.").
Mutability ("We are as clouds that veil the
midnight moon.").
Ode to the West Wind.
On a Painted Woman.
On the Medusa of Leonardo da Vinci in the
Florentine Gallery.
Ozymandias.
Peter Bell the Third, *sels.*
Prometheus Unbound, *sel.*
Queen Mab, *sels.*
Question, The: "I dream'd that, as I wander'd
by the way."
Revolt of Islam, The, *sel.*
Sensitive Plant, The, *sels.*
Song to the Men of England.
Sonnet: Lift Not the Painted Veil.
Sonnet: Political Greatness.
Stanzas Written in Dejection, Near Naples [*or*
—December 1818, near Naples].
Summer and Winter.
To a Skylark.
To Jane: The Invitation.
To Jane: The keen stars were twinkling.
To Jane: The Recollection.
To —: "Music, when soft voices die."
To Night.
To—: "One word is too often profaned."
To the Moon.
To Wordsworth.
Triumph of Life, The, *sels.*
World's Wanderers, The.

Shelton, Richard (b. 1933)
Job the Father.
Letter to a Dead Father.
Promises.

Shelvakh, Aleksey (b. 1948)
Veterans.

Shemer, Naomi (1931–2004)
On Silver Wings.

Shen Chou (1427–1509)
Taoist Huang Has Died of Alcoholism, The.
Written on a Landscape Painting in an Album.

Shen Manyuan (502–56)
Her Tiara Flowers.

Parody of the Other Woman.

Shen Quanqi (c. 650–713)
First Reaching Huanzhou.

Shen Yüeh (441–513)
Green, Green Riverside Grass.
Harmonizing with a Poem by Left Assistant Yu
Kao-chih Requesting Sick Leave.
I Climb High to Look at Spring.
Listening to Gibbons at Rock-Pool Creek.
Night After Night.
Peach.
Returning to My Garden Home: In Respectful
Response to the Master of Hua-yang.
Seeing the Beloved in a Dream.
Spring: "Willows tangle like silk threads."

Shenstone, William (1714–63)
Describing the Sorrow of an Ingenuous Mind
on the Melancholy Event of a Licentious
Amour [*or* Elegy 26], *sels.*
He Repeats the Song of Colin, a Discerning
Shepherd [*or* Elegy 18], *sels.*
Lines Written on a Window at The Leasowes.
Taking a View of the Country from His
Retirement [*or* Elegy 21], *sels.*
Written at [*or* in] an Inn at Henley.

Sheperd, Luke (fl. 1548)
Upcheringe of the Messe, The, *sel.*

Shephard, S. P.
Four and Twenty Soldiers.
Homeless Vets.
Suicides and Fools.

Shepherd, Reginald (b. 1963)
Also Love You.
Another Version of an Ocean.
Boy, Allegorically Deployed.
Difficult Music, The.
Eros in His Striped Blue Shirt.
Gods at Three A.M., The.
Homeric Interim.
Hygiene.
Itinerary.
Lucky One, The.
Man Named Troy, A.
Maritime.
Motive.
Narcissus Learning the Words to This Song.
Objects in Mirror Are Closer Than They
Appear.
Pericles, Prince of Tyre: A Commentary.
Provisional.
Refrain.
Self-Portrait in the New World Order.
Snowdrops and Summer Snowflakes,
Drooping.
That Man.
Three A.M. Eternal.
West Willow.
What Cannot Be Kept.
Where When Was.
White Days.
Who Owns the Night and Lease Stars.

Sheppard, Robert (b. 1955)
Empty Diaries/Twentieth Century Blues 24,
sels.

Sherburne, Sir Edward (1618–1702)
And She Washed His Feet with Her Tear[e]s,
and Wiped Them with the Hairs of Her
Head.
Weeping and Kissing.

Sheridan, Richard Brinsley (1751–1816)
Duenna, The, *sels.*
Lines by a Lady on the Loss of her Trunk.
On Lady Anne Hamilton.
School for Scandal, The, *sels.*

Sheridan, Thomas (1687–1738)
Tom Punsibi's Letter to Dean Swift.

Sherman, Charlotte Watson (b. 1958)
Roots.

Sherman, Joseph (b. 1945)
Aphelion.
For Mordecai Richler's Shalinsky Who Said
"A Jew Is An Idea."
My Father Plaits His Granddaughter's Hair.

Sherman, Maurina
Blackberries.
San Buenaventura.
This Body.
Towards Sunset at Camino Cielo.

Sherrill, Jan-Mitchell
Woodstock.

Sherrill, Steven (b. 1961)
Katyn Forest.

Sherry, James (b. 1946)
Free Radicals.
Hazardous Waste.
In Case, *sel.*
Lepidoptery.
Pay Cash Only.
Radiant.

Sherry, Pearl Andelson
Fermi Lab: Sisyphus of Quarks.

Sherwin, Judith Johnson (b. 1936)
Nightpiece.
To Whom it may concern.

Sherwood, Grace Buchanan (b. 1883)
Love and Life.
Satire against Reason and Mankind, A.

Sherwood, Kate Brownlee (1841–1914)
Albert Sidney Johnston.
Thomas at Chickamauga.

Sherwood, Robert E. (1896–1955)
Old Hokum Buncombe, The.

Sheykhi (d. 1426)
It's the season of spring, let us be.
Your sun-face is a mirror of the soul.

Shi Chong (249–300)
Longing to Return: A Lament.

Shi-wei, Jiang *See* "Mang Ke"

Shields, Ren
In the Good Old Summer Time.

Shih Shu
35.
37.
40.
55.
69.
70.
73.
82.
92.
93.
94.
106.
133.
134.
137.
149.
155.
157.
158.
166.
After Shih-te ("I climb these hills as if walking
on air.").
After Shih-te ("My ragged cloak is streaked
with mountain shadows.").
After Shih-te ("Perfumed springs ripple over
skeletal outcrops.").
Enlightenment.

Shiki, Prince (668–716)
Full moon ringed, The.
In the winter river.
Just when the sermon.
O autumn winds.
Skylark school, The.
Thunderstorm breaks up, The.

Shikibu, Izumi *See* Izumi, Lady

Shillaber, B. P.
Picture, A.
Sagamore, The.

Shimabukuro, Mira Chieko
After the Separation, Dad Takes Me to the
Dance for the Dead.

Shimazaki Toson (1872–1943)
First Love.
Fox's Trick, The.

Shin Kyŏngnim (b. 1936)
Baby, The.
Country Bus Station.
Farmer's Dance.
Graveside Memorial.
Legend.
Market's Closing.
On a Winter's Night.
Road, The.
That Day.
They.

Shin Tongyŏp (1930–69)
Kŭm River, *sels.*

Shinder, Jason (b. 1955)
Changing: "Your unmistakable breasts, plain, finely wrinkled."
Growing Up.
New Year: "Let me dive to the bottom of the hotel pool."
One Secret That Has Carried, The.
Waitress.

Shindo, Ryoko
Puddle.

Shine, Lori (b. 1975)
Union Square.

Shinkichi Takahashi (1901–87)
Absence.
Afterimages.
Beach.
Braggart Duck.
Burning Oneself to Death.
Camel.
Canna.
Clay Image.
Cloud.
Destruction.
Downy Hair.
Drizzle.
Eternity.
Explosion.
Fish.
Flight of the Sparrow.
Four Divine Animals.
Gods.
Hand.
Lap Dog.
Let's Live Cheerfully.
Little Sunlight, A.
Moon.
Moon and Hare.
Mother and I.
Mushroom.
Near Shinobazu Pond.
Peach Blossom and Pigeon (painting by Kiso).
Peach, The.
Pipe, The.
Position of the Sparrow, The.
Quails.
Railroad Station.
Rain.
Raw Fish and Vegetables.
Rocks.
Sea of Oblivion.
Sheep.
Shell.
Sky.
Snowy Sky.
Sparrow and Bird-Net Building.
Sparrow in Withered Field.
Spinning Dharma Wheel.
Spring.
Stitches.
Stone Wall.
Sweet Potato.
Thistles.
Toad.
Urn.
Vimalakirti.
What Is Moving.
Wood in Sound, A.
Words: "I don't take your words."

Shiomi, Mieko
Disappearing Music for Face.
Event for Late Afternoon.
Mirror.

Music For Two Players 2.
Passing Music for a Tree.
Portrait Piece.

Shiphrah, Thandiwe
Grand Diva.
Grandma.
To Adam.

Shipley, Andrea
Mama Said.

Shipley, Vivian
At Fifty.
Birdsong for September 11, 2001.
Birthday Party on Old Orchard Road, A.
Faithful Daughter Dreams of Spring Break While Installing a Bird Feeder for Her Mother by a Window in the Courtyard of Safe Harbour, The.
Heart with Little or No Bedrock for Anchor, A.
Sleeping Soundly Where Lizzie Borden Did.

Shipman, Thomas (1632–80)
Frost, 1654, The: To Mr. W.L, *sel.*
Kiss, The 1656. To Mrs. C.

Shiraishi, Kazuko (b. 1931)
Afternoon of the Sheep, The.
Bear of the Human Family, A.
Donkey Speculates, The.
From the Precious Tears of the Donkey.
Man Root, The.
Residents of the Cocoon, The.
Seven Cats Are Happy, The.
Wild Pigs of Kalimantan, The.

Shirley, Aleda
Hours Musicians Keep, The.
Late Night Radio.
Long Distance.

Shirley, Dorothy, Lady (1600–36)
LD Ansure, The.

Shirley, James (1596–1666)
Contention of Ajax and Ulysses, The, *sels.*
Cupid's Call.
Garden, The.
Lover that Durst Not Speak to His M[istress], A.

Shiroa See Kaya Shirao

Shiseki (1676–1759)
My old thighs / How thin.

Shishin-Goshin (d. 1339)
Talking: seven steps, eight falls.

Shkapskaya, Maria Mikhailovna (1891–1952)
No Dream.

Shockley, Evie (b. 1965)
Bio / *autography* (or, 18th-Century Multiculturalism).
Cause i'm from dixie too.
From The Lost Letters of Frederick Douglass.
My last modernist poem, #2 (or, mugshot).
N-word, The.
Shall become as.

Shockley, Martin Staples (b. 1908)
Armadillo.

Shofu
No dust speck anywhere.

Shoha (Kuroyanagi Shoha) (d. 1771)
Shameful / Dead grass.
When the bush warbler.

Shoha, Kuroyanagi See Shoha

Shōhei (fl. 1844)
Mad Verse.

Shoichi (1202–80)
All-meaning circle, The.

Shokaku
High wind, cold moon.

Shokushi, Princess
Guide me on my way.
O cord of life!

Sholl, Betsy
Autobiography in Third Person.
Dawn.
Distinct Call of the Alligator, The.
Don't Explain.
Four Crows at Dusk.
Girl Named Spring, A.
Good News/Bad News.

Hospital State, The.
Late Psalm.
Midnight Vapor Light Breakdown.
Monkey House.
Outside the Depot.
Past, The.
Postmaster's Children, The.
Redbud.
Small Patch of Ice, A.
Something to Say.
Soup Kitchen.
Thinking of You, Hiroshima.
To the Dregs.
You Figure It Out.

Shoman, Kiren
Cords.
In Explanation to the Mother.
Is Beautiful.
321738.

Shomer, Enid
Falling for Jesus.
First Sunset at Outler's Ranch.
Freestyle, on the First of Tishri.
From the Wailing Wall.
Letter Home from Brooklyn.
My Mother's Body.
Refusing the Call.
Shards.
World Goes Black, The, *sels.*

Shoneyin, Titiola
Bedside Wreaths.
Quiver of Questions, A.

Shore, Jane (b. 1947)
Astronomer's Journal, An.
High Holy Days.
Sawdust.

Short, John (b. 1911)
Leave in Mid-Winter.

Short, Spencer (b. 1972)
Romanticism.

Shorter, Dora Sigerson (1866–1918)
Ireland.
Mother, The.
Skeleton in the Cupboard, The.

Shostakovskaya, Irina (b. 1978)
Boy bears a gray shield, The.
Sailor sailor got ashore.
Today I'm a proper king's daughter.

Shot, Danny
Executive Privilege.

Shoukry, Guiguis
Good Man Talking to Himself, A.
Personal Portrait, A.

Shouman, Mas-oud
Dance with Nothing On, with Nobody Around, A.

Shove, Fredegond Maitland (1889–1949)
Farmer, The.
New Ghost, The.

Shozan (1717–1800)
Guest gone / I stroke the brazier.
No mind, no Buddha.

Shpolyansky, Aminado Petrovich See Aminado, Don

Shreshtha, Bishwabimohan (b. 1956)
Should I Earn My Daily Bread, or Should I Write a Poem?

Shreve, Sandy (b. 1950)
Dance.
Landing.

Shrine Priestess of Ise
My mind is dazzled.

Shu-jen, Chou See "Lu Hsün"

"Shu Ting" (Gong Peiyu) (b. 1952)
Assembly Line.
Bits of Reminiscence.
Brother, I Am Here.
Fairy Tales.
Gifts.
Maple Leaf.
Mirror, The.
Missing You.
Perhaps.

Singing Flower, The.
Shúa, Ana Maria
Golem and Rabbi, *sels.*
Shuford, Gene (b. 1907)
Celebration.
Horse in My Yard, The.
Sam Bass.
Visit, The.
Shukman, Henry
Horses at Christmas.
Shumaker, Peggy (b. 1952)
Ajo Lily.
Bush Navigator: The Last Morning of Hands.
Circle of Totems, The.
First Winter: Joy.
Inupiat Christmas Pageant, The.
Waitress's Kid, The.
Shumyatsher, Esther (1899–1985)
Earth Dream.
My New York Street Sings.
Toye-Voye.
Shunoku (1311–88)
After the spring song, "Vast emptiness, no holiness."
Shunryu Suzuki (1904–71)
Beginner's Mind.
Shunzei (Fujiwara no Shunzei; Toshinari) (1114–1204)
Cormorant-boat, The.
Shall I see it again.
"Shunzei's Daughter" (1171?–1252?)
Brought by the breeze.
Burning in Secret.
Shurbanov, Alexander (b. 1941)
Attractions.
Shurin, Aaron (b. 1947)
Blue Shade.
City of Men.
Forward or Back.
His Promise.
Material's Daughter.
Sailed.
Saturated.
Shushtarī, Alī ibn Abd Allāh (1213–69)
Little shaikh from the land of Meknès sings in the middle of the marketplaces, A.
My beloved has visited me and my moments have become sweet. My beloved listened to me.
Shuster, Dana
Mellow on Morphine.
Shuttle, Penelope (b. 1947)
Angel.
Delicious Babies.
Many creatures don't have one.
Old Man, The.
Passion, *sels.*
Taxing the Rain.
Ultra Sound.
Shwarts [*or* Shvarts], Yelena [*or* Elena] (b. 1948)
Conversation with a Cat.
Dump, The.
Elegies on the Cardinal Points.
Elegy on an X-ray Photo of My Skull.
Imitation of Boileau.
Memorial Candle.
My heart's cloth I shall spread before the Savior's feet.
Parrot at Sea, A.
Portrait of the Blockade through Genre Painting, Still Life, and Landscape, A.
Remembrance of Strange Hospitality.
Sale of a Historian's Library.
What That Street Is Called.
Shy, Shoshauna
Bringing My Son to the Police Station to Be Fingerprinted.
"Shy, Timothy" *See* Lewis, Dominic Bevan Wyndham
Sia, Beau (b. 1976)
Claim to Fame.
Enemy.
Howl.
No Words Empty.

Open Letter to the Entertainment Industry, An.
Things to Do in Holland.
Siamanto (1878–1915)
Dance, The.
Grief.
Sica, Gabriella (b. 1950)
I.
Lightening, The.
Monotomy.
Nudity.
On the Sea.
Poems for a Little Boy, *sel.*
Sicoli, Dan
All Shook Up.
Siddal, Elizabeth (1829–62)
At Last.
Dead Love.
Lust of the Eyes, The.
Sidgwick, Henry
Strenuous Life, The.
Sidney, Sir Philip (1554–86)
Astrophil and Stella, *sels.*
Countesse of Pembroke's Arcadia, The, *sels.*
Dirge: "Ring out your bells [*or* belles], let mourning shows [*or* shewes] be spread."
Leave Me O Love.
Nightingale, The.
Thou Blind Man's Mark.
When, to my deadly [*or* deadlie] pleasure.
White Great Nimble Cat, A.
Sidney, Robert (1563–1626)
Ah dearest limbs, my life's best joy and stay.
Alas, why say you I am rich? when I.
Forsaken woods, trees with sharp storms opressed.
Songe 17: "Sun is set, and masked night, The."
Sonnet 25: "Yow that take pleasure in yowr cruelty."
Siegel, Joan I.
Drought.
How the Tortoise Knew It Was Her Time.
Wild Hyacinth.
Siegel, Marcella
Waiting Wife.
Siegel, Robert (b. 1839)
Air Field.
Hog Heaven.
Silverfish.
Slug.
Turtles.
Sigerson, George (1839–1925)
Love's Despair.
Sigourney, Lydia Huntley (1791–1865)
Advertisement of a Lost Day.
Death of an Infant.
Erin's Daughter.
Indian Names.
Indian's Welcome to the Pilgrim Fathers, The.
Poetry.
Stars, The.
Suttee, The.
To the First Slave Ship.
Western Emigrant, The.
Sík Sándor (1889–1963)
English, The.
Summer and Dawn.
Sikelianos, Eleni (b. 1965)
Heaven: "What was it I saw at the top."
Siken, Richard (b. 1967)
Boot Theory.
Primer for the Small Weird Loves, A.
Saying Your Names.
Sikong Tu (837–908)
Twenty-Four Modes of Poetry, *sels.*
Silano, Martha (b. 1961)
Explaining Current Events to a One-Year-Old.
In Henry Carlile's *Writing 213.*
Moon, The.
Sausage Parade, The.
Such a Way to Go.
Sweet Red Peppers, Sun-Drieds, the Hearts of Artichokes.
Sılay, Celâl (1914–74)
You Will Come to Me.

Silberg, Richard (b. 1940)
Audience, The.
Silesky, Barry
Kingdom, The.
Prime Time.
Screens.
Silex, Edgar
Acts of Love.
Departure.
Elegy: "What remains of the suicide's voice is the last conversation."
Gift, The.
Silkin, Jon (1930–97)
Lilies of the Valley.
Silko, Leslie Marmon (b. 1948)
In Cold Storm Light.
Indian Song: Survival.
It Was a Long Time Before.
Long Time Ago.
Prayer to the Pacific.
Toe'osh; a Laguna Coyote Story.
When Sun Came to Riverwoman.
Where Mountain Lion Lay [*or* Laid] Down with Deer.
Sill, Edward Rowland (1841–87)
California Winter.
Fool's Prayer, The.
Opportunity.
Truth at Last.
Silliman, Ron (b. 1946)
Glimmer of light high over Mount Diablo (silhouette flat across).
Hidden, *sel.*
Ketjak, *sel.*
Paradise, *sels.*
Tjanting, *sels.*
VOG, *sels.*
Sillitoe, Alan (b. 1928)
Synagogue in Prague.
Silook, Susie
Uncle Good Intentions.
"Silurist" *See* Vaughan, Henry
Silva, Clara (1908–76)
In the Darkness of the Other.
Magical Devices.
Moon's Cadaver, The.
Tea at the Magdalene.
Who Will Throw the First Stone?
Silva, José Asunción (1865–96)
Art: "Poem is a holy glass— put, A."
Nocturne: "One night / One night full of perfumes, music of wings and murmurs."
Silva, Luis Andrade (b. 1943)
Emigrant's Son, The.
Island and Europe, The.
Silven, Patrik *See* Sylvain, Patrick
Silverstein, Shel [*or* Shelley] (b. 1932)
Friendship.
Hug o' War.
Jimmy Jet and His TV Set.
Lazy People, The.
Sick.
Slithergadee, The.
Simic, Charles (b. 1938)
Against Whatever It Is That's Encroaching.
Ancient Autumn.
Arctic Voyager, An.
At the Cookout.
Austerities.
Bather, The.
Bestiary for the Fingers of My Right Hand.
Book Full of Pictures, A.
Breasts.
Butcher Shop.
Cameo Appearance.
Charles Simic.
Charon's Cosmology.
Classic Ballroom Dances.
Clouds Gathering.
Club Midnight.
Concerning My Neighbors, the Hittites.
Congress of the Insomniacs, The.
Country Fair.
Crepuscule with Nellie.

December: "It snows."
Devils, The.
Dismantling the Silence.
Dream Avenue.
Eastern European Cooking.
Elders, The.
Empire of Dreams.
Entertaining the Canary.
Errata.
Evening Chess.
Evening Walk.
Eyes Fastened with Pins.
Fear: "Fear passes from man to man."
February: "One who lights the wood stove,
  The."
Fork.
Great Infirmities.
Head of a Doll.
Hundred-Year-Old China Doll's Head, The.
I Was Stolen by the Gypsies.
Immortal, The.
Inner Man, The.
Lesson, The.
Live at Club Mozambique.
Lives of Alchemists, The.
Miracle Glass Co.
Mirrors at 4 A.M.
Modern Sorcery.
Much Dwindled, Starker Annotator, A.
My Beloved.
My Mother was a Braid.
My Noiseless Entourage.
My Shoes.
Night Picnic.
Northern Exposure.
Old Couple.
Old World, The.
Pain.
Partial Explanation, The.
Past-Lives Therapy.
Poem: "Every morning I forget how it is."
Poem without a Title.
Popular Mechanics.
Prodigy.
Psalm: "You've been a long time making up
  your mind."
Scarecrow, The.
Shelley.
Solitude.
Something, The.
Spoons with Realistic Dead Flies on Them.
Spring: "This is what I saw—old snow on the
  ground."
St. Thomas Aquinas.
Stone.
Stone is a mirror which works poorly, The.
Summer Morning.
Sunday Papers.
Tapestry.
To the One Upstairs.
Used Book Store.
Wall, A.
Watch Repair.
Watching the Hearse.
Watermelons.
We Were So Poor.
Winter Night.

Simić, Goran (b. 1952)
Sorrow of Sarajevo, The.

Simidò, Danyèl *See* Simidor, Daniel

Simidor, Daniel
Slippery Ground.
Spring: "Spring afternoon, a lovely sky, bright
  sunshine, A."

Simmerman, Jim (b. 1952)
Child's Grave, Hale County, Alabama.
Take a Hike.

Simmonds, Kevin
New Sestina, The.
White Man and the Judge, A.

Simmons, James (b. 1933)
After Eden.
Archæologist, The.
Birthday Poem, A.
Cavalier Lyric.

Claudy.
Didn't He Ramble.
Eden.
End of the Affair, The.
For Imelda.
For Thomas Moore.
From the Irish.
Honeymoon, The.
In the Wilderness.
Influence of Natural Objects, The.
Join Me in Celebrating.
Long Way After Ronsard, A.
Lullaby for Rachael.
One of the Boys.
Pleasant Joys of Brotherhood, The.
Rogation Day: Portrush.
Stephano Remembers.
West Strand Visions.
Westport House, Portrush.
Written, Directed by and Starring.

Simmons, Naomi Stroud
Black Sunday, April 14, 1935.

Simmons, Sharif
All the shoes are shined and the cotton is
  picked.

Simms, Colin
First English Wildcat, The.
Grey Wagtail on the Tyne.
Pallid Harrier.
Shots at Otters, *sel.*

Simms, William Gilmore (1806–72)
By the Swannannoa.
City of the Silent, The, *sel.*
Lost Pleiad, The.
New Moon, The.
Ode: "Do ye quail but to hear, Carolinians."
Voice of Memory in Exile, from a Home in
  Ashes, The.

Simon, John Oliver (b. 1946)
Caffe Mediterraneum.

Simon, Leslie
Bernice Got Next to Isis.
Hattie Went to Market.
Kali.
Nellie Gives into Blanche.

Simon, Luke Icarus
Measuring Apollo.
Ravine.

Simon, Maurya (b. 1950)
All Soul's Day.
Atomic Psalm.
Blue Movies.
Boy Crazy.
Coward.
Dolphin, The.
Doomsday.
Helsinore, Denmark.
Keeping Track.
Night.
Sea Sprite, Hermosa Beach, The.
Search, The.
Shiva's Prowess.
Snow.
Standing Between Two Ideas.
Tale Before the End of the World.

Simon, Onika
Heat.

Simonides (c.556–468 B.C.)
All things come to one hideous Charybdis.
As whenever.
Because of these men's courage, no smoke
  rose.
Being human, don't ever say what happens
  tomorrow.
Countless birds.
Danae and Perseus.
Distinguishes the fair and the shameful.
For the Spartan Dead at Thermopylai (480
  B.C.)
Greek Dead at Thermopylae, The.
Human strength.
It is hard to become a truly good.
No leaf-shaking blast of winds.
On the Spartan Dead at Thermopylae.
Stranger, when you come to / Lakedaimon.

There is a tale.
Thermopylae.
Thermopylai's dead.
These men lying here were carrying honors to
  Apollo.
They wept for the violet-wreathed [lady's].
When in the skillfully welded chest.
Who, trusting his mind, could praise the man
  of Lindos, Kleoboulos.
Without pleasure.

Simonov, Konstantin Mikhailovich (1915–79)
Death Struck Him.

Simonovic, Ifigenija (b. 1953)
Misere.

Simons, Seymour
All of Me.

Simpson, Anne (b. 1956)
Deer on a Beach.
Lilacs, The.
Möbius Strip.
Name, Many Names, A.
Seven Paintings By Brueghel.
Waking.
White, Mauve, Yellow.

Simpson, Jane Cross (1811–86)
Oh! if thou lov'st me, love me not so well!

Simpson, Joshua McCarter (1820–76)
Away to Canada, *sel.*

Simpson, Louis (b. 1923)
After Midnight.
American Classic.
American Poetry.
Appointment, The.
Arm in Arm.
Battle, The.
Boots and Saddles.
Bower of Roses, A.
Carentan O Carentan.
Chocolates.
Early in the Morning.
Ed.
Heroes, The.
In the Suburbs.
Inner Part, The.
Letter from Brazil, A.
Listeners, The.
Long Afternoon, The.
Man Who Married Magdalene, The.
Memories of a Lost War.
Middleaged Man, The.
My Father in the Night Commanding No.
Old Soldier.
On the Ledge.
Outward.
Physical Universe.
Quiet Desperation.
Riverside Drive.
Runner, The.
Silent Generation, The.
Silent Piano, The.
Story About Chicken Soup, A.
Summer Morning.
Summer Storm.
Sway.
To the Western World.
Variations on a Poem by Reznikoff.
Walt Whitman at Bear Mountain.
White Oxen.
Wind, Clouds, and the Delicate Curve of the
  World.
Working Late.

Simpson, Matt (b. 1936)
Millet's *The Gleaners.*

Simpson, Mercer (b. 1926)
Homo Erectus, Cerne Abbas.

Simpson, Natalie (b. 1975)
Sentencing.

Simpson, Ronald Albert (b. 1929)
All Friends Together.

Sims, George R. (1847–1922)
Beauty and the Beast, *sel.*
Garden Song, A.
Told to the Missionary.

Sims, Hylda
Left Rites.
Sims, Steve
It's night, an extra quilt.
Sin Hŭm (1566–1628)
Don't laugh if my roof beams.
I would draw her face with blood.
Person who made a song, The.
Rain came overnight, A.
Sin Saimdang, Lady (1504–52)
Looking Homeward from a Mountain Pass.
Sin Sukchu
Upon Listening to the Flute.
Sinch'ung (fl. 737–57)
Regret.
Sinclair, Iain (b. 1943)
Ebbing of Kraft, The, sels.
Sinclair, Sue (b. 1972)
Lilacs.
Orpheus Meets Eurydice in the Underworld.
Paddling.
Red Pepper.
Refrigerator, The.
Saturday Afternoon.
Sing, Dorothy Wong Loi
Baap-Nemesthe Reggae Song.
Singer, Burns (James Burns Singer) (1928–64)
Corner Boy's Farewell.
Local Ogres Are Against Me Here, The.
Poem About Death, A.
Poem: "Now absence is a habit it is time."
Still and All.
Your Words, My Answers.
Singer, Elizabeth (1674–1737)
Cant. 5.6 & c.
Singer, James Burns See Singer, Burns
Singleton, Giovanni
Defensive Driving.
For my 27th birthday: a poem longer than 10
lines in which pronouns appear.
Thermometer.
Sinka, István (1897–1969)
Bobbin Stops, The.
Dear Stars, Rock Me to Sleep.
Memories of Mudland-Meadow.
My Mother Dances a Ballad.
Only the Sun.
Shepherd's Wife's Farewell to the Old Pasture,
The.
Siôn Cent (fl. 1400–30)
Vanity of the World, The.
Sioux Oral Tradition
Ghost-Dance Songs, sels.
Sipris, Lenous See Surprice, Lenous
Sirin, Vladimir See Nabokov, Vladimir
Vladimirovich
Sirota, Lyubov
Radiophobia.
Your Glance Will Trip on My Shadow.
Sirowitz, Hal
Cookies for Peace.
Equality.
I Finally Managed to Speak to Her.
Lending Out Books.
Slowing Down for Death.
Sirr, Peter (b. 1960)
Beginnings.
Collector's Marginalia, The.
Few Helpful Hints, A.
Guide to Holland, A.
Understanding Canada.
Sissay, Lemn (b. 1967)
I have a voice in my head that talks
backwards.
Sissle, Noble (1889–1975)
Baltimore Buzz.
I'm Craving for That Kind of Love.
I'm Just Wild about Harry, sel.
Sissman, Louis Edward (b. 1928)
Big Rock-Candy Mountain, The.
Deathplace, A.
Dying: An Introduction, sels.
Upon Finding Dying: An Introduction, by L. E.

Sissman, Remaindered at IS.
Sisson, Charles Hubert (1914–2003)
Carmen Saeculare.
Herb-Garden, The.
In Flood.
Letter to John Donne, A.
Person, The.
Red Admiral, The.
Tristia.
Un-Red Deer, The.
Usk, The.
Sitwell, Dame Edith (1887–1964)
Aubade: "Jane, Jane, / Tall as a crane."
Bird's Song, A.
Colonel Fantock.
Façade, sels.
Gardener Janus Catches a Naiad.
Gold Coast Customs, sel.
Hambone and the Heart, The.
Heart and Mind.
Interlude.
King of China's Daughter, The.
Lament of Edward Blastock, The.
Lullaby: "Though the world has slipped and
gone."
Madwoman in the Park, The.
Mother, The.
Panope.
Poet Laments the Coming of Old Age, The.
Said King Pompey.
Serenade: Any Man to Any Woman.
Sleeping Beauty, The, sels.
Solo for Ear-Trumpet.
Song: "Now that Fate is dead and gone."
Song: "Where is all the bright company gone."
Spinning Song.
Still Falls the Rain.
Swans, The.
Three Poems of the Atomic Bomb, sels.
Trams.
Two Songs of Queen Anne Boleyn.
Sitwell, Sir Osbert (1892–1969)
Elegy for Mr. Goodbeare.
Fountains.
How Shall We Rise to Greet the Dawn?, sel.
In the Potting Shed.
In the Winter.
Judas and the Profiteer.
Next War, The.
On the Coast of Coromandel.
Shaking Hands with Murder.
Sitwell, Sacheverell (1897–1988)
Agamemnon's Tomb, sel.
Fountains.
Kingcups.
"Psittachus Eois Imitatrix Ales ab Indis."
Red-Gold Rain, The.
River God, The.
Tulip Tree.
Sivan, Arye (b. 1929)
Concerning the Rehabilitation of the Disabled
from the Wars of Israel.
To Live in the Land of Israel.
To Wither Like Weeds in an Easterly Wind.
Unpleasantness During a Memorial Service.
Sivudu (b. 1931)
Warrior, Bhaskar!
Sizer, Peter
Old Man on a Bike.
Sjoberg, Leif See Rukeyser, Muriel [and Leif
Sjoberg]
Sjolander, John P.
Last Longhorn's Farewell, The.
Skeeter, Sharyn Jeanne (b. 1945)
California, 1852.
Midwest, Midcentury.
Western Trail Cook, 1880.
Skelley, Jack (b. 1956)
To Marie Osmond.
Skellings, Edmund
Frost to Skellings.
Skelton, John (1460?–1529)
Bouge of Court, The, sels.
Calliope.

Colin Clout, sels.
Garland [or Garlande or Garlands] of
Laurel[l], The, sels.
How the Doughty Duke of Albany like a
Coward Knight Ran Away Shamefully, sel.
Lawde and Prayse Made for Our Sovereigne
Lord the Kyng, A, sels.
Magnificence, sels.
Phyllyp Sparowe [or Philip Sparrow or Phillip
Sparow], sels.
Prayer to the Father of [or in] Heaven, A.
Replycacion, A, sel.
Speak [or Speke] Parrot, sels.
Tunning of Elinour Rumming, The, sel.
Tunnyng [or Tunning] of Elynour [or Elinor]
Rummyng [or Rumming], The, sel.
Upon a Dead Man's Head.
Why Come Ye Not to Court, sel.
Skelton, Robin (b. 1925)
Night Piece.
Skinner, Jeffrey
City Out of the Boy, The.
Earth Angel.
Fetch.
For Stuart Porter, Who Asked for a Poem That
Would Not Depress Him Further.
Late Afternoon, Late in the Twentieth Century.
Objects in Mirror are Closer Than They
Appear.
Restoration.
Silk Robe.
Starling Migration, The.
Skinner, Richard
Conjure with me: three letters.
Skipsey, Joseph (1832–1903)
Get Up!
Skirrow, Desmond (1924–76)
Ode on a Grecian Urn Summarized.
Skirving, Adam (1719–1803)
Johnnie Cope.
Sklarew, Myra (1934–1987?)
After Theresienstadt.
Lithuania, sel.
On Muranowska Street.
Teaching the Children.
Three-Course Meal for the New Year, A.
Skloot, Floyd (b. 1947)
Closer to Home.
Everly Brothers, The.
Flight: "Summer night is flying, The."
Frost.
Hook.
Music Appreciation.
Role of a Lifetime, The.
Twilight Time.
Whitman Pinch Hits, 1861.
Year the Space Age Was Born, The.
Skòt, Jaklin See Scott, Jacqueline
Skovron, Alex (b. 1948)
Election Eve, with Cat.
Skoyles, John (b. 1949)
Academic.
Skrine, Nesta Higginson See O'Neill, Moira
Skrzynecki, Peter (b. 1945)
Buddha, Birdbath, Hanging Plant.
Hunting Rabbits.
Skyrm, Paul (b. 1976)
Book 2: White Rose.
Terrors of the In-Between.
Sladen, Douglas Brook Wheelton (1856–1947)
Summer Christmas in Australia, A.
Slamnig, Ivan (1930–2001)
Sailor, A.
Slater, Eleanor (b. 1903)
Search.
Slauerhoff, J. (1898–1936)
Columbus.
Within My Life.
Slavitt, David R. (b. 1935)
Titanic.
Tryma.
Sleigh, Tom

Augusto Jandolo: On Excavating an Etruscan Tomb.
Field, The: "Once I left the room."
In the Park.
Lamentation on Ur.
Shame: "If only I'd known then what I was reaching for."
Spell Spoken by Suppliant to Helios for Protection.
To the Sun.
Work, The, *sels*.

Slessor, Kenneth (1901–71)
All-night Taxi Stand, The.
Beach Burial.
Bushranger, A.
Choker's Lane.
Five Bells.
Fixed Ideas.
Full Orchestra.
Last Trams.
Metempsychosis.
Nuremberg.
Sleep.
South Country.
To Myself.
Up in Mabel's Room.
Wild Grapes.
William Street.

Slicer, Deborah
Sunflowers, Wyoming.

Slonimski, Antoni (1895–1976)
Elegy: "No more, no more Jewish townships in Poland."

Slugs, Slocum (*fl.* 1857)
I Saw Her in Cabbage Time.

Slutsky [*or* Slutskii], Boris Abramovich (1919–86)
Bathhouse, The.
Burnt.
Coppers.
God.
Horses in the Ocean.
Hospital, The.
How Did They Kill My Grandmother?
How They Killed My Grandmother.
Law, which each citizen knows well.
My Friends.
My old men are dying.

Small, Robin *See* Jerry, Bongo

Smallfield, Edward (b. 1946)
Amazing Grace.

Smallpiece, Anna Maria (*fl.* 1805)
Veil's removed, the gaudy, flimsy veil, The.
Written in Ill Health.

Smart, Christopher (1722–71)
English Bull Dog, Dutch Mastiff, and Quail, The, *sels*.
Hop-Garden, The, *sels*.
Hymn to the Supreme Being.
Hymns and Spiritual Songs for the Fasts and Festivals of the Church of England, *sels*.
Hymns for the Amusement of Children, *sels*.
Jubilate Agno, *sels*.
On a Bed of Guernsey Lilies.
Song to David, A, *sels*.
To the Rev. Mr. Powell.

Smedley, Menella Bute (1820–77)
Cavour.
Contrast, A.
Face from the Past, A.
Irish Fairy, The.
Sorrowful Sea-Gull, The.

Smelcer, John E.
Animal Spirits.
Bonanza Creek.
My Indian Grandmother Speaks to Animals.

Smile (b. 1946)
Nothing Happened.

Smith, Aaron (b. 1974)
Silent Room.

Smith, Alexander (1830–67)
Glasgow, *sel*.

Smith, Ali (b. 1962)
Genesis.

Smith, Anna Deavere
Fires in the Mirror, *sels*.

Smith, Anne K.
Giving Thanks.
Praise.

Smith, Arthur James Marshall (1902–80)
Archer, The.
Lonely Land, The.
News of the Phoenix.
Prothalamium.

Smith, Bessie (1895–1937)
Backwater Blues.
Black Mountain Blues.
Empty Bed Blues.
Young Woman's Blues.

Smith, Beverlyjean
Saturday before Easter, The.

Smith, Bruce (b. 1949)
How Garnett Mims and the Enchanters Came into Your Life.
Song of the Ransom of the Dark.

Smith, Caroline Sprague (1827–88)
Metamorphosis.

Smith, Catherine
New Bride, The.

Smith, Charlie (b. 1947)
Beds.
Essential Story, The.
Religious Art.
Santa Monica.
Still Winter (Spring).

Smith, Charlotte (1749–1806)
Beachy Head, *sels*.
Blessed is yon shepherd on the turf reclined.
By the Same.
By the Same. To Solitude.
Captive Escaped in the Wilds of America, The. Addressed to the Hon. Mrs. O'Neill.
Composed During a Walk on the Downs, in November 1787.
Emigrants, The.
Female Exile, The.
Nepenthe.
Ode to Death.
On Being Cautioned against Walking on an Headland Overlooking the Sea, Because It Was Frequented by a Lunatic.
On the Aphorism "L'Amitié est l'Amour sans Ailes."
On the Departure of the Nightingale.
Partial Muse, has from my earliest hours, The.
Pressed by the Moon, Mute Arbitress of Tides.
Sea View, The.
Should the lone Wanderer, fainting on his way.
Sighing I see yon little troop at play.
Sonnet Written at the Close of Spring [*or* Elegiac Sonnet].
Stanzas: "Ah! think'st thou, Laura, then, that wealth."
Supposed To Be Written by Werter.
Thirty-eight: Addressed to Mrs H—y.
To a Friend.
To a Nightingale.
To Dependence.
To Fancy.
To Friendship.
To Hope.
To Melancholy. Written on the Banks of the Arun, October 1785.
To Miss C—on Being Desired To Attempt Writing a Comedy.
To Mr. Hayley, on Receiving Some Elegant Lines from Him.
To Mrs. G.
To Night.
To Sleep.
To Spring.
To the Countess of A—. Written on the Anniversary of Her Marriage.
To the Earl of Egremont.
To the Insect of the Gossamer.
To the Moon.
To the Naiad of the Arun.
To the River Arun ("Be the proud Thames of trade the busy mart!").

To the River Arun ("On thy wild banks, by frequent torrents worn.").
To the Shade of Burns.
To the South Downs.
Walk by the Water, A.
Where the wild woods and pathless forests frown.
Written at Bignor Park in Sussex, in August, 1799.
Written in Farm Wood, South Downs, in May 1784.
Written in October.
Written near a Port on a Dark Evening.
Written on the Sea Shore.—October, 1784.
Written September 1791, During a Remarkable Thunder Storm, in which the Moon Was Perfectly Clear, While the Tempest Gathered in Various Directions Near the Earth.

Smith, Dave Jeddie (b. 1942)
Allegheny Happiness.
American Roadside Elegy, An.
August, on the Rented Farm.
Bats.
Between the Moon and the Sun.
Black Silhouettes of Shrimpers.
Blowfish and Mudtoad.
Cleaning a Fish.
Cumberland Station.
Dream of the Jacklighter, The.
Egret Tree, The.
Elegy in an Abandoned Boatyard.
Fiddlers.
Fieldswirl, October.
Hole, Where Once in Passion We Swam.
Lake Drummond Dream.
Leafless Trees, Chickahominy Swamp.
Louisiana Sea of Faith, The.
Making a Statement.
Moles in Spring.
Morning Light at Wanship, Utah.
New Orleans Engagement.
Night Traffic Near Winchester, Virginia.
On a Field Trip at Fredericksburg.
Out Whistling.
Pine Cones.
Pink Slip at Tool & Dye.
Pulling a Pig's Tail.
Roundhouse Voices, The.
Sea Owl.
Snapshot of a Crab-Picker among Barrels Spilling Over, Apparently at the End of Her Shift.
Spring Poem, The.
Tire Hangs in the Woods, The.
To Isle of Wight.
2000.
With Walt Whitman at Fredericksburg.
Wreck in the Woods.

Smith, David (b. 1945)
Near Frost's Grave.

Smith, Douglas Burnet (b. 1949)
Bare Places.
Killed, The, *sel*.
Multiple Choice.
Skull.
Walk After Rain.

Smith, Edgar (1857–1938)
Heaven Will Protect the Working-Girl.

Smith, Elizabeth J. (b. 1956)
God in the darkness, God beyond our knowing.

Smith, Ellen McGrath
Shaken, *sels*.

Smith, Gary
Penitential Cries of Jupiter Hammond, The.

Smith, George Jay (1886–1937)
When Helen Keller Spoke.

Smith, Goldie Capers
Ballad of a Bombardier from Texas.

Smith, Harry Bache (1860–1936)
My Angeline.

Smith, Horace (1779–1849)
Cui Bono?
Ozymandias.

Smith, Iain Crichton (b. 1928)
At the Scott Exhibition, Edinburgh Festival.
Clearances, The.
Contrasts.
Deer on the High Hills--a Meditation, *sel.*
Exiles, The.
Gaelic Stories.
Ghost, The.
Herring Girls, The.
John Knox.
Listen.
Nose, The.
Old Woman.
Old Woman, The.
Poem of Lewis.
Returning Exile.
Shall Gaelic Die?
Tinily a Star Goes Down.
Two Girls Singing.
You Are at the Bottom of My Mind.
Smith, J. D. (b. 1953)
Goodsonnet.
Seven Ages of Man.
Smith, Jack
Gimme a Little Kiss (Will Ya, Huh?).
Smith, James (1775–1839)
Baby's Debut, The.
Playhouse Musings.
Smith, James *See* Smith, Horace
Smith, James Gregory
Antonio López and Emily.
Smith, Joan Jobe
Honeybee upon the Tundra.
Philodendron Named Joan, A.
What I Learned From the Movies.
Smith, John (b. 1927)
All Light.
Early Morning Was.
How Could They.
Muted, The.
Unicorn, The.
You Wanted to Hear.
Smith, John (1580–1631)
Sea Marke.
Smith, Kay (b. 1911)
Again with Music.
Annunciation.
Old Women and Love.
On Sundays in Summer.
Remembering Miller.
Smith, Ken (b. 1938)
Being the Third Song of Urias.
Encounter at St. Martin's.
Essential Serbo-Coat.
Here.
Malenki Robot.
Message on the Machine.
1984 Tour of Britain, The.
Part of the Crowd that Day.
Writing in Prison.
Smith, Langdon (1858–1908)
Evolution.
Smith, Larry
Calligraphy of Birds.
Following the Road.
In Muddy Waters.
Into Still Air.
Walking a Field into Evening.
Smith, Laurel
Burial Code.
Smith, Laurence
Christmas Tree.
Smith, Michael (1954–83)
Asleep in the City.
Chimes.
City.
From the Chinese.
Stopping to Take Notes.
Visit to the Village, A.
Smith, Michael S.
Springtime at Twilight.
Sunday Morning Services.
Watering the New Lawn.

Smith, Patricia (b. 1955)
Annie Pearl Smith Discovers Moonlight.
Biting Back.
Blonde White Women.
Building Nicole's Mama.
Dylan, Two Days.
Finding His Fist.
Great Pat Smith American Dreampoem, The.
Jemez Pueblo: December 26.
Meanwhile, in Rwanda.
Meeting Up with the Picaro.
Nickel Wine and Deep Kisses.
San Luis, New Mexico.
Some Reservation Valentines.
Sweet Daddy, *sel.*
They Say That Black People.
What It's Like to Be a Black Girl (For Those
of You Who Aren't).
Woman Who Died in Line, The.
Smith, Patti (b. 1946)
Dream of Rimbaud.
Smith, R. T. (b. 1904)
Brieves from the Book of Kells.
Halcion.
Illumination.
Softball at Julia Tutwiler Prison.
Teresa.
This Is How It Comes.
Smith, Rod (b. 1962)
Ted's Head.
Smith, Rudolph
On Poems.
Smith, Ruth
Bluetits.
Smith, Sam
Rumoured thief.
Smith, Samuel Francis (1808–95)
America.
Smith, Stevie (1902–71)
Admire Cranmer!
After-Thought, The.
Airy Christ, The.
Away, Melancholy.
Black March.
Blue from Heaven, The.
Bog-Face.
Celts, The.
Christmas.
Cock-a-Doo.
Commuted Sentence, The.
Conviction (iv).
Correspondence between Mr. Harrison in
Newcastle and Mr. Sholto Peach Harrison in
Hull.
Dear Female Heart.
Death Sentence, The.
Dirge: "From a friend's friend I taste
friendship."
Donkey, The.
Dream of Comparison, A.
Emily Writes Such a Good Letter.
Exeat.
Fairy Story.
Freddy.
God the Eater.
Grange, The.
Great Unaffected Vampires and the Moon.
Harold's Leap.
He Told His Life Story to Mrs. Courtly.
House of Mercy, A.
How Cruel Is the Story of Eve.
Human Affection.
I Remember.
Infelice.
Is It Wise?
Jungle Husband, The.
Lady "Rogue" Singleton.
Lightly Bound.
Like This (1).
Like This (2).
Lord Barrenstock.
Magna Est Veritas.
Major Macroo.
Mrs Simpkins.
Mother, among the Dustbins.

Mother Love.
Mr. Over.
New Age, The.
No Categories!
Not Waving but Drowning.
On the Death of a German Philosopher.
Our Bog is Dood.
Pad, Pad.
Papa Love Baby.
Pretty.
River God, The.
Scorpion.
Songe d'Athalie.
Souvenir de Monsieur Poop.
Sunt Leones.
Tenuous and Precarious.
This Englishwoman.
Thoughts about the Person from Porlock.
To Carry the Child.
To the Tune of The Coventry Carol.
Wanderer, The.
Was He Married?
Was It Not Curious?
White Thought, The.
Word, The.
Smith, Sydney (1771–1845)
Exemplary Nick.
Smith, Sydney Goodsir (1915–75)
Armageddon in Albyn, *sels.*
Gangrel Rymour and the Pairdon of Sanct
Anne, The, *sel.*
Grace of God and the Meth-Drinker, The.
Kenless Strand, The.
Largo.
Philomel.
Salad, A.
Under the Eildon Tree, *sel.*
Ye Mongers Aye Need Masks for Cheatrie.
Smith, Tracy K.
Duende.
History.
Self-Portrait as the Letter Y.
Spring: "Let's not talk."
Smith, Vivian (b. 1933)
At an Exhibition of Historical Paintings,
Hobart.
Early Arrival: Sydney.
Tasmania.
Smith, Walter Chalmers (1824–1908)
Glenaradale.
Immortal, invisible, God only wise.
Smith, William Jay (b. 1918)
American Primitive.
Around My Room.
Brooklyn Bridge.
Columbus Circle Swing.
Epithalamium in Olive Drab.
Lovers, The.
Pavane for the Nursery, A.
Pidgin Pinch.
Plain Talk.
Polar Bear.
Quail in Autumn.
Robert Frost: The Road Taken.
Tempest, The.
There Was an Old Woman Named Piper.
Toaster, The.
Smith, William Loran
Butchertown.
Family Man, The.
Good Man's Fate, A.
Sole of Dover.
Smith-Soto, Mark (b. 1948)
How It Happened.
Smither, Elizabeth (b. 1941)
Cortège of Daughters, A.
Mission Impossible.
On the Euthanasia of a Pet Dog.
Sea Question, The.
To a friend with osteoporosis.
Smoker, Mandy L.
Another Attempt at Rescue.
Letter to David James Duncan, February 16,
2003.

Smollett, Tobias (1721–71)
To Leven Water.

Smrek, Jan (1898–1982)
December: "God gave a sign—and the."

Smukler, Linda (b. 1954)
Days Inn.
Home in Three Days. Don't Wash.
Marry.
Sign.
Trash.

Sneeden, Ralph (fl. 20th cent.)
Coltrane and My Father.

Snodgrass, William DeWitt ("S. S. Gardons") (b. 1926)
After Experience Taught Me.
Albert Speer.
April Inventory.
As a Child, Sleepless.
Campus on the Hill, The.
Coroner's Inquest.
Diplomacy: The Father.
Flat One, A.
Führer Bunker, The, sels.
Heart's Needle, sels.
Leaving the Motel.
Lobsters in the Window.
Locked House, A.
Love Lamp.
Lying Awake.
Matisse: "The Red Studio."
Mementos, 1.
Men's Room in the College Chapel, The.
Mother, The: "She stands in the dead center like a star."
Old Apple Trees.
Poet Ridiculed by Hysterical Academics, The.
Powwow.
Returned to Frisco, 1946.
Snow Songs, sel.
Song: "Sweet beast, I have gone prowling."
Ten Days Leave.
Viewing the Body.

Snorri Hjartarson
House in Rome.

Snow, A. H. (b. 1910)
Gardener.

Snow, Carol (b. 1949)
Déjeuner, Le.
Positions of the Body, 8.
Tour: "Near a shrine in Japan he'd swept the path."

Snow, Wilbert (1884–1977)
Advice to a Clam-Digger.

Snydal, Laurence
Frost.

Snyder, Gary (b. 1930)
Above Pate Valley.
As for Poets.
August on Sourdough, a Visit from Dick Brewer.
Avocado.
Axe Handles.
Bath, The.
Before the Stuff Comes Down.
Beneath My Hand and Eye the Distant Hills, Your Body.
Breasts.
Building.
Burning Island.
Burning the Small Dead.
Cartagena.
Changing Diapers.
Circumambulating Arunachala.
Coffee, Markets, Blossoms.
Dragonfly.
Earth Verse.
Elwha River, The.
Feathered Robe, The.
For a Far-out Friend.
For a Stone Girl at Sanchi.
For Carole.
For John Chappell.
For Lew Welch in a Snowfall.
For the Children.
Four Poems for Robin, sels.

Gaia.
Geese Gone Beyond.
Getting in the Wood.
Grand Entry, The.
Hay for the Horses.
How Do You Shape an Axe Handle?
How Poetry Comes to Me.
I Went Into the Maverick Bar.
Instructions.
It Pleases.
Late October Camping in the Sawtooths.
Lines on a Carp.
Marin-An.
Meeting the Mountains.
Message from Outside.
Mid-August at Sourdough Mountain Lookout.
Milton by Firelight.
Mountains and Rivers without End: The Market, sels.
Myths and Texts, sels.
Nansen.
Night Herons.
Night Song of the Los Angeles Basin.
No Shadow.
No Shoes No Shirt No Service.
Old Woman Nature.
One Should Not Talk to a Skilled Hunter about What Is Forbidden by the Buddha.
Out of the soil and rock.
Piute Creek.
Plum Blossom Poem, The.
Prayer for the Great Family.
Raven's Beak River at the End.
Really the Real.
Removing the Plate of the Pump on the Hydraulic System of the Backhoe.
Right in the Trail.
Riprap.
Saying Farewell at the Monastery After Hearing the Old Master Lecture on "Return to the Source"
Ship in Yokohama, The.
Smokey the Bear Sutra.
Song of the Taste.
Strategic Air Command.
Things to Do Around San Francisco.
Through the Smoke Hole, sels.
Vapor Trails.
Waiting for a Ride.
Walking through Myoshin-Ji.
What Happened Here Before.
What Have I Learned.
What You Should Know to Be a Poet.
Why Log Truck Drivers Rise Earlier Than Students of Zen.
Wild Edge, The.
Without.
Working on the '58 Willys Pickup.

Snyder, Jennifer
Roses, The.
Train.

Snyder, Maryhelen (b. 1932)
Choreograph of the Robed Sheep.
Painting, The.
Synge's Chair.

Snyder, Richard (b. 1905)
Aging Poet, on a Reading Trip to Dayton, Visits the Air Force Museum and Discovers There a Plane He Once Flew, The.
Mongoloid Child Handling Shells on the Beach, A.

Sŏ Chŏngju (1915–2000)
At a Wine House near Taegu.
Autumn, 1949: At the "Flower" Tea Room.
Beside a Chrysanthemum.
Blue Days.
Cuckoo and Skylark.
Elephants of Thailand.
Floor in Goethe's House, The.
Flower-Patterned Snake.
Grandmother's Verandah.
Great Wave, The.
If I Became a Stone.
In the Old Capital.
Kilimanjaro Sunrise.
Leper.

Like a Wind from Lotus Blossoms.
Midday.
New Year's Prayer: 1976.
Owl.
Peony Afternoon.
"Pine flower's blooming," says.
Self-portrait ("Father was a serf.").
Self-Portrait ("Father was a serf, seldom came home at night.").
Sneeze, A.
Such a Land.
Wanderer's Bouquet.
Winter Sky.

Sŏ Kyŏngdŏk (1489–1546)
My mind is foolish.

Soaba, Russell
Looking Thru Those Eyeholes.

Soan
Sailing on Men River, I heard.

Sobaku (1728–92)
Cherry blossoms.

Sobalvarro, Juan (b. 1966)
I've Seen a Dead Man.

Sobin, Anthony
Driving Home to See the Folks.

Sobin, Gustaf (1935–2005)
Anguish & Metaphor.
Eleven Rock Poems.
Fourteen Irises for J. L.
Girandole.
Irises.
On the Nature of the Iconic.
Out of the Identical.
Sixth Ode: The Grottoes.
What the Music Wants.

Socho See Saiokuken Socho

Södergran, Edith (1892–1923)
Arrival in Hades.
Forest Lake.
Hell.
Homecoming.
Instinct.
My Childhood Trees.
Net, The.
On Foot I Had to Walk Through the Solar Systems.
Question.
There is No One.
Vierge Moderne.

Sodo (fl. c.1868)
Late spring / Paling rose.
Question clear, the answer deep, The.
Sudden shower / Cooling lava.

Soen (1859–1919)
Calm, activity—each has its use. At times.
Master Joshu and the dog.
On Visiting Shorin Temple, Where Bodhidharma Once Lived.

Soga, Keiho (1873–1953)
Beyond the forbidding fence.
Within just ten days.

Sogetsuni (d. c.1804)
After the Dance for the Dead.
Divine mystery.

Sogi See Iio Sogi

Sokan (Yamazaki Sokan) (1465–1553)
Cold, yes / But don't test.

Sokan, Yamazaki See Sokan

Sokol, John
Robert Frost's Books, Ripton, Vermont, 1980.

Sol, Adam (b. 1969)
Conductor, The.

Solari, Rose (b. 1960)
Currents.
December 25, 1991.
Truro.

Soldofsky, Alan
Chin Music.

Solie, Karen
Argument For Small Arms, An.
Beethoven: Op. 95.
Cardio Room, Young Women's Christian Association.

Emergency Response.
Larking.
Lilacs.
Meeting Walter Benjamin.
More Fun In The New World.
Parabola.
Science and the Single Girl.
Sturgeon.
Thrasher.
To Have and Have Not.
Sologuren, Javier (b. 1922)
Oh, Astonishing Love.
Solomon, Mark
Comment on My Host, A.
Solomon ibn Gabirol (1021–58)
My Heart Thinks as the Sun Comes Up.
Pen, The.
Solomos, Dionysios (1798–1857)
Destruction of Psara, The.
Solon (c.635–c.559 B.C.)
Love of Boys, The.
Solonche, J. R.
Chopin Preludes, Opus 28.
Worse.
Solórzano, Laura (b. 1961)
Deluge.
Diluvio.
Early Poem.
Herbario.
Herbarium.
Horizon.
Horizonte.
House Poem.
Incessant Poem.
Mute Poem.
País de la calle.
Poema de casa.
Poema del habla.
Poema incesante.
Poema mudo.
Poema temprano.
Speech Poem.
Street Country.
Zacoalco o paisaje.
Zacoalco or Landscape.
Soloukhin, Vladimir Alekseievich (b. 1924)
Apple, The.
For the Tree to Sing.
How to Drink the Sun.
Wind, The.
Solt, Mary Ellen
Lilac.
Somali Oral Tradition
Woman's Love Song.
Someck, Ronny (b. 1951)
Ballad of Alcohol Valley, The.
Blues for Elliot Sharp.
40.
Ice Cream.
Poem for a Daughter Who Is Already Born.
Short History of Vodka, A.
Sign of the Bite, The.
Testifying to Beauty.
Till When Will We Sleep after the Whore.
Transparent.
Somervile [or Somerville], William (1675–1742)
Chase, The, *sel.*
Sommer, Jason
Last in before Dark.
Mengele Shitting.
Somoza, Joseph (b. 1940)
Day Break.
Fire Ants.
Foreign Game, A.
Late Light.
Temperate.
Sondheim, Stephen (b. 1930)
All I Need Is the Girl.
America.
Another Hundred People.
Children Will Listen.
Comedy Tonight.
Everybody Says Don't.
Everything's Coming Up Roses.

Gee, Officer Krupke.
I Never Do Anything Twice (Madam's Song).
I'm Still Here.
In Buddy's Eyes.
Ladies Who Lunch, The.
Losing My Mind.
Remember?
Send in the Clowns.
Some People.
Somewhere.
Together Wherever We Go.
Sone no Yoshitada (fl. late 10th cent.)
Lower leaves of the trees, The.
Song, Cathy (b. 1955)
Beauty and Sadness.
Easter: Wahiawa, 1959.
Father and Daughter.
Ghost.
Girl Powdering Her Neck.
Heaven.
Ikebana.
Immaculate Lives.
Journey.
Leaf.
Leaving.
Lost Sister ("In China.").
Lost Sister ("In China, / even the peasants.").
Mehinaku Girl in Seclusion, A.
Mother of Us All.
Out of Our Hands.
Poet in the House, A.
Sky-Blue Dress, The.
Small Light, A.
Spaces We Leave Empty.
Sunworshippers.
Vegetable Air, The.
Waterwings.
White Porch, The.
Wind in the Trees, The.
Youngest Daughter, The.
Sŏng Hon (1535–98)
By Chance.
Mountain is silent, The.
Song Ikp'il (1534–99)
Boating at Dusk.
To the Moon.
Sŏng Kan (1427–56)
Fisherman, A.
Sŏng [or Sung] Sammun (1418–56)
At the Execution Ground.
Upon Listening to the Flute.
Were you to ask me what I'd wish to be.
White Banners.
Song Sun (1493–1583)
Do not grieve, little birds.
I discuss with my heart.
I have spent ten years.
Ten Years It Took.
Sŏngjong, King of Chosŏn (1456–94)
Stay: / will you go? Must you go?
Soniat, Katherine
Dog Days.
Harp/Desire.
Last Warm Day, A.
Shared Life, A.
Sonnevi, Göran (b. 1939)
Child is Not a Knife, A.
Demon Colors, Dark.
Sono-Jo, Lady (1649–1723)
How cool / forehead touched.
Shameful / These clothes.
Sontag, Kate
Plum Crazy.
Sontrop Theo (b. 1931)
Acorn Speaks, The.
Park, A.
Sophocles (c.495–c.406 B.C.)
Antigone [Fagles Translation].
Antigone, *sels.*
Lovers of Achilles, The, *sel.*
Oedipus at Colonus, *sels.*
Oedipus the King.
Women of Trachis, *sel.*

Sora (Kaai Sora) (1649–1710)
In the deutzia.
Matsushima.
Shaving my head.
Skylark / Soaring—her young.
Sora, Kaai *See* Sora
Sorby, Angela
Glossolalia.
Gossip.
Land of Lincoln.
Man without a Middle, The.
Synchronized Swimming.
Sorescu, Martin (1936–97)
Arrow, The.
Balls and Hoops.
Don Juan (After He'd Consumed Tons of Lipstick).
Fountains in the Sea.
Fresco.
Map.
Perseverance.
Pond.
Precautions.
Start.
Tear, The.
With a Green Scarf.
Sorley, Charles Hamilton (1895–1915)
All the hills and vales along.
Hundred Thousand Million Mites, A.
Rooks.
Song of the Ungirt Runners, The.
Sonnet, A: "When you see millions of the mouthless dead."
To Germany.
Two Sonnets.
Sornberger, Judith
Wallpapering to Patsy Cline.
When She Can't Sleep.
When She Laughs.
Sorrell, Martin
Time and again we're cut down to size.
Sorrentino, Gilbert (b. 1929)
Good Night!
Handbook of Versification.
Land of Cotton.
Magic Composer.
Oranges Returned, The.
Razzmatazz.
Sosa, Roberto
Most Ancient Names of Fire, The.
Sŏsan, Great Master [Hyujŏng] (1520–1604)
In Praise of the Portrait of My Former Master.
Sosnora, Viktor Aleksandrovich (b. 1936)
Crow.
Do you envy, my comrades-in-arms.
Footsteps of an Owl and His Lament, The.
Letter, A.
Owl and the Mouse, The.
Supreme Hour, The.
There it all was: the gaslamp, drugstore.
Where are our horses.
Soto, Gary (b. 1952)
After Tonight.
Antigua.
Behind Grandma's House.
Black Hair.
Blanco.
Braly Street.
Brown Girl, Blonde Okie.
Chiapas.
Chitchat with the Junior League Women.
Dizzy Girls in the Sixties.
Drought, The.
Effects of Abstract Art, The.
Elements of San Joaquin, The, *sels.*
Envying the Children of San Francisco.
Failing in the Presence of Ants.
Family in Spring, The.
Field Poem.
Graciela.
Harvest.
Heaven.
History.
Hoeing.
How Things Work.

Jungle Café, The.
Making Money: Drought Year in Minkler, California.
Map, The.
Mexicans Begin Jogging.
Morning They Shot Tony Lopez, Barber and Pusher Who Went Too Far, 1958, The.
Not Knowing.
Ode to the Yard Sale.
Oranges.
Practicing Eulogies.
Red Palm, A.
Saturday at the Canal.
Small Town with One Road.
Soup, The.
Street.
Sun.
Tale of Sunlight, The.
Teaching Numbers.
Telephoning God.
Trees that Change Our Lives.
TV in Black and White.
Who Will Know Us?

Soto, Maria Viviana (1823–1916)
Hey, fog, go home.
I dream of you.
See! I am dancing!

Sotoba, Layman (1036–1101)
Mountain—Buddha's body, The.

Soudijn, Karel (b. 1944)
Cleaning.
Régime.

Soupault, Philippe (b. 1897)
Chanson pour des fantômes et pour celles qui ont disparu.
Cinéma-palace.
Comrade.
Condemned.
Epitaph: André Breton.
Epitaph: Tristran Tzara.
Georgia.
Georgia.
Horizon.
Horizon.
Life-Saving Medal.
Movie-house.
One o'Clock.
One Two or Three.
Poems from Saint Pelagia Prison.
Route.
Song for Ghosts and for Those Now Gone.
Sunday.
To Drink.
Twilight.
You Who Sleep.

Sour, Robert
Body and Soul.

Sousa, Noémia da (b. 1927)
Call.
Let My People Go.
Our Voice.
Poem of a Distant Childhood.

Souster, Raymond (b. 1921)
Lagoons, Hanlan's Point.
Memory of Bathurst Street.
Queen Anne's Lace.
Very Short Poem.
Words Before a Statue of Champlain.
Young Girls.

Soutar, William (1898–1943)
Gowk, The.
Permanence of the Young Men, The.
Philosophic Taed, The.
Room, The.
Summer Is By.
Three Puddocks, The.
To Karl Marx.
Tryst [or Trysting Place], The.
Who Are These Children?
Winter Beauty.

Southerland, Ellease
Blue Clay.
Night in Nigeria.
Pale Ant.
Recitation.

Two Fishing Villages.

Southern Bushmen Oral Tradition
Day We Die, The.

Southerne, Thomas (1660–1746)
Song: "Pursuing beauty, men descry."

Southey, Caroline Anne Bowles (1786–1854)
Conte à Mon Chien, sels.
Mariner's Hymn.
On Trust.
Rude Ranger Rebuked.

Southey, Robert (1774–1843)
Battle of Blenheim, The.
Canine Immortality.
Cataract of Lodore, The.
Curse of Kehama, The, sels.
Devil, The.
Devil's Thoughts, The.
Did then the bold slave rear at last the sword.
Hold your mad hands! for ever on your plain.
Inchcape Rock, The.
Joan of Arc, sel.
Oh he is worn with toil! the big drops run.
Old Man's Comforts and How He Gained Them, The.
Poems Concerning the Slave Trade, sels.
Remembrance.
Roderick, The Last of the Goths, sels.
Ship, The.
Soldier's Wife, The.
Thalaba the Destroyer, sel.
'Tis night; the mercenary tyrants sleep.
To a Brook Near the Village of Corston.
To a Goose [or Gosse].
Vision of Judgement, A, sels.
Why dost thou beat thy breast and rend thine hair.
Widow, The.
Wrinkled, crabbèd man they picture thee, A.

Southgate, Christopher
Man.

Southwell, Anne Harris, Lady (1571–1636)
All married men desire to have good wives.
Elegie Written by the Lady A. S. to the Countesse of London Derrye Supposyenge Hir to be Dead by Hir Long Silence, An.
Epitaph, uppon Cassandra Mac Willms Wife to Sr Thomas Ridgway Earle of London Derry by ye Lady A. S., An.
To the Kinges Most Excellent Majestye.

Southwell, Robert (1561?–95)
Burning Babe, The.
Child[e] My Choice [or Choyse], A.
Christ[e]'s Childhood[e].
Content and Ri[t]ch[e].
David's Peccavi.
I Dye Alive.
Look[e] Home.
Loss[e] in Delay[e].
Man's Civil[l] War[re].
Marie [or Mary] Magdalens Complaint at Christs Death.
Nativity of Christ[e], The.
New Heaven, New War[re].
New Prince, New Pomp[e].
Of the Blessed Sacrament of the Altar ("Angels' eyes, whom veils cannot deceive, The.").
Of the Blessed Sacrament of the Altar [or Aulter] ("In paschall feast, the end of a[u]ncient rite.").
Times [or Tymes] Go[e] By Turn[e]s.
Upon the Image of Death, sel.
Vale of Tear[e]s, A.

Southwick, Marcia
Earthly Light.
Magic Broom, The.
Star Is Born in the Eagle Nebula, A.
Waves, The.

Souza, Eunice De (b. 1940)
Conversation Piece.
De Souza Prabhu.
For Rita's Daughter, Just Born.
Landscape.
Sweet Sixteen.
Women in Dutch Painting.

Sowle, Jane (fl. 1680)
Short Testimony for Anne Whitehead, A.

Soyinka, Wole (b. 1934)
Abiku.
After the Deluge.
Apologia (Nkomati).
Around Us, Dawning.
Civilian and Soldier.
Dragonfly at My Windowpane.
Fado Singer.
Funeral in Soweto, sel.
Funeral Sermon, Soweto.
Harvest of Hate.
He escape the lynch days. He survives.
Huge with Time, a wombfruit lanced.
Hunchback of Dugbe, The.
I Think It Rains.
Idanre and Other Poems (1967), sels.
Ikeja, Friday, Four O'Clock.
Massacre, October '66.
"No!" He Said.
Post Mortem.
Rust and silence fill the thatch.
Telephone Conversation.
To My First White Hairs.

Soyo Taeneung (1562–1649)
Deathbed Song.
Man of No Attachments.
To the Old Reverend Monk, Hwasung.

Sozan-Kyonin (fl. 9th cent.?)
Rootless tree, A.

Spacks, Barry (b. 1931)
Assimilation, The.
Film Version, The.
Malediction.
Poetry Bug, The.

Spady, Susan
Push-Pull of This Love, The.
Tending Flowers.

Spafford, Horatio G. (1828–88)
It Is Well with My Soul.

Spahr, Juliana
December 1, 2002.
December 4, 2002.
January 28, 2003.
Localism or t/here.
We, sel.
Write Like One Walks.

Spalding, A. W.
High Adventure.

Spalding, Esta
August.

Spanel, Ann
Pez Dorado.

Spark, Muriel (b. 1918)
Elementary.
Evelyn Cavallo.
Kensington Gardens.
We Were Not Expecting the Prince To-day.
Yellow Book, The.

Sparrow, John (1906–92)
Apology and Explanation.
Epitaph: "This stone, with not unpardonable pride."
To an Angel in the House.

Spatola, Adriano (b. 1941)
Poem Stalin, The.
Risk of Abstraction, The.

Spaulding-Convy, Annette
Why Women Become Water.

Spaziani, Maria Luisa (b. 1924)
Aegean, The.
Comet, The.
Convent in '45, The.
Crossroads, The.
Destiny.
Duomo, The.
Figurehead, The.
Grain of Sand, The.
If it were a sea, this immense wind.
It is Said by Some Sailors, the Old.
Memory's Usefulness.
Merciful Shore, The.
Present, The.

Prison, The.
Pure Dust.
Role Reversal.
Rome has a thousand fountains, and in May
they sing.
Spark of Green.
Star of Free Will, The, *sels.*
Tender heart, hairy muscle.
To the Readers.
To the Victims of Mauthausen.
Ultrasound.
Via Margutta.
White on White.
Your life is a baby not yet born.

Speak, Margaret
Ingredients of Glass.

Speakes, Richard
Heartbreak Hotel Piano-Bar.
Mama Loves Janis Joplin.
Patsy Cline.

Spear, Roberta (b. 1948)
Good Men.
Meditation: "I could sit in this hot bath for
hours."
Nest for Everyone, A.
River Song.

Spears, Rebecca
Marina's Daughters, 1964.

Speckled Red (Rufus Perryman)
Dirty Dozens, The.

Spee, Friedrich (1591–1635)
Spouse of Jesus Laments Her Heart's Flame,
The.

Speed, Samuel
Peace.

Speers, Edith (b. 1949)
Australorp.

Speght, Rachel (b. 1597)
Dream[e], The [*or* A], *sels.*

Spellman, Alfred B. (b. 1935)
Beautiful Day, The. V.
Blues: My Baby's Gone.
Did John's Music Kill Him?
John Coltrane: An Impartial Review.
Truth You Carry Is Very Dark, The.
Twist, The.

Spence, Lewis (1874–1955)
Capernaum.
Portrait of Mary Stuart, Holyrood.
Prows O' Reekie, The.

Spence, Michael
Fig Curtain of Atherton, The.

Spencer, Anne (1882–1975)
At the Carnival.
Before the Feast of Shushan.
Lady, Lady.
Letter to My Sister.
Lines to a Nasturtium.
White Things.

Spencer, Bernard (1909–63)
Blue Arm.
Boat Poem.
Castanets.
Delos.
Egyptian Dancer at Shubra.
Invaders, The.
Night-Time: Starting to Write.
Olive Trees.
Passed On.
Thousand Killed, A.
Yachts on the Nile.

Spencer, Cherie Forman
Desert Symphony, *sels.*

Spencer, William Robert (1770–1834)
Beth Gelert.

Spender, Stephen (1909–95)
Abrupt and Charming Mover.
Air Raid Across the Bay at Plymouth.
Elementary School Classroom in a Slum, An.
Epilogue: "Time is a thing."
Epilogue to a Human Drama.
Express, The.
Farewell in a Dream.
Funeral, The.

History and Reality.
"I" Can Never Be a Great Man, An.
I Think Continually of Those Who Were Truly
Great.
Judas Iscariot.
Landscape near an Aerodrome, The.
Marginal Field, The.
Mask.
Memento.
My Parents.
Not Palaces.
One More New Botched Beginning.
Polar Exploration.
Prisoners, The.
Pylons, The.
Rejoice in the Abyss.
Seascape.
Shapes of Death, The.
Sonnet: "You were born; must die; were loved;
must love."
Statistics.
Thoughts During an Air Raid.
To T.A.R.H.
Two Armies.
Ultima Ratio Regum.
What I Expected.
Whim of Time, A.
Winter and Summer.
Winter Landscape.

Spenser, Edmund (1552?–99)
Amoretti, *sels.*
Commendatory Sonnets, *sels.*
Daphnaïda, *sels.*
Epithalamion: "Ye learned sisters which have
oftentimes."
Faerie Queene, The, *sels.*
Hymn of Heavenly Love, An.
Hymn[e] of Heavenly Beauty [*or* Beautie], An,
sel.
Iambicum Trimetrum.
Merry Cuckoo, The.
Mother Hubbard's Tale, *sels.*
Penelope for her *Ulisses* sake.
Prothalamion, *sel.*
Ruines of Rome: by Bellay, *sel.*
Ruines of Time, The.
Shepherd's Calender, The, *sels.*
Sonnet 12: "I saw an ugly beast come from the
sea."
Sonnet 13: "I saw a woman sitting on a beast."
Sonnet 14: "Then might I see upon a white
horse set."
Sonnet 15: "I saw new Earth, new Heaven,
said Saint John."
Sonnet 73: 'Being my self captived here'
To the Right Worshipfull, My Singular Good
Friend, Master Gabriel Harvey, Doctor of
the Lawes.

Spera, Gabriel
Balkan.

"Speranza" *See* Wilde, Lady Jane Francesca

Speyer, Leonora (1872–1956)
To a Song of Sappho Discovered in Egypt.
Witch!

Spicer, Jack (1925–65)
Army Beach with Trumpets.
Book of Galahad, The.
Book of Music, A.
Cantata.
Cardplayers, The.
Conspiracy: "Violin which is following me,
A."
Duet for a Chair and a Table.
Ghost Song.
Good Friday: For Lack of an Orchestra.
Imaginary Elegies, *sels.*
Improvisations on a Sentence by Poe.
Jungle Warfare.
Lament for the Makers: "No call upon anyone
but the timber drifting in the waves."
Language, *sels.*
Love Poems, *sels.*
Morphemics.
Mummer.
Orfeo.

Phonemics.
Poem Without a Single Bird in It, A.
Red Wheelbarrow, The.
Song of a Prisoner.
Sporting Life.
Textbook of Poetry, 21, A.
Transformations.
Valentine, A.

Spinner, Bettye T.
Harvest Home.

Spireng, Matthew J.
Snowy Owl.

Spires, Elizabeth (b. 1952)
Apology.
Beds, The.
Bodies, The.
Celestial, The.
Cemetery Reef.
Comb and the Mirror, The.
Fabergé's Egg.
First Day, The.
Glass-Bottom Boat.
In Heaven It Is Always Autumn.
Interrogations of the Sparrow.
Mansion Beach.
Robed Heart, The.
Rock, The.
Sunday Afternoon at Fulham Palace.
Woman on the Dump, The.
Worldling.

Spivack, Kathleen (b. 1938)
Dido: Swarming.
Love U.S.A.
Scroll, The.
Sunday.
Yearning throughout Life, The.

Spofford, Harriet Prescott (1835–1921)
Magdalen.
Tryst, The.

Sprackland, Jean (b. 1962)
Ringlet, The.
Translating Birdsong.

Spragins, Anna Word
Farewell to Texas.

Sprague, Achsa W. (c.1828–62)
Poet, The, *sels.*

Spratt, Thomas (1635–1713)
On His Mistress Drown'd [*or* Drowned].

Springer, Eintou Pearl
Freedom Child—Tilla's Lullaby.

**Squire, Sir John Collings ("Solomon Eagle")
(1884–1958)**
Ballade of the Poetic Life.
When I Leapt over Tower Bridge.

Sri Sri (1910–83)
Announcement, An.
Bitter Poem, A.
Call of Poetry.
Myth of Myself.
Really?
Some People Laugh, Some People Cry, *sel.*
Vedantist, The.
Wheels of Jagannatha, The.

Srinivas, Tripuraneni (1963–96)
Chasing Memory.

Sriramulu, Dasu (1846–1908)
Other Tongue, The.

Sruoginis, Laima
Irish Woman Washing.

Ssu-k'ung Shu (740–90?)
In Illness, Dismissing My Singing Girl.
Oxhead Temple.

Ssu-ma Hsiang-ju (c.179–118 B.C.)
Beautiful Person, The.
Cock-Phoenix, Hen-Phoenix.
Mighty One, The.
Sir Fantasy.

StacyLynn
Crushin.
Dirt.
Examination.
Lookin Good.

Stadler, Ernst
On Crossing the Rhine Bridge at Cologne by Night.
Saying, The.
Staff, Leopold (1878–1957)
Duckweed.
Foundations.
Foundations.
Kingdom.
Portrait.
Speech.
Stafford, Kim R.
Inside the Fence: Tule Lake Internment Camp.
Stafford, William (1914–93)
Adults Only.
After Arguing against the Contention That Art Must Come from Discontent.
Archival Print, An.
Ask Me.
At Cove on the Crooked River.
At Fourth and Main in Liberal, Kansas, 1932.
At the Bomb Testing Site.
At the Grave of My Brother: Bomber Pilot.
At the Playground.
At the Robert Frost Memorial.
At the Un-National Monument along the Canadian Border.
August.
British Columbia.
Ceremony.
Chair in the Meadow, The.
Christianite.
Dog Asleep.
Earth Dweller.
Entering a Wilderness Area.
Explaining the Big One.
Fifteen.
For a Lost Child.
For the Barn at Bread Loaf.
For the Grave of Daniel Boone.
For You, Walt Whitman.
Gaea.
Gift, The.
Glimpses.
Growing Up.
Gulls at Cannon Beach.
Holding the Sky.
How the Real Bible Is Written.
How to Regain Your Soul.
Humanities Lecture.
Indian Cave Jerry Ramsey Found, The.
Juncos.
Kolob Canyon.
Light by the Barn, The.
Maybe Alone on My Bike.
Meditation: "Animals full of light."
Men.
Message from the Wanderer, A.
Monuments for a Friendly Girl at a Tenth Grade Party.
Near.
Once in the 40s.
Our Kind.
Owls at the Shakespeare Festival.
Priorities at Friday Ranch.
Report to Crazy Horse.
Rescued Year, The.
Right Time, The.
Ritual to Read to Each Other, A.
Run before Dawn.
Scars.
Shepherd.
Silver Star.
Sky.
Some Remarks When Richard Hugo Came.
Spirit of Place: Great Blue Heron.
Starting with Little Things.
Story That Could Be True, A.
Textures.
Tourist Country.
Traveling Through the Dark.
Vacation.
Visions.
Vocation.
Way It Is, The.
Widow.

Wind from a Wing, A.
With Kit, Age 7, at the Beach.
You Reading This, Be Ready.
Stahl, Christopher
Greyhound.
Polestar.
Stainer, Pauline (b. 1941)
Bleaklow.
Creatures Preach to St Francis, The.
Honeycomb, The.
I am black-browed.
Quanta.
Ringing Chamber, The.
Sarcophagus.
Seals, The.
Sighting the Slave Ship.
This Atomising of Things.
Wound-dresser's Dream, The.
Xochiquetzal.
Stallings, A. E.
Dead Language Lesson.
How the Demons Were Assimilated and Became Productive Citizens.
Postcard from Greece, A.
Stallworthy, Jon (b. 1935)
Almond Tree, The.
Letter from Berlin, A.
Letter to a Friend.
Mother Tongue.
Poem about Poems about Vietnam, A.
Pour Commencer.
Source, The.
Stam, Betty Scott
Ring Sonnet.
Stand Still, and See.
Two Names.
Stanard, Christopher (b. 1967)
Baseball.
Rap Is.
Washington Square Park and a Game of Chess.
Wrong Color.
Standing, Sue
Hopper's Women.
Mouvance.
Stanford, Ann (1916–87)
Beating, The.
Childhood.
Committee, The.
Done With.
Double Mirror.
I Thought Back and.
365 Poems.
Stanford, Frank (1948–78)
I still got hope Tang says.
Stanley, George (b. 1934)
Mountains and Air, *sels*.
Stanley, Thomas (1625–78)
Beauty.
Celia Singing.
Dr. Jack.
Glowworm, The.
Imperialism—The Dancing Do Not Die.
Love Deposed.
Ode XV.
On a Violet in Her Breast.
On S. John the Baptist.
Paraphrase Upon Part of the CXXXIX Psalm, A.
Pythagoric Letter, The.
Relapse, The.
Snow-Ball, The.
Time Recover'd.
Stanley-Wrench, Margaret (1917–74)
Hinterland.
Storm, The.
Stansbury, Joseph (1740–1809)
When Good Queen Elizabeth Governed the Realm.
Stanton, Johnny (b. 1943)
Finger Paintings.
Stanton, Maura (b. 1946)
Ballad of the Magic Glasses.
Comfort.
Conjurer, The.

Drugstore Trolls.
Few Picnics in Illinois, A.
In Ignorant Cadence.
Judith Recalls Holofernes.
Little Ode for X.
Ode to Mozart.
Pole Vaulting.
Posthuman.
Revolt.
Shoplifters.
Short Story.
Sorrow and Rapture.
Space.
Veiled Lady, The.
Visibility.
Voice for the Sirens, A.
Stanton, Will D. (b. 1918)
Dandelions.
Staple, Will
Shen Tao.
Stapleton, Francellina (*fl.* 1655)
Upon a Joynted Ring.
Starbuck, George (b. 1931)
Boston.
Communication to the City Fathers of Boston.
High Renaissance.
Of Late.
On the Antiquity of Warfare.
Prognosis.
Reading the Facts about Frost in *The Norton Anthology*.
Said.
Said ("Agatha Christie to.").
Said ("Dame Edith Evans to.").
Said ("J. Alfred Prufrock to.").
Technologies.
Working Habits.
Starck, Clemens
Job No. 75-14.
Starhawk
Demeter's Song.
Starkey, David
Annunciation, The: "Surely God thought this would be a moment."
Poet Is Like a Church, The.
Scrabble.
Suburban Crimes 3.
Starodubtseva, Natalya (b. 1979)
And it is cold here and a bit strange.
Roundabouts stolidly turn.
Statius, Publius Papinius (c.61–96 A.D.)
Sylvae [*or* Silvae], *sels*.
Thebais [*or* Thebaid], *sels*.
Staveley, Brian
Speak Again.
Stead, Christian Karlson (b. 1932)
Between.
Stead, W. T. (1849–1912)
War against War in South Africa, *sel*.
Stead, William Force (b. 1884)
I Closed My Eyes To-Day and Saw.
Uriel, *sels*.
Steede, Vejay
Reggae.
Steele, Nancy
Diminutive.
Steele, Peter (b. 1939)
Cana.
Marking Time.
Steele, Sir Richard (1672–1729)
Conscious Lovers, The, *sels*.
Steele, Timothy (b. 1948)
At Will Robers Beach.
Au Aubade.
Aubade, An: "As she is showering, I wake to see."
Chanson Philosophique.
Epitaph: "Here lies Sir Tact, a diplomatic fellow."
Eros.
Fae.
In the King's Rooms.
Joseph.
Library, The.

Sapphics Against Anger.
Three Notes Toward Definitions, *sels.*
Timothy.
Waiting for the Storm.
Wartburg, 1521–22, The.

Steensen, Sasha
Spatial Spectacles, *sel.*
This Land.

Steere, Richard (1643–1721)
Monumental Memorial of Marine Mercy, A.

Steeves, Andrew (b. 1970)
Haunting.
Winter Marsh.

Stéfan, Jude (b. 1930)
Butcher's Meat by Loti.
Emma Zola à Wimbledon supposons.
Emma Zola at Wimbledon Let's Say.
Harengs et bouleaux.
Herrings and Birch Trees.
Viande de boucherie par Loti.

Stefanile, Felix (b. 1920)
Answering Robert Frost.
How I Changed My Name, Felice.

Stefans, Brian Kim (b. 1969)
They're Putting a New Door In.

Steffler, John (b. 1947)
Cedar Cove.
Grey Islands, The, *sel.*
Hollis Street Square, Halifax.
That Night We Were Ravenous.

Steiger, Anatoly (1908–43)
Ancient Custom, An.
Dull rattle of shutters being lowered, The.
Friendship.
How do we break the habit of big words.
Nobody waits at the foot of the stairs any
   more.
Not an epilogue, but everything coming to an
   end.
They will not ask us: have you sinned?
Until the sun sinks into a green.
We believe books and music.

Stein, Charles (b. 1944)
My hat vanished.
Parmenides Machine, A.
Provisional Measures.
Virgo Poem, The: Ouspensky Addresses a
   Congress of Virgoes.

Stein, Gertrude (1874–1946)
Book Concluding with As A Wife Has a Cow
   a Love Story, A, *sels.*
Bundles for Them.
Cézanne.
Four Saints in Three Acts, *sel.*
George Hugnet.
Guillaume Apollinaire.
Identity A Poem.
If I Told Him: A Completed Portrait of
   Picasso.
In This Way.
Kneeling.
Leave, A.
Let Us Describe.
Lifting Belly, *sels.*
Mother of Us All, The, *sels.*
On Her Way.
Picasso.
Preciosilla.
Rooms, *sel.*
Sacred Emily.
Scenes from the Door.
Stanzas in Meditation, *sels.*
Suppose an Eyes.
Susie Asado.
Teachers taught her, The.
Tender Buttons, *sels.*
Valentine to Sherwood Anderson, A.
Very Valentine, A.
What Do I See.
White Hunter, A.
Why Do You Feel Differently.
Yet Dish, *sel.*

Stein, Kevin
Because You're American.

Benefit Picnic, Cigar Makers' Strike, August
   1884.
First Performance of the Rock 'n Roll Band
   Puce Exit.
In the Kingdom of Perpetual Repair.
It Didn't Begin with Horned Owls Hooting at
   Noon.
Night Shift, after Drinking Dinner, Container
   Corporation of America, 1972.
Past Midnight, My Daughter Awakened by
   Miles Davis' *Kind of Blue.*
Terms.
Upon Finding a Black Woman's Door Sprayed
   with Swastikas, I Tell Her This Story of
   Hands.
World Without End.

Steinberg, David
Image Was of Me Flowing Through You, The.
Purple is the Color of Longing.
Slowly, slowly.
With you I begin.

Steinberg, Jakov [*or* Jacob] (1887–1947)
All of a Summer.
It has been long since first my fears grew light.
Rain at Night.
Till Evening.
Turn towards the end, be a leaf dying.

Steinbergh, Judith W. (b. 1943)
Burial.
Give Peace a Chance.
Religion.

Steingesser, Martin
Spring Forward.

Steinmar (*fl.* late 13th cent.)
Farmhand lay all hidden, A.
Since She Gives So Little Pay.

Stenhouse, Shelley
Circling.

Stepanchev, Stephen (b. 1915)
Inspiration.
Seven Horizons.

Stepanova, Mariya (b. 1972)
Airman.

Stephen, James Kenneth (1859–92)
England and America, *sels.*
Malines.
Sonnet, A: "Two voices are there: one is of the
   deep."
To R. K.

Stephens, Brunton (1835–1902)
Gentle Anarchist, The.

Stephens, James (1880–1950)
Blue Blood.
Cage, The.
Crest Jewel, The.
Deirdre.
Evening.
Glass of Beer, A.
Good and Bad.
Hate.
In the Night.
In the Poppy Field.
In Waste Places.
Lake, The.
Little Things.
Main-Deep, The.
Odell.
Outcast, The.
Red-haired Man's Wife, The.
Rivals, The.
Shell, The.
To the Four Courts, Please.
Twins, The.
Watcher, The.
What Thomas an Buile Said in a Pub.
Whisperer, The.
Wind, The.

Stephens, Meic (b. 1938)
Elegy for Llywelyn Humphries.
Hooters.
Ponies, Twynyrodyn.

Stephens, Philip (b. 1966)
God Shed His Grace.
Hangman.
Signalmen, The.

Stept, Sam H. (*fl.* 1928)
That's My Weakness Now.

Steptoe, Lamont B. (b. 1949)
Coming Ashore.
Contraband.
Election Time.
For Etheridge Knight.
Hambone Gospel, A.
In Black Churches.
Mississippi Blues.
Notes for a Poem from the Middle Passage of
   Years.
O' Yes.
Spookism.
Such a Boat of Land.
Sweet Brown Rice and Red Bones.
There Is a House.
Three Legged Chairs.
To the Father of Me.
Window Shopping.
Wired In.

Sterling, Andrew B. (1874–1955)
Meet Me in St. Louis, Louis.

Sterling, George (1869–1926)
Aldebaran at Dusk.
Ballad of the Grapes.
Black Vulture, The.
Last Days, The: "Russet leaves of the
   sycamore, The."

Stern, Anatol (1899–1968)
Europa.

Stern, Gerald (b. c.1925)
Adler.
All I Did For Him.
Another Insane Devotion.
Behaving Like a Jew.
Bela.
Birthday.
Bitter Thoughts.
Blue Skies, White Breasts, Green Trees.
Bull-roarer, The.
Cow Worship.
Dancing, The.
December 1, 1994.
Diary.
Dog That I Am.
Dog, The.
Ducks Are for Our Happiness.
Faces I Love, The.
For Song.
Fritz.
Hats.
Hinglish.
Hot Dog, *sels.*
Hydrangea.
I Hate My Moaning.
I Remember Galileo.
Inkspot, The.
June Fourth.
Large Pots.
Lilacs for Ginsberg.
Lucky Life, *sel.*
Mentioning of Souls.
Mimi.
Modern Love.
Night.
96 Vandam.
On the Far Edge of Kilmer.
On the Island.
Peaches.
Pile of Feathers.
Red Bird.
Romania, Romania.
Roses: "There was a rose called Guy de
   Maupassant."
Royal Manor Road.
Samaritans.
Self-Portrait.
She Was a Dove.
Shirt Poem, The.
Soap.
Sounds, The.
Spider: "How you like these threads, said
   white spider."
Stepping Out of Poetry.

Suzanne.
Tashlikh.
Waving Good-Bye.
Sternlieb, Barry (b. 1947)
Right of Way.
Stesichoros (fl. 6th cent. B.C.)
Across from glorious Erytheia.
Don't pile cruel cares upon those griefs.
Helen suddenly saw a divine omen.
Since Tyndareos.
They flung many quinces toward the chariot.
This story is not true.
Stétié, Salah (b. 1929)
Garden of the One, The.
Jardin de l'un, Le.
Steve Gibson *See* Wilkins, Machine
Steven, Kenneth (b. 1968)
Calvinist, The.
Edge.
Lamb.
Long Silence, The.
Stevens, C. J. (b. 1927)
New Blue Bike, A.
Stevens, Cat
Wild World.
Stevens, Meic (b. 1942)
Sylvia.
Stevens, Wallace (1879–1955)
American Sublime, The.
Anecdote of the Jar.
Anecdote of the Prince of Peacocks ("In the
   moonlight / I met Berserk.").
Anglais Mort à Florence.
Annual Gaiety.
Another Weeping Woman.
Asides on the Oboe.
Auroras of Autumn, The, *sels.*
Autumn Refrain.
Bantams in Pine-Woods.
Bird with the Coppery, Keen Claws, The.
Bouquet of Belle Scavoir.
Brave Man, The.
Clear Day and No Memories, A.
Comedian as the Letter C, The.
Connoisseur of Chaos.
Contrary Theses (I).
Course of a Particular, The.
Curtains in the House of the Metaphysician,
   The.
Dance of the Macabre Mice.
Death of a Soldier, The.
Debris of Life and Mind.
Discovery of Thought, A.
Disillusionment of Ten O'Clock.
Domination of Black.
Dry Loaf.
Earthy Anecdote.
Emperor of Ice-Cream, The.
Fabliau of Florida.
Farewell to Florida.
Final Soliloquy of the Interior Paramour.
Flyer's Fall.
Gallant Chateau.
Girl in a Nightgown.
Glass of Water, The.
God is Good. It Is a Beautiful Night.
Gray Stones and Gray Pigeons.
Gubbinal.
High-Toned Old Christian Woman, A.
Homunculus et La Belle Etoile.
House Was Quiet and the World Was Calm,
   The.
Idea of Order at Key West, The.
In the Carolinas.
Indigo Glass in the Grass, The.
Infanta Marina.
Irish Cliffs of Moher, The.
John Smith and His Son, John Smith.
Landscape with Boat.
Large Red Man Reading.
Le Monocle de Mon Oncle.
Less and Less Human, O Savage Spirit.
Lettres d'un Soldat, *sel.*
Life Is Motion.
Lunar Paraphrase.

Man on the Dump, The.
Man Whose Pharynx Was Bad, The.
Man with the Blue Guitar, The, *sels.*
Meditation Celestial & Terrestrial.
Men Made out of Words.
Metaphors of a Magnifico.
Motive for Metaphor, The.
Mozart, 1935.
Nomad Exquisite.
Not Ideas about the Thing but the Thing Itself.
Notes toward a Supreme Fiction, *sels.*
O Florida, Venereal Soil.
Of Heaven Considered as a Tomb.
Of Mere Being.
Of Modern Poetry.
Old Lutheran Bells at Home, The.
On the Adequacy of Landscape.
On [*or* Of] the Manner of Addressing Clouds.
Ordinary Evening in New Haven, An, *sel.*
Ordinary Women, The.
Paltry Nude Starts on a Spring Voyage, The.
Peter Quince at the Clavier.
Phases, *sels.*
Phosphor Reading by His Own Light.
Plain Sense of Things, The.
Planet on the Table, The.
Pleasures of Merely Circulating, The.
Plot Against the Giant, The.
Poem That Took the Place of a Mountain, The.
Poems of Our Climate, The.
Poetry Is a Destructive Force.
Postcard from the Volcano, A.
Quiet Normal Life, A.
Rabbit Is King of the Ghosts, A.
Reader, The.
Reality Is an Activity of the Most August
   Imagination.
River of Rivers in Connecticut, The.
Rock, The, *sel.*
Room on a Garden, A.
Sea Surface Full of Clouds.
Sense of the Sleight-of-Hand Man, The.
Snow Man, The.
Song of Fixed Accord.
Stars at Tallapoosa.
Study of Two Pears.
Sun This March, The.
Sunday Morning.
Table Talk.
Tea at the Palaz of Hoon.
Things of August, *sel.*
Thinking of a Relation between the Images of
   Metaphors.
Thirteen Ways of Looking at a Blackbird.
To an Old Philosopher in Rome.
To the One of Fictive Music.
To the Roaring Wind.
Two Figures in Dense Violet Night.
Ultimate Poem Is Abstract, The.
Vacancy in the Park.
Valley Candle.
Waving Adieu, Adieu, Adieu.
World as Meditation, The.
Worms at Heaven's Gate, The.
Stevenson, Alec Brock (b. 1895)
Death, My Companion.
He Who Loved Beauty.
Hemlock at Sunset, A.
Icarus in November.
Sonnet: "If it be night . . . "
Stevenson, Anne (b. 1933)
After the End of It.
Arioso Dolente.
Ballad for Apothecaries, A.
Cold: "Snow. No roofs this morning, alps,
   ominous message."
Correspondences, *sels.*
Epitaph for a Good Mouser.
Gales.
Himalayan Balsam.
In the Orchard.
Level Cambridgeshire.
Making Poetry.
Marriage, A.
Marriage, The.
Minister.

Mother, The.
Musician's Widow.
On Going Deaf.
Painting It In.
Ragwort.
Re-reading Jane.
Respectable House.
Salter's Gate.
Sous-Entendu.
Spirit is Too Blunt an Instrument, The.
Temporarily in Oxford.
Utah.
Vertigo.
Victory, The.
When the Camel Is Dust it Goes Through the
   Needle's Eye.
Who's Joking with the Photographer?
Willow Song.
Stevenson, Matthew (fl. 1654–85)
Elegy upon Old Freeman, An, *sel.*
Stevenson, Robert Louis (1850–94)
Alcaics; to H. F. B.
At the Seaside [*or* Sea-Side].
Auntie's Skirts.
Autumn Fires.
Bed in Summer.
Block City.
Blows the Wind Today.
Celestial Surgeon, The.
Christmas at Sea.
Cow, The.
Epitaph: "Angler rose, he took his rod, The."
Evensong.
Flowers, The.
From a Railway Carriage.
Gardener, The.
Good and Bad Children.
Happy Thought.
He hears with gladdened heart the thunder.
Home no more home to me, whither must I
   wander.
In the highlands, in the country places.
It's an owercome sooth for age an' youth.
Lamplighter, The.
Land of Counterpane, The.
Land of Story-Books, The.
Last night we had a thunderstorm in style.
Light-Keeper, The.
Looking Forward.
Mile an' a Bittock, A.
Moon, The.
My house, I say. But hark to the sunny doves.
My Shadow.
Nay, but I fancy somehow, year by year.
O to Be Up and Doing.
Pirate Story.
Rain.
Requiem: "Under the wide and starry sky."
Song of a Traveller, The.
Summer Sun.
Swing, The.
Ticonderoga: A Legend of the West Highlands.
To A Gardener.
To Any Reader, *sel.*
To Henry James.
To Mrs. Will H. Low.
To S.C.
Treasure Island, *sels.*
Tropics vanish, and meseems that I, The.
Vagabond, The.
Where Go the Boats?
Whole Duty of Children.
Winter Time [*or* Winter-Time].
Wishes.
Stevenson, William (1530?–75) *and* **John Still**
Gammer Gurton's Needle, *sels.*
Stever, Ed
Her Back to Me.
Stewart, Bob
August Town.
Words Is Not Enough.
Stewart, Douglas (1913–85)
Country Song, A.
Leopard Skin.
Terra Australis.

Stewart, Frank
Black Winter.
Stewart, Harold (b. 1916)
Sage in Unison, The.
Stewart, James
On Seeing Man with a Guitar at the Moma.
On Speed, or How We Murdered Nostalgia.
Stewart, Pamela (b. 1943)
Against Silence.
August.
Estes' Backyard, The.
Martin.
Punk Pantoum.
What's It For.
Stewart, Pauline (b. 1962)
Singing down the Breadfruit.
Stewart, Susan (b. 1952)
Apple.
Arbor 1937, The.
Dark the Star.
Forest, The.
Forms of Forts.
Gypsy, The.
Lost Rules of Usage.
May 1988.
Meadow, The.
Pear.
Seasons, The.
Slaughter.
These Trees in Particular.
Wings.
Zero.
Stickney, Trumbull (1874–1904)
Age in Youth.
And, the last day being come, Man stood
    alone.
As a sad man, when evenings grayer grow.
At Sainte-Marguerite.
Athenian Garden, An.
Autumn's done; they have the golden corn in,
    The.
Be still. The Hanging Gardens were a dream.
Departure, The.
Dramatic Fragments, *sels.*
Eride ("Dull words that swim upon the page."),
    sel.
He said: If in his image I was made.
Here in the North I chase an old despair.
I hear a river thro' the valley wander.
In Ampezzo ("In days of summer let me go.").
In Ampezzo ("Only once more and not
    again—the larches.").
In the Past.
Lakeward.
Live Blindly.
Melancholy year is dead with rain, The.
Mnemosyne.
On Rodin's "L'Illusion, Sœur d'Icare."
On Sandro's Flora.
On Some Shells Found Inland.
On the Concert.
Pity.
Prometheus Pyrphoros, *sel.*
Quiet after the rain of morning.
Requiescam.
Six O'Clock.
Sonnets from Greece, *sels.*
You say, Columbus with his argosies.
Sticman
Police State.
Stidger, William Leroy (1886–1949)
Day, A.
Stieler, Kaspar (1632–1707)
Hatred Surely Does Not Kiss.
Night's Delights.
Stigter, Gerard *See* Schippers, K.
Still, John *See* Stevenson, William
Stillborn, Myra
Trail, The.
Stillman, Al (fl. 1942)
Jukebox Saturday Night.
Stillman, Michael (b. 1940)
In Memoriam John Coltrane.
Lullaby for Suzanne.

Ophelia.
Prospero.
Song: "Love is a green girl."
Songs for the Seasons: A Distant
    Collaboration.
Two Princes, The.
Whiskers Meets Polly.
Stillpoint, Horehound
Form a Band, Goddammit.
This I Whisper.
**Stirling, Sir William Alexander, Earl of (1567–
1640)**
Aurora, *sels.*
Echo, An.
Stock, Norman (b. 1940)
First Time I Robbed Tiffany's, The.
What I Said.
Stockbridge, Patricia
My True Love Hath My Heart and I Have His.
Stoddard, Charles Warren (1843–1909)
Old Monterey.
Stoddard, Elizabeth (1823–1902)
Above the Tree.
Before the Mirror.
House by the Sea, The.
Nameless Pain.
One Morn I Left Him in His Bed.
Wife Speaks, The.
Stoddart, Greta (b. 1966)
Blindfold, The.
Night We Stole a Full-Length Mirror, The.
Stoddart, Thomas Tod (1810–80)
Death-Wake, The; or, Lunacy, *sels.*
Stodghill, Pat
August 1, 1966.
Rattlesnake Roundup.
Traitor.
Stokes, Glenn
Blue Texarkana.
Stokes, Terry (b. 1943)
Elvis Elevator, The.
Stokesbury, Leon (b. 1945)
Bottom's Dream.
Evening's End.
Jaques Lured by Audrey.
Reynaldo in Paris.
Stoller, Michael E. (b. 1933)
Searchin.'
Stoller, Michael E. *See Also* Leiber, Jerry
Stone, Alison
Rocket to Russia.
Spofford Hall.
Stone, John A. (b. 1936)
Bass, The.
Confabulation.
Death: "I have seen come on."
Early Sunday Morning.
Gaudeamus Igitur: A Valediction.
Getting to Sleep in New Jersey.
He Makes a House Call.
Rosemary.
Talking to the Family.
Truck, The.
Stone, Ruth (b. 1915)
Always on the Train.
Cabbage, The.
Cocks and Mares.
Curtains.
Earth Quake.
For My Dead Red-Haired Mother.
Habit.
Hummingbirds.
In an Iridescent Time.
In the Next Galaxy.
It Follows.
Latest Hotel Guest Walks Over Particles That
    Revolve in Seven Other Dimensions
    Controlling Latticed Space, The.
Magnet, The.
Nose, The.
Periphery.
Poems: "When you come back to me."
Reading.
Resonance.

Secondhand Coat.
Seed.
So Be It.
Song of Absinthe Granny, The.
That Winter.
Train Ride.
Up There.
Vernal Equinox.
Winter: "Ten o'clock train to New York, The."
Stone, Samuel John (1602–63)
Church's One Foundation, The.
Storace, Patricia
Archaeology of Divorce, The.
King Lear Bewildered.
Wedding Song.
Storey, Edward (b. 1930)
Wireless Aerial, The.
Storm, Hester G.
Bop for Laotzu.
Storm, Theodor (1817–88)
At the Desk.
Woman's Ritornelle.
Storni, Alfonsina (1892–1938)
Ancestral Burden.
Camp Fire.
Encounter.
I'm Going to Sleep.
Lost Caress, The.
Lyrical Letter to the Other Woman.
Me at the Bottom of the Sea.
Siren, The.
Sorrow.
To Eros.
To Eros.
To My Lady of Poetry.
What Would They Say?
White Claw, The.
Words to My Mother.
World is Bitter, The.
You Want Me White ("You want me pure.").
Story, William Wetmore (1819–95)
Cleopatra.
Contemporary Criticism, A, *sel.*
Stoutenburg, Adrien (1916–82)
Before We Drown.
Cicada: "I lay with my heart under me."
Midnight Saving Time.
Stover, Darrell
Fire/Water Blues.
Stow, Randolph (b. 1935)
Calenture, The.
Enemy, The.
Ghost at Anlaby, The.
Landfall.
My Wish for My Land.
Singing Bones, The.
Stowe, Harriet Beecher (1811–96)
Only a Year.
Stowell, Phyllis
Scales, The.
Stoyanova, Danila (1960–90)
Sea woke up, The.
They say I don't love life.
Three mares.
Strabo, Walafrid (809–49)
Dearest, You Come Suddenly and Suddenly
    You Depart.
Elegy on Reichenau.
Stradling, Sir John (1563–1637)
Abraham's Sacrifice of Isaac.
Stramm, August
Encounter.
Reconnaissance Patrol.
Urdeath.
Strand, Mark (b. 1934)
Always.
A.M.
Black Maps.
Coming to This.
Courtship.
Dark Harbor, *sels.*
Dead, The.
Door, The.
Dreadful Has Already Happened, The.

Dress, The.
Eating Poetry.
Elegy for My Father, *sels.*
End, The.
Five Dogs.
Garden, The.
Here: "Sun that silvers all the buildings here,
  The."
Idea, The.
In Celebration.
In Memory of Joseph Brodsky.
Keeping Things Whole.
Kite, The.
Late Hour, The.
Letter.
Marriage, The.
Morning, A.
Morning, Noon and Night.
My Life.
My Life by Somebody Else.
Night, The Porch, The.
Old Man Leaves Party.
Orpheus Alone.
Philosopher's Conquest, The.
Piece of the Storm, A.
Poor North.
Pot Roast.
Prediction, The.
Reading in Place.
Shooting Whales.
Story of Our Lives, The.
To Himself.
Tunnel, The.
2032.
2002.
When the Vacation Is Over for Good.
Where Are the Waters of Childhood?

Strange, Edward F.
Scorcher, The.

Strange, Sharan (b. 1959)
Acts of Power.
Barbershop Ritual.
Childhood.
Crazy Girl, The.
Hunger.
Night Work.
Offering.
Still Life.
Streetcorner Church.
Transits.

Strangman, Honor (*fl.* **1616**) *et al.*
Yf there be any man that can tell me quicklye.

Strasser, Judith (b. 1944)
Memory Lapse.
Protest at Los Alamos, August 2000.

Stratanovsky, Sergey (b. 1944)
Herostratos and Herostratos.
Leningrad stairwell, A.
Terrorist, The.

Stratidakis, Eileen
Need for Armor, A.

Strato [*or* **Straton] (d. 270 B.C.)**
Begin with Zeus, Aratus said; but, Muse.
Boys' members, Diodorus, come in three.
Despite the ruddy down upon your cheek.
Don't hitch your dear little cunt against that
  wall.
Fitness expert. Big gym-man.
I loathe a boy who won't be hugged and
  kissed.
In the bed are two, submissive.
In years to come, I ask, be kind.
Long hair, and curls woven not by Nature but
  by Art.
To start with, grapple your opponent 'round.
Twelve-year-old looks fetching in his prime, A.
Yesterday in the bath Diodes' penis.
Your rosy-fingered prick that used to charm.

Straus, Austin
All-Purpose Apology Poem.

Straus, Marc J.
Log of Pi, The.
Luck.
Neuroanatomy Summer.
Scarlet Crown.

What I Heard on the Radio Today.

Strauss, Jennifer (b. 1933)
Love Notes.
Tending the Graves.

Strayhorn, Billy (1915–67)
Lonely Coed, A.
Lush Life.
Something to Live For.

"Streamer, Col. D." *See* Graham, Harry

Street, Douglas
Love Letters of the Dead.

Street, Sean (b. 1946)
Shipping Forecast, Donegal.

Strejilevich, Nora
When They Robbed Me of My Name.

Strickland, Agnes (1796–1874)
Forsaken, The.
Infant, The.
Maniac, The.
Self-Devoted, The.

Strickland, Stephanie
Absent from Dances 1925.
FigTree.
Gustave Thibon, How Simone Weil Appeared
  to Me/2.
Gustave Thibon, How Simone Weil Appeared
  to Me/3.
Gustave Thibon, How Simone Weil Appeared
  to Me/4.
Gustave Thibon, How Simone Weil Appeared
  to Me/5.
Intact.
Shadow.

Strobel, Marion (Mrs. James Herbert Mitchell)
(b. 1895)
Encounter.
Pastoral: "This is a place of ease."

Strode, William (1600–43)
Bracelets.
Ear-string, An.
Epitaph on the Monument of Sir William
  Strode.
Girdle, A.
In Commendation of Music.
Justification.
Kisses.
Nightingale, The.
On a Gentlewoman that Sung and Played upon
  a Lute.
On a Good Leg and Foot.
On Chloris Walking in the Snow.
On Fairford Windows.
On the Death of Mistress Mary Prideaux.
On Westwall Downes [*or* On Westwell
  Downs].
Opposite to Melancholy.
Riddle: On a Kiss, A.

Stroffolino, Chris
Lingua Franca.
Love as Fear of Love in Laughter.

Strong, Eithne (b. 1923)
Farewell, A: "I have not won."

Strong, George A. (1832–1912)
Song of Milkanwatha, The, *sels.*

Strong, Leonard Alfred George (1896–1958)
Brewer's Man, The.
Door, The.
Knowledgeable Child, The.
Lowery Cot.
Mad Woman of Punnet's Town, The.
March Evening.
Old Dan'l.
Old Man at the Crossing, The.
Old Woman, Outside the Abbey Theater, An.
Rufus Prays.
Two Generations.
Zeke.

Stroud, Joseph (b. 1943)
Comice.
Directions.
Documentary.
Grandfather.
Hacedor.
Hear That Phone Ringing? Sounds Like a

Long Distance Call.
Homage: Doo-Wop.
Homage: Summer/Winter, Shay Creek.
Homage to Life: Jules Supervielle.
Homage to the *Word-Hoard.*
Manna.
Missing.
Oh Yes.
Provenance.

Stroud, William
Rustler.

Struther, Jan (Joyce Anstruther Maxtone
Graham) (1901–53)
Freedom.

Struthers, Betsy (b. 1951)
Last Days.

Stryk, Lucien (b. 1924)
Awakening.
Black Bean Soup.
Blood.
Child in the City, A.
Cormorant.
Dawn.
Enough.
History.
Oeuvre.
Pit, The.
Return to DeKalb.
Return to Hiroshima.
Sniper.
Winter Storm.

Stuart, Alice V. (1899–1981)
Plait of Hair, The.

Stuart, Dabney (b. 1937)
Desolation: "At the top of the dune."
Figure on the Edge.
Fishing with Elvis.
Palm Reader.
Rumination.
Swinging on the First Pitch.
Where the Deer Go.

Stumbrs, Olafs
Song at a Late Hour.

Sturluson, Snorri (1179?–1241)
Corpsebeach.

Sturm, Frank Pearce (1879–1942)
Still-Heart.

Su, Adrienne (b. 1967)
Address.
Antidepressant.
Four Sonnets About Food.
I Can't Become a Buddhist.
Miss Chang is Missing.
Wedding Gifts.

Su Hsiao-hsiao (*fl.* **late 5th cent.)**
Song of Xiling Lake, A.

Su Man-shu (Hsüan-ying) (1884–1918)
Exile in Japan.

Su Shih *See* Su Tung-p'o (Su Shih)

Su Tung-p'o (Su Shih) (1036–1101)
At Gold Hill Monastery.
At the Temple of Kuan Yin in the Rain.
Black Clouds—Spilled Ink.
Climbing Yun-lung Mountain.
Eastern Slope, *sels.*
Epigram: "I fish for minnows in the lake."
Lament of the Farm Wife of Wu.
Listening to the River.
Lyrics to the Tune "Fairy Grotto"
Lyrics to the Tune "The Charms of Niennu":
  At the Red Cliff I Ponder Over Antiquity.
Mid-Autumn Moon.
On a Painting by Wang the Clerk of Yen Ling.
On the Birth of His Son.
On the Tower of Gathering Remoteness.
Rain During the Cold Food Festival.
Rain in the Aspens.
Reading the Poetry of Meng Chiao: Two
  Poems.
Red Cliff Rhapsodies.
Red Cliff, The.
Remembering Min Ch'e.
Remembering My Wife.

Roadside Flowers, Three Poems with Introduction, *sels.*
Seeking Spring Beyond the city.
Sitting at Night with My Nephew Who Has Just Come from Afar.
Southern Room Over the River, The.
Spring Scene.
Terrace in the Snow, The.
Thoughts in Exile.
To a Traveler.
Tune: "A Riverside Town."
Tune: "Always Having Fun."
Tune: "Butterflies Lingering over Flowers."
Tune: "Calming Windswept Waves."
Tune: "Charming Nien-Nu."
Tune: "Fragrance Fills the Courtyard."
Tune: "Immortal by the River."
Tune: "Immortal by the River"
Tune: "Partridge Sky."
Tune: "River Town."
Tune: "Water Mode Song."
Turning Year, The.
Verses: "I am old, sick and lonely."
Walk in the Country, A.
When Yü-k'o painted bamboo.
White Crane Hill.
Who Says a Painting Must Look Like Life?

Su Wu (*fl.* **2d cent.**)
Drafted.

Suárez, Clementina (**b. 1906**)
Another Poem to My Mother.
Like the Magic Glow of Paradise.
Now That I Have Grown Up, Mother.
Poem for Mankind and Its Hope.
Poem, The: "If you start to write a poem."
Worker Dies, A.
Workwoman's Death, A.

Suárez, Virgil (**b. 1962**)
Aguacero.
Cuban-American Gothic.
Donatilia's Unrequited Love Remedy.
Duende.
Florida, La.
H. Chic.
Rice Comes to El Volcán.
Song for the Sugar Cane.
Song to the Banyan.

Sub-ok
Spring at Yesan Station.

Subbarao, Nanduri (**1895–1957**)
Blow Out the Lamp.
He Didn't Come Back.
Is This All!
My Love.
You in My Dream.

Subbarao, Rayaprolu (**1892–1984**)
Chained.
Waiting.

Subido, Trinidad Tarrosa (**b. 1912**)
Paganly.

Suckling, Sir John (**1609–42**)
Against Absence.
Against Fruition ("Stay here, fond youth, and ask no more.").
Aglaura, *sels.*
Ballad[e] [upon a Wedding], A.
Barley-Break , A.
Candle, A.
Dream, A.
Love and Debt Alike Troublesome.
Love's Clock.
Love's Offence.
Love's Siege.
Loving and Beloved.
Poem with the Answer, A, *sels.*
Soldier, A.
Song: "I prithee spare me, gentle boy."
Sonnet: "Dost see how unregarded now."
Sonnet: "Of thee, kind boy, I ask no red and white."
Sonnet: "O[h]! for some honest lover's ghost."
Summons to Town, A.
Upon My Lady Carlisle's Walking in Hampton Court Garden.
Upon Stephen Stoned.
Wits, The; A Session[s] of the Poets.

Woman's Constancy.

Sudeley, Baron Seymour of *See* Seymour, Sir Thomas

Suermondt, Tim
Briefly Eavesdropping on Walt Whitman, Virginia, 1863.
Missing Supper.
Squad I.

Suessdorf, Karl (*fl.* **1944**)
Moonlight in Vermont.

Suhl, Yuri (**1908–86**)
Kh'hob dikh lib.
My October Song.
Winter: "Now winter's standing at the door."

Suian
Traceless, no more need to hide.

Suk, Julie
From Ruin.

Suk Mumyong
After Getting Drunk in a Hermitage on Chiri Mountain.

Sukhovey, Darya (**b. 1977**)
Spring Scales.

Sulchinskaya, Olga (**b. 1966**)
Crimea.
Kite, The.
Wind paces on the lower branch, The.

Suleyman I, Sultan *See* Muhibbi

Sullivan, Aloysius Michael (**b. 1896**)
Jet Plane.

Sullivan, Breda
Hair.

Sullivan, Mary Louise
Unearth.
Wedding Song: "Where the bridesmaid waits in the vestibule."

Sumangalamata (*fl.* **6th cent. B.C.**)
At last free.

Summerfield, Geoffrey
Washday Battles.

Summers, Paul (**b. 1967**)
If Keir Hardie Was the Man on the Moon.

Sumrall, Amber Coverdale (**b. 1945**)
Silence at the End of the World.

Sun, Phillina
Untitled: "In the living room sit the men."

Sun Ch'o (**320?–80**)
Autumn Day, An.
Orchid Pavilion.
Wandering on Mount Tiantai.

Sund, Robert (**b. 1929**)
Considering Poverty and Homelessness.
Frog I Saved from a Snake, The.
Two Poems for the Good Given.

Sundiata, Sekou (*fl.* **c.1990–95**)
Blink Your Eyes.
Ear Training.
Making Poems; on the road in Minneapolis.
Notes from the Defense of Colin Ferguson.
Open Heart.
Shout Out.
Space. A Prose Poem Monologue.

Sung Fang-hu (*fl.* **c.1317**)
Traveler's Life, A.

Sung Tzu-hou (*fl.* **c.120 A.D.**)
Song: "On the Eastern Way at the city of Lo-yang."

Sung Yu (*fl.* **3d cent. B.C.**)
Gao Tang Rhapsody, The.
Wind, The.

Suntsova, Elena (**b. 1976**)
As old salts know.
As you and I stand long.
Beyond is where the passersby end.
City of summer you inhabit a fluff-light city of little claws.

Supervielle, Jules (**1884–1960**)
Early in the morning.
Earth.
Entangled.
Like an ox.
Missing France.

Poet, A.
Poète, Un.
Rain and the Tyrants.
Regret de la terre, Le.
Regretting the Earth.
Return to Paris.
Some day shall I be.
Sphere.
Traveller, traveller.
Voyages.

Süreya, Cemal *See* Cemal Süreya

Suri, Tenneti (**1911–58**)
Here Comes God.

Surprice, Lenous (**b. 1976**)
If You Want.
Little Love Kiss.
Result of an Observation.

Surrey, Henry Howard, Earl of (**1517?–47**)
Epitaph for [*or* on] Thomas Clere.
Excellent Epitaffe of Syr Thomas Wyat, An.
Golden Mean, The.
Laid in My Quiet Bed.
Paraphrase of Part of the Book of Ecclesiates, A, *sels.*
Prison in Windsor Castle.
Sardanapalus.
Seafarer, The.
When Raging Love.
Windsor Castle, *sels.*
Wyatt Resteth Here.

Sutcliffe, Alice (*fl.* **c.1633**)
Meditations of Man's Mortalitie; or, A Way to True Blessedness, *sels.*

Sute-Jo, Lady Den (**1633–98**)
Are there / Short-cuts in the sky.
Woman.

Sutherland, Fraser (**b. 1946**)
Auden's Face.
On the Beach One Day.
Undergoing: Jewish General Hospital, Montreal 6:35 a.m.

Sutherland, Robert *See* Garioch, Robert

Sutherland-Smith, James
Something you won't ever bring pressure to bear on.

Sutphen, Joyce (**b. 1949**)
Girl on a Tractor.
Household Muse.
Living in the Body.
Not for Burning.
Problem Was, The.
Terra Incognita.
Wishbone USA.

Sutskever [*or* **Sutzkever**], **Abraham** (**b. 1913**)
Between Chimneys.
Cartload of Shoes, A.
Death of an Ox, The.
Honey of a Wild Bee.
How?
Peasant Who Saw God, The.
Poems from a Diary, *sels.*

Sutter, Barton (**b. 1949**)
Hoarfrost and Fog.
Peregrine.
Shoe Shop.
Static.

Sutton, Virginia Chase
Housekeeping.
While Watching *Cops* I Think of You.

Suyemoto, Toyo (**1916–2003**)
Hokku: "Geese flew over, The."
In Topaz.

Suzuki, Mitsu (**b. 1914**)
Monastery gate.
Soft rain.
Summer butterfly.
Swiftly walking away.

Suzuki, Shonan
Moon shadows on internment camp.
Withered grass on ground.

Svankmajerová, Eva (**b. 1940**)
I Don't Know Exactly.
Stunned by Freedom.

Svoboda, Terese (b. 1951)
  Appomattox.
  Death Stayed.
  Epithalamion.
  Goddess Corn Finds Her Dress in
    Disarray,The.
  Report from High School.

Swaanswijk, L. J. *See* "Lucebert"

Swan, E. A. (*fl.* 1931)
  When Your Lover Has Gone.

Swan, Guida
  I pull opposites together.

Swanger, David (b. 1940)
  Knob Pines.
  Natural Disaster.
  Wayne's College of Beauty, Santa Cruz.

Swann, Brian (b. 1940)
  Land at the World's End, The.
  Old Song of the Musk Ox People.
  Walking at Night.

Swann, Roberta
  EFT.

Swartwout, Susan
  Gypsy Teaches Her Grandchild Wolfen Ways,
    The.
  I Wannabe Your Queen.
  Siamese Twins in Love.

Sweeney, Matthew (b. 1952)
  Appointment, The.
  Box, The.
  To the Building Trade.
  Tube Ride to Martha's.

Sweet, Bruce
  "New World" Interview.

Sweet, Denise
  My Mother and I Had a Discussion One Day.

Swensen, Cole (b. 1955)
  Crowd.

Swenson, Karen (b. 1936)
  Ice-Cream Sandwich, The.
  Landlady in Bangkok, The.
  Mother and Son.

Swenson, May (b. 1919)
  Almanac.
  Bison Crossing Near Mt. Rushmore.
  Bleeding.
  Bronco Busting, Event #1.
  Cardinal Ideograms.
  Cat and the Weather.
  Centaur, The.
  Colors Without Objects.
  Couple, A.
  Distance and a Certain Light.
  Electronic Sound.
  Feel Me.
  Fire Island.
  First Walk on the Moon.
  Flying Home from Utah.
  Four-Word Lines.
  Goodbye, Goldeneye.
  He That None Can Capture.
  How Everything Happens (Based on a Study
    of the Wave).
  In Love Made Visible.
  July 4th.
  Last Day.
  Motherhood.
  On Its Way.
  One of the Strangest.
  Painting the Gate.
  Poet to Tiger.
  Question: "Body my house."
  Riding the "A."
  Shape of Death, The.
  Shu Swamp, Spring.
  Something Goes By.
  Southbound on the Freeway.
  Staring at the Sea on the Day of the Death of
    Another.
  Staying at Ed's Place.
  Stone Gullets.
  Strawberrying.
  Stripping and Putting On.
  Teleology.

Unconscious Came a Beauty.
Waking from a Nap on the Beach.
Waterbird.
Wave and the Dune, The.
Weather.
Women.
Written While Riding the Long Island Rail
  Road.

Swift, Joan (b. 1926)
  Anthuriums, Pahoa.
  In Hilo Hospital.
  Spider.
  Steelhead in the Whitehorse Rearing Pond.
  Wild Salmon: Stillaguamish Tribal Hatchery.

Swift, Jonathan (1667–1745)
  Advice to a Dog Painter.
  Beautiful Young Nymph Going to Bed, A.
  Character of Sir Robert Walpole, The.
  Day of Judgement, The.
  Description of a City Shower, A.
  Description of the Morning, A.
  Dick, a Maggot.
  Dogs of Nile, The.
  Epigram on Fasting.
  Epigram on Scolding, An.
  Gentle Echo on Woman, A.
  Holyhead. September 25, 1727.
  Lady's Dressing Room, The.
  Mary the Cook-Maid's Letter to Dr. Sheridan.
  On Poetry: a Rhapsody.
  On the Irish Club.
  Oysters.
  Parson's Case, The, *sel.*
  Pastoral Dialogue, A.
  Phyllis [*or* Phillis] [*or* Progress of Love, The].
  Place of the Damned [*or* Damn'd], The.
  Prometheus: "As, when the squire and tinker,
    Wood."
  Satirical Elegy on the Death of a Late Famous
    General, A.
  Stella's Birthday, 1725.
  Stella's Birthday [1721].
  Stella's Birthday ([March 13,] 1727).
  To the Earl of Oxford, Late Lord Treasurer.
  To Their Excellencies the Lords Justices of
    Ireland, the Humble Petition of Frances
    Harris, Who Must Starve, and Die a Maid if
    It Miscarries.
  Twelve Articles.
  Upon the Horrid Plot Discovered by Harlequin
    the Bishop of Rochester's French Dog.
  Verses Made for the Women Who Cry Apples,
    etc.
  Verses Occasioned by the Sudden Drying Up
    of St. Patrick's Well, *sel.*
  Verses on the Death of Dr. Swift, D.S.P.D,
    Occasioned by Reading a Maxim in
    Rochefoucauld, *sels.*
  Virtue conceal'd within our breast.

Swift, Todd (b. 1966)
  Ballad Of The Solitary Diner.
  Homage To Charlotte Rampling.
  Influence of Anxiety at the Seaside with Tea,
    The.
  Leaving Paris.
  My Radios.
  Tenant Of Wildfeld Hall, The.

Swiggart, Katherine
  Exhaled, The.

Swinburne, Algernon Charles (1837–1909)
  Aholibah.
  Anactoria.
  Atalanta in Calydon, *sels.*
  Ave atque Vale.
  Before the Mirror, *sels.*
  Come into the orchard, Anne.
  Dolores, *sel.*
  Étude Réaliste, *sel.*
  Forsaken Garden, A.
  Free Thought.
  Garden of Proserpine, The.
  Heptalogia, The, *sels.*
  Hymn to Proserpine.
  Itylus.
  Lake of Gaube, The.

Leave-taking, A.
Leper, The.
Love And Sleep.
On the Russian Persecution of the Jews.
Sestina: "I saw my soul at rest upon a day."
Triumph of Time, The, *sels.*
Vision of Spring in Winter, A.

Swingler, Randall (b. 1909)
  Acres of Power.
  Day the War Ended, The.
  Drinking Song.

Swiontkowski, Gale
  Old Moon With Her Youth In Her Arms.

Swir, Anna *See* Swirszczynska, Anna

Swirszczynska [*or* Swir], Anna (1909–84)
  Bitch, A.
  Conversation Through the Door, A.
  Good Lord Saved Her, The.
  Greatest Love, The.
  He Is Gone.
  He Was Lucky.
  I Am Afraid of Fire.
  I Starve My Belly for a Sublime Purpose.
  I Talk to My Body.
  I Wash the Shirt.
  Maternity.
  My Father's Workshop.
  Poetry Reading.
  Same Inside, The.
  Sea and the Man, The.
  Second Madrigal, The.
  She Came to Say Farewell.
  She Does Not Remember.
  Terminally Ill.
  Thank You, My Fate.
  They Lay Dying Side by Side.
  Three Bodies.
  Three Pieces of Candy.
  Troubles with the Soul at Morning
    Calisthenics.
  Very Sad Conversation at Night, A.
  Visit, A.
  We Are Going to Shoot at the Heart.
  We Survived Them.
  White Wedding Slippers.
  Woman Writer Does Laundry, A.

Swiss, Thomas (Thom)
  On a Stanza by Rilke.

Sy, Thich Tue
  Cup of Clear Water, A.
  Hermit Thoughts.
  Stone Walls.

Sykes, Arthur A.
  Splendid Bankrupt, The.

Sykes, Bobbi (b. 1943)
  Cycle.
  One Day.

Sylvain, Patrick (b. 1966)
  Army of Draculas.
  Collective Search.
  Constant Memories.
  Horizon of Gunbutts.
  Palace of Mourners, A.
  Panama.
  Refugees.

Sylvester, Janet (b. 1950)
  Arrowhead Christian Center and No-Smoking
    Luncheonette.

Sylvester, János Edrosi
  To the Hungarian People.

Sylvester, Joshua (1561–1618)
  Aestas.
  Du Bartas: His Divine Weeks and Works, *sels.*
  Father, The.
  Garden, The.
  Job's Epitaph.
  Maidens Blush, The, *sel.*
  Of a Husbandman.
  Saluste du Bartas' Devine Weekes, *sel.*
  Variable.
  War is the mistress of enormity.
  Were I as Base as Is the Lowly Plain.

Sylvester, June
  Palms.

Taggard, Genevieve (Mrs. Kenneth Durant) (1894–1948)
All Around the Town.
At Last the Women are Moving.
Bounding Line.
Demeter.
Dilemma of the Elm.
Doomsday Morning.
Enamel Girl, The.
Everyday Alchemy.
Fructus.
Hymn to Yellow.
Millions of Strawberries.
Solar Myth.
Thirst.
Time Out: "We will put Time to sleep on that warm hill."
To Mr. Maunder Maunder, Professional Poet.
To One Loved Whollly Within Wisdom.
To the Natural World: at 37.
To the Powers of Desolation.
To the Veterans of the Abraham Lincoln Brigade.
Try Tropic.
Weed, The.
With Child.

Taggart, John
Body and Soul: Poem for Two Readers.
Monk.
Never Too Late.
Pen Vine and Scroll.
Sainte-Chapelle.
Slow Song for Mark Rothko.

Tagliabue, John (b. 1923)
Bare Arms of Trees, The.
March Blizzard.
Moderation Is Not a Negation of Intensity, But Helps Avoid Monotony.

Tagore, Rabindranath (1861–1941)
Epigrams, sel.
Final Poems, sels.
Gardener, The.
Gift.
Gitanjali, sels.
Song That I Came to Sing, The.
You Did Not Find Me.

Taha, Ahmed (b. 1948)
Abode of Arrival.
Anwar Kamel Celebrates Le Quatorze Juillet.
Arabesque.
Childhood Wall.
December 31.
State of Butterfly.
Tale, A.
Wall of Dreams (2).
Wall of Genesis, The.

Tahmiscic, Husein
You're Not a Man If You Don't Die.

Tai Shu-lun (732–89)
Su Creek Pavilion.

Tait, George Edward (b. 1910)
U.S.A. Court of No Appeal, The.

Tait, William J. (b. 1918)
Adjustan Mysel tae the Situation.
Contracting Universe, The.
On With the Dance! Let Freud Be Unconfined!

Takagi Kyozo (b. 1903)
How To Cook Women.

Takahashi Mutsuo (b. 1937)
Monkey-eaters.
Self-Portraits, sels.

Takai Kito (1741–89)
Barley-reaping song / Smith's hammer.
Contending / Temple bell.
Nightingale / Rarely seen.
Seaweed / Between rocks—.

Takamura Kotaro (1883–1956)
Bear Fur.
Cathedral in the Thrashing Rain.
Elephant's Piggy Bank, The.
Final Battle for the Ryūkyū Islands, The.
Steak Platter, A.
Whale Spouting.

Takara, Kathryn
Cows and Alabama Folklore.

Takei, Sojin
There is no fence.
While the MP's wait.

Takeshima Hagoromo (1872–1967)
Maiden Called Love, The.

Takomaq (fl late 19th cent.)
Improvised Song of Joy.

Taksa, Mark
Granite Jaw.

Takuan (1573–1645)
Though night after night.

Takushitsu (1290–1367)
Breeze strokes the water of the spring, A.

Talbot, Norman (b. 1936)
Ballad of Old Women & of How They Are Constrained To Simulate Youth In Order To Avoid Shocking the Young.

Talfourd, Sir Thomas N.
'Tis a Little Thing.

"Talhaiarn" See Jones, John

Taliesin (fl. c.550)
Battle of Argoed Llwyfain, The.
Death Song for Owain ab Urien.

Tall, Deborah
Miraculous Mandarin, The.

Talley, Nancy
Vegetables make love above the tenors.

Tallie, Mariahadessa Ekere
Medusa.
Note from a Loving Wife.
Raindrop Women.

Tallmountain, Mary (b. 1918)
Brother Wolverine.
Good Grease.
Hands of Mary Joe, The.
Indian Blood.
Last Wolf, The.
Matmiya.
Peeling Pippins.
There Is No Word for Goodbye.

Talvikki, Ansel
Afterwards: Caliban.
Conversation with the Sun Bittern.
Flemish Beauty.
For Want.
In Fragments, In Streams, sels.
My Shining Archipelago.
Origin Charm Against Uncertain Injuries.
You Don't Know What Happened When You Froze.

Tamer, Ülkü (b. 1937)
You're Not a Man If You Don't Die.

Tammaro, Thom
'Mericn Fst Fd.

Tan Taigi (1709–71)
Barley's season / Dust mutes.
Beyond serenity / Gray kites.
"Don't touch!" my host cried.
Fallen leaves / Raking.
In the boat / Crescent moon's light.
In the melon-patch / Thief, fox.
Swellfish eaten / He chants nembutsu.
Temple in / Deep winter grove.
Thunder / Voices of drowned.
Winter withering.
Zazen / Fat mosquitoes.

Tana, Patti
I Have Touched.
Marvelous Beast.
No.
River, The.
You Bring Me Back.

Tanahashi, Kazuaki (b. 1933)
Can five hundred paintings be created in one stroke?
Does the brush paint, or does the ink? Or does the paper.
One-line poem? Why not one-word poem?
Six Characters from the *Heart Sutra*.

Tanaquil, Paul (J. G. Clemenceau Le Clerq) (b. 1893)
Very Young Man Speaks, A.

Taneda Santoka (1882–1940)
Autumn wind.
Came along / a mountain path.
Dawn coming on.
Deeper I go, The.
Edge of town.
Heaven / doesn't kill me.
Mountain's stillness, The.
No desire to die.
Nothing left of the house.
Road running straight ahead.
Sleep on the ground.
Somewhere / inside my head.
This trip.
Valiantly—that too.
Waiting for what?

Tanfield, Lady Elizabeth (fl. 1565–1628)
Epitaph for Sir Lawrence Tanfield.

T'ang Hsien-tsu (1550–1616)
On the Day of Washing the Buddha in the Year Ting-wei (1607), I Dreamed That My Late Son Shih-ch'ü Was Holding a Book, and Appeared To Be Quite Happy. He Said That He Had Earned His Chin-shih Degree in the Underworld. After We Sighed and La.
Twenty-two Quatrains on Receiving the Obituary Notice for my Son Shih-Chü, sel.

T'ang Yin (1470–1523)
Inscription for a Portrait.

Tanikawa, Shuntaro (b. 1931)
Concerning a Girl.
Cycle of Months (Menstruation).
Dusk.
Family Portrait.
Growth.
Kiss.
Landscape with Yellow Birds.
Nero.
Picnic to the Earth.
Porno-Bach.
Rain Please Fall.
Request.
River.
Sadness.
Stone and Light.
Twenty Billion Light Years of Loneliness.
Two Tokyos.
With Silence My Companion, sel.
Zoo.

Tannahill, Robert (1774–1810)
Eild.
Tap-Room, The.

Tanning, Dorothea
Report from the Field.

Tantan (1674–1761)
Morning frost / Mount Fuji.
On the rock / Waves can't reach.

Tanzan (1819–92)
Madness, the way they gallop off to foreign shores!

T'ao Ch'ien [or T'ao Yuan-ming] (365–427)
After Kuo Chu-Pu's Poems.
Bearers' Song.
Bright sun sinks / beyond the western ridge, The.
Burial Songs, sels.
Days and months do not wish to tarry, The.
Drinking Alone in the Rainy Season.
Drinking Wine, sels.
Elegy for Myself.
Fire, Sixth Month, 408.
Five Poems on Returning to Dwell in the Country.
Four Poems Written While Drunk.
Great men want the four seas. I've only.
Harmonizing with a Poem by the Registrar Guo.
Home Again among Gardens and Fields.
I Return to the Place I Was Born.
In Reply to a Poem by Liu Chaisang.
Lament: "Ways of heaven are mysterious, The."

Miscellaneous Poem.
Passing Through Ch'ien-hsi, Third Month, 405.
Peach Blossom Spring, The ("Ying clan disrupted Heaven's ordinance, The.").
Peach-Blossom Spring ("Ch'in's First Emperor ravaged the sense.").
Picnic by the Xie River, A.
Poem on Returning to Dwell in the Country.
Putting the Blame on His Sons.
Reply to Prefect Liu.
Returning to Fields and Gardens (1) ("When I was young, I did not fit in.").
Return, The.
Returning to Fields and Gardens (2) ("I plant beans below the southern hill.").
Returning to My Fields and Gardens.
Scolding My Sons.
Seeing Off a Guest at Captain Wang's Headquarters.
Substance, Shadow, and Spirit ("Earth and heaven endure forever.").
Substance, Shadow, and Spirit ("Heaven and Earth endure and do not perish.").
Thinking of Impoverished Ancients.
Three Dirges: Written in Imitation of an Ancient Funeral Song.
To My Cousin, Ching-yuan, Twelfth Month, 403.
To-Em-Mei's "The Unmoving Cloud"
Two Poems Written While Drunk.
Written on the First Day of the Fifth Month.
Written on the Ninth Day of the Ninth Month of the Year Yi-you.

T'ao Hung Ching (T'ao T'ung Ming) (452–536)
Poem Written in Answer to His Majesty's Question: "What Is There in the Mountains?"

Tapahonso, Luci (b. 1954)
All I Want.
I Am Singing Now.
Old Salt Woman.
Pay Up or Else.
They Were Alone in the Winter.
Warp is Even, The: Taut Vertical Loops Between Our Father and the Earth.
What Danger We Court.

Tappan, William Bingham (1794–1849)
Last Drunkard, The, sel.
Obey Your Parents.
Song of the Three Hundred Thousand Drunkards in the United States, sel.

Tappenden, Sandra
I'm ugly but I don't know why.

Tardieu, Jean (1903–95)
Cézanne.
Cézanne.
Days.
Fly and the Ocean, The.
Jours, Les.
Mouche et l'Océan, La.
Seine de Paris, La.
Seine in Paris, The.

Tarkos, Christophe (b. 1964)
67 Words with One Vowel and One Consonant.
67 mots d'une voyelle et d'une consonne.

Tarn, Nathaniel (b. 1928)
As If There were any Matter.
Before the Snake.
First Zen Abbess of America, The.
Great Odor of Summer, The.
Hearing about the Virtual Destruction of Pain.
Heart Stumbles in Darkness, The.
Journal of the Laguna de San Ignacio.
Kluane, the Yukon.
Lyrics for the Bride of God, sels.
Man Whose Name Rhymes with Peace, A.
Narrative of the Men and Women Who Became Stars.
Recollections of Being.
Retreat toward the Spring.

Tarpley, Natasha (b. 1971)
Feel Free.

Tarrant, John
Han Shan in Santa Rosa.

Hula Dancers Dance the Hula, Kilauea the Caldera, The.

Tassis y Peralta, Juan de (1582–1622)
Love Is Not Will But Destiny.
To a Lady Combing Her Hair.

Tasso, Torquato (1544–95)
Aminta, sels.
Godfrey of Bulloigne; or, The Recoverie of Jerusalem [Gerusalemme Liberata], sels.
Jerusalem Delivered, sel.

Tatarunis, Paula (b. 1952)
Before the Brain Surgery.
Chest X-Ray.
I Have Two Sons and the One I Love Best Is Robert.

Tate, Allen (1899–1979)
Aeneas at Washington.
Battle of Murfreesboro.
Cross, The.
Ivory Tower, The.
Last Days of Alice.
Mediterranean, The.
Mr. Pope.
Mother and Son.
Non Omnis Moriar.
Oath, The.
Ode to Our Young Pro-consuls of the Air.
Ode to the Confederate Dead.
Seasons of the Soul.
Sonnet: To a Portrait of Hart Crane.
Sonnets at Christmas, sels.
Sonnets of the Blood, sels.
Swimmers, The.
To the Lacedemonians.
Twelve, The.
Wolves, The.

Tate, Garth (1952–92)
Last Instructions.

Tate, Greg S. (b. 1957)
Tonguing.

Tate, James (b. 1943)
Aunt Sophie's Morning.
Blue Booby, The.
Book of Lies, The.
Bounden Duty.
Cages, The.
Chaste Stranger, The.
Coming Down Cleveland Avenue.
Death on Columbus Day.
Descent, The.
Diagnosis, The.
Distance from Loved Ones.
Dream On.
Failed Tribute to the Stonemason of Tor House, Robinson Jeffers.
Figure in the Carpet, The.
Head of a White Woman Winking.
How the Pope is Chosen.
I Am A Finn, sels.
I Know Someone from Another World.
Inspiration.
Intimidations of an Autobiography.
Land of Little Sticks, 1945.
Lost Pilot, The.
Lousy in Center Field.
Manna.
Miss Cho Composes in the Cafeteria.
Motorcyclists, The.
Never Again the Same.
Nirvana.
Non-Stop.
Poem: "Angel kissed my alphabet, The."
Poem to Some of my Recent Poems.
Promotion, The.
Radical Departure, A.
Rescue.
Rooster.
Sadness of My Neighbors, The.
Shadowboxing.
Stray Animals.
Teaching the Ape to Write Poems.
There's a Certain Point Each Evening.
Vagabond, A.
Wedding, A.
Wheelchair Butterfly, The.
When the Nomads Come Over the Hill.

Where Babies Come From.

Tate, Nahum (1652–1715)
Absalom and Achitophel, Part 2.
Ode upon the New Year.
While Shepherds Watched [Their Flocks by Night].

Tatham, John (fl. 1632–64)
Ostella forth of Town: To My Heart.

Tati-Loutard, Jean-Baptiste (b. 1939)
Early.
Man-Myth: Puberty.

Taub, Debra (b. 1954)
Exquisite Alchemy.
Secret Melodies.

Taufer, Veno and Michael Scammell
Prayers and Games of the Water People, The, sel.

Tayankannanar
Overspread with Salty Soil.

Taylor, Andrew (b. 1940)
Beast with Two Backs, The.
Clearing Away.
Fitzroy.
Travelling to Gleis-Binario, sels.

Taylor, Ann (1783–1824)
Air.
Earth.
Fire.
Maniac's Song, The.
Water.

Taylor, Bayard (1825–78)
Bedouin Song.
Echo Club, The, sels.
Gettysburg Ode.
Goblet, The.
Hylas, sels.
Love Returned.
On the Headland.
On the Sea.
Paean to the Dawn, A.
Proposal.
To a Persian Boy in the Bazaar at Smyrna.

Taylor, Bert Leston ("B. L. T.") (1866–1921)
Passionate Professor, The.
Upon Julia's Arctics.

Taylor, Cecil (b. 1929)
Choir.
Da / Phallic mystère.
Scroll No. 1.
Scroll No. 2.

Taylor, Charles S. (b. 1927)
Our texas economy.
Poem to Ma Ferguson.
Renting.
Winterdirge.

Taylor, Cheryl Boyce
Forever Arima.
Like a Dog.
Plenty Time Pass Fast, Fas Dey So.
Round Irving High School.

Taylor, Edward (1645–1729)
Ebb and Flow, The.
Fig for Thee, Oh! Death, A.
God's Determinations [touching his Elect], sels.
Huswifery.
O! what a thing is Love? who can define.
Preparatory Meditations Before My Approach to the Lord's Supper, sels.
Preparatory Meditations: Part 1 (Complete), sels.
Upon a Spider Catching a Fly.
Upon a Wasp Chilled [or Child] with Cold.
Upon Wedlock and Death of Children.

Taylor, Eleanor Ross (b. 1920)
After Twenty Years.
Boiled Peanuts.
Envoy: "Better than any of you, poems."
Few Days in the South in February, A.
This Year's Drive to Appomattox.
Welcome Eumenides.
Woman as Artist.

Taylor, Elizabeth (fl. c.1680)
Off the Dutchesse.

To Mertill Who Desired Her to Speak to
  Clorinda of His Love.
Taylor, Hannah
  Virtue alone can never die. but lives to.
Taylor, Sir Henry (1800–86)
  Philip van Artevelde, *sels.*
Taylor, Henry (b. 1942)
  After a Movie.
  At South Fork Cemetery.
  At the Swings.
  Bargain at Half the Price, A.
  Buildings and Grounds.
  Elevator Music.
  Flying Change, The.
  For William Stafford.
  Goodbye to the Old Friends.
  Hayfork, The.
  Hughesville Scythe, The.
  Landscape with Tractor.
  Riding a One-eyed Horse.
  Riding Lesson.
  Speech.
  View from a Cab, The.
Taylor, Jane (1783–1824)
  Fairies' Song, The.
  My Mother.
  Recreation.
  Squire's Pew, The.
  Star, The.
  Violet, The.
Taylor, Jeremy (1613–67)
  Hymn for Advent.
  Prayer, A: "My soul doth pant towards thee."
  Prayer, A: "O beauteous God! uncircumscribed
    treasure."
  Prayer for Charity, A.
Taylor, John (1580–1653)
  Comparison betwixt a Whore and a Booke, A,
    sel.
  Epigram, A Supposed Construction.
  Epigram: "Fair Beatrice tucks her coat up
    somewhat high."
  Epigram: "Look how yon lecher's legs are
    worn away."
  Epigram: "Lusty wench as nimble as an eel,
    A."
  Epigram: "There chanced to meet together in
    an inn."
  Here followeth the unfashionable fashion, or
    the too too homely Worshipping of God, *sel.*
  Libra, September.
  Sculler, The, *sel.*
  Sir Gregory Nonsense's News from No Place,
    sel.
  Taylor's Arithmetic from One to Twelve, *sel.*
  Virgo, August.
Taylor, Judith (b. 1939)
  Instructions to Her Next Husband.
  Mistakes.
  Natural Woman.
  Remedy for Backache.
Taylor, Kate
  Wheel Building.
Taylor, Livingston (b. 1950)
  Bicycle.
Taylor, Marilyn
  To a Young Diver.
Taylor, Mervyn (b. c.1942)
  Well-Bred Woman, A.
Taylor, Rachel Annand (1876–1960)
  Princess of Scotland, The.
Taylor, Rod (b. 1947)
  Dakota: October, 1822, Hunkpapa Warrior.
Taylor, Susan
  I am true in the land of ancient sounds.
Tayo-jo (1772–1865)
  People, more people.
Tayson, Richard
  Chase, The.
  First Sex.
  Nightsweats.
  Phone Sex.
Tcherni, Carmi See Carmi, T.

Teare, Brian (b. 1974)
  Dead House Sonnet.
  Detail from "Set for a Southern Gothic."
  First person plural is a house.
  Set for a Southern Gothic.
  Trick Noir.
Teasdale, Sara (1884–1933)
  After Love.
  Answer, The.
  Appraisal.
  At Night.
  August Night.
  Barter.
  Broken Field, The.
  Crystal Gazer, The.
  Day's Ending.
  Effigy of a Nun.
  Enough.
  Falling Star, The.
  Flight, The.
  Gift, The.
  I Shall Live To Be Old.
  I Shall Not Care.
  I Would Live in Your Love.
  Jewels.
  Lines.
  Little While, A.
  Long Hill, The.
  Look, The.
  Moods.
  Moon's Ending.
  Mystery, The.
  Night.
  Night Song at Amalfi.
  On the Dunes.
  On the South Downs.
  Open Windows.
  Over the Roofs.
  Sanctuary, The.
  Shrine, The.
  Solitary, The.
  Song: "Let it be forgotten, as a flower is
    forgotten."
  Song: "You bound strong sandals on my feet."
  Spring Night.
  Summer Night, Riverside.
  There Will Come Soft Rains.
  Those Who Love.
  Unchanging, The.
  Water-Lilies.
  Wisdom.
  Wood Song.
Teasley, Lisa (b. 1962)
  As Dancers.
Teddy
  At Terezin.
Teft, Elizabeth (*fl.* 1741–47)
  On a Friend's Taking a Journey.
Teig, Michael (b. 1968)
  When the Time Comes.
Teiga (1744–1826)
  In the poor man's house.
Teika, Fujiwara no See Fujiwara no Teika
Teillier, Jorge (b. 1935)
  Bridge in the South.
  In the Secret House of Night.
  No Sign of Life.
  Portrait of My Father, Militant Communist.
Teitelboim, Dora (1914–92)
  Gambling.
  In Your Eyes.
  Jim the Janitor Is Dead.
  Men.
  Threesome.
  War Lullaby.
  Your Arms.
Tejani, Bahadur (b. 1942)
  Lines for a Hindi Poet.
"Tekahionwake" See Johnson, Emily Pauline
Tekeyan, Vahan
  Country of Dust, The.
  Dream.
  Forgetting.
  Prayer on the Threshold of Tomorrow.

  Sacred Wrath.
Tekkan
  No mind, no Buddha, no being.
Telesilla (*fl.* 5th cent.)
  But Artemis, my girls.
Tellegen, Toon (b. 1941)
  If Just For Once.
  Visit, The.
Templeton, Fiona (b. 1951)
  You: The City, *sels.*
ten Berge, H. C. (b. 1938)
  Lusitanian Variant, The, *sels.*
Tendo-Nyojo (1163–1228)
  Sixty-six years.
Teng Yu-pin (*fl.* late 13th cent.)
  Taoist Song: "Empty bag of skin filling with
    desire."
  Taoist Song: "Heaven and hell are men's
    unhappy inventions."
  Taoist Song: "In white clouds, in green
    mountains."
Tengour, Habib (b. 1947)
  Au pays des morts, *sels.*
  Empedocles' Sandal, *sel.*
  In the Country of the Dead.
  Secret in Broad Daylight.
  Secrète au Grand Jour.
Tennant, Edward Wyndham (1895–1916)
  A Bas la Gloire!
  Mad Soldier, The.
Tennant, William (1784–1848)
  Anster Fair, *sels.*
  Papistry Storm'd, *sels.*
Tennyson, Alfred Tennyson, 1st Baron (1809–92)
  Ancient Sage, The.
  As when with downcast eyes we muse and
    brood.
  Babylon.
  Boädicea, *sel.*
  Break, Break, Break.
  Brook; An Idyl, The.
  Charge of the Light Brigade, The.
  Check every outflash, every ruder sally.
  City Child, The.
  Crossing the Bar.
  Dawn, The.
  Dream of Fair Women, A, *sels.*
  Dying Swan, The.
  Eagle, The.
  Enoch Arden, *sels.*
  Flower in the Crannied Wall.
  Forgiving.
  Frater Ave Atque Vale.
  Gardener's Daughter, The, *sels.*
  Guess well, and that is well. Our age can find.
  Higher Pantheism, The.
  How thought you that this thing could
    captivate?
  Human Cry, The.
  Idylls of the King, *sels.*
  If I were loved, as I desire to be.
  In Memoriam A. H. H, *sels.*
  In the Garden at Swainston.
  In the Valley of Cauteretz.
  Kraken, The.
  Lady of Shalott, The.
  Late, late, so late! and dark the night and chill!
  Lines on Cambridge of 1830.
  Locksley Hall.
  Lord of Burleigh, The.
  Mariana.
  Maud [A Monodrama], *sels.*
  May Queen, The.
  Merman, The.
  Miller's Daughter, The.
  Mine be the strength of spirit fierce and free.
  Morte d'Arthur, *sels.*
  Northern Farmer: New Style.
  Ode on the Death of the Duke of Wellington.
  Ode Sung at the Opening of the International
    Exhibition.
  Old Roä.
  Palace of Art, The.
  Princess, The, *sels.*
  Printed in "The Times," May 1859, *sels.*

Recollections of The Arabian Nights.
Revenge, The, *sel.*
Rizpah.
Sonnet: "She took the dappled partridge flecked [*or* fleckt] with blood."
Spinster's Sweet-Arts, The, *sel.*
St. Agnes' Eve.
Tithonus.
To E. Fitzgerald.
To Virgil [*or* Vergil].
To —. With the Following Poem.
Ulysses.

Tennyson, Frederick (1807–98)
Holy Tide, The.
Incident, An.
Iona.
Poetical Happiness.

Teofilov, Ivan (b. 1931)
Falcon, The! His symmetrical confession.
Hills, The: "Unrepeatable, ever-present mirage."
Old City, The.
Ortamezar—The Jewish Quarter.
Shared Existence.
Teenagers.
Turkish Bath in Ortamezar.

Terán, Víctor (b. 1958)
Biluxe.
Duda.
En la palma de mi mano.
Huadxí que ziyaba.
In the Palm of My Hand.
Indecision.
It Was Early Evening.
It's Over.
Lu ti nagana.
Ndaani' batanaya.'
Se acabó.
Seis variaciones acerca del amor.
Six Variations on Love.
Tarde caía, La.
Xhoopa' diidxa' rui' xiinga guendaranaxhii.

Terranova, Elaine
Needlework.
Self-Examination.
Why Your Father Cried.

Terrazas, Francisco de (1525?–1600?)
To a Lady.
To a Pair of Legs.

Terrio, Chris (b. 1970)
Viola Recalls.

Terris, Susan
Ophelia.

Terry, Lucy (c.1730–1821)
Bars Fight [August 28, 1746].

Teschke, Holger (b. 1958)
Documentary Film.
Massacre of the Innocents, The (after Brueghel).
Minutes of Hasiba, The.

Tessho
Finally out of reach.

Tesshu (*fl.* 14th cent.)
How heal the phantom body of its phantom ill.
On Visiting Sokei, Where the Sixth Patriarch Lived.

Tester, Victoria Edwards (b. 1964)
Broken Glass.
First Horses, 1519.
Histories, The.
Santa Rita Massacre, 1837.

Teton Sioux Oral Tradition
I Sing for the Animals.
You Have No Horses.

Tewa Oral Tradition
Song of the Sky Loom.

Thackeray, William Makepeace (1811–63)
At the Zoo.
Ballad of Bouillabaisse, The.
Damages, Two Hundred Pounds.
Dear Jack.
Due of the Dead, The.
King of Brentford's Testament, The *abr.*
Little Billee.

Mahogany Tree, The.
Napoleon.
Sorrows of Werther, The.
Speculators, The.

Thamnaret
Nightsong.

Thatcher, Charles Robert (1831–82)
Dick Briggs from Australia.
Moggy's Wedding.
Taking the Census.

Thaxter, Celia Laighton (1835–94)
Alone.
Chanticleer.
Imprisoned.

Thayer, Ernest Lawrence (1863–1940)
Casey at the Bat.

The Earl of Longford
Careful Husband, The.
Forgetfulness.

Thế Lữ' (Nguyễn Thứ' Lễ) (b. 1907)
Green Nostalgia.

Thelwall, John (1764–1834)
Anacreontic.
On the Rapid Extension of the Suburbs.
To Ancestry.
To Tyranny.
Vanity of National Grandeur, The.

Theocritus (c.310–c.250 B.C.)
Adonis.
Death of Adonis, The.
Epitaph: Justice.
Idylls, *sels.*

Theodoridas (*fl.* 3d cent. B.C.)
Epitaph, An: "This is a drowned man's tomb. Sail on, stranger."

Theognis (*fl.* c.545 B.C.)
Captive.
Second Book of Theognis, The, *sels.*

Theresa [*or* Teresa], Saint, of Avila (1515–82)
Lines Written in Her Breviary.
Poem: "Nothing move thee."

Thésée, Lucie
Beautiful As.
Buckets in My Head, The.

Thesen, Sharon (b. 1946)
Animals.
Broken Cup, The.
Hello Goodbye.
Mean Drunk Poem.

Thicknesse, Lily (*fl.* early 20th cent.)
Siena.

Thiel, Diane (b. 1967)
Minefield, The.

Thiele, Colin (b. 1920)
Radiation Victim.
Tom Farley.

Thieu, Nguyen Quang
Eleven Parts of Feeling, *sel.*

Thimelby, Gertrude Aston (c.1615–c.1670)
Mrs Thimelby, on the Death of Her Only Child.
To Her Husband, on New Year's Day 1651.
Upon a Command to Write on My Father.

Thom *See* Swiss, Thomas

Thom, William (1799?–1848)
Blind Boy's Pranks, The.

Thomas Aquinas, Saint (c.1225–74)
Thee we adore, O hidden Saviour, thee.

Thomas, Claude Anshin
Alone / with only.
Anyone can.
As / the.
Bullet, A / slams.

Thomas, Delaina (b. 1955)
Turning of the Year, The.

Thomas, Dylan (1914–53)
After the Funeral.
Among Those Killed in the Dawn Raid Was a Man Aged a Hundred.
And Death Shall Have No Dominion.
Author's Prologue.
Ceremony after a Fire Raid.
Conversation of Prayer, The.

Do Not Go Gentle into That Good Night.
Especially When the October Wind.
Fern Hill.
Force That through the Green Fuse Drives the Flower, The.
Ghost Story.
Hand That Signed the Paper, The.
Hunchback in the Park, The.
I Have Longed to Move Away.
If I Were Tickled by the Rub of Love.
In My Craft or Sullen Art.
In The Beginning.
Light Breaks Where No Sun Shines.
Marriage of a Virgin, The.
Me and My Bike, *sel.*
Not from This Anger.
O Make Me a Mask.
Over Sir John's Hill.
Parachutist, *sel.*
Poem in October.
Refusal to Mourn the Death, by Fire, of a Child in London, A.
Should Lanterns Shine.
Song of the Mischievous Dog, The.
Spire Cranes, The.
There Was a Saviour.
This Bread I Break.
Twenty-four Years.
Walking in Gardens.
We Lying by Seasand.
When All My Five and Country Senses See.
You shall not despair.

Thomas, Edith Matilda (1854–1925)
Cries of the Newsboy.
Deep-Sea Pearl, The.
Frost To-night.
Shooting Star, A.

Thomas, Edward ("Edward Eastaway") (1878–1917)
Adlestrop.
And You, Helen.
As the Team's Head-Brass.
Aspens.
Barn and the Down, The.
Birds' Nests.
Celandine.
Cherry Trees, The.
Cock-Crow.
Combe, The.
Digging.
February Afternoon.
Fifty Faggots.
Gallows, The.
Glory, The.
Gone, Gone Again.
Green Roads, The.
Gypsy, The.
Haymaking.
Hollow Wood, The.
I never saw that land before.
If I Should Ever by Chance.
In Memoriam (Easter, 1915).
It Rains.
Lights Out.
New House, The.
No One So Much As You.
October.
Old Man.
Out in the Dark.
Owl, The.
Penny Whistle, The.
Private, A.
Rain: "Rain, midnight rain, nothing but the wild rain."
Roads.
She Dotes.
Snow.
Some Eyes Condemn.
Sun Used to Shine, The.
Swedes.
Tale, A.
Tale, A [Revised Version].
Tall Nettles.
Tears.
Thaw.
This Is No Case of Petty Right or Wrong.

Trumpet, The.
When First.

Thomas, Elizabeth (1675–1731)
Dream, The; An Epistle to Mr. Dryden.
Forsaken Wife, The.
Midnight Thought, A. On the Death of Mrs. E.
   H. and Her Little Daughter.
Remedia Amoris.
To Almystrea, on her Divine Works.
To Clemena.
To Colindra.

Thomas, Evan (c.1710–c.70)
To the Gentlewoman of Llanarth Hall.

Thomas, Evan J. (1903–30)
Return, The.
Spectator, The.

Thomas, F. Richard
Behind the Nationalist's Flag.

Thomas, Graham (b. 1944)
At Ynysddu.
Lessons.

Thomas, Gwyn (b. 1936)
For.
Greetings.
Horses.
Killer Dog.
Last Things, The.
Little Death.
Microscope.
Nativity Play, The.
Welsh-speaking Welsh, The.

Thomas, John L. (Ieuan Ddu) (1795–1871)
Harry Vaughan, *sel.*

Thomas, Larry D.
Great Storm, The.
Red Raging Waters, The.

Thomas, Lorenzo (1944–2005)
Another Poem in English.
Argent, L'
Back in the Day.
Bathers, The.
Blues Variations.
Cameo in Sudden Light.
Clear Channel.
Dangerous Doubts.
Discovering America Again.
Downtown Boom.
Dracula.
Electricity of Blossoms.
Embarkation for Cythera.
Even-Tempered Girl Holds Her Breath, An.
Excitation.
Fit Music.
Flash Point.
Foolish Treasures.
Great Love Duets.
Historiography.
Hurricane Doris.
Inauguration.
Instructions for Your New Osiris.
Liquid City.
Magnetic Charms.
Marvelous Land of Indefinitions, The.
Onion Bucket.
Song: "You asked me to sing."
Souvenir of the Manassah Ball.
Subway Witnesses, The.
Twelve Gates.
MMDCCXIII½.

Thomas, Peter (b. 1939)
Lascars, The.

Thomas, R. Hewett
Evacuee, The.

Thomas, R. S. (1913–2000)
Ancients of the World, The.
Blackbird Singing, A.
Bright Field, The.
Calling, The.
Centuries.
Counterpoint, *sel.*
Cry, The.
Cynddylan on a Tractor.
Echoes.
Empty Church, The.

Evans.
Evening.
Expatriates.
Farm Wife.
Geriatric.
Gifts.
Here.
Hill Farmer Speaks, The.
In a Country Church.
Island, The.
Kneeling.
Line from St. David's, A.
Llanrhaeadr Ym Mochnant.
Lonely Farmer, The.
Lore.
Marriage, A.
Moor, The.
Moorland.
Mother and Child.
Navigation.
Nocturne by Ben Shahn.
On the Farm.
Other.
Pavane.
Peasant, A.
Period.
Pietà.
Pisces.
Raptor.
Reservoirs.
Rhodri.
Sir Gelli Meurig.
Song for Gwydion.
Still.
Taliesin 1952.
Via Negativa.
View from the Window, The.
Village, The.
Welsh Hill Country, The.
Welsh History.
Welsh Landscape.
Welsh Testament, A.
Welshman at St. James' Park, A.
White Tiger, The.

Thomas, Robert (b. 1951)
Ensenada Wedding.
Repairing the Hubble Telescope.
Salamander.

Thomas, Sheree Renée
Road from Khartoum, The.

Thomas, Susan
My Grandmother's Birthday.

Thomas, Thomas Jacob ("Sarnicol") (1873–1945)
Dic Siôn Dayfydd.

Thomas, Yumi
Love Poem to an Avocado from a Tomato.

Thompson, Clara Ann (b. 1887?)
After-Glow of Pain, The.
Angel's Message, The.
Autumn Day, An.
Autumn Leaves.
Christmas Rush, The.
Church Bells.
Doubt.
Drift-Wood.
Dying Year, The.
Easter Bonnet, The.
Easter Light, The.
Empty Tomb, The.
His Answer.
Hope.
Hope Deferred.
If Thou Shouldst Return.
I'll Follow Thee.
Johnny's Pet Superstition.
Lullaby: "Hush ye, hush ye! honey, darlin'."
Memorial Day.
Mrs. Johnson Objects.
Not Dead, but Sleeping.
Oh List to My Song!
Old and the New, The.
Opening Service, An.
Out of the Deep.
Parted.
She Sent Him Away.

Skeptic, The.
Storm-Beaten.
Submission.
To My Dead Brother.
Uncle Rube on the Race Problem.
Uncle Rube to the Young People.
Uncle Rube's Defense.
Watcher, The.

Thompson, Donald
On the Relative Merit of Friend and Foe,
   Being Dead.

Thompson, Dorothy Brown (b. 1896)
Good Will to Men—Christmas Greetings in
   Six Languages.

Thompson, Dorothy Perry (b. 1944)
Blues at 1.
Dancing in Menopause.
Intelligence Quotients.
Laurel Street, 1950.
Sister Lakin and Lally.

Thompson, Douglas
Days of Yore, The.

Thompson, Earle (b. 1950)
Juniper Moon Pulls at My Bones, The.
Love Song: "She is a reed swaying in blue."
Mythology.
No Deposit.
Song: "Woman sits on her porch."

Thompson, Edward Palmer (b. 1924)
Homage to Salvador Allende.
My Study.

Thompson, Eloise Bibb *See* Bibb, Eloise

Thompson, Francis (1859–1907)
Any Saint.
Arab Love-Song, An.
At Lord's.
Counsel of Moderation, A.
Daisy.
Envoy: "Go, songs, for ended is our brief,
   sweet play."
Fallen Yew, A.
Grace of the Way, *sel.*
Heart, The, *sels.*
Heaven and Hell.
Hound of Heaven, The, *sel.*
Judgment in Heaven, A, *sels.*
Kingdom of God, The.
Love's Varlets.
Non Pax—Expectatio.
Ode to the Setting Sun, *sels.*
Past Thinking of Solomon.
Poppy, The.
Sister Songs, *sel.*
To a Snowflake.
To Olivia.

Thompson, John (1938–76)
Ghazal 37: "Now you have burned your books,
   you'll go with nothing."
Horse.
Onion, The.
Stilt Jack, *sels.*
Turnip Field.

Thompson, John Randolph (b. 1838)
Lee to the Rear.
Obsequies of Stuart.

Thompson, John Reuben (1823–73)
Burial of Latané, The.
Music in Camp.

Thompson, Kyle (b. 1922)
Appalachia Novena.

Thompson, Maurice (1844–1901)
Address by an Ex-Confederate Soldier to the
   Grand Army of the Republic, An.
Lincoln's Grave.
To the South.

Thompson, Phyllis
At the Nu'uanu Reservoir Pool.
Erato.
Jade.
Shape of Things, The.
Two Photographs.
Window Washing.

Thompson, Priscilla Jane (b. 1882)
Address to Ethiopia.

Adieu, Adieu, Forever.
Adown the Heights of Ages.
After the Quarrel.
Afternoon Gossip, An.
Alberta.
Athelstane.
Autumn.
Autumn.
Christmas Ghost, A.
Common Occurrence, A.
Consumptive, The.
David and Goliath.
Death and Resurrection.
Domestic Storm, A.
Emancipation.
Evelyn.
Examination, The.
Favorite Slave's Story, The.
Freedom at McNealy's.
Fugitive, The.
Glimpses of Infancy.
Happy Pair, A.
Home Greeting, An.
Husband's Return, The.
Hymn: "Lord, within thy fold I be."
In the Valley.
Inner Realm, The.
Insulted.
Interrupted Reproof, The.
Just How It Happened.
Kindly Deed, A.
King's Favorites, The.
Knight of My Maiden Love.
Lines on a Dead Girl.
Lines to an Old School-House.
Lines to Emma.
Little Wren, A.
Muse's Favor, The.
My Father's Story.
Oh, Whence Comes the Gladness?
Old Freedman, The.
Old Saint's Prayer, The.
Old Year, The.
Prayer, A: "Oh, Lord! I lift my heart."
Precious Pearl, The.
Raphael.
Snail's Lesson, The.
Snow-Flakes, The.
Soft Black Eyes.
Song of the Moon.
Song, The: "Oh, foully slighted Ethiope maid!"
Southern Scene, A.
They Are the Same.
Thwarted.
To a Deceased Friend.
To a Little Colored Boy.
To the New Year.
Tribute to the Bride and Groom, A.
Turncoat, The.
Uncle Ike's Holiday.
Uncle Jimmie's Yarn.
Unromantic Awakening, An.
Valentine, A.
Vineyard of My Beloved, The.
While the Choir Sang.
Winter Night, A.

Thompson, Simon (b. 1962)
All Apologies to L. Cohen.
Thompson, Sue Ellen (b. 1948)
Living at the Frost Place.
Thompson, Will Henry (1848–1918)
High Tide at Gettysburg, The.
Thomson, Derick (b. 1921)
Am bodach-ròcais.
An dàrna eilean.
Coimhthional Hiort.
Herring Girls, The.
Lewis.
St Kildan Congregation.
Scarecrow.
Second Island, The.
Stèidhichean Làidir.
Thomson, Edward William (1849–1924)
Aspiration.

Thomson, James (1700–48)
Alfred: A Masque, *sels.*
Castle of Indolence, The, *sels.*
City of Dreadful Night, The, *sels.*
Doom of a City, The, *sel.*
Of a Country Life, *sel.*
On Beauty [*or* Beauety], *sel.*
On the Death of Mr. William Aikman the
  Painter, *sels.*
Paraphrase of the Latter part of the Sixth
  Chapter of St. Matthew, A.
Seasons, The, *sels.*
Songs in the Desert! songs of husky breath.
**Thomson, James ("B. V." *or* "Bysshe Vanolis")
(1834–82)**
City of Dreadful Night, The, *sels.*
In the Room.
Sunday at Hampstead, *sel.*
Sunday up the River, *sels.*
Thomson, Wilson H. (*fl.* 19th cent.)
Contract Mucker, The.
T'Hooft, Jotie (1956–77)
Death, Dark Agent.
Death, Dark Doer.
Worn-Out Pop Song, A.
Thoreau, Henry David (1817–62)
All things are current found.
Any fool can make a rule.
Brother where dost thou dwell?
Dong, sounds the brass in the east.
Fog.
Guido's Aurora.
I Am a Parcel of Vain Strivings Tied.
I am bound, I am bound, for a distant shore.
Indeed Indeed, I Cannot Tell.
Inspiration ("Whate'er we leave to God, God
  does.").
Light-winged smoke, Icarian bird.
Love Equals Swift and Slow.
Low-anchored cloud.
Men say they know many things.
Music.
My life has been the poem I would have writ.
On fields oer which the reaper's hand has
  passed.
On Ponkawtasset, since, we took our way.
Poet's Delay, The.
Pray to what earth does this sweet cold belong.
Rumors from an Aeolian Harp.
Salmon Brook.
Sympathy.
Though All the Fates Should Prove Unkind.
Walden [prose work], *sel.*
When with pale cheek and sunken eye I sang.
Winter and Spring Scene, A.
Thorley, Wilfrid (b. 1878)
Chant for Reapers.
Thorn, Jas. D.
Sigh of the Old Cattleman, The.
Thorne, Ellin (*fl.* c.1576)
Ellin Thorne Songe.
Thorne, Tim (b. 1944)
High Country.
Whatever Happened to Conway Twitty?
Thornton, Russell (b. 1959)
Cherry Laurel, The.
Thornton, Valerie (b. 1954)
Birds of Passage.
Thorpe, John
Man in a Semi-Detached House.
Thorpe, Michael (b. 1932)
Open-Air Museum.
Presence and Process.
Wishful Fall.
Thorpe, Peter
Take-Off.
Thorpe, Rose Hartwick (1850–1939)
Curfew Must Not Ring Tonight [*or* To-Night].
**Thrale [*later* Mrs. Piozzi], Hester Lynch
Salusbury (1741–1821)**
Winter in Wales, A.
Thribb, E. J. (b. 1960?)
In Memoriam Krishna Menon.
In Memoriam Larry Parnes ("Mr Parnes

Shillings and Pence").
In Memoriam Salvador Dali.
Lines on the Award "Pipe Man of the Year" to
  Magnus Magnusson.
Thrilling, Isobel
Mother.
Thumboo, Edwin (b. 1933)
Exile, The: "He was not made for politics."
Thurayya, Malhas
False...False.
Orphan, An.
Thurman, Judith (b. 1946)
Clockface.
Oil Slick.
Zebra.
Thurston, Harry
Dragging Bottom.
Father on My Shoulders.
Revelations.
River Otters at Play.
Thwaite, Anthony (b. 1930)
At Evening.
Freedom.
Great Foreign Writer Visits Age-Old Temple,
  Greeted by Venerable Abbess, 1955.
On Consulting "Contemporary Poets of the
  English Language"
Throes.
Thwaites, Michael (b. 1917)
Jervis Bay, The, *sel.*
Tibbetts, Elizabeth (b. 1953)
Coming Home.
Tibble, Anne (b. 1912)
Trials of a Tourist.
Tibi, Lina (b. 1963)
Failure.
If Only.
Striding, shuddering.
Suicide.
Voice, A.
Tibullus (Albius Tibullus) (c.59–c.19 B.C.)
Adde Merum Vinoque, *sel.*
Cross the Aegean Without Me, Then, Messalla.
Peace.
Priapus, may this shady roof forever.
Tibullus, Albius *See* Tibullus
Tichborne [*or* Tichbourne], Chidiock (1558–86)
Tichborne's Elegy.
Tickell, Thomas (1686–1740)
Fragment of a Poem on Hunting, A, *sels.*
To the Earl of Warwick, on the Death of Mr.
  Addison.
Ticknor, Francis Orrery [*or* Orray] (1822–74)
Little Giffen.
Virginians of the Valley, The.
Tidjani-Cissé, Ahmed (b. 1947)
Home News.
Tiger, Madeline J.
Lovepoem Writing Me.
Tighe, Mary (1772–1810)
Address to My Harp.
As one who late hath lost a friend adored.
Can I look back, and view with tranquil eye.
1802.
On Receiving a Branch of Mezereon Which
  Flowered at Woodstock, December 1809.
Poor, fond deluded heart! wilt thou again.
Psyche, *sels.*
Sonnet Addressed to My Mother.
To Death.
When glowing Phoebus quits the weeping
  earth.
Wine, I Say! I'll Drink to Madness!
Written at Killarney. July 29, 1800.
Written at Rossana. November 18, 1799.
Written at Scarborough.
Written at the Eagle's Nest, Killarney. July 26,
  1800.
Written in Autumn.
Tikhonov, Nikolai Semionovich (1896–1979)
Fire and Rope, Bullet and Axe.
Tilak, Devarakonda Balagangadhara (1922–66)
Night It Rained Life, The.

Police Report.
Prayer, A: "God / save this country."

Tilden, Stephen (1690–1766)
Song of Braddock's Men, The.

Tillema, Mieke (b. 1944)
Considering Tulips.
So Soon ("So soon, so tired.").
So Soon ("So soon—so without tomorrow.").
Tulips.

Tilley, H. H.
Citizen BOR Speaking, *sel.*

Tillinghast, Richard (b. 1940)
Table.

Tilsley, Gwilym R. (1911–1976)
Ode in Praise of the Coalminer, An, *sel.*

Timoner, Jennifer
Business of Health, The.
Earliest Crows in Mineral.
Eye Occupation, The.
Push the Feathered Glory.

Timpson, Reggie
For Lester.
Verbal gun shots.

Timrod, Henry (1828–67)
Carmen Triumphale.
Carolina.
Charleston.
Christmas.
Cotton Boll, The.
Dreams.
Ethnogenesis.
I know not why, but all this weary day.
La Belle Juive.
Ode: "Sleep sweetly in your humble graves."
Retirement.
Unknown Dead, The.

Tindal, Henrietta (1818–79)
Birth Wail, The.
Cry of the Oppressed, The.

Tindley, Charles A. (1859–1933)
Stand by Me.

Tinódi, Sebestyén (1505 *or* 1510–56)
Call to Lieutenants, *sel.*
Chronicle of Sigismund, The, *sel.*
Fall of Zolnok, The.

"Tipcuca" *See* Wilson, T. P. Cameron

Tipper, Elizabeth (*fl.* 1698–1704)
Pilgrim's Viaticum; or, The Destitute, But Not
    Forlorn, *sels.*
Some Experimental Passages of My Life, with
    Reflections upon Jacob's Words, Few and
    Evil Have the Days of the Years of My Life
    Been.

Tipping, Richard (b. 1949)
Casino.
Just after Michael's Death, the Game of Pool.
Mangoes.
Men at Work.
Poet at Work.
When You're Feeling Kind of Bonkers.

Tipton, James
I Want to Speak With the Blood that Lies
    Down.
I Wanted You in the Kitchen of My Heart.
There Are Rivers of Oranges.

Tiruvalluvar (*fl.* c.500)
Kural, The, *sels.*

Titherage, Dion (1889–1934)
And Her Mother Came Too.

Tjinapirrgarri
Emu Shot.

Tkachenko, Aleksandr Petrovich (b. 1945)
Battle.
Dynamo Stadium, 1980.
Engraving, An.
Like Thousands of Others.

Tkhorzhevskaya, Vitalina (b. 1971)
He wouldn't sign the death warrant.
Silence: "This is addressed to you—A century
    later."
Wild Rose.

Tlingit Oral Tradition
Carrying My Mind Around.

Toadhouse *See* Graham, Allan

Tobin, Daniel
At the Egyptian Exhibit.
Bridge View.
Deep Shit.
Floor Scrapers.
For Christine at the Frost Farm.
Hunt-Cup, The.
Pigeons.

Tobrise, Mabel (b. 1965)
Dyeing.

Todd, Mark
Game Trail, The.
Grandmother's Farm.
Mud Season.
Post Scriptum.
Rigby.
Son et Lumière.
To Kill Stray Dogs.
Wire Song.

Todd, Ruthven (1914–78)
About Scotland, &C.
Of Moulds and Mushrooms.
Personal History; for My Son.

Todhunter, John (1839–1916)
Moment, A.
Song: "Bring from the craggy haunts of birch
    and pine."

Togawa, Akira (b. 1903)
Distorted Sun.

Tohe, Laura
She Was Telling It This Way.

Tokareva, Yana (b. 1976)
Brief reflection on the greatness of God.
On Russian Poetry (1996-2000), *sels.*
Why is she sleeping on some steps.

Tokoku
Mad Verse.

Tokuo (1649–1709)
Town's aflame with summer heat, The.

Toledo, Natalia (b. 1967)
Agrícola.
Agrícola.
Bandaa sti bianni.
Bertha Beninu.
Bertha Beninu.
Bertha Beninu.
Ca gunaa rusianda.
Cadidi Laaga Lua.
Casa de Olga, La.
Cielo Min.
Cielo Min.
Curanderas.
Dxiibi Guidxa.
Espanto tonto.
Guibá xti min.
Healers.
Liidxi na Olga.
Marcelina.
Marcelina.
Marcelina.
Na Agrícola.
Na Aurea.
Na Aurea.
Na Aurea.
Na hermila limón.
Na Hermila Limón.
Na hermila limón.
Na tacha.
Na Tacha.
Na tacha.
Na Victórica litru.
Na Victórica Litru.
Na Victórica litru.
Natalia.
Natalia.
Natalia.
Olga's House.
Revelación.
Revelation.
Shadow That Draws the Light, The.
Silly Ghost.
Sombra que dibuja la luz, La.
Temple.
Templo.

Yudu.
Zenaida.
Zenaida.
Zenaida.

Tolkien, John Ronald Reuel (1892–1973)
Man in the Moon Stayed up To Late, The.

Tollet, Elizabeth (1694–1754)
On Loving Once and Loving Often.
Winter Song.

Tolliver, Imani
Fisher King.
Hardest Part About Love, The.
Those i love are sometimes white.

Tolson, Melvin B. (1898–1966)
African China.
Chitterling King, The.
Dark Laughter.
Dark Symphony, *sel.*
Festus Conrad.
Harlem Gallery, *sels.*
Lena Lovelace.
Libretto for the Republic of Liberia, *sels.*
Note, The.
Old Houses.
Old Pettigrew.
Sootie Joe.
Victor Garibaldi.

Tolson, Nancy D.
Bullet Hole Man.

Tomioka, Taeko (b. 1935)
Will You Marry Me?

Tomlinson, Charles (b. 1927)
Above the Rio Grande.
After a Death.
Against Extremity.
Ararat.
Arizona Desert.
At Barstow.
Cavern, The.
Cézanne at Aix.
Crane, The.
Death in the Desert, A.
Door, The.
Farewell to Van Gogh.
Fiascherino.
For Danton.
In Defence of Metaphysics.
In the Borghese Gardens.
In the Studio.
Jam Trap, The.
John Maydew or The Allotment.
Juliet's Garden.
Las Trampas U.S.A.
Matachines, The.
More Foreign Cities.
Mr. Brodsky.
On a Pig's Head.
Paring the Apple.
Picture of J. T. in a Prospect of Stone, The.
Prometheus.
Radial wheels of the season spiked with
    knives, The.
Santa Fe Railroad, The.
Saving the Appearances.
Second Song.
Sense of Distance, A.
Snapshot.
Snow Signs.
Song: "To enter the real."
Stone Speech.
Swimming Chenango Lake.
Two Views of Two Ghost Towns.
Weather Report.
Word in Edgeways, A.
Zipangu, *sels.*

Tompa, Mihály (1817–68)
Autumn.
Bird, to Its Young, The.
Haven of Rest.
Last Poem.
To the Stork.

Tompson, Benjamin (1642–1714)
On a Fortification at Boston Begun by Women
    [American edition].

"Tomson, Graham R." *See* Watson, Rosamund

Marriott

Tong, Raymond
Then suddenly his brain became the sound.

Tongue, Robert Clarkson (1869–1904)
Invention.

Tonks, Rosemary
Badly-Chosen Lover.
Hydromaniac.
Sofas, Fogs, and Cinemas, The.
Story of a Hotel Room.

Tontongi
Go There.
How?

Toomer, Jean (1894–1967)
Beehive.
Blue Meridian, The, *sels.*
Cotton Song.
Delivered at the Knighting of Lord Durgling
  by Great Bruce-Jean.
Evening Song.
Face.
Georgia Dusk.
Gods Are Here, The.
Gum.
Harvest Song.
Her Lips Are Copper Wire.
I Sit in My Room.
It is Everywhere.
Merl.
Nora.
November Cotton Flower.
Nullo.
Our Growing Day.
People.
Portrait in Georgia.
Reapers.
Seventh Street.
Skyline.
Song of the Son.
Storm Ending.

Too-qua-stee *See* Duncan, DeWitt Clinton

Toplady, Augustus Montague (1740–78)
Hymn: "Inspirer and hearer of prayer."
Rock of Ages.

Torgerson, Eric (b. 1943)
Apple from Walt Whitman, An.

Torneol, Nuño Fernández (*fl.* c.1225)
Lady's Farewell, The.

Tornero, Angélica (b. 1959)
And mainly: the dawn symphony blazes
  sudden, reds.
Arden la torcida, entre mis ojos, y la jerarquía
  intermedia de una imagen esta tarde.
Cempasúchil, copal—en la parte alta de librero
  bajo—libamen, oblación.
Cempasúchil, copal—on the top part of the low
  bookcase—libation, offering.
Cosas que se tocan sonidos materiales
  surcaron.
Lisos al extremo cuando voltearon diurnos.
Lo que penetró tu vida—acedo espectáculo
  incrustado en el sitio del espasmo.
Noise in thousands of fissures my sight.
Por levante, vientos blanquecinos sobre mis
  lindes distribuidos.
Ruido en miles de grietas la vista.
Smooth in the extreme when they turned
  around diurnal.
They blaze, between my eyes, the wick-twist
  and the intermediate hierarchy of an image
  this afternoon.
Things touching each other sounds materials
  furrowed.
To the East, whitish winds on my allotted
  boundary lines.
What penetrated your life—acid spectacle
  encrusted in the site of spasm.
Y de fondo: llamaradas la sinfonía del
  lubricán, rojos.

Tornes, Beth (b. 1955)
Sleep.

Torrance, Chris (b. 1941)
Acrospirical Meanderings in a Tongue of the
  Time.

It Is Difficult to Exaggerate the Importance of
  Mushrooms as Food.
Maen Madoc.

Torre, Mónica de la (b. 1969)
Driven by a Strange Desire.
Golfers in the Family.
How to Look at Mexican Highways.

Torregian, Sotère (b. 1941)
After Mayakovsky.
Attitudes.
Golden Palomino Bites the Clock, The, *sel.*

Torrence, Frederic Ridgely (1875–1950)
Son, The.

Torres, Anabel (b. 1948)
Eskimo's Woman, The.
Kettle Rooted to the Void.
Small Miracle, A.
Smash Your Fist.
These Are the Sweet Girls.
Warmness.

Torres Bodet, Jaime (1902–74)
Exodus.
Labyrinth.
Living.
My Country.
Summary.

Torres, Edwin
Bio-Rodent-Oriole.
Breezy Delicious Day.
Drowning in the Last Days of Luxury.
Elbow in Dumberland, An.
Elder Dubb.
Entrancielo.
Gigabyte Me—How Much RAM in Your
  Summer of Love?
How Long Does the Curator Dance For?
Lipsticktion.
Of My Nipple Ring Halos.
Poetry Detective.
Summertime Late Show.
Theorist Has No Samba!, The.
Vase of the Universe, The.

Toscano, Rodrigo (b. 1964)
Meditatio Lectoris.

Toshinari, Fujiwara no Shunzei; *See* Shunzei

Tostevin, Lola Lemire
Gyno-Text.

Tosui Unkei (d. 1683)
Content with chipped bowl and tattered robe.

Tóth, Árpád (1886–1928)
Berzsenyi.
Elegy on a Broom Bush.
Evening Halo of Light, An.
From Soul to Soul.
Non Piu Leggevano.
Pendulum, The.
Retreat.
Serenade at Dawn.
Soul Woven of Shadows.
Until New Spring or Death.

Toufic, Jalal (b. 1962)
Emperor's New Costume, Or the Case of the
  Missing Mask, The.

Touré, Askia Muhammad (b. 1938)
A*boriginal* Elegy: The Once and Future
  Queen.
Azuri.
Dawnsong!
Frontier of Rage, The.
Imani in Sunburst Summer: A Chant.
JuJu.
O Lord of Light! A Mystic Sage Returns to
  Realms of Eternity!
Palenque Queen by Habana's Shores.
Summer Worlds: A Mythic Landscape.

Tourneur, Cyril (1575?–1626)
Revenger's Tragedy, The, *sels.*

Towers, Tarin
Mission Poem.
Three Observations on Belief.

Towle, Tony (b. 1939)
Diptych.
Immaterial Nocturnes: Hudson and Worth.
Night.

North.
Painting the Eaves.
Poem: "Lead drains from your heart on the left
  side, The."
Postmodern Maturity.
Prospects.
Random (Re-arrangeable) Study for *Views*.
Seasonal Ramble.

Townsend, Alison
Hospital Corners.
Persephone in America.
Western Holly Stove.

Townsend, Ann (b. 1962)
After the End.
Bicycle Racers, The.
Butane, Kerosene, Gasoline.
Comings and Goings.
Date Nut Bread.
Day's End.
Dinner Guest, The.
Eighteenth-Century Medical Illustration: The
  Infant in its Little Room.
First Death.
First Quilt.
Institutional Blue.
Mardi Gras Premortem.
Modern Love.
Night Watch in the Laboratory.
Outdoor Chums in the Forest.
Purple Loosestrife.
Rouge.
Shirt Collar, The.
They Call You Moody.
Touch Me Not.

Townsend, F. H. (b. 1893)
To the Cuckoo.

**Townshend [or Townsend], Aurelian (c.1583–
  c.1651)**
Albion's Triumph, *sels.*
Dialogue betwixt Time and a Pilgrim[e], A.
Let not thy beauty make thee proud.
Song: "Though regions farr divided."
To the Lady May.
Upon Kind[e] and True Love.

Toya, Debra Haaland
Hunter's Dance in Early Fall.

Tozan-Gyoso
Way's not for the blind.

Traherne, Thomas (1636–74)
Amendment.
Anticipation, The.
Apostacy, The.
Centuries of Meditations, *sel.*
Childhood.
Christian Ethics, *sel.*
Demonstration, The.
Eden.
Hosanna.
Hymn upon St. Bartholomew's Day, An.
In Salem Dwelt a Glorious King.
Innocence.
Insatiableness.
Instruction, The.
Meditations on the Six Days of the Creation,
  sels.
On the Bible.
Preparative, The.
Rapture, The.
Salutation [or Salutations], The.
Shadows in the Water.
Third Century, The, *sels.*
To the Same Purpos[e].
Wonder.

Traig, Jannifer
For My Sister.

Trail, C.B.
Sonnet: "This is for the afternoon we lay in the
  leaves."

Trakl, Georg (1887–1914)
Birth: "These mountains: blackness, silence,
  and snow."
De Profundis.
Decline.
Descent and Defeat.
Downfall.

Dream of Evil (First Version).
Elis.
Evening, The.
Evening, The: "With the ghostly shapes of
    dead heroes."
From Revelation and Defeat.
Grodek ("All evening the autumn thickets.").
Grodek ("At evening the woods of autumn are
    full of the sound.").
Grodek ("In the evening the autumn woods
    ring.").
Grodek (Second Version).
Heart, The: "Wild heart grew white in the
    forest, The."
In Hellbrunn.
Mood of Depression, The.
Mourning: "Dark eagles, sleep and death,
    The."
On the Eastern Front.
On the Marshy Pastures.
Revelation and Decline.
Romance to Night, A.
Sleep (Second Version).
Song of the Western Countries.
Summer: "At evening the complaint of the
    cuckoo."
Sun, The: "Each day the gold sun comes over
    the hill."
To the Child Elis.
West, The (Fourth Version).
Winter Night, A.

Trammell, Robert
After Hours.
Light Forms.
Nightclub, A: on the Jacksboro Highway.

Tran, Barbara
From Rosary.
Women Next Door, The.

Tran Nhan-tong
Spring View.

Trần Tế Xu'o'ng (1870–1907)
New Year's Season and Its Poetasters, The.
Women.

Trần Thái-Tông, King
To the Monk Dúc Son at Thanh-phong
    Monastery.

Tranströmer, Tomas (b. 1931)
After a Death.
Allegro.
Alone.
April and Silence.
At Funchal.
Below Freezing.
Black Postcards.
Clearing, The.
December Evening, '72.
Eagle Rock.
Elegy.
Facades.
For Mats and Laila.
From March 1979.
Gallery, The.
Haiku, sels.
Homewards.
Morning Bird Songs.
November: "When the hangman's bored he
    turns dangerous."
Out in the Open.
Outskirts.
Scattered Congregation, The.
Schubertiana.
Signatures.
Sketch in October.
Snow is Falling.
Solitude.
Standing Up, sel.
Start of a Late Autumn Novel.
Syros.
To Friends Behind a Frontier.
Track.
Tracks.
Vermeer.

Tranter, John (b. 1943)
Alphabet Murders, The, sels.
Backyard.

Blackout, sels.
Crying in Early Infancy, sels.
Debbie and Co.
Enzensberger at 'Exiles.'
Glow-boys.
Great Artist Reconsiders the Homeric Simile,
    The.
Having Completed My Fortieth Year.
Lufthansa.
Mark.
Moment of Waking, The.
Moonshine Sonata.
Un-American Women, The.

Trapnell, Anna (c.1622–c.1660)
Cry of a Stone, A [or The], sels.
Having Prayed for, and Made Much Mention
    of the Merchants, She Sings the Following
    Hymn to Them.

Trapnell, N. J.
Lament of a Desert Rat.

Trask, Haunani-Kay
Chant of Lamentation.
Sisters.

Travis, Nancy (b. 1967)
At My Father's House.
Church Ladies.
Sunbathing.

Tree, Iris (Mrs. Curtis Moffat) (b. 1897)
Pity the Slain that Laid Away Their Lives.

Tree-Leaf Woman
Who speaks the sound of an echo?

Treece, Henry (1912–66)
Conquerors.
Three Pleas.
Y Ddraig Goch.

Trefusis, Elizabeth (b. 1763)
Valentine, A, sels.

Tregian, Francis (1548–1608)
Imprisoned Recusant Writes to His Wife, An.

Trejo, Ernesto
Cloud Unfolding, The.
Some Sparrows.

Tremayne, Sydney (b. 1920)
Falls of Falloch, The.
Mixed Weather.
North of Berwick.

Tremblay, Gail (b. 1945)
Indian Singing in 20th Century America.
It Is Important.
Medicine Bearer.
Night Gives Old Woman the Word.
Not Sense.
Reflections on a Visit to the Burke Museum,
    University of Washington, Seattle.
Surviving.
To Grandmother on Her Going.
Urban Indians, Pioneer Square, Seattle.

Trench, Herbert (1865–1923)
Charge, A.
Jean Richepin's Song.
Killary.
She Comes Not When Noon Is on the Roses.

Trench, Richard Chenevix (1807–86)
Lord, Many Times.
What is Man?

Trenet, Charles
I Wish You Love (Que Reste-t-il de Nos
    Amours?).

Trentham, Edwina
Hurricane Season.

Tretheway, Eric
Florilegium.
Green Cadillac.
Homesteading.
Near Dawn.
Reading the Signs.
Resurrection at West Lake.
Text of Evening, The.

Trethewey, Natasha (b. 1966)
Amateur Night.
Bellocq's Ophelia.
Cameo.
Collection Day.
Countess P——'s Advice for New Girls.

Domestic Work, 1937.
Drapery Factory, Gulfport, Mississippi, 1956.
Flounder.
Genus Narcissus.
History Lesson.
Hot Comb.
Housekeeping.
Letter Home.
Limen.
Miscegenation.
Naola Beauty Academy, New Orleans,
    Louisiana, 1943.
Native Guard.
Photograph of a Bawd Drinking Raleigh Rye.
Secular.
Storyville Diary, sels.
Vignette.
White Lies.
Zebra.

Tribal Chieftain (c.10th cent.)
Come here, my love, the crown of my home.

Triem, Eve (b. 1902)
For Paul.
Witness, The.

Trigilio, Tony
Body is Fragile, The.
Five Verses for Shariputra Mugged Outside His
    Building.
Sitting, Wedding Morning.

Trinidad, David (b. 1953)
Adam and Eve on the Hollywood Tread Mill.
Answer Song.
Boy, The.
Doll Not Included.
Double Trouble.
Eighteen to Twenty-One, sels.
For Joe Brainard.
Meet the Supremes.
Monday, Monday.
Moonstones.
Movin' with Nancy.
Of Mere Plastic.
Shower Scene in Psycho, The.
Slicker.
Things to Do in Valley of the Dolls (The
    Movie).
Yvette Mimieux in Hit Lady.

Triplett, Pimone (b. 1965)
Fractal Audition.
Manora.
Next to Last Prayer.
Portraits at the Epicenter.
Spectral Dues.
Spider of Doubt.
Story for the Mother Tongue.
Studies in Desire.
Winter Swim.

Tripp, John (b. 1927)
Armistice Day '77, Honiton.
Capital.
Caroline Street, Cardiff.
Connection in Bridgend.
Diesel to Yesterday.
Eglwys Newydd.
Father.
Headmaster.
In Memory of Idris Davies.
Last at Lucy's, The.
On My Fortieth Birthday.
Ploughman.
Twilight in the Library.
Welcome to Wales.

Tritica, John
Approaching the Equinox.
Not Masterpieces, Planting Astonishments.

Trocchi, Alexander (1925–84)
For John Donne: Master Metaphysical.

Trommer, Rosemerry Wahtola
Climbing the Ridge.
If You Listen.
March.
Sonnet for July.

Tropp, Gloria
Poem for Ernie Henry.

Trouillot, Lyonel
  Clay Pot Broken, A.
  I'm Dreaming of Your Body All Nude.
Troup, Bobby (1910–99)
  Baby, Baby All the Time.
  Daddy.
  (Get Your Kicks On) Route 66!
  You're in Love.
  You're Lookin' at Me.
Troupe, Quincy (b. 1943)
  And Syllables Grow Wings There.
  Avalanche.
  Boomerang: A Blatantly Political Poem.
  Change: "Use to be eye would be laying
    there."
  Conjuring Against Alien Spirits.
  Eye Change Dreams.
  Following the North Star Boogaloo.
  Forty-one Seconds on a Sunday in June, in Salt
    Lake City, Utah.
  Gray Day in January in La Jolla.
  In Jimmy's Garden.
  Old Black Ladies Standing on Bus Stop
    Corners #2.
  Old People Speak of Death, The.
  One for Charlie Mingus.
  Poem for "Magic", A.
  Poem for My Father; for Quincy Trouppe, Sr.
  Reflections on Growing Older.
  River Town Packin House Blues.
  Sense of Coolness, A.
  Signals and Demarcations.
  So What.
  Transcircularities.
  View from Skates in Berkeley, The.
Trowbridge, John Townsend (1827–1916)
  Circumstance.
  Idyl of Harvest Time, An.
  Old Lobsterman, The.
  Recollections of "Lalla Rookh."
Trowbridge, William (b. 1941)
  Bad Birds.
  Curtain Call.
  Kong Breaks a Leg at the William Morris
    Agency.
  O Paradise.
  Stark Weather.
  Viet Kong.
  What We Could Do.
Trubridge, B. A. See Vrepont, Brian
Trudell, Dennis
  Jump Shooter, The.
Truitt, Sam (b. 1960)
  Anamorphosis Eisenhower, *sels.*
Trumbull, John (1750–1831)
  M'Fingal, *sels.*
Trungpa, Chogyam (1940–87)
  Beginner in meditation, The.
  Coming home from work.
  Gentle day's flower.
  His parents are having tea.
  Skiing in a red and blue outfit.
Ts'ai Yen (c.177–c.239)
  Poem of Sorrow.
Ts'ai Yung (133–92)
  Stele for Wang Ziqiao.
Ts'ao Ching-chao (fl. 1620)
  Palace Poem.
Tsaloumas, Dimitris (b. 1921)
  Autumn Supper.
  Consolation.
  Epilogue: "My joys are those of the spare
    autumn birds."
  Falcon Drinking.
  Grudge, The.
  Note.
  Old Friend.
  Old Snapshot.
  Progressive Man's Indignation, A.
  Return of an Ikon.
  Song for My Father, A.
Ts'an, Ts'en See Ts'en Shen
Tsanev, Ivan (b. 1941)
  Archaeological Site, An.

  Bee.
  Cricket.
  Express Train.
  Fine Day.
  Koprivshtitsa.
Tsanev, Stefan (b. 1936)
  Dog: "Why do you watch me so sadly and
    inquisitively."
  Nostalgia, or a Painful Return to Memories.
  Old woman leans against the pine tree, The.
  Penguins.
  Rehearsal for a Parade.
  When a Poet is Born.
Tsang, K'o Chia (b. 1905)
  Street Angel, The.
Tsang, Lori
  Girlfriend.
  Lunching.
Ts'ao Chih (192–232)
  Ballad of the Orioles in the Fields.
  Emotion.
  Far-Off Journey.
  Goddess of the Luo, The.
  In the northwest there is a Weaving-lady.
  In the south country there lives a lovely lady.
  Round the tall towers blow many mournful
    winds.
  Tumbleweed that leaves its root and stock,
    The.
  White Horses.
  Woe Indeed!
Ts'ao P'i (187–226)
  Song of Yan, A.
Ts'ao Ts'ao (155–220)
  Bitter Cold: A Song.
  Drinking Song.
  Graveyard Song.
  Song on Enduring the Cold.
  Variant on the Songs of the East and West
    Gates.
  View of the Blue Sea.
Ts'en Shen (Ts'en Ts'an) (715–70)
  On the West Tower in Guozhou.
  Song for General Zhao.
  Song of the Running Horse River, A: Presented
    on Saying Farewell to the Army Going on
    Campaign to the West.
Tso Ssu (fl. 3d cent.)
  Summoning the Recluse.
Tsogyel, Yeshe (757?–817?)
  Listen.
Tsugen Jakurei (1322–91)
  Not a mote in the light above.
Ts'ui Hao (704–54)
  Yellow Crane Tower.
Tsui, Kitty
  Suzy Wong's Been Dead a Long Time.
Tsujii Takashi
  Woman Singing.
Tsung Ch'en (1525–60)
  Song of Selling Flowers.
**Tsvetayeva [or Tsvetaeva], Marina Ivanovna
  (1892–1941)**
  Ancient Song, An.
  And, Not Crying in Vain.
  Attempt at Jealousy, An.
  Attempt at Jealousy, An.
  Bethlehem.
  Beware.
  Cycle Akhmatova, The, *sel.*
  Fatal Volume, The.
  Garden.
  God (3).
  Gold that was my hair has turned, The.
  Horn of Roland, The.
  I am happy to live correctly and simply.
  I Bless the Daily Labor.
  I bless the everyday labor.
  I know the truth—give up all other truths!
  I opened my veins. Unstoppably.
  If the Soul was Born with Pinions.
  Insomnia, *sels.*
  Magdalene.
  March, *sels.*

  Opened my veins—unhaltable.
  Poem of the End, *sels.*
  Poem: "When I look at the falling leaves."
  Poems to Blok, *sels.*
  Staircase.
  To Kiss a Forehead Is to Erase Worry.
  Verses: "Written so long ago, I didn't even."
  White Low Sun . . . , A.
  You, Walking Past Me.
Tsvetkov, Aleksey [or Aleksei] Petrovich (b. 1947)
  Like a ruddy child you fall asleep in
    september.
  To the apostles of history.
Tu Fu [or Du Fu] (712–76)
  After Rain.
  After Solstice.
  After the Harvest.
  Another Spring ("In all the country.").
  Another Spring ("White birds over the grey
    river.").
  At the Sky's End, Thinking of Li Po.
  At the Thatched Hall of the Ts'ui Family.
  Autumn Meditation: 7.
  Autumn Night.
  Autumn Wastes, The: 1 and 2.
  Ballad of the Army Carts.
  Ballad of the Army Wagons, The.
  Ballad on Seeing a Pupil of the Lady Gongsun
    Dance the Sword Mime.
  Becoming a Farmer.
  Brimmed Whole.
  Brimming Water.
  Broken Boat, A.
  By the Winding River.
  By Yangtze and Han.
  Chaos of mountains upon mountains, A.
  Chengtu.
  Ch'iang Village.
  Clear After Rain ("Autumn, cloud blades on
    the horizon.").
  Clear after Rain ("Long after rainfall, Sorceress
    Hills grow dark.").
  Climbing on the Double Ninth Day.
  Coming Home Late at Night.
  Conscription, The.
  Cricket, The.
  Crooked River Meditation.
  Crossing the Border, First Series, *sel.*
  Dawn Landscape.
  Dawn Over the Mountains.
  Daytime Dream.
  Deep in Winter.
  Déjeuner sur l'herbe.
  Departing from Ch'in-chou.
  Descending Through Dragon Gate.
  Draft Board at Shih-hao, The.
  Dragon Gate Gorge.
  Dreaming of Li Po ("Death at least gives
    separation repose.").
  Dreaming of Li Po ("Death separation: sobs
    hard to swallow.").
  Dreaming of Li Po ("Parted by death, we'd
    strangle on our tears.").
  Drinking at Crooked River.
  Drinking with Elder Cheng the Eighth at
    Crooked River.
  Early Rising.
  Empty Purse.
  Empty Purse, The.
  Evening after Rain.
  Evening near Serpent River.
  Evening Shower in Spring, An.
  Facing Snow ("Enough new ghosts now to
    mourn any war.").
  Facing the Snow ("New ghosts weep over lost
    battles.").
  Facing the Snow ("Northern snows invade the
    city.").
  Facing the Snow ("Weeping over battle, many
    new ghosts.").
  Farewell Rhyme.
  Firefly.
  Flying from Trouble.
  For the Recluse Wei Pa.
  Full Moon ("Above the tower—a lone, twice-
    sized moon.").

Going to the Palace with a Friend at Dawn.
Good Rain: A Night in Spring.
Guest, A.
Guest Arrives, A ("North and south of my cottage, spring waters everywhere.").
Guest Arrives, A ("North of my lodge, south of my lodge, spring rivers all.").
Hawk in a Painting, A.
Heading South.
Hearing of Imperial Forces Retaking Ho-Nan and Ho-Pei.
Heavenly River.
Homage to the Painter General Ts'ao.
Homestead.
Hundred Worries, A.
I Pass the Night at General Headquarters.
I Stand Alone.
Impromptu.
In a Village by the River.
In Praise of Rain.
In Seclusion.
Jade Flower Palace ("Stream swirls, The. The wind moans in.").
Jade Flower Palace ("Where the stream winds pine winds linger.").
Journey North.
Journey North, The.
Kindly Rain, The.
Lament for Ch'en T'ao.
Landscape: "Clear autumn opens endlessly away."
Leaving Ch'in-chou.
Leaving Government Offices.
Listless.
Lone Wild Goose.
Loneliness.
Looking at Mount T'ai.
Looking at Mount T'ai-Shan.
Lovely Lady.
Madman, The.
Midnight.
Moon Festival.
Moon on the Cold Flood Festival.
Moon, Rain, Riverbank.
Moonlit Night ("In Fuzhou, far away, my wife is watching.").
Moonlit Night ("This same moon hangs over Fu-chou.").
Moonlit Night ("Tonight, moon over Fu-chou.").
Moonlit Night Thinking of My Brothers.
My Thatched Roof Is Ruined by the Autumn Wind.
New Moon.
New Year's Eve at the Home of Tu Wei.
Night feast at the Tsos.
Night Feast, Zuo Family Village.
Night in a Room by the River.
Night in the Villa by the River.
Night Thoughts While Traveling.
Night Thoughts While Travelling ("Light breeze rustles the reeds, A.").
Night Up in the Tower.
On a Portrait of a Falcon.
On Climbing the Heights on the Ninth Day of the Ninth Moon.
On the River.
On the Spur of the Moment.
Outside the City.
Overnight at Headquarters.
Passing Mr. Sung's Old House.
Passing the Night.
P'eng-ya Road.
P'eng-Ya Song.
Pluie de Printemps, La.
Poem for Mr. Li in Early Spring.
Poem for My Brother Returning to My Farm.
Prelude: "This fugitive between the Earth and Sky."
Presented to Wei Ba, Gentleman in Retirement.
Pressgang at Shihao Village, The.
Pressgang, The.
Quatrain: "Before you praise Spring's advent note."
Quatrain: In Late Sun.
Random Pleasures, sels.

Recruiting Officer of Shih-hao.
Restless Night.
Restless Night ("As bamboo chill drifts into the bedroom.").
Restless Night in Camp, A.
Return, The.
Rising Spring Waters.
River Jade-Gray.
River Pavilion.
Running from Trouble.
Second Letter to My Nephew Wulang.
Sent to the Magistrate of P'eng-chou.
Servant Boy Delivers, The.
Seven Songs Written During the Qianyuan Era While Staying at Tonggu District, sels.
Seven Songs Written while Living at T'ung-ku in 759.
Shady, Shady.
Sick Horse.
Singing Girls (Written in Jest).
Six Choruses.
Sleepless Nights.
Snow Storm.
Song for a Young General.
Song of Pengya.
Song of the Vermeil Phoenix.
Song of the War Wagons.
Song of the War-Carts.
Song of the War-Chariots (Yueh-Fu).
Song of T'ung-ku.
South Wind.
Spring.
Spring Day: Thinking of Li Po.
Spring Homecoming.
Spring Night, Happy Rain.
Spring Rain.
Spring Scene.
Spring View.
Spring View.
Spring Vigil in the Imperial Chancellery.
Standing Alone.
Summer Night.
Summit, A.
Sun Lengthens.
Sun Rises from Water.
Sunset ("How beautiful the river is in spring.").
Sunset ("Sunset glitters on the beads.").
Taking Leave of Two Officials.
Thatch House.
Thatched Hut, The.
They Say You're Staying in a Mountain Temple.
Thinking of Li Po.
Thinking of My Brothers on a Moonlit Night.
Thinking of My Little Boy.
Thoughts, sels.
Thoughts on a Night Journey.
Thoughts, Traveling at Night.
To a Guest.
To Abbot Min the Compassionate.
To Li Po ("Floating cloud follows the sun, The.").
To Li Po ("When the cold wind visits you from the corners of the earth.").
To Li Po on a Spring Day ("Po, the unrivalled poet.").
To Li Po on a Spring Day ("There's no poet quite like you, Li Po.").
To Li Po on a Winter Day.
To My Younger Brother.
To Pi Ssu Yao.
To Wei Pa, a Retired Scholar.
Traveler at Night Writes His Thoughts, A.
Traveler's Pavilion.
Traveling at Night.
Travelling Northward.
Village by the River.
Visit.
Visiting the Monastery at Lung-men.
Visiting Zan, Abbot of Dayun.
Visitors.
Walking Alone by the Riverbank Seeking Flowers.
Wasteland—Gazing Far Away.
Watching the Distances.
West of Hut.

Winter Dawn.
Word from My Brothers.
Written on the Wall at Chang's Recluse Home.
Written on the Wall at Zhang's Hermitage.
Wu-Chueh.
Wu-Chuen.
Yellow Orioles.
Yen-chou City Wall Tower.

Tu Mo (1900–76)
Mandarins Got Their Raise, The.

Tu Mu (803–53)
Basin Pond.
Departing in Early Morning.
Easing My Heart.
Egrets ("Snowy coats and snowy crests and beaks of blue jade.").
Egrets ("With snowy coats, snowy crests, and sapphire bills.").
Mooring at River Ch'in-Huai.
Mountain Walk, A.
Old Love.
Plantains.
Recalling Former Travels, sels.
Red Embankment.
Spring South of the River.
Take the Bottle, and Ascend.
To Judge Han Chuo at Yangzhou.
Too Late.
Tower by the Yangtze River, A.
Unsent.
Wilderness, A.

Tu Shan-fu (fl. 1230)
Tune: "Shua Hai-erh" Country Cousin at the Theater.

Tu Shen-yen (648–708)
Harmonizing a Spring Poem by Premier Lu of Chin-Ling.

Tucker, Mary E. (b. 1838?)
Adieu.
All Alone.
Apple Dumplings.
Arria to Poetus.
Autumn Thoughts.
Beautiful, The.
Beautiful Sea, The.
Blight of Love, The.
Burial of a Fairy Queen.
Charley du Bignon.
Child Life.
Christmas Eve, South, 1865.
Christmas, South, 1866.
Crazed.
Crushed Flower, The.
"Did You Call Me, Father?"
Disappointment.
Drink On.
Drunkard's Wife, The.
Evanishings.
Family Portraits.
Father's Love, The.
First Grey Hair, The.
Found—Who Lost?
Gone.
Heart's Ease.
Hope.
Hugging the Shore.
Humming-Bird, The.
I Am Fashion's Toy.
I am Weary, Mother.
I Smile, but Oh! My Heart Is Breaking.
I Was a Stranger and Ye Took Me In.
Kindness.
Kiss, A.
Knitting.
Life.
Life for a Life.
Lift Me Higher.
Light in Darkness.
Lines on the Death of the Rev. S. K. Talmage.
Lines to an Old Dress.
Little Bell.
Love-letter, A.
Mail Has Come, The.
Mine.
Mistletoe.

Mother's Lament, The.
Mrs. Myrick's Lecture.
My Mother's Voice.
Mysteries of Life.
No Letter.
Old Crib, The.
Only a Blush.
Opium-Eater, The.
Revenge.
Signal Gun, The.
Silvery Fountain.
Soldier Boy's Dream, The.
Speak to Her Tenderly.
Spring.
That Glove.
To Annie.
To Don Juan Baz.
To Fannie.
To Father.
To Mary.
To One Who Sleepeth.
Tryst, The.
Upon Receipt of a Pound of Coffee in 1863.
Wail of the Divorced.
We Met.
Weariness.

Tucker, St. George (1752–1827)
Cynic, The, *sel.*

Tucker, Seth
Boy Exploded on the Corner Today, A.

Tuckerman, Frederick Goddard (1821–73)
As Sometimes in a Grove.
Coralie.
Cricket, The.
Infatuation.
Question, The.
Refrigerium.
Rhotruda.
Sonnet: "And so, as this great sphere (now turning slow)."
Sonnets: First Series, 1854–1860, *sels.*
Sonnets: Second Series, 1854–1860, *sels.*
Sonnets, *sels.*
Sonnets: "Starry flower, the flower-like stars that fade, The."

Tudur Aled (*fl.* c.1480–c.1525)
Stallion, The.

Tuéni, Nadia (1935–83)
Baalbeck.
Beirut.
Cedars.
Certainties in huge colors.
I think of the land and the wheat.
In the Lebanese Mountains.
Tripoli.

Tufariello, Catherine
In Glass.

Tufts, Carol
We Take the New Young Couple Out to Dinner.

Tuglik (*fl.* 19th cent.)
Tuglik's Song.

Tŭgo [*or* Tŭgogok] (*fl.* 692–702)
Ode to Knight Chukchi.

Tuite, Eliza Cobbe, Lady (1764–1850)
To a Friend, Fearful of Being Forgotten in Absence.

Tukaram (1598–1649)
In My View.

Tung Chieh-yüan (*fl.* c.1190–1208)
Master Tung's Western Chamber Romance, *sels.*

Tupper, Martin Farquhar (1810–89)
Art of Giving, The (1850).
Marriage Market, The.
Poor Relation, The; or, Pious Hope Frustrated.
Portrait of a Victorian Author.

Tuqan [*or* Tuquan], Fadwa (b. 1917)
After Twenty Years.
Behind Bars, Sel.
Elegy of a Knight.
Face Lost in the Wilderness.
Gone Are Those We Love.
I Found It.

I Won't Sell His Love.
Prayer to the New Year, A.
Song of Becoming.
To Etan: An Israeli Child from the Kibbutz Ma'oz Hayim.

Tur-Malka, Ayin (b. 1926)
For the Fighters—A Lament.
Heralds of New Jerusalem.
Memorial Service.
Mirror of the Battle.

Turberville, George (c.1540–c.1610)
Hare's Complaint, The.
Love Me, Love My Dog.
Poor Ploughman to a Gentleman for Whom He Had Taken a Little Pains, A.
To His Friend P. of Courting, Traveling, Dicing, and Tennis.
To Spencer.
Woful Words of the Hart, The.

Turcotte, Mark
Battlefield.
Indian Things.
Reflection.

Turell, Jane Colman (1708–35)
Invitation Into the Country, In Imitation of Horace, An, *sel.*
You Beauteous Dames.

Tureski, L.
Song, The: "It's the tone, not the harp."

Turgeniev, Ivan
Insect, The.
Skulls, The.
Sphinx, The.

Turk, Roy (1892–1934)
Ain't That the Way It Goes?
Are You Lonesome Tonight?
Gimme a Little Kiss (Will Ya, Huh?).
I Don't Know Why (I Just Do).
I'll Get By (As Long As I Have You).
Mean to Me.
Walkin' My Baby Back Home.

Turnbull, Gael (1928–2004)
And I Think it Yours.
For Whose Delight.
Residues: Thronging the Heart.
Takings.
There Are Words.
Transmutation ("Boy is amazed to see his father home from work in the afternoon with a bandaged finger, A.").
Transmutation ("Every evening a mother makes up another episode of the same story for her son.").
Transmutation ("It was as if she couldn't know herself. Only other persons could do that.").
Transmutation ("Take severely ill, he is conscious only at brief intervals.").

Turner, Ann
Clean.
Medusa: "Ageing woman combs her hair, The."
Red Flower.
Red-Dress Girl.

Turner, Brian (b. 1944)
Here, Bullet.
Training on the Peninsula.

Turner, Charles Tennyson (1808–79)
Bliss of Heaven, Maria, shall be thine, The.
Buoy-Bell, The.
Country Dance, A.
Dream, A.
Drowned Spaniel, The.
East or West?
Great Britain Through the Ice: Or, Premature Patriotism.
Hence with your jeerings, petulant and low.
Julius Caesar and the Honey-Bee.
Kiss of Betrothal, The.
Letty's Globe.
No trace is left upon the vulgar mind.
On a Vase of Gold-Fish.
Orion.
Prisoner, The.
Supposed to Be Written By One On Whom the Death of an Excellent Woman Has Forced the Conviction of a Future State, *sels.*

Turner, Frederick (b. 1943)
April Wind.
Early Warning.
On the Pains of Translating Miklós Radnóti.
110 Degrees in Dallas.
Poet Gets Drowsy on the Road, The.
Spring Evening.
Texas Eclogues.

Turner, Godfrey (*fl.* c.1878)
Synchoresis.

Turner, Jack (b. 1947)
Plan, The.
TV Movie.

Turner, James
In cities I'm as rare as I'm unwelcome.

Turner, Nancy Byrd (b. 1880)
First Thanksgiving of All.
When Young Melissa Sweeps.

Turner, Steve (b. 1951)
Christmas Is Really for the Children.

Turner, Walter James (1889–1946)
Dancer, The.
Epithalamium: "Can the lover share his soul."
Hymn to Her Unknown.
In Time like Glass.
India.
Lion, The.
Love-song: "Beautiful, delicate bright gazelle, The."
Magic.
Marriage.
Men Fade Like Rocks.
Music of a Tree, The.
Navigators, The.
Reflection.
Robber, The.
Romance.
Seven Days of the Sun, The.
Silence.
Song: "Lovely hill-torrents are."
Sun, The.
Talking with Soldiers.
Tragic Love.
Word Made Flesh, The.

Turner, William Price (b. 1927)
Full Supporting Programme.
Homely Accommodation, Suit Gent.

Turpin, Mark
Box, The.

Tusser, Thomas (c.1524–80)
Five Hundred Points of Good Husbandry, *sels.*

Tutchin, John (1661?–1707)
Foreigners, The.

Tuwayni, Nadia *See* Tueni, Nadia

Tvardovsky [*or* Tvardovskii], Aleksandr Trifonovich (1910–71)
Poem: "Blue snow is turning black, The."

Twain, Mark (Samuel Langhorne Clemens) (1835–1910)
Adventures of Huckleberry Finn, The, *sels.*

Tweedy, Jeff (b. 1967)
Prayer #3: "I have pondered."

Twichell, Chase (b. 1950)
Aisle of Dogs.
All of It, The.
Animal Languages.
Cat and Mirror.
City Animals.
Condom Tree, The.
Dirt.
Ghost Birches.
Horse.
Hunger for Something.
Immortal Pilots, The.
Kerosene.
Let's Talk.
Marijuana.
My Listener.
My Taste for Trash.
Next and Last.
Paper River, The.
Passing Clouds.
Pine.

Private Airplane.
Quality of Striving, The.
Quality of Striving, The ("Eye-catching as a
  dog on a chain.").
Rain in Ivy.
Saint Animal.
Snow in Condoland.
Soul in Space.
Tea Mind.
Topiary Rooster.
Tutelage.
Twiss, Horace (1786 or 1787–1849)
Our Parodies are Ended.
Patriot's Progress, The.
Twomey, Mary
Exchanges in Italy.
Twouyo, Lyonel *See* Trouillot, Lyonel
Tyfield, Thelma (1906–68)
Gifts.
Tyler, N. P.
My Magic Wheel.
Tyler, Parker (1907–74)
Nijinsky.
Tyler, Royall (1757–1826)
Contrast, The, *sels.*
Tyler, Tanya
Zizwe.
Tymnes (*fl.* 2d cent. B.C.)
Maltese Dog, A.
Stone says that it covers here the white dog,
  The.
Tynan Hinkson, Katharine (1861–1931)
Blind Country.
Dead-Tryst, The.
I Wonder Why.
I would choose to be a doorkeeper.
Lux in Tenebris.
Of an Orchard.
Prayer, A.
Sheep and Lambs.
Tynes, Maxine (b. 1950)
Womanskin.
Tyrwhit, Lady Elizabeth (*fl.* c.1548–82)
Hymne of the Daie of Judgment, The.
Hymne of the State of all Adams Posteritie,
  An.
Tyson, Ian *See* John, Richard Johnny
**Tyutchev, Fyodor [or Feodor] Ivanovich (1803–
73)**
At Vshchizh.
Last Love.
Past, The.
Silentium.
To His Wife.
Tzara, Tristan (1896–1963)
Approximate Man, The, *sels.*
Chanson Dada.
Cheval, Le.
Cosmic Realities Vanilla Tobacco Wakings.
Dada Manifesto on Feeble and Bitter Love,
  sels.
Death of Guillaume Apollinaire, The.
Dompteur de lions se souvient, Le.
For Robert Desnos.
Géant Blanc Lépreux du paysage, Le.
Great Lament of my Obscurity Three, The.
Horse, The.
Lion Tamer Remembers, The.
Maison Aragon.
Metal Coughdrops.
Mort de Guillaume Apollinaire, La.
Poemes Negres, *sels.*
Proclamation without Pretention.
Réalités cosmiques vanille tabac éveils.
Waking.
White Giant Leper of the Countryside.
Zurich Chronicle February 1916.
Tzara, Tristan *See Also* Huelsenbeck, Richard
Tzu Yeh (*fl.* 3d–4th cent.)
Admonition.
All Night.
Bare branches tremble, The.
Bitter Harvest.
Busy in the Spring.

End to Spring, An ("Spring has vanished.").
End to Spring, An ("Your leaving brought an
  end to spring.").
I had not fastened my sash over my gown.
Illusions.
It is night again.
Late Spring.
Lotus Lover, The.
Smile, A.
So soon. Today, love, we.
Song: "Longing, I watch out the open
  window."
Song: "Winter skies are cold and low."
When I started wanting.

U

U Sam Oeur (b. 1936)
Loss of My Twins, The.
U T'ak (1263–1342)
Sticks in one hand.
Wind that melted the spring hills, The.
U Tam'si Tchicaya (b. 1929)
Treasure, The.
Udeozo, Obu (b. 1956)
Slave Boat.
Tomato.
Uflyand [or Ufliand], Vladimir (b. 1937)
It has for ages been observed.
Now, at last, even Nikifor's a suitor.
Peasant, The.
Working week comes to an end, The.
Ujević, Tin (1891–1955)
Green branch with a sadness of yellow fruit.
Ukon, Lady (*fl.* 10th cent.)
Me.
Ulacia, Manuel (1953–2001)
Aegean Sea.
Arabian Knight.
Arabian Knight.
Conrail Wax Museum.
Conrail Wax Museum.
En el Ritz de Meknés.
En la playa.
En un baño de vapor.
Hampstead Heath.
Hampstead Heath.
In the Ritz at Meknes.
In the Steam Bath.
Mar Egeo.
On the Beach.
Regreso a la ciudad.
Return to the City.
Stone at the Bottom, The.
Tenochtitlán Blues.
Tenochtitlán Blues.
Visit to Turk's Head Pub.
Visita al Turk's Head Pub.
Ulku, Alpay (b. 1964)
History.
Lullaby: "You are safe / You are lying in a
  hammock."
Spring Forward, Fall Back.
Ullman, Leslie (b. 1947)
Dreams by No One's Daughter.
History of Women, The.
Hotwire.
Living Near the Plaza of Thieves.
Memo.
1945.
Rain.
Resolve.
Rose Quartz.
Running.
Way Animals Are, The.
Why There are Children.
Ulrich, Anton (1633–1714)
Dying Song.
Umoja, Mbali
Say Something: A Change Is Gonna Come.
Umpierre, Luz Maria (b. 1947)
No Hatchet Job.

Only the Hand That Stirs Knows What's in the
  Pot.
Statue, The.
Unaipon, David *See* Ngunaitponi
Unamuno, Miguel de (1864–1936)
Beside Christ's Lake in Aldehuela de Yeltes,
  on a Night with a Full Moon.
Black Heart.
Cancionero *Diario Poético* 1928–1936, *sels.*
Cristo Yacente de Santa Clara (Iglesia de la
  Cruz) en Palencia, El, *sel.*
Dead Christ Lying in the Church of Santa
  Clara (Church of the Cross) in Palencia,
  The, *sel.*
Delicately Sloping Neck, The.
En Casa Ya, *sels.*
En un Cementerio de Lugar Castellano.
How Quiet under the Earth.
In a Castilian Graveyard.
Incidentes Domésticos, *sels.*
It Is Night, in My Study.
Nevada es silenciosa, La.
On Reading Jules Renard's Diary.
Snowfall Is So Silent, The.
Throw Yourself Like Seed.
Uncho
Forty-nine years / —What a din!
U'ng Binh (1877–1961)
At the Exiled King's River Pavilion.
Ungar, Lynn
Common Prayer.
Groundhog Day.
Ungaretti, Giuseppe (1888–1970)
Babel.
In Memoriam: "His name was / Mohammed
  Sceab."
Morning.
Rivers, The.
Soldiers.
Wake.
Watch.
Where the Light.
Whole night, A.
You Were Broken.
Unger, Barbara
Observance.
Photo Taken in Winter, 1944.
Ungo Kiyo (1583–1659)
Whirled by the three passions, one's eyes go
  blind.
Ungria, Ricardo M. de
Carillonneur.
Commerce and the Man.
Culture Nervous.
Sui Veneris/The Poet of No Return.
Unknown, formerly at. to Homer
Batrachomyomachia; The Battle of the Frogs
  and Mice, *sel.*
Unknown, fr. Egyptian hieroglyphics
He is the love-wolf.
Is there anything sweeter than this hour?
Little sycamore she planted, The.
My lover is a lotus blossom.
Unknown, fr. Sumerian cuneiform
Courtship of Inanna and Dumuzi, The, *sel.*
Unknown, fr. Terezin Concentration Camp
Birdsong.
Birdsong 2.
Closed Town, The.
Concert in the Old School Garret.
Dusk.
Forgotten.
Homesick.
Letter to Daddy, A.
Night in the Ghetto.
On a Sunny Evening.
Pain Strikes Sparks on Me, the Pain of Terezin.
Theresienstadt's Hospital.
Unknown, sometimes at. to Sir Walter Ralegh
As You Came from the Holy Land [of
  Walsingham].
Untermeyer, Jean Starr (1886–1970)
Autumn.
Country of No Lack.
Dew on a Dusty Heart.

False Enchantment.
High Tide.
Sinfonia Domestica.
Untermeyer, Louis (1885–1977)
Caliban in the Coal Mines.
Dark Chamber, The.
Down-hill on a Bicycle.
End of the Comedy.
Food and Drink.
Imperial Airways.
Koheleth.
Last Words before Winter.
Long Feud.
Mother Goose Up-to-Date, *sels.*
Portrait of a Machine.
Prayer: "God, though [*or* although] this life is but a wraith."
Repentance.
Robber, The.
To a Vine-clad Telegraph Pole.
Truce.
Victor, The.
Updike, John (b. 1932)
Air Show.
Child's Calendar, A.
Dea ex Machina.
Dog's Death.
Ex-Basketball Player.
I Missed His Book, but I Read His Name.
In Extremis.
Insomnia the Gem of the Ocean.
Newlyweds, The.
On the Inclusion of Miniature Dinosaurs in Breakfast Cereal Boxes.
Open Letter to Voyager II, An.
Perfection Wasted.
Player Piano.
Richmond.
Saying Goodbye to Very Young Children.
Seagulls.
Snapshots.
Some Frenchmen.
To Two of My Characters.
Two Hoppers.
V. B. Nimble, V. B. Quick.
Upton, Charles
Panic Grass, *sel.*
Upton, Elaine Maria (b. 1945)
Streetwalker Trying to Speak to Sojourner Truth, A.
Upton, Lee
Beatrix Potter.
Bedtime Story.
Civilian Histories.
Contortionist.
Destruction of Daughters.
Ditch, The.
Gertrude to Hamlet.
Happiness: "In the hot white dome of air."
Imagination of Flowers, The.
Jim's Hairball.
Quality of Mercy, The.
Scarlet Letter, The.
Scroll.
Somewhere So Lush.
Table, The.
Window Seat at the Paradise.
Women's Labors.
Urdang, Constance (b. 1922)
All Around Us.
At Frank 'n' Helen's.
Back Far Enough, Down Deep Enough.
Birth of Venus.
Muse Is Always the Other Woman, The.
My Father's Death.
Old Wives' Tales.
Portrait.
Returning to the Port of Authority: A Picaresque.
This Poem.
Urquiza-Vicente, Ivan
Spare Tire *(the atheist's unmailed letter to god).*
Ursachi, Mihai (b. 1941)
Monologue, A.

Urusova, Ekaterina (1747–1816?)
Heroides: Dedicated to the Muses, *sel.*
Usborne, Richard (b. 1910)
Epitaph on a Party Girl.
Uschuk, Pamela
Of Simple Intent.
Usher, Leila (1859–1955)
I Am the Cat.
Utkin, Iosif Pavlovich (1903–44)
Tale of Red-Haired Motele, Mister Inspector, Rabbi Isaiah and Commissar Blokh, The.
Utting, Susan
Spoon Maker's Daughter, The.
Uvavnuk (fl. 19th cent.)
Shaman Song.
Uyematsu, Amy
December 7 Always Brings Christmas Early.
Deliberate.
Fortune Cookie Blues.
Lone Pine.
Near Roscoe and Coldwater.
Same Month They Bombed Cambodia, The.
Tea.
Ten Million Flames of Los Angeles, The.
30 Miles from J-Town.
To All Us Sansei Who Wanted to Be Westside.

V

Vacietis, Ojars
Goodbye to a Spaceman.
Vagura
Love Poem, A.
"Vaidehi" (Janaki Srinivas Murthy) (b. 1945)
Girl in the Kitchen.
Vail, Alice Ewing
Coons in the Corn.
Vajda, János (1827–97)
Comet, The.
In the Forest of Vaal.
Lusitanian Song.
On The Reedy Lake.
Thirty Years After.
Times Gone By.
Twenty Years After.
Vala, Katri (Karen Alice Heikel) (1901–44)
Bridge.
Valachová, Lenka (b. 1973)
Sterile Dish, The.
Valdés, Gina (b. 1943)
English con Salsa.
Valduga, Patrizia (b. 1953)
And This is a Beautiful Night That in the Heart.
I Despair Because I Don't Have Words.
Other Simulation, The.
Why Are Those Who Are Loved So Dull and Leaden?
Word Knows How to Seduce the Flesh, The.
Vale, Edmund (1888–1969)
Bowl Over, Wheel.
Valek, Miroslav
Beating the Drum in Reverse.
Valente, José Ángel (1929–2000)
Con Palabras Distintas.
Elegía Incompleta, Una.
Elegy That Was Never Finished, An.
Empty Place at the Celebration, An.
Evening Before, The.
Lugar Vacío en la Celebración.
Mañana, La.
Morning: "Naked morning, the day's transparent."
No Man's Land.
Tierra de Nadie.
Víspera, La.
With Plain Words.
Valentine, Jean (b. 1934)
American River Sky Alcohol Father.
Annunciation: "I saw my soul become flesh breaking open."
Bit of Rice, A.

Bride's Hours, A.
Death Asphodel.
December 21st.
Drinker's Wife Writes Back, The.
Elegy for Jane Kenyon (2).
Everyone Was Drunk.
First Station, The.
Forces.
Forgiveness Dream, The: Man from the Warsaw Ghetto.
Free Abandonment Blues, The.
In the Burning Air.
Letter: "Hornet holds on to the curtain, winter, The."
Lines in Dejection.
Messenger, The.
Night: "From this night on God let me eat."
Night Lake.
One You Wanted to Be Is the One You Are, The.
Pen, The.
She Would Long.
Skate.
Sleep Drops Its Nets.
Snow Landscape, in a Glass Globe.
Summer Was Not Long Enough, The.
Sunset at Wellfleet.
To My Soul.
Trust Me.
Truth.
Under Voice, The.
Waiting.
X.
Yield Everything, Force Nothing.
Valentine, Jean (b. 1934) *and* Anne Frydman
River at Wolf, The.
Valentine, Stephen
How to Thank God for Your Loneliness.
Valerie, Jean (b. 1953)
Astrology?
Lesson on Braces.
On Apologies.
Valéry, Paul (1871–1945)
Cimetière marin, Le.
Crusoe.
Fileuse, La.
Girl with Mind Wandering.
Graves by the Sea, The.
Graveyard by the Sea, The.
Helen ("I am the blue! I come from the lower world.").
Helen ("It is I, O Azure, come from the caves below.").
Helen ("O Light, 'tis I, who from death's other shores.").
Oarsman, The.
Rameur, Le.
Seaside Cemetery, The.
Spinner, The.
Valiente, Doreen
Charge of the Goddess, The.
Vallejo, César (1892–1938)
Agape.
And What If after So Many Words.
Anger.
Anger that Breaks a Man Down into Boys, The.
Anger that Breaks the Man into Children, The.
Babble.
Black Cup, The.
Black heralds, The.
Black Heralds, The.
Black Messengers, The.
Black Riders, The.
Black Stone Lying on a White Stone.
Black Stone on a White Stone.
Conflict Between the Eyes and the Gaze, The.
Dead Idyll.
Distant Footsteps, The.
Down to the Dregs.
España, Aparta de me Este Caliz, *sels.*
Eternal Dice, The.
Finished the stranger, with whom, late.
Footfalls of a Great Criminal, The.
God: "I feel that God is traveling."

Good Sense.
Have You Anything to Say in Your Defense?
Hungry Man's Wheel, The.
I Am Going to Speak of Hope.
I Am Going to Talk About Hope.
I'm thinking of your sex.
In That Corner Where We Slept Together.
In that corner where we slept together.
In the Moment.
Intensity and Height.
It was Sunday in the fair ears of my burro.
Man Walks By with a Loaf of Bread on His
     Shoulder, A.
Mule Drivers, The.
Need to Die, The.
Our Daily Bread.
Poem to Be Read and Sung ("I know there is a
     person.").
Poem to Be Read and Sung ("I know there is
     someone.").
Right Meaning, The.
Roll Call of Bones, The.
Spain, Take Away This Cup from Me [España,
     Aparta de Mí Este Cáliz], *sels*.
Spain, Take [Away] This Cup from Me
     [España, Aparta de Mí Este Cáliz], *sels*.
Spider, The.
Telluric and Magnetic.
Three hundred womanly states of the Eiffel
     Tower are frozen, The.
To My Brother Miguel.
Today I like life much less.
Trilce, *sels*.
Valley-Fox, Anne *See* Fox, Anne Valley
Van Cleave, Ryan (b. 1972)
Confession #1.
Hamlet at the Paris Aerobleu.
Ophelia on a Graveled Garden Walk in
     Purgatory.
Van Clief-Stefanon, Lyrae
Strip.
Van de Woestijne, Karel (1878–1929)
Fever Tune.
I Am the Hazel-Nut.
Oars Heavy with Seaweed, The.
Van den Bergh, Herman (1896–1967)
Nocturn: "Moon rows burning, The."
Van Doesburg, Theo (1883–1991)
Remembrance of the Founts of Night.
Still Life: The Table.
Van Doren, Mark (1894–1973)
Axle Song.
Distant Runners, The.
Dream of Trains, A.
Escape, The.
First Poem, The.
Former Barn Lot.
Good Appetite.
Immortal.
Midland.
My Brother Lives Too Far Away.
Near House, The.
Orbit.
Pulse, The.
Slowly, Slowly Wisdom Gathers.
So Simple.
This Amber Sunstream.
Where I Saw the Snake.
Whisperer, The.
Van Duyn, Mona (b. 1921)
Causes.
Christmas Card, After the Assassinations, A.
Condemned Site.
Falling in Love at Sixty-Five.
Gardener to His God, The.
Homework.
In Bed with a Book.
Into Mexico.
Late Flight of The Love God.
Letters from a Father.
Mockingbird Month.
Moose in the Morning, Northern Maine.
One Strategy for Loving the World.
Open Letter from a Constant Reader.
Poets in Late Winter.

Relationships.
Sonnet for Minimalists.
Stream, The.
Twins, The.
View, A.
Vision Test, The.
What the Motorcycle Said.
Wish to Be Believed, The.
Van Dyke, Cheryl
Birth, 1975.
Van Dyke, Henry (1852–1933)
America for Me.
Foundation.
Gospel of Labor, The.
Reliance.
Victoria.
Work.
Van Eeden, Frederick (1860–1932)
City Evening.
North Wind, The.
Van Hanh (d. 1018)
Body of Man, The.
Van Haren, Elma (b. 1954)
Stepping Out With Edvard Munch ("When
     from the other world you.").
Stepping Out With Edvard Munch ("When
     from the virile grave.").
Van hee, Miriam (b. 1952)
December.
van Hirtum, Marianne (1935–88)
And I Shall Be the Mouth of Copper.
In Those Rooms.
Naked Truth, The.
Vampiro Nox.
While We Spend Our Lives Ironing.
Van Hoddis, Jakov (1887–1942?)
End of the World.
Van Jordan, A.
Dance Lesson, A.
If I Write a Poem.
My Father's Retirement.
Question: "*What up, brother?* the white teen
     with dreadlocks."
Van Ostaijen, Paul (1896–1928)
Landscape.
Murderers, The.
Ode to Singer.
Song of the Alpine Hunter.
Souvenir.
Van Peenen, H. J.
Insulin Receptor.
Will Campbell Displays His Craniotribe.
Van Riessen, René (b. 1954)
Old in Overijssel.
Van Rooten, Luis d'Antin (1906–73)
Mots d'Heures: Gousses, Rames, *sels*.
Van Sertima, Ivan (b. 1935)
Volcano.
Van Vliet, Eddy (b. 1942)
City, The.
Coastline, The.
Courtyard, The.
Old Champagne Glass.
Party.
Valediction—To My Father.
Van Walleghen, Michael (b. 1938)
Crabapples.
Elephant in Winter, The.
Happiness.
In the Chariot Drawn by Dragons.
More Trouble with the Obvious.
Walking the Baby to the Liquor Store.
Van Winckel, Nance (b. 1951)
Appetite, the Great Painting.
As is His Wont.
Avant-Garde, The.
Back When.
Basket with Blue Ox.
Let Me Remind You You Are Still under Oath.
Nicholas by the River.
Watching the Men Walk.
Vancrevel, Laurens (b. 1941)
About Time ("At dusk the silence by the
     sea.").

About Time ("This silence at the sea's edge, so
     late in the afternoon.").
Vandas, Drahomira (b. 1919)
Egg Hatches Out a Flame, An.
Light Throws Shadows.
Rain Man.
Vander Ven, Tom
Sea Washes Sand Scours Sea.
Vando, Gloria
Blanca's Red Lips.
Commonwealth, Common Poverty.
Father's Day.
In the Crevices of Night.
In the Dark Backward.
Knife.
Lydia's Phantasmagoria.
My Mother Cunning, Yet Innocent.
Ode to Your Back.
Swallows of Salangan.
Vanek, John A.
People's Republic, The.
Vanek, Mary
Homing Instinct.
Summer Begins Outside Dalhart, Texas.
Vanhomrigh, Esther (1690–1723)
Hail, Blushing Goddess, Beauteous Spring!
Vanshenkin, Konstantin Iakovlevich (b. 1925)
Forest in winter, The! From edge to edge.
Girl dreams of her lover at night, The.
Path, The.
Rain.
Sunset fades, and from the little hill, The.
We came back late from visiting.
Varchi, Benedetto (1503–65)
What part of my holiest and most beautiful
     feelings.
Varela, Blanca (b. 1926)
Madonna.
Várnai, Zseni (1890–1981)
To My Soldier Son.
Varon, Lee (b. 1950)
Pink magnolias, the punishment.
Vas, István (1910–91)
Armageddon.
Beethoven's Old Age.
Coventry Cathedral.
Deaf Mute Girl, The.
From the Admonitions of St. Theresa of Avila.
In the Roman Forum.
Invisible Element, The.
Lion, The.
Rhapsody: Keeping Faith.
Romanus Sum.
Santa Maria Antiqua.
Through the Smoke.
Through Time's Segments.
Understanding.
Upon a Drawing.
Xenophon's Song.
Vasalis, M. (b. 1909)
Idiot in the Bath, The.
Sotto Voce.
Vásárhelyi, András (d. 1526)
Song to the Virgin Mary.
Vashon, George Boyer (1824–78)
Vincent Ogé.
Vâsıf, Enderunlu (d. 1824)
Gazelles have bound their hearts, The.
Vasileva, Elena (b. 1964)
I used to be your echo.
I wish I could look.
She's calling God, she wants to ask Him.
Vasquez, Robert
At the Rainbow.
Early Morning Test Light over Nevada, 1955.
For Jose Mercado Vasquez and Frances Roman
     Vasquez.
Pismo, 1959.
Vatsyayan, Sachidananda Hirananda *See*
     "Agyeya"
Vaughan, David Kirk
Lonely Impulse of Delight, A—W.B. Yeats.

Vaughan, Henry ("Silurist") (1622?–95)
Abel's Blood.
And do they so?
Anguish.
Ascension Hymn.
Bird, The.
Book, The.
Charnel-house, The.
Childhood.
Cock-crowing.
Corruption.
Day of Judgement.
Death.
Death.
Disorder and Frailty.
Dwelling-Place, The.
Easter Hymn.
H. Scriptures.
I Walked [or Walkt or Walk'd] the Other Day
   to Spend My Hour.
Incarnation and Passion, The.
Invitation to Brecknock, An, sel.
Isaac's Marriage.
Jacob's Pillow, and Pillar.
Joy of My Life! While Left Me Here.
Kingdom of Heaven Compared to a Grain of
   Mustard-Seed, The.
Knot, The.
Lamp[e], The.
Love and Discipline.
Man.
Midnight.
Morning-Watch, The.
Nativity, The.
Night, The.
Peace.
Pilgrimage, The.
Pursuit[e], The.
Quickness.
Regeneration.
Religion.
Retirement.
Retreat[e], The.
Revival, The.
Rhapsody, A, sel.
Search, The, sel.
Seed Growing Secretly, The.
Shepherds [or Shepheards], The.
Silence and Stealth of Day[e]s!
Son-Days [dayes].
Song to Amoret, A.
Stone, The.
They Are All Gone into the World of Light!
Timber, The.
To His Books.
To His Retired Friend, an Invitation to
   Brecknock, sel.
To the Most Excellently Accomplished Mrs.
   Katherine Philips.
Unprofitablenes.
Upon a Cloak [or Cloke] Lent Him by Mr. J.
   Ridsley, sel.
Vanity of Spirit.
Waterfall [or Water-Fall], The.
World, The (1).

Vaughan, Jane (fl. mid-17th cent.)
Debate between Jane Vaughan of Caergai and
   Cadwaladr the Poet.
O my merciful Lord God, you, who are one in
   three.

Vaughan, Richard Murray (b. 1965)
Insight into private affairs. . .raises certain
   barristers and magistrates to such great
   heights.
Men Together.
Simone Signoret, Beldam.
10 Reasons Why I Fall in Love with
   Inaccessible Straight Boys Every Damn
   Time.

Vaughan, Thomas (1622?–66)
On The Death of an Oxford Proctor, sel.
Stone, The.

**Vaux, Thomas, 2d Baron Vaux of Harrowden
(1510–66)**
Aged Lover Renounceth Love, The.

Vaynper, Zishe (1893–1957)
Whiteness.
Word: "So many bright words covered."

Vaynshteyn, Berysh (1905–67)
America, sel.
Negro Dies, A.

Vays, Shifre (1889–1955)
To Mani Leyb.
Today: "I won't be sitting shiva."

Vaysman, Nokhem (1894–1944)
Anne Pauker.
On the Hudson, sel.

Vazakas, Byron
Epitaph for the Old Howard.
Pavilion on the Pier, The.

Vazirani, Reetika (b. 1962)
Daughter-Mother-Maya-Seeta.
Dedicated to You.
Dream of the Evil Servant.
E-Mail.
It's Me, I'm Not Home.
Lullaby: "I would not sing you to sleep."
Maya to Herself and Then to Her Gardener.
Mrs. Biswas Breaks Her Connection with
   Another Relative.
Mrs. Biswas Goes Through a Photo Album.
Mrs. Biswas of Maryland on the Phone.

Vázquez Montalbán, Manuel (1939–2003)
Gauguin ("His journalist.").
Gauguin ("Periodista / su padre.").
In Memoriam ("Aprendí / la interminable
   lista.").
In Memoriam ("I learned / the interminable
   list.").
Summer and Smoke.
Verano y Humo.
Yramín and the Sea.
Yramín y el Mar.

Veale, Peter (b. 1919)
I put my hat upon my head.

Vecchione, Patrice (b. 1957)
Sugarmother's Daughter Dreams.

Veenendaal, Cornelia
On My Fourteenth Wedding Anniversary I
   Ride on Trains.
Sun-crossed.

Vega (b. 1954)
Brothers Loving Brothers.

Vegin, Pyotr (b. 1939)
Explanation of a Sign.
"Moscow" Pool.

Vehbî, Sünbülzâde
Oh east wind, come, what news from that
   garden.

Veiga, Amélia (b. 1931)
Angola.
Wind of Liberty.

Veinberg, Jon
Last Shot.
Next to Tut.
Owl's Landscape, An.
To an Exeter City Cocktail Waitress.

Veinstein, Alain (b. 1942)
From Far.

Veldeke, Heinrich von (1140?–1210?)
In April when the flowers spring.
Tristan had no choice.
Whoever hurts my favor with my lady.

Vélez, Elizabeth Ash
Elvis P. and Emma B.

Velichansky, A.
Flame's speech is confused, The. The
   muttering of the water is hollow.
In the evil time.
Infant is white, like down, The. And the youth
   dark-complexioned, like shingle.
Kalmyk poppies, horde of pan-Mongol tulips.
Memory of the past grows paler with each day.
Policeman does not blow his whistle, The.
Trunks of birches, like scrolls.

Velter, André (b. 1945)
Autre, L'
Je chante ma femme.

My Wife I Sing.
Other One, The.

Venaille, Franck (b. 1936)
Éloge de Robert Desnos.
In Praise of Robert Desnos.
Maintenant.
Now They Tell Me.

Venclova, Tomas
Canto Eleven.

Venkatarao, Kavikondala (1898–1964)
Home: "Like sapphire and terracotta mingling
   in the Ganga."
Letter, A: "Mail runner carries the bag of mail,
   The."
Workers in Love.
You on My Mind.

Venn, George (b. 1943)
Poem Against the First Grade.

Vere, Adriel
To My Cycle.

Verga, Angelo
My Wife's Therapist.

Verhaeren, Emile (1855–1916)
Spade.

Verlaine, Paul (1844–96)
A la Promenade.
Art of Poetry, The ("Let's hear the music first
   and foremost.").
Art of Poetry, The ("You must have music first
   of all.").
Asleep in the Valley.
Autumn Song ("Long sobs of, The.").
Autumn Song ("Violins complain.").
Autumn Song ("With long sobs.").
Balanide 2.
Beams.
Beauty of women, their weakness, those pale
   hands.
Brussels: Simple Frescos 1.
Brussels: Simple Frescos 2.
Cold wind hurls itself at, A.
Colombine.
Cortège.
Endless sameness.
Exchange of Feelings.
Falling tears in my heart.
Fantoches.
Femme et Chatte.
Green.
Green ("Take this fruit, these flowers, these
   branches and leaves.").
He's an awkward bedfellow and I love to keep.
Hope like a wisp of straw shines in the stable.
Humble life of dull and easy work, The.
In Prison.
It's languor and ecstasy.
Like city's rain, my heart.
Malines.
Mandoline.
Mille e tre.
Moonlight.
Muted Tones.
On the Grass.
Parsifal.
Peaceful eyes my only wealth.
Piano kissed by a slender hand, The.
Sadness, the languor of the human body, The.
Sky above the roof's, The.
Sonnet to the Asshole.
Spleen.
Streets 1.
Streets 2.
Tears Fall in My Heart.
Uneven rows of hedges.
Voice of Pride: shout of blaring trumpets.
Weird as Puppets.
White Moonglow, The.
Without Guile.
Woman and Cat.
Wooden Horses.
You see, we have to be forgiven things.
You Would Have Understood Me.
Young Fools, The.

Vermont, Charlie
Death of Karen Klausner, The.

Verstegan [or Vertegen], Richard (Richardowlands) (1565–1620)
Lullaby: "Upon my lap my sovereign sits."
Times Go by Turns.

Vertinsky [or Vertinskii], Aleksandr [or Viktor Fyodorovich] (1889–1957)
I remember the night.

Vertreace, Martha (b. 1945)
Arc Welder.
Black Tulips.
Caged Stone.

Verwey, Albert (1865–1937)
Beautiful World, The.
North-Sea, The.
Soul and Love, The.

Very, Jones (1831–80)
Autumn Flowers.
Autumn Leaves.
Beauty.
Birds of Passage, The.
Clouded Morning, The ("Morning comes, and thickening clouds prevail, The.").
Columbine, The.
Cottage, The.
Created, The.
Cross, The ("I must go on, till in my tearful line.").
Cup, The.
Dead, The.
Eagles, The.
Earth, The.
Enoch.
Eye and Ear, The.
Fair Morning, The.
Faith ("There is no faith; the mountain stands within.").
Fear not: for they that are with us are more than they that are with them. 2 Kings 6:16.
First Atlantic Telegraph, The.
Forevermore.
Garden, The.
God Not Afar Off.
Hand and Foot, The [or Hand and the Foot, The].
Harvest, The ("They love me not, who at my table eat.").
Hath the Rain a Father?
He Was Acquainted with Grief.
I Was Sick and in Prison.
In Him We Live [and Move and Have Our Being].
Indian's Retort, The.
Jacob Wrestling with the Angel.
John.
Laborers, The.
Lament of the Flowers, The.
Latter Rain, The ("Latter rain, it falls in anxious haste, The.").
Lost, The ("Fairest day that ever yet has shone, The.").
Morning Watch, The.
Moses in Infancy.
Mountain, The.
My Meat and Drink.
My People are destroyed for lack of Knowledge.—Hosea 4:6.
Nature ("Bubbling brook doth leap when I come by, The.").
New Birth, The.
New Man, The.
New World, The.
Night.
One generation passeth away, and another generation cometh: but the earth abideth for ever. Ecclesiastes 1:4.
Origin of Man, The, sel.
Poor, The.
Prayer of Jabez, The.
Prayer, The ("Wilt Thou not visit me?").
Promise, The ("I come the rushing wind that shook the place.").
Robe, The.
Rock, The.
Serpent, The.
Settler, The.
Silent, The.

Slavery.
Slowness of Belief in a Spiritual World, The.
Son, The.
Song, The.
Sower, The.
Spirit, The.
Strangers, The.
Sumach Leaves, The.
Take ye heed, watch and pray: for ye know not when the time is. Mark 13:33.
Thy Better Self.
Thy Brother's Blood.
Wild Rose of Plymouth, The.
Winter Rain, The.
Word, The ("Word! it cannot fail; it ever speaks, The.").
Yourself.

"Vesey, Paul" *See* Allen, Samuel

Vessup, A. Anthony
Mighty Blood, The.

Vest, Jennifer Lisa
In This, the Fifth World.

Vettese, Raymond (b. 1950)
Photograph.
Scottish Mythology.
Scottish Names.

Vian, Boris (1920–59)
Jour, Un.
One Day.
Pourquoi que je vis.
What for Do I Live Then.

Vicinelli, Patrizia (b. 1943)
Foundations of Being, The, *sels.*
I Met the Thieving Miss Magpie.
When time--irreversible--begins to doze.

Vicioso, Chiqui (b. 1948)
Fazal.
Haiti.
Perspectives.
Survival 1.
Survival 2.
Wo/men.

Vicuña, Cecilia (b. 1948)
Fables of the Beginning and Remains of the Origin.
Five Notebooks for Exit Art.
Palabrarmás, *sel.*
Shadow of a Loom, The.
With a Little Notebook at the Met.
Thirst.
Untitled.

Vidya (Vijjika) (fl. c.659)
And What of Those Arbors of Vines.
Fate Is a Cruel and Proficient Potter.
Hiding in the.
Love Poem, A.
On Makeshift Bedding.

Vidyapati (fl. 15th cent.)
First Love.

Viereck, Peter (b. 1916)
Blindman's Buff.
Kilroy.
Love Song to Eohippus.
Poet.
Ripeness Is All.
To Helen of Troy (N.Y.).
Vale from Carthage.

Vietnamese Oral Tradition
Across the Field of the Old Corporal.
Arranged Marriage, The.
Autumn: "Autumn rains blow."
Bare Rocks and Stars.
Body Is Pain, The.
Carp, The.
Cat, The.
Clear Skies, Still Sea.
Coins of Van-Lich.
Colonial Troops Transport, The.
Complaining about the Second Wife.
Concubine, The.
Difficulties at Love.
Egret's Death and Funeral Preparations.
Evening.
From *So* Mountain.

Girl with the Binh Tien Hairdo, The.
Harmony in the Kingdom.
Homesick Bride, The.
Husband and Wife.
Impossible Tasks.
Ke-Mo Village Girl.
King Star, The.
Leaving the Village.
Linked Verses.
Looking Out in All Directions.
Love Lament.
Lullaby: "Little one, go to sleep. Sleep soundly."
Mandarin Who Couldn't Do Anything, The.
Mother Egret.
Outpost Soldier, The.
Painting, The.
Phoenixes and Sparrows.
Pole at the Village Pagoda, The.
Red Cloth, The.
Replies.
Saigon River, The.
Ship of Redemption.
Singer with a Bad Voice, The.
Talking about Birds.
Tao.
Testing the Confucian Ideal.
Tiny Bird, A.
Venturing Out.
Whisky Lovers.
Wicked Women.
Woman's Heart, A.

Vigil, Anthony R. (b. 1968)
As the Beer Trucks Eclipse the Light of Morning.
At the Stop Light, the Braided Blond Man.
Hogarcito de La Madrugada, El.
That's the Way, Uh Huh, Uh Huh, I Liked It.

Viidikas, Vicki (b. 1948)
Future.

Vijghen, Samira
Fallen.

Vijjika *See* Vidya

Viktor, Avrom (1871–1954)
Shadows: "Black-blue shadows on red-brown bricks."

Vilariño, Idea (b. 1920)
Each Afternoon.
How Awful.
How disgusting.
How to shrug off.
If I Died Tonight.
Lifelong farewell.
Like a dog howling endlessly.
Like a Floating Jasmine.
Like that man who kicks off his shoes.
Maybe Then.
No.
No More.
There is no hope.
Visitor, A.
What Was Life.

Villa, Dario (1953–96)
Blades and slime, the limits, The.
In the end.
It is.
Remember the goose that.
Sometimes, Doctor, I awake.
Then if I think about it.
What counts in any action.

Villa, Emilio (b. 1914)
Natus de Muliere, Brevi Vivens.
Words, *sels.*

Villa, José Garcia (b. 1914)
I Was Speaking of Oranges to a Lady.
Inviting a Tiger for the Weekend.
Now I Prize Yellow Strawberries.

Villalobos, Marco
I'm Sayin Though.

Villalongo, José Angel Sr.
In the Good Old U. S. A.

Villani, Luisa
Watching the Mayan Women.

Villanueva, Alma (b. 1944)
Even the Eagles Must Gather.
From the Healing Dark.
Peace #3.
Planet Earth Speaks, The.
Power.
Song of the Self: The Grandmother.
They Didn't Get Me.

Villanueva, Tino (b. 1941)
Day-Long Day.
Haciendo Apenas la Recolección.
Scene from the Movie *Giant.*
Serving of Water, The.

Villaurrutia, Xavier (1903–50)
Los Angeles Nocturne.
Nocturnal Sea.
Nocturne.
Nocturne of the Statue.
Nocturne: The Eternal.
Our Love.
Poetry.
Rose Nocturnal.
They and I.

Villemaire, Yolande (b. 1949)
Quartz and Mica.

Villiers, George, 2d Duke of Buckingham (1628–87)
Cabin-Boy, The.
Epitaph upon Thomas, Lord Fairfax, An.

Villon, François (1431–65)
Ballade: "Tell me where, in what country, where."
Ballad[e] of Dead Ladies, The.
Ballad of Villon and Fat Madge, The.
Ballade of the Ladies of Time Past.
Ballade of the Men Who Were Hanged.
Ballade to End With, A.
Ballade to His Mistress.
Ballat o the Hingit.
Ballat o the Leddies o Langsyne.
Complaint of the Fair Armoress [or Armouress], The.
Dispute of the Heart and Body of François Villon, The.
Gone Ladies.
Grand Testament, *sel.*
I Die of Thirst While at the Fountain Side.
Old Woman's Lamentations, An.
Prayer of the Old Woman.
Quatrain: "France's I am; my lookout's glum."
Remember, Imbeciles and Wits.
Testament, The, *sel.*

Vinal, Harold (1891–1967)
To Persephone.

Vinkenoog, Simon
((((((Hollanditis))))))).

Vinograd, Julia (b. 1943)
In These Dark Times.
Jerusalem Walked thru War.

Vinokurov, Yevgeny [or Evgenii] Mikhailovich (b. 1925)
Adam.
All Grows Old.
Eyes.
Has the time come to draw up the accounts?
History, *sels.*
I do not like the circus.
I don't remember him.
Mother of Judas, The.
When the Parachute Does Not Open.

Vinz, Mark (b. 1942)
Blues, The.
Wall between Us, The.

Violi, Paul (b. 1944)
Appeal to the Grammarians.
Harold and Imogene.
Hazards of Imagery, The.
House of Xerxes.
Index.
Rifacimento.
When to Slap a Woman.

Viorst, Judith (b. 1931)
Honeymoon is Over, The.
Mother Doesn't Want a Dog.

Night Fun.

Virág, Benedek (1754–1830)
Invocation: "O holy Justice! Hiding your puissance."
Spartan Mother, The.

Viray, Manuel A. (b. 1917)
Patio.
Saturday Morning, A.
Two Strangers, The.

Virgil [or Vergil] (Publius Vergilius Maro) (70–19 B.C.)
Aeneid (Dryden translation), *sels.*
Aeneid [or Eneados or Aeneis], The, *sels.*
Death Plucks My Ear.
Eclogues, *sels.*
Fourth Ecologue: Pollio, The.
Georgics, *sels.*
Wave, The.

Viscusi, Robert
Autobiography.

Visick, Mary
Wordsworth on Lloyd George.

Vitale, Marianne
Become Your Face.
I Read That It Was All a Chain.
Joy Island.
Loop, Fleck, Sound *and So On.*
On Justifying Cuckoo La Goose, *sel.*
Patois.
Three Written Poems, Unconnected.
Truth Put It.
You Oh Even.

Vitéz, Mihály Csokonai (1773–1805)
Constantinople.
Evening.
Happiness.
Love Song to the Foal-Hide Flask.
On My Pneumonia.
Once More to Lilla.
Shy Request.
Susie's Lament for Johnny.
To Hope.
To Solitude.
To the Echo of Tihany.

Vitiello, Justin (fl. 20th cent.)
Letter to a Cretan Flute-Maker.

Vivar, Alicia Galaz
Delivery.
Femmemasochism.
Love is Round.
Order and the Days, The.

Vivien, René[e] (1877–1909)
Rançon, La.
Ransom, The.

Vizenor, Gerald (b. 1934)
Seasons in Santa Fe.
Shaman Breaks.
Surrendered Names.
White Earth.

Vlasova, Ekaterina (b. 1976)
Create me a world.
I see / your hands in my nightmares.
Little sympathy, A.
On an old grand piano.
There is a way to sew wings on arms.

Vliet, R. G.
Clem Maverick, *sels.*
Penny Ballad of Elvious Ricks.

Voce, Lello (b. 1957)
Variation 3 (On Love and More), *sel.*

Voeten, Bert (1918–92)
Sun On My Hand, The ("Sun lights my hand writing, The.").
Sun On My Hand, The ("Writing with the sun on my hand.").

Vogel, David (1891–1943)
How Can I See You, Love.
I Saw My Father Drowning.
On autumn nights.
Silently you stand before me.
Single and last carriage is ready for the journey, A.
There Is a Last, Solitary Coach.
Waiting-rooms.

With gentle fingers.

Vogelweide, Walther [or Walter] von der (1170?–1230?)
Alas, all my years, where have they disappeared?
Alas, that wisdom, and youth.
Dancing Girl.
Dearly beloved gentle girl.
I sat down on a rock.
"Lady, take this garland."
Now My Life Has Gained Some Meaning.
Translation from Walter von der Vogelweide, A.
Under the linden.
Under the Lindentree.
Will anyone tell me what Minne is?
You excellent women, you valiant men.
You should bid me welcome.

Vogt, Benjamin (b. 1963)
Uncle with Landscape—Kansas, 1954.

Voigt, Ellen Bryant (b. 1943)
Amaryllis.
At the Movie: Virginia, 1956.
Blue Ridge.
Burial, The.
Claiming Kin.
Daughter.
Effort at Speech.
Exile.
Farmer, The.
For My Mother.
Gobelins.
Harvesting the Cows.
Hen, The.
House.
January: "After days of putting down my poem."
Kyrie, *sel.*
Lotus Flowers, The.
Nocturne.
Song and Story.
Spire, The.
Spring, The.
Stone Pond.
Trust, The.
Two Trees.
Visiting the Graves.
Woman Who Weeps.
Year's End.

Voisine, Connie
Blue Hat.

Voiture, Vincent (1597–1648)
Rondeau: "Lord, I'm done for: now Margot."
You Know Where You Did Despise.

Volach, Yona (1944–85)
Bird.
Hebrew.
I Have a Stage in My Head.
Life You Have, The.
Tefillin.
When You Come Sleep with Me.

Vold, Jan Erik (b. 1939)
Hokusai the Old Master, Who Painted a Wave Like Nobody Ever Painted a Wave Before Him.
Thor Heyerdahl's Mother.

Volkman, Karen (b. 1967)
Although the paths lead into the forest, we are bitter with the bodies of days that end too early.
Case, The.
Create Desire.
Daffodils.
Evening.
I believe there is a song that is stranger than wind, that sips the scald from the telling, toss, toss.
I never wish to sing again as I used to, when two new eyes could always.
I was watching for it, everytime watching, for the neck that was.
I won't go in today, I'll stay out today.
If it be event, I go towards and not back. I go tower, not floor.
Infernal.

Kiss Me Deadly.
Lady of the lake, what does all our weeping
lead to? A pair of keys, paucity of
summer—just because.
May: "In May's gaud gown and ruby
reckoning."
No noise subtracts it. It won't leave, or scatter
jokes or fathoms, no tiny failing.
Now I promise the shriek that the pressure of
days, the pressure of days will be weapon.
Pregnant Lady Playing Tennis, The.
Seasonal.
Shipwreck Poem.
Shrewd star, who crudes our naming: you
should be flame.
Sonnet: "As the dream a consciousness
adored."
Sonnet: "Brown is the flat gestation of a
maze."
Sonnet: "Lease of my leaving, heartfelt lack,
what does."
Sonnet: "Lifting whither, cycle of the sift."
Sonnet: "Never got, and never thought, and
yet."
Sonnet: "Nothing was ever what it claimed to
be."
Sonnet: "Now you nerve. Flurred, avid as the
raw."
Sonnet: "Premise, a solace—deciduous dress,
A."
Sonnet: "Sky we bear on our shoulders,
heaven-height, The."
Sonnet: "This ellipse, slip between seasons."
Sonnet: "Tilt the placeless waver of this
moving."
Sonnet: "What is this witness, the watching
ages."
Theft.
There comes a time to rusticate the numbers.
The way the birds, jug.
We did things more dulcet, more marionette.
Well, You Needn't.
When kiss spells contradiction it spills an
ocean of open clothes.

Volková, Bronislava (b. 1946)
I am not an Amazon—a warrior.
Shoreless bath a fabulous boast, A.

Volkow, Veronica
Arcana 4: The Emperor.
Arcana 8: Justice.
Arcana 10: Fortune.
Arcana 12: The Hanged Man.
Arcano 4: El Emperador.
Arcano 8: La Justicia.
Arcano 10: La Fortuna.
Arcano 12: El Colgado.
En el Valle de Zapata.
Historia del laberinto, La.
Story of the Labyrinth, The.
Valley of Zapata, The.
Varas.
Wands.
Washerwoman, The.

Vollmer, Judith
Canning Cellar, Early Sixties.
Nursing the Sunburn.
On Reporting the Murder of a Young
Prostitute.
Wildsisters Bar.

**Voloshin, Maksimilian Aleksandrovich
(Maksimilian Kirilenko-Voloshin) (1877–
1932)**
Holy Russia.

Voltaire (François Marie Arouet) (1694–1778)
Mountain Mountainous in Parturition, A.
Poem Upon the Lisbon Disaster; or, An Inquiry
into the Adage, "All Is for the Best", *sel.*

Voltskaya, Tatyana
God is the first snow. He is a leaf, a mosquito.
Low clouds, the shreds of dry grass, The.
Rhyme is a woman, trying on clothes.

Von Freytag-Loringhoven, Else (1874–1927)
Affectionate.
Appalling Heart.
Café du Dôme.

Dozen Cocktails—Please, A.
Holy Skirts.
Is It?
Klink—Hratzvenga (Deathwail).
X-Ray.

Von Reis, Siri
Vast Problem Still Obscure.

Vörös, Mátyás Nyéki (1575–1654)
Hell, *sel.*

Vörösmarty, Mihály (1800–55)
Ancient Gypsy, The.
Another for Miss Pardo's Album.
Appeal.
Bitter Cup, A.
Csongor and Tünde, *sels.*
Fair Ilonka.
Flight of Zalán, The.
For Laura.
Gutenberg Inscription.
On Mankind.
One For Miss Pardo's Travel Diary.
Prologue: "I wrote this when the sky was still
serene."
Thoughts in the Library.
To Ferencz Liszt.
To the Day-Dreamer.
Young Pete.

Voss, Fred
Inspection, The.
Making America Strong.
Stud, The.
Sun Worshiper.
Termination.

**Voznesensky [or Voznesenskii], Andrey [or
Andrei] Andreievich (b. 1933)**
Anguish.
Arrow in the Wall.
Autumn Prelude.
Beatnik's Monologue, The.
Bicycles.
Big Fire at the Architectural College, The.
Boat on the Shore.
Call of the Lake, The.
Chorus of Nymphs, A.
Darkmotherscream.
Dead Still.
December Pastures.
Dogalypse.
Edge, The.
First Ice, The.
For a Portrait of Annette Vallon.
Forgive Me!
From the Window of a Plane.
Genealogy of Crosses, The.
I Am Goya.
In the Mountains.
Ironical Elegy, Composed in Those Terribly
Sad Moments When I Cannot Write.
Look Back into the Future.
Mayakovsky in Paris.
Monologue with Commentary.
New Year's Letter in Warsaw, A.
Old Song.
On the Metamorphoses Brought About By
Emotion: The Rebellion of the Eyes.
Poem: "From us, like appendicitis."
Portrait of Plisetskaya.
Public Beach No. 2.
Recommendation.
Someone Is Beating a Woman.
Striptease.
Two Poems.
War Ballad.
Why.

Vrepont, Brian (B. A. Trubridge) (1882–1955)
Bomber, The.

Vroman, Leo (b. 1915)
Flowers.
Regeneration.
Thin Wire.
Wrinkling Together.

Vroomkoning, Victor (b. 1938)
Returning.
Rubbish Bags.
Together Again ("I behold her there.").

Together Again ("You get these thoughts in
melancholy Autumn.").

Vuong-Riddick, Thuong (b. 1940)
My Beloved Is Dead in Vietnam.

Vyazemsky, Petr Andreevich (1792–1878)
Russian God, The.

W

W., A. (*fl.* c.1586)
Hopeless Desire Soon Withers and Dies.

W., C. A.
To have it out or not? that is the question.

Waberi, Abdourahman A.
Between clackstones.

Wachtel, Chuck (b. 1950)
Coriolis Effect, The.
On Class and Desire.
Two Quarters, Two Nickels, and the Jacket of
the One Album He Ever Recorded—
America Welcomes Home the Desert Sax—
Are in the Open Felt-Lined Case On the
Platform of the Astor Place Subway Station:
Gulf War 1.
Workingman's Wife: *Who She Is, Who She Is
Not, What She Buys—And Why.*

Wada, Hakuro
Even the croaking of frogs.
Released Seagull.
Young grass and shriveled.

Waddell, P. Hately (1817–91)
David and Goliath.

Wadding [or Waddinge], Luke (1588–1657)
Christmas Day [Is Come].

Waddington, Miriam (b. 1917)
Advice to the Young.
Old Women of Toronto.
Sea Bells.
Ten Years and More.
Thou Didst Say Me.
Ulysses Embroidered.

Waddleton, Joan
Fatherhood.

Wade-Gayles, Gloria (b. 1940)
Inquisition.
Loving Again.

Wade, Jamila Z.
Runnin.

Wade, Sidney (b. 1951)
Gas.

Wadsworth, Connemara
Desire.

Wadsworth, William
Need for Attention, The.

Wagner, Catherine (b. 1969)
Lover.

Wagner, Maryfrances Cusumano (b. 1947)
Miss Clement's Second Grade.

Wagner, Richard (1813–83)
Tristan and Isolde, *sel.*

Wagner, Shari Miller (b. 1958)
A Cappella.
Rook.
Second Language.
Sunken Gardens (Huntington, IN), The.

Wagoner, David (b. 1926)
Advice to the Orchestra.
Author of American Ornithology Sketches a
Bird, Now Extinct, The.
Best Slow Dancer, The.
By a Waterfall.
Chorus: "That rain-strewn night in the woods,
the chorus, chorus."
Curtains.
Dead Letter From Out of Town.
Elegy for a Forest Clear-Cut by the
Weyerhaeuser Company.
Elegy for Yards, Pounds, and Gallons.
Excursion of the Speech and Hearing Class,
The.
Five Dawn Skies in November.
Loons Mating.

Lost: "Stand still. The trees ahead and bushes beside you."
Making Camp ("When their eyes opened, it was more than morning.").
Making Camp ("You've found the place in time—no permanent shade.").
Man of the House, The.
Meeting a Bear.
My Father's Garden.
Naval Trainees Learn How to Jump Overboard, The.
Nuthatch.
Peacock Display.
Poem about Breath.
Silence of the Stars, The.
Singing Lesson, The.
Source, The.
Their Bodies.
To a Farmer Who Hung Five Hawks on His Barbed Wire.
Trying to Make Music.
Victorian Idyll, A.
Walt Whitman Bathing.
Words, The.
Young Girl with a Pitcher Full of Water, A.

Wah, Fred (b. 1939)
Music At The Heart Of Thinking 22.
Music At The Heart Of Thinking 42.
Music at the Heart of Thinking 52.
Music At The Heart Of Thinking 54.
This Dendrite Map: Father / Mother Haibun, *sels.*
3 Pictograms From The Interior of BC.

Waight, Simone
To the Coming of the Decade.

Wainwright, Jeffrey (b. 1944)
Apparent Colonnades, The.
1815.
Thomas Müntzer.

Wainwright, Kiki (b. 1937)
Changes.
Trouble.

Waits, Tom (b. 1949)
Swordfishtrombone.

Wakayama Bokusui (1885–1928)
Cut off these hands, cut off these feet.
How many mountains.
Sight of my father and mother, The.
They say there lives.
White bird.

Wakoski, Diane (b. 1937)
Belly Dancer.
Black Leather Because Bubmlebees Look Like It.
Blue Monday.
Blue Suede Shoes.
Canoer, The.
Father of My Country, The.
For Craig Who Leapt Off a Cliff in to Hummingbird Light.
For Whitman.
George Washington and the Loss of His Teeth.
Hitchhikers, The.
Hummingbird Light.
Ice Eagle, The.
Imagining Point Dume.
Light.
Mirror of a Day Chiming Marigold, The.
My Trouble.
Night Blooming Jasmine.
Photos, The.
Poet Recognizing the Echo of the Voice, A.
Reading *Bonjour, Tristesse* at the Florence Crittenden Home for Unwed Mothers.
Remembering the Pacific.
Ring of Irony, The.
Ring, The.
Ringless.
Singer, The.
Valentine for Ben Franklin Who Drives a Truck in California, A.

Wakuan-Shitai (1108–69)
Iron tree blooms.

Walafrid Strabo (809–49)
To His Friend in Absence.

With His Book, Of Gardening.

Walcott, Brenda
Much of Your Poetry Is Beautiful.

Walcott, Derek (b. 1930)
Arkansas Testament, The.
Becune Point.
Blues: "Those five or six young guys."
Cloud, The.
Codicil.
Crusoe's Island.
Divided Child, The, *sel.*
Earth.
Eulogy to W.H. Auden.
Far Cry from Africa, A.
Fist, The.
Fortunate Traveller, The.
Frederiksted, Dusk.
Glory Trumpeter, The.
Gulf, The.
Hotel Normandie Pool, The.
Italian Eclogues.
Laventille.
Le Loupgarou.
Letter from Brooklyn, A.
Love after Love.
Man Who Loved Islands, The.
Map of Europe, A.
Menelaus.
Midsummer, *sels.*
Midsummer, Tobago.
Missing the Sea.
Nights in the Gardens of Port of Spain.
Omeros, *sels.*
Polish Rider, The.
Port of Spain.
Ruins of a Great House.
Saddhu of Couva, The.
Sainte Lucie, *sel.*
Schooner Flight, The, *sel.*
Sea Canes.
Sea Grapes.
Sea Grapes.
Sea Is History, The.
Season of Phantasmal Peace, The.
Streams.
Tomorrow, Tomorrow.
Upstate.
Villa Restaurant, The.
Village Life, A.
Virgins, The.
Voice out of the Sabbaths, A.
Winding Up.

Walden, Gale Renée
Misguided Angels.
Oracle.

Walders, Davi
Anniversary.
Kindness of Abishag, The.

Waldinger, Ernst
Lidice.

Waldman, Anne (b. 1945)
Admonitions of the Boudoir.
After-Life, The.
Baby's Pantoum.
Berthe Morisot.
Culture Drift.
De Carlo Lots, The.
Dispersal of It.
Fait Accompli.
Giant Night.
Gonna change my life.
How the Sestina (Yawn) Works.
Icy Rose.
In the Room of Never Grieve.
Iovis XIX: Why That's a Blade Can Float.
Letter S.
Marriage: "Marriage marriage is like you say everything everything in stereo stereo fall fall on the bed bed at dawn dawn because you work work all night."
Nerves.
On Walt Whitman's Birthday.
One Inch of Love Is an Inch of Ashes.
Paul Eluard.
Recalling Former Travels.

Sexy Things.
Sick.
Skin / Meat / BONES
Under My Breath.
Up Thru the Years.
Worry Yr Logos: Conversant You Speak to the Dead, *sel.*
Yum Yab.

Waldner, Liz
Determinate Inflorescence: Ephemera.

Waldrep, G. C. (b. 1968)
Hotel d'Avignon.
Miracles of St. Sebasatian, The.
O Canada!
What Begins Bitterly Becomes Another Love Poem.

Waldrop, Keith (b. 1932)
Chances of Magic, The.
Poet: "Wind dying, I find a city deserted, except for crowds of, The."
Shipwreck in Haven, A, *sel.*
Wandering Curves.
Will to Will.

Waldrop, Rosmarie (b. 1935)
Hölderlin Hybrids, *sels.*
Inserting the Mirror, *sel.*
Key into the Language of America, A, *sels.*
Lawn of Excluded Middle, *sel.*
Reproduction of Profiles, The, *sels.*

Walker, Alice (b. 1944)
Even as I Hold You.
Good Night, Willie Lee, I'll See You in the Morning.
In These Dissenting Times, *sels.*
Kiss, The.
Reassurance.
Remember?
Revolutionary Petunias.

Walker, David
Astronomy.
Daylight.
Home.

Walker, Frank X. (b. 1961)
Crooked Afro.
Sweet Bread.
Wishbone.

Walker, James (b. 1940)
Safe.

Walker, Jeanne Murray (b. 1944)
Coming into History.
Flt #4372.
How Mother Courage Saves Desdemona.
Studying Physics with My Daughter.

Walker, Kath See Oodgeroo of the tribe Noonuccal

Walker, Margaret Abigail (1915–98)
Childhood.
Dark Blood.
Delta.
For Malcolm X.
For Mary McLeod Bethune.
For My People.
Jackson, Mississippi.
Kissie Lee.
Lineage.
Molly Means.
Now.
Since 1619.
Solace.
Southern Song.
Street Demonstration.
We Have Been Believers.
Whores.

Walker, Robert (1958–84)
Solitary Confinement.

Walker, Ted (b. 1934)
Owl.

Walker, William Sidney (1795–1846)
Too solemn for day, too sweet for night.

Wallace, Edgar (1875–1932)
War.

Wallace, Robert (1858–1938)
Dog's Song.

Wallace, Ronald (b. 1945)
At the St. Louis Institute of Music.

Basketball.
Building an Outhouse.
Constipation.
Facts of Life, The.
Fat of the Land, The.
Friday Night Fights, The.
Hell Mural, The: Panel I.
Hot Property, A.
In a Pig's Eye.
Makings of Happiness, The.
Nightline: An Interview with the General.
Sestina for the House.
Smoking.
Sound Systems.
State Poetry Day.
Student Theme, The.
Thirteen.

Wallace, William Ross (1819–81)
Hand That Rocks the Cradle Is the Hand That
    Rules the World, The.

Wallace-Crabbe, Chris (b. 1934)
Abhorring a Vacuum.
And the World was Calm.
Binary.
Bits and Pieces, The, *sels.*
Collective Invention, The.
Dead Cartesian, The.
Double Dactyl.
Life of Ideas, The.
Mental Traveller's Landfall, The.
Nub.
Secular, The.
Shape-Changer, The.
Sonnets to the Left, *sels.*
Sporting the Plaid.
Tribunal, The.
Windows, The.

Wallenstein, Barry (*fl.* 20th cent.)
Blues 1.
Blues 2.

Waller, Edmund (1606–87)
Budd, The.
Fall, The.
Love's Farewell.
Of English Verse.
Of Loving at First Sight.
Of the Last Verses in the Book, *sel.*
Of the Marriage of the Dwarfs.
On a Girdle.
On St. James's Park, as Lately Improved by
    His Majesty.
Song: "Go[e], lovely rose."
Story of Phoebus and Daphne Applied, [etc.],
    The.
To a Fair Lady Playing with a Snake.
To a Lady in a Garden.
Upon Ben Johnson [*or* Jonson].
Upon His Majesty's [*or* Majesties] Repairing
    of Paul's.

Waller, John Francis (1810–94)
Spinning-Wheel, The.

Waller, Kim
On the Road to Homer Noble Farm.

Waller, Marey (*fl.* 1674)
To; Oxon.

Waller, Robert James
Three Poems.

Wallis, Severn Teackle (1816–94)
Prayer for Peace, A.

Walls, Doyle Wesley
Summer the Beatles Went Over Seven Minutes
    on a Single, The.

Walsh, Agnes (b. 1963)
Mike's.
Night in the Ashes.
Tilts, Point Lance, The.
Time That Passes, The.

Walsh, Edward (1805–50)
Dawning of the Day, The.

Walsh, John (1911–72)
Drimin Donn Dílis.
I've Got an Apple Ready.

Walsh, William (1663–1708)
Despairing Lover, The.

Rivals.

Walsh, William (1663–1708) *and* **Sir George
Etherege (1653–91)**
Imperfect Enjoyment, The.
Rivals.

Walsh, Catherine (b. 1964)
Nearly Nowhere.
Pitch, *sel.*

Walters, Elizabeth
Elizabeth Walters is my name.

Walters, Meredith (b. 1973)
Spontaneous Monument.

Walters, Wendy S.
Meridian Hill Terrace.

Waltham, Brian M.
Radio 3.

Waltner-Toews, David (b. 1948)
Coming Up for Air, *sels.*
Coyotes at Eyebrow Lake, Saskatchewan.
How the Earth Loves You.
Request from Tante Tina to the Mennonite
    Women's Missionary Society to Put Salman
    Rushdie on the Prayer List, A.
Roots: "Rudy Weibe, wiping the sweat from
    his brow."
Teilhard de Chardin Surfs the Internet.

Walton, Anthony
Dissidence.
Elegy for Joan.
Encyclopedia of Rhythm and Blues, The.
Gwendolyn Brooks.
McDonald's, Scottsboro, April, 1997.
Third Shift.

Walton, Eda Lou (b. 1896)
In Recompense.

Walton, John
God, the Port of Peace.

Walwicz, Ania (b. 1951)
Abattoir, The.
Big Tease.
Daredevil.
Little Red Riding Hood.
Tattoo, The.
Wonderful.

Wanek, Connie
After Us.
Duluth, Minnesota.

Wang, Jiaosheng
Tune: "Magnolia Flowers."
Tune: "The Charm of a Maiden Singer;"
    Spring Thoughts.

Wang An-shih (1021–86)
At Home.
Bald Mountain.
Confiscating Salt.
Hui-chu Temple, Mount K'un.
In the Style of Han Shan and Shih Te, *sel.*
Night Watch.
On Chung Mountain.
Spring Evening on Pan Mountain.
Working for the Government.

Wang Ch'ang-ling (698–757)
At the Stream's Source in Spring: A Party.
Autumn Evening on the Great Lake.
Chant of the Frontiersman.
Complaint from a Lady's Chamber.
Parting with Hsin Chien at Hibiscus Tavern.
Silent at Her Window.
Song by the Walls.
Under a Border-Fortress.

Wang Chien (768?–833?)
Round Fan.
South, The.
Willow.

Wang Chih-huan (688?–742)
Ascend the Heron Tower.
Climbing the Stork Pavilion.
Hooded Crane Tower.
View from Heron Tower.

Wang Chiu-ssu (1468–1551)
After Reading the Poems of Master Han Shan,
    sels.
Ballad of Selling a Child.

Wang Fan-chih (c.590–c.660)
Drinking Alone.
I have a couple acres of land.
Poem: "When the rich pass proudly by."
Reclusive.
Requiem: "Houses in country and city."

Wang Han (*fl.* 713 A.D.)
Reason Fair, A (Liangzhou Song).
Song of Liang-chou.

Wang Ho-ch'ing
Tune: "Po Pu-tuan" Fat Couple.
Tune: "Po Pu-tuan" Long-Haired Little Dog.
Tune: "Tsui-chung T'ien" To the Giant
    Butterfly.

Wang Hsi-chih (321–79)
Orchid Pavilion.

Wang Hsiao-lung *See* Wang Xiaolong

Wang Ji (585–644)
Drinking Alone.
Farmers.
To a Kill-Joy.
View of the Wilds.
Written on the Tavern Wall.

Wang Kuo-wei (1877–1927)
Tune: "Rouged Lips."
Tune: "Sand of Silk-Washing Brook" ("Faded
    hibiscus and its leaves.").
Tune: "Sand of Silk-Washing Brook" ("Hazy
    mountain temple hides away behind the
    setting sun, A.").

Wang Pin-chih (*fl.* 400)
Orchard Pavilion.

Wang Po (c.650–76)
Departing from Yiyang in the Early Morning.
In the Mountains.
Parting by Moonlight in a River Pavilion.

Wang Po-ch'eng (*fl.* c.1279)
Song of Parting.

Wang Seng-ju (465–522)
Describing a Dream for Someone.

Wang Shih-chieng (1634–1711)
After Snow, Longing for Elder Brother Hsi-
    ch'iao.
Ch'ai-kuan Mountain Pass.
Composed at the West Wall of Tsou-p'ing
    Three Days After the Festival of Pure
    Brightness.
Medicine.
Pure Sound Pavilion.

Wang the Zealot
Bumping on an Ass.
Get Blind Drunk.
Ghosts Clap Hands.
Piece of the Loot, A.

Wang Ts'an (177–217)
Climbing the Tower.
Poem of Seven Sorrows.
Seven Sorrows.

Wang Wan (693–751?)
Stayover at Pei-Ku-Shan.

Wang Wei
Abschied des Freundes, Der.
After Long Rain.
After Source of the Peach Blossom Stream.
Alighting from my horse to drink with you.
Answer to Vice-Prefect Chang.
Army Ballad.
Arriving at Ba Gorge in the Morning.
At a House in the Bamboo Grove.
At Lake Yi.
At Li's Mountain Hermitage.
At Parting.
At the Hermitage of Master Fu.
Autumn Dusk at a Mountain Lodge.
Autumn Mountain Evening.
Autumn Twilight in the Mountains.
Bamboo Grove.
Bamboo Lane House.
Bamboo-Midst Cottage.
Bird and Waterfall Music.
Bird-Cry Creek.
Bird-Singing Stream.
Birdsong Torrent.
Birdsong Valley.

Chi River Gardens and Fields.
Climbing Pien-chueh Temple.
Climbing to the Monastery of Perception.
Cold Mountain, The.
Crossing the Yellow River.
Dawn on the Mountain.
Deep in the Mountain Wilderness.
Deer Camp.
Deer Enclosure.
Deer Park.
Deer Park.
Departure.
Dike of the Cormorants.
Farewell.
Farewell to Spring.
Floating on the River Han.
Four Examples from the Poems of River Wang
    Deer Enclosure.
Goodbye to Meng Haoran.
Hermitage at Chung-nan Mountain.
Hsin-I Village.
In Reply to Vice-Magistrate Chang.
In Retirement at Zhongnan.
In the Hills.
In the Mountain.
Light rain is on the light dust.
Meal for the Monks, A.
Melody of Wei City.
Mission to the Frontier.
Morning.
Mount Chung-Nan.
Mount Zhongnan.
Mourning for Yin Yao.
On the Mountain.
Parting.
Passing Hidden Fragrance Temple.
Passing the Temple of Teeming Fragrance.
Peerless Lady, The.
Playfully Inscribed on a Large Boulder.
Poem: "You who come from my village."
Poor dwelling near valley mouth.
Reply to a Magistrate.
Return to Wang River.
Rill of the House of the Luans.
Sailing Down the Han.
Second Song for the Worship of the Goddess
    at Yu Mountain: "Bidding the Goddess
    Farewell."
Seeing Someone Off.
Sitting Alone on an Autumn Night.
Sitting in mystic bamboo grove, back unseen.
So Farewell. And If for Ever, Still for Ever
    Fare Ye Well.
Song for Wei City, A.
Song of Peach Tree Spring.
Spring Night at Bamboo Pavillion, Presenting a
    Poem to Subprefect Qian about His Staying
    for Good in Blue Field Mountains.
Thinking of My Brother in Shantung on the
    Ninth Day of the Ninth Moon.
To Magistrate Zhang.
To See a Friend Off.
Twilight Comes.
Twilight in the Garden.
Verses: "You who come from the old village."
Villa at the Foot of Mount Chungnan.
Visiting Hsiang-Chi Monastery.
Visiting the Mountain Hermitage of a Monk at
    Gan-hua Monastery.
Walking at Leisure.
Way to the Temple, The.
Weeping for Ying Yao.
Weeping for Ying Yao.
Wheel River, *sels.*
You Come from My Village.
Wang Xiaolong (b. 1955)
    In Memoriam: Dedicated to My Father.
Wang Yang-ming (1472–1529)
    Magic City Monastery.
    Taoist Song.
Wang Yen-Shou (*fl.* 2nd cent. A.D.)
    Nightmare, The.
Wang Yin (b. 1962)
    Walt Whitman: "He is simply chopping wood
    in my front yard."

Wang, Yu (b. 1939)
    My Pain.
Wang Yü-ch'eng (954–1001)
    Song of the Crow Pecking at My Scarred
    Donkey.
Wang Yung (468–85)
    River Song, The.
Waniek, Marilyn Nelson (Lynn Nelson) (b. 1946)
    Abba Jacob and St. Francis.
    Alderman.
    Balance.
    Bali Hai Calls Mama.
    Ballad of Aunt Geneva, The.
    Canticle for Abba Jacob, A.
    Chosen.
    Daughters, 1900.
    Diverne's Waltz.
    Dusting.
    Emily Dickinson's Defunct.
    Freeman Field.
    House on Moscow Street, The.
    Letter to a Benedictine Monk.
    Lonely Eagles.
    Mama I Remember.
    My Grandfather Walks in the Woods.
    Porter.
    Sacrament of Poverty, The.
    Sleepless Nights.
    Source of the Singing, The.
    Star-Fix.
    Three Men in a Tent.
    Tuskegee Airfield.
    Women's Locker Room.
Wanley, Nathaniel (1634–80)
    Resurrection, The.
    Royal[1] Presents.
Warburton, N. J.
    Snake on D. H. Lawrence, The.
Ward, B. J.
    Daily Grind.
    Shakespeare as a Waiter.
Ward, Bert
    Twenty Million Buckets.
Ward, David Scott (b. 1961)
    Hunting in Twilight.
    My Brothers Make a Lantern.
Ward, Diane (b. 1956)
    Absolution.
    Approximately.
    Crossing.
    Glass House.
    Immediate Content Recognition.
    Limit.
    Lovely Stuff.
    Re-Verse.
    Shakeout.
    Tables in Pictures.
Ward, Edward (1667–1731)
    Nuptial Dialogues, *sels.*
    South Sea Ballad, A.
Ward, Frederick (b. 1937)
    Who.
Ward, Geoff (b. 1954)
    Distance Learning.
    English Music, *sels.*
    Horace Belisha.
    Trapped Wind.
    What's Wrong.
Ward, J. P. (b. 1937)
    To Get Clear.
    Unusual View of the Town.
Ward, Jerry W., Jr. (b. 1943)
    After the Report from Iron Mountain.
    Comfort-Maker.
    I Have Felt the Gulf: Mississippi.
    Journey 55.
    Mississippi: Bell Zone 1.
Ward, John Powell (b. 1937)
    Eros: "Valley of the Usk, exactly mid-distant."
    Here, Home.
    In the Box.
    London Welsh v. Bridgend.
    Marathon.
    Wye Below Bredwardine, The.

Ward, Thom (b. 1963)
    At Twenty-Three Weeks She Can No Longer
    See Anything South of Her Belly.
    Dark Underfoot.
    In the Interest of Possibility.
    On Being Kicked Out of the Harold
    Washington Library Center for Napping on
    the Floor.
    Poem Without a Freight Train or a Pocket
    Watch.
    Stray Dogs, Foaming.
    Tacit.
Ward, Whitney
    Montana's Biggest Weekend.
Ward, William Allen
    Texas.
Wardle, Sarah (b. 1969)
    Flight: "Mother blackbird I've been feeding,
    The."
Wardman, Gordon
    I have horns, but am not beast.
    Revisionism.
Wardrop, Daneen (b. 1952)
    Robert Frost at the Net.
Warfield, Catherine Anne (1816–77)
    Forests and Caverns.
    Sun-Struck Eagle, The.
Waring, Anna L. (1823–1910)
    My Times Are in Thy Hand.
Waring, Belle
    Baby Random.
    Back to Catfish.
    Baltazar Beats His Tutor at Scrabble.
    Breeze in Translation.
    Look.
    Nothing Happened.
    Our Lady of the Laundromat.
    Refuge at the One Step Down.
    Reprieve on the Stoop.
    So Get Over It, Honey.
    Tip, The.
    When a Beautiful Woman Gets on the Jutiapa
    Bus.
    You Could Have Been Me.
Warn, Emily
    After Reading the Book of Splendor.
    Dwelling.
    Nuit Blanche, Une.
    Word Between the World and God, The.
Warner, Gary
    Midnight percussion.
Warner, Patrick (b. 1963)
    Crocus (after snow), The.
    Heart, The.
    Poem Without Beginning or End.
Warner, Rex (b. 1905)
    Egyptian Kites.
    Hymn: "Splendid body is private, and calls for
    more, The."
Warner, Sylvia Townsend (1893–1978)
    Absence, The.
    After He Had Gone.
    Alarum, The.
    Astrophysics, *sel.*
    Become as little children.
    Benicasim.
    Building in Stone.
    Clock Plods On, The.
    Country Thought.
    Drawing You, Heavy With Sleep.
    Elizabeth.
    Epitaph: "Her grieving parents cradled here."
    Epitaph: "I, an unwedded wandering dame."
    Epitaph: "I, Richard Kent, beneath these
    stones."
    Epitaph: "John Bird, a laborer, lies here."
    Eyes of [*or* the] body, being blindfold by night,
    The.
    Green Valley, The.
    In April.
    Killing No Murder.
    Modo and Alciphron.
    Nelly Trim.
    Rival, The.

Road 1940.
Sad Green.
Sailor, The.
Since the first toss of gale that blew.
Song from the Bride of Smithfield.
Song: "She has left me, my pretty."
Triumph of Sensibility.
Waiting at Cerbere.

Warner, Val (b. 1946)
Clearing Out.

Warner, William (1558?–1609)
Albion's England, sels.

Warr, Michael
Brain on Ice.
Malcolm Is 'Bout More Than Wearing a Cap.
TV Dinner.

Warren, Harry
Gold Digger's Song (We're in the Money),
    The.
Spring Isn't Everything.

Warren, Robert Penn (1905–89)
Acquaintance with Time in Early Autumn.
After the Dinner Party.
Afterward.
Amazing Grace in the Back Country.
Arizona Midnight.
Aubade for Hope.
Audubon: A Vision, sels.
Ballad: Between the Boxcars [1923], sels.
Ballad of Billie Potts, The.
Bearded Oaks.
Birth of Love.
Blow, West Wind.
Brotherhood in Pain.
Crime.
Dawn.
Day Dr. Knox Did It, The, sels.
Dead Horse in Field.
Death of Time.
Evening Hawk.
Fear and Trembling.
Flaubert in Egypt.
Heart of Autumn.
If.
Island of Summer, sels.
Kentucky Mountain Farm, sels.
Lessons in History.
Letter from a Coward to a Hero.
Letter of a Mother.
Letter to a Friend.
Mexico is a Foreign Country: Five Studies in
    Naturalism, sel.
Mortal Limit.
Muted Music.
Nameless Thing.
Night Walking.
Only Poem, The.
Original Sin [: A Short Story].
Owl, The.
Penological Study: Southern Exposure, sels.
Pondy Woods.
Pro Sua Vita.
Promises, sels.
Pursuit.
Rattlesnake Country.
Red-Tail Hawk and Pyre of Youth.
Return, The: An Elegy.
Revelation.
Sila.
Sitting on Farm Lawn on Sunday Afternoon.
Some Quiet, Plain Poems, sels.
Tale of Time.
There's a Grandfather's Clock in the Hall.
To a Face in a Crowd.
To a Little Girl, One Year Old, in a Ruined
    Fortress, sel.
Two Studies in Idealism: Short Survey of
    American and Human History.
Vermont Ballad: Change of Season.
Vermont Thaw.
Vision.
Was It One of the Long Hunters of Kentucky
    who Discovered Boone at Sunset?
Whole Question, The.
You Sort Old Letters.

Warren, Rosanna (b. 1954)
Cormorant, The.
Daylights.
Funerary Portraits.
Hagar.
His Long Home.
In Creve Coeur, Missouri.
Interior at Petworth: From Turner.
Man, That Is Born of a Woman.
Max Jacob at Saint Benoît.
North, sels.
Renoir.
Snow Day.
Song: "Yellow coverlet, A."

Warren-Moore, Jackie (b. 1950)
All-Night Issue, The.
Dannemora Contraband.
For Etheridge Knight.
For Paula Cooper.
Pink Poem.

Warrior, Emma Lee (b. 1941)
Enemy's Eyes, The.
How I Came to Have a Man's Name.
New Indian Medicine.
Reginald Pugh, The Man Who Came from the
    Army.

Warsh, Lewis (b. 1944)
Before I Was Born.
Downward Mobility.
Dreaming Over a Page.
Elegy: "Leaves have a sense of, The."
Enmeshment.
Free Speech.
Going to Jail.
Good Omen.
Gout.
Halloween 1967.
Inside Long Treks.
Man Escaped, A.
Mistaken Identity.
Moving through Air.
Static, The.
Suicide Rates, The.
To John Ashbery.
Travelogue.
What I've Learned in My Travels.
White Nights.
Year from Monday, A.

Warton, Joseph (1722–1800)
Dying Indian, The.
Ode against Despair, sels.
Ode to Evening.

Warton, Thomas, the Elder (1688–1745)
Fashioned After the Manner of Master
    Geoffrey Chaucer in His Assembly of
    Fowls.
Ode on the Passion.
On the Spirit Adulterated by the Flesh.
Stanzas on the Psalms.

Warton, Thomas, the Younger (1728–90)
Come, gentle sleep, death's image though thou
    art.
On Bathing.
On the Marriage of the King, sels.
Pleasures of Melancholy, The, sel.
Sonnet: To the River Lodon.
While summer-suns o'er the gay prospect
    played.

Wascovich, Matthew
Serial Toxic Teen.
Wolf Packet and Rural America.

Washbourne, Thomas (1606–87)
Casting All Your Care upon God, for He
    Careth for You.
God's Two Dwellings.

Washington, Harriet Wilkes
Good Ole Days, The.

Washington, Ned
Give Me a Heart to Sing To.
Hundred Years from Today, A.
Love Is the Thing.
My Foolish Heart.
Nearness of You, The.
Woman's Intuition, A.

Wastell, Simon (d. 1632)
Microbiblion, sel.

Wat, Aleksander (1900–67)
Facing Bonnard.
From "Songs of a Wanderer."
Imagerie d'Epinal.
Joke, A.
Persian Parables, sels.

Waterhouse, Andrew (1958–2001)
Climbing My Grandfather.
Now the City Has Fallen.
Speaking About My Cracked Sump.

Waterman, Andrew (b. 1940)
Birth Day.

Waters, Chocolate
Singer, The.

Waters, Michael (b. 1949)
American Bandstand.
Burden Lifters, The.
Christ at the Apollo, 1962.
Cognac.
Conversion of Saint Paul, The.
Demonstration: Women's House of Detention,
    1965.
Divine Will.
First Lesson: Winter Trees.
Horse: "First horse I ever saw, The."
Making Love at the Frost Place.
"Night in the Tropics" (1858-59?).

Watkins, Vernon (1906–67)
Collier, The.
Cwmrhydyceirw Elegiacs.
Demands of the Muse.
Foal.
Heron, The.
Mare, The.
Music of Colours: The Blossom Scattered.
Music of Colours—White Blossom.
Ode to Swansea.
Ophelia.
Replica, the.
Returning to Goleufryn.
Taliesin and the Mockers.

Watkins, William Jon (b. 1942)
Mall, The.

Watkins-Cothran, Eunice Juaquina
Beloved Ones, The.

Watkyns, Rowland (fl. 1635–64)
Anabaptist, The.
Blackamoors, The.
Common People, The.
Gardener, The.
Golden Grove, Carmarthen.
Holy Sepulchre, The.
New Illiterate Lay-Teachers, The.
Peace and War.
Periwig, A.
Shrew, The.
To the Reader.
Upon Christ's Nativity or Christmas.
Upon the mournful death of our late Sovereign
    Lord Charles the first, King of England, etc.

Watley, Matthew
For the Man I Met on Georgia Ave.
Negroes.
100 Million.

Watson, Clyde (b. 1947)
Dilly Dilly Piccalilli.
Do the Baby Cake-Walk.
Knickerbocker Knockabout.
Phoebe in a Rosebush.
Rock, Rock, Sleep, My Baby.

Watson, Craig
Currency.
Home Guard, sel.

Watson, Ellen Doré
Battered Toddler, Page B6.
First Date in Twenty-Five Years.
First Sight: "Blind woman—who by some
    miracle can, A."
Natural.

Watson, Miles Garett
Sestina Halted in a Rain Delay.

Watson, Roderick (b. 1943)
Is This Man, Martin Bormann?

Watson, Rosamund Marriott ("Graham R. Tomson"; "R. Armytage") (1863–1911)
Aubade: "Lights are out in the street, and a cool wind swings, The."
Ave atque Vale.
Ballad of the Bird-Bride.
Ballad of the Were-Wolf, A.
Betty Barnes, the Book-Burner.
Cage, The.
Children of the Mist.
Die Zauberflöte.
Enchanted Princess, An.
Hic Jacet.
Midnight Harvest, A.
Moor Girl's Well, The.
Nirvana.
Of the Earth, Earthy.
Ruined Altar, A.
Serenade: "Who is it sings the gypsies' song to-night."
Vespertilia.
White Bird, The.
White Lady, The.

Watson, Thomas (c.1557–92)
My Love is Past.

Watson, Sir William (1858–1935)
Ode in May.
Song: "April, April, / Laugh thy girlish laughter."

Watta, Oumarou (b. 1951)
Cloud Rains.
Stone at the Tip of the Tongue, A.

Watten, Barrett (b. 1948)
Complete Thought I - XXV.
Progress, sels.
Radio.
Real Estate, sels.
Statistics.

Watts, Alaric Alexander (1797–1864)
Ten Years Ago.

Watts, Enos D. (b. 1939)
Crocuses and Crown-of-Thorns.
Longliner at Sunset.
Summer Solstice.

Watts, Isaac (1674–1748)
Cradle Hymn, A.
Day of Judg[e]ment, The; an Ode [Attempted in English Sapphic].
Felicity.
Flying Fowl, and Creeping Things, Praise Ye the Lord.
How Doth the Little Busy Bee.
How sweet and awful is the place.
Hymn: "When I survey the wondrous cross."
Incomprehensible, The.
Jesus shall reign where'er the sun.
Joy to the World.
Launching Into Eternity.
Law Given at Sinai, The.
Man Frail, and God Eternal.
Mr. Gunston is Shown round Heaven [or To the Dear Memory of Thomas Gunston, Esq.].
Mr. Mead, Mr. Bates, and Mr. Gouge [or An Elegy on Mr. Thomas Gouge].
Mrs. Warner Arrives Above [or An Elegiac Thought on Mrs. Anne Warner].
On the Landing of William III [or A Hymn of Praise for Three Great Salvations].
Polyglot in Paradise, A [or On the Death of an Aged and Honoured Relative].
Sluggard, The.

Watts, May Thielgaard (d. 1975)
Vision.

Watts-Dunton, Theodore (1832–1914)
Coleridge.
Sonnet's Voice, The.

Waugh, Arthur (1866–1943)
Ballade of the Devout Husband, The.
Her Majesty.
Old Road Map, The.
Romaunt of Cecilia, The.
Town and Country.

Waugh, Evelyn (1903–66)
Loved One, The, sel.
They told me, Francis Hinsley, they told me you were hung.

Wayman, Tom (b. 1945)
Did I Miss Anything?
Hating Jews.
Long Beach Suite.
Picketing Supermarkets.
Wayman in Love.

Wayne, Jane O. (b. 1938)
By Accident.
Cleaning Indian Dahl.
Eavesdropper, The.
In Praise of Zigzags.

Wearne, Alan (b. 1948)
Go on, tell me the season is over.
Nightmarkets, The, sels.

Weatherford, Carole Boston (b. 1956)
Charleston Baskets.
From Birmingham to Bristol in a Boxcar.
From the Mouth of the Gxara.
Ladies of Dimbaza, The.
Queen Ijo's Blues.
Tan Chanteuse, The.
Tar Baby on the Soapbox, The.

Weatherly, Tom (b. 1942)
Canto 7: First Thesis.
Canto 10: Wooten.
Croatan.
First Monday Scottsboro Alabama.
Fishes / theirs fit.
Gandhabba #5.
P.W.T.
Vocal texts evoke.

Weaver, Afaa Michael (b. 1951)
Afternoon Train.
Appaloosa, The.
Baby Boy.
Baltimore.
Beginnings.
Black and White Galaxie, The.
Black Man's Sonata, A.
Blind Solo.
Borders.
Brooklyn.
Charleston.
Colors—Struck.
Dancers.
Dogs, The.
Easy Living.
Evidence of Life.
Imitation of Life.
Improvisation for Piano.
In C. W.'s Closet.
Left Bank Jazz Society, The.
Lines: "I feel your legs touching."
Luxembourg Garden.
Message on Cape Cod, The.
Michele.
Missing Patriarch, The.
My Father's First Baseball Game.
My Father's Geography.
New Nephilim, A.
Picnic, an Homage to Civil Rights, The.
Poets, The.
Providence Journal V: Israel of Puerto Rico.
Sin, 1969.
Sub Shop Girl.
Thelonius.
Water Song.
Weekend Equestrian, The.

Weaver, Andy (b. 1971)
Were the Bees, sels.

Weaver, Michael S. See Weaver, Afaa Michael

Webb, Charles
Death of Santa Claus, The.
Potato Bug.
Rumpelstiltskin Convention.

Webb, Charles Harper
Amplified Dog.
Arson.
At Summer's End.
At *The Tempest* with a Pregnant Wife.
Biblical Also-Rans.
Coach Class Seats.
Faith.
Identifying with the Buddha.
Invaders from South of the Border Imperil Native Population.
Killing the Animals.
Marrying.
Meat Michelangelo.
Ooh My Soul.
Prayer for the Man Who Mugged My Father, 72.
What We Believe.
You Missed the Earthquake, Bill.

Webb, Charles Henry ("John Paul") (b. 1834)
Revenge.

Webb, Francis (1925–73)
Airliner.
Around Costessey, sels.
Clouds.
Death at Winson Green, A.
End of the Picnic.
Gunner, The.
Hospital Night.
Laid Off.
Port Phillip Night.
Tip for Saturday, A.
Towards the Land of the Composer.
Wild Honey.

Webb, Harri (b. 1920)
Abbey Cwmhir.
Cywydd o Fawl.
Epil y Filiast.
Nightingales, The.
Ode to the Severn Bridge.
Stone Face, The.
Synopsis of the Great Welsh Novel.
Thanks in Winter.
Vive Le Sport.

Webb, Mary (1881–1927)
Why?

Webb, Phyllis (b. 1927)
Breaking.
Marvell's Garden.
Naked Poems, sels.
Patience: "Patience is the wideness of the night."
Second Hand, The.
Sunday Water, sel.
Tall Tale, A; or, A Moral Song.

Webbe, Charles (fl. c.1678)
Against Indifference.

Weber, Richard (b. 1932)
Lady and Gentleman.

Webster, Augusta Davies ("Cecil Home") (1837–94)
By the Looking-Glass.
Castaway, A, sel.
Circe, sels.
Enigma No. 6.
Faded.
Flood of Is in Brittany, The.
Medea in Athens, sel.
Mother and Daughter, sels.
Passing Away.
Where Home Was.

Webster, John (1580?–1625?)
Devil's Law Case, The, sels.
Duchess of Malfi, The, sels.
White Devil, The, sels.

Webster, Paul Francis
Baltimore Oriole.
Black Coffee.
Doctor, Lawyer, Indian Chief.
I Got It Bad and That Ain't Good.
Jump for Joy.
Love Is a Many-Splendored Thing.
Secret Love.
Two Cigarettes in the Dark.
What's Your Story, Morning Glory.

Wechsler, Elina
Child is Born, A.
Lilith, Adam's First Companion.
Once Again, Anne Frank.

Weckherlin, Georg Rudolph (1584–1653)
Concerning the King of Sweden.
Love Is Life and Death.
She Is the Greatest Wealth.
To Breisach, Taken by That Supremely
  Celebrated Hero, Bernhard, Duke of
  Saxony.
To Germany.

Wedderburn, Robert *See* James, John

Wedekind, Frank (1864–1918)
Blind Youth, The.

Wedmore, Suellen
Why I'm Different in Wyoming.

Wee, Rebecca
Hoop Snake.

Weeks, James Eyre (b. 1719?)
Answer by the Lady's Maid [to a Poem Left in
  a Lady's Toilet].
Poem Left in a Lady's Toilet.

Weelkes, Thomas (*fl.* c.1600)
Fara Diddle Dyno.
Madrigal: "Ay me, alas, heigh ho, heigh ho!"

Weems, Mary (b. 1954)
B.B. Blues.
Dime after Dime.
Funk.
Return to Temptation.
Yesterday.

Wei Chuang (836–910)
Against Conscription.
Candle Dies, A.
Green Pond, A.
Hidden Tears.
I Remember.
Lament of the Lady of Qin.
Moon Dips Low, The.
To the Tune: Beautiful Barbarian.
Tune: "The Bodhisattva Foreigner."
Tune: "Thinking of the Imperial Capital."

Wei Feng (*fl.* 10th cent. A.D.)
Staying with Master Heng Chao at Roost of
  the Sages Monastery on Mount Lu.

Wei Ying-wu (b. 736)
At Chuzhou on the Western Stream.
Autumn Night: A Letter Sent to Ch'iu.
Autumn Night Message: To Qiu.
East of the Town.
Milky Way.
Mooring at Twilight in Yuyi District.
Poem to a Taoist Hermit on Quanjiao
  Mountain, A.
Tartar Horse.

Weigl, Bruce (b. 1949)
Burning Shit at An Khe.
Convoy.
Dialectical Materialism.
Hand to Hand.
Her Life Runs Like a Red Silk Flag.
Him, on the Bicycle.
Homage to Elvis, Homage to the Fathers.
Home.
Impossible, The.
Last Lie, The.
May.
Mines.
Monkey.
Oh, Atonement.
On Not Finding Frost's Grave in the Dark.
On the Anniversary of Her Grace.
Our 17th Street Years.
Painting on a T'ang Dynasty Water Vessel.
Red Squirrel.
Regret for the Mourning Doves Who Failed to
  Mate.
River Journal.
Sailing to Bien Hoa.
Self-Portrait at Fifty-Three.
Sky in Daduza Township, The.
Snowy Egret.
Temple Near Quang Tri, Not on the Map.
Temptation.
Three Fish.
Way of Tet, The.
What Saves Us.
Why I Hate Theory.

Why Nothing Changes for Miss Ngo Thi
  Thanh.
Why We Are Forgiven.

Weil, Joe
Ben Hur.

Weinberger, Eliot (b. 1949)
Anecdotal Evidence.
Changs.
Wind: "Wind: what is it? You don't see it but
  you hear it, and you feel its force."

Weinblatt, Jennifer
Marriage Song for Many Voices.

Weiner, Estha
When My Poem Appeared.

Weiner, Hannah (b. 1928)
Clairvoyant Journal, *sels.*
From *Spoke / Aug 19.*
Little Books / 137 / Silence Mar 22 79.
Little Books / Indians, *sels.*
Remembered Sequel.
Sand.
Spoke Aug 19, *sels.*

Weiner, Joshua
Yonder Tree, The.

Weingarten, Roger (b. 1945)
Ghost Frost.
Inquisition, The: A Romance.

Weinstein, Berish *See* Vaynshteyn, Berysh

Weinstein, Norman
Drummond's Lover Sings the Blues.
Ethiopian Apocalypse of Don, The.
Garvey's Head as Value.
Migration of Drummond's Organs (After
  Death), The.

Weinstock, Don
You Don't Want to Hear a Poem, Do You?

Weisburd, Stefi
Sponge Boy.

Weise, Christian (1642–1708)
Upon the Birth of a Young and Highly Desired
  Son.

Weiser, Karen (b. 1975)
How can the day arrest.

Weismiller, Edward (b. 1915)
Crystal Moment.
Hemlocks in Autumn.
Skull.
To the Woman in Bond Street Station.
Vermont: Spring Rains.

Weiss, George David (b. 1921)
Lullaby of Birdland.
Oh! What It Seemed to Be.
Too Close for Comfort.

Weiss, Lynne
Other Tongues.

Weiss, Renée
Conference, A.
For Gil and Other Incurables.
Lost Wood, The.

Weiss, Theodore (b. 1916)
After All.
Clothes Maketh the Man.
Conference, A.
Fire at Alexandria, The.
Flypaper.
For Gil and Other Incurables.
Good Grey Poet, The.
Lost Wood, The.
Pair of Shoes, A.
Shorthand.
Ten Little Rembrandts.
Ultimate Antientropy, The.

Weissbort, Daniel (b. 1935)
Mourning.

Weisz, Olga Klein
Jerusalem, I am a pilgrim.
Sefarad.

Weitsman, Sojun Mel
Mondo.
One third of my life has been spent in this
  practice and you.

Welburn, Ron (b. 1944)
Ben Webster: "Did You Call Her Today?"

Bones and Drums.
Gonsalves.

Welch, James (b. 1940)
Arizona Highways.
Christmas Comes to Moccasin Flat.
Day after Chasing Porcupines.
Grandma's Man.
Harlem, Montana.
Magic Fox.
Man from Washington, The.
Never Give a Bum an Even Break.
Plea to Those Who Matter.
Snow Country Weavers.
Surviving.

Welch, Lew (b. 1920)
Basic Con, The.
Chicago Poem.
Difficulty Along the Way.
Empress Herself Served Tea to Su Tung-Po,
  The.
He Thanks His Woodpile.
I Saw Myself.
In Answer to a Question From P. W.
Large Little Circle.
Not Yet 40, My Beard is Already White.
Redwood Haiku.
Sausalito Trash Prayer.
Small Sentence to Drive Yourself Sane.
Springtime in the Rockies, Lichen.
Step out onto the planet.
Taxi Suite, *sel.*
This Book is for Magda.
Whenever I Make a New Poem.

Welch, Liliane (b. 1937)
Claude Monet's Water Landscapes.
December 1972: First Winter Ascension of the
  Sass Maor.
Dikes on Fundy Bay.
In Cézanne's studio, we're dappled with joy.
Tattoo.

Welish, Marjorie (b. 1944)
Blood or Color.
Casting Sequences.
Crossing Disappearing behind Them.
Detained by Rest.
If I Blindfold You.
Kiss Tomorrow Goodbye.
Macbeth in Battle.
Respected, Feared, and Somehow Loved.
Scalpel in Hand.
Skin.
Textile 9.
Textile 11.
Textile 12.
Textile 13.
Veil.
Wild Sleeve.
Within This Book, Called Marguerite.

Wellburn, Ron
Pitching Coups.

Weller, Archie (b. 1957)
Ngungalari.
Story of Frankie . . . My Man, The.

Welles, Winifred (1893–1939)
Dogs and Weather.

Wellesley, Dorothy, Duchess of Wellington (1891–1956)
Asian Desert.
Deserted House, *sels.*
Fire.
Fishing.
Horses.
Lenin, *sel.*
Maiden Castle.
Matrix, *sel.*
Morning After, The.
Walled Garden.

Wellman, Mac (b. 1945)
Having Led a Charmed Life, He Had to be
  Hanged Twice.
Hollowness, *sel.*
Mad Wolf in Lunar Web, Mad Crow on the
  Beach.
Rat Minaret: Miniaturist-Divan, The, *sels.*
Terminal Hip, *sel.*

Wells, Amos Russel (1862–1935)
Ambitious Ant, The.
By Proxy.

Wells, Carolyn (1862–1942)
Famous Baths and Bathers.
Fate.
How To Tell the Wild Animals.
Limerick: "Tutor who tooted a flute, A."
Of Modern Books.
Original Summer Girl, The.
Pastoral in Posters, A.
Poster Girl's Defence, The.
Problem, A.
Universal Favorite, The.

Wells, Jeanne
July Thirteenth.

Wells, Nigel (b. 1944)
Owl Wives.
Up.

Wells, Robert (fl. 1947)
Christmas Song, The.

Wells, Zachariah (b. 1976)
Fool's Errand.

Welt, Bernard (b. 1952)
I stopped writing poetry.

Wen Chao (fl. 10th cent. A.D.)
Farewell to Master Yu Chao.
Hearing the Gibbons Call in Pa Gorge.

Wen T'ien-hsiang (1236–82)
Chin-ling Post Station.

Wen T'ing-yün (812–72)
Brilliant Moon, A.
Deva-like Barbarian.
Embers of Incense.
Gold Glimmers and Fades.
In Her Moonlit Chamber.
In the Mountains as Autumn Begins.
In the South Courtyard.
Near the Lizhou Ferry.
News So Seldom Comes.
Passing a Ruined Palace.
She Sighs on Her Jade Lute.
Temple of Su Wu, The.
To a Friend Bound East.
To the Tune: Southern Song.
To the Tune: The Water Clock.
Tune: "Beautiful Barbarians."

Wen Yi-tuo [or Wen I-to] (1898–1946)
Dead Water.
Laundry Song, The.
Miracle.

Wenderoth, Joe (b. 1966)
Aesthetics of the Bases Loaded Walk.
All That Really Happens.
As Hour and Year Collapsed.
Billy's Famous Lounge.
Death.
Detailed History of the Western World.
Disfortune.
Each Sentence Is Into the Fast.
First Impression.
January 11, 1997.
Moon River.
Museum.
My Life: "Somehow it got into my room."
Narrative Poem.
Only Fortunate Thing, The.
Outside the Hospital.
Promise.
Send New Beasts.
We Were a Whole Army Underground.
Where I Stand with Regard to the Game.
Writer.

Wendt, Ingrid (b. 1944)
Lady on the Cover of Family Circle, The.
Singing the Mozart Requiem.
Starting from Scratch.

Wenger, Michael
Zen Corners.

Wennrayt, Kiki See Wainwright, Kiki

Wenthe, William
White Settlement.

Wentworth, Anne (fl. 1676–79)
Revelation 5, October 8.
Revelation 8, March 31.

Weöres, Sándor (1913–89)
Another World.
Ars Poetica.
Brambleberry, The.
Clouds.
Coolie.
Dissolving Presence, A.
Dragon-Steed, The.
Eternal Moment.
Eternity.
Four Elements, The.
In Memoriam Gyula Juhász.
Insect.
Lost Parasol, The, sel.
Monkeyland.
Moon and Farmstead.
Never Again Another Garden.
On Death.
Plain, The.
Rain.
Rayflower.
Saturn Declining.
Seventh Symphony,The.
Sheep School.
Song: Boundless Space.
Storm from the Far Heights.
Time's Come Up Pearls.
To Die.
Twentieth Century Fresco.
Valse Triste.
Whisper in the Dark.
Wingless.

Werfel, Franz (1890–1945)
Lasting Things, The.
Man is Dumb, A.

Werner, Judith
Ethel Rosenberg and Me.

Wershler-Henry, Darren (b. 1966)
Ten Out of Ten, or, Why Poetry Criticism
Sucks in 2003, sels.

Wescott, Glenway (b. 1901)
Poet at Night-Fall, The.

Wesley, Charles (1707–88)
Arise, my soul, arise, Shake off thy guilty
fears.
Catholic Love.
Come on, my partners in distress.
Come, Thou Almighty King.
For the Anniversary Day of One's Conversion.
Free Grace.
Hark, how all the welkin rings! Glory to the
King of Kings.
Hark! the herald angels sing, Glory to the
newborn King.
He Shook off the Beast.
Hymns, sel.
Let earth and heaven combine.
Love Divine, All Loves Excelling.
Morning Hymn.
N T.
None is like Jeshuron's God.
On Worldly Prelates.
Rejoice! The Lord is King.
Still, O Lord, for Thee I Tarry.
True Use of Music, The.
Wrestling Jacob.

Wesley, Samuel (1691–1739)
On the Setting Up of Mr. Butler's Monument
in Westminster Abbey.
On Two Souldiers Killing One Another for a
Groat, sel.
Pindaricque on the Grunting of a Hog, A, sel.

Weslowski, Dieter
Dry World.
Heart.
Pablo.
Year I Found, The.
Zoe and the Ghosts.

Wessling, Suki
Angry.

West, Arthur Graeme
Night Patrol, The.

West, Gilbert (1703–56)
Stowe, the Gardens of the Rt. Hon. Richard
Lord Viscount Cobham, sels.

West, Jane (1758–1852)
To May.

West, Jean
I paid a spring-time visit to your country.

West, Kathleene
By Water Divined.
On Track.
To My Twin Sister Who Died at Birth.

West, Robert A. (1809–65)
Two Evangelists.

Westendorf, Thomas P.
I'll Take You Home Again, Kathleen.

Western Brothers
We're Frightfully BBC, sel.

Westheimer, David (1917–2005)
At the Movies.

**Westmorland, Mildmay Fane, 2d Earl of (1602–
65)**
How to Ride Out a Storm.
In Praise of Fidelia.
My Country Audit.
Occasioned by Seeing a Walk of Bay Trees.
Reveille Matin, or Good Morrow to a Friend.
Shamed by the Creature.
To Retiredness.
To Sir John Wentworth, Upon His Curiosities
and Courteous Entertainment at Summerly
in Lovingland.

Weston, Mildred (b. 1900)
Departure.
Primitive Place.

Weston, R. P. (1878–1936)
Epitaph: "Beneath this stone lies William
Burke."
I've Got Rings on My Fingers.

Westphalen, Emilio Adolfo (b. 1911)
You Came to Rest.

Wetzsteon, Rachel (b. 1967)
Coming Back to the Cave.
Dinner at Le Caprice.
Drinks in the Town Square.
Late Show, The.
Learning from the Movies.
Poem for a New Year.
Rival, A.
Surgical Moves.
Thoughts While Walking.
Three Songs.
Three Songs.
Urban Gallery.
Witness.

Wever, Robert (fl. c.1550)
Lusty Juventus, sels.

Whalen, Philip (1923–2002)
Absolute / Reality, namely.
Canoeing Up Cabarga Creek, sel.
Chanson d'Outre Tombe.
Coming Forth By Day.
Complaint: To the Muse.
Damachi.
Dharmakaya.
Elizabethan Phrase, The.
End of the line, The.
Epigrams & Imitations, sels.
For Shunko Enjo.
Grievances.
Hoist great blocks of language into place.
Hymnus Ad Patrem Sinensis.
Imperfect Sonnet, The.
International Date Line, Monday/Monday
27:XI:67.
Never Apologize; Never Explain.
Off . . . / over / that way.
On the Way to the Zendō.
Pathogenesis.
Pet Shop.
Poem: "Like a bird."
Regalia in Immediate Demand!
Saturday.
Simple Life, The.
Slop Barrel, The.
Somewhere Else.
Sourdough Mountain Lookout.

Take dandelions first salad.
Waiting for Claude.
Walking beside the Kamogawa, Remembering Nansen and Fudo and Gary's Poem.
We Sing in Our Sleep. We Converse with the Dead in Our Dreams.

Wharton, Anne (1659–85)
Elegy on the Earl of Rochester.
My Fate.

Wharton, Edith (1862–1937)
Autumn Sunset, An.
Chartres.
Experience.
Last Giustiniani, The.
Life.
Mona Lisa.
Mortal Lease, The: V.
Terminus.
Tomb of Ilaria Giunigi, The.
Two Backgrounds.

Wharton, Thomas Wharton, 1st Marquess of (1648–1715)
Lilli Burleo [A New Song].

Whately, Richard, Archbishop (1787–1863)
There Is a Place in Distant Seas.

Wheatley, David (b. 1970)
Along a Cliff.
Autumn, the Nightwalk, the City, the River.
Backward Glance, A.
Chronicle.
Fourteen.
Gasmask, The.
Moonshine.
Numerology.
Sonnets to James Clarence Mangan, sels.
Verlaine Dying.

Wheatley, Phillis (c.1753–84)
America.
Farewel[l] to America, A. To Mrs. S. W.
On Being Brought from Africa to America.
On Imagination.
On the Death of a Young Gentleman.
On the Death of the Rev. Mr. George Whitefield [1770].
Thoughts on the Works of Providence, sel.
To His Excellency General Washington.
To Maecenas.
To S. M., a Young African Painter.
To the Rev. Dr. Thomas Amory on Reading His Sermons on Daily Devotion.
To the Right Honourable William, Earl of Dartmouth.
To the University of Cambridge, in New-England.

Wheeler, Jackson
Falstaff's Dream.

Wheeler, Post (1869–1956)
Rain Race, The.

Wheeler, Susan (b. 1955)
He or She That's Got the Limb, That Holds Me Out on It.
In Juarez.
Produce, Produce.
Song for the Spirit of Natalie Going.
That Been to Me My Lives Light and Saviour.

Wheelock, C. Webster (b. 1939)
Divorcee.

Wheelock, John Hall (1886–1978)
Afternoon: Amagansett Beach.
Beethoven.
Earth.
Earth.
Earth, Take Me Back.
Fish-Hawk, The.
House in the Green Well, The.
Love and Liberation.
Nirvana.
Sunday Evening in the Common.
This Quiet Dust.
Triumph of Love.

Wheelwright, John (1897–1940)
Abel.
Anathema. Maranatha!
Bread-Word Giver.

Come Over and Help Us; a Rhapsody.
Cross Questions.
Esprit d'Escalier.
Fish Food.
In the Bathtub, to Mnemosyne.
Lion.
Live, Evil Veil.
Poem by David McCord, A.
Slow Curtain.
There Is No Opera like "Lohengrin."
Train Ride.
Why Must You Know?
Would You Think?

Whipple, Laura
My Dad.

Whitaker, John (1735–1808)
Roman Tribute, A.

Whitbread, Thomas (b. 1931)
Alcohol Question, The.
Alpine, Texas.
November 25, 1963.
Whomp and Moonshiver.

White, Artress Bethany
Beelzebub Chronicles, The.
Moon Daughters.

White, Brenda Black
Country Boy, City Girl.
Tolly Masters.

White, Bukka (1909–77)
Fixin' to Die.

White, Dorothy (1630–85)
Epistle of Love and of Consolation unto Israel, An.

White, Elwyn Brooks (1899–1985)
Chairs in Snow.
Commuter.
Definitions, sels.
I Paint What I See.
Listener's Guide to the Birds, A.
Marble-Top.
Natural History.
Red Cow Is Dead, The.
Village Revisited.
Window Ledge in the Atom Age.

White, Gail
Dead Armadillos.
Leopard in Eden, The.
Queen Gertrude's Soliloquy.
Traveling with Cats on a Snowy Evening.
Walt Whitman Encounters the Cosmos with the Cats of New York.

White, Henry Kirke (1785–1806)
Clifton Grove, sels.
Sonnet: "Give me a cottage on some Cambrian wild."
Time: A Poem, sels.
Winter Traveler, The.

White, Howard (b. 1945)
Men There Were Then, The.

White, J. P. (b. 1940)
In Ecclesiastes I Read.

White, James L. (1936–81)
Oshi.

White, Joseph Blanco (1775–1841)
To Night.

White, Kenneth (b. 1936)
Brandan's Last Voyage.
McTaggart.
Song of the Coffin Close.

White, Lawrence L.
Acanthus.
Emetic.
Soundtrack.
Station. He.She.You.Me.
World as I Found It, The.

White, Marvin K.
Foursomes.

White, Michael
Recurrence.

White, Sam (b. 1973)
Loved One: "You were not gone."

White, Viola C.
Child of Adam.

Whitehead, Charles (1804–62)
Lamp, The.

Whitehead, Christiania (b. 1969)
Brutus' Last Song.
Daybreak.
Girls Sitting Together Like Dolls.
Grass Crust, The.
Marian Hymn.
Morning Thesis.

Whitehead, William (1715–85)
Charge to the Poets, A, sel.
On the Late Improvements at Nuneham, the Seat of the Earl of Harcourt.

Whiteman, Roberta Hill (Roberta Hill) (b. 1947)
Climbing Gannett.
For Heather, Entering Kindergarten.
From the Sun Itself.
Horses in Snow.
In the Longhouse, Oneida Museum.
One More Sign.
Patterns.
Reaching Yellow River.
Star Quilt.
Variations for Two Voices.
Waiting for Robinson.
White Land, The.
Woman Seed Player.

Whitfield, James M. (1823–78)
America.
Poem Written for the Celebration of the Fourth Anniversary of President Lincoln's Emancipation Proclamation, A, sel.
To A. H.

Whiting, George (1884–1943)
My Blue Heaven.

Whiting, Richard A.
She's Funny That Way (I Got a Woman, Crazy for Me).

Whitlow, Carolyn Beard
Book of Routh.
Poem for the Children.
Rockin' A Man, Stone Blind.

Whitman, Albery Allson (1851–1901)
Idyll of the South, An, sel.
Lute of Afric's Tribe, The.
Octoroon, The, sels.
Twasinta's Seminoles; Or Rape of Florida, sels.

Whitman-Raymond, Lee Miriam
Quickening.

Whitman, Ruth (b. 1922)
Bubba Esther, 1888.
Cutting the Jewish Bride's Hair.
Hearing a Mozart Duo at 36,000 Feet.
Laughing Gas.
Listening to Grownups Quarreling.
My Greatgreatuncle the Archbishop.
Touro Synagogue.
Uncle Harry at the La Brea Tar Pits.

Whitman, Sarah Helen (1803–78)
Morning-Glory, The.
November Landscape, A.
Past, The.
Raven, The.
Sonnets from the Series Relating to Edgar Allan Poe, sels.
To ———: "Vainly my heart had with thy sorceries striven."

Whitman, Teresa
Hunger and Imagination.
Scissortails.

Whitman, Walt (1819–92)
Aboard at a Ship's Helm.
After the Sea-Ship.
After the Supper and Talk.
America.
Among the Multitude.
Are You the New Person Drawn toward Me?
Army Corps on the March, An.
Artilleryman's Vision, The.
As Adam Early in the Morning.
As I Ebb'd with the Ocean of Life.
As I Lay with My Head in Your Lap Camerado.
As I Sit Writing Here.

As If a Phantom Caress'd Me.
As Toilsome I Wander'd Virginia's Woods.
Ashes of Soldiers.
Base of All Metaphysics, The.
Beat! Beat! Drums!
Beauty.
Beginning My Studies.
Behold This Swarthy Face.
Bivouac on a Mountain Side.
Broadway.
By Blue Ontario's Shore, sels.
By the Bivouac's Fitful Flame.
Cavalry Crossing a Ford.
Chanting the Square Deific.
Chants Democratic and Native Americans: 5.
City of Orgies.
Clear Midnight, A.
Come Up from the Fields Father.
Commonplace, The.
Crossing Brooklyn Ferry.
Dalliance of the Eagles, The.
Death's Valley.
Dirge for Two Veterans.
Dismantled Ship, The.
Earth, My Likeness.
Eidólons.
Europe, the 72d and 73d Year of These States.
Evening Lull, An.
Excelsior.
Facing West from California's Shores.
Fancies at Navesink, sels.
Farm Picture, A.
Fast-Anchor'd Eternal O Love!
For You O Democracy.
From Far Dakota's Cañons (June 25, 1876).
From Pent-up Aching Rivers.
Full of Life Now.
Give Me the Splendid Silent Sun.
Glimpse, A.
Good-Bye, My Fancy!
Good-Bye My Fancy.
Hand-Mirror, A.
Hast Never Come to Thee an Hour.
Here the Frailest Leaves of Me.
Hours Continuing Long.
I Am He That Aches with Love.
I Am the Poet.
I Dream'd in a Dream.
I Hear America Singing.
I Hear It Was Charged against Me.
I Heard You Solemn-Sweet Pipes of the Organ.
I Saw in Louisiana a Live-Oak Growing.
I Sing the Body Electric, sels.
I Sit and Look Out.
In Paths Untrodden.
Italian Music in Dakota.
Joy, Shipmate, Joy!
Last Invocation, The.
Leaf for Hand in Hand, A.
Leaves of Grass [1855 Version], sels.
Live Oak, with Moss.
Mannahatta.
March in the Ranks Hard-Prest, and the Road
    Unknown, A.
Memories of President Lincoln, sels.
Miracles.
My Picture-Gallery.
Native Moments.
No Labor-Saving Machine.
Noiseless Patient Spider, A.
Not Heat Flames Up and Consumes.
Not Heaving from My Ribb'd Breast Only.
Now Precedent Songs, Farewell.
O Tan-Faced Prairie-Boy.
O You Whom I Often and Silently Come.
Of the Terrible Doubt of Appearances.
Old Man's Thought of School, An.
Old Salt Kossabone.
On the Beach at Night.
On the Beach at Night Alone.
On the Same Picture.
Once I Pass'd through a Populous City.
One's-Self I Sing.
Orange Buds by Mail from Florida.
Osceola.
Out of the Cradle Endlessly Rocking.

Passage to India.
Patrolling Barnegat.
Prairie Sunset, A.
Prairie-Grass Dividing, The.
Prayer of Columbus.
Preface to Leaves of Grass [1855].
Promise to California, A.
Proud Music of the Storm.
Reconciliation.
Recorders Ages Hence.
Respondez!
Roots and Leaves Themselves Alone.
Rounded Catalogue Divine Complete, The.
Runner, The.
Scented Herbage of My Breast.
Ship Starting, The.
Sight in Camp [in the Daybreak Gray and
    Dim], A.
Sleepers, The, sels.
Sometimes with One I Love.
Song for All Seas, All Ships.
Song for Occupations, A, sel.
Song of Joys, A, sel.
Song of Myself, sels.
Song of the Broad-Axe [or Broad-Ax], sels.
Song of the Exposition, sels.
Song of the Open Road, sels.
Sparkles from the Wheel.
Spirit Whose Work Is Done.
Spontaneous Me.
Stronger Lessons.
Tears.
Thanks in Old Age.
That Shadow My Likeness.
There Was a Child Went Forth.
These I Singing in Spring.
This Compost.
This Moment Yearning and Thoughtful.
Thought ("Of obedience, faith, adhesiveness.").
To a Certain Cantatrice.
To a Certain Civilian.
To a Common Prostitute.
To a Locomotive in Winter.
To a President.
To a Stranger.
To a Western Boy.
To Him That Was Crucified.
To Old Age.
To the East and to the West.
To the Garden the World.
To the Man-of-War Bird.
To the States.
To the States, To Identify the 16th, 17th, or
    18th Presidentiad.
Torch, The.
Trickle Drops.
Untold Want, The.
Vigil Strange I Kept on the Field One Night.
We Two Boys Together Clinging.
What Am I After All.
What Think You I Take My Pen in Hand?
When I Heard At The Close Of The Day.
When I Heard the Learn'd Astronomer.
When I Peruse the Conquer'd Fame.
When I Read the Book.
Whoever You Are Holding Me Now in Hand.
Woman Waits for Me, A.
World below the Brine, The.
Wound-Dresser, The, sel.
Year That Trembled and Reel'd beneath Me.
Years of the Modern.
Yonnondio.

Whitmore, Susan M. (b. 1962)
    Bird, The.
    Gamelia.
    Lenaia.

Whitney, Helen Hay
    To a Woman.

Whitney, Isabella (b. c.1540, d. after 1580)
    Admonition by the Auctor to All Yong
        Gentilwomen: And to Al Other Maids Being
        in Love, The, sel.
    Aucthour Maketh Her Wyll and Testament,
        The.
    I. W. To Her Unconstant Lover.
    Manner of Her Will and What She Left to

London and to All Those in It, at Her
    Departing, The, sel.
Whitney, Joan
    Candy.
Whitney, Louise Grassi
    Beautiful Eyes.
Whitson, Beth Slater (1879–1930)
    Let Me Call You Sweetheart.
Whittemore, Reed (b. 1919)
    Crow and the Fox, The.
    Farmhouse, The.
    For the Life of Him and Her.
    High School Band, The.
    Mother's Past.
    Psalm: "Lord feeds some of His prisoners
        better than others, The."
    Smiling Through.
**Whitten, Martha E. (Martha Elizabeth
    Hotchkiss) (b. 1842)**
    Beautiful in Death.
Whittier, John Greenleaf (1807–92)
    Abraham Davenport.
    Among the Hills, sels.
    Andrew Rykman's Prayer, sel.
    Angels of Buena Vista, The.
    Anniversary Poem.
    Astræa.
    Barbara Frietchie.
    Barefoot Boy, The.
    Battle Autumn of 1862, The.
    Brewing of Soma, The, sel.
    Brown of Ossawatomie.
    Burning Drift-Wood.
    Changeling, The.
    Christian Slave, The.
    Cities of the Plain, The.
    Dedication: "I would the gift I offer here."
    Ezekiel.
    Farewell, The: "Gone, gone,—sold and gone."
    First-Day Thoughts.
    For Righteousness' Sake.
    Forgiveness.
    Fruit-Gift, The.
    Garden.
    Godspeed.
    Haschish, The.
    Henchman, The.
    Ichabod[!].
    Laus Deo!
    Massachusetts to Virginia.
    Maud Muller.
    Metacom.
    My Playmate.
    My Triumph.
    Official Piety.
    Over-Heart, The.
    Overruled.
    Palm-Tree, The.
    Pipes at Lucknow, The.
    Proem: "I love the old melodious lays."
    River Path, The.
    Robin, The.
    Skipper Ireson's Ride.
    Slave-Ships, The.
    Snow-Bound [or Snow-Bound] [A Winter
        Idyl], sels.
    Song of Slaves in the Desert.
    Telling the Bees.
    Tent on the Beach: [The Dreamer], sels.
    To a Cape Ann Schooner.
    To My Old Schoolmaster.
    Vesta.
    What the Birds Said.
    Word for the Hour, A.
    Worship.
Whitworth, John
    Big sleep, the high window, The.
Whur, Cornelius (1782–1853)
    Armless Artist, The, sels.
    Female Friend, The.
    First-Rate Wife, The.
    Liberality of Sentiment, sels.
    Rose-Covered Grave, The, sel.
    Unfortunate Gentleman, The, sel.
    Village Musings, sels.

Whyte, David (b. 1955)
Sweet Darkness.
Working Together.
Whyte-Melville, George John
Coyotes.
Wickham, Anna (Mrs. Patrick Hepburn) (1884–1947)
Affinity, The.
After Annunciation.
Butler and the Gentleman, The.
Cherry-Blossom Wand, The.
Creatrix.
Dedication of the Cook.
Divorce.
Domestic Economy.
Egoist, The.
Envoi: "God, thou great symmetry."
Fired Pot, The.
Friend Cato.
Last Round, The.
Letter to a Boy at School.
Marriage, The.
Meditation at Kew.
Nervous Prostration.
Nursery Song.
Paradox.
Sehnsucht.
Self-Analysis.
Singer, The.
Slighted Lady, The.
Song: "I was so chill, and overworn, and sad."
Song-Maker, The.
Soul's Liberty.
Sung in a Graveyard.
Tired Woman, The.
To a Crucifix.
To Men.
Weapons.
Wicks, Susan (b. 1947)
Buying Fish.
Clever Daughter, The.
Joy.
Knot.
Moderato.
My Father Is Shrinking.
My Father's Caul.
Night Toad.
On Re-recording Mozart.
Persephone.
Protected Species.
Rain Dance.
Setback.
Stilt-walker.
Voice.
Widdows, P. F.
Minutiae 3.
Widerberg, Siv (b. 1931)
At Annika's Place.
Best?
Once.
Wieder, Laurance (b. 1946)
Tower of Babel, The.
Wieners, John (b. 1934)
Acceptance.
Act #2.
Acts of Youth, The.
After Symond's *Venice*.
Children of the Working Class.
Doll.
Glimpse, A.
High Noon.
Hotels 1970.
Invitation au Voyage 2.
Just an Ordinary Joe.
King Solomon's Magnetic Quiz.
Loneliness, The.
Long Nook.
Morgana La Fay.
My Mother.
Poem for Cocksuckers, A.
Poem for Museum Goers, A.
Poem for Painters, A.
Poem for the Insane, A.
Poem for Trapped Things, A.
Poem for Vipers, A.

Suck, The.
To H.
Two Years Later.
Waning of the Harvest Moon, The.
What Happened?
With Meaning.
Wier, Dara (b. 1949)
Chance Encounter with a Wounded Man
Playing a Theremin.
Wiese, Brooke
Everyone Who Wants to Work Can.
Going Home Madly.
Wiesel, Elie
Ani Maamin, A Song Lost and Found Again,
sel.
Never Shall I Forget.
Wieseltier, Meir (b. 1941)
Again a Drab Khaki Light is Coming Down.
Love is Progressing.
Military Call-up.
Wiesenthal, Christine (b. 1963)
Blues.
Wiesinger, Steve
Snow Climbers.
Wiethüchter, Blanca (b. 1942)
At This Juncture.
Movement.
Song: "Among the clamor the single shout."
Without Histories.
Wife of Chieftain (c. 10th cent.)
Come to me here.
Wigglesworth, Michael (1631–1705)
Day of Doom, The [First Section], *sels.*
Day of Doom, The: Or, A Poetical Description
of the Great and Last Judgment, *sels.*
Farewell to the World, A.
Wilberforce, Samuel (1805–73)
Impromptu.
Wilbur, Richard (b. 1921)
Advice to a Prophet.
After the Last Bulletins.
Alatus.
Another Voice.
April 5, 1974.
Ballade for the Duke of Orléans.
Baroque Wall-Fountain in the Villa Sciarra, A.
Barred Owl, A.
Beacon, The.
Beasts.
Beautiful Changes, The.
Bell Speech.
Black November Turkey, A.
Boy at the Window.
Caserta Garden.
Catch, The.
Ceremony.
Christmas Hymn, A.
Cottage Street, 1953.
Death of a Toad, The.
Digging for China.
Dubious Night, A.
Epistemology.
Exeunt.
Eye, The, *sels.*
Finished Man, A.
First Snow in Alsace.
Flippancies, *sels.*
Grasse: The Olive Trees.
Hamlen Brook.
Icarium Mare.
In a Churchyard.
In the Smoking-Car.
In Trackless Woods.
Juggler.
Junk.
Late Aubade, A.
Leaving.
Lilacs, The.
Looking into History.
Love Calls Us to the Things of This World.
Loves of the Puppets.
Lying.
Man Running.
Marché aux Oiseaux.
Marginalia.

Matthew 8, 28 ff.
Mayflies.
Mind.
Mind-Reader, The.
Mined Country.
Museum Piece.
Objects, *sel.*
October Maples, Portland.
Pangloss's Song: A Comic-Opera Lyric.
Parable.
Pardon, The.
Patriots' Day.
Piazza di Spagna, Early Morning.
Place Pigalle.
Plain Song for Comadre, A.
Playboy.
Praise in Summer.
Prisoner of Zenda, The.
Proof, The.
Ride, The.
Rillons, Rillettes.
Rule, The.
Running.
St. Matthew, *sel.*
Seed Leaves.
Shallot, A.
Shame.
She.
Sleepless at Crown Point.
Someone Talking to Himself.
Sonnet: "Winter deepening, the hay all in,
The."
Still, Citizen Sparrow.
Summer Morning, A.
Teresa.
To an American Poet Just Dead.
To His Skeleton.
Transit.
Trolling for Blues.
Tywater.
Walking to Sleep.
Wall in the Woods, A: Cummington.
What is the opposite of nuts?
World Without Objects Is a Sensible
Emptiness, A.
Writer, The.
Year's End.
Zea.
Wilcox, Carlos (1794–1827)
Age of Benevolence, The, *sel.*
Wilcox, Ella Wheeler (1850–1919)
Attraction.
Burdened.
Come Back Clean.
Communism.
Drops of Water, *sel.*
Engine, The.
Friendship After Love.
In the Night.
Inspiration, An.
King Tommy's Rise and Fall.
My Grave.
No Classes!
Nothing New.
Solitude.
Sonnet, The.
Way of It, The.
Winds of Fate, The.
Woman.
Wilcox, Finn
Nine Flower Mountain.
Wilczek, Frank (b. 1951)
Virtual Particles.
Wild, Robert (1609–79)
Alas Poore Scholler, Whither Wilt Thou Goe,
sel.
Epitaph on Some Bottles of Sack and Claret
Laid in Sand.
**Wilde, Jane Francesca, Lady ("Speranza")
(1820–96)**
Corinne's Last Love-Song.
Désillusion.
Poet's Destiny, The.
Who Will Show Us Any Good?

Wilde, Oscar (1854–1900)
Ave Maria Gratia Plena.
Ballad of Reading Gaol, The, *sels.*
E Tenebris.
Easter Day.
Harlot's House, The.
Hélas!
Impression du Matin.
La Dame Jaune.
Magdalen Walks.
Requiescat.
Santa Decca.
Silentium Amoris.
Sphinx, The, *sels.*
Symphony in Yellow.
Theocritus: A Villanelle.
Wasted Days.

Wilde, Richard Henry (1789–1847)
Hesperia, *sels.*
Lament of the Captive, The.
To the Mocking-Bird.

Wilder, Alec (1907–80)
Did You Ever Cross Over to Sneden's.
I'll Be Around.
It's So Peaceful in the Country.
Photographs.
Trouble Is a Man.

Wilder, Amos Niven (1895–1993)
Battle-Retrospect, *sel.*

Wilder, Rex
Baby, The.

Wilder, Thornton (1897–1975)
Our Town, *sel.*
Sentences.

Wildman, Eugene
Cure, The.

Wiler, Jack
Bensonhurst.

Wilkes, John (1727–97)
Essay on Woman, *sels.*

Wilkes, Kennette
Dolce.

Wilkie, Britton (1944–93)
Intuition, An.
Modern Western History.
Mummification and Space Travel.
Observations of Egyptian Artifacts.
Very Fine Lines.
Virus, The.

Wilkins, Machine
Mobile City.

Wilkinson, Anne (1910–61)
In June and Gentle Oven.
Lens.
Nature Be Damned.
On a Bench in a Park.
Tigers Know from Birth.

Wilkinson, Claude (b. 1959)
Landmarks.

Wilkinson, John (b. 1953)
Funk Qualms.
Grace.
Impatient Man Kills with His Piano-playing, The.
Oiled Sweater.
Rest of It, The.
Sideshow.
Torn Ones, The.

Will, Colin (b. 1942)
Satori in Fauldhouse.

Willard, Carla
To the Station.

Willard, Nancy (b. 1936)
Angels in Winter.
Ballad of Biddy Early, The.
Cat's Second Song, The.
How to Stuff a Pepper.
In Praise of the Puffball.
Little Blessing, A.
Sand Shark.
Speckled Hen's Morning Song to Biddy Early, The.
Wisdom of Geese, The.
Wreath to the Fish, A.

Willerton, Chris
Battle of Adobe Walls.
Campsite.
Our Speaker This Morning.
Winter at the Intersection.

William of Aquitaine (1071–1127)
Spring Song.

Williams, Ann (fl. 1660s)
Greifes Farwell, to an Inherritor of Joy.

Williams, Benin
On the Other Side.

Williams, Beryle
Night Flute, The.
Srategies for Survival.

Williams, Charles (1886–1945)
Dream, A.
Kings Came Riding.
Night Song for a Child.

Williams, Sir Charles Hanbury (1709–57)
Song upon Miss Harriet Hanbury, Addressed to the Revd Mr Birt.
Verses: "Poor fellow, what is it to you."

Williams, C. K. (Charles Kenneth) (b. 1936)
Alzheimer's: The Wife.
Blades.
Bone.
Critic, The.
Dance, The.
Day for Anne Frank, A.
Dog, The.
Doves.
Dress, The.
Fragment: "This time the hold up man didn't know a video-sound camera hidden up in a corner."
From My Window.
Gas Station, The.
Heart, The.
Hearth, The.
It Is This Way with Men.
Loss.
Love: Beginnnings.
Lover, The.
Mistress, The.
Money.
My Fly.
My Mother's Lips.
On Learning of a Friend's Illness.
Poem: "I think I came close to being insane a few months ago."
Question, The.
Racists.
Reading: The Bus.
Repression.
Risk.
Sanctity, The.
Shade, The.
Shock.
Shrapnel.
Singing, The.
Snow: II.
Spit.
Spring: another / joke.
Still Life.
Tar.
That the world / is going.
Vessel, The.
World's Greatest Tricycle-Rider, The.

Williams, Crystal (b. 1970)
For the White Lady Holding Me.
Happiness.
In Search of Aunt Jemima.
Negro Survival 101 or Poem for Tiger Woods and Other Multiethnic *Other's.*
On Forgetting Your Father's Face.
Revolutionary Thoughts.
Ritual.
Shop Sonnet.
Sugar.

Williams, Daniel
Feste and the Fence Post.

Williams, Delores S. (b. 1939)
Little Girl Talk.

Williams, Derrick "Goldie" *See* X, Derrick

Williams, Edward (Iolo Morganwg) (1747–1826)
Happy Farmer, The, *sel.*
Poet's Arbour in the Birchwood, The.
Stanzas Written in London in 1773, *sel.*

Williams, Edward W. (1863–91)
At Harper's Ferry Just before the Attack.

Williams, Eliseus (1867–1926)
Heather Flowers.

Williams, Emmett (b. 1925)
Like Attracts Like.
Red Chair (for three voices), The, *sel.*
Rose is a Rose is a Rose is a Rose is a Rose.
Ultimate Poem, The, *sels.*

Williams, Florence H. (d. 1976)
Reply (crumped on her desk).

Williams, George *See* Awoonor, Kofi

Williams, Gerwyn (b. 1963)
Final Curtain.
Forward March.
My Wales?
Pledge.
Washington.

Williams, Gwyn (b. 1904)
After Reading *Poems to Einhir.*
After the Exam.
Aspects of Now, *sel.*
City Under Snow.
Jet Planes.
Oak Tree.
Saint Ursula of Llangwyryfon.
Wild Night at Treweithan.
Winemaking.

Williams, Helen Maria (1762–1827)
Address to Poetry, An, *sel.*
Bastille, a Vision, The.
Farewell, for Two Years, to England, A. A Poem.
Part of an Irregular Fragment Found in a Dark Passage of the Tower, *sel.*
Poem on the Bill Lately Passed for Regulating the Slave-Trade, A.
Poems, *sels.*
Song, A: "No riches from his scanty store."
Sonnet 6. To the Torrid Zone.
To Dr Moore, in Answer to a Poetical Epistle Written by Him in Wales, *sels.*
To Hope.
To Mrs. K———, On Her Sending Me an English Christmas Plum-Cake at Paris.
To the Curlew.
To the Moon.
To the Strawberry.
To the White Bird of the Tropic.

Williams, Herbert (b. 1932)
Like Father.
Old Tongue, The.

Williams, Hugo (b. 1942)
Last Poem.
Making Friends with Ties.
Prayer.
Saturday Morning.
When I Grow Up.

Williams, John (1761–1818)
On Reading Aloud My Early Poems.

Williams, John Hartley (b. 1942)
Script Conference.

Williams, John Stuart (b. 1920)
Early Days.
In Duffryn Woods.
Pastoral: "You see that forest on the height?"
Rhyfel y Sais Bach.
River Walk.

Williams, Jonathan (b. 1929)
Uncle Iv Surveys His Domain from His Rocker.

Williams, Karen (b. 1962)
From the Spirit of Phillis Wheatley to the Spirit of Thomas Jefferson (A Note 212 Years Later).
Momma in Red.
Wildlife.

Williams, Kimmika L. H.
I Watched.
January 8, 1996.

Snapshot: West Philly.
Williams, Lana C.
Saints.
Williams, Lisa (b. 1966)
Crater.
Interruption of Flight.
Williams, Lorelei
Stranger in the Village.
Williams, M. L.
Astronomy.
First Kill.
152 Into 5, *El Centro Palabra de Fe*.
South.
Williams, Merryn
Heading for the Heights.
Williams, Miller (b. 1930)
Animals.
Caterpillar, The.
Death of Chet Baker, The.
Listen.
Love and How It Becomes Important in Our
Day to Day Lives.
Love Poem with Toast.
Of History and Hope.
Plain.
Poem for Emily, A.
Shrinking Lonesome Sestina, The.
Some Lines Finished Just Before Dawn at the
Bedside of a Dying Student It Has Snowed
All Night.
Thinking about Bill, Dead of AIDS
Why God Permits Evil: For Answers to This
Question of Interest to Many Write Bible
Answers, Dept. E-7.
Williams, Mogg (b. 1928)
Redundant Miners.
Williams, Niama Leslie JoAnn (b. 1962)
Daniel's Hands.
Williams, Oscar (b. 1900)
Golden Fleece, The.
With Me.
Williams, Palorine
Libation.
Williams, Patrick (b. 1950)
Baby in the House, A.
In the Dark.
Lost Seed.
Passing Through.
Rhapsody on Main Street.
Trails.
Williams, R. Bryn (1902–81)
Williams, Rhydwen (b. 1916)
Baboon, The.
Dogs.
Mountain Streams, *sel.*
Williams, Robert (1830–77)
On a Woman.
Williams, Roger (c.1603–83)
Courteous Indian, The.
God makes a path, provides a guide.
Observation Generall from Their Eating, Etc.,
The.
Williams, Sarah (1837–68)
Youth and Maidenhood.
Williams, Sharron K.
Letter to a Black Woman.
Sub Umbra Floreo.
Williams, Sherley Anne (b. 1944)
California Light.
Green Eyed Monsters of the Valley Dusk, The.
Iconography of Childhood, The, *sels.*
If He Let Us Go Now.
Letters from a New England Negro.
She Had Known Brothers.
Straight Talk from Plain Women.
Wishon Line, The.
You Were Never Miss Brown to Me.
Williams, Simon
Inscrutable question, The.
Williams, Stephanie
Coarse rigors.
Drunkard Promise, A.
Duchess of Dogs.

Hope Chest.
Maid of Need, A.
Of Riches.
Peerage.
Williams, T. Arfon (1935–98)
Foam.
May: "Mortality shrinks back—because."
One-day Snow.
Quarry.
Williams, Taliesin (1787–1847)
Cardiff Castle, *sel.*
**Williams, Tennessee (Thomas Lanier Williams)
(1914–83)**
Beanstalk Country, The.
Carrousel Tune.
Shuttle, The, *sels.*
We Have Not Long to Love.
Williams, Thomas Lanier *See* Williams, Tennessee
Williams, Treasure
Nintendo.
Williams, Tyrone
Ask-Vubba: A Decalogue.
Williams, Waldo (1904–72)
After the Mute Centuries.
Bibelforscher, Die.
Daffodil.
In Two Fields.
In Two Fields.
Preseli.
Summer Cloud, A.
Summer Cloud, A.
Three English Poets and England.
Welsh and Wales.
What Is a Man?
Young Girl, A.
Williams, William ("Pantycelyn") (1717–91)
Guide me, O Thou Great Jehovah, *sels.*
Hymn: "Now the shadows flee and vanish."
Hymn: "What is the world, and what is life."
I Gaze across the Distant Hills.
View of Christ's Kingdom, A, *sels.*
Williams, William Carlos (1883–1963)
Act, The.
Adoration of the Kings, The.
Apology.
Artist, The.
Asphodel, That Greeny Flower, *sel.*
At the Ball Game.
At the Faucet of June.
Banner Bearer, The.
Between Walls.
Bird Song.
Black Winds, The.
Botticellian Trees, The.
Breakfast.
Brilliant Sad Sun.
Burning the Christmas Greens.
Catholic Bells, The.
Chicory and Daisies.
Children, The.
Chinese Nightingale.
Complaint.
Complete Destruction.
Coronal, A.
Daisy.
Dance, The: "In Brueghel's great picture, The
Kermess."
Dance, The ("When the snow falls the
flakes.").
Danse Russe.
Dawn.
Death ("He's dead / the dog won't have to.").
Death the Barber.
Descent, The.
Desert Music, The.
Desolate Field, The.
El Hombre.
Elegy for D.H. Lawrence, An.
Exercise No. 2.
Farmer, The.
Fine Work with Pitch and Copper.
Flight to the City.
Flowers by the Sea ("When over the flowery,
sharp pasture's.").
Folded Skyscraper, A, *sels.*

4th of July.
Fragment: "As for him who."
Gift, The.
Good Night.
Goodnight, A.
Great Figure, The.
Great Mullen.
Grotesque.
Heel and Toe to the End.
Illegitimate Things.
Iris.
It Is a Small Plant.
Italian Garden, The.
Ivy Crown, The.
January.
January Morning.
Kora in Hell, *sels.*
Last Words of My English Grandmother, The.
Late Singer, The.
Le Médecin Malgré Lui.
Lear.
Locust Tree in Flower, The.
Lonely Street, The.
Love Song: "Sweep the house clean."
Marriage.
Metric Figure ("There is a bird in the
poplars.").
Mezzo Forte.
Mists Over the River.
Moon, the dried weeds, The.
Mujer.
Nantucket.
Negro Woman, A.
New Clouds, The.
On Gay Wallpaper.
Overture to a Dance of Locomotives.
Parable of the Blind, The.
Pastoral: "Little sparrows, The."
Pastoral: "When I was younger."
Paterson, *sels.*
Paterson: The Falls.
Perpetuum Mobile: The City.
Pictures from Brueghel, *sels.*
Pink Locust, The.
Poem: "As the cat."
Poem: "Rose fades, The."
Poor, The ("It's the anarchy of poverty.").
Portrait of a Lady.
Pot of Flowers, The.
Predicter of Famine, The.
Prelude to Winter.
Proletarian Portrait.
Queen Anne's Lace.
Question and Answer.
Rain: "As the rain falls."
Raleigh Was Right.
Rapid Transit.
Red Wheelbarrow, The.
Revelation, The.
Rigamarole.
Right of Way, The.
Romance Moderne.
Rose, The ("Rose is obsolete, The.").
Sadness of the Sea, The.
Sea-Elephant, The.
Shoot It Jimmy!
Short Poem.
Silence.
Smell.
Sort of a Song, A.
Spring and All.
Spring Strains.
St. Matthew; He also told them a parable, *sels.*
Sympathetic Portrait of a Child.
There are no perfect waves.
These.
This Is Just to Say.
This is the time of year.
Thursday.
To a Dog Injured in the Street.
To a Man Dying on His Feet.
To a Poor Old Woman.
To a Sparrow.
To an Old Jaundiced Woman.
To Close.
To Daphne and Virginia.

To Elsie.
To Flossie.
To Ford Madox Ford in Heaven.
To Greet a Letter-Carrier.
To Mark Anthony in Heaven.
To the Shade of Po Chü-I.
To Waken an Old Lady.
Tract.
Tribute to Neruda the Poet Collector of
  Seashells.
Tulip Bed, The.
Turtle, The.
Waiting.
Wanderer, The: A Rococo Study, *sels.*
Widow's Lament in Springtime, The.
Wild Orchard.
Willow Poem.
Woman Walking.
World Contracted to a Recognizable Image,
  The.
Yachts, The.
Yellow Flower, The.
Yellow Season, The.
Young Housewife, The.
Young Laundryman, The.
Young Love.
Young Sycamore.
Young Woman at a Window.
Williamson, Alan (b. 1944)
Almost at the Horizon.
Arrangements.
Childhood Around 1950, A.
Light's Reading, The.
Minoan Distance, The.
Williamson, Greg (b. 1964)
Annual Returns.
Appalachian Trees Encircled by Police Tape.
Belvedere Marittimo.
Bodies of Water.
Counterfeiter, The.
Dark Days, The.
Drawing Hands.
Italics, Mine.
Junkyard.
Kites at the Washington Monument.
Neighboring Storms.
Nervous Systems.
New Year's: A Short Pantoum.
On His Birthday.
Origami.
Outbound.
Up in the Air.
Walter Parmer.
Waterfall.
Willis, Elizabeth (b. 1961)
Without Pity.
Willis, Humphrey (*fl.* 1647)
Time's Whirligig, Or, The Blue-New-Made-
  Gentleman Mounted.
Willis, Jeanne
Inside Our Dreams.
Willis, Nathaniel Parker (1806–67)
City Lyrics.
Confessional, The.
January 1, 1829.
Lady in the White Dress, Whom I Helped into
  the Omnibus, The.
Melanie, *sel.*
New Year, The.
Psyche, Before the Tribunal of Venus.
To Charles Roux, of Switzerland.
Wills, Jackie (b. 1955)
One Day We'll Be Able to Talk to the Dead.
Willson, Dixie
Tip-Toe Tail.
Willson, Forceythe (1837–67)
Estray, The.
In State, Part 1.
To Hersa.
Willson, Meredith
Seventy Six Trombones.
Till There Was You.
Ya Got Trouble.
Wilmer, Sydney
Mess Boy, The.

Wilmot, Frank *See* Maurice, Furnley
Wilner, Eleanor (b. 1937)
Abstraction.
All the Wide Grin of Him.
Ars Poetica: "They wanted from us."
As soft and as pink as a nursery.
Conversation with a Japanese Student.
Epitaph: "Young then, / we were bored
  already."
Found in the Free Library.
Her Body Is Private.
High Noon at Los Alamos.
Judgment.
Meditation on the *Wen-Fu.*
Miriam's Song.
Muse, The.
Operations: Desert Shield, Desert Storm.
Reading the Bible Backwards.
Sarah's Choice.
Secret Garden, The.
Theory and Practice in Poetry.
When Asked to Lie Down on the Altar.
You, Failed Pronoun.
Wilson, Alan Robert
Antlia the Air Pump.
Lynx.
Octans the Octant.
Particle Limericks.
Pegasus the Winged Horse.
Wilson, Anthony
Everything opaque about us, perhaps.
Wilson, Carletta Carrington (b. 1951)
History of the Quilt That Heaved Life into
  Stars Patched, Circled, Stitched and Square.
Kiss her that she don't know how.
"Wilson, Charlotte" *See* Baker, Karle Wilson
Wilson, Edmund (1895–1972)
Disloyal Lines to an Alumnus.
Easy Exercises in the Use of Difficult Words,
  sels.
Enemies of Promise.
Epitaphs.
Miniature Dialogue.
Past Midnight.
Wilson, Emily (b. 1968)
Coal Age.
Fossil Garden, The.
Relict.
Wind in bare vines.
Wilson, Frances
Bathing My Mother.
Wilson, Imani E.
Fruitbowl 1.
Wilson, Jim (b. 1948)
Death in Venice.
Pruning.
Wilson, Keith (b. 1927)
Arrival of My Mother, The.
Circle, The.
Dusk in My Backyard.
Memory of a Victory.
People from the Valley, The.
Powerhouse, The.
River Girl.
Still Life: "Three old New Mexican men."
Waterfront Bars.
Wilson, Mary
Diary.
Harold Wilson's Selected Poems, *sel.*
Wilson, Ramona (b. 1945)
Dry Rivers—Arizona.
Wilson, Robley, Jr. (b. 1936)
Envoi: "Sun in the mouth of the day."
I Wish in the City of Your Heart.
Mechanical Cow, The.
Military-Industrial Complex, The.
Old Movies.
Rejoicing That Attend the Murder of Famous
  Men, The.
Say Girls in Shoe Ads: "I Go for a Man Who's
  Tall!"
Sparrow Hills.
Wilson, Ronaldo V.
Dungle Sublime.

White.
Wilson, Sandy (b. 1924)
Boy Friend, The.
It's Never Too Late to Fall in Love.
Room in Bloomsbury, A.
Wilson, Steve (b. 1960)
Contemporary Poet, A.
Experiments in the Impersonal.
Home: After a Poem by Frost.
Mad Man.
Picture on the Purple Wall, the.
Recreational Mathematics.
Wilson, T. P. Cameron ("Tipcuca") (1889–1918)
Magpies in Picardy.
Wilson, Ted
And the Saga Continues.
Wiman, Christian (b. 1966)
Hearing Loss.
In Lakeview Cemetery.
Sweet Dreams.
Winbush-David, Wanda
African Sunrunner.
Winch, Terence (b. 1945)
Diagnosis.
Mysteries.
Shadow Grammar.
Six Families of Puerto Ricans.
Social Security.
Winchcombe, Mrs. (*fl.* 1614)
I lovd thee living and lament thee dead.
Winchilsea, Anne Finch, Countess of (1661–1720)
Adam Posed.
All Is Vanity, *sel.*
Answer, The [*To Pope's* Impromptu].
Caesar and Brutus.
Circuit of Apollo, The.
Epistle from Alexander to Hephaestion in His
  Sickness, An.
Friendship Between Ephelia and Ardelia.
Glass.
Introduction, The: "Did I, my lines intend for
  public[k] view."
Letter to Daphnis, A.
Nocturnal Reverie, A.
On Myself.
Petition for an Absolute Retreat, The, *sel.*
Pindaric Poem, A, *sels.*
Sigh, A.
Some Reflections.
Spleen, The: A Pindaric Poem, *sels.*
There's No To-Morrow.
To Death.
To the Nightingale.
Trail All Your Pikes.
Unequal Fetters, The.
Upon My Lord Winchilsea's Converting the
  Mount in His Garden to a Terrace.
White Mouses Petition to Lamira the Right
  Honble the Lady Anne Tufton now Countess
  of Salisbury, The.
Winder, Barbara
Lesson.
On Fourteen Maple Street.
Unaccompanied Suite.
Wine, Maria (b. 1912)
Woman, you are afraid of the forest.
Winged Serpent
Two Rain Songs (Papago).
Wingfield, Sheila (1906–73)
Back.
Beat Drum, Beat Heart, *sels.*
Bird, A.
In a Dublin Museum.
Waking.
Winter.
Winkfield, Trevor
Nature Study.
Winkler Prins, Jacob (1849–1904)
Shower.
Winnebago Oral Tradition
Felix White Sr.'s Introduction to Wakjankaga.
Winner, Robert (b. 1930)
Segregated Railway Diner—1946.

Winner, Septimus ("Alice Hawthorne") (1827–1902)
Listen to the Mocking Bird.

Winslow, Pat
God on a Bike.
Rise: "Marvellous how the house builds itself."

Winslow, Pete
I blink and half my life is over.
O god of spring forgive me.

Winstanley, Gerrard (1609?–76)
Digger's Song, The.

Winstanley, John (1678–1750)
Inventory of the Furniture of a Collegian's Chamber, An.
Last Will and Testament, A.
Upon a Friend's Pet Cat, Being Sick.

Winter, Max (b. 1970)
As If I Knew.
Ascent, The.
Dux Bellorum.
Elegy: "There is a question."
Here and There.
Long Distance.
Space Parable.
That Is the Way.

Winter, Miriam Therese
In the Beginning.

Winters, Anne (b. 1939)
Elizabeth Near and Far, *sels.*
Night Light.

Winters, Yvor (1900–68)
Apollo and Daphne.
At the San Francisco Airport.
Barnyard, The.
Before Disaster.
By the Road to the Air-Base.
Cold, The.
Dream Vision, A.
Elegy on a Young Airedale Bitch Lost Two Years Since in the Salt-Marsh.
Fable, The.
Fall of Leaves, The.
For My Father's Grave.
Fragment: "I cannot find my way to Nazareth."
In Praise of California Wines.
John Sutter.
Magpie's Shadow, The, *sels.*
Marriage, The.
Moonlight Alert.
Much in Little.
Night of Battle.
Nocturne: "Moonlight on stubbleshining."
October.
On a View of Pasadena from the Hills.
On Teaching the Young.
One Ran Before.
Realization, The.
Sir Gawaine and the Green Knight.
Slow Pacific Swell, The.
Solitude of Glass, The.
Static Autumn.
Summer Commentary, A.
Summer Noon: 1941.
Time and the Garden.
To a Military Rifle, 1942.
To a Young Writer.
To My Infant Daughter, *sel.*
To the Holy Spirit.
To the Moon.
Two Songs of Advent.
Vacant Lot.
Wild Sunflower.

Winthrop, Jeanette I.
Couple Having Breakfast in the Deli, The.

Wintu Oral Tradition
Six Dream Songs, *sels.*

Wisdome, Robert (d. 1568)
Religious Use of [Taking] Tobacco, A.

Wise, Nina
To Papaji.

Wise, Suzanne (b. 1965)
Advice.
Closure Opening Its Trap.
Confession.

50 Years in the Career of an Aspiring Thug.
I Was Very Prolific.
Testimony.

Wise, William (b. 1923)
When I Grow Up.

Wiseman, Christopher
April Elegy (Sam Selvon d.1994).
Triolets for Ken.

Wisenberg, S. L.
Casino.
May 28, 1945.

With, Elizabeth (*fl.* 1659)
How Elizabeth Foole and Her Husband Parted by Means of Her Sister in Law.

Wither, George (1588–1667)
Britain's Remembrancer Canto 4, *sel.*
Choice, The.
Collection of Emblemes, Ancient and Moderne, A, *sels.*
Conversion of S. Paul, The.
Epigram: "Women, as some men say, unconstant be."
Fair Virtue, the Mistress of Philarete [Selections from anthologies], *sels.*
First Song of Moses, The.
For a Poet.
Hallelujah; or, Britain's Second Remembrancer, *sel.*
I Loved a Lass.
Ninth Canticle, The.
Prayer for His Wife and Children, Written in Newgate.
Prayer of Hezekiah, The.
Prayer of Nehemiah, The.
Prisoner's Lay, A, *sel.*
Shephe[a]rd's Hunting, The, *sels.*
Vox Pacifica, *sel.*
When We Cannot Sleep.
Widow's Hymn, A.

Witherspoon, Naomi Long *See* Madgett, Naomi Long

Witherup, William (b. 1935)
Lamb of Peace, the Ram of War, The.
Mervyn Clyde Witherup.

Witt, Sam (b. 1970)
Americana.
Everlasting Quail.
Ikonostasis. The Sound of the Sea Filling a Faraway Room.
Michael Masse.
Thermal Signatures ("I sing a place called Newborn.").
Thermal Signatures ("There is nothing to remember but flight. The owl's eyes spoke.").
Waterfowl Descending.

Witte, Francine
Prom.
When You Call Again.

Witting, Amy (b. 1918)
Beauty Is the Straw.
Blinkered Mind, The.
Curse on Herod, A.

Wizlaw von Rügen (c.1265–1325)
Only Love.

Woddis, Roger (b. 1917)
Believers' Best Buy.
Do Not Go Sober.
Doctor, The.
Eat Your Heart Out, Edward Lear!
Final Curtain.
I Shall Vote Centre.
Moral Tale, A.
Rewards and Fairies.
Rolling Chinese Wall, The.

Wodehouse, P. G. (Pelham Grenville) (1881–1975)
Bill.
Bill (Original Version).
Bungalow in Quogue.
Cleopatterer.
It's a Hard, Hard World for a Man.
Land Where the Good Songs Go, The.
Napoleon.

Outcast, The.
Printer's Error.
That Was Before I Met You.
Till the Clouds Roll By.
Tulip Time in Sing Sing.
You Can't Make Love by Wireless.
You Never Knew About Me.

Woessner, Warren
Jungle Music.

Wohlfeld, Valerie (b. 1956)
Quilt.
Sea.
That Which Is Fugitive, That Which Is Medicinally Sweet or Alterable to Gold, That Which Is Substantiated by Unscientific Means.

Wojahn, David (b. 1953)
Allegory: Attic and Fever.
Assassination of Robert Goulet as Performed by Elvis Presley: Memphis, 1968, The.
Buddy Holly.
Distance.
Elvis Moving a Small Cloud: The Desert Near Las Vegas, 1976.
Floating Houses.
Francis Ford Coppola and Anthropologist Interpreter Teaching Gartewienna Tribesmen to Sing "Light My Fire," Philippine Jungle, 1978.
Inside, The.
It's Only Rock and Roll but I Like It: The Fall of Saigon, 1975.
John Berryman Listening to Robert Johnson's "King of the Delta Blues," January 1972.
My Father's Pornography.
Mystery Train: A Sequence, *sels.*
Necromancy: The Last Days of Brian Jones, 1968.
Nixon Names Elvis Honorary Federal Narcotics Agent at Oval Office Ceremony, 1973.
Pharaoh's Palace.
Photo of My Father in a Snowbound Train.
Poison, 1959.
Rajah in Babylon.
Riding the Empire Builder, 1948.
Satin Doll.
Song of the Burning.
W. C. W. Watching Presley's Second Appearance on The Ed Sullivan Show: Mercy Hospital, Newark, 1956.
Wartime Photos of My Father.
Workmen Photographed inside the Reactor.

Wojtyla, Karol (Pope John Paul II) (b. 1920)
Sister.
Wall, The: "I see a wall; but unwhole."

Wolcot, John *See* Pindar, Peter

Wolcott, Roger (1679–1767)
Heart Is Deep, The.

Wolf, Michele
Lucky Smile.

Wolfe, Charles (1791–1823)
Burial of Sir John Moore, The.
Song: "Oh say not that my heart is cold."
To Mary.

Wolfe, Ffrida
Choosing Shoes.

Wolfe, Humbert (1885–1940)
A. E. Housman and a Few Friends.
Blackbird, The.
British Journalist, The.
Gray Squirrel, The.
Green Candles.
Iliad.
Love Is a Keeper of Swans.
Man.
This Is Not Death.
Tulip.
Waters of Life, The.

Wolfe, Marianne
Thaw, The.

Wolfe, Thomas Clayton (1900–38)
For, Brother, What Are We?

Wolff, Rebecca (b. 1967)
Criminal Justice System.
Flame On.
Lamb, Willow: An Arch Dolefulness Has
Taken Me This Far.
Press Play.
Sybil.

Wolfli, Adolf (1864–1930)
From The Cradle to the Graave, or, through
working and sweating, suffering and
hardship, even through prayyer into
damnation, sel.
Nostalgic Song for My Beloved.

Woljo Toan (1638–1715)
Cuckoo.
Deathbed Song.

Wolkenstein, Oswald von (1377–1445)
O Margie, Marge, Dear Margaret.

Wolley, Hannah (c.1621–74)
Queen-Like Closet, The, sel.

Wŏlmyŏng, Master (c.742–65)
Requiem for the Dead Sister.
Song of Tusita Heaven.

Woloch, Cecilia (b. 1956)
Blink.
Ottava Rima: Lear.

Wolverton, Terry
Black Slip.
Dead Stepfather, The.
In China.
Tubes.

Wŏn Ch'ŏnsŏk (c.1390–1410)
Fortune determines rise and fall.

Wong, Janet S. (b. 1962)
Good Luck Gold.

Wong, Nellie (b. 1934)
Can't Tell.
Dreams in Harrison Railroad Park.
Grandmothers' Song.
Heart of Rice Straw, A, sel.
Ironing.
It's in the Blood.
Mama, Come Back.
On Plaza Garibaldi.
On Thinking of Photographing My Fantasies.
Picnic.
When I Was Growing Up.
Where Is My Country?

Wong, Rita (b. 1968)
Leavetaking.

Wong, Telly
Loneliness.

Wŏngam Chungji See Chungji

Wonham, Jonathan (b. 1965)
Emergency Services.

Wonhyo, Great Master (617–86)
Axe without a Handle.
Enlightenment Song.
Pledge.
To Master Monk Nangjee.

Woo, David (b. 1959)
Eden.
Expatriates.
Grandfather's Rockery.
Great Helmsman, The.
Habit.

Woo, Merle
Under a Full Moon.

Wood, Charles Erskine Scott
Poet in the Desert, The, sels.

Wood, Dilys
Christmas Fare.

Wood, Eve (b. 1967)
Recognition.

Wood, Peter
First Job Viper.

Wood, Robert Williams (1868–1955)
Elk, The Whelk, The.
Pecan, The Toucan, The.
Pen-guin. The Sword-fish, The.

Wood, Susan (b. 1946)
Carnation. Lily, Lily, Rose.
Eggs.

Four Roses.
Hollow.

Wood, Victoria (b. 1953)
Saturday Night.

Wood, William (1606–c.1637)
Sea's Abundant Progeny, The.

Woodhouse, Peter
I see a Soldiers service is forgot.

Woods, Donald (1957–92)
Prescription.
Waiting.

Woods, Harry
Over My Shoulder.
Paddlin' Madelin' Home.
Side by Side.
Try a Little Tenderness.
We Just Couldn't Say Good-bye.
When the Red, Red Robin Comes Bob, Bob,
Bobbin' Along.

Woods, Margaret Louisa (b. 1856)
Genius Loci.

Woods, Vincent (b. 1960)
After the American Wake.
Asylum is Water, The.
Blue Cage, A.
Departure.
Fourth World, The.
History Set, The.
House, The.
Lost Masterpiece, The.
Meaning of a Word, The.
Road West, The.
She Replies to the Fat Crimson Bishop.
Song of Lies, A.
Three Gifts.

Woodward, Gerard (b. 1961)
Lighthouse.
Murderer is a Cow, The.

Woodward, Vincent
Cornbread Blues.

Woodworth, Samuel (1784–1842)
Old Oaken Bucket, The.

Woody, Elizabeth
Girlfriends, The.
She-Who-Watches . . . The Names are Prayer.
Speaking Hands.

Woolagoodjah, Sam
Lalai (Dreamtime).

Woolsey, Sarah Chauncey See Coolidge, Susan

Woolson, Constance Fenimore (1840–94)
Detroit River.
Florida Beach, The.
Kentucky Belle.
Love Unexpressed.
Two Women, sels.

Wordsworth, Christopher (1807–85)
All Saints' Day, Nov. 1.
O Day of Rest and Gladness.
See the Conqueror mounts in triumph.

Wordsworth, Dorothy (1771–1855)
Address to a Child during a Boisterous Winter
Evening.
Floating Island at Hawkshead.
Irregular Verses.
Loving and Liking [Irregular Verses Addressed
to A Child].
Peaceful Our Valley, Fair and Green.
Thoughts on my sick-bed.

Wordsworth, William (1770–1850)
Address to My Infant Daughter, Dora on Being
Reminded That She Was a Month Old That
Day, September 16, sel.
Affliction of Margaret, The.
Alice Fell; or, Poverty.
Anecdote for Fathers [Showing how the Art of
Lying may be Taught], sels.
Animal Tranquillity and Decay.
Castle of Indolence Stanzas, The, sel.
Complaint, A.
Composed by the Sea-Side, near Calais,
August, 1802.
Composed in One of the Valleys of
Westmoreland, on Easter Sunday.
Composed upon Westminster Bridge,

September 3, 1802.
Decadence; or, The Umbrella.
Discharged Soldier, The.
Ecclesiastical Sonnets, sels.
1801.
Elegiac Stanzas: Suggested by a Picture of
Peele Castle, in a Storm, Painted by Sir
George Beaumont.
Excursion, The, sels.
Expostulation and Reply.
Extempore Effusion upon the Death of James
Hogg.
Farewell, A: "Farewell thou little Nook of
mountain-ground."
Fidelity.
Fountain, The.
Fragments from Dove Cottage Manuscript, sel.
Goody Blake and Harry Gill, sel.
Gravestone upon the Floor in the Cloisters of
Worcester Cathedral, A.
Great men have been among us; hands that
penned.
Home at Grasmere [1800 version], sel.
How sweet it is, when mother Fancy rocks.
Hymn: "Blest are the moments, doubly blest."
I Wandered Lonely as a Cloud.
I watch, and long have watched, with calm
regret.
Idiot Boy, The.
Inscription for the Moss-Hut at Dove Cottage.
It Is a Beauteous Evening.
Kitten and [the] Falling Leaves, The, sels.
Liberty [sequel to Gold and Silver Fishes in a
Vase], sels.
Lines Composed a Few Miles above Tintern
Abbey on Revisiting the Banks of the Wye
During a Tour, July 13, 1798.
Lines Written in Early Spring.
London 1802 ("Milton! thou shouldst be living
at this hour.").
Lucy, sels.
Lucy Gray; or, Solitude.
Memorials of a Tour in Italy, 1837, sels.
Memorials of a Tour of the Continent; 1820,
sels.
Methought I saw the footsteps of a throne.
Michael [A Pastoral Poem], sel.
My Heart Leaps Up [When I Behold].
November, 1806.
Nutting.
October, 1803 ("When, looking on the present
face of things.").
Ode: Intimations of Immortality from
Recollections of Early Childhood, sels.
Ode to Duty.
Old Man by the Brook, The.
Old Man Travelling [Animal Tranquillity and
Decay, a Sketch].
On the Extinction of the Venetian Republic.
On the Projected Kendal and Windermere
Railway.
Peter Bell, sels.
Poems Composed or Suggested During a Tour,
in the Summer of 1833, sel.
Power of Music, The, sels.
Prelude, The; Growth of a Poet's Mind [1805
version], sels.
Prelude, The; Growth of a Poet's Mind [1850
version], sels.
Primrose of the Rock, The.
Recluse, The, sels.
Resolution and Independence, sels.
River Duddon [A Series of Sonnets], The, sels.
Ruined Cottage, The.
Sailor's Mother, The, sels.
Salisbury Plain, sel.
Scorn Not the Sonnet [Critic, You Have
Frowned].
September 1, 1802.
She Was a Phantom of Delight.
Simon Lee [Original Version], sels.
Simon Lee, the Old Huntsman; with an
incident in which he was concerned.
Simplon Pass, The.
Small Celandine, The.
Solitary Reaper, The.

Sonnet: "Nuns fret not at their convent's narrow room."
Sonnets upon the Punishment of Death, *sel.*
Statue Horse.
Steamboats, Viaducts, and Railways.
Stepping Westward.
Strange Fits of Passion Have I Known.
Surprised by Joy.
Tables Turned, The.
Thorn, The, *sels.*
Those [*or* These] words were uttered as in [*or* in a] pensive mood.
Thought[s] of a Briton on the Subjugation of Switzerland.
To a Butterfly ("I've watched you now a full half-hour.").
To a Butterfly ("Stay near me—do not take thy flight!").
To a Child [Written in Her Album].
To H. C., Six Years Old.
To My Sister.
To the Cuckoo ("O blithe New-comer! I have heard.").
To the Men of Kent (October, 1803).
To Toussaint L'Ouverture.
Tradition of Oker Hill in Darley Dale, Derbyshire, A.
Trosachs, The.
Two April Mornings, The.
Two-Part Prelude, The, *sels.*
Vaudracour and Julia, *sels.*
We Are Seven, *sel.*
When I have borne in memory what has tamed.
Where lies the Land to which yon Ship must go?
With how sad steps, O Moon, thou climb'st the sky.
With Ships the sea was sprinkled far and nigh.
World Is Too Much with Us, The.
Written in London, September, 1802.
Written in March [While Resting on the Bridge at the Foot of Brother's Water].

Work, Henry Clay (1932–84)
Come Home, Father[!].
Grandfather's Clock.
Marching through Georgia.

Worley, Demetrice A. (b. 1960)
Dancing in the Dark.
Las Flores para una Niña Negra.
Sandra.
Tongues in My Mouth.

Wormser, Baron (b. 1948)
By-Products.
Fans.
First Love, Sixteen Years Old.
It's a Party (1959).
January.
Pigeons.
Shoplifting.
Single Urge, The.
Soul Music.

Worpole, Ken (b. 1944)
Sleeper.

Worth, Valerie (b. 1933)
Chairs.
Clock.
Dinosaurs.
Door.
Duck.
Fireworks.
Goldfish in the Garden Pond.
Sun.
Zinnias.

Wotton, Sir Henry (1568–1639)
Character of a Happy Life, The.
De Morte.
Dialogue betwixt God and the Soul, A.
Hymn to My God in a Night of My Late Sickness[e], A.
On a Bank [*or* Banck] as I Sat[e] [a-]Fishing; a Description of the Spring.
On His Mistress [*or* Mistris], the Queen of Bohemia.
Poem Written by Sir Henry Wotton, in His Youth, A.

To John Donne.
Upon the Death of Sir Albert Morton's Wife.
Upon the Sudden Restraint of the Earl[e] of Somerset, Then Falling from Favor [*or* Favour].

Wozek, Gerard
Song to Myself at Seventeen.

Wray, Clyde A.
Private Thoughts.
Star, The.

Wren, Andrea M. (b. 1969)
Day at School, A.
Harmony.
Surrogate Mothers.

Wrigglesworth, Anne (*fl.* 1584)
Yf I had as faire a face as John Williams.

Wright, C.
May God Go with You, Son.

Wright, C. D. (b. 1949)
And it Came to Pass.
Bent Tones.
Deepstep Come Shining, *sels.*
Elements of Night.
Everything Good Between Men and Women.
Flame.
Floating Trees.
Girl Friend Poem # 3.
Grace: "Its hair is a fine weed."
Humidity.
In Our Only Time.
Just Whistle, *sels.*
Key Episodes from an Earthly Life.
Kings' Daughters, Home for Unwed Mothers, 1948.
Lake Echo, Dear.
Morning Star.
Next to Last Draft, The.
Obedience of the Corpse.
On the Eve of Our Mutually Assured Destruction.
Personals.
Petition for Replenishment.
Planks.
Ponds, in Love.
Privacy.
Provinces.
Secret Life of Musical Instruments, The.
So Far Off and Yet Here.
Song of the Gourd.
Spring Street Girl Friend (#8).
Until words turn to moss.
Wages of Love.
What Keeps.
What No One Could Have Told Them.
Why Ralph Refuses to Dance.

Wright, Carolyne (b. 1949)
KZ.
My Last Night in Bahia.
Peace Corps Volunteer Comes Home, The.
Post-Revolutionary Letter.
Prayer: "Bless my life—its inks."
Sierra Walk.
Survivalist.
Wander Luís.

Wright, Celeste Turner (b. 1906)
State of Preservation.

Wright, Charles (b. 1935)
After Reading Tu Fu, I Go Outside to the Dwarf Orchard.
Apologia Pro Vita Sua.
Appalachian Book of the Dead 3, The.
April.
As Our Bodies Rise, Our Names Turn into Light.
Aubade: "Over Govino Bay, looking up from the water's edge, the landscape resembles nothing so much as the hills above Genova."
Autumn: "November the 1st. Gold leaves."
Blackwater Mountain.
California Dreaming.
California Spring.
California Twilight.
Chickamauga.
Chinese Journal.

Christmas East of the Blue Ridge.
Cicada Blue.
Clear Night.
Clinchfield Station.
December Journal.
Disjecta Membra.
Gate City Breakdown.
Hardin County.
Him.
Homage to Claude Lorrain.
Homage to Paul Cézanne.
In Praise of Han Shan.
Laguna Blues.
Looking Outside the Cabin Window, I Remember a Line by Li Po.
Looking West from Laguna Beach at Night.
Mondo Henbane.
Negatives.
Night Journal.
Nightletter.
Other Side of the River, The.
Poet Grows Older, The.
Quotations.
Reading Lao Tzu Again in the New Year.
Relics.
Reunion.
Saturday 6 a.m.
Self-Portrait.
Self-Portrait ("Charles on the Trevisan, night bridge.").
Sitting at Night on the Front Porch.
Sitting Outside at the End of Autumn.
Snow.
Spider Crystal Ascension.
Stone Canyon Nocturne.
Storm.
Stray Paragraphs in February, Year of the Rat.
Tattoos.
Virginia Reel.
Virgo Descending.
Voyage, The: "At first I was overly cautious, procedure being all-important."
Winter-Worship.
Yard Work.

Wright, Charles David
Tours.

Wright, David (b. 1920)
Caleb Barnes.
Cockermouth.
Funeral Oration, A.
Juxtapositions.
Lakes, The.
Musician, The.
On Himself.
Those Walks We Took.
To the Gods the Shades Flavinus of the Cavalry Regiment.
Winter at Gurnard's Head.

Wright, David (b. 1966)
Addison Street.
Beethoven's Romance in G.
Lines on Retirement, after Reading *Lear*.
Map of the Kingdom, A.
New Mennonite Replies to Julia Kasdorf, A.
Protest Poem, A.

Wright, Ernest Vincent (1872–1939)
When Father Carves the Duck.

Wright, Franz (b. 1953)
After Picasso, *sels.*
Alcohol.
August Insomnia.
Blood.
Brother, The.
Brugge.
Circle Drawn in Water.
Flight.
Have You Seen This Child.
Illegibility.
Knife.
Lines Written in the Dark Illegible Next Day.
Loneliness.
Morning.
Only Animal, The.
Publication Date.
Sitting Up Late with My Father, 1977.

Sunday Afternoon.
Thoughts of a Solitary Farmhouse.
Walking to Martha's Vineyard.
Wedding, The.

Wright, Ivan Leonard
Want of You, The.

Wright, James (1643–1713)
Out of Horace.

Wright, James (1927–80)
Against Surrealism.
And Yet I Know.
Angel, The.
Arrangements with Earth for Three Dead
    Friends.
Art of the Fugue, The: A Prayer.
At the Executed Murderer's Grave.
Autumn Begins in Martins Ferry, Ohio.
Beginning.
Blessing, A: "Just off the highway to
    Rochester, Minnesota."
Depressed by a Book of Bad Poetry, I Walk
    toward an Unused Pasture and Invite the
    Insects to Join Me.
Dream of Burial, A.
Eisenhower's Visit to Franco, 1959.
Four Dead Sons.
Handsome Is as Handsome Does.
Honey.
Hook.
Horse, The.
In Response to a Rumor that the Oldest
    Whorehouse in Wheeling, West Virginia,
    Has Been Condemned.
Journey, The.
Lying in a Hammock at William Duffy's Farm
    in Pine Island, Minnesota.
Mad Fight Song for William S. Carpenter,
    1966, A.
Magnificence.
Milkweed.
Minneapolis Poem, The.
Nocturne, Aubade, and Vesper: "To call it a
    wet dream would be too barren."
Northern Pike.
Note Left in Jimmy Leonard's Shack, A.
Old Bud.
Old WPA Swimming Pool in Martins Ferry,
    Ohio, The.
On a Phrase from Southern Ohio.
Poem Written under an Archway in a
    Discontinued Railroad Station, Fargo, North
    Dakota, A.
Presentation of Two Birds to My Son, A.
Regret for a Spider Web.
Romeo, Grown Old.
Saint Judas.
Sappho.
Secret Gratitude, A.
Silent Angel, The.
Sirmione.
Small Frogs Killed on the Highway.
Snowfall; a Poem about Spring.
Song for the Middle of the Night, A.
Sparrows in a Hillside Drift.
Speak.
Sumac in Ohio, The.
To the Evening Star: Central Minnesota.
Trying to Pray.
Two Hangovers, *sels.*
Two Postures beside a Fire.
Winter Daybreak above Vence, A.
You and I Saw Hawks Exchanging the Prey.
Young Don't Want to Be Born.
Young Good Man, The.
Youth.

Wright, Jay (b. 1935)
Albuquerque Graveyard, The.
Annihilation's Trio: Three Irrational Sonnets
    Begging the Question of Being and Act.
Benjamin Banneker Sends His *Almanac* to
    Thomas Jefferson.
Boleros #21.
Boleros #31.
Boleros #36.
Compassion's Bird.
Cradle Logic of Autumn, The.

Death as History.
Desire's Persistence.
Don José Gorostiza Encounters El Cordobés.
End of an Ethnic Dream, The.
Homecoming Singer, The.
Invention of a Garden, The.
Invitation to Madison County, An.
January, Love, and the Galician.
Journey to the Place of Ghosts.
Lake in Central Park, The.
Logbook of Judgments, *sels.*
Love's Dozen, *sels.*
Madrid.
Sketch for an Aesthetic Project.
Wednesday Night Prayer Meeting.
What is Beautiful.
White Deer, The.

Wright, John (*fl.* 1708–27)
Portugal Laurel, The.
Therapy.
Transfiguration.
Walking the Dog.

Wright, Judith (b. 1915)
And Mr. Ferritt.
At Cooloolah.
Australia 1970.
Beanstalk, Meditated Later, The.
Birds.
Black Cockatoos.
Blind Man, The, *sels.*
Bora Ring.
Brother and Sisters.
Bull, The.
Camphor Laurel.
Child, The.
Dove-Love.
Drought Year.
Eli, Eli.
Eve to Her Daughters.
Finale.
Flood Year.
For a Pastoral Family, *sels.*
Gum-trees Stripping.
Half-Caste Girl.
Ishtar.
Killer, The.
Lament for Passenger Pigeons.
Legend.
Love Song in Absence.
Metho Drinker.
Naked Girl and Mirror.
Nigger's Leap, New England.
Night After Bushfire.
Notes at Edge, *sels.*
Old Prison, The.
Pelicans.
Portrait.
Precipice, The.
Rainforest.
Remittance Man.
Request to a Year.
River Bend.
Rosina Alcona to Julius Brenzaida.
Shadow of Fire: Ghazals, The, *sels.*
Sisters, The.
Skins.
Song: "O where does the dancer dance."
Sonnet for Christmas.
To a Child.
To Another Housewife.
Train Journey.
Two Fires, The.
Wings.
Woman to Child.
Woman to Man.

Wright, Kit (b. 1944)
All Purpose Country and Western Self Pity
    Song, The.
Doll's House, A.
Here Come Two Very Old Men.
Hoping It Might Be So.
How the Wild South East Was Lost.
I go through the wood in silence.
Love Song of Tooting, A.
Mantles.
My Version.

New World Symphony, A.
Other Side of the Mountain, The.
Sergeant Brown's Parrot.
Underneath the Archers *or* What's All This
    about Walter's Willy?
Unlikely Obbligato of Andersonstown.
Victorian Family Photograph.

Wright, Lillian
West Texas Suicide.

Wright, Nancy Means
Acrophobia.

Wright, Richard (1908–60)
Between the World and Me.
Bloody knife blade, A.
Bulging yellow clouds.
Bursting ripe plum, A.
Chill autumn dusk, The.
Consumptive man, The.
Crying and crying.
Droning autumn rain.
FB Eye Blues, The.
For you, O gulls.
From a red tile roof.
From the woods at night.
From under the house.
Haiku: "Just enough of rain."
Hokku Poems, *sels.*
I am nobody.
I cannot find it.
I Have Seen Black Hands.
In the falling snow.
O finicky cat.
On winter mornings.
Rustling dry paper.
Sound of the rain, The.
Spring lingers on, The.
Stars are dredging, The.
Twisting tendril, A.
Waking from a nap.
Wild winter wind, A.

Wright, Robert (b. 1914)
And This Is My Beloved.
Baubles, Bangles, and Beads.
It's a Blue World.
Strange Music.
Stranger in Paradise.

Wright, Stephen Caldwell (b. 1946)
And the Birds Sing of Life.
Harvest.
Out of the Wailing.

Wrigley, Ammon
Owdham Footbo.'

Wrigley, Robert
American Manhood.
Ashtray in the Snow.
For the Last Summer.
Letter to a Young Poet.
Milkflowers.
Moon in a Mason Jar.
Other World, The: "So here is the old buck."
Prophecy, The.
Sinking of Clay City, The.
Skull of a Snowshoe Hare, The.
What My Father Believed.

Wronsky, Gail
Sor Juana's Last Dream, *sel.*

**Wroth, Mary Sidney, Countess of Montgomery
(1587?–1651?)**
Pamphilia to Amphilanthus, *sels.*
Railing Rimes Returned upon the Author by
    Mistress Mary Wrothe.
Urania, *sels.*

Wu Chia-chi (1618–84)
Grain-Barge Wife, The.

Wu Li (1632–1718)
Singing of the Source of Holy Church.
Tune: "Happily Flitting Oriole."

Wu of Han, Emperor (155–87 B.C.)
Autumn Wind.
Autumn Wind, The.
Li Furen.
Liu Ch'e.
Oh the sound of her silk sleeves.
Skein, The.

Wu Tsao (*fl.* c.1800)
For the Courtesan Ch'ing Lin.

Wu Wei-yeh (1609–72)
Broken Lampstand, The.

Wu Wen-ying (c.1200–c.60)
Tune: "Rouged Lips" Rain Just Over on the
Night of the Lantern Preview.
Tune: "Sand of Silk-Washing Brook" A
Reminiscence.

Wu Yun (469–520)
Apotheosis.
From the mountain's end, sight of coming
smoke.

Wunderlich, Mark
Amaryllis.
Anchorage, The.
Aubade: "All day I've been searching for
omens, flimsy as they are, and the cat."
Bruise of This, The.
Chapel of the Miraculous Medal.
Continent's Edge.
Difficult Body.
East Seventh Street.
Fourteen Things We're Allowed to Bring to the
Underworld.
From a Vacant House.
Given in Person Only.
On Opening.
One Explanation of Beauty.
Peonies.
Predictions about a Black Car.
Simplify Your Combination Therapy.
Suture.
Take Good Care of Yourself.
Thirst.
Trick, The.
Voluntary Servitude.

Wyat, Hester
What makes me write my dearest Freind you
aske.

Wyatt, Sir Thomas (1503?–42)
Argument, The.
Blame Not My Lute.
Courtier's Life, The.
Divers[e] [*or* Dyvers] doth[e] use, as I have
heard and kno[w].
Farewell, love, and all thy law[e]s forever [*or*
for ever].
Fortune doth frown.
He is not de[a]d that sometime [*or* somtyme]
hath a fall.
His Reward.
Honesty.
I am as I am and so will I be.
If waker care, if sudden [*or* sodayne] pale
colo[u]r.
In aeternum I was once determed.
In mourning wise since daily I increase.
In Spayn.
Introductory Poem to the Penitential Psalms.
Long love that in my thought doth harbo[u]r,
The.
Lover Showeth How He Is Forsaken of Such
as He Sometime Enjoyed, The.
Lover's Appeal, The.
Madame, withouten Many Wordes.
My Lute, Awake!
Penitential Psalms, *sels.*
Pillar [*or* Piller] perished [*or* pearisht] is
whe[a]rto I le[a]nt, The.
Quondam was I in my lady's grace.
Satires, *sels.*
Sighs are my food, drink are my tears.
So unwarely was never no man caught [*or*
cawght].
Sometime I fled the fire that me brent.
Sonnet: "My Galley Charged."
Stand Whoso List.
Steadfastness.
Thenmy of liff decayer of all kynde.
Unstable dream[e] [*or* dreme], according [*or*
accordyng] to the place.
Varium et Mutabile.
What nedeth these thretning wordes and
wasted wynde?

What Once I Was.
What should I say.
Who list his wealth and ease retain.
Whoso List to Hunt.

Wycherley, Lynne
Cat's Cradle.
Earth Man.

Wylie, Elinor (1885–1928)
Atavism.
August.
Beauty.
Birthday Sonnet.
Castilian.
Confession of Faith.
Crowded Trolley Car, A.
Desolation Is a Delicate Thing.
Doomsday.
Drowned Woman.
Eagle and the Mole, The.
Ejaculation.
Epitaph: "For this she starred her eyes with
salt."
Escape.
Felo de Se.
Full Moon.
Golden Bough.
Green Hair.
Hymn to Earth.
Incantation: "White well, A."
King Honour's Eldest Son.
Knight Fallen on Evil Days, The.
Let No Charitable Hope.
Madman's Song.
Malediction upon Myself.
Nebuchadnezzar.
Nineteen Sonnets, *sel.*
Now That Your Eyes Are Shut.
O Virtuous Light.
Parting Gift.
Pastiche.
Pebble, The.
Pegasus Lost.
Peter and John.
Portrait in Black Paint, with a Very Sparing
Use of Whitewash.
Preference.
Prophecy.
Puritan's Ballad, The.
Sanctuary.
Sea Lullaby.
Self-portrait.
Sonnet: "You are the faintest freckles on the
hide."
Spring Pastoral.
This Corruptible.
To a Lady's Countenance.
Twelfth Night.
Velvet Shoes.
Village Mystery.
Where, O, Where?
Wild Peaches, *sels.*

Wyndham, William (1759–1834)
Shipwrecked Tippoo.

Wynne, Frances (1866–93)
Nocturne: "Long day was bright, The."

Wynne, Robert
Revisionist History: Magic Kingdom.

Wyrebek, M. (b. 1960)
Example, An.
Healing Logic, A.
Night Owl.
Recovery.
Trendelenburg Position.

X

X, Derrick
Burn Rubber on Me.

X, Marvin (b. 1944)
Palestine.

Xenophanes
Pythagorean, The.
War Memories.

Xiang Xiu (221–300 A.D.)
Recalling Old Times.

Xiao Zihui (*fl.* 519)
Winter Dawn.

Xu, Haixin *See Also* Barnstone, Tony

Xuan Quynh (1942–88)
Summer: "It's the season of birdsong."

Xuanjian (782–865)
Zen Sermon.

Xuanjing, Zhou (*fl.* 12th cent.)
Meditating at midnight.

Xuanjue (665–713)
Canticle of the Way, *sels.*

Xue Di (b. 1957)
Interplay.
Nostalgia.

Y

Yaba (d. 1740)
Plum Blossom Scent, *sels.*

Yadoyano [*or* Yadoya] **Meshimori** (1753–1830)
When it comes to poets.

Yahya Beg (d. 1582)
Come wander through the city, drink wine.
Poetry holds the written veil across its face,
shyly.

Yahya Efendi, Sheyhülislâm (1553?–1644)
Is there no heart capable of love.
Let the hypocrites practice their way.
Saki, offer the cup, let them call me a
drunkard.

Yakamochi (Otomo no Yakamochi) (718–85)
Late evening finally comes.
[These] meetings in dreams.
When my wife left home.

Yakamochi, Otomo no *See* Yakamochi

Yakusai, Layman
Deafening peal, A.

Yalden, Thomas (1670–1736)
Treacherous Towser.

Yamabe no Akahito (*fl.* 724–49)
Manyo Shu, Part 3 of 4, *sel.*
Manyo Shu, Part 2 of 4, *sel.*

Yamada, Mitsuye (b. 1923)
American Son.
Cincinnati.
Club, The.
Night before Good-Bye, The.

Yamaguchi Seishi (1901–94)
Cleaning yellowtail.
Miserable ant.
On a hook he hangs.
Summer river, The.
Up to summer grass.

Yamamura Bochō (1884–1924)
Dance.
Ecstasy.
Mandala.

Yamani, Ahmed
Streets of Black and White.

Yamanoé [*or* Yamanoué] **no Okura (Okura)**
(660?–733?)
Lament for the Evanescence of Life, A.
Longing for His Son, Furuhi.

Yamei (18th cent.)
Spring plain / Gulped.

Yan Yanzhi (384–456)
Pure Wife, A.

Yana Oral Tradition
Now then.

Yang Chi (c.1334–c.1383)
Five-Color.

Yang Chu-Yuan (*fl.* 800)
Early Spring East of Town.

Yang Fang (*fl.* 4th cent.)
Joy of Union, The.

Yang Hsiung (52 B.C.–18 A.D.)
Sweet Springs Palace, The.

Yang Hsün-chi (1456–1544)
Inscribed on the Doors of My Bookshelves.

Yang Lian (b. 1955)
Crocodile 1–15.
Yang Mu (Wang Ching-hsien) (b. 1940)
Let the Wind Recite.
Yang Na
Tune: "Hung Hsiu-hsieh" To a Flea.
Yang Shen (1488–1559)
To the Tune "Moon Over West River"
Yang Shih-ch'i (1365–1444)
Following the Rhymes of Shao-pao Huang's
Poem on Being Moved while Visiting the
Farmers.
Night Rain: A Wall Collapses—Sent To My
Neighbors.
On the Hall of Precious Virtue.
Yang Wan-li (1127–1206)
Cold Fly, A.
Cold Sparrows.
Don't Read Books!
Moored for the Night at the Lan-chi Riverside
Courier Station.
Night Rain at Luster Gap.
Sailing Through the Gorges.
Songs of Depression, sel.
Watching a Village Festival.
Written on a Cold Evening.
Yang Wei-chen (1296–1370)
Mating.
Yang Wen-li (fl. 16th cent.)
New Year's Eve.
Thinking of My Family on an Autumn Day.
Yao, Brother See Brother Yao
Yao Chen (1448–78)
Ballad on the Investigation of a Disaster.
Yao K'uan
To an Ancient Tune.
Yao Sui (1239–1314)
Tune: "Full Court of Fragrance."
Ya'oz-kest, Itamar (1732–1815)
Smoke Rose.
Yaqoob, Jawad (1966–2002)
Only Choice, The.
Resurrections of Layla Al-Attar, The.
Yardımcı, Mehmet (b. 1945)
Link.
Yasui
In the withering gusts.
Mad Verse, sels.
Who's that?
Yates, David C.
Century Plant.
Sex.
Sunset Along U.S. Highway 90 Between
Langtry and Sanderson.
Washing the Cow's Skull.
Yau, John (b. 1950)
Angel Atrapado 7.
Avila.
Cenotaph.
Chinese Landscape Above Caracas.
Chinese Villanelle.
Corpse and Mirror III.
Domestic Bliss.
Engines of Gloom and Affection.
January 18, 1979.
Late Night Movies I.
Painter Asks, The.
Picadilly or Paradise.
Postcard from Trakl.
Radiant Silhouette I.
Radiant Silhouette II.
Radiant Silhouette III.
Radiant Silhouette IV.
Radiant Silhouette V.
Yauch, Adam (b. 1964)
Bodhisattva Vow.
Update, The.
Yauger, Fay M.
Country Fair.
I Remember.
Planter's Charm.
Yavuz, Hilmi (b. 1936)
Empty Streets.

Windy Windows.
Yayu (1701–83)
One sneeze / Skylark's.
Transplanting rice / He pisses.
Ye, Zi
All night I could not sleep.
Ye Weilian [or Yeh Wei-lien or Wai-lim Yip] (b. 1937)
In and Out of Check Points.
Yearsley, Ann (1752–1806)
Addressed to Sensibility.
On Mrs. Montagu.
On the Inhumanity of the Slave Trade, sels.
Reflections on the Death of Louis XVI.
Rural Lyre, The.
Soliloquy: "What folly to complain."
To———: "Lo! dreary Winter, howling o'er
the waste."
To the Right Hon. and Right Revd. Fredrick,
Earl of Bristol, Bishop of Derry, Etc., Etc.
Yeatman, R. J. (1898–1968) and W. C. Sellar
How I Brought the Good News from Aix to
Ghent (or Vice Versa).
Yeats, William Butler (1865–1939)
Acre of Grass, An.
Adam's Curse.
After Long Silence.
Among School Children.
Apparitions, The.
At Galway Races.
Ballad of Father Gilligan, The.
Beggar to Beggar Cried.
Byzantium.
"Calvary," sel.
Cap and Bells, The.
Cap and Bells, The.
Cat and the Moon, The.
Choice, The: "Intellect of man is forced to
choose, The."
Circus Animals' Desertion, The.
Coat, A.
Cold Heaven, The.
Collarbone [or Collar-Bone] of a Hare, The.
Coming of Wisdom with Time, The.
Coole Park and Ballylee, 1931.
Coole Park, 1929.
Cradle Song, A: "Angels are stooping, The."
Crazy Jane on God.
Crazy Jane Talks with the Bishop.
Cuchulain Comforted.
Dawn, The.
Death.
Dialogue of Self and Soul, A, sel.
Dolls, The.
Down by the Salley Gardens.
Easter 1916.
Fascination of What's Difficult, The.
Fiddler of Dooney, The.
Fisherman, The.
Folly of Being Comforted, The.
For Anne Gregory.
Fragments: "Locke sank into a swoon."
Friends.
Gyres, The.
He Thinks of Those Who Have Spoken Evil of
His Beloved.
He Wishes for the Cloths of Heaven.
Her Anxiety.
High Talk.
Host of the Air, The.
Hosting of the Sidhe, The.
In Memory of Eva Gore-Booth and Con
Markievicz.
In Memory of Major Robert Gregory.
In the Seven Woods.
Indian upon God, The [or An].
Irish Airman Foresees His Death, An.
Lake-Isle of Innisfree, The.
Lamentation of the Old Pensioner, The (1890
version).
Lamentation of the Old Pensioner, The (1925
version).
Land of Heart's Desire, The, sel.
Lapis Lazuli.
Last Confession, A.

Leaders of the Crowd, The.
Leda and the Swan.
Long-Legged Fly.
Lover Mourns for the Loss of Love, The.
Lullaby: "Beloved, may your sleep be sound."
Mad as the Mist and Snow.
Madness of King Goll, The.
Magi, The.
Man and the Echo.
Man Who Dreamed of Faeryland, The.
Meditations in Time of Civil War, sels.
Men Improve with the Years.
Meru.
Michael Robartes Bids His Beloved Be at
Peace.
Mohini Chatterjee.
Mother of God, The.
News for the Delphic Oracle.
Nineteen Hundred and Nineteen.
No Second Troy.
On a Political Prisoner.
On Being Asked for a War Poem.
On Hearing That the Students of Our New
University Have Joined the Agitation against
Immoral Literature.
On Woman.
Politics.
Prayer for My Daughter, A.
Prayer for My Son, A.
Prayer for Old Age, A.
Reprisals.
Resurrection, The, sels.
Ribh Considers Christian Love Insufficient.
Rose of the World, The.
Rose Tree, The.
Sailing to Byzantium.
Scholars, The.
Second Coming, The.
Secret Rose, The.
September 1913.
Sixteen Dead Men.
Solomon and the Witch.
Song of the Happy Shepherd, The.
Song of the Old Mother, The.
Song of Wandering Aengus, The.
Sorrow of Love, The [1892 Version].
Sorrow of Love, The [1927 Version].
Spur, The.
St. Matthew, sels.
Statues, The.
Stick of Incense, A.
Stolen Child, The.
Swift's Epitaph.
Symbols.
Three Things.
To a Friend Whose Work Has Come to
Nothing.
To a Shade.
To a Squirrel at Kyle-Na-No.
To Be Carved on a Stone at Thoor Ballylee.
To Ireland in the Coming Times.
To the Rose upon the Rood of Time.
Tower, The.
Under Ben Bulben, sels.
Vacillation, sels.
Vision, A, sels.
When You Are Old.
Where My Books Go.
Who Goes with Fergus?
Wild Old Wicked Man, The.
Wild Swans at Coole, The.
Yejong, King of Koryŏ (1079–1122)
Dirge for Two Generals.
Yellen, Jack (1892–1991)
Ain't She Sweet?
Are You Havin' Any Fun?
Glad Rag Doll.
Happy Days Are Here Again.
Hard-Hearted Hannah (The Vamp of
Savannah).
Louisville Lou (The Vampin' Lady).
Mamma Goes Where Papa Goes.
Yellen, Samuel (b. 1906)
Nighthawks.
Yen Chen (fl. c.1960)
On the Willow Bank.

Yen Shu (991–1055)
Song: "Old song with new words, An."
Tune: "Sand of Silk-Washing Brook."
Tune: "Spring in the Jade House."
Tune: "Treading on Fragrant Grass."

Yenser, Stephen (b. 1941)
Another Lo-Cal Elegy.
Harmonie du Soir.

Yépez, Heriberto (b. 1974)
Del estilo de vida "poco común" de los indios
cucapá citados por R. W. Haly Hardy,
teniente Británico explorando el Golfo de
California.
En la Calle Coahuila.
Juan Martínez, Juan Nadie, Juan Todos.
Juan Martínez, Juan Nobody, Juan All.
Life of a Cucapá Woman, The.
Maníacos y locos.
Maniacs and crazies.
On Coahuila Street.
On the "Unusual" Lifestyle of the Cucapá
Indians as Recorded by R. W. Hardy, British
Lieutenant, While Exploring the Gulf of
California.
Vida de una mujer cucapá, La.

Yeryomin, Mikhail (b. 1937)
Drake pays court to the duck, The.
Faceted grains of wisdom.
Helioptér of a skyscraper hotel.
House over the garden is a bouquet of evening
windows, The.
Polyhedral kernels of wisdom.
Seamstress stitches on a sewing machine, The.
Street lamp. Something missing. Drugstore.

Yesenin [or Essenin], Sergey [or Sergei] (1895–1925)
All Too Soon.
Blue Mist.
Do You Not Love Me.
Esenin's Suicide Note.
Field Upon Field Upon Field.
For My Sister Shura.
Golden Birch Grove's, The.
Golden Grove, The.
Horn of doom is blaring!, The.
I Regret Nothing.
Letter to My Mother.
Mysterious, Ancient World of Mine.
Sergei Yesenin.
Sleigh, The.
Winds, Winds, Winds.
Yesterday's rain.

**Yevtushenko [or Evtushenko], Yevgeny
Aleksandrovich (b. 1933)**
At Forty.
Babii Yar.
Cemetery of the Whales, The.
Dwarf Birches.
Fear (Extracts).
From a Talk.
Hand-Rolled Cigarettes.
Hundred miles from the capital city of hope,
A.
I am.
John Reed's Monologue.
On a Bicycle.
Saints of Jazz.
Siberian Wooing.
Streetcar Named Poetry, A.

Yezzi, David
Woman Holding a Fox.

Yi Cha (b. 1966)
Neighbors.

Yi Chehyŏn (1287–1367)
After the Snow in the Mountains.
Contemporary Folk Songs, sels.

Yi Chinmyŏng (b. 1955)
Bear, The.
Pure Talk.
Record of a Certain Summer.
Snow: "It snowed. It snowed comfortably. No,
that's not it. In the beginning, it snowed
violently."
Woman Mopping With a Rag Mop.

Yi Chŏngbo (1693–1766)
If flowers bloom, I think of the moon.
May my love become an alder tree.
Memory, A.
When the owl hoots.

Yi Chono (1341–71)
That clouds have no intent.

Yi Chonyŏn (1269–1343)
Moon is white on pear blossoms, The.

Yi Hwang (1501–71)
Twelve Songs of Tosan, sels.

Yi Hyangji (b. 1942)
Acromatic Dawn.
Joy of Love, The.
Leaf Struck by Bird Droppings.
Leaving Home.
March of Dawn, The.
Phoenix, The.
Reply at an Unknown Place.
Ringing in My Ears.
Sea, The: "Ladies, why don't you lift a stone."
Song of a Balloon in Search of Her Mom's
balloon.
Sunrise: "Blood stolen from my body before
dawn."
What Did You Do Yesterday?

Yi I (1536–84)
Nine Songs of Mount Ko, sels.

Yi Illo (1151–1220)
Cicada.
Night Rain on the Rivers Hsiao and Hsiang.
On the River on a Spring Day.
Written on the Wall of Ch'ŏnsu Monastery.

Yi Inbok (fl. 1350)
Drumbeats.

Yi Jang'hi (Jang-hi Lee) (1902–28)
Spring is a Cat, The.

Yi Jung (fl. 16th cent.)
River Darkens on an Autumn Night, The.

Yi Kae (1417–56)
Candle burns in the room, The.
Upon Listening to the Flute.

Yi Kyŏngnim (b. 1947)
Anam Street 1.
Anam Street 2—Outside the Cinema.
At the Grave.
Certain Sickness, Deep Love.
Chirping.
Korean Women.
Oh Life.
Song: "In the world are many roads I haven't
walked, and I have pain."
Time 5.

Yi Kyubo (1168–1241)
Burning My Manuscripts.
Composed Playfully on New Year's Day.
Evening on the Mountain: Song to the Moon in
the Well.
Farmhouse: Three Poems, sels.
Grieving for My Little Girl.
How I Felt Pawning My Coat: Shown to Ch'oe
Chongbon.
Mad Rout of the Rat, The.
Moon in the Well, The.
On Poetry.
Poetry: A Chronic Disease.
Sung Impromptu.
Thoughts on Eyes Growing Dim: Presented to
Chŏn Iji.

Yi Myŏnghan (1595–1645)
If the path of my dreams.
Morning star has set, The. A lark.
With tears I cling to your sleeves.

Yi Saek (1328–96)
Rough clouds gather around the valley.

Yi Sang (1910–37)
Critical Condition, sels.
Crow's-Eye View, sels.
Face.
Flowering Tree.
I Wed a Toy Bride.
Mirror.
Motion.
Noon—A Certain.

Paper Memorial Stone.
Performance Angel.
Publications Law.
Soyŏng Problems.
Two People : 1.
Two People : 2.

Yi Sanghŭi (b. 1960)
As My Will Concurred Not To My Being, It
Were But Right and Equal to Reduce Me to
My Dust.
Dance: "When I wait."
Dickinson's Blue Sleeve.
Dracula.
Farewell, My Youth.
For Men to Tell How Human Life Began Is
Hard, For Who Himself Beginning Knew?
Desire With Thee Still Longer to Converse
Induced Me as New-Waked from Soundest
Sleep Soft on the Flow'ry Herb I Found Me
Laid in Balmy Sweat.
I Ask in Late Evening.
Igloo! Igloo!
Morning Stroll, A.
Night, Work.
Organizing a Drawer.
Van Gogh.

Yi Sanghwa (1901–43)
Will Spring Return to Stolen Fields?

Yi Sŏkhyŏng
Upon Listening to the Flute.

Yi Sunsin (1545–98)
By moonlight I sit all alone.
In the Chinhae Camp.

Yi T'aek (1651–1719)
O roc, don't ridicule the small black birds.

Yi Tal (fl. 1568–1608)
Mountain Temple.

Yi Talch'ung
Neglected Wife, The.

Yi Yŏng (1615–37)
Who sliced the crescent moon so small.

Yi Yŏnju
Bread and I, The.
Clinic in a Dangerous Season 1, A.
Clinic in a Dangerous Season 7, A.
Clinic in a Dangerous Season 8, A.
For the Sake of Two Screws.
Grandmother's Sea.
Holiday Inside an Incubator.
Open-Eyed Blind Man, An.
Our Old Home.
Taking a Watermelon as a Paradigm.

Yi Yuksa (1904–44)
Blue Grapes.
Small Park, A.
Summit, The.
Thatched House.
Twilight.

Yin Luoth (b. 1951)
Phnom Penh Morning.

Yo Inlŏ (c.1050–1100)
Meditating on the Start of a New Era.

Yoketsu
Nothing longed for.

Yolen, Jane (b. 1939)
Caterpillar's Lullaby.
Fat Is Not a Fairy Tale.
First Robin.
Graffiti.
Shepherd's Night Count.
Sky Scrape / City Scape.

Yomono Akara (1749–1823)
In Yoshiwara.
Season greeter, The.

Yonathan, Nathan (b. 1923)
Dust of Poems, The.
Friends: "Joseph is without doubt rent in
pieces an evil beast hath devoured him."
Without the Boy.

Yoneda, Karl
Angel Island—what a beautiful name.
New Year's Day came quietly and left silently.
New Year's Day on Angel Island.

Yŏngjae, Monk (*fl.* 785–98)
  Meeting Bandits.
York, Jake Adam
  Walt Whitman in Alabama.
Yorke, Philip
  Our Gardener here, James Phillips see.
Yosano Akiko (1878–1942)
  And then one morning.
  Are you still longing.
  Beloved, You Must Not Die.
  Certain Country, A.
  Channel Boat, The, *sel.*
  Dancing Girl, The.
  From Paris on a Postcard.
  Half-horse / half-woman.
  Heart of a Thirtyish Woman, The.
  In the First Person.
  Let men pay for their.
  No words for the Way.
  Once, far over the breakers.
  Pressing my breasts.
  Sakai Harbor.
  Spring is short.
  Spring quickly passes.
  Spring Thaw.
  Star that once, A.
  Tangled Hair, *sel.*
  Temple bell, The.
  This hot tide of blood.
  Thousand strands, A.
  What I dreamed was.
Yosano Tekkan (1873–1935)
  Victory Arches.
  Withered Lotus.
Yosef, Hamutal Bar
  Angel on the Beach, An.
  In the Library.
  Jaffa, July 1948.
  Reflections on a Dove.
Yoseph, Reuven ben *See* ben Yoseph, Reuven
Yoshida Issui (1898–1973)
  Swans.
Yoshihara, Sachiko (b. 1932)
  Air Raid.
Yoshioka Minoru (1919–90)
  Pilgrimage.
Yost, Chryss
  California Poem.
  Descano, California.
  Escaping from Autopia.
  From San Diego.
  Lai with Sounds of Skin.
  Last Night: "When the sun sets, and he isn't
    home, she walks."
Youmans, Greg
  Pear's Complaint.
Youn, Monica (b. 1971)
  Flatlanders.
  Naglfar.
  Night Ferry to Naxos 1.
  Night Ferry to Naxos 2.
  Venice, Unaccompanied.
Young, Al (b. 1939)
  Art of Benny Carter, The.
  Blue Monday.
  Blues Don't Change, The.
  California Peninsula: El Camino Real.
  Conjugal Visits.
  Dance of the Infidels.
  Detroit 1958.
  Fifty-Fifty.
  From Bowling Green.
  How Stars Start.
  How the Rainbow Works.
  In the Sierras.
  Jazz as Was.
  Leaving Syracuse.
  Lester Leaps In.
  Mountains of California: Part 1, The.
  Mountains of California: Part 2, The.
  Myself When I Am Real.
  One Snapshot I Couldn't Take in France, The.
  One West Coast.
  Poem for Players, A.

Ravel: Bolero.
Seeing Red.
Song Turning Back into Itself, The, *sels.*
Studio Up Over In Your Ear.
Third Street Promenade; Full Moon, Sunday
  Night, Santa Monica.
Who Am I in Twilight.
Written in Bracing, Gray L.A. Rainlight.
Young, Albert
  And It Shall Come.
Young, Andrew (1885–1971)
  Christmas Day.
  Culbin Sands.
  Dead Mole, A.
  Fairy Ring, The.
  Falls of Glomach, The.
  Fear, The.
  Field-Glasses.
  March Hares.
  Nest, The.
  Stockdoves, The.
  Suilven.
  Wet Day, A.
Young, Andy
  Foxfire.
  Ghost of Me.
  In Anguish, the Heart Finally Prays.
  Vodou Headwashing Ceremony.
Young, Augustus (b. 1943)
  She's My Love.
Young, C. Dale (b. 1969)
  Infidelity.
  Proximity.
  Torn.
Young, Colville N. (b. 1932)
  In the Wilderness.
  Night-Mullins River.
Young, David
  After My Death.
  Four About Apples.
  Four About Heavy Machinery.
  Four About Metaphysics.
  Poem Against the Horizon, The.
  Poem for Adlai Stevenson and Yellow Jackets.
  Project for Freight Trains, A.
Young, Dean
  Business of Love is Cruelty, The.
  Chapped Lips.
  Colophon.
  Cotton in a Pill Bottle.
  Frottage.
  Invention of Heaven, The.
  Only One of My Deaths.
  Pleasure.
  Rothko's Yellow.
  Sources of the Delaware.
  White Crane.
Young, Douglas (1913–73)
  Ballant o' the Laird's Bath, The.
  Deid sall ye ligg, and ne'er a memorie.
  For a Wife in Jizzen.
  For the Old Highlands.
  Kirkyaird by the Sea, The, *sel.*
  Last Lauch.
  Minnie, I canna caa my wheel.
Young, Edward (1683–1765)
  Epistles to Mr. Pope, *sel.*
  Foreign Address, The, *sels.*
  Imperium Pelagi, or, The Merchant, *sels.*
  Last Day, The, *sels.*
  Love of Fame, the Universal Passion, *sel.*
  Night Thoughts, *sels.*
  Ocean, an Ode, *sel.*
  Ode to the King, *sel.*
  One to destroy, is murder by the law.
  Resignation, *sels.*
Young, Gary (b. 1951)
  After Cycling.
  Braver Deeds, *sel.*
  Days, *sels.*
  Eating Wild Mushrooms.
  Four Poems.
  I had never seen her so angry, and her rage
    revealed a measure of love I had missed.
  If He Had, *sels.*

Our Life in California.
Young, George
  Damien.
  Letter to William Carlos Williams, A.
  Miracle, The.
  Night Call.
Young, George W. (1846–1919)
  Lips That Touch Liquor.
Young, Irene
  Mermaid Knows, A.
  Visit to the Palace of Venus.
Young, Jeremy
  True Love.
Young, Joe (1889–1939)
  Dinah.
  Five Foot Two, Eyes of Blue (Has Anybody
    Seen My Girl?).
  How 'Ya Gonna Keep 'Em Down on the
    Farm? (After They've Seen Paree).
  I Wonder Why She Kept on Saying "Si-Si-Si-
    Si-Senor."
  I'm Gonna Sit Right Down and Write Myself a
    Letter.
  I'm Sitting on Top of the World.
  Life Is a Song, Let's Sing It Together.
  Rock-a-Bye Your Baby with a Dixie Melody.
  Was That the Human Thing to Do?
  You're Gonna Lose Your Gal.
Young, Joseph
  Hundred Years from Today, A.
Young, Kevin (b. 1970)
  Almanac, 1939, An.
  Anatomy.
  Boiling, The.
  Campbell's Black Bean Soup.
  Casting.
  Central Standard Time.
  Clyde Peeling's Reptiland in Allenwood,
    Pennsylvania.
  Degrees.
  East Jesus.
  Eddie Priest's Barbershop and Notary.
  Errata.
  Escape Artist, The, *sels.*
  Everywhere Is Out of Town.
  Field Trip.
  Langston Hughes.
  Letters from the North Star.
  Litany: "Dirt grows up, The."
  Negative.
  No Offense.
  Preserving, The.
  Quivira City Limits.
  Revival.
  Reward.
  Rushes, The.
  Song of Smoke.
  Soundtrack.
  Southern University, 1962.
  Wake.
Young, Mary Julia (*fl.* 1789–1809)
  Anxiety.
  Friendship.
  On an Early Spring.
  To Dreams.
  To My Pen.
  To Time.
Young, Patricia (b. 1954)
  Photograph, 1958.
  Third Sex, The.
  Three Point Five Nine.
Young, Sally
  I love your plumpness.
Young, Seth
  River We Are Caried By, *sel.*
Young, Stanley
  Epitaph for a Concord Boy.
Young Bear, Ray A. (b. 1950)
  Drive to Lone Ranger, A.
  Emily Dickinson, Bismarck and the
    Roadrunner's Inquiry.
  First Dimension of Skunk, The.
  From the Spotted Night.
  King Cobra as Political Assassin, The.

Language of Weather, The.
Nothing Could Take Away the Bear-King's
  Image.
Personification of a Name, The.
Race of the Kingfishers.
Significance of a Water Animal, The.
Song Taught to Joseph, The.
Wadasa Nakamoon, Vietnam Memorial.

Youngblom, Tracy
Ophelia Speaks.

Yount, Alan
Sharing.

Yourcenar, Marguerite (Marguerite Antoinette Jeanne Marie Ghislaine Cleenwerke de Crayencour) (1903–87)
Daily Papers.
Epitaph in Time of War.
Épitaphe, temps de guerre.
Journaux Quotidiens.
Poem for a Doll Bought in a Russian Bazaar.
Poème pour une poupée achetée dans un bazar
  russe.

Youssef, Saadi *See* Yusuf, Sa'di

Youssri, Zahrah
Why Are Seaman Always Miserable?

Yoyotte, Simone (c.1910–33)
Half-Season.
Pale Blue Line in a Forced Episode, I Cut a
  Hole in the Flag of the Republic.

Yü, Hsiang *See* Hsiang Chi

Yu Ch'an (c.286–339)
Looking at Stone Drum Mountain.
Third Day of the Third Month at the
  Meandering River, The.

Yu Chao (*fl.* 10th cent. A.D.)
Pine Whisk, The.

Yu Chien-wu (487–550)
On the Third Day I Wait on the Emperor at a
  Banquet and Describe the Reflection of the
  Candles in the Serpentine.
Spring Day.

Yü Ch'ing-tsěng (*fl.* 19th cent.)
To the Tune "Intoxicated with Shadows of
  Flowers."

Yu Hsin (513–81)
Bidding Farewell to Secretary Chou.
Harmonizing with Great Officer Yan's Poem
  "The Start of the Fine Weather."
Harmonizing with the Monk Heling's Poem
  "An Outing to the Kunming Pool."
Knights Errant.
Offered in Thanks for a Present of Wine and a
  Goose.
Running Into Snow While Journeying Through
  the Suburbs.
Season of Shadow, The.

Yü Hsüan-chi (c.843–68)
Living in the Summer Mountains.
On a Visit to Ch'ung Chen Taoist Temple.
Spring Thoughts Sent to Tzu-an.

Yu Mongin (1559–1623)
Poor Woman, A.

Yu Ŭngbu (d. 1456)
Do you say the wind blew last night.

Yu Xuanji
At Home in the Summer Mountains.
Divided by the Han River.
Selling Wilted Peonies.
Spring Passion.
Vanishing Spring Moves to Regret.
Voicing Deepest Thoughts.

Yüan Chěn (779–831)
Bamboo Mat.
Dreaming of My Wife.
Elegy: "O loveliest daughter of Hsieh."
Empty House.
Iranian Whirling Girls.
Letter Smuggled in a Fish.
Nearly a Sky Half Clear, Not Yet Half Light.
Oriole.
Peach Blossoms.
Pitcher, The.
Remembering.
Retirement.

Song of the Pearl-Fishers, The.
Three Dreams in Chiang-ling.
When We Are Apart.
White Dress.
You're No Exception.
Yuan Zhen to Bo Juyi.

Yüan Chieh (719–72)
After the Raiders Have Gone: To Clerks and
  Officials.

Yüan Chiu-ts'ai (*fl.* early 18th cent.)
Warm Invitation, A.

Yüan Chüeh (1266–1327)
Shipboard Song.

Yüan Hao-wen (1190–1257)
Poems on Poetry, *sel.*
With Chang Hung-lüeh, Court Attendant,
  Discussing Literature.

Yüan Hung-tao (1568–1610)
On Receiving My Letter of Termination.
Slowly, Slowly Poem, The.

Yüan Mei (1716–98)
Growing Old (1).
Growing Old (2).
Last Poem: Goodbye to My Garden.
Miscellaneous Feelings in the Sui Garden.
Motto.
Old and Traveling.
On the Road to T'ien-t'ai.
On the Way to Pa-ling.
Writing What I've Seen.

Yüan-ti
Ejected Wife, The.

Yuasa Hangetsu (1858–1943)
Twelve Stones. Chapter 1: Prologue.

Yuishun (d. 1544)
Why, it's but the motion of eyes and brows!

Yujŏng (1544–1610)
Longing for My Hometown.
Sitting at Night at an Old Inn in Silla.

Yün-k'an Tzu (*fl.* first half of 14th cent.)
Out of chaos.

Yün-shang, Hu *See* "Lin Ling"

Yun Sŏndo (1587–1671)
Angler's Calendar, The, *sels.*
At My Study.
Songs of Five Friends, *sels.*

Yun Tongju (1918–45)
Cross, The.
Foreward.
His Last Words.
Hospital.
One Night I Count the Stars.
Poem That Came Easily, A.
Self-portrait.
Yet Another Home.

Yun Tusŏ (b. 1668)
Mud-encrusted piece of jade, A.

Yun'er
Yun'er's Bell.

Yungch'ŏn, Master (c.579–632)
Song of the Comet.

Yup, Paula
Things I Miss, The.

Yuson, Alfred A. (b. 1944)
Andy Warhol Speaks to His Two Filipino
  Maids.
Dead Center.
Love Before Dinner.
World Poetry Circuit.

Yusuf, Sa'di (b. 1943)
America, America, *sels.*
Attention.
Enemies.
Good Morning, Fakhani.
Hamra Night.
How L'Akhdar Ben Youssef Wrote His Last
  Poem.
Mouse, The.
Night in Al-Hamra.
Poetry: "Who broke these mirrors."
Three Bridges.
Trees of Ithaca, The.
Woman, A.

Yüsuf III, King of Granada (1376–1417)
My friend go gently, for Time is as you know
  it to be, since there is no avoiding an easy
  life in spite of the present trace of hardship.
O you who have aimed / At my heart with the
  dart / Of a piercing glance.

Z

Zabel, Morton Dauwen (b. 1901)
Hoar Frost.

Zabolotsky [*or* Zabolotskii], Nikolai Alekseievich (1903–58)
All That My Soul Possessed.
At the Fishmonger's.
Face of a Horse, The.
Loop Canal, The.
Metamorphoses.
Nocturnal Garden.
Poem about Rain.
Poprryshchin.
Signs of the Zodiac are fading, The.
Snakes.
Warning.
Yesterday Reflecting Upon Death.

Zach, Natan (b. 1930)
Against Parting.
Be Attentive.
Be Careful.
Failure.
Greater Courage.
King Solomon's Camel.
On the Desire to Be Precise.
Seven.

Zafrir, Yehoshua (b. 1928)
Forced March in Summer.

Zagajewski, Adam (b. 1945)
At Daybreak.
Auto Mirror.
Betrayal.
Electric Elegy.
Fire: "Probably I am an ordinary middle-
  class."
Flame, A.
Moment ("Clear moments are so short.").
Moths.
On Swimming.
Quick Poem, A.
To Go to Lvov.
Try to Praise the Mutilated World.
Watching Shoah in a Hotel Room in America.
When Death Came.

Zaid, Gabriel
Circe.
Cloister.
Furious Clarity, A.
Mortal Practice.
Song of Pursuit.
Sundial.

Zakama, Kabura
Call of the Fulani Maid.
My Generation.

Zakaria Youssef, Meelaad
Sadder Man, A.

Zamora, Daisy (b. 1959)
Celebration of the Body.
Downpour.
Hand Mirror.
Lineage.
Loyal Housewife.
Mother's Day.
Precisely.
Report on the Protest in Front of the United
  States Embassy by the Pino Grande
  Movement, A.
Vision of Your Body.

Zamora-Linmark, R.
Day 1: Portrait of the Artist, Small-kid Time.
Election Day.

Zand, Rick
Hot House.

Zandvakili, Katayoon (b. 1967)
County.

Love Letter.
No Trespassing (Private Beach).

Zant, Johan van der *See* Andreus, Hans

Zanzotto, Andrea (b. 1921)
Behold the Thin Green.
Campèa.
Distance.
Eclogue 4: "Shell-bursting births, comas, and the mute."
Epiphany.
Existing Psychically.
From a New Height.
How Long.
If It Were Not.
Prophecies or Memories or Display-Board Newspapers, *sel.*
Subnarcosis.
That's How We Are.

Zappala, Robyn
Hope: "She has a way of standing as if a belt of weights."
One Year Later.

Zapruder, Matthew (b. 1967)
Canada.
School Street.
Ten Questions for Mona.
Thank You for Being You.
Whoever You Are.

Zaragoza Clubs (*fl.* 1860)
Héroes del Cinco de Mayo, *sel.*
Homenajes de Gratitud, *sel.*

Zarco, Cyn (b. 1950)
Manila Paper.
My Worst Fear.
Once upon a Seesaw with Charlie Chan.
Saxophonetyx.

Zarifoğlu, Cahit (1940–84)
Tigerish.

Zarin, Cynthia (b. 1959)
Ant Hill, The.
Song: "My heart, my dove, my snail, my sail, my."

Zarou-Zouzounis, Lorene (b. 1958)
Embroidered Memory.
Her Heart Is a Rose Petal and Her Skin Is Granite.

Zarzyski, Paul
How Near Vietnam Came to Us.
Hurley High.

Zati (d. 1546)
Oh heavens, why do you cry? Is your beloved seen.

Zaturenska, Marya Alexandrovna (Mrs. Horace Gregory) (1902–82)
Daisy, The.
Head of Medusa.
Lovers, The.
Tempest, The.
White Dress, The.
Woman at the Piano.

Zavalnyuk [or Zaval'niuk], Leonid Andreievich (b. 1931)
I Love My Enemies.

Zavatsky, Bill (b. 1943)
Bald.
Live at the Village Vanguard.
Walker Evans in Bridgeport.

Zawacki, Andrew (b. 1972)
Ampersonata.
Argument for an Elemental Aesthetic.
Ascension Provisos.
Astrelegy.
Credo.
From the Book of Divine Consolation.
Velocity Among the Ruins of Angel Republic.
Ventriloquy.
Vertigo.
Viatica, *sel.*

Zawgee (1907–90)
Way of the Water-Hyacinth, The.

Zawinski, Andrena
You Touch Me.

Zayyad, Tawfiq (b. 1932)
Here We Will Stay.

Zdanys, Jonas
Angels of Wine, The.

Zehrd [or Zahrad] (b. 1924)
Woman Cleaning Lentils, The.

Zeiger, David
Mostly Mozart at Planting Fields Arboretum.

Zekkai Chushin (1336–1405)
Void has collapsed upon the earth, The.

"Zelda" (1914–84)
Crippled beggar who lives, The.
How Much a Word Could Help.
Place of Fire, A.

Zelenina, Galina (b. 1978)
Shma Yisrael (Hear, O Israel).
With grown-up clever hands.

Zen Center Sangha
Mondo.
One third of my life has been spent in this practice and you.

Zenmaro, Toki
Evidence.
Tanka: "All the young men I know."
Tanka: "In sullen silence."
Tanka: "No news of him."
Tanka: "Nothing / but reason."
Tanka: "Old Japan."
Tanka: "Work on the impossible."

Zepeda, Ofelia
Bury Me with a Band.

Zepeda, Rafael
Philosophical Emancipation, The.
Wreckers, The.

Zephaniah, Benjamin (b. 1958)
According to My Mood.
De Rich Getting Rich.
Speak.
Sun, The.

Zeppa, Mary
Aleatory.

Zesen, Philipp von (1619–89)
Evening Song.
To the Superhuman Adelmund, When She Would Undo the Kiss Already Done.

Zetter, Sharon
Misdemeanor.

Zeyneb (d. c.1481)
Remove your veil and illuminate the earth.

Zhang Hua (232–300)
Emotion.

Zhang Ruoxu (c.660–c.720)
Spring, River, Flowers, Moon, Night.

Zhang Shuai (475–527)
Pining.
Staring.

Zhao, Pan (48–117?)
Needle and Thread.

Zhenkai, Zhao *See* Bei Dao

Zhidun (314–66)
Song of My Mountain Dwelling.

Zhiyuan, Shi
In Praise of Ch'an Master Wang You Who Cares for the Bonnet Monkeys around His Mountain Studio.
Living in Poverty.
Lost Cranes.

Zhou Xingsi (d. 521)
Thousand Character Classic, The, *sels.*

Ziedonis, Imants
At Maruža's.

Ziemianin, Adam (b. 1948)
Heart Attack.

Zilahy, Péter (b. 1970)
Dictators.

Zimmer, Paul (b. 1934)
Another Place.
Because of Duties, Zimmer Had Forgotten the Forest.
Brain of the Spider, The.
But Bird.
Crazy with Love.
Day Zimmer Lost Religion, The.
Duke Ellington Dream, The.

Eisenhower Years, The.
Example, The.
Lester Tells of Wanda and the Big Snow.
Romance.
Romance for the Wild Turkey, A.
Sitting with Lester Young.
What I Know About Owls.
Zimmer Drunk and Alone, Dreaming of Old Football Games.
Zimmer Imagines Heaven.
Zimmer in Fall.
Zimmer in Grade School.
Zimmer's Head Thudding against the Blackboard.

Zimmerman, Robert *See* Dylan, Bob

Zimmerman, Rosamond
Anemia.

Zimunya, Musaemura Bonus
Arrivants.
Kisimiso.
Let It Be.
Mr. Bezuidenthout's Dogs.

Zinger, Gali-Danah (b. 1962)
I'm speaking to make you silent.
Lamentation of the Border-Guard.
Strategy.

Zinnemann-Hope, Pam
Taking Tea with My Father and Mother.

Zinzendorf, Nikolaus [or Nicolaus] Ludwig, Graf von (1700–60)
Jesus, thy blood and righteousness.

Zisquit, Linda (b. 1947)
After Years of Feasting and No Sacrifice.
Unopened Letters, *sels.*
Word before the Last about Loss, A.

Ziyalan, Mustafa (b. 1959)
Night Ride On 21.

Zolotow, Charlotte (b. 1915)
Bridge, The.
Enemies.
Riddle, A: "Once when I was very scared."

Zolynas, Al (b. 1945)
Living with Others.
Love in the Classroom.
Pastorale for Spring.
Same Air, The.
Way He'd Like It, The.
Whistling Woman.
Zen of Housework, The.

Zonas (*fl.* 90 B.C.)
Charon.

Zondberg, Olga (b. 1972)
Cockle-antarctica / has been cast up onto the shore.
There were lots of them.
They all but cry out.
To die. And be born as an inspector of playgrounds for tiny tots.
Variety of animals, said Khlebnikov, The.

"Zozimus" *See* Moran, Michael

Zrínyi, Miklós (1620–64)
Elegy: "Outworn year has altered his apparel, The."
Epilogue: "My monument is done, my task is ended."
Idyll, *sel.*
Sortie, The.
Zrinyiad, The, *sels.*

Zubick, Kelleen
Evolution of Appetite.

Zu-Bolton, Ahmos, II (b. 1935)
Dudley Randall.
Struggle-Road Dance.

Zucker, Rachel (b. 1971)
Avoid.
Cloister or "vietato toccare le rose."
Diary (Underworld).
In Your Version of Heaven I am Younger.
Kind of Catastrophe, A.
Not Knowing Nijinsky or Diaghilev.
Portrait of Unknown.
Post Card (Central Park).
Sacristy.

What I Want You to See Is She When Not
    Here As in Now.
Zuckerman, Marilyn
    In Every Pot and Closet.
Zuian
    Sky-piercing sword, gleaming cold.
Zuiderent, Ad (b. 1944)
    Along the River.
Zukofsky, Louis (1904–78)
    A, *sels*.
    Anew 10.
    Anew 20.
    Anew 21.
    As to How Much.
    For you I have emptied the meaning.
    H. T.
    I Sent Thee Late.
    I's (pronounced *Eyes*).
    It's hard to see but think of a sea.
    "Mantis."
    No it was no dream of coming death.
    Non Ti Fidar.

Poem Beginning "The", *sels*.
    (Ryokan's scroll).
Shang Cup.
Song for the Year's End, A, *sel*.
Songs of Degrees, *sel*.
29 Poems, *sels*.
29 Songs, *sels*.
When the crickets.
Xenophanes.
Zulu, Phumzile
    You are Mad: and I Mean It!
Zuni Oral Tradition
    History Myth of the Coming of the A'shiwi as
        Narrated by 'Kiäklo, *sel*.
    Prayer at the Winter Solstice, A, *sel*.
    Scalp Dance, The, *sel*.
    Shalako, *sels*.
Zurita, Raúl (b. 1951)
    Even Forsaken They'd Flower.
    March of the Cordilleras, The.
    6.

Sparkling Beaches, The.
    Splendor in the Wind.
Zweig, Martha
    Fleshpot.
Zweig, Paul (1935–84)
    Aunt Lil.
    Eternity's Woods.
    Father.
    Life Story.
Zwein, Sabah Al-Kharrat (b. 1954)
    As If in Flaw, or in the Flaw of Space, *sel*.
    Inclined House, The, *sel*.
Zwicky, Fay (b. 1933)
    Jack Frost.
    Reckoning.
    Three Songs of Love and Hate, *sels*.
Zwicky, Jan
    You Must Believe in Spring.
Zych, Adam
    Auschwitz, 1987.

SUBJECT INDEX

*Poems under each subject heading are listed alphabetically by author. Subjects range from specific (*Dublin, Ireland *or* Mandela, Nelson*) to the general (*Faith *or* Imagination).
Some subject headings show cross-references to related subjects. The subject category* Love *is so broad that it appears here only to refer the user to related subjects.*

A

Aachen, Germany
Bowers, E.   Aix-La-Chappelle, 1945.
Aaron (Bible)
Carey, T.   Zohar.
Herbert, G.   Aaron.
Abandonment
Arrillaga.   Mariana II.
  Rosa/Filí.
Atwood.   Beauharnois (1).
  Four Small Elegies.
Aygi, G.   Rustle of Birches.
Basho.   Now I see her face.
  You've heard monkeys crying.
Ben-Lev, D.   Broken Helix.
Berlin.   Supper Time.
Bialik.   At Twilight.
Blake, W.   Love's Secret.
Bradley, J.   Improper Disposal.
Brown, K.   '49 Merc, A.
Bürger, G.   Lass of Fair Wone, The.
Cassian.   Lady of Miracles.
Citino.   Newborn Found Alive in Shallow
  Grave.
Clark, T.   "Like Musical Instruments".
Daley, V.   Mother Doorstep.
Dávila Andrade, C.   Abandoned House, The.
Davis, C.   Belongings.
Davis, C.   Nod.
Dawe, Tom.   Abandoned Outpost.
Derricotte.   Poem for My Father.
Dimitrova.   Interior with Faded Colors.
Dove, R.   Adolescence—3.
Goldberg, B.   Third Body.
González, R.   Death of the Farm Workers' Cat.
Hammerstein.   Don't Ever Leave Me.
Hill, G.   My little son, when you could
  command marvels.
Hô Sugyông.   Butterfly, The.
Hughes, L.   Lament over Love.
Hugo, R.   Degrees of Gray in Philipsburg.
  River Now, The.
Ivey, M.   After You Left.
Jaimes Freyre.   Eternal Farewell.
Kamienska.   On the Cross.
Kim Sowŏl.   Forsaken.
Kimbrell, J.   My Father at the North Street
  Boarding House.
Kingsley, C.   Airly Beacon.
Komunyakaa, Y.   *Bui Doi*, Dust of Life.
  My Father's Love Letters [*or* Loveletters].
Kooser.   Abandoned Farmhouse.
Longfellow, H.   Preamble to a Tale of Acadie.
Macdonagh, T.   John-John.
Madhubuti.   After Her Man Had Left Her for
  the Sixth Time That Year (An Uncommon
  Occurrence).
Meynell, A.   Study, A.
Michelangelo Buonarroti.   It was over here that
  my love, in his mercy.
Mistral, G.   Flower of Air, The.
Moore, L.   Winter 1967.
Nguyễn Gia Thiều.   You were a fool, Old Man
  of the Moon.
Nowlan.   Only When My Heart Freezes.

Orozco.   There Are No Doors.
Ovid.   You who are reading this work without
  malice, may you.
Owen, W.   To Eros.
Pastan.   I Am Learning to Abandon the World.
Propertius.   Ariadne Lay, Theseus' Ship Sailing
  Away.
Randell.   Hard to Place.
Ransom, J.   Lady Lost.
Ratzlaff, K.   Dill.
Realuyo.   La Querida.
Reece, Spencer.   Portofino.
Reznikoff.   Deserter, A.
Rilke.   Olive Garden, The.
Seneca.   Flee every friendship and live: a greater
  truth.
Smith, R.   Bluetits.
Song.   Mother of Us All.
Sorrentino.   Land of Cotton.
Stickney, T.   Departure, The.
Szporluk.   Meteor.
Tellegen.   Visit, The.
Tomlinson, C.   Two Views of Two Ghost
  Towns.
Unknown.   I may wel sike for grevous is my
  peyne.
  Meng: To a Man.
Vando.   My Mother Cunning, Yet Innocent.
Verwey, A.   North-Sea, The.
Weissbort.   Mourning.
Wenderoth, J.   Disfortune.
Wither.   I Loved a Lass.
Wordsworth, W.   Thorn, The.
Wyatt.   Lover Showeth How He Is Forsaken of
  Such as He Sometime Enjoyed, The.
  Lover's Appeal, The.
Yost, C.   Last Night: "When the sun sets, and he
  isn't home, she walks."
Zurita, R.   Even Forsaken They'd Flower.
Abbey Theatre, Dublin
Strong, L.   Old Woman, Outside the Abbey
  Theater, An.
Abbeys
Denham.   Here should my wonder dwell, and
  here my praise.
Landon.   Fountain's Abbey.
See also **Monasteries**
Abelard and Heloise
Pope, A.   Eloisa to Abelard.
Villon.   Ballade of the Ladies of Time Past.
Abolitionists
Benét, S.   Invocation: "American muse, whose
  strong and diverse heart."
  John Brown's body lies a-mouldering in the
  grave.
  John Brown's Prayer.
Dove, R.   David Walker (1785–1830).
Dunbar, P.   Douglass.
Harper, F.   Bible Defence of Slavery.
  Bury Me in a Free Land.
Hayden, R.   Runagate Runagate.
Rukeyser, M.   Soul and Body of John Brown,
  The.
Whittier.   Brown of Ossawatomie.
  For Righteousness' Sake.
Williams, E.   At Harper's Ferry Just before the
  Attack.

Aborigines
Campbell, D.   Lovers, The.
Davis, J.   Desolation.
  First-born, The.
  One Hundred and Fifty Years.
  Warru.
Durack.   Lament for the Drowned Country.
Fogarty, L.   Biral Biral.
  Fuck All Departments.
  Memo to Us (story).
  No Grudge.
  Remember Something Like This.
Marshall-Stoneking.   Passage.
Momaday.   Carriers of the Dream Wheel.
Mudrooroo Narogin.   Peaches and Cream.
  Song Thirty-Four.
Oodgeroo of the tribe Noonuccal.   Last of His
  Tribe.
  No More Boomerang.
  We Are Going.
Sykes, B.   One Day.
Touré, A.   A*boriginal* Elegy: The Once and
  Future Queen.
Unknown.   See there, that tree is a digging stick.
Weller.   Story of Frankie . . . My Man, The.
Wright, J.   Bora Ring.
Abortion
Anderson, A.   Suicide Year, The.
Atkins, R.   Lakefront, Cleveland.
Baumel.   Snow-Day.
Brooks, G.   Mother, The.
Carroll, K.   Truth About Karen, The.
Clifton, L.   Donor.
  Lost baby poem, The.
Cole, H.   Folly.
Finney, Janice.   Lightning and Thunder.
Gillan.   Waiting for the Results of a Pregnancy
  Test.
Hewett, D.   This Version of Love.
Hope, A.   Massacre of the Innocents.
Jess, T.   What does a man do.
Johnson, G.   Motherhood.
Jonson, B.   To Fine Lady Would-Be.
Katz, M.   Her Three Unborn Baby Boys.
Meehan, P.   Child Burial.
Mirsal.   Abortion.
O'Hara, F.   Abortion, An.
Peacock, M.   ChrisEaster.
Sepúlveda-Pulvirenti.   To the Child That Never
  Was.
Sexton.   Abortion, The.
Snodgrass.   Mother, The: "She stands in the
  dead center like a star."
Woddis.   Moral Tale, A.
Yi Hyangji.   Song of a Balloon in Search of Her
  Mom's balloon.
Abraham
Bly, R.   Night Abraham Called to the Stars, The.
Dickinson, E.   Abraham to kill him.
Frost, R.   Luke 16:19–26; "There was a rich
  man".
Hajjaj, N.   Hebron (Al-Khalil).
Muir, E.   Abraham.
Nemerov.   Nicodemus.
Noll.   Abraham's Madness.
Ostriker.   Story of Abraham, The.
Owen, W.   Parable of the Old Men and the

Young, The.

Rilke. Luke 1:39–56: In those days Mary arose.

Schwartz, D. Abraham.

Smart, C. Hymn 1. Faith.

Stradling. Abraham's Sacrifice of Isaac.

Wilner, E. Sarah's Choice.

Zisquit. After Years of Feasting and No Sacrifice.

Absalom

Rosenberg, I. Chagrin.

Absence

Auden. Song: "Stop all the clocks, cut off the telephone."

Azzawi, F. Self-Defeating Poem, The.

Basheva. It Was War.

Basho. It's fall and dusk.

Bécquer, G. They Closed Her Eyes.

Bernard [or Bernart] de Ventadour [or Ventadorn]. To see the lark, delighted, dare.

Bernes, J. Found Missing.

Berryman. Great citadels whereon the gold sun falls.

Bowdan, Janet. Year, The.

Brent, E. Angel Eyes.

Brion, R. Good Friday.

Brown, C. What Her Absence Means.

Buson. Mourning for Hokuju Rosen.

Old cormorant keeper, The.

Tilling the field.

Byron, G. To Thyrza.

Cahn, S. I'll Walk Alone.

Campo, C. Ah that the Tiger.

Cernuda. Shadow, The.

Cervantes. Isla Mujeres.

Chambers, G. If Only for One Night.

Chase, N. He Comes to Lie Down.

Chia Tao. Seeing Off the Monk Ts'ung-Ch'ih Returning to the Capital.

Ching An. Passing by Where Hsu, "The Wine-Flushed Immortal," Used to Live.

Ch'iu Wei. Seeking a Hermit on West Mountain and Not Finding Him.

Cho Hŏn. Rain sprinkles on the pond.

Chou Pang-yen. Tune: "Prince Lan-Ling".

Cobbold, E. Absence.

Coleridge, M. Only a little shall we speak of thee.

Cowley, A. Spring, The: "Though you be absent here, I needs must say."

Crase. Astropastoral.

Creeley. Away.

Turn, The.

Crozier, A. Humiliation in Its Disguises.

Cruz, S. Spiritual Canticle, The.

Cunningham, J. Absence, my angel, presence at my side.

Daive. I rise from the depths.

Nomad, A.

de Burgos. Poem Arrested at Daybreak.

De Coninck, H. If Only.

Dewdney. Radiant Inventory.

Dickinson, E. It was not Death, for I stood up.

My life closed twice before its close.

Dizhur. Silence.

Doan Van Kham. Remembering Priest Quang Tri.

Dooley, M. No, Go On.

Drummond, W. Sonnet: "Slide soft, fair forth, and make a crystal plain."

Duncan, R. Passage over Water.

Faiz. Before You Came.

Florit, E. Elegy for Your Absence.

Fuller, R. Your Absence.

Gallagher, T. I Stop Writing the Poem.

Kidnap[p]er.

Garcilaso de la Vega. I Came to a Valley in the Wilderness.

Gardinier. Memorials: "Walt Whitman I lay on the grass today."

Georgiou, E. Space Between, The.

Gezelle. Little Mother.

Glück, L. Penelope's Song.

Quiet Evening.

Glück, R. Odd to close my eyes during the day and open them at night.

Gomringer, E. [Untitled Concrete Poem].

Graham, W. Beast in the Space, The.

Guest, B. Valorous Vine.

Habington. To Castara, *Being to Take a Journey*: "What's death more than a departure; the dead go."

Hands, E. Epistle, An.

Harburg. When I'm Not Near the Girl I Love.

Hardy, T. Voice, The.

Hashimoto, S. Mirror of Matsuyama, The.

Hass, R. Song: "Afternoon cooking in the fall sun."

Herd. Missing.

Hicok. Absence: "There are men and women huddled in rooms tonight."

Hofmannsthal. Two of Them, The.

Hove. Lost Bird.

Hsieh T'iao. Ascend the Three Mountains Toward the Evening: Looking Back at the Capital.

Hughes, L. Homecoming.

Huidobro. Poetry Is a Heavenly Crime.

Inada. Filling the Gap.

Issa. Moon tonight, The.

Ivanov, Binyo. Tale That's Not a Tale, A.

Izumi. Lying here alone.

Jago. Absence.

Jennings, E. Not at Home.

Juana Inés de la Cruz. Verses Expressing the Feelings of a Lover.

Kabir. Meeting, The: "When my friend is away from me, I am depressed."

Kim Chiha. No One.

Kong Rong. First-Born, A.

Kopland. Natzweiler.

Lewis, A. Song (On Seeing Dead Bodies Floating Off the Cape).

Li Ho. High the Mount of Wu.

Li Po. Song of Ch'ang-Kan (Yueh-Fu), The.

Li Shang-yin. Chamber Music.

Coming was an empty promise, you have gone, and left no footprint.

Hearing a Startled Bird During Stayover at Chin-Ch'ang Pavilion.

Night Rains: A Letter to Go North.

Phoenix tail on scented silk, flimsy layer on layer.

Liu, T. Sunday.

Liu Yung. Tune: "Bells in the Rain".

Lleshanaku, L. Absence.

Lovelace, R. Elinda's [or Ellinda's] Glove.

Lowell, R. Home After Three Months Away.

Lu Yu. Tune: "Hairpin Phoenix".

Mac Low. 27th Dance—Walking—22 March 1964.

MacDiarmid, H. Empty Vessel.

Magrelli. I'm what is missing.

Martínez, V. Absence, Luminescent.

Mathews, A. Letter Following.

Medrano, F. Sonnet 41.

Meng Hao Jan. In Summer at the South Pavilion Thinking of Xing.

Mercer, J. I Thought About You.

Merwin. Separation.

Mew. Absence.

Miedzyrzecki. Can You Imagine.

Millay, E. Oh, Oh, you will be sorry for that word!

Mistral, G. Absence.

Ballad: "He went by with another."

Monro, H. Solitude.

Montague, J. Flowering Absence, A ("How can one make an absence flower.").

Montale. Far away, still I was with you.

Montgomerie, A. Dreame, Ane.

Moroz, S. There's a cinnamon tree that grows on the Moon.

Muldoon, P. Why Brownlee Left.

Nairne. Will Ye No Come Back Again?

Neruda. Poem 15.

Nolens, L. Poetic License.

Nortje. Waiting: "Isolation of exile is a gutted, The."

Your Absence.

Novello, I. We'll Gather Lilacs.

Ó Dálaigh, M. Elegy on Mael Mhedha, his Wife.

O'Callaghan, C. On Re-entering the Lavender City.

Okekwe, P. Two Beautiful Creatures.

Okudzhava. Departure.

Olson, E. Presence, The.

Pao Chao. Do you not see the young men off to war.

Pao Ling-hui. Added to a Letter Sent to a Traveler.

Poem Sent to a Traveler.

Pasos, J. This Is Not Her.

Penna. Lady on Streetcar.

Petrarch. Woods Are Wild and Were Not Made for Man, The.

Raine, K. Angelus.

Ransom, J. Jack's Letter.

Rich, A. Splittings.

Ritsos. Distant, The.

Rochester, J. Song: "Absent from thee, I languish still."

Rome, H. Wish You Were Here.

Romo-Carmona, M. Daylight.

Fish.

Sabines. Entresol.

St. John, D. Hush.

Seed. Sofia.

Shakespeare, W. Sonnet 97: "How like a winter hath my absence been[e]."

Shinkichi Takahashi. Absence.

Sidney. Sonnet 89: "Now that of absence the most irksome night."

Silex, E. Gift, The.

Singer, B. Poem: "Now absence is a habit it is time."

Smukler. Home in Three Days. Don't Wash.

Stevens, W. Gallant Chateau.

Stone, R. Curtains.

Su, A. Miss Chang is Missing.

Suckling, S. Against Absence.

Surrey. Seafarer, The.

Tagore. You Did Not Find Me.

T'ao Ch'ien [or T'ao Yuan-ming]. Return, The.

Tatham. Ostella forth of Town: To My Heart.

Teasdale. At Night.

Tennyson, A. Thy spirit ere our fatal loss.

Tkachenko. Engraving, An.

Tsanev, Stefan. Nostalgia, or a Painful Return to Memories.

Tu Fu [or Du Fu]. Spring Day: Thinking of Li Po.

Tu Mu. To Judge Han Chuo at Yangzhou.

Unknown. At Fifteen I Went to War.

At midnight when the world's at rest.

God, you may render me blind today!

Green is the grass on riverbanks.

I Believe.

Lass A-Laundering.

Love's footprints.

Oh springtime! The pomegranate trees are blooming.

Reed Flowers Turn White.

Shu is away in the hunting-fields.

Summer: "She has done with silkworms and the fieldwork."

Those gone are day by day remote.

Walk on again walk on.

Western Wind.

Velter André. Other One, The.

Villaurrutia. Rose Nocturnal.

Villon. Ballade: "Tell me where, in what country, where."

Warner, S. Absence, The.

Wayman. Did I Miss Anything?

Wei Chuang. Hidden Tears.

Wiesel. Behold, God of Abraham, God of mercy.

Wilbur, R. World Without Objects Is a Sensible Emptiness, A.

Yü Hsüan-chi. Spring Thoughts Sent to Tzu-an.

Yu Xuanji. Divided by the Han River.

Spring Passion.

Zhang Ruoxu. Spring, River, Flowers, Moon, Night.

See also **Isolation; Loneliness; Separation**

Abu-Jamal, Mumia

Espada. Another Nameless Prostitute Says the

Man is Innocent.

Abundance
Bukowski. Sexpot.
Craig, David. Apple Fools.
Granville [or Grenville]. Cloe.
Navajo Oral Tradition. Night Chant, The.
Pankey. Reason, The.
Statius. First of December, The.
Unknown. Peace, Rain, Plenty.
  Yu-li: Fine Fish to Net.

Acacia
Brion, R. If Fortune Smiles.
Field. Leaves.

Academia
Berryman. Professor's Song, A.
Cook, C. It's Just As Well About Heather.
DiPalma. Each Moment is Surrounded.
Drew, G. Apparently Someone in the
  Department.
Glaser, E. Confluences at San Francisco.
Jeffers, H. Instructions for Academic Poets
  Who Talk to God.
Joseph, J. Ant nest.
Kleinzahler. Autumnal Sketch, An.
Mathews, H. Dream-Work, The.
Perelman. Marginalization of Poetry, The.
Skoyles. Academic.
Whitman, W. When I Heard the Learn'd
  Astronomer.
Worley, D. Dancing in the Dark.

Acadia and Acadians
Longfellow, H. This is the forest primeval. The
  murmuring pines and the hemlocks.

Accents
Bennett, L. Dry-Foot Bwoy.
Hare, M. Alfred de Musset.
Joseph, A. On Being Told I Don't Speak Like a
  Black Person.
Kay, J. Old Tongue.
Lees, J. Jone o' Grinfilt.

Acceptance
Blunt, W. As To His Choice of Her.
Bradstreet, A. [Here Follows Some] Verses
  upon the Burning of Our House [July 10th,
  1666. Copied Out of a Loose Paper].
Clifton, L. Praise Song.
Derricotte. Poem for My Father.
  Promise, The.
Dickinson, E. It ceased to hurt me, though so
  slow.
  "Why do I love" You, Sir?
Emerson, R. Terminus ("It is time to be old.").
France, L. North and South.
Frost, R. Acceptance.
Ghalib, M. My Head and My Knees.
Gillespie, N. Bus Driver, The.
Habila, H. After the Obsession.
Herbert, Z. Mr. Cogito Meditates on Suffering.
Hernández, M. Wounded Man, The.
Jacobsen, R. Sunflower.
Johnson, J. We To America.
Kipling, R. Ex-Clerk.
  Refined Man, The.
Levine, P. On My Own.
MacNeice. Selva Oscura.
McDaniel, J. Obvious, The.
McFall, Gardner. Missing.
Mirabai [or Mira Bai]. Heat of Midnight Tears,
  The.
Nathan, L. Ragged Sonnet: When in a Deep
  Depression.
Olson, C. Kingfishers, The.
Peacock, T. Love and Age.
Piercy. I Will Not Be Your Sickness.
Rich, A. Loser, The.
Rossetti, C. Advent: "Come, thou dost say to
  Angels."
Rukeyser, M. Desdichada.
Shelley, P. To—: "One word is too often
  profaned."
Smith, L. Walking a Field into Evening.
Vinokurov. When the Parachute Does Not
  Open.
Whitman, W. Little one sleeps in its cradle,
  The.

To a Common Prostitute.

Accidents
Aytoun [or Ayton], R. Upon Mr Thomas
  Murrays Fall.
Babstock, Ken. What We Didn't Tell the Medic.
Belieu. How the Elderly Drive.
Carruth, H. Wreck of the Circus Train, The.
Coogler. Her charming steel-horse could not
  miss.
Cooper, D. 10 Dead Friends.
Dickey, J. Falling.
Esteves. Lil' Pito.
Feld, Andrew. Boxers, The.
  On Fire.
Frost, R. Objection to Being Stepped On, The.
  Out, Out—.
Gibson, W. White Dust, The.
Godden, J. Lost.
Greenlaw, L. Earliest Known Representation of
  a Storm in Western Art, The.
Gudding, Gabriel. One Petition Lofted into the
  Ginkgos.
Harington [or Harrington]. Ambiguity.
Heaney, S. Summer of Lost Rachel, The.
Herd. Coronach.
Herrick. Casualties.
Hume, C. Helicopter Wrecked on a Hill.
Jones, R. News of the Cranes.
Kipling, R. Destroyers in Collision.
Knight, E. Poem of Attrition, A.
Lansky, B. Oh, Woe Ith Me!
Larkin, P. Whatever Happened?
Laux, D. Nurse, The.
Lawrence, D. H. Collier's Wife, The.
Lee, D. This all happened before.
Lemm, Richard. Perfect Circle.
Lichtman, Risa. Bicycle, The.
Livingstone, D. One Time.
Lysaght, E. Kitty of Coleraine.
Masters, E. "Butch" Weldy.
  Justice Arnett.
Matthews, W. Black Box.
Mayes, J. Pedaling Paranoia.
McElroy, C. Ruth.
McFayden, Stazja. Not My Knees.
McFerren. Metaphor Crosses the Road, A.
McGonagall. Tay Bridge Disaster, The.
McIntyre. Disaster to Steamer Victoria at
  London.
Merrill, C. Diver, The.
Merrill, J. Broken Bowl, The.
Murray, L. Cotton Flannelette.
Plath. Cut.
Rawling. Gas Drill.
Reznikoff. 1. The Sinking.
  2. The Job.
Roethke. Elegy for Jane.
Schnackenberg. Accident, An.
Seshadri. Lifeline.
Shumaker. Circle of Totems, The.
Sivan, A. To Live in the Land of Israel.
Stafford, W. Fifteen.
Townsend, A. Bicycle Racers, The.
Warren, R. I Can't Even Remember the Name.
Wayne, J. By Accident.
Wilcox, E. King Tommy's Rise and Fall.

See also **Airplane Crashes; Automobile
Accidents; Disasters; Nuclear Accidents;
Railroad Wrecks; Shipwrecks**

Accounting and Accountants
Blumenthal, M. Accountant, The.
Nandī Majumdār, R. Mind, I'm talking to you.

Achilles
Alcaeus [or Alkaios]. Story goes, from evil,
  The.
Auden. Shield of Achilles, The.
Chaloner. Unnamed.
Duncan, R. Achilles' Song.
Ewart. Personal Footnote, A.
Glück, L. Triumph of Achilles, The.
Heine, H. Every idle desire has died in my
  breast.
Homer. Achilles and Priam.
  Achilles' Dream.
  Achilles' Lament and the Funeral of Patroclus.
  Achilles Over the Trench.

Achilles with wild fury in his heart.
  Death of Hector, The.
  Embassy to Achilles, The.
  Goddess intervenes between Achilles and
    Agamemnon, The.
  Host set forth, and pour'd his steel waves far
    out of the fleet, The.
  Invocation, The: "Wrath of *Peleus* Son, O Muse,
    resound, The."
  Priam and Achilles.
  Proposition and Invocation.
  Rage of Achilles, The.
  Shield of Achilles, The.
  Then Achilles.
  Vulcan Forges the Shield of Achilles.
Lihn. Goodnight, Achilles.
Longley, M. Ceasefire.
McKay, D. 2. Fates Worse Than Death.
Ryan, G. Achilleus to Odysseus.
Santayana. Before a Statue of Achilles.

Acorns
Nicholls, J. Journey.
Sontrop. Acorn Speaks, The.
Unknown. Acorn Song, The.

Acquiescence
Brooks, G. Speech to the Young Speech to the
  Progress-Toward (Among Them Nora and
  Henry III).
Hammerstein. I Cain't Say No.
Herrick. To Fortune.
MacLeish. What Any Lover Learns.
Unknown. All my hotheaded lovers will be
  pleased with me.
Wroth. Sonnet 7: "Love leave to urge, thou
  know'st thou hast the hand."
  Sonnet 48: "How like a fire doth love increase
    in me[e]."

Acrobatics and Acrobats
Cruz e Sousa. Acrobat of Pain.
Lefevre, A. Halftime.
Ramanujan. Alien.
Redmond. Dance Bodies #1.
Swenson, M. He That None Can Capture.
See also **Circus; Tightropes and Tightrope
Walkers; Trapezes and Trapeze Artists**

Actaeon
Bewe. I Would I Were Actaeon.
Ovid. Actaeon.
  Actaeon and His Hounds.

Acting and Actors
Allston. On Kean's Hamlet.
Artaud. Nerve Meter, The.
Baraka, I. Poem for Willie Best, A.
Bernstein, C. Caught.
Berry, D. Hamlet Off-stage: Laertes Cool.
Borges. Everything and Nothing.
Campert. Theatre.
  Theatre, The.
Chrystos. Soap Bubbles.
Cleary, S. Acting: "I most remember the class
  where we lie."
Coleridge, S. Mrs. Siddons.
Conway, J. Marlo Thomas in Seven Parts and
  Epilogue.
Cook, E. To Charlotte Cushman.
Coward. Regarding yours, dear Mrs
  Worthington.
Cullen, Y. Kabuki.
Donaghy, M. Caliban's Books.
Dunn, S. On the Death of a Colleague.
Garrigue. Movie Actors Scribbling Letters Very
  Fast in Crucial Scenes.
Ginsberg, A. Blue Angel, The.
Goldsmith, O. David Garrick.
Harrison, T. Continuous.
Henley, W. E. Ballade of Dead Actors.
Hershon. Cowboy and the Farmer Should Be
  Friends, The.
Heywood, T. Author to His Book[e], The.
Holman, B. Performance Poem.
Johnson, D. Maybe Desdemona.
Jonson, B. To Edward Alleyn.
Kirby, D. Amazed by Chekhov.
Klipschutz. Funicello at 50.
Koertge. Sidekicks.

LaBarre, M. For Gloucester on Being Newly Blind.
Levy, N. Pelleas and Melisande.
Lindsay, V. To Mary Pickford—Moving Picture Actress.
Mandel, T. Actor, The.
Martial. Traveller on the Flaminian Way.
Mason, D. Spooning.
McKinney, I. Rapt.
Melville, H. Coming Storm, The.
Muske, C. Last Take.
 Ovation.
No Ch'ŏnmyŏng. Performer, Male.
O'Hara, F. To the Film Industry in Crisis.
Oliveira, D. Laurence Olivier's Hamlet.
Parker, D. Actress, The.
 Certain Lady, A.
Redmond, J. Role.
Reid, C. Howl, Howl.
Salter. Video Blues.
Scalise, G. Amiti´ Amoureuse.
 Dora Markus and Her Actors.
Scamell, B. Actor Speaks, An.
Schulman. First Nights.
Shakespeare, W. Sonnet 23: "As an unperfect actor on the stage."
Skloot. Role of a Lifetime, The.
Speakes. Patsy Cline.
Stern, G. Adler.
Szöcs, G. Commentary on an Old Review.
Szymborska, W. Theater Impressions.
Trinidad. Things to Do in Valley of the Dolls (The Movie).
Vaughan, R. Simone Signoret, Beldam.
Volach, Y. I Have a Stage in My Head.
Waters, M. Conversion of Saint Paul, The.
Wheelwright. Slow Curtain.
Wicks, S. Persephone.
Wilbur, R. Prisoner of Zenda, The.
Wilson, R. Old Movies.
Yau. Late Night Movies I.

See also **Show Business**

Adam and Eve
Agee. So it begins. Adam is in his earth.
al-Braikan, M. Empty City, An.
Andrews, N. Notes for a Sermon on the Mount.
Beddoes. Old Adam, the Carrion Crow.
Belli, G. What Might Have Been.
Bingen, Hildegard von. Antiphon for the Angels.
Blake, W. Earth's Answer.
 Ghost of Abel, The.
Booth, P. Original Sequence.
Breton, A. They Tell Me That Over There.
Chaucer. Chaucer's Wordes unto Adam, his Owne Scriveyn.
Clive. Mother, The.
Coolbrith. Woman.
Copus, J. Making of Eve, The.
 Masaccio's *Expulsion from Paradise*.
Crane, H. Garden Abstract.
Davies, S. Why did my parents send me to the schools.
Dharker. Namesake.
Dickey, J. Poisoned Man, The.
Donnelly, S. Eve Names the Animals.
Dove, R. All Souls'.
Dugan, A. Letter to Eve.
Emerson, R. Dæmonic and the Celestial Love, The.
Enright, D. Days of Adam were 930 years, The.
 "Rich soil," remarked the Landlord.
 Why didn't we think of clothes before?
Fichman. Eve.
Frost, C. Fury.
Gibson, M. Just Like Eve.
Graves, R. Apple Island.
Hardy, J. Computer Aided Design: Creation.
Hecht, A. Naming the Animals.
Hirsch, E. Husband and Wife.
Hollander, J. Adam's Task.
Hope, A. Imperial Adam.
 Paradise Saved.
Howe, M. Part of Eve's Discussion.
Hughes, T. Childish Prank, A.
 Theology.

Ilagha, N. Adam's Cry.
Jacob, M. Egg, An.
Jensen, L. To a Stranger (At the End of a Caboose).
Ko Chŏnghŭi. What Is History? 1.
Koertge. Lilith.
Lanier, E. Now Pontius Pilate is to judge the cause.
 Our Mother *Eve,* who tasted of the Tree.
Macpherson, J. Fisherman, The: "World was first a private park, The."
Meddeb, Abdelwahab. I Take the Path.
Meyer, T. Uranium Ore.
Milton. Adam and Eve led out of Paradise.
 Adam Describes His Own Creation and That of Eve; Having Repeated His Warning, the Angel Departs.
 Banquet, The.
 Now had th' Almighty Father from above.
 Prospect of Eden, The.
 Serpent Finds Eve Alone, The.
 So spake the godlike power, and thus our sire.
 So spake the [*or* th'] Archangel Michael; then paused.
 So to the sylvan lodge.
 Thus began / Outrage from lifeless things; but Discord first.
 Uncloistered Virtue.
Mitchell, E. Death of Adam, The.
Muir, E. Adam's Dream.
Paino. Each Bone of the Body.
Reznikoff. As I Was Wandering with My Unhappy Thoughts.
Roethke. Follies of Adam, The.
Sabines. 4: The Animals.
 13: Eve No Longer Exists.
 1: I'm Naked, Bruised, and I Smell of You.
Sassoon, S. Ancient History.
Sewell, L. Expulsion.
Shapcott, J. Rosa Sancta.
Shapiro, K. Lord, I Have Seen Too Much.
Snyder, G. Milton by Firelight.
Thomas, D. Ceremony after a Fire Raid.
Traherne. Eden.
Trinidad. Adam and Eve on the Hollywood Tread Mill.
Tsvetayeva [*or* Tsvetaeva]. Beware.
Unknown. Adam Lay Ybounden [*or* I-bounden].
 What a Trying Time.
 When Adam dalf and Eve span.
Very. Serpent, The.
Vinokurov. Adam.
Walcott. Cloud, The.
Welish. Macbeth in Battle.
White, G. Leopard in Eden, The.
White, V. C. Child of Adam.
Whitman, W. As Adam Early in the Morning.
 To the Garden the World.
Williams, W. Marriage in Eden, The.
Winchilsea. Adam Posed.
Wright, J. Eve to Her Daughters.
Yeats. Adam's Curse.
Yusuf, S. Trees of Ithaca, The.

See also **Eve**

Adams, John
Mac Low. 1797.
 Monks. Twilight's Last Gleaming.

Adams, John Quincy
Mac Low. 1825.

Admiration
Ammons. Still.
Bacon, C. Outlook.
Behn, A. To My Lady Morland at Tunbrige [*or* Tunbridge].
Bell, M. Mystery of Emily Dickinson, The.
Berkson, B. October: "It's odd to have a separate month. It."
Berland, D. Blazon.
Boker. Sonnet 165.
Booth, Kwan. Untitled One.
Bradley, Jerry. For a Texas Beauty.
Bukowski. Eulogy to a hell of a dame.
Burns, R. Of A' the Airts [the Wind Can Blaw].
Byron, G. She Walks In Beauty.
Campert. Futile Poem, A.

Caples, G. Targets and Flowers (Begun with Lines from Breton).
Carew, T. Lips and Eyes.
Casal, J. My Loves.
Catullus. He Seems to Me Almost a God.
Cavalieri. First, The.
Constable, H. Of his Mistress, upon Occasion of her Walking in a Garden.
Cox, M. Moles, the.
Crockett-Smith, D. Rhinemaiden.
Cullen, C. To John Keats, Poet, at Springtime [*or* Spring Time].
Dante Alighieri. Sestina: "I have reached, alas, the long shadow."
Denby. Delos.
Ezekiel. Goodbye Party for Miss Pushpa T. S.
Fenollosa, M. Yuki.
Fischer, N. Slipped Away.
Gay, J. Molly Mog [*or* The Fair Maid of the Inn].
Gerstler. Dear Boy George.
Gex-Breaux, Q. Wisdom Is.
Gilyard, K. Letter.
Gogarty. Perfection.
 Portrait with Background.
Grapes, J. I Like My Own Poems.
Guiney. Salutation, A.
Hamill, S. To Hayden Carruth on His Eightieth Birthday.
Herrick. Upon the Nipples of Julia's Breast.
Hood, T. Parental Ode to My Son, Aged Three Years and Five Months, A.
Huntington, C. Hot Wind, Provincetown Harbor.
Jarnot, L. They Loved These Things Too.
Jian, Y. Thank You Father.
Johnston, E. Lines: To a Young Gentleman of Surpassing Beauty.
Keats. Addressed to Haydon.
 Great Spirits Now on Earth.
Kendrick, D. For Gwendolyn Brooks: As I Civilize a Space.
Koch, K. In Love with You.
 To Marina.
Komunyakaa, Y. Songs for My Father.
Levy, A. To Lallie.
Lindsay, V. To a Golden-Haired Girl in a Louisiana Town.
Linebarger, Jim. Oppa.
Lysaght, E. Garnyvillo.
Madgett. Reluctant Light.
McCarriston. Wrought Figure.
Melville, H. College Colonel, The.
 Sheridan at Cedar Creek.
Neidhardt, Frances E. Street Flower in Big D.
Nicholas, J. Bush, The.
O'Rourke, D. Algren.
Okekwe, P. Two Beautiful Creatures.
Ponsot. A La Une.
Praed. Talented Man, The.
Saloy, M. This Poem Is for You, My Sister.
Schwitters. Anna Blume.
Sidney. Eighth Song: "In a grove most rich of shade."
 Sonnet 37: "My mouth doth water, and my breast doth swell."
 Sonnet 52: "Strife is grown between Virtue and Love, A."
 Sonnet 91: "Stella, while now by honour's cruel might."
 Sonnet 103: "O happy Thames, that didst my Stella bear."
Silex, E. Gift, The.
Sondheim. In Buddy's Eyes.
Song. Father and Daughter.
Unknown. When a Beggar Beholds You.
Waller, E. Song: "Go[e], lovely rose."
Warren, R. Birth of Love.
Whitfield. To A. H.
Wilbur, R. Piazza di Spagna, Early Morning.
 Praise in Summer.
Williams, S. Song upon Miss Harriet Hanbury, Addressed to the Revd Mr Birt.
Wood, E. Recognition.
Wright, K. Unlikely Obbligato of Andersonstown.

Young, A. Mountains of California: Part 1, The.

Adolescence
Alexander, E. Nineteen.
Zodiac.
Arnold, C. Why I Skip My High School Reunions.
Auden. Adolescence.
Ayres, R. Corporeal.
Bandele, A. 1980–1990: A Poet's Personal Review.
Barresi. Vacation, 1969.
Bonazzi, Robert. Houston's Adolescence.
Brainard, J. I Remember.
Brooks, G. Religion.
Burris. Very True Confessions.
Carver, R. Luck.
Clinton, M. I Wanna Be Black.
DeFoe, M. Dream Lover.
Delgado, J. Two Timer.
Dickey, J. Sheep Child, The.
Dove, R. Adolescence—1.
Adolescence—2.
Hully Gully.
Duhamel. Bicentennial Barbie.
Dybek. My Neighborhood.
Ellis, K. N. Girl.
Forché. As Children Together.
Ginsberg, A. Walking into King Sooper after Two-Week Retreat.
Glück, L. From the Suburbs.
Goetsch, D. Beach, The.
Goldbarth. Counterfeit Earth!, The.
Graham, D. Father of the Man.
Hernández Cruz. Three Days/out of Franklin.
Hostetler, A. Priestess of Love.
Howe, M. Sixth Grade.
Jackson, M. L. Blunts.
Jones, R. Carpe Diem: "Though pretty, it rarely worked, lining seduction."
Joseph, A. Adolescence.
Kessler, S. Marty's Mother.
Kunitz, S. Game, The.
La Loca. Why I Choose Black Men for My Lovers.
LaFemina. Her Rose Tattoo.
Lea, S. Paternity.
Long, R. What's So Funny 'bout Peace, Love and Understanding.
Lorde. Hanging Fire.
Lux. Little Tooth, A.
Machan. In 1969.
Manrique, J. Tarzan.
Mariani. Betty.
Matthews, W. Mood Indigo.
McClatchy. First Steps.
McGinley. Portrait of a Girl with Comic Book.
Meinke. Helen.
Murray, L. Burning Want.
Neely, L. Rhonda, Age 15, Emergency Room.
Neruda. Youth: "Odor like an acid sword made, An."
Oles. To a Daughter at Fourteen Forsaking the Violin.
Ondaatje. Burning Hills.
Pape. Street Music.
Rakosi. Young Girl.
Samyn, M. Art of Kissing, The.
Sanchez, S. Norma.
Prelude to Nothing.
Seidman. Gail.
Sexton. Little Girl, My String Bean, My Lovely Woman.
Shapiro, K. Confirmation, The.
Simon, M. Boy Crazy.
Smith, P. So Motown taught me all about men. Men worshipped.
What It's Like to Be a Black Girl (For Those of You Who Aren't).
Soto. Heaven.
Souster. Young Girls.
Souza. Sweet Sixteen.
Stafford, W. Adults Only.
Fifteen.
Stein, K. First Performance of the Rock 'n Roll Band *Puce Exit*.
Trinidad. Double Trouble.

Meet the Supremes.
Movin' with Nancy.
Turner, W. Romance.
Unknown. Song for a Young Girl's Puberty Ceremony.
Uyematsu. To All Us Sansei Who Wanted to Be Westside.
Valerie, J. Lesson on Braces.
Vasquez, R. At the Rainbow.
Wallace, R. Smoking.
Thirteen.
Walls, D. Summer the Beatles Went Over Seven Minutes on a Single, The.
Warren-Moore. For Paula Cooper.
Wilson, R. Say Girls in Shoe Ads: "I Go for a Man Who's Tall!".
Wilson, S. Boy Friend, The.
Wrigley, R. American Manhood.
Zarzyski. Hurley High.

Adonis
Ayres. Death of Adonis, The.
Bion. Lament for Adonis.
Lament for Adonis.
Ovid. Venus and Adonis.
Pessoa. I the roses love in the gardens of Adonis.
Sappho. Delicate Adonis is dying, Kytheria— what should we do?
Shakespeare, W. All swoln with chasing, down Adonis sits.
Shelley, P. One remains, the many change and pass, The.
Spenser, E. There now he lives in everlasting joy.
Theocritus. Adonis.
Death of Adonis, The.

Adoption and the Adopted
Beasley. Hermetic Diary.
Ben-Lev, D. Broken Helix.
Gunn, T. Blank, A.
Hoagland, T. Migration.
Kay, J. Waiting Lists, The.
Keller, D. Man Who Knew the Words to "Louie, Louie", The.
Lavieri, J. Autobiography of John Doe, The.
Masters, E. Constance Hately.
Nikolayeva [or Nikolaeva]. Daughter.
Smith, B. Song of the Ransom of the Dark.
Wren, A. Surrogate Mothers.

Adultery and Adulterers
Beatrice [or Beatritz or Beatriz], Countess de Die [or Dia]. Lover's Prize, A.
Begum, S. Qaus-e Qazah.
Berry, W. Marriage.
Berssenbrugge. Jealousy.
Bloch, C. Discipline of Marriage, The.
Boyd, E. Guess Who I Saw Today.
Cairns, Scott. Adulterer, The.
Castellanos. Parable of the Unfaithful Wife.
Cho-yong. Song: "I carouse all night."
Coleman, W. Chuck Man.
Cope, W. Reading Scheme.
Copus, J. In Defence of Adultery.
Crabbe, G. Three weeks had past, and Richard rambles now.
Creeley. Anger.
Curtis, T. Gambit.
Dickey, J. Adultery.
Erdrich. Leonard Commits Redeeming Adulteries with All the Women in Town.
Ewart. Old Husband Suspects Adultery, An.
Gandlevsky, S. Oh, how the lilacs are this May! Bulging-large bunches fell.
García Lorca. Unfaithful Married Woman, The. Unfaithful Wife, The.
Goetsch, D. Beach, The.
Gregg. Marriage and Midsummer's Night.
Hall, D. When the Young Husband.
Hardy, T. In the Restaurant.
Heaney, S. Punishment.
Hisle, Janeya K. For Fatma and Her Co-Wives.
Hoagland, T. Sweet Ruin.
Hope, A. Gloss to Matthew V 27–28.
Hope, M. Only Days.
Hughes, L. Sister.
Juvenal. Satire 6.

Kasischke. My Heart.
Kochanowski, J. To a Mathematician.
Lewis, G. Advice on Adultery.
Lewis, L. Tracy and Joe.
Lochhead, L. Hickie, The.
Lockward, D. My Husband Discovers Poetry.
Lomax, M. Other Woman, The.
Maguire, S. Spilt Milk.
Martial. For rank, descent and title famed.
Masters, E. Elsa Wertman.
McDaniel, J. First Person Omniscient.
Mora. Bruja: Witch.
More, S. Astrologer, The.
Norris, K. Hester Prynne Recalls a Sunday in June.
Ovid. Elegy 1.4: "Thy husband to a banquet goes with me."
Parra, N. Viper, The.
Petersen, M. What I Would Do.
Pinsky. Street, The.
Popova, O. Curve of your lips, The.
Quarles. On Dinah.
Rhodes, M. Who Knew.
St. John, D. California.
Schwarz, S. Sonnet: "If love is chaste, what bears adultery?"
Shakespeare, W. Sonnet 152: "In loving thee thou know'st I am forsworn."
Simmons, J. End of the Affair, The.
Storni. Lyrical Letter to the Other Woman.
Taylor, J. Remedy for Backache.
Teare, Brian. Set for a Southern Gothic.
Tourneur. Duke: royall letcher; goe, gray hayrde adultery.
Tsvetayeva [or Tsvetaeva]. And, Not Crying in Vain.
Unknown. Come, my beloved, come quickly and be close to me!
Frankie and Johnny [or Johnnie or Albert].
Hurry up, my love, if you want to delight in me.
In the Chung Mode, to the Tune of "P'u T'ien Lo".
Little horror, take your rifle and kill me now.
My love, jump into bed with me and do not fear.
Open a crack in the wall and kiss me on the mouth.
Red Man's Wife, The.
Stretched out I want to take him into me.
These Women Plunder My Husband.
Trial of Renard, The.
Tune: "San-fan Yü-lou Jen".
When you come to our house, my love, the "little horror" grows angry.
Upton, L. Scarlet Letter, The.
Volkman. Case, The.
Williams, C. K. Mistress, The.
Williams, W. Great Mullen.
Witte, Francine. When You Call Again.
Yi Kyôngnim. Time 5.

Advent
Allnutt, G. Silk Light of Advent, The.
Doddridge, P. Hark! the glad sound! the Savior comes.
Meynell, A. Advent Meditation.
Rossetti, C. Advent.
Advent ("This Advent moon shines cold and clear.").

Adventure and Adventurers
Apollinaire. Pretty Redhead, The.
Bandeira. Off to Pasárgada.
Brontë, C. Young Man Naughty's Adventure.
Brown, S. Odyssey of Big Boy.
Cavafy. Ithaka.
Comden, B. Adventure.
Dehn, P. Alternative Endings to an Unwritten Ballad.
Green, A. Adventure.
Hume, C. Explanation.
Nance. Rio Grande Hills.
Nash, O. Adventures of Isabel.
Owen, M. For Emily (Dickinson).
Shakespeare, W. Her father lov'd me; oft invited me.
Stevenson, R. Mile an' a Bittock, A.
Unknown. I Think Over Again My Small

Adventures.

Advertising

Breton, A.   Mystery Corset, The.
Bunting.   Personal Column.
Butlin.   Advertisement for a Scottish Servant.
Cummings, E. E.   Poem, or Beauty Hurts Mr. Vinal.
Dawe, B.   Copy-writer's Dream, The.
Deniz, G.   Classified Ads.
Ofertas.
Francia, L.   Video Victim.
Fuhrman, J.   Personal Ad.
Jiménez, J.   Moon, The.
Lochhead, L.   Promises.
Nash, O.   Song of the Open Road.
Padilla.   Landscapes.
Portnoy, M.   Voucher.
Rouse, A.   Lilies of the Field.
Sakaki.   Top Ten of American Poetry.
Simic.   December: "It snows."
Unknown.   Advertising Agency Song, The.
Burma-Shave Roadside Signs.
Wright, C.   Personals.

See also **Billboards**

Advice

Abbot, E.   Awakening.
Addaeus.   When you meet a young boy, be direct.
Adisa.   Things No One Told Me.
Aristophanes of Byzantium.   On the advice of Praxilla.
Armand.   Word to the Wise, A.
Armstrong, J.   Advice to the Stout.
Berrigan, A.   Advice to a Young Philosopher.
Berry, W.   Manifesto: The Mad Farmer Liberation Front.
Blaisdell, G.   To a Poet (the Pearl).
Bland, P.   Notes for the Park Keeper.
Brown, L.   Button Up Your Overcoat.
Calpurnius Siculus.   Eclogue 5.
Chaucer.   Nun's Priest's [*or* Nonne Preestes] Tale, The.
Cook, E.   Building upon the Sand.
Copeland, J.   Bayonet, The.
Darlington, T.   Field Guide to Western Intimacy.
Davidson, D.   Sanctuary.
Delmore, E.   Such Sweet Sorrow.
DeSylva, B. G.   Button Up Your Overcoat.
Dodge, M.   Early to Bed.
Dufferin and Clandeboye.   Charming Woman, The.
Eichner, Maura.   What My Teachers Taught Me I Try to Teach My Students.
Emerson, R.   Suum Cuique.
To Rhea.
Fan Chung-yen.   Tune: "Trimming the Silver Lamp".
Fearing.   Any Man's Advice to His Son.
Beware.
Fulson, Lowell.   Check Yourself.
Glaukos.   Where once you could win over grasping boys.
Grimké, A.   At April.
Han-shan.   Whoever has Cold Mountain's poems.
Healy, E.   Advice Like That.
Henderson, R.   Button Up Your Overcoat.
Holm, B.   Advice.
Horace.   Ne'er fash your *thumb* what *gods* decree.
Housman.   Carpenter's Son, The.
When I was one-and-twenty.
Jackson, H.   Danger.
Jellicoe.   Advice to a Lover.
Johnson, B.   Advice to a Reckless Youth.
Jonson, B.   Martial. Epigram XLVII, Book X.
Kasdorf.   Eve's Striptease.
Keyes, S.   Advice for a Journey.
Kipling, R.   If.
Kshemendra.   Poet should learn with his eyes, A.
Kydios.   Beware. There are fawns.
Lao Tzu.   Human beings are / soft and supple when alive.
Lewis, G.   Advice on Adultery.
Li Mi-an.   Half-and-Half Song, The.

Massimi.   Advice to Paulinus.
McCallum, S.   What My Mother Taught Me.
Michaux.   Slices of Knowledge.
Millay, E.   If in the years to come you should recall.
Montagu, L.   Summary of Lord Lyttleton's 'Advice to a Lady', A.
Muso Soseki.   For a Monk Going West.
Niedecker.   Poet's Work.
Pessoa.   Segue O Teu Destino.
Piercy.   Seven of Pentacles, The.
Pitter.   Love and the Child.
Ralegh, S.   Sir Walter Ra[u]le[i]gh to His Son[ne].
Rich, A.   1948: Jews.
Ríos, A.   Advice to a First Cousin.
Simmons, J.   Lullaby for Rachael.
Snodgrass.   Diplomacy: The Father.
Sorescu, M.   Balls and Hoops.
Southwick.   Magic Broom, The.
Stroud, J.   Hacedor.
Su Tung-p'o.   Tune: "Calming Windswept Waves".
Taylor, J.   Mistakes.
Tennyson, A.   Check every outflash, every ruder sally.
Thomas, L.   Dangerous Doubts.
Thompson, S.   All Apologies to L. Cohen.
Torre, M.   How to Look at Mexican Highways.
Trethewey, N.   Countess P———'s Advice for New Girls.
Tupper, M.   Marriage Market, The.
Unknown.   Advice to a Young Man.
Cautiously bubbles that spring water.
Good Counsel.
Make quiet, so quiet, your awesome bearing.
Of alle the enemies that I can fynde.
Penny.
Restored Terrace is new and fresh, The.
Seize the moment!—.
Then down the brave man lay with his bolster.
Towering is that southern mountain.
Wise, S.   Advice.
Wotton, S.   To John Donne.
Yang Wan-li.   Don't Read Books!
Zhou Xingsi.   Extracts.

Aegean Sea

Flecker, J.   Santorin.
Spaziani.   Aegean, The.
Ulacia, M.   Aegean Sea.
Mar Egeo.

Aeneas

Tate, A.   Aeneas at Washington.
Virgil [*or* Vergil].   Aeneas Arrives in Carthage.
Aeneas in the Underworld.
Arms, and the Man I sing, who, forc'd by Fate.
Dawn leaves the bed of Dark and climbs the sky.
Death of Turnus, The.
In Heaven, Queen Juno saw. She's trapped.
Passion of the Queen, The.
Prologue.
Shield of Aeneas, The.
Sky rumbles. Gathers. Rain.

Aeneid, The (Virgil)

Lowell, R.   Falling Asleep over the Aeneid.

Aengus

Yeats.   Song of Wandering Aengus, The.

Aeschylus

MacDiarmid, H.   British Leftish Poetry, 1930–40.

Aesop

Crane, H.   Black Tambourine.
Markham, M.   After Aesop.
Marquis.   Aesop Revised by Archy.

Affection

Adamson.   My Tenth Birthday.
Alcman.   Love, again sweetly streaming down.
Alcuin.   Love has pierced my heart with its flame.
Amaru.   Lying in Bed.
Amichai, Y.   Two Songs of Peace.
Two Songs of Peace.
We Have Done Our Duty.
Anacreon.   O Lord, with whom subduer Love.

Soaring again from the Leukadian Rock.
Ancient Sumerian Oral Tradition.   Bridegroom, dear to my heart.
Andrade, E.   Penniless Lovers.
Andreus.   For Some Future Day.
Andrews, C.   Morn's Recompense.
Anguita, E.   Real Moment, The.
Armantrout.   Winter.
Auden.   Fish in the Unruffled Lakes.
Bachmann.   Songs from an Island.
Baldwin, J.   Guilt, Desire and Love.
Barbauld.   Rights of Woman, The.
Barnfield [*or* Barnefield].   Beauty and majesty are fallen at odds.
Sighing, and sadly sitting by my Love.
Sometimes I wish that I his pillow were.
Bawer.   On Leaving the Artists' Colony.
Bécquer, G.   I Know a Strange, Gigantic Hymn.
Bell, M.   To Dorothy.
Bernstein, C.   Poem: "Here. Forget."
Berryman.   He Resigns.
Bishop, E.   Casabianca.
One Art.
Blaga.   I Will Not Crush the World's Corolla of Wonders.
Blake, W.   Clod & the Pebble, The.
Garden of Love, The.
How Sweet I Roamed [*or* Roam'd] from Field to Field.
Blunt, W.   Farewell, then. It is finished. I forego.
Bobis, M.   Driving to Katoomba.
Bobyshev.   Other World, The.
Boland, E.   Ready for Flight.
That the Science of Cartography Is Limited.
Boyd, M.   Fra Bank to Bank, Fra Wood to Wood I Rin.
Bradstreet, A.   Another.
Another.
Before the Birth of One of Her Children.
Letter to Her Husband, Absent upon Public[k] Employment, A.
To Her Father, with Some Verses.
Breton, A.   Free Union.
Brooke, R.   Dining-Room Tea.
Hill, The.
Sonnet: "Oh! Death will find me, long before I tire."
Brooks, G.   Novelle; My Grandmother Is Waiting For Me To Come Home.
Broumas, O.   Privacy.
Brown, L.   Button Up Your Overcoat.
Browning, E.   L.E.L.'s Last Question.
Browning, R.   Lost Mistress, The.
Meeting at Night.
Porphyria's Lover.
Two in the Campagna.
Burns, R.   Highland Mary.
O[h] Wert Thou in the Cauld Blast.
Red, Red Rose, A.
Buson.   Head pillowed on arm.
Butler, S.   She was too kind, wooed too persistently.
Byron, G.   Alas, they were so young, so beautiful.
She Walks In Beauty.
To Thyrza.
Camões [*or* Camõens *or* Camoëns], L.   Do This Favour For Me.
Campion, T.   Follow Thy Fair Sun[ne] [Unhappy Shadow].
When to Her Lute Corinna [*or* Corrina] Sings.
Carew, T.   In Praise of His Mistress.
Song[, A]: "Ask[e] me no more where Jove bestow[e]s."
To My Rival.
Castillo, S.   At the Havana Hilton.
Catullus.   Carmen 5.
Caulfield.   You All Know the Story of the Two Lovers.
Chapman, G.   But dwell in darkness, for your god is blind.
Love flows not from my liver but her living.
Muses that fame's loose feathers beautify.
To living virtues turns the deadly vices.
Chaucer.   Song of Troylus, The.
Cherry, K.   Late Afternoon at the Arboretum.

Ch'iao Chi. Love Song: "Orioles and orioles."
Ch'in Kuan. Song: "Pleading eyebrows, intoxicating eyes!"
Cisneros, S. You Bring Out the Mexican in Me.
Cleveland, J. Antiplatonic[k], The.
Coleridge, M. Blue and White.
Constable, H. Uncivil sickness, hast thou no regard.
Cook, E. Building upon the Sand.
Cope, W. Flowers: "Some men never think of it."
Valentine.
Cory, W. Preparation.
Cottle. Affectionate Heart, The.
Cowley, A. Wish, The.
Crabbe, G. Marriage Ring, The.
Crashaw. Love, thou art absolute sole lord.
Creeley. Act of Love, The.
Cruz Varela. Love Song for Difficult Times.
Cullen, Y. This.
Cummings, E. E. If everything happens that can't be done.
If(touched by love's own secret)we,like homing.
Curbelo. Dreaming Horse.
Tonight I Can Almost Hear the Singing.
Davenant [or D'Avenant]. Countess of Anglesey lead Captive by the Rebels, at the Disforresting of Pewsam, The.
Davie, D. Time Passing, Beloved.
de Burgos. Transmutation.
de Fierro. Secret, The.
De la Mare. Ghost, The ("Who knocks? I, who was beautiful.").
Delmore, A. Girl by the River, The.
Deloney. Long have I lov'd this bonny Lasse.
Desnos. If You Knew.
I've dreamed such dreams of you.
DeSylva, B. G. Button Up Your Overcoat.
Dickinson, E. If I may have it, when it's dead.
Soul selects her own Society, The.
Disch. Clouds, The.
Dixon, M. Great Big Bunch of You, A.
Donne. Canonization, The.
Ecstasy, The.
Funeral[l], The.
Good-Morrow, The.
His Picture.
Nocturnal[l] upon Saint Lucy's [or S. Lucy's or S. Lucies] Day, Being the Shortest Day, A.
Relic, The.
Song: "Sweetest love, I do not go[e]."
Valediction, A: Forbidding Mourning.
Valediction, A: of Weeping.
Dove, R. Mother Love.
Dowson. Non Sum Qualis Eram Bonae sub Regno Cynarae.
Drayton. As Love And I.
Since there's no help, come let us kiss and part.
Duffy, C. Valentine: "Not a red rose or a satin heart."
Duhig, I. From the Irish.
Dunbar, P. Negro Love Song, A.
Dunn, D. France: "Dozen sparrows scuttled on the frost, A."
Dyer, S. Lowest trees have top[p]s, the ant[e] her gall, The.
Elizabeth I. When I Was Fair and Young.
Elizabeth, M. Manon Reassures Her Lover.
Elledge. 14 Reasons Why I Mention Mario Lanza to the Man I Love Every Chance I Get Tonight.
Elmslie, K. One Night Stand.
Elsschot. Mother.
Éluard, P. Woman In Love.
"Ephelia.". In the Person of a Lady, to Bajazet, Her Unconstant Gallant.
Faiz. Don't Ask Me for That Love Again.
We Who Were Executed.
Feirstein. Mark Stern Wakes Up.
Rune-Maker, The.
Fenton, J. In Paris with You.
Ferguson, G. Silent as Roses.
Winter Sunflowers.
Flanner. True Western Summer.
Forbes, D. Recension Day.
Gallagher, T. Hug, The.

García Lorca. Sonnet of Sweet Complaint.
Garcia, R. Los Amantes.
Garcilaso de la Vega. Oh, to my sobs, Galatea, you are harder than a stone.
Sonnet 5.
Gardner, I. In the Museum.
Gascoigne. For That He Looked Not upon Her.
Lullaby [or Lullabie] of a Lover, The.
Gershwin, I. I Can't Get Started.
They All Laughed.
Ghalib, M. Ghazal 25.
Ginsberg, A. To Aunt Rose.
Glück, L. Garden, The: "I couldn't do it again."
Hawk's Shadow.
Gorges. Her Face, Her Tongue, Her Wit.
Gotoba. There Were Those I Loved.
Graves, R. Lost Love.
She Tells Her Love While Half Asleep.
Green, D. R. Names and sorrows.
Greenwald, T. And, Hinges.
I Hear a Step.
Greville, F. I, with whose colors [or colours] Myra dressed [or dress'd or drest] her head.
You little stars that live in skies.
Guevara, M. Buddy Holly Poem, The.
Gunn, T. High Fidelity.
Tamer and Hawk.
Haavikko. One who writes us is now doing four plays a year, The.
Hall, D. Love-Letter-Burning.
Hamill, S. True Illumination Is Habitude.
Hampton. Yugoslav Story.
Hanlo. New Verses for June 7, 1951.
Harbach, O. Love Nest, The.
Harburg. I Like the Likes of You.
Hardy, T. After a Journey.
Church Romance, A.
Going, The.
She Hears The Storm.
Heaney, S. Sunlight.
Henderson, R. Button Up Your Overcoat.
Herbert, E. You well-compacted groves, whose light and shade.
Herbert, G. Affliction (1).
Hikmet. Things I Didn't Know I Loved.
Holmes, O. Tartarus.
Hoornik. To Love a Woman.
Hope, A. Return of Persephone, The.
Hope, L. I Shall Forget.
Horace. Ode 3.9: Dialogue between Horace and Lydia, A ("Donec gratus eram").
Horton, G. Early Affection.
Housman. Because I liked you better.
Huerta, E. This Is a Love.
Hughes, L. Gal's Cry for a Dying Lover.
Ibarbourou. Rainy Night.
Jefferson, B. Long Distance Moan.
Johnson, G. I Want to Die While You Love Me.
Jonson, B. Elegy, An: "Though beauty be the mark of praise."
Her Triumph.
My Picture Left in Scotland.
Song. To Celia ("Come my Celia, let us prove.").
Song. To Celia ("Drink to me only with thine eyes.").
Sonnet to the Noble Lady, the Lady Mary Wroth, A.
Joyce, J. My dove, my beautiful one.
József, A. Attila József.
Kasa. Have I let my love.
I shall think of you.
Look at this keepsake.
Keats. Belle Dame sans Merci, La [A Ballad].
To ———: "Had I a man's fair form, then might my sighs".
To Some Ladies.
Keithley. Thunder Storm.
Kemble. Noonday Vision, A.
Sonnet: "If there were any power in human love."
Kenney. Aubade: "Cold snap. Five o'clock."
King, H. Exequy, The.
Kinnell. Parkinson's Disease.
Koch, K. Permanently.
Korinna [or Corinna]. Wishing to take her son.

Kuan Yün-shih. Love Song: "Fondling and snuggling."
Kupriyanov [or Kuprianov]. Lesson in Natural History, A.
Lamartine. Lake, The.
Lake, The.
Landon. Bonds of Affection.
Lanier, S. Song for "The Jacquerie".
Lawrence, J. Tenderly.
Leithauser. Ghost of a Ghost, The.
Leopardi. To Sylvia.
Levertov. Love Poem: "What you give me is."
Time Past, A.
Woman Meets an Old Lover, A.
Lewis, A. Goodbye.
Post-Script: for Gweno.
Li Po. River Merchant's Wife, The; A Letter.
Lodge, T. Love Guards [or Guides] the Roses of Thy Lips.
Rosalind's [or Rosalynd's] Madrigal[l].
Loesser. Luck, Be a Lady.
Lomax, M. Amor Diving.
Longfellow, H. Children's Hour, The.
Lovelace, R. Gratiana Dancing [or Dauncing] and [or &] Singing.
On Sanazar's being honoured with six hundred Duckets by the Clarissimi of Venice, for composing an Elegiack Hexastick of The City. A Satyre.
To Althea, from Prison.
Lowell, A. Aubade: "As I would free the white almond from the green husk."
Lowell, J. Contrast, A.
Lowell, R. Grandparents.
Lux. Amiel's Leg.
I Love You Sweatheart.
Magrelli. Wood of my thoughts is on fire, The.
Malloch, D. Manly Love.
Mansour, J. Gently stroke a wound.
Tinfoil.
Marlowe. Now ore the sea from her old Love comes she.
Marston, P. Speechless: Upon the Marriage of Two Deaf and Dumb Persons.
Martinez, D. Cole Porter.
In a Duplex Near the San Andreas Fault.
Matisse: Blue Nude, 1952.
Martory, P. Blues.
Marvell. Definition of Love, The.
Fair Singer, The.
Gallery, The.
Mower to the Glowworms [or Glow-Worms or Glo-Worms], The.
Mayer, B. Sonnet: Kamikaze: "Dawn and night of fighting, lovers like actual wars."
McCree, J. Put Your Arms Around Me, Honey.
Mei Yao Ch'en. Dream at Night, A.
Mercer, J. Midnight Sun.
Mhac an tSaoi. Jack.
Mignon, A. One Heart's Enough for Me.
Millay, E. I shall go back.
Mitchison. My True Love Hath My Heart.
Montagu, L. Lover, The; a Ballad.
Montale. Eel, The.
Montgomerie, A. Remembers thou of Æsope of a taill.
Moore, T. Did Not.
Echo ("At the mid hour of night, when stars are weeping, I fly.").
Oft In the Stilly Night.
Muir, E. In Love For Long.
Musgrave. You Didn't Fit.
Nathan, L. Toast.
Neruda. Tonight I Can Write the Saddest Lines.
Nezval. Walker in Prague.
Nims, J. Love Poem: "My clumsiest dear, whose hands shipwreck vases."
Niu Hsi-chi. Where the mist has torn.
Nolla. Troubadour Love.
Odarchenko. Only for you my tea roses.
Olds, S. Knowing, The.
Ondaatje. For you I have slept.
Ovid. So, when she saw Narcissus wandering through the lonely countryside, Echo fell in love with him, and followed secretly in his steps.

Parker, D.   One Perfect Rose.
Parker, M.   Thou knowst I lov'd thee well.
Parra, V.   To Be Seventeen Again.
Pasolini.   Prayer to My Mother.
Petrarch.   Complaint of a Lover Rebuked.
  Long[e] love that in my thought do[e]th [or I]
    harbour [or harber or harbar], The.
Pfeiffer, E.   Nathaniel to Ruth.
Phillips, S.   Apparition, The.
Piatt, S.   Lesson in a Picture, A.
Pique at Parting, A.
This World.
Po Chü-i.   Golden Bells.
Poe.   To One in Paradise.
Poliziano.   To Giovan Battista Buoninsegni.
Pope, A.   Rape of the Lock, The: An Heroi-
  Comical Poem in Five Cantos.
Popova, O.   Lay your head in my lap.
Porter, C.   I Concentrate on You.
Prévert.   Barbara.
Dunce, The.
Ralegh, S.   Thus now I leave my love in
  fortunes {handes / bandes}.
Ramsey, J.   Tally Stick, The.
Ravikovitch, D.   Real Love Isn't What It Seems.
Rich, A.   What homage will be paid to a beauty
  built to last.
Rilke.   O you lovers that are so gentle, step
  occasionally.
Roberts, M.   Magnificat.
Robin, L.   Easy Living.
Rochester, J.   Love And Life.
Roethke.   For An Amorous Lady.
I Knew a Woman.
Roland Holst.   Beggar Love.
Rossetti, C.   I loved you first: but afterwards
  your love.
I wish I could remember the [or that] first day.
L. E. L.
Many in aftertimes will say of you.
O my heart's heart, and you who are to me.
Somewhere Or Other.
Thinking of you, and all that was, and all.
Rowe, E.   Chapter II.
Rumi.   If you're not going to sleep.
Ryan, G.   Orbit.
Salom.   Ghazal on signs of Love and
  Occupation.
Salter.   Summer 1983.
Sanguineti.   At the offset it was calculated.
Sappho.   Gongyla.
I have a beautiful child, her form.
I loved you Atthis once long ago.
Kypris, / May she find you very bitter.
Of love.
Some say an army of horsemen, others.
To me it seems.
Schnackenberg.   Supernatural Love.
Schwitters.   Anna Blume.
Seidman.   Gail.
Seward.   In every breast affection fires, there
  dwells.
Shakespeare, W.   Clown's Song, The.
O[h] Mistress Mine.
Sonnet 20: "Woman's face with nature's own[e]
  hand painted, A."
Sonnet 29: "When, in disgrace with fortune and
  men's eyes."
Sonnet 33: "Full many a glorious morning have
  I seen[e]."
Sonnet 37: "As a decrepit father takes delight."
Sonnet 55: "Not marble, nor the g[u]ilded
  monuments."
Sonnet 91: "Some glory in their birth, some in
  their skill."
Sonnet 98: "From you have I been absent in the
  spring."
Sonnet 108: "What's in the brain[e] that in[c]k
  may character."
Sonnet 124: "If [or Yf] my dear[e] love were
  but the child[e] of state."
Sonnet 135: "Whoever [or Who ever] hath her
  wish, thou hast thy Will."
Shapiro, K.   Twins, The.
Shelley, P.   To Jane: The keen stars were
  twinkling.

To —: "Music, when soft voices die."
Sherwood, G.   Love and Life.
Shwarts [or Shvarts].   What That Street Is
  Called.
Sidney.   Dirge: "Ring out your bells [or belles],
  let mourning shows [or shewes] be spread."
My true love hath my heart [or hart], and I have
  his.
Nightingale, The.
Sonnet 1: "Loving in truth, and fain[e] in verse
  my love to show."
Sonnet 2: "Not at [the] first sight, nor with a
  dribbed shot."
Sonnet 25: "Wisest scholar of the wight most
  wise, The."
Sonnet 31: "With how sad steps, O Moon[e],
  thou climb'st the skies."
Sonnet 48: "Soul's joy, bend not those morning
  stars from me."
Sonnet 49: "I on my horse, and Love on me
  doth try."
Sonnet 63: "O grammar rules, O now your
  virtues show."
Sonnet 72: "Desire, though thou my old
  companion art."
Sonnet 81: "O kiss, which dost those ruddy
  gems impart."
Sonnet 87: "When I was forced from Stella ever
  dear."
Sidney, R.   Sonnet 25: "Yow that take pleasure
  in yowr cruelty."
Silverstein, S.   Hug o' War.
Simic.   My Beloved.
Old Couple.
Simonides.   Without pleasure.
Skelton, J.   To Mistress [or Maystres] Margaret
  Hussey.
Smith, S.   Freddy.
Human Affection.
Snodgrass.   Mementos, 1.
Sorescu, M.   Fountains in the Sea.
Precautions.
Sparrow, J.   To an Angel in the House.
Spenser, E.   By vew of her he ginneth to revive.
Eftsoones they heard a most melodious sound.
Epithalamion: "Ye learned sisters which have
  oftentimes."
May.
Penelope for her *Ulisses* sake.
Sonnet 8: "More than most fair [or fayre], full
  of the living fire [or fyre]."
Sonnet 70: "Fresh Spring the herald of love's
  [or loves] mighty king."
Sonnet 71: "I joy to see how in your drawen
  work."
Strand.   Coming to This.
Strauss, J.   Love Notes.
Suckling, S.   Constant Lover, A [or The].
Swenson, M.   Staying at Ed's Place.
Swift, J.   Stella's Birthday ([March 13,] 1727).
Swirszczynska [or Swir].   Greatest Love, The.
Same Inside, The.
Synge.   In May.
Taggart, J.   Body and Soul: Poem for Two
  Readers.
Taylor, B.   Love Returned.
Proposal.
Tellegen.   If Just For Once.
Tennyson, A.   O [or Oh] that 'twere possible.
Thomas, E.   No One So Much As You.
Thomas, L.   Cameo in Sudden Light.
Clear Channel.
Tipton.   I Wanted You in the Kitchen of My
  Heart.
Tonks.   Story of a Hotel Room.
Traherne.   Salutation [or Salutations], The.
Tranter.   Moonshine Sonata.
Tsaloumas.   Return of an Ikon.
Tsvetayeva [or Tsvetaeva].   Cupolas flame, in
  Moscow where I live.
Den—for the beast, A.
Tuckerman, F.   Coralie.
Rhotruda.
Tuqan, F.   I Won't Sell His Love.
Turk, R.   I'll Get By (As Long As I Have You).
Tyutchev.   Last Love.

Unknown.   Barbara Allan.
Country Lassie, The.
Do not look at me.
I Have a Young Sister.
I Saw My Lady Weep.
Love Me Little, Love Me Long.
Medicine Song of an Indian Lover.
Sweet Polly Oliver.
To G.
To His Love.
Waly, Waly [Love Be Bonny].
We cannot tell now.
Will You Love Me When I'm Old?
Unknown, sometimes at. to Sir Walter Ralegh.
As You Came from the Holy Land [of
  Walsingham].
Vallejo.   Good Sense.
Van Vliet.   City, The.
Vando.   Ode to Your Back.
Verlaine.   Exchange of Feelings.
Green ("Take this fruit, these flowers, these
  branches and leaves.").
Muted Tones.
Spleen.
Streets 1.
Vietnamese Oral Tradition.   Carp, The.
Painting, The.
Saigon River, The.
Waldrop, R.   Lawn of Excluded Middle.
Waller, E.   Love's Farewell.
Warsh.   Enmeshment.
Wayne, J.   By Accident.
Wheelwright.   Slow Curtain.
Whitman, W.   Base of All Metaphysics, The.
I knew a man, a common farmer, the father of
  five sons.
Live Oak, with Moss.
Now what my mother told me one day as we sat
  at dinner together.
When I Heard At The Close Of The Day.
Woman Waits for Me, A.
Whitney, I.   I. W. To her unconstant Lover.
Wieners.   Doll.
Wilcox, E.   Friendship After Love.
Williams, C. K.   Dog, The.
Snow: II.
Williams, M.   Poem for Emily, A.
Williams, W.   Love Song: "Sweep the house
  clean."
Wilson, R.   I Wish in the City of Your Heart.
Winchilsea.   Friendship Between Ephelia and
  Ardelia.
Letter to Daphnis, A.
Wroth.   Song: "Love what art thou? A vain
  thought."
Sonnet 3: "His flames ar[e] joy[e]s, his bands
  true lovers' might."
Wyatt.   Long love that in my thought doth
  harbo[u]r, The.
Lover Showeth How He Is Forsaken of Such as
  He Sometime Enjoyed, The.
My Lute, Awake!
Wylie.   Puritan Sonnet.
Yeats.   Down by the Salley Gardens.
Folly of Being Comforted, The.
Lullaby: "Beloved, may your sleep be sound."
When You Are Old.
Yevtushenko [or Evtushenko].   Siberian Wooing.
Yosano Akiko.   Once, far over the breakers.
Yount, A.   Sharing.
Yuson.   Love Before Dinner.
Zanzotto.   Behold the Thin Green.
Distance.
Zawinski, A.   You Touch Me.
Zolynas.   Love in the Classroom.

Affliction
Davies, S.   Affliction.
Herbert, G.   Affliction (1).
Miedzyrzecki.   29-77-02.
Orr, G.   Who'd Want to Be a Man?

Afghanistan
Allingham, W.   In Snow.
Bhatt, S.   Written After Hearing About the
  Soviet Invasion of Afghanistan.
Espada.   Alabanza: In Praise of Local 100.
Ghazal for Open Hands.

Jones, H.   Emine and Hamide.
  Laments for the Afghan Women.
Pawlak.   All the News—September 23, 2001.
Schreiber, R.   Public Stammer, The.
Unknown.   Beautiful Nahid rose up and in her
  clear voice cried, The.
  Woman in exile never stops dying, The.

Africa and Africans
'Abd al-Hayy.   Ode of Signs.
Abdul Karim.   Nightmare 1.
  Nightmare 3.
Acam-Oturu.   Agony . . . A Resurrection, An.
Acholonu.   Harvest of War.
Acquah.   They're Tearing Up the Old
  Graveyard.
Adisa.   Count Ossie.
Ai.   Calling, The.
Aiyejina.   When the Monuments.
Al-Haidari, B.   Dialogue of the Colours.
Allen, F.   Surveyor's Story, The.
Amadiume.   Nok Lady in Terracotta.
  Oya Now.
Angelou, M.   Africa.
Angira.   Newscast.
  Obbligato from a Public Gallery.
  Old Wharf Canto.
  Symphony from the Balcony.
Anyidoho.   Elegy for the Revolution.
  Tsitsa.
Aworinde.   If a Suite in Praise of the Yoruba
  Oracle.
Baker, H.   Toward Guinea: For Larry Neal,
  1937–1981.
Baraka, I.   Ka 'Ba.
  Kenyatta Listening to Mozart.
Barlow, G.   4½ Months: Halfway Song.
Barlow, J.   Columbiad, The.
Bennett, G.   Heritage.
Bontemps.   Nocturne at Bethesda.
  Nocturne of the Wharves.
Brand, D.   Canto 1: "Ashes head to toes."
Brathwaite, E.   How Europe Underdeveloped
  Africa.
  Mmenson.
Braxton, Joanne M.   Invisibles.
Brew.   Plea for Mercy, A.
Breytenbach.   Dung-beetle.
  Write Off.
Brooks, G.   To the Diaspora.
Browning, R.   Home-Thoughts, from the Sea.
  Through the Metidja to Abd-el-Kadr.
Busia, A.   Exiles.
  Mawu of the Waters.
Césaire, A.   Macumba Word.
  Miraculous Weapons, The.
Cheney-Coker.   Analysis.
  Childhood.
  Peasants.
  Poet Among Those Who Are Also Poets.
Chipasula.   Everything to Declare.
  Singing Drum, The.
Clark Bekedermo.   Epilogue to Casualties.
  New from Ethiopia and the Sudan, The.
Clifton, L.   Driving through new england.
Coleman, W.   Metaphysically Niggerish.
Crouch, S.   Riding Across John Lee's Finger.
Cullen, C.   Heritage.
da Silva.   Along the Banks of the Charles.
  Return to the Homeland.
D'Almeida, F.   By Forty-Sixth.
Davis, H.   Ali, Bomaye.
De Kok.   Our Sharpeville.
Diop, D.   Vultures, The.
Duffy, C.   Comprehensive.
Dumas, H.   Root Song.
Espirito Santo.   To Tania.
Ezenwa-Ohaeto.   I Wan Bi President.
Fuller, R.   In Africa.
Gashe.   Village, The.
Gelman.   Epochs.
Gomes, A.   Martyred Tamarind, The.
Góngora y Argote.   Capture of Larache, The.
Goodison.   Guinea Woman.
  Turn Thanks to Miss Mirry.
Guillén, N.   Sensemayá.
Hardy, T.   Drummer Hodge.

Heffernan, M.   Africa: "I looked out toward the
  pasture at the cows."
Horne, N.   Messages.
  Note to My Liberal Feminist Sister, A.
Hughes, L.   Afro-American Fragment.
  Cubes.
  Danse Africaine.
  Negro.
Ismaili.   Bajji.
  Lagos.
  Solange.
Jackson, B.   Another Impostor.
Jeffers, L.   O Africa, where I baked my bread.
Jordan, J.   Mid-Year Report: For Haruko.
Kadima-Nzuji.   Incantations of the Sea: Moando
  Coast.
Karade, B.   Yemoja.
Kaufman, B.   African Dream.
Kizer, C.   Race Relations.
Knight, E.   Idea of Ancestry, The.
Koch, K.   Geography.
Kombem.   Another Moment.
Laing, K.   Africa Sky.
  Steps.
Lane, P.   Girl at the Window.
Lara, A.   Nights.
Lindsay, V.   Congo, The.
Livingstone, D.   Waste land at Station 14, The.
Lorde.   Dahomey.
Lowell, M.   Africa.
Mabuza.   Love Song, A: "It was good."
  Tired Lizi Tired.
Macgoye.   Letter to a Friend.
Macha, F.   Artist and a Wailing Mother, An.
  Corruption.
Madani.   Here I am Once More.
Madhubuti.   Knocking Donkey Fleas off a Poet
  from the Southside of Chi.
Mandela.   I Have Tried Hard.
Mansour, J.   Desire as Light as a Shuttle.
Mapanje.   After Wiriyamu Village Massacre by
  Portuguese.
  Messages.
  On Being Asked to Write a Poem for 1979.
  These Too Are Our Elders.
  Visiting Zomba Plateau.
Marchera, D.   Desert Crossing.
McKay, C.   Africa.
Mercado, N.   Somalia.
Miller, J.   Africa.
Mirsal.   Abortion.
  Confessions.
  I Usually Look Around Me.
Moore, M.   Jerboa, The.
Moorer.   Africa.
Morales, A.   Other Heritage, The.
Morales, R.   Africa.
Mphande.   I Was Sent For.
  Pain.
  Walking the Plateau.
Mpina.   Reborn.
  Summer Fires of Mulanje Mountain.
Neely, L.   Multiple Assaults.
Neto.   African Poem.
  Grieved Lands, The.
Nortje.   Waiting: "Isolation of exile is a gutted,
  The."
O'Lahsen, M.   Dead Erect, The.
Ofeimun.   New Brooms, The.
Ogundipe-Leslie.   Tendril Love of Africa.
Ojaide.   Fate of Vultures, The.
  Verdict of Stone, A.
  Where Everybody is King.
Okpala, Jude Chudi.   When Africa Speaks.
Opoku-Agyemang.   King Tut in America.
Osofisan.   She Thinks in Song.
Pedro, J.   Homecoming.
Pegram, A.   Deliverance.
  I Will Still Sing.
  Mr. White Discoverer.
Penn, R.E.   Morning Songs.
Phillips, C.   Africa Says.
Rampolekeng.   Welcome to the New
  Consciousness.
Rich, A.   Letters in the Family.
Rocha.   Guerilla Fighter.

Roggeman.   African Queen.
Rothenberg, J.   Praises of the Bantu Kings (1–
  10).
Saïd, A.   Africa of the Statue, The.
  My Woman's Transparence.
  On the Tattered Edges.
  Vultures Grow Impatient, The.
Salaam.   Spiritual Geography.
Sall, A.   Cloak of Dawn.
Sallah, T.   Elders Are Gods, The.
Sanchez, S.   Letter to Ezekiel Mphahlele.
Senghor.   African Image Is Not An Image by
  Equation, The.
  Before Night Comes.
  Kaya-Magan, The.
  Man and Beast.
  Prayer to the Masks.
  Song of the Initiate.
  Taga for Mbaye Dyôb.
  Young Sun's Greeting, The.
Serote.   This Old Woman.
Sexton.   Somewhere in Africa.
Shange.   Bocas: A Daughter's Geography.
Silva, L.   Island and Europe, The.
Sousa, N.   Call.
Southerland.   Pale Ant.
Southey, R.   Did then the bold slave rear at last
  the sword.
  Hold your mad hands! for ever on your plain.
  Oh he is worn with toil! the big drops run.
  'Tis night; the mercenary tyrants sleep.
  Why dost thou beat thy breast and rend thine
  hair.
Steptoe.   Contraband.
  Mississippi Blues.
Taha, A.   Abode of Arrival.
  Arabesque.
  December 31.
  State of Butterfly.
Thomas, L.   Embarkation for Cythera.
Tidjani-Cissé.   Home News.
Tobrise.   Dyeing.
Tolson, M.   Dark Laughter.
  Ti.
Touré, A.   Summer Worlds: A Mythic
  Landscape.
Waberi, A.   Between clackstones.
Walcott.   Far Cry from Africa, A.
Walker, M.   For My People.
Watkins-Cothran, E.   Beloved Ones, The.
Weaver, A.   My Father's Geography.
Wilson, T.   And the Saga Continues.
Winbush-David, W.   African Sunrunner.
Zimunya.   Let It Be.
  Mr. Bezuidenthout's Dogs.

African Americans
Abiyah.   Fatherless Townships.
Addison, L.   Umbra.
Ai.   Chance.
  Endangered Species.
  Riot Act, April 29, 1992.
  Self Defense.
Akiwumi, V.   Different Ones #6—Future
  Possibilities (An Aids Soliloquy).
Alexander, E.   Affirmative Action Blues
  (1993).
  Boston Year.
  Deadwood Dick.
  Feminist Poem Number One.
  Kevin of the N.E. Crew.
  Ladders.
  Today's News.
Algarin.   Broadway Opening.
Allen, J.   Deep Rock.
  Mud Wit.
  Prayer to Eshbu-Elegba.
Allen, S.   Moment Please, A.
  View from the Corner.
Amaker, A.   Roots.
Anderson, J.   13th Letter, The.
Anderson-Thompkins.   brken promises.
  Epitaph for Willie or Little Black Poet with No
  Future.
Angelou, M.   Family Affairs.
  Our Grandmothers.
  Still I Rise.

As-Sabah. I'll Never Know No Sunday in This Weekday Room.
Jubilee.
Asim, J. Dumas.
Askhari. Colorstruck.
Isalutu.
REcreation.
Aubert, A. Opposite of Green, The.
Bandele, A. 1980–1990: A Poet's Personal Review.
Prayer for the Living, A.
Baraka, I. Black Art.
Black Dada Nihilismus.
Clay.
Funk Lore.
Hymn for Lanie Poo.
Ka 'Ba.
Leadbelly Gives an Autograph.
Leroy.
Nation Is Like Ouselves, The.
Pause of Joe, The.
Poem for Black Hearts, A.
Poem Some People Will Have to Understand, A.
Short Speech to My Friends.
W. W.
Wise 1.
Wise 5.
Baraka, R. American Poetry.
Five-0.
For the Brothers Who Aint Here.
I Remember Malcolm.
In the Tradition Too.
Barkan, S. Negro Song.
Barlow, G. Painting Drunken Twilight.
Place Where He Arose, The.
Barras, J. Peace.
Beatty, P. Gription.
I Know You Are, But What Am I?
Independent Study.
New York Newsday: Truth, Justice and Vomit.
That's Not in My Job Description.
Why That Abbott and Costello Vaudeville Mess Never Worked with Black People.
Bennett, G. Heritage.
To a Dark Girl.
Benson, L. Asante.
P Word Poem, The.
Bernie, B. Sweet Georgia Brown.
Berryman. I'm scared a lonely. Never see my son.
Betts, T. Dreadlocks.
Bontemps. God Give to Men.
Boyd, M. Epitaph for Etheridge Knight.
Branch, J. Farewell Queen Mother Moore.
Brand, D. Blues Spiritual for Mammy Prater.
Canto 2: "Ancestor dirt."
Brathwaite, E. Journeys, The.
Braxton, C. Arts Are Black, The.
Braxton, Joanne M. Zoning.
Breedlove, N. Black and Divided or Chittlins and Caviar.
New Miz Praise de Lawd, The.
Brooks, S. Kojo: I Am A Black.
Negro Hero.
Of De Witt Williams on His Way to Lincoln Cemetery.
Primer for Blacks.
Third Sermon on the Warpland, The.
To the Diaspora.
Vacant Lot, The.
We Real Cool.
Brooks, S. Darktown Strutter's Ball, The.
Brooks, S. Grandma Talk.
Sweet molasses.
Brown, J. et al. Say It Loud—I'm Black and I'm Proud.
Brown, M. Survival Motion: Notice.
Brown, S. Memo: For the Race Orators.
Odyssey of Big Boy.
Old Woman Remembers, An.
Scotty Has His Say.
Slim in Atlanta.
Slim Lands a Job?
Southern Cop.
Sporting Beasley.
Strong Men.

To Sallie, Walking.
Browning, E. Runaway Slave at Pilgrim's Point, The.
Buddy. Callin Buddy / Bolden.
Caesar, V. In 5th Grade.
Carroll, K. Laughin at Cha.
Casey, K. Sweet Georgia Brown.
Cassells. Soul Make a Path Through Shouting.
Césaire, A. Islands scars of the water.
Césaire, A. et al. How did you come to develop the concept of Negritude?
Chambers, G. Meditations on Stevie.
Waxing Poetic on Marvin.
Clarke, T. For Babies Unborn.
Clifton, L. 4/30/92 for Rodney King.
Good Times.
In Salem.
In White America.
Light / on my mother's tongue.
Listen Children.
Thirty-Eighth Year, The.
Clinton, M. Black Rape.
I Wanna Be Black.
Warning to Young Bright Sisters / White AM. Culture 101A.
Coleman, H. OK Corral East: Brothers in the Nam.
Coleman, W. African Beneath the American, The.
African Sleeping Sickness.
American Sonnet (10).
Coffee.
Essay on Language.
Metaphysically Niggerish.
Notes on a Departure.
Where I Live.
Collins, J. Big World Look Out.
Collins, K. I Am Africa.
Sisters.
Cornish, S. Brown Bomber.
Corpus. Blkfern-jungal.
Cortez, J. How Long Has Trane Been Gone.
Craighead, L. Whole Truth So Help Me God— Also Known as the Gettin' Rid of Nigguz Business.
Wo/man's Voice Must Be Heard, A.
Crane, H. Black Tambourine.
Crawley, H. Bud.
Poetry for the Goddess.
Cross, T. Complected.
Cullen, C. Brown Girl Dead, A.
Colored Blues Singer.
From the Dark Tower.
Heritage.
Litany of the Dark People, The.
Yet Do I Marvel.
Cuney. No Images.
Cyril. Children's Games.
Jump Black Honey Jump Black.
Just Because I Am.
Damas. Hiccups.
Just Like the Legend.
S.O.S.
Datcher, M. Joseph speaks to gericault in the studio.
de Portalatin. Black Autumn.
DeBerry, J. Plain Ole Brother Blues.
Dent. For Cool Papa Bell.
Derricotte. Blackbottom.
For Black Women Who Are Afraid.
In an Urban School.
St. Peter Claver.
Struggle, The.
Dove, R. Event, The.
La Chapelle. 92nd Division. Ted.
Wingfoot Lake.
DuBois, W. Quadroon, The.
Song of the Smoke, The.
Dumas, H. Zebra Goes Wild Where the Sidewalk Ends, The.
Dunbar, P. Black Samson of Brandywine.
Colored Soldiers, The.
Negro Love Song, A.
Unsung Heroes, The.
We Wear the Mask.
When Dey 'Listed Colored Soldiers.

Eady. Why Do So Few Blacks Study Creative Writing?
Ellis, T. Hush Yo Mouf.
Slow Fade to Black.
Encarnacion. Bulosan Listens to a Recording of Robert Johson.
Fauset. Touché.
Finney, N. Uncles.
Fleming, R. For All Unwed Mothers.
Forman, R. Green Boots n Lil Honeys.
Foster, S. Old Folks at Home.
Gilbert, C. Time with Stevie Wonder in It.
Gilmore, B. Georgia avenue, washington d.c.
To be or not to be.
Giovanni. Beautiful Black Men.
Ego Tripping (There May Be a Reason Why).
Genie in the Jar, The.
Monday.
Nikki-Rosa.
Train Rides.
Giscombe, C. Negromania, Negrophilia, Negrophobia.
1980.
1962 At the Edge of Town.
Gray-Kontar, D. Cuz' mama played jazz.
Not no socialism/communism classical, but some power to the people jazz.
Grimké, A. Black Finger, The.
Fragment.
Grinshpan, Y. Grand Central by Night.
Hairston. Alabama Bus.
Handy, W. Beale Street Blues.
Harland-Watts, J. For a Woman's Rights.
Let It Be Known.
Resist Confinement.
Harper, M. Archives.
Grandfather.
High Modes: Vision as Ritual: Confirmation.
Homage to the Brown Bomber.
Song: I Want a Witness.
Harris, R. Usual Suspects, The.
Harris, W. Rib Sandwich.
Hayden, R. Beginnings.
Frederick Douglass.
Hayes, T. Postcard from Okemah, A.
Talk.
Hemphill. Cordon Negro.
Family Jewels.
Henderson, D. African Burial Ground called Tribeca, The.
Downtown-Boy Uptown.
Sketches of Harlem.
Henderson-Holmes. Failure of an Invention.
Hershon. Light and Dark, East and West.
Hisle, Janeya K. And All the Sisters Said.
Holman, M. Mr. Z.
Holmes, D. Time for Guns, A.
Hope, M. Sacrifice.
Hopkins, L. Nat Love: Black Cowboy.
Hughes, L. Afro-American Fragment.
American Heartbreak.
Aunt Sue's Stories.
Beaumont to Detroit: 1943.
Be-Bop Boys.
Bitter River, The.
Black Clown, The.
Blue Bayou.
Boogie: 1 a.m.
Brass Spittoons.
Christ in Alabama.
Come to the Waldorf-Astoria.
Cross.
Deferred.
Dinner Guest: Me.
Dream Boogie.
Dream Boogie: Variation.
For Russell and Rowena Jelliffe.
Freedom Train.
Good Morning.
Harlem Sweeties.
Harlem ("What happens to a dream deferred?").
High to Low.
I, Too.
Jim Crow Car.
Letter ("Dear Mama, / Time I pay rent and get

my food.").
Letter from Spain.
Low to High.
Merry-Go-Round.
Mulatto.
My People.
Mystery.
Negro.
Negro Speaks of Rivers, The.
Neighbor.
Note on Commercial Theatre.
Projection.
Same in Blues.
Share-Croppers.
Silhouette.
Song for a Dark Girl.
Song to a Negro Wash-woman, A.
Theme for English B.
Trumpet Player.
Uncle Tom ("Within— / The beaten pride.").
Visitors to the Black Belt.
Weary Blues, The.
When Sue Wears Red.
Hummer, T. Ideal, The.
Irvine, W. To be Young, Gifted, and Black.
Iverem, E. Daddy's Friends.
Journalist's Convention 1987.
Jackson, A. Make/n My Music.
Miz Rosa Rides the Bus.
Spinster Song: African-American Woman Guild.
Jackson, B. Another Impostor.
In Exchange for Forty Acres.
Jackson, G. Fugitive Slaves.
Some of Betty's Story Round 1850.
Jackson, R. After the Dance.
Albert James.
Jamal's Lamentation.
Jacobs, A. After the 200th White Person Locks
  Her Car Door at Me.
Jacobs, H. On Growing Up the Darker Berry.
Jeffers, H. Hold it Steady.
Jeffers, L. My Blackness Is the Beauty of This
  Land.
Nina Simone.
When I Know the Power of my Black Hand.
Jemeni. America Eats Its Young.
Jess, T. Letter to an Unconceived Son.
Johnson, F. Tired.
Johnson, H. Bottled [New York].
Sonnet to a Negro in Harlem.
Johnson, J. Creation, The.
Fifty Years.
Lift Every [or Ev'ry] Voice and Sing.
O Black and Unknown Bards.
Johnson, T. Until He Comes.
Jones, I. Echoes of the Murder of Emmett Till.
Haiku for My Brothers.
Jones, R. Small Lower-Middle-Class White
  Southern Male.
Jordan, A. Orientation: Wittenberg University,
  1983.
Jordan, J. DeLiza Spend the Day in the City.
If You Saw a Negro Lady.
Something Like a Sonnet for Phillis Miracle
  Wheatley.
Joseph, A. My Father's Heroes ("Not JFK, not
  MLK.").
Numbers: "My father taught me to measure."
On Being Told I Don't Speak Like a Black
  Person.
Reading Room.
Soul Train.
Kaufman, B. Oregon.
Sun is a negro, the.
Kendrick, D. Solo: The Good Blues.
We are the Writing on the Wall.
Knight, E. Another Poem for Me (after
  Recovering from an O.D.).
Black Poet Leaps to His Death, A.
Bones of My Father, The.
For Black Poets Who Think of Suicide.
Hard Rock Returns to Prison from the Hospital
  for the Criminal Insane.
Idea of Ancestry, The.
Once on a Night in the Delta: A Report From
  Hell.

Warden Said to Me the Other Day, The.
Komunyakaa, Y. Family Tree.
Gift Horse.
Troubling the Water.
Ladd, M. Tragic Mulatto is Neither, The.
Lee, K. On South Africa.
Lima, J. That Black Girl Fulô.
Lindsay, V. Congo, The.
Loftin, E. Black Lady, A.
Weeksville Women.
Loftis, N. Big John.
Long, D. Black Love Black Hope.
Lorde. Between Ourselves.
Coal.
For the Record.
Harriet.
Naturally.
Outside.
Lowell, R. For the Union Dead.
Lukata, B. Rehearsal.
Mack, C. That's Why They Call Me "Shine".
Madgett. Black Woman.
Images.
Madhubuti. B Network, The.
Big Momma.
Gwendolyn Brooks.
Malcolm Spoke / Who Listened?
My Brothers.
Poet: What Ever Happened to Luther?
Possibilities: Remembering Malcolm X.
Maier, J. Timbalero.
Major, C. News Story.
Paragraph from English Speaking World.
Pictures.
McElroy, C. Ghost-Who-Walks, The.
Griots Who Know Brer Fox, The.
Illusion.
This Is the Poem I Never Meant to Write.
Under the Oak Table.
McElroy, D. Present Moments.
McKay, C. Harlem Dancer, The.
If We Must Die.
Negro Spiritual.
Outcast.
White House, The.
McManus, J. Commercials exaggerate.
McManus, K. 450 Years of Selective Memory
  (Smile).
McNeil, R. Angel in the Temple of Luxor, An.
Medina, T. Big House Revisited, The.
Don't Say Goodnight to Etheridge Knight.
Poem for Teacup Mantlepiece Poets Palpitating
  Poot Booty Plagiarists Imprisoned in Ivy
  League White Supremacist Mental Biological
  Warfare Labs.
Way We Move, The.
Melville, H. Formerly a Slave.
Swamp Angel, The.
Mercado, N. Somalia.
Miller, A. My Trip.
Morgenstern, Felicia L. Soul Roots.
Moses, G. Poem for Trish, A.
Moss, T. Raising a Humid Flag.
Mullen, H. Denigration.
Present Tense.
Viejas Locas.
We Are Not Responsible.
Neal, L. Holy Days.
Neely, L. Multiple Assaults.
Rhonda, Age 15, Emergency Room.
Nelson, M. Balance.
Ballad of Aunt Geneva, The.
Chopin.
Obadike, M. Tradition/Abstraction.
Oyewole. We're Not Well Here.
Page, E. To Become Unconscious.
Parker, D. Sand.
Patterson, G. Autobiography of a Black Man.
Patterson, R. Black Power.
Twenty-Six Ways of Looking at a Blackman.
Perdomo, W. Nigger-Reecan Blues.
Phillips, C. Passing.
Piatt, S. Child's Party, A.
Pinkard, M. Sweet Georgia Brown.
Plummer, P. Conversations in the struggle.
Pomeroy, R. Gay Love and the Movies.

Powell, K. Don't Feel No Way.
For Aunt Cathy.
Genius Child.
Mental Terrorism.
Southern Birth.
What the Deal, Son?
Public Enemy. Party for your Right to Fight.
Quigless, H. Concert.
Randall, D. Blackberry Sweet.
Booker T. and W. E. B.
Redmond. 11-Haiku-Poem for a Magnificent
  Million.
Reed, I. Dualism in ralph ellison's invisible
  man.
Railroad Bill, A Conjure Man.
Reynolds, H. Black Maid to the Fair Boy, The.
Richardson, J. My Man Caliban!
Rivers, C. Underground.
Roach. At Guaracara Park.
Roberson, E. American culture is the pot.
Four Lines of a Black Love Letter between
  Teachers.
On the Calligraphy of Black Chant.
Poll.
Roberts, N. Nigger and Some Poofters, A.
Rodgers, C. Mama's God.
Ross, L. Indecent Exposure (A True Story).
James Brown.
Rukeyser, M. George Robinson: Blues.
Rushin. Black Back-Ups, The.
Rykard, R. Whole two weeks after The Million
  Man March; and still, if you'd ask me, this is
  all I could say about it, A.
Sadiq, M. Tuskegee Experiment.
Saint. Heart and Soul.
St. John, P. Benign Neglect / [West Point,]
  Mississippi, 1970.
Violence of Pronoun, The.
Saloy, M. We've Come This Far.
Sanchez, S. Blues.
Reflections After the June 12th March for
  Disarmament.
Song No. 2: "I say. all you young girls waiting
  to live."
Song No. 3: "Cain't nobody tell me any
  different."
This is Not a Small Voice.
To Anita.
Saunders, R. Lawd, Dese Colored Chillum.
Schreiber, R. They Kill Us.
To Be Held.
Shakur, A. Tradition, The.
Shange. About Atlanta.
Sharp, S. Tribal Marks.
Shepherd, R. Difficult Music, The.
Sherman, C. Roots.
Simmons, S. All the shoes are shined and the
  cotton is picked.
Simon, L. Nellie Gives into Blanche.
Smith, D. To Isle of Wight.
Smith, P. Blonde White Women.
Building Nicole's Mama.
They Say That Black People . . . .
What It's Like to Be a Black Girl (For Those of
  You Who Aren't).
Sousa, N. Let My People Go.
Soyinka. Telephone Conversation.
Spellman, A. Did John's Music Kill Him?
Stafford, W. Monuments for a Friendly Girl at a
  Tenth Grade Party.
Stanard, C. Baseball.
Steptoe. In Black Churches.
Window Shopping.
Stokes, G. Blue Texarkana.
Sykes, B. One Day.
Sylvain, P. Collective Search.
Thomas, L. Discovering America Again.
Embarkation for Cythera.
Excitation.
Thompson, C. Mrs. Johnson Objects.
Tolson, M. Dark Symphony.
Despite his caricatures.
Sootie Joe.
They tell us to forget.
Touré, A. Frontier of Rage, The.
Imani in Sunburst Summer: A Chant.

JuJu.
  Palenque Queen by Habana's Shores.
Travis, N. Sunbathing.
Troupe. Following the North Star Boogaloo.
  Poem for My Father; for Quincy Trouppe, Sr.
  River Town Packin House Blues.
Tucker, S. Boy Exploded on the Corner Today, A.
Umoja, M. Say Something: A Change Is Gonna Come.
Van Jordan, A. If I Write a Poem.
Vega. Brothers Loving Brothers.
Voigt. At the Movie: Virginia, 1956.
Wade-Gayles. Inquisition.
Walcott, B. Much of Your Poetry Is Beautiful.
Walker, A. Women.
Walker, M. For My People.
  We Have Been Believers.
Waniek. Balance.
  Ballad of Aunt Geneva, The.
  Diverne's Waltz.
  Three Men in a Tent.
  Tuskegee Airfield.
Watkyns. Blackamoors, The.
Watley, M. Negroes.
  100 Million.
Weatherford, C. Charleston Baskets.
Weaver, A. Afternoon Train.
  Black and White Galaxie, The.
  Black Man's Sonata, A.
  Easy Living.
  Imitation of Life.
  Left Bank Jazz Society, The.
  Luxembourg Garden.
  Picnic, an Homage to Civil Rights, The.
Welburn. Bones and Drums.
Wheatley, P. On Being Brought from Africa to America.
Whitlow. Poem for the Children.
Williams, C. For the White Lady Holding Me.
  In Search of Aunt Jemima.
  Negro Survival 101 or Poem for Tiger Woods and Other Multiethnic Other's.
  Revolutionary Thoughts.
Williams, S. Buildings of the, The.
  Letters from a New England Negro.
  Straight Talk from Plain Women.
  Summer mornings we.
  Wishon Line, The.
  You Were Never Miss Brown to Me.
Wilson, T. And the Saga Continues.
Wordsworth, W. September 1, 1802.
Worley, D. Dancing in the Dark.
Wormser. It's a Party (1959).
Wren, A. Harmony.
Wright, J. Albuquerque Graveyard, The.
  End of an Ethnic Dream, The.
  Homecoming Singer, The.
Wright, R. Between the World and Me.
  I Have Seen Black Hands.
Young, A. Poem for Players, A.
See also **Blacks**

Afterlife
Addonizio. What the Dead Fear.
Ajanta. Dateline Hyderabad.
Akers. Dead, The: "Dead come, looking for their shoes, The."
Ball, A. Premature Burial Gazette.
Bell, J. Poem to Line My Casket with, Ramona.
Belloc. Her Faith.
Boruch. Window, The.
Bruchac. Canticle: "Let others speak."
Buchan, J. Fisher Jamie.
Cairns, Scott. Coming Forth.
Castillo, A. Nani Worries about Her Father's Happiness in the Afterlife.
Chang Heng. Bones of Zhuangzi, The.
Clinton, Robert. Modulation.
Cox, M. At the Crematorium, My Son Asks Why We're All Wearing Black.
  Things My Grandfather Must Have Said.
Crane, H. Circumstance, The.
Cummings, E. E. If there are any heavens my mother will (all by herself) have.
De Mello Breyner. Inscription.
Deanovich. American Avalon.

Eady. Paradiso.
Ekelof. Alone in the quiet night.
Faber, F. After-State.
Fenton, J. Kingfisher's Boxing Gloves, The.
Garcia, M. Mi Mamá, the Playgirl.
Goldberg, B. Whitman's Confession: In the Cleft of Eternity.
González Prada, M. If the Tomb Is Not Oblivion.
Guest, B. Farewell Stairway, The.
Gunn, T. Reassurance, The.
Hill, G. Not as we are but as we must appear.
Hine. Man's Country.
Hristov, Boris. Dandelion Bone.
Jansma, E. Descent.
Kalina, R. Testimonies.
Keckler, W. Wedding, A.
Khayr, A. I'm going to tell you something that is true.
Kleinzahler. Where Souls Go.
Komunyakaa, Y. Ode to the Maggot.
Kumin, M. In the Park.
Lampman. City of the End of Things, The.
Leeke, Kiamsha Madelyn. October Death.
Lewis, W. Some Solace, Some Yearning.
Li Po. Conversation among the Mountains.
MacNeice. This Is the Life.
Mahon. Consolations of Philosophy.
Martineau, J. Life's Success.
Mengham, Rod. Concession to Perpetuity No. 166.
Merrill, J. Voices from the Other World.
Moritz [*or* Morits]. Parting the curtains on the other world.
Mtshali. Voice from the Dead, A.
Nezahualcoyotl. Where Will I Go?
O'Donnell, D. Even Solomon.
O'Hara, F. To John Ashbery.
Oliver, M. Roses, Late Summer.
Pagis, D. Sominex.
Preston, N. When I Leave My Body.
Quevedo y Villegas. From the White Day to Take Me.
  Love Beyond Death.
Rimbaud, A. Night in Hell.
Rogers, P. Dead Never Fight against Anything, The.
Rosenberg, I. Dead Heroes, The.
Sexton. Somewhere in Africa.
Shakespeare, W. Ay[e], but to die, and go we know not where.
Shepherd, R. Also Love You.
Smith, S. Mrs Simpkins.
Sŏng [*or* Sung] Sammun. Were you to ask me what I'd wish to be.
Tennyson, A. O [*or* Oh] that 'twere possible.
  Thy spirit ere our fatal loss.
Turner, C. Bliss of Heaven, Maria, shall be thine, The.
Unknown. Artemisia Village.
  Build a House in Paradise.
  Dead Man Asks for a Song, The.
  Gold Band, The.
  Good News, Member.
  My little ship, three-masted.
  Petelia Tablet, The.
  Soldier stood at the pearly gate.
  Travel On.
  Wake Up, Jacob.
  When We Do Meet Again.
Valentine, J. Skate.
Waldman, A. After-Life, The.
  One Inch of Love Is an Inch of Ashes.
Willis, J. Inside Our Dreams.
Wright, C. Clinchfield Station.
  Nightletter.
Wunderlich, M. Fourteen Things We're Allowed to Bring to the Underworld.
Xue Di. Interplay.

Afternoon
Bevington, L. Afternoon.
Cerruto, O. Love: "Afternoon is offered to us, The."
Cofer, J. Hour of the Siesta, The.
Creeley. Place, The ("Afternoon it changes.").
Darío, R. Tropical Afternoon.

García Lorca. Goring and the Death, The.
Hinsey, E. Roman Arbor, The.
Latouche, J. Lazy Afternoon.
Longfellow, H. Afternoon in February.
Lowell, A. September, 1918.
McAuley, J. One Tuesday in Summer.
Millay, E. Afternoon on a Hill.
Neruda. Leaning into the Afternoons.
Ríos, A. Coffee in the Afternoon.
Serrano, P. Bullfight.
  Corrida.
Stickney, T. Quiet after the rain of morning.
Vallejo. Down to the Dregs.
  Finished the stranger, with whom, late.
Wright, C. Sitting Outside at the End of Autumn.

Agamemnon
Kossman. Cassandra to Agamemnon.

Aggression
Clare, J. Turkeys.
Gilbert, W. Thought from Ruddigore, A.
Griffiths, S. Just a Product of a Certain Situation.
Guiducci. Perhaps One Day There Will Be Ways.
Nash, O. Tweedledee and Tweedledoom.
Pinter, H. American Football (A Reflection upon the Gulf War).

Agincourt, Battle of (1415)
Shakespeare, W. Now entertain conjecture of a time.
Unknown. Song of the English Bowmen.

Aging
Adcock, F. Weathering.
Agathias. Beautiful Melite, in the throes of middle age.
Al-Haidari, B. Premature Elegy.
al-Sayyab, B. Singer Has Aged, The.
Alberti. Homecoming of Love Amongst Illustrious Ruins.
Alcman. No longer, O honeytongued, holyvoiced maidens.
Anderson, M. September Song.
Andreus. Empty Room, The.
  Empty Room, The.
Armantrout. Generation.
Armitage, S. Kid.
Arnold, M. Growing Old.
Atwood. Miss July Grows Older.
Auden. Doggerel by a Senior Citizen.
  Prologue at Sixty.
Ausonius. I used to tell you, "Frances, we grow old".
Ayukawa Nobuo. Last I Heard, The.
Baillie, J. Song: "What voice is this, thou evening gale!"
Baraka, I. Look for You Yesterday, Here You Come Today.
Barker, J. To My Young Lover.
Barnfield [*or* Barnefield]. Sweet Corrall lips, where Nature's treasure lies.
Basho. Another year gone.
  Autumn / Even the birds.
  Gray hairs being plucked.
  Teeth sensitive to the sand.
  This autumn.
  This dark autumn.
  Year's end / All corners.
Baudri of Bourgueil. Your Appearance is Pleasing.
Beckett, S. Saint-Lô.
Beer, P. Middle Age.
Bek, T. I breathed my fill—and then breathed out.
  If a song flies to me from the garden.
Berry, W. Ripening.
Blackburn, M. Before That.
Blake, W. Angel, The.
Blood, B. Late.
Bly, R. Dream of Retarded Children, A.
  For My Son Noah, Ten Years Old.
  My Father at 85.
Bokuo. For seventy-two years / I've kept the ox well under.
Boland, E. Anna Liffey.
Bonnefoy. Book, for Growing Old, The.

Bontemps. To a Young Girl Leaving the Hill Country.
Borges. Limits (or Good-byes).
Bosquet, A. Old Gentleman, An.
Brontë, E. Love and Friendship.
Why do I hate that lone green dell?
Brooks, G. Marie Lucille.
Broumas, O. Sometimes, as a Child.
Brown, Polly. This Is for Megan.
Brown, S. Feminine Intuition.
Browning, R. Rabbi Ben Ezra.
Youth and Art.
Bryan, J. Bindweed.
Buckley, V. In the faint blue light.
Bun-Etsu. Sixty-five years.
Burns, R. John Anderson, My Jo ("John Anderson my jo, John / When we were first acquent.").
Buson. Goodbye. I will go.
Spring Wind on the Riverbank at Kema.
Byron, G. On This Day I Complete My Thirty-sixth Year.
Stanzas for Music ("There's not a joy the world can give like that it takes away.").
Carew, T. Disdain Returned.
Carroll, L. Father William.
Carruth, H. Capper Kaplinski at the North Side Cue Club.
Sonnet: "You rose from our embrace and the small light spread."
Testament.
Cartwright, K. Delta, The / Itch of cayenne.
Castro, R. They Say that the Plants Do Not Speak.
Causley. Nursery Rhyme of Innocence and Experience.
Cavendish, M. Woman Drest by Age, A.
Celan. Your Hand Full of Hours.
Ch'i-chi. White Hair.
Ching An. Crossing the Yang-Chia Bridge Once More.
Cho Wen-chun. Lament of a Graying Woman.
Chou Pang-yen. Tune: "Prince Lan-Ling".
Christopher. Palm Reader, The.
Chrystos. Portrait of Assimilation.
Chu Tun-ju. To an Ancient Tune.
Clarke, A. Martha Blake at Fifty-one.
Claudian. Old Man of Verona, The.
Clifton, L. Climbing.
1994.
Thirty-Eighth Year, The.
Clough. Here am I yet, another twelvemonth spent.
Cole, T. Dial, The.
Coleridge, H. Long Time a Child.
Coleridge, S. Old Man's Sigh, The. A Sonnet.
This Lime-Tree Bower My Prison.
Collins, B. On Turning Ten.
Cooley. Brother Body.
Cooper, J. Childhood in Jacksonville, Florida.
Cope, W. Names: "She was Eliza for a few weeks."
Corn. To Hermes.
Cornford, F. Childhood.
Cowley, H. Departed Youth.
Cowper, W. To Mary.
Cranch. My Old Palette.
Creeley. Age ("Most explicit— / the sense of trap.").
Body.
Faces, The.
Crummey, Michael. Naked Man, The.
Cunningham, J. Epigram: "You wonder why Drab sells her love for gold?"
Moral Poem, A.
To My Wife.
Darío, R. Eheu!
Davis, O. Thirty Years Rising.
Day Lewis. Walking Away.
Dickinson, E. We outgrow love like other things.
Diodes. Somebody said when snubbed, "Is Damon so.
Disch. Entropic Villanelle.
d'Oettingen. To Il y a.
Donne. Autumnal[l], The.

Canonization, The.
Donovan, K. Grooming.
Dransfield. Portrait of the Artist as an Old Man.
Drummond de Andrade. Your Shoulders Hold Up the World.
Dudley, E. Pathologist.
Dyer, J. Now, I gain the Mountain's Brow.
Earle, J. May Tree, The.
Elsschot. Mother.
Emerson, R. Climacteric.
Terminus ("It is time to be old.").
Erdrich, H. Hopi Prophet Chooses a Pop.
Fan Chung-yen. Tune: "Trimming the Silver Lamp".
Feinstein, E. Bathroom.
Getting Older.
Feinstein, S. Blues for Zoot.
Fell, A. Pushing Forty.
Field, E. Little Boy Blue.
Fischer, N. I've Changed.
Fisher, J. Gooseflesh.
Forché. As Children Together.
Frost, R. Span of Life, The.
To Earthward.
Fuller, C. Guests.
Fumi Saito. Palm of the hand, The / Is not aware of dying as.
Fusselman, A. Puffy Jacket.
Fuyo-Dokai. Seventy-six: done.
Gahagan. Colour of the Old Man's Eyes, The.
Galvin, J. Two Horses and a Dog.
Gandlevsky, S. There's our street, let's say.
Garcilaso de la Vega. While There Is Still the Color of a Rose.
Ginsberg, A. Father Death Blues.
Sphincter.
Giovanni. Life I Led, The.
Goldberg, L. Toward Myself.
Góngora y Argote. Whistling arrow flies less eagerly, The.
González Prada, M. How Old Is Pilar?
Goodman, M. Upkeep.
Gray, S. On a Cat Aging.
Greenberg, S. To Dear Daniel.
Greig, A. Ruth Says.
Gruffydd, W. 1914–1918 The Young to the Old.
Guevara, M. Hands of the Old Métis, The.
Hall, D. Dusting.
Hall, Daniel. My Son, My Executioner.
HaNagid. You Mock Me Now in Your Youth.
Hantoosh, G. Glass of Ancient Wine, A.
Hardy, T. Church Romance, A.
Circus-Rider to Ringmaster.
Colonel's Soliloquy, The.
Former Beauties.
Voice of Things, The.
Heaney, S. Fosterling.
Hemingway. Age Demanded, The.
Herbert, G. Answer, The.
Mortification.
Herrick. To His Mistress[es] ("Help[e] me! help[e] me! now I call.").
Heym. Final Vigil.
Hicok. Alzheimer's.
Hikmet. My Lady's Eyes Are Hazel.
Hill, S. My Sister's Jeans.
Hilton, D. I Try to Turn in My Jock.
Hinsey, E. Body in Youth, The.
Ho Ch'e Ch'ang. Written Impromptu upon Returning to My Hometown.
Hồ Xuân Hương. On a Portrait of Two Beauties.
Hollander, J. Carmen Ancillae.
Horace. Late Night Ode.
Ode 1.25: Ribald Romeos Less and Less Berattle ("Parcius iunctas quatiunt fenestras").
Young Men Come Less Often, The—Isn't It So?
Houlihan, J. All the Cold Mechanicals.
Housman. Loveliest of trees, the cherry now.
Howe, J. My Last Dance.
Huang T'ing-chien. To Go with Shih K'o's Painting of an Old Man Tasting Vinegar.
Hugo, R. Flying, Reflying, Farming.
From Altitude, the Diamonds.
Letter to Blessing from Missoula.
Letter to Libbey from St. Regis.

Places and Ways to Live.
Ibarbourou. Wild Root.
Ibn Hazm al-Andalusi. Twice Times Then Is Now.
Ichigen. Seventy-eight awkward years.
Ikuo-Myotan. Seventy-two years I've hung.
Ingelow. Seven Times Three. Love.
Ingram-Roberts, A. Poem 2 (for Duckie Simpson of Black Uhuru).
Issa. As I grow older.
As we grow old / What triumph.
Flies swarming / What do they want of.
In my hidden house.
Moon and the flowers, The.
Ivanova, O. I meet myself each and every day.
Jakushitsu. Refreshing, the wind against the waterfall.
Jarrell, R. Aging.
Face, The.
Island, The.
Next Day.
Player Piano, The.
Jeffers, R. Age in Prospect.
But I Am Growing Old and Indolent.
For Una.
Johnson, J. Girl of Fifteen.
Jones, P. Modris.
Jones, R. Song of the Old Man.
Jonson, B. My Picture Left in Scotland.
Joseph, J. Warning.
Joyce, J. Bahnhofstrasse.
Juan Chi. Elder lives by the side of the river, An.
Juana Inés de la Cruz. On Her Portrait.
Justice, D. Men at Forty.
Juvenal. Satire 10.
Kantaris. Stocking Up.
Kaufman, S. Next Year, in Jerusalem.
Kekova. Having submitted your petition for dismissal.
Kennedy, X. In a Prominent Bar in Secaucus [One Day].
Kenyon, J. Finding a Long Gray Hair.
Kerrigan, T. Elvis Kissed Me.
Kim Suyŏng. Journal Encounter, The.
Kinsella, T. Oldest Place, The.
Kirsanov. Suddenly.
Kizer, C. For Jan as the End Draws Near.
Knoepfle. Dark Spaces: Thoughts on All Souls Day.
Ko Chônghûi. Our Baby is a Living Prayer.
Komunyakaa, Y. Way the Cards Fall, The.
Kort, E. Gardener, The.
Kowit. Cosmetics Do No Good.
Snapshot.
Kuan Han-ch'ing. In the Southern Mode, to the Tune "A Sprig of Flowers" The Refusal to Get Old.
Kunitz, S. Passing Through.
Lamb, C. Gipsy's Malison, The.
Old Familiar Faces, The.
Landor, W. Tears of the Dying.
Larkin, J. My Body.
Larkin, P. Age.
Dockery and Son.
Love Songs in Age.
Old Fools, The.
Lem. Temple City Blvd. and Ellis Ln.
Levertov. Woman Alone, A.
Levine, P. Red Dust.
28.
Li Ch'ing-chao. Hopelessness.
Lyric to the Tune "Immortal by the River".
Tune: "Joy of Eternal Union".
Li Ho. Flying Light.
Li Po. For Meng Hao-Jan.
Springtime South of the Yangtze.
To Meng Hao-jan.
Li Shang-yin. Chance to Meet Is Difficult, The. Without Title.
Li Yü. Tune: "The Beauty of Yü".
Lieberman, M. Regret.
Lihn. Old Man's Monologue with Death, The.
Lingafelter, A. Grandmothers, The.
Lisick, B. Empress of Sighs ("Mom and Dad have abandoned the family home and retired to

Palm.").
Lockhart. Lines: "When youthful faith hath fled."
Locklin. Leader of the Pack, The.
Loftin, E. Weeksville Women.
Longley, M. Ash Keys.
Lowell, A. New Heavens for Old.
Lowell, R. For Sheridan.
Loy. Jules Pascin.
Lum. Riding the North Point Ferry.
Lux. Little Tooth, A.
Lyman Jr., D. B. Eternal Controversy, The.
Lynch, T. Skating with Heather Grace.
MacCaig. No Choice.
MacLeish. Old Men in the Leaf Smoke, The.
Madonick, M. Settled In.
Mallet, D. On an Amorous Old Man.
Mandell, A. Middle Age.
Manrique, J. Barcelona Days.
Marbod of Rennes. This vision of a face, radiant and full of beauty.
Martial. Epigram: Likeness, The.
Marvell. To His Coy Mistress.
Marzán. Emergency.
Masaoka Shiki. Aged nightingale / How sweet.
McClatchy. My Mammogram.
McGinley. Blues for a Melodeon.
McGough, R. Cinders.
Mei Sheng. Beautiful Toilet, The.
Meredith, W. Last Things.
Merrill, J. Kimono, The.
  Mirror.
Merwin. River of Bees, The.
  Waves in August.
Meynell, A. Letter from a Girl to Her Own Old Age, A.
Miles, J. Album: "This is a hard life you are living."
Millar, J. Midlife.
Millay, E. Grown-up.
  Oh, my belovèd, have you thought of this.
  Sonnet 43: "What lips my lips have kissed, and where, and why."
Milton. How soon hath Time the subtle [or suttle] thief [or theef] of youth.
Mistral, G. Dusk.
  Let Him Not Grow Up.
  Serene Words.
Montale. Story of Every Day, The.
Moody, E. To a Friend, Who Gave the Author a Reading Glass.
Moore, H. Girl in a Fur-Trimmed Dress.
Mueller, L. Curriculum Vitae.
Muir, E. Late Wasp, The.
  Myth, The.
Mun Chônghui. Elderly Woman, An.
  Song of a Middle-Aged Woman.
Murray, J. And As I Came Out from the Temples.
Muso Soseki. Green mountains.
Nantembo. On New Year's Day.
Nasir, A. Poem Looking in a Mirror, A.
Nemerov. Boy with Book of Knowledge.
Nguyễn Khuyến. To the Singing Girl Named Luu.
Niedecker. There's a better shine.
Noguchi, R. His Waves.
Nye, N. Boy Removes All Traces from His Room, The.
O'Grady, D. In the valleys of the future we shall walk.
  Purpose.
O'Grady, J. Buster's Last Hand.
Oliveira, D. Paso Robles, San Luis Obispo, San Luis Obispo.
Opitz. Ah Dearest, let us haste us.
Oppen. Resort.
Ormsby, E. My Mother in Old Age.
Ou-yang Hsiu. Old Age.
Ovid. Elegy 3.6: "Either she was foul, or her attire was bad."
Owen, W. Sonnet, to a Child.
Pagis, D. Ein Leben.
Paley, G. Sad Children's Song, The.
Pao Chao. Ballad in Imitation of "The Prince of Huainan".

Rough Road, A.
Parker, D. Ballade at Thirty-Five.
  Indian Summer.
Pasolini. Lines from the Testament.
Pastan. Self-Portrait.
Patchen. Street Corner College.
Pavlova. Life calls us, and we go, massing our courage.
Peacock, T. Love and Age.
Pei Di. Cove of the Wall of Meng, The.
Phillips, C. In the blood, Winnowing.
Pilinszky, J. On the Back of a Photograph.
Pindar. Hyperboreans, The.
Plath. Mirror.
Po Chü-i. At the End of Spring.
  River Flute.
  Song of the P'i-P'a.
Poe. Eldorado.
Porter, P. On This Day I Complete My Fortieth Year.
  What I Have Written I Have Written.
Pound, E. Tea Shop, The.
Pow. Years, The: "Sometimes to get their own back."
Preil, G. From a Late Diary.
Preston, R. Mama.
Queneau. If You Imagine.
Quevedo y Villegas. Ah, What of Life! Does No One Answer Me?
Ralegh, S. Nymph's [or Nimphs] Reply to the [Passionate] Shepherd [or Sheepheard], The.
Randall, D. Haymakers.
Rankin, J. Sea-bundle.
Ransom, J. Blue Girls.
Reed, H. Chard Whitlow.
Reed, I. Turning Pro.
Reid, A. Weathering.
Reid, C. Howl, Howl.
Rexroth, K. I hate this shadow of a ghost.
Reynolds, R. Peridot.
Rich, A. Middle-Aged, The.
  Since we're not young, weeks have to do time.
  Upper Broadway.
Roberson, E. True We Are Two Grown Men.
Robertson, J. George Buchanan in Old Age.
Robinson, E. Isaac and Archibald.
Rochester, J. Disabled Debauchee, The.
Romo-Carmona, M. Signs.
Rosenblatt, S. Mom and Dad Getting Older.
  Second Half of Our Lives, The.
Rossetti, C. Youth gone, and beauty gone if ever there.
St. John, D. My Friend.
Salinas, L. Middle Age.
  My Fifty-Plus Years Celebrate Spring.
Sanchez, S. July.
  Personal Letter No. 3.
Sanders, E. Cutting Prow, The.
Santayana. Sonnet 25: "As in the midst of battle there is room."
Sappho. But as my friend, take to a younger bed.
  Tonight I've watched.
  You / Put success in the mouth.
Scarbrough, G. Letter to Spencer.
Schilpp, M. Non Sequitur.
Schoenberger. Epithalamion.
Schwartz, R. L. Falling in Love after Forty.
  Midnight Supper.
Scott, William B. Garland for Advancing Years, A.
Scott, William T. We Are So Fond of One Another, Because Our Ailments Are the Same.
Scovell. Ghosts, The.
  Listening to Collared Doves.
Seifū. Faces of dolls, The.
Sekishitsu-Soei. Fifty-three years / This clumsy ox has managed.
Shakespeare, W. Sonnet 2: "When forty winters shall besiege thy brow."
  Sonnet 5: "Those hours that with gentle work did frame."
  Sonnet 60: "Like as the waves make toward[s] the pebbled [or pibled] shore."
  Sonnet 73: "That time of year thou may'st in me behold."

Sonnet 104: "To me, fair friend, you never can be old."
Shakhova. Autobiographical Response from a Provincial Wasteland (in Reply to a New Year's Greeting Sent with a Bouquet).
Shapcott, T. Blue Paisley Shirt, The.
  Turning Fifty.
Shiseki. My old thighs / How thin.
Sholl. Autobiography in Third Person.
Singleton, Giovanni. For my 27th birthday: a poem longer than 10 lines in which pronouns appear.
Sisson. Tristia.
Smith, C. Thirty-eight: Addressed to Mrs H—y.
Smith, K. Writing in Prison.
Smith, L. Walking a Field into Evening.
Smith, M. City.
Smith, S. Pad, Pad.
Southey, R. Old Man's Comforts and How He Gained Them, The.
  Remembrance.
Soyinka. To My First White Hairs.
Speakes. Mama Loves Janis Joplin.
Spender, S. What I Expected.
Stafford, W. Growing Up.
  How the Real Bible Is Written.
Stanton, M. Pole Vaulting.
Stephens, P. Hangman.
Stevenson, A. Willow Song.
Stevenson, R. He hears with gladdened heart the thunder.
Strato [or Straton]. Despite the ruddy down upon your cheek.
  Twelve-year-old looks fetching in his prime, A.
Strickland, A. Forsaken, The.
Su Tung-p'o. Rain During the Cold Food Festival.
  Thoughts in Exile.
  Tune: "Immortal by the River".
Sullivan, B. Hair.
Supervielle. Early in the morning.
Swift, J. Stella's Birthday, 1725.
  Stella's Birthday [1721].
Symons, A. 5. At Seventeen.
Synge. I've Thirty Months.
Szécsi. Only with Radiance.
Takushitsu. Breeze strokes the water of the spring, A.
Tallmountain. Hands of Mary Joe, The.
Tanikawa, S. Growth.
T'ao Ch'ien [or T'ao Yuan-ming]. Days and months do not wish to tarry, The.
  Fire, Sixth Month, 408.
  Great men want the four seas. I've only.
  Reply to Prefect Liu.
Tate, A. Last Days of Alice.
Taylor, B. Love Returned.
Tendo-Nyojo. Sixty-six years.
Theocritus. Idyll 29: "Truth in the cups men say, dear youth."
Thomas, E. Gone, Gone Again.
Thomas, R. S. Geriatric.
  Pavane.
Thompson, F. Past Thinking of Solomon.
Thoreau. Music.
Toomer. Delivered at the Knighting of Lord Durgling by Great Bruce-Jean.
Trinidad. Answer Song.
Tripp. On My Fortieth Birthday.
Troupe. Reflections on Growing Older.
Tsvetayeva [or Tsvetaeva]. Gold that was my hair has turned, The.
Tsvetkov. Like a ruddy child you fall asleep in september.
Tu Fu [or Du Fu]. By the Winding River.
  New Year's Eve at the Home of Tu Wei.
  Passing Mr. Sung's Old House.
  Snow Storm.
  Spring Scene.
  To Wei Pa, a Retired Scholar.
  Traveling at Night.
  Winter Dawn.
Tŭgo [or Tŭgogok]. Ode to Knight Chukchi.
U T'ak. Sticks in one hand.
Uncho. Forty-nine years / —What a din!
Unknown. Aging.

Chanting Buddha's name.
Cherished Daughter, The.
In the valley where the stream leaps.
It takes a very stupid dolt.
Life-Parting.
Look what your love has done to me.
Ode to the Seasons.
Old Woman of Beare, The.
Song: "Yellow dust drifts down the road to Ch'ang-an."
Whether I see you now.
Will You Love Me When I'm Old?
Vallejo. Distant Footsteps, The.
It was Sunday in the fair ears of my burro.
Van Duyn. Stream, The.
Van Riessen. Old in Overijssel.
Van Vliet. Party.
Very. Autumn Flowers.
Villaurrutia. Nocturne: The Eternal.
Villon. Now I think I hear the laments.
Vinokurov. All Grows Old.
Volkman. Theft.
Vroman. Wrinkling Together.
Vroomkoning. Together Again ("I behold her there.").
Wah. Father / Mother Haibun #19.
Wakuan-Shitai. Iron tree blooms.
Walcott. Codicil.
Wang Wei. Answer to Vice-Prefect Chang.
Cove of the Wall of Meng, The.
Farewell to Spring.
Sitting Alone on an Autumn Night.
Villa at the Foot of Mount Chungnan.
Waniek. Sleepless Nights.
Warren, R. Acquaintance with Time in Early Autumn.
Vermont Ballad: Change of Season.
Warton, T. Sonnet: To the River Lodon.
Wedekind, F. Blind Youth, The.
Welch, L. Not Yet 40, My Beard is Already White.
Whitman, R. Laughing Gas.
Whittier. To My Old Schoolmaster.
Wicks, S. My Father Is Shrinking.
Wilcox, E. Friendship After Love.
Williams, C. K. Alzheimer's: The Wife.
World's Greatest Tricycle-Rider, The.
Williams, M. Love Poem with Toast.
Shrinking Lonesome Sestina, The.
Williams, W. Descent, The.
To a Man Dying on His Feet.
Wilson, K. Still Life: "Three old New Mexican men."
Wiman, C. Hearing Loss.
Winslow, P. I blink and half my life is over.
Wright, C. After Reading Tu Fu, I Go Outside to the Dwarf Orchard.
Wright, J. Youth.
Wright, J. Brother and Sisters.
I To my Brothers.
Sonnet for Christmas.
Wu of Han [or Wu Ti or Ou-ty or Liu Ch'e or Liu Ch'u]. Autumn Wind.
Wylie. Let No Charitable Hope.
Yeats. Coming of Wisdom with Time, The.
Crazy Jane Talks with the Bishop.
Folly of Being Comforted, The.
Lamentation of the Old Pensioner, The (1890 version).
Men Improve with the Years.
Wild Swans at Coole, The.
Yevtushenko [or Evtushenko]. At Forty.
Yi Hyangji. Sea, The: "Ladies, why don't you lift a stone."
Yujŏng. Sitting at Night at an Old Inn in Silla.
See also **Middle Age; Old Age**

Agnosticism and Agnostics
Abrahams, L. Agnostic's funeral prayer.
Burris. On Living with a Fat Woman in Heaven.
Hardy, T. Impercipient, The.
O'Driscoll, D. Missing God.
Pobo, K. Grand Canyon.
See also **Doubt**

Agriculture
Jordan, J. Notes on the Peanut.

Roscoe, W. To the Harvest Moon.
Unknown. Big rats! Big rats!
Chen-gong: King's Serfs.
Extensive the lands flanking that southern mountain.
In the seventh month, declining is the Fire Star.
One who first gave birth to our people, The.
Zai-shan: Weed Grass.
See also **Farming and Farmers**

AIDS
Addonizio. Conversation in Woodside.
Akiwumi, V. Different Ones #6—Future Possibilities (An Aids Soliloquy).
Alarcon, F. Blues del SIDA / AIDS Blues.
Campo. Allegory.
Her Final Show.
Towards Curing AIDS.
Carruth, H. Your dream: / The letters HIV appear.
Chin, J. Undetectable.
Conway, J. Marlo Thomas in Seven Parts and Epilogue.
Weight Belt.
Cording. Elegy for John, My Student Dead of AIDS.
Corn. Long-Distance Call to Gregg, Who Lived with AIDS as Long as He Could.
Dixon, M. Heartbeats.
DJ Renegade. Father and Son.
Doty, M. Fog.
New Dog.
Tiara.
Drake, N. Very Rich Hours, The.
Elmslie, K. Bare Bones.
Fries, K. I bed next to you, I feel your heartbeat.
Who knows the precise moment when the stream.
Gates, B. Cathy.
Homeless.
Ron.
Triptych.
Gilbert, S. Island of Lost Tears, The.
Gunn, T. In the Post Office.
J Car, The.
Lament: "Your dying was a difficult enterprise."
Man With Night Sweats, The.
Missing, The.
Reassurance, The.
Still Life: "I shall not soon forget."
Terminal.
Hacker, M. Dusk: July.
Hall, H. Palmer. Romeo Is Dead.
Hamer. Different Strokes Bar, San Francisco, The.
Healy, E. Louganis.
Hemphill. Better Days.
Holland, W. Journal of the Plague Years, A.
Howard Jr., W. Memorial Drive.
Howard, R. Man Who Beat Up Homosexuals Reported to Have AIDS Virus.
Larkin, J. Inventory.
Lassell. How to Watch Your Brother Die.
Kissing Ramén.
Sunset Stripping: Visiting L.A.
Three Poems.
Liu, T. Thoreau.
Moore, H. Edward.
Murphy, J. 13.
Neely, L. Multiple Assaults.
Powell, D. A. *Tall and* thin *and young and lovely the* michael with kaposi's sarcoma *goes walking.*
Reynolds, C. Worst of it, The.
Schwartz, R. L. AIDS Education, Seventh Grade.
Grief.
Scott, M. Cave of AIDS, The.
Stein, K. It Didn't Begin with Horned Owls Hooting at Noon.
Vando. Blanca's Red Lips.
Voisine, Connie. Blue Hat.
Waniek. Sacrament of Poverty, The.
Wiese, B. Everyone Who Wants to Work Can.
Williams, M. Thinking about Bill, Dead of AIDS.

Woods, D. Prescription.
Wunderlich, M. Given in Person Only.

Air
Ashbery, J. Melodic Trains.
Atwood. Variation on the Word *Sleep*.
Coates, F. Unconquered Air, The.
Davies, S. Speach of Love persuading men to learn Dancing, The.
Ekelof. If You Ask Me.
If You Ask Me Where I Live.
Field. Nightfall.
Gardelle, C. Air.
Rain.
Guest, B. Roses.
Han Yong'un [or Yongwun]. I Cannot Know.
Jackson, H. Distance.
Johnson, R. Beam 7.
Juana Inés de la Cruz. Since Love is shivering.
Kinzie. In air hard as sand.
Kleinzahler. Poetics.
Lassaw-Paljor, Denise. Counting Breaths.
Levin, P. Citizens and Sky.
Lux. Poem in Thanks.
Maiden. Air.
Mörling, M. For F. M. Who Did Not Get Killed Yesterday on 57th Street.
Nemes Nagy. Between.
Polkowski. World is Only Air, The.
Raine, K. Air.
Robinson, E. For Karen.
Sanchez, S. Haiku: "Was it yesterday".
Serge. Asphyxiated Man, The.
Strand. Marriage, The.
Taylor, A. Air.
Zolynas. Same Air, The.

Air Plants
Crane, H. Air Plant, The.

Air Travel
Alexie. Airplane.
Alexopoulos. Night Flight.
Appleman, P. Landing Pattern.
Beckman, J. Ode to the Air Traffic Controller.
Birney. Twenty-third Flight.
Blumenthal, M. Over Ohio.
Cahn, S. Come Fly with Me.
Cardiff. It has something to do with final words.
Ciardi, J. Back through the Looking Glass to This Side.
Collins, B. Passengers.
Dove, R. Vacation.
Dunn, S. On Hearing the Airlines Will Use a Psychological Profile to Catch Potential Skyjackers.
Grant, J. Planes Landing.
Harjo, J. White Bear.
Hoagland, T. Reading *Moby-Dick* at 30,000 Feet.
Hooper, P. At the Terminal.
Kooser. Flying at Night.
Kumin, M. Our Ground Time Here Will Be Brief.
Leahy, Anna. History of Air Travel, A.
Lenfestey, James P. Landing.
Lustig, Dana Lisa. Plane song.
Makuck. Jet Lag.
McHugh, H. 20-200 on 737.
Meek, Sandra. Windowseat.
Nash, O. Unwinged Ones, The.
Olds, S. Topography.
Rexroth, K. Coming.
Scott, F. Trans Canada.
Stanley, G. Poem wrestles you, The.
Swenson, M. Flying Home from Utah.
Untermeyer, L. Imperial Airways.
Voznesensky [or Voznesenskii]. From the Window of a Plane.
Warren, R. 1. Over Prairie.
Webb, C. Coach Class Seats.
Whitman, R. Hearing a Mozart Duo at 36,000 Feet.
Winters, Y. At the San Francisco Airport.
See also **Airports; Air Warfare; Aviation and Aviators**

Air Warfare
Baker, K. Eagle Youth.

Bayliss.   Reported Missing.
Bowers, E.   Stoic, The: For Laura Von Courten.
Ciardi, J.   Journal.
Dickey, J.   Firebombing, The.
Doolittle, H.   R.A.F.
Duncan, A.   Andy-the-German Servant of Two
   Masters.
Eberhart, R.   Dam Neck, Virginia.
   Fury of Aerial Bombardment, The.
Enright, D.   As You Say.
Everson, W.   Raid, The.
Ewart.   When a Beau Goes In.
Field, E.   World War II.
Fitzgerald, R.   Pacific.
Hamod, S.   Libyan Airliner/Egyptian Acrobats/
   Israeli Air Circus [2004 version].
Jarrell, R.   Dead Wingman, The.
   Death of the Ball Turret Gunner, The.
   Eighth Air Force.
   Field Hospital, A.
   Front, A.
   Losses.
   Pilot from the Carrier, A.
   Pilots, Man Your Planes.
   Range in the Desert, The.
   Second Air Force.
Kipling, R.   R.A.F. (Aged Eighteen).
Lawrence, D. H.   Bombardment.
Lowell, R.   Bomber, The.
   Dead in Europe, The.
MacNeice.   Brother Fire.
McDonald, W.   War in Bosnia, The.
Meredith, W.   Simile: "As when a heavy bomber
   in the cloud."
Nemerov.   IFF.
   Models.
   Night Operations, Coastal Command RAF.
   War in the Air, The.
Nims, J.   Shot Down at Night.
Receveur.   Cobra Pilot.
Rodgers, W.   Raider, The.
Rolfe, E.   City of Anguish.
Sarton, M.   Navigator: "This lazy prince of
   tennis balls and lutes."
Shapiro, H.   Battle Report.
Shinkichi Takahashi.   Wood in Sound, A.
Simpson, L.   On the Ledge.
Sitwell, D.   Still Falls the Rain.
Spender, S.   Air Raid Across the Bay at
   Plymouth.
   Thoughts During an Air Raid.
Stepanova, M.   Airman.
Stephens, M.   Hooters.
Tate, A.   Ode to Our Young Pro-consuls of the
   Air.
Thomas, D.   Ceremony after a Fire Raid.
   Refusal to Mourn the Death, by Fire, of a Child
   in London, A.
Unknown.   Little Friend.
   Pilot's Psalm, The.
Webb, F.   Gunner, The.
Yeats.   Irish Airman Foresees His Death, An.
   Reprisals.
See also **Aviation and Aviators; Bombs and
Bombing**
Airline Stewardesses
Dickey, J.   Falling.
Airplane Crashes
Appleman, P.   Landing Pattern.
Bang, M.   Crossed-Over, Fiend-Snitched, X-ed
   Out.
Berkson, B.   Booster.
Ewart.   When a Beau Goes In.
Hall, D.   Man in the Dead Machine, The.
Hamod, S.   Libyan Airliner/Egyptian Acrobats/
   Israeli Air Circus [2004 version].
Herd.   Survivors, The.
Hugo, R.   Where We Crashed.
Jarrell, R.   Front, A.
   Pilot from the Carrier, A.
Laughlin, J.   Above the City.
Long, J.   Bermuda Triangle.
   Music's Wife.
McFall, Gardner.   Missing.
Mullen, H.   Anthropic Principle, The.
Muñoz, Charles.   Lockerbie.

Reading, P.   Life is too black as he paints it and
   "Reading's nastiness sometimes".
Robbins, R.   Women of Lockerbie, The.
Rukeyser, M.   Ceiling Unlimited.
Schwartz, R. L.   When They Know.
Stainer.   Bleaklow.
Walker, J.   Flt #4372.
Airplanes
Applewhite.   Flight Instructor.
Babcock, H.   Leaf from a Log Book, A.
Bawer.   View from an Airplane at Night, over
   California, The.
Berryman.   Henry sats in de bar and was odd.
Cardenal.   Lights.
Chamberlain, K.   Airlift.
Clarke, G.   No Hands.
Collom.   3-4-00.
Dater, Tony.   Thunderbirds.
Dauer.   Falling.
Deanovich.   Zombie Jet.
Delano, P. L.   Sonnet for an SR-71.
Duncan, A.   Martyrdom and Triumph of Sergei
   Korolev.
Duran, J.   Mere Pleasure of Flying, The.
Enzensberger, H.   In Memory of Sir Hiram
   Maxim (1840–1916).
Ferlinghetti, L.   History of the Airplane.
Frost, R.   Wrights' Biplane, The.
Gach, G.   Inflight.
Gilkes, D.   Thoughts from a 747.
Graham, J.   What the End Is For.
Gunn, T.   Small Plane in Kansas.
Hall, D.   Old Pilot, The.
Herbert, W.   Looking Up from Aeroplanes.
Hugo, R.   Flying, Reflying, Farming.
Hummer, T.   Plate Glass.
Jacobs, B.   Friendly Skies.
Kenyon, J.   At a Motel near O'Hare Airport.
Koch, K.   Airplane Betty in Holland.
Luterman, A.   On Not Flying to Hawaii.
McCabe, C.   Postcard from London, A.
Meredith, C.   Jets.
Meredith, W.   Airman's Virtue.
   Navy Field.
Morrice, K.   Crossing the Alps.
   To a Shy Girl at a Party.
O'Donoghue, B.   Apparition, The.
Olin.   Vanishing Point.
Oppen.   Flight: "Outside the porthole life, or
   what is."
Ortiz.   San Diego Poem, A: January-February
   1973.
Ostroff.   Sparrows at the Airport, The.
Pack, R.   Black Hole, The.
Péret.   Hello.
Pudjipangu.   Aeroplane.
Quade, Mary.   Air Show: F-16s above
   Cleveland.
Rankine.   New Windows.
Rawson, J.   Border, The ("Leaping from the
   eucalyptus branch, the wild desert pigs.").
Revard.   Dragon-Watching in St. Louis.
Reverdy.   Adieu.
Rolfe, E.   About Eyes.
Salaam.   Flying over America.
Sandburg, C.   Bas-Relief.
Snyder, G.   No Shadow.
Snyder, R.   Aging Poet, on a Reading Trip to
   Dayton, Visits the Air Force Museum and
   Discovers There a Plane He Once Flew, The.
Sullivan, A.   Jet Plane.
Thomas, R. S.   Navigation.
Tranter.   Lufthansa.
Unknown.   Pilot's Psalm, The.
   Twats in the Ops Room.
Updike.   Air Show.
Voss, F.   Making America Strong.
Waniek.   Porter.
Weigl.   Sailing to Bien Hoa.
Williams, G.   Jet Planes.
Williamson, G.   Up in the Air.
Young, K.   Central Standard Time.
See also **Aviation and Aviators**
Airports
Appleman, P.   Landing Pattern.
Fickert.   Bad Weather at the Airport.

Hobson, G.   Buffalo Poem #1.
Kramer, A.   Kennedy Airport.
McCarthy, E.   Dulles Airport.
Mead, J.   La Guardia, the Story.
Merwin.   Airport.
Moore, L.   Airport.
Nemerov.   At the Airport.
Richie, E.   Airports of the World.
Shinkichi Takahashi.   Snowy Sky.
Winters, Y.   At the San Francisco Airport.
See also **Air Travel**
Akhmatova, Anna
Balaban.   Anna Akhmatova Spends the Night on
   Miami Beach.
Barskova, P.   Evening at Tsarskoe Selo.
Cheney-Coker.   Letter to a Tormented
   Playwright.
Chimombo.   Messengers, The.
Friesen, P.   Anna.
Khlebnikov, V.   Lonely Masquerader.
Mooney, M.   Anna Akhmatova's Funeral.
Nortje.   Asseverations.
Różewicz.   Proofs.
Sedakova.   In Memory of a Poet.
Tsvetayeva [*or* Tsvetaeva].   . . . In my
   melodious city cupolas burn.
Alabama (state)
Berlin.   When the Midnight Choo-Choo Leaves
   for Alabam'.
Brecht, B.   Alabama Song.
Hairston.   Alabama Bus.
Hughes, L.   Croon.
   Daybreak in Alabama.
Jeffers, H.   Tuscaloosa: Riversong.
Parish.   Stars Fell on Alabama.
Weatherly, T.   First Monday Scottsboro
   Alabama.
Williams, M.   Plain.
York, Jake Adam.   Walt Whitman in Alabama.
Alamo
Bradley, Jerry.   For a Texas Beauty.
Espada.   Other Alamo, The.
Harrigan, S.   Poem Of Adulthood, A.
Hinojosa, Rolando.   Eighth Army at the
   Chongchon, The.
Lind, Michael.   Now Crockett said, "You
   gentlemen are free".
Miller, J.   Defense of the Alamo, The.
Newton, Violette.   Witness, Susanna Dickinson,
   The.
Reposa, Carol Coffee.   Alamo Plaza at Night.
Alaska
Cendrars.   Aleutian Islands.
Corn.   Walrus Tusk from Alaska, A.
Fordham.   Alaska.
Haines, J.   Train Stops at Healy Fork, The.
Harjo, J.   Anchorage.
Paljor, N.   Cars stuck in the snow.
Reed, I.   On the Fourth of July in Sitka,
   1982.
Rose.   Alaskan Fragments June 1981—Summer
   Solstice.
Unknown.   Song of the Alaskero.
Albatrosses
Baudelaire.   Albatross, The.
   Albatross, The.
Coleridge, S.   Rime of the Ancient Mariner
   (1817 version).
   Rime of the Ancient Mariner, The (1798
   version).
Masefield.   Sea Change.
Alberta, Canada
Francis, M.   Sitting with My Uncle.
Albinos
Belieu.   Legend of the Albino Farm.
Alcatraz
Kaufman, B.   No More Jazz at Alcatraz.
Alchemy and Alchemists
Bogan, L.   Alchemist, The.
Chubb, T.   Merlin.
Clifton, L.   Quilting.
Donne.   Love's Alchemy [*or* Alchemie].
Jonson, B.   To Alchemists.
Meyer, T.   Uranium Ore.
Simic.   Lives of Alchemists, The.

Poem without a Title.
Wilder, Thornton. Sentences.

Alcohol
Beckman, J. Canals, The. The liquor coming through.
Berrigan, T. Waterloo Sunset.
Byrd, Bobby. Things You Can't Do in Albuquerque or Santa Fe, #11.
Chang Yüeh. Composition in Drunkenness.
Cisneros, S. Black Lace Bra Kind of Woman.
Crawford, R. Scotch Broth.
Fei Ma. Drunkard, A.
Gardiner, S. Brought Up.
Gizzi, M. Versailles.
Greenberg, A. Letters from Camp.
Hicok. Dropping the Euphemism.
Li Po. Best of Life Is But, The.
Drinking with a Friend, Among the Mountains.
Take Wine.
McDaniel, J. First One, The.
Molloy, D. First Blood.
Mullen, H. Drinking Mojitos in Cuba Libre.
Olin. Don't Let Me Eat Dinner.
Padgett, R. Waterloo Sunset.
Reading, P. These are the days of the horrible headlines.
Rodefer. Stewed and Fraught with Birds.
St. John, D. Gin.
Shuford. Celebration.
Starbuck, G. Working Habits.
Suk Mumyong. After Getting Drunk in a Hermitage on Chiri Mountain.
Valentine, J. American River Sky Alcohol Father.
Wang Ji. To a Kill-Joy.
Written on the Tavern Wall.
Waters, M. Cognac.
Wheatley, D. Moonshine.
Whitbread. Alcohol Question, The.

Alcoholism and Alcoholics
Addonizio. Beer. Milk. The Dog. My Old Man.
Ai. I Can't Get Started.
Anderson, D. Itinerary.
Anstett. Shift.
Becker, R. Riding Lesson.
Berryman. Alcoholic in the 3rd Week of the 3rd Treatment, The.
Dry Eleven Months.
5th Tuesday.
4th Weekend.
Group.
Phase Four.
Bradford, E. His Mother Drinks.
Browne, S. First Drink.
Burkard. How I Shaded the Book.
Sober Ghost.
White City, A: "In the dream, N. is singing "a white city." A teacher he had is wearing a girdle."
Carver, R. Alcohol.
Luck.
NyQuil.
Compton, W. Alley Blues.
Constantine, D. Pity the Drunks.
Coulehan, J. I'm Gonna Slap Those Doctors.
Cunningham, J. Interview with Doctor Drink.
Cuthand, B. She Ties Her Bandanna.
Daniels, J. Hard-Boiled Egg.
Davitt. Shortening the Road.
Dunn, S. On the Death of a Colleague.
Erdrich. Family Reunion.
Eubulus. Benefits and Abuse of Alcohol, The.
Ewart. Sonnet: The Last Things.
Fennelly. Asked for a Happy Memory of Her Father, She Recalls Wrigley Field.
Hafiz, K [or Hafez]. Light of my eyes, there is something to be said.
Harjo, J. Drowning Horses.
Hass, R. Bookbuying in the Tenderloin.
World as Will and Representation, The.
Haug. Tennessee Waltz, The.
Heaney, S. Casualty.
Hirsch, E. Two Suffering Men.
Howe, M. Mother, The.
Larkin, J. Co-alcoholic.
Genealogy.

Good-Bye.
Loesser. Boys in the Backroom, The.
Logau. Drunkenness.
Louis, A. Something About Being an Indian.
Lux. Loudmouth Soup.
MacIntyre, T. Yellow Bittern, The.
Mayer, B. Booze Turns Men into Women.
McDonald, W. I Still Can't Say the Word.
Meredith, W. John and Anne.
Nash, O. Reflections on Ice-breaking.
Which the Chicken, Which the Egg?
Nickelson, C. Three men.
Notley. Jack Would Speak Through the Imperfect Medium of Alice.
Oktavi. At Five.
Olds, S. Waste Sonata.
Olinka, S. Bird of Death.
Parker, A. Another Poem about the Vandals.
Peirce. Alcoholic's Son at Ten, The.
Near Burning.
Rhodes, M. His.
Who Knew.
Roberts, L. Assignment, The.
Roethke. My Papa's Waltz.
Shen Chou. Taoist Huang Has Died of Alcoholism, The.
Smith, W. Good Man's Fate, A.
Someck, R. Ballad of alcohol valley, The.
Starbuck, G. Working Habits.
Stepanova, M. Airman.
Stone, J. Confabulation.
Townsend, A. Mardi Gras Premortem.
Trethewey, N. Photograph of a Bawd Drinking Raleigh Rye.
Trinidad. Tom used spit for lubricant and fucked me.
Troupe. River Town Packin House Blues.
Valentine, J. Drinker's Wife Writes Back, The.
Villa, D. Then if I think about it.
Walker, F. X. Crooked Afro.
Wang Ji. Drinking Alone.
Wetzsteon. Drinks in the Town Square.
Wright, J. Metho Drinker.
See also **Drunkards**

Ale
Blake, W. Little Vagabond, The.
Stevenson, W. *et al.* Back and Side Go Bare, Go Bare.
Unknown. Bring Us In Good Ale.
There was a little man.

Alexander the Great, King of Macedon
Akhmatova, A. Alexander at Thebes.
Dryden, J. Alexander's Feast; or, The Power of Music [or Musique].
Dugan, A. How We Heard the Name.
Flecker, J. Santorin.
Killigrew, A. Alexandreis.
Lee, N. Nay, *Clytus*, you that cou'd advise—.
Moore, R. Ripeness Is Rapid.

Alexandria, Egypt
Weiss, T. Fire at Alexandria, The.

Algeria
al-Mala'ika, N. Jamilah and Us.

Alhambra, The
Ibn Zumruk, M. Question the horizon adorned by the bright stars, for I have entrusted a description of my condition to it.

Ali, Muhammad
Alexander, E. Narrative: Ali.
Davis, H. Ali, Bomaye.
Komunyakaa, Y. Once the Dream Begins.

Alice in Wonderland
Ferlinghetti, L. I am waiting for my case to come up.
Hollander, J. For "Fiddle-De-De".
Tate, A. Last Days of Alice.
White, L. Emetic.

Alienation
al-Braikan, M. Possessed, The.
Allen, P. Kopis'taya.
Anderson, L. Dog Show.
Arnold, M. Buried Life, The.
Bachmann. Exile.
Baraka, I. Invention of Comics, The.
Berryman. Traveller [or Traveler], The.

Bly, R. Snowbanks North of the House.
Cagnone, N. Fifth Book: On Limitation.
Celan. Shibboleth.
Christopher. Far from Home.
Cisneros, A. Hampton Court.
Clare, J. I Am.
Clarke, G. Baby-Sitting.
Creeley. Form of Women, A.
Croft, J. D-Zug.
Dickinson, E. Much Madness is divinest Sense.
Duncan, R. Passage over Water.
Eliot, T. S. Burnt Norton.
Gerontion.
Journey of the Magi.
Love Song of J. Alfred Prufrock, The.
Portrait of a Lady.
Rhapsody on a Windy Night.
Ellis, T. T.A.P.O.A.F.O.M.
Emerson, R. Blight.
Intellect.
Esteban, Claude. Once Evening's Fallen.
Fearing. Dirge: "1-2-3 was the number he played but today the number came 3-2-1."
Forbes, C. Blue Monday.
Fuller, R. Sonnet: "Crumbled rock of London is dripping under, The."
Ginsberg, A. America: "America I've given you all and now I'm nothing."
Glück, R. Invaders from Mars.
Hall, D. Exile.
Harry, J. Honesty-Stones.
Hayden, R. Soledad.
Heaney, S. Guttural Muse, The.
Hernton, C. Poem: "And I went up to that chandeliered place."
Hoagland, T. Reading *Moby-Dick* at 30,000 Feet.
Hongo. Legend, The.
Hopkins, G. To Seem the Stranger.
Housman. Laws of God, the Laws of Man, The.
Komunyakaa, Y. Troubling the Water.
Kuznetsova, I. Seagull shrilly in my head, A.
Litvak, S. I catch the smell of beans.
Lopez, T. Dauntless the slug-horn to my lips I set.
Lovecraft. Alienation.
Lowell, A. Dissonance.
Lowell, J. Street, The.
Madhubuti. Empty Warriors.
'Marnia. I Must be Able to Protect You.
McDonald, R. Incident in Transylvania.
McKay, C. Outcast.
Mistral, G. Stranger, The.
Nelson, M. Wish Fulfillment.
Nortje. All hungers pass away.
Oppen. Anniversary Poem.
I cannot even now.
Now in the helicopters the casual will.
Whether, as the intensity of seeing increases, one's distance from Them, the people , does not also increase.
Paulin. Ulster Unionist Walks the Streets of London, An.
Piñero. This Is Not the Place Where I was Born.
Pinsky. Poem about People.
Pound, E. In a Station of the Metro.
Tea-rose tea-gown, etc., The.
Raffalovich, M. A. Sonnet 120.
World Well Lost 4, The.
Reed, I. Dualism in ralph ellison's invisible man.
Reid, A. Figures on the Frieze, The.
Reznikoff. I walked through the lonely marsh.
Rich, A. Usonian Journals 2000.
Rilke. Panther, The.
Robinson, E. Mr Flood's Party.
Rodriguez, L. We Never Stopped Crossing Borders.
Rukeyser, M. Effort at Speech between Two People.
Samaras, N. Farasa.
Schnackenberg. Paperweight, The.
Seferis. Word for Summer, A.
Senghor. To New York.
Shapiro, K. My Grandmother.

Travelogue for Exiles.
Sharp, S.   Tribal Marks.
Solomon, M.   Comment on My Host, A.
Stanton, M.   Space.
Stevens, W.   Anglais Mort à Florence.
Tennyson, A.   I will not shut me from my kind.
Tomlinson, C.   Mr. Brodsky.
Tranter.   Great Artist Reconsiders the Homeric
   Simile, The.
Unknown.   Chinook Songs.
   Oxaitoq's Song.
   Thus feverish fancies floated in my brain.
Warren, R.   To a Face in a Crowd.
Warsh.   Enmeshment.
Wordsworth, W.   World Is Too Much with Us,
   The.
Wright, C.   Stone Canyon Nocturne.

Aliens
Azzawi, F.   On a Dying Planet.
Campo.   X Files, The.
Carruth, H.   Time, Place, and Parenthood.
Conoley, G.   World, The: "It was just a gas
   station. It was not spectacular carnage."
Delanty.   Alien, The.
Jones, Daryl E.   Triangulation.
Kinsella, J.   Visitant Eclogue.
Kocot, N.   Bad Aliens.
Koertge.   Foolish Earthlings.
McMillan, H.   X Files, The: Bonnybridge,
   October '95.
Michaux.   Future.
Morgan, E.   First Men on Mercury, The.
Nuriddin, J. M.   Children of the Future.
Pugh.   'Do you think we'll ever get to see Earth,
   sir?'.
Raine, C.   Martian Sends a Postcard Home, A.
Tate, J.   I Know Someone from Another World.
Violi.   Harold and Imogene.

All Saints' Day [Day of the Dead]
Jones, P.   All Saints Day, 2001.

All Souls' Day
Atkins, R.   Lisbon.
Bidgood.   All Souls'.
Knoepfle.   Dark Spaces: Thoughts on All Souls
   Day.

All Souls' Night
Glück, L.   All Hallows.

Allende, Salvador
Thompon, E.   Homage to Salvador Allende.

Alligators
Bartolomé, E.   Intermedio con cinco cocodrilos.
   Intermezzo with Five Crocodiles.
Bly, R.   Day We Visited New Orleans, The.
Nash, O.   Purist, The.
"Pindar.".   Pups and the Alligator, The.
Santos Chocano.   Dream of the Caiman, The.
See also **Crocodiles**

Almanacs
Bishop, E.   Sestina: "September rain falls on the
   house."
Unknown.   In the seventh month, declining is
   the Fire Star.

Almond Trees and Almonds
Lawrence, D. H.   Bare Almond-Trees.

Alone in Death
De Kok.   My father would not show us.
   Still life: "Woman is wild, The."
Jensma.   Till no one.
Marcus, A.   Cleopatra.
Marennikova, K.   Don't let me leave you, I may
   die.
Moore, J.   Hic Finis Rapto 1.
O'Connor, U.   Oscar Wilde.
Unknown.   Social Band, The.

Alphabet
Caesar.   Animal Crackers in My Soup.
Crase.   Continent as the Letter M, The.
Diego, G.   Julio Campal ("We were walking to
   your funeral, eleven friends.").
Heaney, S.   Alphabets.
Hughes, Audrey.   Logocyclegram.
Jandl, E.   Big e, The.
Kalina, R.   Cabalistic Rabbis, The.
Kekova.   Running water is cold, the river from
   Eden flows east.

Koehler, T.   Animal Crackers in My Soup.
Kostelanetz.   A / ABA.
Page, P.   Curious concept—*afterwards*, A.
Peacock, M.   Spell, The.
Rakosi.   ZZZZZ.
Rimbaud, A.   Vowels.
   Voyelles.
Roberts, M.   Wireless.
Royet-Journoud.   I.E.
Shapiro, K.   Alphabet, The.
Tritica, J.   Not Masterpieces, Planting
   Astonishments.
Winter, M.   That Is the Way.

Alphabet Poems
Coward.   A. Stands for Absolutely Anything.
Disch.   Abecedary.
   Zewhyexary.
Humphries, B.   Edna's Alphabet.
McGrath, C.   Xena, Warrior Princess.
McLucas, L.   Graph.
Nemerov.   Primer of the Daily Round, A.
Pinsky.   ABC.
Unknown.   Alphabet.

Alps
Bunting.   On the Fly-Leaf of Pound's Cantos.
Byron, G.   Manfred.
Coleridge, S.   Hymn before Sunrise, in the Vale
   of Chamouni.
Dickinson, E.   Our lives are Swiss.
Italicus.   Memories of past struggles were
   expelled by fear.
Meynell, A.   Watershed, The.
Morrice, K.   Crossing the Alps.
   To a Shy Girl at a Party.
Radcliffe, A.   Storied Sonnet.

Alsace, France
Wilbur, R.   First Snow in Alsace.

Altar Boys
Ríos, A.   Purpose of Altar Boys, The.

Altars
Chin.   Altar.
Heaney, S.   Westering.
Herbert, G.   Altar, The.
Lampadius.   As a symbol.
Nossis.   When we go to the temple, let's see
   Aphrodite's.
Sappho.   Full moon was rising, The.
Sobin, B.   On the Nature of the Iconic.
Taylor, B.   Goblet, The.
Taylor, E.   Lord with thine Altars Fire, mine
   Inward man.
   Meditation. Heb. 13.10. We[e] have an Altar.

Alumni
Wilson, E.   Disloyal Lines to an Alumnus.

Alzheimer's
Hicok.   Alzheimer's.
Reitenauer, Vicki L.   Wife Of.
Williams, C. K.   Alzheimer's: The Wife.

Amaryllis (mythology)
Campion, T.   I Care Not for These Ladies.

Amazon Rain Forest
Ashbery, J.   Template, The.

Amazons
Coleridge, M.   White Women, The.
Hartmann, S.   Cyanogen Seas Are Surging.
Killigrew, A.   Alexandreis.
Melinno.   Hail, Roma, daughter of Ares.

Ambition
Ammons.   Play.
Attlee.   Few thought he was even a starter.
Beranová, J.   Mother's Mark.
Berger, B.   Ambition.
Bly, R.   Watering the Horse.
Brock-Broido.   One Thousand Days, The.
Budbill.   Like Smoke from Our Campfire.
Cary, A.   West Country, The.
Clampitt.   Cormorant in Its Element, The.
Clewell.   Going Wrong in the House of
   Neptune.
Clifton, L.   Climbing.
   We are running.
Cornish, S.   Generations 2.
Cunningham, J.   For My Contemporaries.
Davies, W. H.   Ambition.
Gladding.   Fisherman's Wife, The.

Gumilyov [*or* Gumiliov *or* Gumilev].
   Fragments 1920–1921.
Gurney, I.   Old Dreams.
Han Yü.   To Hou Xi.
Hsieh T'iao.   Looking at the Morning Rain.
Hughes, T.   Other, The.
Johnson, M.   Ambition.
Longfellow, H.   Mezzo Cammin.
Mitchell, K.   Monster, The.
Morrissey, S.   Post Mortem.
Nantembo.   On New Year's Day.
Parker, D.   Red Dress, The.
Pietri.   Title of This Poem Was Lost, The.
Pollarolo, G.   S.L.A.M.
Ray, H.   Ambition.
Roth, F.   Just only alive.
Ryokan.   Without a jot of ambition left.
Sahagún, C.   Life in the Provinces.
Sidney.   Sonnet 27: "Because I oft, in dark
   abstracted guise."
Unknown.   Man's ambition is to conquer the
   world, A.
Waniek.   Sleepless Nights.
Warren, R.   He Was Formidable.
Whalen, P.   Waiting for Claude.
Whitman, W.   Hast Never Come to Thee an
   Hour.
Wordsworth, W.   Column Intended by
   Buonaparte for a Triumphal Edifice in Milan,
   Now Lying by the Way-Side in the Simplon
   Pass, The.
Wright, J.   January, Love, and the Galician.

Ambulances
Larkin, P.   Ambulances.
Moore, L.   Tanka.

America
Ai.   Blue Suede Shoes.
   More.
Alexie.   Vision (2).
Allen, P.   Zen Americana.
Appleman, P.   Peace with Honor.
Ashbery, J.   One Thing That Can Save America,
   The.
   Pyrography.
Awoonor.   America.
   American Memory of Africa, An.
   On Having Been an Experimental Sacred Cow
      for Four Years, and a Token African on
      Faculty.
Baca.   How We Carry Ourselves.
Balaban.   After Our War.
Baraka, I.   Das Kapital.
   Hymn for Lanie Poo.
   Nation Is Like Ouselves, The.
   Three Modes of History and Culture.
Baraka, R.   American Poetry.
Baratier, D.   Estrella's Prophecies #18.
Barlow, J.   Columbiad, The.
   From slavery then your rising realms to save.
   From sultry Mobile's gulf-indented shore.
Bates, K.   America the Beautiful.
Behrle.   Charm of the Highway Strip, The.
Bell, J.   Beautiful American Poem, The.
Benét, R. *et al.*   Daniel Boone.
Benét, S.   American Names.
   Ballad of William Sycamore, The.
   Daniel Boone.
Berkeley, G.   On the Prospect of Planting Arts
   and Learning in America.
Berrigan, A.   Drugged and Hooded into a Prose
   Poem.
Berrigan, D.   My Name.
Berryman.   American Lights, Seen from Off
   Abroad.
Bevington, H.   Mrs. Trollope in America.
Bierce.   Rational Anthem, A.
Blake, W.   Visions of the Daughters of Albion.
Bly, R.   After the Industrial Revolution, All
   Things Happen at Once.
   Great Society, The.
Bobyshev.   Other World, The.
Brathwaite, E.   Colombe.
Bromige.   Eastward Ho! A Succession.
Brook, D.   April 27, 1994.
Brown, M.   Survival Motion: Notice.
Bryant, W.   Not Yet.

Byrd, B. Top Stories.
Campo. Battle Hymn of the Republic, The.
Cardenal. Mosquito Kingdom.
Cary, A. West Country, The.
Cary, P. Homes for All.
Cheney-Coker. Analysis.
Cherry, K. Forecast.
Chin. How I Got That Name.
We Are Americans Now, We Live in the Tundra.
Chrystos. I Have Not Signed a Treaty with the United States Government.
Ciardi, J. Box Comes Home, A.
Clover, J. Ceriserie.
Cohan. You're a Grand Old Flag.
Cole, F. America™.
Comden, B. Conga.
Cook, E. Sot-Weed Factor, The.
Costanzo. Everything You Own.
Jeane Dixon's America.
Creeley. America.
Cummings, E. E. Next to of course god america i.
O pr / gress verily thou art m.
Poem, or Beauty Hurts Mr. Vinal.
Darío, R. To Roosevelt.
Davidson, L. America.
Davidson, M. Sensation Type and His Friends, The.
Davis, C. Displaced Person.
Davis, L. Mown Lawn, A.
Dickinson, E. Union.
Djanikian. In the Elementary School Choir.
When I First Saw Snow.
Doina, A. Roof over far away.
Donovan, K. You Meet Yourself.
Drake, J. To a Friend.
DuBois, W. My Country 'Tis of Thee.
Dumas, H. America.
Zebra Goes Wild Where the Sidewalk Ends, The.
Dylan. Lonesome Death of Hattie Carroll, The.
Etter. Green-Eyed Boy after Reading Whitman and Sandburg.
Ferlinghetti, L. I am waiting for my case to come up.
Starting from San Francisco.
Figueroa, J. Cowboynomics.
Finnell. Over *Voice of America*.
Follen, E. For the Fourth of July.
Freneau. On the Emigration to America [and Peopling the Western Country].
Frost, R. America Is Hard to See.
Gift Outright, The.
Fuhrman, J. How Many More Minutes Until We Can Devour Our Breached Contract?
Gibbons, R. American Trains.
Gilmore, B. Bow to Allah.
Ginsberg, A. America: "America I've given you all and now I'm nothing."
Supermarket in California, A.
Who Runs America?
Glazier, L. On TV.
Goll, I. Lackawanna Elegy.
Green, A. Conga.
Greenwald, T. Coordinating cities gulls still gull, and, arms binged with wine, as wine.
Grenier. Wrath to Sadness.
Guignard, M. One morning just like that they arrive.
Guillén, N. National Police Headquarters.
Hagedorn, J. Filipino Boogie.
Hardy, T. On an Invitation to the United States.
Harms. Tomorrow, We'll Dance in America.
Harper, M. American History.
Hayden, R. [American Journal].
Hayes, T. Harryette Mullen Lecture on the American Dream.
Healy, E. From Los Angeles Looking South.
Herbert, G. Religion stands on tip-toe in our land.
Hernández Cruz. Areyto.
It's Miller Time.
Herrera. Cherry Bowl with Blue Revolver: Neo-American Landscape.
Dream of Christopher Columbus, The.

Poetry of America, The.
When He Believed Himself to Be a Young Girl Lifting the Skin of the Water.
Hirsch, E. Edward Hopper and the House by the Railroad.
Holmes, J. Map of My Country.
Hoover, P. American Heaven.
Howe, J. Battle Hymn [or Battle-Hymn] of the Republic, The.
Howe, S. Thorow.
Hughes, L. American Heartbreak.
I, Too.
Let America Be America Again.
Huidobro. Cow Boy.
Hunt, L. Iterating Sonnet.
Jeffers, L. My Blackness Is the Beauty of This Land.
Jeffers, R. Shine, Perishing Republic.
Jemeni. America Eats Its Young.
Johnson, E. Joe.
Johnson, J. We To America.
Keene, J. Captain America at Home.
Key. Star-Spangled Banner, The.
Kipling, R. American, An.
White Man's Burden, The.
Kizer, C. Ashes, The.
Koethe. Morning in America.
Kumin, M. Height of the Season, The.
Larkin, P. Faith Healing.
Lauterbach. Novelist Speaks, The.
Lawrence, D. H. Evening Land, The.
Lazarus, E. 1492.
How Long?
New Colossus, The.
Levertov. Fragrance of Life, Odor of Death.
In Thai Binh (Peace) Province.
Weeping Woman.
Lim, S. Learning to Love America.
Lincoln, A. Gettysburg Address, The.
Lindsay, V. Bryan, Bryan, Bryan, Bryan.
Lloréns [or Lorens] Torres. Ugly Duckling, The.
Llwyd, Iwan. Meet me at the St Francis.
Long, R. Conspiracy, The.
Lourie. Song Embodying What I've Learned in Thirty-Five Years.
Lum. Chinese Hot Pot.
Mabuza. Tired Lizi Tired.
MacLeish. Invocation to the Social Muse.
Major, C. Water USA.
Mathews, C. Masses, The.
Mayer, B. America: "As for me, when I saw you."
McClatchy. 1871.
McClure, M. Reading Frank O'Hara in a Mexican Rainstorm.
McKay, C. America: "Although she feeds me bread of bitterness."
McLaughlin, D. Battle of Johnny Freedom, The.
Meinke. Supermarket.
Melville, H. America.
Mikhail, D. America: "Please don't ask me, America."
Urgent Call, An.
Miller, J. American Odalisque.
Miller, J. Sierras.
Mitchell, A. From Rich Uneasy America to My Friend Christopher Logue.
Moise *et al.* To Persecuted Foreigners.
Moore, M. Love in America.
Morales, A. Immigrants.
Morisseau-Leroy, F. Down with All Candidates.
Mueller, L. American Literature.
Highway Poems.
Not Only the Eskimos.
Myles, E. American Poem, An.
Nash, O. Columbus.
Nemerov. Boy with Book of Knowledge.
Neruda. America, I Do Not Call Your Name Without Hope.
Letter to Miguel Otero Silva, in Caracas.
Stone within stone, and man, where was he?
O'Grady, D. Great Horse Fair, The.
O'Hara, F. Ave Maria.
You at the Pump.

Olds, S. Topography.
Olin. Shark Wrangler Goes to Church, The.
Opoku-Agyemang. King Tut in America.
Ortiz. Travels in the South.
Padgett, R. Early Triangles.
Parkerson. Statistic.
Parra, N. Modern Times.
Paulding. Neglected Muse! of this our western clime.
Piatt, J. Farther.
To the Statue on the Capitol.
Pierman. Apparition, The.
Pietri. Intermission from Wednesday.
Prunty. To be Sung on the Fourth of July.
Ras. In the New Country.
Rekdal, Paisley. Americana.
Résil, C. Walls of Bois-de-Chene Shacks, The.
Rexroth, K. American Century, The.
Roethke. Night Journey.
Romano, R. But My Blood.
Rosten. I am immortal in Cheyenne!
We came during those years.
Rukeyser, M. Blood is Justified, The.
Book of the Dead, The.
St. John, P. We Are Going to Be Here Now.
Salaam. Flying over America.
Sallah, T. Television as God.
Sanchez, S. Morning Song and Evening Walk.
Poem for July 4, 1994.
Right On: White America.
Schulman. American Solitude.
Scott-Heron. Winter in America.
Seay. Johnny B. Goode.
Shapiro, H. National Cold Storage Company.
Shapiro, K. Manhole Covers.
Simpson, L. American Poetry.
Inner Part, The.
To the Western World.
Walt Whitman at Bear Mountain.
Smith, Rod. Ted's Head.
Smith, S. America.
Smith, W. Tempest, The.
Snyder, G. I Went into the Maverick Bar.
What Happened Here Before.
Sondheim. America.
Spacks. Assimilation, The.
Spicer, J. Book of Galahad, The.
Steensen, S. This Land.
Stein, K. Because You're American.
Steptoe. Such a Boat of Land.
Sternlieb. Right of Way.
Stevens, W. Anecdote of the Jar.
Stevenson, R. Ticonderoga: A Legend of the West Highlands.
Su, A. Address.
Supervielle. Some day shall I be.
Taylor, C. Scroll No. 2.
Thomas, L. Discovering America Again.
Thorne, T. Whatever Happened to Conway Twitty?
Tomlinson, C. Word in Edgeways, A.
Tontongi. How?
Toomer. It is Everywhere.
Troup, B. (Get Your Kicks On) Route 66!
Trowbridge, W. Stark Weather.
Unknown. America . . . then.
Toishan Song, A.
Updike. Air Show.
Upton, C. When I was very young.
Vaynshteyn [or Weinstein]. But when one stops to think back a moment.
Very. Slavery.
Voss, F. Making America Strong.
Wainwright, K. Changes.
Walcott. Blues: "Those five or six young guys."
Glory Trumpeter, The.
Gulf, The.
Upstate.
Waldman, A. On Walt Whitman's Birthday.
Weaver, A. My Father's Geography.
Webb, C. What We Believe.
Weiners. Poem for Painters, A.
Welburn. Bones and Drums.
Wheatley, P. America.
Wheelwright. Come Over and Help Us; a Rhapsody.

Whitman, W. America.
By Blue Ontario's Shore.
Chants Democratic and Native Americans: 5.
For You O Democracy.
Full of Life Now.
I celebrate myself, and sing myself.
I Hear America Singing.
Orange Buds by Mail from Florida.
Passage to India.
Prairie-Grass Dividing, The.
Respondez!
Song of Myself.
To the East and to the West.
To the States, To Identify the 16th, 17th, or 18th
Presidentiad.
Wound-Dresser, The.
Years of the Modern.
Yonnondio.
Williams, M. Of History and Hope.
Williams, W. To Elsie.
Willis, N. To Charles Roux, of Switzerland.
Winter, M. Here and There.
Woolson. Detroit River.
Yuson. Dead Center.
Yusuf, S. I too love jeans and jazz and *Treasure
Island.*
Zimmer. Eisenhower Years, The.
Zukofsky, L. Fifth Movement: Autobiography.
See also **United States**
American Revolution
Bailey, A. La Route Jackman.
Davidson, M. Landing of Rochambeau, The.
Dunbar, P. Black Samson of Brandywine.
Emerson, R. Concord Hymn.
Freneau. France aids them now, a desperate
game I play.
Hunt, L. Iterating Sonnet.
Kandel. Spring 61.
Longfellow, H. Paul Revere's Ride [The
Landlord's Tale].
Richards, L. Molly Pitcher.
Young, S. Epitaph for a Concord Boy.
Americans
Allston. America to Great Britain.
Bell, J. Beautiful American Poem, The.
Berrigan, T. London Air.
Buuck, D. Geopolitical, The.
Charara, H. Thinking American.
Chin. Composed Near the Bay Bridge (after a
wild party).
Chrystos. Okeydoekey Tribe, The.
Clay, W. On Me, the Imported Skies.
Crooker. Barbie and Ken Maximize Their
Options.
Di Prima. Les Americains.
Fagan. Charm for What Looks Like.
Ferlinghetti, L. And Pablo Neruda / that
Chilean omnivore of poetry.
Baseball Canto.
Buddha in the Woodpile, A.
Fried, E. Naturalization.
Frost, R. Gift Outright, The.
Gilfillan, M. Horseshoe.
Glazier, L. On TV.
Halliday, M. Reality U.S.A.
Hayes, T. Harryette Mullen Lecture on the
American Dream.
Hejinian. I arrived with biographical context.
Presences that constitute life do so by entering
life, The.
Hoagland, T. America.
Hughes, L. Madam's Calling Cards.
Jeffers, R. Ave Caesar.
Kipling, R. American, An.
Knight, E. Idea of Ancestry, The.
Koch, K. You Were Wearing.
Kress, L. Backyards of America.
Lawrence, D. H. English Are So Nice!, The.
Mathews, C. Masses, The.
McHugh, H. Language Lesson 1976.
McLaughlin, D. Battle of Johnny Freedom,
The.
Morris, J. Life Beside This One, The.
Oppen. Myself I Sing.
Pearson, T. Sound Check.
Pound, E. Soirée.

Ratcliff, C. So Gallantly Streaming: To the
Poet.
Rekdal, Paisley. Americana.
Roberson, E. American culture is the pot.
Rose, R. What the Japanese Perhaps Heard.
What We Heard About the Japanese.
Simic. Crepuscule with Nellie.
Simpson, L. American Classic.
Inner Part, The.
Runner, The.
Smith, W. American Primitive.
Towle. Poem: "Lead drains from your heart on
the left side, The."
Townsend, A. Persephone in America.
Very. Indian's Retort, The.
Walcott. Midsummer.
Walker, M. For My People.
Whitman, W. For You O Democracy.
I Hear America Singing.
Prairie-Grass Dividing, The.
Williams, W. Question and Answer.
Yevtushenko [*or* Evtushenko]. John Reed's
Monologue.
Yusuf, S. I too love jeans and jazz and *Treasure
Island.*
Amish, The
Baggett. Anna: *Rose of Sharon.*
Rachel: *Queen Charlotte's Crown.*
Becker, R. Why We Fear the Amish.
Brunk, J. Papaya: Lancaster County.
Dubie. Peace of Lodi, The.
Falcón, J. Burial Clothes.
Kasdorf. Dying with Amish Uncles.
Green Market, New York.
Grossdaadi's Funeral.
Owen, J. Visitation, The.
Amnesia
Berkson, B. Obvious Tradition, The.
Carver, R. Alcohol.
Hodges, Janice W. Annuals and Perennials.
Nemes Nagy. Like One Who.
Sansom, A. World is everything, The.
Amon Ra
Reed, I. I Am a Cowboy in the Boat of Ra.
Wilde, O. How subtle-secret is your smile! Did
you love none then? Nay, I know.
Amputees
Ai. Back in the World.
Calling, The.
Bierds, L. Phantom Pain.
Coulehan, J. D-Day, 1994.
Crawford, R. Downtown Sunday.
Deniz, O. Superior.
Ditzanny, R. Complicated and Innovative
Orthopedic Surgery.
Legging Behind.
Piggy-back.
Grinshpan, Y. Miner's Family, The.
Hood, T. Faithless Nelly Gray.
Khazak, Y. I saw you. / You were like scarred
stones scattered on the green.
Levertov. Weeping Woman.
MacDiarmid, H. In the Children's Hospital.
Ormond. Lament for a Leg.
Owen, W. Disabled.
Pak Sôwôn. Recurring Nightmare, A: My
Amputation.
Sarajlić, I. Luck in Sarajevo.
Sassoon, S. Does It Matter?
Shapiro, K. Leg, The.
Sutherland, Fraser. Undergoing: Jewish General
Hospital, Montreal 6:35 a.m.
Vinokurov. I don't remember him.
Volkman. I never wish to sing again as I used
to, when two new eyes could always.
Williams, L. Interruption of Flight.
Yi Sang. Poem No. 13.
Amsterdam, Netherlands
Garlick, R. Capitals.
Garrigue. Amsterdam Letter.
Ismail. Van Gogh's Ear.
Amusement Parks
Allbery. Carnies.
Berlin, E. Sea World.
Brouwer, J. Steve's Commando Paintball, San

Adriano, California.
Cooley, N. Diane Arbus, New York.
Foerster. Playland.
Laâbi Abdellatif. Tomorrow Will Be the Same
Day.
Pinsky. Ralegh's Prizes.
Prunty. Ferris Wheel, The.
Powers, S. Eagles at Dollywood.
Wynne, R. Revisionist History: Magic
Kingdom.
Anacreon
Antipater of Sidon. This is Anacreon's grave.
Here lie.
Anarchism and Anarchists
Carruth, H. Republicans? We've got a few. In
fact.
Pietri. 10th Untitled Poem.
Shelley, P. As I lay asleep in Italy.
Mask [*or* Masque] of Anarchy, The.
Ancestry and Ancestors
Acholonu. Going Home.
Adler, F. Voices Are Coming Up, The.
Akhmatova, A. Sister, I have come to take your
place.
Angelou, M. Family Affairs.
Aridjis. Letter from Mexico.
Babstock, Ken. Pragmatist.
Baehr, A. I Will Not Pretend.
Baker, H. Toward Guinea: For Larry Neal,
1937–1981.
Balaban. Riding Westward.
Barkova, A. Tatar Anguish.
Bennett, G. Heritage.
Blaeser. Certificate of Live Birth.
Blunden. Forefathers.
Boland, E. Oral Tradition, The.
Borges. Page to Commemorate Colonel Suárez,
Victor at Junín, A.
Brand, D. Canto 2: "Ancestor dirt."
No Language Is Neutral.
Brathwaite, E. Ancestors.
Brooks, G. Sundays of Satin-Legs Smith, The.
Cabico, R. Mango Poem.
Caesar, V. In 5th Grade.
Campo. Belonging.
Cariaga. Family Tree, The.
Cervantes. Archeology.
Chappell, F. Attending, The.
Chedid, A. Future and the Ancestor, The.
Chin. Barbarian Suite.
Floral Apron, The.
Citino. Sister Mary Appassionata Lectures the
Home Ec Class: The Feast.
Clinton, M. History as Trash.
Cohan. Nothing New Beneath the Sun.
Conran. Death of a Species.
Cortez, J. I See Chano Pozo.
Cullen, C. Heritage.
Davidson, D. Descending Chestnut Ridge.
de Aerenlund, C. Cuando el tecolote canta, el
Indio muere.
DeCormier-Shekejian. Grandmother.
Delmore, E. Willow.
Dixon, M. Tour Guide: La Maison des
Esclaves.
Drayton. Owen Tudor to Queen Katherine.
Drinkwater. Who Were before Me.
E'der, E. Once We Were Farmers.
Emerson, R. Forerunners.
Falcón, J. Indian Locks.
Feldman, I. Simple Outlines, Human Shapes.
Forman, R. Kin.
France de Bravo, B. Unrepentant.
Garlick, R. Ancestors.
Garnett, R. Concerning Violence.
Georges, D. Another Ode to Salt.
Gilbert, C. Sorrow Since Sitting Bull, A.
This Bridge Across.
Glancy. Hides.
González, A. Before I Could Call Myself Ángel
González.
Graves, J. What the Dead Do.
Hacker, M. Squares and Courtyards.
Hamby, B. Invention.
Hamilton, M. Woman Who Jumped, The.
Harryman. Mutations ("Face with red cavernous

gashes a things possibly living in them, A.").
Hayden, R.　Beginnings.
Heaney, S.　Digging.
Henry, J.　Another and another and another.
Hewitt, J.　Search, The.
Hinz-Penner, R.　Once, in Santa Fe.
Hostetler, S.　Woman with the Screw in Her Mouth Speaks, The.
Howe, S.　Thorow.
Hugo, V.　Boaz Asleep.
Humphreys, E.　Ancestor Worship.
Ilkov, Ani.　Dreamsters.
Jacobs, B.　After the 200th White Person Locks Her Car Door at Me.
Jess, T.　Father Country.
Kamenszain.　Mea Shearim.
Kasdorf.　Body Remembers, The.
Kennelly.　My Dark Fathers.
Kenny, M.　Joshua Clark.
Kinsella, T.　Ancestor.
Klein, A.　Heirloom.
Knight, E.　Bones of My Father, The.
Idea of Ancestry, The.
Komunyakaa, Y.　Little Man around the House.
Salt.
Ladd, M.　Tragic Mulatto is Neither, The.
Lemm, Richard.　My Class Draws a Blank on Robbie Burns.
Levertov.　Illustrious Ancestors.
Limburg, J.　Seder Night with My Ancestors.
MacEwen, G.　Letter to a Future Generation.
Manyarrows.　Lakota Sister/Cherokee Mother.
Masters, E.　Archibald Higbie.
Indignation Jones.
Mattawa.　History of My Face.
McGrath, T.　From here it is necessary to ship all bodies east.
Merkureva, V.　Grandmother of Russian Poetry: A Self-Portrait, The.
Merwin.　Unknown Forebear.
Mohiuddin, K.　Birthmark.
Montale.　I repeat I'm ready, but ready for what?
Mora.　Sonrisas.
Morales, A.　1930.
Morales.　Africa.
Muir, E.　Absent, The.
Scotland 1941.
Muldoon, P.　Ancestor, The.
Throwback, The.
Mutis.　You Are a Daughter of the Lagides.
Nolens, L.　Origins.
Place and Date.
Norris, K.　Inheritance.
Oandasan.　Song of Ancient Ways, The.
Okantah.　Black Experience, The.
Olson, C.　Chain of memory is resurrection I am a vain man, The.
Porter, C.　Land of the Lost.
Powell, D. A.　Long line of bohunks and hunyaks, A: we settled in podunk. thirteen consonants.
Press, K.　Ancestors.
Prunty.　Winter's Tale, A.
Raine, K.　Highland Graveyard.
Redmond.　Milestone: The Birth of an Ancestor.
Reid, C.　Stones and Bones.
Rimbaud, A.　Bad Blood.
Robles.　Cutting Back the Ifugao Past.
Rose.　Story Keeper.
Rukeyser, M.　Bubble of Air.
Bunk Johnson Blowing.
For My Son.
Sadeh, P.　At Nightfall, 1/27/91.
Salaam.　Funeraled Fare Well.
Name the Oldest Member of Your Family.
Sanchez, S.　Letter to Ezekiel Mphahlele.
Santos Chocano.　Manifesto, A.
Senghor.　In Memoriam.
Totem.
Sioux Oral Tradition.　Father says so—E'yayo!, The.
Smart, C.　For man is between the pinchers while his soul is shaping and purifying.
Smith, M.　Stopping to Take Notes.
Visit to the Village, A.

Soaba, R.　Looking Thru Those Eyeholes.
Song.　Heaven.
Springer, E.　Freedom Child—Tilla's Lullaby.
Storni.　Ancestral Burden.
Taylor, J.　Squire's Pew, The.
Thelwall.　To Ancestry.
Touré, A.　Summer Worlds: A Mythic Landscape.
Troupe.　Sense of Coolness, A.
Valentine, J.　Forgiveness Dream, The: Man from the Warsaw Ghetto.
Van Winckel, N.　Back When.
Various authors.　Because the wolves wrought havoc.
Your four ancestors never enjoyed peace.
Wagner, S.　A Cappella.
Wah.　Father / Mother Haibun #1.
Father / Mother Haibun #16.
Father / Mother Haibun #21.
Walker, M.　Lineage.
Waltner-Toews, D.　Roots: "Rudy Weibe, wiping the sweat from his brow."
Watkins-Cothran, E.　Beloved Ones, The.
Welburn.　Bones and Drums.
Winchilsea.　Upon My Lord Winchilsea's Converting the Mount in His Garden to a Terrace.
Woods, V.　Meaning of a Word, The.
Worley, D.　Tongues in My Mouth.
Young Bear.　Wadasa Nakamoon, Vietnam Memorial.
Zamora, D.　Lineage.

Anchorage, Alaska
Harjo, J.　Anchorage.

Anchors
Blight.　Anchor, The.
Williamson, G.　Up in the Air.

Andersen, Hans Christian
Lindsay, M.　At Hans Christian Andersen's Birthplace, Odense, Denmark.

Andrea del Sarto.
See **Sarto, Andrea del**

Andromache
Baudelaire.　Swan, The.
Homer.　Andromache's Lamentation.
Hector Returns to Troy.
To this, great Hector said.
Iremonger.　Hector.
Sappho.　Herald came, The.

Andromeda
Fay, J.　Mother of Andromeda, The.
Hopkins, G.　Andromeda.
Sappho.　Atthis, for you the thought of me has become hateful.

Anemones
Copus, J.　Sea-Polyp, The.
Harwood, G.　Sea Anemones, The.

Anesthesia
Centolella.　Woman of Three Minds, The.
Kitahara Hakushū.　Anesthesia of Red Flowers.

Angels
Agüeros.　Psalm for Distribution.
Aichinger.　Correspondence.
Alberti.　Angels of the Ruins, The.
Eviction.
Andrews, N.　That Cold Summer.
Bejerano, M.　Suddenly I was stabbed from behind.
Bingen, Hildegard von.　Antiphon for the Angels.
Blake, W.　Angel, The.
Memorable Fancy, A.
Blickstein, J.　Vision of Salt & Water: Elijah's Horn.
Bly, R.　Eel in the Cave, The.
Bontemps.　Nocturne at Bethesda.
Borges.　Houses like Angels.
Butts, A.　Skin.
Cairns, Scott.　Our Lost Angels.
Carroll.　Ode to the Angels Who Move Perpetually toward the Dayspring of Their Youth.
Carson, C.　Slate Street School.
Causley.　Angel's Song.
Christie.　In My Dream.

Cole, H.　40 Days and 40 Nights.
Countryman, L.　Going to God with the Shepherds.
Cowley, A.　Gabriel's Appearance.
Crashaw.　Flaming Heart, The.
Upon the Book and Picture of the Seraphical Saint Teresa.
Crews, J.　Mullhaven.
Dana, R.　Chanting Cherubs, The [A Group by Greenough].
David, M.　Sinner Kissed an Angel, A.
De Luca, C.　Dancing with Demons.
Di Michele, A.　About the Extinction Of.
Dickinson, E.　God's Residence.
Little East of Jordan, A.
Didsbury, P.　That Old-Time Religion.
Donne.　Air[e] and Angels.
At the round earth's imagined [or imagin'd] corners, blow.
Doyle, S.　Hell to Pay.
Dubin, A.　I'll String Along with You.
Dunn, S.　Guardian Angel, The.
Dylan.　Three Angels.
Elfyn, Menna.　Cell Angel.
Erdrich, H.　Sweeping Heaven.
Erdrich.　Angels.
Gerstler.　Bitter Angel.
Gilbert, J.　It Is Clear Why the Angels Come No More.
Goldbarth.　Talk Show, The.
Gonzalez, R.　Angels of Juárez, Mexico, The.
Graves, R.　Gardener.
Gumilyov [or Gumiliov or Gumilev].　First Canzone.
Habington.　To Castara, upon an Embrace.
Hart, K.　Dark Angel.
Hass, R.　Privilege of Being.
Hawker.　Are They Not All Ministering Spirits?
Hemans.　Vigil of Rizpah, The.
Hölderlin.　Hyperion's Song of Fate.
Schicksalslied.
Howard, R.　Vocational Guidance, with Special Reference to the Annunciation of Simone Martini.
Howitt, M.　Dying Child, The.
Huerta, D.　Baraja.
Deck of Cards.
Huidobro.　Canto I (excerpt).
Hunt, L.　Abou Ben Adhem.
Jacobsen, R.　Guardian Angel.
Jennings, E.　Annuciation, The.
Johnson, L.　Dark Angel, The.
Jones, A.　Communal Living.
Kamienska.　Annunciation.
Luke 1:26–38; In the sixth month the angel Gabriel.
Kandel.　First They Slaughtered the Angels.
Kavanagh, P.　On Raglan Road.
Keble.　Christmas Day: "What sudden blaze of song."
Kelly, B.　Imagining Their Own Hymns.
Kelly, R.　In June.
Khodasevich.　Music.
Killeen, G.　My Father's Angels.
Kimball, H.　Angel of the Rain.
Kimbrell, J.　True Descenders.
Kipling, R.　Hour of the Angel, The.
Klyuyev [or Kliuev or Klyuev].　Mother Sabbath.
Larsen, W.　After: "Once upon a time."
Levertov.　Jacob's Ladder, The.
Where Is the Angel?
Levi, P.　Annunciation.
Levine, P.　Angel Butcher.
Lima, J.　Trumpets, The.
Liu, T.　Vox Angelica.
Longfellow, H.　Sandalphon.
Spanish Jew's Tale: Azrael, The.
Spanish Jew's Tale: The Legend of Rabbi Ben Levi, The.
MacBeth [or Macbeth].　Poem of Death, A.
Machado Ruiz.　And He Was the Evil Spirit of My Dreams.
Mackey, N.　One hand on her hip, one hand.
Winged Abyss.
Mallarmé.　Saint.

McFadden, D. 10. La Traviata.
McIlroy, L. Good-Bye, Valentine.
McPherson, S. Michael.
McQuilkin. Learning the Angels.
Melville, H. Swamp Angel, The.
Menashe. Annunciation, The.
Mengham, Rod. Allegory of Good Government.
Merrill, J. Angel.
Dedication: "Hans, there are moments when the whole mind."
Mew. Trees Are Down, The.
Meynell, A. Thoughts in Separation.
Milosz, C. On Angels.
Milton. Adam Describes His Own Creation and That of Eve; Having Repeated His Warning, the Angel Departs.
March of the Rebel Angels.
Now had th' Almighty Father from above.
So to the sylvan lodge.
Mitchell, S. Annunciation, The.
Morrissey, S. My New Angels.
Moulds, J. When Bad Angels Love Women.
Mulkey, R. Why I Believe in Angels.
Nemes Nagy. Winter Angel.
Neri, G. Inn of Angels, The.
North, C. Air and Angels.
O'Hara, F. In Favor of One's Time.
Padel, R. Angel.
Page, P. Images of Angels.
Parnell, T. Song: "When thy beauty appears."
Phillips, R. Wounded Angel, The.
Pizarnik. Exile.
Poe. Israfel.
Porter, P. Angel in Blythburgh Church, An.
Pound, E. Sandalphon.
Radnóti. Angel of Dread, The.
Reid, C. Fetish.
Rilke. Man Watching, The.
Olive Garden, The.
Rosemurgy, C. Angel Finally Admits What She Knows to Lou Binkler of Bethany, Missouri, An.
Rossetti, C. Advent: "Come, thou dost say to Angels."
Rózewicz. Fight With An Angel.
Homework Assignment on the Subject of Angels.
Ruefle. Evangelical.
Sachs, N. In the Evening Your Vision Widens.
Sáenz. I Wouldn't Even Bleed.
Sanford, C. Rachel's Recovery (Fucking with the Angels).
Schwartz, D. Sarah.
Sears, E. It Came upon the Midnight Clear.
Seaton, M. Wings.
Service. Woman and the Angel, The.
Sewell, L. Expulsion.
Sexton. Consorting with Angels.
Shakespeare, W. Sonnet 144: "Two loves I have of comfort and despair [or dispaire]."
Shapcott, J. Mad Cow in Love, The.
Shuttle. Angel.
Smith, S. No Categories!
Southwell. New Heaven, New War[re].
Spenser, E. Book 2, Canto 8.
Stallings. How the Demons Were Assimilated and Became Productive Citizens.
Starkey, D. Annunciation, The: "Surely God thought this would be a moment."
Strand. I am sure you would find it misty here.
Taggart, J. Body and Soul: Poem for Two Readers.
Tate, J. Poem: "Angel kissed my alphabet, The."
Torres, E. Of My Nipple Ring Halos.
Trakl. De Profundis.
Triplett, P. Fractal Audition.
Unknown. Angels in the House, The.
Brother, Guide Me Home.
I Want To Join the Band.
If the land of the Flowery Flag is occupied by us in turn.
Join the Angel Band.
Social Band, The.
Weatherly, T. Canto 10: Wooten.
Wesley, C. Wrestling Jacob.

Willard, N. Angels in Winter.
Wordsworth, W. She Was a Phantom of Delight.
Wright, J. Angel, The.
Secret Gratitude, A.
Wright, J. Boleros #31.
Yi Sang. Performance Angel.
Yoneda, Karl. Angel Island—what a beautiful name.
Yosef, H. Angel on the Beach, An.
Young, D. Poem Against the Horizon, The.
Zucker, R. Sacristy.

Anger
Allen, S. Moment Please, A.
Andrew, G. Housewife, The.
Arapaho Oral Tradition. He'Yoho'Ho!
He'Yoho'Ho!
Awoonor. To the Eminent Scholar and Meddler.
Baugh, E. Carpenter's Complaint, The.
Baxter, C. Purest Rage, The.
Beckman, J. Canals, The. The liquor coming through.
Blake, W. Poison Tree, A.
Bly, R. Anger Against Children.
Cabañas, S. It's Called Kings.
Carmona. Tenderness.
Cetina, G. Madrigal 1.
Christensen, Paul. Going Postal.
Chu Shu-chen. Spring Joy.
Clifton, L. Fury.
Coleman, W. Wanda Why Aren't You Dead.
Conoley, G. Violence, The.
Creeley. Anger.
Darwish, M. Identity Card.
Sirhan Drinks His Coffee in the Cafeteria.
Davie, D. Devil on Ice.
Derricotte. Promise, The.
Dugan, A. Internal Migration: On Being on Tour.
Erdrich. Mary Kröger.
Estep, M. I Have to Go Now.
Fauset. La Vie C'est la Vie.
Ferré. Ballerina.
Field. Wheat-miners.
Garrison, D. Fight Song.
Glück, L. Labor Day.
Goedicke. My Brother's Anger.
Goethe. Ill Humor.
Goldsmith, K. One pair ridiculous gorilla slippers; 3 pairs of cheap shit sunglasses.
Goodman, P. Open Poem.
Gorbanevskaya. Savage cold of Russian winters, The.
Griffiths, B. For P—Celtic: found text from Machen.
Griffiths, S. Mines in Sepia Tint, The.
Hejinian. Mask of Anger, A.
Hernandez, D. Martin and My Father.
Herrick. Gods Anger without Affection.
Hodgson, R. Gipsy Girl, The.
Homer. Proposition and Invocation.
Rage of Achilles, The.
Hongo. Yellow Light.
Horace. Anger Poem, The (1.16).
Huerta, D. Machinery.
Maquinarias.
Hughes, L. Hard Daddy.
Iverem, E. Daddy's Friends.
Kaufman, S. Mothers, Daughters.
Komunyakaa, Y. Seven Deadly Sins.
Konie, G. In the Fist of Your Hatred.
Koroneu. Funeral Eva.
Laing, K. Many Worlds Are Walked Once.
Lamb, C. Anger.
If From My Lips Some Angry Accents Fell.
Lamb, M. Anger.
Lee, N. Nay, *Clytus*, you that cou'd advise.
Leonard, T. Fathers and Sons.
Levine, P. Fox, The.
Lorde. Question of Climate, A.
Louis, A. Dust World.
MacKenzie, John. My love is strung with the ancient.
Matherne, B. Les Fils (Sons).
Matthews, W. Grief.
Mayer, B. Failures in Infinitives.

Sonnet: "Thousand apples you might put in your theories."
McKay, C. White City, The.
McMillan, H. X Files, The: Bonnybridge, October '95.
Meinke. Rage.
Molina, P. Your Anger.
Myles, E. Maxfield Parrish.
Neruda. Walking Around.
Noël, Bernard. Angers.
Nolla. Greek History.
Olds, S. Clasp, The.
Pak Sôwôn. Lies: "Little bitch!"
Pastorius. Penance, A.
Peacock, M. Anger Sweetened.
Pietri. 9th Untitled Poem.
Rankin, J. Love Affair 36.
Rich, A. Phenomenology of Anger, The.
Rodgers, W. Lovers, The.
Rosenberg, L. Silence of Women, The.
Rumi. Light You Give Off, The.
Samaras, N. Elegy for a Professor.
Sandburg, C. Choose.
Sappho. When anger spreads in the breast.
Scarbrough, G. Hymn for the Sound of Hymns.
Schneider, M. Release: "I'm going to slap my anger onto a wet slab."
Shin Kyŏngnim. They.
Simic. Evening Chess.
Soto. Behind Grandma's House.
Spender, S. Prisoners, The.
Stead, C. Between.
Steele, T. Sapphics Against Anger.
Stesichoros. Since Tyndareos.
Takamura Kotaro. Elephant's Piggy Bank, The.
Tayson, R. Chase, The.
Thomas, D. Do Not Go Gentle into That Good Night.
Not from This Anger.
Torres, E. Vase of the Universe, The.
Troupe. Boomerang: A Blatantly Political Poem.
Tuqan, F. Song of Becoming.
Unknown. Angry Bride, The.
Gu-feng: The Valley Wind.
In the Chung Mode, to the Tune of "P'u T'ien Lo".
Tune: "San-fan Yü-lou Jen".
Warsong of the Kwakiutl.
Valéry. Oarsman, The.
Vallejo. Anger.
Anger that Breaks a Man Down into Boys, The.
Anger that Breaks the Man into Children, The.
Verga, Angelo. My Wife's Therapist.
Wah. Father / Mother Haibun #2.
Warsh. Enmeshment.
Watta. Stone at the Tip of the Tongue, A.
Wetzsteon. Urban Gallery.
Wicks, S. Voice.
X, D. Burn Rubber on Me.
Young, G. I had never seen her so angry, and her rage revealed a measure of love I had missed.
Yüan Mei. Miscellaneous Feelings in the Sui Garden.
Zwicky. Stone Dolphin, The.

See also **Quarrels**

Anglo-Saxons
Unknown. Riddle, A.
Seafarer, The.

Angola
Johnson, J. Saudades.
Veiga. Angola.

Animal Migration
Bryant, W. To a Waterfowl.
Field, R. Something Told the Wild Geese.

Animals
Albrecht, A. Passing Piedras Blancas.
Alcman. All asleep: mountain peaks and chasms.
Alexander, P. Antichromatic.
Amirthanayagam, I. Elephants Are in the Yard, The.
Ammons. Pet Panther.
Amor, P. CXXX.

Anti-Jabobins, The.   Canto First.
Atwood.   Animals in That Country, The.
Auden.   Fish in the Unruffled Lakes.
  Our Hunting Fathers.
Baca.   Thirteen.
Bador, B.   Progress: "Jacaranda blindings."
Benson, G.   Cat and the Pig, The.
Berger, B.   Photo Safari.
Berry, W.   To the Unseeable Animal.
Bishop, E.   Armadillo, The.
Blaser.   Ruler, The.
Blevins, S.   New York.
Blight.   Into the Ark.
Bobrowski.   Latvian Songs.
Brooke, L.   Johnny Crow's Garden.
Bruchac.   Prayer: "Let my words."
Bryant, W.   These are the gardens of the Desert,
  these.
Burke, J.   Swinging on a Star.
Burnham, D.   Maintaining the Species.
Bynner.   Opus 2.
Caesar.   Animal Crackers in My Soup.
Canning, G. *et al.*   Canto First.
Carroll, L.   Lobster Quadrille, A.
Carruth, H.   Little Citizen, Little Survivor.
Castillero, S.   Diminuto Anfibio.
  Minute Amphibian.
Causley.   On Being Asked to Write a School
  Hymn.
Cavendish, M.   Discourse of Beasts, A.
  Sea Similized to Meadows and Pastures, The:
  the Mariners, to Shepherds: the Mast, to a
  May-Pole: the Fish, to Beasts.
Centolella.   Small Acts.
Ceravolo.   Ho Ho Ho Caribou.
  Spring of Work Storm.
Césaire, A.   Day and Night.
Chang, E.   After the Storm.
Clare, J.   Hares at Play.
Clark, P.   Zoo.
Claus.   Woman 12, A.
Clifton, L.   Earth Is a Living Thing, The.
Cooley.   Sleep of Beasts, The.
Coolidge, C.   At the Poem.
Corso.   Mad Yak, The.
Cortez, J.   Heavy Headed Dance, The.
Cortez, Sarah.   Interlude: "I watch a handsome
  young female."
Couzyn.   Spell to Protect Our Love.
Daglarca.   Sultan of the Animals Is the Night,
  The.
Darío, R.   Philosophy.
Darwin.   Ae Fond Kiss, and Then.
Dauer.   Mammals.
Daumal.   Clavicles for a Great Poetic Game.
Davies, W. H.   Dumb World, The.
  Hermit, The.
  Joy and Pleasure.
Davis, H.   Proud Riders.
De Viau.   Ode: "Raven croaks before me, A."
Deerchild, R.   Snag.
DeFrees.   Census of Animal Bodies: Driving
  Home.
Deschamps, E.   Ballade 1.
Deutsch.   Creatures in the Zoo.
Dewdney.   Grid Erectile.
Dickey, J.   Heaven of Animals, The.
Dickinson, E.   Little Dog that wags his tail, A.
Donne.   Why are we[e] by all creatures waited
  on?
Dugan, A.   Letter to Eve.
Duncan, R.   Temple of the Animals, The.
Enzensberger, H.   End of the Owls, The.
Eskimo Oral Tradition.   Magic Words.
Estes, A.   Nocturne.
Evans, A.   Under Cover.
Faigao, B.   Kundiman.
Ferril.   Something Starting Over.
Follain.   Face the Animal.
Frénaud.   Self-Creation.
Galvin, B.   Bullfrog.
Garcia, R.   Death in Larkspur Canyon, A.
Garrigue.   Song in Sligo.
Gelinas, D.   Arca del día, El.
  Ark of Day, The.
Gibbs, Robert J.   Kind of Wakefulness, A.

Godfrey.   Radiant Dog.
Gonzalez, R.   San Jacinto Plaza.
Goodrich.   Higglety, Pigglety, Pop!
Hale, S.   Mary's Lamb [*or* Mary and Her
  Lamb].
Haley, M.   Tropicalia.
Hejinian.   Nights.
Herbert, W.   Slow Animals Crossing.
Hervey, L.   Nature Queries [*or* Epistle to Mr.
  Fox, from Hampton Court].
Heym.   With Pointed Head She Rises.
Hoffenstein.   Serpent has no feet or hands, The.
Hollander, J.   Adam's Task.
Holmes, O.   Questions.
Hope, Andrew, III.   Shagoon 1–4.
Howitt, M.   Cry of the Animals, The.
Hughes, T.   I See a Bear.
Hume, C.   Animal House Shape of God.
Jarnot, L.   Song of the Chinchilla.
  They Loved These Things Too.
  Valley of the Shadow of the Dogs.
Jeffers, R.   Animals.
  Hurt Hawks.
Jenkins, N.   Castration.
Jiménez, J.   Lamb Was Bleating Softly, The.
Johnson, J.   Brer Rabbit, You's de Cutes' of
  'Em All.
Jones, G.   Psalm to the Creatures.
Kearney, M.   Nature Poetry.
Keelan, C.   End is an Animal, The.
Kercheval, J.   Things That Have Escaped Me.
Kipling, R.   Eddi's Service.
Koehler, T.   Animal Crackers in My Soup.
Kumin, M.   Retrieval System, The.
Kyger.   Unexpectedly, from the outside.
Lear, E.   Calico Pie.
Levertov.   Come into Animal Presence.
Levine, P.   Animals Are Passing from Our
  Lives.
Lim, G.   Animal Liberation.
Long, H.   Cobweb.
Lovelace, R.   Her Muffe.
MacCaig.   Byre.
  Feeding Ducks.
  Summer Farm.
MacDiarmid, H.   Parley of Beasts.
Maiden.   Taste.
Marquis.   Archy at the Zoo.
Marsman.   Landscape.
Martial.   People have the oddest kinks.
Martinaitis, M.   Silly Spring.
Masters, E.   Willie Metcalf.
Matthews, W.   Names.
Mazur.   In Houston.
McHugh, H.   Animal Song.
Meredith, W.   On Falling Asleep by Firelight.
Milton.   On the Detraction Which Followed
  upon My Writing Certain Treatises ("I did
  but prompt the age to quit their [*or* thir]
  clogs.").
"Monty Python.".   All Things Dull and Ugly.
Moore, M.   Jerboa, The.
  Like a Bulrush.
  Monkeys, The.
  Pangolin, The.
Moss, S.   Dog, The.
Mueller, L.   Naming the Animals.
Muir, E.   Animals, The.
Murray, L.   Animal Nativity.
Neruda.   Some Beasts.
Nichol.   Scraptures: 7th Sequence.
Nijhoff.   Dancer.
North, C.   Postcard Element in Winter, The.
North, M.   Shap.
Nye, N.   Thinking About Cows at Ten O'Clock
  in the Morning, Abilene.
O'Driscoll, D.   Experimental Animals.
Oppen.   Myth of the Blaze.
  They await / War, and the news.
Palmer, M.   Words, The.
Parry, R.   Strangeness of Dawn, The.
Petersen, P.   Groom of the Animal-Bride.
Piercy.   Moonburn.
Pilinszky, J.   Definition of Your Attraction.
Porta.   Traveler.
Quasimodo.   O my Dear Animals.

  Only if Love Should Pierce You.
Quiller-Couch.   Sage Counsel.
Ransom, J.   Spiel of [the] Three Mountebanks.
Rekdal, Paisley.   Crash of rhinos, A.
Reverdy.   In the Fields or on the Hill.
Rochester, J.   Were I (who to my cost already
  am).
Roethke.   For An Amorous Lady.
Roripaugh, L.   Peony Lover.
Roscoe, W.   Butterfly's Ball [and the
  Grasshopper's Feast], The.
Ryuichi.   Invisible Tree.
Salkeld.   That Corner.
Scammell, W.   Screes, The.
Shapcott, J.   Life.
Sharma, P.   Performance Test.
Shepherd, R.   Itinerary.
Simms, C.   First English Wildcat, The.
Smelcer.   Animal Spirits.
  My Indian Grandmother Speaks to Animals.
Snodgrass.   I get numb and go in.
  Love Lamp.
Soto, Maria Viviana.   I dream of you.
Stainer.   Creatures preach to St Francis, The.
Stein, G.   Much Later.
  What Do I See.
Stephens, J.   Cage, The.
  Little Things.
Stern, G.   Behaving Like a Jew.
Swirszczynska [*or* Swir].   Bitch, A.
  I Talk to My Body.
Szymborska, W.   In Praise of Self-Deprecation.
  Unexpected Meeting.
Tadic.   Dogs Gambol.
Tanikawa, S.   Zoo.
Tate, J.   Descent, The.
Tellegen.   Visit, The.
Thackeray.   At the Zoo.
Theognis.   Man who doesn't love boys and
  single-foot horses and dogs, his heart will
  never know pleasure, The.
Thesen.   Animals.
Tsaloumas.   Epilogue: "My joys are those of the
  spare autumn birds."
Twichell.   Animal Languages.
  City Animals.
Ullman.   Way Animals Are, The.
Ungar.   Groundhog Day.
Unknown.   Allansford Pursuit, The.
  Animal Fair.
  Fowls in the Frith.
  Grass on the Mountain, The.
  Hunters Ask God, The.
  I want the robes, the skins of the game animals,
  the meat of the game animals. Bring them to
  me. Let us enjoy ourselves.
  Incantation Songs of the Klamath Lake People.
  Incantations of Modoc Conjurers.
  Kindness to Animals.
  Little Lamb, A.
  Summer Song.
  Trial of Renard, The.
Vallejo.   In the Moment.
Volkman.   Sonnet: "Tilt the placeless waver of
  this moving."
Weiner, J.   Yonder Tree, The.
Wells, C.   How To Tell the Wild Animals.
Wenderoth, J.   My Life: "Somehow it got into
  my room."
Whitman, W.   I think I could turn and live with
  animals, they are so placid and self-contained.
  World below the Brine, The.
Wilbur, R.   Beasts.
Wilson, R.   White.
Wright, J.   To the Evening Star: Central
  Minnesota.
Wright, J.   Pelicans.
Xuanjue.   Roar of the Lion.
Young Bear.   Significance of a Water Animal,
  The.
Yüan Chĕn.   You're No Exception.
See also **Death of Animals**

Animism

Baudelaire.   Intimate Associations.
Rich, A.   Trees, The.

Anniversaries
Berry, W.   Anniversary, An.
Cofer, J.   Anniversary.
Donne.   Anniversary [or Anniversarie], The.
Ellis, T.   T.A.P.O.A.F.O.M.
García Lorca.   Second Anniversary.
Guidacci.   Anniversary with Agave Plants.
Hewitt, D.   Anniversary.
Merwin.   For the Anniversary of My Death.
Pastan.   25th Anniversary.
Probyn.   Anniversaries.
Schulman.   Psalm for an Anniversary.
Smith, C.   To the Countess of A—. Written on the Anniversary of Her Marriage.

Annunciation of the Virgin
Castellanos.   Nazareth.
Hudgins.   Cestello Annunciation, The.
Kamienska.   Annunciation.
Luke 1:26–38; In the sixth month the angel Gabriel.
Levi, P.   Annunciation.
Menashe.   Annunciation, The.
Messerli.   Annunciation, The.
Mitchell, S.   Annunciation, The.
Muir, E.   Annunciation, The.
Norris, K.   Mysteries of The Incarnation: "She Said Yeah".
Smith, K.   Annunciation.
Zucker, R.   Sacristy.

Antarctica
Holden, C.   Antarctica.
Mahon.   Antarctica.
Wilson, A.   Octans the Octant.

Anteaters
Moore, M.   Pangolin, The.

Anthropology and Anthropologists
Arnett.   Powwow.
Birkelbach, Alan.   Coronado Points.
Cortázar.   Behavior of Mirrors on Easter Island, The.
Kinsella, J.   Visitant Eclogue.
McDonald, W.   Digs in Escondido Canyon, The.
Wojahn.   Francis Ford Coppola and Anthropologist Interpreter Teaching Gartewienna Tribesmen to Sing "Light My Fire," Philippine Jungle, 1978.

Anti-Christ, The
Hummer, T.   Antichrist in Arkansas, The.

Anticipation
Ashbery, J.   At North Farm.
One Thing That Can Save America, The.
Beresford.   Courtship, The.
Boye.   That profound waiting time.
Ch'ien Ch'i.   From My Study at the Mouth of the Valley: A Message to Censor Yang.
Dickinson, E.   Presentiment—is that long Shadow—on the lawn.
Doolittle, H.   At Ithaca.
Everwine.   From the Meadow.
Ferlinghetti, L.   I am waiting for my case to come up.
Fries, K.   Who knows the precise moment when the stream.
Gay, N.   Leaning on a Lamppost.
Gilbert, J.   To See if Something Comes Next.
Gould, J.   Tanana Valley.
Graham, J.   Swarm, The.
Grennan.   Pause.
Groarke, V.   Tonight of Yesterday.
Harnick.   Tonight at Eight.
Hayden, R.   Night-Blooming Cereus, The.
Heaney, S.   From the Canton of Expectation.
Hinsey, E.   Approach of War, The.
Hugo, R.   Skykomish River Running.
Jouve.   After the Deluge.
Larkin, P.   Next, Please.
Lawrence, D. H.   Suspense.
Leigh, C.   Best Is Yet to Come, The.
Levy, A.   Twilight.
Litvak, S.   Shadows of the plane-tree leaves.
Maltby, R.   Today Is the First Day of the Rest of My Life.
Morris, A.   Imani's Song.
Neruda.   Dead Gallop.
Niedecker.   Young girl to marry.

Novello, I.   We'll Gather Lilacs.
Palmer, O.   Wasting Time.
Peacock, M.   Veil of If, The.
Raab, L.   My Life Before I Knew It.
Shoman, K.   In Explanation to the Mother.
Shomer.   Dive from 45,000 Feet.
Smith, P.   Meeting Up with the Picaro.
StacyLynn.   Crushin.
Thompson, F.   Non Pax—Expectatio.
Tritica, J.   Approaching the Equinox.
Unknown.   Juan-er: Curl-Grass.
She Waits for Me.
Venkatarao, K.   Letter, A: "Mail runner carries the bag of mail, The."

Antigone
Nathan, L.   Letter: "Dear Antigone."
Ray, H.   Antigone and Oedipus.
Wilner, E.   Operations: Desert Shield, Desert Storm.

Antiques
Dickinson, E.   We outgrow love like other things.
Krolow.   Wind in the Room, The.
Mathews, H.   Relics, The.
McKinnon, K.   Vintage.
Turner, W.   Homely Accommodation, Suit Gent.
Wright, K.   Mantles.
Zukofsky, L.   Shang Cup.

Anti-Semitism
Becker, R.   Crypto-Jews, The.
Bell, M.   Book of the Dead Man #58, The.
Bruck.   Pretty Soon.
Ezrokhi, Z.   Day at Home, A.
Feinstein, E.   Annus Mirabilis 1989.
Finkelstein, C.   Not Responsible.
Hershon.   Minnesota Farmers Blame Bad Crop on Jews.
Ignatow, D.   Harold.
Jacob, M.   Yellow Star Again, The.
Kumin, M.   In the Absence of Bliss.
Riddle of Noah, The.
Lazarus, E.   1492.
Lifshin.   After the Anti-Semitic Calls on a Local Talk Station.
Plotnick, H. M.   Jewish.
Rakosi.   To an Anti-Semite.
Reznikoff.   It had long been dark, though still an hour before supper-time.
Rosenberg, I.   Jew, The.
Sadeh, P.   At Nightfall, 1/27/91.
Sadoff.   Nazis.
Shapiro, H.   News, The.
Wayman.   Hating Jews.
Yevtushenko [or Evtushenko].   Babii Yar.

Antony (Marc Antony)
Hemans.   Last Banquet of Antony and Cleopatra, The.
Marx, S.   Mark Antony's Valentine.
Pascal.   Tact.
Simpson, L.   Early in the Morning.
Williams, W.   To Mark Anthony in Heaven.

Ants
Adair, V. H.   Ants on the Melon.
Barnard, M.   Fable of the Ant and the Word.
Campbell, D.   Anguish of Ants, The.
Clare, J.   Ants, The.
Collin, Bernard.   Perpetual *Look* Physics: 17/5.
De la Mare.   Immanent.
Empson.   Ants, The.
Faverey.   Its only riddle: *how*.
Frost, R.   Departmental.
İnce.   Wind, Ant, History.
Issa.   Line of ants, The.
This line of black ants.
Jacobsen, R.   Country Roads.
Johnson, S.   Paraphrase.
Joseph, J.   Ant Nest.
Kekova.   Ants, The.
Knott.   Ant Dodger.
Kreymborg.   Ants.
López Velarde.   Ants.
Lovelace, R.   Ant, The.
Masaoka Shiki.   Summer sky / Clear after rain.
Matthews, W.   Vermin.
McGrath, T.   Skull of the Horse.

Moore, M.   Critics and Connoisseurs.
Moss, T.   Ant Farm.
Nash, O.   Emmet, The.
Piccione.   Watching Ants Play Soccer in Central Park.
Simic.   Solitude.
Somoza, J.   Fire Ants.
Soto.   Failing in the Presence of Ants.
Tachibana Akemi.   Gathered Ants.
Wallace, R.   Dog's Song.
Whur.   Poet Questions the Ant, The.
Yamaguchi Seishi.   Miserable ant.
Zarin.   Ant Hill, The.

Anxiety
Ammons.   Anxiety's Prosody.
Ashbery, J.   Problem of Anxiety, The.
Atwood.   Up.
Baillie, J.   Song: Woo'd and married and a'.
Berrigan, T.   (Clarity! clarity!) a semblance of motion, omniscience.
Berry, W.   Peace of Wild Things, The.
Blake, W.   Little Boy Lost, The.
Bukowski.   I Am Dead But I Know the Dead Are Not Like This.
Bulich, V.   Omnibus, The.
Busceti, G.   Dissonances.
Creeley.   Something.
Di Prima.   Abyss.
Dobyns.   Allegorical Matters.
Erb, E.   In the Picture.
Gilyard, K.   Daughter, That Picture of You.
Greenberg, A.   Afterward, There Will Be a Hallway.
Hayden, R.   Ice Storm.
Herrera.   Crack Inside My Breast, A.
Hofer, J.   Of Deaths, Days, Futures, Nations ("Do i need to (need to).").
Hoggard, James.   Dove Hunting Each Labor Day.
Huerta, E.   This Is a Love.
Hugo, R.   In Your Racing Dream.
Hwang Jiwoo.   Mirror 2.
Juan Chi.   It is the middle of the night—I cannot sleep.
Kunitz, S.   Game, The.
Lagier.   Second Class Citizen.
Lifshin.   After the Anti-Semitic Calls on a Local Talk Station.
Lisnyanskaya [or Lisnianskaia].   Wind blows and makes the light tremble, The.
Liu, T.   Mama.
Size of It, The.
Millay, E.   Departure.
Mora.   Elena.
Immigrants.
Morgenstern.   Anxiety for the Future.
Neto.   Saturday in the Sand-Slums.
No Ch'ŏnmyŏng.   Lemon for Me, A.
Oppen.   They await / War, and the news.
Orr, G.   Dark Prayer.
Phillips, R.   Panic Bird, The.
Pietri.   Intermission from Thursday.
Powell, D. A.   Minotaur at Supper, The: Spare the Noritake and the Spode.
Ramanujan.   Snakes.
Reverdy.   That.
Roberson, E.   Any moment (12/4/69 4:30 A.M. chicago).
Robinson, M.   Dreams of a Rival.
Sharaf, M.   Behind the House.
Shepherd, R.   Eros in His Striped Blue Shirt.
Simic.   Clouds Gathering.
Smith, C.   Female Exile, The.
To a Friend.
Stein, G.   Teachers taught her, The.
Weaver, A.   Improvisation for Piano.
Williams, C. K.   Risk.
Williamson, G.   Nervous Systems.
Wright, C.   Laguna Blues.
Young, M. J.   Anxiety.
Yuan Mei.   Old and Traveling.

Apartheid
Afrika, T.   Funeral of Anton Fransch, The.
Hit squad.
Brooks, G.   Music for Martyrs.
Near-Johannesburg Boy, The.

Gwala. Bonk'abajahile.
  Getting off the ride.
  Gumba, gumba, gumba.
Jensma. I come.
Johnson, L. Mi Revalueshanary Fren.
Jonker, I. Child Who Was Shot Dead by
  Soldiers at Nyanga, The.
Motsapi, S. Shak-shak.
Press, K. Tiresias Remembers.
Sepamla. Measure for Measure.
Soyinka. We wish only to bury our dead. Shorn.
Zulu, P. You are Mad: and I Mean It!

Apartments
As-Sabah. I'll Never Know No Sunday in This
  Weekday Room.
Bodenheim. Rear Porches of an Apartment
  Building, The.
Cooper, J. Rent.
Davis, J. Time Bum.
Dunn, D. Modern Love.
Greenlaw, L. Five O'Clock Opera.
Haskins, L. Dearborn North Apartments
  Chicago, Illinois.
Hogan, L. New Apartment.
Hughes, L. Madam and the Rent Man.
Khomin, I. Dike, a flower bed, a bare linden
  tree, A.
Komunyakaa, Y. Ignis Fatuus.
Ku Sang. Spring Chrysanthemums.
Osterhaus, J. New York Minute.
Ponge. Last Simplicity, The.
Rich, A. Living in Sin.

Apathy
Auden. Musée des Beaux Arts.
Carruth, H. California: "To come again into the
  place of revolutionary."
De la Mare. Pooh!
Enzensberger, H. At Thirty-Three.
Holiday, The.
  Song for Those Who Know.
Hugo, R. Last Days.
Lindsay, V. Leaden-eyed, The.
Llwyd, Alan. Our Godless Days.
Milosz, C. Elegy for N. N.
Philodemus. You Cry, Whine, Peer Strangely at
  Me.
Stafford, W. Ritual to Read to Each Other, A.
Stevenson, R. Celestial Surgeon, The.
Troupe. So What.

Apes
Bogen, L. Pygmy Headhunters and Killer Apes,
  My Lover and Me.
Edson, R. Ape.
Faverey. In the Service of the Wheel.
Hayes, T. Goliath Poem.
Jandl, E. Ch[i/o]mp.
Pagis, D. Ready.
Robinson, A. Darwinism.
Sassoon, S. Sporting Acquaintances.
Szymborska, W. Two Apes of Brueghel, The.
Tate, J. Teaching the Ape to Write Poems.

Aphrodisiacs
Lockward, D. Vegetable Love.
McGuckian. Aphrodisiac, The.
Sharpless. In Praise of Cocoa, Cupid's
  Nightcap.

Aphrodite
Anacreon. Not / But near another you have a
  timid.
  O Lord, with whom subduer Love.
Anyte [or Anytes]. This is Kypris' place; it ever
  pleases her.
Field. To the Winter Aphrodite.
  Why should I praise thee, blissful Aphrodite?
Ghiselin. Bath of Aphrodite.
Ibycus. Again Love, glancing meltingly.
Moiro. Beneath Aphrodite's golden portico you
  now lie.
Nossis. It seems that Aphrodite took with joy.
Kallo dedicated her portrait in the house of
  golden.
  Nothing is sweeter than love, all other riches.
  When we go to the temple, let's see Aphrodite's.
Price, V. Three Hymns for Aphrodite.
Sappho. Come to me from Krete to this holy.

Happy bridegroom, the marriage that you
  prayed for.
Horses in Flowers.
Kypris and Nereids, let that brother.
Kypris, / May she find you very bitter.
May I, goldencrowned Aphrodite.
On the throne of many hues, Immortal
  Aphrodite.
On your throne, a marvel of art, immortal.
Prayer to Aphrodite.
Sardis.
Sweet mother, I cannot weave.
Throned in splendor, deathless, O Aphrodite.
Seneca. Medea's Frenzy.
Stesichoros. Since Tyndareos.

See also **Venus (goddess)**

Apocalypse
Baraka, R. After-Word.
Bhatt, S. What Does One Write When the
  World Starts to Disappear?
Bold, A. As if a few odd bombs were bouncing
  around.
Braxton, C. Apocalypse.
Cabral de Melo Neto. End of the World, The.
Clare, J. That time was come, or seemed as it
  was come.
Grabill. Lightning, The.
Hirsch, E. American Apocalypse.
Holmes, O. Latter-Day Warnings.
Ingalls, J. Vision of St. Michael and St. John,
  The.
Kinsella, T. Wormwood.
Longfellow, H. In happy hours, when the
  imagination.
  In the Coliseum.
Lowell, R. Harriet ("Repeating fly, blueback,
  thumbthick—so gross, A.").
McAuley, J. One Tuesday in Summer.
McGrath, T. End of the World, The.
Niedecker. Radio talk this morning, The.
Rothenberg, M. Apocalyptic Yearnings.
Sherry, J. Hazardous Waste.
Unknown. Steal Away to Jesus.
Upton, C. When I was very young.
Wilbur, R. Advice to a Prophet.
Witherup. Lamb of Peace, the Ram of War,
  The.
Wordsworth, W. Simplon Pass, The.
Wylie. Doomsday.

See also **Armageddon; End of the World;
Judgment Day**

Apollinaire, Guillaume
Aragon. Embrace, The.
Berrigan, T. It is night. You are asleep. And
  beautiful tears.
Ginsberg, A. At Apollinaire's Grave.
Kaufman, B. Unhistorical Events.
MacSweeney. Cute Petite.
Stein, G. Guillaume Apollinaire.
Tzara. Death of Guillaume Apollinaire, The.

Apollo
Bourque, D. Durer's *Apollo.*
Byron, G. Or view the Lord of the unerring
  bow.
Davidman. Lament for Evolution.
Doolittle, H. Evadne.
Drayton. Sacrifice to Apollo, The.
Drummond, W. Invocation: "Pheobus, arise! /
  And paint the sable skies."
Field. It was deep April, and the morn.
Fulton, A. Supernal.
Herbert, Z. Apollo and Marsyas.
Hölderlin. Descriptive Poetry.
Homer. Apollo Defeats Patroclus.
Kunitz, S. Flight of Apollo, The.
Masters, E. Webster Ford.
Melville, H. Ravaged Villa, The.
Meredith, G. Phoebus with Admetus.
Ovid. Apollo and Daphne.
  Apollo and Hyacinthus.
  Daphne and Apollo.
Petrarch. Apollo, if the sweet desire is still alive
  that inflamed you beside.
Philpot, T. Road Trip as Clues, A.
Riley, P. 147. 67.

Rilke. Archaic Torso of Apollo.
  Archaic Torso of Apollo.
Robinson, A. Search for Apollo, A.
Robinson, E. Many Are Called.
Shepherd, R. Man Named Troy, A.
Unknown. Stealing of Apollo's Cattle, The.
Waller, E. Story of Phoebus and Daphne
  Applied, [etc.], The.
Winchilsea. Circuit of Apollo, The.
Winters, Y. Apollo and Daphne.

Apostles
Azzawi, F. Lion and the Apostle, The.
Dickinson, E. Of Paul and Silas it is said.
Herrick. Salutation.
Pound, E. Ballad of the Goodly Fere.
Prassinos. Apostle Qualities.
Schwartz, D. Starlight like Intuition Pierced the
  Twelve.
Smart, C. Let Peter rejoice with the Moon Fish
  who keeps up the life in the waters by night.
Tate, A. Twelve, The.

Appalachia
Beecher, J. Appalachian Landscape.
Morgan, R. Grain of Sound, The.
Thompson, K. Appalachia Novena.

Apple Blossoms
Farrar, J. Comparison, A.
Jacobsen, R. Moon and Apple.
Pastan. Apple Shrine, The.

Apple Trees and Apples
Amichai, Y. Inside the Apple.
Armantrout. As We're Told.
Barker, G. How many apples grow on the tree?
Behn, R. Aubade: "After the sadness of apples
  in August."
Bogan, L. Crossed Apple, The.
Booth, P. Original Sequence.
Brown Rosellen. This is no baby skin—.
Causley. Apple-Tree Man, The.
Coiffait, C. Last Apple, The.
Crane, H. Sunday Morning Apples.
Dauenhauer. Tlingit Concrete Poem.
De la Mare. Miss T.
Drinkwater. Moonlit Apples.
Dufault. Burden.
Follain. Red Apple, The.
Freneau. On Observing a Large Red-Streak
  Apple.
Frost, C. Sin: "Tree bore the efflorescence of
  October apples, The."
Frost, F. Deserted Orchard.
Frost, R. After Apple-Picking.
  Unharvested.
  Wood-Pile, The.
Gilbert, J. Hunger.
Glück, L. Nostos.
Guernsey, B. Apple, The.
Heyen. Windfall.
Heynen. Boys Go to Ask a Neighbor for Some
  Apples, The.
Humphreys, E. Apple Tree and a Pig, An.
Kaufman, S. Apples.
Kim Hyesun. Ripe Apple.
Kovaleva, I. And there was beauty.
Lapeyrère, J. Apples.
Larkin, P. As Bad as a Mile.
Lawrence, D. H. Medlars and Sorb-Apples.
  Mystic.
Livesay, D. Eve.
Major, C. Apple Core.
Margolis, G. On the Way to the Sitter's.
Masaoka Shiki. Haiku: "I think I'll die."
Morris, W. Pomona.
Murphy, E. Thank you, Mr Rason, for the
  Apples.
Nemerov. Primer of the Daily Round, A.
Neruda. Oda a la Manzana.
  Ode to the Apple.
Ni Ghallchóir, C. In the Garden of Apples.
Nutter, G. Air War, The.
Okamoto. Tanka: "Stark naked."
Ormond. My Grandfather and His Apple-Tree.
Philips, J. Apple-Culture.
Pogson, P. Apples.
Riordan, M. Apples.
Rivera, D. Under the Apple Tree.

Rossetti, C.   Apple Gathering, An.
Rossetti, D.   Orchard-Pit, The.
Salter.   Young Girl Peeling Apples.
Sappho.   Horses in Flowers.
  Like the sweet-apple.
  Sweet apple reddens on a high branch, The.
Scannell.   Apple-raid, The.
Shimazaki Toson.   First Love.
Snodgrass.   Old Apple Trees.
Soloukhin.   Apple, The.
Spenser, E.   Sonnet 77: "Was it a dream, or did I
  see it plain."
Stewart, S.   Apple.
Tomlinson, C.   Paring the Apple.
Unknown.   Girl threw an apple to a cloud, A.
  Oh send to me an apple that hasn't any kernel.
Williams, W.   Wild Orchard.
Yeats.   Song of Wandering Aengus, The.
Young, D.   Four About Apples.

Apprentices
Malanga.   Apprentice, The.
Muldoon, P.   Sushi.

Approval
Hamill, G.   Limerick: "If you're aristocratic,
  said Nietzsche."
Piercy.   I Will Not Be Your Sickness.

Apricot Trees and Apricots
Eady.   Too Young to Know.

April
Benét, S.   For City Spring.
Browning, R.   Home-Thoughts, from Abroad.
Clare, J.   Last of April, The.
Clarke, George Elliott.   April 19, 19—: A
  Sonnet.
Davies, W. H.   Visitor, The.
DeSylva, B.   April Showers.
Eberhart, R.   This Fevers Me.
Field.   It was deep April, and the morn.
García Lorca.   Spring Song.
Grimké, A.   At April.
Grosholz.   Remembering the Ardèche.
Gurney, I.   April Gale.
Hall, D.   Winter's asperity mollifies.
Harburg.   April in Paris.
Hardie, K.   Rain in April.
Jeffers, R.   Gale in April.
Jiménez, J.   Street Is Waiting for the Night, The.
Johnston, P.   I'll Remember April.
Kenney.   In April.
Keyes, S.   Elegy: "April again, and it is a year
  again."
Lasoen, P.   That April Morning.
Levine, P.   Sleepless Night, A.
Lowell, A.   April.
Masefield.   West Wind, The.
Millay, E.   Spring: "To what purpose, April, do
  you return again?"
Miyazawa Kenji.   Spring & Asura.
Nesbit, E.   Dead to the Living, The.
Oswald, A.   April: "Sheer grip and the push of
  it—growth gets, The."
Pak Mogwŏl [*or* Mokwŏl].   April.
Ray, H.   April.
Raye, D.   I'll Remember April.
Reznikoff.   April.
Shaw, A.   April.
Snodgrass.   April Inventory.
Turner, F.   April Wind.
Watson, S.   Song: "April, April, / Laugh thy
  girlish laughter."

April Fool's Day
Berryman.   47. April Fool's Day, or St. Mary
  Egypt.

Aquariums
Bush, D.   Aquarium du Trocadéro.
Gunn, T.   Aquarium, The.
Hammial.   Petit Guignol.
Lowell, R.   For the Union Dead.
Schiff, Robyn.   At Shedd Aquarium.
Shinkichi Takahashi.   Near Shinobazu Pond.
Voigt.   Effort at Speech.
Wenderoth, J.   Narrative Poem.

Aquinas, St. Thomas
Howe, F.   Catholic.
Simic.   St. Thomas Aquinas.

Arab-Americans
Charara, H.   Here It Is.
  More Than We Dared.
Espada.   Ghazal for Open Hands.
Kronenfeld, J.   Peaceful Sentiment.
Mattawa.   Echo and Elixir 2.
Muhawi, I.   Bad Moon Rising.
Reed, P.   September 18.

Arabia
Merrill, J.   Arabian Night.
Tennyson, A.   Recollections of The Arabian
  Nights.

Arab-Israeli Wars
Alkalay-Gut.   Public Outcry.
Amichai, Y.   Rustle of History's Wings, as They
  Used to Say Then, The.
  Since Then.
Amir, D.   After Fall, 1956.
Back, R.   Gaza, Undated.
Darwish, M.   August, Beirut, 1982.
  On a Canaanite Stone in the Dead Sea.
Ditzanny, R.   My Hand is Extended for the
  Peace of the Galilee.
El Janabi, A.   If Only the Horse Was Left to Its
  Solitude.
Guri, H.   Like Beirut.
Hamod, S.   Libyan Airliner/Egyptian Acrobats/
  Israeli Air Circus [2004 version].
Hurvitz, Y.   Around the Water Near the Birds.
Israeli, A.   Eulogy: "This should be a eulogy
  without words."
Kalinski, E.   Teacher of Defeated Hebrew
  Language.
Kosman, Admiel.   Games.
Nawwab, M.   Bridge of Old Wonders.
Saari, R.   Only Democracy (in the Middle East),
  The.
Shabtai, Aharon.   Nostalgia.
Sheinfeld, I.   War Night 6.
Sivan, A.   To Wither Like Weeds in an Easterly
  Wind.
  Unpleasantness During a Memorial Service.
Tuqan, F.   Gone Are Those We Love.
Yonathan, N.   Friends: "Joseph is without doubt
  rent in pieces an evil beast hath devoured
  him."
Yosef, H.   Jaffa, July 1948.

Arabs
Ali, A.   Ghazal: "Only language of loss left in
  the world is Arabic, The."
  In Arabic.
Bekes Jr.   Picture.
Blind.   Fantasy, A.
Breytenbach.   Write Off.
Browning, R.   Through the Metidja to Abd-el-
  Kadr.
Charara, H.   Holy Water.
Cross, E.   Mandap.
  Mandap.
Darwish, M.   Identity Card.
Hamod, S.   Dying with the Wrong Name.
  So we move now.
Joseph, L.   Curriculum Vitae.
  That's All.
Li'aibi, S.   Stone of the Arabian woman, The.
Mattawa.   Echo and Elixir 2.
Minhinnick.   Twenty-Five Laments for Iraq.
Nye, N.   My Father and the Fig Tree.
  Small Vases from Hebron, The.
Ravikovitch, D.   Blood Heifer.
Samaras, N.   Notes in Jerusalem.
Shabtai, Aharon.   As We Were Marching.
Someck, R.   Transparent.
Taylor, B.   Bedouin Song.
Thompson, F.   Arab Love-Song, An.
Ungaretti.   In Memoriam: "His name was /
  Mohammed Sceab."
Yusuf, S.   Trees of Ithaca, The.
Zolotow.   Enemies.

Arachne
Fletcher, G.   I saw, sweet Licia, when the spider
  ran.

Aran Islands, Ireland
Unknown.   Arran.

Arbor Day
Morris, G.   Woodman, Spare That Tree.

Arbus, Diane
Nemerov.   To D———, Dead by Her Own
  Hand.

Arbutus
Crapsey.   Arbutus.

Arcadia
Sepúlveda, O.   Cuatro.
  Four.
Sidney.   Sestina: "Farewell, O Sun".
Taylor, B.   Paean to the Dawn, A.
Tennyson, A.   Now, sometimes in my sorrow
  shut.

Archaeology and Archaeologists
Abdullatif, Y.   Archeology.
Cervantes.   Archeology.
Gabrielian, N.   Phoenician Statuette, A.
Heaney, S.   Bog Queen.
  Electric Light.
  Punishment.
MacKenzie, John.   Me as an Archaeologist.
Neruda.   Amor America (1400).
Phillips, D.   Maridunum.
Prufer, K.   My Father Recounts a Story from
  His Youth.
Riley, P.   147. 67.
Roggeman.   Archaeological Find.
Stepanchev.   Seven Horizons.
Storace.   Archaeology of Divorce, The.
Tsanev, Ivan.   Archaelogical Site, An.
Yau.   Late Night Movies I.

Archery
Chuang Tzu.   Need to Win, The.
Gascoigne.   Gascoigne's Woodmanship.
Homer.   Suitors watch Ulysses string the bow,
  The.
Longfellow, H.   Arrow and the Song, The.
Unknown.   Song of the English Bowmen.
Various authors.   He hit the backs of forty tailed
  deer.
  Heaven sent a genius.
  His arrow was huge beyond compare.
  On Mount Chorae he struck two roebucks.
  Seven pinecones.

Architecture and Architects
Basho.   Kannon's tiled temple.
Blake, E. J.   Within and Without.
Bobrowski.   Invocation: "High on, above the
  lake, the mute Nowgorod."
Breton, A.   Always for the First Time.
Cabico, R.   Art in Architecture.
Crumpacker, C.   Trans-Relational Love Poem.
Cullen, Y.   Memorial: "There had to be a way of
  making a building talk."
Denney.   Building the Dam.
Emerson, R.   Problem, The.
"Ern Malley.".   Baroque Exterior.
Evans, A.   On Sir John Vanbrugh [Architect].
Garrigue.   Grand Canyon, The.
Gier, J.   Going Baroque.
Hall, J.   Hous-keping's dead, *Saturio:* wot'st
  thou where?
Krivulin.   Crossing the keyboards of the palace.
Maar, Dora.   These Tall Constructions.
Melville, H.   Greek Architecture.
Meyers, B.   Arc de Triomphe.
Morshen.   Andreyevsky Church, The.
Oliphant.   Eugene Wukasch, Texas Architect.
Palmer, M.   I am an architect in Vienna.
Reposa, Carol Coffee.   Alamo Plaza at Night.
Rich, A.   Architect.
Rimbaud, A.   Cities.
Ward, Geoff.   Distance Learning.

Arctic
Booth, P.   Stefansson Island.
Brodsky, J.   Polar Explorer, A.
Lane, P.   Winter 40: "She is a northern woman,
  barely more."
Levertov.   Arctic Spring.
Nicholls, J.   Polar Cub.
Simic.   Arctic Voyager, An.
Spender, S.   Polar Exploration.

Argentina
Borges.   Houses like Angels.

Mythical Founding of Buenos Aires, The.
Cortázar. Normal Behavior of the Famas.
Coward. Nina.
Komunyakaa, Y. Let's Say.
Molinari. Poem of the Girl from Velázquez.
Rosario, M. Latter-day Mother Courage.

Arguments
Bécquer, G. Into Her Eyes a Tear Crept.
Bracho, C. Hipotético espectador, El.
  Hypothetical Spectator, The.
Durcan. Sally.
Gershwin, I. Let's Call the Whole Thing Off.
Goldbarth. *Ancestored-Back* Is the
  Overpresiding Spirit of This Poem.
Gonzalez, N. How the Heart Aches.
Goodge. Smithville Tandem Bike, The.
Guiterman. Three Ponies.
Hezutsu Tosaku. Affluence—define it as.
  On the crest of the hills.
Hill, S. I Know I Ought to Love You.
Kinsella, T. Portrait of the Artist, A.
Lea, S. Paternity.
Muso Soseki. Lodging House in Town, A.
Nowlan. It's Good To Be Here.
O'Callaghan, C. 10 The Salmon.
Page, P. Cross.
Rivard. Cures.
Roberts, L. I Blame It On Him.
Sallah, T. No Argument Tonight.
Unknown. Hebe and Ganymede.
Warren, R. Revelation.
See also **Quarrels**

Ariadne
Cruz, C. Ariadne, waiting.
Propertius. Ariadne Lay, Theseus' Ship Sailing
  Away.

Ariel [Shakespeare]
Hooker, E. Ariel.

Aristocracy
Coward. Stately Homes of England, The.
Graves, R. Cloak, The.
Li Po. Third month in T'ientsin, The.
Marie de France. Wolf and the Lamb, The.
Ronald of Orkney, Saint. Attributes of a
  Gentleman, The.
Ssu-ma Hsiang-ju. Sir Fantasy.
Thomas, R. S. Sir Gelli Meurig.
Unknown. Author of this is Ossian, The.
  Ballad of the Mulberry Road.
  One who first gave birth to our people, The.
  Tu-zhi: Hares.
  Vicar of Bray, The.
Ward, Geoff. Horace Belisha.

Aristotle
Nolla. Greek History.
Stafford, W. Humanities Lecture.

Arithmetic
Adcock, F. Halfway Street, Sidcup.
Brownjohn. Common Sense.
Carroll, L. Sum, A.

Arizona (state)
Johnson, D. Incognito Lounge, The.
Pape. In the Bluemist Motel.
Reyes, C. Arizona Nocturne.
Santos, S. Near the Desert Test Sites.
Teasdale. Day's Ending.
Tomlinson, C. Arizona Desert.
Walden, G. Oracle.
Warren, R. Arizona Midnight.
Zukofsky, L. In Arizona.

Ark, The
Adonis [*or* Adunis]. New Noah, The.
Amichai, Y. Couplets.
Blight. Into the Ark.
Gelinas, D. Arca del día, El.
  Ark of Day, The.
  Jardín de madera.
  Wood Garden.
Kendall, M. Vision of Noah, The.
Levertov. Ache of Marriage, The.
Mansour, J. Beyond the Breakers.
Mengham, Rod. Allegory of Good Government.
Ombres. Ballad of Noah's Daughter.
Thomas, D. Author's Prologue.
Tomlinson, C. Ararat.

Wright, J. Pelicans.
See also **Noah**

Arkansas (state)
Hummer, T. Antichrist in Arkansas, The.
Ortiz. Bend in the River.
Roberts, David Thomas. Toward Mena.
Robin, L. Little Girl from Little Rock.
Unknown. State of Arkansas, The.
Walcott. Arkansas Testament, The.

Armadillos
Cumpian. Armadillo Charm.
Shockley. Armadillo.
White, G. Dead Armadillos.

Armageddon
Dickey, W. Armageddon.
Gioseffi. These are the word wounds.
Huerta, D. Bolero at Armageddon.
  Bolero en Aramgedón.
Ransom, J. Armageddon.
Vas, I. Armageddon.
See also **Apocalypse; End of the World;**
Judgement Day

Armenia and Armenians
Der Hovanessian, D. Shifting the Sun.
Hovanessian, D. Two Voices.
Ishkhan. Armenian Language Is the Home of
  the Armenian, The.
Iskander. Gegard.
Mandelstam [*or* Mandelshtam]. I Am Deaf.
Siamanto. Dance, The.
  Grief.
Tekeyan. Country of Dust, The.

Armies
Arapaho Oral Tradition. *He!* When I met him
  approaching.
Atkins, R. Christophe.
Crane, S. Black riders came from the sea.
Grimke, C. Gathering of the Grand Army, The.
Homer. Night Piece: the Trojans outside Troy.
Joyce, J. I hear an army charging upon the land.
Kao Shih. Ji Gate.
Lu Lun. Black moon geese fly high.
Melville, H. Armies of the Wilderness, The.
Montgomerie, W. Flodden.
Rai San'yo. On a Painting of Kenshin
  Attacking Shingen.
  Stopping at Amakusa Sea.
Sappho. Some say an army of horsemen, others.
Tester, V. Histories, The.
Trakl. Mood of Depression, The.
Ts'ao Ts'ao. Graveyard Song.
  Song on Enduring the Cold.
Tur-Malka, A. Mirror of the Battle.
Wenderoth, J. As Hour and Year Collapsed.
Wieseltier, M. Love is Progressing.

Armistice
Sassoon, S. Everyone Sang.
See also **Peace**

Armstrong, Louis
Allen, S. I Say, Mr. A.
Brock-Broido. Radiating Naïveté.
Fabio. For Louis Armstrong, A Ju-Ju.
Lucca, C. Conversation with Duke Ellington
  and Louis (Pops) Armstrong.
Moerman. Louis Armstrong.
Tolson, M. Lambda.

Army Life
Amichai, Y. Rain on the Battlefield.
  Two Poems about the First Battles.
Anderson, D. Papasan.
  Purification.
Belitt. Spool, The.
Berlin. Oh! How I Hate to Get Up in the
  Morning.
  This Is the Army, Mr. Jones.
Brookes, J. Officers and Gentlemen Down
  Under.
Campo. Battle Hymn of the Republic, The.
Carmichael, H. Don't Forget to Say No, Baby.
Ciardi, J. First Snow on an Airfield.
Clare, J. Soldier, The.
Corfield, J. Morse Lesson.
Dawe, B. Weapons Training.
Day, J. North Sea.
De Forest. In Louisiana.

Donaghy, M. Shibboleth.
Duncan, R. Spring Memorandum, A: Fort
  Knox.
Ellis, R.H. Walk up, walk up, my bonny boys.
Ewart. Officers' Mess.
  Personal Footnote, A.
Freneau. Jeffery, or, the Soldier's Progress.
Gefen, J. Setting-Up Camp.
Guri, H. On a Stone Pillow.
Gurney, I. Bohemians, The.
  First March.
  Laventie.
Hemingway. Riparto d'Assalto.
Herbert, S. General inspecting the trenches,
  The.
Housman. Grenadier.
  New Mistress, The.
Huddle. Haircut.
Hudgins. Road Home, The.
Jackson, F. Elvis Goes to the Army.
Jarmain. Embarkation, 1942.
Jarrell, R. Second Air Force.
Kipling, R. Boots.
  Cholera Camp.
  Danny Deever.
  Gentlemen-Rankers.
  Gunga Din.
  Mandalay.
Kirstein. Rank.
Koch, K. To Carelessness.
Komunyakaa, Y. Fragging.
Kovner, A. My comrades / Inasmuch as they
  are comrades do not need to study the
  map.
Lewis, A. All Day It Has Rained.
  Infantry.
Llwyd, Alan. Chaplin and Others.
Long, H. For Tony, Embarking in Spring.
Meredith, W. Love Letter from an Impossible
  Land.
Omer, H. Squad in the Land, A.
Oppen. Survival: Infantry.
Pagis, D. Twenty Years in the Wadi.
Prince, H. Boogie Woogie Bugle Boy.
Raye, D. Boogie Woogie Bugle Boy.
Razaf, A. My Man o' War.
Rosenberg, I. Soldier: Twentieth Century.
  Troop ship, The.
Saner. They Said.
Scannell. Bayonet Training.
Service. Pot of Tea, A.
Shanks, E. Going In to Dinner.
Shapiro, H. War Stories.
Shapiro, K. Troop Train.
Simpson, L. Memories of a Lost War.
Smith, W. Pidgin Pinch.
Ts'ao Chih. Tumbleweed that leaves its root
  and stock, The.
Tu Fu [*or* Du Fu]. Overnight at Headquarters.
Unknown. Army Dance, The.
  Deserter, The.
  I've lost my rifle and bayonet.
  Sure, a little bit of shrapnel fell from out the sky
    one day.
  We are Fred Karno's army.
Waniek, A. Freeman Field.
  Three Men in a Tent.
West, A. Night Patrol, The.
Whitman, W. Bivouac on a Mountain Side.
  By the Bivouac's Fitful Flame.
  Cavalry Crossing a Ford.
See also **Soldiers**

Arnold, Matthew
Brehm, J. Sea of Faith.
Clark, T. Dover Beach.
Hecht, A. Dover Bitch, The.
Logan, W. Valentine for Matthew Arnold, A.

Arranged Marriage
Nageshbabu, M. What Do I Want?
Unknown. Young men, defend me, defend your
  very honor!

Arrows
Chippewa Oral Tradition. Arrow Song.
Jonson, B. How He Saw Her.
  What He[e] Suffered.
Li Ho. Song of an Arrowhead from Changping.

Art and Artists

Longfellow, H.   Arrow and the Song, The.
Lu Lun.   Grass rustle through dim woods.
MacDiarmid, H.   In Memoriam Dylan Thomas.
Nichol.   Blues.
Senryū, K.   That Tsugunobu.
Sorescu, M.   Arrow, The.
Various authors.   His arrow was huge beyond
  compare.
Voznesensky [*or* Voznesenskii].   Arrow in the
  Wall.
Wilner, E.   Meditation on the *Wen-Fu*.

Art and Artists

Agee.   To Walker Evans.
Ai.   Back in the World.
Akhmadulina.   Lunatics.
Albert-Birot.   In the Paul Guillaume Gallery.
Alberti.   Millares 1965.
Alegría.   Ars Poetica.
Allston.   Art.
  On Rembrant; Occasioned by His Picture of
    Jacob's Dream.
  On Seeing the Picture of Æolus by Pelegrino
    Tibalbi, in the Institute at Bologna.
  On the Group of the Three Angels Before the
    Tent of Abraham, by Raffaelle, in the Vatican.
  On the Statue of an Angel, by Bienaimé, in the
    Possession of J.S. Copley Greene, Esq.
  To My Venerable Friend, the President of the
    Royal Academy.
Aretino.   If famous Apelles with his hand of art.
Arp.   For that Reason We Are Also Not Obliged
  to Polish the Claws, Horns, and Weather
  Vanes.
Ayewanu, S.   Man with a Hat, A.
Baraka, A.   X.
Baraka, I.   Black Art.
  State/meant.
Bartlett, L.   What It Means to be Avant-Garde.
Baudelaire.   Gypsies on the Move.
Bawer.   On Leaving the Artists' Colony.
Becker, R.   Subject / Matter.
Bernlef.   Beatrice.
  Disconcerting Object.
Berrigan, T.   In Joe Brainard's collage its white
  arrow.
Bishop, E.   Monument, The.
  One Art.
Blake, W.   Orator Prigg.
Blaser.   Image-Nation 23 (imago-mundi).
Bogan, L.   To an Artist, to Take Heart.
Boroditskaya, M.   Poor composer.
Bosquet, A.   Celebrities.
Bowering, G.   Swing, The.
Braxton, C.   Arts Are Black, The.
Brouwer, J.   Aesthetics.
Browning, E.   Hiram Powers' "Greek Slave".
Browning, R.   Dîs Aliter Visum; or, Le Byron
  de Nos Jours.
  Fra Lippo Lippi.
  How It Strikes a Contemporary.
  Youth and Art.
Campbell, D.   Lovers, The.
Cendrars.   Head, The.
  My Dance.
Ceravolo.   Sculpture.
Chao Meng-fu.   Admonition to Myself, An.
Cherry, K.   Bride of Quietness, The.
Clark, T.   Suicide with Squirtgun.
Cole, T.   Painter, A.
Coleridge, M.   On a Bas-relief of Pelops and
  Hippodameia.
Connolly, C.   On Geoffrey Grigson.
Copus, J.   Art of Interpretation, The.
Couto.   Flowers and Water.
Creeley.   Figures, The.
Cummings, E. E.   Picasso / you give us Things.
Curdy.   On a Painting by a Member of the
  Northwest Visionary School.
Daniel, S.   Stonehenge.
Datcher, M.   Joseph speaks to gericault in the
  studio.
Davie, D.   Hill Field, The.
  With the Grain.
DeFrees.   Beetle Light.
Delaunay, S.   Greetings, Blaise Cendrars.
Di Michele, A.   Unica Zurn's Loam Bowl.

Doolittle, H..   Strophe.
Drake, N.   Foley Artist, The.
Duchamp.   Speculations.
Durand, M.   Reading Postures 3.
Edson, R.   Performance at Hog Theater, A.
Edwards, K.   About this time streetlamps flicker
  up like.
  Art of definition—is this, An.
Ellis, T.   T.A.P.O.A.F.O.M.
Elmslie, K.   History of France.
Emerson, R.   Art.
Erinna.   Delicate hands fashioned this portrait:
  good Prometheus.
Ernst, M.   Hundred Headless Woman, The.
Fanailova, E.   Frida's Album (*Frida Kahlo's
  Album*).
Fearing.   Art Review.
Ferlinghetti, L.   Monet's Lilies Shuddering.
Field.   La Gioconda; Leonardo Da Vinci, The
  Louvre.
  L'indifférent.
Ford, M.   Early to Bed, Early to Rise.
Fox, S.   Peaches.
Galvin, J.   Art Class.
Gautier.   Art.
Goethe.   Nature and Art.
Goldbarth.   Counterfeit Earth!, The.
Gonzáles Martínez.   Nectar of Ápan, The.
Goodison.   Hungry Belly Kill Daley.
Graves, R.   Epitaph on an Unfortunate Artist.
Griffin, S.   To the Far Corners of Fractured
  Worlds.
Guest, B.   On the Verge of the Path.
  Roses.
  Wild Gardens Overlooked by Night Lights.
Hacker, M.   Ballad of Ladies Lost and Found.
Hahn, K.   Artist's Daughter, The.
Han Yong'un [*or* Yongwun].   Artist, The.
  Artist, The.
Hannan, M.   Life Model.
Hass, R.   Image, The.
  Pornographer, The.
Heaney, S.   Artist, An.
Hecht, A.   Death the Painter.
Herbert, Z.   What Mr. Cogito Thinks About
  Hell.
  What Mr. Cogito Thinks About Hell.
Herlin.   Echo of fireplace, An.
Hernández Cruz.   Art of Hurricanes, The.
Herrera.   Resurrection of the Flesh, The.
Herrick.   Art above Nature, to Julia.
Hill, G.   Pre-Raphaelite Notebook, A.
  Vergine Bella.
Hinz-Penner, R.   Flowers: "I have not missed
  the irony of this magnetism, my being."
  Opening in Santa Fe, The.
Hirschman, J.   Painting, The.
Hirshfield, J.   Stream of It, The.
Hofmann, M.   Late Richard Dadd, 1817–1886,
  The.
Holloway, G.   Bash on Basho: Six of the Best.
Hovey.   Accident in Art.
Howard, R.   Nikolaus Mardruz to his Master
  Ferdinand, Count of Tyrol, 1565.
  Venetian Interior, 1889.
Hsieh Chin.   Song of Cursive Calligraphy.
Hughes, R.   Image, The.
Hugo, V.   More about God (But with Some
  Reservations).
Issa.   Writing shit about new snow.
Jacobsen, R.   Cobalt.
Jeffers, R.   Artist, An.
Jenkins, A.   Barcelona.
Jensma.   Portrait of the artist.
Johnson, J.   Before a Painting.
Juana Inés de la Cruz.   On Her Portrait.
Justice, D.   Anonymous Drawing.
Kates.   No Altarpiece.
Keats.   On Seeing the Elgin Marbles.
Kees.   Round: "Wondrous life! cried Marvell at
  Appleton House."
Keith, Sally.   Gallery, The.
Kinsella, J.   Warhol at Wetlands.
Kinsella, T.   Portrait of the Artist, A.
Kipling, R.   Conundrum of the Workshops, The.
  Evarra and His Gods.

  L'Envoi.
Klassen, S.   Artist and Medium.
Kosugi, T.   Micro 1.
Krivulin.   Crossing the keyboards of the palace.
  Glory to caesar! and glory to God in the
    highest!
Kunze, R.   End of Art, The.
Landor, W.   I Strove With None.
Lanier, S.   Clover.
  To Bayard Taylor.
Lauterbach.   Stones (Istanbul, Robert Smithson).
Lefroy.   Palaestral Study, A.
Levertov.   Dog of Art, The.
  Life of Art, The.
Lezama Lima.   Portrait of José Cemí.
Lindsay, V.   Arts are old, old as the stones, The.
Liu, T.   Vox Angelica.
Livesay, D.   Three Emily's, The.
Loftis, N.   Delirium.
Logue, C.   To My Fellow Artists.
Luzi.   Postscriptum.
Mac Lochlainn, G.   Artists, The.
Macha, F.   Artist and a Wailing Mother, An.
Machado Ruiz.   But art? / It is pure and intense
  play.
Mahon.   Dying Art, A.
  Girls on the Bridge.
Maiden.   New.
Martinez, D.   Matisse: Blue Nude, 1952.
Mason, W.   Alcander's Flower Garden.
Masters, E.   Archibald Higbie.
Mayor, C.   Winter Night.
McDonald, C.   At the Gwen John Exhibition.
Melville, H.   Art: "In placid hours well-pleased
  we dream."
  Attic Landscape, The.
Miedzyrzecki.   Golden Age, The.
Mistral, G.   Decalogue of the Artist.
Monroe, H.   Rubens.
Montale.   Elegy of Our Times.
Moore, M.   When I Buy Pictures.
Mullen, H.   Music for Homemade Instruments.
Murray, G.   Art of a Cold Sun.
Murray, J.   You Talk of Art.
Naden.   Two Artists, The.
Napier, F.   I Do Not Want the Ceiling of the
  Sistine Chapel.
Nemerov.   Intimations.
Ni Tsan.   Inscribed on a Painting by Myself.
Norse.   Business of Poetry, The.
  Picasso Visits Braque.
Nortje.   Newcombe at the Croydon Gallery.
O'Donoghue, M.   Harmony in Blue.
O'Hara, F.   Memorial Day 1950.
  Step Away from Them, A.
  Why I Am Not a Painter.
Ondaatje.   Henri Rousseau and Friends.
Opie.   To Mr. Opie, On His Having Painted for
  Me the Picture of Mrs Twis.
Oppen.   Drawing.
  Fragonard, / Your spiral women.
Ormsby, F.   Apples, Normandy, 1944.
O'Shaughnessy, A.   Ode: "We are the music-
  makers."
Pai, S.   Circle, triangle, square.
  Fall aster with firefly.
Palmer, M.   Dearest Reader.
Parker, D.   Portrait of the Artist.
Peacocke.   Remembrance.
Peterson, L.   Wake Up, My Little Pretties.
Phillips, C.   Luncheon on the Grass.
Pilling.   Ophelia.
Pinkerton, H.   On Vermeer's *Young Woman with
  a Water Jug* (1658) in the Metropolitan
  Museum.
Pinsky.   Their Speech, Compared with Wisdom
  and Poetry.
Polkowski.   Noli Me Tangere.
Porter, P.   And No Help Came.
  It's there, somewhere in the Platonic cold store.
Portugal, Anne.   You really know your art you.
Pound, E.   L'Art, 1910.
  Of Jacopo del Sellaio.
  Rest, The.
Procter, A.   Unexpressed.
Rakosi.   Figures in an Ancient Ink.

Ransom, J. Painted Head.
Ratcliff, C. Big Bad Art Thing, The.
Reddy, Srikanth. Evening with Stars.
Rich, A. Architect.
  At a Bach Concert.
  Aunt Jennifer's Tigers.
  Burning Oneself Out.
  Diamond Cutters, The.
Richardson, L. Poet Sings His Painting, The.
Ríos, A. Death of Anselmo Luna, The.
Robinson, A. Art and Life.
Roland Holst. Quatrain: "We're snug as a bug
  in a heated house."
Rossetti, C. In An Artist's Studio.
Rossetti, D. 74: Old and New Art (St Luke the
  Painter).
Rouse, A. Memo to Auden.
Rukeyser, M. Homage to Literature.
  Käthe Kollwitz.
  Painters.
Ryan, T. Trompe l'oeil.
Sadoleto. Poem of Jacobus Sadoletus on the
  Statue of Laocoon, The.
Salmon, A. Painting.
Salter. Rebirth of Venus, The.
Sanders, E. Cutting Prow, The.
Santayana. On a Piece of Tapestry.
Scalapino. Picasso and Anarchism.
Scammell, W. Eclogue: Clerk of the Weather.
  Retrospective.
Schmitz. Because the Eye Is a Flower Whose
  Root is the Hand.
Schuyler, J. Red Brick and Brown Stone.
Seiffert. Cubist Portrait.
Serote. Hell, well, heaven.
Shapiro, K. Poet.
Sia, B. Open Letter to the Entertainment
  Industry, An.
Slessor. Nuremberg.
Smith, K. Remembering Miller.
Smith, S. New Age, The.
Smith, V. At an Exhibition of Historical
  Paintings, Hobart.
Snodgrass. Matisse: "The Red Studio".
Song. Girl Powdering Her Neck.
Soto. Effects of Abstract Art, The.
Speght. *Disswasion* hearing her assigne my
  helpe.
Stafford, W. After Arguing against the
  Contention That Art Must Come from
  Discontent.
Stevens, W. Anecdote of the Jar.
  Indigo Glass in the Grass, The.
Stickney, T. On the Concert.
  Requiescam.
Swirszczynska [or Swir]. My Father's
  Workshop.
Sylvester, J. Cunning Painter, that with curious
  care, The.
Tanning. Report from the Field.
Tate, A. Sonnet: To a Portrait of Hart Crane.
Taylor, B. Paean to the Dawn, A.
Taylor, E. Woman as Artist.
Tennyson, A. Palace of Art, The.
Thomas, D. In My Craft or Sullen Art.
Thompson, P. At the Nu'uanu Reservoir Pool.
Tranter. Great Artist Reconsiders the Homeric
  Simile, The.
  Having Completed My Fortieth Year.
Troupe. View from Skates in Berkeley, The.
Tu Fu [or Du Fu]. Homage to the Painter
  General Ts'ao.
Tzara. Chanson Dada.
  Proclamation without Pretention.
Unknown. Art.
  Artist, The.
Updike. Two Hoppers.
Upton, L. Happiness: "In the hot white dome of
  air."
Van Duyn. Homework.
Van Haren, E. Stepping Out With Edvard
  Munch ("When from the other world you.").
  Stepping Out With Edvard Munch ("When from
  the virile grave.").
Violi. Hazards of Imagery, The.
Voigt. Gobelins.

Voznesensky [or Voznesenskii]. Mayakovsky in
  Paris.
  Portrait of Plisetskaya.
Wagoner, D. Author of American Ornithology
  Sketches a Bird, Now Extinct, The.
Walcott. Map of Europe, A.
Waters, M. First Lesson: Winter Trees.
Webb, C. Meat Michelangelo.
Weiners. Poem for Painters, A.
Welish. Textile 9.
Werfel. Lasting Things, The.
Whitman, W. Eidólons.
Wilbur, R. Museum Piece.
Williams, H. Blest Poesy! Oh sent to calm.
Williams, T. One-day Snow.
Williams, W. Artist, The.
  Landscape with the Fall of Icarus.
Wilner, E. Conversation with a Japanese
  Student.
  Meditation on the *Wen-Fu*.
Wilson, T. Magpies in Picardy.
Winters, Y. Alas, that I should be.
  To My Infant Daughter.
Wood, S. Carnation. Lily, Lily, Rose.
Woods, V. Lost Masterpiece, The.
Wright, C. Quotations.
Wright, J. Request to a Year.
Yau. January 18, 1979.
Yeats. Lapis Lazuli.
Young, K. Campbell's Black Bean Soup.
Yuson. Andy Warhol Speaks to His Two
  Filipino Maids.
Zukofsky, L. Shang Cup.
See also **Artists' Colonies**

Art Poetry
Bernstein, C. This poem intentionally left blank.

Artaud, Antonin
Artaud. Letter to André Breton.
  Pounding and Gism.
  Ten years that the language is gone.

Artemis
Anacreon. I implore you, deer-shooter.
Bell, J. Sleeping with Artemis.
Broumas, O. Artemis.
Callimachus. Hymn to Artemis.
Healy, E. Moon on the Porch.
Horace. Poem for Artemis (3.22).
Nossis. O Artemis of Delos and lovely Ortygia.
Ovid. Arethusa Saved.
Price, V. Artemis: "Bear mother, supple."
Sappho. To goldenhaired Phoibos whom Leto
  bore.
Telesilla. But Artemis, my girls.

Arthritis
Appleman, P. Birthday Card to My Mother.
Pilling. Nostrum.

Arthurian Legend
Emerson, R. Merlin I.
Frere. I've often wish'd that I could write a
  book.
Hill, G. Merlin.
Layamon. Arthur was mortally wounded,
  grievously badly.
  Arthur's Dream.
Lytton, E. Bloodhounds on Arthur's Track.
Morris, W. Defense of Guenevere, The.
Smith, S. Blue from Heaven, The.
Spicer, J. Book of Galahad, The.
Tennyson, A. Lady of Shalott, The.
  Pelleas and Ettarre.
  Prayer: "Pray for my soul. More things are
  wrought by prayer."
Unknown. Sir Gawain and the Green Knight
  [Marie Borroff Translation].
Wieners. High Noon.
Winters, Y. Sir Gawaine and the Green Knight.

Artichokes
Cortázar. Clocks.
Robertson, R. Artichoke.

Artifacts
Armitage, S. Dead Sea Poems, The.
Doty, M. Green Crab's Shell, A.
Hughes, T. Relic.
Mahon. Dying Art, A.
Martínez, V. Reliquaries, The.

Morgan, R. Jutaculla Rock.
Pound, E. Papyrus.
Sarah, R. Relics.

Artifice
Nathan, L. Ragged Sonnet: So Shall I Live.

Artificial Insemination
StacyLynn. Examination.

Artists' Colonies
Robinson, E. Hillcrest.

Ascension Day
De León, L. At the Ascension.
Lewis, S. Ascension Thursday.
Vaughan, H. They Are All Gone into the World
  of Light!

Ash Trees
Barnes, W. Leaves a-Vallen.
Pei Di. Path of the Ashtrees, The.
Wang Wei. Path of the Ashtrees, The.

Ashbery, John
Clark, T. To John Ashbery.
Duncan, R. At the Poetry Conference: Berkeley
  After the New York Style.
Koch, K. Circus, The ("I remember when I
  wrote The Circus.").
O'Hara, F. To John Ashbery.
Schuyler, J. Dining Out with Doug and Frank.
Warsh. To John Ashbery.

Ashes
Antokolsky. You must dig in black ashes a long
  time.
Bibbins, M. Mud.
Bousoño, C. There's a Miracle Going On in the
  Ashes.
Clanchy, K. Miscarriage, Midwinter.
Daisen. All things come apart.
Edmond, L. Anniversary.
Field. Your Rose is Dead.
Ginsberg, A. On Neal's Ashes.
Hudgins. Ashes.
Khoury, N. People of Fire.
Kizer, C. Ashes, The.
Mahapatra, J. Ash.
Morling, M. Ashes.
Pizarnik. Ashes.
Sears, P. Volcanic Ash.
Simms, W. Voice of Memory in Exile, from a
  Home in Ashes, The.
Unknown. You would be a heap of ashes
  instantly.
Wen T'ing-yün. Embers of Incense.

Asia
Barkova, A. Tatar Anguish.
Carleton, Bob. Ja Da.
Jaimes Freyre. Dawn, The.
Kaufman, S. Poem in November.
Melville, H. My Jacket Old.
Merrill, J. Willoware Cup.
Olin. No Matter What Sign You Are.
Purdy, A. Blue City, The.
Sŏ Chŏngju. Elephants of Thailand.
Tomlinson, C. Epilogue: "This advanced
  frontier."

Asian-Americans
Chang, D. Foreign Ways.
Chin. Floral Apron, The.
  We Are Americans Now, We Live in the
  Tundra.
Chong Xiong. Because I am it's a race thing
  trip.
Davis, K. Searching for Mooncakes.
Divakaruni. Indian Movie, New Jersey.
Hottel, J. Shikata ga nai.
Inada. F.B.I. swooped in early, The.
  It began as truth, as fact.
  Making It Stick.
  Projected Scenario of a Performance to Be
  Given Before the UN.
Lee, L. Cleaving, The.
  He gossips like my grandmother, this man.
  Persimmons.
Lem. So Now You're Chicana.
Lim, S. Lost Name Woman.
  Modern Secrets.
  Riding into California.
Mark, D. Suzie Wong Doesn't Live Here.

Okita. Notes for a Poem on Being Asian
  American.
Pegram, L. Yellah.
Phi, T. Asian Am Anthem, An.
Robles. Remembering the Past.
Sia, B. Open Letter to the Entertainment
  Industry, An.
Su, A. Address.
  Miss Chang is Missing.
Uyematsu. 30 Miles from J-Town.
  To All Us Sansei Who Wanted to Be Westside.
Vazirani, R. Mrs. Biswas Goes Through a Photo
  Album.
  Mrs. Biswas of Maryland on the Phone.
Wong, N. When I Was Growing Up.
See also Chinese, The; Filipinos; Japanese, The

Asians
Alvi, M. Presents from My Aunts in Pakistan.
Divakaruni. Founding of Yuba City, The.
  Leaving Yuba City.
Gorostiza, J. Fireflies.
Sharma, P. Action-Packed Sonnet.

Aspen Trees
Holan. Reminiscence.
Hopkins, G. Binsey Poplars (Felled 1879).
Ivask, Y. Shall we forget the shiver.
Su Tung-p'o. Rain in the Aspens.
Thomas, E. Aspens.
See also Poplar Trees

Aspirations
Benedetti, M. We All Conspire.
Burnside, J. Men's Harbour, The.
Chin. Elegy for Chloe Nguyen.
Cullen, Lisa. Reasons to Meditate.
Duncan, L. Visit, The: "Mary, more than quite
  contrary, bars the door."
Dunn, D. Ships.
Goodell, L. I Was Going to Be.
Hughes, L. Deferred.
Juvenal. Satire 10.
Kennedy, X. Keep a Hand on Your Dream.
Larkin, J. Inventory.
Martial. Ad Quintilianum.
Miyazawa Kenji. November 3rd.
Musa, Y. Where is Tomorrow?
Persius. Satire 5: "From the earliest poets, the
  fashion stands."
Petrarch. Father in heaven, after each lost day.
Pollarolo, G. Sunny Afternoon Dream, The.
Porter, C. Tale of the Oyster, The.
Procter, A. Incompleteness.
Salaam. I Live in the Mouth of History.
Scott, W. Early Aspirations.
Stafford, W. Way It Is, The.
Trethewey, N. Domestic Work, 1937.

Assassinations and Assassins
Addison, L. After MLK: the marksman marked
  leftover kill.
Barrax. For Malcolm: After Mecca.
  King: April 4, 1968.
Berman, D. April 13, 1865.
Bobyshev. Trotsky in Mexico.
Brown, D. Where I Was.
Clifton, L. Malcolm.
Dickinson, E. Apparently with no surprise.
Ellis, T. Zapruder.
Faiz. No Sign of Blood.
Felltham [or Feltham]. On the Duke of
  Buckingham, Slain by Felton, the 23rd August,
  1628.
Gunn, T. Claus von Stauffenberg.
Herd. Pink Rose Rings, The.
Hyneman, R. No. 5, Judith.
Ismaili. Bajji.
Justice, D. Assassination, The.
  Voice of Col. Von Stauffenberg Rising from
  Purgatory, The.
LaMon, J. Sammy Davis, Jr.
Limonov. Japanese restaurant is good in
  autumn—in dank weather—the hot napkins,
  the warm sake, The.
Livingston, M. Arthur Thinks on Kennedy.
Llwyd, Iwan. Disappeared, The.
Luzi. Postscriptum.
Madhubuti. Assassination.

Melville, H. Martyr, The.
Murphy, R. Luttrell.
Ondaatje. Heat of explosions, The.
Randall, B. Be He Ezra Pound, Kennedy, or
  King.
Reed, I. Nov 22, 1988.
Rimbaud, A. Morning of Drunkenness.
Shaler, N. Marksman's Work, The.
Shuford. Visit, The.
Stodghill, Pat. August 1, 1966.
Upton, L. Scroll.
Wachtel. Coriolis Effect, The.
Whitbread. November 25, 1963.
Whitehead, C. Brutus' Last Song.

Asses
Baxter, J. Brother Ass, Brother Ass, you are full
  of fancies.
Prigov. Entry into Jerusalem.
Wang the Zealot. Bumping on an Ass.
See also Donkeys

Assistance
Finlay, I. O.H.M.S.
Hudgins. Colonel.
Issa. Man pulling radishes, The.

Assurance
Crosby, F. Blessed Assurance.

Assyria and Assyrians
Al-Bayati, A. Elegy to Aisha, An.
  Transformations of Aisha: Aisha's Birth and
  Death in the Magical Rituals Inscribed in
  Cuneiform on the Nineveh Tablets.
  Writing on Aisha's Tomb.
Byron, G. Destruction of Sennacherib, The.
Kushner, A. Picture, A.
Moore, M. Is Your Town Nineveh?

Astarte
Doolittle, H. Evil was active in the land.

Asteroids
Cumpian. Estrellitas.

Astrology and Astrologers
Beatty, P. Independent Study.
Kipling, R. Astrologer's Song, An.
Longfellow, H. Poet's Calendar, The.
Manilius. Why do we in worries waste our
  lives, and torture.
McElroy, C. Horoscope.
More, S. Astrologer, The.
Ramke, B. Difference Between Night and Day,
  The.
Robertson, Lisa. Wednesday.
Stein, C. Virgo Poem, The: Ouspensky
  Addresses a Congress of Virgoes.
Valerie, J. Astrology?

Astronauts
Alexander, E. Apollo.
Buchan, T. Everlasting Astronauts, The.
Dickey, J. 2: The Moon Ground.
Emans. Crew of Apollo 8, The.
George, W. Armstrong and Aldrin on the Moon.
Hayden, R. Astronauts.
Morgan, E. From the Domain of Arnheim.
Redmond, J. Let's Not Get Ahead of Ourselves.
Roseliep. EVA Psalm.
Williams, W. Heel and Toe to the End.

Astronomy and Astronomers
Adcock, F. Ex-Queen Among the Astronomers,
  The.
Basho. Clouds come and go, The.
Bowers, E. Astronomers of Mont Blanc, The.
Condee. Mrs. Charles Sanders Peirce, or The
  Solution to the Universe.
Donne. Good Friday [or Goodfriday], 1613.
  Riding Westward.
Espada. Mayan Astronomer in Hell's Kitchen,
  A.
Goldbarth. Talk Show, The.
Griffin, J. Night Sky Hiss.
Hristic. That Night They All Gathered on the
  Highest Tower.
Keyes, S. Greenwich Observatory.
Khosravani. There are four kinds of men who'll
  get no fee from me.
Lea, S. Telescope.
Ortiz. On late-night television, two U.S.
  scientists talk about why the U.S.

Patterson, R. Forerunner.
Ramke, B. Astronomer Works Nights: A
  Parable of Science, The.
Rich, A. Planetarium.
Shore. Astronomer's Journal, An.
Very. Slowness of Belief in a Spiritual World,
  The.
Volkman. Shrewd star, who crudes our naming:
  you should be flame.
Wakoski. For Whitman.
Whitman, W. When I Heard the Learn'd
  Astronomer.
Williams, M. Astronomy.
Young, K. Letters from the North Star.

Astrophysics and Astrophysicists
Hoover, P. Letter to Einstein Beginning Dear
  Albert.
Lumsden, R. Beginning of the End, The.
Salazar. Moulton Transformations.
Wilkie, B. Very Fine Lines.

Atheism
Chesterton. On Reading "God".
Dobell, S. Liberty to M. le Diplomate.
Dunn, S. At the Smithville Methodist Church.
Farrell, F. Credo.
Flynn, N. Emptying Town.
Garrison, D. I Saw You Walking.
Hardy, T. Impercipient, The.
Keelan, C. Secularist, The.
Newman, R. Theology.
O'Driscoll, D. Missing God.
Pobo, K. Grand Canyon.
Réda, Jacques. Amen.
Shapiro, K. I Am an Atheist Who Says His
  Prayers.
Shiki. O autumn winds.
Tukaram. In My View.
Urquiza-Vicente, I. Spare Tire (the atheist's
  unmailed letter to god).
Whittemore, R. Psalm: "Lord feeds some of His
  prisoners better than others, The."

Athena
Alcaeus [or Alkaios]. Having done most
  shameful, unjust things.
Anyte [or Anytes]. Ox-sized cauldron,
  Kleubotos gave, An.
  Stand there, manslaying spear; no longer drip.
Atabay, Cyrus (1929-1996). Pallas.
Clampitt. Athena.
Homer. Goddess intervenes between Achilles
  and Agamemnon, The.
See also Minerva

Athens, Greece
Lefroy. Idler Listening to Socrates Discussing
  Philosophy with His Boy-Friends, An.
Lourie. Three Recent Trips to the Golden Past:
  East Village, Clarksdale Mississippi, Athens.
Milton. Athens.
Ritsos. After the Defeat.
Symonds. In years of old.
Williamson, A. Minoan Distance, The.

Athletics and Athletes
Allen, S. To Satch.
Arif. Twelfth Man, The.
Barresi. Called Up: Tinker to Evers to Chance.
Dean, D. K. Back to Back.
Evans, D. Song of Racquetball.
Guillén, N. Small Ode to a Black Cuban Boxer.
Higgins, F. Tennis in the City.
Hope, A. Massacre of the Innocents.
Housman. To an Athlete Dying Young.
Khalifa, I. No Need to Discourage Dreams.
Lacavaro, A. Advantages of Being a World
  Class Athlete, The.
Matthews, W. Foul Shots: A Clinic.
  In Memory of the Utah Stars.
McManus, J. Commercials exaggerate.
Miller, E. Roy Campanella: January, 1958.
Pahmeier, G. Grief Comes in Smallest Ways.
Piercy. Morning Athletes.
Pushkin, A. On the Statue of a Player at Svaika.
Rexroth, K. Vitamins and Roughage.
Updike. Ex-Basketball Player.
Veinberg, J. Last Shot.
Wellburn, R. Pitching Coups.

Whitman, W. Runner, The.

Atlanta, Georgia
DuBois, W. Litany of [*or* at] Atlanta, A.
Fordham. Atlanta Exposition Ode.
Obadike, M. Tradition/Abstraction.
Shange. About Atlanta.
Touré, A. Imani in Sunburst Summer: A Chant.

Atlantic Ocean
Aiken, C. Hatteras Calling.
Cowper, W. Castaway, The.
Hayley. To Mrs. Hayley, On her Voyage to America. 1784.
Longfellow, H. Seaweed.
Osundare. Goree.
Sargent, E. Rockall.
Sexton. Crossing the Atlantic.

Atlantis
Crane, H. Atlantis.
Fritz, Walter Helmut (b. 1929). Atlantis.
Fuhrman, J. Atlantis.
Hendry, J. Constant North, The.
Retivova, T. Elegy to Atlantis.

Atomic Bomb
"Agyeya.". Hiroshima.
Ai. Chance.
Testimony of J. Robert Oppenheimer, The.
Armour. Hiding Place.
Balaban. Atomic Ghost.
Bradley, J. Sailors Shielding Their Eyes During Atomic Bomb Test, Bikini, 1947.
Brandi. Preparing the Nets at New Stuyahok.
Braun, H. To Fat Boy, the Bomb.
Buckley, C. Why I'm in Favor of a Nuclear Freeze.
Ciardi, J. V-J Day.
Collins, A. Hiroshima Day at the Riviera Coffeeshop.
Corso. Bomb.
Curnow. Pacific 1945-1995.
Daugherty, J. Pack train, stage coach, pony express, climb over the mountain passes.
Davie, D. Rejoinder to a Critic.
Doubiago, S. Ground Zero.
Dougherty, E. Why I Think About Hiroshima and Nagasaki.
Dugan, A. Actual Vision of Morning's Extrusion.
Duncan, A. Ghost of Fusion, The.
Dunn, S. Cocked Finger, The.
Eimers. Another Kimono.
Engels, J. Fish Dream, The.
Engman. Mushroom Clouds.
Fell, A. August 6, 1945.
Forché. Garden Shukkei-en, The.
Frost, R. U. S. 1946 King's X.
Gibson, M. Radiation.
Ginsberg, A. Plutonian Ode.
Glancy. Harry S Truman Library, Independence, Missouri.
Grabill. Dream of the Closeness of Venus, A.
Greenway, W. Atom Bum, The.
Griswold, J. Origami.
Hahn, K. Bath, The: August 6, 1945.
Hahn, O. Vision of Hiroshima.
Herd. Bombshell.
Heyen. N.
Hogan, L. Prayer for Men and Children.
Ignatow, D. Simultaneously.
Johnson, K. Trilobytes.
Kaminsky, M. Questions: "If I shriek."
Kaschnitz. Hiroshima.
Keenan, T. After the Neutron.
Kinnell. Fundamental Project of Technology, The.
Kirkup. No More Hiroshimas.
La Morticella. Liturgy for Trinity, A.
Levertov. Gathered at the River.
Watching "Dark Circle".
Levine, P. Horse, The: "They spoke of the horse alive."
Louis, A. Nevada Red Blues.
Lowell, R. For the Union Dead.
McKain. Opening Day.
Merrill, C. Wipp Protest.
Mura. Hibakusha's Letter (1955), The.
Olds, S. When.

Oresick. In this third year of Reagan, my 27th year.
Ray, D. For Harry S Truman in Hell.
Rich, A. For Ethel Rosenberg.
History.
Trying to Talk with a Man.
Romtvedt. Black Beauty, A Praise.
Eating Dinner at My Sister's.
Roripaugh, L. Hiroshima Maiden.
Sáenz. Creation. Trinity Site, New Mexico. 5:30 A.M. July 16th, 1945.
Sakaki. Memorandum.
Salter. Welcome to Hiroshima.
Sanders, M. Vigil at a Missile Silo, A.
Sankichi, T. At the Makeshift Aid Station.
Dying.
Flames.
Shadow, The: "Cheap movie theaters, saloons, fly-by-night markets."
Santos, S. Near the Desert Test Sites.
Seaton, M. Jubilee for the Bomb.
Sherry, J. Free Radicals.
Hazardous Waste.
Shinkichi Takahashi. Burning Oneself to Death.
Stafford, W. At the Bomb Testing Site.
Stainer. Quanta.
Steensen, S. State of affairs is thinkable, eventually, A.
Strickland. Shadow.
Stryk, L. Return to Hiroshima.
Uschuk, P. Of Simple Intent.
Vasquez, R. Early Morning Test Light over Nevada, 1955.
Wallace, R. Hell Mural, The: Panel I.
Wheelock, J. Earth.
Wilner, E. High Noon at Los Alamos.
Wisenberg, S. May 28, 1945.
Zimmer. But Bird.

See also **Hiroshima, Japan; Nuclear War**

Atoms
Blanco. Quantum Theory.
Teoría cuántica.
Cavendish, M. Of Many Worlds in This World.
Dickinson, E. Choice.
Glenday, J. Concerning the Atoms of the Soul.
Levertov. After "Mindwalk".
Morgan, R. Music of the Spheres.
Pack, R. Proton Decay.
Sherry, P. Fermi Lab: Sisyphus of Quarks.

Atonement
Guiney. Atoning Yesterday, The.
Im Yŏngjo. Soap.
López Velarde. My Heart, Faithful.
Pinsky. Avenue.
Smart, C. Hymn to the Supreme Being.
Unknown. Let the first syllable of PEnelope be followed by the first of DIdo, the first of CAnus by that of REmus.

Attics
Goetsch, D. Walls, The.
Justice, D. In the Attic.
Peacocke. We're Staying at the Castlemount, Western Esplanade.

Attucks, Crispus
Hayden, R. Crispus Attucks.
Tolson, M. Dark Symphony.

Auctions
Brouwer, J. Space Memorabilia Auction, Superior Stamp and Coin, Beverly Hills, California.
Bynner. Highest Bidder, The.
Pow. Favourite Stretch of Disused Railway, A.
Reed, H. Auction Sale, The.
Sandburg, C. Auctioneer.
Scott, D. Kirkwall Auction Mart.
Taylor, H. Bargain at Half the Price, A.

Auden, W. H. (Wystan Hugh)
Booth, P. Seeing Auden Off.
Empson. Just a Smack at Auden.
Haley, V. Miss Gee Meets W. H. Auden in Heaven.
Loftis, N. In Memorium: Robert Hayden.
Muldoon, P. Wystan.
Rouse, A. Memo to Auden.
Sutherland, Fraser. Auden's Face.

Walcott. Eulogy to W.H. Auden.

Audubon, John James
Alexander, P. Reprise.
Warren, R. Audubon: A Vision.
Dream He Never Knew the End of, The.
Love and Knowledge.
Tell Me a Story.
Was Not the Lost Dauphin.

Aughrim, Battle of (1691)
Lawless, E. After Aughrim.
Murphy, R. Rapparees.

August
Alcosser. Approaching August.
Bly, R. August Rain.
Buffoni, F. Partitions.
Eberhart, R. Loon Call, A.
Filkova, Fedya. Friendship: "Death gives way sometimes."
García Lorca. August: "August. / The opposing."
Garland, H. In August.
Halpern, D. Approach, The.
Ipadeola, T. August.
Jacobik, G. Turkeys in August.
Kennedy, X. One Winter Night in August.
Kenyon, J. August Rain, after Haying.
Lux. Hungry Gap-Time, The.
Oliver, M. August: "When the blackberries hang."
Ponge. Trees That Come Undone within a Sphere of Fog.
Prévert. August Bank Holiday.
Ray, H. August.
Sexton. I Remember.
Snyder, G. Mid-August at Sourdough Mountain Lookout.
Spalding, E. August.
Wylie. August.
Zhenkai. August Sleepwalker, The.

Augustine, Saint
Grosholz. Back Trouble.
Kizer, C. Erotic Philosophers, The.

Aunt Jemima
Williams, C. In Search of Aunt Jemima.

Aunts
Alvi, M. Presents from My Aunts in Pakistan.
Blue Cloud. To-ta Ti-om.
Boss, L. Candy Lady, The.
Browning, E. First Book: Young Aurora's Fostermother.
Campo. Aunt Toni's Heart.
Cather, W. Macon Prairie.
Clifton, L. Praise song.
Dittberner-Jax. Blues for Aunt Ruth.
Dybek. Cherry.
Eliot, T. S. Aunt Helen.
Gemin, P. Upper Peninsula Landscape with Aunts.
Ginsberg, A. To Aunt Rose.
Graham, H. Waste.
Gylys, B. Family Reunion—Aunt Vern's Two Cents.
Harrison, T. Study.
Lee, W. Aunt Martha.
Nordhaus. Aunt Lily and Frederick the Great.
Parra, N. Tunnel, The.
Powell, K. For Aunt Cathy.
Rich, A. Aunt Jennifer's Tigers.
Ríos, A. Language of Great-Aunts, The.
Seto, T. Blood Ties.
Sexton. Some Foreign Letters.
Stevenson, R. Auntie's Skirts.
Tolson, M. Old Houses.
Trethewey, N. Flounder.
Unknown. My Aunt Jane.
Wojahn. Satin Doll.

Auschwitz, Poland
Agosin. Traveling Valise.
Aini, L. Shower.
Amichai, Y. All the Generations Before Me.
All the Generations Before Me.
Almost a Love Poem.
Bond, E. If.
Borowski. Night over Birkenau.
Sun of Auschwitz, The.

Australia
Sun of Auschwitz, The.
Brock, V.   Remembering Dresden.
Fainlight, R.   Archive Film Material.
Gershon.   Experiments with God.
Hill, G.   Statesmen have known visions. And,
   not alone.
Levi, P.   Buna.
MacBeth [or Macbeth].   Poem of Death, A.
Porter, P.   Annotations of Auschwitz.
   Your Attention Please.
Quasimodo.   Auschwitz.
Roberts, E.   Primo Levi.
Rózewicz.   Questions about Poetry since
   Auschwitz.
Schiff, H.   Discovery.
Sheinfeld, I.   War Night 6.
Vinokurov.   Adam.
   Objects.
Welch, L.   Tattoo.
Yi Yŏnju.   Holiday Inside an Incubator.
Zych.   Auschwitz, 1987.
Australia
Adamson.   Elm Tree in Paddington, An.
   Stone Curlew, The.
Bobis, M.   Driving to Katoomba.
   Word Gifts for an Australian Critic.
Brookes, J.   Officers and Gentlemen Down
   Under.
Brown, F.   Last of England, The.
Browne, F.   Australian Emigrant, The.
Buckmaster.   Wilpena Pound.
Campbell, D.   Lovers, The.
Catalano.   Australia.
Cataldi.   13 November 1983.
Davidson, R.   Gravy Train, The.
Davis, J.   Desolation.
   First-born, The.
   One Hundred and Fifty Years.
Dransfield.   Minstrel.
   That Which We Call a Rose.
Duggan, L.   Five. One.
   Hearts (1983).
   One. One.
"Ern Malley.".   Dürer: Innsbruck, 1495.
   Sweet William.
Ewart.   Short Time.
Fogarty, L.   Kath Walker.
   Memo to Us (story).
Gray, R.   Journey: the North Coast.
Harris, R.   Sydney.
Hart-Smith.   Nullarbor.
Heaney, S.   Requiem for the Croppies.
Hope, A.   Australia.
Humphries, B.   Edna's Hymn.
Ingamells.   We who are called Australians have
   no country.
Jones, T.   Rhiannon.
Marshall-Stoneking.   Picture Postcard.
McAuley, J.   Envoi.
McAuley, J.   Terra Australis.
Mead, P.   Melbourne or the Bush.
Murphy, E.   Thank you, Mr Rason, for the
   Apples.
Murray, L.   Folklore.
   Now the sun is an applegreen blindness through
      the swells, a white blas on the sea face,
      flaking and shoaling.
   People are eating dinner in that country north of
      Legge's Lake, The.
O'Driscoll, D.   Tomorrow: "Tomorrow I will
   start to be happy."
Oodgeroo of the tribe Noonuccal.   No More
   Boomerang.
   We Are Going.
Page, G.   Jerry's Plains, 1848.
Porter, P.   Australian Garden, An.
   Last of England, The.
   Sydney Cove, 1788.
   Talking to You Afterwards.
Rankin, J.   Old Currawong.
Rodriguez, J.   Mahogany Ship, The.
Sladen.   Summer Christmas in Australia, A.
Slessor.   Five Bells.
   South Country.
Smith, V.   Early Arrival: Sydney.
Stewart, D.   Terra Australis.

Thorne, T.   High Country.
Tranter.   Enzensberger at 'Exiles'.
Unknown.   Hail South Australia!
   Hot Day In Sydney, A.
   See there, that tree is a digging stick.
Wallace-Crabbe.   Collective Invention, The.
   Mental Traveller's Landfall, The.
Webb, F.   Towards the Land of the Composer.
Wright, J.   At Cooloolah.
   Australia 1970.
   I To my Brothers.
Austria
Laughlin, J.   Inn at Kirchstetten, The.
Trakl.   In Hellbrunn.
Authorship and Authors
Artaud.   Civil Status.
Belloc.   On His Books.
Bradstreet, A.   Author to Her Book, The.
Campbell, R.   On the Same.
Chaucer.   Chaucer's Retraction.
Fitzgerald, F.   Obit on Parnassus.
Freneau.   To an Author.
Gilgun, J.   Ars Poetica: "About writing a poem.
   It occurs to me."
Herrick.   Argument of His Book, The.
Holmes, O.   Cacoëthes Scribendi.
Kaminsky, Ilya.   Author's Prayer.
Kaplinski, J.   Shunryu Suzuki.
Kennedy, B.   On ["Who Wrote Icon Basilike"
   by Dr.] Christopher Wordsworth, Master of
   Trinity.
Killigrew, A.   Upon the Saying That My Verses
   Were Made by Another.
Macpherson, J.   Boatman, The.
Nelson, S.   Anti-Foucault Poem, The.
Ondaatje.   Burning Hills.
Pound, E.   Lake Isle, The.
Powell, Robat.   For Jurij Koch.
Jones, R.   Yasnaya Polyana.
Robinson, E.   George Crabbe.
   Verlaine.
Scott, F.   Canadian Authors Meet, The.
Short, Spencer.   Romanticism.
Starbuck, G.   Said ("Agatha Christie to.").
   Working Habits.
Tupper, M.   Portrait of a Victorian Author.
Unknown.   To a Living Author: "Your comedy
   I've read, my friend."
Updike.   I Missed His Book, but I Read His
   Name.
Wagner, Catherine.   Lover.
Wheelwright.   There Is No Opera like
   "Lohengrin".
Automation
Brautigan.   All Watched Over by Machines of
   Loving Grace.
Automobile Accidents
Abbey, L.   Broken Silence.
Afrika, T.   Accident, The.
Burnside, J.   Penitence.
Corob, T.   Either Way.
Delgado, J.   I-5 Incident.
Fearing.   Obituary.
Geiger.   Disproportionate.
Glück, L.   Racer's Widow, The.
Hinojosa, Rolando.   Rest Due and Taken.
Joselow, B.   We Startle Things.
Kimbrell, J.   Salvation.
Kinnell.   Hitchhiker.
Lux.   Wife Hits Moose.
McCarthy, T.   Persephone, 1978.
McKendrick, J.   Beyond.
Mullen, L.   White Paintings I.
Ochester.   Mary Mihalik.
Oness, C.   August 1990.
Prufer, K.   Car Has Fallen from a Bridge, A.
Reznikoff.   Permit me to warn you.
Riordan, M.   Time Out.
Shapiro, K.   Auto Wreck.
Sholl.   Redbud.
Smith, D.   To Isle of Wight.
Snyder, G.   For John Chappell.
Sze.   Ice Floe.
Tranströmer.   Alone.
   Solitude.
Warren, R.   Snow Day.

Williams, W.   Romance Moderne.
Wunderlich, M.   Predictions about a Black Car.
Automobile Racing
Dubie.   Death of the Race Car Driver, The.
Glück, L.   Racer's Widow, The.
Seidel.   Men and Women.
Autumn
Alexander, M.   October Journey.
Apollinaire.   Farewell, The.
   Meadow Saffron.
Argensola, de, L. L.   Damon's Lament for His
   Clorenda, Yorkshire, 1654.
Barker, G.   Gardens of Ravished Psyche, The.
Barnes, W.   Leaves a-Vallen.
Basho.   All along this road.
   Autumn approaches.
   Autumn / Even the birds.
   Autumn going.
   Autumn moon / Tide foams.
   Autumn moonlight.
   Autumn wind / Blasting the stones.
   Autumnal full moon.
   Blowing stones.
   Chilling autumn rains.
   Cool fall night, A.
   Crow, A.
   Crows resting.
   Deep autumn.
   First day of spring.
   Many nights on the road.
   On a withered branch.
   Seeing people off.
   Smell of autumn / Heart longs.
   Solitary, A.
   Spider, if you had a voice.
   This autumn.
   This dark autumn.
   This road.
   Tomb, bend / To autum wind—.
   What voice.
   You could turn this way.
   You've heard monkeys crying.
Baudelaire.   Autumn Song.
Binyon.   Now is the time for the burning of the
   leaves.
Blake, W.   To Autumn.
Bobrowski.   Latvian Autumn, The.
Bogan, L.   Simple Autumnal.
Bonnefoy.   Words of Evening, The.
Bridges, R.   Garden in September, The.
Brock-Broido.   Of the Finished World.
Bronk.   Where It Ends.
Brontë, E.   Song: "Fall, leaves, fall; die, flowers,
   away;."
Bryant, W.   Autumn Woods.
   Death of the Flowers, The.
   November.
   October.
   To the Fringed Gentian.
Buckley, C.   Autumn's End.
Buson.   Autumn breezes.
   Autumn evening.
   Crossing the autumn moor.
   I go.
   I go.
   I go.
   I go out alone.
   Late evening cow, The.
   Sick man passing.
   Slung over a screen.
   Tub with no bottom, A.
   Utter aloneness—.
Campana.   Autumn Garden.
Campbell, R.   Autumn.
Caraion.   Enveloping Echo, The.
Carman, B.   Vagabond Song, A.
Carroll, L.   Humpty Dumpty's Poetic Recitation.
Cary, A.   Autumn.
Ceravolo.   Invisible Autumn.
   Song of Autumn, A.
Chao Shan-ch'ing.   Autumn on the Riverbank.
Chin.   Autumn Leaves.
Ching An.   Dusk of Autumn: Writing What My
   Heart Embraces.
Cho Myŏngni [or Myŏnghŭi].   Sky-geese have
   gone, The.

Wild geese have all flown away.
Chungji.   On Autumn.
Clare, J.   Autumn.
Claudel, P.   October.
Clover, J.   Archive of Confessions, a Genealogy of Confessions, An.
Coolidge, C.   Country Autumns, The.
Corbett, W.   Vermont Apollinaire.
Cranch.   Autumn Rain, The.
Crane, H.   Sunday Morning Apples.
Crapsey.   November Night.
Cristall.   Song: "Through springtime walks, with flowers perfumed."
Crowell, G.   Texas Autumn.
Cummings, E. E.   Always before your voice my soul.
   Wind has blown the rain away and blown, A.
Curry, N.   Anne Hathaway Composes Her 18th Sonnet.
Cushing, J.   Autumn Leaves.
Dana, R.   Figures, The.
   In Heaven.
Darío, R.   Autumn Verses.
   Autumn Verses.
   Autumnal.
Davis, K.   Miracle.
Davison, P.   From the Outland.
Day Lewis.   Stand-To, The.
Dengina, S.   Autumnal Equinox.
Dickinson, E.   Morns are meeker than they were, The.
   Name—of it—is "Autumn," The.
Dobyns.   Music One Looks Back On, The.
Doubleday, T.   No walk today;—November's breathings toss.
Duke, V.   Autumn in New York.
Dunbar, P.   Signs of the Times.
Eberhart, R.   Loon Call, A.
   Spider, The.
Ekelof.   Absentia Animi.
Encarnacion.   Seattle, Autumn, 1933.
Faiz.   When Autumn Came.
Farjeon, E.   Down! Down!
Fell, A.   Pushing Forty.
Field, R.   Something Told the Wild Geese.
Finch, B.   Written in a Shrubbery Towards the Decline of Autumn.
Forrester, S.   Gray autumn sky.
Freneau.   On Observing a Large Red-Streak Apple.
Frost, R.   Clear and Colder.
   My November Guest.
Fuller, M.   Lines Written in Boston on a Beautiful Autumnal Day.
Garland, H.   Plowing: A Memory.
Geng Wei.   Autumn Day.
George, S.   Come to the park they say is dead and see.
Gilliams, M.   Autumn.
Glück, L.   All Hallows.
Gray, D.   Sonnet: "October's gold is dim—the forests rot."
Grenier.   Autumn Moon Rising.
Halpern, D.   Annuals.
Han-shan Te-ch'ing.   Flat Lake's autumn water merges with the winter sky.
Hardie, K.   Autumn Cancer.
Harrison, D.   Collage for Richard Davis—Two Short Forms, A.
Hayne, P.   October.
Hébert, A.   I Am Earth and Water.
Herbert, W.   Smirr.
Hiestand, E.   Witch-Hazel Wood, The.
Hölderlin.   Autumn.
Hong Yunsuk.   That I Can Do This Autumn.
Hood, T.   Autumn: "I saw old Autumn in the misty morn."
   No!
Hopkins, G.   Hurrahing in Harvest.
   Spring and Fall [To a Young Child].
Housman.   Tell Me Not Here [It Needs Not Saying].
Howells, W.   November.
Hsieh T'iao.   Autumn Night, An.
Huai Ku.   Living on the Plain in Early Autumn.
Hulme, T.   Autumn.

Irwin, M.   Autumnal.
Issa.   Autumn evening.
   Autumn evening / Knees in arms.
   Autumn moon.
   Autumn wind / Mountain's shadow.
   Autumn wind / The beggar looks.
   Before this autumn wind.
   Evening clears, The.
   Holes in the wall, The.
   O autumn winds.
   Prostitute's shack, The.
   Tonight you too / Are rushed.
Jackson, H.   September [Days Are Here].
James, J.   Sister Midnight.
Jeffers, R.   Autumn Evening.
Kakei.   Making / the Master of Early Dawn.
Kanchev, Nikolai.   Smile, A.
Keats.   To Autumn: "Season of mists and mellow fruitfulness!"
Kennedy, X.   Landscapes with Set-Screws.
Kenney.   Apples on Champlain.
Kikaku.   Full autumn moon / On the straw mat.
Kinsella, T.   Another September.
Ko Chônghûi.   On the Way to Ch'ôngju.
Ko Ŭn.   Impermanence.
Kunitz, S.   End of Summer.
Kuzmina-Karavayeva.   Ruth.
Kyger.   For Your Birthday, Philip: And upon the Occasion of Becoming Abbot of the Hartford Street Zen Center.
Lady of the Assembly.   Assembly of Ladies, The.
Lamartine.   Autumn.
Larkin, P.   Afternoons.
Lawrence, D. H.   Butterfly.
   Ship of Death, The ("Now it is autumn and the falling fruit.").
Leonard, W.   Indian Summer.
Levine, P.   Zaydee.
Lewis, A.   Autumn, 1939.
Li Ching.   West Wind Ferries Grief, The.
Li Ch'ing-chao.   Long Melancholy Tune, A.
   Sorrow of Departure.
   Tune: "On the Trail of Sweet Incense".
Li Po.   Autumn Lines.
   Climbing Xie Tiao's North Tower at Xuan in Autumn.
   Verses: "Clean is the autumn wind."
Li Yü.   Tune: "Beating Silk Floss".
   Tune: "New Bounty of Royalty".
Li Yu [or Li Hou-Chu].   Silent and Alone.
Linden, M.   Fall Is Here, The.
Liu Yung.   Tune: "Bells Ringing in the Rain".
Loden.   Miss October.
Lodge, G.   Fall.
Longfellow, H.   Aftermath.
   Autumn.
   Harvest Moon, The.
Lorde.   What My Child Learns of the Sea.
Lowell, A.   Hoar-Frost.
   Wind and Silver.
Machado Ruiz.   Amancer de Otoño.
MacLeish.   Autumn.
   Immortal Autumn.
   Old Men in the Leaf Smoke, The.
Maeng Sasŏng.   Autumn comes to rivers and lakes.
Maiden.   Green Side, The.
Malroux.   Octet Before Winter.
Masaoka Shiki.   Autumn come / Cicada husk.
   Autumn wind / Gods, Buddha.
Mathews, H.   Sad Birds, The.
Matveyeva [or Matveieva].   Eggplants Have Pins and Needles, The.
McGrath, T.   Black Train, The.
Melville, H.   Pontoosuce.
Mercer, J.   Early Autumn.
Merwin.   Given Day, A.
Millay, E.   God's World.
Milosz, O.   Bridge, The.
Mistral, G.   Autumn.
Morikawa Kyoroku.   Even the dumplings / Are smaller.
Moses.   Fall, The.
Muir, E.   Late Wasp, The.
Naong.   Song for Late Autumn.

Nara Singde.   Tune: "Butterflies Lingering over Flowers".
Nashe [or Nash].   Autumn.
Nelson, J.   If You Knew September.
Nemerov.   For Robert Frost, in the Autumn, in Vermont.
Neruda.   Autumn Returns.
   I remember you as you were that ultimate autumn.
Ngo Chi Lan.   Autumn.
No Hyangnim.   Autumn Letter.
Noguchi, Yonejiro (Yone).   Leaves blown.
Nukada, P.   Polite Debate, A.
O'Callaghan, C.   Fall.
O'Hara, F.   Poem: "Eager note on my door said 'Call me', The."
Onitsura.   Autumn wind / Across the fields.
Ono no Komachi.   Autumn nights, it seems.
Opie.   On the Approach of Autumn.
O'Reilly, C.   Flames and Leaves.
Ou-yang Hsiu.   Pear Leaves Redden, Cicada's Song is Done, The.
Ozawa Roan.   By the Ōi River.
Pao Hsien.   Autumn Path.
Pastan.   Beall Mountain Seasonal.
Pasternak, B.   Let the Words.
Peterson, R.   Autumn.
Petri.   Morning Coffee.
Po Chü-i.   Autumn Thoughts, Sent Far Away.
   Lonely Night in Early Autumn.
Ponge.   End of Fall, The.
Posey, A.   Autumn.
Pushkin, A.   Autumn (A Fragment).
Radnóti.   Anxiously Autumn Arrives.
Réda, Jacques.   Autumn Distance.
Reece, Spencer.   Autumn Song.
Rexroth, K.   Buddha took some Autumn leaves.
   Half in a dream.
Riley, J.   When the Frost Is on the Punkin.
Rilke.   Autumn Day.
Robertson, R.   Fall: "Leaves are falling, falling from trees, The."
   Flags of Autumn.
   Flags of Autumn from Camera Obscura.
Robinson, A.   Art and Life.
Roland Holst.   Autumn Wind.
Rossetti, C.   Autumn ("I dwell alone—I dwell alone, alone.").
Ryuichi.   October Poem.
Schein, Michael.   Autumn: "On the first day of Autumn."
Schuyler, J.   Master of the Golden Glow, The.
   Verge.
Seward.   Behold that tree, in Autumn's dim decay.
Shakespeare, W.   Sonnet 73: "That time of year thou may'st in me behold."
Shelley, P.   Autumn: A Dirge.
   Ode to the West Wind.
Shiki.   O autumn winds.
Simic.   Ancient Autumn.
Smith, C.   To Melancholy. Written on the Banks of the Arun, October 1785.
   Written in October.
Smith, W.   Quail in Autumn.
Sogetsuni.   Divine mystery.
Spires.   In Heaven It Is Always Autumn.
Steiger.   Until the sun sinks into a green.
Stevens, W.   Last leaf that is going to fall has fallen.
Stevenson, R.   Autumn Fires.
Stickney, T.   Autumn's done; they have the golden corn in, The.
   Mnemosyne.
Su Tung-p'o.   Mid-Autumn Moon.
   Tune: "Water Mode Song".
Sun Ch'o.   Autumn Day, An.
Swenson, M.   On Its Way.
Taneda Santoka.   Waiting for what?
T'ao Ch'ien [or T'ao Yuan-ming].   In Reply to a Poem by Liu Chaisang.
   Written on the Ninth Day of the Ninth Month of the Year Yi-you.
Tate, A.   Seasons of the Soul.
Teiga.   In the poor man's house.
Tesshu.   On Visiting Sokei, Where the Sixth

Patriarch Lived.
Thomas, D.   Poem in October.
Thomas, E.   Digging.
   October.
Thomas, R. S.   Still.
Thompson, C.   Autumn Day, An.
   Autumn Leaves.
Thompson, P.   Autumn.
   Autumn.
Thomson, J.   Evening and Night.
Tighe.   Written in Autumn.
Tsvetayeva [*or* Tsvetaeva].   Poem: "When I look
   at the falling leaves."
Tu Fu [*or* Du Fu].   Autumn Meditation: 7.
   Autumn Wastes, The: 1 and 2.
   Clear After Rain ("Autumn, cloud blades on the
     horizon.").
   Déjeuner sur l'herbe.
   Moon Festival.
   My Thatched Roof Is Ruined by the Autumn
     Wind.
   On the River.
   Traveler's Pavilion.
   Wasteland—Gazing Far Away.
   Watching the Distances.
Tucker, M.   Autumn Thoughts.
Tuckerman, F.   Series 2, Sonnet 18.
Ungaretti.   Soldiers.
Unknown.   Reed Flowers Turn White.
   Words "I love you," The.
Untermeyer, J.   Autumn.
Van de Woestijne.   Fever Tune.
Verlaine.   Autumn Song ("Long sobs of, The.").
   Autumn Song ("Violins complain.").
   Autumn Song ("With long sobs.").
Very.   Autumn Flowers.
   Autumn Leaves.
   Sumach Leaves, The.
Vietnamese Oral Tradition.   Autumn: "Autumn
   rains blow."
Vogel, D.   On autumn nights.
Volkman.   Sonnet: "Premise, a solace—
   deciduous dress, A."
Vroomkoning.   Returning.
   Together Again ("You get these thoughts in
     melancholy Autumn.").
Wakayama Bokusui.   Cut off these hands, cut
   off these feet.
Waller, E.   Fall, The.
Wang Ch'ang-ling.   Song by the Walls.
Wang Kuo-wei.   Tune: "Sand of Silk-Washing
   Brook" ("Faded hibiscus and its leaves.").
Wang Wei.   Autumn Dusk at a Mountain Lodge.
   Autumn Mountain Evening.
   In the Hills.
Warren, R.   Acquaintance with Time in Early
   Autumn.
   Heart of Autumn.
Wei Ying-wu.   Autumn Night Message: To Qiu.
Weismiller.   Hemlocks in Autumn.
Welburn.   Gonsalves.
Wen T'ing-yün.   In the Mountains as Autumn
   Begins.
Wheatley, D.   Autumn, the Nightwalk, the City,
   the River.
Whittier.   Battle Autumn of 1862, The.
   Fruit-Gift, The.
Wieners.   Waning of the Harvest Moon, The.
Wilbur, R.   Alatus.
   October Maples, Portland.
Williams, W.   Prelude to Winter.
   Yellow Season, The.
Winters, Y.   Static Autumn.
Wright, C.   Autumn: "November the 1st. Gold
   leaves."
Wright, J.   Autumn Begins in Martins Ferry,
   Ohio.
Wright, J.   Cradle Logic of Autumn, The.
Wright, R.   Droning autumn rain.
Wu of Han [*or* Wu Ti *or* Ou-ty *or* Liu Ch'e *or*
   Liu Ch'u].   Autumn Wind.
   Autumn Wind, The.
Wylie.   Golden Bough.
Yang Wen-li.   Thinking of My Family on an
   Autumn Day.
Yeryomin.   Helioptér of a skyscraper hotel.

Yesenin [*or* Essenin].   Yesterday's rain.
Yi Hyangji.   Leaf Struck by Bird Droppings.
Yi I.   Where is the seventh bend?
Zimmer.   Zimmer in Fall.

Avalanches
Simon, M.   Keeping Track.

Aviation and Aviators
Alexander, P.   Flight: "Series of white squares,
   each, A."
Allen, D.   Coming of the First Aeroplanes, The.
Crane, H.   Stars scribble on our eyes the frosty
   sagas.
Deutsch.   Flight, The: "Earthen shadow lay on
   men's endeavor, An."
Dias, Robert Vas.   At the Controls.
Ewart.   When a Beau Goes In.
Francis, R.   Buzz Plane, The.
Hall, D.   Old Pilot, The.
Harteis.   Tempus Fugit.
Hoffman, D.   First Flight.
Iremonger.   Icarus.
Jarrell, R.   Dead Wingman, The.
   Death of the Ball Turret Gunner, The.
   Losses.
Kelly, B.   Those Who Wrestle with the Angel
   for Us.
Levine, P.   Poem of Flight, The.
Nemerov.   IFF.
Plumly.   Altitude.
Plutzik.   Airman Who Flew over Shakespeare's
   England, The.
Sandburg, C.   To Beachey, 1912.
Siegel, R.   Air Field.
Snyder, G.   Vapor Trails.
Spender, S.   Landscape near an Aerodrome,
   The.
Vaughan, David Kirk.   Lonely Impulse of
   Delight, A—W.B. Yeats.

See also **Air Travel; Air Warfare; Airports**

Avignon, France
Campert.   Avignon.

Avoca, Ireland
Moore, T.   Meeting of the Waters, The.

Avocados
Rakosi.   Avocado Pit, The.
Snyder, G.   Avocado.
Thomas, Yumi.   Love Poem to an Avocado from
   a Tomato.

Axes
Adamson.   Private, The.
Buson.   Blow of an ax.
   My ax sinks in.
   Thwack of an ax, The.
Evans, M.   Boss Communication.
Morris, G.   Woodman, Spare That Tree.
Pittman, Al.   Echo of the Ax, The.
Plath.   Words.
Snyder, G.   Axe Handles.
Unknown.   How cut haft for an axe?
Wonhyo, Great Master.   Axe without a Handle.

Azaleas
Adams, Cyd.   Azaleas and Dogwoods.
Basho.   Bucket of azaleas, A.
Buson.   Mason's finger, The.
Kang Ŭn'gyo.   Azalea.
Kim Sowŏl.   Azaleas.

Aztecs
Cuetzpaltzin, Ayocuan.   Let the earth last.
Gonzales, R.   Aztec Father.
Nezahualcoyotl.   I, Nezahualcóyotl ask it.

B

Babel, Tower of
Quarles.   On the Babel-Builders.
Wieder.   Tower of Babel, The.

Babies
Adcock, F.   Counting.
Adisa.   Rainbow, The.
Al-Harizi.   Lute, The.
Aldis, D.   Little.
Arcana, J.   Great with Child.
Arsone, S.   Father's Poem, A.

Auden.   Mundus et Infans.
Baggett.   Rachel: *Queen Charlotte's Crown*.
Baillie, J.   Mother to Her Waking Infant, A.
Barbauld.   To a Little Invisible Being Who Is
   Expected Soon to Become Visible.
Barker, C.   Verses for a First Birthday.
Barlow, G.   4½ Months: Halfway Song.
Bartlett, E.   Birth.
Bensley.   Single Parent.
Blake, W.   Cradle Song, A: "Sleep, sleep, beauty
   bright."
   Infant Joy.
   Infant Sorrow.
Bradley, J.   Improper Disposal.
Brooks, F.   New Baby, The.
Brown Rosellen.   This is no baby skin—.
Bruce, D.   Two Couples.
Buffoni, F.   Partitions.
Byrd.   Lulla Lullaby.
Campbell, R.   Zulu Girl, The.
Causley.   Infant Song.
Cerenio.   13 June 1994.
   20 July 1994.
Chernoff.   How Lies Grow.
Clanchy, K.   Love.
Clifton, L.   I am accused of tending to the past.
Coleridge, H.   First Birthday, The.
Coleridge, S.   Frost at Midnight [1798 version].
   Frost at Midnight [1829 version].
   Sonnet to a Friend Who Asked How I Felt
     When the Nurse First Presented My Infant to
     Me.
Cornford, F.   New-Born Baby's Song, The.
Couzyn.   Heartsong.
Dalton, A.   Dad-Baby, The.
Day Lewis.   Carol, A.
Denby.   Out of Bronx subway June forest.
Dickey, J.   Magus, The.
Dougherty.   Double Helix.
Dove, R.   Mother Love.
Dunbar, P.   Little Brown Baby.
Duran, J.   Stillborn.
Feinstein, E.   Mother Love.
Ferguson, G.   Inhaling His Hair.
   Scan.
Friesen, P.   Pa poem 1: firstborn.
Galvin, J.   Station (1).
Garrett, E.   Airborne.
Gerstler.   Seesaw.
Gunn, T.   Baby Song.
Hall, H.   Baby's Dress, A.
Hannan, M.   Tom Passey's Child.
Hardy, T.   New Toy, The.
Harrison, D.   Formula for Blue Blues Babies.
Harrison, J.   Arrival: "I will consider my son
   William."
Harryman.   Again. The. Time.
   Another Artifact.
   Baby. In Three Parts.
   Baby. N. Baseball. Song.
   Knowledge ("White fuzz in the air froze on a
     screen. Baby danced the cancan.").
   Next.
   The. Open. Box.
Harvey, M.   Ideas Go Only So Far.
Harvor, Elisabeth.   Four O'Clock, New Year's
   Morning, New River Beach.
Herrick.   Upon a Child.
Hirshfield, J.   Red Onion, Cherries, Boiling
   Potatoes, Milk.
Houghton, L.   Caustic Soda.
Ingelow.   Little babe, while burns the west.
Issa.   Counting.
   Nursing her child.
Jamie, K.   Child with Pillar Box and Bin Bags.
Jarrell, R.   Bats.
Johnson, S.   Ballad: "Tender infant, meek and
   mild, The."
Kasischke.   Hostess.
Katz, M.   Her Three Unborn Baby Boys.
Kim Namjo.   For Baby.
King, H.   Dream Maiden, A.
Kinzie.   Sound Waves.
Kirby, D.   Search for Baby Combover, The.
Kirchwey.   He Considers the Birds of the Air.
Kirkup.   Baby's Drinking Song.

Ko Un. Baby.
Koch, K. Girl and Baby Florist Sidewalk Pram Nineteen Seventy Something.
Lamb, C. First Tooth, The.
  Gipsy's Malison, The.
Lamb, M. First Tooth, The.
Larkin, P. Born Yesterday.
Lee, M. Child, You New Man.
Leigh, H. Natural Child, The.
Locker-Lampson. Terrible Infant, A.
Lorde. Now That I Am Forever with Child.
Lux. Upon Seeing an Ultrasound Photo of an Unborn Child.
Macdonald, G. Where did you come from, baby dear?
MacKenzie, John. Hearthouse.
Mahon. Unborn Child, An.
Mark, Sabrina Orah. Babies, The.
Mayer, B. Sonnet: "Love is a babe as you know and when you."
McAdams, J. Leaving the Old Gods.
Mercer, J. You Must Have Been a Beautiful Baby.
Morgan, D. Registering the Little One.
Murray, L. Cotton Flannelette.
Nash, O. Reflection on Babies.
  Song to Be Sung by the Father of Infant Female Children.
Nesbit, E. Song: "Oh, baby, baby, baby dear."
Nickerson. Seal's cry has lain against my leg, A.
No Hyegyŏng. Disease That Arrives at Death. Wedding: "Inside the womb-like darkness."
Norris, K. Blue Light, The.
Notley. Incidentals in the Day World.
  Three Strolls.
Ogilvy. Natal Address to My Child, March 19th 1844, A.
  Newly Dead and Newly Born.
Ogiwara Seisensui. Morning with a baby crying with all its might.
Ōkuma Kotomichi. Pinwheel, A.
Orr, G. Hand, The: "Brightness Falls from the Air".
Osgood, F. Ellen Learning to Walk.
Owen, M. All That Glitters.
Pak Sŏwŏn. Lies: "Little bitch!"
Plath. Death and Co.
  Magi.
  Morning Song: "Love set you going like a fat gold watch."
  Nick and the Candlestick.
  Night Dances, The.
Probyn. End of the Journey, The.
Ramanujan. Alien.
Ray, D. At the Washing of My Son.
Riley, J. King of Oo-Rinktum-Jing, The.
Roberson, E. Any moment (12/4/69 4:30 A.M. chicago).
Robinson, M. Sweet baby boy, accept a stranger's song.
Rodriguez, J. Rebeca in a mirror.
Rossetti, C. Why did baby die. . .?
Rukeyser, M. Night Feeding.
Russell, T. Dear Babe, whose meaning by fond looks expressed.
Salter. Summer 1983.
Sanchez, S. To P. J. (2 Yrs Old Who Sed Write a Poem for Me in Portland, Oregon).
Scott, D. Onondaga Madonna, The.
Seiferle, R. Foundling, The.
Senryū, K. Baby at her breast.
Seth. How ugly babies are! How heedless.
Sexton. Dreams.
  Unknown Girl in the Maternity Ward.
Shin Kyŏngnim. Baby, The.
Shuttle. Delicious Babies.
Silano, M. Explaining Current Events to a One-Year-Old.
Smith, P. Dylan, Two Days.
Snyder, G. Changing Diapers.
Sora. Skylark / Soaring—her young.
Stevenson, A. Spirit is too Blunt an Instrument, The.
Swinburne. Baby's feet, like sea-shells pink, A.
Tapahonso. Old Salt Woman.

Tate, J. Where Babies Come From.
Troupe. Change: "Use to be eye would be laying there."
Van Walleghen. Walking the Baby to the Liquor Store.
Waldman, A. Baby's Pantoum.
Waring, B. Baby Random.
Warner, S. Road 1940.
Weatherford, C. Tar Baby on the Soapbox, The.
Whitman, W. From Pent-up Aching Rivers.
Wilder, R. Baby, The.
Williams, W. Poem for Emily, A.
Winters, A. Chair by the Window, The.
  Night Light.
Wordsworth, W. Experiment that Failed, An.
Wright, C. What No One Could Have Told Them.
Wright, J. Song for the Middle of the Night, A.
Yeats. Dolls, The.
Young, K. Almanac, 1939, An.
See also **Death of an Infant**

Baboons
Belloc. Big Baboon, The.
Tranter. Thunder heard—speak to ourselves.
Williams, R. Baboon, The.

Babylon
Aiken, C. And in the Hanging Gardens.
Reznikoff. Babylon: 539 B.C.E.
Sandburg, C. Bilbea.
Sassoon, S. Babylon.
Tennyson, A. Babylon.

Baby-Sitting and Baby-Sitters
Clarke, G. Baby-Sitting.
Gomez, M. Making It.
Hashimoto, S. Eleven A.M. on My Day Off, My Sister Phones Desperate for a Babysitter.
Kunitz, S. Magic Curtain, The.
Prufer, K. Babysitter's Devotion, The.
Rein. Nanny Tanya.
Roethke. Frau Bauman, Frau Schmidt, and Frau Schwartze.

Bacchus
Anacreon. Come, boy, bring us.
Anyte [*or* Anytes]. Behold the horned goat of Bacchos, how lordly.
Donaghy, M. Bacchae, The.
Emerson, R. Bacchus.
Guest, B. Outside of This, That Is.
Ransom, J. Nocturne.
Redi. Bacchus's Opinion of Wine, and Other Beverages.
Sapgir. Dionysus.
Shakespeare, W. Drinking Song, A.
Whitmore, S. Lenaia.
Zukofsky, L. Cocktails / and signs of.

Bach, Johann Sebastian
Bly, R. Six Winter Privacy Poems.
Dacey, P. Musician, The.
Fairley, B. Bach Fugue.
Gurney, I. Bach and the Sentry.
Holm, B. Playing the Goldberg Variations on Sunday Morning.
Max, L. Equal Temperament.
Tanikawa, S. Porno-Bach.
Waltham, B. Radio 3.

Bachelors
Eberhart, R. New England Bachelor, A.
Garrett, E. Bachelors, The.
Goetsch, D. Bachelor Song.
Herrick. Upon the Loss[e] of His Mistresses.
MacKay, R. Rispond Miser, The.
Parra, V. Attention Young Bachelors.
Porter, C. I'm a Gigolo.
Unknown. In al this world nis a murier lyf.

Backs
Groarke, V. Veneer.
Grosholz. Back Trouble.
Portnoy, M. Voucher.
Taylor, J. Remedy for Backache.

Bacon, Sir Francis
Bentley, E. When their lordships asked Bacon.

Badgers
Clare, J. Badger.
  Badger, The.
Clarke, C. Tortoise and Badger.

Heaney, S. Badgers, The.
Muldoon, P. Brock.
Thomas, E. Combe, The.

Baez, Joan
Aubert, A. James Baldwin, 1924–1987.

Bagels
Ignatow, D. Bagel, The.

Baggage
Devara Dasimayya. Tattered Sack, The.
Moore, L. Airport.

Bagpipes
MacNeice. Bagpipe Music.
Sempill, F. Maggie Lauder.
Tomlinson, C. Mr. Brodsky.
Whittier. Pipes at Lucknow, The.

Baiae
Symonds. Midnight at Baiae.

Baker, Chet
Ai. Archangel.
Doty, M. Almost Blue.
Hull, L. Lost Fugue for Chet.
Komunyakaa, Y. Speed Ball.
Williams, M. Death of Chet Baker, The.

Baker, Josephine
Alexander, E. Josephine Baker Museum, The.
Cortez, J. So Many Feathers.

Baking and Bakers
Jackson, A. Loving.
Jones, J. Zen Baker.
Kennelly. Bread.
Kumin, M. Magellan Street, 1974.
Morgan, M. Legend of the Baker and Her Daughter, The.
Mullen, H. Joy, The.
Nye, N. Mind of Squash, The.
Olds, S. Bread: "When my daughter makes bread, a cloud of flour."
Pahmeier, G. Sunday Baking.
Powell, J. First Light.
Sajé, N. What I Want to Make for You.
Townsend, A. Date Nut Bread.
Weaver, A. Evidence of Life.
Woodward, V. Cornbread blues.
Yi Yŏnju. Bread and I, The.

Balaam
Amichai, Y. Thoughts came to him like long lines of freight, The.
Pope, A. Sir Balaam.

Baldness
Bhartrihari. Bald-Headed Man, A.
Chao Meng-fu. Admonition to Myself, An.
Henderson-Holmes. "C" ing in Colors: Red.
Hicok. Bald Truth, The.
LittleDog, Pat. In austin reigns a bald-headed queen.
Po Chü-i. On his Baldness.
Shapcott, J. Hairless.
Zavatsky. Bald.

Baldwin, James
Aubert, A. James Baldwin, 1924–1987.
Troupe. In Jimmy's Garden.

Ballads and Songs
Baingana, D. Song to Come, The.
Bowen, E. Power of Song, The.
Brother Yao. Soledad.
Brown, Laura Soul. Oh! Mercy Mercy Me! A Family Gathers to Marvin Gaye.
Buckley, C. Sleep Walk.
Colosi, David. Sun with Issues.
Davies, J. Hard Song.
Gorbanevskaya. And, having started singing this melody.
Grahame, K. Carol: "Villagers all, this frosty tide."
Hernández Cruz. Song 1 from "Three Songs from the 50's".
Irish Oral Tradition. O Donall Oge : The Grief of a Girl's Heart.
Louise, E. Jesus' Song.
Nguyen, Hoa. Calmly grass becomes a wave.
Redmond. Tune for a Teenage Niece.
Rodríguez, A. Torch.
Satyanarayana, V. Blind Beggar, The.
Sullivan, Mary Louise. Wedding Song: "Where

the bridesmaid waits in the vestibule."
Weiner, J.   Yonder Tree, The.

Ballet
Dickinson, E.   I cannot dance upon my Toes.
Goldberg, B.   Fetish.
Merrill, J.   Watching the Dance.
Russell, B.   Ballerina.
Voznesensky [or Voznesenskii].   Portrait of
  Plisetskaya.
Wright, S.   Out of the Wailing.

Balloons
Bishop, E.   Armadillo, The.
Freneau.   To Mr. Blanchard, the Celebrated
  Aeronaut in America.
Gylys, B.   Balloon Heart.
Kelly, B.   Visitation, The.
Knight, E.   Green Grass and Yellow Balloons.
Pagis, D.   Balloons.
Plath.   Morning Song: "Love set you going like
  a fat gold watch."

Ballrooms
Dickson, J.   Aragon Ballroom, The.
Turgeniev, I.   Skulls, The.

Balls
Berryman.   Ball Poem, The.
Brooks, S.   Darktown Strutter's Ball, The.
Farjeon, E.   Over the Garden Wall.
Harryman.   Baby. N. Baseball. Song.
Matson.   Beach, The.
Praed.   Belle of the Ball-Room, The.
Ryokan.   In my sleeve the colored ball worth a
  thousand in gold.
Wilbur, R.   Juggler.

Ballylee, Ireland
Yeats.   Coole Park and Ballylee, 1931.
  To Be Carved on a Stone at Thoor Ballylee.

Baltimore, Maryland
Cullen, C.   Incident.
Romtvedt.   Glass Canyons.
Sissle, N.   Baltimore Buzz.
Weaver, A.   Baltimore.
  Imitation of Life.
  Weekend Equestrian, The.
Webster, P.   Baltimore Oriole.

Bamboo
Basho.   Moonlight slanting.
  Winter storm, The.
Chunghur Hyujung.   Reply to King Sunjo's
  Poem on Bamboo.
Hagiwara Sakutaro.   Bamboo.
Issa.   My spring is just this.
Jinkag Haesim.   Bamboo Tree.
  For the Great Zen Master Sagum.
Kim Kwanguk.   Bamboo stick, the sight of you.
Mitchell, S.   Bamboo.
Muso Soseki.   Bamboo Garden.
Naong.   Bamboo Forest.
Noguchi, Yonejiro (Yone).   In Japan Beyond.
Pei Di.   Hermitage of the Bamboos, The.
  Hill of the Hatchet-Leaved Bamboos.
Po Chü-i.   Bamboo by Li Ch'e Yun's Window,
  The.
  Eating Bamboo-Shoots.
  Planting Bamboos.
Pou Kuksa.   Bamboo Hermitage.
Rolls.   Bamboo.
Su Tung-p'o.   When Yü-k'o painted bamboo.
Tu Fu [or Du Fu].   Restless Night.
Unknown.   Bamboos Grow Well Under Good
  Rule, The.
Wang Wei.   Bamboo Grove.
  Hermitage of the Bamboos, The.
  Hill of the Hatchet-Leaved Bamboos.
Yun Sŏndo.   You are not a tree.

Bananas
Basho.   Banana tree, The.
Benedikt.   Moralist of Bananas, The.
Edwards [or Edwardes], R.   When I Was Three.
Hernández Cruz.   Tale of Bananas, A.
Unknown.   Pluck, pluck, pluck, the thick
  plantain.

Bandits
Yŏngjae, Monk.   Meeting Bandits.

See also **Highwaymen**

Bands
Berger, B.   Salad Days.
Berlin.   Alexander's Ragtime Band.
Knight, S.   Double Writing.
Stein, K.   First Performance of the Rock 'n Roll
  Band *Puce Exit.*
Stillpoint, H.   Form a Band, Goddammit.
Whittemore, R.   High School Band, The.

Bangkok, Thailand
Clifton, H.   Monsoon Girl.
Swenson, K.   Landlady in Bangkok, The.
Townsend, A.   Comings and Goings.

Bangladesh
Duran, J.   Time Zones.
Heyen.   Grace.

Banjos
Foster, S.   Oh! Susanna.
Morgan, R.   Grain of Sound, The.

Banking and Bankers
Kooser.   At the Office Early.
Lytton, E.   Financial Note.
Masters, E.   Ralph Rhodes.
Mills, D.   Chembank Card.
Olin.   Stick-up.
Shapiro, K.   Girls Working in Banks.
Unknown.   War the Source of Riches.
Wellman, M.   No point mortgages wilt in
  daynights.

See also **Financiers**

Banneker, Benjamin
Wright, J.   Benjamin Banneker Sends His
  Almanac to Thomas Jefferson.

Baptism
Coleridge, S.   My Baptismal Birthday [or Birth-
  Day].
Crashaw.   On the Baptized Ethiopian.
Lewis, G.   Llanbadarn Baptism 1843.
Mulligan.   Shylock.
Willerton, Chris.   Our Speaker This Morning.
Zurita, R.   Sparkling Beaches, The.

See also **Christenings**

Bar Kokba, Simon
Vollmer.   Wildsisters Bar.

Barbarians
Cavafy.   Waiting for the Barbarians.
  Waiting for the Barbarians.
  Waiting for the Barbarians.
Witherup.   Lamb of Peace, the Ram of War,
  The.

Barbecues
Barresi.   How It Comes.
Rivera, D.   Dinner Together.

See also **Picnics and Barbecues**

Barbers and Barbershops
Aridjis.   Self-Portrait at Thirteen Years of Age.
Barnes, S.   Gentleman in the Barber Shop.
Frost, R.   First Haircut.
Huddle.   Haircut.
Kooser.   Self-Portrait at Thirty-Nine.
Laird, N.   Cuttings.
Levine, P.   To a Child Trapped in a Barber
  Shop.
Strange.   Barbershop Ritual.
Williams, C.   Ritual.
Williams, W.   Death the Barber.

Barcelona, Spain
Bly, R.   Eel in the Cave, The.
Cunard.   To Eat To-day.
Jenkins, A.   Barcelona.
Lewis, S.   I Wonder Why She Kept on Saying
  "Si-Si-Si-Si-Senor".
Manrique, J.   Barcelona Days.
Young, J.   I Wonder Why She Kept on Saying
  "Si-Si-Si-Si-Senor".

Bards
Benson, G.   Limerick: "There once was a bard
  of Hong Kong."
Blake, W.   Introduction: "Hear the voice of the
  Bard!"
Boland, E.   My Country in Darkness.
Gray, T.   Bard, The [A Pindaric Ode].
  Progress of Poesy, The.
Johnson, J.   O Black and Unknown Bards.
Keats.   'How Many Bards Gild the Lapses of

Time!'.
Webb, H.   Cywydd o Fawl.
Whitman, W.   By Blue Ontario's Shore.

Barges
Oppen.   On the water, solid.

Barley
Basho.   She cat, The.
Brown, G.   Ballad of John Barleycorn, the
  Ploughman, and the Furrow, The.
Buson.   Green leaves.
  Old man, The.
  Sick man passing.
Kana-jo, Lady.   Quivering together /Ears of
  barley.
Mokusetsu.   Long summer rains / Barley's
  tasteless.
Tan Taigi.   Barley's season / Dust mutes.

Barmaids
Lumsden, R.   Tricks for the Barmaid.
Stephens, J.   Glass of Beer, A.
Toledo, N.   Agricola.
  Agrícola.
  Na Agrícola.

Barns
Blunden.   Barn, The.
Brandt, D.   When i was five i thought heaven
  was located.
Carter, A. B.   Cobb's Barns.
Coatsworth.   Barn, The.
Jiménez, J.   Lamb Was Bleating Softly, The.
MacCaig.   Byre.
Pritchard, N.   Paysagesque.
Thomas, E.   Barn and the Down, The.
Whitman, W.   Big doors of the country barn
  stand open and ready, The.
Yesenin [or Essenin].   Horn of doom is blaring!,
  The.

Baroque
Bogan, L.   Baroque Comment.
Gier, J.   Going Baroque.

Barrel Organs
Baudelaire.   Autumn Lament.

See also **Hurdy-Gurdies**

Bars and Bartenders
Auden.   September 1, 1939.
Berryman.   Henry sats in de bar and was odd.
Bukowski.   Crucifix in a Deathhand.
  Freaky time.
Cisneros, S.   Las Girlfriends.
Corn.   Billie's Blues.
Coxon, W.   Flash Colonial Barman, The.
Croft, J.   Greenhalgh's Pub.
Cummings, E. E.   I was sitting in mcsoreley's.
  outside it was New York and beauti- / fully
  snowing.
Daniels, J.   Ted's Bar and Grill.
Davis, J.   You Turn Around.
Denby.   City Without Smoke.
Des Rochers, A.   City-Hotel.
Dugan, A.   Swing Shift Blues.
Elmslie, K.   Big Bar.
Eluard, P. *et al.*   Diamond He Didn't Give You,
  The.
Espada.   Dándole la mano a Mongo.
  Shaking Hands with Mongo.
Galloway, T.   Whiffenpoof Song.
Gonzales, R.   Paso del Norte.
Guillén, N.   Bars.
Harjo, J.   Deer Dancer.
Harms.   From Now On.
Hecht, A.   Third Avenue in Sunlight.
Henderson, D.   In Williams.
Herrera.   Iowa Blues Bar Spiritual.
Holden, J.   Men in the Hoboken Bar, the.
Hughes, L.   Bar.
Hugo, R.   Milltown Union Bar, The.
Hutchinson, P.   Flames.
Jenkins, A.   Murphy's Law.
Kennedy, X.   In a Prominent Bar in Secaucus
  [One Day].
LaFemina.   Her Rose Tattoo.
Lewis, Emyr.   Drivel.
Lim, S.   Starlight Haven.
Loesser.   Boys in the Backroom, The.
May, D.   Thoughts from a Bar Stool.

McRay.   Performance.
Middleton, C.   Saloon with Birds.
Minhinnick.   Drinking Art, The.
Minnigerode.   Whiffenpoof Song.
Muirhead, Eric.   Closing Time.
Patchen.   State of the Nation, The.
Peacock, M.   Buffalo.
Peterson, R.   September 5.
Pomeroy, G.   Whiffenpoof Song.
Randall, D.   Finney's Bar.
Reynolds, R.   Surplus.
Roberts, K.   Plastic Cup, The.
Rogers, D.   Some Nights I Love Everybody in
   Texas.
Rouse, A.   Glass.
Shepherd, R.   Gods at Three A.M., The.
Snyder, G.   I Went Into the Maverick Bar.
Speakes.   Heartbreak Hotel Piano-Bar.
Stephens, J.   Glass of Beer, A.
Swingler.   Drinking Song.
Tannahill.   Tap-Room, The.
Tate, J.   Failed Tribute to the Stonemason of Tor
   House, Robinson Jeffers.
Trammell, Robert.   After Hours.
   Nightclub, A: on the Jacksboro Highway.
Ulacia, M.   Visit to Turk's Head Pub.
   Visita al Turk's Head Pub.
Upton, L.   Window Seat at the Paradise.
Wenderoth, J.   Billy's Famous Lounge.
Whitman, W.   Glimpse, A.
Williams, W.   Hemmed-in Males.
Wilson, K.   Waterfront Bars.
Wright, K.   Other Side of the Mountain, The.
See also **Barmaids**

Barters
Bahdal, M.   Give me . . . I'll give you.

Baseball
Adler, R.   Heart.
Allen, S.   To Satch.
Applewhite.   Home Team.
Barresi.   Called Up: Tinker to Evers to Chance.
Bilgere, G.   Catch.
Bowering, G.   Kingdome 1974, The.
Byrd, Bobby.   Good Life, The.
   On Karma at 9.11.85.
Campbell, R.   In a Motel in Louisiana I Watch
   the Pirates And the OJ Simpson Freeway
   Chase at the Same Time.
Carlson, D.   Russ Joy Little League.
Cistulli.   42.24.
Clark, T.   Baseball and Classicism.
Corso.   Dream of a Baseball Star.
Dent.   For Cool Papa Bell.
Djanikian.   How I Learned English.
Fagin, L.   New York.
Fairchild.   Body and Soul.
Feinstein, S.   Blues for Zoot.
Fennelly.   Asked for a Happy Memory of Her
   Father, She Recalls Wrigley Field.
Ferlinghetti, L.   Baseball Canto.
Fincke.   Class A, Salem, the Rookie League.
Francis, R.   Base Stealer, The.
   Catch.
   Pitcher, The.
Gallup.   Pretty Beads.
Galvin, B.   Knot Hole Gang, The.
Gilbert, C.   Theory of Curve.
Gildner.   4th Base.
Gregerson.   Line Drive Caught by the Grace of
   God.
Hall, D.   Eighth Inning, The.
   Fifth Inning, The.
   Independence Day Letter.
Hamer.   Allegiance.
Harper, M.   Archives.
Heyen.   Mantle.
Holden, J.   How to Play Night Baseball.
   Poem for Ed "Whitey" Ford, A.
Hoover, P.   Baseball.
Hugo, R.   From Altitude, the Diamonds.
   Letter to Mantsch from Havre.
Lopez, L.   NEHI Strawberry Down-and-Away.
Miller, E.   Boys of Summer, The.
   Players.
   Roy Campanella: January, 1958.
Monroe, H.   Radio.

Moore, M.   Baseball and Writing.
Mosby.   To Josh Gibson (Legendary Slugger of
   the Old Negro Baseball League).
Norworth.   Take Me Out to the Ball Game.
Pastan.   Baseball.
Patchen.   Origin of Baseball, The.
Pinsky.   Night Game, The.
Richter, J.   Nothing but Bad News.
Rosenberg, L.   City Baseball.
Ross, J.   Heart.
Sandburg, C.   Hits and Runs.
Skloot.   Whitman Pinch Hits, 1861.
Smith, D.   Roundhouse Voices, The.
Soldofsky, A.   Chin Music.
Soto.   Black Hair.
Stanard, C.   Baseball.
Stuart, D.   Swinging on the First Pitch.
Tate, J.   Lousy in Center Field.
Thayer, E.   Casey at the Bat.
Trammell, Robert.   Light Forms.
Troupe.   Poem for My Father; for Quincy
   Trouppe, Sr.
Watson, M.   Sestina Halted in a Rain Delay.
Weaver, A.   My Father's First Baseball Game.
Wellburn, R.   Pitching Coups.
Wenderoth, J.   Aesthetics of the Bases Loaded
   Walk.
Williams, W.   At the Ball Game.
Wood, S.   Four Roses.

Basho (Matsuo Basho)
Kang [Grossjean], Ok-Ku [or Ok-Koo].   Were I
   a Flower.
Mahon.   Snow Party, The.
Nooteboom.   Basho ("Old man among the reeds
   mistrust of the poet.").
   Basho ("Oude man tussen het riet achterdocht
   van de dichter.").
Pinsky.   Impossible to Tell.
Ray, D.   Journey with Basho, A.
Shea, James.   Haiku: "Upon Kissing You after
   You Vomited."
Tomlinson, C.   Yamadera.

Basketball
Alexie.   Defending Walt Whitman.
   Father and Farther.
   Penance.
   Why We Play Basketball.
Bowen, K.   Playing Basketball with the Viet
   Cong.
Bowman, C.   My Knicks Are Going to Beat
   Your Spurs—NBA Souvenir Bracelet 1999 for
   My Long Distance Love.
Byrd, Bobby.   Good Life, The.
De Los Santos, M.   Women Watching
   Basketball.
Ellis, T.   Being There.
Fairchild.   Old Men Playing Basketball.
Giovanni.   Basketball.
Harper, M.   Makin' Jump Shots.
Hilton, D.   I Try to Turn in My Jock.
Hirsch.   Fast Break.
Jenkins, L.   Basketball.
Kleinzahler.   Winter Ball.
Komunyakaa, Y.   Slam, Dunk, & Hook.
Kraushaar, M.   Free Throw.
Matthews, W.   Cheap Seats, the Cincinnati
   Gardens, Professional Basketball, 1959.
   Foul Shots: A Clinic.
   In Memory of the Utah Stars.
McKean.   Good "D".
McManus, J.   Commercials exaggerate.
Olstein, L.   We Still Have Basketball, Sara.
Phillips, L.   My Son Shows Me a Photograph of
   Michael Jordan Performing a Slam Dunk.
Rambsy II, H.   Trash Talker, The.
Ridlon.   Fernando.
Schockley, E.   Ballplayer.
Seibles, T.   What It Comes Down To.
Troupe.   Following the North Star Boogaloo.
   Poem for "Magic", A.
Trudell.   Jump Shooter, The.
Updike.   Ex-Basketball Player.

Bastille Day
Taha, A.   Anwar Kamel Celebrates Le Quatorze
   Juillet.

Bastogne, Battle of (1944–45)
Simpson, L.   Battle, The.

Bathrooms
Degentesh.   5-Year-Old Girls Encountered.
Machan.   Hazel Tells LaVerne.
Rochelle, T.   Feeding the Worms.
Rye, L.   Scatological History.
Wallace, R.   Constipation.

Baths and Bathing
Adamson.   Rimbaud Having a Bath.
Africa-Bolasco.   Sauna 2.
Aini, L.   Shower.
Ammons.   Foot-Washing, The.
Becker, R.   Bath, The.
Berkson, B.   Perfect Work.
Butlin.   Bath, The.
Cabalquinto.   Value Added in Smashing a
   German Roach on the Bathroom Door, The.
Campo.   El Curandero.
Carver, R.   Woman Bathing.
Chitsu.   No more head shaving.
Clarke, C.   What Goes Around Comes Around,
   or The Proof is in the Pudding.
Cole, H.   Roman Baths at Nîmes, The.
Davis, T.   Susannah.
Etsujin.   First snow / Head clear.
Fagin, L.   Little Hand.
Feinstein, E.   Bathroom.
Galassi.   Siren.
Giovanni.   Trips.
Godfrey.   Bath.
Graves, R.   I Wonder What It Feels Like to Be
   Drowned?
Harvey, M.   Pity the Bathtub Its Forced
   Embrace of the Human Form.
   Thermae.
Hoagland, T.   Lucky.
Issa.   Bath when you're born.
   One bath / After another.
   With this rising bath-mist.
Kim Hyesun.   Taklamakan.
Kipling, R.   Naaman's Song.
Lawrence, D. H.   Gloire de Dijon.
Mackey, N.   Dream Thief.
Magrelli.   Tomorrow morning I will take a
   shower.
McCabe, C.   Ancutsa, Ancutsa.
Miller, E.   Another Love Affair/Another Poem.
Mookam Choinul.   Bath, A.
Moss, T.   Accessible Heaven.
Nash, O.   Samson Agonistes.
Nichols, G.   Thoughts drifting through the fat
   black woman's head while having a full bubble
   bath.
Nossis.   O Artemis of Delos and lovely Ortygia.
Okamoto.   Tanka: "Stark naked."
Olin.   Wu Gambinos.
Peacocke.   Soap.
Phillips, C.   In the blood, Winnowing.
Pilling.   Ophelia.
Portnoy, M.   Evolution of Lather, The.
Pound, E.   Bathtub [*or* Bath Tub], The.
Rossiter.   Your Body Glistens From the Bath.
Rufinus.   Her foot sparkled like silver.
Schneider, M.   Bath: "Kindness, an Irish lilt in
   her voice."
Shapcott, J.   In the Bath.
Shoman, K.   Is Beautiful.
Slutsky [*or* Slutskii].   Bathhouse, The.
Smukler.   Home in Three Days. Don't Wash.
Snyder, G.   Bath, The.
Spear, R.   Meditation: "I could sit in this hot
   bath for hours."
Spenser, E.   And in the midst of all, a fountaine
   stood.
Sruoginis, L.   Irish Woman Washing.
Steele, T.   Au Aubade.
   Aubade, An: "As she is showering, I wake to
   see."
Teofilov, Ivan.   Turkish Bath in Ortamezar.
Trinidad.   Shower Scene in *Psycho*, The.
Unknown.   Draw a bucket of water.
   Midwife's Invocation, A.
   Wash me in the water.
Vasalis.   Idiot in the Bath, The.
Warton, T.   On Bathing.

Wells, C.   Famous Baths and Bathers.
Wheelwright.   In the Bathtub, to Mnemosyne.
Whitman, W.   Twenty-eight young men bathe by the shore.
Wilson, F.   Bathing My Mother.
Young, D.   Ballant o' the Laird's Bath, The.

Bats
Bennett, R.   Witch of Willowby Wood, The.
Berryman.   Bats have no bankers and they do not drink.
Bierds, L.   Vespertilio.
Buson.   Bat flits, A.
Bats flitting here and there.
Darting here and there.
Carroll, L.   Mad Hatter's Song, The.
Dickinson, E.   Bat, The.
Issa.   Bats flying.
Jarrell, R.   Bats.
Jashuva, G.   Bat Messenger, The.
Kizer, C.   Intruder, The.
Llewellyn-Williams.   Feeding the Bat.
Oliver, M.   Bats.
O'Reilly, C.   Lecture Upon the Bat, A.
Pacheco, J.   Enquiry Concerning the Bat, An.
Pitter.   Bat, The.
Radcliffe, A.   Sonnet: "Now the bat circles on the breeze of eve."
To the Bat.
Roethke.   Bat, The.
Shapcott, J.   Life.
Smith, D.   Bats.
Wicks, S.   Protected Species.
Wilbur, R.   Mind.

Battlefields
al-Sa'igh, Y.   Iraqi Evening, An.
Aldington.   Battlefield.
Alon, E.   If There is a God.
Amichai, Y.   Rain on the Battlefield.
Basho.   Summer grasses.
Boland, E.   How We Made a New Art on Old Ground.
Bridges, T.   Squabbling gods the fight forsake, The.
Bunting.   Loaded with mail of linked lies.
Campbell, T.   Hohenlinden.
Chaucer.   On t'other side there stood destruction bare.
Ch'en Tao.   Turkestan.
Collins, W.   How Sleep the Brave.
Cowley, M.   Chateau de Soupir, 1917.
Darwin.   Eliza at the Battle.
Douglas, K.   Vergissmeinnicht.
Emerson, R.   Concord Hymn.
Fenton, J.   Wind: "This is the wind, the wind in a field of corn."
González, A.   Battlesfield, The.
Hardy, T.   Albuera.
Heóghusa.   Winter Campaign, A.
Hill, G.   Distant Fury of Battle, The.
Pastoral, A: "Mobile, immaculate and austere."
Holub.   Fly, The.
Homer.   Battle.
Priam and Achilles.
Rude Mars had th' ordering of their spirits; of Greeks, the learned Maid.
Then Achilles.
Through the host with this the goddess ran.
Tide of Battle Turns, The.
Italicus.   Give me Maeonian Homer's resonant tongue.
Horses which Titan when discharged for the night, The.
Jarmain.   El Alamein.
Johnstone, P.   High Wood.
Katz, M.   Into a Dead Zone.
Kennedy, B.   Bad Luck to This Marching.
Li Ho.   Arrowhead from the Ancient Battlefield of Ch'ang-p'ing.
Song of an Arrowhead from Changping.
Li Po.   Fighting South of the Wall.
Logue, C.   Battle swayed, The.
Malczewski, A.   After the Battle.
McCrae, J.   In Flanders Fields.
McGrath, T.   Remembering That Island.
Melville, H.   Battle Summers, The.
Inscription: "To them who crossed the flood."

Shiloh (A Requiem).
Muir, E.   Combat, The.
Murray, P.   Redemption.
Olebara, N.   Warrior's Lament, A.
Pastan.   At Gettysburg.
Peacock, T.   War Song of Dinas Vawr, The.
Popa.   Battle on the Blackbird's Field, The.
Pope, A.   "Restore the lock!" she cries; and all around.
Rimbaud, A.   Sleeper in the Valley, The.
Sakaki.   Sugar Loaf Hill.
Sandburg, C.   Grass.
Shakespeare, W.   What bloody man is that? He can report.
Simonides.   For the Spartan Dead at Thermopylai (480 B.C.).
Greek Dead at Thermopylae, The.
On the Spartan Dead at Thermopylae.
Smith, D.   On a Field Trip at Fredericksburg.
Southey, R.   Battle of Blenheim, The.
Stevenson, R.   Ticonderoga: A Legend of the West Highlands.
Szymborska, W.   Reality Demands.
Tkachenko.   Battle.
Towle.   Immaterial Nocturnes: Hudson and Worth.
Tu Fu [or Du Fu].   Travelling Northward.
Tung Chieh-yüan.   Chapter 2: "Stopping before the steps, the young monk gushed."
Tyutchev.   At Vshchizh.
Unknown.   At last these two stout erles did meet.
Gereint Son of Erbin.
Hēr Æþoelstān cyning, eorla drihten.
Hymn to the Fallen.
My sisters, tie your veils around like waistbands.
Wang Ch'ang-ling.   Under a Border-Fortress.
Warren, R.   History among the Rocks.
Whitman, W.   Vigil Strange I Kept on the Field One Night.
Wilson, T.   Magpies in Picardy.
Wingfield.   Where is the lumber-room of what was important?

Battles
Aldrich, T.   Fredericksburg.
Brecht, B.   There is no greater crime than leaving.
Cook, E.   Entry of the Marines [or The Red Cross of England].
Davies, P.   I Was with Ulysses.
French, T.   No Man's Land.
Hudgins.   In Alesia.
Neal, J.   Battle comes again, The. The charging host.
Rai San'yo.   On a Painting of Kenshin Attacking Shingen.
Takamura Kotaro.   Final Battle for the Ryūkyū Islands, The.
Trakl.   On the Eastern Front.
Tu Fu [or Du Fu].   Facing the Snow ("Weeping over battle, many new ghosts.").
Unknown.   Come back to me, riddled with holes from a dark rifle's bullets.
Dust for you, but never my mouth again.
Go and fight in Kabul, my love.
Had I known the time of separation was to come.
Hurry up, my love, and quickly rise to the assault.
If you do not have a wound in the center of your chest.
If you truly love me, my love, go off and liberate our land!
In battle today my lover turned his back to the enemy.
Lament of Maev Leith-Dherg, The.
Little horror, oblivious to combat, sleeps quietly beside me, The.
May you be found cut to pieces by a trenchant sword.
My beloved! If you turn your back upon the enemy, do not come home again!
Oh my love! If in my arms you tremble so.
With my own hands I have sent you off to die.
Wang Han.   Reason Fair, A (Liangzhou Song).

Willerton, Chris.   Battle of Adobe Walls.
Winters, Y.   Night of Battle.
Yüan Chieh.   After the Raiders Have Gone: To Clerks and Officials.

Baucis and Philemon
Ovid.   Baucis and Philemon.

Baudelaire, Charles
Fanning, R.   Baudelaire's Ablutions.
Hochman.   Sphinxes.
Mallarmé.   Tomb of Charles Baudelaire, The.
Manrique, J.   Baudelaire's Spleen.
Swinburne.   Ave atque Vale.
Young, Seth.   *All* says a glass doorknow Parabola ghost.

Bayous
Alcosser.   Pole Boat at Honey Island.
Fox, Skip.   Sic transit ("Kingfisher in highest cypress green.").
Freeman, Jessica.   Houseboat Ferry.
Salaam.   Spiritual Geography.
St. Germain, S.   Cajun.

Beaches
Adam, H.   Pre-Teen Trot.
Agran, R.   Door Thrown Open to Daisies.
Ammons.   Constant, The.
Arnold, M.   Dover Beach.
Basho.   Fall going.
Becker, R.   Incarnate.
Beer, P.   Jane Austen.
Berryman.   Traveller [or Traveler], The.
Betjeman.   East Anglian Bathe.
Bishop, E.   End of March, The.
Bleakney, J.   By Starlight on Narin Strand.
Depending on the Angle.
Boden, C.   Sombreo Beach, Vancouver Island, BC.
Bowers, E.   Afternoon at the Beach, An.
Bridges, R.   Snow Lies Sprinkled on the Beach, The.
Brutus.   Sand Wet and Cool, The.
Buson.   Short night, The.
Caleshu, A.   Collaboration: A Day at the Beach.
Collaboration: Storming the Beaches.
Carroll, J.   Blue Poles.
Ceravolo.   Wind Is Blowing West, The.
Clampitt.   Beach Glass.
Clark, T.   Dover Beach.
On the Beach.
Coccimiglio.   Night Beach.
Corben.   On The Beach.
Cummings, E. E.   How many moments must(amazing each).
Maggie and milly and molly and may.
Cunningham, J.   Night is still, The. The unfailing surf.
Davie, D.   Across the Bay.
de Fréine, C.   Bubbles.
De Mello Breyner.   Beach.
Flute, The.
Denby.   Northern Boulevard.
Sant' Angelo d'Ischia.
Dickinson, E.   By the Sea.
Doty, M.   2. Beach Roses.
Dugan, A.   Memorial Service for the Invasion Beach Where the Vacation in the Flesh Is Over.
Dunn, S.   Because You Mentioned the Spiritual Life.
Eberhart, R.   Ceremony by the Sea, A.
Emerson, J.   Night Blindness.
Espirito Santo.   Far from the Beach.
Fitzgerald, R.   Amphibians.
Gleason, M.   We Are Like These Things.
Goeckel, L.   Wave Falling on the Beach, A.
Goetsch, D.   Beach, The.
Hannon.   Homeless.
Harvor, Elisabeth.   Damp Hips of the Women, The.
Heaney, S.   Strand at Lough Beg, The.
Issa.   From that woman.
Jones, Einir.   Ffynnon Grandis.
Jones, R.   Foam.
Kelley, E.   At the Center, Creator Hourglass.
Kennedy, X.   Emily Dickinson in Southern California.
Kingsley, C.   Sands of Dee, The.

Knighton, R. Ballad of Echolocation, The.
Koch, C. Shelly Beach.
Laird, N. Length of a Wave, The.
Livingstone, D. Isipingo.
Longley, M. Björn Olinder's Pictures.
Martínez, V. Coastal.
Matson. Beach, The.
McGuckian. On Ballycastle Beach.
Menashe. Beachhead.
Meredith, W. Rhode Island.
Millay, E. Eel-Grass.
Mitchell, K. Tree Stillness.
Murphy, P. Learning to Swim at Poverty Beach.
Nemerov. Salt Garden, The.
Noyes, S. Beach House.
  Seascape.
Okigbo. Eyes Watch the Stars.
Orlen. Androgyny.
O'Sullivan, L. Being Free.
Plath. Point Shirley.
Press, K. First thirty-seven years, The.
Richman, L. To Valenton: Impressions circa
  1947.
Robbins, Z. Beaches.
Robinson, M. Haunted Beach, The.
Rossi, T. Beach.
St. John, D. Saffron.
Saleh. Beach, Later.
Santos, S. Midsummer.
  On the Last Day of the World.
Satyamurti. Day Trip.
Schick. Last summer.
Schwartz, D. Far Rockaway.
Schwartz, R. L. Edgewater Park.
Scupham. Beach, The.
Shakespeare, W. Sonnet 60: "Like as the waves
  make toward[s] the pebbled [or pibled] shore."
Shiomi, M. Mirror.
Solari, R. December 25, 1991.
  Truro.
Spenser, E. Sonnet 75: "One day I wrote her
  name upon the strand."
Spires. Mansion Beach.
Stafford, W. Gulls at Cannon Beach.
  With Kit, Age 7, at the Beach.
Stevens, W. Fabliau of Florida.
Stevenson, R. At the Seaside [or Sea-Side].
Stickney, T. At Sainte-Marguerite.
Swenson, M. Goodbye, Goldeneye.
  Waking from a Nap on the Beach.
Szporluk. Duressor.
Teasdale. Unchanging, The.
Tomlinson, C. Stone Speech.
Toomer. Merl.
Tranströmer. At Funchal.
Ulacia, M. En la playa.
  On the Beach.
Unknown. All too soon, I fear.
  O sea-gulls that are crying.
Vander Ven, Tom. Sea Washes Sand Scours
  Sea.
Vasquez, R. Pismo, 1959.
Vinokurov. I do not like the circus.
Voznesensky [or Voznesenskii]. Public Beach
  No. 2.
Wakoski. Imagining Point Dume.
Warsh. Moving through Air.
Wheelock, J. Afternoon: Amagansett Beach.
Whitman, W. As If a Phantom Caress'd Me.
  On the Beach at Night.
  On the Beach at Night Alone.
Winch. Shadow Grammar.
Woolson. Florida Beach, The.
Wright, C. Looking West from Laguna Beach at
  Night.
Wunderlich, M. Continent's Edge.
Zandvakili, K. No Trespassing (Private Beach).
Zappala, Robyn. One Year Later.
Zurita, R. Sparkling Beaches, The.
See also **Shores**

Beads
Barnett, C. Into Perfect Spheres Such Holes Are
  Pierced.
Issa. Flies in the temple, The.
Otomo no Sakanoé, t. Were you a string of
  beads.

Unknown. So it is because.
Beagles
Muldoon, P. Beagles.
Beans
Herbert, W. Coco-de-Mer.
Murray, L. Broad Bean Sermon, The.
Pierpoint, K. Dreaming Bean, The.
Beards
Bachner. Yes, That's the Way Things Are.
Blanco, R. Shaving.
Clarke, J. There was an old man with a beard.
Dove, R. This Life.
Forrester, S. Winter wind.
Korteweg. Sed Non Frustra.
Košek, M. Yes, That's the Way Things Are.
Lear, E. There Was an Old Man With a Beard.
Löwy, H. Yes, That's the Way Things Are.
Martial. Irresolute the down upon your cheek.
Ríos, A. Domingo Limón.
Bears
Austin, M. Grizzly Bear.
Bachmann. Invocation of the Great Bear.
Barnett, R. Taxidermist at the Zoo, The.
Birney. Bear on the Delhi Road, The.
Blue Cloud. Bear: A Totem Dance As Seen by
  Raven.
Bottoms. Sierra Bear.
Butler, S. Bear-Baiting.
Césaire, A. Three for Bear.
Clampitt. Hispaniola.
Crowley, R. Sunday Bear-Baiting.
Davies, B. Berne.
Dubie. Elizabeth's War with the Christmas
  Bear.
Fanning, R. Parable of the Boy and the Polar
  Bear.
Field, R. Dancing Bear, The.
Frost, R. Bear, The.
Gerber. Bear on Main Street, The.
Giorno. Capsule.
Harjo, J. White Bear.
Hogan, L. Bear Fat.
Housman. Infant Innocence.
Hughes, T. I See a Bear.
  That Morning.
Kelen. Rabbit Shoeshine.
Kinnell. Bear, The.
Kirk, Kathleen. Exit, Pursued by a Bear.
Kumin, M. In the Park.
Kyger. Destruction.
Levertov. Arctic Spring.
Matthews, W. Bear at the Dump, The.
McKendrick, J. Six Characters in Search of
  Something.
Merwin. Feast Day.
Momaday. Bear, The.
Moritz [or Morits]. Leader, The.
Nemerov. Goose Fish, The.
Nicholls, J. Polar Cub.
Roberson, E. Sonnet.
Roethke. Lady and the Bear, The.
Saner. This Grizzly.
Schwartz, D. Heavy Bear Who Goes with Me,
  The.
Sears, P. One Polar Bear, The.
Shiraishi. Bear of the Human Family, A.
Smith, W. Polar Bear.
Snyder, G. Right in the Trail.
  This Poem Is for Bear.
Solie, Karen. Parabola.
Stanley, G. Mist rises, The.
Suntsova, E. Beyond is where the passersby
  end.
Unknown. Song of the Black Bear, The.
  Spell, A.
Wagoner, D. Meeting a Bear.
Willard, N. Cat's Second Song, The.
Wright, K. Other Side of the Mountain, The.
Yi Chinmyŏng. Bear, The.
Beatings
Algarin. Trampling.
Baraka, I. Biography.
Carroll, L. Duchess's Lullaby, The.
Kando. It's as if our heads were on fire, the
  way.

Knight, E. Hard Rock Returns to Prison from
  the Hospital for the Criminal Insane.
Larkin, J. Beatings.
Lear, E. Limerick: "There was an old man who
  screamed out."
Morrissey, S. Thoughts in a Black Taxi.
No Hyangnim. Nature: "In a corn field."
Ross, C. Jack.
Shoman, K. In Explanation to the Mother.
Trigilio. Body is Fragile, The.
Unknown. No More Auction Block.
Beatniks
Baraka, I. All is One for Monk.
Bell, M. First Poem: "Bulletin board flutters
  with a flair, The."
Ginsberg, A. America: "America I've given you
  all and now I'm nothing."
  'Back on Times Square, Dreaming of Times
  Square'.
  Howl.
Voznesensky [or Voznesenskii]. Beatnik's
  Monologue, The.
Beatrice Portinari
Dante Alighieri. I have at times seen all the
  eastern sky.
Phillips, C. One sees pictures of Dante.
Beaufort, South Carolina
Heard, J. National Cemetery, Beaufort, South
  Carolina, The.
Beauty
Abu Sa'id. I Asked My Love.
Addison, L. Umbra.
Agathias. Beautiful Melite, in the throes of
  middle age.
Akenside. Amoret.
Alcman. Desire Loosening.
  Polydeukes.
Alexander, C. All Things Bright and Beautiful.
Amaru. You with Your Beautiful Swaying
  Walk.
Amirthanayagam, I. So Beautiful.
Ammuvanar. They Shout Out the Price of Salt.
Anacreon. Ode 3: "Of late, what time the Bear
  turned round."
Apollinaire. Pretty Redhead, The.
Arnold, M. Growing Old.
Baraka, I. Return of the Native.
Barnfield [or Barnefield]. Beauty and majesty
  are fallen at odds.
  Thus was my love, thus was my Ganymed.
Barras, J. Peace.
Basho. Among moon gazers.
  Chilling autumn rains.
  Group of them, A.
  Sad beauty?
Baudri of Bourgueil. Your Appearance is
  Pleasing.
Behn, A. To My Lady Morland at Tunbrige [or
  Tunbridge].
Bek, T. Oh life, long as an epic.
Berlin. Pretty Girl Is Like a Melody, A.
Bernie, B. Sweet Georgia Brown.
Berryman. Astronomies and slangs to find you,
  dear.
  Canto Amor.
Bhartrihari. Sweet Maid.
Bhattācārya, K. How can that black woman be
  so beautiful?
Binyon. Beauty.
Bishop, J. Metamorphoses of M.
Blake, W. Abstinence Sows Sand All Over.
Blane, R. That Face.
Blunden. One among the Roses.
Blunt, W. On Her Vanity.
Bogan, L. Juan's Song.
Boker. Sonnet 188: "My darling's features,
  painted by the light."
Bridges, R. I Love All Beauteous Things.
Brown, L. Maybe This Is Love.
Browning, E. Best Thing in the World, The.
  Hiram Powers' 'Greek Slave'.
Browning, R. Women and Roses.
Burke, J. Moonlight Becomes You.
Burns, R. Bonnie Lesley.
Burrington. Beautiful, The.
Buson. Dewy morn / These saucepans.

Bynner. Lightning.
Byron, G. She Walks In Beauty.
 Sonnet, to the Same.
 Stanzas for Music ("There be none of Beauty's
  daughters.").
Campbell, J. Old Woman, The.
Campion, T. Rose-cheeked Laura[, Come].
Carew, T. Beautiful Mistress, A.
 Disdain Returned.
 Divine Mistress, A.
 Fancy, A.
 Ingrateful[l] Beauty Threatened.
 Song[, A]: "Ask[e] me no more where Jove
  bestow[e]s."
 To a Lady That Desired I Would Love Her.
Carroll, L. Song of the Mock Turtle, The.
Casal, J. My Loves.
Casey, K. Sweet Georgia Brown.
Cassells. Beautiful Signor.
Catulus. Waking Intuitively.
Cavafy. At the Cafe Door.
Cavalcanti. Encounter, An.
Cawein. Beauty.
 Unimaginative, The.
Cepollaro, B. Requiem in C.
Cetina, G. Madrigal 1.
Chao Luan-luan. Cloud Hairdress.
 Red Sandalwood Mouth.
 Willow Eyebrows.
Chapman, G. Love flows not from my liver but
  her living.
Cherokee Oral Tradition. Formula to Secure
  Love.
Chin, J. Cocksucker's Blues.
Chippewa Oral Tradition. Love-Charm Song.
Chivers. To Isa Sleeping.
Chu Hsiang. Pawnshop, The.
Chudleigh. Song: "Why Damon, why, why,
  why so pressing?"
Clare, J. First Love.
Clarke, A. Planter's Daughter, The.
Clarke, G. Everything Is Peaches Down in
  Georgia.
Clifton, L. Song at Midnight.
 To my last period.
Coatsworth. Swift Things Are Beautiful.
Coffman. Cheerleaders.
Cohan. When a Fellow's on the Level with a
  Girl That's on the Square.
Collins, B. Nightclub.
Collins, J. Big World Look Out.
Colonna, S. Disconnections.
Conquest. Rokeby Venus, The.
Constable, H. Of His Mistress, upon Occasion
  of Her Walking in a Garden.
Coralin, J. Rosa's Beauty.
Cowley, H. Departed Youth.
Cranch. Evening Primrose, The.
Crashaw. Bubble, The.
Cristall. Elegy on a Young Lady.
Cross, T. Complected.
Crowell, G. Texas Autumn.
Cullen, C. To John Keats, Poet, at Springtime
  [or Spring Time].
Cummings, E. E. Poem, or Beauty Hurts Mr.
  Vinal.
 Who are you, little i.
Cuney. No Images.
Cunningham, J. Epigram: "You wonder why
  Drab sells her love for gold?"
Dafydd [or David] ap Gwilym. Mirror, The.
Daglarca. Beauty and Mind.
Dante Alighieri. Great Canzon, The.
 Sestina: Of the Lady Pietra degli Scrovigni.
 To Waning Day, To the Wide Round of Shadow.
Darío, R. I Pursue a Form.
Darley. It Is Not Beauty I Demand.
Davenant [or D'Avenant]. Lover and
  Philosopher.
De la Mare. Epitaph, An: "Here lies a most
  beautiful lady."
 Three Cherry Trees, The.
Derricotte. Minks, The.
DeSylva, B. G. Maybe This Is Love.
Devlin, D. Wishes for Her.
Di Prima. After months of sitting.

Dickinson, E. I died for Beauty—but was
  scarce.
Dietz, H. If There Is Someone Lovelier Than
  You.
Diodes. Somebody said when snubbed, "Is
  Damon so."
Dixon, M. Lady in Red, The.
Donne. Autumnal[l], The.
 Undertaking, The.
Doolittle, H. Song: "You are as gold."
Dowson. Villanelle of His Lady's Treasures.
Drake, N. Very Rich Hours, The.
Drayton. If he, from heaven that filched the
  living fire.
 Roundelay Between Two Shepherds, A.
Drosinēs, G. Wild Creeper.
Drummond de Andrade. Diminutive.
Drummond, W. Madrigal: "Like the Idalian
  Queen[e]."
Dubin, A. Dames.
Duffy, C. Medusa.
Duhamel. Bicentennial Barbie.
Duncan, R. Poetry, a Natural Thing.
 Torso, The.
Dunn, D. Thirteen Steps and the Thirteenth of
  March.
Ehrenburg [or Erenburg]. Our Grandsons Will
  Be Astonished.
Eich. Lauras.
Elizabeth I. When I Was Fair and Young.
Éluard, P. Dawn Dissolves the Monsters.
Emanuel, L. Blond Bombshell.
Emerson, R. Each and All.
 Harp, The.
 Rhodora, The [On Being Asked Whence Is the
  Flower].
Empson. Villanelle: "It is the pain, it is the
  pain, endures."
"Ephelia". To a Proud Beauty.
Ettinger, E. Believe Me.
Evelyn, M. Mundus Muliebris.
Field. Elsewhere.
 Girl, A.
 Portrait, A.
 So jealous of your beauty.
Fields, D. Lovely to Look At.
 Way You Look Tonight, The.
 You Couldn't Be Cuter.
Fletcher, G. I saw, sweet Licia, when the spider
  ran.
Fletcher, J. Take, Oh, Take Those Lips Away.
Florián, M. Pastora.
Forché. Kalaloch.
Forman, R. You So Woman.
Forrest, G. And This Is My Beloved.
Freed, R. You Leave Me Breathless.
Garcilaso de la Vega. While There Is Still the
  Color of a Rose.
Garrett, E. Vista.
Gautier. Carmen.
Gay, J. Air: "O ruddier than the cherry!"
Giovanni. Beautiful Black Men.
Glück, L. Mirror, The.
Goldsmith, O. When Lovely Woman Stoops to
  Folly.
Góngora y Argote. O Noble and Most High in
  Beauty, Thou.
 Pride of the Fourth and Liquid Element.
Goran. Woman and Beauty.
Gorges. Her Face, Her Tongue, Her Wit.
Graham, A. Flowers', The.
Graves, R. Down, Wanton, Down!
Greville, F. You little stars that live in skies.
Grimké, A. Mona Lisa, A.
Gudo. It's not nature that upholds utility.
Gullar. Poster.
 Sweet Talk.
Harjo, J. Eagle Poem.
 Woman Who Fell from the Sky, The.
Hart, L. Most Beautiful Girl in the World, The.
 Wait Till You See Her.
 You Are Too Beautiful.
Hayâlî. When dawn hennas her hands with the
  blood.
Hemphill. Soft Targets.
Henderson, R. Maybe This Is Love.

Herbert, E. La Gialletta Gallante, or the
  Sunburned Exotic Beauty.
 Sonnet of Black Beauty.
 To One Black, and Not Very Handsome, Who
  Expected Commendation.
Herbert, Z. Power of Taste, The.
Hernández Cruz. Problems With Hurricanes.
Herrick. Art above Nature, to Julia.
 Delight in Disorder.
 Request to the Graces, An.
 Upon Julia's Clothes.
 Upon the Nipples of Julia's Breast.
Hewett, D. This Version of Love.
Hilary. To an English Boy: "Hail, fair youth,
  who seeks no bribe."
Hill, A. Garden Window, The.
Hồ Xuân Huong. On a Portrait of Two
  Beauties.
Hoagland, E. Anti-Semanticist, The.
Hodgson, R. Gipsy Girl, The.
Hoffman, D. At Provincetown.
Holway, J. Throbbings.
Homer. Helen and the Elders.
Hood, T. Ruth.
Hookes. To Amanda Walking in the Garden.
Hopkins, G. Pied Beauty.
Horace. Ode 1.5: Quis Multa Gracilis.
Hsin Ch'i-chi. Tune: "Partridge Sky" For a
  Friend.
 Tune: "Pure Serene Music" En Route to Po-
  shan.
Huang O [or Huang Ho]. To the Tune "A
  Floating Cloud Crosses Enchanted Mountain".
Hughes, L. Harlem Sweeties.
 My People.
 When Sue Wears Red.
Hull, A. Another Rhythm.
Ibaragi Noriko. When I Was Prettiest in My
  Life.
Ibn 'Ubāda al-Qazzāz, A. I would give my
  father in ransom for a gazelle of imā guarded
  by a lion of the thicket.
Iqbal. Make Your Radiant Twining Curls.
Ismaili. Solange.
Issa. Even a fleabite.
 So many flea bites.
 That pretty girl.
Jaccottet. Daybreak.
Jackson, H. Her Eyes.
Jackson, L. Divestment of Beauty.
 Helen's Burning.
 Mask, The.
Jackson, M. L. Don Pullen at the Zanzibar Blue
  Jazz Café [2006].
Jacobs, H. On Growing Up the Darker Berry.
Jakiela. Personal History of Hands, A.
Jakushitsu. Refreshing, the wind against the
  waterfall.
Jamie, K. Queen of Sheba, The.
Jeffers, L. My Blackness Is the Beauty of This
  Land.
Jeffers, R. Beauty of Things, The.
 Birds and Fishes.
 Divinely Superfluous Beauty.
 Ocean's Tribute, The.
Jennings, E. Ugly Child, The.
Johnson, J. White Witch, The.
Johnston, E. Lines: To a Young Gentleman of
  Surpassing Beauty.
Jones, M. After the Small Pox.
Jones, P. If I Were Rita Hayworth.
Jonson, B. Elegy, An: "Though beauty be the
  mark of praise."
 Fair friend, 'tis true, your beauties move.
 Her Triumph.
 How He Saw Her.
 It was a beauty that I saw.
 To Mary, Lady Wroth ("Madam[e], had all
  antiquity [or antiquitie] been lost.").
Juan Chi. Hibiscus grows lushly on the grave
  mounds, The.
Kahal, I. Night Is Young and You're So
  Beautiful, The.
Kahn, G. You Stepped Out of a Dream.
Kai, N. Beauty Rituals 2000.
Kao Shih. North Tower of Golden Fort, The.

Kasischke. Pall.
Katz, J. Imperfect Is Our Paradise, The.
Keats. Ode on a Grecian Urn.
Kemble. Sonnet: "What is my lady like? thou fain would'st know."
Kenney. Plume.
Kenny, M. Still-Life.
Kim Sujang. Deception.
Kim Suyŏng. Beauty, A.
Kinnell. Saint Francis and the Sow.
Kinsella, T. Portrait of the Artist, A.
Kirchwey. Maculate Beauty.
Kirsch, S. Legend of Lilja.
Kleban, E. One.
Knott. Sonnet: "Way the world is not, The."
Koch, K. Energy in Sweden.
Košek, M. It All Depends on How You Look at It.
Kuzmin. Antinous.
Kynaston. To Cynthia.
Lake, P. Introduction to Poetry.
Lamb, C. Timid grace sits trembling in her eye, A.
Landon. Banquet, The.
Lady, thy face is very beautiful.
Landor, W. Rose Aylmer.
Le Gallienne. Beauty Accurst.
Leapor. Strephon to Celia. A modern Love-Letter.
Leconte de Lisle, C. Venus de Milo.
Lefroy. Palaestral Study, A.
Legaré. To a Lily.
Leigh, R. On a Fair Lady, Looking in the Glass.
Leslie, E. Little Bit Independent, A.
Levertov. Love Song: "Your beauty, which I lost sight of once."
Li Ch'ing-chao. Tune: "Magnolia Flowers".
Li Po. Suite in the Ch'ing-p'ing Mode, A.
Sy-che and the King.
Woman from Ch'ang-kan, The.
Li Yen-nien. Song, A: "In the north there is a lovely woman."
Song: "There's a beautiful woman in the north."
Lochhead, L. Grim Sisters, The.
López Velarde. Purple Spot, The.
Lorde. Naturally.
Lovelace, R. Gratiana Dancing [or Dauncing] and [or &] Singing.
To Amarantha, That She Would Dishevel[l] Her Hair[e].
Lowell, J. In a Copy of Omar Khayyám.
Lux. Gorgeous Surfaces.
Lyly, J. Cupid and My Campaspe Played.
MacDiarmid, H. Milk-Wort and Bog Cotton.
MacLean, S. Turmoil, The.
MacNeice. Circe.
Madgett. Black Woman.
Malé. Glance.
Mandelstam [or Mandelshtam]. Notre Dame.
Mansour, J. Vices of Men, The.
Marbod of Rennes. Horace composed an ode about a certain boy.
This vision of a face, radiant and full of beauty.
Marlowe. His bodie was as straight as Circes wand.
What Is Beauty?
Marston, J. *Pigmalion,* whose hie love-hating minde.
Martí. I am an honest man.
Martial. Did he have eyes and, if so, did he look.
If by chance, Flaccus, someone could offer me for the asking.
Martin, H. That Face.
Martinaitis, M. Kukutis's Swallow's Hymn.
Masefield. On Growing Old.
McCarthy, J. Alice Blue Gown.
McHugh, J. Lovely to Look At.
McKay, C. To O. E. A.
McLain, P. Beauty, That Lying Bitch.
Meinke. Sonnet on the Death of the Man Who Invented Plastic Roses.
Menken. Working and Waiting.
Mercer, J. Jeepers Creepers.
Tangerine.
You Must Have Been a Beautiful Baby.

You Were Never Lovelier.
Merrill, J. Peacock, The.
Michelangelo Buonarroti. From sweet weeping to a painful smile.
I see in your beautiful face, my lord.
Millay, E. Euclid Alone Has Looked on Beauty Bare.
Love is not blind. I see with single eye.
Spring: "To what purpose, April, do you return again?"
When I too long have looked upon your face.
Mistral, G. Decalogue of the Artist.
Song: "Fairest things are those which live, The."
Montagu, L. Between Your Sheets.
Saturday: The Small-Pox.
Moore, T. Believe Me, If All Those Endearing Young Charms.
Morley, H. Parents.
Murray, L. On Removing Spiderweb.
Muso Soseki. On the blue waves.
Myers, J. Mom Did Marilyn, Dad Did Fred.
Nabbes. Song, The: "Beauty no more the subject be."
Nairne. Heiress, The.
Navajo Oral Tradition. Night Chant, The.
Song of the Earth.
Neruda. Body of a Woman.
Ode to a Beautiful Nude.
Nervo. Cowardice.
Nezval. Prague in the Midday Sun.
O'Daniel, Wilbert Lee. Beautiful Texas.
O'Hara, F. Having a Coke with You.
Olson, C. Kingfishers, The.
Thing Was Moving, The.
O'Reilly, C. Weekend in Bodega Bay, A.
Orerulavanar. What He Said.
Orléans, C. Quant Souvenir Me Ramentoit.
Orr, G. Best.
Ovid. Elegy 1.5: "In summer's heat[e] and mid-time of the day."
Page, E. To Become Unconscious.
Paquin, Ethan. Capstone.
Parker, A. God of Pepper, The.
No Fool, the God of Salt.
Parker, D. Prophetic Soul.
P'Bitek. Woman with Whom I Share My Husband, The.
Pearse, P. Wayfarer, The.
Peele. Bethsabe's Song.
Percival. Morning among the Hills.
Petrarch. Loose to the wind her golden tresses streamed.
Sonnet: "When she walks by here."
Petronius Arbiter. Beauty is not enough; who wishes to be fair.
Phillips, C. Toys.
Piatt, S. Lesson in a Picture, A.
Piercy. Barbie Doll.
Pinkard, M. Sweet Georgia Brown.
Po Chü-i. Song of Everlasting Sorrow.
Poe. Al Aaraaf.
Eulalie—A Song.
Israfel.
Lake: To———, The.
Sleeper, The.
Stanzas: "How often we forget all time, when lone."
To Helen ("Helen, thy beauty is to me.").
To Helen ("I saw thee once—once only—years ago.").
Valley of Unrest, The.
Pogson, P. Exits.
Face Mask.
Hairdressing.
Porter, C. All of You.
It's All Right with Me.
Pound, E. Dance Figure.
Study in Aesthetics, The.
Prado, A. Grace.
Serenade.
Praed. Beauty and Her Visitors.
Prestwich. How to Choose a Mistress.
Prévert. River, The.
Prior. To a Lady: She Refusing to Continue a Dispute with Me.

Probyn. Frustrated.
Procter, A. Lost Chord, A.
Queneau. If You Imagine.
Quevedo y Villegas. On Lisi's Golden Hair.
Rafferty, C. Arsonist Tells His Story to the Attorney, The.
Raftery [or Raifteiri]. Mary Hynes.
Rakosi. Sandalwood Comes to My Mind.
Ransom, J. Judith of Bethulia.
Reznikoff. I met in a merchant's place.
Rhianos. To Theodorus et al.
Rich, A. What homage will be paid to a beauty built to last.
Rimbaud, A. Being Beauteous.
Roberson, E. Eclipse.
Robin, L. Louise.
Roethke. I Knew a Woman.
Roffé. Wanted.
Rogow, J. Symmetron: You and Brother Will.
Rohrer, M. Quick Sell the Pig.
Rojas. And to Be Born Is Here an Unnameable Feast.
Beautiful Ones, The.
Romero, L. If Marilyn Monroe.
Ronsard. Roses.
Rose, B. Night Is Young and You're So Beautiful, The.
Rossetti, C. Cousin Kate.
Youth gone, and beauty gone if ever there.
Rossetti, D. 78: Body's Beauty.
77: Soul's Beauty.
Rufinus. Her foot sparkled like silver.
How could I have known.
Russell, G. Great Breath, The.
St. John, P. Pearle's Poem.
Sanchez, S. Song No. 3: "Cain't nobody tell me any different."
Sandburg, C. Flash Crimson.
Murmurings in a Field Hospital.
Santayana. On a Piece of Tapestry.
Sonnet 43: "Candour of the gods is in thy gaze, The."
Sonnet 48: "Of Helen's brothers, one was born to die."
When I discover that the substance of the beautiful is a certain rhythm.
Sappho. And you, Dika, put lovely garlands round your hair.
For you beautiful ones my mind.
Handsome man is good to look at, A.
I have a beautiful child, her form.
Sapphics.
Sardis.
Some there are who say that the fairest thing seen.
Stars around the luminous moon—how soon they.
Sepamla. Odyssey, The.
Sexton. Snow White and the Seven Dwarfs.
Shakespeare, W. O, she doth teach the torches to burn bright!
Phoenix and the Turtle, The.
Sonnet 1: "From fairest creatures we desire increase."
Sonnet 5: "Those hours that with gentle work did frame."
Sonnet 18: "Shall I compare thee to a summer's day?"
Sonnet 20: "Woman's face with nature's own[e] hand painted, A."
Sonnet 53: "What is your substance, whereof are you made."
Sonnet 54: "O[h] how much more doth beauty beauteous seem."
Sonnet 65: "Since brass, nor stone, nor earth, nor boundless sea."
Sonnet 94: "They that have power [or pow'r or powre] to hurt[e], and will do[e] none."
Sonnet 95: "How sweet and lovely dost thou make the shame."
Sonnet 104: "To me, fair friend, you never can be old."
Sonnet 106: "When in the chronicle of wasted time."
Sonnet 127: "In the old age black was not counted fair."

Sonnet 130: "My mistress' eyes are nothing like the sun."
Sonnet 132: "Thine eyes I love, and they, as pitying me."
Shapiro, K.   Cut Flower, A.
Shaughnessy, B.   Your One Good Dress.
Shelley, P.   Conclusion.
Hymn to Intellectual Beauty.
Shen Chou.   Written on a Landscape Painting in an Album.
Sherwin, J.   Nightpiece.
Sholl.   Redbud.
Siddal.   Lust of the Eyes, The.
Sidney.   First Song: "Doubt you to whom my Muse these notes intendeth [or entendeth]."
Sonnet 5: "It is most true that eyes are formed to serve."
Sonnet 9: "Queen Virtue's court, which some call Stella's face."
Sonnet 11: "In truth, O Love, with what a boyish kind."
Sonnet 25: "Wisest scholar of the wight most wise, The."
Sonnet 52: "Strife is grown between Virtue and Love, A."
Simms, C.   Grey Wagtail on the Tyne.
Singer, E.   Cant. 5.6 & c.
Skelton, J.   To Mistress [or Maystres] Isabell Pennell.
To Mistress [or Maystres] Margaret Hussey.
Slessor.   William Street.
Smart, C.   Hymn 11. Beauty.
Smith, P.   Blonde White Women.
Smith, S.   Pretty.
Someck, R.   Testifying to Beauty.
Sophocles.   Colonus' Praise.
Spenser, E.   First was Fancy, like a lovely boy, The.
Sonnet 8: "More than most fair [or fayre], full of the living fire [or fyre]."
Sonnet 15: "Ye tradeful merchants that, with weary toil."
Sonnet 64: "Coming [or Comming] to kiss[e] her lips [or lyps], such grace I found."
Sonnet 79: "Men call you fair [or fayre], and you do[e] credit it."
Sonnet 81: "Fair [or Fayre] is my love, when her fair [or fayre] golden heares."
Stanley, T.   Celia Singing.
Glowworm, The.
Stein, G.   Bundles for Them.
Suppose an Eyes.
Stevens, W.   Peter Quince at the Clavier.
Stevenson, A.   He Who Loved Beauty.
Stevenson, R.   To Henry James.
Strato [or Straton].   Long hair, and curls woven not by Nature but by Art.
Twelve-year-old looks fetching in his prime, A.
Strode.   On a Good Leg and Foot.
On Fairford Windows.
Su Tung-p'o.   Lyrics to the Tune "Fairy Grotto".
Tune: "Butterflies Lingering over Flowers".
Suckling, S.   Sonnet: "Dost see how unregarded now."
Sonnet: "Of thee, kind boy, I ask no red and white."
Swanger.   Wayne's College of Beauty, Santa Cruz.
Swift, J.   Lady's Dressing Room, The.
Stella's Birthday [1721].
Swinburne.   Aholibah.
Symons, A.   Faint Love.
T'ang Yin.   Inscription for a Portrait.
Taylor, B.   Hylas.
Paean to the Dawn, A.
Tennyson, A.   To —. With the Following Poem.
Terrazas.   To a Lady.
To a Pair of Legs.
Thaxter.   Alone.
Thomas, E.   Glory, The.
Thompson, D. P.   Sister Lakin and Lally.
Tikhonov.   Fire and Rope, Bullet and Axe.
Toledo, N.   Natalia.
Natalia.
Natalia.
Tomlinson, C.   Shugakuin Garden.

Traherne.   Salutation [or Salutations], The.
Trethewey, N.   Hot Comb.
Tribal Chieftain.   Come here, my love, the crown of my home.
Ts'ao Ching-chao.   Palace Poem.
Ts'ao Chih.   Goddess of the Luo, The.
In the south country there lives a lovely lady.
Tu Fu [or Du Fu].   South Wind.
Tuckerman, F.   Question, The.
Tzu Yeh.   Bare branches tremble, The.
Unknown.   At sunset I come out of the door.
Ballad of the Mulberry Road, A.
Chaste Maiden, shining scarlet, The.
Filipino Woman, The.
Girl, don't be so haughty.
Go, litel bille, and do me recomaunde.
I have made myself beautiful in my worn clothes.
I have repainted my beauty mark and blackened my eyelids.
I Saw My Lady Weep.
It Is the Third Watch.
Large-headed beauty, head so alluring, The.
Last night with hair unbrushed.
Madrigal: "My Love in her attire doth show her wit."
Mulberry by the Path.
On the offering mound, a dead roe.
Question, A.
Shootingway Ceremony Prayer.
Sun sinks low, The. I.
To me, your beauty.
Whether I see you now.
Unknown, fr. Terezin Concentration Camp.
Birdsong 2.
Unknown, sometimes at. to Sir Walter Ralegh.
As You Came from the Holy Land [of Walsingham].
Vagura.   Love Poem, A.
Vegin, P.   "Moscow" Pool.
Verlaine.   Beauty of women, their weakness, those pale hands.
Moonlight.
White Moonglow, The.
Verwey, A.   Beautiful World, The.
Vicinelli.   I Met the Thieving Miss Magpie.
Vilariño.   Each Afternoon.
Villon.   Complaint of the Fair Armoress [or Armouress], The.
Gone Ladies.
Now I think I hear the laments.
Vogelweide.   Dancing Girl.
Wakoski.   Poet Recognizing the Echo of the Voice, A.
Waller, E.   Song: "Go[e], lovely rose."
Wang, J.   Tune: "Magnolia Flowers".
Wang Kuo-wei.   Tune: "Rouged Lips".
Ward, J.   Journey 55.
Waring, B.   When a Beautiful Woman Gets on the Jutiapa Bus.
Warren, R.   Arizona Midnight.
Wat.   From "Songs of a Wanderer".
Webster, A.   Faded.
That she is beautiful is not delight.
Wells, C.   Poster Girl's Defence, The.
Wen T'ing-yün.   News So Seldom Comes.
To the Tune: Southern Song.
Tune: "Beautiful Barbarians".
Wenderoth, J.   Aesthetics of the Bases Loaded Walk.
Disfortune.
Wescott.   Poet at Night-Fall, The.
Whitman, W.   Beauty.
This is the female form.
Twenty-eight young men bathe by the shore.
Walt Whitman, a kosmos, of Manhattan the son.
Wiese, B.   Going Home Madly.
Wilbur, R.   Beautiful Changes, The.
Caserta Garden.
Piazza di Spagna, Early Morning.
Still, Citizen Sparrow.
Transit.
Wilde, L.   Poet's Destiny, The.
Williams, Sir Charles H.   Song upon Miss Harriet Hanbury, Addressed to the Revd Mr Birt.

Williams, Sherley Anne.   Straight Talk from Plain Women.
Willson, F.   Estray, The.
To Hersa.
Wither.   Ninth Canticle, The.
Witting.   Beauty Is the Straw.
Wodehouse.   Cleopatterer.
Woolson.   Other, The.
Wordsworth, W.   As the black storm upon the mountain top.
Composed upon Westminster Bridge, September 3, 1802.
I Wandered Lonely as a Cloud.
Wright, C.   Night Journal.
Wright, J.   What is Beautiful.
Wright, K.   Unlikely Obbligato of Andersonstown.
Wright, R.   And This Is My Beloved.
Wu Tsao.   For the Courtesan Ch'ing Lin.
Wunderlich, M.   One Explanation of Beauty.
Wylie.   Beauty.
Preference.
Yeats.   Crazy Jane Talks with the Bishop.
Folly of Being Comforted, The.
No Second Troy.
Secret Rose, The.
Symbols.
Yellen, J.   Ain't She Sweet?
Young, D.   Rothko's Yellow.
Zamora, D.   Vision of Your Body.
Zanzotto.   Eva, forma futuri.
Zukofsky, L.   In Arizona.
Not much more than being.

Beauty and the Beast
Brown, E.   Beauty and the Prince Formerly Known as Beast.

Beauty Pageants
Atwood.   Miss July Grows Older.

Beauty Parlors
Dauer.   Lois at the Hair Salon.

Beavers
Rothenberg, J.   Seneca Journal 1: "A Poem of Beavers".

Bedouins
Blind.   Beautiful Beeshareen Boy, The.
James, S.   Sisters of Saida Manoubia, The.
Taylor, B.   Bedouin Song.

Bedrooms
Berger, D.   Lincoln Bedroom, The.
Boruch.   Sewing.
Cornford, F.   Country Bedroom, The.
George, F.   Sudden Tug of the Familiar, The.
Henry, B.   Rooms.
Jacob, M.   Little Poem.
Komunyakaa, Y.   Between Days.
Wright, C.   Floating Trees.

Beds
Agustini.   Shadow Beds.
Alvi, M.   Bed, The.
Armstrong, J.   On Feather Beds.
Benét, S.   For City Spring.
Benserade, I.   Translation of Lines by Benserade.
Blagg, T.   In Bed this Morning.
Blanchfield, B.   Endowment Becoming Less An Institution, The.
Borgmann, K.   Bed.
Cisneros, S.   Man in My Bed Like Cracker Crumbs, A.
Dacey, P.   Squeak.
Debravo, J.   Beds of Purification.
Deltoro, A.   Almohadas.
Pillows.
Field.   Love rises up some days.
Finlay, I.   Bedtime.
Gibson, M.   Reading in Bed.
Hahn, O.   Death Is Sitting at the Foot of My Bed.
Heaney, S.   Settle Bed, The.
Herrick.   Her Bed.
Hope, A.   Bed, The.
Janeczko.   Blanket Hog.
Jewsbury.   Verses: "I am monarch of troubles a host."
Lady Ise.   Pillows know, they say.

Larkin, P.   Sad Steps.
  Talking in Bed.
Lowell, R.   Man And Wife.
Madhubuti.   Loneliness, A.
Matson, C.   Bedside.
Montagu, L.   Between Your Sheets.
Morley, C.   Plumpuppets, The.
Moss, H.   Making a Bed.
Ni Dhomhnaill.   Labasheedy (The Silken Bed).
  Leaba Shíoda.
O'Brien, G.   Bed in the Wilderness, The.
Parker, D.   Inscription for the Ceiling of a
  Bedroom.
Plath.   Most Beds are Beds.
Ramsay, A.   Polwart on the Green.
Reisen, A.   Household of Eight.
Rendra.   Moon's Bed, the Bride's Bed, The.
Ross, A.   Two in Bed.
Schilpp, M.   Non Sequitur.
Shapiro, D.   House (Blown Apart).
Smith, C.   Beds.
Spires.   Beds, The.
Stern, G.   96 Vandam.
Stevenson, R.   Bed in Summer.
  Land of Counterpane, The.
Stillman, M.   Lullaby for Suzanne.
Surrey.   Laid in My Quiet Bed.
Swinburne.   Love And Sleep.
Torres, E.   Entrancielo.
Townsend, A.   Hospital Corners.
Townsend, A.   Day's End.
Unknown.   Get Up, Get Up.
  Lord Randal[l].
Updike.   Insomnia the Gem of the Ocean.
Walsh, Agnes.   Mike's.
Warren-Moore.   All-Night Issue, The.
Wen T'ing-yün.   She Sighs on Her Jade Lute.

Beech Trees and Beechnuts
Longley, M.   Beech Tree, The.

Beer
Addonizio.   Beer. Milk. The Dog. My Old Man.
Alexie.   Reservation Love Song.
Allen, F.   Fall, The.
Braunstein, Evan.   Newark.
Brown, G.   Old Women, The.
Bukowski.   Crucifix in a Deathhand.
Byrd, Bobby.   Good Life, The.
Chavez, L.   After the Prom.
Durcan.   My Belovèd Compares Herself to a
  Pint of Stout.
Feaver.   River God, the.
Gay, J.   Birth of the Squire; an Eclogue, The.
Goff, C.   Drinking Beer with Sir.
Hall, H, Palmer.   Death on Village Creek, A.
Heinowitz, C.   Five Men.
Housman.   Terence, this is stupid stuff.
Leland, C.   Hans Breitmann's Party [*or* Barty].
Leonard, T.   Jist Ti Let Yi No.
Locklin.   Beer.
Marquis.   Archy Interviews a Pharoah.
Nelson, M.   Misunderstanding, A.
Roberts, K.   Plastic Cup, The.
Stephens, J.   Glass of Beer, A.
Swingler.   Drinking Song.
Thackeray.   Dear Jack.
Unknown.   Gud Ber.
Vietnamese Oral Tradition.   Ke-Mo Village Girl.
Webster, A.   Enigma No. 6.
Whitbread.   Alpine, Texas.

Bees and Beekeeping
Alexander, P.   Lightfall.
Ball, A.   Attempt, An.
Basho.   Bee, A.
  Farewell! Like a bee.
  How reluctantly
Baxter, J.   Wild Bees.
Bhattācārya, K.   Bee of my mind, The.
Bierds, L.   In the Beeyard.
Blunden.   Forefathers.
Booth, P.   Bee.
Bukowski.   b.
Clare, J.   To an Angry Bee.
Clarke, George Elliott.   King Bee Blues.
Colonna, S.   Orientation from Afar.
Cooper, Allan.   Worker Bee, The.
Davidkov, Ivan.   Monastery.

Dickinson, E.   Bee, The.
  Bees.
  Come slowly—Eden!
  Could I but ride indefinite.
  Did the Harebell loose her girdle.
  His Feet are shod with Gauze.
  Letter to Bee.
Emerson, R.   Humble-Bee, The.
Field.   Penetration.
Flynn, N.   Hive.
  Swarm.
Forrester, S.   Sun on the windowsill.
Fortini.   Poetry of Roses, The.
Frost, C.   Part of the Bee's Body Embedded in
  the Flesh, The.
  Telling the Bees.
Gerstler.   BZZZZZZZZ.
Glazer, M.   Science.
Graham, H.   Opportunity.
Greene, Jonathan.   Hut Poem #1.
Hughes, H.   At the Teahouse, 6 am.
Im Ŏngnyŏng.   To a Friend.
Levin, P.   Lost Bee, The.
  Planting Roses.
Lewis, L.   May Mowing Clover.
Lodge, T.   Rosalind's [*or* Rosalynd's]
  Madrigal[l].
Magdeburg, Mechthild von.   Of all that God has
  shown me.
Mandelstam [*or* Mandelshtam].   Lightheartedly
  Take from the Palms of My Hands.
Margolis, G.   Autumn Bees on Broccoli
  Blossoms Gone-by.
Martinez, D.   Prodigal Son in His Own Words,
  The: Bees.
McQuade, Molly.   Bees Stumble.
Merrill, C.   Bees, The.
Morgan, R.   Honey.
Mother Goose.   God made the bees.
Orton, B.   Beekeeper.
Pak Tujin.   Song in a Graveyard.
Palmer, M.   I killed a bee on the Street of
  Scissors.
Peck, J.   Mount Bromley Hymn.
Phillips, C.   Rest of Love, The.
Plath.   Arrival of the Bee Box, The.
  Stings.
  Swarm, The.
  Wintering.
Pogson, P.   Bee.
  Resin.
Rakosi.   ZZZZZ.
Reese, L.   Telling the Bees.
Rose, D.   Queen Bee.
Sandburg, C.   In Tall Grass.
Sappho.   For me neither honey nor bee.
Spenser, E.   Sonnet 71: "I joy to see how in
  your drawen work."
Spivack, K.   Dido: Swarming.
Stainer.   Honeycomb, The.
Swenson, M.   Couple, A.
Toomer.   Beehive.
Tsanev, Ivan.   Bee.
Turner, C.   Julius Caesar and the Honey-Bee.
Unknown.   My mistress in a hive of bees.
Watts, I.   How Doth the Little Busy Bee.
Winkfield, T.   Nature Study.
Young, D.   Poem for Adlai Stevenson and
  Yellow Jackets.
Young, D.   Colophon.
Ziemianin A.   Heart Attack.

Beethoven, Ludwig van
Barney, W.   Mr. Watts and the Whirlwind.
Berger, B.   To Answer Your Question.
Clampitt.   Beethoven, Opus 111.
Collins, B.   Another Reason Why I Don't Keep
  a Gun in the House.
Hughes, Daniel.   Too Noble.
Jones, B.   Beethoven's Ears.
Lanier, S.   To Beethoven.
Levy, A.   Sinfonia Eroica.
Millay, E.   On Hearing a Symphony of
  Beethoven.
Ray, H.   Beethoven.
Rich, A.   Ninth Symphony of Beethoven
  Understood at Last as a Sexual Message, The.

Rylander, E.   Dancing on Beethoven's Birthday.
Seaman, E.   Double Dactyls.
Solie, Karen.   Beethoven: Op. 95.
Wheelock, J.   Beethoven.
Wright, D.   Beethoven's Romance in G.
Zolynas.   Pastorale for Spring.

Beetles
Blind.   Scarabaeus Sisyphus.
Breytenbach.   Dung-beetle.
Busceti, G.   Exhausted Inconsistency Floats
  Here, An.
Davies, P.   Dung Beetle, The.
Dickinson, E.   These are the Nights that Beetles
  love.
Gwynn, H.   Welcome / Black beetle.
Merwin.   Rose Beetle, The.
Oliver, M.   How Everything Adores Being
  Alive.
Szymborska, W.   Seen from Above ("On a dirt
  road lies a dead beetle.").
Young, D.   Only One of My Deaths.

Beets
Nash, O.   Parsnip, The.

Begging and Beggars
Aleshire.   Double, The.
Basho.   Dried salmon.
Berry, W.   Guest, The.
Bishop, E.   Pink Dog.
Brines, F.   Beggar, The.
Browning, R.   Twins, The.
Bye.   Dear Mozart.
Coleridge, M.   Insincere Wish Addressed to a
  Beggar, An.
Cummings, E. E.   Right here the other night
  something.
Dana, R.   Mark, The.
Dickinson, E.   I never lost as much but twice.
  Let me not thirst with this Hock at my Lip.
  There comes an hour when begging stops.
Donne.   Lame Beggar, A.
Douglas, K.   Egypt.
Enzensberger, H.   Hôtel Fraternité.
Gander, F.   Sinister.
González, R.   Marías, Old Indian Mothers.
Healy, E.   Advice Like That.
Hippolyte.   So Jah Sey.
Hughes, F.   Foxes.
Issa.   Autumn wind / The beggar looks.
  In the beggar's tin.
Jacob, M.   Beggar Woman of Naples, The.
Johnson, G.   Suppliant, The.
Kleinzahler.   Ebenezer Californicus.
Mattes, L.   On the Street Corner.
Matthews, W.   Grief.
Mikha'il, M.   Beggar, The.
Notley.   Woman came into "a car I rode" "about
  thirty-seven" "maybe", A.
Ozaki Hosai.   I have no bowl.
Parker, M.   Maunding Soldier; or, The Fruits of
  Warre Is Beggery, The.
Penna.   When I don't feel well, I wander among.
Plath.   Applicant, The.
Reznikoff.   Beggar Woman.
Ruden, S.   Beggar Outside Cape Town Station,
  A.
Ryokan.   Done with a long day's begging.
  I've forgotten.
  Picking violets.
Satyanarayana, V.   Blind Beggar, The.
Shushtarī, A.   Little shaikh from the land of
  Meknès sings in the middle of the
  marketplaces, A.
Stephens, J.   Glass of Beer, A.
Swirszczynska [*or* Swir].   Same Inside, The.
Thomas, D.   Hunchback in the Park, The.
Unknown.   Oh Cruel Was the Press-Gang.
Volkman.   Case, The.
Watley, M.   For the Man I Met on Georgia Ave.
Winter, M.   Here and There.
Wroth.   Sonnet 2: "Late in the Forest I did
  Cupid See."
Yeats.   Beggar to Beggar Cried.
"Zelda.".   Crippled beggar who lives, The.

See also **Homeless, The; Vagabonds**

Beginnings
Dao. Landscape Over Zero.
Duncan, R. Returning to Roots of First Feeling.
Eliot, T. S. So here I am, in the middle way, having had twenty years.
Hejinian. Beginner, The.
Hillman, B. Unbeginning, The.
Kennelly. Begin.
Lenfestey, James P. Landing.
Lochhead, D. Nothing: "Now, this beginning."
Metodiev, Ivan. Garden of Questions.
Olson, C. These Days: "Whatever you have to say, leave."
Terrio, Chris. Viola Recalls.

Behn, Aphra
Unknown. Elegy upon the Death of Mrs. A. Behn, the Incomparable Astrea, An.

Beirut, Lebanon
Adonis [or Adunis]. Diary of Beirut Under Siege, 1982, The.
Gebeyli, C. Beirut.
Guri, H. Like Beirut.
Hammad, S. Broken and Beirut.
Tuéni. Beirut.

Belfast, Northern Ireland
Brodsky, J. Belfast Tune.
Carson, C. Belfast Confetti.
Campaign.
Slate Street School.
Causley. HMS Glory.
Grattan, P. Little Night Music, A.
Signs of an Organised Hand.
Mahon. Afterlives.
Spring Vacation, The.
Morrissey, S. Thoughts in a Black Taxi.
Muldoon, P. Aisling.
Paulin. Under the Eyes.

Belgium
Nolens, L. Place and Date.
Rossetti, D. Antwerp to Ghent.
Sassoon, S. On Passing the New Menin Gate.

Belief
Apotheker, A. Burning Bush.
Blumenthal, M. What I Believe.
Cary, P. Hymn: "How dare I in thy courts appear."
Chasin. In Communication with a UFO.
Crane, H. To Brooklyn Bridge.
Crane, S. I saw a man pursuing the horizon.
Cunningham, J. This Humanist whom no beliefs constrained.
Cunningham, P. Cats—A Retrospective.
Dickinson, E. Spirit lasts, but in what mode, The.
Forché. Ancapagari.
Fullerton. John 14:1–2.
Garcia, R. Why I Left the Church.
Gaskill, C. I Can't Believe That You're in Love with Me.
Haavikko. How decisively.
Han Yü. Girl of Mount Hua, The.
Harvey, M. Festival of Giovedo Grasso, The.
Howard, B. Would You Believe It?
Howe, F. Veteran.
Jennings, E. Lord's Prayer, The.
Kenyon, J. Suggestion from a Friend.
Killigrew, A. Upon the Saying That My Verses Were Made by Another.
Kitahara Hakushū. Secret Song of the Heretics.
Kizer, C. Dixit Insipiens.
Krukowski, D. Intellectual Life, The.
Levine, P. Belief.
Lezama Lima. Portrait of José Cemí.
Loden. Gospel According to Clairol, The.
Loesser. I Believe in You.
Morton, J. On Sir Henry Ferrett, M.P.
Nichol. St. Anzas IX.
Pack, R. Proton Decay.
Rexroth, K. Sword in a Cloud of Light, A.
Simon, L. Ravine.
Smith, S. God the Eater.
Steiger. We believe books and music.
Towers, T. Three Observations on Belief.
Weigl. Why I Hate Theory.
Zapruder, M. Whoever You Are.

Zawacki, Andrew. Credo.
See also **Faith**

Belize
Arana, Milton. Birth of a Nation.
Cayetano, E. Roy. Drums of My Fathers.
Faber, Reginal. Forward to Nationhood.
Galvez, Carol Fonesca. Creation Continues.
Godfrey, Glenn. New Spirit, The.
Lewis, P. A Si Wha New Belize.
Dis Da Me.
Morter, L. Belizean Dawn, A.
Muhammad, Sakinah Carol. Rain Lover.
Musa, Y. Imagine a Revolution.
Where Are They?
Parham, Mary Gomez. Belize Cemetery, The.
Parks, R. Dawn of Freedom.
Song of Freedom, A.
Price, G. Belizeans: Unite to Build our Nation.
Ramirez, L. Yet to Come.
Searle, J. Matthew the Bayman.
Shoman, A. 321738.
Waight, S. To the Coming of the Decade.

Bellbirds
Kendall, H. Bell-Birds.

Belloc, Hilaire
Beerbohm, M. After Hilaire Belloc.

Bells
Adams, L. Bell Tower.
Atkins, R. Night and a Distant Church.
Baca. Bells.
Basho. As the sound fades.
Clouds of blossoms.
Clouds of cherry blossoms!
Temple bell / A cloud of cherry flowers.
Temple bell stops, The.
Village without bells, A.
Baudelaire. Cracked Bell, The.
Bevington, L. With the Tide: A Cry of Weakness.
Buson. Butterfly.
Clinging to the bell.
Coolness.
Oh, how cool.
Sound of a bell.
Carroll, L. Fit the Second: The Bellman's Speech.
Castro, R. Bells, The.
Chang Chi. Night-Mooring near Maple Bridge, A.
Chang Yüeh. Hearing Bells at Night in the Mountains.
Collins, B. Japan.
Crane, H. Broken Tower, The.
Cummings, E. E. Anyone lived in a pretty how town.
Curtis, T. To My Father.
Davies, I. Gwalia Deserta XV.
Dickinson, E. When Bells stop ringing—Church—begins.
Ekelof. Greece.
Fordham. Bells of St. Michael.
Forrester, S. Temple bell ringing.
Fuhaku. So very still, even.
García Lorca. My Little Girl Went to the Sea.
Guiney. Sunday Chimes in the City.
Heard, J. Sabbath Bells.
Housman. Bredon Hill.
When the bells justle in the tower.
Ingelow. High Tide on the Coast of Lincolnshire, 1571, The.
Jackson, L. Ding-Donging.
Jiji, Dobashi. My Bicycle Bell.
Jones, R. Bell, The.
Levitt, Peter. Bell, The.
Linden, M. Church Bells, The.
Liu Ch'ang-ch'ing. On Parting with the Buddhist Pilgrim Ling-Ch'ě.
Loesser. If I Were a Bell.
Longfellow, H. Bells of San Blas, The.
Christmas Bells.
Machado Ruiz. Poem: "Frail sound of a tunic trailing, A."
Mant, R. Church Bells, The.
Masaoka Shiki. Evening bell / Persimmons pelt.
I eat a persimmon.

McDonald, W. Christmas Bells, Saigon.
Meynell, A. Chimes.
Nguyen, Hoa. Captive and Able.
Noin. Spring in a Mountain Village.
Ōkuma Kotomichi. Vespers.
Owen, W. Anthem for Doomed Youth.
Pessoa. My smalltown bell.
Poe. Bells, The.
Probyn. Changes.
Reverdy. Secret.
Sidney. Dirge: "Ring out your bells [or belles], let mourning shows [or shewes] be spread."
Slessor. Five Bells.
Smith, M. Chimes.
Stevens, W. Old Lutheran Bells at Home, The.
Takai Kito. Contending / Temple bell.
Tan Taigi. Barley's season / Dust mutes.
Tennyson, A. Ring Out, Wild Bells.
Thompson, C. Church Bells.
Thoreau. Dong, sounds the brass in the east.
Turner, C. Buoy-Bell, The.
Unknown. Bell da Ring.
Heaven Bells, The.
London Bells.
Song of the Gong and Chimes.
Upon Arch-bishop Laud, Prisoner in the Tower. 1641.
Vietnamese Oral Tradition. Ship of Redemption.
Wang Ch'ang-ling. At the Stream's Source in Spring: A Party.
Warsh. Suicide Rates, The.
Whittier. Skipper Ireson's Ride.
Wilbur, R. Bell Speech.
Dubious Night, A.
Williams, W. Catholic Bells, The.
Yosano Akiko. Temple bell, The.
Yun'er. Yun'er's Bell.

Belly Dancing
Wakoski. Belly Dancer.

Belshazzar
Bibb. Belshazzer's Feast.

Ben Bulben, Ireland
Yeats. Under Ben Bulben.

Bengal
Bhattācārya, M. Come, brothers, everyone together.

Beowulf
Borges. Poem Written in a Copy of Beowulf.
De Los Santos, M. Wiglaf.
Unknown. Beowulf.

Bergman, Ingmar
Chaloner. Thicket of Time.

Berkeley, California
Clurman, D. Berkeley Marina at Dusk, The.
Ginsberg, A. Strange New Cottage in Berkeley, A.
Hamer. Berkeley, Late Spring.
Pinsky. In Berkeley.
Reed, I. Going East.
Simon, J. Caffe Mediterraneum.
Troupe. View from Skates in Berkeley, The.

Berkeley, George
Davie, D. Fountain, The.
Reed, I. Going East.

Berkshire Hills, Massachusetts
Ray, H. Among the Berkshire Hills.

Berlin, Germany
Brodsky, J. Berlin Wall Tune, The.
Curbelo. Photograph from Berlin.
Fathy, S. For Heiner Muller: Part 3.
Glazova, A. Berlin.
Holz. In the Thiergarten, on a bench, I'm sitting and smoking.
Kunze, R. Wall, The: For october 3, 1990.
Llywelyn-Williams. In Berlin, August 1945: Lehrte Bahnhof.
Loerke, Oskar (1884-1941). Winter Evening, Berlin.
Sahl. Charter Flight into the Past, A.
Sutskever [or Sutzkever]. Cartload of Shoes, A.
Villanueva, A. Even the Eagles Must Gather.

Bermuda
Koch, K. Airplane Betty in Holland.
Long, J. Bermuda Triangle.

Marvell. Bermudas.
Trentham, E. Hurricane Season.

Berries
Beissel, H. Tanka: "Ice rain coats berries."
Helwig. Cape Breton in Autumn.
Hudgins. Chinaberry Trees, The.
Réda, Jacques. Autumn Distance.

Berrigan, Daniel
Rich, A. Burning of Paper instead of Children, The.

Berrigan, Ted
Duncan, R. At the Poetry Conference: Berkeley After the New York Style.
Notley. April Not an Inventory but a Blizzard.

Berryman, John
Dickey, W. Death of John Berryman,The.
Halpern, D. Bravura Lament.
Harper, M. Tongue-tied in Black and White.
Meredith, W. John and Anne.
Merwin. Berryman.

Bertrand de Born
Pound, E. Near Perigord.
  Sestina: Altaforte.

Bestiality
Dickey, J. Sheep Child, The.
Dobyns. Bowlers Anonymous.
Donovan, K. Entering the Mare.
Lewis, G. Farmer's Evidence, The.

Bethlehem
Brooks, P. O Little Town of Bethlehem.
Longfellow, H. Three Kings, The.
Parker, D. Maid-Servant at the Inn, The.
Roberts, E. Christmas Morning.
Yeats. Second Coming, The.

Betjeman, Sir John
Causley. Betjeman, 1984.

Betrayal
Adcock, F. Things: "There are worse things than having behaved foolishly in public."
Archilochus. Buffeted by the waves.
Bibbins, M. Mud.
Brown, L. (Here Am I) Broken Hearted.
Cabico, R. Gameboy.
Catullus. To Aurelius.
Coleridge, S. Pitt.
Creeley. Anger.
Davidman. And Pilate Said.
Davidson, J. Ballad of Hell, A.
Fainlight, R. Invitation, The.
Galvin, J. Station (4).
Goldsmith, O. When Lovely Woman Stoops to Folly.
Goodman, M. Open Poem.
Graves, R. Not at Home.
Greenwell, D. Fidelity Rewarded.
Grotz, J. Kiss of Judas.
Harbach, O. Poor Pierrot.
Hardy, T. Broken Appointment, A.
Herbert, Z. Matthew 27:3–10; When Judas, his betrayer, saw.
  Speculations on the Subject of Barabbas.
Hill, G. Gasholders, russet among fields. Milldams, marpools.
Housman. Is my team ploughing.
Ignatow, D. Each Day.
Ismaili. Bajji.
  Queue.
Jordan, J. Wasted.
Kirsch, S. I Wanted to Kill My King.
Kisielewsky, Sergio. Cough Drops.
Kossman. John 13:21–30; When Jesus had thus said, he was troubled.
  Judas' Reproach.
Lom. Lament for the State of the Country, A.
Marlowe. Here is the form of Gaveston's exile.
Martinson. Lighthouse Keeper.
Maxwell, G. Nerve, The.
Medina, T. Big House Revisited, The.
Millay, E. Bluebeard.
Muso Soseki. In these mountain villages and harbor towns.
Myles, E. Maxfield Parrish.
Nguyễn Văn Lạc. Shrimps.
Nuccoli. Your promises come to me always together with your betrayals, which you have

more of than the fox.
Ovid. Back from the sea now, back to their sources shall deep rivers.
Pasternak, B. Mark 14:26–42; And when they had sung.
  Matthew 26:47–56; While he was still speaking, Judas came.
"Perse." Nocturne: "Now! they are ripe, these fruits of a jealous fate."
Polkowski. I Don't Know That Man.
Prior. Epigram, An: "To John I ow'd great obligation."
Ralegh, S. Farewell to False Love, A.
Ralin, Radoi. Ideological Tango.
Sappho. Mika / But I will not allow you.
Sen, R. I have learned.
Seneca. Flee every friendship and live: a greater truth.
Seto, T. Blood Ties.
Shakespeare, W. Sonnet 41: "Those pretty [or petty] wrongs that liberty commits."
  Sonnet 151: "Love is too young to know what conscience is."
Sitwell, E. Two Songs of Queen Anne Boleyn.
Sitwell, O. Judas and the Profiteer.
Szymborska, W. Laughter.
Tayson, R. Phone Sex.
Unknown. Frankie and Johnny [or Johnnie or Albert].
  Hughie [the] Gra[e]me [Version from Scott's Minstrelsy].
  I have been brought into darkness.
  In the vale of resteles mynde.
  Kinmont Willie.
  Lamkin.
  Listen to me, you wench!
Ward, BJ. Daily Grind.
Weigl. Oh, Atonement.
Whittier. Ichabod[!].
Wilde, O. Yet each man kills the thing he loves.
Wyatt. Lover Showeth How He Is Forsaken of Such as He Sometime Enjoyed, The.
Yan Yanzhi. Pure Wife, A.
Zagajewski. Betrayal.

Betrothal
Coleridge, S. Keepsake, The.

Biafra
Achebe. Christmas in Biafra (1969).

Bible
Ali, A. Ghazal: "Where are you now? Who lies beneath your spell tonight."
Amichai, Y. Biblical Meditations.
Bishop, E. Over 2000 Illustrations and a Complete Concordance.
Blake, W. Marriage of Heaven and Hell, The.
  Memorable Fancy, A.
Borges. John 1:14 (1969).
Branch, A. In the Beginning Was the Word.
Buffoni, F. De Pisis--Piacenza Papers.
Cowper, W. To Mary Unwin.
Dickinson, E. Bible is an antique Volume, The.
Dickinson, P. Moses and the Princess.
Elfyn, Menna. Cell Angel.
Eliscu, E. Great Day.
Ephraim ben Jacob. Sacrifice of Isaac, The.
Equi. Things to Do in the Bible.
Ettinger, E. Micrographic Manuscript, Miniature (1).
  Micrographic Manuscript, Miniature (2).
Field. Will You Crucify Your King?
Gershwin, I. It Ain't Necessarily So.
Hardy, T. Respectable Burgher, The.
Haxton. Gloss.
Heaney, S. Other Side, The.
Hemans. Vigil of Rizpah, The.
Jabès. Beginning of the Book, The.
  Book, The.
Johnson, J. Creation, The.
Kalina, R. Testimonies.
Kinsella, J. Akbar.
Lanier, E. To the Queen's Most Excellent Majesty.
Lanyer. To the Queen's Most Excellent Majesty.
Lea, S. Still dark when we file like children out on the turf.
Longfellow, H. Sand of the Desert in an Hour-

  Glass.
Madhubuti. Books as Answer.
Merritt, C. Woman of Color.
Merwin. Calling, A.
Milosz, C. Readings.
  With Her.
Moore, M. Is Your Town Nineveh?
Moorer. Bible, The.
  Mountain Tops.
Moss, T. Goodness and the Salt of the Earth.
Oden. Bible Study.
Ostriker. Story of Abraham, The.
Quarles. On The Gospel.
  On the Holy Scriptures.
Rojas. Chapter and Verse.
Rose, B. Great Day.
Rosser, J. Parable of the Cheek.
Smart, C. Hymn 15. Taste.
  Song to David, A.
Stafford, W. How the Real Bible Is Written.
Traherne. On the Bible.
Ullman. Rain.
Unknown. From a London Bookshop.
  In *Bath* a wanton wife did dwell.
  On the Bible.
Vaughan, H. Book, The.
  H. Scriptures.
Warton, T. Stanzas on the Psalms.
Webb, C. Biblical Also-Rans.
  Faith.
Wesley, C. N T.
White, V. C. Child of Adam.
Wilbur, R. Matthew 8, 28 ff.
Wilner, E. Reading the Bible Backwards.
Young, K. Central Standard Time.

Bicycles and Bicycling
Afrika, T. Nightrider.
Alexander, P. Bicycle Sprint.
Allen, W. Away from the Office.
Alpaugh, D. Herbie.
Anna, Glory. Bicycle Glee Song, A.
Aragon, F. Tricycles.
Bateman, C. Bicycle Slow Race, The.
Becker, R. Bicycle Days.
Beeching, H. Going Down Hill on a Bicycle.
Bennett, Alberto A. My Wheel and I.
Berkson, B. Bicycle Thief, The.
Bilgere, G. Like Riding a Bicycle.
Boas, G. Beard and Bicycle.
Bold, A. Engima, The.
Bornholdt, J. Instructions for How to Get Ahead of Yourself While the Light Still Shines.
Boylan, G. Dames of Washington.
  Wooing the Bicycle.
Boyle, M. Silver Creature.
Brackenbury. Cycles.
Brooks, B. Moon in the Mirror.
Broumas, O. Way a Child Might Believe, The.
Brown, J. Sonnet at Three-Speed.
Brown, James. Bicycle, The.
  Lesson, The: "Cleaned, lubed and wiped."
Buchanan, R. Bicycle Song (For Women).
Buddingh'. Ode to the Bicycle.
Cantor, Michael. Tour de France.
Carleton, W. Centurion, A.
  Wheelmen's Song.
Centolella. Zeno's Progress.
Clawson, Jim. Fearless Rider.
Cloves, Jeff. For Fausto Coppi (1916–60) et Tous les Copains de la Bicyclette.
Coogler. Her charming steel-horse could not miss.
deFreese, A. Cycles in Flight: The Racing Bike.
Dodge, C. Wheel Ethics.
Dryden, C. Scorcher's Farewell to His Steed, The.
Dudis, Ellen Kirvin. Riding Their Bikes.
Edmond, L. Bicycle Dream.
  Girls.
Ehrhart. Cycling the Rosental.
Faulkner, D. W. Phoebe on a Bicycle.
Ferguson, G. Bhakti Yogi Buys a Bike, The.
  Puncture Near Wittedrif.
  Puritan against the Wind.
Field, E. New Cycle, A.
Foster, S. Conant. Boycycle, The.

From Out the Heated City.
To Flight.
Toasting Song.
Galef. Bicycle Race in *Beowulf*,The.
Gander, F. Mission Thief.
Gargulinski, Ryn. We.
Gibbens, J. To the Bicycle.
Goodge. Smithville Tandem Bike, The.
Gordon, G. Timothy. At Jhong-Jhou Train
Station.
Grant, Peter. Winter Resolve.
Harrington, Jonathan. Rain of Bicycles, A.
Harvey, James Clarence. At Eventide.
Swiftly We Fly.
Versicle, A.
Harvey, M. By Bicycle.
Heaney, S. Constable Calls, A.
Wheels within Wheels.
Hedrington, William. Bicycling Away from the
Library.
Held, George. Learning to Ride My Bike.
Hughes, Audrey. Logocyclegram.
Hung. I Never Dream of My Father.
Ilton, Phil. No Goalies.
Israeli, H. Bicycle Ride, The.
Jarry. Passion of Jesus Considered as an Uphill
Race, The.
Jiji, Dobashi. My Bicycle Bell.
Kal, Jan. Mont Ventoux.
Kasdorf. Riding Bike with No Hands.
Kendall, Walter G. Men Who Ride for Fun,
The.
Kenyon, J. Noiseless Wheel, The.
Kercheval, J. Your Wife, a Widow, Waits for
You.
Kirchner, F. In Cold February Twilight.
Reasons to Commute by Bicycle.
Kocot, N. Bicycle Poem.
Korteweg. Entirely You.
Laing, K. Race on Gathering Bites.
Lancaster, John. Yellow Bike, The.
Lansky, B. Oh, Woe Ith Me!
Laughlin, J. Our Bicycles.
Lawrence, Arthur H. Song of the Wheel, A.
Lichtman, Risa. Bicycle, The.
Love, R. Puncture Wounds: A Baiku.
MacCarthy, C. Island of Miracles.
Malouf. Bicycle.
Mayes, J. Pedaling Paranoia.
McClure, D. Hampton Lock.
McFayden, Stazja. Not My Knees.
Mitchell, C. Roll On, Shining Wheel!
Monroe, H. Bicyclers, The.
Montale. Buffalo.
Morgan, B. Among Goldfinches.
Morgan, J. Chill summer day, the sky, A.
Neckar, Ninon. On the Road.
Nelson, H. No Hands.
Nelson, M. Minor Miracle.
Neruda. Ode to Bicycles.
Nixon-Roulet, M. Highroller.
Noguchi, R. When for Weeks the Sea is Flat.
Norris, L. Eden.
Nye, N. Rider, The.
Oppen. Bicycles and the Apex, The.
Oswald, A. Bike Ride on a Roman Road.
Painter, F. V. N. (Franklin Verzelius Newton).
Pastoral, A: "Sun looks o'er the mountain fair,
The."
Pantani, Marco. Sometimes We Close Our
Eyes.
Parke. Buying a Cycle.
Pastan. Stationary Bicycle.
Pastnor, Paul. Silent Steed, The.
Paterson, A. Mulga Bill's Bicycle.
Piercy. Cyclist, The.
Pierson, Ernest De Lancey. Flying Wheel, The.
Pike, M. When Gerty Goes A-Wheeling.
Pranses, T. Shovelin' Coal.
Pratt, Charles E. To the Wheel.
Prunty. Learning the Bicycle.
Pryputniewicz, Tania. Dragonfly.
Reaney. Bicycle, The.
Reder, C. Lesson, The: "Stand next to your
bike, like that."
Rexford. Joy: "It's joy to be up in the morning

when the dew's on the grass and clover."
Rhys, K. Interlude.
Rice, S. Bicycle, The.
Richardson, G. Song of the Wheel, The.
Ritsos. Myopic Child, A.
Rosselli. From relief to relief, the white lines,
the white paper.
Rubin, L. North of Amsterdam.
Rudman, M. There was only one problem—the
steepness of the hill.
Sangster, M. Queen of Girlhood, The.
Schein, Michael. Autumn: "On the first day of
Autumn."
Schultz, P. Eight-Mile Bike Ride, The.
Schulz, B. Constellation: Prose Poem.
Scollard. Ballads of the Wheel.
Scott, Mary. At the Crossroads.
Sears, P. Place for Four-Letter Words.
Sizer, P. Old Man on a Bike.
Smith, M. Sunday Morning Services.
Stafford, W. Maybe Alone on My Bike.
Stillborn, Myra. Trail, The.
Strange, E. Scorcher, The.
Tabb. Bicycles! Tricycles!
Taylor, Livingston. Bicycle.
Thomas, D. How stern you appear.
Tongue, R. Invention.
Townsend, A. Bicycle Racers, The.
Turner, B. Training on the Peninsula.
Tyler, N. P. My Magic Wheel.
Tzara. Chanson Dada.
Unknown. Bicycle and I, The.
Bicycler's Song, A.
Birth of the Bike, The.
Companion, The.
Cyclolotry.
Galileo and the Bicycle.
Gol-darned Wheel, The.
Maiden, The.
Morning Ride.
New View of Sunday Cycling, A.
Old Bike, The.
Old Maid's Reverie, An.
On Rainy Days.
Quiet Revery, A.
School lets out for the summer.
She Waits for Me.
Two Sonnets.
Whirling Wheel, The.
Untermeyer, L. Down-hill on a Bicycle.
Vale, Edmund. Bowl Over, Wheel.
Valek. Beating the Drum in Reverse.
Vere, Adriel. To My Cycle.
Voznesensky [or Voznesenskii]. Bicycles.
Waugh, Arthur. Ballade of the Devout Husband,
The.
Her Majesty.
Old Road Map, The.
Romaunt of Cecilia, The.
Town and Country.
Weigl. Him, on the Bicycle.
Wells, A. By Proxy.
Wessling, Suki. Angry.
Wheeler, Post. Rain Race, The.
Wilcox, E. Lying Tommy's Rise and Fall.
Wilkins, Machine. Mobile City.
Williams, C. K. World's Greatest Tricycle-
Rider, The.
Winslow, P. God on a Bike.
Yevtushenko [or Evtushenko]. On a Bicycle.
Young, G. After Cycling.
Zuiderent. Along the River.
Bill of Rights
Barnstone, A. First Amendment.
Billboards
Larkin, P. Sunny Prestatyn.
Nash, O. Song of the Open Road.
Ondaatje. 7 or 8 Things I Know About Her—A
Stolen Biography.
Billiards
Berry, Betsy. Afternoon in Austin.
Keller, B. Major, The.
O'Callaghan, C. Green Baize Couplets.
Willson, M. Ya Got Trouble.
Bin Laden, Osama
Kearney, L. Man with His Kids on a Table,

The.
Bingen, Germany
Norton, C. Bingen on the Rhine.
Biography
Bentley, E. George III.
Buchanan, G. Lyle Donaghy, Poet, 1902-1949.
Burkard. 2 Poems on the Same Theme.
Draycott. Night Tree, The.
Greacen. Captain Fox.
Malé. Poet's Biography.
McFadden, R. Contemplations of Mary.
Menicanti. Biographical News.
Shockley, E. Bio / *autography* (or, 18th-Century
Multiculturalism).
Sholl. Autobiography in Third Person.
Tate, J. Intimidations of an Autobiography.
Violi. Index.
Whitman, W. When I Read the Book.
Biology and Biologists
Bierds, L. Pasteur on the Rue Vauquelin.
Day, L. Cell, The.
Fox, Skip. Economics of Metonymy: sic transit.
Gregerson. Elegant.
Tufariello, C. In Glass.
Birch Trees
Aygi, G. Again: Air in the Tops—Of Birches.
Blasing, R. Refuge.
Coleridge, M. Lady of Trees, The.
Frost, R. Birches.
Young Birch, A.
Meinke. Robert Frost in Warsaw.
Sadoff. Birches, Revisited: October.
Twichell. Ghost Birches.
Velichansky, A. Trunks of birches, like scrolls.
Yevtushenko [or Evtushenko]. Dwarf Birches.
Bird Migration
Chine-Jo, Lady. Wild geese / Fellow travelers.
Glück, L. Parable of Flight.
Heyen. Blackbird Spring.
Hudgins. Chinaberry, The.
Hughes, T. Swifts.
Jarman, M. Chimney Swifts.
Johnson, D. Dust of Mexico, The.
Livingston, M. Birds Know.
Pastan. Birds, The.
Jones, R. Geese at Gregynog.
Rexroth, K. It is the time when.
Schelling. Haibun Flycatcher.
Warren, R. Heart of Autumn.
See also **Animal Migration**
Bird Songs
Andrade, E. Walt Whitman and the Birds.
Berry, W. Where the great trees were felled.
Boden, F. As I Came Home from Labour.
Budbill. What Issa Heard.
Collom. 3-4-00.
Eigner. Noise absorbed.
Eirian, S. Endsong.
Falk. Morning *Minyan*.
Ferguson, S. Lark in the Clear Air, The.
Gibson, W. Prelude: "As one, at midnight
wakened by the call."
Giorno. This is a field book.
Graham, J. In/Silence.
Haewŏn. On Hearing the Song of the Geese.
Hecht, A. Anthem.
Ivanova, S. Bird, start up your moan, your
whine.
Kaufman, S. Waiting: "After the fervor."
Kingston, M. Birds: "I'm living in one place so
long."
Kitahara Hakushū. Birds of spring.
Lauinger, A. Leir.
Levine, Jeffrey. Dawn, with Cardinals.
Longley, M. Echoes.
Morton, C. Twice now this morning I am
wakened by full-throated geese.
Neill. Lark.
Ni Dhomhnaill. Celebration.
Notari, L. Wee bird sang in the wasteland, A.
O'Reilly, C. Hide.
Pyungyang Ungee. On a Cuckoo's Song.
Sadi [or Saadi or Sa'di]. Prayers: "My shoes
are mulberry with dew."
Schelling. Haibun Flycatcher.

Schnackenberg. Heavenly Feast, The.
Shipley, V. Birdsong for September 11, 2001.
Thomas, E. She Dotes.
Unknown. Blackbird, The.
  Kill That Crowing Cock.
  Scribe, The.
Wang Wei. Birdsong Torrent.
Woljo Toan. Cuckoo.
Woods, V. Blue Cage, A.
Wright, S. And the Birds Sing of LIfe.
Yi Kyŏngnim. Chirping.

Birds
Abdul-Salaam, A. Bird Close to Old Houses, A.
Adamson. Southern skua, The.
  Stone Curlew, The.
Addonizio. Bird.
Agustini. In Fields of Sleepdreaming.
Ahmet Hasim. Moonstruck Storks.
Aitchison. Dipper Territory.
Albrecht, A. Below White Cliffs.
  Elkhorn Slough.
Alexander, P. Inventory. Journal.
  Reprise.
Alexander, W. I cannot say that I am
  phenomena by model.
Alterman, N. Householder Departs from the
  City, The.
Alvarez, J. Redwing Sonnets.
Ammons. City Limits, The.
Auden. Bird-Language.
  Epilogue: "'O where are you going?' said reader
    to rider".
  Their Lonely Betters.
Awoonor. Weaver Bird, The.
Axelrod, D. Guide to Urban Birds, A.
Baker, D. Envoi: Waking After Snow.
Bardoloi. Dawn.
Barker, G. Street Ballad.
Barnes, D. Portrait of a Lady Walking.
Basho. Bush warbler.
  Crane's legs, The.
  Crow, A.
  Dusk.
  Even in Kyoto.
  Exciting at first.
  Good house.
  Lightning.
  Midfield.
  Moonlight slanting.
  Moor / Point my horse.
  Not this human sadness.
  On the cow shed.
  Ploughing the land.
  Shrieking plovers / Calling darkness.
  Singing, flying, singing.
  Solitary, A.
  Spring going.
  Spring going.
  Squid seller's call, The.
  This autumn.
  What fish feel.
  Your song caresses.
Beaulieu, D. Summer Triangle.
Bécquer, G. Black Swallows Will Return, The.
Belieu. Radio Nebraska.
Bentley, J. First Bird.
Beranová, J. Mother's Mark.
Berger, B. Plagiarist, The.
  Silver-Paced.
  Transmigration.
Berkson, B. Booster.
  By Halves.
  Head at the Covers, A.
Bhattācārya, M. Screening its face amongst
  lotus stalks.
Bidgood. Safaddan.
Bishop, E. Five Flights Up.
  Rain Towards Morning.
  Some Dreams They Forgot.
Blake, W. How Sweet I Roamed [*or* Roam'd]
  from Field to Field.
Blight. Oyster-Eaters, The.
Blind. Entangled.
Bogan, L. Statue and Birds.
Borisov. What Freedom Said.
Boruch. Camouflage.

Bosley. Bird Sips Water.
Bottomley. Dawn.
Bowen, E. Winged in Gold.
Braxton, J. Conversion.
Bridgeman, P. Cockatoo.
Brodsky, J. September came on Tuesday.
Brontë, A. Captive Dove, The.
Browning, E. First Book: Young Aurora's
  Fostermother.
Bryant, T. Stranger.
Bryant, W. To a Waterfowl.
Budy. On High Street.
Burlingame. After Bird Watching near the
  Mexican Border.
Buson. Behavior of the pigeon, The.
  Dawn.
  Evening wind.
  Flying squirrel, A.
  Gust of wind, A.
  Iris, An.
  Listening to the plovers.
  Mountain cuckoo, The.
  Mountain cuckoo, The.
  Sparrow singing.
  Sudden shower.
  Winter warbler.
Campbell, D. Hear the Bird of Day.
Carbone, L. Flight from the Marriage Bed.
Carroll, L. Little Birds Are Playing.
Carruth, H. In filthy Puerto Rico lives a bird
  with no.
Castro, M. New York City.
Ceni, A. With What Courage.
Ceravolo. Sunset.
Chaucer. Catalogue of the Birds.
  Rondel: "And whan this werk al brought was to
    an ende."
Chiyojo. While I was musing on my theme.
Ch'ôn Yanghûi. At Moments Like This, I
  Always Blush.
  One Day.
  Thoughts on a Bird.
Christie. Hollywood Finch, The.
Clampitt. Syrinx.
  Whippoorwill in the Woods, A.
Clare, J. Birds' Nest.
  Little Trotty Wagtail.
  Nightingale's Nest, The.
  Wren, The.
  Wryneck's Nest, The.
Coatsworth. Swallows, The.
Cohen, M. Evensong.
Cokinos. Earth Movers, The.
Coleridge, S. Answer to a Child's Question.
  Song: "Sunny shaft did I behold, A."
Coles, G. Heron in the Alyn.
Collier, M. Brave Sparrow.
Collom. 3-4-00.
Conyus. Day in the Life of . . . , A.
Cook, E. On Seeing a Bird-Catcher.
  Song of the Imprisoned Bird.
Cording. Peregrine Falcon, New York City.
Corey, S. Complicated Shadows.
Costanzo. In the Aviary.
Cranch. Bird Language.
Crane, S. Little birds of the night.
  Once, I knew a fine song.
Cross, D. All the flutterlings gone.
Cummings, E. E. If everything happens that
  can't be done.
Curry, N. Mute Swans.
  Swallows and Tortoises.
Darío, R. Swan, The.
Davis, O. Panic of Birds, The.
De la Mare. Owl, The.
  Thomas Hardy.
Dean, D. K. Arrival.
DeFoe, M. Aviary.
Dèr Mouw. Audible Still.
Dickinson, E. Before you thought of Spring.
  Bird came down the Walk, A.
  Cat.
  Hope is the thing with feathers.
  Saddest noise, the sweetest noise, The.
Dimitrova. Who Cares for the Blind Stork.
Dissanayake. Freedom.

Doolittle, H. Birds in Snow.
  Where is the nightingale.
Doty, M. Coastal.
  Flit.
Dove, R. In the Old Neighborhood.
Dransfield. Strange Bird, A.
Dunbar, P. Sympathy: "I know what the caged
  bird feels, alas!"
Duo Duo. Wishful Thinking Is the Master of
  Reality.
Eichner, Maura. Eclogue and Elegy.
Eigner. Live /, Bird Which.
Eijkelboom. Town a Bird Sanctuary, The.
Elmslie, K. Feathered Dancers.
Erdrich. I Was Sleeping Where the Black Oaks
  Move.
Everson, W. Canticle to the Waterbirds, A.
Fagan. Weather They Were Written In, The.
Faigao, B. Kundiman.
Farid-uddin Attar. World's birds gathered for
  their conference, The.
Faust, H. After the Storm.
Ferguson, S. Lark in the Clear Air, The.
Field. Goad, The.
Finch, A. Native American Birds, The.
Finch, P. Scaring Hens.
Follain. Taxidermist, A.
Fox, Skip. In Referring to What Does Not
  Exist.
Francis, R. Waxwings.
Frost, R. Last Word of a Bluebird, The.
  Minor Bird, A.
  Never Again Would Birds' Song Be The Same.
  On a Bird Singing in its Sleep.
  Oven Bird, The.
Gallagher, T. Little Invitation in a Hushed
  Voice.
  Not a Sparrow.
  Unsteady Yellow.
Galvin, B. Running.
Gatina, D. I'm being stalked by a bird.
Gerhardt, I. G. M. Buried Birds, The.
  Expectation.
Gerov, Alexander. Birds: "They don't plow, nor
  do they sow."
Ghigna. Lesson of Night, A.
Ghiselin. Food of Birds, The.
Gibson, M. Summer Birds and Flowers (2).
Gilbert, C. African Sculpture.
Giorno. This is a field book.
Giussani, S. Vegetable Calendar.
Glazer, M. Purpose of Design Is to Make the
  Whole Greater Than the Sum of Its Parts, The.
Goldbarth. Seriema Song.
Goldberg, L. In the Jerusalem Hills.
Goyette, Susan. On Building a Nest: St. Peter's,
  Saskatchewan.
Graham, J. Thinking.
Graham, Taylor. Chances.
Greger. Penguin Jane Austen, The.
Grennan. Detail.
  On a 3 1/2 Oz. Lesser Yellowlegs, Departed
    Boston August 28, Shot Martinique
    September 3.
Groarke, V. Flight.
Grosholz. Last of the Courtyard, The.
Gu Cheng. There're Not Many Birds in the
  Village Now.
Guest, B. Geese Blood.
Guevara, M. Once When I Was in the Eighth
  Grade.
Guillén, J. Flight.
Guillén, N. Usurers, The.
Gundy, J. Inquiry into Gifts, or the Indigo
  Bunting.
Gunn, T. On the Move.
Habila, H. Birds in the Graveyard.
Hadfield, J. Staple Island Swing.
Hall, D. Short Circuit.
Hall, H. Listening Macaws, The.
Hamill, S. Seducing the Sparrow.
Hanzlicek, C. Feeding Frenzies.
Hardie, K. Signals.
Hardy, T. Weathers [*or* Weather].
Harris, Ken. Fire After Fire, The.
Harris, W. Practical Concerns.

Harrison, J. Birds That Woke Us: An Urban Pastoral, The.
Swifts at Evening.
Harryman. Allegory.
Hart-Smith. Boomerang.
Hartnett. I Have Exhausted the Delighted Range.
Haslam, M. 84 01.
Hauge. Midwinter. Snow.
Heath-Stubbs. Jays, The.
Hecht, A. Anthem.
Helwig. Sudden risk of birds, A.
Hemans. Written on the Sea-Shore.
Henry, P. Love Birds.
Herlin. Gull inch-perfect over water, The.
Hernandez, D. Pigeons.
Herzberg. Morning.
Heyen. Crane in Reeds.
Derailment.
Heywood, J. Egles byrde hath spred his wings, The.
Hierro, José. Boy with the Empty Cage, The.
Hirshfield, J. Story, A.
Hodgson, R. Birdcatcher, The.
Höllerer. Tarry Awhile, Restless Bird.
Hope, A. Death of the Bird, The.
Hopes. Birdbones.
October: "It's nuthatch on the box elder outside the window."
Hopkins, G. As Kingfishers Catch Fire.
Windhover, The.
Hove. Lost Bird.
Migratory Bird.
Howe, F. This angel clung to boats.
Hughes, F. Bird.
Birds.
Kookaburra.
Hughes, T. Crow and the Birds.
October Robin, An.
Out of the maternal watery blue lines.
Rooks love excitement.
Swifts.
Hugo, V. Be Like the Bird.
Huidobro. Sailor.
Hull, L. Ornithology.
Ibycus. On its highest leaves.
Inez. Monologue of the Falconer's Wife.
Ingoldsby, T. Jackdaw of Rheims, The.
Jackdaw of Rheims, The.
Issa. As the great old trees.
Children imitating cormorants.
Cuckoo singing.
Cuckoo sings, The.
Even on the smallest islands.
Hey, sparrow!
Mountain cuckoo, The.
No doubt about it.
Noon.
O owl!
Pheasant cries, The.
That wren.
Village named Little-Plum-Tree, A.
Woodpecker, The.
Jaccottet. Distances.
Letter of the 26th June.
Swifts.
Jarnot, L. Specific Incendiaries of Springtime, The.
Jarrell, R. Country Life, A.
Mockingbird, The.
Jastrun, T. Seed, The.
Jeffers, R. Birds.
Birds and Fishes.
Jenkins, M. Diver-Bird.
Martins.
Johnson, G. Heart of a Woman, The.
Jones, G. Esyllt.
Kaschock, Kirsten. As Birds in Rain.
Katrovas. Rehab.
Keats. 'How Many Bards Gild the Lapses of Time!'.
Kenyon, J. Insomnia at the Solstice.
Kerouac. Birds singing.
Ki no Tsurayuki. Out in the marsh reeds.
Kim Ku. Until the duck's short legs.
Kimbrell, J. Rooftop.

Kingsolver. Waiting for the Invasion.
Kinnell. Gray Heron, The.
Last Songs.
Kinsella, J. Sick Woman.
Kirchwey. He Considers the Birds of the Air.
Matthew 8:20; And Jesus said to him.
Kirkup. Scarecrows.
Kirsch, S. Mail.
Klyuyev [or Kliuev or Klyuev]. October, A Copper-Crawed Cock.
Krasicki, I. Caged Birds.
Kruit, J. Birds Leaving.
Kyger. Bird family.
Lake, P. Blue Jay.
Laughlin, J. Bird of Endless Time, The.
Lawrence, D. H. Blue Jay, The.
Lear, E. Limerick: "There was an Old Man of Whitehaven."
Lehmann, G. What's that bird, Mr Long?
Leiris, Michel. Miserly.
Lennon, J. Fat Budgie, The.
Lenski, H. Lightly a slight shadow floats on the March snows.
Levertov. Wren, A.
Levine, P. Red Dust.
Levitt, Peter. On my altar.
Lewis, G. Beginning to Forget.
Lewis, N. Footprint on the Air, A.
Li Po. Birds have Vanished, The.
Poem Composed at the Command of the Emperor.
Li Shang-yin. Hearing a Startled Bird During Stayover at Chin-Ch'ang Pavilion.
"Lin Ling.". Footpaths Cross in the Rice Field.
Linden, M. Bird Song, The.
Lindley, D. Nearness.
Liu, T. Highway 6.
Livingstone, D. Lake Morning in Autumn.
Lloyd, J. Thoughts of Boyhood.
Longenbach. What You Find in the Woods.
Lorde. Ballad from Childhood.
Lowenthal, J. Hovering.
Loynaz, D. M. Calm, The.
Ludvigson. Not Swans.
Lyly, J. Trico's Song.
MacBeth [or Macbeth]. Owl.
MacCaig. Blue Tit on a String of Peanuts.
Ringed Plover by a Water's Edge.
MacDiarmid, H. Caledonian Antisyzygy, The.
Ex Vermibus.
Perfect.
Whip-the-World.
Mackey, N. Winged Abyss.
Mahon. Bonn´n Buí, An.
Major, C. Apple Core.
On Trying to Imagine the Kiwi Pregnant.
Makuck. Prey.
Mandel, T. Of Birds.
Mares, E. Wild Birds.
Markham, M. After Aesop.
Obedience / Intention to Hunt.
Petition.
Marshall, J. Air Dagger.
Martinaitis, M. Kukutis in the Reich's Guard House.
Masahide. When bird passes on.
Masalha, Salman. Cage.
Masefield. Sea Change.
Mathias, R. Sanderlings.
Mattawa. Letter to Ibrahim.
Mayer, B. Turning Prose into Poetry.
Mayes, J. Descant.
McAuley, J. Nocturne.
McClure, M. For Marilyn and Stan Brakhage.
McKay, C. Birds of Prey.
Melville, H. Man-of-War Hawk, The.
Meng Hao Jan. Spring Dawn.
Meredith, W. Jain Bird Hospital in Delhi, The.
Meynell, A. Chimes.
October Redbreast, The.
Milán, E. No hay porqué, hay órdenes de canto.
There is no wherefore, there is a command of song.
Miller, J. Bird dressed as solitude and tears.
Moiro. Great Zeus was reared in Krete and no one.

Monro, H. Bird at Dawn, The.
Montale. Bird-Shooting.
Moore, M. Bird-witted.
Smooth Gnarled Crape Myrtle.
Moritz [or Morits]. Crow.
Morley, D. Politicisation of the North Wind, The.
Morshen. At the Lighthouse.
Morton, C. Twice now this morning I am wakened by full-throated geese.
Mother Goose. Who Killed Cock Robin.
Moxon. Loud midnight-soothing melancholy bird.
Murray, L. Equanimity.
Na Hûidôk. Sleeping on the Nail.
That Place Isn't Far.
Nash, O. Grackle, The.
Nemerov. More Joy in Heaven.
Nesbit, E. Vies Manquées.
No Hyegyông. Peace on Earth.
Norton, C. Sonnet 7: "Like an enfranchised bird, who wildly springs."
O'Hehir, D. Home Free.
O'Reilly, M. Small Girl Brings an Injured Bird into the Surgery, A.
Oles. Cedar Waxwing, The.
Oliver, M. Kingfisher, The.
Olson, C. Variations Done for Gerald Van De Wiele.
Oness, C. Climbing.
O'Reilly, C. Augury.
O'Sullivan, M. Giant Yellow.
Hill Figures.
Otomo no Sakanoé, L. Where the plovers cry.
Ou-yang Hsiu. East Wind.
Pack, R. Thrasher in the Willow by the Lake, The.
Padgett, R. Wonderful Things.
Paek Sôk. Sound of the Mountain Bird.
Page, P. Deaf-Mute in the Pear Tree.
Paterson, D. St Brides: Sea-Mail.
Peaux, A. Old Houses on the Quays.
Spring Landscape.
Pei Di. Magnolia Enclosure, The.
Pellicer, C. Flocks of Doves.
Perillo, L. Shrike Tree.
"Perse." Bird, The.
Pessoa. Rather the Bird Flying By and Leaving No Trace.
Petrarch. Ye vales and woods! fair scenes of happier hours.
Pfeiffer, E. Aspiration.
Phillips, C. Custom.
Phylip, S. Seagull, The.
Pinsky. First Early Mornings Together.
Plumly. Cardinals in a Shower at Union Square.
Plumpp. Survivors.
Po Chü-i. Red Cuckatoo, The.
Poe. Romance.
Pogson, P. Deep.
Press, K. Bird.
Prévert. Quartier Libre.
Probyn. Tête-à-Tête.
Pryde, A. I'll See You Down the Lane.
Queneau. Nourishment of Little Birds, The.
Radiguet. Poem: "Red eiderdown at the window, A."
Raine, K. Good Friday.
Rakosi. Good Morning.
Ramanujan. In the Zoo.
Rankin, J. Old Currawong.
Ransom, J. Lady Lost.
Ravikovitch, D. Sound of Birds at Noon, The.
Rexroth, K. It Is a German Honeymoon.
Uguisu sleeps in the bamboo grove, The.
Reznikoff. Dead gull in the road, A.
Riley, J. Few of the Bird-Family, A.
Ritsos. In the white egg.
Roberts, N. Gull's Flight, The.
Robeson, E. Counsel of Birds, The.
Roethke. Rose, The.
Rolle, S. Birds' Refuge, The.
Ronsard. Génèvres Hérissez, et Vous, Houx Espineux.
Rossetti, C. Birthday, A.
Fly Away, Fly Away.

Roux, S.   Aviary, The.
Różewicz.   Questions about Poetry since Auschwitz.
Russell, T.   To the Owl.
Ryan, K.   Paired Things.
St. John, P.   Reading a Story to My Child.
Sanger, Peter.   Kestrel.
Santos Chocano.   Dream of the Condor, The.
Savitz, M.   Bird, The.
  To the Horizon.
Schelling.   Haibun Flycatcher.
Scott, S.   Proud Maisie.
Seed.   During War, the Timeless Air.
Sen, R.   Black clouds have risen in my sky.
Shakespeare, W.   Amiens's Song.
  Phoenix and the Turtle, The.
Shapcott, T.   Shadow of War, 1941.
Shepherd, R.   Provisional.
Shinkichi Takahashi.   Clay Image.
Simic.   Fork.
Sorby.   Man without a Middle, The.
Spenser, E.   Sonnet 73: 'Being my self captived here'.
Sprackland, Jean.   Translating Birdsong.
Stafford, W.   Juncos.
Stanley, G.   Slow.
Stefanile.   Answering Robert Frost.
Stephens, J.   Rivals, The.
Stern, G.   Pile of Feathers.
  Red Bird.
Stevens, W.   Not Ideas about the Thing but the Thing Itself.
  Of Mere Being.
Storni.   Words to My Mother.
Sutter.   Peregrine.
Swenson, M.   Waterbird.
Sylvester, J.   Palms.
Synge.   In Glencullen.
Taggard.   Thirst.
Tarn.   Section: America (2): Seen as a Bird.
Tate, J.   Blue Booby, The.
Taylor, E.   Meditation 8 (First Series).
Teasdale.   Moods.
Thomas, D.   Over Sir John's Hill.
  Spire Cranes, The.
Thomas, E.   Snow.
Tobin, D.   Pigeons.
Torneol.   Lady's Farewell, The.
Torres, A.   Warmness.
Townsend, A.   Butane, Kerosene, Gasoline.
Tranströmer.   Morning Bird Songs.
Tretheway.   Resurrection at West Lake.
Trowbridge, W.   Bad Birds.
Truitt, S.   Kerf, The.
Tsaloumas.   Falcon Drinking.
Ts'ao Chih.   Ballad of the Orioles in the Fields.
Tu Fu [or Du Fu].   Another Spring ("White birds over the grey river.").
  Loneliness.
  Yellow Orioles.
Unknown.   After spring has come.
  Aura Lee.
  Bird and man.
  Bird Starver's Cry.
  Candy-throated Carib, The.
  Chickcharnies.
  Cold Fountain, Cold Fountain.
  Cutty Wren, The.
  Death and Burial of Cock Robbin, The.
  Death Song.
  Examination Question.
  Fowls in the Frith.
  Fowls [or Foweles or Fowles] in the Frith.
  Mango.
  North-East.
  O sea-gulls that are crying.
  On May-day, when the lark began to rise.
  Paddle-song.
  Riddle: "Cuckoo and the gowk, the."
  Song of Summer.
  Treeback.
  Two Seabirds.
Unknown, fr. Terezin Concentration Camp.
  Birdsong.
Van Duyn.   Letters from a Father.
  Mockingbird Month.

Van Vliet.   Courtyard, The.
Vaughan, H.   Bird, The.
Veinberg, J.   Owl's Landscape, An.
Very.   Birds of Passage, The.
Vicinelli.   I Met the Thieving Miss Magpie.
Vietnamese Oral Tradition.   Talking about Birds.
  Tiny Bird, A.
Volach, Y.   Bird.
Volkman.   Sonnet: "Now you nerve. Flurred, avid as the raw."
Wagoner, D.   Author of American Ornithology Sketches a Bird, Now Extinct, The.
  Loons Mating.
  Nuthatch.
Wakayama Bokusui.   White bird.
Walcott.   Season of Phantasmal Peace, The.
Wang Chien.   South, The.
Wang Wei.   Bird-Singing Stream.
  Birdsong Torrent.
  Magnolia Enclosure, The.
Warner, R.   Egyptian Kites.
Warren, R.   Death of Time.
  Heart of Autumn.
  Love and Knowledge.
Warsh.   Gout.
Warton, T.   Fashioned After the Manner of Master Geoffrey Chaucer in His Assembly of Fowls.
Watson, R.   Ballad of the Bird-Bride.
  Cage, The.
  Die Zauberflöte.
  White Bird, The.
Webster, A.   Since first my little one lay on my breast.
Weiss, G.   Lullaby of Birdland.
Whalen, P.   "Never Apologize; Never Explain".
  Pet Shop.
  Poem: "Like a bird."
White, E.   Listener's Guide to the Birds, A.
Whitman, W.   Out of the Cradle Endlessly Rocking.
  To the Man-of-War Bird.
Whitmore, S.   Bird, The.
Wilberforce, S.   Impromptu.
Wilbur, R.   Marché aux Oiseaux.
  Still, Citizen Sparrow.
Williams, C. K.   Shock.
  That the world / is going.
Williams, H.   To the Curlew.
  To the White Bird of the Tropic.
Williams, W.   Breakfast.
  To Waken an Old Lady.
Wingfield.   Bird, A.
Wise, S.   Closure Opening Its Trap.
Witt, S.   Waterfowl Descending.
Wordsworth, W.   Return.
Wright, D.   Juxtapositions.
  Those Walks We Took.
Wright, J.   Presentation of Two Birds to My Son, A.
Wright, J.   Invention of a Garden, The.
Wright, J.   Birds.
  Black Cockatoos.
Yenser, S.   Another Lo-Cal Elegy.
Yeryomin.   Drake pays court to the duck, The.
Yi Hyangji.   Leaf Struck by Bird Droppings.
Yi Illo.   Written on the Wall of Ch'ŏnsu Monastery.
Yi T'aek.   O roc, don't ridicule the small black birds.
Yi Yuksa.   Small Park, A.
Yosano Akiko.   Once, far over the breakers.
Young, A.   Stockdoves, The.
Young Bear.   Song Taught to Joseph, The.
Young, G.   Owl drifts slowly through the canyon where three flickers worry a pitted oak for grubs, An.
Zanzotto.   Subnarcosis.
See also Waterfowl

Birds' Nests
Averill.   Shoplifter Hands.
Blind.   On a Forsaken Lark's Nest.
Clare, J.   Green Woodpecker's Nest, The.
  Nightingale's Nest, The.
  Pewits Nest.
  Sky Lark, The.

Gallagher, T.   Choices.
Kuzma.   Poetry: "Old forms are like birdhouses that, The."
McCollough, Aaron.   Eros, Ethos, Economuos.
Na Hûidôk.   Sleeping on the Nail.
Thomas, E.   Birds' Nests.
Unknown.   Que-chao [Translations].
Williams, C. K.   That the world / is going.
Young, A.   Nest, The.

Birds of Paradise
Coleridge, M.   In London Town.

Bird-watching
Alexander, P.   Mt. Auburn Owl.
Barney, W.   Mr. Bloomer's Birds.
Endrezze.   Birdwatching at Fan Lake.
Fay, J.   Estuary.
Glazer, M.   2 Blinds & a Bittern.
Kinnell.   Gray Heron, The.
Snyder, G.   Really the Real.
Van Duyn.   Letters from a Father.

Birmingham, Alabama
Giscombe, C.   1962 At the Edge of Town.
  Recent Past, The.
Randall, D.   Ballad of Birmingham.

Birmingham, England
MacNeice.   Birmingham.
Seward.   Scene of superfluous grace, and wasted bloom.

Birth
Acholonu.   Nigeria in the Year 1999.
Adcock, F.   Video, The.
Ai.   Country Midwife, The: A Day.
Alexander, E.   Giving birth is like jazz, something from silence.
Andriescu, Radu.   Apple, The.
Aridjis.   To Emerge from a Woman Is to Become Separate.
Barber, D.   Small Hours.
Bartlett, E.   Birth.
Bartlett, M.   Burning of Margaret Moone, The.
Basho.   On Buddha's birthday.
Behlen, Charles.   Two Ice Storms.
Belli, G.   Birth.
Bellman.   Fredman's Epistle No. 23.
Berger, J.   Between Worlds.
Bernstein, C.   Dysraphism.
Berry, W.   Her First Calf.
Berryman.   So squeezed, wince you I scream? I love you & hate.
  Winters close, Springs open, no child stirs, The.
Bingen, Hildegard von.   Alleluia-verse for the Virgin.
Blake, W.   Infant Sorrow.
Blaser.   Ruler, The.
Blind.   Motherhood.
Bradstreet, A.   Before the Birth of One of Her Children.
Brecht, B.   Luke 2:8–20; And in that region there were shepherds.
  Mary.
Brinks, Dave.   Proscenium Moon.
Brooks, G.   Birth in a narrow room, The.
Broumas, O.   Pealing, The.
Bruce, D.   Sonnet 2: "Deep in her seventh month, my sister dozes."
Bryce, Colette.   Lines: "I have given birth to a see-through child."
Buckley, V.   Origins.
Charach, R.   Labour and Delivery.
Chesterton.   Donkey, The.
Ch'oe Sûngja.   About Women.
Clanchy, K.   Driving to the Hospital.
Clifton, L.   June 20.
Copus, J.   Sea-Polyp, The.
Couzyn.   Creation.
  Pain, The.
  Spell for Birth.
  Transformation.
Crawford, R.   Handshakes, The.
Creeley.   River wandering down.
De Kok.   Small passing.
De la Mare.   Birthnight: To F, The.
Deltoro, A.   Anestesia.
  Anesthesia.
Devi.   Birth, A.

Dhompa, T. Body as What Is Remembered.
Drummond de Andrade. Seven-Sided Poem.
Dugan, A. Let Heroes Account to Love.
Durcan. Birth of a Coachman.
Edmond, L. Tempo.
Emmott, K. Labour Pantoum.
Empress. Creation Is a Cycle.
Erdrich. Birth.
Esteves. Celebration of Home Birth: November 15th, 1981, A.
Ettinger, E. Believe Me.
Fanthorpe. Nativities.
Fenton, J. Born Too Soon.
Fisher, M. In Cool, Green Haunts.
Flint, R. 2-26-91.
Foppa. Woman.
Fuller, J. Born Too Soon.
Garrett, E. Airborne.
Gay, J. Birth of the Squire; an Eclogue, The.
Gilbert, C. Midwives, The.
Glück, L. Garden, The: "One sound. Then the hiss and whir."
Luke 2:1–7; In those days a decree went out from Caesar Augustus.
Goffette, Guy. Raising of Icarus, The: Envoi.
Goodison. Birth Stone.
Goodtimes. Learning to Smile.
Haavikko. Bastard Son is born with a tooth in his mouth and hair on his.
Woman raises her garment, rain, wind, darkness rise, The.
Hacker, M. Nearly a Valediction.
Hadewijch. Love's Maturity.
Harjo, J. For Alva Benson, and for Those Who Have Learned to Speak.
White Bear.
Harper, M. Deathwatch.
Love Medley: Patrice Cuchulain.
Hejduk. Sleep of Adam, The.
Herbert, W. Harvest in March, The.
Hernández, M. I Go on in the Dark, Lit from Within.
Heyen. Witness.
Hollis, M. And let us say.
Hope, A. Imperial Adam.
Hopwood, Mereid. Rebirth.
Hughes, T. Examination at the Womb-Door.
February 17th.
Yesterday He Was Nowhere to Be Found.
Issa. Autumn evening.
Bath when you're born.
Jones, B. Women at the Pit-head, The.
Jones, D. On Seeing a Dead Lamb.
Joyce, J. Ecce Puer.
Kamienska. Luke 1:26–38; In the sixth month the angel Gabriel.
Kay, J. What Jenny Knows.
Kazantzis. Midwife.
Kelleher, D. For C. K. at His Christening.
Kim Hyesun. Memories of the Day I Gave Birth to a Daughter.
Remembering the Day I Gave Birth to a Daughter.
Kim Sŭnghŭi. Love Song for the Belly Button 1.
Ko Un. Baby.
Koch, K. To the Roman Forum.
Kuzmin. At noon I must have been conceived.
Le Brun, Annie. Rituals.
Leigh, H. Natural Child, The.
Lleshanaku, L. Half Past Three.
Lorde. Now That I Am Forever with Child.
Luzi. Reflective life separates us from the sources of reflection.
Ly Ngoc Kieu. Birth, old age.
MacDiarmid, H. Lo! A Child Is Born.
Macgoye. August the First; Court Martial. The Mother Speaks.
MacLaine, Brent. 4. Birth Story.
Macphee, K. Night before the last day of January, The.
Madhubuti. Men and Birth: the Unexplainable.
Majorino. Kisses.
Mansour, J. Anti-mnemonic self-vaccination.
McCallum, S. Jamaica, October 18, 1972.
McMichael. Pretty Blue Apron.

Meynell, A. Maternity.
Miles, J. Conception: "Death did not come to my mother."
Miller, E. Jasmine.
Minhinnick. Catching My Breath.
Mistral, G. Like those jars that women put out to catch the dew of night.
Mitchell, S. Havana Birth.
Muldoon, P. Mules.
Murphy, M. Occasions.
Murphy, R. Beehive Cell.
Natural Son.
Navies, K. Birth.
Neruda. Births.
Nickerson. Seal's cry has lain against my leg, A.
No Hyegyông. Memory of Underdevelopment.
Nolens, L. Place and Date.
Nossis. O Artemis of Delos and lovely Ortygia.
Nurkse. Birth Room, The.
Odio, E. Creation.
O'Donoghue, B. Weakness, The.
Ogilvy. Newly Dead and Newly Born.
O'Hara, F. Female Torso.
Olds, S. First Birth.
Language of the Brag, The.
My First Weeks.
Pak Sôwôn. Lies: "Little bitch!"
Parker, D. Maid-Servant at the Inn, The.
Paschen. Birth Day.
Pavlova, V. Mother: "Funniest of all was birth."
Pearlman. Child of Wonder.
Pinchas-Cohen. Remembering Our Fathers.
Plath. Morning Song: "Love set you going like a fat gold watch."
Pleynet. In the Daylight.
Ponsot. Multipara: Gravida 5.
Porteous. Calf.
Pratt, M. Poem for My Sons.
Prunty. Winter's Tale, A.
Quarles. Born in Winter.
Quinn, J. They stand around. They reach into the offing.
Randell. Its this familiar black line from the tops.
Waiting.
Redel, V. Ninth Month.
Ridland. New Person, A.
Rilke. 1. The Birth of Mary.
Robertson, R. New Gravity.
Rogers, P. Elinor Frost's Marble-Topped Kneading Table.
Opus from Space.
Rojas. Chapter and Verse.
Roland Holst. I Who Was Born.
Rome, H. F.D.R. Jones.
Rungano. Labour.
Sachs, N. Someone.
Savageau. Henri Toussaints.
Scupham. First Things, Last Things.
Seminole Oral Tradition. Song for Bringing a Child into the World.
Sen, R. Brother / This world.
Shange. Oh, I'm 10 Months Pregnant.
Shapiro, K. Recognition of Eve, The.
Shinkichi Takahashi. Rocks.
Shell.
Simmons, J. Join Me in Celebrating.
Slessor. Sleep.
Souza. For Rita's Daughter, Just Born.
Spires. First Day, The.
Robed Heart, The.
Stallworthy, J. Almond Tree, The.
Stevenson, A. Victory, The.
Stewart, S. Apple.
Sykes, B. Cycle.
Szymborska, W. Born of Woman.
Tadic. Dogs Gambol.
Taylor, J. Epigram: "Fair Beatrice tucks her coat up somewhat high."
Tindal. Birth Wail, The.
Townsend, A. Eighteenth-Century Medical Illustration: The Infant in its Little Room.
Trakl. Birth: "These mountains: blackness, silence, and snow."
Tsanev, Stefan. When a Poet is Born.

Unknown. Midwife's Invocation, A.
One who first gave birth to our people, The.
Song of Blodeuwedd, The.
Your Thwarts in Pieces, Your Mooring Rope Cut.
Upton, L. Women's Labors.
Van Dyke, C. Birth, 1975.
Van Peenen, H. Will Campbell Displays His Craniotribe.
Vasalis. Idiot in the Bath, The.
Virgil [or Vergil]. Fourth Ecologue: Pollio, The.
Vivar. Delivery.
Waniek. Chosen.
Warren, R. Man, That Is Born of a Woman.
Wechsler, E. Child is Born, A.
White, Brenda Black. Tolly Masters.
Whitman, W. Has any one supposed it lucky to be born?
Out of the Cradle Endlessly Rocking.
Woman Waits for Me, A.
Wilde, O. Ave Maria Gratia Plena.
Williams, O. With Me.
Wohlfeld. That Which Is Fugitive, That Which Is Medicinally Sweet or Alterable to Gold, That Which Is Substantiated by Unscientific Means.
Wordsworth, W. Our birth is but a sleep and a forgetting.
Wright, C. Kings' Daughters, Home for Unwed Mothers, 1948.
Obedience of the Corpse.
Planks.
Yeats. Stick of Incense, A.
Young, D. For a Wife in Jizzen.
Young, P. Three Point Five Nine.
Zucker, R. Not Knowing Nijinsky or Diaghilev.

Birth Control
Jonson, B. To Fine Lady Would-Be.
Miller, E. She Is Flat on Her Back.
Vivar. Femmemasochism.
See also **Contraception**

Birth Defects
Belli, C. Unknown Voice, An.
Charach, R. Labour and Delivery.
Gorey. Limerick: "To his club-footed child said Lord Stipple."
Stallworthy, J. Almond Tree, The.
Van Peenen, H. Will Campbell Displays His Craniotribe.

Birthdays
Adamson. My Tenth Birthday.
Benevento, Joe. May 31, 1989.
Byron, G. On This Day I Complete My Thirty-sixth Year.
Carroll, J. Poem on My Son's Birthday.
Coleridge, H. First Birthday, The.
Edwards, D. Birthday: "I have fallen to the ground."
Geier. On Your Twenty-First Birthday.
Geiger. Soundtracks.
Goodman, P. Birthday Cake.
Grin, B. Morris Winchevsky.
Hadas, R. Twelfth Birthday.
Hahn, K. Hula Skirt, 1959, The.
Hall, D. My mother said, "Of course".
Heard, J. My Husband's Birthday.
Issa. From now on.
Jacobsen, J. Birthday Party, The.
Jewett, S. For a Birthday.
Johnson, S. Short Song of Congratulation, A [or To a Young Heir].
Jordan, J. If You Saw a Negro Lady.
Koch, K. Poem for My Twentieth Birthday.
Komunyakaa, Y. Gift Horse.
Kooser. Happy Birthday, A.
Kunitz, S. Passing Through.
Kusano Shimpei. Birthday Party.
Kuskin. Rose on My Cake, The.
Lancaster, John. Yellow Bike, The.
Lee, D. Jan's Birthday.
Lehman. June 11.
Levine, A. Four November 9ths.
Lorde. Ethiopia.
Madigan. Curtis Fuller.
Menashe. 49th Birthday Trip (What Are You On?).

Moorer. Birthday Wishes to a Husband.
  Birthday Wishes to a Minister of the Gospel.
  Birthday Wishes to a Physician.
Morgan, E. Birthday, The: "I'm driving tonight
  into November."
Mother Goose. Birthdays.
Murphey, John Collin. First Birthday After
  Death, The.
Myles, E. December 9th.
Ogilvy. Grannie's Birthday.
Paschen. Birth Day.
Phillips, Jayne Anne. Pretty.
Porter, P. On This Day I Complete My Fortieth
  Year.
Rago. Child's Birthday, A.
Robinson, M. Birth-Day, The.
Romero, N. New Suit, The.
Rosen, M. Eddie and the Birthday.
Rossetti, C. Birthday, A.
Rouse, A. Birthday, A.
Rukeyser, M. Rondel: "Now that I am fifty-
  six."
Sanfield. Birthday Poem.
Sarton, M. August Third.
Scupham. Birthday Triptych.
Sholl. Thinking of You, Hiroshima.
Simmons, J. Birthday Poem, A.
Steele, T. Epitaph: "Here lies Sir Tact, a
  diplomatic fellow."
Stern, G. Birthday.
Swift, J. Stella's Birthday, 1725.
  Stella's Birthday [1721].
  Stella's Birthday ([March 13,] 1727).
Synge. On a Birthday.
Tagore. Last Poems 10.
Thomas, D. Poem in October.
Tranter. Having Completed My Fortieth Year.
Tripp. On My Fortieth Birthday.
Waterman, A. Birth Day.
Wenderoth, J. Disfortune.
Williamson, G. On His Birthday.

Birthmarks
Kuzmin. Nine delightful birthmarks.

Birthplaces
Alvi, M. Presents from My Aunts in Pakistan.
Blicher, S. My birthplace is the brown heather-
  land.
Hardy, T. Domicilium.
Heaney, S. Birthplace, The.
Jonson, B. To Penshurst.
Kanchev, Nikolai. Birthplace.
Levine, P. I Was Born in Lucerne.
Macari, A. New York, 1927.
Milosz, C. In Szetejnie.
Otero, B. Far Away.
Jones, R. Yasnaya Polyana.
Taneda Santoka. Nothing left of the house.

Bishop, Elizabeth
Doty, M. Elizabeth Bishop, *Croton.*
McClatchy. Bishop Reading.
Valentine, J. Snow Landscape, in a Glass
  Globe.

Bison
Malroux. Every Breath.
See also **Buffaloes**

Bitterness
Amadiume. Bitter.
Amichai, Y. Quick And Bitter.
Anwar, C. Willingness.
Atwood. Beauharnois (3).
Aytoun [*or* Ayton], R. To His Forsaken
  Mistress.
Baudelaire. Autumn Song.
Baugh, E. Nigger Sweat.
Breytenbach. Black City, The.
Brown, S. Bitter Fruit of the Tree.
Browning, R. Dîs Aliter Visum; or, Le Byron
  de Nos Jours.
Carew, T. To Celia, upon Love's Ubiquity.
  To My Inconstant Mistress [*or* Mistris].
Cernuda. Nocturnal, you sword-fight.
Crane, S. In the desert.
Daniel, S. Love Is a Sickness.
Elagin. Amnesty.
Eliot, T. S. Lines for an Old Man.

Gorbanevskaya. It is time to think.
Graves, R. Laureate, The.
Guinness. Forlorn Queen, The.
Hartnett. Small Farm, A.
Hsin Ch'i-chi. Tune: "Moon of the Western
  River".
Hughes, T. Her Husband.
Jones, T. Cwmchwefri.
Jong, E. Colder.
Karim, F. Malice.
Kooser. Widow, A.
Landon. Castle of Chillon, The.
Lau, A. Bittermelon.
Major, C. Isolate.
Millay, E. Scrub.
Montague, J. Cage, The.
Moronelli da Fiorenza. Canzonetta: A Bitter
  Song to His Lady.
Mura. Blueness of the Day, The.
Nortje. All hungers pass away.
Pizarnik. Speaking Your Name.
Rowe, E. Reply to Mr.———, The.
Salaam, K. N.
Sappho. Kypris, / May she find you very bitter.
Seward. Farewell, false Friend!—our scenes of
  kindness close!
Smallpiece, A. M. Veil's removed, the gaudy,
  flimsy veil, The.
Smith, S. Lightly Bound.
Snodgrass. Diplomacy: The Father.
Sri Sri. Bitter Poem, A.
Stern, G. Bitter Thoughts.
Storni. World is Bitter, The.
Taylor, E. After Twenty Years.
Teasdale. After Love.
Teng Yu-pin. Taoist Song: "Empty bag of skin
  filling with desire."
Tennyson, A. O let the solid ground.
Thomas, R. S. Island, The.
Tighe. Poor, fond deluded heart! wilt thou
  again.
Tikhonov. Fire and Rope, Bullet and Axe.
Tzu Yeh. Bitter Harvest.
Unknown. I have lived anxious and hurt.
  Night so.
  Seafarer, The.
Villaurrutia. Nocturnal Sea.
Wen T'ing-yün. Temple of Su Wu, The.

Black (color)
Arrington, L. Untitled: "Tomorrow night."
Breytenbach. Threat of the Sick.
Chinnov. Black bird on a black and snowy
  branch, A.
Coleridge, S. Ne Plus Ultra.
Crosby, H. Photoheliograph (For Lady A.).
Dadié. I Give You Thanks My God.
Donne. Oh my black[e] soul[e]! now thou art
  summoned.
García Lorca. Song of the Rider.
Herbert, E. Another Sonnet to Black It Self [*or*
  Itself].
  Sonnet of Black Beauty.
Levertov. Wings, The.
McClure, M. For Zenshin Ryufu Philip Whalen.
Nichols, G. Black.
Salaam. Spiritual Geography.
Sanchez, S. Haiku: "Was it yesterday".
Sidney. Sonnet 7: "When Nature made her chief
  work, Stella's eyes."
Vertreace, M. Black Tulips.

Black Holes
No Hyangnim. Black Hole.
Riley, P. 119. 3.

Black Power
Baraka, I. Ka 'Ba.
  Last Word, The.
  New Reality Is Better Than a New Movie!, A.
  State/meant.
Clinton, M. I Wanna Be Black.
Edelman, M. I Care and I'm Willing to Serve.
Gilmore, B. Revolution.
Harper, M. High Modes: Vision as Ritual:
  Confirmation.
Hoagland, E. Anti-Semanticist, The.
Hughes, L. I, Too.
Jackson, R. Big Chill Variations.

Jerry. Mabrak.
Knight, E. Dark Prophecy: I Sing of Shine.
Reed, I. Badman of the Guest Professor.
Tolson, M. Dark Symphony.

Blackberries
Heaney, S. Blackberry-Picking.
Kinnell. Blackberry Eating.
Komunyakaa, Y. Blackberries.
Nicholson, N. Blackberry, The.
Oliver, M. August: "When the blackberries
  hang."
Plath. Blackberrying.
Ponge. Blackberries.
Sherman, M. Blackberries.
Turner, J. Plan, The.
Van den Bergh. Nocturn: "Moon rows burning,
  The."

Blackbirds
Baker, D. Works and Days.
Dings, Fred. Redwing Blackbirds.
Dixon, M. Bye Bye Blackbird.
Everson, W. Winter Ploughing.
Forbes, C. Killer Blues.
Forrester, S. Gray autumn sky.
Hardie, K. On Derry's Walls.
Heyen. Blackbird Spring.
Hill, J. That's Good, That's Enough.
Moss, T. Reconsideration of the Blackbird, A.
Mother Goose. Sing a song of sixpence.
Peaux, A. Spring Landscape.
Popa. Battle on the Blackbird's Field, The.
Satyamurti. Where Are You?
Shinkichi Takahashi. Snowy Sky.
Stevens, W. Thirteen Ways of Looking at a
  Blackbird.
Stevenson, A. In the Orchard.
Thomas, R. S. Blackbird Singing, A.
Unknown. Blackbird, The.
  Deserted Home, The.
  Silk-spread Blackbird.
Unknown, fr. Terezin Concentration Camp.
  Birdsong.
Wardle, S. Flight: "Mother blackbird I've been
  feeding, The."
Wolfe, H. Blackbird, The.

Blacks
Adisa. No, Women Don't Cry.
Ai. Riot Act, April 29, 1992.
Alexander, E. Venus Hottentot, The.
Allen, L. Rub a Dub Style inna Regent Park.
Baraka, I. Ka 'Ba.
Blake, W. Little Black Boy, The.
Bontemps. God Give to Men.
Booth, Kwan. Untitled One.
Brand, D. No Language Is Neutral.
Breytenbach. Black City, The.
Brooks, G. Kojo: I Am A Black.
  To Black Women.
  To the Diaspora.
Brown, Sterling A. Strong Men.
Brown, Stewart. Let Them Call It Jazz.
Carroll, K. Domino Theory (or Snoop Dogg
  rules the world), The.
  Something easy for Ultra Black nationalists.
  Upper Marlboro.
Césaire, A. Islands scars of the water.
Searle, C. Balthazar's Poem.
Clinton, M. History as Trash.
  Traditional Post-Modern Neo-HooDoo Afra-
  Centric Sister in a Purple Head Rag Mourning
  Death and Cooking.
Coleman, W. Where I Live.
Corpus. Blkfern-jungal.
Cullen, C. From the Dark Tower.
Dadié. I Give You Thanks My God.
D'Aguiar, F. Dreadtalk.
Damas. Hiccups.
  Just Like the Legend.
  S.O.S.
Davis, F. Christ is a Dixie Nigger.
Derksen, J. Interface.
Derricotte. Black Boys Play the Classics.
  Family Secrets.
  Passing.
Doyle, R. E. Ma Ramon.
DuBois, W. Song of the Smoke, The.

Eady. Running Man.
Ellis, T. T.A.P.O.A.F.O.M.
Evans, M. Black Queen Blues.
Speak the Truth to the People.
Farr, R. At general Electric, where they eat their/young.
Giovanni. Ego Tripping (There May Be a Reason Why).
Nikki-Rosa.
Hamer. Line Up.
Harper, M. Black Cryptogram.
Brother John.
Hayden, R. Beginnings.
Henderson-Holmes. "C" ing in Colors: Red.
Holman, M. Mr. Z.
Hopkins, L. Nat Love: Black Cowboy.
Hughes, L. Black Clown, The.
Cubes.
Dream Variation[s].
Good Morning.
Letter from Spain.
Negro.
Negro Speaks of Rivers, The.
Nightmare Boogie.
Visitors to the Black Belt.
When Sue Wears Red.
Irvine, W. To Be Young, Gifted, and Black.
Jeffers, L. My Blackness Is the Beauty of This Land.
Joans, T. Skip The Byuppie.
Johnson, L. Reggae Sounds.
Jordan, J. Something Like a Sonnet for Phillis Miracle Wheatley.
Joseph, A. On Being Told I Don't Speak Like a Black Person.
Traitor.
Kaufman, B. Sun is a Negro, The.
Keita, N. Black Tax.
King, J. Intercity Dub.
Komunyakaa, Y. Let's Say.
Loftin, E. Weeksville Women.
Lorde. Between Ourselves.
Harriet.
Naturally.
Lowell, R. For the Union Dead.
Madhubuti. B Network, The.
Magnificent Tomorrows.
Mandiela, A. Speshal Rikwes.
Mapun, D. O Myland Woman.
McKay, C. If We Must Die.
McManus, J. Commercials exaggerate.
Morris, T. Just Say No Blues.
Nichols, G. Beverley's Saga.
Okantah. Black Experience, The.
Pomeroy, R. Gay Love and the Movies.
Reynolds, S. F. Open Letter to All Black Poets, An.
Roberts, N. Nigger and Some Poofters, A.
Salaam. I Live in the Mouth of History.
Saloy, M. "N" Word, The.
Sanchez, S. This is Not a Small Voice.
Smith, P. What It's Like to Be a Black Girl (For Those of You Who Aren't).
Sundiata. Notes from the Defense of Colin Ferguson.
Sykes, B. One Day.
Tolson, M. Alpha.
Touré, A. Azuri.
Travis, N. Sunbathing.
Tynes, M. Womanskin.
Valerie, J. On Apologies.
Walker, A. Remember?
Weems, M. Funk.
Wheatley, P. On Being Brought from Africa to America.
See also **African Americans**
Blacksmiths
Anacreon. Again Love struck me like a smith with a giant.
Artmann. Blacksmith's Shop, The.
Dickinson, E. Dare you see a Soul *at the White Heat?*.
Hopkins, G. Felix Randal.
Illyés, G. Work.
Kurtz. Two Songs of a Blacksmith.
Livingstone, D. Mpondo's smithy, Transkei.

Longfellow, H. Village Blacksmith, The.
Martinson. Makers of Perpetuum Mobile, The.
McDonald, W. Heirlooms.
Swift, J. Prometheus: "As, when the squire and tinker, Wood."
Unknown. Blacksmiths, The.
Blake, William
Catling. Pittancer, The.
Kinzie. Engraving of Blake, An.
Nichol. Little song, A.
Oliver, M. Spring Azures.
Rawls, Alex. Marriage of Heaven and Hell by William Blake, The.
Rukeyser, M. Homage to Literature.
Schelling. Tyger Tyger.
Blasphemy
Bentley, E. After dinner Erasmus.
Brooke, R. Sonnet: In Time of Revolt.
Field. Trinity.
Goldsmith, K. One pair ridiculous gorilla slippers; 3 pairs of cheap shit sunglasses.
Blenheim, Battle of (1704)
Addison, J. Poem to His Grace the Duke of Marlborough, A.
Southey, R. Battle of Blenheim, The.
Blessings
Amichai, Y. Psalm: "Psalm on the day, A."
Ben Yitzhak. Blessed Are They That Sow.
Blessed Are They Who Sow and Do Not Reap.
Bible, *N.T.* And seeing the multitudes, he went up into the mountain: and when he was set, his disciples came unto him.
Borges. From an Apocryphal Gospel.
Clare, J. God Looks on Nature With a Glorious Eye.
Clark, T. Blessing on the house, A.
Clifton, L. Blessing the boats.
Craig, David. Brother we are like weeds growing.
Dawe, B. Beatitudes.
Dharker. Blessing.
Dickinson, E. One Blessing had I than the rest.
Dove, R. Testimonial.
Dunmore. Blessing, The.
Everson, W. High Embrace, The.
Frost, R. Answer, An.
George, S. What marvels smiles the morning-earth.
González, Rafael. Grace.
Gonzalez, Ray. For the Other World.
Goodison. Bam Chi Chi Lala.
Griffiths, A. His left hand, in heat of noonday.
Guidacci. Before Our Encounter.
Guri, H. Prayer: "Bestow a blessing on the young men, because the time has come."
Hadewijch. Madness of Love, The.
Herrick. Grace for a Child.
To Dianeme ("Show [*or* Shew] me thy feet; show [*or* shew] me thy legs, thy thighs.").
Wassaile, The.
Herzog, A. God Bless the Child.
Holiday. God Bless the Child.
Howell, C. Blessing's Precision.
Kamienska. Those Who Carry.
Kreitman, N. In Torrett, Minorca.
Landon. Bonds of Affection.
Luterman, A. Justice of the Peace, The.
Martinez, D. Blessing Poem.
Miller, H. Without God's Blessing.
"Rachel." [*or* "Rahel."]. Barn, The.
Reznikoff. Kaddish.
When my grandfather was about fifty, he fell sick.
Robinson, M. Sweet baby boy, accept a stranger's song.
Rossetti, C. O my heart's heart, and you who are to me.
Salzman, E. Spells.
Sappho. Happy bridegroom, the marriage that you prayed for.
Seltzer, D. Blessing Over Bread, A.
Smart, C. For I pray God to bless Polly in the the blessing of Naomi.
Tremblay, G. It Is Important.
Trenet, C. I Wish You Love (Que Reste-t-il de Nos Amours?).

Tsvetayeva [*or* Tsvetaeva]. I Bless the Daily Labor.
I bless the everyday labor.
Unknown. Gentlemen, for this day's work our chance has not been ill.
I See the Moon.
My Darlings' Shoes.
Weingarten Travel Blessing, The.
Whittier. Barefoot Boy, The.
Godspeed.
Wilkes, J. Pleased to the last, she likes the luscious food.
Willard, N. Little Blessing, A.
Wright, C. May God Go with You, Son.
Wright, C. Prayer: "Bless my life—its inks."
Zuni Oral Tradition. House Blessing.
Sayatasha's Night Chant.
Blindness
Baudelaire. Blind, The.
Butts, A. Nature of Braille, The.
Campbell, J. Blind Man at the Fair, The.
Chapman, L. Stevie Wonder.
Coleridge, M. Doubt.
Corbière. Blindman's Cries, The.
Crashaw. Samson to His Delilah.
De la Mare. All but Blind.
Dickinson, E. Before I got my eye put out.
Dimitrova. Who Cares for the Blind Stork.
Dubin, A. I Only Have Eyes for You.
Dunn, D. War Blinded.
Gibson, W. Sight.
Guthrie, W. Blinding of Isaac Woodard, The.
Haley, V. Gangrene.
Hay, G. Homer.
Heym. Why Do You Come, White Moths.
Holmes, O. Prelude to a Volume Printed in Raised Letters for the Blind.
Hŭimyŏng. Hymn to the Thousand-Eyed Sound Observer.
Iskander. Blind Man, The.
Jungkwan Ilson. To an Old, Deaf, and Blind Monk.
Keller, H. In the Garden of the Lord.
Kitahara Hakushū. Completely blind.
Kuusisto, Stephen. Night Seasons.
LaBarre, M. For Gloucester on Being Newly Blind.
Levertov. Uncertain Oneiromancy.
Lover. Whistlin' Thief, The.
Loy. Der Blinde Junge.
Mandelstam [*or* Mandelshtam]. I Am Deaf.
Mapanje. On His Royal Blindness Paramount Chief Kwangala.
Meynell, A. Wind Is Blind, The.
Milton. Hail, Holy Light[!].
On His Blindness.
On His Deceased Wife.
To Mr. Cyriack Skinner upon His Blindness.
Molina, P. Things of the Blind.
Norris, L. Ballad of Billy Rose, The.
Pastan. Apple Shrine, The.
Piper, E. Indian Counsel.
Pratt, S. Blind Man's Dog, The.
Ridler. Corneal Graft.
Rilke. Woman Going Blind.
Ritsos. Unanswered.
Rossetti, C. Sketch, A.
Ruddock, G. To a Blind Mother.
Sassoon, S. Does It Matter?
Saxe, J. Blind Men and the Elephant, The.
Sorescu, M. With a Green Scarf.
Stoddart, G. Blindfold, The.
Tabb. Milton.
Unknown. Blind man carried, A.
God, you may render me blind from here on in.
God, you may render me blind today!
Velichansky, A. Policeman does not blow his whistle, The.
Wakayama Bokusui. They say there lives.
Watson, E. First Sight: "Blind woman—who by some miracle can, A."
Williams, M. Some Lines Finished Just Before Dawn at the Bedside of a Dying Student It Has Snowed All Night.
Williams, W. Luke 6:39.
Parable of the Blind, The.

Parable of the Blind, The.
Yi Kyubo. Thoughts on Eyes Growing Dim: Presented to Chŏn Iji.
Yi Yŏnju. Open-Eyed Blind Man, An.
Young, G. Miracle, The.

Blizzards
"Antler.". Thoughts Breathing in a Blizzard.
Dougherty. Cocoons.
Kumin, M. Notes on a Blizzard.
Levin, P. Blizzard, The: "Now that the worst is over, they predict."
Pasternak, B. Winter Night.
Wells, Z. Fool's Errand.
Yesenin [or Essenin]. Winds, Winds, Winds.
See also **Storms**

Blocks (toys)
Stevenson, R. Block City.

Blood
Acorn. I've Tasted My Blood.
Alberti. Punishments.
Amadiume. Bloody Masculinity.
Amor, P. CXXXIX.
Armstrong, J. Blood.
Baron, S. They Say.
Belli, G. Blood of Others, The.
Benn. Bunch of Drifter Sons Hollered, A.
Berberova. To Shakespeare.
Blunden. Midnight Skaters, The.
1916 Seen from 1921.
Breytenbach. Dreams Are Also Wounds.
Brontë, C. Lonely Lady, The.
Campbell, T. Hohenlinden.
Caraion. Tomorrow the Past Comes.
Castera, G. Blood.
Cavafy. Bandaged Shoulder, The.
Celan. All those sleep shapes.
Tenebrae.
Chin, D. Sterling Williams' Nosebleed.
Chŏng Hyŏnjong. Blood of Daybreak, The.
Clanchy, K. I had my eyes shut the whole time.
Clifton, L. Mississippi river empties into the gulf.
Cowley, A. Yoicks! Gone Away!
Cowper, W. There is a fountain filled with blood.
Crashaw. Love, thou art absolute sole lord.
de Fréine, C. Pints.
Testing, testing.
Dickey, J. Poisoned Man, The.
Dickinson, E. Name—of it—is "Autumn," The.
Donne. Flea, The.
Donovan, K. Underneath Our Skirts.
Doty, M. Fog.
Duncan, R. My Mother Would Be a Falconress.
Dybek. Gradually.
Stain.
Everson, W. Passion Week.
Faiz. No Sign of Blood.
Field. Flaw, A.
Fortini. Perhaps the Time of Blood.
Fries, K. I bed next to you, I feel your heartbeat.
García Lorca. New York.
Gorbanevskaya. Drought, malevolent stepmother.
Gunn, T. Cannibal.
Hachenburg, H. Terezin.
Harper, M. Breaded Meat, Breaded Hands.
Haslam, M. 30 55.
Herbert, Z. Hakeldama.
Speculations on the Subject of Barabbas.
Hernández, M. July 18, 1936–July 18, 1938.
Wounded Man, The.
Herrick. Upon a Child That Died [or Dyed].
Hill, G. On the sixth day, as I rode.
Hô Sugyông. Poem: "Slash my back with a sickle."
Iverem, E. Keeper.
Jackson, R. For Thurman Thomas.
Jarrell, R. Islands, The.
Johnson, L. Red Wind, The.
Khoury, N. People of Olives.
Kim Sŭnghŭi. Growing Pearl 1.
Larsen, L. Red.
Lawrence, D. H. Mosquito Knows, The.
Levin, D. Red Water.

Lope de Vega. Judith.
Macari, A. Counting the Years.
Masaoka Shiki. Swatting mosquitoes.
Mashinskaya, I. So I stood by and watched.
Moore, M. Odor of a Metal Is Not Strong, The.
Naden. Poet and Botanist.
Nepote, M. A esta mujer la sangre se le fuga.
Blood leaks from this woman, The.
Neruda. Almería.
O'Hara, F. Poem: "Eager note on my door said 'Call me'", The."
Okamoto. Tanka: "Having let flow."
Olsen, W. Blood.
Orten. Whispered.
Owen, S. Written in Blood.
Polak, J. Storm, The.
Prévert. Song in the Blood.
Rodriguez, L. Heavy Blue Veins.
Rosselli. Negro blood flowing on his brown.
Rouse, A. Sunday Morning.
Saroyan. Blod.
Satyanarayana, V. Your Chariot.
Scarbrough, G. Cutting Sod-Land.
Serge. Hands.
Serrano, P. Beacon.
Hacho.
Shaw, R. To His Pulse.
Sherry, J. Lepidoptery.
Simic. Butcher Shop.
Sorescu, M. Start.
Stafford, W. Ceremony.
Sternlieb. Right of Way.
Strange. Transits.
Swenson, M. Bleeding.
Takamura Kotaro. Steak Platter, A.
Thomas, L. Subway Witnesses, The.
Thomas, R. S. Welsh Landscape.
Ungaretti. Babel.
Unknown. On our native soil, the martyr's drops of blood.
Unknown, fr. Terezin Concentration Camp. Pain Strikes Sparks on Me, the Pain of Terezin.
Vallejo. Our Daily Bread.
Vaughan, H. Abel's Blood.
Wheelwright. Esprit d'Escalier.
Whitman, W. Trickle Drops.
Wright, F. Blood.
Knife.
Yamaguchi Seishi. Cleaning yellowtail.
Zimmerman, Rosamond. Anemia.

Bloodhounds
Barbour, J. Bruce and the Bloodhound.
Scott, S. Branksome's Heir and the Hound.

Blue (color)
Alberti. Blue.
Ap Hywel, Elin. Blue.
Blue.
Barba-Jacob. Song of the Fleeting Day.
Berlin. Blue Skies.
Carranza, E. Azure Because of You.
Cherry, K. Reading, Dreaming, Hiding.
Davies, B. Blue.
DeCarteret, M. Coloring.
Divakaruni. Indigo.
Edwards [or Edwardes], R. Blue Room, The.
Evans, A. Fringed Gentians.
Forrest, G. It's a Blue World.
Gahagan. Colour of the Old Man's Eyes, The.
Harrison, D. Formula for Blue Blues Babies.
Hart, L. Blue Room, The.
Jacobs, H. Goree.
Keats. Blue! 'Tis the Life of Heaven, the Domain.
Kelly, R. Coming.
Larsen, W. Bluebird in Cutleaf Beech.
Lowry, M. About Ice.
McCarthy, J. Alice Blue Gown.
Morgenstern, Felicia L. Hues of Electric Blue.
Muhammad ibn Ghalib al-Rusafi. Blue River.
Ormond. Certain Questions for Monsieur Renoir.
Phillips, C. Blue: "As through marble or the lining of."
Shapcott, T. Blue Paisley Shirt, The.
Silano, M. Such a Way to Go.
Sŏ Chŏngju. Blue Days.

Stanard, C. Wrong Color.
Stein, K. Past Midnight, My Daughter Awakened by Miles Davis' *Kind of Blue*.
Tate, J. Blue Booby, The.
Touré, A. Azuri.
Volkman. I was watching for it, everytime watching, for the neck that was.
Sonnet: "Nothing was ever what it claimed to be."
Wakoski. Blue Monday.
Warner, S. To no believable blue I turn my eyes.
Wright, C. Cicada Blue.
Wright, R. It's a Blue World.
Yeryomin. Seamstress stitches on a sewing machine, The.

Blue Jays
Blackwell, Holley. New Poem.
Carryl, G. Patrician Peacocks and the Overweening Jay, The.
Clark, T. Elegy: "It's a pity we have to suffer."
Inada. In So Doing.
Wright, J. I Try to Waken and Greet the World Once Again.

Bluebells
Kavanagh, P. Bluebells for Love.

Blueberries
Adair, V. H. Blueberry City.
Layton. Berry Picking.
Moore, L. Indian Girl.

Bluebirds
Blackwell, Holley. New Poem.
Frost, R. Last Word of a Bluebird, The.
Knox, J. God Gave Safe Passage to the Animals through His Forest of Bright Spectrums.
Padgett, R. Big Bluejay Composition.

Bluefish
Wilbur, R. Trolling for Blues.

Blues (mood)
Baraka, I. Funk Lore.
Berlin. Blue Skies.
Brown, L. Sunny Side Up.
Caldwell, A. Left All Alone Again Blues.
Clarke, G. Am I Blue?
Cortez, J. Drying Spit Blues.
Cox, J. Nobody Knows You When You're Down and Out.
Davis, T. Rogue and Jar: 4/27/77.
Derricotte. Blackbottom.
DeSylva, B. G. Sunny Side Up.
DJ Renegade. Subterranean Night-Colored Magus.
Encarnacion. Bulosan Listens to a Recording of Robert Johnson.
Fields, D. Blue Again.
Forrest, G. It's a Blue World.
Gardinier. Blues.
George, D. I Ain't Got Nothin' But the Blues.
Hart, L. Blue Moon.
Henderson, R. Sunny Side Up.
Hernton, C. Long Blues, The.
Hughes, L. Blue Monday.
Blues at Dawn.
Blues, The.
Bound No'th Blues.
Hard Daddy.
Homesick Blues.
Miss Blues'es Child.
Po' Boy Blues.
Weary Blues, The.
Jefferson, B. Easy Rider Blues.
Jones, P. Song: "I have so little sorrow."
Jordan, N. When A Woman Gets Blue.
Kaufman, B. I Have Folded My Sorrows.
Knight, E. Poem for Myself (Or Blues for a Mississippi Black Boy), A.
Koehler, T. I Gotta Right to Sing the Blues.
Komunyakaa, Y. No-Good Blues.
Llwyd, Iwan. Dust Truck Blues.
Medina, T. Rhudine Rhudine.
Morgan, R. Add-Water Instant Blues.
Morton, "Jelly Roll.". Mamie's Blues.
Nichol. Blues.
Perdomo, W. Nigger-Reecan Blues.

Porter, C.   I Concentrate on You.
Pritchard, N.   From Where the Blues?
Randall, D.   Langston Blues.
Robin, L.   In Love In Vain.
St. John, D.   Homage to Robert Johnson.
Segal, J.   When Sunny Gets Blue.
Smith, B.   Empty Bed Blues.
Spellman, A.   Blues: My Baby's Gone.
Unknown.   Railroad Blues, The.
   Southern Blues.
Wright, R.   It's a Blue World.
Young, A.   Blue Monday.
   Blues Don't Change, The.
See also **Melancholy**
Blues (music)
Aubert, A.   Bessie Smith's Funeral.
Baker, H.   Tobacco Warehouse Blues.
Ball, A.   Jazz.
Baraka, A.   To Aretha Franklin from Sparkle.
Baraka, I.   Legacy.
Bauer, G.   So You Want to Hear the Blues.
Blanchard, Mary Loving.   East Texas Blues.
Bottoms.   Homage to Lester Flatt.
Brathwaite, E.   Blues.
Braxton, C.   Bluesman.
Brooks, G.   Queen of the Blues.
Brown, L.   Birth of the Blues, The.
Bukowski.   Last Song, The.
Caldwell, A.   Left All Alone Again Blues.
Carruth, H.   Called him "Big Joe" yes and Joe
   Turner it was his name.
   High above themselves. Above everything, flux,
   ooze.
Cortez, J.   How Long Has Trane Been Gone.
Cox, J.   Nobody Knows You When You're
   Down and Out.
Crockett-Smith, D.   Hell Hound Blues.
Cullen, C.   Colored Blues Singer.
Dameron, Chip.   South Texas Boxcar Blues.
DeSylva, B. G.   Birth of the Blues, The.
Dittberner-Jax.   Blues for Aunt Ruth.
Dumas, H.   Concentration Camp Blues.
Eady.   Muddy Waters and the Chicago Blues.
Encarnacion.   Bulosan Listens to a Recording of
   Robert Johnson.
France, L.   Blues for Bird.
Fulson, Lowell.   Check Yourself.
Gibb.   Paul Butterfield, Dead at 44.
Gilbert, C.   Enclosure.
Hamod, S.   Joe Williams at the Blue Note/
   Chicago, 1955; March 30 1999.
Harper, M.   For Bud.
   Narrative of the Life and Times of John
   Coltrane: Played by Himself, A.
Harris, T.   For Lady and Prez.
Harrison, D.   Formula for Blue Blues Babies.
Hayden, R.   Homage to the Empress of the
   Blues.
Henderson, R.   Birth of the Blues, The.
Hopkins, L.   Death Bells.
Hughes, L.   Weary Blues, The.
Hunter, A. *et al.*   Down-Hearted Blues.
Jackson, A.   Choosing the Blues.
Johnson, R.   Hellhound on My Trail.
   Me and the Devil Blues.
Jordan, J.   Reception, The.
Koehler, T.   I Gotta Right to Sing the Blues.
Komunyakaa, Y.   Villon/Leadbelly.
Lea, S.   One White Face in the Place, The.
Lowe, J.   With Thanks to Eddie Shaw.
McDonald, W.   Honky-Tonk Blues.
McKay, D.   Kinds of Blue #41 Far Hills.
McLaughlin-Carruth, J.   Black Irish Blues.
Moore, L.   Bluesman's Blues, A.
   Haiku.
Morton, "Jelly Roll.".   Mamie's Blues.
Nordhaus.   Bluegrass.
Overton, R.   Blues in "C".
Patterson, R.   Hopping Toad Blues.
   Sundown Blues.
Plumpp.   Remembered.
Powell, J.   It Was Fever That Made the World.
Robson, J.   Blues for the Lonely.
Salaam.   Spiritual Geography.
Smith, B.   Backwater Blues.
   Black Mountain Blues.

Young Woman's Blues.
Smith, P.   So Motown taught me all about men.
   Men worshipped.
Someck, R.   Blues for Elliot Sharp.
Tafolla.   Mi Tía Sofía.
Thomas, L.   Blues Variations.
Unknown.   Railroad Blues, The.
Vinz.   Blues, The.
Walcott.   Blues: "Those five or six young guys."
Wallenstein.   Blues 1.
   Blues 2.
Walton, A.   Encyclopedia of Rhythm and Blues,
   The.
Weinstein, N.   Drummond's Lover Sings the
   Blues.
Wojahn.   John Berryman Listening to Robert
   Johnson's "King of the Delta Blues," January
   1972.
Young, A.   Blues Don't Change, The.
   Who Am I in Twilight.
Zu-Bolton.   Struggle-Road Dance.
Boarding Houses
Dacey, P.   Rules, The.
Larkin, P.   Mr Bleaney.
Van Duyn.   Condemned Site.
Boars
Lee, D.   Loading a Boar.
Yamaguchi Seishi.   On a hook he hangs.
Boasting
Forman, R.   This Poem.
Griffiths, S.   Just a Product of a Certain
   Situation.
McDaniel, J.   Logic in the House of Sawed-Off
   Telescopes.
Sandburg, C.   Primer Lesson.
Unknown.   Tune: "Wu Yeh-erh" Twitting the
   Teller of Tall Tales.
Boats and Boating
Ahern, T.   Unbruised.
Alexander, P.   1. Ipswich.
Armstrong, Tammy.   Boat Builder.
Asekoff, L.   North Star.
Ashbery, J.   Archipelago, The.
Beachy-Quick, Dan.   Prologue: "Editor, / Here
   are the lines my mind fathomed."
Beddoes.   Song on the Water.
Bingxin.   Paper Boat—Sent to Mother.
Bishop, E.   Fish, The.
Blind.   Russian Student's Tale, The.
Bobrowski.   In the Torrent.
Brunk, J.   Letter to Myself as a Child.
Buson.   Mad girl, The.
   Moored boat, A.
Carver, R.   Quiet Nights.
Chang Chi.   Maple Bridge Night Mooring.
   Night-Mooring at Maple Bridge.
   Night-Mooring near Maple Bridge, A.
Ch'in Kuan.   Tune: "Rouged Lips".
Ching An.   Moored at Maple Bridge.
Chute, M.   My Plan.
Clark, T.   Time.
Clifton, L.   Blessing the boats.
Davis, J.   Boat, A.
Davison, P.   Equinox 1980.
Denham, Joe.   Morning Set.
Dickey, J.   Lifeguard, The.
Eberhart, R.   Chart Indent.
   Immortal Picture, The.
Emmett.   Boatman's Dance.
Field.   As two fair vessels side by side.
Finlay, I.   Boat's Blueprint, The.
Frost, R.   Flower-Boat, The.
Garrigue.   Song in Sligo.
Guiney.   Down Stream.
Harryman.   Rowboat was caught in the mudflats,
   The. A few gulls padded around it.
Heyen.   Return, The.
Hirsch, E.   Tristan Tzara.
Hoggard, James.   Anniversary Trip.
Hokushi.   Sailboats in line.
Holmes, O.   Old Ironsides.
Hsieh Ling-yün.   Night: Setting out from Shih-
   Kuan Pavilion.
Hsüeh T'ao [*or* Xue Tao].   Lotus-Gathering
   Boat.
ibn Hariq, A.   Galley Oars.

Ingoldsby, T.   Lines Left at Mr Theodore Hook's
   House in June, 1834.
Issa.   Autumn moon.
Jackson, H.   My Lighthouses.
Jeffers, R.   Boats in a Fog.
Jiménez, J.   Oceans.
Kakinomoto no Hitomaro.   My thoughts are
   with a boat.
Kikaku.   Above the boat.
Komunyakaa, Y.   Boat People.
   Reed Boat, A.
Kunitz, S.   Long Boat, The.
Lady Ise.   If it is you, there / in the light boat on
   the pond.
Lake, P.   In Rough Weather.
Lepson, Ruth.   They Were Gliding.
Levertov.   To Rilke.
Li Po.   Snapshot, A.
Lim-Wilson.   Raising the Dead.
Loesser.   Sit Down, You're Rockin' the Boat.
Lu Yu.   Blue Rapids.
Ma Chih-yüan.   Tune: "Winds of Falling
   Plums".
MacCaig.   So Many Summers.
Marvell.   Bermudas.
Mayer, B.   Boats.
Mei Yao Ch'en.   Dappled Horse, The.
Meng Hao Jan.   Night Mooring on the Jiande
   River, A.
   Stayover at Chien-Teh River.
Milosz, C.   Luke 5:1–11; While the people
   pressed upon him.
Mitchell, S.   Matthew 13:1–9; That same day
   Jesus.
Montale.   Haul Your Paper Boats.
Morgan, E.   At Eighty.
Morley, D.   Enniskillen.
Morrissey, S.   On Waitakere Dam.
Murphy, R.   Last Galway Hooker, The.
Murray, C.   Charon's Song.
Nicholson, N.   From a Boat at Coniston.
Oppen.   Mast / Inaudibly soars; bole-like,
   tapering, The.
   Product.
Ou-yang Hsiu.   Old Fisherman.
   Tune: "Gathering Mulberry Leaves".
Pak Sŏwŏn.   Small Wooden Vessel, A.
Pao Chao.   Ballad: The Boatman's Song.
Pape.   Dinner on the Miami River.
Pilling.   You and You, In the Pink.
Plath.   Crossing the Water.
Ponge.   Boat, The.
Porteous.   Decommissioning.
Prasad, V.   Hades.
Rafferty, P.   Passage.
Rimbaud, A.   Drunken Boat.
   Drunken Boat, The.
   Drunken Boat, The.
   Hearing the thunder of the intransitive weirs.
Ríos, A.   Domingo Limón.
Robinson, M.   Describes her Bark.
Rollings.   For Dear Life.
Saigyō.   Out in the high waves.
Samaras, N.   Crossing the Strait.
Sen, R.   My Mind, my helmsman.
Sexton.   Boat, The.
Shakespeare, W.   Sonnet 80: "O, how I faint
   when I of you do write."
Shaku, S.   En Route to America.
Share, D.   Divorced.
Shokushi.   Guide me on my way.
Shunzei.   Cormorant-boat, The.
Sidney.   Sonnet 103: "O happy Thames, that
   didst my Stella bear."
Song Ikp'il.   Boating at Dusk.
Souster.   Lagoons, Hanlan's Point.
Spencer, B.   Boat Poem.
Spires.   Glass-Bottom Boat.
Stevenson, R.   Where Go the Boats?
Synková, A.   To Olga.
Tennyson, A.   Fair ship, that from the Italian
   shore.
Toledo, N.   Na Hermila Limón.
   Na hermila limón.
Tranströmer.   Humming in the mist.
   Start of a Late Autumn Novel.

Tu Fu [or Du Fu]. Broken Boat, A.
Déjeuner sur l'herbe.
Tu Mu. Mooring at River Ch'in-Huai.
Unknown. Boat floats over shadow, two boys were aboard, A.
Cypress Boat.
Girl and Her Companion, The.
Song of the Viet Boatman.
Vietnamese Oral Tradition. Ship of Redemption.
Voznesensky [or Voznesenskii]. Boat on the Shore.
Wang Ch'ang-ling. Autumn Evening on the Great Lake.
Watts, Enos D. Longliner at Sunset.
Wei Chuang. Green Pond, A.
Wordsworth, W. Hymn for the Boatmen, as They Approach the Rapids under the Castle of Heidelberg.
Yang Wan-li. Moored for the Night at the Lan-chi Riverside Courier Station.
Yasui. Man pulling the boat, A.
Yu Hsin. Harmonizing with the Monk Heling's Poem "An Outing to the Kunming Pool".
See also **Ferry Boats; Freighters; Ships and Shipbuilding; Tugboats; Yachts**

Bobolinks
Dickinson, E. No Bobolink—reverse His Singing.

Bodhidharma
Anderson, Tenshin Reb. To Bodhidharma.
Dogen. Western Patriarch's doctrine is transplanted!, The.
Hirshfield, J. Why Bodhidharma Went to Howard Johnson's.
Muso Soseki. Cloud Mountain.
Reply to Reizan Osho.
Reply to Suzan Osho's Snow Poem.
Reito. Ox bridle tossed, vows taken.
Soen. On Visiting Shorin Temple, Where Bodhidharma Once Lived.

Bodies
Abdullah, F. Small Bodies That Cannot Be Healed.
Abrahams, L. Flesh.
Abse. Lunch and Afterwards.
Pathology of Colours.
Aldana. Sonnet 12: "Which is the reason my Damon that although."
Aleixandre. Body and the Soul, The.
Alvi, M. Sari, The.
Amichai, Y. Two Songs of Peace.
Two Songs of Peace.
Amorosi. Good Teacher, The.
Aridjis. Decomposition with Laughter.
To Emerge from a Woman Is to Become Separate.
Armand. Poem with Skin.
Armantrout. Plan, The.
Winter.
Armstrong, J. Gastric Muse, The.
Auden. Prime.
Ayres, R. Corporeal.
Azuah, U. Forbidden.
Babu, S. Sound of Silence, The.
Bador, B. Evil Port.
Baldwin, Sandy. [Basic system code].
Ball, J. And This Is So.
Barnett, R. Anorexic, The.
Bass, E. To Praise.
Baudelaire. Snake that Dances, The.
Belli, C. Poem: "Our love is not found in our respective."
Belli, G. Brief Lessons in Eroticism 1.
Benn. Monologue.
Berlin. Heat Wave.
Bethel, M. Reggae Prophecy.
Bible, *O.T.* Each inmost peece in me is thine.
Psalm 139. Domine, Probasti.
Bidart. Ellen West.
Blagg, T. In Bed this Morning.
Bogan, L. Cartography.
Bonset. Remembering the Night Fountains.
Borthwick, P. Scan.
Bousoño, C. How Am I To Tell You.
Bracho, C. En esta oscura mezquita tibia.

In This Warm Dark Mosque.
Braun, H. To Fat Boy, the Bomb.
Breton, A. Free Union.
Breytenbach. Padmapani.
Bringhurst. Parśvanatha.
Brooks, G. Still Do I Keep My Look, My Identity.
Still Do I Keep My Look, My Identity.
Broumas, O. Masseuse, The.
With the clear.
Brownstein. Oracle night / the porch is frozen.
Brunk, J. On This Earth.
Brutus. Let not this plunder be misconstrued.
Budbill. This Shining Moment in the Now.
Budde, R. Anorexia.
Bui-Burton. Look at Me.
My Love is Like a Lily.
Bunting. Remember, imbeciles and wits.
Burgess, F. On Digital Extremities.
Busceti, G. Eight Phases of Contemplation.
Butts, A. Skin.
Cabico, R. Antonio Banderas in His Underwear.
Art in Architecture.
Caldwell, E. Love Poem: "Olfactory paradise."
Campert. Futile Poem, A.
Campo. What the Body Told.
Carrera Andrade. Your body is a garden, a bush of flowers.
Your body is a golden temple.
Your body is bathed eternally.
Cartelli, Mary Anne. Water.
Cavafy. At the Cafe Door.
Return.
Cavendish, M. Body, The: A Fancy.
Dialogue betwixt the Body and the Mind, A.
Of the Animal Spirits.
Celaya, G. After a Native Poem from the Solomon Islands that Begins: "Your Shameful Parts Are the White Man's Gramophone".
Cendrars. Great Fetishes, The.
Cernuda. Speaking Other Than with Words.
Césaire, A. Batouque.
Charach, R. Question of Vitamins, A.
Chazal, M. Plastic Sense (1948 version).
Chedid, A. Stepping Aside.
Child, A. Squeeze.
Ching An. Laughing at Myself 2.
Ch'oe Sŭngja. About Women.
Chubb, R. Song of My Soul.
Transfiguration.
Citino. Sister Mary Appassionata Lectures the Eighth Grade Boys and Girls on the Nature of the Candle.
Clarke, A. Martha Blake at Fifty-one.
Clarke, C. Rondeau: "They are bodies left unburied."
Clary. Camellia, It's that Moist and Sensitive.
Clifton, L. 11/10 Again.
Homage to my hips.
Love the Human.
Poem to my uterus.
Clover, J. There Is the Body Lying in State.
Cohen, L. Suzanne [Takes You Down].
Colby, T. Dear, I Love.
Colonna, V. Without muscles without slipping.
Comer, Carrie St. George. Long Goodbye.
Comte de Lautréamont. I am filthy. Lice gnaw me. Swine, when they look at me, vomit. The scabs.
Cooley. Brother Body.
Coolidge, C. One of Essence's Entrances.
Cott, J. Enjoyment Body.
Couani. Map of the World, The.
Coulehan, J. Anatomy Lesson.
Coultas, B. Human Museum, The.
Couzyn. Creation.
Mystery, The.
Cowley, A. Platonic[k] Love.
Creeley. Body.
Crenner, Jim. Out-of-Body Experience.
Cross, E. Form.
Forma.
Crowley, A. Rondels.
Cruz Varela. Love Song for Difficult Times.
Cucchi, M. Hibernation.
Cuddihy. This Body.

D'Aquino, A. Hotel.
Hotel.
Daumal. Clavicles for a Great Poetic Game.
Davies, P. Ave Atque Vale.
Davis, T. Loving the Flesh.
Dawes, K. Some Tentative Definitions 4.
De Angelis. Every Metaphor.
Reasons for the Beginning.
There's a Hand that Nails Down.
DeNiord, C. Soul as a Body, The.
Derricotte. Invisible Dreams.
Dickinson, E. I am afraid to own a Body.
Prison gets to be a friend, A.
These—saw Visions.
Donne. Ecstasy, The.
Love's Progress.
Resurrection, Imperfect.
Dooley, M. Does It Go Like this?
Doty, M. Michael's Dream.
Douskey. Wet Bodies.
Drieu la Rochelle. Roundness.
Dudley, E. Pathologist.
Dugan, A. Actual Vision of Morning's Extrusion.
Let Heroes Account to Love.
Duggan, L. One xxxvii.
Duncan, R. I Am a Most Fleshly Man.
Torso, The / Passages 18.
Dunmore. Three Ways of Recovering a Body.
Dyer, E. Painting the Nude.
Ehret, T. Lost Body.
Elburg. Wanting To.
Elizabeth, M. She Teaches Him to Reach Out.
Elmslie, K. Circus Nerves and Worries.
Emanuel, L. She.
Equi. Autobiographical Poem.
Erdrich, H. Fat in America.
Erdrich. Lady in the Pink Mustang, The.
"Ern Malley.". Egyptian Register.
Eyton, F. Body and Soul.
Fatchen. Hullo, Inside.
Feinfeld, D. Wound Man, The.
Felltham [or Feltham]. To Phryne.
Fermini, L. Moments that hands without a vine . . . laughter.
Field. Sweet-Briar in Rose.
Fisk, M. Late Afternoon.
Follain. Mirror, A.
Taxidermist, A.
Ford, Katie. Flesh.
Fortini. Poetry of Roses, The.
Fox, S. Miss Pimberton Of.
Foy, J. Autopsy.
France, L. Body Language.
Fried, E. One Kind of Freedom Speaks.
Gallagher, T. Sea Inside the Sea.
Garcia, R. Brief Entanglements.
Gilliams, M. Tristitia Ante.
Ginsberg, A. Change, The: *Kyoto-Tokyo Express.*
Looking over my shoulder.
On Neal's Ashes.
Sphincter.
Gizzi. Another Day on the Pilgrimage.
Goldberg, B. God Body.
Lilies at Night.
González, A. Before I Could Call Myself Ángel González.
Graham, A. Hands and feet.
Graham-Pole, J. Venipuncture.
Grahn. Fortunately the skins.
Greenberg, U. Song of the Great Mind.
Greenlaw, L. Skin Full.
Greenwald, T. Open mouth open through.
Gregerson. Bicameral.
Grimké, A. Black Finger, The.
Groarke, V. Veneer.
Guidacci, M. Madame X.
Guiducci, A. Brevity of Embraces.
Gullar. Poster.
Gunn, T. Man With Night Sweats, The.
Ha-Levi, J. Poem in Parts.
Hacker, M. Year's End.
Hadas, R. Winged Words.
Hagiwara Sakutaro. One Who's in Love with Love, The.

Hall, D.   Winged Torso of Eros.
Halpern, D.   Her Body.
Hamill, S.   Ten Thousand Sutras.
Harding, S.   Noblest bodies are but gilded clay.
Harper, M.   Studs.
Harvey, M.   Pity the Bathtub Its Forced
  Embrace of the Human Form.
Heaney, S.   Bog Queen.
Hecht, A.   Feast of Stephen, The.
Heine, H.   Song of Songs, The.
Henderson, Donna.   Transparent Woman.
Herbert, Z.   Hygiene of the Soul, The.
Hernández, M.   My heart can't go on any
  longer.
Waltz Poem of Those in Love and Inseparable
  Forever.
Herrera.   Resurrection of the Flesh, The.
Heyman, E.   Body and Soul.
Hilberry.   Body and Mind.
Hill, M.   Sleep.
Holst-Warhaft.   In the End Is the Body.
Holt, R.   Pleasure of Feeling Inside Your Body,
  The.
Holub.   Vanishing Lung Syndrome.
Hume, C.   Birthday.
Hunter, T.   Wanting You.
Hwang Jiwoo.   Out of the Winter-Tree Into the
  Spring-Tree.
Ibarbourou.   Hour, The.
Ilagha, N.   Adam's Cry.
Istarú, A.   To the cove of my breasts your
  forehead will return.
Jackson, L.   Starved.
Jiménez, J.   Night Piece.
Jones, A.   Anorexia.
Tap.
Josefowitz, N.   Music.
Joseph, A.   Learning to Laugh.
Pleasure.
Kalendek, Julie.   Take Five of These.
Kekova.   Sky is covered with stars, like a body
  with sores, The.
Kennedy, L.   Moonburn.
Khlebnikov, V.   Me and Russia.
Kim Hyesun.   Taklamakan.
Kim Sŭnghŭi.   Love Song for the Belly Button
  1.
Kizer, C.   Food of Love.
Klinger, A.   Transformation.
Your fingers circle.
Klugman, S.   God's Body.
Komunyakaa, Y.   Anodyne.
Jeanne Duval's Confession.
Slam, Dunk, & Hook.
Kowit.   In the Morning.
What Chord Did She Pluck.
Kruchyonykh [or Kruchionykh or Kruchenykh].
Sahara to America, The.
Kuzmin.   Nine delightful birthmarks.
Lacavaro, A.   Advantages of Being a World
  Class Athlete, The.
LaFemina.   White Dwarf.
Lamantia.   There Are Many Pathways to the
  Garden.
Larkin, J.   Legacy.
My Body.
Larkin, P.   Mr Bleaney.
Laughlin, J.   Rhyme.
Laux, D.   China.
Lawrence, D. H.   Body of God, The.
Eloi, Eloi, Lama Sabachthani?
Lee, L.   Interrogation, The.
This Room and Everything in It.
Lee, W.   Lovers' Duet.
Leiris, Michel.   Vertical.
Levertov.   Our Bodies.
Levin, D.   Red Water.
Levis.   Morning After My Death, The.
Levitt, Peter.   My robe hangs in the garden.
Liu, T.   Size of It, The.
Livesay, D.   Other.
Logan, W.   Song: "Her nose is like a satellite."
Logau.   Best Medecines, The.
Longley, M.   Casualty.
Loy.   Three Moments in Paris.
Luca, Gherasim.   End of the World, The: To

Embody.
Lux.   Swimming Pool, The.
Macari, A.   Counting the Years.
MacDiarmid, H.   Scunner.
Mackowski, Joanie.   Self-Portrait, Double
  Exposed.
MacLeish.   What the Serpent Said to Adam.
MacLeod, Sue.   This is the body, consoling
  itself.
Magrelli.   Like ground that's been walked over,
  it echoes.
Mahadevi.   On Her Decision to Stop Wearing
  Clothes.
When the body becomes Your mirror.
Maiden.   In the Gloaming.
Majorino.   My Flesh in its Sweat.
Scene-Script.
Malroux.   Octet Before Winter.
Manhire.   Distance between Bodies, The.
Mansour, J.   Tinfoil.
Marcus, J.   Justice.
Markham, M.   Compendium Notes.
Marks, G.   All of Me.
Marlowe.   His bodie was as straight as Circes
  wand.
Martial.   Chrestus, your balls are depilated.
Martinez, D.   Pain.
Martínez, V.   It Is Not.
Night of Fathers.
Marvell.   Dialogue between the Soul and [the]
  Body, A.
Marzán.   Emergency.
Mathews, H.   Comatas.
Matthews, W.   Descriptive Passages.
Mayr, S.   Watching a Dance Rehearsal in a
  Calgary Theatre with a Concrete Floor.
Mays, M.   #4, In Red.
McClatchy.   My Mammogram.
McClure, M.   Canticle: "Sharks tooth is perfect
  for biting, The. The Intent."
McGuckian.   On Not Being Your Lover.
McMorris, M.   Some Days in the City.
McOrlan.   Weighing-machine, The.
McPherson, S.   His Body.
Merrill, J.   Body [or B o d y].
Merwin.   Some Last Questions.
Metras, G.   Vanishing Point.
Miller, J.   Bird dressed as solitude and tears.
Mirabai [or Mira Bai].   O friend, understand: the
  body.
Mishol, A.   Shopping.
Mistral, G.   Final Tree.
Molloy, D.   Envelope of Skin.
Mooney, M.   In the Parlour.
Morgan, R.   As it was in the beginning.
Morley, H.   Made Out of Links.
Moro, C.   Battle at the Edge of the Falls.
Moulds, J.   Renoir's Bathers.
Mouré.   Toxicity.
Mugrón, Abbot of Iona.   Christ's Cross.
Muldoon, P.   Hard Drive.
Mulkey, R.   Why I Believe in Angels.
Mullen, H.   Anatomy.
Mullen, L.   Catch, The.
Muske, C.   Our Kitty.
Nagai, M.   Histories of Bodies.
Naong.   Auspicious Cloud.
Needell.   Not a Balancing Act.
Nelson, M.   Vallejo.
Neruda.   Ode to a Beautiful Nude.
Nichols, G.   Come up and see me sometime.
Noguere.   Soma.
Novikov, N.   In our world it's unusual.
O'Lahsen, M.   It Took One Hundred Years.
O'Hara, F.   Female Torso.
Olds, S.   Language of the Brag, The.
Palmer, M.   Eighth Sky.
Erolog.
Pastan.   After Minor Surgery.
Patmore, C.   To the Body: "Creation's and
  Creator's crowning good."
Paz.   Crystal willow, a poplar of water, A.
I travel your body as I would travel the world.
Penna.   Shadowless sun on male bodies.
When I don't feel well, I wander among.
Perelman.   Cliff Notes.

Perillo, L.   Body Mutinies, The.
Phillips, C.   As from a Quiver of Arrows.
Loose Hinge.
Luna Moth.
Parable: "There was a saint once."
Recumbent.
Toys.
Piercy.   Friend, The.
Pollitt.   Mind-Body Problem.
Porter, C.   All of You.
Ports, K.   Desire.
Powell, D. A.   How his body stood against a
  thicket. rich in hardwood gentry: ponderous
  and gloomy.
Prados, E.   Song of Taking Leave.
Pratt, M.   Elbows.
Praxilla.   Peeking in through.
Press, K.   Humus.
Raine, K.   Love-Poem: "Yours is the face that
  the earth turns to me."
Ralegh, S.   Lie, The.
Ramanujan.   Elements of Composition.
Hindu to His Body, A.
Ranaldo, L.   Five Weeks.
Rankin, J.   Tale.
Rayl, J.   Spring Storm.
Rebolledo.   Sapho's Kiss.
Rehm, Pam.   Thus I Find My Legs.
Reichard, W.   Monster's Dream, The.
Reverdy.   Squares.
Rexroth, K.   Vitamins and Roughage.
Reynolds, R.   Peridot.
Rhianos.   To Theodorus et al.
Rich, A.   Splittings.
Ricks, D.   Variation on a Theme of Baudelaire.
Rilke.   Birth of the Smile, The.
Tombs of the Hetaerae.
Rimbaud, A.   Being Beauteous.
Our Assholes Are Different.
Roberts, N.   Max Factor Pink.
Robinson, K.   Intent to consider.
Robinson, Matt.   Body as dictionary, as bible,
  The.
Snow; a fear of dying.
Rollings.   Dirty Dreams and God Smiling.
Ronci, Seido R.   Becoming a Buddha.
Rosenberg, L.   Lesson in Anatomy, A.
Ross, Martin.   Body Cavity.
Royet-Journoud.   Locality.
Rufinus.   Her foot sparkled like silver.
Ryan, G.   Cruising.
Salinas, P.   Do You Hear How They Beg for
  Realities?
Scalise, G.   Passion circles round our body, A.
Schneiders, J.   Weight.
Schwartz, R. L.   Late Summer.
Possible.
Seibles, T.   Who.
Senghor.   Song of the Initiate.
Serrano, P.   Beacon.
Hacho.
Rosario.
Rosary.
Sexton.   In Celebration of My Uterus.
Shatalov, A.   Age of aquarius mineral water
  taking a bath, The.
Shepherd, R.   Boy, Allegorically Deployed.
Sherman, M.   This Body.
Shih Shu.   Enlightenment.
Shinkichi Takahashi.   Eternity.
Vimalakirti.
Shozan.   No mind, no Buddha.
Shwarts [or Shvarts].   Elegy on an X-ray Photo
  of My Skull.
Simons, S.   All of Me.
Smith, A.   Praise.
Smith, S.   This Englishwoman.
Snyder, G.   Bath, The.
Södergran.   Instinct.
Solomon, M.   Comment on My Host, A.
Sorescu, M.   Fresco.
Map.
Soupault.   One o'Clock.
Sour, R.   Body and Soul.
Spender, S.   Abrupt and charming mover.
Spires.   Bodies, The.

Stein, G.   Kiss my lips. She did.
Steinberg, D.   Image Was of Me Flowing
   Through You, The.
   With you I begin.
Stevenson, A.   Spirit is too Blunt an Instrument,
   The.
   Vertigo.
Stever, E.   Her Back to Me.
Strand.   Old Man Leaves Party.
Strato [or Straton].   Long hair, and curls woven
   not by Nature but by Art.
Strode.   On a Good Leg and Foot.
Suárez.   Like the Magic Glow of Paradise.
Sutphen, J.   Living in the Body.
Swenson, M.   Question: "Body my house."
Swirszczynska [or Swir].   I Starve My Belly for
   a Sublime Purpose.
   I Talk to My Body.
Tadic.   Man from the Death Institute.
Tana, P.   I Have Touched.
   Marvelous Beast.
   You Bring Me Back.
Tanikawa, S.   Request.
Trigilio.   Body is Fragile, The.
Triplett, P.   Spectral Dues.
   Studies in Desire.
Truitt, S.   Kerf, The.
Unknown.   Because of this love.
   God, what are you doing to me?
   I Found My Love by the Secret Canal.
   I Have a Gentle Cock [or Gentil Cok].
   I Know Moon-Rise [or Moonrise].
   Marsh's Plants Bewilder, The.
   O'er the Crossing.
Unknown, fr. Terezin Concentration Camp.   Pain
   Strikes Sparks on Me, the Pain of Terezin.
Updike.   In Extremis.
Upton, L.   Contortionist.
Van Hanh.   Body of Man, The.
Van Peenen, H.   Insulin Receptor.
Vasalis.   Idiot in the Bath, The.
Verlaine.   Balanide 2.
   Mille e tre.
   Sadness, the languor of the human body, The.
   Sonnet to the Asshole.
Vietnamese Oral Tradition.   Body Is Pain, The.
Voce, L.   Your eyes stolen.
Volkman.   I was watching for it, everytime
   watching, for the neck that was.
Vroman.   Wrinkling Together.
Waldman, A.   Skin / Meat / BONES.
Waller, E.   Of the Last Verses in the Book.
   On a Girdle.
Wanley.   Resurrection, The.
Ward, D.   Absolution.
   Limit.
Wat.   Facing Bonnard.
Weinstein, N.   Migration of Drummond's
   Organs (After Death), The.
Wenderoth, J.   First Impression.
Westphalen, E.   You Came to Rest.
Wheelwright.   Esprit d'Escalier.
Whitman, W.   I am the poet of the Body and I
   am the poet of the Soul.
   I Sing the Body Electric.
   Walt Whitman, a kosmos, of Manhattan the son.
Wiesinger, S.   Snow Climbers.
Wilbur, R.   Shallot, A.
Williamson, G.   Nervous Systems.
Wilner, E.   Muse, The.
Woods, D.   Prescription.
Wright, C.   Grace: "Its hair is a fine weed."
Wright, J.   What is Beautiful.
Wu Tsao.   For the Courtesan Ch'ing Lin.
Wylie.   This Corruptible.
Yakusai, Layman.   Deafening peal, A.
Yeats.   Crazy Jane Talks with the Bishop.
Yi Sang.   Poem No. 5.
Young, Andy.   Ghost of Me.
Young, C.   Proximity.
Zamora, D.   Celebration of the Body.
   Vision of Your Body.
Zucker, R.   Portrait of Unknown.

See also Nudity and Nudists

Bodybuilding
Katz, J.   Women Must Put Off Their Rich

   Apparel.
Nilsson, H.   My Least Skirtable Deficiency.

Boer War
Davidson, J.   Battle.
Hardy, T.   Christmas Ghost-Story, A.
   Colonel's Soliloquy, The.
   Drummer Hodge.
   Embarcation.
   Wife in London, A.
Kipling, R.   Absent-Minded Beggar, The.
   Bridge-Guard in the Karroo.
   Return, The.
Morant, H.   Last Rhyme and Testament of Tony
   Lumpkin.

Boethius, Anicius Manlius Severinus
Bell, J.   Meditation on The Consolation of
   Philosophy.

Bogs
Claus.   Tollund Man.
Heaney, S.   Bog Queen.
   Bogland.
   Tollund Man, The.
Smith, S.   Our Bog is Dood.

Bohemian Life
Deschamps, E.   Rondeau: "Fleas, stink, pigs,
   mold."
Gurney, I.   Bohemians, The.
Padgett, R.   Ode to Bohemians.
Parker, D.   Bohemia.
Rimbaud, A.   My Bohemia (Fantasy).

Boleyn, Anne
Banks, J.   Short Curse.
Bernheim, Erica.   Anne Boleyn.
Bibb.   Anne Boleyn.
Wyatt.   Whoso List to Hunt.

Bolsheviks
Shkapskaya [or Shkapskaia].   No Dream.
Unknown.   Harry Pollit Was a Bolshie.

Bombay, India
Cain, Justin.   My Required Tool.
Dharker.   Living Space.

Bombs and Bombing
Alkalay-Gut.   Instead of his leash.
   So we begin to plan.
   Think of the children in Baghdad.
   Tonight we wait for the alarm.
   Unable to move.
Amichai, Y.   Diameter of the Bomb, The.
   Radius of the bomb was twelve inches, The.
Back, R.   You ask.
Boulus.   Entries for a Possible Poem.
Brathwaite, E.   Irae.
Brecht, B.   This Summer's Sky.
Brock, V.   Remembering Dresden.
Cherry, K.   Forecast.
Corso.   Bomb.
Crozier, A.   Blank Misgivings.
Cunard.   To Eat To-day.
Cunningham, P.   Dog Called Chance, A.
   Hats.
   Red Wine Stain from Malin to Mizen Head, A.
De la Mare.   Immanent.
Dickey, J.   Firebombing, The.
Ditzanny, R.   My Hand is Extended for the
   Peace of the Galilee.
Fiacc.   Intimate Letter 1973.
Fisher, R.   Entertainment of War, The.
Garioch.   Phooie!
   Wire, The.
Graham, J.   What the End Is For.
Hefer, H.   Sappers, The.
Hoagland, E.   From Ground Zero.
Hoagland, T.   Kind of Shadow That Calls Out
   Fate, The.
Holden, J.   Why We Bombed Haiphong.
Ignatow, D.   All Quiet.
Jarrell, R.   Truth, The.
Juma'h, J.   Thus my brother.
Kaminsky, Ilya.   Maestro.
Kim, Suji Kwock.   Flight.
Kingsolver.   Waiting for the Invasion.
Kipling, R.   Bombed in London.
Kossman.   Bomb said to a city, A.
Lam Thi My Da.   Garden Fragrance.
   Night Harvest.

Lehman.   World Trade Center, The.
Levertov.   Fragrance of Life, Odor of Death.
Lindsay, M.   'Tis Sixty Years Since.
Lowell, R.   Bomber, The.
Major, C.   News Story.
Margolis, G.   Town Meeting.
Michelson, P.   Enduring Witness, the Mosques
   of Kattankudi.
Miller, V.   Light Reading.
Montale.   Frost on the windowpanes; the sick.
O'Callaghan, C.   Coventry.
O'Keefe, E.   Chords.
Peake.   Babe was born in the reign of George,
   A.
Randall, D.   Ballad of Birmingham.
Reed, H.   Chard Whitlow.
Rodenko.   Bombing.
Rolfe, E.   Casualty.
   City of Anguish.
   Paris—Christmas 1938.
Sanders, M.   Vigil at a Missile Silo, A.
Seifert.   Never Again.
Shapiro, K.   Full Moon: New Guinea.
Smith, Goldie Capers.   Ballad of a Bombardier
   from Texas.
Smith, W.   Columbus Circle Swing.
Spender, S.   Epilogue to a Human Drama.
   Rejoice in the Abyss.
Stafford, W.   Some Remarks When Richard
   Hugo Came.
Szymborska, W.   One Twenty Pub, The.
   Terrorist, He Watches, The.
   Terrorist Is Watching, A.
Thiel, D.   Minefield, The.
Weigl.   Her Life Runs Like a Red Silk Flag.
Wilbur, R.   Mined Country.
Williams, C. K.   Shrapnel.
Yoshihara.   Air Raid.

See also Air Warfare

Bones
Abse.   Origin of Music, The.
Basho.   Weathered bones.
Beath, M.   Solid Ground.
Bly, R.   Counting Small-Boned Bodies.
Bousoño, C.   Three Poems on Death.
Broumas, O.   On Earth.
Buson.   Flying squirrel, A.
Chang Heng.   Bones of Zhuangzi, The.
Ciardi, J.   Elegy for a Cave Full of Bones.
Coultas, B.   Capitalist Projections.
   Lecture #1.
Coyote, Peter.   Do you think.
Demetre, S.   Woman Is Running for Her Life,
   A.
Donne.   Relic, The.
Evans, C.   Lucy's Bones.
Garcia, R.   Los Amantes.
Gehrke, S.   Near the Mississippi.
Geiger.   Dry Spell of Faith, A.
Hannan, M.   Bone Die, The.
Harries, E.   Bone Prison, The.
Harwood, G.   Bone Scan.
Herd.   Hyperion's Bones.
Hollander, J.   Lady's-Maid's Song, The.
Hope, A.   Meditation on a Bone.
Hopes.   Birdbones.
Hughes, T.   Relic.
Ilagha, N.   Adam's Cry.
Koertge.   What She Wanted.
Kumin, M.   Seeing the Bones.
Leslie, E.   T'ain't No Sin to Dance Around in
   Your Bones.
Lilley, Gary.   Meetin the Conjure Woman.
Lorde.   Ethiopia.
Milton.   On Shakespear[e].
Moritz [or Morits].   Memorandum.
Neruda.   Nothing but Death.
O'Brien, G.   Aubade 2.
O'Reilly, C.   Six.
Perillo, L.   Floating Rib, The.
Pinsky.   Want Bone, The.
Ramke, B.   Paul Verlaine at the Grave of Lucien
   Létinois.
Roy, L.   Suffering The Sea Change: All My
   Pretty Ones.
Scofield, G.   His Flute, My Ears.

Shakespeare, W. Full Fathom Five.
Smith, K. Remembering Miller.
Smither. To a friend with osteoporosis.
Stow. Singing Bones, The.
Takushitsu. Breeze strokes the water of the spring, A.
Tester, V. Histories, The.
Unknown. Outlaws stripped everyone down to the bone, The.
Tie up my bones and walk them away.
Valley of Dry Bones, The.
Upton, L. Contortionist.
Waltner-Toews, D. Roots: "Rudy Weibe, wiping the sweat from his brow."
Wat. By a great, swift water.
Williams, C. K. Bone.
Yun Tongju. Yet Another Home.
See also **Skeletons**

Bonn, Germany
Garlick, R. Capitals.

Bonnard, Pierre
Carver, R. Bonnard's Nudes.

Bonney, William H.
Cesaire, A. *et al.* How did you come to develop the concept of Negritude?

"Bonnie Dundee".
See **Dundee, John Graham of Claverhouse, 1st Viscount ("Bonnie Dundee")**

Boobies
Tate, J. Blue Booby, The.

Books
Adams, F. To a Thesaurus.
Alféri, Pierre. Library.
An Jung-Sŏp. Drinking Alone on a Spring Night.
Davies, A. Books.
Bancquart. I Walk in the Solitude of Books.
Beer, P. Footbinding.
Belloc. On His Books.
Berrigan, T. London Air.
Bogan, L. Man Alone.
Boland, E. Other Woman, The.
Bonnefoy. Book, for Growing Old, The.
Bradstreet, A. Author to Her Book, The.
Brown, S. Marginalia.
Brownell, H. Suspiria Noctis.
Budy. First Books.
Burkard. How I Shaded the Book.
Burns, J. How.
Reading.
Carew, T. Fancy, A.
Cavendish, M. Common Fate of Books, The.
Poetresses Petition, The.
Cerenio. 13 June 1994.
Char. Every Life.
Chaucer. Conclusion.
Collins, B. Marginalia.
Tomes.
Coolidge, C. This Garden Being: The Hanging of Books.
Corso. I Held a Shelley Manuscript.
Crane, S. I met a seer.
Cummings, E. E. If everything happens that can't be done.
Dana, R. Pleasure Boat, The [*or* Pleasure-Boat, The].
Davenant [*or* D'Avenant]. There, when they thought they saw in well sought Books.
Davidson, M. Dream Dream, The.
Deltoro, A. Libro de Segunda Mano.
Secondhand Book.
Dickinson, E. He ate and drank the precious Words.
Precious—moldering pleasure—'tis, A.
There is No Frigate Like a Book.
Disch. Bookmark, A.
Dove, R. First Book, The.
Drummond, W. Book, The.
Earle, J. Saturday in the '20s, A.
Fearing. Literary.
Garcia, R. Book of Dreams, The.
Glaser, M. Changing Address Books.
Gorenko, A. Houses like piles of children's books.
Guiducci. Readings.

Upon Closing the Book.
Guiney. In the Reading-Room of the Brtish Museum.
Hadas, R. Moments of Summer.
Hale, S. Blessing on the printer's art!, A.
HaNagid. One Who Works and Buys Himself Books.
Harmon, B. E. Chanson Delice.
Hass, R. Bookbuying in the Tenderloin.
Herlin. So many traces.
Herrick. Argument of His Book, The.
To God ("If any thing delight me for to print.").
To His Book[e] ("Have I not blessed [*or* blest] thee? Then go forth; nor fear.").
To the Most Illustrious and Most Hopeful[l] Prince, Charles, Prince of Wales.
Heyen. Where.
Hicok. Active Reader, The.
Holmes, O. Iris, Her Book.
Huerta, D. Baroque Cell, A.
Celda barroca, Una.
Ignatow, D. 1905.
Im Yŏngjo. Textbook.
Jabès. To be in the book. To figure in the book of questions, to be part of it.
Jackson, L. Troubles of a Book, The.
James, N. I Had No Books.
Joseph, A. In the Bookstore.
Reading Room.
Searching for *Melinda's Magic Moment.*
Keyes, S. War Poet.
Khlebnikov, V. One Book, The.
Kirby, D. To a French Structuralist.
Klink, J. Apology: "Lately, too much disturbed, you stay breathing in me."
Kornblith, M. Books of the Dead, The.
Lamb, C. In My Own Album.
Larkin, P. Fiction and the Reading Public.
Study of Reading Habits, A.
Laughlin, J. Inn at Kirchstetten, The.
Lawrence, A. Robert Penn Warren's Book.
Le Gallienne. Library in a Garden, A.
Lewis, Emyr. This Is My Book.
Lewis, G. Farmer's Evidence, The.
Lockwood. Bookshop in Winter.
Madhubuti. Books as Answer.
So Many Books, So Little Time.
Mallarmé. End / conscience.
Martial. Slipshod writing, premature publication.
Masaoka Shiki. Amid a jumble of.
Swatting mosquitoes.
McOrlan. Modern circus, The.
Mei Yao Ch'en. Offering for the Cat, An.
Milosz, C. And Yet the Books.
Milton. On the Detraction Which Followed upon My Writing Certain Treatises ("Book was writ[t] of late called [*or* call'd] *Tetrachordon*, A.").
Moore, M. He Wrote the History Book.
Mörike [*or* Möricke]. Forest Murmurs.
Motion, A. Lines, The: "November, and the Sunday twilight fallen."
Muldoon, P. Making the Move.
Muñiz Huberman. Manuscript.
Ní Chuilleanáin. Secret, The.
Nooteboom. Basho 1.
Norton, C. To My Books.
Ovid. Little book—no, I don't begrudge you— you're off to the City.
Padgett, R. Famous Flames.
Pak Tujin. Book of Poems.
Palis, Y. Waking Up.
Pilling. Fran.
Pinsky. Book: "Its leaves flutter, they thrive or wither, its outspread."
Prado, A. Fluency.
Reese, L. Love, Weeping, Laid This Song.
Reverdy. Spirit Escapes, The.
Rich, A. Burning of Paper instead of Children, The.
Novel, The.
Sanguineti. And now a few questions to end with.
Schelling. Perfection of Wisdom Suite, A: Hymns for the Perfection of Wisdom in

Paradise.
Seyburn, P. First Bookshelf.
Shapiro, D. Book of Glass, A.
Shwarts [*or* Shvarts]. Sale of a Historian's Library.
Sirowitz, H. Lending Out Books.
Sissman. Upon Finding Dying: An Introduction, by L. E. Sissman, Remaindered at 1s.
Sosnora. Do you envy, my comrades-in-arms.
Spenser, E. To His Booke.
Stadler. Saying, The.
Statius. Jocular Lines to Plotius Grypus.
Stevenson, R. Land of Story-Books, The.
Strand. Eating Poetry.
Swirszczynska [*or* Swir]. He Was Lucky.
Taylor, J. Me thinks I heare some Cavillers object.
Thomas, L. Dracula.
Tipping. Poet at Work.
Tranter. Enzensberger at 'Exiles'.
Trowbridge, J. Recollections of "Lalla Rookh".
Unknown. To the Lady with a Book.
Upton, L. Ditch, The.
Vaughan, H. Book, The.
To His Books.
Veenendaal. On My Fourteenth Wedding Anniversary I Ride on Trains.
Wakoski. Light.
Walafrid Strabo. With His Book, Of Gardening.
Waller, E. Of the Last Verses in the Book.
Watson, R. Betty Barnes, the Book-Burner.
Weiss, T. Fire at Alexandria, The.
Weitsman, Sojun Mel. One third of my life has been spent in this practice and you.
Wells, C. Of Modern Books.
Whitman, W. Whoever You Are Holding Me Now in Hand.
Williams, C. K. Critic, The.
Williams, Gerwyn. My Wales?
Williams, T. Quarry.
Williams, W. Coronal, A.
Wordsworth, W. Expostulation and Reply.
Tables Turned, The.
Yang Hsün-chi. Inscribed on the Doors of My Bookshelves.
Yang Shih-ch'i. Night Rain: A Wall Collapses—Sent To My Neighbors.
Yang Wan-li. Don't Read Books!
Yeats. When You Are Old.
Yeryomin. Faceted grains of wisdom.
Zen Center Sangha. One third of my life has been spent in this practice and you.

Books of Hours
Peralta Family Oral Tradition. O Blanca Virgen.

Bookstores
O'Donoghue, M. This is Sunday.
Simic. Used Book Store.

Bookworms
Cynewulf. Old English Riddle.
Unknown. Bookworm.
Moth ate words; a marvellous event, A.

Boone, Daniel
Benét, R. *et al.* Daniel Boone.
Benét, S. Daniel Boone.
Stafford, W. For the Grave of Daniel Boone.
Warren, R. Was It One of the Long Hunters of Kentucky who Discovered Boone at Sunset?

Booth, Edwin
Melville, H. Coming Storm, The.

Bootlegging and Bootleggers
Toomer. Seventh Street.

Boots
Batraville, D. Paper 43.
Mouré. 8 Little Theatres of the Cornices.
Rowlands, D. Little Boots, The.
Siken, Richard. Boot Theory.

Borden, Lizzie
Shipley, V. Sleeping Soundly Where LIzzie Borden Did.

Boredom
Auden. Turn off the wireless; we are tired.
Baudelaire. To the Reader.
To the Reader.
Belieu. Radio Nebraska.
Belloc. Ballade of Hell and of Mrs. Roebeck.

Brownstein. War.
Buzbee. Sunday, Tarzan in His Hammock.
Clampitt. Meridian.
Dermée. Poem.
Elliott, A. Stay Behind, The.
Fanning, R. Baudelaire's Ablutions.
Giovanni. Forced Retirement.
Hope, A. Observation Car.
Huidobro. Quiet Spaces.
Hummell, A. I Never Saw a Goddess Go.
Isherwood. Turn off the wireless; we are tired.
Jiménez, J. Yes, If I Could Only Smash.
Kirby, D. Moderation Kills (Excusez-Moi, je Suis Sick as a Dog).
Kyger. Duncan's class met last night and more talk.
Laâbi Abdellatif. Tomorrow Will Be the Same Day.
Lawrence, D. H. Last Lesson of the Afternoon.
Leonard, T. Song: "Yi surta."
Li Yü. Tune: "Joy of Encounter".
Lleshanaku, L. Out of Boredom.
Machado Ruiz. Memory from Childhood.
MacSweeney. Cute Petite.
Malanga. Apprentice, The.
Martos. Casti Connubi.
Mayer, B. Inventing Stasis.
McDaniel, J. Leonard.
Moss, H. Ménage à Trois.
Nash, O. Spring Comes to Murray Hill.
Neruda. Walking Around ("It happens that I am tired of being a man.").
O'Driscoll, D. Lads, The.
Palés Matos. Pueblo.
Pollarolo, G. They All Think.
Ryan, G. Pure and Applied.
Sabines. I Love You at Ten in the Morning.
Simic. Book Full of Pictures, A.
Sondheim. I Never Do Anything Twice (Madam's Song).
Some People.
Wickham. Nervous Prostration.
Wordsworth, W. Methinks 'twere no unprecedented feat.
Yang Wan-li. I don't feel like reading another book.

Bores
Betjeman. Reproof Deserved; or After the Lecture.
De la Mare. Pooh!

Borges, Jorge Luis
Borges. Borges and I.
Borges and Myself.
Cairns, Scott. In Praise of Darkness.
Dalton, R. From a Revolutionary to J. L. Borges.

Borgia, Lucretia
Landor, W. On Seeing a Hair of Lucretia Borgia.

Borneo
Shiraishi. Wild Pigs of Kalimantan, The.

Bosch, Hieronymus
MacGreevy [orMcGreevy]. Homage to Hieronymus Bosch.

Bosnia and Herzegovina
Spera, G. Balkan.
Suk, J. From Ruin.

Boston, Massachusetts
Behrle. Beacon Arms.
White Album.
Bossidy. Boston.
Brouwer, J. History: "In Boston, a tongue of red paint traces the city's history, from Massacre to Tea Party to Faneuil Hall."
Cording. Elegy for John, My Student Dead of AIDS.
Doty, M. Days of 1981.
Espada. Bully.
Hall, D. Independence Day Letter.
Woolworth's.
Harnick. Boston Beguine, The.
Houghton, F. Mr. Frost Goes South to Boston.
Jiménez, J. Lavender Windowpanes and White Curtains.
Laird, N. Evening forecast for the region, The.

Lowell, R. For the Union Dead.
Public Garden, The.
Where the Rainbow Ends.
Plath. Winter's Tale, A.
Robinson, E. Boston.
Starbuck, G. Boston.
Communication to the City Fathers of Boston.
Whitman, W. Boston Ballad, A.
Wieners. After Symond's *Venice*.

Botany and Botanists
Foss, P. Anascesis and Wreckage.

Botticelli, Sandro
Hass, R. Against Botticelli.
Hudgins. Cestello Annunciation, The.
Outram, R. Tourist Stricken at the Uffizi.
Rossetti, D. For Spring, by Sandro Botticelli, in the Accademia of Florence.

Bottles
Noguchi, R. His Waves.

Bottom (Shakespeare)
Hooker, E. What Bottom Said When He Came Home.
Stokesbury. Bottom's Dream.

Bottoms
Ginsberg, A. Sphincter.
Iorwerth, D. New Bottom.
Ronci, Seido R. Becoming a Buddha.

Bouillabaisse
Thackeray. Ballad of Bouillabaisse, The.

Boundaries
Akhmatova, A. There Is A Boundary.
Alarcon, F. Frontera / Border.
Back, R. You ask.
Bejerano, M. States of War.
Borges. Limits.
Creeley. Edge, The ("Long over whatever edge.").
Davis, T. Building Walls.
Dharker. Minority.
France, L. North and South.
Gonzalez, R. Angels of Juárez, Mexico, The.
Hsi Chou. Sent to Huai Ku.
Ivanov, G. On the boundary of snow and melting.
James, D. E. Horizon.
Krivulin. Idea of Russia, The.
Lomax, M. Kith.
McGrath, C. Prose Poem, The.
Mtshali. Boy on a Swing.
Muso Soseki. All worries and troubles.
Beyond the World.
Reagon. Greed.
Rose. Long Division; a Tribal History.
Spahr, J. December 1, 2002.
Tsang, L. Girlfriend.
Unknown. I have only yielded you the privilege of my mouth.
Vest, Jennifer Lisa. In This, the Fifth World.
Ye Weilian. In and Out of Check Points.
Zisquit. Because passion is the silence we share.

Bourgeoisie
Andrade, M. Ode to the Bourgeois Gentleman.
Auden. Unknown Citizen, The.
Belli, G. Bosses of Rome, The.
Bunina. Though poverty's no stain.
Corso. Marriage.
Cummings, E. E. Cambridge ladies who live in furnished souls, The.
Dalton, R. Petty Bourgeoisie, The.
Enzensberger, H. At Thirty-Three.
Middle Class Blues.
Short History of the Bourgeoisie.
Feirstein. Mark Stern.
Friedman, E. Isolated Bourgeoisie.
Larkin, P. Toads.
Lawrence, D. H. How Beastly the Bourgeois Is.
Worm Either Way.
Levertov. Tenebrae.
Lihn. Revolution.
Myles, E. Merk.
Nemerov. Life Cycle of Common Man.
Parra, N. Litany of the Little Bourgeois.
Reid, C. Whole School of Bourgeois Primitives, A.

Saarikoski. Potato Thief.
Wickham. Fired Pot, The.
See also **Proletariat**
Bowlers.
See **Bowling and Bowlers**
Bowling and Bowlers
Costanzo. Old Neighborhood, The.
Dobyns. Bowlers Anonymous.
Moore, M. Bowls.
Skloot. Hook.

Bowls
Boruch. Simple Machines.
Follain. One Day I Suddenly Notice.
Forrester, S. Monk's bowl.
Winter afternoon.
Kyoriku. Scent of plum blossoms.
Mukai Kyorai. On a veranda.
Ozaki Hosai. I have no bowl.

Boxing and Boxers
Addonizio. Event.
Late Round.
Alexander, E. Narrative: Ali.
Today's News.
Barlow, G. Dream of the Ring: The Great Jack Johnson, A.
Cornish, S. Brown Bomber.
Davis, H. Ali, Bomaye.
Davis, O. Moorer Denies Holyfield in Twelve.
Dugan, A. On Hurricane Jackson.
Dybek. My Father's Fights.
Espada. Man Who Beat Hemingway, The.
Feld, Andrew. Boxers, The.
Guillén, N. Small Ode to a Black Cuban Boxer.
Harper, M. Homage to the Brown Bomber.
Hayden, R. Free Fantasia: Tiger Flowers.
Hernton, C. Ballad of the Life and Times of Joe Louis, A.
Ignatow, D. Boxing Match, The.
Jackson, M. Old Mongoose, The—*for Mac*.
San Diego Goodbye—*1944, Jacksaw Arena*.
Komunyakaa, Y. Boxing Day.
Levine, P. Right Cross, The.
March, S. Knockout, The.
Pindar. Olympia 11—For Agesidamus of the Westwind Locrians: Winner in the Boys' Boxing Match.
Reed, I. White Hope.
Rodriguez, L. Meeting the Animal in Washington Square Park.
Tate, J. Shadowboxing.
Wallace, R. Friday Night Fights, The.

Boyne (river), Ireland
Higgins, F. Father and Son.

Boys
Adams, S. Rough Boys.
Aldis, D. Hiding.
Ammons. Widespread Implications.
Baker, H. Advice to a Man Who Lost a Dog.
Beeching, H. Going Down Hill on a Bicycle.
Behn, R. Yellow House Writes a Story for the Boy, The.
Betjeman. False Security.
Bishop, E. Casabianca.
Blind. Beautiful Beeshareen Boy, The.
Brecht, B. Three Fragments.
Burroughs, W. My Legs Señor.
Calderón, T. "From Your Depths and Kneeling . . .".
Campert. Silver Talk.
Carroll, L. Duchess's Lullaby, The.
Carver, R. Happiness.
Cernuda. Boy Behind a Window.
Cheng Hsieh. Song of Surfing on the Bore.
Ciardi, J. All about Boys and Girls.
Clifton, L. Those boys that ran together.
Cornish, S. Generations 1.
Cuadra, P. Horses in the Lake.
de Gillies, G. De Puerorum osculis.
De la Mare. Tired Tim.
Derricotte. Furious Boy, The.
Duncan, R. Preface to the Suite: "Childhood, boyhood, young manhood."
Duran, J. Spanish Peasant Boy.
Eberhart, R. Horse Chestnut Tree, The.
Euripides. Fragment 652.

Fanning, R. In the Barn.
Field, E. Little Boy Blue.
Greppi, C. Boy's Afraid of the Live Tiger, The.
Gunn, T. Allegory of the Wolf Boy, The.
Hamer. Allegiance.
Hanu. Four Songs Calling a Boy.
Hartwig. Above Us.
Healy, E. Toltecs.
Heynen. Bloating and Its Remedies.
Higgins, F. Tennis in the City.
Hogg, J. Boy's Song, A.
Holmes, J. Four and a Half.
Howes, B. Portrait of the Boy as Artist.
Inada. 4. The Legend of Lost Boy.
Issa. Asked how old he was.
Jewett, S. Country Boy in Winter, A.
Kinnell. First Song.
Kipling, R. If.
Komunyakaa, Y. Boys in Dresses.
Lamb, M. Two Boys, The.
Larcom. Little Cavalier, A.
Lauterbach. Boy Sleeping.
Longfellow, H. My Lost Youth.
Martial. Breath of balm from foreign branches
  pressed.
  Cure of my unquietness.
  Did he have eyes and, if so, did he look.
  Why, Hyllus, do you deny to me today.
Martinez, D. Cultivation of Orchids, The.
McDonald, C. Nightfishing.
McHugh, H. Fence, The.
Morejón. To a Boy.
Nutter, G. Boy Leading a Horse.
Olds, S. Good Will.
  One Girl at the Boys Party, The.
Ovid. Iphis and Ianthe.
Patchen. Street Corner College.
Penna. Always boys in my poems!
Found—my little angel.
Po Chü-i. Realizing the Futility of Life.
Praed. School and Schoolfellows.
Ratzlaff, K. Group Portrait with Ukuleles.
Reznikoff. Testimony: The United States
  (1901–1910) Recitative/The South.
Rivard. 1966.
Robinson, E. Meshes.
Rumi. Has Anyone Seen the Boy?
Shakespeare, W. Song: "When that I was and a
  little tiny boy."
Shepherd, R. Boy, Allegorically Deployed.
  Refrain.
Solari, R. December 25, 1991.
  Truro.
Solon. Love of Boys, The.
Souster. Memory of Bathurst Street.
Strato [or Straton]. Twelve-year-old looks
  fetching in his prime, A.
Taylor, C.B. Round Irving High School.
Theognis. Boy and horse, a similar brain: the
  horse doesn't cry when its rider lies in the
  dust.
Tuqan, F. Song of Becoming.
Unknown. One Little Boy.
  Sad Story of a Little boy That Cried, The.
Walwicz. Tattoo, The.
Warren, R. He Was Formidable.
Whitman, W. We Two Boys Together Clinging.
Wilmer, S. Mess Boy, The.
Wise, W. When I Grow Up.
Wright, R. In the falling snow.
See also **Childhood and Children; Youth**

Bradstreet, Anne
Berryman. So squeezed, wince you I scream? I
  love you & hate.
  Winters close, Springs open, no child stirs, The.
Unknown. Anagram, An.

Brahma
Bhattācārya, K. Unperturbed at the battle.
Dèr Mouw. I am Brahman.
Emerson, R. Brahma.
Jones, S. Hymn to Na'a'yena, A.
Rāy, D. Wake up, wake up, Mother!

Brahms, Johannes
Berger, B. Stout Brahms.
Derricotte. Black Boys Play the Classics.
Stevens, W. Anglais Mort à Florence.

Brains
Abse. In the Theatre.
Akhmadulina. In the Botkin Hospital.
Auden. Ode to the Diencephalon.
Beasley. Lord Brain.
Buffoni, F. Song of Diamond Eyes, The.
Bye. On the Rails.
Coviello, M. Self-Portrait.
Dickinson, E. Brain, within its Groove, The.
Enquist, A. Invasion.
Ferguson, G. In Hospital-land.
Harburg. If I Only Had a Brain (If I Only Had a
  Heart) (If I Only Had the Nerve).
Lowell, J. Darkened Mind, The.
Lux. Walt Whitman's Brain Dropped on
  Laboratory Floor.
Magrelli. I have a brain populated by women.
Mouré. Toxicity.
Mullen, H. Fancy Cortex.
Rowe, V. MRI of a Poet's Brain.
Shapcott, J. Mad Cow in Love, The.
Shinkichi Takahashi. Railroad Station.
Straus, M. Neuroanatomy Summer.
Vroman. Thin Wire.

Brancusi, Constantin
Loy. Brancusi's Golden Bird.

Brandy
Fallon, P. Flask of Brandy, A.
Kinoshita Mokutarō. Gold Leaf Brandy.

Braque, Georges
Jacob, M. Meeting.
Norse. Picasso Visits Braque.

Brazil
Andrade, M. Inspiration.
  Nocturne.
  Processions, The.
Andrade, O. Babbling.
  Election.
  Good Luck.
  Portuguese Mistake.
Bandeira. Evocation of Recife.
  Portrait.
Carson, A. He She We They You You.
Eliscu, E. Flying Down to Rio.
Gordon, M. I, Yi, Yi, Yi, Yi (I Like You Very
  Much).
Gullar. Oswald Dead.
Hilliard, B. Coffee Song (They've Got an
  Awful Lot of Coffee in Brazil), The.
Kahn, G. Flying Down to Rio.
Lima, J. That Black Girl Fulô.
Manhire. Brazil.
Oden. Private Letter to Brazil, A.
Parry-Williams. Girl on the Quay at Rio, The.
Wright, C. My Last Night in Bahia.
  Peace Corps Volunteer Comes Home, The.

Bread
Aleshire. Fingers in the Bread.
Arp. Snakebread.
Hamhur Kiwha. Pine Bark Bread.
Hauge. Dream, The: "Let us slip into."
Heyen. Bread: "I'm standing in elm shadow."
Keller, D. Joining the Circus.
Kogawa. Bread to Stone.
Olds, S. Bread: "When my daughter makes
  bread, a cloud of flour."
Powell, J. First Light.
Silberg, Richard. Audience, The.
Yi Yônju. Bread and I, The.

Breakfast
Basho. Breakfast enjoyed.
Byrd, Bobby. Steak and Eggs.
Denham, Joe. Breakfast.
Dove, R. Quaker Oats.
Edson, R. Wounded Breakfast, The.
Jernigan, Marla. Put together how it will.
Kikaku. I begin each day.
Kinnell. Oatmeal.
Lowry, M. Eye-Opener.
Mayer, B. Incorporation of Sophia's Cereal,
  The.
Morabito, F. Piazza Gimma.
  Piazza Gimma.
Peacock, M. Breakfast with Cats.
Prévert. Breakfast.

Rankine. Man. His Bowl. His Raspberries, The.
Vallejo. Our Daily Bread.

Breast-Feeding
Factor, J. On Nursing.
Griffin, S. I Sit.
Jerningham, Edward. Latte, Il.

Breasts
Adcock, F. Soho Hospital for Women, The.
Addonizio. First Kiss: "Afterwards you had that
  drunk, drugged look."
Anton, S. Milky Way, The.
Bernstein, C. Caught.
Bible, *N.T.* Blessed be the Paps which Thou
  hast Sucked.
Brion, R. Love Song: "One long and humid
  afternoon."
Chao Luan-luan. Creamy Breasts.
Chernoff. Breasts.
Cistulli. 42.24.
Clifton, L. Lumpectomy Eve.
  1994.
Coleman, W. Breast Examination.
Copus, J. Breast.
Dunn, S. Routine Things Around the House,
  The.
Farish, H. Look at These.
Feld, Andrew. Intermission.
Fennelly. Latching On, Falling Off.
Griffin, S. I Sit.
Hacker, M. Cancer Winter.
Hahn, K. Shower, The.
Hass, R. Story about the Body, A.
Herman, G. Clinic, The.
Herrick. Fresh Cheese and Cream.
  How Roses Came Red ("Roses at first were
  white.").
  Upon Julia's Breasts.
  Upon the Nipples of Julia's Breast.
Hill, S. Small Hotel, A.
Kasischke. My Heart.
Majorino. Kisses.
Martinez, D. In a Duplex Near the San Andreas
  Fault.
McClatchy. My Mammogram.
Miller, E. Bringing Back the Draft.
  Rebecca.
Mistral, G. Like those jars that women put out
  to catch the dew of night.
Ozaki Hosai. Splendid breasts.
Péret. Wink.
Pratt, M. Poem for My Sons.
Prévert. River, The.
Rankine. Short Narrative of Breasts and Wombs
  in Service of Plot Entitled, A.
Ruefle. Perpetually Attempting to Soar.
Satyamurti. Out-Patients.
Schwartz, R. L. Possible.
Shuttle. Ultra Sound.
Simic. Breasts.
Smith, S. This Englishwoman.
Snyder, G. Breasts.
Spenser, E. Sonnet 76: "Fair bosom! fraught
  with virtue's richest treasure."
Stainer. This Atomising of Things.
Terranova. Self-Examination.
Torregian. After Mayakovsky.
Unknown. Between his hands.
  Do not crush me in your arms.
  Gently slide your hand inside my sleeves.
  You were hiding behind the door.
Waring, B. You Could Have Been Me.
Wilkinson, J. Funk Qualms.
Wrigley, R. Milkflowers.

Breath
Antler. One Breath.
Biespiel, D. Heat Sours, The.
Burkard. Foolish Thing.
Cox, M. Garglers, The.
Dickey, J. Basics.
Dupin. He Breathes before Writing.
Engle, P. Look! The air shudders when you
  breathe it in.
Freed, R. You Leave Me Breathless.
Garnett, R. Dealing Scraps.
Gehrke, S. Mouth to Mouth.
Gerner, K. House of Breath.

Gotlieb. Death's Head.
Harjo, J. Call It Fear.
Herrick. To Julia ("Julia, when thy Herrick dies.").
Holub. Vanishing Lung Syndrome.
Kenyon, J. In and Out.
Kikaku. Sacred night / Through masks.
Kinsella, J. Chess Piece Cornered.
Kinzie. But her arm—damp, small.
Lassaw-Paljor, Denise. Counting Breaths.
Levitt, Peter. It's easy to die.
Mahadevi. So long as this breath fills your nostrils.
Mays, M. #2, In Alabaster.
Nathan, L. Breathing Exercises.
Noguchi, R. Breath He Holds, The.
Price, V. Balancing Zero.
Reichard, W. Monster's Dream, The.
Rimbaud, A. Common Nocturne.
Triplett, P. Next to Last Prayer.
Unknown. As the thread of my breath.
Wagoner, D. Poem about Breath.

Brecht, Bertolt
Brecht, B. Of Poor B.B.
Mueller, L. Triage.
Müller, Heiner (1929-1995). Brecht.
Shafiq, H. Mirage.

Breughel, Pieter.
See **Brueghel, Pieter**

Bricks and Bricklayers
Bruce, W. Holland Brick, A.
Ginsberg, A. Bricklayer's Lunch Hour, The.
Griffiths, B. Fragment 13: "Maple."
Rybicki, J. For Daniel Beels, Third Generation Bricklayer.
This Sun.
Wylie. Sanctuary.

Brides
Akhmadulina. Bride, The.
Anyte [*or* Anytes]. Instead of bridal bed and holy wedding songs.
Bang, M. Constant Bride, The.
Bayly. We Met.
Cary, A. Bridal Veil, The.
Chŏng Hwajin. Water in a Gourd.
Cruz, S. Spiritual Canticle.
Spiritual Canticle, The.
D'Aquino, A. Boda, La.
Wedding, The.
Dubrava. Miraculous Marriage of Zarife Dominquez.
Dyer, C. My Dearest Dust: Epitaph on the Monument of Sir William Dyer at Colmworth, 1641.
Erinna. Girls / Brides / Tortoise.
I'm the tomb of Baukis, a bride; passing the deeply lamented.
Goldberg, B. My Husband's Bride.
Groarke, V. Trousseau.
Hemans. Bride of the Greek Isle, The.
Bride's Farewell, The.
Kaschnitz. Genazzano.
Levine, M. Wedding Day.
MacDiarmid, H. O wha' the bride that cairries the bunch.
McClanahan, R. Bridal Rites.
Meleager. Upon a Maid That Died [*or* Dyed] the Day She Was Married [*or* Marryed].
Mew. Farmer's Bride, The.
Poe. Bridal Ballad.
Praxilla. You who look lovely from the windows.
Rendra. Moon's Bed, the Bride's Bed, The.
Ríos, A. They Said I Was a Crying Bride.
Rosenberg, L. Big White Dress, The.
St. John, D. Portrait: "There is in his daughter's gaze."
Sappho. Bride: Virginity, virginity, where have you gone leaving me behind?
Scott, S. Lochinvar.
Smedley, M. Contrast, A.
Smith, S. I Remember.
Spenser, E. Epithalamion: "Ye learned sisters which have oftentimes."
Unknown. Angry Bride, The.
It Is the Third Watch.

Que-chao [Translations].
Tao-yao: Like the Slender Peach.
Valentine, J. Bride's Hours, A.
Veenendaal. On My Fourteenth Wedding Anniversary I Ride on Trains.
Vietnamese Oral Tradition. Homesick Bride, The.
Volkman. Sonnet: "Lifting whither, cycle of the sift."
Yi Sang. I Wed a Toy Bride.
See also **Weddings**

Bridges
Alegría. From the Bridge.
Alexander, M. River and Bridge.
Anderson, S. Song of the Soul of Chicago.
Armantrout. Getting Warm.
Basho. First snow.
Beranová, J. Williamsbridge.
Berkson, B. Bridge.
Buson. No bridge.
Carpenter, W. Ghosts.
Crane, H. To Brooklyn Bridge.
Dickey, J. At Darien Bridge.
Dickinson, E. How brittle are the Piers.
Dromgoole. Building the Bridge.
Gregerson. Waterborne.
Greville, F. Peace is the next in order, first in end.
Hammond, M. GWB in the Rain, The.
Hugo, R. Bridge, The.
Jiménez, J. To the bridge of love.
Keith, Sally. Mechanics.
Kikaku. Evening bridge / A thousand hands.
Kinnell. Under the Williamsburg Bridge.
Longfellow, H. Bridge, The.
Marcus, M. Picnic on the Bay Bridge.
McGonagall. Beautiful new railway bridge of the Silvery Tay.
Beautiful Railway Bridge of the Silvery Tay!
Railway Bridge of the Silvery Tay, The.
Tay Bridge Disaster, The.
McPherson, S. Suspension: Junior Wells on a Small Stage in a Converted Barn.
Mikhail, D. Jewel, The.
Minhinnick. Catching My Breath.
Mitcham. On the Otis Redding Bridge.
Mother Goose. London Bridge.
Muso Soseki. Bridge Where the Moon Crosses, The.
Norris, L. Bridges.
Ravenna Bridge.
Nortje. At Lansdowne Bridge.
Otomo no Sakanoé, L. Where the plovers cry.
Plumpp. Poem: "Poems are not places."
Red Hawk. 2 Ways of Crossing the Creek.
Reyes, C. Bridges: "My first bridge was a log— a slippery one across a muddy creek."
Reznikoff. Bridge, The.
On Brooklyn Bridge I saw a man drop dead.
Shapiro, D. For the Princess Hello.
Smith, W. Brooklyn Bridge.
Tabb. Bridge, The.
Teillier, J. Bridge in the South.
Tobin, D. Bridge View.
Tsvetayeva [*or* Tsvetaeva]. Last bridge I won't.
Vietnamese Oral Tradition. Leaving the Village.
Voznesensky [*or* Voznesenskii]. Mayakovsky in Paris.
Webb, H. Ode to the Severn Bridge.
Wordsworth, W. Composed upon Westminster Bridge, September 3, 1802.
Yusuf, S. Three Bridges.
Zolotow. Bridge, The.

Bridges, Robert
Hopkins, G. To R. B.

Brighton, England
Collins, M. Winter in Brighton.

Bristol, England
Lloyd, C. Written at the Hotwells, near Bristol.

British Columbia, Canada
Boden, C. Sombreo Beach, Vancouver Island, BC.
Stafford, W. British Columbia.

British Empire
Aytoun, W. Royal Banquet, The.

Sonnet to Britain.
Blake, W. Song of Liberty, A.
Cardenal. Mosquito Kingdom.
Chesterton. Geography.
Ellis, R.H. Walk up, walk up, my bonny boys.
Kipling, R. Arithmetic on the Frontier.
Ballad of East and West, The.
Boots.
Cholera Camp.
Christmas in India.
Gunga Din.
Mandalay.
New Knighthood, The.
Recessional.
Screw-Guns.
When first under fire an' you're wishful to duck.
Widow at Windsor, The.
Lee, D. 1838.
Logue, C. Song of the Dead Soldier, The.
Magee, W. British Garden, A.
Muldoon, P. Meeting the British.
Murphy, E. Thank you, Mr Rason, for the Apples.
Shenstone. Home Industries First: The Song of Colin, a Discerning Shepherd, Lamenting the State of the Woollen Manufactory.
Sheppard, R. Empty Diary 1944.
Sitwell, O. Shaking Hands with Murder.
Tate, N. Ode upon the New Year.
White, H. Britannia Rejecta.
Young, E. Who sings the source.

British Museum, London
Empson. Homage to the British Museum.
Guiney. In the Reading-Room of the Brtish Museum.
Levy, A. To Lallie.
MacNeice. British Museum Reading Room, The.

Brittany, France
James, J. Idyl: "Tiny fish."
Webster, A. Flood of Is in Brittany, The.

Broadway, New York City
Algarín. Broadway Opening.
Cohan. Down by the Erie Canal.
Forty-five Minutes from Broadway.
Give My Regards to Broadway.
Dubin, A. Lullaby of Broadway.
Elfyn, Menna. Broadway Morning.
Elmslie, K. Girl Machine.
Freed, A. Broadway Melody.
Freed, R. Babes on Broadway.
Gardinier. To Peace.
Jackson, B. Another Impostor.
Jiménez, J. Moon, The.
Masters, E. Flossie Cabanis.
Rich, A. Upper Broadway.
Whitman, W. Broadway.

Brodsky, Joseph
Strand. In Memory of Joseph Brodsky.

Brontë, Anne
Brontë, C. On the Death of Anne Brontë.
Carson, A. Kitchen.
Prismanova. Brontë Sisters, The.

Brontë, Charlotte
Carson, A. Kitchen.
Well there are many ways of being held prisoner.
Hayne, P. Charlotte Brontë.
Prismanova. Brontë Sisters, The.

Brontë, Emily
Brontë, C. On the Death of Emily Jane Brontë.
Carson, A. Kitchen.
Prismanova. Brontë Sisters, The.
Wright, J. Rosina Alcona to Julius Brenzaida.

Bronx, The, New York City
Di Prima. April Fool Birthday Poem for Grandpa.
Donaghy, M. Repertoire, A.
Drake, J. Bronx.
Esteves. For South Bronx.
South Bronx Testimonial.
Figueroa, J. Boricua.
Foerster. Bronx Park.
Ginsberg, A. Your last night in the darkness of the Bronx—I phonecalled—thru hospital to

secret police.
Henderson-Holmes.　My First Riot: Bronx, NYC.
Morales.　Getting Out Alive.

Brooke, Rupert
Gibson, W.　Golden Room, The.

Brooklyn Bridge
Al-Rihani.　It Was All for Him.
Crane, H.　Bridge, The.
　To Brooklyn Bridge.
Denby.　New York Face, A.
García Lorca.　City That Does Not Sleep.
Hernández Cruz.　Side 4.
Oppen.　Great stone, The / Above the river.
Reznikoff.　On Brooklyn Bridge I saw a man drop dead.
Rohrer, M.　Brooklyn Bridge.
Shapiro, H.　National Cold Storage Company.
Smith, W.　Brooklyn Bridge.

Brooklyn, New York City
Berrigan, T.　It's 8:54 a.m. in Brooklyn it's the 28th [or 26th] of July [and].
Blackburn, P.　Brooklyn Narcissus.
Di Prima.　Backyard.
Espada.　Moon Shatters on Alabama Avenue, The.
　Owl and the Lightning, The.
Freeman, Jessica.　November 1st.
Jarnot, L.　Brooklyn Anchorage.
Liu, T.　Brooklyn Botanic Garden, The.
Loftin, E.　Bkln.
Meitner, E.　Job: "My mother sold life insurance."
Pearlberg, G.G.　Loop-the-Loop in Prospect Park (1905).
Shapiro, H.　National Cold Storage Company.
Shomer.　Letter Home from Brooklyn.
Waters, M.　Horse: "First horse I ever saw, The."
Weaver, A.　Brooklyn.
Whitman, W.　Crossing Brooklyn Ferry.

Brooks and Streams
Arnold, M.　Below the Surface-Stream.
Baxter, J.　Buried Stream, The.
Burn.　Welsh Love Letter.
Buson.　May rains.
Castro, R.　Spring Does Not Flow Now, The.
Chien Chang.　Given to Master Ch'ing-lun of Hsia Mountain.
Chiun.　Nameless / Weed quickening.
Chou Pang-yen.　Peach Blossom Stream.
Ch'u Ch'uang I.　Mountain Spring, A.
Clough.　Highland Glen near Loch Ericht, A.
Frost, R.　Hyla Brook.
　West-Running Brook.
Hopkins, G.　Inversnaid.
　Winter with the Gulf Stream.
Hwang Chini.　Blue mountains speak of my desire.
　Do not boast of your speed.
　Mountains are steadfast.
Ibn Hamdîs, A.　I remember a certain brook that offered the impiety of drunkenness to the topers [sitting] along its course, with [its] cups of golden [wine].
Janzen, J.　At Summer's End.
Lee, L.　Interrogation, The.
Muso Soseki.　Clear Valley.
　Gem Creek.
　Old Creek.
　Snow Valley.
Roethke.　Lady and the Bear, The.
Seward.　Scene of superfluous grace, and wasted bloom.
Sonnet: "Stranger, when o'er yon slant, warm field no cloud."
Smollett.　To Leven Water.
Southey, R.　To a Brook Near the Village of Corston.
Spratt.　On His Mistress Drown'd [or Drowned].
Thoreau.　Salmon Brook.
Twichell.　Paper River, The.
Unknown.　Zhu-gan: This Rod.
Various authors.　Tree, whose roots are deep, The.
Vietnamese Oral Tradition.　Painting, The.

Wagoner, D.　Source, The.
Wang Pin-chih.　Orchard Pavilion.
Wang Wei.　Bird-Singing Stream.
Wilbur, R.　Hamlen Brook.
Wordsworth, W.　Old Man by the Brook, The.
Yi I.　Nine Songs of Mount Ko.
Yi Yŏng.　Who sliced the crescent moon so small.
See also **Rivers**

Brooks, Gwendolyn
Kendrick, D.　For Gwendolyn Brooks: As I Civilize a Space.
Madhubuti.　Gwendolyn Brooks.
Sanchez, S.　For Sister Gwen Brooks.
Walton, A.　Gwendolyn Brooks.

Brooms
Buson.　Short night, The.
Digges.　Broom.
Johnston, G.　Cathleen Sweeping.
Lear, E.　Limerick: "There was an old Lady of Winchelsea."
Na Hûidôk.　Five A.M.
Pitcher, O.　Tango.

Brotherhood
Baraka, I.　Return of the Native.
Blake, W.　Divine Image, The.
　Little Black Boy, The.
Burns, R.　For A' That and A' That ["Is there, for honest poverty"].
Campos Cervera, H.　Sent.
Ceravolo.　Wild Provoke of the Endurance Sky.
Clifton, L.　Listen Children.
Cornish, S.　We Have Never Loved.
Cronin, J.　Motho Ke Motho Ka Batho Babang (A Person Is a Person Because of Other People).
Dame.　Seder, The.
Dodson, O.　Open Letter.
Encarnacion.　Bulosan Listens to a Recording of Robert Johson.
Frost, R.　Tuft of Flowers, The.
Hogan, L.　New Apartment.
Hopkins, G.　Epithalamion: "Hark, hearer, hear what I do; lend a thought now, make believe."
Hughes, L.　I Dream a World.
　Projection.
Hunt, L.　Abou Ben Adhem.
Jensma.　Ring da till.
Jones, I.　Haiku for My Brothers.
Keller, B.　One Million Men Marching 2.
Kinsella, T.　Brotherhood.
Kipling, R.　Ballad of East and West, The.
Lindsay, J.　It Has Happened.
Lum.　Chinese Hot Pot.
MacDiarmid, H.　Farewell to Dostoevski.
Machado Ruiz.　You say nothing is created new?
Moore, M.　In Distrust of Merits.
Muir, E.　Brothers, The.
Plumpp.　Daybreak.
Ransom, J.　Armageddon.
Rolfe, E.　First Love.
Rukeyser, M.　Hostages, The.
Saint.　Heart and Soul.
Sandburg, C.　Long Shadow of Lincoln: A Litany, The.
Shelley, P.　Over the utmost hill at length I sped.
Symonds.　Love and Death: A Symphony.
　Thou dost establish—and our hearts receive—.
Unknown.　Fraternitas.
Whitman, W.　Full of Life Now.
　I believe in you my soul, the other I am must not abase itself to you.
　I Dream'd in a Dream.
　I Hear It Was Charged against Me.
　To Him That Was Crucified.
　To the East and to the West.
Wylie.　Pebble, The.

Brothers
Ai.　Blue Suede Shoes.
Aldis, D.　Little.
Alegría.　Have Pity.
Amadiume.　Be Brothers.
Anderson, A.　Licking Wounds.
Bangaramma, C.　My Brother.
Bly, R.　Things My Brother and I Could Do.

Bödvarsson, G.　Brother.
Bryan, M.　To My Brother ("O, thou art far away from me—dear boy!").
　To My Brother ("Oh transient sorrows, light as morning dews.").
　To My Brother ("Once in our customed walk a wounded bird.").
Burkard.　Weather.
Carroll, L.　Brother and Sister.
Catullus.　By strangers' coasts and waters, many days at sea.
Ch'i-chi.　Autumn Evening: To Send to my Nieces and Nephews.
Chipasula.　My Blood Brother.
Craig, David.　Brother we are like weeds growing.
Creeley.　World, The.
Dalton, Mary.　My One Brother.
de Vries, H.　My Brother.
Enzensberger, H.　Hôtel Fraternité.
Forbes, C.　Hand Me Down Blues.
Geiger.　Soundtracks.
Goedicke.　My Brother's Anger.
Gonzáles Martínez.　Like Sister and Brother.
Gunn, T.　Cannibal.
Harper, M.　Drowning of the Facts of a Life, The.
Heaney, S.　Mid-Term Break.
Hemans.　To My Eldest Brother, With the British Army in Portugal.
Herrick.　To His Dying Brother, Master William Herrick.
Hicok.　Heroin.
Im Hwa.　My Brother and the Brazier.
Kapovich, K.　Green One over There, The.
Kinnell.　Another Night in the Ruins.
Kizer, C.　Amusing Our Daughters.
Lake, P.　In Rough Weather.
Lamb, C.　If From My Lips Some Angry Accents Fell.
Lassell.　How to Watch Your Brother Die.
Lee, L.　This Hour and What Is Dead.
Lersch, H.　Brothers.
Levine, P.　You Can Have It.
MacDonald, Hugh.　Shingle Flies.
MacKay, R.　Rispond Miser, The.
Mapanje.　Making Our Clowns Martyrs.
Mattawa.　Letter to Ibrahim.
Max, L.　When the Tules Are Peppered with Red-winged Blackbirds.
Melville, H.　Timoleon.
Motsapi, S.　Brotha saul.
Muir, E.　Brothers, The.
Naimy, M.　My Brother.
Norton, C.　Recollections: "Do you remember all the sunny places."
Nutter, G.　Pond and Peace.
Nye, N.　Little Brother Poem, The.
Orr, G.　Gathering the Bones Together.
Redmond, J.　Charlie and Joe.
Robinson, A.　Scape-Goat, The.
Robinson, E.　Prodigal Son, The.
Ross, A.　Two in Bed.
Rybicki, J.　Brother Ben.
Samaras, N.　After the Children Have Gone to Bed.
Sanchez, S.　To P. J. (2 Yrs Old Who Sed Write a Poem for Me in Portland, Oregon).
Sappho.　Kypris and Nereids, let that brother.
Scamell, B.　My Lost Brother.
Scarbrough, G.　Letter to Spencer.
Serge.　Constellation of Dead Brothers.
Shapiro, K.　Two-Year-Old Has Had a Motherless Week, The.
"Shu Ting.".　Brother, I Am Here.
Skloot.　Everly Brothers, The.
　Year the Space Age Was Born, The.
Soto.　Not Knowing.
Stafford, W.　At the Grave of My Brother: Bomber Pilot.
Su Tung-p'o.　Tune: "Water Mode Song".
Thompson, C.　To My Dead Brother.
Thoreau.　Brother where dost thou dwell?
Tu Fu [or Du Fu].　All day, all night, I worry.
　I have brothers, younger brothers in a place far away.

Poem for My Brother Returning to My Farm.
They Say You're Staying in a Mountain Temple.
To My Younger Brother.
Turner, F. On the Pains of Translating Miklós
  Radnóti.
Unknown. King and Hermit.
Last Words of the Prophet.
Vallejo. To My Brother Miguel.
Van Doren. My Brother Lives Too Far Away.
Van Duyn. Twins, The.
Various authors. Brothers rebelled against one
  another, The.
Vaughan, H. Silence and Stealth of Day[e]s!
Walker, F. X. Crooked Afro.
Wang Shih-chieng. After Snow, Longing for
  Elder Brother Hsi-ch'iao.
Ward, D. My Brothers Make a Lantern.
Wordsworth, W. Tradition of Oker Hill in
  Darley Dale, Derbyshire, A.
Yosano Akiko. Beloved, You Must Not Die.

Brown (color)
Grimké, A. At April.
Partridge, E. Vuillard Interior.
Stein, G. Brown, A.

Brown, John
Atkins, R. Narrative.
Benét, S. John Brown's body lies a-mouldering
  in the grave.
Brownell, H. John Brown's Body.
Costello, R. Battle hymn.
Lindsay, V. John Brown.
Melville, H. Portent, The.
Rukeyser, M. Soul and Body of John Brown,
  The.
Whittier. Brown of Ossawatomie.

Browning, Elizabeth Barrett
Blagden. To George Sand on her Interview with
  Elizabeth Barrett Browning.
Browning, R. Lost Mistress, The.
Dickinson, E. Her—"last Poems".
Greenwell, D. To Elizabeth Barrett Browning,
  in 1851.
To Elizabeth Barrett Browning, in 1861.
Lowell, A. Sisters, The.
Parkes, B. To Elizabeth Barrett Browning.
Shapcott, J. Elizabeth Looks at Robert.
Robert Watches Elizabeth Knitting.

Browning, Robert
Chesterton. From a Spanish Cloister.
Landor, W. To Robert Browning.
Shapcott, J. Elizabeth Looks at Robert.
Robert Watches Elizabeth Knitting.

Brueghel, Pieter
Auden. Musée des Beaux Arts.
Berryman. Winter Landscape.
Dubie. February: The Boy Breughel.
Kopland. Breughel's Winter.
Simpson, A. Seven Paintings By Brueghel.
Teschke, H. Massacre of the Innocents, The
  (after Brueghel).
Williams, W. Dance, The: "In Brueghel's great
  picture, The Kermess."
Dance, The ("When the snow falls the flakes.").
Parable of the Blind, The.

Brutus (Marcus Junius Brutus)
Cowley, A. Brutus.
Whitehead, C. Brutus' Last Song.

Bubbles
Bacon, F. Life of Man, The.
Crashaw. Bubble, The.
Drummond, W. Madrigal: "This life, which
  seems so fair."
Greenberg, S. Glass Bubbles, The.

Buber, Martin
Harris, M. Martin Buber in the Pub.

Buccaneers
Prys-Jones. Henry Morgan's March on Panama.

Buckets
Ward, B. Twenty Million Buckets.

Buckingham, George Villiers, 2d Duke of
Felltham [*or* Feltham]. On the Duke of
  Buckingham, Slain by Felton, the 23rd August,
  1628.
Unknown. Epitaph: "Fortune's darling, king's
  content."

Epitaph on the Duke of Buckingham.
Upon the Duke of Buckingham.

Budapest, Hungary
Jamie, K. Flower-sellers, Budapest.

Buddha and Buddhism
Adams, H. Buddha and Brahma.
Alexander, W. Let us recall the illusion.
Anbun. Years keeping that in mind.
Andrews, N. Crossing.
Nirvana: "After you left me, I was so lonely and
  sad, I became but an apparition, a ghost of
  who I had been."
Zen 101.
Baiho. On Entering His Coffin.
Basho. Behind Ise Shrine.
Buddha's death-day / Old hands.
Dried salmon.
On Buddha's birthday.
On Buddha's deathday.
Temple bell / A cloud of cherry flowers.
To the willow.
Year's end / Still in straw hat.
Berrigan, D. Assembled sirs. The courtesies
  afforded us by the Dali Lama.
Betsugen. All night long I think of life's
  labyrinth.
Bokuo. For seventy-two years / I've kept the ox
  well under.
Boryu. Cloud above lotus / It too.
Brehm, J. When My Car Broke Down.
Breytenbach. Padmapani.
Bun-Etsu. Sixty-five years.
Bunan. Moon's the same old moon, The.
When you're both alive and dead.
Buson. At a roadside shrine.
Flowers offered to the Buddha.
Priestly poverty—.
Ten holy nights / Even tea.
This cold winter night.
Casey, M. On What the Army Does with
  Heads.
Chajang. Hymn to Sarira.
Chalfi, R. Reading the I Ching.
Champ, Amy. Buddha is neither asian nor male.
  she could be an african woman.
Ch'ang Chien. Buddhist Retreat Behind
  Broken-Mountain Temple, A.
Chifu. No mind, no Buddhas, no live beings.
Chikusen. He's part of all, yet all's transcended.
Chinese Oral Tradition. Transformation Text on
  Mahāmaudgalyāyana Rescuing His Mother
  from the Underworld.
Ching An. Laughing at Myself 2.
Chitsu. No more head shaving.
Cho Chihun. Ancient Temple.
Chungji. Instructing Fellow Buddhists after
  Picking Brackens.
Collins, B. Shoveling Snow with Buddha.
Daegak Euchon. Retreat at Haein Temple.
Daichi. Thoughts arise endlessly.
Daichu. Fiery unicorn snapped, The.
Daie-Soko. Life's as we / Find it—death too.
Daigu. Here none think of wealth or fame.
Who dares approach the lion's.
Daisen. All things come apart.
Daito. At last I've broken Unmon's barrier!
To slice through Buddhas, Patriarchs.
Dangai. Earth, river, mountain.
Dankyo-Myorin. Coming, I clench my hands.
Dey, Atanu. Buddha and I, The.
Dhompa, T. How Thubten Sang His Songs.
Di Prima. Death Sunyata Chant: A Rite for
  Passing Over.
I Fail as a Dharma Teacher.
Summer Retreat: Pema Osel Ling.
Three "Dharma Poems".
Dogen. Coming, going, the waterfowl.
Western Patriarch's doctrine is transplanted!,
  The.
Duncan, R. For the Assignment of the Spirit.
Eian. Joshu's "Oak in the courtyard".
Eichu. My eyes eavesdrop on their lashes!
Emperor Kōkō. Word at last, The.
Ferguson, G. Bhakti Yogi Buys a Bike, The.
Ferlinghetti, L. Buddha in the Woodpile, A.
Fields, R. Very Short Sutra on the Meeting of

the Buddha and the Goddess, The.
Forrester, S. Meditation hall.
Melting into pure water the snow buddha.
Monk's bowl.
Morning light.
Temple ruin.
Fugai. Only the Zen-man knows tranquillity.
Fumon. Magnificent! Magnificent!
Fuyo-Dokai. Seventy-six: done.
Gasan. Invaluable is the Soto Way.
Gekko-Sojo. How Zenists carry on.
Gekkutsu-Sei. I set down the emerald lamp.
Genko. Unaware of illusion or enlightenment.
Gertler, P. Standing with Chiyo-Ni.
Gesshu Soko. Seven seas sucked up together,
  The.
Getsudo. I moved across the Dharma-nature.
Gibson, M. Strange Altars.
Gido. Inscription over His Door.
Gilgun, J. Buddha Is Lord of Our Town.
 Lights Out.
 Zen Frost.
 Zen Sky.
Ginsberg, A. Reflections at Lake Louise.
Gojusan. Seamless.
Guchu. Men without rank, excrement spatulas.
Guest, B. Walking Buddha.
Guevara, M. Buddy Holly Poem, The.
Haavikko. Don't smile. So you won't become a
  Buddha.
Hakugai. Last year in a lovely temple in
  Hirosawa.
Hakuin. How lacking in permanence the minds
  of the sentient.
Past, present, future: unattainable.
Priceless is one's incantation.
You no sooner attain the great void.
Hakuyo. Over the peak spreading clouds.
Hamill, S. Ten Thousand Sutras.
Han-shan. Ever since I left home.
Whoever reads my poems.
Han Yü. Girl of Mount Hua, The.
Han-shan Te-ch'ing. Through a few splinters of.
Hirshfield, J. Studying Wu Wei, Muir Beach.
Hoge. How long the tree's been barren.
Hoin. On the rocky slope, blossoming.
Hoitsu. Buddha / Cherry flowers.
Homyo. Wino, always stumbling.
Hsieh Ling-yün. On My Way from South
  Mountain to North Mountain, I Glance at the
  Scenery from the Lake.
Hsüeh T'ao [*or* Xue Tao]. Listening to a Monk
  Play the Reed Pipes.
Hueung Powoo. Taking Pleasure in Myself.
Ichigen. Joshu exclaimed, "Dog's no Buddha".
Seventy-eight awkward years.
Ikkyu Sojun. Form in Void.
Void in Form.
Ikuo-Joun. This fellow, perfect in men's eyes.
Ikuo-Myotan. Seventy-two years I've hung.
Issa. All the time I pray to Buddha.
Buddha Law / Shining.
Buddha's Nirvana / Beyond flowers.
Come what may.
Farmer / Pointing the way.
From the end of the nose.
From the Great Buddha's.
Here in Shinano.
Night is so long, The.
Not yet become a Buddha.
Under the image of Buddha.
Where there are humans / you'll find flies.
Winter lull / No talents.
Zealous flea.
Izumi. In the Autumn, on Retreat at a Mountain
  Temple.
Jaewol Kyunghun. To a Fellow Monk.
Jakushitsu. Refreshing, the wind against the
  waterfall.
Jien. Too Much to Ask.
Jinkag Haesim. Fan.
On Arriving at Oeo Temple.
Sitting and Teaching at Night.
Jinzu. In serving, serve.
Juo. Beyond the snatch of time, my daily life.
Kaigen. Old master held up fluff, The.

Kando. It's as if our heads were on fire, the way.

Kanemitsu-Kogun. My hands released at last, the cliff soars.

Kanzan-Shigyo. Where is the dragon's cave?

Karasumaru-Mitsuhiro. Beware of gnawing the ideogram of nothingness.

Katagiri, Dainin. Peaceful Life.

Kaufman, S. Buddha of Sŏkkuram, The.

Keppo. Searching Him took.

Kikaku. O Great Buddha.

On Buddha's birthday.

Kiko. Mount Sumeru—my fist!

Kim Sŭnghŭi. Female Buddha.

Kishu. Once the goal's reached.

Ko Un. Annihilation.

Asking the Way.

Kodo. Serving the Shogun in the capital.

Koeppel, M. While the Wolf Walks the Edge of the Woods.

Kokai. Taking hold, one's astray in nothingness.

Komunyakaa, Y. 2527th Birthday of the Buddha.

Korean Oral Tradition. Abandoned Princess, The.

Song of Entertaining the Holy One.

Kosen. Blind horse trotting up an icy ledge, A.

Kuchu. Joshu's word—Nothingness.

Kuhar, M. On the death of philip whalen.

On the galloping cusp of the new now.

Suburban buddha, coffeehouse christ.

You can't blow up the buddha.

Kukoku. Riding backwards this wooden horse.

Kwangdŏk. Prayer to Amitāyus.

Kyger. Dream: "I'm doing this poetry reading with Simone."

Kyunyŏ, Great Master. Eleven Poems on the Ten Vows of the Universally Worthy Bodhisattva.

Kyurin-Eki. Eighty-three years—at last.

Lanier, S. Nirvâna.

Leighton, Taigen Dan. All of Us So Close to Buddha.

Li Po. In Praise of a Gold and Silver Painted Scene of the Buddha Manifestation in the Pure Land of the West, with a Preface.

Lieberman, L. God's Measurements.

Lindsay, V. Buddha.

Liu Tsung-yüan. Reading Buddhist Classics with Chao at His Temple in the Early Morning.

Lloyd, C. Gate Gate Paragate Parasmgate Bodhi Svaha.

Lojowski, M. Big Fort Island Buddha.

In the Cage of Doves.

Makusho, Layman. Loving old priceless things.

Manan. Unfettered at last, a traveling monk.

Manzan. One minute of sitting, one inch of Buddha.

Masaoka Shiki. Autumn wind / Gods, Buddha.

Buddha too.

McNiece, R. Kerouac, we knock.

Letter Left On the Porch of the Kerouac House.

McNulty, T. Bodhidharma Crossing the Graywolf River on a Ry-Krisp.

Meyerhoff, J. Resounding echo of the buddha's words, The.

Miller, E. Morning Buddhism.

Mo Shih-lung. To the Monk Wu-hsia on the Occasion of His Editing the Lotus Sutra.

Moan. Clear, clear—clearest!

Mokusen. On Climbing the Mountain Where Buddha Trained.

Monju-Shindo. Joshu's "Oak in the courtyard".

Mueller, John. Rubber Eraser.

Mullen, H. Kamasutra Sutra.

Mumon Gensen. Life: a cloud crossing the peak.

Munom-Ekai. Thunderbolt—eyes wide, A.

Muso Soseki. Among rocks and valleys.

Ancient Origin.

At the Nachi Kannon Hall.

Bamboo Garden.

Buddha's Satori.

Cave of the Thousand Pines.

Clear Valley.

Curtain of cloud hangs, A.

Digging Out the Buddha Relic.

East of the strait.

For a Monk Going West.

For Myo's Departure for Shofuku-ji.

For Sho the New Head Priest of Erin-ji.

For Taihei Osho.

For Tetsu the New Head Priest of Erin-ji.

For the Death of a Monk.

Fragrance of the Udumbara, The.

Free Old Man.

Garden at the General's Residence, The.

Gate of Universal Light, The.

Green mountains.

Hall of the Guardian God.

Hui-neng's Pond.

I wake from my noon nap.

I'm not so deep in it.

In this small hut.

Inauguration of Fukusan Dormitory.

Incomparable-Verse Valley.

Lamenting the Civil War.

Many times the mountains have turned from green to yellow.

Moon Tree Cliff.

Mugoku Osho's Snow Poem.

No Precedent.

Old Man of Few Words.

Old Man To-The-Point.

One Hut.

Peak of the Held-Up Flower, The.

People's abuse.

Plum Window.

Reply to Bukko Zenji's Poem at Seiken-ji.

Snow at Rohatsu Sesshin.

Snow Garden.

Snow Valley.

Spring Cliff.

Suzan Osho's Visit.

Suzan Oshos's Visit to My West Mountain Hut.

Temple of Eternal Light.

Three-Step Waterfall.

Toki-no-Ge (Satori Poem).

Truth Hall.

Turtle Head Stupa.

Vainly I dug for a perfect sky.

With compassionate hands.

Myoyu. Defying the power of speech, the Law Commission on Mount Vulture!

Nan-o-myo. Not falling, not ignoring.

Nanei. Splitting the void in half.

Nantembo. On New Year's Day.

Naong. Song of the Pure Land.

Nensho. Only genuine awakening results in that.

O'Connor, M. On the Road to Denver in a Coat and Tie, I Think of My Old Friend Master Red Pine and the Example He Inspires.

Soliloquy of the Danish Cloister.

Pai, S. Milkstone.

Paljor, N. Way, The.

Wish of my Amala, The.

Pendell, D. Amra: The Neuropharmacology of Nirvana.

Pinsky. Hearts, The.

Piper, P. Morning Star, The.

Po Chü-i. Flower No Flower.

Idle Song.

Rakan-Keinan. Today Rakan, riding an iron horse.

Ray, N. Last Flower, The.

Reed, I. Going East.

Reito. Ox bridle tossed, vows taken.

Reizan. Myriad differences resolved by sitting, all doors opened, The.

Reps, Paul. Open here.

Rexroth, K. Buddha took some Autumn leaves.

Empty Mirror.

It Is a German Honeymoon.

Rilke. Buddha Inside the Light.

Ronci, Seido R. Becoming a Buddha.

Old Monks Drinking.

Ryokan. In my begging bowl.

Without a jot of ambition left.

Ryushu Shutaku. For all these years, my certain Zen.

Mind set free in the Dharma-realm.

Why bother with the world?

Ryuzan. Clear in the blue, the moon!

Sagan. South Ridge Zendo.

Saijo, A. Bodhisattva Vows.

St. John, D. Saffron.

Saisho. On Joshu's Nothingness.

Sansom, A. Cross Country.

Schelling. Perfection of Wisdom Suite, A: Hymns for the Perfection of Wisdom in Paradise.

Seigen-yuiin. How vast karma.

Seiho. Sky's not high, earth not solid.

Seiken-Chiju. Twenty years a pilgrim.

Sekioku-Seikyo. This body won't pollute.

Sekishitsu-Soei. Fifty-three years / This clumsy ox has managed.

Senryū, K. Judging by the pictures.

Shaku Chōkū. Tanka: "Somewhere around."

Shinkichi Takahashi. Spinning Dharma Wheel.

Vimalakirti.

Shofu. No dust speck anywhere.

Shoichi. All-meaning circle, The.

Shozan. No mind, no Buddha.

Shunoku. After the spring song, "Vast emptiness, no holiness,".

Sikong Tu. Twenty-Four Modes of Poetry.

Skrzynecki. Buddha, Birdbath, Hanging Plant.

Snyder, G. Avocado.

Circumambulating Arunachala.

Soan. Sailing on Men River, I heard.

Sodo. Question clear, the answer deep, The.

Soen. Calm, activity—each has its use. At times.

Master Joshu and the dog.

On Visiting Shorin Temple, Where Bodhidharma Once Lived.

Sogetsuni. Divine mystery.

Sokan. Cold, yes / But don't test.

Sotoba, Layman. Mountain—Buddha's body, The.

Soyo Taeneung. Man of No Attachments.

Sozan-Kyonin. Rootless tree, A.

Su, A. I Can't Become a Buddhist.

Suian. Traceless, no more need to hide.

Suzuki, M. Soft rain.

Takuan. Though night after night.

Tan Taigi. Fallen leaves / Raking.

Swellfish eaten / He chants nembutsu.

Tanahashi, Kazuaki. Six Characters from the Heart Sutra.

Tanzan. Madness, the way they gallop off to foreign shores!

Tekkan. No mind, no Buddha, no being.

Tendo-Nyojo. Sixty-six years.

Tessho. Finally out of reach.

Tesshu. How heal the phantom body of its phantom ill.

On Visiting Sokei, Where the Sixth Patriarch Lived.

Tokuo. Town's aflame with summer heat, The.

Tosui Unkei. Content with chipped bowl and tattered robe.

Tozan-Gyoso. Way's not for the blind.

Tsugen Jakurei. Not a mote in the light above.

Twichell. Rain in Ivy.

Uncho. Forty-nine years / —What a din!

Ungo Kiyo. Whirled by the three passions, one's eyes go blind.

Unknown. Blind man carried, A.

Buddhist Ruminations.

Chanting Buddha's name.

Chapter 3: Parable.

Gathas.

Ode to Yangji.

Queen wept but thought: It is not appropriate to show such grief, The.

Story of How the Monk Tripiṭaka of the Great Country of T'ang Brought back the Sūtras, The.

Take apart your cassock and make a coat.

Wakuan-Shitai. Iron tree blooms.

Waldman, A. Recalling Former Travels.

Wang Wei. At the Hermitage of Master Fu.

Meal for the Monks, A.

Sitting Alone on an Autumn Night.

Webb, C. Identifying with the Buddha.

Whalen, P.   Actions of Buddha.
Dharmakaya.
Walking beside the Kamogawa, Remembering Nansen and Fudo and Gary's Poem.
White, J.   Oshi.
Will, C.   Satori in Fauldhouse.
Wŏlmyŏng.   Song of Tuṣita Heaven.
Wonhyo, Great Master.   Enlightenment Song.
Pledge.
Wright, C.   Disjecta Membra.
Wu Wei-yeh.   Broken Lampstand, The.
Xuanjue.   One Moon Seen, The.
Yakusai, Layman.   Deafening peal, A.
Yauch, Adam.   Bodhisattva Vow.
Yoketsu.   Nothing longed for.
Yüan Mei.   Motto.
Yuishun.   Why, it's but the motion of eyes and brows!
Zekkai Chushin.   Void has collapsed upon the earth, The.
Zuian.   Sky-piercing sword, gleaming cold.
See also **Zen Buddhism**
Buds and Blossoms
Baqi.   If only the bud would open like the beloved's ruby lips.
Ch'i-chi.   Early Plum Blossoms.
Darwish, M.   I am the witness of the massacre.
Kinnell.   Flower of Five Blossoms.
Lee, L.   From Blossoms.
My Indigo.
Li Ch'ing-chao.   Fading Plum Blossoms.
To the Tune "Clear Peace Happiness".
McClure, M.   For Diane di Prima.
For Jack Kerouac.
Sanger, Peter.   Crabapple Blossoms.
Schevill.   Love Song in Summer's Furnace Heat.
Sobin, G.   Fourteen Irises for J. L.
Sze.   Earthstar.
Yomono Akara.   In Yoshiwara.
Buenos Aires, Argentina
Phillips, E.   Ties.
"Buffalo Bill" (William Frederick Cody)
Cummings, E. E.   Buffalo Bill's Lament.
Buffaloes
Andal.   O sister of wealth.
Arapaho Oral Tradition.   Spirit Host Is Advancing, They Say, The.
Belloc.   Bison, The.
Dobyns.   Nouns of Assemblage.
Edelman, B.   Buffalo Dreams.
Eiseley.   Prairie Spring.
Heyen.   Words: "Wind in the fur of living buffalo dead."
Hobson, G.   Buffalo Poem #1.
Hume, C.   Dirty Money.
Lindsay, V.   Flower-fed Buffaloes, The.
Ghosts of the Buffaloes, The.
McDonald, W.   In Fields of Buffalo.
Nance.   Old Fort Griffin.
Salisbury.   After Heart-Bypass Surgery, Another Ritual for Continuing Struggle.
Sandburg, C.   Buffalo Dusk.
Sioux Oral Tradition.   Give Me Back My Bow. Whole world is coming, The.
Swenson, M.   Bison Crossing Near Mt. Rushmore.
Unknown.   Buffalo are coming. We will feed and feast. We wish to be fortunate and we expect it, The.
Song of the Promise of the Buffalo.
Bugles and Buglers
Day, J.   Picket before Bull Run, The.
Fallon, P.   Bit of Brass, A.
LeFlore, S. B.   Rayboy Blk & Bluz.
Merwin.   Second Psalm: The Signals.
Prince, N.   Boogie Woogie Bugle Boy.
Raye, D.   Boogie Woogie Bugle Boy.
Tennyson, A.   Splendour [*or* Splendor] Falls, The.
Whitman, W.   Beat! Beat! Drums!
Buildings and Builders
Bernes, J.   Sonnet with Lock and Key.
Bertrand.   Mason, The.
Mason, The.
Boruch.   Hammer Falls, Is Falling, The.

Brooks, G.   Building.
Browning, R.   Apparent Failure.
Ch'en Lin.   Horses at a Breach in the Great Wall.
Ch'ien T'ao.   Written While Drunk.
Ch'ôn Yanghûi.   One Day.
Creeley.   Invitation, The.
Crowe, T.   Saw-Mill Shack, The.
Damacion, K.   Canciones.
Dugan, A.   Love Song: I and Thou.
Dunn, S.   Stairway, The.
Eguren.   Towers, The.
Esteves.   Ahora.
Graves, R.   Fallen Tower of Siloam, The.
Hacker, M.   Squares and Courtyards.
Harbach, O.   Love Nest, The.
Hartnett.   Visit to Castletown House, A.
Heaney, S.   Roof it again. Batten down. Dig in. Scaffolding.
Herlin.   Morning space.
Hernández Cruz.   Man Who Came to the Last Floor, The.
Huerta, D.   Cancellation of a Construction Project.
Suspensión de una obra.
Hulme, T.   Image.
Ignatova, E.   I have encountered a valley, in ragged bast matting.
Jonson, B.   To Penshurst.
Jungkwan Haean.   Ridiculing the Monk Who Builds a Stupa.
Kelly, R.   Bittersweet Growing Up the Red Wall.
Komunyakaa, Y.   Instructions for Building Straw Huts.
Lampadius.   As a symbol.
Larkin, J.   Housework.
Lear, E.   There Was an Old Man With a Beard.
Macdonald, G.   Song.
Machado Ruiz.   Plaza Has a Tower, The.
MacLeish.   Burying Ground by the Ties.
Marvell.   Upon Appleton House [To My Lord Fairfax].
Minton, Helena.   Building the Compost.
Moore, H.   Window at Key West, A.
Mother Goose.   House That Jack Built, The.
Murphy, R.   Roof-Tree.
Murray, L.   Flight from Manhattan, The.
Musa, Y.   Zinc.
Oden.   Review from Staten Island.
Ormond.   Cathedral Builders.
O'Shaughnessy, A.   Ode: "We are the music-makers."
Pietri.   7th Untitled Poem.
Pope, A.   Epistle to Lord Burlington.
Price, G.   Belizeans: Unite to Build our Nation.
Rafferty, C.   Man on the Tower, The.
Scovell.   Workers in Metal.
Sidney.   Sonnet 9: "Queen Virtue's court, which some call Stella's face."
Skeeter.   Midwest, Midcentury.
Snyder, G.   Building.
Song Sun.   I have spent ten years.
Staff.   Foundations.
Foundations.
Starck, Clemens.   Job No. 75-14.
Stein, K.   It Didn't Begin with Horned Owls Hooting at Noon.
Stevenson, R.   Block City.
Stryk, L.   Oeuvre.
Sweeney, M.   To the Building Trade.
Sze.   Ice Floe.
Tomlinson, C.   Crane, The.
Tranströmer.   Outskirts.
Tu Fu [*or* Du Fu].   Jade Flower Palace ("Stream swirls, The. The wind moans in.").
Unknown.   By curvèd bank.
Fort of Rathangan, The.
Mian: The House of Zhou.
Stanza: "What, my Lord, shall I do with."
Wang Chih-huan.   Ascend the Heron Tower.
Watts, I.   How Doth the Little Busy Bee.
Wei Ying-wu.   East of the Town.
Williams, C. K.   Sanctity, The.
Yahya Efendi, Sheyhülislâm.   Saki, offer the cup, let them call me a drunkard.

Bulgaria
Ilkov, Ani.   Of Stone.
Ivanov, Binyo.   Wind Is Coming and I Love You, The.
Meredith, W.   Two Masks Unearthed in Bulgaria.
Teofilov, Ivan.   Hills, The: "Unrepeatable, ever-present mirage."
Old City, The.
Turkish Bath in Ortamezar.
Tsanev, Ivan.   Archaelogical Site, An.
Koprivshtitsa.
Bull Run, Battles of (1861, 1862)
Benét, S.   Congressmen Came Out To See Bull Run.
Day, J.   Picket before Bull Run, The.
Melville, H.   March into Virginia, The.
Bullets
Ahl, L.   Ammo.
Baraka, I.   Heavy, The.
Beatty, A.   Memorization.
Cabral de Melo Neto.   Knife All Blade, A.
Dove, R.   Teach Us to Number Our Days.
Ehrhart.   How It All Comes Back.
Harte, B.   What the Bullet Sang.
Nye, N.   For Mohammed Zeid, Age 15.
Ritsos.   Audible and Inaudible.
Simic.   Poem without a Title.
Tolson, N.   Bullet Hole Man.
Turner, B.   Here, Bullet.
Bullfights and Bullfighters
Beckman, J.   Lament for the Death of a Bullfighter.
Frost, C.   Custom.
García Lorca.   Goring and the Death, The.
Lament for Ignacio Sánchez Mejías.
Lament for Ignacio Sánchez Mejías.
Herrera.   Hallucinogenic Bullfighter.
Serrano, P.   Bullfight.
Corrida.
Bulls
Alberti.   To the Sun of the War.
Baehr, A.   Ritual.
Bunting.   Autobiography, An.
Gillies, V.   Summer Bull.
Heaney, S.   Outlaw, The.
Hirshfield, J.   Earthly Beauty, An.
Hodgson, R.   Bull, The.
Khlebnikov, V.   Lonely Masquerader.
Layton.   Bull Calf, The.
Lovibond.   Bull-Baiting.
Ovid.   Europa and Jove.
Phelp.   Duke Of Buccleuch, The.
Wright, J.   Bull, The.
Bullying and Bullies
Awoonor.   Songs of Abuse: To Stanislaus the Renegade.
Cramer.   For the Bullies of West Morris High.
Jordan, A.   Debt is Paid, A.
Parker, D.   When Mark Deloach Ruled the World.
Rector.   First Grade.
Reiter, T.   Class Bully.
Sirowitz, H.   Cookies for Peace.
Smith, Rod.   Ted's Head.
Spender, S.   My Parents.
Taksa, M.   Granite Jaw.
Walsh, J.   I've Got an Apple Ready.
Bunker Hill, Battle of (1775)
Pierpont, J.   Warren's Address at Bunker Hill [*or* to the American Soldiers].
Bureaucracy and Bureaucrats
Ashbery, J.   On The Empress's Mind.
Auden.   Unknown Citizen, The.
Davie, D.   Pilate.
Fogarty, L.   Fuck All Departments.
Frost, R.   Departmental.
Hughes, L.   Madam and the Census Man.
Miles, J.   Bureau 2.
Morgenstern.   Summons.
Tu Fu [*or* Du Fu].   Leaving Government Offices.
Various authors.   Even though they were rebellious.
Wang An-shih.   Working for the Government.

Burglars
Bhattācārya, M. You can't catch the thief, Mind.
Delgado, Alvin. When I Was a Kid in Nueva York.
Tate, J. There's a Certain Point Each Evening.

Burial
Akhmatova, A. In 1940.
Anyte [or Anytes]. Youth buried you, Captain; as sons for their mother, The.
Ball, A. Premature Burial Gazette.
Basho. Come, let's go / snow-viewing.
Brock, E. And another thing.
Busia, A. Exiles.
Carson, J. I Am Asking You to Come Back Home.
Carver, R. My Dad's Wallet.
Ciardi, J. Box Comes Home, A.
Clarke, C. Rondeau: "They are bodies left unburied."
Currey. Burial Flags.
Davies, D. At Branwen's Grave.
Dickey, J. Sled Burial, Dream Ceremony.
Drummond, W. If of the dead save good nought should be said.
France de Bravo, B. Unrepentant.
Freneau. Indian Burying Ground, The.
Frost, R. Home Burial.
Gerhardt, I. G. M. Buried Birds, The.
Giovanni. Women Gather, The.
Goodison. For Don Drummond.
Grimké, A. Grass Fingers.
Guevara, M. Magic Carpet, The.
Gwyer, J. Heap on more grass was his request.
Hardy, T. I Found Her Out There.
Harper, F. Bury Me in a Free Land.
Herbert, E. Epitaph on Sir Philip Sidney Lying in St Paul's without a Monument, to be Fastned upon the Church Door.
Herrick. Upon a Child That Died [or Dyed].
Upon Himselfe Being Buried.
Upon Prue [or Prew], His Maid.
Hill, G. Strange church smelled a bit 'high,' of censers, The.
Hooks. As they bury the dead.
Hudgins. Burial Detail.
Hughes, L. Stony Lonesome.
Hwang Tonggyu. Wind Burial 1.
Jamie, K. Inhumation.
Meadowsweet.
Jeffers, R. Shane O'Neill's Cairn.
Kreymborg. To W. C. W. M. D.
Lane, M. Travis. Codicil: Including the cost of a monument and inscription.
Lee, L. Little Father.
Liu Tsung-yüan. On Covering the Bones of Chang Chin, the Hired Man.
Lochhead, D. John Thompson.
MacNeice. Canto XX: "To Wales once more, though not on holiday now."
Mayne, S. Hail.
McKinney, I. Visiting My Gravesite: Talbott Churchyard, West Virginia.
Meehan, P. Child Burial.
Millay, E. Burial.
Mistral, G. To the Children.
Mitchell, K. On the Anniversary Of Your Death.
Nash, O. Tweedledee and Tweedledoom.
Ni Ghallchóir, C. Under the Sod.
O'Donoghue, B. Concordiam in Populo.
Pasternak, B. Magdalene (I).
Peacock, M. Fare, The.
Pegram, A. Burials.
Piñero. On The Day They Buried My Mother.
Powell, D. A. Always Returning: Holidays and Burials. Not Every Week.
Jones, R. For Ewan McLachlan.
Rein. Nanny Tanya.
Ross, L. Requiescat.
Requiescat.
Shakespeare, W. Pray you fetch him hither.
Smith, L. Burial Code.
Southerland. Blue Clay.
Stevenson, A. Temporarily in Oxford.
Stroud, J. Documentary.

Sutskever [or Sutzkever]. Honey of a Wild Bee.
T'ao Ch'ien [or T'ao Yuan-ming]. Bearers' Song.
Unknown. Lay This Body Down.
Rhyme from Lincolnshire, A.
Romance of Love.
Shades of the Newly Buried Complain to the Gods, The.
Voigt. Burial, The.
Volkman. Case, The.
Webster, J. Call for the Robin-Redbreast and the Wren.
Wenderoth, J. As Hour and Year Collapsed.
Whitman, W. Vigil Strange I Kept on the Field One Night.
Wright, D. Caleb Barnes.
To the Gods the Shades Flavinus of the Cavalry Regiment.
Wright, J. Dream of Burial, A.
See also **Cemeteries; Funerals; Graves; Interment; Mausoleums; Tombs**

Burial Mounds
Cherokee Oral Tradition. Formula to Cause Death.
Macari, A. Burial Mound.
Newton, Violette. Caddo Mounds, The.

Burke, Edmund
Coleridge, S. Burke.
Goldsmith, O. Edmund Burke.
Wilbur, R. Marché aux Oiseaux.

Burlesque
Atwood. Victory Burlesk, The.
Voznesensky [or Voznesenskii]. Striptease.
See also **Striptease**

Burma
Kipling, R. Mandalay.

Burne-Jones, Edward
Rossetti, D. For 'The Wine of Circe' by Edward Burne Jones.

Burns, Robert
Smith, C. To the Shade of Burns.

Burros
Lezama Lima. Rhapsody for the Mule.
Vallejo. It was Sunday in the fair ears of my burro.
See also **Donkeys**

Burroughs, William
Glück, R. Burroughs.

Bus Terminals
Arnold, C. Your friend's arriving on the bus.
Butson, D. Tuesday 9:00 AM.
Christopher. Through the Window of the All-Night Restaurant.
Johnson, J. Unmarked Stop in Front of Westmond General Store, Westmond, Idaho.
Reznikoff. Highway I was walking on, The.
Shin Kyŏngnim. Country Bus Station.

Buses
Atkins, R. Late Bus (After a Series of Hold-Ups).
Bishop, E. Moose, The.
Bremer, C. Metro Taxqueña.
Metro Taxqueña.
Bulich, V. Omnibus, The.
Caleshu, A. Collaboration: Between Countries.
Chŏng Hyŏnjong. Country Bus at Night.
Clarke, C. Passing.
Cohen, L. Bus, The.
Cope, W. Bloody Men.
Cross, D. Big words.
Bus poems, The.
Turn-on (with most of a line by Spicer).
Dove, R. Enactment, The.
Freedom Ride.
Flint, J. Metropolitan Metaphysics.
Gillespie, N. Bus Driver, The.
Gilmore, B. Georgia avenue, washington d.c.
Goodwin, Eli. Untitled: "Number 1 bus jerks to a stop at Mass. Ave., The."
Hirschman, J. Tremor, The.
Jackson, A. Miz Rosa Rides the Bus.
Jordan, J. Bus Window.
Kaddour, Hédi. Bus Driver, The.
Kalamaras, G. Mud.

Levy, A. Ballade of an Omnibus.
Loftin, E. Black Lady, A.
Long, R. Muse Is Gone, The.
MacSweeney. I Looked Down on a Child Today.
Mattawa. Bus Driver Poem, The.
Morgan, F. Busses, The.
Morley, D. Exact Fares.
Na Hûidôk. For Five Minutes.
Okudzhava. Ah, Nadya, Nadyenka.
Prunty. Downtown Bus, The.
Scalapino. Man getting on a bus carrying a huge sack of crushed cans, A.
Shapiro, H. Bus Ride.
Silliman. Glimmer of light high over Mount Diablo (silhouette flat across).
Sirowitz, H. I Finally Managed to Speak to Her.
Williams, S. Wishon Line, The.
Willis, N. Lady in the White Dress, Whom I Helped into the Omnibus, The.

Bush, George W.
Dana, R. In Heaven.
Kearney, L. Man with His Kids on a Table, The.
Kyger. Deeply Immoral Arrogant and Ignorant.
Lourie. Theological.
Pawlak. Official Versions.
Richardson, J. First Lady Challenges a Loa-as-Poem.

Business and Businessmen
Atkins, R. Furious'd Garb.
Baca. So Mexicans Are Taking Jobs from Americans.
Barbir, A. Ah, Mr Businessman!
Berlin. There's No Business Like Show Business.
Betjeman. Business Girls.
Ciardi, J. Back through the Looking Glass to This Side.
Clary. Mr. Dooms would meet us across the Bay Bridge at a restaurant that featured "Dancing Waters".
Crabbe, G. Business Man's Lair, A.
Dickinson, E. I asked no other thing.
Farr, R. At general Electric, where they eat their/young.
Fearing. Dirge: "1-2-3 was the number he played but today the number came 3-2-1."
Fuertes. Scrawny Women, The.
Gibbons, R. Cash or Turtle or Heaven.
Ginsberg, A. Who Runs America?
Hashmi. Pro Bono Publico.
Hicok. Dropping the Euphemism.
Hughes, L. Madam's Past History.
Leonard, T. Opting for Early Retirement.
London, R. Folk Form.
Martinson. Letter from a Cattleboat.
O'Callaghan. Managing the Common Herd: Two Approaches for Senior Management.
Ochester. Pocahontas.
Pobo, K. Stormy Lear.
Unknown. Coffee Rancher, The.
Williams, Gerwyn. Forward March.
See also **Accounting and Accountants; Advertising; Banking and Bankers; Capitalism; Financiers; Commerce**

Butchering and Butchers
Brathwaite, E. Ancestors.
Bremer, C. Butcher Shop.
Carnicería.
Duggan, L. Hearts (1983).
Evans, D. Pig Killing Day.
Hampton. Crafty Butcher, The.
Janzen, J. Chicken Guts.
Krause, K. Eid Al-Fitr.
Lee, L. Cleaving, The.
He gossips like my grandmother, this man.
Levine, P. Angel Butcher.
Animals Are Passing from Our Lives.
Lewis, G. Ritual.
Makuck. Story of Sound.
Parry, R. Spring: "After the bitter weather."
Robinson, E. Reuben Bright.
Simic. Butcher Shop.
Smith, W. Butchertown.
Stern, G. Bull-roarer, The.

Tipping. Casino.
Tomlinson, C. On a Pig's Head.
Unknown. Butcher of Abbeville, The.
Walwicz. Abattoir, The.
Warner, Patrick. Heart, The.
Webb, C. Meat Michelangelo.
Williams, C. K. Racists.

Butler, Samuel (1612–80)
Oldham, J. On Butler who can think without rage.

Butter
Calverley. Ballad: "Auld wife sat at her ivied door, The."
Heaney, S. Churning Day.
Lakshminkara. Lay your head on a block of butter and chop.
Moore, O. Taste of Life Going On, The.
Nash, O. Arthur.
Unknown. Butter Charm.

Buttercups
Sanfield. Hills of buttercups.

Butterflies
Arakida Moritaké. Falling flower, The.
  Haiku: "Falling flower, The."
Avison. Butterfly Bones; or, Sonnet against Sonnets.
  Butterfly, The.
Basho. Caterpillar, A.
Bayly. I'd Be a Butterfly.
Becker, R. Monarchs of Parque Tranquilidad.
Bensko. Butterfly Net, The.
Boruch. Camouflage.
Buson. Butterfly.
  Clinging to the bell.
Caleshu, A. Collaboration: Migration Patterns.
Chang Pi. Butterfly.
Cho Chihun. Spring Day.
Cole, H. Cabbage Butterfly, The.
Coleridge, M. September.
Cullen, Y. Not a Letter.
Daichi. Thoughts arise endlessly.
Davies, W. H. Example, The.
De la Tierra. Butterflying.
Densmore. Song of the Butterfly, The.
Dickinson, E. Butterfly upon the Sky, The.
  My Cocoon tightens—Colors tease.
Duncan, R. Roots and Branches.
Dunn, S. Instead of You.
Ermakova, I. Toward morning around seven.
Friedmann. Butterfly, The.
  Butterfly, The.
Frost, C. Papilio.
Frost, R. Tuft of Flowers, The.
Fuller, J. Butterfly, The.
Fumi Saito. With wings that will not ever.
González, R. Mariposa.
Gould, H. Butterfly's Dream, The.
Grace, P. Butterflies.
Grimké, A. Butterflies.
Hagiwara Sakutaro. So Terrifyingly Melancholy.
Hô Sugyông. Butterfly, The.
Humes. Butterfly Effect, The.
Hurbak Myungjo. Dream of a Butterfly, The.
Inagaki Chikai. Butterflies.
Issa. From burweed / Such a butterfly.
  Garden butterfly.
  In this world / Even butterflies.
Kana-jo, Lady. Quivering together /Ears of barley.
Katz, M. To a Butterfly.
Kim Ch'unsu [*or* Chun-soo]. Lilac Petals.
Kowit. Whitman Portrait, A.
Lawrence, D. H. Butterfly.
Layton. Butterfly on Rock.
Lee, K. Haiku #3.
Levertov. Dead Butterfly, The.
Levin, D. Ars Poetica: "Six monarch butterfly cocoons."
Li'aibi, S. Butterfly frozen in stone, A.
Lim, S. Monarchs Steering.
Liu, T. Poem: "Late butterflies gliding through the air."
Lowell, A. Nuance.
Masaoka Shiki. White butterfly / Darting among pinks.

Milosz, C. Abundant Catch (Luke 5:4–10).
Moore, M. To a Steam Roller.
Moritake. Those falling blossoms.
Muldoon, P. Milkweed and Monarch.
Neri, G. Natural History.
Nomura Akitari. Butterflies.
Noyes, A. Butterfly Garden, The.
Olds, S. Monarchs.
Ozaki Hosai. All day long.
Pope, A. Then thick as locusts black'ning the ground.
Rossetti, C. Caterpillar, The.
Sachs, N. Butterfly.
Sherry, J. Lepidoptery.
Simic. Much Dwindled, Starker Annotator, A.
Suzuki, M. Summer butterfly.
Swenson, M. Unconscious Came a Beauty.
Unknown. Butterfly Song.
Wang Ho-ch'ing. Tune: "Tsui-chung T'ien" To the Giant Butterfly.
Wieners. Poem for Trapped Things, A.
Wilde, O. Symphony in Yellow.
Wordsworth, W. To a Butterfly ("I've watched you now a full half-hour.").
  To a Butterfly ("Stay near me—do not take thy flight!").
Wright, J. Wings.
Yang Chi. Five-Color.
Yi Sang. Poem No. 10: Butterfly.

Buttocks
L'Abbé, Sonnet. Theory My Natural Brown Ass.
Wenderoth, J. January 11, 1997.
Wilbur, R. Shallot, A.

Buzzards
Curtis, T. Pembrokeshire Buzzards.
Rossetti, C. Sketch, A.
Warren, R. Pondy Woods.
See also **Vultures**

Byron, George Gordon Noel Byron, 6th Baron
Arnold, M. Memorial Verses.
Auden. You lived and moved among the best society.
Byron, G. On This Day I Complete My Thirty-sixth Year.
Chesterton. Sea Replies to Byron, The.
Coogler. Byron.
Nash, O. Very Like a Whale.
Parker, D. Lives and Times of John Keats, Percy Bysshe Shelley, and George Gordon Noel, Lord Byron, The.
Porter, P. On This Day I Complete My Fortieth Year.
Praed. Chancery Morals.
Unknown. Among the yeomen's sons on my estate.
  Chance led me once, when idling through the street.
  Sometimes I sauntered from my lone abode.
  Thus feverish fancies floated in my brain.
  Women as women, me had never charmed.

Byzantium
Nordbrandt. Our Love Is Like Byzantium.
Notley. Where Leftover Misery Goes.
Unknown. Thus feverish fancies floated in my brain.
Yeats. Byzantium.
  Sailing to Byzantium.

C

Cabala
Borges. Golem, The.
Kalina, R. Cabalistic Rabbis, The.
Muñiz Huberman. Cabalists, The.

Cabbages
Oliver, M. Skunk Cabbage.
Ormsby, E. Skunk Cabbage.
Slugs, M. I Saw Her in Cabbage Time.
Swenson, M. Shu Swamp, Spring.
Unknown. Mid-West, The.

Cabins and Cottages
Bruce, C. Nova Scotia Fish Hut.
Edson, R. Cottage in the Wood, A.

Cactus
Burlingame. Desert, Not Wasteland.
Collier, M. Landscape: "Stupid. But each of us took turns."
Gardiner, S. Cactus.
Rabéarivelo [*or* Rebéarivelo]. Cactuses.
Towle. Diptych.

Cadavers
Abse. Carnal Knowledge.
Coulehan, J. Anatomy Lesson.
Dudley, E. Pathologist.
Foy, J. Autopsy.
Ramanujan. Death and the Good Citizen.
Schley, J. Inquest, By Hand.
Sepúlveda, O. Three ("She is of the continent, around her everything is light and I observe her atop the slab in the image of her body.").
  Tres ("Es del continente, alrededor de ella todo es luz y yo la observo sobre la plancha en la imagen de su cuerpo.").
Wagoner, D. Their Bodies.
See also **Corpses**

Cads
Bowen, C. Rain It Raineth, The.

Caedmon
Levertov. Caedmon.

Caesar, Julius
Auden. Fall of Rome, The.
Bukowski. b.
Jonson, B. To Clement Edmonds, on His *Caesar's Commentaries* Observed, and Translated.
Lamartine. Lizard, The.
Marlowe. This said, the restles generall through the darke.
Masefield. Night on the Downland.
Murray, J. Here We Stand Before the Temporal World.
Shakespeare, W. Antony's Oration [over Caesar's Body].
  I cannot tell what you and other men.
Turner, C. Julius Caesar and the Honey-Bee.
Whitehead, C. Brutus' Last Song.

Cafés
Al-Bayati, A. To Naguib Mahfouz.
Bhatt, S. Fischerhude, 2001.
Eliot, T. S. Sweeney among the Nightingales.
Gotera. Manong Chito Tells Manong Ben about His Dream over Breakfast at the Manilatown Cafe.
Johnson, J. View Café, The.
Komunyakaa, Y. Yellow Dog Café.
Lewis, S. Scene in a Café.
Tripp. Connection in Bridgend.
Von Freytag-Loringhoven. Café du Dôme.
Wetzsteon. Drinks in the Town Square.

Cage, John
Fox, Skip. Most Notoriously Absent North American Bird in Her Face, The.

Cain and Abel
Back, R. After Eden.
Blake, W. Ghost of Abel, The.
Byron, G. Oh! thou dead / And everlasting witness! whose unsinking.
Clifton, L. Cain.
Dobyns. Long Story.
Ghazoul, F. Abel's Brothers.
Hope, A. Imperial Adam.
Hugo, V. Conscience.
McKay, D. 1. The Man from Nod.
Pagis, D. Autobiography.
  Autobiography.
  Autobiography.
  Written in Pencil in the Sealed Railway-Car.
Vaughan, H. Abel's Blood.
Very. Thy Brother's Blood.
Wheelwright. Abel.

Cakes
Adair, V. H. Cutting the Cake.
Agran, R. Cakes Continue to Rise.
Brodey. Stone Free.
Cook, T. Mouse and the Cake, The.
Hume, C. Birthday.
Prior-Pitt. Fitting.
St. John, D. Wedding Preparations in the

Country.
Williams, H.   To Mrs. K———, On Her Sending Me an English Christmas Plum-Cake at Paris.
Wright, J.   Against Surrealism.

Calcutta, India
Nye, N.   At Mother Teresa's.

Caliban
Brathwaite, E.   Caliban.
Browning, R.   Caliban upon Setebos; or, Natural Theology in the Island.
Dancing Bear, J. P.   Caliban.
Donaghy, M.   Caliban's Books.
Namjoshi, S.   Caliban's Journal.
Porter, P.   Radio Caliban.
Richardson, J.   My Man Caliban!
Talvikki, A.   Afterwards: Caliban.
Webb, C.   At *The Tempest* with a Pregnant Wife.

California (state)
Alarcon, F.   Viernes Santo / Good Friday.
Berlin.   White Christmas.
Buckley, C.   Leaving the West Coast.
Cervantes.   Como lo Siento.
Freeway 280.
Poema para los Californios Muertos.
Cross, D.   Sterling Park.
Davie, D.   Across the Bay.
In California.
Davis, G.   August Fires.
DeSylva, B. G.   California, Here I Come.
Fagan.   California, *She Replied*.
In California.
Gier, J.   California Coast.
Gilman, C.   California Colors: A Song.
Gioia.   California Hills in August.
In Chandler Country.
Gomez, Cynthia.   San José: A Poem.
Gould, J.   Easter Sunday.
Gunn, T.   Flying Above California.
Harms.   Dogtown.
When You Wish Upon a Star That Turns into a Plane.
Hass, R.   Concerning the Afterlife, the Indians of Central California Had Only the Dimmest Notions.
Late Spring.
On the Coast near Sausalito.
Palo Alto: the Marshes.
Spring Rain.
Tahoe in August.
Hearle, K.   Politics of Memory, The.
Hillman, B.   Foghorn, A.
Geology, A.
Recycling Center.
Hongo.   Confession of the Highway / The Hermit Speaks.
Mendocino Rose.
Off from Swing Shift.
Porphyry of Elements, A.
Hoover, P.   California.
Houellebecq, Michel.   In the Limpid Air.
Inada.   Fresno Truth, The.
Jarnot, L.   Specific Incendiaries of Springtime, The.
Jeffers, R.   Carmel Point.
Clouds of Evening.
Return.
Jolson, A.   California, Here I Come.
Kizer, C.   Afternoon Happiness.
For Jan as the End Draws Near.
Kramer, L.   Strong Winds Below the Canyons.
Kyger.   And with March a Decade in Bolinas.
Lem.   California Dreaming.
Levine, P.   Waking in March.
Lim, S.   In California with Neruda.
Lockett.   Oaktown CA.
Locklin.   California: "What the hell am i doing anyway?"
Luschei, G.   Here.
Water Song, The.
Maio, Samuel.   In Memoriam: "On this coast where they once arrived destined."
Martin, C.   Metaphor of Grass in California.
McCann, Anthony.   Confessions: "Before money and California."
Miller, J.   California Christmas, A.

Mullen, H.   Bilingual Instructions.
Nameroff, R.   California Dreaming.
Oliveira, D.   San Joaquin.
Oppen.   And Their Winter and Night in Disguise.
Quintana.   Poem for Pancho Gonzales.
Reed, I.   Oakland Blues.
Rexroth, K.   Vitamins and Roughage.
Rich, A.   Walking Down the Road.
Ridge, J.   Mount Shasta: "Behold the dread Mt. Shasta, where it stands."
Rozga, M.   To California Where Rhymes Fail.
St. John, D.   California.
I will tell you. Maybe.
Salazar.   Hotel Fresno.
Salinas, L.   Nights in Fresno.
Sherman, M.   Towards Sunset at Camino Cielo.
Sill.   California Winter.
Snyder, G.   Before the Stuff Comes Down.
Burning the Small Dead.
Hay for the Horses.
Marin-An.
Somoza, J.   Temperate.
Song.   Beauty and Sadness.
Soto.   Elements of San Joaquin, The.
Stroud, J.   Grandfather.
Voigt.   Blue Ridge.
Wakoski.   Imagining Point Dume.
Night Blooming Jasmine.
White, L.   World as I Found It, The.
Whitman, W.   Facing West from California's Shores.
Promise to California, A.
Williams, S.   Buildings of the, The.
Winters, Y.   John Sutter.
Wright, C.   California Dreaming.
Looking West from Laguna Beach at Night.
Yost, C.   California Poem.
Descano, California.
Young, A.   California Peninsula: El Camino Real.
One West Coast.

Callas, Maria
Field, E.   Callas.

Calligraphy
Gillespie, N.   Seated in a Chinese Painting, He Speaks.
Hsieh Chin.   Song of Cursive Calligraphy.
Lloyd, C.   Nightfall.
Mitchell, S.   Bamboo.
Pak Tujin.   Inscription Etched by Water.
Paljor, N.   Way, The.
Reps, Paul.   Pine needling.
Segalen.   Out of Respect.
Shunryu Suzuki.   Beginner's Mind.
Tanahashi, Kazuaki.   Six Characters from the *Heart Sutra*.
Zukofsky, L.   (Ryokan's scroll).

Calling Cards
Hughes, L.   Madam's Calling Cards.

Calliope (muse)
Skelton, J.   Calliope.

Calm
Afrika, T.   Respite.
Agustini.   Night Came in the Drowsy Living Room, The.
Ajanta.   Sleep: "Nobody nowhere they've all gone home."
Baxter, J.   Morning and Evening Calm.
Bynner.   All tempest.
Clough.   It is most curious to see what a power a few calm words.
Cucchi, M.   Like the Chinese, I too am going to.
Donne.   Calm[e], The.
Doty, M.   Parable of a Marriage (Chi Gong).
Hayden, R.   Islands, The.
Hsi K'ang.   Song of Disillusionment, A.
Hughes, T.   Horses, The.
Jiménez, J.   Immense Hour.
L'Abbé, Sonnet.   Reaction To What You Said.
Lisnyanskaya [or Lisnianskaia].   Quiet days and quiet evenings.
Lugones.   Rain Psalm.
Masuri, S.   Day's End.
McAuliffe, J.   Calm, The.

Mistral, G.   Serene Words.
Morgan, R.   Honey.
Nyunai, J.   Hour of Life, An.
Pak Chaesam.   Nothing.
Parry-Williams.   Return.
Rossetti, C.   In Progress.
Unknown.   Kadavu.
Verlaine.   Brussels: Simple Frescos 1.
Sky above the roof's, The.
Uneven rows of hedges.
Vietnamese Oral Tradition.   Clear Skies, Still Sea.
Warren, R.   Masts at Dawn.
Wordsworth, W.   It Is a Beauteous Evening.
Wunderlich, M.   One Explanation of Beauty.

Calvary
Dickinson, E.   That I did always love.
Levertov.   Calvary Path, A.
Miller, M.   Calvary Way.
Robinson, E.   Calvary.
See also **Crucifixion, The**

Calves
Berry, W.   Her First Calf.
Parry, E.   I Would Like You for a Comrade.
Porteous.   Calf.

Calvinism
Clough.   Latest Decalogue, The.
Hall, D.   Impossible Marriage, The.
Howard, B.   For the Calvinists.
Lowell, R.   Mr. Edwards and the Spider.
Millay, E.   To a Calvinist in Bali.
Steven, K.   Calvinist, The.
Tennant, W.   Sang First.

Calypso Music
Brathwaite, E.   Calypso.
McCallum, S.   Calypso.

Calypso (mythology)
Broumas, O.   Calypso.
McCallum, S.   Calypso.

Cambodia and Cambodians
Bowman, C.   Jackie in Cambodia.
Fenton, J.   Cambodia.
Dead Soldiers.
Glazier, L.   On TV.
Long, R.   Conspiracy, The.

Cambridge, Massachusetts
Alexander, E.   Boston Year.
O'Grady, D.   Professor Kelleher and the Charles River.
See also **Harvard University**

Cambridge University
Ewart.   Semantic Limerick According to Dr. Johnson's Dictionary (Edition of 1765), The.
Semantic Limerick According to the Shorter Oxford English Dictionary (1933), The.
Levy, A.   Cambridge in the Long.
Tennyson, A.   Lines on Cambridge of 1830.

Cambridgeshire, England
Brooke, R.   Old Vicarage, Grantchester, The.

Camden, William
Jonson, B.   To William Camden.

Camellias
Akutagawa Ryunosuke.   Unable to stand.
Basho.   Heard, not seen.
Buson.   Camellia, The.
Camellia tips, The.
Cho Chihun.   Spring Day.
Kakei.   At the break of dawn.
Kistler, W.   Kyoto 1—Kinkaku-ji.
Lisboa.   Camellia.
Moore, M.   Camellia Sabina.
Roscoe, W.   Camellia, The.
Snow, C.   Tour: "Near a shrine in Japan he'd swept the path."

Camelot
Chubb, T.   Merlin.
Lerner, A.   Camelot.
Tennyson, A.   Lady of Shalott, The.
Unknown.   Since the siege and the assault upon Troy were finished.

Camels
Kamienska.   Matthew 19:16–24; And behold, one came up to him.
Things of This World.

Kipling, R.   Hump, The.
Lewis, J.   How to Tell a Camel.
Sarton, M.   August Third.
Shinkichi Takahashi.   Camel.
Unknown.   Camel.

Cameras
Andrews, T.   Cinema Vérité: The Death of Alfred, Lord Tennyson.
Bernes, J.   South Central: Notes toward a Shooting Script.
Dunn, D.   I Am a Cameraman.
"Ern Malley.".   Documentary Film.
Herd.   Marilyn Climbs Out of the Pool.
Shoukry, G.   Good Man Talking to Himself, A.
Tomlinson, C.   Snapshot.
Vando.   Lydia's Phantasmagoria.
Williams, Gerwyn.   Final Curtain.
See also **Photography and Photographers**

Camões, Luis de
Campbell, R.   Luis de Camões.

Campaigns, Political
Lindsay, V.   Bryan, Bryan, Bryan, Bryan.
See also **Voting and Voters**

Camping
Blackwell, Holley.   Message No. 32.
Fisher, J.   Camp.
Kittredge.   Tenting on the Old Camp Ground.
Kumin, M.   Despair.
Lux.   Poem in Thanks.
Olds, S.   Summer-Camp Bus Pulls Away from the Curb, The.
Reed, P.   Container of Stars.
Rexroth, K.   Floating.
Saner.   Camping Clean.
Snyder, G.   August on Sourdough, a Visit from Dick Brewer.
Late October Camping in the Sawtooths.
Solie, Karen.   Parabola.
Stafford, W.   At Cove on the Crooked River.
Storni.   Camp Fire.
Wagoner, D.   Making Camp ("When their eyes opened, it was more than morning.").
Making Camp ("You've found the place in time—no permanent shade.").
Waltner-Toews, D.   Coyotes at Eyebrow Lake, Saskatchewan.
Willerton, Chris.   Campsite.
Wright, C.   Other Side of the River, The.
Young, A.   Third Street Promenade; Full Moon, Sunday Night, Santa Monica.

Canaan
Holmes, O.   To Canaan: A Puritan War-Song.
Wechsler, E.   Child is Born, A.

Canada
Alexander, P.   Inventory. Journal.
Atwood.   At the Tourist Centre in Boston.
Thoughts from Underground.
Bowling, T.   Morenz.
Deerchild, R.   This is a small northern town.
Fiorentino, J.   Mission Street Song.
Holden, C.   Biblical Winnipeg.
Layton.   From Colony to Nation.
Lee, D.   1838.
Mayor, C.   Driving Away.
Moore, T.   Canadian Boat Song, A.
Nowlan.   Canadian Love Song.
Simpson, J.   Grieve not, my wife—grieve not for me.
Sirr.   Understanding Canada.
Smith, I.   Exiles, The.
Waldrep, G. C.   O Canada!
Zapruder, M.   Canada.

Canals
Ch'in Kuan.   Along the Grand Canal.
Freneau.   On the Great Western Canal of the State of New York.
Lowell, A.   Spring Longing.
McClure, D.   Hampton Lock.
Melville, H.   In a Bye-Canal.
Verlaine.   Streets 2.
Wainwright, J.   1815.
Zabolotsky [*or* Zabolotskii].   Loop Canal, The.

Canaries
Heard, J.   My Canary.
Heyen.   Canary.

Jewett, S.   Caged Bird, A.
Simic.   Entertaining the Canary.

Canberra, Australia
Rowland.   Canberra in April.

Cancer (disease)
Adcock, F.   Soho Hospital for Women, The.
Agard, J.   For Bob Marley.
Agran, R.   Swimming with Seiger.
Ai.   Chance.
More.
Ammons.   Improvisation for the Stately Dwelling, An.
Auden.   Miss Gee.
Bartlett, M.   Only Death.
Benn.   Man and Woman Go Through the Cancer Ward.
Blaser.   Ruler, The.
Bradley, J.   Sailors Shielding Their Eyes During Atomic Bomb Test, Bikini, 1947.
Campo.   Her Final Show.
Carruth, H.   Pittsburgh.
Carver, R.   What the Doctor Said.
Charara, H.   Holy Water.
Clifton, L.   Dialysis.
Lumpectomy Eve.
Coulehan, J.   D-Day, 1994.
Craven, Jerry.   Midsummer Farewell.
Curbelo.   Tourist Weather.
Darling, J.   Chemotherapy.
Dickey, J.   For the Death of Vince Lombardi.
Dubie.   Funeral, The.
Dugan, A.   For Euthanasia and Pain-Killing Drugs.
Dunn, D.   Sundial, The.
Espada.   Ghazal for Open Hands.
Shiny Aluminum of God, The.
Spanish of Our Out-Loud Dreams, The.
Fathy, S.   For Heiner Muller: Poem 2.
Gardiner, S.   Flight.
Geiger.   Dry Spell of Faith, A.
Glatt.   Amanda.
What We Did After My Mother's Mastectomy.
Graham-Pole, J.   Candor.
Hacker, M.   Cancer Winter.
Invocation: "This is for Elsa, also known as Liz."
Year's End.
Hahn, K.   Shower, The.
Hall, D.   Last Days.
Hardie, K.   Autumn Cancer.
Henderson-Holmes.   "C" ing in Colors: Blue.
"C" ing in Colors: Red.
Herman, G.   Clinic, The.
Hodgins.   Death Who.
Huffstickler.   In the Compound.
Kenyon, J.   Pharaoh.
Kessler, S.   Jack's Last Words.
Kimbrell, J.   My Father at the North Street Boarding House.
Kizer, C.   American Beauty, An.
La Morticella.   Liturgy for Trinity, A.
Lewis, G.   It looks like she's drowning.
Loydell, R.   Flesh and Fluids.
Lucas, J.   Nes From Nowhere.
Maddox, M.   Cancer Diagnosis.
Martinez, D.   In a Duplex Near the San Andreas Fault.
Matthews, W.   Dire Cure.
McClatchy.   My Mammogram.
Miller, E.   Rebecca.
Mohr, B.   Why the Heart Never Develops Cancer.
Moore, O.   Eulogy for Sister.
Mosquera, A.   Tamoxifen.
Norgate, S.   Water on the Moon.
Olds, S.   Glass, The.
In the Hospital Near the End.
Orlowsky, D.   Losing My Hair.
Paino.   Matter of Division, A.
Peacock, M.   Raptor, The.
Perillo, L.   Needles.
Satyamurti.   Diagnosis.
Out-Patients.
Shaw, A.   Bird Nests.
Shuttle.   Ultra Sound.
Spires.   Cemetery Reef.

Terranova.   Self-Examination.
Thomas, G.   Last Things, The.
Van Walleghen.   Crabapples.
Waring, B.   You Could Have Been Me.
Witherup.   Mervyn Clyde Witherup.
Wunderlich, M.   On Opening.
Wyrebek, M.   Healing Logic, A.
Young, A.   Seeing Red.

Candlemas
Clampitt.   Procession at Candlemas, A.
Herrick.   Ceremony upon Candlemas Eve.

Candles
Adams, F.   If.
Aini, L.   Liquidation.
Aygi, G.   People Are a Temple, The.
Blanco.   Set Theory.
Teoría de conjuntos.
Brown Rosellen.   Storm high.
Buson.   Lighting one candle.
Cavafy.   Candles.
Citino.   Sister Mary Appassionata Lectures the Eighth Grade Boys and Girls on the Nature of the Candle.
Creeley.   Warning, The.
Drake, E.   Just for Today.
Dunmore.   Candle Poem.
Empson.   Legal Fiction.
Gilgun, J.   Lights Out.
Hsiao Yen [*or* Emperor Wu of Liang].   Candle, The.
Hudgins.   Supper.
Jones, M.   Candle's Fly, The.
Leithauser.   Haunted, The.
Light, K.   Idea of Love Between Us, The.
Millay, E.   First Fig.
Second Fig.
Ponge.   Candle, The.
Candle, The.
Reese, L.   War Memory, A.
Ruefle.   Search Party.
Seifert.   Candlestick, The.
Shwarts [*or* Shvarts].   Memorial Candle.
Snodgrass.   Love Lamp.
Stevens, W.   Valley Candle.
Suckling, S.   Candle, A.
Unknown.   Riddle: "Little trotty hetty coat."
Warsh.   Static, The.
Wei Chuang.   Candle Dies, A.
Willard, N.   Cat's Second Song, The.
Wilson, K.   Dusk in My Backyard.
Yi Kae.   Candle burns in the room, The.
Yo Inlŏ.   Meditating on the Start of a New Era.
Yu Chien-wu.   On the Third Day I Wait on the Emperor at a Banquet and Describe the Reflection of the Candles in the Serpentine.
Yusuf, S.   Hamra Night.
Night in Al-Hamra.

Candy
Bang, M.   Crossed-Over, Fiend-Snitched, X-ed Out.
Bidart.   Ellen West.
Bricusse, L.   Candy Man, The.
Clare, S.   On the Good Ship Lollipop.
David, M.   Candy.
Ferlinghetti, L.   Pennycandystore beyond the El, The.
Follain.   Marshmallow Man, The.
González, R.   Day of the Dead.
Kramer, A.   Candy.
Lingafelter, A.   Candy Poem, The.
Mataka.   Licorice.
Nash, O.   Reflections on Ice-breaking.
Pak Chaesam.   Sound of the Taffy-Seller's Shears.
Reynolds, A.   Rock Candy.
Simpson, L.   Chocolates.
Swirszczynska [*or* Swir].   Three Pieces of Candy.
Whitney, J.   Candy.
Williams, C. K.   Reading: The Bus.

Candy Stores
Ferlinghetti, L.   Pennycandystore beyond the El, The.

Cannibalism and Cannibals
Brion, R.   One Morning Beside a Pond.

Canning
Byron, G.   Shipwreck, The.
Chase, K.   Venison.
Gilbert, W.   Yarn of the *Nancy Bell*, The.
Goodison.   Jamaica 1980.
Hajjaj, N.   Man Who Devoured Himself, The.
Jemeni.   America Eats Its Young.
Reid, C.   Perversion, A.
Segovia, F.   No acabamos nunca.
  We Never Come.
Sepúlveda, O.   Three ("She is of the continent, around her everything is light and I observe her atop the slab in the image of her body.").
  Tres ("Es del continente, alrededor de ella todo es luz y yo la observo sobre la plancha en la imagen de su cuerpo.").
Unknown.   Arere, Eiroworowin and Eomakan.
Vietnamese Oral Tradition.   Woman's Heart, A.
Webb, C.   At *The Tempest* with a Pregnant Wife.
Wright, J.   Dove-Love.

Canning
Cervantes.   Cannery Town in August.
Sontag, K.   Plum Crazy.
Van Duyn.   Homework.
Vollmer.   Canning Cellar, Early Sixties.
Young, K.   Preserving, The.

Cannons and Cannonballs
Espada.   Thanksgiving.

Canoes and Canoeing
Edson, R.   Canoeing, The.
Johnson, E.   Wave-Won.
Lux.   Can Tie Shoes but Won't.
Revard.   Birch Canoe.
Rexroth, K.   Floating.
Sinclair, S.   Paddling.
Unknown.   My dugout flibbles.
Woods, H.   Paddlin' Madelin' Home.

Canyons
Farley, Estelle E.   Grand Canyon.
Meng Chiao.   Laments of the Gorges ("Long ago, everyone laughed together.").
Stafford, W.   Kolob Canyon.
Strand.   There is a road through the canyon.

Cape Breton Island, Nova Scotia
Bishop, E.   Cape Breton.

Cape Cod, Massachusetts
Huntington, C.   Hot Wind, Provincetown Harbor.
Santayana.   Cape Cod.
Weaver, A.   Message on Cape Cod, The.

Cape Horn
Masefield.   Rounding the Horn.

Capital Punishment
Akhmatova, A.   Fear turns objects over in the darkness.
Alexie.   Capital Punishment.
Bartee.   Beginning at the End: Capital/Capitol Punishment.
Cendrars.   Head, The.
Hammad, S.   On the state-sanctioned murder of shaka sankofa.
Montrose.   On Himself, upon Hearing What Was His Sentence.
Padilla.   Question for the Frankfurt School, A.
Peterson, R.   San Quentin 1968.
Pound, E.   Nor can who has passed a month in the death cells.
Roberts, A.   Epistle to the Revolutionary Bible, An.
Shkapskaya [*or* Shkapskaia].   No Dream.
Warren-Moore.   For Paula Cooper.
Wilde, O.   There is no chapel on the day.
See also **Executions and Executioners**

Capitalism
Andrade, O.   Babbling.
Brecht, B.   Late Lamented Fame of the Giant City of New York.
Chrystos.   Okeydoekey Tribe, The.
Clampitt.   Hispaniola.
Codrescu.   Circle Jerk.
Cole, F.   America™.
Consuegra, D.   You and I.
Cumpian.   No Deposit Returns.
Dailey.   Ride the High Country.
Davies, I.   Gwalia Deserta XXVI.
Drake, N.   Man in the White Suit, The.

Eliot, T. S.   4. Death by Water.
Ginsberg, A.   Kral Majales.
Goetz.   Pianist looks like an airline pilot who's afraid to land, The.
Hahn, K.   Rockhopper, The.
Harland-Watts, J.   Resist Confinement.
Hughes, L.   Goodbye Christ.
Joseph, L.   That's All.
Kandel.   First They Slaughtered the Angels.
Knight, S.   Eyeball Works, The.
Kyger.   Deeply Immoral Arrogant and Ignorant.
Larkin, P.   Homage to a Government.
Lawrence, D. H.   Mosquito Knows, The.
Logue, C.   Know Thy Enemy.
Lopez, T.   No Transport.
Lowther, John.   Asleeping: a kind of rendezvous.
McNair.   Big Cars.
McNeill, A.   Saint Ras.
Merrill, J.   Clearing the Title.
Mills, D.   Chembank Card.
Mullen, H.   Land of the Discount Price, Home of the Brand Name.
Mullen, L.   Series of Failures So That I'm Sick of the Word, A.
Owen, M.   Topography.
Palmer, M.   Flower of Capital, The.
Parra, V.   At the Center of Injustice.
Pawlak.   East-West Dialog 2002.
Reed, I.   El Paso Monologue.
Rich, A.   In Those Years.
San Juan.   Owl of Minerva Takes Flight in the Evening, The.
Teillier, J.   No Sign of Life.
Thomas, R. S.   Other.
Umpierre.   Statue, The.
Vanek, J.   People's Republic, The.
Walcott.   Chapter 38, Part 3.
Watson, C.   Then the old fruit-and-vegetable economy dried up and blew away but self-defense gave us a way.
See also **Banking and Bankers; Business and Businessmen; Financiers**

Capriciousness
Mhac an tSaoi.   Finit.

Captivity
Amalrik.   Lake Baskunchak.
Belieu.   Sleeping Man Must Be Awakened to Be Killed, A.
Bryant, W.   African Chief, The.
Bulich, V.   Omnibus, The.
Chippewa Oral Tradition.   Song of the Captive Sioux Woman.
Coleman, W.   Prisoner of Los Angeles (2).
Davenant [*or* D'Avenant].   Countess of Anglesey lead Captive by the Rebels, at the Disforresting of Pewsam, The.
Dickinson, E.   Prison gets to be a friend, A.
Dugan, A.   Prison Song.
Dunbar, P.   Sympathy: "I know what the caged bird feels, alas!"
Gumilyov [*or* Gumiliov *or* Gumilev].   Baby Elephant, The.
Hierro, José.   Boy with the Empty Cage, The.
Hooker, E.   Ariel.
Jara, V.   Estadio Chile.
Jewett, S.   Caged Bird, A.
Karp.   Captivity.
Kipling, R.   Half-Ballad of Waterval.
Knight, S.   Mermaid Tank, The.
Komunyakaa, Y.   Chastity Belt.
Landon.   Castle of Chillon, The.
Levy, A.   Captivity.
Lowell, A.   Captured Goddess, The.
Milton.   But peace, I must not quarrel with the will.
Mu'tamid, King of Seville.   Stranger, captive in the lands of the West, will be mourned by a certain pulpit and throne, A.
Myrddin ap Dafydd.   Gwenllian.
Noguchi, R.   His Waves.
Rilke.   Panther, The.
  Panther, The.
Rohrer, M.   Last Look at the Mutineers, A.
Rowe, E.   Expostulation, The.
Sen, R.   Death, get out of here!

Sholl.   Monkey House.
Steptoe.   Wired In.
Struther.   Freedom.
Szporluk.   Occupant of the Hose.
Thwaite, A.   Freedom.
Tretheway, N.   Bellocq's Ophelia.
Turner, C.   Prisoner, The.
Unknown.   Franks come down the hill with a random course, The.
  Song of the Breaking of the Willow.
  To chain me down he takes charge of the chains.
  Tune: Magpie on the Branch.
Very.   I Was Sick and in Prison.
Wilde, R.   Lament of the Captive, The.
Wroth.   Did I boast of liberty?
  Sonnet 14: "Am I thus conquered [*or* conquer'd]? have I lost the powers."

Caravaggio, Michelangelo Merisi da
Beasley.   Witness.
Gunn, T.   In Santa Maria del Popolo.
Levis.   Caravaggio: Swirl and Vortex.

Card Games
Boland, E.   Game, The.
Cataldi.   Advice.
Davis, T.   Playing Solitaire.
Frost, R.   In Divés' Dive.
Hitchcock.   Solitaire.
Kavanagh, P.   Cards are shuffled and the deck, The.
Laraque, P.   My Broad Back.
Larkin, P.   Card-Players, The.
Leiris, Michel.   Misdeal.
Lyly, J.   Cupid and My Campaspe Played.
O'Grady, J.   Buster's Last Hand.
Pope, A.   "Restore the lock!" she cries; and all around.
Rossetti, C.   Queen of Hearts, The.
Rutsala.   House of Cards, The.
Spicer, J.   Cardplayers, The.
Wagner, S.   Rook.
Webster, A.   Enigma No. 6.

Cardiff, Wales
Abse.   Return to Cardiff.
Garlick, R.   Capitals.
Tripp.   Capital.
Williams, T.   Tourist, as he views the place, The.

Cardinals (ornithology)
Harvey, M.   Translation.
Plumly.   Cardinals in a Shower at Union Square.
Stern, G.   Red Bird.

Cargoes
Masefield.   Cargoes.
Steptoe.   Contraband.
See also **Freighters**

Caribbean Islands
Brathwaite, E.   Calypso.
  How Europe Underdeveloped Africa.
Davis, Cortney.   What Man Might Kill.
Esteves.   From Fanon.
  It Is Raining Today.
Hernández Cruz.   Islandis.
  It's Miller Time.
Hyppolite, M.   Caribbean Islands.
Soto.   Antigua.
Walcott.   Adios, Carenage.
See also **West Indies**

Caribbean Sea
Barrax.   Scuba Diver Recovers the Body of a Drowned Child, The.
Mistral, G.   Caribbean Sea.
See also **West Indies**

Caring
Ackerman, J.   First Night.
Bart, L.   As Long As He Needs Me.
Craig, David.   Nursing Home, 3rd Shift.
Foster, A.   Starting School.
Klein, M.   Guardian Life.
Loesser.   Somebody, Somewhere.
McGuire, Virginia.   Leaning into the Tilt.
Prufer, K.   Babysitter's Devotion, The.
Unknown.   Oshun, the River Goddess.
Wright, J.   Arrangements with Earth for Three Dead Friends.

Carlyle, Thomas
Lowell, J.   Emerson.
Parker, D.   Thomas Carlyle.
Carmel, California
Jeffers, R.   Carmel Point.
 Tor House.
Santos, S.   Jeffers Country.
Schmitz.   Carmel.
Tate, J.   Failed Tribute to the Stonemason of Tor House, Robinson Jeffers.
Carnivals
Bishop, E.   Pink Dog.
Brown, G.   Hamnavoe Market.
Kasischke.   Fatima.
Keplinger, D.   Distance Between Zero and One, The.
Kitchener.   Miss Tourist.
Morejón.   Will-o'-Wisp.
Rafferty, P.   After Carnival.
St. John, P.   Carnival.
Spencer, A.   At the Carnival.
Weatherford, C.   Queen Ijo's Blues.
Caroline of Ansbach
Pope, A.   On Queen Caroline's Deathbed.
Carp
Martinez, D.   Carp.
Quinn, J.   7. Bohemian Carp.
Spires.   Celestial, The.
Tomlinson, C.   Pines at Hakone, The.
Vietnamese Oral Tradition.   Carp, The.
Carpe Diem
Alcaeus [or Alkaios].   Come tip a few with me.
Drink...with me, Melanippos. Why (think that).
Alcuin.   Love has pierced my heart with its flame.
Angelou, M.   Come, And Be My Baby.
Browning, R.   Youth and Art.
Budbill.   Tomorrow: "Tomorrow / we are."
Carson, J.   I Am Asking You to Come Back Home.
Catullus.   Carmen 5.
Chŏng Ch'ŏl.   Let's drink a cup of wine; let's drink another!
Cohan.   If I'm Going to Die I'm going to Have Some Fun.
 I'm Mighty Glad I'm Living and That's All.
Coslow, S.   (Up on Top of a Rainbow) Sweepin' the Clouds Away.
Cummings, E. E.   My father moved through dooms of love.
 Ponder, darling, these busted statues.
 What If a Much of a Which of a Wind.
De Vries, P.   Bacchanal.
Dowson.   Villanelle of the Poet's Road.
Dubin, A.   Young and Healthy.
Emre.   Whole universe is full of God, The.
Foley, H.   Touch Wood.
Furey, T.   Verse for First.
Gershwin, I.   One Life to Live.
Goethe.   Haste Not! Rest Not!
Harte, B.   California Madrigal.
Herman, J.   Before the Parade Passes By.
Herrick.   Corinna's Going a-Maying.
 To the Virgins, to Make Much of Time.
Horace.   Ne'er fash your *thumb* what *gods* decree.
 Ode 1.2: To Leuconoë.
 Young Men Come Less Often, The—Isn't It So?
Jamal, P.   Edge, The.
Jonson, B.   Song. To Celia ("Come my Celia, let us prove.").
Keats.   Fancy.
Lodge, T.   Pluck the Fruit and Taste the Pleasure.
Lovelace, R.   To Amarantha, That She Would Dishevel[l] Her Hair[e].
MacLeish.   Speech to a Crowd.
Mahon.   Dog Days.
Marlowe.   Passionate Shepherd to His Love, The.
Marvell.   To His Coy Mistress.
 Young Love.
Masefield.   Laugh and Be Merry.
Melville, H.   Rosary Beads.
Millay, E.   I shall forget you presently, my dear.

Moore, T.   Young May Moon, The.
Morley, T.   Sing We and Chant It.
Motsapi, S.   Andif.
Opitz.   Ah Dearest, let us haste us.
Pak Nohae.   Road to Corruption, The.
Pessoa.   I the roses love in the gardens of Adonis.
 Segue O Teu Destino.
Plato.   Apple, The.
Pongnim, Prince.   What amuses you in the sound.
Ralegh.   Nymph's [or Nimphs] Reply to the [Passionate] Shepherd [or Sheepheard], The.
Ramsay, A.   Thou Were My Ain Thing, An.
Ransom, J.   Blue Girls.
Rich, A.   Floating Poem, Unnumbered, The.
Ronsard.   Corinna In Vendome.
 When you are old, at evening candle-lit.
Rossetti, D.   71: The Choice ("Eat thou and drink; to-morrow thou shalt die").
 73: The Choice ("Think thou and act; to-morrow thou shalt die").
 72: The Choice ("Watch thou and fear; to-morrow thou shalt die").
 86: Lost Days.
Shakespeare, W.   O[h] Mistress Mine.
Shaoxuan.   Black hair and red cheeks: for how long?
Sidney.   Fourth Song: "Only joy, now here you are."
Southwell.   Loss[e] in Delay[e].
Spenser, E.   Song of Bliss.
Stafford, W.   You Reading This, Be Ready.
Stickney, T.   Live Blindly.
Su Tung-p'o.   Turning Year, The.
T'ao Ch'ien [or T'ao Yuan-ming].   In Reply to a Poem by Liu Chaisang.
 Picnic by the Xie River, A.
Tennyson, A.   Now Sleeps the Crimson Petal.
Unknown.   Advice to a Young Man.
 Harper's Song for Inherkhawy, The.
 Ladies, you see time flieth.
 Sister, Awake!
 Take a Lamp and Wander Forth.
 West Gate Ballad.
 White-haired, but wanton still.
Vays, S.   Today: "I won't be sitting shiva."
Waller, E.   Song: "Go[e], lovely rose."
Washington, N.   Hundred Years from Today, A.
Winchilsea.   There's No To-Morrow.
Yosano Akiko.   Spring is short.
Young, J.   Hundred Years from Today, A.
Carpentry and Carpenters
Baugh, E.   Carpenter's Complaint, The.
Brathwaite, E.   Ogun.
Carroll, L.   Walrus and the Carpenter, The.
Carter, M.   Bitter Wood.
Davie, D.   With the Grain.
Dickinson, E.   Props assist the House, The.
Dove, R.   Genie's Prayer Under the Kitchen Sink.
Garza, E.   Why I Make the Best Barrels.
Im Yŏngjo.   Carpenter's Song, A.
Masters, E.   Indignation Jones.
Stein, K.   In the Kingdom of Perpetual Repair.
Zepeda, R.   Philosophical Emancipation, The.
Carpets
Calvino.   Eudoxia.
Hauge.   Carpet, The.
Morejón.   Carpet.
See also **Rugs and Carpets**
Carriages
Hammerstein.   Surrey with the Fringe on Top, The.
Jiménez, J.   Oxcarts Are Now on Their Way, The.
Rimbaud, A.   Common Nocturne.
Shelley, P.   As in that trance of wondrous thought I lay.
Vogel, D.   Single and last carriage is ready for the journey, A.
Carrots
Crozier, L.   Carrots.
Cars
Apollinaire.   Little Car, The.

Aragon.   Partial.
Armitage, S.   Very Simply Topping Up the Brake Fluid.
Bauer, G.   On Seeing a '57 Chevy Cruising 16th and O.
Berger, B.   Silver-Paced.
Boas, G.   Beard and Bicycle.
Bottoms.   In the Black Camaro.
Brehm, J.   When My Car Broke Down.
Brown, K.   '49 Merc, A.
Bryce, Colette.   Day: "That was the day that went too far."
Bye.   Car Music.
Coleman, W.   I Live for My Car.
Conoley, G.   Walt Whitman in the Car Lot, Repo or Used.
Countryman, Jeremy.   Woman with Chrysler.
Dacey, P.   Four Men in a Car.
Daniels, J.   Wheels: "My brother kept."
Edson, R.   Automobile, The.
Erdrich.   Lady in the Pink Mustang, The.
Espada.   Jeep Driver, The.
Fetherston, K.   Hating.
Göransson.   Last Instrument, The.
Grieves, C.   Indian Car.
Hajjaj, N.   Three Cows in Hamra Street.
Hall, H. Palmer.   Requiem for James Byrd, Jr.
Halliday, M.   Pink Car, The.
Haskins, L.   Jacked.
Healy, E.   Changing the Oil.
Jackson, M. L.   Some Kind of Crazy.
Jacobik, G.   Turkeys in August.
Jacobs, B.   Jeep Cherokee.
Kennedy, X.   Close Call.
Lifshin.   Child We Won't Have Is Crowding Us in the Front, The.
Llwyd, Iwan.   Automobiles.
McCabe, C.   Postcard from London, A.
McMahon, L.   Barbie's Ferrari.
McNair.   Big Cars.
Minhinnick.   She Drove a 'Seventies Plymouth.
Monroe, H.   Meeting, The.
Monsour.   Parking Lot.
Moore, H.   Edward.
Morgan, R.   Rearview Mirror.
Morris, H.   Duesenberg, 1929.
Olds, S.   Necking.
Oppen.   Closed car—closed in glass.
 Evening, water in a glass, The.
Paljor, N.   Cars stuck in the snow.
Parnell, P.   Sile Na gCioch.
Pau-Llosa.   Kendall Gulls.
Pearlberg, G.G.   Dog Star.
Rabkin, S.   Wheels.
Restifo, Elaine.   Jealousy: "I've watched a young woman fondling three strands of her own hair."
Rhodes, M.   How Fast.
Savageau.   Trees.
Savitz, M.   Sweetness.
Seidel.   Men and Women.
Simpson, L.   American Classic.
Smith, D.   Wreck in the Woods.
Snyder, G.   Instructions.
 Night Song of the Los Angeles Basin.
Stein, K.   Because You're American.
Whalen, P.   Perpetuum Mobile.
White, G.   Traveling with Cats on a Snowy Evening.
Williams, C. K.   Shock.
Wormser.   January.
Wyrebek, M.   Night Owl.
Cartoons
Ahern, T.   Popeye in the 19th Century.
 Popeye's Last Words.
Flynn, N.   Cartoon Physics, Part 1.
 Cartoon Physics, Part 2.
Carts
Jiménez, J.   Lumber Wagons, The.
Carving and Carvers
Yi Chehyŏn.   I carve a small rooster from wood.
Casanova, Giovanni
Livingstone, D.   Giovanni Jacopo meditates.
Casement, Roger David
Murphy, R.   Casement's Funeral.

Cassady, Neal
Ginsberg, A.　Elegy for Neal Cassady.
Green Automobile, The.
On Neal's Ashes.

Cassandra
Bogan, L.　Cassandra.
Chizhova.　Cassandra.
Dickey, W.　Cassandra.
Jeffers, R.　Cassandra.
Kossman.　Cassandra to Agamemnon.
Robinson, E.　Cassandra.
Ronsard.　Fragment of a Sonnet.

Caste System, Indian
Apparao, G.　Comet, The.
Chandar, M.　Birth Postponed, A.
Jashuva, G.　Bat Messenger, The.

Castles
Bowles, W.　Written at Bamborough Castle.
Burn.　Welsh Love Letter.
Carr, M.　Castle in the Fire, The.
Corben.　Harlech Castle.
Cotton, C.　Chatsworth.
Derricotte.　Exits from Elmina Castle: Cape
Coast, Ghana.
Dunn, S.　Happiness.
Holloway, G.　Ford Castle: The Borders.
Hugo, R.　Ferniehirst Castle.
Ingram, A.　Castle Howard, the Seat of the Rt.
Hon. Charles, Earl of Carlisle.
Landon.　Castle of Chillon, The.
Lang, A.　Romance.
Li Po.　At Ch'ang-men Palace.
Neri, G.　Inn of Angels, The.
Page, P.　Castle, The.
Pau-Llosa.　Paredón.
Poe.　Haunted Palace, The.
Reed, H.　Château, The.
Rothenberg, J.　At the Castle.
Simon, M.　Helsinore, Denmark.
Sitwell, D.　Trams.
Spires.　Robed Heart, The.
Stevenson, R.　Song of a Traveller, The.
Tennyson, A.　Splendour [orSplendor] Falls,
The.
Unknown.　Bonnie House o' Airlie, The.
Edom o' Gordon [Foulis Version].
Wheatley, D.　Along a Cliff.
Wordsworth, W.　Elegiac Stanzas: Suggested by
a Picture of Peele Castle, in a Storm, Painted
by Sir George Beaumont.

Castration
Grotz, J.　Last Living Castrato, The.
Jenkins, N.　Castration.
Mun Chônghui.　To You, My Beloved Ssuma
Ch'ien.
Sharp, S.　In the Tradition of Bobbitt.

Castro, Fidel
Espada.　Fidel in Ohio.
Esteves.　For Fidel Castro.
Guevara, E.　Song to Fidel.

Caterpillars
Basho.　Caterpillar, A.
Buson.　Morning breeze.
Short night, The.
Dickinson, E.　Caterpillar ("How soft a
Caterpillar steps—.").
Fisher, A.　Caterpillars.
Foster, A.　Caterpillar.
Ivanova, S.　O caterpillar, daughter of the
butterfly.
Johnson, K.　Query: "Who left / this wooly
caterpillar."
Kunitz, S.　Hornworm: Autumn Lamentation.
Hornworm: Summer Reverie.
Levertov.　On the dream sidewalk.
Ransetsu.　Without a sound.
Rossetti, C.　Caterpillar, The.
Caterpillar, The.
Serraillier.　Tickle Rhyme, The.
Unknown.　Woman Who Married a Caterpillar,
The.
Williams, M.　Caterpillar, The.
Yolen.　Caterpillar's Lullaby.

Catfish
Engels, J.　Bullhead.

Catharine of Aragon
Wodehouse.　It's a Hard, Hard World for a Man.

Cathedrals
Carrera Andrade.　Your body is a golden temple.
Chester, T.　Candle at Canterbury, A.
Fields, J.　Citizen.
Hicok.　Arch of Sanctification, The.
Johnson, J.　Before a Painting.
Linett, D.　Cathedral: "For hours I held one of
my son's infant twins."
Martin, Steve.　Demolition of the Cathedral at
Chartres.
Milosz, C.　Abundant Catch (Luke 5:4–10).
Oppen.　Chartres.
Ormond.　Cathedral Builders.
Phillips, R.　At the Summit.
Pulido, A.　Historia / debe tener.
History / the cathedral.
Ramírez, J.　Ficción y las Cosas, La.
Of Fiction and Things.
Wharton, E.　Chartres.

Catholicism and Catholics
Apollinaire.　Zone.
Zone.
Citino.　Cleveland, Angels, Ogres, Trolls.
Coles, R.　Christmas, Belfast.
Craig, David.　Peter pumped Dorothy's hand.
Crashaw.　To the Noblest and Best of Ladies, the
Countess of Denbigh.
Derricotte.　High School.
St. Peter Claver.
Donne.　Show me dear[e] Christ, thy spouse, so
bright and clear[e].
Eliot, T. S.　Hippopotamus, The.
Gildner.　They Have Turned the Church Where I
Ate God.
Higgins, R.　Middle-aged Irish Mothers.
Power of Prayer, The.
LaFemina.　Her Rose Tattoo.
Lehmann, G.　Pope Alexander VI.
Lim-Wilson.　Explaining the Origin of My
Name.
Myles, E.　Eileen's Vision.
Ní Chuilleanáin.　Real Thing, The.
Paino.　Each Bone of the Body.
Parra, N.　Poems of the Pope, The.
Pau-Llosa.　Segovia.
Ramírez, J.　Ficción y las Cosas, La.
Of Fiction and Things.
Scates.　Going to Mass after Fifteen Years.
Sheperd.　Who hath not knowne or herd.
Skelton, J.　Over this the foresayd lay.
Waters, M.　Conversion of Saint Paul, The.
Williams, W.　Catholic Bells, The.
Woods, V.　She Replies to the Fat Crimson
Bishop.

Cats
al-Rahim, A.　Shadow, A.
Alegría.　Savoir Faire.
Algarin.　Tiger Lady.
Arnold, M.　Atossa.
Bancquart.　Woman asleep.
Basho.　Cats making love.
Cat's wife, A.
Girl cat / So thin.
She cat, The.
Baudelaire.　Cats.
Clock, The.
Baxter, J.　Tomcat.
Benson, G.　Cat and the Pig, The.
Bodecker.　Cats and Dogs.
Bone, K.　Catlike.
Brown, L.　Sonnet Around Stephanie.
Bukowski.　Mockingbird, The.
Startled into Life Like Fire.
Buson.　Old post town, two or three houses.
Cavalli.　When suddenly, you're hit with good
health.
Chaucer.　Lat take a cat, and fostre him [or
hym] wel[l] with milk.
Coatsworth.　On a Night of Snow.
Open Door, The.
Collins, B.　Putting Down the Cat.
Cranch.　Old Cat's Confessions, An.
Crane, H.　Chaplinesque.
Cunningham, P.　Cats—A Retrospective.

D'Aquino, A.　Amoroso.
Amorous.
Denby.　Domestic Cat, A.
Old age, lookit, it's stupid, a big fart.
Deniz, G.　Superior.
Superior.
Di Prima.　Black and white cat.
Dickinson, E.　Cat.
Du Bellay.　Epitaph on a Pet Cat.
Eliot, T. S.　Bustopher Jones: The Cat About
Town.
Macavity: The Mystery Cat.
Mr Mistoffelees.
Naming of Cats, The.
Rum Tum Tugger, The.
Erb, E.　Inedible.
Erdrich.　Angels.
Ewart.　14-Year-Old Convalescent Cat in the
Winter, A.
Jubilate Matteo.
Who Likes the Idea of Guide Cats?
Fanning, R.　In the Barn.
Farjeon, E.　Cats.
Faverey.　Muffled thud with which the strange
cat, The.
Field, E.　Duel, The.
Fisher, A.　Cat in the Snow.
Listening.
Flatman.　Appeal to Cats in the Business of
Love, An.
Fuhrman, J.　Watching Trains.
Fyleman.　Cat, The.
Gallico, P.　Application.
Confession.
Garrigue.　Dialog.
Georges.　Alley Cat.
Gilbert, W.　Gilbertian Cats.
Gioia.　Alley Cat Love Song.
Goetsch, D.　What Keeps Animals Sane?
González, R.　Death of the Farm Workers' Cat.
Gray, S.　On a Cat Aging.
Gray, T.　Ode on the Death of a Favo[u]rite Cat,
Drowned in a Tub [or Bowl] of Gold Fishes.
Grimes, A.　Alice's Cat, New Year's Eve 1990.
Hagiwara Sakutaro.　Corpse of a Cat, The.
Halpern, D.　Dance, The.
Han-shan.　Cold Mountain Poem No. 158.
Hare, M.　Alfred de Musset.
Harris, W.　Samantha Is My Negro Cat.
Hass, R.　Elegy Residence on Earth.
Heine, H.　Memory, A.
Hemingway.　Earnest Liberal's Lament, The.
Hirsch, E.　Wild Gratitude.
Hirshfield, J.　Against Certainty.
Hood, T.　Choosing Their Names.
Huddle.　Perspective.
Hudgins.　Two Ember Days in Alabama.
Hughes, T.　Esther's Tomcat.
Issa.　After a long nap.
Flopped on the fan.
Goes out.
Having slept, the cat gets up.
My cat.
Winter fly, The.
Johnston, E.　Nelly's Lament for the Pirnhouse
Cat.
Kanik.　Erol Güney's Cat.
Karim, F.　Robin (The bird that was devoured by
the cat in the garden of the house).
Keats.　To a Cat.
Khodasevich.　On the Death of My Tomcat
Murr.
Kikaku.　Her mate devoured.
Kizer, C.　Widow in Wintertime, A.
Klassen, S.　Act of Mercy.
Kopland.　Ulumbo, a Cat.
Kumin, M.　Plans.
Kupriyanov [or Kuprianov].　Everything gets
forgotten.
La Fontaine.　Young mouse, poor, no
experience, A.
Lane, M. Travis.　Poem Upon the Forcible Entry
by Cat into a Poem Originally Upon Trilliums.
Larsen, L.　Lips.
Lear, E.　Children of the Owl and the Pussy-Cat,
The.

Owl and the Pussy-Cat [*or* Pussycat], The.
Levertov. Scenes from the Life of the Peppertrees.
Loncar, M. As My Cat Eats the Head of a Field Mouse He Has Caught.
Marquis. I had some romantic.
Mehitabel S Extensive Past.
Song of Mehitabel, The.
Mayes, F. Sister Cat.
Mei Yao Ch'en. Offering for the Cat, An.
Merrill, J. Maisie.
Merwin. Burning the Cat.
Miller, M. Cat.
Molony. Cat Washing.
Monro, H. Cat's Meat.
Milk for the Cat.
Moore, M. Peter.
Moore, R. Catalog [*or* Catalogue].
Morley, C. In Honour of Taffy Topaz.
Mother Goose. As I was going to St. Ives.
Ding, dong, bell.
Myer, M. Cool Cat.
Nash, O. Cat, The.
Natsume Soseki. Is it showering?
Nemes Nagy. Proportions of the Street, The.
Neruda. Ode to the Cat.
Oliver, M. Morning.
Parkinson, Thomas. Homage to a Tom-Cat.
Peacock, M. Breakfast with Cats.
Petrie. Indoor Cat, The.
Piercy. Cat's song, The.
Pitcher, O. Formula for tragedy.
Pratt, E. Prize Cat, The.
Rands. Cat of Cats, The.
Reid, A. Curiosity.
Propinquity.
Robinson, E. New England.
Sackville-West. Greater Cats, The.
Saroyan. Leaf, A / left.
Sayers, D. War Cat.
Seward. Old Cat's Dying Soliloquy, An.
Shamaqmaq, A. Hungry Master and Hungry Cat.
Sharaf, M. Dali.
Shinkichi Takahashi. Drizzle.
Shiraishi. Seven Cats Are Happy, The.
Shwarts [*or* Shvarts]. Conversation with a Cat.
Sidney. White Great Nimble Cat, A.
Smart, C. My Cat Jeoffry.
Smith, J. Philodendron Named Joan, A.
Sosnora. Owl and the Mouse, The.
Stern, G. Another Insane Devotion.
Stevenson, A. Epitaph for a Good Mouser.
Straus, M. Neuroanatomy Summer.
Swenson, M. Cat and the Weather.
Townsend, A. Day's End.
Tretheway. Near Dawn.
Twichell. Cat and Mirror.
Unknown. Cats of Kilkenny, The.
Pangur Bán.
Scholar and the Cat, The.
Usher, L. I Am the Cat.
Vegin, P. Explanation of a Sign.
Verlaine. Femme et Chatte.
Woman and Cat.
Vietnamese Oral Tradition. Cat, The.
Ward, J. To Get Clear.
Wenderoth, J. Detailed History of the Western World.
Whalen, P. Walking beside the Kamogawa, Remembering Nansen and Fudo and Gary's Poem.
White, G. Traveling with Cats on a Snowy Evening.
Walt Whitman Encounters the Cosmos with the Cats of New York.
Wilde, O. Fin-de-Siècle Cat.
Williams, W. Complete Destruction.
Mujer.
Poem: "As the cat."
Winstanley, J. Upon a Friend's Pet Cat, Being Sick.
Wordsworth, W. Kitten at Play, The.
Yeats. Cat and the Moon, The.
Yesenin [*or* Essenin]. For My Sister Shura.
Yi Jang'hi. Spring is a Cat, The.

See also **Kittens**
Cattle
Avianus. Calf and the Ox, The.
Benedikt. Meat Epitaph, The.
Chandar, M. Child Is Born, A.
Colum, P. Drover, A.
Davis, H. Proud Riders.
Keener, LuAnn. Dehorning the Yearlings.
Mackay-Warna. Cattle Loading.
Martinson. Letter from a Cattleboat.
Murray, L. Death Words.
Unknown. Cattle-count.
Corrido of "Gregorio Cortez".
Kansas 1.
Stealing of Apollo's Cattle, The.
See also **Bulls; Cowboys; Cows; Meat**
Catullus
Huxley, A. Second Philosopher's Song.
Kushner, A. As Catullus wrote, a man's voice deserts him.
Landor, W. On Catullus.
MacLeish. You Also, Gaius Valerius Catullus.
Millay, E. Passer Mortuus Est.
Nichol. From Catullus Poem LI.
Shockley, E. My last modernist poem, #2 (or, mugshot).
Tennyson, A. Frater Ave Atque Vale.
Caution
Brown, L. Button Up Your Overcoat.
Cassian. Orbits.
Creeley. I Know a Man.
DeSylva, B. G. Button Up Your Overcoat.
Gascoigne. For That He Looked Not upon Her.
Henderson, R. Button Up Your Overcoat.
Hewitt, J. Search, The.
Ivanov, Binyo. Bulletin.
Jabeen, M. Act of Caution, An.
Lewis, A. To a Comrade in Arms.
Montagu, L. Lover, The; a Ballad.
Moore, T. Duke Is the Lad [to Frighten a Lass], The.
Press, K. Rotten fish.
Roethke. Monotony Song, The.
Sappho. When anger spreads in the breast.
Slessor. Up in Mabel's Room.
Sorescu, M. Precautions.
Washington, N. My Foolish Heart.
Weigl. Mines.
Whitney, I. Ye virgins that from Cupid's tents.
Wroth. Sonnet 34: "Take heed mine eyes, how you your foe[s] do[e] cast."
Cavafy, Constantine P.
Jarman, M. Cavafy in Redondo.
Cavaliers
Larcom. Little Cavalier, A.
Cavalry
Bierds, L. Van Leeuwenhoek: 1675.
Davidson, D. Sequel of Appomattox.
Housman. Lancer.
Tennyson, A. Charge of the Light Brigade, The.
Whitman, W. Cavalry Crossing a Ford.
Cavemen
Cullar, Carol. 12,000 Years Is Not Too Long.
Eshleman, C. Placements I.
Kipling, R. King, The.
Mahon. Hunt by Night, The.
Pratt, E. From Stone to Steel.
Rukeyser, M. Painters.
See also **Man, Primitive**
Caves
Bierds, L. Altamira: What She Remembered.
Cary, A. Sea-Side Cave, The.
Cawein. Caverns.
Crashaw. Come See the Place Where the Lord Lay.
Daigu. Who dares approach the lion's.
Dodd, E. Like Memory, Caverns.
Dorantes, D. En la profunda cueva.
In the deep cave.
Eshleman, C. Notes on a Visit to Le Tuc d'Audoubert.
Field. Maidenhair.
Hedin, R. At Betharram.
Hopes. 2. The Cave.
Hueung Powoo. Deciding to Live in an Empty

Cave on Kumgang Mountain.
Jeffers, R. Hands.
Lee, E. Forests and Caverns.
McMorris, M. More Than Once in Caves.
Merwin. Bread.
Moraes, D. Kanheri Caves.
Morris, S. Here in these fretted caverns whence the sea.
Muso Soseki. Cave of the Thousand Pines.
Peterson, J. Cody. La Jolla. In 3 Acts.
Rukeyser, M. Ajanta.
Stafford, W. Indian Cave Jerry Ramsey Found, The.
Tomlinson, C. Cavern, The.
Tu Mu. Red Embankment.
Warfield. Forests and Caverns.
Wetzsteon. Coming Back to the Cave.
Cecilia, Saint
Dryden, J. Alexander's Feast; or, The Power of Music [*or* Musique].
Song for St Cecilia's Day, 1687, A.
Mallarmé. Saint.
Cedar Trees
Miller, M. Gift from Kenya.
Reid-Marr, David Tokuyu. Cedar.
Celan, Paul
Brasfield, J. Celan.
Halperin. Two Lines from Paul Celan.
Hirsch, E. In Memoriam Paul Celan.
Celandine
Thomas, E. Celandine.
Wordsworth, W. Small Celandine, The.
Celebrations
Allen, F. First-born.
Basho. In the mountain village.
Guest, B. Outside of This, That Is.
Hantoosh, G. Celebration.
Leeke, Kiamsha Madelyn. October Death.
Pitter. Victory Bonfire.
Sanfield. Birthday Poem.
Schneider, M. When It's All Over.
Celibacy
Clarke, A. Celibacy.
Hubbell, L. W. Birth-Hour.
Ramanujan. Pleasure.
See also **Bachelors; Virgins**
Cellars
Hope, M. Bare Floors.
Roethke. Root Cellar.
Cellists and Cellos
Winder. Unaccompanied Suite.
Celtic Mythology
Hull, E. Sleep-Song of Grainne over Dermuid, The.
Celts
Smith, S. Celts, The.
Cemeteries
Aldington. Battlefield.
Amichai, Y. Is all this sorrow? I don't know.
Behar, R. Jewish Cemetery in Guanabacoa, The.
Bunting. Now that sea's over that island.
Cabral de Melo Neto. Cemetery in Pernambuco: Our Lady of Light.
Castera, G. Cemetery Gate.
Causley. At the British War Cemetery, Bayeux.
By St. Thomas Water.
Cernuda. Cemetery in the City.
Cervantes. Meeting Mescalito at Oak Hill Cemetery.
Clifton, L. At the cemetery, walnut grove plantation, south carolina, 1989.
Creeley. Stairway to Heaven.
Crummey, Michael. Loom: Burnt Woods Cemetery, Western Bay, Newfoundland.
Daiches, J. Jewish Cemetery, Frankfurt.
Dickinson, E. Cemetery, A.
Dobyns. Cemetery Nights.
Fairfax, J. Forest of the Dead, The.
Flecker, J. Town without a Market, The.
Fordham. Magnolia.
Freneau. Indian Burying Ground, The.
Frost, R. Home Burial.
Fuertes. Unknown Also Attracts Cowards, The.

Goethe.   Anacreon's Grave.
Gray, T.   Elegy Written in a Country
    Churchyard.
Gu Cheng.   Forever Parted: Graveyard.
Hardy, T.   Friends Beyond.
    Voices from Things Growing in a Churchyard.
Heard, J.   National Cemetery, Beaufort, South
    Carolina, The.
Hernández, M.   Cemetery Lies Near, The.
Hill, G.   Distant Fury of Battle, The.
Howe, F.   Seeking Out His face in a Cup.
Hugo, R.   Graves at Elkhorn.
Iofe, Y.   Olsanski Cemetery, The.
Kaufman, S.   Mount of Olives, The.
Lihn.   Cemetery in Punta Arenas.
Lochhead, D.   Cemetery at Loch End, Catalone,
    Cape Breton, The.
Longfellow, H.   In the Churchyard at
    Cambridge.
    Jewish Cemetery at Newport, The.
Lowell, R.   Quaker Graveyard in Nantucket,
    The.
Lukata, B.   Rehearsal.
Lynch, T.   At the Opening of Oak Grove
    Cemetary Bridge.
Masters, E.   Hill, The.
McCrae, J.   In Flanders Fields.
Mew.   In Nunhead Cemetery.
Miller, J.   In Père La Chaise.
Momaday.   Rainy Mountain Cemetery.
Moore, L.   Again.
Neruda.   Nothing but Death.
Olds, S.   Leningrad Cemetery, Winter of 1941.
Parham, Mary Gomez.   Belize Cemetery, The.
Pelletiere, M.   Under Her Crib.
Ratzlaff, K.   My Students against the Cemetery
    Pines.
Rifat.   Flute, The.
Robinson, M.   After Eighteen Years of This Sort
    of Thing.
Ryan, A.   Lines: "Gather the sacred dust."
Salaam.   St. Louis Cemetery Crypt.
Sandburg, C.   Cool Tombs.
Smith, C.   Pressed by the Moon, Mute Arbitress
    of Tides.
Smith, S.   Great Unaffected Vampires and the
    Moon.
Stevenson, R.   Blows the Wind Today.
Tate, A.   Ode to the Confederate Dead.
Timrod.   Ode: "Sleep sweetly in your humble
    graves."
Tomlinson, C.   After a Death.
Unknown.   Of Sir Frauncis Walsingham Sir
    Phillipp Sydney, and Sir Christopher Hatton,
    Lord Chancelor.
Valéry.   Graves by the Sea, The.
    Graveyard by the Sea, The.
    Seaside Cemetery, The.
Vallejo.   Our Daily Bread.
Wilbur, R.   In a Churchyard.
Williams, W.   Children, The.
Wiman, C.   In Lakeview Cemetery.
Winters, Y.   To the Holy Spirit.
Wright, J.   Albuquerque Graveyard, The.
Yeats.   Under bare Ben Bulben's head.
Yevtushenko [*or* Evtushenko].   Cemetery of the
    Whales, The.
See also **Burial; Graves; Mausoleums; Tombs**

Censorship
Akao, A.   Zombies Arise.
Benedetti, M.   With Your Permission.
Brecht, B.   Burning of the Books, The.
Brodsky, J.   Will a mouth that's muttered its
    goodbyes.
Clarke, A.   Penal Law.
Dana, R.   Radiance.
Dharker.   They'll say, "She must be from
    another country".
Duchamp.   SURcenSURE.
Hirschman, J.   Painting, The.
Kramer, L.   Night Bird, The.
Kunze, R.   Low Volume.
    Need for Censorship, The.
Large, J.   Text XXX.
Lawrence, D. H.   Broadcasting to the G.B.P.
    Innocent England.

Long, N.   Now the BBC once wrote to me and
    said 'Dear Norman Long'.
Paulin.   Where Art Is a Midwife.
Ritsos.   They tagged you an illiterate, those idle
    bureaucrats.
Tranströmer.   To Friends Behind a Frontier.
Waltner-Toews, D.   Request from Tante Tina to
    the Mennonite Women's Missionary Society to
    Put Salman Rushdie on the Prayer List, A.

Centaurs
Swenson, M.   Centaur, The.

Centipedes
Dove, R.   Centipede.
Hwang Insuk.   Beneath Her Ribs.
Kendall, M.   Education's Martyr.

Central America
Mac Low.   Central America.
Ritsos.   Guatemala, Nicaragua, Salvador.
Rose.   Day They Cleaned Up the Border, The:
    El Salvador, February, 1981.
See also **Latin America and Latin Americans**

Central Park, New York City
Brouwer, J.   Conservatory Pond, Central Park,
    New York, New York.
Cooley, N.   Diane Arbus, New York.
Denby.   Summer: "I stroll on Madison in
    expensive clothes, sour."
Halpern, M.   In Central Park.
Schuyler, J.   Dining Out with Doug and Frank.
Takamura Kotaro.   Elephant's Piggy Bank, The.
Wright, J.   Lake in Central Park, The.
Zucker, R.   Post card (central park).

Ceres
Ovid.   Ceres and Proserpina.
Paz.   Solo for Two Voices.
See also **Demeter**

Cereus, Night-blooming
Hayden, R.   Night-Blooming Cereus, The.

Certainty
Calvino.   Octavia.
Delanty.   Goat, the.
Hirshfield, J.   Against Certainty.
Jiménez, J.   Ship, Solid and Black, The.
Milán, E.   No hay porqué, hay órdenes de canto.
    There is no wherefore, there is a command of
    song.
Stevens, W.   It feels good as it is without the
    giant.
Van Vliet.   Coastline, The.
Zaid.   Furious Clarity, A.

Cervantes, Miguel de
Borges.   Soldier of Urbina, A.

Ceylon
Nishiwaki Junzaburo.   Ceylon.
See also **Sri Lanka**

Cézanne, Paul
Brutus.   Under House Arrest.
Kees.   Round: "Wondrous life! cried Marvell at
    Appleton House."
Salmon, A.   Painting.
Stein, G.   Cézanne.
Strange.   Still Life.
Tardieu Jean.   Céanne.
Tomlinson, C.   Cézanne at Aix.
Welch, L.   In Cézanne's studio, we're dappled
    with joy.

Chagall, Marc
Cendrars.   Prose of the Trans-Siberian and of
    Little Jeanne of France, The.
Kim Ch'unsu [*or* Chun-soo].   Snow over
    Chagall's Village.
McGinley.   On the Farther Wall, Marc Chagall.

Chairs
Blanco.   Metamorfosis de la silla.
    Metamorphosis of a Chair.
Borson.   After a Death.
Campbell, S.   Chairmaker, The.
Forbes, L.   Turning a Fresh Eye.
Guillén, J.   Happy Armchair.
Hagiwara Sakutaro.   Chair.
Haviaras, Stratis.   Tree.
Herbert, Z.   Armchairs.
Howe, S.   Plain chair or two back.
Jandl, E.   Chanson.

Klein, A.   Rocking Chair, The.
Masaoka Shiki.   Wicker chair / In pinetree's
    shade.
Metras, G.   Robert Frost's Chair.
Morgan, M.   Conversation.
Pietri.   3rd Untitled Poem.
Pilling.   Affair With a Chair, An.
Snyder, M.   Synge's Chair.
Townsend, A.   Rouge.
White, E.   Chairs in Snow.
Worth, V.   Chairs.

Challenger Space Shuttle
Ackerman, D.   Elegy for *Challenger*.
Ahl, L.   Defining Moment.
Estess.   Sunset on the Bayou.
Sagay-Lights, V.   Space.

Chameleons
Belchenko, N.   Chameleons are fine.
Cofer, J.   Chameleon, The.
Kinnell.   Gray Heron, The.
Menicanti.   Chameleon.
Moore, M.   To a Chameleon.
Prior.   Chameleon, The.
Unknown.   Cameleon Lover, The.

Chamois
Hemans.   Chamois Hunter's Love, The.

Champions
Preston, R.   Champion Chant.

Chance
Aiken, C.   Chance Meetings.
Amichai, Y.   Almost a Love Poem.
Andrade, O.   Frontier.
    Good Luck.
Armantrout.   As We're Told.
Baldwin, Sandy.   Artificial Terra-cotta Skin
    Mutagen Mask of Humbaba/Humwawa.
Bandeira.   Interview.
Bawer.   On Leaving the Artists' Colony.
Bécquer, G.   Arrow Flying Past, An.
Bond, E.   If.
Bone, K.   What Might Have Been.
Brandi.   Perhaps.
Burke, J.   It Could Happen to You.
Cassity.   Why Fortune Is the Empress of the
    World.
Cataldi.   We Could Have Met.
Charara, H.   On the Murder of an Ice Cream
    Man.
Creeley.   Way, The.
Cunningham, P.   Dog Called Chance, A.
Duhamel.   Art.
Elizabeth I.   Ah silly pug wert thou so sore
    afraid.
Fetter, T.   Taking a Chance on Love.
Gioia.   Summer Storm.
Gyatso, T.   Lover met by chance on the road.
Gylys, B.   Fat Chance.
Herrick.   Casualties.
Hunter, K.   Accident in a naked place.
Kalmar *et al.*   Nevertheless (I'm in Love with
    You).
Knott.   At the Crossroads.
Latouche, J.   Taking a Chance on Love.
Lewis, S.   Chance Child.
MacNeice.   Close and slow, summer is ending in
    Hampshire.
Melville, H.   Guide and Guard.
Merwin.   One of the Lives.
Mulkey, R.   Blind-Sided.
Nelson, H.   Journey, The: "I am wearing my
    gray wool pants, and my brown boots."
Phillips, D.   Hounds are either the work of wind,
    The.
Ralegh.   Thus now I leave my love in fortunes
    {handes / bandes}.
Ruby, H.   Nevertheless (I'm in Love with You).
Smith, John.   Unicorn, The.
Szymborska, W.   Love at First Sight.
    Terrorist, He Watches, The.
    Terrorist Is Watching, A.
Tuqan, F.   I Won't Sell His Love.
Vallejo.   Eternal Dice, The.
Volkow.   Arcana 10: Fortune.
    Arcano 10: La Fortuna.
Wotton, S.   Upon the Sudden Restraint of the

Wen T'ing-yün. Temple of Su Wu, The.
Whittier. My Playmate.
Wilbur, R. Beautiful Changes, The.
Williams, M. Animals.
Williams, W. Why go further? One might
 conceivably rectify the rhythm.
Williamson, A. Almost at the Horizon.
Wordsworth, W. Mutability.
Worth, V. Door.
Wright, D. Cockermouth.
Wright, J. On a Phrase from Southern Ohio.
Wu Wen-ying. Tune: "Sand of Silk-Washing
 Brook" A Reminiscence.
Wunderlich, M. On Opening.
Wyatt. Divers[e] [or Dyvers] doth[e] use, as I
 have heard and kno[w].
Yeats. Lamentation of the Old Pensioner, The
 (1890 version).
 Lamentation of the Old Pensioner, The (1925
 version).
Young, A. California Peninsula: El Camino
 Real.
Zabolotsky [or Zabolotskii]. Metamorphoses.
Zondberg, O. Variety of animals, said
 Khlebnikov, The.
See also **Transience**

Changelings
Cofer, J. Changeling, The.
Unknown. Tam Lin.

Channing, William Henry
Emerson, R. Ode, Inscribed to W. H. Channing.

Chaos
Aiken, C. Room, The.
Artaud. Spurt of Blood, The.
Ashbery, J. Hotel Lautréamont.
Benn. Fragments.
Bernstein, C. Gradation.
Berrigan, A. Looking Up My Balance.
Blind. Chaunts of Life.
Breton, A. "Factory".
 Mystery Corset, The.
Brown, L. Impulse to Call & Spring Upon, The.
Brownstein. Glass Enclosure, The.
Byron, G. Darkness.
Daumal. Short Revelation Concerning Death
 and Chaos.
Desnos. Language Event Two.
Drieu la Rochelle. Roundness.
Eich. Old Postcards.
Ekelof. Absentia Animi.
Fisher, R. Rules and Ranges for Ian Tyson.
Glatstein, J. To a Friend Who Wouldn't Bother
 to Strain His Noodleboard Because Even So It
 Is Hard to Go Hunting When Your Rifle Is
 Blunt and Love Is Soft as an Old Blanket.
John, R. *et al.* Two Songs About a Dead Person
 or a Mole—Whichever It Was.
Kelly, R. Looking.
Kharms. Symphony No. 2.
Kowit. Notice.
Levin, D. Ars Poetica (the idea).
Lowell, R. For the Union Dead.
Mac Low. Mani-Mani Gatha.
Marlowe, A. He Does Not Give the Reader One
 Line of Information.
Mengham, Rod. Allegory of Good Government.
Messerli. Essay on Concrete, An.
Phillips, D. Five.
Pope, A. Yet, yet a moment, one dim ray of
 light.
Ribemont-Dessaignes. Artichokes.
Riley, J. Silence.
Robinson, K. First Thing.
 Severance.
Rolfe, E. City of Anguish.
Rothenberg, J. That Dada Strain.
St. John, P. Carnival.
Shakespeare, W. Go bind thou up young
 dangling apricots.
Sorley. Hundred Thousand Million Mites, A.
Stein, G. Scenes from the Door.
Szymborska, W. Seen from Above ("On a dirt
 road lies a dead beetle.").
Van Doesburg. Remembrance of the Founts of
 Night.
 Still Life: The Table.

Yeats. Second Coming, The.

Chaplin, Charlie
Crane, H. Chaplinesque.
Llwyd, Alan. Chaplin and Others.
Mandelstam [or Mandelshtam]. Charlie Chaplin
 Poem, The.
Orlovsky. Collaboration: Letter to Charlie
 Chaplin.
Sharshar, S. Charlie Chaplin.

Chapman, George
Keats. On First Looking into Chapman's
 Homer.

Chariots
George, F. Charioteer, The.
Satyanarayana, V. Your Chariot.

Charity
Berry, W. Guest, The.
Bishop, E. Miracle for Breakfast, A.
Browning, R. Twins, The.
Campo. Begging for Change in Winter.
Chatterton. Excelente Balade of Charitie, An.
Chesterton. From a Spanish Cloister.
Crashaw. C[h]aritas Nimia; or, The Dear[e]
 Bargain.
de Portalatin. Second Elegy.
Dickinson, E. If I can stop one Heart from
 breaking.
Euenus. To the Swallow.
Hopes. Invalid of Park Street, The.
Kelly, B. Imagining Their Own Hymns.
Klappert. To Whom.
MacKay, R. Rispond Miser, The.
McDonald, W. After the Random Tornado.
Mirville, E. Don't give me food.
Moore, M. Charity Overcoming Envy.
Mukand, J. First Payment.
Pritchard, N. Cloak, The.
Ray, H. Charity.
 Triple Benison, The.
Robinson, E. Karma.
Unknown. Good King Wenceslas.
 I Shall Not Pass This Way Again.
Wright, J. Hook.
See also **Philanthropy and Philanthropists**

Charlemagne
Tuckerman, F. Rhotruda.
Unknown. Charles the King, our Emperor, the
 great.
 Marsilion sees his people's martyrdom.
 Night passes on, and the bright day appears.
 They arm themselves with Saracen hauberks.

Charles I, King of England
Herrick. Bad Season Makes the Poet Sad, The.
 To the King and Queen[e], upon Their Unhappy
 Distances.
 To the King; Upon His Com[m]ing with His
 Army into the West.
 To the King; Upon His Taking of Leicester.
Johnson, L. By the Statue of King Charles [or
 I] at Charing Cross.
Llwyd, A. Law was ever above kings, The.
Lovelace, R. To My Worthy Friend Mr. Peter
 Lely [or Lilly].
Philips, K. Upon the Double Murther of King
 Charles I.

Charles II, King of England
Dryden, J. Absalom and Achitophel.
 In pious times ere [or e'r] priest-craft did begin.
 Return of Charles II, The.
Herrick. To the Most Illustrious and Most
 Hopeful[l] Prince, Charles, Prince of Wales.
Rochester, J. Epitaph on Charles II.
 Impromptu on Charles II.
 Satire on Charles II, A.
Unknown. Me thinks I see our mighty monarch
 stand.

Charles, Prince of Wales
Davies, T. Caernarfon, 2 July [or July 2] 1969.

Charles, Ray
Berrigan, T. Personal Poem # 8.
Cecil. Richard's Blues.

Charles River, Massachusetts
Hyde, L. Goldfish in the Charles River.
O'Grady, D. Professor Kelleher and the Charles
 River.

Rosen, K. Along the Charles.
Share, D. Divorced.

Charleston, South Carolina
Derricotte. 1994 Inventory.
Heard, J. New Organ, The.
Mack, C. Charleston.
 Charleston.
Timrod. Charleston.
 Ode: "Sleep sweetly in your humble graves."
Weaver, A. Charleston.

Charm
Burke, J. Personality.
Greenberg, S. East River's Charm.
Hutchinson, P. Bright after Dark.
Plomer. French Lisette: A Ballad of Maida
 Vale.
Ransom, J. Vision by Sweetwater.
Sansom, M. Honour, that Guardian Angel, can
 alone.
Schnackenberg. Accident, An.
Zanzotto. Eva, forma futuri.

Charms (genre)
Campion, T. Thrice Toss[e] These Oaken Ashes
 in the Air [or Ayre].
Fagan. Little Bad Dream Charm.
Orozco. To Make a Talisman.
Sleigh. Spell Spoken by Suppliant to Helios for
 Protection.
Talvikki, A. Origin Charm Against Uncertain
 Injuries.
Unknown. Butter Charm.
 Charm Rhyme, A.

Charon
Belloc. To Dives.
Ficowski. 5.8.1942 / In Memory of Janusz
 Korczak.
Field. It was deep April, and the morn.
Landor, W. Dirce.
López Colomé, P. Dolor de corazón.
 Heartache.
MacNeice. Charon.
Rossetti, D. Sonnet is a moment's monument,
 A.
Simic. Charon's Cosmology.
Virgil [or Vergil]. Charon.
 Charon.
Zonas. Charon.

Chartism
Jenkins, M. Chartist Meeting.

Chartres, France
Bowen, E. In Chartres.
Martin, Steve. Demolition of the Cathedral at
 Chartres.
Molloy, D. Chacun à son goût.
Oppen. Chartres.
Wharton, E. Chartres.

Chastity
Ausonius. I used to tell you, "Frances, we grow
 old".
Barnfield [or Barnefield]. Thus was my love,
 thus was my Ganymed.
Blake, W. Abstinence Sows Sand All Over.
Carolan [or O'Carolan]. Gracey Nugent.
Field. Tragic Mary Queen of Scots, The.
Juvenal. Satire 6.
Komunyakaa, Y. Chastity Belt.
Montagu, L. Lover, The; a Ballad.
Ovid. Arethusa Saved.
Paz. Better the crime, / the suicides of lovers,
 the incest committed.
Philips, K. Answer to Another Persuading a
 Lady to Marriage, An.
Robinson, M. 2. The Temple of Chastity.
Ssu-ma Hsiang-ju. Beautiful Person, The.
Storni. You Want Me White ("You want me
 pure.").
Theocritus. Idyll 27: Daphnis.
Thomas, E. Remedia Amoris.
Unknown. Song of Summer.
 Ye-you si-jun: Lies a Dead Deer.
Wroth. Sonnet 2: "Is to leave all, and take the
 thread of love."

Chattahoochee River, Georgia
Lanier, S. Song of the Chattahoochee.

Chatterton, Thomas
Keats.   To Chatterton.
Chaucer, Geoffrey
Breeze.   Wife of Bath Speaks in Brixton Market.
Greene, R.   Description of Sir Geoffrey Chaucer,
   The.
Longfellow, H.   Chaucer.
Silliman.   When that april with his sure as soot
   the draft of March has pierced it to the root.
Waller, E.   Of English Verse.
Cheating and Cheaters
Unknown.   Village Burglar, The.
Cheerfulness
Creeley.   Be of Good Cheer.
Harvey, James Clarence.   Versicle, A.
Cheese
Alcman.   But often on the mountain peaks
   when.
Crooker.   Grating Parmesan.
Herrick.   Fresh Cheese and Cream.
Hughes, T.   Cheese for the Archdeacon, A.
Landesman.   Say "Cheese!".
McGrath, C.   Capitalist Poem #36.
McIntyre.   Ancient poets ne'er did dream, The.
   Prophecy of a Ten Ton Cheese.
Murray, G.   American Cheese.
Unknown.   Sukey [or Suky], you shall be my
   wife.
Chekhov, Anton
Berg, S.   Prayer: "Nobody understands so let the
   Rabbi."
Bolton, J.   Fin de Siècle.
Hirshfield, J.   In Praise of Coldness.
Kirby, D.   Amazed by Chekhov.
Mueller, L.   Late Hours.
Simpson, L.   Chocolates.
Vazirani, R.   It's Me, I'm Not Home.
Chemical Warfare
Kipling, R.   Gethsemane.
Merwin.   Asians Dying, The.
Owen, W.   Dulce et Decorum Est.
Chemistry and Chemists
Bentley, E.   Sir Humphry Davy.
Bierds, L.   Quickly and Fully.
Lehrer.   Elements, The.
Masters, E.   Trainor, the Druggist.
Wilkie, B.   Very Fine Lines.
Cheney, Dick
Friedlander, B.   Dick Cheney's Heart.
Chernobyl
Bhatt, S.   Wine from Bordeaux.
Chadwick, J.   Eight-Legged Colt, Chernobyl.
Marshall, J.   In the Shadow of the Poisoned
   Wind.
Salter.   Chernobyl.
Sirota, L.   Radiophobia.
Stainer.   Xochiquetzal.
Wojahn.   Workmen Photographed inside the
   Reactor.
See also **Nuclear Accidents**
Cherry Trees and Cherries
Akutagawa Ryunosuke.   Sick and feverish.
Basho.   Cedar umbrella / Off to Mount Yoshino.
   Temple bell / A cloud of cherry flowers.
Blumenthal, M.   Cherries.
Brown, L.   Life Is Just a Bowl of Cherries.
Burrows, S.   Time of Cherries, A.
Fenollosa, M.   Yuki.
Herrick.   Cherry-ripe [or Cherrie-ripe].
Hezutsu Tosaku.   On the crest of the hills.
Hoitsu.   Buddha / Cherry flowers.
Hokushi.   My house gutted.
Housman.   Loveliest of trees, the cherry now.
Issa.   Cherry blossoms? / In these parts.
   Under cherry trees / There are.
Jenkins, N.   Wild Cherry.
Ki no Tsurayuki.   Wind that scatters, The.
Lawrence, D. H.   Cherry Robbers.
Lowry, M.   Wild Cherry, The.
McClure, M.   For Diane di Prima.
Nishiyama Soin.   Cherry blossoms / dizzying.
O'Connor, M.   Sakura.
Okamoto.   Tanka: "Ten years ago."
Patchen.   Only Cherries?
Rossetti, C.   Let's Be Merry.

Let's Be Merry.
Sobaku.   Cherry blossoms.
Thomas, E.   Cherry Trees, The.
Thornton, R.   Cherry Laurel, The.
Unknown.   Whatever the cost.
Ward, T.   In the Interest of Possibility.
Wickham.   Cherry-Blossom Wand, The.
Chesapeake Bay
Kendrick, D.   Drowned River, The.
Wylie.   Wild Peaches.
Chess
Borges.   Chess.
Breton, N.   Chess Play, The.
Goodman, P.   Chess Game, A.
Harwood, G.   Game of Chess, A.
Kirsch, S.   I Wanted to Kill My King.
Lake, P.   Pieces.
Li K'ai-hsien.   Sent to the Master Physician,
   "Almond Orchard" Shih.
Rossetti, D.   On the Poet, Arthur
   O'Shaughnessy—.
Sánchez, K.   Porcelain Childhood.
Seidman.   Demonstration.
Simic.   Evening Chess.
   Prodigy.
Stanard, C.   Washington Square Park and a
   Game of Chess.
Yüan Mei.   Miscellaneous Feelings in the Sui
   Garden.
Chesterton, Gilbert Keith
Belloc.   Lines to a Don.
Chestnut Trees and Chestnuts
Akera Kanko.   Chased round and round.
Aldrich, T.   Song: "Chestnuts shine through the
   cloven rind, The."
Basho.   Chestnut by the eaves.
Eberhart, R.   Horse Chestnut Tree, The.
Jones, B.   Chestnut Tree Deciding to Fly in
   May, The.
Longfellow, H.   Village Blacksmith, The.
Masaoka Shiki.   Storm—chestnuts / Race along.
Meyer, C.   Blackshadow Chestnut.
Neufeldt, L.   Tree with a hole in our front yard,
   The.
Unknown, fr. Terezin Concentration Camp.   On a
   Sunny Evening.
Chicago, Illinois
Alexander, M.   Chicago.
Anderson, S.   Evening Song.
   Evening Song.
   Song of the Soul of Chicago.
Carruth, H.   Scrambled Eggs and Whiskey.
Coleman, T.   Chicago on the Day Brother
   Increases His Chances of Reaching Age 21.
Coolbrith.   Captive of the White City, The.
Dobyns.   Freight Cars.
Fordham.   Chicago Exposition Ode.
Fujita, Jun.   Chicago River.
   Michigan Boulevard.
Hamod, S.   Joe Williams at the Blue Note/
   Chicago, 1955; March 30 1999.
Harris, D.   Landscapes.
Harte, B.   Chicago.
Hernandez, D.   Rooftop Piper.
Hirsch, E.   American Apocalypse.
Hughes, L.   Visitors to the Black Belt.
Jordan, J.   For Beautiful Mary Brown: Chicago
   Rent Strike Leader.
Loftis, N.   Big John.
Marshall, Susan.   Chicago.
Martinez, D.   Hysteria.
Masters, E.   This is the city of great doges
   hidden.
McGrath, C.   Spring Comes to Chicago.
Nichols, Travis.   Wild is the Wind.
Piatt, J.   Fires in Illinois.
Ramanujan.   Chicago Zen.
Rexroth, K.   Bad Old Days, The.
Ridge, L.   Chicago.
Rodriguez, L.   Fire.
Sandburg, C.   Chicago.
   Mamie.
Schmitz.   Climbing Sears Tower.
   Making Chicago.
Seaton, M.   Nostradamus Predicts the

Destruction of Chicago.
   Tagging.
Shepherd, R.   Maritime.
Walcott.   Chicago's avenues, as white as Poland.
Welch, L.   Chicago Poem.
Chicanos and Chicanas
Anzaldúa.   Horse.
Encarnacion.   Bulosan Listens to a Recording of
   Robert Johnson.
Lem.   Office Hour.
Mora.   Depression Days.
   La Migra.
Salinas, R.   Trip Through the Mind Jail, A.
Soto.   Black Hair.
   Mexicans Begin Jogging.
Chickadees
Balakian, P.   Idyll: "I lived behind a window."
McKay, D.   Chickadee Encounter.
Chickens
Addonizio.   Chicken.
Bly, R.   As a Child.
Brown, G.   Hawk, The.
Buson.   From outside a hedge, a hen calls her
   chicks.
Corben.   In the eggs.
Dobyns.   Spiritual Chickens.
Finch, P.   Scaring Hens.
Frémon, Jean.   Autumn: "Shogun, always on the
   lookout for ways to increase his glory, The."
Garcia, R.   Chickens Everywhere.
   Nobody Here But Us.
Herbert, Z.   Hen.
Hernández Cruz.   If Chickens Could Talk.
Ignatow, D.   No Theory.
Jacob, V.   Water-Hen, The.
Knox, J.   Chicken Bucket.
Nash, O.   Experiment Degustatory.
Orton, B.   Bacchanal.
Rankine.   Eden.
Ryan, K.   Home to Roost.
Shange.   Ancestral Messengers / Composition
   13.
Stein, G.   Chicken.
   Chicken ("Alas a doubt in case of more go to
   say what it is cress. What is it. Mean. Potato.
   Loaves.").
   Chicken ("Pheasant and chicken, chicken is a
   peculiar bird.").
   Chicken ("Stick stick call then, stick stick
   sticking, sticking with a chicken. Sticking in a
   extra succession, sticking in.").
Unknown.   I went down to my garden patch.
Williams, W.   Red Wheelbarrow, The.
Wilson, R.   Dungle sublime.
Wright, J.   Presentation of Two Birds to My
   Son, A.
Child Abuse
Addonizio.   Broken Sonnets.
Anderson, A.   Suicide Year, The.
Bass, E.   Bearing Witness.
Bradley, J.   Improper Disposal.
Brooks, G.   Merle; Uncle Seagram.
Budbill.   What I Heard at the Discount
   Department Store.
Bursk.   What a Boy Does Not Say.
Carroll, L.   Duchess's Lullaby, The.
Cary, P.   Granny's House.
Chin, J.   Why a Boy.
Citino.   In the Bedroom of Fear.
   Newborn Found Alive in Shallow Grave.
Dove, R.   Taking in Wash.
Duhamel.   Four Hours.
Espada.   When the Leather Is a Whip.
Gregerson.   For the Taking.
Hayden, R.   Whipping, The.
Hodges, Janice W.   Bruised Children.
Holloway, G.   Non-Accidental Injury Slides.
Larkin, J.   Origins.
Lawrence, D. H.   Discord in Childhood.
McCarriston.   Billy.
   Castle in Lynn, A.
Meinke.   This is a poem to my son Peter.
Mouré.   Thirteen Years.
O'Reilly, M.   Abused Child.
Potos.   Twenty Years Later, to a Friend.
Russell, T.   In Simili Materia.

Child Labor
Santos, S. Talking Cure, The.
Smith, S. Lord Barrenstock.
 Papa Love Baby.
Thiel, D. Minefield, The.
Watson, E. Battered Toddler, Page B6.
Child Labor
Blake, W. Chimney Sweeper, The ("Little black
 thing among the snow, A.").
 Chimney Sweeper, The ("When my mother died
 I was very young.").
Cook, E. Our Father.
Landon. Factory, The.
Reznikoff. 2. The Job.
Childhood and Children
Abad, G. Toys.
Abbot, E. Awakening.
Adams, A. Cooking.
Adams, F. Those Two Boys.
Adams, L. Kids!
Adcock, F. Halfway Street, Sidcup.
Addonizio. Broken Sonnets.
Adkins, G. Children in Armour.
Aguilar-Cariño. Familiar.
Ai. Good Shepherd, The: Atlanta, 1981.
Aiken, C. Senlin, walking before us in the
 sunlight.
Albert-Birot. Who is that blond child laughing
 as he runs after his colored marbles?
Aldis, D. Hiding.
Alexander, E. Aspirin.
 Minnesota Fats Describes His Youth.
Alexander the Wild. Strawberry Picking.
 When We Were Children.
Algarin. Meeting Gaylen's 5th Grade Class.
Allbery. Offering.
Alley, R. Growing Days, The.
Amichai, Y. Anniversaries of War.
 My Child Blossoms Sadly.
 My Son.
 We Have Done Our Duty.
 What is it? An airplane at dawn. No.
Anderson, A. Licking Wounds.
Angela, F. Old Stone Age.
Angus. Blue Jacket, The.
Anyte [or Anytes]. Putting red reins on you,
 goat, with a noseband.
Ashbery, J. Young Son, The.
Atwood. Fainting.
 Making Poison.
 Sad Child, A.
Aygi, G. Going to Sleep in Childhood.
Baca. Book 5: Rebirth; Poem Twenty-Eight.
Bachhuber, D. Mozart in a Classroom of
 Children.
Bachmann. Firstborn Land, The.
Baehr, A. Christina.
Baillie, J. Child to His Sick Grandfather, A.
Barber, D. Spirit Level, The.
Barber, M. Written for My Son, and Spoken by
 Him at His First Putting on Breeches.
Barlow, G. Painting Drunken Twilight.
Barrax. Scuba Diver Recovers the Body of a
 Drowned Child, The.
 Strangers Like Us: Pittsburgh, Raleigh, 1945–
 1985.
 Visit.
 Whose Children Are These?
Basheva. N. N.
Basho. Peasant's child, The.
Bass, F. Garden, The.
Baton, M. Childhood in the Country, A.
Beeching, H. Going Down Hill on a Bicycle.
Behn, R. Origin.
Bekes Jr. Picture.
Belev. Dream: "When the trees began to calcify,
 and the birds to coalesce with the branches."
 Love: "What do you scrawl."
Belieu. Against Writing about Children.
 Radio Nebraska.
Bell, M. We Have Known.
 Who I am is a short person with small feet.
Belli, C. Father, Mother.
 My Parents, Know It Well.
Belloc. Jim Who Ran Away from His Nurse,
 and Was Eaten by a Lion.
Bennett, K. 99.9 FM Radio Nostalgia.

Benson, S. Beaten Track, The.
Berg, S. Don't Forget.
Berger, B. Without.
Berggolts [or Bergholts]. To My Sister.
Bergland, B. Up Yonder in the Meadow of
 Children.
Bernes, J. Found Missing.
Berry, W. To Tanya at Christmas.
Berryman. Ball Poem, The.
 Henry sats in de bar and was odd.
Betjeman. False Security.
Beveridge. Catching Webs.
Bevington, L. One More Bruised Heart!
Binyon. Little Dancers, The.
Bishop, E. In the Waiting Room.
Bishop, M. Sales Talk for Annie.
Blake, W. Holy Thursday [1].
 Holy Thursday [2].
 Infant Joy.
 Infant Sorrow.
 Nurse's Song ("When the voices of children are
 heard on the green.").
 Nurse's Song ("When the voices of children are
 heard on the green / And whisperings [or
 whisprings] are in the dale.").
Blumenthal, M. Disappointments of Childhood,
 The.
Bly, R. Anger Against Children.
 As a Child.
 Things My Brother and I Could Do.
Bogan, L. Kept.
Boland, E. Game, The.
Bonnefoy. All, the Nothing, The.
Borthwick, P. Out of Bounds.
Boruch. Sewing.
Boyle, K. What Parents Do Not Yet Know.
Bradstreet, A. Author to Her Book, The.
 In Reference to Her Children, 23 June, 1659 [or
 1659].
 To My Dear Children.
Braithwaite. City Garden, A.
Brandt, D. Little one, black angel.
Breytenbach. Black City, The.
Brines, F. Beggar, The.
Brontë, C. Orphan Child, The.
Brooks, G. Bronzeville Woman in a Red Hat.
 Children of the Poor, The.
 Mother, The.
 Parents: People Like Our Marriage Maxie and
 Andrew, The.
Brown, M. Survival Motion: Notice.
Brown, S. Children's Children.
 Chillen Get Shoes.
 Conjured.
Browning, E. Cry of the Children, The.
Bruck. Childhood.
Brunk, J. All Sweet Things, Like Forgiveness,
 Are a Falling.
 Letter to Myself as a Child.
Bryan, S. Lunch with Girl Scouts.
Bryner. Part of a Larger Country.
Buddingh'. Some Biographical Data.
Bukowski. Me against the world.
Burns, J. Marble surfaces.
Burnside, J. Anstruther.
Burroughs, W. Cold Lost Marbles.
Butts, A. Nature of Braille, The.
Cabalquinto. Depths of Fields.
Caesar. Animal Crackers in My Soup.
Caldwell, A. Raggedy Ann.
Campert. Message About the Times.
 Sign of the Times.
Campo. Lost Plaza Is Everywhere, The.
 My Childhood in Another Part of the World.
Carbó, N. Civilizing the Filipino.
 In Tagalog Ibon Means Bird.
 When the Grain Is Golden and the Wind Is
 Chilly, Then It Is the Time to Harvest.
Carroll, L. Duchess's Lullaby, The.
 Jabberwocky.
Carroll. In the Shakespeare Garden at
 Northwestern University.
Casey, M. On What the Army Does with
 Heads.
Cassells. From the Theater of Wine.
Cassian. Part of a Bird.

Castillo, S. Letter to Yeni on Peering into Her
 Life.
Cawthorn. Wit was a strange unlucky child.
Ceravolo. Indian Suffering.
 Lighthouse.
Cerenio. 13 June 1994.
 20 July 1994.
Chamberlain, K. Airlift.
Cheney-Coker. Childhood.
Chippewa Oral Tradition. Sioux Woman
 Defends Her Children, The.
Ch'oe Sûngja. From Early On I Was.
Chông Hwajin. Monsoon Season Opens
 Children's Eyes.
 Suddenly, the Yard Where Rice and Yeast Brew.
Ciardi, J. Sometimes Even Parents Win.
Clampitt. Imago.
Clanchy, K. Men From the Boys.
Clarke, G. Baby-Sitting.
Clements, S. Matinee.
 Reservation, The.
 Susans.
Clifton, L. C. C. Rider.
 Listen Children.
 Sorrow Song.
Cofer, J. How to Get a Baby.
Cole, H. Childlessness.
Coleman, W. Coffee.
 Three Trees.
Coleridge, H. Long Time a Child.
Coleridge, M. In London Town.
Coleridge, S. Youth and Age.
Coles, R. Goddam Street, The.
Collins, B. First Reader.
 On Turning Ten.
 Writing in the Afterlife.
Cook, E. Our Father.
 Song of the Rushlight.
Cooley, N. Arson.
 Diane Arbus, New York.
Coolidge, C. Album—A Runthru.
Cooper, D. After School, Street Football, Eighth
 Grade.
Cope, J. Solstice for John.
Copus, J. Back Seat of My Mother's Car, The.
Corn. Conch from Sicily, A.
Cornford, F. Childhood.
 Ode on the Whole Duty Of Parents.
Cornwall. To My Child.
Coultas, B. Human Museum, The.
Creeley. Company, The.
Crucefix. Air-Waves.
Cruickshank, H. Shy Geordie.
Csoori. Visitor's Memories, The.
Cullen, C. Incident.
Cummings, E. E. Hist whist / little ghostthings.
 In Just.
 Little tree / little silent Christmas tree.
 Who are you,little i.
Dalton, A. How to Disappear.
Damas. Hiccups.
Daniel, G. It Makes Me Sad.
Daniels, K. Prayer for My Children.
 War Photograph.
Darío, R. Far Away and Long Ago.
Daryush. Children of Wealth.
Davis, G. Children in the Arbor.
De Cristoforo, Violet Kazue. Konchu Kazu Aru
 Yube Ako Iyo-Iyo Seicho Shitari.
De Kok. Al Wat Kind Is.
De la Selva. Tropical Childhood.
Dean, D. K. In the Way Back.
Deltoro, A. Viaje.
 Voyage.
Denby. People on Sunday.
Deniz, G. Childish.
 Pueril.
Derricotte. Fears of the Eighth Grade.
Deutsch. "To an Amiable Child".
Dharker. Namesake.
Dickey, R. Father.
 Mulatto Lullaby.
Dickey, W. Memoranda.
Dickinson, E. Little Dog that wags his tail, A.
Dietz, H. Triplets.
Divakaruni. Childhood.

Yuba City School.
Djanikian. How I Learned English.
  In the Elementary School Choir.
  When I First Saw Snow.
Dodd, W. Of His Life.
Doty, M. Coastal.
Dove, R. Breathing, the Endless News, The.
  Quaker Oats.
Doyle, S. This Shade.
Drummond de Andrade. Infancy.
Dubie. Of Politics, & Art.
  Poem: "Mule kicked out in the trees, A. An
    Early."
Duffy, C. Close.
Duhig, I. First Second, The.
Dunbar, P. Little Brown Baby.
Duncan, L. Visit, The: "Mary, more than quite
    contrary, bars the door."
Duncan, R. Ark for Lawrence Durrell, An.
  Childhood's Retreat.
Duran, J. Pyrenees, The.
Durcan. Weeping Headstones of the Isaac
    Becketts, The.
Earle, J. Saturday in the '20s, A.
E'der, E. La Puente.
Edmond, L. Jardin des Colombières.
Edwards [or Edwardes], R. When I Was Three.
El-Gabry, M. Child Hunting Tales, A.
Elliot, A. Latitudes of Home, The.
Elliott, G. Poem About Myself.
Ellis, T. Star Child.
Elmslie, K. Sibling Rivalry.
Emerson, R. Awed I behold once more.
  Motto to "The Poet".
Erdrich. Windigo.
Esteves. Take the Hearts of Children.
Ezekiel. Night of the Scorpion.
Factor, J. Mother to Son.
Fagan. Charm for What Looks Like.
Falcón, J. Sycamore.
Farjeon, E. Over the Garden Wall.
Feld, Andrew. On Fire.
Ferlinghetti, L. Pennycandystore beyond the El,
  The.
Field, E. Jest 'fore Christmas.
  Little Boy Blue.
  Sugar-Plum Tree, The.
Field, Miranda. Childhood's House.
Fitzgerald, R. Figlio Maggiore.
Flynn, N. Cartoon Physics, Part 1.
Fogarty, L. By Accident, Blinked.
Follen, E. Children in Slavery.
Fontanella. For Emma.
Forbes, C. Picture of a Man.
Forché. As Children Together.
Foster, A. Gap, The.
Francis, R. Farm Boy after Summer.
Frost, R. Birches.
  Home Burial.
Fuller, C. Guests.
Gallup. Backing into the Future.
  Guard Duty.
Galvin, B. Knot Hole Gang, The.
Galvin, J. Station (1).
  Station (2).
García Lorca. Little Mute Boy, The.
  1910.
Gardiner, S. Brought Up.
Garrett, E. Vista.
Geiger. Soundtracks.
Gilbert, C. Pushing.
Gilmore, B. Revolution.
Giovanni. Always There Are the Children.
  Legacies.
  Nikki-Rosa.
Glickman. But till that morning, ain't no one
    gonna harm you.
Gloria. Assimilation.
Glück, L. Descending Figure.
  Drowned Children, The.
  Firstborn.
  Gift, The.
  Illuminations.
  School Children, The.
  Time: "There was too much, always, then too
    little."

Goethe. When you tell me that you were
    unpopular as a child.
Goldbarth. Poem of the Praises, The.
Goldberg, B. Bedtime Story.
  Retro Lullaby.
  Third Body.
  Twentieth Century Children.
  Twentieth Century Children (2).
Goodison. Songs of the Fruits and Sweets of
  Childhood.
Goodman, M. Cobwebs.
Gordon, J. Love.
Goyette, Susan. True Names of Birds, The.
Graham, D. Wireless, The.
Graham, H. L'Enfant Glacé.
  Tender-Heartedness.
Graham, W. Loch Thom.
Graham-Pole, J. Candor.
Graves, R. I'd Love to Be a Fairy's Child.
  Warning to Children.
Gray, T. Ode on a Distant Prospect of Eton
  College.
Greacen. Carnival at the River.
Greenberg, A. Berlin Series.
Greening, T. My Children Visit the Zendo.
Greger. Prince of the Powers of the Air.
Gregory, H. Cage of Voices, The.
Grennan. Pause.
Grey, C. Hallelujah!
Griffin, S. This Is Not Love's Offering.
Griffiths, B. Fragment 9: "I go to Zoo."
Grosholz. Eden.
Grubb, D. Windows of Sarajevo, The.
Gu Cheng. Holy Child Descends, The.
Guest, B. Hungry Knight, The.
Guevara, M. Once When I Was in the Eighth
  Grade.
Gumilyov [or Gumiliov or Gumilev].
  Childhood.
Gunn, T. Blank, A.
Gwala. One small boy longs for summer.
Gwynn, R. Drive-In, The.
Haavikko. Woman raises her garment, rain,
  wind, darkness rise, The.
Hachenburg, H. Terezin.
Hadas, R. Moments of Summer.
  Red Hat, The.
Hagedorn, J. Souvenirs.
Hagiwara Sakutaro. Chair.
Hale, S. Mary's Lamb [or Mary and Her
  Lamb].
Hall, D. Goggles and Helmet.
Hardy, T. Oxen, The.
Harms. Sky.
Harmsen van Beek. Introduction to a Prayer.
Harris, D. What we have lost.
Harris, J. Fever.
Harrison, G. Playground, The.
Harryman. Note.
Harte, B. Miss Edith's Modest Request.
Hartwig. Matthew 2:16–18; Then Herod, when
  he saw.
Hashimoto, S. Standing in the Doorway, I
  Watch the Young Child Sleep.
Hass, R. Late Spring.
Hauge. Leaf Huts and Snow Houses.
Hawaiian Oral Tradition. With one woven
  basket.
Hayden, R. Those Winter Sundays.
  Whipping, The.
Hayes, T. At Pegasus.
Healey, S. My Wrist Split Open.
Heaney, S. Alphabets.
  Clearances.
  Death of a Naturalist.
  Follower.
  Hazel Stick for Catherine Ann, A.
  Personal Helicon.
  Railway Children, The.
  Sofa in the Forties, A.
  Wheels within Wheels.
Hecht, A. Book of Yolek, The.
  It Out-Herods Herod. Pray You, Avoid It.
  Sarabande on Attaining the Age of Seventy-
    Seven.
Heine, H. Mein Kind, wir waren Kinder.

Hemans. Return, The.
Henderson-Holmes. Friendly Town #1.
  Friendly Town #3.
  To Hell and Back, with Cake.
Herbert, G. Holy Baptism (2).
Herbert, W. Praise of Italian Chip-Shops.
Herd. Bathing Girls, The.
  Survivors, The.
Hernández, M. Lullabies of the Onion.
Herrick. Grace for a Child.
Herschberger. Page Torn from a Notebook.
Heyen. Blue.
Heym. With Pointed Head She Rises.
Hill, G. Princes of Mercia were badger and
  raven, The. Thrall.
Hirsch, E. Magic Mirror, The.
Hoagland, E. Big Zeb Johnson.
Hogg, J. Boy's Song, A.
Holan. Children at Christmas in 1945.
  You're Thinking of Children.
Holland, J. Spin-Cycle.
Holloway, G. Non-Accidental Injury Slides.
Hongo. Winnings.
Hood, T. I Remember, I Remember.
  Parental Ode to My Son, Aged Three Years and
    Five Months, A.
Hopes. Holy Innocents.
Hopkins, G. Handsome Heart, The.
  Spring and Fall [To a Young Child].
Houlihan, J. And Everywhere Offering Human
  Sound.
Housman. African Lion, The.
  Fragment of an English Opera.
  Infant Innocence.
  Purple William or The Liar's Doom.
Hove. Child's Parliment.
Howe, M. Sixth Grade.
Howitt, M. Dying Child, The.
Hudgins. Adoration of the Magi, The.
  Childhood of the Ancients.
  Gospel.
  Tree.
Hughes, L. Children's Rhymes ("By what
  sends.").
  Genius Child.
Hugo, R. White Center.
Hugo, V. At Villequier.
  Jeanne was holed up (pitch darkness; bread and
    water).
Ilio, D. Children of the Atomic Age.
Ilkov, Ani. Ram.
Iofe, Y. Thing or Two about Childhood, A.
Iorwerth, D. House of Teletubbies, The.
Issa. Bedbugs, The.
  Children / Don't harm the flea.
  Children imitating cormorants.
  Her row veering off.
  I envy.
  It once happened.
  Melting snow.
  Snow is melting, The.
  This stupid world.
Jaccottet. Glimpses.
Jacinto, J. Heaven Is Just Another Country.
Jacob, M. Little Poem.
Jacobsen, J. Birthday Party, The.
  Primer, The.
Jamie, K. Mother-May-I.
Jammes. Five Sorrowful Mysteries, The.
Janzen, J. Learning to Sing in Parts.
Jarnot, L. Girl Who Couldn't Be Loved, The.
Jarrell, R. Cinderella.
  Lost Children, The.
  Sick Child, A.
  Thinking of the Lost World.
  Truth, The.
Jeffers, L. My Children.
Jennings, E. Child's Story, The.
  Ugly Child, The.
Jones, Ceri Wyn. Honour.
Jones, P. In the Formal Garden.
Jordan, J. Test of Atlanta 1979, The.
Joseph, A. On Sidewalks, on Streetcorners, as
  Girls.
  Searching for *Melinda's Magic Moment.*
Joyce, J. Ecce Puer.

On the Beach at Fontana.
Juarroz. Bottom of things is neither life nor death, The.
Justice, D. Children Walking Home from School through Good Neighborhood.
In the Attic.
Nostalgia of the Lakefronts.
Poet at Seven, The.
Sonatina in Yellow.
Kahn, G. All God's Chillun Got Rhythm.
Kalina, R. *Dayeinu*—they said.
Kaminsky, Ilya. Dancing in Odessa.
Kaneko. Bailey Gatzert: The First Grade, 1945.
Kasdorf. First TV in a Mennonite Family.
Grossdaadi's Funeral.
Leftover Blessings.
Kaufman, S. Accuser, The.
Kavanagh, P. Long Garden, The.
Kees. 1926.
Keeshig-Tobias. I Grew Up.
Mother with Child.
Kelly, B. To the Lost Child.
Kendall, M. In the Toy Shop.
Kennedy, X. Help!
Poets.
Kennelly. Poem from a Three Year Old.
Kenyon, J. From the Nursery.
Kercheval, J. Children's Book of Knowledge, The.
Kerouac. 127th Chorus.
Khoury-Gata. Autumn Preceded Summer.
Kim Ch'unsu [*or* Chun-soo]. Lilac Petals.
Kim Sŭnghŭi. Institutions.
Kinnell. First Song.
Lackawanna.
Kinsella, J. Fall, The.
Kinzie. Boy.
Kitahara Hakushū. Ailing child, An.
Kizer, C. Children.
Not Writing Poems about Children.
Kleinzahler. Lunatic of Lindley Meadow, The.
Knight, E. Green Grass and Yellow Balloons.
Poem of Attrition, A.
Knight, S. In Case of Monsters.
Knott. Two Vietnam Poems: (1966).
Ko Ŭn. Into the Woods.
Koch, K. You Were Wearing.
Koehler, T. Animal Crackers in My Soup.
Koethe. From the Porch.
Komunyakaa, Y. Looking for Choctaw.
Sunday Afternoons.
Toys in a Field.
Venus's-flytraps.
Kumin, M. Height of the Season, The.
Nuns of Childhood, The: Two Views.
Kunitz, S. Testing-Tree, The.
Kurtz. Spanish Lullaby.
Kuskin. I Woke Up This Morning.
Question, The.
Rose on My Cake, The.
Lamb, C. Childhood Fled.
O! I Could Laugh to Hear the Midnight Wind.
Lamb, M. Parental Recollections.
Landon. Little Shroud, The.
Lane, P. Children.
Langford. Speak Gently.
Lapierre, B. Tomorrow's Hope.
Larcom. What the Train Ran Over.
Larkin, P. I Remember, I Remember.
This Be The Verse.
Larsen, L. Red.
Laughlin, J. Our Bicycles.
Lauterbach. Boy Sleeping.
Laux, D. Children's Train, The.
Lawrence, D. H. Piano.
Piano, The.
Lea, S. Clouded Evening, Late September.
Leader, M. Her Door.
Lee, L. Gift, The: "To pull the metal splinter from my palm."
Out of Hiding.
Tearing the Page.
Leeflang. 1945.
Lees, G. Waltz for Debby.
Lemm, Richard. Metamorphosis.
Levin, P. Dark Horse.

Levine, P. Belle Isle, 1949.
Old Testament, The.
On My Own.
To a Child Trapped in a Barber Shop.
Levison, B. Eighth Symphony Interruptus.
Lewis, J. For the Father of Sandro Gulotta.
Lewis, N. Footprint on the Air, A.
Li Po. Ballad of Long Bank, The.
Lihn. Dark Room, The.
Lim-Wilson. Alphabet Soup.
Limonov. And it's the summer civil war.
Lincoln, A. My Childhood-Home I See Again.
Liu, T. Echoes.
Livingston, M. Coming from Kansas.
Lemonade Stand.
Llewellyn-Williams. Making Babies.
Lloyd, C. My pleasant home! where erst when sad and faint.
Oh, I have told thee every secret care.
Lodeizen. Ode: In a Few Hours.
Loftis, N. Ruth.
Logan, J. Picnic, The: "It is the picnic with Ruth in the spring."
Longfellow, H. Children's Hour, The.
My Lost Youth.
Lope de Vega. Ice and Fires Contend with My Child.
Lorde. Ballad from Childhood.
Song for a Thin Sister.
What My Child Learns of the Sea.
Love, M. Initiation.
Lowell, R. My Last Afternoon with Uncle Devereux Winslow.
Lu Yu. Night Thoughts.
Lumsden, R. Show and Tell.
Lux. Amiel's Leg.
Men with Small Heads.
There Were Some Summers.
MacCaig. Intruder in a Set Scene.
MacDiarmid, H. Of John Davidson.
MacDonald, Hugh. Shingle Flies.
MacEwen, G. Child Dancing, The.
Children Are Laughing, The.
Macgoye. August the First: The Shadow. Patel Speaks.
Machado Ruiz. Memory from Childhood.
Portrait.
Mackenzie, K. Children Go, The.
Mackey, N. Phantom Light of All Our Day, The.
MacLeish. Eleven.
MacNeice. Soap Suds.
Madgett. Offspring.
Mahapatra, J. Main Temple Street, Puri.
Major, C. Doll Believers, The.
Mapanje. On Being Asked to Write a Poem for 1979.
Maraini. Plaza de Mayo.
Marennikova, K. Mother, squatting hurts.
Markham, M. Of Children on Wood.
Markus, P. Black Light.
Light.
Marlatt, D. Summer of the New Well.
Martínez, V. Children of the Disappeared.
Martinson. No Name for It.
Marvell. Picture of Little T. C. in a Prospect of Flowers, The.
Matthews, W. Housework.
McCabe, C. Ancutsa, Ancutsa.
McCallum, S. In My Other Life.
Perfect Heart, The.
McCarriston. Billy.
McClatchy. First Steps.
McCombs, J. Epithet.
McDaniel, J. First One, The.
Leonard.
McDonald, W. Children of Saigon, The.
McFadden, D. 12. Shantideva.
McFadden, R. Stringer's Field.
McGough, R. Cinders.
McGrath, C. Delphos, Ohio.
McLagan, Elizabeth. At Twelve.
McLain, P. Connor in the Wind and Rain with His Coat on.
McMahon, L. Barbie's Ferrari.
Mei Yao Ch'en. Excuse for Not Returning the

Visit of a Friend, An.
Meinke. Vincent.
Meireles. Sketch.
Meredith, W. Country Stars.
Merrill, J. Broken Home, The.
Days of 1935.
World and the Child, The.
Merwin. Windows, The: "Here is a child who presses his head to the ground."
Metodiev, Ivan. River: "River, River."
Mew. Ne Me Tangito.
Meynell, A. Cradle-Song at Twilight.
Parentage.
Mhlophe. Sometimes When It Rains.
Michaelis. I Was About Three Years of Age.
Miles, J. Doll.
Millay, E. Childhood Is the Kingdom Where Nobody Dies.
From a Very Little Sphinx.
Miller, A. My Trip.
Milligan, S. Bad Report—Good Manners.
Minhinnick. Children, The.
Mistral, G. Close to Me.
Let Him Not Grow Up.
Piececitos.
Rocking.
To the Children.
Mitchell, A. Dumb Insolence.
Mitchelson, T. Circa.
Mitchison. Hartmanswillerkopf.
Mitsui. Photograph of a Child, Japanese-American Evacuation, Bainbridge Island, Washington, March 30, 1942.
Moffett. Reaching Around.
Mok, J. Winter Mirror.
Momaday. To a Child Running with Outstretched Arms in Canyon de Chelly.
Montague, J. Locket, The.
Welcoming Party, A.
Moore, B. Child's Thought, A.
Moore, H. First Time: 1950.
Moore, T. Oft In the Stilly Night.
Morales, A. Child's Christmas in Puerto Rico, A.
Morgan, F. Busses, The.
Morgan, R. Code, The.
Morris, G. Woodman, Spare That Tree.
Morse, B. Day on the Planet, A.
Muir, E. Childhood.
Myth, The.
Muldoon, P. Right Arm, The.
Muske, C. Dulce Lignum, Dulces Clavos.
Field Trip.
Myers, J. Jake Addresses the World from the Garden.
Nash, O. Grandpa Is Ashamed.
Parent, The.
Nemerov. Icehouse in Summer, The.
Snow Globe, The.
Nesbit, E. Dead to the Living, The.
Haunted.
Nguyễn Chí Thiện. Model Children of the Regime, The.
Ní Chuilleanáin. Tale of Me, The.
Nims, J. Tennis Trophy.
No Hyangnim. Nursery.
Noguchi, R. Not Surfing Some Days.
Norris, L. Ravenna Bridge.
Nossis. Melinna herself is re-created: notice the face.
Notley. California Girlhood, A.
Nutter, G. Pond and Peace.
Nye, N. Shoulders.
Yellow Glove.
O'Reilly, M. Small Girl Brings an Injured Bird into the Surgery, A.
Oakes-Smith, E. Insect Affection.
Odio, E. Memory of My Private Childhood.
Ogilvy. Natal Address to My Child, March 19th 1844, A.
O'Hara, F. Autobiographia Literaria.
Blocks.
Cornkind.
Olds, S. Seventh Birthday of the First Child.
Try-Outs, The.
Ome Shushiki. Frost of separation / Father,

child.
Ondaatje. Bearhug.
Oppen. Exodus.
  Pedestrian.
Orr, G. Father's Song.
Ortiz, D. Ladders.
O'Sullivan, L. Prayer, The.
Owen, M. Topography.
Owen, W. To ———: "Three rompers run
  together, hand in hand."
Pagis, D. Ein Leben.
  Souvenir, The.
Paino. Matter of Division, A.
  1965.
Paley, G. Sad Children's Song, The.
Palgrave. Eutopia.
Pankey. As We Forgive Those.
Parker, D. When Mark Deloach Ruled the
  World.
Parnok, S. Childhood memory: those pears, A.
Parry, E. I Would Like You for a Comrade.
Patmore, C. Toys, The.
Patterson, G. Autobiographia.
Paulin. Peacetime.
Peacock, M. Buffalo.
  Dogged Persistence.
Peacock, T. Love and Age.
Pedretti, Erica. Dogs Are Supposed.
Peters, L. Isatou Died.
Philips, A. Ode: To Miss Margaret Pulteney
  [Daughter of Daniel Pulteney, Esq., in the
  Nursery].
Philpot, T. It Was a Boy.
Piatt, S. Answering A Child.
  Child's Party, A.
  Lesson in a Picture, A.
  Palace-Burner, The.
Pierpoint, K. Cuckoo-spit.
Pinsky. From the Childhood of Jesus.
  Street, The.
  Woman, A.
Pitter. Love and the Child.
Plath. Child.
  Getting There.
Poe. Alone.
Pollarolo, G. During Recess.
  Sunny Afternoon Dream, The.
Pomerantz, A. My Father the Foundryman.
Popa. Little Box, The.
Porter, A. Perfect Child, The.
Porzecanski. Every Month.
Prado, A. Stained Glass Window.
Praed. School and Schoolfellows.
Preston, R. Mama.
Prior. Letter to the Honourable Lady Margaret
  Cavendish Holles-Harley, A.
  To a Child of Quality, Five Years Old, the
    Author Suppos'd Forty.
Priory, J. Emma and the Radio.
Prunty. Winter's Tale, A.
Ramsey, J. Ontogeny.
Randell. Hard to Place.
Ravikovitch, D. You Can't Kill a Baby Twice.
Ray, H. On the Picture of a Child.
Reaney. Bicycle, The.
Reeves, J. Others.
Reid, C. In the Echoey Tunnel.
Rexroth, K. Homer in Basic.
Reyes, A. Monterrey Sun.
Reznikoff. Beggar Woman.
Rich, A. Children Playing Checkers at the Edge
  of the Forest.
  Memory lifts her smoky mirror: 1943.
  Not Like That.
Richman, L. Rue de Rosiers: To My Brother
  Fred.
Richter, H. Round Room, The.
Ridge, L. Because you are four years old.
Ridler. For a Child Expected.
Riley, J. Days Gone By, The.
  Little Orphant Annie.
  Old Sweetheart of Mine, An.
Rilke. Imaginary Career.
  Spring Has Returned.
Ríos, A. Language of Great-Aunts, The.
Ritsos. Myopic Child, A.

Robertson, R. Waves: "I have swum too far."
Robin, L. Hallelujah!
Robinson, E. For Karen.
  Meshes.
Roethke. Child on Top of a Greenhouse.
  My Papa's Waltz.
Rohrer, M. Childhood Stories.
Rontsh, Y. Ballad of the Night.
Roripaugh, L. Pearls.
Rosenberg, L. No Boundaries.
  Offpsring, The.
  Suburban Childhood, A.
  Which One Is the Grown-up? Haiku.
Rossetti, C. Frisky Lamb, A.
Roy, L. Suffering The Sea Change: All My
  Pretty Ones.
Rozhdestvensky [or Rozhdestvenskii]. Winter
  of Thirty-Eight, The.
Rukeyser, M. Boy with His Hair Cut Short.
  In adolescence I knew travellers.
Russell, G. Frolic.
  Germinal.
Russell, N. Message of the Rain, The.
Russell, T. In Simili Materia.
St. John, P. Reading a Story to My Child.
Salter. Half a Double Sonnet.
Sánchez, K. Porcelain Childhood.
Sanchez, S. Song No. 3: "Cain't nobody tell me
  any different."
Sanders, E. Leaves of Heaven, The.
Scalapino. Or a Play.
Scalise, S. Days pass on that face, The.
Scamell, B. For a Six Year Old.
Scammell, W. Nicola.
Scannell. Hide and Seek.
Schiff, H. When It Happened.
Schultz, P. Stories.
Schwartz, D. I Am Cherry Alive.
Scott, D. Dreadwalk.
Scovell. Child Waking.
Seale, J. Playing the Flute for the TMR Class.
Seiferle, R. What We Need Words For.
Serraillier. Anne and the Field-Mouse.
Sexton. Fury of Overshoes.
  Fury of Overshoes, The.
  Red Roses.
Seyburn, P. First Bookshelf.
Shakespeare, W. Song: "When that I was and a
  little tiny boy."
Shapiro, D. Book of Glass, A.
Shehadeh, Mohammed. Letters to Childhood.
Sherman, M. San Buenaventura.
Sholl. Dawn.
Silverstein, S. Sick.
Simic. Austerities.
  Book Full of Pictures, A.
  Prodigy.
Simon, M. Sea Sprite, Hermosa Beach, The.
Simpson, L. My Father in the Night
  Commanding No.
Slavitt. Tryma.
Smith, C. I once was happy, when while yet a
  child.
  Sighing I see yon little troop at play.
Smith, D. Roundhouse Voices, The.
Smith, K. On Sundays in Summer.
Smith, K. Being the Third Song of Urias.
Smith, P. Biting Back.
Smith, S. Bog-Face.
  Our Bog is Dood.
  To Carry the Child.
Snodgrass. Child between them on the street.
  Child between them on the street, The.
Snyder, G. Dragonfly.
Sŏ Chŏngju. New Year's Prayer: 1976.
Södergran. Homecoming.
  My Childhood Trees.
Sondheim. Children Will Listen.
Song. Wind in the Trees, The.
Soto. Behind Grandma's House.
  Black Hair.
Soupault. Poems from Saint Pelagia Prison.
Sousa, N. Poem of a Distant Childhood.
Soutar. Who Are These Children?
Spears, Rebecca. Marina's Daughters, 1964.
Spender, S. Elementary School Classroom in a

Slum, An.
My Parents.
Spires. First Day, The.
Stefanile. How I Changed My Name, Felice.
Steffler, J. Hollis Street Square, Halifax.
Stein, G. Teachers taught her, The.
Stevens, C. J. New Blue Bike, A.
Stevenson, A. Mother, The.
Stevenson, R. Auntie's Skirts.
  Bed in Summer.
  Cow, The.
  Good and Bad Children.
  Lamplighter, The.
  Land of Counterpane, The.
  Land of Story-Books, The.
  Looking Forward.
  My Shadow.
  Pirate Story.
  Swing, The.
  Where Go the Boats?
  Whole Duty of Children.
  Winter Time [or Winter-Time].
Strand. Where Are the Waters of Childhood?
Strange. Acts of Power.
  Childhood.
Strickland, A. Infant, The.
Stroud, J. Missing.
Stryk, L. Child in the City, A.
Suárez, V. Rice Comes to El Volcán.
Sullivan, B. Hair.
Surrey. Prison in Windsor Castle.
Swenson, M. Centaur, The.
Szymborska, W. Laughter.
"Tabitha.". Sweet it is to be a child.
Tarrant, J. Han Shan in Santa Rosa.
Taylor, C.B. Plenty Time Pass Fast, Fas Dey
  So.
Tayson, R. First Sex.
Tennyson, A. City Child, The.
  Sweet and Low.
Thomas, D. Conversation of Prayer, The.
  Fern Hill.
Thomas, R. S. Song for Gwydion.
Thompson, C. Mrs. Johnson Objects.
Tomlinson, C. Picture of J. T. in a Prospect of
  Stone, The.
Torgerson. Apple from Walt Whitman, An.
Traherne. Corn was Orient and Immortal
  Wheat, which never should, The.
Trakl. To the Child Elis.
Trethewey, N. Genus Narcissus.
Troupe. Boomerang: A Blatantly Political
  Poem.
Tsanev, Ivan. Fine Day.
Tsvetkov. Like a ruddy child you fall asleep in
  september.
Tucker, M. Old Crib, The.
  We Met.
Tuckerman, F. How Oft in Schoolboy Days.
Tuqan, F. To Etan: An Israeli Child from the
  Kibbutz Ma'oz Hayim.
Turner, C. Letty's Globe.
Ulacia, M. Regreso a la ciudad.
  Return to the City.
Ullman. Why There Are Children.
Unknown. Bitter Withy, The.
  By curvèd bank.
  Crows on City Walls.
  Foxes move in pairs.
  Hou Ji (Lord Millet), Progenitor of Zhou.
  Little Rose.
  Lullabies, 2:174.
  Old Folks' Room, The.
  On the Death of Mr. Persall's Little Daughter, in
    the Beginning of the Spring, at Amsterdam.
  Young children do not yet know worry, The.
Updike. Saying Goodbye to Very Young
  Children.
Valente, J. Empty Place at the Celebration, An.
Valerie, J. On Apologies.
Van Dyke, C. Birth, 1975.
Van Jordan, A. If I Write a Poem.
Vanek, Mary. Summer Begins Outside Dalhart,
  Texas.
Vaughan, H. Childhood.
  Retreat[e], The.

Veinstein. From Far.

Verlaine. You see, we have to be forgiven things.

Vietnamese Oral Tradition. Complaining about the Second Wife.

Lullaby: "Little one, go to sleep. Sleep soundly."

Villanueva, A. They Didn't Get Me.

Voeten. Sun On My Hand, The ("Sun lights my hand writing, The.").

Sun On My Hand, The ("Writing with the sun on my hand.").

Wagner, M. Miss Clement's Second Grade.

Walcott. Camps hold [or held] their distance— [of] brown chestnuts and grey smoke, The.

Waldman, A. De Carlo Lots, The.

Walker, M. Childhood.

Wallace, R. Facts of Life, The.

Walsh, J. I've Got an Apple Ready.

Wang Chiu-ssu. Ballad of Selling a Child.

Wang, Y. My Pain.

Waniek. Sacrament of Poverty, The.

Warner, S. Become as little children.

Warren, R. Gold Glade.

Wet Hair: If Now His Mother Should Come.

Watson, E. Battered Toddler, Page B6.

Watson, R. Children of the Mist.

White Lady, The.

Weaver, A. Improvisation for Piano.

Webster, A. Little child she, half defiant came, A.

Since first my little one lay on my breast.

Sometimes, as young things will, she vexes me.

There's one I miss. A little questioning maid.

Weems, M. Yesterday.

Weigl. Last Lie, The.

Werner, Judith. Ethel Rosenberg and Me.

Wessling, Suki. Angry.

Whitehead, C. Girls Sitting Together Like Dolls.

Whitman, W. There Was a Child Went Forth.

Whittemore, R. Farmhouse, The.

Whittier. Barefoot Boy, The.

My Playmate.

Wilbur, R. Boy at the Window.

Digging for China.

Pardon, The.

Williams, C. K. Blades.

My Mother's Lips.

Still Life.

Williams, C. For the White Lady Holding Me.

Williams, M. Of History and Hope.

Williams, P. Baby in the House, A.

Williams, R. Listen. / The rejoicing of waters fills my ears this evening.

Williams, S. Summer mornings we.

Williams, W. Sympathetic Portrait of a Child.

Waiting.

Williamson, A. Childhood Around 1950, A.

Williamson, G. Drawing Hands.

Origami.

Wilner, E. As soft and as pink as a nursery.

Wojahn. Poison, 1959.

Wong, N. Ma, my heart must be made of rice straw.

Wonham, J. Emergency Services.

Wordsworth, W. Anecdote for Fathers [Showing how the Art of Lying may be Taught].

I have seen / A curious child, who dwelt upon a tract.

My Heart Leaps Up [When I Behold].

Ode: Intimations of Immortality from Recollections of Early Childhood.

To a Child [Written in Her Album].

To H. C., Six Years Old.

We Are Seven.

Work. Come Home, Father[!].

Wright, C. Poet Grows Older, The.

Wright, F. Have You Seen This Child.

Wright, J. Note Left in Jimmy Leonard's Shack, A.

Sappho.

Song for the Middle of the Night, A.

Wright, J. To a Child.

Wright, K. How the Wild South East Was Lost.

Wyrebek, M. Healing Logic, A.

Yates, D. Washing the Cow's Skull.

Yeats. Among School Children.

Cradle Song, A: "Angels are stooping, The."

Prayer for My Daughter, A.

Yi Hyangji. What Did You Do Yesterday?

Yi Sang. Poem No. 1.

Yosano Tekkan. Victory Arches.

Yost, C. From San Diego.

Young, D. Chapped Lips.

Sources of the Delaware.

Young, K. No Offense.

Young, P. Photograph, 1958.

Zamora-Linmark. Day 1: Portrait of the Artist, Small-kid Time.

Zarco. Manila Paper.

Once upon a Seesaw with Charlie Chan.

Zarin. Ant Hill, The.

Zimmer. Zimmer's Head Thudding against the Blackboard.

Zimmerman, Rosamond. Anemia.

Zondberg, O. To die. And be born as an inspector of playgrounds for tiny tots.

Zurita, R. Even Forsaken They'd Flower.

See also **Adolescence; Boys; Death of a Child; Girls; Youth**

Children's Poetry

Giussani, S. Abel and Abel.

Hahn, O. Little Phantoms.

Mother Goose. As I was going to St. Ives.

Baa, baa, black sheep, have you any wool?

Birthdays.

Boys and girls come out to play.

Bye, baby bunting.

Daffadowndilly.

Dance to your [or thee] daddy.

Ding, dong, bell.

Dingty diddlety.

Flying-Man.

Forehead, Eyes, Cheeks, Nose, Mouth, and Chin.

God made the bees.

House That Jack Built, The.

Humpty Dumpty sat on a wall.

Hush-a-bye, baby, on the tree-top.

I saw a ship a-sailing.

Intery, mintery, cutery corn.

Ladybird, Ladybird fly away home.

Little Bo-Peep.

Little Jack Horner/ Sat in a corner.

Little Jumping Joan.

London Bridge.

Old Mother Twitchett had [or has] but one eye.

Rain, rain, go to Spain.

Sing a song of sixpence.

Solomon Grundy.

Teeth and Gums.

They That Wash on Monday.

This is the House that Jack Built.

This Little Pig Went to Market.

Three blind mice, see how they run!

Three wise men of Gotham.

Two Legs Sat Upon Three Legs.

What Are Folks Made Of.

When the wind is in the east.

Who Killed Cock Robin.

Olin. Like Beatrix Potter.

Yang Hsün-chi. Inscribed on the Doors of My Bookshelves.

Chile

Agüeros. Psalm for the Damnation of Pig Pino Oink Ochet, Who Unlike His Victims Will Neither Die nor Disappear, Because He Was Never Human.

Ali, A. I See Chile in My Rearview Mirror.

Davies, G. Chilean People, The.

de Jesús. Flag of Chile, The.

Proverbs.

Jara, V. Estadio Chile.

Larsen, L. Peach.

Lihn. Cemetery in Punta Arenas.

Mitchell, A. Victor Jara of Chile.

Neruda. I did not touch your night, or your air, or dawn.

They Receive Instructions Against Chile.

Parra, N. Modern Times.

Teillier, J. No Sign of Life.

Portrait of My Father, Militant Communist.

Thompon, E. Homage to Salvador Allende.

Zurita, R. Even Forsaken They'd Flower.

March of the Cordilleras, The.

Chile's distant and it's a lie.

Sparkling Beaches, The.

Chimney Sweepers

Blake, W. Chimney Sweeper, The ("Little black thing among the snow, A.").

Chimney Sweeper, The ("When my mother died I was very young.").

Tolson, M. Sootie Joe.

Chimneys

Bidgood. Chimneys.

Jarman, M. Chimney Swifts.

Sachs, N. O the Chimneys.

Sutskever [or Sutzkever]. Between Chimneys.

Chimpanzees

Sassoon, S. Sporting Acquaintances.

China

Auden. Spain [1937].

Beer, P. Footbinding.

Benét, W. Merchants from Cathay.

Brodsky, J. Letters from the Ming Dynasty.

Bynner. Tiles.

Ch'en Lin. Song: "I watered my horse at the Long Wall caves."

Chin Ho. Ballad of the Maiden of Lan-ling.

Chin. Barbarian Suite.

Prelude.

Ch'iu Chin. To the Tune "The River Is Red".

Chu Yün-ming. Fan from Korea, A.

Clifton, H. Monsoon Girl.

Dao. End or a Beginning, An.

Résumé.

Engle, P. Chinese Courtesy.

Torture.

Fenton, J. Tiananmen.

Fried, Michael. Send-Off, The.

Glass, Jesse. Lecturing on Walt Whitman and Emily Dickinson in China.

Gu Cheng. Forever Parted: Graveyard.

Han Yü. Song of the Stone Drums.

Hovey. Sea Gypsy, The.

Kao Shih. Ji Gate.

Kaufman, S. Emperor of China, The.

Keckler, W. Wedding, A.

Kizer, C. Ashes, The.

Koch, K. To Old Age.

Krivulin. Crossing the keyboards of the palace.

Li Ho. Chang'gu: A Poem Written on the Twenty-Seventh Day of the Fifth Month.

Farewell Song of Magic Strings.

Under the Walls of Ping City.

Li Po. Early Departure from White Emperor Fortress.

Intoxication of Love.

Song of the Heavenly Horse.

Summer Song ("Mirror Lake, The.").

Xiangyang Song.

Lindsay, V. Chinese Nightingale, The.

Lu Chao-lin. Chang'an.

Lu Yu. To Show to My Sons.

Mao Tse-tung [or Mao Zedong]. Glitter of a northern kingdom.

I stand alone in the cold autumn.

Return to Shaoshan.

Merrill, S. Ballade of the Chinese Lover.

Merwin. Rose Beetle, The.

Messerli. Angry with China.

Nordbrandt. China Observed Through Greek Rain in Turkish Coffee.

O'Hara, F. Poem: "At night Chinamen jump."

Pathabhi. Moon in China Bazaar.

Piccione. With Whitman at the Friendship Hotel.

Po Chü-i. Everlasting Wrong, The.

Song of Lasting Regret, The.

Wu.

Roberts, N. Mona Lisa Tea Towel, The.

Rojas. Bed with Mirrors.

Ryan, K. Masterworks of Ming.

Rylander, E. Midnight Rocker, Tiananmen Square, May 27, 1989.

Sanfield. Concern.

Silko. Prayer to the Pacific.

Song. Heaven.
Lost Sister ("In China.").
Ssu-ma Hsiang-ju. Mighty One, The.
Su Man-shu. Exile in Japan.
Sze. Spring Smoke.
Torre, M. Driven by a Strange Desire.
Ts'ai Yen. Poem of Sorrow.
Ts'ao Ts'ao. Graveyard Song.
Tu Fu [or Du Fu]. Autumn Meditation: 7.
Ballad on Seeing a Pupil of the Lady Gongsun
Dance the Sword Mime.
Pressgang at Shihao Village, The.
Tu Mu. Spring South of the River.
Unknown. Being idle in the wooden building, I
opened a window.
My grief, like dense clouds, cannot be
dispersed.
Xishi always lives in golden houses.
Wang Chien. South, The.
Wang Wei. Climbing to the Monastery of
Perception.
Wei Chuang. Lament of the Lady of Qin.
Weinberger, E. Changs.
Wilbur, R. Digging for China.
Wolverton, T. In China.
Chinaware
Hugo, V. Broken Vase, The.
Merrill, J. Willowware Cup.
Moore, M. No Swan So Fine.
Probyn. China Maniacs.
Ryan, K. Masterworks of Ming.
Weigl. Painting on a T'ang Dynasty Water
Vessel.
Chinese Poetry
Segalen. Out of Respect.
Chinese, The
Addonizio. China Camp, California.
Barnstone, W. Jiang Yuying, Famous Professor
at Beijing University, Who Daringly Rendered
into Chinese the First Complete Walt Whitman.
Carruth, H. Of Distress Being Humiliated by
the Classical Chinese Poets.
Cendrars. Frisco-City.
Chan Fang-sheng. Sailing into the South Lake.
Ch'en Lin. Horses at a Breach in the Great
Wall.
Chin. Chinese Quatrains (The Woman in Tomb
44).
Composed Near the Bay Bridge (after a wild
party).
How I Got That Name.
Chinn. Not Translation, Not Poetry.
Ch'u Yüan. Ying from "The Nine
Declarations".
Gillespie, N. Seated in a Chinese Painting, He
Speaks.
Harte, B. Plain Language from Truthful James.
Hsieh Ling-yün. From Chin-Chu Creek, Past
the Ridge, Along the Stream.
Inada. Chinks.
Kerouac. Thrashing Doves, The.
Kingston, M. Idea!: Four-word poems!
K'ung Chih-kuei. Trip on Mount T'ai-P'ing.
Lau, A. Upside Down Basket, The.
Lazutkina, E. Ruined so many romances.
Li Po. Ascend the Phoenix Terrace.
Crossing Ching-Men to See a Friend Off.
Olinka, S. Chinese Man in Smyrna, A.
Pao Chao. Do you not see the riverside grass.
Do you not see the young men off to war.
Splash water on level ground.
To you, fine wine in gold cup.
Rai San'yo. Stopping at Amakusa Sea.
Rich, A. Catch if you can your country's
moment, begin.
Song. Ghost.
Heaven.
Lost Sister ("In China, / even the peasants.").
Su, A. Address.
Suárez, V. Rice Comes to El Volcán.
T'ao Ch'ien [or T'ao Yuan-ming]. Bearers'
Song.
Tate, J. Miss Cho Composes in the Cafeteria.
Ts'ao Chih. Woe Indeed!
Ts'ao Ts'ao. Bitter Cold: A Song.
Tu Fu [or Du Fu]. Wu-Chueh.

Unknown. At Fifteen I Went to War.
At sunset I come out of the door.
Ballad of the Mulberry Road.
Chen and Wei are brimming, The.
East Gate, The.
Fighting, south of the ramparts.
Fragrance is due to perfumes.
Green beyond green, the grass along the river.
Him I'm thinking of.
In the wilds, a dead doe.
It was four days before the Chongyang Festival.
Kuan-kuan, the ospreys.
Last night with hair unbrushed.
Long night: unable to sleep.
Millets in full rows.
My parents are old; my family is poor.
O Heavens!
Old Song.
Pick ferns, pick ferns.
Sad Song.
Song of the Little Miss by the Green Rill.
South of the Yangtze.
Spring Song from "Tzu-Yeh" Songs of the Four
Seasons.
Tchirek Song (Northern Yueh-Fu).
Those gone are day by day remote.
Walk on again walk on.
Water the Horses at a Breach in the Great Wall.
What grass not yellowed?
Wah. Father / Mother Haibun #20.
Wang Chih-huan. Ascend the Heron Tower.
Wang Wei. After Source of the Peach Blossom
Stream.
Answer to Vice-Prefect Chang.
Autumn Dusk at a Mountain Lodge.
Bamboo Grove.
Bird-Singing Stream.
Floating on the River Han.
Four Examples from the Poems of River Wang
Deer Enclosure.
Hsin-I Village.
In the Mountain.
Mount Chung-Nan.
Passing the Temple of Teeming Fragrance.
Rill of the House of the Luans.
To See a Friend Off.
Villa at the Foot of Mount Chungnan.
Wei Ying-wu. Autumn Night: A Letter Sent to
Ch'iu.
Weinberger, E. Wind: "Wind: what is it? You
don't see it but you hear it, and you feel its
force."
Wen Yi-tuo [or Wen I-to]. Laundry Song, The.
Whalen, P. Hymnus Ad Patrem Sinensis.
Wong, N. When I Was Growing Up.
Chipmunks
Melville, H. Chipmunk, The.
Wilbur, R. Wall in the Woods, A: Cummington.
Chirico, Giorgio di
Guest, B. Nostalgia of the Infinite.
Pagis, D. Devotion.
Chivalry
Black, S. Hoopla.
Melville, H. Rusty Man, The.
Chocolates
Gomez, M. Chocolate Confessions.
Simpson, L. Chocolates.
Sissle, N. I'm Just Wild About Harry.
Choices
Baraka, I. Kenyatta Listening to Mozart.
Belloc. Child, Do Not Throw This Book About.
Cassells. Marathon.
Citino. Situation No. 33: The Feast.
Di Prima. Abyss.
Dickinson, E. I'm ceded—I've stopped being
Theirs.
Elizabeth, M. She Teaches Him to Reach Out.
Emanuel, L. Like God.
Finch, A. Intellect of Woman, The.
Frost, R. Lovely Shall Be Choosers, The.
Garrett, E. Tyranny of Choice.
Gibson, M. Woman Resting on a Bundle of
Kindling.
Gonzalez, R. For the Other World.
Graves, R. Down, Wanton, Down!

Gregg. Edge of Something, The.
Grennan. Pause.
Hands, E. Perplexity: A Poem.
Harpur, J. I stretch my arms.
Healy, E. Changing What We Mean.
Hirshfield, J. Cedary Fragrance, A.
Joseph, L. When One Is Feeling One's Way.
Kasischke. Bike Ride with Older Boys.
Kenyon, J. Otherwise: "I got out of bed."
Larkin, P. Dockery and Son.
Maxwell, G. Nerve, The.
Meredith, W. Consequences.
Myself, Rousseau, a Few Others.
Merwin. Air: "Naturally it is night."
Norris, K. Blue Light, The.
Olson, C. In Cold Hell, in Thicket.
Otomo no Sakanoé, t. When we could have
met.
Revell, D. What Can Stop This.
Riley, P. 1134. 39.
Sandburg, C. Choose.
Santos Chocano. Who Knows?
Schwartz, D. All Clowns Are Masked [and All
Personae].
Smith, Douglas Burnet. Multiple Choice.
Sund. Considering Poverty and Homelessness.
Szymborska, W. Woman's Portrait, The.
Turner, C. East or West?
Unknown. My friends, which of these two to
choose?
Williams, H. Prayer.
Wordsworth, W. Glad Preamble, The.
Yeats. Choice, The: "Intellect of man is forced
to choose, The."
Youn, Monica. Venice, Unaccompanied.
Zagajewski. Betrayal.
Choking
Char. Man flees suffocation.
Hartman, J. Petition Hecate at the seal.
Moore, J. Hic Finis Rapto 6.
Serge. Asphyxiated Man, The.
Voigt. Daughter.
Cholera
al-Mala'ika, N. Cholera.
Kipling, R. Cholera Camp.
Chopin, Frédéric François
Downie. Some Poetry.
Solonche. Chopin Preludes, Opus 28.
Chopsticks
Jenkins, A. Chopsticks.
Christchurch, New Zealand
Curnow. Skeleton of the Great Moa in the
Canterbury Museum, Christchurch, The.
Christenings
McCord, D. When I Was Christened.
See also **Baptism**
Christianity and Christians
Abad, G. Holy Order.
"Ada.". Appeal to Women, An.
Scroll is open, The.
Adams, F. To the Christians: "Take, then, your
paltry Christ."
Adams, S. Nearer, My God, to Thee.
Ai. Charisma.
Mother's Tale, The.
Alarcon, F. Viernes Santo / Good Friday.
Alexie. Crow Testament.
Artaud. I Spit on the Innate Christ.
Baxter, J. Brother Ass, Brother Ass, you are full
of fancies.
Colin, you can tell my words are crippled now.
Morning and Evening Calm.
Beeching, H. Prayers.
Bertrand. Tulip Merchant, The.
Bible, *O.T.* Psalme 91.
Bishop, E. Brazil, January 1, 1502.
Blake, W. Vision of Christ that thou dost see,
The.
Blunden. Report on Experience.
Bly, R. Empty Place, An.
Breedlove, N. New Miz Praise de Lawd, The.
Buchanan, G. Pope from penance purgatorial,
The.
Bulich, V. From My Diary, 3.
Caballero-Robb, M. Dear Rosario.

Camões [or Camõens or Camoëns], L.   With glad reception our Commander meets.
Cardenal.   León.
 Prayer for Marilyn Monroe.
 Psalm 5: "Give ear to my words, O Lord."
Carrera Andrade.   Perfect Life, The.
 Sunday.
Chesterton.   Donkey, The [1920 version].
Clarke, A.   Martha Blake at Fifty-one.
Cleyre, V.   Love's Compensation.
Cofer, J.   Campesino's Lament, The.
 Las Magdalenas.
Cole, H.   White Spine.
Cooke, R.   Schemhammphorasch.
Coolidge.   My Rights.
Corbet [or Corbett].   Proper New Ballad Entitled [or Intituled] The Fairies' [or Faeryes] Farewell, or God-a-Mercy Will, A.
Cortázar.   Very Real Story, A.
Crosby, F.   Blessed Assurance.
 I Am Thine, O Lord.
 Thoughts in Midnight Hours.
Cruz e Sousa.   Good Friday.
Cruz, S.   I Entered Where I Did Not Know.
 I Live and Do Not Live in Myself.
de Folgar.   Irreverent Epistle to Jesus Christ.
De Villagrá.   Canto 1.
Delgado, J.   Mexican Fire Breather, A.
Depestre.   Ballad of a Little Lamp.
Dickinson, E.   I'm ceded—I've stopped being Theirs.
Dizhur.   Eve's Monologue.
Donne.   Satire 3 [Religion].
 Show me dear[e] Christ, thy spouse, so bright and clear[e].
Doty, M.   Homo Will Not Inherit.
Duhig, I.   Fundamentals.
Dunn, S.   At the Smithville Methodist Church.
Dwight.   I Love Thy Kingdom, Lord.
Eichner, Maura.   Litany for the Living.
Elytis, O.   Even when they destroy you it will still be beautiful.
 I was late in understanding the meaning of humility.
Epictetus.   Pleasd with thy Place.
Erdrich.   Immaculate Conception.
Ferlinghetti, L.   Sometime During Eternity.
Field.   Lovers.
Florit, E.   Martyrdom of Saint Sebastian, The.
Fuller, M.   Meditations.
 One in All, The.
Galvin, J.   Station (4).
Gilman, C.   Christian Virtues.
Gippius.   Wedding Ring, The.
Glaser, M.   Magnificat!
Gomez, M.   Lost Daughter.
 Troubled Awakening.
Harper, F.   Bible Defence of Slavery.
Harwood, G.   Bone Scan.
Heath-Stubbs.   For the Nativity.
Herbert, G.   British Church, The.
Herrick.   On Himself[e] ("Here down my wearied [or wearyed] limbs I'll [or Ile] lay.").
Heynen.   Clean People, The.
Hope, M.   INRI.
Horovitz, F.   Brigomaglos, a Christian, Speaks.
Howe, J.   Lost Jewel, The.
Hudgins.   At the Piano.
Hughes, L.   Madam and the Minister.
Hugo, R.   Letter to Hill from St. Ignatius.
Huxley, A.   Christlike is my behaviour.
Hyneman, R.   Woman's Rights.
Jackson, H.   Distance.
 Opportunity.
Jennings, E.   Annuciation, The.
Jones, D.   A, a, a, Domine Deus.
 In the middle silences of this night's course the blackthorn.
Jones, R.   Blasphemy, A.
Jonson, B.   Carol.
Kanchev, Nikolai.   Glory: "Sky with reddened eyelids foretells windy weather, The."
Kekova.   Ants, The.
 Everything has come true. The punishment fits the crime.
Kelly, B.   Imagining Their Own Hymns.

Kumin, M.   Living Alone with Jesus.
Levin, P.   Third Day, The.
Lezama Lima.   Rhapsody for the Mule.
Lihn.   Mud.
Lim-Wilson.   Raising the Dead.
Lima, J.   Stranger, Stranger.
Lisboa.   Idyll: "Lord, forgive me if I do not look for you."
Lochhead, D.   John Thompson.
Logau.   Faith.
Lope de Vega.   Stranger to Love, Whoever Loves Not Thee.
Lourie.   Theological.
Machado Ruiz.   Siesta.
Markotić, N.   Try book-ending punctuation vouchers.
Mary Stuart.   My lord and my God, I have hoped in Thee.
McLaughlin-Carruth, J.   Introducing New Year's SOLUTIONS, from Saint Terri's Inc.
McVeigh, J.   Eve Falling.
Melville, H.   Symphonies.
Meynell, A.   To Conscripts.
Milosz, C.   Lecture 5.
 Poor Christian Looks at the Ghetto, A.
Milton.   On His Blindness.
Mistral, G.   Decalogue of the Artist.
Montrose.   On Himself, upon Hearing What Was His Sentence.
Moritz [or Morits].   My apple-tree, my willow.
Muldoon, P.   Our Lady of Ardboe.
Nikolayeva [or Nikolaeva].   Daughter.
Obejas, A.   Sunday.
O'Curry, E.   Litany to Our Lady.
Odio, E.   Prologue to a Time That Is Not Itself.
Osherow.   9 (Looking through the Window: Psalm 121).
Otero, B.   Censored.
Owen, W.   Maundy Thursday.
Pacheco, J.   Job 18, 2.
Pavlich.   Black Flower.
Pizarnik.   Ashes.
 Awakening, The.
Plath.   Medusa.
Plato.   True Friend, The.
Plotnick, H. M.   Jewish.
Prado, A.   Fluency.
 Grace.
 In Portuguese.
 Siesta.
Pratt, E.   Highway, The.
Ragan, J.   Child Christ at the Top of the Stairs.
Reese, L.   Trust.
Rexroth, K.   Wednesday of Holy Week, 1940.
Ritsos.   End of Dodona II, The.
Robinson, E.   Christmas Sonnet, A.
Ryman.   Have mynde how I mankynde have take.
 Sancta Maria, ora pro nobis.
Ryuichi.   My Imperialism.
Saarikoski.   Winter solstice.
Sachs, H.   Fair Melody, A: To Be Sung by Good Christians.
Saloy, M.   We've Come This Far.
Sandburg, C.   Washerwoman.
Shkapskaya [or Shkapskaia].   No Dream.
Shomer.   Falling for Jesus.
Silva, C.   Who Will Throw the First Stone?
Smart, C.   Nativity of Our Lord and Saviour Jesus Christ, The.
 Song to David, A.
Smith, S.   Sunt Leones.
Sorby.   Glossolalia.
Stein, G.   In the Kingdom of Perpetual Repair.
Stevens, W.   High-Toned Old Christian Woman, A.
 Old Lutheran Bells at Home, The.
 Sunday Morning.
Swinburne.   On the Russian Persecution of the Jews.
Taylor, E.   Another Meditation at the same Time.
 Fiery Darts of Satan stob my heart, The.
 Here is a Mudwall tent, whose Matters are.
 Lord with thine Altars Fire, mine Inward man.
 Meditation. Numb. 28.4.9. One Lamb shalt thou

offer in the Morning, and the other at Even.
 And on the Sabbath day two Lambs etc.
Thomas, R. S.   Navigation.
Traherne.   Corn was Orient and Immortal Wheat, which never should, The.
Troupe.   Signals and Demarcations.
Unknown.   A! Sone, tak hede to me whos sone thou wast.
 Christian Epigram.
 Evermore, wher-so-evere I be.
 God send euerie Preist ane wyfe.
 Gospel Train, The.
 Hand by Hand We Shall Us Take.
 I Will Bow and Be Simple.
 King Emanuel.
 Litany to Our Lady.
 Lonesome Valley, The.
 Ne hath my soule but fyr and yse.
 Now thise foweles syngen and maken her blisse.
 Nowel, el, el, el, el!
 Of a rose, a lovely rose.
 On hire is al my lyf ylong.
 Psalm 23: "Lord to me [or mee] a shepherd is, The."
 Religion So Sweet.
 Sith al that in this world hath ben in rerum natura.
 That mayden mylde hir childe dide kepe.
 Ther bloweth a cold wynd to-day, to-day.
 Trouble of the World, The.
 Whan I thenke on the rode.
 Who Is on the Lord's Side.
 Whoso saw on rode.
 With huntis vp, with huntis vp.
Vaughan, H.   Nativity, The.
Viray, M.   Saturday Morning, A.
Voloshin.   Holy Russia.
Wesley, C.   Let earth and heaven combine.
Wheatley, P.   On Being Brought from Africa to America.
 On the Death of a Young Gentleman.
 Thoughts on the Works of Providence.
Whitman, W.   To Him That Was Crucified.
Wilbur, R.   Rule, The.
Williams, W.   Hymn: "Now the shadows flee and vanish."
 Hymn: "What is the world, and what is life."
Yeats.   Ribh Considers Christian Love Insufficient.

Christmas
Achebe.   Christmas in Biafra (1969).
Anderson, D.   Executive Geochrone.
Appleman, P.   Matthew 1:18–25: Now the birth of Jesus Christ took place.
Babstock, Ken.   Palindromic.
Bampfylde.   On Christmas.
Belloc.   Noël.
Berlin.   White Christmas.
Berrigan, T.   For You.
Berry, W.   To Tanya at Christmas.
Betjeman.   Christmas.
Bishop, M.   Dark Christmas on Wildwood Road, The.
Blane, R.   Have Yourself a Merry Little Christmas.
Bottoms.   Boy Shepherds' Simile, The.
Bridges, R.   Noel; Christmas Eve, 1913.
Calil, A.   Blouse of Felt.
Carruth, H.   Essay on Death.
Causley.   Sailor's Carol.
Chesterton.   House of Christmas, The.
Chittenden.   Cowboys' Christmas Ball, The.
Chute, M.   Day before Christmas.
Clare, J.   December.
Coatsworth.   Barn, The.
Coleridge, M.   I saw a stable, low and very bare.
Coleridge, S.   Christmas Carol, A: "Shepherds went their hasty way, The.
Cooley.   Incantation.
Corn.   Navidad, St. Nicholas Ave.
Cortes, F.   Fish 2.
Couzyn.   One autumn afternoon when I was nine.
Crashaw.   In the Holy Nativity of Our Lord God.
Cullen, C.   Christus Natus Est.

Cummings, E. E.   Little tree / little silent Christmas tree.

Dafydd [or David] Bach ap Madog Wladaidd. Christmas Revel, A.

Deniz, G.   Christmas.

Navidades.

Dickinson, P.   Advent; a Carol.

Dillard, A.   Thanksgiving—Christmas 3.

Djanikian.   When I First Saw Snow.

Donne.   Nativity [or Nativitie].

Duncan, L.   Festive Tolls.

Dunn, G.   Journey Back to Christmas.

Edwards J.   Christmas in Europe: 1945.

Falkner.   Christmas Day; the Family Sitting.

Fanthorpe.   BC:AD.

What the Donkey Saw.

Field, E.   Jest 'fore Christmas.

Finch, R.   Crib, The.

Fordham.   Nativity, The.

Gibson, C.   There's a straw in the manger and babies in danger.

Gillespie, H.   Santa Claus Is Comin' to Town.

Gilmore, B.   Bow to Allah.

Glück, L.   Nativity Poem.

Godolphin.   Hymn: "Lord, when the wise men came from far[r]."

Graves, R.   Carol of Patience.

Christmas Robin, The.

Gregory.   Christmas Lullaby for a New-Born Child.

Hardy, T.   Oxen, The.

Reminder, The.

Heaney, S.   Turkeys Observed.

Heard, J.   Birth of Jesus, The.

Heber.   Brightest and Best of the Sons of the Morning.

Hecht, A.   Christmas Is Coming.

Heine, H.   Wise Men Ask the Children the Way, The.

Herbert, G.   Christmas.

Herrick.   Ceremonies for Christmas[se].

Ode on the Birth of Our Saviour, An.

Holan.   Children at Christmas in 1945.

Holland, J.   Christmas Carol, A: "There's a song in the air!"

Hopkins, G.   Moonless darkness stands between.

Hopkins, J.   We Three Kings of Orient Are.

Horne, F.   Kid Stuff.

Hudgins.   Adoration of the Magi, The.

Image.   Meditation for Christmas, A.

Jacob, M.   Horrible Today, The.

Jennings, E.   Afterthought.

Johnson, M.   Christmas Times.

Krismas Dinnah.

Jonson, B.   Hymn[e] on the Nativity [or Nativitie] of My Saviour, A.

Masque of Christmas, The.

Kennelly.   Story, The.

Kinnell.   To Christ Our Lord.

Kipling, R.   Christmas in India.

Eddi's Service.

Kirkup.   Shepherd's Tale, The.

Kleinzahler.   Ebenezer Californicus.

Knott.   Christmas at the Orphanage.

Levertov.   Advent 1966.

Christmas 1944.

Lewis, C.   Nativity, The.

Longfellow, H.   Christmas Bells.

Three Kings, The.

MacIntyre, S.   Christmas Present for My Mother.

MacNaughton.   Season, The.

Martin, H.   Have Yourself a Merry Little Christmas.

McClatchy.   Old Song Ended, An.

McDaniel, J.   Multiple Floor, The.

McDonald, W.   Christmas Bells, Saigon.

McGinley.   City Christmas.

McGrath, T.   And we, of the damned poor, trot our frost-furred horses.

Bread of this World; Praises III, The.

Mendes, M.   Christmas 1961.

Middleton, R.   Carol of the Poor Children, The.

Mikhail, D.   Christmas.

Millay, E.   To Jesus on His Birthday.

Miller, J.   California Christmas, A.

Miller, V.   Christmas Mourning.

Milton.   On the Morning of Christ's Nativity.

Mitchell, A.   Nothingmas Day.

Moore, C.   Visit from St Nicholas, A.

Moore, L.   Gifts.

Moorer.   Christmas Eve.

Morales, A.   Child's Christmas in Puerto Rico, A.

Morgan, E.   Computer's First Christmas Card, The.

Morris, W.   French Noel.

Newton, Violette.   Mythology of Snow, A.

Nicholson, N.   Shepherds' Carol.

Niedecker.   Will You Write Me a Christmas Poem?

Nims, J.   Christmas.

Norris, L.   Mice in the Hay.

Shepherd's Dog, The.

Paman.   On Christmas Day to My Heart.

Parry-Williams.   Christmas Carol, A: "It is close to a quarter of a century since then."

Christmas Carol: "Close to a quarter of a century since then."

Pasternak, B.   Christmas Star, The.

Plath.   Winter's Tale, A.

Randell.   Jetty, The.

Ray, H.   At Christmas-Tide.

Revard.   Christmas Shopping.

Roberts, E.   Christmas Morning.

Robinson, E.   Karma.

Rodgers, W.   White Christmas.

Rossetti, C.   Christmas Carol, A: "In the bleak mid-winter."

Christmas Eve.

Rossetti, D.   My Sister's Sleep.

Sansom, C.   Innkeeper's Wife, The.

Scammell, W.   Christmas at Bristol.

Schnackenberg.   Advent Calendar.

Scott, S.   Heap on more wood!—the wind is chill.

Sears, E.   It Came upon the Midnight Clear.

Shapiro, A.   Christmas Story, A.

Shorter.   Skeleton in the Cupboard, The.

Shukman, H.   Horses at Christmas.

Smart, C.   Nativity of Our Lord and Saviour Jesus Christ, The.

Southwell.   Burning Babe, The.

Child[e] My Choice [or Choyse], A.

Nativity of Christ[e], The.

New Prince, New Pomp[e].

Stevenson, R.   Christmas at Sea.

Tate, A.   Sonnets at Christmas.

This is the day His hour of life draws near.

Tate, N.   While Shepherds Watched [Their Flocks by Night].

Tennyson, A.   Time draws near the birth of Christ, The.

Time draws near the birth of Christ, The.

Thackeray.   Mahogany Tree, The.

Thomas, G.   Nativity Play, The.

Thompson, C.   Christmas Rush, The.

Thomson, J.   Hymn on the Seasons, A.

Timrod.   Christmas.

Tucker, M.   Christmas, South, 1866.

Turner, S.   Christmas Is Really for the Children.

Unknown.   Carol, for Candlemas Day.

First Nowell, The.

God Rest Ye Merry, Gentlemen.

Here We Come A-wassailing.

Holly and the Ivy, The.

I Sing of a Maiden.

Song Bewailing the Time of Christmas, So Much Decayed in England, A.

Van Duyn.   Christmas Card, After the Assassinations, A.

Vaughan, H.   Shepherds [or Shepheards], The.

Wadding [or Waddinge].   Christmas Day [Is Come].

Waldman, A.   Baby's Pantoum.

Watkyns.   Upon Christ's Nativity or Christmas.

Watts, I.   Cradle Hymn, A.

Wells, R.   Christmas Song, The.

Whalen, P.   Damachi.

Wilbur, R.   Christmas Hymn, A.

Williams, W.   Burning the Christmas Greens.

Wood, D.   Christmas Fare.

Wright, C.   Christmas East of the Blue Ridge.

Yeryomin.   Street lamp. Something missing. Drugstore.

Young, A.   Christmas Day.

Christmas Cards

McGinley.   Lady Selecting Her Christmas Cards.

Morgan, E.   Computer's First Christmas Card, The.

Christmas Carols

Brooks, P.   O Little Town of Bethlehem.

Clare, J.   December.

Pierpont, J.   Jingle Bells.

Sears, E.   It Came upon the Midnight Clear.

Tate, N.   While Shepherds Watched [Their Flocks by Night].

Unknown.   First Nowell, The.

Good King Wenceslas.

Here We Come A-wassailing.

I Saw Three Ships Come Sailing In.

Nowell Sing We.

Twelve Days of Christmas, The.

Watts, I.   Joy to the World.

Christmas Eve

Algarin.   Christmas Eve: Nuyorican Café.

Anderson, D.   Executive Geochrone.

Davie, D.   Devil on Ice.

De la Mare.   Christmas Eve.

Feinstein, S.   Christmas Eve.

Hardy, T.   Oxen, The.

Moore, C.   Visit from St Nicholas, A.

Piper, P.   Christmas Eve, 2003.

Rexroth, K.   Sword in a Cloud of Light, A.

Tennyson, A.   Tonight ungathered let us leave.

Thompson, P.   Christmas Ghost, A.

Tucker, M.   Christmas Eve, South, 1865.

Christmas Trees

Berry, W.   Our Christmas Tree.

Burford, W.   Christmas Tree, A.

Cook, S.   Christmas Tree.

Cummings, E. E.   Little tree / little silent Christmas tree.

Day Lewis.   Christmas Tree, The.

Moorer.   Christmas Tree, The.

Morris, J.   Untrimming the Tree.

Smith, L.   Christmas Tree.

Tate, J.   Miss Cho Composes in the Cafeteria.

Williams, W.   Burning the Christmas Greens.

Chrysanthemums

An Minyŏng.   Speak, chrysanthemum, why do you you shun.

Basho.   Chrysanthemum scent.

Monk sips morning tea, A.

Sickly.

When the winter chrysanthemums go.

White chrysanthemums.

Buson.   Before the white chrysanthemum.

Chrysanthemum growers.

Lighting the lantern.

Grin, B.   Dead Chrysanthemums.

Ishikawa Jōzan.   Gardening Chrysanthemums, I Think of [T'ao] Yüan-Ming.

Ku Sang.   Spring Chrysanthemums.

Kyoriku.   Next to even.

Lee, L.   Between Seasons.

McKinney, I.   Chrysanthemums.

Po Chü-i.   Chrysanthemums in the Eastern Garden, The.

Pou Kuksa.   Untitled: "Unmoving, it presents itself in a thousand shapes."

Sampu.   Moving / Deep into mist.

Scovell.   Shadows of Chrysanthemums.

Sŏ Chŏngju.   Beside a Chrysanthemum.

T'aego, National Preceptor.   Nothingness.

Unknown.   Girl, don't be so haughty.

To learn how to die.

Yi Kyubo.   Loom importunes, The.

Chuang-tzu

Chunggwan, Great Master.   Upon Reading Chuang Tzu.

Jungkwan Haean.   On Reading Namwha Sutra.

Church of England

Herbert, G.   British Church, The.

Herrick.   Persecutions Purifie.

Knox, R.   Anglican curate in want, An.

Moore, T.   Scene from a Play, Acted at Oxford,

Called "Matriculation".
Unknown. Vicar of Bray, The.

Churches
Akhmatova, A. We Do Not Know How to Say
  Goodbye.
Alun Cilie. Old Chapel, The.
Andrade, M. Sunday.
Aubert, A. Whispers in a Country Church.
Baraka, I. A, B, C's, The.
Belieu. At St. Sulpice.
Berkeley, S. Mass is Over, The.
Bertrand. Mason, The.
  Mason, The.
Betjeman. St. Saviour's, Aberdeen Park,
  Highbury, London, N.
  Undenominational.
Blake, W. Little Vagabond, The.
Booth, P. Within.
Brown, L. Call for Vertical Integration in the
  Eye of the Storm, A.
Burns, R. Tam o' Shanter; A Tale.
  To a Louse [On Seeing One on a Lady's Bonnet
  at Church].
Caleshu, A. Church Full of Objections.
Cardenal. León.
Carrera Andrade. Sunday.
Catacalos. Swallow Wings.
Char. On the Bell Frieze of a Roman Church.
Clifton, L. In White America.
Corbet [or Corbett]. Upon Fairford Windows.
Crane, H. Broken Tower, The.
Dana, R. A Capella.
Davie, D. Rodez.
Dickinson, E. Some keep the Sabbath going to
  Church.
  When Bells stop ringing—Church—begins.
Doolittle, H.. Trance.
Durcan. Divorce Referendum, Ireland, 1986,
  The.
Ekelof. Greece.
Foust, G. On the Evening of a Wedding.
Garcia, R. Why I Left the Church.
Gibbons, R. Cash or Turtle or Heaven.
Graham, D. Jesus Never Sleeps.
Gruffydd, W. Yew of Llanddeiniolen, The.
Hardy, T. Church Romance, A.
Harper, F. Church Building.
Hart, S. Sundays.
Hayden, R. Those Winter Sundays.
Herbert, G. Prayer (1): "Prayer the Church's
  banquet, Angels' age."
Hughes, R. Sermon, The.
Ikeda, P. Three Churches.
Iskander. Gegard.
Jewett, S. At Home from Church.
Kanchev, Nikolai. Church: "I've come to kneel
  before you, while you're falling down."
Kantaris. Airing the Chapel.
Kendall, M. Church Echoes.
Kendrick, D. Where the Grieved Ones Sat.
Krivulin. Glory to caesar! and glory to God in
  the highest!
Larkin, P. Broadcast.
  Church Going.
Lawrence, D. H. Tabernacle.
Lea, S. Do not trust in these deceptive words.
Lee, D. Benediction.
Leithauser. Old Bachelor Brother.
Lieberman, L. Organist's Black Carnation, The.
Lochhead, D. John Thompson.
Lowell, A. Meeting-House Hill.
Mahapatra, J. Taste for Tomorrow.
Mangan, G. Kirkintilloch Revisited.
Mathias, R. Brechfa Chapel.
Matthews, W. Old Folsom Prison.
McKinney, I. Sunday Morning, 1950.
Melville, H. In a Church of Padua.
Moore, L. Bad Times.
  Tanka.
Morgan, R. Bellrope.
Morshen. Andreyevsky Church, The.
Mullen, H. Dance She Does, The.
Nguyen, Hoa. Mission Dolores.
Olds, S. Wedding Vow, The.
Orlovsky. Dream May 18, 1958.
Paino. 1965.

Palazzeschi. Nuns Go Walking.
Pessoa. Inside, the church lights up today's rain.
Philipott. To Sir Henry Newton, upon His Re-
  edifying the Church of Charleton in Kent.
Pook. In Chapel.
Porter, P. Angel in Blythburgh Church, An.
Prufer, K. Rise of Rome, The.
Ragan, J. St. Jacob's Church of the Hanging
  Hand.
Rilke. Sometimes a Man Stands Up During
  Supper.
Rogers, D. Customs of the Country.
Scott, D. Church Boiler, The.
  Locking the Church.
Scupham. Service.
Seward. Eyam.
Shannon, A. Sunday: "It could have been the
  way the Southern."
Simic. Winter Night.
Spires. Comb and the Mirror, The.
Starkey, D. Poet Is Like a Church, The.
Steptoe. In Black Churches.
Stevens, W. Gray Stones and Gray Pigeons.
Synge. Dread.
Tate, A. Sonnets at Christmas.
Taylor, Jane. Squire's Pew, The.
Taylor, John. Gods *Houses,* almost like *Troyes
  Ilion,*.
Tennant, W. Sang First.
Thomas, Larry D. Red Raging Waters, The.
Thomas, R. S. In a Country Church.
  Kneeling.
Thompson, C. Opening Service, An.
Tolson, M. Lena Lovelace.
Tomlinson, C. Las Trampas U.S.A.
Tranströmer. Scattered Congregation, The.
Travis, N. Church Ladies.
Unknown. Building of a New Church, The.
  Oranges and lemons, say the bells of St.
  Clement's.
  Preston.
Vegin, P. "Moscow" Pool.
Waller, E. Upon His Majesty's [or Majesties]
  Repairing of Paul's.
Warner, S. Building in Stone.
  Country Thought.
Weigl. Temple Near Quang Tri, Not on the
  Map.
Whitman, W. March in the Ranks Hard-Prest,
  and the Road Unknown, A.
Wilbur, R. Dubious Night, A.
  Plain Song for Comadre, A.
Wordsworth, W. KIRK OF ULPHA to the pilgrim's
  eye, The.
Wright, J. Wednesday Night Prayer Meeting.
Wrigley, R. Prophecy, The.
Young, K. Wake.
Zagajewski. Auto Mirror.
Zakaria Youssef, M. Sadder Man, The.
Zucker, R. Cloister or "vietato toccare le rose".

Churchill, Winston Leonard Spencer
Scott, D. Winston Churchill.

Churchyards
Clampitt. Palm Sunday.
Collins, W. Ode on the Poetical Character.
Fane, V. In an Irish Churchyard.
Góngora y Argote. Ruins of Time, The.
Gray, T. Elegy Written in a Country
  Churchyard.
Mahon. In Carrowdore Churchyard.
McKinney, I. Visiting My Gravesite: Talbott
  Churchyard, West Virginia.
Pierpoint, K. Steeplejack.
Scott, D. Churchyard under Snow.

Cicadas
Anyte [or Anytes]. For the cricket (nightingale
  of the field) and oak.
Basho. Cicada shell, A.
  It's quiet, all right.
  Lonely silence.
  Nothing in the cry.
  Stillness.
  Stillness.
  Such stillness.
  They don't live long.
Ch'i-chi. Start of Autumn: Hearing a Cicada

While Sick in Bed.
Chia Tao. Sick Cicada, A.
Eady. Dance, The.
Hsüeh T'ao [or Xue Tao]. Cicadas.
Issa. First cicada / Life is.
  Shush, cicada / Old Whiskers.
Kikaku. Cicada chirp / Fan peddler.
  Sprinkle water wide / For the sparrow.
Masaoka Shiki. Autumn come / Cicada husk.
Shiki. Thunderstorm breaks up, The.
Stoutenburg. Cicada: "I lay with my heart under
  me."
Warner, S. Waiting at Cerbere.
Yi Illo. Cicada.

Cigarettes
Ai Ch'ing. Chilean Cigarette Pack, The.
Beck, Art. Nicotine.
Campo. Lost in the Hospital.
Cortez, Sarah. Interlude: "I watch a handsome
  young female."
Enzensberger, H. Vending Machine.
Ferrari, M. Eternity!
Gibbons, R. "Luckies".
Iozia, J. Last Night at the Flamingo.
Kim Sowŏl. Cigarette.
Loncar, M. Picasso Shag.
Mitchell, S. Smoke.
Pearlberg, G.G. Marianne Faithfull's Cigarette.
Pollard, C. And Another Bloody Thing.
Popa. In the Ashtray.
Rodgers, C. Group Therapy.
Shaw, A. Crepuscule.
Torregian. Attitudes.
Webster, P. Two Cigarettes in the Dark.
Yevtushenko [or Evtushenko]. Hand-Rolled
  Cigarettes.
See also **Smoking and Smokers**

Cigars
Harryman. Baby. (For B and T).
Sáenz. I Wouldn't Even Bleed.
Wrigley, R. Ashtray in the Snow.

Cinderella
Alvarez, J. Against Cinderella.
Duhamel. Ugly Step Sister, The.
Jarrell, R. Cinderella.
Reed, Tennessee. Disney's Cinderella.
Sexton. Cinderella.
Shcherbina. Stepmother, The.

Circe
Duffy, C. Circe.
Glück, L. Circe's Power.
Gunn, T. Moly.
MacNeice. Circe.
Rossetti, D. For 'The Wine of Circe' by
  Edward Burne Jones.
Webster, A. Circe.
Zaid. Circe.

Circumcision
Herrick. To His Savior [or Saviour]. The New
  Years [or yeers] Gift.
Lowell, R. New Year's Day.
Milton. Upon the Circumcision.
Okigbo. Elegy of the Wind.
Ostriker. Story of Abraham, The.
Rafat. Circumcision.

Circus
Al-Aziz, M. Fall, The.
Alexander, E. Venus Hottentot, The.
Brouwer, J. Kelly, Ringling Bros. Oldest
  Elephant, Goes On Rampage.
Brownstein. Monkey Blues.
Buddingh'. Hyena, The.
Bursky, R. Decisions, The.
Cable, G. Song of Cayetano's Circus, The.
Carruth, H. Wreck of the Circus Train, The.
Cendrars. Medrano Academy.
Dickinson, E. I've known a Heaven, like a
  Tent.
Fallon, P. Flask of Brandy, A.
Ferlinghetti, L. Constantly Risking Absurdity.
Goldbarth. Book of Human Anomalies, The.
Heaney, S. Wheels within Wheels.
Koch, K. Circus, The ("We will have to go
  away, said the girls in the circus.").
Larkin, P. For Sidney Bechet.

Lim-Wilson. Ringmaster's Wife.
Lima, J. Big Mystical Circus, The.
McOrlan. Modern circus, The.
Ondaatje. Driving with Dominic in the Southern
    Province We See Hints of the Circus.
Padgett, R. First Drift.
Ratushinskaya [or Ratushinskaia]. Thus you
    lived your life without regret.
Shapcott, T. Litanies of Julia Pastrana (1832-
    1860), The.
Turnbull. For Whose Delight.
Vinokurov. I do not like the circus.
Williams, W. Artist, The.
Young, K. Escape Artist, The.

Cities
Abrahams, L. Thoughts on Johannesburg's
    centenary.
Aguilar, M. Pall Hanging over Manila.
al-Braikan, M. Empty City, An.
Al-Rihani. Lilatu Laili.
Albert-Birot. City is free of sin, The.
Ali, M. Condition.
Ammons. City Limits, The.
Andrade, M. Nocturne.
Annensky. Capitol, The.
Apollinaire. Voyager, The.
    Windows.
Aridjis. Letter from Mexico.
Armantrout. View.
Arp. Cities Have Been Cut Off at the Feet, The.
Asekoff, L. Invisible Hand.
Ashbery, J. Meaningful Love.
    Rain.
    Rivers and Mountains.
    These Lacustrine Cities.
Auden. Paysage Moralisé.
Axelrod, D. Guide to Urban Birds, A.
Bancquart. Town.
Barot, R. Portishead Suite.
    Riffing.
Bateman, E. Cockney's Garden, The.
Belchenko, N. I'd happily survey the world.
Bell, M. Street Fair: The Quartet.
Bernard, A. Praise Psalm of the City-Dweller.
Bernstein, C. Matters of Policy.
Betjeman. City.
Bierce. Passing Show, The.
Bishop, E. From the Country to the City.
    One Art.
Blanco, R. Perfect City Code.
Blind. Manchester by Night.
Borges. Mythical Founding of Buenos Aires,
    The.
Borisov. And when the winter wind rushed
    straight into my heart.
Braithwaite. City Garden, A.
Brannon, J. Evolution on 38th Street.
Brecht, B. Of Poor B.B.
Broumas, O. Next to the *Café Chaos*.
Brutus. Nightsong: City.
Bryant, W. Hymn of the City.
Buffoni, F. When he was far away from those
    evenings.
Bulich, V. Omnibus, The.
Burich. Precepts for City Living.
Burkard. I have a silence in the rain.
Buscani. Barefoot in the City.
Busceti, G. Suddenly on a day in July.
Cabalquinto. Ordinance, The.
Calvino. Argia.
    Armilla.
    Eudoxia.
    Fedora.
    Octavia.
Campana. Genoa.
Carroll, J. Love Rockets.
Cavafy. City, The.
    City, The.
Cavalli. And to see the city again and to see it
    again.
    When suddenly, you're hit with good health.
Cawein. Dead Cities.
Cendrars. Hammock.
Christensen, Paul. What the Citizens of Corpus,
    Rockport, Palacios, or Bryan Need.
Ch'u Kuang-hsi. Streets of Ch'ang-an.

Clarke, C. 14th Street Was Gutted in 1968.
Clifton, H. Eccles Street, Bloomsday, 1982.
    Euclid Avenue.
Clifton, L. In the Inner City.
Clover, J. Archive of Confessions, a Genealogy
    of Confessions, An.
Coe, C. Possibility.
Coleridge, M. Day-dream, A.
Corn. Water: City Wildlife and Greenery.
Cortes, F. Poem Composed During a Brownout.
Costanzo. Jeane Dixon's America.
    Washington Park.
Coviello, M. This hour is made of iron grates
    where the underground.
Cowley, A. Wish, The.
Craighead, L. Dancin' Our Lives Away.
Crane, H. To Brooklyn Bridge.
Crawford, R. Love Song of Tommo Frogley.
Crow, C. City Park.
Crow, M. Cityscape.
Davies, A. Thirty East Forty-Second Street.
DeFoe, M. Aviary.
Denby. City Without Smoke.
Derricotte. Whitman, Come Again to the Cities.
Dewdney. She is liquid darkness occult with
    desire.
"Dhoomil.". City, Evening, and an Old Man:
    Me, The.
Di Prima. Montezuma.
Disch. Crumbling Infrastructure, The.
Donne. To Sir Henry Wotton ("Sir, more than
    kisses, letters mingle souls.").
Doty, M. Homo Will Not Inherit.
Dougherty. Puerto Rican Girls of French Hill,
    The.
Douglas, L. Impression de Nuit; London.
Dransfield. Day at a Time.
Drummond de Andrade. Motionless Faces.
Drummond, W. Content and Resolute.
Dumdum. Li Pos of the Polis.
Dunn, D. On Roofs of Terry Street.
"Eliot.". In a London Drawingroom.
Eliot, T. S. *Boston Evening Transcript*, The.
    Morning at the Window.
    Preludes: "Winter evening settles down, The."
    Rhapsody on a Windy Night.
Ellis, T. Break of Dawn, The.
Esteves. Ahora.
    For South Bronx.
Evans, R. Buttons and Bows.
Fenton, J. German Requiem, A.
Fields, J. Citizen.
Fleckenstein, M. Getting Even.
Follain. Buying.
Forman, R. We Are the Young Magicians.
Fructuoso, E. Astig.
Gamalinda, E. Denials.
Gandlevsky, S. There's our street, let's say.
Garlick, R. Capitals.
Georgiou, E. Week in the Life of the Ethnically
    Indeterminate, A.
Godfrey. What It Takes.
    What Say.
Goetsch, D. Urban Poem.
González, A. City.
Gonzalez, R. San Jacinto Plaza.
Greenberg, A. City Life.
Greenwald, T. Coordinating cities gulls still
    gull, and, arms binged with wine, as wine.
Gregerman, D. Silent Globe.
Guest, B. Bleat.
Guilpin. What more variety of pleasures can.
Gunn, T. Map of the City, A.
    Night Taxi.
Haines, J. Nocturnal.
Han-shan. I live in a little country village.
Harwood, G. Nightfall.
Hausman. September City.
Hearne, B. Commuters.
Hecht, A. Third Avenue in Sunlight.
Hemans. Illuminated City, The.
Herbert, Z. Report from the Besieged City.
Herlin. Gull inch-perfect over water, The.
Hernández Cruz. Energy.
    Entering Detroit.
    Man Who Came to the Last Floor, The.

Mountain Building.
    Side 18.
    Side 4.
    Slick.
    Swans' Book, The.
Heym. Demons of the Cities, The.
Hill, M. City in You.
Hogan, L. Heartland.
Hollander, J. Lion Named Passion, A.
Hubbell, P. Streetcleaner's Lament, The.
Huerta, E. Declaration of Hate.
Huidobro. Express.
Hume, C. Sampler City.
Huws, Meirion MacIntyre. City, The.
Hwang Tonggyu. Wind Burial 3.
Ignatova, E. I have encountered a valley, in
    ragged bast matting.
Ilio, D. Children of the Atomic Age.
    Prokosch in Tehran, 1978.
Inada. Fresno Truth, The.
Inez. Courtyard Noises from the North, Twenty-
    fourth Precinct.
Irby. January 1965, Looking on.
Ismaili. Lagos.
Iverem, E. Earth Screaming.
Jackson, L. City Seems, A.
Jacobsen, R. Gaslight.
Jordan, J. Speculations on the Present through
    the Prism of the Past.
Kanik. I Am Listening to Istanbul.
Kaplinski, J. My Wife and Children.
Kaufman, B. Battle Report.
    Late Lamented Wind, Burned in Indignation,
    The.
Kearney, M. Nature Poetry.
Kees. City as Hero, The.
Kefala. Industrial City.
Kenjeev. And a fool, and a smart one, a miser.
Kimbrell, J. Rooftop.
Kooser. City Limits.
    Interchange.
Korican, L. City Goddess.
Kovner, A. Far, Far a City Lies.
Kramer, L. Strong Winds Below the Canyons.
Krivulin. Southwest.
Lane, P. Wind Thoughts.
Lee, L. City in Which I Love You, The.
Lehman. Towards the Vanishing Point.
Lenski, L. Sing a Song of People.
Levertov. World Outside, The.
Levin, P. Citizens and Sky.
Levy, A. London Plane-Tree, A.
Li K'ai-hsien. Parable, A.
Li Po. City of Choan, The.
    Poem Composed at the Command of the
    Emperor.
    Xiangyang Song.
Lihn. Cemetery in Punta Arenas.
Liu, T. Brooklyn Botanic Garden, The.
Livingston, J. Buttons and Bows.
Lo Pin-Wang. Mooring by Jiangzhen in the
    Evening.
Lodge, G. Lower New York.
Lowell, J. Street, The.
Lu Chao-lin. Chang'an.
Lueck, D. You want to climb the steps.
MacNeice. Birmingham.
    Close and slow, summer is ending in
    Hampshire.
    Morning Sun.
Madani. Here I am Once More.
Mangan, G. Glasgow 1956.
Masters, E. Cities of the Plain.
Mattawa. Bus Driver Poem, The.
Mayor, C. Driving Away.
McGrath, C. Smokestacks, Chicago.
McKay, C. White City, The.
Meléndez. Oye Mundo/Sometimes.
Mew. Not for That City.
Miliauskaite. Temporary City.
Milosz, C. Temptation.
Morejón. Love, Attributed City.
Morgan, E. Glasgow Sonnets.
Mueller, L. Commuter.
Nemes Nagy. Four-Light Window, A.
Neruda. I'm Explaining a Few Things.

Noguere. Whirling Round the Sun.
Noyes, A. Barrel-Organ, The.
Nyka-Niliunas. Winter Landscape.
Okantah. African Morning.
Oldham, J. London.
O'Loughlin. Posthumous.
Oppen. Amor fati / The love of fate.
Bicycles and the Apex, The.
I cannot even now.
Impossible Poem, The.
Now in the helicopters the casual will.
Obsessed, bewildered / By the shipwreck.
Pedestrian.
So spoke of the existence of things.
We are pressed, pressed on each other.
O'Shaughnessy, A. Ode: "We are the music-makers."
Paloff, B. On Transportation.
Pao Chao. Desolate City, The: A Rhapsody.
Ruined City, The.
Parfi, R. Today I dreamed all day. I dreamed.
Parra, N. Vices of the Modern World.
Patchen. 23rd Street Runs into Heaven.
Paz. I Speak of the City.
Penn, R.E. Morning Songs.
Piercy. Learning Experience.
Pietri. Intermission from Monday.
Piñero. La Bodega Sold Dreams.
Running Scared.
Pinsky. Avenue.
City Dark, The.
Plumpp. Another Mule.
Survivors.
Po Chü-i. Hangzhou.
Jiangnan.
Poe. City in the Sea, The.
Pope, A. Epistle to Miss [*or* Miss Teresa] Blount, on Her Leaving the Town after the Coronation.
Popova, O. Curve of your lips, The.
Powell, J. Now in the tight trench you go.
Prufer, K. End of the City, The.
Purdy, A. Blue City, The.
Radiguet. Map.
Ramsey, L. That Which Hovers.
Rattenbury, A. Rain Falls on Utopia Too.
Reverdy. Post.
Reznikoff. [Winter Sketches II: Subway].
Rich, A. Rusted Legacy.
Rimbaud, A. Cities.
City.
Rivard. Consolation.
Robles. Remembering the Past.
Rosenberg, L. City Baseball.
Roy, T. Nowadays.
Rumsey, Tessa. More Important Than the Design of Cities Will Be the Design of Their Decay.
Rutsala. Sunday Morning Walk.
Rux, C. H. Asphalt Musings.
Asylum of Gestures.
Salazar. Hotel Fresno.
Sandburg, C. Blue Island Intersection.
Cahoots.
Chicago.
Prayers of Steel.
Skyscraper.
Scalapino. Considering How Exaggerated Music Is.
Schwartz, D. Mind Is an Ancient and Famous Capital, The.
Seferis. Word for Summer, A.
Senghor. Porte Dorée.
Shapcott, T. City of Home, The.
Shcherbina. Whole city seductively lit up, The.
Shen Yüeh. I Climb High to Look at Spring.
Shepherd, R. Provisional.
Sherwin, J. Nightpiece.
Shreve, S. Landing.
Shwarts [*or* Shvarts]. What That Street Is Called.
Simic. Dream Avenue.
Sitwell, D. Trams.
Skinner, J. City Out of the Boy, The.
Smith, M. Asleep in the City.
Visit to the Village, A.
Snyder, G. Cartagena.
Sŏ Chŏngju. In the Old Capital.
Sondheim. Another Hundred People.
Stevenson, R. Block City.
Stewart, P. Estes' Backyard, The.
Stryk, L. Child in the City, A.
Sutter. Peregrine.
Swift, J. Description of the Morning, A.
Taggard. All Around the Town.
Taylor, A. Fitzroy.
Tennyson, A. City Child, The.
Teofilov, Ivan. Hills, The: "Unrepeatable, ever-present mirage."
Old City, The.
Thomas, E. Cries of the Newsboy.
Thomas, R. S. Rhodri.
Thurman. Zebra.
Tkachenko. Like Thousands of Others.
Tomlinson, C. More Foreign Cities.
Toomer. Gum.
Trowbridge, W. Bad Birds.
Tsanev, Stefan. Nostalgia, or a Painful Return to Memories.
Turner, A. Clean.
Red Flower.
Twichell. City Animals.
Ungria, R. Carillonneur.
Unknown. Cid Enters Burgos, The.
How doth the city sit solitary that was full of people.
Valente, J. No Man's Land.
Van Vliet. City, The.
Villaurrutia. Los Angeles Nocturne.
Voigt. Nocturne.
Wakoski. Night Blooming Jasmine.
Walcott. Tomorrow, Tomorrow.
Waldrop, K. Poet: "Wind dying, I find a city deserted, except for crowds of, The."
Wanek. Duluth, Minnesota.
Wang Chien. South, The.
Wang Wei. Melody of Wei City.
Waterhouse, A. Now the City Has Fallen.
Weiners. With Meaning.
Weston, M. Primitive Place.
Wetzsteon. Urban Gallery.
Wharton, E. Two Backgrounds.
Whitman, W. Once I Pass'd through a Populous City.
Sparkles from the Wheel.
Wilbur, R. After the Last Bulletins.
Shame.
Williams, Gerwyn. Forward March.
Williams, G. City Under Snow.
Williams, W. Grotesque.
Perpetuum Mobile: The City.
Predicter of Famine, The.
Wordsworth, W. Composed upon Westminster Bridge, September 3, 1802.
London Images.
Wormser. Pigeons.
Wunderlich, M. Chapel of the Miraculous Medal.
Yeats. Coole Park, 1929.
Yeryomin. Street lamp. Something missing. Drugstore.
Yin Luoth. Phnom Penh Morning.
Yolen. Sky Scrape / City Scape.
Zagajewski. At Daybreak.
Zanzotto. How Long.
Zhenkai. Discovery.
Zukofsky, L. Cocktails / and signs of.
See also **Towns; Villages**
Citizenship
Ashbery, J. One Thing That Can Save America, The.
Cabalquinto. Ordinance, The.
Rich, A. Late summers, early autumns, you can see something that binds.
Yeats. Road at My Door, The.
Civil Defense
Hofer, J. Tactics ("Will not tolerate will expend offer known facts armed with knives.").
Civil Rights Movement
Abner, P. Lest We Forget.
Addison, L. After MLK: the marksman marked leftover kill.
Baraka, I. Courageousness.
Branch, J. Farewell Queen Mother Moore.
Carroll, K. Theory on Extinction or what happened to the dinosaurs?
Espada. Other Alamo, The.
Fay, S. Back in My Day.
Fogarty, L. Kath Walker.
Gilmore, B. Georgia avenue, washington d.c.
Johnston, G. Blood Is the Argument.
Jones, P. Glad All Over.
Sepúlveda-Pulvirenti. September 11, 1973.
Walker, M. Street Demonstration.
See also **Social Protest**
Civil Service
Chernoff. Dead Letter Office, The.
Civil War, Spain
Auden. Spain [1937].
Campbell, R. Toledo.
Cornford, J. Full Moon at Tierz: Before the Storming of Huesca.
Letter from Aragon, A.
Éluard, P. November 1936.
García Lorca. Quarrel, The.
Hernández, M. July 18, 1936–July 18, 1938.
Hughes, L. Letter from Spain.
Madrid [—1937].
Jeffers, R. Sinverguenza.
Levine, P. On the Murder of Lieutenant José del Castillo by the Falangist Bravo Martinez, July 12, 1936.
Machado Ruiz. Today's Meditation.
MacNeice. And I remember Spain.
Millay, E. Say that We Saw Spain Die.
Neruda. I Explain a Few Things.
Orwell. Italian soldier shook my hand, The.
Rich, A. Letters in the Family.
Rolfe, E. City of Anguish.
Rukeyser, M. Sestina: "Coming to Spain on the first day of the fighting."
Spender, S. Two Armies.
Taggard. To the Veterans of the Abraham Lincoln Brigade.
See also **Spain**
Civil War, United States
Adcock, B. Kaiser's Burnout.
Aldrich, T. By the Potomac.
Fredericksburg.
Ball, C. Jacket of Gray, The.
Beers, E. All Quiet Along the Potomac.
Bell, J. Though Tennyson the Poet King.
Benét, S. Song of the Riders.
Bierce. Confederate Flags, The.
Death of Grant, The.
Hesitating Veteran, The.
To E. S. Salomon.
Bishop, E. From Trollope's Journal.
Breckenridge. General John Cabell Breckinridge.
General John Cabell Breckinridge.
Bristol. Crime of the Ages, The.
Brown, S. Memo: For the Race Orators.
Brownell, H. Bay Fight, The.
Bryant, W. Death of Slavery, The.
Not Yet.
Burlingame. Walking Past the Dugout of Felix McKittrick.
Chittendon. Old Fort Phantom Hill.
Davidson, D. Lee in the Mountains.
Sequel of Appomattox.
De Forest. I heard the bullet's hiss.
In Louisiana.
Storming Column, The.
Di Piero. Walt, the Wounded.
Dickey, J. Hunting Civil War Relics at Nimblewill Creek.
Dickinson, E. Aurora.
Dugan, A. Fabrication of Ancestors.
Dunbar, P. Colored Soldiers, The.
Robert Gould Shaw.
Unsung Heroes, The.
When Dey 'Listed Colored Soldiers.
Emerson, R. Boston Hymn.
Voluntaries.
Emmett. Dixie [*or* Dixie's Land].
Evans, Mayme. Whiskey-Bomb Battle.

Farrow, S.   Civil War, The.
Finch, F.   Blue and the Gray, The.
Foss, S.   House by the Side of the Road, The.
Frost, R.   Black Cottage, The.
Gilmore, P.   When Johnny Comes Marching
 Home.
Grimke, C.   Gathering of the Grand Army, The.
Harper, F.   Deliverance, The.
Harrison, J.   Ghazal 39: "If you laid out all the
 limbs from the Civil War hospital."
Harte, B.   John Burns of Gettysburg.
 Second Review of the Grand Army, A.
Hayden, R.   Dream, The.
Hayne, P.   Vicksburg.
Hightower, S.   Tontine.
Hill, G.   Shiloh Church, 1862: Twenty-Three
 Thousand.
Holmes, O.   To Canaan: A Puritan War-Song.
Horgan.   Tintype of a Private in the Fifteenth
 Georgia Infantry.
Horton, G.   General Grant—the Hero of the
 War.
Howe, J.   Battle Hymn [or Battle-Hymn] of the
 Republic, The.
 Robert E. Lee.
Hudgins.   After the Wilderness.
 Around the Campfire.
 Burial Detail.
 Road Home, The.
 Serenades in Virginia.
 Soldier on the Marsh, A.
Ignatow, D.   Walt Whitman in the Civil War
 Hospitals.
Irving, M.   Marching Still.
Jarrell, R.   Description of Some Confederate
 Soldiers, A.
Jordan, J.   Grand Army Plaza.
Kenyon, J.   Gettysburg, July 1, 1863.
Kittredge.   Tenting on the Old Camp Ground.
Krapf.   Civil War Veteran from Indiana Recalls
 Visiting with Walt Whitman in a Washington
 Hospital, A.
Lanier, S.   Dying Words of Stonewall Jackson,
 The.
Lazarus, E.   South, The.
Lincoln, A.   Gettysburg Address, The.
Longfellow, H.   Arsenal at Springfield, The.
 Building of the Ship, The.
 Cumberland, The.
 Killed at the Ford.
Lowell, J.   Memoriae Positum R. G. Shaw.
 Ode Recited at the Harvard Commemoration
 (July 21, 1865).
Lowell, R.   For the Union Dead.
 March 1, The.
Masters, E.   Battle of Gettysburg, The.
 Veterans of the Wars.
McDonald, W.   Heirlooms.
Melville, H.   Apparition, The—A Retrospect.
 Armies of the Wilderness, The.
 Ball's Bluff.
 Battle Summers, The.
 College Colonel, The.
 Dirge for McPherson, A.
 House-Top, The.
 Malvern Hill.
 March into Virginia, The.
 Meditation, A.
 Memorial on the Slain at Chickamauga.
 Portent, The.
 Requiem[:] for Soldiers Lost in Ocean
 Transports, A: "When, after storms that
 woodlands rue."
 Sheridan at Cedar Creek.
 Shiloh (A Requiem).
 Stonewall Jackson.
 Swamp Angel, The.
 Uninscribed Monument on One of the
 Battlefields of the Wilderness, An.
 Utilitarian View of the Monitor's Fight, A.
Meredith, W.   Farragut, Farragut.
Mitchell, S.   How the Cumberland Went Down.
Moody, W.   Ode in Time of Hesitation, An.
Moolten, D.   Brandy Station, Virginia.
Morgan.   Road from Elmira, The.
Nowlan.   In Those Old Wars.

O'Brien, F.   Soldier's Letter, A.
Olson, C.   Anecdotes of the Late War.
Oppen.   Civil war photo.
Osgood, K.   Driving Home the Cows.
Palmer, J.   Stonewall Jackson's Way.
Preston, M.   Hymn to the National Flag.
Randall, D.   Memorial Wreath.
Randall, J.   My Maryland.
Randolph, I.   Rebel, The.
Ray, H.   Robert G. Shaw.
Read, T.   Sheridan's Ride.
Reese, L.   Old Belle, An.
 War Memory, A.
Reposa, Carol Coffee.   Hill County Rest Home.
Rhodenbaugh.   Civil War, The.
Root, G.   Battle-Cry of Freedom, The.
Ryan, A.   Lines: "Gather the sacred dust."
 Sword of Robert Lee, The.
Shaler, N.   Marksman's Work, The.
 Merry Truce, The.
 Near the Front.
Sherwood, K.   Albert Sidney Johnston.
 Thomas at Chickamauga.
Simms, W.   Ode: "Do ye quail but to hear,
 Carolinians."
Smith, D.   Night Traffic Near Winchester,
 Virginia.
Stodghill, Pat.   Traitor.
Suermondt, Tim.   Briefly Eavesdropping on
 Walt Whitman, Virginia, 1863.
Tate, A.   Battle of Murfreesboro.
 Ode to the Confederate Dead.
Taylor, B.   Gettysburg Ode.
Taylor, E.   Few Days in the South in February,
 A.
 This Year's Drive to Appomattox.
Thompson, John Randolph.   Lee to the Rear.
 Obsequies of Stuart.
Thompson, John Reuben.   Burial of Latané, The.
 Music in Camp.
Thompson, M.   Address by an Ex-Confederate
 Soldier to the Grand Army of the Republic,
 An.
 Lincoln's Grave.
 To the South.
Ticknor.   Little Giffen.
 Virginians of the Valley, The.
Timrod.   Carolina.
 Charleston.
 Christmas.
 Cotton Boll, The.
 Ethnogenesis.
 Ode: "Sleep sweetly in your humble graves."
 Unknown Dead, The.
Trethewey, N.   Native Guard.
Tucker, M.   Men swell the current,—many of
 them wear.
Unknown.   Battle Cry of Freedom, The.
 Confederate Memorial Day.
 Enlisted Today.
 Hospital Duties.
Updike.   Richmond.
Van Jordan, A.   Question: "*What up, brother?*
 the white teen with dreadlocks."
Wallis, S.   Prayer for Peace, A.
Warren, R.   History among the Rocks.
 Two Studies in Idealism: Short Survey of
 American and Human History.
Whitfield.   From Year to Year the Contest Grew.
Whitman, W.   Army Corps on the March, An.
 Artilleryman's Vision, The.
 As I Lay with My Head in Your Lap Camerado.
 As Toilsome I Wander'd Virginia's Woods.
 Bearing the bandages, water and sponge.
 Beat! Beat! Drums!
 Bivouac on a Mountain Side.
 By the Bivouac's Fitful Flame.
 Cavalry Crossing a Ford.
 Come Up from the Fields Father.
 Dirge for Two Veterans.
 Give Me the Splendid Silent Sun.
 March in the Ranks Hard-Prest, and the Road
 Unknown, A.
 Reconciliation.
 Sight in Camp [in the Daybreak Gray and Dim],
 A.

 Spirit Whose Work Is Done.
 To a Certain Civilian.
 Vigil Strange I Kept on the Field One Night.
 Wound-Dresser, The.
 Year That Trembled and Reel'd beneath Me.
Whittier.   Anniversary Poem.
 Barbara Frietchie.
 Battle Autumn of 1862, The.
 Laus Deo!
 What the Birds Said.
 Word for the Hour, A.
Williams, E.   At Harper's Ferry Just before the
 Attack.
Woolson.   Kentucky Belle.
Work.   Marching through Georgia.

Civil Wars, England
Brome.   Saints' Encouragement, The.
Cowley, A.   Powers of Darkness.
Herrick.   Bad Season Makes the Poet Sad, The.
 Upon the Troublesome Times.
Milton.   On the Lord Gen[eral] Fairfax at the
 Siege of Colchester.
 On the New Forcers of Conscience Under the
 Long Parliament.
 To the Lord General Cromwell.
 When the Assault Was Intended to the City.
Shakespeare, W.   Ill blows the wind that profits
 nobody.
Stevenson, A.   Ballad for Apothecaries, A.
Unknown.   Eccho, An.

Civilization
Baraka, I.   I Am.
Bible, Apocrypha.   Steel Usurps the Forests;
 Silence Dethrones Dialogue.
Bowman, C.   Demographics.
Brooks, G.   First Fight. Then Fiddle.
Campbell, D.   Anguish of Ants, The.
Cavafy.   Waiting for the Barbarians.
 Waiting for the Barbarians.
Char.   Disdained Apparitions.
Ch'u Yüan.   Heavenly Questions.
Dickey, W.   For Easter Island or Another Island.
Dransfield.   Day at a Time.
 That Which We Call a Rose.
Duncan [Too-qua-stee], DeWitt Clinton.   Dead
 Nation, The.
Durcan.   Wife Who Smashed Television Gets
 Jail.
Elfyn, Menna.   May in My Lai.
Eliot, T. S.   Waste Land, The.
Emerson, R.   Water: "Water understands /
 Civilization well, The."
 World-Soul, The.
"Ern Malley.".   Dürer: Innsbruck, 1495.
Fink, Robert A.   Mesquite.
Freneau.   On the Civilization of the Western
 Aboriginal Country.
Griffin, S.   Summer Night.
Halliday, M.   Population.
Harris, W.   We Live in a Cage.
Hilliard, B.   Civilization (Bongo, Bongo,
 Bongo).
Hine.   Northwest Passages.
Hope, A.   Australia.
 Under Sedation.
Hughes, L.   Letter to the Academy.
Iverem, E.   Earth Screaming.
Jeffers, R.   New Mexican Mountain.
Johnson, F.   Tired.
Johnstone, R.   Eden Says No.
 Not from our dreams, not from our daft cadres.
Jones, D.   Angle-Land.
Kil Chae.   I return on horseback.
Kipling, R.   White Man's Burden, The.
Kushner, B.   Civilization.
Longley, M.   All of These People.
Mahon.   Image from Beckett, An.
Miller, E.   Tomorrow.
Milosz, C.   Tidings.
Moore, R.   Personal Atlas.
Nagnamuni.   Wooden Horse.
Neruda.   Walking Around.
Oodgeroo of the tribe Noonuccal.   No More
 Boomerang.
Ormond.   Ancient Monuments.

Padgett, R.   Second Why.
Pak Illo.   Song of Peace.
Perillo, L.   Skin: "Back then it seemed that wherever a girl took off her clothes the police would find her."
Pinsky.   Figured Wheel, The.
Prunty, Randy.   Trigger D'evolution.
Raine, C.   Martian Sends a Postcard Home, A.
Rakosi.   Journey Away, A.
Rimbaud, A.   After the Flood.
Shange.   Ancestral Messengers / Composition 13.
Stafford, W.   At Cove on the Crooked River.
Stephen, J.   On a Rhine Steamer.
Stevens, W.   Anecdote of the Jar.
Thomas, R. S.   Period.
Trakl.   West, The (Fourth Version).
Unknown.   Money, Money.
Wright, J.   Horse, The.
Yeats.   Long-Legged Fly.
   Meru.

Clairvoyance and Clairvoyants
Weiner, H.   How can I describe anything when all these interruptions keep *arriving* and then.

Clams and Clamming
Basho.   Autumn going.
   Fall going.
Snow, W.   Advice to a Clam-Digger.
See also **Oysters; Shells**

Clans
Blue Cloud.   Wolf.
See also **Culloden, Battle of (1746)**

Classicism
Agüeros.   Psalm for the Next Millennium.
Cole, H.   Harvard Classics.
Cortez, J.   There It Is.
Derricotte.   Black Boys Play the Classics.
Hardy, T.   Liddell and Scott.
Higgins, R.   Some People.
Jonson, B.   Fit of Rhyme against Rhyme, A.
Pinkney, E.   Italy.
Poe.   To Helen ("Helen, thy beauty is to me.").
Porter, P.   It's there, somewhere in the Platonic cold store.
Pound, E.   Return, The.
Sanchez, S.   Morning Song and Evening Walk.
Sandburg, C.   Southern Pacific.
Shapiro, K.   University.
Tate, A.   Aeneas at Washington.
   Mediterranean, The.
Wachtel.   On Class and Desire.
Walcott.   Sea Grapes.
Wickham.   Butler and the Gentleman, The.
Wilde, R.   Saint Augustine, thy praise was sung by one.

Cleanliness
Alvarez, J.   How I Learned to Sweep.
Berlin, M.   Fungus Considered.
Brown, E.   Jezebel to the Eunuchs.
Burgess, F.   Table Manners: "Goops they lick their fingers, The."
Carroll, J.   Love Rockets.
Dèr Mouw.   I am Brahman.
Dove, R.   Great Palaces of Versailles, The.
Ficke.   Opus 118.
Gorbanevskaya.   Rhymes picked me in a ditch, The.
Graves, R.   It Was All Very Tidy.
Henderson-Holmes.   Goodhousekeeping #17.
Heynen.   Clean People, The.
Housman.   Oh, when I was in love with you.
Hubbell, P.   Streetcleaner's Lament, The.
Hudgins.   Grandmother's Spit.
Kovacic, K.   Brick.
Kwŏn Homun.   Nature makes clear the windy air.
Laux, D.   Idea of Housework, The.
Locke, A.   So Foul Is Sin and Loathsome in Thy Sight.
Monsour.   Sweeping.
Mookam Choinul.   Bath, A.
November, Deena.   Clean that god damned room already.
Reed, H.   Naming of Parts.
Rochester, J.   Song: "By all love's soft, yet

mighty powers."
Silano, M.   Such a Way to Go.
Soudijn.   Cleaning.
   Régime.
Tolson, M.   Old Houses.
Trethewey, N.   Domestic Work, 1937.
Turner, A.   Clean.
Wilbur, R.   Plain Song for Comadre, A.
Yi Chinmyông.   Woman Mopping With a Rag Mop.

Cleopatra
Aiken, C.   Dead Cleopatra lies in a crystal casket.
Akhmatova, A.   Cleopatra.
Hemans.   Last Banquet of Antony and Cleopatra, The.
Hughes, T.   Cleopatra to the Asp.
Marcus, A.   Cleopatra.
Marx, S.   Mark Antony's Valentine.
Pascal.   Tact.
Rossetti, C.   Study (A Soul), A.
Shakespeare, W.   Death of Cleopatra.
Simpson, L.   Early in the Morning.
Story, W.   Cleopatra.
Wodehouse.   Cleopatterer.

Clergy
Arnold, M.   In Harmony with Nature.
Bly, R.   Scandal, The.
Bowering, G.   Grandfather.
Browning, R.   Bishop Orders His Tomb at Saint Praxed's Church, The.
   Soliloquy of the Spanish Cloister.
Burroughs, W.   My Legs Señor.
Citino.   Sitting in the Sixth Grade at Ascension of Our Lord School in Cleveland, Ohio, Reading a Pamphlet Entitled "Possession in Iowa".
Cook, E.   Idiot-Born, The.
Corbet [*or* Corbett].   On Mr. Rice the Manciple of Christ Church in Oxford.
Crashaw.   Upon Bishop Andrewes's [*or* Andrewes His] Picture before His Sermons.
Daumal.   Jesus Before Pilate.
Didsbury, P.   Priest in the Sabbath Dawn Addresses His Somnolent Mistress, A.
Fenton, J.   Staffordshire Murderer, A.
Hardy, T.   In Church.
Heaney, S.   Cleric, The.
Herbert, G.   Aaron.
   Collar, The.
   Windows, The.
Hopkins, G.   Habit of Perfection, The.
Hughes, T.   Cheese for the Archdeacon, A.
Ingoldsby, T.   Jackdaw of Rheims, The.
   Jackdaw of Rheims, The.
Jones, D.   Queen of the differentiated sites, administratrix of the.
Ken.   Priest of Christ, The.
Kipling, R.   Eddi's Service.
Knox.   Anglican curate in want, An.
Lloyd, E.   Portrait of a Bishop.
Marvell.   Flecknoe, an English Priest at Rome.
Merriman [*or* Merryman].   Unmarried Clergy, The.
Milton.   Lycidas.
Moorer.   Birthday Wishes to a Minister of the Gospel.
Norse.   Believing in the Absurd.
Praed.   Vicar, The.
Quarles.   On Those That Deserve It.
Scott, D.   Hopkins Enters the Roman Catholic Church.
   Locking the Church.
   Surplice, The.
Stevens, W.   Gray Stones and Gray Pigeons.
Swift, J.   Thy curate's place, thy fruitful wife.
Tate, J.   Vagabond, A.
Unknown.   Butcher of Abbeville, The.
   Heriger and the False Prophet.
   Humble Petition of a Beautiful Young Lady, The.
   On a Clergyman's Horse Biting Him.
   Ring That Controlled Erections, The.
   Vicar of Bray, The.
   What Really Goes on in the College of Cardinals.

Wheatley, P.   To the Rev. Dr. Thomas Amory on Reading His Sermons on Daily Devotion.
Whittier.   Official Piety.
Woods, V.   She Replies to the Fat Crimson Bishop.
Yeats.   Ballad of Father Gilligan, The.
See also **Rabbis**

Clerks
Davidson, J.   Thirty Bob a Week.
DeCarteret, M.   Town Clerk, The.
Ho Ching-ming.   Ballad of the Government Granary Clerk.
Reece, Spencer.   Clerk's Tale, The.
Robinson, E.   Clerks, The.
Roethke.   Dolor.
Unknown.   Quiet Revery, A.
Weaver, A.   Sub Shop Girl.
See also **Office Workers**

Cleveland, Ohio
Atkins, R.   Lakefront, Cleveland.
Kinsley, R.   Walk Along the Old Tracks, A.

Clichés
Guiterman.   Everything in Its Place.
Muldoon, P.   Symposium.
Schwartz, L.   Proverbs from Purgatory.

Cliffs
Arguelles, Ivan.   I Danced with You Once Only Onliest One.
Coleridge, S.   Blest is the tarn which towering cliffs o'ershade.
Curry, N.   St Kilda.
Han-shan.   In a Tangle of Cliffs.
Hardy, T.   Beeny Cliff.
Loewinsohn.   Siv, With Ocean (Pacific).
Millay, E.   Ragged Island.
Muso Soseki.   Spring Cliff.
Orr, G.   Cliff, The.
Paz.   Landscape.
Robinson, E.   Salisbury Plain.
Shakespeare, W.   Come on, sir; he[e]re's the place: stand still.
Tennyson, A.   Splendour [*or* Splendor] Falls, The.
Yi I.   Where is the seventh bend?

Climbing
Balbulus, N.   Hymn to Holy Women, A.
Benjamin, P.   Press On.
Ch'ôn Yanghûi.   Mountain Stroll.
Dīnrām.   O Baba! Look at this Cadak tree.
Hall, D.   Surface.
Herd.   Coronach.
Hsieh Ling-yün.   On Climbing the Highest Peak of Stone Gate Mountain.
Koontz, T.   Bending the Light.
Li Shang-yin.   From the Heights.
MacCaig.   Climbing Suilven.
Mokusen.   On Climbing the Mountain Where Buddha Trained.
Oness, C.   Climbing.
Pierpoint, K.   Steeplejack.
Rafferty, C.   Man on the Tower, The.
Schmitz.   Climbing Sears Tower.
Shinkichi Takahashi.   Sky.
Stafford, W.   After Arguing against the Contention That Art Must Come from Discontent.
Trommer, R.   Climbing the Ridge.
Tu Fu [*or* Du Fu].   Descending Through Dragon Gate.
   Night in a Room by the River.
Unknown.   Makeme.
   Monkey knows, The.

Clinton, Bill (William Jefferson Clinton)
Shot, D.   Executive Privilege.

Clocks
Aiken, C.   North Infinity Street.
Atwood.   Beauharnois (1).
Barnes, W.   Wold Clock, The.
Baudelaire.   Clock, The.
Bishop, E.   Paris, 7 A.M.
Cabral de Melo Neto.   Knife All Blade, A.
Carrera Andrade.   Clock, The.
Cortázar.   Clocks.
Dickinson, E.   Clock stopped, A.
Graves, R.   Counting the Beats.

Greenlaw, L.   Five O'Clock Opera.
Hsüan-yeh.   Lines in Praise of a Self-Chiming Clock.
Jackson, L.   Wind, the Clock, the We, The.
Kharms.   Death of the Wild Warrior.
Kim Hyesun.   Bloody Clock, A.
Longfellow, H.   Old Clock on the Stairs, The.
Lowell, R.   Fall 1961.
Machado Ruiz.   Clock Struck Twelve Times, The.
Mansfield, K.   Meeting, The.
McMaster, R.   Clockface.
Medard, B.   Tonton Macoutes Steal Dreams.
Niedecker.   There's a better shine.
Nietzsche.   Against the Laws.
O'Rourke, D.   Clockwork.
Pellicer, C.   Studies.
Pietri.   3rd Untitled Poem.
Ponge.   Rain.
Poulin, A.   Red Clock.
Radiguet.   Handless Clock.
Reznikoff.   Heart and Clock.
Rich, A.   Clock in the Square, A.
Sosnora.   Owl and the Mouse, The.
Thurman.   Clockface.
Warner, S.   Alarum, The.
Warren, R.   There's a Grandfather's Clock in the Hall.
Webb, P.   Second Hand, The.
Wilbur, R.   Bell Speech.
Work.   Grandfather's Clock.
Worth, V.   Clock.
Zaid.   Sundial.
See also Watches
Clonmacnoise, Ireland
O'Gillan.   Dead at Clonmacnois [or Clonmacnoise], The.
Unknown.   End of Clonmacnois, The.
Clothing
Adair, T.   Violets for Your Furs.
Alvarez, J.   Naming the Fabrics.
Alvi, M.   Presents from My Aunts in Pakistan.
Annand.   Fur Coats.
Arnold, C.   Party She Outdid Herself, The.
Ball, C.   Jacket of Gray, The.
Bang, M.   It Says, I Did So.
Barber, M.   Written for My Son, and Spoken by Him at His First Putting on Breeches.
Basho.   I would like to use.
  My summer robes.
Bell, M.   Uniform, The.
Brown, S.   Sporting Beasley.
Brownstein.   Ninth Symphony.
Buson.   Bamboo hat, straw coat—.
  Slung over a screen.
Carson, A.   Father's Old Blue Cardigan.
Cerenio.   My Mother.
Chester, T.   Running Hares.
Cho Hwi.   In Peking to a Woman with a Veil.
Clarke, G.   Second Hand Rose.
Cliff.   History of Costume, A.
Cofer, J.   Spring.
Cole, W.   Robert Herrick.
Collins, B.   Taking Off Emily Dickinson's Clothes.
Conway, J.   Clothes Make the Man.
Copus, J.   Clothes, The.
Crane, S.   Youth in apparel that glittered, A.
Crozier, A.   Driftwood and Seacoal.
Davies, S.   Sacred muse that first[e] made love divine [or devine], The.
Dickinson, E.   We outgrow love like other things.
Donegan, P.   Half-Open.
Dubin, A.   Lulu's Back in Town.
Dybek.   Windy City.
Enright, D.   Why didn't we think of clothes before?
Espada.   My Native Costume.
Feaver.   Coat.
Feldman, I.   Se Aprovechan.
Fergusson.   Braid Claith.
Ferlinghetti, L.   Underwear.
Fishman, C.   Diagnosis: My Mother's Breast.
Gallagher, T.   Black Silk.
Gillilan, P.   Four Years.

Goodman, M.   Lullabye for a Butch.
Hadas, R.   House Beside the Sea, The.
Hagedorn, J.   Vulva Operetta.
Hahn, K.   Hula Skirt, 1959, The.
Heaney, S.   Suit, The.
Hendriks.   Will the Real Me Please Stand Up?
Herrick.   Art above Nature, to Julia.
  Clothes Do But Cheat and Cozen [or Cousen] Us.
  Delight in Disorder.
  Upon Julia's Clothes.
Hill, S.   My Sister's Jeans.
Hipponax.   Still Waiting for My Winter Coat: A Sequence of Fragments.
Hoberman.   Let's Dress Up.
Hoffenstein.   You buy yourself a new suit of clothes.
Hudgins.   At Chancellorsville.
Hughes, L.   What?
  When Sue Wears Red.
Huws, Meirion MacIntyre.   Coat.
Issa.   Changing clothes / But not.
Jackson, L.   Because of Clothes.
  One Self.
  Only Daughter, The.
Jacobik, G.   Skirts.
Jenkins, N.   Shirts.
Johnson, M.   Wintah Styles, De.
Jones, D.   Coat, The.
Jonson, B.   Sweet Neglect, The.
Katz, J.   Women Must Put Off Their Rich Apparel.
Kendrick, D.   Alone for a Week.
Kennelly.   Scarf, The.
Kinzie.   Bolt, The.
Klyuyev [or Kliuev or Klyuev].   Fourth Rome, The.
Kowit.   Notice.
Lapeyrère, J.   Skirt, The.
Lawson, H.   When Your Pants Begin to Go.
Lee, D.   Coat, The.
Levitt, Peter.   My robe hangs in the garden.
Lochhead, L.   Neckties.
  Sorting Through.
Lovelace, R.   To a Lady with Child that Asked [or Ask'd] an Old Shirt.
Lowell, A.   Bright Sunlight.
Lux.   Fisherman's Pants, The.
Lynes, Jeanette.   Valley, After Blossoms, The.
Mahadevi.   On Her Decision to Stop Wearing Clothes.
Majorino.   Hints.
Martial.   He scanned me closely, Rufus, just as.
McAuley, J.   Cloak, The.
McPherson, S.   Sock, A.
Melville, H.   My Jacket Old.
Merritt, C.   Woman of Color.
Morales.   My Revolution.
Moss, H.   Persistence of Song, The.
Mother Goose.   Daffadowndilly.
Nash, O.   Requiem: "There was a young belle of old Natchez."
Nelson, H.   Journey, The: "I am wearing my gray wool pants, and my brown boots."
Neruda.   Ode to My Socks.
  Ode to My Socks.
Notley.   Latticed Culotte and Starry Blouse.
O'Donoghue, M.   Textures, The.
Oguma Hideo.   Long, Long Autumn Nights.
O'Hara, F.   Raspberry Sweater, A.
Olds, S.   Good Will.
Ono no Komachi.   When longing for you.
Ouwens.   New Sweater.
Padgett, R.   Tell Us, Josephine.
Pak Mogwŏl [or Mokwŏl].   Hanbok.
Peacock, M.   How I Had to Act.
Peacocke.   Final reductions.
Pei Di.   Hill of Huazi, The.
Petit, P.   My Father's Clothes.
  My Mother's Clothes.
Phillips, C.   Cotillion.
Pierson, J.   Thrift Shop Ladies.
Pinsky.   Shirt.
Po Chü-i.   Ease.
Portnoy, M.   Dinogon.
Powell, D. A.   My Father and Me Making

Dresses: Together.
Probyn.   After.
  Before.
Ravikovitch, D.   Dress of Fire, A.
Redmond.   Poetic Reflections Enroute To, and During, The Funeral and Burial of Henry Dumas, Poet.
Reece, Spencer.   Clerk's Tale, The.
Remoto.   Black Silk Pajamas.
Ritsos.   Underneath Oblivion.
Robinson, M.   Modern Female Fashions.
  Modern Male Fashions.
Romero, N.   New Suit, The.
Romo-Carmona, M.   Signs.
Rosenblatt, S.   Should I Stay or Should I Go?
Ryan, G.   Cruising.
Sansom, A.   Cross Country.
Schiff, Robyn.   House of Dior.
Shakespeare, W.   Thy gown? Why, ay. Come, tailor, let us see't.
Shaughnessy, B.   Your One Good Dress.
Shih Shu.   After Shih-te ("My ragged cloak is streaked with mountain shadows.").
Snyder, G.   No Shoes No Shirt No Service.
Sono-Jo, Lady.   Shameful / These clothes.
Stein, G.   Waist, A.
Steptoe.   Window Shopping.
Stevenson, R.   Auntie's Skirts.
Stillman, M.   Whiskers Meets Polly.
Strand.   Dress, The.
Swenson, M.   Question: "Body my house."
Tobrise.   Dyeing.
Townsend, A.   Shirt Collar, The.
Trinidad.   Doll Not Included.
Tucker, M.   Lines to an Old Dress.
Tzu Yeh.   Song: "Longing, I watch out the open window."
Unknown.   Brian O'Linn.
  Clothes.
  Gao-yang: In His Lambskin Coat.
  Inscription on a Robe.
  Lü-yi: Green Robe.
  Madrigal: "My Love in her attire doth show her wit."
  Silvery red shirt is half covered with dust, The.
  Su-guan [Translations].
  Visitors.
  With a mere glance at the fur coat.
  You, wild hawk.
Waller, E.   On a Girdle.
Wang Wei.   Hill of Huazi, The.
Weiss, T.   Clothes Maketh the Man.
Wiesenthal, C.   Blues.
Wilbur, R.   Catch, The.
  Love Calls Us to the Things of This World.
Williams, C.   Dress, The.
Williams, H.   Making Friends with Ties.
Wolverton, T.   Black Slip.
Wu of Han [or Wu Ti or Ou-ty or Liu Ch'e or Liu Ch'u].   Li Furen.
Wunderlich, M.   Take Good Care of Yourself.
Young, A.   Wet Day, A.
See also Jewelry
Clouds
al-Rahim, A.   My Heart.
Atkins, R.   Dark Area.
Basho.   Clouds come and go, The.
  Clouds of blossoms.
  Clouds, The.
  Crossing half the sky.
  This autumn.
  To the capital / Snow-clouds forming.
Baudelaire.   Soup and the Clouds, The.
  Stranger, The.
Bogan, L.   Train Tune.
Boryu.   Cloud above lotus / It too.
Brooke, R.   Clouds.
Buson.   Mountains of Yoshino / Shedding petals.
  They swallow clouds.
Cardona-Hine.   Acquaintances.
Cavalli.   That white cloud in its contrast.
Charry Lara, F.   I Would Have Loved You.
Ch'i-chi.   Up after Illness, I Watch the Idle Clouds.
Ching An.   Returning Clouds.
Coleridge, S.   Fancy in Nubibus.

Crane, H.   To the Cloud Juggler.
DeSylva, B. G.   Look for the Silver Lining.
Disch.   Clouds, The.
Edgar, C.   Cloud of Unknowing, The.
Evance, S.   To the Clouds.
Feng Yen-ssu.   Cloud That Drifted, The.
Figueroa, J.   Confessions from the Last Cloud.
Finlay, I.   Cloud's Anchor, The.
Flanders, J.   Cloud Painter.
Fletcher, J.   Over the roof-tops race the shadows
   of clouds.
Forrester, S.   Backyard sun shower.
   Plum blossom breeze.
Frost, R.   Lost in Heaven.
Fuller, M.   Meditations.
Galassi.   Argument.
Gorham.   White Tiger Leaps, The.
Gumilyov [or Gumiliov or Gumilev].   Moon at
   Sea.
Han-shan Te-ch'ing.   After late spring rain the
   falling petals swirl.
Hauge.   Evening Clouds.
Herrick.   Her Bed.
Holden, J.   Face Up.
Hsü Pen.   To a Hermit in the Mountains.
Ignatow, D.   Cloud Creates, A.
Iosifovna, Ekaterina.   Cloud, The: "It's darker
   and cooler."
Issa.   Let's take / The duckweed way.
   Toad! It looks like, The.
Jacobsen, R.   Meadowsweet.
Kalidasa.   High on the Mount of Rama a yaksha
   dwelt, who for.
Kaya Shirao.   Mountain mist / Torches dropped.
Kruit, J.   Way of the Water, The.
Levertov.   Clouds.
Levin, P.   Citizens and Sky.
Li Ch'ing-chao.   "Fisherman's Honor," The.
Lowell, A.   Night Clouds.
Loynaz, D. M.   Cloud, The.
Machado Ruiz.   Clouds Ripped Open.
McCarthy, J.   Cloudy Morning.
Mirabai [or Mira Bai].   Clouds, The.
Monk, G.   AC.
   CS.
Morgan, E.   King Billy.
Moss, S.   Clouds.
Muso Soseki.   With compassionate hands.
Onitsura.   Leaping trout sees, The.
Pastan.   Last Train, The.
Pou Kuksa.   Cloudy Mountain.
Pulido, A.   De la ventana.
   Out of the window.
Radnóti.   Clouded Sky.
Ray, H.   Cloud Song.
Reichard, W.   Cloud Game, The.
Reznikoff.   [Winter Sketches II: Subway].
Romo-Carmona, M.   Fish.
Seibles, T.   4AM.
Shelley, P.   Cloud, The.
Shin Tongyŏp.   Scene 9.
Shinkichi Takahashi.   Cloud.
Stevens, W.   On [or Of] the Manner of
   Addressing Clouds.
   Pleasures of Merely Circulating, The.
   Sea Surface Full of Clouds.
Strand.   Marriage, The.
Sundiata.   Making Poems; on the road in
   Minneapolis.
T'ao Ch'ien [or T'ao Yuan-ming].   To-Em-Mei's
   "The Unmoving Cloud".
Thoreau.   Low-anchored cloud.
Tomlinson, C.   Above the Rio Grande.
Unknown.   If the clouds come good, our tobacco
   will grow. We will be happy.
   Rain Song of the Quer'ränna Chai' än, A.
Very.   Clouded Morning, The ("Morning comes,
   and thickening clouds prevail, The.").
Warren, R.   1. Over Prairie.
Watta.   Cloud Rains.
Williamson, G.   Up in the Air.
Wodehouse.   Till the Clouds Roll By.
Woljo Toan.   Deathbed Song.
Wordsworth, W.   I Wandered Lonely as a Cloud.
Wu of Han [or Wu Ti or Ou-ty or Liu Ch'e or
   Liu Ch'u].   Autumn Wind, The.

Yi Chono.   That clouds have no intent.
Clough, Arthur Hugh
   Arnold, M.   Thyrsis.
Clover
   Basho.   Along the shore.
   Bell, M.   White Clover.
   Heine, M.   Memory, A.
   Higginson, E.   Four-Leaf Clover.
   Lanier, S.   Clover.
   Lewis, L.   May Mowing Clover.
   Ōshima Ryōta.   Pure brush-clover / Basket of
      flowers.
Clowns
   Beer, P.   Ninny's Tomb.
   Cendrars.   Medrano Academy.
   Cruz e Sousa.   Acrobat of Pain.
   Darío, R.   Nicaraguan Triptych.
   Gregorio, R.   Clown, The.
   Hughes, L.   Black Clown, The.
   Sondheim.   Send in the Clowns.
See also **Circus**
Clumsiness
   Lowell, A.   Bungler, The.
   Nims, J.   Love Poem: "My clumsiest dear,
      whose hands shipwreck vases."
Coal Mining and Coal Miners
   Avison.   Balancing Out.
   Ballowe, J.   Coal Miners, The.
   Bush, D.   Pneumoconiosis.
   Collier, M.   North Corridor.
   Davies, G.   Wild Geese, The.
   Dickson, J.   Fossil Fuel.
   Grin, B.   Strike of the Coal Miners.
   Heaney, S.   She taught me what her uncle once
      taught her.
   Henry, J.   Two hundred men and eighteen killed.
   Hughes, T.   Her Husband.
   Kay, J.   Close Shave.
   Lawrence, D. H.   Collier's Wife, The.
   Lewis, Emyr.   Above us, where the clouds'.
   Lopez, L.   To a Coal Miner in Madrid, New
      Mexico.
   Lorde.   Coal.
   Menai.   Pieces of Coal.
   Morgan, R.   Blood Donor.
   Morris, L.   Miner's Ballad, The.
   Nagy, L.   Coalmen, The.
   Owen, W.   Miners.
   Parini.   Coal Train.
   Pettit.   Self-Portrait Approaching Promontory,
      Utah.
   Tilsley, G.   Boy strides boldly from his June of
      youth, The.
   Untermeyer, L.   Caliban in the Coal Mines.
   Watkins, V.   Collier, The.
Cobain, Kurt
   Avellán, H.   Declaration of Love to Kurt Cobain.
Coca Cola
   Cumpian.   No Deposit Returns.
   Dacey, P.   Coke.
   Erdrich, H.   Hopi Prophet Chooses a Pop.
   Espada.   Coca-Cola and Coco Frío.
   Fusselman, A.   Mother Nature.
   Hiestand, E.   Moon Winx Motel.
   Hollander, R.   You Too? Me Too—Why Not?
      Soda Pop.
   O'Hara, F.   Having a Coke with You.
   Stillman, A.   Jukebox Saturday Night.
Cocaine
   Ai.   Self Defense.
   Clifton, L.   White Lady.
   Espada.   Prisoners of Saint Lawrence, The.
   France, L.   What I Know Now.
   Harper, M.   Elvin's Blues.
   Morton, A.   Cokaigne Fantasy.
Cockfighting
   Ai.   Cockfighter's Daughter, The.
   Garrett, E.   Grandfather's Mint.
   Hernández Cruz.   Side 26.
   Liu Cheng.   Cockfight.
See also **Roosters**
Cockroaches
   Clifton, L.   At last we killed the roaches.
   Cruelty.   Don't talk to me about cruelty.

Espada.   Cockroaches of Liberation.
   My Cockroach Lover.
   Greenlaw, L.   Love from a Foreign City.
   Marquis.   Expression is the need of my soul.
      Song of Mehitabel, The.
   Rukeyser, M.   St. Roach.
Cocks
   Basho.   On the cow shed.
   Jacobik, G.   Turkeys in August.
   Raine, K.   Good Friday.
   Unknown.   I Have a Gentle Cock [or Gentil
      Cok].
See also **Roosters**
Cocoa
   La Fontaine.   Saddled Ass, The.
   Sharpless.   In Praise of Cocoa, Cupid's
      Nightcap.
Coconuts
   Espada.   Coca-Cola and Coco Frío.
   Unknown.   First Coconut Tree, The.
Cocoons
   Levin, D.   Ars Poetica: "Six monarch butterfly
      cocoons."
   Shiraishi.   Residents of the Cocoon, The.
Cocteau, Jean
   Tagliabue.   Moderation Is Not a Negation of
      Intensity, But Helps Avoid Monotony.
Coercion
   Flanders, M.   Have Some Madeira, M'dear?
   Kalagoe, C.   This johnny / is Mr Strong from
      Strongtown.
Coffee
   Akhmadulina.   Coffee Imp, The.
   Alegría.   Documentary.
   Berlin.   Let's Have Another Cup of Coffee.
   Bernstein, C.   Cup of Coffee, The.
   Brown, L.   You're the Cream in My Coffee.
   Burke, S.   Black Coffee.
   Coleman, W.   Coffee.
   Cunningham, J.   Coffee.
   DeSylva, B. G.   You're the Cream in My
      Coffee.
   Henderson, R.   You're the Cream in My Coffee.
   Hilliard, B.   Coffee Song (They've Got an
      Awful Lot of Coffee in Brazil), The.
   Hoagland, E.   Time Break.
   Iozia, J.   Last Night at the Flamingo.
   Kemp, A.   100 Times.
   Loncar, M.   Picasso Shag.
   Nordbrandt.   China Observed Through Greek
      Rain in Turkish Coffee.
   Nye, N.   Arabic Coffee.
   Padgett, R.   Prose Poem: "Morning coffee, The.
      I'm not sure why I drink it."
   Peacock, M.   Breakfast with Cats.
   Petri.   Morning Coffee.
   Ríos, A.   Coffee in the Afternoon.
   Saffoti.   Espresso.
   St. John, D.   Coffee.
   Sears, P.   Good Morning Coffee Makes Vivid of
      the Vague; Suddenly You Have Hands and
      Eyes and Legs!
   Stein, G.   Piece fo Coffee, A.
   Tucker, M.   Upon Receipt of a Pound of Coffee
      in 1863.
   Unknown.   Coffee Rancher, The.
   Vian, Boris.   What for Do I Live Then.
   Walcott.   Gulf, The.
   Webster, P.   Black Coffee.
Coffins
   Adonis [or Adunis].   Mirror for the Twentieth
      Century, A.
   Alon, E.   Coffins.
   Baiho.   On Entering His Coffin.
   Baugh, E.   Carpenter's Complaint, The.
   Celan.   Night Ray.
   Cendrars.   Frisco-City.
   Ciardi, J.   Box Comes Home, A.
   Hernández, M.   War.
   Kim Hyesun.   Not Knowing He's Dead.
   Kovner, A.   What's Not in the Heart.
   Monsour.   Emily's Words.
   Postnikova, O.   Archangel Cathedral.
   Ruefle.   Furtherness.
   Ryuichi.   Standing Coffin.

White, K.   Song of the Coffin Close.

Coins

Hartman, J.   Petition Hecate at the seal.
Hill, G.   Coins handsome as Nero's; of good substance and.
Hughes, L.   Fact.
Hume, C.   Dirty Money.
Issa.   In the beggar's tin.
Jiménez, J.   Song: "Setting sun left my heart, The."
Kramer, L.   Strong Winds Below the Canyons.
Nemerov.   Money.
Slutsky [or Slutskii].   Coppers.
Swift, J.   Prometheus: "As, when the squire and tinker, Wood."
Vietnamese Oral Tradition.   Coins of Van-Lich.
Weems, M.   Dime after Dime.
Weinstein, N.   Garvey's Head as Value.

Cold

Abse.   Hunt the Thimble.
Ammons.   First Cold.
Atwood.   You Are Happy.
Bacon, C.   Outlook.
Basho.   All this foolishness.
  Awake at night.
  Chilling autumn rains.
  Cold night: the wild duck.
  Cold rain starting, A.
  In the fish shop.
  Winter leeks,The.
  Withering winds.
Bates, C.   Hard-Hearted Hannah (The Vamp of Savannah).
Berlin.   I've Got My Love to Keep Me Warm.
Bigelow, B.   Hard-Hearted Hannah (The Vamp of Savannah).
Brown, L.   Turn On the Heat.
Bryant, W.   November.
Burns, R.   O[h] Wert Thou in the Cauld Blast.
Buson.   Walking on dishes.
  With a runny nose.
Bynner.   Wintry Mind, The.
Ceravolo.   Stolen Away.
Chiao-jan.   Cold Mountain.
Clary.   Camellia, It's that Moist and Sensitive.
Corfield, J.   Morse Lesson.
Dalton, Mary.   Conkerbells.
De Roux, Paul.   Cold Again, The.
DeSylva, B. G.   Turn On the Heat.
Devi.   Cold Meat.
Dickinson, A.   Cryo.
Dickinson, E.   'Twas warm—at first—like Us.
Doolittle, H.   You come late.
Du Bouchet.   Light of the Blade, The.
Dugan, A.   Glad at the Cold (1955).
Enquist, A.   December Offensive.
Frazier, John Alexander, Jr.   Guard, A.
Galvin, J.   Two Horses and a Dog.
Gbadamosi.   Death of the Polar Explorers.
Gilliams, M.   Tristitia Ante.
González Prada, M.   Into the Hearth They Are Tossing Logs.
Guest, B.   Nebraska.
Han-shan.   In the Mountains.
  Rough and Dark.
Hanu.   Some said the northern window was bright.
  Why should you freeze to sleep?
Heath, R.   On the Unusual Cold and Rainy [or Rainie] Weather in the Summer, 1648.
Henderson, R.   Turn On the Heat.
Hesiod.   Beware of the month Lenaion, bad days.
Holtby, W.   Man Who Hated the Spring, The.
Hulme, T.   Embankment, The (The fantasia of a fallen gentleman on a cold, bitter night).
Issa.   Closer, closer / to paradise—.
  Crescent moon.
  Even considered.
  Where.
Jackson, H.   Found Frozen.
Jacobsen, R.   Crust on Fresh Snow.
Kavanagh, P.   Fields were bleached white, The.
Keithley.   First Morning.
Kenney.   Aubade: "Cold snap. Five o'clock."
Kim Chiha.   Truth.

Loesser.   Baby, It's Cold Outside.
Masaoka Shiki.   Hands so cold.
Matthews, W.   Pissing off the Back of the Boat into the Nivernais Canal.
McCarriston.   January, Anchorage.
McFee.   Cold Quilt.
Merrill, J.   David's Night in Veliès.
Moore, L.   Winter 1967.
Morgan, E.   Shilpit dog fucks grimly by the close, A.
Na Hûidôk.   Cold Rain Comes, A.
Nash, O.   Samson Agonistes.
Niedecker.   Popcorn-can cover.
Paek Sŏk.   Sound of the Mountain Bird.
Peaux, A.   Cold Landscape.
Randell.   Our hands crushed.
Rosemurgy, C.   Why God Invented the Cold.
Sansom, A.   Confinement.
Schley, J.   Inquest, By Hand.
Scovell.   Light the Fire.
Scupham.   After Ovid, Tristia.
Service.   Cremation of Sam McGee, The.
Simic.   Winter Night.
Smith, S.   Like This (2).
Snyder, G.   Late October Camping in the Sawtooths.
Sokan.   Cold, yes / But don't test.
Sorescu, M.   Tear, The.
Stevenson, A.   Cold: "Snow. No roofs this morning, alps, ominous message."
Strand.   Poor North.
Suhl.   Winter: "Now winter's standing at the door."
Szymborska, W.   Words ("La Pologne? La Pologne? It's awfully cold there, isn't it? she asked.").
T'ao Ch'ien [or T'ao Yuan-ming].   Thinking of Impoverished Ancients.
Teiga.   In the poor man's house.
Thomas, E.   Frost To-night.
Thomson, J.   For, see! where Winter comes, himself, confest.
Ts'ao Ts'ao.   Bitter Cold: A Song.
  Song on Enduring the Cold.
Ts'en Shen.   Song for General Zhao.
Unknown.   My loved one is far away.
Ward, D.   Hunting in Twilight.
Warner, S.   After He Had Gone.
Williams, C. K.   Snow: II.
Winters, Y.   Cold, The.
Wormser.   January.
Yellen, J.   Hard-Hearted Hannah (The Vamp of Savannah).
Yi Sanghûi.   Morning Stroll, A.

Cold War

Baggott, J.   Kitchens: 1959.
Burns, J.   Confessions of an Old Believer.
Fell, A.   Women in the Cold War.
Ginsberg, A.   America: "America I've given you all and now I'm nothing."
Gorbanevskaya.   Notes of a Cold War Veteran.
Kazantzis.   Thatcher, A.
Lopez, T.   Dint.
MacBeth [or Macbeth].   Crab-Apple Crisis, The.
Revell, D.   Last.
Smith, K.   1984 Tour of Britain, The.
Snodgrass.   Child between them on the street, The.
Stewart, S.   May 1988.
Troupe.   So What.
Wright, C.   On the Eve of Our Mutually Assured Destruction.

Colds (illness)

Akhmadulina.   Chills.
Williams, C. K.   Shade, The.

Cole, Thomas

Bryant, W.   To Cole, the Painter, Departing for Europe.

Coleridge, Samuel Taylor

Barbauld.   To Mr. S. T. Coleridge.
Breytenbach.   Constipation.
Clampitt.   Cure at Porlock, A.
Coleridge, H.   Dedicatory Sonnet to S. T. Coleridge.
Coleridge, Sara.   Father! no amaranths e'er shall wreathe my brow.

Dubie.   Coleridge Crossing the Plain of Jars [1833].
Fanthorpe.   Person's Tale, The.
Frost, R.   Most of It, The.
McGuckian.   Coleridge.
Smith, S.   Thoughts about the Person from Porlock.
Watts-Dunton.   Coleridge.
Wordsworth, W.   Mind Debarred, A.
  With him there often walked in friendly wise.

Colleges and Universities

Berman, D.   Community College in the Rain.
Brown, L.   Varsity Drag, The.
Cook, C.   Anthelmintic.
DeSylva, B. G.   Varsity Drag, The.
Dugan, A.   Internal Migration: On Being on Tour.
Espada.   Community College Revises Its Curriculum in Response to Changing Demographics, The.
Frost, R.   Lucretius versus the Lake Poets.
Henderson, R.   Varsity Drag, The.
Holmes, J.   Old Professor, The.
Hughes, L.   Theme for English B.
Khali, S.   Walking On: A Declaration of Wholeness.
Kirby, D.   Dear Derrida.
Kizer, C.   Twelve O'Clock.
McNair.   Goodbye to the Old Life.
Moore, M.   Student, The.
Moorer.   Claflin's Alumni.
  Dedication Day Poem.
  What We Teach at Claflin.
Nazario, A.   Kevin and Nicole.
Olds, S.   I Go Back to May 1937.
Rich, A.   1948: Jews.
Samaras, N.   Elegy for a Professor.
Shapiro, K.   University.
Song.   Sunworshippers.
Spender, S.   One More New Botched Beginning.
Strayhorn, B.   Lonely Coed, A.
Travis, N.   At My Father's House.
Voznesensky [or Voznesenskii].   Big Fire at the Architectural College, The.
Waniek.   Letter to a Benedictine Monk.
Wheatley, P.   To the University of Cambridge, in New-England.
Wilbur, R.   Finished Man, A.
Wilson, E.   Disloyal Lines to an Alumnus.
Wodehouse.   Tulip Time in Sing Sing.

See also **Students**

Collies

MacCaig.   Praise of a Collie.

Cologne, Germany

Coleridge, S.   Cologne.
Gier, J.   Examining the I.

Colonialism

Abad, G.   Light in One's Blood, The.
Adisa.   No, Women Don't Cry.
Aguilar, M.   Pall Hanging over Manila.
Allingham, W.   In Snow.
Andrade, O.   Babbling.
  Good Luck.
  Portuguese Mistake.
Barlow, J.   Progress of the Colonies. Troubles with the Natives.
Baxter, J.   New Zealand.
Bhattācārya, M.   Come, brothers, everyone together.
Borges.   Mythical Founding of Buenos Aires, The.
Bradstreet, A.   Dialogue between Old England and New, A.
Chrystos.   I Bring You Greetings: How. Okeydoekey Tribe, The.
Creeley.   America.
D'Aguiar, F.   Mama Dot.
Damas.   On Sale.
Daniel, S.   Theare be great Prince, such as will tell you howe.
Diop, D.   Vultures, The.
Duhig, I.   Fundamentals.
Dunbar, P.   Conquerors, The: The Black Troops in Cuba.
Esteves.   From Fanon.

Gier, J.   California Coast.
  Going Baroque.
Gilfillan, M.   Horseshoe.
Gloria.   Touch.
Góngora y Argote.   Capture of Larache, The.
González Prada, M.   Inca's Arrows, The.
  Mitayo, The.
Guignard, M.   One morning just like that they
  arrive.
Hagedorn, J.   Souvenirs.
Hemans.   England's Dead.
Hernández Cruz.   New/Aguas Buenas/Jersey.
Hugo, V.   Inquisition, The.
Im Hwa.   Pier of Yokohama under the Umbrella,
  The.
Islām, N.   Don't go back, Ma, don't go back,
  Mother.
Kipling, R.   White Man's Burden, The.
Landor, W.   To Arthur de Noé Walker.
Lazarus, E.   1492.
  How Long?
Lim-Wilson.   Alphabet Soup.
Livingstone, D.   Sleep of my lions, The.
Lopez, T.   Path Marked with Breadcrumbs, A.
Mateo.   There Is No Word for Sex in Taglog.
Maunick.   Seven Sides and Seven Syllables.
Motsapi, S.   Ityopia phase-in.
Neruda.   United Fruit Co., The.
Nichols, G.   Beverley's Saga.
Pietri.   Intermission from Wednesday.
Putnam.   Words of an Old Woman.
Robles.   Feasting with Etang a Hundred Times
  Around.
Salaam.   Flying over America.
San Juan.   Owl of Minerva Takes Flight in the
  Evening, The.
Schoolcraft.   Otagamiad.
Schulman.   New Netherland, 1654.
Seferis.   Days of April '43.
Senghor.   Camp 1940.
Senior.   Meditation on Yellow.
Sylvain, P.   Constant Memories.
Vando.   Commonwealth, Common Poverty.
Vietnamese Oral Tradition.   Colonial Troops
  Transport, The.
Wainwright, K.   Changes.
Walcott.   Adios, Carenage.
  Far Cry from Africa, A.
Yi Sanghwa.   Will Spring Return to Stolen
  Fields?
See also **British Empire; Imperialism**
Colorado (state)
Griswold, J.   Origami.
Holden, J.   September: Nederland, Colorado.
Saner.   Indian Peaks, Colorado.
Stafford, W.   Holding the Sky.
Colors
Abse.   Pathology of Colours.
Albert-Birot.   Balalaïka.
Alberti.   Going Back Through Color.
Alexander, E.   Stravinsky in L.A.
Alexander, P.   Antichromatic.
Ap Hywel, Elin.   Understanding Light.
Apollinaire.   Windows.
Avison.   Present From Ted.
Basho.   Seas slowly darken.
Belchenko, N.   Chameleons are fine.
Berkson, B.   Blue Is the Hero.
Bhattācārya, K.   Is my black Mother Syama
  really black?
Borges.   Houses like Angels.
Bowen, E.   In Chartres.
Brown, G.   Shroud.
Browne, W.   Golden Age: Flower-weaving, The.
  Happyer those times were, when the Flaxen
  clew.
Buson.   Only the shoots.
  Pure white plum blossoms.
Bynner.   Tiles.
Clark, T. J.   Landscape with a Calm.
Clifton, L.   Gift, The.
Cowper, W.   Winter Walk at Noon, The.
Craven, Jerry.   Spring in Palo Duro Canyon.
Cruz e Sousa.   Antiphony.
D'Aquino, A.   Sol abre los labios y nos dice, El.
  Sun opens its lips and says to us, The.

de Jesús.   Flag of Chile, The.
DeCarteret, M.   Coloring.
Depero.   Colors.
Dickinson, E.   Yellow Man, Purple Man.
Dubie.   February: The Boy Breughel.
Ebb, F.   My Coloring Book.
Eguren.   Towers, The.
Esteves.   Weaver.
Ficke.   Opus 131.
Follain.   Useful, The.
Fried, E.   Naturalization.
Gilman, C.   California Colors: A Song.
Goodman, P.   I planned to have a border of
  lavender.
Gray-Kontar, D.   Not no socialism/communism
  classical, but some power to the people jazz.
Guest, B.   River Road Studio.
Halliday, M.   Pink Car, The.
Hamadani.   Quatrain.
Ikkyu Sojun.   Oh green green willow
  wonderfully red flower.
Ilagha, N.   Nora.
Jacobsen, R.   Cobalt.
Jones, Einir.   Grey.
Kruit, J.   Giving Way.
Lima, M.   Marketwoman of Luanda.
Madhubuti.   Poem Looking for a Reader, A.
Martial.   You were a swan, you're now a crow.
Marvin, C.   Alba: Aberdeen.
Mathews, A.   Spectrum.
Mathews, H.   Ring, The.
McPherson, S.   Quilt of Rights.
Merritt, C.   Woman of Color.
Morley, H.   Curve of the Water.
  For Elaine de Kooning.
Mukai Kyorai.   After the green storm / True
  color.
Nichols, G.   Black.
  White.
Nijhoff.   Light.
  Light, The.
Novikov, N.   White on white's a flatness.
Okamoto.   Tanka: "Flower blooms, A."
Orlowsky, D.   To Our Cosmeticians.
Pellicer, C.   Flocks of Doves.
  Wishes.
Pilling.   You and You, In the Pink.
Pound, E.   Song of the Degrees, A.
Randell.   Jetty, The.
Ratcliffe, S.   Diagonal plane of low grey white
  cloud moving.
Riley, D.   Lure, 1963.
Salaam.   Height, Breadth, Depth.
  New Orleans Rainbow.
Seidman.   Making of Color, The.
Snyder, G.   Gaia.
Stanard, C.   Wrong Color.
Stein, G.   Box, A ("Large box is handily made
  of what is necessary to replace any substance,
  A.").
  Glazed glitter.
  Little Bit of Tumbler, A.
Steinberg, D.   Purple is the Color of Longing.
Steptoe.   Sweet Brown Rice and Red Bones.
Stern, G.   She Was a Dove.
Stevens, W.   Domination of Black.
Tanikawa, S.   Landscape with Yellow Birds.
Tengour, H.   Secret in Broad Daylight.
Toomer.   People.
Verlaine.   Brussels: Simple Frescos 1.
Wakayama Bokusui.   White bird.
Watkins, V.   Music of Colours: The Blossom
  Scattered.
  Music of Colours—White Blossom.
Weaver, A.   Colors—Struck.
Wolverton, T.   Tubes.
Wylie.   Green Hair.
Yang Chi.   Five-Color.
Yi Yuksa.   Blue Grapes.
Young, D.   Project for Freight Trains, A.
Colosseum, Rome
Byron, G.   Stars are forth, the moon above the
  tops, The.
Lamartine.   Lizard, The.
Poe.   Coliseum, The.

Coltrane, John
Baker, H.   Set Piece.
Baraka, I.   Am/Trak.
  John Coltrane (1926–1967).
  Monk's World.
Brathwaite, E.   Naima.
  Trane.
Early, G.   Country or Western Music.
Etter.   Monk's Dream.
Gordon, G.   Gas.
Graham, M.   After the War; When Coltrane
  Only Wanted to Play Dance Tunes.
Greenlee.   Memorial for Trane.
Harjo, J.   Healing Animal.
Harper, M.   Brother John.
  Dear John, Dear Coltrane.
  Here Where Coltrane Is.
  Narrative of the Life and Times of John
  Coltrane: Played by Himself, A.
Hayes, T.   Boxcar.
Henderson, D.   Elvin Jones Gretsch Freak.
Kgositsile.   Acknowledgement.
Levine, P.   Soloing.
Madhubuti.   Don't Cry, Scream.
Mor.   Coming of John, The.
Okantah.   Afreeka Brass.
Rodgers, C.   Written for Love of an
  Ascension—Coltrane.
Sneeden.   Coltrane and My Father.
Spellman, A.   Did John's Music Kill Him?
  John Coltrane: An Impartial Review.
Stillman, M.   In Memoriam John Coltrane.
Touré, A.   JuJu.
Colts
Chadwick, J.   Eight-Legged Colt, Chernobyl.
Frost, R.   Runaway, The.
See also **Horses**
Columba, Saint
Morgan, E.   Columba's Song.
Unknown.   Colum Cille's Greeting to Ireland.
Columbia University
Ferlinghetti, L.   And Pablo Neruda / that
  Chilean omnivore of poetry.
Columbine Massacre
Armitage, S.   Meanwhile, somewhere in the
  state of Colorado, armed to the teeth.
Bugeja, M.   Littleton.
Goldbarth.   Columbine High School / Littleton,
  CO.
Columbus, Christopher
Barlow, J.   There reigns a prince, whose hand
  the sceptre claims.
Brathwaite, E.   Colombe.
Crane, H.   Ave Maria.
Durham.   Columbus Day.
Fritz, Walter Helmut (b. 1929).   Columbus.
Frost, R.   America Is Hard to See.
Gardinier.   Admirals (Columbus).
Lazarus, E.   1492.
Miller, J.   Columbus: "Behind him lay the gray
  Azores."
Nash, O.   Columbus.
Robertson, J.   Discovery of America, The.
Rukeyser, M.   Columbus.
Slauerhoff.   Columbus.
Smith, W.   Columbus Circle Swing.
Stickney, T.   You say, Columbus with his
  argosies.
Sylvain, P.   Constant Memories.
Whitman, W.   Passage to India.
  Prayer of Columbus.
Comas
Ai.   Sleeping Beauty.
Heise, Thomas.   Zombie.
Khalvati.   Coma.
Combs
Buson.   It pierces through me.
Cardiff.   Combing.
Kasa.   Have I let my love.
Li Ho.   Song: A Lovely Girl Combing Her Hair.
Tassis y Peralta.   To a Lady Combing Her Hair.
Trethewey, N.   Hot Comb.
Comedians
Bernstein, C.   Of Time and the Line.
Hathaway, W.   Why That's Bob Hope.

Norris, K.   Luke 14: A Commentary.

Comets
Abrahams, L.   To Halley's Comet.
Apparao, G.   Comet, The.
Lewis, G.   Second time the comet swung by, The.
Marvell.   Mower to the Glowworms [*or* Glow-Worms *or* Glo-Worms], The.
Nicholson, N.   Comet Come.
  Halley's Comet.
Noguere.   Soma.
Ortiz.   On late-night television, two U.S. scientists talk about why the U.S.
Ramsey, J.   Comet and Treefrog.
Riordan, M.   Comet, The.
Yungch'ŏn, Master.   Song of the Comet.

Comfort
Adler, L.   You: "When afternoon."
Angus.   Blue Jacket, The.
Baraka, I.   Political Poem.
Bauer, G.   She Calms the Savage Beast with Her Aubade.
Berry, W.   In Rain.
  Wild Geese, The.
Bible, *O.T.*   Psalm 92. Bonum Est Confiteri.
Bock, J.   Too Close for Comfort.
Browning, E.   Comfort.
  Thought for a Lonely Death-Bed, A.
Cairns, Scott.   Lucifer's Epistle to the Fallen.
Cixous.   I urgency, I begged. *Give me your dish,* I said, icy.
Clark, T.   Some Details of Hebridean House Construction.
Cuthbert, J.   Memories of St. George's Caye.
Dowson.   Vesperal.
Enzensberger, H.   Short History of the Bourgeoisie.
Foster, A.   Starting School.
Hammerstein.   My Favorite Things.
Harbach, O.   Love Nest, The.
Hardy, T.   At the Railway Station, Upway.
Haskins, L.   To Play Pianissimo.
Herrick.   Comfort to a Youth That Had Lost His Love.
Holofcener, L.   Too Close for Comfort.
Hopkins, G.   No Worst, There Is None. Pitched Past Pitch of Grief.
Howe, M.   Kiss, The.
Ivey, M.   Subterranean Business.
Johnson, H.   Fringe-Area Reception.
Keats.   Why Did I Laugh Tonight?
Keita, N.   My Sleeping Husband.
Kirsch, S.   I Am Very Gentle.
Lerner, A.   I've Grown Accustomed to Her Face.
Liu, T.   Ikon.
MacCaig.   Of You.
Martial.   Ad Quintilianum.
McDaniel, J.   Hunting for Cherubs.
Melville, H.   Herba Santa.
Monnier, Pascalle.   Winter.
Mun Chônghui.   Letter, The.
Murphy, P.   Manifesto.
Parker, D.   Words of Comfort to Be Scratched on a Mirror.
Philips, K.   Retired Friendship, To Ardelia, A.
Pollitt.   Small Comfort.
Razran, Gregory.   Jade's Iguanas Are Dead.
Robbins, Z.   December 12th.
Ryokan.   All my life I've had no interest in worldly success.
  Too Lazy to Be Ambitious.
Samaras, N.   First Nightmare Waking.
Stern, G.   Mentioning of Souls.
Synge.   With One Long Kiss.
Talfourd.   'Tis a Little Thing.
Unknown.   As in thee resteth my joye and confort.
Walders, D.   Anniversary.
Weiss, G.   Too Close for Comfort.
Williams, N.   Daniel's Hands.
Yi Sanghûi.   Night, Work.

Comic Strips
Ashbery, J.   Farm Implements and Rutabagas in a Landscape.
Mueller, J.   Life in the Comics.

Olin.   Shark Wrangler Goes to Church, The.
Wallace-Crabbe.   Collective Invention, The.

Comics and Comic Books
Clifton, L.   Note, Passed to Superman.
Keene, J.   Captain America at Home.
Koertge.   Dear Superman.
Machan.   No, Superman Was Not the Only One.
Powell, D. A.   My neck a toothsome feeding ground. vespered swarms had drunk of me before this new batman.

Coming of Age
Cox, M.   At the Crematorium, My Son Asks Why We're All Wearing Black.
Finch, A.   Perdita's Song.
Gloeggler, T.   Fowler Street.
Healy, E.   Toltecs.
Joseph, A.   Poem for the Purchase of a First Bra.
Moss, T.   One for All Newborns.
Thomas, L.   Back in the Day.

Commerce
Brown, L.   Best Things in Life Are Free, The.
DeSylva, B. G.   Best Things in Life Are Free, The.
Dyer, J.   Insensible Hottentot, The.
  Leeds for Pleasure.
Edwards, K.   De—um majorettes.
Elliott, K.   Fatal Birth, The.
Eveleigh, G.   Divine Mission, A.
Ginsberg, A.   Studying the Signs.
Grainger, J.   Shame of France, The.
Griffith, L.   Office Window.
Gwynn, R.   Classroom at the Mall, The.
Hacker, M.   Elysian Fields.
Hall, D.   Hermit with Landscape.
Henderson, R.   Best Things in Life Are Free, The.
Hofer, J.   Of Deaths, Days, Futures, Nations ("On the corner of plato and national army a man early.").
Jensma.   Confidentially Yours.
Juan Chi.   Whether one is eminent or humble depends on Fate.
Knight, S.   Eyeball Works, The.
Koch, K.   You Were Wearing.
Machado Ruiz.   Wind, One Brilliant Day, The.
Martin, C.   Victoria's Secret.
McLaughlin-Carruth, J.   Introducing *New Year's SOLUTIONS,* from Saint Terri's Inc.
Mirabai [*or* Mira Bai].   It's True I Went to the Market.
Quarles.   What is the *World?* A great *Exchange* of ware.
Ridge, L.   Morning Ride.
Spender, S.   Ultima Ratio Regum.
Spenser, E.   Sonnet 15: "Ye tradeful merchants that, with weary toil."
Wellman, M.   United bolt and screw.
Zukofsky, L.   Song for the Year's End, A.
See also **Barters; Business and Businessmen**

Communes
Jones, A.   Communal Living.
Piatt, S.   Palace-Burner, The.

Communication
Aiken, C.   Annihilation.
Ashbery, J.   Train Rising Out of the Sea.
Beatty, A.   Memorization.
Behn, A.   Love's Witness.
Bermeo, O.   Oda para Leticia.
Bowers, M.   Answer.
Bowes-Lyon.   Feather, The.
Bronk.   Mayan Glyphs Unread, The.
Carruth, H.   Sonnet: "Well, she told me I had an aura. "What?" I said."
Creeley.   Act of Love, The.
Cummings, E. E.   May i feel said he.
Davidson, D.   Utterance.
Dimitrova.   Blind woman was more intimate with it, The.
Dooley, M.   No, Go On.
Dow, R.   How Should I Say This?
Dunn, S.   Little Essay on Communication.
Fritz, Walter Helmut (b. 1929).   Almost Bashfully.
Gaspar.   Part of What I Mean.

Ginsberg, A.   Stroke.
Goodell, L.   Human Non-Sequitur.
Graham, W.   Beast in the Space, The.
Hacker, M.   And I shout at Iva, whine at you. Easily.
Harwood, G.   In the Park.
Hauge.   I Stand Here, Do You Understand.
Higgins, R.   Almost Communication.
Hunt, L.   Domestic Chat.
Imbriglio, C.   Motive.
Jackson, L.   Summary for Alastor.
  World and I, The.
Kipling, R.   Fabulists, The.
Lee, James R.   Stranger at Home.
Lloyd, M.   Simplest and the Hardest, The.
Lukata, B.   Interpretations.
Lum.   Going Home.
Lustig, Dana Lisa.   Big guns go boom! (for Mark Prejsnar).
Maguire, S.   Communion.
Mansfield, K.   Meeting, The.
Matthews, T.   Even the Whales.
Matthews, W.   Cloister, The.
McGuire, Jerry.   Cages, The.
Millay, E.   Hearing Your Words, and Not a Word Among Them.
Morgan, E.   First Men on Mercury, The.
Padgett, R.   Joe Brainard's Painting "Bingo".
Palmer, M.   I Do Not.
  Voice and Address.
Pantani, Marco.   Sometimes We Close Our Eyes.
Pearlman.   Staying in Touch.
Piercy.   You Don't Understand Me.
Ranaldo, L.   Wrong #.
Rich, A.   Cartographies of Silence.
  Implosions.
  In the Evening.
  That conversation we were always on the edge.
  Valediction Forbidding Mourning, A.
Robinson, E.   Tact.
Rosselli.   From relief to relief, the white lines, the white paper.
Rukeyser, M.   Effort at Speech between Two People.
Rushin.   Bridge Poem, The.
Sexton.   From the Garden.
Sexton, M.   Marriage Patois.
Shapiro, K.   Funeral of Poetry, The.
Sinclair, I.   Snow Lip.
Singer, B.   Your Words, My Answers.
Stafford, W.   Ritual to Read to Each Other, A.
Sukhovey, D.   Spring Scales.
Valentine, J.   Snow Landscape, in a Glass Globe.
Van Duyn.   Wish to Be Believed, The.
Voznesensky [*or* Voznesenskii].   Dogalypse.
Watta.   Stone at the Tip of the Tongue, A.
Whitman, W.   Past and present wilt—I have filled them, emptied them, The.
Whittemore, R.   For the Life of Him and Her.
Williams, C. K.   Singing, The.
Woolson.   Love Unexpressed.

Communion
Andrade, M.   Sunday.
Barnstone, A.   Wild With It.
Craig, David.   John Says Mass on All Souls' Day.
Emanuel, L.   Walt, I Salute You!
Gibson, M.   One Body.
Gilgun, J.   Zen Sky.
Kabir.   Owl and the Moon, The.
Kennelly.   Big Words, The.
Levertov.   This Day.
Portugal, Anne.   Seen from Over Here ("From the horizon there.").
Spahr, J.   December 4, 2002.
Teofilov, Ivan.   Shared Existence.
See also **Eucharist**

Communism
Ackland.   Communist Poem, 1935.
Astley, N.   East of Easter.
Basheva.   N. N.
Bobyshev.   Trotsky in Mexico.
Brecht, B.   Late Lamented Fame of the Giant City of New York.

Breeze. Red Rebel Song.
Brook, D. Pink Diapers.
Burns, J. Confessions of an Old Believer.
Cardenal. Unrighteous Mammon (Luke 16:9).
Connolly, C. M is for Marx.
Cornford, J. Full Moon at Tierz: Before the
    Storming of Huesca.
Dalton, R. Looking for Trouble.
    My Neighbor.
Duff, V. Letters from an Exile.
Eastman, M. To John Reed.
France, L. Stateless.
Galanskov. Last Platform, The.
Ginsberg, A. America: "America I've given you
    all and now I'm nothing."
    Kral Majales.
Gu Cheng. Forever Parted: Graveyard.
Guest, B. Eating Chocolate Ice Cream: Reading
    Mayakovsky.
Hikmet. Angina Pectoris.
Hughes, L. Goodbye Christ.
Jones, R. End of Communism, The.
Kavulu. Forces of Production.
Kay, J. Shoes of Dead Comrades, The.
    Waiting Lists, The.
Kunze, R. Wall, The: For October 3, 1990.
Mayakovsky [or Maiakovskii]. Last Page of the
    Civil War.
    My most respected / comrades of posterity!
Mitchison. To Some Young Communists from
    an Older Socialist.
Nguyễn Chí Thiện. Party holds you down and
    you lie still, The.
Nicholas, T. To a Sparrow.
Pavlov, Konstantin. Adaptation.
    End of Mythology, The.
    Interview from the Belly of a Whale.
    Wonderful in Poetry, or a Victim of Goldfish,
    The.
Pawlak. East-West Dialog 2002.
Petri. By an Unknown Poet from Eastern
    Europe, 1955.
Ponge. Silent World Is Our Only Homeland,
    The.
Rich, A. For Ethel Rosenberg.
Rosen, M. Fighters For Life.
Ryuichi. My Imperialism.
Saarikoski. Winter solstice.
"Sagittarius.". Stalin Moy Golubchik.
Salkey. Clearsightedness.
Sapgir. Psalm 1.
Scharpenberg, Margot (b. 1924). Field of Red
    Tulips.
Serge. Asphyxiated Man, The.
    Dialectic.
Sims, H. Left Rites.
Teillier, J. Portrait of My Father, Militant
    Communist.
Tomlinson, C. Prometheus.
Vanek, J. People's Republic, The.
Werner, Judith. Ethel Rosenberg and Me.
Wilcox, E. Communism.
Worley, D. Las Flores para una Niña Negra.
Worpole, K. Sleeper.
Yevtushenko [or Evtushenko]. John Reed's
    Monologue.
Young, A. And It Shall Come.
Zilahy, P. Dictators.

Commuting and Commuters
As-Sabah. Transition #2.
Bulich, V. Omnibus, The.
Clarke, C. Passing.
Dunmore. To Virgil.
Elledge. Duckling, Swan.
Hearne, B. Commuters.
Hopkins, L. Subways Are People.
Kirchner, F. Reasons to Commute by Bicycle.
Manrique, J. Baudelaire's Spleen.
Mercado, N. Going to Work.
Rodriguez, L. Reflection on El Train Glass.
Ross, L. Indecent Exposure (A True Story).
Rouse, A. Her Retirement.
White, E. Commuter.

See also **Suburbs and Suburban Life**

Companionship and Companions
Adamson. Action Would Kill It / A Gamble.

Adler, L. Traveling Out, The.
Ai. Why Can't I Leave You?
Aird, T. Fellowship in Grief.
Alford, H. You and I.
Ali, A. Stars.
Amadiume. Union, The.
Amichai, Y. Couplets.
    Two of Us Together, Each of Us Alone, The.
Anderson, J. Waking Up Twice.
Andrew, G. O That Summer.
Atwood. Is / Not.
Auden. Glad.
    Lullaby: "Lay your sleeping head, my love."
Belieu. Part of the Effect of the Public Scene Is
    to Importune the Passing Viewer.
Bell, M. Nature: "Hand that tries to shake a
    hand, A."
Bendall, M. Matinée Idylls.
Berrigan, A. Various multitudes contained by
    the loves of my love, The.
Berry, W. To Tanya at Christmas.
Blacklock, T. To a Young Lady's Dog.
Blanchfield, B. Endowment Becoming Less An
    Institution, The.
Blaser. Ah.
Bowdan, Janet. Year, The.
Bracho, C. Sediment of Lukewarm and Radiant
    Rain.
Brock-Broido. Soul Keeping Company.
Brooke, R. Dining-Room Tea.
Broughton, J. Twin Flames.
Broumas, O. Amazon Twins.
    Way a Child Might Believe, The.
Brown, E. What do I have, when I contemplate
    this.
Browning, R. Dîs Aliter Visum; or, Le Byron
    de Nos Jours.
Bruce, G. Love in Age.
    Soup and Sherry.
Bryden, Diana Fitzgerald. Always, Not Always.
Buchanan, G. I Suddenly.
Bunting. Personal Column.
Burns, R. O[h] Wert Thou in the Cauld Blast.
    Red, Red Rose, A.
Bykova, Z. At the Stop.
Bynner. If I were only dafter.
Carroll, J. Blue Poles.
Carruth, H. Little Citizen, Little Survivor.
Carter, J. Adagio at Twilight.
Castellanos. Poetry Is Not You.
    You Are Not Poetry.
Castro, R. He Who Weeps Goes Not Alone.
Cataldi. We Could Have Met.
Ceravolo. I Like to Collapse.
Chester, T. Buttons.
Ch'i-chi. Written on a Summer Day in the City.
Chia Tao. Auspicious Arrival of Yung T'ao.
Ch'in Kuan. Farewell Song.
Cixous. I urgency, I begged. *Give me your dish,*
    I said, icy.
Colby, T. Boy and the Girl, The.
    Think Eight.
Cooper, J. Faithful, The.
    Rent.
Coslow, S. Cocktails for Two.
Creeley. For Love.
Cunningham, J. Aged Lover Discourses in the
    Flat Style, The.
Curbelo. Among Strangers.
Dao. Bouquet, A.
Davie, D. Time Passing, Beloved.
Davis, W. On Lookout: Guadalupe River
    Ranch.
Dickinson, E. Wild Nights—Wild Nights!
Dienstfrey, Patricia. Arrival.
Dietz, H. Alone Together.
DJ Renegade. Thursday Poem.
Donne. Canonization, The.
Dooley, M. Does It Go Like this?
    Up on the Roof.
Doty, M. New Dog.
Dugan, A. Glad at the Cold (1955).
Duncan, R. And If He Had Been Wrong for
    Me.
Elliott, E. My Only Friends.
Etherege. To a Lady Asking Him How Long He

    Would Love Her.
Evans, R. Never Let Me Go.
Everson, W. Stone Face Falls.
Factor, J. Scotch and Soda.
Fitzgerald, J. There Is But One True Friend.
Foppa. Your Hand in Mine.
Frost, R. Pasture, The.
Garshman, B. Keys.
Gates, B. Cathy.
Gay, J. Song: "Were I laid on Greenland's
    coast."
Gelman. Man and a Woman, A.
Ginsberg, A. Green Automobile, The.
Giovanni. World Is Not a Pleasant Place to Be,
    The.
Gogarty. To a Boon Companion.
González, A. Whatever You Want.
Goodman, M. Open Poem.
Gunn, T. Problem, The.
    Touch.
Hamby, B. Mr. Pillow.
Harnick. Matchmaker.
Hart, L. There's a Small Hotel.
Heaney, S. Dream of Jealousy, A.
Heine, H. To the World We Must Appear.
Herd. On the Glittering Beaches.
Heyman, E. You're Mine, You!
Hirshfield, J. Music Like Water, The.
Hollander, J. Some Walks With You.
Homer. Achilles' Dream.
Hoornik. To Love a Woman.
Hovanessian, D. On Commonwealth Avenue
    and Brattle Street.
Hughes, T. Bride and Groom Lie Hidden for
    Three Days.
    Other, The.
Hugo, R. Letter to Libbey from St. Regis.
Im Hwa. Pier of Yokohama under the Umbrella,
    The.
Istarú, A. To the cove of my breasts your
    forehead will return.
Jackson, A. Moment.
Jacob, M. Shady Soul.
Jennings, K. Just the Two of Us.
Josefowitz, N. Foreplay.
Joyce, J. Though I thy Mithridates were.
Kahn, G. No, No, Nora.
    Toot, Toot, Tootsie! (Good-bye).
Kefala. Sunday Visit.
Kendall, Walter G. Men Who Ride for Fun,
    The.
Kennelly. We Are Living.
Kenyon, J. Man Eating.
Kherdian. Couple that walked, The.
Kim Ch'unsu [or Chun-soo]. Flower.
King, H. Exequy, The.
Kinnell. Rapture.
    Waking, The.
Kizer, C. For Jan as the End Draws Near.
Klein, M. Guardian Life.
Klink, J. Lodestar.
Koehler, T. Good for Nothin' Joe.
Korean Oral Tradition. Transplanting Song.
Kuan Han-ch'ing. Tune: "Four Pieces of Jade".
Kuan Yün-shih. Love Song: "Fondling and
    snuggling."
Kunitz, S. Science of the Night, The.
Lamar. Carmelita.
Lanier, S. To Bayard Taylor.
Lawrence, J. Other Half of Me, The.
Lees, G. Right to Love, The.
Lerner, A. Heather on the Hill, The.
Levchev. Front Line.
Levertov. Don't You Hear that Whistle Blowin'.
    Everything That Acts Is Actual.
    Losing Track.
Li Po. Night with a Friend, A.
Light, K. Idea of Love Between Us, The.
Livingston, J. Never Let Me Go.
Lleshanaku, L. Out of Boredom.
Lockwood. Bookshop in Winter.
Lorde. Memorial 1: "If you come as softly."
Loy. One O'Clock at Night.
Loynaz, D. M. Sea Surrounded.
Marion, G. There's a Man in My Life.
Masters, E. Benjamin Pantier.

Mathews, A.   Spectrum.
Matson, C.   Bedside.
McGrath, T.   Celebration: "How wonderful, Tomasito!"
McGuckian.   War Ending, The.
McKay, C.   Wild Goat, The.
Merrill, B.   People.
Morozov, S.   Poem about the Blue Horse.
Mueller, L.   Alive Together.
Naimy, M.   My Brother.
Nash, O.   Which the Chicken, Which the Egg?
Nelson, J.   Our Love.
Nelson, M.   56 Westervelt.
Nemerov.   Blue Suburban.
Nemes Nagy.   Terraced Landscape.
Niedecker.   Wilderness.
Nye, N.   Kindness: "Before you know what kindness really is."
Olson, C.   Telesphere, The.
Ou-yang Hsiu.   Cutting, A.
Owen, W.   Apologia Pro Poemate Meo.
Palés Matos.   Calling, The.
Parker, A.   Magpie.
Parker, D.   Ballade at Thirty-Five.
Danger of Writing Defiant Verse, The.
Fighting Words.
General Review of the Sex Situation.
Prophetic Soul.
Parnok, S.   Through a Window-Light.
Peacock, T.   Love and Age.
Penn, R.E.   Hand.
Piccione.   With Whitman at the Friendship Hotel.
Piercy.   Implications of One Plus One.
To Have without Holding.
Po Chü-i.   To Yuan Chen.
Porter, C.   From This Moment On.
Price, R.   Hawk Hill.
Radden, V.   Our Second Night.
Rakosi.   Old Lovers.
Ramsdell, H.   Where Things of a Kind.
Ramsey, J.   Tally Stick, The.
Rashad, J.   Place Setting.
Rees-Jones.   I Know Exactly the Sort of Woman I'd Like to Fall in Love With.
It Will Not Do.
Rexroth, K.   How long, long ago.
Night without end. Loneliness.
Some day in six inches of.
Without me you can only.
Reznikoff.   Though our thoughts often, we ourselves.
Rich, A.   After Twenty Years.
I wake up in your bed. I know I have been dreaming.
In the Evening.
Living in Sin.
Marriage in the Sixties, A.
No one's fated or doomed to love anyone.
Paula Becker to Clara Westhoff.
Rain on the West Side Highway.
Ríos, A.   Chance Meeting of Two Men, A.
Ritchie.   Sorting Laundry.
Robin, L.   For Every Man There's a Woman.
Robinson, E.   Companion, The.
Firelight.
Ruefle.   Suburb of Long Suffering.
Safford, J.   Very Floor of Our Existence, The.
Satir, V.   Making Contact.
Scamell, B.   Working for British Telecom.
Shelley, P.   From the Arabic: An Imitation.
Simic.   Old Couple.
Smith, S.   Like This (1).
Sondheim.   Together Wherever We Go.
Sousa, N.   Poem of a Distant Childhood.
Swift, J.   Stella's Birthday, 1725.
Twelve Articles.
Sykes, B.   One Day.
Taggard.   Everyday Alchemy.
Tate, J.   Blue Booby, The.
Motorcyclists, The.
Teasley, L.   As Dancers.
Tennyson, A.   I know that this was Life—the track.
Path by which we twain did go, The.
Thompson, D. P.   Sister Lakin and Lally.

Unknown.   Coming of Enkidu, The.
Companion, The.
Death of Enkidu, The.
Lament of Gilgamesh for Enkidu, The.
Silk Cotton Tree.
Tu-zhi: Hares.
Valentine, J.   Under Voice, The.
Vallejo.   Finished the stranger, with whom, late.
Vietnamese Oral Tradition.   Autumn: "Autumn rains blow."
From *So* Mountain.
Whisky Lovers.
Vilariño.   Visitor, A.
Walcott.   Village Life, A.
Waller, Robert James.   Three Poems.
Warren, R.   After the Dinner Party.
In Moonlight, Somewhere, They Are Singing.
Wei Feng.   Staying with Master Heng Chao at Roost of the Sages Monastery on Mount Lu.
Williams, M.   Love Poem with Toast.
Winthrop, Jeanette I.   Couple Having Breakfast in the Deli, The.
Wodehouse.   You Never Knew About Me.
Woods, H.   Side by Side.
Wray, C.   Star, The.
Wright, C.   Girl Friend Poem # 3.
Wright, F.   Alcohol.
Wright, J.   Transfiguration.
Yellen, J.   Mamma Goes Where Papa Goes.
Yi Chehyŏn.   At a wash place by the stream under a drooping willow.
Zapruder, M.   Ten Questions for Mona.
Thank You for Being You.
See also **Friendship**

Compassion
Bhattācārya, K.   Tell me, Syama.
Brecht, B.   World's One Hope, The.
Brontë, A.   Song.
Brooks, G.   Children of the poor, The (1).
Brown, L.   Never Swat a Fly.
Byron, G.   Tear, The.
Crane, H.   Chaplinesque.
Creeley.   World, The.
Cristall.   Noon. Lysander.
DeSylva, B. G.   Never Swat a Fly.
Dickinson, E.   This Is My Letter to the World.
Donne.   What if this present were the world's last night?
Faiz.   Fragrant Hands.
Ginsberg, Allen.   Is About.
Ginsberg, Arthur.   Line Drive.
Hahn, O.   With Passion without Compassion.
Hamburger, M.   Between the Lines.
Hedyla.   Either cockleshells from the Erythraian reef as gifts.
Henderson, R.   Never Swat a Fly.
Herbert, Z.   Mr. Cogito and the Imagination.
Islām, N.   Let's be girls, Ma.
Knott.   Two Vietnam Poems: (1966).
Kyger.   Once Again Another Century Ahead.
Kyunyŏ, Great Master.   King of the bodhi tree, The.
Lao Tzu.   Person of superior integrity, The.
Levine, P.   Coming Home, *Detroit*, 1968.
Levitt, Peter.   Before falling to the scythe.
Mandal, B.   I'm not a child any more, Syama.
McClure, M.   For Zenshin Ryufu Philip Whalen.
Mukand, J.   Lullaby.
Muso Soseki.   No Gain.
North, C.   Few Facts about Me, A.
O'Reilly, M.   Small Girl Brings an Injured Bird into the Surgery, A.
Peck, J.   Metal Denser Than, and Liquid, A.
Ponge.   Frog, The.
Raab, E.   Today I am modest like an animal.
Sāheb, A.   Victory to Yogendra's Wife, Great Illusion!
Sanguineti.   And now a few questions to end with.
Sen, R.   Can someone / Called Daughter of a Stone.
Let me tell You a thing or two, Tara.
Spender, S.   History and Reality.
Spivack, K.   Yearning throughout Life, The.
Storni.   Lost Caress, The.
Tsvetayeva [*or* Tsvetaeva].   Tonight—I am alone

in the night.
Unknown.   Homage to Tara Our Mother.
Vietnamese Oral Tradition.   Red Cloth, The.
Vlasova, E.   Little sympathy, A.
Williams, C. K.   Day for Anne Frank, A.
Witt, S.   Americana.
Wright, James.   Saint Judas.
Wright, Jay.   Compassion's Bird.
Wright, Judith.   Ishtar.
Wunderlich, M.   From a Vacant House.
Yun Tongju.   Foreward.
Zapruder, M.   Canada.
Zukofsky, L.   Song for the Year's End, A.

Competition
Arif.   Twelfth Man, The.
Calpurnius Siculus.   Eclogue 2.
Eclogue 6.
Ch'en Tzu-ang.   I dwell in seclusion and observe the creative process.
Cooley.   Fathers and Sons.
Emerson, R.   Fable: "Mountain and the squirrel, The."
Hein.   Noble Funerals Arranged.
Holden, J.   Saturday Afternoon, October.
Holland, J.   Baize Queens.
Jarry.   Passion of Jesus Considered as an Uphill Race, The.
Johnson, J.   Brer Rabbit, You's de Cutes' of 'Em All.
Juan Chi.   Whether one is eminent or humble depends on Fate.
Kumin, M.   400-Meter Freestyle.
Lund.   Wrist-wrestling father.
Nekrasov, V.   So who of us.
O'Callaghan, C.   Green Baize Couplets.
Ramanujan.   At Forty.
Suckling, J.   Wits, The; A Session[s] of the Poets.
Unknown.   Foot Race Song.
Vietnamese Oral Tradition.   Phoenixes and Sparrows.
Wardrop, D.   Robert Frost at the Net.
Winchilsea.   Circuit of Apollo, The.
See also **Rivalry**

Complacency
Bradley, G.   E Pur Si Muove.
Browning, E.   Loved Once.
Creeley.   Warning, The.
Ingalls, J.   Apprehension.
Shapiro, K.   Buick.
Ulku, A.   Lullaby: "You are safe / You are lying in a hammock."

Complaints and Complainers
Cotton, C.   Litany: "From a ruler that's a curse."
Field, E.   New Yorkers.
Li Ch'ing-chao.   Spring Fades.
Ramirez, L.   Why I Do It.
Unknown.   New View of Sunday Cycling, A.

Composers
Jones, B.   Beethoven's Ears.
Keene, J.   After C (3): Tayloriana.
Livesay, D.   Bartok and the Geranium.
Martinez, D.   Moto Perpetuo.
Waltham, B.   Radio 3.

Computers
Baldwin, Sandy.   Artificial Terra-cotta Skin Mutagen Mask of Humbaba/Humwawa.
Brautigan.   All Watched Over by Machines of Loving Grace.
Budde, R.   Bodiless.
Tattoo.
Davies, Mererid Puw.   Computers Are Poets Too.
Ewing, B.   Stealth-pirates of Cyberia.
Flynn, L.   Perl Poem.
García Lorca.   Romance Somnambulo by Garcia Lorca.
Grumman, Bob.   Cryptographiku for Jim L5ftwich.
Cryptographiku No. 1.
Hardy, J.   Computer Aided Design: Creation.
Lisnyanskaya [*or* Lisnianskaia].   Ode to the Computer.
Martin, Camille.   Pseudo slammer.
Morgan, E.   Computer's First Christmas Card,

The.

Comraderie [or Camaraderie]
Afrika, T.   Maqabane.
Amrane.   You Called to Me, Prison Windows.
Clifton, L.   Lost Women, The.
de Folgar.   Monday.
Djanikian.   How I Learned English.
Gottlieb, L.   Greeting Shekinah.
Gréki.   Future is for Tomorrow, The.
Jarmain.   Embarkation, 1942.
Kay, J.   Shoes of Dead Comrades, The.
Kovner, A.   My comrades / Inasmuch as they
   are comrades do not need to study the map.
November, Yehoshua.   Brotherhood: "First boy
   to fall in, The."
Owen, W.   Apologia Pro Poemate Meo.
Pittman, Al.   Another Night in Crawley's Cove.
Reznikoff.   Four sailors on the bus, dressed in
   blue denim shirts.
Sousa, N.   Poem of a Distant Childhood.
Stone, J.   Confabulation.
Storni.   Camp Fire.
Whitman, W.   Past and present wilt—I have
   filled them, emptied them, The.
Williams, C. K.   Sanctity, The.
Yu Hsin.   Harmonizing with the Monk Heling's
   Poem "An Outing to the Kunming Pool".

Concentration
Kopland.   Natzweiler.
Meredith, W.   Traveling Boy.
Noguchi, R.   Not Surfing Some Days.
Patacara.   When they plow their fields.
Su Tung-p'o.   When Yü-k'o painted bamboo.

Concentration Camps
Aini, L.   Shower.
Alkalay-Gut.   Kitzbuhl Church.
Bachner.   Yes, That's the Way Things Are.
Berg, S.   Desnos Reading the Palms of Men on
   Their Way to the Gas Chambers.
Bienek.   Our Ashes.
   Vorkuta.
Carruth, H.   Camps, The.
Dubie.   Aubade of the Singer and Saboteur,
   Marie Triste: 1941.
Durcan.   Death by Heroin of Sid Vicious, The.
Fenton, J.   German Requiem, A.
Ficowski.   5.8.1942 / In Memory of Janusz
   Korczak.
Filkova, Fedya.   Buchenwald.
Fogel, E.   Shipment to Maidanek.
Forché.   Elegy.
Fried, E.   My Girlfriends.
Hachenburg, H.   Terezin.
Hecht, A.   Book of Yolek, The.
   More Light! More Light!
Helfgott, S.   Trains, The.
Henderson, D.   Alvin Cash/Keep on Dancin'.
Heyen.   Blue.
Inada.   Concentration Constellation.
F.B.I. swooped in early, The.
It began as truth, as fact.
Legend of Home, The.
Jarrell, R.   Camp in the Prussian Forest, A.
In the Camp There Was One Alive.
Protocols.
Kalina, R.   To Anne Frank.
Kirsch, S.   Legend of Lilja.
Košek, M.   It All Depends on How You Look at
   It.
Yes, That's the Way Things Are.
Levi, P.   Buna.
Lindtová, A.   Campfire.
Löwy, H.   Yes, That's the Way Things Are.
Mif.   Terezin.
Pagis, D.   Roll Call, The.
Roll-Call in the Concentration Camp.
Pilinszky, J.   On the Wall of a KZ-Lager.
Passion of Ravensbrück.
Passion of Ravensbrück, The.
Popa.   Be Seeing You.
Quasimodo.   Auschwitz.
Radnóti.   Seventh Eclogue ("Do you see?
   Evening falls, fringed with barbed-wire.").
Roberts, E.   Primo Levi.
Rowlands, D.   Schutzstaffeln 45326.
Schulzová, E.   Evening in Terezin, An.

Spender, S.   Memento.
Teddy.   At Terezin.
Unger, B.   Photo Taken in Winter, 1944.
Unknown, fr. Terezin Concentration Camp.
   Closed Town, The.
   On a Sunny Evening.
   Pain Strikes Sparks on Me, the Pain of Terezin.
   Theresienstadt's Hospital.
Wada, Hakuro.   Even the croaking of frogs.
Wilkie, B.   Intuition, An.
Williams, C. K.   Day for Anne Frank, A.
Wright, C.   KZ.

See also **Auschwitz, Poland; Holocaust;
Internment**

Conception
Berrigan, T.   Poem upon the page is as massive
   as, The.
Chiasson, D.   Purple Blouse.
Dickinson, E.   Solemn thing—it was—I said, A.
Erdrich.   Immaculate Conception.
Kasdorf.   Streak, The.
Kearney, M.   Goodnight, Goodbye.
Max, L.   Stone Fruit.
Olds, S.   Good Will.
Pavlova, V.   Juice.
Rouse, A.   Birthday, A.
Ryan, M.   When I Was Conceived.
Sepúlveda-Pulvirenti.   To the Child That Never
   Was.
Stevens, W.   Major abstraction is the idea of
   man, The.

Concerts
Aiken, C.   At a Concert of Music.
Blunden.   Concert Party: Busseboom.
North, C.   Hospital.
Sagay-Lights, V.   Savannah Brass.
Zavatsky.   Live at the Village Vanguard.

Concord, Massachusetts
Emerson, R.   Concord Hymn.
   Musketaquid.
Unknown.   Irishman's Epistle to the Officers and
   Troops at Boston, The.
Young, S.   Epitaph for a Concord Boy.

Concubines
Po Chü-i.   Everlasting Wrong, The.

Condors
Reid-Marr, David Tokuyu.   Condor.
Santos Chocano.   Dream of the Condor, The.

Coney Island, New York City
Eichner, Maura.   Imagist at Coney Island.
Rohrer, M.   I went out one night with people
   from work.

Confederacy
Ball, C.   Jacket of Gray, The.
Bierce.   Confederate Flags, The.
Davidson, D.   Lee in the Mountains.
   Sequel of Appomattox.
Emmett.   Dixie [or Dixie's Land].
Preston, M.   Grave in Hollywood Cemetery,
   Richmond, A.
   Hymn to the National Flag.
Randall, J.   My Maryland.
Tate, A.   Battle of Murfreesboro.
   Ode to the Confederate Dead.
Thompson, M.   To the South.
Timrod.   Charleston.
   Ethnogenesis.
   Ode: "Sleep sweetly in your humble graves."
Unknown.   Confederate Memorial Day.
Van Jordan, A.   Question: "What up, brother?
   the white teen with dreadlocks."
Walcott.   Arkansas Testament, The.

See also **Civil War, United States**

Confessions
Berg, S.   On This Side of the River.
Berry, W.   Purification, A.
Bible, O.T.   Psalm 139. Domine, Probasti.
Blunt, W.   To One Who Would Make a
   Confession.
Chiasson, D.   Stealing from Your Mother.
Clover, J.   Archive of Confessions, a Genealogy
   of Confessions, An.
Creeley.   Hill, The.
Dauer.   Lois at the Hair Salon.
Davis, O.   Unbosoming, The.

Derricotte.   Weakness, The.
Dunn, S.   On Hearing the Airlines Will Use a
   Psychological Profile to Catch Potential
   Skyjackers.
   What They Wanted.
Eady.   Birthing.
Faber, F.   Confessional, The.
Figueroa, J.   Confessions from the Last Cloud.
Gomez, M.   Chocolate Confessions.
Goodwin, Eli.   Confession: "I held your sins
   against you for so long."
Hahn, S.   Confession.
Hudgins.   Praying Drunk.
Komunyakaa, Y.   Jeanne Duval's Confession.
Kowit.   Lurid Confessions.
Langland, W.   Confession of Gluttony.
Leonard, T.   Jist Ti Let Yi No.
Melville, H.   In a Church of Padua.
Milosz, C.   Task, A.
Muldoon, P.   Cuba.
Ortiz, D.   Again.
Pankey.   Confession of Cleopas, The.
Pavlov, Konstantin.   Adaptation.
Purser, J.   Love Poem: "No nightfall in June."
Rumi.   Night full of talking that hurts, A.
Tobin, D.   Deep Shit.
Unknown.   Archpoet's Confession, The.
   Confession for Forgiveness, A.
Ward, J.   In the Box.
Whitman, W.   As I Lay with My Head in Your
   Lap Camerado.
   Trickle Drops.
Whitney, I.   Aucthour Maketh Her Wyll and
   Testament, The.
   Manner of Her Will and What She Left to
   London and to All Those in It, at Her
   Departing, The.
Wilbur, R.   Mind-Reader, The.
Wise, S.   Confession.
Wodehouse.   That Was Before I Met You.

Confidence
Bairagi.   Give Me Confidence.
Edmond, L.   Girls.
Fields, D.   Pick Yourself Up.
Levertov.   Variation on a Theme by Rilke.
Murray, L.   Performance.
Sastri, C.   Born for Poetry.
Tennyson, A.   Mine be the strength of spirit
   fierce and free.
Townshend [or Townsend].   Upon Kind[e] and
   True Love.
Troup, B.   You're Lookin' at Me.
Wilcox, E.   King Tommy's Rise and Fall.
Zolynas.   Whistling Woman.

Conflict
Berg, S.   On This Side of the River.
Berryman.   Recognition, The.
Brandt, D.   There are no words in me for Gaza,
   for what i saw.
Busceti, G.   Dissonances.
Cleary, B.   Slouch.
Creeley.   Whip, The.
Cunningham, J.   Jack and Jill.
De Angelis.   Main Idea, The.
Denby.   On the Home Front—1942.
Derricotte.   Invisible Dreams.
Dunn, S.   At the Smithville Methodist Church.
   In the House.
Foster, A.   No Dice.
Glaser, E.   And in the Afternoons I Botanized.
Hardy, J.   Difference, The.
Harryman.   Tragedy. Reconsidered.
Hirsch, E.   Self-Portrait.
Huddle.   Music.
Hunter, C.   Two Thousand and Two.
Johnson, M. F.   Widow's Remarriage, The.
Keithley.   Thunder Storm.
Klink, J.   Mariana Trench.
MacGowan.   Description of an Irish Feast, The.
Mapanje.   On Being Asked to Write a Poem for
   1979.
Melville, H.   After the Pleasure Party [Lines
   Traced under an Image of Amor Threatening].
   America.
   Armies of the Wilderness, The.
Merry.   Tiff, The [or The Interview].

Nolens, L.   Poetic License.
O'Brien, L.   Diabolus in Musica.
Ovid.   Elegy 3.1: "Old wood stands uncut, of long years' space, An."
Pasolini.   Redefining "Orthodoxy".
Pollitt.   Mind-Body Problem.
Porta.   Dialogue with Herz.
Rutsala.   Summer: "There is no breeze, sounds travel far in the dead air."
Seaton, M.   Fiddleheads.
Shabtai, Aharon.   Hope: "It's hopeless, you told me."
  Our Land.
Southwell.   Man's Civil[l] War[re].
Turner, G.   Synchoresis.
Vinograd.   Jerusalem Walked thru War.
Ward, J.   After the Report from Iron Mountain.
Wilder, A.   Trouble Is a Man.

Conformity
Auden.   Unknown Citizen, The.
Boland, E.   Self-Portrait on a Summer Evening.
Crane, S.   Think as I think, said a man.
Crozier, A.   Driftwood and Seacoal.
Dickinson, E.   Much Madness is divinest Sense.
Egerton, S.   Emulation, The.
  Liberty, The.
Graves, R.   It Was All Very Tidy.
Harland-Watts, J.   Resist Confinement.
Joseph, J.   Warning.
Laing, K.   Huge Car with the Sad Voice, The.
Lindsay, V.   Congo, The.
McGrath, T.   Ode for the American Dead in Korea.
Melville, H.   Enthusiast, The.
Musgrave.   You Didn't Fit.
Ofeimun.   Let Them Choose Paths.
Schuyler, J.   Yorkville.
Shapiro, K.   University.
Snodgrass.   Poet Ridiculed by Hysterical Academics, The.
Stevens, W.   Disillusionment of Ten O'Clock.
Tkachenko.   Like Thousands of Others.
Wilson, S.   Contemporary Poet, A.

Confucius and Confucianism
Byrd, Bobby.   Things You Can't Do in Albuquerque or Santa Fe, #11.
Chin.   Chinese Quatrains (The Woman in Tomb 44).
Li Po.   Great Bird, The.
Senryū, K.   Each time footsteps.
Vietnamese Oral Tradition.   Testing the Confucian Ideal.

Confusion
Adams, L.   But Alive.
Ashbery, J.   Chapter 2, Book 35.
Beckett, S.   Saint-Lô.
Behn, A.   Song: On Her Loving Two Equally.
Berrigan, J.   Astonishment.
  Wonder / why illness.
Cacciatore, E.   Where do I stand and where do you? Seems like.
Cadiot, Oliver.   Why I Became a Saint.
Dauer.   Bewilderment is Love.
Davis, J.   Fire Barns.
Delmore, E.   Such Sweet Sorrow.
Dragomoschenko.   Instructing Clarity in a Confusion.
Ford, M.   Early to Bed, Early to Rise.
Forhan, C.   Big Jigsaw.
Frost, R.   Cabin in the Clearing, A.
Gallagher, T.   3 A.M. Kitchen: My Father Talking.
Graves, R.   In Broken Images.
Guidacci.   Madame X.
Hadas, R.   Lair, The.
Hamer.   Because We Need Good Maps.
Hollander, J.   Carmen Ancillae.
Hooker, E.   What Bottom Said When He Came Home.
Howe, S.   Cannot Be.
  Gabion / Parapet.
Huang T'ing-chien.   Tune: "Joy of Returning to the Fields" ("Evening rain drips on the steps.").
Israeli, H.   Bicycle Ride, The.
Izumi.   Lying down alone.

Kassabova, K.   Mirages.
Koch, K.   To World War Two.
Lee, P.   I Don't Know Enough About You.
Levin, P.   Lost Bee, The.
Nash, O.   What's in a Name? Some Letter I Always Forget.
Nasir.   Loneliness.
Nolens, L.   Origins.
Ouwens.   Some Tears.
Pietri.   Intermission from Friday.
  Intermission from Saturday.
Portnoy, M.   Hints at Distance.
  Instant Control.
  Of of Titmouse.
Rojas.   Bed with Mirrors.
Rossi, T.   Pot.
Shepherd, R.   Another Version of an Ocean.
Shinkichi Takahashi.   Beach.
Shrine Priestess of Ise.   My mind is dazzled.
Smedley, M.   Irish Fairy, The.
Supervielle.   Voyages.
Szporluk.   Holy Ghost.
  Occupant of the Hose.
Toomer.   I Sit in My Room.
Torres, E.   Breezy Delicious Day.
  Poetry Detective.
Unknown.   Drinking Wine.
  Whatever the cost.
Vitale, M.   You Ouh Even.
Volkman.   We did things more dulcet, more marionette.
Von Freytag-Loringhoven.   Café du Dôme.
  Dozen Cocktails—Please, A.
Waniek.   Bali Hai Calls Mama.
Wellman, M.   Lost from an airy.
Wetzsteon.   Three Songs.
  Urban Gallery.
Williams, M.   Listen.
Winchilsea.   Adam Posed.

Congo River
Bethune, L.   For Singing In Good Mood.
Kgositsile.   Gods Wrote, The.
Martinson.   On the Congo.
Sanchez, S.   Haiku: "Your voice unwrapping."

Congratulations
Kyger.   For Your Birthday, Philip: And upon the Occasion of Becoming Abbot of the Hartford Street Zen Center.

Congreve, William
Dryden, J.   To My Dear Friend Mr Congreve [on His Comedy Called "The Double-Dealer"].

Conjugal Love
Beachy-Quick, Dan.   Nightbook.
Durcan.   Difficulty That Is Marriage, The.
Eyuboǧlu, B.   Black Mulberries.
Kelly, M.   Half Century.
Mock, Jeff.   Epithalamion for Sarah and Tony.
Muhibbi.   My very own queen, my everything.
Murphy, P.   Sequence: "Standing in her basement."
Pahmeier, G.   Sunday Baking.
Rifat.   To My Wife: "Anterooms keep nice and cool with you."
Unknown.   Oh Lord! Once again your long and dismal night is here.
Wife of Chieftain.   Come to me here.

Connecticut (state)
Branch, A.   Connecticut Road Song.
Stevens, W.   River of Rivers in Connecticut, The.
Tate, J.   Chaste Stranger, The.

Conquistadors
Brathwaite, E.   Colombe.
Chilam Balam.   Flight of the Itzás.
De Villagrá.   Canto 1.
González Prada, M.   Inca's Arrows, The.
Lane, P.   Pissaro's Tomb.
Nathaniel, Isabel.   Weepers, The.
Nezhukumatathil, A.   Tallahassee.

Conrad, Joseph
Borges.   Manuscript Found in a Book of Joseph Conrad.

Conscience
Dewdney.   Immaculate Perception, The.
Dunn, S.   With No Experience in Such Matters.

Heaney, S.   From the Republic of Conscience.
Herrick.   Sabbaths.
  To His Conscience.
  To Oenone ("What conscience, say, is it in thee.").
Hopkins, G.   Candle Indoors, The.
Huws, Meirion MacIntyre.   Conscience.
Langland, W.   Dreamer Meets Conscience and Reason.
  Thus I awoke, God knows, when I lived in Cornhill.
Mikha'il, M.   Voice of Conscience, The.
Morgan, Elin Llwyd.   Contemporary Jezebel, The.
Nash, O.   Inter-Office Memorandum.
Ramsdell, H.   Nearly Circle.
Shakespeare, W.   Sonnet 151: "Love is too young to know what conscience is."
Szymborska, W.   In Praise of Self-Deprecation.
Ungria, R.   Culture Nervous.
Wilbur, R.   Mind-Reader, The.
Wilner, E.   Judgment.

Conscientious Objectors
Kees.   June 1940.
Lowell, R.   After the Surprising Conversions.
  Memories of West Street and Lepke.
Shapiro, K.   Conscientious Objector, The.
Stafford, W.   Wind from a Wing, A.
See also **Pacifism and Pacifists**

Consciousness
Baraka, I.   Minute of Consciousness, The.
Brand, D.   Then it is this simple. I felt the unordinary romance of.
Ching An.   On the Spot Where Shih-chia Tzu Sits in Meditation.
Collins, B.   Going Out for Cigarettes.
Darío, R.   Fatality.
Deming, A.   Tilden Park.
Denby.   Old age, lookit, it's stupid, a big fart.
Dickinson, E.   My Cocoon tightens—Colors tease.
  We learned the Whole of Love.
Edwards, K.   Unconsciously.
Frost, R.   Silken Tent, The.
Glück, L.   Wild Iris, The.
Greenberg, U.   I thirst for water; wine is my need no longer.
Grosjean, Jean.   Trial Desert.
Han-shan Te-ch'ing.   After late spring rain the falling petals swirl.
  Hard cold rain a forest of wind, A.
  Who can be a wild deer among deserted mountains.
Hardy, T.   New Year's Eve.
Jiménez, J.   Full Consciousness.
Kabir.   Only Woman Awake, The.
  What Made Kabir a Servant.
  Why Arrange the Pillows.
Levitt, Peter.   On my altar.
Mac Low.   Galactic anachronisms enslave assessments.
Machado Ruiz.   Beyond living and dreaming.
Muso Soseki.   Mugoku Osho's Snow Poem.
Shiomi, M.   Event for Late Afternoon.
Shunryu Suzuki.   Beginner's Mind.
Sisson.   Person, The.
Sorrentino.   Handbook of Versification.
Stafford, W.   Ritual to Read to Each Other, A.
Tagliabue.   Moderation Is Not a Negation of Intensity, But Helps Avoid Monotony.
Volkman.   Sonnet: "As the dream a consciousness adored."
Whalen, P.   End of the line, The.

Conservation
Chaloner.   Unnamed.
Enzensberger, H.   Poison, The.
Unknown.   Careful!
Wang An-shih.   Bald Mountain.
See also **Ecology and Ecologists**

Consolation
Amichai, Y.   Is all this sorrow? I don't know.
Atwood.   People come from all over to consult me, bringing their limbs.
Bek, T.   Oh life, long as an epic.
Berg, S.   Prayer: "Nobody understands so let the

Rabbi."
Brontë, E.   To Imagination.
Brooke, R.   Busy Heart, The.
Buscani.   Miss Mary Mack.
Cook, E.   To My Lyre.
Csoori.   Somebody Consoles Me with a Poem.
Davis, C.   Belongings.
Fanning, M.   Consolation: "I wend to the sea."
Fishman, L.   Promiscuity.
Giovanni.   Women Gather, The.
Hooks.   Woman's Mourning Song, The.
Ibn Hamdīs, A.   Fortune that is wont to stumble often brought you honor, and a time in which you succored us has done you wrong, A.
Kocot, N.   Consolations Before an Affair, Upper West Side.
Kushner, A.   Oak, The.
Landor, W.   Tears of the Dying.
Mahon.   Consolations of Philosophy.
Mew.   May, 1915.
Porter, C.   I Concentrate on You.
  It's All Right with Me.
Rivard.   Consolation.
Steiger.   We believe books and music.
Tsaloumas.   Consolation.
Unknown.   Beguines who hear these words.
Van Duyn.   Open Letter from a Constant Reader.
White, D.   Epistle of Love and of Consolation unto Israel, An.

Conspiracy
Komunyakaa, Y.   Fragging.
Marlowe.   Ah, wicked King! Accursed Gaveston!
  Here is the form of Gaveston's exile.
  My father is deceas'd. Come, Gaveston.
Nuriddin, J. M.   Children of the Future.
Webb, C.   What We Believe.
Wise, S.   I Was Very Prolific.

Constancy
Ahmed Arif.   Your Love Never Left.
Armantrout.   Almost.
Cagnone, N.   General names, no other.
Darley.   Song: "Streams that wind amid the hills, The."
Fitnet Khanim.   In a heart that bears the image.
Juana Inés de la Cruz.   In Containing a Thought Satisfied with Chaste Love.
Moore, T.   Away with this Pouting.
  Love Thee, Dearest? Love Thee?
O'Callaghan, C.   On Re-entering the Lavender City.
Yun Sŏndo.   Songs of Five Friends.
See also **Fidelity**

Constellations
Alcaeus [*or* Alkaios].   Come to me, leaving the Peloponnesos.
Barnard, M.   Pleiades, The.
Basho.   Seventh Month, The.
Berssenbrugge.   Constellation Quilt, The.
Bleakney, J.   By Starlight on Narin Strand.
Bryant, W.   Constellations, The.
De la Mare.   Ride-by-Nights, The.
Eliot, T. S.   Sweeney among the Nightingales.
Frost, R.   Canis Major.
Graves, R.   Star-Talk.
Grennan.   Conjunctions.
Healy, R.   Size of This Universe, The.
Hollander, J.   Great Bear, The.
  Lion Named Passion, A.
Nijhoff.   New Stars, The.
Reese, Rita Mae.   Remembering Emily.
Rich, A.   Orion.
  Planetarium.
Russell, G.   Continuity.
Schulz, B.   Constellation: Prose Poem.
Seiho.   Sky's not high, earth not solid.
Shen Yüeh.   Night After Night.
Sigourney.   Stars, The.
Stevenson, A.   Sonnet: "If it be night . . . ".
Storace.   Wedding Song.
Tuckerman, F.   Sonnets: "Starry flower, the flower-like stars that fade, The."
Turner, C.   Orion.
Unknown.   [Version 1].
  [Version 2].

Wilson, A.   Pegasus the Winged Horse.
Yoshida Issui.   Swans.
See also **Sky; Stars**

Constitution (ship)
Holmes, O.   Old Ironsides.

Construction Workers
Adams, Cyd.   Rock Pickers.
Delgado, J.   Con Los Pájaros.
Griffiths, B.   Fragment 12: "For example, taking the cement onto palettes, for the hoist."
Grover, Dorys Crow.   Ranch on the Limpia, The.
Huerta, D.   Cancellation of a Construction Project.
  Suspensión de una obra.
Zepeda, R.   Wreckers, The.
See also **Buildings and Builders**

Consumerism
Chrystos.   Real Indian Leans Against, The.
Cole, F.   America™.
Cummings, E. E.   Poem, or Beauty Hurts Mr. Vinal.
Doty, M.   Letter to Walt Whitman.
Francia, L.   Video Victim.
Goetz.   Pianist looks like an airline pilot who's afraid to land, The.
Lazard.   In Answer to Your Query.
Moore, T.   Announcement of a New Grand Acceleration Company for the Promotion of the Speed of Literature.
Nemerov.   Life Cycle of Common Man.
Olsen, W.   Winter, Voyeurism.
Parker, A.   Sears Catalogue, The.
Thomas, R. S.   Period.
Unknown.   Lydia Pinkham.
Warr, M.   Malcolm Is 'Bout More Than Wearing a Cap.

Contempt
Ch'i-chi.   Song of the Insolent Air.
Herbert, Z.   Hen.
Hölderlin.   No Pardon.
Horace.   To a Randy Old Woman.
Hughes, L.   Ballad of the Girl Whose Name Is Mud.
Loseff [*or* Losev].   I know—the Mongol yoke, the years of famine.
Millay, E.   Oh, Oh, you will be sorry for that word!
Petri.   Electra.
Rochester, J.   Ramble in St. James's Park, A.
Shakespeare, W.   My liege, I did deny no prisoners.
Sia, B.   Things to Do in Holland.

Contentment
Anderson, S.   American Spring Song.
Assultani, F.   Van Gogh.
Baraka, I.   Song Form.
Berlin.   I Got the Sun in the Morning.
  Little Things in Life, The.
Blane, R.   I Never Felt Better.
Blumenthal, M.   Squid.
Bontemps.   God Give to Men.
Brines, F.   There Is a Light That Shrouds the Whole Field.
Brodsky, J.   Six Years Later.
Brown, L.   Life Is Just a Bowl of Cherries.
Brown, S.   Odyssey of Big Boy.
Bryan, J.   Contentment: "Strung along back elm."
Bunyan.   Shepherd Boy Sings [in the Valley of Humiliation], The.
Buson.   My arm for a pillow.
Byrom.   Careless Content.
Castro, R.   I Know Not What I Seek Eternally.
Cernuda.   Boy Behind a Window.
Chalkhill.   Coridon's Song.
Chudleigh.   Resolve, The.
Collins, B.   Osso Buco.
Cowper, W.   Contentment.
Crane, S.   Youth in apparel that glittered, A.
Creeley.   Rain, The: "All night the sound had."
David, M.   I'm Just a Lucky So-and-So.
Davies, W. H.   Truly Great.
De Mello Breyner.   I Feel the Dead.
De Vere, E.   Poem: "Were I a king, I could

command content."
Dekker, T.   Art thou poore yet hast thou golden Slumbers.
Dekker, T. *et al.*   Happy Heart, The.
Dickinson, E.   I'm sorry for the Dead—Today.
  Their Height in Heaven comforts not.
Dixon, M.   Great Big Bunch of You, A.
Dubin, A.   Cup of Coffee, a Sandwich, and You.
Duo Duo.   Looking Out from Death.
Dyer, S.   My Mind to Me a Kingdom Is.
Dyer, J.   Grongar Hill.
Emerson, R.   Day's Ration, The.
Emmens, J.   Lion of Judah, The.
Epictetus.   Pleasd with thy Place.
Esposito, Nancy.   Doing Good.
Francis, R.   Part for the Whole.
Gershwin, I.   I Got Plenty o' Nuthin'.
  I Got Rhythm.
  Nice Work If You Can Get It.
Hafiz, K [*or* Hafez].   Deciding Not to Go to India (147).
  Gabriel's News (37).
Haines, J.   To Turn Back.
Han Kwak.   Don't Bring Out the Straw Mat.
Hardie, K.   Hunter Home from the Hill, The.
Herbert, G.   Jesu.
Herrick.   His Content in the Country.
  His Grange, or Private Wealth.
Hikmet.   Letters from a Man in Solitary.
Hilliard, B.   Civilization (Bongo, Bongo, Bongo).
Holmes, O.   Contentment.
Hsieh Ling-yün.   Written on the Lake on My Way Back to the Retreat at Stone Cliff.
  Written on the Lake While Returning to Stone Cliff Hermitage.
Hughes, H.   Mind Wanting More.
Hwansung Jian.   Silly Song, A.
Inada.   Nice Place, A.
Iosifova, Ekaterina.   Beneath Winter's Roof.
Ishikawa Jōzan.   Gardening Chrysanthemums, I Think of [T'ao] Yüan-Ming.
Jackson, M. L.   Some Kind of Crazy.
Joseph, J.   Inland sea, The.
Kanchev, Nikolai.   Seventh Heaven Can Be Seen at First Glance.
Kinnell.   Why Regret?
Kyger.   And with March a Decade in Bolinas.
Lampman.   In November: "Hills and leafless forests slowly yield, The."
Lanier, S.   Nirvâna.
Latouche, J.   Not a Care in the World.
Lerner, A.   Wouldn't It Be Luverly?
Levitt, Peter.   Where you are going.
Lewis, S.   I'm Sitting on Top of the World.
Li Po.   Conversation among the Mountains.
Liu Tsung-yüan.   Dwelling by a Stream.
Longfellow, H.   Day Is Done, The.
Lowell, A.   Decade, [A].
Lu Yu.   Idleness.
MacGuigan, B.   Contentment: "Why am I."
Martial.   Happy Life, A.
  How to Do It.
  My carefree Namesake, this the art.
Martin, H.   I Never Felt Better.
Marvell.   Garden, The.
Milosz, C.   Gift: "Day so happy, A."
Munro, N.   Heather, The.
Nguyễn Trãi.   Bamboo Hut, The.
  Plough and a Spade, A.
No Ch'ŏnmyŏng.   Nameless Woman.
Patterson, G.   Autobiographia.
Peacock, T.   Love and Age.
Po Chü-i.   Lodging with the Old Man of the Stream.
  Old, and a Fever.
Poe.   Eulalie—A Song.
Poliziano.   Love Song for Chrysokomos (Goldenlocks).
Postell, T.   Harmony.
Rivera, D.   Under the Apple Tree.
Roberts, S.   Poem # 3: "Today, I'm wearing new love."
Robinson, E.   Firelight.
Rose, B.   Cup of Coffee, a Sandwich, and You.
Ryokan.   Too Lazy to Be Ambitious.

Sagan. Contentment: "Woke up to the finches crowing."
Sexton. I Remember.
Shakespeare, W. Sonnet 29: "When, in disgrace with fortune and men's eyes."
Sidney. Sonnet 39: "Come Sleep! O sleep the certain knot of peace."
Sill. California Winter.
Smith, C. To Spring.
  To the Moon.
  Written September 1791, During a Remarkable Thunder Storm, in which the Moon Was Perfectly Clear, While the Tempest Gathered in Various Directions Near the Earth.
Staple, W. Shen Tao.
Stern, G. Red Bird.
Swenson, M. Staying at Ed's Place.
T'ao Ch'ien [or T'ao Yuan-ming]. Great men want the four seas. I've only.
  Returning to My Fields and Gardens.
Teillier, J. In the Secret House of Night.
Tennyson, A. If I were loved, as I desire to be.
Tu Fu [or Du Fu]. Listless.
  Shady, Shady.
  Village by the River.
Turk, R. I'll Get By (As Long As I Have You).
Unknown. Another Little Boy.
  Farmer's Pride, The.
  Quiet Mind, The.
Van Riessen. Old in Overijssel.
Verwey, A. North-Sea, The.
Vietnamese Oral Tradition. Harmony in the Kingdom.
Washington, N. Love Is the Thing.
Whiting, G. My Blue Heaven.
Whitman, W. Glimpse, A.
  Who goes there? hankering, gross, mystical, nude.
Wilbur, R. Ballade for the Duke of Orléans.
Wilson, S. Room in Bloomsbury, A.
Winchilsea. Give me, O indulgent fate!
Wordsworth, D. Peaceful Our Valley, Fair and Green.
Wordsworth, W. Return, Content! for fondly I pursued.
  Sonnet: "Nuns fret not at their convent's narrow room."
Wotton, S. Character of a Happy Life, The.
Wylie. Wild Peaches.
Yeats. Lake-Isle of Innisfree, The.
Young, G. Owl drifts slowly through the canyon where three flickers worry a pitted oak for grubs, An.
Young, J. I'm Sitting on Top of the World.
Zhidun. Song of My Mountain Dwelling.
See also **Happiness**

Continuity
Amichai, Y. Instructions for a Waitress.
Anderson, J. Re-member Us.
Bell, M. Drawn by Stones, by Earth, by Things That Have Been in the Fire.
Clampitt. Procession at Candlemas, A.
Creeley. Again.
Eliot, T. S. Dry Salvages, The.
  Little Gidding.
Ganev, Nedelcho. Further.
Hardy, T. Heredity.
Harper, M. High Modes: Vision as Ritual: Confirmation.
Kumin, M. Excrement Poem, The.
Marshall-Stoneking. Passage.
Meynell, A. Song of Derivations, A.
Murray, L. Mitchells, The.
Nemerov. Dependencies, The.
Neruda. My love, if I die and you don't.
Oliver, M. In Blackwater Woods.
Seferis. Memory 2.
Snodgrass. Leaving the Motel.
Vitale, M. I Read That It Was All a Chain.
Young, A. How Stars Start.

Contraception
Twichell. Condom Tree, The.

Contrariness
Dowden, E. Love's Chord.
Melville, H. Parthenon, The.
Salmon, A. Prikaz.

Unknown. Writing on an Ink-Stone, A.
Contrition
Di Michele, A. Solstice / Surgery.
Erdrich. Leonard Refuses to Atone.
Parker, D. Little Old Lady in Lavender Silk, The.
Smith, C. Santa Monica.
Unknown. In *Bath* a wanton wife did dwell.
Convalescence
Chester, T. Running Hares.
Emerson, R. Give All to Love.
McCarriston. Healing the Mare.
Pak Chaesam. Spring's Path.
Conventionality
Ransom, J. Nocturne.
Snodgrass. Poet Ridiculed by Hysterical Academics, The.
Thomas, L. Electricity of Blossoms.
Convents
Brownjohn. In a Convent Garden.
Davidson, J. Ballad of a Nun, A.
DeFrees. Going Back to the Convent.
Hugo, R. Montesano Unvisited.
Mew. At the Convent Gate.
St. John, D. Coffee.
See also **Nuns**
Conversation
Adamson. Action Would Kill It / A Gamble.
Adesuyi, N. Rains.
Albert-Birot. In the Paul Guillaume Gallery.
Ashbery, J. Life As a Book That Has Been Put Down.
  Path to the White Moon, The.
Austin, M. Grizzly Bear.
Basho. Long conversations.
Berg, S. On This Side of the River.
Berryman. Dream Song 55.
Bottke, A. How to Approach Your Lover's Wife.
Bunina. Conversation between Me and the Women.
Celan. Leaf, Treeless for Bertolt Brecht, A.
  Zurich, at the Stork.
Crane, H. Praise for an Urn.
Cuadra, A. Brief Letter to Donald Walsh (in memoriam).
Dailey. Right Away.
Deltoro, A. Submarine.
Dickinson, A. Cryo.
Dixon, M. Would You Like to Take a Walk?
Donne. . . . Then, as if he would have sold.
Eliot, T. S. Conversation Galante.
Fearing. How Do I Feel?
Frost, R. Meeting and Passing.
Green, M. Sometimes I dress, with women sit.
Hacker, M. Villanelle: Late Summer.
Harvey, M. Abandoned Conversation with the Senses.
Heine, H. Words, Words, Words, and Nothing Doing.
Hierro, José. Meeting, The.
Hodgins. Death Who.
Hunt, L. Domestic Chat.
Jackson, M. L. Blunts.
Kasdorf. Green Market, New York.
Keith, Sally. Subtraction Song.
Kirby, D. Nosebleed, Gold Digger, KGB, Henry James, Handshake.
Larkin, P. Talking in Bed.
Levchev. Weasel.
Longfellow, H. Fire of Drift-Wood, The.
Machado Ruiz. To talk with someone.
Martinez, D. Room itself, The. The women. The absence of women.
Menashe. Annunciation, The.
Merrill, J. Charles on Fire.
Millay, E. I, Being Born A Woman [And Distressed].
More, H. Long was Society o'er-run.
Morgan, M. Conversation.
Morley, H. For Elaine de Kooning.
Oden. Bible Study.
O'Grady, D. In the valleys of the future we shall walk.
Pagis, D. Conversation.

Po Chü-i. To a Talkative Guest.
Prior. To a Lady: She Refusing to Continue a Dispute with Me.
Rich, A. Dialogue.
Richardson, J. Retort Perfect, The.
Rilke. Going Blind.
Rose, B. Would You Like to Take a Walk?
Schuyler, J. Master of the Golden Glow, The.
Scott, D. Dreadwalk.
Shurin. Sailed.
Sidney. Sonnet 30: "Whether the Turkish new moon minded be."
Simpson, L. Chocolates.
Sirowitz, H. I Finally Managed to Speak to Her.
Sitwell, E. Said King Pompey.
Soto. Chitchat with the Junior League Women.
Stevenson, A. Sous-Entendu.
Szporluk. Elsewhere.
Talvikki, A. Conversation with the Sun Bittern.
Taylor, J. Recreation.
Thomas, D. Conversation of Prayer, The.
Thomas, E. Sun Used to Shine, The.
Tomlinson, C. Word in Edgeways, A.
Turner, G. Synchoresis.
Valéry. Girl with Mind Wandering.
Van Vliet. Party.
Waldrop, R. Feverish Propositions.
Webb, F. Tip for Saturday, A.
Welish. Blood or Color.
Whur. And So Home.
Conversion
Crashaw. To the Noblest and Best of Ladies, the Countess of Denbigh.
Heywood, J. Wilt thou use turners craft still? ye by my trouth.
McCarthy, J. You Made Me Love You (I Didn't Want to Do It).
Merton. St. Paul.
Ritsos. End of Dodona II, The.
Sorby. Glossolalia.
Unknown. Vicar of Bray, The.
Voznesensky [or Voznesenskii]. Old Song.
Wheatley, P. On Being Brought from Africa to America.
Williamson, G. Dark Days, The.
Wither. Conversion of S. Paul, The.
Conviction
Belli, G. Night of Terror.
Celaya, G. Poetry Is a Weapon Loaded with the Future.
Convoys
Kipling, R. Convoy Escort.
Cooking and Cooks
Aguilar-Cariño. Dinakdakan.
Aiken, J. Palace Cook's Tale.
Alexie. Capital Punishment.
Ap Hywel, Elin. Thing.
Blumenthal, M. Squid.
Cager, Chezia Thompson. Callaloo.
Clampitt. Gooseberry Fool.
Clifton, L. Cutting greens.
Comden, B. I Can Cook, Too.
Crooker. Grating Parmesan.
Daniels, J. Short-Order Cook.
Delmore, E. Marmalade.
Dove, R. Crab-Boil.
Dunn, D. Ratatouille.
Farley, Estelle E. Home Cookin.
Follon, C. Love Rats.
Forbes, C. Potlicker Blues.
Forché. Skin Canoes.
Gaspar de Alba. Making Tortillas.
Gilbert, W. Ferdinando and Elvira; or, The Gentle Pieman.
Green, A. I Can Cook, Too.
Hamod, S. Leaves.
Hardie, K. Things That Are Lost.
Harper, M. Breaded Meat, Breaded Hands.
Hoffenstein. You hire a cook, but she can't cook yet.
Holmes, J. Mediterranean Cooking for Two.
Iglesias, H. Thursday Afternoon: Life Is Sweet.
Ishikawa Jōzan. Eating Roasted *Matsutake* Mushrooms.
Jackson, A. Cayenne.
Keplinger, D. Another Century.

Kercheval, J.   Ham and the Moon.
Kim Hyesun.   Titanic, Reincarnate, The.
Kleinschmidt.   Cooking to Music.
Lorde.   From the House of Yemanjá.
Lumsden, R.   Piquant.
Marlatt, D.   Bruce and the Bluegills.
Martial.   Did he have eyes and, if so, did he look.
Massinger.   Men May Talk of Country-Christmasses.
McCallum, S.   What Lies Beneath.
McDonald, C.   Fresh Mussels.
McGrath, T.   Bread of this World; Praises III, The.
Moore, L.   Tanka.
Morales, A.   Kitchens.
Morales.   Dinner, The.
Muhammad, Mursalata.   Last Days of a Slow Cooker.
Muldoon, P.   Sushi.
Mullen, H.   Joy, The.
Mun Chônghui.   Little Kitchen Song, A.
Pahmeier, G.   Grief Comes in Smallest Ways.
Penn, P.   Soup, The: "On the day of your scan, I make a soup."
Pereira, P.   Pot of Red Lentils, A.
Piercy.   What's That Smell in the Kitchen?
Plath, Z.   Cooking Lesson.
Renshaw, Edyth.   Pantoum: In a Texas Farm-House Kitchen.
Rogers, P.   Elinor Frost's Marble-Topped Kneading Table.
Rossetti, C.   Mix a Pancake.
Saffoti.   Espresso.
Sajé, N.   Song of the Cook.
Salaam.   Everywhere You Eat.
Seaton, M.   Furious Cooking.
Shabtai, Aharon.   Rosh HaShanah.
Shange.   Different Love Poem, A. / We Need a Change.
Simic.   Lives of Alchemists, The.
Sioux Oral Tradition.   Give me my knife.
Skeeter.   Western Trail Cook, 1880.
Stein, G.   Eggs.
   Mutton.
   Sugar.
Strange.   Offering.
Sutton, V.   Housekeeping.
Tafolla.   Allí Por La Calle San Luis.
Takagi Kyozo.   How To Cook Women.
Tapahonso.   All I Want.
Taylor, C.B.   Forever Arima.
Townsend, A.   Western Holly Stove.
Townsend, A.   Dinner Guest, The.
Umpierre, L.   Only the Hand That Stirs Knows What's in the Pot.
Unknown.   Song of the Pestle.
"Vaidehi.".   Girl in the Kitchen.
Willard, N.   How to Stuff a Pepper.
Zabolotsky [*or* Zabolotskii].   At the Fishmonger's.

Coole, Ireland
Yeats.   Coole Park and Ballylee, 1931.
   Coole Park, 1929.
   In the Seven Woods.
   Wild Swans at Coole, The.

Cooper, James Fenimore
Lowell, J.   Cooper.

Copenhagen, Denmark
Padgett, R.   Fairy Tale: "Little elf is dressed in a floppy cap, The."

Copernicus, Nicholas
Leapor.   Epistle to a Lady, An.

Coral
Cardona-Hine.   Listen Galaxea.
Donovan, K.   Coral.
Fuller, H.   To a Tropic Reef.
Percival.   Coral Grove, The.
Spires.   Cemetery Reef.

Cordelia
Howe, S.   WHITE FOOLSCAP / Book of Cordelia.
Lauinger, A.   Cordeilla.
Raymund, J.   Ordeal of Love, The.
Staveley, B.   Speak Again.

Corinth, Greece
Elytis, O.   This Wind That Loiters.

Cormorants
Basho.   Exciting at first.
Buson.   Dawn.
Clampitt.   Cormorant in Its Element, The.
Isherwood.   Common Cormorant [*or* Shag], The.
Issa.   Children imitating cormorants.
Kinsella, J.   Cormorants.
O'Grady, Thomas.   Cormorants.
Preece.   Cormorant.
Stryk, L.   Cormorant.
Wang Wei.   Dike of the Cormorants.

Corn
Apache Oral Tradition.   Corn Ceremony.
Benn.   Before a Cornfield.
Cook, W.   Corn, corn, sweet Indian corn.
Craig, M.   Good Night, Star.
Equi.   Lesbian Corn.
Kuzmina-Karavayeva.   Ruth.
Lanier.   Waving of the Corn, The.
Mayer, B.   Corn.
Mouré.   8 Little Theatres of the Cornices.
Nelson, G.   Stare Decisis.
No Hyangnim.   Nature: "In a corn field."
Paz.   Reliefs.
   Relieves.
Riggs, L.   Santo Domingo Corn Dance.
Sandburg, C.   Early Copper.
Stone, R.   Seed.
Unknown.   Corn Song.
   Lo! ye children of men and the Mother.
   Mother with the life-giving power now comes.
Wilbur, R.   Zea.
Willard, N.   Speckled Hen's Morning Song to Biddy Early, The.

Cornell, Joseph
Mullen, L.   Sandbox. 1952.—*Homage to Joseph Cornell.*

Cornwall, England
Strong, L.   March Evening.

Corpses
Aiken, C.   All Death, All Love.
Ajanta.   Dateline Hyderabad.
Alegría.   From the Bridge.
Annensky.   One Second.
Avison.   Whole Story, The.
Bador, B.   Hand, The.
Baudelaire.   Carcass, A.
Bialik.   Only a single ray, but suddenly.
Bly, R.   Counting Small-Boned Bodies.
Breytenbach.   Asylum.
Byron, G.   At the Siege of Corinth.
Campo.   Jane Doe #2.
Celan.   Night Ray.
Derricotte.   On the Turning Up of Unidentified Black Female Corpses.
Dickinson, E.   Do People moulder equally.
Djogo.   National Hero, The.
Ferguson, G.   Grey Kirk in the Mearns.
Foerster.   Failure of Similes, The.
Grin, B.   Man Falls at Work, A.
   Sacco and Vanzetti.
Guevara, M.   Postmortem.
Heaney, S.   Grauballe Man, The.
Herd.   Exhibits, The.
Hood, T.   Mary's Ghost.
Horace.   Satire 1.8: "Once I was wood from a worthless old fig tree."
Housman.   Some can gaze and not be sick.
Hughes, F.   Kookaburra.
Hughes, T.   View of a Pig.
Hwang Insuk.   Huge Mouth.
Kasischke.   Pall.
Kim Hyesun.   Not Knowing He's Dead.
Kinnell.   Quick and the Dead, The.
MacBeth [*or* Macbeth].   Ward, The.
MacDiarmid, H.   Dead Liebknecht, The.
Marlowe.   His bodie was as straight as Circes wand.
Matthews, W.   Sentence: "Bloated and mesmerized by rasberries."
Neruda.   Nothing but Death.
   Only Death.
Paloff, B.   My Corpses.

Pedretti, Erica.   What Difference Does It Make.
Phillips, C.   As from a Quiver of Arrows.
Radnóti.   Picture Postcards.
Rilke.   Matthew 27:57–61; When it was evening, there came a rich man.
   Tombs of the Hetaerae.
Rodgers, Gordon.   On the Ice.
Roeske, P.   Preparing the Dead.
Rosenberg, I.   Dead Man's Dump.
Ryuichi.   Standing Coffin.
Shinkichi Takahashi.   Moon.
Snodgrass.   Old Apple Trees.
   Viewing the Body.
Sobalvarro, J.   I've Seen a Dead Man.
Southerland.   Blue Clay.
Soyinka.   Post Mortem.
Stryk, L.   Pit, The.
Taylor, H.   Landscape with Tractor.
Unknown.   We love the daylight.
Vallejo.   Mass.
Young, G.   Damien.
Zenmaro.   Evidence.
See also **Necrophilia**

Corruption
Ba.   Seen to be Done.
Baraka, I.   Three Modes of History and Culture.
Blake, W.   London: "I wander through [*or* thro'] each chartered [*or* charter'd] street."
Boadiba.   Madam President.
Bock, J.   Little Tin Box.
Boethius.   Lib. 2. Metrum 5.
Castera, G.   Both Yesterday and Today.
Chaucer.   Pardoner's Prologue, The.
Ch'u Yüan.   On Encountering Trouble.
Citino.   Situation No. 13: City Hall.
Dede, J.   Bits.
Donne.   Satire 3 [Religion].
   Then, as if he would have sold.
Drake, N.   Man in the White Suit, The.
Duffy, C.   Medusa.
Gandlevsky, S.   There's our street, let's say.
Hemphill.   Family Jewels.
Hitchman-Britton, O.   Road to the Presidency.
Holmes, O.   Latter-Day Warnings.
Hughes, L.   Bad Man.
   Goodbye Christ.
   Un-American Investigators.
Jeffers, R.   Sinverguenza.
   Stars Go over the Lonely Ocean, The.
Johnson, F.   Minister, The.
Jonson, B.   On English Monsieur.
Kim Suyông.   Ha . . . No Shadows.
Lamb, C.   Gipsy's Malison, The.
Machado Ruiz.   Young Spain, A.
Mandelstam [*or* Mandelshtam].   I Drink to the Asters of War.
Marlowe.   Nephew, I must to Scotland. Thou stay'st here.
Massimi.   Advice to Paulinus.
McClure, M.   Senate Hearings.
Milosz, C.   You Who Wronged.
Milton.   Lycidas.
Ovid.   Elegy 3.13: "Seeing thou art fair[e], I bar[re] not thy false playing."
Pawlak.   East-West Dialog 2002.
Prejsnar, Mark.   Ode to Toge.
Ríos, A.   Advice to a First Cousin.
Shakespeare, W.   Sonnet 35: "No more be[e] grieved [*or* greev'd] at that which thou hast done."
   Sonnet 54: "O[h] how much more doth beauty beauteous seem."
   Sonnet 94: "They that have power [*or* pow'r *or* powre] to hurt[e], and will do[e] none."
Sheeler, J.   This Old Man.
Shot, D.   Executive Privilege.
Spenser, E.   Legend of the Knight of the Red Crosse, or of Holinesse, The.
Taylor, C.   Scroll No. 2.
Tu Mo.   Mandarins Got Their Raise, The.
Unknown.   Epitaph on the Duke of Buckingham.
   Statesmen, in your exalted station know.
Vaughan, H.   Town believes thee lost, and didst thou see, The.
Wilner, E.   Found in the Free Library.

Corso, Gregory
Elmslie, K.   Venus Preserved.

Coruña, La, Spain
Wolfe, C.   Burial of Sir John Moore, The.

Cosmetics
Borthwick, P.   Out of Bounds.
Brooks, A.   Here is the queen.
Chao Luan-luan.   Willow Eyebrows.
Clarke, C.   Make-Up.
Fanning, R.   In the Barn.
Jonson, B.   Sweet Neglect, The.
Kowit.   Cosmetics Do No Good.
Masterson, R.   Chinese Stripper.
Miles, J.   Government Injunction [Restraining Harlem Cosmetic Co.].
Naden.   Two Artists, The.
Olin.   Wu Gambinos.
Orlowsky, D.   To Our Cosmeticians.
P'Bitek.   Woman with Whom I Share My Husband, The.
Pope, A.   Sol through white curtains shot a tim'rous ray.
Riley, D.   Shantung.
Smith, B.   Saturday before Easter, The.
Trinidad.   Slicker.
Unknown.   Fragrance is due to perfumes.
  People, kind people, please buy my powder and rouge.
Ward, T.   At Twenty-Three Weeks She Can No Longer See Anything South of Her Belly.
Wen T'ing-yün.   Tune: "Beautiful Barbarians".
Wolverton, T.   Tubes.

Cosmology
Buckley, C.   Presocratic, Surfing, Breathing Cosmology Blues, The.
Ch'en Tzu-ang.   Men in the market pride themselves on their knowledge and craft, The.
Ch'u Yüan.   Heavenly Questions.
Fox, S.   Almagest, Last Letter to Zakarias.
Healy, R.   Size of This Universe, The.
Kyunyŏ, Great Master.   With tongs I trim the lamp.
Mullen, H.   Anthropic Principle, The.
Muso Soseki.   Cave of the Thousand Pines.
  House of Spring.
  Peak of the Held-Up Flower, The.
  Temple of Eternal Light.
  Three-Step Waterfall.
Unknown.   Cosmology.
  Rain Song of the Shu'-wi Chai' än (Snake Society), A.

Cosmos
Amor, P.   CXLII.
Cortes.   Space Song.
Fabian, C.   On Reading the New Physics— Creation and Cosmology.
González Prada, M.   Cosmos Shows His Power, The.
Gottlieb, A.   Meditation on the Feminine Nature of Shekinah, A.
Hildebrandt, Z.   In Hecate's Garden.
Hillman, B.   Black Series.
Hixon, L.   My Blissful Mother Exists Fully through Every Creature!
Kiko.   Mount Sumeru—my fist!
Munom-Ekai.   Thunderbolt—eyes wide, A.
Mutén, B.   Queen Hera.
  Urania.
Olson, C.   Celestial Evening, October 1967.
Rakan-Keinan.   Today Rakan, riding an iron horse.
Sornberger.   When She Laughs.
Storni.   World Is Bitter, The.
Tuckerman, F.   Sonnet: "And so, as this great sphere (now turning slow)."
Villanueva, A.   Planet Earth Speaks, The.
Von Reis, Siri.   Vast Problem Still Obscure.

See also **Creation**

Cotswold Hills, England
Gurney, I.   Felling a Tree.
  High Hills, The.
Thomas, E.   Adlestrop.

Cotton
Allen, S.   Apple Trees in Sussex, The.
Angelou, M.   Miss Scarlet, Mr. Rhett and other

Latter-Day Saints.
Blanchard, Mary Loving.   Picking Cotton.
Bontemps.   Southern Mansion.
Brown, S.   Old King Cotton.
Lahey, Joy.   Cotton and Gladiolas.
Martinson.   Cotton.
Timrod.   Cotton Boll, The.
Toomer.   Cotton Song.
  November Cotton Flower.
Whittier.   Haschish, The.

Count Ossie (Oswald Williams)
Adisa.   Count Ossie.

Counterfeiting and Counterfeiters
Goldbarth.   Counterfeit Earth!, The.
Williamson, G.   Counterfeiter, The.

Counting
Adcock, F.   Counting.
Justice, D.   Counting the Mad.
Kendrick, D.   Sophie, Climbing the Stairs.
Lehrer.   Wernher von Braun.
Prévert.   Inventory.
Reznikoff.   Her work was to count linings.
Robinson, E.   Fountain.
Soto.   Teaching Numbers.
Unknown.   Cattle-count.
Yolen.   Shepherd's Night Count.

Country Life
Adams, L.   Country Summer.
Anderson, M.   Country Wisdoms.
Anderson, T.   I Think You Got Me Confused.
Applewhite.   Map of Simplicities, A.
  Road Down Home.
Ashbery, J.   Interesting People of Newfoundland.
  Ode to Bill.
Baillie, J.   Disappointment, A.
Baton, M.   Childhood in the Country, A.
Berry, W.   At a Country Funeral.
  First time I remember waking up.
  History.
Bishop, E.   From the Country to the City.
Blunt, W.   Old Squire, The.
Breton, N.   Merry Country Lad, The.
Brewster, E.   Return of the Native: "This is the true land of fairy tales."
Brinks, Dave.   Please the Carrots.
Brown, S.   Virginia Portrait.
Budbill.   Irrelevant and Useless.
Burns, R.   Cotter's Saturday Night [nscribed to Robert Aiken [*or* R. A****], Esq.], The.
Cairncross, A.   Covenanting Country.
Chan Fang-sheng.   Poem about My Study at the Back of the House.
Ch'u Yüan.   After Ch'u Yuan.
Clare, J.   Noon.
  Thou far-fled pasture, long evanished scene.
Clarke, G.   Field-Mouse, The.
Claudian.   Old Man of Verona, The.
Clough.   There Is No God.
Cohan.   Forty-five Minutes from Broadway.
Colman, G.   London Rurality.
Coolidge, C.   Country Autumns, The.
Cornford, F.   Country Bedroom, The.
Cowley, A.   Wish, The.
Cunningham, J.   Montana Pastoral.
Cynan.   It was all go with the jazz-band and all go with the dance.
Davidkov, Ivan.   Villages Like Ghosts.
Davies, O.   Urban.
DeFoe, M.   Aviary.
Dehmel.   Quiet Town, The.
Denham.   Cooper's Hill.
Donne.   To Sir Henry Wotton ("Sir, more than kisses, letters mingle souls.").
Dunn, D.   In the Grounds.
Erb, E.   This and That.
Evans, A.   Old Yellow Shop, The.
Evans, R.   Buttons and Bows.
Fairchild.   Dumka, The.
Frost, R.   Directive.
  Hill Wife, The.
  Need of Being Versed in Country Things, The.
Gale, N.   Country Faith, The.
Garrigue.   After Reading "The Country of the Pointed Firs."

Gashe.   Village, The.
Gizzi.   Last Cigar.
Goldsmith, O.   Deserted Village, The.
Goodman, M.   Poems from a Country House.
Greenaway.   Three Little Girls.
Greenberg, A.   Letters from Camp.
Greenlaw, L.   Zombies.
Gregg.   Adult.
Guest, B.   If So, Tell Me [1999].
Hall, D.   Names of Horses.
  Ox Cart Man.
Hardy, T.   In Time of "The Breaking of Nations".
Hart, S.   Mountain Greenery.
Hennen.   Soaking Up Sun.
Herrick.   His Content in the Country.
  His Grange, or Private Wealth.
Hogg, J.   Boy's Song, A.
Höllerer.   Particularly Effortless He Lay.
Horace.   Praises of a Country Life, The.
Jackson, M. L.   Urban Renewal 12.
Jarrell, R.   Country Life, A.
Jewett, S.   Country Boy in Winter, A.
Johnson, J.   Unmarked Stop in Front of Westmond General Store, Westmond, Idaho.
Jones, D.   Adrift.
Jonson, B.   To Penshurst.
Justice, D.   Poem to Be Read at 3 a.m.
Kavanagh, P.   Epic.
  Spraying the Potatoes.
Keats.   To One Who Has Been Long in City Pent.
  Where Be You [*or* Ye] Going, You [*or* Ye] Devon Maid?
Keller, D.   After Supper.
Kennedy, Sarah.   How My Mother-in-Law Instructed Me in Slaughter.
Kinsley, R.   Walk along the Old Tracks, A.
Kinsella, J.   Rust Eclogues, The: Radnoti, Poetry, and the Strains of Appropriation.
Kuusisto, Stephen.   Summer at North Farm.
Langgässer, E.   Daphne.
Lanier, E.   Description of Cooke-ham [*or* Cookham], The.
Lawrence, D. H.   Love on the Farm.
  Whether or Not.
Layton.   Aubade, An.
Leopardi.   Saturday Night in the Village.
Livingston, J.   Buttons and Bows.
Logghe.   Española Pantoum.
Longfellow, H.   Fire of Drift-Wood, The.
Longley, M.   Gorse Fires.
  West, The.
Lux.   There Were Some Summers.
  View from a Porch.
Mahon.   Woods, The.
Marlatt, D.   Summer of the New Well.
Martial.   Happy Life, A.
  While unquiet, *Juvenal*, you haunt.
Martinson.   Dusk in the Country.
Marvell.   And now to the ab[b]yss I pass.
  Garden, The.
Mason, W.   Heroic Epistle to Sir William Chambers, An.
McGrath, T.   And we, of the damned poor, trot our frost-furred horses.
McGuckian.   Gateposts.
McMorris, M.   Evening.
Meehan, P.   My Love about His Business in the Barn.
Melville, H.   Immolated.
Millay, E.   Return, The.
Miller, J.   Which Religion Vouchsafes.
Mother Goose.   This Is the House That Jack Built.
Mukai Kyorai.   Even while chopping.
Murray, C.   Dockens afore His Peers.
Murray, L.   Noonday Axeman.
Neilson, S.   Rural Gothic.
No Ch'ŏnmyŏng.   Nameless Woman.
  Nameless Woman, A.
Nordhaus.   Adirondack Return.
Nye, N.   Endurance of Poth, Texas, The.
O'Donoghue, B.   Nun Takes the Veil, A.
Orr, T.   Soybeans.
Phelps, D.   Ordinary Country Girl, An.

Philips, K.   Country Life, A.
Plumpp.   I wonder.
Pope, A.   Epistle to Miss [or Miss Teresa]
   Blount, on Her Leaving the Town after the
   Coronation.
   Happy Life of a Country Parson, The.
Purdy, A.   Country North of Belleville, The.
Rattenbury, A.   Rain Falls on Utopia Too.
Ravenscroft, E.   In Derision of a Country Life.
Rawlins, C.   Living in at Least Two Worlds.
Reverdy.   Heavier.
Riley, J.   When the Frost Is on the Punkin.
Rogers, S.   Wish, A.
Rohrer, J.   In the Kitchen before Dinner.
Sage, C.   Retired Postman Recalls the Old
   Route, A.
Sanelli, M.   Swansonville.
Scarbrough, G.   Eastward in Eastanalle.
   Letter to Spencer.
Schuyler, J.   Korean Mums.
Sen, S.   Solitary.
Shakespeare, W.   Amiens's Song.
Shomer.   First Sunset at Outler's Ranch.
Smith, I.   John Knox.
Soniat.   Shared Life, A.
Stafford, W.   Light by the Barn, The.
Strobel.   Pastoral: "This is a place of ease."
Sutphen, J.   Girl on a Tractor.
Sylvester, J.   Of a Husbandman.
T'ao Ch'ien [or T'ao Yuan-ming].   Five Poems
   on Returning to Dwell in the Country.
   Harmonizing with a Poem by the Registrar Guo.
   Peach Blossom Spring, The ("Ying clan
   disrupted Heaven's ordinance, The.").
Tate, J.   Land of Little Sticks, 1945.
Tennyson, A.   City Child, The.
Thomas, E.   Haymaking.
Thomas, R. S.   Farm Wife.
   Village, The.
Townsend, A.   They Call You Moody.
Tu Fu [or Du Fu].   In a Village by the River.
Turell, J.   Though my small incomes never can
   afford.
Unknown.   Country Lassie, The.
Untermeyer, J.   Country of No Lack.
Vaughan, H.   Retirement.
Verlaine.   Malines.
Walcott.   Upstate.
Walker, M.   Childhood.
Waller, K.   On the Road to Homer Noble Farm.
Wang Wei.   Arriving at Ba Gorge in the
   Morning.
Warner, S.   Waiting at Cerbere.
Warren, R.   Sitting on Farm Lawn on Sunday
   Afternoon.
Warren, R.   Renoir.
Wascovich, M.   Wolf Packet and Rural America.
Waugh, Arthur.   Town and Country.
Weöres.   Plain, The.
Westmorland.   My Country Audit.
   To Retiredness.
Whitman, W.   Farm Picture, A.
Whittemore, R.   Farmhouse, The.
Wilder, A.   It's So Peaceful in the Country.
Williams, W.   Raleigh Was Right.
   Woman Walking.
Wodehouse.   Bungalow in Quogue.
Wordsworth, W.   Inscription for the Moss-Hut at
   Dove Cottage.
Wright, C.   December Journal.
Wright, J.   Country Dance.
Wright, K.   How the Wild South East Was Lost.
Yeats.   Lake-Isle of Innisfree, The.
Yesenin [or Essenin].   Sergei Yesenin.
Yi Kyubo.   Farmhouse: Three Poems.
Yi Yuksa.   Thatched House.

County Antrim, Northern Ireland
MacNeice.   Carrickfergus.
Mahon.   Rathlin.

County Cork, Ireland
Mahon.   Garage in Co. Cork, A.

County Galway, Ireland
Murphy, R.   Sailing to an Island.

County Kerry, Ireland
Synge.   In Kerry.

County Mayo, Ireland
Flavell [or Lavell].   County of Mayo, The.

County Meath, Ireland
Higgins, F.   Father and Son.

County Monaghan, Ireland
Kavanagh, P.   Shancoduff.
   Stony Grey Soil.

County Sligo, Ireland
Yeats.   Lake-Isle of Innisfree, The.

Courage
Amis, K.   Autobiographical Fragment.
Anstett.   Man Saves Own Life.
Archilochus.   Be Bold! That's One Way.
   Ideal General, The.
Babcock, M.   Be Strong.
Barkan, S.   Bring Me Your Woes.
Brontë, E.   No Coward Soul Is Mine.
Brooke, R.   Hill, The.
Bunyan.   Pilgrim Song, The.
Butler, C. E.   Other Places, The.
Cary, P.   Leak in the Dike, The.
Castillo, O.   Distances.
Cavalli.   Who ever again will be able to say.
Ceni.   With What Courage.
Char.   Fighters.
Clough.   Say Not the Struggle Nought Availeth.
Coffman.   Courage, or One of Gene Horner's
   Fiddles.
Creeley.   Dishonest Mailmen, The.
de la Parra Jr., J.   Courage!
Delgado, J.   Dandelion.
Dickinson, E.   I think to Live—may be a Bliss.
   I took my Power in my Hand.
Douglas, K.   Gallantry.
Dryden, J.   'Tis war again, and I am glad 'tis so.
Earhart, Amelia.   Courage: "Courage is the price
   that life exacts for granting peace."
Emerson, R.   In an Age of Fops and Toys.
Gilbert, J.   Abnormal Is Not Courage, The.
Harburg.   If I Only Had a Brain (If I Only Had a
   Heart) (If I Only Had the Nerve).
Hardy, T.   Certain sort of bravery, A.
Horace.   Brave Dog's Challenge, The [Epode 6].
Hyppolite, M.   Woman: "Women carry life."
Jonson, B.   On Playwright ("Playwright convict
   of public wrongs to men.").
Kakkai Patiniyar Naccellaiyar.   Many Said.
Kao Shih.   Ji Gate.
Karr.   Hubris.
Kaschnitz.   Not Courageous.
Katz, M.   Brave Coward, The.
Kay, J.   Twelve Bar Bessie.
Kipling, R.   When first under fire an' you're
   wishful to duck.
Konie, G.   In the Fist of Your Hatred.
Legaré.   Tallulah.
Lewis, G.   And this, too, is love.
Lynes, Jeanette.   Brave.
Marlowe.   Bastardly boy, sprung from some
   coward's loins.
McKay, C.   Baptism.
   If We Must Die.
Millay, E.   Courage that my mother had, The.
Nossis.   Shields Bruttians threw from their
   doomed shoulders.
Nyhart.   Playing the Part.
Palmer, R. F.   Conchie, The.
Parker, D.   Penelope.
Patterson, R.   You Are the Brave.
Rich, A.   Trying to Talk with a Man.
Rumi.   Where is a foot worthy to walk a
   garden,.
Salter.   Frost at Midnight.
Sassoon, S.   Hero, The.
Schwartz, R. L.   Can Pigeons Be Heroes?
Sexton.   Courage.
Shakespeare, W.   Great lords, wise men ne'er sit
   and wail their loss.
Skirving.   Johnnie Cope.
Slutsky [or Slutskii].   How Did They Kill My
   Grandmother?
   How They Killed My Grandmother.
Smith, S.   Harold's Leap.
Tennyson, A.   Charge of the Light Brigade, The.
Thomas, R. S.   Lore.
Unknown.   Come and kiss me without thinking

of the danger. What does it matter if they kill
   you?
   Courage shall grow keener, clearer the will.
   I love! I love! I shall not hide it. I'll not deny it.
   If the hour has not rung, death will not be
   coming.
   Little horror, oblivious to combat, sleeps quietly
   beside me, The.
   Oliver's climbed upon a hilly crest.
Vallejo.   Masses.
Vaysman, N.   Anne Pauker.
Walwicz.   Daredevil.
Webb, F.   Art.
Whittier.   Barbara Frietchie.
Wright, J.   Mad Fight Song for William S.
   Carpenter, 1966, A.
Wright, J.   Legend.
Yevtushenko [or Evtushenko].   From a Talk.
Yuan Mei.   Old and Traveling.
Zach, N.   Greater Courage.

Courtesy
Darling, J.   How to Behave with the Ill.
De León, L.   O Courtesy, O Harborage Most
   Sweet.
Du Bellay.   To walk with sober step, to raise the
   eyebrow.
Huddle.   Mouth of Him, The.
Robinson, E.   Flammonde.
Sansom, A.   From the Moment I Picked Up
   Your Book.
Ts'ao Ching-chao.   Palace Poem.
Unknown.   When Adam dalf and Eve span.
Zhiyuan, S.   In Praise of Ch'an Master Wang
   You Who Cares for the Bonnet Monkeys
   around His Mountain Studio.

Courtiers
Donne.   Satire 4.
   Then, as if he would have sold.
   To Sir Henry Wotton ("Here's no more news,
   than virtue, I may as well.").
   To Sir Henry Wotton ("Sir, more than kisses,
   letters mingle souls.").
Holub.   Polonius.
Li Po.   Ascend the Phoenix Terrace.
   Remembering Our Excursion in the Past.
   River Song.
Li Shang-yin.   Without Title (1).
Steele, T.   Epitaph: "Here lies Sir Tact, a
   diplomatic fellow."
Unknown.   Mode of France, The.
Wyatt.   Of the Courtier's Life.

Courts
Burford, W.   South, Southwest.
Butler, S.   Law, The.
Han Yü.   Song of the Stone Drums.
Irish Oral Tradition.   John McGoldrick's Trial
   for the Quaker's Daughter.
Po Chü-i.   Everlasting Wrong, The.
Simmonds, Kevin.   White Man and the Judge,
   A.
Tait, G.   U.S.A. Court of No Appeal, The.
Tu Fu [or Du Fu].   Ballad on Seeing a Pupil of
   the Lady Gongsun Dance the Sword Mime.

Courtship
Alexie.   Reservation Love Song.
Amis, K.   Aberdarcy: The Main Square.
Anderson, M.   September Song.
Anderson-Thompkins.   brken promises.
Angus.   Doors of Sleep, The.
Anthony, M.   Ugly Heart, The.
Anyte [or Anytes].   I mourn maiden Antibia:
   desiring her, many.
Auden.   As I Walked Out One Evening.
Aytoun [or Ayton], R.   Answer, The.
   Rejection, The.
   Song: "What means this strangeness now of
   late."
   There is none, no none but I.
   To His Coy Mistress.
   Upon His Unconstant Mistress.
Baillie, J.   Song: Woo'd and married and a'.
Beckett, S.   Song: "Age is when to a man."
Behn, A.   Dream, The.
   To Lysander, on Some Verses Be Writ, and
   Asking More for His Heart.
Betjeman.   Subaltern's Love-Song, A.

Blake, W. How Sweet I Roamed [or Roam'd] from Field to Field.
Love's Secret.
Brooks, G. Lovely Love, A.
Brooks, S. Some of These Days.
Brown, L. You Are Not Gorgeous and I Am Coming Anyway.
Brown, S. Scotty Has His Say.
Browning, E. Lord Walter's Wife.
Man's Requirements, A.
Year's Spinning, A.
Burns, R. Comin[g] thro' [or through] the Rye.
Halloween.
I Once Was a Maid.
Mary Morison.
Whistle, and I'll Come to You, My Lad.
Butler, S. She was too kind, wooed too persistently.
Caesar. Too Many Rings around Rosie.
Calverley. In the Gloaming.
Campion, T. I Care Not for These Ladies.
Now Winter Nights Enlarge.
Shall I Come, Sweet Love.
Think'st thou to seduce me then.
What Fair[e] Pomp[e].
Cannon, H. Bill Bailey, Won't You Please Come Home.
Carew, T. To a Lady That Desired I Would Love Her.
Carmichael, H. Don't Forget to Say No, Baby.
Castro, R. I Love You . . . Why Do You Hate Me?
Chaucer. Franklin's Tale, The.
Chippewa Oral Tradition. Love-Charm Song.
Chudleigh. Song: "Why *Damon*, why, why, why so pressing?"
Clarke, A. Envy of Poor Lovers, The.
Cobbold, E. Veil, The.
Cohan. Twentieth-Century Love.
Cook, E. Song of the Ugly Maiden.
Corso. Love Poem for Three for Kaye & Me.
Marriage.
Coward. Irish Song [Rosie O'Grady].
Craighead, L. Whole Truth So Help Me God—Also Known as the Gettin' Rid of Nigguz Business.
Crawley, W. Poetry for the Goddess.
Cruz, C. Briar Rose Waltz.
Cunningham, J. Ars Amoris.
Dante Alighieri. New Love and the Gentle Heart.
Darío, R. Marguerite.
Davies, S. Faith (Wench) I Cannot Court Thy Sprightly Eyes.
De la Mare. Some One.
Delmore, A. Girl by the River, The.
DeSylva, B. G. I'll Say She Does.
Dickinson, E. Death is the supple Suitor.
God is a distant—stately Lover.
Her Sweet turn to leave the Homestead.
Donne. Nature's lay idiot [or ideot], I taught thee to love.
Prohibition, The.
Dove, R. Adolescence—3.
Drummond, W. All Changeth.
Du Bois. Song: "Scholar first my Love implor'd, A."
Duffy, M. Semi-Skilled Lover.
"Ephelia.". On a Bashful Shepherd.
"Ern Malley.". Boult to Marina.
Perspective Lovesong.
Fenollosa. Wood Dove, The.
Fields, D. Have Feet, Will Dance.
Fleming, R. Long Walk Home, The.
Garrigue. Cracked Looking Glass.
Grenoble Café.
To Speak of My Influences.
Gay, J. To a Young Lady, with Some Lampreys.
Gershwin, I. Embraceable You.
Gilbert, W. Ferdinando and Elvira; or, The Gentle Pieman.
Godfrey. Our Lady.
Greger. Penguin Jane Austen, The.
Grimké, A. Caprichosa.
Hall, J. Call, The.
Hammerstein. Surrey with the Fringe on Top,

The.
Hands, E. Favourite Swain, The.
Perplexity: A Poem.
Widower's Courtship, The.
Harbach, O. Let's Begin.
Poor Pierrot.
Hardy, T. Epitaph on a Pessimist.
Harland-Watts, J. Let It Be Known.
Heard, J. To Clements' Ferry.
Hecht, A. Ghost in the Martini, The.
Samuel Sewall.
Herrick. Corinna's Going a-Maying.
To the Virgins, to Make Much of Time.
Holmes, O. Ballad of the Oysterman, The.
Hookes. To Amanda Walking in the Garden.
Housman. Along the field as we came by.
Oh see how thick the goldcup flowers.
Hupfeld, H. Are You Makin' Any Money?
Jellicoe. Advice to a Lover.
Jerome, W. Row, Row, Row.
Jolson, A. I'll Say She Does.
Jonson, B. Song. To Celia ("Drink to me only with thine eyes.").
Juana Inés de la Cruz. I Can Neither Hold You Nor Let You Go.
Verses Against the Inconsequence of Men's Taste and Strictures.
Kahn, G. I'll Say She Does.
Kaschnitz. Girl thinks if I can only manage, The.
Kavanagh, P. On Raglan Road.
Keats. To ———: "Had I a man's fair form, then might my sighs."
Where Be You [or Ye] Going, You [or Ye] Devon Maid?
Larcom. Little Cavalier, A.
Lawrence, D. H. Cherry Robbers.
Leapor. Strephon to Celia. A Modern Love-Letter.
Livingstone, D. One Time.
Loesser. Luck, Be a Lady.
Murder, He Says.
Logan, J. Picnic, The: "It is the picnic with Ruth in the spring."
López Velarde. In the Dying Afternoon.
MacCaig. Wild Oats.
Mack, C. He's a Cousin of Mine.
Madden, E. By the Light of the Silvery Moon.
Madhubuti. My Brothers.
Marlowe. Passionate Shepherd to His Love, The.
Marvell. To His Coy Mistress.
McDaniel, W. Realist of 1939–40, A.
Meredith, G. Love in the Valley.
Merrill, S. Ballade of the Chinese Lover.
Miller, E. Another Love Affair/Another Poem.
Monck. On A Romantic Lady.
Montagu, L. To a Lady Making Love.
Moore, T. Time I've Lost in Wooing, The.
Naden. Love Versus Learning.
Natural Selection.
Scientific Wooing.
Nairne. Heiress, The.
Laird o' Cockpen, The.
North, D. Platonic.
O'Hara, G. K-K-K-Katy.
O'Neill. Grand Match, The.
Oppian [of Corycus]. Loves of the Tortoise, The.
Orléans, C. Go forth myn hert wyth my lady.
Orozco. Miss Havisham.
Palmer, O. Wasting Time.
Parker, D. Indian Summer.
One Perfect Rose.
Social Note.
Unfortunate Coincidence.
Patchen. Figure Motioned with Its Mangled Hand toward the Wall behind It, The.
We Go Out Together.
Pathabhi. Sita.
Pearlberg, G.G. Sailor.
Petrarch. Complaint of a Lover Rebuked.
Long[e] love that in my thought do[e]th [or I] harbour [or harber or harbar], The.
Philips, K. Answer to Another Persuading a Lady to Marriage, An.

Popova, O. Among black trees.
Porter, C. Brush Up Your Shakespeare.
Red, Hot and Blue.
Prior. Ode, An: "Merchant, to secure his treasure, The."
Ralegh, S. Nymph's [or Nimphs] Reply to the [Passionate] Shepherd [or Sheepheard], The.
Sir Walter Ralegh to the Queen.
Ramsay, A. Polwart on the Green.
Rankin, J. Man Is Following Me, A.
Ransom, J. Piazza Piece.
Rexroth, K. Aspen Meadows.
Roethke. For an Amorous Lady.
Rossetti, C. Amor Mundi.
Cousin Kate.
No, Thank You, John.
Noble Sisters.
Triad, A.
Rowe, E. To Orestes.
Sabines. I Do Not Know It for Sure.
Safie, D. Danger, Men in Trees.
Salter. Young Girl Peeling Apples.
Scarlatti. Lanza 51.
Scott, A. Return Thee, Heart.
Sedley. Song: "Love still has something of the sea."
Shakespeare, W. Blossom, The.
Country Song.
Sidney. My true love hath my heart [or hart], and I have his.
Fourth Song: "Only joy, now here you are."
Eleventh Song: "Who is it that this dark[e] night."
Eighth Song: "In a grove most rich of shade."
Sonnet 6: "Some lovers speak, when they their Muses entertain."
Sonnet 61: "Oft with true sighs, oft with uncalled tears."
Sonnet 69: "O joy, too high for my low style to show."
Sonnet 107: "Stella, since thou so right a Princess art."
Smith, C. On the Aphorism "L'Amitié est l'Amour sans Ailes."
Stanzas: "Ah! think'st thou, Laura, then, that wealth."
Soto. Oranges.
Trees That Change Our Lives.
Spenser, E. Book 3, Canto 11.
Sonnet 67: "Like a huntsman after weary chase."
Stevenson, R. Song of a Traveller, The.
Stirling, S. Echo, An.
Strand. Courtship.
Su Hsiao-hsiao. Song of Xiling Lake, A.
Suckling, S. Barley-Break , A.
Love's Siege.
Loving and Beloved.
Song: "I prithee spare me, gentle boy."
Song: "Why so pale and wan, fond lover?"
Sonnet: "Of thee, kind boy, I ask no red and white."
Tennant, W. My pulse beats fire—my pericranium glows.
Tennyson, A. Come into the Garden, Maud.
Teton Sioux Oral Tradition. You Have No Horses.
Theocritus. Idyll 27: Daphnis.
Tibullus. Priapus, may this shady roof forever.
Titherage. And Her Mother Came Too.
Touré, A. Frontier of Rage, The.
Unknown. Aura Lee.
Bei-feng: Cold Is the North Wind.
Bonny Barbara Allan.
Chance led me once, when idling through the street.
Chen and Wei are brimming, The.
Chung Tzu.
Do you carrot all for me?
Dowie Dens of Yarrow, The [Version from Blackwood's Magazine].
Faire, fresshest erthly creature.
Four on a Sidewalk.
Fressh lusty beautee joyned wyth gentilesse.
Go, litel ryng, to that ilke swete.
Guan-ju.

I go before, my darling.
In the wilds, a dead doe.
Kuan-kuan, the ospreys.
Lord Thomas and Fair Annet.
Pao-you ku-ye: Bitter Blade.
Piao-you-mei: Like Falling Fruit.
Polly Perkins.
Qian-shang: Gird Your Loins.
So faire, so fressh, so goodly on-to see.
Song Inscribed on an Earthenware Vessel.
Sound of my lover, The.
Three Things Come Without Seeking.
Vallejo. Poem to Be Read and Sung ("I know there is a person.").
Wade-Gayles. Inquisition.
Waugh, Arthur. Ballade of the Devout Husband, The.
  Romaunt of Cecilia, The.
Weber, R. Lady and Gentleman.
Whalen, P. Slop Barrel, The.
Whitman, W. Dalliance of the Eagles, The.
Willis, N. City Lyrics.
Wyatt. If waker care, if sudden [or sodayne] pale colo[u]r.
  Long love that in my thought doth harbo[u]r, The.
  Madame, withouten Many Wordes.
Yeats. Cap and Bells, The.
Young, J. You're Gonna Lose Your Gal.
Zarzyski. How near Vietnam Came to Us.

Cousins
Brooks, G. Rites for Cousin Vit, The.
Browning, E. Aurora Leigh.
Buhyu Sunsoo. Biding Farewell to My Cousin, Haeil, on His Return Home.
Clanchy, K. For a Wedding.
Jacobsen, J. Poems for My Cousin.
Jordan, J. Through These Halls.
López Velarde. My Cousin Agueda [or Agatha].
Mack, C. He's a Cousin of Mine.
Paino. Matter of Division, A.
Tu Shan-fu. Tune: "Shua Hai-erh" Country Cousin at the Theater.
Winder. On Fourteen Maple Street.

Coventry, England
Larkin, P. I Remember, I Remember.
O'Callaghan, C. Coventry.

Cowardice and Cowards
Archilochus. Some Thracian exults in an excellent shield.
Benjamin, P. Press On.
Boker. Oh! craven, craven! while my brothers fall.
Crosland. White Feather Legion, The.
Dalton, A. Kitchen Beast.
Eliot, T. S. Gerontion.
  Love Song of J. Alfred Prufrock, The.
France, L. Body Language.
Ingalls, J. Apprehension.
Katz, M. Brave Coward, The.
Kim Suyŏng. Emerging from the Old Palace One Day.
Kipling, R. Coward, The.
  Dead Statesman, A.
Nossis. Shields Bruttians threw from their doomed shoulders.
Praxilla. Learning from the tale of Admetos, my friend, love the brave.
Unknown. Dust for you, but never my mouth again.
  In battle today my lover turned his back to the enemy.
  Martyr is like lightning that glitters and is then snuffed out, A.
  My beloved! If you turn your back upon the enemy, do not come home again!

Cowboys
Alexander, E. Deadwood Dick.
Baker, K. Texas Cowboy.
Barney, W. Ballad for Bill Pickett, A.
Byrd, Bobby. Things You Can't Do in Albuquerque or Santa Fe, #11.
Campbell, D. Song for the Cattle.
Chittenden. Cowboys' Christmas Ball, The.
Clarke, G. Rag Time Cowboy Joe.
Cole, Maude E. Over Texas Hills.

Craven, Jerry. Last Running, The.
Craven, Sherry. Garden City Diner: Loving Back.
Crowell, N. Texas Trails.
Dailey. Call Me 'Shortchange'.
Dorn, E. Idle Visitation, An.
Elmslie, K. Experts at Veneers.
Hopkins, L. Nat Love: Black Cowboy.
Huidobro. Cow Boy.
LittleDog, Pat. Cowgirl.
Major, C. I Was Looking for the University.
McDonald, W. Honky-Tonk Blues.
  Songs We Fought For, The.
McElroy, C. Mae West Chats It Up with Bessie Smith.
Michie. Arizona Nature Myth.
Nance. Frontier Mystery.
Reed, I. I Am a Cowboy in the Boat of Ra.
Robertson, Lexie Dean. Aunt Gilly.
Seale, J. Travel North: The Rules.
Swenson, M. Bronco Busting, Event #1.
Thorn, Jas. D. Sigh of the Old Cattleman, The.
Tomlinson, C. At Barstow.
Unknown. Corrido of "Gregorio Cortez."
  Cowboy Sayings.
  Cowboy's Lament, The.
  Gol-darned Wheel, The.
  Kansas 1.
  New Corrido of Laredo.
  O I'm a jolly old cowboy.
Waller, Robert James. Three Poems.
Ward, William Allen. Texas.
Warren, R. Rattlesnake Country.
Yauger, Fay M. I Remember.

Cowper, William
Browning, E. Cowper's Grave.
North, C. For a Cowper Paperweight.

Cows
Ahern, T. Titled.
Alberti. Buster Keaton Looks in the Woods for His Love Who Is a Real Cow.
Alvarez, J. Cows.
Barnes, K. Night Light.
Basho. On the cow shed.
Berry, W. Her First Calf.
Brooks, G. Jamal; Nineteen Cows in a Slow Line Walking.
Burgess, F. Cinq Ans Après.
  Purple Cow, The.
  Purple Cow, The: Suite.
Carruth, H. Cows at Night, The.
Carryl, G. Harmonious Heedlessness of Little Boy Blue, The.
Chŏng Chiyong. Paengnokdam: White Deer Lake.
Clarke, A. Lost Heifer, The.
Clifton, L. My Dream About the Cows.
Crozier, A. Heifer, The.
D'Aguiar, F. Cow *Perseverance*,The.
Duhig, I. Lammas Hireling, The.
Frost, R. Cow in Apple Time, The.
Gaspar, Lorand. Flute Player.
Graves, R. Dead Cow Farm.
Halbur, A. 4-H.
Heynen. Bloating and Its Remedies.
Hill, J. Economics of Gererosity, The.
Hill, S. Cow.
Johnson, J. Music for the Cows.
Kinsley, R. Those Mornings.
Kocan. Cows.
Labid. Tent marks in Mínan are worn away, The.
Lewis, G. Farmer's Evidence, The.
  In the Open Air.
Llwyd, Alan. Bull of Bryncelyn, The.
MacCaig. Fetching Cows.
MacDiarmid, H. Cloudburst and Soaring Moon.
Martin, Steve. Cows in Trouble.
McDonald, W. Wind and Hardscrabble.
McNair. Mina Bell's Cows.
Mishol, A. Sacred Cow of Hardship, The.
Moore, Robert John. We are nowhere near as calm as we probably appear.
Moore, T. Response to Rimbaud's Later Manner.
Musgrave. I Am Not a Conspiracy Everything

Is Not Paranoid the Drug Enforcement Administration Is Not Everywhere.
Nash, O. Cow, The.
Nicholson, N. Tune the Old Cow Died Of, The.
O'Donoghue, B. Weakness, The.
Ovid. Io and Jove.
Porteous. Calf.
Randell. O house, o sloping field, o poplar trees whose tall arms salute.
  Waiting.
Rector. My Grandfather Always Promised Us.
Reeves, J. Cows.
Roberson, E. Blue Horses.
Ruffin. Burying.
Santos, S. Dairy Cows of Maria Cristina Cortes.
Shapcott, J. Mad Cow in Love, The.
Sjolander. Last Longhorn's Farewell, The.
Stern, G. Cow Worship.
Stevenson, R. Cow, The.
Takara, Kathryn. Cows and Alabama Folklore.
Tate, J. Intimidations of an Autobiography.
Unknown. Muiveyo Cow, The.
  Sukey [or Suky], you shall be my wife.
Voigt. Harvesting the Cows.
Walsh, J. Drimin Donn Dílis.
White, E. Red Cow Is Dead, The.
Woodward, G. Murderer Is a Cow, The.
Zabolotsky [or Zabolotskii]. Face of a Horse, The.

Coyote (mythology)
Blue Cloud. Coyote Makes the First People.
Ortiz. Telling about Coyote.
Silko. Toe'osh; a Laguna Coyote Story.

Coyotes
Goodtimes. Roadkill Coyote.
Hannon. Beneath Cold Mountain.
Hanzlicek, C. What I Want Is.
Navajo Oral Tradition. Coyote, Skunk, and the Prairie Dogs.
Silko. Toe'osh; a Laguna Coyote Story.
Waltner-Toews, D. Coyotes at Eyebrow Lake, Saskatchewan.
Warren, R. Arizona Midnight.
Whyte-Melville. Coyotes.

Crab Apple Trees and Crab Apples
Feaver. Crab Apple Jelly.
Sanger, Peter. Crabapple Blossoms.
Unknown. That Shady Crab.
Van Walleghen. Crabapples.
Wright, J. Young Good Man, The.

Crabbe, George
Robinson, E. George Crabbe.

Crabs and Crabbing
Atwood. Landcrab I.
  Landcrab II.
Basho. Clear water.
Bishop, E. Strayed Crab.
Dove, A. Crab.
Dove, R. Crab-Boil.
Fuller, R. Crustaceans.
Gotera. Pacific Crossing.
O'Donnell, D. Crab, The.
Saleh. Crabs.
Smith, D. Fiddlers.
Szporluk. Duressor.
See also **Hermit Crabs; Horseshoe Crabs**

Cracow, Poland
See **Krakow [or Cracow], Poland**

Craftsmanship
Beachy-Quick, Dan. Prologue: "Editor, / Here are the lines my mind fathomed."
Borgmann, K. Bed.
Garrett, E. Unguentarium.
Guevara, M. Miniaturist, The.
Howe, S. Plain chair or two back.
Nye, N. Man Who Makes Brooms, The.
Snyder, G. Axe Handles.
Tohe. She Was Telling It This Way.

Crane, Hart
Doty, M. Almost Blue.
Gilfillan, M. Proposed Elegy for Hart Crane.
North, C. Landscape and Chardin.
Wheelwright. Fish Food.

Cranes (ornithology)
Aalfs, J. Sewing the Torn Sleeve.

Akhmatova, A. 1915.
Basho. Crane's legs, The.
  In the shallows.
Celan. When you lie.
Cody, James. Whooping Crane.
Daegak Euchon. For Sanje, a Hermit.
Faust, H. Six Cranes at Dusk.
Gregerson. Cranes on the Seashore.
Harper, Cynthia. Water Birds.
Heyen. Crane in Reeds.
Jones, R. News of the Cranes.
Kagami Shiko. Arid fields / The only life.
Kasa. As one hears the cry.
Po Chü-i. Cranes, The.
Ritterbusch. Thousand Cranes, A.
Snyder, G. Really the Real.
Unknown. Crane Calls.
Young, D. White Crane.
Zhiyuan, S. Lost Cranes.

Cranmer, Thomas
Smith, S. Admire Cranmer!

Crashaw, Richard
Cowley, A. On the Death of Mr. Crashaw.

Crazy Horse (Oglala Sioux Chief)
Blue Cloud. Crazy Horse Monument.
Clifton, L. Death of Crazy Horse, The.
Heyen. Steadying, The.
Le Guin. His Daughter.
MacLeish. Wildwest.
Stafford, W. Report to Crazy Horse.
  Right Time, The.

Creation
Addison, J. Ode: "Spacious firmament on high,
  The."
Addonizio. Theodicy.
Alexander, C. All Things Bright and Beautiful.
Amadiume. Creation.
Andrews, T. Cinema Vérité: Jacques Derrida
  and God's *Tsimtsum.*
Anti-Jabobins, The. Canto First.
Apuleius, L. I who am Nature, mother of all.
Aridjis. Poem, The.
Azzawi, F. In a magic land.
Baraka, I. How People Do.
Beausoleil, B. Traces.
Bedregal. Nocturne of Hope.
Bell, M. Sevens (Version 3): In the Closed Iris
  of Creation.
Berman, C. Poem for the Shechina.
Bible, *O.T.* In the beginning God created the
  heaven and the earth.
Bidart. Lament for the Makers.
Blake, W. Tyger, The.
Blind. Chaunts of Life.
Blood, B. Late.
Blue Cloud. Spring Equinox.
  Turtle.
Browning, R. Johannes Agricola in Meditation.
Bryant, W. Song of the Stars.
Budapest. Medea speaks: / This is God,
  children, listen up well. The.
Budbill. First Green of Spring, The.
Canning, G. *et al.* Canto First.
Carson, A. God's Woman.
Castillero, S. Hare, The.
Castro, R. Glowworm Scatters Flashes, A.
Causley. Forest of Tangle, The.
Celan. Psalm: "No one kneads us again out of
  earth and clay."
Ceravolo. Data.
Cherry, K. In the Garden by the Sea: Easter.
Chesterton. Donkey, The.
Cibber. Let there be light!
Clare, J. I Feel I Am.
Copus, J. Making of Eve, The.
Couzyn. Creation.
  Mystery, The.
Cowley, A. Hymn to Light.
Crawford, R. Fiat Lux.
Cross, E. Shakti.
De la Mare. Scribe, The.
Di Prima. Loba as Eve.
Dickinson, E. It's easy to invent a Life.
  Just as He spoke it from his Hands.
Doyle, S. To an Undiscerning Critic.
Drake, N. Foley Artist, The.

Eclipse. Cicada.
El-Dinasouri, O. If I Were a God.
El Janabi, A. Against Ibn Arabi.
Elijio, C. Hummingbird at Dawn.
Emerson, R. Rhodora, The [On Being Asked
  Whence Is the Flower].
Empress. Creation Is a Cycle.
Essbaum, J. In the Beginning.
Evans, D. Creation.
Fabian, C. On Reading the New Physics—
  Creation and Cosmology.
Farid-uddin Attar. Invocation to the Conference
  of the Birds.
Ford, Katie. Flesh.
Fordham. Creation.
Francis of Assisi. Canticle of the Creatures.
Fuller, J. Whole New Scene, A.
George, W. Armstrong and Aldrin on the Moon.
Gerov, Alexander. Mice.
Gidlow. Creed for Free Women, A.
Glück, L. Lamentations.
Goldberg, B. God Body.
Goodtimes. Sartor Resartus.
Gottlieb, A. Meditation on the Feminine Nature
  of Shekinah, A.
Gould, J. Coyotismo.
Grahn. Grand Grand Mother Is Returning.
Graves, R. Dead Cow Farm.
Griffin, S. Our Mother.
Gurr. Creation.
Hadewijch II. All things.
Hamburger, M. Treblinka.
Hardy, J. Computer Aided Design: Creation.
Harjo, J. Anniversary: "When the world was
  created wasn't it like this?"
  Perhaps the World Ends Here.
Harper, M. Black Cryptogram.
Harvey, A. Prayer to the Divine Mother, A.
Harvey, M. Image Cast by a Body Intercepting
  Light.
Heford, Will. That God Made.
Herbert, G. Man.
  Pulley, The.
Hesiod. Vision.
Hildebrandt, Z. In Hecate's Garden.
  Kali.
Hill, G. Genesis.
Hillman, B. Formation of Soils, The.
Hollander, J. What the Lovers in the Old Songs
  Thought.
Hollander, V. Rosh Chodesh Tisheri.
Hoogerhuis. Search, The.
Howe, J. Kosmos.
Hugo, V. At the Window in the Dark.
  More about God (But with Some Reservations).
Hummell, A. Sculpture Garden.
Ibáñez, S. Empty Page, The.
Ironbiter, S. Song to the Mother of the World.
Jabès. Notebook, Two.
Jackson, A. Transformable Prophecy.
Jennings, E. Identity.
Johnson, J. Creation, The.
Johnson, Peter. Genesis: A Retrospective.
Karade, B. Yemoja.
Kilmer, J. Trees.
Kim Chŏngnan. Images: "Scene 1. Front angle,
  dark sky, or the middle of the universe."
Klugman, S. God's Body.
Ko Un. Baby.
Koertge. Redondo.
Kreymborg. Ants.
Lao Tzu. When thirty spokes join the wheel-
  hole.
Lawrence, D. H. Let There Be Light!
Lejeune, Claire. So Where.
Levine, P. Rain Downriver.
Lewis, S. Et Homo Factus Est. Crucifixus.
Logghe. Madonna of the Peaches.
Longfellow, H. Kéramos.
Løvgreen, G. First Day, The.
Lowenthal, J. Hovering.
Lu Chi. Music of Words, The.
  Satisfaction, The.
Lucretius. Darling of Gods and Men, beneath
  the gliding stars.
Machado Ruiz. You say nothing is created new?

Macpherson, J. Fisherman, The: "World was
  first a private park, The."
Magrelli. If you melt some lead.
Martí. I know: from flesh.
Martinson. Creation Night.
McAuley, J. Seventh Day, The.
McVeigh, J. Eve Falling.
Meador, B. Fields Belong to Woman, The.
Meddeb, Abdelwahab. I Take the Path.
Melville, H. Venice.
Miller, V. Morning Person.
Milton. Adam Describes His Own Creation and
  That of Eve; Having Repeated His Warning,
  the Angel Departs.
  For man to tell how human life began.
  Forthwith the sounds and seas, each creek and
  bay.
  Heaven opened wide / Her ever during gates,
  harmonious sound.
  So spake the godlike power, and thus our sire.
Monaghan. Persephone's Journey.
Montgomery, R. Request, A.
Moore, M. Book of How, The.
Morgan, R. As it was in the beginning.
Morozov, S. Poem about the Blue Horse.
Muñiz Huberman. Eye of Creation, The.
Navajo Oral Tradition. Creation of the Earth,
  The.
Nemerov. Creation Myth on a Moebius Band.
Odio, E. Creation.
Olds, S. Early Images of Heaven.
Olson, C. Added to / making a Republic.
  Celestial Evening, October 1967.
Olson, T. Hypothesis.
Ormsby, E. Origins.
Ortiz. Creation.
O'Shaughnessy, A. Ode: "We are the music-
  makers."
Ovid. Deucalion and Pyrrha, sole survivors of
  the Flood, renew Creation by casting stones
  behind them.
Pastan. Imperfect Paradise, The.
Patmore, C. To the Body: "Creation's and
  Creator's crowning good."
Pavlova, V. Heaven and Earth.
Piatt, S. If I Had Made the World.
Pratt, E. Highway, The.
Ragan, J. Birth of God (from an Early
  Photograph), The.
Raine, K. Spell of Creation.
Reis, P. Ancient Ones, The.
Richter, H. Beginning.
Roberts, John. One.
Rooney-Céspedes, A. Retro Creation.
Rukeyser, M. Gyroscope, The.
Sixth Night: Waking, The.
Sadler, L. Why God Chose Robert Frost Over
  Elvis.
Saïd, A. And We Were Born.
  Earth, The.
Sassoon, S. Power and the Glory, The.
Schwartz, R. L. Talking to God on the Seventh
  Day.
Seidman. Making of Color, The.
Serpas, M. Finishing Touch.
Shange. We Need a God Who Bleeds Now.
Shapiro, K. Recognition of Eve, The.
Sherman, J. For Mordecai Richler's Shalinsky
  Who Said "A Jew Is An Idea."
Shúa, A. Golem and Rabbi 5.
Smith, D. Jemez Pueblo: December 26.
Smith, Tracy K. History.
Someck, R. Sign of the Bite, The.
Southwell. Vale of Tear[e]s, A.
Souza. For Rita's Daughter, Just Born.
Starhawk. Demeter's Song.
Stenhouse, S. Circling.
Stevenson, A. Spirit Is Too Blunt an Instrument,
  The.
Swinburne. Aholibah.
Thomas, R. S. Echoes.
Traherne. Third Day.
Tuckerman, F. Sonnets: "Starry flower, the
  flower-like stars that fade, The."
Unknown. Before light became time.
  Cosmogony.

Creation Hymn.
Holy Goddess Tellus.
Lo! ye children of men and the Mother.
Songs of Spirits.
That the earth be made safer for men, and more
  stable.
Truly now.
Valéry. Crusoe.
Valiente. Charge of the Goddess, The.
Very. Man has forgot his Origin; in vain.
Villanueva, A. Planet Earth Speaks, The.
Volach, Y. Life You Have, The.
Wesley, C. Let earth and heaven combine.
Wilbur, R. Praise in Summer.
Williams, Stephanie. Duchess of Dogs.
Winter, M. In the Beginning.
Woody. Girlfriends, The.
Wright, C. Night Journal.
Yeats. Rose of the World, The.
Yi Sanghûi. For Men to Tell How Human Life
  Began Is Hard.
See also **Cosmology**

Creativity
Allston. Art.
Ammons. Anxiety's Prosody.
Bidart. For the Twentieth Century.
Breton, A. On the Road to San Romano.
Brown, L. Birth of the Blues, The.
Creeley. Figures, The.
Deguy. Ballad, The: "In those days, wasy of
  feinting and of tenderness."
  Grey Pier.
DeSylva, B. G. Birth of the Blues, The.
Donnelly, T. Birdsong from Inside the Egg.
Einzig *et al.* Reading for Pleasure.
Esteves. Motherseed.
Ferlinghetti, L. Adieu À Charlot.
Ginsberg, A. Mescaline.
Harrison, D. Yellow.
Henderson, R. Birth of the Blues, The.
Hovey. Accident in Art.
Khlebnikov, V. Russia, I give you my divine.
Le Guin. Stanza 4.
Levertov. For Those Whom the Gods Love
  Less.
  To the Muse.
Malanga. Apprentice, The.
Maulpoix, Jean-Michel. Giving Birth, The.
Meddeb, Abdelwahab. I Take the Path.
Miller, J. Rise of the Afternoon is a Wide
  Glory, The.
Mohr, B. In Line at Pancho's Tacos.
Molodovsky [*or* Molodowsky]. Merciful God.
Morejón. Carpet.
Mörike [*or* Möricke]. Forest Murmurs.
Rich, A. Diamond Cutters, The.
St. John, P. Reading a Story to My Child.
Snodgrass. Matisse: "The Red Studio".
Su Tung-p'o. Who Says a Painting Must Look
  Like Life?
Tanning. Report from the Field.
Tsvetayeva [*or* Tsvetaeva]. Opened my veins—
  unhaltable.

Creatures
Alexander, C. All Things Bright and Beautiful.
Brown, M. Little Black Bug.
Copus, J. Topsell's Beasts.
Jones, M. Living Spring, The.
Morgan, E. First Men on Mercury, The.
Nerval. Golden Sayings.
Stephens, J. Little Things.
Traherne. Demonstration, The.
Yeats. High Talk.
See also **Animals**

Credit
Kocot, N. Gypsy Summer.
See also **Installment Buying**

Cremation
Ali, A. Cremation.
Betjeman. Crematorium.
Bibbins, M. Mud.
Borowski. Night over Birkenau.
Chinnov. In the land of Schlaraffenland.
Cox, M. At the Crematorium, My Son Asks
  Why We're All Wearing Black.

Dāsdatta, R. Because You love cremation
  grounds.
Fogel, E. Shipment to Maidanek.
Harrison, T. Marked with D.
Hesketh. Dilemma.
Hudgins. Ashes.
Islām, N. Syama wakes on the cremation
  grounds.
Jeffers, R. Cremation.
Lane, M. Travis. Codicil: Including the cost of
  a monument and inscription.
Mahapatra, J. Ash.
Morling, M. Ashes.
Ormsby, F. Passing the Crematorium.
Service. Cremation of Sam McGee, The.
Williams, W. Complete Destruction.

Cressida.
See **Troilus and Cressida**

Crete
Constantine, D. Lasithi.
Duran, J. Time Zones.
Purdy, A. On the Decipherment of "Linear B".
Vitiello. Letter to a Cretan Flute-Maker.
Williamson, A. Minoan Distance, The.

Cricket (game)
Bhattacharya, K. Cricketer, The.
Brathwaite, E. Look wha' happen las' week at
  de Oval!
Ewart. Radio Cricket.
Lang, A. Brahma.
Moore, J. When Mr. Dennis does well play.
Petty. There's a Breathless Hush.
Rowlands, D. Cricket.
Shanahan, D. Morning Radio.
Thompson, F. At Lord's.
Wodehouse. Outcast, The.

Crickets
Anyte [*or* Anytes]. For the cricket (nightingale
  of the field) and oak.
Basho. Gray hairs being plucked.
  How pitiful!
  Ungraciously, under.
Bishop, E. Behind Stowe.
Bly, R. Listening to a Cricket in the
  Wainscoting.
Citino. Sister Mary Appassionata Proves to the
  Entomology Class That Woman and Man
  Descended from the Cricket.
Etter. Roma Higgins.
García Lorca. Boy Unable to Speak, The.
  Little Mute Boy, The.
Heath-Stubbs. Winter Cricket.
Hughes, H. Invitation to the Cricket.
Hunt, L. To the Grasshopper and the Cricket.
Hwang Tonggyu. Cricket, The.
Issa. Cricket.
  Cricket, be.
  I'm going to roll over.
Ivanov, Binyo. Crickets, green-faced.
Izumi. In the Autumn, on Retreat at a Mountain
  Temple.
Keats. On the Grasshopper and [the] Cricket.
Kikaku. Her mate devoured.
Klein, A. Rocking Chair, The.
Lear, E. Incidents in the Life of My Uncle Arly.
Lovelace, R. Ant, The.
McCord, D. Crickets.
Oliver, M. Poem 12.
Pak Hyogwan. If my lovesick dream.
Ronci, Seido R. Cricket.
Sachs, N. In the Blue Distance.
Salazar. Cricket at Central California Women's
  Facility.
Sandburg, C. Splinter.
Sedakova. Grasshopper and the Cricket, The.
Tsanev, Ivan. Cricket.
Tu Fu [*or* Du Fu]. Cricket, The.
Tuckerman, F. Cricket, The.
Unknown. And then night fell.
Zukofsky, L. When the crickets.

Crime and Criminals
Adamson. O to be in the news again—now as
  fashion runs.
Atkins, R. Imaginary Crimes in a Real Garden.
Late Bus (After a Series of Hold-Ups).

Ba. Seen to be Done.
Bart, L. Fings Ain't Wot They Used t'Be.
  Reviewing the Situation.
Benbow. Larson Arson.
Bloem, R. Amsterdam Chronicle.
Butts, A. Poe Story, A.
Caesar. Spanish Jake.
Calloway, C. Minnie, the Moocher.
Celan. Leaf, Treeless for Bertolt Brecht, A.
Dickinson, E. I know some lonely Houses off
  the Road.
Doyle, B. Our Man.
Duncan, A. Andy-the-German Servant of Two
  Masters.
Eady. How I Got Born.
Eliot, T. S. Macavity: The Mystery Cat.
Enright, D. Since Then.
Fisher, J. Life, A.
Gaskill, C. Minnie, the Moocher.
Ginsberg, A. Mugging.
Graham, Taylor. Pieces of Henry.
Guillevic. When He'd Looked Hard.
Hamer. Line Up.
Hardy, T. In the Servants' Quarters.
Harington [*or* Harrington]. Of honest Theft. To
  my good friend Master Samuel Daniel.
Harris, R. Usual Suspects, The.
Haskins, L. Jacked.
Hattersley, G. Remembering Dennis's Eyes.
Hayes, T. Postcard from Okemah, A.
Henley, W. E. Villon's Straight Tip to All Cross
  Coves.
Housman. Oh who is that young sinner with the
  handcuffs on his wrists?
Huerta, E. Men of Dawn, The.
Katrovas. Doggerel for the Great Czech
  Phallometer.
Kaufman, B. No More Jazz at Alcatraz.
Kingston, M. Absorption of Rock.
Lerner, S. Spanish Jake.
Matthews, W. Old Folsom Prison.
McGuire. Streets of Forbes, The.
Meredith, W. Effort at Speech.
Mills, I. Minnie, the Moocher.
Muldoon, P. More a Man Has the More a Man
  Wants, The.
Myrddyn (Merlin). Yscolan.
Newbolt. He Fell among Thieves.
Noyes, A. Highwayman, The.
Obradović, B. Intrusion, The.
Orlen. Happy As I Am.
Pope, A. Rape of the Lock, The: An Heroi-
  Comical Poem in Five Cantos.
Ransome-Davies. Raymond Chandler: The Big
  Sleep.
Raworth. Future Models May Have Infra-Red
  Sensors.
Saarikoski. Potato Thief.
Sandburg, C. Cahoots.
  People, yes, the people, The.
Service. Shooting of Dan McGrew, The.
Sondheim. Gee, Officer Krupke.
Stephens, M. Elegy for Llywelyn Humphries.
Tennyson, A. Rizpah.
Thomas, S. My Grandmother's Birthday.
Unknown. Claude Allen.
  Jesse James.
  John Gilbert Was a Bushranger.
  New Corrido of Laredo.
Valente, J. With Plain Words.
Walsh, C. Nearly Nowhere.
Warren, R. Crime.
Webb, C. Prayer for the Man Who Mugged My
  Father, 72.
Whittier. Slave-Ships, The.
Williams, C. K. Fragment: "This time the hold
  up man didn't know a video-sound camera
  hidden up in a corner."
Young, C. Torn.
See also **Prisons and Prisoners**

Crimean War
Landor, W. Crimean Heroes, The.
Tennyson, A. Charge of the Light Brigade, The.
Thackeray. Due of the Dead, The.

Cripples
Désiré, J. Philosophy, A.

Gerstler. True Bride, The.
HaNagid. One Who Works and Buys Himself
 Books.
Hand, M. Tattooed Girl.
Hudgins. Colonel.
Kipling, R. Dead Statesman, A.
Lemm, Richard. Metamorphosis.
McGough, R. Poem with a Limp.
McIntyre. Wooden Leg.
Owen, W. Disabled.
Page, P. Selves, The.
Sassoon, S. Does It Matter?
Unknown. Oh Cruel Was the Press-Gang.
Whur. Catastrophe.
See also **Handicaps and the Handicapped**

Criticism and Critics
"Alta.". Judy Comes to Visit.
Antiphanes. Strange race of critics, A.
Barnett, A. Critique.
Barskova, P. Evening at Tsarskoe Selo.
Belloc. Lines to a Don.
Berger, M. Constrained Response.
Bierce. Rational Anthem, A.
Browning, R. Dialogue between Father and
 Daughter.
Bukowski. Black Poets, The.
 Comments upon my last book of poesy.
Byron, G. Oh! Southey! Southey! cease thy
 varied song!
Collins, B. Workshop.
Cope, W. Emily Dickinson.
 Serious Concerns.
Cunningham, J. Epigram: "Here lies New Critic
 who would fox us."
Daniel, S. Poet and Critic.
Davie, D. Rejoinder to a Critic.
Doyle, S. To an Undiscerning Critic.
Drayton. His Defence against the Idle Critic.
Elliott, E. Criticism.
Enright, D. Evil Days, The.
Ewart. Black Box, The.
Ezekiel. In the Garden: "It seemed to me so
 much like you."
Foley, Jack. Poet's Tango, The.
Frankau, R. Thoughts While Broadcasting.
Han-shan. Some critic tried to put me down.
Hartnett. Man Who Wrote Yeats, the Man Who
 Wrote Mozart, The.
Hemingway. Valentine.
Herrick. To the Detracter.
Hewitt, J. Because I Paced My Thought.
Hinz-Penner, R. Once, in Santa Fe.
Johnson, S. Prologue to Hugh Kelly's *A Word
 to the Wise*.
Jonson, B. To Censorious Courtling.
 To Fool or Knave.
 To John Donne ("Who shall doubt, Donne,
 where [*or* whe'er] I a poet be[e].").
Kirby, D. Dear Derrida.
Lehman. One Size Fits All: a Critical Essay.
Lu Chi. Rhymeprose on Literature.
Luzi. Postscriptum.
Marston, J. Fy Satyre fie, shall each mechanick
 slave.
Martial. Who deem epigrams mere trifles.
Maule. To Cotton Mather, from a Quaker.
Meredith, G. Camelus Saltat.
 Camelus Saltat: Continued.
Nemerov. Sacrificed Author, A.
 To My Least Favorite Reviewer.
Nirmala, K. Birds Love the Net.
O'Hara, F. Critic, The.
Osterhaus, J. Gambier.
Palmer, R. Sterling Brown.
Pavlova, V. And God saw.
Pope, A. But most by numbers judge a poet's
 song. Essay on Criticism, An.
Pound, E. Tenzone.
Prior. In Imitation of Anacreon.
Ramirez, L. Why I Do It.
Rochester, L. Song: "Give me leave to rail at
 you."
Roethke. Pipling.
Salaam. Directions for Understanding Modern
 Jazz Criticism.
Schjeldahl. Reading, The.

Shakespeare, W. Sonnet 140: "Be wise as thou
 art cruel; do not press."
Swift, J. Epigram on Scolding, An.
Unknown. What the Listener Thinks.
Weinstock, D. You Don't Want to Hear a Poem,
 Do You?
Wershler-Henry, D. Ten Out of Ten, or, Why
 Poetry Criticism Sucks in 2003.
Whalen, P. Chanson d'Outre Tombe.
Williams, C. K. Critic, The.
Williams, K. From the Spirit of Phillis
 Wheatley to the Spirit of Thomas Jefferson (A
 Note 212 Years Later).
Wordsworth, W. Scorn Not the Sonnet [Critic,
 You Have Frowned].
Yüan Hao-wen. I know my foolishness, a mere
 ant trying to shake a tree.
 With Chang Hung-lüeh, Court Attendant,
 Discussing Literature.

Crockett, Davy (David Crockett)
Lind, Michael. Now Crockett said, "You
 gentlemen are free".
Unknown. Davy Crockett.

Crocodiles
Armstrong, K. Cuba, Crocodiles, Rain.
Bartolomé, E. Intermedio con cinco cocodrilos.
 Intermezzo with Five Crocodiles.
Beddoes. Crocodile, A.
Carroll, L. Crocodile, The.
Nash, O. Purist, The.
Rossetti, C. My Dream.
Santos Chocano. Dream of the Caiman, The.
Speyer. To a Song of Sappho Discovered in
 Egypt.
See also **Alligators**

Crocuses
Filkova, Fedya. Friendship: "Death gives way
 sometimes."
Rossetti, C. 83: Barren Spring.
Warner, Patrick. Crocus (after snow), The.
Watts, Enos D. Crocuses and Crown-of-Thorns.

Cromwell, Oliver
Brome. Come a *brimmer* (my bullies) drink
 whole ones or nothing.
 On Sir G. B. his defeat.
Marvell. First Anniversary of the Government
 under His Highness the Lord Protector, 1655,
 The.
 Horatian Ode upon Cromwell's Return from
 Ireland, An.
 'Is this, said one, the Nation that we read'.
Milton. To the Lord General Cromwell.
Unknown. Character of a Roundhead, The.
Wright, C. State of Preservation.

Croquet
MacNeice. Soap Suds.

Cross, The
Berrigan, D. Crucifix, The.
Clephane. Beneath the cross of Jesus.
Everson, W. Making of the Cross, The.
Garrett, E. Lost Property.
Herebert. Steddefast cross, inmong alle other.
Ikeda, P. Wood.
Jacob, M. Visitation.
Kamienska. On the Cross.
Knott. Crux.
Melville, H. Inscription, The: "While yet
 Rolfe's foot in stirrup stood."
Moritz [*or* Morits]. My apple-tree, my willow.
Rayes, M. Stigmata.
Sanchez, S. Father and Daughter.
Sexton. With Mercy for the Greedy.
Tate, A. Cross, The.
Transtromer. Out in the Open.
Unknown. Hail, Mary.
Yun Tongju. Cross, The.
See also **Crucifixion, The**

Crowds
Abrahams, L. Song for the new order.
Afrika, T. Accident, The.
Alvi, M. Houdini.
Berlin. Manhattan Madness.
Brontë, C. Obscure and little seen my way.
Clough. It is most curious to see what a power
 a few calm words.

Denby. Snoring in New York: An Elegy.
Gorbanevskaya. Square of the Holy Passion,
 gaze on the demonstrators.
Hudgins. Ecce Homo.
Lafleur, W. Wedding Party.
Lowell, J. Street, The.
Mew. Fame.
Perkins, S. Common Road, The.
Poloskey, M. Encounter.
Pound, E. In a Station of the Metro.
Ramanujan. Some People.
Romtvedt. Glass Canyons.
Ruefle. Kiss of the Sun.
Sandburg, C. I Am the People, the Mob.
Shepherd, R. Self-Portrait in the New World
 Order.
Smith, K. Part of the crowd that day.
Sommer, J. Last in before Dark.
Sondheim. Another Hundred People.
Swensen, C. Crowd.
Williams, W. At the Ball Game.
Wordsworth, W. London Images.
Zabolotsky [*or* Zabolotskii]. Loop Canal, The.

Crowns
Marvell. Coronet, The.
Shen Manyuan. Her Tiara Flowers.

Crows
Alexie. Crow Testament.
Basho. Crow, A.
 Crows resting.
 Solitary, A.
Beddoes. Old Adam, the Carrion Crow.
Berger, B. Transmigration.
Bogan, L. Crows, The.
Buson. Late evening cow, The.
Butcher. Crow Is Walking.
Chippewa Oral Tradition. Song of the Crows.
Eady. Crows in a Strong Wind.
Foerster. Clearing, The: "Always in that
 clearing."
Francis, M. West Nile Crow.
Frost, R. Dust of Snow.
Garrett, G. Crows at Paestum.
Glück, R. Pasolini.
Graham, J. Thinking.
Grenier. Crow.
Harjo, J. Path to the Milky Way Leads through
 Los Angeles, The.
Hughes, T. Childish Prank, A.
 Crow and the Birds.
 Crow's First Lesson.
 Crow's Last Stand.
 Crow's Theology.
 Examination at the Womb-Door.
 That Moment.
Issa. About the field / Crow moves.
 Crow, The.
Jones, D. In a Beautiful Glass.
La Fontaine. Fox and the Crow, The.
Langille. Crows.
MacCaig. Solitary crow.
MacDiarmid, H. In Memoriam Dylan Thomas.
Markus, P. Shooting Crows.
McCord, D. Crows.
McNiece, R. After its caw.
Menai. Rooks: December.
Metodiev, Ivan. This Crow.
Moritz [*or* Morits]. Crow.
Oliver, M. Crows.
O'Reilly, C. Weekend in Bodega Bay, A.
Ortiz. Telling About Coyote.
Reese, L. Crows.
Rexroth, K. In the park a crow awakes.
Rimbaud, A. Blackcurrant River.
Roethke. Night Crow.
Romo-Carmona, M. Crows.
Seiferle, R. Mythology of Heavenly
 Messengers, The.
Shapiro, K. Crossing Lincoln Park.
Shinkichi Takahashi. Sheep.
Sholl. Four Crows at Dusk.
Sioux Oral Tradition. Whole world is coming,
 The.
Sorley. Rooks.
Sosnora. Crow.
Stanford, A. Committee, The.

Taneda Santoka. Somewhere / inside my head.
Unknown. Doodle durdle.
Omens on the Road to Burgos.
Twa Corbies, The.
Vinokurov. Has the time come to draw up the accounts?
Volkman. Seasonal.
Wang Yü-ch'eng. Song of the Crow Pecking at My Scarred Donkey.

Crucifixion, The
Alabaster, W. Of the Reed That the Jews Set in Our Saviour's Hand.
Upon the Ensigns of Christ's Crucifying.
Auden. Luke 23:26–38; And as they led him away.
Shield of Achilles, The.
Barnes, D. Chuang Tzu and Hui Tzu.
Beasley. What Did You Come to See.
Beaumont, J. Garden, The.
Bell, M. Sounds of the Resurrected Dead Man's Footsteps (#3).
Berrigan, D. Facing It.
Bevington, L. Dreamers?
Bond, B. Transparencies.
Borges. John 1:14 (1964).
Brewer, G. Christ, the End.
Burnside, J. Parousia.
Carmichael, A. Yet Listen Now.
Carruth, H. Crucifixion.
Causley. I Am the Great Sun.
Celan. Tenebrae.
Colman, H. On the Inscription Over the Head of Christ on the Cross.
On the Strange Apparitions at Christ's Death.
Cowley, A. Christ's Passion.
Craig, David. Christ Bearing the Cross by El Greco.
Gospel Poem #2.
Gospel Poem #3.
Crashaw. To Our Blessed Lord upon the Choice of His Sepulchre.
Cullen, C. Simon the Cyrenian Speaks.
Daumal. Matthew 27:11–24; Now Jesus stood before.
Dickinson, E. I should have been too glad, I see.
One Crucifixion is recorded—only.
"Remember me" implored the Thief!
Donne. Good Friday [or Goodfriday], 1613.
Riding Westward.
Dove, R. On Veronica.
Everson, W. Zone of Death.
Fletcher, P. Ocean of Light.
Fordham. Crucifixion, The.
Uranne.
Herrick. Cross-tree, The.
His Saviour[']s Words, Going to the Cross[e].
Observation ("Virgin-Mother stood at distance (there), The.").
Hill, G. Canticle for Good Friday.
Hill, S. Small Hotel, A.
Hine. Here is another poem in a picture.
Hudgins. Crucifixion (Montgomery, Alabama).
Ecce Homo.
Hughes, T. God, A.
Matthew 27:45–56; Now from the sixth hour there was darkness.
Jammes. Five Sorrowful Mysteries, The.
Kamienska. On the Cross.
Kates. No Altarpiece.
Knott. Crux.
Lanier, S. Ballad of Trees and the Master, A.
Levertov. Ikon: The Harrowing of Hell.
On a Theme from Julian's Chapter 20.
Lewis, S. To the Good Thief.
Livingstone, D. One Golgotha.
Melville, H. Via Crucis.
Meynell, A. Crucifixion, The.
Miller, M. Calvary Way.
Milman. Crucifixion, The.
Mitchell, E. Crucifixion Will Not Take Place, The.
Mugrón, Abbot of Iona. Christ's Cross.
Muir, E. Killing, The.
Muske, C. Dulce Lignum, Dulces Clavos.
Nijhoff. Last Day.

New Stars, The.
Soldier Who Crucified Jesus, The.
Patchen. Pastoral: "Dove walks with sticky feet, The."
Pound, E. Ballad of the Goodly Fere.
Prince, F.T. Soldiers Bathing.
Quarles. Crucified.
They Gave Him Vinegar and Gall (Matt. 27) and Wine Mingled with Myrrh (Mark 15).
Rayes, M. Stigmata.
Robinson, E. Calvary.
Rodgers, W. It was a lovely night.
Rossetti, C. Good Friday ("Am I a stone and not a sheep.").
Rukeyser, M. Gates, The.
Sandburg, C. Early Lynching.
Sexton. In the Deep Museum.
Sitwell, D. Still Falls the Rain.
Smith, P. San Luis, New Mexico.
Smither. Mission Impossible.
Snow, C. Positions of the Body, 8.
Thomas, R. S. Mother and Child.
Thompson, P. Death and Resurrection.
Unknown. Dream of the Rood, The.
He Never Said a Mumblin' Word.
'O, My Heart Is Woe.'
Seven Virgins, The.
Sinner Won't Die No More.
Were You There When They Crucified My Lord?
Very. Cross, The ("I must go on, till in my tearful line.").
Warton, T. Ode on the Passion.
Watts, I. Hymn: "When I survey the wondrous cross."
Yeats. I am Judas.
Zakaria Youssef, M. Sadder Man, The.

See also **Cross, The; Calvary**

Cruelty
Ager, M. Louisville Lou (The Vampin' Lady).
Al-A'mā at-Tuṭīlī, A. Tears that are shed and a breast that is burned Water and fire! / Things never joined save for matters of moment!
Allen, S. Moment Please, A.
Barnes, D. Every Man His Own Cross.
Bates, C. Hard-Hearted Hannah (The Vamp of Savannah).
Bigelow, B. Hard-Hearted Hannah (The Vamp of Savannah).
Breytenbach. Constipation.
Carroll, L. Alice's Recitation.
Ciardi, J. Faces.
Cleary, B. Slouch.
Clifton, L. Cruelty. Don't talk to me about cruelty.
Collier, M. Robert Wilson.
Creeley. Hill, The.
Delgado, J. Lame Boy Returns, The.
Dickey, W. Memoranda.
Dickinson, E. She dealt her pretty words like Blades.
Dixon, S. Request of Alexis, The.
Fitnet Khanim. In a heart that bears the image.
Fox, A. Why She Suffers.
Fuzuli. Oh God, don't let anyone be like me.
Gumilyov [or Gumiliov or Gumilev]. Baby Elephant, A.
Herrera y Reissig. Heraldic Decoration.
Herrick. Cruelties.
Holden, J. Liberace.
Issa. First cicada / Life is.
Jackson, G. Some of Betty's Story Round 1850.
Jensma. I come.
Johnston, E. Address to Nature on Its Cruelty, An.
Kim Suyŏng. Vinegar of Cruelty.
Koehler, T. Good for Nothin' Joe.
Kuan Hsiu. Bad Government.
Lane, P. On Being Head of the English Department.
Lawrence, D. H. Cherry Robbers.
Lumsden, R. Show and Tell.
Lux. Swimming Pool, The.
Marbod of Rennes. This vision of a face, radiant and full of beauty.
Mayakovsky [or Maiakovskii]. Good Attitude

to Horses, A.
McKay, D. 2. Fates Worse Than Death.
Meinke. Vincent.
Morris, W. Haystack in the Floods, The.
Muhibbi. No end to this separation, no limit to this cruel pain.
Parker, A. Cruelty, the Vandals Say.
Piercy. Friend, The.
Reynolds, S. F. Whipping, The.
Santos, S. Of Haloes & Saintly Aspects.
Shakespeare, W. Sonnet 94: "They that have power [or pow'r or powre] to hurt[e], and will do[e] none."
Shange. It's Not So Good to Be Born a Girl / Sometimes.
Smith, S. How Cruel Is the Story of Eve.
Southey, R. Did then the bold slave rear at last the sword.
Oh he is worn with toil! the big drops run.
'Tis night; the mercenary tyrants sleep.
Terrazas. To a Lady.
Teschke, H. Minutes of Hasiba, The.
Tikhonov. Fire and Rope, Bullet and Axe.
Tsvetayeva [or Tsvetaeva]. I know the truth—give up all other truths!
Turk, R. Mean to Me.
Ulku, A. History.
Unknown. Ballad of the Orphan Boy, The.
Wetzsteon. Three Songs.
Yellen, J. Hard-Hearted Hannah (The Vamp of Savannah).
Louisville Lou (The Vampin' Lady).
Young, J. Was That the Human Thing to Do?
Zach, N. On the Desire to Be Precise.

Cruelty to Animals
Addonizio. Bird.
al-Braikan, M. Monkey's Journey, The.
Chaucer. Pitiful Prioress, The.
Clare, J. Badger.
Derricotte. From a Letter: About Snow.
Dillard, A. Observations and Experiments.
Espada. Do Not Put Dead Monkeys in the Freezer.
Garioch. Nemo Canem Impune Lacessit.
Harington [or Harrington]. To His Wife, for Striking Her Dog.
Hodgson, R. Bells of Heaven, The.
Kinnell. Bear, The.
Porcupine, The.
Krasicki, I. Master and the Dog, The.
Kumin, M. Heaven as Anus.
Levertov. Watching "Dark Circle".
Merwin. Fly.
Nowlan. Bull Moose, The.
Pulido, A. Meanwhile / a young man.
Mientras / un hombre joven.
Straus, M. Neuroanatomy Summer.
Thomas, E. Gallows, The.
Xenophanes. Pythagorean, The.

Crusades
Chesterton. Lepanto.
Kumin, M. In the Absence of Bliss.
Lourie. Theological.

Crystals
Bishop, E. Vague Poem.
Césaire, A. Automatic Crystal, The.
MacDiarmid, H. Crystals like Blood.

Cuba
Ai. Cuba, 1962.
Armstrong, K. Cuba, Crocodiles, Rain.
Baraka, I. Cuba Libre.
Behar, R. Jewish Cemetery in Guanabacoa, The.
Campo. Belonging.
My Voice.
Castillo, S. Cuba.
En el Sol de Mi Barrio.
Monday Night at Pedro's.
Rincón.
Doty, M. Elizabeth Bishop, *Croton.*
Dunbar, P. Conquerors, The: The Black Troops in Cuba.
Esteves. 1st Poem for Cuba.
For Fidel Castro.
García Lorca. Song of the Cuban Blacks.
Grinshpan, Y. In Any Case.

Guevara, E. Song to Fidel.
Guillén, N. National Police Headquarters.
  Small Ode to a Black Cuban Boxer.
Gullar. Sweet Talk.
Hupfeld, H. When Yuba Plays the Rumba on
  the Tuba.
Lowell, R. Fall 1961.
Martí. Two Countries.
Menes, O. Raspa.
Morejón. Havana Harbor.
Mullen, H. Drinking Mojitos in Cuba Libre.
Padilla. Landscapes.
Pau-Llosa. Frutas: "Growing up in Miami any
  tropical fruit I ate."
Rollings. For Dear Life.
Salkey. Remember Haiti, Cuba, Vietnam.
Stevens, W. On a blue island in a sky-wide
  water.
Suarez, V. Aguacero.
Suárez, V. Cuban-American Gothic.
  Rice Comes to El Volcán.
  Song for the Sugar Cane.
  Song to the Banyan.
Touré, A. Palenque Queen by Habana's Shores.
Cuchulain (Irish legendary hero)
Yeats. Cuchulain Comforted.
Cuckoldry and Cuckolds
Bishop, M. My Friend the Cuckold.
Catullus. Carmen 5.
Gandlevsky, S. Oh, how the lilacs are this May!
  Bulging-large bunches fell.
Montagu, L. Epitaph: "Here lies John Hughes
  and Sarah Drew."
Ovid. Elegy 1.4: "Thy husband to a banquet
  goes with me."
Shakespeare, W. Spring.
Unknown. Open a crack in the wall and kiss me
  on the mouth.
See also **Adultery and Adulterers**
Cuckoos
Akimine. Beloved person must I think, The.
Alcuin. Lament for the Cuckoo.
Basho. Cuckoo, A.
  Cuckoo cries, A.
  Cuckoo, The.
  Even in Kyoto.
  Lead my pony.
  Moonlight slanting.
  Not this human sadness.
  Singing, flying, singing.
  Squid seller's call, The.
Buson. Behavior of the pigeon, The.
  Mountain cuckoo, The.
Chiyojo. While I was musing on my theme.
Davies, W. H. Great Time, A.
Desnos. Cuckoo.
Dugan, M. Coolun, The.
Hopkins, G. Cuckoo, The.
Issa. Cuckoo singing.
  Cuckoo sings, The.
  Cuckoo sings / To me, to the mountain.
  Cuckoo's crying / Nothing special to do.
  Mountain cuckoo, The.
Kim Sowŏl. Cuckoo, The.
Masaoka Shiki. Aged nightingale / How sweet.
McAuley, J. Late Winter.
Pak Mogwŏl [*or* Mokwŏl]. April.
Pierpoint, K. Cuckoo-spit.
Ray, H. Cuckoo Song.
Sanpu. First cherry blossoms.
Shiki. Just when the sermon.
Sŏ Chŏngju. Cuckoo and Skylark.
Sora. Matsushima.
Soutar. Gowk, The.
Spenser, E. Merry Cuckoo, The.
Townsend, F. To the Cuckoo.
Unknown. Cuckoo, The.
  I have lived anxious and hurt.
  I live at the foot of the mountain.
  Song of the Pigeon.
  Sumer Is Icumen [*or* Ycomen] In.
  Wee Jenny Wren, The.
Warner, S. In April.
Woljo Toan. Cuckoo.
Woods, V. Blue Cage, A.
Wordsworth, W. To the Cuckoo ("O blithe

New-comer! I have heard.").
Cucumbers
Ap Glyn, Ifor. Cucumbers of Wolverhampton,
  The.
Crozier, L. Cucumbers.
Hikmet. Cucumber, The.
Unknown. Cautionary Limerick.
Culloden, Battle of (1746)
Campbell, T. Wizard.
Cults
Ai. Charisma.
Huffstickler. In the Compound.
Webb, C. What We Believe.
Culture
Abad, G. Jeepney.
Agustini. Vision.
Andrade, M. Nocturne.
  Sunday.
Anzaldúa. Cultures.
Bandeira. Evocation of Recife.
  Portrait.
Basho. Culture's beginnings.
Blanco, R. Letter to El Flaco on His Birthday.
Borges. Witness, The.
Braxton, Joanne M. Zoning.
Burns, J. Revisionism.
Cabico, R. Check One.
  Gameboy.
Campo. Belonging.
Collins, K. I Am Africa.
Corn. Contemporary Culture and the Letter
  "K".
Dacey, P. Coke.
Davies, G. Incomers.
de Aerenlund, C. Cuando el tecolote canta, el
  Indio muere.
DeCormier-Shekekjian. Snow.
Divakaruni. Indian Movie, New Jersey.
"Ern Malley.". Culture as Exhibit.
Evasco, M. Heron-Woman.
Ezekiel. In India.
Fenton, J. This Octopus Exploits Women.
Georgiou, E. Week in the Life of the Ethnically
  Indeterminate, A.
Gertler, P. Right Thing, The.
Ginsberg, A. Studying the Signs.
Gonzales, R. Praise the Tortilla, Praise the
  Menudo, Praise the Chorizo.
Gotera. Pacific Crossing.
Gwynn, R. Oprah Out of Control.
Hewitt, J. Once Alien Here.
Hovanessian, D. Mixed Marriage.
Hufana, A. Contemporary.
Ilio, D. Marikudo in Kalibo, 1979.
Joe, R. You, I, Love, Beauty, Earth.
Joseph, L. Curriculum Vitae.
Katagiri, Dainin. You are nearly as old as the
  number of years it has been since I came to
  America.
Koch, K. You Were Wearing.
Lara, A. Nights.
Lauterbach. After Mahler.
Lee, L. Cleaving, The.
Lewis, P. Dis Da Me.
Li Po. Ku Feng (After the Style of Ancient
  Poems).
López Velarde. Provincial Sundays.
M'Baye d'Erneville. Kassacks.
McLaughlin, D. Battle of Johnny Freedom,
  The.
Meléndez. Oye Mundo/Sometimes.
Melo, M. Red Lipstick on a Straw.
Mueller, L. Highway Poems.
Nazareno, C. Bohol's Tarsier Population.
Okita. Notes for a Poem on Being Asian
  American.
Older. Two Worlds.
Olson, C. Kingfishers, The.
Opoku-Agyemang. King Tut in America.
P'Bitek. Woman with Whom I Share My
  Husband, The.
Peri Rossi. Tired of women.
Pinsky. Figured Wheel, The.
Pollarolo, G. In My Days.
Redmond. 11-Haiku-Poem for a Magnificent
  Million.

Retallack, J. Western CIV, 4 and 5.
Robles. Manong with a Thousand Tribal
  Visions, The.
Rome, H. Who Knows?
Sakaki. Top Ten of American Poetry.
Salazar. Taking It Back.
Samuels, I. Escapology.
Santos Chocano. Manifesto, A.
Shabtai, Aharon. Hebrew Culture.
Smith, I. Shall Gaelic Die?
Snyder, G. Axe Handles.
Souza. Conversation Piece.
St. Germain, S. Cajun.
Taha, A. Tale, A.
Troupe. Following the North Star Boogaloo.
Ungria, R. Culture Nervous.
Weaver, A. Brooklyn.
Weems, M. Funk.
Wolff, Rebecca. Press Play.
Yuson. Dead Center.
Yusuf, S. I too love jeans and jazz and *Treasure
  Island*.
Zamora-Linmark. Day 1: Portrait of the Artist,
  Small-kid Time.
Cumberland, England
Nicholson, N. To the River Duddon.
Cumberland, Virginia
Smith, D. Cumberland Station.
Unknown. Cumberland Gap.
Cummings, E. E. (Edward Estlin)
Niedecker. If I Were a Bird.
Cunningham, Merce
Olson, C. Merce of Egypt.
Cupboards
De la Mare. Cupboard, The.
Cupid
Asclepiades. 105: On a Happy Love.
Baillie, J. To Cupid.
Behn, A. On Her Loving Two Equally.
Boroditskaya, M. Now I am a fan of silence.
Bridges, R. Eros.
Elizabeth I. When I Was Fair and Young.
Greene, R. Night Visitor, A.
Herrick. Cheat of Cupid; or, The Ungentle
  Guest, The.
  How Roses Came Red ("Tis said, as Cupid
  danced [*or* danc't] among.").
  Hymne to Love, An.
  Wounded Cupid, The.
Hilary. To an English Boy: "Beautiful boy,
  flower fair."
Jonson, B. How He Saw Her.
Lodge, T. Rosalind's [*or* Rosalynd's]
  Madrigal[l].
Lyly, J. Cupid and My Campaspe Played.
Mistral, G. I Love, Love.
North, D. Platonic.
Rossini, C. Cupid.
Shakespeare, W. O! And I forsooth in love!
Sidney. Epithalamium: "Let mother Earth".
  Sonnet 20: "Fly, fly, my friends."
  Sonnet 54: "Because I breathe not love to every
  one."
Spenser, E. Book 3, Canto 12.
  There now he lives in everlasting joy.
Tighe. Glimpse of Love, A.
Wroth. Song: "Love a child is ever crying [*or*
  criing]."
  Sonnet 1: "When night's black mantle could
  most darknes[s] prove."
  Sonnet 2: "Late in the Forest I did Cupid
  See."
  Sonnet 3: "His flames ar[e] joy[e]s, his bands
  true lovers' might."
  Sonnet 5: "And burn[e], yet[t] burning you will
  love the smart."
Cups
Darío, R. Fount, The.
Hafiz, K [*or* Hafez]. Ghazal 24: For Years My
  Heart Asked Me for Jamshid's Cup.
Harwood, G. Cups.
Hsin Ch'i-chi. Tune: "Spring in the Ch'in
  Garden".
Ishikawa Takuboku. Tanka: "Accidentally /
  having broken a teacup."

Machado Ruiz. You say nothing is created new?
Palmer, M. Painted Cup, The.
Roberts, K. Plastic Cup, The.
Ryokan. In my begging bowl.
  I've forgotten.
  Picking violets.
Schuyler, J. Shimmer.
Theocritus. Idyll 1: "Whisper of the wind in, The."
Thesen. Broken Cup, The.
Vallejo. Black Cup, The.
Whalen, P. Imperfect Sonnet, The.
Zukofsky, L. Shang Cup.

Curfew
Espada. Toque de queda: Curfew in Lawrence.
Thorpe, R. Curfew Must Not Ring Tonight [or To-Night].

Curie, Marie
Bierds, L. Thinking of Red.
Boruch. Way the Dying Hear Things, The.
Brock-Broido. Radiating Naïveté.
Rich, A. Power.

Curiosity
Citino. Whole Wheat, Decaf Black, a Morbid Curiosity.
Davies, Grahame. Rough Guide.
de Fierro. Speak to Me.
DeSylva, B. G. Somebody Loves Me.
Hadas, P. Curious Experiments.
Johnson, K. Query: "Who left / this wooly caterpillar."
Lorde. Ballad from Childhood.
MacDonald, B. Somebody Loves Me.
Olds, S. Connoisseuse of Slugs, The.
Page, P. Landlady, The.
Reid, A. Curiosity.
Robinson, M. Sappho's Conjectures.
Sidney. Sonnet 92: "Be your words made (good sir) of Indian ware."
Wither. Shall I, Wasting in Despair.

Curses
Bidart. Curse.
Browning, E. Curse for a Nation, A.
Coleman, W. Three-Headed Woman Song.
Coleridge, S. I fear thee, ancient Mariner!
  Rime of the Ancient Mariner (1817 version).
  Rime of the Ancient Mariner, The (1798 version).
Didsbury, P. Malediction, A.
Gibson, W. Parrot, The.
Graves, R. Travel[l]er's Curse after Misdirection[, The].
Herrick. To the Sour[e] Reader.
Maitland, T. Sir Thomas Maitland's Satyr upon Sir Niel Laing.
Parra, V. I Curse in the Highest Sky.
Rûhî. Curse the Thorns of Fate.
Salzman, E. Spells.
Sedley. On a Cock at Rochester.
Smith, S. Thoughts about the Person from Porlock.
Stephens, J. Glass of Beer, A.
  Odell.
Synge. Curse, The.
Unknown. Bonny Barbara Allan.
  In the early hours of the next morning dawning.
  May God prohibit you from any pleasure as you travel.
  Nell Flaherty's Drake.
  Son, if you desert our war.
  Then Job spoke and cursed his day and chanted and said.
Wright, J. Song for the Middle of the Night, A.

Custer, George Armstrong
Alexie. Crazy Horse Speaks.
Coolbrith. Captive of the White City, The.
Kelen. Rabbit Shoeshine.
MacLeish. Wildwest.
Whitman, W. From Far Dakota's Cañons (June 25, 1876).

Custom
Curry, N. St Kilda.
Eich. Salt.
Emerson, R. Him strong Genius urged to roam.
France de Bravo, B. Unrepentant.

Keller, G. Venus de Milo.
P'Bitek. Woman with Whom I Share My Husband, The.

Cyclamen
Field. Cyclamens.
Lawrence, D. H. Sicilian Cyclamens.

Cycles of Life
Adler, L. On the Night of the Day the Worlds Ends.
Ammons. In View of the Fact.
Barrows, A. How many million years before wood turns to stone?
Bell, M. Ars Poetica at the Window.
Buhyu Sunsoo. Deathbed Song.
Burnside, J. History.
Dao. Rose of Time, The.
Davies, P. Ave Atque Vale.
Davies, W. H. Money.
Fennelly. Latching On, Falling Off.
Flores, M. Whenever something dies.
Forman, R. Wedding.
Garrett, G. Pastoral: "Ghosts of summer learn, The."
Gogarty. Palinode.
Hahn, K. Firsts in No Particular Order.
Hancock, Butch. Circumstance.
Hierro, José. Accelerando.
Howard, R. Like Most Revelations.
"Hsiung Hung.". Who Stops the Dance?
Hyecho. Elegy: "Lamp lost its master at home, The."
Jacobs, B. It's a Dog's Life.
Jinkag Haesim. On the Death of the Most Reverend Priest.
Kercheval, J. Things That Have Escaped Me.
Kim Chôngnan. Poetry: "Many entrances. Open. Everywhere. But reaching nowhere. Wandering."
Kingston, M. Saturday April 8 Swansea, where Dylan Thomas was born on October 27th, the same day I was born.
Koch, K. Proverb.
Lauterbach. Hum.
Lee, L. Become Becoming.
Løvgreen, G. Life's Dovey Junctions.
Mezey. Touch It.
Miller, A. Forever Afternoon.
Morales. Old.
Muske, C. Crack the Whip.
New, W. Acoustics.
Nhat Hanh. Journey: "Here are words written down."
Oliver, M. Where Does the Dance Begin, Where Does it End?
Oswald, A. Prayer: "Here I work in the hollow of God's hand."
Parry, R. Hedd Wyn.
Parry-Williams. Life: "O the blessedness of life! It's lucky, no doubt."
Paz. Response and Reconciliation.
Prasad, V. First Blood.
Pulido, A. It is not known.
  No se sabe.
Radnóti. Unnoticed.
Reynolds, M. This World.
Rossetti, D. Sonnet is a moment's monument, A.
Smith, J. D. Seven Ages of Man.
Stafford, W. Ask Me.
Stevens, W. Pleasures of Merely Circulating, The.
Stone, R. Train Ride.
Strand. Five Dogs.
Tilak, D. Police Report.
Tomioka. Will You Marry Me?
Unknown. You Never Ask.
Weaver, A. Evidence of Life.
Williams, W. What Is a Man?
Woljo Toan. Deathbed Song.

Cycles of Nature
Antler. Trees Seen Now.
Aygi, G. Day—Towards Evening.
Berry, W. 1979 II.
Bonitto-Burwell, T. Going Home.
Clark, T. Elegy: "It's a pity we have to suffer."
Cummins, Deborah. To the Days Lost in

  August.
Davis, T. Ripe.
DeNiord, C. I Stand Beneath the Mountain with an Illiterate Heart.
Fargas. Out of Time.
Funkhouser. Lilies.
Gibbs, Robert J. This Catching of Breath at the Top.
Hidalgo, J. Flowers Under the Dead.
Hurbak Myungjo. Dream of a Butterfly, The.
Jandl, E. Summer Song, A.
Jones, D. Harvest and Spring.
Jones, T. Argoed.
Keita, N. Cycles.
Li Po. Red sun comes out of the Eastern corner, The.
Madgett. Last Happy Day, The.
Maihiot, Michelle M. Playing Fields.
Merriam, E. Summer's End.
Meyerhoff, J. On Impermanence.
Noguchi, Yonejiro (Yone). Suppose the stars.
Parini. Some Compensation.
Rice, D. Remains.
Richter, H. Round Room, The.
Robinson, Matt. Snow; a fear of dying.
Rodríguez, A. Lexicon of Exile.
Rosenberg, L. End of Winter.
Tueni, N. Certainties in huge colors.
Unknown. Last Survivor's Speech, The.
Waltner-Toews, D. How the Earth Loves You.
Wright, C. Mondo Henbane.
Young, G. Four Poems.

Cyclops
Homer. Cave we found, but vacant all within, The.
Ovid. Cyclops.
Theocritus. Idyll 11: The Cyclops.

Cymon
Dryden, J. Cymon and Iphigenia.

Cynicism and Cynics
Berrigan, A. Four Minute History of Getting It Together in Order to Be Fabulous, Briefly, A.
Brooks, G. Speech to the Young Speech to the Progress-Toward (Among Them Nora and Henry III).
Bukowski. Secret, The.
Daniel, S. Love Is a Sickness.
Doyle, S. To an Undiscerning Critic.
Hardy, T. Christmas: 1924.
  He Never Expected Much.
Hughes, J. Knowingness.
Lowell, R. As a Plane Tree by the Water.
McDonald, P. Totalled.
Ojaide. Launching Our Community Developement Fund.
Parker, D. Certain Lady, A.
  Comment.
  Inscription for the Ceiling of a Bedroom.
  Symptom Recital.
  Unfortunate Coincidence.
Raleigh, W. Lines Suggested by an Edition of Blake's Poems.
Southey, R. Battle of Blenheim, The.
Stafford, W. Meditation: "Animals full of light."
Wedekind, F. Blind Youth, The.
Wilbur, R. Matthew 8, 28 ff.

Cypress Trees
Francis, R. Cypresses.
Jeffers, R. Granite and Cypress.
Kelly, R. Life of Intimate Fleeing, A.
Kushner, A. Cypress.
Lawrence, D. H. Cypresses.

Cyprus
Brackenbury. Produce of Cyprus.

Czars
Dubie. Czar's Last Christmas Letter, The: A Barn in the Urals.

Czech Republic [formerly Czechoslovakia]
Harwood, L. Czech Dream.
Hirsch, E. Milena Jesenká.
Holan. Children at Christmas in 1945.
Osherow. Villanelle from a Sentence in a Poet's Brief Biography.
Rumens. Geography Lesson.

Seifert. Never Again.
Tsvetayeva [or Tsvetaeva]. They took quickly, they took hugely.
Walker, A. Kiss, The.

D

Dachau, Germany
Dubie. Aubade of the Singer and Saboteur, Marie Triste: 1941.
Merwin. Dachau Shoe, The.

Dachshunds
Meredith, G. Islet the Dachs.

Daedalus
Oppen. Daedalus: The Dirge.
Ovid. Daedalus.

Daffodils
Davies, I. In Gardens in the Rhondda.
Goodison. Quartet of Daffodils, A.
Herrick. To Daffodils.
To Daffodils [or Daffadills].
Hughes, T. Daffodils.
Majer. Spring.
McGrath, T. Black Train, The.
Mother Goose. Daffadowndilly.
Shakespeare, W. When Daffodils Begin to Peer.
Trethewey, N. Genus Narcissus.
Williams, W. Daffodil.
Wordsworth, W. I Wandered Lonely as a Cloud.

Daggers
Tamer, Ü. You're Not a Man If You Don't Die.

Daisies
Burns, R. To a Mountain Daisy [On Turning One Down, with the Plough, in April—1786].
Frazier, John Alexander, Jr. Audre's Son.
Herrick. To Daisies, Not to Shut So Soon[e].
Meynell, A. To a Daisy.
Morris, W. Love Is Enough.
Probyn. Blossom.
Rossetti, C. Where Innocent Bright-Eyed Daisies Are.
Williams, W. Chicory and Daisies.
Daisy.
Wordsworth, W. To a Child [Written in Her Album].
Zaturenska. Daisy, The.

Dalai Lama
Anderson, L. Wild White Horses.
Zapruder, M. Canada.

Dali, Salvador
Muldoon, P. Salvador.
Oppenheim, M. Dream in Barcelona.
Thribb. In Memoriam Salvador Dali.

Damascus, Syria
MacEwen, G. Damascus.

Damnation and the Damned
Cairns, Scott. Lucifer's Epistle to the Fallen.
Empson. This Last Pain.
Erdrich. Angels.
Graves, R. Song: Lift-Boy.
Hill, G. Ovid in the Third Reich.
Iofe, Y. Thing or Two about Childhood, A.
Mardi, Jas. Good-bye Summer.
Odarchenko. Path I'm following, The.
Raffalovich, M. A. World Well Lost 18, The.
Rimbaud, A. Night in Hell.
Swift, J. Place of the Damned [or Damn'd], The.

Dams
Alexie. Powwow at the End of the World, The.
Guiney. Reason for Silence, A.
Woody. She-Who-Watches . . . The Names Are Prayer.

Danae
Simonides. When in the skillfully welded chest.

Dance of Death
Hwang Insuk. Dance of Death.
Jeffers. Five Note Range of Sorrow.
Tait. On With the Dance! Let Freud Be Unconfined!

Dancing and Dancers
Acorn. Completion of the Fiddle, The.
Adamson, H. Make with the Feet.

Afrika, T. Dancing in my city.
Agosin. Dance, The.
Aini, L. One Girl's Dance.
al-Sa'igh, Y. Tune, The.
Alden, J. Sleepy Time Gal.
Algarin. Dante Park.
El Jibarito Moderno.
Prologue.
Allen, L. Rub a Dub Style inna Regent Park.
Altizer. Sonnet 5: "No, I'll not, carrion, comfort you. Comfort."
Auden. Turn off the wireless.
Automedon. Turkish. Belly-dancer. Sexy tricks.
Baehr, A. I Am Dancing with My Mennonite Father.
Barlow, G. Nook.
Belloc. Tarantella.
Bendall, M. Conversation with Isadora Duncan.
Berke. Fifties Rock Party, 1985.
Berlin. Change Partners.
Cheek to Cheek.
Heat Wave.
Let's Face the Music and Dance.
Bernes, J. Rave.
Bernstein, J. Tango'd Love.
Berry, W. Wheel, The.
Berryman. King David Dances.
Binyon. Little Dancers, The.
Birney. Bear on the Delhi Road, The.
Blue Cloud. Bear: A Totem Dance as Seen by Raven.
Wolf.
Bond, S. Tuesday Night Affair.
Bontemps. Dark Girl.
Brooks, S. Darktown Strutter's Ball, The.
Walkin' the Dog.
Brown, L. Turn On the Heat.
Varsity Drag, The.
Buchanan, G. Theatrical Venus.
Buckley, C. Sleep Walk.
Burris, J. Ballin' the Jack.
Bynner. Snake Dance.
Caddel. Against Numerology.
Caldwell, A. Raggedy Ann.
Campbell, J. Dancer, The.
Caples, G. Targets and Flowers (Begun with Lines from Breton).
Carroll, L. Lobster Quadrille, A.
Cendrars. My Dance.
Chaloner. Waste.
Cho Chihun. Nun's Dance, The.
Chông Hwajin. Dance: "Billions of maggots are being sucked into a whirlpool."
Clampitt. Dancers Exercising.
Clanchy, K. Stance.
Coffman. Cheerleaders.
Comden, B. Conga.
Cooper, A. Stepping to da Muse/Sic.
Cortázar. Normal Behavior of the Famas.
Cortez, J. Heavy Headed Dance, The.
So Many Feathers.
Coward. Nina.
Coyote, Peter. Do you think.
Craighead, L. Dancin' Our Lives Away.
Craven, Jerry. Spring in Palo Duro Canyon.
Cristall. Song: "Come, let us dance and sing."
Crouch, S. Riding across John Lee's Finger.
Cruz e Sousa. Acrobat of Pain.
Cuthand, B. Dancing with Rex.
Cyril. Jump Black Honey Jump Black.
D'Aguiar, F. Now the Two Are One.
Davies, S. Orchestra; or, A Poem[e] of Da[u]ncing.
Speach of Love Persuading Men to Learn Dancing, The.
Davis, T. Boppin' Is Safer Than Grindin'.
Dawes, K. Some Tentative Definitions 4.
Trickster 4 (for Sister Patra).
Deerchild, R. Snag.
DeSylva, B. G. Turn On the Heat.
Varsity Drag, The.
Di Prima. I Ching.
Dickinson, E. I cannot dance upon my Toes.
Dietz, H. Dancing in the Dark.
Dobell, S. Timely Hint, A.
Dorfman, A. Last Waltz in Santiago.

Dove, R. American Smooth.
Planning the Perfect Evening.
Drayton. Dancing Dog, The.
Dubin, A. Forty-second Street.
She's a Latin from Manhattan.
Duncan, R. Presence of the Dance, The / The Resolution of the Music.
Dunn, S. Dancing with God.
Eady. Jazz Dancer.
Johnny Laces Up His Red Shoes.
My Mother, If She Had Won Free Dance Lessons.
Egan, R. Sleepy Time Gal.
Ellington, D. It Don't Mean a Thing (If It Ain't Got That Swing).
Elmslie, K. Girl Machine.
Evasco, M. Dancing a Spell.
Eyen, J. New Dream, A (Wuski A-Baw-Tan).
Ferlinghetti, L. Retired Ballerinas, Central Park West.
Ferré. Ballerina.
Field, R. Dancing Bear, The.
Fields, D. Bojangles of Harlem.
Have Feet, Will Dance.
I Won't Dance.
Never Gonna Dance.
Fusselman, A. Puffy Jacket.
García, D. Turns at the Dance.
Gilbert, C. Directions, The.
Giovanni. Three/Quarters Time.
Glazer, J. Final Disposition.
Green, A. Conga.
Gregg. Dark Thing Inside the Day, A.
Grenfell, J. Stately as a Galleon.
Gurevitch. Everyone's dancing where I live.
Gwala. Attempt at Communication, An.
Jive, The.
Hagedorn, J. Latin Music in New York.
Hahn, K. Izu Dancer, The.
Hahn, S. Nijinsky's Dog.
Halpern, D. Dance, The.
Hamilton, K. At the Frenchman's.
Hammerstein. Shall We Dance?
Hancock, Butch. Circumstance.
Hardy, T. By Her Aunt's Grave.
Harechavi. 1 x 2.
Hart, L. Dancing on the Ceiling.
Ten Cents a Dance.
Hayes, T. At Pegasus.
Healy, E. What It Was Like the Night Cary Grant Died.
Heath, R. Seeing Her Dancing.
Henderson, D. Alvin Cash/Keep on Dancin'.
Henderson, R. Turn On the Heat.
Varsity Drag, The.
Herman, J. Tap Your Troubles Away.
Hernández Cruz. Ironing Goatskin.
Latin and Soul for Joe Bataan.
Loíza Aldea.
Poem: "Think with your body."
Side 12.
Hippolyte. Antonette's Boogie.
Holst-Warhaft. Old Men of Athens, The.
Hopes. Planxty Irwin.
HSü Ling. Dance, The.
Hughes, L. College Formal: Renaissance Casino.
Danse Africaine.
Dream Boogie.
Dream Variation[s].
Jazzonia.
Sunday by the Combination.
Hummell, A. Saraband.
Ilio, D. Marikudo in Kalibo, 1979.
Isherwood. Turn off the wireless.
Ivask, Y. Ode for the Dancing Khlysty.
Iverem, E. Journalist's Convention 1987.
Jacobsen, J. Limbo Dancer, The.
Janzen, J. Chicken Guts.
Jeffers. New Mexican Mountain.
Johnson, A. Joint Is Jumpin', The.
Johnson, H. Bottled [New York].
Johnson, J. Joint is Jumpin', The.
Johnson, J. Saudades.
Johnson, L. Spirit of the Dancer.
Jonson, B. Masque of Christmas, The.

Joseph, A. Junior High Dance.
Soul Train.
Wedding Party.
Kendrick, D. Jenny in Love.
Kennelly. I See You Dancing, Father.
Khazak, Y. Dead in a Bereft Horah.
Kikaku. Sacred night / Through masks.
Koehler, T. Truckin'.
Lal Ded [or Lalla]. Soul, like the moon, The.
Landon. Dancing Girl, The.
Laurencin, M. Zebra, The.
Lear, E. Limerick: "There was an old lady of Chertsey."
Limerick: "There was an Old Man of Whitehaven."
Owl and the Pussy-Cat [or Pussycat], The.
Lerner, A. I Could Have Danced All Night.
Leslie, E. T'ain't No Sin to Dance Around in Your Bones.
Lewis, S. I Wonder Why She Kept on Saying "Si-Si-Si-Si-Senor".
Li Po. For the Dancer of the King of Wu, When She Is Half Drunk.
Intoxication of Love.
Sy-che and the King.
Lightburn, S. Dancing after Sanchez.
Lovelace, R. Gratiana Dancing [or Dauncing] and [or &] Singing.
Lustig, Dana Lisa. Barefoot / Extinguish at Will.
MacEwen, G. Child Dancing, The.
Mack, C. Charleston.
MacKenzie, R. Square.
Magdeburg, Mechthild von. I cannot dance, O Lord.
Magidson, H. Continental (You Kiss While You're Dancing), The.
Major, C. Large Room with Wood Floor.
Majorino. My Flesh in Its Sweat.
Marais. Dance of Sister Rain.
Martí. I am an honest man.
Martinez, D. Death of Isadora Duncan, The.
Mayr, S. Watching a Dance Rehearsal in a Calgary Theatre with a Concrete Floor.
Watching a Dance Rehearsal in a Calgary Theatre with a Concrete Floor 2.
McDonald, W. Songs We Fought For, The.
McKay, C. Harlem Dancer, The.
McKinney, I. Dance, The.
McRay. Performance.
Meireles. Ballad of the Ten Casino Dancers.
Mercer, J. Arthur Murray Taught Me Dancing in a Hurry.
Satin Doll.
Merrill, B. Music That Makes Me Dance.
Merrill, J. Watching the Dance.
Meyer, T. Dancing There.
Mistral, G. Those Who Do Not Dance.
Morton, J. To Hilda Dancing.
Moss, T. Tornados.
Mottram. Zuni Dancers.
Mueller, L. Deaf Dancing to Rock, The.
Mullen, H. Dance She Does, The.
Munom-Ekai. Thunderbolt—eyes wide, A.
Mutén, B. Urania.
Naden. Natural Selection.
Navajo Oral Tradition. Prayer of First Dancers.
Nijhoff. Dancer.
Nye, N. Whole Self, The.
Obejas, A. Dancing in Paradise.
Ogundipe-Leslie. Rain at Noon-time.
Olson, C. Merce of Egypt.
Osterhaus, J. New York Minute.
Page, G. Road Show.
Palmer, M. Noche, Una.
Philp, G. Dance Hall.
Pittman, Al. Another Night in Crawley's Cove.
Pound, E. Dance Figure.
Pratt, M. Other Side, The.
Preston, R. Deep-Sea Bathing (Inna Reggae Dancehall).
Ragan, J. Child Christ at the Top of the Stairs.
Rajendra, C. Prince of the Dance.
Razaf, A. Joint Is Jumpin', The.
Stompin' at the Savoy.
Redmond. Ballad of Black/Essence.

Dance Bodies #1.
Reed, I. Black Cock, The.
Reuental, Neidhart von. "Sing, my golden cock, I'll give thee grain!".
Reynolds, O. Spanish Dancer.
Rhodes, M. Sweeping the Floor.
Riggs, L. Santo Domingo Corn Dance.
Rilke. Spanish Dancer.
Rimbaud, A. In Tsegihi.
Roethke. Four for Sir John Davies.
Rohrer, J. Hotel.
Roland Holst. Being.
Rome, H. Doing the Reactionary.
Rose. Ta Tiopa Maza Win / Iron Door Woman.
Roseliep. EVA Psalm.
Rossiter. Your Body Glistens from the Bath.
Rumaker. Fairies Are Dancing All Over the World, The.
Rumi. Daylight, full of small dancing particles.
Music Master.
Russell, B. Ballerina.
Rylander, E. Dancing on Beethoven's Birthday.
Ryokan. Breeze is fresh, The.
St. John, D. Slow Dance.
Salaam. All Nite Long.
Sappho. In the young spring evening.
Satyanarayana, V. Song of Krishna.
Savageau. Heart.
Seibles, T. Who.
Seiferle, R. Music We Dance To, The.
Sellers, H. In the Kitchen Dancing to Kitty Wells.
Sempill, F. Maggie Lauder.
Sexton. How We Danced.
Shange. Dream of Pairing.
Shepherd, R. Gods at Three A.M., The.
Narcissus Learning the Words to This Song.
Shin Kyŏngnim. Farmer's Dance.
Shouman, M. Dance with Nothing On, with Nobody Around, A.
Shreve, S. Dance.
Siamanto. Dance, The.
Simic. Classic Ballroom Dances.
Sissle, N. Baltimore Buzz.
Smith, P. They Say That Black People.
Soto, Maria Viviana. See! I am dancing!
Spellman, A. Twist, The.
Spencer, B. Castanets.
Egyptian Dancer at Shubra.
Stein, G. Susie Asado.
Stevens, W. Dance of the Macabre Mice.
Life Is Motion.
Synge. On an Island.
Tarpley. Feel Free.
Teasley, L. As Dancers.
Thomas, R. Ensenada Wedding.
Thompson, D. P. Dancing in Menopause.
Tu Fu [or Du Fu]. Ballad on Seeing a Pupil of the Lady Gongsun Dance the Sword Mime.
Coming Home Late at Night.
Turner, C. Country Dance, A.
Tyler, P. Nijinsky.
Unknown. Dancer.
Figaro.
Great War Dance, The.
Mode of France, The.
Old Maid's Reverie, An.
To-morrow shall be my dancing day.
Wooyeo Ball, The.
Van Haren, E. Stepping Out with Edvard Munch ("When from the other world you.").
Van Jordan, A. Dance Lesson, A.
Vasquez, R. At the Rainbow.
Venaille, Franck. In Praise of Robert Desnos.
Verlaine. Streets 1.
Vigil, A. That's the Way, Uh Huh, Uh Huh, I Liked It.
Vogelweide. Dancing Girl.
Voznesensky [or Voznesenskii].
Darkmotherscream.
Portrait of Plisetskaya.
Wagoner, D. Best Slow Dancer, The.
Wakoski. Belly Dancer.
Wallenstein. Blues 2.
Waniek. Diverne's Waltz.
Waters, M. American Bandstand.

Weaver, A. Dancers.
Thelonius.
Wicks, S. Joy.
Rain Dance.
Williams, C. K. Dance, The.
Williams, W. Artist, The.
Dance, The: "In Brueghel's great picture, The Kermess."
Dance, The ("When the snow falls the flakes.").
Danse Russe.
Heel and Toe to the End.
Overture to a Dance of Locomotives.
Wright, C. Why Ralph Refuses to Dance.
Wright, J. Country Dance.
Wright, S. Out of the Wailing.
Wunderlich, M. Take Good Care of Yourself.
Yeats. Fiddler of Dooney, The.
Yi Inbok. Drumbeats.
Yi Sanghûi. Dance: "When I wait."
Yosano Akiko. Dancing Girl, The.
Young, A. Ravel: Bolero.
Young, J. I Wonder Why She Kept on Saying "Si-Si-Si-Si-Senor".
See also **Ballet; Ghost Dances and Ghost Dancers; Waltzes and Waltzing**

Dandelions
Acorn. Ballad of the Pink-Brown Fence, The.
Buson. Dandelions blooming in fives and threes.
Softly she breaks off.
Curry, N. Dandelion.
Flanders, J. Dandelion Greens.
Friedmann. Butterfly, The.
Gerov, Alexander. Dandelion.
Holloway, G. Virtue of Slovenliness, The.
Hoogs, Rebecca. Lion's Teeth.
Mayer, G. Dandelions.
Stanton, W. Dandelions.
Taneda Santoka. This trip.
Whalen, P. Take dandelions first salad.
Wintu Oral Tradition. Dandelion Puffs.

Danger
Antipater of Thessalonica. I've Never Feared.
Aragon. Partial.
Atwood. Daphne and Laura and So Forth.
Auden. Legend.
Belli, G. Night of Terror.
Benjamin, P. Press On.
Borisova, M. Dry birch tree stood, The.
Castillero, S. Jeopard, The.
Jeopardo, El.
Crabbe, G. Delay Has Danger.
Davis, T. Letter to My Mother, Sixteen Years after the Fact.
Denham, Joe. Scotchman Salvage.
Dybek. Daredevil.
Genoways, Ted. Under the Big Top.
Glickman. But till that morning, ain't no one gonna harm you.
Hofer, J. Of Deaths, Days, Futures, Nations ("On the corner of plato and national army a man early.").
Hofmannsthal. Traveller's Song.
Jamie, K. Mother-May-I.
Lomax, M. Gulf.
Meng Chiao. Risks.
Noguchi, R. From Rooftops, Kenji Takezo Throws Himself.
O'Lahsen, M. Dead Erect, The.
Rollings. For Dear Life.
Shakespeare, W. Her father lov'd me; oft invited me.
Snyder, R. Aging Poet, on a Reading Trip to Dayton, Visits the Air Force Museum and Discovers There a Plane He Once Flew, The.
Tu Fu [or Du Fu]. Descending Through Dragon Gate.
Udeozo, O. Tomato.
Unknown. Dangerous Things.
Fish Weeps, The.
I have braided my hair but it has come undone.
Message from your distant lover is the smell of gunpowder, The.
My Army Cross Over.
Volkman. Infernal.
Waldman, A. Admonitions of the Boudoir.

Yesenin [or Essenin]. Horn of doom is blaring!, The.

Daniel (Bible)
Glück, L. Gretel in Darkness.
Rowbotham. Nebuchadnezzar's Kingdom-Come.
Unknown. Didn't My Lord Deliver Daniel?
Lean on the Lord's Side.
O Daniel.

Dante Alighieri
Akhmatova, A. Dante.
Borges. Inferno 1, 32.
Bryant, W. Dante.
Dante Alighieri. But tell me if the man whom I see here.
I have at times seen all the eastern sky.
Inferno.
To course across more kindly waters now.
Eady. Paradiso.
Freeman, Jessica. Part Evil.
Goetsch, D. Nobody's Hell.
Longfellow, H. Dante.
Phillips, C. One sees pictures of Dante.
Ray, H. Dante.
St. John, D. From the Lake.

Danube
Garcilaso de la Vega. Song 3: "Surrounded by the gentle sound."

Daphne
Boland, E. Daphne with Her Thighs in Bark.
Cowley, A. Yoicks! Gone Away!
Fulton, A. Supernal.
Glück, L. Mythic Fragment.
Pound, E. Tree, The.
Waller, E. Story of Phoebus and Daphne Applied, [etc.], The.
Winters, Y. Apollo and Daphne.

Daredevils
Clawson, Jim. Fearless Rider.
Teofilov, Ivan. Teenagers.

Darkness
Addison, L. Umbra.
Adler, L. Geranium Flame.
Aiken, J. Rhyme for Night.
al-Rahim, A. Shadow, A.
Aldis, D. No One Heard Him Call.
Alexander, P. Lightfall.
Alterman, N. First Smile.
Mole, The.
Asekoff, L. Crowdoll.
Barber, D. Small Hours.
Basho. Lightning.
Shrieking plovers / Calling darkness.
Berry, W. 1980 VI.
1985 III.
Bialik. Stars shine and go out.
Bible, *O.T.* Song: "I am dark, daughters of Jerusalem."
Bobrowski. Latvian Songs.
Brodsky, J. I Sit by the Window.
Brontë, E. Spellbound.
Bush, D. Sunday the Power Went Off, The.
Buson. Camellia, The.
Field of mustard, A.
Old well.
Butler, C. E. Darkness, The.
Other Places, The.
Byron, G. Darkness.
Cagnone, N. It lies--when urged to, it lies.
Carew, T. Beautiful Mistress, A.
Ceni, A. Reconciled Flame.
Chapman, G. But dwell in darkness, for your god is blind.
Ch'u Yüan. In the beginning of old.
Cleyre, V. Out of the Darkness.
Cogswell, Fred. Edge, The.
Coleridge, M. Doubt.
Corbière. It's getting dark, little thief of starlight!
Cortes, F. Poem Composed During a Brownout.
Creeley. Anger.
I Know a Man.
Somewhere.
Crevel, R. Nighttime.
Cruz, S. I Know Full Well the Water's Flowing

Power.
Cucchi, M. Like the Chinese, I too am going to.
Cullen, Y. Signals.
Curzon, D. Instructions to a Seed.
Dickinson, E. Lightning is a yellow Fork, The.
Presentiment—is that long Shadow—on the lawn.
We grow accustomed to the Dark.
Dunbar, P. Slow Through the Dark.
Duo Duo. At Parting.
Ellis, T. Shooting Back.
Evans, R. No Moon at All.
Everwine. Perhaps It's as You Say.
Fall, M. Nightstart.
Field. They Shall Look on Him.
Fisher, R. Rules and Ranges for Ian Tyson.
Freneau. Dark was the sky, and not one friendly star.
O'er a dark field I held my dubious way.
Gioia. Insomnia.
Gore-Booth. Vision of Niamh, The.
Greenlaw, L. Five O'Clock Opera.
Guiducci. Delivery.
Gunn, T. Feel of Hands, The.
Gustafsson, L. Ballad of the Dogs.
Gyodai. Inching / From dark to dark—.
Harjo, J. White Bear.
Hart, K. Dark Angel.
Haslam, M. 84 01.
Hatubou, S. Night 1.
Hecht, A. Christmas Is Coming.
Hemphill. Where Seed Falls.
Henry, B. Look Around.
Herd. Survivors, The.
Hickey, E. For Richer, For Poorer.
Hill, G. Masque of Blackness, The.
Hill, J. That's Good, That's Enough.
Hippolyte. Reggae Cat (for Boston Jack).
Hugo, V. Bridge, The.
Izumi. From one darkness.
Way I must enter, The.
Japicx, G. Lovelight.
Jarrell, R. 90 North.
Justice, D. Insomnia of Tremayne, The.
Kim Namjo. Evening Primrose.
Knott. Funny Poem.
Kojijū. On the Spirit of the Heart as Moon-Disk.
Kooser. Late Lights in Minnesota.
Krivulin. Two in a Room.
Kruit, J. Birds Leaving.
Kulishova, I. Total darkness / The light's off in the kitchen.
Lane, P. Lake Murry.
Lao Tzu. Boundless shaping Power, A.
Lawrence, D. H. Young Wife, A.
Lenski, H. Light, my light, who commanded, 'Disappear!
Levertov. Closed World, The.
Lezama Lima. Fragments of the Night, The.
Lindtová, A. Campfire.
Long, H. In the Dark World.
Longfellow, H. Children's Hour, The.
Lowell, J. Darkened Mind, The.
Lux. Dark Comes On in Blocks, in Cubes, The.
MacCaig. Likenesses.
Mann, D. No Moon at All.
Marsman. Polderland.
Martin, C. What the Dark Proposes.
Meinke. Unnatural Light.
Milton. Il Penseroso.
Samson's Complaint.
Miyoshi Toyoichiro. Shadow 1.
Morshen. At the Lighthouse.
Moss, H. Long Island Night, The.
Neruda. Nothing but Death.
Novakovich. Shadow.
O'odham. In the great night my heart will go out.
Songs for the Four Parts of the Night.
Palmer, M. O you in that little bark.
Peck, J. Metal Denser Than, and Liquid, A.
Peterson, J. Stand Still.
Pinsky. City Dark, The.
Poole, R. Dark, The.
Probyn. More Than They That Watch for the

Morning.
Pushkin, A. Lines Written at Night During Insomnia.
Roethke. In a Dark Time.
Rossetti, C. Remember [Me].
Santos Chocano. Indignation.
Satchell. Velvet Blanket.
Schultz, P. Dark Between, The.
Shelley, P. As in that trance of wondrous thought I lay.
Shumyatsher, E. Toye-Voye.
Silva, C. In the Darkness of the Other.
Simic. Night Picnic.
Snyder, G. How Poetry Comes to Me.
Spender, S. Abrupt and charming mover.
Stafford, W. Traveling Through the Dark.
Stoutenburg. Midnight Saving Time.
Strand. Dress, The.
Subbarao, N. Blow Out the Lamp.
Swinburne. Lake of Gaube, The.
Szymborska, W. Four in the Morning.
Thomas, E. Out in the Dark.
Thomas, R. S. Still.
Torres, E. Elbow in Dumberland, An.
Tsvetayeva [or Tsvetaeva]. Last bridge I won't.
Unknown. Mouse, The.
Silk Cotton Tree.
Unknown, fr. Terezin Concentration Camp.
Night in the Ghetto.
Vallejo. Footfalls of a Great Criminal, The.
Van Eeden, F. North Wind, The.
Van Ostaijen. Souvenir.
Villa, E. It is world of the back hune wone it is.
Welch, L. Empress Herself Served Tea to Su Tung-Po, The.
White, J. To Night.
Whitman, S. Past, The.
Raven, The.
Whitman, W. I wander all night in my vision.
Wilbur, R. Beacon, The.
Wright, J. Beginning.
Wroth. Sonnet 8: "Led by the pow'r [or powre] of grief[e], to wailings [or waylings] brought."
Sonnet 19: "Come darkest night, be[e]coming sorrow best."
Sonnet 22: "Like to the Indians, scorched with the sun[ne]."
Wunderlich, M. On Opening.
Wylie. Incantation: "White well, A."
Zukofsky, L. Anew 21.

Darwin, Charles
Bierds, L. Hunter.
Melville, H. Epilogue: "If Luther's day expand to Darwin's year."
Naden. Natural Selection.
Solomon Redivivus, 1886.
Newman, A. Darwin's Unfinished Notes to Emma.
Niedecker. Darwin.
Robinson, A. Darwinism.
Schnackenberg. Darwin in 1881.
See also **Evolution**

Dating
Aytoun [or Ayton], R. Rejection, The.
Song: "What means this strangeness now of late."
Upon His Unconstant Mistress.
Behn, A. On Her Loving Two Equally.
Bouwers. Final Signs, The.
Brown, E. Bitcherel.
Brown, L. Don't Bring Lulu.
Chrystos. I Bought a New Red.
Cooper, D. David Cassidy Then.
Cope, W. Exchange of Letters.
DeFoe, M. Dream Lover.
Dove, R. Planning the Perfect Evening.
Dunbar, P. Negro Love Song, A.
Foerster. Playland.
Goodman, M. Lullabye for a Butch.
Gylys, B. Family Reunion—Aunt Vern's Two Cents.
Harnick. Tonight at Eight.
Mariani. Betty.
Niedecker. Fancy Another Day Gone.
North, D. Platonic.
Parker, D. News Item.

Pollard, C.   I enjoy dancing.
Ralin, Radoi.   Seduced and Abandoned.
Robin, L.   My Cutey's Due at Two-to-Two
  Today.
Rose, B.   Don't Bring Lulu.
Stillman, A.   Jukebox Saturday Night.
Wallace, R.   Sound Systems.
Watson, E.   First Date in Twenty-Five Years.
Wilson, S.   Boy Friend, The.
Wright, C.   Personals.

Daughters
Abu Khalid.   Two Little Girls.
Acholonu.   Dissidents, The.
Addonizio.   Gravity.
Adewale, T.   Olayimika.
Agosin.   When she showed me her photograph.
Ai.   Cockfighter's Daughter, The.
Anyte [or Anytes].   Throwing her arms around
  her dear father.
Arrillaga.   Mariana II.
Bailey, J.   Ceasefire.
Balamani Amma.   To My Daughter.
Baraka, I.   Preface to a Twenty Volume Suicide
  Note.
Barresi.   Prodigal Daughter, The.
Basu, R.   How are you faring, Uma.
Baton, M.   Flight of the Daughter, The.
Belli, G.   Birth.
Ben-Lev, D.   Broken Helix.
Betjeman.   Old Land Dog, The.
Bhāndārī, S.   Menaka says, Hey listen,
  Mountain King.
Bhattācārya, K.   Consulting the omens.
  From her autumn-lotus mouth.
  Here, Queen of the Mountains.
  Hey, Hara, Ganges-Holder.
  Jaya, tell him that Uma will not be sent.
  King of the Mountains is on his way to Hara's
    abode, The.
  My Gauri / You've come home!
  My Uma has come!
  Tell me / What can I do?
  You ask me, Queen, time after time.
Boland, E.   Blossom, The.
  Pomegranate, The.
Booth, P.   First Lesson.
Brooks, G.   Jessie Mitchell's Mother.
Byron, G.   Jephtha's Daughter.
Campbell, D.   Mothers and Daughters.
Campbell, S.   Constant Welcome, The.
Candī, A.   Bring Tara quickly, Mountain.
Carruth, H.   Essay on Death.
  Pittsburgh.
Clarke, A.   Planter's Daughter, The.
Clifton, L.   Admonitions.
  Here is another bone to pick with you.
  I was born with twelve fingers.
  Quilting.
Cofer, J.   Unspoken.
Coleman, H.   Poem for a "Divorced" Daughter.
Coleman, W.   Cousin Mary.
Copus, J.   Second Home.
Cruz, C.   Persephone.
Curtis, T.   Games with My Daughter.
Dove, R.   After Reading *Mickey in the Night
  Kitchen* for the Third Time Before Bed.
Dufferin and Clandeboye.   Mother's Lament,
  The.
Edmond, L.   Tempo.
Eliot, T. S.   Marina.
Evans, E.   Gadafi's Little Daughter.
Fairchild.   Machinist, Teaching His Daughter to
  Play the Piano, The.
Fay, J.   Santorini Daughter.
Galvin, B.   For a Daughter Gone Away.
García, D.   Green Corn Season.
Garcia, R.   Note Folded Thirteen Ways.
Gardinier.   Ghost of Santo Domingo, The.
Garrett, G.   Envoy: "Little poem, the two of us
  know too much."
Garza, E.   Why I Make the Best Barrels.
Gibbons, R.   For My Daughter.
Gilyard, K.   Daughter, That Picture of You.
Gioia.   Counting the Children.
Gomez, M.   Lost Daughter.
Goodison.   I Am Becoming My Mother.

Goyette, Susan.   Peonies, The.
Graves, R.   Frosty Night, A.
Griffin, S.   Daughter.
Hacker, M.   No better lost than any other
  woman.
Hamill, S.   Natural History: "Late afternoon,
  autumn equinox."
Han-shan.   Raise girls but not too many.
Hardie, K.   Young Woman Stands on the Edge
  of Her Life, The.
Harper, M.   Eve (Rachel).
Hashimoto, S.   Standing in the Doorway, I
  Watch the Young Child Sleep.
Herd.   Exhibits, The.
Hogg, J.   Thirteenth Bard's Song, The.
Hope, M.   Praise the Daughter.
Ishikawa Takuboku.   What prompted her.
Issa.   In a dream.
Jackson, L.   Only Daughter, The.
Jamie, K.   Mother-May-I.
Jarrell, R.   Lost Children, The.
Johnson, J.   What Is There For Us?
Jonson, B.   On My First Daughter.
  To Elizabeth, Countess of Rutland.
Joseph, A.   Numbers: "My father taught me to
  measure."
Joyce, J.   Flower Given to My Daughter, A.
Kabysh, I.   Whenever the prodigal son returns
  home.
Kao Ch'i.   Written on Seeing the Flowers, and
  Remembering My Daughter.
Kaufman, S.   Mothers, Daughters.
  Notes to my Daughters.
Kay, E.   Phoenix.
Kees.   For My Daughter.
Kgositsile.   To My Daughter.
Khalvati.   Blue Moon.
Kim Hyesun.   Remembering the Day I Gave
  Birth to a Daughter.
Kingsolver.   Middle Daughter, The.
Kinnell.   Parkinson's Disease.
Kipling, R.   Merrow Down.
Kishkan, T.   Spell for a Daughter.
Kizer, C.   Amusing Our Daughters.
  Thrall.
Knight, E.   Circling the Daughter.
Ko Ŭn.   No-More-Daughters's.
Korinna [or Corinna].   Of your daughters: Zeus,
  Father.
Krysl.   Persephone, to Demeter.
Kumin, M.   Envelope, The.
  Making the Jam without You.
  Seeing the Bones.
Landor, W.   Mother, I Cannot Mind My Wheel.
Larkin, J.   Cold River.
  Legacy.
Laux, D.   Finding What's Lost.
Layton.   Song for Naomi.
Le Guin.   His Daughter.
Livingston, M.   Working with Mother.
Lomax, M.   July.
Longfellow, H.   Wreck of the Hesperus, The.
Lowell, R.   Home After Three Months Away.
Lux.   Little Tooth, A.
Lynch, T.   Skating with Heather Grace.
MacCaig.   Intruder in a Set Scene.
Macpherson, J.   Beauty of Job's Daughters, The.
Madgett.   Offspring.
Martinaitis, M.   Kukutis's Lament under the
  Heavens.
Mayer, G.   Make Believe.
McElroy, C.   In My Mother's Room.
  To Welcome a Changeling.
Meogo.   Cossante.
Metz, R.   Father of the Bride.
Meyer, B.   Ferry to South Baymouth, The.
Meynell, A.   Girl on the Land, The.
Michie, S.   Connecting Light.
Mikha'il, M.   Don't Despair.
Molloy, D.   Looking for Mother.
Moon, K.   Daughter-to-Father Talk.
Moraes, V.   Song: "Never take her away."
Moss, T.   Undertaker's Daughter Feels Neglect,
  The.
Msham.   Daughter, take this amulet.
Mullen, H.   Saturday Afternoon, When Chores

  Are Done.
Muñiz Huberman.   Prodigal Daughter.
Murphy, M.   Occasions.
Mutén, B.   Queen Hera.
Mutis.   You Are a Daughter of the Lagides.
Nikolayeva [or Nikolaeva].   Daughter.
Norris, K.   Persephone.
Ochiai Naobumi.   Song of the Faithful Daughter
  Shiragiku.
Odio, E.   Memory of My Private Childhood.
O'Grady, Thomas.   Prayer for My Daughters, A.
Olds, S.   Her List.
  Quake Theory.
  Quest, The.
Oppen.   Exodus.
  From a Photograph.
Ovid.   Myrrha and Cinyras.
Partnoy, A.   To *El Mingo* (with Whom I Share
  Eva Victoria and Anahi Paz).
Pastan.   To a Daughter Leaving Home.
Paterson, E.   Griselda.
Pelizzon, V.   Wedding Day, The.
Po Chü-i.   Golden Bells.
Prunty.   Learning the Bicycle.
Ransom, J.   Bells for John Whiteside's
  Daughter.
Rexroth, K.   American Century, The.
  Wheel Revolves, The.
Rich, A.   Woman Mourned by Daughters, A.
Rodgers, C.   It Is Deep.
Ruefle.   Public Garden with a Weeping Tree.
St. John, D.   Portrait: "There is in his daughter's
  gaze."
Sappho.   It's no use.
Satyamurti.   Broken Moon.
Seaton, M.   Blonde Ambition.
  Fear of Shoplifting.
Sexton.   Little Girl, My String Bean, My Lovely
  Woman.
Shafiq, H.   Destinies.
Shumaker.   Waitress's Kid, The.
Shurin.   Material's Daughter.
Siddal.   At Last.
Smith, S.   Human Affection.
Someck, R.   Poem for a Daughter Who Is
  Already Born.
Song.   Lost Sister ("In China, / even the
  peasants.").
  Youngest Daughter, The.
Stead, C.   Between.
Steinbergh.   Burial.
Stern, G.   Waving Good-Bye.
Stone, R.   Cabbage, The.
  Seed.
Suárez.   Now That I Have Grown Up, Mother.
Tallmountain.   Brother Wolverine.
Tanikawa, S.   Zoo.
Tennyson, A.   Gardener's Daughter, The.
Thomas, E.   If I Should Ever by Chance.
Unknown.   Hush, little baby, don't say a word.
  Mother-in-law, do not stamp.
  Mu-Lan.
Upton, L.   Destruction of Daughters.
Utting, S.   Spoon Maker's Daughter, The.
Valerie, J.   Astrology?
Van Dyke, C.   Birth, 1975.
Van hee.   December.
Vazirani, R.   Daughter-Mother-Maya-Seeta.
Vertreace, M.   Caged Stone.
Waniek.   Daughters, 1900.
Webster, A.   Her father lessons me I at times am
  hard.
Weems, M.   Dime after Dime.
Whittier.   Farewell, The: "Gone, gone,—sold
  and gone."
Wicks, S.   My Father Is Shrinking.
Wilbur, R.   Writer, The.
Williams, M.   Caterpillar, The.
  Poem for Emily, A.
Wilson, K.   Dusk in My Backyard.
Winters, Y.   Alas, that I should be.
  To My Infant Daughter.
Wright, J.   Eve to Her Daughters.
Yeats.   Prayer for My Daughter, A.
Young, I.   Mermaid Knows, A.

David (Bible)
Abelard. David's Lament for Jonathan.
Benét, S. King David.
Berryman. King David Dances.
Byron, G. Harp the Monarch Minstrel Swept, The.
Drayton. Our sacred Muse, of Israel's Singer sings.
Graves, R. Goliath and David.
Jarrell, R. Bronze David of Donatello, The.
Lamb, C. David in the Cave of Adullam.
Lindsay, V. In Which Roosevelt Is Compared to Saul.
Moore, M. That Harp You Play So Well.
Naylor. Authorship.
Quarles. On Saul and David.
Reznikoff. David.
I Do Not Believe That David Killed Goliath.
Smart, C. Song to David, A.
Steele, T. In the King's Rooms.
Thompson, P. David and Goliath.
Traherne. In Salem Dwelt a Glorious King.
Waddell, P. David and Goliath.

Davis, Bette
Kay, J. Birth and Death of Bette Davis, The.

Davis, Miles
Brathwaite, E. Blues.
DJ Renegade. Subterranean Night-Colored Magus.
Ford, W. Of Miles Davis.
Gordon, G. Tercios del Muerte.
Harper, M. Alone.
Brother John.
Hayes, T. Boxcar.
Hoagland, E. Kinda Blue Miles Davis Died Today.
Jauss. Black Orchid.
Jordan, A. Kind of Blue.
Kaufman, B. Round About Midnight.
Kelly, R. Ode to Language.
Komunyakaa, Y. Boxing Day.
Redmond. Milestone: The Birth of an Ancestor.
Rux, C. H. Shunning an Imperative.
Sundiata. Open Heart.
Whitlow. Poem for the Children.
Williams, B. On the Other Side.

Dawn
Angeles, C. Light Invested.
Bardoloi. Dawn.
Barrow, Raymond. Dawn Is a Fisherman.
Basho. Early dawn.
More than ever I want to see.
Silhouette, A.
Belloc. Early Morning, The.
Bible, O.T. Glory Glory / Psalm 19.
Blue Cloud. Spring Equinox.
Buson. Dawn.
Pure white plum blossoms.
Camões [or Camõens or Camoëns], L. Sonnet: That Sad and Joyful Dawn.
Campbell, R. Mass at Dawn.
Sisters, The.
Ch'in Kuan. Tune: "Sand of Silk-Washing Brook".
Chiyojo. While I was musing on my theme.
Chŏng Hyŏnjong. Blood of Daybreak, The.
Citino. Situation No. 9: The Corposant.
Crapsey. Triad.
Cynewulf. When stars are hid in the western wave, dimmed at dawn.
Dana, R. Daybreak.
Davenant [or D'Avenant]. Lark Now Leaves His Watery [or Wat'ry] Nest.
Davison, P. Equinox 1980.
Dickinson, E. It was a quiet way—.
Drummond, W. Invocation: "Pheobus, arise! / And paint the sable skies."
Dunbar, P. Dawn: "Angel, robed in spotless white, An."
Duo Duo. None.
Ellis, T. Break of Dawn, The.
Fulton, R. Forecast for a Quiet Night.
Gander, F. Macula of Light, A.
Ginsberg, A. Fourth Floor, Dawn, Up All Night Writing Letters.
Graves, R. Return of the Goddess [Artemis].

Grimké, A. Dawn.
Gyodai. Whales / Bellowing dawn.
Hearn, M. At Dawn.
Herlin. Light brush of dawn, A.
Herrera y Reissig. Grey Dawn.
Higginson, E. Dawn.
Dawn on the Willamette.
Homer. Now all day long until the sun went down.
Housman. Reveille.
Howe, F. Edge of the dome is slipping, The.
Hsieh Ling-yün. From Chin-Chu Creek, Past the Ridge, Along the Stream.
Hudgins. Two Ember Days in Alabama.
Huerta, E. Men of Dawn, The.
Hughes, L. Daybreak in Alabama.
Hughes, T. Roe-Deer.
Ibarbourou. Hour, The.
Issa. With my father.
Jaccottet. Dawn.
Daybreak.
Swifts.
Wishes.
Jaimes Freyre. Dawn, The.
Jiménez, J. Dawn brings with it, The.
Dawn Outside the City Walls.
Moon Was Gliding the River, The.
Vigil.
Jones, G. Morning.
Kakei. At the break of dawn.
Kerouac. Birds singing.
Kipling, R. Hunting-Song of the Seeonee Pack.
Lane, P. Spring.
Lewis, A. Dawn on the East Coast.
Li'aibi, S. My days pass with the beads of the rosary.
Soul of a pebble on top of the mountain, The.
Lodge, G. Lower New York.
Loesser. Two Sleepy People.
Longfellow, H. Children's Hour, The.
Daybreak.
Lope de Vega. If You Leave at Daybreak.
Machado Ruiz. Amancer de Otoño.
Mandelstam [or Mandelshtam]. Because I Let Go Your Hands.
Marlowe. Now ore the sea from her old Love comes she.
McKay, C. Dawn in New York.
Meng Hao Jan. Spring Dawn.
Springtime Dawn.
Merwin. How We Are Spared.
Millay, E. Recuerdo.
Mistral, G. Dawn.
Montgomerie, A. Night Is Near [or Neir] Gone, The.
Morris, W. Summer Dawn.
Morter, L. Belizean Dawn, A.
Mullen, L. Alba.
North, C. Dawn, The: "TO BE / Immortal."
Sunrise with Sea Monster.
Parry, R. Miraculous Dawn.
Paz. Dawn.
Percival. Morning among the Hills.
Po Chü-i. On his Baldness.
Starting Early from the Ch'u-ch'ĕng Inn.
Prados, E. I Look into the Sky.
Ray, H. Dawn's Carol.
Reposa, Carol Coffee. Dawn in El Paso.
Rimbaud, A. Dawn.
Rossetti, C. "Kookoorookoo! kookoorookoo!" / Crows the cock before the morn.
St. John, D. Saffron.
Salaam. Sunrise on the River.
Sassoon, S. Invocation: "Come down from heaven to meet me when my breath."
Seferis. Last Day, The.
Shakespeare, W. Hark, hark! the lark at heaven's gate sings.
Sidney. Sonnet 99: "When far-spent night persuades each mortal eye."
Skloot. Closer to Home.
Soyinka. Death in the Dawn.
Stevens, W. Brave Man, The.
Stryk, L. Dawn.
Taneda Santoka. Dawn coming on.
Taylor, B. Paean to the Dawn, A.

Tennyson, A. Dawn, The.
Thomas, D. Light Breaks Where No Sun Shines.
Thomas, E. Cock-Crow.
Trumpet, The.
Thoreau. Guido's Aurora.
Togawa, Akira. Distorted Sun.
Trần Thái-Tông, King. To the Monk Đúc Son at Thanh-phong Monastery.
Tu Fu [or Du Fu]. Dawn Landscape.
Evening Shower in Spring, An.
Going to the Palace with a Friend at Dawn.
Kindly Rain, The.
Spring Night, Happy Rain.
Unknown. Alba ("When the nightingale to his mate").
Alba, With a Refrain from the Provençal.
Aubade.
Dawn Has Arisen, Our Welfare Is Assured.
En un Vergier Soiz Folha D'Albespi.
First Daylight Song.
I Think Over Again My Small Adventures.
Kill That Crowing Cock.
Last Daybreak Song.
Last Song of the Exploding Stick.
Rooster is already announcing dawn, The.
She likes it, the conjugal act.
White light of dawn grows wider, The.
Unknown, fr. Terezin Concentration Camp.
Night in the Ghetto.
Vanshenkin. We came back late from visiting.
Vaughan, H. Cock-crowing.
Very. Fair Morning, The.
Wagoner, D. Five Dawn Skies in November.
Walsh, E. Dawning of the Day, The.
Wang Wei. Dawn on the Mountain.
Warren, R. Dawn.
Masts at Dawn.
Watson, R. Aubade: "Lights are out in the street, and a cool wind swings, The."
Westmorland. Reveille Matin, or Good Morrow to a Friend.
Whitehead, C. Daybreak.
Morning Thesis.
Williams, W. Chinese Nightingale.
Dawn.
Wright, C. Saturday 6 a.m.
Xiao Zihui. Winter Dawn.
Yeats. Dawn, The.
Yi Hyangji. Acromatic Dawn.
March of Dawn, The.
Sunrise: "Blood stolen from my body before dawn."
Yüan Chĕn. Nearly a Sky Half Clear, Not Yet Half Light.
Zagajewski. At Daybreak.

See also **Morning; Sunrise**

Day
Adamson, H. It's a Most Unusual Day.
Azzawi, F. Unknown Man, The.
Barba-Jacob. Song of the Fleeting Day.
Barbauld. Tomorrow.
Barbour, D. It's a Good Day.
Belloc. Early Morning, The.
Beranová, J. Williamsbridge.
Bourdillon. Night Has a Thousand Eyes, The.
Bu-er. Cut brambles long enough.
Buson. Day slow in going, A.
In the white plum blossoms.
Spring sea rising, The.
Cahn, S. Day by Day.
Carroll, J. Burning of Bustin's Island, The.
Cummings, E. E. Hours rise up putting off stars and it is, The.
Out of midsummer's blazing most not night.
Darío, R. Tropical Afternoon.
De Mello Breyner. Day of Sea.
Dickinson, E. First Day's Night had come, The.
Doolittle, H. Mid-day.
Dowson. Vesperal.
Drummond de Andrade. Elegy: "I've won (lost) my day."
Emerson, R. Days.
Eskimo Oral Tradition. Song: "And I thought over again."
Groarke, V. Tonight of Yesterday.

Guidacci. Before Our Encounter.
Hennen. Life of a Day, The.
Hernández Cruz. Thursday.
Herrick. Dream[e]s.
Hesketh. Love's Advocate.
Issa. No talent.
 Spring day, The.
 Treated shabbily / by fleas, by flies.
Jiménez, J. Daybreak.
Kagawa Kageki. While reading.
Kimball, H. In Reverie.
Kipling, R. Morning Song in the Jungle.
Lanier, S. Song for "The Jacquerie".
Larkin, P. Days.
Lee, P. It's a Good Day.
Levertov. Celebration.
 Variation on a Theme by Rilke.
Martí. I Dream Awake.
Molina, E. As the Great Days Flow.
Motherwell. Jeanie Morrison.
Neruda. If Each Day Falls.
 Leaning into the Afternoons.
Owen, G. Gathering in the Days.
Petrarch. For Whatever Animals Dwell On Earth.
Porta. Dialogue with Herz.
Prynne. Of Movement towards a Natural Place.
Robertson, Lisa. Tuesday.
Romo-Carmona, M. Daylight.
Rossetti, C. "Kookoorookoo! kookoorookoo!" / Crows the cock before the morn.
Rumi. This is such a day: the sun is dazzling twice as before.
Salaam. Height, Breadth, Depth.
Schierbeek. Sun, The: Day.
Sigourney. Advertisement of a Lost Day.
Somoza, J. Day Break.
Stevenson, R. Bed in Summer.
 Moon, The.
Stidger. Day, A.
Thoreau. Guido's Aurora.
Volkman. Sonnet: "Tilt the placeless waver of this moving."
Wilbur, R. Death of a Toad, The.

Daydreams
Ashbery, J. Instruction Manual, The.
 Mixed Feelings.
Bishop, E. End of March, The.
Brontë, E. Little while, a little while, A.
Coleridge, M. Day-dream, A.
Crapsey. Laurel in the Berkshires.
Cross, E. Fabulación.
 Fabulation.
Denham, Joe. Setting.
Foster, S. Jeanie with the Light Brown Hair.
Hahn, S. Her Purse, at the Winter Solstice.
Harrison, G. Playground, The.
Hecht, A. Hill, A.
Jones, J. Watching the Wheat.
Lehman. November 19.
Machado Ruiz. Daydreams Have Endlessly Turning Paths.
Nash, O. Spring Comes to Murray Hill.
Robinson, E. Miniver Cheevy.
Safie, D. Meditation by the Xerox Machine.
"Shu Ting.". Bits of Reminiscence.
Unknown. Drinking Wine.
"Vaidehi.". Girl in the Kitchen.
Valéry. Girl with Mind Wandering.
Wright, C. Poet Grows Older, The.

See also **Dreams and Dreaming**

de Beauvoir, Simone
Perillo, L. Deuxieme Sexe, La.

De Hooch, Pieter
Tomlinson, C. Paring the Apple.

De la Mare, Walter
Untermeyer, L. Walter de la Mare Tells the Listener about Jack and Jill.

De Soto, Hernando
Harjo, J. New Orleans.
Van Doren. Distant Runners, The.

Dead Sea, The
Armitage, S. Dead Sea Poems, The.

Deafness
Baranczak, S. N. N. Tries to Remember the

 Words of a Prayer.
Davies, E. Portrait of Auntie Blodwen.
DeNiord, C. This Is a Blessing, This Is a Curse.
Jones, B. Beethoven's Ears.
 Conversation of the Deaf, The.
Jungkwan Ilson. To an Old, Deaf, and Blind Monk.
Levitt, Peter. Though she is deaf.
Mandelstam [*or* Mandelshtam]. I Am Deaf.
Marston, P. Speechless: Upon the Marriage of Two Deaf and Dumb Persons.
Mueller, L. Deaf Dancing to Rock, The.
Murray, L. Hearing Impairment.
Nguyễn Khuyến. Man Who Feigns Deafness, The.
Page, P. Deaf-Mute in the Pear Tree.
Ryan, R. Deafness.
Salzman, E. Conch.
Smith, George Jay. When Helen Keller Spoke.
Stevenson, A. On Going Deaf.
Wiman, C. Hearing Loss.
Wright, D. On Himself.

Dean, James
Jones, R. James Dean.
Like, J. James Dean and the Pig.
Oliphant. Too talented to give a hot damn.

Death and the Dead
Aafjes. Last Letter, The.
Abbey, L. Broken Silence.
Abdul Karim. Nightmare 1.
 Nightmare 3.
Abercrombie. Epitaph: "Sir, you should notice me: I am the Man."
Abse. Carnal Knowledge.
 Lunch and Afterwards.
 Millie's Date.
 Pathology of Colours.
 Peachstone.
 Winter Visit, A.
Abu Dhu'ayb al-Hudhali. Lament for Five Sons Lost in a Plague.
Acholonu. Going Home.
Adams, L. Death and the Lady.
Adamson. My House.
Adcock, F. Poem Ended by a Death.
Addonizio. Night of the Living, Night of the Dead.
Adnan. There is a word that never.
Adonis [*or* Adunis]. New Noah, The.
 Tree of Fire.
Aeschylus. For Ares, gold-exchanger for the dead.
Agard, J. For Bob Marley.
Agosin. Disappeared Woman V.
Ågren, G. Death's Secret.
Agustini. Ineffable, The.
 Shadow Beds.
 To Death, from the Genie of My Poetry.
"Agyeya.". Hiroshima.
Ai. Deserter, The.
 Mortician's Twelve-year-old Son, The.
Aichinger. Enumeration.
Aiken, C. Tetélestai.
Aini, L. In Their House.
 Liquidation.
Akers. Dead, The: "Dead come, looking for their shoes, The."
Akhmatova, A. Dedication.
 In Memory of M. B.
 Requiem.
 So, I Remained Alone.
 We Do Not Know How to Say Goodbye.
al-Mala'ika, N. Elegy for a Woman of No Importance.
al-Rahim, A. Who Are You?
al-Saygh, S. White Sleep.
Alarcon, F. Blues del SIDA / AIDS Blues.
Alberti. Punishments.
Aldington. Choricos.
Aldrich, T. Lycidas.
 Memory.
Alegría. Desire.
 From the Bridge.
 Have Pity.
 I Am Root.
 Silence.

 We Were Three.
Alexie. One Stick Song.
 Theology.
Allingham, W. Dream, A [*or* The].
 No funeral gloom, my dears, when I am gone.
Alterman, N. First Smile.
 Mole, The.
Alvarez, J. How I Learned to Sweep.
Amichai, Y. Death of My Father, The.
 I have nothing to say about the war.
 Is all this sorrow? I don't know.
 Lips of the dead once thoughtlessly.
 Little Ruth.
 Summer or Its Ending.
Amiel. Death Is a Matter of Mathematics.
Amir, D. I Have Longings for My Dead.
 Thoughts about Sari's Jump.
Amis, K. Last War, The.
Ammianus. Epitaph of Nearchos.
Ammons. Play.
Anderson, J. Re-member Us.
Anderson-Thompkins. To Love a Stranger.
Andrews, M. Elegy on the Death of Mr Sterne.
Aneirin. Gorcheanu: The Three Laments.
Antokolsky. You share your mourning with all Moscow. There.
Anwar, C. Me.
 Twilight at a Little Harbor.
Anyte [*or* Anytes]. I mourn maiden Antibia: desiring her, many.
 Instead of bridal bed and holy wedding songs.
 This Manes alive once was a slave; now dead.
 Throwing her arms around her dear father.
 Youth buried you, Captain; as sons for their mother, The.
Argensola, de, L. L. Damon's Lament for His Clorenda, Yorkshire, 1654.
Aridjis. Epitaph for a Poet.
Arnold, M. Memorial Verses.
 Requiescat.
 Thyrsis.
Arp. Kaspar Is Dead.
Asclepiades. Here Lies Archeanassa.
Asekoff, L. Will.
Aston, A. Everything in the Garden Is Lovely.
Atkins, R. Narrative.
Atwood. Dufferin, Simcoe, Grey (4).
 Four Small Elegies.
 This Is a Photograph of Me.
Auden. As I Walked Out One Evening.
 Death's Echo.
 In Memory of W. B. Yeats.
 O What Is That Sound [Which So Thrills the Ear].
 Song: "Stop all the clocks, cut off the telephone."
Austin, A. Go away, Death!
Awoonor. Song of War.
 Songs of Sorrow.
Aytoun [*or* Ayton], R. On the Prince's Death, to the King.
Bachmann. Early Noon.
Baiho. On Entering His Coffin.
Baker, D. Puritan Way of Death, The.
Balaban. News Update.
Bancquart. Baroque.
 Counterfable of Orpheus.
 Epitaph.
 Town.
 Vanished, The.
Bang, M. Crossed-Over, Fiend-Snitched, X-ed Out.
Baraka, I. Clay.
 Incident.
 Invention of Comics, The.
Baraka, R. For the Brothers Who Aint Here.
Barbauld. Life's "Good-Morning".
Bard, W. E. Seventh Seal, The.
Barkova, A. Few Autobiographical Facts, A.
Barlow, G. Mingus Speaks: Found Poems.
Barnes, W. Mater Dolorosa.
 Wife a-Lost, The.
Barrax. Scuba Diver Recovers the Body of a Drowned Child, The.
Basho. Buddha's death-day / Old hands.
 Fish shop.

Many nights on the road.
Sick on a journey.
Sick on my journey.
Summer grasses / All that remains.
Tomb, bend / To autumn wind—.
Tremble, oh my gravemound.
Battin, Wendy (b. 1953). Mondrian's Forest.
Baudelaire. Carcass, A.
Carcass, A.
Cracked Bell, The.
Spleen LXXVI.
Baugh, E. Carpenter's Complaint, The.
Baxter, J. East Coast Journey.
Ikons, The.
Beaumont, F. *et al.* Aspatia's Song.
Beaver. Three images of dying stick in my mind like morbid transfers.
Becker, R. Crypto-Jews, The.
Beckett, S. Song: "Age is when to a man."
Beckman, J. Lament for the Death of a Bullfighter.
Bedient, C. When the Gods Put on Meter.
Beer, P. Grave Doubts.
Lemmings.
Beerbohm, M. On the Imprint of the First English Edition of "The Works of Max Beerbohm".
Behn, A. On the Death of the Late Earl of Rochester.
Behn, R. Like a Horse.
On Being Asked My Opinion About an Autopsy.
Bejerano, M. I Made a New Memory for You.
Oh spare me, spare me.
Bek, T. I breathed my fill—and then breathed out.
Belieu. Nocturne: My Sister Life.
Sleeping Man Must Be Awakened to Be Killed, A.
Bell, C. Lying in Small Pieces.
Bell, M. Book of the Dead Man #33, The.
Book of the Dead Man #43, The.
Book of the Dead Man #87, The.
Book of the Dead Man (#13), The.
Someone Is Probably Dead.
Belli, C. Why Have They Moved Me.
Belloc. Obiter Dicta.
Statue, The.
Bendall, M. Conversation with Isadora Duncan.
Bensko. Bones of Lazarus.
Last Look in the Sambre Canal, A.
Bently, S. River Dove, The: a Lyric Pastoral.
Berg, S. Nostalgia.
Berger, J. Between Worlds.
Berggolts [*or* Bergholts]. Don't turn around, don't look back.
Wish, A.
Bernlef. Uncle Charles: A Home Movie.
Bernstein, C. Cup of Coffee, The.
Profaning the Dead.
Berrigan, T. Dear Margie, hello. It is 5:15 a.m.
Last Poem.
Sonnet I: "His piercing pince-nez. Some dim frieze."
Berry, W. Dark with power.
Morning's News, The.
Ripening.
Slip, The.
Sparrow.
Sycamore, The.
Wheel, The.
Berryman. 324. Elegy for W. C. W., the Lovely Man, An.
Henry sats in de bar and was odd.
89. Op. Posth. No. 12.
To My Father.
Bertrans de Born. Planh for the Young English King.
Bethune, L. For Singing In Good Mood.
Harlem Freeze Frame.
Betjeman. Before the Anæsthetic; or, A Real Fright.
City.
Cottage Hospital, The.
Death in Leamington.
House of Rest.

Inevitable.
Remorse.
Bevington, L. Twilight.
Bhattācārya, K. Who is this enchantress.
Bhattācārya, M. Ma, are you really dead?
Bialik. Orphanhood.
Bibbins, M. Mud.
Bidart. Sacrifice, The.
To the Dead.
Yoke, The.
Bidgood. Burial Path.
Bienek. Exodus.
Our Ashes.
Vorkuta.
Bierce. General B. F. Butler.
Here Stanford lies, who thought it odd.
Year's "Casualties", A.
Binyon. Now is the time for the burning of the leaves.
Unreturning Spring, The.
Bion. Lament for Adonis.
Bishop, E. First Death in Nova Scotia.
Man-Moth, The.
Bishop, J. Dream, The: "And once again I was within that house."
Blagden. To George Sand on Her Interview with Elizabeth Barrett Browning.
Blake, W. Epitaph, An: "I was buried near this dyke [*or* Dike]."
Little Boy Lost, The.
Sick Rose, The.
Blaser. Ruler, The.
Blaustein, N. Water and Light.
Blight. Death of a Whale.
Blind. Dead, The.
Blue Cloud. Ochre Iron.
Bluger, M. In Oak.
Bly, R. Looking at New-Fallen Snow from a Train.
Things My Brother and I Could Do.
Week after Your Death, A.
Bodenheim. Death.
Bodman. What rich profusion here.
Bogan, L. My Voice Not Being Proud.
Boland, E. Anna Liffey.
Bolton, J. In Memory of the Boys of Dexter, Kentucky.
Boncho. Piled for burning/ Brushwood.
Bond, B. Transparencies.
Bonnefoy. De Natura Rerum.
Booth, P. Sixty-Six.
Borges. Enigmas, The.
Limits.
Limits (or Good-byes).
Borson. After a Death.
Boruch. Elegy: "Before the basil blackened. Before plates."
Boss, L. Candy Lady, The.
Boutens. Lonely Night.
Bowers, E. Elegy, An: December, 1970.
Bowers, N. Dead Man Interview.
Bowles, W. On the Death of William Linley, esq.
Bowling, T. Morenz.
Boyle, K. To a Seaman Dead on Land.
Bracho, C. Sediment of Lukewarm and Radiant Rain.
Bradstreet, A. Before the Birth of One of Her Children.
Epitaph on my Dear and Ever Honored Mother Mrs. Dorothy Dudley.
Here sleeps the Queen, this is the royall bed.
In Memory of My Dear Grandchild Anne Bradstreet Who Deceased June 20, 1669, Being Three Years and Seven Months Old.
To My Dear and Loving Husband.
To the Memory of My Dear and Ever Honored Father Thomas Dudley Esq. Who Deceased July 31, 1653, and of His Age 77.
Braithwaite. House of Falling Leaves, The.
Brant, B. Stillborn Night.
Braschi. Final Manuscript.
Brass. There Isn't Any Death.
Brathwaite, E. Ancestors.
Breidenbach, T. Confessional.
Brewer, G. Teen Drowns in Rehabilitation

Camp Days Before 17th Birthday, Questions Persist.
Transport of the Dead.
Breytenbach. Out There.
Threat of the Sick.
Bridges, R. When Death to Either Shall Come.
Bringhurst. For the Bones of Josef Mengele, Disinterred June 1985.
Brontë, A. Night.
Brontë, C. Diving.
Is this my tomb, this humble stone.
On the Death of Anne Brontë.
On the Death of Emily Jane Brontë.
Reason.
Young Man Naughty's Adventure.
Brontë, E. Aye there it is! It wakes tonight.
Come, walk with me.
Death Scene, A.
Long Neglect Has Worn Away.
Night Wind, The.
No Coward Soul is Mine.
Remembrance: "Cold in the earth—and the deep snow piled above thee!"
Song: "Linnet in the rocky dells, The."
Brooke, R. Great Lover, The.
Hill, The.
Peace.
Soldier, The: "If I should die, think only this of me."
Sonnet: "Oh! Death will find me, long before I tire."
Brooks, G. Boy Died in My Alley, The.
In Honor of David Anderson Brooks, My Father.
Last Quatrain of the Ballad of Emmett Till, The.
Medgar Evers.
Mentors.
Of De Witt Williams on His Way to Lincoln Cemetery.
Old Relative.
Rites for Cousin Vit, The.
Still Do I Keep My Look, My Identity.
We Real Cool.
White Troops Had Their Orders but the Negroes Looked Like Men.
Broumas, O. Choir, The.
On Earth.
Brown, A. Assassination of Charlie Parker, The.
Brown, E. Jezebel to the Eunuchs.
Brown, G. Kirkyard.
Brown, S. Conjured.
Sister Lou.
Browne, E. When I Am Dead.
Browne, W. On the Countess Dowager of Pembroke.
Browning, E. Grief.
L. E. L.'s Last Question.
Mother and Poet.
Sleep, The.
Thought for a Lonely Death-Bed, A.
Browning, R. Bishop Orders His Tomb at Saint Praxed's Church, The.
Evelyn Hope.
Lost Leader, The.
Prospice.
Brutus. Endurance.
Bryan, M. To———: "O timeless guest!—so soon returned art thou."
Bryan, S. Beyond Recall.
Bryant, W. Death of Lincoln, The.
Death of the Flowers, The.
So live, that when thy summons comes to join.
Thanatopsis.
To the Fringed Gentian.
Buchanan, G. Jill's Death.
Buckley, V. In the faint blue light.
Buckmaster. Seed.
Buffoni, F. And in the end, the entire earth may answer to a single name.
Bukowski. Eulogy to a hell of a dame.
I Am Dead But I Know the Dead Are Not Like This.
Bulich, V. From My Diary, 3.
Bun-Etsu. Sixty-five years.
Bunan. When you're both alive and dead.
Bunin. Flowers, and tall-stalked grasses, and a

bee.
Bunting. Remember, imbeciles and wits.
  To Violet.
Burns, Ralph. Fishing in Winter.
Burns, Robert. Highland Mary.
  Man Was Made to Mourn, a Dirge.
  Prayer, in the Prospect of Death, A.
Busia, A. Exiles.
Buson. It pierces through me.
  Mourning for Hokuju Rosen.
  Scattering bloom, The.
  Sudden chill, A / In our room my dead wife's.
  Winter rain on moss.
  Winter warbler.
Bynner. Donald Evans.
Byrd, Bobby. On Karma at 9.11.85.
Byron, G. Aristomenes.
  Destruction of Sennacherib, The.
  If Sometimes in the Haunts of Men.
  Last Words on Greece.
  Love and Death.
  Manfred.
  One Struggle More, and I Am Free.
  To Thyrza.
Caballero-Robb, M. Memoranda for Rosario.
Cabral de Melo Neto. Cemetery in Pernambuco:
  Our Lady of Light.
  Two of the Festivals of Death.
Caddel. Against Numerology.
Cagnone, N. General names, no other.
Cakrabartī, N. Can you claim to win.
Callimachus. Here Philip the father buried.
  Someone told me, Heraclitus.
  Would that there had never been swift ships!
Cami, B. You Stand.
Camões [or Camoëns or Camoëns], L. Battle's
  uncertain work begins; and move.
  Do This Favour For Me.
  On a Shipmate, Pero Moniz, Dying at Sea.
Campbell, J. Dancer, The.
Campbell, T. Hohenlinden.
  Last Man, The.
Campert, J. Eighteen Dead, The.
Campert. Avignon.
Campo. El Día de los Muertos.
  Her Final Show.
  Jane Doe #2.
Carbó, N. Verso Libre.
Cardenal. For Those Dead, Our Dead.
Carew, T. Another [On the Duke of
  Buckingham].
  Elegy upon the Death of the Dean of [St.]
    Paul's, Dr. John Donne, An.
  Maria Wentworth.
Carrera Andrade. Second Life of My Mother.
Carroll, J. Maybe I'm Amazed.
Carruth, H. Bearer, The.
  Crucifixion.
  Essay on Death.
  Paragraph 36.
  Quality of Wine.
Carson, A. Epitaph: Zion.
Casey, M. LZ Gator Body Collector, The.
Cassells. Courtesy, A Trenchant Grace, A.
Castellanos. Origin.
  Return, The.
Castillo, A. Nani Worries about Her Father's
  Happiness in the Afterlife.
Caston, A. Burden, The.
Castro, R. Ailing Woman Felt Her Forces Ebb,
  The.
  Feeling Her End Would Come with Summer's
    End.
Cather, W. Macon Prairie.
Catullus. Sun May Set, The.
Causley. By St. Thomas Water.
  Death of a Poet.
  Song of the Dying Gunner A.A.1.
Cavalli. Ah, yes, to your misfortune.
Cavendish, M. Common Fate of Books, The.
  Woman drest by Age, A.
Cawein. Uncalled.
Celan. Aspen Tree.
  Death Fugue.
  Death Fugue, A.
  Deathfugue.

Fugue of Death.
  Profuse announcement.
  When you lie.
  You were my death.
Ceraman Kottampalattut. Great It May Be.
Ceravolo. Autumn-Time, Wind and the Planet
  Pluto.
Cernuda. I don't want to return a sad spirit.
  Nocturnal, you sword-fight.
  You were a tender desire, an insinuating cloud.
Césaire, A. In Memory of a Black Union
  Leader.
Chamberlain, B. Dead Ponies.
  Islandman.
Chang Chi. Elegy: "We carved our names."
Chang, E. Bamboo Elegy: Two.
Chapman, G. Death Described by His True
  Effects.
  Homer and the Brazen Head of Rumour.
Chaucer. Experience, though noon auctoritee.
  Song of Troylus, The.
Chedid, A. Imagine.
Chenette, S. Ritual.
Cheney-Coker. Letter to a Tormented
  Playwright.
Cherokee Oral Tradition. Formula to Cause
  Death.
Chester, T. Candle at Canterbury, A.
Chesterfield. On Lord Ila's Improvements, near
  Hounslow Heath.
Chimombo. Four Ways of Dying.
Chin. Elegy for Chloe Nguyen.
Chinnov. Instance of fore-ordained harmony,
  An.
Chisholm, A. Contact.
Chitsu. No more head shaving.
Chiu Tsz-yung. Lament for Fortune's Frailty, A.
Chivers. Avalon.
Chock. Poem for George Helm: Aloha Week
  1980.
Ch'oe Kinam. Elegy to Myself.
Chŏnggam, Great Master. At the Moment of
  My Death.
Chu Yohan. Life, Death.
Ch'u Yüan. Summons of the Soul, The.
Chudakov. Suicide is a duel with yourself.
Ciardi, J. Death's the Classic Look.
Cisneros, A. To a Dead Lady.
Cisneros, S. I Am on My Way to Oklahoma to
  Bury the Man I Nearly Left My Husband For.
Clanchy, K. Deadman's Shoes.
Clare, J. I Am.
  To the Memory of John Keats.
Clark Bekedermo. Death of a Lady.
  Family Procession, A.
  Order of the Dead, The.
Clark, P. Kleptomaniac.
Clarke, G. Marged.
Claus. Tollund Man.
Clementelli. Moviola.
Clifton, H. Death of Thomas Merton.
Clifton, L. Death of thelma sayles, The.
  Sam.
  Sorrow Song.
Clough. *Dulce* it is, and *decorum,* no doubt, for
  the country to fall, to.
  Epi-strauss-ium.
Clover, J. There Is the Body Lying in State.
Cofer, L. Lesson of the Teeth, The.
  My Grandfather's Hat.
Coleridge, M. But in That Sleep of Death What
  Dreams May Come?
  Death.
  I envy not the dead that rest.
  Witch, The.
Coleridge, S. Epitaph: "Stop, Christian passer-
  by!—Stop, child of God."
  Koskiusko.
  Ne Plus Ultra.
Coleridge, S. Father! no amaranths e'er shall
  wreathe my brow.
Collier, M. Robert Wilson.
Collins, B. Dead, The.
  Memento Mori.
  Tomes.
  Writing in the Afterlife.

Collins, W. How Sleep the Brave.
Conway, J. Weight Belt.
Cook, E. Song of the Rushlight.
  Written at the Couch of a Dying Parent.
Cook-Lynn. My Grandmother's Burial Ground.
Cooke, P. Florence Vane.
Cooper, D. Dreamt Up.
  Drugs.
  10 Dead Friends.
Cooper, J. Faithful, The.
  Hotel de Dream.
  Long, Disconsolate Lines.
Cope, J. Solstice for John.
Copus, J. Clothes, The.
Corbet [or Corbett]. On the Lady Arabella.
Corcoran. When Suzy Was.
Cording. Elegy for John, My Student Dead of
  AIDS.
Cornford, F. Watch, The.
Corso. Mad Yak, The.
Cothi. Lament for Siôn y Glyn.
Cotton, C. Epitaph on M. H., An.
Coulehan, J. Azalea Poem, The.
Cowley, A. It was a dismal and a fearful night.
  On the Death of Mr. Crashaw.
  On the Death of Mr. William Hervey [or
    Harvey].
Cowper, W. Epitaph on a Hare.
Crabbe, G. Peter Grimes.
Crane, H. Broken Tower, The.
  Circumstance, The.
  Praise for an Urn.
Crane, S. Behold, the grave of a wicked man.
  If I should cast off this tattered coat.
  There is a grey thing that lives in the tree-tops.
Crapsey. Lonely Death, The.
  Moon-Shadows.
Crase. There Is No Real Peace in the World.
Crashaw. Epitaph upon Husband and Wife Who
  Died and Were Buried Together, An.
Crawford, R. Downtown Sunday.
Creeley. After Lorca.
  For My Mother: Genevieve Jules Creeley.
  Heroes.
  Mother's Voice.
  Road, The.
  World, The.
Cristall. Elegy: "Wander, my troubled soul, sigh
  mid the night thy pain."
  Song: "Both gloomy and dark was the shadowy
  night."
Crozier, A. Blank Misgivings.
Cruz, S. I Live and Do Not Live in Myself.
Csoori. Thin, Black Band, A.
Cucchi, M. Like the Chinese, I too am going to.
  You said: it's hot tonight.
Cullar, Carol. He's Crossed the River.
Cullen, C. Brown Girl Dead, A.
  For Hazel Hall, American Poet.
Cummings, E. E. Buffalo Bill's Lament.
  Nobody loses all the time.
  Since feeling is first.
  Sonnet IV.
  When God Lets My Body Be.
Cuney. Death Bed, The.
Cunningham, J. Epigram: "Here lies my wife.
  Eternal peace."
  Life flows to death as rivers to the sea.
Curry, N. St Kilda.
Cust. Non Nobis.
Cynddelw Brydydd Mawr. Poem on His Death-
  Bed.
Daichu. Fiery unicorn snapped, The.
Daie-Soko. Life's as we / Find it—death too.
Daisen. All things come apart.
Dalton, A. Dad-Baby, The.
Dalton, R. Soldier's Rest.
Dana, R. Dying Raven, The.
  Husband's and Wife's Grave, The.
Daniels, K. Ethiopia.
Dankyo-Myorin. Coming, I clench my hands.
Darío, R. Marguerite.
Darley. Pass of Death, The.
Darr. At Sixteen.
Darwish, M. Guests on the Sea.
Daumal. Short Revelation Concerning Death

and Chaos.
Davidson, D. Lines for a Tomb.
Redivivus.
Davidson, L. Charnel Ship, The.
Davies, I. At Branwen's Grave.
Davies, W. H. Bed-Sitting Room, The.
Davitt. Mirror, The.
Dawe, B. Family Man, The.
Going.
On the Death of Ronald Ryan.
Day, J. Man's Natural Infirmity.
Day Lewis. Reconciliation.
De Angelis. July Has Come for the Dead.
de Burgos. Poem of My Sleeping Sorrow.
Poem to My Death.
De Coninck, H. Ballad of Indolence.
de Folgar. Nocturnal.
Panorama.
De Kok. Al Wat Kind Is.
Our Sharpeville.
Small passing.
Transfer.
De la Mare. Autumn.
Epitaph, An: "Here lies a most beautiful lady."
Fare Well.
Motley.
Shubble, The.
Silver Penny, The.
Slim Cunning Hands.
De Mello Breyner. I Feel the Dead.
Small Square, The.
De Vere, E. Poem: "Were I a king, I could
command content."
Deane, S. Burial, A.
DeFrees. Census of Animal Bodies: Driving
Home.
Letter to an Absent Son.
Degentesh. 5-Year-Old Girls Encountered.
Delgado, J. Winter Fruit.
Denham. Song, A: "Morpheus, the humble god,
that dwells."
Dennis, C. St. Francis and the Nun.
Désiré, J. Dream: "Last night in sleep."
Philosophy, A.
Desnos. Epitaph: "I lived in those times. For a
thousand years."
Di Prima. Death Poems in September.
Death Sunyata Chant: A Rite for Passing Over.
For the Dead Lecturer.
Diaz-Duque. Why Don't I?
Dickey, J. Hospital Window, The.
Sled Burial, Dream Ceremony.
Dickey, W. Cassandra.
Death of John Berryman,The.
Plot, The.
Dickinson, E. Admirations—and Contempts—
of time, The.
After a hundred years.
Bereavement in their death to feel.
Brain, within its Groove, The.
Bustle in a House, The.
By a departing light.
Choice.
Color, Caste, Denomination.
Death is a Dialogue between.
Death is the supple Suitor.
Do People moulder equally.
Dropped into the Ether Acre.
Dust is the only Secret.
Flags Vex a Dying Face.
He fought like those Who've nought to lose.
He fumbles at your Soul.
Heart asks Pleasure—first, The.
How many times these low feet staggered.
I died for Beauty—but was scarce.
I Felt a Funeral in My Brain.
I heard a Fly buzz—when I died.
I know that He exists.
I like a look of Agony.
I never lost as much but twice.
If any sink, assure that this, now standing.
If I may have it, when it's dead.
It was not Death, for I stood up.
I've seen a Dying Eye.
Last Night that She Lived, The.
More than the Grave is closed to me.

My life closed twice before its close.
My Triumph lasted till the Drums.
Oh give it Motion—deck it sweet.
Promise This, When You be Dying.
Shade upon the mind there passes, A.
Some things that fly there be.
Somehow myself survived the Night.
Sun kept setting—setting—still, The.
That after horror that was us.
There comes an hour when begging stops.
There's a certain Slant of light.
There's been a Death, in the Opposite House.
They put Us far apart.
This Consciousness that is aware.
This docile one inter.
Throe upon the features, A.
Tie the Strings to my Life, My Lord.
To know just how He suffered—would be dear.
'Twas warm—at first—like Us.
Two swimmers wrestled on the spar.
Under the Light, yet under.
Visitor in Marl, A.
We don't [or dont] cry—Tim and I.
What care the Dead, for Chanticleer.
Word is dead, A.
You're right—"the way is narrow".
Diop, B. Vanity.
Dixon, M. Grandmother: Crossing Jordan.
Dobson, R. Being Called For.
Dobyns. Allegorical Matters.
Cemetery Nights.
Counterparts.
Fragments: "Now there is a slit in the blue
fabric of air."
Tomatoes.
Dodd, E. Like Memory, Caverns.
Dodd, W. Of His Life.
d'Oettingen. Kilimanjaro.
Donne. Blossom[e], The.
Computation, The.
Death be not proud, though some have called
thee.
Funeral[l], The.
Hero and Leander.
Hymn[e] to God My God, In My Sickness[e],
A.
Hymn to the Saints, and to Marquis Hamilton,
An.
Oh my black[e] soul[e]! now thou art
summoned.
Paradox, The.
Since she whom[e] I loved [or lov'd or lovd]
hath paid [or payd] her last debt.
Song: "Sweetest love, I do not go[e]."
Valediction, A: Forbidding Mourning.
Valediction, A: of Weeping.
Dooley, M. Heart.
Doolittle, H. Epigram: "Golden one is gone
from the banquets, The."
Epitaph: "So I may say."
Fragment 68: "I envy you your chance of
death."
Helen.
Wine Bowl.
D'Orleans. Oft in My Thought.
Doty, M. Michael's Dream.
New Dog.
Tiara.
Doubleday, T. Friends, when my latest bed of
rest is made.
Douglas, K. How to Kill.
Offensive, The.
Prisoner, The.
Simplify Me When I'm Dead.
Dove, R. Event, The.
Political.
Teach Us to Number Our Days.
Tou Wan Speaks to Her Husband Liu Sheng.
Dowson. Dregs.
Extreme Unction.
Last Word, A.
Dragomoschenko. March Elegy.
Dressel. You, Benjamin Jones.
Drummond de Andrade. Motionless Faces.
Drummond, W. Madrigal: "Daedal of my death,
A."

Dryden, J. Epilogue to Tyrannic[k] Love.
To the Memory of Mr Oldham.
To the Pious Memory of the Accomplished [or
Accomplisht] Young Lady, Mrs. Anne
Killigrew, [Excellent in the Two Sister-Arts of
Poesie and Painting. An Ode].
Whil'st Alexis lay prest [or press'd].
Du Maurier. Music.
Du Tū' Lě. What I Leave to My Son.
Dubie. Death of the Race Car Driver, The.
Genesis Text for Larry Levis, Who Died Alone,
A.
Sanctuary.
Sky Harbor.
Dudley, E. Pathologist.
Dufault. First Night, A.
Dugan, A. Memorial Service for the Invasion
Beach Where the Vacation in the Flesh Is
Over.
Duhamel. How Much Is This Poem Going to
Cost Me?
Duhig, I. Fred.
Dunbar, P. Compensation.
Death Song, A.
Frederick Douglass.
Paradox, The.
To Alice Dunbar.
When All Is Done.
Dunbar, W. Lament for the Makaris [or Makars
or Makers].
Duncan, R. After a Long Illness.
In Blood's Domaine.
Dunn, D. Kaleidoscope, The.
Thirteen Steps and the Thirteenth of March.
Dunn, S. Routine Things Around the House,
The.
Duo Duo. Looking Out from Death.
Morning.
No More Than One Allowed.
Durcan. Ireland 1972.
Tullynoe: Tête-à-Tête in the Parish Priest's
Parlour.
We resided in a Loreto convent in the centre of
Dublin city.
Dyer, C. My Dearest Dust: Epitaph on the
Monument of Sir William Dyer at Colmworth,
1641.
Earle, J. Tea Party, The.
Eastman, M. To John Reed.
Eberhart, R. Ceremony by the Sea, A.
Horse Chestnut Tree, The.
I Walked over the Grave of Henry James.
Edmond, L. Anniversary.
Edson, R. Bringing a Dead Man Back into Life.
Egan, T. Drover's Boy, The.
Eguren. Dead, The.
Ehrenburg [or Erenburg]. Our Grandsons Will
Be Astonished.
Eich. Seminar for Backward Pupils.
Eigner. Letter for Duncan.
Ekelof. Alone in the quiet night.
Eliot, T. S. Aunt Helen.
Hollow Men, The.
Marina.
Song for Simeon, A.
"Eliza.". To My Husband.
Ellis, T. Star Child.
Elsschot. Mother.
Éluard, P. Dawn Dissolves the Monsters.
Elytis, O. Even when they destroy you it will
still be beautiful.
Emerson, R. Dirge: "I reached the middle of the
mount."
Terminus ("It is time to be old.").
Visit, The.
Emmett. Blue Tail Fly or Jimmy Cracked Corn,
The.
Emperor Kōkō. Word at last, The.
Empson. Ignorance of Death.
Teasers, The.
Engels, J. Bullhead.
Engle, P. Hart Crane.
Enquist, A. Invasion.
Enzensberger, H. For the Grave of a Peace-
Loving Man.
Erdrich, H. Future Debris.

Quiet Earth, The.
Erinna.   I'm the tomb of Baukis, a bride; passing the deeply lamented.
Stele and my sirens and mournful urn.
"Ern Malley.".   Egyptian Register.
Eshleman, C.   Lich Gate, The.
Espada.   Latin Night at the Pawnshop.
Espinet, R.   Merchant of Death.
Espirito Santo.   Where Are the Men Chased Away by that Mad Wind?
Etter.   Drink and Agriculture.
Roma Higgins.
Eugenius Vulgarius.   Metrum Parhemiacum Tragicum.
Evance, S.   Written at Netley Abbey.
Written in Ill Health at the Close of Spring.
Evans, G.   Horse on a Fence.
Everson, W.   Poet Is Dead, The.
Ewart.   Sonnet: The Last Things.
Faber, F.   After-State.
Faiz.   Day Death Comes, The.
So Bring the Order for My Execution.
When Autumn Came.
Fane, V.   In an Irish Churchyard.
Fearing.   Dirge: "1-2-3 was the number he played but today the number came 3-2-1."
Obituary.
Feinfeld, D.   Carmelita.
Feldman, A.   Contemporary American Poetry.
Fenton, J.   Cambodia.
Dead Soldiers.
God, A Poem.
Ferguson, G.   Swimming Pool Ghost, The.
Ferlinghetti, L.   Sometime During Eternity.
Ferry.   Cythera.
Fiacc.   Saint Coleman's Song for Flight / An Ite Missa Est.
Ficowski.   Girl of Six from the Ghetto Begging in Smolna Street in 1942, A.
Field, E.   Little Boy Blue.
Field.   Almoner, An.
Dying Viper, A.
Lo, my loved is dying, and the call.
Picture, A.
Portrait, A.
Your Rose Is Dead.
Finch, A.   Reply from His Coy Mistress, A.
Finch, R.   Epitaph: "Here lies a man who was so bright."
Fingueret, M.   86 Pasteur Corner.
Fisher, J.   There are only so many words.
Fisher, R.   As He Came Near Death.
Occasional Poem 7.1.72.
Fitzgerald, F.   Obit on Parnassus.
Flatman.   Thought of Death, A.
Flecker, J.   Prologue: "We Who with Songs Beguile Your Pilgrimage".
Fletcher, J.   Blue Symphony.
Lincoln.
Fletcher, P.   Dying Husband's Farewell, The.
Florit, E.   Elegy for Your Absence.
Flynn, E.   After Grave Deliberation.
Foerster.   Mozart's Death.
Follain.   Hardware Store.
Foot, E.   Captain scans the ruffled zone, The.
Lisp in Numbers, A.
Forbes, J.   Death, an Ode.
Fordham.   Dying Girl, The.
Magnolia.
On Parting with a Friend.
To My Mother.
Twilight Musings.
Forrest-Thomson.   Garden of Proserpine, The.
Fortini.   Poetry of Roses, The.
Foster, A.   Ashes.
Nest of Hats, A.
Fox, Skip.   Sic transit gloria mundi.
Sic transit ("Kingfisher in highest cypress green.").
France, P.   Death.
Francia, L.   Is There There in Dying.
Francis, R.   While I Slept.
Freneau.   And from within the howls of Death I heard.
Before the hearse Death's chaplain seem'd to go.

Dim burnt the lamp, and now the phantom Death.
Hills sink to plains, and man returns to dust.
Indian Burying Ground, The.
Trembling, across the plain my course I held.
What is this Death, ye deep read sophists, say?
When Nature bids thee from the world retire.
Fried, E.   One Kind of Freedom Speaks.
Frost, R.   Death of the Hired Man, The.
Departmental.
Fire and Ice.
Home Burial.
Out, Out—.
Stopping by Woods on a Snowy Evening.
Fuller, M.   Let Me Gather from the Earth.
Fuller, R.   Death.
Fumon.   Magnificent! Magnificent!
Futuransky, L.   Jerusalem, Timeless.
Fuyo-Dokai.   Seventy-six: done.
Gallagher, T.   Wake.
Galvin, J.   Shadow-Casting.
García Lorca.   Absence of the Soul.
Ballad of One Doomed to Die.
Elegy for Joan the Mad One.
Quarrel, The.
Garcia, R.   Dangerous Hats.
Death in Larkspur Canyon, A.
Garcilaso de la Vega.   Nemoroso.
Gardinier.   Ghost of Santo Domingo, The.
Two Girls.
Garioch.   Elegy: "They are lang deid, folk that I used to ken."
Gascoyne.   De Profundis.
Gay, J.   My Own Epitaph.
Gbadamosi.   Death of the Polar Explorers.
Gehrke, S.   Mouth to Mouth.
Gekko-Sojo.   How Zenists carry on.
George, D.   Wreck of the Old 97.
Gerhardt, I. G. M.   Remembrance Day.
Gerlach, E.   Turn and Turn About.
Gertsyk, A.   Spring.
Gervitz, G.   Life is nothing but time.
Maybe we are the same darkness the same words.
Gezelle.   Little Mother.
Ghalib, M.   Ghazal 15: "Almost none."
Ghazal 34: "He's going around with your letter.".
Not All, Only a Few, Return as the Rose or the Tulip.
Gibb, B.   Vigil.
Gibbons, O.   Silver Swan, The.
Gilbert-Lecomte.   Son of the Bone Speaks, The.
Gilbert, S.   Elegy: "Pages of history open, The. The dead enter."
Gilliams, M.   Autumn.
Gillilan, P.   Four Years.
Ginsberg, A.   At Apollinaire's Grave.
Death News.
Elegy for Neal Cassady.
Father Death Blues.
Kaddish.
O mother / what have I left out.
On Neal's Ashes.
Ginsberg, A.   Line Drive.
Giorno.   Scum & Slime.
Gioseffi.   American Sonnets for My Father.
Giovanni.   Women Gather, The.
Glaser, E.   Coroner.
Glaser, M.   Changing Address Books.
Glatt.   Amanda.
Gleim.   To Death.
Glück, L.   Descending Figure.
Drowned Children, The.
Fantasy, A.
Firstborn.
Garden, The: "One sound. Then the hiss and whir."
Hyacinth.
Lullaby: "My mother's an expert at one thing."
Racer's Widow, The.
Godfrey.   Air.
Goethe.   Anacreon's Grave.
Ecstatic Longing.
Erl-King, The.
Holy Longing, The.

Gogarty.   Per Iter Tenebricosum.
To Death.
Goldbarth.   Complete with Starry Night and Bourbon Shots.
Goldberg, B.   Nights in the Constellation of the Tree Stepping from its Robe.
Goldberg, L.   In the Jerusalem Hills.
Goldsmith, O.   When Lovely Woman Stoops to Folly.
Goll, I.   Ferry of Lead, The.
Last River, The.
Your Sleep.
Gomes, A.   Martyred Tamarind, The.
Gonzáles Martínez.   Last Journey.
González, A.   Diatribe Against the Dead.
González Prada, M.   Living and Dying.
To Be with the Dead.
Your Lily Eyes Said Yes.
Gonzalez, R.   At the Rio Grande Near the End of the Century.
Without Villages.
González, R.   Day of the Dead.
Goodison.   For Don Drummond.
Goodtimes.   Roadkill Coyote.
Gordon, G.   Tercios del Muerte.
Gorges.   Written upon the Death of the Most Noble Prince Henrie.
Gorostiza, J.   Filled with myself, walled up in my skin.
Gotlieb.   Death's Head.
Graham, A.   Life and death.
Graham, H.   Opportunity.
Tender-Heartedness.
Waste.
Graham-Pole, J.   Candor.
Graves, R.   Down.
It Was All Very Tidy.
Gray, D.   Sonnet: "October's gold is dim—the forests rot."
Gray, T.   Descent of Odin, The.
Elegy Written in a Country Churchyard.
Ode on the Death of a Favo[u]rite Cat, Drowned in a Tub [or Bowl] of Gold Fishes.
Sonnet [on the Death of Mr. Richard West].
Greacen.   Summer Day, A.
Greening, M.   Missing — Believed Drowned.
Greenlee.   Memorial for Trane.
Greenwell, D.   Christina.
To Christina Rossetti.
Gregerson.   Safe.
Gregg.   Past Perfect.
Singers Change, the Music Goes On, The.
Grimald.   From A Funeral Song, Upon the Decease of Annes His Mother.
I, in your frutefull woomb conceyved, born was.
Grimké, A.   Epitaph on a Living Woman.
Grobman, M.   In mass graves the bodies of plants.
Grossman, A.   Enough Rain for Agnes Walquist.
Gruffydd, W.   In Memoriam.
Guarini.   Shepherd Thirsis longed to die, The.
Guevara, M.   Abuelo, Answers and Questions.
Magic Carpet, The.
Postmortem.
Tuesday Shaman.
Guidacci.   Anniversary with Agave Plants.
First to feast is love, The. On the scraps of love the fever feasts.
Guillory, D.   Retinal burn of warm November light.
Guiney.   Open, Time.
Gullar.   Oswald Dead.
Gumilyov [or Gumiliov or Gumilev].
Childhood.
Gunn, T.   Death's Door.
Gas-poker, The.
In the Post Office.
J Car, The.
Lament: "Your dying was a difficult enterprise."
My Sad Captains.
Reassurance, The.
Unsettled Motorcyclist's Vision of His Death, The.
Victim, The.
Gurney, I.   Silent One, The.

Gwynn, R. Approaching a Significant Birthday, He Peruses The Norton Anthology of Poetry.
Haavikko. You can't take with you.
Hachenburg, H. Terezin.
Hacker, M. Autumn 1980.
  Ballad of Ladies Lost and Found.
  Dusk: July.
  Year's End.
Hadas, R. In the Grove.
Hadrian. Adriani Morientis ad Animam Suam.
  Emperor Hadrian on His Soul.
Hahn, O. Death Is Sitting at the Foot of My Bed.
Hahn, S. Perennial.
Halfe, L. Pähkahkos.
Hall, Daniel. Dusting.
Hall, Donald. Eleanor's Letters.
  Her Long Illness.
  Last Days.
  Letter with No Address.
  Man in the Dead Machine, The.
  My Son, My Executioner.
  Small Fig Tree, A.
  Snow, The: "Snow is in the oak."
  White Apples.
Hall, H. Palmer. Death on Village Creek, A.
  Requiem for James Byrd, Jr.
Hall, H. Woman Death.
Halleck, F. On the Death of Joseph Rodman Drake.
Halswell. Upon Mr. Hopton's Death.
Hamburger, M. Treblinka.
Hammial. Petit Guignol.
Hamod, S. After the Funeral of Assam Hamady.
  Dying with the Wrong Name.
Han-shan. Wrecked Town, The.
Han Yong'un [or Yongwun]. Come to Me.
Hanson, M. Occasioned by Reading Mrs. M. Robinson's Poems.
Hanzlicek, C. Sierra Noon.
Hardy, T. Afterwards.
  At Castle Boterel.
  Beeny Cliff.
  By Her Aunt's Grave.
  Channel Firing.
  Drummer Hodge.
  During Wind and Rain.
  Friends Beyond.
  Going, The.
  I Found Her Out There.
  Neutral Tones.
  She Hears the Storm.
  Subalterns, The.
  Thoughts of Phena.
  Transformations.
  Voice, The.
  Wife in London, A.
  Your Last Drive.
Harechavi. Already Night, Already Day.
Harington, L. Elegy: "Death be not proud, thy hand gave not this blow."
Harms. Soon.
Harper, M. Nightmare Begins Responsibility.
  Reuben, Reuben.
  We Assume: On the Death of Our Son, Reuben Masai Harper.
Harries, E. Bone Prison, The.
Harrison, T. Heartless Art, The.
  Long Distance II.
  Study.
  Timer.
Harry, J. Honesty-Stones.
Harter. Sister Death.
  Turtle Blessing.
Hartnett. Death of an Irishwoman.
  Last Vision of Eoghan Rua Ó Súilleabháin, The.
Harwood, G. Death Has No Features of His Own.
Havergal. Just When Thou Wilt.
Hawkesworth, P. Two Statues.
Hay, G. Bizerta.
Hayden, R. Broken Dark, The.
  Mourning Poem for the Queen of Sunday.
  Paul Laurence Dunbar.
Healy, E. What It Was Like the Night Cary Grant Died.

Heaney, S. Badgers, The.
  Be literal a moment. Recollect.
  Casualty.
  Clearances.
  Funeral Rites.
  Grauballe Man, The.
  In Memoriam Francis Ledwidge.
  Mid-Term Break.
  Ship of Death, A.
  Summer of Lost Rachel, The.
  When all the others were away at Mass.
Heard, J. Message to a Loved One Dead, A.
  Resting.
Hecht, A. Death the Painter.
  More Light! More Light!
Hedin, R. Wreck of the Great Northern, The.
Heine, H. Ah, Death Is Like the Long Cool Night.
  Death and Morphine.
  Every idle desire has died in my breast.
  Memory, A.
  My zenith was luckily happier than my night.
Heithaus. What a Little Moonlight Can Do.
Hemans. Bring Flowers.
  Effigies, The.
  England's Dead.
  Grave of a Poetess, The.
  Graves of a Household, The.
  Hour of Death, The.
  Image in Lava, The.
  Imelda.
  Indian Woman's Death-Song, The.
  Juana.
  Magic Glass, The.
  Properzia Rossi.
  Statue of the Dying Gladiator, The.
  To a Departed Spirit.
Hemingway. Champs d'Honneur.
Henderson, H. We Show You That Death as a Dancer.
Henley, W. E. Madam Life's A Piece in Bloom.
  Margaritae Sorori.
Henry, J. Two hundred men and eighteen killed.
Heraclitus of Halicarnassus. Soil is freshly dug, the half-faded wreaths of leaves, The.
Herarty, T. Cyclus.
Herbert, E. Elegy over a Tomb.
Herbert, G. Ah Mater, quo te deplorem fonte?
  Dolores.
  Death: "Death, thou wast once an uncouth hideous thing."
  Life.
  Mortification.
  Redemption.
  Virtue [or Vertue].
Herbert, J. Dossers at the Imperial War Museum.
Herbert, Z. Elegy of Fortinbras.
  Envoy of Mr. Cogito, The.
  Meditations of Mr. Cogito on Redemption.
  Our Fear.
Herd. Coronach.
  Exhibits, The.
  Gia.
  Hyperion's Bones.
  Missing.
Hernández, M. I Go On in the Dark, Lit from Within.
Herrera. Atavistic: Traces after the Rain.
  Yellow Room, The.
Herrick. Comfort to a Youth That Had Lost His Love.
  Dirge of Jephthah's Daughter, The.
  Funeral[l] Rites of the Rose, The.
  Gods Keyes.
  Grace for a Child.
  His Winding-Sheet.
  On Himself[e] ("I will no longer kiss.").
  On Himselfe ("Weepe for the dead, for they have lost this light.").
  To Julia ("Julia, when thy Herrick dies.").
  To Perilla.
  Upon a Child.
  Upon Ben Jo[h]nson.
  Upon Prue [or Prew], His Maid.
  Widow's Tears [or Widdowes Teares]: or, Dirge

of Dorcas, The.
Hesketh. Death of a Gardener.
  Dilemma.
Hewitt, J. Father's Death, A.
  Scar, The.
Heyen. Crane in Reeds.
  Derailment.
Hicok. Goodbye in the Shape of a Knot.
Hill, G. Guardians, The.
  In Memory of Jane Fraser [or Frazer].
  Merlin.
  Not as we are but as we must appear.
  Statesmen have known visions. And, not alone.
  Two Formal Elegies.
Hillyer. Dead Man's Corner.
Hirsch, E. Fast Break.
Hirschhorn, N. Number Our Days.
Hirshfield, J. Story, A.
Hodgins. Death Who.
Hoffmann, H. Story of Augustus Who Would Not Have Any Soup, The.
Hofmannsthal. Evanescence.
Hogg, J. Kilmeny.
Holden, M. Seaman, 1941.
Höllerer. Held Back, Like a Bow Drawn Tight.
Holst-Warhaft. In the End Is the Body.
Holub. Death in the Evening.
  On the Origin of the Contrary.
Homer. Achilles and Priam.
  Achilles' Dream.
  Achilles' Lament and the Funeral of Patroclus.
  Achilles Over the Trench.
  Execution of the faithless maids.
  We bore down on the ship at sea's edge.
Homyo. Wino, always stumbling.
Hongo. Legend, The.
Honig, E. Now, My Usefullness Over.
Hood, T. Bridge of Sighs, The.
  Death in the Kitchen.
  Death-Bed, The.
  Jack Hall.
Hooks. Body Inside the Soul, The.
Hoornik. To Love a Woman.
Hope, A. Death of the Bird, The.
  Inscription for a War.
Hopkins, G. Felix Randal.
  No Worst, There Is None. Pitched Past Pitch of Grief.
Horace. Ode 4.7: "Snows dissolving, grass returns to meadow."
  Ode 4.7 To L. Manlius Torquatus.
Horan. Soft Swimmer, Winter Swan.
Horovitz, F. Rain—Birdoswald.
Houghton, L. Caustic Soda.
Housman. Along the field as we came by.
  Because I liked you better.
  Bredon Hill.
  Crossing Alone the Nighted Ferry.
  Epitaph: "Here dead lie we because we did not choose."
  If truth in hearts that perish.
  Is my team ploughing.
  Isle of Portland, The.
  Night Is Freezing Fast, The.
  Some can gaze and not be sick.
  To an Athlete Dying Young.
  When I watch the living meet.
  When smoke stood up from Ludlow.
  With rue my heart is laden.
Howard, R. 1915: A Pre-Raphaelite Ending, London.
Howe, F. Doubt.
  Seeking Out His face in a Cup.
Howe, M. What the Living Do.
Howe, S. In its first dumb form.
Howe, W. Funeral Hymn.
Howell, J. Elegy upon His Tomb in Herndon-Hill Church, Erected by His Wife, Who Speaks, An.
Howes, B. Death of a Vermont Farm Woman.
Howitt, M. Dying Child, The.
Huchel. Roads.
Hudgins. After the Wilderness.
  Burial Detail.
  Dead Christ.
  Elegy for My Father, Who Is Not Dead.

Hereafter, The.
Hufana, A. Floating Epitaphs, Their Possible Explanations in Poro Point.
Hughes, F. In the Shadow of Fire.
Kookaburra.
Hughes, L. As Befits a Man.
Dead in There.
Drum.
Gal's Cry for a Dying Lover.
Madam and the Wrong Visitor.
Stony Lonesome.
Sylvester's Dying Bed.
Wake.
Hughes, T. Day He Died, The.
Examination at the Womb-Door.
Heptonstall.
Suddenly his poor body.
View of a Pig.
Hugo, R. Death in the Aquarium.
Elegy: "I expected him to look dead in the casket."
Hugo, V. At Villequier.
Djinns, The.
Huidobro. Midnight.
Hummer, T. Train Wreck, 1890: My Grandmother Lies Down with the Dead.
Humphreys, E. From Father to Son.
Hwang Jiwoo. Mirror 1.
Hwang Tonggyu. Wind Burial.
Hywel ab Owain Gwynedd. Exultation.
Ibáñez, S. Island in the Light.
You, for My Meditation.
Ibarbourou. Life-Hook.
Ibn Ezra, Moses. And Where Are the Graves.
Ichigen. Seventy-eight awkward years.
Ignatow, D. Walt Whitman in the Civil War Hospitals.
Ikuo-Joun. This fellow, perfect in men's eyes.
Ikuo-Myotan. Seventy-two years I've hung.
Ingelow. High Tide on the Coast of Lincolnshire, 1571, The.
Iofe, Y. Olsanski Cemetery, The.
Islām, N. Oh hey, All-Destroyer.
Syama wakes on the cremation grounds.
Issa. Bath when you're born.
Closer, closer / to paradise—.
When I go / Guard my tomb well.
Why did the wild pink break?
Windy fall.
Istarú, A. To the cove of my breasts your forehead will return.
Ivanov, G. Old man shuffles to the fish market, The.
Ivanov, V. Winter Sonnets, The.
Ivask, Y. Emily Dickinson.
Ives, G. With Whom, Then, Should I Sleep?
Jabès. Desert, II, The.
Jaccottet. These wood-shadows.
Jacinto, J. Absence.
Jackson, F. Death of Gladys Presley, The.
Jackson, G. Some of Betty's Story Round 1850.
Jackson, H. Found Frozen.
Jackson, L. Death as Death.
Elegy in a Spider's Web.
Jacobsen, J. Limbo Dancer, The.
Poems for My Cousin.
Jakushitsu. Refreshing, the wind against the waterfall.
James, T. Lines on His Companions Who Died in the Northern Seas.
Jammes. Prayer to Go to Paradise with the Donkeys, A.
Jarman, M. Ground Swell.
Jarrell, R. Death of the Ball Turret Gunner, The.
In the Camp There Was One Alive.
Islands, The.
Knight, Death, and the Devil, The.
Losses.
Say Good-bye to Big Daddy.
Truth, The.
Jeffers, R. Bed by the Window, The.
Cremation.
Deer Lay Down Their Bones, The.
May-June, 1940.
Original Sin.
Purse-Seine, The.

Vulture.
Where I?
Jewsbury. Summer Eve's Vision, A.
Jiménez, J. Zenith.
Johnson, F. Song of the Whirlwind.
Johnson, G. I Want to Die While You Love Me.
Johnson, J. Color Sergeant, The.
Go Down Death (A Funeral Sermon).
Johnson, L. Collins.
Dark Angel, The.
Johnson, S. On the Death of Dr [or Mr] Robert Levet [a Practiser in Physic].
Johnston, E. Mother's Love, A.
Nelly's Lament for the Pirnhouse Cat.
Johnston, M. In Memoriam.
Johnstone, R. Robot Camera.
Undertakers.
Jones, G. Merthyr.
Jones, S. Community.
Jones, T. My Grandmother Died in the Early Hours of the Morning.
Jonson, B. By this time had they reached the Stygian pool.
Epitaph on Elizabeth, L. H.
Ode to Himself, An ("Where dost [or; do'st] thou careless[e] lie.").
Of Life and Death.
Juan Chi. Hibiscus grows lushly on the grave mounds, The.
Juarroz. Any movement kills something.
Life Draws a Tree.
Look First at the Air and Its Black Element Which Never Stops.
To die, but far away.
Justice, D. First Death.
In Memory of the Unknown Poet, Robert Boardman Vaughn.
Invitation to a Ghost.
On the Death of Friends in Childhood.
Psalm and Lament.
Kao Ch'i. Written on Seeing the Flowers, and Remembering My Daughter.
Kaplinski, J. Death does not come from outside.
Kasdorf. Dying with Amish Uncles.
Grossdaadi's Funeral.
Kavanagh, P. In Memory of My Mother.
Keats. Bright Star.
To Chatterton.
When I Have Fears [That I May Cease to Be].
Kees. For My Daughter.
If This Room Is Our World.
Robinson.
Kekova. Having submitted your petition for dismissal.
Kelen. Gods Ash Their Cigarettes, The.
Kendrick, D. Inpatient.
26th Person, The.
Kennedy, X. Epitaph for a Postal Clerk.
Kennelly. Glimpse of Starlings, A.
I See You Dancing, Father.
Poem from a Three Year Old.
Kenyon, J. Travel: After a Death.
Kerim. Mother.
Kessler, S. Jack's Last Words.
Keyes, S. Elegy: "April again, and it is a year again."
Kgositsile. Acknowledgement.
Khayr, A. For men and women soon the day draws near.
His absence is the knife that cuts your throat?
If I've been dead for twenty years or so.
I'm going to tell You something that is true.
Khazak, Y. Dead in a Bereft Horah.
Wake.
Khodasevich. Bride, The.
Music.
On the Death of My Tomcat Murr.
Khoury, N. Death Is Your Salvation.
Kiko. Mount Sumeru—my fist!
Killigrew, A. On Death.
King, H. Exequy, The.
Kinnell. Quick and the Dead, The.
Kinsella, T. Death Bed.
Tear.
Kinzie. Lunar Frost.
Kipling, R. Harp Song of the Dane Women.

Song to Mithras, A.
Kizer, C. Food of Love.
On a Line from Valéry.
Klappert. In Memory of H. F.
Klein, M. Guardian Life.
Scenes for an Elegy.
Kleist. Song at Graveside.
Kloos, W. Trees, Late in the Season.
Klyuyev [or Kliuev or Klyuev]. You Twist Your Death in Nooses.
Knevet. Navigation.
Knight, E. Poem of Attrition, A.
Knott. At the Crossroads.
Death: "Going to sleep, I cross my hands on my chest."
Funny Poem.
Two Vietnam Poems: (1966).
Koch, K. Circus, The ("We will have to go away, said the girls in the circus.").
Komrij. Park of the Dead.
Komunyakaa, Y. April Fools' Day.
Between Days.
Seven Deadly Sins.
You and I Are Disappearing.
Kopland. Natzweiler.
Thanks to the Things.
Ulumbo, a Cat.
Korean Oral Tradition. Abandoned Princess, The.
Kornblith, M. Books of the Dead, The.
Mirrors.
Košek, M. It All Depends on How You Look at It.
Kozameh, A. Presence. Opposites. Absence.
Forces exercising pressure against.
Kruit, J. Post Heads.
Kumin, M. How It Is.
Retrieval System, The.
Thinking of Death and Dogfood.
Kunene. Elegy for My Friend E. Galo.
Kunitz, S. Dragonfly, The.
Kupriyanov [or Kuprianov]. Everything gets forgotten.
For a long time he tried to survive.
Kushner, A. Memoirs.
Kyurin-Eki. Eighty-three years—at last.
Lacavaro, A. Advantages of Being a World Class Athlete, The.
Laforgue. Complaint on the Oblivion of the Dead.
Laing, K. I Am the Freshly Dead Husband.
Lake, P. Blue Jay.
Lamartine. Autumn.
Lamb, C. Hester.
Old Familiar Faces, The.
Lampman. City of the End of Things, The.
Landon. Child Screening a Dove from a Hawk, A.
Felicia Hemans.
Little Shroud, The.
Marriage Vow, The.
Stanzas on the Death of Mrs Hemans.
Landor, W. Age.
Alas! 'Tis Very Sad to Hear.
Death of the Day.
I Strove With None.
Maid's Lament, The.
Rose Aylmer.
Tears of the Dying.
To Arthur de Noé Walker.
Lane, P. Rain Ditch.
Lanier, S. Nirvâna.
Larkin, J. Inventory.
Larkin, P. Ambulances.
Aubade: "I work all day, and get half-drunk at night."
Church Going.
Dublinesque.
Next, Please.
Lasoen, P. That April Morning.
Lassell. Brady Street, San Francisco.
How to Watch Your Brother Die.
Sunset Stripping: Visiting L.A.
Three Poems.
Laurencin, M. Horse, The.
Lawrence, D. H. Bride, The.

Cherry Robbers.
Hymn to Priapus.
Ship of Death, The ("Now it is autumn and the falling fruit.").
Layton. Cold Green Element, The.
Street Funeral.
Le Guin. Child on the Shore, The.
Le Pan. Incident, An.
Lea, S. At the Flyfisher's Shack.
Feud, The.
Wrong Way Will Haunt You, The.
Leapor. Epistle to a Lady, An.
Mira's Will.
Lee, L. Between Seasons.
Eating Together.
Visions and Interpetations.
Leithauser. Haunted, The.
Lejeune, Claire. Death, I Speak of It.
Leopardi. To Himself.
Levertov. By the gas-fire, kneeling.
Change, The.
Clouds.
Dead Butterfly, The.
Death in Mexico.
Note to Olga (1966), A.
Olga Poems.
What Were They Like?
Levin, P. Shadow Returns, The.
Levine, P. And the Trains Go On.
Angel Butcher.
Baby Villon.
Belief.
Death of Saul, The.
On a Drawing by Flavio.
On the Birth of Good and Evil During the Long Winter of '28.
On the Murder of Lieutenant José del Castillo by the Falangist Bravo Martinez, July 12, 1936.
Red Dust.
Water's Chant, The.
Levis. Morning After My Death, The.
Levy, A. Cross-Road Epitaph, A.
Epitaph: "This is the end of him, here he lies."
Felo de Se.
In the Mile End Road.
London Poets.
Magdalen.
Old House, The.
On the Threshold.
Reminiscence, A.
Sequel to "A Reminiscence", The.
Straw in the Street.
Twilight.
Lewis, A. All Day It Has Rained.
Autumn, 1939.
Easter at Christmas.
Song (On Seeing Dead Bodies Floating Off the Cape).
Unknown Soldier, The.
Lewis, C. Ballade of Dead Gentlemen.
Epitaph, An: "Erected by her sorrowing brothers."
Lewis, G. And this, too, is love.
Chernobyl Icon.
Flyover Elegies.
It looks like she's drowning.
Last suppers, I fancy, are always wide-screen.
What is her vanishing point?
Lewis, M. Alonzo the Brave and the Fair Imogine.
Li K'ai-hsien. Earthquake covered Shansi and Shensi, The.
Li Kuang-t'ien. Dead Turk, A.
Li Po. Old Tai's Wine Shop.
Li Shang-yin. Without Title (2).
Lichtenstein. Morning.
Lieberman, L. Compass of the Dying.
Lieberman, M. Los Olivos.
On the Anniversary of My Father's Death.
Lifshin. Yahrtzeit Light, The.
Lightfoot. Wreck of the Edmund Fitzgerald, The.
Lihn. Cemetery in Punta Arenas.
Goodnight, Achilles.
Of All Despondencies.

Lima, J. Words of Departure.
Limburg, J. Return, The.
Lincoln, A. My Childhood-Home I See Again.
Lisboa. Elegy: "At first the dead."
Liu, T. Vox Angelica.
Wellfleet.
Liu Tsung-yüan. On Covering the Bones of Chang Chin, the Hired Man.
Livesay, D. Going to Sleep.
Llywelyn Goch ap Meurig Hen. Lament for Lleucu Llwyd.
Lochhead, D. John Thompson.
Lockhart. Lines: "When youthful faith hath fled."
Loesser. Boys in the Backroom, The.
Loftis, N. In Memorium: Robert Hayden.
Lomax, M. Amor Diving.
July.
Longenbach. What You Find in the Woods.
Longfellow, H. Cross of Snow, The.
Dante.
Excelsior.
Jewish Cemetery at Newport, The.
Nature.
Spanish Jew's Tale: Azrael, The.
Longley, M. In Memoriam.
In Memory of Gerard Dillon.
Linen Workers, The.
Third Light, The.
Wounds.
Lope de Vega. Down in the orchard.
Lorde. Day They Eulogized Mahalia, The.
Father Son and Holy Ghost.
Hanging Fire.
Memorial 1: "If you come as softly."
Lourie. Letters to the Dead: Denise Levertov.
Lovecraft. Well, The.
Lowell, J. First Snowfall [or Snow-Fall], The.
Memoriae Positum R. G. Shaw.
Lowell, R. Falling Asleep over the Aeneid.
Harriet ("Repeating fly, blueback, thumbthick— so gross, A.").
History.
Mr. Edwards and the Spider.
Quaker Graveyard in Nantucket, The.
Sailing Home from Rapallo.
Where the Rainbow Ends.
Lowry, M. Epitaph: "Malcolm Lowry."
Strange Type.
Volcano Is Dark, The.
Loynaz, D. M. Sea Surrounded.
Lu Yu. To Show to My Sons.
Lucilius. Lean Gaius, who was thinner than a straw.
Lumsden, R. Mercy.
Lux. Plague Victims Catapulted Over Walls into Besieged City.
Luzi. Reflective life separates us from the sources of reflection.
Lydgate. O thow Minstral that cannest so note and pipe.
Lynch, T. Death, A: "In the end you want the clean dimensions of it mentioned."
Lyte. Abide With Me.
Mabuza. Back to the Gold Mine!
Macaulay, T. Horatius [or Horatius at the Bridge].
MacCaig. So Many Summers.
MacDiarmid, H. At My Father's Grave.
Dead Liebknecht, The.
Empty Vessel.
Of John Davidson.
Under the Greenwood Tree.
Watergaw, The.
Yet Ha'e I Silence Left.
Macgoye. Freedom Song, A.
MacKay, R. Rispond Miser, The.
Mackenzie, K. Door Swung Open, The.
Sick Men Sleeping.
MacLean, S. Ebb.
Heroes.
MacLeish. Burying Ground by the Ties.
Epistle to Be Left in the Earth.
Prologue: "And the way goes on in the worn earth."
MacNeice. Charon.

Sunlight on the Garden, The.
This Is the Life.
Magrelli. I prefer to come from silence to talk.
We go through life this way.
Maguire, S. Invisible Mender, The.
Mahapatra, J. Ash.
Mahon. Bonn´n Buí, An.
In Carrowdore Churchyard.
Māhtābcānd, M. Who is this, all alone? Whose woman is She.
Maiden. Air.
Climbing.
Major, C. Swallow the Lake.
Mallarmé. Fine suicide fled victoriously, The.
Tomb.
Tomb of Edgar Poe, The.
With her pure nails offering their onyx high.
Mandelstam [or Mandelshtam]. I Hate the Light.
I Was Washing Outside in the Darkness.
Lamarck.
Mounds of Human Heads.
Mounds of Human Heads Are Wandering into the Distance.
Tristia.
Mangan, J. O'Hussey's Ode to the Maguire.
Manguso, S. Rider, The.
Manley, R. Bob Marley's Dead.
Mansfield, K. To L. H. B.
Mansour, J. Gently stroke a wound.
Last night I saw your corpse.
Regulation equipment.
March, A. Let others hail the holidays with laughter.
Out scouting for sound counsels? How to prosper?
Markham, E. In Death Valley.
Lincoln, the Man of the People.
Marlatt, D. Summer of the New Well.
Marshall-Stoneking. On the Death of Muriel Rukeyser.
Martí. I am an honest man.
I want, in the shade of a wing.
In the shadow of a wing.
Martial. Aulus, my girlfriend's in a dreadful plight.
De Cœnatione Micae.
Pre-eminent among scholars.
Rome, I am Scorpus, foremost in the race.
This was the young Camonus; this his face.
Why is it modern books are little read.
You gave Bithynicus thousands yearly; still.
Martin, C. Easter Sunday, 1985.
Martin, P. Tongues.
Martinaitis, M. Last Farewell to Kukutis.
Martinez, D. Altruism.
Death of Isadora Duncan, The.
Discreet Prayer, A.
Standard Time: Novena for My Father.
Martínez, V. Absence, Luminescent.
Tesoro.
Martinson. Peonies.
Marvell. Damon the Mower.
To His Coy Mistress.
Marzials. Tragedy, A.
Masefield. Sorrow of Mydath.
To-morrow.
Massey. And thou hast stolen a jewel, Death.
Masters, E. Amanda Barker.
Hill, The.
Matherne, B. Les Fils (Sons).
Mathias, R. Departure in Middle Age.
Maxton. Elegies.
M'Baye d'Erneville. Requiem.
McAuley, J. Cloak, The.
Pietá.
McAuliffe, J. Vision of Rahoon, A.
McCabe, C. In Memory of My Mother.
McClatchy. Landing, The.
Tattoos.
McGonagall. Alas! Lord and Lady Dalhousie are dead, and buried at last.
As the procession passes the palace the blinds are drawn.
By taking the impressions of watch-cases he discovered, one day.

Calamity in London; Family of Ten Burned to Death.
Late Sir John Ogilvy, The.
McGough, R. Survivor.
McGrath, C. First Trimester, The.
Jeffrey Lee Pierce.
McGrath, T. Blues for Warren.
Epitaph: "Again, traveller, you have come a long way led by that star."
Go Ask the Dead.
McHugh, H. Or Else.
McKay, C. If We Must Die.
My Mother "Dawn departs, the morning is begun, The."
My Mother "Reg wished me to go with him to the field."
McLaughlin-Carruth, J. Black Irish Blues.
McOrlan. Wood merchant's parlour, The.
Mei Yao Ch'en. Dream at Night, A.
On the Death of a New Born Child.
Sad Remembrance.
Sorrow.
Meilyr Brydydd. Poem on His Death-Bed.
Meireles. Vigil.
Meleager. Upon a Maid That Died [or Dyed] the Day She Was Married [or Marryed].
Meltzer, D. 17:II:82.
Melville, H. Ball's Bluff.
Dirge: "Stay, Death. Not mine the Christus-wand."
Haglets, The.
Monody: "To have known him, to have loved him."
Time's Betrayal.
Menai. Pieces of Coal.
To One Who Died in a Garret in Cardiff.
Mengham, Rod. Concession to Perpetuity No. 166.
Smitten.
Menicanti. If.
Menken. Dying.
Resurgam.
Meredith, G. Dirge in Woods.
Meredith, W. Dying Away.
For His Father.
To the Thoughtful Reader.
Merrill, C. Diver, The.
Merrill, J. Annie Hill's Grave.
Broken Home, The.
Country of a Thousand Years of Peace, The.
Hôtel de l'Univers et Portugal.
Merwin. Ballad of John Cable and Three Gentlemen.
For the Anniversary of My Death.
Hydra, The.
Strawberries.
Mew. À Quoi Bon Dire.
At the Convent Gate.
Beside the Bed.
In Nunhead Cemetery.
Meynell, A. Maternity.
Parentage.
Mezey. Touch It.
Michelson, J. Rings.
Michelson, P. Enduring Witness, the Mosques of Kattankudi.
Miles, J. Conception: "Death did not come to my mother."
Millay, E. Buck in the Snow, The.
Childhood Is the Kingdom Where Nobody Dies.
Conscientious Objector.
Elegy before Death.
I Dreamed I Moved among the Elysian Fields.
Passer Mortuus Est.
Miller, E. Players.
Miller, M. Closing, A.
Mills, R. For Lorine Niedecker in Heaven.
Milosz, C. Dedication: "You whom I could not save."
Mark 5:21–43; And when Jesus had crossed.
With Her.
Milosz, O. Bridge, The.
Milton. Lycidas.
On His Blindness.
On His Deceased Wife.
On Shakespear[e].

On the University Carrier Who Sick'n'd [or Sickened] in the Time of His Vacancy [, Being Forbid to go to London, by Reason of the Plague].
On Time.
Sin and Death.
Sonnet: On the Religious Memorie of Mrs. Catherine Thomason My Christian Friend Deceas'd Decem. 1646.
Mirikitani. Fisherman, The.
Shadow in Stone.
Mishol, A. Gravity, Death.
Sacred Cow of Hardship, The.
Mistral, G. Empty Walnut, The.
Martha and Mary.
My Mother.
Mitchell, K. On the Anniversary Of Your Death.
Mitchell, S. Parable of the Sower, The.
Mitchell, S. Dead, The: "At night the dead come down to the river to drink."
Mitchison. Hartmanswillerkopf.
Momaday. Colors of Night, The.
Rainy Mountain Cemetery.
Two Figures.
Monck. Verses Written on Her Death-bed at Bath to Her Husband in London.
Monsour. Emily's Words.
Montagu, L. Epitaph: "Here lies John Hughes and Sarah Drew."
On the Death of Mrs. Bowes.
Montague, J. Family Conference.
Montale. Fan, The.
I repeat I'm ready, but ready for what?
Montgomerie, W. Epitaph: "My brother is skull and skeleton now."
Montgomery, W. Death Rode a Pinto Pony.
Moolten, D. Brandy Station, Virginia.
Moore, M. Grave, A.
What Are Years?
Moore, R. Dirge for the Living.
Shipwreck: "Watching, watching from the shore."
Still without Life.
Moore, T. Echo ("At the mid hour of night, when stars are weeping, I fly.").
Moorer. In Memoriam of E. B. Clark.
Morabito, F. Compared to the condos of the living.
Junto a los condominios de los vivos.
Morgan, R. Blood Donor.
Mori. Speaking Through White: For My Mother.
Mörike [or Möricke]. Remember It, My Soul.
Morisseau-Leroy, F. Zombies.
Moritz [or Morits]. Leader, The.
Parting the curtains on the other world.
Mörling, M. In a Motel Room at Dawn.
Morris, W. Death Song, A.
Morrissey, S. Post Mortem.
To Look Out Once from High Windows.
Moss, H. Elegy for My Sister.
Water Island.
Moss, T. Fisher Street.
Mother Goose. Who Killed Cock Robin.
Muir, E. Child Dying, The.
Muldoon, P. Soap-Pig, The.
Mumon Gensen. Life: a cloud crossing the peak.
Muñiz Huberman. Cascades of Death.
Mura. Grandfather-in-law.
Murphey, John Collin. First Birthday After Death, The.
Re-stringing 100 Year Old Wire.
Murray, G. Rounds, The.
Murray, L. Corniche.
Lament for the Country Soldiers.
Muske, C. Eulogy, The.
Muso Soseki. At Gen's Embarkation for Yuan China.
For the Death of a Monk.
Mourning for the Layman Named Cloud Peak.
Reizan Osho Visits Me.
Mutis. Amen.
Myles, E. December 9th.

Na'car, P. Foreigner Who Died in Juchitán, The.
Naimy, M. My Brother.
Nairne. Land o' the Leal, The.
Napier, F. I Have Taken the Suits and Shoes to Oxfam.
Narihira. Facing His Own Death.
Nash, O. Tweedledee and Tweedledoom.
Nashe [or Nash]. Adieu, Farewell, Earth's Bliss[e].
Negroni, M. Theory of a Good Death.
Nelson, H. My Father Went to Funerals.
Nemerov. Easter: "Even this suburb has overcome Death."
Grace to Be Said at the Supermarket.
Nemes Nagy. Lazarus.
To a Poet.
Neruda. Absence of Joaquín.
Different Ship, A.
Final.
Nothing but Death.
Nervo. Gift, The.
Nesbit, E. Dead to the Living, The.
Nezahualcoyotl. Flowers of Red and Blue.
Nezval. Trap Door.
Nguyễn Chí Thiện. This Land's No Joy.
Ni Dhomhnaill. Labasheedy (The Silken Bed).
Nichol. Ferry Me Across.
Nichols, G. Tropical Death.
Nicholson, N. Five Minutes.
Nims, J. Trainwrecked Soldiers.
Noguchi, R. I, the Neighbor Mr. Uskovich, Watch Every Morning Kenji Takezo Hold His Breath.
Noguchi, Yonejiro (Yone). Lines: "Sun I worship, The."
Nonnus. But Dionysos had no healing physic for his comrade fallen, of dancing he thought no more.
Where Carpos wandered and died, I will fall headlong.
Nordbrandt. Our Love Is Like Byzantium.
Norris, J. Meditation, The.
Norris, L. Elegy for Lyn James.
Nortje. Autopsy.
Norton, C. Obscurity of Woman's Worth.
Notley. Back.
Beginning with a Stain.
How the Dead Women May Operate from Negative Space.
Poem: "You hear that heroic big land music?"
"Novalis.". Longing for Death.
Yearning for Death.
Nowlan. Aunt Jane.
Noyes, A. Highwayman, The.
Ó Dálaigh, M. Elegy on Mael Mhedha, His Wife.
O'Hehir, D. Bedside.
O'Reilly, M. Abused Child.
Small Girl Brings an Injured Bird into the Surgery, A.
O'Lahsen, M. Dead Erect, The.
O'Connell, E. Your Grave Disfigures Me.
Odarchenko. Claudia Petrovna.
Only for you my tea roses.
Ogilvy. Newly Dead and Newly Born.
O'Grady, D. Dying Gaul, The.
Reading the Unpublished Manuscripts of Louis MacNeice at Kinsale Harbour.
O'Hara, F. Day Lady Died, The.
Elegy: "Ecstatic and in anguish over lost days."
Ode to Joy.
Poem: "And tomorrow morning at 8 o'clock in Springfield, Massachusetts."
Poem: "Eager note on my door said 'Call me', The."
Okudzhava. Not About Death.
Olds, S. His Smell.
Leningrad Cemetery, Winter of 1941.
Lifting, The.
Moment of My Father's Death, The.
Race, The.
Oliver, D. Little Night, A.
Oliver, M. Black Snake, The.
When Death Comes.
Wings.

O'Loughlin. Irish Requiem, An.
Posthumous.
Olson, C. As the Dead Prey upon Us.
At Yorktown.
La Préface.
Newly Discovered "Homeric" Hymn, A.
Thing Was Moving, The.
Variations Done for Gerald Van De Wiele.
Omer, H. To the Memory of a Comrade.
Oodgeroo of the tribe Noonuccal. Dawn Wail for the Dead.
O'odham. No. 77. His Heart Is Almost Covered with Night.
Oppen. Survival: Infantry.
Taste, The.
They await / War, and the news.
O'Reilly, C. Envoi: "And although it will be."
Orléans, C. Las! Mort Qui T'a Fait Si Hardie.
Quant Souvenir Me Ramentoit.
Ormond. At His Father's Grave.
My Dusty Kinsfolk.
Ormsby, F. Day in August, A.
Orozco. Miss Havisham.
Olga Orozco.
Orr, G. City of Salt, The.
Gathering the Bones Together.
Gray Fox, The.
Orten. Whispered.
Ovid. Apollo and Hyacinthus.
Death of Orpheus, The.
Elegy 1.15: "Envy, why carp'st [or carpest] thou my time is spent so ill."
Venus and Adonis.
Owen, G. Elegy for His Daughter Ellen.
Owen, W. End, The.
Futility.
Miners.
Strange Meeting.
To My Friend (With an Identity Disc).
Unreturning, The.
Pack, R. Fathering the Map.
Padgett, R. Something or Other.
Padilla. Legacies.
Page, G. Elegist, The.
Inscription at Villers-Bretonneux.
Page, P. About Death.
Pagis, D. Autobiography.
Balloons.
Battle, The.
Draft of a Reparations Agreement.
Ein Leben.
Evidence.
Paino. Matter of Division, A.
Truth, The.
Pak Mogwŏl [or Mokwŏl]. Bare Wind, A.
Paley, G. Some days I am lonesome I want to talk to my mother.
Palmer, M. Notes for Echo Lake 3.
Said the Speaker.
Pankey. Resurrection of the Body, The.
Paquet. It Is Monsoon at Last.
Parker, Bonnie. Story of Bonnie and Clyde, The.
Parker, Dominque. Foxfire.
Parker, Dorothy. Résumé.
Parkerson. Statistic.
Parra, N. Anti-Lazarus, The.
Parry, R. Two Hearts Divided.
Parry-Williams. These Bones.
Pasolini. Day of My Death, The.
John 12:24–25; Truly, truly, I say to you.
Pastan. Death's Blue-Eyed Girl.
Departures.
Hat Lady, The.
Turnabout.
Pasternak, B. To Love.
Patchen. Body beside the Ties, The.
Do the Dead Know What Time It Is?
From My High Love.
In Memory of Kathleen.
O All Down within the Pretty Meadow.
Religion Is That I Love You.
Paul, C. Georgina.
Paulinus of Nola. To Ausonius.
Pavlova. Life calls us, and we go, massing our courage.

Paz. And the banquet, the exile, the first crime.
Small Variation.
Peacock, M. Dream Come True.
Fare, The.
Peacocke. In Memoriam.
Pegram, A. Burials.
Towards Abraham's Bosom.
Péret. Nungesser und Coli Sind Verreckt.
Peters, L. Isatou Died.
Peterson, M. I Kissed Pa Twice after His Death.
Petrarch. Go, grieving rimes of mine, to that hard stone.
He Understands the Great Cruelty of Death.
Philips, K. Epitaph on her Son H. P. at St. Syth's Church [where her body also lies Interred].
Piatt, S. Army of Occupation.
Giving Back the Flower.
Her Word of Reproach.
Picasso. Bottle of Suze, A.
Picková, E. Fear.
Pickthall, M. Resurgam.
Piercy. Barbie Doll.
Pietri. Night Is out of Sight, The.
Pilinszky, J. Harbach 1944.
Pilling. Ophelia.
Pinchas-Cohen. Remembering Our Fathers.
Ping. No cloud or rain all night long.
Pinsky. At Pleasure Bay.
Dying.
Impossible to Tell.
Piontek. In the Woods.
Pitcher, O. Pale Blue Casket, The.
Pizarnik. Poem for the Father.
Silences.
Pizarnik. Shadow of Days to Come.
Plath. Bee Meeting, The.
Daddy.
Death and Co.
Edge.
Getting There.
Lady Lazarus.
Last Words: "I do not want a plain box, I want a sarcophagus."
Point Shirley.
Stings.
Plato. Aster.
Po Chü-i. Last Poem.
Song of Lasting Regret, The.
Poe. Annabel Lee.
City in the Sea, The.
Conqueror Worm, The.
For Annie.
Lenore.
Monody on Doctor Olmsted.
Raven, The.
Sleeper, The.
To My Mother.
To One in Paradise.
Ulalume [or Ulalume—a Ballad].
Pogson, P. Bee.
Pollarolo, G. In My Days.
Popa. Heaven's Ring.
Pope, A. Epitaph for One Who Would Not Be Buried in Westminster Abbey.
Ode: The Dying Christian to His Soul.
Poplavsky [or Poplavskii]. Another Planet.
Porta. Dialogue with Herz.
Portal. Watch of Time.
Porter, D. Lollies Noir.
Porter, P. Exequy, An.
Talking to You Afterwards.
Portugal, Anne. Seen from Over Here ("Seen from over here.").
Porzecanski. Every Month.
Pound, E. Sandalphon.
When, when, and whenever death closes our eyelids.
Powell, D. A. Darling can you kill me: with your mickeymouse pillows.
Sleek mechanical dart: the syringe noses into the blue vein marking the target of me.
Thicknesses of victor decreased: blanket->sheet->floss. Until no material would do, The.
Powell, J. Lines Written for a Friend on the

Death of His Brother, Caused by a Railway Train Running Over Him Whilst He Was in a State of Inebriation.
Prado, A. Successive Deaths.
Pratt, M. Red String.
Praxilla. Fairest thing I leave behind is sunlight, The.
Prévert. Familial.
Last Supper, The.
Probyn. Kyrielle.
Rondelet: "Which way he went?"
Procter, A. Philip and Mildred.
Three Evenings in a Life.
Propertius. Night's best of all. Night brings delight.
When Thou Must Home.
Prufer, K. For the Dead.
Prys-Jones. Unfortunate Occurrence at Cwm-Cadno.
Purdy, A. Winter Walking.
Quarles. David's Epitaph on Jonathan.
I saw him dead; I saw his Body fall.
Quasimodo. Dead of Winter.
To the Fifteen of Piazzale Loreto.
Quevedo y Villegas. He Points Out the Brevity of Life, Unthinking and Suffering, Surprised by Death.
Love beyond Death.
Love Constant beyond Death.
Raboni, G. Alibi of a Dead Man.
For C., Who Died of Childbirth at the Age of One Year and Eleven Months.
Moon.
"Rachel." [or "Rahel."]. In my great loneliness.
Messenger came in the night, The.
My Dead.
Radcliffe, A. Storied Sonnet.
Radnóti. Forced March.
Peace, Horror.
Picture Postcards.
Postcard (Found on His body after He Was Killed by the Nazis).
Ragan, J. Huckster at Noontime.
Raine, K. Highland Graveyard.
Instrument, The.
Rakan-Keinan. Today Rakan, riding an iron horse.
Ralegh, S. Authours Epitaph, Made by Himself, The.
Even Such Is Time.
Passionate Man[']s Pilgrimage, The.
Sir Walter Ra[u]le[i]gh to His Son[ne].
Ramanujan. Breaded Fish.
Death and the Good Citizen.
Hindu to His Body, A.
Some People.
Randall, Deborah. Blue Dome, The.
Randall, Dudley. Old Witherington.
Randell. Temperament is related to physique.
Randolph, T. On Sir Robert Cotton the Antiquary.
Rankin, J. Forever the Snake.
Ransom, J. Here Lies a Lady.
Piazza Piece.
Ravikovitch, D. Blood Heifer.
You Can't Kill a Baby Twice.
Ray, D. Eskimo Girl, The.
Rāy, R. Who is this.
Rāy, T. Wait a moment, Death.
Rector. Showing.
Redmond. Milestone: The Birth of an Ancestor.
Poetic Reflections Enroute to, and during, The Funeral and Burial of Henry Dumas, Poet.
Reed, I. I Am Not the Walrus.
Oakland Blues.
Reese, L. Telling the Bees.
Regan, J. In Flight.
Reid, A. Curiosity.
Rexroth, K. Andrée Rexroth ("Now once more gray mottled buckeye branches.").
Andrée Rexroth ("Years have gone, The. It is spring.").
Delia Rexroth ("California rolls into.").
Delia Rexroth ("Under your illkempt yellow roses.").
Reynolds, C. Worst of It, The.

Reznikoff. Dead gull in the road, A.
Epitaph: "Not the five feet of water to your chin."
Epitaphs: "Drowning / I felt for a moment reaching towards me."
My grandfather, dead long before I was born.
Of course, we must die.
On Brooklyn Bridge I saw a man drop dead.
She who worked patiently.
1. The Sinking.
Testimony: The United States (1901–1910) Recitative/The South.
Rich, A. From a Survivor.
I Dream I'm the Death of Orpheus.
Paula Becker to Clara Westhoff.
Phantasia for Elvira Shatayev.
Tattered Kaddish.
Woman Mourned by Daughters, A.
Rickword. Moonrise Over Battlefield.
Ridge, L. Fifth-Floor Window, The.
Rilke. Death.
Orpheus, Eurydice, Hermes.
Rimbaud, A. Being Beauteous.
Decidedly we are out of the world. No longer any sound.
Sleeper in the Valley, The.
Ríos, A. Mi Abuelo.
Ritsos. Afternoon.
Miniature.
Unanswered.
Robinson, A. Dead Friend, The.
Pallor.
To a Dead Friend.
Venetian Nocturne.
Robinson, E. Exit.
For a Dead Lady.
Luke 15:20–32; And he arose and came.
Luke Havergal.
Many Are Called.
Old Story, An.
Walt Whitman: "Master-songs are ended, and the man, The."
Robinson, M. Foresees her Death.
Her Reflections on the Leucadian Rock Before She Perishes.
Resolves to Take the Leap of Leucata.
To the Muses.
Rochester, J. Song: "Absent from thee, I languish still."
Rock, D. Mother.
Rodgers, C. Written for Love of an Ascension—Coltrane.
Roeske, P. Preparing the Dead.
Roethke. Elegy for Jane.
Judge Not.
Rogers, S. Boy of Egremond, The.
Roggeman. Fata Morgana in Flanders.
Rojas. And to Be Born Is Here an Unnameable Feast.
Chapter and Verse.
Roland Holst. Autumn Wind.
Night Visit.
Rolfe, E. Paris—Christmas 1938.
Rolleston. Grave of Rury, The.
Root, W. Sonnet 20: Remembering, from a Nazi Prison, a Teacher Years Before.
Rose, P. Terminus.
Rose. Truganinny.
Ross, L. Requiescat.
Rossetti, C. After Death.
Amen.
At Home.
Before the Beginning.
Cardinal Newman.
Chilly Night, A.
Convent Threshold, The.
Dead before Death.
Dirge, A: "Why were you born when the snow was falling?"
Eve.
Gone Before.
Heaviness May Endure for a Night, But Joy Cometh in the Morning.
Iniquity of the Fathers upon the Children, The.
Passing Away, Saith the World, Passing Away.
Pause, A.

Remember [Me].
Rest.
Sappho.
Sleeping at Last.
Song: "Oh roses for the flush of youth."
Song: "When I am dead, my dearest."
Triad, A.
Two Thoughts of Death.
Under Willows.
Uphill [or Up-Hill].
Verse III.
Rossetti, D. Blessed Damozel, The.
My Sister's Sleep.
Orchard-Pit, The.
Sudden Light.
Rothenberg, J. Water of the Flowery Mill (II), The.
Rowbotham. Bus-Stop on the Somme, The.
Rózewicz. Busy with Many Jobs.
Larva, The.
Posthumous Rehabilitation.
Ruefle. Furtherness.
Rukeyser, M. Book of the Dead, The.
Death and the Dancer.
Iris.
Madboy's Song.
Outer Banks, The.
Power of Suicide, The.
Rumi. In the shambles of love, they kill only the best.
Rungano. Mother.
Russell, G. Immortality.
Ryan, G. Achilleus to Odysseus.
Elegy for 6 So Far.
Ryan, M. Talking About Things.
Ryan, R. At the End.
Ryan, T. Eclipse, Kenwick, 1974.
Trompe l'Oeil.
Ryuichi. October Poem.
Standing Coffin.
Sachs, N. Chorus of the Dead.
How Long Have We Forgotten How to Listen!
O Sister.
You.
Sáenz. Benjamín.
St. John, D. Elegy: "It's true such reckless grace should never die."
Elegy: "Who keeps the owl's breath? Whose eyes desire?"
Saitō Mokichi. From far off I have brought medicines, she watches me because I am her son.
Salaam. Funeraled Fare Well.
I Just Heard John Buffington Died.
Our World Is Less Full Now That Mr. Fuller Is Gone.
Secondline Send Off.
Salazar. E Is in Heaven.
Piñon Nuts.
Salinas, L. For Larry Levis in Memory.
Sanchez, S. Blues.
Philadelphia: Spring, 1985.
Sandburg, C. Bones.
Cool Tombs.
Grass.
Haze.
Illinois Farmer.
Losers.
Murmurings in a Field Hospital.
People, yes, the people, The.
Right to Grief, The.
Southern Pacific.
Sanguineti. I tell you it was a hard punch to my brain.
Sankichi, T. Dying.
Santayana. Sonnet 25: "As in the midst of battle there is room."
Sappho. Delicate Adonis is dying, Kytheria— what should we do?
Gongyla.
On a Lady Indifferent to Poetry.
Their souls became cold.
When you die you'll lie dead, no memory of you.
Sargant, J. A. How gladly would I lay my aching head.

'Lo, on her dying couch, the sufferer lies.
Sarson, H. Shell, The.
Sarton, M. Letter from Chicago.
Sassoon, S. Conclusion: "Image dance of change, An."
Counter-Attack.
Death-Bed, The.
General, The.
Grandeur of Ghosts.
In Heytesbury Wood.
Rear-Guard, The.
To His Dead Body.
Working Party, A.
Scammell, W. Inventions.
Schechter. What Were You Patching?
Schelling. Run My Hand Under.
Schnackenberg. Nightfishing.
Schwartz, D. Now He Knows All There Is to Know: Now He Is Acquainted with the Day and Night.
Schwartz, R. L. Grief.
When They Know.
Scott, D. Forsaken, The.
Scott, S. Breathes there the [or a] Man with soul so dead.
Proud Maisie.
Scott, W. My Mother.
Scott, W. U.S. Sailor with the Japanese Skull, The.
Seale, J. To a Late Local Environmentalist.
Seeger, A. I Have a Rendezvous with Death.
Seeger, P. Where Have All the Flowers Gone?
Seferis. Day was cloudy, The. No one could come to a decision.
Euripides the Athenian.
Last Day, The.
Our Sun.
Seiho. Sky's not high, earth not solid.
Sekioku-Seikyo. This body won't pollute.
Sekishitsu-Soei. Fifty-three years / This clumsy ox has managed.
Seminole Oral Tradition. Song for the Dying.
Sempill, R. Life and Death of [Habbie Simson] the Piper of Kilbarchan, The.
Sen, R. Death, get out of here!
This time, Kali.
Wait a minute, Death.
What a joke!
Seneca. After Death Nothing Is.
Deaths of Orphues and Hercules, The.
Trojan Women.
Voracious Time, uprooting all, consumes it.
Serge. Constellation of Dead Brothers.
Seward. On a Lock of Miss Sarah Seward's Hair Who Died in Her Twentieth Year.
Sonnet 31.
Sexton. All My Pretty Ones.
Dreams.
Elizabeth Gone.
Jesus Dies.
Moss of His Skin, The.
Somewhere in Africa.
Starry Night, The.
Truth the Dead Know, The.
Wanting to Die.
Shakespeare, W. Ay[e], but to die, and go we know not where.
Clown's Song, The.
Dirge for Fidele.
Full Fathom Five.
Ophelia's Song.
Sonnet 5: "Those hours that with gentle work did frame."
Sonnet 64: "When I have seen by Time's fell hand defac'd [or defaced]."
Sonnet 66: "Tired [or Tyr'd or Tir'd] with all these, for restful[l] death I cry."
Sonnet 71: "No longer mourn for me when I am dead."
Sonnet 72: "O, lest the world should task you to recite."
Sonnet 73: "That time of year thou may'st in me behold."
Sonnet 74: "But be contented: when that fell arrest."
Sonnet 81: "Or I shall live your epitaph to

make."
Sonnet 86: "Was it the proud full sail[e] of his
  great verse."
Sonnet 107: "Not mine own[e] fear[e]s, nor the
  prophetic[k] soul[e]."
Sonnet 110: "Alas, 'tis true, I have gone here
  and there."
Sonnet 146: "Poor[e] soul[e], the centre [or
  center] of my sinful[l] earth."
What saies my brother?
Shapiro, K.   Auto Wreck.
Cut Flower, A.
My Grandmother.
Scyros.
Shelley, P.   Adonais; An Elegy on the Death of
  John Keats.
Mask [or Masque] of Anarchy, The.
One remains, the many change and pass, The.
To Night.
Shen Chou.   Taoist Huang Has Died of
  Alcoholism, The.
Sherrill, S.   Katyn Forest.
Shinkichi Takahashi.   Canna.
Drizzle.
Eternity.
Four Divine Animals.
Hand.
Let's Live Cheerfully.
Little Sunlight, A.
Moon.
Mother and I.
Near Shinobazu Pond.
Sheep.
Shell.
Sparrow in Withered Field.
Urn.
Shishin-Goshin.   Talking: seven steps, eight
  falls.
Shokaku.   High wind, cold moon.
Shozan.   No mind, no Buddha.
Shuford.   Sam Bass.
Sia, B.   Howl.
Siamanto.   Dance, The.
Grief.
Siddal.   At Last.
Dead Love.
Sidney.   Dirge: "Ring out your bells [or belles],
  let mourning shows [or shewes] be spread."
Leave Me O Love.
Since wailing is a bud of causeful sorrow.
Sigourney.   Death of an Infant.
Silesky.   Kingdom, The.
Silva, C.   Moon's Cadaver, The.
Simic.   Eyes Fastened with Pins.
Simmons, J.   From the Irish.
Simonides.   For the Spartan Dead at
  Thermopylai (480 B.C.).
Greek Dead at Thermopylae, The.
On the Spartan Dead at Thermopylae.
Thermopylae.
These men lying here were carrying honors to
  Apollo.
Simonov.   Death Struck Him.
Simpson, L.   On the Ledge.
Siôn Cent.   Vanity of the World, The.
Sioux Oral Tradition.   Whole world is coming,
  The.
Sirowitz, H.   Slowing Down for Death.
Sirr.   Beginnings.
Sissman.   Bruisingly cradled in a Harvard chair.
Deathplace, A.
Upon Finding Dying: An Introduction, by L. E.
  Sissman, Remaindered at IS.
Skeeter.   Western Trail Cook, 1880.
Skelton, J.   Pla ce bo.
Upon a Dead Man's Head.
Slutsky [or Slutskii].   My old men are dying.
Smedley, M.   Cavour.
Face from the Past, A.
Smith, A.   Archer, The.
Smith, C.   By the Same.
Ode to Death.
Pressed by the Moon, Mute Arbitress of Tides.
To the Shade of Burns.
To the South Downs.
Smith, D.   Roundhouse Voices, The.

Smith, P.   Building Nicole's Mama.
Woman Who Died in Line, The.
Smith, S.   Black March.
Death Sentence, The.
Exeat.
Harold's Leap.
Mr. Over.
Mrs Simpkins.
Not Waving but Drowning.
Snodgrass.   Flat One, A.
Viewing the Body.
Snyder, G.   Dragonfly.
For John Chappell.
For Lew Welch in a Snowfall.
Södergran.   Arrival in Hades.
Sogetsuni.   After the Dance for the Dead.
Sophocles.   Torn between griefs, which grief
  shall I lament.
Sorby.   Land of Lincoln.
Sorley.   All the hills and vales along.
Sosnora.   There it all was: the gaslamp,
  drugstore.
Soupault.   Epitaph: André Breton.
One o'Clock.
Southern Bushmen Oral Tradition.   Day We Die,
  The.
Southey, R.   Did then the bold slave rear at last
  the sword.
Southwell.   I Dye Alive.
Souza.   Landscape.
Sowle, J.   Short Testimony for Anne Whitehead,
  A.
Soyinka.   Around Us, Dawning.
Civilian and Soldier.
Death in the Dawn.
Funeral Sermon, Soweto.
Massacre, October '66.
Post Mortem.
We wish only to bury our dead. Shorn.
Sozan-Kyonin.   Rootless tree, A.
Sparrow, J.   Epitaph: "This stone, with not
  unpardonable pride."
Spellman, A.   Did John's Music Kill Him?
Spender, S.   Funeral, The.
Spires.   First Day, The.
Spragins, Anna Word.   Farewell to Texas.
Stainer.   Bleaklow.
Sarcophagus.
Xochiquetzal.
Stanley, T.   On S. John the Baptist.
Stanton, M.   Few Picnics in Illinois, A.
Starbuck, G.   Prognosis.
Statius.   In Memory of His Father.
Steinberg, J.   Turn towards the end, be a leaf
  dying.
Stephens, P.   Signalmen, The.
Steptoe.   Notes for a Poem from the Middle
  Passage of Years.
Stern, G.   Behaving Like a Jew.
Pile of Feathers.
Stesichoros.   Don't pile cruel cares upon those
  griefs.
Stevens, W.   Death of a Soldier, The.
Emperor of Ice-Cream, The.
Flyer's Fall.
Of Heaven Considered as a Tomb.
Postcard from the Volcano, A.
Sunday Morning.
Worms at Heaven's Gate, The.
Stevenson, Alec Brock.   Death, My Companion.
Stevenson, Anne.   Epitaph for a Good Mouser.
Minister.
Stevenson, R.   Celestial Surgeon, The.
Epitaph: "Angler rose, he took his rod, The."
He hears with gladdened heart the thunder.
It's an owercome sooth for age an' youth.
Pirate Ditty.
Requiem: "Under the wide and starry sky."
Ticonderoga: A Legend of the West Highlands.
To Mrs. Will H. Low.
Tropics vanish, and meseems that I, The.
Stewart, S.   Apple.
Stone, J.   Death: "I have seen come on."
Truck, The.
Stone, R.   Curtains.
Habit.

Stowe.   Only a Year.
Strand.   Dead, The.
End, The.
Prediction, The.
Strauss, J.   Tending the Graves.
Strejilevich.   When They Robbed Me of My
  Name.
Strickland, A.   Forsaken, The.
Strode.   Epitaph on the Monument of Sir
  William Strode.
Stryk, L.   Black Bean Soup.
Su Tung-p'o.   Remembering Min Ch'e.
Tune: "River Town".
Suárez.   Another Poem to My Mother.
Worker Dies, A.
Suckling, S.   Song: "I prithee spare me, gentle
  boy."
Suermondt, Tim.   Missing Supper.
Supervielle.   Like an ox.
Surrey.   Epitaph for [or on] Thomas Clere.
Excellent Epitaffe of Syr Thomas Wyat, An.
Wyatt Resteth Here.
Swenson, M.   Feel Me.
Question: "Body my house."
Shape of Death, The.
Staring at the Sea on the Day of the Death of
  Another.
Swift, J.   Satirical Elegy on the Death of a Late
  Famous General, A.
To the Earl of Oxford, Late Lord Treasurer.
Swinburne.   Forsaken Garden, A.
Garden of Proserpine, The.
Sonnet for a Picture.
Swirszczynska [or Swir].   Conversation Through
  the Door, A.
I Wash the Shirt.
They Lay Dying Side by Side.
Symonds.   Midnight at Baiae.
Synge.   On an Anniversary.
Patch-Shaneen.
Question, A.
Synková, A.   I'd Like to Go Alone.
Szymborska, W.   Seen from Above ("On a dirt
  road lies a dead beetle.").
Tabb.   Echoes.
Tadic.   Man from the Death Institute.
Taggard.   To the Powers of Desolation.
Tagore.   Echo always mocks the sound, The.
Takushitsu.   Breeze strokes the water of the
  spring, A.
Taliesin.   Death Song for Owain ab Urien.
Tallmountain.   Hands of Mary Joe, The.
Tan Taigi.   Thunder / Voices of drowned.
T'ang Hsien-tsu.   My son, you loved telling the
  story of Prince Nata.
On the Day of Washing the Buddha in the Year
  Ting-wei (1607), I Dreamed That My Late
  Son Shih-ch'ü Was Holding a Book, and
  Appeared to Be Quite Happy. He Said That
  He Had Earned His Chin-shih Degree in the
  Underworld.
T'ao Ch'ien [or T'ao Yuan-ming].   Bearers'
  Song.
Tasso.   Drearie trumpet blew a dreadfull blast,
  The.
Tate, A.   Cross, The.
Non Omnis Moriar.
Oath, The.
Tate, G.   Last Instructions.
Tate, J.   Death on Columbus Day.
Diagnosis, The.
Distance from Loved Ones.
Taylor, E.   Fig for Thee, Oh! Death, A.
Upon a Spider Catching a Fly.
Teasdale.   Answer, The.
I Shall Live to Be Old.
On the Dunes.
Tekeyan.   Forgetting.
Tendo-Nyojo.   Sixty-six years.
Tengour, H.   In the Country of the Dead.
Secret in Broad Daylight.
Tennyson, A.   Be near me when my light is low.
Crossing the Bar.
Danube to the Severn gave, The.
Dear friend, far off, my lost desire.
Dying Swan, The.

Fair ship, that from the Italian shore.
I held it truth, with him who sings.
In the Garden at Swainston.
In the Valley of Cauteretz.
Lady of Shalott, The.
Lord of Burleigh, The.
Love is and was my Lord and King.
Now, sometimes in my sorrow shut.
O [or Oh] that 'twere possible.
O Sorrow, cruel fellowship.
Old yew, which graspest at the stones.
Path by which we twain did go, The.
Sonnet: "She took the dappled partridge flecked [or fleckt] with blood."
Sweet after showers, ambrosial air.
Tears of the widower, when he sees.
Thy spirit ere our fatal loss.
Thy voice is on the rolling air.
Tithonus.
Yet if some voice that man could trust.
Terry, L.   Bars Fight [August 28, 1746].
Tessho.   Finally out of reach.
Thackeray.   Dear Jack.
Sorrows of Werther, The.
Theocritus.   Epitaph: Justice.
Theognis.   Captive.
Thomas, D.   After the Funeral.
Among Those Killed in the Dawn Raid Was a Man Aged a Hundred.
And Death Shall Have No Dominion.
Conversation of Prayer, The.
Do Not Go Gentle into That Good Night.
Force That through the Green Fuse Drives the Flower, The.
Hand That Signed the Paper, The.
Thomas, E.   Gallows, The.
Lights Out.
Rain: "Rain, midnight rain, nothing but the wild rain."
Snow.
Thomas, E.   Spectator, The.
Thomas, G.   Little Death.
Thomas, R. S.   Pisces.
Still.
Thompson, C.   Not Dead, but Sleeping.
To My Dead Brother.
Thompson, P.   Afternoon Gossip, An.
Consumptive, The.
Lines on a Dead Girl.
Song, The: "Oh, foully slighted Ethiope maid!"
To a Deceased Friend.
Thomson, J.   Part 2: "Because he seemed to walk with an intent."
T'Hooft.   Death, Dark Agent.
Death, Dark Doer.
Tichborne [or Tichbourne].   Tichborne's Elegy.
Tighe.   As one who late hath lost a friend adored.
1802.
To Death.
Tikhonov.   Fire and Rope, Bullet and Axe.
Timrod.   Ode: "Sleep sweetly in your humble graves."
Tipping.   Just after Michael's Death, the Game of Pool.
Tolson, M.   Festus Conrad.
Old Pettigrew.
Tomlinson, C.   After a Death.
Death in the Desert, A.
Torres Bodet.   Summary.
Townsend, A.   First Death.
Tozan-Gyoso.   Way's not for the blind.
Trakl.   De Profundis.
To the Child Elis.
Tranströmer.   After a Death.
Black Postcards.
Track.
Tranter.   Burden of noise, of infections, A.
Some sports are odious, but.
Triem.   For Paul.
Tripp.   Armistice Day '77, Honiton.
In Memory of Idris Davies.
Troupe.   Conjuring against Alien Spirits.
Old People Speak of Death, The.
Tsvetayeva [or Tsvetaeva].   Garden.
Gentle ghost.

I know the truth—give up all other truths!
They thought: Human!
Who sleeps at night? No one is sleeping.
Tsvetkov.   Like a ruddy child you fall asleep in september.
Tu Fu [or Du Fu].   Dreaming of Li Po ("Parted by death, we'd strangle on our tears.").
Song of the War-Chariots (Yueh-Fu).
Tucker, M.   "Did You Call Me, Father?".
Gone.
Lift Me Higher.
Tuckerman, F.   Coralie.
Turner, C.   Bliss of Heaven, Maria, shall be thine, The.
Julius Caesar and the Honey-Bee.
Twichell.   Aisle of Dogs.
Tzara.   Death of Guillaume Apollinaire, The.
For Robert Desnos.
Waking.
Ulacia, M.   Stone at the Bottom, The.
Uncho.   Forty-nine years / —What a din!
Ungaretti.   Wake.
Watch.
Unger, B.   Photo Taken in Winter, 1944.
Unknown.   Al worldly welthe passed me fro.
Barbara Allan.
Bells of hell go ting-a-ling-a-ling, The.
Blowflies Buzz, The.
Bonny Earl of Murray, The [Version from Tea-Table Miscellany].
Cowboy's Lament, The.
Dead Man Asks for a Song, The.
Death.
Death.
Death Is Before Me Today.
Death of Enkidu, The.
Death of Yesugei, The.
Elegy upon the Death of Mrs. A. Behn, the Incomparable Astrea, An.
Epitaph.
Epitaph on the Duke of Buckingham.
Evermore, wher-so-evere I be.
Farewell, this world! I take my leve for ever.
Feltons Epitaph.
Fighting, south of the ramparts.
Finnegan's Wake.
Grave, The.
Graves the rain makes wet and sleek, The.
How Death Comes.
I Know Moon-Rise [or Moonrise].
I wende to deeth, knight stith in stour.
If I might offer.
In the early hours of the next morning dawning.
In the vale of resteles mynde.
John Henry.
Lament for the Death of Guillén Peraza.
Lament of Gilgamesh for Enkidu, The.
Last Survivor's Speech in Old English, The.
Limerick.
Lonesome Valley.
Lord, Remember Me!
Lullabies, 2:174.
Lyke-Wake Dirge, The [or A].
Message to the Living.
My Boy Willie.
No More Auction Block.
On Bond the Usurer.
On the Death of Mr. Persall's Little Daughter, in the Beginning of the Spring, at Amsterdam.
Peacock Southeast Flew, A.
Perle, plesaunte to prynces paye.
Petelia Tablet, The.
Romance of Love.
Ruin, The.
Shades of the Newly Buried Complain to the Gods, The.
Since Bonny-Boots Was Dead.
Sith al that in this world hath ben in rerum natura.
Sodeynly affrayed, half wakyng, half slepyng.
Springfield Mountain.
Steal Away to Jesus.
Stormalong!
There were two royal children.
They Fought South of the Wall.
Three Ravens, The.

Timor Mortis.
To learn how to die.
Tune: Eternal Longing.
Twa Corbies, The.
Unquiet Grave, The.
Wel, who shal thise hornes blowe.
Which is worse.
Wife of Usher's Well, The.
With the first light of the early morning dawning.
You all by yourself fulfilled.
You intend, it seems.
Your Thwarts in Pieces, Your Mooring Rope Cut.
Unknown, fr. Terezin Concentration Camp.
Birdsong 2.
Closed Town, The.
Concert in the Old School Garret.
Homesick.
On a Sunny Evening.
Theresienstadt's Hospital.
Untermeyer, L.   To a Vine-Clad Telegraph Pole.
Updike.   Perfection Wasted.
Urdang.   My Father's Death.
Usborne.   Epitaph on a Party Girl.
Vallejo.   Black Messengers, The.
Black Riders, The.
Black Stone Lying on a White Stone.
Black Stone on a White Stone.
Eternal Dice, The.
Masses.
Our Daily Bread.
To My Brother Miguel.
Trilce.
Van Duyn.   Stream, The.
Van Vliet.   Party.
Van Walleghen.   More Trouble with the Obvious.
Vando.   In the Crevices of Night.
Vaughan, H.   Death.
Death.
Easter Hymn.
Pursuit[e], The.
They Are All Gone into the World of Light!
Waterfall [or Water-Fall], The.
Veinberg, J.   Next to Tut.
Owl's Landscape, An.
Venclova.   Canto Eleven.
Verlaine.   Asleep in the Valley.
Verwey, A.   Beautiful World, The.
Very.   Cup, The.
Dead, The.
Yourself.
Vietnamese Oral Tradition.   Egret's Death and Funeral Preparations.
Red Cloth, The.
Vilariño.   Each Afternoon.
If I Died Tonight.
Like a Dog Howling Endlessly.
Villiers.   Epitaph upon Thomas, Lord Fairfax, An.
Villon.   Ballad[e] of Dead Ladies, The.
Ballade to End With, A.
Remember, Imbeciles and Wits.
Vinal.   To Persephone.
Vinokurov.   When the Parachute Does Not Open.
Virgil [or Vergil].   Aeneas in the Underworld.
Death Plucks My Ear.
Sleep of Palinurus, The.
Voce, L.   Your eyes stolen.
Vogel, D.   Single and last carriage is ready for the journey, A.
There Is a Last, Solitary Coach.
Voigt.   Visiting the Graves.
Volkman.   Infernal.
Voznesensky [or Voznesenskii].   Call of the Lake, The.
Recommendation.
Vroman.   Thin Wire.
Vroomkoning.   Together Again ("You get these thoughts in melancholy Autumn.").
Wagoner, D.   Author of American Ornithology Sketches a Bird, Now Extinct, The.
Wainwright, J.   1815.

Wakuan-Shitai. Iron tree blooms.
Walcott. Letter from Brooklyn, A.
  Sea Canes.
  Village Life, A.
Waldman, A. Death is all things we see awake.
Walker, A. Good Night, Willie Lee, I'll See
  You in the Morning.
Wallace-Crabbe. Dead Cartesian, The.
Walton, A. Elegy for Joan.
Wang Wei. Mourning for Yin Yao.
  Weeping for Ying Yao.
Wanley. Resurrection, The.
Warren, R. After the Dinner Party.
  Confederate Veteran Tries to Explain the Event,
    A.
  Dream He Never Knew the End of, The.
  School Lesson Based on Word of Tragic Death
    of Entire Gillum Family.
  Tale of Time.
  There's a Grandfather's Clock in the Hall.
Warren, R. Cormorant, The.
  In Creve Coeur, Missouri.
  Max Jacob at Saint Benoît.
Warsh. Gout.
Watson, E. Battered Toddler, Page B6.
Waugh, E. They told me, Francis Hinsley, they
  told me you were hung.
Weaver, A. Water Song.
Webb, C. You Missed the Earthquake, Bill.
Webb, F. Death at Winson Green, A.
Webster, A. Passing Away.
  That some day death who has us all for jest.
Webster, J. Call for the Robin-Redbreast and
  the Wren.
Weems, M. Return to Temptation.
Weigl. Temple Near Quang Tri, Not on the
  Map.
Weinstein, N. Migration of Drummond's
  Organs (After Death), The.
Weismiller. Skull.
Welish. Kiss Tomorrow Goodbye.
Weston, R. Epitaph: "Beneath this stone lies
  William Burke."
Whalen, P. Walking beside the Kamogawa,
  Remembering Nansen and Fudo and Gary's
  Poem.
Wheatley, P. On the Death of a Young
  Gentleman.
  On the Death of the Rev. Mr. George Whitefield
  [1770].
Wheelock, J. Earth, Take Me Back.
White, B. Fixin' to Die.
White, D. Epistle of Love and of Consolation
  unto Israel, An.
White, G. Dead Armadillos.
Whitlow. Rockin' a Man, Stone Blind.
Whitman, W. As If a Phantom Caress'd Me.
  As Toilsome I Wander'd Virginia's Woods.
  Ashes of Soldiers.
  Come Up from the Fields Father.
  Death's Valley.
  Has any one supposed it lucky to be born?
  Hush'd Be the Camps To-Day.
  Joy, Shipmate, Joy!
  Last Invocation, The.
  O Captain! My Captain!
  Old Salt Kossabone.
  On the Same Picture.
  Osceola.
  Out of the Cradle Endlessly Rocking.
  Sight in Camp [in the Daybreak Gray and Dim],
    A.
  This Compost.
  Vigil Strange I Kept on the Field One Night.
  When Lilacs Last in the Dooryard Bloom'd.
Whitten, Martha E. (Martha Elizabeth Hotchkiss).
  Beautiful in Death.
Whittier. Telling the Bees.
Whur. In a dark and trying hour.
Wicks, S. On Re-recording Mozart.
Wigglesworth. Farewel to the World, A.
Wilbur, R. Another Voice.
  Bell Speech.
  Finished Man, A.
  In a Churchyard.
  Lilacs, The.

Pardon, The.
To an American Poet Just Dead.
To His Skeleton.
Tywater.
Year's End.
Wild, R. Epitaph on Some Bottles of Sack and
  Claret Laid in Sand.
Wilde, O. For oak and elm have pleasant
  leaves.
  Requiescat.
  There is no chapel on the day.
Willard, N. Angels in Winter.
Williams, M. Death of Chet Baker, The.
Williams, O. With Me.
Williams, Stephanie. Drunkard Promise, A.
Williams, W. Complete Destruction.
  Death ("He's dead / the dog won't have to.").
  Death the Barber.
  Last Words of My English Grandmother, The.
  Rapid Transit.
  To a Dog Injured in the Street.
  Why go further? One might conceivably rectify
    the rhythm.
  Widow's Lament in Springtime, The.
Wills, J. One Day We'll Be Able to Talk to the
  Dead.
Winchilsea. *Bolder Youth*, grown of capable
  arms, A.
  To Death.
  Trail All Your Pikes.
Winner, S. Listen to the Mocking Bird.
Winters, Y. Before Disaster.
  For My Father's Grave.
  Realization, The.
  Time and the Garden.
  To the Holy Spirit.
Wiseman. April Elegy (Sam Selvon d.1994).
Wojahn. Buddy Holly.
  John Berryman Listening to Robert Johnson's
    "King of the Delta Blues," January 1972.
  Riding the Empire Builder, 1948.
Wolfe, C. To Mary.
Wolverton, T. Dead Stepfather, The.
Wong, N. Mama, Come Back.
Woods, D. Waiting.
Woody. She-Who-Watches . . . The Names Are
  Prayer.
Wordsworth, W. Methought I saw the footsteps
  of a throne.
  No record tells of lance opposed to lance.
  She Dwelt among the Untrodden Ways.
  She Was a Phantom of Delight.
  Slumber Did My Spirit Seal, A.
  Strange Fits of Passion Have I Known ("Strange
    fits of passion have I known.").
  Surprised by Joy.
  Two April Mornings, The.
Wotton, S. De Morte.
Wright, C. D. Obedience of the Corpse.
Wright, Charles. Homage to Paul Cézanne.
  Quotations.
  Sitting at Night on the Front Porch.
Wright, F. Thoughts of a Solitary Farmhouse.
Wright, J. Angel, The.
  Arrangements with Earth for Three Dead
    Friends.
  At the Executed Murderer's Grave.
  Dream of Burial, A.
  Minneapolis Poem, The.
  Northern Pike.
  Note Left in Jimmy Leonard's Shack, A.
  Old WPA Swimming Pool in Martins Ferry,
    Ohio, The.
  Saint Judas.
  Small Frogs Killed on the Highway.
  Speak.
Wright, J. Don José Gorostiza Encounters El
  Cordobés.
  Journey to the Place of Ghosts.
Wright, J. Eli, Eli.
  Metho Drinker.
Wu of Han [*or* Wu Ti *or* Ou-ty *or* Liu Ch'e *or*
  Liu Ch'.]. Li Furen.
Wunderlich, M. East Seventh Street.
Wyatt. In mourning wise since daily I increase.
  Stand Whoso List.

Wylie. Prophecy.
Yeats. Byzantium.
  Circus Animals' Desertion, The.
  Cold Heaven, The.
  Death.
  Irish Airman Foresees His Death, An.
  Last Confession, A.
  Man and the Echo.
  Man Who Dreamed of Faeryland, The.
  Sailing to Byzantium.
  Three Things.
  To a Shade.
  Vacillation.
Yesenin [*or* Essenin]. Blue Mist.
  Esenin's Suicide Note.
  For My Sister Shura.
  Mysterious, Ancient World of Mine.
Yoketsu. Nothing longed for.
Yorke. Our Gardener here, James Phillips see.
Yosef, H. In the Library.
Young, D. After My Death.
Young, D. White Crane.
Young, G. It's Sunday, October ninth, and the
  earth here is barren after harvest.
Young, G. Damien.
Young, K. Clyde Peeling's Reptiland in
  Allenwood, Pennsylvania.
  Escape Artist, The.
Young, Seth. *All* says a glass doorknob
  Parabola ghost.
Young, S. Epitaph for a Concord Boy.
Yüan Chên. Three Dreams in Chiang-ling.
Zabolotsky [*or* Zabolotskii]. At the
  Fishmonger's.
  Metamorphoses.
  Yesterday Reflecting upon Death.
Zach, N. Seven.
Zagajewski. When Death Came.
Zepeda, O. Bury Me with a Band.
Zuian. Sky-piercing sword, gleaming cold.
Zukofsky, L. H. T.

Death in Old Age
De Kok. Leavetaking.
Huffstickler. Passing of the Old Man, The.
Machado Ruiz. For Don Francisco Giner de
  Los Ríos.
Olin. My Boyfriend, the Infidel.

Death in War
Abelard. More than a brother to me, Jonathan.
Allen, H. Dragon's Breath.
Allingham, W. In Snow.
Alon, E. If There Is a God.
  Leave-Taking ("Death in a war.").
Amichai, Y. God Has Mercy on Kindergarten
  Children.
Antipater of Sidon. Amyntor.
Antokolsky. We are not always dependent on
  memory.
  You must dig in black ashes a long time.
  You share your mourning with all Moscow.
    There.
Anyte [*or* Anytes]. This Lydian earth covers
  Amyntor, Philip's son.
  Youth buried you, Captain; as sons for their
    mother, The.
ben Yoseph, R. On the Readiness for Sacrifice.
Bendall, F. Outposts.
Bishop, J. Young Men Dead.
Boker. Dirge for a Soldier.
Borges. Juan Lopez and John Ward.
Brecht, B. What Did the Nazi Send His Wife?
Buck, H. Mort, Le.
Ch'en Tao. Turkestan.
De Forest. I heard the bullet's hiss.
Denney. Death in an ancient country was a
  simple passport.
Đỗ Tấn Xuân. Twenty Years.
Fink, Robert A. At Our Backs.
George, P. Battle Won Is Lost.
Graham, W. Conscript Goes, The.
Graves, R. Escape.
  When I'm Killed.
Grimm, R. Assault.
Gudzenko. Before the Attack.
Gumilyov [*or* Gumiliov *or* Gumilev]. Worker,
  The ("Grizzly squab comrade, A.").

Hardy, T.   Albuera.
 What are you thinking, that you speak no word?
Heaney, S.   Requiem for the Croppies.
Hemingway.   Champs d'Honneur.
Hernández, M.   Sitting on Top of Corpses.
Hinojosa, Rolando.   Jacob Mosqueda Wrestles
 with the Angels.
Homer.   Death of Hector, The.
 Patroclus Fights and Dies.
 So mourn'd Pelides his late loss, so weighty
  were his moans.
 Then rash Patroclus with new fury glows.
Jěn Jui.   Midnight.
Kakkai Patiniyar Naccellaiyar.   Many Said.
Kharms.   Death of the Wild Warrior.
Kipling, R.   Destroyers in Collision.
 Nativity, A.
Komunyakaa, Y.   We Never Know.
Lersch, H.   Brothers.
Levis.   Caravaggio: Swirl and Vortex.
Logue, C.   Song of the Dead Soldier, The.
Malroux.   There's War or There's Peace.
Masters, E.   Harry Williams.
McDonald, W.   Flying Dutchman, The.
Meddemmen, J. G.   L.R.D.G.
Merwin.   Asians Dying, The.
Monroe, H.   These Two.
Nabokov.   When he was small, when he would
 fall.
Nims, J.   Shot Down at Night.
Nisbet, H.   Isandula.
Nowlan.   In Those Old Wars.
Nye, J.   Dead Weight.
Ofek, U.   Hagomel.
Raine, K.   Heroes.
Rawling.   Gas Drill.
Rimington, J.   God of the Flies.
Saner.   Flag Memoir.
Shakespeare, W.   Doth Fortune play the huswife
 with me now?
Siegel, Marcella.   Waiting Wife.
Southey, R.   Soldier's Wife, The.
Spencer, B.   Passed On.
 Thousand Killed, A.
Stafford, W.   At the Grave of My Brother:
 Bomber Pilot.
Stevens, W.   Death of a Soldier, The.
Stramm.   Reconnaissance Patrol.
Tasso.   Who first of Christian warriors now did
 chance.
Taylor, E.   After Twenty Years.
Thompson, D.   On the Relative Merit of Friend
 and Foe, Being Dead.
Ts'ao Chih.   White Horses.
Tu Fu [or Du Fu].   Draft Board at Shih-hao,
 The.
Unknown.   At last these two stout erles did
 meet.
 Battle of Inverlochy, The.
 Last Battle and Death of Chingis Khan, The.
 Marsilion sees his people's martyrdom.
 Now Roland feels that he is at death's door.
Velichansky, A.   In the evil time.
Virgil [or Vergil].   Death of Turnus, The.
Warner, S.   Become as little children.
Yosano Akiko.   Beloved, You Must Not Die.
Yosano Tekkan.   Victory Arches.

See also **War Dead**

Death of a Child
Al-Mansouri, A.   Abandonment.
Antipater of Sidon.   Amyntor.
Anyte [or Anytes].   Often keening on her
 daughter's tomb, Kleina.
Atwood.   Death of a Young Son by Drowning.
Austen, K.   Dec. 5th 1644 upon Robin Austins
 Recovery of the Smal Pox and General
 Popams Son John Diing of Them.
Behn, A.   Epitaph on the Tombstone of a Child,
 the Last of Seven That Died Before.
Belev.   Tale: "Children's poet's own child is
 dying, A."
Bigelow, M.   Come, lowly ones, and take your
 places now.
 Two Smothered Children.
Bishop, E.   First Death in Nova Scotia.
Bishop, J.   Young Men Dead.

Bourdillon.   Night Has a Thousand Eyes, The.
Bradstreet, A.   In Memory of My Dear
 Grandchild Anne Bradstreet Who Deceased
 June 20, 1669, Being Three Years and Seven
 Months Old.
 In Memory of My Dear Grandchild Elizabeth
  Bradstreet Who Deceased August, 1665,
  Being a Year and Half Old.
 On My Dear Grandchild Simon Bradstreet,
  [Who Died on 16TH November, 1669, Being
  but a Month and One Day Old].
Bridges, R.   On a Dead Child.
Browning, E.   Mother and Poet.
Callimachus.   Here Philip the father buried.
Carew, T.   Epitaph on the Lady Mary Villiers
 ("Lady Mary Villiers lies, The.").
Carey, M.   Wretten by Me at the Death of My
 4th Sonne and 5th Child Perigrene Payler.
Castro, R.   Mild Was the Air.
Clifton, L.   Sorrow Song.
Coleman, W.   Having Lost My Son, I Confront
 the Wreckage.
 Notes on a Departure.
Coleridge, S.   On an Infant Which Died before
 Baptism.
Collier, M.   Robert Wilson.
Cothi.   On the Death of His Son.
Dawe, B.   Elegy for Drowned Children.
Dawe, Tom.   Daedalus.
Dubie.   Annual of the Dark Physics, An.
Duran, J.   Stillborn.
Egerton, E.   On My Boy Henry.
Eichendorff.   On My Child's Death.
Emerson, R.   Threnody: "South-wind brings,
 The."
Esteves.   Lil' Pito.
Field, E.   Little Boy Blue.
Fordham.   In Memoriam. Alphonse Campbell
 Fordham.
 Queenie.
 To an Infant.
French, T.   Touching the River.
Frost, R.   Home Burial.
 Out, Out—.
Gioia.   Pentecost: "Neither the sorrows of
 afternoon, waiting in the silent house."
Glück, L.   Mount Ararat.
Goethe.   Erl-King.
 Erl-King, The.
Gregg.   Poet Goes about Her Business, The.
Gryphius.   Epitaph for Mariana Gryphius, His
 Brother Paul's Little Daughter.
Habila, H.   Birds in the Graveyard.
Harper, M.   Nightmare Begins Responsibility.
 Reuben, Reuben.
Heaney, S.   Limbo.
 Mid-Term Break.
Heard, J.   Solace.
Hecht, A.   Book of Yolek, The.
Hemans.   Wreck, The.
Herrick.   Upon a Child That Died [or Dyed].
Holmes, O.   Iris, Her Book.
Honig, E.   1925.
Howell, C.   New Orpheus, The.
Howitt, M.   Dying Child, The.
Hugo, V.   Night of the Fourth: A Recollection,
 The.
Jarrell, R.   Lost Children, The.
 Protocols.
Jennings, E.   Unknown Child, The.
Jones, Ceri Wyn.   Legacy.
Jones, R.   Portrait of My Father and His
 Grandson.
Jonson, B.   Epitaph on S. P. [or Salomon Pavy],
 a Child of Queen Elizabeth's Chapel.
 On My First Daughter.
 On My First Son.
Jordan, J.   Test of Atlanta 1979, The.
Justice, D.   On the Death of Friends in
 Childhood.
Kearney, L.   Man with His Kids on a Table,
 The.
Keelan, C.   Secularist, The.
Kennedy, X.   Little Elegy.
Khurshid-Banu.   To My Son, Abbas.
Landon.   Dying Child, The.

Leopardi.   To Sylvia.
Levine, P.   Detroit, Tomorrow.
Li K'ai-hsien.   Thanking Doctor Jen.
Liu, T.   Kindertotenlieder.
Luce, N.   Poor little Ada Queetie has departed
 this life.
MacEwen, G.   Children Are Laughing, The.
MacSweeney.   I Looked Down on a Child
 Today.
Martial.   Epitaph on Erotion.
 Fronto, Father, Flaccilla, Mother, extend.
Martinez, D.   Discreet Prayer, A.
Massey.   And thou hast stolen a jewel, Death.
McClure, M.   Madame Secretary.
McDonald, W.   I Still Can't Say the Word.
Meehan, P.   Child Burial.
Mew.   To a Child in Death.
Meynell, A.   Maternity.
Mikha'il, H.   Demonstration.
Mirville, E.   Nine months in the belly.
Mistral, G.   Woman, A.
Moore, J.   Hic Finis Rapto 3.
 Hic Finis Rapto 6.
 Hiram Helsel.
 One morning in April, a short time ago.
 She had blue eyes and light flaxen hair.
 William House and Family.
Moorer.   Russia's Resentment.
Muir, E.   Child Dying, The.
Muske, C.   Wish Foundation, The.
Norris, L.   Elegy for David Beynon.
O'Reilly, M.   Abused Child.
Ondaatje.   Strange Case, The.
Peacock, M.   Raptor, The.
Peters, L.   Isatou Died.
Philips, K.   On the Death of My First and
 Dearest Child, Hector Philips.
Piatt, S.   Her Blindness in Grief.
Po Chü-i.   Remembering Golden Bells.
Porter, A.   For My Son Johnny.
Randall, D.   Ballad of Birmingham.
Ransom, J.   Bells for John Whiteside's
 Daughter.
 Dead Boy.
Reznikoff.   Children.
 2. The Job.
Rilke.   Requiem for the Death of a Boy.
Rossetti, C.   Why Did Baby Die. . .?
Ryan, M.   First Exercise.
Sachs, N.   Already Embraced by the Arm of
 Heavenly Solace.
 Dead Child Speaks, A.
Salaam.   Threnody: "What's your story Atlanta/
 America?"
Shorter.   Mother, The.
Simmerman.   Child's Grave, Hale County,
 Alabama.
Sitwell, D.   Mother, The.
Smith, P.   Meanwhile, in Rwanda.
Soyinka.   Abiku.
Spellman, A.   Blues: My Baby's Gone.
Stafford, W.   For a Lost Child.
Stein, K.   Benefit Picnic, Cigar Makers' Strike,
 August 1884.
Strode.   On the Death of Mistress Mary
 Prideaux.
Taylor, E.   Upon Wedlock and Death of
 Children.
Thimelby, G.   Mrs Thimelby, on the Death of
 Her Only Child.
Thomas, D.   Refusal to Mourn the Death, by
 Fire, of a Child in London, A.
Thompson, D. P.   Laurel Street, 1950.
U Sam Oeur.   Loss of My Twins, The.
Unknown.   Babes in the Wood, The.
 Kū' siut Song.
 Papa's Letter.
Valentine, J.   She Would Long.
Voigt.   Year's End.
Wang Shih-chieng.   Medicine.
Whittier.   Vesta.
Wilde, O.   Requiescat.
Wilson, S.   Home: After a Poem by Frost.
Wordsworth, W.   Lucy Gray.
 Lucy Gray; or, Solitude.
 Surprised by Joy.

Three Years She Grew [in Sun and Shower]. We Are Seven.
Wright, J.   Flood Year.
Yamanoé [or Yamanoué] no Okura.   Longing for His Son, Furuhi.
Yi Kyubo.   Grieving for My Little Girl.
Zonas.   Charon.

Death of a Family Member
Alcosser.   Glory Monster.
Baggett.   Rachel: *Crown of Thorns*.
Bangaramma, C.   My Brother.
Bartlett, J.   From a Paris Hotel Room. When I Got My First Tattoo I Was.
Benbow.   Larson Arson.
Bödvarsson, G.   Brother.
Bykova, Z.   Potatoes in flower.
Davis, C.   Jojo's.
Dhompa, T.   Bardo.
Eichner, Maura.   Letter from Santa Cruz.
Fortini.   Seed, The.
Gilboa, A.   And My Brother Was Silent.
Ginsberg, A.   Your last night in the darkness of the Bronx—I phonecalled—thru hospital to secret police.
Gould, J.   Going Home.
Gregorio, R.   Long Hill of Garrapata, The.
Harding, R.   Brother Is a Star.
Howe, M.   Kiss, The.
Hudgins.   Mostly My Nightmares Are Dull.
Janzen, J.   These Words Are for You, Grandmother.
Johnson, F.   Aunt Jane Allen.
Jones, R.   Uncle Fenster's Grave.
Juhász, F.   Biography of a Woman, The.
Mark, Sabrina Orah.   Transylvania, 1919.
Max, L.   When the Tules Are Peppered with Red-Winged Blackbirds.
McDowell.   Elegy in August.
Monette.   No Goodbyes.
Montgomerie, W.   Epitaph: "My brother is skull and skeleton now."
Newton, Violette.   Going Back to Ireland.
Nickel, B.   For Peter, My Cousin.
Parry-Williams.   Christmas Carol, A: "It is close to a quarter of a century since then."
Press, K.   First Thirty-seven Years, The.
Reznikoff.   When my grandfather was about fifty, he fell sick.
Richter, J.   Everywhere the Earth Is Opening.
Rowlands, D.   Little Boots, The.
Savageau.   Heart.
Unknown.   Edom o' Gordon [Foulis Version].
Watts, Enos D.   Summer Solstice.
Watts, I.   Polyglot in Paradise, A [or On the Death of an Aged and Honoured Relative].
Williams, Stephanie.   Peerage.
Zucker, R.   What I Want You to See Is She When Not Here as in Now.

Death of a Father
Addonizio.   Beer. Milk. The Dog. My Old Man.
Alexander, R.   For Years My Father.
Beasley.   Witness.
Behn, R.   Vigil: Dwindle.
Bell, M.   Ending with a Line from *Lear*.
Benson, J.   Columbarium.
Cairns, Scott.   Translation of Raimundo Luz, The: My Good Luck.
Corbet [or Corbett].   Elegy upon the Death of His Own Father, An.
De Kok.   My father would not show us.
Dimitrova.   Interior with Faded Colors.
DJ Renegade.   Father and Son.
Fanthorpe.   Fanfare.
Feinstein, E.   Dad.
Gibbs, Robert J.   Death of My Father, The.
Glück, L.   Terminal Resemblance.
Harnik, R.   And at Night.
Herd.   Shadowed by your father.
Hicok.   Radical Neck.
Hristov, Boris.   My Mother's Wedding.
Kim, Suji Kwock.   Fragments of the Forgotten War.
Komunyakaa, Y.   [Excerpts].
Kopland.   Johnson Brothers Ltd.
Laâbi Abdellatif.   Portrait of the Father, The.
Leeke, Kiamsha Madelyn.   October Death.

Livesay, D.   Lament: "What moved me, was the way your hand."
MacDiarmid, H.   At My Father's Grave.
Martinez, D.   Bad Alchemy.
Matthews, W.   Men at My Father's Funeral.
Murray, L.   Last Hellos, The.
Olds, S.   Beyond Harm. This Hour.
Ondaatje.   7 or 8 Things I Know about Her—A Stolen Biography.
Orban, O.   Chile. Letter, The.
Paino.   Truth, The.
Ponge.   Sage's Family, The.
Stroud, J.   Provenance.
Thomas, D.   Do Not Go Gentle into That Good Night.
Thurston, H.   Father on My Shoulders.
Townsend, A.   Touch Me Not.
Waddington, M.   Sea Bells.
Williamson, A.   Arrangements.
Wilson, A.   Pegasus the Winged Horse.
Wright, J.   Honey.
Yun Tongju.   His Last Words.

Death of a Friend
Aviram, A.   Pictures of Maurice among Funeral Flowers.
Bly, R.   Yellow Dot, The.
Bottoms.   Recording the Spirit Voices.
Brock-Broido.   Periodic Table of Ethereal Elements.
Cairns, Scott.   After the Last Words.
Chatterton.   Mr. Smith is Dead.
Close, J.   Mentem Mortalia Tangunt.
Clurman, D.   To David.
Cooper, J.   Long, Disconsolate Lines.
Dana, R.   Figures, The.
Dobyns.   When a Friend.
Fenton, J.   For Andrew Wood.
Funkhouser.   Lilies.
Garrett, G.   Rugby Road.
Hernández, M.   Each Time I Pass.
Heyen.   Sake Gold.
Hoagland, T.   Migration.
Hyecho.   Elegy: "Lamp lost its master at home, The."
Jensma.   In Memoriam Akbar Babool.
Kan, T.   And He Whispered Stolen Words.
Kaufman, S.   Waiting: "After the fervor."
Lepson, Ruth.   October 7, 1994.
Levchev, Vladimir.   Beacon.
Levy, D.   Honey.
Martinson.   No Name for It.
Millay, E.   To Elinor Wylie ("Oh, she was beautiful in every part!").
Montale.   Visit to Fadin.
Philpot, T.   What There Is, Today.
Reagon.   They Are All Falling around Me.
Rodríguez, C.   Eugenio de Luelmo.
Rossetti, C.   My Friend.
Seiferle, M.   Music We Dance To, The.
Stern, G.   Lilacs for Ginsberg.
Taylor, H.   For William Stafford.
Valentine, J.   Elegy for Jane Kenyon (2).
Vázquez Montalbán, M.   In Memoriam ("I learned / the interminable list.").
Walcott.   Sea Canes.
Watts, I.   Mr. Gunston Is Shown round Heaven [or To the Dear Memory of Thomas Gunston, Esq.].
Mrs. Warner Arrives Above [or An Elegiac Thought on Mrs. Anne Warner].
Wunderlich, M.   Fourteen Things We're Allowed to Bring to the Underworld.
Xiang Xiu.   Recalling Old Times.

Death of a Lover
Aiken, C.   All Death, All Love.
Baudelaire.   Autumn Lament.
Bolger.   I drifted into sleep.
Buson.   Piercing chill.
Char.   Lied of the Fig Tree.
Chivers.   In the Rosy Bowers of Aiden.
Davison, P.   Under the Roof of Memory.
Dunn, D.   Dining.
Gallagher, T.   Crazy Menu.
Gibson, W.   Parrot, The.

Grainger, J.   Bryan and Pereene.
Gregorio, R.   Long Hill of Garrapata, The.
Groarke, V.   Folderol.
Habington.   *Upon* Castara's *Departure*.
Hall, D.   Ardor. Letter after a Year.
Harnik, R.   And at Night.
Hikmet.   Three Storks Restaurant.
Lytton, E.   Count and the Lady, The.
Machado Ruiz.   Eyes, The.
Monette.   Half Life.
Moore, J.   Hic Finis Rapto 4. Hic Finis Rapto 5.
Morling, M.   Ashes.
O'Connell, E.   Dirge on the Death of Art O'Leary.
P'an Yüeh.   In Mourning for His Dead Wife.
Procter, A.   Envy.
Sabines.   13: Eve No Longer Exists.
Shakespeare, W.   Come night! come, Romeo! come, thou day in night!
Simmonds, Kevin.   New Sestina, The.
Thomas, E.   She Dotes.
Tuckerman, F.   Refrigerium.
Tynan Hinkson, K.   I Wonder Why.
Unknown.   Come quickly, my love, so I can give you my mouth!
Deirdre's [or Deidre's] Lament for the Sons of Usnach.
If my lover dies, let me be his shroud!
Meng Jiangnü at the Long Wall.
My lover rests near where the flowers are.
Oh ruined tomb, oh scattered bricks, my beloved is no more than dust.
Song of Crede, Daughter of Guare, The.
Vermont, C.   Death of Karen Klausner, The.
Vuong-Riddick, T.   My Beloved Is Dead in Vietnam.
Wilson, A.   Lynx.

Death of a Mother
Abbott, K.   Windy clear day, A.
Ali, A.   Lenox Hill.
Ap Hywel, Elin.   In My Mother's House.
Aragon, F.   Tricycles.
Assultani, F.   My Mother, in memoriam.
Barresi.   Bad Joke.
Darwin.   Eliza at the Battle.
Frost, R.   First Haircut.
Glatt.   Leash.
Goldberg, B.   Wren.
Hahn, S.   Baobab Tree 1996, The.
Hammond, M.   3. Paying Respects.
Howard Jr., W.   Memorial Drive.
Kizer, C.   Great Blue Heron, The.
Kroetsch.   Sounding the Name.
Levi, J.   Tuscarora.
Masefield.   C. L. M.
McCabe, C.   In Memory of My Mother.
McKinnon, K.   Moving My Mother.
Muller, R.   16 Year-Old Girl Who's Standing, A.
Newman, J.   **Fall under.** To succumb to; come under an influence or power.
O'Donoghue, M.   Bova.
Prufer, K.   Car Has Fallen from a Bridge, A.
Reznikoff.   Kaddish.
Rich, A.   Woman Mourned by Daughters, A.
Rohrer, J.   Mennonite Funeral in the Shenandoah Valley.
Sabok.   At My Mother's Funeral.
Steptoe.   There Is a House.
Stevenson, A.   Marriage, A.
Swirszczynska [or Swir].   She Came to Say Farewell.
Wells, Jeanne.   July Thirteenth.

Death of an Infant
Bawer.   Grand Central Station, 20 December 1987.
Crashaw.   To the Infant Martyrs. Upon the Infant Martyrs.
Davies, W. H.   Inquest, The.
Geier.   On Your Twenty-First Birthday.
Harper, M.   We Assume: On the Death of Our Son, Reuben Masai Harper.
Hewett, D.   Anniversary.
Hopwood, Mereid.   Rebirth.
Jackson, G.   1619. Virginia.

Jonson, B.   On My First Daughter.
Kakei.   By an unfaded stupa.
Kong Rong.   First-Born, A.
Lamb, C.   On an Infant Dying as Soon as Born.
Landon.   Little Shroud, The.
Marvell.   Picture of Little T. C. in a Prospect of
    Flowers, The.
McAuley, J.   Pietá.
Mei Yao Ch'en.   On the Death of a New Born
    Child.
Melville, H.   Chipmunk, The.
Muir, E.   Child Dying, The.
Muske, C.   Intensive Care.
O'Rahilly.   Lament for Tadhg Cronin's Children.
Philips, K.   Epitaph on her Son H. P. at St.
    Syth's Church [where her body also lies
    Interred].
    On the Death of My First and Dearest Child,
    Hector Philips.
Piatt, S.   No Help.
Rao, S.   Memories: "My name is Lila."
Sigourney.   Death of an Infant.
Simonides.   They wept for the violet-wreathed
    [lady's].
Stoddard, E.   One Morn I Left Him in His Bed.
West, K.   To My Twin Sister Who Died at Birth.
See also **Death of a Child**

Death of Animals
Ai.   I Have Got to Stop Loving You. So I Have
    Killed My Black Goat.
Algarin.   Tiger Lady.
Ammons.   Widespread Implications.
Anyte [or Anytes].   Damis erected this mound
    for his dead steadfast.
    For the cricket (nightingale of the field) and oak.
    No longer, as before, plying with whirring
    wings.
    No longer will I fling up my neck, exulting.
    You, too, perished by a bush with tangled roots.
Armantrout.   Traveling Through the Yard.
Avidan, D.   Life of a Dead Dog.
Barham, R.   Cynotaph, The.
Basho.   Nothing in the cry.
Bly, R.   Dead Seal [near McClure's Beach], The.
Braun, R.   Goose.
    Lilies, The.
Bremer, C.   Metro Taxqueña.
Brown, L.   Never Swat a Fly.
Brown, S.   Marriage.
Burnside, J.   Penitence.
Cassian.   Sacrilege.
Chamberlain, B.   Dead Ponies.
Chandar, M.   Child Is Born, A.
Coccimiglio.   St. Francis Speaks to Me at a
    Young Age.
Coleman, W.   Dog Suicide.
Collier, M.   Real-Life Drama, A.
    Snake, The.
Collins, B.   Putting Down the Cat.
Collins, M.   Tory, a Puppy.
Cooper, Allan.   Worker Bee, The.
Cowper, W.   Epitaph on a Hare.
Cummings, E. E.   Me Up at Does.
Davis, C.   Murderer, The.
DeSylva, B. G.   Never Swat a Fly.
Dickey, J.   Heaven of Animals, The.
Du Bellay.   Epitaph on a Pet Cat.
Dubie.   Obscure, The.
Dugan, A.   Plague of Dead Sharks.
Eberhart, R.   For a Lamb.
Eichner, Maura.   Eclogue and Elegy.
Espada.   Cada Puerco Tiene Su Sábado.
Evans, D.   Pig Killing Day.
Faust, H.   After the Storm.
Frost, R.   Draft Horse, The.
Fry, C.   Dog of St. Bernard's, The.
García Lorca.   New York.
George, S.   Do Not Ponder Too Much.
Gerber.   Bear on Main Street, The.
Gibson, M.   Strange Altars.
Gillespie, N.   Road Kill.
Glazer, M.   Matter.
Glenday, J.   Hydrodamalis Gigas.
González, R.   Death of the Farm Workers' Cat.
Gray, T.   Ode on the Death of a Favo[u]rite Cat,
    Drowned in a Tub [or Bowl] of Gold Fishes.

Grennan.   One Morning: "Looking for
    distinctive stones, I found the dead otter."
Harmsen van Beek.   Introduction to a Prayer.
Hartley, M.   As the Buck Lay Dead.
Hartman, J.   Petition Hecate at the seal.
Hayden, R.   Plague of Starlings, A.
Henderson, R.   Never Swat a Fly.
Herrick.   Upon His Spaniel[l] Tracie [or Tracy].
Heyen.   Witness.
    Yellowjackets.
Hoagland, T.   Candlelight.
Horsfield, K.   Old Rocket.
Hughes, F.   Different Voice, The.
    Kookaburra.
Hughes, R.   Glaucopis.
Hughes, T.   February 17th.
    Old Age Gets Up.
    View of a Pig.
Ibáñez, S.   Island in the Light.
Issa.   Don't kill that poor fly!
Jeffers, R.   Hurt Hawks.
Johnson, D.   Road-Kill.
Jones, D.   On Seeing a Dead Lamb.
Kikaku.   Her mate devoured.
Klassen, S.   Act of Mercy.
Kumin, M.   Requiem on I-89.
    Thinking of Death and Dogfood.
Kunitz, S.   Robin Redbreast.
    Wellfleet Whale, The.
Labid.   Tent marks in Mínan are worn away,
    The.
Larsen, L.   Lips.
Lavender, Bill.   Note to Skip on Max and
    Maxine, A.
Lawrence, A.   Cro-Kill.
Lee, D.   First Turtle.
Leggott, M.   Thoroughfares await them.
Lewis, G.   White Horse.
Lindsay, V.   Eagle That Is Forgotten, The.
Lux.   So You Put the Dog to Sleep.
Mahon.   Bonn´n Buí, An.
Marinho, T.   Ear of a Goat, The.
Marlatt, D.   Bruce and the Bluegills.
Marvell.   Nymph Complaining for the Death of
    Her Faun [or Fawn], The.
Mattawa.   Letter to Ibrahim.
McNair.   Killing the Animals.
Meads, K.   Dogs.
Mei Yao Ch'en.   Offering for the Cat, An.
Meireles.   Dead Horse, The.
Meredith, G.   Islet the Dachs.
Millay, E.   Buck in the Snow, The.
Mitford.   Fleet Marmion.
    Manx.
Moir, D.   Dying Oscar.
Moran, R.   Cross Country.
Morshen.   At the Lighthouse.
Mother Goose.   Who Killed Cock Robin.
Murray, L.   Death Words.
Musgrave.   Burial of the Dog.
Nicholson, N.   Tune the Old Cow Died Of, The.
Nowlan.   Bull Moose, The.
Olds, S.   Forty-one, Alone, No Gerbil.
Parrington, G.   Sweet Dog! now cold and stiff in
    death.
Payn.   Our Dog Jock.
Peacock, M.   Lull, The.
Perillo, L.   Shrike Tree.
Phillips, P.   Doe, The.
Randolph, T.   On the Death of a Nightingale.
Ransom, J.   Janet Waking.
Razran, Gregory.   Jade's Iguanas Are Dead.
Rohrer, M.   Winged Snake Found on a Path.
Rossetti, C.   Last Rites.
Sarton, M.   Death and the Turtle.
Scott, S.   Maida.
Sharah.   Package for Another World.
Shiki.   In the winter river.
Simon, M.   Dolphin, The.
Simpson, A.   Deer on a Beach.
Slutsky [or Slutskii].   Horses in the Ocean.
Smither.   On the Euthanasia of a Pet Dog.
Snodgrass.   Coroner's Inquest.
Soto.   Practicing Eulogies.
Stafford, W.   Meditation: "Animals full of light."
    Traveling Through the Dark.

Steinbergh.   Burial.
Stern, G.   Bull-roarer, The.
    Dog, The.
Strong, G.   Modern Hiawatha, The.
Sutskever [or Sutzkever].   Death of an Ox, The.
Tanikawa, S.   Nero.
Thomas, E.   Gallows, The.
Thomas, G.   Killer Dog.
Thurston, H.   Dragging Bottom.
Townsend, A.   After the End.
Turner, C.   Drowned Spaniel, The.
Tymnes.   Stone says that it covers here the white
    dog, The.
Unknown.   Candy-throated Carib, The.
    Lord Orrery's Hector.
Updike.   Dog's Death.
Van Walleghen.   More Trouble with the
    Obvious.
Vietnamese Oral Tradition.   Egret's Death and
    Funeral Preparations.
Voigt.   Harvesting the Cows.
    Hen, The.
    Trust, The.
Warren, R.   Dead Horse in Field.
    Love and Knowledge.
    Sila.
    Was Not the Lost Dauphin.
Weelkes.   Madrigal: "Ay me, alas, heigh ho,
    heigh ho!"
White, G.   Dead Armadillos.
Wilbur, R.   Death of a Toad, The.
    Pardon, The.
Williams, M.   Animals.
Wingfield.   Bird, A.
Wright, J.   Small Frogs Killed on the Highway.
    Sparrows in a Hillside Drift.
Wrigley, R.   Other World, The: "So here is the
    old buck."

Death Poetry
Basho.   Sick on my journey.
Buson.   Winter rain on moss.
Ruefle.   Furtherness.
Winchilsea.   To Death.

Debauchery
Awoonor.   To the Eminent Scholar and Meddler.
Brooks, G.   Rites for Cousin Vit, The.
Chipasula.   Dusk.
Giorno.   Pornographic Poem.
Graves, R.   Blue-Fly, The.
Johnson, S.   Short Song of Congratulation, A
    [or To a Young Heir].
Jonson, B.   On Gut.
Juvenal.   Northward beyond the Lapps to the
    world's end, the frozen.
Kuan Han-ch'ing.   To the Tune "A Spray of
    Flowers" (Not Giving In to Old Age).
Lesley, G.   Behold, how Sodom swaggers in its
    Pride.
Meleager.   To Diodorus, Dorotheus, Callicrates
    et al.
Nortje.   Sonnet two: "I have drunk up nights and
    spent the days."
Ovid.   Elegy 3.1: "Old wood stands uncut, of
    long years' space, An."
Rochester, J.   Disabled Debauchee, The.
    Ramble in St. James's Park, A.
Strato [or Straton].   In the bed are two,
    submissive.
Symonds.   Midnight at Baiae.
Unknown.   Advice to a Young Man.
    What Really Goes On in the College of
    Cardinals.
Verlaine.   Mille e tre.
Whitman, W.   Hand-Mirror, A.
Wyatt.   Courtier's Life, The.

Debt
Bayly.   Out, John.
Bryan, J.   I've Looked Everywhere.
Cardenal.   Luke 16:1–9; He also said to the
    disciples.
Coward.   Stately Homes of England, The.
De Vries, P.   To His Importunate Mistress.
Dickinson, E.   I gave myself to Him—.
Dunbar, P.   Debt, The.
Emerson, R.   Suum Cuique.
Gellis, W.   City of No Reprieve.

Ishikawa Takuboku.   He sees me.
Jordan, A.   Debt Is Paid, A.
Meyer, T.   Uranium Ore.
Prejsnar, Mark.   Composition with Wire.
Suckling, S.   Love and Debt Alike Troublesome.
Westmorland.   My Country Audit.
Wrigley, R.   Moon in a Mason Jar.

Decadence
Baudelaire.   To the Reader.
Cummings, E. E.   Come,gaze with me upon this
  dome.
  Space being(don't forget to remember)Curved.
El-Hadi, S.   Drama, The.
Eliot, T. S.   Burnt Norton.
  Mr. Apollinax.
  Portrait of a Lady.
  Sweeney among the Nightingales.
  Waste Land, The.
  Whispers of Immortality.
Ewart.   One for the Anthologies.
Juvenal.   Northward beyond the Lapps to the
  world's end, the frozen.
MacNeice.   Individualist Speaks, The.
Martial.   Bearded Callistratus wedded rugged
  Afer.
  Chrestus, your balls are depilated.
Pack, R.   Fathering the Map.
Pound, E.   Portrait d'une Femme.
Stratanovsky.   Herostratos and Herostratos.
  Terrorist, The.
Warren, R.   Bearded Oaks.

Decay
Auden.   Paysage Moralisé.
Awoonor.   Songs of Sorrow.
Bador, B.   Hand, The.
  Journey to the End of Night.
Bateman, M.   Decline of Gaelic, The.
Baudelaire.   Carcass, A.
Benn.   Monologue.
Blue Cloud.   Deeper Than a Dream.
Boland, E.   My Country in Darkness.
Bolt, T.   Meditation in Loudoun County.
Breytenbach.   Asylum.
Brooks, G.   Throwing Out the Flowers.
Cabral de Melo Neto.   Landscape of the
  Capibaribe River.
Ceravolo.   Song of Autumn, A.
Churchyard.   That humor now, declines for age
  drawes on.
Comte de Lautréamont.   I am filthy. Lice gnaw
  me. Swine, when they look at me, vomit. The
  scabs.
Cook, Geoffrey.   Lorne, Nova Scotia.
Dickinson, E.   Crumbling is not an instant's Act.
Disch.   Entropic Villanelle.
Donne.   Thou hast made me, and shall thy
  work[e] decay?
  When that rich soul[e] which to her heaven is
  gone.
Dooley, M.   Does It Go Like This?
Dransfield.   War of the Roses, The.
Eberhart, R.   Groundhog, The.
Eijkelboom.   A Nos Glorieux Morts.
  Sometimes.
Eliot, T. S.   Burnt Norton.
  Gerontion.
  Hollow Men, The.
  Waste Land, The.
Frost, R.   Range-finding.
  Wood-Pile, The.
Georgiev, Marin.   Riverbend.
Gilliams, M.   Autumn.
Ginsberg, A.   Sunflower Sutra.
Graham, J.   Opulence.
Greger.   Notre Dame, Sainte Chapelle, Sacré
  Coeur by foot—.
Guidacci.   First to feast is love, The. On the
  scraps of love the fever feasts.
Gwynn, R.   Approaching a Sentimental Birthday,
  He Peruses The Norton Anthology of Poetry.
Hall, D.   Old Pilot, The.
Heath-Stubbs.   Footnote to Belloc's "Tarantella".
Herbert, Z.   To Marcus Aurelius.
Hidalgo, J.   You Have to Go Down.
Hsiao Kang.   Spiders' Spun Threads.
Ignatova, E.   I have encountered a valley, in

ragged bast matting.
Jeffers, R.   For Una.
  Prescription of Painful Ends.
Jünger, F. G.   Ultima Ratio.
Kefala.   Freedom Fighter.
Kelly, R.   Recessional.
Lane, M. Travis.   For Brigid.
Lawrence, A.   Robert Penn Warren's Book.
Li Po.   On Climbing the Phoenix Tower at
  Chinling.
Long, H.   Our Spring Needs Shoveling.
Lowell, R.   As a Plane Tree by the Water.
McAuley, J.   Wet Day.
McCarthy, J.   Alice Blue Gown.
Merwin.   Losing a Language.
Olson, C.   Kingfishers, The.
Pack, R.   Proton Decay.
Pao Chao.   Desolate City, The: A Rhapsody.
  Ruined City, The.
Petri.   By an Unknown Poet from Eastern
  Europe, 1955.
Pierpoint, K.   In the Outhouse.
Portnoy, M.   Evolution of Lather, The.
Powell, D. A.   Sleek mechanical dart: the
  syringe noses into the blue vein marking the
  target of me.
Press, K.   Humus.
Quevedo y Villegas.   Sonnet: Death Warnings.
Ramanujan.   Elements of Composition.
Rich, A.   Diving into the Wreck.
Robinson, E.   Ballade of Broken Flutes.
  House on the Hill, The.
Rodefer.   Pretext.
Scott, D.   Skiddaw House.
Seed.   'From Escomb, County Durham': July
  1990.
Shelley, P.   Ozymandias.
Simpson, L.   Inner Part, The.
Sitwell, D.   Hambone and the Heart, The.
Slessor.   Choker's Lane.
Stevens, W.   Worms at Heaven's Gate, The.
Trakl.   Revelation and Decline.
Unknown.   Shades of the Newly Buried
  Complain to the Gods, The.
  Song Bewailing the Time of Christmas, So
  Much Decayed in England, A.
Vaughan, H.   They Are All Gone into the World
  of Light!
Verhaeren.   Spade.
Wanley.   Resurrection, The.
Ward, T.   Stray Dogs, Foaming.
Wilbur, R.   Junk.
Williams, H.   Sonnet 6. To the Torrid Zone.
Williams, W.   Raleigh Was Right.
Wordsworth, W.   Decadence; or, The Umbrella.
  Her cottage, then a cheerful object, wore.
  I watch, and long have watched, with calm
  regret.
Zenmaro.   Tanka: "No news of him."

December
Bleakney, J.   Winter Solstice.
Cane.   Tree in December.
Clare, J.   December.
Clark, L.   Singing in the Streets.
Cranch.   December.
Enquist, A.   December Offensive.
Fergusson.   Daft Days, The.
Giovanni.   December of My Springs, The.
Heard, J.   December.
Herford.   I Heard a Bird Sing.
Housman.   Night Is Freezing Fast, The.
Ignatova, E.   Then there was the rose I fell in
  love with.
Keats.   In [a] Drear-nighted December.
Kenny, M.   December.
Lovelace, R.   Grasshopper, The [To My Noble
  Friend Mr Charles Cotton: Ode].
Quintana.   Poem for Salt.
Ray, H.   December.
Smith, Douglas Burnet.   Walk After Rain.
Smrek, J.   December: "God gave a sign—and
  the."
Van hee.   December.
Waldman, A.   Giant Night.
Whittier.   Snow-Bound [A Winter Idyl].

Deception
Agali, A.   Sister: "House, A. A car. Sweet
  things. Gold."
Allen, Gilbert.   Good Duke Speaks, The.
Barbauld.   Tomorrow.
Bayly.   Out, John.
Bhattācārya, M.   Oh Ma Kali, for a long time
  now.
Boruch.   Camouflage.
Brecht, B.   From a German War Primer.
Buson.   Fox disguised, The.
Carew, T.   Deposition from Love, A.
Carroll, L.   Crocodile, The.
Carryl, G.   Sycophantic Fox and the Gullible
  Raven, The.
Cartwright, W.   Falsehood.
Chaucer.   Miller's Prologue, The.
Chesterton.   Aristocrat, The.
Clark, T.   Society.
Coulehan, J.   Dynamizer and the Oscilloclast,
  The.
Creeley.   If You.
  Song: "What I took in my hand."
Davis, T.   Playing Solitaire.
Derricotte.   Passing.
Dickey, W.   Plot, The.
Dōyaku Sensei, Master Artery.   Housemaid's
  Ballad, The.
Donne.   On His Mistress [or Mistris].
Drayton.   Three Sorts of Serpents Do Resemble
  Thee.
Dunbar, P.   Made to Order Smile, The.
  We Wear the Mask.
Dunn, S.   Grudges.
  On Hearing the Airlines Will Use a
  Psychological Profile to Catch Potential
  Skyjackers.
  What They Wanted.
Duo Duo.   Thousands of images have suddenly
  brightened in the emptiness.
Elizabeth I.   On Monsieur's Departure.
Emerson, R.   Maia.
"Ephelia.".   In the Person of a Lady, to Bajazet,
  Her Unconstant Gallant.
Frost, R.   Revelation.
Garrett, E.   Double.
Gates, B.   Homeless.
Graves, R.   Beauty in Trouble.
  Sick Love.
Hare, P.   Deceit in the Park.
Heffernan, M.   Message, The.
Horan.   Soft Swimmer, Winter Swan.
Hughes, T.   Childish Prank, A.
Jackson, L.   You or You.
Johnson, J.   White Witch, The.
Kim Sujang.   Deception.
Lauinger, A.   Edgar.
Loftis, N.   Brief Encounter.
MacBeth [or Macbeth].   Alsatian.
Martial.   You were a swan, you're now a crow.
Masterson, R.   Chinese Stripper.
Matveyeva [or Matveieva].   I'm no fighting
  man, he says.
McElroy, C.   Horoscope.
Mikha'il, M.   Three Flags.
Mirabai [or Mira Bai].   Coffer with the
  Poisonous Snake, The.
Montalvan, J.   Self-Deceaver, The.
Muso Soseki.   Laughing Mountain.
Navajo Oral Tradition.   Coyote, Skunk, and the
  Prairie Dogs.
Nolla.   Troubadour Love.
Ojaide.   When Tomorrow Is Too Long.
Osgood, F.   Maiden's Mistake, The.
Ostriker.   Lamenting the Inevitable.
Ovid.   Elegy 3.13: "Seeing thou art fair[e], I
  bar[re] not thy false playing."
Parry-Williams.   Two Poems.
Peacock, M.   Have You Ever Faked an Orgasm?
Peire Cardenal.   Clerks pretend to be shepherds,
  and under, The.
Phillips, C.   Clearing, The.
Plomer.   French Lisette: A Ballad of Maida
  Vale.
Pope, J.   Word of Encouragement, A.
Prescod.   Vicious Circle.

Prior. Ode, An: "Merchant, to secure his treasure, The."
Prunty. Note of Thanks, A.
Sen, R. Tara, what more are You planning?
Senryū, K. Even in the time of gods.
Shakespeare, W. Sonnet 95: "How sweet and lovely dost thou make the shame."
Silverstein, S. Sick.
Stanton, M. Shoplifters.
Stephens, J. Blue Blood.
Thomas, L. Instructions for Your New Osiris.
Unknown. Men Only Pretend.
Three Hunchbacks, The.
Westphalian Song.
Welch, J. Man from Washington, The.
Whitehead, C. Brutus' Last Song.
Whitlow. Book of Routh.
Whitney, I. Ye virgins that from Cupid's tents.
Williams, W. Great Mullen.
Wroth. Song: "Love a child is ever crying [or criing]."
Sonnet 2: "Love like a jugler, comes to play his prize [or prise]."
Sonnet 35: "False [or Faulce] hope which feeds but[t] to destroy, and spill."
Yeats. Matthew 24:15–31.

Decisions
Atwood. I made no choice / I decided nothing.
Brooks, G. Do Not Be Afraid of No.
Burrell. Chloe and Myra.
Carew, T. Mediocrity in Love Rejected.
Corbin, A. Love Me At Last.
Field. Second Thoughts.
Frost, R. Road Not Taken, The.
Harechavi. 1 x 2.
Herrick. Neutrality Loathsome.
Jamme, Franck André. Life of a Beetle, The.
Lazutkina, E. I stand and inspect the phenomena drawn up.
Marcus, M. Poem for Gonzales, California, The.
Muyong Sooyon. To the Reverend Bagam.
See also **Free Will**

Declaration of Independence
Bye. Indiana.
Hopkins, L. John Hancock.

Decorum
Kinnell. To William Carlos Williams.
Meynell, A. Shepherdess, The.

Deer
Addonizio. Alone in Your House.
Arreola, Juan José. Deer.
Baker, D. Deer, The.
Benét, R. *et al.* Daniel Boone.
Benét, S. Daniel Boone.
Benét, W. Fawn in the Snow, The.
Biespiel, D. There Were No Deer in the Thicket.
Booth, P. How to See Deer.
Burnside, J. Penitence.
Buson. Deer in rain / Three cries.
It cried three times.
Conyus. Upon Leaving the Parole Board Hearing.
Crawford, I. Dark Stag, The.
Davidson, J. Runnable Stag, A.
Davis, T. Ripe.
Dickinson, E. Wounded Deer Leaps Highest, A.
Erdrich. Strange People, The.
Fisher, M. In Cool, Green Haunts.
Flanner. Fern Song.
Moment: "I saw a young deer standing."
Frost, C. Being.
To Kill a Deer.
Frost, R. Two Look at Two.
Glück, L. Messengers.
Hamill, S. Midsummer: "Two yearling deer."
Han-shan Te-ch'ing. Who can be a wild deer among deserted mountains.
Hartley, M. As the Buck Lay Dead.
Hass, R. Image, The.
Hicok. Once a Green Sky.
Hughes, H. At the Teahouse, 7 am.
Hughes, T. Roe-Deer.
Issa. Deer licking.

Jeffers, R. Deer Lay Down Their Bones, The.
Fawn's Foster-Mother.
Jouve. Lament for the Stag.
Kipling, R. Hunting-Song of the Seeonee Pack.
Kirchner, F. In Cold February Twilight.
Kyger. On the Other Side.
Lewis, J. Grandmother Remembers, A.
Lilburn, Tim. Contemplation Is Mourning.
Lovelace, R. La Bella Bona-Roba.
MacIntyre, D. To the Air of a Pibroch.
Martial. New Point of View, A.
Marvell. Nymph Complaining for the Death of Her Faun [or Fawn], The.
McCallum, S. Deer, The.
Meogo. Cantiga de Amigo.
Millay, E. Buck in the Snow, The.
More, S. Child's Song.
Morley, D. Air Street.
No Ch'ŏnmyŏng. Deer.
O'Callaghan, C. 100 The Stag.
Oliver, M. Picking Blueberries, Austerlitz, New York, 1957.
Oppen. Psalm: "In the small beauty of the forest."
Otsuyu. Cry of the deer / Where at its depths.
Pak Mogwŏl [or Mokwŏl]. Blue Deer.
Papago. There was a mountain, over its black roots [the deer].
Patchen. Deer and the Snake, The.
Phillips, P. Doe, The.
Pinchas-Cohen. Journey of a Doe.
Simpson, A. Deer on a Beach.
Smith, I. Deer looks through you to the other side, A.
Snyder, G. This Poem Is for Deer.
Spenser, E. Sonnet 67: "Like a huntsman after weary chase."
Stafford, W. Traveling through the Dark.
Stuart, D. Where the Deer Go.
Tester, V. Histories, The.
Tu Fu [or Du Fu]. Dawn over the Mountains.
Turberville. Woful Words of the Hart, The.
Unknown. Lone Buck.
Warren, R. Sila.
Weismiller. Crystal Moment.
Wright, J. White Deer, The.
Wyatt. Whoso List to Hunt.
See also **Hunting and Hunters**

Defeat
Akhmatova, A. Cleopatra.
Archilochus. Heart, my heart churning with fathomless cares.
Azzawi, F. Self-Defeating Poem, The.
Bible, *O.T.* David's Lament.
Bly, R. Defeated.
Bynner. What though they conquer us?
Cagnone, N. Fifth Book: On Limitation.
Dickinson, E. I took my Power in my Hand.
My Portion is Defeat—today.
Success is counted sweetest.
Ezekiel. I met a man once.
Foley, M. On the Waterfront.
Gascoigne. Soldiers, behold, and captains, mark it well.
Gryphius. My Country Weeps.
Heine, H. Grenadiers, The.
Hsiang Chi. Hegemon's Lament, The.
Hugo, R. Degrees of Gray in Philipsburg.
Hugo, V. Russia 1812.
Waterloo! Waterloo! Waterloo! dismal plain!
Ibn al-Labbānah, M. Heavens weep with their morning and evening rain clouds over those excellent lords, the Banū 'Abbād, The.
Italicus. Death comes in strange forms and contrasting images.
Furiously along the banks stormed Hannibal.
Jones, R. My Manhood.
Keyes, S. Dunbar, 1650.
Komunyakaa, Y. After the Fall [of Saigon].
Nicarchus of Alexandria. Mighty Runner, A.
Padilla. Discourse on Method, The.
Quasimodo. From the Willow Branches.
Queneau. Reinforcements [1].
Ramanujan. At Forty.
Ransom, J. Prelude to an Evening.
Rilke. Man Watching, The.

Ritsos. After the Defeat.
Rundĭ, A. Everything declines after reaching perfection, therefore let no man be beguiled by the sweetness of a pleasant life.
Spencer, B. Invaders, The.
Thayer, E. Casey at the Bat.
Wright, J. Speak.

Deformities
Baudelaire. Seven Old Men, The.
Volkman. I never wish to sing again as I used to, when two new eyes could always.
Yevtushenko [or Evtushenko]. Dwarf Birches.

Degas, Edgar
Fourcade, Dominique. Ensembles.
Wilbur, R. Museum Piece.

Degradation
Notley. Woman came into "a car I rode" "about thirty-seven" "maybe", A.

Dehumanization
Agosin. Most Unbelievable Part, The.
Amadiume. Nok Lady in Terracotta.
Carmona. Tenderness.
Djabali. For My Torturer, Lieutenant D.
M'Baye d'Erneville. Labane.
Mitsui. Destination: Tule Lake Relocation Center, May 20, 1942.
Owen, W. Anthem for Doomed Youth.
Plath. Applicant, The.
Vilariño. Like That Man Who Kicks Off His Shoes.
Maybe Then.
See also **Bureaucracy and Bureaucrats**

Deirdre
Stephens, J. Deirdre.

Deism
Addison, J. Ode: "Spacious firmament on high, The."
Kerouac. Did I create that sky? Yes, for, if it was.

Déjà Vu
Hart, L. Where or When.
Kalidasa. Even the man who is happy.
Ransom, J. Vision by Sweetwater.

Dejection
Baudelaire. Spleen LXXV.
Spleen LXXVII.
Coleridge, S. Dejection: An Ode.
Letter to Sara Hutchinson.
Mahon. Dejection [Ode].
Mallarmé. Sea Breeze.
Shelley, P. Stanzas Written in Dejection, Near Naples [or —December 1818, near Naples].
Unknown. Arjuna sat dejected.
Valentine, J. Lines in Dejection.
See also **Melancholy**

Delaware River
Odell. Song for a Fishing Party.

Delaware (state)
Kinnell. Memory of Wilmington.
Scott, D. Delaware.

Delft, Holland
Mahon. Courtyards in Delft.

Delight
Basho. Delight, then sorrow.
Bridges, R. My Delight and Thy Delight.
Thou Didst Delight My Eyes.
Dickinson, E. Oh Sumptuous moment.
Follain. Bliss.
Freed, A. Fit as a Fiddle.
Harvey, James Clarence. Swiftly We Fly.
Herrera, F. Sonnet 32.
Johnston, G. Cathleen Sweeping.
Kloos, W. Evening.
Lugones. Slow Delight.
Oliver, M. Summer Day, The.
Porter, C. It's De-Lovely.
Shakespeare, W. O[h] Mistress Mine.
Soloukhin. Apple, The.
Swinburne. Sestina: "I saw my soul at rest upon a day."
Traherne. Anticipation, The.
Verlaine. Without Guile.

Deliverance
Jarrell, R. Jews at Haifa.

Jeffers, R. Home.
Merwin. How We Are Spared.
Sachs, N. Someone Will Take the Ball.
Unknown. Didn't My Lord Deliver Daniel?

Delphi, Oracle of
Friman. Trip to Delphi.
Lindsay, C. Love or Fame.
Merrill, J. Charioteer of Delphi, The.
Unknown. Last Oracle from Delphi.
Yeats. News for the Delphic Oracle.

Demeter
Doolittle, H. Mysteries, The.
Dove, R. Demeter, Waiting.
  Persephone Underground.
  Political.
Greenwell, D. Demeter and Cora.
Krysl. Persephone, to Demeter.
Mutén, B. Demeter's Blessing.
Starhawk. Demeter's Song.
Taggard. Demeter.

Democracy
"Ada.". Scroll is open, The.
Anderson, S. Song of the Soul of Chicago.
Anene, L. Democracy.
Belloc. On a General Election.
Dede, J. Bits.
Freneau. On Mr. Paine's Rights of Man.
Hall, D. Impossible Marriage, The.
Hitchman-Britton, O. Road to the Presidency.
Katz, E. In Praise of the Seattle Coalition.
Kim Chiha. In Burning Thirst.
Kim Suyŏng. Ha . . . No Shadows.
London, R. Folk Form.
McClatchy. 1871.
McClure, M. Madame Secretary.
Mendelssohn Anna. Franked.
Ngoma. Demockery.
Ruhani, G. Gaffer Speaks.
Scott-Heron. Winter in America.
Skovron. Election Eve, with Cat.
Tilley, H. Democracy, my grannie's foot!
Whitman, W. Commonplace, The.
  For You O Democracy.
  One's-Self I Sing.
  Walt Whitman, a kosmos, of Manhattan the son.

See also **Campaigns, Political; Voting and Voters**

Demons
Boadiba. Autozobop.
Brecht, B. Mask of Evil, The.
Brown, K. Good Devil, The.
Burns, R. De'il's [*or* Deil's] Awa wi' th' [*or* the] Exciseman, The.
Cagnone, N. Book Three: On Preparation.
Ch'ŏyong. Song of Ch'ŏyong.
Citino. Sitting in the Sixth Grade at Ascension of Our Lord School in Cleveland, Ohio, Reading a Pamphlet Entitled "Possession in Iowa".
Crane, S. I stood upon a high place.
De Luca, C. Dancing with Demons.
Della Cruscans. Moods 1.
Emerson, R. Dæmonic and the Celestial Love, The.
Heym. Demons of the Cities, The.
Huerta, D. Baraja.
  Deck of Cards.
Kimbrell, J. True Descenders.
McClure, M. Madame Secretary.
Milosz, C. Readings.
Pushkin, A. Demons.
Simic. Head of a Doll.
Stallings. How the Demons Were Assimilated and Became Productive Citizens.
Tranströmer. Chill-to-the-bone, A.
Unknown. No longer will I draw water from the spring at dusk.
  Song of Ch'ŏyong.
  With the first light of the early morning dawning.
Wright, J. Killer, The.

See also **Monsters**

Dempsey, William Harrison ("Jack")
Ignatow, D. Boxing Match, The.

Denial
Carrington, H. Woo's People.

Cernuda. I'll Tell You How You Were Born.
Clifton, L. At the cemetery, walnut grove plantation, south carolina, 1989.
Cooley, N. Good Friday, Alice Liddell.
Dickinson, E. Renunciation—is a piercing Virtue.
Dove, R. Poem in Which I Refuse Contemplation.
Gamalinda, E. Denials.
Graves, R. Cool Web, The.
  Nobody.
Hardy, T. In the Servants' Quarters.
Ismaili. Solange.
Larkin, J. Origins.
MacNeice. Canto XX: "To Wales once more, though not on holiday now."
Martial. Why, Hyllus, do you deny to me today.
Martinaitis, M. Forbid!
Meynell, A. Renouncement.
Paulus [*or* Paulos] Silentiarius. Tantalos.
Ransom, J. Good Ships.
  Nocturne.
Rich, A. What Kind of Times Are These.
St. John, P. Benign Neglect / [West Point,] Mississippi, 1970.

Dentistry and Dentists
Brown, S. Her lips disclosed to view.
Kay, J. Crown and Country.
Marzán. Emergency.
Quevedo y Villegas. Toothpuller Who Wanted to Turn a Mouth into a Grinding Machine, The.
Valerie, J. Lesson on Braces.

Dentures
Dickey, W. Poet's Farewell to His Teeth, The.

Denver, Colorado
Ferril. Waltz against the Mountains.
Foster, T. Folktale, A: "Father stands on a walkway talking, A."
Ginsberg, A. Green Automobile, The.

Department Stores
Alexander, E. Ladders.
Derricotte. Weakness, The.
Irwin, M. Woolworth's.
McHugh, H. What Could Hold Us.

Deportation
Im Hwa. Pier of Yokohama under the Umbrella, The.
Lavieri, J. Autobiography of John Doe, The.
Unknown. Deported.
  For one month I was imprisoned; my slippers never moved forward.
  Insects chirp outside the four walls, The.
Yoneda, Karl. New Year's Day on Angel Island.

Depression (economic)
Cooper, J. Wanda's Blues.
Justice, D. Pantoum of the Great Depression.
Oppen. Bad times: / The cars pass.
Walker, M. Delta.
Weatherford, C. From Birmingham to Bristol in a Boxcar.

See also **Great Depression**

Depression (psychological)
Agustini. Ineffable, The.
Alley, R. Dissecting Uncle Sorrow.
Butler, C. E. Darkness, The.
Cardenal. Prayer for Marilyn Monroe.
Cleyre, V. Out of the Darkness.
Darío, R. Sonatina.
Gerstler. Fan Letter, A.
Glück, L. Matins: "Sun shines; by the mailbox, leaves, The."
González, A. Death in the Afternoon.
Gross, P. I'm fat, look, *fat.*
Hadas, R. Humble Herb Is Rival to Prozac.
Hayden, R. Ice Storm.
Hierro, José. Any Afternoon.
Holmes, J. Depressive Episode.
Howe, F. Doubt.
Kabir. Meeting, The: "When my friend is away from me, I am depressed."
Kenyon, J. Back: "We try a new drug, a new combination."
  Having It Out with Melancholy.
Lake, P. Crime and Punishment.

McGough, R. Survivor.
Murray, L. Corniche.
Nathan, L. Ragged Sonnet: When in a Deep Depression.
O'Hara, F. Lines to a Depressed Friend.
Orozco. Miss Havisham.
Parker, D. Symptom Recital.
Pizarnik. Exile.
Randall, D. His Favourite Seat.
Rosenberg, L. Poems of Delight.
Ross, W. Another Song.
Sadoff. Depression, The.
Sanchez, S. Depression.
Schmitt, Kate. Prelude to the Fall.
Sears, P. One Polar Bear, The.
"Shu Ting.". Brother, I Am Here.
Smith, A. Silent Room.
Smith, C. To Night.
Stadler. On Crossing the Rhine Bridge at Cologne by Night.
Stoddard, E. Nameless Pain.
Su, A. Antidepressant.
Szymborska, W. Four in the Morning.
Thomas, R. S. Evans.
Trakl. Mood of Depression, The.
Trinidad. Things to Do in Valley of the Dolls (The Movie).
Tuckerman, F. Series 3, Sonnet 10.
Vallejo. I Am Going to Talk About Hope.
Van de Woestijne. Oars Heavy with Seaweed, The.
Warren, R. Pursuit.
Yang Wan-li. I don't feel like reading another book.
Yosano Akiko. Spring Thaw.

See also **Melancholy; Mental Illness**

Dereliction
Walcott. Ajax, / lion-coloured stallion from Sealey's stable.

Descartes, René
Kyger. Descartes and the Splendor of *a Real Drama of* Everyday Life. In Six Parts.

Desdemona
Beck, R. Interlude: "Sing together."
Bishop, J. Speaking of Poetry.
Walker, J. How Mother Courage Saves Desdemona.

Deserters and Desertion
Freneau. Jeffery, or, the Soldier's Progress.
Unknown. Son, if you desert our war.

Deserts
al-Rahim, A. Who?
Al-Wahaybi. Desert, The.
Ali, A. Leaving Sonora.
  Snow on the Desert.
Benton, S. Lilith.
Blind. Fantasy, A.
Broda, Martine. I Wash.
Bryner. Desert Flowers.
Césaire, A. Blank to Fill in on the Visa of Pollen.
Clover, J. Bathtub Panopticon.
Collobert. For Which the Sun.
Crane, S. I walked in a desert.
  In the desert.
Cullar, Carol. Heat.
Currey. Burial Flags.
Dove, R. Desert Backyard.
  Other Side of the House, The.
Fingueret, M. Games at the Hour of the Desert.
Forbes, C. Dark Mirror.
Gardiner, S. Colorado Desert Night.
Garioch. Property.
Goldberg, B. Since I Have Lived.
Greenberg, S. African Desert.
Hadewijch. Knowing Love in Herself.
Hartog, D. Oasis.
Hope, A. Australia.
Illyés, G. Logbook of a Lost Caravan.
Jabès. Desert, II, The.
Jackowska. Proud Shore For Legends, A.
Jarrell, R. Range in the Desert, The.
Khoury, N. Death Is Your Salvation.
Kizer, C. Food of Love.
Kulishova, I. Till now / I've not been able to

imagine.

Kunitz, S.   Old Cracked Tune, An.

Leopardi.   Upon the arid shoulder.

Longfellow, H.   Sand of the Desert in an Hour-Glass.

Magdeburg, Mechthild von.   Desert Has Many Teachings, The.

Major, C.   Lost in the Desert.

Marchera, D.   Desert Crossing.

Markham, E.   In Death Valley.

Martínez, V.   It Is Not.

Matthews, W.   Moving Again.

McAuley, J.   Envoi.

Melville, H.   In the Desert.

Merrill, C.   Erosion.

Mora.   La Migra.

Morgan, E.   Dowser, The.

Murphy, M.   Al-Khamasin.

Neruda.   Broken Glish.

Pagis, D.   Snake.

Prigov.   In the Desert.

Raine, K.   Moment, The.

Ramke, B.   Difference Between Night and Day, The.

Rawson, J.   Border, The ("Leaping from the eucalyptus branch, the wild desert pigs.").

Rich, A.   On this earth, in this life, as I read your story, you're lonely.

Richter, H.   Surfaces.

Robinson, A.   Oasis, An.

Sachs, N.   Your Eyes, O My Beloved.

Sandburg, C.   People know what the land knows, The.

Saner.   Desert Wisdom.

Santos, S.   Near the Desert Test Sites.

Seneca.   O barbarous Corsica, locked in by crags.

Shelley, P.   Ozymandias.

Stafford, W.   At the Bomb Testing Site.

Teasdale.   Day's Ending.

Togawa, Akira.   Distorted Sun.

Tomlinson, C.   Arizona Desert.

Death in the Desert, A.

Trapnell, N.   Lament of a Desert Rat.

Uschuk, P.   Of Simple Intent.

Weslowski.   Dry World.

Whittier.   Song of Slaves in the Desert.

Woo, D.   Eden.

Zukofsky, L.   In Arizona.

Desire

Abbott, W.   Quite Mercenary He Stalked Her.

Abdal.   Ilahi.

Abu-l-Hasan Ibn Al-Qabturnuh.   In Battle.

Adamson.   Action Would Kill It / A Gamble.

Addonizio.   For Desire.

Them.

Adler, R.   Whatever Lola Wants (Lola Gets).

Ager, M.   Louisville Lou (The Vampin' Lady).

Agustini.   Intruder, The.

Wild for Love.

Akhmatova, A.   Visitor, The.

Al-A'mā at-Tuṭīlī, A.   Laughing out of pearls, / A full moon appears.

Al-Bayati, A.   Shiraz Moon.

Al-Mushafi.   Yellow Its Color.

Al-Rihani.   Lilatu Laili.

Alberti.   Homecoming of Love Amongst Illustrious Ruins.

Alcman.   Desire Loosening.

Olympian [Muses], round my mind.

Polydeukes.

With limb-loosening desire; and her glances are more melting than sleep or death.

Aldana.   Sonnet 12: "Which is the reason my Damon that although."

Alegría.   Savoir Faire.

Alford, H.   You and I.

Amadiume.   Union, The.

Amaru.   Much Too Close.

Amichai, Y.   Quick and Bitter.

Amis, K.   Dream of Fair Women, A.

Sight Unseen.

Ammons.   Love Song: "Like the hills under dusk you."

Spit.

Anacreon.   Fragment 360.

Lad, glancing like a virgin.

Thracian filly, why do you.

Tossing a crimson ball.

Ancient Sumerian Oral Tradition.   Word they had spoken, The.

Andal.   We rose before dawn.

Anderson, M.   It Never Was You.

Angus.   Invitation.

Anwar, C.   Ordinary Song, An.

Tuti's Ice Cream.

Archilochus.   Hold back completely.

Miserable I lie in desire.

My friend, limb-loosening.

Archpoet.   His Confession.

Asclepiades.   Dorkion, sweet little tomboy.

Ashbery, J.   Blessing in Disguise, A.

Atwood.   Variation on the Word Sleep.

Ayres, R.   Corporeal.

Baldwin, B.   Field of Poppies, A.

Baldwin, J.   Guilt, Desire and Love.

Baqi.   Fountain of my spirit thirsts for your ruby, The.

Baratier, D.   She Wants.

Barker, J.   To My Young Lover.

Barnes, B.   Sestine 4.

Barnett, A.   Music of the Spheres.

Barnfield [or Barnefield].   Sighing, and sadly sitting by my Love.

Sometimes I wish that I his pillow were.

Baron, R.   Diner.

Barrows, A.   Pleasures of the Flesh.

Bartlett, J.   Man and a Woman Standing in the Rain in Front of a Candy Store, A.

Basho.   To the willow.

Bataille, Georges.   Night Is My Nudity.

Bates, C.   Hard-Hearted Hannah (The Vamp of Savannah).

Bathurst, B.   To Marthe.

Baudri of Bourgueil.   Your Appearance Is Pleasing.

Beatrice [or Beatritz or Beatriz], Countess de Die [or Dia].   Lover's Prize, A.

Becker, R.   Story I Like to Tell, The.

Beckett, S.   Cascando.

Begley, T.   Sappho's Gymnasium ("For healthy cells please remember.").

Behn, A.   In Imitation of Horace.

On Desire. A Pindarick.

Thousand Martyrs I Have Made, A.

To the Fair Clarinda [or Clorinda], Who Made Love to Me, Imagin'd [or Imagined] More than Woman.

Bell, M.   Book of the Dead Man #43, The.

Belli, C.   Poem: "Our love is not found in our respective."

Berlin.   Change Partners.

Fools Fall in Love.

Heat Wave.

How Deep Is the Ocean? (How High Is the Sky?).

I Got Lost in His Arms.

Isn't This a Lovely Day (To Be Caught in the Rain?).

It's a Lovely Day Today.

I've Got My Love to Keep Me Warm.

Let's Face the Music and Dance.

Remember.

They Say It's Wonderful.

What'll I Do?

You'd Be Surprised.

You're Laughing at Me.

Bernard [or Bernart] de Ventadour [or Ventadorn].   Good time of the year, The.

Berrigan, A.   Various multitudes contained by the loves of my love, The.

Berry, W.   Marriage.

Berryman.   Desires of Men and Women.

Beveridge.   Dining Out.

Bhartrihari.   Bearing the lustre of a full moon.

Sweet Maid.

Bhatt, S.   White Asparagus.

Bhattācārya, K.   So, forgetful Mahadeva.

Bibbins, M.   Bluebeard.

Whitman on the Beach.

Bible, O.T.   How beautiful are thy feet with shoes.

Bigelow, B.   Hard-Hearted Hannah (The Vamp of Savannah).

Blackburn, T.   Now Light Congeals.

Blagg, T.   In Bed this Morning.

Blake, W.   Abstinence Sows Sand All Over.

Question Answered, The [or A].

Blind.   Fantasy, A.

Once We Played.

Blok.   Visitor.

Bly, R.   French Generals, The.

Bogan, L.   Dream, The.

Boker.   Sonnet 24: "Farewell once more,—and yet again farewell!"

Sonnet 42: "If she should give me all I ask of her."

Boland, E.   Daphne with Her Thighs in Bark.

In Her Own Image.

Breton, A.   Free Union.

They Tell Me That Over There.

Bridie, J.   West End Perk, The.

Brion, R.   Love Song: "One long and humid afternoon."

Broumas, O.   Sappho's Gymnasium ("For healthy cells please remember.").

Brown, E.   Beauty and the Prince Formerly Known as Beast.

Tell me I'm beautiful, and bring me flowers.

What do I have, when I contemplate this.

Brown, L.   (Here Am I) Broken Hearted.

If I Had a Talking Picture of you.

It All Depends on You.

Magnolia.

Maybe This Is Love.

Never Swat a Fly.

That Old Feeling.

You're the Cream in My Coffee.

Browning, E.   Man's Requirements, A.

Brownstein.   Oracle night / the porch is frozen.

Brutus.   Let not this plunder be misconstrued.

Bryan, M.   To———: "O thou unknown disturber of my rest."

Buchanan, S.   Alone in Belize.

Burns, R.   Green Sleeves [and Tartan Ties].

Mary Morison.

O Were My Love Yon Lilac[k] Fair.

Butler, S.   She was too kind, wooed too persistently.

Butts, A.   Nature of Braille, The.

Caesar.   What a Perfect Combination.

Cagnone, N.   Book Three: On Preparation.

Caldwell, A.   I Know That You Know.

Calpurnius Siculus.   Eclogue 3.

Cambridge, A.   Dream.

Camlan.   Lady Charlotte Guest.

Campion, T.   Fain Would I Wed.

Fire, fire, fire, fire!

Campo.   For J. W.

Cardenal.   For me to lose you and for you to lose me, we both lose.

I offer these verses to you, Claudia, because you are their mistress.

Carew, T.   Mediocrity in Love Rejected.

Second Rapture, The.

Carpenter, E.   Through the Long Night.

Casal, J.   My Loves.

Catullus.   Carmen 5.

He Seems to Me Almost a God.

Ipsithilla, my pet, my favorite dish.

Lesbia's sparrow!

Catulus.   Waking Intuitively.

Caulfield.   For Albert, the Terrible.

Cavafy.   At the Cafe Door.

Return.

When They Come Alive.

Cavalli.   But first one must free oneself.

Far from kingdoms.

Cendrars.   Newspaper.

Cernuda.   If Man Could Name.

Speaking Other Than with Words.

That Which Is Enough for Love.

Cerruto, O.   Love: "Afternoon is offered to us, The."

Cervantes.   A un Desconocido.

Chandidas.   Why Tell Me What to Do?

Charry Lara, F.   I Would Have Loved You.

Chaucer.   Song of Troylus, The.

Cheney-Coker. On Being a Poet in Sierra Leone.
Chesterton. Joseph.
Ch'ôn Yanghûi. Thoughts on a Bird.
Chudleigh. Song: "Why *Damon*, why, why, why so pressing?"
Cisneros, S. You Called Me *Corazón*.
Clare, J. First Love.
Clarke, A. Young Woman of Beare, The.
Clarke, George Elliott. Monologue for Selah Bringing Spring to Whylah Falls.
Clifton, L. Scar.
We are running.
Cobbold, E. Reproach.
Coffman. Girl/Spit.
Cohan. When a Fellow's on the Level with a Girl That's on the Square.
Colonna, S. Disconnections.
Comden, B. Not Mine.
Party's Over, The.
Cooley, N. Undine.
Corey, S. Complicated Shadows.
Countryman, Jeremy. Woman with Chrysler.
Coviello, M. This hour is made of iron grates where the underground.
Creamer, H. If I Could Be with You.
Creeley. Ballad of the Despairing Husband.
For W. C. W ("Rhyme is after, The.").
Crevel, R. Nighttime.
Crews, J. Essence.
Cross, D. Turn-On (with Most of a Line by Spicer).
Cross, E. Fabulación.
Fabulation.
Pabellón.
Pavilion.
Crowley, A. Rondels.
Cruz, S. Dark Night, The.
Cuadra, P. Manuscript in a Bottle.
Cullen, C. Timid Lover.
Cummings, E. E. Goodby Betty,don't remember me.
Item.
My sweet old etcetera.
Thy fingers make early flowers of.
Cummins, J. Sestina: "He wanted to tell her the weekend idea was "neat"."
Cutts. To a Lady, Who Desired Me Not To Be in Love with Her.
Dacre, C. Power of Love, The.
Sappho; or, The Resolve.
Daigu. Here none think of wealth or fame.
Dailey. Rio.
Damas. Through the Half-Opened Window.
Daniel, A. Firm desire which enters, The.
Resolute Desire That Enters, The.
D'Aquino, A. Amoroso.
Amorous.
Darío, R. Autumn Verses.
Darr. At Sixteen.
Davidson, J. Ballad of a Nun, A.
Davidson, M. Century of Hands.
Davies, M. Love Song: "There is a strong wall about me to protect me."
Davis, C. Little Crisis Framed in My Window.
Davis, J. You Turn Around.
Davis, T. Desire 1.
de Burgos. Transmutation.
de Gillies, G. De Puerorum osculis.
De Vere, E. Lively lark stretched forth her wing, The.
DeBerry, J. Plain Ole Brother Blues.
Debravo, J. Beds of Purification.
Degenaar. Phenomenon, A.
Delgado, J. Dandelion.
Denby. Delos.
DeNiord, C. There Is an Error at the Heart of Desire.
Dermée. Silver Clasps.
These apples.
des Forêts Louis-René. It Is High Time.
Desbordes-Valmore. Memory, A.
DeSylva, B. G. If I Had a Talking Picture of you.
If You Knew Susie (Like I Know Susie).
It All Depends on You.

Magnolia.
Maybe This Is Love.
Never Swat a Fly.
You're the Cream in My Coffee.
Dewdney. She is liquid darkness occult with desire.
Dickinson, E. I cannot live with You.
Wild Nights—Wild Nights!
Dillard, A. Man Who Wishes to Feed on Mahogany, The.
Ditlevsen. Eternal Three, The.
Dixon, M. I Found a Million Dollar Baby (In a Five and Ten Cent Store).
Dixon, S. Request of Alexis, The.
Dobyns. Tenderly.
Donaldson, W. Little White Lies.
You're Driving Me Crazy (What Did I Do?).
Donne. Canonization, The.
Lovers' Infiniteness[e].
Donovan, K. Watermelon Man.
Doolittle, H. Helmsman, The.
Doubiago, S. How to Make Love to a Man.
Douskey. Dog Days and Delta Nights.
Wet Bodies.
Dove, R. Secret Garden, The.
Sunday Greens.
Dowson. Exchanges.
Flos Lunae.
Non Sum Qualis Eram Bonae sub Regno Cynarae.
Dransfield. Epiderm.
Memoirs of a Velvet Urinal.
Dryden, J. Whil'st Alexis lay prest [or press'd].
Dubin, A. Cup of Coffee, a Sandwich, and You.
I Only Have Eyes for You.
I'll String Along with You.
Lulu's Back in Town.
Young and Healthy.
You're Getting to Be a Habit with Me.
Duffy, C. Mrs Midas.
Words, Wide Night.
Duffy, M. I Am Beset with a Dream of Fair Woman.
Semi-Skilled Lover.
Duhamel. Kinky.
Dunbar-Nelson. You! Inez!
Duncan, R. Preface to the Suite: "Childhood, boyhood, young manhood."
Torso, The.
Dunn, S. Landscape at the End of the Century.
Tenderness.
Edwards, D. Not Having.
Elder daughter.
Were you a string of beads: Otomo no Sakanoé.
"Eliot.". How Lisa Loved the King.
Eliot, T. S. Love Song of J. Alfred Prufrock, The.
Elizabeth I. When I Was Fair and Young.
Elizabeth, M. She Teaches Him to Reach Out.
Éluard, P. *et al.* Loving.
Emerson, R. To Rhea.
Emre. Your love has wrested me away from me.
"Ephelia.". To J.G. on the News of His Marriage.
Erdrich. Leonard Commits Redeeming Adulteries with All the Women in Town.
"Ern Malley.". Night Piece.
Eskimo Oral Tradition. Love Song: "I cannot bear it, I cannot bear it at all."
Estes, A. You Stand There Fishing.
Etter. Andy Hasselgard.
Ettinger, E. Excerpts from the Sabbath Dream Book.
Evans, D. Dinner at the Hotel de la Tigresse Verte.
Faber, F. Dream of Blue Eyes, A.
Fabian, C. Qadesha (Sacred Whore).
Fagan. Desire.
Faiz. Before You Came.
Farish, H. Look at These.
Faverey. Train scarcely slackens speed, The.
Field. Ebbtide at Sundown.
Fields, D. I'm in the Mood for Love.
Make the Man Love Me.
Fishman, L. V's Farmhouse.

Fletcher, J. Take, Oh, Take Those Lips Away.
Fletcher, J. Blue Symphony.
Florián, M. Pastora.
Flynn, N. Cartoon Physics, Part 2.
Forman, R. Someone.
Fournier, R. Encounter.
Freed, A. All I Do Is Dream of You.
Fit as a Fiddle.
I Cried for You.
I've Got a Feelin' You're Foolin'.
This Heart of Mine.
You Were Meant for Me.
Frost, R. Fire and Ice.
Gaitán Durán. They Unite Naked.
García Lorca. Sleepwalkers' Ballad.
Sleepwalking Ballad, The.
Garcilaso de la Vega. Nemoroso.
Garrigue. Grenoble Café.
To Speak of My Influences.
Gascoigne. For That He Looked Not upon Her.
Lullaby [or Lullabie] of a Lover, The.
Gaskill, C. I Can't Believe That You're in Love with Me.
Prisoner of Love.
Gay, J. Air: "O ruddier than the cherry!"
I rage, I melt, I burn.
George, D. It Shouldn't Happen to a Dream.
Gershwin, I. I Can't Get Started.
Gerstler. Unforeseen, The.
Ghalib, M. Ghazal: "If you've given your heart away.".
Gibbons, S. Truce, The.
Gillespie, H. You Go to My Head.
Gillies, V. Look-Alike, The.
Ginsberg, A. Green Automobile, The.
Malest Cornifici Tuo Catullo.
Why Is God Love, Jack?
Written in My Dream by W. C. Williams.
Giorno. Life Is a Killer.
Scum & Slime.
Gladding. Fisherman's Wife, The.
Glatt. Amanda.
Glazer, M. All That in the Voice I Have Adopted for This Lie.
Science.
Sonnet: "Invisible in vernal pools."
Gleason, K. After Fighting for Hours.
Glück, L. Aubade: "World was very large, The. Then."
Elms.
Mirror, The.
Godfrey. One or More Together.
Wings.
Goese, M. Love Ghost.
Goldberg, B. Fetish.
He Said Discipline Is the Highest Form of Love.
Nights in the Constellation of the Tree Stepping from Its Robe.
Twentieth Century Children (5): Blood-Kissing.
Golffing. Higher Empiricism, The.
Gomez de Avellaneda. Imitating an Ode by Sapho.
Góngora y Argote. Sonnet 103.
Sonnet 82.
Gonzalez, R. Beyond Having.
Göransson. Last Instrument, The.
Gray, S. Fine Fechtin Mouse, The.
Green, A. Not Mine.
Party's Over, The.
Greene, R. Palmer's Ode, The.
Gregg. What Is Kept.
Grey, C. If You Were the Only Girl in the World.
Grimké, A. Beso, El.
Want of You, The.
Guidacci. It Is like a Shortness of Breath.
Guillén, N. Don't Know No English.
Guiney. Borderlands.
Guinicelli. Canzone: Of the Gentle Heart.
Gunn, T. In the Post Office.
Ha-Levi, J. Poem in Parts.
Hacker, M. Conclusion: "Did you love well what very soon you left?"
Hadas, R. Mars and Venus.
Three Silences.
Hadewijch II. If I desire something, I know it

not.
Hafiz, K [or Hafez]. Gabriel's News (37).
  Ghazal: Half-Way Through the Night.
  I cease not from desire till my desire.
Hagiwara Sakutaro. One Who's in Love with
  Love, The.
Hahn, K. Izu Dancer, The.
  Pine.
Hall, D. Mangosteens.
Hamilton, K. At the Frenchman's.
Han Yong'un [or Yongwun]. Artist, The.
Handy, J. Mata Hari Blues or Why I Will Never
  Be a Spy.
Harbach, O. Let's Begin.
  She Didn't Say "Yes".
Harechavi. 1 x 2.
Harford, L. I Count the Days Until I See You,
  Dear.
Harms. Tomorrow, We'll Dance in America.
Harryman. Matter.
Harwood, L. As Your Eyes Are Blue.
Hass, R. Story about the Body, A.
Hattersley, G. Frank O'Hara Five, Geoffrey
  Chaucer Nil.
Hatun. My heart burns in flames of sorrow.
Heine, H. Young Man Loves a Maiden, A.
Henderson, R. If I Had a Talking Picture of
  You.
  It All Depends on You.
  Magnolia.
  Maybe This Is Love.
  Never Swat a Fly.
  You're the Cream in My Coffee.
Henry, B. Skin: "Never mind the fantasy about
  the tweezers and the tongue."
Herd. Bathing Girls, The.
  Marilyn Climbs Out of the Pool.
Hernández, M. Final Sonnet.
Herrera. After All.
Herrera y Reissig. Sadistic Love.
Herrick. Hymne to Love, An.
  Night-Piece, to Julia, The.
  To Electra ("I dare not ask a kiss[e].").
  To His Mistress[es] ("Help[e] me! help[e] me!
    now I call.").
  Upon Julia's Clothes.
Hervey, L. Nature Queries [or Epistle to Mr.
  Fox, from Hampton Court].
Hewett, D. Sunset flames over the city, The.
  You Gave Me Hyacinths First a Year Ago.
Hilary. To an English Boy: "Beautiful boy,
  flower fair."
Hill, M. Bad Karma.
Hill, S. Desire's a Desire.
  Please Can I Have a Man.
Hirshfield, J. Adamantine Perfection of Desire,
  The.
  Half-sleeping, / my body pulls toward yours.
  Of Gravity and Angels.
  To Drink.
Homer. "Here," said the Cloud-gatherer Zeus,
  "that is a journey you may well postpone."
Horace. Ode 1.5: Quis Multa Gracilis.
  Ode 1.25: Ribald Romeos Less and Less
    Beattle ("Parcius iunctas quatiunt fenestras").
Housman. Others, I am not the first.
Hovey. Song by the Shore, A.
Huang T'ing-chien. Tune: "Joy of Returning to
  the Fields" ("Evening rain drips on the
  steps.").
Huerta, D. Machinery.
  Maquinarias.
Hughes, H. Mind Wanting More.
Hughes, L. Desire.
  Preference.
  When Sue Wears Red.
Hugo, V. Words in the Shadow.
Hunter, T. Wanting You.
Ibn Quzman, A. To a Beauty, White, Pure, and
  Constant.
Ibn 'Ubāda al-Qazzāz, A. I would give my
  father in ransom for a precious possession that
  clings to [my] soul!
Ichigen. Joshu exclaimed, "Dog's no Buddha".
Imr el [or ul] Kais. Ode of Imr El-Qais, The.
Irwin, M. Five Panels.

Issa. After a long nap.
  I wish she were here.
Istarú, A. Moon became mired on our bed, The.
Izumi. Lying down alone.
Jackson, H. Tides.
Jacob, V. Tam i' the Kirk.
James, J. Shakin All Over.
Jaramillo Agudelo, D. Some Day.
Jarnot, L. Still Life.
Jeffers, R. Divinely Superfluous Beauty.
Jennings, E. First Love.
  Thinking of Love.
Johnston, C. I know thee not, bright creature,
  ne'er shall know.
Jones, R. Loft, The.
Jones, R. Carpe Diem: "Though pretty, it rarely
  worked, lining seduction."
Jonson, B. Another Lady's Exception, Present
  at the Hearing.
  Her Man Described by Her Own[e] Dictamen.
  Song. To Celia ("Come my Celia, let us
    prove.").
  Urging Her of a Promise.
  What He[e] Suffered.
Josefowitz, N. Foreplay.
Joseph, A. Pure Pop.
József, A. Freight Trains.
Juana Inés de la Cruz. Elusive Shadow of My
  Substance, Stay.
Kahal, I. I Can Dream, Can't I?
Kahn, G. Guilty.
  I'll See You in My Dreams.
  It Had to Be You.
  Love Me or Leave Me.
  My Baby Just Cares for Me.
  Okay, Toots.
  One I Love (Belongs to Someone Else), The.
  Pretty Baby.
  Yes, Sir! That's My Baby.
  You Stepped Out of a Dream.
Kalmar et al. Nevertheless (I'm in Love with
  You).
  What a Perfect Combination.
Kantaris. Body Language.
Kasa. I love and fear him.
  White drops of dew, The.
Katz, J. Concerning the Islands Newly
  Discovered.
Kennedy, L. I am in the most exquisite distress.
Kenyon, J. August Rain, after Haying.
Khlebnikov, V. Once More, Once More.
Kinzie. Want, predation, sleep.
Kloos, W. Sonnet.
Klyuyev [or Kliuev or Klyuev]. Fourth Rome,
  The.
Koehler, T. As Long As I Live.
  Let's Fall in Love.
  Sing, My Heart.
  Stop! You're Breakin' My Heart.
Kool, M. Different.
Korteweg. Sed Non Frustra.
Kowit. What Chord Did She Pluck.
Kuan Yün-shih. Tune: "Rapt with Wine, Loudly
  Singing; Joy in Spring's Coming".
Kunitz, S. Touch Me.
Labé. Long-Felt Desires.
LaFemina. White Dwarf.
Lamb, H. She Said / He Said.
Langille. Through a Slit in the Tent.
Lasker-Schüler. Only for You.
  To The Barbarian.
Laux, D. Fast Gas.
  Laundromat, The.
Lawrence, D. H. Grasshopper Is a Burden.
  In Trouble and Shame.
Leapor. Strephon to Celia. A Modern Love-
  Letter.
Lee, L. Irises.
Lefroy. Idler Listening to Socrates Discussing
  Philosophy with His Boy-Friends, An.
Lehman. On the Nature of Desire.
Leifso, B. What Do You Want?
Leslie, E. Kansas City Kitty.
  Little Bit Independent, A.
Leto. Anna Magnani at the Castro.
Levertov. Quest, The.

Sea's Wash in the Hollow of the Heart, The.
Variation and Reflection on a Theme by Rilke
  (The Book of Hours, Book 1, Poem 7).
Lewis, S. Dinah.
  Five Foot Two, Eyes of Blue (Has Anybody
    Seen My girl?).
  For All We Know.
  I Wonder Why She Kept on Saying "Si-Si-Si-Si-
    Senor".
Lezama Lima. Call of the Desirous.
Li'aibi, S. Stone of the Arabian woman, The.
Lihn. Dark Room, The.
Lodeizen. Ode: In a Few Hours.
Lomax, M. Gruoch.
Long, H. Daphnis and Chloe.
Lope de Vega. And you my spent heart's
  treasure.
  Pentecost Castle, The.
López-Adorno, P. Throbs for the Instructress.
López Velarde. Purple Spot, The.
Lorde. Burning the Water Hyacinth.
Lovelace, R. Love Made in the First Age[: To
  Chloris].
Lowell, A. Opal.
Luca, Gherasim. End of the World, The: To
  Embody.
Lum. Urban Love Songs.
Lumbreras, E. Reunión de violonchelos.
  Reunion of Cellos.
Lumsden, R. Piquant.
Lyly, J. Cupid and My Campaspe Played.
Lyons, S. Loving along Western Rivers.
Mackay, J. Tomorrow.
Mackenzie, K. Fool, The.
Maclean, A. Question and Answer.
Magdeburg, Mechthild von. God Speaks to the
  Soul.
  How God Answers the Soul.
Maguire, S. Divorce Referendum, The.
Mandel, T. Say Ja.
Mandelstam [or Mandelshtam]. Tristia.
Mansfield, K. Secret Flowers.
Mansour, J. Desire as Light as a Shuttle.
  I Want to Sleep with You.
March, A. Know what I'm like? Some captain
  moors his ship.
Marlatt, D. Working Girl.
Marlowe. Amorous Leander, beautiful and
  young.
  Men of wealthy Sestos, every year, The.
Martí. I want, in the shade of a wing.
Martial. Cure of my unquietness.
  If by chance, Flaccus, someone could offer me
    for the asking.
  Out of the house or be the wife I want.
  People have the oddest kinks.
  When you say, "Quick, I'm going to come,".
Martin, D. Clock.
Martínez, V. Into the Next One.
  New World, The.
  Traveler.
Marvell. Mower's Song, The.
Masini. Two Men, Two Grapefruits.
Massimi. Love Song for Marcus, A.
Mathews, H. Comatas.
Mattawa. Heartsong.
Maxwell, G. Helene and Heloise.
McAuley, J. Legendary.
McCarthy, J. You Made Me Love You (I Didn't
  Want to Do It).
McDaniel, J. D.
McLain, P. Beauty, That Lying Bitch.
  Willing.
McNally, L. Lass of Richmond Hill, The.
Melville, H. After the Pleasure Party [Lines
  Traced under an Image of Amor Threatening].
  In a Bye-Canal.
Mercer, J. Laura.
  Something's Gotta Give.
Merrill, J. Kimono, The.
  Octopus, The.
Merritt, C. Mute Swan, The.
Merry. Adieu and Recall to Love, The.
Merwin. Vixen.
Mew. On the Road to the Sea.
Michelangelo Buonarroti. Love's Justification.

You know that I know, my lord, that you know.
Miller, R.   Aspects of Love.
Mirabai [or Mira Bai].   His Hair.
Miron, Gaston.   Walk toward Love, The.
Monk, M.   Fire Us with Ice, Burn Us with Snow.
Monsour.   Nimis Compos Mentis.
Montagu, L.   Man in Love, A.
Receipt to Cure the Vapours, A.
To a Lady Making Love.
Montgomerie, A.   Dreame, Ane.
Moore, T.   Did Not.
Moraes, D.   Snow on a Mountain.
Morungen, H.   Wound of Love, The.
Muldoon, P.   Something of a Departure.
Mun Chônghui.   For the Sake of Man Again.
Murphy, M.   When you say no.
Muske, C.   Red Trousseau.
Muso Soseki.   Withered Zen.
Myŏngok.   Dreams.
Na'ili [or Yeni-Zada Mustafa Efendi].   What witch are you, that entangles our hearts.
Nazario, A.   Kevin and Nicole.
Nelson, M.   Proposal.
Nesimi.   Oh my idol of the temple, in the dark of night.
Nguyễn Khuyên.   To the Singing Girl Named Luu.
Noble, R.   Touch of Your Lips, The.
Nordbrandt.   Our Love Is Like Byzantium.
North, C.   From the French.
O Cham.   Turkish Bakery, The.
Obejas, A.   Public Place (After Olga Broumas), The.
O'Hara, F.   Poem: "I don't know as I get what D.H. Lawrence is driving at."
Ojaide.   What They Said.
Omer, H.   Word from the Gray Soldiers.
Ondaatje.   Nine Sentiments, The.
Oommen, G.   Private Sorrow, A.
Oppen.   Forms of Love, The.
O'Reilly, J.   White Rose, A.
Orerulavanar.   What He Said.
Orléans, C.   Balade.
Go forth myn hert wyth my lady.
Orozco.   Reality and Desire.
Orr, G.   We Must Make a Kingdom of It.
Orton, B.   Love Poem.
Otomo no Sakanoé, Lady.   Where the plovers cry.
Ovid.   Elegy 1.5: "In summer's heat[e] and mid-time of the day."
Pygmalion.
Owen, W.   Music.
Oyake.   Hidden in the clouds.
Paisley, J.   Intellectual, The.
Paley, G.   Here.
Parra, N.   Pilgrim, The.
Pastan.   What We Want.
Paulus [or Paulos] Silentiarius.   Take off your clothes, my love!
Paz.   I travel your body as I would travel the world.
Peacock, M.   Desire.
Wheel, The.
Pearse, P.   Naked I Saw You.
Peele.   Bethsabe's Song.
Penna.   Shadowless sun on male bodies.
Peruñcattan.   What Her Girl-Friend Said.
Petrarch.   Apollo, if the sweet desire is still alive that inflamed you beside.
Blest be the day, and blest the month and year.
Clear, fresh, sweet waters, where she who alone seems lady.
Father in heaven, after each lost day.
Go, grieving rimes of mine, to that hard stone.
Sonnet: "When she walks by here."
When Simon received the high idea which, for my sake, put his.
Woods Are Wild and Were Not Made for Man, The.
Petronius Arbiter.   Long may our hearts, Nealce, guard that night.
Phillips, C.   Cotillion.
Pleasure.
Pietri, P.   January Hangover.

Pindar.   Ode on Theoxenos.
Poe.   Dream within a Dream, A.
To F——.
To Helen ("I saw thee once—once only—years ago.").
Poliziano.   On the Love of Two Boys.
Pollard, C.   And Another Bloody Thing.
Pope, J.   Beau Ideal, The.
Porete.   Beloved, what do you want of me?
Porter, C.   All of You.
At Long Last Love.
Get Out of Town.
In the Still of the Night.
It's All Right with Me.
It's De-Lovely.
I've Got You Under My Skin.
Laziest Gal in Town, The.
Let's Do It, Let's Fall in Love.
Porter, D.   Lollies Noir.
P. M. T.
Porter, P.   Now it's in all the novels, what's pornography to do?
Ports, K.   Desire.
Pound, E.   Δωρια.
Pozzi, C.   Nyx.
Pratt, M.   Done.
Elbows.
Praxilla.   You who look lovely from the windows.
Prévert.   River, The.
Prunty.   Pyromaniac, The.
Quevedo y Villegas.   Love Beyond Death.
On Lisi's Golden Hair.
Rabinowitz.   Of Joy Illimited: Polyphonic Soundings: Shore to Ship.
Rakosi.   Young Girl.
Ramsay, A.   Thou Were My Ain Thing, An.
Ranaldo, L.   Flash me.
Randall, D.   Haymakers.
Nightwatchman.
Rankin, J.   Love Affair 36.
Ravikovitch, D.   Surely You Remember.
Trying Again.
Razaf, A.   My Special Friend (Is Back in Town).
Rexroth, K.   Aspen Meadows.
Come to me, as you come.
Every morning, I.
Making love with you.
Scorched with love, the cicada.
Rhianos.   To Theodorus et al.
Rich, A.   Two Songs.
Two Songs.
Ricketts, W.   Scout.
Ridge, J.   Cherokee Love Song, A.
Stolen White Girl, The.
Riesco.   When I Passed in the Afternoon.
Rilke.   Birth of the Smile, The.
I Believe in All That Has Never Yet Been Spoken.
Roberts, K.   How Late Desire Looks.
Robin, L.   Louise.
Love Is Just Around the Corner.
My Ideal.
Prisoner of Love.
Robinson, C.   We Who Have Loved.
Robinson, E.   John Evereldown.
Tavern, The.
Robinson, K.   On the Corner.
Robinson, M.   Describes Phaon.
Laments the Volatility of Phaon.
Phaon Awakes.
Rejects the Influence of Reason.
She Endeavors to Fascinate Him.
Rochester, E.   Song: "Nothing ades to Loves fond fire."
Roethke.   Four for Sir John Davies.
I Knew a Woman.
Rose, The.
Rojas.   Beautiful Ones, The.
Rome, H.   Nobody Makes a Pass at Me.
Ronsard.   By looking too long on your perfect face.
Roripaugh, L.   Peony Lover.
Rose, B.   Cup of Coffee, a Sandwich, and You.
I Found a Million Dollar Baby (In a Five and Ten Cent Store).

Rose, J.   Marisel.
Rosenberg, L.   Lesson in Anatomy, A.
Ross, J.   Whatever Lola Wants (Lola Gets).
Rossetti, C.   Come back to me, who wait and watch for you.
Trust me, I have not earned your dear rebuke.
What Would I Give?
Rowe, E.   To Orestes.
Ruby, H.   Nevertheless (I'm in Love with You).
What a Perfect Combination.
Rudaki.   Prayer.
Ruiz, J.   Charms of Small Women.
Rukeyser, M.   Meeting, The.
Rumi.   Edge of the Roof, The.
Great Wagon, A.
Mill, the Stone, and the Water, The.
That moon which the sky never saw.
Russell, G.   Desire.
Rux, C. H.   Shunning an Imperative.
Ryushu Shutaku.   Why bother with the world?
Saarikoski.   I lived in a ruin called The Lion.
Sackville-West.   No Obligation.
Sadi [or Saadi or Sa'di].   He glanced at me one day—but then his mean.
St. John, D.   Desire: "There is a small wrought-iron balcony."
Salter.   Video Blues.
Salzman, E.   Alex, Tiffany, Meg.
Samyn, M.   Art of Kissing, The.
Sandburg, C.   Adelaide Crapsey.
Sanders, T.   Temporary Insanity.
Sansom, M.   Honour, that Guardian Angel, can alone.
To My Heavenly Charmer.
Santos, S.   Midsummer.
Sappho.   Anaktoria.
Arbor, The.
But as my friend, take to a younger bed.
For you beautiful ones my mind.
Honestly I'd as soon be dead!
I urge you.
Like the sweet-apple.
Like the very gods in my sight is he who.
Of love.
Once again Love [Eros], the looser of limbs, shakes me.
Once again that looosener of limbs, Love.
Percussion, salt and honey.
Sapphics.
Sardis.
Sweet apple reddens on a high branch, The.
Sweet mother, I cannot weave.
You came and did (well); I felt for you.
Schwartz, D.   Heavy Bear Who Goes with Me, The.
Schwartz, R. L.   Falling in Love after Forty.
Possible.
Schwitters.   Anna Blossom Has Wheels.
Desire.
Scythinus.   Calamity and conflagration! Strife!
Seifert.   Candlestick, The.
Sen, S.   Love.
Senghor.   Nocturne (I Accompanied You).
Song of the Initiate.
Serrano, P.   Inventario.
Inventory.
Sexton.   Jesus Asleep.
Seyburn, P.   Persuasion.
Shakespeare, W.   Country Song.
Sonnet 46: "Mine eye and heart are at a mortal war."
Sonnet 52: "So am I as the rich, whose blessed key."
Sonnet 56: "Sweet love, renew thy force; be it not said."
Sonnet 129: "Expense [or Expence] of spirit in a waste of shame, The [or Th']."
Sonnet 144: "Two loves I have of comfort and despair [or dispaire]."
Sonnet 147: "My love is as a fe[a]ver, longing still."
Sonnet 150: "O, from what power hast thou this powerful might."
Shaughnessy, B.   Rise.
Shaw, A.   Rear Window.
Small Pleasures.

Shelley, M. Stanzas: "Oh, come to me in dreams, my love!"
Shinkichi Takahashi. Downy Hair.
Lap Dog.
Stone Wall.
Shirley, J. Lover That Durst Not Speak to His M[istress], A.
Shofu. No dust speck anywhere.
Shurin. Forward or Back.
Sidney. Second Song: "Have I caught my heav'nly jewel."
Sonnet 14: "Alas, have I not pain enough, my friend."
Sonnet 39: "Come Sleep! O sleep the certain knot of peace."
Sonnet 52: "Strife is grown between Virtue and Love, A."
Sonnet 56: "Fie, school of Patience, fie; your lesson is."
Sonnet 71: "Who will in fairest book of Nature know."
Sonnet 72: "Desire, though thou my old companion art."
Thou Blind Man's Mark.
Simon, O. Heat.
Sissle, N. I'm Craving for That Kind of Love.
I'm Just Wild about Harry.
Sitwell, D. Heart and Mind.
King of China's Daughter, The.
Smith, B. Empty Bed Blues.
Smith, J. Gimme a Little Kiss (Will Ya, Huh?).
Smith, P. Dream of Rimbaud.
Smith, W. Family Man, The.
Snyder, G. Beneath My Hand and Eye the Distant Hills, Your Body.
For a Far-out Friend.
Four Poems for Robin.
Sŏ Chŏngju. Flower-Patterned Snake.
Södergran. Instinct.
Solie, Karen. Emergency Response.
Solon. Love of Boys, The.
Song. White Porch, The.
Soniat. Harp/Desire.
Sophocles. This disease is an evil bound upon the day.
Soto. Chitchat with the Junior League Women.
Spalding, E. August.
Spencer, B. Egyptian Dancer at Shubra.
Spender, S. Abrupt and charming mover.
Spenser, E. Eftsoones they heard a most melodious sound.
Legend of the Knight of the Red Crosse, or of Holinesse, The.
Sonnet 73: 'Being my self captived here'.
Stanton, M. Voice for the Sirens, A.
Steele, T. Aubade, An: "As she is showering, I wake to see."
Eros.
Stevens, W. Peter Quince at the Clavier.
Poems of Our Climate, The.
Stewart, S. Apple.
Stokesbury. Jaques Lured by Audrey.
Stone, J. Rosemary.
Stramm. Encounter.
Strand. Courtship.
Strato [or Straton]. I loathe a boy who won't be hugged and kissed.
Strauss, J. Love Notes.
Suárez, V. Donatilia's Unrequited Love Remedy.
Suckling, S. Against Absence.
Sonnet: "Dost see how unregarded now."
Sonnet: "Of thee, kind boy, I ask no red and white."
Suhl. Kh'hob dikh lib.
Surprice, L. If You Want.
Swinburne. Love And Sleep.
Sonnet for a Picture.
Swiontkowski, G. Old Moon with Her Youth in Her Arms.
Sylvester, J. But, fair Iĕmpsar (wife of Potiphar).
Symonds. What Cannot Be.
Sze. Great White Shark, The.
Szporluk. Axiom of Maria.
Grass and the Sin, The.

Libido.
Tall, Deborah. Miraculous Mandarin, The.
Tassis y Peralta. To a Lady Combing Her Hair.
Taylor, B. Goblet, The.
Hylas.
Teitelboim, D. Your Arms.
Tennyson, A. I envy not in any moods.
If I were loved, as I desire to be.
Terrazas. To a Pair of Legs.
Thomas, D. If I Were Tickled by the Rub of Love.
Thomas, E. Remedia Amoris.
To Colindra.
Thomas, L. Souvenir of the Manassah Ball.
Tibullus. Priapus, may this shady roof forever.
Timoner, J. Eye Occupation, The.
Timrod. La Belle Juive.
Tollet. On Loving Once and Loving Often.
Tornero, A. Lo que penetró tu vida—acedo espectáculo incrustado en el sitio del espasmo.
What penetrated your life—acid spectacle encrusted in the site of spasm.
Torre, M. Driven by a Strange Desire.
Tosui Unkei. Content with chipped bowl and tattered robe.
Traherne. Insatiableness.
Trethewey, N. Photograph of a Bawd Drinking Raleigh Rye.
Trinidad. More than anything, I wanted Charlie.
Of Mere Plastic.
Triplett, P. Studies in Desire.
Trouillot, L. I'm Dreaming of Your Body All Nude.
Tuckerman, F. Question, The.
Tufts, C. We Take the New Young Couple Out to Dinner.
Turell, J. You Beauteous Dames.
Turk, R. Ain't That the Way It Goes?
Gimme a Little Kiss (Will Ya, Huh?).
I Don't Know Why (I Just Do).
Mean to Me.
Tzu Yeh. When I started wanting.
Uflyand [or Ufliand]. It has for ages been observed.
Ulacia, M. Arabian Knight.
Arabian Knight.
Conrail Wax Museum.
Ungo Kiyo. Whirled by the three passions, one's eyes go blind.
Unknown. As night succeeds night.
Being helpless.
Bitter Cold.
Body's Speech, The.
Come, come, my companion.
CRUEL, you pull away too soon your lips whenas you kiss me.
De Ramis Cadunt Folia (Love in Winter).
Do You Remember That Night.
Do You Remember That Night?
Faire, fresshest erthly creature.
Fragrance Comes from the Scent I Wear, The.
Fressh lusty beautee joyned wyth gentilesse.
Go, litel bille, and do me recomaunde.
Here in my garden.
Hidden-in-winter.
How far from enough.
I love thee for thy fickleness.
Is there not a single madman in this village?
Kuan-kuan call the ospreys.
Lady, those cherries plenty.
Love of women leaves me cold; desire, The.
Love Song.
Love Song: "I will walk into some one's dwelling."
Love-Song, A: "Such a heart!"
Marsh's Plants Bewilder, The.
My love, open my tomb and see.
My pants, the hue of fire, are slipping down my thighs.
My perfume?
One is dying of desire to see me if only for a moment.
Pomelo, The.
Quickly, my love, I want to offer you my mouth!

So faire, so fressh, so goodly on-to see.
Sometimes I sauntered from my lone abode.
Things the Bigger the Better.
Those Women.
Thus feverish fancies floated in my brain.
To His Love.
To the Lady with a Book.
Tomorrow those who hunger for my love will be satisfied.
Unhappy pedophiles, cease your inane.
Were I to send word.
Whan the nyghtengale syngeth the wodes waxen grene.
When I Think About Why.
Wonders.
You intend, it seems.
You, wild hawk.
Yue-chu [Translations].
Unknown, fr. Egyptian hieroglyphics. Is there anything sweeter than this hour?
Unknown, fr. Sumerian cuneiform. Word they had spoken, The.
Vallejo. Poem to Be Read and Sung ("I know there is someone.").
Vanhomrigh. Hail, Blushing Goddess, Beauteous Spring!
Verlaine. Green.
Young Fools, The.
Vicinelli. When time--irreversible--begins to doze.
Vidya. Hiding in the.
Villalobos, M. I'm Sayin Though.
Villanueva, A. Peace #3.
Villaurrutia. Los Angeles Nocturne.
Nocturne.
Vivar. Love is Round.
Vivien. Ransom, The.
Vogelweide. Dancing Girl.
Volkman. Create Desire.
We did things more dulcet, more marionette.
W., A. Hopeless Desire Soon Withers and Dies.
Wachtel. On Class and Desire.
Wadsworth, C. Desire.
Waldrep, G. C. What Begins Bitterly Becomes Another Love Poem.
Waldrop, R. Feverish Propositions.
Waller, E. On a Girdle.
Walls, D. Summer the Beatles Went Over Seven Minutes on a Single, The.
Walsh, E. Dawning of the Day, The.
Walton, E. In Recompense.
Walwicz. Tattoo, The.
Wang Wei. Passing Hidden Fragrance Temple.
Warn. Nuit Blanche, Une.
Warren, R. Birth of Love.
Washington, N. Nearness of You, The.
Wearne. Division of O'Dowd, The.
Elise.
Terri.
Welish. Veil.
Wetzsteon. Dinner at Le Caprice.
Three Songs.
Whitman, W. As Adam Early in the Morning.
Fast-Anchor'd Eternal O Love!
From Pent-up Aching Rivers.
I Heard You Solemn-Sweet Pipes of the Organ.
Is this then a touch? . . . quivering me to a new identity.
Not Heat Flames Up and Consumes.
O You Whom I Often and Silently Come.
To the Garden the World.
When I Heard at the close of the Day.
Whitson, B. Let Me Call You Sweetheart.
Whittier. Henchman, The.
Widdows. Minutiae 3.
Wieners. Invitation au Voyage 2.
Wiesenthal, C. Blues.
Wilbur, R. Playboy.
She.
Wilcox, E. Attraction.
William of Aquitaine. Spring Song.
Williams, C. K. Love: Beginnnings.
Mistress, The.
Williams, Stephanie. Maid of Need, A.
Williams, W. Woman Walking.
Willis, N. Lady in the White Dress, Whom I

Helped into the Omnibus, The.
Witt, S. Everlasting Quail.
  Michael Masse.
Wodehouse. Bill.
  Bill (Original Version).
  That Was Before I Met You.
Wohlfeld. Sea.
Wormser. Single Urge, The.
Wright, C. On the Eve of Our Mutually
  Assured Destruction.
Wright, J. Angel, The.
  Sappho.
Wright, J. Cradle Logic of Autumn, The.
  Desire's Persistence.
  Meta-A and the A of Absolutes.
Wright, J. Metho Drinker.
  To a Child.
Wroth. Song: "Love a child is ever crying [or
  criing]."
  Sonnet 2: "Love like a jugler, comes to play his
    prize [or prise]."
  Sonnet 5: "And burn[e], yet[t] burning you will
    love the smart."
  Sonnet 7: "How blest be[e] they then, who his
    favo[u]rs prove."
  Sonnet 11: "Unprofitably pleasing, and
    unsound."
  Sonnet 34: "Take heed mine eyes, how you your
    look[e]s do[e] cast."
  Sonnet 35: "False [or Faulce] hope which feeds
    but[t] to destroy, and spill."
Wunderlich, M. From a Vacant House.
Wyatt. Divers[e] [or Dyvers] doth[e] use, as I
  have heard and kno[w].
  Long love that in my thought doth harbo[u]r,
    The.
  Lover Showeth How He Is Forsaken of Such as
    He Sometime Enjoyed, The.
  So unwarely was never no man caught [or
    cawght].
  Sometime I fled the fire that me brent.
Wylie. Pastiche.
Yahya Beg. Come wander through the city,
  drink wine.
Yeats. Politics.
Yellen, J. Ain't She Sweet?
  Hard-Hearted Hannah (The Vamp of Savannah).
  Louisville Lou (The Vampin' Lady).
Yi Sanghûi. As My Will Concurred Not To My
  Being, It Were But Right and Equal to Reduce
  Me to My Dust.
Yosano Akiko. Thousand lines, A.
Young, Andy. Foxfire.
Young, J. Dinah.
  Five Foot Two, Eyes of Blue (Has Anybody
    Seen My girl?).
  I Wonder Why She Kept on Saying "Si-Si-Si-Si-
    Senor".
Young, K. Song of Smoke.
Yüan Chĕn. Peach Blossoms.
Zaid. Song of Pursuit.
Zandvakili, K. County.
Zeyneb. Remove your veil and illuminate the
  earth.

See also **Erotic Love; Lust**

Desks
Graham, D. Robert Frost's Writing Desk.
Thompon, E. My Study.

Desolation
Aiken, C. Music I heard with you was more
  than music.
Anwar, C. Light Leaving a Small Harbour.
Azzawi, F. Crossing the Valley.
Behn, A. Paraphrase on Oenone to Paris, A.
Belloc. Ha'nacker Mill.
Bontemps. Blight.
Brontë, E. Remembrance: "Cold in the earth—
  and the deep snow piled above thee!"
Byron, G. Darkness.
Cassian. Bread and Wine.
Celan. There was earth inside them, and.
Ch'i-chi. Stopping at Night at Hsiang-yin.
Chŏng Ch'ŏl. Continued Song of Longing.
  Song of Longing.
Clare, J. Thou far-fled pasture, long evanished
  scene.

Creeley. Marriage, A.
Dalton, Mary. Down the Bay.
Delmore, E. Marmalade.
Eguren. Dead, The.
Faiz. Tyrant, The.
Follain. School and Nature.
Forrest-Thomson. In This House.
Gil de Biedma, J. In the Forties.
Ginsberg, A. In Back of the real.
Gordon, Roxy. West Texas Mid-Century.
Hesse. How Heavy the Days.
Hughes, T. That Moment.
Im Che. Deep among the green valley grasses.
Jeffers, R. Place for No Story, The.
Jordan, N. When a Woman Gets Blue.
Joseph, L. Do What You Can.
Kim Sowŏl. Cigarette.
Knight, E. Feeling Fucked/Up Up.
Li Ch'ing-chao. Boat of Stars.
Liu Yung. Song: "Because spring brings
  miserable green and painful red."
Lowry, M. Delirium in Vera Cruz.
Lux. Grim Town in a Steep Valley.
Mengham, Rod. Allegory of Good Government.
Milosz, C. Temptation.
Monnier, Pascale. Summer ("These are the first
  fine days.").
Muir, E. Milton.
Oppen. Myth of the Blaze.
Paz. Native Stone.
Rexroth, K. Chilled through, I wake up.
  Once I shone afar like a.
Sin Hŭm. I would draw her face with blood.
Stanton, M. Shoplifters.
Stevens, W. Dry Loaf.
Stuart, D. Desolation: "At the top of the dune."
Teasdale. Over the Roofs.
Thomas, D. Hand That Signed the Paper, The.
Thomas, R. S. Reservoirs.
Trakl. West, The (Fourth Version).
Unknown. Like a hen pheasant.
  War Lament: "Every plant is burnt yellow."
Very. Lament of the Flowers, The.
Wu of Han [or Wu Ti or Ou-ty or Liu Ch'e or
  Liu Ch'u]. Skein, The.
Yeats. Meru.
Yi Sunsin. By moonlight I sit all alone.
Zimmer. Eisenhower Years, The.

Despair
Abercrombie. Hope and Despair.
Ai. Man with the Saxophone, The.
Akhmatova, A. Twenty-First. Night. Monday.
Al-A'mā at-Tuṭīlī, A. Laughing out of pearls, /
  A full moon appears.
Alexie. Exaggeration of Despair, The.
Arnold, M. To Marguerite—Continued.
Atkins, R. Irritable Songs.
Awoonor. Agosu if you go tell them.
Baraka, I. Poem Some People Will Have to
  Understand, A.
Baudelaire. Spleen LXXVIII.
Beckett, S. Cascando.
Berg, S. Nostalgia.
Berryman. Despair: "It seems to be DARK all
  the time."
  Sonnet 115: "As usual I'm up before the sun."
Blake, W. Sick Rose, The.
  Song: "My silks and fine array."
Bly, R. Snowbanks North of the House.
Borson. Save Us From.
Bremer, C. En la ventana.
  In the Window.
Brines, F. Having Sunk His Chin in His Hand.
Bronk. World, The.
Brontë, E. F. de Samara to A. G. A.
Browning, E. Loved Once.
  Mask, The.
Brunk, J. Where My Mother Cries.
Brutus. Endurance.
Burns, R. Despondency, an Ode.
Byron, G. One Struggle More, and I Am Free.
Cairns, Scott. Translation of Raimundo Luz,
  The: My Amusing Despair.
Campbell, S. Big John's Tears Fall to the River.
Campo, C. Indian Summer.
Campo. Manuel.

Cary, A. In Bonds.
Cassian. Morning Exercises.
Castro, R. Black Mood.
Ceccoli. Sir, I have remained so overcome, that
  I can no longer suffer your attacks.
Cervantes. Poet Is Served Her Papers, The.
Chin. We Are Americans Now, We Live in the
  Tundra.
  Year Passes in My Morning Teacup, The.
Chitre. My Father Travels.
Chudakov. When the cry goes up.
Colby, T. Captain's Log.
Coleridge, M. Awake.
  Doubt.
  Other Side of a Mirror, The.
Coleridge, S. Work without Hope.
Congreve, W. Music.
Cowper, W. Castaway, The.
  Lines Written During a Period of Insanity.
Creeley. Ballad of the Despairing Husband.
  For Love.
Crunk, T. Leaving.
Cussrooee. My Grief on the Sea.
Dalton, A. How to Disappear.
  Nest.
Dalton, A. Praying-Mantis, The.
D'Aquino, A. Metempsicosis del perro.
  Metempsychosis of the Dog.
Deane, S. Roots.
Dickinson, E. I cannot live with You.
  It might be lonelier.
  It was not Death, for I stood up.
  There's a certain Slant of light.
Disch. Zewhyexary.
Doolittle, H. Fragment 40: "Keep love and he
  wings."
  Fragment 68: "I envy you your chance of
    death."
Dowson. Last Word, A.
Drayton. O breake my hart quoth he, O breake
  and dye.
  Why doe I quake my down-fall to reporte?
Drummond, W. Madrigal: "My thoughts hold
  mortal[l] strife."
Dugan, A. American Variation on How Rilke
  Loved a Princess and Got to Stay in Her
  Castle.
Dunbar, P. Ships That Pass in the Night.
Duo Duo. Night.
Empson. This Last Pain.
Ferlinghetti, L. In Golden Gate Park that day.
Field. Maidenhair.
Ghalib, M. Ghazal 25: "If it ever occurs to her
  to be kind to me.".
  My Spiritual State.
Giorno. Life Is a Killer.
Godfrey. Where the Weather Suits My Clothes.
Gomez, M. Desert Cry, A.
Gonzalez, N. Deepest Well in Madras, The.
Gryphius. Misery.
Gu Cheng. Ark.
Gumilyov [or Gumiliov or Gumilev]. Streetcar
  That Lost Its Way, The.
Hardy, T. Darkling Thrush, The.
Hays, M. Ah! let not hope fallacious, airy, wild.
Hemans. Indian Woman's Death-Song, The.
Herbert, G. Affliction (4).
  Collar, The.
  Denial[l].
  Longing.
Hoffenstein. You buy some flowers for your
  table.
Hope, A. Return of Persephone, The.
Hopkins, G. Carrion Comfort.
  I Wake and Feel the Fell of Dark, Not Day.
  Leaden Echo and the Golden Echo, The.
  No Worst, There Is None. Pitched Past Pitch of
    Grief.
  Thou Art Indeed Just, Lord.
Housman. Shot? so quick, so clean an ending?
Hove. Red Hills of Home.
Hughes, L. Bad Luck Card.
Hugo, R. My Buddy.
Ibn Baqī, A. I have no wine other than sorrows
  mixed in the cup with flowing tears.
Ifowodo, O. Homeland.

Iosifova, Ekaterina. If the Silence Should Suddenly Return.
Jabès. Desert, II, The.
Jacobsen, R. Light Pole.
Jenkins, L. In a Tavern.
Johnson, J. We to America.
Kaufman, S. Security.
Kavanagh, P. Memory of Brother Michael.
Keats. Belle Dame sans Merci, La [A Ballad].
Day Is Gone and All Its Sweets Are Gone, The.
Khurshid-Banu. To My Son, Abbas.
Kumin, M. Despair.
Laing, K. Senior Lady Sells Garden Eggs.
Lamartine. Isolation.
Lansdown. Golgotha.
Lasker-Schüler. O God.
Le Brun, Annie. Festivals.
Lear, E. Limerick: "There was an old man whose despair."
Levis. Rhododendrons.
Levy, A. To Vernon Lee.
Lewis, A. Karanje Village.
Mountain over Aberdare, The.
Li Ch'ing-chao. Butterflies Love Flowers.
Li Ho. Under the Walls of Ping City.
Lihn. Of All Despondencies.
Locke, A. Sin and Despair Have So Possess'd My Heart.
Lodeizen. Ode: In a Few Hours.
Lodge, G. Lower New York.
Lowell, M. Africa.
Luca, Gherasim. My Folly of Being.
Macaulay, T. Jacobite's Epitaph, A.
Machado Ruiz. Close to the Road.
MacKay, I. Meeting, The.
Magidson, H. T'Ain't No Use.
Mangan, J. Twenty Golden Years Ago.
March, A. Day's in dread of losing her bright features, The.
Marlowe. He's gone, and for his absence thus I mourn.
Masters, E. Mrs. Benjamin Pantier.
McAuley, J. Tomb of Heracles, The.
McAuley, J. Winter Drive.
McCarthy, T. Quatrain without Sparrows, Helpful Bells or Hope.
McCord, D. Five Chants.
McGrath, T. End of the Line, The.
Nuclear Winter.
Melville, H. Island, The.
Meng Chiao. Despair.
Mew. Quiet House, The.
Mezey. How Much Longer?
Michelangelo Buonarroti. I live in sin, and dying to myself I live.
Mikha'il, M. Don't Despair.
Mirabai [or Mira Bai]. Dark one, / how can I sleep?
O friends, I am mad.
Mistral, G. Autumn.
Molina, E. Way It Must Be, The.
Molinari. Ode to a Long Sorrow.
Mörike [or Möricke]. Forsaken Girl, The.
Morris, W. Apology, An.
Nemerov. Redeployment.
Nerval. El Desdichado.
Nguyễn Gia Thiều. You were a fool, Old Man of the Moon.
Niedecker. I married.
Notley. Poem: "You hear that heroic big land music?"
Nuccoli. You have the light of my life, in your clear and pleasing face, and don't see me.
Your promises come to me always together with your betrayals, which you have more of than the fox.
O'Hara, F. Meditations in an Emergency.
Oliver, M. Wild Geese.
Otero, B. Chap. 10 Book 2.
Ovid. So, when she saw Narcissus wandering through the lonely countryside, Echo fell in love with him, and followed secretly in his steps.
Pak Inhwan. Sleepless Night, A.
Papaionnou. Nights without Hope (Rebetiko Song).

Parker, D. Coda: "There's little in taking or giving."
Pasolini. Redefining "Orthodoxy."
Petrarch. My ship laden with forgetfulness passes through a harsh sea, at.
Piñero. Running Scared.
Pizarnik. Exile.
Plath. Moon and the Yew Tree, The.
Street Song.
Popova, O. What's left for me to say? God.
Porzecanski. What Matters.
Preseren, F. Where?
Raab, L. Being a Monster.
Ralegh, Sir. Fortune Hath Taken Away.
Rankine. Short Narrative of Breasts and Wombs in Service of Plot Entitled, A.
Rao, A. Longing, A.
Rexroth, K. Chilled through, I wake up.
Requiem for the Spanish Dead.
Reznikoff. She sat by the window opening into the airshaft.
Rimbaud, A. Cheated Heart.
Ritsos. Not Even Mythology.
Rivard. For Michaela.
Rivera-Garza, C. Tercer Mundo.
Third World.
Robinson, M. Her Address to the Moon.
Her Confirmed Despair.
Sappho Discovers Her Passion.
Sappho Rejects Hope.
Stanzas: "In this vain, busy world, where the good and the gay."
Roethke. In a Dark Time.
Roland Holst. Time, Please.
Rossetti, C. Better Resurrection, A.
If Only.
L. E. L.
Old-World Thicket, An.
What Would I Give?
Rossetti, D. 97: A Superscription.
51: Willowwood ("O ye, all ye that walk in Willowwood").
Woodspurge, The.
Rutsala. Summer: "There is no breeze, sounds travel far in the dead air."
Sabines. Lovers, The.
Sadi [or Saadi or Sa'di]. Last night without sight of you my brain was ablaze.
St. John, D. No Heaven.
Sappho. Gongyla.
Sassoon, S. Lamentations.
Sepamla. Silence: 2.
Sexton. Her Kind.
Shabtai, Aharon. Hope: "It's hopeless, you told me."
Shakespeare, W. To-morrow, and to-morrow, and to-morrow.
Shelley, P. England in 1819.
Stanzas Written in Dejection, Near Naples [or —December 1818, near Naples].
Shumyatsher, E. Toye-Voye.
Sidney. Sonnet 19: "On Cupid's bow how are my heart-strings bent."
Sonnet 108: "When sorrow (using mine own fire's might)."
Simic. Dream Avenue.
Smith, C. Composed During a Walk on the Downs, in November 1787.
Nepenthe.
Ode to Death.
Should the lone Wanderer, fainting on his way.
To Fancy.
To Spring.
Where the wild woods and pathless forests frown.
Written at Bignor Park in Sussex, in August, 1799.
Smith, M. City.
Smith, S. Bog-Face.
Sŏng [or Sung] Sammun. White Banners.
Spender, S. Memento.
Spenser, E. Cave of Despair, The.
Spicer, J. Transformations.
Stickney, T. At Sainte-Marguerite.
Storni. Ancestral Burden.
Su Tung-p'o. Lament of the Farm Wife of Wu.

Swift, J. Phyllis [or Phillis] [or Progress of Love, The].
Tate, J. Lost Pilot, The.
Teillier, J. No Sign of Life.
Tennyson, A. Mariana.
Thomson, J. In the Room.
Trakl. Mourning: "Dark eagles, sleep and death, The."
Tsvetayeva [or Tsvetaeva]. Ancient Song, An.
You, Walking Past Me.
Unknown. Am I to go on.
Ballad of the Orphan Boy, The.
Great God of the exiled!
Romance of Love.
Sometimes I feel like a motherless child.
To G.
Untermeyer, L. Koheleth.
"Vaidehi.". Girl in the Kitchen.
Valente, J. No Man's Land.
Vaughan, H. Anguish.
Verlaine. Autumn Song ("Long sobs of, The.").
Very. Forevermore.
Villaurrutia. Nocturne: The Eternal.
They and I.
Voznesensky [or Voznesenskii]. Monologue with Commentary.
W., A. Hopeless Desire Soon Withers and Dies.
Walcott. Laventille.
Wallace-Crabbe. Sonnet IV.
Walsh, W. Despairing Lover, The.
Wang Ts'an. Poem of Seven Sorrows.
Warton, J. Spleen, Le.
Weissbort. Mourning.
Weller. Story of Frankie . . . My Man, The.
Wen T'ing-yün. Deva-like Barbarian.
Wieners. Waning of the Harvest Moon, The.
Williams, C. K. Loss.
Williams, W. These.
Woods, D. Prescription.
Wordsworth, W. Written in London, September, 1802.
Wright, J. Lying in a Hammock at William Duffy's Farm in Pine Island, Minnesota.
Wroth. Song 2: "All night I weep[e], all day I cry, Ay me[e]."
Sonnet 6: "My pain[e], still smothered [or smother'd] in my grieved bre[a]st."
Sonnet 8: "Led by the pow'r [or powre] of grief[e], to wailings [or waylings] brought."
Sonnet 9: "Be[e] you all pleased [or pleas'd]? your pleasures grieve not[t] me[e]."
Sonnet 11: "You endless torments that my rest opress."
Sonnet 25: "Poor[e] eyes be[e] blind, the light behold no[e] more."
Sonnet 42: "If ever love had force in huma[i]ne bre[a]st?"
Wu of Han [or Wu Ti or Ou-ty or Liu Ch'e or Liu Ch'u]. Oh the sound of her silk sleeves.
Wunderlich, M. Bruise of This, The.
Wyatt. Pillar [or Piller] perished [or pearisht] is whe[a]rto I le[a]nt, The.
Sonnet: "My Galley Charged".
Wylie. Full Moon.
Yamada. Cincinnati.
Yi Kyôngnim. Anam Street 2—Outside the Cinema.
Young, Andy. In Anguish, the Heart Finally Prays.
Zabolotsky [or Zabolotskii]. Yesterday Reflecting Upon Death.
Zakama, K. My Generation.

Destiny
Atwood. It's the story that counts.
Blumenthal, M. Forces, The.
Borges. Chess.
Inferno 1, 32.
Limits.
Brouwer, J. Hamartia Symbolized by the Stray.
Castellanos. Destiny.
Nazareth.
Cernuda. From What Country.
Frost, R. Gift Outright, The.
Gelbtrunk, A. God said to Abraham.
Ghalib, M. My Destiny.
Gilman, C. What Will Be Your Destiny?

Harjo, J.   Woman Who Fell from the Sky, The.
Hecht, A.   Jason.
Jacob, M.   Egg, An.
Jones, T.   Humanity.
Kimbrell, J.   My Psychic.
Kunina, Y.   I'm trying to fit my destiny into.
Lauture, D.   Our Destiny.
Mahon.   Last of the Fire Kings, The.
Moore, M.   Those Various Scalpels.
Nguyen, Hoa.   Shred.
Pinsky.   Hearts, The.
Simon, M.   Standing between Two Ideas.
Stesichoros.   Don't pile cruel cares upon those griefs.
Towle.   Seasonal Ramble.
Turner, C.   Julius Caesar and the Honey-Bee.
Vietnamese Oral Tradition.   King Star, The.
See also **Fate**

Destruction
Afrika, T.   Hit squad.
Aiken, C.   Summer.
Akhmatova, A.   Alexander at Thebes.
Arapaho Oral Tradition.   I'yehe! my children— Uhi'yeye'heye!
Atwood.   Beauharnois, Glengarry (2).
  Four Small Elegies.
  It Is Dangerous to Read Newspapers.
Ausländer, R.   So That No Light Would Remain to Love Us.
Awoonor.   Sea Eats the Land at Home, The.
Back, R.   Gaza, Undated.
Baratier, D.   Fall of Because, The.
Berry, W.   Against the War in Vietnam.
  Dark with power.
Borawski.   Power of One.
Brecht, B.   Friends, The.
  To Those Born Later.
Brooks, G.   Boy Breaking Glass.
Brown, S.   Schadenfreude.
Cavafy.   City, The.
Chaloner.   Spring and Other Places.
Chaucer.   On t'other side there stood destruction bare.
Ch'i-chi.   After the Rebellion, Visiting West Mountain Temple.
Chilam Balam.   Flight of the Itzás.
Cho Chihun.   At Toriwpn.
Crane, H.   Eternity.
Crews, J.   Rejoice.
Cross, E.   Kali.
Cucchi, M.   I wouldn't know what it's like to be a pawn.
Davies, I.   Gwalia Deserta XXII.
de Fierro.   Heart of Time.
Dede, Esrâr.   In the ruins, in the tavern.
Di Prima.   Brief Wyoming Meditation.
Djogo.   Black Sheep, The.
Donne.   Broken Heart, The.
Duncan, R.   Passage over Water.
Dupin.   Begin Like Tearing.
Elliott, E.   War.
Éluard, P.   November 1936.
Emerson, R.   Water: "Water understands / Civilization well, The."
Fenton, J.   Wind: "This is the wind, the wind in a field of corn."
Fogarty, L.   Fuck All Departments.
Fulton, R.   End of an Age, The.
Gallagher, T.   Unsteady Yellow.
Goldsmith, O.   Cause and Effect.
González Prada, M.   Cosmos Shows His Power, The.
Gould, A.   Demolisher.
Graves, R.   Twins.
Greenlaw, L.   What's Going On.
Griffin, J.   Emperor, The.
Gwangwa'a.   Leaking Roof.
Hahn, O.   Vision of Hiroshima.
  With Passion without Compassion.
Hamhur Kiwha.   Lament: "I heard that many temples were destroyed."
Harjo, J.   Returning from the Enemy, Part 6.
Hawoldar.   Destruction.
Hine.   Northwest Passages.
Hirsch, E.   In the Midwest.
Hoagland, T.   Sweet Ruin.

Holub.   Brief Thoughts on Cracks.
Houellebecq, Michel.   In the Limpid Air.
Hughes, T.   That Moment.
Ibáñez, S.   Island in the Light.
Ishikawa Takuboku.   Tanka: "Accidentally / having broken a teacup."
İzzet Molla.   Everyone knows this world will not be ruined.
Jabès.   Desert, The.
Jeffers, R.   Summer Holiday.
Jones, D.   Angle-Land.
Kanchev, Nikolai.   Church: "I've come to kneel before you, while you're falling down."
Kees.   City as Hero, The.
Kinsella, J.   Pig Melons.
Kirsch, S.   Pictures.
Kocbek.   Dialectics.
Komunyakaa, Y.   Urban Renewal.
Kooser.   Shooting a Farmhouse.
Kowit.   Notice.
Kuhar, M.   All Holyroadz Home.
  You Can't Blow Up the Buddha.
Kunitz, S.   Last Picnic, The.
Kyger.   Destruction.
Kyle, C. J.   Fire in Early Morning.
Lazutkina, E.   Ruined so many romances.
LeFlore, S. B.   Dream/Eaters.
Lesley, G.   Behold, how Sodom swaggers in its Pride.
Lewis, A.   Raiders' Dawn.
Manyarrows.   See No Indian, Hear No Indian.
Mapanje.   Glory Be to Chingwe's Hole.
Marlowe.   Bastardly boy, sprung from some coward's loins.
  Grecian soldiers, tired with ten years' war.
Martin, Steve.   Demolition of the Cathedral at Chartres.
Martinaitis, M.   Kukutis's Sermon to the Pigs.
McFadden, D.   4. Love's Two Hemispheres.
McLain, P.   Beauty, That Lying Bitch.
Melville, H.   Iris.
  Ravaged Villa, The.
Merrill, J.   Urban Convalescence, An.
Meynell, A.   Messina, 1908.
Michaelis.   I Was about Three Years of Age.
Mikha'il, M.   Three Flags.
Mikhail, D.   War Works Hard, The.
Milosz, C.   Poor Christian Looks at the Ghetto, A.
Momaday.   Burning, The.
Moore, H.   Spuyten Duyvil.
Mother Goose.   Three Wise Men of Gotham.
Moulds, J.   When Bad Angels Love Women.
Mukai Kyorai.   On a veranda.
Narovchatov.   In Those Years.
Nichol.   Some Nets.
Oliphant.   Eugene Wukasch, Texas Architect.
Oppen.   It is the air of atrocity.
  Survival: Infantry.
Orientius.   Bulk of these years is already gone out of mind, The.
Owen, W.   To Eros.
Pagis, D.   Lesson in Observation, A.
Poe.   Sonnet—To Science.
Porter, P.   May, 1945.
Powell, J.   Now in the tight trench you go.
Prior.   Dutch Proverb, A.
Pugh.   'Do you think we'll ever get to see Earth, sir?'.
Rāy, D.   Who is this black.
Rich, A.   For the Record.
Rukeyser, M.   Sand-Quarry with Moving Figures.
Sandburg, C.   Prayers of Steel.
Saunders, R.   Empty Glen, The.
Seferis.   Last Stop.
Seifert.   Never Again.
Seyburn, P.   Good Water.
Shabtai, Aharon.   Basel Square.
  Hebrew Culture.
Shakespeare, W.   How yet resolves the Governor of the town?
Shinkichi Takahashi.   Destruction.
Slonimski.   Elegy: "No more, no more Jewish townships in Poland."
Snodgrass.   Mother, The: "She stands in the

dead center like a star."
Solomos, D.   Destruction of Psara, The.
Stanford, A.   Done With.
Stratanovsky.   Herostratos and Herostratos.
  Terrorist, The.
Su Tung-p'o.   Lament of the Farm Wife of Wu.
Szymborska, W.   End and Beginning.
  End and the Beginning, The.
Tate, J.   Death on Columbus Day.
Teare, Brian.   Dead House Sonnet.
Tennyson, A.   Babylon.
Thelwall.   On the Rapid Extension of the Suburbs.
Thomas, G.   Greetings.
Tuqan, F.   Song of Becoming.
Unknown.   Bonnie House o' Airlie, The.
  Elephant.
  End of Clonmacnois, The.
  How doth the city sit solitary that was full of people.
  Kilcash.
  Tell me.
Vaughan, H.   Charnel-house, The.
Virgil [*or* Vergil].   How They Took the City.
Waldinger, E.   Lidice.
Waldrop, K.   Wandering Curves.
Watts, I.   Day of Judg[e]ment, The; an Ode [Attempted in English Sapphic].
Webb, P.   Breaking.
Wei Chuang.   Lament of the Lady of Qin.
Williams, C. K.   Shock.
Williamson, G.   Walter Parmer.
Wilner, E.   Abstraction.
Winter, M.   Elegy: "There is a question."
Winters, Y.   Summer Noon: 1941.
Wylie.   Doomsday.
Zenmaro.   Tanka: "Old Japan."

Detectives
Carter, C.   Parts of a Mystery.
Gerstler.   Unexpected Adventure, An.
Mathews, H.   Cassation on a Theme by Jacques Dupin.
Nielsen, K.   Self Portrait as Nancy Drew, Girl Sleuth.
Orlovsky.   Dick Tracy's Yellow Hat.
Ransome-Davies.   Raymond Chandler: The Big Sleep.
Szporluk.   Eohippus.

Determination
Angelou, M.   Still I Rise.
Brooks, G.   Song of Winnie.
Creeley.   En Famille.
Grimké, A.   Black Runner, The.
Guillevic.   I Don't Speak.
Lefevre, A.   Halftime.
Moore, M.   I May, I Might, I Must.
Ni Ghallchóir, C.   Refusal.
Oliver, M.   Journey, The.
Rich, A.   Power.
Rivas, J.   Thalassa.
  Thalassa.
Thomas, L.   Magnetic Charms.
Williams, W.   To an Old Jaundiced Woman.

Detroit, Michigan
Butts, A.   Belle Isle Men, The.
Charara, H.   Thinking American.
Cornish, S.   Work to Be Done.
Daniels, J.   Time, Temperature.
Davis, O.   Thirty Years Rising.
Gustafson, J.   Idea of Detroit, The.
Hernández Cruz.   Entering Detroit.
Jackson, M.   Detroit Addendum.
Joseph, L.   Then.
Levine, P.   Belle Isle, 1949.
  Coming Home, *Detroit*, 1968.
  Snow: "Today the snow is drifting."
  You Can Have It.
Pape.   Birds of Detroit.

Developing Countries
Hove.   Country Life.
Ojaide.   Ward 6.
Salkey.   Remember Haiti, Cuba, Vietnam.

Development
Seyburn, P.   What I Disliked about the Pleistocene Era.

Swenson, M. Goodbye, Goldeneye.
Unknown. God, what are you doing to me?
Vest, Jennifer Lisa. In This, the Fifth World.

Devil
Alberti. Bosch.
Brown, K. Good Devil, The.
Chinnov. Do you think we might go to hell too?
Dante Alighieri. And so from bridge to bridge
we went, talking.
El-Shawwaf, H. Devil's Symbol, The.
Fisher, D. That Old Devil Called Love.
Johnson, R. Me and the Devil Blues.
Komunyakaa, Y. Devil's Workshop, The.
Peacock, T. Legend of Manor Hall, The.
Roberts, A. That Old Devil Called Love.
Roethke. To an Anthologist.
Simic. Scarecrow, The.
Simpson, L. Silent Generation, The.
Tranter. Burden of noise, of infections, A.
Weatherly, T. Canto 10: Wooten.
See also **Satan**

Devotion
Ahti, Risto. Beloved's Face, The.
Barnes, J. Passion at Forty.
Bonnefoy. Voice, A.
Brandi. In What Disappears.
Bryce, Colette. Deposition, The.
Calder, R. Love in the Abstract.
Coleman, W. I Live for My Car.
Davis, O. You Art a Scholar, Horatio, Speak to
It.
Desnos. I've Dreamt of You So Often.
Never Anyone but You.
Fulton, A. Fix.
Fuzuli. Oh God, don't let anyone be like me.
Gorges. Sonnet: "Your selfe the Sonne, and I
the meltinge froste."
Hafiz, K [*or* Hafez]. As Rich as Solomon (21).
Fish in Deep Water, The (144).
Hayâlî. We are among those who came to be
moths.
Hernández, M. Letter: "Pigeon-house of letters,
The."
Hicok. Whither Thou Goest.
Hristov, Boris. At Night: "Our tree's shadow is
green at night."
Hunter, C. Two Thousand and Two.
İzzet Molla. I am a nightingale in the garden of
grief.
Jackson, R. Sonata of Love's History.
Lahey, Joy. White Soil.
Lennox, C. Ardelia to Flavia, an Epistle.
Meier, Richard. Eclipsed.
Merrill, C. Love Poem: "Your silver hair, a
galaxy."
Mirabai [*or* Mira Bai]. Faithfulness.
Music, The.
Miron, Gaston. Walk toward Love, The.
Muhibbi. Till the day I die, I shall never leave
her beauty's sun.
Mullen, H. Omnivore.
Nev'î. Help me, oh sapling of the tulip cheek.
O'Sullivan, V. By the Sea-Wall.
Rosenberg, L. Susquehanna.
Sepúlveda, O. Three ("She is of the continent,
around her everything is light and I observe
her atop the slab in the image of her body.").
Tres ("Es del continente, alrededor de ella todo
es luz y yo la observo sobre la plancha en la
imagen de su cuerpo.").
Spenser, E. Sonnet 22: "This holy season, fit to
fast and pray."
Stern, G. Another Insane Devotion.
Teasdale. Song: "You bound strong sandals on
my feet."
Unknown. Come Go with Me.
If my lover dies, let me be his shroud!
If you kiss my mouth, you must give me your
heart.
If you truly love me, my love, go off and
liberate our land!
Yi Kyŏngnim. Certain Sickness, Deep Love.

Dew
Basho. Coolness of melons.
Melon / In morning dew.
Wet with morning dew.

With dewdrops dripping.
Bell, M. Dew at the Edge of a Leaf.
Bryant, W. To a Waterfowl.
Buson. Dew on the bramble / Thorns.
Dewy morn / These saucepans.
Short night, The.
White dew.
Clare, J. Clock-A-Clay.
Guidacci. Tiny dew reinvigorates the tiny grass,
The.
Hsüeh T'ao [*or* Xue Tao]. Cicadas.
Ikkyu Sojun. Void in Form.
Issa. Buddha Law / Shining.
Dew spread / The seeds of hell.
Good world, A.
On the Death of the Poet's Daughter Sato.
This world of dew.
This world of dew's.
Were it sweet.
World of dew, A.
World of dew, The.
Kakei. Morning glory / So pure.
Kasa. White drops of dew, The.
Magdeburg, Mechthild von. How God Comes
to the Soul.
Marvell. On a Drop of Dew.
Masaoka Shiki. Dew, clinging / To potato
field.
Pine needles.
Miles, J. Fields of Learning.
Nishiyama Soin. Settling, white dew.
Noguchi, Yonejiro (Yone). Are the fallen stars.
Ōshima Ryōta. Pure brush-clover / Basket of
flowers.
Unknown. Dew on the Shallot.
I Sing of a Maiden.
Yi Myŏnghan. Morning star has set, The. A
lark.

Diabetes
Haley, V. Gangrene.
Hoagland, E. Big Zeb Johnson.

Dialects
Herbert, W. To a Mousse.
Porteous. Charlie Douglas.
Torres, E. Elder Dubb.

Diallo, Amadou
Agüeros. Psalm for Amadou Diallo.
Cherry, J. Amadou.
Dufflar, C. Amadou Diallo from Guinea to the
Bronx Dead on Arrival.
Moore, M. Another Scream.

Diamonds
Feld, Andrew. Intermission.
Metodiev, Ivan. This Crow.
Rich, A. Diamond Cutters, The.

Diana (mythology)
De [*or* Du] Guillet. But if he came straight for
me.
Jonson, B. Hymn[e] to Cynthia.
Killigrew, A. On a Picture Painted by Herself
[*or* Her self], Representing Two Nymphs [*or*
Nimphs] of Diana's, One in a Posture to Hunt,
the Other Bath[e]ing.
Kulman. To Diana.
Motion, A. Mythology.
Ovid. Actaeon.
Ralegh, S. Homage to Diana.
Reznikoff. I met in a merchant's place.
Simms, W. New Moon, The.
Unknown. Dum Diana Vitrea.

Diaries
Abse. New Diary, A.
Bishop, E. From Trollope's Journal.
Brewer, G. Journals, The.
Colby, T. Captain's Log.
Erb, E. Diary Entry, January Seven.
Fusselman, A. Ticker.
Kingston, M. Write before other people get up.
Dress.
Larkin, P. Forget What Did.
Monette. Half Life.
Procter, A. My Journal.
Scamell, B. Diaries.
Webster, A. Poor little diary, with its simple
thoughts.

Wilson, M. Diary.

Diaspora
Baytelman, S. My Name is Shlomit.
Becker, R. Crypto-Jews, The.
Behar, R. Survivals.
Brathwaite, E. Journeys, The.
Brooks, G. To the Diaspora.
Carruth, H. Little Citizen, Little Survivor.
Southey, R. Did then the bold slave rear at last
the sword.
Hold your mad hands! for ever on your plain.
Oh he is worn with toil! the big drops run.
'Tis night; the mercenary tyrants sleep.
Why dost thou beat thy breast and rend thine
hair.

Dice
Leiris, Michel. Misdeal.

Dickens, Charles
Duffy, C. Havisham.

Dickinson, Emily
Bell, M. Mystery of Emily Dickinson, The.
Bly, R. Visiting Emily Dickinson's Grave with
Robert Francis.
Brown, L. Encyclopedia Botanica.
Carson, A. Sumptuous Destitution.
Collins, B. Taking Off Emily Dickinson's
Clothes.
Cope, W. Emily Dickinson.
Crane, H. To Emily Dickinson.
Finch, A. Dickinson.
Finnell. Over *Voice of America.*
Fulton, A. Wonder Bread.
Glass, Jesse. Lecturing on Walt Whitman and
Emily Dickinson in China.
Ivask, Y. Emily Dickinson.
Jones, R. Comment on This: in the Real
Scheme of Things, Poetry Is Marginal.
Kennedy, X. Emily Dickinson in Southern
California.
Lowell, A. Sisters, The.
Peacock, M. Desire.
Rich, A. I Am in Danger—Sir.
Rubin, L. Houses of Emily Dickinson, The.
Ruefle. Furtherness.
Valentine, J. Elegy for Jane Kenyon (2).
Waniek. Emily Dickinson's Defunct.
Yi Sanghûi. Dickinson's Blue Sleeve.
Young Bear. Emily Dickinson, Bismarck and
the Roadrunner's Inquiry.

Dictionaries
Alvi, M. Throwing Out My Father's Dictionary.
Darragh. Numb to Number.
DuPlessis, R. Draft 55: Quiptych.
Hardy, T. Liddell and Scott.
Inman, P. Numb to Number.
Mullen, H. Sleeping with the Dictionary.
Shapcott, J. Motherland.

Dido
Ausonius. I am that Dido which thou here do'st
see.
Hilary. To an English Boy: "Beautiful boy,
flower fair."
Italicus. At the city's heart stood the shrine to
Dido's ghost.
Unknown. Let the first syllable of PEnelope be
followed by the first of DIdo, the first of
CAnus by that of REmus.
Virgil [*or* Vergil]. Aeneas Arrives in Carthage.
Dawn leaves the bed of Dark and climbs the
sky.
In Heaven, Queen Juno saw. She's trapped.
Passion of the Queen, The.
Priests, prophets, helpless. She's beside herself.
Sky rumbles. Gathers. Rain.

Dieting
Mansour, J. Your Figure or the War Against
Fat.
Prys-Jones. Wife of Carcassonne, The.

Digging and Diggers
Celan. There was earth inside them, and.
Ford, Katie. Hands of the Body without the
Body, and Nothing to Hold, The.
Gildner. Digging for Indians.
Gruffydd, P. Digging Soil.
Hall, D. Digging.

Ismail. Buried Poem, The.
Levertov. Re-Rooting.
MacDonald, Hugh. Digging of Deep Wells, The.
McDonald, W. Digs in Escondido Canyon, The.
Muso Soseki. For years I dug in the earth.
Nietzsche. Undiscouraged.
Parker, A. Alchemy.
Rumi. Someone Digging in the Ground.
Rux, C. H. Excavation, The.
Stephens, P. Signalmen, The.
Stevenson, R. At the Seaside [or Sea-Side].
Stewart, S. Zero.
Su Tung-p'o. White Crane Hill.
Unknown. Digging Sing, A.
Waltner-Toews, D. Roots: "Rudy Weibe, wiping the sweat from his brow."
Wilbur, R. Digging for China.

Dikes
Cary, P. Leak in the Dike, The.
Kipling, R. Dykes, The.
Welch, L. Dikes on Fundy Bay.
Winters, Y. By the Road to the Air-Base.

Diners
Atwood. They Eat Out.
Baron, R. Diner.
Hudgins. Loose Change.
Johnson, M. All-Night Diner, The.
Justice, D. Poem to Be Read at 3 a.m.
Liu, T. Ikon.
Snow, C. Déjeuner, Le.
Waring, B. Tip, The.

Dinosaurs
Alegría. Toward the Jurassic Age.
Armour. Pachycephalosaurus.
Couto. Living in the La Brea Tar Pits.
Updike. On the Inclusion of Miniature Dinosaurs in Breakfast Cereal Boxes.
Worth, V. Dinosaurs.

Diogenes
Karr. Diogenes Tries to Forget.

Dionysus
Anacreon. O Lord, with whom subduer Love.
Anyte [or Anytes]. Behold the horned goat of Bacchos, how lordly.
Moiro. Beneath Aphrodite's golden portico you now lie.
Nonnus. But Dionysos had no healing physic for his comrade fallen, of dancing he thought no more.
Dionysus and Ampelos.
Sapgir. Dionysus.

Diplomacy and Diplomats
Barrington, P. I Had a Duck-billed Platypus.
Lao Tzu. Large state is like a low-lying estuary, A.
Martinez, D. Prodigal Son Considers a Diplomatic Career, The.
Nakano Shigeharu. Paul Claudel.

Dirt
Bell, M. To an Adolescent Weeping Willow.
Calvino. Argia.
Olson, C. These Days: "Whatever you have to say, leave."
StacyLynn. Dirt.
Taneda Santoka. Sleep on the ground.

Disabilities
Clare, Eli. Learning to Speak.
Hopes. Invalid of Park Street, The.
Lim, S. Pantoun for Chinese Women.
Mistral, G. Those Who Do Not Dance.
Owen, W. Disabled.

Disappointment
Acorn. I've Tasted My Blood.
Behn, A. Disappointment, The.
Bibbins, M. Groupie.
Burt, S. Morningside Park.
Cassian. Bread and Wine.
Clifton, L. Thirty-Eighth Year, The.
Comden, B. Party's Over, The.
Davis, O. Small Number, A.
Dickinson, E. I showed her Heights she never saw.
It would never be Common—more—I said.
Dietz, H. I Guess I'll Have to Change My Plan.

Gershwin, I. But Not for Me.
Man That Got Away, The.
Glatt. One Night with a Stranger at 30.
Green, A. Party's Over, The.
Hafiz, K [or Hafez]. Where is my ruined life, and where the fame.
Hardy, T. Broken Appointment, A.
Heyman, E. Blame It on My Youth.
Holan. She Asked You.
Howe, F. Doubt.
Hurreh, I. Pardon Me.
Jamie, K. Mrs McKellar, Her Martyrdom.
Joseph, A. Wedding Party.
Kyle, C. J. Argument, The.
Latouche, J. Love Turned the Light Out.
Lazard. Ordinance on Arrival.
Lummis, Suzanne. Femme Fatale.
Martí. Two Countries.
McCarthy, J. I'm Always Chasing Rainbows.
McDaniel, J. Play It Again, Salmonella.
Meinke. Noreen.
Meynell, A. Modern Mother, The.
Nash, O. Round About.
Norton, C. Laura was lightsome, gay, and free from guile.
Ntiru. Listen—listen.
Orozco. Miss Havisham.
Parker, D. One Perfect Rose.
Rafferty, C. Story of the Man Whose Tastes Were Too Refined.
Ralegh, S. Farewell to False Love, A.
Rich, A. Snapshots of a Daughter-in-Law.
Rosenberg, I. Chagrin.
Smith, C. To Mrs. G.
T'ao Ch'ien [or T'ao Yuan-ming]. Putting the Blame on His Sons.
Scolding My Sons.
Trinidad. More than anything, I wanted Charlie.
Troup, B. You're Lookin' at Me.
Unknown. America. . .then.
Cruel people, who see how an old man leads me to his bed.
Fate brought me as husband a child I must raise.
It takes a very stupid dolt.
Young once / and dreaming.
Violi. Appeal to the Grammarians.
Whitehead, C. Morning Thesis.
Wroth. Sonnet 27: "Fie [or Fy] tedious Hope, why do[e] you still rebel[l]?"
Zeyneb. Remove your veil and illuminate the earth.

Disarmament
Ap Hywel, Elin. Disarmed.
Rumens. Memo about the Green Oranges, A.
See also **Militarism; Pacifism and Pacifists**

Disasters
Balaban. Hurricane.
Brewer, G. Transport of the Dead.
Byrne, Elena Karina. In Particular.
Flynn, N. Cartoon Physics, Part 1.
Foot, E. Disaster at Sea.
Graves, R. Fallen Tower of Siloam, The.
Hudspith, V. Nodding Cranes.
Kasischke. Grace.
Khlebnikov, V. Once More, Once More.
Kramer, L. Images of the San Francisco Disaster.
Larkin, P. Explosion, The.
Longfellow, H. Disasters.
McGonagall. Tay Bridge Disaster, The.
Moore, J. Ashtabula Disaster, The.
Oppen. From Disaster.
Shinkichi Takahashi. Beach.
Sleigh. Lamentation on Ur.
Swanger. Natural Disaster.
Sze. Ox-Head Dot.
Urdang. All around Us.
Voltaire. Woeful mankind, born to a woeful earth!
Warren, R. School Lesson Based on Word of Tragic Death of Entire Gillum Family.
Yao Chen. Ballad on the Investigation of a Disaster.
Zolynas. Way He'd Like It, The.

Discipline
Berlin. This Is the Army, Mr. Jones.

Ellis, T. Sticks.
Gilmore, B. Revolution.
Han-shan. Raise girls but not too many.
Herbert, G. Discipline.
Knox, J. My Big German Bra.
Martial. You rocked my cradle, Charidemus, once.
Matthews, W. Foul Shots: A Clinic.
Porter, P. Soliloquy at Potsdam.
Ross, C. Jack.
Russell, G. Self-Discipline.
Stevenson, R. Good and Bad Children.

Discontent
Aiken, C. At a Concert of Music.
Akhtar-ul-Iman. Compromise.
Alcaeus [or Alkaios]. I long for the call to council.
Auden. Roman Wall Blues.
Bernheim, Erica. I Love How Your Eyes Close Every Time You Kiss Me.
Bidart. Self-Portrait [1969].
Boland, E. Night Feed.
Brathwaite, E. Naima.
Coleman, W. African Sleeping Sickness.
Creeley. Something for Easter.
Dobyns. How to Like It.
Dunmore. When You've Got.
Enzensberger, H. Middle Class Blues.
Song for Those Who Know.
Fagan. Desire.
Fagin, L. Women.
Fanthorpe. Not My Best Side.
Fields, D. Fine Romance, A.
Glancy. Kemo Sabe.
Han Yü. Discontent.
Herbert, G. Affliction (1).
Jennings, E. Afterthought.
Keats. There Was a Naughty Boy.
Lear, E. O dear! How disgusting is life!
MacNeice. Nature Morte.
Wolves.
Malroux. There's War or There's Peace.
Mathew. Poem in Time of Winter.
McCord, D. Five Chants.
McGough, R. Prayer to Saint Grobianus.
Millay, E. Hearing Your Words, and Not a Word among Them.
Rendezvous.
Nordbrandt. No Matter Where We Go.
O'Brien, S. In Residence: A Worst Case View.
Plath. Spinster.
Porter, P. Consumer's Report, A.
Sewell, L. Release.
Smith, C. Pressed by the Moon, Mute Arbitress of Tides.
Stafford, W. After Arguing against the Contention That Art Must Come from Discontent.
Thomas, D. I Have Longed to Move Away.
Toomer. I Sit in My Room.
Trapnell, N. Lament of a Desert Rat.
Unknown. Have you with your white beard no shame?
Volkman. Well, You Needn't.
Wang Wei. At Parting.
Parting.
Wickham. Nervous Prostration.
Williams, W. Raleigh Was Right.
Zinger, G. Lamentation of the Border-Guard.

Discothèques
Ginsberg, A. Chances "R."
Lowe, J. Club House.
Merrill, J. Watching the Dance.

Discovery
Adamson, H. I Just Found Out about Love.
Aizenberg, M. Look what's come to light.
Amir, D. What Seeps In.
Auden. Legend.
Avison. Voluptuaries and Others.
Campo. Our Country of Origin.
Carew, T. Ingrateful[l] Beauty Threatened.
Carson, A. HE SHE WE THEY YOU YOU YOU I HER SO PRONOUNS BEGIN THE DANCE CALLED WASHING.
Coleridge, S. On a Discovery Made Too Late.
Gershwin, I. How Long Has This Been Going

On?
Graham, J. Dream of the Unified Field, The.
Gunn, T. Discovery of the Pacific, The.
Hall, D. Poem, The: "It discovers by night."
Hass, R. After I Seized the Pentagon.
Heffernan, M. Message, The.
Henry, B. Discovery.
Hernández Cruz. Discovery.
Katz, J. Concerning the Islands Newly
  Discovered.
Keats. But there are.
  There Was a Naughty Boy.
Laughlin, J. Deep Pool, the.
Levertov. Overland to the Islands.
  Pleasures.
  Secret, The.
Lorde. Ballad from Childhood.
MacEwen, G. Discovery, The.
MacLeish. Voyage West.
MacNeice. Truisms, The.
Merwin. Thing of Beauty, A.
Millay, E. Euclid Alone Has Looked on Beauty
  Bare.
Owen, W. Music.
Porta. Traveler.
Shapiro, K. Leg, The.
Slauerhoff. Columbus.
Stern, G. For Song.
Tuqan, F. I Found It.

Disdain
Akhtar-ul-Iman. Compromise.
Arapaho Oral Tradition. He'Yoho'Ho!
  He'Yoho'Ho!
Betham-Edwards. Urge me no more! nor think,
  because I seem.
Boker. Oh! craven, craven! while my brothers
  fall.
Cahn, S. Put 'Em in a Box, Tie 'Em with a
  Ribbon (And Throw 'Em in the Deep Blue
  Sea).
Campion, T. Follow Thy Fair Sun[ne]
  [Unhappy Shadow].
Chesterton. World State, The.
Damas. Through the Half-Opened Window.
Florian. Send My Spinach.
Follain. Face the Animal.
Nguyễn Văn Lạc. Shrimps.
Plath. Daddy.
Rafferty, C. Story of the Man Whose Tastes
  Were Too Refined.
Unknown. Bo-zhou: That Boat of Cypress
  Wood.
  Mode of France, The.
Wyatt. Farewell, love, and all thy law[e]s
  forever [or for ever].
  My Lute, Awake!

Disease
Abse. X-Ray.
Becker, R. Medical Science.
Beckett, S. Ooftish.
Bruce, D. Prognosis.
Cavalli. Outside, in fact, there wasn't any
  change.
Chimombo. Derailment: A Delirium.
Cloves, Jeff. For Fausto Coppi (1916–60) et
  Tous les Copains de la Bicyclette.
Coulehan, J. Azalea Poem, The.
  Lovesickness: A Medieval Text.
Crosby, F. Mandan Chief, The.
Crucefix. Air-Waves.
Cummings, E. E. Come,gaze with me upon this
  dome.
Dickson, J. Poemectomy.
Duncan, R. In Blood's Domaine.
Dyer, J. Pastoral ("In cold stiff soils the bleaters
  oft complain.").
Elliott, A. Angel.
García, D. Tísica.
Hicok. Alzheimer's.
Holub. Teaching about Disease.
Kees. For My Daughter.
Kinnell. Parkinson's Disease.
Lux. Plague Victims Catapulted over Walls into
  Besieged City.
MacBeth [or Macbeth]. Worst Fear, The.
Martínez, V. Tesoro.

Mukand, J. First Payment.
Muldoon, P. Aisling.
No Hyegyông. Disease That Arrives at Death.
O'Reilly, M. House Call to a Man with
  Parkinson's Disease, A.
  Potter.
Perillo, L. Body Mutinies, The.
Picková, E. Fear.
Piercy. Crabs.
Pitchford. Surgery.
Po Chü-i. Wind Sickness Strikes.
Powell, D. A. When you touch down upon this
  earth. little reindeers.
Scott, D. Apocalypse Dub.
Senryū, K. Doctor disrobed, The.
  What a miracle.
Shapcott, J. Mad Cow in Love, The.
Stone, J. Gaudeamus Igitur: A Valediction.
Straus, M. Luck.
Teddy. At Terezin.
Unknown. As in thee resteth my joye and
  confort.
Wilbur, R. Pangloss's Song: A Comic-Opera
  Lyric.
Williams, C. K. Alzheimer's: The Wife.
Williams, M. Thinking about Bill, Dead of
  AIDS.
Williams, W. Pathology literally speaking is a
  flower garden.
Wilson, J. Pruning.
Woods, D. Waiting.

Disgrace
Char. Faction Du Muet.
Hughes, L. Ballad of the Girl Whose Name Is
  Mud.
Masters, E. Doctor Meyers.
Mu'tamid, King of Seville. Rest your heart; let
  your cares not overcome you. What good will
  grief and apprehension do you?
Sadi [or Saadi or Sa'di]. Until you can correct
  and heal yourself.
Sidney. Sonnet 21: "Your words my friend
  (right healthful caustics) blame."
Thackeray. Napoleon.
Unknown. I disgraced myself in my lover's
  eyes.

Disguise
Basheva. Not long ago a whole sun.
Brown, T. Disguises.
Kenny, Melanie. Hungry as the Sea.
Kyger. To Live in This World Again.
Osgood, F. Maiden's Mistake, The.
Page, P. Disguises, The.
Paquin, Ethan. Capstone.
Tranströmer. Hold on, nightingale!
Unknown. Make yourself a beggar and a fool,
  then come in search of me.

Dishonesty
Cary, P. When Lovely Woman.
Dunn, S. Shame Place, The.
Hjern, K. To My Love.
Nesbit, E. Appeal.

Dishonor
Jonson, B. To Captain Hungry.
Melville, H. Stonewall Jackson.
Surrey. Sardanapalus.
Unknown. May you be found cut to pieces by a
  trenchant sword.

Disillusion
Adair, T. Will You Still Be Mine?
Bishop, J. Return, The.
Blunden. Report on Experience.
Carew, T. Ingrateful[l] Beauty Threatened.
Ceravolo. Caught in the Swamp.
Coleridge, S. On a Discovery Made Too Late.
Comden, B. If You Hadn't—But You Did.
Conley, L. Cottage for Sale, A.
Dickinson, E. Loss of something ever felt I, A.
  Split the Lark—and you'll find the Music.
Ginsberg, A. America: "America I've given you
  all and now I'm nothing."
Gippius. Seamstress, The.
Goethe. Three Stanzas.
Green, A. If You Hadn't—But You Did.
Hall, D. Hardy's "Shelley's Skylark."

HaNagid. First War.
Hart, L. Falling in Love with Love.
Hass, R. Story about the Body, A.
Hsi K'ang. Song of Disillusionment, A.
Kochanowski, J. I'd Buy You, Wisdom.
Leopardi. To Himself.
Lo Pin-Wang. On the Cicada: In Prison.
Macaulay, T. Jacobite's Epitaph, A.
Manrique, J. Barcelona Days.
Maturaikkataiayattar Makan Vennakan. What
  She Said to Her Girl-Friend.
Mercer, J. I Wonder What Became of Me.
Mew. Rooms.
Mills, I. Sophisticated Lady.
Oliver, M. House, The.
Owen, W. Dulce et Decorum Est.
  Sonnet, to a Child.
To ——: "Three rompers run together, hand
  in hand."
Parish. Sophisticated Lady.
Raine, K. Star, The.
Ransom, J. Blackberry Winter.
Ras. Sadness of Couples, The.
Reese, L. Lyric on the Lyric, A.
Shelley, P. Alastor; or, The Spirit of Solitude.
Shen Yüeh. Harmonizing with a Poem by Left
  Assistant Yu Kao-chih Requesting Sick Leave.
Stevens, W. Disillusionment of Ten O'Clock.
  Plain Sense of Things, The.
Swan, E. When Your Lover Has Gone.
Tomlinson, C. Jam Trap, The.
Unknown. Long Time Back, A.
  Oxaitoq's Song.
Wilbur, R. Someone Talking to Himself.
Wright, C. May God Go with You, Son.
Wyatt. Of the Courtier's Life.

Disorder
Anacreon. Dice of Love are, The.
Bishop, E. Filling Station.
Herrick. Delight in Disorder.
Hofer, J. Of Deaths, Days, Futures, Nations
  ("Question, the action, the speech, the taxi, the
  proof, the reference, forgotten, The.").
Lyndsay [or Lindsay], D. Complaynt [or
  Compleynt or Complaint] of the Comoun [or
  Common] Weill of Scotland, The.
Merrill, J. Broken Bowl, The.
Shearin, F. Entropy.
Spicer, J. Thing Language.
Stevens, W. Connoisseur of Chaos.
Suntsova, E. As old salts know.
Wang Ts'an. Poem of Seven Sorrows.
  Seven Sorrows.
Welish. Blood or Color.
  Wild Sleeve.
Whitman, W. Beat! Beat! Drums!

Displacement
Dean, D. K. Stitches.
Dharker. Postcards from god (1).
Griffiths, J. Migration.
Kamenszain. Return 2.
Scliar-Cabral. Sephirot.
Senghor. All Day Long.
Valente, J. Empty Place at the Celebration, An.
Vanshenkin. We came back late from visiting.
Yi Saek. Rough clouds gather around the
  valley.

Distrust
Amis, K. Last War, The.
Campert. Message about the Times.
  Sign of the Times.
Dunn, S. Man Who Closed Shop, The.
Halpern, M. Bird, The.
Morgan, E. Cinquevalli.
Padilla. Prayer for the End of the Century, A.
Piercy. Air Like Stained Glass Cuts Me, The.
The Earl of Longford. Careful Husband, The.
Williams, C. K. Question, The.

Diversity
Dunbar, P. Accountability.
Kipling, R. We and They.
Longfellow, H. Kéramos.
Razaf, A. Tan Manhattan.
Salaam. Height, Breadth, Depth.

Divine Love

Abercrombie. Hymn to Love.
Afrika, T. Glimpse of God.
  To God.
Berryman. Master of beauty, craftsman of the
  snowflake.
Carson, A. God's Bouquet of Undying Love.
  Town of Finding Out about the Love of God.
Citino. Analysis, The.
Craig, David. Hyperbole.
Daglarca. Beyond: "Whenever I love a
  woman."
Dennis, C. God Who Loves You, The.
Doyle, S. Spark Divine, A.
Gundy, J. Cookie Poem, The.
Hafiz, K [or Hafez]. Fish in Deep Water, The
  (144).
  Night and Dawn.
Herbert, G. Call, The.
  Discipline.
  Love Unknown.
  Pearl, The. Matth. 13:45.
  Providence.
  Temper (1), The.
  World, The.
Lumbreras, E. Keys of the Saint.
  Llaves de santo.
Machado Ruiz. From the Doorsill of a Dream.
Mehmedinović, Semezdin. Essay, An.
Murray, L. Chimes of Neverwhere, The.
  Man with the Hoe, The.
Rumi. Ecstatic Love Is an Ocean.
Scott, G. All Our Joy Is Enough.
Serpas, M. As If There Were Only One.
Traherne. Amendment.
Unknown. Ox.
Vallejo. God: "I feel that God is traveling."

Diving and Divers

Anacreon. Soaring again from the Leukadian
  Rock.
Biespiel, D. Tower.
Brontë, C. Diving.
Broumas, O. Sometimes, as a Child.
Davis, T. Letter to My Mother, Sixteen Years
  after the Fact.
Ferlinghetti, L. Ecolog.
Garcia, R. Diver for the NYPD Talks to His
  Girlfriend, A.
Garrett, E. Reprieve, The.
Goese, M. Dive, The.
Hayden, R. Diver, The.
Healy, E. Louganis.
Hemans. Diver, The.
Kang Ŭn'gyo. Woman.
Knight, E. Poem of Attrition, A.
Livingstone, D. One Time.
Merrill, C. Diver, The.
Mole, J. Taking the Plunge.
Ono no Komachi. Diver does not abandon, A.
Quennell. Divers, The.
Rich, A. Diving into the Wreck.
Smith, I. You Are at the Bottom of My Mind.
Taylor, M. To a Young Diver.

Divining and Diviners

Chalfi, R. Reading the I Ching.
Griffiths, J. Rosa Mystica.
Iroquois Oral Tradition. Dancing Speech of O-
  No'-Sa, The.
Jarman, M. Astragaloi.
Kunitz, S. Day of Foreboding.
Meyer, T. Dancing There.
O'odham. No. 78. I See Spirit-Tufts of White
  Feathers.
Rawls, Alex. April 19, 1999.
  August 29, 1999.
  December 31, 1999.
  February 18, 1999.
  January 1, 1999.
  July 10, 1999.
  June 9, 1999.
  March 12, 1999.
  May 26, 1999.
  November 20, 1999.
  October 1, 1999.
  September 25, 1999.

Divorce

Amichai, Y. Pity, A. We Were Such a Good
  Invention.
Boss, L. My Ringless Fingers on the Steering
  Wheel Tell the Story.
Brouwer, J. Divorce.
Coleman, H. Poem for a "Divorced" Daughter.
Copus, J. Back Seat of My Mother's Car, The.
Dryden, J. Why should a foolish marriage vow.
Durcan. Divorce Referendum, Ireland, 1986,
  The.
  Pietà's Over, The.
Elliott, A. X-Ray, The.
Enzensberger, H. Divorce, The.
Feld, Andrew. Intermission.
Ferlinghetti, L. People Getting Divorced.
Fleming, R. Long Walk Home, The.
Fraser, K. History of My Feeling, The.
Gewanter, D. Divorce and Mr. Circe.
Goff, C. Turning into an Oak Tree.
Gylys, B. Family Reunion—Aunt Vern's Two
  Cents.
Hillman, B. Shared Custody.
Hoagland, T. Sweet Ruin.
Hollander, J. For Both of You, the Divorce
  Being Final.
Kunitz, S. River Road.
Levertov. Divorcing.
  Wedding-Ring.
Levine, Jeffrey. Dawn, with Cardinals.
Lynch, T. Custody.
Maguire, S. Divorce Referendum, The.
Mathis. Getting Out.
McCarriston. Kitchen Terrarium.
  To Judge Faolain, Dead Long Enough: A
    Summons.
Merrill, J. Broken Home, The.
  My Father's Irish Setters.
Mew. Madeleine in Church.
Moulds, J. Late Summer Litany.
Ni Ghallchóir, C. Divorce 19th-century Style.
Nimmo, D. Ill-Wishing Him.
Olds, S. Victims, The.
Realuyo. Sojourners, The.
Rodriguez, L. Victory, Victoria, My Beautiful
  Whisper.
Snodgrass. Mementos, 1.
Storace. Archaeology of Divorce, The.
Tucker, M. Wail of the Divorced.
Wickham. Divorce.
Williams, K. Wildlife.

Doctors

Abse. Carnal Knowledge.
  Case History.
  Doctor, The.
  Lunch and Afterwards.
  Origin of Music, The.
  Stethoscope, The.
  X-Ray.
Alon, E. If There Is a God.
Alvarez, J. Papi Working.
Auden. Give Me a Doctor.
Belloc. Henry King, Who Chewed Bits of
  String, and Was Early Cut Off in Dreadful
  Agonies.
  On Hygiene.
Borges. Conjectural Poem.
Browning, R. Epistle Containing the Strange
  Medical Experience of Karshish, the Arab
  Physician, An.
Campo. El Curandero.
  Lost in the Hospital.
  S. W.
Coles, R. On Dutch's Death.
Coulehan, J. Dynamizer and the Oscilloclast,
  The.
  I'm Gonna Slap Those Doctors.
Dalton, Mary. Doctor, The.
Darling, J. Too Heavy.
Dauenhauer. Grandmother Eliza.
Davis, Cortney. It Is August 24th.
de Fréine, C. Testing, testing.
Donze, R. Vermont Has a High Suicide Rate.
Dyer, E. Painting the Nude.
  'Round Killar.
Edson, R. Dr. Nigel Bruce Watson Counting.

Enzensberger, H. In Memory of William Carlos
  Williams.
Feinstein, P. Health Check.
Fitzgerald, R. Wind at Your Door, The.
Fusselman, A. Ticker.
Ginsberg, A. Chief of Medicine, The.
  Line Drive.
Graham-Pole, J. Venipuncture.
Guevara, M. Postmortem.
Hicok. Angels of Mercy.
Hirsch, E. Two Suffering Men.
Hirschhorn, N. Number Our Days.
Hoagland, T. Medicine: "Black hair of my
  Chinese doctor, The."
Johnson, S. On the Death of Dr [or Mr] Robert
  Levet [a Practiser in Physic].
Jonson, B. To Doctor Empiric[k].
Khosravani. There are four kinds of men who'll
  get no fee from me.
Li K'ai-hsien. Sent to the Master Physician,
  "Almond Orchard" Shih.
  Thanking Doctor Jen.
Logau. Best Medecines, The.
  Physicians' Fortune, The.
Mersaal, E. Too Many Times.
Miles, J. Doctor Who Sits at the Bedside of a
  Rat, The.
Moorer. Birthday Wishes to a Physician.
Mukand, J. Lullaby.
Norris, K. Lilith and the Doctor.
O'Reilly, M. Small Girl Brings an Injured Bird
  into the Surgery, A.
O'Neill, A. Dr Hanagan.
Palmer, R. F. Conchie, The.
Phillips, C. Going Under.
Pinsky. Doctor Frolic.
Platt, F. Coincidentally.
Powell, D. A. You don't have syphilis. the
  doctor says.
Robinson, E. How Annandale Went Out.
Ronci, Seido R. Diamond Cutter.
Rouse, A. Anaesthetist, The.
Rowe, V. Time Heals All Wounds—But One.
Sadiq, M. Tuskegee Experiment.
Satyamurti. Diagnosis.
Senryū, K. Doctor has prepared, The.
  There'll soon be.
Shafer, A. Gurney Tears.
  Monday Morning.
Smith, K. Here.
Stainer. Wound-Dresser's Dream, The.
Stallworthy, J. Letter from Berlin, A.
Stone, J. Gaudeamus Igitur: A Valediction.
  Getting to Sleep in New Jersey.
  Talking to the Family.
Straus, M. Log of Pi, The.
Van Peenen, H. Will Campbell Displays His
  Craniotribe.
Villa, D. Sometimes, Doctor, I awake.
Williams, W. Complaint.
  Le Médecin Malgré Lui.
  To Close.
  Young Love.
Wright, J. Portugal Laurel, The.
Young, G. Letter to William Carlos Williams,
  A.
  Miracle, The.
  Night Call.
See also **Hospitals; Medicine; Nurses**

Dogs

Aesop. Dog and the Shadow, The.
  Dog in the Manger, The.
Aird, T. Fellowship in Grief.
Alkalay-Gut. Instead of his leash.
Anderson, J. Ye Bruthers Dogg.
Anderson, L. Dog Show.
Anyte [or Anytes]. You, too, perished by a bush
  with tangled roots.
Ariosto. Mastiff-Worrying Fly, The.
  Trial of Endurance, A.
  Tumbler, The.
Armitage, S. Before You Cut Loose.
Arnold, S. Mercy's Reward.
Arnold, M. Kaiser Dead.
Avidan, D. Life of a Dead Dog.
Baker, H. Advice to a Man Who Lost a Dog.

Bangs, J. My Dog.
Barham, R. Cynotaph, The.
Beddoes. Sonnet: To Tartar, a Terrier Beauty.
Beerbohm, M. Brave Rover.
Berners. Properties of a Good Greyhound, The.
Bertolino. Baying, The.
Bishop, E. Five Flights Up.
  Pink Dog.
Blacklock, T. To a Young Lady's Dog.
Blake, W. Proverbial Philosophy.
Bloomfield. To Err Is Human.
  Trouncer, the Foxes Foe.
Bly, R. Resemblance between Your Life and a
  Dog, The.
Bodecker. Cats and Dogs.
Boece [or Boethius], H. Battle about a Dog,
  The.
Bowles, W. Grown Old Together.
Brent. I Think I Know No Finer Things Than
  Dogs.
Brooke, H. Fox Hunt, The.
Brown, H. Dogs: "We humans talk."
Brown, Polly. This Is for Megan.
Browne, W. Comedy, A.
Browning, E. Flush or Faunus.
  To Flush, My Dog.
Burkard. Dogs on the Cliffs, The.
Buson. Dog barking, A.
Butler, S. Agrippa's Pug.
  Bear-Baiting.
Byron, G. Abdiel.
  At the Siege of Corinth.
  Don Juan's Spaniel.
Camerarius, P. Faithfullest Beast, The.
Catacalos. One Man's Family.
Chase, K. Before She Died.
Chaucer. Fawning Whelp, The.
  Pitiful Prioress, The.
  Rape of Chanticleer, The.
Chavez, L. Woman Who Raised Dogs, The.
Ch'ŏn Kŭm. Night draws near in a mountain
  village.
Chute, M. My Dog.
Ciardi, J. Suburban.
Clare, J. Frolicsome Old Dog, The.
  Guardian at the Gate, A.
  Teased Pet, The.
Coleman, W. Dog Suicide.
Collier, M. Real-Life Drama, A.
Collins, B. Another Reason Why I Don't Keep
  a Gun in the House.
  Dharma.
  Dog.
Cornford, F. Child's Dream, A.
Cowper, W. Beau's Reply.
Creeley. Messengers, The.
Cross, D. Sterling Park.
Crowley, R. Sunday Bear-Baiting.
D'Aquino, A. Metempsicosis del perro.
  Metempsychosis of the Dog.
Davenant [or D'Avenant]. Lombard Stag-Hunt,
  The.
Davies, S. In Cineam.
Dawe, B. Dogs in the Morning Light.
  Drifters.
Dawe, Tom. If Sonnets Were in Fashion.
Day Lewis. Sheepdog Trials in Hyde Park.
  Stand-To, The.
De Kok. Transfer.
Delmore, E. Difference, The.
Derricotte. From a Letter: About Snow.
Doty, M. New Dog.
  Retrievers in Translation.
Drayton. Dancing Dog, The.
  Farewell to Whitefoot.
Drummond, W. Dog Star, The.
  Melampus' Epitaph.
Dugan, A. Memorial Service for the Invasion
  Beach Where the Vacation in the Flesh Is
  Over.
Edson, R. Neighborhood Dog, The.
Elliott, E. My Only Friends.
Erskine, T. Deserted Died.
Fanthorpe. Our Dog Chasing Swifts.
Ferlinghetti, L. Dog.
Field, E. Duel, The.

Fielding. Revenge.
Finkel. Hound Song.
Fouilloux, J. Blazon Pronounced by the
  Huntsman, The.
Frost, R. Canis Major.
  One More Brevity.
  Span of Life, The.
Fry, C. Dog of St. Bernard's, The.
Galvin, J. Little Dantesque.
Garcilaso de la Vega. I Came to a Valley in the
  Wilderness.
Garrigue. Dialog.
Gay, J. Babbling Ringwood.
  Dogs on Strike, The.
  Meddling Mastiff, The.
  Plain Words to the Spaniel.
  Rural Sports.
  Tray, the Exemplar.
  Turnspit Taught, The.
  Yelping Nuisance of the Way, The.
Geddes, A. Infallible Doussiekie.
Gilbert, C. Glimpses.
Giscombe, C. 1978, Remembering 1962.
Goldsmith, O. Elegy on the Death of a Mad
  Dog, An.
Graham, D. Dogs in Dutch Paintings, The.
Grattius, F. Roman Tribute, A.
Greenwell, D. Fidelity Rewarded.
Grue. Dogs of New York, The.
Guiterman. Little Lost Pup.
Gunn, T. Yoko.
Hadas, P. Lion of God in Vermont in May.
Hahn, S. Nijinksy's Dog.
Hallam. Scott's Dogs at Melrose Abbey.
Hamilton, D. O. Ajax.
Hamilton, W. Bonny Heck.
Hardy, T. Ah, Are You Digging on My Grave?
Harington [or Harrington]. Ambiguity.
  In Praise of Bungey.
  To His Wife, for Striking Her Dog.
Harper, M. Sandra: At the Beaver Trap.
Heaney, S. Dog Was Crying Tonight in
  Wicklow Also, A.
Henry the Minstrel. On Wallace's Track.
Hirshfield, J. Theology.
Hoagland, T. Benevolence.
Hodgins. Shooting the Dogs.
Hoffman, D. In the Days of Rin-Tin-Tin.
Hogg, J. Deep-Toned Jowler, The.
Hoggard, James. My Auld Hector.
Holmes, O. Welcoming the Dawn.
Holub. Distant Howling.
Homer. Odysseus and Argus.
  Odysseus and the Swineherd.
Horace. Brave Dog's Challenge, The [Epode 6].
Horne, R. Beth Gelert.
Horsfield, K. Old Rocket.
Howitt, M. Tobias's Dog.
Hsüeh T'ao [or Xue Tao]. Dog Parted from Her
  Master.
Hudgins. In the Well.
  Two Ember Days in Alabama.
Hughes, T. Roger the Dog.
Hutchinson, P. Flames.
Ishikawa Takuboku. Tanka: "On the roadside."
Issa. Going to Tend Our Family Graves.
  Mokuboji Temple.
  Old dog bends his head listening, The.
  Old dog listens, The.
  Old dog, The.
  Visiting the graves.
Johnson, E. Train Dogs, The.
Johnson, J. Midnight Run.
Johnson, M. Old Dog.
Jong, E. Jubilate Canis.
Jonker, I. Dog.
Jordan, J. July 4, 1984: For Buck.
József, A. Dog, The.
Karpowicz. Dog Which Barked Itself Out, The.
Kearney, M. First Blow-Job.
Keller, D. After the First Snow.
Kelly, B. Orchard, The.
Kemble. On an Irish Retriever.
Kim Sujang. Of all the dogs around me,
  spotted, black, and hairy.
Klee. Wolf Speaks, The.

Kooser. Dog's Grave, A.
Krasicki, I. Master and the Dog, The.
Landor, W. To a Spaniel.
Larsen, W. Surrender.
Lĕ Thánh-tông. Stone Dog, The.
Lea, S. Wrong Way Will Haunt You, The.
Leonard, H. Lost Friend, A.
Levertov. Dog of Art, The.
  Overland to the Islands.
  Shlup, shlup, the dog.
Lewis, J. Stories.
Lovibond. Bull-Baiting.
Lux. So You Put the Dog to Sleep.
Lyndsay [or Lindsay], D. Bagsche's Complaint.
MacBeth [or Macbeth]. Alsatian.
MacCaig. Praise of a Collie.
MacInnes, Mairi. I Object, Said the Object.
MacLean, S. Dogs and Wolves.
Macleod, N. Waggin' O' Our Dog's Tail, The.
MacNaughton. Feast Day Dog.
Mallock. Questions: "Where are you now, little
  wandering."
Mariani. Landscape with Dog.
Markell, Jennifer. Veterinary Student, The.
Martial. Gallic Lap-Dog, The.
  New Point of View, A.
Massey. Dead Boy's Portrait and His Dog, The.
Masters, E. Benjamin Pantier.
Matthews, W. Dogs of Montone, The.
McFerren. Metaphor Crosses the Road, A.
McLagan, Elizabeth. At Twelve.
McLeod. Lone Dog.
McNiece, R. Old Joe the stray dog.
Meads, K. Dogs.
Mengham, Rod. Names in the Bark.
Merrill, J. My Father's Irish Setters.
  Victor Dog, The.
Messer, S. Rendered Dog.
Middleton, C. Wooden Dog.
Miller, L. Triangle.
Mitford. Manx.
  To Tray—Stolen.
Mnookin. Signs.
Moir, D. Dying Oscar.
Moller, V. Faithfullest Beast, The.
Momaday. Two Figures.
Monro, H. Dog.
Montgomerie, A. Remembers Thou in Æsope
  of a Taill.
More, S. De Principe Bono et Malo.
  Good Princes and Bad.
Morgan, E. Shilpit dog fucks grimly by the
  close, A.
Morris, L. To the Tormentors.
Mueller, L. What the Dog Perhaps Hears.
Muldoon, P. All I Did for Him.
Musgrave. Burial of the Dog.
Nash, O. Dog, The.
  Please Pass the Biscuit.
Nasr, M. With meek eyes.
Nemerov. Walking the Dog.
Nokhem, Y. Hounds Howl at the Moon.
Norris, L. Shepherd's Dog, The.
Nossis. This portrait captures Thaumareta's
  form—it renders.
Ondaatje. Biography: "Dog scatters her body in
  sleep, The."
Oppenheim, M. My Friend's Dog.
Oppian of Apamea [or Pella]. Greek
  Compliment, A.
Ovid. Actaeon and His Hounds.
Paljor, N. I woke up early.
Payn. Our Dog Jock.
Pedretti, Erica. Dogs Are Supposed.
Perry, S. Fugue.
Phillips, D. Hounds are either the work of wind,
  The.
"Peter Pindar.". Old Friends.
  Pups and the Alligator, The.
Pope, A. Argus.
  Bounce to Fop.
  Epigram Engraved on the Collar of a Dog Given
   [or Which I Gave] to His Royal Highness.
  Lo, the poor Indian! whose untutor'd mind.
Praed. Dogs' Welcome, The.
Pratt, S. Blind Man's Dog, The.

Prior. Home-Loving Dog, The.
Procter, A. Homeless.
Ramsay, A. Lover's Logic.
Rees, Elizabeth. Rockstar Poet.
Retallack, J. Woman Dragged by Welsh Corgis.
Reznikoff. Highway I was walking on, The.
Salisbury. After Heart-Bypass Surgery, Another Ritual for Continuing Struggle.
Salom. Winter.
Schaeffer. Dog, The.
Schelling. Run My Hand Under.
Schwartz, D. Dogs Are Shakespearean, Children Are Strangers.
Scott, S. Baffled Staghounds, The.
 Jealous Twain, The.
 Lufra Avenged.
 Maida.
 Poor Yarrow.
 Wanderer's Dog, The.
Senryū, K. Now that he has a child.
Shakespeare, W. Differences in Dogs.
 Helena's Humble Petition.
 Lear and the Dogs.
 Misanthropos.
 Music of the Hound, The.
 Venus with Adonis' and Hounds.
Sheppard, R. Empty Diary 1990.
Shinkichi Takahashi. Lap Dog.
Sims. Told to the Missionary.
Skinner, J. Fetch.
Smart, C. Insular Prejudice.
Smith, S. Exemplary Nick.
Smither. On the Euthanasia of a Pet Dog.
Somervile [or Somerville]. All-Accomplished Rover.
 First let the kennel be the huntsman's care.
Soniat. Dog Days.
Southey, C. On Trust.
 Rude Ranger Rebuked.
Southey, R. Canine Immortality.
 Roderick's Faithful Theron.
Spencer, W. Beth Gelert.
Stafford, W. Dog Asleep.
Stein, G. Dog, A.
 Identity A Poem.
Stern, G. All I Did for Him.
 Dog That I Am.
 Dog, The.
Strand. Five Dogs.
Svoboda. Death Stayed.
Swift, J. Advice to a Dog Painter.
 Dogs of Nile, The.
Tanikawa, S. Nero.
Tate, J. Promotion, The.
Taylor, E. Woman as Artist.
Tennyson, A. Old Roä.
Thomas, D. Song of the Mischievous Dog, The.
Thomas, G. Killer Dog.
Thompson, P. Unromantic Awakening, An.
Tickell. Fragment on Hunting-Dogs, A.
Todd, M. To Kill Stray Dogs.
Toomer. Nora.
Tsanev, Stefan. Dog: "Why do you watch me so sadly and inquisitively."
Turberville. Love Me, Love My Dog.
Tymnes. Maltese Dog, A.
 Stone says that it covers here the white dog, The.
Unknown. Dog Latin.
 Doubt as to Identity.
 Dumb Advocate, A.
 Friend of Man, The.
 Indian Hero's Creed, The.
 Lord Orrery's Hector.
 Of flying birds and beasts that craw.
 Old Mother Hubbard.
 On Some Elegies on a Lap-Dog.
Updike. Dog's Death.
Van Walleghen. Happiness.
Vietnamese Oral Tradition. Cat, The.
Vilariño. Like a dog howling endlessly.
Viorst. Mother Doesn't Want a Dog.
Virgil [or Vergil]. Uses of the Dog, The.
Voigt. Trust, The.
Voznesensky [or Voznesenskii]. December Pastures.

Wallace, R. Dog's Song.
Wang Ho-ch'ing. Tune: "Po Pu-tuan" Long-Haired Little Dog.
Ward, T. Stray Dogs, Foaming.
Warren, R. Sila.
Webb, C. Amplified Dog.
Weigl. May.
Welch, J. Day after Chasing Porcupines.
Welles. Dogs and Weather.
Whalen, P. Saturday.
Whitaker, J. Roman Tribute, A.
Whitehead, W. Waning Honeymoon, The.
Wilbur, R. Pardon, The.
Williams, C. K. Dog, The.
Williams, M. Listen.
Williams, R. Dogs.
Williams, W. Banner Bearer, The.
 To a Dog Injured in the Street.
Wilner, E. Theory and Practice in Poetry.
Winters, Y. Elegy on a Young Airedale Bitch Lost Two Years Since in the Salt-Marsh.
Wordsworth, W. Fidelity.
Wright, J. Walking the Dog.
Wyndham, W. Shipwrecked Tippoo.
Xenophanes. Pythagorean, The.
Yalden. Treacherous Towser.
 Treacherous Towser.
Zimunya. Mr. Bezuidenthout's Dogs.
See also **Puppies**

Dolls
Alviso, M. Barbies, Las.
Basho. Time even for the grass hut.
Black, J. Paper Doll.
Boland, E. Dolls Museum in Dublin, The.
Buson. Lights are going out, The.
Caldwell, A. Raggedy Ann.
Couzyn. One autumn afternoon when I was nine.
Dubie. Poem: "Mule kicked out in the trees, A. An Early."
Duhamel. Barbie's Molester.
 Bicentennial Barbie.
 Kinky.
Gioia. Counting the Children.
González, R. Perla at the Mexican Border Assembly Line of Dolls.
Harryman. Another Artifact.
Hemphill. Soft Targets.
Lees, G. Waltz for Debby.
Livingston, M. Doll.
Major, C. Doll Believers, The.
McMahon, L. Barbie's Ferrari.
Miles, J. Doll.
Mole, J. Song of the Hat-Raising Doll.
Mori. Barbie Says Math is Hard.
Palmer, M. Of This Cloth Doll Which.
Paterson, E. Griselda.
Ravikovitch, D. Clockwork Doll.
Reedy, C. Doll Museum, The.
St. John, D. Dolls.
 Hush.
Seifū. Faces of dolls, The.
Simic. Head of a Doll.
 Hundred-Year-Old China Doll's Head, The.
Trinidad. Of Mere Plastic.
Yeats. Dolls, The.
Yourcenar, Marguerite. Poem for a Doll Bought in a Russian Bazaar.

Dolphins
Anyte [or Anytes]. No longer will I fling up my neck, exulting.
Constantine, D. Watching for Dolphins.
Faverey. Seldom has a panther's leap.
Griffiths, B. Dolphins.
Gunn, T. Aquarium, The.
Simon, M. Dolphin, The.
Zwicky. Stone Dolphin, The.

Domestic Abuse
Addonizio. From Then to Now.
Ai. Finished.
 Mother's Tale, The.
Baker, D. More Rain.
Bennett, N. Ghost of His Hand, The.
Brooks, G. Battle, The.
Castillo, S. Voyeur.
Cox, M. Style.

Daniels, J. 911.
Duhamel. Crater Face.
Hahn, K. Open Kitchen, The.
Hershon. Woman Strangles, A.
Joseph, A. Learning to Drive at 32.
Lundberg, J. Chivalry.
Mattson, N. Her Other Language.
Morrissey, S. Sea Stone.
Nasrin. Happy Marriage.
Pegram, L. Perspective.
Rash, R. Devil Beating His Wife.
Rekdal, Paisley. What Was There to Bring Me to Delight but to Love and Be Loved?
Ruffin. Redneck with Hair on His Back.
Rushin. Coward, The.
St. John, P. Violence of Pronoun, The.
Sellers, H. Some Poems Aren't for You.
Sholl. You Figure It Out.
Starkey, D. Suburban Crimes 3.
Unknown. I love! I love! I shall not hide it. I'll not deny it.
 See the dreadful tyranny of husbands.
Williams, B. On the Other Side.
Wright, C. Tours.
X, D. Burn Rubber on Me.

Dominican Republic
Dove, R. Parsley.

Don Juan
Apollinaire. Always.
Byron, G. Alas, they were so young, so beautiful.
 Don Juan's Spaniel.
 Juan and Haidee [from Cantos 2-4].
Jouve. More and More Woman.
Sorescu, M. Don Juan (After He'd Consumed Tons of Lipstick).

Don Quixote
Borges. Soldier of Urbina, A.
Fathy, S. Don Quixote and the Flour Mills.
Melville, H. Rusty Man, The.
Queneau. That Don't Scare Me.
Wilbur, R. Parable.

Donkeys
al-Rahim, A. Everyday.
Baudelaire. Joker, A.
Baxter, J. Brother Ass, Brother Ass, you are full of fancies.
Chesterton. Donkey, The.
 Donkey, The [1920 version].
Coleridge, S. To a Young Ass.
Dubie. Elegy for Wright & Hugo.
Fanthorpe. What the Donkey Saw.
Gibson, W. Advice to Travelers.
Gonzalez, R. Calling the White Donkey.
Howe, F. From a donkey, excuse me, one lesson is given.
Ismail. Donkeys in Anantapur.
Jammes. Prayer to Go to Paradise with the Donkeys, A.
La Fontaine. Donkey and the Lapdog, The.
Montgomerie, A. Remembers thou in Æsope of a taill.
Paek Sŏk. Natasha, the White Donkey, and I.
Pasternak, B. Matthew 21:1–11.
Phillips, C. Minotaur.
Roethke. Monotony Song, The.
Shiraishi. Donkey Speculates, The.
 From the Precious Tears of the Donkey.
Smith, S. Donkey, The.
Thomas, D. After the Funeral.
Wang Yü-ch'eng. Song of the Crow Pecking at My Scarred Donkey.

Donne, John
Caird, J. John Donne, You Were Wrong.
Carew, T. Elegy upon the Death of the Dean of [St.] Paul's, Dr. John Donne, An.
Coleridge, S. On Donne's Poetry.
Jonson, B. To John Donne ("Donne, the delight of Phoebus, and each Muse.").
 To John Donne ("Who shall doubt, Donne, where [or whe'er] I a poet be[e].").
Kenyon, J. Travel: After a Death.
King, H. Upon the Death of My Ever Desired Friend Doctor [or Dr] Donne Dean of Paul's.
Maxton. Elegies.

Doorbells
Rukeyser, M.   Homage to Literature.
Sisson.   Letter to John Donne, A.
Thomas, L.   Another Poem in English.
Trocchi, A.   For John Donne: Master Metaphysical.
Wotton, S.   To John Donne.

Doorbells
al-Sa'igh, Y.   Habitude.

Doors
Aini, L.   In Their House.
Allen, S.   In My Father's House.
Andal.   O sister of wealth.
  O you who guard over.
Baron, S.   Tenebrae.
Barrington, J.   Villanelle VI.
Bei Dao.   Rose of Time, The.
Bible, O.T.   Song: "I was asleep but my heart stayed awake."
Bousoño, C.   Door, The.
Budenz.   Poeta Fui.
Clark, T.   You (I).
Coleridge, M.   Broken Friendship.
  Witch, The.
Creeley.   Door, The: "It is hard going to the door."
Davis, W.   In a Room.
Frost, R.   Lockless Door, The.
García Lorca.   Casida of Sobbing.
Hart, K.   Room, The.
Hill, M.   Sleep.
Holub.   Door, The.
Hwang Insuk.   Two Doors.
Ibáñez, S.   I Cannot.
Jamie, K.   Rooms.
Jiménez, J.   Leave the Doors Standing Open.
Kafka.   Before the Law.
Kassabova, K.   Door, The: anticipation of wisdom.
Kerouac.   Missing a kick.
Larkin, P.   Mr Bleaney.
Levy, A.   Minor Poet, A.
Li Shang-yin.   High Noon.
Mackenzie, K.   Door swung open, The.
Mackey, N.   Dream Thief.
Maiden.   In the Gloaming.
McKay, C.   White House, The.
Miller, M.   Closing, A.
Moore, R.   Doors.
Odio, E.   Memory of My Private Childhood.
Ponge.   Delights of the Door, The.
  Pleasures of a Door.
  Pleasures of the Door, The.
Rabi'a al-Adawiyya.   I am fully qualified to work as a doorkeeper, and for this reason.
  O my Lord.
Ramsdell, H.   In Spite of How.
Reed, H.   Door and the Window, The.
Reed, I.   Why I Often Allude to Osiris.
Reznikoff.   House-wreckers, The.
Shorter.   Skeleton in the Cupboard, The.
Sorby.   Gossip.
Stefans, Brian Kim.   They're Putting a New Door In.
Tomlinson, C.   Door, The.
Tranströmer.   Elegy.
Unknown.   Song Inscribed on an Earthenware Vessel.
  Writing on a Door, A.
Yeats.   Road at My Door, The.
Yi Yônju.   For the Sake of Two Screws.

Dormice
Eich.   Huge Person, The.

Dorset, England
Hardy, T.   Domicilium.
  Roman Road, The.

Dostoyevsky, Feodor
Bukowski.   Dostoevsky.
MacDiarmid, H.   Farewell to Dostoevski.
Tagliabue.   Moderation Is Not a Negation of Intensity, but Helps Avoid Monotony.

Doubt
Anwar, C.   Heaven.
Arnold, M.   Dover Beach.
Basheva.   Fifth Floor.
Beasley.   Witness.

Bei Dao.   Answer, The.
Bellerby.   Night.
Brontë, A.   Doubter's Prayer, The.
Brownjohn.   Looking at Her.
Cairns, Scott.   Theology of Doubt, The.
Citino.   Man Who Couldn't Believe, The.
Clarke, George Elliott.   Prelude: "Shelley's a garden."
Coleridge, M.   Doubt.
Daryush.   You should at times go out.
Davies, W. H.   Inquest, The.
Dickinson, E.   Split the Lark—and you'll find the Music.
  This World Is Not Conclusion.
  Those—dying then.
Drayton.   Sonnet 35: Some, misbelieving and profane.
Dunn, S.   Guardian Angel, The.
Gallagher, T.   On Your Own.
Green, D. R.   Names and Sorrows.
Herbert, G.   Affliction (1).
Hewitt, J.   Substance and Shadow.
Hope, A.   Luke 24:36–49; As they were saying this, Jesus.
Howe, F.   Doubt.
Hristic.   That Night They All Gathered on the Highest Tower.
Hudgins.   Elegy for My Father, Who Is Not Dead.
Johnson, S.   Lines Contributed to Hawkesworth's "The Rival".
Juarroz.   Every word is a doubt.
Lakshminkara.   Lay your head on a block of butter and chop.
McGuckian.   Aviary.
Moore, T.   Away with this Pouting.
O'Hara, F.   To the Harbormaster.
Ostriker.   Story of Abraham, The.
Pankey.   Confession of Cleopas, The.
Petri.   By an Unknown Poet from Eastern Europe, 1955.
Piatt, S.   Doubt, A.
  We Two.
Press, K.   Rotten fish.
Reese, L.   Prayer of an Unbeliever.
Rexroth, K.   Did you take me because you loved me?
Rilke.   5. The Suspicions of Joseph.
Robinson, A.   Sibyl, The.
Robinson, E.   Christmas Sonnet, A.
Rossetti, C.   After Communion.
Roubaud.   It Is Raining.
Sabines.   I Do Not Know It for Sure.
Serrano, P.   Acotamiento.
  Boundary.
Shapiro, D.   House (Blown Apart).
Smart, C.   St. Thomas.
Spenser, E.   Sonnet 65: "Doubt which ye misdeeme, fayre love, is vaine, The."
Thomas, L.   Dangerous Doubts.
Thompson, C.   Doubt.
  Skeptic, The.
Tuckerman, F.   As Sometimes in a Grove.
Unknown.   Twelfth Song of the Thunder.
Wilbur, R.   Dubious Night, A.
Williams, C. K.   Question, The.

See also **Agnosticism and Agnostics**

Douglass, Frederick
Bibb.   In Memoriam Frederick Douglass.
Dunbar, P.   Douglass.
  Frederick Douglass.
Hayden, R.   Frederick Douglass.
Heard, J.   Welcome to Hon. Frederick Douglass.
Hughes, L.   Frederick Douglass: 1817–1895.
Ray, H.   In Memoriam Frederick Douglass.
Seibles, T.   Douglass, a Last Letter.
Shockley, E.   From The Lost Letters of Frederick Douglass.

Dover, England
Arnold, M.   Dover Beach.
Ruefle.   Seven Postcards from Dover.
Shakespeare, W.   Come on, sir; he[e]re's the place: stand still.

Doves
Armantrout.   Traveling Through the Yard.
Bible, O.T.   I Am the Rose of Sharon.

Brontë, A.   Captive Dove, The.
Crapsey.   Pledge, The.
De la Mare.   Dove, The.
Dove, R.   Ta Ta Cha Cha.
Fenollosa.   Wood Dove, The.
Field.   I sing thee with the stock-dove's throat.
  Trinity.
Florit, E.   Martyrdom of Saint Sebastian, The.
García Lorca.   Casida of the Dark Doves.
Ha-Levi, J.   Distant Dove.
Hall, D.   Short Circuit.
Ifan, W.   In Porthcawl.
Irish Oral Tradition.   Pearl of the White Breast.
Kerouac.   Thrashing Doves, The.
Miller, E.   What the Women Told Me.
Moiro.   Great Zeus was reared in Krete and no one.
Moldaw.   Nest, The.
Muldoon, P.   Inkspot, The.
Nepote, M.   Visitación.
  Visitation.
Pellicer, C.   Flocks of Doves.
Piatt, S.   Shapes of a Soul.
Probyn.   Lai.
Ray, H.   My Easter Dove.
Robertson, A.   Song of the Dove, The.
Robinson, A.   Song: "Oh for the wings of a dove."
Saigyō.   In a tree standing.
Scovell.   Listening to Collared Doves.
Stainer.   Sarcophagus.
Stern, G.   Inkspot, The.
  She Was a Dove.
Stevens, W.   Song of Fixed Accord.
  Thinking of a Relation between the Images of Metaphors.
Unknown.   Thousand doves, A.
Weigl.   Regret for the Mourning Doves Who Failed to Mate.
Williams, C. K.   Doves.
Wright, J.   Dove-Love.
Wright, S.   And the Birds Sing of LIfe.
Yosef, H.   Reflections on a Dove.
Young, A.   Stockdoves, The.
Zakaria Youssef, M.   Sadder Man, The.

Down's Syndrome
Alpaugh, D.   Herbie.
Snyder, R.   Mongoloid Child Handling Shells on the Beach, A.
Stallworthy, J.   Almond Tree, The.

See also **Mental Retardation**

Dowries
Ramsay, A.   Lass with a Lump of Land.
Vietnamese Oral Tradition.   Arranged Marriage, The.

Dowsing and Dowsers
Morgan, E.   Dowser, The.

Drag
Brooks, A.   Here is the queen.
Campo.   Her Final Show.
Olds, S.   His Costume.
White, J.   Oshi.
Wieners.   Poem for Cocksuckers, A.

Dragonflies
Aygi, G.   Dream: Flight of a Dragonfly.
Basho.   Dragonfly, The.
Bogan, L.   Dragonfly, The.
Buson.   My village / Dragonflies.
Chông Hwajin.   I'm a Dragonfly Caught in a Net.
Fourcade, Dominique.   Ensembles.
Holley, M.   Dancer, The.
Hughes, T.   To Paint a Water Lily.
Issa.   Distant mountains, The.
  Dragonfly, The.
  Reflected / In the dragonfly's eye.
Kunitz, S.   Dragonfly, The.
Lowell, A.   In Time of War.
Masaoka Shiki.   Indian summer / Dragonfly shadows seldom.
Natsume Soseki.   It comes to my shoulder.
Paloff, B.   On Transportation.
Rossetti, D.   19: Silent Noon.
Snyder, G.   Dragonfly.
Soyinka.   Dragonfly at My Windowpane.

Unknown. I wish I was.

Dragons
Al-Bayati, A. Dragon, The.
Allen, P. Tattoo #47, "Happy Dragon".
Arp. Dragon Carries the Inscription "Kunigundula" and Is Led on a Leash, The.
Bottoms. Chinese Dragons.
Carroll, L. Jabberwocky.
Chalfi, R. Reading the I Ching.
Fanthorpe. Not My Best Side.
Kuan Hsiu. Nacreous land had no dust, The.
Lipton, Lenny. Puff the Magic Dragon.
Malveisin, W. Fergus Attempts to Make Off with the Sheild of Dunottar.
Moore, M. O to Be a Dragon.
Muso Soseki. Don't ask suspiciously. From My Hut in Miura.
Old Creek.
Nash, O. Tale of Custard the Dragon, The.
Nicholls, J. Storytime.
Pepler. Concerning Dragons.
Revard. Dragon-Watching in St. Louis.
Ryuzan. Clear in the blue, the moon!
Smith, W. Toaster, The.
Sutphen, J. Terra Incognita.
Tu Fu [or Du Fu]. To the south there is a dragon living in a mountain pool.
Unknown. Ch'ien (Heaven).
Unknown Beowulf.
Upton, L. Imagination of Flowers, The.

Drake, Sir Francis
Newbolt. Drake's Drum.

Drawing
Ap Hywel, Elin. Understanding Light.
Arber, Carol. Sketching in Barnstable.
Bailey, Peter. Practice.
Behn, H. Circles.
Cowper, W. To George Romney, Esq.
Forbes, C. Picture of a Man.
Hass, R. Spring Drawing 2.
Juarroz. Life Draws a Tree.
Levine, P. On a Drawing by Flavio.
Merrill, J. Graffito.
Oppen. Drawing.
Rago. Childhood Painting Lesson.
Rector. David's Rumor.
Reps, Paul. Open here.
Who is.

Dreams and Dreaming
Adcock, F. Dreaming.
Addison, M. Names.
Adonis [or Adunis]. Passage, The.
Agustini. Vision.
Ai. More.
Aini, L. One Girl's Dance.
Akhmatova, A. Dream, A.
al-Sa'igh, Y. Wake Up, Yousif.
al-Saygh, S. White Sleep.
Alberti. Coming Back of an Assassinated Poet, The.
Good Angel, The.
Punishments.
Aleixandre. Life: "Paper bird I have in my chest, A."
Alexander, E. Feminist Poem Number One.
Overture: Watermelon City.
Alexander, P. Scherzo.
Ali, A. Dream of Glass Bangles, A.
I See Chile in My Rearview Mirror.
Allingham, W. Dream, A [or The].
Alvi, M. Bed, The.
Fish.
Amis, K. Against Romanticism.
Dream of Fair Women, A.
Anderson, L. Dog Show.
Arnold, M. Longing.
Arturo, A. Song of the Silent Night.
Ashbery, J. Improvement, The.
Ato Tobira. Only one fleeting.
Atwood-Fukuda. Ballybunion.
Atwood. Dream 1: the Bush Garden.
Variation on the Word *Sleep.*
Aygi, G. Dream: Flight of a Dragonfly.
Dream: Queue for Paraffin.
From Lines in a Dream.
Baca. Voz de la Gente.

Work We Hate and Dreams We Love.
Baillie, J. Reverie, A.
Ballagas. Of Another Fashion.
Bampfylde. On a Frightful Dream.
Bang, M. Like a Fire in a Fire.
Baraka, I. New World, The.
Barer, M. Here Come the Dreamers.
Barnfield [or Barnefield]. Sweet Corrall lips, where Nature's treasure lies.
Basho. Autumn approaches.
Jars of octopus, The.
Sick on a journey.
Sick on a journey / Over parched fields.
Sick on my journey.
Summer grass.
Summer grasses / All that remains.
Bataille, Georges. I Dreamed of Touching.
Night Is My Nudity.
Becker, R. Dreaming at the Rexall Drug.
Bécquer, G. I Lay Awake, Wandering in that Limbo.
Beddoes. Dream-Pedlary.
Behn, A. Dream, The.
Belev. Dream: "When the trees began to calcify, and the birds to coalesce with the branches."
Belieu. Sleeping Man Must Be Awakened to Be Killed, A.
Bellerby. Night.
Benedetti, M. We All Conspire.
Berkson, B. Fourth Street, San Rafael.
Berrigan, T. Sonnet: "My dream a drink with Lonnie Johnson we discuss the code."
Bevington, L. Dreamers?
Bidart. Another Life.
Bishop, J. Dream, The: "And once again I was within that house."
Blaisdell, G. After the Symbols.
Blake, W. Angel, The.
Dream, A.
Little Girl Found, The.
Blue Cloud. Deeper Than a Dream.
Bly, R. Dream of Retarded Children, A.
Bobrowski. East.
Bogan, L. Dream, The.
Meeting, The.
Bona. Dream Poem.
Bonitto-Burwell, T. Leaving Winston-Salem.
Bonnefoy. De Natura Rerum.
Stone, A.
Borges. Dreamtigers.
Everything and Nothing.
Soldier of Urbina, A.
Boruch. Hammer Falls, Is Falling, The.
Bowering, M. Madrigal, a Lullaby for Xan.
Brecht, B. I, the Survivor.
Breckenridge. General John Cabell Breckinridge.
Breton, A. Vigilance.
Breytenbach. Dreams Are Also Wounds.
Brinks, Dave. Story Pillow, The.
Brock, V. Mary's Dream.
Brontë, C. Again I find myself alone.
Dream that stole o'er us in the time.
Pilate's Wife's Dream.
What does she dream of.
Brontë, E. Day Dream, A.
Stars.
Brooke, R. Sonnet: "Oh! Death will find me, long before I tire."
Brooks, G. Kitchenette building.
My dreams, my works must wait till after hell.
Broumas, O. After *The Little Mariner.*
Old Wives' Tale.
Browning, E. True Dream, A.
Browning, R. Women and Roses.
Brydges. On Dreams, October 15, 1782.
Buckley, C. Sycamore Canyon Nocturne.
Buffoni, F. On Poetry.
Burkard. White City, A: "In the dream, N. is singing "a white city." A teacher he had is wearing a girdle."
Burke, J. I've Got a Pocketful of Dreams.
Polka Dots and Moonbeams.
Welcome to My Dream.
Busch, T. Heartland.
Bynner. Wistaria.

Byron, G. Darkness.
Campbell, T. Soldier's Dream, The.
Campo. Allegory.
Carson, A. Short Talk on the Truth to Be Had from Dreams.
Cartwright, K. In / dreams / diving deeper / than my disbelief.
Cartwright, W. Dream Broke, A.
Cavalieri. Grandmother.
Cavalli. In that small dark fever of every reawakening.
Chalfi, R. Night Hair.
Chen Zi'ang. Just now in wild, free mood I yearn.
Cherry, K. Reading, Dreaming, Hiding.
Ch'ien Ch'i. Dedicated to the Hermit Cui.
Chin, D. Sleeping Father.
Chin, J. Night.
Ch'in Kuan. From a Dream.
Ch'oe Sŭngja. Instead of a Dream.
Christie. In My Dream.
Overture.
Chu Ŭisik. What is life, I ponder.
Chu Yohan. To Catch the Moon.
Chunghur Hyujung. Song for Three Dreams.
Clark, T. "Before Dawn.."
Clifton, L. Death of Crazy Horse, The.
Mary's Dream.
My Dream about the Poet.
Night Vision.
Powell (officer charged with the beating of rodney king).
Women You Are Accustomed To, The.
Cocteau. Young Girl Sleeping.
Cole, H. Original Face.
Coleridge, M. But in That Sleep of Death What Dreams May Come?
Coleridge, Samuel. Kubla Khan: or, A Vision in a Dream.
Coleridge, Sara. Blest is the tarn which towering cliffs o'ershade.
Collin, Bernard. Perpetual *Look* Physics: 17/5.
Colonna, S. So it tries to reach her inside her mind.
Without muscles without slipping.
Conkling, G. I Will Not Give Thee All My Heart.
Conoley, G. Beckon.
Cooper, J. Estrangement.
Cornford, F. Child's Dream, A.
Corso. Dream of a Baseball Star.
30th Year Dream.
Cortes. Great Prayer.
Cortes, F. Poem Composed During a Brownout.
Cott, J. He Dreams What Is Going On inside His Head.
Couzyn. Morning.
Creeley. Edges.
I Know a Man.
Place, The ("Afternoon it changes.").
Cullen, C. For a Poet.
Cummings, E. E. My sweet old etcetera.
Curbelo. Bedtime Stories.
Lake Has Swallowed the Whole Sky, The.
Daichi. Thoughts arise endlessly.
Daive. She does not move.
Daley, V. Vision of Sunday in Heaven, A.
Darío, R. Melancholy.
Story for Margarita.
Darwish, M. On Our Last Evening on This Land.
Davies, W. H. Sluggard, The.
Davis, T. C. T. at the Five Spot.
Dawe, B. Copy-writer's Dream, The.
De Angelis. Reasons for the Beginning.
de Burgos. Seawall.
De Kok. Dream of a trophy.
De' Medici. (To the Virgin).
De Vries, R. On Alabama Ave., Paterson, NJ, 1954.
DeLange, E. Darn That Dream.
Delgado, J. I-5 Incident.
Denham, Joe. Fo'c'sle Dreams.
Desbordes-Valmore. Intermittent Dream of a Sad Night.
Désiré, J. Dream: "Last night in sleep."

Desnos. I Have So Often Dreamed of You.
I've Dreamed of You So Much.
I've Dreamed Such Dreams of You.
I've Dreamt of You So Often.
No, Love Is Not Dead.
Dey, Atanu. Buddha and I, The.
Di Prima. For Suzuki Roshi.
Dickey, J. Sled Burial, Dream Ceremony.
Dickinson, E. In Winter in my Room.
Digges. Rough Music.
Dodge, M. Poor Crow!
Dolben. One night I dreamt that in a gleaming hall.
Donne. Dream[e], The.
Doolittle, H. At Baia.
Doty, M. Michael's Dream.
Douglas, L. Dead Poet, The.
Two Loves.
Dove, R. This Life.
Dransfield. That Which We Call a Rose.
Driscoll, L. Hold Fast Your Dreams.
Dubie. Sanctuary.
Duhamel. Sex with a Famous Poet.
Dunbar, P. Ere Sleep Comes Down to Soothe the Weary Eyes.
He Had His Dream.
Duncan, R. Often I Am Permitted to Return to a Meadow.
Rites of Participation.
Sentinels, The.
Duo Duo. Morning.
Thousands of images have suddenly brightened in the emptiness.
Eady. Success.
Early, G. Innocency or Not Song X.
Elledge. Their Hats Is Always White.
Eluard, P. I've Told You.
Emerson, R. Memory.
Engels, J. Fish Dream, The.
Equi. In a Monotonous Dream.
Erdrich. Strange People, The.
Espada. My Cockroach Lover.
Etter. Monk's Dream.
Ettinger, E. Excerpts from the Sabbath Dream Book.
Fagan. Little Bad Dream Charm.
Faigao, B. Balitaw.
Fairchild. Flight.
Faiz. Prison Daybreak, A.
Fan Chung-yen. Tune: "Sumuche Dancers".
Feinstein, E. Aviation.
Ferguson, G. In Hospital-land.
Field, E. Little Boy Blue.
Sugar-Plum Tree, The.
Wynken, Blynken, and Nod.
Field. Elsewhere.
Figueroa, J. Pablo Neruda.
Flynn, L. My Dream Mentor.
Foppa. Nocturne.
Foster, S. Conant. From Out the Heated City.
Freed, A. All I Do Is Dream of You.
Frénaud. Self-Creation.
Frost, R. After Apple-Picking.
Frumkin. Bad Dream and the Friend.
Fugai. Only the Zen-man knows tranquillity.
Fuller, C. My Father's Dreams.
Gandlevsky, S. Is it time to change the record? But I'm dreaming again.
Gannon, K. Dreamer's Holiday, A.
Garcia-Camarillo, C. Dream 8.
Garcia, R. Book of Dreams, The.
Gardinet, C. Wet Dream.
Garrett, E. Moules à la Marinière.
Gelinas, D. Dream of the Just, The.
Sueño de los justos, El.
George, D. Asenath.
George, D. It Shouldn't Happen to a Dream.
Gershwin, I. Long Ago (And Far Away).
Man I Love, The.
Gervitz, G. Life is nothing but time.
Gibbs, Robert J. Kind of Wakefulness, A.
Gilbert, C. Kite-Flying.
Gilbert, W. Nightmare, [A or The].
Giscombe, C. 1980.
Recent Past, The.
Giussani, S. Hot and Cold.

Glancy. Kemo Sabe.
Glück, L. Condo.
Seven Ages, The.
Siren.
Goethe. To Belinda.
Goldstein, Stephanie. At Night: "Worries creep like insects."
González Prada, M. If the Tomb Is Not Oblivion.
Goodtimes. Sartor Resartus.
Gotera. Manong Chito Tells Manong Ben about His Dream over Breakfast at the Manilatown Cafe.
Graves, R. Pinch of Salt, A.
Greenlaw, L. Shape of Things, The.
Grimké, A. Little Grey Dreams.
Guevara, M. Reader of This Page.
Guillén, J. Shadows, The.
Gunn, T. Reassurance, The.
Small Plane in Kansas.
Haavikko. Bastard Son is born with a tooth in his mouth and hair on his.
Hachenburg, H. Terezin.
Hacker, M. Wagers.
Hadas, R. Journey Out.
Haines, Anne. Catching the Scent.
Hall, D. White Apples.
Woolworth's.
Hamill, S. Abstract.
Hammerstein. Happy Talk.
Han-shan Te-ch'ing. Single cloud envelops ten-thousand streamside pines, A.
Hardy, T. Self-Unseeing, The.
Harms. Los Angeles, The Angels.
My Own Little Piece of Hollywood.
Harris, J. Dream of the Hair Burning Smell.
Hart, L. Blue Room, The.
Harte, B. Second Review of the Grand Army, A.
Harvey, M. Our Square of Lawn.
Hass, R. Palo Alto: the Marshes.
Pornographer, The.
Hassaan, Y. I Considered Myself.
Hauge. It Is That Dream.
Hayden, R. Bone-Flower Elegy.
Heaney, S. Dream of Jealousy, A.
Hébert, A. Earth at Its Origin.
Hemans. Dreaming Child, The.
Herbert, Z. Emperor's Dream, The.
Trial, The.
Herrera y Reissig. Heraldic Decoration.
Heraldic Decoration.
Herrick. Dream[e]s.
Vine, The.
Vision, The ("Methought I saw (as I did dream[e] in bed).").
Vision, The ("Sitting alone (as one forsook).").
Heyen. Bread: "I'm standing in elm shadow."
Higginson, E. Dream of Sappho, A.
Hill, M. Sleep.
Hô Sugyông. One White Dream.
Hoekstra. Cedar, The.
Hogg, J. Thirteenth Bard's Song, The.
Hollo. Le Jazz Hot.
Howe, M. Dream, The.
Hu Shih. Dream and Poetry.
Hughes, L. Dream Boogie.
Dream Dust.
Dream Keeper, The.
Dream Variation[s].
Dreams.
Harlem ("What happens to a dream deferred?").
I Dream a World.
Morning After.
Nightmare Boogie.
Same in Blues.
Water-Front Streets.
Hugo, R. In Your Dream after Falling in Love.
In Your Racing Dream.
Hugo, V. Boaz Asleep.
Hunt, L. Nile, The.
Hwang Insuk. All Dreams Are Sexual.
Ilkov, Ani. Dreamsters.
Imbriglio, C. Gospel According to How We Throw Stones.
Ishikawa Takuboku. Better Than Crying.

Iskrenko. How to Live through This Night (A Dream).
Issa. In a dream.
Not yet become a Buddha.
Istarú, A. From where you have come.
Jabès. Mirror and Scarf.
Jackson, H. Dreams.
Jarrell, R. Dead Wingman, The.
Girl in a Library, A.
Jenkins, P. Six Small Fires.
Jewsbury. Summer Eve's Vision, A.
Jiménez, J. I Pulled on the Reins.
Johnson, M. Dream, A.
Jones, E. Dream, A.
Jonson, B. Dream, The.
Jordan, A. Beggar's Song.
Joseph, J. Instead of a Mystery.
Kahn, G. I'll See You in My Dreams.
You Stepped Out of a Dream.
Kane, P. Disciples Asleep at Gethsemane.
Kang Ün'gyo. In the Fog.
Sound 8.
Kapovich, K. Something from an untidy Russian life.
Kasa. Have I let my love.
Kasischke. Housekeeping in a Dream.
Kaufman, B. African Dream.
Keats. Fall of Hyperion, The; A Dream.
Sudden a thought came like a full-blown rose.
Kelly, B. Orchard, The.
Kendall, M. Pure Hypothesis, A.
Kennelly. Dream of a Black Fox.
Kim Ch'unsu [or Chun-soo]. Masks.
Kim Hyesun. Daybreak in Seoul.
Inside the Iris.
Kim Sangyong. Love Is False.
King, H. Dream Maiden, A.
Kinsella, T. Nuchal, a Fragment.
Wormwood.
Kipling, R. If.
Koehler, T. Wrap Your Troubles in Dreams.
Kossman. Pilate's Wife.
Kuan Hsiu. I came in a dream to a mountain in the sea.
Kumin, M. Making the Jam without You.
Kyle, C. J. Fire in Early Morning.
Lane, P. Girl at the Window.
Nuclear Peril.
Langland, W. Dreamer Meets Conscience and Reason.
Thus I awoke, God knows, when I lived in Cornhill.
Layamon. Arthur's Dream.
Lazutkina, E. Wind's mane, The.
Leconte de Lisle, C. Jaguar's Dream, The.
Lee, L. Pillow.
Lehmann, G. Roses.
Lenski, H. There broke into my cell last night.
Leong, R. What Does the Body Dream at Rest?
Lermontov. Dream.
Levertov. Don't You Hear that Whistle Blowin'.
To Rilke.
Levi, P. Reveille.
Levine, P. Soloing.
Waking in March.
Levy, A. Cambridge in the Long.
Old House, The.
On the Threshold.
Lewis, S. Street of Dreams.
Li Ch'ing-chao. Tune: "Airing Inmost Feelings".
Tune: "Dream Song".
Li Po. My Trip in a Dream to the Lady of Heaven Mountain A Farewell to Several Gentlemen of Eastern Lu.
Li Yu [or Li Hou-Chu]. Immeasurable Pain.
My Idlest Dreams.
One Dream.
Lilley, Gary. Funeral: "Naked in eastern mournin sun."
Lim, S. Modern Secrets.
Llwyd, Iwan. Harley Davidson.
Loden. Gospel According to Clairol, The.
Loesser. Sit Down, You're Rockin' the Boat.
Longfellow, H. Golden Mile-Stone, The.
Lopez, L. To a Coal Miner in Madrid, New

Mexico.
Louise, E.   Swinging doors of knocking-wood cowards: 8 for us.
Lowell, J.   Aladdin.
Lu Yu.   Night Thoughts.
Lum.   Chinese Hot Pot.
Mabuza.   Dream Cloud.
Machado Ruiz.   And He Was the Evil Spirit of My Dreams.
Between living and dreaming.
Clouds Ripped Open.
From the Doorsill of a Dream.
I go on dreaming.
It Doesn't Matter Now.
It's Possible That While We Were Dreaming.
Last Night.
Last night while I was sleeping.
Parables, I.
Yesterday, dreamed He was near me.
Mackenzie, K.   Sick Men Sleeping.
Mackey, N.   Winged Abyss.
MacNeice.   Bad Dream.
Mallarmé.   Afternoon of a Faun, The.
Mandelstam [or Mandelshtam].   I Am Deaf.
Mansour, J.   I Saw You through My Closed Eye.
Martí.   I Dream Awake.
Martinaitis, M.   Kukutis's Consciousness Becomes Alienated.
McAuley, J.   Dialogue.
McClure, M.   PLEASURE FEARS ME, FOOT ROSE, FOOT BREATH.
McFadden, D.   2. Night Bus to Montreal.
McKinnon, K.   Vintage.
Mehmedinović, Semezdin.   Only Dream, The.
Mei Yao Ch'en.   Dream at Night, A.
Melançon, Robert.   Wakening.
Meleager.   Epigram: "At 12 o'clock in the afternoon."
Night Alone, The.
Melville, E.   Upon one day as I did mourn full sore.
Melville, H.   Rose Window.
To ———: "Ah, wherefore, lonely, to and fro."
Meng Hao Jan.   Spring Dreams.
Mengham, Rod.   Names in the Bark.
Menken.   Dreams of Beauty.
Meredith, W.   Bachelor.
Merrill, J.   Mad Scene, The.
Merwin.   Carol: "On vague hills the prophet bird."
Mew.   Ne Me Tangito.
Not for That City.
Michaelis.   I Was About Three Years of Age.
Miles, J.   Dear Frank, Here is a poem.
Dream: "I see you displaced, condensed, within my dream."
Miljkovic.   Sleepers.
Milton.   On His Deceased Wife.
Mitchell, K.   Monster, The.
Mitchell, N.   Incognito.
Miyazawa Kenji.   Daydreaming on the Trail.
Mok, J.   Winter Mirror II.
Momaday.   Carriers of the Dream Wheel.
Montale.   In the Greenhouse.
Prisoner's Dream, The.
Montgomerie, A.   Dreame, Ane.
Moore, H.   Window at Key West, A.
Moxley, Jennifer.   From a Distance I Can See.
Muir, E.   Adam's Dream.
Brothers, The.
Labyrinth, The.
Myŏngok.   Dreams.
They say dream visits.
Nara Singde.   Tune: "As If in a Dream".
Negroni, M.   Theory of a Good Death.
Nelson, M.   Motel Story.
Nguyễn Chí Thiện.   Party holds you down and you lie still, The.
Niedecker.   Subliminal.
Nikolic, G.   Key to Dreams.
No Hyangnim.   Dream: "Sea was in front of me, The."
Nordbrandt.   Streets.
Norton, C.   Dreams: "Surely I heard a voice—surely my name."
Notley.   Where Leftover Misery Goes.

Noyes, S.   Dream Painter, The.
Oldham, J.   One night, as I was pondering of late.
Ome Shushiki.   After dream / How real.
Ono no Komachi.   Although my feet.
Thinking about him.
Though I go to you.
Oppen.   Resort.
Orlovsky.   Dream May 18, 1958.
I Dream of St. Francis.
Orpingalik.   Alcheringa Definitions.
Orr, G.   All Morning.
O'Shaughnessy, A.   Ode: "We are the music-makers."
Otomo no Sakanoé, L.   Till the rough-gem moon.
Owen, W.   Strange Meeting.
Padgett, R.   Light as Air.
Pak Hyogwan.   If my lovesick dream.
She came to my dream.
Pak Sŏwŏn.   Recurring Nightmare, A: My Amputation.
Palmer, M.   Dream of a Language that Speaks.
Erolog.
Parfi, R.   Today I dreamed all day. I dreamed.
Parker, A.   Vandals, Horses.
Parker, P.   I Have a Dream.
Parkes, B.   Dream Fears.
Pastan.   September.
Phillips, C.   As a Blow, from the West.
Phillips, D.   On Entries Emptiness.
Pietri.   Intermission from Saturday.
Night Is out of Sight, The.
Plumpp.   Daybreak wakes.
Po Chü-i.   Dream of Mountaineering, A.
Dreaming of Yuan Zhen.
Night Duty in the Palace, Dreaming of a Hsien-yu Temple.
Sleeping on Horseback.
Poe.   Dream within a Dream, A.
Dream-Land [or Dreamland].
Dreams: "Oh! That my young life were a lasting dream!"
Fairyland [or Fairy-Land].
To One in Paradise.
Pogson, P.   In Dreams.
Pollak, F.   Dream, The.
Popa.   Dream of the Quartz Pebble, The.
Pound, E.   To Kalon.
Powell, D. A.   Nicholas the ridiculous: you will always be 27 and impossible. No more expectations.
Powell, K.   What the Deal, Son?
Prados, E.   I Locked the World Out.
Rafferty, P.   Personal.
Rakosi.   Journey Away, A.
Ramke, B.   Difference between Night and Day, The.
Ransom, J.   Prelude to an Evening.
Rees-Jones.   Making for Planet Alice.
Reverdy.   Internal Travels.
Rexroth, K.   Poem: "As the full moon rises."
Rich, A.   I wake up in your bed. I know I have been dreaming.
Jerusalem.
Riley, J.   As one who cons at evening o'er an album, all alone.
Rimbaud, A.   Runt of a Dream, A.
Robinson, A.   Pallor.
Robinson, E.   Miniver Cheevy.
Robinson, M.   Dreams of a Rival.
Visions Appear to Her in a Dream.
Rodney.   Bardo of Sleep and Dream.
Roethke.   Dream, The.
Roland Holst.   Being.
Rossetti, C.   Echo.
I dream of you to wake: would that I might.
My Dream.
Old-World Thicket, An.
On the Wing.
Reflection.
Rossetti, D.   Orchard-Pit, The.
Rózewicz.   Memory of a Dream from the Year 1963.
Return, The.
Ruefle.   Before Bed.

Rukeyser, M.   Burning the Dreams.
Nevertheless the Moon.
Rumi.   Night and Sleep.
Sachs, N.   Sleepwalker, The.
St. John, D.   Opal Trees, The.
Salaam.   Round Midnight, Place de Congo.
Salom.   World of Dreams, The.
Samawi, S.   Quartets of Inner Whispering.
Sanchez, S.   Blues.
Sandburg, C.   Among the Red Guns.
Mamie.
Murmurings in a Field Hospital.
Portrait of a Motorcar.
Prayers of Steel.
Sanguineti.   What you're reading (if you're reading me) are the effects.
Santayana.   Sonnet 5: "Dreamt I today [or to-day] the dream of yesternight."
When I discover that the substance of the beautiful is a certain rhythm.
Sappho.   Black Dream, you come.
Sarton, M.   Nursery Rhyme.
Schjeldahl.   Adventures with Nick & Cindy.
David's Sister.
Dynamite.
Reading, The.
Talking to Arlene.
Schwartz, D.   O Child, Do Not Fear the Dark and Sleep's Dark Possession.
Segovia, F.   Ahí Donde Duermes.
There Where You Sleep.
Seibles, T.   4AM.
Seuss, D.   Purpose.
Seward.   Invocation, To the Genius of Slumber Written Oct. 1787.
Sexton.   Author of the Jesus Papers Speaks, The.
Dreams.
Sexton, M.   Marriage Patois.
Shakespeare, W.   Sonnet 27: "Weary with toil, I haste me to my bed."
Shange.   Dream of Pairing.
Sharma, P.   Action-Packed Sonnet.
Shelley, M.   Stanzas: "Oh, come to me in dreams, my love!"
Shelley, P.   Indian Serenade, The.
Poet wandering on, through Araby, The.
Shen Yüeh.   Seeing the Beloved in a Dream.
Shinkichi Takahashi.   Sea of Oblivion.
Sparrow and Bird-Net Building.
Shrine Priestess of Ise.   My mind is dazzled.
"Shu Ting.".   Singing Flower, The.
Shumyatsher, E.   Earth Dream.
"Shunzei's Daughter.".   Brought by the breeze.
Silberg, Richard.   Audience, The.
Simic.   Empire of Dreams.
Simon, L.   Kali.
Skelton, R.   Night Piece.
Smith, C.   To Sleep.
Where the wild woods and pathless forests frown.
Smith, S.   Songe d'Athalie.
Snyder, G.   For a Stone Girl at Sanchi.
Soto, Maria Viviana.   I dream of you.
Stadler.   Saying, The.
Stafford, W.   Vocation.
Stern, G.   Lucky Life.
Stepping Out of Poetry.
Stevens, W.   Disillusionment of Ten O'Clock.
Stoddard, C.   Old Monterey.
Stokesbury.   Bottom's Dream.
Su Tung-p'o.   Southern Room over the River, The.
Subbarao, N.   You in My Dream.
Suckling, S.   Dream, A.
Swinburne.   Love And Sleep.
Synková, A.   To Olga.
Tada.   Odyssey or "On Absence," The.
Taggard.   Demeter.
Taha, A.   Wall of Genesis, The.
Talvikki, A.   You Don't Know What Happened When You Froze.
Taylor, H.   Buildings and Grounds.
Tekeyan.   Dream.
Timrod.   Dreams.
Todd, M.   To Kill Stray Dogs.

Toomer. Evening Song.
Tree-Leaf Woman. Who speaks the sound of an echo?
Tsvetayeva [or Tsvetaeva]. In my enormous city it is—night.
Tu Fu [or Du Fu]. Daytime Dream.
  Dreaming of Li Po ("Death at least gives separation repose.").
  Dreaming of Li Po ("Death separation: sobs hard to swallow.").
Tu Mu. Easing My Heart.
Turner, C. Dream, A.
Turner, W. Romance.
Unamuno. Delicately Sloping Neck, The.
Unknown. And in the mountains of Kiev, Sviatoslav.
  Come quickly, my love, so I can give you my mouth!
  Dream of the Rood, The.
  Girl with the Dark Hair.
  In the early hours of the next morning dawning.
  Last night I had a dream.
  Last night I had a dream that has come true.
  Limerick: "There was an old man of [or from] Peru / Who dreamt [or dreamed] he was eating his shoe."
  Message of King Sakis and the Legend of the Twelve Dreams He Had in One Night, The.
  Poet Dreamt of Heaven, The.
  So it is because.
  Those Women.
  Wild Dreams, The.
  You intend, it seems.
Valentine, J. Sleep Drops Its Nets.
Valéry. Spinner, The.
Van Doren. Dream of Trains, A.
Van Walleghen. In the Chariot Drawn by Dragons.
Vanshenkin. Girl dreams of her lover at night, The.
Verwey, A. North-Sea, The.
Villaurrutia. Nocturne of the Statue.
Volkman. Sonnet: "As the dream a consciousness adored."
Wang Ch'ang-ling. Autumn Evening on the Great Lake.
Wang Ji. Written on the Tavern Wall.
Wang Kuo-wei. Tune: "Rouged Lips".
Wang Seng-ju. Describing a Dream for Someone.
Warsh. Dreaming over a Page.
Watson, R. Nirvana.
Weaver, A. Blind Solo.
Wen T'ing-yün. In Her Moonlit Chamber.
Whalen, P. We Sing in Our Sleep. We Converse with the Dead in Our Dreams.
Wheeler, Jackson. Falstaff's Dream.
Whitman, W. I wander all night in my vision.
Whitmore, S. Bird, The.
Whittier. Tent on the Beach: [The Dreamer].
Wieners. King Solomon's Magnetic Quiz.
Wilbur, R. Beasts.
  In the Smoking-Car.
  Walking to Sleep.
Wilde, L. Corinne's Last Love-Song.
Williams, Stephanie. Hope Chest.
Williams, W. Revelation, The.
  Thursday.
Williamson, G. Annual Returns.
Willis, J. Inside Our Dreams.
Wiman, C. Sweet Dreams.
Winner, S. Listen to the Mocking Bird.
Winter, M. Elegy: "There is a question."
Wintu Oral Tradition. Six Dream Songs.
Wojahn. Allegory: Attic and Fever.
Wordsworth, W. Expostulation and Reply.
  Strange Fits of Passion Have I Known ("Strange fits of passion have I known.").
Wright, F. Brugge.
Wright, J. Dream of Burial, A.
  I slouch in bed.
  Old Bud.
Wright, J. Compassion's Bird.
Wyatt. Lover Showeth How He Is Forsaken of Such as He Sometime Enjoyed, The.
Yeats. He Wishes for the Cloths of Heaven.

Host of the Air, The.
Rose of the World, The.
To the Rose upon the Rood of Time.
Yen Shu. Tune: "Treading on Fragrant Grass".
Yi Myŏnghan. If the path of my dreams.
Yi Sang. Poem No. 15.
Yi Yŏnju. Clinic in a Dangerous Season 7, A.
Yosano Akiko. Once, far over the breakers.
  What I dreamed was.
Young, M. J. To Dreams.
Yüan Chĕn. Pitcher, The.
  Three Dreams in Chiang-ling.

Dress
Addonizio. What Do Women Want?
Chrystos. I Bought a New Red.
Collins, B. Taking Off Emily Dickinson's Clothes.
Dixon, M. Lady in Red, The.
Duran, J. For the Woman Who Dressed Up to Listen to Gigli on the Radio.
Emanuel, L. White Dress, The.
Hall, H. Baby's Dress, A.
McCarthy, J. Alice Blue Gown.
Mirville, E. Pretty little dress,. . .stockings full of holes.
Muske, C. Epith.
O'Donoghue, M. Textures, The.
Parker, D. Red Dress, The.
Pearlberg, G.G. Loop-the-Loop in Prospect Park (1905).
Rosenberg, L. Big White Dress, The.
Satyanarayana, V. Song of Krishna.
Sondheim. All I Need Is the Girl.
Tzu Yeh. I had not fastened my sash over my gown.
Unknown. Others dress up in their new clothes for the feast, The.
Weeks, J. Answer by the Lady's Maid [to a Poem Left in a Lady's Toilet].
  Poem Left in a Lady's Toilet.
See also **Clothing**

Driftwood
Bynner. Driftwood.

Drinking Water
Bishop, E. Under the Window: Ouro Prêto.
De Kok. To Drink Its Water.
Goldbarth. Complete with Starry Night and Bourbon Shots.
Tranter. Tell me we will drink water, and drink to me.
Wagoner, D. Young Girl with a Pitcher Full of Water, A.

Drinks and Drinking
Ade. R-E-M-O-R-S-E.
Ai. I Can't Get Started.
Alcaeus [or Alkaios]. Come tip a few with me.
  Wet your lungs with wine—the dogstar rises.
Aldrich, H. Catch, A.
Ali Hsiying. Lazy Cloud's Nest 1.
Allen, P. Tattoo #47, "Happy Dragon".
Anacreon. Come, boy, bring us.
  Elegy 2.
Antipater of Thessalonica. I've Never Feared.
"Anvari.". Drunkenness.
Arlen, H. One for My Baby (And One More for the Road).
Barnes, B. Something Cool.
Belloc. West Sussex Drinking Song.
Bitar. Happy Hour.
Brecht, B. Three Fragments.
Brome. Come a *brimmer* (my bullies) drink whole ones or nothing.
Brooks, G. We Real Cool.
Bukowski. Crucifix in a Deathhand.
  Not Much Singing.
Burns, R. Auld Lang Syne.
  Scotch Drink.
  Tam o' Shanter; A Tale.
Carver, R. Drinking While Driving.
Celan. I Am the First.
Ceravolo. Geological Hymn.
Chang Yang-hao. Ch'ü Yüan's "sorrow".
Chavez, L. After the Prom.
Ch'en Yü-yi. Tune: "Immortal at the Riverbank".

Ch'ien T'ao. Blaming Sons.
Ch'in Kuan. Tune: "Happiness Approaches".
  Tune: "Rouged Lips".
Cho Chonsŏng. Boy, lead a cow to the northern village.
Cho-yong. Song: "I carouse all night."
Chŏng Ch'ŏl. Let's drink a cup of wine; let's drink another!
Claman, E. Show Biz Parties.
Cleary, B. Boys' Own.
Coolidge, C. Some Glow on the Sill.
Cope, W. Usquebaugh.
Cornish, S. His Fingers Seem to Sing.
Cornwall. For a Fountain.
Coslow, S. Cocktails for Two.
Cowley, A. Drinking.
Crane, H. Wine Menagerie, The.
Cunningham, J. Interview with Doctor Drink.
Curbelo. Drinking Song.
  Last Call.
Davis, J. Desolation.
De Vries, P. Bacchanal.
Dickinson, E. I Taste a Liquor Never Brewed.
  Strong Draughts of Their Refreshing Minds.
Doyle, S. Hell to Pay.
Dressel. Dai, Live.
Drummond de Andrade. Seven-Sided Poem.
Dugan, A. Drunken Memories of Anne Sexton.
Dumas, H. Knees of a Natural Man.
Elizabeth, M. On the Porch—Denton, Texas.
Etter. Drink and Agriculture.
Eubulus. Benefits and Abuse of Alcohol, The.
Ewart. Yorkshiremen in Pub Gardens.
Faiz. Prison Daybreak, A.
Fergusson. Daft Days, The.
Fincke. Class A, Salem, the Rookie League.
Flanders, M. Have Some Madeira, M'dear?
Forbes, C. Potter's Wheel, The.
Foster, S. Conant. Toasting Song.
Gannon, K. Moonlight Cocktail.
Gillespie, H. You Go to My Head.
Glaser, E. Blues for the Nightowl.
Gorey. Limerick: "From the bathing machine came a din."
  Limerick: "Some Harvard men, stalwart and hairy."
Greenwell, D. To Christina Rossetti.
Gregerman, D. High Speed.
Guillén, N. Wake for Papa Montero.
Gunn, T. Donahue's Sister.
Gwyer, J. Intoxicating draughts he never does drink.
Hafiz, K [or Hafez]. Light of my eyes, there *is* something to be said.
Halliday, M. Questmale.
Harms. From Now On.
Hass, R. Our Lady of the Snows.
Haug. Tennessee Waltz, The.
Heaney, S. Drink of Water, A.
  Sloe Gin.
Hecht, A. Ghost in the Martini, The.
Hernández Cruz. Perlas.
Herrick. To Live Merrily, and to Trust to Good Verses.
  Wassaile, The.
Ho Ch'i-fang. Get Drunk.
Homyo. Wino, always stumbling.
Hsin Ch'i-chi. Tune: "Spring in the Ch'in Garden".
Hudgins. Praying Drunk.
Hughes, L. Bar.
  Morning After.
  Neighbor.
Hugo, V. After the Battle.
Ibn Hamdîs, I. I remember a certain brook that offered the impiety of drunkenness to the topers [sitting] along its course, with [its] cups of golden [wine].
Ibn Quzman, A. I am madly in love despite the angry behavior of one who finds fault [with me]!
Iozia, J. Last Night at the Flamingo.
Johnston, M. Café of Situations, The.
  Drinking Sappho Brand Ouzo.
  Sea-Cucumber, A.
Jonson, B. Song. To Celia ("Drink to me only

with thine eyes.").

Kasischke. Grace.

Kendrick, D. 26th Person, The.

Kennedy, X. In a Prominent Bar in Secaucus [One Day].

Komunyakaa, Y. White Port and Lemon Juice.

Lal Ded [or Lalla]. I searched for my Self.

Larkin, J. Good-Bye.

Larkin, P. Aubade: "I work all day, and get half-drunk at night."

Lewis, G. Hedge, The.

Li Ch'ing-chao. To the Tune: Bodhisattva's Headdress.

Li Ho. Drinking All Night, Sleeping All Day. King Ch'in Drinks Wine.

Li Po. Awakening from Drunkenness on a Spring Day.
Best of Life Is But, The.
Drinking Alone in Moonlight.
Drinking Alone in the Moonlight.
Drinking Alone under Moonlight.
Drinking Alone with the Moon.
Drinking Wine with a Mountain Hermit.
Drinking with a Friend, Among the Mountains.
For the Dancer of the King of Wu, When She Is Half Drunk.
Mountain Drinking Song.
Night with a Friend, A.
Remembering Our Excursion in the Past.
Solitary Carouse on a Day in Spring, A.

Livingston, M. Lemonade Stand.

Lopez, L. NEHI Strawberry Down-and-Away.

Lowry, M. Eye-Opener.

Lu Chih. Tune: "Drunk in the East Wind".

Lyly, J. Serving Men's Song, A.

Mallarmé. Toast.

Mandelstam [or Mandelshtam]. I Drink to the Asters of War.

Masefield. Captain Stratton's Fancy.

Mathias, R. Testament.

McDaniel, J. First One, The.

McIlroy, L. Siesta.

Mei Yao Ch'en. Necessities.

Mercer, J. One for My Baby (And One More for the Road).

Messerli. Actually Swallowed.

Mihalic. Drinking Spree Beneath the Open Sky.

Montague, J. Drink of Milk, A.

Moorer. Circle, The.
Social Glass, The.

Morton, T. Song, The: "Drink and be merry, merry, merry boys."

Nabi. When we watch the spinning of the sky.

Nash, O. Reflections on Ice-breaking.

Nedim. At the gathering of desire you made me a wine-cup.

Okudzhava. Ruispiri—A Comic Ballad.

O'odham. No. 81. We Will Join Them.
No. 83. The Women Are Singing.

Otomo no Tabito. To sit silent.

Padel, R. Scotch.

Pak Inhwan. Rocking Horse and the Lady, The.

Paschen. Confederacy.

Patchen. Great-Sledmakers, The.

Peacock, M. Say You Love Me.

Péret. Fountain.

Po Chü-i. After Getting Drunk, Becoming Sober in the Night.

Pollard, C. I enjoy dancing.

Rafferty, C. Man on the Tower, The.

Ramsay, A. Up in the Air.

Randall, D. Old Witherington.

Redi. Bacchus's Opinion of Wine, and Other Beverages.

Rimbaud, A. Thirst.

Robinson, A. Oasis, An.

Robinson, E. Miniver Cheevy.
Mr Flood's Party.

Rochester, J. Ramble in St. James's Park, A.

Roethke. My Papa's Waltz.

Rohrer, M. I went out one night with people from work.

Rossetti, C. Better Resurrection, A.

Rouse, A. England Nil.
Glass.

Rumi. Two strong impulses: One.

St. John, D. Gin.

Salaam. All Nite Long.

San Juan. Entelechy on the Libidinal Fringe.
Three for the Road.

Sanders P. Tripoli.

Sapgir. Dionysus.

Sappho. There a bowl of ambrosia.

Scott, J. Plato's Dog.

Sen, R. Hey, it's not wine I drink.

Shen Yüeh. Green, Green Riverside Grass.

Sheridan, R. Drinking Song.

Smith, S. Grace of God and the Meth-Drinker, The.

Snyder, G. I Went into the Maverick Bar.

Solie, Karen. Larking.

Soupault. To Drink.

Starbuck, G. Working Habits.

Stein, K. Terms.

Stephens, J. Glass of Beer, A.
What Thomas an Buile Said in a Pub.

Stevenson, W. et al. Back and Side Go Bare, Go Bare.

Strayhorn, B. Lush Life.

Su Tung-p'o. Tune: "A Riverside Town."
Tune: "Immortal by the River."
Tune: "Water Mode Song."

Suárez, V. Donatilia's Unrequited Love Remedy.

Szymborska, W. Drinking Wine ("He looked, and gave me beauty.").

T'ao Ch'ien [or T'ao Yuan-ming]. Putting the Blame on His Sons.
Two Poems Written While Drunk.
Written on the Ninth Day of the Ninth Month of the Year Yi-you.

Tranter. Hang up a yellow shirt—you cause joy.

Tu Fu [or Du Fu]. Crooked River Meditation.
Drinking at Crooked River.
Drinking with Elder Cheng the Eighth at Crooked River.
Guest Arrives, A ("North of my lodge, south of my lodge, spring rivers all.").
Snow Storm.

Tu Mu. Take the Bottle, and Ascend.

Unknown. Finnegan's Wake.
I have no pain, dear mother, now.
Judged by the Company One Keeps.
Love.
Riddle: "As I went through yon guttery gap / I met my Uncle Davy."

Valentine, J. Night Lake.

Vietnamese Oral Tradition. Whisky Lovers.

Villa, D. then if I think about it.

Voznesensky [or Voznesenskii].
Darkmotherscream.

Wang Ch'ang-ling. At the Stream's Source in Spring: A Party.

Wang Fan-chih. Drinking Alone.

Wang Han. Reason Fair, A (Liangzhou Song).

Webster, A. Circe.

Winch. Shadow Grammar.

Wright, J. Journey to the Place of Ghosts.

Yevtushenko [or Evtushenko]. Siberian Wooing.

Young, G. Lips That Touch Liquor.

Zappala, Robyn. Hope: "She has a way of standing as if a belt of weights."

See also **Alcoholism and Alcoholics; Drunkards**

Driving and Drivers

Allen, P. Pickup.

Anania. Interstate 80.

Andrew, G. Rolls-Royce Dreams.

Belieu. How the Elderly Drive.

Blackburn, P. El Camino Verde.

Bowering, G. Do Sink.

Brown, K. First Time at the Wheel.

Bryce, Colette. Day: "That was the day that went too far."
Epilogue: "Journey back was a nightmare, The."

Burnside, J. Out of Exile.

Bye. Car Music.

Ceni, A. Atrium.

Cherry, K. Late Afternoon at the Arboretum.

Christensen, Paul. Driving Towards Houston.

Clanchy, K. Driving to the Hospital.

Clary. Restless before the canary, wave of traffic on an inhale, I can just barely see on a

dark blue ground black arabesques.

Cofer, J. Seizing the Day.

Coolidge, C. Miss ship.

Creeley. I Know a Man.

Cummings, E. E. She being Brand.

Cunningham, J. I drive Eastward. The ethics of return.
I drive Westward. Tumble and loco weed.
On either side of the white line.

Dauenhauer, R. Driving in a Snowstorm, King Salmon to Naknek.

Davis, G. August Fires.

Dove, R. Nigger Song: An Odyssey.

Draycott. Night Driving.

Dunn, A. Radio.

Egatz, R. Into First.

Elfyn, Menna. Driver.

Erdrich. Lady in the Pink Mustang, The.

Espada. Fidel in Ohio.
Jeep Driver, The.

Freeman, Jessica. Mourning dove ragpicks bargemen.

Gillespie, N. Bus Driver, The.
Road Kill.

Ginsberg, A. Green Automobile, The.

Gioia. Cruising with the Beach Boys.

Giovanni. Monday.

Gloria. Touch.

Heaney, S. From the Frontier of Writing.
Peninsula, The.
Postscript.

Hejinian. Nostalgia is the elixir drained.

Herbert, W. Slow Animals Crossing.

Jackson, F. Highway 5.

Jernigan, Marla. Kind of Ransom.

Jones, B. Engine Driver.

Joseph, A. Learning to Drive at 32.

Justice, D. Poem to Be Read at 3 a.m.

Keller, D. After Supper.

Kim Hyesun. Driving During a Shower.

Kinnell. Sheffield Ghazal 4: Driving West.

Kyger. News bulletin from Keith Lampe.

Laux, D. Singing Back the World.

Lea, S. Tempted by the Classical on Returning from the Store at Twenty Below Zero.

Lehman. First Offense.

Levine, P. I Caught a Glimpse.
Return, The: "All afternoon my father drove the country roads."

London, S. Cold War.

Lux. Black Road Over Which Green Trees Grow.
Wife Hits Moose.

Mateo. Jeepneyfying.

McFerren. Metaphor Crosses the Road, A.

McNiece, R. Driving the Midwest.

Miles, J. Reason: "Said, Pull her up a bit will you, Mac, I want to unload there."

Millar, J. Poem for a New Girlfriend.

Mitchison. Nettlebed Road.

Morgan, E. Birthday, The: "I'm driving tonight into November."

Morgan, R. Rearview Mirror.

Morris, H. Duesenberg, 1929.

Muldoon, P. Hard Drive.

Muske, C. Coming Over Coldwater.

Orr, G. Lament: "I thought of you."

O'Sullivan, L. Getaway Car.

Parker, A. Driving Past My Exit.

Phillips, R. Drive Friendly.

Prunty. Elderly Lady Crossing on Green.

Revard. Driving in Oklahoma.

Rohrer, J. Gearshift Poem, The.

Ruefle. Perpetually Attempting to Soar.

Rukeyser, M. Sand-Quarry with Moving Figures.

Sabry, M. Marionette.

Seibles, T. 4AM.

Serros, M. Mr. BOOM BOOM Man.

Singleton, Giovanni. Defensive Driving.

Smukler. Home in Three Days. Don't Wash.

Sobin, Anthony. Driving Home to See the Folks.

Stevens, W. Reality Is an Activity of the Most August Imagination.

Sundiata. Blink Your Eyes.

Sze. Bajada, La.
Teitelboim, D. Threesome.
Turner, F. Poet Gets Drowsy on the Road, The.
Unknown. When I start my fast driving.
Upton, L. Somewhere So Lush.
Van Duyn. Vision Test, The.
Vanek, Mary. Homing Instinct.
Voigt. Stone Pond.
Volkman. Now I promise the shriek that the pressure of days, the pressure of days will be weapon.
Wallace, R. Smoking.
Ward, J. Eros: "Valley of the Usk, exactly mid-distant."
Whalen, P. Perpetuum Mobile.
Williams, M. 152 Into 5,*El Centro Palabra de Fe.*
South.
Williams, W. Right of Way, The.
Yost, C. Escaping from Autopia.
Zagajewski. Quick Poem, A.

Drought
Brathwaite, E. Prelude: "Drum skin whip."
Caraion. Remember.
Crews, J. It Is Not Golgotha—It Is.
Davison, P. Frozen Drought.
Dressel. Drouth, The.
Duncan, E. Drought.
Fink, Robert A. Drought: Sure Signs in Merkle, Texas.
Gorbanevskaya. Drought, malevolent stepmother.
Grin, B. Rain: "Little ears of corn are parched, The."
Hannon. Subterranean.
Hummell, A. Salt Longing.
Keeler, C. Drouth, The.
Lewis, A. Mahratta Ghats, The.
Mocoancoeng, J.G. Drought.
Murphy, M. Al-Khamasin.
Murray, L. Craze Field, The.
Osundare. Who Says That Drought Was Here?
Siegel, J. Drought.
Simmons, N. Black Sunday, April 14, 1935.
Soto. Drought, The.
Su Tung-p'o. Little stream used to cross my land, A.
Wright, J. Drought Year.

Drowning
Aiken, C. Solitaire.
Atwood. Death of a Young Son by Drowning. This Is a Photograph of Me.
Barrax. Scuba Diver Recovers the Body of a Drowned Child, The.
Behn, R. Drownproofing Lesson.
Benn. Little Aster.
Bierds, L. Safe.
Bloch, C. Kiss, The.
Brewer, G. Teen Drowns in Rehabilitation Camp Days Before 17th Birthday, Questions Persist.
Cavafy. Supplication.
Claus. Ten Ways of Looking at P.B. Shelley. Tien manieren om P.B. Shelley te zien.
Cofer, J. Drowned Sailor, The.
Cowper, W. Castaway, The.
Crane, S. Man adrift on a slim spar, A.
Dawe, B. Elegy for Drowned Children.
Dawe, Tom. Daedalus.
Delgado, J. La Llorona.
Dickinson, E. Drowning is not so pitiful.
Dobson, R. Three Fates, The.
Donne. Burnt Ship, A.
Hero and Leander.
Doolittle, H. So I would rather drown, remembering.
Doty, M. Death of Antinoüs.
Eliot, T. S. 4. Death by Water.
Field, E. Icarus.
Friman. Ophelia.
Glück, L. Drowned Children, The.
Gonzalez, R. Angels of Juárez, Mexico, The.
Gray, T. Ode on the Death of a Favo[u]rite Cat, Drowned in a Tub [or Bowl] of Gold Fishes.
Greening, M. Missing — Believed Drowned.
Hauge. Across the Swamp.

Heaney, S. Limbo.
Holden, M. Seaman, 1941.
Holmes, O. Ballad of the Oysterman, The.
Hopkins, G. Wreck of the Deutschland, The.
Houlihan, J. Incarnation.
Hugo, R. Lady in Kicking Horse Reservoir, The.
Janzen, J. At Summer's End.
Johnson, J. Midnight Run.
Jones, R. Portrait of My Father and His Grandson.
Kendrick, D. Drowned River, The.
Kingsley, C. Sands of Dee, The.
Kinsella, J. Drowning in Wheat.
Komunyakaa, Y. Let's Say.
Kumin, M. Junior Life Saving.
Lux. Tarantulas on the Lifebuoy.
Magdeburg, Mechthild von. Fish cannot drown in water, A.
Millay, E. Burial.
Milton. Lycidas.
Montrose, Percy. My Darling Clementine.
Moss, H. Water Island.
Mother Goose. Ding, dong, bell.
Motion, A. Close.
Norwood, Nick. For the Drowned.
Oliver, D. Oracle of the Drowned, The.
Olson, C. Pacific Lament.
Parker, D. Résumé.
Parry-Williams. From a Travel Diary.
Petrushevskaya, L. Poor Ruth.
Ramanujan. Breaded Fish.
Rendra. Baby at the Bottom of the River.
Rodgers, Gordon. Drowned.
On the Ice.
Salom. Winter.
Santos, S. Still Life with Minnows.
Schjeldahl. Ocean Liner.
Shakespeare, W. Full Fathom Five.
Slutsky [or Slutskii]. Horses in the Ocean.
Smith, S. Not Waving but Drowning.
Sŏ Chŏngju. Great Wave, The.
Stillman, M. Ophelia.
Stoutenburg. Before We Drown.
Synge. 'Mergency Man, The.
Theodoridas. Epitaph, An: "This is a drowned man's tomb. Sail on, stranger."
Thomas, E. Midnight Thought, A. On the Death of Mrs. E. H. and Her Little Daughter.
Twain. Emmeline Grangerford's Ode to Stephen Dowling Bots, Dec'd.
Unknown. Clementine.
Sir Patrick Spens [or Spence].
Tweed and Till.
Vogel, D. I Saw My Father Drowning.
Watts, Enos D. Summer Solstice.
Wheelwright. Fish Food.
Wilbur, R. Marginalia.
Williams, W. Landscape with the Fall of Icarus.
Wright, J. In Response to a Rumor that the Oldest Whorehouse in Wheeling, West Virginia, Has Been Condemned.
Note Left in Jimmy Leonard's Shack, A.
Wright, J. Eli, Eli.
Wylie. Drowned Woman.
Sea Lullaby.

Drowsiness
Brunk, J. All Sweet Things, Like Forgiveness, Are a Falling.

Drug Addiction
Adamson. Passing through Experiences.
Ai. Archangel.
Self Defense.
Akhmadulina. Coffee Imp, The.
Anderson, D. Itinerary.
Baraka, I. Babylon Revisited.
Barresi. Venice Beach: Brief Song.
Beatty, P. Doggin the Rockman.
Brooks, G. Coora Flower, The.
Brown, P. I Remember Dexedrine. 1970.
Campo. Jane Doe #2.
Carroll, J. Paregoric Babies.
Withdrawal Letter.
Clifton, L. White Lady.
Cuthand, B. She Ties Her Bandanna.
DJ Renegade. Father and Son.

Dransfield. Fix.
Dubin, A. You're Getting to Be a Habit with Me.
Fanthorpe. Person's Tale, The.
Forbes, J. Speed, a Pastoral.
Goff, C. Addiction.
Gould, J. I Learn a Lesson about Our Society.
Gunn, T. Street Song.
Hicok. Heroin.
Hirsch, E. Art Pepper.
Hope, A. Under Sedation.
Howe, M. Recovery.
Hull, L. Adagio.
Visiting Hour.
Jarrell, R. Say Good-bye to Big Daddy.
Jauss. Black Orchid.
Jones, J. Drugs.
Jordan, A. Kind of Blue.
Knight, E. Another Poem for Me (after Recovering from an O.D.).
Idea of Ancestry, The.
Welcome Back, Mr. Knight: Love of My Life.
Komunyakaa, Y. Addiction.
McLaughlin-Carruth, J. Black Irish Blues.
Mead, J. Fall: "This morning I found."
Memory, The.
On the Lawn at the Drug Rehab Center.
Medina, T. Rhudine Rhudine.
Moore, H. Blues: "I meet you again in public. I."
Murray, L. Drugs of War, The.
Roberts, C. Leopard, The.
Sanchez, S. Summer Words of [or for] a Sistuh [or Sister] Addict.
St. Germain, S. Addiction.
Stone, A. Spofford Hall.
Thomas, L. Historiography.
Tucker, M. Opium-Eater, The.
Unknown. Face haggard turning yellow and puffy.
Waring, B. Refuge at the One Step Down.
Warsh. White Nights.
Weisburd, S. Sponge Boy.
Williams, K. Snapshot: West Philly.
Worley, D. Sandra.

Drugs
Anderson, D. Itinerary.
Beckman, J. I like your handsome drugs. Your pleasant.
Berrigan, T. Dear Margie, hello. It is 5:15 a.m. Personal Poem # 7.
Cafagña, M. Lithium.
Carroll, J. Maybe I'm Amazed.
Clampitt. Cure at Porlock, A.
Cooper, D. Drugs.
Espinet, R. Merchant of Death.
Fisher, J. Life, A.
Galvin, J. Station (4).
Ginsberg, A. Mescaline.
Goodtimes. Learning to Smile.
Gunn, T. Painkillers.
Victim, The.
Harding, D. Intelligence Quotient, The.
Herrera. Future Martyr of Supersonic Waves.
Howe, M. Certain Light, A.
Iozia, J. Last Night at the Flamingo.
Jackson, M. L. Euphoria.
Jackson, R. Tee.
Jarman, M. Black Riviera, The.
Jones, J. Drugs.
Katz, J. Falling.
Kenyon, J. Back: "We try a new drug, a new combination."
Knight, E. Feeling Fucked/Up Up.
Idea of Ancestry, The.
Knox, J. Chicken Bucket.
Kolodny, S. Tsuneko—Psychiatric Medications Clinic.
Kyger. Joanne.
Lopez, T. Path Marked with Breadcrumbs, A. Studies in Classic American Literature.
Mayer, B. Maple Syrup Sonnet ("Syrup's up again.").
McCaslin, S. Triolet for the Amphetamine Afflicted.
McClure, M. Clear—the senses bright—sitting

in the black chair—Rocker.
McDaniel, J.   Friends and High Places.
Mercredi, D.   Coffee Table Blues.
Muldoon, P.   Gathering Mushrooms.
O'Hara, F.   Poem: "Green things are flowers too."
Phillips, C.   Somewhere Holy.
Pietri.   How Do Your Eggs Want You (?).
Sanchez, S.   Answer to yo / question / of am I not yo / woman / even if you went on shit again.
Schjeldahl.   Drugstore.
Selman, R.   Exodus.
Tranter.   Wild stinking fire, love and death.
Waldman, A.   How the Sestina (Yawn) Works.
Weiners.   Act #2.
   Poem for Vipers, A.
Weisburd, S.   Sponge Boy.
White, J.   Oshi.
White, M.   Foursomes.
Wojahn.   Necromancy: The Last Days of Brian Jones, 1968.

Drugstores
Anstett.   Pharmacy.
Doty, M.   Crêpe de Chine.
Goldstein, Stephanie.   At Night: "Worries creep like insects."
Schjeldahl.   Drugstore.

Druids
Nichols, G.   Long-Man.

Drummers and Drums
Adisa.   Count Ossie.
Andal.   We rose before dawn.
Andrews, L.   Time Signature.
Baca.   Voz de la Gente.
Barlow, G.   4½ Months: Halfway Song.
Baron, S.   Tom-Tom Talk.
Bethune, L.   For Singing in Good Mood.
Bontemps.   Dark Girl.
Brathwaite, E.   Making of the Drum, The.
   Wings of a Dove.
Casiano, A.   Puente.
Chipasula.   Singing Drum, The.
Dacey, P.   Drummer, The.
Dryden, J.   Trumpet's loud clangor, The.
Etter.   Stuffy Turkey.
Fearing.   Old Story.
Giovanni.   Drum, The.
Gould, R.   Amateur Drummer.
Hardy, T.   Drummer Hodge.
Hernández Cruz.   Ironing Goatskin.
Hernton, C.   Distant Drum, The.
Hughes, L.   Danse Africaine.
   Drum.
Kaufman, B.   There is a silent beat in between the drums.
Komunyakaa, Y.   Back Then.
MacLeish.   End of the World, The.
Maier, J.   Timbalero.
Momaday.   Eagle-Feather Fan, The.
Nichol.   Cycle #22.
Okara.   Piano and Drums.
Pegram, A.   I Will Still Sing.
Quasimodo.   Anno Domini MCMXLVII.
Saint-Natus, C.   Poet, The: "Voice of the drum slowly unravels, The."
Scott of Amwell.   Ode: "I hate that drum's discordant sound."
Smith, P.   They Say That Black People . . . .
Unknown.   Wizard's Chant, The.
Whitman, W.   Beat! Beat! Drums!
Yi Inbok.   Drumbeats.
Young, K.   Escape Artist, The.

Drunkards
Baillie, J.   Hooly and Fairly.
Berryman.   Alcoholic.
Bhattācārya, M.   I've gone mad drinking nectar.
Brome.   New-Courtier, The.
Burns, R.   Poor Merry-Andrew, in the neuk.
Cambridge, G.   Drunken Lyricist, The.
Cary, A.   Telling Fortunes.
Chesterton.   Rolling English Road, The.
Ch'in Kuan.   From a Dream.
Cho Wen-chun.   Poet's Wife, A.
Chŏng Ch'ŏl.   Boys have gone out to gather bracken.

Cunningham, J.   Interview with Doctor Drink.
Dickinson, E.   I Taste a Liquor Never Brewed.
Dove, R.   Genie's Prayer under the Kitchen Sink.
Drayton.   Love, in a humour, played the prodigal.
Endrezze.   Song-Maker.
Evans, G.   Renaissance Drunk, A.
Fenton, J.   Skip, The.
Gizzi, M.   Versailles.
Goodell, L.   History of Myself.
Hafiz, K [or Hafez].   As Rich as Solomon (21).
Hattersley, G.   New Mr Barnsley Something, The.
Hernández Cruz.   Scarlet Skirt.
Herrick.   Vision, The ("Methought I saw (as I did dream[e] in bed).").
Hô Sugyông.   One at Rest, The.
   Sober, Remaining.
Housman.   Could man be drunk for ever.
   Terence, this is stupid stuff.
Hsin Ch'i-chi.   Tune: "Moon of the Western River".
Hugo, R.   Neighbor.
Ibn Quzman, A.   My life is spent in dissipation and wantonness!
Khomin, I.   They drank. They ate. They smoked.
Kipling, R.   Cells.
Kochanowski, J.   In Defence of Drunkards.
Le Fanu.   Drunkard's Address to a Bottle of Whiskey, A.
Leland, C.   Wein Geist.
Levine, P.   Sweet Will.
Li Po.   Drinking in the Mountains with a Recluse.
   Drinking Together.
   Rising Drunk on a Spring Day.
Liu Ling.   Hymn to the Virtue of Wine.
Lu Yu.   Wild Flower Man, The.
MacAdams.   Pockets of Haze.
Masters, E.   Oscar Hummel.
McGrath, T.   On the Head of a Pin.
Meltzer, D.   For Jack Spicer.
Meng Hao Jan.   Late Spring.
Merwin.   Drunk in the Furnace, The.
Molloy, D.   Pascual the Shepherd.
Myers, J.   Lightweight.
Nef'i.   That black drunken eye has become a tavern.
Neruda.   Fable of the Mermaid and the Drunks.
Neto.   Saturday in the Sand-Slums.
Notley.   Jack Would Speak Through the Imperfect Medium of Alice.
Oles.   For the Drunk.
Paul, L.   Cynical Portraits.
Powell, J.   Lines Written for a Friend on the Death of His Brother, Caused by a Railway Train Running Over Him Whilst He Was in a State of Inebriation.
Ramírez, J.   Corazón mecánico.
   Mechanical Heart.
Randall, D.   Old Witherington.
Reverdy.   Internal Travels.
Rimbaud.   Morning of Drunkenness.
Robinson, E.   Miniver Cheevy.
   Mr Flood's Party.
Rumi.   Drunkards, The.
   Who Says Words with My Mouth.
Sen, R.   Mind, don't be duped by others' sneers.
Shin Kyŏngnim.   Legend.
Skelton, J.   With Lullay, Lullay, Like a Child.
Smith, S.   Grace of God and the Meth-Drinker, The.
Smith, W.   Butchertown.
   Sole of Dover.
Södergran.   Question.
Stevenson, R.   Pirate Ditty.
Tappan.   He stood, the last—the last of all.
   Onward! though ever in our march.
Thatcher, C.   Moggy's Wedding.
Tu Mu.   Take the Bottle, and Ascend.
Tucker, M.   Drunkard's Wife, The.
Unknown.   Chinook Songs.
   Drunk Man, The.
   Limerick.

Pig, The.
   Shickered as He Could Be.
   To the Tune "The Drunken Young Lord".
Valentine, J.   Everyone Was Drunk.
Wang the Zealot.   Get Blind Drunk.
Williams, K.   Snapshot: West Philly.
Work.   Come Home, Father[!].
Wright, J.   I slouch in bed.
   Note Left in Jimmy Leonard's Shack, A.
Yüan Chên.   Nearly a Sky Half Clear, Not Yet Half Light.
Zimmer.   Zimmer Drunk and Alone, Dreaming of Old Football Games.
See also Alcoholism and Alcoholics

Dryden, John
Thomas, E.   Dream, The; An Epistle to Mr. Dryden.

Du Bois, W. E. B. (William Edward Burghardt)
Randall, D.   Booker T. and W. E. B.
Rushin.   Looking for W. E. B.

Dublin, Ireland
Aled, Sion.   Weather Forecast.
Garlick, R.   Capitals.
Kavanagh, P.   Canal Bank Walk.
   Elegy for Jim Larkin.
Kennelly.   Clearing a Space.
Larkin, P.   Dublinesque.
McAuliffe, J.   North Brunswick Street Lullaby.
Quinn, J.   High and Dry.

Duchamp, Marcel
Kennedy, X.   Nude Descending a Staircase.

Ducks
Allingham, W.   Four Ducks on a Pond.
Barnard, M.   Solitary, The.
Basho.   Cold night: the wild duck.
   Sea darkening, The.
   Sea grows dark, The.
   Seas slowly darken.
   Warmly wrapped.
Bottoms.   Armored Hearts.
Buson.   Washing the hoe.
Davison, P.   From the Outland.
Dupree, E.   At Present I Am Working as a Security Guard.
Grahame, K.   Duck's Ditty.
Hardie, K.   Daniel's Duck.
Heaney, S.   Widgeon.
Ibycus.   On its highest leaves.
Iio Sogi.   Night frost / Pulsing wings.
Issa.   Ducks bobbing on the water.
   New Year's morning.
Lea, S.   Late Season.
Masaoka Shiki.   Such silence / Snow tracing wings.
Murray, L.   It is good to come out after driving and walk on the bare grass.
Nan-o-myo.   Not falling, not ignoring.
Oles.   For the Drunk.
Oliver, M.   Look and See.
Putnam.   Ship of State and Grandpa.
Shinkichi Takahashi.   Braggart Duck.
Stern, G.   Ducks Are for Our Happiness.
Unknown.   Nell Flaherty's Drake.
Upton, L.   Beatrix Potter.
Worth, V.   Duck.
Yeryomin.   Drake pays court to the duck, The.

Dudevant, Baronne
See "Sand, George" (Amandine Aurore Lucie Dupin, Baronne Dudevant)

Duels
Field, E.   Duel, The.
Unknown.   Dowie Houms o' Yarrow, The [Hogg Version from Scotch Ballads, Materials for Border Minstrelsy; Scott's Minstrelsy].

Dullness
Dryden, J.   Mac Flecknoe [or, A Satire upon the True-Blue Protestant Poet T. S.].
Greig, A.   Pre-Breakfast Rant, A.
Pope, A.   Reign of Chaos, The.
   Triumph of Dullness, The.
Pound, E.   Les Millwin.

Dumps
Khlebnikov, V.   Burning Field, The.
McHugh, H.   What Could Hold Us.
Nemerov.   Town Dump, The.

Shwarts [or Shvarts]. Dump, The.
Spires. Woman on the Dump, The.
Stevens, W. Man on the Dump, The.

Dunbar, Paul Laurence
Cullen, C. For Paul Laurence Dunbar.
Hayden, R. Paul Laurence Dunbar.
Linden, M. Paul Laurence Dunbar.
Ray, H. In Memoriam Paul Laurence Dunbar.
Reed, I. Paul Laurence Dunbar in The Tenderloin.

Duncan, Isadora
Bendall, M. Conversation with Isadora Duncan.
Martinez, D. Death of Isadora Duncan, The.

Dundee, John Graham of Claverhouse, 1st Viscount ("Bonnie Dundee")
Scott, S. Bonny [or Bonnie] Dundee.

Dunes
Ammons. Corsons Inlet.
So I Said I Am Ezra.
Frost, R. Sand Dunes.
Stuart, D. Desolation: "At the top of the dune."
Swenson, M. Wave and the Dune, The.
Teasdale. On the Dunes.
Young, C. Infidelity.

Dunkirk, France
Aragon. Night at Dunkirk.

Duns Scotus
Hopkins, G. Duns Scotus's Oxford.

Dürer, Albrecht
Bourque, D. Durer's *Apollo.*
Dove, R. Dissolve.
Great Piece of Turf, The.
"Ern Malley.". Dürer: Innsbruck, 1495.
Hill, N. Dürer's 'Young Hare.'
Jarrell, R. Knight, Death, and the Devil, The.
Moore, M. Steeple-Jack, The.

Dusk
Basho. Dusk.
Village without bells, A.
Borges. Patio.
Dunn, D. Land Love.
Everwine. Distance.
Faust, H. Six Cranes at Dusk.
Florit, E. Present Evening, The.
Gray, R. Dusk, The.
Grimké, A. Dusk.
Hewett, D. Sunset flames over the city, The.
Issa. From that woman.
Jamie, K. Skeins o Geese.
Jiménez, J. Moguer ("Dusk. Enormous clouds press down on the town.").
Tenebrae.
Kang Ŭn'gyo. Rotation 1.
Klink, J. River in Dusk.
Longfellow, H. Afternoon in February.
McMorris, M. Evening.
Merwin. Dusk in Winter.
Rohrer, M. Quick Sell the Pig.
Smith, C. Written near a Port on a Dark Evening.
Smith, L. Into Still Air.
Song Ikp'il. Boating at Dusk.
Unknown. Kadavu.
Woodcutter on His Way Home, A.
Unknown, fr. Terezin Concentration Camp. Dusk.
Voigt. Nocturne.
Volkman. Evening.
Wang Wei. Autumn Dusk at a Mountain Lodge.
Twilight in the Garden.
Ward, D. Hunting in Twilight.
My Brothers Make a Lantern.
Whitman, W. Hours Continuing Long.
Wilson, K. Dusk in My Backyard.
See also **Twilight**

Dust
Berry, W. Dust.
Blanco, R. How It Begins / How It Ends.
Borges. John 1:14 (1964).
Brooke, R. Dust.
Cather, W. Prairie Spring.
Chesterton. Praise of Dust, The.
Chin. Altar.
Dickinson, E. Death is a Dialogue between.

Dragomoschenko. Footnotes.
Faiz. No Sign of Blood.
Field. Mummy Invokes His Soul, The.
Finch, A. Sapphics for Patience.
Forrester, S. How quickly.
Frost, R. Meeting and Passing.
Gascoyne. Yves Tanguy.
Gunn, T. Elegy on the Dust.
Hall, D. Dusting.
Han-shan Te-ch'ing. Mountains stand unmoving just the way they are, The.
Janzen, J. Claiming the Dust.
Johnson, G. Common Dust.
Kanchev, Nikolai. Glory: "Sky with reddened eyelids foretells windy weather, The."
Komunyakaa, Y. *Bui Doi,* Dust of Life.
Levertov. Laying the Dust.
Manning, Maurice. O boss of ashes boss of dust.
Mistral, G. To the Children.
Murphy, M. Al-Khamasin.
Negar. Dust: "Dead ringing of distant steps, The."
Osherow. Dust on the Mantel: Sonnet.
Rakha, Y. Dust Storm, The.
Rukeyser, M. George Robinson: Blues.
Santos Chocano. Indignation.
Simmons, N. Black Sunday, April 14, 1935.
Tan Taigi. Barley's season / Dust mutes.
Tekeyan. Country of Dust, The.
Unknown. My love, open my tomb and see.
Wu-jiang da-ju: Don't Walk Beside the Big Carriage.
Wang Chiu-ssu. Floating, floating, the river waters.
Waniek. Dusting.
Wheelock, J. This Quiet Dust.

Dutch, The
Bruce, W. Holland Brick, A.
Song. Immaculate Lives.

Dutch Wars
Dryden, J. Now van to van the foremost squadrons meet.
Marvell. Character of Holland, The.
Sackville, C. Song Written at Sea in the First Dutch War (1665), the Night before an Engagement.

Duty
Aguero, Kathleen. Working Mother.
Amichai, Y. We Have Done Our Duty.
We Have Done Our Duty.
Boker. Brave comrade, answer! When you joined the war.
Chinese Oral Tradition. Transformation Text on the Boy Shun's Extreme Filial Piety.
Cornford, F. Ode on the Whole Duty Of Parents.
Emerson, R. Voluntaries.
Farley, Estelle E. Home Cookin.
Frost, R. Stopping by Woods on a Snowy Evening.
Han Yü. This morning I can't seem to get out of bed.
Hay, J. Jim Bludso of the Prairie Belle.
Herrick. Duty to Tyrants.
Hisle, Janeya K. For Fatma and Her Co-Wives.
Holub. Polonius.
Kipling, R. Eddi's Service.
McCrae, J. In Flanders Fields.
Milton. How soon hath Time the subtle [or suttle] thief [or theef] of youth.
On His Blindness.
Monck. Verses Written on Her Death-bed at Bath to Her Husband in London.
Moorer. Duty, or Truth at Work.
Nash, O. Kind of an Ode to Duty.
Po Chü-i. Planting Bamboos.
Ralegh, S. Sir Walter Ralegh to the Queen.
Sabry, M. Harem, The.
Stafford, W. Traveling through the Dark.
Stevenson, A. In the Orchard.
Tennyson, A. Charge of the Light Brigade, The.
Tu Fu [or Du Fu]. On the River.
Unknown. Ox.
Si-mu: Request for Furlough.
Van Jordan, A. My Father's Retirement.

Wang Ts'an. Climbing the Tower.
Watts, I. How Doth the Little Busy Bee.
Whittier. Abraham Davenport.
Anniversary Poem.
Wordsworth, W. Ode to Duty.

Dwarfs
Darío, R. Nicaraguan Triptych.
Karr. Hubris.
Unknown. Say, Dwarf, for it seems to me.
Words of the All-Wise, The.
Wallace-Crabbe. Windows, The.
Waller, E. Of the Marriage of the Dwarfs.
Yevtushenko [or Evtushenko]. Dwarf Birches.

Dying and Death Throes
Aleixandre. Old Man and the Sun, The.
Andrews, N. Crossing.
Assultani, F. RS Thomas.
Bierds, W. White Bears: Tolstoy at Astapovo.
Blackburn, T. Now Light Congeals.
Bly, R. Prayer for My Father.
Bonnefoy. Voice, A.
Boruch. Way the Dying Hear Things, The.
Bowers, N. Dead Man Interview.
Clare, J. Wish, A ("Be where I may when death brings in his bill.").
Copus, J. Breast.
Crapsey. Triad.
Dickinson, E. 'Twas Crisis—All the length had passed.
Dillard, A. This is too tight; loosen it a little. I pray.
Dubie. Pendulum, The.
Erb, E. Inedible.
Felipe, L. Now I Am Going.
Fisher, R. As He Came Near Death.
Goldberg, B. Blossom at the End of the Body.
Since I Have Lived.
González, A. Battlesfield, The.
Gould, J. Going Home.
Greenway, W. Anniversary.
Gunn, T. Lament: "Your dying was a difficult enterprise."
Hall, D. My mother said, "Of course."
Heaney, S. Polished linoleum shone there. Brass taps shone.
Hegley. Dreaming My Dad.
Hidalgo, J. Sun of Death.
Holub. Dead, The.
Howell, C. Blessing's Precision.
Irby. Record.
Jansma, E. Descent.
Jouve. Lament for the Stag.
Lewis, G. Last Minutes, The.
Longley, M. Björn Olinder's Pictures.
Loydell, R. Flesh and Fluids.
Lynch, T. Death, A: "In the end you want the clean dimensions of it mentioned."
Mackenzie, K. Caesura.
Matthews, W. Last Words.
Max, L. When the Tules Are Peppered with Red-Winged Blackbirds.
McClatchy. Aden.
McKendrick, J. Beyond.
Meyer, B. Diet, The.
Monette. No Goodbyes.
Motion, A. Close.
Murray, L. Last Hellos, The.
Muske, C. Call, The: "When I heard the voice on the telephone."
Request Radio.
Noël, Bernard. Portrait.
Norris, K. Blue Light, The.
Nowlan. This Is What I Wanted to Sign Off With.
O'Donoghue, B. Going Without Saying.
O'Driscoll, D. Someone.
Oresick. In this third year of Reagan, my 27th year.
Pinsky. ABC.
Dying.
Ponge. Last Simplicity, The.
Press, K. This, too.
Prévert. At the Florist's.
Rich, A. Final Notations.
Riordan, M. Comet, The.
Routh, J. Pale.

Sanford, C. Rachel's Recovery (Fucking with the Angels).
Scarbrough, G. Hymn for the Sound of Hymns.
Scott, M. Cave of AIDS, The.
Scupham. First Things, Last Things.
Shapiro, A. Soul.
Sims. Told to the Missionary.
Sleigh. 6. The Current.
Smith, A. Silent Room.
Snodgrass. As a Child, Sleepless.
Stone, J. Death: "I have seen come on."
Struthers, B. Last Days.
Tagliabue. March Blizzard.
Unknown. Death of Old Men, The.
Voigt. For My Mother.
Volkow. Arcana 12: The Hanged Man.
  Arcana 12: El Colgado.
Walton, A. Elegy for Joan.
Wheatley, D. Verlaine Dying.
Wicks, S. Setback.
Wilkie, B. Intuition, An.
Williams, M. Some Lines Finished Just Before Dawn at the Bedside of a Dying Student It Has Snowed All Night.

E

Eagles
Archilochus. Here is a fable men tell.
Asim, J. Dumas.
Cook, William. Endangered Species.
Darley. Free-booter, The.
Dickey, J. Eagles.
Dodge, M. Taking Time to Grow.
Duncan, R. Letting the Beat Go.
Fordham. To the Eagle.
Harburg. Eagle and Me, The.
Harjo, J. Eagle Poem.
Hughes, L. Fact.
Jamme, Franck André. Recitation of Forgetting, The.
Jeffers, R. Beaks of Eagles, The.
  Fire on the Hills.
Kavanagh, P. Goldie Sapiens.
Lee, E. Sun-Struck Eagle, The.
Lindsay, V. Eagle That Is Forgotten, The.
McWhirter. Era of Easy Meat at Locarno, An.
Moiro. Great Zeus was reared in Krete and no one.
Momaday. Eagle-Feather Fan, The.
  Story of a Well-made Shield, The.
Ortiz. Vision Shadows.
Pfeiffer, E. Aspiration.
Sioux Oral Tradition. Whole world is coming, The.
Powers, S. Eagles at Dollywood.
Sylvain, P. Panama.
Tennyson, A. Eagle, The.
Unknown. Eagle Above Us, The.
  Eagle of Pengwern.
  Ha-Kon-E-Crase, the Eagle Dance.
Very. Eagles, The.
Villanueva, A. Even the Eagles Must Gather.
Wakoski. Ice Eagle, The.
Warfield. Sun-Struck Eagle, The.
Whitman, W. Dalliance of the Eagles, The.
Wylie. Eagle and the Mole, The.

Earhart, Amelia
Alexander, P. Flight: "Series of white squares, each, A."
Hall, D. Goggles and Helmet.

Ears
Dickinson, A. Cryo.
Edson, R. Dr. Nigel Bruce Watson Counting.
Forché. Colonel, The.
Hannan, M. Tap.
Herbert, Z. Rosy Ear.
Martinaitis, M. Pony in Kukutis's Ear, A.
Powell, D. A. Studs and Rings: Favors of the Piercing Party.
Sirowitz, H. Equality.
Smith, P. Finding His Fist.
Wellman, M. Endowed fiction of a mouse ear.

Earth
Allen, S. Moment Please, A.
Atwood. You Begin.
Azzawi, F. Leave the earth behind you!
  On a Dying Planet.
Ballav, I. Stride On.
Baranda, M. Epistle of the Shipwreck.
  Epistola del náufrago.
Begay. Mother's Lace.
Belli, C. Why Have They Moved Me.
Berry, W. Enriching the Earth.
Betsugen. All night long I think of life's labyrinth.
Bingen, Hildegard von. Earth is at the same time mother, The.
  I am the one whose praise.
Blake, W. And every Space that a Man views around his dwelling-place.
  Earth's Answer.
  Introduction: "Hear the voice of the Bard!"
Blandiana. Covered with Dew.
Bleakney, J. Black and White.
Blind. Chaunts of Life.
Bradstreet, A. Contemplations.
Bright, S. Makes Them Wild.
Bruchac. Canticle: "Let others speak."
Bryant, W. Thanatopsis.
Buckley, C. Concerning Paradise.
Budapest. Medea speaks: / This is God, children, listen up well. The.
Buffoni, F. And in the end, the entire earth may answer to a single name.
Cavendish, M. Of the Animal Spirits.
Césaire, A. Bucolic.
Channing. Hymn of the Earth.
  Then spoke the Spirit of the Earth.
Chia Tao. Evening View as the Snow Clears.
Clifton, L. Earth Is a Living Thing, The.
Cortes. Space Song.
Couzyn. Spell for Birth.
Craven, Jerry. Spring in Palo Duro Canyon.
Cummings, E. E. Bigness of cannon, The.
  O sweet spontaneous.
De la Mare. Snow.
Deloney. Weavers Song, The.
Desnos. There once was a leaf.
D'Haen. Mole, The.
DiPrima, C. Her Eyes a Thousand Times Over.
Donne. Valediction, A: of Weeping.
  When that rich soul[e] which to her heaven is gone.
Donnelly, T. Purgatory Chasm.
Dransfield. Strange Bird, A.
Dumas, H. If I Were Earth.
Eberhart, R. Hard Structure of the World, The.
  Under the Hill.
Emerson, R. Hamatreya.
Empson. To an Old Lady.
Enheduanna. Lady of Largest Heart.
Everson, W. Winter Ploughing.
Faverey. Aarde; uit aardewerk bestaande, De.
  Earth; consisting of earthenware, The.
Fel-Yelin, S. Breath of Spring.
Fletcher, G. As when the cheerfull Sunne, elamping wide.
Fuertes. Birds Nest.
Fulton, A. Fix.
Gilbert, W. To the Terrestrial Globe.
Gilkes, D. Rain Making.
Götter-Abendroth. Thou Gaia Art I.
Graham, J. Erosion.
Greenberg, U. Song of Earth.
Gregg. Fish Tea Rice.
Griffin, J. One's Country.
Griffin, S. Our Mother.
Harington [or Harrington]. Thus all that day, they spent in divers talke.
Harjo, J. My House Is the Red Earth.
Hedd Wyn. Black Blot, The.
Herrera. Earth Chorus.
Herrick. White Island, The: or Place of the Blest.
Hewitt, J. Because I Paced My Thought.
Hidalgo, J. You Have to Go Down.
Hill, G. Genesis.
  I was invested in mother-earth, the crypt of roots.
Hillman, B. Formation of Soils, The.
Hollo. Shed the Fear.
Hoogerhuis. Search, The.
Hopkins, G. God's Grandeur.
Howe, J. Kosmos.
Hughes, T. River.
Hummell, A. Salt Longing.
Ibáñez, S. Island in the Earth.
Ignatow, D. Kaddish.
Issa. Never forget / We walk on hell.
Iverem, E. Earth Screaming.
Ivsic Radovan. Mavena.
Jaccottet. In the Steps of the Moon.
Jeffers, R. Autumn Evening.
  Eye, The.
  Shine, Perishing Republic.
Jiménez, J. Night Piece.
Juana Inés de la Cruz. Since Love is shivering.
Kanchev, Nikolai. Miracle.
Kekova. Sky is covered with stars, like a body with sores, The.
Kelber, M. Pledge of Allegiance to the Family of Earth, A.
Kinnell. Quick and the Dead, The.
Kipling, R. Sestina of the Tramp-Royal.
Kocbek. Earth, I Get Everything from You.
Koch, K. Geography.
Kusano Shimpei. Skylarks and Fuji.
Lao Tzu. Valley Spirit never dies, The.
Leiris, Michel. Vertical.
Levertov. O Taste and See.
Levine, P. On a Drawing by Flavio.
  Rain Downriver.
  Snow: "Today the snow is drifting."
  They Feed They Lion.
Li Ho. Ravine on a Cold Evening.
Lindsay, S. World Truffle.
MacDiarmid, H. Bonnie Broukit Bairn, The.
  Little White Rose, The.
MacLeish. Speech to a Crowd.
Meador, B. Fields Belong to Woman, The.
Merrill, J. Childlessness.
Michaels, D. Returning from Italy.
Mikha'il, M. Talk.
Miles, J. On Inhabiting an Orange.
Millay, E. God's World.
Milosz, C. Goddess, A.
Muir, E. One Foot in Eden.
Murray, P. Conquest.
Muso Soseki. Cave of the Thousand Pines.
  For years I dug in the earth.
  Many times the mountains have turned from green to yellow.
Mutén, B. Queen Hera.
Nanei. Splitting the void in half.
Navajo Oral Tradition. Song of the Earth.
Neidjie. This earth.
Nemes Nagy. Between.
  Earth Remembers, The.
Nichols, G. Sugar Cane.
Noguere. Whirling Round the Sun.
Ortiz. Earth and Rain, the Plants & Sun.
O'Sullivan, L. Earth.
Osundare. Eyeful Glances.
  Goree.
  I Sing of Change.
  Our Earth Will Not Die.
  We called the statue.
  Who Says That Drought Was Here?
Ovid. Deucalion and Pyrrha, Sole Survivors of the Flood, Renew Creation by Casting Stones behind Them.
Pack, R. Watchers.
Padilla. Fountain, a House of Stone, A.
Page, P. Planet Earth.
Perelman. China.
"Perse." Anabasis.
Philpot, T. Clump of Gods, The.
Pilling. Earth, The.
Polkowski. World Is Only Air, The.
Popa. Burning Shewolf.
Popova, O. Lay your head in my lap.
Prévert. Song in the Blood.
Puttenham. O mightye Muse.
Quarles. What is the *World?* A great *Exchange*

of ware.
Ralin, Radoi. Home-Study Course in Freedom.
Reynolds, S. F. Moon/light quarter/back sack.
Rilke. Spring Has Returned.
Roberts, E. People, The.
Robinson, A. Sibyl, The.
 Unum est Necessarium.
Robinson, K. Nursery Rhyme.
Rossetti, C. Advent.
 Advent ("This Advent moon shines cold and
  clear.").
 Horses of the Sea, The.
 Later Life: A Double Sonnet of Sonnets.
Rossi, T. Law.
 System.
Sahn, Seung. Mountain sinks into the sea, The.
St. John, P. Lynching and Burning.
Sandburg, C. Be Ready.
 Early Copper.
Schevill, Margaret Erwin. Desert Center.
Shumyatsher, E. Earth Dream.
Sidney. Epithalamium: "Let mother Earth".
Snyder, G. Earth Verse.
 Gaia.
Sornberger. When She Laughs.
Southwell. Vale of Tear[e]s, A.
Southwick. Earthly Light.
Stafford, W. Earth Dweller.
Strand. A.M.
Supervielle. Earth.
 Regretting the Earth.
 Voyages.
Suyemoto, Toyo. In Topaz.
Sylvester, J. "Were I as Base as Is the Lowly
  Plain".
Sze. Before Completion.
 Every Where and Every When.
Szymborska, W. Ball, The.
T'ao Ch'ien [or T'ao Yuan-ming]. Substance,
  Shadow, and Spirit ("Earth and heaven endure
  forever.").
Tarrant, J. Hula Dancers Dance the Hula,
  Kilauea the Caldera, The.
Taylor, A. Earth.
Tewa Oral Tradition. Song of the Sky Loom.
Thomas, D. This Bread I Break.
Tomlinson, C. Ararat.
Tsanev, Stefan. Old woman leans against the
  pine tree, The.
Tsvetayeva [or Tsvetaeva]. Fatal Volume, The.
Tuckerman, F. Sonnet: "And so, as this great
  sphere (now turning slow)."
Unamuno. How Quiet under the Earth.
 This Spanish Christ that hasn't lived.
Ungaretti. You Were Broken.
Unknown. I Came from Under the Earth.
 We love the daylight.
Vacietis. Goodbye to a Spaceman.
Vaughan, H. World, The (1).
Vietnamese Oral Tradition. From So Mountain.
Vigil, A. Hogarcito de La Madrugada, El.
Villanueva, A. From the Healing Dark.
 Planet Earth Speaks, The.
Volkman. Sonnet: "Nothing was ever what it
  claimed to be."
Walcott. Earth.
Waldrep, G. C. What Begins Bitterly Becomes
  Another Love Poem.
Waltner-Toews, D. How the Earth Loves You.
Ward, T. Dark Underfoot.
Watson, R. Of the Earth, Earthy.
Weston, M. Departure.
Wheelock, J. Earth.
White, J. In Ecclesiastes I Read.
Whitman, S. November Landscape, A.
Whitman, W. Earth, My Likeness.
 I am the poet of the Body and I am the poet of
  the Soul.
 This Compost.
Whitmore, S. Gamelia.
Wilbur, R. Caserta Garden.
Williams, W. Bibelforscher, Die.
 What Is a Man?
Wordsworth, W. Composed upon Westminster
  Bridge, September 3, 1802.
Wright, J. Arrangements with Earth for Three

Dead Friends.
 Horse, The.
 Wylie. Hymn to Earth.
Earthquakes
Darío, R. Nicaraguan Triptych.
De Kok. Ground Wave.
Dickinson, E. Still—Volcano—Life, A.
Gould, J. Earthquake Weather.
Griffiths, J. There Are Limits to Brotherly
  Love.
Guevara, M. After the Colombian Earthquake.
Heard, J. Earthquake of 1886, The.
Kramer, L. Images of the San Francisco
  Disaster.
Kuo Mo-jo. Earthquake.
Li K'ai-hsien. Earthquake covered Shansi and
  Shensi, The.
Olds, S. Quake Theory.
Reed, I. Earthquake Blues.
Rothenberg, J. At Tsukiji Market Tokyo.
Salzman, E. English Earthquake, The.
Sharp, S. Good Nights.
Unknown. Earthquake.
Webb, C. You Missed the Earthquake, Bill.
East Wind
Johnson, L. Red Wind, The.
"Eastaway, Edward".
See **Thomas, Edward ("Edward Eastaway")**
Easter
Ammons. Easter Morning.
Astley, N. East of Easter.
Berlin. Easter Parade.
Bulich, V. From My Diary, 3.
Burns, E. Jesus Speaks to the Church at
  Eastertime.
Carr, S. Easter Outing.
Cherry, J. Bird.
Clampitt. Easter Morning.
De la Selva. Tropical Town.
Elmslie, K. Easter for Joe.
Gibbons, R. Life Everlasting, The.
Hadas, R. Easter Afternoon.
Heard, J. Easter Morn.
Herbert, G. Easter ("Rise heart; thy Lord is
  risen. Sing his praise.").
 Easter Wings.
Hope, A. Easter Hymn.
Hopkins, G. That Nature Is a Heraclitean Fire
  and of the Comfort of the Resurrection.
Housman. Easter Hymn.
 Loveliest of trees, the cherry now.
Jeffers, R. Another Easter Poem.
Kalina, R. Dayeinu—they said.
Mathews, H. Invitation to a Sabbath.
Melville, H. Easter.
Meynell, A. Easter Night.
Miller, V. Whitewash of Houston.
Moorer. Easter; or, Spring-Time.
Mörling, M. Three-Card Monte.
Nemerov. Easter: "Even this suburb has
  overcome Death."
Nichol. Easter Pome.
Peacock, M. ChrisEaster.
Ray, H. Easter Carol.
Spenser, E. Sonnet 68: "Most glorious Lord of
  Life that on this day."
Thompson, C. Easter Light, The.
Turner, S. Christmas Is Really for the Children.
Vaughan, H. Easter Hymn.
Waters, M. Divine Will.
Wilde, O. Easter Day.
Wordsworth, W. Composed in One of the
  Valleys of Westmoreland, on Easter Sunday.
Yeats. Easter 1916.
Easter Island
Cortázar. Behavior of Mirrors on Easter Island,
  The.
Dickey, W. For Easter Island or Another
  Island.
Elmslie, K. Easter for Joe.
Easter Rebellion (1916)
Yeats. Easter 1916.
 Rose Tree, The.
 Sixteen Dead Men.

Eatherly, Claude R.
Crashaw. Luke 11: Blessed Be the Paps Which
  Thou Hast Sucked.
Eating
Aesop. Dog in the Manger, The.
Agosin. Mi Estomago / My Belly.
Armstrong, J. Rustic Interior.
Barrax. In the Restaurant.
Belloc. Vulture, The.
Benedikt. Meat Epitaph, The.
Beveridge. Dining Out.
Blanco, P. Soldiers.
Boruch. Simple Machines.
Brooks, G. Bean Eaters, The.
 Sunday Chicken.
Burgess, F. Table Manners: "Goops they lick
  their fingers, The."
Byron, G. At the Siege of Corinth.
Carroll, L. Walrus and the Carpenter, The.
Cassian. Sacrilege.
Cendrars. Menus.
Chase, K. Venison.
Chông Hwajin. Bowl of Mul Kimch'i, A.
Citino. Sister Mary Appassionata Lectures the
  Home Ec Class: The Feast.
Clough. Le Diner.
Cohen, Lynne. Body Doubled.
Collins, B. Osso Buco.
Crane, S. In the desert.
De la Mare. Miss T.
Dizhur. Here is an island. Here is a house on
  stilts.
Dobyns. Spiritual Chickens.
Evasco, M. Baked Oysters Rockefeller.
Floyd-Miller, C. Roots 2: the conjure woman
  replies.
France, L. Eater of Wives, The.
Frost, C. Scorn.
Gonzalez, R. Brown Pot.
Greiffenberg. On the Fruit-Providing Autumn
  Season.
Gunn, T. J Car, The.
Hajjaj, N. Man Who Devoured Himself, The.
Hanzlicek, C. Feeding Frenzies.
Harjo, J. Perhaps the World Ends Here.
Harper, M. Fireplace, The.
Herbert, G. Love (3): "Love bade me welcome:
  yet my soul drew back."
Herrick. Upon Jack and Jill: Epigram.
Highfill, M. Rebis.
Hirshfield, J. Red Onion, Cherries, Boiling
  Potatoes, Milk.
Hoffmann, H. Story of Augustus Who Would
  Not Have Any Soup, The.
Hughes, F. Foxes.
Janzen, J. Wild Grapes.
Jaques, F. There Once Was a Puffin.
Joans, T. Overloaded Horse, The.
Jonson, B. Inviting a Friend to Supper.
 On Gut.
Keller, D. After Supper.
Kenyon, J. Eating the Cookies.
 Man Eating.
King, Julie. Giving the House Away.
Kinzie. Heat-heavy creatures.
Kizer, C. Food of Love.
Kossman. Judas' Reproach.
Larsen, L. Peach.
 Red.
Lau, A. Eating Habits of the Old Man.
Lee, L. Eating Together.
MacCaig. Fetching Cows.
Maguire, S. Communion.
Markham, E. Petition.
Masterson, R. Making Love in the Meat
  Locker.
McLaughlin-Carruth, J. Existentially Speaking.
Merriam, E. How to Eat a Poem.
Mirikitani. Soul Food.
Mother Goose. Little Jack Horner/ Sat in a
  corner.
Myles, E. Merk.
Nash, O. Experiment Degustatory.
 Termite, The.
Nikolayeva [or Nikolaeva]. Here, everything
  gets eaten: drippings, marinade.

No Hyegyông. Fish and Sauce.
O'Callaghan. Federal Case.
O'Hara, F. Blocks.
Oliver, M. Kingfisher, The.
Pai, S. Fruit They Had in Common.
Peacock, M. Anger Sweetened.
  Devolution.
Péret. Fountain.
Peseroff. Raptor in the Kitchen.
Po Chü-i. Eating Bamboo-Shoots.
Rakosi. Good Morning.
Romero, N. New Suit, The.
Rukeyser, M. Night Feeding.
Salaam. Everywhere You Eat.
Sen, R. This time, Kali.
Serrano, P. Prurito.
  Ticklish Moments.
Shaughnessy, B. Rise.
Southey, R. To a Goose [or Gosse].
Stein, G. This is this dress, aider.
Stevenson, R. Cow, The.
Strand. Eating Poetry.
Swift, T. Ballad of the Solitary Diner.
Tallmountain. Good Grease.
Tanikawa, S. Family Portrait.
Torres, E. Bio-Rodent-Oriole.
Unknown. Limerick: "There was an old man of
  [or from] Peru / Who dreamt [or dreamed] he
  was eating his shoe."
  There was a young lady of Riga.
Valentine, J. Night: "From this night on God let
  me eat."
Van Winckel, N. Appetite, the Great Painting.
Wallace, R. Fat of the Land, The.
White, E. Marble-Top.
Williams, W. This Is Just to Say.
  To a Poor Old Woman.
Wright, D. Addison Street.
Wright, E. When Father Carves the Duck.
Yao Sui. Tune: "Full Court of Fragrance".
See also **Food; Gluttony and Gluttons**
Eating Disorders
Bandele, A. After diana died.
Barnett, R. Anorexic, The.
Bidart. Ellen West.
Boland, E. Anorexic.
Bryce, Colette. Form.
Hoffmann, H. Story of Augustus Who Would
  Not Have Any Soup, The.
Jones, A. Anorexia.
Maiden. Anorexia.
Nash, O. Curl Up and Diet.
Olin. Don't Let Me Eat Dinner.
O'Reilly, C. Thin.
Stowell, P. Scales, The.
Echo (mythology)
Ausonius. Echo.
Chappell, F. Narcissus and Echo.
Glazer, M. Echo to Narcissus.
Jones, A. M. To Echo.
Milton. Echo.
Ovid. So, when she saw Narcissus wandering
  through the lonely countryside, Echo fell in
  love with him, and followed secretly in his
  steps.
Ray, H. Echo's Complaint.
Rossetti, C. Echo.
Spenser, E. Epithalamion: "Ye learned sisters
  which have oftentimes."
See also **Narcissus (mythology)**
Echoes
Ashbery, J. Late Echo.
Bishop, E. Chemin de Fer.
Buson. Day slow in going, A.
Cawein. Echo.
Cofer, J. Life of an Echo, The.
De la Mare. Echo.
Lazarus, E. Echoes.
Lisboa. Echo.
Longley, M. Echoes.
Lorde. Echoes.
Madgett. Echoes.
Nekrasov, V. I repeat.
Popa. Echo.
Reid, C. In the Echoey Tunnel.

Saitō Mokichi. At daybreak.
Segalen. Faithful Betrayal.
Swift, J. Gentle Echo on Woman, A.
Tabb. Echo.
Tennyson, A. Splendour [or Splendor] Falls,
  The.
Thoreau. Dong, sounds the brass in the east.
Tree-Leaf Woman. Who speaks the sound of an
  echo?
Eclipses
Bly, R. Seeing the Eclipse in Maine.
Hummell, A. Sculpture Garden.
McGrath, Carmelita. Solar Eclipse, St. John's,
  Newfoundland.
Petit, P. During the Eclipse.
Robbins, Mary Susannah. Eclipse of the Moon.
Roberson, E. Eclipse.
Ryan, T. Eclipse, Kenwick, 1974.
  Lunar Eclipse.
Unknown. Moon Eclipse Exorcism.
Ecology and Ecologists
Baker, D. Works and Days.
Barry, Quan. Asylum.
Bradley, Jerry. How the Big Thicket Got
  Smaller.
Buckmaster. End to Myth, An.
Cole, T. Lament of the Forest, The.
Cowper, W. Poplar Field, The.
De Kok. Ecotone.
Fulton, A. Fix.
Healey, S. As Western Culture Declined without
  Its Knowing.
Hopkins, G. Binsey Poplars (Felled 1879).
  Inversnaid.
Kunitz, S. War against the Trees, The.
Levertov. Gathered at the River.
Lindsay, V. Flower-fed Buffaloes, The.
Marshall, J. Wing and Prayer.
Morgenstern. Blueprint for Disaster.
Morris, G. Woodman, Spare That Tree.
Rabinowitz. Ecosystem.
Roethke. Moss-Gathering.
Snyder, G. Smokey the Bear Sutra.
Spacks. Malediction.
Spender, S. I Think Continually of Those Who
  Were Truly Great.
Stephens, J. Little Things.
See also **Conservation; Pollution**
Economics and Economists
Ai. Riot Act, April 29, 1992.
Bentley, E. Intrepid Ricardo, The.
Dunn, D. Ballad of the Two Left Hands.
Huerta, J. Toward a Portrait of the
  Undocumented.
Kavulu. Forces of Production.
Kumar, A. Primary Lessons in Political
  Economy.
London, R. Folk Form.
McGrath, C. Capitalist Poem #36.
Nash, O. What Do You Want: A Meaningful
  Dialogue, or a Satisfactory Talk?
Rich, A. Here is a map of our country.
Taylor, C. Our texas economy.
Ecstasy
Aygi, G. Dream: Flight of a Dragonfly.
Baudelaire. Get High.
Bhattācārya, M. There's a huge hullabaloo in
  my lotus heart.
Browning, R. Now.
Cavafy. Passing Through.
Donne. Ecstasy, The.
Ferlinghetti, L. Extasis.
Fullerton. Poetry.
Kabir. Music without Strings, The.
Lux. Ecstasy Notebook.
Nervo. Ecstasy.
Pellicer, C. To Poetry.
Piercy. Raisin Pumpernickel.
Rimbaud, A. Morning of Drunkenness.
Rumi. Ecstatic Love Is an Ocean.
  When the heart bursts into flame.
Sanguineti. Wind shoves my New Year's Day
  sun in my face, The.
Stratanovsky. Herostratos and Herostratos.
Traherne. On News.

Eden
Aisenberg, N. Leaving Eden.
Armantrout. Plan, The.
Auchterlonie. Tree, The.
Back, R. After Eden.
Beaumont, J. Garden, The.
Chin. Disorder, The.
Coolbrith. Longing.
Cotton, N. On Lord Cobham's Garden.
Crane, H. Garden Abstract.
Dickey, J. Poisoned Man, The.
Dickinson, E. Did the Harebell loose her girdle.
  Eden is that Old-Fashioned House.
  Wild Nights—Wild Nights!
Dobyns. Utopian Melodies.
Donnelly, S. Eve Names the Animals.
Dugan, A. Letter to Eve.
Frost, C. Fury.
Goodison. Jamaica 1980.
Grey, C. If You Were the Only Girl in the
  World.
Grosholz. Eden.
Higginson, E. Eve.
Hopkins, G. Spring: "Nothing is so beautiful as
  Spring."
Housman. When Adam walked in Eden young.
Howitt, M. Cry of the Animals, The.
Hughes, T. Theology.
Ignatova, E. Then there was the rose I fell in
  love with.
Kavanagh, P. Long Garden, The.
Kendrick, D. Gethsemane A. D.
Kipling, R. L'Envoi.
Kovaleva, I. And there was beauty.
Larkin, P. High Windows.
Lawrence, D. H. Paradise Re-entered.
Lisnyanskaya [or Lisnianskaia]. Like the earth
  turning, I creak, and dream.
Milton. Now had th' Almighty Father from
  above.
  So spake the [or th'] Archangel Michael; then
  paused.
  Tempter Disarmed, The.
  To whom thus also th' Angel last repli'd.
Muir, E. Adam's Dream.
  One Foot in Eden.
Pastan. Imperfect Paradise, The.
Polkowski. World Is Only Air, The.
Probyn. Ballade of Lovers.
Rabi'a al-Adawiyya. O my Lord.
Raine, K. On its way I see.
Richter, H. Beginning.
Robinson, A. Unum est Necessarium.
Rochester, J. Fall, The.
Rossetti, C. Blessed that flock safe penned in
  Paradise.
  Later Life: A Double Sonnet of Sonnets.
Tarn. Before the Snake.
Thomas, R. S. Mother and Child.
Unknown. Adam Lay Ybounden [or I-
  bounden].
Vaughan, H. Corruption.
Very. Garden, The.
Vinokurov. Adam.
Voigt. Two Trees.
Walcott. Crusoe's Island.
Wallace-Crabbe. And the World was Calm.
White, G. Leopard in Eden, The.
Whitman, W. To the Garden the World.
Whittier. Garden.
Youmans, Greg. Pear's Complaint.
See also **Adam and Eve**
Edgar [Shakespeare]
Lauinger, A. Edgar.
Edinburgh, Scotland
Adamson. Edinburgh.
Calder, A. Greeting, Not Greeting.
Fergusson. Auld Reikie.
  Daft Days, The.
Jamie, K. One of Us.
Sullivan, Mary Louise. Unearth.
Editors
Beachy-Quick, Dan. Afterword.
  Prologue: "Editor, / Here are the lines my mind
  fathomed."
Betjeman. Ballad of George R. Sims, The.

Buson.   End of spring, The.
Byron, G.   To Mr. Murray.
Cummings, E. E.   Mr U.
Fogel, A.   Printer's Error, The.
Masters, E.   Editor Whedon.
Mo Shih-lung.   To the Monk Wu-hsia on the
   Occasion of His Editing the Lotus Sutra.
Moore, J.   Poet Is Scornful, The.
Shapiro, K.   Editing *Poetry*.
Stanley, T.   Dr. Jack.
Zucker, R.   Not Knowing Nijinsky or Diaghilev.

Education
Amichai, Y.   Anniversaries of War.
   We Have Done Our Duty.
Awoonor.   On Having Been an Experimental
   Sacred Cow for Four Years, and a Token
   African on Faculty.
Belloc.   Lines to a Don.
Bentley, E.   On Education, December 1789.
Berkeley, G.   On the Prospect of Planting Arts
   and Learning in America.
Black, D.   Educators, The.
Brownjohn.   Common Sense.
Bunina.   Though poverty's no stain.
Butler, S.   When civil fury [*or* dudgeon] first
   grew high.
Cabral de Melo Neto.   Education by Stone.
Camlan.   Education in Wales.
Chung-ch'ang T'ung.   Speaking My Mind.
Collins, B.   First Reader.
Cortázar.   Loss and Recovery of the Hair, The.
Dickinson, E.   Through the Dark Sod—as
   Education.
   Water, is taught by thirst.
Dodge, M.   Shepherd John.
Dove, R.   Flash Cards.
Finney, N.   Fishing among the Learned.
Flores, J.   Last Visit to Chestnut Middle School.
Fogarty, L.   Kath Walker.
Follain.   First Grade.
Forbes, J.   Speed, a Pastoral.
Gandlevsky, S.   Dear God, allow me to recall
   my works.
   There's our street, let's say.
Gregory, H.   Cage of Voices, The.
Gwynn, R.   Classroom at the Mall, The.
Heaney, S.   Alphabets.
Heard, J.   Advance of Education, The.
Heath-Stubbs.   One.
Hecht, A.   Mysteries of Caesar, The.
Hill, J.   Season with Angels.
Holmes, J.   Old Professor, The.
Jordan, A.   Orientation: Wittenberg University,
   1983.
Lilley.   Sewing Lesson, The.
Lorde.   Learning to Write.
Machado Ruiz.   Memory from Childhood.
Martin, C.   E. S. L.
McCord, D.   History of Education.
McLucas, L.   Negotiation.
Milton.   To Cyriack Skinner.
Naden.   Love Versus Learning.
Nowlan.   Warren Pryor.
Nye, N.   Rain: "Teacher asked Paul, A."
Palmer, T.   Try, Try Again.
Pollarolo, G.   During Recess.
   Grocer's Dream, The.
Praed.   Talented Man, The.
Prelutsky.   Homework! Oh, Homework!
Samaras, N.   Elegy for a Professor.
Sanchez, S.   This Is Not a Small Voice.
Schwartz, R. L.   AIDS Education, Seventh
   Grade.
Silva, L.   Emigrant's Son, The.
Snodgrass.   Campus on the Hill, The.
Speght.   Dream[e], The [*or* A].
Spender, S.   Elementary School Classroom in a
   Slum, An.
Tranter.   Wild stinking fire, love and death.
Travis, N.   At My Father's House.
Urusova, E.   O Muses! I beseech you, fire my
   heart with song.
Villalongo.   In the Good Old U. S. A.
Whitman, W.   When I Heard the Learn'd
   Astronomer.
Whitney, Louise Grassi.   Beautiful Eyes.

Wordsworth, W.   When the third summer freed
   us from restraint.
See also **Colleges and Universities; Scholarship
   and Scholars; Students; Teaching and Teachers**

Edward II, King of England
Drayton.   And thus like slaves we sell our soules
   to sinne.
   O breake my hart quoth he, O breake and dye.
   This Edward in the Aprill of his age.
   Why doe I quake my down-fall to reporte?
Marlowe.   Ah, wicked King! Accursed
   Gaveston!
   Here is the form of Gaveston's exile.
   He's gone, and for his absence thus I mourn.
   My father is deceas'd. Come, Gaveston.
   Nephew, I must to Scotland. Thou stay'st here.

Edward IV, King of England
Sidney.   Sonnet 75: "Of all the kings that ever
   here did reign."

Edward VII, King of England
Beerbohm, M.   Addition to Kipling's "The Dead
   King (Edward VII), 1910".
Murphy, E.   Thank you, Mr Rason, for the
   Apples.

Edwards, Jonathan
Lowell, R.   After the Surprising Conversions.
   Mr. Edwards and the Spider.
McGinley.   Theology of Jonathan Edwards, The.

Eels
Bly, R.   Eel in the Cave, The.
Diaper.   Sex-life of Fish, The.
Montale.   Eel, The.
Muldoon, P.   Briefcase, The.
   Eugenio Montale: The Eel.
Nash, O.   Eel, The.
Oppian [of Corycus].   Loves of the Eel [*or*
   Fishes], The.
Petit, P.   Embrace of the Electric Eel.
Unknown.   Lord Randal[l].
Vietnamese Oral Tradition.   Mother Egret.
See also **Lampreys**

Eggs
Arp.   Domesticated Egg, A.
Blanco, R.   Tía Olivia Serves Wallace Stevens a
   Cuban Egg.
Blind.   On a Forsaken Lark's Nest.
Brooks, G.   Egg Boiler, The.
Cabico, R.   Afternoon in Pangasinan with No
   Electricity, An.
Caston, A.   Blowing Eggs.
Chazal, M.   Logic.
Day, C.   Egg, The.
Deltoro, A.   Eggs Laid by a Tiger.
   Huevos puestos por un tigre.
Garrett, E.   History Goes to Work.
Gogarty.   Leda and the Swan.
Grass.   In the Egg.
Hanzlicek, C.   Egg.
Herrick.   Her Legs.
Hoban.   Egg Thoughts.
Hughes, L.   Bar.
Kim Sŭnghŭi.   Life in the Egg 3.
   Life within an Egg.
Klyuyev [*or* Kliuev *or* Klyuev].   October, A
   Copper-Crawed Cock.
Lamport.   Eggomania.
Laskey, M.   Tray of Eggs, A.
Lear, E.   Limerick: "There was an old man of
   Thermopylae."
Okita.   Notes for a Poem on Being Asian
   American.
Olds, S.   Eggs.
Pastan.   Egg.
Pietri.   How Do Your Eggs Want You (?).
Ritsos.   In the white egg.
Spires.   Fabergé's Egg.
Upton, L.   Beatrix Potter.
Yeryomin.   Drake pays court to the duck, The.

Egotism and Egotists
Barker, G.   O Pearl and Breasted World.
Berlin.   Couple of Swells, A.
Bierce.   Egotist.
Carew, T.   Ingrateful[l] Beauty Threatened.
Davie, D.   In the Stopping Train.
Dōyaku Sensei, Master Artery.   Kyoto Minor

Retainer.
Ewart.   It's Hard to Dislike Ewart.
Frumkin.   Life of Eternity, The.
Giovanni.   Ego Tripping (There May Be a
   Reason Why).
González, A.   Diatribe against the Dead.
Komrij.   Poet, The.
Landon.   Gifts Misused.
Martial.   You've told me, Maro.
Meredith, G.   Lucifer in Starlight.
Sia, B.   Claim to Fame.
Tarn.   As If There Were Any Matter.
Tillema, M.   Considering Tulips.
Torres, E.   Drowning in the Last Days of
   Luxury.
Wickham.   Egoist, The.
See also **Individualism and Individualists**

Egrets
Smith, D.   Egret Tree, The.
Tu Mu.   Egrets ("Snowy coats and snowy crests
   and beaks of blue jade.").
   Egrets ("With snowy coats, snowy crests, and
   sapphire bills.").
Unknown.   Fluid as water that all tones reflects.
Vietnamese Oral Tradition.   Egret's Death and
   Funeral Preparations.
   Mother Egret.
Weigl.   Snowy Egret.

Egypt
al-Mala'ika, N.   Cholera.
Bringhurst.   Song of Ptahhotep, The.
Coolidge, C.   I came here. I don't know you
   here.
   New hunt / the morning bent, A.
Crawford, R.   Saltcoats Structuralists, The.
Doolittle, H.   Egypt.
Douglas, K.   Egypt.
   On a Return from Egypt.
Dufault.   Mud Dauber Wasp, The.
"Ern Malley.".   Egyptian Register.
Fyleman.   Cat, The.
Giovanni.   Ego Tripping (There May Be a
   Reason Why).
Hill, S.   Questioning Mr Bonnet.
Hunt, L.   Nile, The.
Kipling, R.   Naaman's Song.
Kuzmin.   Were I a general of olden times.
López Mills, T.   Advertisement.
   Anuncio.
Martial.   If by chance, Flaccus, someone could
   offer me for the asking.
McKay, C.   Africa.
McNeil, R.   Angel in the Temple of Luxor, An.
Mendes, M.   Everything happens / In an Egypt
   of aerial corridors.
Mutis.   You Are a Daughter of the Lagides.
Reed, I.   I Am a Cowboy in the Boat of Ra.
   Why I Often Allude to Osiris.
Seferis.   Days of April '43.
Shelley, P.   Ozymandias.
Tobin, D.   At the Egyptian Exhibit.
Touré, A.   Summer Worlds: A Mythic
   Landscape.
Unknown.   Go Down, Moses.
   Shari Wag El Burka.
Warner, R.   Egyptian Kites.
Warren, R.   Flaubert in Egypt.
Wodehouse.   Cleopatterer.

Eichmann, Adolf
Levi, P.   For Adolf Eichmann.

Eiffel Tower
Huidobro.   Eiffel Tower.
Vallejo.   Three hundred womanly states of the
   Eiffel Tower are frozen, The.

Einstein, Albert
Crawford, R.   Alba Einstein.
Feinstein, E.   Annus Mirabilis 1989.
Hoover, P.   Letter to Einstein Beginning Dear
   Albert.
Kizer, C.   Twelve O'Clock.
Moss, H.   Einstein's Bathrobe.
Nemerov.   Einstein & Freud & Jack.
Wilson, A.   Antlia the Air Pump.

Eisenhower, Dwight David
Lowell, R.   Inauguration Day: January 1953.

Stafford, W.   Explaining the Big One.
Wright, J.   Eisenhower's Visit to Franco, 1959.

El Dorado
Poe.   Eldorado.

El Greco (Domenikos Theotokopoulos)
Birney.   El Greco: Espolio.
Craig, David.   Christ Bearing the Cross by El Greco.
Ryan, K.   Bad Time for the Sublime, A.
Starbuck, G.   High Renaissance.

El Salvador
Alegría.   Documentary.
   Toward the Jurassic Age.
Dalton, R.   Looking for Trouble.
Forché.   Colonel, The.
Healy, E.   From Los Angeles Looking South.
Rose.   Day They Cleaned Up the Border, The: El Salvador, February, 1981.

Electric Appliances
Townsend, A.   Western Holly Stove.

Electricity
Allnutt, G.   Notes on Living inside the Lightbulb.
Bartlett, M.   Spring in Placitas.
Cranch.   Spirit of the Age, The.
Duchamp.   Electricity Breadthwise.
Duncan, A.   Ghost of Fusion, The.
Durkin, Kevin.   American Pylons.
Edwards, K.   About this time streetlamps flicker up like.
Greenlaw, L.   Electricity.
Lawrence, D. H.   Storm in the Black Forest.
Lleshanaku, L.   Electrolytes.
McOrlan.   Battery Woman.
Murray, L.   Powerline Incarnation, The.
Ritchie, E.   Electroconvulsive Therapy.
Thomas, L.   Electricity of Blossoms.
Wellman, M.   United bolt and screw.

Elegance
Connolly, G.   New House.

Elements
Davis, T.   Skin of Clouds.
Jinkag Haesim.   May Day.
Lleshanaku, L.   Half Past Three.
Naong.   Illusory Hermitage.
Parra, N.   Note on the Lessons of Antipoetry.
Stover, D.   Fire/Water Blues.
Unknown.   Your love is water and it is fire.
Wilkie, B.   Very Fine Lines.

Elephants
Amirthanayagam, I.   Elephants Are in the Yard, The.
Belloc.   Elephant, The.
Bradley, G.   Electrocuting an Elephant.
Brooks, G.   Pete at the Zoo.
Brouwer, J.   Kelly, Ringling Bros. Oldest Elephant, Goes On Rampage.
Chiasson, D.   Elephant, The.
Cole, H.   Cleaning the Elephant.
Drummond de Andrade.   Elephant, The.
Edson, R.   Elephant Tears.
   Retirement of the Elephant, The.
Gumilyov [*or* Gumiliov *or* Gumilev].   Baby Elephant, A.
Hayes, T.   Elegant Tongue, The.
Lakshminkara.   Lay your head on a block of butter and chop.
Le Guin.   Stanza 4.
Link, L.   Holding Hands.
Mahadevi.   Like an elephant.
McFadden, D.   7. Elephants.
Moore, M.   Black Earth.
Morabito, F.   Elefantes nacen viejos, Los. Elephants are born old.
Mosquera, A.   Tamoxifen.
Richards, I.   Eletelephony.
Sandburg, C.   Elephants Are Different to Different People.
Saxe, J.   Blind Men and the Elephant, The.
Schley, J.   Cradle Song: "Reapers and sowers, gleaners and drovers."
Sŏ Chŏngju.   Elephants of Thailand.
Soupault.   Twilight.
Takamura Kotaro.   Elephant's Piggy Bank, The.
Unknown.   Elephant.

Water pouring from clouds.
Van Walleghen.   Elephant in Winter, The.

Elevators
Bierce.   Safety-Clutch.
Fraser, S.   Elevator: "Passing my floor."
Holan.   Meeting in a Lift.
Taylor, H.   Elevator Music.

Elgin Marbles
Keats.   On Seeing the Elgin Marbles.

Elijah (Bible)
Blickstein, J.   Vision of Salt & Water: Elijah's Horn.
Dickinson, E.   Elijah's Wagon knew no thill.

Eliot, T. S. (Thomas Stearns)
Al-Bayati, A.   To TS Eliot.
Cope, W.   Waste Land Limericks.
Crawford, R.   Love Song of Tommo Frogley.
Eliot, T. S.   Lines for Cuscuscaraway and Mirza Murad Ali Beg.
Levi, P.   New Year's Eve Poem 1965.
Lowell, R.   T. S. Eliot.
Starbuck, G.   Said ("J. Alfred Prufrock to.").
Wallace-Crabbe.   Double Dactyl.
Webb, M.   Thanks in Winter.
Zukofsky, L.   First Movement: "And out of olde bokes, in good feith".

Elizabeth I, Queen of England
Bradstreet, A.   Here lies the pride of Queens, pattern of Kings.
   In Honour of that High and Mighty Princess Queen Elizabeth of Happy Memory.
Dubie.   Elizabeth's War with the Christmas Bear.
Elizabeth I.   Doubt of Future Foes.
   Written with a Diamond on Her Window at Woodstock.
Kipling, R.   Looking Glass, The.
Ondaatje.   Elizabeth.
Peele.   Write write yow Croniclers of Tyme and Fame.
Pembroke, M.   Dialogue between Two Shepherds, Thenot and Piers, in Praise of ASTRÆA.
   To the Thrice-Sacred Queen Elizabeth.
Puttenham.   Her Majestie Resembled to the Crowned Piller. Ye Must Read Upward.
Seager, J.   To Queen Elizabeth.
Unknown.   Short and Sweet Sonnet Made by One of the Maids of Honour, upon the Death of Queen Elizabeth, Which She Sewed upon a Sampler, in Red Silke, A.

Elizabeth, Queen of Bohemia
Wotton, S.   On His Mistress [*or* Mistris], the Queen of Bohemia.

Elk
Ceravolo.   Ho Ho Ho Caribou.
Dugan, A.   On the Elk, Unwitnessed.
Nash, O.   Wapiti, The.
Pack, R.   Elk in Winter.
Unknown.   Song of the Elk.

Ellington, Edward Kennedy (Duke)
Baraka, I.   Duke's World.
Dana, R.   Elegy for the Duke.
Fabio.   Tribute to Duke.
Jackson, R.   For Duke Ellington.
Komunyakaa, Y.   Twilight Seduction.
Lucca, C.   Conversation with Duke Ellington and Louis (Pops) Armstrong.

Elm Trees
Ayres, R.   Neighbor's Elm, The.
Clare, J.   Fallen Elm, The.
Elliott, E.   Drone *v.* Worker.
Field.   Leaves.
Gibbons, R.   Affect of Elms, The.
Kessler, R.   Elm Tree on Lafayette Street, The.
Melville, H.   Malvern Hill.
Mueller, L.   Triage.
Plath.   Elm.
Simpson, A.   Waking.
Taggard.   Dilemma of the Elm.
Thomas, E.   October.

Elopement
Campbell, T.   Lord Ullin's Daughter.
Derricotte.   Family Secrets.
Keats.   Eve of St. Agnes, The.

Longfellow, H.   Skeleton in Armor [*or* Armour], The.
Mu, King of Paekche.   Song of Sŏdong.
Scott, S.   Jock of Hazeldean.
   Lochinvar.
Unknown.   Bleeding Nun, The.
   To His Love.

Elves
Bangs, J.   Little Elf, The.
Bishop, E.   Behind Stowe.
Chaucer.   Wife of Bath's Tale, The.
Keats.   Belle Dame sans Merci, La [A Ballad].
Mayer, B.   Corn.
Ray, H.   Dream of Elfland, A.
Unknown.   Tam Lin.
See also **Fairies**

Elysian Fields
Boullosa, C.   Elysian Garden.
   Jardín Elíseo.

Emancipation (1863–65)
Heard, J.   General Robert Smalls.
Howe, J.   Battle Hymn [*or* Battle-Hymn] of the Republic, The.
Johnson, J.   Fifty Years.
Moorer.   Emancipation Day.
Thompson, P.   Emancipation.
   Freedom at McNealy's.
   Hymn: "Lord, within thy fold I be."
Unknown.   No More Auction Block.
Whittier.   Laus Deo!

Embarrassment
Akera Kanko.   Under a ragged loincloth.
Birnbaum, M.   By the River.
Burkard.   Woman in the Red House.
Johnson, D.   Honor, The.
McDonald, E.   Uncle: "Sam was a family embarrassment."
Olds, S.   Once.
Rosenthal, G.   Wild Hooves.
Williams, H.   Saturday Morning.
Witte, Francine.   Prom.
Wright, C.   Why Ralph Refuses to Dance.

Embryos
Dunmore.   Scan at 8 Weeks.
Macphee, K.   Ultrasound at 13 Weeks.
Muldoon, P.   Sonogram, The.
Traherne.   Preparative, The.
Walker, J.   Coming into History.
Wright, J.   Woman to Man.

Emerson, Ralph Waldo
Cooke, R.   R. W. Emerson.
Grumman, Bob.   Mathemaku No. 16.
Lee, L.   Cleaving, The.
Lowell, J.   Emerson.
Ray, H.   Emerson.

Emigration and Emigrants
Bennett, L.   Colonization in Reverse.
Boucicault, D.   I'm Very Happy Where I Am: A Peasant Woman's Song, 1864.
Brodsky, J.   Mary, the Scots are sots in any case.
Browne, F.   Australian Emigrant, The.
Caird, J.   Emigrants.
Chinese Oral Tradition.   Song of the Wife of a Gold Mountain Man.
Dufferin and Clandeboye.   Lament of the Irish Emigrant.
Dunn, D.   Landscape with One Figure.
Griffiths, J.   Emigrants.
Hall, D.   Sister on the Tracks, A.
Hemans.   Song of Emigration.
Hernández Cruz.   New/Aguas Buenas/Jersey.
Hill, S.   Masters.
Iofe, Y.   Olsanski Cemetery, The.
Jackson, H.   Emigravit.
Mak.   Farewell to Russia.
McCarthy, T.   Emigration Trains, The.
Milosz, C.   Bypassing Rue Descartes.
Nichols, G.   Wherever I Hang.
Rumens.   Emigrée, The.
Sigourney.   Western Emigrant, The.
Weisz, O.   Sefarad.
See also **Immigration and Immigrants**

Emilia
Beck, R.   Epilogue for Emilia.
   Interlude: "Sing together."

Emmet, Robert
Moore, T.　She Is Far from the Land.
Emotions
Adisa.　Fennel.
Ayukawa Nobuo.　Love: "I'm Japanese."
Bayly.　Soldier's Tear, The.
Bingxin.　Myriad Stars, Part 132.
Brown, S.　Agapé.
Brown, T.　Pain.
Cărtărescu, Mircea.　Happy Day in My Life, A.
Clark, T.　What I've Learned in My Travels.
Cullen, Y.　Kabuki.
Davies, W. H.　Joy and Pleasure.
Dorantes, D.　Meter todas las manos en el agua.
　To put all hands into the water.
Duncan, R.　Returning to Roots of First Feeling.
Finch, A.　Landing under Water, I See Roots.
Hamby, B.　Beriberi.
Horace.　Bring Roses and Cardamom (2.3).
Hyde, E.　About Poems.
Ikkyu Sojun.　I Like My Anger My Grouchy
　Furious Love.
Kim Sünghŭi.　Floating Metonymy 5.
Lummis, Suzanne.　Sea Chanty.
Mitchell, N.　Love Story in Subtitles.
Mullen, H.　Omnivore.
Nance.　State Song.
Nester, Daniel.　Third Maisie Poem.
Nichol.　Love song 2.
Ono no Yoshiki.　My love / Is like the grasses.
Prasad, V.　Liberation.
Redmond.　Highflown: Love.
Rilke.　We Must Die Because We Have Known
　Them.
Rosenberg, L.　Poems of Delight.
Royet-Journoud.　I.E.
Sappho.　In my eyes he matches the gods, that
　man who.
Shannon, A.　Hands.
Warsh.　What I've Learned in My Travels.
Willis, Elizabeth.　Without Pity.
Winters, Y.　Summer Commentary, A.
Empedocles
Gregory, H.　Death and Empedocles 444 B.C..
Emperors and Empresses
Chinese Oral Tradition.　How Liu Chih-yüan
　Bade San-niang Good-bye and Joined the
　Army in T'ai-yüan.
　Scroll 1: "From the Three Emperors and Five
　Kings down to Hsia, Shang, and Chou."
Herbert, Z.　Emperor's Dream, The.
Liu Pang.　Song of the Great Wind.
Segalen.　Funerary Edict.
Unknown.　Song of the Peasants in the Time of
　Yao.
Empire State Building, New York City
Berrigan, T.　Bean Spasms.
Emptiness
Andreus.　Empty Room, The.
Armstrong, Tammy.　Presque Isle, Maine.
Bobrowski.　Deserted Village.
Budbill.　Thirty-Five Miles to a Traffic Light.
Cabral de Melo Neto.　Emptiness of Being a
　Man, The.
　Emptiness of Man, The.
Cagnone, N.　Book Three: On Preparation.
Cavalli.　I remember little of myself.
Ceravolo.　Warmth.
Clark, T.　Like Musical Instruments.
Creeley.　Dishonest Mailmen, The.
　Language, The.
　Long road of it all, The.
Dabney.　Earth's Bondman.
Dalton, A.　Almost Bird.
Davis, K.　Animal Zen.
Domin.　Remigration.
Eliot, T. S.　Conversation Galante.
　Gerontion.
　Hollow Men, The.
　Waste Land, The.
Forrester, S.　Plum blossom breeze.
Gallagher, T.　Coming Home.
Galvin, J.　On Exploration.
Graves, R.　Not at Home.
Guillén, J.　I Want to Sleep.

Han Yü.　Losing a Tooth.
Hardy, T.　Exeunt Omnes.
Harms.　After Yes.
Harris, Ken.　Poem in Progress.
Herbert, G.　Dotage.
Herbert, Z.　Drawer.
Herrera.　House Is Empty Now.
Howard, R.　Among the Missing.
Hughes, L.　Summer Night.
Hughes, T.　You are a wild look—out of an egg.
Ivey, M.　After You Left.
Johnson, D.　Incognito Lounge, The.
Juarroz.　Emptiness of the day, The.
Kassabova, K.　Preparation for the Big
　Emptiness.
Kerouac.　113th Chorus.
Kimbrell, J.　Empty House.
Kipling, R.　Derelict, The.
Kupriyanov [or Kuprianov].　Lesson in Natural
　History, A.
Kyle, C. J.　Argument, The.
Lal Ded [or Lalla].　Coursing in emptiness.
Larbaud.　Gift of Oneself, The.
Lindsay, V.　Leaden-eyed, The.
Magdeburg, Mechthild von.　Desert Has Many
　Teachings, The.
Magrelli.　I'm what is missing.
Maré, N.　You Can Say That the Bird as the
　Saying Goes.
McGrath, T.　After Tomasito's Departure.
Merwin.　"Prodigal Son," The.
Mew.　I Have Been through the Gates.
Millay, E.　Bluebeard.
Nolens, L.　Poetic License.
Oppen.　Population.
Ouwens.　Farmer, The.
Padgett, R.　Nothing in That Drawer.
Prados, E.　Song: "Bridge of my solitude."
Prasad, V.　Empty.
Quarles.　Nahum 2.10.
Robinson, E.　Undoing, The.
Sagan.　Yojimbo.
Sahn, Seung.　Mountain sinks into the sea, The.
Salinas, P.　Not in Marble Palaces.
Simic.　Mirrors at 4 A.M.
Smith, Douglas Burnet.　Bare Places.
Tagore.　Last Poems 10.
Towers, T.　Mission Poem.
Tsvetayeva [or Tsvetaeva].　Horn of Roland,
　The.
Tu Fu [or Du Fu].　Facing Snow ("Enough new
　ghosts now to mourn any war.").
Valéry.　Seaside Cemetery, The.
Van de Woestijne.　I Am the Hazel-Nut.
Wang Wei.　On the Mountain.
Williams, C. K.　Spring: another / joke.
Williams, W.　These.
Wright, C.　Disjecta Membra.
Zukofsky, L.　Anew 20.
Emus
Tjinapirrgarri.　Emu Shot.
Enchantment
Brontë, E.　Spellbound.
Carew, T.　In Praise of His Mistress.
Disch.　Rapist's Villanelle, The.
Fletcher, G.　I saw, sweet Licia, when the spider
　ran.
Hardy, T.　First Sight of Her and After.
Keats.　Belle Dame sans Merci, La [A Ballad].
Landon.　Enchanted Island, The.
Mickiewicz.　Mushroom Gatherers, The.
Spenser, E.　Eftsoones they heard a most
　melodious sound.
Wright, R.　Depiction of Childhood.
Yeats.　Sorrow of Love, The [1892 Version].
End of the World
Akhmatova, A.　Land not mine, still, A.
Bishop, M.　Eschatology.
Bottomley.　End of the World, The.
Brown, S.　Allegory of the Supermarket.
Browning, R.　Childe Roland to the Dark Tower
　Came.
Byron, G.　Darkness.
Crane, S.　God lay dead in Heaven.
　Should the wide world roll away.
Cummings, E. E.　What If a Much of a Which

　of a Wind.
Derricotte.　Fears of the Eighth Grade.
Donne.　At the round earth's imagined [or
　imagin'd] corners, blow.
Eady.　Dance, The.
Figueroa, J.　Confessions from the Last Cloud.
Frost, R.　Fire and Ice.
　Once by the Pacific.
Graves, R.　Warning to Children.
Hinz-Penner, R.　Prayer for the End of the
　World.
Jackson, A.　Transformable Prophecy.
Jauss.　After the End of the World.
Kinnell.　Fundamental Project of Technology,
　The.
Lieberman, M.　Prediction.
MacLeish.　End of the World, The.
Mahon.　Morning Radio.
McGrath, T.　End of the World, The.
Milosz, C.　Song on the End of the World, A.
Nuriddin, J. M.　Children of the Future.
Otero, B.　Children of the Planet.
Pack, R.　Proton Decay.
Pagis, D.　Lesson in Observation, A.
Pinsky.　Uncreation, The.
Puttenham.　O mightye Muse.
Shapiro, K.　Scyros.
Simic.　December: "It snows."
Simon, M.　Tale Before the End of the World.
Spires.　Sunday Afternoon at Fulham Palace.
Sri Sri.　Announcement, An.
Stafford, W.　For You, Walt Whitman.
Stickney, T.　And, the Last Day Being Come,
　Man Stood Alone.
Sumrall.　Silence at the End of the World.
Thurston, H.　Revelations.
Van Winckel, N.　Watching the Men Walk.
Wade-Gayles.　Loving Again.
Wilbur, R.　Advice to a Prophet.
Williams, C. K.　That the world / is going.
Winters, Y.　Summer Noon: 1941.
Woods, V.　Lost Masterpiece, The.
Wylie.　Doomsday.
See also **Apocalypse; Armageddon; Judgment
Day**
Endangered Species
Merwin.　For a Coming Extinction.
　Shore, The.
Wojahn.　Rajah in Babylon.
Endurance
Archilochus.　No townsman, Perikles, will
　blame us for groaning.
Aua.　To Lighten Heavy Loads.
Baca.　Cloudy Day.
Bek, T.　Beneath the flakes of Russian snow.
Bowles, W.　Time and Grief.
Brathwaite, E.　Prelude: "Drum skin whip."
Brutus.　Endurance.
Cameron, N.　Unfinished Race, The.
Campbell, T.　Lines Written on Visiting a Scene
　in Argyleshire.
Carruth, H.　At Seventy-Five: Rereading an Old
　Book.
Cervantes.　Archeology.
Coleridge, S.　Forbearance.
Delgado, J.　I-5 Incident.
Di Prima.　For H. D.
Hewitt, J.　If I had given you that love and care.
Humphrey, D.　Hope.
Jeffers, R.　Granite and Cypress.
Justice, D.　Pantoum of the Great Depression.
Kipling, R.　Old Men, The.
Kittredge.　Tenting on the Old Camp Ground.
Lawrence, D. H.　Race and Battle.
Livingstone, D.　Darwinian Preface, A.
MacLeish.　Snowflake Which Is Now and Hence
　Forever, The.
Merrill, J.　After Greece.
O'Hara, F.　Poem: "Light clarity avocado salad
　in the morning."
Porteous.　I Envy the Cracked, Black Basalt.
Radnóti.　Forced March ("He is a fool who,
　collapsed on the ground, gets up and walks
　on.").
Serote.　Introit.
Shokushi.　O cord of life!

Strange. Still Life.
Warren, R. To a Face in a Crowd.
Westmorland. Occasioned by Seeing a Walk of Bay Trees.
See also **Fortitude**

Endymion
Elytis, O. As Endymion.
Kinsella, T. Endymion.

Enemies
Ali, Taha Muhammad. Abd El-Hadi Fights a Superpower.
Barrax. In the Restaurant.
Benson, T. Enemies.
Blake, W. Poison Tree, A.
Coleridge, M. Gifts.
Hannah, S. My Enemies.
Hardy, T. Man He Killed, The.
Harjo, J. Returning from the Enemy, Part 6.
Hejinian. Presences that constitute life do so by entering life, The.
Henderson, H. Ninth Elegy: Fort Capuzzo.
Iman. Love Your Enemy.
Juan Chi. In the Shadow of Death.
Logue, C. Know Thy Enemy.
Marcus, B. Battle at Horizon.
Matveyeva [*or* Matveieva]. I'm no fighting man, he says.
Millay, E. First Fig.
Reznikoff. I will write songs against you.
Robinson, E. New Tenants, The.
Shostakovskaya, I. Boy bears a gray shield, The.
Sia, B. Enemy.
Thompson, D. On the Relative Merit of Friend and Foe, Being Dead.
Unknown. Approaching Dance, The.
Seven, The.
Song of the Lenape Warriors Going against the Enemy, The.
Whitman, W. Reconciliation.
Zarco. My Worst Fear.
Zavalnyuk [*or* Zaval'niuk]. I Love My Enemies.
Zolotow. Enemies.

Energy
Avison. Prospecting.
Bingen, Hildegard von. Antiphon for Divine Wisdom.
Bloch, C. Conservation of Energy, The.
Cacciatore, E. Let's try another hand, let's redo the count.
Ceravolo. Dangers of the Journey to the Happy Land.
Césaire, A. Laughable.
Citino. Principles of Scarcity, Doctrines of Growth.
Georgiou, E. Intimate Mixture.
Gunn, T. My Sad Captains.
Hernández Cruz. Energy.
Kendall, M. Ether Insatiable.
Koch, K. Energy in Sweden.
MacCaig. Blue Tit on a String of Peanuts.
Mirabai [*or* Mira Bai]. All I Was Doing Was Breathing.
Mookam Choinul. Sitting Alone.
Pai, S. Office Feng Shui.
Sorrentino. Razzmatazz.
Whitman, W. I celebrate myself, and sing myself.
Wilbur, R. Star System, The.

Energy Crisis
Morley, C. Elegy Written in a Country Coal-Bin.

Engineers
Bolt, T. Glimpse of Terrain.
Cope, W. Engineers' Corner.
Crawford, R. Saltcoats Structuralists, The.
Elliott, G. Poem about Myself.
Kipling, R. Nurses, The.
Whitman, W. O the engineer's joys! to go with a locomotive!

England
Agard, J. Palm Tree King.
Allingham, W. In Snow.
Allnutt, G. About Benwell.

Alvi, M. Laughing Moon, The.
Auden. On This Island.
Beer, P. Millennium.
Belloc. Ha'nacker Mill.
Imitation.
South Country, The.
Berrigan, T. Waterloo Sunset.
Betjeman. Christmas.
In Westminster Abbey.
Blake, W. Fields from Islington to Marybone, The.
Preface: "And did those feet in ancient time."
Bond, E. If.
Bradstreet, A. Dialogue between Old England and New, A.
Brome. On Sir G. B. his defeat.
Brooke, R. Old Vicarage, Grantchester, The.
Soldier, The: "If I should die, think only this of me."
Browning, E. Sweetness of England, The.
Browning, R. Home-Thoughts, from Abroad.
Home-Thoughts, from the Sea.
Burns, R. Such a Parcel of Rogues in a Nation.
Causley. Armistice Day.
At the British War Cemetery, Bayeux.
Chesterton. Elegy in a Country Churchyard.
Rolling English Road, The.
World State, The.
Cisneros, A. Hampton Court.
Coleridge, S. To the Honourable Mr. Erskine.
Collins, W. How Sleep the Brave.
Coward. Stately Homes of England, The.
Croft, A. Beasts of England, The.
D'Aguiar, F. English Sampler, An.
Darwin. Kew.
Day Lewis. You That Love England.
Drayton. *Satyr* O never ask how I came to this place.
What spirit can lift you up, to that immortall praise.
Dryden, J. Mac Flecknoe [*or*, A Satire upon the True-Blue Protestant Poet T. S.].
Duffy, C. In Your Mind.
Duo Duo. In England.
"Ern Malley.". Sweet William.
Furber, D. Lambeth Walk.
Garrick. Heart of Oak.
Gay, N. Lambeth Walk.
Gilbert, W. Utopia Anglicized.
Gorges. Written upon the Death of the Most Noble Prince Henrie.
Gurney, I. Behind the Line.
To the Prussians of England.
Hanson, M. How proudly Man usurps the power to reign.
Hardy, T. On an Invitation to the United States.
Harrison, T. Classics Society.
Durham.
Earthen Lot, The.
Harry, J. Shot of War, A.
Heath-Stubbs. One.
Hemans. England's Dead.
Homes of England, The.
Herbert, G. British Church, The.
Religion stands on tip-toe in our land.
Hewitt, J. Once Alien Here.
Hill, G. Laurel Axe, The.
To the High Court of Parliament ("Where's probity in this.").
Hopkins, G. To Seem the Stranger.
Housman. 1887.
New Mistress, The.
On Wenlock Edge the wood's in trouble.
Hunt, L. Iterating Sonnet.
Hutchinson, P. Fleadh Cheoil.
Jones, D. In the middle silences of this night's course this night.
Jonson, B. To Penshurst.
Keats. Happy Is England! I Could Be Content.
There Was a Naughty Boy.
Kinsella, T. Foot of the tower. An angle where the darkness, The.
Kipling, R. Absent-Minded Beggar, The.
Broken Men, The.
Brown Bess.
Glory of the Garden, The.

Land, The.
Return, The.
Kyffin. Adore November's sacred seventeenth day.
Landon. Factory, The.
Lanier, E. Description of Cooke-ham [*or* Cookham], The.
Larkin, P. MCMXIV.
Lawrence, D. H. English Are So Nice!, The.
Innocent England.
Lindsay, J. Voice of the Wheat, The.
Lopez, T. No Transport.
MacDiarmid, H. We must look at the harebell as if.
MacNeice. I ought to be glad.
Mallet, D. Rule, Britannia!
Marvell. First Anniversary of the Government under His Highness the Lord Protector, 1655, The.
Is this, saith one, the Nation that we read.
Upon Appleton House [To My Lord Fairfax].
Meynell, A. Summer in England, 1914.
Miller, J. At Our Golden Gate.
Mure. O Heavens! O Earth! heer I must pause a space.
Nichols, G. Long-Man.
Wherever I Hang.
Norton, C. Voice from the Factories, A.
Padel, R. Icicles Round a Tree in Dumfriesshire.
Padgett, R. Waterloo Sunset.
Peake. Babe was born in the reign of George, A.
Peele. Write write yow Croniclers of Tyme and Fame.
Pembroke, M. To the Thrice-Sacred Queen Elizabeth.
Philips, K. On the 3 of September, 1651.
"Pindar.". Hymn to the Guilotine.
Plutzik. Airman Who Flew over Shakespeare's England, The.
Porter, P. Last of England, The.
Pound, E. Tudor indeed is gone and every rose.
Prior. Fable, A: "In Æsop's tales an honest wretch we find."
Retallack, J. Secret Life of Gilbert Bond, The.
Riley, P. Another damp Sunday morning up and walk over.
Riordan, M. England, His Love.
Rosenberg, I. Worm Fed on the Heart of Corinth, A.
Salzman, E. English Earthquake, The.
Scammell, W. Act, The.
Scott, D. Playing for England.
Shakespeare, W. Henry V at the Siege of Harfleur.
Now is the winter of our discontent.
Shapcott, J. Motherland.
Shelley, P. England in 1819.
Song to the Men of England.
Skelton, J. Laud and Praise Made for Our Sovereign Lord the King.
Smith, C. Beachy Head.
Spenser, E. Ruines of Time, The.
Stansbury, J. When Good Queen Elizabeth Governed the Realm.
Stevenson, A. Level Cambridgeshire.
Swinburne. Forsaken Garden, A.
Thelwall. To Ancestry.
Thomas, E. Adlestrop.
Thomson, J. Rule, Britannia!
Tighe. Written at Scarborough.
Tomlinson, C. John Maydew or The Allotment.
Unknown. Diggers' Song, The.
I Don't Want to Be a Soldier.
Of Sir Frauncis Walsingham Sir Phillipp Sydney, and Sir Christopher Hatton, Lord Chancelor.
Song Bewailing the Time of Christmas, So Much Decayed in England, A.
Vaughan, H. Charnel-house, The.
Waight, S. To the Coming of the Decade.
Walcott. Far Cry from Africa, A.
Warton, T. While summer-suns o'er the gay prospect played.
Watts, I. Mr. Mead, Mr. Bates, and Mr. Gouge

[or An Elegy on Mr. Thomas Gouge].
Wheatley, P. Farewel[l] to America, A. To Mrs. S. W.
Williams, H. Farewell, for Two Years, to England, A. A Poem.
Wither. If by mischance the people in the street.
Wordsworth, W. Composed by the Sea-Side, near Calais, August, 1802.
I Travelled among Unknown Men.
London 1802 ("Milton! thou shouldst be living at this hour.").
When I have borne in memory what has tamed.
Yeats. On a Political Prisoner.
See also **Civil Wars, England**
English Channel
Smith, C. Beachy Head.
English, The
Allston. America to Great Britain.
Brooke, R. Soldier, The: "If I should die, think only this of me."
Campbell, T. Ye Mariners of England.
Chapman, G. And, for our tongue, that still is so empayr'd.
Cleveland, J. How? 'Providence', and yet a Scottish crew?
Rebel Scot, The.
Coleridge, S. Fears in Solitude [Written in April, 1798, during the Alarm of an Invasion].
Cook, E. Entry of the Marines [or The Red Cross of England].
Coward. Mad Dogs and Englishmen.
Cowley, A. London Subverted by the Furies.
D'Aguiar, F. Dreadtalk.
Defoe, D. Wherever God erects a house of prayer.
Della Cruscans. Notice to Tourists.
Dryden, J. In pious times ere [or e'r] priestcraft did begin.
Finch, P. Why Do You Want to Be English?
Hardy, T. Certain sort of bravery, A.
Kay, J. English Cousin Comes to Scotland.
Kipling, R. Absent-Minded Beggar, The.
Fuzzy-Wuzzy.
Gentlemen-Rankers.
Ladies, The.
Lawrence, D. H. Broadcasting to the G.B.P.
English Are So Nice!, The.
How Beastly the Bourgeois Is.
Lees, J. Jone o' Grinfilt.
Leonard, T. This is thi.
Limburg, J. Barton in the Beans.
Longfellow, H. Rhyme of Sir Christopher, The.
Macaulay, T. Jacobite's Epitaph, A.
Milligan, S. Teeth.
Milton. To the Lord General Cromwell.
Morgan, E. Sir James Murray.
Nichols, G. Beverley's Saga.
Nisbet, H. Isandula.
Pembroke, M. To the Thrice-Sacred Queen Elizabeth.
Pfeiffer, E. Fight at Rorke's Drift, The.
Robinson, M. After Eighteen Years of This Sort of Thing.
Rouse, A. England Nil.
Sackville, C. My Opinion.
Shapcott, J. Phrase Book.
Shelley, P. Song to the Men of England.
Simpson, L. Runner, The.
Smith, S. Celts, The.
This Englishwoman.
Unknown. Song of the English Bowmen.
To Buonaparte.
Western Brothers. Connected with County, and landed estates.
Williams, W. Three English Poets and England.
Wolfe, H. British Journalist, The.
Engraving and Engravers
Gibbs, Robert J. Death of My Father, The.
Kinzie. Engraving of Blake, An.
Klassen, S. Artist and Medium.
Tkachenko. Engraving, An.
Enkidu
Unknown. Coming of Enkidu, The.
Death of Enkidu, The.
Lament of Gilgamesh for Enkidu, The.

Envy
Adams, F. Rich Man, The.
Archilochus. What Gyges so golden has doesn't matter to me.
You see that high crag.
Bertrans de Born. Protestation.
Cagnone, N. No place is extreme.
Catullus. Carmen 5.
Ch'oe Sûngja. Portrait of the Marginalized.
Cole, H. Horses: "Setting out on my bicycle alone."
Coleridge, M. I envy not the dead that rest.
Cook, E. Lines / Suggested by the Song of a Nightingale.
Fauset. La Vie C'est la Vie.
Fenton, J. Skip, The.
Field. So jealous of your beauty.
Gerov, Alexander. Birds: "They don't plow, nor do they sow."
Hass, R. Envy of Other People's Poems.
Hecht, J. September.
Ishikawa Takuboku. Tanka: "On the roadside."
Issa. I envy.
Komunyakaa, Y. Seven Deadly Sins.
Langland, W. Envy with heavy heart asked for shrift.
Lochhead, L. My Rival's House.
Moore, M. Charity Overcoming Envy.
Moritz [or Morits]. Memorandum.
Morshen. Andreyevsky Church, The.
No Hyegyông. Triangle, Mirror.
Porteous. I Envy the Cracked, Black Basalt.
Procter, A. Envy.
Serchuk. My Other Life.
Shakespeare, W. Sonnet 70: "That thou art blam'd shall not be thy defect."
Soto. Envying the Children of San Francisco.
Spenser, E. Envy.
Synge. Dread.
Thomas, L. Foolish Treasures.
Tibbetts. Coming Home.
Unknown. He is handsome.
Wakayama Bokusui. They say there lives.
Yü Hsüan-chi. On a Visit to Ch'ung Chen Taoist Temple.
Yüan Mei. Growing Old (2).
See also **Jealousy**
Epic Poetry
Browning, E. Critics say that epics have died out, The.
Callimachus. Prologue to the Aetia.
De Villagrá. Canto 1.
Kavanagh, P. Epic.
Epictetus
Arnold, M. To a Friend.
Epicureanism
Davies, J. Author Loving These Homely Meats, The.
Epigrams
Coleridge, S. What Is an Epigram?
Erinna. Stele and my sirens and mournful urn.
Jonson, B. To My Book.
Menicanti. Epigram for a Worm.
Parker, D. Oscar Wilde.
Epiphany
Ashbery, J. Evening in the Country.
Beaumont, J. Of the Epiphany.
Cairns, Scott. Surprise.
Collins, M. Epiphany.
D'Haen. Epiphany.
Fitzgerald, R. Epiphany: "Unearthly lightning of presage."
Garrett, E. Reprieve, The.
Johnson, J. Silent Promise, A.
Kyle, C. J. Season of Locking-In, The.
Naong. Auspicious Cloud.
Nijhoff. Light.
Light, The.
Rumi. Walking with Others.
Seferis. Epiphany, 1937.
Smith, W. Sole of Dover.
Whitman, W. Hast Never Come to Thee an Hour.
See also **Twelfth Night**

Epitaphs
Anyte [or Anytes]. No longer will I fling up my neck, exulting.
Youth buried you, Captain; as sons for their mother, The.
Asclepiades. Here Lies Archeanassa.
Behn, A. Epitaph on the Tombstone of a Child, the Last of Seven that Died Before.
Benedikt. Meat Epitaph, The.
Bliss, D. Epitaph of John Jack.
Bloem, J. C. Writing on a Tombstone.
Bradstreet, A. Epitaph on my Dear and Ever Honored Mother Mrs. Dorothy Dudley.
Davidson, D. Lines for a Tomb.
Drummond, W. Melampus' Epitaph.
Freneau. Epitaph for Jonathan Robbins.
Gay, J. My Own Epitaph.
Gray, T. Elegy Written in a Country Churchyard.
Gryphius. Epitaph for Mariana Gryphius, His Brother Paul's Little Daughter.
Herbert, E. Epitaph on Sir Philip Sidney Lying in St Paul's without a Monument, to be Fastned upon the Church Door.
Jackson, L. Dimensions.
Levy, A. Epitaph: "This is the end of him, here he lies."
Lochhead, D. Cemetery at Loch End, Catalone, Cape Breton, The.
Martial. Epitaph on Erotion.
Masters, E. Trainor, the Druggist.
Nossis. When you've laughed out loud and said a friendly.
Owen, E. Epitaph: On the Near-Death Experience.
Plato. Epitaph, An: "I am a drowned man's tomb. There is a farmer's."
Ralegh, S. Authours Epitaph, Made by Himself, The.
Rochester, J. Epitaph on Charles II.
Shirley, J. Garden, The.
Simonides. Thermopylae.
Unknown. Dog Latin.
Whitman, W. As Toilsome I Wander'd Virginia's Woods.
Wordsworth, W. Gravestone upon the Floor in the Cloisters of Worcester Cathedral, A.
Wylie. Epitaph: "For this she starred her eyes with salt."
Equality
Adams, Joan. Yellow Is Me, But All the Same Are We.
Adisa. Women at the Crossroad / (May Elegba Forever Guard the Right Doors).
Anyte [or Anytes]. This Manes alive once was a slave; now dead.
Barbauld. Rights of Woman, The.
Burns, R. For A' That and A' That ["Is there, for honest poverty"].
Carew, T. Rapture, A.
Carroll, L. Alice's Recitation.
Chaucer. Franklin's Tale, The.
Wife of Bath's Tale, The.
Cowper, W. Negro's Complaint, The.
Dickey, J. Basics.
Dickinson, E. Color, Caste, Denomination.
Eady. Why Do So Few Blacks Study Creative Writing?
Giscombe, C. Black River, The.
Ibn az-Zaqqāq, A. My two friends, the love of one's two sons is not heresy, so surely you will both establish my innocence concerning the matter.
Iskrenko. Hair.
Jackson, R. Smile.
Jordan, J. What Would I Do White?
Kelber, M. Pledge of Allegiance to the Family of Earth, A.
Kim Sujang. Standing in your lofty tower.
Konie, G. We Are Equals.
Korinna [or Corinna]. But I sing the excellence of heroes.
Lincoln, A. Gettysburg Address, The.
Martí. I grow a white rose.
Martial. *Ligurra's* fearful I'll contrive.
Pollarolo, G. Good Marriage, A.

Public Enemy. Party for Your Right to Fight.
Reznikoff. Four sailors on the bus, dressed in blue denim shirts.
Rouweler. Silent Time.
Sanchez, S. Poem for July 4, 1994.
Shakespeare, W. I cannot tell what you and other men.
Simonides. Human strength.
Sirowitz, H. Equality.
Spender, S. Not Palaces.
Symonds. Love and Death: A Symphony.
Unknown. I married an emancipated woman.
In all earnestness, I speak to all my sisters.
Whitman, W. America.
Song for Occupations, A.
Yevtushenko [*or* Evtushenko]. Dwarf Birches.
See also **Social Class**

Erie Canal
Allen, W. Erie Canal, The.
Cohan. Down by the Erie Canal.
Unknown. E-ri-e, The.

Erie, Lake
Weems, M. Dime after Dime.

Erne (river), Ireland
Allingham, W. Winding Banks of Erne, The[: Or, The Emigrant's Adieu to His Birthplace].
Muldoon, P. Yggdrasill.

Eros
Agustini. Another Race.
Alcman. It isn't Aphrodite, but wild Eros.
Anacreon. Weaving a garland long ago.
Darío, R. Nicaraguan Triptych.
Goldberg, B. Hound and Leper.
Greger. Psyche and Eros in Florida.
Hall, D. Winged Torso of Eros.
Levertov. Eros.
Mueller, L. Romantics: Johannes Brahms and Clara Schumann.
Rossini, C. Cupid.
Sappho. [Eros] came from heaven wearing a purple cloak.
Once again Love [Eros], the loosener of limbs, shakes me.
Percussion, salt and honey.
Shepherd, R. Eros in His Striped Blue Shirt.
Storni. To Eros.
To Eros.
See also **Cupid**

Erosion
Basho. Autumn wind / Blasting the stones.
Borges. Labyrinth, The.
Coleridge, M. On a Bas-Relief of Pelops and Hippodameia.
Freneau. Towering Alps, the haughty Appenine, The.
Hejinian. Erosion of rocks blooms, The. The world.
Pastan. Erosion.

Erotic Love
Abbott, D. All Day at Work.
Ackerman, D. Sweep Me through Your Many-Chambered Heart.
Adair, T. Night We Called It a Day, The.
Will You Still Be Mine?
Adams, F. If.
Adamson, H. Everything I Have Is Yours.
I Just Found Out about Love.
Time on My Hands.
Adler, R. Hey There.
There Once Was a Man.
Aguilar, M. Sunshine.
Ahmed Pasha. Is there any heart not bleeding.
Akhmatova, A. There Is a Boundary.
Altizer. Sonnet 2: "My own heart let me have. More pity on."
Amaru. You with Your Beautiful Swaying Walk.
Amichai, Y. Quick And Bitter.
To My Love, Combing Her Hair.
Amis, K. Ever-Fixed Mark, An.
Ammons. Love Song: "Like the hills under dusk you."
Anacreon. Count, if you can, every leaf on every tree.
Fragment 360.

Ancient Sumerian Oral Tradition. Bridegroom, dear to my heart.
Word they had spoken, The.
Anday, M. 6. Love: "Forest would start when you held my hand, The."
Andrews, C. Morn's Recompense.
Angus. Invitation.
Apollinaire. My darling little Lou how I love you.
Argentarius. I can't bear to watch your hips.
Armantrout. Language of Love.
Plan, The.
Arnold, C. My Love Is Sick.
Arnold, M. To Marguerite—Continued.
Asclepiades. Didyme waved an olive branch at me.
Think how unspeakably sweet.
Ashbery, J. My Erotic Double.
Atwood-Fukuda. Wreck of the *Platonic*, The.
Auden. As I Walked Out One Evening.
Legend.
Bâkî. Oh Beloved, Since the Origin We Have Been.
Ball, J. And This Is So.
Bangs, C. Touching Each Other's Surfaces.
Barba-Jacob. Song of the Fleeting Day.
Barer, M. Beyond Compare.
On Such a Night as This.
Barker, G. O Golden Fleece.
Barnes, B. Love, for Europa[e]s love took[e] shape of bull.
Sestina: "Then first with locks dishevelled and bare."
Barnfield [*or* Barnefield]. But if thou wilt not pittie my complaint.
Daphnis to Ganymede.
Oh would to God he would but pitty mee.
Scarce had the morning starre hid from the light.
Sporting at fancie, setting light by love.
Sweet Corrall lips, where Nature's treasure lies.
Thus was my love, thus was my Ganymed.
When will my May come, that I may embrace thee?
Barot, R. Three Amoretti.
Baudelaire. Snake That Dances, The.
Beatty, J. Modern Love: "Early evening, five minutes before."
Becker, R. Sonnet to the Imagination.
Bécquer, G. Black Swallows Will Return, The.
Behn, A. On a Juniper-Tree, Cut Down to Make Busks.
Song: "I led my Silvia to a grove."
Song. Love Arm'd [*or* Armed].
To Damon. To Inquire of Him If He Cou'd Tell Me by the Style, Who Writ Me a Copy of Verses That Came to Me in an Unknown Hand.
To the Fair Clarinda [*or* Clorinda], Who Made Love to Me, Imagin'd [*or* Imagined] More Than Woman.
Belev. Love: "What do you scrawl."
Benjamin, B. Oh! What It Seemed to Be.
Bergman, A. Summer Me, Winter Me.
Bergman, M. Summer Me, Winter Me.
Berk, İ. Poem: "Yellow, Loveliest, enters my city."
Berlin. Always.
Say It Isn't So.
You're Just in Love.
Bernstein, J. Tango'd Love.
Berrigan, A. Various multitudes contained by the loves of my love, The.
Berry, W. To Tanya at Christmas.
Berryman. Great citadels whereon the gold sun falls.
Betjeman. Licorice Fields at Pontefract, The.
Potpourri from a Surrey Garden.
Bible, *O.T.* How beautiful are thy feet with shoes.
I am come into my garden, my sister, my spouse.
Song of Solomon, The.
Bihari. *What she said to her companion.*
Bilhana. Even now.
Black, S. Hoopla.
Blackhawk, Terry. Dawn of the Navajo Woman,

The.
Blake, W. Garden of Love, The.
Look of love alarms, The.
Visions of the Daughters of Albion.
Blane, R. Love: "Love can be a moment's madness."
Blind. Many Will Love You.
Bly, R. Listening to the Köln Concert.
Bock, J. Too Close for Comfort.
Bogan, L. Juan's Song.
Breton, A. On the Road to San Romano.
Breton, N. Olden Love-making.
Bricusse, L. What Kind of Fool Am I?
Bridges, R. Eros.
Brinson, C. Sextet.
Brodsky, J. Love Song: "If you were drowning, I'd come to the rescue."
Brooke, R. Dust.
Broughton, J. Twin Flames.
Broumas, O. Caritas.
Privacy.
Brown, L. Best Things in Life Are Free, The.
Browne, W. Shall I tell you whom I love?
Browning, E. Romance of the Swan's Nest, The.
Browning, R. Last Ride Together, The.
Meeting at Night.
Bui-Burton. My Love Is Like a Lily.
Poem for R.
Burke, J. But Beautiful.
Like Someone in Love.
Misty.
You May Not Love Me.
Burns, R. Patriarch, The.
Red, Red Rose, A.
Bynner. Lovers: "From somewhere over the houses, through the silence."
Byron, G. Alas, they were so young, so beautiful.
As boy, I thought myself a clever fellow.
Cornelian, The.
How long in his damp trance young Juan lay.
Last Words on Greece.
Love and Death.
On This Day I Complete My Thirty-sixth Year.
One Struggle More, and I Am Free.
So We'll Go No More A-Roving.
To Thyrza.
Caesar. Sometimes I'm Happy.
Cahn, S. All the Way.
Day by Day.
I Fall in Love Too Easily.
(Love Is) The Tender Trap.
Put 'Em in a Box, Tie 'Em with a Ribbon (And Throw 'Em in the Deep Blue Sea).
Second Time Around, The.
Time After Time.
Until the Real Thing Comes.
Caldwell, E. Love Poem: "Olfactory paradise."
Campbell, J. Good Night, Sweetheart.
If I Had You.
Campion, T. I Care Not for These Ladies.
Carew, T. Rapture, A.
Second Rapture, The.
Song[, A]: "Ask[e] me no more where Jove bestow[e]s."
Carle, F. Oh! What It Seemed to Be.
Carpenter, E. Summer Heat.
Through the Long Night.
Carroll, K. Short Poem.
Carruth, H. Sonnet: "You rose from our embrace and the small light spread."
Cartwright, W. No Platonic [*or* Platonique] Love.
Song of Dalliance, A.
Carver, R. Waiting.
Woman Bathing.
Castellanos. Love: "Only the voice, the skin, the polished."
Catullus. Carmen 5.
He Seems to Me Almost a God.
To Juventius.
Cavalcanti. Encounter, An.
Celan. Corona.
Cemal Süreya. Yellow Blight.
Cempulappeyanirar. What He Said.

Centamputan. What She Said.
Cernuda. For Two Voices.
Lover Digresses, The.
That Which Is Enough for Love.
Chao Luan-luan. Creamy Breasts.
Chapman, G. Bridal Song: "O come, soft rest of cares, come Night."
Chase, K. Venison.
Chatterton. Ode to Miss Hoyland.
Chaucer. Double sorwe of Troilus to tellen, The.
This Troilus in armes gan hir streyne.
Chubb, R. Song of My Soul.
Citino. 6. The Nature of Love.
Walt Whitman in New Orleans, 1848.
Clare, J. First Love.
Clark, C. Border Affair, A.
Clarke, A. Envy of Poor Lovers, The.
Penal Law.
Clarke, C. Rondeau: "They are bodies left unburied."
Clarke, George Elliott. Love Poem / Song Regarding Weymouth Falls.
Cleage. Confession.
Clifton, H. Monsoon Girl.
Clover, J. Map Room, The.
Comden, B. Adventure.
Just in Time.
Little Bit in Love, A.
Connelly, R. Good Night, Sweetheart.
If I Had You.
Cook, E. 'Tis Well to Wake the Theme of Love.
Cortez, J. Pray for the Lovers.
Cory, W. Desiderato.
Deteriora.
Parting.
Coslow, S. (I'm In Love With) The Honorable Mr. So and So.
It's Love Again.
My Old Flame.
Couzyn. Spell to Protect Our Love.
Coward. Let's Do It.
Crane, S. Should the wide world roll away.
Crashaw. Bubble, The.
Crowley, A. Ballad of Passive Paederasty, A.
Dedicace.
Go into the Highways and Hedges, And Compel Them to Come In.
Rondels.
Cullen, C. Wind Bloweth Where It Listeth, The.
Cummings, E. E. I like my body when it is with your.
May i feel said he.
My sweet old etcetera.
Cunningham, P. Aubade: "Man is squeezing oranges in my kitchen, A."
Cushing, J. Lover Man.
Dacre, C. Kiss, The: "Greatest bliss, The."
Dafydd [or David] ap Gwilym. Rattle Bag, The.
Daglarca. Day Within a Day.
Daniel, A. Art of Love, The.
Firm desire which enters, The.
Dante Alighieri. Love and Poetry.
Sestina: Of the Lady Pietra degli Scrovigni.
Darío, R. I Love, You Love.
Darley. It Is Not Beauty I Demand.
Song: "Sweet in her green dell the flower of beauty slumbers."
Darlington, T. Field Guide to Western Intimacy.
David, M. Candy.
Davies, S. Sacred muse that first[e] made love divine [or devine], The.
Davies, M. Love Song: "There is a strong wall about me to protect me."
de Gillies, J. De Puerorum osculis.
DeLange, E. Shake Down the Stars.
Densmore. I Have Found My Lover.
Dermée. Silver Clasps.
These apples.
DeSylva, B. G. Best Things in Life Are Free, The.
Somebody Loves Me.
Dickey, J. Cherrylog Road.
Dickinson, E. Wild Nights—Wild Nights!
Dietz, H. Dancing in the Dark.
Haunted Heart.

You and the Night and the Music.
Diophanes of Myrina. On Love.
Donaldson, W. Because My Baby Don't Mean Maybe Now.
Donne. Air[e] and Angels.
Anniversary [or Anniversarie], The.
Bait[e], The.
Canonization, The.
Confined Love.
Dream[e], The.
Ecstasy, The.
Farewell to Love.
Flea, The.
Good-Morrow, The.
Indifferent, The.
Love's Alchemy [or Alchemie].
Love's Deity [or Deitie].
Love's Growth.
Love's Progress.
Nature's lay idiot [or ideot], I taught thee to love.
Sun Rising, The.
To His Mistress Going to Bed.
Donovan, K. These Last Days.
Doolittle, H. So I would rather drown, remembering.
When in the company of the gods.
Dorcey. Night.
Douglas, L. Two Loves.
Dove, R. Persephone Underground.
Dransfield. Memoirs of a Velvet Urinal.
Drayton. And thus like slaves we sell our soules to sinne.
O breake my hart quoth he, O breake and dye.
Since there's no help, come let us kiss and part.
This Edward in the Aprill of his age.
Why doe I quake my down-fall to reporte?
Drieu la Rochelle. Tennis.
Drummond de Andrade. Don't Kill Yourself.
Dubie. At Midsummer.
Duhamel. Sex with a Famous Poet.
Dunbar, P. Negro Love Song, A.
Durand, M. Reading Postures 3.
Elder daughter of Otomo no Sakanoé: When we could have met.
Elizabeth I. On Monsieur's Departure.
Elledge. Triptych.
Éluard, P. Lady Love.
Éluard, P. et al. 32 Positions of Love, The.
Emerson, R. Eros.
Give All to Love.
Engle, P. Look! The air shudders when you breathe it in.
"Ephelia.". On a Bashful Shepherd.
Erdrich. Woods, The.
"Ern Malley.". Perspective Lovesong.
Evans, D. Dinner at the Hotel de la Tigresse Verte.
Evans, R. To Each His Own.
Faiz. Any Lover to Any Beloved.
Fetter, T. Taking a Chance on Love.
Field, A. Eros Doth Not Always Smite.
As two fair vessels side by side.
Constancy.
Lovers.
Palimpsest, A.
Unbosoming.
Field, T. Compass Room, The: East.
Fields, D. Don't Blame Me.
I Can't Give You Anything but Love.
Remind Me.
There Must Be Somethin' Better Than Love.
Figani Ramazan Çelebi. Your kiss does not satisfy the heart.
Fisher, D. That Old Devil Called Love.
Flaccus, G. Book 7.
Flatman. Appeal to Cats in the Business of Love, An.
Follain. Taxidermist, A.
Forrest, G. And This Is My Beloved.
Strange Music.
Fowler, W. Ship-Broken Men Whom Stormy Seas Sore Toss.
Francis, R. Swimmer.
Freeman, J. Fifteen.
Furber, D. Me and My Girl.

Galvin, P. With My Little Red Knife.
Gangopadhyay. Blindfold.
Gannon, K. Reciprocity.
García Lorca. Ah secret voice of dark love! Ah bleating without wool! Ah wound! Ah prick of gall, sunken camellia!
Poet Speaks the Truth, The.
Gay, N. Leaning on a Lamppost.
Me and My Girl.
Genet. Man Condemned to Death, The.
George, D. I'm Beginning to See the Light.
Gershwin, I. But Not for Me.
Do, Do, Do.
Fun to Be Fooled.
I Got Rhythm.
Isn't It a Pity?
Long Ago (And Far Away).
Love Is Here to Stay.
Love Is Sweeping the Country.
Man I Love, The.
Nice Work If You Can Get It.
Of Thee I Sing.
'S Wonderful.
Someone to Watch over Me.
Who Cares?
Gilyard, K. Portraits of a Moment.
Ginsberg, A. Malest Cornifici Tuo Catullo.
Glück, L. Balcony, The.
Garden, The: "One sound. Then the hiss and whir."
Happiness.
Mirror, The.
Godolphin. Faire Friend, 'tis true, your beauties move.
Thou Joy of my Life.
Goetz, E. For Me and My Gal.
Goldsmith, O. Gift, The. To Iris, in Bow Street, Covent Garden.
When Lovely Woman Stoops to Folly.
Gonzalez, R. Beyond Having.
Gordon, I. Be Anything (But Be Mine).
Unforgettable.
Gordon, M. Head Over Heels in Love.
Mam'selle.
There Will Never Be Another You.
There's a Lull in My Life.
Time on My Hands.
You Hit the Spot.
Graham, D. Varied Carol, The.
Graham, J. Salmon.
Graves, R. Down, Wanton, Down!
Not at Home.
She Tells Her Love While Half Asleep.
Green, A. Adventure.
Just in Time.
Little Bit in Love, A.
Green, B. That's My Weakness Now.
Grimké, A. Beso, El.
Grossmith, G. You Can't Make Love by Wireless.
Grunke, A. Learning to Live with the Piano.
Guinicelli. Canzone: Of the Gentle Heart.
Gunn, T. Hug, The.
Gyatso, T. I sought my lover at twilight.
Lover met by chance on the road.
White teeth smiling.
Wild horses running in the hills.
Habila, H. After the Obsession.
Hacker, M. Ballad of Ladies Lost and Found.
Eight Days in April.
Rondeau after a Transatlantic Telephone Call.
Villanelle: "Every day our bodies separate."
Villanelle: Late Summer.
Hadewijch. Cult of Love, The.
Love has seven names.
Hafiz, K [or Hafez]. Night Visit, The (22).
Hahn, K. Reckless Sonnet.
Hall, D. Winged Torso of Eros.
Hamilton, N. How High the Moon.
Hammerstein. All er Nothin'.
All the Things You Are.
Can't Help Lovin' Dat Man.
Dat's Love (Habanera).
Don't Ever Leave Me.
Hello, Young Lovers.
If I Loved You.

I'll Take Romance.
I've Told Ev'ry Little Star.
Make Believe.
Many a New Day.
Mister Snow.
People Will Say We're in Love.
Some Enchanted Evening.
Song Is You, The.
Who?
Wonderful Guy, A.
Younger Than Springtime.
Han Yong'un [or Yongwun]. Artist, The.
Embroidery's Secret, The.
Love's Reasons.
Master's Sermon, The.
Your Touch.
Harbach, O. Who?
Harburg. Down with Love.
Fun to be Fooled.
Happiness Is Just a Thing Called Joe.
If This Isn't Love.
Last Night When We Were Young.
Old Devil Moon.
Springtime Cometh, The.
Then I'll Be Tired of You.
What Is There to Say?
When I'm Not near the Girl I Love.
Hardy, T. Beeny Cliff.
Neutral Tones.
Harnick. She Loves Me.
Hart, L. Bewitched, Bothered and Bewildered.
Blue Moon.
Falling in Love with Love.
Have You Met Miss Jones?
I Didn't Know What Time It Was.
It's Got to Be Love.
I've Got Five Dollars.
Most Beautiful Girl in the World, The.
My Funny Valentine.
My Heart Stood Still.
My Romance.
Ship Without a Sail, A.
This Can't Be Love.
To Keep My Love Alive.
Where or When.
You Took Advantage of Me.
Hatun. At one glance.
Heath, R. Seeing Her Dancing.
Hecht, A. Gardens of the Villa D'Este, The.
Hemans. Chamois Hunter's Love, The.
Properzia Rossi.
To a Wandering Female Singer.
Henderson, R. Best Things in Life Are Free,
The.
Herbert, G. Love (3): "Love bade me welcome:
yet my soul drew back."
Herbert, Z. Rosy Ear.
Herrick. Her Bed.
Her Legs.
To Anthea, Who May Command Him Anything.
To Dianeme ("Show [or Shew] me thy feet;
show [or shew] me thy legs, thy thighs.").
Upon Julia's Breasts.
Upon Julia's Clothes.
Vine, The.
Hesketh. Love's Advocate.
Heyman, E. Blame It on My Youth.
Easy Come, Easy Go.
Ho Hum.
I Wanna Be Loved.
When I Fall in Love.
You're Mine, You!
Hilary. To an English Boy: "Beautiful boy,
flower fair."
Hill, B. Glory of Love, The.
Hill, S. Don't Let's Talk about Being in Love.
Hirsch, E. Lectures on Love, The.
Hirshfield, J. Painting.
Hogg, J. When Maggy Gangs Away.
Hölderlin. No Pardon.
Holiner, M. Until the Real Thing Comes.
Why Shouldn't It Happen to Us?
You Can't Stop Me from Lovin' You.
Holofcener, L. Too Close for Comfort.
Hongnang. I send you, my love.
Hope, A. Blason, A.

Horace. Ode 4.7: "Snow dissolv'd no more is
seen, The."
Old Malediction, An.
Horton, G. Early Affection.
Housman. Because I liked you better.
He would not stay for me; and who can
wonder?
If truth in hearts that perish.
Look not in my eyes, for fear.
Shake hands, we shall never be friends, all's
over.
When I was one-and-twenty.
Howard, B. Fly Me to the Moon (In Other
Words).
Who Besides You.
Would You Believe It?
Year After Year.
Howe, F. Once on a summer night.
Huddle. Music.
Huerta, D. Thirteen Propositions against Trivial
Love.
Trece intenciones contra el amor trivial.
Hughes, L. Juke Box Love Song.
Lament over Love.
Lover's Return.
Hughes, T. Bride and Groom Lie Hidden for
Three Days.
Hung Hung. Helas!
Hupfeld, H. As Time Goes By.
Huxley, A. Armour.
Hwang Chini. Blue mountains speak of my
desire.
Ibycus. Again Love, glancing meltingly.
In Spring.
Ignatow, D. Each Day.
Im Che. Woman's Sorrow, A.
Izumi. If you love me.
Jacinto, A. Letter from a Contract Worker.
Jackson, A. Cayenne.
Jackson, D. Nice Sister-Scholars Need Loving,
Too.
Jackson, L. O Vocables of Love.
Take Hands.
You or You.
Jackson, R. Sonata of Love's History.
James, J. Sister Midnight.
James, J. Can This Be Love?
Fine and Dandy.
Japicx, G. Lovelight.
Jaufré Rudel. Love Song.
Jeffers, R. For Una.
Jiménez, J. Faster, Earth, Faster.
To the bridge of love.
Jobim, A. Quiet Nights of Quiet Stars
(Corcovado).
Johnson, G. I Want to Die While You Love Me.
Jones, S. Force of Love, The.
Jonson, B. Song. To Celia ("Come my Celia, let
us prove.").
Jordan, A. Beggar's Song.
Kind of Blue.
Jordan, J. Grand Army Plaza.
Joyce, J. Though I thy Mithridates were.
Kabir. I Cherish That Love.
Kahal, I. When I Take My Sugar to Tea.
Kahn, G. I'm Through with Love.
Kalmar et al. Three Little Words.
Kang Ŭn'gyo. Love's Way.
Kasdorf. Eve's Striptease.
Keats. Bright Star.
Sudden a thought came like a full-blown rose.
Kennelly. Wings.
Kenny, Melanie. Hungry as the Sea.
Khayr, A. If I've been dead for twenty years or
so.
Kikaku. In the Emperor's bed.
Kim Ch'unsu [or Chun-soo]. Masks.
Kim Namjo. Love's Cursive.
Kim Sangyong. Love Is False.
Kinnell. Perch, The.
Rapture.
That Silent Evening.
Waking, The.
Kizer, C. Copulating Gods, The.
Food of Love.
Glass, The.

Kramer, A. Candy.
Kunitz, S. Touch Me.
Kuzmin. Ah, those lips, kissed by so many.
Antinous.
At noon I must have been conceived.
At the Party.
Leaving my house in the morning.
Not for nothing did we read the theologians.
People see gardens and houses.
Were you apprenticed to a fortune teller?
Labé. Kiss me again, and kiss me still, and kiss.
Lady Ise. Pillows know, they say.
Lamantia. Winter Day, A.
Landon. Girl at Her Devotions, A.
Proud Ladye, The.
Landor, W. Mother, I Cannot Mind My Wheel.
Rose Aylmer.
Latouche, J. Honey in the Honeycomb.
Love Turned the Light Out.
Maybe I Should Change My Ways.
Taking a Chance on Love.
Laughlin, J. Bird of Endless Time, The.
Inn at Kirchstetten, The.
O Best of All Nights, Return and Return Again.
Rhyme.
Laurencin, M. Present, The.
Lawrence, D. H. Gloire de Dijon.
Young Wife, A.
Lawrence, J. All or Nothing at All.
Foolin' Myself.
Sleepy Lagoon.
What's Your Story, Morning Glory.
Ledwidge. Spring Love.
Lee, P. I Love Being Here with You.
Lee, W. Lovers' Duet.
Lees, G. Right to Love, The.
Leigh, C. How Little We Know (How Little It
Matters).
It Amazes Me!
I've Got Your Number.
Rules of the Road, The.
Lerner, A. Almost Like Being in Love.
Leslie, E. For Me and My Gal.
Levchev. Dénouement.
Levchev, Vladimir. Athens.
Levertov. Eros at Temple Stream.
Hymn to Eros.
Love Poem: "What you give me is."
Poem Unwritten, The.
Levy, A. Sinfonia Eroica.
Lewis, G. Ménage à Trois.
Li Ch'ing-chao. To the Tune: Sands of the
Washing Stream.
Li Po. Take Wine.
Limonov. As if a quiet branch drew a line.
Liu Yung. Song: "After the eating, the drinking,
the singing."
Song: "She lowers her fragrant curtain."
Livingston, J. To Each His Own.
Livingstone, D. One Time.
Lodge, T. Rosalind's [or Rosalynd's]
Madrigal[l].
Loesser. I Wish I Didn't Love You So.
Lady's in Love with You, The.
Once in Love with Amy.
Two Sleepy People.
López Velarde. Ants.
Lorde. Echo.
Love Poem: "Speak earth and bless me with
what is richest."
On a Night of the Full Moon.
Recreation.
Lovelace, R. Love Made in the First Age[: To
Chloris].
To Lucasta, [on] Going to the War[re]s.
Lowe, J. With Thanks to Eddie Shaw.
Lowell, A. April.
Aubade: "As I would free the white almond
from the green husk."
Bungler, The.
Vespers.
Lowell, R. Man and Wife.
Lowry, M. Volcano is Dark, The.
Mabuza. Love Song, A: "It was good."
Macari, A. Even Love.
MacDonald, B. Somebody Loves Me.

Mackay, J. Nameless Love, The.
Tomorrow.
MacKenzie, John. Sledgehammer.
MacNeice. Shelley and jazz and lieder and love
and hymn-tunes.
Madan. Abelard to Eloisa.
Magidson, H. (I'm Afraid) The Masquerade Is
Over.
Maguire, S. Perfect Timing.
Mallarmé. Afternoon of a Faun, The.
Maltby, R. Little Bit Off, A.
Marbod of Rennes. This vision of a face,
radiant and full of beauty.
Marino. Out of the Italian.
Marion, G. Love Is a Random Thing.
My Future Just Passed.
There's a Man in My Life.
Marks, G. All of Me.
Marlowe. Amorous Leander, beautiful and
young.
By this Leander being near the land.
Here is the form of Gaveston's exile.
My father is deceas'd. Come, Gaveston.
Passionate Shepherd to His Love, The.
Martí. In the shadow of a wing.
Martin, H. Love: "Love can be a moment's
madness."
Marvell. To His Coy Mistress.
Marx, S. Mark Antony's Valentine.
Maschwitz, E. Nightingale Sang in Berkeley
Square, A.
Massimi. Love Song for Marcus, A.
On Happiness.
Mayakovsky [or Maiakovskii]. Cloud in
Trousers, A.
McDaniel, J. D.
McQuilkin. Learning the Angels.
Meinke. Love Poem 1990.
Meleager. Epigram: "At 12 o'clock in the
afternoon."
To Aristogoras.
Meogo. Cantiga de Amigo.
Cossante.
Mercer, J. Come Rain or Come Shine.
Day In—Day Out.
How Little We Know.
I Remember You.
P.S. I Love You.
That Old Black Magic.
Meredith, W. Crossing Over.
Metras, G. Vanishing Point.
Mew. À Quoi Bon Dire.
Michelangelo Buonarroti. Flee, lovers, from
Love, flee from his fire.
From sweet weeping to a painful smile.
I live in sin, and dying to myself I live.
I see in your beautiful face, my lord.
It was over here that my love, in his mercy.
Like dry wood in a burning fire.
Soul tries a thousand remedies in vain, The.
Violent burning for prodigious beauty, A.
Why should I still pour out my intense desire.
You know that I know, my lord, that you know.
Millay, E. I think I should have loved you
presently.
Night is my sister, and how deep in love.
Milosz, C. After Paradise.
Mistral, G. I Love, Love.
Montague, J. All Legendary Obstacles.
Montemayor, C. Cytherea.
Moore, G. Rondo: "Did I love thee? I only did
desire."
Moore, H. Green Place, A.
Moraes, D. Snow on a Mountain.
Moronelli da Fiorenza. Canzonetta: A Bitter
Song to His Lady.
Nabokov. Lolita.
Nash, O. I'm a Stranger Here Myself.
Speak Low.
Nashe [or Nash]. Choise of Valentines, The.
Nedim. When the east wind leaves that curl.
Nelson, J. Our Love.
Neruda. Drunk as drunk on turpentine.
Nesbit, E. Vies Manquées.
Newley, A. What Kind of Fool Am I?
Nichols, G. Configurations.

Noble, R. Good Night, Sweetheart.
I Hadn't Anyone Till You.
Very Thought of You, The.
Nonnus. But Dionysos had no healing physic
for his comrade fallen, of dancing he thought
no more.
Dionysus and Ampelos.
Eros came near in the horned shape of a shaggy
Silenos.
Where Carpos wandered and died, I will fall
headlong.
Norman, P. When I Take My Sugar to Tea.
Noyes, A. Highwayman, The.
Nuccoli. Since I abandoned and tied my soul to
your sweet appearance and manners oh Sir,
guide and light of my life, will I ever see you
before I die?
You have the light of my life, in your clear and
pleasing face, and don't see me.
Your promises come to me always together with
your betrayals, which you have more of than
the fox.
Nŭngun. Waiting for My Love.
Olds, S. Last Night.
True Love.
Wellspring, The.
Olin. My Boyfriend, the Infidel.
Olson, C. Boats' lights in the dawn going so
swiftly the, The.
Ondaatje. Cinnamon Peeler, The.
Ono no Komachi. Autumn nights, it seems.
Diver does not abandon, A.
Thinking about him.
Though I go to you.
Yielding to a love.
Orr, G. We Must Make a Kingdom of It.
Orton, B. Love Poem.
Ostriker. Idea of Making Love, The.
Otomo no Sakanoé, Lady. Don't you cut the
brush.
Ovid. Amores (after Ovid).
Apollo and Hyacinthus.
Ovid in Love.
Owen, W. Music.
To Eros.
Oyake. Hidden in the clouds.
Parini. To His Dear Friend, Bones.
Parish. Stars Fell on Alabama.
Sweet Lorraine.
Parker, D. Anecdote: "So silent I when Love
was by."
Pour Prendre Congé.
Unfortunate Coincidence.
Parra, N. Viper, The.
Pasolini. Southern Dawn.
Pasternak, B. Don't Touch.
To Love.
Patchen. Character of Love Seen as a Search
for the Lost, The.
In Memory of Kathleen.
Religion Is That I Love You.
Paz. All is transformed and is sacred.
As One Listens to the Rain.
Madrid, 1937, / in the Plaza del Angel the
women.
Peele. Song: "Whenas [or When as] the Rye [or
Rie] reach to the chin."
Penna. Pitiless war of love I fought, A.
Petrarch. He Understands the Great Cruelty of
Death.
It was the day when the sun's rays turned pale
with grief for his.
You who hear in scattered rhymes the sound of
those sighs with.
Petronius Arbiter. Doing, a filthy pleasure is,
and short.
My bed was soft, the early night was bliss.
Philodemus. I Loved—Who Hasn't?
Xanthippe, singing at her lyre.
Pickard, T. Bush Telegram.
Piercy. Raisin Pumpernickel.
Pilkington, L. Dol and Roger.
Fair and Softly Goes Far or, The Wary
Physician.
Pindar. Ode on Theoxenos.
Pinkerton, H. For an End.

Pizarnik. Silences.
Politziano, A. Splendor and pride I celebrate.
Poliziano. Love Song for Chrysokomos
(Goldenlocks).
Porter, C. Let's Not Talk About Love.
Love for Sale.
Ridin' High.
So in Love.
What Is This Thing Called Love?
Porter, P. Affair of the Heart.
Pound, E. Speech for Psyche in the Golden
Book of Apuleius.
To Kalon.
Virginal, A.
Powell, Dannye Romine. Woman Who Allowed
Light to Have Its Way with Her, The.
Pratt, E. Lee-Shore, The.
Praxilla. Peeking in through.
Previn, D. Morning After, The.
Prior. Question, to Lisetta, The.
Probyn. After.
Barcarolle.
Before.
Blossom.
China Maniacs.
Lai.
Love in Mayfair.
Procter, A. Philip and Mildred.
Woman's Answer, A.
Woman's Last Word, A.
Propertius. Night's best of all. Night brings
delight.
Pushkin, A. I Loved You.
Imitation of the Arabic.
Ode on the Hills of Georgia.
Quevedo y Villegas. Amorous Sonnet Defining
Love.
Continues in the Same State of Feeling.
Raffalovich, M. A. Rose Leaves When the Rose
Is Dead.
World Well Lost 18, The.
Raine, K. Love-Poem: "Yours is the face that
the earth turns to me."
Ralegh, S. Nymph's [or Nimphs] Reply to the
[Passionate] Shepherd [or Sheepheard], The.
Randall, D. Blackberry Sweet.
Rankine. Testimonial.
Ransom, J. Equilibrists, The.
Rashad, J. Morning After, The.
Raye, D. You Don't Know What Love Is.
Razaf, A. Guess Who's in Town? (Nobody but
That Gal of Mine).
Keepin' Out of Mischief Now.
Porter's Love Song to a Chambermaid, A.
S'posin'.
You're Lucky to Me.
Rendra. Tall Weeds.
Rexroth, K. Did you take me because you loved
me?
Frost covers the reeds of the marsh.
How many lives ago.
Night is too long to the sleepless, The.
Oh the anguish of these secret meetings.
Quietly.
Uguisu sing in the blossoming trees.
Void Only.
Who is there? Me.
You ask me what I thought about.
Rich, A. Floating Poem, Unnumbered, The.
I wake up in your bed. I know I have been
dreaming.
My mouth hovers across your breasts.
Riley, P. E Questa Vita Un Lampo.
Roberts, A. That Old Devil Called Love.
Roberts, E. Old Love in Song, An.
Robin, L. Hooray for Love.
In Love In Vain.
Robinson, A. Posies.
Tuscan Olives.
Rochester, J. Imperfect Enjoyment, The.
Rodgers, W. Net, The.
Roethke. I Knew a Woman.
Rohrer, M. Gliding toward the Lamps.
Rollings. Dirty Dreams and God Smiling.
Rome, H. Who Knows?
Ronsard. Génèvres Hérissez, et Vous, Houx

Espineux.
When you are old, at evening candle-lit.
Rose, B.   I Wanna Be Loved.
More Than You Know.
Ross, J.   Hey There.
There Once Was a Man.
Rossetti, C.   Bed of Forget-Me-Nots, A.
Birthday, A.
"Love me, for I love you"—and answer me.
Many in aftertimes will say of you.
Rossetti, D.   Blessed Damozel, The.
Insomnia.
Sudden Light.
52: Willowwood ("So sang he: and as meeting rose and rose").
Ruby, H.   Three Little Words.
Rukeyser, M.   Nevertheless the Moon.
Rumi.   Caring for My Lover.
I, you, he, she, we.
Like This.
Minute I heard my first love story, The.
This night there are no limits to what may be given.
Rungano.   This Morning.
Russell, B.   Crazy She Calls Me.
I Didn't Know About You.
St. John, D.   My Friend.
St. John, P.   Obsessions Are Important.
Salaam.   Haiku # 135: "My butterfly breaths."
Our Natures Rise.
Why I Dont Leave the Apartment Until After Ten Some Mornings.
Salihoğlu, M.   Smoke upon Smoke.
Sappho.   Eros seizes and shakes my very soul.
He is almost a god, a man beside you.
I love / love's delicacy.
I simply wish to die.
It's no use.
Night / Virgins.
With his venom.
Scarlatti.   Lanza 51.
Schwartz, R. L.   Falling in Love after Forty.
Scott, A.   Rondel of Luve [or Love], A.
Sedley.   Song: "Phillis, let's shun the common fate."
Segal, J.   Nothing Ever Changes My Love for You.
Sexton.   Us.
Shakan, J.   Soft.
Shakespeare, W.   All swoln with chasing, down Adonis sits.
Come night! come, Romeo! come, thou day in night!
Phoenix and the Turtle, The.
Sonnet 15: "When I consider every thing that grows."
Sonnet 61: "Is it thy will thy image should keep open."
Sonnet 66: "Tired [or Tyr'd or Tir'd] with all these, for restful[l] death I cry."
Sonnet 80: "O, how I faint when I of you do write."
Sonnet 87: "Farewell! thou art too dear[e] for my possessing."
Sonnet 88: "When thou shalt be dispos'd to set me light."
Sonnet 116: "Let me not to the marriage of true minds."
Sonnet 130: "My mistress' eyes are nothing like the sun."
Sonnet 138: "When my love swear[e]s that she is made of truth."
Shange.   If I Go All the Way without You Where Would I Go!
Where the Mississippi Meets the Amazon.
Sharkey.   Hots, The.
Shaughnessy, B.   You Love, You Wonder.
Shaw, A.   April.
Shelley, P.   Indian Serenade, The.
Shrine Priestess of Ise.   My mind is dazzled.
Sidney.   My true love hath my heart [or hart], and I have his.
Second Song: "Have I caught my heav'nly jewel."
Sonnet 1: "Loving in truth, and fain[e] in verse my love to show."

Sonnet 31: "With how sad steps, O Moon[e], thou climb'st the skies."
Sonnet 54: "Because I breathe not love to every one."
When, to my deadly [or deadlie] pleasure.
Siken, Richard.   Primer for the Small Weird Loves, A.
Simic.   Breasts.
My Beloved.
Simons, S.   All of Me.
Sin Hŭm.   Rain came overnight, A.
Smith, C.   On the Aphorism "L'Amitié est l'Amour sans Ailes".
Smith, K.   Old Women and Love.
Smith, W.   Pavane for the Nursery, A.
Snodgrass.   Love Lamp.
Sŏ Chŏngju.   Winter Sky.
Sologuren.   Oh, Astonishing Love.
Song.   White Porch, The.
Soutar.   Tryst [or Trysting Place], The.
Spahr, J.   December 4, 2002.
Spender, S.   Abrupt and Charming Mover.
To T. A. R. H.
Spenser, E.   Epithalamion: "Ye learned sisters which have oftentimes."
First was Fancy, like a lovely boy, The.
Sonnet 54: "Of this world's Theatre in which we stay."
Sonnet 75: "One day I wrote her name upon the strand."
There now he lives in everlasting joy.
Stainer.   Honeycomb, The.
Stept, S.   That's My Weakness Now.
Steptoe.   Sweet Brown Rice and Red Bones.
Stevenson, R.   Nay, but I fancy somehow, year by year.
Storni.   To Eros.
Strabo, W.   Dearest, You Come Suddenly and Suddenly You Depart.
Strato [or Straton].   Despite the ruddy down upon your cheek.
In years to come, I ask, be kind.
Long hair, and curls woven not by Nature but by Art.
Strayhorn, B.   Something to Live For.
Suckling, S.   Constant Lover, A [or The].
Love's Clock.
Love's Siege.
Song: "Why so pale and wan, fond lover?"
Sonnet: "O[h]! for some honest lover's ghost."
Upon My Lady Carlisle's Walking in Hampton Court Garden.
Swinburne.   Love And Sleep.
Swirszczynska [or Swir].   Second Madrigal, The.
Thank You, My Fate.
Symonds.   In years of old.
Love and Death: A Symphony.
Symons, A.   Faint Love.
Nerves.
White Heliotrope.
Synge.   In May.
Sze.   Apache Plume.
Szymborska, W.   Love at First Sight.
Tana, P.   River, The.
Tassis y Peralta.   Love Is Not Will but Destiny.
Teasdale.   Enough.
Summer Night, Riverside.
Unchanging, The.
Tennyson, A.   Deep in the night I woke: she, near me, held.
I envy not in any moods.
Yet if some voice that man could trust.
Thamnaret.   Nightsong.
Theocritus.   Idyll 29: ""Truth in the cups" men say, dear youth."
Theognis.   Boy and horse, a similar brain: the horse doesn't cry when its rider lies in the dust.
It's a thrill to love a boy: even Kronos' son, king of immortals, once longed for Ganymede.
Thomas, D.   In My Craft or Sullen Art.
Tibullus.   Fill up my glass again! The anodyne.
Tiger.   Lovepoem Writing Me.
Torneol.   Lady's Farewell, The.

Trail, C.   Sonnet: "This is for the afternoon we lay in the leaves."
Tremblay, G.   Not Sense.
Trenet, C.   I Wish You Love (Que Reste-t-il de Nos Amours?).
Trocchi, A.   For John Donne: Master Metaphysical.
Troup, B.   You're in Love.
Tsvetayeva [or Tsvetaeva].   Last bridge I won't.
Tzu Yeh.   Smile, A.
Song: "Winter skies are cold and low."
Unknown.   After spring has come.
All Year Long.
Among the yeomen's sons on my estate.
At daybreak I dropped in on a beauty.
At night the verandah is dark, the beds too numerous.
Aubade.
Because of this love.
Black Hair.
Brightlines.
By your side I am beautiful with my mouth extended and my open arms.
Chance led me once, when idling through the street.
Come be with me like jewelry around my neck.
Come close to me, my love.
Come, my love, let us go to bed together.
Come to me so I can touch you and embrace you.
Cripple Creek.
En un Vergier Soiz Folha D'Albespi.
Epithalamium: "By good luck I was granted a meeting with you."
Gather some wood and make a great fire!
Give me your hand, my love, and let us go into the fields.
Go first, my love, to avenge the martyrs' blood.
Hark, All Ye Lovely Saints.
Here in my garden.
I Have a Gentle Cock [or Gentil Cok].
I have only yielded you the privilege of my mouth.
I loathe them, I loathe them.
I shall bend toward you with my entire body.
If it is but sleep.
If you kiss my mouth, you must give me your heart.
Inanna spoke.
It's you puts the green sprig in my hatband.
Just because of you.
Last night I was close to my lover, oh evening of love not to return again!
Last night was the strangest night.
Long Time Back, A.
Love Me Not [for Comely Grace].
Love, Why Don't You Come.
Loveburn.
Monk that slept here must, after all, have been a man, The.
Moon shines on valley.
My lover was dozing on armfuls of flowers.
Now Is the Month of Maying.
O love, round as the watermelon.
Oh for the love of God, sleep, don't let it come to this!
Oh my love! If in my arms you tremble so.
One by one I've gathered up my feelings of love.
Pass where the winds pause before they cross.
Pitman's Lovesong, A.
Pleasant Songs of the Sweetheart Who Meets You in the Fields.
Plucking the Rushes.
Sometimes I sauntered from my lone abode.
Spring Overflows the Pavilion.
This Morning Our Boat Left.
Though you made me think.
Thus feverish fancies floated in my brain.
Unquiet Grave, The.
Was I Not Made for Love?
What is love, what is it?
Whatever the cost.
While I asked myself.
White light of dawn grows wider, The.
White Rejoice with Ganymede, The.

Women as women, me had never charmed.
You Love Her.
Young once / and dreaming.
Your love is water and it is fire.
Unknown, fr. Egyptian hieroglyphics. Is there anything sweeter than this hour?
Unknown, fr. Sumerian cuneiform. Word they had spoken, The.
Van Duyn. Falling in Love at Sixty-Five.
Vidya. Hiding in the.
Love Poem, A.
Villaurrutia. Our Love.
Villon. Ballad of Villon and Fat Madge, The.
Virgil [*or* Vergil]. Eclogue 2: The Lament of Corydon for His Faithless Alexis.
Wave, The.
Vogelweide. Under the Lindentree.
Voznesensky [*or* Voznesenskii]. Dead Still.
Wade-Gayles. Loving Again.
Walafrid Strabo. To His Friend in Absence.
Walker, F. X. Sweet Bread.
Waller, E. Budd, The.
Waltner-Toews, D. How the Earth Loves You.
Waniek. Ballad of Aunt Geneva, The.
Warren-Moore. Pink Poem.
Washington, N. Hundred Years from Today, A.
Love Is the Thing.
Woman's Intuition, A.
Weaver, A. Lines: "I feel your legs touching."
Webster, A. By the Looking-Glass.
Webster, P. Doctor, Lawyer, Indian Chief.
Love Is a Many-Splendored Thing.
Secret Love.
Two Cigarettes in the Dark.
What's Your Story, Morning Glory.
Weigl. What Saves Us.
Weiss, G. Lullaby of Birdland.
Oh! What It Seemed to Be.
Too Close for Comfort.
Wharton, E. Mortal Lease, The: V.
White, A. Beelzebub Chronicles, The.
Whiting, R. She's Funny That Way (I Got a Woman, Crazy for Me).
Whitman, W. Among the Multitude.
As Adam Early in the Morning.
From Pent-up Aching Rivers.
Live Oak, with Moss.
Spontaneous Me.
This is the female form.
When I Heard at the Close of the Day.
Whoever You Are Holding Me Now in Hand.
Whitney, J. Candy.
Wilbur, R. Late Aubade, A.
Loves of the Puppets.
Pangloss's Song: A Comic-Opera Lyric.
Someone Talking to Himself.
Wilde, L. Corinne's Last Love-Song.
Wilde, O. Silentium Amoris.
Williams, C. Sugar.
Williams, M. Love Poem with Toast.
Williams, W. Queen Anne's Lace.
Willson, M. Till There Was You.
Wilson, S. It's Never Too Late to Fall in Love.
Wodehouse. You Can't Make Love by Wireless.
Woods, H. Over My Shoulder.
Paddlin' Madelin' Home.
We Just Couldn't Say Good-bye.
Woodward, V. Cornbread Blues.
Wordsworth, W. I Travelled among Unknown Men.
Wright, C. So Far Off and Yet Here.
Wright, J. Sappho.
Wright, R. And This Is My Beloved.
Strange Music.
Wroth. Sonnet 1: "In this strang[e] labyrinth [*or* labourinth] how shall I turn[e]?"
Sonnet 14: "Am I thus conquered [*or* conquer'd]? have I lost the powers."
Sonnet 22: "Like to the Indians, scorched with the sun[ne]."
Wu Tsao. For the Courtesan Ch'ing Lin.
Wyatt. His Reward.
Lover Showeth How He Is Forsaken of Such as He Sometime Enjoyed, The.
Varium et Mutabile.
Wylie. Confession of Faith.

Yang Shen. To the Tune "Moon Over West River".
Yeats. Last Confession, A.
Lullaby: "Beloved, may your sleep be sound."
Yesenin [*or* Essenin]. Yesterday's rain.
Yi Chŏngbo. May my love become an alder tree.
Yosano Akiko. Spring is short.
Young, J. Hundred Years from Today, A.
Yü Ch'ing-tsĕng. To the Tune "Intoxicated with Shadows of Flowers."
Yüan Chĕn. Bamboo Mat.
Remembering.
Zarco. Saxophonetyx.
See also **Sex**

Error
Buchsbaum, Julianne. Thrillsville.
Carson, A. Essay on What I Think about Most.
Eady. How I Got Born.
Heise, Thomas. Corrections.
Issa. Thus spring begins: old.
Karim, F. Crumbled Paper for Future Poems.
Komunyakaa, Y. Please.
Mueller, John. Rubber Eraser.
Pavlova, V. On the way to you.
Peacock, M. How I Had to Act.
Preston, K. Lapsus Linguae.
Probyn. Masquerading.
Ranaldo, L. Wrong #.
Ransom, J. Parting, without a Sequel.
Ruskin, H. I May Be Wrong (But I Think You're Wonderful).
Simic. Errata.
Souza. Conversation Piece.
White, Brenda Black. Country Boy, City Girl.
Yeryomin. House over the garden is a bouquet of evening windows, The.
Young, K. Errata.

Escalators
Frumkin. Escalator.

Escape
Adcock, F. Way Out, A.
Addonizio. Chicken.
Adler, F. Riding the Eye.
Ai. Kid, The.
Aizenberg, M. So where is that guy who left us piles.
Alexander, E. Passage.
Alvi, M. Houdini.
Balaban. Heading Out West.
Bayly. Out, John.
Bennett, R. Gingerbread Man, The.
Bonnefoy. What House Would You Build For Me.
Brathwaite [*or* Brathwait], R. Vandunk's Four Humours, in Quality and Quantity.
Brecht, B. There is no greater crime than leaving.
Brouwer, J. Kelly, Ringling Bros. Oldest Elephant, Goes On Rampage.
Buson. He's on the porch.
Causley. What Has Happened to Lulu?
Ciardi, J. Sometimes Even Parents Win.
Cleary, B. Sealink.
Collin, J. Layman's Lament, The.
Corn. Kimchee in Worchester (Mass.).
Cruz, S. One Dismal Night.
Deerchild, R. This is a small northern town.
Dickinson, E. Escape is such a thankful Word.
I never hear the word "escape".
Drennan, J. Not Gone Yet.
Durcan. Death by Heroin of Sid Vicious, The.
Eich. Marketplace.
Erdrich. Indian Boarding School: The Runaways.
Glaser, M. Magnificat!
Gonzalez, R. There.
Greenway, W. Ophelia Writes Home.
Gumilyov [*or* Gumiliov *or* Gumilev]. Baby Elephant, A.
HaNagid. Prison, The.
Hardi, C. Escape Journey, 1988.
Harechavi. Already Night, Already Day.
Harjo, J. Drowning Horses.
Harper, F. Eliza Harris.
Slave Mother, The: A Tale of the Ohio.

Hartman, J. So harmless and regal in the hieratic dark.
Hayden, R. Runagate Runagate.
Hernández Cruz. Swans' Book, The.
Holzer, R. Current "Now, Voyager" Fantasy.
Housman. Shot? so quick, so clean an ending?
Ivanov, Binyo. Man, A.
Jackson, G. Fugitive Slaves.
Jamie, K. One of Us.
Kay, J. Dressing Up.
Keats. There Was a Naughty Boy.
Kendrick, D. Sadie Snuffs a Candle.
Klyuyev [*or* Kliuev *or* Klyuev]. Sky Lies Blue—Like a Sea, The.
Korean Oral Tradition. Wretched Married Life (Folk Song from Koch'ang).
Kunitz, S. Route Six.
Kuzmina-Karavayeva. Ruth.
Lazard. Ordinance on Arrival.
"Leadbelly.". Take this Hammer.
Lear, E. Limerick: "There was an Old Person of Basing."
Levine, P. And the Trains Go On.
Lezama Lima. Ah, That You Escape.
Longfellow, H. Slave in the Dismal Swamp, The.
Lucilius. Lean Gaius, who was thinner than a straw.
MacNeice. Cradle Song: "Sleep, my darling, sleep."
Mandel, E. Houdini.
McLain, P. Residue.
Morales. Getting Out Alive.
Neruda. Ambassador, The.
Ni Ghallchóir, C. Escape.
Nichols, R. Beginning when I was six I became my father's accomplice.
No Ch'ŏnmyŏng. Nameless Woman.
Nolens, L. Origins.
O'Sullivan, L. Being Free.
Pagis, D. Footprints.
Instructions for Crossing the Border.
Last Ones, The.
Probyn. Anniversaries.
Reznikoff. When the Second World War began.
Robinson, A. To My Muse.
Rodriguez, L. Always Running.
Rolfe, E. City of Anguish.
Rumsey, Tessa. Big Rig the Baroque Sky.
Salzman, E. Double Crossing.
Samuels, I. Escapology.
Sen, S. Solitary.
Seward. Eyam.
Stokesbury. Reynaldo in Paris.
Suyemoto, Toyo. Hokku: "Geese flew over, The."
Torres Bodet. Exodus.
Tsanev, Stefan. Dog: "Why do you watch me so sadly and inquisitively."
Unknown. Hey diddle diddle.
I leap into the river, the current doesn't carry me away.
Jock o' the Side [Version from Poetical Museum; Albyn's Anthology 2].
Kinmont Willie.
Verlaine. Brussels: Simple Frescos 2.
Villanueva, A. They Didn't Get Me.
Waldman, A. In the Room of Never Grieve.
Wang the Zealot. Get Blind Drunk.
Wang Ts'an. Poem of Seven Sorrows.
Wong, N. Can't Tell.
Wylie. Escape.
Where, O, Where?
Yamada. Club, The.
Yesenin [*or* Essenin]. Winds, Winds, Winds.
Yost, C. Escaping from Autopia.
Young, K. Escape Artist, The.
Eschatology.
See **End of the World**
Eskimos
Berg, S. Orpingalik's My Breath: Eskimo Song.
Brown, L. Turn On the Heat.
DeSylva, B. G. Turn On the Heat.
Dylan. Quinn the Eskimo.
Henderson, R. Turn On the Heat.
Koch, K. Geography.

Pinsky. Samba.
Purdy, A. Lament for the Dorsets.
Ray, D. Eskimo Girl, The.
Rodriguez, J. Eskimo Occasion.
Silook, Susie. Uncle Good Intentions.
Tallmountain. Indian Blood.
Torres, A. Eskimo's Woman, The.
Warren, R. Sila.
Watson, R. Ballad of the Bird-Bride.

Esther, Book of (Bible)
Harper, F. Vashti.
Spencer, A. Before the Feast of Shushan.

Estrangement
Bendall, M. After Estrangement.
Byron, G. Lines on Hearing That Lady Byron
  Was Ill.
Cooper, J. Estrangement.
Cope, W. At 3 A.M.
Crane, H. Stark Major.
Crown, K. Necklace: Rich Pink Corona Round
  a Flashing Yellow Heart.
Crozier, L. So This Is Love.
Eliot, T. S. Love Song of J. Alfred Prufrock,
  The.
Ghos, G. You're home, Uma! Stay here.
Godfrey. Where the Weather Suits My Clothes.
Guiducci. In Emily's Manner.
Harrison, T. Book Ends.
Helwig. Departures.
Hogan, L. Heritage.
Ibn al-Khaṭīb. May the rain cloud be bountiful
  to you when the rain cloud pours, O time of
  love union in al-Andalus!
Ibn Baqī, A. I have no wine other than sorrows
  mixed in the cup with flowing tears.
Ibn Shuhayd, A. I observe certain eyes gazing
  steadily at me as if speckled snakes [issuing
  from them] were attacking me from both sides.
Jeffers, R. Birth-Dues.
Jong, E. Colder.
Kantaris. Body Language.
Light, K. My Worst Nightmare.
Lowell, R. Man And Wife.
  To Speak of Woe That Is in Marriage.
Mackey, N. Sound and Cerement.
MacNeice. Selva Oscura.
Major, C. Isolate.
Mansfield, K. Meeting, The.
'Marnia. Accoutrement.
McFadden, D. 14. The CN Tower.
Merrill, J. Renewal, A.
Mollineux. Another Letter to a Friend.
Motsapi, S. Missa joe.
Po Chü-i. Dreaming of Long Ago.
Rich, A. In the Evening.
  Rain on the West Side Highway.
Rumens. Double Bed.
Sahagún, C. Photograph of a Boy.
St. John, D. Winter Fires.
Scott, L. Ettrick.
Shakespeare, W. Sonnet 89: "Say that thou
  didst forsake me for some fault."
  Sonnet 120: "That you were once unkind,
  befriends me now."
Shcherbina. Whole city seductively lit up, The.
Stanley-Wrench. Storm, The.
Unknown. One I Love, The.
  Since First I Saw Your Face.
  Year Draws to Its End, The.
  Zun-da-lu: If Along the Highroad.
Viorst. Honeymoon is Over, The.
Walker, F. X. Wishbone.
Whitehead, C. Grass Crust, The.
Young, A. Dance of the Infidels.

Eternity
Achterberg. Across the Jarbok.
Amor, P. CXXXIX.
Beaumont, S. Description of Love, A.
Berlin. Always.
Blake, W. Eternity.
Bonnefoy. To the Voice of Kathleen Ferrier.
Bradstreet, A. Contemplations.
  There is a path no vulture's eye hath seen.
Brontë, E. I'm happiest when most away.
  No Coward Soul is Mine.
Browning, R. Last Ride Together, The.

Bursk. Tearing Up the Tracks.
Cami, B. You Stand.
Castro, R. Mild Was the Air.
Chinnov. Gust of memory stirs faded letters, A.
Clare, J. Vision, A.
Coleridge, M. Some in a child would live, some
  in a book.
Cornwall. Address to the Ocean.
Dèr Mouw. Does Anyone Know This Feeling.
Dickinson, E. It was a quiet way—.
  Only News I know, The.
  Our journey had advanced.
Donne. Anniversary [or Anniversarie], The.
Emerson, R. Days.
  Spiritual Laws.
Ferlinghetti, L. Cro-Magnons.
  River Still To Be Found, A.
Frumkin. Life of Eternity, The.
Gershwin, I. Love Is Here to Stay.
Gezelle. Ego Flos.
Glück, L. White Lilies, The.
Hannon. Beyond Freedom.
Heard, J. Eternity.
Herrick. Sabbaths.
  White Island, The: or Place of the Blest.
Heyman, E. When I Fall in Love.
Hill, G. Not as we are but as we must appear.
Horace. Ode 3.30: This Monument Will Outlast
  (Exegi monumentum aere perennius).
Housman. Immortal Part, The.
Hugo, V. At the Window in the Dark.
Kabir. Eternity.
Kasa. I shall think of you.
Kaufman, B. Private Sadness.
Keats. Bright Star.
Kim Ku. Until the duck's short legs.
Kinnell. Quick and the Dead, The.
Klyuyev [or Kliuev or Klyuev]. You Twist
  Your Death in Nooses.
Lao Tzu. Valley Spirit never dies, The.
  Ways that can be walked are not the eternal
  Way, The.
  Whenever all the world declares fair "fair".
Leopardi. Infinite, The.
  Upon the arid shoulder.
Loynaz, D. M. Futile Flight, Futile Fugue.
Machado Ruiz. It Doesn't Matter Now.
Magdeburg, Mechthild von. How God Answers
  the Soul.
Mengham, Rod. To the Soviet Embalmers.
Meynell, A. To a Daisy.
Montale. I repeat I'm ready, but ready for
  what?
Moore, T. Response to Rimbaud's Later
  Manner.
Nemerov. John 3:1–15; Now there was a man.
Otero, B. Eternal, The.
Ovid. Elegy 1.15: "Envy, why carp'st [or
  carpest] thou my time is spent so ill."
Pak Mogwŏl [or Mokwŏl]. Eternity of Pure
  Color.
Pasolini. John 12:24–25; Truly, truly, I say to
  you.
Poplavsky [or Poplavskii]. Another Planet.
Procter, A. Address to the Ocean.
Rands. Cat of Cats, The.
Riley, J. Eternity.
Rilke. To praise is the whole thing! A man who
  can praise.
Rist. Eternity, thou thunderous word.
Rochester, J. Song: "Absent from thee, I
  languish still."
Roethke. I Knew a Woman.
Rossetti, C. Bed of Forget-Me-Nots, A.
  Life's Parallels, A.
  Rest.
Shakespeare, W. Sonnet 15: "When I consider
  every thing that grows."
  Sonnet 109: "O, never say that I was false of
  heart."
  Sonnet 116: "Let me not to the marriage of true
  minds."
Simic. Mirrors at 4 A.M.
Smith, W. Pavane for the Nursery, A.
Spender, S. To T. A. R. H.
Spenser, E. Sonnet 75: "One day I wrote her

name upon the strand."
Sylvester, J. Father, The.
Tennyson, A. Thy voice is on the rolling air.
Tsvetkov. Like a ruddy child you fall asleep in
  september.
Unknown. I am I, but also the other.
  Tell me.
Vallejo. Today I like life much less.
Varchi. What part of my holiest and most
  beautiful feelings.
Vaughan, H. World, The (1).
Verwey, A. North-Sea, The.
Very. Forevermore.
Vilariño. How to Shrug Off.
Wordsworth, W. Simplon Pass, The.
Young, A. Blues Don't Change, The.
See also **Immortality**

Ethiopia
Adisa. Ethiopia Unda a Jamaican Mango Tree.
Clark Bekedermo. New from Ethiopia and the
  Sudan, The.
Crashaw. On the Baptized Ethiopian.
Cumberbatch, L. In the Early Morning Breeze.
Lorde. Ethiopia.
Touré, A. Dawnsong!

Etiquette
Betjeman. How to Get On in Society.
Bishop, E. Manners.
Brownjohn. Sonnet of a Gentleman.
Burgess, F. Table Manners: "Goops they lick
  their fingers, The."
Guiterman. Of Courtesy.
Lao Tzu. Person of superior integrity, The.
Macklin. House Style, The.
Probyn. Mésalliance, A.
Stevenson, R. Good and Bad Children.
  Whole Duty of Children.
Waniek. Daughters, 1900.

Eton College
Connolly, C. On Himself.
Gray, T. Ode on a Distant Prospect of Eton
  College.
Mathews, H. Sense of Responsibility, The.

Etruscan Civilization
Lawrence, D. H. Cypresses.

Eucharist
Behrle. Beacon Arms.
Clarke, A. Martha Blake.
Constable, H. To the Blessed Sacrament.
Herbert, G. Agony [or Agonie], The.
  Holy [or H.] Communion, The ("Not in rich
  furniture, or fine array.").
  Love (3): "Love bade me welcome: yet my soul
  drew back."
  Superliminare.
Hopkins, G. Bugler's First Communion, The.
Lyon, G. Foot-Washing, The.
Ryman. Song of the Eucharist, A.
Southwell. Of the Blessed Sacrament of the
  Altar [or Aulter] ("In paschall feast, the end of
  a[u]ncient rite.").
Thomas, D. This Bread I Break.
Unknown. Sacrament of the Altar, The.
See also **Last Supper**

Euclid
Lovelace, R. Snail [or Snayl], The.
Martinson. Hades and Euclid (first version).
Millay, E. Euclid Alone Has Looked on Beauty
  Bare.

Eunuchs
Cannell. King, The.
Martial. Surrounded by eunuchs and limp as a
  tissue.

Euripides
Morgan, E. Euripides' Cave.

Europa
Ovid. Europa and Jove.

Europe
Apollinaire. Zone.
Barlow, J. From slavery then your rising realms
  to save.
Bolton, K. In Ferrara.
Brown, L. You Are Not Gorgeous and I Am
  Coming Anyway.

Bryant, W.　To Cole, the Painter, Departing for Europe.
Clampitt.　Imago.
Dischell.　Yellow Slicker, The.
Douglas, K.　On a Return from Egypt.
Gascoyne.　Snow in Europe.
Goethe.　United States, The.
Gustafson, R.　In the Yukon.
Hollander, J.　Late August on the Lido.
Jenkins, J. *et al.*　In Ferrara.
Juana Inés de la Cruz.　In Acknowledgment of the Praises of European Writers.
Kaplinski, J.　East-West border, The.
Larbaud.　Ode: "Lend me your great sound, your fine smooth speed."
Lassell.　Going to Europe.
Lewis, G.　Pentecost.
MacSweeney.　Seared to the echo.
Maguire, S.　Liminal.
Martinaitis, M.　Kukutis's Sermon to the Pigs.
Milosz, C.　Child of Europe.
Oliver, D.　Walnut and Lily.
Rimbaud, A.　Hearing the thunder of the intransitive weirs.
Silva, L.　Island and Europe, The.
Sirr.　Guide to Holland, A.
Whitman, W.　Europe, the 72d and 73d Year of These States.
　Europe the 72nd and 73rd Years of These States.

Eurydice
Bancquart.　Counterfable of Orpheus.
Doolittle, H.　So you have swept me back.
Glück, L.　Eurydice.
Henryson.　Syne nethir-mare he went quhare Pluto was.
Hill, G.　Orpheus and Eurydice.
Klink, J.　Orpheus. Eurydice. Hermes.
Poliziano.　What song will ever be so sorrowful.
Raine, K.　What substance had Euridice.
Rilke.　Orpheus, Eurydice, Hermes.
Sinclair, S.　Orpheus Meets Eurydice in the Underworld.

Euthanasia
Belli, C.　Unknown Voice, An.
Berger, J.　Between Worlds.
Collins, B.　Putting Down the Cat.
Dugan, A.　For Euthanasia and Pain-Killing Drugs.
Jeffers, R.　Hurt Hawks.
Karr.　Patient, The.
Lumsden, R.　Mercy.
Markell, Jennifer.　Veterinary Student, The.
Randall, D.　To the Mercy Killers.
Smither.　On the Euthanasia of a Pet Dog.
Weigl.　May.

Evangelism and Evangelists
Hayden, R.　Witch Doctor.
Pardo, P.　I was on the couch when the jehova's witnesses came.
Rossetti, D.　74: Old and New Art (St Luke the Painter).
Ryman.　Matthew, Mark, Luke and John, / She chanted.
Strange.　Streetcorner Church.
Unknown.　There's a Meeting Here To-Night.
Warren, R.　Amazing Grace in the Back Country.
West, R.　Two Evangelists.

Eve
Copus, J.　Masaccio's *Expulsion from Paradise.*
Dizhur.　Eve's Monologue.
Frost, R.　Never Again Would Birds' Song Be the Same.
Harper, M.　Eve (Rachel).
Hecht, J.　History.
Hejduk.　Sleep of Adam, The.
Higginson, E.　Eve.
Hildebrandt.　O Eve.
Hodgson, R.　Eve.
Hope, A.　Imperial Adam.
Howe, M.　Part of Eve's Discussion.
Hughes, T.　Theology.
Marzán.　Eve.
McVeigh, J.　Eve Falling.
Milton.　As when of old some orator renowned.

To whom thus also th' Angel last repli'd.
Nasrin.　Eve Oh Eve.
Norris, K.　Mrs. Adam.
　Prayer to Eve, A.
Pagis, D.　Written in Pencil in the Sealed Railway-Car.
Probyn.　Ballade of Lovers.
Ray, H.　Vision of Eve, The.
Rossetti, C.　Eve.
Sharpless.　*Paradise Lost* as a Haiku.
Smith, S.　Dream of Comparison, A.
　How Cruel Is the Story of Eve.
Triplett, P.　Fractal Audition.
Wechsler, E.　Lilith, Adam's First Companion.
Wells, C.　Original Summer Girl, The.
Wilbur, R.　She.
Wright, J.　Eve to Her Daughters.
Yeats.　Adam's Curse.

Evening
Adams, L.　Home-Coming.
Aldington.　Evening.
Allen, W.　Away from the Office.
Applewhite.　Village After Sunset, The.
Auden.　As I Walked Out One Evening.
Balingit, J.　Quiet Evening, Home Away.
Basho.　All along this road.
　As the sound fades.
　Crow, A.
　Plates and bowls.
　Solitary, A.
　This road.
　You could turn this way.
Baudelaire.　Harmony of Evening, The.
Blake, W.　To the Evening Star.
Borges.　Patio.
Bowles, W.　Sonnet 5: "Evening, as slow thy placid shades descend."
Bridges, R.　Evening Darkens Over, The.
　Winter Nightfall.
Buffoni, F.　When he was far away from those evenings.
Buson.　Along the roadside.
　Autumn evening.
　Evening cloudburst, An.
　Evening wind.
　Lighting one candle.
　Misty grasses.
Campana.　Window, The.
Clare, J.　Gypsy's Evening Blaze, The.
　Mist in the Meadows.
Coleridge, S.　Pensive at eve on the hard world I mus'd [*or* mused].
Collins, W.　Ode to Evening.
Cooley.　Vespers: "Now it is evening, the light rushes to fall."
Cowper, W.　Just when our drawing-rooms begin to blaze.
　Winter Evening, The: A Brown Study.
Creeley.　Buffalo Evening.
Daive.　I Rise from the Depths.
　Under the Wind.
De la Mare.　Summer Evening.
　Thomas Hardy.
Dickinson, E.　Lightly stepped a yellow star.
Doolittle, H.　Evening.
Dowson.　Vesperal.
Ema Saikō.　Evening Stroll.
Fargue.　In Yellow Towns.
Florit, E.　Present Evening, The.
Frost, R.　Stopping by Woods on a Snowy Evening.
Gascoigne.　Gascoigne's [*or* Gascoygnes] Good-Night.
Gensei.　Distant View from a Grass Hill.
　Evening View from Grass Hill.
Gerhardt.　Evensong.
Giussani, S.　Abel and Abel.
Glück, L.　Quiet Evening.
Gray, T.　Elegy Written in a Country Churchyard.
Guest, B.　Otranto.
Guiney.　When on the Marge of Evening.
Haines, J.　Evening Change.
Hammerstein.　Some Enchanted Evening.
Harrison, J.　Swifts at Evening.
Harvey, James Clarence.　At Eventide.

Healy, E.　Pope at 7:00 P.M., The.
Herrick.　Evensong.
Hodgson, R.　Late, Last Rook, The.
Hughes, T.　Full Moon and Little Frieda.
Issa.　Autumn evening.
　Autumn evening / Knees in arms.
　Bats flying.
　Evening clears, The.
　Evening moon.
　Holes in the wall, The.
　In the beggar's tin.
　Under the evening moon.
Izumi.　If Someone Would Come.
Jaccottet.　Wishes.
Jauss.　Quotations for a Winter Evening.
Jeffers, R.　Autumn Evening.
Johnson, M. F.　Second Evening.
Jordan, J.　San Juan.
Kahn, G.　Tomorrow Is Another Day.
Kaplan, L.　I wait for him by the subway exit.
　It's night, the.
Kenyon, J.　Let Evening Come.
Kimbrell, J.　Rooftop.
Kloos, W.　Evening.
Koster, E. B.　Shoal of Silver Angelfish, A.
Lampman.　Winter Evening.
Langille.　Prayer: "Every hour I am disappearing."
Larkin, P.　Coming.
　Going.
Lazarus, E.　Evening.
Leiter, Deborah.　Midsummer's Eve.
Lezama Lima.　Fragments of the Night, The.
Longfellow, H.　Curfew.
　Fire of Drift-Wood, The.
López Velarde.　Wet Earth.
Lovelace, R.　Another.
Machado Ruiz.　I go on dreaming.
Magrelli.　Every evening, bent over the bright.
Masaoka Shiki.　Evening bell / Persimmons pelt.
Masuri, S.　Day's End.
Meng Hao Jan.　At the Mountain-Lodge of the Buddhist Priest Ye Waiting in Vain for My Friend Ding.
　Steering my little boat towards a misty islet.
Merriam, E.　Lullaby "Purple".
Meynell, A.　November Blue.
Mezey.　Evening, An.
Miller, T.　Evening.
Miller, W.　Willie Winkie.
Mills, R.　Evening Song.
Moss, H.　Persistence of Song, The.
Pei Di.　Magnolia Enclosure, The.
Petrarch.　For Whatever Animals Dwell on Earth.
Po Chü-i.　Evening Rain.
Porter, F.　Island in the Evening, The.
Quasimodo.　And Suddenly It Is Evening.
Radnóti.　Seventh Eclogue ("Do you see? Evening falls, fringed with barbed-wire.").
Sachs, N.　In the Evening Your Vision Widens.
Sarton, M.　Light Left On, A.
Segovia, F.　Evening Star.
　Lucero de la Tarde.
Senghor.　Man and Beast.
Shapiro, D.　Tracing of an Evening.
Shaw, A.　Crepuscule.
Simic.　Evening Walk.
Stephens, J.　Evening.
Stevenson, R.　Evensong.
Terán, V.　Huadxí que ziyaba.
　It Was Early Evening.
　Tarde caía, La.
Toomer.　Georgia Dusk.
Trakl.　De Profundis.
Tran Nhan-tong.　Spring View.
Tretheway.　Text of Evening, The.
Tu Fu [*or* Du Fu].　Evening near Serpent River.
Turner, F.　Spring Evening.
Unknown.　In the evening / The mists trail.
　Work's end.
Unknown, fr. Terezin Concentration Camp.　On a Sunny Evening.
Van Eeden, F.　City Evening.
Vietnamese Oral Tradition.　Evening.
Wang Wei.　Autumn Twilight in the Mountains.

Magnolia Enclosure, The.
Warren, R. Evening Hawk.
Wordsworth, W. It Is a Beauteous Evening.
Zesen. Evening Song.
See also **Twilight**

Evening Star
Blake, W. To the Evening Star.
Bogan, L. Evening-Star.
Cuadra, P. Evening Star, The.
Doolittle, H. In the field-furrow.
Jeffers, R. Evening Ebb.
Longfellow, H. Evening Star, The.
Sappho. Star of Evening.
Segovia, F. Evening Star.
Lucero de la Tarde.
Stevens, W. Homunculus et La Belle Etoile.
See also **Venus (planet)**

Evers, Medgar
Brooks, G. Medgar Evers.
Ignatow, D. For Medgar Evers.

Evictions
Clinton, M. Eviction.
Espada. Imagine the Angels of Bread.
Korman, N. Eviction Fight.

Evil
Addonizio. Theodicy.
Archilochus. Attribute all to the gods: often they raise.
Baudelaire. To the Reader.
Bible, *O.T.* Psalm 52. Quid Gloriaris?
Blake, W. Marriage of Heaven and Hell, The.
Brecht, B. When Evil-Doing Comes Like Falling Rain.
Byrom. On the Origin of Evil.
Chaucer. Pardoner's Tale, The.
Coleridge, S. Christabel.
de Folgar. Panorama.
Doolittle, H. Evil was active in the land.
Dowriche, A. So him at first *De Nance* commanded was to kill.
Duncan, R. Fire, The.
El-Hadi, S. Drama, The.
Field. Dying Viper, A.
Frost, R. Bearer of Evil Tidings, The.
Design.
George, S. Antichrist, The.
Gray, T. Tophet.
Hamer. Crossroads.
Hecht, A. It Out-Herods Herod. Pray You, Avoid It.
Herrick. Neutrality Loathsome.
Holan. To the Enemies.
Hope, A. Möbius Strip-Tease.
Howe, F. Little Wrongs.
Ivanov, G. Oh, how fastidious you once were.
Jackson, M. L. Don Pullen at the Zanzibar Blue Jazz Cafe, 1994 [1997].
Johnston, C. Spirit of evil, with which the earth is rife.
Kaufman, S. Emperor of China, The.
Kearney, L. Man with His Kids on a Table, The.
Kendall, M. Legend of the Crossing-Sweeper.
Lawrence, D. H. Root of Our Evil, The.
Snake.
Longfellow, H. Rhyme of Sir Christopher, The.
Mandelstam [*or* Mandelshtam]. Notre Dame.
McClure, M. Black Dahlia.
Merwin. Stranger, The.
Millay, E. Not to Be Spattered by His Blood.
Min, N. M. Deep in the Pit.
Neihardt. In vain against the formless wolves of air.
Osundare. Madding moon, A.
Picková, E. Fear.
Poe. Sonnet—Silence.
Polkowski. Noli Me Tangere.
Raine, K. Pythoness, The.
Różewicz. What Happens.
Shakespeare, W. Now is the winter of our discontent.
Shapiro, K. Lord, I Have Seen Too Much.
Puritan, The.
Silva, C. In the Darkness of the Other.

Smith, S. Lord Barrenstock.
To the Tune of The Coventry Carol.
Snodgrass. Mother, The: "She stands in the dead center like a star."
Soto. Who Will Know Us?
Trakl. Sun, The: "Each day the gold sun comes over the hill."
Unknown. Seven, The.
Vaughan, H. Kingdom of Heaven Compared to a Grain of Mustard-Seed, The.
Vinokurov. Adam.
Walcott. Camps hold [*or* held] their distance— [*of*] brown chestnuts and grey smoke, The.
Wesley, C. He Shook Off the Beast.
Wheelwright. Live, Evil Veil.
Whitman, W. I Sit and Look Out.
Rounded Catalogue Divine Complete, The.
Williams, M. Why God Permits Evil: For Answers to This Question of Interest to Many Write Bible Answers, Dept. E-7.
Wright, K. Hoping It Might Be So.
Young, D. Business of Love Is Cruelty, The.

Evolution
Bevington, L. Midnight.
Morning.
Bierds, L. Hunter.
Davidman. Lament for Evolution.
Day, C. Yesterday explorers found.
Emerson, R. Nature [1836].
Fulton, A. Doing the Evolution Shuffle.
Garner, P. Lucy, *Lucie.*
Goldbarth. Closer.
Graham, J. Exit Wound.
Hahn, S. Incontinence.
Hicok. Active Reader, The.
Hiestand, E. Day Lily and the Fox, The.
Howe, J. Kosmos.
Kendall, M. Lay of the Trilobite.
Lower Life, The.
Lawrence, D. H. Self-Protection.
Mandelstam [*or* Mandelshtam]. Lamarck.
Melville, H. Epilogue: "If Luther's day expand to Darwin's year."
Naden. Solomon Redivivus, 1886.
Pagis, D. Ready.
Peskett. Inheritors, The.
Question of Time, The.
Saïd, A. Earth, The.
Sandburg, C. Wilderness.
Schelling. Haibun.
Schnackenberg. Darwin in 1881.
Shapiro, A. Natural Selection.
Smith, L. Evolution.
Stoutenburg. Midnight Saving Time.
Very. Man has forgot his Origin; in vain.
Viereck, P. Love Song to Eohippus.
See also **Darwin, Charles; Extinction; Genetics and Geneticists**

Examinations
Fainlight, R. Sheba's Tests.
Hahn, K. Shower, The.
Williams, G. After the Exam.

Excavations
Phillips, D. Maridunum.
Rux, C. H. Excavation, The.
Unknown. Clementine.
Weston, M. Primitive Place.

Excrement
Benn. Monologue.
Bhatt, S. Muliebrity.
Brecht, B. Three Fragments.
Breytenbach. Constipation.
Buson. Fallen red blossoms.
Castillo, R. Ode to the Urge.
Ciardi, J. Suburban.
Comte de Lautréamont. I am filthy. Lice gnaw me. Swine, when they look at me, vomit. The scabs.
Davies, P. Dung Beetle, The.
Forrester, S. Dog shit.
Grainger, J. Of composts shall the Muse disdain to sing?
Herbert, S. General inspecting the trenches, The.
Holan. To the Enemies.

Issa. Just beyond the gate.
Kumin, M. Excrement Poem, The.
Longchamps, G. O Luxury.
Mansour, J. From an Ass to an Analyst and Back.
Nathan, L. Bladder Song.
Nemerov. Walking the Dog.
Plumly. Human Excrement.
Ward, T. In the Interest of Possibility.
Weigl. Burning Shit at An Khe.
Yi Hyangji. Leaf Struck by Bird Droppings.

Executions and Executioners
Acosta. Apparition (ca. 1896).
Aguilera Díaz, G. Does Anyone Know Where Roque Dalton Spent His Final Night?
Akhmatova, A. Requiem.
Aytoun, W. Morning dawned full darkly, The.
Bartee. Beginning at the End: Capital/Capitol Punishment.
Bell, J. Meditation on *The Consolation of Philosophy.*
Brodsky, J. That which ripped an amazed scream.
Bruchac. Let the Midnight Special.
Bukowski. Dostoevsky.
Cable, G. Dirge of St. Malo, The.
Deguy. Here Often I Am.
Dove, R. Revenant.
Elagin. My murderer is no thief.
Engle, P. Chinese Courtesy.
Enzensberger, H. Rich, The.
Espirito Santo. Where Are the Men Chased Away by That Mad Wind?
Fairfax of Cameron. On the Fatal Day January 30, 1648.
Shortness of Life.
Faiz. So Bring the Order for My Execution.
We Who Were Executed.
Frankau. Deserter, The.
Galanskov. Last Platform, The.
Murder.
Garlick, R. Anthem for Doomed Youth.
Genet. Man Condemned to Death, The.
Gwynn, R. Among Philistines.
Hammad, S. On the State-Sanctioned Murder of Shaka Sankofa.
Harington [*or* Harrington]. Tragicall Epigram, A.
Hecht, A. More Light! More Light!
Herbert, Z. Five Men.
Heym. Clearer Now the Days Are Passing.
Housman. Carpenter's Son, The.
Eight O'Clock.
Kipling, R. Danny Deever.
Lowenfels. Execution, The.
Martínez, V. Children of the Disappeared.
McKendrick, J. Shortened History in Pictures, A.
Melville, H. Billy in the Darbies.
Mendelssohn Anna. Franked.
Newbolt. He Fell among Thieves.
Nowlan. Execution, The.
Weakness.
Ojaide. State Executive.
Pau-Llosa. Paredón.
Peterson, R. San Quentin 1968.
Popa. Be Seeing You.
Ralegh, S. Sir Walter Ra[u]le[i]gh to His Son[ne].
Reznikoff. Jewish women were lined up by German troops in charge of the territory.
Ritsos. Underneath Oblivion.
Roberts, A. Epistle to the Revolutionary Bible, An.
Ruefle. Execution Poster, The.
Shakespeare, W. Fortune is Bardolph's foe, and frowns on him.
Smith, S. Death Sentence, The.
Sŏng [*or* Sung] Sammun. At the Execution Ground.
Tekeyan. Sacred Wrath.
Tennyson, A. Rizpah.
Thorpe, R. Curfew Must Not Ring Tonight [*or* To-Night].
Tichborne [*or* Tichbourne]. Tichborne's Elegy.
Unknown. Edict Against Christianity (Section

12).
Frankie and Johnny [or Johnnie or Albert].
John Hardy.
Mary Hamilton.
Mary [or Marie] Hamilton [Version from
  Motherwell's Manuscript].
Night before Larry Was Stretched, The.
Queen's Marie, The [Version from Scott's
  Minstrelsy].
Villon.   Quatrain: "France's I am; my lookout's
  glum."
Wat.   Imagerie d'Epinal.
Wilde, O.   Ballad of Reading Gaol, The.
Wyatt.   In mourning wise since daily I increase.
See also Capital Punishment; Hanging

Exercise
Goedicke.   American Exercises.
Pastan.   Stationary Bicycle.
Rouse, A.   Uni-Gym, The.
Ryan, M.   First Exercise.
Solie, Karen.   Cardio Room, Young Women's
  Christian Association.
Swirszczynska [or Swir].   Troubles with the
  Soul at Morning Calisthenics.

Exhilaration
Browning, R.   Now.
Elytis, O.   Sun the First.
Neruda.   Dead Gallop.
Sılay, C.   You Will Come to Me.
Tennyson, A.   Ode Sung at the Opening of the
  International Exhibition.

Exile
Adonis [or Adunis].   Elegy for the Time at
  Hand.
Aisenberg, N.   Leaving Eden.
Al-Bayati, A.   I am Born and I Burn in My
  Love.
  Nine Ruba'iyat.
  Two Poems for My Son, Ali.
Al-Haidari, B.   Death in Four Voices.
  So That We Do Not Forget.
Alcaeus [or Alkaios].   I long for the call to
  council.
  Wretched me / I live a rustic live.
Alcott, L.   Lay of a Golden Goose, The.
Alegría.   We Were Three.
Ali, M.   Expatriation.
  Homeland.
  Upside Down Picture, An.
Araidi, N.   Return to the Village.
Bachmann.   Exile.
Back, R.   Notes: From the Wait.
Bancquart.   Town.
Basho.   Wild sea, A.
Bat-Miriam.   Monasteries Lift Gold Domes,
  The.
Bécquer, G.   Arrow Flying Past, An.
Békes.   I Who Have Nothing.
Bekri, Tahar.   Return to Tunisia.
Bienek.   Exodus.
Bly, R.   Dream of Retarded Children, A.
Brecht, B.   1940.
Breeze.   Riddym Ravings (The Mad Woman's
  Poem).
Breytenbach.   Dar es-Salaam: Harbour of Peace.
  Eavesdropper.
  Exile, Representative.
Brodsky, J.   In the Lake District.
  Mary, the Scots are sots in any case.
  May 24, 1980.
Brontë, E.   Visionary, The.
Brooke, R.   Old Vicarage, Grantchester, The.
Burns, R.   My Heart's in the Highlands.
Burnside, J.   Lost: "Fog walks down the hill and
  finds our yard, The."
Busia, A.   Exiles.
Cairns, Scott.   Exile: "Here exactly—a little
  elbow room. Here, in this margin of poor
  housing."
Calderón, T.   Exile.
Campion, T.   As by the stream[e]s of Babylon
  [or Babilon].
Castillo, S.   Letter to Yeni on Peering into Her
  Life.
  Primos.
Catacalos.   Letter to a Brother in Exile.

Cavalcanti.   Ballata II: Last Song: from Exile.
Cherokee Oral Tradition.   Formula to Cause
  Death.
Chŏng Sŏ.   Regret.
Ch'u Yüan.   Ying from "The Nine
  Declarations].
Cleary, B.   Sealink.
  Slouch.
Clover, J.   El periférico, or Sleep.
Crane, H.   Purgatorio.
Cuadra, A.   In Brief.
Curnow.   House and Land.
Dafydd [or David] Benfras.   From Exile.
Darwish, M.   Give Birth to Me Again That I
  May Know.
  Guests on the Sea.
  Identity Card.
  Sirhan Drinks His Coffee in the Cafeteria.
  We Travel Like Other People.
De Kok.   Shadows behind, Before.
  Transfer.
Dharker.   Minority.
Dib, M.   To a Voyager.
Dorfman, A.   Vocabulary.
Doty, M.   Elizabeth Bishop, Croton.
Drayton.   Why doe I quake my down-fall to
  reporte?
Duff, V.   Letters from an Exile.
Duffy, C.   Foreign.
Duo Duo.   In England.
Duran, J.   Pyrenees, The.
Fordham.   Exile's Reverie, The.
France, L.   Stateless.
Fried, E.   Exile.
Galeano, J.   Eraser.
Gilfillan, R.   Exile's Song, The.
Griffith, L.   Exile: Welsh Service from Daventry.
Griffiths, J.   Emigrants.
  Migration.
Guillén, J.   Last Land of Exile.
Halpern, M.   Long for Home.
Hamilton, S.   Farewell to France.
Healy, E.   From Los Angeles Looking South.
Hecht, A.   Alceste in the Wilderness.
Hemans.   Ancient Greek Song of Exile.
Herbert, G.   Religion stands on tip-toe in our
  land.
Herrera.   Exiles: "At the greyhound bus stations,
  at airports, at silent wharfs."
Hŏ Nansŏrhŏn.   For My Brother Hagok.
Hovanessian, D.   Exiles.
Hove.   Red Hills of Home.
Huchel.   Aristeas 2.
Hugo, V.   Conscience.
Ingalls, J.   For the Intellectuals.
Ivanov, G.   Quarter century of exile has passed,
  A.
  Should I tell of all the absolute fools.
  Unharnessed, the white horse ambles along.
Jastrun, T.   Scrap.
Jones, T.   Welshman in Exile Speaks, The.
Kalidasa.   High on the Mount of Rama a yaksha
  dwelt, who for.
Karim, F.   What Was My Choice?
Kipling, R.   Broken Men, The.
  St. Helena Lullaby, A.
Kizer, C.   Ingathering.
Kolmar.   Judith.
Kouchag, N.   I Was Suffering Exile.
Laraque, P.   Exile Is Stale Bread.
Lazard.   Ordinance on Arrival.
Lenski, H.   Lightly a slight shadow floats on the
  March snows.
Levertov.   Contraband.
Li Ch'ing-chao.   Banana Trees.
Li Po.   Fall River Song.
  Return of the Banished.
Liu Chi-hsün.   Lament.
Liu Tsung-yüan.   Dwelling by a Stream.
Macleod, M.   Blue Song.
Marlowe.   Here is the form of Gaveston's exile.
Martinez, D.   Altruism.
Masters, E.   Archibald Higbie.
Mattawa.   Before.
Maunick.   Seven Sides and Seven Syllables.
McDonald, C.   Asdrubral Jiménez.

Medina, P.   Exile, The.
Meng Chiao.   Laments of the Gorges ("Long
  ago, everyone laughed together.").
Milosz, C.   My Faithful Mother Tongue.
Milton.   Adam and Eve led out of Paradise.
  So spake the [or th'] Archangel Michael; then
  paused.
Muñiz Huberman.   Obsession.
Nasir, A.   Poet's Fate, A.
Neruda.   Ode to César Vallejo.
Nurkse.   Olmos.
Ovid.   Back from the sea now, back to their
  sources shall deep rivers.
  Dipped now in Ocean, the She-Bear's stellar
  guardian.
  Every letter you've read in this whole book was
  written.
  Friend, henceforth to be reckoned the foremost
  among my comrades.
  Friend of the arts and artists, scholar, generous
  patron.
  If you're one who keeps a bust made in my
  likeness.
  Little book—no, I don't begrudge you—you're
  off to the City.
  Nagging reminders: the black ghost-melancholy
  vision.
  You gods of sea and sky—what's left me now
  but prayer?
Padilla.   In Trying Times.
  Nuclear Umbrella.
Pagis, D.   Instructions for Crossing the Border.
Pau-Llosa.   Frutas: "Growing up in Miami any
  tropical fruit I ate."
Pembroke, M.   Psalm 114: In Exitu Israel.
"Perse."   Doors open on the sands, doors open
  on exile.
Phillips, D.   From Arena.
Pinchas-Cohen.   Journey of a Doe.
Pizarnik.   Exile.
Po Chü-i.   After Collecting the Autumn Taxes.
  Dreaming that I Went with Li and Yu to Visit
  Yuan Zhen.
  Rain.
  Song of the P'i-P'a.
Ralegh, S.   Farewell to the Court.
Remoto.   Exile.
Robinson, E.   Aaron Stark.
Rocha.   Poem of Return.
Salganicoff.   Nightmare.
Sappho.   My mother / In her youth it was a
  great.
Schiff, H.   German Frontier at Basel: 1942 and
  1992, The.
Seneca.   O barbarous Corsica, locked in by
  crags.
Sepúlveda-Pulvirenti.   From Now Until Chile.
Shafiq, H.   Mirage.
Shapiro, K.   Travelogue for Exiles.
Shauqi.   Andalusian Exile, An.
Shen Quanqi.   First Reaching Huanzhou.
Smith, C.   Female Exile, The.
Smith, I.   Exiles, The.
  Returning Exile.
Solomon, M.   Comment on My Host, A.
Soyinka.   Massacre, October '66.
Stewart, F.   Black Winter.
Strabo, W.   Elegy on Reichenau.
Su Man-shu.   Exile in Japan.
Suárez, V.   Song to the Banyan.
Supervielle.   Regretting the Earth.
Swiggart, Katherine.   Exhaled, The.
Thumboo.   Exile, The: "He was not made for
  politics."
Tibullus.   Cross the Aegean without Me, Then,
  Messalla.
Tidjani-Cissé.   Home News.
Torres Bodet.   Exodus.
Tu Fu [or Du Fu].   Blown by winds, the
  thistledown.
  Broken Boat, A.
  By Yangtze and Han.
  Dreaming of Li Po ("Parted by death, we'd
  strangle on our tears.").
  Heading South.
  Running from Trouble.

U'ng Bình. At the Exiled King's River Pavilion.
Ungaretti. In Memoriam: "His name was / Mohammed Sceab."
Unknown. Cid Calls His Vassals Together, The. They'll Go into Exile with Him.
Edward [*or* Edward, Edward].
Exile of Erin, The.
Exiles.
God, do not let any woman die in exile!
Great God of the exiled!
I have a fading flower in my hand.
It is springtime, here the leaves are sprouting on the trees.
Living in this land of exile is ravaging my heart.
My beloved, my sun, rise above the horizon and obliterate my nights of exile.
My friends, which of these two to choose?
My love, capture me, embrace me!
Now mountains are separating us.
Song Bewailing the Time of Christmas, So Much Decayed in England, A.
Tears are streaming down my face.
Wanderer, The.
Woman in exile never stops dying, The.
Voigt. Exile.
Walcott. Hotel Normandie Pool, The.
Wang Wei. Second Song for the Worship of the Goddess at Yu Mountain: "Bidding the Goddess Farewell".
Wat. From "Songs of a Wanderer".
Watkins, V. Returning to Goleufryn.
Weisz, O. Sefarad.
Woods, V. Departure.
Wyatt. Of the Courtier's Life.
Yi Sang. Poem No. 7.

Existentialism and Existentialists
Basho. Along my journey.
Crane, S. Man said to the universe, A.
Hillman, B. Black Series.
 Dark Existence.
Issa. In the midst of this world.
 This year on, forever.
Katz, J. Imperfect Is Our Paradise, The.
Mattawa. Before.
 Heartsong.
McLaughlin-Carruth, J. Existentially Speaking.
McNeil, R. It Just Doesn't Matter.
Pietri. 7th Untitled Poem.
Roethke. Duet.
Schwartz, R. L. Why I Forgive My Younger Self Her Transgressions.
Talvikki, A. My Shining Archipelago.
Tomlinson, C. Juliet's Garden.
Torres Bodet. Summary.
Williams, C. K. Gas Station, The.

Ex-lovers
Adamson, H. It's Been So Long.
Adcock, F. Advice to a Discarded Lover.
Akhmatova, A. I wrung my hands under my dark veil.
Alegría. Erosion.
Amichai, Y. Rustle of History's Wings, as They Used to Say Then, The.
Anania. Judy Travaillo Variations, The.
Andrew, G. Prayer: "God bless the chick in Alaska."
Baillie, J. Storm-Beat Maid, The.
Ballagas. Nocturne and Elegy.
Bang, M. It Says, I Did So.
Barber, W. Gay Poet, The.
Barker, G. To Whom Else.
Becker, R. Bicycle Days.
Bedregal. Pointless Journey.
Behn, A. Paraphrase on Oenone to Paris, A.
Berggolts [*or* Bergholts]. Indian Summer.
Blanco, R. Elegant Endings.
Bolton, J. Parthenon at Nashville, The.
Brooke, R. Busy Heart, The.
Brown, E. Sonnet: "Not if you crawled from there to here, you hear?"
 What do I have, when I contemplate this.
 When I recall you—as I often do.
Brown, L. That Old Feeling.
Cardenal. For me to lose you and for you to lose me, we both lose.
Carnevali. Serenade.

Cavafy. In Despair.
Chin, J. Ex-Boyfriends Named Michael.
Clare, J. Ballad: "Mary, fate lent me a moment of pleasure."
Clark, P. Walk in the Rain.
Corn. Billie's Blues.
Cunningham, J. I write only to say this.
 Love's Progress.
Denis, J. Zombie.
Duffy, C. Mrs Lazarus.
 Mrs Midas.
Eluard, P. *et al.* Shared Nights.
Engvick, W. Who Can I Turn To?
Estep, M. I Have to Go Now.
Fenton, J. Let's Go Over It All Again.
Flower. At Parting: "False love, since thou and I must sever."
Frost, R. Fifteen: "Late that summer my girlfriend's boyfriend."
García Lorca. Ah secret voice of dark love! Ah bleating without wool! Ah wound! Ah prick of gall, sunken camellia!
 Night of Sleepless Love.
 Poet Asks His Love about the Enchanted City of Cuenca, The.
 Poet Asks His Love to Write to Him, The.
 Poet Speaks the Truth, The.
 Poet Speaks with Love by Telephone, The.
 Sonnet of Sweet Weeping.
Ghalib, M. Ghazal 13: "Where are your woo-trysts and your heart-wreches now, Ghalib?"
Gilbert, M. Friendless Blues.
Gregory, A. Day Draws Near, The.
Groarke, V. Riverbed, The.
Hacker, M. Who would divorce her lover with a phone.
Han Yong'un [*or* Yongwun]. Your Silence.
Hart, L. He Was Too Good to Me.
Hass, R. Sonnet: "Man talking to his ex-wife on the phone, A."
Hoffenstein. Maid of Gotham, ere we part.
Ignatow, D. Each Day.
James, P. Can't We Be Friends?
Joyce, J. Tutto è Sciolto.
Killeen, G. Rewind.
Kizer, C. Bitch.
Koehler, T. Don't Worry 'Bout Me.
 Tess's Torch Song (I Had a Man).
Koertge. Dear Superman.
Kunitz, S. After the Last Dynasty.
Lahey, Joy. U-Turn.
Leggott, M. Dark torch.
Lewis, M. Hearts.
Lewis, S. Just Friends.
Lumsden, R. Yeah Yeah Yeah.
Martínez, V. Absence, Luminescent.
Menicanti. What's Left of You.
Mew. I Have Been through the Gates.
Moore, H. Blues: "I meet you again in public. I."
Moss, H. Shorelines.
Necatigil, B. Secret Love: "It was seven or eight years ago."
Negar. Forgive me that I opened your door silently.
Nimmo, D. Ill-Wishing Him.
Norton, C. First Love.
Pak Chaesam. Autumn River in Burning Tears.
Pak Inhwan. When Seasons Pass.
Parker, D. Healed.
 Sonnet for the End of a Sequence.
Phillips, R. Changed Man, The.
Piercy. Air Like Stained Glass Cuts Me, The.
Porter, C. Just One of Those Things.
Praed. Belle of the Ball-Room, The.
Rainger, R. Thanks for the Memory.
Ramke, B. Paul Verlaine at the Grave of Lucien Létinois.
Rees-Jones. And Please Do Not Presume.
Rich, A. Seven Skins.
Roberts, K. Darkness Was upon the Face of the Deep.
 Tilt, The.
Robin, L. Thanks for the Memory.
Rosser, J. Lover Release Agreement.
Rouse, A. Timing.

Rozhdestvensky [*or* Rozhdestvenskii]. In the Night.
Sappho. Atthis, for you the thought of me has become hateful.
Segal, J. I Keep Going Back to Joe's.
Şeyh Galib. You are my effendi, if I have any respect in the world.
Soupault. Song for Ghosts and for Those Now Gone.
Stevenson, A. After the End of It.
Strong, E. Farewell, A: "I have not won."
Sutphen, J. Not for Burning.
Sutter. Static.
Teasdale. After Love.
 Jewels.
The Earl of Longford. Forgetfulness.
Thomas, D. You shall not despair.
Tonks. Badly-Chosen Lover.
Tsvetayeva [*or* Tsvetaeva]. Ancient Song, An.
Unknown. Now that the fragrance.
 We cannot tell now.
Upton, L. Quality of Mercy, The.
Vallejo. In That Corner Where We Slept Together.
Vilariño. No More.
Warren, R. You Sort Old Letters.
Waters, M. Divine Will.
Wei Chuang. Candle Dies, A.
Williams, K. January 8, 1996.
Wilson, S. Recreational Mathematics.
Wright, C. Post-Revolutionary Letter.
Wright, K. My Version.
Wu of Han [*or* Wu Ti *or* Ou-ty *or* Liu Ch'e *or* Liu Ch'u]. Skein, The.
Wyatt. What Once I Was.
Yesenin [*or* Essenin]. Do You Not Love Me.

Exodus
Belli, G. Revenge 1.
Dunbar, P. Ante-Bellum Sermon, An.
Keene, J. Exodus.
Moore, T. Sound the Loud Timbrel.
Oppen. Exodus.
Reznikoff. Exodus.
Torres Bodet. Exodus.
Unknown. Go Down, Moses.
 Let My People Go.
Zelenina, G. Shma Yisrael (Hear, O Israel).

Experience
Akhmadulina. I was so buoyant.
Anania. On the Conditions of Place.
Apollinaire. Pretty Redhead, The.
Berrigan, T. Last Poem.
Blake, W. Piping Down the Valleys Wild.
 What is the price of Experience? Do men buy it for a song.
Blunden. Report on Experience.
Brontë, E. Old Stoic, The.
 Why do I hate that lone green dell?
Browne, S. First Drink.
Bruce, D. Plunder.
Cavafy. Ithaka.
 Passing Through.
 Their Beginning.
Ceravolo. May: "I am lost. / I had swum before."
Chaucer. Wife of Bath's Prologue, The.
Chubb, R. Song of My Soul.
Clary. In this wind, the sharp blue cut of the San Gabriels flattens against the neon east.
Cohan. I'm Mighty Glad I'm Living and That's All.
Cole, H. Buddha and the Seven Tiger Cubs.
Coleridge, S. Christabel.
Conway, J. Odd Years, The.
Coolidge, C. He walked around and couldn't think of anything.
 There Is a Caterpillar That Makes a Very Complicated Hammock.
Cortez, J. Guitars I Used to Know, The.
Crane, S. Little birds of the night.
Cross, D. Trilogy.
Cummings, E. E. If everything happens that can't be done.
 Since feeling is first.
Denby. People on Sunday.
Devi. Distance.

Dickinson, E.   Far from Love the Heavenly Father.
I stepped from Plank to Plank.
Driscoll, Frances.   Real Life.
Dunn, S.   Tenderness.
Dylan.   Desolation Row.
Emerson, R.   Experience.
Empson.   Let It Go.
Evans, Brett.   K-Doe Codas.
Gandlevsky, S.   Dear God, allow me to recall my works.
García, D.   Serpentine Voices.
Gelbtrunk, A.   Empty House, The.
Ginsberg, A.   Howl.
Giovanni.   Alabama Poem.
Guest, B.   Blurred Edge.
Gumilyov [or Gumiliov or Gumilev].   First Canzone.
Halliday, M.   Credentials.
Han-shan Te-ch'ing.   I wake up a novice and ask him to make tea.
Harris, Allison.   Nothing Much.
Hébert, A.   I Am Earth and Water.
Hecht, A.   To Fortuna Parvulorum.
Hirshfield, J.   Lives of the Heart,The.
Hope, A.   Observation Car.
Hughes, L.   Aesthete [or Esthete] in Harlem.
Jackson, A.   Fitting Room, The.
Jones, R.   Nudes.
Kabir.   How Much Is Not True.
Kerouac.   Poem: "Anyway the time has come to explain."
Kipling, R.   Bonfires, The.
Nurses, The.
Sestina of the Tramp-Royal.
Koch, K.   To the Roman Forum.
Kyger.   It's a great day. Last night I visited my old.
Lazer, Hank.   Teshuva: Heading South.
Levertov.   In Mind.
Levine, P.   Never Before.
28.
Lund.   Wrist-Wrestling father.
Madgett.   Old Women, The.
Majorino.   Doing.
Martí.   I am an honest man.
Merwin.   Given Day, A.
Mills, I.   Sophisticated Lady.
Nervo.   Ecstasy.
Okudzhava.   I never soared, and never did I soar.
Parish.   Sophisticated Lady.
Philodemus.   Demo and Thermion Both Slay Me.
Prescod.   Vicious Circle.
Ransom, J.   Blue Girls.
Rich, A.   Diving into the Wreck.
Richardson, J.   Vectors: Forty-five Aphorisms and Ten-Second Essays.
Rimbaud, A.   Departure.
O seasons, o châteaux.
Robinson, E.   Isaac and Archibald.
Rolle, S.   Keeping Watch.
Rosemurgy, C.   Angel Finally Admits What She Knows to Lou Binkler of Bethany, Missouri, An.
Ryan, M.   Reminder.
Saïd, A.   Paths of Light.
Schultz, P.   My Friend Is Making Himself.
Seferis.   Memory 2.
Seidman.   Gail.
Shunryu Suzuki.   Beginner's Mind.
Sobin, Anthony.   Driving Home to See the Folks.
Sondheim.   I Never Do Anything Twice (Madam's Song).
I'm Still Here.
Stafford, W.   Vocation.
Stern, G.   Royal Manor Road.
Szymborska, W.   View with a Grain of Sand.
Trejo.   Some Sparrows.
Troupe.   Old Black Ladies Standing on Bus Stop Corners #2.
Unknown.   Song of an Old Gray Wolf.
Vallejo.   Today I like life much less.
Van Duyn.   Moose in the Morning, Northern

Maine.
Walcott.   Tomorrow, Tomorrow.
Walsh, C.   Matter / of fact.
Wharton, E.   Experience.
Whitman, W.   Houses and rooms are full of perfumes, the shelves are crowded with perfumes.
Stronger Lessons.
Trippers and askers surround me.
When I Heard the Learn'd Astronomer.
Winner, R.   Segregated Railway Diner—1946.
Wordsworth, W.   World Is Too Much with Us, The.

Exploring and Explorers
Ackerman, D.   Elegy for *Challenger*.
Apollinaire.   Always.
Atwood.   Further Arrivals.
Booth, P.   Stefansson Island.
Brodsky, J.   Polar Explorer, A.
Cairns, Scott.   Prospect of the Interior.
Clewell.   Going Wrong in the House of Neptune.
Crist-Evans, C.   No Guarantee.
Curry, N.   Galapagos.
Donne.   Calm[e], The.
Storm[e], The.
Drayton.   To the Virginian Voyage.
Dryden, J.   By viewing nature, nature's handmaid, art.
Frost, R.   America Is Hard to See.
Gonzales, R.   Roberto Meets Cabeza de Vaca in the Desert.
Heifetz-Tussman.   Keep Me.
Hinsey, E.   *Planisféria*, Map of the World, Lisbon, 1554.
Lane, P.   Winter 40: "She is a northern woman, barely more."
Lux.   Ultima Thule.
MacLeish.   Voyage West.
Marvell.   Bermudas.
Melville, H.   To Ned.
Merton.   Place Names.
Merwin.   Gardens of Zuñi, The.
Miller, J.   Columbus: "Behind him lay the gray Azores."
Nathaniel, Isabel.   Weepers, The.
Parini.   Ruined House, The.
Simpson, L.   To the Western World.
Slauerhoff.   Columbus.
Souster.   Words before a Statue of Champlain.
Stafford, W.   For the Grave of Daniel Boone.
Thomas, L.   Flash Point.
Unknown.   Wonders.
Waniek.   Star-Fix.
Whitman, W.   Passage to India.

Explosions
Amichai, Y.   What is it? An airplane at dawn. No.
Fingueret, M.   86 Pasteur Corner.
Groarke, V.   To Smithereens.
Hinojosa, Rolando.   Jacob Mosqueda Wrestles with the Angels.
Komunyakaa, Y.   Fragging.
Larkin, P.   Explosion, The.
Oktenberg, A.   It Was an Open-Air Market.
Ondaatje.   Heat of explosions, The.
Pelizzon, V.   Feast of San Silvestro, The.
Portugal, Anne.   Every Shack.
Sankichi, T.   Flames.
Thiel, D.   Minefield, The.
Whalen, P.   Silence in the middle of traffic.

Exposure
Field, Miranda.   Subway.
Hughes, L.   Strange Hurt.
Reverdy.   In the Fields or on the Hill.

Exterminating and Exterminators
Browning, R.   Pied Piper of Hamelin, The.
Jacobsen, J.   Blue-Eyed Exterminator, The.
Matthews, W.   Vermin.

Extinction
Blight.   Death of a Whale.
Buckmaster.   End to Myth, An.
Burnham, D.   Maintaining the Species.
Carroll, K.   Theory on Extinction or What Happened to the dinosaurs?

Darwish, M.   On Our Last Evening on This Land.
Davis, J.   First-born, The.
Dransfield.   Endsight.
Dunn, D.   St Kilda's Parliament: 1879–1979.
Enzensberger, H.   End of the Owls, The.
Vanished Work.
Huchel.   Psalm: "That from the seed of men."
Hughes, T.   Orf.
Kendall, M.   Ballad of the Ichthyosaurus.
MacBeth [or Macbeth].   Bedtime Story.
Matthews, W.   Names.
Menicanti.   Felines.
Merwin.   For a Coming Extinction.
Oodgeroo of the tribe Noonuccal.   Last of His Tribe.
We Are Going.
Pack, R.   Mountain Ash without Cedar Waxwings.
Perillo, L.   For the Pileated Woodpecker and Its Cousin, the Ivory-Billed, Who May or May Not Be Extinct.
Porteous.   Charlie Douglas. Decommissioning.
Sandburg, C.   Buffalo Dusk.
Teasdale.   There Will Come Soft Rains.

Extrasensory Perception
Bécquer, G.   I Lay Awake, Wandering in that Limbo.
Graves, R.   Foreboding, The.
Wilbur, R.   Mind-Reader, The.

Extraterrestrial Intelligence
Tanikawa, S.   Twenty Billion Light Years of Loneliness.

Extreme Unction
Dowson.   Extreme Unction.
Wilbur, R.   Rule, The.
See also **Last Rites**

Eyeglasses
Evans, D.   En Monocle.
Fanthorpe.   Relief of Myopia, The.
Parker, D.   News Item.
Ritsos.   Myopic Child, A.

Eyes
Acconci, H.   Placable Caps, The.
Agustini.   Night Came in the Drowsy Living Room, The.
Alberti.   Angel of Sand, The.
Atwood.   You Fit into Me.
Bador, B.   Transparent Man, The.
Basho.   Spring going.
Baudelaire.   Owls.
Birney.   Slug in Woods.
Bogan, L.   Medusa.
Bourdillon.   Night Has a Thousand Eyes, The.
Breytenbach.   Threat of the Sick.
Broda, Martine.   I Wash.
Buson.   Makes the eye happy.
Cagnone, N.   It lies--when urged to, it lies.
Cairns, Scott.   Martyr, The.
Carpenter, E.   Through the Long Night.
Celan.   Language Mesh.
Cernuda.   For Two Voices.
Cetina, G.   Madrigal 1.
Madrigal: Eyes of Clear Serenity.
Clanchy, K.   Recognition.
Clarke, George Elliott.   To Selah.
Coleridge, M.   Moment, A.
Coulehan, J.   Man with a Hole in His Face, The.
Crashaw.   Weeper, The.
Curtis, L.   Only One Eye.
de la Parra Jr., J.   Courage!
Dickinson, E.   I like a look of Agony.
Diego, G.   Your Eyes Are Always Open.
Dowson.   Extreme Unction.
Flos Lunae.
Dubin, A.   I Only Have Eyes for You.
Fiallo, F.   Silence of Eyes, A.
Field, E.   Wynken, Blynken, and Nod.
Field.   Already to Mine Eyelids' Shore.
Dying Viper, A.
La Gioconda; Leonardo Da Vinci, The Louvre.
Field, R.   Dancing Bear, The.
Gahagan.   Colour of the Old Man's Eyes, The.
Gelman.   Eyes.

Gilbert-Lecomte. Wink.
González Prada, M. Your Lily Eyes Said Yes.
González, R. Perla at the Mexican Border Assembly Line of Dolls.
Greenlaw, L. Millefiori.
Grenier. Wrath to Sadness.
Gu Cheng. Generation, A.
Halpern, D. Her Body.
Harburg. Old Devil Moon.
Harwood, G. Naked Vision.
Holland, J. Pulse.
Hovanessian, D. Inside Green Eyes, Black Eyes.
Huidobro. Canto 2 (excerpts).
Hummell, A. I Never Saw a Goddess Go.
Jackson, H. Her Eyes.
Jonson, B. Song. To Celia ("Drink to me only with thine eyes.").
Joseph, A. Chalazion.
Kandinsky [or Kandinskii]. Sounds.
Kaufman, B. Would You Wear My Eyes?
Kendrick, D. Note to the Ophthalmologist.
Kim Hyesun. Inside the Iris.
Knight, E. He Sees Through Stone.
Knight, S. Eyeball Works, The.
Lowell, R. Eye and Tooth.
MacCaig. Instrument and Agent.
MacDiarmid, H. Milk-Wort and Bog Cotton.
Machado Ruiz. Eye you see is not, The.
Eye You See Isn't, The.
Eyes, The.
MacMuireadach. Farewell for ever to last night.
Macpherson, J. Third Eye, The.
Mandelstam [or Mandelshtam]. Eyesight of Wasps.
Marvell. Eyes and Tears.
McClure, M. For Zenshin Ryufu Philip Whalen.
Mercer, J. Jeepers Creepers.
Meyer, B. Ferry to South Baymouth, The.
Meynell, A. Cradle-Song at Twilight.
Mirabai [or Mira Bai]. O friends on this Path.
Moses. Hands, The.
Mullen, H. Eyes in the Back of Her Head.
Mun Chônghui. Stare, The.
Nelson, M. Shiner.
Neufeldt, L. Man with the Glass Eye, The.
Okamoto. Tanka: "As I gaze upon."
Okigbo. Eyes Watch the Stars.
Olds, S. Knowing, The.
Pack, R. Thrasher in the Willow by the Lake, The.
Paterson, D. Eyes, The.
Paz. Lake.
Mystery.
Pfeiffer, E. Any Husband to Many a Wife.
Prassinos. Loving Poem.
Rabi'a al-Adawiyya. O my Lord.
Roberts, L. Window of Our Soul.
Rolfe, E. About Eyes.
Rosenblatt, S. Visiting New York.
Roubaud. Way I, A.
Ruskhan. In Praise of Krishna.
Sachs, N. Your Eyes, O My Beloved.
Salter. Half a Double Sonnet.
Sandburg, C. Under a Hat Rim.
Sastri, D. Her Eyes.
Shakespeare, W. Sonnet 130: "My mistress' eyes are nothing like the sun."
Siddal. Lust of the Eyes, The.
Sidney. Sonnet 7: "When Nature made her chief work, Stella's eyes."
Sonnet 48: "Soul's joy, bend not those morning stars from me."
Solórzano, L. House Poem.
Poema de casa.
Sondheim. In Buddy's Eyes.
Steensen, S. State of affairs is thinkable, eventually, A.
Stein, G. Suppose an Eyes.
Swenson, M. Four-Word Lines.
Thomas, L. Some Eyes Condemn.
Thompson, P. Soft Black Eyes.
Timoner, J. Eye Occupation, The.
Toledo, N. Temple.
Templo.
Yudu.

Tsaloumas. Return of an Ikon.
Unknown. My heart said this to me: "I have no role to play".
My lover prefers sky-colored eyes.
Vinokurov. Eyes.
Ward, D. Approximately.
Wilson, K. River Girl.
Wroth. Sonnet 34: "Take heed mine eyes, how you your look[e]s do[e] cast."
Wylie. Now That Your Eyes Are Shut.
Yeats. Cat and the Moon, The.
Yi Jang'hi. Spring Is a Cat, The.
Yi Sang. Performance Angel.
Zaid. Cloister.
Mortal Practice.

Ezra
Ammons. So I Said I Am Ezra.

F

Faces
Akhmatova, A. Alone.
al-Braikan, M. Face, The.
Aled, Sion. Tracks of Longing.
Allingham, W. Everything passes and vanishes.
Bandeira. Portrait.
Basho. Lightning flash.
Wintry wind.
Year after year.
Blane, R. That Face.
Bogan, L. Song for the Last Act.
Bremer, C. Cena de un 10 de Abríl.
Dinner on an April 10th.
Bridges, R. Eros.
Bringhurst. Parśvanatha.
Brontë, A. Fragment, A: "Maiden, thou wert thoughtless once."
Campbell, J. Old Woman, The.
Carew, T. Lips and Eyes.
Chedid, A. Naked Face, The.
Chin. Altar.
Clare, J. First Love.
Colonna, S. He spins about (laughing) then shows.
Coulehan, J. Man with a Hole in His Face, The.
Creeley. Faces, The.
Oh my god—you.
Daglarca. Shadow: "Person we love, The."
Dickinson, E. These—saw Visions.
Diego, G. Hostility.
Dietz, H. I See Your Face before Me.
Duhamel. Crater Face.
Dunn, S. Criminal.
Eguren. Peregrin, Wandering Hunter of Faces.
Eigner. In Imitation.
Field. Elsewhere.
Fyleman. (Mice).
Gallagher, T. Even Now You Are Leaving.
Not There.
Gascoyne. Ecce Homo.
Gogarty. With a Coin from Syracuse.
Graves, R. Face in the Mirror, The.
Griffiths, J. Rosa Mystica.
Harryman. Mutations ("Face with red cavernous gashes a things possibly living in them, A.").
Hayati. Before there was a trace of this world of men.
Is this darkness the night of Power, or the black falling of your hair?
Hughes, L. 125th Street.
Subway Face.
Issa. Blossoms at night.
Last time, I think.
Morning glories, yes.
Ivanova, O. I meet myself each and every day.
Jackson, L. With the Face.
Jones, T. Meal, The.
Kay, J. Pride.
Khlebnikov, V. It Has the Unassuming Face of a Burnt-Out Candle.
Kooser. Self-Portrait at Thirty-Nine.
Kuzmin. People see gardens and houses.
When it was I first encountered you.
Lerner, A. I've Grown Accustomed to Her

Face.
Lewis, A. Unknown Soldier, The.
Li Ch'ing-chao. Hopelessness.
Lindsay, C. To My Own Face.
Liu, T. Ikon.
Loden. Reconstructed Face.
Lorde. From the House of Yemanjá.
Lovelace, R. Another.
Majorino. Scene-Script.
Marbod of Rennes. Horace composed an ode about a certain boy.
This vision of a face, radiant and full of beauty.
Marcus, B. Plagiarism.
Martin, H. That Face.
Mattawa. History of My Face.
McGuckian. On Not Being Your Lover.
McPherson, S. Ability to Make a Face Like a Spider While Singing Blues, The: Junior Wells.
Meireles. Portrait.
Milán, E. Do you care to remedy the faces of the gods? Make white.
He sends word for them not to be in His place.
Manda decir que no estén en Su lugar.
One's alone in this: making masks.
¿Quieres curar las caras de los dioses? Haz máscaras.
Uno está solo frente a esto: haciendo máscaras.
Milosz, C. Esse.
Moses. Hands, The.
Mutis. You Are a Daughter of the Lagides.
No Hyegyông. Face: "Suddenly below my ankles."
Onitsura. Autumn wind / Across the fields.
Patterson, R. Sundown Blues.
Pinkerton, H. On Dorothea Lange's Photograph "Migrant Mother" (1936).
Pound, E. In a Station of the Metro.
Probyn. Model, The.
Rehm, Pam. Vow 2.
Rodgers, C. Poem No. 1.
Sandburg, C. Halsted Street Car.
Under a Hat Rim.
Secundus, J. Kisses, The.
Sheykhi. Your sun-face is a mirror of the soul.
Shockley, E. My last modernist poem, #2 (or, mugshot).
Sidney. Sonnet 9: "Queen Virtue's court, which some call Stella's face."
Simon, L. Nellie Gives into Blanche.
Smedley, M. Face from the Past, A.
Stevenson, A. Who's Joking with the Photographer?
Suckling, S. Constant Lover, A [or The].
Sutherland, Fraser. Auden's Face.
Swensen, C. Crowd.
Vitale, M. Become Your Face.
Wah. Father / Mother Haibun #2.
Webster, A. By the Looking-Glass.
Faded.
Wellman, M. Blue sky in a human face.
Whitman, W. Faces.
Williams, C. On Forgetting Your Father's Face.
Wylie. To a Lady's Countenance.
Yi Hyangji. March of Dawn, The.
Yi Sang. Face.
Soyông Problems.
Zabolotsky [or Zabolotskii]. Face of a Horse, The.
Zandvakili, K. Love Letter.
Zanzotto. If It Were Not.

Factories
Ackland. Communist Poem, 1935.
Alexander, M. Chicago.
"Antler.". Machines waited for me, The.
Cafagña, M. Hawthorne Metal, Detroit, 1939.
Dent, A. Restricting Gate, The.
Fisher, J. Back on the Job.
Flynn, L. What You Get.
Galanskov. It shames one to look.
Hollander, J. Back to Town.
Johnston, E. Lines to Ellen, the Factory Girl.
Kelly, R. Bittersweet Growing Up the Red Wall.
Klassen, S. Making the Rate (factory journals).
Knight, S. Eyeball Works, The.
Landon. Factory, The.

Lindsay, V.   Factory Windows Are Always Broken.
Longfellow, H.   Ropewalk, The.
McGrath, C.   Smokestacks, Chicago.
Mueller, I.   Night Shift at the Fruit Cannery.
Nicholson, N.   On the Closing of Millom Ironworks.
Norton, C.   Voice from the Factories, A.
Reznikoff.   Girls outshout the machines, The.
   2. The Job.
   Shopgirls leave their work, The.
   They have built red factories along Lake Michigan.
Shepherd, R.   What Cannot Be Kept.
Stein, K.   Night Shift, after Drinking Dinner, Container Corporation of America, 1972.
Unknown.   Factory Workers' Song.
Voss, F.   Making America Strong.
Zavatsky.   Walker Evans in Bridgeport.

Faerie Queene, The
Ralegh, S.   Vision upon This Concei[p]t of the Faerie [or Faery] Queen[e], A.
Spenser, E.   Sonnet 80.

Failure
Altizer.   Sonnet 5: "No, I'll not, carrion, comfort you. Comfort."
Bly, R.   August Rain.
Cavendish, M.   Poetresses Petition, The.
Citino.   Principles of Scarcity, Doctrines of Growth.
Coleridge, H.   He Lived amidst th' Untrodden Ways.
Colonna, S.   But what an idea she'd gotten into her head.
Cummings, E. E.   Nobody loses all the time.
Dickinson, E.   Success is counted sweetest.
Dunn, S.   Instead of You.
Eady.   Hank Mobley's.
Eidenier, Elon G.   Failure of Language, The.
Ficowski.   I Did Not Manage To Save.
Ginsberg, A.   Last Night in Calcutta.
   Ode to Failure.
Gioia.   Failure.
   Guide to the Other Gallery.
Gleason, K.   After Fighting for Hours.
Glück, L.   Legend.
Guillén, N.   Don't Know No English.
Gwynn, R.   Anacreontic.
Gylys, B.   Fat Chance.
Halperin.   Tulips.
Henry, B.   Discovery.
Housman.   Shake hands, we shall never be friends, all's over.
Hughes, T.   Crow's First Lesson.
Hunt, L.   Rondeau: "Jenny kissed [or kiss'd] me when we met."
Ibn Ezra, A.   My Stars.
James, C.   Book of My Enemy Has Been Remaindered, The.
Jonson, B.   Ode to Himself, An ("Where dost [or; do'st] thou careless[e] lie.").
Kendall, M.   Failures.
Kooser.   Abandoned Farmhouse.
Kraushaar, M.   Dear Mr. Whitman.
Lake, P.   Crime and Punishment.
Masefield.   Consecration, A.
Masters, E.   Flossie Cabanis.
   Ralph Rhodes.
Mayer, B.   Failures in Infinitives.
Meng Chiao.   On Failing the Examination.
Neilson, S.   Rural Gothic.
Oakes-Smith, E.   Unattained, The.
Rafferty, P.   Back End.
Ray, H.   Failure.
Rekdal, Paisley.   Strawberry.
Robinson, E.   Bewick Finzer.
   Shadrach O'Leary.
Rossetti, C.   Symbols.
Rukeyser, M.   Paper Anniversary.
Russell, G.   Tragedy.
Ryan, K.   Failure.
Sassoon, S.   Counter-Attack.
Silano, M.   In Henry Carlile's Writing 213.
Updike.   Player Piano.
Wilbur, R.   In the Smoking-Car.
Yeats.   To a Friend Whose Work Has Come to

Nothing.
Zimmer.   Zimmer in Grade School.

Fairies
Allingham, W.   Fairies, The.
Bangs, J.   Little Elf, The.
Beddoes.   Song by Isbrand.
Burgess, F.   Trapping Fairies.
Cavendish, M.   Pastime of the Queen of Fairies, The.
Corbet [or Corbett].   Proper New Ballad Entitled [or Intituled] The Fairies' [or Faeryes] Farewell, or God-a-Mercy Will, A.
Fyleman.   Goblin, The.
Graves, R.   I'd Love to Be a Fairy's Child.
Hardy, T.   On a Midsummer Eve.
Herrick.   Oberon's Feast.
Keats.   Belle Dame sans Merci, La [A Ballad].
More, H.   Inscription in a Beautiful Retreat Called Fairy Bower.
Morley, C.   Plumppuppets, The.
Moultrie.   Fairy Maimounè, The.
Peake.   O here it is! And there it is!
Poe.   Fairyland [or Fairy-Land].
Ray, H.   On a Nook Called Fairyland.
Riley, J.   Little Orphant Annie.
Rumaker.   Fairies Are Dancing All Over the World, The.
Shakespeare, W.   Ariel's Song: "Come unto these yellow sands".
   Where the Bee Sucks.
Smedley, M.   Irish Fairy, The.
Taylor, J.   Fairies' Song, The.
Unknown.   Thomas the Rhymer.
Wordsworth, W.   Faery Chasm, The.
Yeats.   Stolen Child, The.
See also **Elves; Goblins**

Fairs
Andrews, T.   Cinema Vérité: William Makepeace Thackeray Follows His Bliss.
Blind.   Beautiful Beeshareen Boy, The.
Davidkov, Ivan.   Returning from the Fair.
Davidson, J.   Contraption,—that's the bizarre, proper slang.
Gay, J.   Two Monkeys, The.
Giorno.   Capsule.
Hardie, K.   Sheep Fair Day.
MacDiarmid, H.   Cattle Show.
McLaughlin-Carruth, J.   Parents They Would Be, The.
Simic.   Country Fair.
Stafford, W.   Adults Only.
Williams, P.   Rhapsody on Main Street.
Williams, W.   Dance, The: "In Brueghel's great picture, The Kermess."
Yauger, Fay M.   Country Fair.

Fairy Tales
Aguilar-Cariño.   Gabi.
Aichinger.   Winter Answer.
Bennett, B.   True Story of Snow White, The.
Boychuk.   Fairy Tale, A.
Clementelli.   I'd Like to Try Telling You of Spring.
Cooley, N.   Family History, The.
Dacey, P.   Jack, Afterwards.
Draycott.   Night Driving.
Ferrell, M.   Stories from the Tower.
Galvin, J.   Independence Day, 1956: A Fairy Tale.
Glück, L.   Gretel in Darkness.
Graves, R.   To Juan at the Winter Solstice.
Jacobsen, J.   Primer, The.
Jarrell, R.   Märchen, The.
Khlebnikov, V.   Iranian Song.
Lindsay, M.   At Hans Christian Andersen's Birthplace, Odense, Denmark.
Lochhead, L.   Rapunzstiltskin.
Machan.   Hazel Tells LaVerne.
Mörike [or Möricke].   Forest Murmurs.
Nesbit, E.   Goose-Girl, The.
Padgett, R.   Fairy Tale: "Little elf is dressed in a floppy cap, The."
   Prose Poem: "Morning coffee, The. I'm not sure why I drink it."
Ransom, Jane R.   This Is Just a Fairy Tale.
Reznikoff.   Beggar Woman.
Seshadri.   Wolf Soup.

Sexton.   Briar Rose (Sleeping Beauty).
Smith, S.   Fairy Story.
Unknown, fr. Terezin Concentration Camp. Forgotten.
Yolen.   Fat Is Not a Fairy Tale.

Fairyland
Alexander, C.   Dreams.
More, H.   Inscription in a Beautiful Retreat Called Fairy Bower.

Faith
Afsar.   Prayer: "We praise only you. We cringe with shame like crumbs."
Anwar, C.   At the Mosque.
Arghezi.   Psalm.
Arnold, M.   Dover Beach.
Askew, A.   Ballad Which Anne Askew[e] Made and Sang When She Was in Newgate, The.
Barbir, A.   Ah, Mr Businessman!
Baxter, R.   Now it belongs not to my care.
Beachy-Quick, Dan.   Psalm (Traherne).
Bedell, J.   Mains du Bon Dieu, Les.
Bek, T.   Oh life, long as an epic.
Bell, J.   Zombie Sunday (Had We but World Enough and Time).
Ben-Lev, D.   Sensualist Speaks on Faith, A.
Berman, C.   Mother Lakshmi's Poem.
Bibbins, M.   Just Yesterday.
Bible, Apocrypha.   Jeremie .17.
Blake, W.   Divine Image, The.
   Lamb, The.
   Mock On, Mock On, Voltaire, Rousseau.
   Night.
Bonar.   Thy Way, Not Mine.
Brehm, J.   Sea of Faith.
Brontë, A.   Doubter's Prayer, The.
Brontë, E.   No Coward Soul Is Mine.
   Visionary, The.
Brooke, R.   Heaven.
Bryant, W.   To a Waterfowl.
Bryce, Colette.   Full Indian Rope Trick, The.
Buffoni, F.   And in the end, the entire earth may answer to a single name.
Byrom.   My Spirit Longeth for Thee.
Byron, G.   Stanzas to Augusta ("Though the day of my destiny's over.").
Cairns, Scott.   Theology of Doubt, The.
   Translation of Raimundo Luz, The: My Good Luck.
Cane.   Tree in December.
Cary, A.   My Creed.
Chesterton.   Convert, The.
Clough.   There Is No God.
Coleridge, S.   Hexameters[; Paraphrase of Psalm XLVI].
Coolbrith.   Sea-Shell, The.
Coverdale.   Song of the Virgin Mary, The.
Cowper, W.   Light Shining out of Darkness.
Creeley.   En Famille.
Crunk, T.   Visiting the Site of One of the First Churches My Grandfather Pastored.
Cummings, E. E.   I Thank You God.
Dalton, A.   Almost Bird.
   In Love.
Dharker.   Honour Killing.
   Living Space.
Dias, Robert Vas.   At the Controls.
Dickinson, E.   Faith is a fine invention.
   Faith—is the Pierless Bridge.
   How brittle are the Piers.
   I know that He exists.
   I never lost as much but twice.
   I never saw a Moor.
   I think to Live—may be a Bliss.
   Nearest Dream recedes—unrealized, The.
   On a Columnar Self.
   This World Is Not Conclusion.
   Those—dying then.
   To lose one's faith—surpass.
   To pile like Thunder to its close.
Dobell, S.   Liberty to M. le Diplomate.
Donne.   Batter my heart, three-personed [or three person'd] God; for you.
Drayton.   Other Song of the Faithful, for the Mercies of God, An.
   Song of the Faithful, A.

Dunbar, P. Resignation.
  Slow through the Dark.
Dunn, S. At the Smithville Methodist Church.
  Guardian Angel, The.
Emerson, R. Problem, The.
  Worship.
Esrefoğlu. O My God Do Not Part Me from
  Thee.
Farrell, F. Credo.
Fenton, J. God, a Poem.
Fields, J. Ballad of the Tempest.
Fitzgerald, J. God in Hiding, God of Faith.
Frost, R. Sitting by a Bush in Broad Daylight.
Fuertes. Prayer: "You are here on earth, our
  Father."
Gale, N. Country Faith, The.
Gelbtrunk, A. All Illusion Is a Form of Hope.
Gilbert, C. Directions, The.
Gippius. Wedding Ring, The.
Glück, L. Celestial Music.
Graham, J. Prayer: "Over a dock railing, I
  watch the minnows, thousands, swirl."
Greenlaw, L. Earliest Known Representation of
  a Storm in Western Art, The.
Griffiths, J. Parasites.
Guiney. Wild Ride, The.
Hall, J. Praise of Faith, The.
Han-shan. Someone sits in a mountain gorge.
Hardie, K. Avatar, The.
Hardy, T. Impercipient, The.
Harris, R. Isaiah by Kerosene Lantern Light.
Hartnett. There Will Be a Talking.
Hayes, T. Postcard from Okemah, A.
Herbert, G. Affliction (1).
  Affliction (2).
  Artillery [or Artillerie].
  Church-Floor[e], The.
  Collar, The.
  Complaining.
  Discipline.
  Divinity.
  Elixir [or Elixer], The.
  Flower, The.
  Forerunners, The.
  Grace.
  Holy Baptism (2).
  Love Unknown.
  Peace.
  Pearl, The. Matth. 13:45.
  Pilgrimage, The.
  Quidditie [or Quiddity], The.
  Sin (1).
  Sonnet: "My God, where is that ancient heat
    towards Thee."
  Superliminare.
  Temper (1), The.
  Windows, The.
Herbert, Z. Envoy of Mr. Cogito, The.
Herrick. His Litany to the Holy Spirit.
Hill, G. So what is faith if it is not.
Hirsch, E. For the Sleepwalkers.
Hirshfield, J. Theology.
Holmes, O. Our Limitations.
Hopes. When the wolf moon howls, when the
  juncos.
Hopkins, G. Carrion Comfort.
  God's Grandeur.
Hostetler, A. Resisting Geometry.
Housman. If it chance your eye offend you.
Howard, R. Vocational Guidance, with Special
  Reference to the Annunciation of Simone
  Martini.
Howe, F. White Lines.
Howe, S. Silence Wager Stories.
Hughes, R. Lover's Reply to Good Advice.
Hunt, L. Abou Ben Adhem.
  Faith, Hope, and Charity Are the Prospects of
    Manhood.
Jeffers, H. Instructions for Academic Poets
  Who Talk to God.
Jeffers, R. Credo: "My friend from Asia has
  powers and magic, he plucks a blue leaf from
  the young blue-gum."
Johnson, F. Song of the Whirlwind.
Johnson, L. Spirit of the Dancer.
Keats. O Thou Whose Face Hath Felt the

Winter's Wind.
Keble. See Lucifer Like Lightning Fall.
Kemble. V.
Kipling, R. Recessional.
Knevet. Harp, The.
Koertge. Redondo.
Komunyakaa, Y. Instructions for Building Straw
  Huts.
Kumin, M. Getting the Message.
Landon. Bonds of Affection.
Laux, D. Dust.
Lawrence, D. H. Hills, The.
Lea, S. Do not trust in these deceptive words.
Levertov. Flickering Mind.
Levine, P. 28.
Lim-Wilson. Raising the Dead.
Lisboa. Idyll: "Lord, forgive me if I do not look
  for you."
Llwyd, Alan. Our Godless Days.
Llwyd, M. What? summer now? divisions ring.
Lochhead, L. Noises in the Dark.
Locke, A. Sin and Despair Have So Possess'd
  My Heart.
Logan, W. Valentine for Matthew Arnold, A.
Longfellow, H. Bells of San Blas, The.
Lope de Vega. Where Are You Going, Maiden.
Lowell, J. In a Copy of Omar Khayyám.
Lowell, R. As a Plane Tree by the Water.
Lux. Wife Hits Moose.
McAuley, J. In the Twentieth Century.
McLaughlin-Carruth, J. Introducing *New Year's
  SOLUTIONS*, from Saint Terri's Inc.
Mehmedinović, Semezdin. Essay, An.
Melville, H. Conflict of Convictions, The.
  Epilogue: "If Luther's day expand to Darwin's
    year."
  Swamp Angel, The.
Meyerhoff, J. Million times, A.
Michelangelo Buonarroti. I see in your
  beautiful face, my lord.
Milosz, C. Faith.
  Veni Creator.
Milton. On His Blindness.
  On Time.
Montale. Little Testament.
Moore, O. Eulogy for Sister.
More, H. Patient Joe; or, The Newcastle Collier.
More, S. Prayer, A.
Morter, L. Sunset on the River.
Murray, J. There Has Been More Than
  Beginning and End to Face.
Murray, P. Canticle of the Void, The.
Neruda. Hero, The.
Newman, J. Pillar of the Cloud, The.
Newman, R. Theology.
Newton, J. Amazing Grace.
Noll. Abraham's Madness.
Norris, K. Washing Dishes Late at Night.
Palmer, R. My Faith Looks Up to Thee.
Parker, R. Above the Timberline.
Pfeiffer, E. Any Husband to Many a Wife.
Powers, J. Garments of God, The.
Procter, A. Incompleteness.
  Strive, Wait, and Pray.
Ralegh, S. Even Such Is Time.
Ray, H. Triple Benison, The.
Reichard, W. Cloud Game, The.
Rekdal, Paisley. Stupid.
Riach, A. Sankey Hymns.
Rilke. I Have Faith.
Ríos, A. If I Leave You.
Roberts, L. Window of Our Soul.
Robinson, E. Children of the Night, The.
  Christmas Sonnet, A.
  Credo: "I cannot find my way."
Rossetti, C. O my heart's heart, and you who
  are to me.
  Somewhere Or Other.
  Thinking of you, and all that was, and all.
Rouse, A. Faith Healers.
Rowbotham. Nebuchadnezzar's Kingdom-
  Come.
Rumi. Keep walking, though there's no place to
  get to.
Ryan, T. Spin.
Sachs, N. Someone Will Take The Ball.

Sedakova. Rain: "It's raining, / and still people
  say there's no God!"
Serpas, M. Faith in Florida.
Sexton. Small Wire.
Sharp, S. How to Build a Prayer.
"Shu Ting.". Fairy Tales.
Sigourney. Poetry.
Simic. Psalm: "You've been a long time making
  up your mind."
Smart, C. Conclusion of the Matter, The.
  Hymn 1. Faith.
  Hymn 8. Fortitude.
  Strength.
Smith, P. Annie Pearl Smith Discovers
  Moonlight.
Smith, S. Dream of Comparison, A.
  God the Eater.
Stafford, W. Spirit of Place: Great Blue Heron.
Steele, T. 2. Of Faith.
Stevenson, R. Evensong.
Stradling. Abraham's Sacrifice of Isaac.
Swinburne. Higher Pantheism in a Nutshell,
  The.
Swiss. On a Stanza by Rilke.
Synková, A. I've met enough people.
Tabb. Sisters, The.
  Tenebrae.
Tanaquil. Very Young Man Speaks, A.
Taylor, E. Meditation 8 (First Series).
  Meditation 16 (First Series).
  State, a state, oh! dungeon state indeed, A.
Taylor, H. Goodbye to the Old Friends.
Tennyson, A. Be near me when my light is
  low.
  O[h], yet we trust that somehow good.
  That which we dare invoke to bless.
  You say, but with no touch of scorn.
Thomas, L. Electricity of Blossoms.
Thomas, R. S. In a Country Church.
  Island, The.
Thompson, F. Hound of Heaven, The.
Thomson, D. St Kildan Congregation.
Thomson, J. Part 2: "Because he seemed to
  walk with an intent."
Traherne. Innocence.
Tranströmer. Scattered Congregation, The.
Tuckerman, F. As Sometimes in a Grove.
Unknown. Angels in the House, The.
  Bell da Ring.
  Bound to Go.
  Children Do Linger.
  Come Along, Moses.
  Graveyard, The.
  Gwine Follow.
  Heaven Bell A-Ring.
  Hold Out to the End.
  Hold Your Light.
  Hunting for a City.
  Hunting for the Lord.
  I an' Satan Had a Race.
  I Believe.
  I Can't Stand the Fire.
  I grow crazier with each passing day.
  I Wish I Been Dere.
  I'm A-Trouble in de Mind.
  Jine 'Em.
  Lonesome Valley.
  Lonesome Valley, The.
  My Body Rock 'Long Fever.
  O Shout Away.
  O'er the Crossing.
  On the Flightiness of Thought.
  On to Glory.
  Praise, Member.
  Religion So Sweet.
  Rock o' Jubilee.
  Roll, Jordan, Roll.
  Sail, O Believer.
  Sometimes I feel like a motherless child.
  Who Is on the Lord's Side.
Valentine, J. *et al.* River at Wolf, The.
Vallejo. In the Moment.
Vaughan, H. Retreat[e], The.
Very. Nature ("Bubbling brook doth leap when
  I come by, The.").
  Night.

Rock, The.
Slavery.
Slowness of Belief in a Spiritual World, The.
Vitale, M.　Three Written Poems, Unconnected.
Walker, M.　We Have Been Believers.
Wallace-Crabbe.　Secular, The.
Warton, T.　On the Spirit Adulterated by the Flesh.
Watts, I.　Incomprehensible, The.
Webb, C.　Faith.
Wee, R.　Hoop Snake.
Wesley, C.　Come On, My Partners in Distress.
Whitehead, C.　Daybreak.
Whittemore, R.　Psalm: "Lord feeds some of His prisoners better than others, The."
Wilcox, E.　Nothing New.
Wild, R.　In a melancholly studdy.
Williams, M.　Some Lines Finished Just before Dawn at the Bedside of a Dying Student It Has Snowed All Night.
Why God Permits Evil: For Answers to This Question of Interest to Many Write Bible Answers, Dept. E-7.
Wright, J.　Cradle Logic of Autumn, The.
Wroth.　Song: "O[h] me[e], the time is [or has] come to part."
Sonnet 6: "My pain[e], still smothered [or smother'd] in my grieved bre[a]st."
Wyatt.　Steadfastness.
What should I say.
Yauch, Adam.　Bodhisattva Vow.
Young, K.　Revival.
Yūsuf III.　My friend go gently, for Time is as you know it to be, since there is no avoiding an easy life in spite of the present trace of hardship.
Zurita, R.　6.

Faith Healers
García, D.　Curandera, La.
Larkin, P.　Faith Healing.

Falcons
Cording.　Peregrine Falcon, New York City.
Cruz, C.　Praying ("In the middle of the night.").
Duncan, R.　My Mother Would Be a Falconress.
Han Yü.　Wounded Falcon, The.
Hopkins, G.　Windhover, The.
Inez.　Monologue of the Falconer's Wife.
Jamme, Franck André.　Often You Come.
Rossetti, C.　Noble Sisters.
Sutter.　Peregrine.
Teofilov, Ivan.　Falcon, The! His symmetrical confession.
Tu Fu [or Du Fu].　On a Portrait of a Falcon.
Unknown.　I trained me a falcon, for more than a year.
Lover Compareth Himself to the Painful Falconer, The.
Timor Mortis.
Winters, Y.　God of Roads.
Yenser, S.　Another Lo-Cal Elegy.

Falkland Islands
Borges.　Juan Lopez and John Ward.

Fall
Ammons.　Improvisation for the Stately Dwelling, An.
Basho.　Caterpillar, A.
Early fall.
It's fall and a full moon.
It's late fall.
Campo, C.　White Summer Clothes Are Folded Away, The.
Crapsey.　November Night.
Edson, R.　Fall, The: "There was a man who found two leaves and came indoors holding them out saying to his parents that he was a tree."
Jabeen, M.　Fall: "He always did that."
Thorpe, M.　Wishful Fall.

See also **Autumn**

Falling
Anania.　Fall, The.
Berlin.　I Got Lost in His Arms.
Cherry, K.　Pines without Peer, The.
Cross, E.　Balancing Act.
Equilibrismo.

Curbelo.　Bedtime Stories.
Fall: "It was a wing, it was a kiss."
Davidkov, Ivan.　Meteor.
Davis, T.　Boppin' Is Safer than Grindin'.
Dickey, J.　Falling.
Dickinson, E.　It Dropped So Low in My Regard.
Du Bouchet.　Fraction.
Faulkner, D. W.　Phoebe on a Bicycle.
Greger.　Prince of the Powers of the Air.
Greppi, C.　If you dropped me on the table.
Hayes, T.　Goliath Poem.
Held, George.　Split.
Hooks.　Body Inside the Soul, The.
Issa.　Here.
Kimbrell, J.　True Descenders.
Kinsella, J.　Fall, The.
Lal Ded [or Lalla].　This world.
Lam, F.　Loop.
MacInnes, Mairi.　Mass.
Magdeburg, Mechthild von.　Fish cannot drown in water, A.
Makeda (Queen of Sheba).　I fell.
Martinez, D.　Discreet Prayer, A.
Molodovsky [or Molodowsky].　Prayers: I.
Mother Goose.　Humpty Dumpty sat on a wall.
O'Callaghan, C.　Fall.
O'Malley, M.　Shoeing the Currach.
O'Reilly, C.　Six.
Otero, B.　Last Judgement.
Pagis, D.　Footprints.
Reibetanz, D.　Norgberto Hernandez—Photographed Falling September Eleventh.
Robinson, E.　Snow: "Purpose of the blanket, The."
Rózewicz.　Homework Assignment on the Subject of Angels.
Sewell, L.　Denied, The.
Sharma, P.　Transit.
Smith, S.　Harold's Leap.
Unknown.　Haida Cradle-Song.
Volkman.　Sonnet: "Lease of my leaving, heartfelt lack, what does."
Warren, R.　He Was Formidable.
Williams, W.　Luke 6:39.
Wiseman.　Triolets for Ken.

Falstaff
Wheeler, Jackson.　Falstaff's Dream.

Fame
Ai.　Paparazzi, The.
Barkova, A.　Few Autobiographical Facts, A.
Barney, W.　Ballad for Bill Pickett, A.
Berlin.　There's No Business Like Show Business.
Bibbins, M.　Groupie.
Bible, Apocrypha.　Our Fathers.
Bradstreet, A.　In Honour of that High and Mighty Princess Queen Elizabeth of Happy Memory.
Brontë, E.　Old Stoic, The.
Budbill.　Dilemma.
Burkard.　Woman in the Red House.
Butler, S.　There is a tall long-sided dame.
Byron, G.　Stanzas Written on the Road between Florence and Pisa.
What is the end of fame? 'Tis but to fill.
Cardenal.　Prayer for Marilyn Monroe.
Carey, S.　Fames Away.
Castro, R.　As I Composed This Little Book.
Chang Chiu-ling.　Climbing a Tall Building on an Autumn Evening: I Gaze to Where the South River Touches the Shixing Road.
Chudleigh.　Resolve, The.
Clover, J.　Feral Floats the Form in Heaven and of Light.
Coleridge, S.　Epitaph: "Stop, Christian passer-by!—Stop, child of God."
Coward.　Mad About the Boy.
Cowley, A.　Motto, The.
Davies, I.　Consider Famous Men, Dai Bach.
De Tabley.　Sonnet: "Record is nothing, and the hero great."
Dickinson, E.　Aurora.
Fame is a bee.
Fame is a fickle food.
I'm Nobody! Who are you?

Publication—is the Auction.
To fight aloud, is very brave.
Dietz, H.　Rhode Island Is Famous for You.
Doan Van Kham.　Remembering Priest Quang Tri.
Finnell.　Over *Voice of America*.
Flexner, H.　Contemporary.
Foley, Jack.　Poet's Tango, The.
Freneau.　To a New England Poet.
Frost, R.　Provide, Provide.
Greenhalgh, C.　Night I Met Marilyn, The.
Heard, J.　Fame.
Hemans.　Woman and Fame.
Herrick.　Pillar of Fame, The.
To His Book[e] ("Have I not blessed [or blest] thee? Then go forth; nor fear.").
Horace.　Exegi Monumentum.
Ode 3. 30.
Jackson, R.　One More Once.
Jewsbury.　Summer Eve's Vision, A.
Jonson, B.　To Sir Henry Cary.
Juan Chi.　Last Rays of the Sun.
Keats.　Addressed to Haydon.
Great Spirits Now on Earth.
On Fame.
To Kosciusko.
When I Have Fears [That I May Cease to Be].
Kemble.　Sonnet: "Thou poisonous laurel leaf, that in the soil."
Killigrew, A.　Upon the Saying That My Verses Were Made by Another.
Kinsella, J.　Warhol at Wetlands.
Kizer, C.　Ashes, The.
Landon.　Felicia Hemans.
Lazarus, E.　Success.
Li Po.　For Meng Hao-Jan.
There was a sojourner in Ying who intoned "White Snows".
Lihn.　Favorite Little Shrine, A.
Lindsay, V.　She is madonna in an art.
Lindsay, C.　Love or Fame.
Lowell, J.　Sonnet: "Amid these fragments of heroic days."
Machado Ruiz.　I Have Never Wanted Fame.
Martial.　Post-Obits and the Poets.
Slipshod writing, premature publication.
Why is it modern books are little read.
Why is it modern poets are ignored.
McClure, M.　Mad Sonnet: Fame.
Mew.　Fame.
Milton.　On Shakespear[e].
Nathan, L.　So?
Nemerov.　Modern Poet, A.
Norton, C.　Picture of Sappho, The.
Nye, N.　Art of Disappearing, The.
Famous.
O'Brien, S.　Welcome, Major Poet!
Okereke, C.　Starlette.
Ovid.　And now my work is done: no wrath of Jove.
Elegy 1.15: "Envy, why carp'st [or carpest] thou my time is spent so ill."
Friend of the arts and artists, scholar, generous patron.
Owen, W.　To My Friend (With an Identity Disc).
Parkes, B.　To an Author Who Loved Truth More Than Fame.
Parra, N.　Poems of the Pope, The.
Pasternak, B.　To Be Famous Isn't Decent.
Pettit.　Vanna White's Bread Pudding.
Pietri.　Intermission from Sunday.
Po Chü-i.　On Hearing Someone Sing a Poem by Yuan Zhen.
Robinson, E.　Three Quatrains.
Robinson, M.　[Sonnet] Conclusive.
Sonnet Introductory.
Rosselli.　Worthless as was her itinerary to fame.
Sandburg, C.　Soup.
Shakespeare, W.　Sonnet 125: "Were't aught to me I bore the canopy."
Shelley, P.　Ozymandias.
Sia, B.　Open Letter to the Entertainment Industry, An.
Sidney.　Sonnet 15: "You that do search for every purling spring."

Sonnet 27: "Because I oft, in dark abstracted guise."

Sonnet 90: "Stella, think not that I by verse seek fame."

Simonides. Thermopylai's dead.

Troupe. Poem for "Magic", A.

Tu Fu [or Du Fu]. To Pi Ssu Yao.

Traveler at Night Writes His Thoughts, A.

Unknown. [Last Survivor's Speech in Old English, The].

Updike. Newlyweds, The.

Villon. Ballade of the Ladies of Time Past.

Virgil [or Vergil]. Fame.

Wang Chiu-ssu. This crazy man has escaped the world.

Whalen, P. International Date Line, Monday/ Monday 27:XI:67.

Whitman, W. When I Heard at the Close of the Day.

Wyatt. Stand Whoso List.

Young, E. Love of Fame, the Universal Passion.

See also **Greatness**

Family

Abrahams, L. Family man.

Ai. Blue Suede Shoes.

Family.

Alabaú. Sister.

Alegría. Grandmother, The.

Alexander, E. Who I Think You Are.

Alexie. One Stick Song.

Ali, A. Cracked Portraits.

Lost Memory of Delhi, A.

Return to Harmony 3.

Anderson, A. Suicide Year, The.

Arrillaga. Dream.

Like Raquel.

Ashbery, J. History of My Life, The.

Awoonor. I Rejoice.

Babstock, Ken. Pragmatist.

Barresi. How It Comes.

Vacation, 1969.

Becker, R. Dreaming at the Rexall Drug.

Bensko. Bones of Lazarus.

Last Look in the Sambre Canal, A.

Bernstein, C. Memories.

Berryman. Henry's Fate.

When by me in the dusk my child sits down.

Bertrand. Five Fingers of the Hand, The.

Bishop, E. Poem: "About the size of an old-style dollar bill."

Blaeser. Rituals, Yours—and Mine.

Bobrowski. Latvian Songs.

Bowering, G. Do Sink.

Brainard, J. I remember living on the Lower East Side.

Brant, B. Stillborn Night.

Brooks, G. Parents: People Like Our Marriage Maxie and Andrew, The.

Broumas, O. Landscape with Next of Kin.

Brown, E. Out.

Buckley, V. Origins.

Bukowski. Me against the World.

Burkard. Breathless Storm.

Weather.

Burns, R. Memory.

Buson. He's on the porch.

Byrd, Bobby. Breaking and Entering: A Very Short Novel in Verse.

Cager, Chezia Thompson. Callaloo.

Campo. S. W.

Carbó, N. Verso Libre.

Carson, C. Dresden.

Castillo, S. Monday Night at Pedro's.

Primos.

Caston, A. Blowing Eggs.

Chase, N. Plenty.

Chester, L. Search to get lost in a great big coat, The.

Chin. How I Got That Name.

Chinese Oral Tradition. Transformation Text on the Boy Shun's Extreme Filial Piety.

Chrystos. Old Indian Granny, The.

Chu Yün-ming. Fan from Korea, A.

Citino. Sister Mary Appassionata Lectures the Home Ec Class: The Feast.

Clark Bekedermo. Abiku.

Death of a Lady.

Family Procession, A.

Order of the Dead, The.

Clifton, L. Light / on my mother's tongue.

Clover, J. Family Romance.

Cofer, J. They Never Grew Old.

Collin, J. Layman's Lament, The.

Cook, E. Written at the Couch of a Dying Parent.

Cooley, N. Family History, The.

Copus, J. Back Seat of My Mother's Car, The.

Cornwall. To My Child.

Couzyn. Transformation.

Creeley. En Famille.

Won't It Be Fine?

Crunk, T. Leaving.

Visiting the Site of One of the First Churches My Grandfather Pastored.

Cuthand, B. Dancing with Rex.

Dacey, P. Drummer, The.

Dalton, A. Dad-Baby, The.

Davidson, D. Sanctuary.

Davies, J. Visitor's Book, 9, The.

De Vries, R. On Alabama Ave., Paterson, NJ, 1954.

Dean, D. K. In the Way Back.

Deane, S. Fording the River.

DeCormier-Shekejian. Snow.

DeFrees. Family Group, The.

Delgado, J. Flora's Plea to Mary.

Dooley, M. Dancing at Oakmead Road.

Dove, R. Fifth Grade Autobiography.

Drummond de Andrade. Motionless Faces.

Portrait of a Family.

Traveling as a Family.

Dunn, S. That Saturday without a Car.

Durcan. Wife Who Smashed Television Gets Jail.

E'der, E. La Puente.

El-Gabry, M. Child Hunting Tales, A.

El-Hadi, S. Drama, The.

Ennis. Drink of Spring, A.

Essbaum, J. When the Kingdom Comes.

Fay, J. Flowers.

Ferré. Message.

Firer. 1956, the Year My Sister, Using Her Ill Health Once Again, Blackmailed My Parents into an Accordion.

Fitzpatrick, K. Highland, 1955.

Forhan, C. Taste of Wild Cherry, The.

Forman, R. Abraham Got All the Stars N the Sand.

Foster, T. Folktale, A: "Father stands on a walkway talking, A."

Fried, E. My Girlfriends.

Garcia-Camarillo, C. Family Photographs.

Garrett, G. For a Bitter Season.

Gay, Garry. Family reunion.

George, E. Family.

Gewanter, D. Xenia: Stranger/Guest.

Gillilan, P. Mistress, The.

Giussani, S. Abel and Abel.

Glück, L. Brown Circle.

From the Suburbs.

Gomez, M. Lost Daughter.

Gonzalez, N. How the Heart Aches.

Goodman, M. Upkeep.

Gordon, C. Calling Out the Names.

Gotera. Pacific Crossing.

Groarke, V. Family.

Family Photograph, The.

History of My Father's House, The.

Guillén, N. My Last Name.

Gwala. Children of Nonti, The.

Gylys, B. Family Reunion—Aunt Vern's Two Cents.

Hacker, M. And I shout at Iva, whine at you. Easily.

Hagedorn, J. Smokey's Getting Old.

Hahn, K. Hula Skirt, 1959, The.

Hai-Jew, S. Three Gypsies.

Hall, D. X.

Hannan, M. Coming Down from Derry Hill.

Hardy, T. During Wind and Rain.

Harms. Sky.

Harper, M. Kin.

Hart, J. Only Applebaum Can Make a Tree.

Hawkesworth, P. Two Statues.

Hawoldar. You.

Hayden, R. Beginnings.

Heaney, S. Clearances.

Hemans. Graves of a Household, The.

Herrera. Portrait of Woman in Long Black Dress / Aurelia.

Hertz, D. Return, The.

Hippolyte. So Jah Sey.

Hirshfield, J. Picnic.

Hogan, L. Heritage.

Hongo. Hilo: First Night Back.

Hopkins, G. Epithalamion: "Hark, hearer, hear what I do; lend a thought now, make believe."

Hovanessian, D. Two Voices.

Hsin Ch'i-chi. Tune: "Pure Serene Music" Rural Life.

Hudgins. Telling, The.

Hughes, T. Walt.

Ignatova, E. To sob, pressing oneself against the officer's greatcoat.

Ingelow. Seven Time Six. Giving in Marriage.

Johnson, M. F. Idiot Girl, The.

Jones, S. New World.

Jones, T. Llanafan Unrevisited.

Jordan, A. Public Radio Plays Eddie Harris.

Jordan, J. Through These Halls.

Joseph, A. My Father's Heroes ("Not JFK, not MLK.").

Numbers: "My father taught me to measure."

Juhász, F. Biography of a Woman, The.

Kaplinski, J. My Wife and Children.

Kasdorf. Grossdaadi's Funeral.

Kavulu. Me?

Kawano, Y. Climbing the mountain pass.

Kay, J. English Cousin Comes to Scotland.

Kenny, M. Joshua Clark.

Kenyon, J. From Room to Room.

Kinzie. Boy.

Kirsch, S. Pictures.

Kizer, C. Amusing Our Daughters.

Knight, E. My Uncle Is My Honor and a Guest in My House.

Koch, K. You Were Wearing.

Kollar. Late Arrivals.

Komunyakaa, Y. Family Tree.

Kumin, M. Family Reunion.

For My Great-Grandfather: A Message Long Overdue.

Retrieval System, The.

Kunitz, S. Father and Son.

Quinnapoxet.

Three Floors.

Kushner, D. Grandma in the Shower.

Laird, N. Layered, The.

Larkin, P. Ambulances.

Lee, L. Eating Together.

Persimmons.

Levin, D. Wind.

Levine, P. I Was Born in Lucerne.

Lewis, M. My Mother.

Lilley. Sewing Lesson, The.

Lim-Wilson. Wave, The.

Lisella. Song of the Third Generation.

Liu, T. Kindertotenlieder.

Livingston, M. Coming from Kansas.

Invitation.

Lloyd, C. My pleasant home! where erst when sad and faint.

Oh, I have told thee every secret care.

Lomax, M. Amor Diving.

Lopez, L. Tomás.

Ludvigson. Inventing My Parents.

Lum. Picture of my Mother's Family, A.

Lux. Large Branch Splintering off a Tree in a Storm, A.

Mahon. Achill.

Maroon, B. Neighbor.

Matherne, B. La Fabrique de Tabac (Tobacco Harvest).

Les Fils (Sons).

Mathews, A. Letter Following.

Matthews, W. Moving Again.

McDaniel, J. 1977.

McGrath, C. Delphos, Ohio.

First Trimester, The.
McGrath, T.   And we, of the damned poor, trot our frost-furred horses.
McGuckian.   Lychees.
McGuire, Virginia.   Leaning into the Tilt.
Melville, H.   Fragments of a Lost Gnostic Poem of the Twelfth [or 12th] Century.
Meredith, W.   For His Father.
Mersaal, E.   Neutrality.
Merwin.   Ballad of John Cable and Three Gentlemen.
Miles, J.   Belief.
Miller, A.   My Trip.
Miller, E.   My Father's Girlfriend.
Million, D.   Housing Poem, The.
Mills, B.   Ballad: Of Motion.
Montague, J.   Family Conference.
  Point, The.
  Silver Flask, The ("Sweet, though short, our.").
Moolten, D.   Bio 7.
Moore, L.   Haiku.
Morales.   Old.
Morgan, J.   My Welsh Home.
Muir, E.   Scotland 1941.
Murray, L.   Cotton Flannelette.
Myles, E.   American Poem, An.
Nicholson, N.   Epithalamium for a Niece.
Nickel, B.   Lines: "Empty foolscap, The."
Niedecker.   Paean to Place.
Noguchi, R.   Breath He Holds, The.
  I, the Neighbor Mr. Uskovich, Watch Every Morning Kenji Takezo Hold His Breath.
O'Brien, L.   Diabolus in Musica.
Olds, S.   Clasp, The.
O'Loughlin.   Glasnevin Cemetery.
Ondaatje.   Light.
O'Reilly, C.   Possession.
Orton, B.   Beekeeper.
Pak Mogwŏl [or Mokwŏl].   Family.
Paschen.   Two Standards.
Pastan.   Old Photograph Album.
Peck, J.   Woods Burial.
Penn, M.   Calling Up the Spirit of the Lost Child.
Petillar, T.   Generation Gap.
Philp, G.   Heirlooms.
Piercy.   My Rich Uncle, Whom I Only Met Three Times.
Pilling.   Specimen.
Pollarolo, G.   In My Days.
  While My Father.
Popa.   In the Village of My Forefathers.
Porter, A.   Five Wishes.
Powell, K.   For Aunt Cathy.
Prado, A.   Successive Deaths.
Preil, G.   Eternal Present, The.
Prévert.   Whale Hunt, The.
Ramanujan.   Extended Family.
  In the Zoo.
Rebelo.   Poem of a Militant.
Rich, A.   Letters in the Family.
Richman, L.   To Valenton: Impressions circa 1947.
Ridl.   Video Mama.
Roberts, L.   My Father's Whistle.
Rodney.   Bardo of the Threshold.
Rodrigues J. P.   Half-.
Rogers, P.   Family Is All There Is, The.
Rosenblatt, S.   Leaving Home.
Rossetti, C.   Gone Before.
Rózewicz.   Return, The.
Rukeyser, M.   Absalom.
  Ceiling Unlimited.
Rungano.   Labour.
Rybicki, J.   This Sun.
Saffoti.   Espresso.
Saito, Brynn Noelle.   Turkey People.
Salzman, E.   Physics.
Sanguineti.   Wind shoves my New Year's Day sun in my face, The.
Savageau.   At the Powwow.
  Like the Trails of Ndakinna.
  Looking for Indians.
  Trees.
Scamell, B.   My Lost Brother.
Scammell, W.   Poem for a Younger Son.

Schnackenberg.   Returning North.
Schultz, P.   Free Mercy.
Scott, J.   Illness.
Self, Joan.   Quill Holler Waller.
Sereni.   Each Time That Almost.
Seto, T.   Blood Ties.
Seward.   On a Lock of Miss Sarah Seward's Hair Who Died in her Twentieth Year.
Sexton.   All My Pretty Ones.
Shapcott, T.   Turning Fifty.
Shapiro, D.   Father Knows Best.
Sheehan, M.   My Father's Singing.
Shepherd, R.   Difficult Music, The.
Simpson, L.   Ed.
Slutsky [or Slutskii].   Burnt.
Smith, S.   Tenuous and Precarious.
Smith, W.   Family Man, The.
Snyder, G.   Waiting for a Ride.
Sŏ Chŏngju.   Grandmother's Verandah.
  Self-Portrait ("Father was a serf, seldom came home at night.").
Song.   Spaces We Leave Empty.
Soto.   Braly Street.
  Family in Spring, The.
Speak, M.   Ingredients of Glass.
Stanton, M.   Pole Vaulting.
Stead, C.   Between.
Stétié, Salah.   Garden of the One, The.
Stevenson, A.   Arioso Dolente.
Stone, J.   Talking to the Family.
Strickland, A.   Infant, The.
Suárez, V.   Cuban-American Gothic.
  Song for the Sugar Cane.
Sun, Phillina.   Untitled: "In the living room sit the men."
Suntsova, E.   As you and I stand long.
Tanikawa, S.   Family Portrait.
T'ao Ch'ien [or T'ao Yuan-ming].   Return, The.
Tapahonso.   I Am Singing Now.
  Warp Is Even, The: Taut Vertical Loops between Our Father and the Earth.
Tate, J.   Land of Little Sticks, 1945.
Tennyson, A.   Sweet and Low.
Tidjani-Cissé.   Home News.
Townsend, A.   First Death.
Tran, B.   From Rosary.
Tu Shan-fu.   Tune: "Shua Hai-erh" Country Cousin at the Theater.
Tucker, M.   We Met.
Ullman.   Why There Are Children.
Unknown.   Ballad of Mulan, The.
  Crows on City Walls.
  Girl threw an apple to a cloud, A.
  Large-headed beauty, head so alluring, The.
  Peacock Southeast Flew, A.
  Si-mu: Request for Furlough.
  Swallow flies away, The.
  That peachtree so frail.
  Zhi-hu: Young Soldier Thinks of Home.
Valentine, J.   American River Sky Alcohol Father.
Vazirani, R.   Daughter-Mother-Maya-Seeta.
  Mrs. Biswas Breaks Her Connection with Another Relative.
Vertreace, M.   Black Tulips.
Vietnamese Oral Tradition.   Mother Egret.
  Testing the Confucian Ideal.
Walcott.   Glory Trumpeter, The.
Waldman, A.   De Carlo Lots, The.
Waniek.   Porter.
Warren, R.   Ballad of Billie Potts, The.
Watkins, V.   Returning to Goleufryn.
Weller.   Ngungalari.
  Story of Frankie . . . My Man, The.
Wenderoth, J.   January 11, 1997.
Wickham.   Letter to a Boy at School.
Winder.   On Fourteen Maple Street.
Wong, N.   It's in the Blood.
  Ma, my heart must be made of rice straw.
  Picnic.
Wright, C.   Virginia Reel.
Wright, J.   I to My Brothers.
Yamada.   American Son.
Yang Hsün-chi.   Inscribed on the Doors of My Bookshelves.
Yang Wen-li.   Thinking of My Family on an

Autumn Day.
Young, K.   Anatomy.
Zarco.   Manila Paper.
Zukofsky, L.   H. T.

Family Life
Akhmatova, A.   Northern Elegies.
Andrew, G.   Down on My Knees.
Barker, W.   Trying To.
Barrax.   Domestic Tranquility.
Behn, R.   Vigil: Dwindle.
Berlin.   Supper Time.
Berman, D.   From His Bed in the Capital City.
Bloch, C.   Conservation of Energy, The.
Brissenden.   Verandahs.
Brooks, G.   Jamal; Nineteen Cows in a Slow Line Walking.
  Religion.
  Vacant Lot, The.
Brown, Laura Soul.   Oh! Mercy Mercy Me! A Family Gathers to Marvin Gaye.
Bye.   Not Tyrants.
Carrara, Carli.   On Weekends.
Cervantes.   Beneath the Shadow of the Freeway.
Clifton, L.   Cigarettes.
  Good Times.
Cortez, Sarah.   Reunion.
Davis, Cortney.   Smoke We Make Pictures Of, The.
Dawe, Tom.   Riddle: "I see them in summer."
Derricotte.   Poem for My Father.
Di Prima.   Poem in Praise of My Husband (Taos).
Dienstfrey, Patricia.   Let the Raspberry Jam in the Crystal Jar Stand for It.
Digges.   Broom.
Dove, R.   Daystar.
  Taking in Wash.
Dugan, A.   Nomenclature.
Duran, J.   Conversations with Louis.
Eshleman, C.   Deeds Done and Suffered by Light.
Factor, J.   Song beside a Sippy Cup.
Flanders, J.   Dandelion Greens.
Foley, M.   Provincial Adolescence, A.
Forman, R.   Abraham Got All the Stars N the Sand.
Gemin, P.   Upper Peninsula Landscape with Aunts.
Gildner.   Nails.
Giovanni.   Nikki-Rosa.
Goeckel, L.   Short Hand.
Gorlanova, N.   Three-Liners.
Gwala.   One small boy longs for summer.
Hands, E.   On an Unsociable Family.
Hartnett.   Small Farm, A.
Harwood, G.   In the Park.
Hass, R.   Concerning the Afterlife, the Indians of Central California Had Only the Dimmest Notions.
  Song: "Afternoon cooking in the fall sun."
Hayden, R.   Those Winter Sundays.
Hicok.   Man of the House.
Hierro, José.   Accelerando.
Hoch, James.   Riding Backwards on a Train.
Hogan, L.   Heritage.
Hood, T.   Parental Ode to My Son, A.
Hughes, L.   Piggy-back.
Ivanov, Binyo.   Tale That's Not a Tale, A.
Jackson, M.   Gifts.
Jarnot, L.   Girl Who Couldn't Be Loved, The.
Joseph, L.   Sand Nigger.
Kaufman, S.   Mothers, Daughters.
Kay, J.   Dressing Up.
Knight, E.   Idea of Ancestry, The.
Kuo.   Then they are young and on vacation, their camera.
Kutchins, L.   Clothesline.
Lane, P.   Children.
Laux, D.   Nurse, The.
Locklin.   Learning to See Crooked.
London, S.   Cold War.
Lopez, T.   No Transport.
Lowell, R.   My Last Afternoon with Uncle Devereux Winslow.
Mayer, B.   Spring House.
McCarriston.   Hotel Nights with My Mother.

To Judge Faolain, Dead Long Enough: A Summons.
Mezey. She thinks if she puts out, her sainthood will be recognized.
Miller, E. Father's Day.
Miller, N. My Family.
Muldoon, P. Mixed Marriage, The.
Mura. Nisei Picnic: From an Album, A.
Niedecker. Fancy Another Day Gone.
Nowlan. Britain Street: Saint John, New Brunswick.
O'Hara, F. Ave Maria.
Olin. "Colors" Starring Patti, Grandma, & Me at Twenty-five.
Oomen, A. Peaches: "In the only moment of ecstasy I have."
Ortiz. My Mother and My Sisters.
Pastan. Who Is It Accuses Us?
Peacock, M. Those Paperweights with Snow Inside.
Prévert. Familial.
Ramanujan. Routine Day Sonnet.
Reddy, S. Generations.
Rhodes, M. All the Soups.
Rich, A. Woman Mourned by Daughters, A.
Riley, J. King of Oo-Rinktum-Jing, The.
Roberts, L. Assignment, The.
Roethke. My Papa's Waltz.
Ruefle. American Dream, An.
Salter. Frost at Midnight.
Home Movies: A Sort of Ode.
Sellers, H. In the Kitchen Dancing to Kitty Wells.
Sexton. Boat, The.
Funnel.
Simpson, L. My Father in the Night Commanding No.
Physical Universe.
Smith, S. Emily Writes Such a Good Letter.
Song. Sky-Blue Dress, The.
Stafford, W. Rescued Year, The.
Stanford, A. Childhood.
Swirszczynska [or Swir]. Three Pieces of Candy.
Teare, Brian. First person plural is a house.
Unknown. Nü-yue ji-ming: The Cock Is Crawin' (scoticè).
Van Duyn. Relationships.
Waldman, A. De Carlo Lots, The.
Williams, C. K. Sanctity, The.
Williams, W. Shrinking Lonesome Sestina, The.
Williams, W. This Is Just to Say.
Wright, E. When Father Carves the Duck.
Wright, F. Sunday Afternoon.
Wright, K. Victorian Family Photograph.

Famine
Achebe. Christmas in Biafra (1969).
Boland, E. Famine Road, The.
Bryan, T. Planting Potatoes during Chernobyl.
Byron, G. Abdiel.
Clark Bekedermo. New from Ethiopia and the Sudan, The.
Dupin. Let Us Salute.
Griffin, S. This Is Not Love's Offering.
Khlebnikov, V. Trumpet, Shout, Carry!
McClure, M. Madame Secretary.
Olds, S. Photograph of the Girl.
Ryan, R. Father of Famine.
Shwarts [or Shvarts]. Portrait of the Blockade through Genre Painting, Still Life, and Landscape, A.
Unknown. War Lament: "Autumn flowers."
Wickham. Nursery Song.

Fancy.
Burns, R. Mary Morison.
Lowell, A. Free Fantasia on Japanese Themes.
Opie. Stanzas Written Under Aeolus' Harp.
Smith, C. To Fancy.
See Imagination

Fans
Boland, E. Black Lace Fan My Mother Gave Me, The.
Buson. Makes the eye happy.
Gerstler. Fan Letter, A.
Jinkag Haesim. Fan.
Major, C. 1915 Interior.

Momaday. Eagle-Feather Fan, The.
Pan Chieh-yû. Fan-Piece, for Her Imperial Lord.
Present from the Emperor's New Concubine, A.
Song of Regret.
Probyn. Tête-à-Tête.
Unknown. Fluid as water that all tones reflects.
When I Think About Why.
Yi Talch'ung. Neglected Wife, The.

Fantasies
Agustini. Swan, The.
Amichai, Y. Ideal Woman, An.
Arnold, M. Longing.
Barlow, G. Dream of the Ring: The Great Jack Johnson, A.
Blanco, R. Perfect City Code.
We're Not Going to Malta.
Boyd, M. Fra Bank to Bank, Fra Wood to Wood I Rin.
Browning, E. Romance of the Swan's Nest, The.
Cavafy. In Despair.
When They Come Alive.
Christie. Dusk and the Wife.
Coleridge, S. Frost at Midnight [1829 version].
Cooper, D. David Cassidy Then.
Crane, S. Youth in apparel that glittered, A.
Cummings, E. E. My sweet old etcetera.
Davidkov, Ivan. Some Day.
Doolittle, M. At Baia.
Dove, R. Adolescence—3.
Duhamel. I'm Dealing with My Pain.
Eliot, T. S. Rhapsody on a Windy Night.
Elledge. Duckling, Swan.
Elmslie, K. Sibling Rivalry.
Field. And on My Eyes Dark Sleep by Night.
Guest, B. Hungry Knight, The.
Harms. Los Angeles, the Angels.
Hart, L. Dancing on the Ceiling.
Henry, B. Skin: "Never mind the fantasy about the tweezers and the tongue."
Hughes, L. As Befits a Man.
Huws, Meirion MacIntyre. City, The.
Jacob, M. Spanish Generosity.
Juana Inés de la Cruz. Elusive Shadow of My Substance, Stay.
Katz, M. Suicide: "As if a wood of oaks gave."
Kizer, C. For Jan as the End Draws Near.
Krolow. In the Rearview Mirror.
Lipton, Lenny. Puff the Magic Dragon.
Locklin. Leader of the Pack, The.
Mathews, H. Spell.
Merrill, J. Arabian Night.
Mihaiu, Virgil. Ultimate Luxury Woman, The.
Mitchell, A. Celia Celia.
Naden. Love's Mirror.
Nerval. Fantasy.
North, C. For Dorothy Wordsworth.
Ortiz. Travelling.
Padgett, R. Symbols of Transformation.
Pound, E. Dance Figure.
Powell, D. A. Writing for a young man on the redline train: "to his boy mistress".
Prescod. Women Are Different.
Ragan, J. Child Christ at the Top of the Stairs.
Reed, I. Poetry Makes Rhythm in Philosophy.
Roberts, L. Problem, The.
Robin, L. My Ideal.
Rossetti, C. Echo.
In an Artist's Studio.
Rukeyser, M. Along History.
Sarton, M. Nursery Rhyme.
Spencer, Cherie Forman. Night.
Spivack, K. Love U.S.A.
Steptoe. Window Shopping.
Stevenson, A. Sous-Entendu.
Stock, N. First Time I Robbed Tiffany's, The.
Strange. Hunger.
Suckling, S. Upon My Lady Carlisle's Walking in Hampton Court Garden.
Turnbull. Transmutation ("Every evening a mother makes up another episode of the same story for her son.").
Unknown. Pitman's Lovesong, A.
Weems, M. B.B. Blues.
Wilbur, R. Baroque Wall-Fountain in the Villa

Sciarra, A.
Williams, W. Good Night.
Winter, M. Space Parable.
Wong, N. On Thinking of Photographing My Fantasies.
Woo, M. Under a Full Moon.
Wu Yun. Apotheosis.
Wylie. Wild Peaches.

Farewell
Basho. Farewell! Like a bee.
From deep within.
Bruce, G. Departure and Departure And.
Buhyu Sunsoo. Biding Farewell to My Cousin, Haeil, on His Return Home.
Chia Tao. Seeing Off the Mountain Monk Ch'u, Returning to Japan.
Clare, J. Song: "Sad was the day when my Willie did leave me."
Eminescu, M. Goodbye: "From now till never, goodbye."
Field, E. Farewell, The: "They say the ice will hold."
French, Nora May. Ave Atque Vale: "It gathers where the moody sky is bending."
Goeckel, L. Message from the Photo-Mat.
Gorges. Tell me my harte how wilte thow doe.
Guest, B. Farewell Stairway, The.
Housman. I hoed and trenched and weeded.
Kang Ŭn'gyo. Leaves of Grass.
Kaschnitz. Outside the Door.
Kirstein. P.O.E.
Lamar. Carmelita.
McNair. Goodbye to the Old Life.
Merwin. Good-Bye Shirts, The.
Murray, L. Last Hellos, The.
O'Donoghue, B. Going Without Saying.
St. John, D. After Esenin.
Strong, E. Farewell, A: "I have not won."
Unknown. Deported.
Good-bye, Brother.
Goodnight Irene.
Streamers of farewell.
Texas Corrido.
You were still waving, beloved.
Yauger, Fay M. I Remember.
Yi Sanghûi. Farewell, My Youth.

Farming and Farmers
Adams, L. Country Summer.
Alexander, M. Iowa Farmer.
Ammons. Silver.
Applewhite. Wilson County Farmer, A.
Arnold, B. No Tool or Rope or Pail.
Baillie, J. Hay Making.
Balaban. Riding Westward.
Bampfylde. Written at a Farm.
Basho. By the old temple.
Culture's beginnings.
Beaver. Silo Treading.
Belieu. Legend of the Albino Farm.
Berrigan, D. Crucifix, The.
Berry, W. Enriching the Earth.
Mad Farmer Revolution, The.
Man Born to Farming, The.
Bishop, E. Prodigal, The.
Blunden. Country God, A.
Bly, R. Warning to the Reader.
Bontemps. Black Man Talks of Reaping, A.
Boston, B. By All Lights: 1959.
Bowen, G. Poet's Prelude, The.
Brown, B. Taxman.
Brown, K. Good Devil, The.
Brown, S. After Winter.
Bruce, C. Orchard in the Woods.
Burns, R. Cotter's Saturday Night [nscribed to Robert Aiken [or R. A****], Esq.], The.
Burnside, J. Home Farm.
Busch, T. Heartland.
Calverley. Ballad: "Auld wife sat at her ivied door, The."
Cary, P. Harvest Gathering.
Casey, M. Bummer, A.
Chappell, F. My Mother's Hard Row to Hoe.
Char. Alberto Giacometti.
Ch'i-chi. Old Farmer, The.
Clampitt. Beethoven, Opus 111.
Stacking the Straw.

Cofer, J. Campesino's Lament, The.
Cogswell, Fred. George Burroughs.
Coles, G. Dornier, The.
Colum, P. Drover, A.
Conn. Todd.
Cook, Geoffrey. Lorne, Nova Scotia.
Coultas, B. Third Farming Poem.
Croft, A. Beasts of England, The.
Cummings, E. E. Nobody loses all the time.
Divakaruni. Founding of Yuba City, The.
Dorn, E. On the Debt My Mother Owed to Sears Roebuck.
Dove, R. Small Town.
E'der, E. Once We Were Farmers.
Emerson, R. Musketaquid.
Ennis. Coyne's.
Etter. Drink and Agriculture.
Evans, C. Callers.
Fallon, P. Meadow, The.
Farjeon, E. F is for Forecast.
Finch, A. For Grizzel McNaught (1709–1792).
Francis, R. Curse, The.
Frost, R. Code, The.
  Impulse, The.
  Mowing.
  Oft-Repeated Dream, The.
  Pasture, The.
  Putting in the Seed.
  Range-finding.
  Strong Are Saying Nothing, The.
Garland, H. Plowing: A Memory.
Genoways, Ted. Under the Big Top.
Gerov, Alexander. Birds: "They don't plow, nor do they sow."
Gilbert, C. Glimpses.
Goldberg, N. Two Iowa Farmers.
Grainger, J. Call to the Muse.
  Crescendo.
Halbur, A. 4-H.
Hall, D. Ox Cart Man.
Hanu. Four Songs Calling a Boy.
Hartnett. Retreat of Ita Cagney, The.
  Small Farm, A.
Heaney, S. Constable Calls, A.
  Follower.
  Harvest Bow, The.
Hedin, R. At the Olive Grove of the Resistance.
Herrera y Reissig. Return, The.
Herrick. His Grange, or Private Wealth.
Heynen. Boys Go to Ask a Neighbor for Some Apples, The.
Hiebert. Farmer and the Farmer's Wife, The.
Hochman. Cannon Hill.
Holmes, O. Ploughman, The.
Hostetler, A. Female Ancestor.
  Iconoclast.
Howes, B. Death of a Vermont Farm Woman.
Huddle. Work.
Hughes, T. February 17th.
  Tractor.
Isfoel. Tractor, The.
Issa. Farmer / Pointing the way.
  Man pulling radishes, The.
  Skylarks singing / The farmer.
Ivanov, Binyo. Summer: "On this long farm facing Rila Mountain."
Johnson, J. Music for the Cows.
Johnson, M. F. Village Maid, The.
Johnston, A. To Robert Baron.
Jones, Ceri Wyn. Legacy.
Jones, D. Reaping.
Jones, E. Song of the Banana Man, The.
Jones, R. Nell.
Kauffman, J. Working Tobacco.
Kavanagh, P. Fields were bleached white, The.
  Spraying the Potatoes.
Kim Ch'anghyŏp. Mountain Folk.
Kinsley, R. Those Mornings.
Kinsella, J. Visitant Eclogue.
  Wild Radishes.
Ko Ŭn. Crossing Rice Fields at Nightfall.
Komunyakaa, Y. Banking Potatoes.
  Buried Light.
Kooser. Abandoned Farmhouse.
Korean Oral Tradition. Transplanting Song.
Kort, E. Letter from McCarty's Farm.

Kumin, M. Family Reunion.
Kupala, I. Yelling-alive.
Lanier, S. Waving of the Corn, The.
Lawrence, D. H. Love On the Farm.
Lee, D. For Jan, with Love.
  Hired Hand.
  Jan's Birthday.
Leithauser. At an Island Farm.
Lewis, G. In the Open Air.
Lewis, S. How 'Ya Gonna Keep 'Em Down on the Farm? (After They've Seen Paree).
Li Shen. Pitying the Farmer.
Longfellow, H. Preamble to a Tale of Acadie.
Lovecraft. Well, The.
Lux. Commercial Leech Farming Today.
  Hungry Gap-Time, The.
  View From a Porch.
Lynes, Jeanette. Brave.
MacCaig. Summer Farm.
MacLaine, Brent. 4. Birth Story.
MacLeish. Eleven.
Mar, Y. Between Sickle and Sword.
Markham, E. Man with the Hoe, The.
Matherne, B. La Fabrique de Tabac (Tobacco Harvest).
Mccann, S. Robert Frost as Father.
McGrath, C. Prose Poem, The.
McKay, D. 1. The Man from Nod.
Meinke. Rage.
Meredith, G. Phoebus with Admetus.
Messerli. Harrowing.
Mhac an tSaoi. Jack.
Millay, E. From a Train Window.
Mitchison. Farm Woman, The: 1942.
  House of the Hare, The.
Mitsui. Picture of a Japanese Farmer, Woodland, California, May 20, 1942.
Montague, J. Drink of Milk, A.
Morgan, R. Man and Machine.
  Working in the Rain.
Muldoon, P. Cauliflowers.
  Why Brownlee Left.
Murray, L. Man with the Hoe, The.
  Misery Cord (In Memory of F. S. Murray), The.
Muske, C. Ideal.
Muso Soseki. Jewel Field.
Neufeldt, L. Dyke View Berry Farm.
Nowlan. Warren Pryor.
Ou-yang Hsiu. Reading the Poems of an Absent Friend.
Ouwens. Farmer, The.
Paek Sŏk. Samch'ŏnp'o.
Peacock, T. Legend of Manor Hall, The.
Peirce. Farmers.
Pellicer, C. To Poetry.
Powell, D. A. Long line of bohunks and hunyaks, A: we settled in podunk. thirteen consonants.
Prys-Jones. Ploughman: In Welsh Uplands, The.
Rao, A. Farmer's Song, The.
Rawson, J. Map Burnt Through.
Redcloud. Farmer.
Reed, I. White Hope.
Riley, J. Raggedy Man, The.
Roberts, S. Sower, The.
Roberts, T. Apotheosis of the Kitchen Goddess 2.
Sandburg, C. Illinois Farmer.
  Onion Days.
Scheele. Wake of Plenty, The.
Sen, R. Oh Mind, you don't know how to farm.
Shin Kyŏngnim. Farmer's Dance.
Simmons, J. Rogation Day: Portrush.
Skeeter. Midwest, Midcentury.
Snyder, G. Hay for the Horses.
Soto. Field Poem.
  Hoeing.
Spender, S. Marginal Field, The.
Stafford, W. Light by the Barn, The.
Su Tung-p'o. Lament of the Farm Wife of Wu.
Sylvester, J. Aestas.
Takai Kito. Barley-reaping song / Smith's hammer.
T'ao Ch'ien [or T'ao Yuan-ming]. Home Again among Gardens and Fields.
  Miscellaneous Poem.

Tate, J. Bounden Duty.
Taylor, H. Hayfork, The.
Tennyson, A. Northern Farmer: New Style.
Thomas, E. As the Team's Head-Brass.
  Haymaking.
Thomas, R. S. Cynddylan on a Tractor.
  Hill Farmer Speaks, The.
  Lonely Farmer, The.
  On the Farm.
  Peasant, A.
Thurston, H. Revelations.
Todd, M. Grandmother's Farm.
Torrence. Son, The.
Tripp. Ploughman.
Trowbridge, J. Idyl of Harvest Time, An.
Tu Fu [or Du Fu]. Becoming a Farmer.
  Poem for My Brother Returning to My Farm.
  West of my hut, I grow mulberry.
Turberville. Poor Ploughman to a Gentleman for Whom He Had Taken a Little Pains, A.
Unknown. Barren grassland, A.
  Bugs.
  Farmer's Pride, The.
  Ground-Thumping Song.
  He's to the War.
  Home to Farm.
  Hou Ji (Lord Millet), Progenitor of Zhou.
  Jun-zi yu-yi [Translations].
  Qui-yue: In the Seventh Month.
  Shi-shu: Rats.
  Song of the Peasants in the Time of Yao.
  Synge we alle and seye we thus.
  Yi-xi: Halloa!
Vietnamese Oral Tradition. Leaving the Village.
  Mandarin Who Couldn't Do Anything, The.
Virgil [or Vergil]. What crops the region will bear.
Voigt. Amaryllis.
  Farmer, The.
Wallace, R. Makings of Happiness, The.
Wang Ji. Farmers.
Warner, S. Rival, The.
Weigl. Home.
Whitman, W. Farm Picture, A.
Wilbur, R. Sonnet: "Winter deepening, the hay all in, The."
Williams, C. K. Loss.
Williams, E. I live on my farm in a beautiful vale.
Williams, J. Pastoral: "You see that forest on the height?"
Williams, W. Farmer, The.
Wilson, K. People from the Valley, The.
Wither. Planting.
  Spade, The.
Wodehouse. Bungalow in Quogue.
Wordsworth, W. Solitary Reaper, The.
Wright, J. Milkweed.
Yang Shih-ch'i. Following the Rhymes of Shao-pao Huang's Poem on Being Moved While Visiting the Farmers.
Yi Myŏnghan. Morning star has set, The. A lark.
Young, J. How 'Ya Gonna Keep 'Em Down on the Farm? (After They've Seen Paree).

Farmworkers
Cornish, S. In Mr. Turner's Fields.
Espada. Water, White Cotton, and the Rich Man.
Frost, R. Death of the Hired Man, The.
García, D. Orchard of Figs in the Fall, An.
Hausman. Appaloosa Hail Storm.
Irwin, T. Potato-Digger's Song, The.
Kenyon, J. Twilight: After Haying.
Kinsella, J. Rust Eclogues, The: Radnoti, Poetry, and the Strains of Appropriation.
  Wild Radishes.
Lee, D. Hired Hand.
Marcus, M. I Think of Those Mornings.
Nowlan. Day's End.
Orr, T. Soybeans.
Prunty. Haying.
Ratzlaff, K. Necessity.
Sutphen, J. Girl on a Tractor.
Taylor, H. Hayfork, The.
See also **Migrant Workers**

Farragut, David Glasgow
Meredith, W. Farragut, Farragut.
Fascism and Fascists
Haavikko. Plant trees. Exactly against this tree.
Hill, G. Christmas Trees.
Reed, I. Why I Often Allude to Osiris.
Teillier, J. No Sign of Life.
Fashion
Barlow, G. Place Where He Arose, The.
Berlin. Puttin' on the Ritz (Original Version).
Puttin' on the Ritz (Revised Version).
Top Hat, White Tie, and Tails.
Cavendish, M. Woman Drest by Age, A.
Dickinson, E. Morns are meeker than they were, The.
Frishberg, D. I'm Hip.
Herd. Bathing Girls, The.
Hughes, L. What?
Jonson, B. On English Monsieur.
Kelly, R. Rainmakers, The.
Pope, A. Epistle [II,] to a Lady[: Of the Characters of Women].
Epistle [II,] to a Lady[: Of the Characters of Women].
Robinson, M. Modern Female Fashions.
Modern Male Fashions.
Rossetti, C. If a Pig Wore a Wig.
Wunderlich, M. Take Good Care of Yourself.
Yellen, J. Glad Rag Doll.
See also **Clothing**
Fate
Adams, F. Those Two Boys.
Akhmadulina. Snow Maiden, The.
Ashbery, J. Brute Image.
Barker, J. Necessity of Fate, The.
Barkova, A. Tatar Anguish.
Beckett, S. Je suis ce cours de sable qui glisse.
My way is in the sand flowing.
Bécquer, G. Where Do I Come From?
Bedient, C. When the Gods Put on Meter.
Benjamin, P. Press On.
Bevington, L. 'Egoisme à Deux'.
Measurements.
Bibb. Destiny.
Blaser. Finder, The.
Bogan, L. Cartography.
Didactic Piece.
Borges. Borges and Myself.
Bradstreet, A. [Here Follows Some] Verses upon the Burning of Our House [July 10th, 1666. Copied Out of a Loose Paper].
Brown, S. Schadenfreude.
Burns, R. To a Mountain Daisy [On Turning One Down, with the Plough, in April—1786].
Butler, S. Love.
Campbell, T. Lines Written on Visiting a Scene in Argyleshire.
Carew, T. To Celia, upon Love's Ubiquity.
Castellanos. Nazareth.
Return, The.
Char. Unbending Prayer.
Chia Yi. Owl, The.
Clare, J. Ballad: "Mary, fate lent me a moment of pleasure."
Clifton, L. Kali.
Cooke, R. Arachne.
Creeley. Kore.
Oh No.
Song: "What I took in my hand."
Window, The.
Cruickshank, H. Fate: "Fate fell upon a man."
Cucchi, M. Every season has its dead.
Dickinson, E. Belshazzar had a Letter.
Ended, ere it begun.
He fumbles at your Soul.
It Dropped So Low in My Regard.
Dunbar, P. Robert Gould Shaw.
Duncan, R. Poem Beginning with a Line by Pindar, A.
Rites of Participation.
Emerson, R. Day's Ration, The.
Fate.
"Ephelia.". To One That Asked Me Why I Loved J.
Ferry. Cythera.
Embarkation for Cythera, The.

Fitzgerald, E. War begets Poverty.
Forbes, C. Hand Me Down Blues.
Freed, A. You Were Meant for Me.
Frost, R. Design.
Draft Horse, The.
Gift Outright, The.
Fulton, A. A.M.: The Hopeful Monster.
Gertsyk, A. Silent, draped in the garments of sacrifice.
Gizzi. Another Day on the Pilgrimage.
Glück, L. Mount Ararat.
Goethe. To Charlotte von Stein.
González, A. Future, The.
Greig, A. Ruth Says.
Grossman, A. Enough Rain for Agnes Walquist.
Gurney, I. Ballad of the Three Spectres.
Old Dreams.
Haavikko. Twice, three times.
Hardy, T. Hap.
Hecht, A. Jason.
Henley, W. E. Invictus.
Hölderlin. To the Fates.
Hood, T. Miss Kilmansegg's Birth.
Hope, A. Beyond Phigalia.
Fafnir.
Hughes, L. Bad Luck Card.
Ibn Abdūn, A. It is Fate [alone] that causes us distress, first by the blow itself and then by the traces it leaves; so what is the use of weeping over illusions and vain imagings?
Issa. O autumn winds.
Ivask, Y. Ode for the Dancing Khlysty.
Jackson, H. Crossed Threads.
Kahn, G. It Had to Be You.
Kenyon, J. Otherwise: "I got out of bed."
Khlebnikov, V. Once More, Once More.
Zangezi: R, K, L, G.
King, H. Sonnet: "Tell me[e] no more how fair[e] she[e] is."
Kunitz, S. Approach to Thebes, The.
Landon. Stern Truth.
Li Po. Leave-taking Near Shoku.
Lieberman, M. Los Olivos.
Lleshanaku, L. Betrayed.
Lumelli, A. They could be reservoirs for water.
MacCarthy, C. To the Same.
Manilius. Why do we in worries waste our lives, and torture.
Marlowe. Love at First Sight.
Martial. Rome, I am Scorpus, foremost in the race.
Marvell. Definition of Love, The.
McAuley, J. Blue Horses, The.
Melville, H. Haglets, The.
Immolated.
Meredith, W. Consequences.
Mew. Call, The.
Mihalic. Atlantis.
Millay, E. Buck in the Snow, The.
Montale. Dora Markus.
Fan, The.
Nash, O. Necessary Dirge, A.
Nasir, A. Poet's Fate, A.
Negar. Dust: "Dead ringing of distant steps, The."
Okigbo. On the New Year.
Oppen. Amor fati / The love of fate.
Pao Chao. Water Spilt.
Pasternak, B. Mary Magdalene (I).
Peacock, M. Wheel, The.
Piatt, S. We Two.
Rattray, D. They Don't Have to Have That Look.
Reading, P. Fates of Men.
Rein. Monastery.
Robin, L. For Every Man There's a Woman.
Robinson, E. Eros Turannos.
Karma.
Roethke. Waking, The ("I wake to sleep, and take my waking slow.").
Rûhî. Curse the Thorns of Fate.
Sandburg, C. Mamie.
Seeger, A. I Have a Rendezvous with Death.
Seneca. This said, she twirled the thread on an ugly spool.
Shapiro, K. Auto Wreck.

"Shu Ting.". Assembly Line.
Shwarts [*or* Shvarts]. Sale of a Historian's Library.
Simon, M. Standing between Two Ideas.
Simonides. Distinguishes the fair and the shameful.
Sissle, N. I'm Just Wild about Harry.
Soloukhin. For the Tree to Sing.
Sparrow, J. Apology and Explanation.
Stesichoros. Don't pile cruel cares upon those griefs.
Stevenson, R. Ticonderoga: A Legend of the West Highlands.
Swirszczynska [*or* Swir]. Thank You, My Fate.
Tannahill. Tap-Room, The.
T'ao Ch'ien [*or* T'ao Yuan-ming]. Substance, Shadow, and Spirit ("Heaven and Earth endure and do not perish.").
Tardieu Jean. Days.
Tassis y Peralta. Love Is Not Will But Destiny.
Thrale [*later* Mrs. Piozzi]. Winter in Wales, A.
Trowbridge, J. Circumstance.
Unknown. Dragon Speaks, The.
Hebe and Ganymede.
Omens.
Vidya. Fate Is a Cruel and Proficient Potter.
Vietnamese Oral Tradition. Bare Rocks and Stars.
Replies.
Voznesensky [*or* Voznesenskii].
Recommendation.
Ward, D. Crossing.
Wells, C. Fate.
Wilbur, R. Marginalia.
Wilcox, E. Way of It, The.
Winds of Fate, The.
Wordsworth, W. Column Intended by Buonaparte for a Triumphal Edifice in Milan, Now Lying by the Way-Side in the Simplon Pass, The.
Yeats. Leda and the Swan.
Yesenin [*or* Essenin]. Horn of doom is blaring!, The.
See also **Fortune; Chance**
Fathers
Abinader, E. Letters from Home.
Abiyah. Fatherless Townships.
Acholonu. Dissidents, The.
Ai. Cockfighter's Daughter, The.
Alexander, E. Who I Think You Are.
Alexie. Father and Farther.
Penance.
Allen, Alma Stacey. Road Trip.
Allen, G. Poem for My Father.
Alvi, M. Throwing Out My Father's Dictionary.
Amichai, Y. Death of My Father, The.
Letter of Recommendation.
My Father.
My father fought their war four years or so.
Song of Lies on Sabbath Eve, A.
Antokolsky. You share your mourning with all Moscow. There.
Anyte [*or* Anytes]. Throwing her arms around her dear father.
Arapaho Oral Tradition. My Son, Let Me Grasp Your Hand.
Arends, J. I.
Armitage, S. Poem: "And if it snowed and snow covered the drive."
Arrillaga. Rosa/Filí.
Arsone, S. Father's Poem, A.
Atwood. Flowers: "Right now I am the flower girl."
Baehr, A. I Am Dancing with My Mennonite Father.
Bailey, R. Father's Things.
Balaban. Words for My Daughter.
Barer, M. Very Soft Shoes.
Barrax. Visit.
Bartlett, E. Smile for Daddy.
Becker, R. Incarnate.
Beer, P. John Milton and My Father.
Benedict, E. At Ease.
Berlin, M. Fungus Considered.
Berry, J. Girls Can We Educate We Dads?
Berryman. Scholars at the Orchid Pavilion.

To My Father.
Bhattācārya, K.   King of the Mountains is on his way to Hara's abode, The.
Bialik.   Orphanhood.
Biespiel, D.   Lilacs.
Bilgere, G.   Catch.
  Like Riding a Bicycle.
Blake, W.   Little Boy Lost, The.
Blanco, R.   El Malibú.
  Shaving.
Blue Cloud.   Ochre Iron.
Bly, R.   My Father at 85.
  My Father's Neck.
  My Father's Wedding.
  Prayer for My Father.
  When My Dead Father Called.
Borgmann, K.   Bed.
Borthwick, P.   Forest.
Boss, L.   At the Nuclear Rally.
Bottoms.   Desk, The.
Bowering, G.   My Father in New Zealand.
Bowers, N.   Tenth-Year Elegy.
Bradstreet, A.   To Her Father, with Some Verses.
  To the Memory of My Dear and Ever Honored Father Thomas Dudley Esq. Who Deceased July 31, 1653, and of His Age 77.
Broumas, O.   On Earth.
Brown, L.   Thank Your Father.
Buckley, C.   Father, 1952.
Bukowski.   My Old Man.
Burns, R.   Fishing in Winter.
Carlson, D.   Russ Joy Little League.
Carroll, J.   Poem on My Son's Birthday.
Carson, A.   Father's Old Blue Cardigan.
Carver, R.   My Dad's Wallet.
Cashdan.   Laughing All the Way.
Castillo, A.   Toltec, The.
Chappell, F.   My Father's Hurricane.
Charara, H.   My Father Breaks the Neighbor's Nose.
Chin, D.   Sleeping Father.
Chisholm, A.   Contact.
Chitre.   My Father Travels.
Chrystos.   Portrait of Assimilation.
Clampitt.   Beethoven, Opus 111.
Cleveland, T.   Our Fathers.
Clifton, L.   Sam.
Clover, J.   Family Romance.
Coleman, H.   Poem for a "Divorced" Daughter.
Coleman, W.   Cousin Mary.
Coleridge, S.   Sonnet Composed on a Journey Homeward; the Author Having Received Intelligence of the Birth of a Son, 20 September 1796.
Coleridge, S.   Father! no amaranths e'er shall wreathe my brow.
Coles, G.   Ithaca-Liverpool.
Cook-Lynn.   Grandfather at the Indian Health Clinic.
Cooley, N.   Family History, The.
Cooley.   Fathers and Sons.
Copus, J.   Pulling the Ivy.
  Second Home.
Cox, M.   Moles, the.
Creeley.   Fathers.
Crucefix.   Pietá.
Cullen, Y.   With Me.
Cummings, E. E.   My father moved through dooms of love.
Curtis, T.   To My Father.
Dalton, A.   Dad-Baby, The.
Davis, O.   Moorer Denies Holyfield in Twelve.
Davitt.   Mirror, The.
Deane, S.   Fording the River.
Delgado, J.   Con Los Pájaros.
  Visiting Father.
DeNicola, D.   My Father's First Fight.
Derricotte.   Poem for My Father.
DeSylva, B. G.   Thank Your Father.
Der Hovanessian, D.   Shifting the Sun.
Dickens.   Joe Gargery's Epitaph on His Father.
Dickey, J.   Bee, The.
  Hospital Window, The.
Dickey, R.   Father.
Dodd, W.   Of His Life.
Donaghy, M.   Caliban's Books.

Dooley, M.   Dancing at Oakmead Road.
  Heart.
  Mansize.
Dove, A.   Crab.
Dove, R.   Taking in Wash.
Drummond de Andrade.   Infancy.
Dugan, A.   Elegy: "I know but will not tell."
  For Euthanasia and Pain-Killing Drugs.
Duhig, I.   First Second, The.
Dumas, H.   Zebra Goes Wild Where the Sidewalk Ends, The.
Dunbar, P.   Little Brown Baby.
Duo Duo.   Morning.
Duran, J.   Pyrenees, The.
  Spanish Peasant Boy.
Dybek.   My Father's Fights.
Earle, J.   At the South Pole.
Eichner, Maura.   Father, The.
Eimers.   Another Kimono.
Eirian, S.   My Dad Versus Ginsberg.
Eldan, A.   When You Grow Up.
Ellis, T.   Sticks.
Emanuel, L.   Of Your Father's Indiscretions and the Train to California.
Ennis.   Road to Patmos, The.
Fairchild.   Machinist, Teaching His Daughter to Play the Piano, The.
Fanthorpe.   Fanfare.
Farley, P.   Laws of Gravity.
Faruqi, M.   Return, The: "After washing Paddington loos."
Fearing.   Any Man's Advice to His Son.
Feinstein, E.   Dad.
Fennelly.   Asked for a Happy Memory of Her Father, She Recalls Wrigley Field.
Ferguson, G.   In Hospital-land.
Field, E.   New Cycle, A.
Fingueret, M.   My Father.
Fisher, J.   There are only so many words.
Fleming, R.   For All Unwed Mothers.
Foley, K.   My Father, Counting Sheep.
Fontanella.   Father-Sequence.
Foreman, Paul.   Brazos de Dios.
Friesen, P.   Pa poem 1: firstborn.
  Pa poem 4: naked and nailed.
Friman.   Trip to Delphi.
Frost, K.   Winners.
Fuller, C.   My Father's Dreams.
Fyfe, A.   Upturn.
Gallagher, T.   Even Now You Are Leaving.
  Heart-Mirror.
  3 A.M. Kitchen: My Father Talking.
Galvin, J.   Shadow-Casting.
Garcia, R.   Note Folded Thirteen Ways.
Garrett, G.   Envoy: "Little poem, the two of us know too much."
Garza, E.   Why I Make the Best Barrels.
Gibson, W.   Old Skinflint.
Gillan.   Arturo.
Gillilan, P.   Looking North.
Gilmore, B.   Hazing (for Tony New and Albee).
  Revolution.
Gilyard, K.   Daughter, That Picture of You.
Gioseffi.   American Sonnets for My Father.
Glazer, J.   Point of No Return.
Glen, D.   My Father: "Staunin noo aside his braw bress-haunled coffin."
Glück, L.   Departure.
  First Memory.
  Mirror Image.
  Mythic Fragment.
Goethe.   Erl-King.
  Erl-King, The.
Golding, N.   My Father Makes a Lightbox for Vivienne Westwood.
Gonzales, R.   Aztec Father.
González Prada, M.   Forced Labour.
Gotera.   Dance of the Letters.
Graham, D.   Father of the Man.
Grennan.   Pause.
Groarke, V.   History of My Father's House, The.
Grosholz.   Legacies.
  Life of a Salesman.
Grossberg, B.   Advice to a Coming Child.
Hall, D.   White Apples.
Hamill, S.   Natural History: "Late afternoon,

autumn equinox."
Hamilton, L.   My Father's Words.
Hamlett, J.   Therapist's Comment, The.
Hannan, M.   Coming Down from Derry Hill.
Harris, D.   For My Father.
  What We Have Lost.
Harryman.   Baby. In Three Parts.
Harwood, G.   At Mornington.
Hayden, R.   Those Winter Sundays.
Heaney, S.   Digging.
  Follower.
Hegley.   Dreaming My Dad.
Held, George.   Learning to Ride My Bike.
Henderson, R.   Thank Your Father.
Henry, J.   Son's a poor, wretched, unfortunate creature, The.
Herbert, Z.   Remembering My Father.
Hernández Cruz.   Ruskie's Boy.
Herrera.   Atavistic: Traces after the Rain.
Hershon.   Sentimental Moment or Why Did the Baguette Cross the Road?
Hewitt, J.   Father's Death, A.
Hicok.   Sudden Movements.
Higgins, F.   Father and Son.
Higgins, R.   Almost Communication.
Hill, N.   Dürer's 'Young Hare.'
Hippolyte.   So Jah Sey.
Hirsch, E.   My Father's Back.
Hoagland, T.   Benevolence.
  Sweet Ruin.
Hoffenstein.   Now, alas, it is too late.
Hollo.   Le Jazz Hot.
Holmes, E.   Fathers, The: "Something's familiar about that villain."
Holub.   End of the World, The.
Hongo.   Hilo: First Night Back.
  O-Bon: Dance for the Dead.
Horst, C.   Everything I Know.
Houghton, L.   Caustic Soda.
  Saturday with Dad.
Howe, M.   How Many Times.
Huddle.   My Daddy, Whenever He Went Some Place.
Hudgins.   At the Piano.
  Childhood of the Ancients.
  Elegy for My Father, Who Is Not Dead.
  Tree.
Hughes, L.   Cross.
Hughes, T.   Out.
Hugo, V.   After the Battle.
Humphreys, E.   From Father to Son.
Hung.   I Never Dream of My Father.
Hurvits.   Autobiographical Moment, An.
Hwang Insuk.   Two Doors.
Ignatow, D.   1905.
  Rightful One, The.
  Time Comes When You Are Facing Him, The.
Ilio, D.   Site of My Grandfather's House, The.
Irwin, M.   My Father's Hats.
Israeli, H.   Bicycle Ride, The.
Issa.   Last time, I think.
  With my father.
Jacinto, J.   Absence.
  Heaven Is Just Another Country.
Jackowska.   Woman Who Mistook Her Father for an Irishman, The.
Jagger, B.   Anyway.
Jarman, Geraint.   Dad and Me.
Jastrzebska.   Cracking Walnuts.
Jeffers, H.   Eyes of Soon Children.
  To Keep from Shouting Something.
Jenkins, A.   Visiting.
Jess, T.   Father Country.
  Father's Shoes.
  Letter to an Unconceived Son.
  What does a man do.
Jian, Y.   Thank You Father.
Johnson, Peter.   Socrates.
Johnstone, R.   He's a high clear forehead.
Jones, R.   Portrait of My Father and His Grandson.
  Son.
Jonson, B.   On My First Son.
Joseph, A.   My Father's Heroes ("Not JFK, not MLK.").
Justice, D.   Men at Forty.

Karr. Patient, The.
Kasdorf. Streak, The.
  Vesta's Father.
Kay, E. Phoenix.
Kazantzis. My Dada.
Kennedy, Sarah. Maid.
Kennelly. I See You Dancing, Father.
Kessler, M. Secret Love.
Kessler, S. Jack's Last Words.
Kgositsile. To My Daughter.
Khodasevich. Dactyls.
Kimbrell, J. My Father at the North Street
  Boarding House.
Kinnell. When I come back to my father's
  house,.
Kinsella, T. Death Bed.
Kipling, R. Common Form.
Kizer, C. Thrall.
Klein, A. Heirloom.
Klein, M. Range of It, The.
Komunyakaa, Y. Banking Potatoes.
  [Excerpts].
  My Father's Love Letters [or Loveletters].
  Songs for My Father.
Kramer, L. Non-Emigrant, The.
Kunitz, S. Father and Son.
  Quinnapoxet.
Kunze, R. Reply.
Laâbi Abdellatif. Portrait of the Father, The.
Laird, N. Length of a Wave, The.
Lasoen, P. That April Morning.
Lassell. Going to Europe.
Lea, S. Paternity.
Lee, L. Eating Together.
  Gift, The: "To pull the metal splinter from my
    palm."
  Little Father.
  Mnemonic.
  Story, A.
  Weight of Sweetness, The.
  Words for Worry.
Lehman. Difference between Pepsi and Coke,
  The.
  Drowning, The.
Leivick, H. Lament at Night.
Leonard, T. Fathers and Sons.
Levi, J. Not Bad, Dad, Not Bad.
Levin, P. Planting Roses.
Levine, P. Return, The: "All afternoon my
  father drove the country roads."
  Starlight.
Levis. Winter Stars.
Lieberman, M. On the Anniversary of My
  Father's Death.
Lim, S. Black and White.
  Father from Asia.
Limburg, J. Return, The.
Linebarger, Jim. Coyote.
Liu, T. Thoreau.
Livingston, M. Father.
Longley, M. In Memoriam.
  Wounds.
Lopez, L. Images of San Luis.
Lorde. Father Son and Holy Ghost.
  Love Poem: "Speak earth and bless me with
    what is richest."
Lowell, R. Commander Lowell.
  Home After Three Months Away.
Lund. Wrist-Wrestling father.
Lux. Upon Seeing an Ultrasound Photo of an
  Unborn Child.
Macari, A. New York, 1927.
MacDiarmid, H. At My Father's Grave.
MacKenzie, John. My love is strung with the
  ancient.
MacNeice. Truisms, The.
Maiden. Air.
Mangan, G. Ailsa Craig.
Marcus, B. Delaying Relevance.
Marcus, M. My Father's Hobby.
Markus, P. Black Light.
  Light.
  Shooting Crows.
Marsh, B. Papa.
Martinez, D. Standard Time: Novena for My
  Father.

Martínez, V. Night of Fathers.
Mathews, A. Letter Following.
Matos-Teixera, N. My Father's House.
Mayer, G. Make Believe.
McCuaig. Au Tombeau de Mon Père.
McGrath, T. Offering.
  Poem: "My little son comes running with open
    arms!"
McLaughlin-Carruth, J. Black Irish Blues.
Meinke. This Is a Poem to My Son Peter.
Meredith, W. For His Father.
Merrill, J. Midnight Snack, The.
Merwin. Calling, A.
  On the Subject of Poetry.
  Strawberries.
  Yesterday: "My friend says I was not a good
    son."
Meynell, A. Father of Women, A [Ad Sororem
  E. B.].
Michie, S. Connecting Light.
Millar, J. Midlife.
Miller, E. Father's Day.
  Jasmine.
  My Father's Girlfriend.
  Night Before the First Day of School, The.
Mishol, A. Gravity, Death.
Mitsui. At Bon Odori.
  Because of My Father's Job.
Montague, J. At Last.
  Cage, The.
Moon, K. Daughter-to-Father Talk.
Mooney, M. Painting the Angel.
Moore, L. Gifts.
  Winter 1967.
Moore, M. Silence.
Moritz [or Morits]. Parting the curtains on the
  other world.
Morley, D. Errand.
Moss, T. Lynching, The.
Mueller, J. Fisher Towers.
  Portrait of My Father as the Boy of Winander.
Muldoon, P. Wishbone, The.
Mullen, H. Father (Part 1).
Mun Chônghui. For the Sake of Man.
Murphey, John Collin. Texas Boomer.
Murray, C. Mickey Mouse.
Murray, G. Rounds, The.
Musgrave. You Didn't Fit.
Napier, F. I Have Taken the Suits and Shoes to
  Oxfam.
Nelson, H. My Father Went to Funerals.
Nemerov. Sacrificed Author, A.
Nesbit, E. Song: "Oh, baby, baby, baby dear."
Newbolt. Clifton Chapel.
Ni Dhomhnaill. Labasheedy (The Silken Bed).
Nichols, R. Beginning when I was six I became
  my father's accomplice.
Nicholson, N. Halley's Comet.
Niedecker. Death of my poor father, The.
  He lived—childhood summers.
  Museum man!, The.
Nimmo, D. My Father's Shadow.
Norris, L. His Father, Singing.
North, M. Pheasant Plucker's Son, The.
  Poems to My Father.
Nowlan. Only When My Heart Freezes.
Nye, N. Last Day of August, The.
  My Father and the Fig Tree.
  Shoulders.
O'Rourke, D. Clockwork.
  Letter from My Father, A.
Olds, S. Guild, The.
  His Smell.
  Last Acts.
  Lifting, The.
  Moment of My Father's Death, The.
  Once.
  Race, The.
  Saturn.
  Victims, The.
  Waste Sonata.
Ombres. Morning Hours.
Ome Shushiki. Frost of separation / Father,
  child.
Ondaatje. Letters & Other Worlds.
Oppen. From a Photograph.

Orr, G. Father's Song.
Ortiz. My Father's Song.
  What I Tell Him.
Orton, B. Beekeeper.
Ovid. Myrrha and Cinyras.
Padgett, R. Morning.
Pak Mogwŏl [or Mokwŏl]. Family.
Pankey. As We Forgive Those.
Patterson, G. I Used to Go to Church.
Peacock, M. Buffalo.
  Dream Come True.
Perillo, L. Skin: "Back then it seemed that
  wherever a girl took off her clothes the police
  would find her."
Petit, P. During the Eclipse.
  Embrace of the Electric Eel.
  Fish Daughter, The.
  My Father's Clothes.
  Self-Portrait as a Warao Violin.
  Strait-Jackets, The.
Pietri. Night Is out of Sight, The.
Pinchas-Cohen. Remembering Our Fathers.
Pizarnik. Poem for the Father.
Pizarnik. Poem for My Father.
Plath. Colossus, The.
  Daddy.
Pogson, P. Bo Tree.
Pollarolo, G. While My Father.
Pomerantz, A. My Father the Foundryman.
Pope, A. Father's Day.
Powell, D. A. My Father and Me Making
  Dresses: Together.
Prufer, K. My Father Recounts a Story from
  His Youth.
Prunty. Reading Before We Read, Horoscope
  and Weather.
Rafferty, P. Passage.
Rakosi. L'Chayim.
Ramanujan. Self-Portrait.
Randall, M. Borders.
Ray, D. In the Third Month.
Ray, H. To My Father.
Redgrove, P. My Father's Trapdoors.
Reznikoff. Idiot, The.
Rilke. Sometimes a Man Stands Up during
  Supper.
Riordan, M. Time Out.
Rivard. Fall River.
  Firestone.
Roberts, L. My Father's Whistle.
Rodriguez, L. Victory, Victoria, My Beautiful
  Whisper.
Roethke. My Papa's Waltz.
  Premonition, The.
Rosen, M. This Morning.
Rospigliosi. Leavetaking.
Rozhdestvensky [or Rozhdestvenskii]. Winter
  of Thirty-Eight, The.
Ruefle. Public Garden with a Weeping Tree.
Ryan, M. This Is a Poem for the Dead.
Ryan, R. Father of Famine.
Rybicki, J. In Directions.
St. John, D. Six/Nine/Forty-Four.
  Twin memory, we all seek it.
Samaras, N. First Nightmare Waking.
Sanchez, S. Father and Daughter.
  Poem for My Father, A.
Satyamurti. Erdywurble.
Savageau. Looking for Indians.
  To Human Skin.
Schnackenberg. Supernatural Love.
Schneider, M. Soup and Slavery.
Sen, R. It's silly to hope for Father's wealth.
Seward. Eyam.
Sexton. All My Pretty Ones.
  And One for My Dame.
  How We Danced.
  Moss of His Skin, The.
Shakespeare, W. Full Fathom Five.
  Ill blows the wind that profits nobody.
Shapiro, D. Father Knows Best.
Sharman, R. By Heart.
Sheehan, M. My Father's Singing.
Shelton, R. Letter to a Dead Father.
Sholl. Don't Explain.

Silex, E.   Acts of Love.
Departure.
Simic.   Evening Chess.
Simpson, L.   My Father in the Night
Commanding No.
Working Late.
Skloot.   Hook.
Smith, C.   Essential Story, The.
Smith, D.   Dream of the Jacklighter, The.
Smith, K.   Being the Third Song of Urias.
Smith, R.   Bluetits.
Smith, S.   Correspondence between Mr.
Harrison in Newcastle and Mr. Sholto Peach
Harrison in Hull.
Smith, W.   American Primitive.
Snodgrass.   Diplomacy: The Father.
Someck, R.   40.
Sorescu, M.   Balls and Hoops.
Soto.   Blanco.
Red Palm, A.
Stafford, W.   Rescued Year, The.
With Kit, Age 7, at the Beach.
Statius.   In Memory of His Father.
Steptoe.   To the Father of Me.
Stevens, W.   Irish Cliffs of Moher, The.
Stewart, P.   Singing down the Breadfruit.
Stewart, S.   Gypsy, The.
Stone, J.   Bass, The.
Storace.   King Lear Bewildered.
Strand.   Dreadful Has Already Happened, The.
Stryk, L.   Black Bean Soup.
Suarez, V.   Aguacero.
Swenson, M.   Feel Me.
Swirszczynska [or Swir].   I Wash the Shirt.
My Father's Workshop.
Tate, J.   Lost Pilot, The.
Taylor, E.   Few Days in the South in February,
A.
Tayson, R.   Chase, The.
Teillier, J.   Portrait of My Father, Militant
Communist.
Thomas, D.   Do Not Go Gentle into That Good
Night.
Tipping.   Just after Michael's Death, the Game
of Pool.
Travis, N.   At My Father's House.
Trethewey, N.   Amateur Night.
Tripp.   Father.
Troupe.   Poem for My Father; for Quincy
Trouppe, Jr.
Tsaloumas.   Song for My Father, A.
Tucker, M.   To Father.
Turnbull.   Transmutation ("Boy is amazed to see
his father home from work in the afternoon
with a bandaged finger, A.").
Ulacia, M.   Stone at the Bottom, The.
Unknown.   Dad is busy.
Edward [or Edward, Edward].
Good and Better.
Hush, little baby, don't say a word.
Unknown, fr. Terezin Concentration Camp.
Letter to Daddy, A.
Urdang.   My Father's Death.
Utting, S.   Spoon Maker's Daughter, The.
Valentine, J.   American River Sky Alcohol
Father.
Van Duyn.   Letters from a Father.
Van Jordan, A.   My Father's Retirement.
Van Vliet.   Valediction—To My Father.
Van Walleghen.   Walking the Baby to the Liquor
Store.
Vando.   Father's Day.
Vogel, D.   I Saw My Father Drowning.
Volach, Y.   When You Come Sleep with Me.
Waddleton, J.   Fatherhood.
Wagoner, D.   Man of the House, The.
Wah.   Father / Mother Haibun #7.
Father / Mother Haibun #9.
Wakoski.   Father of My Country, The.
Walcott.   Letter from Brooklyn, A.
Walker, A.   Good Night, Willie Lee, I'll See
You in the Morning.
Wallace, R.   Friday Night Fights, The.
Wang Xiaolong.   In Memoriam: Dedicated to
My Father.
Waniek.   Daughters, 1900.

Warren, R.   Lullaby: Moonlight Lingers.
Night Walking.
Watley, M.   For the Man I Met on Georgia Ave.
Weaver, A.   My Father's First Baseball Game.
My Father's Geography.
Webster, A.   Her father lessons me I at times am
hard.
Weems, M.   Dime after Dime.
Whipple, L.   My Dad.
Whitman, W.   Dirge for Two Veterans.
Wicks, S.   Clever Daughter, The.
My Father Is Shrinking.
My Father's Caul.
Stilt-walker.
Williams, C.   On Forgetting Your Father's Face.
Wilson, K.   Powerhouse, The.
Witherup.   Mervyn Clyde Witherup.
Wojahn.   My Father's Pornography.
Photo of My Father in a Snowbound Train.
Riding the Empire Builder, 1948.
Wong, N.   Ironing.
Wordsworth, W.   Anecdote for Fathers [Showing
How the Art of Lying May Be Taught].
Work.   Come Home, Father[!].
Wright, E.   When Father Carves the Duck.
Wright, F.   Sitting Up Late with My Father,
1977.
Wright, J.   Two Postures beside a Fire.
Youth.
Wrigley, R.   What My Father Believed.
Wycherley, L.   Earth Man.
Yi Sang.   Face.
Poem No. 2.
Young, D.   White Crane.
Young, G.   Miracle, The.
Young, K.   Field Trip.
Young, P.   Photograph, 1958.
Zdanys.   Angels of Wine, The.
Zweig, P.   Father.

Fathers-in-Law
Ciardi, J.   Censorship.
Unknown.   Mother-in-law, do not stamp.
Zukofsky, L.   H. T.

Fatigue
Georgiev, Marin.   Native Soil.
Twichell.   Quality of Striving, The ("Eye-
catching as a dog on a chain.").
Unknown.   Jehovah, Hallelujah.
With me you have done all you ever wanted.
Young, D.   Poem against the Horizon, The.

See also **Weariness**
Faults
Brown, E.   Sonnet 43.
Costello, R.   When My Sister Was Fifteen.
Larkin, P.   This Be The Verse.
Shakespeare, W.   Sonnet 88: "When thou shalt
be dispos'd to set me light."
Unknown.   Oh send to me an apple that hasn't
any kernel.
Wakoski.   My Trouble.

Fauns
Mallarmé.   Afternoon of a Faun, The.
Favn in the Afternoon, A.

Faust
Crane, H.   For the Marriage of Faustus and
Helen.
Marlowe.   Had I as many souls as there be stars.

Fawkes, Guy
Raine, C.   For Hans Keller.

Fear
Agosin.   Fear.
Fear 2.
Akhmatova, A.   Fear turns objects over in the
darkness.
al-Saygh, S.   Dread.
Alcosser.   Pole Boat at Honey Island.
Alexander, P.   First Relations.
Alkalay-Gut.   Some people terrified for their
lives cut.
Unable to move.
Amis, K.   Autobiographical Fragment.
Anacreon.   Already my temples are grey.
Angel.   Breaking the Rock Down.
Angelou, M.   Life Doesn't Frighten Me.
Antin.   List of the Delusions of the Insane /

What They Are Afraid Of, A.
Antipater of Thessalonica.   I've Never Feared.
Archilochus.   Glaukos, look: already the deep
sea is troubled.
Arnold, C.   My Love Is Sick.
Ashbery, J.   Young Son, The.
Atkins, R.   Late Bus (After a Series of Hold-
Ups).
Auden.   Leap Before You Look.
Azuah, U.   Frame of Fear.
Baca.   Like an Animal.
Barkan, S.   I Have Not Woven My Poems.
Baugh, E.   Nigger Sweat.
Belieu.   Against Writing about Children.
Nocturne: My Sister Life.
Berryman.   Despair: "It seems to be DARK all
the time."
I'm scared a lonely. Never see my son.
Bibbins, M.   Just Yesterday.
Blake, W.   Little Boy Lost, The.
Bourne, Lesley-Anne.   Teaching My Husband to
Swim.
Brass.   Only Silly Faggots Know.
Brett, L.   La Pathétique.
Brines, F.   Beggar, The.
Brontë, C.   Again I find myself alone.
Brooks, G.   Michael Is Afraid of the Storm.
Brown, D.   When I Am 19 I Was a Medic.
Browning, R.   Prospice.
Bryan, M.   To ———: "O timeless guest!—so
soon returned art thou."
Buchsbaum, Julianne.   Slowly, Slowly, Horses.
Burke, M.   Former WWII Paratrooper Dreams
of Suicide, 1977, A.
Burns, R.   Prayer, in the Prospect of Death, A.
To a Mouse; On Turning Her up in Her Nest,
with the Plough, November, 1785.
Buson.   In seasonal rain.
Byron, G.   Love and Death.
Cagnone, N.   No place is extreme.
Cankoçak, Gülten Akın.   Not the Fear of
Shivering.
Carson, A.   Longing, a Documentary.
New Rule.
Carver, R.   River, The: "I waded, deepening,
into the dark water."
Cassian.   Other Life, The.
Cepollaro, B.   Requiem in C.
Chappell, F.   Cleaning the Well.
Chimombo.   Four Ways of Dying.
Chudakov.   When the cry goes up.
Clifton, L.   Night Vision.
Powell (Officer Charged with the Beating of
Rodney King).
Cofer, J.   What We Feared.
Cogswell, Fred.   Edge, The.
Coleridge, M.   Master and Guest.
Colonna, S.   Orientation from Afar.
Cooley.   Vespers: "Now it is evening, the light
rushes to fall."
Crane, S.   Man feared that he might find an
assassin, A.
Crapsey.   Warning, The.
Creeley.   Form of Women, A.
Cummings, E. E.   Right here the other night
something.
Cunningham, J.   Epitaph for Anyone, An.
Dalton, A.   Kitchen Beast.
Darío, R.   Nicaraguan Triptych.
Daryush.   You should at times go out.
Davidson, L.   Fear of Madness, The.
Debravo, J.   Beds of Purification.
Delgado, Alvin.   When I Was a Kid in Nueva
York.
Derricotte.   Fears of the Eighth Grade.
From a Letter: About Snow.
Dharker.   Postcards from God (1).
Dickey, J.   Sheep Child, The.
Dickinson, E.   Snake, The.
Dīnrām, L.   Ma, I've drunk Your poisoned nectar.
Dixon, M.   Getting Your Rocks Off.
Douglas, K.   On a Return from Egypt.
Eberhart, R.   New England Bachelor, A.
Edson, R.   Crumble-Knees, The.
Eliot, T. S.   2. A Game of Chess.
Elizabeth I.   Ah silly pug wert thou so sore

afraid.
Doubt of Future Foes.
Fall, M. Nightstart.
Ferguson, G. Fear of the Future.
Fletcher, J. River[-]God's Song, The.
Follain. Marshmallow Man, The.
Forché. Return.
Foster, A. Wythop Mill.
Freeman, J. To End Her Fear.
Freneau. Nor look'd I back, till to a far off wood.
Frost, R. Storm Fear.
Fulton, A. A.M.: The Hopeful Monster.
Galanskov. I am in pain.
Galvin, B. Cougar.
Garcia-Camarillo, C. Chivo.
García, D. Matter of Control, A.
García Lorca. Sonnet of Sweet Complaint.
Gassner, Herbert. Fear: "Fear of the icy moon."
Glück, L. Garden, The: "One sound. Then the hiss and whir."
Gretel in Darkness.
Goethe. Erl-King.
Erl-King, The.
Goll, I. In Age-Old Lakes.
Gould, H. Apprehension.
Greppi, C. Boy's Afraid of the Live Tiger, The.
Grinshpan, Y. Vanzetti's Ghost.
Guillén, J. Without Lights.
Gunn, T. Man with Night Sweats, The.
Gwangwa'a. Leaking Roof.
Hall, D. Footnote.
Hammerstein. I've Told Ev'ry Little Star.
Harechavi. And It Is Still That Way.
Harjo, J. Call It Fear.
I Give You Back.
Harms. Tomorrow, We'll Dance in America.
Harryman. Baby. In Three Parts.
Hartnett. Quicksand.
Hayden, R. Soledad.
Hecht, A. Hill, A.
Henderson-Holmes. My First Riot: Bronx, NYC.
Herbert, Z. Meditations of Mr. Cogito on Redemption.
Our Fear.
Herrick. On Himself[e] ("I fear[e] no Earthly Powers.").
Hogan, L. Return: Buffalo.
Holland, N. Grey Rider, The.
Horne, R. Beth Gelert.
Hostetler, S. Woman with the Screw in Her Mouth Speaks, The.
Housman. Others, I am not the first.
Hudgins. Hereafter, The.
Hughes, F. Different Voice, The.
Hummell, A. Panic.
Jara, V. Estadio Chile.
Jennings, E. Fear, A.
Jensma. I Come.
Johnston, M. Gorey at the Biennale.
Jonson, B. To Fine Lady Would-Be.
Kannan. What Her Girl Friend Said to Him.
Keats. When I Have Fears [That I May Cease to Be].
Kennelly. Dream of a Black Fox.
Killigrew, A. On Death.
Kim Sŭnghŭi. Na Hyesŏk's Complex.
Kingsolver. Waiting for the Invasion.
Knight, S. In Case of Monsters.
Komunyakaa, Y. Venus's-flytraps.
Kovner, A. To Myself.
Kumin, M. Getting the Message.
Laing, K. Many Worlds Are Walked Once.
Laing, R. Sonnet 4: "When I consider what you mean to me."
Lawrence, D. H. Snake.
Song of a Man Who Has Come Through.
Levertov. Age of Terror.
Clouds.
Li K'ai-hsien. Colorful frames are erected beside the Yellow River, The.
Lihn. Of All Despondencies.
Lochhead, L. Noises in the Dark.
Loftis, N. Fights After School.
Loynaz, D. M. Futile Flight, Futile Fugue.

Lucas, J. Good Sunday.
Lux. Large Branch Splintering off a Tree in a Storm, A.
Maassen, Ruth. Confessions of a Pisciphobe.
MacBeth [or Macbeth]. Worst Fear, The.
MacDiarmid, H. Two Memories.
Machado Ruiz. People Possess Four Things.
Mandelstam [or Mandelshtam]. I Hate the Light.
March, A. Day's in dread of losing her bright features, The.
Matthews, W. Misgivings.
Mayakovsky [or Maiakovskii]. Listen!
Mayer, B. Easy Puddings.
McDowell. Origin of Fear, The.
McGinley. Women of Jericho, The.
Melville, H. To ———: "Ah, wherefore, lonely, to and fro."
Merrill, J. Midnight Snack, The.
Moore, H. Spuyten Duyvil.
Moore, R. Doors.
Moritz [or Morits]. Eternally to be waiting for bloody news.
Mouré. Thirteen Years.
Myles, E. Sadness of Leaving, The.
Nasir. Loneliness.
Neill. Are You There, Mr Punch?
Nervo. Cowardice.
Niccolai. Careful that these *Frisbees*.
Nilsson, H. How Came What Came Alas.
Noguchi, R. I, the Neighbor Mr. Uskovich, Watch Every Morning Kenji Takezo Hold His Breath.
Nolens, L. Poetic License.
Nowlan. Thief, The.
Okamoto. Tanka: "As I gaze upon."
Ormsby, E. Jaham Sings of the Fear of the Moon.
Pack, R. Black Hole, The.
Palis, Y. Waking Up.
Parker, D. When Mark Deloach Ruled the World.
Parra, N. Song for a Seed.
Petrarch. Complaint of a Lover Rebuked.
Picková, E. Fear.
Piñero. Running Scared.
Pinsky. Woman, A.
Ponge. Frog, The.
Poole, R. Dark, The.
Pope, A. Epistle to Dr. Arbuthnot.
Prigov. Imagine this: a mighty giant asleep.
Purdy, J. Do You Wonder Why I Am Sleepy.
Queneau. That Don't Scare Me.
Quevedo y Villegas. Now Great and Awesome in My Heart.
Radnóti. Angel of Dread, The.
Ramanujan. Snakes.
Reed, H. Château, The.
Reeves, J. Others.
Rekdal, Paisley. Crash of Rhinos, A.
Robinson, E. Eros Turannos.
Poem for Max Nordau, A.
Rolfe, E. Casualty.
Rumi. Keep walking, though there's no place to get to.
Rumsey, Tessa. Assembling My Shepherd.
Samawi, A. Neighing of the Fingers.
Sappho. Arbor, The.
That one seems to me to be like the gods, the man whosoever sits facing you and listens nearby to your sweet speech an desirable laughter.
There's a man, I really believe, compares with.
Satyamurti. How Are You?
Schmitt, Kate. Fallen.
Schulman. Home Movie.
Seaton, M. Fear of Subways.
Seidman. New York: "I read over my lines."
Sereni. First Year.
Shakespeare, W. Sonnet 23: "As an unperfect actor on the stage."
Sonnet 64: "When I have seen by Time's fell hand defac'd [or defaced]."
Shange. Where the Heart Is.
Shinder. One Secret That Has Carried, The.
Shoman, K. In Explanation to the Mother.

Shorter. Mother, The.
Simic. Fear: "Fear passes from man to man."
Old Couple.
Smith, C. Captive Escaped in the Wilds of America, The. Addressed to the Hon. Mrs. O'Neill.
Smith, S. Word, The.
Spicer, J. Cantata.
Stanley, G. What am I forgetting?
Stanton, M. Little Ode for X.
Starodubtseva, N. And it is cold here and a bit strange.
Steele, T. Eros.
Steinberg, D. With you I begin.
Stephens, J. In the Night.
In Waste Places. .
Stone, R. That Winter.
Swinburne. Lake of Gaube, The.
Szirtes. My Father Carries Me across a Field.
Szporluk. Holy Ghost.
Occupant of the Hose.
Talvikki, A. Conversation with the Sun Bittern.
You Don't Know What Happened When You Froze.
Tatarunis, P. Before the Brain Surgery.
Tayson, R. Nightsweats.
Teasdale. Sanctuary, The.
Teitelboim, D. In Your Eyes.
Thomas, P. Lascars, The.
Toledo, N. Dxiibi Guidxa.
Espanto tonto.
Silly Ghost.
Toufic, J. Emperor's New Costume, Or the Case of the Missing Mask, The.
Turberville. Woful Words of the Hart, The.
Turgeniev, I. Insect, The.
Unknown. At midnight when the world's at rest.
Evermore, wher-so-evere I be.
Hold me tight and very close to you.
Oh my love! If in my arms you tremble so.
Silk Cotton Tree.
Timor Mortis.
Vando. Father's Day.
Warr, M. Brain on Ice.
Watson, E. First Date in Twenty-Five Years.
Weigl. Mines.
Weslowski. Zoe and the Ghosts.
Wetzsteon. Drinks in the Town Square.
Poem for a New Year.
Whitman, R. Listening to Grownups Quarreling.
Whitman, W. Sometimes with One I Love.
Whittier. Song of Slaves in the Desert.
Williams, C. K. Risk.
Williams, G. Wild Night at Treweithan.
Wilner, E. Found in the Free Library.
Winch. Social Security.
Wojahn. Inside, The.
Wordsworth, W. Slumber Did My Spirit Seal, A.
Wright, J. Brother and Sisters.
Woman to Man.
Wyatt. Long love that in my thought doth harbo[u]r, The.
Wylie. Atavism.
Confession of Faith.
Xuanjue. Roar of the Lion.
Ya'oz-kest. Smoke Rose.
Yeats. Who Goes with Fergus?
Yevtushenko [or Evtushenko]. Fear (Extracts).
Yi Hyangji. Reply at an Unknown Place.
Yi Sang. Poem No. 1.
Yi Sanghŭi. Dracula.
Young, A. Fear, The.
Zarco. My Worst Fear.

Fear of Death
Angel. Vigil, The.
Browning, R. Prospice.
Buckley, C. Catechism of the Sea.
Foerster. Petit Mal.
Harris, D. For My Mother.
Harrison, T. Flood.
Hicok. Small Purchase.
Kan, T. Prayer for a Good Death, A.
Katz, E. Weather Seems Different, The.
Klassen, S. Repenting.

Krolow. Fear.
Machado Ruiz. And He Was the Evil Spirit of My Dreams.
Manning, Maurice. On Death.
McCabe, C. Postcard from London, A.
Morisseau-Leroy, F. Shooshoon.
Pastan. I Am Learning to Abandon the World.
Stenhouse, S. Circling.
Unamuno. It Is Night, in My Study.
Unknown. I Know When I'm Going Home.
I'm in Trouble.
My beautiful lover, one day you will be killed.
Shall I Die?
Young, Andy. Ghost of Me.

Feasts and Feasting
Aytoun, W. Royal Banquet, The.
Basho. Good house.
Coleridge, M. Unwelcome.
Didsbury, P. In Britain.
Dupin. Let Us Salute.
Fisher, A. Thanksgiving Dinner.
Hall, D. Eating the Pig.
Herrick. Ceremonies for Christmas[se].
Humphreys, E. On the Guincho.
Lamb, C. To Dora W[ordsworth]; *On Being Asked By Her Father to Write in Her Album.*
Landon. Banquet, The.
MacGowran. Description of an Irish Feast, The.
MacNeice. This Is the Life.
Nash, O. Private Dining Room, The.
Pelletiere, M. Under Her Crib.
Robinson, A. Celia's Home-Coming.
Rueflе. Feast, The.
"Sagittarius.". Passionate Profiteer to His Love, The.
Spenser, E. Sonnet 77: "Was it a dream, or did I see it plain."
Statius. First of December, The.
Tu Fu [*or* Du Fu]. Night Feast, Zuo Family Village.
Winter Dawn.
Unknown. Buffalo are coming. We will feed and feast. We wish to be fortunate and we expect it, The.
Franks come down the hill with a random course, The.
Lu-ming: Salt Lick!
Red Stove Warms the Room, The.
Zisquit. After Years of Feasting and No Sacrifice.

February
Davies, B. Consideration.
Fisher, J. It's February But.
Given. Song for February, A.
Heath-Stubbs. February.
Kenyon, J. February: Thinking of Flowers.
Kinsella, T. Mirror in February.
Kirchner, F. In Cold February Twilight.
Longfellow, H. Afternoon in February.
Morrissey, S. February: "There is no kindness in me here. I ache to be kind, but the weather."
Neri, G. Seasons.
Ray, H. February.
Rodenko. February Sun.
Simic. February: "One who lights the wood stove, The."

Federal Bureau of Investigation
Di Prima. Fragmented Address to the FBI.
Inada. F.B.I. swooped in early, The.

Feebleness
Heine, H. To the World We Must Appear.

Feeling
Becker, R. Subject of Our Lives, The.
Duncan, R. Returning to Roots of First Feeling.
Frazier, John Alexander, Jr. Guard, A.
Hillman, B. Spark, The.
Jabeen, M. Act of Caution, An.
Liu Yu Hsi. Looking at My Knife-Hilt, a Song.
Magee, T. Home Thoughts.
Naong. Haesunja Asks for an Enlightenment Song.
Sexton. Black Art, The.
Sy, T. Stone Walls.
Tornero, A. Lo que penetró tu vida—acedo espectáculo incrustado en el sitio del espasmo.

What penetrated your life—acid spectacle encrusted in the site of spasm.
Waldman, A. In the Room of Never Grieve.
Yearsley. Addressed to Sensibility.

Feet
Adamson, H. Make with the Feet.
Allingham, W. Everything passes and vanishes.
Ammons. Foot-Washing, The.
Buscani. Barefoot in the City.
Buson. Cover my head.
Wading through it.
Deltoro, A. Eggs Laid by a Tiger.
Huevos puestos por un tigre.
Dugan, A. Barefoot Homiletics, after Wittgenstein and Boswell.
Forrester, S. Summer afternoon.
Gardinier. Democracy.
Herrera y Reissig. Heraldic Decoration.
Herrick. To Dianeme ("Show [*or* Shew] me thy feet; show [*or* shew] me thy legs, thy thighs.").
Jacobsen, J. Limbo Dancer, The.
Kassiane. Troparion.
Lyon, G. Foot-Washing, The.
Major, C. Large Room with Wood Floor.
Mistral, G. Piececitos.
Neruda. Ode to My Socks.
Walking Around.
O'Donnell, C. Footprints.
O'Malley, M. Shoeing the Currach.
Ozaki Hosai. When I wash the soles of my feet.
Patmore, C. To the Body: "Creation's and Creator's crowning good."
Probyn. After.
Before.
Ramke, B. Famous Poems of the Past Explained.
Rilke. Pietà.
Sappho. Doorkeeper has feet seven fathoms long, The.
Many-colored sandal, A.
Sutskever [*or* Sutzkever]. Cartload of Shoes, A.
Swinburne. Baby's feet, like sea-shells pink, A.
Tsvetayeva [*or* Tsvetaeva]. Magdalene.
Unknown. My Darlings' Shoes.
Spell against Twisting an Ankle.
Whittier. Barefoot Boy, The.
Williams, W. Overture to a Dance of Locomotives.
Poem: "As the cat."
Yevtushenko [*or* Evtushenko]. Siberian Wooing.
See also **Toes**

Fellowship
Neruda. Ode to Walt Whitman.
Whitman, W. Song of the Answerer.
See also **Brotherhood**

Feminism and Feminists
Allen, P. He Na Tye Woman.
Amadiume. Oya Now.
Arrillaga. Dream.
Atwood. Loneliness of the Military Historian, The.
Barbauld. Rights of Woman, The.
Bartlett, E. Stretchmarks.
Breeze. Wife of Bath Speaks in Brixton Market.
Bunina. Conversation between Me and the Women.
Cahun, C. Sadistic Judith.
Canan. Radioactive.
Chaucer. Wife of Bath's Prologue, The.
Wife of Bath's Tale, The.
Ch'iu Chin. To the Tune "The River Is Red".
Chudleigh. To the Ladies.
Cisneros, S. Las Girlfriends.
Loose Women.
Clifton, L. Wishes for Sons.
Cunningham, P. On Being the Least Feminist Woman You've Ever Met.
Di Cicco. Male Rage Poem.
Dodge, M. Note.
Egerton, S. Emulation, The.
Esteves. One Woman.
Gertler, P. Right Thing, The.
Goodison. Nanny.
Grahn. I Have Come to Claim Marilyn Monroe's Body.

Hacker, M. Ballad of Ladies Lost and Found.
Elegy for a Soldier.
Graffiti from the Gare Saint-Manqué.
Invocation: "This is for Elsa, also known as Liz."
Harland-Watts, J. For a Woman's Rights.
Healy, E. Changing the Oil.
Horne, N. Note to My Liberal Feminist Sister, A.
Hugo, R. To Women.
Keita, N. Rising.
Kizer, C. One: "From Sappho to myself, consider the fate of women."
Three.
Two.
Ko Chônghûi. It Will Be a New World.
Let's Open the Dam: "Let's open the dam."
Study of Women's History 4, A.
Study of Women's History 6, A.
Korican, L. Her Story.
Lanier, E. To the Queen's Most Excellent Majesty.
Levertov. Hypocrite Women.
Lindamichellebaron. I'm the Man.
Love, M. Objects of Desire.
Loy. Effectual Marriage, The.
Love Songs to Joannes.
Malé. Women Don't Die on the Front Lines.
Markotić, N. Try book-ending punctuation vouchers.
Mendelssohn Anna. On being reproached by saintly mediators for bad budgeting.
Millay, E. To Inez Milholland.
Morgan, R. Damn You, Lady.
Nickelson, C. Angry sisters.
Nolla. Manifest, The.
Paisley, J. Feminist.
Perrine. Janus.
Polwhele. Thou, who with all the poet's genuine rage.
Prado, A. Time.
Rich, A. Ninth Symphony of Beethoven Understood at Last as a Sexual Message, The.
Snapshots of a Daughter-in-Law.
Translations.
Riley, D. Affections Must Not.
Robertson, Lexie Dean. Aunt Gilly.
Rodgers, C. Feminism.
Rukeyser, M. Myth.
Salkey. Clearsightedness.
Schwartz, P. Snapshots of the Chameleon Woman.
Shange. We Need a God Who Bleeds Now.
Shaughnessy, B. Postfeminism.
Tompson. On a Fortification at Boston Begun by Women [American edition].
Trinidad. Answer Song.
Unknown. Cloe to Artimesa.
I married an emancipated woman.
In all earnestness, I speak to all my sisters.
Urusova, E. O Muses! I beseech you, fire my heart with song.
Vivar. Femmemasochism.
Vollmer. Wildsisters Bar.
Welish. Textile 13.
Wells, C. Poster Girl's Defence, The.
Yamada. Club, The.

Fences
Blue Cloud. Old Man's Lazy, The.
Edson, R. Good Son Jim.
Frost, R. Mending Wall.
Jensma. Blue 2.
McCord, D. Pickety fence, The.
McHugh, H. Fence, The.
Murphey, John Collin. Re-stringing 100 Year Old Wire.
Oliver, M. Rain: "All afternoon it rained, then."
Stow. Singing Bones, The.
Williams, Daniel. Feste and the Fence Post.
Yosef, H. Jaffa, July 1948.
See also **Walls**

Ferns
Bunno [Wen Wang or King Wen]. Song of the Bowmen of Shu [1954].
Cho Chonsŏng. Boy, gather your straw basket.

Geoghegan, A. Mountain Fern, The.
Lynes, Jeanette. Fern Kidnappings, The.
Seaton, M. Fiddleheads.
Tarrant, J. Hula Dancers Dance the Hula, Kilauea the Caldera, The.
Unknown. Pick ferns, pick ferns.

Ferry Boats
Bartlett, B. 2. To a Northern Gannet.
Buson. Ferry departs, The.
Dibdin, C. Jolly Young Waterman, The.
Goll, I. Ferry of Lead, The.
Grosholz. On the Ferry, Toward Patras.
Han Yong'un [*or* Yongwun]. Ferryboat and the Traveler.
Housman. Crossing Alone the Nighted Ferry.
Imbriglio, C. Block Island Ferry.
Jackson, G. Alice.
Kinnell. Memory of Wilmington.
Millay, E. Recuerdo.
Nelson, H. Reading "Crossing Brooklyn Ferry" on a Summer Morning.
Parnell, P. Sile Na gCioch.
Rossetti, C. Ferry Me across the Water. Ferry Me across the Water.
Wen T'ing-yün. Near the Lizhou Ferry.
Whitman, W. Crossing Brooklyn Ferry.
Youn, Monica. Night Ferry to Naxos 2.

Fertility
Bryden, Diana Fitzgerald. Fertility Test.
Huff, S. Sperm Count.
Lifshin. Child We Won't Have Is Crowding Us in the Front, The.
McGuire, Jerry. Feeling Rosemary.
Nortje. Episodes with Unusables.
"Perse." Song: "Under the bronze leaves a colt was foaled."
Piercy. Kneeling Here, I Feel Good.
Wronsky, G. Be a child forever.
Zuni Oral Tradition. Sayatasha's Night Chant.

Fertilizer
Bryan, J. Rich Ink, Still Slightly Moist.
Ibarbourou. Rainy Night. Wild Root.

Feste
Feinstein, Sandy. Catch, The.
Williams, Daniel. Feste and the Fence Post.

Festivals
Alkalay-Gut. So we begin to plan.
Bhattācārya, M. Everyone's flocking to Gajan.
Bremer, C. Festival of Izcalli or Eighteenth Month. Fiesta de izcalli o décimo octavo mes.
Faiz. Tyrant, The.
Ginsberg, A. Kral Majales.
Goldsmith, O. Entry of the Villagers.
Harvey, M. Festival of Giovedo Grasso, The.
Issa. Dragonfly, The.
Le Brun, Annie. Festivals.
Leopardi. Village Saturday, The.
Li K'ai-hsien. Colorful frames are erected beside the Yellow River, The.
On the Cold Food Festival, Entertaining at the Southern Estate—the Guests Were Li Chiu-ho, Ma Nan-yeh, Wei Tung-kao, Li Hu-ch'uan, Huang K'ung-ts'un, Li Lung-t'ang, and Hu Hu-shan.
Li Yü. Tune: "New Bounty of Royalty".
Machado Ruiz. Poem: "We think to create festivals".
Maiden. Taste.
Ofeimun. Naming Day, A.
Pelizzon, V. Feast of San Silvestro, The.
Seely, Shane. Walt Whitman at the Irish Festival, Syracuse, New York: Four Snapshots.
Shannon, J. Imbolc.
Su Tung-p'o. Rain During the Cold Food Festival.
Tomlinson, C. Matachines, The.
Unknown. Festal Song.
Wang Shih-chieng. Composed at the West Wall of Tsou-p'ing Three Days After the Festival of Pure Brightness.
Yang Wan-li. Watching a Village Festival.

Feuds
Cortázar. Normal Behavior of the Famas.

Lea, S. Feud, The.
Lom. Lament for the State of the Country, A.
Prys-Jones. Cors-y-Gwaed: Fenland of Blood.
Unknown. Lads of Wamphray, The.

Fever
Akutagawa Ryunosuke. Sick and feverish.
Alexander, E. Aspirin.
Bottoms. Daughter's Fever, A.
Guidacci. First to feast is love, The. On the scraps of love the fever feasts.
Harris, J. Fever.
Masefield. Port of Holy Peter.
Pilkington, L. Fair and Softly Goes Far or, The Wary Physician.
Plath. Fever 103°.
Shakespeare, W. Sonnet 147: "My love is as a fe[a]ver, longing still."
Wojahn. Allegory: Attic and Fever.

Fiddles and Fiddlers
Acorn. Completion of the Fiddle, The.
Angus. Fiddler, The.
Burns, R. Green Sleeves [and Tartan Ties].
Coffman. Courage, or One of Gene Horner's Fiddles.
Freed, A. Fit as a Fiddle.
Hardy, T. At the Railway Station, Upway.
Kinnell. First Song.
Lax. Alley Violinist.
Masters, E. Fiddler Jones.
Randall, D. Finney's Bar.
Yeats. Fiddler of Dooney, The.
See also **Violinists and Violins**

Fidelity
Auden. Legend. Lullaby: "Lay your sleeping head, my love."
Aue, Hartmann von. I said I would always live for her.
Barresi. How It Comes.
Beer, P. Faithful Wife, The.
Black, J. Paper Doll.
Blamire. Siller Croun, The.
Boker. Sonnet 165.
Brontë, E. Visionary, The.
Browning, E. Man's Requirements, A.
Burns, R. Red, Red Rose, A.
Carmichael, H. Don't Forget to Say No, Baby.
Carpenter, E. To a Stranger.
Cary, P. Samuel Brown.
Cisneros, A. Dedicatory (to My Wife).
Coleridge, M. Punctilio.
Cooper, J. Faithful, The.
Curtis, T. Gambit.
Delgado, J. Two Timer.
Donne. Anniversary [*or* Anniversarie], The. Indifferent, The. Lovers' Infiniteness[e]. On His Mistress [*or* Mistris]. Relic, The.
Dowson. Non Sum Qualis Eram Bonae sub Regno Cynarae.
Duhamel. Sex with a Famous Poet.
"Ern Malley." Perspective Lovesong.
Field. Constancy.
Ford, T. There Is a Lady Sweet and Kind.
Greenwell, D. Fidelity Rewarded.
Hammerstein. All er Nothin'. Don't Ever Leave Me.
Harms. Soon.
Harwood, G. Wine Is Drunk, The.
Hemans. Gertrude; or, Fidelity till Death.
Herrera y Reissig. Heraldic Decoration.
Herrick. Bracelet to Julia, The. To Anthea, Who May Command Him Anything.
Homer. Odyssey, The.
Housman. Shades of Night, The. Shake hands, we shall never be friends, all's over.
Hwang Chini. When was I unfaithful to you?
Leigh, C. When in Rome (I Do as the Romans Do).
Lewis, A. Post-Script: for Gweno.
Lisboa. Idyll: "Lord, forgive me if I do not look for you."
Lodge, T. Love Guards [*or* Guides] the Roses of Thy Lips.
Mao Tse-tung [*or* Mao Zedong]. Chinese

Ballad.
McAuley, J. In a Late Hour.
Metastasio. On thy grey bark, in witness of my flame.
Mullen, H. Roadmap.
Nesbit, E. Wife of All Ages, The.
Petrarch. Complaint of a Lover Rebuked. Long[e] love that in my thought do[e]th [*or* I] harbour [*or* harber *or* harbar], The. Oh! place me where the burning noon.
Petronius Arbiter. However, Eumolpus, our champion in time of trouble and the author of the present harmony.
Phaedrus. Widow and the Soldier or: The Measure of a Woman's Inconstancy and Lust, The.
Poe. Annabel Lee.
Ponsot. A La Une. Matins and Lauds.
Prassinos. Hair Tonic.
Procter, A. Woman's Answer, A.
Ralegh, S. Fortune Hath Taken Away.
Razaf, A. Keepin' Out of Mischief Now.
Rist. She Boasts of Her Constancy.
Robin, L. My Cutey's Due at Two-to-Two Today. No Love, No Nothin'.
Robinson, E. Luke Havergal.
Robinson, M. Suspects His Constancy.
Rochester, J. Love and Life.
Rossetti, C. Many in aftertimes will say of you.
Sackville-West. Greater Cats, The.
Sajé, N. I Am Peeling Four Pink Grapefruit.
Shakespeare, W. Sonnet 15: "When I consider every thing that grows." Sonnet 31: "Thy bosom is endeared with all hearts." Sonnet 116: "Let me not to the marriage of true minds."
Sherwood, G. Love and Life.
"Shu Ting.". Brother, I Am Here.
Sidney. My true love hath my heart [*or* hart], and I have his. Sonnet 91: "Stella, while now by honour's cruel might."
Strabo, W. Dearest, You Come Suddenly and Suddenly You Depart.
Suckling, S. Constant Lover, A [*or* The].
Tanaquil. Very Young Man Speaks, A.
Taylor, B. Bedouin Song.
Trefusis. Valentine, A.
Tuqan, F. I Won't Sell His Love.
Unknown. Ballad of the Mulberry Road. Bo-zhou: Like a Lonely Bark. Frail, frail, lone-growing bamboo. Ge-sheng: The Kudzu Spreads Till It Darkens the Brier. Love Me Little, Love Me Long. Love Me Not [for Comely Grace]. O Heavens! Peacock Southeast Flew, A. Southeast the Peacock Flies. Winter.
Vaughan, H. Song to Amoret, A.
Veldeke, Heinrich von. Tristan had no choice.
Volkow. Washerwoman, The.
Walafrid Strabo. To His Friend in Absence.
Wickham. Paradox. Slighted Lady, The.
Winchilsea. Letter to Daphnis, A.
Wordsworth, W. Who swerves from innocence, who makes divorce.
Wyatt. Long love that in my thought doth harbo[u]r, The. *Quondam* was I in my lady's grace. Steadfastness.
Yeats. Folly of Being Comforted, The.
Young, M. J. To My Pen.

Field-Glasses
Young, A. Field-Glasses.

Fields and Pastures
Alley, R. Cleaning.
An Jung-Söp. Drinking Alone on a Spring Night.
Apollinaire. Meadow Saffron.
Ausonius. Fields of Sorrow, The.

Aygi, G. Beginning from the Field.
Fields of this Summer.
House in the Field.
Basho. Early fall.
Field of cotton, A.
Long rains, The.
Sick on a journey.
Winter rain.
Benn. Before a Cornfield.
Berry, W. Stay Home.
Betjeman. Licorice Fields at Pontefract, The.
Bible, *O.T.* Song: "Come, my beloved."
Brown, G. Ballad of John Barleycorn, the Ploughman, and the Furrow, The.
Browning, R. Meeting at Night.
Two in the Campagna.
Buchanan, O. Only Yak in Batesville, Virginia, The.
Busch, T. Heartland.
Buson. Field of bright mustard.
Field of mustard, A.
Flying squirrel, A.
Gleaning the rice field.
In the drained fields.
Listening to the moon.
Not quite dark yet.
Owner of the field, The.
They end their flight.
Tilling the field.
Cabalquinto. Depths of Fields.
Cavendish, M. Sea Similized to Meadows and Pastures, The: the Mariners, to Shepherds: the Mast, to a May-Pole: the Fish, to Beasts.
Ch'ŏn Yanghûi. Millet Field in My Mind.
Clare, J. Hares at Play.
Conyus. Day in the Life of, A.
Cowper, W. Poplar Field, The.
Cruz, C. Praying ("When I was set in that field.").
Davidkov, Ivan. Returning from the Fair.
Davie, D. Hill Field, The.
Doolittle, H. I go where I love and where I am loved.
Duncan, R. Often I Am Permitted to Return to a Meadow.
Everson, W. Muscat Pruning.
Foster, A. Field.
Francis, R. Onion Fields.
Frost, R. Cow in Apple Time, The.
Pasture, The.
Gehrke, S. Walking Fields at Night South of Hampton, Iowa.
Griffiths, A. His left hand, in heat of noonday.
Herrick. To Meadows [or Meddowes].
Ibn 'Iyad. Grainfield.
Ingelow. Dappled sky, a world of meadows, A.
Issa. Crow, The.
Even on the smallest islands.
With my father.
Withered fields, The.
Jones, D. Reaping.
Kagami Shiko. Arid fields / The only life.
Levin, D. Field.
Lezama Lima. Dark Meadow Invites Me, A.
"Lin Ling.". Footpaths Cross in the Rice Field.
Lovelace, R. Ant, The.
Lux. Grain Burning Far Away.
Machado Ruiz. Poem: "Figures in the fields against the sky!"
Marlowe. Passionate Shepherd to His Love, The.
Martial. Artemidorus sold his land to buy a boy.
Marvell. And now to the ab[b]yss I pass.
Mower's Song, The.
Masaoka Shiki. Dew, clinging / To potato field.
Mew. In the Fields.
Mickiewicz. Ackermann Steppe, The.
Miles, J. Fields of Learning.
Millay, E. I Dreamed I Moved among the Elysian Fields.
Miller, D. In the Field.
Milton. Lycidas.
Moss, H. Summer Thunder, The.
Paterson, D. Chartres of Gowrie, The.
Pilling. Field, The.
Pritchard, N. Paysagesque.

Pugh. Frozen Field, The.
Ray, H. Pastoral: "Annette came through the meadows."
Reddy, Srikanth. Scarecrow Eclogue.
Roethke. All the Earth, All the Air.
Far Field, The.
Meadow Mouse, The.
Scarbrough, G. Field beyond the Ridge.
Sharma, P. Potter's Field.
Sleigh. Field, The: "Once I left the room."
Tarpley. Feel Free.
Teasdale. Broken Field, The.
Thoreau. On fields oer which the reaper's hand has passed.
Tsogyel. Listen.
Unknown. Millets in full rows.
Van Doren. Immortal.
Weöres. Plain, The.
Wilbur, R. Exeunt.
Wilcox, E. Attraction.
Williams, W. In Two Fields.
Williams, W. Desolate Field, The.
Wordsworth, W. Solitary Reaper, The.
Wright, J. To the Evening Star: Central Minnesota.
Yi Sanghwa. Will Spring Return to Stolen Fields?
Young, A. Field-Glasses.

Fig Trees and Figs
Causley. Figgie Hobbin.
Char. Lied of the Fig Tree.
Dove, R. This Life.
García, D. Orchard of Figs in the Fall, An.
Hajjaj, N. Honey Fig.
Hall, D. Small Fig Tree, A.
Khoury, N. People of Figs.
Lawrence, D. H. Bare Fig-trees.
Figs.
Nye, N. My Father and the Fig Tree.
Paredes, E. Gathering the Wild Figs—Vizcaina, Gomera.
Pilling. Encounter at the Post Office Counter.
Toledo, N. Na Victórica litru.
Ulacia, M. Arabian Knight.
Warren, R. Where the Slow Fig's Purple Sloth.

Fights
Algarin. Always Throw the First Punch.
Belieu. Part of the Effect of the Public Scene Is to Importune the Passing Viewer.
Blake, W. Preface: "And did those feet in ancient time."
Brome. Riddle, The: "No more, no more."
Browning, R. Woman's Last Word, A.
Cameron, N. Fight with a Water-Spirit.
Camões [or Camõens or Camoëns], L. Battle's uncertain work begins; and move.
Carroll, L. Brother and Sister.
Cisneros, S. Las Girlfriends.
Coleridge, M. Mortal Combat.
DeNicola, D. My Father's First Fight.
Fielding. Revenge.
Gay, J. Meddling Mastiff, The.
Homer. Then to th' extremest heat of fight he did his valour turn.
Jones, R. My Manhood.
Loftis, N. Fights After School.
Logue, C. Battle swayed, The.
Mattawa. Bus Driver Poem, The.
McKay, C. If We Must Die.
Millay, E. Hearing Your Words, and Not a Word among Them.
Muldoon, P. All I Did for Him.
Mulkey, R. Blind-Sided.
Myers, J. Lightweight.
Nowlan. Britain Street: Saint John, New Brunswick.
Nye, N. Site of the Indian Fights of 1871, Abilene.
Ransom, J. Captain Carpenter.
Rich, A. Implosions.
Shakespeare, W. What bloody man is that? He can report.
Stern, G. All I Did for Him.
Unknown. At last these two stout erles did meet.
Fight with Grendel.

Rookhope Ryde.
Valerie, J. On Apologies.
Weigl. Hand to Hand.
Weismiller. To the Woman in Bond Street Station.
Whitman, R. Listening to Grownups Quarreling.
Williams, C. K. Blades.
Williamson, G. Neighboring Storms.
Figureheads (ship)
Adams, L. Figurehead, The.
Filipinos
Abad, G. Holy Order.
Jeepney.
Light in One's Blood, The.
Toys.
Africa-Bolasco. Sauna 2.
Aguilar-Cariño. Dinakdakan.
Familiar.
Gabi.
Aguilar, M. Pall Hanging over Manila.
Poem from Sierra Madre.
Balce, N. Pizza and Pretense.
Balingit, J. Quiet Evening, Home Away.
Bobis, M. Driving to Katoomba.
Word Gifts for an Australian Critic.
Brion, R. Good Friday.
If Fortune Smiles.
Love Song: "One long and humid afternoon."
Caballero-Robb, M. Dear Rosario.
Memoranda for Rosario.
Cabalquinto. Depths of Fields.
Cabico, R. Afternoon in Pangasinan with No Electricity, An.
Check One.
Mango Poem.
Carbó, N. Civilizing the Filipino.
I Found Orpheus Levitating.
Little Brown Brother.
Cariaga. Family Tree, The.
Cerenio. My Mother.
13 June 1994.
20 July 1994.
23 October 1992.
Cortes, F. Dolce Far Niente.
Fish 2.
Palace of Fine Arts in San Francisco, The.
Poem Composed during a Brownout.
Duhamel. Yes.
Dumdum. Li Pos of the Polis.
Some Die of Light.
To My Mother.
E'der, E. La Puente.
Once We Were Farmers.
Escandor, V. Summer Nostalgia.
Evasco, M. Baked Oysters Rockefeller.
Dancing a Spell.
Elemental.
Heron-Woman.
Faigao, B. Balitaw.
Kundiman.
Francia, L. In Gurgle Veritas.
Secret in the Roar, The.
Fructuoso, E. Astig.
Gamalinda, E. Denials.
La Naval De Manila: Selim Sot as a Modern Political Observer.
Lament Beginning w/a Line after Cavafy.
Garrett, E. Bachelors, The.
Grandfather's Mint.
Gier, J. California Coast.
Examining the I.
First View of the Islands, A.
Going Baroque.
Gloria. Aleng Maria.
Assimilation.
Rizal's Ghost.
Touch.
Gonzalez, N. Deepest Well in Madras, The.
How the Heart Aches.
I Made Myself a Path.
Wanderer in the Night of the World, A.
Gotera. First Mango.
Madarika.
Manong Chito Tells Manong Ben about His Dream over Breakfast at the Manilatown

Cafe.
Pacific Crossing.
Hagedorn, J.   Souvenirs.
Hufana, A.   Contemporary.
Floating Epitaphs, Their Possible Explanations in Poro Point.
From the Raw.
Insides of Alfred Hitchcock, The.
Humphrey, D.   April in Houston.
Ilio, D.   Children of the Atomic Age.
Marikudo in Kalibo, 1979.
Prokosch in Tehran, 1978.
Site of My Grandfather's House, The.
Jacinto, J.   Absence.
Heaven Is Just Another Country.
Visitation.
Lim-Wilson.   Alphabet Soup.
Raising the Dead.
Mateo.   Jeepneyfying.
There Is No Word for Sex in Taglog.
Melo, M.   Red Lipstick on a Straw.
Scrambled Eggs and Garlic Pork.
Unlearning English.
Nazareno, C.   Bohol's Tarsier Population.
Cortes Swamp, The.
Palis, Y.   Floor, The.
Waking Up.
Pardo, P.   I was on the couch when the jehova's witnesses came.
Remoto.   Black Silk Pajamas.
Exile.
Images of John (1967–92).
Robles.   Cutting Back the Ifugao Past.
Feasting with Etang a Hundred Times Around.
Manong with a Thousand Tribal Visions, The.
Remembering the Past.
San Juan.   Owl of Minerva Takes Flight in the Evening, The.
Ungria, R.   Carillonneur.
Commerce and the Man.
Culture Nervous.
Unknown.   Filipino Woman, The.
Song of the Alaskero.
Then why did I have to make.
Viray, M.   Patio.
Yuson.   Andy Warhol Speaks to His Two Filipino Maids.
World Poetry Circuit.
Zamora-Linmark.   Day 1: Portrait of the Artist, Small-Kid Time.
Election Day.
Zarco.   Manila Paper.
Once upon a Seesaw with Charlie Chan.
See also **Philippines**

Film and Filmmakers
Abse.   Welsh Valley Cinema, 1930s.
Andrews, T.   Cinema Vérité: The Death of Alfred, Lord Tennyson.
Six One-Line Film Scripts.
Bernlef.   Uncle Charles: A Home Movie.
Bierds, L.   Muybridge.
Bowers, N.   On the Elvis Mailing List.
Brown, L.   If I Had a Talking Picture of You.
Carbó, N.   Little Brown Brother.
Dauer.   Woman in the Film, The.
DeFoe, M.   Red Salamander—Video Store Parking Lot.
DeSylva, B. G.   If I Had a Talking Picture of You.
Divakaruni.   Indian Movie, New Jersey.
Dubie.   Sanctuary.
Duhig, I.   I prayed to the ghost of Carrie.
Dunn, D.   I Am a Cameraman.
Eirian, S.   Learning.
Ellis, T.   Zapruder.
Equi.   Being Sick Together.
Flynn, L.   What You Get.
Forhan, C.   Without Presumptions.
Garioch.   Phooie!
Glück, R.   Invaders from Mars.
Goldbarth.   Meop.
Guest, B.   Motion Pictures: 15.
Motion Pictures: 4.
Healy, E.   What It Was Like the Night Cary Grant Died.
Heaney, S.   Shooting Script, A.

Henderson, R.   If I Had a Talking Picture of You.
Hicok.   Over Coffee.
Hill, G.   Violent contrariety of men and days; calm.
Holzer, R.   Current "Now, Voyager" Fantasy.
Hufana, A.   Insides of Alfred Hitchcock, The.
Joseph, A.   Teenage Interplanetary Vixens Run Wild on Bikini Beach.
Lindsay, V.   She is madonna in an art.
Majorino.   Scene-Script.
Malanova, M.   Many films begin with a funeral.
Miller, J.   Topos.
Muske, C.   Last Take.
Notley.   Where Leftover Misery Goes.
Oliveira, D.   Laurence Olivier's Hamlet.
Parra, N.   I Move the Meeting Be Adjourned.
Rich, A.   History.
Rossman, E.   Double Features.
Saroyan.   Film Noir.
Scott, D.   For Norman Nicholson.
Simon, M.   Blue Movies.
Stanton, M.   Sorrow and Rapture.
Trinidad.   As one young guy screwed another young guy.
Shower Scene in *Psycho*, The.
Things to Do in Valley of the Dolls (The Movie).
Villanueva, T.   Scene from the Movie *Giant*.
Vinokurov.   I do not like the circus.
Warsh.   White Nights.
Wojahn.   Francis Ford Coppola and Anthropologist Interpreter Teaching Gartewienna Tribesmen to Sing "Light My Fire," Philippine Jungle, 1978.
Zucker, R.   In Your Version of Heaven I am Younger.
See also **Movies**

Financiers
Ryan, G.   Penserosa, La.
See also **Banking and Bankers**

Finches
Beeson, M.   Flight.
Christie.   Hollywood Finch, The.
Huddle.   Perspective.
MacNaughton.   Cassin's Finch.
Schiff, Robyn.   Vampire Finch.
Woodpecker Finch.

Fingers
Bertrand.   Five Fingers of the Hand, The.
Buson.   Mason's finger, The.
Buzzi.   Finger-nails.
Chao Luan-luan.   Slender Fingers.
Fouad, I.   Truth: I Have Five Fingers on Each Hand!
Halpern, D.   Her Body.
Issa.   Asked how old he was.
Kay, J.   Finger.
Khodasevich.   Dactyls.
Kitasono Katsue.   Words.
Malroux.   Fingers probe.
Milán, E.   ¿Cuál coro?
What chorus?
Nezval.   City with Towers.
Randolph, T.   Upon the Loss[e] of His Little Finger.
Satyamurti.   I Shall Paint My Nails Red.
Simic.   Bestiary for the Fingers of My Right Hand.
Vlasova, E.   On an old grand piano.
Wisenberg, S.   Casino.

Finland
Brecht, B.   1940.
Hacker, M.   Rune of the Finland Woman.
Kuusisto, Stephen.   Summer at North Farm.
Loden.   My Test Market.
Lönnrot.   It is my desire, it is my wish.
Tate, J.   I Am a Finn.

Finns
Tate, J.   I Am Still a Finn.

Fir Trees
Jay, T.   Fir.

Fire and Fires
Adcock, B.   Kaiser's Burnout.
Adonis [*or* Adunis].   Passage, The.

Tree of Fire.
Ai.   Family.
New Crops for a Free Man.
Akhmadulina.   Snow Maiden, The.
Alexander, E.   Overture: Watermelon City.
Ali, A.   Of Fire.
Alipiev, Petar.   Warmth, The.
Ap Gwilym, Gwynn.   Penyberth.
Atwood.   Morning in the Burned House.
Bal, W.   Fire!
Balaban.   Thoughts Before Dawn.
Bartlett, M.   Burning of Margaret Moone, The.
Baxter, J.   Firemen, The.
Wild Bees.
Benbow.   Larson Arson.
Bernheim, Erica.   Like a Face.
Binyon.   Now is the time for the burning of the leaves.
Bishop, E.   Armadillo, The.
Casabianca.
Bobrowski.   Latvian Autumn, The.
Place of Fire.
Bonnefoy.   Remember the Island Where They Build the Fire.
Bradstreet, A.   [Here Follows Some] Verses upon the Burning of Our House [July 10th, 1666. Copied Out of a Loose Paper].
Brathwaite, E.   Prelude: "Drum skin whip."
Bremer, C.   Festival of Xócotl Huetzi or Tenth Month.
Fiesta de xócotl huetzi o décimo mes.
Bromige.   Log.
Point, The.
Brown, J.   Fire: "What makes a fire burn."
Brown, L.   Call for Vertical Integration in the Eye of the Storm, A.
Brown, S.   Schadenfreude.
Buckley, V.   Man, a Woman, A.
Busceti, G.   One Hundred Eighty.
Buson.   Short night, The.
Byron, G.   Darkness.
Campbell, D.   Man in the Honeysuckle, The.
Carberry.   It takes a mighty fire.
Cardiff.   Where Fire Burns.
Carr, M.   Castle in the Fire, The.
Celan.   Alchemical.
Night Ray.
Ceni, A.   Reconciled Flame.
Chao Meng-fu.   To a Pyrotechnist.
Clare, J.   Gypsy's Evening Blaze, The.
Clifton, L.   Fury.
Move.
Coleridge, M.   Fire, the lamp, and I, were alone together, The.
Conoley, G.   World, The: "It was just a gas station. It was not spectacular carnage."
Cooley, N.   Arson.
Copeland, J.   Ed.
Couzyn.   Way Out, The.
Crashaw.   O sweet incendiary! shew here thy art.
Cruz, S.   O Living Flame of Love.
Dalton, Mary.   Conkerbells.
Dancing Bear, J. P.   Making Fire.
Daryush.   Children of Wealth.
Davis, C.   Years, The.
Davis, G.   August Fires.
Demetre, S.   Woman Is Running for Her Life, A.
Dickinson, E.   Dare you see a Soul *at the White Heat?*.
Dodge, M.   Fire in the Window.
Donne.   I am a little world made cunningly.
Doolittle, H.   In no wise is the pillar-of-fire.
Sea Violet.
Drayton.   If he, from heaven that filched the living fire.
Duncan, R.   Fire, The.
For the Assignment of the Spirit.
Tribal Memories.
Elfyn, Menna.   Burning Multitude, The.
Espada.   Mayan Astronomer in Hell's Kitchen, A.
Fermini, I.   Detouring through the rooms were men and fumes.
Field, Miranda.   Housefire.

Fisher, R. Burning Graves at Netherton, The.
Flynn, N. Bag of Mice.
French, T. Asperger Child.
Frost, R. Fire and Ice.
Ganev, Nedelcho. Soul, The: "Flame is full, The."
Garland, H. Fighting Fire.
Geiger. Soundtracks.
Ghalib, M. Freely in Hidden Fire.
González Prada, M. Into the Hearth They Are Tossing Logs.
Graham, H. Tender-Heartedness.
Grimké, A. Epitaph on a Living Woman.
Hall, D. Love-Letter-Burning.
Hamburger, M. Treblinka.
Harper, M. Fireplace, The.
Harte, B. Chicago.
Heaney, S. Tinder.
Hemphill. Soft Targets.
Henderson, D. Blackman in the Desecrated Synagogue—Living in the Last Days.
Henderson-Holmes. My First Riot: Bronx, NYC.
Herlin. Echo of Fireplace, An.
Hirsch, E. American Apocalypse.
 Man on a Fire Escape.
Hooson, I. Flame, The.
Hudgins. Fire and St. Francis.
Hughes, F. In the Shadow of Fire.
Hutchinson, P. Flames.
Jaccottet. Right at the end of night.
Jarnot, L. What in Fire Did I, Firelover, Starter of Fires, Love?
Jeffers, R. Fire on the Hills.
Jones, R. Remembering Fire.
Kagawa Kageki. Buy it! But it!
Kamenetz. Lighter Fluid.
Kang Ŭn'gyo. Becoming Water.
Kaya Shirao. Mountain mist / Torches dropped.
Kennedy, X. Lighting a Fire.
Khlebnikov, V. I Went Out.
 It Has the Unassuming Face of a Burnt-out Candle.
Khoury, N. People of Fire.
Kim Sŭnghŭi. Song of Children in the Land of Ice Who Love the Sun.
King, H. Sonnet: "Tell me[e] no more how fair[e] she[e] is."
Kinnell. Another Night in the Ruins.
Koller. Sitting Alone One Cold June Night before an Empty Whiskey Bottle a Coffee Pot & an Oil Stove with a Window through Which I Watched the Flames.
Komunyakaa, Y. How I See Things.
 You and I Are Disappearing.
Kovner, A. I sat upon the ground, and the ground was fire.
Kreitman, N. Bonfire in April.
Kuong Viet. Wood and Fire.
Kyle, C. J. Fire in Early Morning.
Laux, D. Firestarter.
Leggott, M. Dark Torch.
Lesley, G. Behold, how Sodom swaggers in its Pride.
Levine, P. Coming Home, *Detroit*, 1968.
Lindley, D. By Fire or Flood.
Lindtová, A. Campfire.
Longfellow, H. Golden Mile-Stone, The.
Lope de Vega. Ice and Fires Contend with My Child.
Lorde. Day They Eulogized Mahalia, The.
Lowell, J. Darkened Mind, The.
Lux. Grain Burning Far Away.
Machado Ruiz. But art? / It is pure and intense play.
MacNeice. Brother Fire.
Magdeburg, Mechthild von. Fish cannot drown in water, A.
Marcinkevičius, J. Prelude to 'Blood and Ash.'
Masahide. Barn's burnt down.
McClatchy. Method, The.
McDaniel, J. Leonard.
McGrath, T. Coal Fire in Winter, A.
Merrill, J. Charles on Fire.
Merwin. Burnt Child, The.
Monk, M. Fire Us with Ice, Burn Us with

Snow.
Moore, H. Spuyten Duyvil.
Moore, M. To a Chameleon.
Morley, D. On Fire.
Morrissey, S. There Was Fire in Vancouver.
Mortimer. Wolves.
Moss, T. Lynching, The.
Neruda. Poetry.
Neto. African Poem.
North, C. Leap Year.
O'Connor, M. Fire.
Overton, R. Fire and Ice by Robert Frost: An Early Draft.
Padgett, R. Love Poem: "We have plenty of matches in our house."
Paul, C. Flame.
Paulin. Peacetime.
Peele. Bethsabe's Song.
Peseroff. After the Argument.
Piatt, J. Fires in Illinois.
Piatt, S. Palace-Burner, The.
Pinsky. Shirt.
Piper, E. Indian Counsel.
Pitter. Victory Bonfire.
Polley, J. Smoke.
Prunty. Pyromaniac, The.
Rabinowitz. Of Joy Illimited: Polyphonic Soundings: Shore to Ship.
Rafferty, C. Arsonist Tells His Story to the Attorney, The.
Ramsdell, H. Bright Receding.
Ravikovitch, D. Dress of Fire, A.
Rawson, J. Map Burnt Through.
Redmond. Distance.
 My Tongue Paints a Path.
Rexroth, K. On the bridges.
Rhodes, M. How Fast.
Rich, A. Burning Oneself Out.
Rilke. Birth of the Smile, The.
Rivard. Firestone.
Rizal, J. Water and Fire.
Rodriguez, L. Fire.
Rohrer, M. Short History of Illumination, A.
Rosenfeld, M. Memorial to Triangle Fire Victims.
Ross, Grace. Oil Well Fire.
Rossetti, C. Flint.
Roy, L. Ride, The.
Ruefle. Suburb of Long Suffering.
Rukeyser, M. Burning the Dreams.
Rybicki, J. This Sun.
Sachs, N. Rushing at Times Like Flames.
St. John, D. Winter Fires.
Sanchez, S. Elegy (for MOVE and Philadelphia).
 Philadelphia: Spring, 1985.
Scliar-Cabral. Fire and Embers.
Seyburn, P. Good Water.
Shinkichi Takahashi. Burning Oneself to Death.
Simic. February: "One who lights the wood stove, The."
Slutsky [or Slutskii]. Burnt.
Snyder, G. Burning the Small Dead.
Sokan. Cold, yes / But don't test.
Sologuren. Oh, Astonishing Love.
Sorrentino. Land of Cotton.
Southwell. Burning Babe, The.
Speyer. Witch!
Stevenson, R. Autumn Fires.
Storni. Camp Fire.
Sutskever [or Sutzkever]. Death of an Ox, The.
Swirszczynska [or Swir]. I Am Afraid of Fire.
Tan Taigi. Temple in / Deep winter grove.
Taylor, A. Fire.
Taylor, J. As Gold is better that's in fire tride.
Todd, M. Grandmother's Farm.
Townsend, A. Butane, Kerosene, Gasoline.
Tsvetaeva [or Tsvetaeva]. Staircase.
Unknown. Edict against Christianity (Section 12).
 Edom o' Gordon [Foulis Version].
 Fire.
 First Song of the Exploding Stick.
 Gather some wood and make a great fire!
 Hidden-in-winter.
 I Can't Stand the Fire.

 Match That Darkened the Sun, The.
Uyematsu. Ten Million Flames of Los Angeles, The.
Velichansky, A. Flame's speech is confused, The. The muttering of the water is hollow.
Vigil, A. Hogarcito de La Madrugada, El.
Virgil [or Vergil]. Pyres, The.
Volkman. Create Desire.
Voznesensky [or Voznesenskii]. Big Fire at the Architectural College, The.
Warren, R. In Creve Coeur, Missouri.
Watson, R. Ballad of the Were-Wolf, A.
 Betty Barnes, the Book-Burner.
Webb, C. Arson.
Weigl. Burning Shit at An Khe.
Weiss, T. Fire at Alexandria, The.
Whitman, W. By the Bivouac's Fitful Flame.
Whittier. Burning Drift-Wood.
Williams, C. K. Hearth, The.
Williamson, G. Walter Parmer.
Wolff, Rebecca. Flame On.
Wright, C. Flame.
Wright, C. State of Preservation.
Wright, J. Night After Bushfire.
 To a Child.
 Two Fires, The.
Wright, R. Between the World and Me.
Zagajewski. Fire: "Probably I am an ordinary middle-class."
 Flame, A.
Zawacki, Andrew. Credo.
Zu-Bolton. Struggle-Road Dance.

Fire Engines
Baxter, J. Firemen, The.
Williams, W. Great Figure, The.

Fire Island
Harwood, L. Seaside, The.
O'Hara, F. True Account of Talking to the Sun at Fire Island, A.
Swenson, M. Fire Island.

Firearms
Gorbanevskaya. Hurry, take pleasure in the oblique caress of rain while the sun shines.
See also **Guns**

Fire-eaters
Delgado, J. Mexican Fire Breather, A.

Firefighters
Baxter, J. Firemen, The.
Brown, A. Ash Wednesday, 2002.
Hampton. Fire Station's Delight, The.
Harris, R. Ambition, The.
Holland, J. Three Tests for Darwin Duke.
Suermondt, Tim. Squad I.

Fireflies
Basho. Seen in plain daylight.
Buson. At a roadside shrine.
Channing. Chant to the Fire-fly.
Fleischman. Fireflies.
Forrester, S. Daylight. . . / no one notices.
Frost, R. Fireflies in the Garden.
Gorostiza, J. Fireflies.
Gu Cheng. Words: "My dream won't last long."
Issa. Fireflies / Entering my house.
 First firefly / Why turn away.
 In my house / Mice and fireflies.
 Mokuboji Temple.
 Owls are calling / "Come, come".
 Watch it—you'll bump / Your heads.
Izumi. So forlorn am I.
Kinzie. Canicula.
Lemm, Richard. Spark.
Lowell, A. Lover, A.
Marvell. Mower to the Glowworms [or Glow-Worms *or* Glo-Worms], The.
Mercer, J. Glow-Worm, The.
Onitsura. Come! Come! Though I call.
Pai, S. Fall Aster with Firefly.
Ransetsu. Each morn / From the straw raincoat.
Rexroth, K. How long, long ago.
 Now the fireflies of our youth.
Roberts, E. Firefly.
Strange. Childhood.
Tu Fu [or Du Fu]. Firefly.

Unknown. Chant to the Fire-Fly.
Ward, D. My Brothers Make a Lantern.
See also **Glowworms**

Fireworks
Chu Yohan. Fireworks.
Jordan, J. July 4, 1984: For Buck.
Ni Ghallchóir, C. Spark of Joy, The.
Peck, R. Four of July.
Swenson, M. July 4th.
Voigt. Blue Ridge.
Worth, V. Fireworks.

Firpo, Luis
Ignatow, D. Boxing Match, The.

First Love
Berman, D. Classic Water.
Breton, A. Always for the First Time.
Creeley. First Love.
Halliday, M. First: "For me it was Robin
  Hentz."
Ode: The Capris.
Jiménez, J. Adolescence: "We were alone
  together."
Luu Trong Lu. Autumn End.
Norton, C. First Love.
Savage-Armstrong, G. Wee Lassie's First Luve,
  The.
Shimazaki Toson. First Love.
Stallings. Dead Language Lesson.
Wei Chuang. I Remember.
Wormser. First Love, Sixteen Years Old.

First World War
Blunden. Two Voices.
Gibson, W. Breakfast.
See also **World War I**

Fish
Adams, S. Gwbert: Mackerel Fishing.
Adamson. Gutting the Salmon.
Ahern, T. Unbruised.
Albrecht, A. Below White Cliffs.
Alvi, M. Fish.
Barker, G. How many apples grow on the tree?
Barry, Quan. Asylum.
Basho. Bucket of azaleas, A.
  Early dawn.
  Exciting at first.
  Fish shop.
  Fishy smell, A.
  In the fish shop.
  Snowy morning, A.
  Spring going.
  What fish feel.
  Whitebait, The.
Bishop, E. Fish, The.
Blight. Garfish.
Boland, E. Woman Turns Herself into a Fish,
  The.
Bracho, C. Fish of Fleeting Skin.
  From Their Eyes Adorned with Vitreous Sands.
  Peces de piel fugaz.
Brooke, R. Heaven.
Buson. At the ancient well.
  Autumn breezes.
  Dawn.
  Leaves some trout.
  Old well.
Carroll, L. Crocodile, The.
  Humpty Dumpty's Poetic Recitation.
Carroll. Ode on a Bicycle on Halsted Street in a
  Sudden Summer Thunderstorm.
Catherine of Siena. We were enclosed.
Cendrars. Fish Cove.
Chuang Tzu. Man Is Born in Tao.
Cortes, F. Fish 2.
Couzyn. Spell to Protect Our Love.
Crummey, Michael. Capelin Scull.
De la Mare. Alas, Alack!
Donne. Bait[e], The.
Doty, M. Display of Mackerel, A.
  Fish R Us.
Dove, R. Fish in the Stone, The.
Drinan. Men on the Rocks, The.
Dumas, H. Knees of a Natural Man.
Eigner. Letter for Duncan.
Einzig *et al.* Slide Show, The.
Elfyn, Menna. Sardines.

Engels, J. Fish Dream, The.
Erinna. Escort fish, Pompilos, sending sailors a
  fair sailing.
Feinstein, E. Aviation.
Finlay, I. O.H.M.S.
Giussani, S. Hot and Cold.
Graham, J. My Garden, My Daylight.
  Prayer: "Over a dock railing, I watch the
  minnows, thousands, swirl."
Gray, T. Ode on the Death of a Favo[u]rite Cat,
  Drowned in a Tub [*or* Bowl] of Gold Fishes.
Guest, B. Twilight Polka Dots.
Hannan, M. Lamper, The.
Hartley, M. Fishmonger.
Harwood, G. Mid-Channel.
Hayes, T. Ohio River Region.
Hidalgo, J. Fish.
Hughes, T. Pike.
Hugo, R. Death in the Aquarium.
Hunt, L. Fish Answers, A.
  Fish, the Man, and the Spirit, The.
  To a Fish.
Ingelow. Pups and the Fish, The.
Issa. Not knowing.
Jaques, F. There Once Was a Puffin.
Jeffers, R. Birds and Fishes.
  Purse-Seine, The.
Kelly, B. Leaving, The.
Kirby, D. Moderation Kills (Excusez-Moi, Je
  Suis Sick as a Dog).
Koster, E. B. Shoal of Silver Angelfish, A.
Kunitz, S. King of the River.
Lawrence, D. H. Little Fish.
Lowell, R. Fishnet.
"Lucebert.". Fishermen from Ma Yuan.
Lummis, Suzanne. Fish I Remember.
Maassen, Ruth. Confessions of a Pisciphobe.
MacCaig. Kingfisher.
Major, C. Beaulieu.
Marlatt, D. Bruce and the Bluegills.
McAuley, J. Legendary.
McCaffery. Little Hans.
McFadden, D. Shouting Your Name Down the
  Well.
Melville, H. Maldive Shark, The.
  Song from *Mardi*.
  We Fish.
Metodiev, Ivan. River: "River, River."
Milosz, C. Abundant Catch (Luke 5:4–10).
Mok, J. Winter Mirror II.
Montague, J. Trout, The.
Moore, M. Egyptian Pulled Glass Bottle in the
  Shape of a Fish, An.
  Fish, The: "Wade / through black jade."
Moritz [*or* Morits]. Fisherman, The.
Musgrave. Lure.
Muso Soseki. In these mountain villages and
  harbor towns.
Myles, E. School of Fish.
Nemerov. Goose Fish, The.
Nepote, M. Image of the Fish.
  Imagen del Pez.
Neruda. Flag, The.
Niatum. Salmon, The.
No Hyegyông. Fish and Sauce.
Noguere. Soma.
Novak, H. Freezing Pan, The.
O'Hara, F. Elegy: "Ecstatic and in anguish over
  lost days."
Okamoto. Tanka: "Having let flow."
Oppian [of Corycus]. Then from the teeming
  Filth, and putrid Heap.
Paek Sôk. Sound of the Mountain Bird.
Pastan. Shadblow.
Phillips, C. Parable: "There was a saint once."
Plumly. In Answer to Amy's Question What's a
  Pickerel.
Pollitt. Two Fish.
Quinn, J. 7. Bohemian Carp.
Rafferty, P. View from the Bathysphere.
Ramanujan. Breaded Fish.
Ramke, B. Difference between Night and Day,
  The.
Romo-Carmona, M. Fish.
Rosen, K. Along the Charles.
Rothenberg, J. At Tsukiji Market Tokyo.

Saimaro. Mirrored by stream / Swallow darts.
Satyamurti. Erdywurble.
Shinkichi Takahashi. Fish.
  Near Shinobazu Pond.
Siegel, R. Silverfish.
Smedley, M. Sorrowful Sea-Gull, The.
Smith, C. Walk by the Water, A.
Smith, D. Blowfish and Mudtoad.
Snyder, G. Lines on a Carp.
Stein, G. Fish.
Storni. Me at the Bottom of the Sea.
Swift, J. Steelhead in the Whitehorse Rearing
  Pond.
Sze. In Your Honor.
Thomas, R. S. Pisces.
  Song for Gwydion.
Thoreau. Salmon Brook.
Tomlinson, C. Heron.
Unknown. Fish Weeps, The.
  Fisherman's Rhyme.
  Fowls [*or* Foweles *or* Fowles] in the Frith.
  When a fish.
  Withered Fish, A.
  Yu-li: Fine Fish to Net.
Valentine, J. Skate.
Vian, Boris. What for Do I Live Then.
Vietnamese Oral Tradition. Girl with the Binh
  Tien Hairdo, The.
  Husband and Wife.
Voigt. Effort at Speech.
Wakayama Bokusui. They say there lives.
Waring, B. Back to Catfish.
Weatherly, T. Fishes / theirs fit.
Weigl. Three Fish.
Wicks, S. Buying Fish.
Willard, N. Wreath to the Fish, A.
Wintu Oral Tradition. Minnows and Flowers.
Wood, W. Sea's Abundant Progeny, The.
Wright, D. Juxtapositions.
Wright, J. Northern Pike.
Yu Ch'an. Third Day of the Third Month at the
  Meandering River, The.
Zabolotsky [*or* Zabolotskii]. At the
  Fishmonger's.

Fishing and Fishermen
Adams, S. Gwbert: Mackerel Fishing.
Addonizio. China Camp, California.
Barrax. Visit.
Basho. Cormorant fishing / How stirring.
  Delight, then sorrow.
Basse [*or* Bas]. Angler's Song, The.
Bedell, J. Mains du Bon Dieu, Les.
Berg, S. Ritual.
Bierds, L. Desire.
Bishop, E. At the Fishhouses.
  Fish, The.
Bourque, D. Old Women Fishing from Bridges.
Brown, G. Haddock Fishermen.
  Net, The.
Burns, R. Fishing in Winter.
Buson. Avoiding fishnet.
Carver, R. Catch, The.
  River, The: "I waded, deepening, into the dark
  water."
Chamberlain, B. Islandman.
Chang Chi. Coming at Night to a Fisherman's
  Hut.
Ching An. Written on the Painting "Cold River
  Snow".
Chiyojo. Grazing.
Cho Chonsông. Boy, bring my sedge cape and
  bamboo hat.
Chock. Bait, The.
Cochran, J. To Keep the Spirits.
Cooley, N. Undine.
Delp. Fishing the Dream.
Donne. Bait[e], The.
Dunbar, P. Boy's Summer, A.
D'Urfey [*or* Durfey]. Fisherman's Song, The.
Eigner. Letter for Duncan.
Engels, J. Bullhead.
Espirito Santo. Far from the Beach.
Estes, A. You Stand There Fishing.
Ferlinghetti, L. Ecolog.
Field, E. Wynken, Blynken, and Nod.
Finney, N. Fishing among the Learned.

Galvin, J.   Shadow-Casting.
Glenday, J.   Day at the Seaside, A.
Gomez, M.   Looking Deep.
Greenlaw, L.   World Where News Travelled Slowly, A.
Grosholz.   Old Fisherman, The.
Hall, R.   How oft, ere morning lit the eastern steep.
Hamill, S.   Each word carefully.
Hamilton, G.   Don's Holiday.
Hammerstein.   Mister Snow.
Han Yü.   To Hou Xi.
Harwood, G.   Mid-Channel.
Hass, R.   San Pedro Road.
Hay, G.   Old Fisherman, The.
Holmes, O.   Ballad of the Oysterman, The.
Hughes, L.   Catch.
Hugo, R.   Langaig.
Jeffers, R.   Purse-Seine, The.
 Salmon Fishing.
Jinkag Haesim.   Fisherman's Song, A.
Kagami Shiko.   Small fish-boats / After what.
Kao Shih.   Song of the Fisherman, The.
Kennedy, X.   Curse on a Thief, A.
Kinnell.   Angling, a Day.
Kunitz, S.   Catch, The.
 Quinnapoxet.
Lea, S.   At the Flyfisher's Shack.
Lee, P.   I'm Gonna Go Fishin'.
Leonidas of Tarentum.   Theris, the old man who lived by his fish traps.
Leslie, K.   Sonnet: "Silver herring throbbed thick in my seine, The."
Lewis, G.   Poet Fishing, The.
Li K'ai-hsien.   Parable, A.
Li Tung-yang.   On a Painting of Fish Being Caught, A Song.
Lieberman, L.   Lobsters in the Brain Coral.
Liu Tsung-yüan.   Old Fisherman, The.
 River Snow.
River Snow ("These thousand peaks cut off the flight of birds.").
 River-Snow.
 Snowy River.
Livingstone, D.   Sonatina of Peter Govender, Beached.
Lorde.   Fishing the White Water.
Lowell, R.   Drunken Fisherman, The.
"Lucebert.".   Fishermen from Ma Yuan.
Lux.   Fisherman's Pants, The.
MacDiarmid, H.   With the Herring Fishers.
Marlatt, D.   Ghost.
Martinson.   Cable Ship, The.
McDonald, C.   Nightfishing.
McDonald, W.   Losing a Boat on the Brazos.
McLain, P.   Fishing.
McMichael.   Lutra, the Fisher.
 My parents had teased that if I ever.
Merrill, J.   Pier: Under Pisces, The.
Milosz, C.   Luke 5:1–11; While the people pressed upon him.
Mirikitani.   Fisherman, The.
Mitchison.   Dick and Colin at the Salmon Nets.
 To a Fisherman with the Present of a Knife.
Montague, J.   Trout, The.
Morejón.   Havana Harbor.
Moritz [or Morits].   Fisherman, The.
Morris, L.   Fishing Lass of Hakin, The.
Mullen, L.   Catch, The.
Muso Soseki.   East of the strait.
 From the beginning.
In these mountain villages and harbor towns.
Muyong Sooyon.   Fisherman at Byolam.
Nairne.   Caller Herrin'.
Niedecker.   Dusk— / He's spearing from a boat.
 River-marsh-drowse.
Odell.   Song for a Fishing Party.
O'Hara, F.   Captains Courageous.
 Elegy: "Salt water. and faces dying."
Orr, G.   Sweater, The.
Oswald, A.   Pilchard-Curing Song, The.
Ou-yang Hsiu.   Fisherman.
 Old Fisherman.
Paschen.   Angling.
Porteous.   Charlie Douglas.
 Decommissioning.

Wrecked Creeves.
Price, C.   Night Fishing.
Ray, H.   Fisherman's Story, The.
Roethke.   Lady and the Bear, The.
 Pike, The.
St. John, P.   Song.
Schnackenberg.   Nightfishing.
Seiferle, R.   Face in the Depths of the Desert, The.
Shumaker.   Circle of Totems, The.
Södergran.   Net, The.
Solie, Karen.   Sturgeon.
Sŏng Kan.   Fisherman, A.
Spires.   Glass-Bottom Boat.
Stevens, W.   Thinking of a Relation between the Images of Metaphors.
Stevenson, R.   Epitaph: "Angler rose, he took his rod, The."
Stone, J.   Bass, The.
Stuart, D.   Fishing with Elvis.
Su Tung-p'o.   Epigram: "I fish for minnows in the lake."
Synge.   Beg-Innish.
Thoreau.   Salmon Brook.
Tolliver, I.   Fisher King.
Trethewey, N.   Flounder.
Trowbridge, J.   Old Lobsterman, The.
Twichell.   All of It, The.
Unknown.   Angling.
Van Winckel, N.   Nicholas by the River.
Vietnamese Oral Tradition.   Leaving the Village.
 Mandarin Who Couldn't Do Anything, The.
Voznesensky [or Voznesenskii].   Call of the Lake, The.
Wang Pin-chih.   Orchard Pavilion.
Whitman, W.   Torch, The.
Whittier.   Skipper Ireson's Ride.
Wilbur, R.   Trolling for Blues.
Wu Chia-chi.   Grain-Barge Wife, The.
Yao Sui.   Tune: "Full Court of Fragrance".
Yeats.   Fisherman, The.
Yevtushenko [or Evtushenko].   Hand-Rolled Cigarettes.
Yi I.   Where is the sixth bend?
Yi Jung.   River Darkens on an Autumn Night, The.
Young, K.   Casting.
Yu Ch'an.   Third Day of the Third Month at the Meandering River, The.
Yu Hsin.   Harmonizing with Great Officer Yan's Poem "The Start of the Fine Weather".
Yun Sŏndo.   Angler's Calendar, The.

See also **Clams and Clamming; Crabs and Crabbing**

Fitzgerald, Edward
Browning, R.   To Edward FitzGerald.
Tennyson, A.   To E. Fitzgerald.

Fitzgerald, Ella
Welish.   Textile 11.

Fitzgerald, F. Scott
Davie, D.   Garden Party, The.
Levine, P.   Two, The.

Flags
Atkins, R.   Christophe.
Bell, M.   Primer about the Flag, A.
Berry, W.   Let Us Pledge.
Bidgood.   Dragon.
Bierce.   Confederate Flags, The.
Cohan.   You're a Grand Old Flag.
Coleridge, M.   Blue and White.
Coolidge, C.   Though in should flags.
de Jesús.   Flag of Chile, The.
Fletcher, J.   Flag let loose for a day of festivity, The.
Key.   Star-Spangled Banner, The.
Mikha'il, M.   Three Flags.
Morgan, E.   Itinerary.
Neruda.   Flag, The.
Pawlikowska-Jasnorzewska, M.   Polish Colours.
Robertson, R.   Flags of Autumn.
 Flags of Autumn from Camera Obscura.
Saint.   Heart and Soul.
Thomas, F.   Behind the Nationalist's Flag.
Thomas, L.   Subway Witnesses, The.

Flags, United States
Anderson, J.   American Flag.
Berkson, B.   Gloria.
Cohan.   You're a Grand Old Flag.
Drake, J.   American Flag, The.
Fordham.   Stars and Stripes.
Key.   Star-Spangled Banner, The.
Masters, E.   Harry Williams.
Unknown.   Our Flag.
Whittier.   Barbara Frietchie.

Flamenco
Rilke.   Spanish Dancer.
Schwartz, R. L.   Flamenco Guitar.

Flamingos
Goldbarth.   Seriema Song.
Hudgins.   Flamingos Have Arrived in Ashtabula.
Rilke.   Flamingos, The.
Swenson, M.   One of the Strangest.

Flanders, Belgium
Grenfell, J.   Into Battle.
McCrae, J.   In Flanders Fields.
Roggeman.   Fata Morgana in Flanders.

Flattery
Anderson, W.   I'm Naebody Noo.
Carryl, G.   Sycophantic Fox and the Gullible Raven, The.
Donne.   Oh, let me not serve so, as those men serve.
Ewart.   It's Hard to Dislike Ewart.
Howitt, M.   Spider and the Fly, The.
Jordan, T.   Double Acrostich on Mrs Svsanna Blvnt, A.
Juana Inés de la Cruz.   On Her Portrait.
Kahn, G.   Pretty Baby.
La Fontaine.   Fox and the Crow, The.
Lee, N.   Nay, *Clytus*, you that cou'd advise.
Osgood, F.   Maiden's Mistake, The.
Porter, C.   You're the Top.
Shakespeare, W.   Sonnet 138: "When my love swear[e]s that she is made of truth."
Statius.   Thanksgiving to the Emperor Augustus Germanicus Domitianus.

Flaubert, Gustave
Hejinian.   Constantly I write this happily.
Warren, R.   Flaubert in Egypt.

Fleas
Bachner.   Little Mouse, The.
Basho.   Fleas, lice.
Donne.   Flea, The.
Issa.   Children / Don't harm the flea.
 Counting.
 Even a fleabite.
 Fleas in my hut.
 For you too, my fleas.
 For your fleas too.
 O flea! whatever you do.
 Poor quarter, A.
 So many flea bites.
 This stupid world.
 Treated shabbily / by fleas, by flies.
 Zealous flea.
Issahakian.   For you fleas too.
Košek, M.   Little Mouse, The.
Lindsay, V.   Little Turtle, The.
Löwy, H.   Little Mouse, The.
Unknown.   Poem to Answer the Question: How Old Are Fleas?
Yang Na.   Tune: "Hung Hsiu-hsieh" To a Flea.

Flies
Amichai, Y.   Course of a Life, The.
Blake, W.   Little Fly.
Bremer, C.   En la ventana.
 In the Window.
Buson.   Brushing flies.
Christopher.   Trópico.
Clare, J.   Clock-A-Clay.
D'Aquino, A.   Amoroso.
 Amorous.
Daumal.   Poetry and Thought.
Dickinson, E.   I heard a Fly buzz—when I died.
Dobson, A.   In Town.
Emmett.   Blue Tail Fly or Jimmy Cracked Corn, The.
Forrester, S.   Dog shit.

Ginsberg, A. Not a word! Not a word!
Graves, R. Blue-Fly, The.
Hirshfield, J. Theology.
Ho Ch'i-fang. Get Drunk.
Hoffman, D. Ephemeridae.
Holub. Fly, The.
  On the Origin of the Contrary.
Howitt, M. Spider and the Fly, The.
Hume, C. Million Futures of Late, A.
  True and Obscure Definitions of *Fly*, Domestic
    and Otherwise.
Issa. Don't kill that fly!
  Don't kill that poor fly!
  Flies in the temple, The.
  Flies swarming / What do they want of.
  Hey, don't swat the fly!
  If the times were good.
  I'm going out.
  I'm leaving / Now you can make love.
  Last time, I think.
  Now we are leaving.
  One human being.
  Poor quarter, A.
  Treated shabbily / by fleas, by flies.
  Where there are humans / you'll find flies.
  Winter fly, The.
Jones, M. Candle's Fly, The.
Kay, J. Virus².
Kees. What the Spider Heard.
Kerouac. In my medicine cabinet.
Kilbride, Jerry. Harpist, The.
Larkin, J. Housework.
Levis. Morning After My Death, The.
Lowell, R. Harriet ("Repeating fly, blueback,
    thumbthick—so gross, A.").
MacNeice. Mayfly.
Neruda. United Fruit Co.
Nokhem, Y. Fly, The.
Nowlan. And He Wept Aloud, So That the
    Egyptians Heard It.
Oldys. On a Fly Drinking out of [*or* from] His
    Cup.
Otten, W. J. All Soul's Day.
Ransetsu. Fly, dare take / The rice grain.
Rimington, J. God of the Flies.
Taylor, E. Upon a Spider Catching a Fly.
Teddy. At Terezin.
Tomlinson, C. Jam Trap, The.
Tranströmer. I've been in that place.
Wilbur, R. Mayflies.
Williams, C. K. My Fly.
Yang Wan-li. Cold Fly, A.
Yeats. Long-Legged Fly.

Flight
Ackerman, D. Climbing Out.
Agustini. Wings, The.
Alcott, L. Lay of a Golden Goose, The.
Allingham, W. Swing Song, A.
Basho. Singing, flying, singing.
Bishop, E. Invitation to Miss Marianne Moore.
Boland, E. Ready for Flight.
Branch, A. Ere the Golden Bowl Is Broken.
Brownstein. Stepping Out.
Brutus. Prayer: "O let me soar on steadfast
    wing."
Carroll, L. Mad Hatter's Song, The.
Char. Room in Space.
Coates, F. Unconquered Air, The.
Cocteau. Young Girl Sleeping.
Crane, H. Stars scribble on our eyes the frosty
    sagas.
De la Mare. Ride-by-Nights, The.
Dickey, J. Eagles.
Dickinson, E. Bees.
Dimitrova. Units of Measurement.
Doty, M. Flit.
Dransfield. Flying.
Duncan, R. Letting the Beat Go.
Dunn, Rhoda Hero. Aeronauts, The.
Glück, L. Parable of Flight.
Grennan. On a 3 1/2 Oz. Lesser Yellowlegs,
    Departed Boston August 28, Shot Martinique
    September 3.
Groarke, V. Flight.
Guillén, J. Flight.
Gunn, T. Flying above California.

Small Plane in Kansas.
Tamer and Hawk.
Hall, D. Old Pilot, The.
Harpur, J. I stretch my arms.
Hass, R. Our Lady of the Snows.
Hogg, J. Witch o' Fife, The.
Hopes. Birdbones.
Howes, B. Wild Geese Flying.
Hudgins. Hawk above the House, The.
Hughes, T. Swifts.
Hugo, V. Be Like the Bird.
Issa. Bats flying.
  Garden butterfly.
Jenkins, L. Flight.
Ku Sang. Wings.
Kushner, A. Airman, The.
Levine, P. Poem of Flight, The.
Lindbergh. Ascent.
Lindley, D. Nearness.
MacCaig. Solitary Crow.
Magee, J. High Flight.
Markham, M. Obedience / Intention to Hunt.
  To Understand Flight.
Mastin. Flying.
Mataka. Ornithology.
McLoughland. Crazy Boys.
Melville, H. Man-of-War Hawk, The.
Meredith, W. June: Dutch Harbor.
Moolten, D. Ode for Orville and Wilbur
    Wright.
Morgan, B. Among Goldfinches.
Morshen. Andreyevsky Church, The.
Mother Goose. Flying-Man.
Motion, A. Letter, The: "If I remember right,
    his first letter."
Nepote, M. Visitación.
  Visitation.
Noguere. Barney Bigard.
Padgett, R. Light as Air.
Pellicer, C. Flocks of Doves.
Pessoa. Rather the Bird Flying By and Leaving
    No Trace.
Pietri. How Do Your Eggs Want You (?).
Probyn. As the Flower of the Grass.
Raboni, G. Moon.
Regan, J. In Flight.
Reverdy. Adieu.
Rilke. Woman Going Blind.
Roberts, N. Gull's Flight, The.
Rodney. Bardo of the Threshold.
Rossetti, C. Fly Away, Fly Away.
Sappho. Beneath its wings.
Scott, F. Trans Canada.
Serrano, P. Flying.
  Vuelo.
Sexton. To a Friend Whose Work Has Come to
    Triumph.
Skloot. Flight: "Summer night is flying, The."
Smith, S. No Categories!
Sora. Skylark / Soaring—her young.
Ssu-ma Hsiang-ju. Mighty One, The.
Stanley, G. Hamlet says, this is a place.
  Slow.
Stevenson, R. Swing, The.
Stewart, S. Wings.
Tennyson, A. Thy spirit ere our fatal loss.
Thorpe, Peter. Take-Off.
Tranter. Lufthansa.
Unknown. Paddle-song.
Very. Birds of Passage, The.
Voigt. Effort at Speech.
Warren, R. Evening Hawk.
Witt, S. Thermal Signatures ("There is nothing
    to remember but flight. The owl's eyes
    spoke.").
Woo, M. Under a Full Moon.
Wright, J. Presentation of Two Birds to My
    Son, A.
Yeryomin. Helioptér of a skyscraper hotel.
Young, G. After Cycling.

Flirtation
Ager, M. Louisville Lou (The Vampin' Lady).
Asclepiades. Dorkion, sweet little tomboy.
  We were having fun, that devil Hermione and I.
Aytoun [*or* Ayton], R. Song, A: On His
    Mistress.

Brautigan. It's Raining in Love.
Browning, E. Lady's "Yes," The.
Campbell, D. Small-Town Gladys.
Cockburn, C. Caution, The.
Congreve, W. Doris.
Cullen, C. Timid Lover.
Dougherty. Long Coats with Deep Pockets.
Dove, R. Flirtation.
Gascoigne. For That He Looked Not upon Her.
Godfrey. Our Lady.
  Wings.
Grimké, A. Caprichosa.
Handy, J. Mata Hari Blues or Why I Will Never
    Be a Spy.
Harbach, O. She Didn't Say "Yes."
Herrick. Silken Snake, The.
Ilhami, Sultan Selim III. Coy like a lovebird,
    she flirts with hundreds, she with that lovely
    face.
Jandl, E. Romance, A.
Jordan, J. Reception, The.
Juana Inés de la Cruz. In Containing a Thought
    Satisfied with Chaste Love.
Koehler, T. Between the Devil and the Deep
    Blue Sea.
Landor, W. Alciphron and Leucippe.
Lennox, C. Art of Coquetry, The.
Logan, J. Picnic, The: "It is the picnic with
    Ruth in the spring."
Lumsden, R. Tricks for the Barmaid.
Montagu, L. To a Lady Making Love.
O'Callaghan, C. Green Baize Couplets.
Pegram, L. Yellah.
Petrarch. Complaint of a Lover Rebuked.
Porter, C. My Heart Belongs to Daddy.
Prior. Ode, An: "Merchant, to secure his
    treasure, The."
Razaf, A. Ain't Misbehavin'.
Rome, H. Nobody Makes a Pass at Me.
Shostakovskaya, I. Today I'm a proper king's
    daughter.
Smith, J. Gimme a Little Kiss (Will Ya, Huh?).
Smith, P. Nickel Wine and Deep Kisses.
Stevenson, A. Sous-Entendu.
Symons, A. At the Cavour.
Szymborska, W. Drinking Wine ("He looked,
    and gave me beauty.").
Teitelboim, D. Men.
Turk, R. Gimme a Little Kiss (Will Ya, Huh?).
Turner, C. Country Dance, A.
Unknown. Girl's Song.
  To the Tune: Beautiful Barbarian.
Verlaine. On the Grass.
Voss, F. Inspection, The.
Walwicz. Big Tease.
Wetzsteon. Urban Gallery.
Wyatt. Long love that in my thought doth
    harbo[u]r, The.
  Lover Showeth How He Is Forsaken of Such as
    He Sometime Enjoyed, The.
Yellen, J. Louisville Lou (The Vampin' Lady).

Flodden Field, Battle of (1513)
Aytoun, W. Then the Provost he uprose.
Elliot, J. Flowers of the Forest, The.
Unknown. Battle of Flodden, The.

Flood, The
Beer, P. Flood, The.
Bible, *O.T.* And God saw that the wickedness
    of man was great.
Fingueret, M. Genesis (Chapter 7, Verse 5).
Jouve. After the Deluge.
Kendall, M. Vision of Noah, The.
Lewis, C. Late Passenger, The.
Merwin. Noah's Raven.
Milton. Flood, The.
Reid, C. Stones and Bones.
Synge. 'Mergency Man, The.
Szporluk. Grass and the Sin, The.
Ullman. Rain.
Unknown. Noye, to me thou arte full able.
Ward, Geoff. What's Wrong.
Yosef, H. Reflections on a Dove.

Floods
al-Mala'ika, N. Lover River, The.
Bierds, L. Safe.
Burnside, J. Swimming in the Flood.

Dixon, M.　River, Stay 'Way from My Door.
Emerson, Claudia.　Flood: "This had happened before: rain that began."
Erdrich.　I Was Sleeping Where the Black Oaks Move.
Foulcher.　After the Flood.
Guevara, M.　After the Flood.
Holub.　Brief Thoughts on Floods.
Joyce, J.　Flood.
Khvostova, O.　Flood Songs.
Knight, E.　Poem to Galway Kinnell, A.
Lim-Wilson.　Wave, The.
Marks, Corey.　Three Bridges.
Marvell.　Eyes and Tears.
McAuley, J.　Song of Shem.
McAuliffe, J.　Flood.
Merwin.　Dictum: For a Masque of Deluge.
Murray, L.　Transposition of Clermont, The.
Niedecker.　Well, spring overflows the land.
Otten, W. J.　Mud-Flat.
Ovid.　Deucalion and Pyrrha, sole survivors of the Flood, renew Creation by casting stones behind them.
　Floods, by nature enemies to land, The.
Patton, C.　High Water Everywhere.
Pinsky.　Uncreation, The.
Powell, D. A.　Mule-drawn Scraper Packed this Earth, A: Levees.
Quarles.　On the Two Great Floods.
Rāy, D.　It's no one else's fault, Syama Ma.
Rimbaud, A.　After the Flood.
Ríos, A.　Wet Camp.
Solari, R.　Currents.
Swanger.　Natural Disaster.
Tu Fu [or Du Fu].　Rising Spring Waters.
Turner, C.　Dream, A.
Wei Ying-wu.　At Chuzhou on the Western Stream.
Wright, J.　Beanstalk, Meditated Later, The.
　Flood Year.

Florence, Italy
Agoos, J.　Portinaio.
Akhmatova, A.　Dante.
Campana.　Florence.
Hamby, B.　St. Clare's Underwear.
Levy, A.　Reminiscence, A.

Florida (state)
Becker, R.　In Pompano Beach, Florida.
Blanco, R.　Silver Sands, The.
Cross, D.　Vote, The.
Greger.　Psyche and Eros in Florida.
Haskins, L.　Prayer for the Everglades.
Hilles, R.　Yom HaShoah in Florida.
Hughes, L.　Florida Road Workers.
Lewis, G.　Pentecost.
McElroy, C.　End of Civilization as We Know It, The.
McGrath, C.　Florida.
　Florida Anasazi, The.
Moss, H.　Miami Beach.
Nezhukumatathil, A.　Tallahassee.
Serpas, M.　Faith in Florida.
Sholl.　Distinct Call of the Alligator, The.
Stevens, W.　Fabliau of Florida.
　Nomad Exquisite.
　O Florida, Venereal Soil.
Suárez, V.　Florida, La.
Vollmer.　Nursing the Sunburn.
Woolson.　Florida Beach, The.

Florists
Koch, K.　Girl and Baby Florist Sidewalk Pram Nineteen Seventy Something.
Roethke.　Old Florist.

Flour
Unknown.　Twist of hair, A.

Flowers
Abrahams, L.　After winter '76.
Aiken, C.　Letter from the Grass, A.
Al-Mushafi.　Yellow Its Color.
Alcman.　It isn't Aphrodite, but wild Eros.
Apollinaire.　Fete.
Arakida Moritaké.　Falling flower, The.
Archilochus.　She delighted to hold a slip of myrtle.
Armitage, S.　Meanwhile, somewhere in the

state of Colorado, armed to the teeth.
Ashbery, J.　Archipelago, The.
Picture of Little J. A. in a Prospect of Flowers, The.
Atkins, R.　Lines in Recollection.
Atwood.　Flowers: "Right now I am the flower girl."
Baranda, M.　Bodas de las Flores se Dan Sobre el Estigma, Las. El polen se desprende al comenzar la aurora y en un solo momento la vida se redime y entonces se retira.
Con sólo dos o tres estambres revientan las flores masculinas. Ascienden desde el fondo de sí mismas, candentes y jugosas. A mano suelta se revuelcan, se crían bajo este cielo a medias entre luz y sombra.
Weddings of flowers take place upon the stigma, The. Pollen unfastens when aurora begins, and in a moment life redeems itself and then withdraws.
With only two or three stamens, masculine flowers burst. They rise from their own depths, glistening and moist. Loosely turning over, they bring themselves up under the sky midway between light and shadow. Voiceless they wilt. Sluggish they die.
Basho.　All this foolishness.
As for the hibiscus.
As the sound fades.
Bee, A.
Breakfast enjoyed.
Bucket of azaleas, A.
Clouds of blossoms.
Clouds of cherry blossoms!
Come out to view.
From all these trees.
From every direction.
Hollyhocks, The.
Kannon's tiled temple.
Long conversations.
Lovely spring night, A.
Monk sips morning tea, A.
More than ever I want to see.
Morning glories, The.
Morning glory also, The.
On the way to the outhouse.
Petal shower, A.
Polished and polished.
Sad beauty?
Sickly.
Spring we don't see, The.
Tired.
Traveling this high.
Very brief.
When the winter chrysanthemums go.
Bécquer, G.　Black Swallows Will Return, The.
Bedregal.　Poppies.
Belieu.　My Field Guide.
　Nocturne: My Sister Life.
Beltrán, Carmen Celia.　Dried Flowers.
Benn.　Little Aster.
Betham-Edwards.　To a Llangollen Rose, the Day after It Had Been Given by Miss Ponsonby.
Bethell.　Discipline.
Betjeman.　Licorice Fields at Pontefract, The.
Bevan, M.　Confrontation with a Bouquet.
Binyon.　Harebell and Pansy.
Blake, W.　Garden of Love, The.
Bleakney, J.　Be Careful of the Lilies!
Blumenthal, M.　Deep Ecology.
Blunden.　Vlamertinghe.
Bodecker.　Garden Calendar.
Bowen, E.　Nettles in May.
Bridges, R.　I Have Loved Flowers.
Brooke, R.　Old Vicarage, Grantchester, The.
Brooks, G.　Coora Flower, The.
Browne, W.　Golden Age, The: Flower-weaving.
Bryant, W.　Death of the Flowers, The.
　Painted Cup, The.
Scene on the Banks of the Hudson, A.
When breezes are soft and skies are fair.
Bui-Burton.　My Love Is Like a Lily.
Burns, R.　O Were My Love Yon Lilac[k] Fair.
Buson.　Along the roadside.
　Around the small house.

Bat flits, A.
Before the white chrysanthemum.
Camellia, The.
Chrysanthemum growers.
Cut the peony.
End of spring, The.
Evening primrose.
Fallen petals of red plum.
Fallen red blossoms.
Flowers offered to the Buddha.
Having reddened the plum blossoms.
Heavy cart rumbles by, A.
I went down the bank to pick fragrant plants.
In the white plum blossoms.
Iris, An.
Lighting the lantern.
Mason's finger, The.
Not cherry blossoms.
Peonies scattering.
Peony petals scatter, The.
People visiting all day.
Plum blossoms here and there.
Plum blossoms in bloom.
Plum blossoms scent.
Pure white plum blossoms.
Short night, The.
Sleeping late.
Tea flowers.
They swallow clouds.
White blossoms of the pear.
Calil, A.　Blouse of Felt.
Campbell, C.　When midst the summer-roses the warm bees.
Carruth, H.　Of Distress Being Humiliated by the Classical Chinese Poets.
Sonnet: "To see a woman long oppressed by fear."
Celan.　Psalm.
Psalm: "No one moulds us again out of earth and clay."
Ceravolo.　Dangers of the Journey to the Happy Land.
Chase, N.　My Mother, Listening to Flowers.
Chatterton.　There Lackethe Somethynge Stylle.
Chazal, M.　It was / so hot.
Chiu Tsz-yung.　Lament for Fortune's Frailty, A.
Chiyojo.　From the mind.
Cho Chihun.　Falling Petals.
Ch'ŏn Yanghŭi.　At Moments Like This, I Always Blush.
　Black Cove.
Chŏng Chiyong.　Paengnokdam: White Deer Lake.
Chu Shu-chen.　Plaint.
Clare, J.　First Love.
　Primrose, The.
Cobbold, E.　On Some Violets Planted in My Garden by a Friend.
Coleridge, M.　Poison Flower, The.
　September.
Coleridge, S.　Keepsake, The.
Constable, H.　Of His Mistress, upon Occasion of Her Walking in a Garden.
Coolbrith.　My Cloth of Gold.
Cope, W.　Flowers: "Some men never think of it."
Couto.　Flowers and Water.
Cowper, W.　Winter Walk at Noon, The.
Crane, H.　To Emily Dickinson.
Crapsey.　Guarded Wound, The.
Creeley.　Flower, The: "I think I grow tensions."
Crouch, S.　Chops Are Flyin.
Cucchi, M.　Like the Chinese, I too am going to.
Cummings, E. E.　If everything happens that can't be done.
Curry, N.　Poppy Heads.
Curtis, T.　Queen's Tears.
Davies, W. H.　Hill-Side Park, The.
Day Lewis.　Two Songs.
De la Mare.　Two Gardens.
Delgado, J.　Chuparosa.
DeSylva, B. G.　April Showers.
Dickinson, E.　Apparently with no surprise.
　Clover's simple Flame, The.
　Come slowly—Eden!
　Daisy follows soft the Sun, The.

Did the Harebell loose her girdle.
My nosegays are for Captives.
Divakaruni. Alley of Flowers, The.
Dobell, S. Chanted Calendar, A.
Doolittle, H. At Baia.
Evening.
Garden.
Sea Rose.
Sea Violet.
White World.
Doty, M. Fog.
Lilacs in NYC.
Doubleday, T. Poppies, that scattered o'er this arid plain.
Douglas, K. Desert Flowers.
Douglas, L. Two Loves.
Dove, R. In the Old Neighborhood.
Dowson. Villanelle of Marguerites.
Duncan, R. Glimpse, A.
Eberhart, R. Ceremony by the Sea, A.
Eichner, Maura. Summer: "Fills the white enamel bucket, overflows."
Elmslie, S. Forecast: Nadja.
Emerson, R. Humble-Bee, The.
Rhodora, The [On Being Asked Whence Is the Flower].
Engels, J. Garden.
Enright, D. Flowers.
Evance, S. To a Violet.
Fainlight, R. Archive Film Material.
Faiz. Fragrant Hands.
Fay, J. Flowers.
Ferguson, G. Fear of the Future.
Scan.
Field. Irises.
Penetration.
Sullenness.
Tiger-Lilies.
Unbosoming.
Fishman, L. Promiscuity.
Foley, K. Matching Flowers.
Follain. This Plant, So Exceptional.
Forrester, S. Only one flower.
Foster, A. Field.
Francis, R. Bouquets.
Freneau. And by that light around the dome appear'd.
Wild Honey Suckle, The.
Frost, R. Subverted Flower, The.
Tuft of Flowers, The.
Wind and Window Flower.
Fu. Flower.
Fuhaku. So very still, even.
Gandlevsky, S. Oh, how the lilacs are this May!
Bulging-large bunches fell.
Gerhardt, I. G. M. Rejected Gift, The.
Rejected Gift, The.
Gezelle. Ego Flos.
Ghalib, M. Not All, Only a Few, Return as the Rose or the Tulip.
Ginsberg, A. In back of the real.
Looking over my shoulder.
Glück, L. Mock Orange.
Goethe. Found.
Goldberg, B. Blossom at the End of the Body.
Lilies at Night.
Góngora y Argote. Allegory of the Brevity of Things Human.
Goodison. Kenscoff.
Graham, J. Opulence.
Graves, R. Gardener.
Troll's Nosegay, The.
Greenberg, A. Wintering Over at the End of the Century.
Groarke, V. Way It Goes, The.
Guest, B. Heavy Violets.
Valorous Vine.
Gunn, T. Messenger, The.
Moly.
Hadas, R. Humble Herb Is Rival to Prozac.
Hahn, O. Gladioli by the Sea.
Hahn, S. Perennial.
Hall, H. Things That Grow.
Hamburger, M. Weeding.
Hamilton, S. Poppy, The.
Harnick. Someone's Been Sending Me Flowers.

Harter. Tulip.
Harwood, G. Sea Anemones, The.
Hayden, R. Night-Blooming Cereus, The.
Healy, R. Primula veris.
Heath, R. On Clarastella Walking in Her Garden.
Hecht, A. Illumination.
Hemans. Bring Flowers.
Night-Blooming Flowers.
Henry, B. Look Around.
Herbert, G. Flower, The.
Life.
Herrick. Meditation for His Mistress[e], A.
To Blossoms.
To Daffodils [or Daffadills].
To Violets.
Hidalgo, J. Flowers under the Dead.
Hildebrandt, Z. Persephone.
Hodges, Janice W. Annuals and Perennials.
Hoffenstein. You buy some flowers for your table.
Hoitsu. Buddha / Cherry flowers.
Hope, A. Flower Poem.
Hopes. If the flowers could ask me.
Housman. I hoed and trenched and weeded.
Hsüeh T'ao [or Xue Tao]. Gazing at Spring.
Hughes, T. Daffodils.
Humphrey, D. April in Houston.
No Immunity.
Hunt, L. Noble range it was, of many a rood, A.
Hwang Tonggyu. One Flower and Another Flower.
Ibarbourou. Life-Hook.
Iio Sogi. Spring.
Ikkyu Sojun. Nobody told the flowers to come up nobody.
Ilkov, Ani. Green and Gold.
Islām, N. Talk to me, javas, talk to me.
Issa. Blossoming plum!
Flowering plum, A.
In the midst of this world.
In this world.
Moon and the flowers, The.
Moon, plum blossoms.
Never forget / We walk on hell.
New foal, The.
Sheet of rain, A.
Short night / Scarlet flower.
Under the image of Buddha.
What a strange thing!
Windy fall.
World of trials, A.
Izumi. I cannot say.
Jackson, R. Lady's Way.
Jacobsen, R. Meadowsweet.
Jamie, K. Flower-sellers, Budapest.
God Almighty the First Garden Made.
Jarmain. El Alamein.
Jones, P. In the Formal Garden.
In the Park.
Juan Chi. Mujin Flowers Blossom on the Rolling Graves, The.
Kang [Grossjean], Ok-Ku [or Ok-Koo]. Were I a Flower.
Kaya Shirao. Moonlit night / By melon flowers.
Kelly, B. Arguments of Everlasting.
Kennelly. Poem from a Three Year Old.
Kenyon, J. Peonies at Dusk.
Khlebnikov, V. Hey . . . y! Uh . . . hm!, covered with sweat.
Ki no Tsurayuki. Hue is as rich, The.
On a spring hillside.
Wind that scatters, The.
Kikaku. May he who brings / Flowers tonight.
Kim Ch'unsu [or Chun-soo]. Flower.
Kim Ku. I Spy the Three-Colored Peach Blossom.
Kim Sowŏl. Mountain Flowers.
King, H. Contemplation upon Flowers, A.
Kinnell. Flower Herding on Mount Monadnock.
Kistler, W. Kyoto 1—Kinkaku-ji.
Kitahara Hakushū. Spider Lilies.
Komunyakaa, Y. Venus's-flytraps.
Kuan Han-ch'ing. To the Tune "A Spray of Flowers" (Not Giving In to Old Age).

Lady Ise. Flower of waves, A.
Landon. Death in the Flower.
Landor, W. Hearts-Ease.
Lawrence, D. H. Andraitx—Pomegranate Flowers.
Bavarian Gentians.
Le Gallienne. Library in a Garden, A.
Lee, L. Irises.
Leopardi. Upon the arid shoulder.
Levertov. Métier of Blossoming, The.
Li Ch'ing-chao. To the Tune: Partridge Sky.
Tune: "Airing Inmost Feelings".
Tune: "Magnolia Flowers".
Tune: "Partridge Sky".
Li'aibi, S. Soul of a pebble on top of the mountain, The.
Lili'u-o-ka-lani. Ku'u Pua I Paoakalani.
Sanoe.
Liu, T. Brooklyn Botanic Garden, The.
Liu Yu Hsi. Red Blossoms.
Long, H. Day and Night.
Lowell, A. Afterglow.
Weather-Cock Points South, The.
Lu Yu. Wild Flower Man, The.
Luschei, G. Arrangement.
Mackenzie, K. Ginger-flowers.
Madgett. Woman with Flower.
Magdeburg, Mechthild von. How God Comes to the Soul.
Mahadevi. So long as this breath fills your nostrils.
Mahapatra, A. Tamburā.
Man Giac. Rebirth.
Mansfield, K. Secret Flowers.
Martínez, V. Into the Next One.
Marvell. Picture of Little T. C. in a Prospect of Flowers, The.
Masaoka Shiki. Thing long forgotten.
Masters, E. Serepta Mason.
McGuckian. Flower Master, The.
Orchid House, The.
Meenakshi. If Hot Flowers Come to the Street.
Middleton, David. Embertide in Advent.
Mistral, G. Flower of Air, The.
Mitford. Forget-Me-Not, The.
Moritake. Those falling blossoms.
Mun Chônghui. Single Blossom, A.
Muske, C. Fault, The.
Jacaranda.
Muso Soseki. Dry Tree.
Fragrance of the Udumbara, The.
House of Spring.
Peak of the Held-Up Flower, The.
Plum Window.
Myles, E. Flowers.
Maxfield Parrish.
Naden. Poet and Botanist.
Naito Joso. How green— / Flowering slopes.
These branches.
Newburn, L. Office Geraniums.
Nezahualcoyotl. Flowers of Red and Blue.
Nezval. Lilac by the Museum on St. Wenceslas Square, The.
Niedecker. Something in the water.
Nishiyama Soin. Cherry blossoms / dizzying.
Notley. White Peacock, The.
O'Hara, F. Poem: "Green things are flowers too."
Ohnishi, T. Blossoms in the Wind.
Okamoto. Tanka: "Flower blooms, A."
Oliver, D. Walnut and Lily.
Oliver, M. How Everything Adores Being Alive.
Olson, C. Perfume, The / of flowers! A haw.
Ombres. Twelve.
Onitsura. Cherry blossoms, The.
True obedience.
Osborne, J. Naming of Flowers, The.
Ōshima Ryōta. Pure brush-clover / Basket of flowers.
Ovid. Venus and Adonis.
Padgett, R. Flower's Escape.
Page, P. Metal and the Flower, The.
Pak Sŏwôn. Plantain.
Perk. Iris.
Pittman, Al. Lupines.

Po Chü-i. Buying Flowers.
Flower, A.
Flower Market, The.
Planting Flowers on the Eastern Embankment.
Pogson, P. Amaryllis Belladonna.
In Dreams.
Pope, A. Garden, The.
Then thick as locusts black'ning the ground.
Pound, E. Ts'ai Chi'h.
Prévert. At the Florist's.
Prince, F.T. Babiaantje, The.
Pyungyang Ungee. Flowers in the Garden.
Radiguet. Poem: "Red eiderdown at the window, A."
Rakosi. Menage, The.
ZZZZZ.
Ramsdell, H. Moveable Figures.
Ransetsu. On the old plum tree.
Ray, N. Last Flower, The.
Renk, Charlotte. Mistletoe Kills.
Rexroth, K. Blues: "Tops of the higher peaks, The."
Reyes, A. Menace of the Flower, The.
Rice, D. Ambrosia.
Riley, J. At the Stanley Spencer Exhibition.
Roberts, K. Cantata, 8: "Early March, trickle and rush of ice melt in mountains."
Robertson, Lexie Dean. Memorabilia.
Robinson, A. Posies.
Unum est Necessarium.
Rodriguez, J. Nasturtium Scanned.
Roethke. Carnations.
Geranium, The.
Shape of the Fire, The.
Roscoe, W. Camellia, The.
Rossetti, C. Why did baby die. . .?
Rossetti, D. Woodspurge, The.
Sakhltkhutsishvili, U. Soldiers: "Crossing the mountains."
Samara, M. Door of Roses.
Samawi, S. Dream of a Snow Flower, The.
Sanpu. First cherry blossoms.
Sappho. And you, Dika, put lovely garlands round your hair.
Satyamurti. In-Patient.
Scalise, G. Dora Markus and Her Actors.
Schilpp, M. Triage.
Schubert, D. Kind Valentine.
Schuyler, J. Korean Mums.
Roof Garden.
Scott, S. Flowers and Trees.
Seward. To the Poppy.
Shakespeare, W. Sonnet 99: "Forward violet thus did I chide, The."
Shapiro, K. Cut Flower, A.
Editing *Poetry*.
Shen Manyuan. Her Tiara Flowers.
Shepherd, R. White Days.
Shumaker. Ajo Lily.
Shunzei. Shall I see it again.
"Shunzei's Daughter." Brought by the breeze.
Siegel, J. Wild Hyacinth.
Sitwell, Dame Edith. Swans, The.
Sitwell, Sir Osbert. Kingcups.
Skelton, J. To Mistress Margery Wentworth.
To Mistress [*or* Maystres] Isabell Pennell.
Slater, E. Search.
Smart, C. For the doubling of flowers is the improvement of the gard'ner's talent.
Smith, C. Sonnet Written at the Close of Spring [*or* Elegiac Sonnet].
Sŏ Chŏngju. Peony Afternoon.
Wanderer's Bouquet.
Sobaku. Cherry blossoms.
Steele, T. Fae.
Stein, G. She may count three little daisies very well.
Stern, G. December 1, 1994.
Stesichoros. They flung many quinces toward the chariot.
Stevens, W. Room on a Garden, A.
Stevenson, A. Himalayan Balsam.
Stevenson, R. Flowers, The.
To A Gardener.
Storm, T. Woman's Ritornelle.
Su Tung-p'o. Roadside flowers are blooming,

butterflies on the wing.
Wealth and honor in life were dew on the grass leaf.
Wild roadside flowers, blooming in boundless numbers.
Subbarao, R. Chained.
Sung Tzu-hou. Song: "On the Eastern Way at the city of Lo-yang."
Swinburne. Before the Mirror.
Sylvester, J. Garden, The.
Taggard. Weed, The.
Tan Taigi. "Don't touch!" my host cried.
T'ang Yin. Inscription for a Portrait.
Taylor, J. Violet, The.
Teasdale. Summer Night, Riverside.
Tennyson, A. City Child, The.
Come into the Garden, Maud.
Flower in the Crannied Wall.
Tighe. Written at Rossana. November 18, 1799.
Tillema, M. Considering Tulips.
Tulips.
Todhunter. Moment, A.
Townsend, A. Purple Loosestrife.
Tretheway. Florilegium.
Tsung Ch'en. Song of Selling Flowers.
Tu Fu [*or* Du Fu]. Another Spring ("White birds over the grey river.").
Shady, Shady.
Spring Night, Happy Rain.
Sunset ("Sunset glitters on the beads.").
Walking Alone by the Riverbank Seeking Flowers.
Tuckerman, F. Coralie.
Unknown. At the wind that blew last night.
Chalcan Female Song.
Dedication: "If you would let me leave."
I have a fading flower in my hand.
Just because of you.
Of a rose, a lovely rose.
Spring Blossoms into Flower.
To learn how to die.
Wind Last Night Blew Down.
Upton, L. Imagination of Flowers, The.
Vaughan, H. I Walked [*or* Walkt *or* Walk'd] the Other Day to Spend My Hour.
Velichansky, A. Kalmyk poppies, horde of pan-Mongol tulips.
Very. Autumn Flowers.
Columbine, The.
Lament of the Flowers, The.
Vilariño. Like a Floating Jasmine.
Waldner, Liz. Determinate Inflorescence: Ephemera.
Wang, J. Tune: "Magnolia Flowers".
Wang Wei. Hsin-I Village.
Wat. Joke, A.
Watkins, V. Music of Colours: The Blossom Scattered.
Music of Colours—White Blossom.
Watts, Enos D. Crocuses and Crown-of-Thorns.
Wellesley. Walled Garden.
Whitman, S. Morning-Glory, The.
Whitman, W. Orange Buds by Mail from Florida.
These I Singing in Spring.
Wilbur, R. In a Churchyard.
Williams, K. January 8, 1996.
Williams, W. Chicory and Daisies.
Flowers by the Sea ("When over the flowery, sharp pasture's.").
For What It's Worth.
Iris.
It Is a Small Plant.
Ivy Crown, The.
Locust Tree in Flower, The.
Pathology literally speaking is a flower garden.
Pink Locust, The.
Pot of Flowers, The.
Yellow Flower, The.
Winters, Y. Cool Nights.
Wintu Oral Tradition. Minnows and Flowers.
Strange Flowers.
There Above.
Wood, S. Carnation. Lily, Lily, Rose.
Wordsworth, W. Primrose of the Rock, The.
Wright, J. Therapy.

Wunderlich, M. Amaryllis.
Yi Sang. Flowering Tree.
Precipice.
Yi Yŏnju. Clinic in a Dangerous Season 1, A.
Yu Ŭngbu. Do you say the wind blew last night.
Zabolotsky [*or* Zabolotskii]. All That My Soul Possessed.
Zanzotto. Eva, forma futuri.
Zawgee. Way of the Water-Hyacinth, The.
Zenmaro. Tanka: "No news of him."
Zucker, R. Portrait of Unknown.

Flutes
Browning, E. Musical Instrument, A.
Cho Chihun. As I Play the Flute.
Citino. Neanderthal, with Help from Cave and Bear, Invents the Flute.
De Mello Breyner. Flute, The.
Dryden, J. Song for St Cecilia's Day, 1687, A.
Gaspar, Lorand. Flute Player.
Hongo. Something Whispered in the *Shakuhachi*.
Issa. Holes in the wall, The.
Li Ho. Song: Dragons at Midnight.
Song of the Magic Strings.
Li Po. Listening to a Flute on a Spring Night in Lo-yang.
Li Yi. Listening to a Flute at Night near the City Wall.
On Hearing a Flute at Night from the Wall of Shouxiang.
Lowell, A. Music.
Mirabai [*or* Mira Bai]. Song of the flute, O sister, is madness, The.
Muldoon, P. Lass of Aughrim, The.
Okudzhava. How the young flutist smiles.
Pak P'aengnyŏn. Upon Listening to the Flute.
Pindar. For Midas, the Man from Akragas First in the Flute Match.
Rifat. Flute, The.
Rumi. Listen to the reed-flute telling its tales.
Sama, B. Song, The.
Sastri, D. In Search of Krishna.
Scofield, G. His Flute, My Ears.
Seale, J. Playing the Flute for the TMR Class.
Sin Sukchu. Upon Listening to the Flute.
Sŏng [*or* Sung] Sammun. Upon Listening to the Flute.
Unknown. Old [*or* Ould] Orange Flute, The.
Watson, A. Die Zauberflöte.
Williams, B. Night Flute, The.
Yi Kae. Upon Listening to the Flute.
Yi Sŏkhyŏng. Upon Listening to the Flute.
Flying Dutchman (ship)
Livingstone, D. Vanderdecken.
Flying Saucers
Kinsella, J. Bright Cigar-Shaped Object Hovers over Mount Pleasant, A.
Foals
Hughes, T. Yesterday He Was Nowhere to Be Found.
Issa. Its mother on guard.
New foal, The.
Juhász, F. Birth of the Foal.
Kavanagh, P. Consider the Grass Growing.
Watkins, V. Foal.
See also **Horses**
Fog
Bachmann. Fog Land.
Bartlett, B. 2. To a Northern Gannet.
Berssenbrugge. Fog: "Hundreds of millions of years ago, days were many hours shorter."
Booth, P. Fog-Talk.
Clampitt. Fog.
Clarke, G. Foghorns.
Dickinson, E. Sun and Fog Contested, The.
Doty, M. 2. Beach Roses.
1. Jade.
Drinan. Florence: Sleeping in Fog.
Eichner, Maura. Message from Inland.
Feldman, A. This Fog.
Gershwin, I. Foggy Day (in London Town), A.
Gonzales, Jacinta. Hey, fog, go home.
Greenwald, T. And, Hinges.
Guiney. Fog.

Gunn, T.   Night Piece, The: "Fog drifts slowly down the hill, The."
Hudgins.   In.
Issa.   Seen.
Jarrell, R.   Front, A.
Jeffers, R.   Boats in a Fog.
Kang Ŭn'gyo.   In the Fog.
Merwin.   Fog-Horn.
Montague, J.   Point, The.
Moore, L.   In the Fog.
Oppen.   Forms of Love, The.
Ponge.   Trees That Come Undone within a Sphere of Fog.
Rexroth, K.   I am sad this morning.
Reznikoff.   I like this secret walking.
Sandburg, C.   Fog: "Fog comes, The."
Soto, Maria Viviana.   Hey, fog, go home.
Sutter.   Hoarfrost and Fog.
Thoreau.   Fog.
Unknown.   Northern har, A.
Young, D.   Cotton in a Pill Bottle.
Young, G.   Fog descends over the tidal surge and the shallow lagoons.
Zukofsky, L.   Ferry.

Folk Singers
Aubert, A.   James Baldwin, 1924–1987.
Mitchell, A.   Victor Jara of Chile.

Folly
Deloney.   Long have I lov'd this bonny Lasse.
Drayton.   As Love and I.
Fan Chung-yen.   Tune: "Trimming the Silver Lamp".
Goldsmith, O.   When Lovely Woman Stoops to Folly.
Han-shan.   Yesterday I went to a cloud observatory.
Juan Chi.   Elder lives by the side of the river, An.
Mapanje.   On His Royal Blindness Paramount Chief Kwangala.
Pope, A.   Of all the causes which conspire to blind.
Prior.   Fable, A: "In Æsop's tales an honest wretch we find."
Sandburg, C.   They have yarns / Of a skyscraper so tall they had to put hinges.
Suckling, S.   Barley-Break , A.
Thomas, E.   Some Eyes Condemn.
Traherne.   To the Same Purpos[e].
Unknown.   Rakes of Mallow, The.
Winnebago Oral Tradition.   Felix White Sr.'s Introduction to Wakjankaga.
Yeats.   Down by the Salley Gardens.

Food
Adamo.   Roches Moutonnees.
Agran, R.   Cakes Continue to Rise.
Aguilar-Cariño.   Dinakdakan.
Alexander, E.   Minnesota Fats Describes His Youth.
  Who I Think You Are.
Ap Glyn, Ifor.   Englyns.
Armstrong, J.   Advice to the Stout.
  Gastric Muse, The.
Baratier, D.   She Wants.
Barkan.   Two Grandmas.
Barker, G.   How Many Apples Grow on the Tree?
Barrows, A.   Pleasures of the Flesh.
Basho.   Wrapping dumplings in.
Belloc.   On Jam.
Bentley, J.   Dead Mouth, High Weather, Mixture.
Berrigan, A.   Looking Up My Balance.
Blount, R.   Song to Onions.
Bond, S.   Tuesday Night Affair.
Brinks, Dave.   Please the Carrots.
Brown, L.   Encyclopedia Botanica.
Brown, S.   After Winter.
Brownstein.   Jet Set Melodrama.
Budy.   On High Street.
Burns, R.   To a Haggis.
Bush, N.   Noodling.
Cabico, R.   Afternoon in Pangasinan with No Electricity, An.
Cartwright, K.   ALL-YOU-CAN-EAT / catfish houses.

Cavendish, M.   Dissert, A.
Cendrars.   Menus.
Cisneros, S.   Good Hot Dogs.
Cleary, B.   Chicken & Sex.
Cohen, Lynne.   Body Doubled.
Colby, T.   Labor Day Picnic Poem.
Coward.   Any Part of Piggy.
Cross, D.   Massimo del Panino, Il.
  Painted Ladies, The.
Dailey.   S'what Up.
Dangel.   After Forty Years of Marriage, She Tries a New Recipe for Hamburger Hot Dish.
Dauenhauer.   How to Make Good Baked Salmon from the River.
Davidson, M.   Framing.
Davies, Grahame.   Red.
Davies, J.   Author Loving These Homely Meats, The.
Davis, K.   Searching for Mooncakes.
De la Mare.   Miss T.
Delgado, J.   Two Timer.
Denby.   Summer: "I stroll on Madison in expensive clothes, sour."
Deschamps, E.   Ballade 2.
Dickinson, E.   Art thou the thing I wanted?
Dizhur.   Here is an island. Here is a house on stilts.
Dunn, D.   Ratatouille.
Eady.   Chittlin's.
Elfyn, Menna.   Sardines.
Elmslie, K.   History of France.
Erdrich.   Windigo.
Evans, M.   When in Rome.
Evasco, M.   Baked Oysters Rockefeller.
Fergusson.   To the Principal and Professors of the University of St Andrews, on Their Superb Treat to Dr Samuel Johnson.
Flanders, J.   Dandelion Greens.
Foreman, Paul.   Pecans.
Freeman, Jessica.   Customer #!
  Ewe's Candy Canes Red Sea Outerbank.
Gaspar de Alba.   Making Tortillas.
Gloria.   Assimilation.
  Milkfish.
Gonzales, R.   Praise the Tortilla, Praise the Menudo, Praise the Chorizo.
González, R.   Grace.
Greenwald, T.   Coordinating cities gulls still gull, and, arms binged with wine, as wine.
Grieves, C.   Connuche.
Griffin, S.   I Sit.
Groarke, V.   Imperial Measure.
Han-shan.   Unfortunate human disorder, The.
Hass, R.   Feast, The.
Herbert, W.   To a Mousse.
Herrick.   To His Book[e] ("Make haste away, and let one be.").
  Upon Jack and Jill: Epigram.
Hirschman, J.   Tremor, The.
Hoffman, D.   Lobsterpot Labyrinths.
Hudgins.   Gift, The: "They hung the lambs and cut their white throats. Blood."
Iglesias, H.   Feeding Frenzy.
Issa.   Here in Shinano.
Jackson, B.   Riot at Winchell's.
Jarnot, L.   They Loved These Things Too.
Johns.   Salon de Vers.
Jones, Einir.   Cockles.
Jones, T.   Meal, The.
Jonson, B.   Inviting a Friend to Supper.
Kasdorf.   When Our Women Go Crazy.
Keller, G.   Now Have I Fed and Eaten Up the Rose.
King, B.   Pessimist, The.
Kinzie.   Heat-heavy creatures.
Kleinschmidt.   Cooking to Music.
Kollar.   Sunday Matinee.
Kovacic, K.   Covered Dish.
Lavut, N.   About Love.
Lee, L.   Eating Alone.
Leonard, T.   Song: "Yi surta."
Levine, P.   Simple Truth, The.
LittleDog, Pat.   Crossing the River to juárez.
Liu, T.   Sunday.
Llewellyn-Williams.   Feeding the Bat.
Lyly, J.   Serving Men's Song, A.

MacDiarmid, H.   In the Pantry.
Magrelli.   We go through life this way.
Major, C.   Beaulieu.
Martial.   You sold a slave just yesterday.
McDonald, C.   Fresh Mussels.
McDonald, W.   Children of Saigon, The.
McKay, C.   Tropics in New York, The.
McOrlan.   Horse Butcher, The.
Merrill, J.   Midnight Snack, The.
Mistral, G.   House, The.
Mitchell, A.   Giving Potatoes.
Moore, M.   To a Chameleon.
Moore, T.   Oh Dick! You may talk of your writing and reading.
Morikawa Kyoroku.   Even the dumplings / Are smaller.
Naito Joso.   Gruel heaped / In a perfect bowl.
Nash, O.   Parsnip, The.
  Private Dining Room, The.
Nelson, M.   Brightness.
Nemerov.   Grace to Be Said at the Supermarket.
Nichols, G.   Like a Beacon.
North, M.   Red Desiré.
November, Deena.   Always Secondary.
Nye, N.   Lunch in Nablus City Park.
O'Callaghan.   Federal Case.
Olds, S.   Unswept, The.
Orton, B.   Bacchanal.
Padgett, R.   Lucky Strikes.
Parker, A.   God of Pepper, The.
Parra, N.   Inflation.
Peacock, M.   Devolution.
Phillips, C.   Sunday.
Piercy.   Attack of the Squash People.
Pierpoint, K.   In the Outhouse.
Po Chü-i.   Eating Bamboo-Shoots.
Pogson, P.   Fifteen.
Powell, D. A.   Minotaur at Supper, The: Spare the Noritake and the Spode.
Ransetsu.   Five rice dumplings.
Ransom, J.   Survey of Literature.
Reznikoff.   Showing a torn sleeve, with stiff and shaking fingers the old man.
Robles.   Feasting with Etang a Hundred Times Around.
Rosen, M.   Christmas Dinner.
"Sagittarius.".   Passionate Profiteer to His Love, The.
St. John, P.   Biological Light.
Salaam.   Makes You Go Oohhh!
Sallah, T.   No Argument Tonight.
Schwartz, R. L.   Midnight Supper.
Scott, S.   Fire, The.
Seltzer, D.   Blessing over Bread, A.
Silano, M.   Sweet Red Peppers, Sun-Drieds, the Hearts of Artichokes.
Smith, S.   Salad, A.
Snyder, G.   Song of the Taste.
Soto.   Soup, The.
Steele, T.   Joseph.
Stein, G.   Mutton.
Strand.   Pot Roast.
Su, A.   Four Sonnets about Food.
Swift, J.   Epigram on Fasting.
Swirszczynska [*or Swir*].   White Wedding Slippers.
Tallmountain.   Good Grease.
Tammaro.   'Merican Fst Fd.
Tate, J.   Sadness of My Neighbors, The.
Taylor, C.B.   Forever Arima.
Taylor, E.   Meditation 150 (Second Series).
Tripp.   Caroline Street, Cardiff.
Tsang, L.   Lunching.
Unknown.   Dish for a Poet, A.
  Elegant Things.
  I Had But Fifty Cents.
  Miss Foggerty's Cake.
  On Tomato Ketchup.
  Scones.
  Spring from the earth, food for our children. Give us good health. Let us grow up, and become ripe.
Yu-li: Fine Fish to Net.
Untermeyer, L.   Food and Drink.
Updike.   On the Inclusion of Miniature Dinosaurs in Breakfast Cereal Boxes.

Van de Woestijne.　I Am the Hazel-Nut.
Very.　My Meat and Drink.
Vietnamese Oral Tradition.　Across the Field of the Old Corporal.
Wah.　Father / Mother Haibun #20.
Weigl.　Last Lie, The.
Wells, C.　Universal Favorite, The.
Wilbur, R.　Rillons, Rillettes.
Williams, F.　Reply (Crumped on Her Desk).
Yana Oral Tradition.　Now then.
Yang Shih-ch'i.　Following the Rhymes of Shao-pao Huang's Poem on Being Moved While Visiting the Farmers.
Yao Sui.　Tune: "Full Court of Fragrance".
Young, K.　Everywhere Is out of Town.
Yuson.　Love Before Dinner.
See also **Cooking and Cooks; Eating; Gluttony and Gluttons**

Food Poisoning
Foster, J.　Seder.
Kirby, D.　Moderation Kills (Excusez-Moi, Je Suis Sick as a Dog).

Fools
Adcock, F.　Things: "There are worse things than having behaved foolishly in public."
Adler, R.　Hey There.
Baudelaire.　Joker, A.
Berlin.　Fools Fall in Love.
Bernard [*or* Bernart] de Ventadour [*or* Ventadorn].　To see the lark, delighted, dare.
Berrigan, D.　We Will Now Hear the Word of God from Each of Our Beloved Chaplains.
Bhartrihari.　Man May Tear a Jewel, A.
Blake, W.　Lacedemonian Instruction.
Bricusse, L.　What Kind of Fool Am I?
Browne, W.　Love Who Will, for I'll Love None.
Burns, R.　Holy Fair, The.
Chénier.　Happy is he given to sage disciplines.
Collins, B.　Nightclub.
Dobell, S.　Liberty to M. le Diplomate.
Donne.　Triple Fool, The.
Egerton, S.　Liberty, The.
"Ephelia.".　To a Proud Beauty.
Farquhar.　Song, A.
Feinstein, Sandy.　Catch, The.
Gershwin, I.　Fun to be Fooled.
Hammerstein.　Gentleman Is a Dope, The.
Harburg.　Fun to Be Fooled.
Hart, L.　You Are Too Beautiful.
Jonson, B.　On Don Surly.
　To Fool or Knave.
Landor, W.　Plays.
Levertov.　Man Wearing Bird.
Logau.　Fools and Wise Men.
Mackenzie, K.　Fool, The.
Meredith, G.　Camelus Saltat: Continued.
Newley, A.　What Kind of Fool Am I?
Passerat.　Sonnet Addressed to Henry III on the Death of Thulène, the King's Fool.
Ralegh, S.　Sir Walter Ra[u]le[i]gh to His Son[ne].
Ristovic.　Untitled.
Ross, J.　Hey There.
Shakespeare, W.　Motley's the Only Wear.
Sill.　Fool's Prayer, The.
Thoreau.　Any fool can make a rule.
Tranter.　Some sports are odious, but.
Unknown.　Bungle-man, The.
　Silly Boy.
Waddington, M.　Thou Didst Say Me.
Washington, N.　My Foolish Heart.
Yeats.　Symbols.
See also **Jesters**

Football
Alexie.　At Navajo Monument Valley Tribal School (from the Photograph by Skeet Mcauley).
Beatty, P.　Independent Study.
Coates, T.　Gale Sayers.
Conway, J.　This Is What Happens When You Let Hamlet Play Quarterback.
Cooper, D.　After School, Street Football, Eighth Grade.
Davis, T.　Elkhart, Indiana.

Dickey, J.　Bee, The.
　For the Death of Vince Lombardi.
González, R.　Crush.
House, Boyce.　Mocking-bird, A.
Jackson, R.　For Thurman Thomas.
Jarrell, R.　Say Good-bye to Big Daddy.
Jenkins, L.　Football: "I take the snap from center, fake to the right, fade back."
Komunyakaa, Y.　White Port and Lemon Juice.
MacDonald, C.　Kilgore Rangerette Whose Life Was Ruined, The.
Pinter, H.　American Football (A Reflection upon the Gulf War).
Sale, Richard.　Delayed Love Poem to Odem, Texas.
Wright, J.　Autumn Begins in Martins Ferry, Ohio.
Wrigley, A.　Owdham Footbo'.
See also **Soccer**

Forbidden Fruit
Cernuda.　I'll Tell You How You Were Born.
Garrett, E.　Moules à la Marinière.
Millay, E.　Never May the Fruit Be Plucked.
Milton.　As when of old some orator renowed.
Shakespeare, W.　Take, O Take Those Lips Away.
Sharpless.　*Paradise Lost* as a Haiku.

Forbidden Love
Baggett.　Anna: *Rose of Sharon.*
Brown, L.　After Sappho.
Byron, G.　Juan and Haidee [from Cantos 2-4].
Cummings, P.　Hamlet to Ophelia.
McFadden, D.　1. Il Vecchio Is Our Love.
Moore, T.　Fire-Worshippers, The.
Phaire, D.　Irresistible Light, An.
Ramireddy, D.　Tryst.
Stern, G.　Another Insane Devotion.
Thomas, L.　Souvenir of the Manassah Ball.
Trench, H.　Killary.
Unknown.　Come and kiss me without thinking of the danger. What does it matter if they kill you?
　Do not hold me too closely in your arms.
　Give me your hand, my love, and let us go into the fields.
　I love! I love! I shall not hide it. I'll not deny it.
　If you are looking for the warmth of my arms, you will have to risk your life.
　In secret I burn, in secret I weep.
　Make yourself a beggar and a fool, then come in search of me.
　My lover is Hindu and I am a Muslim.
　My lover wants me to kiss him in the foliage of the blackberry bush.
Young, K.　Rushes, The.

Ford, Ed ("Whitey")
Holden, J.　Poem for Ed "Whitey" Ford, A.
Pinsky.　Night Game, The.

Ford, Ford Madox
Williams, W.　To Ford Madox Ford in Heaven.

Forest Fires
Deb, A.　I started a fire with Kali's name.
Lux.　Man Gets Off Work Early, A.
Melville, H.　Uninscribed Monument on One of the Battlefields of the Wilderness, An.
Ríos, A.　Wet Camp.

Foresters
Roberts, S.　Solitary Woodsman, The.

Forests
Alexander, P.　Crossing.
　Lightfall.
　Northeast Suite.
Allen, H.　In the Forest.
Anday, M.　6. Love: "Forest would start when you held my hand, The."
Barnett, A.　Forest Utilization.
Bentley, N.　Iron Man of the Hoh.
Birney.　Slug in Woods.
Bishop, E.　Chemin de Fer.
Blake, W.　Tyger, The.
　When the Green Woods Laugh.
Blind.　Entangled.
Bobrowski.　Woodland God.
Bopp, R.　Begins here, the ciphered forest.
　I pass the swamp borders.

This is the rotten-breathed forest.
Brecht, B.　Of Poor B.B.
Bryant, W.　Forest Hymn.
　Forest Hymn, A.
　Inscription for the Entrance to a Wood.
Buson.　That axe that I hear.
Carruth, H.　Bearer, The.
Césaire, A.　Virgin Forest, The.
Chipasula.　Double Song.
Cole, T.　Lament of the Forest, The.
Coleridge, M.　Witches' Wood, The.
Dafydd [*or* David] ap Gwilym.　Woodland Mass, The.
Davenant [*or* D'Avenant].　Countess of Anglesey lead Captive by the Rebels, at the Disforresting of Pewsam, The.
Davie, D.　Tunstall Forest.
Duffy, C.　Little Red-Cap.
Emerson, R.　Waldeinsamkeit.
Frost, R.　Come In.
　In winter in the woods alone.
　Stopping by Woods on a Snowy Evening.
Glück, L.　Trillium.
Graham, W.　Imagine a Forest.
Greenberg, U.　Song of My People-Forest, People-Sea.
Hagiwara Sakutaro.　So Terrifyingly Melancholy.
Harwood, L.　That Evening Pierre Insisted That I Had Two Roast Pigeons at Dinner.
Henderson, D.　Song of Devotion to the Forest.
Herbert, E.　Sonnet Made upon the Groves near Merlou [*or* Merlow] Castle.
Hill, M.　Abomination.
Holub.　Forest, The.
Hughes, T.　Modest Proposal, A.
Hummell, A.　Panic.
Inada.　Clearing.
Issa.　Withered fields, The.
Kenyon, J.　Depression in Winter.
Kharabarov, I.　Taiga, The.
Kipling, R.　Way through the Woods, The.
Ko Ŭn.　Into the Woods.
Kushner, A.　Star burns out over the tree tops, The.
Lanier, S.　Ballad of Trees and the Master, A.
Lee, E.　Forests and Caverns.
Lewis, G.　Woods: "Midwinter and this beech wood's mind."
Li Po.　On Visiting a Taoist Master in the Daitian Mountains and Not Finding Him.
Longenbach.　What You Find in the Woods.
MacLean, S.　Hallaig.
Mahon.　Going Home.
Mandelstam [*or* Mandelshtam].　Shy speechless sound, The.
　Whoever Finds a Horseshoe.
Merwin.　Asians Dying, The.
Mezey.　At the Point.
Minhinnick.　Sap.
Moiro.　Tree nymphs, daughters of River, ambrosial.
Mörike [*or* Möricke].　Forest Murmurs.
Murray, L.　Noonday Axeman.
Muso Soseki.　Gem Forest.
Nelson, J.　If a Fish Fell in a Forest.
Ni Ghallchóir, C.　Big Glen, The.
Oliver, M.　Sleeping in the Forest.
Preston, R.　Chicago Blues.
Pritchard, N.　Cassandra and Friend.
　Landscape with Nymphs and Satyrs.
　Narrow Path, The.
Ray, H.　Wood Carols.
Reading, P.　Salopian.
Roberts, S.　Solitary Woodsman, The.
Rolls.　Rain Forest.
Rukeyser, M.　Then I Saw What the Calling Was.
Sandy.　Survivor, Walking.
Segovia, F.　Ánimo vegetal.
　Chrysalis.
　Claridad del silencio.
　Clarity of Silence.
　Crisálida.
　No acabamos nunca.
　Premonición.

Premonition.
Vegetal Animus.
We Never Come.
Shelley, P. To Jane: The Recollection.
Simmerman. Take a Hike.
Smith, D. Wreck in the Woods.
Södergran. Forest Lake.
Stafford, W. Entering a Wilderness Area.
Stewart, S. Forest, The.
Thomas, E. Green Roads, The.
Todhunter. Song: "Bring from the craggy
  haunts of birch and pine."
Tranströmer. Clearing, The.
Unknown. Deep in the Forest.
  Glyn Cynon Wood.
  Mauberes, The.
Vanshenkin. Forest in winter, The! From edge
  to edge.
Very. Indian's Retort, The.
Vietnamese Oral Tradition. Outpost Soldier,
  The.
Wagoner, D. Lost: "Stand still. The trees ahead
  and bushes beside you."
Waltner-Toews, D. Woods.
Wang Wei. Visiting the Mountain Hermitage of
  a Monk at Gan-hua Monastery.
Warfield. Forests and Caverns.
Warren, R. Fear and Trembling.
Watson, R. Enchanted Princess, An.
Wieners. Invitation au Voyage 2.
Wilner, E. Abstraction.
Wright, C. Privacy.
Wright, J. Rainforest.
Zimmer. Because of Duties, Zimmer Had
  Forgotten the Forest.

Forges
Heaney, S. Forge, The.

Forgetfulness
Amir, D. Thoughts about Sari's Jump.
Bensley. One's Correspondence.
Berlin. Remember.
Bromige. Log.
Browning, R. Memorabilia.
Cardona-Hine. Enough Horses.
Collins, B. Forgetfulness.
  Lines Lost among Trees.
Comer, Carrie St. George. Arbor.
Crane, H. Forgetfulness.
Crummey, Michael. What's Lost.
Davidson, M. Sensation Type and His Friends,
  The.
Dooley, M. Does It Go Like this?
Doubleday, T. Poppies, that scattered o'er this
  arid plain.
Ehrhart. Finding My Old Battalion Command
  Post.
Fields, D. Remind Me.
Follain. One Day I Suddenly Notice.
Forbes, D. Recension Day.
Hall, D. Exile.
Hancock, Butch. My Mind's Got a Mind of Its
  Own.
Hardy, T. Tess's Lament.
Hikmet. Three Storks Restaurant.
Ho Ch'i-fang. Get Drunk.
Hope, L. I Shall Forget.
Ivanov, Binyo. Summer: "On this long farm
  facing Rila Mountain."
Jackson, H. Two Truths.
Jamme, Franck André. Recitation of Forgetting,
  The.
Karr. Diogenes Tries to Forget.
Kasa. I shall think of you.
Kasdorf. Body Remembers, The.
Kennedy, X. To Someone Who Insisted I Look
  up Someone.
Kim Sowŏl. Day Long After, A.
  Years from Now.
Kupriyanov [*or* Kuprianov]. Everything gets
  forgotten.
Lemm, Richard. My Class Draws a Blank on
  Robbie Burns.
Levertov. Woman Meets an Old Lover, A.
Lewis, G. Beginning to Forget.
Lisboa. Beyond the Image.
Maltby, R. I Don't Remember Christmas.

Masaoka Shiki. Thing long forgotten.
McCarthy, J. I'm Gonna Laugh You Right Out
  of My Life.
Merwin. Losing a Language.
Michie, S. Connecting Light.
Millay, E. I Forgot for a Moment.
  Sonnet 43: "What lips my lips have kissed, and
  where, and why."
Mura. Natives, The.
Nemes Nagy. Like One Who.
Neruda. There Is No Forgetting (Sonata).
O'Neill, R. I Made a House of Houselessness.
Ou-yang Hsiu. Old Age.
Parra, N. Poems of the Pope, The.
Pietri. Intermission from Friday.
  Intermission from Saturday.
Postnikova, O. Archangel Cathedral.
Pritchard, N. From Where the Blues?
Ramsdell, H. Thank you for saying pathos
  instead of pathetic, keeping us the same size as
  before.
Rossetti, C. I wish I could remember the [*or*
  that] first day.
Ryokan. I've forgotten.
  Picking violets.
Salinas, P. Deaths ("First thing I forgot was
  your voice, The.").
Sinch'ung. Regret.
Smith, C. Nepenthe.
Stephens, P. Hangman.
Stickney, T. Pity.
Strand. Always.
Swirszczynska [*or* Swir]. She Does Not
  Remember.
Szymborska, W. End and the Beginning, The.
Teasdale. Water-Lilies.
The Earl of Longford. Forgetfulness.
Tranströmer. Clearing, The.
Ukon. Me.
Unknown. Though you made me think.
  We cannot tell now.
Velichansky, A. Memory of the past grows
  paler with each day.
Wakoski. Remembering the Pacific.
Weiss, T. Ten Little Rembrandts.
White, L. Acanthus.
Williams, C. K. Alzheimer's: The Wife.
Woodhouse, P. I see a Soldiers service is forgot.
Wyatt. Steadfastness.
Yusuf, S. Attention.

Forgiveness
Alberti. Coming Back of an Assassinated Poet,
  The.
Alexie. Penance.
  Powwow at the End of the World, The.
Ammons. Foot-Washing, The.
Angel. Evolving Similarities.
Barnes, D. Few and Far Between.
Benét, W. Brazen Tongue.
Brebner, D. 1. The Golden Lotus.
Cairns, Scott. On Slow Learning.
Coleridge, S. Epitaph: "Stop, Christian passer-
  by!—Stop, child of God."
Davidson, J. Ballad of a Nun, A.
Davis, C. How Can I Turn Off This Engine
  Now?
Dickinson, E. "Remember me" implored the
  Thief!
Donne. Hymn[e] to God the Father, A.
  If poisonous [*or* poysonous] mineral[l]s, and if
  that tree.
Dunn, S. After the Argument.
Eichner, Maura. Father, The.
Frost, R. Forgive, O Lord, my little jokes on
  Thee.
Glatstein, J. Matthew 5:38–48; "You have heard
  that it was said, 'An eye.'"
Goldberg, L. Prodigal Son, The.
Hamill, S. What the Water Knows.
Herbert, G. Love (3): "Love bade me welcome:
  yet my soul drew back."
Herrick. His Prayer for Absolution.
Hölderlin. No Pardon.
Hope, A. Easter Hymn.
Hurreh, I. Pardon Me.
Jackson, H. Two Truths.

Klink, J. Apology: "Lately, too much disturbed,
  you stay breathing in me."
Komunyakaa, Y. Please.
  Seven Deadly Sins.
Kunitz, S. Magic Curtain, The.
Levitt, Peter. Walking the path.
Marcus, M. Forgiveness.
Markham, E. Outwitted.
Matveyeva [*or* Matveieva]. Ginger-Haired Girl,
  The.
Meads, K. Dogs.
Meynell, A. Beyond Knowledge.
Millay, E. And must I then, indeed, Pain, live
  with you.
Milton. To whom the Tempter impudent
  replied.
Morrissey, S. And Forgive Us Our Traspasses.
Mu'tamid, King of Seville. Rest your heart; let
  your cares not overcome you. What good will
  grief and apprehension do you?
Negar. Forgive me that I opened your door
  silently.
Neruda. Forgive me if my eyes see.
O'Hara, F. Poem: "Light clarity avocado salad
  in the morning."
Oppen. They await / War, and the news.
Pankey. As We Forgive Those.
Parra, N. I Take Back Everything I've Said.
Perry, L. Quatrain: Forgive Me Not.
Pollok. Happiness.
Preston, R. Ten Seconds.
Reznikoff. Day of Atonement.
Rich, A. Rusted Legacy.
Roberts, C. Enough: "Moon the color of an
  empty movie screen, A."
Robinson, E. Unforgiven, The.
Rózewicz. Posthumous Rehabilitation.
Russell, G. Forgiveness.
Shephard, S. Suicides and Fools.
Shiphrah, T. To Adam.
Smart, C. Hymn to the Supreme Being.
Stein, K. Upon Finding a Black Woman's Door
  Sprayed with Swastikas, I Tell Her This Story
  of Hands.
Straus. All-Purpose Apology Poem.
Szymborska, W. Under a Certain Little Star.
Tennyson, A. Forgiving.
Trench, R. Lord, Many Times.
Tsvetayeva [*or* Tsvetaeva]. Ancient Song, An.
Unknown. Confession for Forgiveness, A.
Various authors. Even though they were
  rebellious.
Verlaine. You see, we have to be forgiven
  things.
Voznesensky [*or* Voznesenskii]. Forgive Me!
Waddington, M. Ten Years and More.
Waniek. Abba Jacob and St. Francis.
Webster, A. Sometimes, as young things will,
  she vexes me.
Whittier. Forgiveness.
Williams, W. This Is Just to Say.
Young, J. Was That the Human Thing to Do?

Forks
Boruch. Simple Machines.
McKay, D. Setting the Table.
Simic. Fork.

Fort McHenry, Maryland
Key. Star-Spangled Banner, The.

Fort Sumter, South Carolina
Simms, W. Ode: "Do ye quail but to hear,
  Carolinians."
Timrod. Charleston.

Fortitude
Guest, E. Don't Quit.
Kipling, R. If.
Moore, M. Nevertheless.
Porteous. I Envy the Cracked, Black Basalt.
Smart, C. Hymn 8. Fortitude.
Wilcox, E. Solitude.

See also **Endurance**

Fortune
Barnfield [*or* Barnefield]. Philomel.
Benjamin, P. Press On.
Bethell. Fortune.
Borisov. Horse, The: "Up the moss-grown."

Brion, R.   If Fortune Smiles.
Brown, K.   Money As Water.
Calderón de la Barca.   Those Which Were Pomp and Delight.
Chudleigh.   Wish, The.
Cristall.   Song: "Wandering in the still of eve."
Cunningham, J.   Epigram: "Good Fortune, when I hailed her recently."
Davies, W. H.   Money.
Dekker, T. *et al.*   Fortune and Virtue.
Du Bellay.   Las, Où Est Maintenant Ce Mespris de Fortune.
Forman, R.   We Are the Young Magicians.
Hardy, T.   Hap.
Henry, B.   Discovery.
Herrick.   To Fortune.
Horace.   Ode 1.5: Quis Multa Gracilis.
Housman.   Lads in their hundreds to Ludlow come in for the fair, The.
Hughes, L.   Luck ("Sometimes a crumb falls.").
Kahn, G.   When My Ship Comes In.
Kim Sisŭp.   Now Shine, Now Rain.
Li Po.   Bring On the Wine.
Manilius.   Why do we in worries waste our lives, and torture.
Moramarco, F.   Fortune Cookies.
Nâbî.   In the Garden of Time and Destiny.
Pao Chao.   Grass by the River, The.
Rózewicz.   What Luck.
Shakespeare, W.   Sonnet 29: "When, in disgrace with fortune and men's eyes."
ten Berge.   Fortunes in knee breeches.
Unknown.   Ch'ien (Heaven).
  I've returned to Hong Kong from America.
  K'un (Earth).
  Wei-chi (Not yet across the stream).
Wŏn Ch'ŏnsŏk.   Fortune determines rise and fall.
Wyatt.   Fortune doth frown.
See also **Fate; Luck; Chance**

Fortunetelling and Fortunetellers
Broumas, O.   Calypso.
Carruth, H.   Sonnet: "Well, she told me I had an aura. "What?" I said."
Cary, A.   Telling Fortunes.
Chalfi, R.   Reading the I Ching.
Christopher.   Palm Reader, The.
Hughes, L.   Bad Luck Card.
Justice, D.   Variations on a Text by Vallejo.
Kimbrell, J.   My Psychic.
Kocot, N.   Gypsy Summer.
Kuzmin.   Were you apprenticed to a fortune teller?
Morris, J.   Reading the Writing.
Qabbani.   Fortune Teller, The.
Rifqa [*or* Rifka].   Fortune Teller, The.
Ríos, A.   Madre Sofía.
Williamson, G.   On His Birthday.

Fossils
Citino.   Sister Mary Appassionata Lectures the Science Class: Fossils, Physics, Apple, Heart.
Dickson, J.   Fossil Fuel.
Dove, R.   Fish in the Stone, The.
Ferlinghetti, L.   Cro-Magnons.
Kendall, M.   Fossil, A.
Ranaldo, L.   HIS:STORY.
Randell.   Digging up weeds by the little hedge.
Smith, John.   All Light.
Webb, P.   Tall Tale, A; or, A Moral Song.
Wilson, Emily.   Fossil Garden, The.

Fountains
al-Rahim, A.   My Heart.
Bogan, L.   Roman Fountain.
Bonset.   Remembering the Night Fountains.
Cornwall.   For a Fountain.
Darío, R.   Fount, The.
Davie, D.   Fountain of Cyanë, The.
  Fountain, The.
Duncan, R.   Drinking Fountain, The.
Eberhart, R.   Garden God, The.
Fisher, R.   Memorial Fountain, The.
Grant, A.   Nymph of the Fountain to Charlotte, The.
Herrick.   To the Water Nymphs, Drinking at the Fountain.
Lowell, A.   Bright Sunlight.

Lowell, J.   Fountain, The.
Muso Soseki.   Clear Valley.
Pound, E.   Ts'ai Chi'h.
Rapin.   Of Gardens.
Reznikoff.   Winter Sketches III.
Rilke.   Roman Fountain.
Robinson, E.   Fountain.
Sitwell, S.   Fountains.
Spaziani.   Rome has a thousand fountains, and in May they sing.
Traherne.   Anticipation, The.
Unknown.   Cold Fountain, Cold Fountain.
Wilbur, R.   Ballade for the Duke of Orléans.
  Baroque Wall-Fountain in the Villa Sciarra, A.
Wordsworth, W.   Fountain, The.

Fourth of July
Baker, D.   Patriotics.
Berry, W.   Independence Day.
Daugherty, B.   Nightfire.
Djanikian.   Immigrant Picnic.
Follen, E.   For the Fourth of July.
Jacobik, G.   Under the Sign of Walt Whitman.
Jelus, S.   Factory Town on the 4th of July.
Jordan, J.   July 4, 1984: For Buck.
McGrath, T.   End of the Line, The.
Mitchell, R.   To Walt Whitman on America's Birthday.
Moore, J.   Noble Structure, A.
Mullen, L.   White Paintings IV (Independence Day).
Peck, R.   Four of July.
Reed, I.   On the Fourth of July in Sitka, 1982.
Sanchez, S.   Poem for July 4, 1994.
Sharp, S.   Good Nights.
Shipley, V.   Birthday Party on Old Orchard Road, A.
Swenson, M.   July 4th.
Unknown.   Independence Bell—July 4, 1776.
  Independence Day.
Williams, W.   4th of July.

Fox, Charles James
Scott, S.   Nelson, Pitt, Fox.

Foxes
Alexander, P.   Foxlight.
Archilochus.   Fox knows many things, The.
  Here is a fable men tell.
  Strategy.
Basho.   Calm moon, A.
Bierds, L.   It.
Brooke, H.   Fox Hunt, The.
Carryl, G.   Sycophantic Fox and the Gullible Raven, The.
Ceni, A.   With What Courage.
Chaucer.   Rape of Chanticleer, The.
Dafydd [*or* David] ap Gwilym.   Fox, The.
Davies, E.   Wily Fox, The.
Dubie.   February: The Boy Breughel.
Galina, M.   I said to him—Just don't throw me into that briar patch.
Gibran.   Fox, The.
Grennan.   Conjunctions.
Hudgins.   Homage to the Fox.
Hughes, F.   Different Voice, The.
  Foxes.
Hughes, T.   Thought-Fox, The.
Kaya Shirao.   Moonlit night / By melon flowers.
Kennelly.   Dream of a Black Fox.
Kirchwey.   Matthew 8:20; And Jesus said to him.
La Fontaine.   Fox and the Crow, The.
Levine, P.   Fox, The.
Llwyd, H.   Fox's Counsel, The.
Masefield.   Fellow Mortal, A.
Murray, L.   Gods, The.
Oliver, M.   Fox, The.
  Foxes in Winter.
  Wings.
Orr, G.   Gray Fox, The.
Padel, R.   Scotch.
Parry, R.   Fox, The.
Rich, A.   Fox.
Shimazaki Toson.   Fox's Trick, The.
Snyder, G.   One Should Not Talk to a Skilled Hunter about What Is Forbidden by the Buddha.
Tan Taigi.   In the melon-patch / Thief, fox.

Unknown.   Foxes move in pairs.
  Trial of Renard, The.
  With huntis vp, with huntis vp.
  You-hu: There's Fox.
Vidya.   Hiding in the.
Ward, J.   Here, Home.
Williams, J.   In Duffryn Woods.
Yezzi, David.   Woman Holding a Fox.

Foxgloves
Cambridge, G.   Foxgloves.
Lowell, A.   Vespers.

France
Apollinaire.   Little Car, The.
  Stanzas against Forgetting.
Aragon.   Richard II Forty.
Barbauld.   Sonnet to France On Her Present Exertions.
Baudelaire.   Joker, A.
Beckett, S.   Dieppe.
  Dieppe.
Byron, G.   Napoleon's Farewell.
Cannan.   Rouen.
Caraion.   Song from the Occupation Time.
Cendrars.   Back then I was still young.
Davie, D.   Rodez.
Dehn, P.   St. Aubin d'Aubigne.
Desnos.   Night Watchman of Pont-au-Change, The.
Dove, R.   Great Palaces of Versailles, The.
Du Bellay.   Heureux Qui, Comme Ulysse, A Fait un Beau Voyage.
Elmslie, K.   History of France.
Fargue.   Fragrance of Night, A.
Fisher, J.   Pearls.
Flecker, J.   Rioupéroux.
Gardelle, C.   Air.
  Rain.
Grosholz.   Remembering the Ardèche.
Gurney, I.   Behind the Line.
Hacker, M.   Graffiti from the Gare Saint-Manqué.
  Squares and Courtyards.
Hamilton, S.   Farewell to France.
Heine, H.   Grenadiers, The.
Hill, G.   Violent contrariety of men and days; calm.
Hopkins, G.   Duns Scotus's Oxford.
Jacob, M.   Rooster and the Pearl, The.
Jonson, B.   On English Monsieur.
Martial.   Gallic Lap-Dog, The.
McCarthy, J.   Riviera, The.
McOrlan.   Hairdresser's, The.
Merwin.   Tide Line Garden.
Munro, N.   Heather, The.
Nerval.   Fantasy.
Nordhaus.   Aunt Lily and Frederick the Great.
O'Loughlin.   Bunkers, The.
Péret.   Hymn of the Patriotic War Veterans.
  Nungesser und Coli Sind Verreckt.
"Perse."   Doors open on the sands, doors open on exile.
Ponge.   Silent World Is Our Only Homeland, The.
Prévert.   Barbara.
Rimbaud, A.   Bad Blood.
  Evil.
Rodefer.   Stewed and Fraught with Birds.
Seeger, A.   Aisne, The (1914–15).
Shepherd, R.   Lucky One, The.
Silva, L.   Emigrant's Son, The.
Smith, I.   John Knox.
Supervielle.   Some Day Shall I Be.
Unknown.   Humble Petition of the British Jacobins to Their Brethren of France, The.
  Mode of France, The.
  Roncevalles.
Updike.   Some Frenchmen.
Weaver, A.   Luxembourg Garden.
  My Father's Geography.
Wordsworth, W.   Great men have been among us; hands that penned.
Wright, J.   Winter Daybreak above Vence, A.

Francis of Assisi, Saint
Citino.   Francis Meets a Leper.
Craig, David.   Francis Helps a Brother Who Is in Sin.

Dennis, C. St. Francis and the Nun.
Hecht, A. At the Frick.
Hirsch, E. Simone Weil: In Assisi.
Hudgins. Fire and St. Francis.
Kinnell. Saint Francis and the Sow.
Lahey, Joy. Habitat Photo.
Matthews, W. Wolf of Gubbio, The.
Orlovsky. I Dream of St. Francis.
Stainer. Creatures Preach to St Francis, The.

Franco, Francisco
Wright, J. Eisenhower's Visit to Franco, 1959.

Franco-Prussian War
Rimbaud, A. Poster of Our Dazzling Victory at Saarbrucken, A.

Frank, Anne
Derry, A. Anne.
Kalina, R. To Anne Frank.
Meredith, W. John and Anne.
Motion, A. Anne Frank Huis.
Wechsler, E. Once Again, Anne Frank.
Williams, C. K. Day for Anne Frank, A.

Frankenstein
Barlow, G. Painting Drunken Twilight.
Deanovich. Frankenstein.
Field, E. Bride of Frankenstein, The.
Griffith, K. Hamlet Meets Frankenstein.
Lochhead, L. Dreaming Frankenstein.
Young, D. Business of Love Is Cruelty, The.

Franklin, Aretha
Baraka, A. To Aretha Franklin from Sparkle.

Fraternity
Gilmore, B. Hazing (for tony new and albee).
Shaler, N. Merry Truce, The.

See also **Brotherhood**

Fratricide
Very. Thy Brother's Blood.

Free Will
Crosby, E. Military Creed, The.
Frost, R. Road Not Taken, The.
Herrick. Predestination.
Kekova. Everything has come true. The punishment fits the crime.
Rumi. Deliberation.
Wise teacher tell me.
Spaziani. To the Readers.
Whittier. Overruled.
Wroth. Sonnet 48: "How like a fire doth love increase in me[e]."

Freedom
"Ada.". Slave, The.
Agustini. Break, The.
In Fields of Sleepdreaming.
Akhmadulina. I was so buoyant.
Alegría. From the Bridge.
Angelou, M. Caged Bird.
"Antler.". Ungag our souls!! Unstrangle our souls!! Unsmother our souls!!
Arundel, H. Adam.
Auden. They wondered why the fruit had been forbidden.
Bandeira. Off to Pasárgada.
Poetics.
Baranczak, S. February 8, 1980: And No One Has Warned Me.
Barbauld. Eighteen Hundred and Eleven, a Poem.
Barbour, J. Freedom [or Fredome].
Barnstone, A. First Amendment.
Barry, M. Hymn of Freedom.
Bei Dao. Accomplices.
Bekes Jr. Separation.
Bennett, L. Jamaica Oman.
Berry, W. He goes free of the earth.
Independence Day.
Bible, O.T. Psalm 114: "When Isr'el, freed from Pharoh's hand."
Bierce. Freedom.
To the Bartholdi Statue.
Bishop, E. Sonnet: "Caught—the bubble."
Blake, W. How Sweet I Roamed [or Roam'd] from Field to Field.
Song of Liberty, A.
Bloem, J. C. After Liberation.
Borisov. What Freedom Said.
Borowski. Two Countries.

Branch, A. Ere the Golden Bowl Is Broken.
Brathwaite, E. Citadel.
Breeze. Mother. . .Sister. . .Daughter.
Breton, A. Marquis de Sade, The.
Brontë, E. To Imagination.
Browning, E. Hiram Powers' "Greek Slave". Part II.
Runaway Slave at Pilgrim's Point, The.
Brutus. Prayer: "O let me soar on steadfast wing."
Bryant, W. Conjunction of Jupiter and Venus, The.
Damsel of Peru, The.
Brydges. No more by cold philosophy confined.
Buchanan, R. Bicycle Song (For Women).
Burns, R. De'il's [or Deil's] Awa wi' th' [or the] Exciseman, The.
For A' That and A' That ["Is there, for honest poverty"].
Scots Wha Hae.
Butler, C. E. Other Places, The.
Byron, G. Sonnet on Chillon.
Stanzas: "When a man hath no freedom to fight for at home."
Campert, J. Eighteen Dead, The.
Campo. Superman Is Dead.
Castellanos. Farewell, The.
Cavalli. But first one must free oneself.
Now that the time seems all mine.
Cavendish, M. Claspe, The.
Cernuda. If Man Could Name.
Char. Argument.
Disdained Apparitions.
Room in Space.
Chin. Composed Near the Bay Bridge (after a wild party).
Chubb, R. Transfiguration.
Chung-ch'ang T'ung. Speaking My Mind.
Clare, J. I Feel I Am.
Clark, T. Free Speech.
Cohan. You're a Grand Old Flag.
Coleridge, S. La Fayette.
To the Honourable Mr. Erskine.
Collins, W. How Sleep the Brave.
Comfort, A. Notes for My Son.
Cornish, S. Mississippi on the Doorstep.
Couzyn. Way Out, The.
Cowper, W. Negro's Complaint, The.
Crane, H. To Brooklyn Bridge.
Creeley. Ballad of the Despairing Husband.
Cross, E. Visions.
Crouch, S. Like a Blessing.
Cullen, C. Wind Bloweth Where It Listeth, The.
Cummings, E. E. If(touched by love's own secret)we,like homing.
Darwish, M. Guests on the Sea.
de Gonz'les, Merced J. Mexico Will Be Free.
Densmore. Sound Is Fading Away, The.
Derieva, R. I don't feel at home where I am.
Dickinson, E. Could I but ride indefinite.
No Rack can torture me.
They shut me up in Prose.
Donne. Batter my heart, three-personed [or three person'd] God; for you.
Canonization, The.
Doolittle, H. Helmsman, The.
Dove, R. Geometry.
Lady Freedom Among Us.
Dumas, H. Root Song.
Dunbar, P. Ante-Bellum Sermon, An.
Sympathy: "I know what the caged bird feels, alas!"
Duo Duo. Thousands of images have suddenly brightened in the emptiness.
Egerton, S. Liberty, The.
Eliot, T. S. Burnt Norton.
Éluard, P. To Her of Whom They Dream.
Emerson, R. Freedom.
Give All to Love.
Merlin II.
Feaver. Coat.
Ferlinghetti, L. Dog.
France, L. Blues for Bird.
Fried, E. One Kind of Freedom Speaks.
Garrett, E. Miser.

Tyranny of Choice.
Gibran. Madman (Prologue), The.
Gibson, W. Music Stole In.
Gillespie, H. Breezin' Along with the Breeze.
Gippius. Incantation.
Glück, L. Legend.
Godfrey, Glenn. New Spirit, The.
Gorbanevskaya. And, having started singing this melody.
Gréki. Future Is for Tomorrow, The.
Guevara, M. Buddy Holly Poem, The.
Gullar. There Are Many Traps in the World.
Gunn, T. Aquarium, The.
Tamer and Hawk.
Gwala. Beyond Fences.
Children of Nonti, The.
Han-shan. Like a Drifting Boat.
Han Yong'un [or Yongwun]. Preface.
Haraway. Midnight Vigil.
Harburg. Eagle and Me, The.
Hardy, T. At the Railway Station, Upway.
Harper, F. Slave Mother, The: A Tale of the Ohio.
Hawoldar. I Have Gone into My Prison Cell.
In the Fist of Your Hatred.
Hayden, R. Frederick Douglass.
Runagate Runagate.
Heissenbüttel. Fragment 3: "All horizons are round."
Herbert, G. Religion stands on tip-toe in our land.
Herdi, A. God's Freedom Lovers.
Hernández Cruz. Puerta Rica.
Hernández, M. Wounded Man, The.
Hierro, José. Boy with the Empty Cage, The.
Ho Chi Minh. Two Prison Poems.
Hoagland, E. Time Break.
Holdsworth, E. Freedom.
Howe, F. Crossing Out.
Howe, J. Battle Hymn [or Battle-Hymn] of the Republic, The.
Hucks, J. To Freedom.
Hughes, L. Freedom Train.
Let America Be America Again.
Hughes, T. Jaguar, The.
Irtenev. At the Pavelets radial-line station.
Iwan, D. Why Snow Is White.
Jarrell, R. Emancipators, The.
Woman at the Washington Zoo, The.
Jeffers, L. How High the Moon.
When I Know the Power of my Black Hand.
Jensma. Fear Freedom.
Johnson, J. Fifty Years.
Lift Every [or Ev'ry] Voice and Sing.
Joseph, J. Warning.
Kao Shih. Song of the Fisherman, The.
Kefala. Freedom Fighter.
Kendrick, D. Sidney, Looking for her Mother.
Kennelly. Restoration, A.
Key. Star-Spangled Banner, The.
Khlebnikov, V. Me and Russia.
Khoury, N. People of Pomegranates.
Kipling, R. Ex-Clerk.
Klyuyev [or Kliuev or Klyuev]. You Twist Your Death in Nooses.
Krasicki, I. Caged Birds.
Lazarus, E. In Exile.
Levy, A. Magdalen.
Lewis, J. Time and Music.
Li Po. Lu Mountain Song For the Palace Censor Empty-Boat Lu, A.
Lincoln, A. Gettysburg Address, The.
Lisnyanskaya [or Lisnianskaia]. Two carousing hawk moths, their wings like nervous silk.
Logau. Freedom.
Lovelace, R. To Althea, from Prison.
To Lucasta, from Prison.
Lowell, J. Letter Six—The Pious Editors' Creed.
MacNeice. Sunlight on the Garden, The.
Mandela. Saviour.
Mandelstam [or Mandelshtam]. [Last Poems].
Martial. Were lives of ease, dear Namesake, ours.
Martin, A. Who among Common Men of Their Time?

Martinaitis, M. Forbid!

Masalha, Salman. On Artistic Freedom in the Nationalist Era.

Masters, E. Unknown, The.

Mayer, B. Test 1 How to design freedom. How fine does the.

Meinke. Supermarket.

Milton. On the Detraction Which Followed upon My Writing Certain Treatises ("I did but prompt the age to quit their [or thir] clogs.").

Mkangelwa. Women Sing, The.

Moise *et al.* To Persecuted Foreigners.

Mok, J. Winter Mirror II.

Moore, T. Harp That Once through Tara's Halls, The.

Sound the Loud Timbrel.

Morgan, M. Red High-Heeled Shoes.

Muso Soseki. Wandering.

Nasrin. Border.

Character.

Nemes Nagy. Sincerity.

To Freedom.

Neruda. Poet's Obligation.

Nikolayeva [*or* Nikolaeva]. You can go on holiday now, you can dabble in verse.

Nolens, L. Saint Vitus's Dance in October 10.

Norris, L. Pit Ponies, The.

Norton, C. Sonnet 7: "Like an enfranchised bird, who wildly springs."

Voice from the Factories, A.

O'Brien, G. Techniques of Mass Persuasion.

Ofeimun. Handle for the Flutist, A.

O'Sullivan, L. Being Free.

Paine, T. Liberty Tree.

Pak Sŏwŏn. Highway, The.

Palmer, M. Noche, Una.

Parks, R. Song of Freedom, A.

Parra, N. Inflation.

Patterson, R. Black Power.

Paulding. Neglected Muse! of this our western clime.

Pegram, A. Deliverance.

Persius. Satire 5: "From the earliest poets, the fashion stands."

Philips, K. Answer to Another Persuading a Lady to Marriage, An.

Plumpp. Daybreak.

Polkowski. Noli Me Tangere.

Porta. Nearby creatures of the air.

White bars from the window.

Potos. One Red-Haired Summer, The.

Ralin, Radoi. Home-Study Course in Freedom.

Ransford, Tessa. Stable Relationship, A.

Ray, H. To My Father.

Rebelo. Poem of a Militant.

Reed, I. Railroad Bill, A Conjure Man.

Rich, A. History.

Ritsos. Seek not, want not, be not.

Roethke. I Knew a Woman.

Roland Holst. Outside in the Open.

Rossetti, C. Promises Like Pie-Crust.

Ruhani, G. Gaffer Speaks.

Rukeyser, M. Long Enough. Long Enough.

St. John, D. Essay on Liberation, An.

Sall, A. Cloak of Dawn.

Sandburg, C. Harbor, The.

Limited.

Sapgir. Dionysus.

Sidney. Sonnet 47: "What, have I thus betrayed my liberty?"

Skeeter. California, 1852.

Midwest, Midcentury.

Smith, P. Meanwhile, in Rwanda.

Woman Who Died in Line, The.

Sousa, N. Call.

Let My People Go.

Our Voice.

Stafford, W. Message from the Wanderer, A.

Stevens, W. What shall we say to the lovers of freedom.

Struther. Freedom.

Sumangalamata. At last free.

Swenson, M. Stripping and Putting On.

Swinburne. Free Thought.

Sykes, B. Cycle.

Sylvain, P. Refugees.

Tagore. Let My Country Awake.

Tejani, B. Lines for a Hindi Poet.

Thelwall. To Ancestry.

To Tyranny.

Thompson, P. Emancipation.

Fugitive, The.

Prayer, A: "Oh, Lord! I lift my heart."

Tolson, M. Festus Conrad.

Torres, A. Smash Your Fist.

Unknown. Death of Saint Marinus, The.

Freedom a Come Oh!

Go Down, Moses.

Home on the Range.

Let My People Go.

My island spirit.

No Man Can Hinder Me.

No More Auction Block.

Tomorrow those who hunger for my love will be satisfied.

Vashon. Vincent Ogé.

Veiga. Wind of Liberty.

Villanueva, A. Even the Eagles Must Gather.

Waldman, A. Icy Rose.

Walker, M. For My People.

Warsh. Free Speech.

Watson, R. White Bird, The.

Weller. Ngungalari.

Wheatley, P. To the Right Honourable William, Earl of Dartmouth.

Whitman, W. Commonplace, The.

I take to the open road.

Old Salt Kossabone.

To the States.

Years of the Modern.

Whittier. Laus Deo!

Proem: "I love the old melodious lays."

Wilbur, R. Still, Citizen Sparrow.

Williams, H. France 1792.

Willis, N. To Charles Roux, of Switzerland.

Wordsworth, W. Thought[s] of a Briton on the Subjugation of Switzerland.

Wright, J. Wednesday Night Prayer Meeting.

Wroth. Did I boast of liberty?

Sonnet 14: "Am I thus conquered [or conquer'd]? have I lost the powers."

Wyatt. Farewell, love, and all thy law[e]s forever [or for ever].

Zagajewski. Fire: "Probably I am an ordinary middle-class."

Zu-Bolton. Struggle-Road Dance.

Freedom Train

Hughes, L. Freedom Train.

Freezers

Armour. Hiding Place.

Quinn, J. 2. Icebox.

Freighters

Greenberg, A. Freight Train, Freight Train.

Levertov. Don't You Hear That Whistle Blowin'.

See also **Cargoes**

French and Indian War

Barlow, J. Hostilities between France and England Extended to America. Braddock's Defeat.

Tilden. Song of Braddock's Men, The.

French (language)

Acosta. Dangereux avril.

Molloy, D. Conversation Class.

Ponge. *Assiette*, The (The Plate).

Crate, The.

French Poetry

Cistulli. 34.57.

Stein, G. George Hugnet.

French Revolution

Coleridge, S. Fears in Solitude [Written in April, 1798, during the Alarm of an Invasion].

To the Honourable Mr. Erskine.

Justice, D. Man of 1794, A.

Nartsissov, B. Marated Bastilled age, A.

"Pindar.". Hymn to the Guilotine.

Serge. Dialectic.

Tomlinson, C. For Danton.

Williams, H. France 1792.

To Dr Moore, in Answer to a Poetical Epistle Written by Him in Wales.

French, The

Cadiot, Oliver. Psst!

Datcher, M. Joseph Speaks to Gericault in the Studio.

Desnos. Like.

Hughes, L. Cubes.

O'Hara, F. Ode: Salute to the French Negro Poets.

Osofisan. Paris Latin Quarter.

Ramke, B. Enter Celia, with a Writing.

Sanford, C. Rachel's Recovery (Fucking with the Angels).

Savageau. Like the Trails of Ndakinna.

Torres, A. Kettle Rooted to the Void.

Unknown. Charles the King, our Emperor, the great.

Epigram: "Says a Reverend Priest to a less Rev'rend friend."

Marsilion sees his people's martyrdom.

Night passes on, and the bright day appears.

Oliver's climbed upon a hilly crest.

They arm themselves with Saracen hauberks.

Freud, Sigmund

Auden. In Memory of Sigmund Freud.

Bang, M. Crossed-Over, Fiend-Snitched, X-ed Out.

Dugan, A. Nomenclature.

Field, E. Whatever Became Of: Freud?

Goetsch, D. First Time Reading Freud.

Hannan, M. Life Model.

Howe, F. Doubt.

Meredith, W. Dying Away.

Nemerov. Einstein & Freud & Jack.

In the Beginning.

Sigmund Freud.

Wayman. Wayman in Love.

Friars

Ransom, J. Necrological.

Friends, Society of

Whittier. Anniversary Poem.

First-Day Thoughts.

Friendship

Abelard. More than a brother to me, Jonathan.

Agustini. Miraculous Ship, The.

Alberti. Coming Back of an Assassinated Poet, The.

Aldrich, H. Catch, A.

Alexander, E. At the Beach.

Amirthanayagam, I. There Are Many Things I Want to Tell You.

Angel. Breaking the Rock Down.

Annand. I Winna Let On.

Archilochus. Buffeted by the waves.

Armstrong, P. Sunderland Nights.

Ashbery, J. Operators Are Standing By.

Some Trees.

Train Rising Out of the Sea.

Awoonor. First Circle, The.

Aygi, G. Dream: Queue for Paraffin.

Aytoun [*or* Ayton], R. Upon Platonic Love: To Mistress Cicely Crofts, Maid of Honour.

Barker, J. To My Friends Against Poetry.

Baxter, J. In Auckland it was the twelve days' garland.

Beatty, P. Doggin the Rockman.

Beckman, J. Canals, The. The liquor coming through.

Beer, P. In Memory of Stevie Smith.

Berrigan, T. Personal Poem # 7.

Sonnet XXX: "Into the closed air of the slow."

Sonnet LXXVI: "I wake up back aching from soft bed Pat."

Berry, W. Marriage.

Berryman. Dream Song 45.

Bevington, L. Am I to Lose You?

Bishop, E. Letter to N.Y.

Shampoo, The.

Blake, W. Poison Tree, A.

Bowers, E. Afternoon at the Beach, An.

Bowles, W. To a Friend.

Boyle, D. M. Curtain, The.

Boyle, K. Ode to a Maintenance Man and His Family.

Brett, L. My Mother's Friend.

Brontë, E. Love and Friendship.

Brooke, R. Dining-Room Tea.

Brown, E.   Bitcherel.
Browning, E.   L. E. L.'s Last Question.
  Sleep, The.
Browning, R.   Waring.
Brutus.   They Hanged Him, I Said Dismissively.
Burns, R.   Auld Lang Syne.
  Second Epistle to Davie.
Buson.   With a woman friend.
Caddel.   For Tom.
Cagnone, N.   General names, no other.
Cairns, Scott.   After the Last Words.
Callimachus.   Someone told me, Heracleitus.
Carver, R.   Old Days, The.
Cheney-Coker.   Letter to a Tormented
  Playwright.
Ch'iao Lai.   Tune: "Partridge Sky" I Rejoice to
  Meet a Friend Visting at My Rustic Study.
Chipasula.   Friend, Ah You Have Changed!
Chunghur Hyujung.   To My Old Friend Lee.
Ciardi, J.   What Johnny Told Me.
Cisneros, A.   Paris Cinquième.
Clark Bekedermo.   Abiku.
Cleary, B.   Boys' Own.
Cobbold, E.   On Some Violets Planted in My
  Garden by a Friend.
Coleridge, H.   To a Friend.
Coleridge, M.   Contents of an Ink-bottle, The.
  Friends—With a Difference.
  Gifts.
  Gone.
  Mortal Combat.
Coleridge, S.   Duty Surviving Self-Love.
  To William Wordsworth [1817 version].
Collins, K.   Sisters.
Converse.   Friendship.
Cook, E.   To the Late William Jerdan.
Coolidge, C.   There Is a Caterpillar That Makes
  a Very Complicated Hammock.
Cooper, D.   Dreamt Up.
Cooper, J.   Long, Disconsolate Lines.
Cording.   Elegy for John, My Student Dead of
  AIDS.
Cory, W.   Deteriora.
Cowley, A.   It was a dismal and a fearful night.
  On the Death of Mr. William Hervey [or
  Harvey].
Cox, M.   Barbells of the Gods, The.
Craik.   Friendship.
Creeley.   For Friendship.
  Won't It Be Fine?
Csoori.   Somebody Consoles Me with a Poem.
Cuadra, A.   Brief Letter to Donald Walsh (in
  memoriam).
Cullen, C.   Tableau.
Dante Alighieri.   Love and Poetry.
Daugherty, B.   Nightfire.
Davis, J.   Warru.
Delaunay, S.   Greetings, Blaise Cendrars.
Derricotte.   Friendship, The.
Dickinson, E.   I showed her Heights she never
  saw.
Dooley, M.   Letters from Yorkshire.
Doty, M.   Michael's Dream.
Doubleday, T.   Friends, when my latest bed of
  rest is made.
Drake, E.   Friendliest Thing (Two People Can
  Do), The.
Dubie.   Genesis Text for Larry Levis, Who Died
  Alone, A.
Duncan, R.   Among My Friends.
Dunn, S.   Men Talk.
E'der, E.   La Puente.
Edwards [or Edwardes], R.   When I Was Three.
Ehrhart.   Cycling the Rosental.
Elmslie, K.   Bare Bones.
Emerson, R.   Friendship.
English, T.   Ben Bolt.
Faugeres, M.   Friendship.
Field.   Ah, Eros doth not always smite.
Field, R.   Some People.
Foss, S.   House by the Side of the Road, The.
Fulton, A.   What I Like.
Gallagher, T.   Hug, The.
Garcia, R.   Dangerous Hats.
Gates, B.   Triptych.
Gershwin, I.   Babbitt and the Bromide, The.

Gibb.   Letter to Russel Barron.
Gibson, W.   Golden Room, The.
Ginsberg, A.   Elegy for Neal Cassady.
Glück, L.   Triumph of Achilles, The.
Gonzáles Martínez.   Like Sister and Brother.
Googe.   Of Money.
Graham, W.   Lines on Roger Hilton's Watch.
Green, M.   Sometimes I dress, with women sit.
Green, M.   For My D.C. Girlfriends.
Greshoff, J.   Friendship for a Woman of Grace.
  I Greet You.
Gunn, T.   J Car, The.
  Terminal.
Hacker, M.   Eight Days in April.
Hafiz, K [or Hafez].   Desire's destroyed my life;
  what gifts have I.
  Each friend turned out to be an enemy.
  My friend, hold back your heart from enemies.
Hands, E.   Epistle, An.
Hartnett.   Person as Dreamer, The: We Talk
  about the Future.
Harwood, G.   In the Park.
Hass, R.   Letter to a Poet.
Haynes, C.   Any Wife or Husband.
Herbert, G.   Unkindness.
Herrick.   To His Honoured and Most Ingenious
  Friend Mr. Charles Cotton.
Hill, G.   Gasholders, russet among fields.
  Milldams, marpools.
Hirshfield, J.   Heart's Counting Knows Only
  One, The.
Houlihan, J.   All the Cold Mechanicals.
Housman.   Shake hands, we shall never be
  friends, all's over.
Howard, R.   Keeping.
Hsieh Ling-yün.   Replying to a Poem from My
  Cousin Huilian.
Hsieh T'iao.   I Sit in My Lofty Study.
  In a Provincial Capital Sick in Bed.
Hughes, L.   Poem [2]: "I loved my friend."
Hughes, T.   Six Young Men.
Jackson, H.   Friends.
James, P.   Can't We Be Friends?
Jonson, B.   Epistle Answering to One That
  Asked to Be Sealed of the Tribe of Ben, An.
  Epistle to Master John Selden, An.
  To the Immortal Memory and Friendship of
  That Noble Pair, Sir Lucius Cary and Sir H.
  [or Henry] Morison.
Jordan, J.   Grand Army Plaza.
Kaprow, Allan.   Suppose you telephone your
  own answering.
Keats.   Bright Star.
  But there are.
  To a Friend Who Sent Me Some Roses.
Kemble.   To Mrs. Norton.
Kercheval, J.   Ham and the Moon.
Kessler, S.   Cigarette Case.
King, H.   Change, The.
  Exequy, The.
Kinsella, T.   Talent and Friendship.
Kizer, C.   American Beauty, An.
Klee.   Friend, A.
Knott.   Unsubscriber, The.
Koch, K.   Circus, The ("I remember when I
  wrote The Circus.").
Koehler, T.   Tess's Torch Song (I Had a Man).
Kushner, B.   Friends.
Langhorne.   Studley Park.
Lansana, Q.   Woolworth's Poem, The.
Lars.   Recollection of Gabriela Mistral.
Leapor.   To Artemisia.—'Tis to her we sing.
Lee, K.   Haiku #3.
Lennox, C.   Ardelia to Flavia, an Epistle.
Levin, P.   Meeting of Friends, A.
Levis.   Those Graves in Rome.
Levy, A.   To Vernon Lee.
Lewis, N.   Footprint on the Air, A.
Lewis, S.   Just Friends.
Li K'ai-hsien.   Earthquake covered Shansi and
  Shensi, The.
Li Po.   Remembering Our Excursion in the Past.
  Rhymeprose on the Sword Gallery.
  To a Friend.
  To Wang Lun.
Lisboa.   Camellia.

Liu Ch'ang-ch'ing.   On Seeing Wang Leave for
  the South.
Liu Yung.   Tune: "Bells in the Rain".
Lloyd, C.   Erst when I wandered far from those
  I loved.
  Written at the Hotwells, near Bristol.
Llwyd, Alan.   Chaplin and Others.
Logue, C.   To My Fellow Artists.
Longfellow, H.   Arrow and the Song, The.
Lope de Vega.   What Do I Have, That You Seek
  Out My Friendship?
Lovelace, R.   Grasshopper, The [To My Noble
  Friend Mr Charles Cotton: Ode].
Lucilius.   Lean Gaius, who was thinner than a
  straw.
Lux.   Man Gets Off Work Early, A.
MacCaig.   Chauvinist.
MacDiarmid, H.   To a Friend and Fellow Poet.
MacGill.   Matey.
Macgoye.   Omera.
Machado Ruiz.   When I am alone.
Malouf.   Judas Touch, The.
Martial.   Just half our three score years and ten.
Masahide.   When bird passes on.
Maurus.   To Grimold, Abbot of St. Gall.
Mayer, B.   Birthday Sonnet for Grace.
Mayfield, C.   Thinking of a Friend.
Menai.   To One Who Died in a Garret in
  Cardiff.
Meng Hao Jan.   In Passing an Old Friend's
  Farm.
  In Summer at the South Pavilion Thinking of
  Xing.
  Taking Leave of Wang Wei.
Menicanti.   To the Readers Who Write to Me.
Merrill, J.   Clearing the Title.
Miles, S.   Hares, The.
Milton.   Lycidas.
Minhinnick.   After a Friendship.
Mollineux.   Another Letter to a Friend.
Montagu, L.   Lover, The; a Ballad.
Moody, E.   To a Friend, Who Gave the Author a
  Reading Glass.
  To a Lady, Who Was a Great Talker.
Moore, T.   Meeting of the Waters, The.
Morales, A.   Tita's Poem.
Morley, H.   For Elaine de Kooning.
Moss, S.   Exchange of Hats, An.
Moss, T.   Anointing, An.
Muldoon, P.   Soap-Pig, The.
Muso Soseki.   For a Monk Going West.
  Reizan Osho Visits Me.
  Reply to a Friend's Poem.
  Reply to Gen'no Osho's Poem.
  Tengan Osho's Visit to Erin-ji.
Nemerov.   Blue Suburban.
O'Hara, F.   Aus Einem April.
Osgood, F.   Garden of Friendship, The.
Ovid.   Back from the sea now, back to their
  sources shall deep rivers.
  Friend, henceforth to be reckoned the foremost
  among my comrades.
  You who are reading this work without malice,
  may you.
Pao Chao.   Imitating the Old Poems.
Pao Hsien.   Written on the Wall at Master Wei
  Feng's.
Parra, N.   Who are my friends / the sick / the
  weak / the poor in spirit.
Parry, J.   New Friends and Old Friends.
Patchen.   State of the Nation, The.
Paulinus of Nola.   To Ausonius.
Pearlberg, G.G.   Think Back.
Philips, K.   Friendship in Emblem[e], or the
  Seal[e], to my dearest Lucasia.
  Friendship's Mystery[s], to my dearest Lucasia.
  L'Amitié: To Mrs M Awbrey.
  Retired Friendship, To Ardelia, A.
  To Mrs M. A. at Parting.
  To My Excellent Lucasia, On Our Friendship.
  To the Queen of Inconstancy, Regina Collier, in
  Antwerp.
Phillips, C.   As a Blow, from the West.
Piercy.   Friend, The.
  Morning Athletes.
Planché.   Self-Evident.

Plato. True Friend, The.
Po Chü-i. At the End of Spring.
  Dreaming That I Went with Li and Yu to Visit
  Yuan Zhen.
  Poem for Yuan Zhen.
Poliziano. To Giovan Battista Buoninsegni.
Pollarolo, G. When We Meet Again.
Porta. I'm walking out on Rome.
Porter, C. Friendship.
Prado, A. In Portuguese.
Reverdy. On the Threshold.
  That.
Rexroth, K. For Eli Jacobson.
Rich, A. For a Friend in Travail.
  Ghazal.
Roberts, C. Enough: "Moon the color of an
  empty movie screen, A."
Robinson, A. To a Dead Friend.
Robinson, C. We Who Have Loved.
Robinson, E. How Annandale Went Out.
  Old Story, An.
Rochester, J. Platonic Lady, The.
Rodríguez, C. Who Will Be My Friend Always.
Rosenblatt, S. Second Half of Our Lives, The.
Rossetti, C. After Communion.
  From Sunset to Star Rise.
  Promises like Pie-Crust.
Ruden, S. Stubble Burning, The.
Rutsala. Reunion: A Scenario.
St. John, D. My Friend.
Sanchez, S. Song No. 3: "Cain't nobody tell me
  any different."
Sanders, James. From the Mark Prejsnar
  Playbook.
Sanelli, M. Swansonville.
Scott, S. Wanderer's Dog, The.
Seneca. Flee every friendship and live: a greater
  truth.
Seward. Invocation, To the Genius of Slumber
  Written Oct. 1787.
  To a Friend, Who Thinks Sensibility a
  Misfortune.
Shakespeare, W. Sonnet 30: "When to the
  sessions of sweet silent thought."
  Sonnet 42: "That thou hast her, it is not all my
  grief[e]."
  Sonnet 104: "To me, fair friend, you never can
  be old."
  Sonnet 133: "Beshrew that heart that makes my
  heart to groan."
  Sonnet 134: "So now I have confess'd that he is
  thine."
Shwarts [or Shvarts]. Remembrance of Strange
  Hospitality.
Silverstein, S. Friendship.
  Hug o' War.
Sinch'ung. Regret.
Smallpiece, A. M. Veil's removed, the gaudy,
  flimsy veil, The.
Smith, C. Captive Escaped in the Wilds of
  America, The. Addressed to the Hon. Mrs.
  O'Neill.
  On the Aphorism "L'Amitié est l'Amour sans
  Ailes".
  To Friendship.
Smith, S. Dirge: "From a friend's friend I taste
  friendship."
  Freddy.
Sommer, J. Last in before Dark.
Sosnora. There it all was: the gaslamp,
  drugstore.
Sousa, N. Poem of a Distant Childhood.
Steiger. Friendship.
Stevenson, R. It's an owercome sooth for age
  an' youth.
  Mile an' a Bittock, A.
  My Shadow.
Stone, J. He Makes a House Call.
Su Tung-p'o. To a Traveler.
Swift, J. Twelve Articles.
  Verses on the Death of Dr. Swift, D.S.P.D.
  Occasioned by Reading a Maxim in
  Rochefoucauld.
Talfourd. 'Tis a Little Thing.
Teft. On a Friend's Taking a Journey.
Tennyson, A. In the Garden at Swainston.

Path by which we twain did go, The.
  To E. Fitzgerald.
Thoreau. Sympathy.
Tighe. As one who late hath lost a friend
  adored.
Troupe. View from Skates in Berkeley, The.
Tsaloumas. Old Friend.
Tu Fu [or Du Fu]. At the Sky's End, Thinking
  of Li Po.
  Dreaming of Li Po ("Death separation: sobs
  hard to swallow.").
  Presented to Wei Ba, Gentleman in Retirement.
  To Abbot Min the Compassionate.
  To Li Po on a Winter Day.
  Visitors.
  West of Hut.
Unknown. And Yet the Earth Remains
  Unchanged.
  Cypress on the Mound, The.
  Epitaph: "My friend, judge not me."
  Nü-yue ji-ming: The Cock Is Crawin' (scoticè).
  Pick a pomegranate.
  Plucking the Rushes.
  To me nothing seems as splendid nor as
  praiseworthy.
  Two Cherokee Songs of Friendship.
Vietnamese Oral Tradition. Evening.
  Linked Verses.
Voznesensky [or Voznesenskii]. From the
  Window of a Plane.
Walcott. Village Life, A.
Wang Wei. Autumn Mountain Evening.
  Goodbye to Meng Haoran.
  Melody of Wei City.
Weaver, A. Left Bank Jazz Society, The.
Wei Ying-wu. Poem to a Taoist Hermit on
  Quanjiao Mountain, A.
Welch, L. Large Little Circle.
Wen T'ing-yün. To a Friend Bound East.
Whitman, W. As Toilsome I Wander'd
  Virginia's Woods.
  I Dream'd in a Dream.
  I Saw in Louisiana a Live-Oak Growing.
  In Paths Untrodden.
  Live Oak, with Moss.
  Not Heat Flames Up and Consumes.
  Recorders Ages Hence.
Whur. Female Friend, The.
Wilcox, E. Friendship After Love.
Wilkinson, C. Landmarks.
Williams, M. Thinking about Bill, Dead of
  AIDS.
Winchilsea. Friendship between Ephelia and
  Ardelia.
Wordsworth, W. Tables Turned, The.
  To a Child [Written in Her Album].
Yearsley. To ———: "Lo! dreary Winter,
  howling o'er the waste."
Yeats. Friends.
Yi Chŏngbo. If flowers bloom, I think of the
  moon.
Young, M. J. Friendship.
Yüan Chĕn. Yuan Zhen to Bo Juyi.
Yun Sŏndo. Songs of Five Friends.
Zavalnyuk [or Zaval'niuk]. I Love My
  Enemies.

Frietchie, Barbara
Whittier. Barbara Frietchie.

Frogs
Basho. Ancient silent pond.
  At the ancient pond.
  Old Pond, An.
  Old pond / Leap-splash.
  Old pond, The.
  Old pond—frogs jumped in—sound of water.
  Old silent pond, An.
  Old-time pond, from off whose shadowed depth,
  An.
  Still old pond, The.
  There is the old pond!
Belloc. Frog, The.
Brion, R. One Morning beside a Pond.
Bruchac. Birdfoot's Grampa.
Buson. At the old pond.
  How awkward it looks.
  Listening to the moon.

Char. Tree Frog, The.
Dodge, M. Moon Came Late, The.
Flanner. Frog Song.
Greger. Frog in the Swimming Pool, The.
Grunberger, A. Swimming Upstream.
Heaney, S. Death of a Naturalist.
Hoban. Tin Frog, The.
Issa. Frog.
  Huge frog and I, A.
  Lanky frog, hold.
  Leaping for the river, the frog.
  Now listen, you watermelons.
  Skinny frog.
Jamie, K. Hill-track, The.
Khlebnikov, V. Hey . . . y! Uh . . . hm!, covered
  with sweat.
Kikaku. Riding the wide leaf.
Kinnell. First Song.
La Fontaine. Aesop's Fable of the Frogs.
Lampman. Frogs, The.
Layton. Cain.
Leonidov, Rumen. Another Stone in the
  Swamp.
MacCaig. Frogs.
Machan. Hazel Tells LaVerne.
Metodiev, Ivan. River: "River, River."
Mitchell, S. From the Journals of the Frog
  Prince.
Montale. Elegy of Our Times.
Naito Joso. No need to cling.
Niedecker. Frog noise / suddenly stops.
Ponge. Frog, The.
  Frog, The.
Rexroth, K. Once again I hear.
Rossetti, C. Hopping frog, hop here and be
  seen.
Rothenberg, J. Song of Quavering, A.
Scarbrough, G. Cutting Sod-Land.
Sengai Gibon. On Basho's "Frog".
Shapcott, J. Life.
Shiki. Skylark school, The.
Shoha. When the bush warbler.
Sund. Frog I Saved from a Snake, The.
Takara, Kathryn. Cows and Alabama Folklore.
Unknown. Frog, The.
Unknown, formerly at. to Homer. Ascend my
  shoulders, firmly keep thy seat.
Wallace-Crabbe. Nub.
Wright, J. Small Frogs Killed on the Highway.
Young Bear. Wadasa Nakamoon, Vietnam
  Memorial.

Frontiers
Arnold, C. Extravagance of Zoos, The.
Heaney, S. From the Frontier of Writing.
Kaplinski, J. East-West Border, The.
Lars. Sketch of the Frontier Woman.
Wang Wei. Mission to the Frontier.
Wei Ying-wu. Tartar Horse.

Frontiersmen
Ferril. Jupiter at Beer Springs.
Nance. Moonlight.
Wang Ch'ang-ling. Chant of the Frontiersman.

Frost
Barnes, D. Portrait of a Lady Walking.
Basho. I would like to use.
  It would melt.
  Midnight frost.
Begay. Mother's Lace.
Buson. Miles of frost / On the lake.
Castro, R. When the Frosts Cover Them.
Coleridge, M. September.
Coleridge, S. Frost at Midnight [1829 version].
Davis, C. Years, The.
Dickinson, E. Apparently with no surprise.
Doolittle, H. Blue-geese, white-geese, you may
  say.
Elfyn, Menna. Welsh Ice.
Fisher, C. Frozen Tarn.
Goetsch, D. Nobody's Hell.
Iio Sogi. Night frost / Pulsing wings.
Issa. Deer licking.
Lovelace, R. Grasshopper, The [To My Noble
  Friend Mr Charles Cotton: Ode].
Mangan, J. O'Hussey's Ode to the Maguire.
McCarriston. January, Anchorage.
Norris, L. Early Frost.

Pugh.   Frozen Field, The.
Sandburg, C.   Splinter.
Shipman.   Streams are fettered, and with us as rare, The.
Tantan.   Morning frost / Mount Fuji.
Zabel.   Hoar Frost.
Zwicky.   Jack Frost.

Frost, Robert
Aimone, J.   Second-Grade Incident from Robert Frost's Childhood, A.
Barnstone, W.   Late December, Where Are You, Robert Frost?
Bell, M.   Unable to Sleep in Frost's Bed in Franconia.
Berryman.   37: Three around the Old Gentleman.
Bly, R.   Frost and His Enemies.
Brewka, N.   Elinor White Frost Speaks.
Bridgford, K.   Robert Frost.
Brooks, G.   Of Robert Frost.
Cohen, B.   Ghosts of Luxury, The.
Cooper, W.   Postcard from Robert Frost's Grave.
Davis, T.   Building Walls.
Davison, P.   Getting over Robert Frost.
Dawe, Tom.   If Sonnets Were in Fashion.
Drew, G.   Apparently Someone in the Department.
Eberhart, R.   Worldly Failure.
Espaillat.   For Robert Frost.
Etter.   Farm in the Green Mountains, A.
Finch, A.   Night Call.
Firer.   Mrs. Post's 6th-Hour English Class.
Francis, R.   On a Theme by Frost.
Gibson, W.   Golden Room, The.
Gilberg, G.   Poetry's Beginning.
Glaser, M.   Quarreling with Robert Frost.
Higgins, L.   Re: Robert.
Hillyer.   Letter to Robert Frost, A.
Houghton, F.   Mr. Frost Goes South to Boston.
Ingebretsen, E.   Unlettered.
Jackson, R.   Sprites.
Jacobik, G.   From the Porch of the Frost Place.
Kennedy, X.   Robert Frost Discovers Another Road Not Taken.
Keplinger, D.   Robert Frost.
Kinnell.   For Robert Frost.
Koch, K.   Mending Sump.
Krapf.   Dark and Deep.
Kumin, M.   Final Poem, The.
Lifshin.   Night Robert Frost Died, The.
Lowell, R.   Robert Frost.
   Robert Frost.
Marion, P.   Found Poem, North of Boston.
Mason, D.   Winter, 1963.
Matthews, W.   On the Porch at the Frost Place, Franconia, NH.
Maxwell, G.   Poem to Mr Thomas and Mr Frost.
Mccann, S.   Robert Frost as Father.
Meinke.   Robert Frost in Warsaw.
Meredith, W.   In Memory of Robert Frost.
Metras, G.   Robert Frost's Chair.
Nemerov.   For Robert Frost, in the Autumn, in Vermont.
Olsen, W.   Frost's Last Lecture: A Tape: His Audience—1963.
Overton, R.   Fire and Ice by Robert Frost: an early draft.
Paljor, N.   Robert Frost and I.
Pastan.   Remembering Frost at Kennedy's Inauguration.
Peseroff.   Stray Moth, Asleep.
Ray, D.   Thanks, Robert Frost.
Ridland.   Blue Plate Tea Room: Sestina, The.
Ruark.   Robert Frost to Ezra Pound's Daughter from His Deathbed.
Rukeyser, M.   Double Dialogue: *Homage to Robert Frost.*
Runciman, L.   Robert Frost.
Sadler, L.   Why God Chose Robert Frost Over Elvis.
Salter.   Frost at Midnight.
Schmitt.   Frost in Miami.
Schwartz, D.   Now He Knows All There Is to Know: Now He Is Acquainted with the Day and Night.
Skellings, E.   Frost to Skellings.

Skloot.   Frost.
Smith, D.   Near Frost's Grave.
Smith, W.   Robert Frost: The Road Taken.
Snydal, L.   Frost.
Sokol, J.   Robert Frost's Books, Ripton, Vermont, 1980.
Stafford, W.   At the Robert Frost Memorial.
Starbuck, G.   Reading the Facts about Frost in *The Norton Anthology.*
Thompson, S.   Living at the Frost Place.
Tobin, D.   For Christine at the Frost Farm.
Vinz.   Wall between Us, The.
Wardrop, D.   Robert Frost at the Net.
Weigl.   On Not Finding Frost's Grave in the Dark.
Weingarten.   Ghost Frost.
Weiss, T.   After All.

Fruit Trees and Fruit
Adisa.   Discover Me.
Agard, J.   English Girl Eats Her First Mango.
Basho.   Don't imitate me.
Belitt.   Orange Tree, The.
Bilgere, G.   Madeleine, A.
Buson.   By flowering pear.
Cacciatore, E.   Where do I stand and where do you? Seems like.
Chiyojo.   Whether astringent.
Clampitt.   Gooseberry Fool.
Clarke, George Elliott.   Haligonian Market Cry.
Coleman, W.   Three Trees.
D'Aguiar, F.   Airy Hall Icongraphy.
Dooley, M.   At Les Deux Magots.
Eian.   Joshu's "Oak in the courtyard".
Elmslie, K.   Fruit.
Evasco, M.   Elemental.
Field.   She Is Singing to Thee, *Domine!.*
Fuller, J.   Wild Raspberries.
Garrett, E.   Ribes rubrum.
Gibson, M.   Just Like Eve.
Gomes, A.   Martyred Tamarind, The.
Gonzalez, R.   Beyond Having.
Goodison.   Songs of the Fruits and Sweets of Childhood.
Gorham.   Empress Receives the Head of a Taiping Rebel, The.
Grass.   Transformation.
Greiffenberg.   On the Fruit-Providing Autumn Season.
Hadewijch.   Love's Maturity.
Hall, D.   Mangosteens.
Harpur, J.   Basket Of Summer Fruit, A.
Harrison, T.   Kumquat for John Keats, A.
Hernández, M.   Your Heart?—It Is a Frozen Orange.
Hudgins.   Chinaberry, The.
Huelsenbeck, R.   "We Hardly".
Issa.   In a dream.
Jaccottet.   Fruit.
Kang [Grossjean], Ok-Ku [or Ok-Koo].   Garden: "Space, The."
Keats.   To Autumn: "Season of mists and mellow fruitfulness!"
Kelly, B.   Leaving, The.
Kinsella, J.   Plumburst.
Kyger.   Caption for a Miniature.
Lau, A.   Eating habits of the old man.
Levertov.   O Taste and See.
Levy, A.   At a Dinner Party.
Lima, M.   Marketwoman of Luanda.
Logghe.   Madonna of the Peaches.
Lynes, Jeanette.   What We Learned on the Highway Near St. John's.
MacLeish.   Ars Poetica: "Poem should be palpable and mute, A."
Maguire, J.   Fall, The.
Mahadevi.   Vein of sapphires, A.
Masini.   Two Men, Two Grapefruits.
Max, L.   Stone Fruit.
Mayer, G.   Bilberries.
McKay, C.   Tropics in New York, The.
Millay, E.   Never May the Fruit Be Plucked.
Moore, M.   Nevertheless.
Naimy, M.   Hunger.
Nelson, J.   Never Eat Oranges!
Nelson, M.   Brightness.
Neruda.   United Fruit Co.

Orléans, C.   Ballade: "I was in blossom when I was a child."
Padel, R.   Yew Berries.
Pai, S.   Fruit They Had in Common.
Pau-Llosa.   Frutas: "Growing up in Miami any tropical fruit I ate."
Peacock, M.   Veil of If, The.
"Perse."   Nocturne: "Now! they are ripe, these fruits of a jealous fate."
Piercy.   September Afternoon at Four O'Clock.
Ponge.   Blackberries.
Praxilla.   Fairest thing I leave behind is sunlight, The.
Queneau.   Nourishment of Little Birds, The.
Rankine.   Man. His Bowl. His Raspberries, The.
Rilke.   Where in what ever-blissfully watered gardens, upon what trees.
Rossetti, C.   Goblin Market.
Simonovic, I.   Misere.
Solórzano, L.   Early Poem.
   Poema temprano.
Strange.   Still Life.
Sung Tzu-hou.   Song: "On the Eastern Way at the city of Lo-yang."
Taggard.   Fructus.
Tipping.   Mangoes.
Unknown.   Fruit Plummets from the Plum Tree.
   Piao-you-mei: Like Falling Fruit.
   Pluck, pluck, pluck, the thick plantain.
   Pomelo, The.
   Throw me a quince.
Whitman, T.   Hunger and Imagination.
Whittier.   Fruit-Gift, The.
Williams, W.   This Is Just to Say.
Wilson, Imani E.   Fruitbowl 1.
Wright, C.   Wages of Love.

Frustration
Acorn.   I've Tasted My Blood.
Auden.   Minnelied.
Bartlett, J.   Man and a Woman Standing in the Rain in Front of a Candy Store, A.
Blair, H.   Bloody Orkneys, The.
Bolton, J.   Lights at Newport Beach, The.
Cabico, R.   Gameboy.
Ezekiel.   I met a man once.
Garrison, D.   Fight Song.
Gullar.   There Are Many Traps in the World.
Hope, M.   Sacrifice.
Hugo, V.   Words in the Shadow.
Hyde, E.   Explaining.
Jones, Tudur Dylan.   Gardening.
Lassell.   Kissing Ramén.
Orozco.   Reality and Desire.
Pao Chao.   Folded Wings.
Parker, D.   Frustration.
Powell, K.   Don't Feel No Way.
Reznikoff.   I have not even been in the fields.
Rosemurgy, C.   Why God Invented the Cold.
Scythinus.   Calamity and conflagration! Strife!
Shepherd, R.   That Man.
Stryk, L.   Cormorant.
Unknown.   Disagreeable Things.
   Things One Would Like to Send Away.
   Unhappy pedophiles, cease your inane.
Vallejo.   Intensity and Height.
Wilde, O.   Wasted Days.
Wren, A.   Harmony.

Fuchsia
Pedretti, Erica.   Heimgarten.

Fugitives
Rago.   4. Terror and Love as Fugitives.

Fujiyama
Fenollosa.   Fuji at Sunrise.
Kaneko Mitsuharu.   Mount Fuji.
Kusano Shimpei.   Skylarks and Fuji.
Tantan.   Morning frost / Mount Fuji.

Fulfillment
Blake, W.   Question Answered, The [or A].
Bontemps.   God Give to Men.
Browning, R.   Now.
Chuang Tzu.   Man Is Born in Tao.
Creeley.   Song: "What's in the body you've forgotten."
Cullen, C.   From the Dark Tower.
Donne.   Good-Morrow, The.

Eriksen, Mariane Baggers. I dropped something. I picked it up.
Espada. Tony Went to the Bodega but He Didn't Buy Anything.
Kuzmin. Nine delightful birthmarks.
Mackay, J. Tomorrow.
Massimi. On Happiness.
McGough, R. Away from you.
Owen, W. Music.
Robinson, E. Three Quatrains.
Rodriguez, L. Hungry.
Slauerhoff. Within My Life.
Symonds. In years of old.
Unknown. Chance led me once, when idling through the street.
Things the Bigger the Better.
Verlaine. Sonnet to the Asshole.

Fuller, Margaret
Masters, E. Margaret Fuller Slack.

Fun
Berlin. Pack Up Your Sins and Go to the Devil.
Brown, L. I Want to Be Bad.
Burke, J. Good Time Charlie.
Cohan. If I'm Going to Die I'm going to Have Some Fun.
Coward. Bar on the Piccola Marina, A.
DeSylva, B. G. I Want to Be Bad.
Ebb, F. Nowadays.
Egan, R. Ain't We Got Fun.
Henderson, R. I Want to Be Bad.
Kahn, G. Ain't We Got Fun.
Kindman, S. Fight and Play.
Peacock, M. Next Afternoon.
Russell, B. I Didn't Know About You.
Russell, G. Frolic.
Sondheim. Some People.
Unknown. West Gate Ballad.
Viorst. Night Fun.
Yellen, J. Are You Havin' Any Fun?
See also **Play; Pleasure**

Funerals
Abbott, K. Windy clear day, A.
Abbott, W. Funeral, The: "I see, under the canopy of death."
Abrahams, L. Agnostic's funeral prayer.
Afrika, T. Funeral of Anton Fransch, The.
Funeral, The: "Her smile drains."
Annensky. One Second.
Antiphilus [or Antiphilos]. On the Death of the Ferryman, Glaucus.
Auden. Song: "Stop all the clocks, cut off the telephone."
Awoonor. I Rejoice.
Baker, D. Mercy.
Bancquart. Epitaph.
Barlow, G. Salt.
Bateman, M. After the Funeral.
Beaumont, S. Upon a Funeral.
Bécquer, G. They Closed Her Eyes.
Berkson, B. Variation.
Bernstein, C. Profaning the Dead.
Berry, W. At a Country Funeral.
Bidgood. Burial Path.
Bluger, M. Leafsmoke.
Booth, P. Sixty-Six.
Carmi, T. Military Funeral in the Heat of Day.
Casiano, A. Puente.
Catullus. By strangers' coasts and waters, many days at sea.
Chinnov. Instance of fore-ordained harmony, An.
Clover, J. There Is the Body Lying in State.
Cope, David. Labor Day.
Cullen, C. Brown Girl Dead, A.
Dawe, B. At Shagger's Funeral.
Going.
De Roche. Aunt Laura Moves toward the Open Grave of Her Father.
Dhompa, T. Bardo.
Dickinson, E. I Felt a Funeral in My Brain.
I heard a Fly buzz—when I died.
Diego, G. Julio Campal ("We were walking to your funeral, eleven friends.").
Dobyns. Counterparts.
Donne. Funeral[1], The.
Dove, R. Tou Wan Speaks to Her Husband Liu

Sheng.
Dubie. Funeral, The.
Of Art & Memory.
Duffy, C. Funeral.
Dunn, D. Thirteen Steps and the Thirteenth of March.
Erdrich, H. Future Debris.
Espada. Shiny Aluminum of God, The.
Falcón, J. Burial Clothes.
Ferlinghetti, L. Green Street Mortuary Marching Band, The.
Fisher, J. It's February But.
Forman, R. Wedding.
Graves, R. 1805.
Greacen. St. Andrew's Day.
Summer Day, A.
Gwala. From the Outside.
Hall, J. Twelve Minutes.
Heaney, S. Funeral Rites.
Hein. Noble Funerals Arranged.
Herbert, Z. Elegy of Fortinbras.
Herrick. Funeral[l] Rites of the Rose, The.
Hierro, José. Requiem ("Manuel del Río, born.").
Hoagland, T. Migration.
Holub. Funeral, The.
Homer. Achilles' Lament and the Funeral of Patroclus.
Housman. Bredon Hill.
Hughes, L. As Befits a Man.
Ballad of the Man Who's Gone.
Dead in There.
Night Funeral in Harlem.
Justice, D. First Death.
Kasischke. Pall.
Kees. For H. V. (1901–1927).
Keita, N. Black Tax.
King, H. Exequy, The.
Knut. Woman from the Book of Genesis, A.
Komunyakaa, Y. April Fools' Day.
Kovner, A. Far, Far a City Lies.
Layton. Street Funeral.
Longley, M. Detour.
Lowell, R. Death of the Sheriff, The.
Lynch, T. At the Opening of Oak Grove Cemetary Bridge.
Matthews, W. Men at My Father's Funeral.
M'Baye d'Erneville. Requiem.
McKinney, I. Chrysanthemums.
Meleager. Upon a Maid That Died [or Dyed] the Day She Was Married [or Marryed].
Melville, H. Dirge for McPherson, A.
Merrill, J. Annie Hill's Grave.
Millay, E. Dirge Without Music.
Mitchell, K. On the Anniversary Of Your Death.
Mooney, M. Anna Akhmatova's Funeral.
Neanderthal Funeral.
Morisseau-Leroy, F. Testament.
Mother Goose. Who Killed Cock Robin.
Mukai Kyorai. Returning from a funeral.
Mullen, L. White Paintings III.
Murphy, Jack E. Heave Me a Mountain, Lord! (Prayer from the Plainview Rest Home).
Murphy, K. Girl with the Bad Rep, The.
Muske, C. Eulogy, The.
Page, P. Funeral Mass.
Pagis, D. Souvenir, The.
Parry, R. Old Boatman, The.
Pezoa Velíz, C. Country Funeral.
Pizarnik. Shadow of Days to Come.
Plath. Bee Meeting, The.
Poe. Lenore.
Porteous. Decommissioning.
Prévert. Song of the snails on their way to a funeral.
Probyn. Changes.
Ransom, J. Bells for John Whiteside's Daughter.
Redmond. Poetic Reflections Enroute To, and During, The Funeral and Burial of Henry Dumas, Poet.
Roeske, P. After the Funeral.
Roethke. On the Road to Woodlawn.
Rohrer, J. Mennonite Funeral in the Shenandoah Valley.

Romero, E. *Nuestro* Marine.
Rouse, A. Sacrificial Wolf.
Ruefle. Furtherness.
Salaam. Funeraled Fare Well.
Our World Is Less Full Now That Mr. Fuller Is Gone.
Sexton. Truth the Dead Know, The.
Shapiro, K. My Father's Funeral.
Shin Kyŏngnim. That Day.
Smither. Cortège of Daughters, A.
Snodgrass. Old Apple Trees.
Viewing the Body.
Soyinka. Funeral Sermon, Soweto.
We wish only to bury our dead. Shorn.
Spender, S. Funeral, The.
StacyLynn. Lookin Good.
Stevens, W. Emperor of Ice-Cream, The.
Synge. Question, A.
T'ao Ch'ien [or T'ao Yuan-ming]. Elegy for Myself.
Thomas, D. After the Funeral.
Thomas, E. Spectator, The.
Tranströmer. Snow is Falling.
Umoja, M. Say Something: A Change Is Gonna Come.
Unknown. Cowboy's Lament, The.
Dead on the War Path.
Finnegan's Wake.
Vietnamese Oral Tradition. Egret's Death and Funeral Preparations.
Virgil [or Vergil]. Pyres, The.
Weaver, A. Colors—Struck.
Williams, K. Momma in Red.
Williams, W. Tract.
Wolfe, C. Burial of Sir John Moore, The.
Wright, D. Funeral Oration, A.
Young, K. Wake.

Furnaces
MacBeth [or Macbeth]. Poem of Death, A.
Merwin. Drunk in the Furnace, The.

Furniture
Appleman, P. Birthday Card to My Mother.
Ashbery, J. Melodic Trains.
Atwood. Manet's Olympia.
Chitwood, Michael. Division.
Davidson, M. Feeling Type and His Friends, The.
DiPalma. Table, The.
Guillén, J. Happy Armchair.
Nature Alive.
Heaney, S. Sofa in the Forties, A.
Kearns, J. Moving Furniture.
Maiden. In the Gloaming.
McGuckian. Presence, The.
McHugh, H. What Could Hold Us.
Padgett, R. Nothing in That Drawer.
Pietri. Intermission from Thursday.
7th Untitled Poem.
Prospere. Heart of the Matter.
Rich, A. Dreamwood.
Thomson, J. In the Room.
Tsaloumas. Autumn Supper.
Winstanley, J. Inventory of the Furniture of a Collegian's Chamber, An.

Future
Adams, F. Those Two Boys.
Amichai, Y. Don't prepare for tomorrow, enter the narrow lane.
Ashbery, J. Brute Image.
Crossroads in the Past.
Atwood. Up.
Auden. Gare du Midi.
Benson, S. Blue Book 18 Pages 1–4.
Berry, W. To Tanya at Christmas.
Broumas, O. Song / for Sanna.
Calderón, T. Exile.
Chedid, A. Future and the Ancestor, The.
Coleridge, M. Unwelcome.
Cummings, E. E. If(touched by love's own secret)we,like homing.
Dao. Answer, The.
Davidson, D. Randall, My Son.
de Fierro. Oracle.
Desnos. Trance Event.
Dunn, Rhoda Hero. Aeronauts, The.
Emerson, J. Architecture.

Enzensberger, H. Poem about the Future.
Evans, R. Whatever Will Be, Will Be (Que Sera, Sera).
Everwine. From the Meadow.
Fanning, R. Space Needle, The.
Fenton, J. Born Too Soon.
Frénaud. Toast in Response.
Fuller, J. Born Too Soon.
Gallup. Backing into the Future.
Gilbert, C. Sorrow Since Sitting Bull, A.
Gilman, C. What Will Be Your Destiny?
Giovanni. Always There Are the Children.
González, A. Future, The.
Gray, R. Flames and Dangling Wire.
Gréki. Future is for Tomorrow, The.
Halliday, M. My Moral Life.
Harms. My Androgynous Years.
Hartnett. There Will Be a Talking.
Hawthorne, N. Oh Could I Raise the Darken'd Veil.
Herbert, C. Everything Changes.
Hill, G. Processes of generation; deeds of settlement.
Hölderlin. All the fruit is ripe, plunged in fire, cooked.
Housman. Lads in their hundreds to Ludlow come in for the fair, The.
Jaccottet. Reason.
Jarrell, R. On the Railway Platform.
Jastrun, T. Scrap.
Jeffers, R. Granite and Cypress.
Kahn, G. Tomorrow Is Another Day.
Kao Ch'i. Silkworm Song of Torchlit Fields.
Kelly, R. Recessional.
Kenyon, J. Otherwise: "I got out of bed."
Kim Sowŏl. Years from Now.
King, H. Exequy, The.
Kipling, R. Storm Cone, The.
Kyger. Never talk ahead.
Landor, W. Twenty Years Hence.
Larkin, P. Arundel Tomb, An.
Next, Please.
Levine, P. Clouds above the Sea.
Livingston, J. Whatever Will Be, Will Be (Que Sera, Sera).
Loesser. Make a Miracle.
Lumsden, R. ITMA.
MacEwen, G. Letter to a Future Generation.
Madhubuti. Union of Two, The.
Marinetti. Correction of proofs + desires in speed.
Futurism Wants to Transform the Variety Theater into a Theater of Amazement, Record-setting, and Body-madness.
We had stayed up all night, my friends and I, under hanging mosque lamps.
Marion, G. My Future Just Passed.
Martial. You say, *Postumus*, you'll live tomorrow.
Mayakovsky [*or* Maiakovskii]. My most respected / comrades of posterity!
McFadden, D. 18. Blue Irises.
Meehan, P. Autobiography.
Michaux. Future.
Montale. Soliloquy.
Morgenstern. Anxiety for the Future.
Muso Soseki. Truth Hall.
Obadike, M. Protest Poem.
O'Driscoll, D. Tomorrow: "Tomorrow I will start to be happy."
Ofeimun. Let Them Choose Paths.
Osundare. I Sing of Change.
Padilla. History.
Pasolini. Day of My Death, The.
Patterson, R. Forerunner.
Polak, J. Storm, The.
Pollard, C. On the first of January.
Pollarolo, G. Foretold Futures.
S.L.A.M.
Porter, C. From This Moment On.
Raab, E. Today I am modest like an animal.
Radoev, Ivan. Ballad for the Future.
Rich, A. Prospective Immigrants Please Note.
Richardson, K. Aubade: "Geese flew by as you entered me, The."
Ríos, A. Mi Abuelo.

Roggeman. Archaeological Find.
Rosselli. From relief to relief, the white lines, the white paper.
Rossetti, C. Cobwebs.
Sagan. Prayer Flag.
Salaam. I Live in the Mouth of History.
Sánchez Peláez. Portrait of the Beautiful Unknown Woman.
Sandburg, C. Broken-Face Gargoyles.
Haze.
Shcherbina. Where are the future's clawlets?
Spender, S. Pylons, The.
Spicer, J. Textbook of Poetry, 21, A.
Strand. Prediction, The.
Thoreau. Life in us is like the water in the river, The.
Toomer. It is Everywhere.
Trakl. Evening, The: "With the ghostly shapes of dead heroes."
Tu Fu [*or* Du Fu]. To Pi Ssu Yao.
Unknown. Song of a Marriageable Girl.
Wallace-Crabbe. Nub.
Washington, N. Hundred Years from Today, A.
Whitman, W. Full of Life Now.
Recorders Ages Hence.
Years of the Modern.
Williams, M. Of History and Hope.
Winchilsea. There's No To-Morrow.
Winter, M. Space Parable.
Wunderlich, M. Suture.
Young, J. Hundred Years from Today, A.
Zukofsky, L. I Sent Thee Late.

G

Gabriel
Brooke, R. Mary and Gabriel.
Cowley, A. Archangel's Toilet, An.
Jennings, E. Annunciation, The.
Unknown. Blow Your Trumpet, Gabriel.
Gaea (goddess)
Milosz, C. Goddess, A.
Stafford, W. Gaea.
Galatea
Góngora y Argote. Dedication: to the Count of Niebla.
Polyphemus' Love Song.
Gorbanevskaya. Savage cold of Russian winters, The.
Galilee, Israel
Barnes, D. Chuang Tzu and Hui Tzu*.
Galileo
Cardona-Hine. Listen Galaxea.
Greenlaw, L. Galileo's Wife.
Jackson, A. Confessio.
Jarrell, R. Emancipators, The.
Moore, H. To Janet, on Galileo.
Sanders, B. For What It's Worth.
Stern, G. I Remember Galileo.
Unknown. Galileo and the Bicycle.
Gallantry
Scott, S. Lochinvar.
Gallows
Clampitt. Palm Sunday.
Gibson, W. Old Skinflint.
Unknown. Such Is the Grief of the Grey-Haired Man.
See also **Hanging**
Galoshes
Bacmeister. Galoshes.
Galveston, Texas
Babb, Stanley E. Galveston.
Howes, B. On Galveston Beach.
Miller, V. On a Weekend in September.
Thomas, Larry D. Great Storm, The.
Gambling and Gamblers
Berry, D. After Finding a One Hundred Dollar Bill.
Cavafy. Days of 1908.
Dickinson, E. We lose—because we win.
Frost, R. In Divés' Dive.
Gotera. Gambling.
Hacker, M. Wagers.

Heighton, S. Blackjack.
Hongo. Off from Swing Shift.
Winnings.
Hughes, L. Saturday Night.
Situation.
Knox, J. Daycare in a Doublewide.
Leiris, Michel. Misdeal.
Lyly, J. Cupid and My Campaspe Played.
Ortiz. Telling About Coyote.
Rochester, J. Ramble in St. James's Park, A.
Roggeman. Archaeological Find.
Sandburg, C. Cahoots.
Teitelboim, D. Gambling.
Ts'en Shen. Song for General Zhao.
Unknown. Hurry up, my love, and quickly rise to the assault.
New Corrido of Laredo.
Vallejo. Eternal Dice, The.
Wisenberg, S. Casino.
Young, A. Studio Up Over In Your Ear.
Zeppa, M. Aleatory.
Games
Anderson, L. Red Hot.
Ayhan, E. Epitafio.
Barnett, C. Return, 2, The.
Blind. Once We Played.
Bracho, C. Piedra en la arena.
Stone in the Sand.
Brouwer, J. Steve's Commando Paintball, San Adriano, California.
Caesar. Too Many Rings Around Rosie.
Clare, J. Shepherd Boy, The.
Colonna, S. Disconnections.
Cummings, E. E. May i feel said he.
Curtis, T. Games with My Daughter.
De la Selva. Tropical Childhood.
Dent. For Cool Papa Bell.
Dermée. Poem.
Dunn, S. Competition.
Fulton, A. Fierce Girl Playing Hopscotch.
Gilbert, C. This Bridge Across.
Graves, R. Hide and Seek.
Greenberg, A. Analogies.
Greenlaw, L. Spirit of the Staircase, The.
Hammerstein. Make Believe.
Hannan, M. Bone Die, The.
Harper, M. Makin' Jump Shots.
Holland, J. Baize Queens.
Jackson, R. For Thurman Thomas.
Jarman, M. Astragaloi.
Jonas, S. For LeRoi Jones.
Koehler, T. Between the Devil and the Deep Blue Sea.
Lumelli, A. Candid Camera.
You first, shift your attention (that is, if you withdraw).
Mosby. To Josh Gibson (Legendary Slugger of the Old Negro Baseball League).
Mother Goose. Intery, mintery, cutery corn.
Mullen, H. Zen Acorn.
Muso Soseki. Poem on Dry Mountain (A Zen Garden).
Niccolai. Careful that these *Frisbees*.
Ōkuma Kotomichi. Pinwheel, A.
Pak Chaesam. Immortals' Paduk Game.
Patterson, G. Letter from Home.
Popa. He.
Nail, The.
Riordan, M. Some Sporting Motifs.
Roderick, D. Curlers at Dusk.
Roland Holst. Outside in the Open.
Roy, L. Triple Overtime.
Ryokan. In my sleeve the colored ball worth a thousand in gold.
On a long misty.
Sachs, N. Someone.
Sanders, James. Poem with Referees.
Scalise, J. Man comes last: he's got to.
Sen, R. I came to this world.
Sia, B. No Words Empty.
Somoza, J. Foreign Game, A.
Starkey, D. Scrabble.
Stevenson, R. Pirate Story.
Tate, G. Tonguing.
Troupe. Poem for "Magic", A.
Unknown. Children's Ball-Bouncing Song.

Foot Race Song.
Inter, mitzy, titzy, tool.
Wagner, S. Rook.
Wenderoth, J. Where I Stand with Regard to the Game.
Williams, T. Nintendo.
See also **Card Games; Sports**

Ganges River, India
Kistler, W. Standing Near the Ghats Along the Ganges.
McNiece, R. Skinny-Dipping the Ganges.
Sen, K. Oh Kali Full of Brahman!
Shange. Where the Mississippi meets the Amazon.

Gangs and Gangsters
Brooks, G. Gang Girls.
Fructuoso, E. Astig.
Gilbert, S. Mafioso.
Gunn, T. Black Jackets.
Johns, L. Pink Triangles.
Muldoon, P. Sightseers, The.
Weepies, The.
Muske, C. Field Trip.
Rodriguez, L. To the Police Officer Who Refused to Sit in the Same Room as My Son because He's a "Gang Banger".
Smith, J. D. Goodsonnet.
Soto. Morning They Shot Tony Lopez, Barber and Pusher Who Went Too Far, 1958, The.
Tolson, N. Bullet Hole Man.
Yi Sang. Two People : 1.
Two People : 2.
Young, K. Rushes, The.

Gannets
Bartlett, B. 2. to a northern gannet.
See also **Boobies**

Ganymede
Homer. Dardanus...was son of Zeus the Lord of the clouds.
Marlowe. What is't, sweet wag, I should deny thy youth?
Meleager. Hot day. Dying of thirst. Slake myself.
Ovid. Zeus and Ganymede.
Theognis. It's a thrill to love a boy: even Kronos' son, king of immortals, once longed for Ganymede.
Unknown. Hebe and Ganymede.
Wise Rejoice with Ganymede, The.
Zeus as an eagle came to Ganymede.

Garages
Mahon. Garage in Co. Cork, A.

Garbage and Garbage Men
Alley, R. Cleaning.
Axelrod, D. Guide to Urban Birds, A.
Bolton, D. Schiehallion.
Bryan, J. Rich Ink, Still Slightly Moist.
Coe, C. Possibility.
Grennan. Wing Road.
Hillman, B. Recycling Center.
Kenjeev. You envied the flying birds and stones.
Krivulin. Glory to caesar! and glory to God in the highest!
Matthews, W. Bear at the Dump, The.
Nemerov. Town Dump, The.
North, C. Little Cape Cod Landscape.
Shwarts [*or* Shvarts]. Dump, The.
Simpson, L. Physical Universe.
Tranter. Glow-boys.
Vroomkoning. Rubbish Bags.
Wilbur, R. After the Last Bulletins.
Junk.
Wormser. Pigeons.

Garbo, Greta
Berkson, B. Obvious Tradition, The.

García Lorca, Federico
Duncan, R. Drinking Fountain, The.
García Lorca. Romance Somnambulo by Garcia Lorca.
Hughes, T. After Lorca.
Jackson, R. Eight Ball.
Kaufman, B. Lorca.
Machado Ruiz. Crime Was in Granada, The.
Manrique, J. My Night with Frederico García

Lorca (As Told by Edouard Roditi).
Neruda. Ode to Federico García Lorca.
Suarez, V. Duende.

Garda, Lake, Italy
Tennyson, A. Frater Ave Atque Vale.

Gardens and Gardening
Adcock, F. Unexpected Visit.
Aiken, C. And in the Hanging Gardens.
Akenside. For a Grotto.
Alberti. Going Back Through Color.
Allnutt, G. Bringing the Geranium in for Winter.
Anzaldúa. Cultures.
Arkell. What is a Garden?
Armstrong, J. But if through genuine tenderness of heart.
Aston, A. Everything in the Garden is Lovely.
Atkins, R. Imaginary Crimes in a Real Garden.
Atwood. Dream 1: the Bush Garden.
Auden. Their Lonely Betters.
Baker, D. Yard, The.
Balakian, P. Back Yard, The.
Baranda, M. Ecstasy.
Éxtasis.
Barker, G. Gardens of Ravished Psyche, The.
Basho. Winter garden.
Bass, F. Garden, The.
Bateman, E. Cockney's Garden, The.
Beaver. Déjeuner Sur l'Herbe.
Bethell. Time.
Bible, *O.T.* Song of Solomon, The.
Black, S. Hoopla.
Blake, W. Garden of Love, The.
Bodecker. Garden Calendar.
Boileau-Despéaux. Epistle to My Gardener.
Boruch. Perennial Garden.
Boullosa, C. Elysian Garden.
Jardín Elíseo.
Bridges, R. Garden in September, The.
To Francis Jammes.
Brooke, L. Johnny Crow's Garden.
Brown, T. My Garden.
Browning, R. Sordello.
Brownjohn. In a Convent Garden.
Bullock, M. Garden.
Buson. Cut the peony.
Campana. Autumn Garden.
Carrera Andrade. Your body is a garden, a bush of flowers.
Carroll. In the Shakespeare Garden at Northwestern University.
Chang, E. After the Storm.
Chase, N. Plenty.
Chaucer. With that mine hand in his he took anon.
Cherry, K. In the Garden By the Sea: Easter.
Chesterfield. On Lord Ila's Improvements, near Hounslow Heath.
Chiasson, D. Spade.
Ch'u Ch'uang I. Evening in the Garden, Clear after Rain.
Chungji. Casual Line, A.
Ciardi, J. Suburban.
Clampitt. Palm Sunday.
Clare, J. Wish, The.
Cocteau. Young Girl Sleeping.
Coleridge, M. Poison Flower, The.
Coleridge, S. Garden Year, The.
Collier, M. Consider the Garden.
Cooke, R. Che Sara Sara.
Coolbrith. Ownership.
Cooley, N. Family History, The.
Cope, David. Labor Day.
Cotton, N. On Lord Cobham's Garden.
Cowley, A. Wish, The.
Cowper, W. Shrubbery, The.
Stricken Deer, The.
Crane, H. Garden Abstract.
Creeley. Door, The: "It is hard going to the door."
Cross, E. Pabellón.
Pavilion.
Crozier, L. Dirty Thirties, The.
Cummings, E. E. Sonnet IV.
Curry, N. Gardens.
Darwin. Kew.

Davies, W. H. No Man's Wood.
Dawe, B. Homo Suburbiensis.
Day Lewis. Snowfall on a College Garden.
De la Mare. Two Gardens.
de Lille. Gardens, The.
Dean, D. K. Taproot.
Deanovich. My Favorite Monk Is.
Delgado, J. Dandelion.
Deming, A. Tilden Park.
Denby. Villa d'Este.
Dobson, A. Garden Song, A.
Doddridge, P. Meditations on the Sepulchre in the Garden.
Dodge, M. Someone in the Garden.
Donne. Twickenham [*or* Twicknam] Garden.
Doolittle, H. Garden.
Heat.
Sheltered Garden.
Douglas, L. Two Loves.
Dove, R. Dog Days, Jerusalem.
Drinkwater. Cottage Song.
Druce. Apropos of Garden Statuary: A Disquisition upon a Minor Genre.
Dunn, D. Gardeners.
In the Grounds.
Durrell. In the Garden: Villa Cleobolus.
Edmond, L. Jardin des Colombières.
Elmslie, S. Forecast: Nadja.
Emerson, R. Days.
Enright, D. Kyoto Garden, A.
Erdrich. Fence, The.
Erlich, S. Garden of Shanah.
Evasco, M. Elemental.
Ezekiel. In the Garden: "It seemed to me so much like you."
Farjeon, E. Over the Garden Wall.
Finney, N. Uncles.
Flanders, J. Planting Onions.
Forché. Garden Shukkei-en, The.
Foster, A. Caterpillar.
Fujiwara no Yasusue. Nothing Whatsoever.
Gardner, J. Feat of Gardening, The.
Gilbert, S. Florist's Vade-Mecum, The.
Giles, J. Leasowes: Or, A Poetical Description of the Late Mr. Shenstone's Rural Retirement, The.
Ginsberg, A. Strange New Cottage in Berkeley, A.
Gioia. Alley Cat Love Song.
Glazer, M. Early Romance, Japanese Garden (*In the Heart of the City*).
Glenday, J. Garden, The: "Just for a quarter of a day, I'd have you."
Glück, L. Garden, The: "I couldn't do it again."
Garden, The: "One sound. Then the hiss and whir."
White Lilies, The.
Goethe. Here my garden is growing, the flowers of Eros I tend here.
Goyette, Susan. Peonies, The.
Graves, R. Gardener.
Gregory, H. Chinese Garden, The.
Greppi, C. Like a handful of leaves.
Grigson. Landscape Gardeners, The.
Guest, B. Wild Gardens Overlooked by Night Lights.
Guiney. Garden Chidings.
Gunn, T. Last Days at Teddington.
Martial.
Pope's Carnations Knew Him.
Hafiz, K [*or* Hafez]. On the Way to the Garden (77).
Hall, D. Digging.
Her Garden.
Hamburger, M. Garden, Wilderness.
Weeding.
Hamill, S. Reply to T'ao Ch'ien.
Harvey, M. In Defense of Our Overgrown Garden.
Hawes, S. Pastime of Pleasure, The.
Healy, R. Primula veris.
Hecht, A. Gardens of the Villa D'Este, The.
Herbert, E. You well-compacted groves, whose light and shade.
Herbert, G. Paradise.
Herlin. Warmth of the wind-break wall, The.

Hesketh. Death of a Gardener.
Hildebrandt, Z. In Hecate's Garden.
Hill, A. Garden Window, The.
Hines, P. My Garden.
Hochman. Cannon Hill.
Hoekstra. Cedar, The.
Homer. Gardens of Alcinous, The.
Howard, R. Mrs. Eden in Town for the Day.
Howells, W. November.
Huchel. Garden of Theophrastus, The.
Hudgins. Christ as a Gardener.
Hugo, R. Way a Ghost Dissolves, The.
Hunt, L. Noble range it was, of many a rood,
   A.
Ifan, W. Nant yr Eira.
Ignatova, E. Summer Garden, The.
Imbriglio, C. Gospel According to One Who
   Always Needs an Audience.
Ingram, A. Castle Howard, the Seat of the Rt.
   Hon. Charles, Earl of Carlisle.
Iorwerth, D. Garden.
Israeli, H. Sway.
Issa. Garden butterfly.
Ivask, Y. Emily Dickinson.
İzzet Molla. I am a nightingale in the garden of
   grief.
Jacinto, J. Visitation.
Jago. Instructions on landscaping.
Jarrell, R. In a Hospital Garden.
Jiménez, J. Nightfall. The Coolness of My
   Watered Garden.
Jones, R. Times Like This.
Jones, Tudur Dylan. Gardening.
   Great Glasshouse at the National Botanic
   Garden of Wales.
Jordan, B. This Poem.
Kassid, A. Leaves.
Kaufman, S. Emperor of China, The.
Kavanagh, P. Long Garden, The.
Kendrick, D. Gethsemane A. D.
Kinzie. Sun and Moon.
Kipling, R. Glory of the Garden, The.
Kirkup. Scarecrows.
Kistler, W. Kyoto 2—Ryoanji.
Knight, R. Landscape, The.
Kort, E. Gardener, The.
Kumin, M. Insider's View of the Garden, The.
Kunitz, S. Snakes of September, The.
   Touch Me.
Lady of the Arbour. Flower and the Leaf, The.
Lady of the Assembly. Assembly of Ladies,
   The.
Lawrence, D. H. Trees in the Garden.
Layton. Cold Green Element, The.
Layzer. Lawn Roller, The.
Le Gallienne. Library in a Garden, A.
Lehman. Greenhouses and Gardens.
Leithauser. In a Japanese Moss Garden.
Levertov. Death in Mexico.
Levin, P. Planting Roses.
Lewis, J. Garden Note II, March.
   Winter Garden.
Li Po. Late Bloomer at the Front of My
   Garden.
Liu, T. Brooklyn Botanic Garden, The.
Lowell, R. Public Garden, The.
Lucas, T. Town Garden, A.
Lydgate. Complaint of the Black Knight, The.
MacNeice. Sunlight on the Garden, The.
Magee, W. British Garden, A.
Malroux. Appointment in June.
Marvell. At the demolishing, this seat.
   Garden, The.
   Mower Against Gardens, The.
Marzán. In the Backyard.
Masaoka Shiki. Evening bell / Persimmons pelt.
Mason, W. To a Gravel Walk.
Matveyeva [or Matveieva]. Eggplants Have
   Pins and Needles, The.
Maurice. Chiswick.
Mayer, B. Garden, The.
McClanahan, R. Burial: "Like a sister who
   borrows."
McDonald, C. Oxford Gardens.
McMaster, R. Back Steps Lookout.
Meinke. Love Poem 1990.

Meireles. Sketch.
Melville, H. Ravaged Villa, The.
Merrick, A. Hartwell Gardens.
Merwin. Tide Line Garden.
Milton. Adam and Eve led out of Paradise.
Minhinnick. Grandfather in the Garden.
Mirabai [or Mira Bai]. O friend, understand: the
   body.
Mole, J. Trick, The.
Monroe, H. Garden, The.
Montague, J. 11 rue Daguerre.
Moraes, D. Gardener.
More, S. Child's Song.
Morrissey, S. Jo Gravis in His Metal Garden.
Morton, C. Twice now this morning I am
   wakened by full-throated geese.
Muso Soseki. Among rocks and valleys.
   Garden at the General's Residence, The.
   Snow Garden.
Nâbî. In the Garden of Time and Destiny.
Nedîm. Take Yourself to the Rose-Garden.
Nemerov. Salt Garden, The.
Nesbit, E. At Parting.
Noyes, A. Butterfly Garden, The.
O'Brien, S. Amateur God, The.
O'Shaughnessy, A. Song: "I made another
   garden, yea."
Ovid. Golden Age, The.
Page, P. After Rain.
Pasternak, B. Mirror, The.
Paz. Stanzas for an Imaginary Garden.
Peacocke. Railway Allotments.
Pedretti, Erica. Heimgarten.
   No, That Can't Be.
Phillips, C. Minotaur.
Piercy. Seven of Pentacles, The.
Pitter. Diehards, The.
   Other People's Glasshouses.
Plath. Manor Garden, The.
Po Chü-i. Chrysanthemums in the Eastern
   Garden, The.
   Planting Flowers on the Eastern Embankment.
Pope, A. Garden, The.
Porter, C. Old-Fashioned Garden.
Porter, P. Australian Garden, An.
Pound, E. Garden, The: "Like a skein of loose
   silk blown against a wall."
Pratt, S. Cottage Pictures.
Prunty. Vegetable Garden, The.
Quigless, H. Concert.
"Rachel." [or "Rahel."]. At the Window.
Radiguet. Poem: "Red eiderdown at the
   window, A."
Raine, C. Gardener, The.
Ratzlaff, K. Dill.
Raymond, M. June: "You can't hang a heavy
   mirror."
Redgrove, P. Negotium Perambulans.
Reed, H. Naming of Parts.
Rice, D. Taproots.
Riley, J. At the Stanley Spencer Exhibition.
Riordan, M. Topiary.
Roberts, L. Another Spring on Olmstead Street.
Rodríguez, A. Extracted.
Roethke. Cuttings.
   Cuttings (later) ("This urge, wrestle, resurrection
   of dry sticks.").
   Otto.
   Weed Puller.
Rossetti, C. Shut Out.
Rossetti, D. 19: Silent Noon.
Rowlands, D. Little Boots, The.
Rumi. Drunkards, The.
Sackville-West. Garden, The.
St. John, D. In the Sulphur Garden.
Sassoon, S. In Heytesbury Wood.
Schuyler, J. Roof Garden.
Shakespeare, W. Go bind thou up young
   dangling apricots.
Shen Yüeh. Returning to My Garden Home: In
   Respectful Response to the Master of Hua-
   yang.
Shirley, J. Garden, The.
Sims. Garden Song, A.
Sisson. Herb-Garden, The.
   Red Admiral, The.

Sitwell, E. Gardener Janus Catches a Naiad.
Sitwell, O. In the Potting Shed.
   In the Winter.
Smith, K. Writing in Prison.
Smith, R. Bluetits.
Snow, A. Gardener.
Sosnora. Letter, A.
Southerland. Night in Nigeria.
Spady, S. Tending Flowers.
Spark. Kensington Gardens.
Spenser, E. Bower of Bliss, The.
   Gardin of Adonis, The.
Stanley-Wrench. Hinterland.
Steele, T. Wartburg, 1521–22, The.
Stein, G. In This Way.
Stevens, W. Room on a Garden, A.
Stevenson, R. Autumn Fires.
   Gardener, The.
   To A Gardener.
Stewart, P. Estes' Backyard, The.
Stickney, T. Athenian Garden, An.
Strand. Garden, The.
Straus, M. Scarlet Crown.
Suckling, S. Upon My Lady Carlisle's Walking
   in Hampton Court Garden.
Sun Ch'o. Orchid Pavilion.
Swinburne. Forsaken Garden, A.
   Garden of Proserpine, The.
Sylvester, J. Garden, The.
T'ao Ch'ien [or T'ao Yuan-ming]. Returning to
   Fields and Gardens (2) ("I plant beans below
   the southern hill.").
   Returning to My Fields and Gardens.
Tarrant, J. Han Shan in Santa Rosa.
Taylor, E. Woman as Artist.
Tennyson, A. Come into the Garden, Maud.
   Gardener's Daughter, The.
   Recollections of The Arabian Nights.
   So sang the gallant glorious chronicle.
   Unwatched, the garden bough shall sway.
   Witch-elms that counterchange the floor.
Thomas, D. Walking in Gardens.
Thomas, Edith Matilda. Frost To-night.
Thomas, Edward. Digging.
Thomas, G. Lessons.
Tomlinson, C. In the Borghese Gardens.
   Juliet's Garden.
   Shugakuin Garden.
Trakl. In Hellbrunn.
Tsvetayeva [or Tsvetaeva]. Garden.
Tu Fu [or Du Fu]. Peach and plum I planted
   were my own, The.
   Servant Boy Delivers, The.
Unknown. God, is this then a sin?
   Here in my garden.
   My lover prefers well mannered garden flowers.
   Richmond Gardens: A Poem.
   Rise and Progress of the Present Taste in
   Planning Parks, Pleasure Grounds, Gardens,
   etc, The.
   What business, this? What reason should we
   give.
Van Duyn. Gardener to His God, The.
Vazirani, R. Maya to Herself and Then to Her
   Gardener.
Vidya. On Makeshift Bedding.
Wagner, S. Sunken Gardens (Huntington, IN),
   The.
Waller, E. On St. James's Park, as Lately
   Improved by His Majesty.
   To a Lady in a Garden.
Wang Hsi-chih. Orchid Pavilion.
Wang Wei. Twilight in the Garden.
Webb, P. Marvell's Garden.
Wellesley. Walled Garden.
West, G. Stowe, the Gardens of the Rt. Hon.
   Richard Lord Viscount Cobham.
Whitehead, W. On the Late Improvements at
   Nuneham, the Seat of the Earl of Harcourt.
Whittier. Garden.
Wilbur, R. Caserta Garden.
Williams, P. Lost Seed.
Williams, W. Italian Garden, The.
   Tulip Bed, The.
   Widow's Lament in Springtime, The.
Wilner, E. Secret Garden, The.

Winchilsea. Upon My Lord Winchilsea's Converting the Mount in His Garden to a Terrace.
Winters, Y. Time and the Garden.
Wordsworth, W. Her cottage, then a cheerful object, wore.
Wright, C. Song of the Gourd.
Wright, J. Invention of a Garden, The.
Wright, K. Love Song of Tooting, A.
Yeats. Ancestral Houses.
   Down by the Salley Gardens.
Yeryomin. House over the garden is a bouquet of evening windows, The.
Yorke. Our Gardener here, James Phillips see.
Yuan Mei. Last Poem: Goodbye to My Garden.
Zabolotsky [or Zabolotskii]. Nocturnal Garden.

Gargoyles
Hernández Cruz. Milagrosa, La.
Sandburg, C. Broken-Face Gargoyles.
   Gargoyle.

Garibaldi, Giuseppe
MacDiarmid, H. Why I Choose Red.

Garland, Judy
Seaton, M. Story of Stonewall, A.

Garlic
Horace. Counterblast against Garlic, A.
Meyers, B. Garlic, The.

Garrick, David
Johnson, S. Prologue Spoken by Mr[.] Garrick at the Opening of the Theatre in Drury Lane, 1747.

Garrison, William Lloyd
Ray, H. William Lloyd Garrison.

Gasoline Stations
Bishop, E. Filling Station.
Corn. Reading *Pericles* in New London.
Dye, Jeffrey. Copyright Renewal Under the Texaco Star.
Gilmore, B. Gas Station Attendant.
Grass. Gasco.
Hillman, B. Cheap Gas.
Laux, D. Fast Gas.
Mirosevich, T. Hygiene.
Tapahonso. Pay Up or Else.
Wade, S. Gas.

Gates
Andal. O you who guard over.
Awoonor. At the Gates.
Barnes, W. Turnstile, The.
Borisov. Gates.
Daigu. Who dares approach the lion's.
Dante Alighieri. Through me come into the city full of pain.
Dickinson, E. Soul selects her own Society, The.
Garioch. Nemo Canem Impune Lacessit.
Gorham. Princess Parade.
Homer. Gardens of Alcinous, The.
Jackson, H. Opportunity.
Lu Chao-lin. Old Idea of Choan by Rosoriu.
Macaulay, T. Horatius [or Horatius at the Bridge].
Mew. At the Convent Gate.
Mo Shih-lung. Saying Good-bye to a Singing Girl Who Has Decided to Become a Nun.
Probyn. Blossom.
Reddy, S. Generations.
Stevenson, A. Salter's Gate.
Suzuki, M. Monastery gate.
Unknown. Chu-qi dong-men: At the Great Gate.
   Curse on a Closed Gate, A.

Gauguin, Paul
Hearne, V. Gauguin's White Horse.
Molina, E. To Vahine (Painted by Gaugin).
Vázquez Montalbán, M. Gaugin ("His journalist.").
Walcott. Gauguin.

Gawaine, Sir
Lytton, E. Gawaine and the Hound.
Unknown. Since the siege and the assault upon Troy were finished.
   Sir Gawain and the Green Knight [Marie Borroff Translation].
Winters, Y. Sir Gawaine and the Green Knight.

Gay and Lesbian Poetry
Aguilar, M. Sunshine.
Alviso, M. Barbies, Las.
Anderson, T. I Think You Got Me Confused.
Angguish, D. Arrythmia (1–10).
Aragon, F. Doubletalk.
   Earplugs.
Arroyo, R. Longing: "It wasn't just about sex, but about."
   My Mysterious Body.
B., L. After School Commute with My Girl.
Bailey, S. Hide-n-Seek.
Banzon, K. Here's a Match.
Boden, C. Sombreo Beach, Vancouver Island, BC.
Brannan, J. Texas Sunrise, A.
Coccia, M. We Are Not Vegetarians.
Conway, J. Odd Years, The.
Costello, R. Uncertain Geometry.
   When My Sister Was Fifteen.
Dalby, L. MacArthur High School.
Daugherty, B. Lilac.
   Nightfire.
de la Parra Jr., J. Awakening.
   Courage!
De la Tierra. Butterflying.
Evans, A. Playing for Love.
   Something More Obvious.
Gomez. My Chakabuku Mama: A Comic Tale.
González, R. Crush.
   Mariposa.
Healey, T. Bubble.
   Ode to DJ.
Helfand, J. Girl in the Boy's Dressing Room, The.
Hightower, S. Cruising a Hungry World.
   Spending the Night.
Holland, W. Black Water Creek.
Mann, R. Elegy for the Hurdler.
Martin, D. Clock.
   If We Were in a Gregg Araki Movie.
Murray, C. I Got Beat Up A Lot in High School.
   Mickey Mouse.
Pafunda, Danielle. Saltbox Brothel.
Palmer, R. Logic of Queerness, The: (Releasing Your Ivy Evening Within).
Pickering, R. Untitled: "First thought in my head waking up was, oh no."
Rachel, T. You Can't Go Back to Sleep.
Richard, B. My Sixth Grade Sex Life: Milne Elementary, New Orleans.
Rumens. Stealing the Genre.
Schneiderman, J. Last Ditch.
Shakan, J. Soft.
Shipley, A. Mama Said.
Simon, O. Heat.
Stahl, C. Greyhound.
   Polestar.
Stillpoint, H. Form a Band, Goddammit.
   This I Whisper.
Trinidad. Boy, The.
   Slicker.
Wascovich, M. Serial Toxic Teen.
   Wolf Packet and Rural America.
Wozek, G. Song to Myself at Seventeen.
Zetter, S. Misdemeanor.

Gazelles
HaNagid. Gazelle, The.
Moore, T. Gazelles, The.
Rilke. Gazelle, The.

Geese
Alcott, L. Lay of a Golden Goose, The.
Berry, W. Wild Geese, The.
Braun, R. Goose.
   Lilies, The.
Buson. Calligraphy of geese.
   Tears.
Caleshu, A. Collaboration: Between Countries.
Carroll, J. Withdrawal Letter.
Carruth, H. No Matter What, After All, and That Beautiful Word So.
Chamberlain, K. Stepping in the Same River.
Chine-Jo, Lady. Wild geese / Fellow travelers.
Davies, G. Wild Geese, The.
Davis, J. He Is Lightning.

Doolittle, H. In resurrection, there is confusion.
Field, R. Something Told the Wild Geese.
Fujiwara no Teika. Weary wild geese who came.
Glück, L. Messengers.
Haewŏn. On Hearing the Song of the Geese.
Howes, B. Wild Geese Flying.
Hsiao Kang. Watching a Lonely Wild Goose at Nightfall.
Issa. Cries of wild geese.
   Geese, fresh greens / Wait for you.
Jamie, K. Skeins o Geese.
Kenney. Concrete Delivery Delayed by Goose and Gosling Crossing, Late March, Mallett's Bay.
Kikaku. Above the boat.
Lady Ise. Seeing the Returning Geese.
Nesbit, E. Goose-Girl, The.
Norris, L. Hudson's Geese.
Oliver, M. Wild Geese.
   Wild Geese: "You do not have to be good."
Ortiz. 8:50 AM Ft. Lyons VAH.
Parry, R. Geese, The.
Piercy. Last Scene in the First Act.
   Postcard from the Garden.
Plath. Rhyme.
Jones, R. Geese at Gregynog.
Richardson, K. Aubade: "Geese flew by as you entered me, The."
Sandburg, C. Bas-Relief.
Southey, R. To a Goose [or Gosse].
Stallworthy, J. Poem about Poems about Vietnam, A.
Strand. Poor North.
Suyemoto, Toyo. Hokku: "Geese flew over, The."
Tu Fu [or Du Fu]. Lone Wild Goose.
Unknown. Faint moon in a heavy frost, The.
   What Do We Geese Wear For Clothes?
Villa, D. Remember the goose that.
Waniek. Bali Hai Calls Mama.
Warren, R. Heart of Autumn.
   Tell Me a Story.
Willard, N. Wisdom of Geese, The.
Wunderlich, M. Predictions about a Black Car.

Geisha
Ishikawa Takuboku. Better Than Crying.

Gems
Bat-Miriam. Precious stones that my mother.
Byron, G. Cornelian, The.
De Kok. Salamander.
Dickinson, E. 'Tis little I— could care for Pearls.
Douglas, L. Impression de Nuit; London.
Kasa. Look at this keepsake.
Muso Soseki. Gem Mountain.
Rossetti, C. Flint.
Spenser, E. Sonnet 15: "Ye tradeful merchants that, with weary toil."
Taylor, J. Star, The.
Timoner, J. Earliest Crows in Mineral.
Young, A. Suilven.

Gender
Adonis [or Adunis]. Woman and a Man, A.
Basheva. Fast train, The? The express?
   Not long ago a whole sun.
Crawford, R. Masculinity.
Gordon, G. Timothy. At Jhong-Jhou Train Station.
Helfand, J. Boy Girl Game, The.
   Girl in the Boy's Dressing Room, The.
Komunyakaa, Y. Homo Erectus.
Leonard, T. Four of the Belt.
Markotić, N. Repeat the capitalism of narrative.
Milán, E. Esto no puede seguir así: sé sincero, uno.
   We can't go on like this: be truthful, empty.
Needell. Not a Balancing Act.
O'Donoghue, M. She-Machines, The.
Putnam. Sonnets to Some Sexual Organs.
Ransom, Jane R. This Is Just a Fairy Tale.
Trinidad. Slicker.
White, A. Moon Daughters.
Williams, T. Nintendo.
Wise, S. Testimony.
Young, P. Third Sex, The.

Generals
Archilochus. Ideal General, The.
Betjeman. Old Land Dog, The.
Bierce. General B. F. Butler.
Garman. Bury the Great Horse.
Hồ Xuân Hương. General's Plaque, The.
Ibn Hāni' al-Andalusi, A. Sons of al-'Abbās say, The: "Has Egypt been conquered?" Therefore reply to the sons of al-'Abbās: "The matter has already been accomplished".
Ivanov, G. Old man shuffles to the fish market, The.
Kirstein. Patton.
Kuzmin. Were I a general of olden times.
Landor, W. Crimean Heroes, The.
Lindsay, V. General William Booth Enters into Heaven.
Maraini. Plaza de Mayo.
Marvell. Upon Appleton House [To My Lord Fairfax].
Upon the Hill and Grove at Bilbrough.
Nowlan. In Those Old Wars.
Sassoon, S. General, The.
Good-morning, good-morning! the General said.
Sherwood, K. Albert Sidney Johnston.
Wallace, R. Nightline: An Interview with the General.
Yejong, King of Koryŏ. Dirge for Two Generals.

Generosity
Adamson, H. Everything I Have Is Yours.
Akst, H. Straw Hat in the Rain.
Bhattācārya, M. Your behavior proves how stingy You are, Ma.
Brown, L. Straw Hat in the Rain.
Davies, O. Urban.
Dunn, S. From the Manifesto of the Selfish.
Farrow, S. Civil War, The.
Gilbert, W. There Lived a King.
Hart, L. I've Got Five Dollars.
Hill, J. Economics of Gererosity, The.
Hughes, L. Preference.
Levertov. Métier of Blossoming, The.
Martial. You want me to call you generous.
O'Connor, M. Sakura.
Persius. Satire 6: "Has Sabine winter brought you to your fireside."
Jones, R. Nurse, The.
Salaam. Sharing is Hereditary.
Sanchez, S. This is Not a Small Voice.
Tiruvalluvar. Kindness and Generosity.
Unknown. Hymn to the Virgin.
Wang Wei. Peerless Lady, The.

Genetics and Geneticists
Cassity. Meaner Than a Junkyard Dog; or, Turner's Evil Twin.
Fulton, A. Doing the Evolution Shuffle.
MacKenzie, R. Category Mistakes in Biochemistry.
Moolten, D. Bio 7.
Morrissey, S. Genetics.
See also **Evolution**

Geneva, Switzerland
Truitt, S. Old World Monkeys.

Genghis Khan
Unknown. Last Battle and Death of Chingis Khan, The.
Temujin Becomes Chingis Khan.

Genitalia
Andrews, N. Notes for a Sermon on the Mount.
Antipater of Thessalonica. Priapus, seeing Cimon's rigid rod.
Auden. Mad to be had, to be felt and smelled. My lips.
Behn, A. In a cottage by the mountain.
Broumas, O. Tryst.
With the clear.
Burns, R. Wat ye what my Minnie did.
Citino. Sister Mary Appassionata Lectures the Eighth Grade Boys and Girls: The Family Jewels.
Constantine, D. Pleasure.
Crowley, A. Ballad of Passive Paederasty, A.
Dafydd [or David] ap Gwilym. Penis, The.
Dorantes, D. Iguana láctea.

Lacteal iguana.
Field, E. Street Instructions at the Crotch.
Giorno. Pornographic Poem.
Goodison. On Becoming a Mermaid.
Guerra, T. Canto Twenty-Four: "Cunt is a spiderweb, The."
Hagedorn, J. Vulva Operetta.
Harrison, J. God's Penis.
Ibn Kamal. How an Old Man Can Regain His Youth Through Sexual Potency.
Koertge. All Suffering Comes from Attachment.
Liu, T. Size of It, The.
Martial. Chrestus, your balls are depilated.
Lydia is as wide and slack.
Your slave boy's cock is aching, Naevolus.
McCombs, J. Epithet.
McHugh, H. I Knew I'd Sing.
Mechain, G. Female Genitals, The.
Mooney, M. In the Parlour.
Neely, L. Eight Ways of Looking at Pussy.
Olds, S. Early Images of Heaven.
Pope's Penis, The.
Paquet. Basket Case.
Purdy, J. From rivers, and from the earth itself.
Putnam. Sonnets to Some Sexual Organs.
Rankine. Short Narrative of Breasts and Wombs in Service of Plot Entitled, A.
Redel, V. Singing to Tony Bennett's Cock.
Rimbaud, A. Obscur et froncé.
Our Assholes Are Different.
Rochester, J. Song: "Oh gentle Venus, ease a tarse."
Rouse, A. Queynt.
Rufinus. Her foot sparkled like silver.
Shinder. Growing Up.
Smukler. Trash.
Strato [or Straton]. Boys' members, Diodorus, come in three.
Don't hitch your dear little cunt against that wall.
Yesterday in the bath Diodes' penis.
Your rosy-fingered prick that used to charm.
Unknown. Corpus Inscriptionum Latinarum 14.3565.
Having left behind its cutting.
I ask you to witness, Priapus.
My mistress in a hive of bees.
No Balls at All.
Ring That Controlled Erections, The.
Romans, I appeal to you.
Substituted Poem of Laureate Quynh, The.
To your question: why are my private parts.
Wild Dreams, The.
Vallejo. I'm thinking of your sex.
Verlaine. Balanide 2.
Mille e tre.
Wilkes, J. He who the hoop's immensity can pierce.
Pleased to the last, she likes the luscious food.
Then, in the scale of Pricks, 'tis plain.
Then, say not Man's imperfect, Heaven in fault.

Genius
Bécquer, G. Dark in a Corner of the Room.
Blake, W. All Religions Are One.
Browning, E. To George Sand: A Recognition.
Campos, A. Tobacco Shop, The.
Emerson, R. Him strong Genius urged to roam.
Hughes, L. Genius Child.
Kizer, C. Twelve O'Clock.
Menken. Genius.
My Heritage.
Merry. Genius, or Muse, whate'er thou art! whose thrill.
Robinson, E. Ben Jonson Entertains a Man from Stratford.

Genocide
Auden. Refugee Blues.
Balakian, P. After the Survivors Are Gone.
Brett, L. I Keep Forgetting.
Celan. Death Fugue.
Fainlight, R. Archive Film Material.
Fenton, J. German Requiem, A.
Hamburger, M. Treblinka.
Huchel. Roads.
Reznikoff. When the Second World War began.
Sachs, N. O the Chimneys.

Spender, S. History and Reality.
Watson, R. Is This Man, Martin Bormann?
Zych. Auschwitz, 1987.

Gentians
Bryant, W. To the Fringed Gentian.
Evans, A. Fringed Gentians.
Lawrence, D. H. Bavarian Gentians.

Geodes
Dodd, E. Like Memory, Caverns.

Geography and Geographers
Campo. Our Country of Origin.
Cavendish, M. Body, The: A Fancy.
Chesterton. Geography.
Clements, Brian. Historia.
Crase. Continent as the Letter M, The.
Donne. Hymn[e] to God My God, In My Sickness[e], A.
Goldbarth. Letter to Friends East and West.
Koch, K. Geography.
Lomax, M. Kith.
Osbey. Geography.
Rimbaud, A. Promontory.
St. John, D. I will tell you. Maybe.
Sampley. Coronado at Rio Grande Del Norte.
Sharp, S. Good Nights.
Whitman, W. Passage to India.

Geology and Geologists
Blumenthal, M. Geologist, The.
Copus, J. Widower.
Day, C. Yesterday explorers found.
Hillman, B. Geology, A.
Hongo. Porphyry of Elements, A.
Mulford. Nevrazumitelny.
Neruda. Amor America (1400).
Ramke, B. Art, Love, Geology.
Rexroth, K. Lyell's Hypothesis Again.
Schelling. Haibun.
Seyburn, P. What I Disliked About the Pleistocene Era.
Snyder, G. What Happened Here Before.
Tennyson, A. Guess well, and that is well. Our age can find.

Geometry
Bibbins, M. Geometry Class.
Bremer, C. Cena de un 10 de Abríl.
Dinner on an April 10th.
Collins, M. Lines: "Draw a line. Write a line. There."
Daiches, J. Geometry.
Dickinson, A. Contributors to Geometry: Cold Hands.
Dove, R. Geometry.
Harnick. Ballad of the Shape of Things, The.
Hostetler, A. Resisting Geometry.
McMorris, M. Geometry of the Figure.
Novikov, N. In our world it's unusual.
Roberts, K. Tilt, The.
Vallejo. Three hundred womanly states of the Eiffel Tower are frozen, The.
Wayne, J. In Praise of Zigzags.
See also **Euclid**

George I, King of England
Browne, W. Epigram: "King to Oxford sent a troop of horse, The."

George II, King of England
Carey, H. Lilliputian Ode on Their Majesties' Accession, A.

George III, King of England
Bentley, E. George III.
Byron, G. Vision of Judgment, The ("Saint Peter sat by the celestial gate.").
Carey, H. Lilliputian Ode on Their Majesties' Accession, A.
Freneau. France aids them now, a desperate game I play.
Koch, K. You Were Wearing.
Southey, R. George III Enters Paradise.
Whitman, W. Boston Ballad, A.

George V, King of England
Betjeman. Death of King George V.
Hayward, C. King George V.

Georgia (state)
Bernie, B. Sweet Georgia Brown.
Bottoms. In a U-Haul North of Damascus.
Broonzy. Southern Blues, The.

Brown, S. Slim in Atlanta.
Burris, J. Ballin' the Jack.
Casey, K. Sweet Georgia Brown.
Clarke, G. Everything Is Peaches Down in Georgia.
Dickey, J. In the Marble Quarry.
Dove, R. Planning the Perfect Evening.
Gorrell, S. Georgia on My Mind.
Lanier, S. Song of the Chattahoochee.
McElroy, C. This Is the Poem I Never Meant to Write.
Pinkard, M. Sweet Georgia Brown.
Ríos, A. Purpose of Altar Boys, The.
Toomer. Georgia Dusk.
  Portrait in Georgia.
Work. Marching through Georgia.
Wright, C. Chickamauga.

Geraniums
Adler, L. Geranium Flame.
Allnutt, G. Bringing the Geranium in for Winter.
Baker, D. Heavenly.
Dorn, E. Geranium.
Fagin, L. New York.
Lawrence, D. H. Red Geranium and Godly Mignonette.
Livesay, D. Bartok and the Geranium.
Newburn, L. Office Geraniums.
Roethke. Geranium, The.

German (language)
Buckley, V. Teaching German Literature.
Graham, V. Ein Complaint.
Redmond, J. Daumenbreite.

Germans, The
Caraion. Song from the Occupation Time.
Coward. Don't Let's Be Beastly to the Germans.
Fenton, J. German Requiem, A.
Heyen. Riddle: "From Belsen a crate of gold teeth."
Hölderlin. To the German People.
Jacob, M. In Search of the Traitor.
Knox, J. My Big German Bra.
Leeflang. 1945.
Leland, C. Breitmann in Paris.
  There's a liddle fact of hishdory vitch few hafe oondershtant.
  Wein Geist.
Milosz, O. La Berline Arrêtée Dans la Nuit.
Rohrer, M. Precision German Craftsmanship.
Smith, S. On the Death of a German Philosopher.
Tsvetayeva [or Tsvetaeva]. They took quickly, they took hugely.

Germany
Alkalay-Gut. Kitzbuhl Church.
Bachmann. Early Noon.
Bowers, E. Prince, The.
Brecht, B. From a German War Primer.
  War Has Been Given a Bad Name.
Brock, V. Remembering Dresden.
Celan. Death Fugue.
  Death Fugue, A.
  Deathfugue.
  Fugue of Death.
Eich. Seminar for Backward Pupils.
Éluard, P. Nazi Song.
Fenton, J. His wife nods, and a secret smile.
Gershon. Race.
Heine, H. Night Thoughts.
  Silesian Weavers, The.
Huelsenbeck, R. "We Hardly".
Kramer, L. Immigrants.
Levine, A. Four November 9ths.
Logau. Booty from the German War.
  German Language, The.
MacNeice. Munich Agreement, The.
Martin. Dreams in German.
Maxton. Deutschland.
Merton. Dark Morning, The.
Milosz, C. With Her.
Norton, C. Bingen on the Rhine.
Olin. Warner Bros. Newest Thriller *Valentine*.
Porter, P. May, 1945.
Prufer, K. On Finding a Swastika Carved on a Tree in the Hills above Heidelberg.

Schiff, H. German Frontier at Basel: 1942 and 1992, The.
Shanks, E. High Germany.
Sorley. To Germany.
Tranter. Enzensberger at 'Exiles'.
  Lufthansa.
Weckherlin. To Germany.
Yevtushenko [or Evtushenko]. Babii Yar.

Germs
Gerstler. Seesaw.
Nash, O. Germ, The.

Gertrude [Hamlet]
Upton, L. Gertrude to Hamlet.
White, G. Queen Gertrude's Soliloquy.

Gethsemane
Cairns, Scott. More Earnest Prayer of Christ, The.
Craig, David. Gethsemane: "Damp wind, the innocent."
Ermakova, I. Gethsemane: "Moon swims to the fore in the pale heavens, The."
Kane, P. Disciples Asleep at Gethsemane.
Kipling, R. Gethsemane.
Pasternak, B. Garden of Gethsemane, The.
  Mark 14:26–42; And when they had sung.
Pratt, E. From Stone to Steel.
Unknown. Christ's Prayer in Gethsemane.

Gettysburg, Battle of (1863)
Harte, B. John Burns of Gettysburg.
Kenyon, J. Gettysburg, July 1, 1863.
Masters, E. Battle of Gettysburg, The.
  Gettysburg.
Pastan. At Gettysburg.
Taylor, B. Gettysburg Ode.
Thompson, W. High Tide at Gettysburg, The.

Ghana
Derricotte. Exits from Elmina Castle: Cape Coast, Ghana.
Gerov, Alexander. Accra.
Laing, K. Same Corpse, The.

Ghettos
Algarin. Taos Pueblo Indians: 700 strong according to Bobby's last census.
Brody. Ghetto Twilight.
Dumas, H. Concentration Camp Blues.
Ettinger, E. Micrographic Manuscript, Miniature (2).
Friedmann. Butterfly, The.
  Butterfly, The.
Jenkins, P. Six Small Fires.
Klein, A. Autobiographical.
Košek, M. It All Depends on How You Look at It.
Meléndez. Oye Mundo/Sometimes.
Milosz, C. Poor Christian Looks at the Ghetto, A.
Picková, E. Fear.
Robles. Remembering the Past.
Schulzová, E. Evening in Terezin, An.
Slonimski. Elegy: "No more, no more Jewish townships in Poland."
Steptoe. Three Legged Chairs.
  Wired In.
Unknown, fr. Terezin Concentration Camp. Homesick.
  Night in the Ghetto.
Voznesensky [or Voznesenskii]. Call of the Lake, The.

Ghost Dances and Ghost Dancers
Arapaho Oral Tradition. Father, have pity on me.
  He'Yoho'Ho! He'Yoho'Ho!
  I'yehe! my children—Uhi'yeye'heye!
  My Son, Let Me Grasp Your Hand.
  Spirit Host Is Advancing, They Say, The.
  When I Met Him Approaching.
Sioux Oral Tradition. Give Me Back My Bow.

Ghosts
Alberti. Ghost, The.
Alegría. Nocturnal Visits.
Alexie. Tourists.
Graves, A. Song of the Ghost, The.
Baillie, J. Ghost of Fadon, The.
Baker, H. Toward Guinea: For Larry Neal, 1937–1981.

Balaban. After Our War.
Barry, C. Finding.
Beddoes. Old Adam, the Carrion Crow.
  Phantom-Wooer, The.
  Song by Isbrand.
Bell, J. Poem to Line My Casket with, Ramona.
Bellerby. Voices.
Berger, B. Haunts of the Mirage.
Blair, R. Oft in the lone church-yard at night I've seen.
Bloch, C. Kiss, The.
Bonnefoy. De Natura Rerum.
  Passer-by, these are words.
Bontemps. Southern Mansion.
Brooks, G. Mentors.
Burkard. Sober Ghost.
Cameron, N. Fight with a Water-Spirit.
Cassian. Ghost.
Causley. By St. Thomas Water.
Chittendon. Old Fort Phantom Hill.
Clanchy, K. Deadman's Shoes.
Cofer, J. Drowned Sailor, The.
de Folgar. Panorama.
De la Mare. Ghost, The ("Peace in thy hands / Peace in thine eyes.").
  Ghost, The ("Who knocks? I, who was beautiful.").
  Listeners, The.
Dietz, H. Haunted Heart.
Digges. Rough Music.
Dillard, R. Ghosts in the Stacks.
Donne. Apparition, The.
Dove, R. Revenant.
Dryden, J. Epilogue to *Tyrannic[k] Love.*
Dunn, S. Father, Mother, Robert Henley, who hanged himself in the ninth grade, et al.
Edwards [or Edwardes], R. Recollections of an Old Spook.
Eguren. Dead, The.
"Ern Malley." Coda: "We have lived as ectoplasm."
Eyen, J. New Dream, A (Wuski A-Baw-Tan).
Ferguson, G. Swimming Pool Ghost, The.
French, T. Ghost Ship.
Frost, R. Witch of Coös, The.
Gilbert, C. This Bridge Across.
Gioia. All Souls'.
Gloria. Rizal's Ghost.
Graham, J. Underneath (2).
Graves, R. Corporal Stare.
  Welsh Incident.
Gregg. Adult.
Grinshpan, Y. Vanzetti's Ghost.
Gurney, I. Ballad of the Three Spectres.
Hall, D. Mount Kearsarge.
Hamilton, M. Midnight in Mississippi.
Hardy, T. My Spirit Will Not Haunt the Mound.
Heaney, S. I had come to the edge of the water.
Heath-Stubbs. Simcox.
Hecht, A. Ghost in the Martini, The.
  Still Life.
Heinemann, M. Ringstead Mill.
Hernández Cruz. Discovery.
  Spirits.
Hill, G. And it seemed, while we waited, he began to walk to- / wards us.
  To the High Court of Parliament ("Where's probity in this.").
Hogg, J. Wife of Crowle, The.
Homer. Achilles' Dream.
Housman. When I watch the living meet.
Howard, R. Among the Missing.
Hugo, R. Way a Ghost Dissolves, The.
Hugo, V. Bridge, The.
  Djinns, The.
Huws, Meirion MacIntyre. Window.
Jiménez, J. Leave the Doors Standing Open.
Johnson, M. F. Invocation to the Spirit Said to Haunt Wroxall Down.
Justice, D. Invitation to a Ghost.
Keesing. Queer Thing, A.
Kim Chŏngnan. Veronica, a Double Life.
Kinsella, T. Thinking of Mr D.
Kipling, R. Looking Glass, The.
Lee, L. This Hour and What Is Dead.
Leithauser. Ghost of a Ghost, The.

Levertov. Another Revenant.
Levi, P. Survivor, The.
Levin, D. Red Water.
Levy, A. Old House, The.
Lindsay, L. Auld Robin Gray.
Lingche. Spending the Night at East Forest
 Temple.
Lisboa. Elegy: "At first the dead."
Livesay, D. Uninvited, The.
Long, J. Bermuda Triangle.
Longfellow, H. Cross of Snow, The.
 Haunted Houses.
Macdonald, G. Song.
MacLean, S. Hallaig.
Macpherson, J. Some Ghosts and Some Ghouls.
Maiden. Air.
 Foundations, The.
Mallet, D. William and Margaret.
Marlatt, D. Ghost.
Masefield. No man takes the farm.
Merrill, J. Correct but cautious, that first night,
 we asked.
Millay, E. Little Ghost, The.
Montague, J. Family Conference.
Mtshali. Voice from the Dead, A.
Murphy, P. New Boy, The.
Nemes Nagy. Ghost, The.
Nesbit, E. Gray Folk, The.
 Haunted.
 Villeggiature.
Noyes, A. Highwayman, The.
Olson, C. As the Dead Prey upon Us.
 At Yorktown.
Otero, B. Cloister of the Shades, The.
Peacock, T. Ghosts, The.
Perillo, L. Ghost Shirt, The.
Phillips, D. Hounds are either the work of wind,
 The.
Phillips, S. Apparition, The.
Piatt, S. Army of Occupation.
Poe. Conqueror Worm, The.
 Haunted Palace, The.
Propertius. Ghost, The.
Ramanujan. Some People.
Ransom, J. Spectral Lovers.
Reese, L. Day Before Spring, The.
Robinson, A. Dead Friend, The.
Robinson, E. Lingard and the Stars.
 Why He Was There.
Robinson, M. Haunted Beach, The.
Roethke. She.
Roland Holst. Visitation.
Rose. Poet Haunted, The.
Rossetti, C. Chilly Night, A.
Sassoon, S. Presences Perfected.
Scovell. Ghosts, The.
Seiferle, R. Foundling, The.
Shakespeare, W. Angels and ministers of grace
 defend us!
Shapcott, J. When I Died.
Smith, I. Ghost, The.
Smith, S. Wanderer, The.
Soupault. Song for Ghosts and for Those Now
 Gone.
Soyinka. Abiku.
 Civilian and Soldier.
Stanton, M. Few Picnics in Illinois, A.
Stevens, W. Rabbit Is King of the Ghosts, A.
Stoddard, E. House by the Sea, The.
Tennyson, A. I shall not see thee. Dare I say.
Thomas, D. Ghost Story.
Trakl. Evening, The: "With the ghostly shapes
 of dead heroes."
 In Hellbrunn.
Trench, H. She Comes Not When Noon Is on
 the Roses.
Tsvetayeva [or Tsvetaeva]. Gentle ghost.
Tu Fu [or Du Fu]. Snow Storm.
Tynan Hinkson, K. Dead-Tryst, The.
Unknown. Dark House, The.
 Three Ghostesses.
 Wife of Usher's Well, The.
Van Haren, E. Stepping Out With Edvard
 Munch ("When from the other world you.").
Wang the Zealot. Ghosts Clap Hands.
Waniek. House on Moscow Street, The.

Weaver, A. Appaloosa, The.
Weingarten, J. Ghost Frost.
Wells, Jeanne. July Thirteenth.
Whitman, W. As If a Phantom Caress'd Me.
Wordsworth, W. Lucy Gray; or, Solitude.
 She Was a Phantom of Delight.
Wright, J. Youth.
Wylie. Village Mystery.
Yeats. All Souls' Night.
 Apparitions, The.
 To a Shade.
Young Bear. Emily Dickinson, Bismarck and
 the Roadrunner's Inquiry.
Zurita, R. Splendor in the Wind.

Giacometti, Alberto
Char. Alberto Giacometti.

Giants
Campbell, S. Big John's Tears Fall to the River.
Major, C. Giant Red Woman.
Mayer, G. Count Carrots.
Millay, E. Bean-Stalk, The.
Prigov. Imagine this: a mighty giant asleep.
Riley, J. Jack the Giant-Killer.
Shapiro, D. Giants.
Volkman. Sonnet: "Sky we bear on our
 shoulders, heaven-height, The."

Gibbons
Wen Chao. Hearing the Gibbons Call in Pa
 Gorge.

Gibraltar
Blunt, W. Gibraltar.
Muhammad ibn Ghalib al-Rusafi. Were you to
 go to the fire of the Guidance on the side of
 Mount Sinai, you could take all the knowledge
 and light you wish.

Gifts and Giving
Abu Madi. Holiday Present.
Adebajo, K. Moonlight on the Lake.
Anderson, D. Executive Geochrone.
"Anvari.". Take What He GIves You.
Anyte [or Anytes]. Lone Theudotos placed this
 gift beneath the mountain.
 Ox-sized cauldron, Kleubotos gave, An.
Avison. Present From Ted.
Betjeman. Christmas.
Bible, O.T. Song: "Come, my beloved."
Bishop, M. Dark Christmas on Wildwood Road,
 The.
Borges. Poem of the Gifts.
Byron, G. Cornelian, The.
Carruth, H. Impossible Indispensability of the
 Ars Poetica, The.
Causley. Nursery Rhyme of Innocence and
 Experience.
Clark, P. Kleptomaniac.
Coleridge, M. Broken Friendship.
Comden, B. Thanks a Lot, but No Thanks.
Davenant [or D'Avenant]. For the Lady Olivia
 Porter; a Present upon a New Year's Day.
Dickinson, E. 'Tis customary as we part.
Doolittle, Hilda. Wine Bowl.
Dowson. Exchanges.
Eliot, T. S. Matthew 2:1–12; Now when Jesus
 was born.
Emerson, R. Give All to Love.
Ewing, J. Gifts.
Finlay, I. Gift: "How silly and how dear, how
 very dear."
Fisher, A. Fair Exchange.
Fiskin. Magi, The.
Frishberg, D. Peel Me a Grape.
Frost, R. Gift Outright, The.
Gan Bao. Rare Wedding of Lu Chong.
Garcilaso de la Vega. Sonnet 10: "Oh, sweet
 gifts brought forth for my misfortune."
 Sweet Gifts.
Gay, J. To a Young Lady, with Some Lampreys.
Glück, L. Retreating Wind.
Goldsmith, O. Gift, The. To Iris, in Bow Street,
 Covent Garden.
Green, A. Thanks a Lot, but No Thanks.
Hart, K. Gift, The.
Hedyla. Either cockleshells from the Erythraian
 reef as gifts.
Herrick. Primrose, The.

To His Saviour, a Child; a Present, by a Child.
Hirshfield, J. Each Moment a White Bull Steps
 Shining into the World.
Holthaus, G. Unexpected Manna.
Huddle. My Daddy, Whenever He Went Some
 Place.
Hughes, L. Shepherd's Song at Christmas.
Irvine, W. To be Young, Gifted, and Black.
Keats. To a Friend Who Sent Me Some Roses.
Knott. Christmas at the Orphanage.
Komunyakaa, Y. Gift Horse.
Kruit, J. Giving Way.
Lamantia. Time Traveler's Potlatch.
Lamb, H. Evidence: "He brought her presents."
Landon. Gifts Misused.
Lee, D. Jan's Birthday.
Lewis, G. Watch, The.
Loesser. Take Back Your Mink.
MacIntyre, S. Christmas Present for My
 Mother.
Madhubuti. Mothers.
Martial. Roman Presents.
 Roman Thank-You Letter, A.
 You want me to call you generous.
Masters, E. In Memory of Bryan Lathrop.
Milton. On His Blindness.
Momaday. Gift, The: "Older, more generous."
Moore, L. Gifts.
Moorer. Accompanying a Gift.
 Accompanying a Gift.
Murillo. Conversation in Front of a Helicopter.
Nervo. Gift, The.
Nimmo, D. Good Gifts.
Nossis. It seems that Aphrodite took with joy.
Odio, E. Letter to Carlos Pellicer.
Ormond. Gift, The.
Pan Chieh-yû. Present from the Emperor's New
 Concubine, A.
Po Chü-i. Red Cuckatoo, The.
Raine, K. Heirloom.
Rilke. Three Kings, The.
Roethke. Her Reticence.
Satir, V. Making Contact.
Senior. Tropic Love.
Shange. You are Sucha Fool.
Shelley, P. To—: "One word is too often
 profaned."
"Shu Ting.". Gifts.
Snyder, M. Painting, The.
Sorrentino. Oranges Returned, The.
Stafford, W. At Fourth and Main in Liberal,
 Kansas, 1932.
Statius. Jocular Lines to Plotius Grypus.
Tagore. Gift.
Teasdale. Gift, The.
Tomlinson, C. Picture of J. T. in a Prospect of
 Stone, The.
Troup, B. Daddy.
Tsvetayeva [or Tsvetaeva]. Bethlehem.
Unknown. Dedication: "If you would let me
 leave."
 Him I'm thinking of.
 I have a fading flower in my hand.
 I Went Downtown.
Verlaine. Green ("Take this fruit, these flowers,
 these branches and leaves.").
Walafrid Strabo. With His Book, Of Gardening.
Williams, W. Gift, The.
Woods, V. Three Gifts.
Wright, J. Request to a Year.
Wunderlich, M. Given in Person Only.
Wylie. Parting Gift.
Yi Hyangji. Leaving Home.
Zondberg, O. There were lots of them.

Gilgamesh
Meister, Ernst (1911-1979). In That Place Was
 Another House.
Unknown. Coming of Enkidu, The.
 Death of Enkidu, The.
 Lament of Gilgamesh for Enkidu, The.

Gillespie, Dizzy
Adcock, B. Poem for Dizzy.
Eady. Chittlin's.
Goodwin, Everett. John Birks Gillespie: An
 Appreciation and Reflection.

Ginkgo Trees
Bell, M.   These Green-Going-to-Yellow.
Ginsberg, Allen
Derricotte.   Allen Ginsberg.
Duncan, R.   At the Poetry Conference: Berkeley After the New York Style.
Eirian, S.   My Dad Versus Ginsberg.
Hass, R.   Futures in Lilacs.
Howell IV, T.   Ginsburg.
Keelan, C.   Instead of Reading Marcus Aurelius.
Kennedy, X.   For Allen Ginsberg.
Lewis, Emyr.   Once-in-a-Lifetime, Never-to-Be-Repeated, A.
Lloyd, C.   Gate Gate Paragate Parasmgate Bodhi Svaha.
Lopez, T.   In Memory.
Ping.   No cloud or rain all night long.
Sanfield.   Concern.
Sia, B.   Howl.
Stern, G.   Lilacs for Ginsberg.
Waldman, A.   One Inch of Love Is an Inch of Ashes.
Giotto (Giotto di Bondone)
Alberti.   Giotto.
Giraffes
Beveridge.   Domesticity of Giraffes, The.
Plumly.   Giraffe.
Sŏ Chŏngju.   Kilimanjaro Sunrise.
Villa.   I Was Speaking of Oranges to a Lady.
Girdles
Harding, R.   Ezili Impending.
Waller, E.   On a Girdle.
Girl Scouts
Bryan, S.   Lunch with Girl Scouts.
Perillo, L.   Dangerous Life.
Girls
Agosin.   Obedient Girl, The.
Alcman.   Polydeukes.
Andreus.   Song: "All roocoogirls."
Armstrong, Tammy.   Horse Girls.
Ashbery, J.   Thoughts of a Young Girl.
Bell, M.   Mystery of Emily Dickinson, The.
Blake, W.   Little Girl Found, The.
Bontemps.   Dark Girl.
Bourne, W.   Heart's Fine Gold, The.
Brooks, G.   Narcissa.
Brown, L.   Don't Bring Lulu.
Brownstein.   Jet Set Melodrama.
Buchanan, O.   Girls, The.
Buson.   Mad girl, The.
Campbell, D.   Small-town Gladys.
Campert.   Silver Talk.
Cassells.   Soul Make a Path Through Shouting.
Ciardi, J.   All about Boys and Girls.
Clark, P.   My Life with Horses.
Clifton, L.   Night Vision.
Cocteau.   Fairy Scene.
Cofer, J.   Changeling, The.
Coffman.   Cheerleaders.
 Girl/Spit.
 Likely.
Davis, J.   You Turn Around.
Desnos.   St Merri District, The.
Dougherty.   Puerto Rican Girls of French Hill, The.
Edmond, L.   Girls.
Eguren.   Girls of the Light, The.
Eliot, T. S.   La Figlia Che Piange.
Ellis, K. N.   Girl.
Espino, J.   Sweet Pale Girl.
Field.   Girl, A.
Fu Hsüan.   Pity Me!
Fulton, A.   Fierce Girl Playing Hopscotch.
Furber, D.   Me and My Girl.
Garcia, Edward H.   Chicana.
Gay, N.   Me and My Girl.
Greenaway.   Three Little Girls.
Gullar.   Poster.
Han-shan.   Raise girls but not too many.
Hardy, T.   Former Beauties.
Harris, D.   What we have lost.
Hart, L.   Little Girl Blue.
Heaney, S.   New Song, A.
Hemans.   Evening Prayer, at a Girls' School.
Herd.   Bathing Girls, The.

Hogg, J.   When Maggy Gangs Away.
Höllerer.   'Held Back, Like a Bow Drawn Tight'.
Howe, M.   Practicing.
Hull, A.   Another Rhythm.
Hume, C.   Sampler City.
Issa.   In spring rain.
 So many flea bites.
Jacobs, J.   Two Varieties of the Bitter Orange.
Johnson, J.   Girl of Fifteen.
Joseph, A.   On Sidewalks, on Streetcorners, as Girls.
Kennedy, Sarah.   Maid.
Koch, K.   Circus, The ("We will have to go away, said the girls in the circus.").
Laforgue.   Sunday Piece.
Landon.   Dancing Girl, The.
Langworthy, C.   Why I Look at Girls.
Leigh, C.   Real Live Girl.
Lewis, J.   Girl Help.
Li Ch'ing-chao.   Tune: "Rouged Lips".
Li Po.   Girl of Yueh, The.
 Girls of Yueh, The.
Li Shang-yin.   Without Title.
Lima, J.   That Black Girl Fulô.
Longfellow, H.   There Was a Little Girl.
Mahon.   Girls on the Bridge.
Maiden.   New.
Mansour, J.   Regulation equipment.
Marlatt, D.   Working Girl.
Martínez, V.   Coastal.
McGinley.   Portrait of a Girl with Comic Book.
McLain, P.   Fishing.
Mercer, J.   Tangerine.
Molinari.   Poem of the Girl from Velázquez.
Moore, H.   Girl in a Fur-Trimmed Dress.
Morales, A.   Tita's Poem.
Mori.   Barbie Says Math is Hard.
Morus.   In Praise of a Girl.
Moss, T.   Anointing, An.
Nash, O.   Adventures of Isabel.
Obadike, M.   Tradition/Abstraction.
Olds, S.   One Girl at the Boys Party, The.
 Photograph of the Girl.
O'Sullivan, L.   When We Were Good.
Ou-yang Hsiu.   Tune: "Drunk in Fairyland".
Ovid.   Iphis and Ianthe.
Page, P.   Young Girls.
Parry-Williams.   Girl on the Quay at Rio, The.
Pasternak, B.   At dusk you appear, a school-girl still.
Paz.   Girl.
Peacock, M.   Good Girl.
Penn, M.   Calling Up the Spirit of the Lost Child.
Phylip, S.   Seagull, The.
Pogson, P.   Going Home.
Pollarolo, G.   Foretold Futures.
Potos.   One Red-haired Summer, The.
Pound, E.   Girl, A.
Rafferty, C.   Arsonist Tells His Story to the Attorney, The.
Randall, D.   Blackberry Sweet.
Rose, B.   Don't Bring Lulu.
Sanchez, S.   Song No. 2: "I say. all you young girls waiting to live."
Sandburg, C.   Little girl saw her first troop parade and asked, "What are those?", The.
Shipley, A.   Mama Said.
Shurin.   Blue Shade.
Smith, P.   What It's Like to Be a Black Girl (For Those of You Who Aren't).
Sondheim.   All I Need Is the Girl.
Soto.   Dizzy Girls in the Sixties.
Souza.   Sweet Sixteen.
Spires.   Bodies, The.
Tanikawa, S.   Concerning a Girl.
Timoner, J.   Push the Feathered Glory.
Torres, A.   These Are the Sweet Girls.
Tuckerman, F.   Coralie.
Tuglik.   Tuglik's Song.
Van Jordan, A.   Dance Lesson, A.
Venaille, Franck.   In Praise of Robert Desnos.
Vietnamese Oral Tradition.   Ke-Mo Village Girl.
Volkman.   Daffodils.
Walwicz.   Little Red Riding Hood.

Whitehead, C.   Girls Sitting Together Like Dolls.
Williams, W.   Lonely Street, The.
Wordsworth, W.   Solitary Reaper, The.
Wright, F.   Depiction of Childhood.
Yeats.   Politics.
Zandvakili, K.   Love Letter.
See also **Adolescence; Childhood and Children; Youth**
Giving
Berman, C.   Mother Lakshmi's Poem.
Hauge.   Midwinter. Snow.
Kerouac.   And What Do I Owe You, God.
Leighton, Taigen Dan.   Giving Buddha to all beings is giving to oneself.
Patterson, G.   Saint's First Wife Said, The.
Tupper, M.   Art of Giving, The (1850).
Unknown.   Him I'm thinking of.
See also **Gifts and Giving**
Glaciers
Du Bouchet.   Light of the Blade, The.
Hopes.   Glacier's Daughters, The.
Merwin.   Footprints on the Glacier.
Mooney, M.   Neanderthal Funeral.
Ransom, W.   Message from Ohanapecosh Glacier.
Glasgow, Scotland
Daiches, J.   Horse in Glasgow.
Dunn, D.   Glasgow Schoolboys, Running Backwards.
Leonard, T.   Evidence, The.
Mangan, G.   Glasgow 1956.
Mitchison.   Scottish Renaissance in Glasgow, The: 1935.
Morgan, E.   Glasgow Green.
 Glasgow Sonnets.
 King Billy.
Smith, A.   Sing, Poet, 'tis a merry world.
Glass and Glassblowers
Baldwin, A.   Glass Box Puzzle No. 1.
Brownstein.   Glass Enclosure, The.
Clampitt.   Beach Glass.
Copus, J.   Forgiveness.
Draycott.   Prince Rupert's Drop, The.
Ettinger, E.   Glass, The.
France, L.   Blues for Bird.
Garrett, E.   Unguentarium.
Gorham.   White Tiger Leaps, The.
Gorostiza, J.   Filled with myself, walled up in my skin.
Jarnot, L.   What In Fire Did I, Firelover, Starter of Fires, Love?
Jones, Tudur Dylan.   Great Glasshouse at the National Botanic Garden of Wales.
Martial.   After her wedding-night, the nymph.
Merrill, J.   Octopus, The.
Moore, M.   Egyptian Pulled Glass Bottle in the Shape of a Fish, An.
Morgan, E.   Glass, The.
Ritsos.   One Skit, Then Another.
Shapiro, D.   Book of Glass, A.
Stein, G.   Carafe, that is a blind glass, A.
Supervielle.   Earth.
Ward, D.   Glass House.
Winters, Y.   Solitude of Glass, The.
Glasses
Cortázar.   Very Real Story, A.
Grotz, J.   First Glasses.
Jandl, E.   Pockets.
Kharms.   Optical Illusion, An.
See also **Eyeglasses**
Globalization
Clay, W.   On Me, the Imported Skies.
Cortez, J.   What's Your Take.
Hashmi.   Pro Bono Publico.
Hoagland, E.   How Could All That Have Happened Here?
Ward, J.   After the Report from Iron Mountain.
Globes
Donne.   Valediction, A: of Weeping.
Turner, C.   Letty's Globe.
Glory
Amichai, Y.   And That Is Your Glory.
Borges.   John 1:14; And the Word became flesh and dwelt among us.

Tenebrae.
Tenebrae.
Zurich, at the Stork.
Zürich, the Stork Inn.
Ceravolo. Data.
Fill and Illumined.
Chernoff. God: "God is in the high notes."
Chesterton. Holy of Holies, The.
Chubb, T. Merlin.
Citino. Sister Mary Appassionata Lectures the Eighth Grade Boys and Girls: The Family Jewels.
Clare, J. First Love.
God Looks on Nature With a Glorious Eye.
Clark, T. Bun.
Clarkson. Behold, the King of glory now is come.
Clough. There Is No God.
Though to the vilest things beneath the moon.
With Whom Is No Variableness, Neither Shadow of Turning.
Clurman, D. To David.
Cole, H. 40 Days and 40 Nights.
Coleridge, S. To Nature.
Collymore. Ballad of an Old Woman.
Colonna, V. I see in my mind, surrounding God.
Columba. Maker on High, The.
Conoley, G. Violence, The.
Coogler. God Correctly Understood.
Cook, E. Song for the Workers, A.
Coolbrith. Longing.
Copus, J. Making of Eve, The.
Masaccio's Expulsion from Paradise.
Cornish, W. Pleasure It Is.
Cowper, W. Just when our drawing-rooms begin to blaze.
Light Shining out of Darkness.
Lines Written During a Period of Insanity.
Craig, David. Apple Fools.
Our Father.
Presence of God, The.
Cranch. Correspondences.
Crane, H. Broken Tower, The.
Crane, S. Battle Hymn, The.
In Heaven, / Some little blades of grass.
Livid lightnings flashed in the clouds, The.
Crashaw. Love, thou art absolute sole lord.
Song: "Lord, when the sense of Thy sweet grace."
Cruz, C. Praying ("In the middle of the night.").
Cruz, S. Dark Night, The.
Cruz Varela. Invocation.
Cullen, C. For a Mouthy Woman.
Yet Do I Marvel.
Cummings, E. E. I Thank You God.
Cunningham, J. History of Ideas.
Cust. Non Nobis.
Davenant [or D'Avenant]. Praise and Prayer.
Davie, D. Ordinary God.
Davies, J. Acclamation, An.
Reasons drawn from Divinity.
Davies, S. One Thing Needful Generally Neglected, The.
Davis, J. God's Cutt-Off TV Screen's Vanishing Mirror Seems an Unshared Point.
Day, J. Man's Natural Infirmity.
de Gillies, G. De Puerorum osculis.
De la Mare. Last Chapter, The.
De Vere, S. Reality.
Dennis, C. God Who Loves You, The.
Dèr Mouw. Does Anyone Know This Feeling.
Dharker. Grace.
Dickinson, E. All Circumstances are the Frame.
Alter! When the Hills do—.
Drowning is not so pitiful.
God is a distant—stately Lover.
He fumbles at your Soul.
"Heavenly Father"—take to thee.
I am afraid to own a Body.
I gave myself to Him—.
I got so I could take his name.
I never saw a Moor.
Infinite a sudden Guest, The.
It was a quiet way—.
It was too late for Man.

It would have starved a Gnat.
One who could repeat the Summer day, The.
Only News I know, The.
Publication—is the Auction.
Struck, was I, not yet by Lightning.
There comes an hour when begging stops.
This was a Poet—It is That.
To know just how He suffered—would be dear.
Trees like Tassels—hit—and swung, The.
Truth—is as old as God.
Wild Nights—Wild Nights!
Didsbury, P. That Old-Time Religion.
Dillard, A. God: "Numbers from one to ten, however, are called."
Thanksgiving—Christmas 3.
You go down the hall.
Dodson, O. Black Mother Praying.
Donne. Batter my heart, three-personed [or three person'd] God; for you.
Good Friday [or Goodfriday], 1613. Riding Westward.
Hymn[e] to God My God, In My Sickness[e], A.
Hymn[e] to Christ, at the Author's Last Going into Germany, A.
I am a little world made cunningly.
Satire 3 [Religion].
Doolittle, Hilda. Evil was active in the land.
Helen.
Or anywhere.
Dorsey, T. Take My Hand, Precious Lord.
Dove, R. Breathing, the Endless News, The.
Drayton. Song of the Faithful, A.
Drummond de Andrade. Seven-Sided Poem.
Drummond, W. Book, The.
Dugan, A. Against a Sickness: To the Female Double Principle God.
Dunbar, P. Compensation.
Hymn, A: "Lead gently, Lord, and slow."
Hymn: "When storms arise."
Night.
Resignation.
Spiritual, A.
Duncan, R. This Place Rumord to Have Been Sodom.
Torso, The / Passages 18.
Dunn, D. Gardeners.
Dunn, S. Dancing with God.
Eady. My Mother is a God Fearing Woman.
Eberhart, R. Fury of Aerial Bombardment, The.
On a Squirrel Crossing the Road in Autumn, in New England.
Eichner, Maura. Back Porch Fundamentalist.
Eliot, T. S. O Light Invisible, we praise Thee!
Elizabeth, Queen of Bohemia. Verses by the Princess Elizabeth, Given to Lord Harington, of Exton, Her Preceptor.
Elliott, E. Plaint.
Emanuel, L. Like God.
Emerson, R. Dæmonic and the Celestial Love, The.
Dear Brother, Would You Know the Life.
History.
Threnody: "South-wind brings, The."
Emre. Whole universe is full of God, The.
Enzensberger, H. Poison, The.
Essbaum, J. In the Beginning.
Post-Communion Striptease.
When the Kingdom Comes.
Everson, W. Canticle to the Waterbirds, A.
Ewer. Chosen People, The.
Faber, F. Eternity of God, The.
My God, how wonderful Thou art.
Fairfax of Cameron. On the Fatal Day January 30, 1648.
Fallon, P. Holy Well.
Fargas. If There Is a.
Farid-uddin Attar. Invocation to the Conference of the Birds.
Fenton, J. God, A Poem.
Ferguson, G. Slugs.
Field. Beloved, Now I Love God First.
Fields, J. Jolly Fat Widows, The.
Fishman, L. Diagnosis: My Mother's Breast.
Fletcher, G. As when the cheerfull Sunne, elamping wide.

Flynn, N. God Forgotten.
Foster, A. God and the Holy Stones.
France, P. Death.
Francis of Assisi. Canticle of the Creatures.
Prayer of St. Francis of Assisi for Peace.
Frost, R. Bereft.
Forgive, O Lord, my little jokes on Thee.
Sitting by a Bush in Broad Daylight.
Fuller, J. Whole New Scene, A.
Fuller, M. Sistrum.
Fullerton. John 14:1–2.
Poetry.
Garren, Christine. Figure and Ground.
Gascoigne. Gascoigne's Good-Morrow.
Gascoigne's Woodmanship.
Gascoyne. Rex Mundi.
Gaspar. Tree, The.
Gershon. Experiments with God.
Gilbert, J. White Heart of God, The.
Gilbert-Lecomte. Preface or The Drama of Absence in an Eternal Heart.
Gilmore, J. He Leadeth Me.
Ginsberg, A. Why Is God Love, Jack?
Gioia. Prayer: "Echo of the clocktower, footstep."
Glazier, L. On TV.
Glück, L. Baskets.
Gift, The.
Lamentations.
Gorenko, A. Translated from the European.
Grahn. They Say She Is Veiled.
Greenberg, S. God.
Greenwell, D. Christina.
Gregg. Fishing in the Keep of Silence.
Greiffenberg. I look.
On the Fruit-Providing Autumn Season.
Zealous Admonition to Praise.
Griffiths, A. His left hand, in heat of noonday.
Grobman, M. In mass graves the bodies of plants.
Grosholz. Eden.
Gunn, T. Pope's Carnations Knew Him.
Gurney, I. To God.
Hafiz, K [or Hafez]. Cries We Make, The (64).
Night Visit, The (22).
Hall, D. Small Fig Tree, A.
Hall, John. Praise of Godly Love Out of 1 John. 4, The.
Proverb, XXX.
Hall, Joseph. Anthem for the Cathedral of Exeter.
Hamadani. Quatrain.
Hardie, K. Sheep Fair Day.
Hardy, J. Computer Aided Design: Creation.
Hardy, T. Agnosto Theo [To an Unknown God].
Bedridden Peasant, The.
God-Forgotten.
New Year's Eve.
Harrison, J. God's Penis.
Haught, K. God Says Yes to Me.
Heard, J. Hope Thou in God.
I Will Look Up.
Heber. Holy, Holy, Holy.
Hedge. Mighty Fortress Is Our God, A.
Herbert, G. Affliction (1).
Altar, The.
Artillery [or Artillerie].
Call, The.
Church-Floor[e], The.
Collar, The.
Denial[l].
Discipline.
Easter Wings.
Elixir [or Elixer], The.
Forerunners, The.
Grace.
Hope.
Invitation, The.
Jordan (1).
Jordan (2).
L'Envoy.
Man.
Paradise.
Pearl, The. Matth. 13:45.
Posy [or Posie], The.
Praise (2).

Prayer (1): "Prayer the Church's banquet, Angels' age."
Providence.
Pulley, The.
Redemption.
Sion.
Unkindness.
Vanity [or Vanitie] (1).
Windows, The.
World, The.
Herrick. Evensong.
Gods Anger without Affection.
Gods Keyes.
Gods Presence ("God's evident, and may be said to be.").
Neutrality Loathsome.
No Coming to God without Christ.
Right Hand, The.
To Find[e] God.
To God ("Come to me God; but do not come.").
To God ("God's undivided, One in Persons Three.").
To God ("If any thing delight me for to print.").
To His Ever-Loving God.
To His Saviour.
What God Is.
Heyen. Simple Truths.
Hidalgo, J. You Came Down.
Hirsch, E. American Apocalypse.
Hodgson, R. Mystery, The.
Holan. Resurrection.
To the Enemies.
Hölderlin. In the Days of Socrates.
Holland, H. Judge eternal, throned in splendours.
Holmes, O. Living Temple, The.
Our Limitations.
Questions.
Tartarus.
Holst-Warhaft. John 1:1 and 14.
Hopes. Jack Rhymer.
Under the Drumlin.
Hopkins, G. As Kingfishers Catch Fire.
Carrion Comfort.
God's Grandeur.
In the Valley of the Elwy.
Let me be to Thee as the circling bird.
Pied Beauty.
Spring and Fall [To a Young Child].
Thou Art Indeed Just, Lord.
Hopkins, J. Ye people all in one accord.
Housman. Mark 16:19–20; So then the Lord Jesus, after.
Howe, S. Silence Wager Stories.
Hudgins. Crucifixion (Montgomery, Alabama).
Isaiah ate the blood-red ember.
Southern Crescent Was on Time, The.
Hughes, T. After Lorca.
Crow's First Lesson.
Gog.
Hugo, V. At Villequier.
Bridge, The.
More about God (But with Some Reservations).
Huidobro. Ars Poetica.
Hunt, L. Abou Ben Adhem.
To Percy Shelley.
To the Same.
Jabès. To be in the book. To figure in the book of questions, to be part of it.
Jackson, M. L. Blunts.
Jacob, M. 1914.
Jammes. Prayer to Go to Paradise with the Donkeys, A.
Jana Bai. Cast off all shame.
Jarnot, L. Valley of the Shadow of the Dogs.
Jeffers, R. Birds and Fishes.
Birth-Dues.
Noon.
Pearl Harbor.
Shine, Perishing Republic.
Jerrold, S. John in Prison.
Jiménez, J. Name Drawn from the Names, The.
Johnson, F. Song of the Whirlwind.
Johnson, J. Creation, The.
Go Down Death (A Funeral Sermon).
Lift Every [or Ev'ry] Voice and Sing.

Jones, E. Genesis.
Jones, S. Hymn to Na'a'yena, A.
Jonson, B. Hymn[e] to God the Father, A.
To Heaven.
Juana Inés de la Cruz. Because my Lord was born to suffer.
Kamienska. Prayer That Will Be Answered, A.
Kavanagh, P. Canal Bank Walk.
Kelly, R. Rainmakers, The.
Kenyon, J. Bat, The.
Briefly It Enters, and Briefly Speaks.
Kerouac. And What Do I Owe You, God.
Flies.
Kipling, R. Evarra and His Gods.
Rabbi's Song, The.
Recessional.
Kitahara Hakushū. Secret Song of the Heretics.
Kizer, C. Dixit Insipiens.
Klein, A. For the Sisters of the Hôtel Dieu.
Kolmar. Sacrifice, The.
Kowit. Cosmetics Do No Good.
Kumin, M. Getting the Message.
Lal Ded [or Lalla]. At the end of a crazy-moon night.
I drag a boat over the ocean.
I was passionate.
This world.
Lamartine. Infinite in the Skies, The.
Lanier, S. To Beethoven.
Lasker-Schüler. And Look for God.
O God.
Lawrence, D. H. Body of God, The.
Eloi, Eloi, Lama Sabachthani?
Hands of God, The.
Living Quetzalcoatl, The.
Matthew 6:7–15; "And in praying do not heap up empty".
Pax.
When Wilt Thou Teach the People?
Levertov. Flickering Mind.
Task, The.
This Day.
Levin, P. Night Coach.
Levine, P. On a Drawing by Flavio.
Levy, A. Ballad of Religion and Marriage, A.
Lima, J. Enormous Hand, The.
Linden, M. God's Electric Power.
Llwyd, M. Come Wisdome Sweet.
Locke, A. So Foul Is Sin and Loathsome in Thy Sight.
Longfellow, H. Galaxy, The.
López Mills, T. Dead Weight of the Land, The.
Peso muerto de la tierra, El.
Lowell, R. Mr. Edwards and the Spider.
Watchmaker God.
Luther. In the Very Midst of Life.
Mighty Fortress Is Our God, A.
Lux. Perfect God, The.
Lydgate. Thank God for All.
MacDiarmid, H. With the Herring Fishers.
Macdonald, G. Where did you come from, baby dear?
Machado Ruiz. Lord, You Have Ripped Away.
Magdeburg, Mechthild von. Fish cannot drown in water, A.
God Speaks to the Soul.
God's Absence.
How the Soul Speaks to God.
Of all that God has shown me.
True love in every moment praises God.
Magee, J. High Flight.
Mahon. Ecclesiastes.
Maksimovic. For the Barren Woman.
Matthew 22:15–22; Then the Pharisees went and.
Mandela. Saviour.
Mandelstam [or Mandelshtam]. Your image, tormenting and elusive.
Manning, Maurice. O boss of ashes boss of dust.
On God.
Mant, R. House of God, The.
Social Worship.
Marckant. Lamentation, The.
Martin, C. His Eye Is on the Sparrow.
Martin, Gail. God Packs Lunches.

God Scrubs the Tub.
God Vacuums the Pool.
Marvell. Bermudas.
Mayakovsky [or Maiakovskii]. Listen.
McGinley. Day After Sunday, The.
Meinke. Poet, Trying to Surprise God, The.
Melville, H. Conflict of Convictions, The.
In the Desert.
Ribs and Terrors, The.
Merwin. Leviathan.
Metodiev, Ivan. Garden of Questions.
Sometimes: "Sometimes God resembles a kitten."
Meynell, A. To a Daisy.
Mezey. Silence, The.
Michelangelo Buonarroti. I see in your beautiful face, my lord.
Violent burning for prodigious beauty, A.
Mikha'il, M. Imprisoned God, The.
Talk.
Miller, T. Evening.
Milton. But now I feel hunger, which declares.
How soon hath Time the subtle [or suttle] thief [or theef] of youth.
Just are the ways of God.
Now had th' Almighty Father from above.
On His Blindness.
To Cyriack Skinner.
Mirabai [or Mira Bai]. Song of the flute, O sister, is madness, The.
Mistral, G. Like those jars that women put out to catch the dew of night.
Mitchell, A. Quite Apart from the Holy Ghost.
Montale. In the Greenhouse.
"Monty Python.". All Things dull and Ugly.
Moore, M. Book of How, The.
Moore, T. Sound the Loud Timbrel.
More, S. Prayer, A.
Morrissey, S. After the Hurricane.
Moss, T. Rapture of Dry Ice Burning off Skin as the Moment of the Soul's Apotheosis, The.
Murray, J. Lullaby: "Sleep, little architect. It is your mother's wish."
Murray, P. Canticle of the Void, The.
Muske, C. Applause.
Muyassar. Lost.
Nag Hammadi Library. Sent from the Power.
Nahman [or Nachman] of Bratzlav. From "The Torah of the Void".
Na'mani. Love Poem: "In your quest or request God is remote."
Nasir. Loneliness.
Nelson, M. Cover Photograph.
Nemerov. Primer of the Daily Round, A.
Nichol. Ferry Me Across.
Nijhoff. Musician, The.
Nims, J. Knowledge of God.
Norris, K. Naming the Living God.
Notari, L. Wee bird sang in the wasteland, A.
"Novalis.". Yearning for Death.
Nowlan. Sacrament.
Okudzhava. François Villon.
Olivers, T. God of Abraham praise, The.
Olson, T. Hypothesis.
Omar, I. Not Quiet.
O'Reilly, C. Brief History of Light, A.
Ormond. Cathedral Builders.
To a Nun.
Orten. Last Poem, The.
Ostriker. Story of Abraham, The.
Padgett, R. Bun.
Lucky Strikes.
Pagis, D. Evidence.
Testimony.
Parker, A. Above the Timberline.
Parra, N. Lord's Prayer.
Parra, V. Why Is It This Way, Almighty God?
Pastan. Imperfect Paradise, The.
Pasternak, B. Let the Words.
Patchen. Deer and the Snake, The.
Lions of fire, The.
Origin of Baseball, The.
Patrick, S. St Patrick's Breastplate.
Saint Patrick's Breastplate; or, The Deer's Cry.
Pavlova, V. Heaven and Earth.
Peacock, M. Good Girl.

Pessoa. No One in the Wide Wilderness of the Wood.

Petrarch. Father in heaven, after each lost day.

Pfeiffer, E. Cruse of Tears, The. A Russian Legend.

O Nature! thou whom I have thought to love.

Phillips, C. Sunday.

Piatt, S. Answering A Child.

If I Had Made the World.

No Help.

Pique at Parting, A.

Sad Spring-Song.

We Two.

Pierpont, J. O Thou, to Whom in Ancient Time.

Pinsky. Hearts, The.

Pope, A. Messiah [a Sacred Eclogue, in Imitation of Virgil's Pollio].

Universal Prayer, The [Deo Opt. Max.].

Porete. Beloved, what do you want of me?

Pound, E. Ballad for Gloom.

Night Litany.

Powers, J. Garments of God, The.

Prabhu. For the Lord of Caves.

Prados, E. I Look into the Sky.

Probyn. More than They that Watch for the Morning.

Procter, A. Divine Presence, The.

Judge not; the workings of his brain.

Three Evenings in a Life.

Words.

Prudentius. Of the Father's love begotten Ere the worlds began to be.

Purdy, A. Wilderness Gothic.

Quarles. On God's Law.

On the Life of Man.

Quevedo y Villegas. Love Constant Beyond Death.

Ragan, J. Birth of God (from an Early Photograph), The.

Ralegh, S. Authours Epitaph, Made by Himself, The.

Ravitch. Twelve Lines about the Burning Bush.

Ray, H. God's Ways, Not Our Ways.

Rein. Monastery.

Reznikoff. If you cannot look at the sun.

Ridler. Corneal Graft.

Rilke. I Find You, Lord, All Things and In All.

Just as The Watchman.

Just as the Winged Energy of Delight.

Rinckhart [or Rinkhart]. Now Thank We All Our God.

Ríos, A. Anselmo's Moment with God.

Robertson, R. Three Ways of Looking at God.

Robinson, A. Idea, The.

Valley, The.

Robinson, R. Come, thou Fount of ev'ry blessing.

Rodgers, W. Lent.

Rogers, P. Before the Beginning: Maybe God and a Silk Flower Concubine Perhaps.

Moving God.

Rojas. What Do We Love When We Love?

Rosenberg, I. God.

Rossetti, C. Advent: "Come, thou dost say to Angels."

After Communion.

Before the Beginning.

Blessed that flock safe penned in Paradise.

Christmas Carol, A: "In the bleak mid-winter."

Long Barren.

O my heart's heart, and you who are to me.

St. Michael and all Angels.

Trust me, I have not earned your dear rebuke.

Twice.

Rossetti, D. 72: The Choice ("Watch thou and fear; to-morrow thou shalt die").

Rothenberg, J. Realtheater Piece Two.

Rowe, E. Chapter II.

Expostulation, The.

Rukeyser, M. Akiba.

Rumi. Answers from the Elements.

Drunkards, The.

Say Yes Quickly.

Ryan, M. God Hunger.

Sachs, N. Chorus of the Stars.

Sargent, E. Planet Jupiter, The.

Schiff, H. Discovery.

Schulzová, E. Evening in Terezin, An.

Schwartz, R. L. Talking to God on the Seventh Day.

Sexton. Author of the Jesus Papers Speaks, The.

Small Wire.

Welcome Morning.

Shapiro, K. 151st Psalm, The.

Shcherbina. Tell me, Comrade God, how can life, over this stretch.

Shwarts [or Shvarts]. Elegy on an X-ray Photo of My Skull.

Simic. Night Picnic.

To the One Upstairs.

Simmons, J. Eden.

Singer, E. Cant. 5.6 & c.

Sizer, P. Old Man on a Bike.

Slutsky [or Slutskii]. God.

Smart, C. Conclusion of the Matter, The.

For I pray God to bless Polly in the the blessing of Naomi.

For the word of God is a sword on my side—no matter what other weapon a stick or a straw.

Hymn to the Supreme Being.

My Cat Jeoffry.

Smith, G. Penitential Cries of Jupiter Hammond, The.

Smith, Samuel Francis. America.

Smith, Stevie. Away, Melancholy.

God the Eater.

Mother, among the Dustbins.

No Categories!

Smith, W. Immortal, invisible, God only wise.

Södergran. Question.

"There is no one . . . ".

Souster. Very Short Poem.

Southerland. Pale Ant.

Southey, R. Old Man's Comforts and How He Gained Them, The.

Ship, The.

Sowle, J. Short Testimony for Anne Whitehead, A.

Spellman, A. Twist, The.

Spenser, E. May.

Spicer, J. God must have a big eye to see everything.

God's other eye is good and gold. So bright.

Steinberg, J. Rain at Night.

Stephens, J. What Thomas an Buile Said in a Pub.

Stevenson, R. Epitaph: "Angler rose, he took his rod, The."

Last night we had a thunderstorm in style.

Stickney, T. He said: If in his image I was made.

Stowe. Only a Year.

Strange. Offering.

Subido, T. Paganly.

Swinburne. Leper, The.

Sylvester, J. Cunning Painter, that with curious care, The.

Father, The.

Symonds. Lux Est Umbra Dei.

Tadic. Antipsalm.

Tate, G. Last Instructions.

Taylor, Edward. Meditation 3 Can. 1.3. Thy Good Ointment.

Meditation 8 (First Series).

Meditation 42 (First Series).

Meditation 16 (First Series).

Meditation 22 (First Series).

Meditation. Rom. 9.5. God blessed forever.

Preface [to God's Determinations], The.

Reflexion, The.

Upon a Spider Catching a Fly.

Taylor, Eleanor Ross. After Twenty Years.

Taylor, Jane. My Mother.

Taylor, Jeremy. Hymn for Advent.

Prayer, A: "O beauteous God! uncircumscribed treasure."

Taylor, John. Gods *Houses,* almost like *Troyes Ilion,*.

Tennyson, A. Flower in the Crannied Wall.

Higher Pantheism, The.

O[h], yet we trust that somehow good.

That which we dare invoke to bless.

Wish, that of the living whole, The.

Theresa [or Teresa]. Poem: "Nothing move thee."

Thomas, D. In The Beginning.

Thomas, R. S. Echoes.

Island, The.

Kneeling.

Pisces.

Via Negativa.

Thompson, F. Heaven and Hell.

Hound of Heaven, The.

Thompson, P. In the Valley.

Thomson, J. Hymn on the Seasons, A.

Thoreau. Inspiration ("Whate'er we leave to God, God does.").

Tindley, C. Stand by Me.

Tokareva, Y. Brief reflection on the greatness of God.

Toomer. Gods Are Here, The.

Toplady. Hymn: "Inspirer and hearer of prayer."

Traherne. Demonstration, The.

Salutation [or Salutations], The.

To the Same Purpos[e].

Wonder.

Tranter. Backyard.

Trapnell, A. O he is a rest that requires.

Tsvetayeva [or Tsvetaeva]. God (3).

I am happy to live correctly and simply.

I bless the everyday labor.

Tucker, M. Mysteries of Life.

Tuckerman, F. As Sometimes in a Grove.

Sonnets: "Starry flower, the flower-like stars that fade, The."

Tukaram. In My View.

Unknown. All Is Phantom.

As in thee resteth my joye and confort.

Beguines who hear these words.

Beulah Railway, The.

Chants to the Deity.

Didn't My Lord Deliver Daniel?

God and Man Set as One.

God Knows Why.

Good and Better.

Good Lord in That Heaven.

Harper's Song for Inherkhawy, The.

He was the Word that Spake it.

He's Jus' de Same Today.

Hospital Duties.

I Believe.

I have been brought into darkness.

I See the Moon.

I Sing of a Maiden.

Little Black Train Is A-Comin'.

Loom of Time, The.

Madrigal: "If that a sinner's sighs be angels' food."

Make Me Loathe Earthly Likings.

My Hope Is in God.

Nobody Knows the Trouble I've Had.

Petition to Father and Son and Holy Ghost, A.

Psalm 137.

Steal Away to Jesus.

Thanksgivings, The.

Timor Mortis.

Valley of Dry Bones, The.

You and I.

You Never Ask.

Valéry. Crusoe.

Vallejo. Black Messengers, The.

Eternal Dice, The.

Have You Anything to Say in Your Defense?

Van Doren. Near House, The.

Van Duyn. Gardener to His God, The.

Vaughan, H. Anguish.

Book, The.

Cock-crowing.

Knot, The.

Love and Discipline.

Midnight.

Night, The.

Regeneration.

Vanity of Spirit.

Verlaine. Cold wind hurls itself at, A.

Very. Created, The.

Cup, The.

Earth, The.
Eye and Ear, The.
First Atlantic Telegraph, The.
Hand and Foot, The [*or* Hand and the Foot, The].
In Him We Live [and Move and Have Our Being].
Lost, The ("Fairest day that ever yet has shone, The.").
Mountain, The.
My Meat and Drink.
My People are destroyed for lack of Knowledge.—Hosea 4:6.
Night.
Prayer, The ("Wilt Thou not visit me?").
Promise, The ("I come the rushing wind that shook the place.").
Rock, The.
Silent, The.
Slavery.
Spirit, The.
Word, The ("Word! it cannot fail; it ever speaks, The.").
Yourself.
Vilariño. How Awful.
Vitale, M. I Read That It Was All a Chain.
Volach, Y. When You Come Sleep with Me.
Voltskaya, T. God is the first snow. He is a leaf, a mosquito.
Waltner-Toews, D. Request from Tante Tina to the Mennonite Women's Missionary Society to Put Salman Rushdie on the Prayer List, A.
Waniek. Canticle for Abba Jacob, A.
Warton, T. Stanzas on the Psalms.
Washbourne. God's Two Dwellings.
Watts, I. Day of Judg[e]ment, The; an Ode [Attempted in English Sapphic].
Man Frail, and God Eternal.
Webb, F. Art.
Wesley, C. Come on, my partners in distress.
My God! I know, I feel thee mine.
None is like Jeshuron's God.
Wheatley, P. On Being Brought from Africa to America.
Thoughts on the Works of Providence.
Whitman, W. Chanting the Square Deific.
I believe in you my soul, the other I am must not abase itself to you.
Prayer of Columbus.
Whittemore, R. Psalm: "Lord feeds some of His prisoners better than others, The."
Whittier. Garden.
Over-Heart, The.
Overruled.
Palm-Tree, The.
River Path, The.
Wickham. To Men.
Wiesel. Behold, God of Abraham, God of mercy.
Never Shall I Forget.
Wilbur, R. Dubious Night, A.
Proof, The.
Tywater.
Wilkes, J. Pleased to the last, she likes the luscious food.
Williams, C. K. Loss.
Spit.
Williams, M. Why God Permits Evil: For Answers to This Question of Interest to Many Write Bible Answers, Dept. E-7.
Williams, P. In the Dark.
Williams, R. God makes a path, provides a guide.
Wilson, E. Disloyal Lines to an Alumnus.
Winslow, P. God on a Bike.
Wither. Prayer of Hezekiah, The.
When We Cannot Sleep.
Wolfli. And now: And now: here begins Our Voyage, hunters and naturalists of indefatigable enthusiasm.
Nostalgic Song for My Beloved.
Wordsworth, W. It Is a Beauteous Evening.
Our birth is but a sleep and a forgetting.
Wright, Carolyne. Prayer: "Bless my life—its inks."
Wright, Charles. Clear Night.

Disjecta Membra.
Wright, James. Speak.
Wright, Jay. Meta-A and the A of Absolutes.
Wyatt. Argument, The.
Ya'oz-kest. Smoke Rose.
Yeats. Crazy Jane on God.
Indian upon God, The [*or* An].
Rose of the World, The.
Young, A. Myself When I Am Real.
Zabolotsky [*or* Zabolotskii]. Poem about Rain.
"Zelda.". Crippled beggar who lives, The.
Zukofsky, L. For you I have emptied the meaning.

Gods and Goddesses
Acholonu. Dissidents, The.
Water Woman.
al-Saygh, S. Sanctions.
Alarcon, F. Prayer: "I want a god."
Alcman. But often on the mountain peaks when.
Polydeukes.
Amor, P. CXXXIV.
Antipater of Thessalonica. Priapus, seeing Cimon's rigid rod.
Ap Hywel, Elin. Goddesses.
Goddesses.
Apuleius, L. I who am Nature, mother of all.
Archilochus. Attribute all to the gods: often they raise.
Ashur-Nasir-Pal. Hymn to Ishtar.
Awoonor. At the Gates.
Azzawi, F. In a magic land.
Baring, A. Song, The: "Beehive source."
Barnes, B. Jove, for Europa[e]s love took[e] shape of bull.
Basho. More than ever I want to see.
Basu, R. How are you faring, Uma.
I had a good dream last night.
Basu Rāy, S. Three Kalis appeared in Daksinesvar.
Bedient, C. When the Gods Put on Meter.
Benton, S. Lilith.
Second Coming, The.
Berezan, J. Hail Mother full of grace power is with thee.
Berman, C. Deep inside me at my core.
Mother Lakshmi's Poem.
Poem for the Shechina.
Bhāndārī, S. Ma, You are Brahmani in the world of Brahma.
Menaka says, Hey listen, Mountain King.
Bhattācārya, A. Get up, get up, Mountain: no more sleep for you!
Bhattācārya, K. Bee of my mind, The.
Consulting the omens.
Crazy Mind.
Ever-blissful Kali.
External rituals mean nothing.
From her autumn-lotus mouth.
From now on.
Go, my Lord of the Mountains.
Hara came and made off with my Gauri.
Here, Queen of the Mountains.
Hey, Hara, Ganges-Holder.
Hey, Mountain King, Gauri is sulking.
How can that black woman be so beautiful?
How could you have forgotten her.
How will You rescue me, Tara?
I know, I know, Mother.
Is my black Mother Syama really black?
Jaya, tell him that Uma will not be sent.
Kali / Is everything You do misleading?
Kali! / Today in the dark grove.
Kali, what family are You from?
Kali, you have removed all my difficulties.
King of the Mountains is on his way to Hara's abode, The.
Mother / You're always finding ways to amuse Yourself.
My Gauri / You've come home!
My Uma has come!
Other than Your two red feet, Syama.
Queen asks, The.
So, forgetful Mahadeva.
Stay within yourself, Mind.
Tara, Mother / Lift me out by the hair.

Tell me, Syama.
Tell me / What can I do?
Turn back, Uma.
Unperturbed at the battle.
What a dream I had last night!
What happened? / The ninth night is over.
What's the fault of the poor mind?
Who can describe the waves of Mother Syama's world?
Who is this.
Who is this enchantress.
Withered tree doesn't blossom, The.
You ask me, Queen, time after time.
Bhattācārya, M. Look at all these waves.
Ma, are you really dead?
Oh Ma Kali, for a long time now.
There's a huge hullabaloo in my lotus heart.
What shall I say to You, Sankari?
Your behavior proves how stingy You are, Ma.
Bible, *O.T.* Psalm 100.
Bingen, Hildegard von. Earth is at the same time mother, The.
I am the one whose praise.
Bobrowski. Woodland God.
Boullosa, C. Elysian Garden.
Jardín Elíseo.
Brontë, C. Dream that stole o'er us in the time.
Budapest. Medea speaks: / This is God, children, listen up well. The.
Bukowski. Not Much Singing.
Burnside, J. Old Gods, The.
Bynner. But for these apertures.
Cakrabartī, N. Can you claim to win.
Cakrabarttī, M. Ma, if You wore a Benarasi sari.
Wherever there's a woman in any Bengali home.
Canan. Goddesses, The.
Inanna's Chant.
Mother Dawning.
Oh Kali.
Candī, A. Bring Tara quickly, Mountain.
Catullus. Accept, O Priapus, the moister.
Ceni, A. Fragment.
Césaire, A. In Order to Speak.
Chabbi, F. Blind Goddess, The.
Chénier. When the Euxine goddess with astonished eyes.
Chimombo. Obituary.
Chizhova. Cassandra.
Ch'u Yüan. Nine Songs, The.
Clifton, L. Calming Kali.
Good Friday.
Kali.
Close, J. Haloes, Not Hats [*or* A Vision of the Gods].
Coleridge, S. Visit of the Gods, The.
Corn. To Hermes.
Cott, J. Isis (Lady of Petals).
Couzyn. Spell for Birth.
Craveirinha. 3D.
Cross, E. Kali.
Shakti.
Shakti.
Uma Worshipping Shiva (On a Kangra miniature).
Daryush. I saw the daughter of the sun.
Dās, R. Now I will see whether Siva.
Dāsdatta, R. Because You love cremation grounds.
Davies, S. Cosmus hath more discoursing in his head.
Davis, T. Skin of Clouds.
De [*or* Du] Guillet. But if he came straight for me.
de Portalatin. Humble Litany.
Deb, A. I started a fire with Kali's name.
Debī, T. Tara, this is why I call upon You.
Dharker. Postcards from god (1).
Di Prima. If he did not come apart in her hands, he fell.
Loba as Eve.
Dīnrām. Being the child of a Mad Mother.
From the time of the womb.
I've given up wanting.
Ma, I've drunk Your poisoned nectar.

O Baba! Look at this Cadak tree.
Out of love for You.
Renunciation's agonies.
DiPrima, C.   Her Eyes a Thousand Times Over.
Disch.   Ballade of the New God.
Dizhur.   Here is an island. Here is a house on stilts.
Dobson, R.   Three Fates, The.
Donovan, K.   Entering the Mare.
Doolittle, Hilda.   Evadne.
Evil was active in the land.
Splintered the crystal of identity.
Dove, R.   Demeter, Waiting.
Duhig, I.   Fundamentals.
Duncan, R.   Chords Passages 14.
Structure of Rime XVIII.
Eclipse.   Cicada.
Elfyn, Menna.   Cell Angel.
Eliot, T. S.   Dry Salvages, The.
Elledge.   Household Gods.
Enheduanna.   From The Hymn to Inanna.
Lady of Largest Heart.
Fabian, C.   Prayer of Dedication.
Qadesha (Sacred Whore).
Fanthorpe.   Nativities.
Fields, R.   Very Short Sutra on the Meeting of the Buddha and the Goddess, The.
Forrest-Thomson.   Garden of Proserpine, The.
Fuhrman, J.   Atlantis.
Ghos, G.   I plaster myself with ashes.
Who said / If you took the name All-Destroyer.
You're home, Uma! Stay here.
Gidlow.   Creed for Free Women, A.
Glover, S.   Power of the Soul.
Goddess, R.   Why I Be a Goddess.
Goldberg, L.   God Once Commanded Us, A.
Goode, S.   Lady of Pazardzik.
Goodman, P.   Woman eternal my muse, lean toward me.
Gottlieb, A.   Meditation on the Feminine Nature of Shekinah, A.
Gottlieb, L.   Greeting Shekinah.
Grahn.   Grand Grand Mother is returning.
Graves, R.   Return of the Goddess [Artemis].
Weather of Olympus, The.
White Goddess, The.
Gupta, I.   I got some news from Kailasa!
Hannon.   Real Estate.
Harvey, A.   Prayer to the Divine Mother, A.
Heine, H.   My zenith was luckily happier than my night.
Hildebrandt, Z.   In Hecate's Garden.
Kali.
Hill, S.   Elegy for the Bee-god.
Hinckley, P.   New Our Father, The.
Hirshfield, J.   Each Moment a White Bull Steps Shining into the World.
Osiris.
Painting.
Hixon, L.   My blissful Mother exists fully through every creature!
Who can keep a blazing fire tied in a cotton cloth?
Hogan, L.   Chambered Nautilus.
Return: Buffalo.
Hölderlin.   But speech.
Homer.   Goddess intervenes between Achilles and Agamemnon, The.
Now Here of the Golden Throne, looking out from where she stood on the summit of Olympus, was quick to observe two things.
Rude Mars had th' ordering of their spirits; of Greeks, the learned Maid.
Then Achilles.
Through the host with this the goddess ran.
Vulcan Forges the Shield of Achilles.
Hope, A.   Fafnir.
Horace.   Satire 1.8: "Once I was wood from a worthless old fig tree."
Hsieh Chin.   Song of Cursive Calligraphy.
Huai Ku.   Rotten Axe-Handle Mountain.
Ibycus.   They destroyed the famous and wealthy.
Ironbiter, S.   Song to the Mother of the World.
Islām, N.   Don't go back, Ma, don't go back, Mother.
He who has seen my Mother.

Let's be girls, Ma.
Now there'll be a new mantra, Mother.
Oh hey, All-Destroyer.
Syama Mother's lap a-climbing.
Syama wakes on the cremation grounds.
Talk to me, javas, talk to me.
Wake up, Syama, wake up, Syama!
Wherever are the lowly, the suffering, and the poor.
Issa.   Kites shriek / Together—.
Six Ways, The.
Jaimes Freyre.   Eternal Farewell.
Jones, R.   Foam.
Jones, S.   Hymn to Indra, A.
Jonson, B.   Hymn[e] to Cynthia.
Kalu, U.   Extended Relations (1).
Karade, B.   Yemoja.
Kinnell.   Last Gods.
Kipling, R.   Gods of the Copybook Headings, The.
Song to Mithras, A.
Kizer, C.   Copulating Gods, The.
Muse of Water, A.
Klee.   Wolf Speaks, The.
Klugman, E.   She Who Listens.
Klugman, S.   God's Body.
Klyuyev [or Kliuev or Klyuev].   Conversational Melody, A Good Verse, A.
Kolatkar.   Low Temple, A.
Korican, L.   City Goddess.
Korinna [or Corinna].   Are you, happy man, grandson of Kronos.
Kouretes hid the goddess's, The.
Of your daughters: Zeus, Father.
Koroneu.   Funeral Eva.
Kulman.   To Diana.
Kuo P'o.   Poem on the Wandering Immortal.
Kürenberg.   "Late at night I stood on a battlement".
Laing, K.   Godhorse.
Lawrence, D. H.   Maximus.
Leftwich, Jim.   Eleusis.
Levertov.   Death in Mexico.
Eros.
Li Ho.   Farewell Song of Magic Strings.
Li Po.   Old Style Poem.
Li Shang-yin.   Ch'ang-O.
Logghe.   Madonna of the Peaches.
Lorde.   125th Street and Abomey.
Lowell, A.   Captured Goddess, The.
Lucretius.   Gods, by right of Nature, must possess, The.
Māhtābcānd, M.   Who is this, all alone? Whose woman is She.
Majumdār, H.   Jaya / Don't wake up Hara's wife.
Mandal, B.   I'm not a child any more, Syama.
Marlowe.   What is't, sweet wag, I should deny thy youth?
Marvell.   Mower Against Gardens, The.
Masaoka Shiki.   Autumn wind / Gods, Buddha.
McAdams, J.   Leaving the Old Gods.
McFerrin, B.   23rd Psalm, The: "Lord is my Shepherd, I have all I need, The."
McKay, D.   2. Fates Worse Than Death.
Melinno.   Hail, Roma, daughter of Ares.
Melville, H.   Cypriote, The.
Merrill, J.   After Greece.
Milán, E.   Do you care to remedy the faces of the gods? Make white.
¿Quieres curar las caras de los dioses? Haz máscaras.
Milton.   On the Morning of Christ's Nativity.
Monaghan.   Venus of Laussel.
Morgan, Elin Llwyd.   Schizo de Picasso.
Morgan, R.   As it was in the beginning.
Mukhopādhyāy, K.   Am I afraid of the tenth day?
Is there any treasure like the Mother's name?
Ma, the mail train is leaving now.
Mukhopādhyāy, N.   Use your mental eye.
Mukhopādhyāy, R.   Why should I sit alone, eyes closed.
Murray, L.   Gods, The.
Muske, C.   Epith.
Mutén, B.   Hesperides, The.

Queen Hera.
Queen Medusa.
Urania.
Namjoshi, S.   Caliban's Journal.
Nandī Majumdār, R.   Mind, I'm talking to you.
Nandī, R.   I understand now, Tara, I understand.
Mind, let's go to an estate that's decent.
Nerval.   To J—Y Colonna.
Nolla.   Reencounrter with the Goddess.
Norris, K.   Prayer to Eve, A.
Nossis.   O Honored Hera, who often descending from heaven.
O'Curry, E.   Litany to Our Lady.
Okigbo.   Overture.
Olson, C.   In Cold Hell, in Thicket.
Ono.   Mother of the Universe.
Ovid.   You gods of sea and sky—what's left me now but prayer?
Palladas [or Pallades].   Where the Three Roads Meet.
Parnell, P.   Apotheosis of Medusa.
Medusa and Perseus III: Lilith.
Sheila the Hat.
Sile Na gCioch.
Pāthak, G.   I'll worship You with tears, Ma.
Pātunī, N.   Ma, Hara's Beloved, Tara.
Peacocke.   Goddess, The.
Philpot, T.   Clump of Gods, The.
Pinsky.   Uncreation, The.
Pound, E.   Return, The.
Rakosi.   Origins.
Ralegh, S.   Homage to Diana.
Rāy, D.   It's no one else's fault, Syama Ma.
Wake up, wake up, Mother!
Who is this black.
Rāy, K.   Tara, You are Cintamayi, Full of Thought.
Rāy, M. N.   You've enchanted the world.
Rāy, M. R.   Give me food.
Moon flashes in Her blessed face, The.
Rāy, N.   Everything is Your wish, Tara.
Rāy, Raghunath.   Who is this.
Rāy, Rasikcandra.   Mountain / Whose woman have you brought home to our mountain city?
Rāy, T.   Wait a moment, Death.
Reed, I.   I Am a Cowboy in the Boat of Ra.
Reilly, P.   Imagine a woman who honors the face of the Goddess in her own changing face.
Reis, P.   Ancient Ones, The.
Riley, P.   149. Thesis.
Ritsos.   End of Dodona II, The.
Marpessa's Choice.
Requiem on Poros.
Rochester, J.   Song: "Oh gentle Venus, ease a tarse."
Rupp.   Sophia.
Ruskhan.   In Praise of Krishna.
Saarikoski.   No, Quetzalcoatl, don't come back.
Sāheb, A.   Victory to Yogendra's Wife, Great Illusion!
Santayana.   Sonnet 43: The Candour of the gods is in thy gaze: "Candour of the gods is in thy gaze, The."
Sappho.   Equal to the Gods.
In the young spring evening.
Prayer to my lady of Paphos.
Queen Hera, may your [graceful form].
Sardis.
Sen, R.   At last I have a way to understand.
Brother / This world.
Can someone / Called Daughter of a Stone.
Death, get out of here!
Her face / Is a spotless moon.
Hey, it's not wine I drink.
Hey! Who is She, dark as clouds.
How wonderful! Look what.
I have learned.
I'll die of mental anguish.
It's not Siva.
It's silly to hope for Father's wealth.
Kali, Ma.
Kulakundalini, Goddess Full of Brahman, Tara.
Let me tell You a thing or two, Tara.
Look here.
Love Her, Mind.
Ma, You're inside me.

Meditate on Kali! Why be anxious?
Mind, don't be duped by others' sneers.
Mind, how do you think you'll find Her?
Mind, why this separation from the Mother's feet?
Mind, you're still not rid of your illusions.
Mother, make *me* Your treasurer.
My Mind, my helmsman.
Oh Kali Full of Brahman!
Oh Mind, you don't know how to farm.
Oh my Mind, worship Kali.
Oh my Mind! You're just spinning.
So, Mind / You've decided to go on pilgrimage?
Supreme Savior of Sinners.
Tara, what more are You planning?
Tell me.
This is a fine mess.
This time I've realized the essence.
This time, Kali.
Tongue, call out.
Wait a minute, Death.
What a joke!
What's the fault of the poor mind?
Who can understand Kali?
Who is that Syama woman.
World-Mother's police chief, The.
World's a shoreless ocean, The.
Shange. We Need a God Who Bleeds Now.
Shapiro, A. Old Joke.
Shepherd, R. Gods at Three A.M., The.
Shinkichi Takahashi. Gods.
Simonides. Distinguishes the fair and the shameful.
It is hard to become a truly good.
Who, trusting his mind, could praise the man of Lindos, Kleoboulos.
Slessor. Fixed Ideas.
Smith, S. River God, The.
Snyder, G. Gaia.
Sornberger. When She Can't Sleep.
Souza. Conversation Piece.
Soyinka. Huge with Time, a wombfruit lanced.
Ssu-ma Hsiang-ju. Mighty One, The.
Stainer. Xochiquetzal.
Stesichoros. Across from glorious Erytheia.
Don't pile cruel cares upon those griefs.
Swinburne. Garden of Proserpine, The.
Taggard. Demeter.
Tasso. Drearie trumpet blew a dreadfull blast, The.
Unknown. Coming of Enkidu, The.
Corpus Inscriptionum Latinarum 14.3565.
Cosmology.
Death of Enkidu, The.
First Merseburg Spell.
Get up, Mountain, get up!
Hebe and Ganymede.
Holy Goddess Tellus.
Holy Priestess of Heaven, The.
Homage to Tara Our Mother.
Hymn to Nut.
I was sent forth from the power.
Lady of the Morning, The.
Lady Who Ascends into the Heavens, The.
Litany to Our Lady.
May Isis heal me.
Oshun, the River Goddess.
Prayer to the Gods of the Night.
Proud Queen of the Earth Gods, Supreme Among the Heaven Gods.
Second Merseburg Spell.
Sky is a dark bowl, the stars die and fall, The.
Tantric Praise of the Goddess.
Tell me.
To your question: why are my private parts.
Twelfth Song of the Thunder.
Wait!
Valiente. Charge of the Goddess, The.
Vietnamese Oral Tradition. Whisky Lovers.
Villanueva, A. From the Healing Dark.
Volkman. Sonnet: "Sky we bear on our shoulders, heaven-height, The."
Wade-Gayles. Loving Again.
Warn. Word Between the World and God, The.
Welish. Respected, Feared, and Somehow Loved.

Wilde, O. Santa Decca.
Wingfield. Back.
Winter, M. In the Beginning.
Wright, D. To the Gods the Shades Flavinus of the Cavalry Regiment.
Wright, J. Ishtar.
Young, I. Mermaid Knows, A.
Visit to the Palace of Venus.
Yüan Mei. On the Way to Pa-ling.

God's Protection
Bates, K. America the Beautiful.
Buchanan, R. Wanderers, The.
Colman, H. On the Three Children in the Fiery Furnace.
Drummond, R. As Zeus.
Emerson, R. Worship.
Feldman, A. This Fog.
Herbert, G. Affliction (4).
Invitation, The.
L'Envoy.
Providence.
Hyman, A. Surrender.
Kersch. Soldier, A: His Prayer.
Kipling, R. Hymn before Action.
Kosman, Admiel. Something Hurt.
MacNeice. Prayer Before Birth.
Mirabai [or Mira Bai]. Ankle Bells.
Molodovsky [or Molodowsky]. Merciful God.
O'Daly, M. Consecration.
Smith, E. God in the darkness, God beyond our knowing.
Suri, T. Here Comes God.
Tilak, D. Prayer, A: "God / save this country."
Unknown. All Other Love Is Like the Moon.
Got a Home in That Rock.
Jehovah, Hallelujah.
My Army Cross Over.
Whittemore, R. Psalm: "Lord feeds some of His prisoners better than others, The."
Wordsworth, W. Hymn for the Boatmen, as They Approach the Rapids under the Castle of Heidelberg.
Wylie. Birthday Sonnet.

Goethe, Johann Wolfgang von
Arnold, M. Memorial Verses.
Kunert. Sestri Levante / Liguria 2.
Merry. Elegy Written after Reading the "Sorrows of Werter".
Simic. Eastern European Cooking.
Sŏ Chŏngju. Floor in Goethe's House, The.
Thackeray. Sorrows of Werther, The.
Welish. Textile 9.

Gogol, Nikolai Vasilyevich
Burkard. Personal Histories, The.
Zabolotsky [or Zabolotskii]. Popryshchin.

Gold
Bricusse, L. Goldfinger.
Buddingh'. Hyena, The.
Crabbe, G. Marriage Ring, The.
Doolittle, Hilda. Song: "You are as gold."
Frost, R. Nothing Gold Can Stay.
Gogarty. Good Luck.
Gray, T. Ode on the Death of a Favo[u]rite Cat, Drowned in a Tub [or Bowl] of Gold Fishes.
Greenwell, D. Broken Chain, The.
Greiffenberg. I look.
Hopkins, G. My Own Heart Let Me More Have Pity On.
Kipling, R. Runes on Weland's Sword, The.
Lee-Hamilton. Sunken Gold.
Oppen. Gold on Oak Leaves.
Po Chü-i. Lodging with the Old Man of the Stream.
Wen T'ing-yün. Gold Glimmers and Fades.
Wong, J. Good Luck Gold.

Gold Mining and Gold Miners
Compton, W. Jump Rope Rhyme of the 49er Daughters.
Galich. Goldminers' Waltz, The.
Service. Cremation of Sam McGee, The.
Skeeter. California, 1852.
Winters, Y. John Sutter.
Yost, C. California Poem.

Golden Age
Browne, W. Golden Age, The.

Calpurnius Siculus. Eclogue 1.
Ovid. Golden Age, The.
Tasso. Golden Age, The.
Golden Age, The. A Paraphrase on a Translation out of French.
Whittier. My Triumph.

Golden Rule, The
Gannon, K. Reciprocity.

Goldenrod
Oliver, M. Goldenrod.

Goldfinches
Hardy, T. Caged Goldfinch, The.
Morgan, B. Among Goldfinches.
Thomas, E. Hollow Wood, The.

Goldfish
Doty, M. Brilliance.
Duhig, I. Fred.
Hyde, L. Goldfish in the Charles River.
Ivory, H. Sleeping with the Fishes.
Morgan, F. Busses, The.
Morrissey, S. Goldfish.
Paris, T. Memory Span of a Goldfish Is Three Seconds, The.
Pavlov, Konstantin. Wonderful in Poetry, or a Victim of Goldfish, The.
Turner, C. On a Vase of Gold-Fish.
Worth, V. Goldfish in the Garden Pond.

Goldilocks
Gibson, M. Goldilocks.

Golem
Borges. Golem, The.
Muñiz Huberman. Circle of the Golem, The.
Shúa, A. Golem and Rabbi 5.
Golem and Rabbi 4.
Golem and Rabbi 3.

Golf
Hamill, S. Another Duffer.
Harrison, J. Hitting Golfballs off the Bluff.
Torre, M. Golfers in the Family.
Wheatley, D. Moonshine.

Golgotha
Lansdown. Golgotha.
Livingstone, D. One Golgotha.
Tolson, M. They tell us to forget.

Goliath
Dressel. Let's Hear It for Goliath.
Graves, R. Goliath and David.
Thompson, P. David and Goliath.

Goneril
Patton, L. When Everything Is Goneril.

Good
Allen, Gilbert. Good Duke Speaks, The.
Blake, W. Marriage of Heaven and Hell, The.
Hardy, T. Unkept Good Fridays.
Polkowski. Noli Me Tangere.
Sahn, Seung. Good and Bad are eminent teachers.
Simonides. It is hard to become a truly good.
Trakl. Sun, The: "Each day the gold sun comes over the hill."
Vinokurov. Adam.
Wright, James. Trying to Pray.
Wright, Jay. Meta-A and the A of Absolutes.

Good Friday
Auden. Terce.
Brion, R. Good Friday.
Bulich, V. From My Diary, 3.
Clifton, L. Good Friday.
Cruz e Sousa. Good Friday.
D'Aguiar, F. Mama Dot Warns Against an Easter Rising.
Davie, D. Rodez.
Donne. Good Friday [or Goodfriday], 1613. Riding Westward.
Hardy, T. Unkept Good Fridays.
Herrick. Good Friday: Rex Tragicus, or, Christ Going to His Cross[e].
Hill, G. Canticle for Good Friday.
Petrarch. It was the day when the sun's rays turned pale with grief for his.
Rossetti, C. Good Friday ("Am I a stone and not a sheep.").
Thomas, R. S. Pisces.

Good Samaritan
Cummings, E. E.   Man who had fallen among thieves, A.

Gore-Booth, Eva
Yeats.   In Memory of Eva Gore-Booth and Con Markievicz.

Gospel Music
Evans, M.   And the Old Women Gathered.
Grey, C.   Hallelujah!
Hughes, L.   Tambourines.
Ratzlaff, K.   Gospel.
Robin, L.   Hallelujah!
Thomas, L.   Downtown Boom.
Unknown.   Down by the Riverside.
Waters, M.   Burden Lifters, The.

Gospels, The
Imbriglio, C.   Gospel According to How We Throw Stones.
   Gospel According to One Who Always Needs an Audience.
   Gospel According to the Middle.
Smith, R.   Brieves from the Book of Kells.

Gossip and Gossips
Aubert, A.   Whispers in a Country Church.
Auden.   Love Feast, The.
Berlin.   Say It Isn't So.
Borthwick, P.   Ward Mouth.
Burke, C.   Motor Oil Queen.
Fraser, G.   Lean Street.
Glatt.   Talking About Boys.
Hammerstein.   People Will Say We're in Love.
Kanik.   People Will Talk.
Leapor.   Headache, The.
Leon, R.   Have you not heard the gossip and the rumour going around.
Linden, M.   Gossip.
Neiburg, A.   It's the Talk of the Town.
O'Hara, F.   Personal Poem.
Parker, M.   Whither away good neighbour.
Patterson, G.   Lament.
Shakespeare, W.   Sonnet 121: "Tis better to be vile than vile esteemed."
Sidney.   Sonnet 92: "Be your words made (good sir) of Indian ware."
Sorby.   Gossip.
Symes, M.   It's the Talk of the Town.
Taylor, J.   Recreation.
Unknown.   Jiang Zhong-zi: Hep-Cat Chung.
Wright, K.   Underneath the Archers *or* What's All This about Walter's Willy?

See also **Rumor; Reputation**

Govan, Saint
Prys-Jones.   St. Govan.

Government
Berry, W.   Against the War in Vietnam.
Bierce.   Statesmen, The.
Bly, R.   Johnson's Cabinet Watched by Ants.
Butler, S.   When civil fury [*or* dudgeon] first grew high.
Bye.   Indiana.
Cabico, R.   Check One.
Calpurnius Siculus.   Eclogue 4.
Chŏng Ch'ŏl.   Magistrate.
Chrystos.   I Have Not Signed a Treaty with the United States Government.
Ch'ungdam, Master.   Statesmanship.
Daumal.   Jesus Before Pilate.
Elmslie, K.   Experts at Veneers.
Emerson, R.   Ode, Inscribed to W. H. Channing.
Ennis.   Coyne's.
Espada.   Cockroaches of Liberation.
Eveleigh, G.   Divine Mission, A.
Ezenwa-Ohaeto.   I Wan Bi President.
Freneau.   On Mr. Paine's Rights of Man.
Góngora y Argote.   Roistering I'll Chaff.
Herbert, Z.   Elegy of Fortinbras.
Hernández Cruz.   It's Miller Time.
Herrick.   Ill Government.
   Power in the People, The.
   Shame, No Statist.
Holman, B.   1990.
Hsieh T'iao.   In a Provincial Capital Sick in Bed.
Hughes, L.   Un-American Investigators.
Hugo, V.   Jeanne was holed up (pitch darkness;

bread and water).
Kipling, R.   Death-Bed, A.
Kuan Hsiu.   Bad Government.
Lowell, J.   Letter Six—The Pious Editors' Creed.
Markotić, N.   Verbatim begins with this decade's hit and miss.
Marvell.   First Anniversary of the Government under His Highness the Lord Protector, 1655, The.
More, S.   Quis Optimus Reipublicae Status.
Morgenstern.   Summons.
Mphande.   I Was Sent For.
Mullen, H.   Xenophobic Nightmare in a Foreign Language.
Orban, O.   Chile.
Parra, N.   Discourse of the Good Thief, The.
Po Chü-i.   After Collecting the Autumn Taxes.
   Chancelor's Gravel-Drive, The.
Pound, E.   Great Digest of Confucius, The.
Prejsnar, Mark.   Government and Binding.
   Ode to Toge.
Rein.   Secret Agent, A.
Sall, A.   Cloak of Dawn.
Schneider, I.   History of the Caesars, A.
Shelley, P.   England in 1819.
Silva, L.   Island and Europe, The.
Steptoe.   Election Time.
Taylor, C.   Poem to Ma Ferguson.
Tu Fu [*or* Du Fu].   Sent to the Magistrate of P'eng-chou.
Various authors.   Because his bright nature.
   Because robbers poisoned the people.
   Because the govenment burdened the people.
   Millennium ago, A.
Wheelwright.   Anathema. Maranatha!
Zimunya.   Mr. Bezuidenthout's Dogs.

Goya, Francisco de
Duncan, R.   Poem Beginning with a Line by Pindar, A.
Ferlinghetti, L.   In Goya's greatest scenes we seem to see.
Meredith, W.   Bachelor.
Voznesensky [*or* Voznesenskii].   I Am Goya.
Weiss, T.   Clothes Maketh the Man.

Grace
Askew, A.   Ballad Which Anne Askew[e] Made and Sang When She Was in Newgate, The.
Bin Hassan, U.   Grace.
Bontemps.   God Give to Men.
Borges.   John 1:14; And the Word became flesh and dwelt among us.
Brown, S.   To Sallie, Walking.
Campion, T.   Author of light, revive my dying spright.
   View Mee, Lord.
Cullen, C.   Atlantic City Waiter.
Dickinson, E.   Day that I was crowned, The.
Donne.   Oh my black[e] soul[e]! now thou art summoned.
   Thou hast made me, and shall thy work[e] decay?
Emerson, R.   Grace.
Glück, L.   Gift, The.
Greshoff, J.   Friendship for a Woman of Grace.
Herbert, G.   Grace.
   Love (3): "Love bade me welcome: yet my soul drew back."
Hopkins, G.   Handsome Heart, The.
   Windhover, The.
Jewsbury.   Verses: "I am monarch of troubles a host."
Jones, D.   Last Window.
Kasischke.   Grace.
Kelly, R.   Holy Sonnet.
Kendrick, D.   Gethsemane A. D.
Landor, W.   Rose Aylmer.
Lanier, E.   To the Lady Arabella.
Prado, A.   Grace.
Ralegh, S.   Passionate Man[']s Pilgrimage, The.
Shakespeare, W.   Sonnet 53: "What is your substance, whereof are you made."
Starkey, D.   Scrabble.
Stroud, J.   Directions.
Taylor, E.   Here is a Mudwall tent, whose Matters are.

Meditation 8 (First Series).
   Meditation 42 (First Series).
   Meditation 16 (First Series).
Thompson, F.   Hound of Heaven, The.
Unknown.   Love Me Not [for Comely Grace].
Very.   Promise, The ("I come the rushing wind that shook the place.").
Warren, R.   Amazing Grace in the Back Country.
Williams, C. K.   Dance, The.
Wright, C.   Grace: "Its hair is a fine weed."

Grackles
Nash, O.   Grackle, The.

Graffiti
Alexander, E.   Kevin of the N.E. Crew.
Cárdenas, B.   Sonido Ink(quieto).
Espada.   Courthouse Graffiti for Two Voices.
Field, E.   Graffiti.
Goldbarth.   Counterfeit Earth!, The.
Hamer.   Charlene-N-Booker 4Ever.
Healy, E.   Moroni on the Mormon Temple / Angel on the Wall.
Larkin, P.   Sunny Prestatyn.
Lux.   I Love You Sweatheart.
Martin, C.   Speech Against Stone.
Meinke.   Helen.
Murphy, K.   Eighties Meditation.
November, Deena.   Melba Street.
Philips, K.   Upon the graving of her Name upon a Tree in Barnelmes Walks.
Quinn, J.   12. Graffiti.
Ramke, B.   Art, Love, Geology.
Rodriguez, A.   Sonido Ink(quieto).
Rojas, S.   Creed of a Graffiti Writer, The.
Seaton, M.   Tagging.
Snodgrass.   Men's Room in the College Chapel, The.
Unknown.   I ask you to witness, Priapus.
Viereck, P.   Kilroy.
Yolen.   Graffiti.

Grammar
Berger, B.   Misconstrued, The.
Berkson, B.   By Halves.
Cope, J.   Dementia.
Cope, W.   Uncertainty of the Poet, The.
Cox, M.   Style.
De Coninck, H.   Your Sweaters.
Disch.   Agreement of Predicate Pronouns, The.
Fischer, N.   Favorable Prospects.
Ganev, Nedelcho.   Verb, The.
Herbert, Z.   Transformations of Livy.
Hoagland, T.   Grammar.
Hocquard.   Three Moral Tales.
Hollander, J.   Coordinating Conjunction.
Koch, K.   Permanently.
Kowit.   Grammar Lesson, The.
Lavender, Bill.   Note to Skip on Max and Maxine, A.
Macklin.   House Style, The.
McLagan, Elizabeth.   Reading the Names.
North, C.   Eye Reflecting the Gold of Fall.
Palladas [*or* Pallades].   Having Slept with a Man.
Robertson, Lisa.   Wednesday.
Royet-Journoud.   Locality.
Sale, Richard.   Farm-to-Market #4.
Sidney.   Sonnet 63: "O grammar rules, O now your virtues show."
Simic.   Charles Simic.
Wallace, R.   Student Theme, The.
Welish.   Textile 12.

Grampian Mountains, Scotland
Bruce, G.   Kinnaird Head.

Grand Canyon
Garrigue.   Grand Canyon, The.
Milán, E.   I mean *you* as though referring to two furies because.
   Me refiero a ti como a dos fieras porque.
Pobo, K.   Grand Canyon.

Grand Pré, Nova Scotia
Carman, B.   Low Tide on Grand Pré.

Grandchildren
Allen, F.   Two-day-old Grandchild.
Bensko.   Butterfly Net, The.
Bradstreet, A.   On My Dear Grandchild Simon

Bradstreet, [Who Died on 16TH November, 1669, Being But A Month And One Day Old].
Clifton, L.   Photograph.
Giovanni.   Legacies.
Jones, R.   Portrait of My Father and His Grandson.
Khalvati.   Stone of Patience.
Sanchez, S.   Father and Daughter.

Granddaughters
Boss, L.   When You Are Grown, Amanda Rose.
Bradstreet, A.   In Memory of My Dear Grandchild Elizabeth Bradstreet Who Deceased August, 1665, Being a Year and Half Old.
Sherman, J.   My Father Plaits His Granddaughter's Hair.

Grandfathers
Alexander, E.   Who I Think You Are.
Allbery.   Offering.
Bachner.   Yes, That's the Way Things Are.
Baillie, J.   Child to His Sick Grandfather, A.
Baraka, I.   Why Didnt He Tell Me the Whole Truth.
Berssenbrugge.   Chronicle.
Bishop, E.   Manners.
Bowering, G.   Grandfather.
Bruchac.   Birdfoot's Grampa.
Chappell, F.   Cleaning the Well.
Child, L.   Thanksgiving Day.
Chŏng Hwajin.   I'm a Dragonfly Caught in a Net.
Clarke, G.   Taid's Grave.
Clements, A.   Elegy.
Coccimiglio.   Night Beach.
Cofer, J.   My Grandfather's Hat.
Cox, M.   Things My Grandfather Must Have Said.
Delgado, J.   Phone Booth at the Corner, The.
Di Prima.   April Fool Birthday Poem for Grandpa.
Dove, R.   Musician Talks about "Process," The.
Dubie.   Grandfather's Last Letter, A.
Fox, S.   Grandmother.
Garrett, E.   Grandfather's Mint.
Gloria.   Whisper, The.
Glück, L.   Legend.
Goldbarth.   Gallery.
Graham, H.   Grandpapa.
Grin, B.   Morris Winchevsky.
Guevara, M.   Abuelo, Answers and Questions.
Hall, D.   Maple Syrup.
Harper, M.   Grandfather.
Harris, W.   Grandfather Poem, A.
Heaney, S.   Digging.
Hennen.   Soaking Up Sun.
Henson, L.   Grandfather.
Hirsch, E.   My Grandfather's Poems.
Inada.   Father of My Father.
Jacinto, J.   Visitation.
Janzen, J.   Wild Grapes.
Jenkins, A.   Inheritance.
Khalvati.   Baba Mostafa.
Košek, M.   Yes, That's the Way Things Are.
Kumin, M.   For My Great-Grandfather: A Message Long Overdue.
Levine, P.   Zaydee.
Lewis, W.   Some Solace, Some Yearning.
Linebarger, Jim.   Oppa.
Loftis, N.   Big John.
Longley, M.   Self-Portrait.
Löwy, H.   Yes, That's the Way Things Are.
Mahon.   Grandfather.
Mason, D.   Spooning.
Milosz, O.   La Berline Arrêtée Dans la Nuit.
Minhinnick.   Grandfather in the Garden.
Mosby.   To Josh Gibson (Legendary Slugger of the Old Negro Baseball League).
Mura.   Grandfather-in-law.
Niedecker.   Poet's Work.
Nowlan.   And He Wept Aloud, So That the Egyptians Heard It.
Ormond.   My Grandfather and His Apple-Tree.
Ortiz.   On late-night television, two U.S. scientists talk about why the U.S.
Paley, G.   Here.
Pizarnik.   Suspicion.
Putnam.   Ship of State and Grandpa.

Rector.   My Grandfather Always Promised Us.
Reznikoff.   My grandfather, dead long before I was born.
Ríos, A.   Mi Abuelo.
St. John, D.   Grandfather's Cap, My.
Satchell.   Grandfather Grandfather.
Schaeffer.   Yahrzeit.
Sexauer, T.   Well, The.
Sexton.   Funnel.
Song.   Easter: Wahiawa, 1959.
Wagoner, D.   Curtains.
Waniek.   My Grandfather Walks in the Woods.
Warren, R.   Confederate Veteran Tries to Explain the Event, A.
Waterhouse, A.   Climbing My Grandfather.
Wheatley, D.   Chronicle.
Williams, D.   Little Girl Talk.
Woo, D.   Grandfather's Rockery.
Work.   Grandfather's Clock.
Zuckerman, M.   In Every Pot and Closet.

Grandmothers
Abinader, E.   Letters from Home.
Agosin.   Questions.
Aini, L.   Shower.
Alegría.   Grandmother, The.
Allbery.   Offering.
Baca.   Green Chile.
Barkan.   Two Grandmas.
Becker, R.   Selective Memory.
Berkson, B.   Instinct.
Bernstein, C.   Caught.
When My Grandmother Said "Pussy".
Berssenbrugge.   Chronicle.
Bishop, E.   Sestina: "September rain falls on the house."
Bona.   Dream Poem.
Brooks, G.   Novelle; My Grandmother Is Waiting For Me To Come Home.
Brooks, S.   Grandma Talk.
Caballero-Robb, M.   Dear Rosario.
Memoranda for Rosario.
Caston, A.   Blowing Eggs.
Cavalieri.   Grandmother.
Cervantes.   Beneath the Shadow of the Freeway.
Refugee Ship.
Chŏng Hwajin.   South Yard, The.
Chula, M.   This Winter's Night.
Corwin, N.   Grandmother Living in Fear of Free Verse.
Crane, H.   My Grandmother's Love Letters.
Cullen, C.   For My Grandmother.
Dauenhauer.   Grandmother Eliza.
De la Mare.   Cupboard, The.
DeCormier-Shekejian.   Grandmother.
Derricotte.   Weakness, The.
Divakaruni.   Quilt, The.
Dixon, M.   Grandmother: Crossing Jordan.
Donovan, K.   Stitching.
Dubie.   Of Art & Memory.
Espirito Santo.   Grandma Mariana.
Field, E.   Both My Grandmothers.
Figueroa, J.   Felipa, La Filosofa de Rincon que Nació a los 98 Años.
Finney, N.   Fishing Among the Learned.
Forché.   Morning Baking, The.
Fox, S.   Grandmother.
Giovanni.   Legacies.
Goldbarth.   Recipe.
Goldberg, L.   From My Mother's Home.
Gonzalez, R.   Cabato.
Goodison.   Guinea Woman.
Grahn.   Grand Grand Mother is returning.
Harris, D.   Water from the Well.
Hartnett.   For My Grandmother, Bridget Halpin.
Helfand, J.   Girl in the Boy's Dressing Room, The.
Herd.   Big Girls.
Horst, C.   Everything I Know.
Hudgins.   Grandmother's Spit.
Hugo, V.   Grandmother, The.
Hummer, T.   Train Wreck, 1890: My Grandmother Lies Down with the Dead.
Iverem, E.   Murmur.
Jackson, D.   Grandmother Jackson.
Janzen, J.   These Words Are for You, Grandmother.

Jennings, E.   My Grandmother.
Jones, T.   My Grandmother Died in the Early Hours of the Morning.
Justice, D.   First Death.
Kageyama, C.   Mama.
Khalvati.   Rubaiyat.
Stone of Patience.
Kilbride, Jerry.   Still in the taste.
Kinsella, T.   Tear.
Komunyakaa, Y.   Little Man around the House.
Kooser.   Dishwater.
Kovacic, K.   Brick.
Kushner, D.   Grandma in the Shower.
Lau, A.   Upside Down Basket, The.
Livesay, D.   Green Rain.
Lloyd, C.   Oh, I have told thee every secret care.
Mabuza.   Tired Lizi Tired.
Maloney, F.   Grandmothers in Green and Orange.
Marlatt, D.   Katherine's Hair.
Matthews, W.   Grandmother, Dead at 99 Years and 10 Months.
McElroy, C.   This Is the Poem I Never Meant to Write.
Mercado, N.   Milla.
Merkureva, V.   Grandmother of Russian Poetry: A Self-Portrait, The.
Moore, L.   Tanka.
Morales, A.   1930.
Muldoon, P.   Ancestor, The.
Throwback, The.
Ogilvy.   Grannie's Birthday.
O'Loughlin.   Glasnevin Cemetery.
Paley, G.   Here.
Plath.   Point Shirley.
Pollarolo, G.   In My Days.
While My Father.
Ponge.   Last Simplicity, The.
Potter, Carol.   White Hotel.
Redmond.   Love Necessitates.
Reis, P.   Ancient Ones, The.
Rice, D.   Taproots.
Rich, A.   Grandmothers.
Ríos, A.   Advice to a First Cousin.
Rosario, M.   Curing.
Rossman, E.   Double Features.
St. John, D.   Iris.
Salzman, E.   Grandmother.
Sapia.   Grandmother, a Caribbean Indian, Described by My Father.
Schaeffer.   May Levine.
Sewell, L.   Denied, The.
Shange.   Different Love Poem / We Need a Change, A.
Shapiro, K.   My Grandmother.
Shiphrah, T.   Grandma.
Silko.   In Cold Storm Light.
It Was a Long Time Before.
Long Time Ago.
Sioux Oral Tradition.   Give me my knife.
Slutsky [or Slutskii].   How Did They Kill My Grandmother?
How They Killed My Grandmother.
Sŏ Chŏngju.   Grandmother's Verandah.
Soto.   Behind Grandma's House.
Southerland.   Pale Ant.
Suntsova, E.   City of summer you inhabit a fluff-light city of little claws.
Sutskever [or Sutzkever].   Peasant Who Saw God, The.
Tallmountain.   Matmiya.
Thomas, S.   My Grandmother's Birthday.
Todd, M.   Grandmother's Farm.
Trethewey, N.   Drapery Factory, Gulfport, Mississippi, 1956.
Turnbull.   Transmutation ("Every evening a mother makes up another episode of the same story for her son.").
Unger, B.   Observance.
Unknown.   Old Bike, The.
Walker, M.   Lineage.
Williams, W.   Last Words of My English Grandmother, The.
Wong, N.   Grandmothers' Song.
Wright, J.   Request to a Year.
Yesenin [or Essenin].   For My Sister Shura.

Yi Yônju.   Grandmother's Sea.
Zamora, D.   Hand Mirror.

Grandparents
Carroll, L.   Poeta Fit, Non Nascitur.
Ellis, K. N.   Tougaloo Blues.
Emanuel, L.   Outside Room Six.
Forché.   Morning Baking, The.
Gioseffi.   Bicentennial Anti-Poem for Italian-
   American Women.
González, R.   Day of the Dead.
Grace, P.   Butterflies.
Grimberg.   Reflection of a wet finger that
   slipped over the faded oil-cloth, The.
Jones, R.   End of Communism, The.
Kletke, G.   O Grandfather Dust.
Lowell, R.   Grandparents.
Lux.   Night above the Town.
Madonick, M.   Settled In.
McElroy, D.   Present Moments.
Rimbaud, A.   Thirst.
Salazar.   Piñon Nuts.
Sŏ Chŏngju.   Great Wave, The.

Grandsons
Mason, D.   Spooning.

Grant, Cary
Healy, E.   What It Was Like the Night Cary
   Grant Died.

Grant, Ulysses Simpson
Bierce.   Death of Grant, The.
Harrison, J.   Ghazal 39: "If you laid out all the
   limbs from the Civil War hospital."
Horton, G.   General Grant—the Hero of the
   War.
Sandburg, C.   Cool Tombs.

Grapes
Adams, L.   Grapes Making.
Brackenbury.   Produce of Cyprus.
Levis.   Picking Grapes in an Abandoned
   Vineyard.
Moiro.   Beneath Aphrodite's golden portico you
   now lie.
Shimazaki Toson.   Fox's Trick, The.
Slessor.   Wild Grapes.
Sterling, G.   Ballad of the Grapes.
Yi Yuksa.   Blue Grapes.

Grass
Aiken, C.   Letter from the Grass, A.
Babu, S.   Blade of Grass, A.
Barnstone, T. et al.   Hair of the Field.
Basho.   Dragonfly, The.
   Heat waves shimmering.
   Summer grass.
   Summer grasses.
   Summer grasses / All that remains.
   When I looked under the hedge.
   Withered grass / Under piling.
Beveridge.   In the Park.
Buson.   Coming back.
   Misty grasses.
   Rain falls on the grass.
   Sudden shower.
Byok Namkung.   Grass.
Chŏng Hyŏnjong.   Greenly the Earth.
Corn.   Grass.
Crane, S.   In Heaven, / Some little blades of
   grass.
Dickinson, E.   Grass, The.
   Snake, The.
Dietz, H.   Blue Grass.
Dimitrova.   Grass.
Dragomoschenko.   Footnotes.
Grimké, A.   Grass Fingers.
Haines, J.   To Turn Back.
Holtby, W.   Man Who Hated the Spring, The.
Issa.   Cherry blossoms? / In these parts.
   Faint yellow rose, A.
   Plumes of pampas grass.
Jacobsen, R.   Green Light.
Jones, B.   Landscape without a Hat.
Kang Ŭn'gyo.   Rise, Grass.
Kavanagh, P.   Consider the Grass Growing.
Kim Suyŏng.   Grass.
Kremer.   Epiphany.
Larkin, P.   Cut Grass.
Layton.   Song for Naomi.

Levitt, Peter.   No life but this one.
Lovelace, R.   Grasshopper, The [To My Noble
   Friend Mr Charles Cotton: Ode].
Lowell, A.   Shore Grass.
MacCaig.   Fetching Cows.
Madhubuti.   Loneliness, A.
Martin, C.   Metaphor of Grass in California.
Masaoka Shiki.   Heath grass / Sandals.
Merrill, J.   Grass.
Na Hûidôk.   Song of Grass.
Nguyen, Hoa.   Calmly grass becomes a wave.
Ni Dhomhnaill.   Labasheedy (The Silken Bed).
   Leaba Shíoda.
Nutter, G.   Pastoral: "We're passing the whole
   summer, all of us."
Obejas, A.   Public Place (After Olga Broumas),
   The.
Ono no Yoshiki.   My love / Is like the grasses.
Orban, O.   Blade of Grass, A.
Pavlova, V.   Grass: "Oh praise the lowly stalk."
Reese, L.   Trust.
Ruffin.   Storm Cellar, The.
Sandburg, C.   Grass.
   In Tall Grass.
Suyemoto, Toyo.   In Topaz.
Swenson, M.   Cardinal Ideograms.
Szporluk.   Grass and the Sin, The.
Unknown.   Cai-bin: I Pluck the Grass.
   Do not look at me.
   Grass on the Mountain, The.
   Green, green riverside grass.
   On a Clergyman's Horse Biting Him.
   Two Spring Charms.
   What grass not yellowed?
   Ye-you man-cao: Mid the Bind-Grass.
Untermeyer, L.   Long Feud.
Van Doren.   Former Barn Lot.
Warner, S.   Sad Green.
Whitman, W.   Child said What is the grass?
   fetching it to me with full hands, A.
Winters, Y.   By the Road to the Air-Base.

Grasshoppers
Anacreon.   Grasshopper, The.
Cowley, A.   Grasshopper, The.
Cummings, E. E.   R-P-O-P-H-E-S-S-A-G-R.
Georges, D.   Grasshopper.
Hunt, L.   To the Grasshopper and the Cricket.
Issa.   When I go / Guard my tomb well.
Kawai Chigetsu [orChigetsu-Ni].   Chirping /
   Grasshopper.
Keats.   On the Grasshopper and [the] Cricket.
Lovelace, R.   Grasshopper, The [To My Noble
   Friend Mr Charles Cotton: Ode].
Mathias, R.   Grasshoppers.
Sedakova.   Grasshopper and the Cricket, The.
Zabolotsky [or Zabolotskii].   All That My Soul
   Possessed.

Gratitude
Abse.   Thankyou Note.
Auden.   Glad.
Brodsky, J.   May 24, 1980.
Brown, L.   Thank Your Father.
Buson.   Old calendar, The.
   Spring Wind on the Riverbank at Kema.
Byron, G.   Stanzas to Augusta ("Though the day
   of my destiny's over.").
Comden, B.   Thanks a Lot, but No Thanks.
Congreve, W.   False Though She Be.
DeSylva, B. G.   Thank Your Father.
Dunn, S.   Routine Things Around the House,
   The.
Everson, W.   Canticle to the Waterbirds, A.
Gay, J.   Tray, the Exemplar.
Glück, L.   Gratitude.
Green, A.   Thanks a Lot, but No Thanks.
Gregorio, R.   Solitude Dinner.
Henderson, R.   Thank Your Father.
Issa.   Gratitude for gifts.
Kirsch, S.   Thank-You Note.
Lawrence, D. H.   Wild Common, The.
Merwin.   Stranger, The.
Ovid.   I have been looking these pages over, my
   dearest wife.
Praxilla.   Learning from the tale of Admetos, my
   friend, love the brave.
Prunty.   Note of Thanks, A.

Scully, M.   Variations.
Smith, A.   Giving Thanks.
Snyder, G.   Prayer for the Great Family.
Statius.   Thanksgiving to the Emperor Augustus
   Germanicus Domitianus.
Thomas, E.   No One So Much As You.
Voznesensky [or Voznesenskii].
   Recommendation.
Waring, B.   You Could Have Been Me.
Whitman, W.   Thanks in Old Age.
Yu Hsin.   Offered in Thanks for a Present of
   Wine and a Goose.
Zavalnyuk [or Zaval'niuk].   I Love My
   Enemies.
See also **Thankfulness**

Graves
Akhmatova, A.   We Do Not Know How to Say
   Goodbye.
Anyte [or Anytes].   Damis erected this mound
   for his dead steadfast.
Bachner.   Man Proposes, God Disposes.
Barkova, A.   Few Autobiographical Facts, A.
Basho.   Visting the graves.
Beer, P.   Ballad of the Underpass.
   Grave Doubts.
Behn, A.   Epitaph on the Tombstone of a Child,
   the Last of Seven that Died Before.
Bei Dao.   Accomplices.
Belloc.   Statue, The.
Bierce.   For those this mausoleum is erected.
Brontë, A.   Night.
Broumas, O.   On Earth.
Brown, L.   Sonnet Around Stephanie.
Browning, R.   Bishop Orders His Tomb at Saint
   Praxed's Church, The.
   Childe Roland to the Dark Tower Came.
Bryant, W.   Disinterred Warrior, The.
Buchan, J.   Alastair Buchan (1917).
Bynner.   Idols.
Carver, R.   Walk, A.
Celan.   Profuse announcement.
Cernuda.   To Larra with Some Violets.
Chesterton.   Elegy in a Country Churchyard.
   English Graves, The.
Christensen.   Poem on Death.
Citino.   Last Rites.
Clarke, G.   Taid's Grave.
Coleridge, S.   Knight's Tomb, The.
Cotton, C.   Epitaph on M. H., An.
Crashaw.   Epitaph Upon Husband and Wife
   Who Died and Were Buried Together, An.
Creeley.   Fathers.
Crosby, F.   Let Me Die on the Prairie.
Cullen, C.   In Memory of Colonel Charles
   Young.
Davidson, D.   Lines for a Tomb.
Dickinson, E.   Ample make this Bed.
   Mine—by the Right of the White Election!
   Not any higher stands the Grave.
   We do not play on Graves.
Dobell, S.   Timely Hint, A.
Doddridge, P.   Meditations on the Sepulchre in
   the Garden.
Donne.   Relic, The.
Durcan.   Weeping Headstones of the Isaac
   Becketts, The.
Eberhart, R.   Ceremony by the Sea, A.
   I Walked over the Grave of Henry James.
Elledge.   Strangers: An Essay.
Ellis, K. N.   Tougaloo Blues.
Field.   After Soufrière.
   Sometimes I do despatch my heart.
Glück, L.   Mount Ararat.
Goedicke.   At the Center.
González, A.   Diatribe Against the Dead.
Goodman, P.   Connary, Blodgett, Day, Hapgood.
   Gravestone, August 8, 1968, A.
Gray, T.   Elegy Written in a Country
   Churchyard.
Hajjaj, N.   Hebron (Al-Khalil).
Hall, D.   Maple Syrup.
   Sister on the Tracks, A.
Hardy, T.   Ah, Are You Digging on My Grave?
   Poet, A.
   Rain on a Grave.
Harper, F.   Bury Me in a Free Land.

Harper, M.   Alice.
Harrison, T.   Earthen Lot, The.
Hayden, R.   Paul Laurence Dunbar.
Hemingway.   Champs d'Honneur.
Hernández, M.   I Go on in the Dark, Lit from Within.
Herrick.   Upon Ben Jo[h]nson.
Hooks.   As they bury the dead.
Housman.   Because I liked you better.
   With rue my heart is laden.
Hudgins.   Burial Detail.
Hwang Insuk.   Dance of Death.
Ibarbourou.   Life-Hook.
Ibn Ezra, Moses.   And Where Are the Graves.
Issa.   Evening moon.
   Going to Tend Our Family Graves.
   Visiting the graves.
Ivanov, Binyo.   Summer: "On this long farm facing Rila Mountain."
Ivey, M.   Golden, New Mexico.
Jones, B.   Bilbao Churchyard.
Jones, R.   Uncle Fenster's Grave.
Juhász, F.   Rainbow-Colored Whale, The.
Khoury, N.   People of Fire.
Ki Joon.   Elegy for Myself.
King, H.   Exequy, The.
Kinnell.   Middle Path.
Kitahara Hakushū.   Spider Lilies.
Ko Ŭn.   Memory of the Graves.
Kooser.   Dog's Grave, A.
Košek, M.   Man Proposes, God Disposes.
Kramer, L.   Red Cross Telegram, The.
Kwŏn P'il.   Leaves fall with rain in these vacant mountains.
Landon.   Song: "Farewell!—and never think of me."
Leithauser.   Buried Graves, The.
Levertov.   By the gas-fire, kneeling.
Levis.   Those Graves in Rome.
Levy, A.   Sequel to 'A Reminiscence," The.
Lieberman, L.   Compass of the Dying.
Longfellow, H.   Jewish Cemetery at Newport, The.
Lorde.   Father Son and Holy Ghost.
Lowell, R.   Sailing Home from Rapallo.
Löwy, H.   Man Proposes, God Disposes.
MacNeice.   Introduction, The: "They were introduced in a grave glade."
Mahon.   Image from Beckett, An.
Mallock.   Questions: "Where are you now, little wandering."
Martinez, D.   Death of Isadora Duncan, The.
McKinney, I.   Visiting My Gravesite: Talbott Churchyard, West Virginia.
Mew.   Here Lies a Prisoner.
Millay, E.   In the Grave No Flower.
Mitchell, N.   Runaway.
Moore, M.   Grave, A.
Morabito, F.   Compared to the condos of the living.
   Junto a los condominios de los vivos.
Morgan, E.   King Billy.
Muldoon, P.   Milkweed and Monarch.
Naito Joso.   About the grave / Waves of spring mist.
Niedecker.   Graves, The.
Nijhoff.   At a Grave.
Orlovsky.   Snail Poem.
Ormond.   Lament for a Leg.
Orten.   Whispered.
Pankey.   Resurrection of the Body, The.
Parker, D.   Actress, The.
Parra, N.   Discourse of the Good Thief, The.
Pickthall, M.   Ebb Tide.
Pitter.   Coffin Worm, The.
Po Chü-i.   On an Ancient Tomb East of the Village.
Preston, M.   Grave in Hollywood Cemetery, Richmond, A.
Ramke, B.   Paul Verlaine at the Grave of Lucien Létinois.
Reitenauer, Vicki L.   Wife Of.
Rich, A.   Mark of Resistance, A.
Rossetti, C.   Song: "When I am dead, my dearest."
   Two Thoughts of Death.

Under Willows.
Saigyō.   I don't even know.
Salaam.   St. Louis Cemetery Crypt.
Sandburg, C.   Cool Tombs.
Sassoon, S.   Prehistoric Burials.
Shin Kyŏngnim.   Graveside Memorial.
Simmerman.   Child's Grave, Hale County, Alabama.
Sitwell, E.   Hambone and the Heart, The.
Slessor.   Beach Burial.
Smith, C.   By the Same.
Smith, D.   Near Frost's Grave.
Smith, S.   Exemplary Nick.
Snow, C.   Positions of the Body, 8.
Soto.   Blanco.
Stevenson, A.   Temporarily in Oxford.
Stevenson, R.   Requiem: "Under the wide and starry sky."
Storni.   I'm Going to Sleep.
Stowe.   Only a Year.
Thompson, M.   Lincoln's Grave.
Timrod.   Unknown Dead, The.
Tomlinson, C.   Death in the Desert, A.
Trakl.   Decline.
   Downfall.
Trethewey, N.   Collection Day.
Unknown.   Deirdre's [*or* Deidre's] Lament for the Sons of Usnach.
   Epitaph for Thomas Johnson, Huntsman. Charlton, Sussex.
   No Road Back.
   Unquiet Grave, The.
Valentine, J.   Forces.
Voigt.   Visiting the Graves.
Warner, S.   Elizabeth.
Weigl.   On Not Finding Frost's Grave in the Dark.
Whitman, W.   As Toilsome I Wander'd Virginia's Woods.
   Dirge for Two Veterans.
Whur.   Morning arose, and its beauties were beaming, The.
Wilcox, E.   My Grave.
Wilde, O.   Requiescat.
Wilson, A.   Lynx.
Winters, Y.   For My Father's Grave.
Wordsworth, W.   Gravestone upon the Floor in the Cloisters of Worcester Cathedral, A.
Wright, J.   Albuquerque Graveyard, The.
Yi Kyŏngnim.   At the Grave.
Zimmer.   Because of Duties, Zimmer Had Forgotten the Forest.
Zukofsky, L.   I Sent Thee Late.
See also **Burial; Cemeteries; Mausoleums; Tombs**
Graves, Morris
Montague, J.   Woodtown Manor.
Graves, Robert
Blaser.   Image-Nation 22 (in memoriam).
Ewart.   Robert Graves.
Graves, R.   Face in the Mirror, The.
   My Name and I.
Graveyards
Acquah.   They're Tearing Up the Old Graveyard.
Alexander, P.   Mt. Auburn Owl.
Carver, R.   Walk, A.
Collins, B.   No Time.
Cook, E.   Thought, A [*or* Sunshine].
Goff, C.   Addiction.
Guillén, J.   City Life.
   Last Land of Exile.
Hardie, K.   On Derry's Walls.
Henderson, D.   African Burial Ground called Tribeca, The.
James, S.   Sisters of Saida Manoubia, The.
Kunert.   Jewish Cemetery at Berlin-Weissensee, The.
McAuliffe, J.   Vision of Rahoon, A.
Pak Tujin.   Song in a Graveyard.
Pittman, Al.   Lupines.
Raine, K.   Highland Graveyard.
Randall, D.   Blue Dome, The.
Ruan Yu.   Driving My Chariot Through the Northern Suburbs Gate.
Sutskever [*or* Sutzkever].   Honey of a Wild Bee.
Taneda Santoka.   Edge of town.

Taylor, H.   At South Fork Cemetery.
Unamuno.   In a Castilian Graveyard.
Unknown.   Graveyard, The.
   Lay This Body Down.
   Man's Life a Sojourning.
Valentine, J.   She Would Long.
Weigl.   Convoy.
Wright, R.   Crying and crying.
Wunderlich, M.   Voluntary Servitude.
See also **Cemeteries**
Gravity
Farley, P.   Laws of Gravity.
Garrett, E.   Miser.
Glenday, J.   Concerning the Atoms of the Soul.
Graham, J.   Philosopher's Stone.
Gustafson, R.   In the Yukon.
Jacobsen, J.   Limbo Dancer, The.
Meredith, W.   Airman's Virtue.
Mishol, A.   Gravity, Death.
Porteous.   Calf.
Robertson, R.   New Gravity.
Soloukhin.   Apple, The.
Wilbur, R.   Juggler.
Gray, Thomas
Smith, C.   To the South Downs.
Wilbur, R.   In a Churchyard.
Great Britain
Acconci, H.   Placable Caps, The.
Alvi, M.   Arrival 1946.
Aytoun, W.   Sonnet to Britain.
Davies, I.   Do You Remember 1926?
Dibdin, T.   Origins of Naval Artillery.
Didsbury, P.   In Britain.
Gillilan, P.   Looking North.
Goldsmith, O.   Britain.
Logue, C.   I Shall Vote Labour.
Pickard, T.   Devil's Destroying Angel Exploded, The.
Seneca.   Britannia, free from foes and foreign kings.
Smith, K.   1984 Tour of Britain, The.
Turner, C.   Great Britain Through the Ice: Or, Premature Patriotism.
Zephaniah.   Sun, The.
See also **England; Northern Ireland; Scotland; Wales**
Great Depression
Crozier, L.   Dirty Thirties, The.
Etter.   Elwood Collins: Summer of 1932.
Glaser, I.   Depression.
Hughes, L.   Madam's Past History.
Jones, R.   End of Communism, The.
McDaniel, W.   First Spring in California, 1936.
Moore, M.   Americans in 1933–4–5–6–7–8–, Etc.
Wright, J.   Old WPA Swimming Pool in Martins Ferry, Ohio, The.
Great Lakes
Niedecker.   Lake Superior.
Reznikoff.   They have built red factories along Lake Michigan.
Shepherd, R.   Maritime.
Great Wall, China
Ch'en Lin.   Horses at a Breach in the Great Wall.
   Song: "I watered my horse at the Long Wall caves."
Unknown.   Water the Horses at a Breach in the Great Wall.
Williams, W.   World Contracted to a Recognizable Image, The.
Greatness
Abu-I-Salt Umayyah.   White Stallion, The.
Barnfield [*or* Barnefield].   Beauty and majesty are fallen at odds.
Bible, Apocrypha.   Our Fathers.
Greville, F.   What is the cause, why states, that war and win.
Guiterman.   On the Vanity of Earthly Greatness.
Holloway.   Hand for Some Others, A.
Homer.   Sarpedon's Speech to Glaucus.
Howard, R.   Nadar.
Hughes, L.   Shame on You.
Huidobro.   Canto 2 (excerpts).
Jonson, B.   To the Memory of My Beloved, the

Author Mr [*or* Master] William Shakespeare: And What He Hath Left Us.
Kuzmin. Were I a general of olden times.
mac Lenini, C. In Praise of a Sword Given Him by His Prince.
Montale. Soliloquy.
Scève, M. Every Wide and Long Expanse of Sea.
Seaton, M. Fiddleheads.
Simonides. There is a tale.
Spender, S. I Think Continually of Those Who Were Truly Great.
Taggard. To the Natural World: at 37.
Thackeray. Napoleon.
Unknown. Praise Song for the Oba of Benin.
Whitman, W. By Blue Ontario's Shore.
  Great Are the Myths.
Wordsworth, W. Great men have been among us; hands that penned.

See also **Fame**

Greece
Alcaeus [*or* Alkaios]. Come! Put by Pelops' Isle.
Baker, H. Sappho's Leap.
Bök, Christian. Greek schemers seek egress *en ténèbres*, then enter the melee.
Booth, P. Relations: Old Light / New Sun / Postmistress / Earth / 04421.
Brecht, B. On Reading a Recent Greek Poet.
Broumas, O. On Earth.
  Sometimes, as a Child.
Bryant, W. Conjunction of Jupiter and Venus, The.
Byron, G. Isles of Greece, the isles of Greece!, The.
  On This Day I Complete My Thirty-sixth Year.
  Written After Swimming from Sestos to Abydos.
Cavafy. Ithaka.
  Ithaka.
Chénier. When the Euxine goddess with astonished eyes.
Davidson, D. On a Replica of the Parthenon.
De Angelis. There's a Hand that Nails Down.
Denby. Delos.
  Mykonos.
Doolittle, Hilda. Islands, The.
  Lais.
  This is the spread of wings.
Dryden, J. What Greece, when learning flourished, only knew.
Duncan, R. Chords Passages 14.
Durrell. Delos.
Ekelof. Greece.
Elytis, O. Aegean Melancholy.
England, A. Art of the Snake Story, The.
Gaspar, Lorand. Late Minoan I: (Ewers of Hagia Triada).
Glück, L. Roman Study.
Golding, A. . . . This Damsell was not famous for the place.
Grosholz. On the Ferry, Toward Patras.
Hemans. Bride of the Greek Isle, The.
Hölderlin. Patmos.
Korinna [*or* Corinna]. Thespia, bearing a beautiful race, stranger-loving, Muse-beloved.
Lawrence, D. H. Argonauts, The.
Leftwich, Jim. Eleusis.
Malé. Greek Metamorphosis.
Melville, H. Attic Landscape, The.
Merrill, J. After Greece.
  Charioteer of Delphi, The.
  Correct but cautious, that first night, we asked.
Nolla. Greek History.
O'Grady, D. Here, because of the shock, the sudden.
Petri. Electra.
Rakosi. Origins.
Seferis. Last Stop.
Shelley, P. World's Great Age, The.
Simonides. Thermopylai's dead.
Spenser, E. *Penelope* for her *Ulisses* sake.
Spicer, J. Transformations.
Stallings. Postcard from Greece, A.
Statius. Book 10.
Stickney, T. Sonnets from Greece.

Tada. Odyssey or "On Absence," The.
Taggart, J. Never Too Late.
Taylor, B. Paean to the Dawn, A.
Thornton, R. Cherry Laurel, The.
Tranströmer. Syros.
Unknown. Chance led me once, when idling through the street.
  Sometimes I sauntered from my lone abode.
  Thus feverish fancies floated in my brain.
Williams, Stephanie. Of Riches.
Youn, Monica. Night Ferry to Naxos 1.

Greed
Adams, J. Wants of Man, The.
Agüeros. Psalm for the Next Millennium.
Baratier, D. Estrella's Prophecies #18.
Belli, C. Down with the Money-Exchange.
Belli, G. Greed.
Berryman. Desires of Men and Women.
Bricusse, L. Goldfinger.
Burns, R. Such a Parcel of Rogues in a Nation.
Chaucer. Pardoner's Prologue, The.
  Pardoner's Tale, The.
Clare, J. Look backward on the days of yore.
Coleman, W. Aunt Jessie.
Cowley, A. Against Fruition.
Crabbe, G. Procrastination.
Croft, A. Beasts of England, The.
Cummings, E. E. Greedy the people, The.
Cunningham, J. Epigram: "You wonder why Drab sells her love for gold?"
Dante Alighieri. Natural thirst that never can be quenched.
Davies, W. H. Songs of Joy.
Day Lewis. Consider These, for We Have Condemned Them.
Duffy, C. Making Money.
Edwards, D. Not Having.
Emerson, R. Hamatreya.
  Hamatreya.
  Wealth.
Field. Wheat-miners.
Friedlander, B. Dick Cheney's Heart.
Holmes, O. Contentment.
Horace. Ode 2.18: "Gold or iv'ry's not intended."
Jonson, B. Volpone.
Juvenal. Satire 10.
Marie de France. Wolf and the Lamb, The.
Melville, H. Time's Betrayal.
Meynell, A. To 'A Certain Rich Man'.
Montale. Soliloquy.
Naong. Mosquito.
Quarles. Philippians 1.23.
Reagon. Greed.
Rickword. Luxury.
Robinson, E. Aaron Stark.
Samwell. Negro Boy, The.
Scammell, W. Act, The.
Sexton. With Mercy for the Greedy.
Soto. Failing in the Presence of Ants.
Stickney, T. You say, Columbus with his argosies.
Tennyson, A. Northern Farmer: New Style.
Torres, E. How Long Does the Curator Dance For?
Traherne. Insatiableness.
Unknown. Money, Money.
  War the Source of Riches.
Wang Fan-chih. Requiem: "Houses in country and city."
Wang the Zealot. Piece of the Loot, A.
Warner, R. Hymn: "Splendid body is private, and calls for more, The."
Wesley, S. Full doeful Tales have oft been told.
Whittier. Haschish, The.
Wilbur, R. Matthew 8, 28 ff.
Williams, C. K. Money.
Williams, W. Question and Answer.
Wordsworth, W. Written in London, September, 1802.
Yi Kyubo. Moon in the Well, The.
Zephaniah. De Rich Getting Rich.

Greek Poetry, Classical
Bogardus. Narcissus to Echo.
Carson, A. Homo Ludens.
Unknown. Earthquake.

Green (color)
Armstrong, J. Green: "Green silence softly."
Basho. Early fall.
Boucicault, D. Wearing of the Green, The.
Buson. Green leaves.
Chŏng Hyŏnjong. Greenly the Earth.
Clampitt. Green.
Clare, J. Maple Tree, The.
Espada. Green and Red, Verde y Rojo.
García Lorca. Sleepwalkers' Ballad.
  Sleepwalking Ballad, The.
  Somnambulist Ballad.
Goldstein, Stephanie. At Night: "Worries creep like insects."
Heaney, S. Fosterling.
Konishi Raizan. Green, green, green / Herbs splash.
Lawrence, D. H. Green.
Li Shang-yin. Chamber Music.
Majorino. Hints.
McSweeney, Joyelle. Still Life w/Influences.
Merrill, J. Green Eye, The.
Moffitt. To Look at Any Thing.
Naito Joso. How green— / Flowering slopes.
Pagis, D. Twelve Faces of the Emerald.
Raz, H. For Barbara, Who Brings a Green Stone in the Shape of a Triangle.
Rodgers, C. Black Heart as Ever Green, The.
Scott, W. Come Green Again.
Tu Fu [*or* Du Fu]. Wu-Chuen.
Yeryomin. Seamstress stitches on a sewing machine, The.

Greenhouses
Hardy, T. Frozen Greenhouse, The.
Lehman. Greenhouses and Gardens.
Morgan, E. My Greenhouse.
O'Brien, S. HMS Glasshouse.
Pitter. Other People's Glasshouses.
Roethke. Big Wind.
  Child on Top of a Greenhouse.
Updike. To Two of My Characters.

Greenland
Gay, J. Song: "Were I laid on Greenland's coast."

Greenwich Village, New York City
Daugherty, B. Lilac.

Gregory, Robert
Yeats. In Memory of Major Robert Gregory.

Greyhounds
Barnes, W. Heäre, The.
Berners. Properties of a Good Greyhound, The.
Ovid. Procris' Immortal Lelaps: Cephalus' Story.
Philips, K. Irish Greyhound, The.
Unknown. Greyhound Snowball, The.
  Dog and the Adder, The.
  Murder Will Out.

Grief
Abbott, K. Grief counselor, The.
Abelard. David's Lament for Jonathan.
  More than a brother to me, Jonathan.
Adonis [*or* Adunis]. Elegy for the Time at Hand.
Ai. Cuba, 1962.
Aird, T. Fellowship in Grief.
Akhmatova, A. Dedication.
Alberti. Amparo.
Antipater of Sidon. Never again, Orpheus.
Anyte [*or* Anytes]. Throwing her arms around her dear father.
Aragon, F. Tricycles.
Archilochus. No townsman, Perikles, will blame us for groaning.
Aygi, G. Poppies of This Year.
Baker, D. Mercy.
Baqi. Sparks from my heart rise.
Baraka, I. How People Do.
Barker, G. Summer Song I.
Barker, W. Trying To.
Barnes, W. Wind at the Door, The.
Barot, R. Eight Elegies.
Bécquer, G. Great Waves Breaking with a Roar.
  When They Told Me I Felt the Cold.
Bedregal. Pointless Journey.
Blake, W. On Another's Sorrow.

Blind. Mourning Women.
Bloem, J. C. Honeysuckle.
Blok. On the Plain of Kulikovo.
Bogan, L. Juan's Song.
Bowles, W. On the Death of William Linley, esq.
Time and Grief.
Bracho, C. Sediment of Lukewarm and Radiant Rain.
Breton, N. Wearie thoughts doe waite upon me.
Bridges, R. Elegy on a Lady, Whom Grief for the Death of Her Betrothed Killed.
Brock-Broido. Periodic Table of Ethereal Elements.
Brock, E. And another thing.
Brody. Lamentations.
Brontë, E. Day Dream, A.
Stanzas: "Often rebuked, yet always back returning."
Brown, T. Pain.
Browning, E. Bereavement.
Grief.
Bryant, W. Death of the Flowers, The.
Burns, R. Red, Red Rose, A.
Buson. No poem you send.
Callimachus. Here Philip the father buried.
Camões [or Camõens or Camoëns], L. Do This Favour For Me.
Castro, R. Mild Was the Air.
Celan. All those sleep shapes.
Ceraman Kottampalattut. Great It May Be.
Chenette, S. Ritual.
Chivers. Avalon.
Cho Chihun. Falling Petals.
Chu Yohan. Fireworks.
Clark, P. Kleptomaniac.
Cofer, J. Campesino's Lament, The.
Cruz, S. Shepherd, Young and Mournful, Grieves Alone, A.
Csoori. Postponed Nightmare.
De Kok. Small passing.
De Vere, A. Sorrow.
Dermée. Poem: "I play tennis with the shells."
Dickey, W. Shortest Day, The.
Dickinson, E. Bereavement in their death to feel.
Bustle in a House, The.
Butterfly upon the Sky, The.
I Can Wade Grief.
I measure every Grief I meet.
Dobyns. When a Friend.
Dodson, O. Sorrow Is the Only Faithful One.
Donne. O might those sigh[e]s and tear[e]s return[e] again[e].
Triple Fool, The.
Valediction, A: Forbidding Mourning.
Donnelly, T. Three Panels Depending on the Heart.
Dorfman, A. I Just Missed the Bus and I'll Be Late for Work.
D'Orleans. Oft in My Thought.
Dove, R. "Blown Apart By Loss . . .".
Demeter, Waiting.
Dryden, J. To the Memory of Mr Oldham.
Duncan, R. Structure of Rime XXIII.
Dunn, D. Kaleidoscope, The.
Dunn, S. Sweetness.
Elizabeth I. On Monsieur's Departure.
Erinna. Girls / Brides / Tortoise.
Espaillat. Find Work.
Feinstein, E. Dad.
Ferrell, M. Myths of the Disappearance.
Field. After Soufrière.
Beloved, My Glory in Thee is Not Ceased.
Foster, S. Old Folks at Home.
Frost, R. Hill Wife, The.
García Lorca. Ballad of Black Grief.
Casida of Sobbing.
Gascoigne. For That He Looked Not upon Her.
Geng Wei. Autumn Day.
Gerstler. Sinking Feeling, A.
Ghalib, M. I'm Neither the Loosening of Song nor the Close-Drawn Tent of Music.
Gibb, B. Vigil.
Gibbons, R. We Say.
Gioia. Pentecost: "Neither the sorrows of

afternoon, waiting in the silent house."
Glück, L. Trillium.
Triumph of Achilles, The.
Gorbanevskaya. Sukhanovo.
Gray, T. Sonnet [on the Death of Mr. Richard West].
Gregg. Night Music.
Grimald. From A Funeral Song, Upon the Decease of Annes His Mother.
I, in your frutefull woomb conceyved, born was.
Gumilyov [or Gumiliov or Gumilev]. Streetcar That Lost Its Way, The.
Gunn, T. Blank, A.
Ha Jin. Ways of Talking.
Hardy, T. Bereft.
Hawkesworth, P. Two Statues.
Hawoldar. Destruction.
Heaney, S. Mid-Term Break.
Heard, J. Bereft.
Heinemann, M. Ringstead Mill.
Hemphill. Homocide.
Herbert, G. Affliction (1).
Affliction (3).
Ah Mater, quo te deplorem fonte? Dolores.
Herrick. Observation ("Virgin-Mother stood at distance (there), The.").
Hikmet. On Living.
Hine. Apart from You.
Hirshfield, J. Room, A.
Holmes, J. Four and a Half.
Hopkins, G. Felix Randal.
No Worst, There Is None. Pitched Past Pitch of Grief.
Spring and Fall [To a Young Child].
Horace. Grieving Too Long (2.9).
Horsley, K. Winter Grieving Poem.
Housman. Bredon Hill.
Howard, A. Elegy on the Death of Her Husband.
Huang E. Pearl-teardrops roll and gather.
Huddle. Snow Monkey Argues with God, The.
Huerta, D. Machinery.
Maquinarias.
Hughes, L. Gal's Cry for a Dying Lover.
Lament over Love.
Ilkov, Ani. Muses.
Ishikawa Takuboku. Tanka: "Just for fun."
Ismaili. Bajji.
Jones, R. Apology to Andrew.
Jonson, B. Echo's [or Eccho's] Song.
On My First Son.
Juana Inés de la Cruz. Describes Rationally the Irrational Effects of Love.
Verses Expressing the Feelings of a Lover.
Kan, T. And He Whispered Stolen Words.
Kaufman, S. Job's Wife.
Waiting: "After the fervor."
Kavanagh, P. In Memory of My Mother.
Keble. Rainbow, The.
Kendrick, D. Where the Grieved Ones Sat.
Kim Sangyong. Listlessly I hear the rain.
King, H. Exequy, The.
Kipling, R. Son, A.
Knight, E. As You Leave Me.
Knut. Woman from the Book of Genesis, A.
Kochanowski, J. Where Is That Gate for Grief.
Kong Rong. First-Born, A.
Kopland. Johnson Brothers Ltd.
Kroetsch. Sounding the Name.
Lawrence, D. H. Hymn to Priapus.
Sorrow.
Levine, P. Detroit, Tomorrow.
Li Ching. West Wind Ferries Grief, The.
Li Ch'ing-chao. To the Tune: Lips Painted Red.
To the Tune: Partridge Sky.
Li Hsun. To the Tune: The Wine Spring: "Rain falls on fallen flowers."
Li Po. Farewell Dinner for My Uncle Li Yun, the Collator, at Xie Tiao's Tower in Xuan Prefecture.
Moon over the Mountain Pass, The.
Li Shang-yin. Chamber Music.
Li Yü. Tune: "The Crow's Nocturnal Cry".
Li Yu [or Li Hou-Chu]. To the Tune: Beautiful Lady Yu.
Lilley, Gary. Funeral: "Naked in eastern

mournin sun."
Limonov. As if a quiet branch drew a line.
Lindsay, C. To My Own Face.
Littledale. When My Dog Died.
Liu, T. Poem.
Lomax, M. July.
Longfellow, H. Cross of Snow, The.
Lorde. Memorial 1: "If you come as softly."
Lysohorsky. 22.6.1941.
Ma Chih-yüan. Tune: "Heaven-Cleansed Sands".
MacDiarmid, H. At My Father's Grave.
Marks, S. November Woods.
Martin, Gail. Lemons.
Martinez, D. Bad Alchemy.
Cole Porter.
Masefield. C. L. M.
Matherne, B. Les Fils (Sons).
Matthews, W. Grief.
McDonald, W. I Still Can't Say the Word.
Melville, H. Martyr, The.
Monody: "To have known him, to have loved him."
Mew. June, 1915.
Mihalic. Large Grieving Women.
Millay, E. Sonnet 2: "Time does not bring relief; you all have lied."
Wood Road, The.
Milton. On His Deceased Wife.
Monro, H. Solitude.
Monroe, H. Farewell, A: "Good-bye!—no [or nay] do not grieve that it is over."
Montagu, L. Receipt to Cure the Vapours, A.
Morley, H. Lizard, The.
Mueller, L. Another Version.
When I Am Asked.
Nabi. At the gathering of joy, the wine cup.
Neruda. My love, if I die and you don't.
Nesimi. Oh my idol of the temple, in the dark of night.
Neto. Grieved Lands, The.
Nev'î. Help me, oh sapling of the tulip cheek.
Nguyễn Chí Thiện. Travel with Grief—Goodbye to Joy.
Nikonova, R. I sit over grief.
Nokhem, Y. Fly, The.
O'Connell, E. Your Grave Disfigures Me.
Ofek, U. Hagomel.
Okamoto. Tanka: "Innately reserved."
Okolo, M. Suspended Elegy, A.
Owen, W. Hospital Barge at Cérisy.
Pastan. Five Stages of Grief, The.
Patchen. 'O Now the Drenched Land Wakes'.
Patmore, C. Farewell, A.
Pegram, A. Burials.
Pembroke, M. If Ever Hapless Woman Had a Cause.
Philips, K. Epitaph on her Son H. P. at St. Syth's Church [where her body also lies Interred].
Piatt, S. Her Blindness in Grief.
Her Word of Reproach.
No Help.
Po Chü-i. Remembering Golden Bells.
To the Distant One.
Poe. Annabel Lee.
For Annie.
Porter, P. Exequy, An.
What I Have Written I Have Written.
Prado, A. Successive Deaths.
Ralegh, S. Farewell to the Court.
Ratzlaff, K. Dill.
Reese, L. In Time of Grief.
Rexroth, K. Andrée Rexroth ("Years have gone, The. It is spring.").
In the park a crow awakes.
Richardson, M. Sonnet: "I still shall smile and go my careless way."
Robinson, E. Reuben Bright.
Rodriguez, J. In-flight Note.
Roethke. Elegy for Jane.
Rosales. Locked with a Tear.
Rose, R. What the Japanese Perhaps Heard.
Rose. Long Division; a Tribal History.
Rossetti, C. Gone Before.
Remember [Me].

Song: "When I am dead, my dearest."
Rossetti, D. Woodspurge, The.
Rowe, E. Parthenea, an Elegy.
Ruark. Postscript to an Elegy.
Ruefle. From Here to Eternity.
Sandburg, C. Right to Grief, The.
Schwartz, R. L. Grief.
Shafer, A. Gurney Tears.
Shakespeare, W. Clown's Song, The.
Sonnet 28: "How can I then return in happy
plight."
Sonnet 40: "Take all my loves, my Love, yea,
take them all."
Sonnet 50: "How heavy do I journey on the
way."
Sonnet 90: "Then hate me when thou wilt; if
ever, now."
Shaku Chōkū. Tanka: "Imagining / the grassy
ground not shown."
Shelley, P. Dirge, A: "Rough wind, that
moanest loud."
Sherburne. Weeping and Kissing.
Sheykhi. Your sun-face is a mirror of the soul.
Sidney. Nightingale, The.
Smith, C. New Bride, The.
Song Sun. Do not grieve, little birds.
Sophocles. Torn between griefs, which grief
shall I lament.
Stevens, W. Another Weeping Woman.
Su Tung-p'o. Tune: "Always Having Fun".
Suárez. Another Poem to My Mother.
Suermondt, Tim. Missing Supper.
Synková, A. Tears.
Tabenkin, M. Eulogy: "Bereavement revolves
in our garden like a sword."
Tekeyan. Forgetting.
Tennyson, A. Break, Break, Break.
Calm is the morn without a sound.
Dark house, by which once more I stand.
I held it truth, with him who sings.
I sometimes hold it half a sin.
O [or Oh] that 'twere possible.
Sweet after showers, ambrosial air.
Tears, Idle Tears.
Thomas, D. In My Craft or Sullen Art.
Townsend, A. Touch Me Not.
Tsanev, Stefan. Old woman leans against the
pine tree, The.
Tu Fu [or Du Fu]. Crooked River Meditation.
Drinking at Crooked River.
Flying from Trouble.
Grieved, I idle and doze.
Lovely Lady.
Snow Storm.
Tuckerman, F. Refrigerium.
Tur-Malka, A. Memorial Service.
Tzu Yeh. End to Spring, An ("Spring has
vanished.").
Unknown. Arjuna, his war flag a rampant
monkey.
Deserted Home, The.
Grief.
Kilcash.
Lily bud floating, yellow as sorrow.
Moon Is Rising, The.
My lover rests near where the flowers are.
Oh ruined tomb, oh scattered bricks, my
beloved is no more than dust.
Such Is the Grief of the Grey-Haired Man.
Su-guan [Translations].
Tears are streaming down my face.
Unquiet Grave, The.
Wanderer, The.
Wife's Lament, The.
Valentine, J. She Would Long.
Vallejo. Down to the Dregs.
Vando. In the Dark Backward.
Verlaine. Autumn Song ("Violins complain.").
Autumn Song ("With long sobs.").
Falling tears in my heart.
Vietnamese Oral Tradition. Homesick Bride,
The.
Voznesensky [or Voznesenskii]. I Am Goya.
Walton, A. Elegy for Joan.
Wang Wei. Return to Wang River.
Weeping for Ying Yao.

Webster, A. That some day death who has us all
for jest.
Wen T'ing-yün. Deva-like Barbarian.
Wharton, A. Elegy on the Earl of Rochester.
Whitman, W. Come Up from the Fields Father.
O Captain! My Captain!
Whitney, I. I. W. To her unconstant Lover.
Whittier. Telling the Bees.
Vesta.
Wilde, O. Requiescat.
Williams, Gerwyn. Washington.
Williams, T. My Love Was Light.
Williams, W. Widow's Lament in Springtime,
The.
Wright, J. Poem Written under an Archway in a
Discontinued Railroad Station, Fargo, North
Dakota, A.
Wroth. Sonnet 8: "Led by the pow'r [or powre]
of grief[e], to wailings [or waylings] brought."
Wyatt. Blame Not My Lute.
Lover's Appeal, The.
Sighs are my food, drink are my tears.
Yearsley. Soliloquy: "What folly to complain."
To———: "Lo! dreary Winter, howling o'er the
waste."
Yeats. Down by the Salley Gardens.
Yi Kyubo. Grieving for My Little Girl.
Yüan Chěn. Three Dreams in Chiang-ling.
See also **Sorrow; Mourning and Mourners**
Grim Reaper
al-Rahim, A. Who Are You?
Ch'oe Sŭngja. Untitled 2.
Stroud, J. Hear That Phone Ringing? Sounds
Like a Long Distance Call.
Wakoski. Black Leather Because Bubmlebees
Look Like It.
Grocers
Brunk, J. Papaya: Lancaster County.
Chesterton. Song against Grocers, The.
Davies, I. Angry Summer, The ("Mrs. Evans
fach, you want butter again.").
Espada. Tony Went to the Bodega but He
Didn't Buy Anything.
Rosenblatt, S. Procession, The.
Stanton, M. Shoplifters.
Suárez, V. Song for the Sugar Cane.
Williams, C. K. Racists.
Groundhogs
Eberhart, R. Groundhog, The.
Frost, R. Drumlin Woodchuck, A.
Kumin, M. Woodchucks.
Plath. Incommunicado.
Grouse
Baillie, J. Blackcock, The [or The Black Cock].
Growth
Adonis [or Adunis]. Beginning Speech.
Allen, P. Weed.
Ashbery, J. Spring Day.
Young Son, The.
Bangs, J. Little Elf, The.
Behlen, Charles. Two Ice Storms.
Berry, W. Sycamore, The.
Boyle, K. What Parents Do Not Yet Know.
Byrd, Bobby. Gabachos in the Photograph, The.
Cabral de Melo Neto. Canefield and the Sea,
The.
Celan. I am the first.
Clanchy, K. Men From the Boys.
Clare, J. Maple Tree, The.
Cocteau. Cape of Good Hope, The.
Cummings, E. E. If everything happens that
can't be done.
Curzon, D. Instructions to a Seed.
De Cristoforo, Violet Kazue. Konchu Kazu Aru
Yube Ako Iyo-Iyo Seicho Shitari.
Dickinson, E. Her Sweet turn to leave the
Homestead.
We outgrow love like other things.
Dodge, M. Taking Time to Grow.
Duncan, R. Preface to the Suite: "Childhood,
boyhood, young manhood."
Favery. Bit by Bit.
Field, R. General Store.
Fischer, N. I've Changed.
Hadas, R. Red Hat, The.

Haines, J. Sun on Your Shoulder, The.
Hall, H. Things That Grow.
Herbert, G. Paradise.
Hoekstra. Cedar, The.
Holmes, O. Chambered Nautilus, The.
Hughes, L. For Russell and Rowena Jelliffe.
Ismail. Poetry: "Beautiful woman, A."
Le Guin. Stanza 4.
Lehman. Drowning, The.
Limburg, J. Queen of Swords, The.
MacDiarmid, H. To a Friend and Fellow Poet.
Major, C. Giant Red Woman.
McFadden, D. 15. My Grandmother Learns to
Drive.
Meredith, W. John and Anne.
Merwin. Last One, The.
Mörike [or Möricke]. Remember It, My Soul.
Neruda. Men grow with all that grows.
Ngai, S. Discredit.
Nicholas, J. Bush, The.
O'Hara, F. Cornkind.
Oliver, M. Rain: "All afternoon it rained, then."
Palma. Coming of Age.
Paz. Reliefs.
Relieves.
Pierpoint, K. Dreaming Bean, The.
Plath. Mushrooms.
Rimbaud, A. Being Beauteous.
Roethke. Cuttings.
Cuttings (later) ("This urge, wrestle, resurrection
of dry sticks.").
Shcherbina. Still-Life.
Sinclair, S. Red Pepper.
Smith, M. Watering the New Lawn.
Snodgrass. I thumped on you the best I could.
Song. Mehinaku Girl in Seclusion, A.
Southwell. Times [or Tymes] Go[e] By
Turn[e]s.
Stevenson, R. Looking Forward.
My Shadow.
Nay, but I fancy somehow, year by year.
Thompson, S. Living at the Frost Place.
Unknown. Planting Initiation Song.
Ring That Controlled Erections, The.
Spring from the earth, food for our children.
Give us good health. Let us grow up, and
become ripe.
Wells, N. Up.
Wilbur, R. Seed Leaves.
Winkler Prins. Shower.
Wise, W. When I Grow Up.
Wordsworth, W. My Heart Leaps Up [When I
Behold].
Guadalajara, Mexico
Ashbery, J. Instruction Manual, The.
Guards
Clare, J. Guardian at the Gate, A.
Dupree, E. At Present I Am Working as a
Security Guard.
Fuzuli. For long years we have been haunting
the quarter.
Harte, B. Relieving Guard.
Horace. Satire 1.8: "Once I was wood from a
worthless old fig tree."
Krivulin. Guard.
Li Po. Lament of the Frontier Guard.
Liu Pang. Song of the Great Wind.
Piercy. On Guard.
Reverdy. Nocturne: "Street is pure black and
there are no seasonal traces, The."
Salzman, E. Bargain with the Watchman.
Scupham. Guard-Room.
Tennyson, A. Love is and was my Lord and
King.
Unknown. If you sleep you will have nothing
but dust.
Weigl. Convoy.
Wenderoth, J. As Hour and Year Collapsed.
Zinger, G. Lamentation of the Border-Guard.
Guatemala
Castillo, O. Distances.
Espada. Green and Red, Verde y Rojo.
Guerrillas
Fuller, H. Multiple-Theater.
Guevara, E. Song to Fidel.
Kipling, R. Arithmetic on the Frontier.

Rocha. Guerilla Fighter.

Guests

Barbauld. Washing-Day.
Berry, W. Guest, The.
Bruce, D. Two Couples.
Cairns, Scott. After the Last Words.
Child, L. Thanksgiving Day.
Coleridge, M. Master and Guest.
Dickinson, E. Infinite a sudden Guest, The.
Haynes, C. Any Wife or Husband.
Jonson, B. Inviting a Friend to Supper.
Kasischke. Hostess.
Lane, P. Winter 6: "Guests have arrived at last, The. The old."
McNair. Visit, The: "We were at the camp, it must have been."
Muso Soseki. For Taihei Osho.
O'Hara, F. Poem: "Eager note on my door said 'Call me'", The."
Po Chü-i. Invitation to Hsiao Ch'u-shih. Lodging with the Old Man of the Stream. To a Talkative Guest.
Pugh. Guest, The.
Robinson, E. Matthew 22:1–14; And again Jesus spoke to them.
Rossetti, D. 63: Inclusiveness.
Sze. In Your Honor.
Takomaq. Improvised Song of Joy.
Townsend, A. Dinner Guest, The.
Tu Fu [or Du Fu]. Guest, A. To a Guest.
Unknown. Guest, The. May God let him be invited to our home!
Villa. Inviting a Tiger for the Weekend.
Watson, R. White Bird, The.
Yeats. Secret Rose, The.
See also **Hospitality; Visiting and Visitors**

Guggenheim, John Simon

Hollander, J. No Foundation.

Guides and guiding

Gilgun, J. Lights Out.
Jiménez, J. Road: "They are all asleep, below."
Psaila, K. Polestar.
Sorescu, M. Arrow, The.

Guilt

Balaban. After Our War.
Baldwin, J. Guilt, Desire and Love.
Barnfield [or Barnefield]. Sporting at fancie, setting light by love.
Bek, T. If a song flies to me from the garden.
Berrigan, D. My Name.
Bidart. Sacrifice, The.
Blake, W. Sick Rose, The.
Bowering, G. My Father in New Zealand.
Brontë, C. Again I find myself alone.
Byron, G. Prayer of Nature, The.
Campo. Our Country of Origin.
Cary, A. Sea-Side Cave, The.
Ceccoli. Oh, and yet I see that I will return to you anyway, and throw myself at your feet and cry a lot over my sins, until my crime will be pardoned.
Clampitt. Cormorant in Its Element, The.
Cruz Varela. Kaleidoscope.
Dauer. Philip the Store Policeman.
Dickinson, E. These—saw Visions.
Dunbar, P. Debt, The.
Eich. Geometrical Place.
Field. Flaw, A.
Fields, D. Don't Blame Me.
Fisher, D. Put the Blame on Mame.
Fried, E. What Happens.
Frost, R. Home Burial.
Glazier, L. On TV.
Goldsmith, O. When Lovely Woman Stoops to Folly.
Gorbanevskaya. That time I did not save Warsaw, nor Prague later.
Gunn, T. High Fidelity.
Hill, S. Prawns de Jo.
Jarrell, R. Eighth Air Force.
Jennings, E. My Grandmother.
Kahn, G. Guilty.
Kamenetz. Lighter Fluid.
Kaufman, S. Accuser, The.

Kees. After the Trial.
Landor, W. Maid's Lament, The.
Levi, P. For Adolf Eichmann. Survivor, The.
Lihn. Revolution.
Liu, J. Mama.
Mayfield, C. When I Moved into the Neighborhood.
Meredith, W. Effort at Speech.
Merrill, J. Renewal, A.
Merwin. Yesterday: "My friend says I was not a good son."
Miles, J. Belief.
Moon, Susan. Unintended.
Nash, O. Inter-Office Memorandum.
Oness, C. August 1990.
Oppen. Confession.
Orr, G. Gathering the Bones Together.
Pavlov, Konstantin. Adaptation.
Riley, D. I Take Two of These Tablets Tonight and in the Morning Go on Living.
Roberts, A. Put the Blame on Mame.
Rózewicz. Lament: "I turn to you high priests." Posthumous Rehabilitation.
Rozhdestvensky [or Rozhdestvenskii]. Winter of Thirty-Eight, The.
Sarton, M. Tortured, The.
Stafford, W. Some Remarks When Richard Hugo Came.
Stryk, L. Return to Hiroshima.
Szymborska, W. Under a Certain Little Star.
Thomas, R. S. Here.
Very. Slavery. Thy Brother's Blood.
Voznesensky [or Voznesenskii]. Anguish.
Warren, R. Amazing Grace in the Back Country. Crime. Mango on the Mango Tree, The. Revelation.
Weigl. Her Life Runs Like a Red Silk Flag.
Wright, C. California Spring.

Guitarists and Guitars

Cornford, F. Guitarist Tunes Up, The.
Cortez, J. Guitars I Used to Know, The.
Eady. Photo of Ron Carter, Playing His Bass.
Foreman, Paul. Huddie Ledbetter.
García Lorca. Guitar, The. Six Strings, The.
Hernández Cruz. Two Guitars.
Machado Ruiz. Deep Song. Tavern Guitar Playing a *Jota* Today.
St. John, D. Guitar.
Someck, A. Blues for Elliot Sharp.
Stewart, J. On Seeing Man with a Guitar at the Moma.
Stroud, J. Hacedor.
Sullivan, Mary Louise. Wedding Song: "Where the bridesmaid waits in the vestibule."
Sweeney, M. Appointment, The.

Gulls

Adams, L. Gull Goes Up, A.
Axelrod, D. Guide to Urban Birds, A.
Dafydd [or David] ap Gwilym. Seagull, The.
Dawe, Tom. Daedalus.
De la Mare. Storm, The.
Delanty. Williams Was Wrong.
Graham, J. Gulls.
Hoffman, D. At Provincetown.
Hooker, J. Gull on a Post.
Kherdian. Wing-set lone seagull, The.
MacLeod, Sue. Especially after rain, the gulls.
Murray, J. Even the Gulls of the Cool Atlantic.
Muso Soseki. Reply to Bukko Zenji's Poem at Seiken-ji.
Nash, O. Sea-Gull, The.
Neruda. Ode to the Seagull.
Oliver, M. Look and See.
Pau-Llosa. Kendall Gulls.
Phylip, S. Seagull, The.
Roberts, N. Gull's Flight, The.
Sandburg, C. Harbor, The.
Schwartz, D. Ballet of the Fifth Year, The.
Smedley, M. Sorrowful Sea-Gull, The.
Stafford, W. Gulls at Cannon Beach.
Transt.römer. Sea is a wall, The.

Unknown. O sea-gulls that are crying.
Updike. Seagulls.
Warsh. Moving through Air.

Guns

Ahl, L. Ammo.
Aridjis. Self-Portrait at Age Ten. Wounded Self-Portrait, A.
Armitage, S. Shout, The.
Asim, J. 1st Lt. John R. Fox: Rain of Fire.
Baraka, I. Heavy, The.
Belloc. Maxim Gun, The.
Berger, J. Gun, The.
Berlin. You Can't Get a Man with a Gun.
Bishop, W. Evidence of Death's Voodoo— Inside and Outside the "Gun As Art Exhibit".
Blunden. Vlamertinghe.
Bond, B. Aim.
Brouwer, J. Steve's Commando Paintball, San Adriano, California.
Brown, G. Hawk, The.
Bugeja, M. Shooter Rules.
Carson, C. Bloody Hand.
Chernoff. News, The.
Coleman, T. Chicago on the Day Brother Increases His Chances of Reaching Age 21.
Coleridge, M. In London Town.
Copeland, J. Bayonet, The.
Cummings, E. E. Bigness of cannon, The.
Dalton, Mary. She.
Day, J. Picket before Bull Run, The.
Deming, A. Arboretum.
Duncan, A. Andy-the-German Servant of Two Masters.
Enzensberger, H. In Memory of Sir Hiram Maxim (1840–1916).
Feinstein, S. Blues Villanelle for Sonny Criss.
Fitzgerald, R. Amphibians.
Flynn, N. Fragment (Found Inside My Mother).
Galvin, J. Independence Day, 1956: A Fairy Tale.
Goyette, Susan. This Contradiction of Passion.
Gwynn, R. S. At Rose's Range.
Hanh *et al.* Witness Remains, The.
Hardy, T. Channel Firing.
Heaney, S. From the Frontier of Writing.
Holmes, D. Time for Guns, A.
Housman. Shot? so quick, so clean an ending?
Joans, T. .38, The.
Johnson, Peter. Tattoo.
Jones, D. Across upon this undulated board of verdure chequered bright.
Karpowicz. Rifle, The.
Keene, J. Black Revolver.
Kipling, R. Screw-Guns.
Knorr, J. Wreckage along the River, The.
Kunitz, S. Careless Love.
Lazar. My Gun Has So Many Places to Hide.
Manifold. Defensive Position.
Martin, Camille. Pseudo slammer.
Martinaitis, M. Kukutis in the Reich's Guard House.
Meeks, B. Twin Barrel Bucky: A Kingston 12 Dub, The.
Melville, H. Swamp Angel, The.
Montgomery, W. Outlaws.
Mörling, A. For F. M. Who Did Not Get Killed Yesterday on 57th Street.
Owen, W. Anthem for Doomed Youth. Arms and the Boy.
Péret. Hello.
Quasimodo. Anno Domini MCMXLVII.
Reed, H. Naming of Parts. Unarmed Combat.
Robinson, E. Richard Cory.
Rodriguez, L. Rainfall Piano.
Rolfe, E. Casualty. City of Anguish.
Saitō Sanki. Machine gun, A. Machine gun, A. Machine gun, A. Machine gun soars, A.
Sandburg, C. A. E. F.
Sassoon, S. General, The.
Service. Fulmars.
Sharma, P. Action-Packed Sonnet.
Sivan, A. To Live in the Land of Israel.

Solie, Karen. Argument For Small Arms, An.
Sorescu, M. Start.
Spender, S. Ultima Ratio Regum.
Sylvain, P. Horizon of Gunbutts.
Unknown. Epigram: "Says a Reverend Priest to a less Rev'rend friend."
Riddle: "Long slick black feller."
Riddle: "Wooden belly iron back."
Wadsworth, W. Need for Attention, The.
Wagoner, D. Dead Letter From Out of Town.
Whitman, W. Artilleryman's Vision, The.
Wilson, R. Military-Industrial Complex, The.
Wright, C. Survivalist.
Yeats. To a Squirrel at Kyle-Na-No.
Yi Sang. Poem No. 9.
Young, K. Casting.

Gypsies
Baudelaire. Gypsies on the Move.
Clare, J. Gipsies [*or* The Gipsy Camp]: "Snow falls deep; the forest lies alone, The."
Gypsy's Evening Blaze, The.
Cofer, J. What the Gypsy Said to Her Children.
Galich. Hospital Gypsy Song.
García Lorca. Preciosa and the Wind.
Gautier. Carmen.
Glazer, J. Final Disposition.
Hodgson, R. Gipsy Girl, The.
Hovey. Sea Gypsy, The.
Hughes, L. Bad Luck Card.
Hughes, R. Gipsy-Night.
Keats. Meg Merrilies [*or* Merrilees].
Levertov. Gypsy's Window, The.
Monsour. Emily's Words.
Pound, E. Gypsy, The.
Sagan. Gypsy Hand.
Schjeldahl. Ocean Liner.
Simic. I Was Stolen by the Gypsies.
Swartwout. Gypsy Teaches Her Grandchild Wolfen Ways, The.
Thomas, E. Gypsy, The.
Watson, R. Serenade: "Who is it sings the gypsies' song to-night."

H

Doolittle, H. (Hilda Doolittle)
Niedecker. If I Were a Bird.

Habits
Akhtar-ul-Iman. Compromise.
Barney, N. Habit.
Bejerano, M. From morning slumber a stir a shift a spinning motion of tossing.
Centolella. Small Acts.
Dooley, M. Mansize.
Dubin, A. You're Getting to Be a Habit with Me.
Guiterman. Routine.
Kuzma. Poetry: "Old forms are like birdhouses that, The."
La Fontaine. Shrimp and Her Daughter, The.
McCarthy, J. Why Try to Change Me Now?
O'Reilly, C. Envoi: "And although it will be."
Peacock, M. Breakfast with Cats.
Plath. Love Letter.
Starbuck, G. Working Habits.
Zucker, R. Cloister or "vietato toccare le rose".

Hades
Alcaeus [*or* Alkaios]. Drink...with me, Melanippos. Why (think that).
Anacreon. Already my temples are grey.
Erinna. From here an empty echo penetrates to Hades.
Haavikko. Hades is an even worse place.
Homer. And then went down to the ship.
Ulysses Describes His Visit to the Underworld.
We bore down on the ship at sea's edge.
Hope, A. Return of Persephone, The.
Mandelstam [*or* Mandelshtam]. When Psyche, Who Is Life, Descends Among the Shades.
Martinson. Hades and Euclid (first version).
Ovid. Ceres and Proserpina.
Patterson, G. Lament.
Rukeyser, M. In the Underworld.
Salaam. Secondline Send Off.

Sappho. Gongyla.
When you die you'll lie dead, no memory of you.
Södergran. Arrival in Hades.
Swinburne. Garden of Proserpine, The.
Venclova. Canto Eleven.
Vettese. Scottish Mythology.
Virgil [*or* Vergil]. Aeneas in the Underworld.

Hafiz
Taylor, B. To a Persian Boy in the Bazaar at Smyrna.

Hagar
Bibb. Expulsion of Hagar, The.

Haggard, Sir Henry Rider
Stephen, J. To R. K.

Haggis
Burns, R. To a Haggis.

Haiku (form)
Abbott, K. Billygoat watches me work.
Grief counselor, The.
Our honest neighbor's rolled.
What she thought was.
Windy clear day, A.
Collins, B. Japan.
Cope, W. Cherry blossom, The.
Corn. Long-Distance Call to Gregg, Who Lived with AIDS as Long as He Could.
Forrester, S. Writing a haiku.
Gertler, P. Standing with Chiyo-Ni.
Ginsberg, A. Gray-haired man, The.
Stood on the porch in.
Holloway, G. Bash on Basho: Six of the Best.
Kerouac. Birds singing.
Bottoms of my shoes, The.
In my medicine cabinet.
Missing a kick.
Moon had, The.
Kilbride, Jerry. Cool surface, The.
Harpist, The.
Nurse speaks of christmas, The.
Still in the taste.
Wheelchair child, The.
Milosz, C. Reading the Japanese Poet Issa (1762–1826).
Sagan. Reading Chiyo-Ni, 1703-1775, Japanese Woman Haikuist.
Tranströmer. Haiku.
Trungpa, Chogyam. Beginner in meditation, The.
Coming home from work.
His parents are having tea.
Skiing in a red and blue outfit.
Wilbur, R. Sleepless at Crown Point.

Hail
Basho. Hailstones.
Hopkins, G. Hailstorm in May.
Izumi. On nights when hail / falls noisily.
Mayne, S. Hail.

Hair
Adam, H. I Love My Love.
Agard, J. For Bob Marley.
Amaker, A. Roots.
Amichai, Y. To My Love, Combing Her Hair.
Archilochus. She delighted to hold a slip of myrtle.
Basho. Gray hairs being plucked.
Having to Hide.
Wrapping the rice cakes.
Baudelaire. Head of Hair.
Her Hair.
Betjeman. Licorice Fields at Pontefract, The.
Betts, T. Dreadlocks.
Bishop, E. Shampoo, The.
Bogan, L. Medusa.
Bomani, M. Roots.
Voudou Mama.
Borgmann, K. Rodeo Tangent.
Cardiff. Combing.
Carrera Andrade. Your body is bathed eternally.
Chalfi, R. Night Hair.
Ch'i-chi. White Hair.
Chin. Is It Snowing in Guangzhou?
Coralin, J. Rosa's Beauty.
Cortázar. Loss and Recovery of the Hair, The.
Cott, J. Natural Functions.

Crews, J. Mullhaven.
Dafydd [*or* David] ab Edmwnd. Girl's Hair, A.
D'Aguiar, F. Dread.
Damas. Just Like the Legend.
Dauer. Lois at the Hair Salon.
Dickinson, E. 'Tis customary as we part.
Donegan, P. Tonight / while shampooing my hair.
Donovan, K. Grooming.
Dove, R. "Blown Apart By Loss . . . ".
Elfyn, Menna. Theology of Hair, The.
Erdrich. Butcher's Wife, The.
Ferguson, G. Inhaling His Hair.
Fernandez, M. Broken Ends Broken Promises.
Field. Embalmment.
Flanner. Dumb.
Fujiwara no Teika. Those long black tresses.
Gardiner, S. Flight.
Georgiou, E. From Where I Stand.
Getsi. Washing Your Hair.
Giovanni. Wrong Kitchen, The.
Glatt. World in My Mother's Hair, The.
Greenlaw, L. Three: "Your shaved head on my thigh."
Gunn, T. Skateboard.
Harris, J. Dream of the Hair Burning Smell.
Hayati. Before there was a trace of this world of men.
Henderson-Holmes. "C" ing in Colors: Red.
Herrick. Art above Nature, to Julia.
Hill, S. Hairbrush.
Hjern, K. On the Growth of Hair in Middle Age.
Hochman. Hairbrush, The.
Housman. Oh who is that young sinner with the handcuffs on his wrists?
Ilkov, Ani. Scene, A.
Iqbal. Make Your Radiant Twining Curls.
Iskrenko. Hair.
Izumi. Lying down alone.
Tangled Hair.
Jackson, A. Choosing the Blues.
Jacob, M. Wallpaper of Mr. R. K., The.
Kamenszain. Torah Braids.
Keeshig-Tobias. Mother with Child.
Landor, W. On Seeing a Hair of Lucretia Borgia.
Lee, L. Early in the Morning.
Li Ho. Song: A Lovely Girl Combing Her Hair.
Lochhead, L. Empty Song, The.
Love, M. Initiation.
Lovelace, R. To Amarantha, That She Would Dishevel[l] Her Hair[e].
Mallarmé. Fine suicide fled victoriously, The.
Marlatt, D. Katherine's Hair.
Martial. You were a swan, you're now a crow.
Mayer, B. Steps.
McOrlan. Hairdresser's, The.
Miko, C. Mississippi Girls, Plaited.
Miliauskaite. In the Damp Places.
Mirabai [*or* Mira Bai]. His Hair.
Moss, T. Raising a Humid Flag.
Tornados.
Mullen, H. Saturday Afternoon, When Chores Are Done.
Muso Soseki. Old Man To-The-Point.
Niedecker. There's a better shine.
No Hyegyông. Triangle, Comb.
Orlowsky, D. Losing My Hair.
Patmore, C. To the Body: "Creation's and Creator's crowning good."
Piercy. Hello Up There.
Po Chü-i. On his Baldness.
Pogson, P. Hairdressing.
Poniewaz. Why Young Men Wore Their Hair Long in the Sixties.
Pope, A. Rape of the Lock, The: An Heroi-Comical Poem in Five Cantos.
"Restore the lock!" she cries; and all around.
Probyn. As the Flower of the Grass.
Quevedo y Villegas. On Lisi's Golden Hair.
Quinn, J. Strand of Hair, A.
Rexroth, K. I cannot forget.
Rich, A. Suppose you want to write.
Rózewicz. Pigtail.
Rukeyser, M. Boy with His Hair Cut Short.

Sappho. My mother / In her youth it was a great.

Shaoxuan. Black hair and red cheeks: for how long?

Sherman, C. Roots.

Sherman, J. My Father Plaits His Granddaughter's Hair.

Smith, D. Making a Statement.

Song. White Porch, The.

Sora. Shaving my head.

Spenser, E. Sonnet 37: "What guile [or guyle] is this, that those her golden tresses."

Sprackland, Jean. Ringlet, The.

Sullivan, B. Hair.

Tallie, M. Medusa.

Tassis y Peralta. To a Lady Combing Her Hair.

Taylor, C.B. Like a Dog.

Toomer. Face.
   Portrait in Georgia.

Trethewey, N. Naola Beauty Academy, New Orleans, Louisiana, 1943.

Tsvetayeva [or Tsvetaeva]. Gold that was my hair has turned, The.

Tucker, M. First Grey Hair, The.

U T'ak. Sticks in one hand.

Unknown. At Sunset I Strolled.
   Black Hair.
   Girl with the Dark Hair.
   Last night with hair unbrushed.
   My lover cannot take a joke.
   Night after night, I do not.
   Twist of hair, A.
   Was I Not Made for Love?
   Youth and Age.

Upton, L. Jim's Hairball.

Vietnamese Oral Tradition. Across the Field of the Old Corporal.
   Girl with the Binh Tien Hairdo, The.

Wang Chiu-ssu. This crazy man has escaped the world.

Watkyns. Periwig, A.

Wingfield. In a Dublin Museum.

Wylie. Green Hair.

Yeats. For Anne Gregory.

Yosano Akiko. Star that once, A.
   Thousand lines, A.

Young, K. Eddie Priest's Barbershop and Notary.

Zavatsky. Bald.

Hairdressers

Dauer. Lois at the Hair Salon.

Jackson, A. Choosing the Blues.

Jackson, R. Smile.

Kuzmin, D. Our hairdresser friend.

Laird, N. Cuttings.

Limburg, J. Queen of Swords, The.

Love, M. Initiation.

O'Donoghue, M. Stylist, The.

Smith, B. Saturday before Easter, The.

Strange. Barbershop Ritual.

Swanger. Wayne's College of Beauty, Santa Cruz.

Swift, T. Leaving Paris.

Trethewey, N. Naola Beauty Academy, New Orleans, Louisiana, 1943.

Young, K. Eddie Priest's Barbershop and Notary.

Haiti

Akao, A. Zombies Arise.

Baron, S. They Say.

Batraville, D. Paper 43.

Boadiba. Madam President.

Castera, G. Both Yesterday and Today.
   I Have a Comrade.

Daniel, G. My Mother Tongue.
   What Have We Done.

Dede, J. Bits.

Denis, J. Women of My Country.

Depestre. Ballad of a Little Lamp.

Eugene, E. Wongòl Poem.

Guignard, M. One morning just like that they arrive.

Laraque, P. Mardi Gras.

Large, J. Snowcone Vendor.

Lauture, D. Zaps of Zombifying Powder.

Lerner, A. I Left My Hat in Haiti.

Martineau, J. Haiti Tomorrow.
   Viejo.

Medard, B. Tonton Macoutes Steal Dreams.

Mirville, E. In the land of Haiti.
   Liberty.

Morisseau-Leroy, F. Down with All Candidates.

Philoctete, R. I'm Rooted.

Porter, C. Katie Went to Haiti.

Résil, J. Walls of Bois-de-Chene Shacks, The.

Salkey. Remember Haiti, Cuba, Vietnam.

Simidor, D. Slippery Ground.

Surprice, L. Result of an Observation.

Sylvain, P. Army of Draculas.
   Horizon of Gunbutts.
   Palace of Mourners, A.

Tontongi. How?

Vicioso. Haiti.

Wainwright, K. Changes.

Hallam, Arthur Henry

Tennyson, A. Dear friend, far off, my lost desire.
   Fair ship, that from the Italian shore.
   I held it truth, with him who sings.
   I know that this was Life—the track.
   Love is and was my Lord and King.
   Now, sometimes in my sorrow shut.
   Path by which we twain did go, The.
   Tears of the widower, when he sees.
   Thy spirit ere our fatal loss.
   Thy voice is on the rolling air.

Halloween

Burns, R. Halloween.

Cummings, E. E. Hist whist / little ghostthings.

Glück, L. All Hallows.

Guevara, M. Rhyme for Halloween, A.

Livingston, M. Lazy Witch.

Moorer. Hallowe'en.

Nims, J. Trick or Treat.

Prelutsky. It's Halloween.
   Skeleton Parade.

Stephens, P. Hangman.

Warsh. Halloween 1967.

Ham

Hood, T. Sonnet to Vauxhall.

McGinley. Notes for a Southern Road Map.

Unknown. Riddle: "Riddlum riddlum ranty pole."

Hamer, Fannie Lou

Harris, D. On the uptown lexington avenue express: Martin Luther King Day 1995.

Hamlet

Akhmatova, A. Reading Hamlet.

Alexie. After the Trial of Hamlet, Chicago.

Allston. On Kean's Hamlet.

Applewhite. On the Mississippi.

Bell, M. Sounds of the Resurrected Dead Man's Footsteps (#1).

Berry, D. Hambone Two Tongue.
   Hamlet Off-stage: Laertes Cool.

Conway, J. This Is What Happens When You Let Hamlet Play Quarterback.

Cooley. For Hamlet.

Cummings, P. Hamlet to Ophelia.

Derieva, R. On the sea-shore, smell of iodine.

Dobie, K. King Claudius.

Feinstein, Sandy. Tendered.

Friman. Diapers for My Father.

Gilmore, B. To be or not to be.

Greenway, W. Ophelia Writes Home.

Griffith, K. Hamlet Meets Frankenstein.

Hedderman, R. First Player's Monologue, The.

Herbert, Z. Elegy of Fortinbras.

Holan. Night with Hamlet, A.

Holub. Polonius.

Kates. Nothing in Art.

McNaughtan, A. Oor Hamlet.

Oliveira, D. Laurence Olivier's Hamlet.

Pasternak, B. Hamlet.

Sharpless. Hamlet.

Simon, M. Helsinore, Denmark.

Stokesbury. Reynaldo in Paris.

Tolson, M. Despite his caricatures.

Upton, L. Gertrude to Hamlet.

Van Cleave, M. Hamlet at the Paris Aerobleu.

Vliet. Goodnight sweet prince.

White, G. Queen Gertrude's Soliloquy.

Hammers and Hammering

Bataille, Georges. Night Is My Nudity.

Behlen, Charles. My Grandfather's Hammer.

Bogan, L. Roman Fountain.

Brown, S. Southern Road.

Chevremont. Symphony of the Hammers.

Gustafson, R. Of Green Steps and Laundry.

Herbert, Z. Passion of Our Lord painted by an anonymous hand from the Circle of Rhenish Masters, The.

Hooks. Body Inside the Soul, The.

"Leadbelly.". Take this Hammer.

Ono. Painting To Hammer a Nail.

Hammocks

Alexander, P. Scherzo.

Monsour. Dream of Dying, A.

Pilling. Earth, The.

Toledo, N. Casa de Olga, La.
   Liidxi na Olga.
   Olga's House.

Hampstead Heath, London

Hunt, L. To Hampstead ("Sweet upland, to whose walks, with fond repair.").
   To Hampstead ("Winter has reached thee once again at last.").

Handball

Dunn, S. Day and Night Handball.

Feldman, I. Handball Players at Brighton Beach, The.

Handicaps and the Handicapped

Cook, E. Idiot-Born, The.

Delgado, J. Lame Boy Returns, The.

Donne. Lame Beggar, A.

Ginsberg, A. Stroke.

Hugo, R. Freaks at Spurgin Road Field, The.

Owen, W. Disabled.

Sassoon, S. Does It Matter?

Simic. Great Infirmities.

Stanton, M. Space.

Thomas, D. Hunchback in the Park, The.

Vasalis. Idiot in the Bath, The.

Wordsworth, W. Idiot Boy, The.

See also **Amputees; Birth Defects; Blindness; Cripples; Deafness; Mental Retardation**

Hands

Afrika, T. Fist, The.

Agosin. Your Hands.

Alley, R. Canary Man and You, The.

Arghezi. Flowers of Mildew.

Atwood. You Begin.

Bancquart. Curriculum vitae.

Beatty, P. Gription.

Behn, A. Oh, How the Hand the Lover Ought to Prize.

Belloc. Child, Do Not Throw This Book About.

Bertrand. Five Fingers of the Hand, The.

Bly, R. Taking the Hands of Someone You Love.

Bogan, L. Heard by a Girl.

Born, A. End of the Row.

Boyle, F. Hand Game.

Bracho, C. Desde esta luz.
   From This Light.

Braid, K. 6. Glenn Gould's Hands: A Sonnet.

Brooks, G. Medgar Evers.

Brown, S. Conjured.

Cassian. Sand.

Cavalli. When I listen for the sound of.

Celan. Matière de Bretagne.
   Matière de Bretagne.

Chisholm, A. Contact.

Clementelli. Your Hands, My Love.

Clifton, L. I was born with twelve fingers.

Collins, A. Hiroshima Day at the Riviera Coffeeshop.

Crane, H. Episode of Hands.

Crapsey. Amaze.

Creeley. Figures, The.
   For Friendship.

De Angelis. There's a Hand that Nails Down.

Dickinson, A. Contributors to Geometry: Cold Hands.

Dickinson, E. Caterpillar ("How soft a Caterpillar steps—.").

Dorsey, T. Take My Hand, Precious Lord.
Dunn, D. Ballad of the Two Left Hands.
Fagin, L. Little Hand.
Feinstein, S. Sonnets for Stan Gage (1945–1992).
Ferebee, Gideon. Fallen Bodies.
Finch, A. Sapphics for Patience.
Foppa. Your Hand in Mine.
Fumi Saito. Palm of the hand, The / Is not aware of dying as.
Gates, E. My Mother's Hands.
González, R. Perla at the Mexican Border Assembly Line of Dolls.
Gregerman, D. Strictly Speaking.
Guevara, M. Hands of the Old Métis, The.
Gunn, T. Feel of Hands, The.
Man With Night Sweats, The.
Herrick. Right Hand, The.
Hidalgo, J. Shore of Night.
Huerta, D. Descender.
Descent.
Hwang Insuk. Walk, A.
Ishigaki. Hands.
Ishikawa Takuboku. Tanka: "I work."
Issa. Flies in the temple, The.
Zealous flea.
Jackson, L. Take Hands.
Jakiela. Personal History of Hands, A.
Jeffers, R. Hands.
Johnson, S. Ballad: "I put my hat upon my head."
Keats. This Living Hand, Now Warm and Capable.
Knott. Death: "Going to sleep, I cross my hands on my chest."
Kooser. Hands in the Wind.
Kort, E. Gardener, The.
Kosugi, T. Chironomy.
Lima, F. Hand, The.
Livesay, D. Lament: "What moved me, was the way your hand."
Loftis, N. In Memorium: Robert Hayden.
Lovelace, R. Her Muffe.
Merwin. Dead Hand.
Gardens of Zuñi, The.
Montes de Oca, Marco Antonio. Hands, The.
Moore, F. For a Working Woman.
Muldoon, P. They That Wash on Thursday.
Ngafua, Z. Nommo.
Nickelson, C. Untitled: "I don't get."
Nishiwaki Junzaburo. Hand.
Orr, G. Hand, The: "Brightness Falls from the Air".
Ozaki Hosai. I have no bowl.
Penn, R.E. Hand.
Phillips, C. As from a Quiver of Arrows.
Piercy. Friend, The.
Radoev, Ivan. Ballad for the Future.
Ramsdell, H. In Spite of How.
Randolph, T. Upon the Loss[e] of His Little Finger.
Reverdy. Web, The.
Ríos, A. Anselmo's Moment with God.
Rolle, S. Hands in the Motion of Prayer.
Rossetti, C. Twice.
Ruefle. Hand, The: "Teacher asks a question, The."
Sabines. Capriccios.
St. John, P. Ocean of the Streams of Story.
Schwartz, C. Hands: "Hands were purified in fire."
Serge. Hands.
Serpas, M. Finishing Touch.
Shannon, A. Hands.
Shepherd, R. West Willow.
Shinkichi Takahashi. Hand.
Simic. Bestiary for the Fingers of My Right Hand.
Stein, G. Leave, A.
Stuart, D. Palm Reader.
Tallmountain. Hands of Mary Joe, The.
Thomas, D. Hand That Signed the Paper, The.
Thomas, R. S. Here.
Toledo, N. Na tacha.
Townsend, A. Touch Me Not.
Tsaloumas. Return of an Ikon.

Unknown. Midwife's Invocation, A.
Vallejo. Poem to Be Read and Sung ("I know there is someone.").
Vlasova, E. I see / your hands in my nightmares.
Ward, D. Glass House.
Whitman, W. Leaf for Hand in Hand, A.
Williams, N. Daniel's Hands.
Woody. Speaking Hands.
Wright, R. I Have Seen Black Hands.
In the falling snow.

Handwriting
Barbauld. On a Lady's Writing.
Hume, C. Various Readings of an Illegible Postcard.
Nemerov. Writing.
Unknown. Copier.

Hanging
Auden. Terce.
Aytoun, W. Morning dawned full darkly, The.
Baudelaire. Voyage to Cythera, A.
Birnbaum, M. Man Who Hanged Himself, The.
Borges. Luke 23:39–43; One of the criminals.
Boruch. Window, The.
Brutus. They Hanged Him, I Said Dismissively.
Cutler, Y. Neckst.
Denby. Domestic Cat, A.
Dunqul. Scaffold, The.
Getsi. Woman Hanging from Lightpole, Illinois Route 136.
Hayes, T. Postcard from Okemah, A.
Housman. Carpenter's Son, The.
Eight O'Clock.
Kalamaras, G. Lamps Are Brought In, The.
Kipling, R. Danny Deever.
Lowell, J. Boss, The.
Melville, H. Portent, The.
Parker, D. Résumé.
Plath. Hanging Man, The.
Shakespeare, W. Fortune is Bardolph's foe, and frowns on him.
Shkapskaya [or Shkapskaia]. No Dream.
Stephens, P. Hangman.
Unknown. Night before Larry Was Stretched, The.
Villon. Ballade of the Men Who Were Hanged.
Quatrain: "France's I am; my lookout's glum."
Vinokurov. Mother of Judas, The.
Volkow. Arcana 12: The Hanged Man.
Arcano 12: El Colgado.
Waugh, E. They told me, Francis Hinsley, they told me you were hung.
Wilde, O. Ballad of Reading Gaol, The.
Wilkinson, J. Impatient Man Kills with his Piano-playing, The.
Young, A. Wet Day, A.

See also **Executions and Executioners; Lynching**

Hangovers
Conway, J. Hangover.
Gerov, Alexander. Problem, A.
Lu Yu. At Ta-an I Got Sick from Wine and Had to Lay Over for Half a Day. Governor Wang Invited Me to His Place Again.
Norris, K. Throne of Grace, The.
Nortje. Hangover.
P'i Jih-hsiu. Impromptu on a Hangover.
Pollard, C. Breakfast Poem.
Rohrer, M. I went out one night with people from work.
Sanders P. Tripoli.

Hansel and Gretel
Blackwell, Holley. New Poem.
Glück, L. Gretel in Darkness.
Noel-Scott. Hansel and Gretel.

Han-shan
Crowe, T. After Reading Han-Shan.

Hanukkah
Chaikin. Light Another Candle.

Happiness
Adamson, H. It's a Most Unusual Day.
Agustini. Intruder, The.
Atwood. You Are Happy.
Auden. Glad.
Bateman, M. Thank You, My Little Son.
Berger, B. Ballad of the Bright Angel.

Berlin. Cheek to Cheek.
Let Me Sing and I'm Happy.
Song Is Ended (But the Melody Lingers On), The.
Blake, W. Echoing [or Ecchoing] Green, The.
When the Green Woods Laugh.
Blane, R. Have Yourself a Merry Little Christmas.
Bloem, J. C. Dapper Street.
Brecht, S. Thanksgiving (1974).
Brown, L. Sunny Side Up.
Brown, S. Schadenfreude.
Browne, W. Happyer those times were, when the Flaxen clew.
Buson. Makes the eye happy.
Butler, S. Love.
Caesar. I Want to Be Happy.
Sometimes I'm Happy.
Cairns, Scott. Translation of Raimundo Luz, The: My Amusing Despair.
Carew, T. Second Rapture, The.
Carver, R. Happiness.
Cassian. Part of a Bird.
Celaya, G. Great Moments.
Chang Yüeh. Composition in Drunkenness.
Chasin. Joy Sonnet in a Random Universe.
Chen Zi'ang. Entering Quiao Gorge and Anju Creek.
Ch'u Ch'uang I. Evening in the Garden, Clear after Rain.
Clifton, L. Good Times.
Comden, B. Make Someone Happy.
Coslow, S. (Up on Top of a Rainbow) Sweepin' the Clouds Away.
Cowley, A. Wish, The.
Craig, David. Apprentice Prophecies, The.
Creeley. Air: "The Love of a Woman".
En Famille.
Cummings, E. E. You Shall Above All Things Be Glad and Young.
Curzon, D. Proverbs 6:6.
Davies, W. H. Example, The.
Delmore, E. Is It Not Strange?
DeSylva, B. G. Sunny Side Up.
Doolittle, Hilda. White World.
Doty, M. Embrace, The.
Dove, R. Bistro Styx, The.
Wiederkehr.
Drummond de Andrade. Diminutive.
Du Bellay. Heureux Qui, Comme Ulysse, A Fait un Beau Voyage.
Duncan, A. Shield of Perseus, The.
Dunn, S. Happiness.
Durcan. Sally.
Ebb, F. Happy Time, The.
Quiet Thing, A.
Egan, R. Ain't We Got Fun.
El-Iryaan, S. Thermometer of Happiness.
Eluard, P. et al. Loving.
Erdrich, H. Fat in America.
Evans, R. Haven't Got a Worry.
Feinstein, E. Getting Older.
Ferlinghetti, L. 21.
Freed, A. Singin' in the Rain.
Frost, R. Happiness Makes Up in Height for What It Lacks in Length.
Gershwin, I. Long Ago (And Far Away).
Things Are Looking Up.
Glück, L. Happiness.
Goodman, P. Dreams Are the Royal Road to the Unconscious.
Little Ode.
Gordon, M. You Make Me Feel So Young.
Green, A. Make Someone Happy.
Grey, C. Spread a Little Happiness.
Hammerstein. Happy Talk.
It Might As Well Be Spring.
Han-shan. Happy Among These Cliffs.
Harburg. Happiness Is Just a Thing Called Joe.
Hass, R. Happiness: "Because yesterday morning from the steamy window."
Hattersley, G. Singing.
Hayden, R. Islands, The.
Heard, J. Happy Heart, A.
Henderson, R. Sunny Side Up.
Herrick. Four[e] Things Make Us Happy Here.

Holmes, O. Illustration of a Picture.
Horace. Ode 3.29: To Maecenas.
Hughes, H. At the Teahouse, 7 am.
Hughes, L. Dream Boogie.
Inahata Teiko. As if happiness.
Inuit Oral Tradition. Utitia'q's Song.
Jackson, M. L. Euphoria.
James, P. Fine and Dandy.
Jaramillo Agudelo, D. Some Day.
Justice, D. But That Is Another Story.
Kahn, G. Ain't We Got Fun.
Keble. Happiness.
Kemble. Whene'er I recollect the happy time.
Kenyon, J. Happiness.
Kim Ku. Until the duck's short legs.
Kim Sŭnghŭi. Mother's Feet.
Kinnell. Crying.
Kizer, C. Afternoon Happiness.
Klee. Happy One, The.
Koehler, T. Happy As the Day Is Long.
I've Got the World on a String.
Wrap Your Troubles in Dreams.
Kuznetsova, I. Breadcrumbs falling from the table.
Landon. Mask of Gaiety, The.
Larkin, P. High Windows.
Layton. Birth of Tragedy, The.
Levine, M. Everybody.
Levine, P. Starlight.
Levy, A. First Extra, The.
Li Po. Bring On the Wine.
Lisick, B. Pantoumstone for a Dying Breed.
Livingston, J. Haven't Got a Worry.
Loesser. If I Were a Bell.
Lovelace, R. Grasshopper, The [To My Noble Friend Mr Charles Cotton: Ode].
Lux. Amiel's Leg.
Mansour, J. Remember.
Marlowe. Passionate Shepherd to His Love, The.
Martial. Happy Life, The.
Martin, H. Have Yourself a Merry Little Christmas.
Martinaitis, M. Kukutis's Song.
Massimi. On Happiness.
McAuley, J. Seventh Day, The.
Menicanti. I Don't Know.
If.
Mhlophe. Sometimes When It Rains.
Milán, E. ¿Cuál coro?
What chorus?
Milne, A. Happiness.
Milosz, C. Gift: "Day so happy, A."
Milton. L'Allegro.
Muso Soseki. Poem on Dry Mountain (A Zen Garden).
Tengan Osho's Visit to Erin-ji.
Mutis. East Song.
Nemes Nagy. Sincerity.
Nijhoff. At a Grave.
Nye, N. So Much Happiness.
Oliver, M. Hummingbird Pauses at the Trumpet Vine.
Morning Poem.
Paman. On Christmas Day to My Heart.
Parini. Bliss.
Parker, D. Comment.
Pastan. Obligation to Be Happy, The.
Poe. Dreams: "Oh! That my young life were a lasting dream!"
Poliziano. Love Song for Chrysokomos (Goldenlocks).
To Giovan Battista Buoninsegni.
Pollok. Happiness.
Pope, A. Ode on Solitude.
Porter, C. Ridin' High.
Porter, P. 'In the New World Happiness is Allowed'.
Pound, E. Salutation.
Prévert. Dunce, The.
Quevedo y Villegas. Continues in the Same State of Feeling.
Happy and Contented in Your Hut.
Raboni, G. Madrigal.
Ravenscroft, T. Sing we now merily.
Reverdy. Head Filled with Beauty, The.

Rexroth, K. For Eli Jacobson.
On the bridges.
Rimbaud, A. O seasons, o châteaux.
Robinson, E. Cliff Klingenhagen.
Rodriguez, J. Eskimo occasion.
Roethke. Waking, The.
Rogers, S. Wish, A.
Rome, H. Call Me Mister.
Rosenberg, L. No Boundaries.
Rouse, A. Narrows, The.
Ryokan. First Days of Spring.
Salinas, P. Trouble with the Light, The.
Sandburg, C. Happiness.
Shepherd, R. West Willow.
Shurin. Saturated.
Slauerhoff. Within My Life.
Smith, C. Sonnet Written at the Close of Spring [or Elegiac Sonnet].
To the Countess of A—. Written on the Anniversary of Her Marriage.
Smith, S. Conviction (iv).
Stafford, W. Gift, The.
Once in the 40s.
Stevenson, R. Happy Thought.
Stickney, T. Athenian Garden, An.
Stroud, J. Manna.
Subbarao, N. My Love.
Tachibana Akemi. Happiness is when.
Tanikawa, S. Zoo.
Teasdale. On the South Downs.
Tennyson, F. Poetical Happiness.
Thomas, E. Glory, The.
Toledo, N. Na Aurea.
Tu Fu [or Du Fu]. Hearing of Imperial Forces Retaking Ho-Nan and Ho-Pei.
Visitors.
Unknown. Cypress on the Mound, The.
Goodland.
How do you cut an ax-handle?
It's you puts the green sprig in my hatband.
Myrie a tyme I telle in May.
Utitia' q's Song.
Upton, L. Happiness: "In the hot white dome of air."
Van Walleghen. Happiness.
Vancrevel. About Time ("At dusk the silence by the sea.").
Vanshenkin. Rain.
Verlaine. He's an awkward bedfellow and I love to keep.
You see, we have to be forgiven things.
Vietnamese Oral Tradition. Tao.
Vitale, M. *Who trusteth in hilarity.*
Wallace-Crabbe. Sonnet IV.
Wang Wei. Farewell to Spring.
West, K. On Track.
Whitman, W. Beginning My Studies.
Live Oak, with Moss.
To be in any form, what is that?
When I Heard At The Close Of The Day.
Wilbur, R. What's Good for the Soul is Good for Sales.
Williams, C. Happiness.
Winchilsea. Give me, O indulgent fate!
Woolson. Florida Beach, The.
Wotton, S. Character of a Happy Life, The.
To John Donne.
Wright, James. Out of Horace.
Wright, James. Blessing, A: "Just off the highway to Rochester, Minnesota."
Northern Pike.
Wynne, F. Nocturne: "Long day was bright, The."
Yellen, J. Happy Days Are Here Again.
Yüan Hung-tao. Slowly, Slowly Poem, The.
Zurita, R. Splendor in the Wind.

See also **Contentment**

Harbors and Ports
Acorn. Charlottetown Harbour.
Baxter, J. Bay, The.
Channing. Harbor, The.
Chester, T. Candle at Canterbury, A.
Crane, H. Harbor Dawn, The.
Hardy, T. Harbour Bridge, The.
Heaney, S. Deserted harbour stillness. Every stone.

Heyman, E. I Cover the Waterfront.
Hwang Tonggyu. Port of Call.
Mathews, H. Lateral Disregard.
Mayer, B. Poem: "I am beginning to alter."
Meade, G. In Eyemouth Harbour.
Ni Dhomhnaill. Shannon Estuary 1988.
O'Hara, F. Blocks.
Pau-Llosa. Paredón.
Quiller-Couch. Harbour of Fowey, The.
Sandburg, C. Harbor, The.
Tranströmer. Syros.
Wilkinson, J. Oiled Sweater.
Yosano Akiko. Sakai Harbor.

Hardware Stores
Follain. Hardware Store.

Hardy, Thomas
Beerbohm, M. Luncheon, A.
Cooley. For Jude the Obscure.
De la Mare. Scholars.
Thomas Hardy.
Dubie. Thomas Hardy.
Hall, D. Hardy's "Shelley's Skylark".
Heaney, S. Birthplace, The.

Hares
Castillero, S. Hare, The.
Liebre, La.
Clare, J. Hares at Play.
Clarke, G. Hare, The.
Cowper, W. Epitaph on a Hare.
Davies, G. Dance, The.
Earle, J. Jugged Hare.
Lear, E. Limerick: "There was an old man whose despair."
Miles, S. Hares, The.
Porta. Dialogue with Herz.
Shinkichi Takahashi. Moon and Hare.
Smart, C. To the Rev. Mr. Powell.
Suermondt, Tim. Briefly Eavesdropping on Walt Whitman, Virginia, 1863.
Turberville. Hare's Complaint, The.
Unknown. Names of the Hare, The.
Riddle: "Hopper o'ditches, A."
Young, A. March Hares.

See also **Rabbits**

Harlem, New York City
Asim, J. Harlem Haiku: A Scrapbook.
Baraka, I. Return of the Native.
Beatty, P. Independent Study.
Berlin. Puttin' on the Ritz (Original Version).
Bethune, L. Harlem Freeze Frame.
Brown, S. Harlem Happiness.
Cortez, J. Under the Edge of February.
Dana, R. Elegy for the Duke.
Davis, T. Zoom (The Commodores).
Dove, R. Claudette Colvin Goes to Work.
Espada. Dándole la mano a Mongo.
Shaking Hands with Mongo.
Fields, D. Bojangles of Harlem.
Gilbert, M. Friendless Blues.
Henderson, D. Sketches of Harlem.
Hughes, L. Aesthete [or Esthete] in Harlem.
College Formal: Renaissance Casino.
Comment on Curb.
Dive.
Good Morning.
Harlem Sweeties.
Harlem ("What happens to a dream deferred?").
Island ("Between two rivers.").
Jazzonia.
Juke Box Love Song.
Night Funeral in Harlem.
125th Street.
Passing.
Projection.
Summer Night.
Theme for English B.
Visitors to the Black Belt.
Weary Blues, The.
Johnson, H. Sonnet to a Negro in Harlem.
Koehler, T. Truckin'.
McKay, C. Harlem Dancer, The.
Harlem Shadows.
Morales, A. Other Heritage, The.
Patterson, R. Harlem Suite.
Pitcher, O. Man, in some lan.

Powell, K. Harlem: Neo-Image.
Razaf, A. Stompin' at the Savoy.
Rukeyser, M. Ballad of Orange and Grape.
Simidor, D. Spring: "Spring afternoon, a lovely sky, bright sunshine, A."
Sousa, N. Let My People Go.
Tolson, M. African China.
 Alpha.
 Hideho Heights, / a black Gigas.
 Lambda.
 Mu.
 Nu.
Williams, C. Shop Sonnet.

Harper's Ferry, West Virginia
Atkins, R. Narrative.
Williams, E. At Harper's Ferry Just before the Attack.

Harps and Harpists
Bécquer, G. Dark in a Corner of the Room.
Coleridge, S. Aeolian [or Eolian] Harp, The.
Cook, E. 'Tis Well to Wake the Theme of Love.
Emerson, R. Merlin I.
Fane, V. Siren, The.
Gumilyov [or Gumiliov or Gumilev]. First Canzone.
Hölty. Legacy.
Lamb, L. Let the harp be mute for ever.
Melville, H. Aeolian Harp, The.
Moore, T. Harp That Once through Tara's Halls, The.
 Minstrel Boy, The.
Opie. Stanzas Written Under Aeolus' Harp.
Orr, G. Lament: "I thought of you."
Pitter. Military Harpist, The.
Po Chü-i. Harp, The.
Soniat. Harp/Desire.
Tighe. Address to My Harp.

Harrison, Benjamin
Hollander, J. Historical Reflections.

Hartford, Connecticut
Rossini, C. Cupid.

Harvard University
Cummings, E. E. Little joe gould has lost his teeth and doesn't know where.
Rich, A. Seven Skins.
Wheatley, P. To the University of Cambridge, in New-England.

Harvest
Adair, V. H. Blueberry City.
Akers, E. Bringing Our Sheaves with Us.
Alford, H. Harvest Home.
Auden. As I Walked Out One Evening.
Beaver. Silo Treading.
Blanchard, Mary Loving. Picking Cotton.
Brock-Broido. Of the Finished World.
Brown, S. Master and Man.
Buson. Harvest moon.
Cary, P. Harvest Gathering.
Cendrars. Harvest.
Char. Restore to Them.
Cho Chonsŏng. Boy, gather your straw basket.
Clampitt. Stacking the Straw.
De la Mare. Scarecrow, The.
Everson, W. 8. Advent.
Fallon, P. Meadow, The.
Glück, L. All Hallows.
Hauge. Harvest Time.
Heaney, S. Blackberry-Picking.
 Harvest Bow, The.
Herrick. Hock-Cart, or Harvest Home, The.
Hood, T. Ruth.
Hope, A. Hay Fever.
Hopkins, G. Hurrahing in Harvest.
Hwang Hŭi. Are chestnuts falling.
Ipadeola, T. August.
Jones, D. Harvest and Spring.
Kenyon, J. Twilight: After Haying.
Khlebnikov, V. It Has the Unassuming Face of a Burnt-out Candle.
Kingston, M. Spring Harvest of Snow Peas.
Kleinschmidt. Giorni.
Lawrence, D. H. Youth Mowing, A.
Llwyd, M. Harvest, The.
Longfellow, H. Aftermath.
Lope de Vega. White Was I.

Lux. Hungry Gap-Time, The.
Magdeburg, Mechthild von. I cannot dance, O Lord.
Matherne, B. La Fabrique de Tabac (Tobacco Harvest).
Melville, H. Afterward.
Pardlo, G. Harvest: A Line Drawing.
Pellicer, C. To Poetry.
Prunty. Vegetable Garden, The.
Raymond, M. First Harvest.
Read, T. Summer Shower, The.
Roberts, S. Potato Harvest, The.
Roscoe, W. To the Harvest Moon.
Rossetti, C. Amen.
Scheele. Wake of Plenty, The.
Schwartz, R. L. Late Summer.
Soyinka. Harvest of Hate.
Spalding, E. August.
Spinner, B. Harvest Home.
Takai Kito. Barley-reaping song / Smith's hammer.
Taneda Santoka. Dawn coming on.
Tanikawa, S. Concerning a Girl.
Thoreau. On fields oer which the reaper's hand has passed.
Toomer. Harvest Song.
 Reapers.
Trowbridge, J. Idyl of Harvest Time, An.
Tu Fu [or Du Fu]. After the Harvest.
Tzu Yeh. Bitter Harvest.
Unknown. Feng-nian: Good Year.
 Great hand King Wu.
 Hymn for Seedtime and a Safe Harvest (Arval Hymn).
 Sang-zhong: Hunting the Dodder.
Wordsworth, W. Solitary Reaper, The.

Harvey, Gabriel (1545?–1630)
Spenser, E. To the Right Worshipfull, My Singular Good Frend, Master Gabriell Harvey, Doctor of the Lawes.

Hashish
Whittier. Haschish, The.

Hate
Amichai, Y. Half of the people in the world.
 Quick And Bitter.
Ammianus. Epitaph of Nearchos.
Ballard, B. Hate Crime.
Baraka, I. Agony, An. As Now.
 Poem Some People Will Have to Understand, A.
Basho. To the willow.
Bennett, G. Hatred.
Berry, W. Morning's News, The.
Bowers, E. In the Last Circle.
Browning, R. Soliloquy of the Spanish Cloister.
Buffoni, F. Partitions.
Campbell, S. Constant Welcome, The.
Castellanos. Destiny.
Castro, R. I Love You . . . Why Do You Hate Me?
Catullus. Odi et Amo.
Chesterton. World State, The.
Chudakov. Suicide is a duel with yourself.
Creeley. Self-Portrait.
Cruz e Sousa. Sacred Hatred.
Darwish, M. He Embraces His Murderer.
Dickey, W. Cassandra.
Dickinson, E. I had no time to Hate.
Domina, L. Pharoah's Army Got Drowned.
Duncan, R. Up Rising.
"Ephelia.". To One That Asked Me Why I Loved J.G G.
Evans, M. World I See, The.
Field. As two fair vessels side by side.
Frost, R. Beyond Words.
 Fire and Ice.
Glaser, I. Last Good War—and Afterward, The.
Gotoba. There Were Those I Loved.
Griffiths, B. For P—Celtic: found text from Machen.
Hachenburg, H. Terezin.
Harjo, J. Transformations.
Herbert, E. Ditty: "Why dost thou hate return instead of love."
Hope, A. Fafnir.
Housman. When I watch the living meet.
Huerta, E. Declaration of Hate.

Islām, N. He who has seen my Mother.
Karim, F. Crumbled Paper for Future Poems.
 Malice.
Kaufman, S. Mothers, Daughters.
Kees. For My Daughter.
Kombem. Another Moment.
Konie, G. In the Fist of Your Hatred.
Lawrence, D. H. Eloi, Eloi, Lama Sabachthani?
 History.
Lowery, J. Hate Crimes.
Lowry, M. Wild Cherry, The.
Lux. People of the Other Village, The.
McElroy, C. Illusion.
McKay, C. White House, The.
Michaux. Future.
Nadir, M. My Heart.
Neruda. Dictators, The.
Ostriker. Lamenting the Inevitable.
 Window, at the Moment of Flame, The.
P'Bitek. My Husband's Tongue Is Bitter.
Petri. Night Song of the Personal Shadow.
Piatt, S. Pique at Parting, A.
Plath. Daddy.
Plotnick, H. M. Jewish.
Prelutsky. Homework! Oh, Homework!
Quintana. Poem for Pancho Gonzales.
Raab, L. My Life Before I Knew It.
Ryan, G. If I Had a Gun.
Sepamla. Odyssey, The.
Shore. High Holy Days.
Soyinka. Harvest of Hate.
Stephens, J. Hate.
Stillman, M. Prospero.
Suckling, S. Barley-Break , A.
Unknown. Edward [or Edward, Edward].
 Mother-in-law, do not stamp.
 Oh Lord! Once again your long and dismal night is here.
 Oh my God! Once again you send me the dark night.
Wickham. Paradox.
Wildman, E. Cure, The.
Wyatt. Varium et Mutabile.

Hate Crimes
Wozek, G. Song to Myself at Seventeen.

Hats
Akst, H. Straw Hat in the Rain.
Basho. Cold rain starting, A.
Berlin. Easter Parade.
Bevington, H. Mr. Rockefeller's Hat.
Bishop, E. Exchanging Hats.
Brown, L. Straw Hat in the Rain.
Burns, R. To a Louse [On Seeing One on a Lady's Bonnet at Church].
Cleage. Confession.
Cofer, J. My Grandfather's Hat.
Cunningham, P. Hats.
Durcan. Hat Factory, The.
Foster, A. Nest of Hats, A.
Garcia, R. Dangerous Hats.
Harper, M. Bandstand.
Irwin, M. My Father's Hats.
Jastrun, T. Hat.
Johnson, S. Ballad: "I put my hat upon my head."
Kyger. Philip Whalen's Hat.
Lě Thánh-tông. Stick and Hat.
Lear, E. Limerick: "There was an Old Man who supposed."
Lerner, A. I Left My Hat in Haiti.
Little, L. My Yellow Straw Hat.
Mole, J. Song of the Hat-Raising Doll.
Moss, S. Exchange of Hats, An.
Muldoon, P. Hats.
Parnell, P. Sheila the Hat.
Pastan. Hat Lady, The.
Probyn. Frustrated.
Reznikoff. Millinery District ("Clouds, piled in rows like merchandise, The.").
 Millinery District ("Many fair hours have been buried here.").
Smith, S. Magna Est Veritas.
Stein, C. My hat vanished.
Stern, G. Hats.
Thompson, C. Easter Bonnet, The.
Travis, N. Church Ladies.

Unknown. It's you puts the green sprig in my hatband.
Van Ostaijen. Song of the Alpine Hunter.
Webb, C. Marrying.
Wellman, M. Silvery tells no sphere to go and. Who lowers the unseen hat from on high.
Yasui. Who's that?

Haunted Houses
Bontemps. Southern Mansion.
Donne. Apparition, The.
Edwards [*or* Edwardes], R. Recollections of an Old Spook.
Longfellow, H. Haunted Houses.
Mansour, J. Empty Black Haunted House.
Nesbit, E. Haunted.
Péret. Wink.

Havana, Cuba
Blanco, R. Last Night in Havana.
Bogen, L. Havana.
Castillo, S. En el Sol de Mi Barrio.
Crane, H. Eternity.
Komunyakaa, Y. Boxing Day.
Pau-Llosa. Paredón.

Hawaii
Birney. Twenty-third Flight.
Boruch. Year in Hawaii.
Dean, D. K. In the Way Back.
Hahn, K. Hula Skirt, 1959, The.
Hawaiian Oral Tradition. Hana-Hana: Working. My Mother Dear. Should I return to Japan?
Hernández Cruz. Borinkins in Hawaii.
Lili'u-o-ka-lani. Aloha'oe.
Luterman, A. On Not Flying to Hawaii.
Trask, H. Chant of Lamentation.

Hawks
Axelrod, D. Guide to Urban Birds, A.
Basho. Dusk.
Blackburn, P. Net of Place, The.
Brodsky, J. Hawk's Cry in Autumn, The.
Brouwer, J. Conservatory Pond, Central Park, New York, New York.
Brown, G. Hawk, The.
Buson. Iris, An.
Corey, S. Complicated Shadows.
Crozier, L. Inventing the Hawk.
"Ern Malley.". Sonnets for the Novachord.
Gerner, K. Prey.
Greene, A. C. Hawk Over Inwood Road, A.
Gregg. Skylord.
Gunn, T. Tamer and Hawk.
Hopkins, G. Windhover, The.
Huddle. Visit of the Hawk.
Hudgins. Hawk above the House, The.
Hughes, T. Hawk in the Rain, The. Hawk Roosting.
Jeffers, R. Hurt Hawks. Rock and Hawk.
Jonson, B. To Sir Henry Goodyere.
Lea, S. Fish Pond, The [1993] ("Not full of fish—that's imprecise—but full.").
Lemm, Richard. Perfect Circle.
Llwyd, Alan. Hawk Above Felindre, The.
Masters, E. Unknown, The.
McDonald, W. Hawks in a Bitter Blizzard.
McKay, D. Close-up on a Sharp-shinned Hawk.
Melville, H. Man-of-War Hawk, The.
Montag, T. April 30, 2001 (1).
Oliver, M. Hawk.
Ortiz. Earth and Rain, the Plants & Sun.
Rumi. Hawk, The.
Sadoff. Red Tail Sonnet.
Thomas, D. Over Sir John's Hill.
Townsend, A. After the End.
Tu Fu [*or* Du Fu]. Hawk in a Painting, A.
Unknown. Hawk Chant of the Saginaws.
Warren, R. Evening Hawk. Mortal Limit. Red-Tail Hawk and Pyre of Youth.
Wheelock, J. Fish-Hawk, The.

Hawthorn (botany)
Bidgood. Hawthorn at Digiff.
Brown, T. I Bended unto Me.
Heaney, S. Haw Lantern, The.

Hawthorne, Nathaniel
Hightower, S. Tontine.
Lowell, J. Hawthorne.
Melville, H. Monody: "To have known him, to have loved him."
Noguere. Secret, The.

Hay and Haymaking
Clampitt. Stacking the Straw.
Clarke, G. Hay-Making.
Dickinson, E. I'm sorry for the Dead—Today.
Groarke, V. Thistle.
Hodgins. Making Hay.
Prunty. Haying.
Steele, T. Timothy.
Stewart, S. Forms of Forts.

Hayden, Robert
Gilbert, C. And, Yes, Those Spiritual Matters.

Haydn, Franz Joseph
Ghigna. Lesson of Night, A.
Tranströmer. Allegro.

Haydon, Benjamin Robert
Browning, E. On a Portrait of Wordsworth by B. R. Haydon.
Keats. Great Spirits Now on Earth. To B.R. Haydon, with a Sonnet Written on Seeing the Elgin Marbles.

Hayworth, Rita
Herd. Bombshell.

Haze
Henley, W. E. At Queensferry.
Lowell, A. Moon Haze.
See also **Fog**

Hazlitt, William
Guiney. W. H.

Heads
Bradstreet, A. Letter to Her Husband, Absent upon Public[k] Employment, A.
Buson. Cover my head.
Davidson, M. Troth.
Donegan, P. Tonight / while shampooing my hair.
Gorey. Limerick: "From Number Nine, Penwiper Mews."
Haavikko. When you go to the tyrant. Keep your head on a platter.
Johnson, S. Ballad: "I put my hat upon my head."
Knoepfle. Harpe's Head.
Lux. Men with Small Heads.
Major, C. Balance and Beauty.
Mandelstam [*or* Mandelshtam]. Mounds of Human Heads. Mounds of Human Heads Are Wandering into the Distance.
Meredith, W. Thoughts on One's Head.
Skelton, J. Upon a Dead Man's Head.
Sparrow, J. To an Angel in the House.
Toledo, N. Na Victórica litru.
Webb, H. Stone Face, The.
Wieners. Glimpse, A.

Healing
Atwood. Romantic.
Back, R. Abu Salim, Healer.
Barnes, S. Back to the Blues.
Bishop, E. Sonnet: "I am in need of music that would flow."
Blamire. O Bid Me Not to Wander.
Bly, R. Looking into a Tide Pool.
Broumas, O. Etymology.
Chester, T. Buttons.
Cortázar. Therapies.
Couzyn. Spell to Soften the Hard Heart of a Woman.
Dauenhauer. Grandmother Eliza.
Fisher, Diane G. Sweet Hour.
Futuransky, L. Twenty Years From Auschwitz, Bergen-Belsen and Other Camps.
Goodison. Heartease 3. Jah Music.
Hearle, K. Lesson, The.
Heynen. Bloating and Its Remedies.
Howe, M. Recovery.
Kees. Small Prayer.
Lambert, A. Prayer: "Bones in your foot that were shattered, The."

Larkin, J. Good-Bye. How the Healing Takes Place.
McCabe, C. Jastrzebia Góra.
Mead, J. However.
Mengham, Rod. Smitten.
Meynell, A. Messina, 1908.
Montague, J. Same Gesture, The.
Parker, D. Healed.
Pastan. Apple Shrine, The.
Plumly. Reading with the Poets.
Raz, H. For Barbara, Who Brings a Green Stone in the Shape of a Triangle.
Rooney-Céspedes, A. Cure, The.
Rosario, M. Curing.
Rouse, A. Faith Healers.
Schneider, M. When It's All Over.
Scott, W. Come Green Again.
Sexauer, T. Ambivalent Nature of Healing, The. Poem for Tết.
Stone, A. Spofford Hall.
Taylor, E. Fiery Darts of Satan stob my heart, The.
Tesshu. How heal the phantom body of its phantom ill.
Thomas, R. H. Evacuee, The.
Toledo, N. Ca gunaa rusianda. Curanderas. Healers. Marcelina. Marcelina. Marcelina.
Turnbull. Transmutation ("Take severely ill, he is conscious only at brief intervals.").
Unknown. May Isis heal me.
Volach, Y. Life You Have, The.
Walker, A. Remember?
Wilson, J. Pruning.
Wordsworth, W. Course Prescribed, The.

Health
Huff, S. Sperm Count.
McGough, R. Health Forecast, The.
Stein, G. Centre in a table, A.
Timoner, J. Business of Health, The.
Unknown. Two Sonnets.

Health Clubs
Hillman, B. Y, The.
Rouse, A. Uni-Gym, The.

Heaney, Seamus
Williamson, G. Bodies of Water.

Heart Attacks
Carruth, H. Memory.
Greenway, W. Anniversary.
Lewis, G. Her End.
O'Dwyer, Caley. Texas.
O'Donoghue, B. Concordiam in Populo.
Prévert. At the Florist's.
Schreiber, R. To Be Held.
Ziemianin A. Heart Attack.

Heartbreak
Adler, L. Smike.
Al-Bayati, A. I am Born and I Burn in My Love.
al-Saygh, S. Dread.
Andrews, N. Nirvana: "After you left me, I was so lonely and sad, I became but an apparition, a ghost of who I had been."
Baraka, I. Lefty.
Barnes, S. Back to the Blues.
Bayly. Oh, No! We Never Mention Her.
Bey, Râsih. Don't lower your languid eyes, don't aim.
Blanco, R. Perfect City Code.
Christensen, Paul. What the Citizens of Corpus, Rockport, Palacios, or Bryan Need.
De Kok. Mending.
Dede, Esrâr. You left, but don't forget, my heart.
Denis, J. Zombie.
Dîranas, A. Oblivion: "Twilight hours are always gruff and gory."
Dorgan, T. Up All Night.
Étienne, Marie. Nightmares.
Fanning, M. Consolation: "I wend to the sea."
Fevrî. Arrow of your glance pierces my wounded, The.

Figani Ramazan Çelebi. My sad heart is burnt black in the fire.
Filkova, Fedya. Vulnerability.
Forhan, C. Gouge, Adze, Rasp, Hammer.
Fraser, K. Change of Address.
Fuertes. Love Turns You into a Rosebush.
Fuzuli. I reap no gains but trouble at your place when I come near.
Gan Bao. Grave Wedding of Lu Chong.
Glück, L. Midnight.
Gregory, A. Donal[l] Oge [or Og]: Grief of a Girl's Heart.
Hantoosh, G. Take Me, Loneliness.
Harper, M. Last Affair: Bessie's Blues Song.
Hatun. At times, my longing for the beloved slays me.
Hô Sugyông. One White Dream.
Ibn Zuhr, M. O cupbearer, our complaints are addressed to you; we have called upon you even though you do not listen!
Jordan, J. Poem about heartbreak that go on and on.
Kimbrell, J. Letters to a Vanishing Fiancée.
My Psychic.
Kostyleva, E. Vacancy instead of you, A.
Large, J. Snowcone Vendor.
Li Po. Autumn Lines.
Longing.
Li Yu [or Li Hou-Chu]. Shaken, They Cling Again.
López Colomé, P. Dolor de corazón.
Heartache.
Lustig, Dana Lisa. And I am lonely and small in all this, goodnight.
MacKay, C. Earl and the Girl, The.
Merry. Elegy Written after Reading the "Sorrows of Werter".
Passerat. Villanelle: "I've lost her now, my turtle-dove."
Pierpoint, K. This Dead Relationship.
Press, K. Heart's Hunger.
Ricard, R. Party Crash.
Rosenthal, G. Wild Hooves.
SamanoĞlu, Gültekin. Come So Far as You Can Feel.
Schultz, P. Free Mercy.
Sepúlveda, O. Cuatro ("Pero luego, en el trayecto imaginario de un automóvil blanco.").
Four ("But then, in the imaginary trajectory of a white automobile.").
Shen Yüeh. Green, Green Riverside Grass.
Sigerson, G. Love's Despair.
Siken, Richard. Boot Theory.
Solie, Karen. Larking.
Stanley, T. Love Deposed.
Steele, S. Love-Sick Maid, The.
Subbarao, R. Waiting.
Teasdale. Song: "You bound strong sandals on my feet."
Terán, V. En la palma de mi mano.
In the Palm of My Hand.
Ndaani' batanaya'.
Tonks. Badly-Chosen Lover.
Ts'ao Chih. Round the tall towers blow many mournful winds.
Unknown. Do Not Pluck Me.
First Time I Set Eyes on You, The.
God, you may render me blind from here on in.
Loveshock.
Meng: To a Man.
Stars Stand Up, The.
Suliko.
Year Draws to Its End, The.
Yesterday Morning.
Yue-chu [Translations].
Vogelweide. Translation from Walter von der Vogelweide, A.
Wright, K. All Purpose Country and Western Self Pity Song, The.
Yauger, Fay M. Country Fair.
Yosano Tekkan. Withered Lotus.
Yūsuf III. O you who have aimed / At my heart with the dart / Of a piercing glance.
Yusuf, S. Woman, A.

Hearts
Achterberg. Departure.

al-Rahim, A. My Heart.
Who?
Altizer. Sonnet 2: "My own heart let me have. More pity on."
Alvarez, J. Woman's Work.
Arreola, Juan José. Toad, The.
Aygi, G. Rose of Silence.
Bang, M. Louise in Love.
Binyon. Harebell and Pansy.
Blanvillain, J. (All of a Sudden) My Heart Sings.
Bloem, J. C. After Liberation.
Bogan, L. Song for the Last Act.
Bond, B. Host.
Bourdillon. Night Has a Thousand Eyes, The.
Breton, A. Poem-Object.
Browning, E. My Heart and I.
To George Sand: A Recognition.
Browning, R. Meeting at Night.
Bu-er. Late Indian summer's.
Burke, J. My Heart Is a Hobo.
Burns, R. My Heart's in the Highlands.
Buson. Mourning for Hokuju Rosen.
Bynner. Wintry Mind, The.
Campo, C. Canon 4.
Campo. Aunt Toni's Heart.
Carbó, N. Robo.
Carman, B. World Voice, The.
Ceni, A. Fragment.
Reconciled Flame.
Char. Swift, The.
Chu Hsiang. Pawnshop, The.
Cisneros, S. Heart, My Lovely Hobo.
Clare, J. First Love.
Coleridge, M. Broken Friendship.
Gone.
Cope, W. Valentine.
Couzyn. Heartsong.
Crane, S. In the desert.
Crashaw. Flaming Heart, The.
Love, thou art absolute sole lord.
To the Noblest and Best of Ladies, the Countess of Denbigh.
Cummings, E. E. I carry your heart with me(i carry it in).
Cunningham, J. To My Wife.
Dancing Bear, J. P. Heart-Shaped Island, A.
Davis, T. Playing Solitaire.
De Cristoforo, Violet Kazue. Stockade prisoners on hunger strike: Nani Mo Mite Inai Kokoro No Hi Ga Tsuzuki Kogen Natsu Takenawa.
Derieva, R. Theory of Recruiting.
Devi. Cold Meat.
Dickinson, E. Heart asks Pleasure—first, The.
This dirty—little—Heart.
Dietz, H. Haunted Heart.
Donne. Blossom[e], The.
Broken Heart, The.
Dooley, M. Heart.
Doolittle, Hilda. Antistrophe.
O heart, small urn.
Drayton. Crier, The.
Heart, The.
Love, in a humour, played the prodigal.
Duggan, L. Hearts (1983).
Dunn, S. That Saturday Without a Car.
Emre. Hear me out, my dear friends.
My Lord granted me such a heart.
Engvick, W. Crazy in the Heart.
Field. Love rises up some days.
Sometimes I do despatch my heart.
Unbosoming.
Freed, A. This Heart of Mine.
Frost, R. Dust of Snow.
Garrett, E. Mimesis.
Ghalib, M. Ghazal.
Gibson, M. Woman Resting on a Bundle of Kindling.
Gilbert, J. Getting Ready.
Gordon, M. Meet the Beat of My Heart.
Gylys, B. Balloon Heart.
Fat Chance.
Haewŏn. Regarding the Heart.
Han-shan. People ask about Cold Mountain Way.
Hanley, J. Zing! Went the Strings of My Heart.

Hannah, S. Where is Talcott Parsons Now?
Harburg. If I Only Had a Brain (If I Only Had a Heart) (If I Only Had the Nerve).
Hart, L. My Heart Stood Still.
Nobody's Heart.
With a Song in My Heart.
Hass, R. Forty Something.
Hemans. Stranger's Heart, The.
Herbert, G. Altar, The.
Hernández, M. Your Heart?—It Is a Frozen Orange.
Herrera. Crack Inside My Breast, A.
Herrick. To Oenone ("What conscience, say, is it in thee.").
Hikmet. Angina Pectoris.
Hô Sugyông. Sober, Remaining.
Hope, A. Wandering Islands, The.
Hopes. Holy Innocents.
Hopkins, G. My Own Heart Let Me More Have Pity On.
Hwang Insuk. Beneath Her Ribs.
Jabeen, M. Fall: "He always did that."
Jewsbury. My heart's in the kitchen, my heart is not here.
To My Own Heart.
Jiménez, J. My Feet, So Deep in the Earth.
Johnson, G. Heart of a Woman, The.
Juarroz. There Are Points of Silence Circling the Heart.
Kambala. KYE HO! Wonderful!
Kasischke. My Heart.
Kaufman, S. Emperor of China, The.
Kawai Suimei. Living Voice.
Kim Hyesun. Bloody Clock, A.
Old Hotel, The.
Kim Yŏngnang. Endless River Flows, An.
Someone Who Knows My Heart.
King, H. Sonnet: "Tell me[e] no more how fair[e] she[e] is."
Kirsanov. New Heart, The.
Kloos, W. Evening.
Kojijū. On the Spirit of the Heart as Moon-Disk.
Landor, W. Heart's Abysses, The.
Lee, W. Sex Has a Way.
Leigh, C. Young at Heart.
Levin, D. Glass Heart.
Li Yu [or Li Hou-Chu]. Nightlong I Wander.
López Velarde. My Heart, Faithful.
Lovelace, R. To Lucasta.
Lowell, R. Colloquy in Black Rock.
MacAdams. Pockets of Haze.
Machado Ruiz. Last Night.
Last night while I was sleeping.
Lord, You Have Ripped Away.
Pay attention now.
MacKenzie, John. Hearthouse.
Mackenzie, K. Caesura.
Magdeburg, Mechthild von. How God Answers the Soul.
Magee, T. Home Thoughts.
Mayes, J. Descant.
McCallum, S. Perfect Heart, The.
Mew. I Have Been through the Gates.
Mignon, A. One Heart's Enough for Me.
Millay, E. My Heart, Being Hungry.
Mirabai [or Mira Bai]. O friends on this Path.
Mistral, G. Rose, The.
Mitchison. To Some Young Communists from an Older Socialist.
Mohr, B. Why the Heart Never Develops Cancer.
Nadir, M. My Heart.
Nedim. As the morning wind blows, you are disheveled.
Nef'i. Heart is both the cup and the wine, The.
Nelson, D. Our Love.
Nepote, M. Piensa en esa estatua abierta en el corazón de la ciudad.
Think of that statue open in the heart of the city.
Nezahualcoyotl. Be Indomitable, O My Heart.
Norton, C. Sonnet 7: "Like an enfranchised bird, who wildly springs."
Onitsura. Plum blossoms / One's nose.
Orléans, C. Go forth myn hert wyth my lady.
Orozco. To Make a Talisman.

Ossip, K.   Nature of Things, The.
Parker, D.   Autumn Valentine.
Paschen.   Confederacy.
Peeradina, S.   Testament.
Pelizzon, V.   Late Apostasy, A.
Philips, K.   Friendship in Emblem[e], or the
　Seal[e], to my dearest Lucasia.
　Friendship's Mystery[s], to my dearest Lucasia.
　Wiston Vault.
Pinsky.   Hearts, The.
Poulin, A.   Red Clock.
Rabi'a al-Adawiyya.   I am fully qualified to
　work as a doorkeeper, and for this reason.
Raboni, G.   Hospital Interiors.
Rexroth, K.   Heart of Herakles, The.
Reynolds, T.   To a Bad Heart.
Richardson, K.   Aubade: "Geese flew by as you
　entered me, The."
Riley, J.   As one who cons at evening o'er an
　album, all alone.
　Old Sweetheart of Mine, An.
Rilke.   O you lovers that are so gentle, step
　occasionally.
Roberts, K.   Postcard from the Coast.
Rodgers, C.   Black Heart as Ever Green, The.
Roland Holst.   Outside in the Open.
Rome, H.   (All of a Sudden) My Heart Sings.
Rosales.   I Know Too Well and Sadly Enough.
Rossetti, C.   Birthday, A.
　Twice.
Rózewicz.   What Luck.
Scott, D.   Heart.
Scott, J.   Man in Petersham.
Shakespeare, W.   Sonnet 141: "In faith, I do[e]
　not love thee with mine eyes."
Shelley, P.   From the Arabic: An Imitation.
　Lines: "When the lamp is shattered [or
　shatter'd]."
Shwarts [or Shvarts].   My heart's cloth I shall
　spread before the Savior's feet.
Sidney.   My true love hath my heart [or hart],
　and I have his.
Sitwell, E.   Heart and Mind.
Smith, K.   Here.
Solomon ibn Gabirol.   My Heart Thinks as the
　Sun Comes Up.
Sorby.   Man without a Middle, The.
Spenser, E.   Sonnet 37: "What guile [or guyle]
　is this, that those her golden tresses."
Spires.   Robed Heart, The.
Sundiata.   Open Heart.
Supervielle.   Sphere.
Sylvester, J.   "Were I as Base as Is the Lowly
　Plain".
Teasdale.   Shrine, The.
Thomas, D.   When All My Five and Country
　Senses See.
Thomas, R. S.   Lonely Farmer, The.
Tipton.   I Wanted You in the Kitchen of My
　Heart.
Trakl.   Heart, The: "Wild heart grew white in
　the forest, The."
Trench, H.   Jean Richepin's Song.
Unknown.   Cypress Boat.
　If you kiss my mouth, you must give me your
　heart.
　See! Here, My Heart.
　Thy Heart.
　Woman's Love.
Unknown, fr. Terezin Concentration Camp.
　Birdsong.
Volkman.   Sonnet: "What is this witness, the
　watching ages."
Walcott.   Fist, The.
Washington, N.   Give Me a Heart to Sing To.
　My Foolish Heart.
Watson, R.   Cage, The.
Williams, C. K.   Heart, The.
Williams, S.   Youth and Maidenhood.
Wohlfeld.   Quilt.
Wroth.   Sonnet 13: "Free from all fogs but[t]
　shining fair[e], and clear [or cleere]."
Wylie.   Felo de Se.
　This Corruptible.
Yahya Efendi, Sheyhülislâm.   Is there no heart
　capable of love.

Saki, offer the cup, let them call me a drunkard.
Yang Shen.   To the Tune "Moon Over West
　River".
Yosano Akiko.   Heart of a Thirtyish Woman,
　The.
Zach, N.   Failure.

Heat
Alcaeus [or Alkaios].   Wet your lungs with
　wine—the dogstar rises.
Barnes, B.   Something Cool.
Basho.   Heat waves shimmering.
　This hot day swept away.
　Withered grass / Under piling.
Berlin.   Heat Wave.
　I've Got My Love to Keep Me Warm.
Bernard, A.   Praise Psalm of the City-Dweller.
Biespiel, D.   Heat Sours, The.
Bracho, C.   Desde esta luz.
　From This Light.
Brown, L.   Turn On the Heat.
Bryant, W.   Midsummer.
Buson.   Brushing flies.
Chazal, M.   It was / so hot.
Ching An.   Beating the Heat at Jade Lake.
Cho, P.   One Wintry Day.
Ch'u Ch'uang I.   Tea.
Crowell, G.   Summer Nights in Texas.
Dancing Bear, J. P.   Making Fire.
Densmore.   Song of the Butterfly, The.
DeSylva, B. G.   Turn On the Heat.
Dickey, J.   Basics.
Dimitrova.   Sunstroke.
Divakaruni.   Alley of Flowers, The.
Dooley, M.   Heat.
Doolittle, Hilda.   Heat.
Eigner.   It Sounded.
Erb, E.   Stove Problem, The.
Foreman, Paul.   Impressionist.
Gorbanevskaya.   Hold out a handful of snow.
Graves, R.   Cool Web, The.
Hakuin.   Priceless is one's incantation.
Hampton.   In Andrea's Garden.
Hass, R.   Late Spring.
Henderson, R.   Turn On the Heat.
Hudgins.   Heat Lightning in a Time of Drought.
Johnson, D.   Heat.
Koch, K.   Boiling Water, The.
Kusano Shimpei.   4 Or 5 Tadpoles.
Lampman.   Heat.
Loftin, E.   Weeksville Women.
Luschei, G.   Arrangement.
MacKenzie, John.   Hearthouse.
Mackenzie, K.   Heat.
Mardi, Jas.   Good-bye Summer.
Markus, P.   Black Light.
Masaoka Shiki.   Buddha too.
McDonald, W.   Last Still Days in a Bunker, The.
McIlroy, L.   Siesta.
Monnier, Pascalle.   Summer ("Good, it's hot.").
Myles, E.   Milk.
Nishiwaki Junzaburo.   Ceylon.
Oden.   Riven Quarry, The.
Olds, S.   Space Heater, The.
Ondaatje.   Dates.
Ovid.   Elegy 1.5: "In summer's heat[e] and mid-
　time of the day."
Porter, C.   Too Darn Hot.
Powell, J.   It Was Fever That Made the World.
Rabinowitz.   Of Joy Illimited: Polyphonic
　Soundings: Shore to Ship.
Remizov, Alexei.   Without Heat.
Ruefle.   Rising Bodies.
Scott, D.   Church Boiler, The.
Shurin.   Saturated.
Souza.   Landscape.
Tomlinson, C.   Las Trampas U.S.A.
Turner, F.   110 Degrees in Dallas.
Tzu Yeh.   Song: "Winter skies are cold and
　low."
Unknown.   Hot Day In Sydney, A.
　Red Stove Warms the Room, The.
Vando.   Ode to Your Back.
Voigt.   January: "After days of putting down my
　poem."
Walcott.   Midsummer, Tobago.
Warren, R.   Rattlesnake Country.

Witt, S.   Thermal Signatures ("I sing a place
　called Newborn.").
Wright, C.   Bent Tones.
　Humidity.
Heather
Lerner, A.   Heather on the Hill, The.
Munro, N.   Heather, The.
Williams, E.   Heather Flowers.
Heaven
Agee.   Description of Elysium.
Anwar, C.   Heaven.
Balbulus, N.   Hymn to Holy Women, A.
Bandeira.   Mozart in Heaven.
Baraka, I.   Dope.
Baranczak, S.   N. N. Tries to Remember the
　Words of a Prayer.
Berlin.   Cheek to Cheek.
Berrigan, D.   In Memoriam (2): "Young priest,
　dead suddenly, A."
Betsugen.   All night long I think of life's
　labyrinth.
Bible, O.T.   Psalm 58: "Judges, who rule the
　world by laws."
Bishop, E.   Seascape.
Blake, W.   Marriage of Heaven and Hell, The.
　Marriage of Heaven and Hell, The.
Bradstreet, A.   As Weary Pilgrim, Now at Rest.
　Contemplations.
Brandt, D.   When i was five i thought heaven
　was located.
Brontë, E.   No Coward Soul is Mine.
　Stanzas: "Often rebuked, yet always back
　returning."
Brooke, R.   Heaven.
Brooks, G.   Hunchback Girl: She Thinks of
　Heaven.
Brown, S.   Sister Lou.
Bryant, W.   These are the gardens of the Desert,
　these.
Burris.   On Living with a Fat Woman in
　Heaven.
Byron, G.   Vision of Judgment, The ("Saint
　Peter sat by the celestial gate.").
Campion, T.   O Come Quickly!
Cary, P.   Nearer Home.
Castro, R.   I in My Bed of Thistles.
Cavendish, W.   Love's Sun.
Chapman, G.   Peace of Death, The.
Clare, J.   Vision, A.
Coleridge, M.   Friends—With a Difference.
Coleridge, S.   Kubla Khan: or, A Vision in a
　Dream.
Cranch.   Spirit of the Age, The.
Crane, H.   And Bees of Paradise.
Crashaw.   I Am the Door [or Doore].
　To the Infant Martyrs.
　Upon the Infant Martyrs.
Crosby, F.   We Are Going.
Cullen, C.   For a Lady I Know.
Cummings, E. E.   If there are any heavens my
　mother will (all by herself) have.
Dante Alighieri.   Middle of life's journey; I,
　The.
　Virgin Mary, daughter of your Son.
Davenant [or D'Avenant].   Praise and Prayer.
DeSylva, B. G.   Stairway to Paradise.
Dickey, J.   Heaven of Animals, The.
Dickinson, E.   God's Residence.
　Heaven has different Signs—to me.
　"Heaven"—is what I cannot reach!
　I dwell in Possibility.
　I never saw a Moor.
　I reason, Earth is short.
　I've known a Heaven, like a Tent.
　My life closed twice before its close.
　My nosegays are for Captives.
　Pit—but Heaven over it, A.
　There is a Zone whose even Years.
　What mystery pervades a well!
　You're right—"the way is narrow".
Disch.   Garage Sale as a Spiritual Exercise, The.
Doddridge, P.   Hymn: "Ye golden lamps of
　heaven, farewell."
　Meditations on the Sepulchre in the Garden.
Donne.   Hymn to the Saints, and to Marquis
　Hamilton, An.

Dryden, J. Song for St Cecilia's Day, 1687, A.
Dunbar, P. Theology.
Dunbar, W. Amendis [or Amends] to the Telyouris [or Tailors] and Sowtaris [or Soutaris or Soutars or Shoemakers].
Egerton, S. Blasphemous wretch! How canst thou think or say.
Emerson, R. Spiritual Laws.
Enheduanna. Lady of Largest Heart.
Erdrich, H. Sweeping Heaven.
Ficowski. Assumption of Miriam from the Street in the Winter of 1942, The.
Francis, A. Stairway to Paradise.
Freneau. When Nature bids thee from the world retire.
Ghalib, M. Clay Cup, The.
Gibbons, R. Cash or Turtle or Heaven.
Goethe. Mignon Aspiring to Heaven.
Greenberg, U. Song of Earth.
Song to Heaven.
Hakuin. Tea-kettle / Hooked in mid-air.
Hall, D. Sister on the Tracks, A.
Hartnett. Wounded Otter, The.
Herbert, G. Heaven.
Herrick. Comfort to a Youth That Had Lost His Love.
To Heaven.
To His Ever-Loving God.
White Island, The: or Place of the Blest.
Hoover, P. American Heaven.
Hopkins, G. Handsome Heart, The.
Heaven-Haven.
Housman. Easter Hymn.
Mark 16:19–20; So then the Lord Jesus, after.
Howard, R. Giovanni da Fiesole on the Sublime.
Hudgins. Elegy for My Father, Who Is Not Dead.
Hughes, T. River.
Issa. Six Ways, The.
Jammes. Prayer to Go to Paradise with the Donkeys, A.
Jewsbury. To My Own Heart.
Jonson, B. Pleasures of Heaven, The.
To Heaven.
Kaufman, B. SUN IS A NEGRO, THE.
Kavanagh, P. Sanctity.
Keats. Ode: "Bards of passion and of mirth."
Kendall, M. Legend of the Crossing-Sweeper.
Kumin, M. Heaven as Anus.
Kushner, Tony. Happily I turn the earth.
Lao Tzu. Valley Spirit never dies, The.
Lasker-Schüler. Chronica.
Li Shang-yin. High Noon.
Lindsay, V. General William Booth Enters into Heaven.
Lodge, T. Minde through thee divines on endlesse things, The.
Loesser. Sit Down, You're Rockin' the Boat.
Longley, M. Björn Olinder's Pictures.
Lowry, R. Beautiful River.
March, A. Let others hail the holidays with laughter.
Martinaitis, M. Kukutis's Lament under the Heavens.
Masefield. Port of Many Ships.
Maulpoix, Jean-Michel. Giving Birth, The.
Maurus. To Grimold, Abbot of St. Gall.
Melville, H. Spirit Appeared to Me, A.
Michelangelo Buonarroti. From sweet weeping to a painful smile.
Montgomerie, A. Royall Palice of the Heichest Hewin, The.
Moore, T. This World Is All a Fleeting Show.
Morley, D. Enniskillen.
Morris, W. Apology, An.
Muso Soseki. Cave of the Thousand Pines.
Nairne. Land o' the Leal, The.
Ocampo. Report on Heaven and Hell.
Oliver, M. Roses, Late Summer.
Parra, N. Lord's Prayer.
Patmore, C. 'Twas When the Spousal Time of May.
Phillips, C. Sunday.
Plath. Sheep in Fog.
Polak, J. Storm, The.

Popa. Heaven's Ring.
Pope, A. Universal Prayer, The [Deo Opt. Max.].
Powell, D. A. [Coda & discography].
Procter, A. Lost Chord, A.
Philip and Mildred.
Quarles. On a Feast.
Raffalovich, M. A. World Well Lost 18, The.
Ralegh, S. Passionate Man['] Pilgrimage, The.
Riley, J. Eternity.
Ríos, A. If I Leave You.
Robinson, E. Credo: "I cannot find my way."
Matthew 22:1–14; And again Jesus spoke to them.
Supremacy.
Rohrer, M. Hummock in the Malookas, A.
Rosenberg, I. Dawn Behind Night.
Rossetti, C. Convent Threshold, The.
Gone Before.
Hark! the Alleluias of the great salvation.
Heaviness May Endure for a Night, But Joy Cometh in the Morning.
Pause, A.
Two Thoughts of Death.
Uphill [or Up-Hill].
Rossetti, D. Blessed Damozel, The.
St. John, D. No Heaven.
Salaam. Secondline Send Off.
Sanders, E. Leaves of Heaven, The.
Sappho. I don't expect to touch heaven.
Senryū, K. Judging by the pictures.
Serote. Hell, well, heaven.
Shakespeare, W. Sonnet 94: "They that have power [or pow't or powre] to hurt[e], and will do[e] none."
Shelley, P. To—: "One word is too often profaned."
Shin Tongyŏp. We have seen heaven.
Siegel, R. Hog Heaven.
Sigourney. Stars, The.
Sikelianos, Eleni. Heaven: "What was it I saw at the top."
Smith, P. Annie Pearl Smith Discovers Moonlight.
Song. Heaven.
Southey, C. Mariner's Hymn.
Southwell. New Heaven, New War[re].
Southwick. Earthly Light.
Spires. In Heaven It Is Always Autumn.
Spofford. Tryst, The.
Stevens, W. Of Heaven Considered as a Tomb.
Sylvester, J. "Were I as Base as Is the Lowly Plain".
Taneda Santoka. Heaven / doesn't kill me.
T'ao Ch'ien [or T'ao Yuan-ming]. Substance, Shadow, and Spirit ("Earth and heaven endure forever.").
Taylor, E. Meditation 8 (First Series).
Tekeyan. Dream.
Traherne. Innocence.
Unknown. Archangel Open the Door.
Beulah Railway, The.
Brother Moses Gone.
Dream of the Rood, The.
Elegy upon the Death of Mrs. A. Behn, the Incomparable Astrea, An.
Fare Ye Well.
God Got Plenty o' Room.
Golden Altar, The.
Good Lord in That Heaven.
Good-bye, Brother.
Heaven conserve thy course in quietness.
Holy Priestess of Heaven, The.
I Can't Stay Behind.
In Bath a wanton wife did dwell.
In the Mansions Above.
Lady Who Ascends into the Heavens, The.
Little Children, Then Won't You Be Glad!
My Body Rock 'Long Fever.
My Father, How Long!
O Brothers, Don't Get Weary.
Old Ship of Zion, The [North Carolina version].
Poet Dreamt of Heaven, The.
Poor Rosy.
Soldier stood at the pearly gate.
Sometimes I feel like a motherless child.

Soul's Desire, The.
Travel On.
Unknown, fr. Terezin Concentration Camp. On a Sunny Evening.
Vaughan, H. Peace.
Pilgrimage, The.
They Are All Gone into the World of Light!
Very. Birds of Passage, The.
Vietnamese Oral Tradition. From So Mountain.
Looking Out in All Directions.
Tao.
Waller, E. Of the Last Verses in the Book.
Watts, I. Mr. Gunston is Shown round Heaven [or To the Dear Memory of Thomas Gunston, Esq.].
Mrs. Warner Arrives Above [or An Elegiac Thought on Mrs. Anne Warner].
Whiting, G. My Blue Heaven.
Wilbur, R. Icarium Mare.
Wolfli. And now: And now: here begins Our Voyage, hunters and naturalists of indefatigable enthusiasm.
Wright, D. Map of the Kingdom, A.
Wright, K. Hoping It Might Be So.
Yeats. He Wishes for the Cloths of Heaven.
Young, A. Written in Bracing, Gray L.A. Rainlight.
Young, D. Invention of Heaven, The.
Zimmer. Zimmer Imagines Heaven.
Zucker, R. In Your Version of Heaven I am Younger.

Hebe
Unknown. Hebe and Ganymede.

Hebrew
Ali, A. In Arabic.
Amichai, Y. National Thoughts.
Caulfield. Merci Bien, Monsieur.
Gertler, P. Right Thing, The.
Kalinski, E. Teacher of Defeated Hebrew Language.
Moore, M. Past Is the Present, The.
Reznikoff. How difficult for me is Hebrew.
I have learnt the Hebrew blessing before eating bread.
Shabtai, Aharon. Hebrew Culture.
Volach, Y. Hebrew.

Hebrides
Clark, T. Some Details of Hebridean House Construction.
Longley, M. Hebrides, The.
Pfeiffer, E. Among the Hebrides.
Rosen, K. Kildan Women, The.

Hector
Berkson, B. Instinct.
Carson, A. TV is presocial, like Men.
Deguy. Here Often I Am.
Homer. Achilles with wild fury in his heart.
Death of Hector, The.
Hector Arms.
Hector Returns to Troy.
Night Piece: the Trojans outside Troy.
Then rash Patroclus with new fury glows.
To this, great hector said.
Iremonger. Hector.
Longley, M. Ceasefire.
Muir, E. Ballad of Hector in Hades.
Sappho. Herald came, The.

Hedgehogs
Archilochus. Fox knows many things, The.
Strategy.
Imbriglio, C. Aubade: "Dead woodchuck in the dog's mouth drooped, The."
Jones, D. Hedgehog, The.
Muldoon, P. Hedgehog.

Hedonism
Cummings, E. E. Since feeling is first.
MacNeice. Shelley and jazz and lieder and love and hymn-tunes.
Melville, H. After the Pleasure Party [Lines Traced under an Image of Amor Threatening].
Parker, D. Flaw in Paganism, The.
San Juan. Entelechy on the Libidinal Fringe.
Three for the Road.
Sapgir. Dionysus.
Weaver, A. Providence Journal V: Israel of

Puerto Rico.

Heine, Heinrich
Lazarus, E.   Venus of the Louvre.

Heirs and Heiresses
Donaghy, M.   Inheritance.
Fortini.   Seed, The.

Helen of Troy
Alcaeus [or Alkaios].   And excited the heart of Argive.
Her heart so stricken, Helen.
Story goes, from evil, The.
Crane, H.   For the Marriage of Faustus and Helen.
Doolittle, Hilda.   Helen.
I am not nor mean to be.
This is the spread of wings.
Euripides.   And Pergamos, / City of the Phrygians.
Homer.   Helen and the Elders.
Jackson, L.   Helen's Burning.
Landor, W.   Ianthe.
Lewis, J.   Helen Grown Old.
Lloyd, E.   Helen like the Rose.
Marlowe.   End of Doctor Faustus, The.
Was This the Face.
Poe.   To Helen ("Helen, thy beauty is to me.").
Sappho.   Anaktoria.
Some prefer a glory of horsemen; warships.
Some say an army of horsemen, others.
Some there are who say that the fairest thing seen.
Some think a fleet, a troop of horse.
Starodubtseva, N.   And it is cold here and a bit strange.
Stesichoros.   Helen suddenly saw a divine omen.
Valéry.   Helen ("I am the blue! I come from the lower world.").
Helen ("It is I, O Azure, come from the caves below.").
Walcott.   Menelaus.
Yeats.   Leda and the Swan.

Helicopters
Hume, C.   Helicopter Wrecked on a Hill.
Ritterbusch.   Choppers.
Senghor.   Young Sun's Greeting, The.

Heliogabalus
Hollander, J.   Heliogabalus.

Hell
Auden.   Hell.
Babu, S.   Let's Go to Hell.
Belloc.   Ballade of Hell and of Mrs. Roebeck.
To Dives.
Berlin.   Pack Up Your Sins and Go to the Devil.
Blake, W.   Marriage of Heaven and Hell, The.
Marriage of Heaven and Hell, The.
Boland, E.   Pomegranate, The.
Brecht, B.   Contemplating Hell.
Brontë, E.   Stanzas: "Often rebuked, yet always back returning."
Cernuda.   Lover Digresses, The.
Chinnov.   Do you think we might go to hell too?
Coleridge, M.   Wilderspin.
Cowley, H.   Invocation. To Horror.
Crashaw.   But Men loved Darkness[e] Rather Than [or Then] Light.
Dante Alighieri.   And so from bridge to bridge we went, talking.
Inferno.
Inferno: Canto 1.
Through me come into the city full of pain.
Dawe, B.   Only the Beards Are Different.
Dickinson, E.   My life closed twice before its close.
Pit—but Heaven over it, A.
You're right—"the way is narrow".
Dove, R.   Political.
Doyle, S.   Hell to Pay.
Dunbar, P.   Theology.
Eliot, T. S.   3. The Fire Sermon.
Elizabeth, Queen of Bohemia.   Verses by the Princess Elizabeth, Given to Lord Harington, of Exton, Her Preceptor.
Finkelstein, C.   Persephone's Notes.
Ford, F.   That Exploit of Yours.
Freeman, Jessica.   Part Evil.

Glück, L.   Day Without Night.
Gray, T.   Descent of Odin, The.
Greenwell, D.   Demeter and Cora.
Greer, J.   Rodin's "Gates of Hell".
Gryphius.   Hell.
Herbert, Z.   What Mr. Cogito Thinks About Hell.
What Mr. Cogito Thinks About Hell.
Herrick.   Hell ("Hell is no other, but a soundlesse pit.").
Hill, G.   Ovid in the Third Reich.
Housman.   Hell Gate.
Howard, R.   Giovanni da Fiesole on the Sublime.
Hummer, T.   Walt Whitman in Hell.
Issa.   Blossoming plum!
Dew spread / The seeds of hell.
In this world.
Never forget / We walk on hell.
O autumn winds.
Six Ways, The.
When plum / Blooms—.
Jacob, M.   Wallpaper of Mr. R. K., The.
Jin.   Judgement.
Johnson, Peter.   Hell.
Kelen.   First Circle, The.
Kimbrell, J.   True Descenders.
Kowit.   Hell: "I died & went to Hell & it was nothing like L.A.."
I Attend a Poetry Reading.
Langland, W.   Wool-chafed and wet-shoed I went from after.
Mandel, T.   Jews in Hell.
Merry.   Poet is Piqued, The [or Anna Matilda].
Milosz, C.   On the Other Side.
Milton.   Anon out of the earth a fabric huge.
Occupations of Hell.
Montale.   You know, I must leave you again and I can't.
Muir, E.   Good Man in Hell, The.
Naden.   Pessimist's Vision, The.
Nesbit, E.   Great Industrial Centre, A.
Nietzsche.   Undiscouraged.
Ocampo.   Report on Heaven and Hell.
Olson, C.   In Cold Hell, in Thicket.
Orr, G.   Insomnia Song.
Owen, W.   Strange Meeting.
Parker, D.   Coda: "There's little in taking or giving."
Parra, N.   Journey Through Hell.
Putnam.   Bill Gets Burned.
Rabi'a al-Adawiyya.   O my Lord.
Rich, A.   Lucifer in the Train.
Rimbaud, A.   Decidedly we are out of the world. No longer any sound.
Night in Hell.
Robinson, E.   Supremacy.
Seneca.   After Death Nothing Is.
Serote.   Hell, well, heaven.
Shelley, P.   Hell is a city much like London.
Södergran.   Hell.
Sorescu, M.   Fresco.
Swinburne.   Sonnet for a Picture.
Tate, A.   Cross, The.
Taylor, E.   Pit indeed of Sin: No water's here:, A.
Tendo-Nyojo.   Sixty-six years.
Unknown.   Dere's No Hidin' Place Down Dere.
Harrowing, The.
Petelia Tablet, The.
Vietnamese Oral Tradition.   Looking Out in All Directions.
Wallace, R.   Hell Mural, The: Panel I.
Winters, Y.   Summer Noon: 1941.

Hell's Angels
Ginsberg, A.   First Party at Ken Kesey's with Hell's Angels.
Gunn, T.   Black Jackets.

Help
Dickinson, E.   These Strangers, In a Foreign World.
Dorsey, T.   Take My Hand, Precious Lord.
Ezekiel.   Family.
Gallagher, T.   Little Invitation in a Hushed Voice.
Graves, R.   Grotesques.

Grosholz.   Eden.
Jacobs, B.   Lost.
Kocot, N.   Ordinary Evening, An.
Mead, J.   Memory, The.
Osherow.   9 (Looking through the Window: Psalm 121).
Shokushi.   Guide me on my way.
Unknown.   Hail, Mary.
Noble, enduring, ever-renewed peace do I attribute exclusively to his highness, the best of Caliphs, A.
Weitsman, Sojun Mel.   Mondo.
Zen Center Sangha.   Mondo.

Hemingway, Ernest
Dabydeen, C.   Hemingway.
Espada.   Man Who Beat Hemingway, The.
Feaver.   Hemingway's Hat.

Hemlocks
Ammons.   Improvisatin for Jerald Bullis, An.
Dickinson, E.   I think the Hemlock likes to stand.
Stevenson, A.   Hemlock at Sunset, A.
Weismiller.   Hemlocks in Autumn.

Hendrix, Jimi
McManus, J.   Two Songs for Hendrix.
Seibles, T.   Manic: A Conversation with Jimi Hendrix.

Henry I, King of England
Rossetti, D.   White Ship, The.

Henry, Prince of England (the Young King)
Bertrans de Born.   Planh for the Young English King.

Henry V, King of England
Shakespeare, W.   Henry V at the Siege of Harfleur.

Henry VIII, King of England
Harington, J.   Groom of the Chamber's Religion in King Henry the Eighth's Time, A.
Harington [or Harrington].   Groome of the Chambers religion in King Henry the eights time, A.
Skelton, J.   Laud and Praise Made For Our Sovereign Lord the King.

Hens
Caston, A.   Blowing Eggs.
Gehrke, S.   Walking Fields at Night South of Hampton, Iowa.
Jacobik, G.   Turkeys in August.
Martinson.   Henhouse.
McGonagall.   Hen It Is a Noble Beast, The.
Ransom, J.   Janet Waking.
Ssu-ma Hsiang-ju.   Cock-Phoenix, Hen-Phoenix.
Voigt.   Hen, The.
Wilbur, R.   Black November Turkey, A.
Willard, N.   Speckled Hen's Morning Song to Biddy Early, The.
See also **Chickens**

Heraclitus
Cory, W.   Heraclitus.
Dugan, A.   From Heraclitus.
Fore.   They Told Me, Heraclitus.
Hanlon, G.   They Told Me, Heraclitus.
Hopkins, G.   That Nature Is a Heraclitean Fire and of the Comfort of the Resurrection.
MacNeice.   Variation on Heraclitus.
Rondin, Leslie.   Heraclitus.

Herbs
Blue Cloud.   To-ta Ti-om.
Buson.   Rocks rising from the rushing water.
Char.   Dowry of Maubergeonne, The.
Duncan, R.   Glimpse, A.
Emerson, R.   Blight.
Goodison.   From the Garden of the Women Once Fallen.
Hadas, R.   Humble Herb is Rival to Prozac.
Hufana, A.   From the Raw.
Jacobs, J.   Snakeroot.
Konishi Raizan.   Green, green, green / Herbs splash.
Kumin, M.   Magellan Street, 1974.
Lindley, D.   Fennel.
Martinez, D.   Remedios.
Mathews, H.   Relics, The.
Miliauskaite.   In the Damp Places.
Milosz, C.   Goddess, A.

Rafferty, P. Willowherb.
Rohrer, M. Short History of Illumination, A.
Samara, M. Door of Roses.
Sisson. Herb-Garden, The.
Thomas, E. Old Man.
Unknown. Charm of the Nine Healing Herbs.
White, L. Acanthus.

Hercules
Rogers, S. To the Fragment of a Statue of
  Hercules, Commonly Called the Torso.
Rose, J. Suicide, The.
Seneca. Deaths of Orpheus and Hercules, The.
Stesichoros. Across from glorious Erytheia.

Herding
Duhig, I. Lammas Hireling, The.
Qunanbaev, A. Summer: "Summer climbs the
  mountains."
Sappho. Herdsmen crush under their feet.
Zakama, K. Call of the Fulani Maid.

See also **Shepherds and Shepherdesses**

Heresy and Heretics
Kendall, M. Fossil, A.
Kitahara Hakushū. Secret Song of the Heretics.
Lysohorsky. Ballad of Jan Palach, Student and
  Heretic.
McHugh, H. What He Thought.
Reading, P. This is unclean: to eat turbots on
  Tuesdays.

Heritage and Heredity
Abu Khalid. Mother's Inheritance.
  Tattoo Writing.
Ali, M. Heritage.
Alvi, M. Backgrounds.
Aubert, A. Blood to Blood.
Bapiraju, A. Steps.
Behar, R. Survivals.
Behlen, Charles. My Grandfather's Hammer.
Bermeo, O. Oda para Leticia.
Bialosky, J. Silver.
Blackwell, Holley. Law of Trichotomy.
Blanchard, Mary Loving. Bloodlines.
Bridges, C. Gordian Knot.
Cager, Chezia Thompson. Callaloo.
Cariaga. Family Tree, The.
Carroll, K. For Brothas That Like to Holla.
Chandar, M. Birth Postponed, A.
Chunghur Hyujung. Looking Back at My
  Shadow.
Cisneros, S. You Bring Out the Mexican in Me.
Clifton, L. I was born with twelve fingers.
Cooper, A. Stepping to da Muse/Sic.
De Trejo, Angela. Farewell San Miguel,
  splendid with your harvested fields.
Dumas, H. Afro-American.
  Son of Msippi.
Ferebee, Gideon. Refugee.
Fisher, L. Child of the Sun.
Forbes, C. Gone.
Foreman, Paul. Brazos de Dios.
Gelbtrunk, A. Coincidence.
Goodison. Turn Thanks to Miss Mirry.
Harrison, T. Heredity.
Hayes, T. Blue Terrance, The.
  What I Am.
Humphreys, E. Poughkeepsie.
Jashuva, G. I Was One of Them.
Jeffers, H. To Keep from Shouting Something.
Jeffers, L. O Africa, where I baked my bread.
Johnson, J. What Is There For Us?
Jones, Ceri Wyn. Influence.
Kalina, R. I Am of the Tribe of Yehuda.
Kay, J. Pride.
Kerlikowske. Acceptance Speech.
King, R. Another day.
Larkin, J. Legacy.
Lewis, M. Gullah Women.
  My Mother.
Lewis, S. Vineyard Place in My Care, A.
Limburg, J. Seder Night with My Ancestors.
Llwyd, Iwan. Sure, You Can Ask Me a Personal
  Question.
Martinez, D. Temporary Losses.
Mason, Keith Antar. I Am a Creature of the
  Obvious.
McDowell, Garrett. Blooming in the Valley, A.

McGrath, T. Last Will and Testament.
McGuckian. Slips.
Mercado, N. Milla.
Miller, M. Gift from Kenya.
Morales, A. Ending Poem.
  Other Heritage, The.
Morales. Ending Poem.
Morgenstern, Felicia L. Soul Roots.
Moscona. Naturalization Papers.
Muldoon, P. Grand Conversation, The.
Neal, L. Holy Days.
Neruda. I come to speak through your dead
  mouth.
Newton, Violette. Going Back to Ireland.
Ondaatje. House on a Red Cliff.
Owen, Gerallt Lloyd. Inheritance: "We had a
  country to keep."
Penn, M. Calling Up the Spirit of the Lost
  Child.
Petillar, T. Generation Gap.
Piñero. This Is Not the Place Where I was
  Born.
Platner, I. We Are the Heirs.
Preston, R. Italist Chant.
Ramanujan. Drafts.
  Self-Portrait.
Rogers, D. Near the Rio Grand.
Rosario, M. Latter-day Mother Courage.
Roth, F. Marriage.
Saito, Brynn Noelle. Turkey People.
Savageau. Like the Trails of Ndakinna.
  To Human Skin.
Schwartz, R. L. Flamenco Guitar.
Shannon, A. Sunday: "It could have been the
  way the Southern."
Shcherbina. Still-Life.
Silook, Susie. Uncle Good Intentions.
Song. Spaces We Leave Empty.
Spahr, J. December 4, 2002.
St. Germain, S. Cajun.
Stone, R. For My Dead Red-Haired Mother.
Sun, Phillina. Untitled: "In the living room sit
  the men."
Tafolla. This River Here.
Tallie, M. Raindrop Women.
Thomas, R. S. Gifts.
Williams, Stephanie. Peerage.
Wong, N. It's in the Blood.

Hermes
Klink, J. Orpheus. Eurydice. Hermes.

Hermit Crabs
Oliver, M. Hermit Crab, The.

Hermits
Bibb. Hermit, The.
Birney. Bushed.
Bishop, E. Chemin de Fer.
Ch'i-chi. Written on a Summer Day in the City.
Chia Tao. Looking for a Recluse but Failing to
  Find Him.
  Looking for the Recluse and Not Finding Him.
  Meng Jung, Gainfully Unemployed.
  Seeking but Not Finding the Recluse.
  Written at the Dwelling of a Recluse.
Ch'ien Ch'i. Dedicated to the Hermit Cui.
  Visit to the Hermit Ts'ui.
Ching An. Night Sitting.
Ch'iu Wei. Seeking a Hermit on West Mountain
  and Not Finding Him.
Cho Sik. Wearing hemp clothes in the coldest
  winter.
Chŏng Ch'ŏl. Little Odes on Mount Star.
Chungji. Hermit's Life, A.
Daegak Euchon. For Sanje, a Hermit.
Davies, W. H. Hermit, The.
Drayton. With solitude what sorts, that here's
  not wondrous rife?
Gunn, T. Last Man, The.
Hamhur Kiwha. Higher Living Away from the
  World.
Hsü Pen. To a Hermit in the Mountains.
Hueung Powoo. Spring on the Mountain.
K'ung Chih-kuei. Proclamation on North
  Mountain.
Kuo P'o. First Poem of Wandering Immortals.
Li Po. Looking for Master Yung Ts'un near His
  Hermitage.

  On Visiting a Taoist Master in the Daitian
    Mountains and Not Finding Him.
  Questions Answered.
Lleshanaku, L. Awakening of the Eremite, The.
Lowell, R. Skunk Hour.
Mahon. Mayo Tao, The.
Matthews, T. Private But Sulphurous.
Melville, H. Recluse, The.
Meng Hao Jan. Returning at Night to Lumen
  Mountain.
  Returning Late to Lu-men Shan.
Mookam Choinul. Living at Eunjok Hermitage.
Muso Soseki. Old Mountain.
  On the Wall of Cloud-Friend Hut.
Naong. Lonely Hermitage.
Ní Chuilleanáin. Studying the Language.
Po Chü-i. Invitation to Hsiao Ch'u-shih.
Pyŏn Wŏngyu. To a Friend.
Ray, H. Hermit and the Soul, The.
Shih Shu. After Shih-te ("Perfumed springs
  ripple over skeletal outcrops.").
Sŏ Kyŏngdŏk. My mind is foolish.
Sŏng Hon. By Chance.
Song Sun. I have spent ten years.
Stevenson, A. He Who Loved Beauty.
Sy, T. Cup of Clear Water, A.
  Hermit Thoughts.
Tate, J. Radical Departure, A.
Trần Thái-Tông, King. To the Monk Dúc Son at
  Thanh-phong Monastery.
Tu Fu [*or* Du Fu]. Written on the Wall at
  Chang's Recluse Home.
Unknown. I live at the foot of the mountain.
  In the valley where the stream leaps.
  King and Hermit.
  Made his hut in the vale, a tall man stretched
    out.
  Song of Manchan the Hermit, The.
Walcott. Winding Up.
Wang Chiu-ssu. Floating, floating, the river
  waters.
Wang Wei. At Li's Mountain Hermitage.
  Hermitage at Chung-nan Mountain.
Wang Yang-ming. Taoist Song.
Wei Ying-wu. Poem to a Taoist Hermit on
  Quanjiao Mountain, A.
White, H. Sonnet: "Give me a cottage on some
  Cambrian wild."
Wilcox, F. Nine Flower Mountain.
Yasui. My grass hut.
Yüan Hung-tao. On Receiving My Letter of
  Termination.

Hero and Leander
Byron, G. Written After Swimming from Sestos
  to Abydos.
Chapman, G. New light gives new directions,
  Fortunes new.
Donne. Hero and Leander.
Keats. On a Leander Gem which Miss
  Reynolds, My Kind Friend, Gave Me.
Marlowe. Amorous Leander, beautiful and
  young.
  By this Leander being near the land.
  His bodie was as straight as Circes wand.
  Love at First Sight.
  Men of wealthy Sestos, every year, The.

See also **Leander**

Herod the Great
Causley. Innocent's Song.
Duffy, C. Queen Herod.
Hanzlik. Clap Your Hands for Herod.
Longfellow, H. Three Kings, The.
Mendes, M. Christmas 1961.
Witting. Curse on Herod, A.
Wylie. Twelfth Night.

Heroes and Heroines
Adkins, G. Arthur.
Afrika, T. Funeral of Anton Fransch, The.
Aneirin. Youth.
Anstett. Man Saves Own Life.
Arnold, M. To the Hungarian Nation.
Auden. O What Is That Sound [Which So
  Thrills the Ear].
Beer, P. In Memory of Stevie Smith.
Benjamin, P. Press On.
Bentley, N. Iron Man of the Hoh.

Berkson, B. Blue Is the Hero.
Brooks, G. Negro Hero.
Browning, E. Critics say that epics have died out, The.
Bunting. Remember, imbeciles and wits.
Camões [or Camõens or Camoëns], L. Feats of Arms, and famed heroick Host, The.
Campbell, T. Hohenlinden.
Carroll, L. Jabberwocky.
Ch'ien T'ao. In Praise of Ching K'o.
Collins, W. How Sleep the Brave.
Comfort, A. Song for the Heroes.
Creeley. Heroes.
Crosby, E. Hail to the hero!
Cummings, E. E. My father moved through dooms of love.
De Tabley. Sonnet: "Record is nothing, and the hero great."
Djogo. National Hero, The.
Dryden, J. 'Tis war again, and I am glad 'tis so.
Dumas, H. Saba.
Dylan. Quinn the Eskimo.
Emerson, R. Forerunners.
Encarnacion. Threading the Miles.
Evans, D. People, The.
Flaccus, G. Book 7.
Ford, F. For the white-limbed heroes of Hellas ride by upon their horses.
Gilboa, A. And My Brother Was Silent.
Graves, R. Leveller, The.
Greenberg, S. Conduct.
Gunn, T. Byrnies, The.
Harrison, J. This matted and glossy photo of Yesenin.
Hemans. Casabianca.
Heóghusa. Winter Campaign, A.
Herbert, Z. Elegy of Fortinbras.
Envoy of Mr. Cogito, The.
Homer. But Jove against the Greeks sent forth his son.
Invocation, The: "Wrath of *Peleus* Son, O Muse, resound, The."
Hwang Chini. Mountains are steadfast.
Ibycus. They destroyed the famous and wealthy.
Italicus. Death comes in strange forms and contrasting images.
Furiously along the banks stormed Hannibal.
Joseph, A. My Father's Heroes ("He gloried in the feats.").
My Father's Heroes ("Not JFK, not MLK.").
Keats. To Kosciusko.
Kefala. Party, The.
Koertge. Sidekicks.
Korinna [or Corinna]. But I sing the excellence of heroes.
Lamar. San Jacinto.
Longfellow, H. Skeleton in Armor [or Armour], The.
Lowell, R. For the Union Dead.
Lysohorsky. Ballad of Jan Palach, Student and Heretic.
MacLean, S. Heroes.
Mangan, J. O'Hussey's Ode to the Maguire.
Markham, E. Lincoln, the Man of the People.
Marvell. At the demolishing, this seat.
Mehmedinović, Semezdin. Hero.
Montague, J. Old Mythologies.
Moore, M. Hero, The.
Nichols, G. Wha Me Mudder Do.
Olds, S. Language of the Brag, The.
Owen, Gerallt Lloyd. Man on the Horizon, The.
Padgett, R. Talking to Vladimir Mayakovsky.
Phillips, C. Loose Hinge.
Raine, K. Heroes.
Rich, A. Letters in the Family.
Richards, L. Molly Pitcher.
Rilke. We Must Die Because We Have Known Them.
Rosenberg, I. Dead Heroes, The.
Sassoon, S. Glory of Women.
Seferis. Last Stop.
Simonides. Thermopylai's dead.
Simpson, L. Heroes, The.
Spender, S. I Think Continually of Those Who Were Truly Great.
Seascape.

Stafford, W. At the Grave of My Brother: Bomber Pilot.
Su Tung-p'o. Tune: "Charming Nien-Nu".
Szymborska, W. Pietà.
Thayer, E. Casey at the Bat.
Unknown. Beowulf [Heaney Translation].
Combat of Ferdia and Cúchulainn.
Hēr Æ???oelstān cyning, eorla drihten.
Heroes are always alive.
Indian Hero's Creed, The.
May you perish on the field of honor, my beloved!
One son of God, The.
What else can he do but behave like a hero.
Various authors. He battled against the king's enemy.
He hit the backs of forty tailed deer.
Heaven sent a genius.
Seeing the bodies lying in heaps.
Wishing to entrust him with a great task.
Zealous to deliver the suffering people.
Wadsworth, W. Need for Attention, The.
Wallace-Crabbe. Collective Invention, The.
Yejong, King of Koryŏ. Dirge for Two Generals.

Heroin
Durcan. Death by Heroin of Sid Vicious, The.
Gould, J. I Learn a Lesson About Our Society.
Groves. Heroine.
Herd. Gia.
Hicok. Heroin.
Hull, L. Adagio.
Matthews, W. Bud Powell, Paris, 1959.
Sleigh. In the Park.
St. Germain, S. Addiction.
Warsh. White Nights.
See also **Drug Addiction**

Herons
Alcosser. Glory Monster.
Annand. Heron.
Basho. Lightning.
Lightning-gleam, A.
Brannon, J. Evolution on 38th Street.
Buson. Evening wind.
Chiyojo. Were it not for / Cries in snow.
Coles, G. Heron in the Alyn.
Evasco, M. Heron-Woman.
Henson, S. Heron, The.
Kizer, C. Great Blue Heron, The.
Lowell, A. Hoar-Frost.
MacCaig. Heron.
Moore, R. Height.
Murphy, K. Meditation on the Great Blue Heron.
Roethke. Heron, The.
Rogers, D. Great Blue Heron.
Sanger, Peter. Heron.
Smith, D. Out Whistling.
Stafford, W. Spirit of Place: Great Blue Heron.
Tomlinson, C. Heron.
Watkins, V. Heron, The.
Yasui. My grass hut.

Herrick, Robert
Cole, W. Robert Herrick.
Robert Herrick.
Herrick. On Himself[e] ("I fear[e] no Earthly Powers.").
On Himself[e] ("I will no longer kiss.").
On Himselfe ("Weepe for the dead, for they have lost this light.").
Upon the Loss[e] of His Mistresses.

Herring
Leslie, K. Sonnet: "Silver herring throbbed thick in my seine, The."
MacDiarmid, H. With the Herring Fishers.
Nairne. Caller Herrin'.
Novak, H. Packing Herring.
Smith, I. Herring Girls, The.
Stéfan, Jude. Herrings and Birch Trees.
Thomson, D. Herring Girls, The.

Heston, Charlton
Weil, J. Ben Hur.

Hiawatha
Jones, Nesta Wyn. Beaches.
Longfellow, H. Hiawatha: The White Man's

Foot.
On the fourth day of his fasting.

Hibiscus
Bangaramma, C. Hibiscus on the Lake.
Pei Di. Bank of the Magnolias, The.
Wang Wei. Bank of the Magnolias, The.

Highlands of Scotland
Raine, K. Highland Graveyard.
Young, D. For the Old Highlands.
See also **Scottish Highlands**

Highwaymen
Kumin, M. Highwaymen, The.
Noyes, A. Highwayman, The.
Pastan. Bess.

Highways
Anania. Fall, The.
Interstate 80.
Balaban. Heading Out West.
Beer, P. Ballad of the Underpass.
Behrle. Charm of the Highway Strip, The.
Bukowski. Last song, The.
Cassity. Other-Directed.
Davis, G. August Fires.
Davis, W. I-35, South of Waco.
Fraser, S. Looking Out to Sea Again on the Uptown Express.
Getsi. Woman Hanging from Lightpole, Illinois Route 136.
Healy, E. Artemis in Echo Park.
Hongo. Confession of the Highway / The Hermit Speaks.
Porphyry of Elements, A.
Inada. High-Five for I-5, A.
Keller, D. Melancholy.
Kooser. Interchange.
Kumin, M. Requiem on I-89.
Lewis, B. Flyover Elegies.
McDaniel, W. California Entertainment, 1936.
Mueller, L. Highway Poems.
Pak Sŏwŏn. Highway, The.
Paloff, B. On Transportation.
Shepherd, R. Itinerary.
Troup, B. (Get Your Kicks On) Route 66!
Yates, D. Sunset Along U.S. Highway 90 Between Langtry and Sanderson.
See also **Roads**

Hiking and Hikers
Atwood-Fukuda. Ballybunion.
Betjeman. Hike on the Downs, A.
Fischer, N. Tuesday, 17 April.
Glazer, M. Map.
Kenyon, J. Depression in Winter.
Kinsella, T. Route of the Táin, The.
McPherson, S. Wings and Seeds: For My Birth Mother.
Merwin. Hearing.
Revard. October, Isle of Skye.
Simmerman. Take a Hike.

Hills and Mountains
Ammons. Close-up.
Mountain Talk.
Atkins, R. Lines in Recollection.
Barnes, W. Hill-Shade, The.
Bogan, L. Last Hill in a Vista.
Bontemps. To a Young Girl Leaving the Hill Country.
Borges. Matthew 5:1–12; Seeing the crowds, he went up on the mountain.
Brontë, E. Stanzas: "Often rebuked, yet always back returning."
Chan Fang-sheng. Sailing into the South Lake.
Ch'ŏn Kŭm. Night draws near in a mountain village.
Chŏng Chiyong. Paengnokdam: White Deer Lake.
Rain.
Chŏng Ch'ŏl. Little Odes on Mount Star.
Coleridge, M. Lady of Trees, The.
Coleridge, S. Blest is the tarn which towering cliffs o'ershade.
Creeley. Hill, The.
Di Prima. I Ching.
Dickinson, E. Alter! When the Hills do—.
Mountains grow—unnoticed, The.
Douglas, L. Two Loves.

Dyer, J. Grongar Hill.
Emerson, R. Fable: "Mountain and the squirrel, The."
Field. Eros.
Frost, R. Meeting and Passing.
Garner. Summer Solstice.
Hammerstein. Folks Who Live on the Hill, The.
  Sound of Music, The.
Hannon. Temporary Heart.
Hanzlicek, C. Sierra Noon.
Hecht, A. Hill, A.
Helton. Lonesome Water.
Hemans. Mountain Sanctuaries.
Hove. Red Hills of Home.
Hsieh Ling-yün. Scene from South Hill to North Hill Passing the Lake.
Huntington, W. Lowlands.
Hwang Chini. Blue mountains speak of my desire.
Jackson, H. Cheyenne Mountain.
Kavanagh, P. Shancoduff.
Ki Joon. Elegy for Myself.
Kim Ch'anghyŏp. Mountain Folk.
Kim Sowŏl. Mountain Flowers.
Kooser. City Limits.
K'ung Chih-kuei. Trip on Mount T'ai-P'ing.
Lanier, S. From the Flats.
Leopardi. Antistrophe.
  Infinite, The.
Li Ho. High the Mount of Wu.
Lu Chi. Song of Mount T'ai.
Luschei, G. Water Song, The.
MacLean, S. Kinloch Ainort.
Manning, Maurice. First.
Meynell, A. Watershed, The.
Milton. On the Late Massacre [or Massacher] in Piedmont [or Piemont].
Mirabai [or Mira Bai]. All I Was Doing Was Breathing.
Muir, E. Childhood.
Paek Sŏk. Mountain Rain.
Pak Tujin. Tobong Mountain.
Pao Chao. Ascend Lu-Shan.
Pei Di. Hill of Huazi, The.
Pettit. Self-Portrait Approaching Promontory, Utah.
Po Chü-i. Madly Singing in the Mountains.
  Passing Tianmen Street in Chang'an and Seeing a Distant View of Zhongnan Mountains.
Raine, K. To My Mountain.
Robinson, E. Dark Hills, The.
Rohrer, M. Hummock in the Malookas, A.
Rossetti, C. Uphill [or Up-Hill].
Rossetti, D. 70: The Hill Summit.
Rukeyser, M. Alloy.
Sin Hŭm. Don't laugh if my roof beams.
Sissman. Big Rock-Candy Mountain, The.
Smith, C. To the South Downs.
Snyder, G. Mid-August at Sourdough Mountain Lookout.
Sŏ Chŏngju. Kilimanjaro Sunrise.
Spender, S. Pylons, The.
Stafford, W. Holding the Sky.
Stickney, T. Mt. Lykaion.
Tennyson, A. Unwatched, the garden bough shall sway.
Thomas, R. S. Lonely Farmer, The.
  Pietà.
Ts'ao Ts'ao. Bitter Cold: A Song.
Tu Fu [or Du Fu]. Chaos of mountains upon mountains, A.
  Looking at Mount T'ai-Shan.
Unknown. Pass where the winds pause before they cross.
  Song of Green Mountain.
Wang Wei. Hill of Huazi, The.
  In the Mountain.
  Mount Chung-Nan.
Winters, Y. By the Road to the Air-Base.
Wordsworth, W. Trosachs, The.
Wu Yun. From the mountain's end, sight of coming smoke.
Yeats. Matthew 28:16–20; Now the eleven disciples went to Galilee.
Yi Hwang. Twelve Songs of Tosan.
Yi I. Nine Songs of Mount Ko.

Yi Tal. Mountain Temple.
Yüan Hung-tao. Slowly, Slowly Poem, The.
See also Mountain Climbing

Himalayas
Lea, S. Hundred Himalayas, A.
Szymborska, W. Notes from a Nonexistent Himalayan Expedition.

Hinduism and Hindus
Basu, R. How are you faring, Uma.
  I had a good dream last night.
Basu Rāy, S. Three Kalis appeared in Daksinesvar.
Bhāndārī, S. Ma, You are Brahmani in the world of Brahma.
  Menaka says, Hey listen, Mountain King.
Bhatt, S. Parvati.
Bhattācārya, A. Get up, get up, Mountain: no more sleep for you!
Bhattācārya, K. Bee of my mind, The.
  Consulting the omens.
  Crazy Mind.
  Ever-blissful Kali.
  External rituals mean nothing.
  From her autumn-lotus mouth.
  From now on.
  Go, my Lord of the Mountains.
  Hara came and made off with my Gauri.
  Here, Queen of the Mountains.
  Hey, Hara, Ganges-Holder.
  Hey, Mountain King, Gauri is sulking.
  How can that black woman be so beautiful?
  How could you have forgotten her.
  How will You rescue me, Tara?
  I know, I know, Mother.
  Is my black Mother Syama really black?
  Jaya, tell him that Uma will not be sent.
  Kali / Is everything You do misleading?
  Kali! / Today in the dark grove.
  Kali, what family are You from?
  Kali, you have removed all my difficulties.
  King of the Mountains is on his way to Hara's abode, The.
  Mother / You're always finding ways to amuse Yourself.
  My Gauri / You've come home!
  My Uma has come!
  Other than Your two red feet, Syama.
  Queen asks, The.
  So, forgetful Mahadeva.
  Stay within yourself, Mind.
  Tara, Mother / Lift me out by the hair.
  Tell me, Syama.
  Tell me / What can I do?
  Turn back, Uma.
  Unperturbed at the battle.
  What a dream I had last night!
  What happened? / The ninth night is over.
  What's the fault of the poor mind?
  Who can describe the waves of Mother Syama's world?
  Who is this.
  Who is this enchantress.
  Withered tree doesn't blossom, The.
  You ask me, Queen, time after time.
Bhattācārya, M. Everyone's flocking to Gajan.
  I've gone mad drinking nectar.
  Look at all these waves.
  Ma, are you really dead?
  Oh Ma Kali, for a long time now.
  Screening its face amongst lotus stalks.
  Tell me, what are you doing now, Mind.
  There's a huge hullabaloo in my lotus heart.
  What shall I say to You, Sankari?
  You can't catch the thief, Mind.
  Your behavior proves how stingy You are, Ma.
Bringhurst. Parśvanatha.
Cakrabartī, N. Can you claim to win.
Cakrabarttī, M. Ma, if You wore a Benarasi sari.
  Wherever there's a woman in any Bengali home.
Candī, A. Bring Tara quickly, Mountain.
Cross, E. Shakti.
  Shakti.
Dās, R. Now I'll see whether Siva.
Dāsdatta, R. Because You love cremation

grounds.
Deb, A. I started a fire with Kali's name.
Debī, T. Tara, this is why I call upon You.
Dharker. Purdah, 1.
Dīnrām. Being the child of a Mad Mother.
  From the time of the womb.
  I've given up wanting.
  Ma, I've drunk Your poisoned nectar.
  O Baba! Look at this Cadak tree.
  Out of love for You.
  Renunciation's agonies.
Ghos, G. I plaster myself with ashes.
  Who said / If you took the name All-Destroyer.
  You're home, Uma! Stay here.
Gupta, I. I got some news from Kailasa!
Hannon. Real Estate.
Hass, R. To Phil Dow, in Oregon.
Hemans. Indian City, The.
Hirshfield, J. Painting.
Islām, N. Don't go back, Ma, don't go back, Mother.
  He who has seen my Mother.
  Let's be girls, Ma.
  Now there'll be a new mantra, Mother.
  Oh hey, All-Destroyer.
  Syama Mother's lap a-climbing.
  Syama wakes on the cremation grounds.
  Talk to me, javas, talk to me.
  Wake up, Syama, wake up, Syama!
  Wherever are the lowly, the suffering, and the poor.
Jayadeva. Song of Krishna: The Fourth Song, Sung with Raga "Ramakari".
Kabir. Clay Jug, The.
  Hopeful Spiritual Athlete, The.
  Lamp without Oil, The.
  Meeting, The: "When my friend is away from me, I am depressed."
  Music without Strings, The.
  My First Marriage.
  Only Woman Awake, The.
  Owl and the Moon, The.
  Thirsty Fish, The.
  To Be a Slave of Intensity.
  What Made Kabir a Servant.
  Why Arrange the Pillows.
Kalamaras, G. Banaras Is Another Name for the World.
  Lamps Are Brought In, The.
Kolatkar. Low Temple, A.
Lewis, G. Ménage à Trois.
Māhtābcānd, M. Who is this, all alone? Whose woman is She.
Majumdār, H. Jaya / Don't wake up Hara's wife.
Mandal, B. I'm not a child any more, Syama.
Mirabai [or Mira Bai]. Clouds, The.
  Music, The.
Mukhopādhyāy, K. Am I afraid of the tenth day?
  Is there any treasure like the Mother's name?
  Ma, the mail train is leaving now.
Mukhopādhyāy, N. Use your mental eye.
Mukhopādhyāy, R. Why should I sit alone, eyes closed.
Nandī Majumdār, R. Mind, I'm talking to you.
Nandī, R. I understand now, Tara, I understand.
  Mind, let's go to an estate that's decent.
Pāthak, G. I'll worship You with tears, Ma.
Pātunī, N. Ma, Hara's Beloved, Tara.
Ramanujan. Death and the Good Citizen.
Rāy, D. It's no one else's fault, Syama Ma.
  Wake up, wake up, Mother!
  Who is this black.
Rāy, K. Tara, You are Cintamayi, Full of Thought.
Rāy, M. N. You've enchanted the world.
Rāy, M. R. Give me food.
  Moon flashes in Her blessed face, The.
Rāy, N. Everything is Your wish, Tara.
Rāy, R. Who is this.
Rāy, R. Mountain / Whose woman have you brought home to our mountain city?
Rāy, T. Wait a moment, Death.
Ruskhan. In Praise of Krishna.
Sāheb, A. Victory to Yogendra's Wife, Great

Illusion!
Sama, B. Song, The.
Sen, R. At last I have a way to understand.
  Brother / This world.
  Can someone / Called Daughter of a Stone.
  Death, get out of here!
  Her face / Is a spotless moon.
  Hey, it's not wine I drink.
  Hey! Who is She, dark as clouds.
  How wonderful! Look what.
  I have learned.
  I'll die of mental anguish.
  It's not Siva.
  It's silly to hope for Father's wealth.
  Kali, Ma.
  Kulakundalini, Goddess Full of Brahman, Tara.
  Let me tell You a thing or two, Tara.
  Look here.
  Love Her, Mind.
  Ma, You're inside me.
  Managing the house is a big problem.
  Meditate on Kali! Why be anxious?
  Mind, don't be duped by others' sneers.
  Mind, how do you think you'll find Her?
  Mind, why this separation from the Mother's
    feet?
  Mind, you're still not rid of your illusions.
  Mother, make *me* Your treasurer.
  My Mind.
  My Mind, my helmsman.
  Oh Kali Full of Brahman!
  Oh Mind, you don't know how to farm.
  Oh my Mind, worship Kali.
  Oh my Mind! You're just spinning.
  So, Mind / You've decided to go on pilgrimage?
  Supreme Savior of Sinners.
  Tara, what more are You planning?
  Tell me.
  This is a fine mess.
  This time I've realized the essence.
  This time, Kali.
  Tongue, call out.
  Wait a minute, Death.
  What a joke!
  What's the fault of the poor mind?
  Who can understand Kali?
  Who is that Syama woman.
  World-Mother's police chief, The.
  World's a shoreless ocean, The.
Sharma, P. Action-Packed Sonnet.
Snyder, G. No Shoes No Shirt No Service.
Unknown. Get up, Mountain, get up!
  My lover is Hindu and I am a Muslim.
Yeats. Indian upon God, The [*or* An].

Hip-Hop
Asim, J. Hip Hop Bop.
Chavis, N. Enter(f*#@ckin)tained.
Cousins, L. Ms. Cousins' Rap.
Gaines, R. Kill the dj.
Johnson, L. Flow, The.
Jordan, J. Owed to Eminem.
Kearney, D. Rep/resent.
Kwabena, A. Doin'.
L'Abbé, Sonnet. Freestyle (Why They Don't
  Like Rap).
Lynch, C. Ancestral Echoes/Rap Music.
Maxwell, D. All Up in There.
Moore, J. I'm a Hip Hop Cheerleader.
Payne, F. Conjugation of the verb: to blow.
Stanard, C. Rap Is.

Hippies
Hirsch, E. Days of 1968.
Lothamer. Allen.
Mayer, B. Test 1 How to design freedom. How
  fine does the.
Seale, J. Travel North: The Rules.
Umpierre, L. Statue, The.

Hippopotamuses
Barrington, P. I Had a Hippopotamus.
Cole, J. Hippopotamus.
Eliot, T. S. Hippopotamus, The.
Jones, B. Pregnant Woman.
Tellegen. If Just For Once.

Hips
Clifton, L. Homage to my hips.
Jacobs, H. About our hips.

Hiroshige, Ando
Ruefle. Intended, The.

Hiroshima, Japan
"Agyeya.". Hiroshima.
Collins, A. Hiroshima Day at the Riviera
  Coffeeshop.
Dougherty, E. Why I Think About Hiroshima
  and Nagasaki.
Eich. Geometrical Place.
Fell, A. August 6, 1945.
Forché. Garden Shukkei-en, The.
  Testimony of Light,The.
Hahn, K. Bath, The: August 6, 1945.
Hahn, O. Vision of Hiroshima.
Johnson, K. High Altitude Photo of Hiroshima
  (Circa 1944).
Kaminsky, M. Questions: "If I shriek."
Kaschnitz. Hiroshima.
Kinnell. Fundamental Project of Technology,
  The.
Kirkup. No More Hiroshimas.
Kurihara Sadako. When We Say "Hiroshima".
Levertov. Gathered at the River.
Levine, P. Horse, The: "They spoke of the horse
  alive."
Mirikitani. Shadow in Stone.
Roripaugh, L. Hiroshima Maiden.
Sakaki. Memorandum.
Salter. Welcome to Hiroshima.
Sankichi, T. At the Makeshift Aid Station.
  August 6, 1950.
  Flames.
  Shadow, The: "Cheap movie theaters, saloons,
    fly-by-night markets."
Steensen, S. State of affairs is thinkable,
  eventually, A.
Strasser, J. Protest at Los Alamos, August 2000.
Stryk, L. Return to Hiroshima.

Hispanics
Blanco, R. El Malibú.
Boss, L. When You Are Grown, Amanda Rose.
Castillo, A. Me and Baby.
Clark, C. Border Affair, A.
Delgado, J. Awakened in a Field.
  Campesinos.
  Chuparosa.
  Dandelion.
  I-5 Incident.
Dougherty. Puerto Rican Girls of French Hill,
  The.
Dubin, A. She's a Latin from Manhattan.
Espada. Beloved Spic.
González, R. Death of the Farm Workers' Cat.
  Perla at the Mexican Border Assembly Line of
  Dolls.
Guevara, M. Doña Josefina Counsels Doña
  Concepción Before Entering Sears.
Healy, E. Moroni on the Mormon Temple /
  Angel on the Wall.
  Two Centuries in One Day.
Herández-Ávila. Presente.
Horst, C. Ugly Poem.
Meléndez. ¡Hey Yo / Yo Soy!
Norte, M. Peeping Tom Tom Girl.
Perdomo, W. New Boogaloo.
Riggs, L. Santo Domingo Corn Dance.
Suárez, V. Donatilia's Unrequited Love
  Remedy.
Vigil, A. As the Beer Trucks Eclipse the Light
  of Morning.
  At the Stop Light, the Braided Blond Man.
  Hogarcito de La Madrugada, El.
  That's the Way, Uh Huh, Uh Huh, I Liked It.
See also **Chicanos and Chicanas**

History and Historians
Acam-Oturu. Agony . . . A Resurrection, An.
Aiyejina. When the Monuments.
Alexander, E. West Indian Primer.
Ali, A. Dacca Gauzes, The.
  Farewell: "At a certain point I lost track of
    you."
Alvi, M. Backgrounds.
Ama Ata Aidoo. Gynae One.
Amichai, Y. Rustle of History's Wings, as They
  Used to Say Then, The.
Angelou, M. Family Affairs.

Antler. American History in Context.
Anzaldúa. Cultures.
Atwood. Loneliness of the Military Historian,
  The.
Auden. Fall of Rome, The.
Baca. Mi Tío Baca el Poeta de Socorro.
Baker, K. Nacogdoches Speaks.
Ballowe, J. Starved Rock.
Baraka, I. Three Modes of History and Culture.
Baraka, R. In the Tradition Too.
Beer, P. Millennium.
Benét, R. *et al.* So we march into the present.
Benét, S. So we march into the present.
Berry, W. History.
  Let Us Pledge.
  Meditation in the Spring Rain.
Berryman. Boston Common.
Bly, R. After the Industrial Revolution, All
  Things Happen at Once.
Boland, E. That the Science of Cartography Is
  Limited.
Bond, E. If.
Borges. Compass.
  Page to Commemorate Colonel Suárez, Victor at
  Junín, A.
Brathwaite, E. Citadel.
  Mmenson.
Broughton, J. Aglow in Nowhere.
Brouwer, J. History: "In Boston, a tongue of
  red paint traces the city's history, from
  Massacre to Tea Party to Faneuil Hall."
Brown, S. Let Them Call It Jazz.
Bunting. Loaded with mail of linked lies.
Burlingame. Walking Past the Dugout of Felix
  McKittrick.
Bynner. What though they conquer us?
Canan. Mother Dawning.
Cardenal. Mosquito Kingdom.
Carson, C. Turn Again.
Casey, M. Learning.
Castro, R. Hour After Hour, Day After Day.
Chang K'o-chiu. Tune: "Unbroken".
Cherry, K. History.
Ch'ien T'ao. In Praise of Ching K'o.
  Poems After Drinking Wine.
Chin. Floral Apron, The.
  Prelude.
Chinn. Not Translation, Not Poetry.
Chinnov. In the land of Schlaraffenland.
Cleveland, N. Epitaph on the Earl of Strafford.
Cliff. History of Costume, A.
Clifton, L. Driving through new england.
  I am accused of tending to the past.
  Sorrow Song.
  Why some people be mad at me sometimes.
Clinton, M. Traditional Post-Modern Neo-
  HooDoo Afra-Centric Sister in a Purple Head
  Rag Mourning Death and Cooking.
Coke, A. Change, The.
Collins, B. History Teacher, The.
  Tomes.
Cooley, N. John Winthrop, "Reasons to be
  Considered for...the Intended Plantation in New
  England," 1629.
  Mary Warren's Sampler.
  Mother: Dorcas Good, The.
  Publick Fast on Account of the Afflicted: March
  31, 1692.
Cope, W. Not only marble, but the plastic toys.
Cronin, A. Responsibilities.
Cuadra, P. Horses in the Lake.
Cummings, E. E. All nearness pauses,while a
  star can grow.
Darwish, M. On Our Last Evening on This
  Land.
Davidson, D. On a Replica of the Parthenon.
Davidson, M. Landing of Rochambeau, The.
  Thinking the Alps.
Davis, J. One Hundred and Fifty Years.
Davis, W. Texas: Sesquicentennial.
De Tabley. Sonnet: "Record is nothing, and the
  hero great."
Deane, S. History Lessons.
Deloney. Weavers Song, The.
Dennis, C. History.
  World History.

Dobyns. Where We Are.
Dooley, M. History.
Doolittle, Hilda. Evil was active in the land.
Drayton. What spirit can lift you up, to that immortall praise.
Du Bellay. Rome.
Duggan, L. Town on the Ten Dollar Note, The.
Durham. Columbus Day.
Eirian, S. Learning.
Eliot, T. S. Little Gidding.
Emerson, R. History.
Enzensberger, H. Poem about the Future.
Espirito Santo. Grandma Mariana.
Ettinger, E. Micrographic Manuscript, Miniature (1).
Fearing. 1933.
Feldman, I. Simple Outlines, Human Shapes.
Ferlinghetti, L. Cro-Magnons.
Fife, C. Dear Webster.
Fried, Michael. Next Bend in the Road, The.
Frost, R. Peaceful Shepherd, The.
Galvin, J. Two Horses and a Dog.
Gardinier. Admirals (Columbus).
Gelman. History.
Gerhardt, I. G. M. Rejected Gift, The.
Gilbert, S. Elegy: "Pages of history open, The. The dead enter."
Giovanni. Ego Tripping (There May Be a Reason Why).
Gizzi. Ding Repair.
Goodison. Annie Pengelly.
Gould, J. Easter Sunday.
Graham, J. Fission.
History.
Grenier. Has Faded in Part But Magnificent Also Late for RC / Mirrors.
Gu Cheng. Forever Parted: Graveyard.
Gunn, T. Claus von Stauffenberg.
Gustafson, R. In the Yukon.
Hardy, T. One We Knew.
Harper, M. American History.
Harry, J. Poem Films Itself, The.
Hass, R. Palo Alto: the Marshes.
Healy, E. City Beneath the City, The.
Herbert, Z. Mr. Cogito and the Imagination.
Rain, The.
Transformations of Livy.
Herd. Bombshell.
I stopped the car and stepped out onto gravel.
Hernández Cruz. New/Aguas Buenas/Jersey.
Herrera. Mexican World Mural / 5 x 25.
Poetry of America, The.
Resurrection of the Flesh, The.
Hill, G. Crack of a starting pistol. Jean Jaurès.
Hirsch, E. Simone Weil: In Assisi.
Hooker, J. Take a long view from Mynydd Bach.
Housman. On Wenlock Edge the wood's in trouble.
Houston, Margaret Bell. Old Oak Speaks, The.
Howe, S. Revisionist work in.
Hughes, J. Dog Day Lesson.
Hughes, L. Goodbye Christ.
Negro Speaks of Rivers, The.
Hugo, R. Ferniehirst Castle.
On Hearing a New Escalation.
Ivanov, G. Should I tell of all the absolute fools.
Joe, R. Expect Nothing Else from Me.
Johnson, L. Reggae Sounds.
Jonson, B. To Sir Henry Savile [upon His Translation of Tacitus].
Juarroz. Tenth.9.
Katz, J. Taxonomy.
Kenney. Battle of Valcour Island, The.
Khlebnikov, V. To Everyone.
Kildibekova, M. Everybody was going on talking the same talk.
Kinsella, J. Radnoti Quarantine: Razglednicas.
Kipling, R. Land, The.
Ko Chônghûi. Study of Women's History 4, A.
Study of Women's History 6, A.
Koch, C. Shelly Beach.
Koordada, M. You Can't Escape Your Life Record.
Krivulin. And the silver age, unattainable.

Kunitz, S. Night Letter.
Kusano Shimpei. Skylarks and Fuji.
Landon. History of the Lyre, A.
Larkin, P. Arundel Tomb, An.
Lauterbach. Novelist Speaks, The.
Lear, E. Limerick: "There was a young person whose history."
Lee, E. Forests and Caverns.
Li Ho. Arrowhead from the Ancient Battlefield of Ch'ang-p'ing, An.
Lindley, D. Cromwell: The Last Portrait.
Lloréns [or Lorens] Torres. Ugly Duckling, The.
Lopez, T. Studies in Classic American Literature.
Lowell, R. History.
Lumsden, R. ITMA.
Lux. Bodo.
MacCaig. Chauvinist.
Crossing the Border.
Double Life.
Machado Ruiz. On the Banks of the Duero.
MacNeacail. Proper Schooling, A.
Madhubuti. Possibiliites: Remembering Malcolm X.
Maguire, S. Liminal.
Manning, Maurice. Condensed History of Beauty, A.
Martinaitis, M. Kukutis's Fruitless Bread.
Kukutis's Sermon to the Pigs.
Marvell. Upon Appleton House [To My Lord Fairfax].
Matthews, M. By a Ways.
Mazur. Common, The.
McCann, Anthony. Confessions: "Before money and California."
McGlashan, J. Island of Women, The.
Merrill, J. Self-Portrait in Tyvek(TM) Windbreaker.
Midge, T. Written in Blood.
Milosz, C. Bypassing Rue Descartes.
Child of Europe.
Moolten, D. Brandy Station, Virginia.
Morejón. Requiem for the Left Hand.
Morgan, E. Coin, The.
Morris, B. Dinas Emrys.
Morris, S. Salt sprays deluge it, wild waves buffet it, hurricanes rave.
Moxley, Jennifer. Easter Lesson, The.
Mr. Social Control. History Never Happened.
Muldoon, P. Grand Conversation, The.
Mullen, H. Present Tense.
Mun Chônghui. To You, My Beloved Ssuma Ch'ien.
Nemerov. Historical Judas, The.
Ultima Ratio Reagan.
Ní Chuilleanáin. Real Thing, The.
Nolla. Greek History.
O'Lahsen, M. It Took One Hundred Years.
O'Hara, F. In Memory of My Feelings.
Olson, C. At Yorktown.
I, Maximus of Gloucester, to You ("Off-shore, by islands hidden in the blood.").
Kingfishers, The.
Ondaatje. Gentleman Compares His Virtue to a Piece of Jade, A.
Opoku-Agyemang. King Tut in America.
Osofisan. She Thinks in Song.
Padilla. History.
Legacies.
Prayer for the End of the Century, A.
Promise, The.
Paz. And the banquet, the exile, the first crime.
I Speak of the City.
Perelman. Cliff Notes.
Perillo, L. Ghost Shirt, The.
Piatt, S. Hundred Years Ago, A.
Pickard, T. Devil's Destroying Angel Exploded, The.
Pinsky. At Pleasure Bay.
Figured Wheel, The.
Serpent Knowledge.
Shirt.
Plumpp. Turf Song.
Po Chü-i. Iranian Whirling Girls.
Porter, C. They Couldn't Compare to You.

Porter, P. And No Help Came.
Preston, R. Music.
Rakosi. Figures in an Ancient Ink.
Ramsey, J. Tally Stick, The.
Ranaldo, L. Time Presses Me.
Redmond. River of Bones and Flesh and Blood.
Reed, I. Dualism in ralph ellison's invisible man.
Rendon. You See This Body.
Rexroth, K. August 22, 1939.
Rich, A. Catch if you can your country's moment, begin.
Culture and Anarchy.
In Those Years.
Letters in the Family.
Living Memory.
Mathilde in Normandy.
No one's fated or doomed to love anyone.
Riley, P. 175. 123.
Roberson, E. Ideas Gray Suits Bowler Hats Baal.
Rodefer. Pretext.
Rodriguez, J. Mahogany Ship, The.
Rosselli. Worthless as was her itinerary to fame.
Roth, F. Marriage.
Rózewicz. What Happens.
Rukeyser, M. Book of the Dead, The.
Rux, C. H. Asphalt Musings.
Asylum of Gestures.
Rylander, E. Midnight Rocker, Tiananmen Square, May 27, 1989.
Saïd, A. Africa of the Statue, The.
Salaam. French Quarter Intimacies.
I Live in the Mouth of History.
Sandburg, C. Bilbea.
I Am the People, the Mob.
Old Timers.
Schwartz, D. Lincoln.
Seidman. Making of Color, The.
Shin Tongyǒp. We have seen heaven.
Shwarts [or Shvarts]. Sale of a Historian's Library.
Sidney. Sonnet 30: "Whether the Turkish new moon minded be."
Simic. Eastern European Cooking.
Simpson, L. Silent Generation, The.
Story About Chicken Soup, A.
Slessor. Five Bells.
Smith, C. Beachy Head.
Smith, S. How Cruel Is the Story of Eve.
Snyder, G. Building.
What Happened Here Before.
Stryk, L. History.
Sze. Every Where and Every When.
Szymborska, W. Century's Decline, The.
Once we knew the world well.
Reality Demands.
Two Apes of Brueghel, The.
Talvikki, A. Along the road, the bright painted crosses.
At night, coolness like water lapping.
Before first light, we would open the nets.
Halley's Comet crossed the jungle sky.
Teatro Amazonas, remnant, the.
Waking, months after I leave the jungle.
Tate, A. Mediterranean, The.
Taylor, E. This Year's Drive to Appomattox.
Tennyson, A. Guess well, and that is well. Our age can find.
Thomas, R. S. Centuries.
Thorpe, M. Open-Air Museum.
Tranter. Alphabet Murders, The.
Tsvetkov. To the apostles of history.
Tu Fu [or Du Fu]. Autumn Meditation: 7.
Turner, C. Julius Caesar and the Honey-Bee.
Unknown. Cyclolotry.
Upton, C. When I was very young.
Vando. Commonwealth, Common Poverty.
Vaughan, H. Charnel-house, The.
Villon. Ballade of the Ladies of Time Past.
Walcott. Chapter 38, Part 3.
Sea Is History, The.
Warfield. Forests and Caverns.
Warren, R. Lessons in History.
Two Studies in Idealism: Short Survey of American and Human History.

Wei Chuang.　Lament of the Lady of Qin.
Weinberger, E.　Changs.
Whitman, W.　On the Same Picture.
Wilbur, R.　Looking into History.
Williams, M.　Of History and Hope.
Wright, C.　Chickamauga.
Wright, D.　Cockermouth.
Wright, J.　At Cooloolah.
Yeats.　Lapis Lazuli.
Yevtushenko [or Evtushenko].　Hand-Rolled
　Cigarettes.
Young, K.　Quivira City Limits.
Yüan Chěn.　Iranian Whirling Girls.

Hitchhiking and Hitchhikers
Allen, P.　Pickup.
Balaban.　Daddy Out Hitch-Hiking at 3:30 A.M.
　Heading Out West.
Boyle, F.　Hand Game.
Ciardi, J.　Faces.
Corso.　Poets Hitchhiking on the Highway.
Grahn.　Detroit Annie, Hitchhiking.
Harms.　When You Wish Upon a Star That
　Turns into a Plane.
Kinnell.　Hitchhiker.
　Memory of Wilmington.
Stafford, W.　Once in the 40s.
Taylor, C.　Renting.
Wakoski.　Hitchhikers, The.

Hitler, Adolf
Aragon, F.　Century, The.
Auden.　Refugee Blues.
Brecht, B.　In Dark Times.
Davis, C.　Displaced Person.
Enzensberger, H.　Portrait of a House Detective.
Gunn, T.　Claus von Stauffenberg.
Llwyd, Alan.　Chaplin and Others.
Nemerov.　IFF.
Pitter.　Victory Bonfire.
Rukeyser, M.　Traditional Tune.
Snodgrass.　Adolf Hitler ———1 April, 1945.
　Adolf Hitler ———20 April, 1934; 1900 hours.
　Eva Braun.
Troupe.　Signals and Demarcations.

Hobbes, Thomas
Cowley, A.　To Mr. Hobs: "Vast *Bodies* of
　Philosophie."
Hass, R.　Concerning the Afterlife, the Indians
　of Central California Had Only the Dimmest
　Notions.

Hoboes
Brownstein.　Who Knows Where the Time
　Goes?
Coelho, A.　Drifter's Brand, A.
Shin Kyŏngnim.　Legend.
See also **Vagabonds**

Hogg, James
Wordsworth, W.　Extempore Effusion upon the
　Death of James Hogg.

Hokusai, Katsushika
Frémon, Jean.　Autumn: "Shogun, always on the
　lookout for ways to increase his glory, The."
Rakosi.　ZZZZZ.
Vold, J.　Hokusai the Old Master, Who Painted a
　Wave Like Nobody Ever Painted a Wave
　Before Him.

Holbein, Hans
MacKellar, D.　Fancy Dress.

Holes
Bador, B.　Birth: "Camels pregnant."
Glazer, M.　Purpose of Design Is to Make the
　Whole Greater Than the Sum of Its Parts, The.
Harris, W.　Practical Concerns.

Holiday, Billie
Corn.　Billie's Blues.
Dove, R.　Canary.
Heithaus.　What a Little Moonlight Can Do.
Jackson, A.　Billie in Silk.
Jones, P.　Birth of Rhythm and Blues, The.
Levis.　1974: My Story in a Late Style of Fire.
May, K.　Valentine's Day.
Neal, L.　Lady's Days.
O'Hara, F.　Day Lady Died, The.
Plumpp.　Be-Bop.
　Billie Holiday.

Holidays
Abu Madi.　Holiday Present.
Berman, D.　From His Bed in the Capital City.
Buchanan, G.　May Morning.
Chesterton.　Certain Evening, A.
Dame.　Seder, The.
Durham.　Columbus Day.
Glaser, M.　Preparations for Seder.
González, R.　Day of the Dead.
Hall, D.　Independence Day Letter.
Harper, M.　Studs.
Maltby, R.　I Don't Remember Christmas.
Petri.　Gratitude.
Statius.　First of December, The.
Wilbur, R.　Patriots' Day.

Holland
Koch, K.　Airplane Betty in Holland.
Marsman.　Holland.
　Memory of Holland.
Sia, B.　Things to Do in Holland.
See also **Netherlands**

Holly
Davies, G.　Holly Gone.
Unknown.　Holly and Ivy.
　Holly and the Ivy, The.

Hollyhocks
Basho.　Hollyhocks, The.
　June rain / hollyhocks turning.

Hollywood, California
Coleman, W.　April in Hollywood.
Disch.　Hooray for Hollywood.
Elmslie, K.　Shirley Temple Surrounded by
　Lions.
Harms.　My Own Little Piece of Hollywood.
Jarrell, R.　Thinking of the Lost World.
Klipschutz.　Funicello at 50.
Mercer, J.　Hooray for Hollywood.
Rodríguez, A.　Torch.
Self, Joan.　Quill Holler Waller.

Holmes, Oliver Wendell
Lowell, J.　Holmes.

Holocaust
Agosin.　Traveling Valise.
Aini, L.　Shower.
Alkalay-Gut.　Kitzbuhl Church.
Amichai, Y.　All the Generations Before Me.
　All the Generations Before Me.
　Little Ruth.
Bell, M.　Book of the Dead Man #58, The.
　Extermination of the Jews, The.
Berg, S.　Desnos Reading the Palms of Men on
　Their Way to the Gas Chambers.
Blumenthal, M.　Cherries.
Bobrowski.　Kaunas 1941.
Bond, E.　How We See.
Borowski.　Farewell to Maria.
　Night over Birkenau.
Brett, L.　I Keep Forgetting.
　La Pathétique.
　Leaving You.
　My Mother's Friend.
Breytenbach.　Lullaby.
Brock, V.　Remembering Dresden.
Bruck.　Childhood.
　Pretty Soon.
Carruth, H.　Camps, The.
Celan.　Aspen Tree.
　Aspen Tree . . .
　Death Fugue.
　Death Fugue, A.
　Deathfugue.
　Fugue of Death.
　In Prague.
　Shibboleth.
　Tenebrae.
　Tenebrae.
Charles, J. B.　Polish Girl Standing on a Chair,
　A.
Derry, A.　Anne.
Dorsett, T.　Survivor, The.
Ettinger, E.　Micrographic Manuscript,
　Miniature (2).
Fainlight, R.　Archive Film Material.
Feldman, I.　Pripet Marshes, The.
Fenton, J.　German Requiem, A.

Ficowski.　Assumption of Miriam from the
　Street in the Winter of 1942, The.
　Both Your Mothers.
　Execution of Memory, The.
　5.8.1942 / In Memory of Janusz Korczak*.
　Girl of Six from the Ghetto Begging in Smolna
　Street in 1942, A.
　I Did Not Manage To Save.
Florsheim.　Jewish Singles Event, The.
Fogel, E.　Shipment to Maidanek.
Fogel, E.　Shipment to Maidanek.
Forché.　Ourselves or Nothing.
Fried, E.　My Girlfriends.
Friedmann.　Butterfly, The.
Futuransky, L.　Twenty Years From Auschwitz,
　Bergen-Belsen and Other Camps.
Gardinier.　Two Girls.
Gershon.　I Was Not There.
　Race.
Glaser, M.　English-Speaking Persons Will Find
　Translations.
Graham, J.　History.
Guri, H.　Heritage.
Hamburger, M.　Treblinka.
Harris, R.　Riding Over Belmore Park.
Hecht, A.　Book of Yolek, The.
　It Out-Herods Herod. Pray You, Avoid It.
　More Light! More Light!
　Room, The.
Helfgott, S.　Trains, The.
Herbert, Z.　Biology Teacher.
Heyen.　Blue.
　Passover: the Injections.
　Riddle: "From Belsen a crate of gold teeth."
　Simple Truths.
Hill, G.　Ovid in the Third Reich.
　September Song.
　Two Formal Elegies.
Hilles, R.　Yom HaShoah in Florida.
Hirsch, E.　Paul Celan: A Grave and Mysterious
　Sentence.
Hirschhorn, N.　Number Our Days.
Holan.　To the Enemies.
Howe, F.　White Lines.
Huchel.　Roads.
Jarrell, R.　Camp in the Prussian Forest, A.
　In the Camp There Was One Alive.
　Protocols.
Jenkins, P.　Six Small Fires.
Kirsch, S.　Legend of Lilja.
Klein, A.　Upon the Heavenly Scarp.
Klepfisz.　Perspectives on the Second World
　War.
Kolmar.　Judith.
Kovner, A.　Far, Far a City Lies.
Kramer, L.　Non-Emigrant, The.
　Red Cross Telegram, The.
Levi, P.　Buna.
　For Adolf Eichmann.
　Reveille.
　Shemà.
　Survivor, The.
Lifshin.　I Remember Haifa Being Lovely But.
MacBeth [or Macbeth].　Poem of Death, A.
　Ward, The.
MacLean, S.　Death Valley.
Mahón.　Disused Shed in Co. Wexford, A.
Martin.　Dreams in German.
Meltzer, D.　What Do I Know of Journey.
Merwin.　Dachau Shoe, The.
Mihalic.　Under the Microscope.
Milosz, C.　Child of Europe.
　Poor Christian Looks at the Ghetto, A.
Moraes, D.　Rendezvous.
Muñiz Huberman.　Cascades of Death.
Murray, L.　Dog Fox Field.
Nelson, M.　I Decide Not to Have Children.
Olson, C.　La Préface.
Oppen.　It is the air of atrocity.
Orban, O.　Letter, The.
Pagis, D.　Autobiography.
　Autobiography.
　Autobiography.
　Draft of a Reparations Agreement.
　Europe, Late.
　Footprints.

Instructions for Crossing the Border.
Roll Call, The.
Roll-Call in the Concentration Camp.
Scrawled in Pencil in a Sealed Car.
Testimony.
Written in Pencil in the Sealed Railway-Car.
Paterson, E. History Teacher in the Warsaw
  Ghetto Rising.
Pilinszky, J. Frankfurt.
French Prisoner, The.
Harbach 1944.
On the Wall of a KZ-Lager.
Passion of Ravensbrück.
Passion of Ravensbrück, The.
Pillen [or Pillin]. Ascensions, The.
Plath. Daddy.
Mary's Song.
Plotnick, H. M. Jewish.
Porter, P. Annotations of Auschwitz.
Pound, E. Nor can who has passed a month in
  the death cells.
Quasimodo. Auschwitz.
Radnóti. Postcard (Found on His body after He
  Was Killed by the Nazis).
Replansky. Six Million, The.
Reznikoff. Children.
Entertainment.
Jewish women were lined up by German troops
  in charge of the territory.
Massacres.
When the Second World War began.
Rich, A. Letters in the Family.
Memory lifts her smoky mirror: 1943.
1948: Jews.
Rothenberg, J. Dos Oysleydikn (The
  Emptying).
Rowlands, D. Schutzstaffeln 45326.
Rózewicz. In the Middle of Life.
Pigtail.
She Looked At the Sun.
Survivor, The.
Warning.
Sachs, N. Already Embraced by the Arm of
  Heavenly Solace.
Chorus of the Dead.
Chorus of the Stars.
Dead Child Speaks, A.
How Long Have We Forgotten How to Listen!
O Sister.
O the Chimneys.
Oh Those Smokestacks.
Salganicoff. Shame.
Sapgir. Psalm 137.
Schiff, H. German Frontier at Basel: 1942 and
  1992, The.
When It Happened.
Sillitoe. Synagogue in Prague.
Simon, M. Snow.
Simpson, L. Story About Chicken Soup, A.
Sklarew. After Theresienstadt.
Teaching the Children.
Slonimski. Elegy: "No more, no more Jewish
  townships in Poland."
Slutsky [or Slutskii]. Burnt.
How Did They Kill My Grandmother?
How They Killed My Grandmother.
Spender, S. History and Reality.
Memento.
Stallworthy, J. Letter from Berlin, A.
Stern, G. Adler.
Soap.
Strand. There is a road through the canyon.
Sutskever [or Sutzkever]. Cartload of Shoes, A.
How?
1980.
Peasant Who Saw God, The.
Szymborska, W. Still.
There But for the Grace.
Teofilov, Ivan. Ortamezar—The Jewish Quarter.
Thomas, R. H. Evacuee, The.
Vinokurov. Adam.
Objects.
Vogel, D. How Can I See You, Love.
Voznesensky [or Voznesenskii]. Call of the
  Lake, The.
Warren, R. Max Jacob at Saint Benoît.

Weiss, T. Pair of Shoes, A.
Wiesel. Behold, God of Abraham, God of
  mercy.
Never Shall I Forget.
Wilkie, B. Intuition, An.
Williams, C. K. Spit.
Wright, C. KZ.
Yevtushenko [or Evtushenko]. Babii Yar.
I am.
Zach, N. Against Parting.
Zagajewski. Watching Shoah in a Hotel Room
  in America.
Zukofsky, L. Song for the Year's End, A.

Holy Family
Rukeyser, M. Holy Family.
Unknown. Cherry-Tree Carol, The.

Holy Ghost
Audelay [or Awdelay]. Seven Gifts of the Holy
  Ghost, The.
Crown, K. Holy Ghost Flies into Second
  Baptist on Airline Highway in Baton Rouge,
  The.
Herrick. His Litany to the Holy Spirit.
Sassoon, S. Christ and the Soldier.
Unknown. Petition to Father and Son and Holy
  Ghost, A.
To-morrow shall be my dancing day.

Holy Spirit
Bingen, Hildegard von. Antiphon for the Holy
  Spirit.
Constable, H. To God the Holy Ghost.
Craig, David. Pentecost.
Donne. Show me dear[e] Christ, thy spouse, so
  bright and clear[e].
Field. Sweet-Briar in Rose.
Hicok. Arch of Sanctification, The.
Milosz, C. Veni Creator.
Very. Lost, The ("Fairest day that ever yet has
  shone, The.").
Yeats. Matthew 28:16–20; Now the eleven
  disciples went to Galilee.

Holy Thursday
Blake, W. Holy Thursday [1].
Holy Thursday [2].

Home
Adamson. Home, The Spare Room, The.
Alabaú. Sister.
Aldis, D. No One Heard Him Call.
Alexander, E. Who I Think You Are.
Ali, A. Postcard from Kashmir.
Alvi, M. Bed, The.
Arends, J. I Have.
Ashbery, J. Rain Moving In.
Awoonor. Sea Eats the Land at Home, The.
Back, R. Gaza, Undated.
Notes: From the Wait.
Bancquart. Vanished, The.
Barker, S. There was not loveliness nor fortune
  there.
Bass, F. Home.
Beck, R. Epilogue for Emilia.
Berger, B. Trophy Homes.
Berry, W. Stay Home.
Berssenbrugge. Tan Tien.
Blomer, Y. Landscapes and Home / Ghazal 22.
Brodsky, J. October Tune.
Brontë, A. Home.
Brooks, C. Our Island Home.
Brown, E. Out.
Brunk, J. All Sweet Things, Like Forgiveness,
  Are a Falling.
Where My Mother Cries.
Brutus. I Am Alien in Africa and Everywhere.
Burns, R. My Heart's in the Highlands.
Buson. Going home.
Byron, C. Minding You.
Cariaga. Plantings.
Catacalos. Letter to a Brother in Exile.
Channing. Harbor, The.
Clare, J. After Reading in a Letter Proposals for
  Building a Cottage.
Wish, A ("Be where I may when death brings in
  his bill.").
Clark, S. Some Details of Hebridean House
  Construction.

Claudian. Old Man of Verona, The.
Cleary, B. Sealink.
Clifton, H. Distaff Side, The.
Clifton, L. In the Inner City.
Clinton, N. Eviction.
Clover, J. Alas, That Is the Name of Our Town;
  I Have Been Concealing It All This Time.
Colum, P. Old Woman of the Roads, The.
Coolidge. Home, A.
Cowley, M. Long Voyage, The.
Winter Tenement.
Creeley. Away.
En Famille.
Cunningham, A. Hame, Hame, Hame.
da Silva. Return to the Homeland.
Dana, R. A Capella.
Davies, A. Thirty East Forty-Second Street.
De Kok. To drink its water.
Dharker. Name of god, The.
"Dhoomil.". City, Evening, and an Old Man:
  Me, The.
Di Prima. Backyard.
Notes on the Art of Memory.
Donne. To Sir Henry Wotton ("Sir, more than
  kisses, letters mingle souls.").
Doolittle, Hilda. Take me home.
Dove, R. Dusting.
Doyle, S. This Shade.
Duffy, C. Plainsong.
Dunmore. Domestic Poem.
Edwards [or Edwardes], R. Recollections of an
  Old Spook.
Eich. Where I Live.
Elliot, A. Latitudes of Home, The.
Figueroa, J. Cowboynomics.
Fong, H. Asylum.
Forbes, C. Home.
Foster, S. My Old Kentucky Home.
Old Folks at Home.
Fraser, G. Home Town Elegy.
Frost, R. Death of the Hired Man, The.
Gallagher, T. Coming Home.
Gandlevsky, S. Is it time to change the record?
But I'm dreaming again.
Gilman, C. Homes.
Gioia. In Cheever Country.
Giscombe, C. Home Avenue.
Glaser, M. Quarreling with Robert Frost.
Goldberg, L. Song of the Strange Woman.
Gregg. Night Music.
Griffiths, J. Emigrants.
Migration.
Guest, E. Home.
Han-shan. Cold Mountain.
House Without Walls.
Settled at Cold Mountain.
Harbach, O. Love Nest, The.
Harms. Sky.
Harris, W. Rib Sandwich.
Healy, E. Moroni on the Mormon Temple /
  Angel on the Wall.
Heard, J. Welcome Home.
Heffernan, M. Africa: "I looked out toward the
  pasture at the cows."
Herbert, Z. In a.
Herrick. Thanksgiving to God for His House,
  A.
Hewitt, J. Substance and Shadow.
Ho Ch'e Ch'ang. Written Impromptu upon
  Returning to My Hometown.
Hochman. Cannon Hill.
Holan. Resurrection.
Hove. Red Hills of Home.
Hugo, R. Living Alone.
Hunt, L. To Hampstead ("Winter has reached
  thee once again at last.").
Ikkyu Sojun. My Real Dwelling.
Inada. Legend of Home, The.
Ishkhan. Armenian Language Is the Home of
  the Armenian, The.
Issa. Give me a homeland.
Just to say the word.
My dear old village.
My old village lies.
Jackson, R. Sunday Brunch.
Janzen, J. Claiming the Dust.

Johnson, L.   Mystic and Cavalier.
Jones, J.   Now slowly winding from the mountain's head.
Jones, T.   Llanafan Unrevisited.
Kaplinski, J.   We started home, my son and I.
Kay, J.   In my country.
Keeshig-Tobias.   I Grew Up.
Kilmer, J.   House with Nobody in It, The.
Kyle, C. J.   Fire in Early Morning.
Lal Ded [or Lalla].   I was passionate.
Lanier, E.   Description of Cooke-ham [or Cookham], The.
Lanyer.   Description of Cooke-ham [or Cookham], The.
Larkin, P.   Home Is So Sad.
Lawrence, D. H.   End of Another Home Holiday.
Levitt, Peter.   Where you are going.
Li Po.   Quiet Night Thoughts.
Written on a Wall at Hsiu-Ching Monastery in Wu-Ch'ang.
Lisick, B.   Empress of Sighs ("Mom and Dad have abandoned the family home and retired to Palm.").
Liu Tsung-yüan.   From the City-Tower of Liuzhou To My Four Fellow-Officials at Zhang, Ding, Feng, and Lian Districts.
Llawdden.   No Place Like Home.
Longfellow, H.   Golden Mile-Stone, The.
Longley, M.   Remembering Carrigskeewaun.
West, The.
Lueck, D.   You want to climb the steps.
Luschei, G.   Here.
MacCaig.   Kingfisher.
Macdonald, G.   Baby-Sermon, A.
Mahon.   Afterlives.
Ford Manor.
Marvin, C.   House, Garden, Madness.
Masefield.   West Wind, The.
Mathews, A.   Two Months Married.
Merwin.   Odysseus.
Million, D.   Housing Poem, The.
Montague, J.   Hearth Song.
Morgan, J.   My Welsh Home.
Moriarty, L.   Beautiful House, The.
Mphahlele.   Homeward Bound.
Mun Chônghui.   Seeing Snow.
Murphy, M.   47° 28' N, 19° 1' E.
Murphy, P.   Manifesto.
Muso Soseki.   My thatched hut.
Old Hut.
Wandering.
Neruda.   I Explain a Few Things.
Nguyen, Hoa.   House on fire my mom's.
Nichols, G.   Beverley's Saga.
Like a Beacon.
Nilsson, H.   On Inheriting Departure.
We Are Easily Reduced.
Nolens, L.   Address.
Nooteboom.   Basho 3.
O'Driscoll, D.   Home.
Oliveira, D.   San Joaquin.
Pahmeier, G.   Sunday Baking.
Paschen.   Confederacy.
12 East Scott Street.
Patterson, G.   Letter from Home.
Pavese.   Words from Confinement.
Payne, J.   Home, Sweet Home!
Pei Di.   Cove of the Wall of Meng, The.
Pietri.   7th Untitled Poem.
Pinsky.   Street, The.
Pogson, P.   Going Home.
Pook.   Weekend at Home.
Pope, A.   Revelation.
Pou Kuksa.   Cloudy Mountain.
Radnóti.   Forced March ("He is a fool who, collapsed on the ground, gets up and walks on.").
Seventh Eclogue ("Do you see? Evening falls, fringed with barbed-wire.").
Rhys, E.   Ballad of the Homing Man, The.
Riley, J.   Travel Notes.
Ritsos.   Our Land.
Robinson, E.   House on the Hill, The.
Roethke.   Return, The.
Rosenblatt, S.   Leaving Home.

Mom and Dad Getting Older.
Rukeyser, M.   Book of the Dead, The.
Rybicki, J.   In Directions.
Sabines.   Capriccios.
St. John, P.   All the Way Home.
Shapcott, T.   City of Home, The.
Shapiro, M.   To Jerusalem, 1990.
Shaw, J.   Revelation.
Shen Yüeh.   Returning to My Garden Home: In Respectful Response to the Master of Hua-yang.
Shoukry, G.   Personal Portrait, A.
Sigourney.   Western Emigrant, The.
Simmons, J.   Westport House, Portrush.
Simms, W.   Voice of Memory in Exile, from a Home in Ashes, The.
Slamnig, I.   Sailor, A.
Södergran.   Homecoming.
Stevenson, R.   Blows the Wind Today.
Stickney, T.   Quiet after the rain of morning.
Swenson, M.   Staying at Ed's Place.
Swift, J.   Holyhead. September 25, 1727.
Talvikki, A.   For Want.
T'ao Ch'ien [or T'ao Yuan-ming].   Poem on Returning to Dwell in the Country.
Tennyson, A.   We leave the well-beloved place.
Thompson, D.   Days of Yore, The.
Thorne, T.   High Country.
Troupe.   Conjuring Against Alien Spirits.
Tu Fu [or Du Fu].   Village by the River.
Turner, C.   Hence with your jeerings, petulant and low.
Unknown.   Behind the Mountain.
Deep River.
Fare Ye Well.
Good Lord in That Heaven.
Harper's Song for Inherkhawy, The.
Home to Farm.
Hunting for a City.
I thought for ten years, then I made my house.
I Want to Go Home.
Jehovah, Hallelujah.
Steal Away to Jesus.
That Mountain Far Away.
Those gone are day by day remote.
Wa-Sissica, the War Song.
Xishi always lives in golden houses.
Zion me wan go home.
Unknown, fr. Terezin Concentration Camp.
Homesick.
Untermeyer, J.   Autumn.
Vietnamese Oral Tradition.   Saigon River, The.
Voznesensky [or Voznesenskii].   Old Song.
Walker, D.   Home.
Wang An-shih.   At Home.
Wang Fan-chih.   I have a couple acres of land.
Wang Wei.   Cove of the Wall of Meng, The.
You Come from My Village.
Waniek.   House on Moscow Street, The.
Ward, J.   To Get Clear.
Ward, J.   Here, Home.
Watkins, V.   Returning to Goleufryn.
Watson, R.   Ruined Altar, A.
Webster, A.   Where Home Was.
Weigl.   Home.
Williams, G.   Wild Night at Treweithan.
Williams, M.   Shrinking Lonesome Sestina, The.
Williams, W.   Summer Cloud, A.
Wilson, Emily.   Relict.
Wilson, K.   Dusk in My Backyard.
Wordsworth, D.   Peaceful Our Valley, Fair and Green.
Wordsworth, W.   Farewell, A: "Farewell thou little Nook of mountain-ground."
Ruined Cottage, The.
Wright, C.   Virgo Descending.
Wroth.   Sonnet 35: "False [or Faulce] hope which feeds but[t] to destroy, and spill."
Xiang Xiu.   Recalling Old Times.
Yi Yônju.   Our Old Home.
Young, A.   Third Street Promenade; Full Moon, Sunday Night, Santa Monica.
Yu Xuanji.   At Home in the Summer Mountains.
Yun Tongju.   Yet Another Home.
Zolynas.   Zen of Housework, The.

Homecoming
Allnutt, G.   Road Home, The.
Ammons.   I Went Back.
Aridjis.   Self-Portrait in the Doorway.
Awoonor.   On the Way to Durham, N.C.
Bailey, A.   La Route Jackman.
Bancquart.   Return of Ulysses.
Baxter, J.   Homecoming, The.
Berlin.   When the Midnight Choo-Choo Leaves for Alabam'.
Bhattācārya, K.   Consulting the omens.
My Uma has come!
Bible, *O.T.*   Psalm 114.
Psalm 114: "When Isr'el, freed from Pharoh's hand."
Bishop, J.   Return, The.
Blake, W.   Dream, A.
Bonitto-Burwell, T.   Going Home.
Bowering, G.   My Father in New Zealand.
Buson.   Raising my head, I make out my house in the twilight.
Butterfield, F. G.   For Services Rendered.
Byron, G.   Watch-Dog's Honest Bark, The.
Caleshu, A.   Homecoming.
Catullus.   31.
Chimi Sucho.   Returning to My Hometown.
Chŏng Chiyong.   Home.
Clare, J.   Returned Soldier, The.
Daniels, J.   Blessing the House.
De Kok.   Shadows behind, Before.
DeSylva, B. G.   California, Here I Come.
Dobyns.   Freight Cars.
Du Bellay.   Heureux Qui, Comme Ulysse, A Fait un Beau Voyage.
Dubin, A.   Lulu's Back in Town.
Eliot, T. S.   2. A Game of Chess.
Ellis, K. N.   Tougaloo Blues.
Fisher, S.   Hometown.
Ford Lena, Guilbert.   Keep the Home Fires Burning (Till the Boys Come Home).
Goldberg, L.   Prodigal Son, The.
Graham, W.   What's the News?
Green, B.   Sentimental Journey.
Gurney, I.   After War.
Hardy, T.   His Visitor.
Herman, J.   Hello, Dolly!
Herrera y Reissig.   Return, The.
Hierro, José.   Meeting, The.
Ho Ch'e Ch'ang.   Homecoming: "I was a boy when I left home."
Returning after I left my home in childhood.
Hogg, J.   Charlie is my Darling.
Homer.   Laertes.
Odyssey, The.
Hudgins.   Road Home, The.
Hughes, L.   Lover's Return.
Jarrell, R.   Transient Barracks (1944).
Jeffers, R.   Return.
Johnson, A.   Oil on Troubled Waters.
Jolson, A.   California, Here I Come.
Joshu, K.   Whenever I hear.
Kim Hyesun.   Ripe Apple.
Kim Kwanguk.   Bundle the piles of verbose missives.
Kim Suyŏng.   Lonely Journey, A.
Kipling, R.   Return, The.
Kizer, C.   Ingathering.
Knight, E.   Poem for Myself (Or Blues for a Mississippi Black Boy), A.
Welcome Back, Mr. Knight: Love of My Life.
Levine, P.   Water's Chant, The.
Lewis, S.   How 'Ya Gonna Keep 'Em Down on the Farm? (After They've Seen Paree).
Rock-a-Bye Your Baby with a Dixie Melody.
Liu Ch'ang-ch'ing.   Snow on Lotus Mountain.
López Velarde.   Baleful Return.
Loseff [or Losev].   Conversation with a New York Poet.
Louis, A.   At the House of Ghosts.
MacBeth [or Macbeth].   Shotts.
MacCaig.   Return to Scalpay.
Mapanje.   Making Our Clowns Martyrs.
McGrath, T.   Homecoming: "After the cries of gulls and the fogbound island."
Merwin.   Home for Thanksgiving.
Meynell, A.   At Night.

Muñiz Huberman.   Prodigal Daughter.
Nathan, L.   Circlings.
Neruda.   Homecomings.
Nystrom.   Regardless of the Final Score.
Oness, C.   Of All There Is.
Owen, W.   Send-Off, The.
Peterson, R.   Now and Then.
Press, K.   Hope for refugees.
   I who live here, it is I.
Ransom, J.   Prelude to an Evening.
Rein.   Return, The.
Robin, L.   My Cutey's Due at Two-to-Two
   Today.
Robinson, A.   Celia's Home-Coming.
Robinson, E.   Prodigal Son, The.
Rosenblatt, S.   Mom and Dad Getting Older.
Ross, A.   En Route.
Rossetti, C.   Italia, Io Ti Saluto!
Ryan, G.   Achilleus to Odysseus.
Salaam.   Funeraled Fare Well.
Salkey.   Dry River Bed.
Samaras, N.   Farasa.
Sen, R.   How wonderful! Look what.
Shin Kyŏngnim.   Country Bus Station.
Smith, I.   Returning Exile.
Smith, P.   Dylan, Two Days.
Snodgrass.   Returned to Frisco, 1946.
   Ten Days Leave.
Stryk, L.   Return to DeKalb.
Su Tung-p'o.   Roadside flowers are blooming,
   butterflies on the wing.
   Wild roadside flowers, blooming in boundless
   numbers.
T'ao Ch'ien [or T'ao Yuan-ming].   I Return to
   the Place I Was Born.
   Poem on Returning to Dwell in the Country.
   Returning to Fields and Gardens (1) ("When I
   was young, I did not fit in.").
Thomas, C.   Alone / with only.
Tripp.   Diesel to Yesterday.
Tsvetayeva [or Tsvetaeva].   And, Not Crying in
   Vain.
Tu Fu [or Du Fu].   Outside the City.
   Spring Homecoming.
   Thatched Hut, The.
Ulacia, M.   Regreso a la ciudad.
   Return to the City.
Unknown.   At Fifteen I Joined the Army.
   Bracelets on my arms, jewelry around my neck.
   Ge-tan: Shade o' the Vine.
   Jun-zi yang-yang: The Gudeman's Come Hame
   (scoticè).
   Ru-fen: Along Yew's Banks.
Walcott.   He yawned and watched the lilac
   horns of his island.
Wei Ying-wu.   Mooring at Twilight in Yuyi
   District.
Wetzsteon.   Coming Back to the Cave.
Wright, J.   Homecoming Singer, The.
Yesenin [or Essenin].   Blue Mist.
Young, J.   How 'Ya Gonna Keep 'Em Down on
   the Farm? (After They've Seen Paree).
   Rock-a-Bye Your Baby with a Dixie Melody.
Zimunya.   Arrivants.
   Kisimiso.

Homeless, The
Agodon, K.   What Comes after Because.
Agüeros.   Psalm for the Next Millennium.
Aleshire.   Double, The.
Ashbery, J.   Street Musicians.
Baraka, I.   Legacy.
Berryman.   Boston Common.
Bibbins, M.   Pathology of Proximity, The.
Bowman, C.   1-800-HOT-RIBS.
Brendan-Brown, S.   Dark Side of Dazzle, The.
Brooks, G.   To An Old Black Woman, Homeless
   and Indistinct.
Campo.   John Doe.
Cardiff.   Grey Woman.
Clifton, L.   Miss Rosie.
Colum, P.   Old Woman of the Roads, The.
Coolidge.   Home, A.
Dana, R.   Mark, The.
de Fréine, C.   Skills.
Dobyns.   Frenchie.
Dressel.   Dai, Live.

Gates, B.   Homeless.
   Triptych.
Ginsberg, A.   Homeless Compleynt.
   New Stanzas for Amazing Grace.
Hannon.   Homeless.
Haug.   Tennessee Waltz, The.
Hecht, A.   Christmas Is Coming.
Hirschman, J.   X L E B.
Hopkins, L.   En-vi-RON-ment.
Hughes, L.   Advertisement for the Waldorf-
   Astoria.
Hussein, H.   Room of One's Own, A.
Jackson, M. L.   How to Listen.
MacSweeney.   Pearl Says.
Mandelstam [or Mandelshtam].   Where Can I
   Hide in January.
McKay, C.   Castaways, The.
Medina, T.   Rhudine Rhudine.
Mueller, L.   Triage.
Myles, E.   School of Fish.
O'Brien, S.   HMS Glasshouse.
Overton, R.   Two Stories.
Powers, Arthur.   Bag Lady's Body in the
   Financial District, A.
Procter, A.   Homeless.
Randall, D.   Bag Woman.
Rimbaud, A.   My Bohemia (Fantasy).
Rodriguez, L.   Rant, Rave and Ricochet.
Ryman.   Matthew, Mark, Luke and John, / She
   chanted.
Serote.   This Old Woman.
Shephard, S.   Homeless Vets.
Sholl.   Soup Kitchen.
Spires.   Woman on the Dump, The.
Thomas, D.   Hunchback in the Park, The.
Tokareva, Y.   Why is she sleeping on some
   steps.
Tu Fu [or Du Fu].   Moon on the Cold Flood
   Festival.
Unknown.   Soup Kitchen Song.
Williams, W.   To a Poor Old Woman.

Homer
Adams, Cyd.   River Road.
Byron, G.   Oh, thou eternal Homer! I have now.
Coffey.   Homer where born where buried of
   whom the son.
Cunningham, J.   Homer was poor. His scholars
   live at ease.
Eberhart, R.   Garden God, The.
Fox, Skip.   Economics of Metonymy
   ("Balancing as metal, its sound, the metal in its
   sound.").
Garlick, R.   Note on the Iliad.
Hay, G.   Homer.
Homer.   And then went down to the ship.
Kavanagh, P.   Epic.
Keats.   On First Looking into Chapman's
   Homer.
   To Homer.
Lang, A.   Odyssey, The.
Mandelstam [or Mandelshtam].   Insomnia.
   Insomnia. Homer. Taut Sails.
   Sleeplessness. Homer. The sails tight.
Nishiwaki Junzaburo.   Man Who Reads Homer,
   A.
Reese, L.   Love, Weeping, Laid This Song.
Rexroth, K.   Homer in Basic.
Shepherd, R.   Homeric Interim.
Stephens, P.   God Shed His Grace.
Upton, L.   Women's Labors.
Walcott.   Ajax, / lion-coloured stallion from
   Sealey's stable.

Homesickness
al-Rahim, A.   Road, The.
Alexander, E.   Letter: Blues.
Ali, M.   Homeland.
Ammons.   Alligator Holes Down Along About
   Old Dock.
Běkeš.   I Who Have Nothing.
Berry, J.   Lucy's Letter.
Blomer, Y.   Landscapes and Home / Ghazal 22.
Borges.   John 1:14 (1969).
Brooke, R.   Old Vicarage, Grantchester, The.
Browning, R.   Home-Thoughts, from Abroad.
Buhyu Sunsoo.   On Hearing a Pipe.
Bunno [Wen Wang or King Wen].   Song of the

Bowmen of Shu [1954].
Buson.   Spring breeze.
Byron, G.   Lachin y Gair.
Carmichael, H.   Hong Kong Blues.
Chen Zi'ang.   Staying in Luoxiang County for
   the Evening.
Chia Tao.   Spring Travel.
Cho Myŏngni [or Myŏnghŭi].   Wild geese have
   all flown away.
Chŏng Chiyong.   Homesickness.
Clare, J.   Flitting, The.
   Soldier, The.
Cunningham, A.   Hame, Hame, Hame.
D'Aguiar, F.   Home: "These days whenever I
   stay away too long."
Donovan, K.   Prayer of the Wanderer.
Du Shenyan.   Lodging in Annam.
Fitz-Simon, E.   Woods of Kylinoe, The: Song of
   the Irish Emigrant in North America.
Glück, L.   Legend.
Gorrell, S.   Georgia on My Mind.
Haewŏn.   On Hearing the Song of the Geese.
Halpern, M.   Long for Home.
Heissenbüttel.   Homesick.
Hernández, M.   My heart can't go on any
   longer.
Homer.   Odyssey, The.
Hsieh T'iao.   Ascend the Three Mountains
   Toward the Evening: Looking Back at the
   Capital.
Hughes, L.   Homesick Blues.
Jarrell, R.   Island, The.
Jones, E.   Lament of the Banana Man, The.
Kefala.   Sunday Visit.
Kipling, R.   Broken Men, The.
Kolsson, K.   For five loathsome weeks.
Lewis, A.   In Hospital: Poona (1).
Li Ch'ing-chao.   End to Spring, An.
   To the Tune: Bodhisattva's Headdress.
   To the Tune "The Bodhisattva's Headdress".
Li Kuang-t'ien.   Dead Turk, A.
Li Po.   Barbarian pass is filled with windblown
   sand, The.
   Calm Night Thought.
   Fall River Song.
   Hearing the Flute in the City of Loyang in a
   Spring Night.
   Listening to a Flute on a Spring Night in Lo-
   yang.
   Quiet Night Thought.
   Quiet Night Thoughts.
   Remembering East Mountain.
   Spring Night in Luoyang—Hearing a Flute.
   Still Night Thoughts.
   Thoughts in Night Quiet.
Li Yi.   Listening to a Flute at Night near the
   City Wall.
   On Hearing a Flute at Night from the Wall of
   Shouxiang.
Li Yü.   Tune: "Beauty Yu".
Lin, D.   Nostalgia: "O, fruitful district Corozal!"
Liu Ch'ang-ch'ing.   Climbing in Autumn for a
   View from the Temple on the Terrace of
   General Wu.
Macleod, M.   Blue Song.
MacNeice.   Nostalgia.
Masefield.   West Wind, The.
Masters, E.   Reuben Pantier.
McKay, C.   Outcast.
   Tropics in New York, The.
Meng Hao Jan.   From a Mooring on the Tonglu
   to a Friend in Yangzhou.
Muhammad, Sakinah Carol.   Rain Lover.
Muldoon, P.   Homesickness.
No Ch'ŏnmyŏng.   Nostalgia.
P'an Yüeh.   Homeward.
Pao Chao.   Rough Road, A.
Pilinszky, J.   One Fine Day.
Porter, P.   'In the New World Happiness is
   Allowed'.
Pyungyang Ungee.   On a Cuckoo's Song.
Ransom, J.   Amphibious Crocodile.
Ryan, R.   Winter in Minneapolis.
Shen Quanqi.   First Reaching Huanzhou.
Sin Saimdang, Lady.   Looking Homeward from
   a Mountain Pass.

Strabo, W.   Elegy on Reichenau.
T'ao Ch'ien [or T'ao Yuan-ming].   Passing Through Ch'ien-hsi, Third Month, 405.
Trakl.   On the Marshy Pastures.
Ts'ao Ts'ao.   Bitter Cold: A Song.
Variant on the Songs of the East and West Gates.
Tu Fu [or Du Fu].   After Solstice.
Chengtu.
Moonlit Night ("In Fuzhou, far away, my wife is watching.").
Moonlit Night ("Tonight, moon over Fu-chou.").
Spring Scene.
Tu Mu.   Plantains.
Tu Shen-yen.   Harmonizing a Spring Poem by Premier Lu of Chin-Ling.
Unknown.   Cai-wei: We Pick Ferns, We Pick Ferns.
God, do not let any woman die in exile!
Insects chirp outside the four walls, The.
Living in this land of exile is ravaging my heart.
My Heart Is in Merioneth.
Old Song.
Sad Song.
Sad Song.
With eyes filled with tears.
Wu-jiang da-ju: Don't Walk Beside the Big Carriage.
Zhu-gan: This Rod.
Vietnamese Oral Tradition.   Homesick Bride, The.
Wang Po.   In the Mountains.
Wang Ts'an.   Climbing the Tower.
Wang Wei.   Thinking of My Brother in Shantung on the Ninth Day of the Ninth Moon.
Williams, E.   Why, Cambria did I quit thy shore.
Yujŏng.   Longing for My Hometown.

Homesteaders
Catacalos.   Homesteaders.
Nystrom.   Homesteaders.
Press, K.   Reclaiming our land.
Salzman, E.   Homesteading.

Homophobia
Bibbins, M.   Geometry Class.
Borawski.   Some of Us Wear Pink Triangles.
Brass.   Only Silly Faggots Know.
Cernuda.   I'll Tell You How You Were Born.
Domina, L.   Pharoah's Army Got Drowned.
Doty, M.   Homo Will Not Inherit.
Everhard.   Curing Homosexuality.
Liu, T.   Strange Fruit.
Mackay, J.   Nameless Love, The.
Parker, P.   Where Will You Be?
Pitchford.   Surgery.
Pratt, M.   Crime Against Nature.
Raffalovich, M. A.   Sonnet 120.
World Well Lost 18, The.
World Well Lost 4, The.
Reynolds, C.   Worst of it, The.
Van Jordan, A.   Dance Lesson, A.
Wilmer, S.   Mess Boy, The.
Young, C.   Torn.

Homosexuality and Homosexuals
Adamson.   Action Would Kill It / A Gamble.
Addaeus.   When you meet a young boy, be direct.
Amis, K.   Ever-Fixed Mark, An.
Anacreon.   Elegy 2.
Fragment 17.
Fragment 360.
Auden.   Aubade: "At break of dawn."
Glad.
Legend.
Mad to be had, to be felt and smelled. My lips.
Minnelied.
Aviram, A.   Pictures of Maurice Among Funeral Flowers.
Ayres, R.   Corporeal.
Bailey, S.   Hide-n-Seek.
Barber, W.   Explanation.
Gay Poet, The.
Barnfield [or Barnefield].   But if thou wilt not pittie my complaint.
Daphnis to Ganymede.
Oh would to God he would but pitty mee.
Scarce had the morning starre hid from the light.

Sighing, and sadly sitting by my Love.
Sometimes I wish that I his pillow were.
Sporting at fancie, setting light by love.
Sweet Corrall lips, where Nature's treasure lies.
Thus was my love, thus was my Ganymed.
When will my May come, that I may embrace thee?
Becker, R.   History of Sexual Preference, A.
Sad Sestina.
Behn, A.   To the Fair Clarinda [or Clorinda], Who Made Love to Me, Imagin'd [or Imagined] More than Woman.
Bibbins, M.   Bluebeard.
Whitman on the Beach.
Blaser.   Even on Sunday.
Borawski.   Power of One.
Some of Us Wear Pink Triangles.
Talking to Jim.
Brainard, J.   I Remember.
Brass.   I Have This Vision of Madness.
Only Silly Faggots Know.
Brooks, A.   Here is the queen.
Broumas, O.   Amazon Twins.
Caritas.
With the clear.
Bursk.   What a Boy Does Not Say.
Byron, G.   Cornelian, The.
One Struggle More, and I Am Free.
To Thyrza.
Cabico, R.   Antonio Banderas in His Underwear.
Art in Architecture.
Gameboy.
Cady.   After Hearing Heterosexual Poets in October 1974: What It Seems Like To Write a Male Homosexual Love Poem Now.
Campo.   Asylum.
Aunt Toni's Heart.
Battle Hymn of the Republic, The.
El Día de los Muertos.
Manuel.
Medical Student Learns Love and Death, A.
Our Country of Origin.
Carpenter, E.   Summer Heat.
Through the Long Night.
Cassells.   Beautiful Signor.
Marathon.
New Song of Solomon.
Cataldi.   13 November 1983.
We Could Have Met.
Catullus.   To Aurelius.
To Aurelius and Furius.
To Juventius.
Cavafy.   In Despair.
Cernuda.   I'll Tell You How You Were Born.
Chin, J.   Cocksucker's Blues.
Ex-Boyfriends Named Michael.
Undetectable.
Why a Boy.
Why He Had to Go.
Chubb, R.   Song of My Soul.
Transfiguration.
Cole, H.   Childlessness.
Conway, J.   Hangover.
Marlo Thomas in Seven Parts and Epilogue.
Modern English.
Weight Belt.
Cooper, D.   After School, Street Football, Eighth Grade.
No God.
Teen Idols.
Corn.   Billie's Blues.
Long-Distance Call to Gregg, Who Lived with AIDS as Long as He Could.
Marriage in the Nineties, A.
To Hermes.
Cox, M.   Barbells of the Gods, The.
Crane, H.   Modern Craft.
Creeley.   All That Is Lovely in Men.
Crowley, A.   Ballad of Passive Paederasty, A.
Rondels.
de Gillies, G.   De Puerorum osculis.
Diodes.   Somebody said when snubbed, "Is Damon so.
Domina, L.   Pharoah's Army Got Drowned.
Doty, M.   Days of 1981.
Homo Will Not Inherit.

Letter to Walt Whitman.
Lilacs in NYC.
Michael's Dream.
Douglas, L.   Two Loves.
Drayton.   And thus like slaves we sell our soules to sinne.
O breake my hart quoth he, O breake and dye.
This Edward in the Aprill of his age.
Why doe I quake my down-fall to reporte?
Duffy, C.   Oppenheim's Cup and Saucer.
Elmslie, K.   Venus Preserved.
Euripides.   Fragment 652.
Fanning, R.   In the Barn.
Fisher, S.   Hometown.
Gates, B.   Homeless.
Triptych.
Genet.   Man Condemned to Death, The.
Ginsberg, A.   At 4:00 a.m. the two.
Chances "R".
Howl.
Please Master.
Sphincter.
This Form of Life Needs Sex.
Giorno.   Pornographic Poem.
Glaukos.   Where once you could win over grasping boys.
Gunn, T.   Blank, A.
San Francisco Streets.
Hacker, M.   Ballad of Ladies Lost and Found.
Dusk: July.
Eight Days in April.
Graffiti from the Gare Saint-Manqué.
Harms.   My Androgynous Years.
Hayes, T.   At Pegasus.
Healy, E.   Louganis.
What It Was Like the Night Cary Grant Died.
Hecht, A.   Feast of Stephen, The.
Hemphill.   Homocide.
Where Seed Falls.
Holden, J.   Why We Bombed Haiphong.
Holland, W.   Christopher Street 1979.
Horace.   Late Night Ode.
Iozia, J.   Fag Art.
Last Night at the Flamingo.
Juvenal.   Northward beyond the Lapps to the world's end, the frozen.
Klein, M.   Letters from the Front.
Tides, The.
Klyuyev [or Kliuev or Klyuev].   Fourth Rome, The.
Knight, E.   For Freckle-Faced Gerald.
Koestenbaum, W.   1980.
1992.
1977.
Tea Dance.
Komunyakaa, Y.   Troubling the Water.
Lassell.   Brady Street, San Francisco.
Going to Europe.
Kissing Ramén.
Sunset Stripping: Visiting L.A.
Three Poems.
Lefroy.   Idler Listening to Socrates Discussing Philosophy with His Boy-Friends, An.
Leon, R.   Have you not heard the gossip and the rumour going around.
Lesley, G.   Behold, how Sodom swaggers in its Pride.
Light, K.   2. San Francisco.
Liu, T.   Highway 6.
Reading Whitman in a Toilet Stall.
Thoreau.
Mackay, J.   Nameless Love, The.
Malloch, D.   Manly Love.
Manrique, J.   My Night with Frederico García Lorca (As Told by Edouard Roditi).
Tarzan.
Marlowe.   Ah, wicked King! Accursed Gaveston!
Here is the form of Gaveston's exile.
He's gone, and for his absence thus I mourn.
My father is deceas'd. Come, Gaveston.
Nephew, I must to Scotland. Thou stay'st here.
What is't, sweet wag, I should deny thy youth?
Martial.   Artemidorus sold his land to buy a boy.
Bearded Callistratus wedded rugged Afer.
Breath of balm from foreign branches pressed,

The.
Chrestus, your balls are depilated.
Cure of my unquietness.
Did he have eyes and, if so, did he look.
Gaurus, you have a fault for which.
If by chance, Flaccus, someone could offer me
  for the asking.
Why, Hyllus, do you deny to me today.
Your slave boy's cock is aching, Naevolus.
Massimi.   Advice to Paulinus.
Love Song for Marcus, A.
On Happiness.
McClatchy.   First Steps.
Meleager.   To Aristogoras.
  To Diodorus, Dorotheus, Callicrates et al.
Mew.   On the Road to the Sea.
Moore, H.   Edward.
Morgan, R.   Damn You, Lady.
Nonnus.   Dionysus and Ampelos.
  Eros came near in the horned shape of a shaggy
    Silenos.
  Where Carpos wandered and died, I will fall
    headlong.
Norse.   I Would Not Recommend Love.
Nuccoli.   Since I abandoned and tied my soul to
  your sweet appearance and manners oh Sir,
  guide and light of my life, will I ever see you
  before I die?
O'Hara, F.   Homosexuality.
Ovid.   Apollo and Hyacinthus.
Parker, P.   For Willyce.
  Where Will You Be?
Pearlberg, G.G.   Dog Star.
  Loop-the-Loop in Prospect Park (1905).
  Sailor.
Penna.   Pitiless war of love I fought, A.
Phillips, C.   Cotillion.
  Kill, The.
  Undressing for Li Po.
Pindar.   Ode on Theoxenos.
Pitchford.   Surgery.
Poliziano.   Love Song for Chrysokomos
  (Goldenlocks).
  On the Love of Two Boys.
  What song will ever be so sorrowful.
Pomeroy, R.   Gay Love and the Movies.
Powell, D. A.   When you touch down upon this
  earth. little reindeers.
  Writing for a young man on the redline train:
    "to his boy mistress".
Pratt, M.   Other Side, The.
Pushkin, A.   Imitation of the Arabic.
Raffalovich, M. A.   Rose Leaves When the Rose
  Is Dead.
  Sonnet 120.
  World Well Lost 18, The.
  World Well Lost 4, The.
Rainey.   Prove It on Me Blues.
Redel, V.   Bedecked.
Reece, Spencer.   Clerk's Tale, The.
Rhianos.   To Theodorus et al.
Richard, B.   My Sixth Grade Sex Life: Milne
  Elementary, New Orleans.
Ricketts, W.   Scout.
Roberts, M.   Magnificat.
Roberts, N.   Nigger and Some Poofters, A.
Rochester, J.   Song: "Love a woman? You're [or
  Y'are] an ass."
Sadi [or Saadi or Sa'di].   O I repented, wore my
  pious cloak.
Saint.   Heart and Soul.
Scannell.   Protest Poem.
Scarlatti.   Lanza 51.
Schreiber, R.   Chant.
  Gay Life.
  They Kill Us.
  To Be Held.
Scythinus.   Calamity and conflagration! Strife!
Seaton, M.   Story of Stonewall, A.
Shakespeare, W.   Sonnet 20: "Woman's face
  with nature's own[e] hand painted, A."
Shatalov, A.   Age of aquarius mineral water
  taking a bath, The.
Shepherd, R.   Eros in His Striped Blue Shirt.
  Gods at Three A.M., The.
  Narcissus Learning the Words to This Song.

That Man.
Three A.M. Eternal.
Shurin.   City of Men.
  His Promise.
Siken, Richard.   Primer for the Small Weird
  Loves, A.
  Saying Your Names.
Simon, L.   Bernice Got Next to Isis.
Smith, S.   Lord Barrenstock.
Solon.   Love of Boys, The.
Strato [or Straton].   Begin with Zeus, Aratus
  said; but, Muse.
  Boys' members, Diodorus, come in three.
  Despite the ruddy down upon your cheek.
  Fitness expert. Big gym-man.
  I loathe a boy who won't be hugged and kissed.
  In the bed are two, submissive.
  In years to come, I ask, be kind.
  Long hair, and curls woven not by Nature but
    by Art.
  To start with, grapple your opponent 'round.
  Twelve-year-old looks fetching in his prime, A.
  Yesterday in the bath Diodes' penis.
  Your rosy-fingered prick that used to charm.
Symonds.   In years of old.
  Love and Death: A Symphony.
  Midnight at Baiae.
  Thou dost establish—and our hearts receive—.
  What Cannot Be.
Taylor, B.   Hylas.
  Paean to the Dawn, A.
Tayson, R.   First Sex.
  Nightsweats.
  Phone Sex.
Teare, Brian.   Detail from "Set for a Southern
  Gothic".
  Set for a Southern Gothic.
  Trick Noir.
Theocritus.   Idyll 29: ""Truth in the cups" men
  say, dear youth."
Theognis.   It's a thrill to love a boy: even
  Kronos' son, king of immortals, once longed
  for Ganymede.
  Man who doesn't love boys and single-foot
    horses and dogs, his heart will never know
    pleasure, The.
Trinidad.   As one young guy screwed another
  young guy.
  Boy, The.
  Doll Not Included.
  For Joe Brainard.
  He said his name was Nick; later I learned.
  Monday, Monday.
  More than anything, I wanted Charlie.
  Tom used spit for lubricant and fucked me.
Twichell.   Horse.
Unknown.   Among the yeomen's sons on my
  estate.
  Chance led me once, when idling through the
    street.
  Hebe and Ganymede.
  Love of women leaves me cold; desire, The.
  Sometimes I sauntered from my lone abode.
  Song of the Viet Boatman.
  Statesmen, in your exalted station know.
  Surprise, Surprise.
  Thou ermined judge, pull off that sable cap!
  Thus feverish fancies floated in my brain.
  Tree we plant will, when its boughs are grown,
    The.
  Unhappy pedophiles, cease your inane.
  What Really Goes on in the College of
    Cardinals.
  Wise Rejoice with Ganymede, The.
  Women as women, me had never charmed.
  Zeus as an eagle came to Ganymede.
Vaughan, R.   10 Reasons Why I Fall in Love
  with Inaccessible Straight Boys Every Damn
  Time.
Verlaine.   He's an awkward bedfellow and I love
  to keep.
  Mille e tre.
Villaurrutia.   Los Angeles Nocturne.
Virgil [or Vergil].   Eclogue 2: The Lament of
  Corydon for His Faithless Alexis.
Voss, F.   Stud, The.

Weiners.   Act #2.
Whitman, W.   Earth, My Likeness.
  Glimpse, A.
  In Paths Untrodden.
  Live Oak, with Moss.
  Not Heat Flames Up and Consumes.
  Recorders Ages Hence.
  When I Heard At The Close Of The Day.
  Whoever You Are Holding Me Now in Hand.
Wieners.   Acceptance.
  Doll.
  King Solomon's Magnetic Quiz.
  Loneliness, The.
  Poem for Cocksuckers, A.
  To H.
Williams, S. A.   She Had Known Brothers.
Williams, Stephanie.   Of Riches.
Wilmer, S.   Mess Boy, The.
Wright, J.   Sappho.
Wunderlich, M.   Continent's Edge.
  East Seventh Street.
  Given in Person Only.
  Take Good Care of Yourself.
  Trick, The.

Honesty
Abbott, K.   Our honest neighbor's rolled.
Armand.   Sonnet: "I am an honest man."
Brown, E.   Bitcherel.
Campion, T.   Heart's Music.
Cleage.   Confession.
de Fierro.   Speak to Me.
Duhamel.   Yes.
Dunn, S.   On the Death of a Colleague.
Joyce, J.   Though I thy Mithridates were.
Larkin, P.   Talking in Bed.
Nesbit, E.   Appeal.
Rukeyser, M.   Poem as Mask, The.
Shcherbina.   Eros Poesis.
Vitale, M.   Three Written Poems, Unconnected.
Whitman, W.   Past and present wilt—I have
  filled them, emptied them, The.
Wyatt.   Honesty.

Honey
Brooks, G.   My dreams, my works must wait till
  after hell.
Doolittle, Hilda.   Fragment 113: "Not honey, /
  not the plunder of the bee."
Kelly, R.   In June.
Khoury, N.   People of Figs.
Latouche, J.   Honey in the Honeycomb.
Levy, D.   Honey.
Lima, J.   Distribution of Poetry.
Mandelstam [or Mandelshtam].   Lightheartedly
  Take from the Palms of My Hands.
Morgan, R.   Honey.
Mother Goose.   God made the bees.
Polley, J.   Jar of Honey, A.
Sandburg, C.   In Tall Grass.
Sappho.   For me neither honey nor bee.
Toomer.   Beehive.
Unknown.   Peas.
Watts, I.   How Doth the Little Busy Bee.

Honeymoons
Cahn, S.   Come Fly with Me.
Corso.   Marriage.
Dubie.   Buffalo Clouds over the Maestro Hoon.
Dubin, A.   Shuffle Off to Buffalo.
Durcan.   Honeymoon Postcard.
Friman.   Honeymoon.
Kahn, G.   Okay, Toots.
Rendra.   World's First Face, The.
Rexroth, K.   It Is a German Honeymoon.
Updike.   Newlyweds, The.
Whitehead, W.   Waning Honeymoon, The.

Honeysuckle
Bécquer, G.   Darkling Swallows Will Come
  Again, The.
Belieu.   Nocturne: My Sister Life.
Bloem, J. C.   Honeysuckle.
Freneau.   Wild Honey Suckle, The.
Hudgins.   Flag of Honeysuckle, A.
Razaf, A.   Honeysuckle Rose.

Hong Kong
Carmichael, H.   Hong Kong Blues.
Webster, P.   Love Is a Many-Splendored Thing.

Honor
Bass, F.   I am a Jew.
Belloc.   Love and Honour.
Berryman.   Scholars at the Orchid Pavilion.
Browne, W.   Shall I tell you whom I love?
Chapman, G.   Nor riches to the virtues of my love.
Collins, W.   How Sleep the Brave.
Daniel, S.   Ulysses and the Siren [or Syren].
DeNicola, D.   My Father's First Fight.
Dickinson, E.   Sown in dishonor!
Gezelle.   Little Mother.
Goldsmith, O.   When Lovely Woman Stoops to Folly.
Greenlee.   Memorial for Trane.
Haavikko.   I always bow down deep before a small tree and a great tyrant.
Hồ Xuân Hương.   General's Plaque, The.
Jonson, B.   Song. To Celia ("Drink to me only with thine eyes.").
  To Sir Henry Cary.
Korinna [or Corinna].   But I sing the excellence of heroes.
Lao Tzu.   Weapons are the tools of violence.
Legaré.   Tallulah.
Levine, P.   On the Murder of Lieutenant José del Castillo by the Falangist Bravo Martinez, July 12, 1936.
Lovelace, R.   To Lucasta, [on] Going to the War[re]s.
Lynch, Peggy Zuleika.   True Texan, A.
MacNeice.   Elegy for Minor Poets.
McKay, C.   If We Must Die.
Melville, H.   College Colonel, The.
Murray, L.   Lament for the Country Soldiers.
Nerval.   Golden Sayings.
Nossis.   O Honored Hera, who often descending from heaven.
Owen, W.   S.I.W.
Philips, K.   On the Welsh Language.
Platner, I.   We Are the Heirs.
Shakespeare, W.   O! that we now had here.
  Sonnet 25: "Let those who are in favour with their stars."
Smith, A.   Praise.
Stanley, T.   Pythagoric Letter, The.
Suckling, S.   Loving and Beloved.
Sze.   In Your Honor.
Unknown.   Down to the Mire.
  Elegy upon the Death of Mrs. A. Behn, the Incomparable Astrea, An.
  If you do not have a wound in the center of your chest.
  Introduction: History and Praise of the Danes; Account of Grendel's Attacks on Heorot.
Vega.   Brothers Loving Brothers.
Villiers.   Epitaph upon Thomas, Lord Fairfax, An.
Weinblatt, J.   Marriage Song for Many Voices.
Whitman, W.   To a Certain Cantatrice.
Wilde, L.   Désillusion.

Hooch, Pieter de
Mahon.   Courtyards in Delft.

Hoover, John Edgar
Starbuck, G.   Said.

Hope
Abercrombie.   Hope and Despair.
Akhmatova, A.   Dedication.
Al-Haidari, B.   Will, The.
Alegría.   Ars Poetica.
Alves, R.   Tomorrow's Child.
Aytoun [or Ayton], R.   Upone Tabacco.
Baca.   Book 5: Rebirth; Twenty-Nine.
  Oppression.
Baudelaire.   Spleen LXXVIII.
Beer, P.   Flood, The.
Bell, C.   Where Hope Lives.
Bly, R.   Things to Think.
Bonnefoy.   Task of Hope, The.
Brass.   I Have This Vision of Madness.
Brecht, B.   World's One Hope, The.
Brontë, E.   Hope.
  Prisoner, The. A Fragment.
  Still let my tyrants know, I am not doomed to wear.
Castro, R.   Now that the Sunset of Hope.

Ceravolo.   Wild Provoke of the Endurance Sky.
Chimombo.   Death Song, A.
Clifton, L.   Hag Riding.
Cogswell, Fred.   Edge, The.
Coleridge, H.   All nature ministers to Hope. The snow.
Coleridge, S.   On a Discovery Made Too Late.
  To the Autumnal Moon.
  Work without Hope.
Collins, A.   Song.
Coulehan, J.   Azalea Poem, The.
Crane, H.   Ave Maria.
Cruz, S.   Not Without Hope Pulsing My Breast.
Cullen, C.   From the Dark Tower.
Cunningham, J.   Time heals not: it extends a sorrow's scope.
Dame.   Seder, The.
Demy, J.   You Must Believe in Spring.
Depestre.   Ballad of a Little Lamp.
Di Prima.   Revolutionary Letter #1.
Dickinson, E.   Hope is the thing with feathers.
  I dwell in Possibility.
Diop, D.   Vultures, The.
Divakaruni.   Restroom.
Driscoll, L.   Hold Fast Your Dreams.
Ercilla, M.   Oysters and Zarzuelas.
Faiz.   Prison Evening, A.
Fries, K.   Who knows the precise moment when the stream.
García Lorca.   Poet Speaks with Love by Telephone, The.
Garcilaso de la Vega.   One Moment My Hope Rises Up On Wings.
Giovanni.   Poem For My Nephew.
Graves, R.   Love Without Hope.
Halperin.   Tulips.
Hammerstein.   You'll Never Walk Alone.
Hardy, T.   Darkling Thrush, The.
Hauge.   Evening Clouds.
Heard, J.   Hope.
Hemans.   Despondency and Aspiration.
Herbert, G.   Hope.
Herd.   Bathing Girls, The.
Hernández Cruz.   Today Is a Day of Great Joy.
Hewitt, G.   Sailor, The.
Hikmet.   Rubai.
Hood, T.   Time, Hope, and Memory.
Hopkins, G.   Leaden Echo and the Golden Echo, The.
Horton, G.   On Liberty and Slavery.
Hristov, Boris.   Evening Trumpet.
Hudgins.   Hereafter, The.
Humphrey, D.   Hope.
Iosifova, Ekaterina.   March: "I'm going to your fair."
Jacobsen, R.   Sunflower.
Jarrell, R.   Hope ("Week is dealt out like a hand, The.").
  Jews at Haifa.
Jensma.   Cry Me a River.
József, A.   Encouraging.
Juana Inés de la Cruz.   Hope.
  Perpetual Infirmity of Hope.
Kenyon, J.   Let Evening Come.
  Once There Was Light.
King, J.   Intercity Dub.
Knight, E.   Green Grass and Yellow Balloons.
Ko Chônghûi.   Sisters, Now We Are the Path and the Light.
Kovur Kilar.   We Hope For Patrons.
Landon.   Farewell, The.
Lapierre, B.   Tomorrow's Hope.
Leigh, C.   I Walk a Little Faster.
Levy, E.   Gradually.
Llwyd, Iwan.   Meet me at the St Francis.
Locklin.   Where we are.
Lodge, G.   Fall.
Logghe.   From *Rice.*
Lucas, J.   Good Sunday.
Mahon.   Everything Is Going to Be All Right.
Mathews, H.   Out of Bounds.
Melville, H.   Immolated.
  Shelley's Vision.
Menken.   Aspiration.
Merrill, C.   Wipp Protest.
Merwin.   Hope for Her.

Mikha'il, M.   Don't Despair.
  Three Flags.
Miller, H.   Without God's Blessing.
Momaday.   Gift, The: "Older, more generous."
Montale.   Little Testament.
Moorer.   Door of Hope, The.
Mora.   Immigrants.
Moss, J.   On the Other Side of the Door.
Motsapi, S.   Kulu.
Moxley, Jennifer.   Transom Over Death's Door, A.
Mueller, L.   Hope.
Muir, E.   Good Man in Hell, The.
  Horses, The.
Naimy, M.   Hope is agony.
Neruda.   America, I Do Not Call Your Name Without Hope.
Nicholson, N.   From a Boat at Coniston.
O'Daly, W.   Naturalist, A.
O'Grady, Thomas.   Prayer for My Daughters, A.
Okigbo.   On the New Year.
Oppen.   From Disaster.
Papaionnou.   Nights Without Hope (Rebetiko Song).
Paz.   After: "After chopping off all the arms that reached out to me."
Pitter.   But for Lust.
Poe.   Dreams: "Oh! That my young life were a lasting dream!"
Pollard, C.   On the first of January.
Pollarolo, G.   Foretold Futures.
Pugh.   Sometimes.
Rafferty, P.   Back End.
Ransom, J.   Blackberry Winter.
Ratushinskaya [or Ratushinskaia].   Try to Cover Your Shivering Shoulders.
Ray, D.   Thanks, Robert Frost.
Ray, H.   Aspiration.
  Quest of the Ideal, The.
  Triple Benison, The.
Reeve, F.   Hope.
Rogers, S.   Boy of Egremond, The.
Roland Holst.   Time, Please.
Rosnay, J.   Piazza San Marco.
Rossetti, C.   Aloof.
  If Only.
  Song: "She sat and sang alway."
  Thinking of you, and all that was, and all.
Rukeyser, M.   Who in One Lifetime.
Ryan, R.   Lake of the Woods, The.
Sachs, N.   Someone Will Take The Ball.
Sagan.   Open the Door.
Sakhltkhutsishvili, U.   Soldiers: "Crossing the mountains."
Sall, A.   Cloak of Dawn.
Sanchez, S.   Anthem, An.
Sassoon, S.   Everyone Sang.
Scott, W.   Continuity of Life.
Senghor.   Suddenly Startled.
Shabtai, Aharon.   Hope: "It's hopeless, you told me."
Shelley, P.   England in 1819.
Shin Tongyŏp.   We have seen heaven.
"Shu Ting.".   Fairy Tales.
Simmons, J.   For Thomas Moore.
Smart, C.   Hymn 2. Hope.
Smith, C.   To Hope.
Sondheim.   Somewhere.
Stafford, W.   Way It Is, The.
Suárez.   Poem for Mankind and Its Hope.
Synková, A.   I've met enough people.
Tekeyan.   Country of Dust, The.
Thomas, E.   To Colindra.
Thompson, C.   Hope.
  Hope Deferred.
Thorpe, M.   Wishful Fall.
Tucker, M.   Hope.
Unknown.   America. . .then.
  Day of vast dreaming.
  Elegy upon the Death of Mrs. A. Behn, the Incomparable Astrea, An.
Vallejo.   I Am Going to Talk About Hope.
Verlaine.   Cold wind hurls itself at, A.
  Hope like a wisp of straw shines in the stable.
Vietnamese Oral Tradition.   Pole at the Village Pagoda, The.

Vilariño.   There is no hope.
Walker, A.   Remember?
Walker, J.   How Mother Courage Saves
  Desdemona.
Walker, M.   For My People.
Warren, R.   Aubade for Hope.
Whitehead, C.   Daybreak.
Williams, H.   To Hope.
Williams, Stephanie.   Hope Chest.
Wright, J.   Arrangements with Earth for Three
  Dead Friends.
Wroth.   Sonnet 27: "Fie [or Fy] tedious Hope,
  why do[e] you still rebel[l]?"
Yevtushenko [or Evtushenko].   Hundred miles
  from the capital city of hope, A.
Yi Kyŏngnim.   Anam Street 1.

See also **Optimism**

Hope, Bob
Hathaway, W.   Why That's Bob Hope.

Hopi, The
Rose.   Naayawva Taawi.
  Story Keeper.
Tomlinson, C.   Arizona Desert.
  Death in the Desert, A.

Hopper, Edward
Bonds, D.   Life of the Body, The.
Boruch.   Light.
Carpenter, W.   Evening Wind.
  Night Shadows.
Carter, A. B.   Cobb's Barns.
Cutts, S.   On parquet.
Dunn, S.   Impediment.
Elton, W.   Hopper: In the Cafe.
Greger.   Man on the Bed, The.
Hirsch, E.   Edward Hopper and the House by
  the Railroad.
Hollander, J.   Edward Hopper's Seven A.M.
  Sunday A.M. Not in Manhattan.
Levis.   Edward Hopper, "Hotel Room," 1931.
Ludvigson.   Inventing My Parents.
Mezey.   Evening Wind.
Mueller, L.   American Literature.
  Nude by Edward Hopper, A.
Quagliano.   Edward Hopper Retrospective, The.
  Edward Hopper's "Lighthouse at Two Lights".
Raab, L.   After Edward Hopper.
Ray, D.   Automat.
  Midnight Diner by Edward Hopper, A.
Rudolf.   Edward Hopper.
Sadoff.   Hopper's "Nighthawks" (1942).
Schulman.   American Solitude.
Standing.   Hopper's Women.
Stone, J.   Early Sunday Morning.
Wade, S.   Gas.
Williamson, A.   Light's Reading, The.
Yellen.   Nighthawks.

Horace
Laughlin, J.   I Know How Every Poet.
Marbod of Rennes.   Horace composed an ode
  about a certain boy.
Perelman.   Room.

Horatio
Cohen, N.   Horatio.
Gwynn, R.   Horatio's Philosophy.

Horatius
Macaulay, T.   Horatius [or Horatius at the
  Bridge].

Horn, Cape.
See **Cape Horn**

Hornets
Valentine, J.   Letter: "Hornet holds on to the
  curtain, winter, The."

Horse Racing
Bukowski.   No. 6.
Hart, K.   Flemington Racecourse.
Hayward, D.   To the Man Saying "Come on
  Seis" at Hollywood Park.
Herd.   Hyperion's Bones.
  Pat Taffe and Arkle.
Ibycus.   Again Love, glancing meltingly.
Larkin, P.   At Grass.
Loesser.   Fugue for Tinhorns.
Moore, M.   Tom Fool at Jamaica.
Paterson, A.   Father Riley's Horse.
Philpot, T.   Louisa's Wedding.

Yeats.   At Galway Races.

Horse Shows
Sidney.   Sonnet 41: "Having this day my horse,
  my hand, my lance."

Horseback Riding
Anacreon.   Thracian filly, why do you.
Armstrong, Tammy.   Horse Girls.
Becker, R.   Riding Lesson.
Betjeman.   Hunter Trials.
Bly, R.   Pitzeem and the Mare.
Browning, R.   How They Brought the Good
  News from Ghent to Aix.
  Last Ride Together, The.
Buson.   Toward Toba Palace.
Campbell, R.   Sisters, The.
Cummings, E. E.   All in green went my love
  riding.
Daegak Euchon.   Riding a Horse in the Rain.
Galvin, J.   Stories Are Made of Mistakes.
Gelinas, D.   Caballo de acero, El.
  Steel Horse.
Guiney.   Wild Ride, The.
Hardy, T.   Circus-Rider to Ringmaster.
Harwood, L.   Landscape with 3 People.
King, H.   Moonlight Ride, A.
Kizer, C.   Horseback.
Longfellow, H.   Paul Revere's Ride [The
  Landlord's Tale].
Manguso, S.   Rider, The.
Morris, W.   Haystack in the Floods, The.
Myers, J.   Training Horses.
O'Callaghan, C.   20 The Horse.
Roethke.   Elegy for Jane.
Sarah, R.   Courtney, Mentioned in Passing,
  Years After.
Sidney.   Sonnet 41: "Having this day my horse,
  my hand, my lance."
  Sonnet 49: "I on my horse, and Love on me
  doth try."
Simpson, M.   Millet's *The Gleaners*.
Swenson, M.   Bronco Busting, Event #1.
Taylor, H.   Riding Lesson.
Twichell.   Horse.
Weaver, A.   Weekend Equestrian, The.
Wilbur, R.   Ride, The.

Horses
Abu-I-Salt Umayyah.   White Stallion, The.
Agustini.   In Fields of Sleepdreaming.
Ai.   Before You Leave.
Alberti.   Ghost, The.
Alcaeus [or Alkaios].   Come! Put by Pelops'
  Isle.
Alexie.   I Would Steal Horses.
Ammons.   Silver.
Anacreon.   Thracian filly, why do you.
Anyte [or Anytes].   Damis erected this mound
  for his dead steadfast.
Apollinaire.   Horse Calligram.
Ayres.   Cynthia on Horseback.
Baca.   Mantanza to Welcome Spring.
Bandeira.   Rondeau of the Little Horses.
Barnes, K.   Night Light.
Basho.   As for the hibiscus.
  Farmer's roadside, The.
  Fleas, lice.
  Winter sun, The.
Behn, R.   Like a Horse.
  Yellow House Writes a Story for the Boy, The.
Bierds, L.   Muybridge.
Blaser.   Suddenly.
Bly, R.   Watering the Horse.
Boland, E.   War Horse, The.
Borisov.   Horse, The: "Up the moss-grown."
Browning, R.   How They Brought the Good
  News from Ghent to Aix.
Buchsbaum, Julianne.   Slowly, Slowly, Horses.
Burkard.   I have a silence in the rain.
Burns, R.   Tam o' Shanter; A Tale.
Buson.   Fallen petals of red plum.
  Going home.
  Riding.
  Tethered horse, A.
Bynner.   Horses.
Campbell, R.   Sisters, The.
Cardona-Hine.   Enough Horses.
Chamberlain, B.   Dead Ponies.

Chuilleanáin, E.   Horses of Meaning, The.
Clark, P.   My Life with Horses.
Clark, T.   Lake, The.
Clifton, L.   C. C. Rider.
Coatsworth.   Circus-Postered Barn, The.
  Daniel Webster's Horses.
  Old Mare, The.
Cole, H.   Horses: "Setting out on my bicycle
  alone."
Conn.   Todd.
Creeley.   Rescue, The.
Cuadra, P.   Horses in the Lake.
Cummings, E. E.   All in green went my love
  riding.
Daiches, J.   Horse in Glasgow.
Dalton, Mary.   Sterricky.
Davidkov, Ivan.   Meteor.
Davis, H.   Proud Riders.
Dickey, J.   Dusk of Horses, The.
Dietz, H.   Blue Grass.
Dodge, M.   Wooden Horse, The.
Donovan, K.   Entering the Mare.
Dove, R.   Horse and Tree.
  Revenant.
Espaillat.   Metrics.
Frost, R.   Draft Horse, The.
  Runaway, The.
García Lorca.   Song of the Rider.
Getsi.   Washing Your Hair.
Gill, K.   Ghazal 5: "My white mare on the
  Punjabi plains, the stamp of her hooves."
Glück, L.   Horse.
Goodge.   How We Drove the Trotter.
Gould, H.   Apprehension.
Guiney.   Wild Ride, The.
Gyatso, T.   Wild horses running in the hills.
Hall, D.   Names of Horses.
Harjo, J.   Drowning Horses.
  She Had Some Horses.
Harris, J.   Sending the Mare to Auction.
Harte, B.   Tale of a Pony, The.
Hausman.   Appaloosa Hail Storm.
Haviaras, Stratis.   Still Life.
Hearne, V.   Gauguin's White Horse.
Herd.   Hyperion's Bones.
  Pat Taffe and Arkle.
Hershon.   Unless You Are a Horse.
Hirshfield, J.   Studying Wu Wei, Muir Beach.
Hogan, L.   Celebration: Birth of a Colt.
Hopkins, G.   Felix Randal.
Hsiang Chi.   Hegemon's Lament, The.
Hughes, T.   Bones.
  Horses, The.
  Yesterday He Was Nowhere to Be Found.
Ibycus.   Again Love, glancing meltingly.
Issa.   Hey, sparrow!
  Naked.
  No doubt about it.
Ivanov, G.   Unharnessed, the white horse ambles
  along.
Jeffers, R.   Roan Stallion.
Joans, T.   Overloaded Horse, The.
Jones, R.   Nell.
Juhász, F.   Birth of the Foal.
Kenyon, J.   In the Nursing Home.
Kumin, M.   Grace of Geldings in Ripe Pastures,
  The.
  Thinking of Death and Dogfood.
Labid.   Tent marks in Mínan are worn away,
  The.
Larkin, P.   At Grass.
Laurencin, M.   Horse, The.
Lazutkina, E.   Wind's mane, The.
Levin, P.   Dark Horse.
Levine, P.   Horse, The: "They spoke of the horse
  alive."
Levis.   Anastasia and Sandman.
  Elegy with a Bridle in Its Hand.
Lewis, G.   White Horse.
Li Po.   Song of the Heavenly Horse.
Longley, M.   Horses, The.
Lumbreras, E.   Reunión de violoncelos.
  Reunion of Cellos.
Manguso, S.   Rider, The.
Masaoka Shiki.   Sudden rain / Rows of horses.
Mayakovsky [or Maiakovskii].   Good Attitude

to Horses, A.
McAuley, J.　Blue Horses, The.
McCarriston.　Coursier de Jeanne d'Arc, Le.
　Healing the Mare.
　Riding Out at Evening.
McGrath, T.　End of the Line, The.
Mei Yao Ch'en.　Dappled Horse, The.
Merrill, J.　Charioteer of Delphi, The.
Mitchell, F.　12th Horse Song of Frank Mitchell
　(Blue), The.
Moore, L.　Eternal Landscape, The.
Moore, M.　Tom Fool at Jamaica.
Muir, E.　Horses, The.
Na Hûidôk.　Dirty Nylons.
Nance.　Rio Grande Hills.
Nelson, J.　For Whom the Bells Toll and Toll
　and Toll.
Nemes Nagy.　Sincerity.
Neruda.　Horses.
Norris, L.　Pit Ponies, The.
Nowlan.　Weakness.
Nutter, G.　Boy Leading a Horse.
O Riordain.　Switch.
O'Connell, E.　Dirge on the Death of Art
　O'Leary.
O'Grady, D.　Great Horse Fair, The.
O'Grady, Thomas.　Dark Horses.
Ortiz.　8:50 AM Ft. Lyons VAH.
Parker, A.　Vandals, Horses.
Patchen.　Horses of Yilderin, The.
Peacocke.　Remembrance.
"Perse."　Song: "Under the bronze leaves a colt
　was foaled."
Purdy, A.　Cariboo Horses, The.
Ransford, Tessa.　Stable Relationship, A.
Reeves, J.　Four Horses, The.
Rendall, R.　Horse-Mill, The.
Reznikoff.　What are you doing in our street
　among the automobiles, horse?
Roberson, E.　Blue Horses.
Romtvedt.　Glass Canyons.
Rossetti, C.　Horses of the Sea, The.
　Horses of the sea, The.
Roy, L.　Ride, The.
Sabina.　13th Horse Song of Frank Mitchell,
　The.
Sabry, M.　Troy.
Sappho.　Horses in Flowers.
Shuford.　Horse in My Yard, The.
Shukman, H.　Horses at Christmas.
Slutsky [or Slutskii].　Horses in the Ocean.
Stephens, J.　To the Four Courts, Please.
Stephens, M.　Ponies, Twynyrodyn.
Stoyanova, Danila.　Three mares.
Swenson, M.　Bronco Busting, Event #1.
　Centaur, The.
Taylor, H.　Flying Change, The.
　Riding a One-eyed Horse.
Tester, V.　First Horses, 1519.
Teton Sioux Oral Tradition.　You Have No
　Horses.
Theognis.　Boy and horse, a similar brain: the
　horse doesn't cry when its rider lies in the
　dust.
Thomas, G.　Horses.
Thompson, J.　Horse.
Tkachenko.　Battle.
Tomlinson, C.　Saving the Appearances.
Tu Fu [or Du Fu].　Sick Horse.
Tudur Aled.　Stallion, The.
Ullman.　Hotwire.
Unknown.　Gereint Son of Erbin.
　My horse / thickens.
　On a Clergyman's Horse Biting Him.
　On Buying a Horse.
Van Doren.　Distant Runners, The.
Various authors.　Heaven gave him courage and
　wisdom.
Verlaine.　Wooden Horses.
Viereck, P.　Love Song to Eohippus.
Walcott.　Polish Rider, The.
Warren, R.　Dead Horse in Field.
Waters, M.　Horse: "First horse I ever saw,
　The."
Watkins, V.　Foal.
　Mare, The.

Weaver, A.　Appaloosa, The.
Wei Ying-wu.　Tartar Horse.
Wellesley.　Horses.
Wilbur, R.　Ride, The.
Williams, C. K.　On Learning of a Friend's
　Illness.
Woo, M.　Under a Full Moon.
Woolson.　Kentucky Belle.
Wordsworth, W.　Statue Horse.
　Strange Fits of Passion Have I Known ("Strange
　fits of passion have I known.").
Wright, F.　Morning.
Wright, J.　Blessing, A: "Just off the highway to
　Rochester, Minnesota."
　Horse, The.
Wunderlich, M.　One Explanation of Beauty.
Yavuz, Hilmi.　Windy Windows.
Yeats.　Michael Robartes Bids His Beloved Be
　at Peace.
Zabolotsky [or Zabolotskii].　Face of a Horse,
　The.
See also Colts; Foals; Horse Racing; Horse
　Shows; Horseback Riding

Horseshoe Crabs
Price, R.　Horseshoe Crab in Flagrante Delicto.

Horseshoes
Bottoms.　Horseshoes.
Hopkins, G.　Felix Randal.
Philpot, T.　Louisa's Wedding.

Hospitality
Belloc.　On a Dead Hostess.
Chŏng Ch'ŏl.　Magistrate.
Dickinson, E.　Soul that hath a Guest, The.
Góngora y Argote.　Sonnet 103.
Goodyear, Dana.　Umbra.
Gurney, I.　La Gorgue.
Han Kwak.　Don't Bring Out the Straw Mat.
Hugo, R.　Places and Ways to Live.
Jonson, B.　Inviting a Friend to Supper.
Kipling, R.　Ballad of East and West, The.
Michelson, P.　Enduring Witness, the Mosques
　of Kattankudi.
Robinson, E.　Cliff Klingenhagen.
Tu Fu [or Du Fu].　Guest Arrives, A ("North
　and south of my cottage, spring waters
　everywhere.").
Unknown.　Butcher of Abbeville, The.
　No One Will Put the Cid up. Only a Small Girl
　Addresses Him and That to Tell Him to Go
　Away. The Cid Finds He Has to Make Camp
　Outside of Town, on the Sand of the
　Riverbank.
　Three Hunchbacks, The.
Yüan Chiu-ts'ai.　Warm Invitation, A.
See also Guests

Hospitals
Adcock, F.　Soho Hospital for Women, The.
Akhmadulina.　In the Botkin Hospital.
Atkins, R.　While Waiting for a Friend to Come
　to Visit a Friend in a Mental Hospital.
Atwood.　Flowers: "Right now I am the flower
　girl."
Bartlett, E.　Neurosis.
Bibbins, M.　Counting.
Bloch, C.　Visiting Hours Are Over.
Borthwick, P.　Ward Mouth.
Buckley, V.　In the faint blue light.
Byard, O.　In Intensive Care.
Campo.　Lost in the Hospital.
Charach, R.　Labour and Delivery.
　MRI.
Clampitt.　From a Clinic Waiting Room.
Clifton, L.　Dialysis.
Conn.　Visiting Hour.
Conoley, G.　Masters, The.
Constantine, D.　Common and Particular.
Cooke, R.　Hospital Soliloquy, A.
Daniels, K.　Not Singing.
Darling, J.　My Old Friend Hospital.
Dickey, J.　Hospital Window, The.
Ditzanny, R.　Brand Plucked from the Anti-tank
　Fire, A.
Dransfield.　Visiting Hour (Repatriation
　Hospital).
Dunmore.　Domestic Poem.

Fanthorpe.　After Visiting Hours.
　Children Imagining a Hospital.
　Unprofessionals, The.
　Waiting Room.
Fusselman, A.　Mother Nature.
Garza, D.　Act One.
Gittins, C.　There Are Things I Must Realise
　You Can No Longer Do.
Godley, E.　Ninety-Nine.
Goldbarth.　Edgewater Hospital.
Gunn, T.　Still Life: "I shall not soon forget."
Hamilton, I.　Visit, The.
Harper, M.　This Is My Son's Song: "Ungie, Hi
　Ungie".
Harwood, G.　Hospital Evening.
Hayden, R.　Broken Dark, The.
Holan.　In the Yard of the Policlinic.
Holloway, G.　Monitors.
Ignatow, D.　Harold.
　Sunday at the State Hospital.
　Walt Whitman in the Civil War Hospitals.
Jarrell, R.　Field Hospital, A.
　In a Hospital Garden.
Kavanagh, P.　Hospital, The.
Kim Sŭnghŭi.　Growing Pearl 1.
Kinsella, T.　Lady of Quality, A.
Kleinzahler.　Watching Dogwood Blossoms Fall
　in a Parking Lot Off Route 46.
Lamb, H.　Intensive Care.
Levertov.　Malice of Innocence, The.
Lewis, A.　In Hospital: Poona (1).
MacDiarmid, H.　In the Children's Hospital.
McCord, D.　Convalescence.
McGuckian.　From the Dressing-room.
Meredith, W.　Jain Bird Hospital in Delhi, The.
Mersaal, E.　Repetition.
Merwin.　St. Vincent's.
Muldoon, P.　Field Hospital, The.
Muske, C.　Call, The: "When I heard the voice
　on the telephone."
　Pediatrics.
North, C.　Hospital.
Olds, S.　Space Heater, The.
Oliver, M.　University Hospital, Boston.
Ortiz.　8:50 AM Ft. Lyons VAH.
O'Sullivan, L.　Being Free.
Owen, W.　Conscious.
　Disabled.
　Hospital Barge at Cérisy.
　Mental Cases.
Parker, A.　Vandals Dying, The.
Parker, J.　Foxfire.
Peacock, M.　ChrisEaster.
Petrova, A.　Again sick. / Just now somehow
　paler.
Pilling.　Triptych.
Plath.　Face Lift.
　Morning in the Hospital Solarium.
　Tulips.
Porter, P.　Happening at Sordid Creek.
Powell, D. A.　You're thin again handsome. in
　our last.
Raboni, G.　Hospital Interiors.
Randall, D.　George.
Riley, D.　Cruelty Without Beauty.
Roeske, P.　Preparing the Dead.
Rohrer, J.　Room 703.
Routh, J.　Pale.
Sassoon, S.　Death-Bed, The.
Satyamurti.　Knowing Our Place.
Serge.　Asphyxiated Man, The.
Sexton.　Unknown Girl in the Maternity Ward.
　You, Doctor Martin.
Shafer, A.　Monday Morning.
Shapcott, J.　Lovebirds.
Sholl.　Hospital State, The.
Simidor, D.　Spring: "Spring afternoon, a lovely
　sky, bright sunshine, A."
Sissman.　Deathplace, A.
Slutsky [or Slutskii].　Hospital, The.
Snodgrass.　Flat One, A.
Steinbergh.　Give Peace a Chance.
Taylor, E.　Welcome Eumenides.
Thwaite, A.　Freedom.
Ulacia, M.　Stone at the Bottom, The.
Unknown, fr. Terezin Concentration Camp.

Theresienstadt's Hospital.
Wagoner, D.   Curtains.
Wardle, S.   Flight: "Mother blackbird I've been feeding, The."
Waring, B.   Baby Random.
Warner, S.   Benicasim.
Webb, F.   Hospital Night.
Whitman, W.   Sight in Camp [in the Daybreak Gray and Dim].
Williams, W.   Between Walls.
  Spring and All.
Wojahn.   W. C. W. Watching Presley's Second Appearance on The Ed Sullivan Show: Mercy Hospital, Newark, 1956.
Wyrebek, M.   Example, An.
  Trendelenburg Position.
Yi Sang.   Paper Memorial Stone.
Young, C.   Torn.
Zagajewski.   When Death Came.

Hotels
Auden.   John Milton.
Bell, M.   True Story, A.
Betjeman.   Arrest of Oscar Wilde at the Cadogan Hotel, The.
Brown, G.   Lodging, The.
Campbell, D.   Hotel Marine.
Christopher.   Far from Home.
Dimitrova.   Hotel Room.
Emanuel, L.   Outside Room Six.
Espada.   Transient Hotel Sky at the Hour of Sleep.
Hart, L.   There's a Small Hotel.
Hughes, L.   Advertisement for the Waldorf-Astoria.
  Come to the Waldorf-Astoria.
Jones, R.   Key, The.
Kim Hyesun.   Old Hotel, The.
  Very Old Hotel, A.
Klein, A.   For the Sisters of the Hôtel Dieu.
Lindsay, V.   Jazz of This Hotel, The.
Lowry, M.   Delirium in Vera Cruz.
McClatchy.   What They Left Behind.
Merrill, J.   Hôtel de l'Univers et Portugal.
Mueller, L.   Highway Poems.
Nakano Shigeharu.   Imperial Hotel.
No Hyegyông.   Children on Top of the Hill.
Polito.   Overheard in the Love Hotel.
Rohrer, M.   Hotel de L'Etoile.
Rosemurgy, C.   Hard Put.
Rossetti, C.   Uphill [or Up-Hill].
Ryan, G.   In the Purple Bar.
St. John, D.   California.
Salazar.   Hotel Fresno.
Seidel.   Racine.
Shenstone.   Written at [or in] an Inn at Henley.
Simon, M.   Sea Sprite, Hermosa Beach, The.
Smukler.   Days Inn.
Stone, R.   Latest Hotel Guest Walks Over Particles That Revolve in Seven Other Dimensions Controlling Latticed Space, The.
Tonks.   Story of a Hotel Room.
Tranströmer.   Homewards.
Wieners.   Hotels 1970.
Winter, M.   As If I Knew.
Zagajewski.   Watching Shoah in a Hotel Room in America.
See also **Motels**

Hottentots
Breytenbach.   First Prayer for the Hottentotsgod.
Dyer, J.   Insensible Hottentot, The.

Houdini, Harry
Alvi, M.   Houdini.
Mandel, E.   Houdini.
Quintana.   Poem for Harry Houdini.

Hourglasses
Carruth, H.   Testament.
Clare, J.   To an Hour-Glass.
Jones, M.   Sand-time Measuring.
Jonson, B.   Hour-Glass, The.
Shaw, R.   4. Hourglass.

Housekeeping
Alvarez, J.   How I Learned to Sweep.
Andrew, G.   Hurricane Sisters Work Regardless, The.
Annucci, Marilyn.   Wrecked World.

Atwood.   Romantic.
Baggott, J.   Poetry Despises Your Attempts at Domesticity.
Barresi.   Prodigal Daughter, The.
Beatty, J.   Modern Love: "Early evening, five minutes before."
Blaeser.   Dictionary for the New Century.
Brown Rosellen.   I have a neighbor.
Campbell, R.   On the Same.
Cerenio.   My Mother.
Christie, J.   Solvent.
Cisneros, S.   Man in My Bed Like Cracker Crumbs, A.
Connolly, G.   New House.
Curry, N.   Anne Hathaway Composes Her 18th Sonnet.
Dove, R.   Dusting.
Erdrich, H.   Sweeping Heaven.
Follain.   She Stops Short.
Fordham.   Coming Woman, The.
Gallagher, T.   I Stop Writing the Poem.
Gilman, C.   Mother's Charge, The.
Henderson-Holmes.   Goodhousekeeping #17.
Huntington, C.   Virtue: "All the houses are white."
Issa.   Bedbugs, The.
Joseph, A.   Domestic Humiliation.
Kasischke.   Housekeeping in a Dream.
Kearns, J.   Moving Furniture.
Kenyon, J.   Finding a Long Gray Hair.
Larkin, J.   Housework.
Lauter, S.   Spots.
Laux, D.   Idea of Housework, The.
  Reetika Arranges My Closet.
Loy.   Effectual Marriage, The.
Martin, Gail.   God Scrubs the Tub.
McGrath, T.   Probable Cause.
Mead, J.   Third Stair, Seventh Stair, Landing.
Niedecker.   Popcorn-can cover.
North, M.   Portrait in a Brass Gong.
Radoev, Ivan.   Parable of the Poet's Reward.
Razaf, A.   My Handy Man.
  Porter's Love Song to a Chambermaid, A.
Rock, D.   Mother.
Satterfield, J.   Duties and Vocations.
Schuyler, J.   Things to Do.
Shearin, F.   Entropy.
  Sinking, The.
Sŏ Chŏngju.   Floor in Goethe's House, The.
Song.   Immaculate Lives.
  Poet in the House, A.
Sontag, K.   Plum Crazy.
Sutphen, J.   Household Muse.
Taylor, E.   Huswifery.
Townsend, A.   Day's End.
Trethewey, N.   Housekeeping.
Turner, N.   When Young Melissa Sweeps.
Unknown.   Behind the Mountain.
  Ge-tan: Shade o' the Vine.
  Wee Cooper of Fife, The.
Waldman, A.   Baby's Pantoum.
Walker, A.   Women.
Wayne, J.   In Praise of Zigzags.
Wong, N.   Ironing.
Yi Chinmyông.   Woman Mopping With a Rag Mop.
Yuson.   Andy Warhol Speaks to His Two Filipino Maids.
See also **Housewives**

Houses
Adamson.   My House.
Adler, L.   Plaisir.
Al-Haidari, B.   So That We Do Not Forget.
Ali, A.   Rooms Are Never Finished.
Ap Hywel, Elin.   In My Mother's House.
  In My Mother's House.
Armitage, S.   Zoom!
Ashbery, J.   Old Complex, The.
Atwood.   Morning in the Burned House.
Aygi, G.   House in the Field.
Baggott, J.   Poetry Despises Your Attempts at Domesticity.
Basho.   Good house.
Berggolts [or Bergholts].   To My Sister.
Bible, *O.T.*   Psalm 84.
Bishop, E.   End of March, The.

Blumenthal, M.   Marriage, A.
Bobyshev.   Indifference.
Bonnefoy.   What House Would You Build For Me.
Borges.   Houses like Angels.
  Patio.
Bradstreet, A.   [Here Follows Some] Verses upon the Burning of Our House [July 10th, 1666. Copied Out of a Loose Paper].
Braithwaite.   House of Falling Leaves, The.
Bronk.   Strong Room of the House, The.
Brooks, G.   Vacant Lot, The.
Brouwer, J.   Development: "I learned to fuck one summer in a burgeoning subdivision."
Browning, R.   House.
  Love in a Life.
Budy.   First Night in the New House.
Buson.   Around the small house.
  Early summer rain.
  Harvest moon.
Carew, T.   To Saxham.
Cary, A.   Window Just Over the Street, The.
Catacalos.   Casa, La.
Cawein.   Deserted.
Cecil.   Some Terms in Real Estate Defined.
Chang Chi.   Coming at Night to a Fisherman's Hut.
Ch'ien T'ao.   Written While Drunk.
Clare, J.   After Reading in a Letter Proposals for Building a Cottage.
Coleridge, S.   Aeolian [or Eolian] Harp, The.
Colum, P.   Old Woman of the Roads, The.
Conley, L.   Cottage for Sale, A.
Cook, Geoffrey.   Watermarks.
Coward.   Stately Homes of England, The.
  Stately Homes of England, The.
Cowley, A.   Wish, The.
Crabbe, G.   Business Man's Lair, A.
Creeley.   House, The ("Mas-Soñer / Restaurat— Any.").
  This House.
Crowe, T.   Saw-Mill Shack, The.
Daniels, J.   Blessing the House.
Davies, Grahame.   DIY.
Davies, W. H.   No Man's Wood.
Dávila Andrade, C.   Abandoned House, The.
Davis, K.   Green Noise of Ohio Hardwoods, The.
De Kok.   Ground wave.
De la Mare.   Sleeper, The ("As Ann came in one summer's day.").
De Mello Breyner.   Night and the House.
Delgado, J.   Con Los Pájaros.
Dickinson, E.   Eden is that Old-Fashioned House.
  God's Residence.
  I know some lonely Houses off the Road.
  Props assist the House, The.
Dodd, W.   Of Rain and Air.
Dodge, M.   Fire in the window.
Dooley, M.   Dancing at Oakmead Road.
Dransfield.   Portrait of the Artist as an Old Man.
Dugan, A.   Love Song: I and Thou.
  On Being a Householder.
Dumdum.   Some Die of Light.
Dunn, D.   Modern Love.
  On Roofs of Terry Street.
Dunn, S.   In the House.
Edson, R.   Canoeing, The.
Elfyn, Menna.   Couplings.
Field, Miranda.   Housefire.
Finlay, I.   Finlay's House (in Rousay).
Fisher, A.   Houses.
Flynn, N.   Hive.
Follain.   Eclogue: "In the closed house."
Forbes, C.   My Father's House.
Forrest-Thomson.   In This House.
Frost, R.   Black Cottage, The.
  Directive.
Fyleman.   (Mice).
Gerner, K.   House of Breath.
Ginsberg, A.   Strange New Cottage in Berkeley, A.
Goetsch, D.   Walls, The.
Gorenko, A.   Houses like piles of children's books.

Gould, A. Demolisher.
Graham, J. San Sepolcro.
Grass. Saturn.
Graves, R. Not at Home.
Gray, T. On Lord Holland's Seat near Margate, Kent.
Greenberg, A. Nostalgia, Cheryl, Is the Best Heroin.
Grennan. Woman at Lit Window.
Groarke, V. Glasshouse, The.
History of My Father's House, The.
Grosholz. Legacies.
Guest, B. Defensive Rapture.
Prairie Houses.
Guillén, J. Happy Armchair.
Gunn, T. Last Days at Teddington.
Gwangwa'a. Leaking Roof.
Hadas, R. House Beside the Sea, The.
Hagiwara Sakutaro. Chair.
Hall, J. Hous-keping's dead, *Saturio:* wot'st thou where?
Hammerstein. Folks Who Live on the Hill, The.
Han-shan. House Without Walls.
Han-shan Te-ch'ing. Tiny hut in a world of plants, A.
Hardy, T. Domicilium.
Harjo, J. My House Is the Red Earth.
Hart, K. Room, The.
Hart, L. Blue Room, The.
Hartnett. Visit to Castletown House, A.
Harwood, G. Andante.
Hass, R. House.
Hauge. Leaf Huts and Snow Houses.
Heaney, S. Be literal a moment. Recollect.
Skylight, The.
Summer Home.
Hemans. Homes of England, The.
Herbert, G. Redemption.
World, The.
Herrick. Thanksgiving to God for His House, A.
Hill, S. House.
Hokushi. My house gutted.
Hoover, P. Whitman in a Corner.
Hopkins, G. In the Valley of the Elwy.
Howe, J. House of Rest, The.
Howells, W. Empty House, The.
Huddle. Gregory's House.
Hulme, T. Image.
Hume, C. Dialogue of Thunder.
Ilio, D. Site of My Grandfather's House, The.
Iorwerth, D. House of Teletubbies, The.
Issa. Borrowing my house / From insects.
Under my house.
Iverem, E. Murmur.
Jackson, H. My House Not Made with Hands.
Jensma. Till no one.
Jiménez, J. Remembrance Is Moving, A.
Jones, D. Diptych.
House, The.
Jonson, B. To Penshurst.
Juntoku, Emperor. Royal Dwellings.
Justice, D. Men at Forty.
Kanchev, Nikolai. Birthplace.
Kapos, M. Pulse, The.
Kees. Villanelle: "Crack is moving down the wall, The."
When the Lease Is Up.
Kennelly. We Are Living.
Kenyon, J. From Room to Room.
Khalvati. Blue Moon.
Kilmer, J. House with Nobody in It, The.
Kim, Suji Kwock. Occupation.
Koch, K. Variations on a Theme by William Carlos Williams.
Kooser. Shooting a Farmhouse.
Kovacic, K. Brick.
Lane, M. Travis. For Brigid.
Larkin, P. Home Is So Sad.
Leithauser. In Minako Wada's House.
Levchev. Rooftops.
Levertov. Invocation: "Silent, about-to-be-parted-from house."
Levy, A. Old House, The.
Li Po. Inscribed on the Wall of Hsü Hsüan-Ping's Retreat.

Lihn. Memories of Marriage.
Llywelyn-Williams. On a Visit.
Lochhead, L. My Rival's House.
Louis, A. At the House of Ghosts.
Macdonald, G. Song.
MacNeice. Château Jackson.
House on a Cliff.
Selva Oscura.
Maiden. Foundations, The.
Malouf. For Two Children.
Mansour, J. Empty Black Haunted House.
Masaoka Shiki. Tenement house.
Matos-Teixera, N. My Father's House.
Matthews, W. Housework.
Mayer, B. House Cap.
Spring House.
McKinnon, K. Moving My Mother.
Mead, P. There.
Meredith, W. American Living Room, The: A Tract.
Merwin. Tide Line Garden.
Messer, S. Some women marry houses.
Mew. Quiet House, The.
Millay, E. Second Fig.
Miller, M. Closing, A.
Minhinnick. House, The.
Mistral, G. House, The.
Morabito, F. Master of an Expanse.
Moss, H. Water Island.
Mother Goose. House That Jack Built, The.
This is the House that Jack Built.
Muso Soseki. Visiting My Old Hut in Late Spring.
Nash, O. No Wonder Our Fathers Died.
Turtle, The.
Navajo Oral Tradition. Night Chant, The.
Nesbit, E. Gray Folk, The.
Ní Chuilleanáin. House Remembered, The.
Niedecker. New-sawed.
November, Deena. Melba Street.
Noyes, S. Beach House.
Osgood, F. Lines: "Oh, ye who in those Houses hold."
Padilla. Fountain, a House of Stone, A.
Paley, G. Sad Children's Song, The.
Palis, Y. Floor, The.
Parini. Ruined House, The.
Pinsky. Round.
Plath. Point Shirley.
Plumly. For Esther.
Po Chü-i. Winter Night.
Polley, J. Moving House.
Pope, A. Revelation.
Rago. Distances, The.
Rakosi. Founding of New Hampshire, The.
Ransom, J. Old Mansion.
Reid, A. Manse, The.
Reznikoff. House-wreckers, The.
Ritsos. Evening Walk.
Roberson, E. Poor Houses, The.
Robinson, E. House on the Hill, The.
Rubin, L. Houses of Emily Dickinson, The.
Rudolf. Edward Hopper.
Rutsala. House of Cards, The.
Reunion: A Scenario.
Sabines. Capriccios.
Schiff, Robyn. House of Dior.
Schuyler, J. Along Overgrown Paths.
Scott, D. Skiddaw House.
Selman, R. 21 East 10th, 2BR, WBF, EIK.
Shange. Where the Heart Is.
Shaw, J. Revelation.
Sheridan, T. Tom Punsibi's Letter to Dean Swift.
Silliman. Revolving door.
Smith, S. Grange, The.
Song Sun. Ten Years It Took.
Soutar. Room, The.
Stanford, A. Done With.
Stanley-Wrench. Hinterland.
Statius. Thanksgiving to the Emperor Augustus Germanicus Domitianus.
Steeves, Andrew. Haunting.
Stevens, W. Gallant Chateau.
Stevenson, R. *My house,* I say. But hark to the sunny doves.

Stoddard, E. House by the Sea, The.
Swenson, M. Question: "Body my house."
Sze. Silence, The.
Takomaq. Improvised Song of Joy.
Tate, J. Failed Tribute to the Stonemason of Tor House, Robinson Jeffers.
Taylor, A. Fitzroy.
Teare, Brian. Dead House Sonnet.
Thamnaret. Nightsong.
Thomas, E. New House, The.
Tale, A [Revised Version].
Tranströmer. Start of a Late Autumn Novel.
Tsvetayeva [*or* Tsvetaeva]. Staircase.
Tu Fu [*or* Du Fu]. Visitors.
West of Hut.
Turpin, Mark. Box, The.
Unknown. Bound to Go.
Build a House in Paradise.
Planting Initiation Song.
Vallejo. Babble.
Van Doren. Near House, The.
Vasquez, R. For Jose Mercado Vasquez and Frances Roman Vasquez.
Vaughan, H. They Are All Gone into the World of Light!
Villa, D. It is.
Voigt. House.
Walcott. Ruins of a Great House.
Waldrop, K. Poet: "Wind dying, I find a city deserted, except for crowds of, The."
Wallace, R. Sestina for the House.
Warn. After Reading the Book of Splendor. Dwelling.
Weaver, A. Beginnings.
Water Song.
Wellman, M. Moth house is taking over, Sir Footfall.
Whitlow. Book of Routh.
Williamson, G. Nervous Systems.
Wojahn. Floating Houses.
Woods, V. House, The.
Wordsworth, W. Her cottage, then a cheerful object, wore.
Inscription for the Moss-Hut at Dove Cottage.
Ruined Cottage, The.
Wright, C. Virgo Descending.
Wright, D. Protest Poem, A.
Wyrebek, M. Example, An.
Yeats. Ancestral Houses.
Yi Chinmyông. Record of a Certain Summer.
Yi Sanghûi. Igloo! Igloo!
Zappala, Robyn. One Year Later.
Zapruder, M. School Street.
Zawacki, Andrew. Ventriloquy.
Zuni Oral Tradition. House Blessing.

See also **Home**

Housewives
Alexander, E. Female seer will burn upon this pyre, The.
Andrew, G. Housewife, The.
Armstrong, Tammy. Mother's Winter Guests.
Barresi. In Waking Words.
Berkson, B. October: "It's odd to have a separate month. It."
Blaeser. What They Did by Lamplight.
Bodecker. Hurry, Hurry, Mary Dear!
Boland, E. Woman in Kitchen.
Bryner. Part of a Larger Country.
Cakrabarttî, M. Wherever there's a woman in any Bengali home.
Çelebi, A. My Little Woman.
Chang, V. Five-Year Plan.
Daniels, K. Prayer to the Muse of Ordinary Life.
Dove, R. Daystar.
Erdrich, H. Good Woman.
Erdrich. Mary Kröger.
Gilbert, S. Ladies' Home Journal, The.
Harwood, G. Long After Heine.
Hostetler, A. Female Ancestor.
Jarrell, R. Next Day.
Jewell, Terri L. Sistah Flo.
Keita, N. Dedicated to the domestics.
Martin, Gail. God Packs Lunches.
God Scrubs the Tub.
God Vacuums the Pool.

McLain, P.   Home Remedy.
Mew.   Farmer's Bride, The.
Mills, L.   Days of My Mother, The.
Mishol, A.   Shopping.
Pande, M.   Two Women Knitting.
Pastan.   Marks.
Poetker-Thiessen, A.   She tries to tell him.
Riley, D.   Affections Must Not.
Sergi, P.   One Quick Quiz.
Seuss, D.   Purpose.
Sexton.   Housewife.
Soudijn.   Cleaning.
Tibbetts.   Coming Home.
Unknown.   Epitaph.
  What's that in which good housewives take
  delight.
Williams, W.   Young Housewife, The.
Young, A.   California Peninsula: El Camino
  Real.
Zamora, D.   Loyal Housewife.
See also **Housekeeping**
Housman, Alfred Edward
Auden.   A. E. Housman.
Parry, R.   A E Housman.
Hudson River, New York
Alexander, M.   River and Bridge.
Bryant, W.   Scene on the Banks of the Hudson,
  A.
Corn.   Water: City Wildlife and Greenery.
Freneau.   Two hulks on Hudson's stormy bosom
  lie.
Goodman, P.   Lordly Hudson, The.
Lowell, R.   Mouth of the Hudson, The.
Schuyler, J.   Dining Out with Doug and Frank.
Teasdale.   Summer Night, Riverside.
Vaysman, N.   Sail me.
Hughes, Langston
Brooks, G.   Langston Hughes.
D'Aguiar, F.   Langston.
Forbes, C.   Reading Walt Whitman.
Loftis, N.   Changes—Eight.
Madgett.   Simple.
Major, C.   Petition for Langston Hughes, A.
Plumpp.   Saturday Night Decades.
Powell, K.   Genius Child.
Randall, D.   Langston Blues.
Young, K.   Langston Hughes.
Hughes, Ted
Evans, D.   Wales '99.
Larkin, P.   Limerick: "There was an old fellow
  of Kaber."
Hugs and Hugging
Collins, B.   Embrace.
Gallagher, T.   Hug, The.
Gunn, T.   Hug, The.
Ondaatje.   Bearhug.
Unknown.   Do not crush me in your arms.
  One time only, just one time hold my bosom
  against yours.
Huguenots
Coleridge, M.   Huguenot, A.
Human Folly
Bensley.   Bloomsbury Snapshot.
Blake, W.   Human Abstract, The.
Bradstreet, A.   Contemplations.
  Contemplations.
Burns, R.   Poor Merry-Andrew, in the neuk.
Cairns, Scott.   Salvation.
De Vries, P.   Sacred and Profane Love, or,
  There's Nothing New under the Moon Either.
Dove, R.   All Souls'.
Ferlinghetti, L.   25.
Fleming, R.   This mortal coil.
Gilbert, A.   Relative Heat Index.
Gogarty.   Colophon.
Gumilyov [*or* Gumiliov *or* Gumilev].
  Fragments 1920–1921.
Hall, D.   Grace, A.
Hart, L.   I Wish I Were in Love Again.
Henry, B.   Pyramid, The.
Herbert, G.   Dotage.
Hirsch, E.   History of My Stupidity, The:
  Volume 3, Chapter 5.
Hodgeon, G.   In Conference.
Huchel.   Psalm: "That from the seed of men."

Ibáñez, S.   I Cannot.
Jackson, A.   Worstest Beast, The.
Jeffers, R.   Advice to Pilgrims.
  Original Sin.
  Roan Stallion.
Kerouac.   Poem: "I demand that the human
  race."
Kessler, R.   Elm Tree on Lafayette Street, The.
Kloefkorn.   News.
Masefield.   Passing Strange, The.
McClure, M.   Black Dahlia.
McGough, R.   Prayer to Saint Grobianus.
Mikha'il, M.   Imprisoned God, The.
Muktibodh.   Void, The.
Murray, L.   Quality of Sprawl, The.
Owen, W.   Arms and the Boy.
Parra, N.   Vices of the Modern World.
Patchen.   Origin of Baseball, The.
Pitter.   But for Lust.
Rumi.   Strange Business.
Sahagún, C.   Life in the Provinces.
Scott, S.   Lucy Ashton's Song.
Shapiro, K.   Fly, The.
Shiraishi.   Wild Pigs of Kalimantan, The.
Simonides.   It is hard to become a truly good.
Sri Sri.   Really?
Stanton, J.   Finger Paintings.
Stenhouse, S.   Circling.
Swift, J.   Verses on the Death of Dr. Swift,
  D.S.P.D, Occasioned by Reading a Maxim in
  Rochefoucauld.
Troupe.   Transcircularities.
Unknown.   Cameleon's Defence, The.
Uschuk, P.   Of Simple Intent.
Van Duyn.   Causes.
Williams, C. K.   That the world / is going.
Wright, F.   Only Animal, The.
Xuanjian.   Zen Sermon.
Zach, N.   On the Desire to Be Precise.
Human Nature
Atwood.   Moment, The.
Avison.   Cycle of Community.
Baekoon Kyunghan.   Twelve More Songs for
  Master Jikong.
Baingana, D.   Song to Come, The.
Barker, J.   Invitation to my Friends at
  Cambridge, An.
Blanco.   Accuracy of the Scale, The.
  Fiel de la balanza, El.
Brandi.   Yagul.
Brother Yao.   Science of Forgetting, The.
Canan.   Mother Dawning.
Cărtărescu, Mircea.   Happy Day in My Life, A.
Castellanos.   Destiny.
  Other, The.
  Return, The.
Clifton, L.   Love the Human.
Cortes, F.   Fish 2.
Dabney.   Earth's Bondman.
de Folgar.   Irreverent Epistle to Jesus Christ.
Drummond de Andrade.   Ox Looks at Man, An.
Ekelof.   If You Ask Me Where I Live.
Finkelstein, C.   Afterthought.
Fitzgerald, J.   Being (Human).
Forhan, C.   Without Presumptions.
Gerber.   Afterwords.
Gibson, W.   Prelude: "As one, at midnight
  wakened by the call."
Giovanni.   Crutches.
Glover, S.   Power of the Soul.
Glück, L.   Matins: "Unreachable father, when
  we were first."
Gogarty.   Marcus Curtius.
Griffin, S.   Our Mother.
Gwynn, H.   Welcome / Black beetle.
Haewŏn.   Regarding the Heart.
Hanson, M.   How proudly Man usurps the
  power to reign.
Hedd Wyn.   War.
Howe, F.   Catholic.
Hunt, L.   Fish Answers, A.
Hussein, H.   I Can Talk to Them.
Ibáñez, S.   I Cannot.
Issa.   One human being.
  Where there are humans / you'll find flies.
Jabeen, M.   Relationships.

Jackson, L.   Because of Clothes.
Jackson, R.   Other Day, The.
Jefferson, T.   Passage from a Letter to William
  Charles Jarvis, September 28, 1820.
Jones, H.   Mannyelanong.
Kekova.   Ants, The.
Kingston, M.   Restaurant.
Klein, M.   Guardian Life.
Klink, J.   And Having Lost Track.
Kurtz.   No Pasarán.
Laux, D.   If This Is Paradise.
Lazarus, E.   Success.
Levin, D.   Chill Core.
Lewis, S.   Et Homo Factus Est. Crucifixus.
Logghe.   Española Pantoum.
Lux.   Solo Native.
Mandela.   Saviour.
McNeil, R.   It Just Doesn't Matter.
Merrill, B.   People.
Metwalli, M.   Untitled: "We are two straw
  dolls."
Mipham, Sakyong.   Snow Fell Twice, the Sun
  Always Shone.
Mkangelwa.   Observations.
Morejón.   Tame and Ferocious Animal, A.
Murray, J.   Even the Gulls of the Cool Atlantic.
  There Has Been More Than Beginning and End
  to Face.
Muyong Sooyon.   To the Reverend Bagam.
Nash, O.   Necessary Dirge, A.
O'Reilly, C.   Envoi: "And although it will be."
Otero, B.   Eternal, The.
Owen, Gerallt Lloyd.   To the Death.
Paino.   Each Bone of the Body.
Parham, Mary Gomez.   Chasm.
Parry, R.   Pagan.
  Strangeness of Dawn, The.
Parry-Williams.   Life: "O the blessedness of life!
  It's lucky, no doubt."
Quevedo y Villegas.   Birds Are in the Air at
  Ease.
Ragosta, R.   Excursions.
Rampolekeng.   Welcome to the New
  Consciousness.
Reagon.   Greed.
Rexroth, K.   Long lifetime, A.
Reyes, A.   Scarcely.
Ruefle.   Merengue.
Rumi.   Come, come, for the rosebower has
  blossomed; come, come, for the beloved has
  arrived.
Rux, C. H.   Just Asking.
Sachs, N.   If the Prophets Broke in.
Sahn, Seung.   Good and Bad are eminent
  teachers.
Scott, G.   All Our Joy Is Enough.
Soutar.   To Karl Marx.
Spofford.   Tryst, The.
Storni.   World is Bitter, The.
Suárez.   Poem for Mankind and Its Hope.
Synková, A.   I've met enough people.
Tate, J.   Cages, The.
Teofilov, Ivan.   Falcon, The! His symmetrical
  confession.
Thomas, L.   Dangerous Doubts.
Torres Bodet.   Living.
Tsanev, Stefan.   Penguins.
Uyematsu.   Deliberate.
Valiente.   Charge of the Goddess, The.
Vietnamese Oral Tradition.   Mother Egret.
  Talking about Birds.
Villa, E.   Natus de Muliere, Brevi Vivens.
Villanueva, A.   Planet Earth Speaks, The.
Warren, R.   Whole Question, The.
Wesley, C.   Let earth and heaven combine.
Wiethüchter.   Movement.
Wilbur, R.   Man Running.
Williamson, G.   Bodies of Water.
Willis, Elizabeth.   Without Pity.
Yu Xuanji.   Selling Wilted Peonies.
See also **Humankind**
Humankind
Abdul-Salaam, A.   In Front of the House.
Abdullah, F.   On the Declaration of Joy.
Aiken, C.   Tetélestai.
Aleixandre.   Man Doesn't Exist.

Allen, S. Lingering Doubt, The.
Allston. Word: Man, A.
Amichai, Y. Man in His Life, A.
Andrade, M. Processions, The.
Arnold, M. In Harmony with Nature.
Arp. People.
Ashbery, J. Hotel Lautréamont.
 How to Continue.
 Scheherazade.
Awwad, B. Declining Sun.
Aygi, G. Quietness with a Happening.
Baraka, I. Balboa, the Entertainer.
Barot, R. Many Are Called.
Beaver. Day 20.
Benn. Fragments.
Berry, W. Morning's News, The.
 Peace. Let men, who cannot be brothers.
 Slip, The.
Berryman. Traveller [or Traveler], The.
Bishop, E. In the Waiting Room.
Blake, W. And every Space that a Man views
 around his dwelling-place.
 Divine Image, A.
 Divine Image, The.
 Human Abstract, The.
Blumenthal, M. Meditation on Politics at the
 Quabbin Reservoir.
Bonhoeffer. Who Am I?
Browning, R. Parting at Morning.
Bryant, W. Crowded Street, The.
Burns, R. For A' That and A' That ["Is there,
 for honest poverty"].
Cabral de Melo Neto. Emptiness of Man, The.
Campbell, T. Last Man, The.
Cassity. Why Fortune Is the Empress of the
 World.
Cavendish, M. Dialogue betwixt Man, and
 Nature, A.
Champ, Amy. Buddha is neither asian nor male.
 she could be an african woman.
Char. Man flees suffocation.
Chuang Tzu. Man: "Consider: if we measured
 the Four Oceans."
Coates, F. Unconquered Air, The.
Couani. Obvious, The.
Cowley, M. Ernest.
Cummings, E. E. Pity This Busy
 Monster,Manunkind.
Davies, S. I know my soul hath power to know
 all things.
Davies, P. I Was with Ulysses.
De la Mare. All That's Past.
Drummond de Andrade. Boi Vě os Homens,
 Um.
Dunbar, P. Slow Through the Dark.
Duncan, R. Returning to Roots of First Feeling.
Duo Duo. Wishful Thinking Is the Master of
 Reality.
Éluard, P. Dawn Dissolves the Monsters.
Éluard, P. et al. Of One and Two, of All.
Eskimo Oral Tradition. Magic Words.
Faiz. Love I Gave You Once, The.
Fearing. X Minus X.
Felipe, L. I Have Not Come to Sing.
Fischer, N. Model of the Universe, A.
Flecknoe. Ant, The.
Frost, C. Homo Sapiens.
Gardiner, S. No Title.
Gibson, M. One Body.
Goodell, L. Human Non-Sequitur.
Goodman, P. Little Ode.
Gray, T. Ode on a Distant Prospect of Eton
 College.
Greville, F. Chorus Sacerdotum.
Griffiths, J. There Are Limits to Brotherly
 Love.
Grosjean, Jean. Ancestor, The.
Guilpin. What more variety of pleasures can.
Gunn, T. Last Man, The.
 Last Man, The.
Hahn, O. Man.
Hardy, T. Heredity.
Henry, B. Garage Sale.
Herbert, G. Man.
 Pulley, The.
Herrera. We Are Made.

Hewitt, J. Ram's Horn, The.
Hicok. Team Effort.
Hirsch, E. Song Against Natural Selection.
Hoffenstein. Sexes, The.
Holan. In the Yard of the Policlinic.
Hölderlin. Hyperion's Song of Fate.
 Schicksalslied.
Holmes, O. 3. Sympathies.
Holub. Wings.
Hood, T. Last Man, The.
Hopkins, G. Epithalamion: "Hark, hearer, hear
 what I do; lend a thought now, make believe."
 Lantern Out of Doors, The.
 Sea and the Skylark, The.
 To His Watch.
Howe, F. What We Learned.
Hughes, R. Walking Road, The.
Hughes, T. After Lorca.
Hunt, L. Fish, the Man, and the Spirit, The.
Ishikawa Takuboku. At my words, "Christ was
 a man".
Jackson, M. L. To Afaa Michael S. Weaver.
Jacobsen, R. Some People.
Jarrell, R. Islands, The.
Jeffers, R. Inquisitors, The.
Jinkag Haesim. May Day.
Johnson, G. Common Dust.
Jones, D. Dead, The.
Jones, E. Genesis.
Jones, G. Quiet Valley, The.
Jones, T. Humanity.
Kahn, G. All God's Chillun Got Rhythm.
Kerouac. Orlanda Blues: 24th Chorus.
 Two Hundred and Twenty-Eighth Chorus.
Khlebnikov, V. Suppose I Make a Timepiece of
 Humanity.
King, H. Sic Vita.
Kipling, R. If.
Knevet. Habitation, The.
Koertge. Foolish Earthlings.
Kyger. Oh Man is the highest type of animal
 existing.
Lattany, K. Question of Identity, The.
Lawrence, D. H. Elemental.
 When Wilt Thou Teach the People?
Levi, P. Shemà.
Levine, P. Animals Are Passing from Our
 Lives.
 Poem of Flight, The.
Lewis, G. Half.
Lewis, S. Chance Child.
Li Po. Red sun comes out of the Eastern corner,
 The.
Lima, J. Stranger, Stranger.
 Trumpets, The.
Longfellow, H. Kéramos.
Lowry, Brigid. In the World.
Lowry, M. Volcano is Dark, The.
MacCaig. Basking Shark.
MacDiarmid, H. Glass of Pure Water, The.
 With the Herring Fishers.
Markham, E. Man with the Hoe, The.
Merwin. For a Coming Extinction.
Millay, E. Apostrophe to Man.
Milton. For man to tell how human life began.
 On the Detraction Which Followed upon My
 Writing Certain Treatises ("I did but prompt
 the age to quit their [or thir] clogs.").
Mitchell, S. Sense of Proportion, The.
Moxley, Jennifer. Easter Lesson, The.
Muir, E. Animals, The.
Muktibodh. Void, The.
Nagnamuni. Wooden Horse.
Neill. Are You There, Mr Punch?
Neruda. Dead Woman.
 Men grow with all that grows.
 Oda a la Manzana.
 Ode to the Apple.
 Still, I am here.
 Stone within stone, and man, where was he?
 Walking Around.
 We Are Many.
Nikolayeva [or Nikolaeva]. Daughter.
Oliver, M. Wild Geese.
 Wild Geese: "You do not have to be good."
Olson, C. Chain of memory is resurrection I am

a vain man, The.
 In Cold Hell, in Thicket.
 Thing Was Moving, The.
Padgett, R. Lucky Strikes.
Parra, N. Man, A.
Pennar, Meirion. Ecce Homo: "On the threshold
 of the black cave."
Po Chü-i. Lodging with the Old Man of the
 Stream.
Pope, A. Of all the causes which conspire to
 blind.
 Placed on this isthmus of a middle state.
 What would this Man? Now upward will he
 soar.
Pound, E. Meditatio.
Pratt, E. From Stone to Steel.
Quasimodo. Only if Love Should Pierce You.
Raleigh, W. Wishes of an Elderly Man[, Wished
 at a Garden Party, June 1914].
Redmond. Highflown: Love.
Reeve, F. Hope.
Rich, A. For the Record.
Roberts, John. One.
Robinson, K. Pontoon.
Rochester, J. Were I (who to my cost already
 am).
Rojas. Chapter and Verse.
Rózewicz. What Luck.
Ruefle. Kiss of the Sun.
Rukeyser, M. Myth.
Sakaki. North America.
Sandburg, C. People, Yes, The.
 Wilderness.
Scalapino. Considering How Exaggerated
 Music Is.
 Or a Play.
Senghor. Man and Beast.
Shakespeare, W. Seven Ages of Man, The.
Sherwood, G. Satire against Reason and
 Mankind, A.
Shih Shu. Enlightenment.
Smith, B. Black Mountain Blues.
Smith, S. Away, Melancholy.
 New Age, The.
Southwell. Look[e] Home.
Sri Sri. Man walks on the bridge and gives
 away the change in his, A.
 Myth of Myself.
 Wheels of Jagannatha, The.
Subbarao, N. Is This All!
Sundiata. Space. A Prose Poem Monologue.
Supervielle. Earth.
Swift, J. Day of Judgement, The.
Swirszczynska [or Swir]. Same Inside, The.
 Sea and the Man, The.
Szymborska, W. Ball, The.
Taggard. Fructus.
Tate, A. Ivory Tower, The.
Taylor, J. Natural Woman.
Tennyson, A. I will not shut me from my kind.
Thomas, L. Inauguration.
Tranströmer. For Mats and Laila.
Tzara. Horse, The.
Unknown. And then night fell.
 Bird and man.
 I have to go.
 Love Is a Mortal Disease.
 Rat, The.
 Sans Equity and sans Poise.
 Valley of Dry Bones, The.
Vallejo. Roll Call of Bones, The.
Vaughan, H. Corruption.
 Man.
 World, The (1).
Very. Created, The.
Ward, J. After the Report from Iron Mountain.
Weaver, A. New Nephilim, A.
Whitman, W. Has any one supposed it lucky to
 be born?
 I am of old and young, of the foolish as much
 as the wise.
 I celebrate myself, and sing myself.
 I think I could turn and live with animals, they
 are so placid and self-contained.
 On the Same Picture.
 One's-Self I Sing.

Wickham. To Men.
Wilbur, R. Ceremony.
Williams, W. What Is a Man?
Wilner, E. High Noon at Los Alamos.
Winchilsea. Spleen, The: A Pindaric Poem.
Wolfe, H. Man.
Wordsworth, W. Lines Written in Early Spring.
  Those [or These] words were uttered as in [or in
  a] pensive mood.
Wright, F. Only Animal, The.
Wright, J. Secret Gratitude, A.
Yauch, Adam. Update, The.
Yeats. Sorrow of Love, The [1927 Version].
Yi Sanghûi. For Men to Tell How Human Life
  Began Is Hard, For Who Himself Beginning
  Knew? Desire With Thee Still Longer to
  Converse Induced Me as New-Waked from
  Soundest Sleep Soft on the Flow'ry Herb I
  Found Me Laid in Balmy Sweat.
Young, P. Third Sex, The.

Humility
Astell. In Emulation of Mr Cowleys Poem
  Call'd The Motto.
Blake, W. Clod & the Pebble, The.
Bunyan. Shepherd Boy Sings [in the Valley of
  Humiliation], The.
Chaucer. Franklin's Prologue, The.
Chudleigh. Resolve, The.
Coleridge, S. Forbearance.
Crane, S. In Heaven, / Some little blades of
  grass.
Curzon, D. Proverbs 6:6.
de Portalatin. Humble Litany.
Di Piero. Near Damascus.
Durcan. Kilfenora Teaboy, The.
Elytis, O. I was late in understanding the
  meaning of humility.
Emerson, R. Experience.
Forbes, C. Plea, The.
Foss, S. House by the Side of the Road, The.
Herbert, G. Humility.
  Posy [or Posie], The.
Hubert. Joseph in Carcere.
Ibn Quzman, A. My life is spent in dissipation
  and wantonness!
Inp'yŏng, Prince. Don't mock a pine.
Johnson, S. Paraphrase.
Kerouac. And What Do I Owe You, God.
Kim Sujang. Standing in your lofty tower.
Kipling, R. If.
  Recessional.
Knevet. Contrition.
Magdeburg, Mechthild von. God's Absence.
Mitchell, A. Icarus Schmicarus.
Norris, K. Luke 14: A Commentary.
Pasternak, B. To Be Famous Isn't Decent.
Pawlak. Ace.
Po Chü-i. Inscription Written by Me in My
  Small Garden.
Porter, A. Oaks and Squirrels.
"Rachel." [or "Rahel."]. Surrender.
Ransom, J. Amphibious Crocodile.
Robinson, E. Cliff Klingenhagen.
Rochester, J. Rochester Extempore.
Simonides. Who, trusting his mind, could praise
  the man of Lindos, Kleoboulos.
Stanley, T. Paraphrase Upon Part of the
  CXXXIX Psalm, A.
Steinberg, J. It has been long since first my
  fears grew light.
Surrey. When that repentant tears hath cleansed
  clear from ill.
Taylor, E. Meditation. Heb. 13.10. We[e] have
  an Altar.
  State, a state, oh! dungeon state indeed, A.
Taylor, J. Violet, The.
Unknown. Dedication: "If you would let me
  leave."
I love thee for thy fickleness.
I Will Bow and Be Simple.
Various authors. He did not boast of his natural
  gifts.
Verlaine. Humble life of dull and easy work,
  The.
Wilbur, R. Finished Man, A.
Wright, C. Chinese Journal.

Night Journal.
Wright, J. Out of Horace.
Hummingbirds
Corbett, W. Vermont Apollinaire.
de Fierro. Grain of Sand.
Delgado, J. Chuparosa.
Dickinson, E. Hummingbird, A.
Dubie. Hummingbirds.
Elijio, C. Hummingbird at Dawn.
Fried, Michael. Send-Off, The.
Gallagher, T. Sah Sin.
Hall, D. Her Garden.
Huddle. Inside the Hummingbird Aviary.
Kennedy, X. Hummingbird.
Kingston, M. Birds: "I'm living in one place so
  long."
Lawrence, D. H. Humming-Bird.
Oliver, M. Hummingbird Pauses at the Trumpet
  Vine.
Paz. Exclamation.
Petit, P. Strait-Jackets, The.
Trungpa, Chogyam. Gentle day's flower.
Tucker, M. Humming-Bird, The.

Humorous and Nonsense Verse
Alexie. Theology.
Beatty, P. That's Not in My Job Description.
Buson. This cold winter night.
Dailey. Poetry fro Dummies.
Desnos. Like.
Fĕng Mĕng-lung. Feeling the Itch.
  Fooling Mom.
  My Old Man's Small.
  No Old Lady.
  Smart.
Healy, R. Mutability Checkers.
Holmes, O. After-Dinner Poem (Terpsichore),
  An.
Issa. For you too, my fleas.
  From the Great Buddha's.
  People working fields.
Jensma. Chant of praise for the idi amin dada.
Kuznetsova, I. Wand, A.
Lear, E. Table and the Chair, The.
Longchamps, G. O Luxury.
McDaniel, J. Disasterology.
Mullen, H. Blah-Blah.
Myer, M. Cool Cat.
Noguchi, R. Turn of Privacy, The.
Poe. Monody on Doctor Olmsted.
Pritchard, N. Junt.
Prys-Jones. Unfortunate Occurrence at Cwm-
  Cadno.
Tzara. Cosmic Realities Vanilla Tobacco
  Wakings.
  Lion Tamer Remembers, The.
  White Giant Leper of the Countryside.
Unknown. Polly Wolly Doodle.
  Tune: "Wu Yeh-erh" Twitting the Teller of Tall
  Tales.
Von Freytag-Loringhoven. Klink—Hratzvenga
  (Deathwail).
Wang Ho-ch'ing. Tune: "Po Pu-tuan" Fat
  Couple.
  Tune: "Po Pu-tuan" Long-Haired Little Dog.
Williamson, G. Appalachian Trees Encircled by
  Police Tape.
  Belvedere Marittimo.
Young, K. Clyde Peeling's Reptiland in
  Allenwood, Pennsylvania.

Hunchbacks
Brooks, G. Hunchback Girl: She Thinks of
  Heaven.
Soyinka. Hunchback of Dugbe, The.
Thomas, D. Hunchback in the Park, The.
Unknown. Three Hunchbacks, The.
Hundred Years War
Holub. Fly, The.
Hungary
Arnold, M. To the Hungarian Nation.
Csoori. My Masters.
  We Were Good, Good and Obedient.
Feinstein, E. Annus Mirabilis 1989.
Petri. Christmas 1956.
  Electra.

Hunger
Addonizio. First Kiss: "Afterwards you had that
  drunk, drugged look."
Adisa. Fennel.
Ai. Starvation.
Al-Jawahiri, M. Lullaby for the Hungry, A.
al-Saygh, S. Sanctions.
Alexander, P. Northeast Suite.
Allen, J. Hunger.
Arapaho Oral Tradition. Father, have pity on
  me.
Atwood. More and More.
Auden. Healthy Spot, A.
Barnett, R. Anorexic, The.
Bass, F. I am a Jew.
Berry, W. Sparrow.
Blackman, P. Sometimes all night I kept vigil
  with men stripped of their flesh.
Blake, W. Proverbial Philosophy.
Bonset. Remembering the Night Fountains.
Bourne, W. Heart's Fine Gold, The.
Bunno [Wen Wang or King Wen]. Song of the
  Bowmen of Shu [1954].
Cader. Promise, A.
Cambridge, A. Desire.
Ceravolo. Ho Ho Ho Caribou.
Chin. Disorder, The.
Ch'oe Kinam. Elegy to Myself.
Chungji. Mountain Life.
Clifton, L. Scar.
Collins, B. Osso Buco.
D'Aguiar, F. Sound Bite.
D'Aquino, A. Metempsicosis del perro.
  Metempsychosis of the Dog.
Dickinson, E. I had been hungry, all the Years.
  It would have starved a Gnat.
Dīnrām. From the time of the womb.
Dodge, M. Poor Crow!
Doolittle, Hilda. Satisfied, unsatisfied.
Field. Eros.
Fisher, J. Camp.
Fyleman. Punch and Judy.
Gibran. Fox, The.
Gilbert, J. Hunger.
Goedicke. American Exercises.
Goodison. Hungry Belly Kill Daley.
Grass. Saturn.
Greppi, C. Rain of hollow malice, A.
Hadewijch. Love's Constancy.
Hajjaj, N. Man Who Devoured Himself, The.
Haviaras, Stratis. Checkmark.
Hernández, M. Lullaby of the Onion.
Ho Ching-ming. Ballad of the Government
  Granary Clerk.
Howell, C. Christian Science Minotaur, The.
Hueng Guobin. Mountain Life.
Hughes, F. Foxes.
Im Yŏngjo. Textbook.
Inber. Teeth are bared, the mouth drawn tight,
  the face, The.
Jones, A. Anorexia.
Katz, M. Hungerdance, The.
Kaufman, S. Bread and Water.
Khlebnikov, V. To Everyone.
  Trumpet, Shout, Carry!
Kinsella, J. Archetypal Chillies.
Komunyakaa, Y. Banking Potatoes.
Kumar, A. Primary Lessons in Political
  Economy.
Levertov. O Taste and See.
Levine, P. They Feed They Lion.
Longfellow, H. On the fourth day of his fasting.
Lucan. O wastfull riot, never well content.
MacNaughton. Feast Day Dog.
Mahadevi. When I am hungry.
Major, C. Lost in the Desert.
Mansour, J. Seated on her bed legs spread open.
McFadden, D. 5. Visit to the Zoo, A.
Mei Yao Ch'en. Dappled Horse, The.
Merwin. Bread.
Mif. Terezin.
Milton. But now I feel hunger, which declares.
Mirville, E. Don't give me food.
Mistral, G. House, The.
Motion, A. Wall, A.
Muller, R. 16 Year-Old Girl Who's Standing, A.

Naimy, M. Hunger.
Natsume Soseki. Once I was a poor man's son.
Neihardt. In vain against the formless wolves of air.
Olds, S. Photograph of the Girl.
Oliver, L. Empty Kettle.
Oliver, M. Foxes in Winter.
Pegram, A. Towards Abraham's Bosom.
Pilinszky, J. Frankfurt.
 French Prisoner, The.
Pilling. Cast Away.
Potts. Comrade Laugher.
Powers, Arthur. Bag Lady's Body in the Financial District, A.
Press, K. Heart's Hunger.
 She brought home poppies.
Reed, H. Château, The.
Rodriguez, L. Hungry.
Rontsh, Y. Wolves.
Rothenberg, J. Hunger.
Saltman. Hunger, A.
Sandburg, C. Galoots.
Schwartz, D. Heavy Bear Who Goes with Me, The.
Scott, J. Hatching Thunder.
Shamaqmaq, A. Hungry Master and Hungry Cat.
Shin Tongyŏp. Scene 8.
Short, J. Leave in Mid-Winter.
Shreshtha, B. Should I Earn My Daily Bread, or Should I Write a Poem?
Shuttle. Delicious Babies.
Shwarts [or Shvarts]. Portrait of the Blockade through Genre Painting, Still Life, and Landscape, A.
Sora. Skylark / Soaring—her young.
Suri, T. Here Comes God.
Swirszczynska [or Swir]. I Starve My Belly for a Sublime Purpose.
Thomas, E. Owl, The.
Toomer. Harvest Song.
Tsaloumas. Autumn Supper.
Tsang, L. Lunching.
Tsung Ch'en. Song of Selling Flowers.
Unknown. Lily bud floating, yellow as sorrow.
Unknown, fr. Terezin Concentration Camp. Theresienstadt's Hospital.
Vallejo. Hungry Man's Wheel, The.
Various authors. Zealous to deliver the suffering people.
Vietnamese Oral Tradition. Homesick Bride, The.
Wheeler, S. Produce, Produce.
Wickham. Sehnsucht.
Woodward, V. Cornbread blues.
Yang Shih-ch'i. Following the Rhymes of Shao-pao Huang's Poem on Being Moved while Visiting the Farmers.
Yao Chen. Ballad on the Investigation of a Disaster.
Zabolotsky [or Zabolotskii]. At the Fishmonger's.

Hunt, Leigh
Keats. Written on the Day That Mr. Leigh Hunt Left Prison.

Hunting and Hunters
Amirthanayagam, I. Elephants Are in the Yard, The.
Ariosto. Tumbler, The.
Baker, H. Advice to a Man Who Lost a Dog.
Barker, G. Street Ballad.
Berg, S. Orpingalik's My Breath: Eskimo Song.
Berlin. You Can't Get a Man with a Gun.
Bernstein, M. Manly Sports.
Berryman. Winter Landscape.
Bierds, L. Hunter.
 Ritual for the Dead, Lake Sakami, Quebec, 1980.
Black, S. Hunt, The: "To be in the way, belonging. To wait."
Bloomfield. To Err Is Human.
Blue Cloud. Yellowjacket.
Blunt, W. Old Squire, The.
Bowman, C. Dove at Sundown.
Brontë, A. Song.
Brontë, C. Young Man Naughty's Adventure.

Bryant, W. Indian Story, An.
Cader. Season for Hunting, A.
Carroll, L. Hunting of the Snark, The.
Carter, S. Passing of Arthur, The.
Causley. I Saw a Jolly Hunter.
Cavendish, M. Hunting of the Hare, The.
Chase, K. Venison.
Chaucer. Fawning Whelp, The.
 Lycurgus' Alauns.
Clare, J. Badger.
Clarke, C. Tortoise and Badger.
Cowley, M. Ernest.
Cummings, E. E. All in green went my love riding.
Daniel, G. After a Storm, Going a Hawking.
Davenant [or D'Avenant]. Lombard Stag-Hunt, The.
Davidson, J. Runnable Stag, A.
Davis, C. Little Crisis Framed in My Window.
Davis, J. Warru.
De la Mare. Hi!
Dickinson, E. Cat.
Doty, M. Retrievers in Translation.
Erdrich. Jacklight.
 Strange People, The.
Esquinca, Jorge. Fable of the Hunter.
Faiz. Once Again the Mind.
Follain. Black Meat.
Fouilloux, J. Blazon Pronounced by the Huntsman, The.
Frost, C. To Kill a Deer.
Gascoigne. Gascoigne's Woodmanship.
Gascoyne. Rex Mundi.
Gay, J. Rural Sports.
Gibson, M. One Body.
Graham, H. It was a winter's morning.
Grattius, F. Roman Tribute, A.
Harris, R. Literary Excellence.
Hartley, M. As the Buck Lay Dead.
Helwig. Departures.
Hemans. Chamois Hunter's Love, The.
Herbert, G. Affliction (4).
Hilary. To an English Boy: "Beautiful boy, flower fair."
Hogan, L. Skin.
Hogg, J. Deep-Toned Jowler, The.
 Deep-Toned Jowler, The.
Hoggard, James. Dove Hunting Each Labor Day.
Hopkinson, F. O'er the Hills.
Howe, J. Soul-Hunter, The.
Hughes, T. Modest Proposal, A.
Jamme, Franck André. Often You Come.
Jonson, B. To Sir Henry Goodyere.
Jouve. Lament for the Stag.
Karpowicz. Hunting.
Kennelly. Love-Cry.
Killigrew, A. On a Picture Painted by Herself [or Her self], Representing Two Nymphs [or Nimphs] of Diana's, One in a Posture to Hunt, the other Bath[e]ing.
Kinnell. Bear, The.
 Perch, The.
 To Christ Our Lord.
Kipling, R. Hunting-Song of the Seeonee Pack.
Kumin, M. Woodchucks.
Laforgue. Mystery of the Three Horns, The.
Lanier, S. Revenge of Hamish, The.
Lawrence, D. H. Mountain Lion.
Layton. Black Huntsmen, The.
Lea, S. Late Season.
Linebarger, Jim. Coyote.
Lovelace, R. La Bella Bona-Roba.
Lowbury. Huntsman, The.
MacIntyre, D. To the Air of a Pibroch.
Mahon. Hunt by Night, The.
Markus, P. Shooting Crows.
Martial. You want me to call you generous.
Marvell. Nymph Complaining for the Death of Her Faun [or Fawn], The.
Masters, E. Unknown, The.
McDonald, W. After the Noise of Saigon ("If where we hunt defines us.").
 In Fields of Buffalo.
Merwin. Avoiding News by the River.
Miller, J. Dead in the Sierras.

Nelson, H. Journey, The: "I am wearing my gray wool pants, and my brown boots."
Oliver, L. Empty Kettle.
Orr, G. Gathering the Bones Together.
Ovid. Actaeon.
 Procris' Immortal Lelaps: Cephalus' Story.
Page, P. Stories of Snow.
Preil, G. Tired Hunter, The.
Pritchard, N. Junt.
Sadoff. On the Job.
 Red Tail Sonnet.
Scott, S. Baffled Staghounds, The.
Senghor. Nocturne (She Flies She Flies).
Shakespeare, W. Rival Favourites.
Sioux Oral Tradition. Give Me Back My Bow.
Sisson. Un-Red Deer, The.
Skrzynecki. Hunting Rabbits.
Smith, D. Dream of the Jacklighter, The.
Smith, I. Deer looks through you to the other side, A.
Snyder, G. One Should Not Talk to a Skilled Hunter about What Is Forbidden by the Buddha.
Spenser, E. Sonnet 67: "Like a huntsman after weary chase."
Ssu-ma Hsiang-ju. Sir Fantasy.
Stein, G. Valentine to Sherwood Anderson, A.
 White Hunter, A.
 White Hunter, A.
Stewart, S. Meadow, The.
Su Tung-p'o. Tune: "A Riverside Town".
Sung Yu. Gao Tang Rhapsody, The.
Talvikki, A. You Don't Know What Happened When You Froze.
Tallmountain. Good Grease.
ten Berge. Fortunes in knee breeches.
Tobin, D. Hunt-Cup, The.
Turberville. Hare's Complaint, The.
 Woful Words of the Hart, The.
Unknown. Carmen Possum.
 Epitaph for Thomas Johnson, Huntsman. Charlton, Sussex.
 Finn and Ossian Hunting.
 Hunters Ask God, The.
 Hunter's Song.
 I want the robes, the skins of the game animals, the meat of the game animals. Bring them to me. Let us enjoy ourselves.
 Lone Buck.
 Scholar and the Cat, The.
 Song of the Fallen Deer.
 Song to a Child.
 With huntis vp, with huntis vp.
Van Ostaijen. Song of the Alpine Hunter.
Various authors. He hit the backs of forty tailed deer.
 He shot six roebucks.
 On Mount Chorae he struck two roebucks.
Vietnamese Oral Tradition. Mother Egret.
Virgil [or Vergil]. Dawn leaves the bed of Dark and climbs the sky.
Wang Ch'ang-ling. Song by the Walls.
Warren, R. Love and Knowledge.
 Red-Tail Hawk and Pyre of Youth.
 Was Not the Lost Dauphin.
Webb, C. Killing the Animals.
Weismiller. Skull.
Welish. Textile 9.
Whitaker, J. Roman Tribute, A.
Wordsworth, W. Simon Lee, the Old Huntsman; with an incident in which he was concerned.
Wright, C. Blackwater Mountain.
Wright, J. White Deer, The.
Wyatt. Whoso List to Hunt.
Yesenin [or Essenin]. Mysterious, Ancient World of Mine.
Zanzotto. Eva, forma futuri.

Hurdy-Gurdies
Noyes, A. Barrel-Organ, The.

Huron, Lake
Herschberger. Huron, The.

Hurricanes
Balaban. Hurricane.
Baldwin, Sandy. Heralds of the hurricane.
Batraville, D. Paper 8.
Chappell, F. My Father's Hurricane.

Crane, H.   Hurricane, The.
Freneau.   Hurricane, The.
Glatt.   Amanda.
Guglielmoni, Linda M. Rodriguez.   Hurakán: A Two Way Poem.
Hernández Cruz.   Art of Hurricanes, The.
  Problems With Hurricanes.
Miller, V.   On a Weekend in September.
Morejón.   I Never Saw Great Lakes.
Morrissey, S.   After the Hurricane.
Musa, Y.   Zinc.
Nordhaus.   Protecting the Children from Hurricanes.
Phillips, R.   Houston Haiku.
Philp, G.   Heirlooms.
Thomas, Larry D.   Great Storm, The.
Thomas, L.   Hurricane Doris.
See also **Storms**
Husbands
Alvi, M.   Backgrounds.
  Carrying My Wife.
  Man Impregnated.
Ap Hywel, Elin.   Treasure.
Armitage, S.   Poem: "And if it snowed and snow covered the drive."
Bachinsky, E.   ATM.
Bang, M.   Crossed-Over, Fiend-Snitched, X-ed Out.
Barber, M.   Advice to Her Son on Marriage.
Berry, W.   Marriage.
Bly, R.   French Generals, The.
Bradstreet, A.   Letter to Her Husband, Absent upon Public[k] Employment, A.
  To My Dear and Loving Husband.
Browning, R.   Any Wife to Any Husband.
Cerenio.   23 October 1992.
Chaucer.   My fourthe housbonde was a revelour.
Christie.   Possible Man, The.
Chudleigh.   Unhappy they, who by their duty led.
  Wish, The.
Corcadail, A. I.   O rosary that recalled my tear.
DeFrees.   Letter to an Absent Son.
Egerton, S.   Emulation, The.
"Eliza.".   To My Husband.
Erdrich.   Mary Kröger.
Ferch Gruffyd, A.   Verses Written by Alis Daughter of Gryffydd Son of Iefan When Her Father Asked Her What Sort of Husband She Would Like.
Graves, R.   Slice of Wedding Cake, A.
Harris, M.   Trial Separation.
Haynes, C.   Any Wife or Husband.
Heard, J.   My Husband's Birthday.
Hirsch, E.   Husband and Wife.
Homer.   Ulysses Reunited with Penelope.
Istarú, A.   Crescent moon, A.
Keita, N.   My Sleeping Husband.
Kendrick, D.   Sadie Snuffs a Candle.
King, H.   Dream Maiden, A.
Kirby, D.   Dance of Husbands in Bathrobes, The.
Lee, L.   Gift, The: "To pull the metal splinter from my palm."
Lewis, C.   Ballade of Dead Gentlemen.
Lowell, R.   To Speak of Woe That Is in Marriage.
Macdonagh, T.   John-John.
MacGregor, Mrs., of Glenstrae.   Lament for MacGregor of Glenstrae.
Masini.   Two Men, Two Grapefruits.
McBride, M.   Knife-Thrower's Wife, The.
McGinley.   5:32, The.
Mei Sheng.   Beautiful Toilet, The.
Mugo, M. G.   Wife of the Husband.
Nash, O.   Word to Husbands, A.
Nesbit, E.   Husband of To-Day, The.
Pape.   Minotaur Next Door, The.
Parker, D.   Social Note.
P'Bitek.   My Husband's Tongue Is Bitter.
  Woman with Whom I Share My Husband, The.
Remoto.   Images of John (1967–92).
Rungano.   Woman, The.
Sawyer, A.   Lines, / Written on Seeing My Husband's Picture, painted when he was young: "Those are the features, those the

smiles."
Sexton.   And One for My Dame.
Shaw, A.   Crepuscule.
Simic.   Scarecrow, The.
Stepanova, M.   Airman.
Stoddard, E.   Wife Speaks, The.
Taylor, J.   Instructions to Her Next Husband.
Thompson, P.   Husband's Return, The.
Unknown.   God, provide the "little horror" with an eternal sleep!
  God, take this old husband away.
  Jun-zi yang-yang: The Gudeman's Come Hame (scoticè).
  Let this rock crush me with its weight.
  Little horror does nothing—does not make love, does not make war, The.
  Little horror, oblivious to combat, sleeps quietly beside me, The.
  Meng: To a Man.
  My Husband, Before Leaving.
  Oh Lord! Once again your long and dismal night is here.
  Oh my God! Once again you send me the dark night.
  See the dreadful tyranny of husbands:.
  Substituted Poem of Laureate Quynh, The.
  Tell Me, Wight in the Broom.
  These Women Plunder My Husband.
  They tell me that the "little horror" have fled the face of the earth.
  Too Late for a Husband.
Vietnamese Oral Tradition.   Bare Rocks and Stars.
  Colonial Troops Transport, The.
  Husband and Wife.
Waddington, M.   Thou Didst Say Me.
Walcott.   Menelaus.
Williams, F.   Reply (crumped on her desk).
Winchilsea.   Letter to Daphnis, A.
Zucker, R.   Avoid.
Hyacinths
Brown, L.   My Uncruel April, My Totally Equal Unfortold April Unfolded.
Eliot, T. S.   Song for Simeon, A.
Glück, L.   Hyacinth.
Hacker, M.   Thought thrusts up, homely as a hyacinth.
Prince, F.T.   Babiaantje, The.
Sappho.   Herdsmen crush under their feet.
Siegel, J.   Wild Hyacinth.
Zawgee.   Way of the Water-Hyacinth, The.
Hyacinthus
Ovid.   Apollo and Hyacinthus.
Hydrangeas
Houlihan, J.   Hydrangeas.
Muldoon, P.   Hydrangea.
Stern, G.   Hydrangea.
Hyenas
Buddingh'.   Hyena, The.
Kipling, R.   Hyaenas [*or* Hyenas], The.
Hymns
Abercrombie.   Hymn to Love.
Bécquer, G.   I Know a Strange, Gigantic Hymn.
Bryant, W.   Forest Hymn.
Fletcher, J.   Hymn to Pan.
Foerster.   Tantum Ergo.
Glaser, M.   Magnificat!
Hughes, T.   Hymn: "You, who gave colour to the dawn."
Smallfield, Edward.   Amazing Grace.
Thomson, J.   Hymn on the Seasons, A.
Unknown.   Limerick.
Wagner, S.   A Cappella.
Hypocrisy and Hypocrites
Barnes, W.   False Friends-like.
Berry, D.   Hambone Two Tongue.
Bly, R.   Johnson's Cabinet Watched by Ants.
Browning, E.   Man's Requirements, A.
Browning, R.   Soliloquy of the Spanish Cloister.
Burns, R.   Address to the Unco Guid, or the Rigidly Righteous.
  Holy Willie's Prayer.
Butler, S.   For his religion it was fit.
Carroll, L.   Alice's Recitation.
Clampitt.   Palm Sunday.

Clough.   Latest Decalogue, The.
Congreve, W.   Hue and Cry after Fair Amoret, A.
Connolly, C.   To Osbert Sitwell.
Cummings, E. E.   Come,gaze with me upon this dome.
  Next to of course god america i.
Dalton, R.   Petty Bourgeoisie, The.
Dickinson, E.   Mine—by the Right of the White Election!
Graves, R.   Sick Love.
Han-shan.   His mind is as high as a mountain.
Harington [*or* Harrington].   Groome of the Chambers religion in King Henry the eights time, A.
Harper, F.   Double Standard, A.
Hemingway.   Chapter Heading.
Hughes, L.   Children's Rhymes ("By what sends.").
  Dinner Guest: Me.
Hutchinson, P.   Look, No Hands.
Jonson, B.   On Don Surly.
  On the Town's Honest Man.
Juvenal.   Northward beyond the Lapps to the world's end, the frozen.
Kabir.   Ascetic Dyes His Robes, The.
Kipling, R.   Tommy.
Levertov.   Hypocrite Women.
Lindsay, V.   Why I Voted the Socialist Ticket.
Mapanje.   Cheerful Girls at Smiller's Bar, 1971, The.
Martial.   Chrestus, your balls are depilated.
Montagu, L.   Epistle from Mrs. Yonge to Her Husband.
Mudrooroo Narogin.   Peaches and Cream.
Perrine.   Janus.
Pope, A.   Sporus.
Praed.   Chancery Morals.
Robinson, M.   Stanzas: "In this vain, busy world, where the good and the gay."
Sadi [*or* Saadi *or* Sa'di].   Until you can correct and heal yourself.
Shakespeare, W.   Sonnet 121: "Tis better to be vile than vile esteemed."
Sidney.   Sonnet 31: "With how sad steps, O Moon[e], thou climb'st the skies."
Swinburne.   Higher Pantheism in a Nutshell, The.
Unknown.   Hypocrite and the Concubine, The.
  O Daniel.
  Statesmen, in your exalted station know.
  What Really Goes on in the College of Cardinals.
Vietnamese Oral Tradition.   Wicked Women.
Whittier.   Christian Slave, The.
Yahya Efendi, Sheyhülislâm.   Let the hypocrites practice their way.
Yeats.   On Hearing That the Students of Our New University Have Joined the Agitation against Immoral Literature.

I

Iago
Bernick, J.   Iago.
Dancing Bear, J. P.   Iago, the Poet.
Germain, Carmen.   Literature 100.
Gwynn, R.   Iago to His Torturers.
Powers, Arthur.   Iago.
Ibsen, Henrik
Bentley, E.   "Susaddah!" exclaimed Ibsen.
Ibycus
Lazarus, E.   Cranes of Ibycus, The.
Icarus
Abse.   Brueghel in Naples.
Auden.   Musée des Beaux Arts.
Benét, S.   Winged Man.
Field, E.   Icarus.
Goffette, Guy.   Raising of Icarus, The: Envoi.
Iremonger.   Icarus.
Mitchell, A.   Icarus Schmicarus.
Nowlan.   I, Icarus.
Ovid.   Daedalus.
Rukeyser, M.   Waiting for Icarus.

Sexton. To a Friend Whose Work Has Come to Triumph.
Stevenson, A. Icarus in November.
Stickney, T. On Rodin's "L'Illusion, Sœur d'Icare".
Wilbur, R. Icarium Mare.
Williams, W. Landscape with the Fall of Icarus.

Ice
Acorn. That Corrugated Look To Water.
Basho. Awakened at midnight.
Beissel, H. Tanka: "Ice rain coats berries."
Buchanan, O. Term, The.
Dickey, W. Arrival of the Titanic, The.
Elfyn, Menna. Welsh Ice.
Field, E. Farewell, The: "They say the ice will hold."
Field. To the Winter Aphrodite.
Fletcher, J. Skaters, The.
Fontanella. Image of the frozen lake, The.
Frost, R. Fire and Ice.
Greenlaw, L. Reading Akhmatova in Midwinter.
Hayden, R. Ice Storm.
Hristov, Boris. Sign from Heaven, A.
Johnson, J. Midnight Run.
Kenney. Sailing.
Lane, P. I walk to the river in deep snow. The ice is thick.
Livesay, D. Uninvited, The.
London, S. Cold War.
Longley, M. Freeze-Up.
Lope de Vega. Ice and Fires Contend with My Child.
Lowry, M. About Ice.
MacCaig. Sleet.
Mallarmé. Virginal, vibrant, and beautiful dawn, The.
McCarriston. January, Anchorage.
Meredith, W. Crossing Over.
Mok, J. Winter Mirror.
Monk, M. Fire Us with Ice, Burn Us with Snow.
Nabhan, G. Coming Out on Solid Ground After the Ice Age.
Nemerov. Icehouse in Summer, The.
Overton, R. Fire and Ice by Robert Frost: an early draft.
Quinn, J. 2. Icebox.
Rafferty, P. 66°7' N/22°17' W.
Ransom, W. Message from Ohanapecosh Glacier.
Rector. My Grandfather Always Promised Us.
Rothman, D. Whistling in January.
Roubaud. Ice In.
Sepúlveda, O. Cuatro ("Pero luego, en el trayecto imaginario de un automóvil blanco.").
Four ("But then, in the imaginary trajectory of a white automobile.").
Sexton, T. Skimming the Ice.
Siegel, J. Wild Hyacinth.
Sophocles. This disease is an evil bound upon the day.
Voznesensky [or Voznesenskii]. First Ice, The.
Wakoski. Ice Eagle, The.
Wyrebek, M. Trendelenburg Position.
Yi Sanghûi. Igloo! Igloo!

Ice Cream
Anwar, C. Tuti's Ice Cream.
Charara, H. On the Murder of an Ice Cream Man.
Ginsberg, A. Walking into King Sooper after Two-Week Retreat.
Joseph, A. Good Humor.
Kaplinski, J. My Wife and Children.
Laing, A. Grace for a Ice-Cream, A.
Someck, R. Ice Cream.
Stanard, C. Washington Square Park and a Game of Chess.
Stevens, W. Emperor of Ice-Cream, The.
Swenson, K. Ice-Cream Sandwich, The.

Ice Floes
Maggs, Randall. Night Crossing in Ice.

Ice Skating and Ice Skaters
Calder, A. Curling: Old Murrayfield Ice Rink.
Dunn, S. Criminal.
Erb, E. Stove Problem, The.
Herbert, Z. Georg Heym—The Almost

Metaphysical Adventure.
Kuzma. Ice Skating.
Salter. Sunday Skaters.
See also **Skating and Skaters**

Icebergs
Bishop, E. Imaginary Iceberg, The.
Hardy, T. Convergence of the Twain, The.
Melville, H. Berg, The.

Iceland
Auden. Journey to Iceland.
Enzensberger, H. Reprieve, The.
Holm, B. Icelandic Language, The.
McKendrick, J. Six Characters in Search of Something.
Rafferty, P. 66°7' N/22°17' W.

Icicles
Frost, R. Beyond Words.
Issa. From the end of the nose.
Mueller, J. Year.
Roberson, E. Poor Houses, The.

Idaho (state)
Crase. There Is No Real Peace in the World.
Johnson, J. Unmarked Stop in Front of Westmond General Store, Westmond, Idaho.
Rutsala. Sunday Morning Walk.

Ideal Love
Bass, E. All the Trees.
Crashaw. Wishes. To His (Supposed) Mistress[e].
Dowden, E. Love's Chord.
Dunn, S. Blind Date with the Muse.
Emre. Love is minister to us, our flock is the inmost soul.
Faiz. Love I Gave You Once, The.
Hill, S. Please Can I Have a Man.
Lochhead, L. Rapunzstiltskin.
Luschei, G. Highway.
Mayer, B. America: "As for me, when I saw you."
O'Grady, D. In the Greenwood.
O'Rahilly. Enchanted Mistress, The.
Rohrer, M. Credo: "I believe there is something else."
Rosemurgy, C. Love, with Trees and Lightning.
Rumi. So long as I am alive, love enlivens each day.
Shcherbina. Except for love everything.
Shelley, P. Poet wandering on, through Araby, The.
Takeshima Hagaromo. Maiden Called Love, The.
Tynan Hinkson, K. Blind Country.
Unknown. Almighty on High!
Vasileva, E. I used to be your echo.
Warner, R. Hymn: "Splendid body is private, and calls for more, The."
Wizlaw von Rügen. Only Love.
Young, J. True Love.

Idealism and Idealists
Abrahams, L. To the idealistic killers.
Chen Huan. Presented to the Taoist Paragon Mao.
Collins, M. If.
Cucchi, M. I wouldn't know what it's like to be a pawn.
Greppi, C. Those quiet little feet in the reflected room.
Hughes, L. Let America Be America Again.
Lux. Neighborhood of Make-Believe, The.
Muske, C. Ideal.
Nolla. Troubadour Love.
Nutter, G. Pastoral: "We're passing the whole summer, all of us."
Pitcher, O. Iconoclast's Closet, The.
Ray, H. Quest of the Ideal, The.
Robin, L. My Ideal.
Sanchez, S. Poem for July 4, 1994.
Wyatt. *In aeternum* I was once determed.

Identity
Adonis [or Adunis]. Woman and a Man, A.
Ajanta. Me on the Wall.
Alegría. Accounting.
Aleixandre. In Front of the Mirror.
Alvi, M. Sari, The.
Anderson, S. American Spring Song.

Ap Glyn, Ifor. Cucumbers of Wolverhampton, The.
Aridjis. Self-Portrait at Fifty-Four Years Old.
Armantrout. Up to Speed.
Arrillaga. Dream.
Like Raquel.
Rosa/Filí.
Arroyo, R. My Mysterious Body.
Avison. Prospecting.
Beachy-Quick, Dan. Halt (Naïve).
Unworn.
Bernheim, Erica. I Love How Your Eyes Close Every Time You Kiss Me.
Like a Face.
Bernstein, C. Solidarity Is the Name We Give to What We Cannot Hold.
Berrigan, A. Bloodletting.
Ode to Election Day.
Bibbins, M. Now the sea moves up the lawn for him as those nearby view his life passing before their eyes.
Sinking.
Bitsui, Sherwin. Northern Sun, The.
Bly, R. Man Who Didn't Know What Was His, The.
Borawski. Some of Us Wear Pink Triangles.
Borges. Borges and I.
Brainard, J. Aug. 29, 1967.
Braschi. Final Manuscript.
Brecht, B. Of Poor B.B.
Brinson, C. Haiku: "Black, brother, nigga."
Brock-Broido. Am Moor.
Brooks, G. To the Diaspora.
Brown, E. Out.
Brown, L. I Want to Be Bad.
Brutus. I Am Alien in Africa and Everywhere.
Budy. Ellis Island, September 1907.
Buscani. Downtime.
Cameron, N. Meeting My Former Self.
Chedid, A. Who Remains Standing?
Chin. Is It Snowing in Guangzhou?
We Are Americans Now, We Live in the Tundra.
Clifton, L. Scar.
Cofer, J. Changeling, The.
Comden, B. Lucky to Be Me.
Coolidge, C. By a I.
Cortez, J. Flame.
Coultas, B. Human Museum, The.
Couzyn. House of Changes.
Crapsey. Amaze.
Creeley. Feeling, A.
Davis, O. Unbosoming, The.
de Aerenlund, C. Cuando el tecolote canta, el Indio muere.
de Fierro. Oblivion.
DeFrees. Going Back to the Convent.
DeSylva, B. G. I Want to Be Bad.
Dietz, H. Triplets.
Dimitrova. Hotel Room.
Donnelly, T. Three Panels Depending on the Heart.
Doyle, B. Forensics.
Dumas, H. Afro-American.
Ekelof. Questionnaire.
Éluard, P. Mirror of a Moment, The.
Emanuel, L. Walt, I Salute You!
Espada. My Native Costume.
Esteves. Here.
Ferrell, M. Myths of the Disappearance.
Fisher, A. Diary Theme, The.
Fitts, Susan Love. Anonymous: "To the Department of Motor Vehicles."
Florit, E. Elegy for Your Absence.
Flynn, N. Swarm.
Fogarty, L. Am I.
Fuhrman, J. Personal Ad.
García Lorca. Casida of the Rose.
Ginsberg, A. Sitting crosslegged on a wooden floor.
Goedicke. For Walt Whitman.
Goese, M. I slowly crack my joints to ready and steady myself. Sharpen my mind on.
You Are.
Gomez, M. To the Latin Lover I Left at the Candy Store.

Gonzalez, N.   I Made Myself a Path.
Gordon, I.   Be Anything (But Be Mine).
Graham, J.   Philosopher's Stone.
Green, A.   Lucky to Be Me.
Greenberg, A.   Afterward, There Will Be a
   Hallway.
Greenwald, T.   Who / 'd / of / thought / the /
   morning / 'd / be / so / late.
Halliday, M.   Case Against Mist, The.
Hamer.   Origins.
Harper, M.   Brother John.
Harrison, T.   Self Justification.
   Turns.
Haviaras, Stratis.   Easter Feast.
Hawoldar.   To Be a Woman.
Hayes, T.   What I Am.
Healey, S.   As Western Culture Declined
   Without Its Knowing.
Helfand, J.   Boy Girl Game, The.
Henderson, R.   I Want to Be Bad.
Hendriks.   Will the Real Me Please Stand Up?
Henry, B.   Garage Sale.
Highfill, M.   Marginalization of Poetry, The.
Hillman, B.   Left Eye.
Hirshfield, J.   It Was Like This : You Were
   Happy.
Hovanessian, D.   Inside Green Eyes, Black
   Eyes.
   Mixed Marriage.
   Two Voices.
Hristov, Boris.   Solitary Man.
Hughes, L.   Theme for English B.
Hume, C.   Hume's Suicide of the External
   World.
   Lies Concerning Speed.
   Sampler City.
Hyde, E.   Super High.
Jackson, B.   In Exchange for Forty Acres.
Jackson, L.   One Self.
   Postponement of Self.
   Reasons of Each, The.
   Tiger, The.
   With the Face.
Jaffee, Marc.   King of Repetition.
Jernigan, Marla.   Who are you.
Jinkag Haesim.   Facing the Shadow.
Jones, Nesta Wyn.   Scream!
Jones, R.   Comment on this: in the real scheme
   of things, poetry is marginal.
Joseph, A.   Adolescence.
Joseph, L.   That's All.
Kavulu.   Me?
Kay, J.   Chapter 7: Black Bottom.
   In my country.
   Pride.
   Somebody Else.
Kearney, M.   Goodnight, Goodbye.
Keith, Sally.   Gallery, The.
Kim, Suji Kwock.   Monologue for an Onion.
Klyuyev [or Kliuev or Klyuev].   Fourth Rome,
   The.
Kolsson, K.   I have nine principal talents.
Korteweg.   Entirely You.
Kunitz, S.   Layers, The.
Lasheen, M.   Nearly Three Million Years Ago.
Lattany, K.   Question of Identity, The.
Lavieri, J.   Autobiography of John Doe, The.
Lem.   So Now You're Chicana.
Leong, R.   Threads.
Levin, D.   Chill Core.
Lezama Lima.   Ah, That You Escape.
Lim, S.   Modern Secrets.
Liu K'o-hsiang.   Choice.
Llwyd, Iwan.   Sure, You Can Ask Me a Personal
   Question.
Lorde.   Outside.
Manning, Maurice.   On God.
Mansour, J.   I Opened Your Head.
Mark, Sabrina Orah.   Experiments Lasted
   Through the Winter, The.
   Hello: "I am one anatomy and take turns.
      Sometimes after dinner I wrap them in a
      newspaper."
Mason, Keith Antar.   I Am a Creature of the
   Obvious.
Mattawa.   Echo and Elixir 1.

Echo and Elixir 2.
McSweeney, Joyelle.   Persuasion.
Merwin.   Whoever You Are.
Messer, S.   Rendered Dog.
Mohiuddin, K.   Birthmark.
Morales, A.   Ending Poem.
   Puertoricanness.
Morales.   Ending Poem.
Morgenstern.   Summons.
Morter, L.   Lost: "African drumbeat."
Mtshali.   Boy on a Swing.
Mullen, L.   Applications of.
Neruda.   Amor America (1400).
Nguyen, Hoa.   Unorthodox and impractical one
   not led.
Niedecker.   My life is hung up.
Nooteboom.   Midday.
O'Callaghan, C.   Anon.
Oppen.   Myself I Sing.
Orozco.   Olga Orozco.
Palmer, M.   Song of the Round Man.
   This Time.
Paquin, Ethan.   Capstone.
Pasos, J.   This Is Not Her.
Pinsky.   In Berkeley.
Plotnick, H. M.   Jewish.
Po Chü-i.   For the Beach Gulls.
Pound, E.   Portrait d'une Femme.
Powell, D. A.   House Face.
Prado, A.   Heart's Desire.
Radoev, Ivan.   Tiny Man, The.
Raffalovich, M. A.   Sonnet 120.
   World Well Lost 4, The.
Ramanujan.   Alien.
Ravikovitch, D.   Blood Heifer.
Reps, Paul.   who is.
Reverdy.   Internal Travels.
Rimbaud, A.   O Saisons, O Châteaux.
Rodas.   Poems from the Erotic Left.
Rodrigues J. P.   Half-.
Rossetti, D.   98: He and I.
Rumsey, Tessa.   Big Rig the Baroque Sky.
Russell, P.   Be Careful When You Go Looking
   for a Madonna Cuz You Just Might Find a
   Woman.
Sabry, M.   Marionette.
Sajé, N.   I am peeling four pink grapefruit.
Salaam.   Call of the Wild, The.
Saloy, M.   "N" Word, The.
Samson, J.   Liminal Highway.
Savageau.   At the Powwow.
   Like the Trails of Ndakinna.
   Looking for Indians.
   To Human Skin.
Schilpp, M.   Triage.
Serchuk.   My Other Life.
Sharma, P.   Poorly Matched.
   Principles, When I Felt Them.
Shipley, A.   Mama Said.
Sia, B.   Claim to Fame.
Simic.   Charles Simic.
Singer, B.   Still and All.
Sisson.   Person, The.
Sŏ Chŏngju.   Self-Portrait ("Father was a serf,
   seldom came home at night.").
Solie, Karen.   Science and the Single Girl.
Song.   Lost Sister ("In China, / even the
   peasants.").
Souza.   De Souza Prabhu.
Spahr, J.   Story goes like this: the light, The.
Sri Sri.   Myth of Myself.
St. Germain, S.   Cajun.
Stafford, W.   Story That Could Be True, A.
Steptoe.   Hambone Gospel, A.
Su, A.   Address.
Tarn.   Man Whose Name Rhymes with Peace,
   A.
Towle.   Seasonal Ramble.
Tranströmer.   Schubertiana.
   Solitude.
Trethewey, N.   Flounder.
   White Lies.
Unknown.   Doubt as to Identity.
   I Came from Under the Earth.
   Tree we plant will, when its boughs are grown,
      The.

Uyematsu.   To All Us Sansei Who Wanted to Be
   Westside.
Van Doren.   Midland.
Viray, M.   Patio.
   Two Strangers, The.
Volach, Y.   Bird.
Wallace, R.   Hot Property, A.
Watley, M.   Negroes.
Webb, C.   Coach Class Seats.
Welch, L.   Large Little Circle.
Weöres.   Song: Boundless Space.
Whitman, W.   Song of Myself.
   There Was a Child Went Forth.
Wiethüchter.   Movement.
Williams, C.   In Search of Aunt Jemima.
Williams, W.   Summer Cloud, A.
Witt, S.   Ikonostasis. The Sound of the Sea
   Filling a Faraway Room.
Wright, C.   As Our Bodies Rise, Our Names
   Turn into Light.
Wright, F.   Brother, The.
Wright, S.   Harvest.
Zawacki, Andrew.   One of me stuttered and one.
   Velocity Among the Ruins of Angel Republic.
Zucker, R.   Avoid.

Identity Crisis
Arroyo, R.   Longing: "It wasn't just about sex,
   but about."
Baraka, I.   Agony, An. As Now.
Bona.   Amazone.
Bronk.   I Thought It Was Harry.
Dame.   On the Road to Damascus, Maryland.
de Aerenlund, C.   Cuando el tecolote canta, el
   Indio muere.
Dennis, C.   God Who Loves You, The.
Derricotte.   Struggle, The.
Dickinson, E.   I'm Nobody! Who are you?
Ekelof.   Monologue with Its Wife.
El-Shawwaf, H.   Devil's Symbol, The.
Gamalinda, E.   Opposite of Nostalgia, The.
Gardiner, S.   Identity Crisis.
   Second Person.
Gier, J.   Examining the I.
Hagedorn, J.   Filipino Boogie.
Hayden, R.   Names.
Healy, E.   Changing What We Mean.
Hewitt, J.   Colony, The.
Hogan, L.   Truth Is, The.
Hughes, T.   Wodwo.
Hwang Jiwoo.   Mirror 3.
Ikkyu Sojun.   Don't worry please please how
   many times do I have to say it.
Jarrell, R.   Woman at the Washington Zoo, The.
Mark, Sabrina Orah.   Babies, The.
McDaniel, J.   Dear America.
Messer, S.   With this change to indoor lighting.
Mirikitani.   Doreen.
Mullen, L.   Series of Failures So That I'm Sick
   of the Word, A.
Olson, C.   In Cold Hell, in Thicket.
Peacock, M.   Spell, The.
Rodgers, C.   Group Therapy.
Rose.   Endangered Roots of a Person.
St. John, P.   We Are Going to Be Here Now.
Schiff, Robyn.   At Shedd Aquarium.
Schneiderman, J.   Last Ditch.
Shomer.   Falling for Jesus.
Sŏ Chŏngju.   Self-portrait ("Father was a serf.").
Spires.   Interrogations of the Sparrow.
Stephens, J.   Twins, The.
Torres Bodet.   Labyrinth.
Wong, N.   When I Was Growing Up.
   Where Is My Country?

Idleness
Izumi.   In My Idleness.
Keats.   Ode on Indolence.
Kinsella, T.   Chrysalides.
Maeng Sasŏng.   Four Seasons by the Rivers and
   Lakes.
Mahon.   Dejection [Ode].
Muso Soseki.   To Kengai Osho of Engaku-ji.
Po Chü-i.   After Collecting the Autumn Taxes.
   Autumn Pool.
Sidney.   Sonnet 18: "With what sharp checks I
   in myself am shent."
Silverstein, S.   Jimmy Jet and His TV Set.

Simic.　Against Whatever It Is That's Encroaching.
Tu Fu [*or* Du Fu].　On the Spur of the Moment.
Watts, I.　Sluggard, The.
Welch, L.　This Book is for Magda.
Whalen, P.　Chanson d'Outre Tombe.
Yu Xuanji.　Voicing Deepest Thoughts.
See also **Sloth**

Idolatry
Andrade, O.　Hierofant.
Cooper, D.　Teen Idols.
Haavikko.　Don't say this to an old idol that's lost its nose.
Hollo.　Italics.
Kaufman, S.　After.
Kipling, R.　Evarra and His Gods.
Laing, R.　Sonnet 4: "When I consider what you mean to me."
Lindsay, V.　To a Golden-Haired Girl in a Louisiana Town.
Mistral, G.　Flower of Air, The.
Souza.　Conversation Piece.
Wigglesworth.　Thus everyone before the throne.
Young, C.　In the Wilderness.

Ignorance
Aiken, C.　Annihilation.
Baraka, I.　How People Do.
Brooks, G.　"Pygmies Are Pygmies Still, Though Percht on Alps".
Bunting.　To Violet.
Carroll, K.　Laughin at Cha.
Cary, A.　In Bonds.
Chapman, G.　But dwell in darkness, for your god is blind.
Chinn.　Skin Color from the Sun.
Ch'oe Sŭngja.　Portrait of the Marginalized.
Cornford, F.　To a Fat Lady Seen from the Train.
Crozier, A.　Blank Misgivings.
Darío, R.　Doom.
　Fatality.
Deniz, G.　Ignorance.
　Ignorancia.
Derricotte.　Blackbottom.
Dobell, S.　Liberty to M. le Diplomate.
Gorostiza, J.　Filled with myself, walled up in my skin.
Hacker, M.　Autumn 1980.
Hayâlî.　They do not know how to search for the World-Adorner.
Heffernan, M.　Message, The.
Hewitt, J.　From the Tibetan.
Hillman, B.　On the Pier.
Hoffenstein.　You hire a cook, but she can't cook yet.
Hope, M.　Bare Floors.
　Sixth Grade.
Hughes, L.　Different Voice, The.
Hughes, T.　Childish Prank, A.
Ingalls, J.　Apprehension.
Komunyakaa, Y.　Salt.
Leigh, C.　How Little We Know (How Little It Matters).
Madgett.　Images.
Mezey.　Reaching the Horizon.
Montale.　What you knew of me.
Muso Soseki.　For Ko Who Has Come Back from China.
　Strange Peak.
Pagis, D.　Homily.
Prys-Jones.　Unfortunate Occurrence at Cwm-Cadno.
Rossetti, C.　Sketch, A.
Sen, R.　Managing the house is a big problem.
Souza.　Sweet Sixteen.
Tkachenko.　Battle.
Ts'ao Ching-chao.　Palace Poem.
Vinokurov.　Adam.
Wetzsteon.　Coming Back to the Cave.
Yeats.　Dawn, The.

Iguanas
Razran, Gregory.　Jade's Iguanas Are Dead.
Shapcott, J.　Life.

Illegitimacy
Haavikko.　Bastard Son is born with a tooth in his mouth and hair on his.

Hughes, L.　Mulatto.
Leigh, H.　Natural Child, The.
Masters, E.　Elsa Wertman.
　Willie Metcalf.
Sexton.　Unknown Girl in the Maternity Ward.
Unknown.　Limerick.

Illinois (state)
Bradbury, R.　Byzantium I Come Not From.
Brooks, G.　Lovers of the Poor, The.
Getsi.　Woman Hanging from Lightpole, Illinois Route 136.
Goldbarth.　Letter to Friends East and West.
Kinnell.　First Song.
Knoepfle.　Confluence.
　Late Winter in Menard County.
Loncar, M.　Peoria.
Mueller, L.　Another Version.
Rivers, J.　Illinois: At Night, Black Hawk's Statue Broods.
Sandburg, C.　Illinois Farmer.
Schmitz.　Making Chicago.
Sorby.　Land of Lincoln.
Stanton, M.　Few Picnics in Illinois, A.
　Sorrow and Rapture.
Stryk, L.　Return to DeKalb.

Illiteracy
Alarcon, F.　X in My Name, The.
Jacinto, A.　Letter from a Contract Worker.
　Letter From a Contract Worker.
Meredith, W.　Illiterate, The.
Murphy, R.　Reading Lesson, The.

Illness
Abse.　Doctor, The.
Akhmadulina.　Chill, A.
Andrew, G.　Hurricane Sisters Work Regardless, The.
Aygi, G.　During a Friend's Illness.
Baillie, J.　Child to His Sick Grandfather, A.
Bass, F.　Illness.
Bell, M.　Book of the Dead Man #1, The.
　Someone Is Probably Dead.
Belloc.　Henry King, Who Chewed Bits of String, and Was Early Cut Off in Dreadful Agonies.
Berg, S.　Orpingalik's My Breath: Eskimo Song.
Berland, D.　Blazon.
Berryman.　Recognition, The.
Betjeman.　Devonshire Street W.1.
Bibbins, M.　Counting.
Blake, W.　Sick Rose, The.
Boland, E.　Fever.
Borawski.　Talking to Jim.
Bottoms.　Bronchitis.
Bradstreet, A.　For Deliverance from a Fever.
Broumas, O.　Touched.
Brouwer, J.　Spots, The.
Bush, D.　Pneumoconiosis.
Byron, G.　Lines on Hearing That Lady Byron Was Ill.
Campo.　Lost in the Hospital.
Carroll, J.　Paregoric Babies.
Carver, R.　What the Doctor Said.
Cavalli.　Outside nothing's really changed.
Ch'en Tzu-ang.　I dwell in the forest nursing a long illness.
Chimombo.　Derailment: A Delirium.
Clampitt.　Cure at Porlock, A.
Clifton, L.　Dialysis.
　Donor.
　Poem to my uterus.
Cofer, J.　Counting.
Cohan.　If I'm Going to Die I'm going to Have Some Fun.
Colby, T.　Dear, I Love.
Coleman, W.　Aunt Jessie.
Conn.　Visiting Hour.
Conoley, G.　Masters, The.
Cornford, F.　Watch, The.
Cortázar.　Therapies.
Coulehan, J.　Lovesickness: A Medieval Text.
　Rule of Thirds, The.
Cowper, W.　To Mary.
Crabbe, G.　Procrastination.
da Todi.　Praise of Diseases.
D'Aguiar, F.　Obeah Mama Dot.
Daniel, S.　Love Is a Sickness.

Darling, J.　How to Behave with the Ill.
Davidson, R.　Fear of Madness, The.
Day, J.　Man's Natural Infirmity.
Disch.　Convalescing in London.
Dixon, M.　Heartbeats.
Donaghy, M.　My Flu.
Donne.　Canonization, The.
　Hymn[e] to God My God, In My Sickness[e], A.
　Oh my black[e] soul[e]! now thou art summoned.
Doty, M.　Brilliance.
　Embrace, The.
　Tiara.
Dugan, A.　Against a Sickness: To the Female Double Principle God.
Duncan, R.　After a Long Illness.
Dunn, D.　France: "Dozen sparrows scuttled on the frost, A."
Eskimo Oral Tradition.　Magic Words to Cure a Sick Child.
Evance, S.　Written in Ill Health at the Close of Spring.
Ewart.　Sonnet: How Life Too Is Sentimental.
Ezekiel.　Family.
Fay, J.　Estuary.
Feilding, F.　One the Morening the King was Taken Ill My Dreame of Him.
Field.　Almoner, An.
　Picture, A.
Filkova, Fedya.　Frost: "Hospital garden on Sunday, A."
Frost, C.　Laws.
Frost, K.　Remission.
Fuller, R.　Your Absence.
Gerstler.　Fan Letter, A.
Gilbert, W.　Nightmare, [A *or* The].
Glück, L.　Descending Figure.
Godley, E.　Ninety-Nine.
Goldberg, B.　Since I Have Lived.
Goodman, P.　Sentences After *Defence of Poetry.*
Graham-Pole, J.　Leaving Mother, 1954.
Graves, R.　Down.
Green, M.　Epistle to Mr. Cuthbert Jackson, An.
Gunn, T.　Man With Night Sweats, The.
　Missing, The.
Hagiwara Sakutaro.　Sickly Face at the Bottom of the Ground.
Hahn, S.　Her Purse, at the Winter Solstice.
Hall, D.　Goggles and Helmet.
　Her Long Illness.
Hanson, M.　To Fancy.
Hardy, T.　Sleep-Worker, The.
Harper, M.　This Is My Son's Song: *"Ungie, Hi Ungie".*
Hart, L.　It's Got to Be Love.
Hayden, R.　Broken Dark, The.
Hernández Cruz.　Spirits.
Herrera.　Weaning of Furniture-Nutrition.
Herrick.　To Music, to Becalm His Fever.
　Upon Prudence Baldwin Her Sickness[e].
Hewitt, J.　Scar, The.
Hikmet.　Angina Pectoris.
Hirshfield, J.　Spell to Be Said After Illness.
Hoagland, T.　Medicine: "Black hair of my Chinese doctor, The."
Holloway, G.　Hypochondriac.
　Monitors.
Holtby, M.　Answer to a Kind Enquiry.
Hopkins, G.　Felix Randal.
Hove.　Other Syllabus, The.
Howard, R.　1915: A Pre-Raphaelite Ending, London.
Howe, M.　Certain Light, A.
Hughes, L.　Madam and the Wrong Visitor.
Hughes, T.　Walt.
Ishikawa Takuboku.　Suddenly forgetting my illness one day.
Jarrell, R.　Sick Child, A.
Jewsbury.　Verses: "I am monarch of troubles a host."
Jones, Patricia.　If I Were Rita Hayworth.
Jones, Peter Thabit.　Modris.
Jordan, A.　Public Radio Plays Eddie Harris.
Kavanagh, P.　Hospital, The.

Kendrick, D. Inpatient.
Kinnell. Parkinson's Disease.
Kinsella, J. Sick Woman.
Kinsella, T. Lady of Quality, A.
  Tear.
Kinzie. Orchard dying, The.
Kitahara Hakushū. Ailing child, An.
Kodama Kagai. Suicide of an Unemployed
  Person, The.
Larkin, J. Inventory.
Larkin, P. Matthew 10:1.
Lawrence, D. H. Healing.
Lee, D. Lazy.
Lewis, G. Flyover Elegies.
Li Yeh. Greeting to Lu Yu, A.
Lleshanaku, L. Chronic Appendicitis.
Loesser. Adelaide's Lament.
Lowell, M. Sick-Room, The.
Lowell, R. My Last Afternoon with Uncle
  Devereux Winslow.
Ly Ngoc Kieu. Birth, old age.
MacBeth [or Macbeth]. Worst Fear, The.
Machado Ruiz. Look, our Spaniard's yawning.
Mackenzie, K. Sick Men Sleeping.
Marvell. Dialogue between the Soul and [the]
  Body, A.
McCarriston. Healing the Mare.
McGuire, Virginia. Leaning into the Tilt.
McOrlan. Horse butcher, The.
Mei Sheng. Seven Exhortations to Rise, The.
Merrill, J. Country of a Thousand Years of
  Peace, The.
Miller, V. Bout with Burning.
Milosz, C. With Her.
Mueller, J. Fisher Towers.
Mukand, J. Lullaby.
Nashe [or Nash]. Adieu, Farewell, Earth's
  Bliss[e].
Ni Tsan. Inscribed on a Painting by Myself.
No Hyangnim. Nursery.
Oliver, M. University Hospital, Boston.
Olson, C. Librarian, The.
Ormsby, F. Day in August, A.
Pak Chaesam. Sound of the Taffy-Seller's
  Shears.
Parnok, S. Through a Window-Light.
Paulin. Anastasia McLaughlin.
Peruñcattan. What Her Girl-Friend Said.
Plath. Fever 103°.
Platt, F. Coincidentally.
Po Chü-i. Last Poem.
  Sitting Quietly: Written During My Illness.
Powell, D. A. In the course of travel: strychnine
  every few hours. some italian art.
  Sleek mechanical dart: the syringe noses into
    the blue vein marking the target of me.
  You don't have syphilis. the doctor says.
  You're thin again handsome. in our last.
Price, R. Hawk Hill.
Reed, I. I am not the walrus.
Rogers, S. Written in a Sick Chamber.
Rukeyser, M. Absalom.
  George Robinson: Blues.
Ryokan. I lie alone in my grass hut.
Saitō Mokichi. From far off I have brought
  medicines, she watches me because I am her
  son.
Sargant, J. A. 'Lo, on her dying couch, the
  sufferer lies.
Satyamurti. How Are You?
Schwartz, R. L. AIDS Education, Seventh
  Grade.
  Midnight Supper.
Scott, David. Illness.
Scott, Dennis. Apocalypse Dub.
Seth. Soon.
Shapcott, T. Post Operative.
Shaw, A. Bird Nests.
Sherman, J. My Father Plaits His
  Granddaughter's Hair.
Shinkichi Takahashi. Vimalakirti.
Sissman. Bruisingly cradled in a Harvard chair.
Smart, C. Hymn to the Supreme Being.
Smither. To a friend with osteoporosis.
Snodgrass. Flat One, A.
  I get numb and go in.

Stevenson, R. Land of Counterpane, The.
Stow. Calenture, The.
Strickland, A. Self-Devoted, The.
Sutton, V. Housekeeping.
Swirszczynska [or Swir]. Terminally Ill.
  Visit, A.
Symons, A. Nerves.
Szporluk. Triage.
Taggard. Try Tropic.
Tagliabue. March Blizzard.
Tate, A. Mother and Son.
Teasdale. Open Windows.
Thomas, R. S. Evans.
Tu Fu [or Du Fu]. Visitors.
Turnbull. Transmutation ("Take severely ill, he
  is conscious only at brief intervals.").
Unknown. Little horror will not die of his own
  fever, The.
Vallejo. Have You Anything to Say in Your
  Defense?
  Man Walks By with a Loaf of Bread on His
    Shoulder, A.
Van Duyn. Letters from a Father.
Voigt. Year's End.
Volkman. Theft.
Wang Chien. Round Fan.
Ward, T. Stray Dogs, Foaming.
Watson, E. Natural.
Wenderoth, J. Narrative Poem.
Whitman, W. Evening Lull, An.
Winch. Diagnosis.
Winchilsea. Spleen, The: A Pindaric Poem.
Winder. Unaccompanied Suite.
Winstanley, J. Upon a Friend's Pet Cat, Being
  Sick.
Wolverton, T. In China.
Woods, D. Prescription.
Wordsworth, D. Thoughts on my sick-bed.
Wordsworth, W. Idiot Boy, The.
Wotton, S. Hymn to My God in a Night of My
  Late Sickness[e], A.
Wunderlich, M. Bruise of This, The.
Wyrebek, M. Healing Logic, A.
Yüan Hung-tao. On Receiving My Letter of
  Termination.

Illusion
Ashbery, J. Forties Flick.
  Illustration.
Bhattācārya, M. Everyone's flocking to Gajan.
Boker. Sonnet 188: "My darling's features,
  painted by the light."
Bryan, S. BE-.
Crane, S. I saw a man pursuing the horizon.
Cucchi, M. Every season has its dead.
Dalton, A. In Love.
Darío, R. Melancholy.
Dickinson, E. I many times thought Peace had
  come.
  I met a King this afternoon!
Dunbar, P. We Wear the Mask.
Dunn, S. Happiness.
Emerson, R. Maia.
Fisher, R. Rules and Ranges for Ian Tyson.
Fuertes. Painted Windows.
Genko. Unaware of illusion or enlightenment.
Ghalib, M. Some Exaggerations.
Gier, J. First View of the Islands, A.
Glück, L. Circe's Power.
  Earthly Love.
Guest, B. Emphasis Falls on Reality, An.
Guillevic. When He'd Looked Hard.
Han Wo. Letter to a Zen Master.
Hughes, H. At the Teahouse, 6 am.
Jarman, M. Black Riviera, The.
Juana Inés de la Cruz. Hope.
Kharms. Optical Illusion, An.
Koch, K. One Train May Hide Another.
Kosen. Blind horse trotting up an icy ledge, A.
Laughlin, J. Inn at Kirchstetten, The.
Levine, P. Old Testament, The.
Loftis, N. Changes—Five.
Montale. I repeat I'm ready, but ready for
  what?
Muso Soseki. Ashikaga Tadayoshi's Palace.
  Reply to Reizan Osho.
Raffalovich, M. A. World Well Lost 4, The.

Reeve, F. Illusion, The.
Rojas. And to Be Born Is Here an Unnameable
  Feast.
  Bed with Mirrors.
Rowlands, D. Sawing His Wife in Half.
Russell, G. Illusion.
Sanguineti. And now a few questions to end
  with.
Sen, R. Brother / This world.
Slessor. Choker's Lane.
Stevens, W. Seventy Years Later.
Troup, B. You're Lookin' at Me.
Volkman. If it be event, I go towards and not
  back. I go tower, not floor.
Whitman, W. Are You the New Person Drawn
  toward Me?
  Eidólons.
  Of the Terrible Doubt of Appearances.
Zukofsky, L. Anew 20.

Imagination
Adcock, F. Bogyman.
Adkins, G. Children in Armour.
Ai. Man with the Saxophone, The.
Ammons. He Held Radical Light.
  Laser.
  Play.
  Triphammer Bridge.
Andrew, G. Rolls-Royce Dreams.
Aridjis. Borders, Cages and Walls.
Ashbery, J. Template, The.
Becker, R. Sonnet to the Imagination.
Bernstein, C. Let's Just Say.
Berrigan, T. Mid-Friday morn, 10 o'clock, I go
  to India.
Bishop, E. Little Exercise.
  Sleeping on the Ceiling.
Bobyshev. White Peacock, The.
Brinks, Dave. Secret Brain, The.
Brontë, E. Aye there it is! It wakes tonight.
  Little while, a little while, A.
  To Imagination.
Brooks, G. Lovers of the Poor, The.
Brownstein. Paris Visitation.
  War.
Bryan, M. To———: "O timeless guest!—so
  soon returned art thou."
Burke, J. Imagination.
Calverley. In the Gloaming.
Carr, M. Castle in the Fire, The.
Carroll, L. Mad Gardener's Song, The.
Cavafy. Passing Through.
  When They Come Alive.
Cavendish, M. Discourse of Melancholy, A.
  Imagination.
Ceravolo. Spring in This World of Poor Mutts.
Césaire, A. Automatic Crystal, The.
Char. Poet, conserver of the infinite faces of the
  living, The.
Chedid, A. Imagine.
Cherches, P. Where is She?
Coleridge, S. Fancy in Nubibus.
Colonna, S. But your imagining was wrong.
Creeley. Again.
  Edges.
  Wicker Basket, A.
Cuadra, P. Manuscript in a Bottle.
Dacre, C. Power of Love, The.
Dalton, A. Dad-Baby, The.
Davidson, J. Imagination.
Davies, W. H. Mind's Liberty, The.
Davis, J. Boat, A.
  Kids on Television Imagine Me, The.
Day, J. Moving Object.
Dickinson, E. I cannot dance upon my Toes.
  I never saw a Moor.
d'Oettingen. Outcries.
Donne. Sappho to Philaenis.
Dorfman, A. Vocabulary.
Dove, R. Banneker.
  Geometry.
Dragomoschenko. Instructing Clarity in a
  Confusion.
Driscoll, L. Hold Fast Your Dreams.
Duncan, R. Often I Am Permitted to Return to
  a Meadow.
Dunn, S. Instead of You.

Landscape at the End of the Century.
Durcan.   Backside to the Wind.
Edson, R.   Fall, The: "There was a man who found two leaves and came indoors holding them out saying to his parents that he was a tree."
Eijkelboom.   Town a Bird Sanctuary, The.
Eliot, T. S.   La Figlia Che Piange.
Evance, S.   To the Clouds.
  Written at Netley Abbey.
Galindo.   Short Story, A.
Ganev, Nedelcho.   Height.
Ginsberg, A.   Green Automobile, The.
Giovanni.   Poem For My Nephew.
Giussani, S.   In the Distance.
Glissant.   For Mycea.
Goese, M.   Love Ghost.
Graham, W.   Imagine a Forest.
Graves, R.   Warning to Children.
Grubb, D.   Windows of Sarajevo, The.
Guest, B.   Wild Gardens Overlooked by Night Lights.
Gumilyov [or Gumiliov or Gumilev].   Moon at Sea.
Hale, S.   Blessing on the printer's art!, A.
Han-shan.   I can't stand these bird-songs.
Hanson, M.   To Fancy.
Harjo, J.   Post-colonial Tale, A.
Hass, R.   Heroic Simile.
  Interrupted Meditation.
Heaney, S.   Pitchfork, The.
  Railway Children, The.
  Sofa in the Forties, A.
Herbert, Z.   Mr. Cogito and the Imagination.
Hernández Cruz.   Poem: "Think with your body."
Hernández, M.   Tomb of the Imagination.
Herrick.   Upon Julia's Clothes.
Hewitt, J.   Substance and Shadow.
Hill, G.   Imaginative Life, The.
Holub.   Vanishing Lung Syndrome.
Howe, S.   In its first dumb form.
Hume, C.   Hume's Suicide of the External World.
Hutchinson, P.   Amhrán na mBréag.
Jandl, E.   Pockets.
Jarrell, R.   Cinderella.
  Girl in a Library, A.
  Sick Child, A.
Johnson, M. F.   Thunder Storm.
Johnstone, R.   Robot Camera.
Joseph, A.   Plenty.
Juarroz.   Somewhere There's a Man.
Kaufman, B.   Solitary thoughts on death and other illegal mysteries carried off.
Keats.   Ode on a Grecian Urn.
Kloos, W.   Self-Transformation.
Lamb, C.   O! I Could Laugh to Hear the Midnight Wind.
Lasker-Schüler.   George Grosz.
Lazarus, E.   City Visions.
Lee, D.   Billy Batter.
Levertov.   In Mind.
Lodge, T.   Minde through thee divines on endlesse things, The.
Longfellow, H.   Children's Hour, The.
Lopez, L.   Tomás.
Lovecraft.   Alienation.
Lowell, R.   Epilogue: "Those blessèd structures, plot and rhyme."
Lux.   Neighborhood of Make-Believe, The.
Madhubuti.   Books as Answer.
Markham, E.   After Reading Shakspere.
McDonald, P.   Christmas.
  Pleasures of the Imagination.
Mercer, J.   Laura.
Merriam, E.   Wonderful Whale, The.
Merwin.   Animals, The.
  On the Subject of Poetry.
  Windows, The: "Here is a child who presses his head to the ground."
Millay, E.   From a Very Little Sphinx.
Miller, A.   Eye Behind the I, The.
Minhinnick.   Sax.
Mitsui.   Photograph of a Child, Japanese-American Evacuation, Bainbridge Island,

Washington, March 30, 1942.
Moore, M.   Those Various Scalpels.
Moore, T.   Fancy.
Morse, B.   Day on the Planet, A.
Muir, E.   Childhood.
Muirhead, Eric.   Reflection on the Paintings of Mark Rothko's Chapel, A.
Murray, L.   Milk Lorry, The.
Mutis.   Word, A.
Nims, B.   On a Cold Autumn Day.
Oldham, J.   One night, as I was pondering of late.
Oliver, M.   Spring Azures.
Ondaatje.   Gentleman Compares His Virtue to a Piece of Jade, A.
Orlovsky.   Dick Tracy's Yellow Hat.
Orr, G.   Insomnia Song.
Padgett, R.   Wonderful Things.
Pape.   In the Bluemist Motel.
Paz.   Stanzas for an Imaginary Garden.
Perelman.   Let's Say.
Plath.   Most Beds are Beds.
Porter, P.   Annotations of Auschwitz.
Radcliffe, A.   To the Visions of Fancy.
Radiguet.   Poem: "Horizon line."
Rakosi.   Unswerving Marine.
Ray, H.   Fancy and Imagination.
Rees-Jones.   Making for Planet Alice.
Rich, A.   Architect.
Robinson, E.   Miniver Cheevy.
Rodenko.   February Sun.
Romo-Carmona, M.   Fish.
Rossetti, C.   Somewhere Or Other.
Rózewicz.   Transformations.
Salaam.   SOUND is ProFound Sense.
Sanguineti.   What you're reading (if you're reading me) are the effects.
Schuyler, J.   Greetings from the Chateau.
Seaton, M.   Fiddleheads.
Seward.   When Life's realities the Soul perceives.
Shakespeare, W.   Casket Song, A.
  Lunatic, the Lover, and the Poet, The.
Shapcott, J.   In the Bath.
Simic.   Bather, The.
Simpson, L.   My Father in the Night Commanding No.
Smith, J.   What I Learned From the Movies.
Smith, S.   Fairy Story.
  Our Bog is Dood.
Sŏ Chŏngju.   "Pine flower's blooming," says.
Sosnora.   Do you envy, my comrades-in-arms.
Stevens, W.   Final Soliloquy of the Interior Paramour.
  High-Toned Old Christian Woman, A.
  Plain Sense of Things, The.
Stevenson, R.   Block City.
  Land of Counterpane, The.
  Land of Story-Books, The.
  Pirate Story.
Stone, R.   Secondhand Coat.
Suckling, S.   Upon My Lady Carlisle's Walking in Hampton Court Garden.
Swenson, M.   Centaur, The.
Thomas, D.   Turning of the Year, The.
Tighe.   When glowing Phoebus quits the weeping earth.
Timrod.   I know not why, but all this weary day.
Tomlinson, C.   Sense of Distance, A.
Turner, C.   No trace is left upon the vulgar mind.
Turner, W.   Romance.
  Talking with Soldiers.
Unknown.   If All the World Were Paper.
  Mr Nobody.
Viray, M.   Patio.
Vlasova, E.   Create me a world.
Warsh.   Downward Mobility.
Whalen, P.   Hoist great blocks of language into place.
Wheatley, P.   On Imagination.
Whitman, W.   Child said *What is the grass?* fetching it to me with full hands, A.
Wieners.   Glimpse, A.
Wilbur, R.   Walking to Sleep.
Williams, W.   There is neither beginning nor end

to the imagination.
Wise, W.   When I Grow Up.
Wood, E.   Recognition.
Wordsworth, W.   Decadence; or, The Umbrella.
  Strange Fits of Passion Have I Known ("Strange fits of passion have I known.").
Wright, D.   Lakes, The.
Wylie.   Pastiche.
Yau.   Radiant Silhouette IV.
Young, K.   Degrees.
Young, M. J.   To Dreams.
Zukofsky, L.   Anew 20.
  To my wash-stand.

Immaculate Conception

Lowell, R.   On the Eve of the Feast of the Immaculate Conception: 1942.

Immigration and Immigrants

Abinader, E.   Letters from Home.
Adcock, F.   Immigrant.
Alarcon, F.   Viernes Santo / Good Friday.
Alvarez, J.   Papi Working.
Alvi, M.   Arrival 1946.
Atwood.   Further Arrivals.
Baca.   Immigrants in Our Own Land.
Blanco, R.   El Malibú.
Boadiba.   We Pass through a Foreigner's House.
Brion, R.   Good Friday.
Budy.   Ellis Island, September 1907.
Burnshaw.   House in St. Petersburg.
Capone.   In Answer to Their Questions.
Cariaga.   Family Tree, The.
Cerenio.   My Mother.
  13 June 1994.
Chin.   We Are Americans Now, We Live in the Tundra.
Clements, A.   Elegy.
Cofer, J.   Idea of Islands, The.
Corn.   Photographs of Old New York.
Cortes, F.   Dolce Far Niente.
Dean, D. K.   Immigrants.
Delgado, J.   Chuparosa.
Dharker.   They'll say, "She must be from another country".
Divakaruni.   Founding of Yuba City, The.
  Yuba City School.
Djanikian.   How I Learned English.
  Immigrant Picnic.
  In the Elementary School Choir.
Doina, A.   Roof over far away.
Duffy, C.   Comprehensive.
Espada.   David Leaves the Saints for Paterson.
  Green and Red, Verde y Rojo.
  La tormenta.
  Toque de queda: Curfew in Lawrence.
Field, E.   Both My Grandmothers.
Fingueret, M.   Eve in Eden.
Frazier, John Alexander, Jr.   Deposed.
Freneau.   On the Emigration to America [and Peopling the Western Country].
Frost, R.   Immigrants.
Gilbert, S.   Mafioso.
Ginsberg, A.   O mother / what have I left out.
Gioseffi.   Bicentennial Anti-Poem for Italian-American Women.
Glück, L.   Legend.
Goldbarth.   Gallery.
Gonzalez, N.   I Made Myself a Path.
Gonzalez, R.   Angels of Juárez, Mexico, The.
  At the Rio Grande Near the End of the Century.
Gotera.   Madarika.
  Manong Chito Tells Manong Ben about His Dream over Breakfast at the Manilatown Cafe.
  Pacific Crossing.
Gu Cheng.   Crossing the Border.
Hamod, S.   Dying with the Wrong Name.
  So we move now.
Healy, E.   From Los Angeles Looking South.
Hernández Cruz.   Ruskie's Boy.
  Snaps of Immigration.
Hernandez, D.   Welcome.
Hewitt, J.   Once Alien Here.
Hofmann, M.   Machine That Cried, The.
Huerta, J.   Toward a Portrait of the Undocumented.
Ilio, D.   Site of My Grandfather's House, The.

Jacinto, J.   Heaven Is Just Another Country.
Jones, E.   Lament of the Banana Man, The.
Joseph, L.   Curriculum Vitae.
Kageyama, C.   Mama.
Klassen, S.   Russian Fables.
Kramer, L.   Immigrants.
Lavieri, J.   Autobiography of John Doe, The.
Lazarus, E.   In Exile.
 New Colossus, The.
Lee, L.   Cleaving, The.
Lim, S.   Riding into California.
LittleDog, Pat.   Love letter sent south.
Lochhead, L.   Something I'm Not.
Long, R.   Conspiracy, The.
Luschei, G.   Arrangement.
MacLeish.   Burying Ground by the Ties.
Macrae, J.   Sleep Softly.
Mathews, E. K.   Indian, The.
Mattawa.   Growing Up with a Sears Catalog in
 Benghazi, Libya.
Melnyczuk.   Usual Immigrant Uncle Poem, The.
Melo, M.   Scrambled Eggs and Garlic Pork.
 Unlearning English.
Mikhail, D.   America: "Please don't ask me,
 America."
Milligan, Bryce.   Copano, 1834.
Mitsui.   Katori Maru, October 1920.
 Nisei: Second Generation Japanese-American.
Mora.   Immigrants.
 La Migra.
Morales, A.   Immigrants.
 Old Countries.
Morales.   I Am the Reasonable One.
 I Recognize You.
Moscona.   Naturalization Papers.
Mullen, H.   Bilingual Instructions.
 Xenophobic Nightmare in a Foreign Language.
Mura.   Once near the Border.
Nichols, G.   Wherever I Hang.
Norman, L.   SpaNglisH.
Nortje.   Immigrant.
Papaleo.   American Dream: First Report.
Porter, P.   Last of England, The.
Powell, D. A.   Long line of bohunks and
 hunyaks, A: we settled in podunk. thirteen
 consonants.
Praitis, I.   Anthems.
Prunty.   To be Sung on the Fourth of July.
Ras.   In the New Country.
Regier, G.   Where We All Went.
Reznikoff.   3. The Immigrants.
Rich, A.   Catch if you can your country's
 moment, then.
 Prospective Immigrants Please Note.
Ridge, L.   Phyllis.
Robles.   Feasting with Etang a Hundred Times
 Around.
Rogers, D.   Customs of the Country.
Rollings.   For Dear Life.
Rose, P.   Wind Debates Asian Immigration, The.
Salganicoff.   Being an Immigrant.
Salzman, E.   Physics.
Seale, J.   Travel North: The Rules.
Seiler.   Digging in the Streets of Gold.
Shaku, S.   En Route to America.
Shapiro, K.   My Grandmother.
Sigourney.   Erin's Daughter.
Silva, L.   Emigrant's Son, The.
Smith, K.   Malenki Robot.
Song.   Ghost.
 Lost Sister ("In China, / even the peasants.").
Soto.   Mexicans Begin Jogging.
Suárez, V.   Cuban-American Gothic.
Teitelboim, D.   In Your Eyes.
Thomas, S.   Road from Khartoum, The.
Unknown.   Being idle in the wooden building, I
 opened a window.
 Corrido of the Uprooted Ones.
 Day of vast dreaming.
 Family treasures.
 If the land of the Flowery Flag is occupied by
 us in turn.
 Leaving behind my writing brush and.
 Low building with three beams merely shelters
 the body, The.
 Mid-West, The.

My grief, like dense clouds, cannot be
 dispersed.
Once a Meiji Voice.
 Registration of 1918.
This is a message to those who live here not to
 worry excessively.
This place is called an island of immortals.
 Toishan Song, A.
 With eyes filled with tears.
Uyematsu.   Near Roscoe and Coldwater.
 Same Month They Bombed Cambodia, The.
Vazirani, R.   Mrs. Biswas Breaks Her
 Connection with Another Relative.
Villanueva, T.   Day-Long Day.
Viray, M.   Two Strangers, The.
Wada, Hakuro.   Even the croaking of frogs.
Weiss, Lynne.   Other Tongues.
Weiss, T.   Pair of Shoes, A.
Woods, V.   After the American Wake.
Yoneda, Karl.   Angel Island—what a beautiful
 name.

Immortality
Akers.   Dead, The: "Dead come, looking for
 their shoes, The."
Anwar, C.   Me.
Arnold, M.   Shakespeare: "Others abide our
 question. Thou art free."
Atwood.   They Eat Out.
Barskova, P.   Poet has passed away, The. Or
 rather, snuffed.
Belli, C.   Poem: "Our love is not found in our
 respective."
Borges.   Poem Written in a Copy of *Beowulf*.
Bradstreet, A.   When I behold the heavens as in
 their prime.
Busceti, G.   Suddenly on a day in July.
Campo.   Superman Is Dead.
Cardenal.   From those theaters, Claudia, from
 those feasts.
Clare, J.   Invite to Eternity, An.
Cope, W.   Not only marble, but the plastic toys.
Cowley, A.   Muse, The.
 To Mr. Hobs: "Vast *Bodies* of *Philosophie*."
Dickinson, E.   My life closed twice before its
 close.
 Only News I know, The.
 Soul's Superior instants, The.
Dobell, S.   Liberty to M. le Diplomate.
Donne.   Death be not proud, though some have
 called thee.
 Good-Morrow, The.
Drayton.   How Many Paltry, Foolish, Painted
 Things.
Duggan, L.   Ten ii.
Emerson, R.   Eros.
Enright, D.   Days of Adam were 930 years, The.
Freneau.   Too nearly join'd to sickness, toils,
 and pains.
 When Nature bids thee from the world retire.
Gautier.   Art.
Graves, R.   To Bring the Dead to Life.
Greig, A.   Interlude on Mustagh Tower.
Gutiérrez Nájera.   Non Omnis Moriar.
Hall, D.   My Son, My Executioner.
Hamhur Kiwha.   Lament: "I heard that many
 temples were destroyed."
Han-shan.   Yesterday I went to a cloud
 observatory.
Hannon.   Real Estate.
Hardy, T.   Shelley's Skylark.
Hejinian.   There was once an angel who had a
 neighbor, and this neighbor was ambitious.
Hemans.   Woman and Fame.
Herbert, G.   Death: "Death, thou wast once an
 uncouth hideous thing."
 Virtue [*or* Vertue].
Herrick.   To His Peculiar Friend Master Thomas
 Shapcott, Lawyer.
Horace.   Ode 3. 30.
Housman.   If truth in hearts that perish.
Howard, R.   After 65.
Ignatow, D.   Witness.
Issa.   Poor quarter, A.
Jackson, L.   Poet's Corner, The.
Jeffers, R.   Post Mortem.
Jones, A.   Communal Living.

Juan Chi.   Lucent dew congeals into frost, The.
Keats.   Ode: "Bards of passion and of mirth."
Kim Chôngnan.   Phone Call From
 Immortality—From Agnes to Mr. Kundera, A.
Kuo P'o.   Vision: Second Poem of Wandering
 Immortals.
Landor, W.   Ianthe.
Li Po.   Inscribed on the Wall of Hsü Hsüan-
 Ping's Retreat.
 Late Bloomer at the Front of My Garden.
Marshak.   Immortality.
Mengham, Rod.   To the Soviet Embalmers.
Meynell, A.   Song of Derivations, A.
Michelangelo Buonarroti.   My lady, how comes
 it about—what all can see.
Milton.   On Shakespear[e].
Moorer.   Immortality.
Naden.   Pantheist's Song of Immortality, The.
Okudzhava.   Save us, the poets, save us, we
 have but.
Ovid.   Elegy 1.15: "Envy, why carp'st [*or*
 carpest] thou my time is spent so ill."
 I have been looking these pages over, my
 dearest wife.
Pak Chaesam.   Immortals' Paduk Game.
Pao Chao.   Magic Cinnabar.
Paulinus of Nola.   To Ausonius.
Pindar.   Their boon is life forever freed from
 toil.
Pinkney, E.   Voyager's Song, The.
Porter, A.   Four Poems in One.
Pound, E.   Shades of Callimachus, Coan ghosts
 of Philetas.
Quevedo y Villegas.   Love Constant Beyond
 Death.
Ramanujan.   Hindu to His Body, A.
Reese, L.   Love, Weeping, Laid This Song.
Ritsos.   Marpessa's Choice.
Robinson, E.   Man against the Sky, The.
 Walt Whitman: "Master-songs are ended, and
 the man, The."
Rodriguez, J.   Lifetime devoted to literature, A.
Rossetti, D.   77: Soul's Beauty.
Russell, G.   Immortality.
Shakespeare, W.   Sonnet 55: "Not marble, nor
 the g[u]ilded monuments."
 Sonnet 81: "Or I shall live your epitaph to
 make."
 Sonnet 107: "Not mine own[e] fear[e]s, nor the
 prophetic[k] soul[e]."
Simic.   Immortal, The.
Southey, R.   Canine Immortality.
Spenser, E.   Sonnet 75: "One day I wrote her
 name upon the strand."
Teasdale.   Little While, A.
Tennyson, A.   Dear friend, far off, my lost
 desire.
 Tithonus.
Theognis.   Captive.
Ts'ao Chih.   Far-Off Journey.
Unknown.   Arjuna sat dejected.
 Heroes are always alive.
 Inscription at Mount Vernon.
 Man's Life a Sojourning.
Vaughan, H.   Easter Hymn.
 Waterfall [*or* Water-Fall], The.
Verlaine.   Beauty of women, their weakness,
 those pale hands.
Very.   Cross, The ("I must go on, till in my
 tearful line.").
 New Birth, The.
 New World, The.
Waller, E.   Of English Verse.
Whitman, W.   Joy, Shipmate, Joy!
 On the Beach at Night.
 Woman Waits for Me, A.
Wolfe, H.   Iliad.
Wolff, Rebecca.   Lamb, Willow: An Arch
 Dolefulness Has Taken Me This Far.
Wordsworth, W.   Ode: Intimations of
 Immortality from Recollections of Early
 Childhood.
Yeats.   Sailing to Byzantium.
Zabolotsky [*or* Zabolotskii].   Metamorphoses.

Impending Death
Ahern, T.   Popeye's Last Words.

Davies, A.   I Looked You in the Face Last Night.
Bellerose, Sally.   Bye Bye Barbara.
Blake, W.   London.
Chunghur Hyujung.   Deathbed Song.
Cornett, S.   Lear Expands His Last Words to Cordelia.
Eliot, T. S.   2. A Game of Chess.
Fraser, S.   Elevator: "Passing my floor."
García Lorca.   Song of the Rider ("Córdoba. / Distant and alone.").
Griffin, S.   Born into a World Knowing.
Hsieh Ling-yün.   Last Poem.
Hueung Powoo.   Deathbed Song.
Ibn Shuhayd, A.   When I observed that life had turned away its head and I became assured beyond doubt that death would seize me.
Ishikawa Takuboku.   Suddenly forgetting my illness one day.
Issa.   This, I guess, is.
Janzen, J.   Wild Grapes.
Jones, I.   Alley Games 6/The Ascension.
Keita, N.   Back road.
Kercheval, J.   Ham and the Moon.
Koertge.   Seven Dwarfs, Each on His Deathbed, Remember Snow White, The.
Lewis, G.   Final Minutes, The.
Lewis, S.   Prayer at the End.
Mun Chônghui.   Letter, The.
Nadir, M.   Third, A.
Po Chü-i.   Sick and Old, Same as Ever: A Poem to Figure It All Out.
Poe.   Prone.
Pou Kuksa.   Deathbed Song.
Robertson, J.   George Buchanan in Old Age.
Rossetti, D.   91: Lost on Both Sides.
Saitō Mokichi.   As I lie beside my mother.
Swirszczynska [or Swir].   Visit, A.
Taneda Santoka.   This trip.
Thomas, G.   Last Things, The.
Tkhorzhevskaya, V.   He wouldn't sign the death warrant.
Unknown.   Good-Bye.
Walker, M.   Solace.
Whitman, W.   After the Supper and Talk.
Woljo Toan.   Deathbed Song.

Imperfection
Carlson, E.   Imperfection.
Cunningham, J.   Innocent to innocent.
Hammerstein.   Can't Help Lovin' Dat Man.
Kirchwey.   Maculate Beauty.
Lanier, S.   Crystal, The.
Mansour, J.   Men's Vices.
Reynolds, R.   Object of Burial Is Intent, The.
Zagajewski.   Try to Praise the Mutilated World.

Imperialism
Appleman, P.   Peace with Honor.
Brathwaite, E.   Citadel.
  How Europe Underdeveloped Africa.
Cardenal.   Mosquito Kingdom.
Clampitt.   Hispaniola.
Consuegra, D.   You and I.
Conyus.   Day in the Life of . . . , A.
Crouch, A. L.   Mirabeau B. Lamar.
Dixon, B.   Remembering the invasion of Grenada by the USA.
French, W.   Queen's After-Dinner Speech, The.
Gardinier.   Admirals (Columbus).
Herbert, Z.   Transformations of Livy.
Hughes, L.   Letter from Spain.
Kipling, R.   Recessional.
  White Man's Burden, The.
Lowell, A.   Down, down, down, to the bottom of hte map.
Mayer, B.   Sea: "It's he, it's sea. the sea is continuous; a continuous body."
McGrath, T.   Fresco: Departure for an Imperialist War.
McOrlan.   Produce from the colonies.
Montague, J.   Deer Park.
Muir, E.   Combat, The.
Ryuichi.   My Imperialism.
Sylvain, P.   Panama.
Tontongi.   How?
Tsvetkov.   To the apostles of history.
Wainwright, K.   Changes.

Impermanence
Anwar, C.   Tuti's Ice Cream.
Basho.   Octopus traps.
Du Bellay.   Rome.
Du Bouchet.   Stone or Water.
Forrester, S.   How quickly.
  Writing a haiku.
Guiterman.   Elegy: "Jackals prowl, the serpents hiss, The."
Hakuin.   How lacking in permanence the minds of the sentient.
Horovitz, F.   Visit to the British Museum.
Ibn Abdūn, A.   It is Fate [alone] that causes us distress, first by the blow itself and then by the traces it leaves; so what is the use of weeping over illusions and vain imagings?
Kino Sadamaru.   Though this body, I know.
Machado Ruiz.   I Have Never Wanted Fame.
Martínez, V.   Tesoro.
Meyerhoff, J.   On Impermanence.
Piper, P.   There is no ripple on the world.
Ramanujan.   Elements of Composition.
Sedakova.   Sant'Alessio, Roma.
Smith, L.   Calligraphy of Birds.
Spires.   In Heaven It Is Always Autumn.
Sze.   String Diamond, The.
Tanzan.   Madness, the way they gallop off to foreign shores!
Unknown.   We cannot tell now.
Williams, T.   We Have Not Long to Love.
See also **Transience**

Impotence
Adcock, F.   Happy Ending.
Behn, A.   Disappointment, The.
Djogo.   Wooden Handle, The.
Herrick.   To His Mistress[es] ("Help[e] me! help[e] me! now I call.").
Hope, A.   Paradise Saved.
Levy, A.   On the Threshold.
Martial.   Surrounded by eunuchs and limp as a tissue.
Montagu, L.   Reasons That Induced Dr. Swift to Write a Poem Called "The Lady's Dressing-Room", The.
Ovid.   Elegy 3.6: "Either she was foul, or her attire was bad."
  She'd looks, she'd style.
Porter, C.   Too Darn Hot.
Rochester, J.   Against Constancy.
  Disabled Debauchee, The.
  Imperfect Enjoyment, The.
  Song of a Young Lady to Her Ancient Lover, A.
Unknown.   Bailiff, why your useless plaints about.
  One Writing against His Prick.

Impressionism and Impressionists
Crowell, Elizabeth.   Portraits of the Ladies.
Foreman, Paul.   Impressionist.
Mueller, L.   Monet Refuses the Operation.
Waldman, A.   Berthe Morisot.
Wilde, O.   Impression du Matin.

Impulse
Clark, T.   Time.
Han-shan Te-ch'ing.   I follow my impulsive feet wherever they might go.

Incantations
Buson.   Ten holy nights / Even tea.
Couzyn.   Spell to Soften the Hard Heart of a Woman.
Di Michele, A.   About the Extinction Of.
Gippius.   Incantation.
Hakuin.   Priceless is one's incantation.
Tan Taigi.   Swellfish eaten / He chants nembutsu.
Wŏlmyŏng.   Song of Tuṣita Heaven.

Incas
Lane, P.   Pissaro's Tomb.
  Winter 9: "Each day the time grows less, the hours."
Llwyd, Iwan.   Fingerprints.

Incense
Doolittle, Hilda.   Amen.
Garrett, E.   Lost Property.
Ginsberg, A.   After Yeats.
Kyunyŏ, Great Master.   With tongs I trim the lamp.

Incest
Campo.   Kelly.
Fallon, P.   Airs and Graces.
García Lorca.   Thamar and Amnon ("Moon turns in the sky, The.").
Garcia, R.   Note Folded Thirteen Ways.
Howe, M.   How Many Times.
Macphee, K.   No Fairy Story.
Olds, S.   My Father Speaks to Me from the Dead.
Ovid.   Myrrha and Cinyras.
Ruffin.   Female Cousins at Thanksgiving.
Speckled Red (Rufus Perryman).   Dirty Dozens, The.
Winkfield, T.   Nature Study.

Incomprehensibility
Leigh, C.   It Amazes Me!
Whiting, R.   She's Funny That Way (I Got a Woman, Crazy for Me).
Wright, C.   December Journal.

Inconstancy
Behn, A.   To Alexis in Answer to His Poem Against Fruition.
Brown, T.   Oaths.
Bukowski.   Sexpot.
Burns, R.   Banks o' Doon, The ("Ye banks and braes o' bonie [or bonnie] Doon.").
  Banks o' Doon, The ("Ye flowery banks o' bon[n]ie Doon.").
Congreve, W.   Song: "I tell thee, Charmion, could I time retrieve."
Harpur, J.   Young Man of Galway's Lament, The.
Hood, T.   Faithless Nelly Gray.
Kuzmin.   Ah, those lips, kissed by so many.
Liu Yu Hsi.   Red Blossoms.
Maguire, S.   Fall, The.
Pilkington, L.   Song, A: "Strephon, your breach of faith and trust."
Poliziano.   On the Love of Two Boys.
Stevenson, R.   To Henry James.
Tabb.   Shadow, The.
Theocritus.   Idyll 29: ""Truth in the cups" men say, dear youth."
Theognis.   Boy and horse, a similar brain: the horse doesn't cry when its rider lies in the dust.
Thomas, E.   Forsaken Wife, The.
Tollet.   On Loving Once and Loving Often.
Unknown.   Gu-feng [Translations].
  One I Love, The.
Waddington, M.   Thou Didst Say Me.
Wyatt.   What Once I Was.
Zati.   Oh heavens, why do you cry? Is your beloved seen.

Indecision
Behn, A.   On Her Loving Two Equally.
Cooley.   For Hamlet.
Gershwin, I.   Saga of Jenny, The.
Juana Inés de la Cruz.   I Can Neither Hold You Nor Let You Go.
Koehler, T.   Between the Devil and the Deep Blue Sea.
Maltby, R.   Little Bit Off, A.
Porter, C.   At Long Last Love.
Sappho.   I don't know what I should do—I'm of two minds.
Taneda Santoka.   No desire to die.
Terán, V.   Duda.
  Indecision.
Lu ti nagana.
See also **Decisions**

Independence
Auden.   Glad.
Bennett, L.   Independance.
  Independence Dignity.
Bobyshev.   Return.
Chrystos.   You Know I Like to Be.
Cofer, J.   Learning to Walk Alone.
Frost, R.   Silken Tent, The.
Galvez, Carol Fonesca.   Creation Continues.
Galvin, J.   Independence Day, 1956: A Fairy Tale.
Henley, W. E.   Invictus.

Jabeen, M. Ideal Wife.
  Physical Geography.
Lars. Sketch of the Frontier Woman.
Leslie, E. Little Bit Independent, A.
Miles, J. In the town where every man is king.
Mora. Cortez's Horse.
Nikolayeva [or Nikolaeva]. Party on Women's
  Day, A.
  Seven Beginnings.
Nolla. Manifest, The.
November, Deena. Clean that god damned
  room already.
Ogilvy. Grannie's Birthday.
Oppen. Great stone, The / Above the river.
Parker, D. Indian Summer.
Pegram, L. Yet another epiphany.
Prado, A. Easter.
Preston, M. Erinna's Spinning.
Scott, A. Return thee, heart.
Senghor. Camp 1940.
Smith, B. Young Woman's Blues.
Smith, C. To Dependence.
Unknown. Ground-Thumping Song.
  Path of Independence, The.
Wordsworth, W. Resolution and Independence.

India
Ali, A. Dacca Gauzes, The.
  Lenox Hill.
  Lost Memory of Delhi, A.
Alvi, M. Country at My Shoulder, The.
Berrigan, T. Mid-Friday morn, 10 o'clock, I go
  to India.
Berryman. Henry sats in de bar and was odd.
Bhatt, S. Looking Through a French
  Photographer's Portrayal of Rajasthan with
  Extensive Use of Orange Filters.
Bhattācārya, M. Come, brothers, everyone
  together.
Birney. Bear on the Delhi Road, The.
Bringhurst. Parśvanatha.
Brooks, C. Lines: Composed at the Old
  Temples of Maralipoor.
Coward. I Wonder What Happened to Him.
Divakaruni. Indian Movie, New Jersey.
Ezekiel. In India.
  Night of the Scorpion.
Gay, J. Song: "Were I laid on Greenland's
  coast."
Gill, K. Ghazal 5: "My white mare on the
  Punjabi plains, the stamp of her hooves."
Ginsberg, A. Describe: The Rain on
  Dasaswamedh Ghat.
Greenberg, A. Man in the Moon, The.
Groarke, V. To Smithereens.
Hemans. Indian City, The.
Islām, N. Now there'll be a new mantra,
  Mother.
Kalamaras, G. Mud.
Kamala Das. Introduction: "I don't know
  politics but I know the names."
Kipling, R. Cholera Camp.
  Christmas in India.
  Gunga Din.
  Mandalay.
Lewis, A. Karanje Village.
  Mahratta Ghats, The.
Mahapatra, J. Main Temple Street, Puri.
  Monsoon Day Fable, A.
  Sanskrit.
  Summer Poem, A.
  Taste for Tomorrow.
Meenakshi. If Hot Flowers Come to the Street.
Meredith, W. Jain Bird Hospital in Delhi, The.
Ramanujan. In the Zoo.
Rukeyser, M. Ajanta.
Souza. Landscape.
Stroud, J. Documentary.
Turner, W. India.
Unknown. Some push us around, some curse us.
  Why do these prudes fear Prakrit poetry.
Vazirani, R. Mrs. Biswas Goes Through a Photo
  Album.
  Mrs. Biswas of Maryland on the Phone.
Waldman, A. Culture Drift.
Whitman, W. Passage to India.

Indian Summer
Basho. Taking a midday nap.
Berggolts [or Bergholts]. Indian Summer.
Campo, C. Indian Summer.
Chamberlain, K. Indian Summer.
Deniz, G. Act.
  Acto.
Dickinson, E. Indian Summer.
Garland, H. Indian Summer.
Georgiev, Marin. Silence: "In the afternoon
  hours of autumn heading home."
Lindsay, V. Indian Summer Day on the Prairie,
  An.
Masaoka Shiki. Indian summer / Dragonfly
  shadows seldom.
Reese, L. Indian Summer.
Rilke. Day in October.

Indiana (state)
Byrne, Edward. Envying the Art of the
  Cartographer.
Giscombe, C. Negromania, Negrophilia,
  Negrophobia.

Indifference
Agodon, K. What Comes after Because.
Baraka, I. Preface to a Twenty Volume Suicide
  Note.
Baudelaire. Way her silky garments undulate,
  The.
Bobyshev. Indifference.
Byrom. Careless Content.
Cabral de Melo Neto. End of the World, The.
Castillo, O. Apolitical Intellectuals.
Cernuda. Shadow, The.
Chudakov. When the cry goes up.
Cisneros, S. I Am So in Love I Grow a New
  Hymen.
Cruz Varela. Invocation.
Csoori. We Were Good, Good and Obedient.
Cummings, E. E. Anyone lived in a pretty how
  town.
Davie, D. Rejoinder to a Critic.
Dowson. Flos Lunae.
Fetherston, K. Hating.
Gershwin, I. Who Cares?
Glazier, L. On TV.
Greville, F. Prayer for Indifference, A.
Hands, E. On an Unsociable Family.
Hughes, L. Hard Daddy.
Hugo, R. Last Days.
Ivanov, G. Should I tell of all the absolute
  fools.
Levine, P. Coming Home, *Detroit*, 1968.
Lucretius. *Gods,* by right of Nature, must
  possess, The.
Melville, H. Pebbles.
Montagu, L. Lover, The; a Ballad.
Moritz [or Morits]. Leader, The.
Pfeiffer, E. If we be fools of chance, indeed,
  and tend.
Rozhdestvensky [or Rozhdestvenskii]. They
  Killed the Lad.
Santos Chocano. Who Knows?
Steele, T. In the King's Rooms.
Thackeray. Sorrows of Werther, The.
Troupe. So What.
Verlaine. Streets 1.
Wenderoth, J. Death.
Yesenin [or Essenin]. Do You Not Love Me.

Indigestion
Byron, G. To be or not to be! That is the
  question.

Individualism and Individualists
Berry, J. One.
Clough. *Dulce* it is, and *decorum,* no doubt, for
  the country to fall, to.
Coleridge, S. Phantom.
Crane, S. Think as I think, said a man.
Davies, A. This evening / Is the only evening.
Emerson, R. Ode, Inscribed to W. H. Channing.
Ferlinghetti, L. Adieu À Charlot.
Frost, R. Road Not Taken, The.
Ginsberg, A. Is About.
Giovanni. Drum, The.
Housman. Laws of God, the Laws of Man, The.
Huxley, A. Fifth Philosopher's Song.
Kao Ch'i. Song of the Man of Green Hill, The.

Kreymborg. Culture.
Lear, E. Jumblies, The.
MacNeice. Individualist Speaks, The.
Madgett. Offspring.
Montale. Ours is group solitude.
O'Hara, F. My Heart.
Piercy. I Will Not Be Your Sickness.
Schuyler, J. Yorkville.
Steinberg, D. Slowly, slowly.
Whitman, W. By Blue Ontario's Shore.
  One's-Self I Sing.
  Torch, The.
Wyatt. I am as I am and so will I be.
Yeats. Coat, A.
Zukofsky, L. Song for the Year's End, A.
See also **Egotism and Egotists**

Indonesia and Indonesians
Fenton, J. Dead Soldiers.
See also **Borneo**

Indulgences
Douglas, K. Cairo Jag.
Lugones. Indulgence.
Sheridan, R. On Lady Anne Hamilton.

Industrial Revolution
Bhatt, S. Parvati.
Seward. Scene of superfluous grace, and wasted
  bloom.

Industrial Workers of the World (IWW)
Hill, J. There Is Power in a Union.

Industrialization
Aguilar, M. Pall Hanging over Manila.
Blind. Red Sunsets, 1883, The.
Bobyshev. Other World, The.
Cendrars. My Dance.
Cranch. Spirit of the Age, The.
Davies, I. In Gardens in the Rhondda.
Dransfield. Endsight.
Eberhart, R. Hard Structure of the World, The.
Hopkins, G. God's Grandeur.
Howard, B. Break.
Joseph, L. Here.
Klyuyev [or Kliuev or Klyuev]. Conversational
  Melody, A Good Verse, A.
Kumin, M. Chain, The.
Kunitz, S. War against the Trees, The.
Larkin, P. Going, going.
Lawrence, D. H. Evening Land, The.
Levine, P. They Feed They Lion.
Mandelstam [or Mandelshtam]. In This Cool
  Transparent Spring.
Morales, A. South.
Nesbit, E. Great Industrial Centre, A.
Pinsky. Haunted Ruin, The.
Riley, P. 147. 67.
Rosenfeld, M. Memorial to Triangle Fire
  Victims.
Spender, S. Landscape near an Aerodrome,
  The.
Thomas, R. S. Cynddylan on a Tractor.
Tomlinson, C. John Maydew or The Allotment.
Voznesensky [or Voznesenskii]. Beatnik's
  Monologue, The.
Welch, L. Chicago Poem.
Zabolotsky [or Zabolotskii]. Nocturnal Garden.

Ineptitude
Curbelo. Listening to a White Man Play the
  Blues.
Kizer, C. Election Day, 1984.

Infant Jesus
Chandar, M. Child Is Born, A.
Fitzgerald, J. Great Little One.
Unknown. O come, thou Wisdom from on high.
  Virgin's Lullaby, The.
Varela. Madonna.

Infanticide
Brecht, B. Concerning the Infanticide, Marie
  Farrar.
Browning, E. Runaway Slave at Pilgrim's Point,
  The.
Davies, W. H. Inquest, The.
Delgado, J. La Llorona.
France de Bravo, B. Unrepentant.
Rendra. Baby at the Bottom of the River.
Rogers, P. Infanticide.
Unknown. Mary Hamilton.

Mary [or Marie] Hamilton [Version from Motherwell's Manuscript].
Queen's Marie, The [Version from Scott's Minstresy].
Van Walleghen. In the Chariot Drawn by Dragons.
Wordsworth, W. Thorn, The.

Infants
Allen, F. First-born.
  Two-day-old Grandchild.
Asim, J. Baby's Breath.
Bryce, Colette. Lines: "I have given birth to a see-through child."
Clanchy, K. Love.
  Stance.
Couzyn. Heartsong.
Ewart. Sonnet: How Life Too Is Sentimental.
Farish, H. Newly Born Twins.
Ferrell, M. Geburt des Monicakinds.
Figueroa, J. Taino.
Fletcher, J. Not noisily, but solemnly and pale.
Kahn, G. Pretty Baby.
Linett, D. Cathedral: "For hours I held one of my son's infant twins."
Okolo, M. Still Burn.
Olds, S. Her First Week.
  My First Weeks.
Ortiz. Speaking.
Ossip, K. Nursling.
Pitcher, O. Infant, The.
Stevenson, A. Victory, The.
Velichansky, A. Infant is white, like down, The.
  And the youth dark-complexioned, like shingle.
Voigt. Daughter.
Weöres. Song: Boundless Space.
Williams, Gerwyn. Pledge.
Winters, A. Night Light.

See also **Babies**

Infatuation
Anwar, C. Tuti's Ice Cream.
Behn, A. To the Fair Clarinda [or Clorinda], Who Made Love to Me, Imagin'd [or Imagined] More than Woman.
Berlin. Pretty Girl Is Like a Melody, A.
  They Say It's Wonderful.
Blane, R. Trolley Song, The.
Blanvillain, J. (All of a Sudden) My Heart Sings.
Burke, J. Imagination.
Cahn, S. Call Me Irresponsible.
Clark, P. Excitement.
Cope, W. Two Cures for Love.
Coward. Mad About the Boy.
Cuadra, P. Manuscript in a Bottle.
  Manuscript in a Bottle.
DeSylva, B. G. If You Knew Susie (Like I Know Susie).
  I'll Say She Does.
  You're an Old Smoothie.
Dett. Conjured.
Dietz, H. I Guess I'll Have to Change My Plan.
Durcan. Nessa.
Engvick, W. Crazy in the Heart.
Freed, R. How About You.
Fuzuli. Pointed reproach of the enemy, The.
Gillespie, H. You Go to My Head.
Gippius. Seamstress, The.
González, R. Crush.
Gordon, M. Meet the Beat of My Heart.
  You Make Me Feel So Young.
Griffiths, J. Two Are Embracing.
Hanley, J. Zing! Went the Strings of My Heart.
Hart, L. Thou Swell.
Herrera y Reissig. Heraldic Decoration.
Housman. Oh, when I was in love with you.
Iskander. Once a girl, all April-fresh.
Jolson, A. I'll Say She Does.
Kahn, G. I'll Say She Does.
  My Baby Just Cares for Me.
Kemal, Y. Tryst: "My eyes transfixed on the road, I strained in their light to see."
Kleban, E. One.
Koch, K. In Love with You.
  To Marina.
  To You: "I love you as a sheriff searches for a

walnut."
Koehler, T. Let's Fall in Love.
Kushner, A. As Catullus wrote, a man's voice deserts him.
Lawrence, J. Linda.
Leigh, C. Real Live Girl.
  You Fascinate Me So.
Lerner, A. On the Street Where You Live.
Lloyd, C. Whether thou smile or frown, thou beauteous face.
Lockward, D. On First Reading *Romeo and Juliet*.
Madeira, P. I'm Glad There Is You (In This World of Ordinary People).
Marlowe. "O Hero, Hero!" thus he cried full oft.
Martin, H. Trolley Song, The.
Mercer, J. Out of This World.
  Satin Doll.
  You Were Never Lovelier.
Porter, C. At Long Last Love.
  I Get a Kick Out of You.
Raftery [or Raifteirí]. Shining Posy, The.
Robinson, Matt. Winter's affection, A; radiomimetic.
Rome, H. (All of a Sudden) My Heart Sings.
Ruskin, H. I May Be Wrong (But I Think You're Wonderful).
Salinas, J. Trouble with the Light, The.
Sidney. Eleventh Song: "Who is it that this dark[e] night."
Sonnet 16: "In nature apt to like when I did see."
Sonnet 21: "Your words my friend (right healthful caustics) blame."
Sonnet 47: "What, have I thus betrayed my liberty?"
Sonnet 49: "I on my horse, and Love on me doth try."
Sonnet 53: "In martial sports I had my cunning tried."
Sonnet 54: "Because I breathe not love to every one."
Sonnet 61: "Oft with true sighs, oft with uncalled tears."
Sonnet 69: "O joy, too high for my low style to show."
Sonnet 92: "Be your words made (good sir) of Indian ware."
Sonnet 107: "Stella, since you so right a Princess art."
Sonnet 108: "When sorrow (using mine own fire's might)."
Sondheim. Losing My Mind.
Suckling, S. Upon My Lady Carlisle's Walking in Hampton Court Garden.
Tuckerman, F. Infatuation.
Unknown. At Mass.
  Dancer.
  Just to see you I invent circuitous walks.
  Ringleted Youth of My Love.
  You have consumed my mouth but are not satisfied.
Weaver, A. Sub Shop Girl.
Webster, P. I Got It Bad and That Ain't Good.

Infertility
Baudelaire. Way her silky garments undulate, The.
Cogswell, Fred. George Burroughs.
Macphee, K. IVF.
Martínez, V. Children of the Disappeared.
Pak Sôwôn. Menstrual Irregularities.
Poetker-Thiessen, A. Symbols of Fertility.
Stein, K. Terms.

Infidelity
Alexander, E. Nineteen.
Andrew, G. Prayer: "God bless the chick in Alaska."
Angelou, M. Pickin Em Up and Layin Em Down.
Auden. Lullaby: "Lay your sleeping head, my love."
Beath, M. Oregon Inlet.
Behn, A. To Alexis in Answer to His Poem Against Fruition. Ode.
Bernard [or Bernart] de Ventadour [or

Bernard [or Bernart] de Ventadorn]. Men, a word of wisdom. Give.
Berssenbrugge. Jealousy.
Bottke, A. How to Approach Your Lover's Wife.
Brooks, G. Vacant Lot, The.
Browning, E. Bertha in the Lane.
Browning, R. Any Wife to Any Husband.
Byron, G. Remember Thee! Remember Thee!
  When We Two Parted.
Carew, T. Deposition from Love, A.
Catullus. Carmen: 11.
  Unto no body my woman saith she had rather a wife be [or bee].
Chaucer. Miller's Prologue, The.
  Miller's [or Milleres] Tale, The.
Christie. Dusk and the Wife.
Chuo Wen-chün. Song of White Hair, A.
Cisneros, S. I Am on My Way to Oklahoma to Bury the Man I Nearly Left My Husband For.
Cleveland, J. Antiplatonic[k], The.
Dancer. Variety, The.
De Vries, P. To His Importunate Mistress.
Deloney. Long have I lov'd this bonny Lasse.
Dickey, J. Adultery.
Donne. Indifferent, The.
  Nature's lay idiot [or ideot], I taught thee to love.
  Song: "Go and catch a falling star."
  Woman's Constancy.
Dowson. Non Sum Qualis Eram Bonae sub Regno Cynarae.
Elizabeth I. Doubt of Future Foes.
"Ephelia.". In the Person of a Lady, to Bajazet, Her Unconstant Gallant.
Feirstein. Mark Stern Wakes Up.
  Rune-Maker, The.
France, L. In Kind.
García Lorca. Faithless Wife, The.
  Unfaithful Wife, The.
  Unfaithful Wife, The.
Grosholz. Legacies.
Handy, W. Yellow Dog Blues.
Harrington, J. Inconstancy.
Hass, R. Forty Something.
Hecht, A. Dover Bitch, The.
Heffernan, M. Message, The.
Hoagland, T. My Country.
Homer. "Here," said the Cloud-gatherer Zeus, "that is a journey you may well postpone.
Housman. Along the field as we came by.
Hunter, A. *et al.* Down-Hearted Blues.
Hwang Chini. When was I unfaithful to you?
Jong, E. Parable of the Four-Poster.
King, H. Exequy, The.
Kisielewsky, Sergio. Cough Drops.
Koch, K. To Marina.
Kollar. Late Arrivals.
Korean Oral Tradition. Chôngsôn Arirang.
Kshetrayya. Courtesan to Her Lover, A.
  Wife to a Friend, A.
Lomax, M. Other Woman, The.
Lovelace, R. To Lucasta, [on] Going to the War[re]s.
MacDiarmid, H. O wha' the bride that cairries the bunch.
Masini. Two Men, Two Grapefruits.
Mataka. Next Door.
McCorkle. Infidelities.
McDonald, W. Honky-Tonk Blues.
McElroy, C. Horoscope.
McFadden, D. 1. Il Vecchio Is Our Love.
McFadden, R. Bigamy.
Meehan, P. My Love about his Business in the Barn.
Meleager. Love's night and a lamp.
Millay, E. Oh, think not I am faithful to a vow!
Mistral, G. Ballad: "He went by with another."
Montagu, L. Epistle from Mrs. Yonge to Her Husband.
Nesbit, E. Husband of To-Day, The.
Parker, D. Certain Lady, A.
  Social Note.
Parker, M. Thou knowst I lov'd thee well.
Phaedrus. Widow and the Soldier or: The Measure of a Woman's Inconstancy and Lust, The.

Polito.   Overheard in the Love Hotel.
Porter, C.   Always True to You in My Fashion.
Pound, E.   Temperaments, The.
Rainey.   See, See Rider.
Ralegh, S.   Farewell to False Love, A.
Realuyo.   La Querida.
Reznikoff.   Deserter, A.
Rochester, J.   Against Constancy.
Shakespeare, W.   Balthasar's Song.
  Sonnet 110: "Alas, 'tis true, I have gone here
    and there."
  Sonnet 138: "When my love swear[e]s that she
    is made of truth."
  Spring.
Shakur, Tupac.   Why Must U Be Unfaithful (4
  Women).
Sidney.   Sonnet 91: "Stella, while now by
  honour's cruel might."
Suckling, S.   Constant Lover, A [or The].
  Song: "Why so pale and wan, fond lover?"
Tanikawa, S.   Kiss.
Taylor, A.   Beast with Two Backs, The.
Tranter.   Thunder heard—speak to ourselves.
Unknown.   Demon Lover, The.
  Frankie and Albert.
  Frankie and Johnny [or Johnnie or Albert].
  Hughie [the] Gra[e]me [Version from Scott's
    Minstrelsy].
  I am constantly wounded.
  I like sleeping with somebody.
  Listen to me, you wench!
  Moon, round moon, moon that shines.
  Shickered As He Could Be.
  Substituted Poem of Laureate Quynh, The.
Vliet.   Penny Ballad of Elvious Ricks.
Waring, B.   Our Lady of the Laundromat.
Wickham.   Slighted Lady, The.
Williams, C. K.   Lover, The.
  Mistress, The.
  Question, The.
Wither.   I Loved a Lass.
Wordsworth, W.   Who swerves from innocence,
  who makes divorce.
Wroth.   Song: "Love what art thou? A vain
  thought."
Wyatt.   Lover Showeth How He Is Forsaken of
  Such as He Sometime Enjoyed, The.
  Unstable dream[e] [or dreme], according [or
    accordyng] to the place.
  Whoso List to Hunt.
Yauger, Fay M.   Planter's Charm.
Yeats.   Host of the Air, The.
See also Adultery and Adulterers
Infinity
Dickinson, E.   Infinite a sudden Guest, The.
Dowden, E.   Two Infinities.
Hadewijch II.   All things.
Juarroz.   Tenth.9.
Lamartine.   Infinite in the Skies, The.
Lerner, A.   On a Clear Day You Can See
  Forever.
Muso Soseki.   Green mountains.
Novikov, N.   In our world it's unusual.
Rilke.   Initiation.
Salinas, P.   Do You Hear How They Beg for
  Realities?
Inflation
Gilbert, W.   There Lived a King.
Parra, N.   Inflation.
Ingratitude
Hayden, R.   Those Winter Sundays.
Herbert, G.   Unkindness.
Seward.   Sonnet: Ingratitude.
Inheritance
Aitchison.   Inheritance, The.
Brown, G.   Ikey: His Will in Winter Written.
Bruce, G.   Inheritance.
Dryden, J.   Crown Prince of Dullness, The.
Hogan, L.   Truth Is, The.
Jenkins, A.   Inheritance.
Johnson, S.   Short Song of Congratulation, A
  [or To a Young Heir].
Marlowe.   Bastardly boy, sprung from some
  coward's loins.
Nairne.   Heiress, The.

Norris, K.   Inheritance.
Olds, S.   Guild, The.
Pei Di.   Cove of the Wall of Meng, The.
Persius.   Satire 6: "Has Sabine winter brought
  you to your fireside."
Tupper, M.   Poor Relation, The; or, Pious Hope
  Frustrated.
Twichell.   Dirt.
Unknown.   Sons and grandsons are dearest to
  one's heart.
Wah.   Father / Mother Haibun #14.
Wang the Zealot.   Piece of the Loot, A.
Wang Wei.   Cove of the Wall of Meng, The.
Wolfe, T.   For, Brother, What Are We?
Injuries
Alegría.   Nocturnal Visits.
Amichai, Y.   Ibn Gabirol.
Ammons.   Silver.
Armitage, S.   Shout, The.
Bell, M.   Uniform, The.
Bergman, M.   Sore Thumb.
Berrigan, T.   My Autobiography.
Blue Cloud.   Wolf.
Breton, N.   Let mee thinke no more on thee.
Breytenbach.   Dreams Are Also Wounds.
Budde, R.   Bruise.
Campo.   S. W.
Coulehan, J.   Man with a Hole in His Face, The.
Crane, H.   Episode of Hands.
Crapsey.   Guarded Wound, The.
Cruz, C.   Praying ("In the middle of the night.").
Dugan, A.   Fabrication of Ancestors.
Duhamel.   Crater Face.
Espada.   Who Burns for the Perfection of Paper.
Faiz.   You Tell Us What to Do.
Feinfeld, D.   Wound Man, The.
Frost, R.   Not to Keep.
Galvin, J.   Station (2).
Gibson, W.   In the Ambulance.
Grosholz.   Back Trouble.
Gudding, Gabriel.   One Petition Lofted into the
  Ginkgos.
Gunn, T.   Wound, The.
Hernández, M.   Wounded Man, The.
Highfill, M.   Rebis.
Hô Sugyông.   Poem: "Slash my back with a
  sickle."
Homer.   This said, divine Talthybius he call'd,
  and bad him haste.
Im Yŏngjo.   Carpenter's Song, A.
Jaccottet.   Wound seen from afar.
Kooser.   Very Old, The.
Larkin, J.   My Body.
Lermontov.   Dream.
Mansfield, K.   Man with the Wooden Leg, The.
Mansour, J.   Gently stroke a wound.
Mashinskaya, I.   So I stood by and watched.
Moolten, D.   Motorcycle Ward.
Moss, T.   Rapture of Dry Ice Burning off Skin
  as the Moment of the Soul's Apotheosis, The.
Muldoon, P.   Hard Drive.
Nelson, M.   Shiner.
Orr, G.   Father's Song.
Paquet.   Basket Case.
Platke, S.   Gut Catcher.
Riley, D.   Cruelty Without Beauty.
Ritsos.   Audible and Inaudible.
Schneider, M.   Bath: "Kindness, an Irish lilt in
  her voice."
Shuster, D.   Mellow on Morphine.
Stafford, W.   Ceremony.
Stein, K.   Night Shift, after Drinking Dinner,
  Container Corporation of America, 1972.
Swenson, M.   Bleeding.
Talvikki, A.   Origin Charm Against Uncertain
  Injuries.
Turnbull.   Transmutation ("Boy is amazed to see
  his father home from work in the afternoon
  with a bandaged finger, A.").
Unknown.   Come back to me, riddled with holes
  from a dark rifle's bullets.
  If you do not have a wound in the center of
    your chest.
  Spell against Twisting an Ankle.
Various authors.   Wishing to entrust him with a
  great task.

Wier.   Chance Encounter with a Wounded Man
  Playing a Theremin.
Wilkinson, J.   Rest of It, The.
  Sideshow.
Yamani, A.   Streets of Black and White.
Zarco.   Once upon a Seesaw with Charlie Chan.
Injustice
Agosin.   Disappeared Woman V.
  Most Unbelievable Part, The.
Agüeros.   Psalm for the Next Millennium.
Alexander, E.   Affirmative Action Blues (1993).
Amadiume.   We Have Even Lost our Tongues!
Bandele, A.   After diana died.
Berry, J.   Fantasy of an African Boy.
Bierce.   Hesitating Veteran, The.
Blackman, P.   Sometimes all night I kept vigil
  with men stripped of their flesh.
Bontemps.   Black Man Talks of Reaping, A.
Brecht, B.   World's One Hope, The.
Brown, S.   Master and Man.
Carmona.   Tenderness.
Carroll, L.   Long Tale, A.
  Mouse's Tale, The.
Célestin-Mégie, E.   I'm Writing a Poem.
Cherry, J.   Amadou.
Chrystos.   I Walk in the History of My People.
Clifton, L.   1. at nagasaki.
  4/30/92 for Rodney King.
Cortez, J.   There It Is.
Day Lewis.   Consider These, for We Have
  Condemned Them.
de Portalatin.   Black Autumn.
Dufflar, C.   Amadou Diallo from Guinea to the
  Bronx Dead on Arrival.
Dunbar, P.   Haunted Oak, The.
Dylan.   Lonesome Death of Hattie Carroll, The.
Ezenwa-Ohaeto.   I Wan Bi President.
Felipe, L.   I am no one: a man.
Gahan, Carmel.   Asking for it.
García Lorca.   Arrest of Antoñito el Camborio.
Grahn.   Ella, in a Square Apron, Along
  Highway 80.
Hall, D.   Small Fig Tree, A.
Hardy, J.   Objection Overruled.
Harper, F.   Slave Auction, The.
Hayes, T.   Postcard from Okemah, A.
Hoilette, A.   Blooming Death. . .Blossoms.
Horne, N.   Note to My Liberal Feminist Sister,
  A.
Housman.   Oh who is that young sinner with the
  handcuffs on his wrists?
Howell IV, T.   Ginsburg.
Hughes, L.   Advertisement for the Waldorf-
  Astoria.
  Ballad of the Landlord.
  Bitter River, The.
Ismaili.   Yet Still.
Li Po.   Song of the Heavenly Horse.
Lindsay, V.   Abraham Lincoln Walks at
  Midnight.
Mabuza.   Death to the Gold Mine!
MacCaig.   Red and the Black, The.
Macgoye.   Muffled Cry, A.
Millay, E.   Justice Denied in Massachusetts.
Mkangelwa.   Observations.
Moore, M.   Another Scream.
Moorer.   Injustice of the Courts.
Nadal, L.   Warrior Womb.
Nelson, M.   Wreath for Emmett Till, A.
Nolla.   Thoughts on Innocence.
Owen, W.   Parable of the Old Men and the
  Young, The.
Phaedrus.   Wolf and the Lamb, The.
Pollarolo, G.   At Breakfast.
Powell, K.   Don't Feel No Way.
Prado, A.   Murmur.
Preston, R.   Lift Every Fist and Swing.
Raffalovich, M. A.   Sonnet 120.
Roberts, A.   Epistle to the Revolutionary Bible,
  An.
Robinson, M.   January, 1795.
  Stanzas: "In this vain, busy world, where the
    good and the gay."
Rodriguez, L.   Speaking with Hands.
Rungano.   Woman, The.
Shakespeare, W.   Sonnet 66: "Tired [or Tyr'd or

Tir'd] with all these, for restful[l] death I cry."
Stanley, T.   Ode XV.
Steensen, S.   This Land.
Steptoe.   Notes for a Poem from the Middle Passage of Years.
Tait, G.   U.S.A. Court of No Appeal, The.
Taylor, M.   Well-Bred Woman, A.
Tontongi.   Go There.
Tree.   Pity the Slain that Laid Away Their Lives.
Tupper, M.   Poor Relation, The; or, Pious Hope Frustrated.
Unknown.   Lay of the Lash, The.
Statesmen, in your exalted station know.
Thou ermined judge, pull off that sable cap!
Wang An-shih.   Confiscating Salt.
Whittier.   For Righteousness' Sake.
Massachusetts to Virginia.
Wiethüchter.   Without Histories.
Winchilsea.   Unequal Fetters, The.
Wrigley, R.   What My Father Believed.
Zulu, P.   You are Mad: and I Mean It!

See also **Justice; Social Protest**

Ink and Inkwells
Coleridge, M.   Contents of an Ink-bottle, The.
Mays, M.   #3, In Black Ink.

Innisfree, Ireland
Yeats.   Lake-Isle of Innisfree, The.

Innocence
Atkins, R.   New Storefront.
Aytoun [*or* Ayton], R.   On the Prince's Death, to the King.
Barker, J.   To Her Lover's Complaint.
Bass, F.   Garden, The.
Blake, W.   Auguries of Innocence.
Lily, The.
Piping Down the Valleys Wild.
Brock-Broido.   Radiating Naïveté.
Brontë, E.   Tell me, tell me, smiling child.
Bryant, W.   Oh [*or* O] Fairest of the Rural Maids.
Buckley, C.   Sleep Walk.
Campbell, D.   Small-town Gladys.
Carruth, H.   Cows at Night, The.
Cassian.   Part of a Bird.
Caulfield.   Merci Bien, Monsieur.
Chubb, R.   Transfiguration.
Coleridge, H.   Long Time a Child.
Coleridge, S.   Christabel.
Collins, B.   History Teacher, The.
Cruz Varela.   Kaleidoscope.
Cunningham, J.   Innocent to innocent.
Curbelo.   Listening to a White Man Play the Blues.
Drake, N.   Man in the White Suit, The.
Drayton.   Since there's no help, come let us kiss and part.
Egerton, S.   Blasphemous wretch! How canst thou think or say.
Eliot, T. S.   Hippopotamus, The.
Fagin, L.   Little Hand.
García Lorca.   1910.
Garcia, R.   Note Folded Thirteen Ways.
Garrett, E.   Womanhood.
Gertsyk, A.   Silent, draped in the garments of sacrifice.
Glazier, L.   On TV.
Gunn, T.   Innocence.
Hart, L.   I Didn't Know What Time It Was.
Held, George.   Split.
Herbert, G.   Holy Baptism (2).
Hilary.   To an English Boy: "Hail, fair youth, who seeks no bribe."
Hill, G.   Holy Thursday.
Holmes, O.   Iris, Her Book.
Hugo, V.   Shepherds and Flocks.
Jackson, L.   Only Daughter, The.
Summary for Alastor.
Jarman, M.   Supremes, The.
Jones, Ceri Wyn.   Honour.
Jordan, J.   All the World Moved.
Kalina, R.   *Dayeinu*—they said.
Kavanagh, P.   Innocence.
Knight, E.   Circling the Daughter.
Kunitz, S.   Testing-Tree, The.
Lamb, C.   Timid grace sits trembling in her eye, A.

Lanier, E.   Our Mother *Eve,* who tasted of the Tree.
Lanyer.   Our Mother *Eve,* who tasted of the Tree.
Lea, S.   Clouded Evening, Late September.
Levertov.   In Mind.
Overland to the Islands.
Lewis, A.   Sentry, The.
Loftis, N.   Ruth.
MacEwen, G.   Child Dancing, The.
MacNeice.   Autobiography.
Mahon.   Girls on the Bridge.
Maturaikkataiayattar Makan Vennakan.   What She Said to Her Girl-Friend.
Mew.   June, 1915.
Molina, P.   Events Like Palaces.
Montague, J.   Welcoming Party, A.
Nemerov.   Snow Globe, The.
Nolla.   Thoughts on Innocence.
Oakes-Smith, E.   'Tis the summer prime, when the noiseless air.
Ofeimun.   Naming Day, A.
Olds, S.   I Go Back to May 1937.
Padel, R.   Trial.
Palgrave.   Eutopia.
Pearlman.   Child of Wonder.
Philips, K.   To My Excellent Lucasia, On Our Friendship.
Pollard, C.   Heavy-Petting Zoo, The.
Prado, A.   Stained Glass Window.
Ransom, J.   Janet Waking.
Necrological.
Rich, A.   Children Playing Checkers at the Edge of the Forest.
Robin, L.   Little Girl from Little Rock.
Robinson, E.   Souvenir.
St. John, P.   Violence of Pronoun, The.
Salmon, A.   Prikaz.
Scamell, B.   For a Six Year Old.
Simic.   Prodigy.
Smith, C.   Sighing I see yon little troop at play.
To Fancy.
To Mrs. G.
Written in Farm Wood, South Downs, in May 1784.
Sorrentino.   Razzmatazz.
Thomas, D.   Fern Hill.
Refusal to Mourn the Death, by Fire, of a Child in London, A.
Thompson, F.   To Olivia.
Traherne.   Corn was Orient and Immortal Wheat, which never should, The.
Innocence.
On News.
Unknown.   Now for that slawnders sake.
Under the Linden Tree.
Van Jordan, A.   If I Write a Poem.
Vando.   My Mother Cunning, Yet Innocent.
Verlaine.   Green ("Take this fruit, these flowers, these branches and leaves.").
Vicioso.   Haiti.
Wallace-Crabbe.   Windows, The.
Waller, E.   To a Fair Lady Playing with a Snake.
Weaver, A.   Michele.
Whitehead, C.   Girls Sitting Together Like Dolls.
Whittier.   Changeling, The.
Wilde, O.   Wasted Days.
Williams, C. K.   Gas Station, The.
Zukofsky, L.   It's hard to see but think of a sea.

Inns
Basho.   Staying at an inn.
Chungji.   Watching the Rain at Hoeduk Inn.
Fairfax of Cameron.   Upon the New Building at Appleton.
Heath-Stubbs.   Footnote to Belloc's "Tarantella".
Knight, S.   Double Writing.
Laughlin, J.   Inn at Kirchstetten, The.
Longfellow, H.   Prelude: The Wayside Inn.
Mechain, G.   Hostess of the Ferry Inn, The.
Neri, G.   Inn of Angels, The.
Rossetti, C.   Uphill [*or* Up-Hill].
Warren, R.   Ballad of Billie Potts, The.
Wharton, E.   Terminus.

See also **Hotels; Motels**

Inquisition, The
Hugo, V.   Inquisition, The.

Insanity
Arapaho Oral Tradition.   I'yehe! my children—Uhi'yeye'heye!
Artaud.   Ten years that the language is gone.
Black, S.   Asylum.
Bracho, C.   Piedra en el agua de la cordura, Una.
Stone in the Water of Sanity, A.
Bradford, Perry.   Crazy Blues.
Burkard.   Foolish Thing.
Calloway, C.   Minnie, the Moocher.
Constantine, D.   New Year Behind the Asylum.
Cowper, W.   Crazy Kate.
Early, G.   Innocency or Not Song X.
Gaskell, C.   Minnie, the Moocher.
Gibran.   Madman (Prologue), The.
Gibson, W.   In the Ambulance.
Gurney, I.   To God.
Heine, H.   To the World We Must Appear.
Hill, S.   Hairbrush.
Hinojosa, Rolando.   January-May 1951 Slaughter, The.
Hofmann, M.   Late Richard Dadd, 1817–1886, The.
Justice, D.   Counting the Mad.
Ko Chônghûi.   Prague Spring 8.
Liu, T.   Mama.
McGough, R.   Snipers.
Mills, I.   Minnie, the Moocher.
O'odham.   No. 82. My Feathers.
Pietri.   How Do Your Eggs Want You (?).
Intermission from Friday.
Ritsos.   Naked Face.
Rodriguez, L.   Rant, Rave and Ricochet.
Rumi.   There is a light seed grain inside.
Saitō Mokichi.   In my calling.
Sanders, T.   Temporary Insanity.
Simpson, L.   Old Soldier.
Tester, V.   Broken Glass.
Unknown.   I grow crazier with each passing day.
I have repainted my beauty mark and blackened my eyelids.
Whalen, P.   Waiting for Claude.
Williams, D.   Little Girl Talk.
Wilson, S.   Mad Man.
Yépez, H.   Maníacos y locos.
Maniacs and crazies.

See also **Madness**

Insects
Ariosto.   Mastiff-Worrying Fly, The.
Avison.   Nameless One, A.
Basho.   Winter garden.
Belli, C.   My Parents, Know It Well.
Bly, R.   Exhausted Bug, The.
Brooks, G.   Birth in a Narrow Room, The.
Brown, M.   Little Black Bug.
Browning, R.   Song: "Moth's kiss, first, The!".
Cabalquinto.   Value Added in Smashing a German Roach on the Bathroom Door, The.
Chông Hwajin.   Hidden Path, The.
Clampitt.   Imago.
Clare, J.   Clock-A-Clay.
DeFrees.   Beetle Light.
Dickinson, E.   Further in Summer than the Birds.
DJ Renegade.   Fireflies in a Jar.
Dufault.   Mud Dauber Wasp, The.
Dybek.   Summer Afternoon in Solon, Iowa.
Giussani, S.   Vegetable Calendar.
Gorostiza, J.   Fireflies.
Grainger, J.   Crescendo.
Hahn, K.   Reckless Sonnet.
Haley, M.   Tropicalia.
Heyen.   Yellowjackets.
Hughes, T.   To Paint a Water Lily.
Huntington, C.   Virtue: "All the houses are white."
Issa.   Bedbugs, The.
Borrowing my house / From insects.
Don't kill that fly!
Even with insects.
From the bough.
Insects.
Insects on a bough.

Issahakian. Even with insects—.
Kaya Shirao. Forty years / How sharp.
Laing, K. Race on Gathering Bites.
Matthews, W. Vermin.
Mayer, B. Corn.
McIntyre. When we do trace out nature's laws.
Merwin. After the Alphabets.
Montale. Murder's not my forte.
No Hyegyŏng. Memory of Underdevelopment.
Oakes-Smith, E. Insect Affection.
Ortiz. Speaking.
Pfeiffer, E. Chrysalis, A.
Raine, C. For Hans Keller.
Roethke. Minimal, The.
Shapiro, K. Fly, The.
Shcherbina. About Limits.
Sogetsuni. After the Dance for the Dead.
Spenser, E. Sonnet 71: "I joy to see how in your drawen work."
Tardieu Jean. Fly and the Ocean, The.
Taylor, E. Upon a Spider Catching a Fly.
Turgeniev, I. Insect, The.
Unknown. Bugs.
Webb, C. Potato Bug.
Whalen, P. Coming Forth By Day.
Wright, James. Depressed by a Book of Bad Poetry, I Walk toward an Unused Pasture and Invite the Insects to Join Me.
Wright, Jay. Invention of a Garden, The.
Yang Na. Tune: "Hung Hsiu-hsieh" To a Flea.
Zukofsky, L. "Mantis".

Insomnia and Insomniacs
Afrika, T. Sleepless.
Akhmadulina. Lines Written During a Sleepless Night in Tbilisi.
Alley, R. Dissecting Uncle Sorrow.
Bairagi. Who Is Awake in the Dead of Night?
Berryman. Henry by Night.
Sonnet 115: "As usual I'm up before the sun."
Borson. Save Us From.
Bukowski. I Am Dead But I Know the Dead Are Not Like This.
Ch'in Kuan. Sleepless.
Chinnov. Gust of memory stirs faded letters, A.
Cho Chihun. Apparition.
Coleridge, M. Awake.
Corbière. Insomnia.
Cortez, J. Indelible.
Crane, H. Meticulous, past midnight in clear rime.
Curbelo. Last Call.
Cushman, S. Make the Bed.
Darío, R. Nocturne.
Davidkov, Ivan. Monastery.
Davis, W. Sleep of the Insomniac, The.
Dett. Conjured.
Diego, G. Sleeplessness.
García Lorca. Ballad of One Doomed to Die.
Gioia. Insomnia.
Glatt. What We Did After My Mother's Mastectomy.
Hamill, S. After a Winter of Grieving.
Hardy, T. Lying Awake.
Hayden, R. Broken Dark, The.
Ice Storm.
Heise, Thomas. Zombie.
Hicok. Busy Days of My Nights, The.
Hilliard, B. In the Wee Small Hours of the Morning.
Hughes, L. Summer Night.
Ibn al-Hammarah, A. A. Insomnia.
Jarman, M. Psalm: The New Day.
Jĕn Jui. Midnight.
Juan Chi. It is the middle of the night—I cannot sleep.
Sleepless at Midnight.
Justice, D. Insomnia of Tremayne, The.
Kenyon, J. Insomnia at the Solstice.
Kirsch, M. Sleep's Underside.
Lea, S. Insomnia: The Distances.
Li Po. Longing.
Night Thoughts.
Li Yü. Tune: "Beating Silk Floss".
Lindsay, V. Abraham Lincoln Walks at Midnight.
Logghe. Insomnia Litany.

Loncar, M. Insomniac.
Lu Yu. Insomnia: "Even when I fall asleep early."
Night Thoughts.
Makuck. Jet Lag.
Mandelstam [or Mandelshtam]. Because I Let Go Your Hands.
Insomnia.
Insomnia. Homer. Taut Sails.
Margulies, S. Relentlessly Lovelorn, the Non-Sleeper Whispers and Re-Whispers a Magic Charm Against His Wound's Roar.
Meleager. Night Alone, The.
Mirabai [or Mira Bai]. Dark one, / how can I sleep?
Montagu, L. Between Your Sheets.
Montague, J. 11 rue Daguerre.
Mullen, H. Sleeping with the Dictionary.
Myles, E. Sleepless.
Nystrom. Insomnia.
Oates. Insomnia.
Orr, G. Insomnia Song.
Pak Inhwan. Sleepless Night, A.
Pak Tujin. Sun.
Patumanār. What She Said.
Petronius Arbiter. My bed was soft, the early night was bliss.
Plath. Insomniac.
Po Chü-i. Cold Night.
Palace Song.
Prunty. Insomnia.
Pushkin, A. Lines Written at Night During Insomnia.
Quasimodo. Insomnia.
Quinn, J. Insomnia.
Randell. Tomorrow I shall.
Rossetti, D. Insomnia.
Rossi, T. Insomnia.
Rumi. When I am with you, we stay up all night.
When I have you, the passions of love make me stay awake.
Ryokan. Late at night, listening to the winter rain.
Saba, U. Insomnia on a Summer Night.
Sappho. Moon and the Pleiades have set, The.
Pleiades disappear, The.
Seyburn, P. You and Them.
Shakespeare, W. Sonnet 27: "Weary with toil, I haste me to my bed."
Sonnet 28: "How can I then return in happy plight."
Sonnet 61: "Is it thy will thy image should keep open."
Sidney. Sonnet 40: "As good to write as for to lie and groan."
Simic. Congress of the Insomniacs, The.
Smith, R. Halcion.
Statius. To Sleep.
Stryk, L. Dawn.
T'ao Ch'ien [or T'ao Yuan-ming]. Bright sun sinks / beyond the western ridge, The.
Tu Fu [or Du Fu]. Night in a Room by the River.
Restless Night.
Sleepless Nights.
Tzu Yeh. All Night.
Illusions.
Unknown. As night succeeds night.
At midnight the memory of you is the only visitor.
Bright Moon, The.
Go to sleep inside my eyes.
If it is but sleep.
My / wide eyes watch.
Night so.
Night so.
So it is because.
Updike. Insomnia the Gem of the Ocean.
Van de Woestijne. Oars Heavy with Seaweed, The.
Vanshenkin. Rain.
Wang An-shih. Night Watch.
Wen T'ing-yün. She Sighs on Her Jade Lute.
Wilbur, R. Walking to Sleep.
Wilder, Thornton. Sentences.

Wojahn. Distance.
Wright, F. August Insomnia.
Yi Chonyŏn. Moon is white on pear blossoms, The.
Yi Sunsin. In the Chinhae Camp.

Inspiration
Akhmatova, A. Sister, I have come to take your place.
Alegría. Summing Up.
Amrane. You Called to Me, Prison Windows.
Anderson, Tenshin Reb. To Bodhidharma.
Andrade, M. Inspiration.
Aridjis. Poem, The.
Self-Portrait at Thirteen Years of Age.
Baraka, R. In the Tradition Too.
Berrigan, T. On the 15th day of November in the year of the motorcar.
Sonnet LV: "Grace to be born and live as variously as possible."
Berryman. Henry's Fate.
Bevington, H. Ballade of Poetic Material.
Blake, W. Piping Down the Valleys Wild.
Brecht, B. Bad Time for Poetry.
Bryant, W. I Cannot Forget with What Fervid Devotion.
Brydges. No more by cold philosophy confined.
Bukowski. So you want to be a writer?
Caedmon. Caedmon's Hymn.
Chapman, G. For words want art and art wants words to praise her.
Ching An. Third Time Wandering to Cloud Sluice Peak.
Chunbong Manwoo. On the Mountain.
Creeley. Door, The: "It is hard going to the door."
De León, L. Ode to Francisco Salinas.
Delaunay, S. Greetings, Blaise Cendrars.
Devi. Invocation.
Dimitrova. Ars Poetica.
Drayton. Ode Written in the Peak[e], An.
Dufault. Mud Dauber Wasp, The.
Duhamel. How Much Is This Poem Going to Cost Me?
Elliott, E. Criticism.
Emerson, R. Art.
Merlin I.
Fanthorpe. Person's Tale, The.
Gilbert, S. Retrun of the Muse, The.
Gullar. There Are Many Traps in the World.
Haavikko. How decisively.
Hannah, S. Symptoms.
Hanson, M. To Mrs. Charlotte Smith.
Herrick. Departure of the Good Daemon, The.
To the Most Illustrious and Most Hopeful[l] Prince, Charles, Prince of Wales.
Hirshfield, J. Inspiration: "Think of those Chinese monks' tales."
Holmes, O. 3. Sympathies.
Hyde, E. About Poems.
Ismail. Poetry: "Beautiful woman, A."
Keats. 'How Many Bards Gild the Lapses of Time!'.
On Sitting Down to Read *King Lear* Once Again.
To B.R. Haydon, with a Sonnet Written on Seeing the Elgin Marbles.
Korinna [or Corinna]. I blame even clear-voiced.
Lazarus, E. Echoes.
Lederer, K. In Las Vegas.
Lee, E. Sun-Struck Eagle, The.
Levertov. Cancion: "When I am the sky."
Longfellow, H. Broken Oar, The.
Monroe, A. To W. S. M.
Montale. My Muse.
Morejón. Love, Attributed City.
Muldoon, P. Mimi.
Neruda. Every Day, Matilde.
Norton, C. To My Books.
Ovid. Elegy 3.1: "Old wood stands uncut, of long years' space, An."
Parker, A. Another Poem about the Vandals.
Vandals, The.
Powell, D. A. Sonnet: "Morsels of my lifework: the story of a professional party hostess."
Rankine. Testimonial.

Reynolds, Elinor Wyn. I Had a Really Good Idea for a Poem in Cynwil Elfed.
Robinson, E. Sonnet: "Oh for a poet—for a beacon bright."
Rodriguez, J. How to Be a Street Poet.
Sappho. Come, divine lyre, speak to me.
Service. Inspiration.
Shakespeare, W. Sonnet 78: "So oft have I invok'd thee for my muse."
Sia, B. Howl.
Sidney. Sonnet 1: "Loving in truth, and fain[e] in verse my love to show."
Sonnet 15: "You that do search for every purling spring."
Sonnet 28: "You that with allegory's curious frame."
Sonnet 41: "Having this day my horse, my hand, my lance."
Sonnet 74: "I never drank of Aganippe well."
Sonnet 90: "Stella, think not that I by verse seek fame."
Silberg, Richard. Audience, The.
Sri Sri. Call of Poetry.
Stafford, W. How the Real Bible Is Written.
Stepanchev. Inspiration.
Stern, G. Mimi.
Stevenson, R. Happy Thought.
Strand. Idea, The.
Strayhorn, B. Something to Live For.
Sutphen, J. Household Muse.
Szporluk. Holy Ghost.
Tate, J. Poem to Some of my Recent Poems.
Thoreau. Inspiration ("Whate'er we leave to God, God does.").
Turner, C. No trace is left upon the vulgar mind.
Very. Promise, The ("I come the rushing wind that shook the place.").
Waniek. Source of the Singing, The.
Warfield. Sun-Struck Eagle, The.
Watts-Dunton. Coleridge.
Whalen, P. Complaint: To the Muse.
Wheatley, P. To S. M., a Young African Painter.
Wilbur, R. Love Calls Us to the Things of This World.
Williams, S. Letter to a Black Woman.
Winder. Lesson.
Young, K. Langston Hughes.

Installment Buying
Trethewey, N. Collection Day.

Instinct
Cowper, W. Beau's Reply.
Hemphill. Better Days.
Hervey, L. Nature Queries [or Epistle to Mr. Fox, from Hampton Court].
Wilkinson, A. Tigers Know from Birth.

Institutionalization
Bogan, L. Evening in the Sanitarium.
Delgado, J. Recommitted.
Visiting Father.
Dowson. To One in Bedlam.
Lanzilloti, Das. In the Boobiehatch.
Ornate Iron Gates.
Lowell, R. Waking in the Blue.
Plath. Face Lift.
Rector. David's Rumor.
Schmitt, Kate. I Told Them I Should Be Here.
Sexton. Music Swims Back to Me.
You, Doctor Martin.

Insults
Beatty, P. Stall Me Out.
Belloc. Frog, The.
Bunting. What the Chairman Told Tom.
Coleman, W. Three-Headed Womon Song.
Crawley, W. Poetry for the Goddess.
Ivask, Y. Shall we forget the shiver.
Lee, N. Nay, *Clytus*, you that cou'd advise—.
Maitland, T. Sir Thomas Maitland's Satyr upon Sir Niel Laing.
Martial. Lydia is as wide and slack.
You are a stool pigeon and.
You often say my work is coarse. It's true.
Miranda, Deborah A. Stories I Tell My Daughter.
North, C. Postcard Element in Winter, The.
Speckled Red (Rufus Perryman). Dirty Dozens,

The.
Sutherland, Fraser. On the Beach One Day.
Unknown. Bonny Barbara Allan.

Integrity
Archilochus. I don't like a tall general, swaggering.
Creeley. Like They Say.
Lao Tzu. Know masculinity, / Maintain femininity.
Person of superior integrity, The.
While you / Cultivate the soul and embrace unity.
Pak Nohae. Road to Corruption, The.
Rich, A. Integrity.
Sappho. Handsome man is good to look at, A.
Shakespeare, W. Sonnet 125: "Were't aught to me I bore the canopy."
Various authors. He had many to help him.

Intellect and Intellectuals
Ammons. Pet Panther.
Berry, W. 1980 VI.
Castillo, O. Apolitical Intellectuals.
Chin. Elegy for Chloe Nguyen.
Coleridge, M. Clever Woman, A.
Cummings, E. E. Since feeling is first.
Dobyns. Why Fool Around?
Doty, M. Coastal.
Drummond, W. Content and Resolute.
Dyer, S. My Mind to Me a Kingdom Is.
Eberhart, R. Centennial For Whitman.
Eliot, T. S. Mr. Apollinax.
Emerson, R. Intellect.
Farawell, M. Everything I Need to Know I Learned in Kindergarten.
Fraire. Minute the sun comes out, The.
Frost, R. At Woodward's Gardens.
Galanskov. Intellectual, The.
Gilbert, W. Bunthorne's Song.
Graham, J. Mind.
Harding, D. Intelligence Quotient, The.
Hart, L. Zip.
Heinemann, M. For R. J. C. (Summer, 1936).
Hill, G. Let mind be more precious than soul; it will not.
Ingalls, J. For the Intellectuals.
Kendall, M. Woman's Future.
Kirby, D. Dear Derrida.
Lear, E. Limerick: "There was an Old Person of Basing."
Moore, M. Mind Is an Enchanting Thing, The.
More, H. Strange power of song! the strain that warms the heart.
Nash, O. Just How Low Can a Highbrow Go When a Highbrow Lowers His Brow?
Nemerov. Blue Swallows, The.
Brainstorm.
Ochester. Working at the Wholesale Curtain Showroom.
Paisley, J. Intellectual, The.
Porter, C. Let's Not Talk About Love.
Rexroth, K. Vitamins and Roughage.
Shelley, P. Hymn to Intellectual Beauty.
Stern, G. I Remember Galileo.
Su Tung-p'o. On the Birth of His Son.
Traherne. Preparative, The.
Villa, E. Lend me a battle of unavoidable suggestions.
Ugly season of putrifying buzzards, An.
Wheelock, J. Earth.
Wilbur, R. Mind.
Wright, J. End of an Ethnic Dream, The.

See also **Mind; Rationalism and Rationalists; Reason**

Interment.
Kaschnitz. Genazzano.
Norwood, Nick. For the Drowned.
Ondaatje. To be buried in times of war.
Salzman, E. Conch.
Takei, Sojin. There is no fence.
Togawa, Akira. Distorted Sun.

See also **Burial**

International Brigade
Hughes, L. Letter from Spain.

See also **Civil War, Spain**

Internationalism
Cocteau. Fairy Scene.
Cross, D. Massimo del Panino, Il.
Loseff [/or Losev]. Conversation with a New York Poet.

See also **United Nations**

Internet
Elmslie, K. Diddly Squat From Cyberspace.
Waltner-Toews, D. Teilhard de Chardin Surfs the Internet.

Internment
Gensui. Birds.
Hakkaku. Days when I laughed, The.
Hokko. Hay spread for.
Sprinkling.
Hongo. Redness: Thinking it Through.
Hottel, J. Shikata ga nai.
Inada. Concentration Constellation.
F.B.I. swooped in early, The.
It began as truth, as fact.
Legend of Home, The.
Picking Up Stones.
Katay, Taro. Shouldering.
Komuro, Kyotaro. Passed guard tower.
Want to be with children.
Kyokusui. Thorns of the iron fence.
Mura. Argument: on 1942, An.
Blueness of the Day, The.
Letters from Poston Relocation Camp (1942–45).
Okita. Nice Thing About Counting Stars, The.
Oshio. Stepping through snow.
Pzaki, Muin. Prisoner.
Sasabune. Dimples.
Since the day of internment.
Soga, Keiho. Beyond the forbidding fence.
Within just ten days.
Suzuki, Shonan. Moon shadows on internment camp.
Withered grass on ground.
Uyematsu. December 7 Always Brings Christmas Early.
Wada, Hakuro. Even the croaking of frogs.
Released Seagull.
Young grass and shriveled.
Wong, N. Can't Tell.

Interracial Love and Marriage
Agustini. Another Race.
Clark, C. Border Affair, A.
Clinton, M. Warning to Young Bright Sisters / White AM. Culture 101A.
Eady. Sherbet.
Hughes, L. Cross.
Joseph, A. Noon Talk at Georgia's Coffee Shop.
King, H. Boy's Answer to the Blackmoor, The.
Mattawa. History of My Face.
Maunick. Seven Sides and Seven Syllables.
Press, K. Causality and Chance in Love.
Ridge, J. Stolen White Girl, The.
Sholl. Midnight Vapor Light Breakdown.
Tolliver, I. Those i love are sometimes white.
Tolson, M. African China.
Trethewey, N. Miscegenation.
Williams, C. K. Dog, The.
Williams, C. For the White Lady Holding Me.

Intimacy
Agran, R. Door Thrown Open to Daisies.
Alvi, M. Fish.
Amichai, Y. Inside the Apple.
To My Love, Combing Her Hair.
Anderson, J. Waking Up Twice.
Berger, J. Getting to Know Her.
Berrigan, A. Bloodletting.
Biespiel, D. There Were No Deer in the Thicket.
Bracho, C. En esta oscura mezquita tibia.
In This Warm Dark Mosque.
Misterios del tacto, Los.
Mysteries of Touch, The.
Byron, G. To Thyrza.
Caesar. Tea for Two.
Cerruto, O. Love: "Afternoon is offered to us, The."
Clark, P. Kleptomaniac.
Colby, T. Boy and the Girl, The.

Davis, C.   Any Nest I Can't Sleep in Should Be Burned.
De Burine, Claude.   Greet You.
De Kok.   Inner note.
Doolittle, Hilda.   Presence was spectrum-blue, The.
Dougherty.   Double Helix.
Elizabeth, M.   Manon Reassures Her Lover.
Farley, Estelle E.   Grand Canyon.
Fisk, M.   Late Afternoon.
  Red River.
Flynn, N.   God Forgotten.
Gaitán Durán.   They Unite Naked.
Garcilaso de la Vega.   Sonnet 5.
Gelman.   Man and a Woman, A.
Glatt.   One Night With a Stranger at 30.
Glazova, A.   Solo.
Gregerman, D.   Strictly Speaking.
Joseph, A.   Pleasure.
Kennelly.   Bread.
Klinger, A.   Transformation.
Kuzmin.   Were you apprenticed to a fortune teller?
Laing, R.   Sonnet 16: "Now all our guests have come and gone away."
Laughlin, J.   Deep Pool, the.
Lifshin.   Curling on the Bottom of My Mother's Bed.
Light, K.   Because.
Loesser.   My Darling, My Darling.
López Velarde.   In the Dying Afternoon.
Lowell, A.   Shower, A.
Lumsden, R.   Incident in a Filing Cupboard.
Lyons, S.   Remembering.
Marcus, B.   Battle at Horizon.
  Justice.
Mayes, J.   Orchestration.
McCombs, J.   Love Poem, Later.
McLain, P.   Fishing.
Mistral, G.   Intimate.
Montejo, E.   Marina.
Morse, G.   He kneels on the rumpled bed.
Nelson, M.   Proposal.
Neruda.   Drunk as drunk on turpentine.
  Poem 15.
Nortje.   Episodes with unusables.
Nowlan.   Word, The: "Though I have the gift of tongues."
O'Hara, F.   Poetry.
Paulinus of Nola.   To Ausonius.
Petronius Arbiter.   Coition's brief, a nasty cheat.
Porter, C.   From This Moment On.
Pushkin, A.   Imitation of the Arabic.
Raffalovich, M. A.   World Well Lost 18, The.
Rexroth, K.   Just us. / In our little house.
  Lyell's Hypothesis Again.
  Who is there? Me.
Rossiter.   Nostalgia.
  Your Body Glistens From the Bath.
Safford, J.   Very Floor of Our Existence, The.
Samyn, A.   Art of Kissing, The.
  Poem with Light on Its Shoulder.
Sappho.   May you sleep on the breast of a tender companion.
Schilpp, M.   Devotions in Confidence.
Sissle, N.   I'm Craving for That Kind of Love.
Smith, M.   Springtime at Twilight.
Storni.   Lost Caress, The.
Swiontkowski, G.   Old Moon With Her Youth In Her Arms.
Tennyson, A.   Now Sleeps the Crimson Petal.
  Now, sometimes in my sorrow shut.
  Path by which we twain did go, The.
Torres, E.   Summertime Late Show.
Turk, R.   Walkin' My Baby Back Home.
Unknown.   Chance led me once, when idling through the street.
  Come and be a flower on my chest.
  Even He Was Abashed.
  First take me into your arms and hold me close.
  God, let me be with him if only for a moment.
  One time only, just one time hold my bosom against yours.
Vietnamese Oral Tradition.   Husband and Wife.
Waters, M.   Cognac.
Weeks, J.   Answer by the Lady's Maid [to a

Poem Left in a Lady's Toilet].
  Poem Left in a Lady's Toilet.
Westphalen, E.   You Came to Rest.
Wetzsteon.   Late Show, The.
Whitehead, C.   Grass Crust, The.
Whitney, H.   To a Woman.
Wiesinger, S.   Snow Climbers.
Williams, T.   We Have Not Long to Love.
Yi Chŏngbo.   May my love become an alder tree.
Yount, A.   Sharing.

Introspection
Aridjis.   Self-Portrait at Age Sixteen.
Berg, S.   Writing Class.
Brontë, E.   All hushed and still within the house.
Carver, R.   This Morning.
Creeley.   Rain, The: "All night the sound had."
Crews, J.   Essence.
Davie, D.   In the Stopping Train.
Dunbar, P.   Ere Sleep Comes Down to Soothe the Weary Eyes.
Dunn, S.   Impediment.
Edmond, L.   3 A.M.
Garrigue.   Bad Times Song.
Goodell, L.   History of Myself.
Harjo, J.   Call It Fear.
Hill, J.   Season with Angels.
Hong Yunsuk.   That I Can Do This Autumn.
Hsieh Ling-yün.   On Cimbing Mount Green Crag in Yongjia.
Ivey, M.   Subterranean Business.
Kerouac.   Buddha.
Kim Ch'ŏnt'aek.   Having given my clothes to a boy.
Kim Sujang.   In my quiet grass hut.
Lodge, G.   Pastoral: "Slopes of the sun and vine, and thou dark stream."
MacCaig.   Double Life.
Melville, H.   Afterward.
  Of Mortmain.
Milton.   Il Penseroso.
Moody, W.   Harmonics.
Na Hûidôk.   Women Within Me.
Nemerov.   Salt Garden, The.
November, Yehoshua.   How a Place Becomes Holy.
Olson, C.   Added to / making a Republic.
  Celestial Evening, October 1967.
  Maximus, to Himself.
Pack, R.   Elk in Winter.
Paek Sŏk.   On the White Wall.
Paljor, N.   Exhausted by jogging.
Rexroth, K.   Signature of All Things, The.
Rich, A.   Storm Warnings.
Richter, H.   Self in Variation, The: Scenes From Meditation.
Robbins, Z.   Beaches.
Rumi.   Who Says Words with My Mouth.
St. John, D.   Meditation: "Quiet now, sorrow; relax. Calm down, fear."
Smith, S.   After-Thought, The.
Snyder, M.   Synge's Chair.
Somoza, J.   Day Break.
Stickney, T.   Here in the North I chase an old despair.
Very.   Lost, The ("Fairest day that ever yet has shone, The.").
Walcott.   Hotel Normandie Pool, The.
Wickham.   Self-Analysis.
Williams, C. K.   On Learning of a Friend's Illness.
Wordsworth, W.   Most Sweet It Is with Unuplifted Eyes.
Wright, J.   Annihilation's Trio: Three Irrational Sonnets Begging the Question of Being and Act.
  January, Love, and the Galician.
Yi Hwang.   Twelve Songs of Tosan.

Invective
Catullus.   To Aurelius and Furius.
Jeffers, R.   Advice to Pilgrims.

Inventions and Inventors
Blumenthal, M.   Inventors.
Citino.   Neanderthal, with Help from Cave and Bear, Invents the Flute.
Crosby, E.   I am a great inventor, did you but

know it.
Cucchi, M.   It's over now, the time for observation, for.
Day, J.   Reservation.
Fenton, J.   Born Too Soon.
Fuller, J.   Born Too Soon.
Gibbens, J.   To the Bicycle.
Hamby, B.   Invention.
Holub.   Inventions.
McLoughland.   Crazy Boys.
Meinke.   Sonnet on the Death of the Man Who Invented Plastic Roses.
Moolten, D.   Ode for Orville and Wilbur Wright.
Rich, A.   Rules break like a thermometer, The.
Schjeldahl.   Dynamite.
Tongue, R.   Invention.

Investment and Investors
Beecher, J.   Report to the Stockholders.
Sanguineti.   At the offset it was calculated.

Invocation
Alberti.   To the Sun of the War.
Anacreon.   I implore you, deer-shooter.
  O Lord, with whom subduer Love.
Chaucer.   Conclusion.
Coleridge, M.   Lord of the winds, I cry to Thee.
Gertsyk, A.   Spring.
Hacker, M.   Invocation: "This is for Elsa, also known as Liz."
Herrick.   His Prayer to Ben Jonson.
Hesiod.   Vision.
Homer.   Proposition and Invocation.
Kalina, R.   To Anne Frank.
Kulman.   To Diana.
Lucretius.   Darling of Gods and Men, beneath the gliding stars.
Marais.   Dance of Sister Rain.
Milton.   Invocation to Urania.
Moiro.   Tree nymphs, daughters of River, ambrosial.
Naong.   Song of the Pure Land.
Ovid.   Prologue.
Pope, A.   Yet, yet a moment, one dim ray of light.
Sappho.   On the throne of many hues, Immortal Aphrodite.
  Prayer to Aphrodite.
  Throned in splendor, deathless, O Aphrodite.
Unknown.   Wait!
Virgil [*or* Vergil].   Arms, and the Man I sing, who, forc'd by Fate.
  Prologue.

Io (mythology)
Mathews, H.   Spell.

Iona, Scotland
Tennyson, F.   Iona.

Iowa (state)
Alexander, M.   Iowa Farmer.
Dybek.   Summer Afternoon in Solon, Iowa.

Iphigenia
Dryden, J.   Cymon and Iphigenia.

Iran and Iranians
Khalvati.   Persian Miniature, A.
See also **Persians**

Iraq and Iraqis
Al-Bayati, A.   Who Owns the Homeland?
Al-Haidari, B.   City Ravaged by Silence, The.
  From Behind the Closed Door.
  So That We Do Not Forget.
  Will, The.
al-Sa'igh, Y.   Iraqi Evening, An.
Ali, M.   Homeland.
  Upside Down Picture, An.
Anton, S.   Prism, A: Wet With Wars.
Assultani, F.   Incomplete Anthem.
  RS Thomas.
Azzawi, F.   Every Morning The War Gets Up From Sleep.
  Last Iraq, The.
  Political Prisoner.
Bĕkes.   I Who Have Nothing.
Braun, V.   Desert Storm.
Hantoosh, G.   Celebration.
Juma'h, J.   Thus my brother.
Karim, F.   What Was My Choice?

McClure, M. Souls.
Peshew, A. Fratricide.
Samawi, A. Iraqi Sorrows.
  Mountain of Dreams.
  Neighing of the Fingers.
  Suns in the Night of the Massacre.
Yaqoob, J. Resurrections of Layla Al-Attar,
  The.
Yusuf, S. Enemies.
  I too love jeans and jazz and *Treasure Island*.
  I too love jeans and jazz and *Treasure Island*.
  Night in Al-Hamra.

Ireland
Allingham, W. Winding Banks of Erne, The[:
  Or, The Emigrant's Adieu to His Birthplace].
Berryman. 324. Elegy for W. C. W., the Lovely
  Man, An.
Boland, E. Famine Road, The.
  Fever.
  Mise Eire.
  Mother Ireland.
  My Country in Darkness.
  That the Science of Cartography Is Limited.
Boucicault, D. Wearing of the Green, The.
Carson, C. Turn Again.
Clifton, H. Distaff Side, The.
Davitt. Shortening the Road.
Dawe, G. Names.
Deane, S. Return.
Donovan, K. You Meet Yourself.
Drennan, W. Eire.
Durcan. Backside to the Wind.
  Birth of a Coachman.
  Bloomsday Murders, 16 June 1997, The.
  Going Home to Mayo, Winter, 1949.
  Irish Hierarchy Bans Colour Photography.
Ennis. Alice of Daphne, 1799.
  Coyne's.
Fallon, P. Yeats at Athenry Perhaps.
Fane, V. In an Irish Churchyard.
Ferguson, S. Lament for the Death of Thomas
  Davis.
Fordham. Song to Erin.
French, W. Queen's After-Dinner Speech, The.
Harburg. How Are Things in Glocca Morra?
Heaney, S. At Toomebridge.
  Bogland.
  Broagh.
  I had come to the edge of the water.
  In Memoriam Francis Ledwidge.
  New Song, A.
  Postscript.
  Strand at Lough Beg, The.
Heóghusa. On Maguire's Winter Campaign.
Hewitt, J. Colony, The.
  Irishman in Coventry, An.
Hutchinson, P. Fleadh Cheoil.
  Frost is All Over, The.
  Gaeltacht.
  True Story Ending in False Hope, A.
Kavanagh, P. Long Garden, The.
  Memory of Brother Michael.
Kennelly. Limerick Train, The.
Kinsella, T. Foot of the tower. An angle where
  the darkness, The.
  In the Ringwood.
  Route of the Táin, The.
  Tao and Unfitness at Inistiogue on the River
  Nore.
Lawless, E. In Spain.
Lindley, D. Potato Blight.
Longley, M. Wounds.
Lysaght, E. Our Dear Native Island.
MacNeice. Nightmare leaves fatigue.
MacWard *et al.* Dark Rosaleen.
Marvell. Horatian Ode upon Cromwell's Return
  from Ireland, An.
Maxton. Ode.
  Urgent Letter, An.
McAuliffe, J. Vision of Rahoon, A.
McCarthy, T. Toast.
McFadden, R. First Letter to an Irish Novelist.
McGuckian. To a Cuckoo at Coolanlough.
Montague, J. Windharp.
Moore, M. Spenser's Ireland.
Moore, T. Harp That Once through Tara's Halls,

The.
Minstrel Boy, The.
Oh! blame not the bard, if he fly to the bowers.
Pastoral Ballad by John Bull, A.
Muldoon, P. Cauliflowers.
  Ireland.
  Ma.
  Sightseers, The.
Murphy, R. Gate Lodge.
  Luttrell.
Newton, Violette. Going Back to Ireland.
O'Gnive [*or* O'Gnimh]. Downfall of the Gael,
  The.
O'Grady, D. Here, because of the shock, the
  sudden.
O'Loughlin. Glasnevin Cemetery.
  Irish Requiem, An.
Ormsby, F. Home.
Paulin. Desertmartin.
  Impossible Pictures, The.
Pearse, P. I Am Ireland.
Rolleston. Grave of Rury, The.
Smedley, M. Irish Fairy, The.
Stevens, W. Irish Cliffs of Moher, The.
Street, S. Shipping Forecast, Donegal.
Swift, J. On the Irish Club.
Synge. Beg-Innish.
  Prelude: "Still south I went and west and south
  again."
Thomas, D. Fern Hill.
Tighe. Written at Killarney. July 29, 1800.
  Written at the Eagle's Nest, Killarney. July 26,
  1800.
Trench, H. Killary.
Unknown. Arran.
  Colum Cille's Greeting to Ireland.
  Fair Hills of Ireland, The.
  I Am of Ireland.
Westendorf. I'll Take You Home Again,
  Kathleen.
Wilde, S. Who Will Show Us Any Good?
Woods, V. Road West, The.
Wright, J. Remittance Man.
Yeats. Easter 1916.
  Hosting of the Sidhe, The.
  Lake-Isle of Innisfree, The.
  On a Political Prisoner.
  Prayer for My Daughter, A.
  Rose Tree, The.
  September 1913.
  To Ireland in the Coming Times.
See also **Northern Ireland**

Ireland, Northern
Cunningham, P. Dog Called Chance, A.
  Hats.
  Red Wine Stain from Malin to Mizen Head, A.
Muldoon, P. Third Epistle to Timothy.
See also **Northern Ireland**

Iris (flower)
Buson. Iris, An.
Doolittle, Hilda. Sea Iris.
Field. Irises.
Glück, L. Wild Iris, The.
Grossman, A. Enough Rain for Agnes Walquist.
Hardie, K. Stranger.
Ikeda, P. Wild Iris.
Issa. New foal, The.
Kang [Grossjean], Ok-Ku [*or* Ok-Koo]. Iris.
Lowell, A. Nuance.
Martien, J. In Wild Iris Time.
Perk. Iris.
Rukeyser, M. Iris.
St. John, D. Iris.
Sobin, G. Fourteen Irises for J. L.
  Irises.
Williams, W. Iris.

Irish Poetry
Bartlett, E. Stretchmarks.
Boland, E. Irish Poetry.

Irish Republican Army
Berry, C. Uascán.
Durcan. Bloomsday Murders, 16 June 1997,
  The.
Myrddin ap Dafydd. War Cabinet, The.
Ward, Geoff. Horace Belisha.

Irish, The
Graves, A. Irish Spinning-Wheel, The.
Barnes, F. I've Got Rings on My Fingers.
Boland, E. Emigrant Irish, The.
Cleary, B. Slouch.
Degenaar. Irish Sheep, The.
Donovan, K. Entering the Mare.
Fitz-Simon, E. Woods of Kylinoe, The: Song of
  the Irish Emigrant in North America.
Hardie, K. She Goes with her Brother to the
  Place of their Forebears.
Hartnett. Death of an Irishwoman.
  Pity the Man Who English Lacks.
Heaney, S. Broagh.
  Docker.
  Requiem for the Croppies.
Hewitt, J. Irishman in Coventry, An.
  Once Alien Here.
  Scar, The.
Higgins, R. Middle-aged Irish Mothers.
Hutchinson, P. Gaeltacht.
Irish Oral Tradition. Irish Sailor, The.
Jamie, K. Meadowsweet.
Kickham. Irish Peasant Girl, The.
Mac Lochlainn, G. Irish-speaking Mynah, The.
  Rite of Passage.
Macphee, K. My People.
Maloney, F. Grandmothers in Green and
  Orange.
McCarthy, T. Emigration Trains, The.
Milligan, Bryce. Copano, 1834.
Montague, J. Grafted Tongue, A.
  Like Dolmens Round My Childhood.
Morrissey, S. Clocks.
Muldoon, P. Anseo.
  Cuba.
  More a Man Has the More a Man Wants, The.
  Quoof.
Ní Chuilleanáin. Secret, The.
Ni Dhomhnaill. Deep-Freeze.
O'Callaghan, C. East.
Onassis, Jacqueline Kennedy. Meanwhile in
  Massachusetts.
Philips, K. Irish Greyhound, The.
Unknown. Battle of Inverlochy, The.
  Finnegan's Wake.
  Irishman's Epistle to the Officers and Troops at
  Boston, The.
  Poor Paddy Works on the Railway.
Weston, R. I've Got Rings on My Fingers.
Williams, C. For the White Lady Holding Me.
Woods, V. Meaning of a Word, The.

Iron
Lawrence, D. H. Things Made by Iron.
Moore, M. Odor of a Metal Is Not Strong, The.
Yamaguchi Seishi. Summer river, The.

Iron Lungs
Greenlaw, L. Iron Lung.

Irony
Bukowski. Way it is now, The.
Hattersley, G. Frank O'Hara Five, Geoffrey
  Chaucer Nil.
Hemingway. Age Demanded, The.
Howard, R. Man Who Beat Up Homosexuals
  Reported to Have AIDS Virus.
Matthews, T. Robert Sat.
Ryan, M. Your Own Image.
Sidney. Sonnet 63: "O grammar rules, O now
  your virtues show."
  What Length of Verse?
Southwick. Earthly Light.
Whitney, I. Manner of Her Will and What She
  Left to London and to All Those in It, at Her
  Departing, The.
Wilbur, R. Parable.

Isaac
Clough. Genesis XXIV.
Cole, P. Isaac: a Poise.
Ephraim ben Jacob. Sacrifice of Isaac, The.
Guri, H. Heritage.
No Hyegyông. Disease That Arrives at Death.
Owen, W. Parable of the Old Men and the
  Young, The.
Stradling. Abraham's Sacrifice of Isaac.
Vaughan, H. Isaac's Marriage.
Wilner, E. Sarah's Choice.

When Asked to Lie Down on the Altar.

Isaiah
Yesenin [or Essenin]. Field Upon Field Upon
  Field.

Ishmael
Palmer, H. Ishmael.

Ishtar
Al-Bayati, A. Nightmare, The.
Ashur-Nasir-Pal. Hymn to Ishtar.
Levertov. Song for Ishtar.

Isis
Anaya, R. Isis in the Heart.
Doolittle, H.. Evil was active in the land.
Simon, L. Bernice Got Next to Isis.

Islam
Dharker. Grace.
Espada. Ghazal for Open Hands.
Ibn Hāniʼ al-Andalusi, A. Sons of al-ʼAbbās
  say, The: "Has Egypt been conquered?"
  Therefore reply to the sons of al-ʼAbbās: "The
  matter has already been accomplished".
Jones, H. Emine and Hamide.
Kuhar, M. You can't blow up the buddha.
Rundī, A. Everything declines after reaching
  perfection, therefore let no man be beguiled by
  the sweetness of a pleasant life.
Taha, A. Childhood Wall.
See also **Muslims and Islam**

Islands
Acorn. Island, The.
Albrecht, A. Anacapa.
Arnold, M. To Marguerite—Continued.
Auden. On This Island.
Aygi, G. Quietness with a Happening.
Bailey, A. Isosceles Lighthouse, The.
Barnes, F. I've Got Rings on My Fingers.
Basho. Wild sea, A.
Baudelaire. Voyage to Cythera, A.
  Voyage to Cythera, A.
Bernes, J. Desiderata on a Desert Island.
Berrigan, T. Sonnet III: "Stronger than alcohol,
  more great than song."
Bishop, E. Crusoe in England.
Blane, R. Occasional Man, An.
Bogan, L. Night: "Cold remote islands, The."
Bonnefoy. Remember the Island Where They
  Build the Fire.
Brathwaite, E. Citadel.
Brooks, C. Our Island Home.
Brown, G. Kirkyard.
Campbell, R. Tristan da Cunha.
Cendrars. Aleutian Islands.
Cervantes. Isla Mujeres.
Césaire, A. Islands scars of the water.
  Lagoonal Calendar.
  On the Islands of All Winds.
Cofer, J. Idea of Islands, The.
Crummey, Michael. Painting the Islands.
  What's Lost.
Cuadra, P. Manuscript in a Bottle.
Cummins, Deborah. To the Days Lost in
  August.
Curry, N. Galapagos.
Dancing Bear, J. P. Heart-Shaped Island, A.
Dumas, H. Island within Island.
Dunn, D. St Kilda's Parliament: 1879–1979.
Elmslie, K. Island Celebration.
Fortes, C. Island.
Gier, J. First View of the Islands, A.
Groarke, V. Rainbearers.
Hadfield, J. Staple Island Swing.
Hall, D. Without.
Harms. Elegy as Evening, as Exodus.
Hartley, M. This Crusty Fragment.
Heaney, S. Disappearing Island, The.
Highfill, M. Sea Breeze.
Hokushi. Sailboats in line.
Hölderlin. Patmos.
Hong Yunsuk. My Sea Has One Island.
Hope, A. Wandering Islands, The.
Ibáñez, S. Island in the Earth.
  Island in the Light.
Issa. Even on the smallest islands.
Kennelly. Island, The.
Ko Ŭn. For an Island.

Koehler, T. Spreadin' Rhythm Around.
Landon. Enchanted Island, The.
Lawrence, J. Sleepy Lagoon.
Leithauser. At an Island Farm.
Liu Yu Hsi. Parrot Island.
Livingstone, D. Traffic interlude: Descent from
  the Tower.
Lowry, M. About Ice.
Lysaght, E. Our Dear Native Island.
Mahon. Achill.
  Rathlin.
Martin, H. Occasional Man, An.
McGrath, Carmelita. How to Leave an Island.
McNeill, A. Saint Ras.
Melville, H. Archipelago, The.
  Enviable Isles, The.
  Island, The.
  Rolfe and the Palm.
Millay, E. Ragged Island.
Mistral, G. Caribbean Sea.
Nathaniel, Isabel. Elegy at Mustang Island.
No Hyangnim. Apʼae Island 45—Once Upon a
  Time.
Ojaide. Verdict of Stone, A.
Oswald, A. Sea Sonnet.
Phillips, C. You Are Here.
Pilling. Cast Away.
Rankin, J. Sea-bundle.
Rose. Alaskan Fragments June 1981—Summer
  Solstice.
Rosser, J. Message: Bottle #32.
Rowlands, D. Archipelago.
Russell, T. Sonnet: Suppos'd to Be Written at
  Lemnos.
Sargent, R. Rockall.
Sexton, T. Seal Island.
Stern, G. On the Island.
Steven, K. Edge.
Stevenson, R. To S.C.
Talvikki, A. My Shining Archipelago.
Tate, J. Where Babies Come From.
Thomson, D. Second Island, The.
Walcott. Crusoe's Island.
Weaver, A. Easy Living.
Weston, R. I've Got Rings on My Fingers.
Wordsworth, D. Floating Island at Hawkshead.
Yeats. Lake-Isle of Innisfree, The.
  Sorrow of Love, The [1892 Version].
Youn, Monica. Night Ferry to Naxos 1.

Isolation
Amichai, Y. What drove young Joseph to
  interpret dreams.
Budbill. Thirty-Five Miles to a Traffic Light.
Byron, G. Prisoner Scolds, The.
Chavarría, L. Lone Tree.
Citino. Man Who Couldn't Believe, The.
Cortez, J. Indelible.
Costanzo. Old Neighborhood, The.
Crowe, T. Saw-Mill Shack, The.
Davies, A. This evening / Is the only evening.
Davies, Lynn. On the Train.
Friedman, E. Isolated Bourgeoisie.
Han-shan. Pole your three winged galleons.
Hidalgo, J. Sun of Death.
Hong Yunsuk. My Sea Has One Island.
Huai Ku. Living at a Monastery, Sent to Chien
  Chang.
Juan Chi. My steps lead me to a junction of
  three roads.
Kinsella, J. Fall, The.
Koertge. Lazarus.
Lamartine. Isolation.
Li Chʼing-chao. Tune: "Joy of Eternal Union".
  Tune: "On the Trail of Sweet Incense".
Li Yü. Tune: "Sand Washed by Waves".
  Tune: "Sand Washed by Waves".
Liu Tsung-yüan. River Snow.
  River Snow ("Thousand peaks: no more birds in
  flight, A.").
  Thousand mountains without a bird, A.
Lojowski, M. Big Fort Island Buddha.
Martinson. Lighthouse Keeper.
Meng Hao Jan. Returning Home to Deer-Gate
  Mountain at Night.
Morabito, F. I do not wish, in spite of all.
  No quiero, pese a todo.

Myŏngok. Snow falls on the mountain village.
O'Connor, M. Overnight at a Buddhist
  Mountain Temple.
Oppen. Myself I Sing.
Pao Hsien. Sent to Yuan Chen at White Cabin
  Peak.
Parker, D. Portrait of the Artist.
  Sanctuary.
Pinsky. Poem about People.
Pizarnik. Existing.
Ralin, Radoi. Safety Pins (excerpts).
Rein. Moscow Station, The.
Revell, D. Last.
Rich, A. I Am in Danger—Sir.
Ritsos. Evening Walk.
Rosales. I Know Too Well and Sadly Enough.
Samawi, S. Solo for the Lone Intuition, A.
Smith, S. Like This (1).
Stanton, M. Space.
Stratanovsky. Leningrad stairwell, A.
Tʼao Chʼien [or Tʼao Yuan-ming]. To My
  Cousin, Ching-yuan, Twelfth Month, 403.
Tzara. Horse, The.
Unknown. Home to Farm.
Vallejo. Agape.
Vietnamese Oral Tradition. Outpost Soldier,
  The.
Villaurrutia. They and I.
Wah. Father / Mother Haibun #6.
Zarco. My Worst Fear.
See also **Absence; Loneliness; Separation**

Israel
Ali, A. Land.
Alkalay-Gut. Instead of his leash.
  Public Outcry.
  So we begin to plan.
  Some people terrified for their lives cut.
  Think of the children in Baghdad.
  Tonight we wait for the alarm.
  Unable to move.
Alterman, N. Around the Campfire.
  Silver Platter, The.
Amichai, Y. Almost a Love Poem.
  From the Songs of the Land of Zion and
  Jerusalem.
  Jews in the Land of Israel.
  National Thoughts.
Amir, D. What Seeps In.
Bible, O.T. David's Lament.
  Psalm 114: "When Isrʼel, freed from Pharoh's
  hand."
Byron, G. Oh! Weep for Those.
Curzon, D. Tour of Ein Kerem, A.
Futuransky, L. Israel Revisited.
Ginsberg, A. Galilee Shore.
Greenberg, U. Ones Living by Their Virtue Say,
  The.
  Poem of Blessing.
  Splendor from the Splendid.
Guri, H. Current Account.
Hahn, S. X: October 1 *(morning)*.
Hajjaj, N. Hebron (Al-Khalil).
Hefer, H. Paratroopers are Weeping, The.
Hurvitz, Y. Around the Water Near the Birds.
Jarrell, R. Jews at Haifa.
Kaufman, S. Déjà Vu.
  Security.
Khoury, N. People of Olives.
Kumin, M. In the Absence of Bliss.
Mar, Y. Anonymous Squad, An.
Muhawi, I. Bad Moon Rising.
Nye, N. Small Vases from Hebron, The.
Omer, H. Squad in the Land, A.
Rakosi. Israel.
Ravikovitch, D. Unusual Autumn, An.
  You Can't Kill a Baby Twice.
Rawson, J. Border, The ("Leaping from the
  eucalyptus branch, the wild desert pigs.").
Reznikoff. Kaddish.
Rich, A. Memory says: Want to do right? Don't
  count on me.
Riordan, M. Holy Land, The.
Samaras, N. Notes in Jerusalem.
Shabtai, Aharon. Our Land.
  Sharon Resembles a Person.
  War.

Shapiro, M.　To Jerusalem, 1990.
Shemer, N.　On Silver Wings.
Sillitoe.　Synagogue in Prague.
Sivan, A.　Concerning the Rehabilitation of the Disabled from the Wars of Israel.
To Live in the Land of Israel.
Someck, R.　Transparent.
Tuqan, F.　To Etan: An Israeli Child from the Kibbutz Ma'oz Hayim.
Tur-Malka, A.　Heralds of New Jerusalem.
Mirror of the Battle.
Unknown, fr. Terezin Concentration Camp.
Dusk.
White, D.　Epistle of Love and of Consolation unto Israel, An.
X, M.　Palestine.
Yosef, H.　Jaffa, July 1948.
Reflections on a Dove.
"Zelda.".　Place of Fire, A.

Israeli Poetry
Bat-Tzion, Ellla.　Peace.

Issa (Kobayashi Issa)
Budbill.　What Issa Heard.
Milosz, C.　Reading the Japanese Poet Issa (1762–1826).
Williams, C. K.　Spring: another / joke.
That the world / is going.
Wright, C.　Night Journal.

Italian Poetry
Cacciatore, E.　First Warning Sign: Epiphany.

Italians, The
Barolini.　Having the Wrong Name for Mr. Wright.
Bona.　Amazone.
Browning, R.　Italian in England, The.
Capone.　In Answer to Their Questions.
Clements, A.　Why I Don't Speak Italian.
Downie.　Italians Are Excited, The.
Elledge.　14 Reasons Why I Mention Mario Lanza to the Man I Love Every Chance I Get Tonight.
Gillan.　Arturo.
Growing Up Italian.
Public School No. 18: Paterson, New Jersey.
Gioseffi.　Bicentennial Anti-Poem for Italian-American Women.
Leto.　Anna Magnani at the Castro.
For Talking.
Mary Morelle Show, The.
Palma.　Coming of Age.
Repetto.　6th Grade—Our Lady of Pompeii.
Romano, R.　Bucket, The.
But My Blood.
So I Lost My Temper.
Rossetti, C.　Enrica, 1865.
Saffoti.　Espresso.
Stefanile.　How I Changed My Name, Felice.
Viscusi.　Autobiography.
Wagner, M.　Miss Clement's Second Grade.

Italy
Aretino.　If famous Apelles with his hand of art.
Ash, J.　Memories of Italy (Broken Sestina).
Bona.　Dream Poem.
Browning, E.　I heard last night a little child go singing.
Part II.
Browning, R.　Fra Lippo Lippi.
Love among the Ruins.
Sordello.
Bush, N.　Noodling.
Campana.　Faenza.
Genoa.
Clampitt.　From a Clinic Waiting Room.
Clements, A.　Why I Don't Speak Italian.
Collins, B.　By a Swimming Pool Outside Siracusa.
Coward.　Bar on the Piccola Marina, A.
Cranch.　In the Palais Royal Garden.
Della Cruscans.　Notice to Tourists.
Denby.　Trastevere: A Dedication.
Villa d'Este.
Dickinson, E.　Our lives are Swiss.
Divakaruni.　Outside Pisa.
Doty, M.　Retrievers in Translation.
Fitzgerald, R.　Figlio Maggiore.

Flanagan, D. B.　Three Years from Sorrento.
Fortini.　Italy 1942.
Garrett, G.　Crows at Paestum.
Gilbert, S.　Mafioso.
Glück, L.　Vita Nova.
Graham, J.　Scirocco.
Swarm, The.
Guest, B.　Otranto.
Hayes, A.　City of Beggars, The.
Hecht, A.　Hill, A.
Hemingway.　Riparto d'Assalto.
Hugo, R.　Letter to Libbey from St. Regis.
Map of Montana in Italy, A.
Montesano Unvisited.
Spinazzola: *Quella Cantina Là.*
View from Cortona, A.
Jacobsen, R.　Catacombs in San Callisto, The.
Kemble.　Farewell to Italy.
Kirsch, S.　Thank-You Note.
Kunert.　Sestri Levante / Liguria 2.
Lawrence, D. H.　Cypresses.
Levine, P.　I Was Born in Lucerne.
Marinetti.　Correction of proofs + desires in speed.
Mayröcker.　Ostia Will Receive You.
McHugh, H.　What He Thought.
Milton.　On the Late Massacre [*or* Massacher] in Piedmont [*or* Piemont].
Montale.　You know this: I must lose you again and cannot.
O'Hara, F.　Rogers in Italy.
Older.　Two Worlds.
Pasolini.　Day of My Death, The.
Pelizzon, V.　Late Apostasy, A.
Pinkney, E.　Italy.
Porta.　I'm walking out on Rome.
Quasimodo.　From the Willow Branches.
19 January 1944.
Robinson, A.　To My Muse.
Rogers, S.　Ginevra.
Rossetti, C.　Italia, Io Ti Saluto!
Scammell, W.　One Man.
Sereni.　Each Time That Almost.
Stickney, T.　Autumn's done; they have the golden corn in, The.
In Ampezzo ("Only once more and not again— the larches.").
Tennyson, A.　Frater Ave Atque Vale.
Twomey, M.　Exchanges in Italy.
Walcott.　Italian Eclogues.
Wright, J.　Journey, The.
Zanzotto.　Campèa.

Itching
Nash, O.　Requiem: "There was a young belle of old Natchez."
Unknown.　As I Was A-walking by Yon Green Garden.

Ivy
Brontë, A.　Home.
Copus, J.　Pulling the Ivy.
Cross, E.　Hiedra.
Ivy.
Unknown.　Holly and Ivy.
Holly and the Ivy, The.

J

Jack and the Beanstalk
Dacey, P.　Jack, Afterwards.
Millay, E.　Bean-Stalk, The.
Riley, J.　Jack the Giant-Killer.

Jack the Ripper
Miller, V.　Light Reading.

Jackals
Macari, A.　Even Love.

Jackdaws
Bobrowski.　Trakl.
Dobie, James Frank.　Vanitas.
Earle, J.　Visiting Light.

Jackson, Andrew
Davidson, D.　Twilight on Union Street.
Mac Low.　1829.

Jackson, Mahalia
Lorde.　Day They Eulogized Mahalia, The.

Jackson, Michael
Komunyakaa, Y.　Never Land.

Jackson, Thomas Jonathan ("Stonewall")
Beecher, J.　One More River to Cross.
Lanier, S.　Dying Words of Stonewall Jackson, The.
Melville, H.　Stonewall Jackson.
Palmer, J.　Stonewall Jackson's Way.

Jacob (Bible)
Burns, R.　Patriarch, The.
Dickinson, E.　Little East of Jordan, A.
Levertov.　Jacob's Ladder, The.
Quarles.　On Jacob's Purchase.
Schwartz, D.　Jacob.
Unknown.　Wrestle on, Jacob.
Vaughan, H.　Jacob's Pillow, and Pillar.
Very.　Jacob Wrestling with the Angel.
Wesley, C.　Wrestling Jacob.

Jacob, Max
Goffette, Guy.　Max Jacob.
Warren, R.　Max Jacob at Saint Benoît.

Jacques Derrida
Andrews, T.　Cinema Vérité: Jacques Derrida and God's *Tsimtsum.*

Jade
O'Reilly, C.　Qing Dish, A.
Segalen.　In Praise of Jade.
Thompson, P.　Jade.
Yun Tusŏ.　Mud-encrusted piece of jade, A.

Jaguars
Hughes, T.　Jaguar, The.
Second Glance at a Jaguar.
Leconte de Lisle, C.　Jaguar's Dream, The.

Jails
Haavikko.　Soul against the state, The.
Hannan, M.　Inmates.
Unknown.　Deserter, The.
Midnight Special.
Wilde, O.　Ballad of Reading Gaol, The.
See also **Prisons and Prisoners**

Jam- and Jelly-making
Belloc.　On Jam.
Dienstfrey, Patricia.　Let the Raspberry Jam in the Crystal Jar Stand for It.
Feaver.　Crab Apple Jelly.
Kabysh, I.　Making Jam in July.
Kumin, M.　Making the Jam without You.

Jamaica, West Indies
Asservero, V.　Lock and Key, The.
Baugh, E.　Nigger Sweat.
Bennett, L.　Independance.
Independence Dignity.
Jamaica Oman.
Giscombe, C.　Black River, The.
Goodison.　Annie Pengelly.
Bam Chi Chi Lala.
Jamaica 1980.
Nanny.
Jones, E.　Song of the Banana Man, The.
Mackey, N.　Go Left Out of Shantiville.
Maxwell-Hall.　Jamaica Market.
McCallum, S.　Calypso.
In My Other Life.
Jamaica, October 18, 1972.

James, Henry
Kees.　Henry James at Newport.
Ransom, J.　Old Mansion.

James IV (1473–1513), King of Scotland
Aytoun, W.　Then the Provost he uprose.

James, Jesse
Benét, W.　Jesse James.
Unknown.　Jesse James.

January
Bishop, E.　Brazil, January 1, 1502.
Gibson, D.　January.
Goyette, Susan.　In This January.
Heath-Stubbs.　January.
Issa.　January.
Lewis, Emyr.　Hayes, The.
Macphee, K.　Night before the last day of January, The.
McCarriston.　January, Anchorage.
Nishiwaki Junzaburo.　January in Kyoto.
Rakosi.　January of a Gnat, The.

Ray, H. January.
Robinson, M. January, 1795.
Rothman, D. Whistling in January.
Voigt. January: "After days of putting down my poem."
Williams, W. January.

Japan
Blunden. Eastern Tempest.
Burn. In Japan.
Buson. Flash of lightning.
DiPalma. Annotations Tropes and Lacunae of the Itoku Master.
Donegan, P. Something Happened.
Eimers. Another Kimono.
Fenollosa. I remember an ancient Chinese picture kept over there in Daitokuji.
Separated East, The.
French, T. Holding the Line.
Glazer, M. Early Romance, Japanese Garden (*In the Heart of the City*).
Hawaiian Oral Tradition. Should I return to Japan?
Hoagland, E. From Ground Zero.
Inada. Father of My Father.
Kaneko Mitsuharu. Mount Fuji.
Kumin, M. How to Survive Nuclear War.
Kurihara Sadako. When We Say "Hiroshima".
Leithauser. In a Japanese Moss Garden.
In Minako Wada's House.
Lloyd, C. Looking at a Portrait Sculpture of the Indian Holy Man, Asanga, (Japanese, Mujaku, Flowered about 350 C.E.—Stands in the Kofukuji Treasure Hall of Nara Japan.
Lowell, A. Down, down, down, to the bottom of hte map.
Free Fantasia on Japanese Themes.
Mahon. Snow Party, The.
Milosz, C. Reading the Japanese Poet Issa (1762–1826).
Miyazawa Kenji. Pictures of the Floating World.
Snow on Saddle Mountain, The.
Morrissey, S. February: "There is no kindness in me here. I ache to be kind, but the weather."
Goldfish.
Nishiwaki Junzaburo. January in Kyoto.
Noguchi, Yonejiro (Yone). In Japan Beyond.
Oguma Hideo. Long, Long Autumn Nights.
Radden, V. When You Talk That Talk.
Retallack, J. Japanese Presentation I and II.
Ryuichi. My Imperialism.
Snyder, G. Feathered Robe, The.
Song. Girl Powdering Her Neck.
Su Man-shu. Exile in Japan.
Tesshu. On Visiting Sokei, Where the Sixth Patriarch Lived.
Thwaite, A. Great Foreign Writer Visits Age-Old Temple, Greeted by Venerable Abbess, 1955.
Tomlinson, C. Epilogue: "This advanced frontier."
Zipangu.
Zenmaro. Tanka: "Old Japan."
Tanka: "Work on the impossible."

Japanese Poetry
Schelling. Haibun the migration of haibun.

Japanese, The
Ayukawa Nobuo. Love: "I'm Japanese."
Calil, A. Blouse of Felt.
Dickey, J. Performance, The.
Elmslie, K. Japanese City.
Inada. Japs.
Issa. These sea slugs.
Kageyama, C. Mama.
Kaneko. Bailey Gatzert: The First Grade, 1945.
Mitsui. Nisei: Second Generation Japanese-American.
Mura. Argument: on 1942, An.
Argument: On 1942, An.
Blueness of the Day, The.
Robles. Ryokan the Crazy Snow Poet.
Rose, R. What the Japanese Perhaps Heard.
What We Heard About the Japanese.
Shimabukuro, Mira Chieko. After the Separation, Dad Takes Me to the Dance for the Dead.

Song. Ikebana.
Takamura Kotaro. Final Battle for the Ryūkyū Islands, The.
Unknown. Eager to become.
Once a Meiji Voice.
Uyematsu. Fortune Cookie Blues.
30 Miles from J-Town.
Wada, Hakuro. Even the croaking of frogs.
Wilner, E. Conversation with a Japanese Student.
Yamada. American Son.
Cincinnati.
Club, The.
Yoneda, Karl. New Year's Day on Angel Island.

Jaques
Stokesbury. Jaques Lured by Audrey.

Jasmine
Lorde. Night-Blooming Jasmine, The.
McKay, C. Jasmine.
Wakoski. Night Blooming Jasmine.

Jason
Dickinson, E. Finding is the first Act.
Flaccus, G. Book 7.
Williams, O. Golden Fleece, The.

Jays
Dickinson, E. No Brigadier throughout the Year.
Field. Flaw, A.
Hall, D. Short Circuit.
Lawrence, D. H. Blue Jay, The.
Stroud, J. Homage: Summer/Winter, Shay Creek.

See also **Blue Jays**

Jazz
Adcock, B. Poem for Dizzy.
Ai. Archangel.
Alexander, E. Giving birth is like jazz, something from silence.
Allen, S. I Say, Mr. A.
Andrews, L. Time Signature.
Arguelles, Ivan. I Danced with You Once Only Onliest One.
Ashanti. Just Another Gig.
Asim, J. Hip Hop Bop.
Aubert, A. Bessie.
Bessie Smith's Funeral.
Babb, Stanley E. Galveston.
Baker, H. Of Walter White's Father in the Rain.
Tobacco Warehouse Blues.
Ball, A. Jazz.
Baraka, I. All is One for Monk.
Am/Trak.
Monk's World.
Barlow, G. In My Father's House.
Mingus Speaks: Found Poems.
Barrax. Singer, The.
Barresi. Venice Beach: Brief Song.
Bauer, G. So You Want to Hear the Blues.
Brathwaite, E. Trane.
Brooks, G. Third Sermon on the Warpland, The.
We Real Cool.
Brooks, S. (That's the Way) Dixieland Started Jazz.
Brown, A. Assassination of Charlie Parker, The.
Brown, S. Cabaret.
Ma Rainey.
Buckley, C. Nostalgia.
Playing for Time.
Buddy. Callin Buddy / Bolden.
Carruth, H. Day very solid February 12th, 1944, A.
Exact beat from, The.
Fantastic Names of Jazz, The.
High above themselves. Above everything, flux, ooze.
Scrambled Eggs and Whiskey.
Castro, M. Blew It.
Cecil. Richard's Blues.
Chase, K. What You Can't See.
Collins, B. Man Listening to Disc.
Nightclub.
Collins, K. Trio.
Cooper, J. Wanda's Blues.
Cortez, J. How Long Has Trane Been Gone.

Jazz Fan Looks Back.
Crouch, S. Revelation, The.
Up on the Spoon.
Cummings, E. E. God pity me whom (god distinctly has).
Cushing, J. Autumn Leaves.
Every Time We Say Goodbye.
Lover Man.
Dana, R. Elegy for the Duke.
Davis, F. Jazz Band.
Davis, T. C. T. at the Five Spot.
Rogue and Jar: 4/27/77.
Deanovich. Requirements for Suggesting Fats Waller.
Doty, M. Almost Blue.
Dove, R. Canary.
Claudette Colvin Goes to Work.
Listen to the Sound of My Horn.
Eady. Chittlin's.
Hank Mobley's.
Jazz Dancer.
William Carlos Williams.
Ebb, F. And All That Jazz.
Nowadays.
Ellington, D. It Don't Mean a Thing (If It Ain't Got That Swing).
Espada. Majeski Plays the Saxophone.
Etter. Monk's Dream.
Stuffy Turkey.
Evans, M. Boss Communication.
Fabio. For Louis Armstrong, A Ju-Ju.
Feinstein, S. Blues Villanelle for Sonny Criss.
Christmas Eve.
Sonnets for Stan Gage (1945–1992).
Summerhouse Piano.
Ford, W. Of Miles Davis.
France, L. If Love Was Jazz.
Gex-Breaux, Q. Jazz Rain.
Gilbert, C. Resonance.
Gilyard, K. On Top of It All.
Giovanni. Genie in the Jar, The.
Goodwin, Everett. John Birks Gillespie: An Appreciation and Reflection.
Mom Used to Listen to Erroll Garner.
Gordon, G. Gas.
Tercios del Muerte.
Graham, M. After the War; When Coltrane Only Wanted to Play Dance Tunes.
Harjo, J. Healing Animal.
Harper, M. Alone.
Bandstand.
Brother John.
Dear John, Dear Coltrane.
For Bud.
Narrative of the Life and Times of John Coltrane: Played by Himself, A.
Reuben, Reuben.
Harris, Ken. You Don't Know What Love Is.
Harvey, S. Mighty Tropicale Orchestra, The.
Hayden, R. Soledad.
Hayes, T. Boxcar.
Henderson, D. Elvin Jones Gretsch Freak.
In Williams.
Lee Morgan.
Heyward, D. Jasbo Brown.
Highfill, M. Sea Breeze.
Hirsch, E. Art Pepper.
Hoagland, E. Love Jam.
Hollo. Le Jazz Hot.
Holm, B. Scott Joplin.
Hughes, L. Be-Bop Boys.
Jam Session.
Jazz Band in a Parisian Cabaret.
Jazzonia.
Neon Signs.
Hull, L. Lost Fugue for Chet.
Ornithology.
Hummer, T. Poem in the Shape of a Saxophone.
Jackson, A. Make/n My Music.
Ohnedaruth.
Jackson, M. L. Don Pullen at the Zanzibar Blue Jazz Cafe, 1994 [1997].
Don Pullen at the Zanzibar Blue Jazz Café [2006].
Jackson, R. 63rd and broadway.
Thelonious.

Jackson, R.   Shadows.
Jacobs, H.   Imagination in flight: an
    improvisational duet.
Jauss.   After the End of the World.
    Black Orchid.
    Last Solo: Charlie Parker, Hotel Stanhope,
        March 12, 1955.
Jeffers, L.   How High the Moon.
Jenkins, Joyce.   Piano Man.
Johnston, P.   Blaupunkt (choruses Pepper Adams
    never took).
Joseph, A.   My Father's Heroes ("He gloried in
    the feats.").
Kaliba, L.   Bebop Trumpet.
Kaufman, B.   Battle Report.
    No More Jazz at Alcatraz.
    Round About Midnight.
    Walking Parker Home.
Kelly, R.   Ode to Language.
Kessler, R.   Elm Tree on Lafayette Street, The.
Kgositsile.   Acknowledgement.
    For Art Blakey and the Jazz Messengers.
Komunyakaa, Y.   Copacetic Mingus.
    Elegy for Thelonious.
    February in Sydney.
    Speed Ball.
    Twilight Seduction.
Lagrone.   I Heard the Byrd.
Larkin, P.   For Sidney Bechet.
Lazer, Hank.   8 / (in transit).
Lindsay, V.   Jazz of This Hotel, The.
Long, D.   Black Love Black Hope.
Longley, M.   Words for Jazz Perhaps.
Loy.   Widow's Jazz, The.
Lux.   Night above the Town.
Madgett.   Echoes.
    Plea for My Heart's Sake.
Madhubuti.   Don't Cry, Scream.
    Knocking Donkey Fleas off a Poet from the
        Southside of Chi.
Madigan.   Curtis Fuller.
    Stereo Time with Booker Little.
Matthews, W.   Accompanist, The.
    Bud Powell, Paris, 1959.
    Buddy Bolden Cylinder, The.
    Mingus at The Showplace.
May, K.   Valentine's Day.
McClure, M.   For Monk.
    Jazz at the Intergalactic Nightclub.
McGrath, T.   Guiffre's Nightmusic.
McPherson, S.   Some Metaphysics of Junior
    Wells.
    Suspension: Junior Wells on a Small Stage in a
        Converted Barn.
Meltzer, D.   17:II:82.
Miller, V.   Dirge in Jazz Time.
Mitchell, A.   From Rich Uneasy America to My
    Friend Christopher Logue.
Moerman.   Louis Armstrong.
Mor.   Coming of John, The.
Moskowitz, F.   Bird Lives.
Neal, Gaston.   Monk.
O'Hara, F.   Day Lady Died, The.
Okantah.   Afreeka Brass.
    Southern Road.
Oliphant.   Denton.
Powell, N.   Coda: Thelonius Monk, d. 17
    February 1982.
Prejsnar, Mark.   Abusive! that's the word!
Redmond.   Distance.
Rivard.   Baby Vallejo.
Rivers, C.   Underground.
Rodgers, C.   Written for Love of an
    Ascension—Coltrane.
Rukeyser, M.   Bunk Johnson Blowing.
    Homage to Literature.
Rux, C. H.   Suite Repose.
Sadiq, M.   Tuskegee Experiment.
Salaam.   Directions for Understanding Modern
    Jazz Criticism.
    I Just Heard John Buffington Died.
Sandburg, C.   Jazz Fantasia.
Senghor.   To New York.
Seyburn, P.   You and Them.
Shirley, A.   Hours Musicians Keep, The.
Simic.   Crepuscule with Nellie.

Simmons, J.   Didn't He Ramble.
Sneeden.   Coltrane and My Father.
Someck, R.   Blues for Elliot Sharp.
Spellman, A.   Did John's Music Kill Him?
    John Coltrane: An Impartial Review.
Stein, K.   Past Midnight, My Daughter
    Awakened by Miles Davis' *Kind of Blue*.
Thomas, L.   Historiography.
Tolson, M.   Lambda.
    Mu.
    Nu.
Troupe.   One for Charlie Mingus.
    Poem for My Father; for Quincy Trouppe, Sr.
Van Cleave, R.   Hamlet at the Paris Aerobleu.
Venaille, Franck.   In Praise of Robert Desnos.
Vian, Boris.   One Day.
Walton, A.   Dissidence.
Weaver, A.   Left Bank Jazz Society, The.
    Thelonius.
Welburn.   Ben Webster: "Did You Call Her
    Today?".
Williams, M.   Death of Chet Baker, The.
Williams, W.   Shoot It Jimmy!
Wojahn.   Satin Doll.
Wright, J.   End of an Ethnic Dream, The.
Yenser, S.   Harmonie du Soir.
Yevtushenko [or Evtushenko].   Saints of Jazz.
Young, A.   Art of Benny Carter, The.
    Jazz as Was.
    Lester Leaps In.
Zavatsky.   Live at the Village Vanguard.
Zimmer.   But Bird.
    Duke Ellington Dream, The.
    Romance.
    Sitting with Lester Young.

Jealousy
Archilochus.   What Gyges so golden has doesn't
    matter to me.
Berssenbrugge.   Jealousy.
Brown, E.   Bitcherel.
Brown, S.   Chillen Get Shoes.
Browning, R.   My Last Duchess.
Catullus.   He Seems to Me Almost a God.
    To Aurelius.
Coleridge, M.   Jealousy.
    Other Side of a Mirror, The.
Comden, B.   Not Mine.
Couzyn.   Spell for Jealousy.
Davies, W. H.   J is for Jealousy.
    No Man's Wood.
Doolittle, Hilda.   At Ithaca.
"Ephelia.".   To J.G. on the News of His
    Marriage.
    To My Rival.
Frost, C.   Sexual Jealousy.
Ghalib, M.   Ghazal 25.
Glück, L.   Horse.
Gomez de Avellaneda.   Imitating an Ode by
    Sapho.
Graham, D.   Robert Frost's Writing Desk.
Green, A.   Not Mine.
Hass, R.   Forty Something.
Hausen, F.   When I parted from my Good.
Heaney, S.   Dream of Jealousy, A.
Howard, B.   Who Besides You.
Juana Inés de la Cruz.   Pleaure Given by
    Suspicion with the Rhetoric of Crying, The.
Kahal, I.   When I Take My Sugar to Tea.
Kahn, G.   No, No, Nora.
Kemble.   Petition, A.
Kuzmin.   Ah, those lips, kissed by so many.
Lamb, C.   First Tooth, The.
Lamb, M.   First Tooth, The.
Larkin, P.   Love Again.
Lisnyanskaya [or Lisnianskaia].   Jealousy: "I
    look out of the window at the retreating back."
Lope de Vega.   In Santiago.
Mayer, B.   Sonnet: "Beauty of songs your
    absence I should not show."
Mistral, G.   Ballad: "He passed by with
    another."
    Ballad: "He was strolling with another woman."
Nguyen, Hoa.   Captive and Able.
Norman, P.   When I Take My Sugar to Tea.
O'Hara, F.   For Grace, after a Party.
Ovid.   Elegy 1.4: "Thy husband to a banquet

goes with me."
"Perse."   Nocturne: "Now! they are ripe, these
    fruits of a jealous fate."
Poe.   Annabel Lee.
Porter, C.   Always True to You in My Fashion.
Prior.   Answer to Cloe [or Chloe] Jealous.
Restifo, Elaine.   Jealousy: "I've watched a
    young woman fondling three strands of her
    own hair."
Robinson, M.   Thousand Torments, A.
Sappho.   Arbor, The.
    Like the very gods in my sight is he who.
    To me it seems.
Scott, S.   Jealous Twain, The.
Service.   Shooting of Dan McGrew, The.
Shakespeare, W.   Now is the winter of our
    discontent.
    Sonnet 29: "When, in disgrace with fortune and
        men's eyes."
    Sonnet 41: "Those pretty [or petty] wrongs that
        liberty commits."
    Sonnet 61: "Is it thy will thy image should keep
        open."
    Sonnet 80: "O, how I faint when I of you do
        write."
Shen Manyuan.   Parody of the Other Woman.
Troupe.   Change: "Use to be eye would be
    laying there."
Tsaloumas.   Grudge, The.
Tsvetayeva [or Tsvetaeva].   Attempt at Jealousy,
    An.
    Attempt at Jealousy, An.
Turner, C.   Country Dance, A.
Unknown.   Frankie and Johnny [or Johnnie or
    Albert].
    Oh lute that I would like to see demolished!
    These Women Plunder My Husband.
Vliet.   Penny Ballad of Elvious Ricks.
Waniek.   Women's Locker Room.
Wroth.   Sonnet 13: "Free from all fogs but[t]
    shining fair[e], and clear [or cleere]."
    Sonnet 14: "Except my hart which you
    beestow'd before."
Yi Cha.   Neighbors.
Yi Chöngbo.   When the owl hoots.
Yi Sanghûi.   As My Will Concurred Not To My
    Being, It Were But Right and Equal to Reduce
    Me to My Dust.
See also **Envy**

Jeffers, Robinson
Everson, W.   Man-Fate, The.
    Poet Is Dead, The.
Hass, R.   Return of Robinson Jeffers, The.
Santos, S.   Jeffers Country.
Schmitz.   Carmel.
Tate, J.   Failed Tribute to the Stonemason of Tor
    House, Robinson Jeffers.

Jefferson, Thomas
Katz, J.   Taxonomy.
Mac Low.   1801.
Monks.   Twilight's Last Gleaming.
Niedecker.   Thomas Jefferson.
Williams, K.   From the Spirit of Phillis
    Wheatley to the Spirit of Thomas Jefferson (A
    Note 212 Years Later).

Jehovah's Witnesses
Pardo, P.   I was on the couch when the jehova's
    witnesses came.

Jellyfish
Kendall, M.   Philanthropist and the Jelly-fish,
    The.
Moore, M.   Jellyfish, A.

Jericho
Hugo, V.   Sound, sound forever, trumpet-calls of
    thought!
McGinley.   Women of Jericho, The.

Jerome, Saint
Dubie.   Elegy for Wright & Hugo.

Jerusalem
Alon, E.   In the Mount of Final Repose.
Amichai, Y.   I have nothing to say about the
    war.
    Jerusalem.
    Letter.
    Mayor.

Rustle of History's Wings, as They Used to Say Then, The.

Baxter, J.   I am dying now because I do not die.

Bible, *O.T.*   Song: "I am dark, daughters of Jerusalem."

Song: "I was asleep but my heart stayed awake."

Blake, W.   But turning toward Ololon in terrible majesty Milton.

Preface: "And did those feet in ancient time."

Celan.   You be like you, ever.

Ceni, A.   With What Courage.

Deloney.   Christs Prophesie of the destruction of this Cittie.

Description of the horrible Famine within *the Cittie of* Jerusalem.

Dove, R.   Dog Days, Jerusalem.

Erlich, S.   Jerusalem.

Fenton, J.   Jerusalem.

Fichman.   Jerusalem.

Fingueret, M.   Jerusalem.

Psalms (Chapter 137, Verse 5-6).

Futuransky, L.   Jerusalem, a Whirling Glass.

Jerusalem, Timeless.

More Chagall than Chagall.

Goldberg, L.   Heavenly Jerusalem, Jerusalem of the Earth.

Goldensohn, B.   Arch of Titus.

Hahn, S.   X: October 1 *(morning)*.

Jones, H.   Caught, April 2002—A Prayer for Peace.

Kaufman, S.   Mount of Olives, The.

Next Year, in Jerusalem.

Stones.

Melville, H.   Hostel, The.

Via Crucis.

Morley, D.   Jerusalem.

Nye, N.   Jerusalem.

Paley, G.   Warning, A.

Pasolini.   Southern Dawn.

Pasternak, B.   Evil Days, The.

Matthew 21:1–11.

Pere, V.   At the Wall.

Pinchas-Cohen.   Journey of a Doe.

Prigov.   Entry into Jerusalem.

Rich, A.   Jerusalem.

Rukeyser, M.   Traditional Tune.

Samaras, N.   Notes in Jerusalem.

Seferis.   Stratis the Sailor by the Dead Sea.

Shapiro, M.   To Jerusalem, 1990.

Shwarts [*or* Shvarts].   My heart's cloth I shall spread before the Savior's feet.

Tuqan, F.   Face Lost in the Wilderness.

Unknown.   Hierusalem.

Vinograd.   Jerusalem Walked thru War.

Weisz, O.   Jerusalem, I am a pilgrim.

"Zelda.".   Place of Fire, A.

See also **Zion**

Jesters

Beer, P.   Ninny's Tomb.

Sill.   Fool's Prayer, The.

Storace.   King Lear Bewildered.

Yeats.   Cap and Bells, The.

Cap and Bells, The.

See also **Fools**

Jesuits

Quarles.   I wish a greater knowledge, then t'attaine.

Scott, F.   Brébeuf and His Brethren.

Jesus Christ

Abrahams, L.   Writer in sand, The.

Achterberg.   Trinity.

Adams, F.   To the Christians: "Take, then, your paltry Christ."

Adams, J.   Lord of all worlds, let thanks and praise.

Alabaster, W.   Divine Sonnet, A.

Of the Reed That the Jews Set in Our Saviour's Hand.

To Christ.

Upon the Ensigns of Christ's Crucifying.

Amis, K.   New Approach Needed.

Anatolius.   Fierce was the wild billow, Dark was the night.

Andrade, E.   Fable.

Appleman, P.   Mary.

Matthew 1:18–25: Now the birth of Jesus Christ took place.

Arnold, M.   Progress.

Artaud.   I Spit on the Innate Christ.

To be Christ is not to be Jesus Christ.

Askew, A.   Ballad Which Anne Askew[e] Made and Sang When She Was in Newgate, The.

Auden.   From "The Prolific and the Devourer".

Terce.

Austin, J.   Love of Christ, The.

Avison.   Dumbfounding, The.

Baraka, I.   When We'll Worship Jesus.

Barnes, D.   Chuang Tzu and Hui Tzu*.

Baxter, C.   Diptych: Jesus and the Stone.

Baxter, R.   Good Shepherd, The.

Beasley.   What Did You Come to See.

Witness.

Bell, M.   Sounds of the Resurrected Dead Man's Footsteps (#3).

Berkeley, S.   Mass is Over, The.

Bernard of Clairvaux.   Jesus, Thou Joy of Loving Hearts.

Berrigan, D.   Assembled sirs. The courtesies afforded us by the Dali Lama.

Prayer: "I left Cornell / with half a wit; six mismated socks."

Berryman.   Carpenter's Son, The.

Bevington, L.   Dreamers?

Bible, *N.T.*   Blessed be the Paps which Thou hast Sucked.

Luke 7; She Began To Wash His Feet with Teares and Wipe Them with the Haires of Her Head.

Birnbaum, M.   Visiting Jesus.

Birney.   El Greco: Espolio.

Blake, W.   How Sweet I Roamed [*or* Roam'd] from Field to Field.

Lamb, The.

Memorable Fancy, A.

Night.

Piping Down the Valleys Wild.

Preface: "And did those feet in ancient time."

To Tirzah.

Was Jesus Humble? or did he.

Blok.   Making tracks.

Bly, R.   French Generals, The.

Bonar.   Here, O my Lord, I see Thee face to face.

Borges.   John 1:14 (1969).

Luke 23:39–43; One of the criminals.

Matthew 5:1–12; Seeing the crowds, he went up on the mountain.

Braxton, C.   Apocalypse.

Brecht, B.   Luke 2:8–20; And in that region there were shepherds.

Mary.

Brewer, G.   Christ, the End.

Breytenbach.   There Is Life.

Brontë, C.   Pilate's Wife's Dream.

Brooks, P.   O Little Town of Bethlehem.

Brooks, W.   Pilate Remembers.

Brown, T.   Disguises.

Browning, E.   Thought for a Lonely Death-Bed, A.

Browning, R.   Epistle Containing the Strange Medical Experience of Karshish, the Arab Physician, An.

Bunyan.   Christian Loses His Burden.

Burns, E.   Jesus Speaks to the Church at Eastertime.

Burnside, J.   Parousia.

Byrd.   Lulla Lullaby.

Byrom.   Christians, awake, salute the happy morn.

Cairns, Scott.   More Earnest Prayer of Christ, The.

Translation of Raimundo Luz, The: My Imitation.

Cardenal.   Unrighteous Mammon (Luke 16:9).

Carmichael, A.   Do We Not Hear Thy Footfall?

Carson, A.   God's Christ Theory.

Cary, P.   Hymn: "How dare I in thy courts appear."

Causley.   I Am the Great Sun.

Cendrars.   Newspaper.

Chesterton.   Donkey, The.

Chichester.   Day by Day.

Citino.   Situation No. 33: The Feast.

Clare of Assisi.   Blessing Attributed to Saint Clare, The.

Clarkson.   Behold, the King of glory now is come.

Cleghorn.   Comrade Jesus.

Clephane.   Beneath the cross of Jesus.

Clifton, L.   How Is He Coming Then.

Spring Song.

Clough.   Across the Sea, Along the Shore.

Coffin, C.   Advent of our God With eager hearts we greet, The.

Cohen, L.   Suzanne [Takes You Down].

Coleridge, M.   He Came unto His Own, and His Own Received Him Not.

I saw a stable, low and very bare.

Coleridge, S.   My Baptismal Birthday [*or* Birth-Day].

Collier, M.   Robert Wilson.

Columba.   Maker on High, The.

Cowper, W.   Stricken Deer, The.

There is a fountain filled with blood.

Crabbe, G.   Resurrection.

Craig, David.   Gospel Poem #1.

Crashaw.   Christ's Victory.

Come See the Place Where the Lord Lay.

In the Holy Nativity of Our Lord God.

Love thou art absolute, sole Lord.

Luke 11: Blessed Be the Paps Which Thou Hast Sucked.

Neither Durst Any Man From That Day Ask Him Any More Questions.

On the Wounds of Our Crucified Lord.

To Our Blessed Lord upon the Choice of His Sepulchre.

To the Noblest and Best of Ladies, the Countess of Denbigh.

Upon the Asse That Bore Our Saviour.

Cruz e Sousa.   Good Friday.

Cullen, C.   Christus Natus Est.

Daumal.   Jesus Before Pilate.

Matthew 27:11–24; Now Jesus stood before.

Davie, D.   Pilate.

Davis, D.   Christmas Poem, A.

Davis, F.   Christ is a Dixie Nigger.

De León, L.   At the Ascension.

Denby.   Mykonos.

Dickey, J.   Magus, The.

Dickinson, E.   At least—to pray—is left—is left.

God is a distant—stately Lover.

I shall know why—when Time is over.

One crown that no one seeks.

Savior must have been, The.

So well that I can live without.

Word made Flesh is seldom, A.

Dimitrova.   Units of Measurement.

Doddridge, P.   Hark, the glad sound! the Saviour comes.

Donne.   Oh my black[e] soul[e]! now thou art summoned.

Resurrection, Imperfect.

Spit in my face ye [*or* you] Jew[e]s, and pierce my side.

What if this present were the world's last night?

Why are we[e] by all creatures waited on?

Donovan, K.   Underneath Our Skirts.

Doolittle, Hilda.   Splintered the crystal of identity.

Dove, R.   On Veronica.

Drummond, W.   Miserable Estate of the World Before the Incarnation of God.

Dunbar, W.   Done is a battell [*or* battle] on the dragon blak [*or* black].

Duncan, R.   What I Saw.

Eliot, T. S.   Luke 2:21–40; And at the end of eight days, when he was circumcised.

Matthew 2:1–12; Now when Jesus was born.

Elliott, E.   Three Marys at Castle Howard, in 1812 and 1837, The.

Elmslie, K.   Easter for Joe.

Erdrich.   Christ's Twin.

Etheridge, K.   Annunciation.

Fanthorpe.   Nativities.

Ferlinghetti, L.   Sometime During Eternity.

Field. Constancy.
They Shall Look on Him.
Fletcher, G. Crucify Him!
Fletcher, P. Hymn, An: "Wake, O my soul; awake, and raise."
Ocean of Light.
Flynn, L. Miracle of F6/18, The.
Flynn, N. Emptying Town.
Fordham. Christ Child, The.
Nativity, The.
Galvin, J. Station (4).
Gascoigne. Gloze Upon This Text, *Dominus iis opus habet*, A.
Gascoyne. Ecce Homo.
Gerhardt. Commit thy way unto the Lord.
Glatstein, J. Matthew 5:38–48; "You have heard that it was said, 'An eye'".
Glück, L. Luke 2:1–7; In those days a decree went out from Caesar Augustus.
Nativity Poem.
Grant, S. O worship the King all glorious above.
Graves, R. In the Wilderness.
Griffiths, A. Lo, between the Myrtles Standing.
Grotz, J. Kiss of Judas.
Guevara, M. To Christ Crucified.
Hall, D. Carol, A.
Matthew 21:18–22; In the morning.
Small Fig Tree, A.
Hall, J. For Christmas Day.
Hardy, T. Unkept Good Fridays.
Harris, R. Call, The.
Hartwig. Who Says.
Havergal. Just When Thou Wilt.
Trusting Jesus.
Haviaras, Stratis. Easter Feast.
Hayden, R. Full Moon.
Heard, J. Birth of Jesus, The.
Heath-Stubbs. For the Nativity.
Hemans. Mary at the Feet of Christ.
Olive Tree, The.
Herbert, G. Aaron.
Affliction (2).
Affliction (3).
Agony [or Agonie], The.
Bunch of Grapes, The.
Dawning, The.
Dialogue, A.
Easter Wings.
Holdfast, The.
Iesu.
Jesu.
Longing.
Love (3): "Love bade me welcome: yet my soul drew back."
Mary [or Marie] Magdalene.
Paradise.
Redemption.
Son[ne], The.
Herbert, Z. Matthew 27:3–10; When Judas, his betrayer, saw.
Meditations of Mr. Cogito on Redemption.
Passion of Our Lord painted by an anonymous hand from the Circle of Rhenish Masters, The.
Speculations on the Subject of Barabbas.
Herebert. My Folk, What Have I Done Thee?
Who is This that Cometh from Edom?
Herrick. Good Friday: Rex Tragicus, or, Christ Going to His Cross[e].
His Offering, with the Rest, at the Sepulcher.
His Saviour['] Words, Going to the Cross[e].
No Coming to God without Christ.
Hill, G. Lachrimae Verae.
Hillman, B. Little Furnace.
Höllerer. Particularly Effortless He Lay.
Holst-Warhaft. In the End Is the Body.
Hope, A. Easter Hymn.
Gloss to Matthew V 27–28.
Luke 24:36–49; As they were saying this, Jesus.
Hope, M. INRI.
Hopkins, G. As Kingfishers Catch Fire.
Lantern Out of Doors, The.
Moonless darkness stands between.
Myself unholy, from myself unholy.
Soldier, The.

Spring: "Nothing is so beautiful as Spring."
Starlight Night, The.
Windhover, The.
Housman. Carpenter's Son, The.
Easter Hymn.
Mark 16:19–20; So then the Lord Jesus, after.
Hristic. That Night They All Gathered on the Highest Tower.
Hristov, Boris. Sign from Heaven, A.
Hudgins. Christ as a Gardener.
Consider.
Dead Christ.
Hughes, L. Christ in Alabama.
Feet o' Jesus.
Goodbye Christ.
Shepherd's Song at Christmas.
Hughes, T. God, A.
Matthew 27:45–56; Now from the sixth hour there was darkness.
Ingelow. And didst thou love the race that loved not thee?
Ishikawa Takuboku. At my words, "Christ was a man".
Jarry. Passion of Jesus Considered as an Uphill Race, The.
Jeffers, H. Five Note Range of Sorrow.
Jennings, E. Annuciation, The.
Christ Seen by Flemish Painters.
Johnson, J. Go Down Death (A Funeral Sermon).
Johnson, L. Church of a Dream, The.
Jones, D. In the middle silences of this night's course the blackthorn.
Jonson, B. Carol.
Hymn[e] on the Nativity [or Nativitie] of My Saviour, A.
Jordan, J. All the World Moved.
"K.". How Firm a Foundation.
Kamienska. Luke 10:38–42; Now as they went on their way.
Kane, P. Disciples Asleep at Gethsemane.
Kelly, T. Head That Once Was Crowned with Thorns, The.
Second Advent, The.
We sing praise of him who died.
Kipling, R. Nativity, A.
Sons of Martha, The.
Kirchwey. Matthew 8:20; And Jesus said to him.
Kizer, C. Oration, The.
Kossman. John 13:21–30; When Jesus had thus said, he was troubled.
Pilate's Wife.
Kuhar, M. Suburban buddha, coffeehouse christ.
Kunitz, S. He.
Lanier, E. Now Pontius Pilate is to judge the cause.
Lanier, S. Ballad of Trees and the Master, A.
Crystal, The.
Larkin, P. Matthew 10:1.
Laux, D. Prayer: "Sweet Jesus, let her save you, let her take."
Levertov. Ikon: The Harrowing of Hell.
On a Theme from Julian's Chapter 20.
Salvator Mundi: Via Crucis.
Lewis, G. Chernobyl Icon.
Lillenas, H. Wonderful grace of Jesus, Greater than all my sin.
Llwyd, M. Excuse, The.
What? summer now? divisions ring.
Lope de Vega. Lachrimae Amantis.
Shepherd Who With Your Tender Calls.
What Do I Have, That You Seek Out My Friendship?
López Colomé, P. Cachorros, Los.
Cubs, The.
Love, C. Modern Love Poem, A.
Lowell, R. Drunken Fisherman, The.
Lowry, R. Up from the Grave He Arose.
Luther. From Heaven Above to Earth I Come.
MacDiarmid, H. Innumerable Christ, The.
O Jesu Parvule.
MacDonald, C. And Cause His Countenance to Shine upon You: *Corpus Christi, Texas*.
Machado Ruiz. I love Jesus, who said to us.

Maksimovic. Matthew 22:15–22; Then the Pharisees went and.
Mangan, J. Christ, as a light.
Marks, Corey. Portrait of a Child.
Martin, C. Easter Sunday, 1985.
Marvell. Coronet, The.
Mason, R. On the Swag.
Maurus. To Grimold, Abbot of St. Gall.
McAuley, J. In the Twentieth Century.
Jesus.
Melville, H. Arch, The.
Mendelssohn Anna. Footsteps climb whereas they decend.
Merton. Cana.
Mew. Madeleine in Church.
Meynell, A. Advent Meditation.
Christ in the Universe.
Unto Us a Son Is Given.
Milman. Crucifixion, The.
For thou didst die for me, O Son of God!
Hymn: "When our heads are bowed with woe."
O help us, Lord! Each hour of need.
Milosz, C. Luke 5:1–11; While the people pressed upon him.
Mark 5:21–43; And when Jesus had crossed.
Matthew 28:1–6; Now after the sabbath.
Matthew 4:1–11; Then Jesus was led up by the spirit.
Milton. Athens.
Hymn on the Morning of Christ's Nativity.
On the Morning of Christ's Nativity.
Mitchell, S. Luke 10:25–37; And behold, a lawyer.
Matthew 13:1–9; That same day Jesus.
Mohr, J. Silent Night.
Silent Night! Holy Night!
Montgomery, J. Come to Calvary's holy mountain.
Moorer. Benefits of Sorrow.
Sympathy.
Mordecai. Jesus Is Condemned to Death.
Mugrón, Abbot of Iona. Christ's Cross.
Muir, E. Killing, The.
Muske, C. Coming Over Coldwater.
Neander, J. Praise to the Lord the Almighty.
Nemerov. John 3:1–15; Now there was a man.
Nicodemus.
Sacrificed Author, A.
Newman, J. Desolation.
Newton, J. "In Evil Long I Took Delight".
Nijhoff. Soldier Who Crucified Jesus, The.
Noyes, A. Resurrection.
Okigbo. On the New Year.
Olson, E. Ballad of the Scarecrow Christ.
Oswald, H. S. O let him whose sorrow.
Owen, W. At a Calvary near the Ancre.
Palmer, R. Hymn: "Jesus these eyes have never seen."
Pankey. Luke: 24:13–32; That very day two of them.
Parker, D. Maid-Servant at the Inn, The.
Parra, N. Who are my friends / the sick / the weak / the poor in spirit.
Pasternak, B. Christmas Star, The.
Evil Days, The.
Garden of Gethsemane, The.
Hamlet.
Magdalene (I).
Mark 14:26–42; And when they had sung.
Matthew 21:1–11.
Matthew 26:47–56; While he was still speaking, Judas came.
Miracle, The.
Patterson, R. Harlem Suite.
Peacock, M. Devolution.
Pembroke, M. He placed all rest, and had no resting place.
Perillo, L. Urban Legend.
Perronet. All Hail the Power of Jesus' Name.
Pestel [or Pestell]. Psalm for Christmas Day.
Pfeiffer, E. Cruse of Tears, The. A Russian Legend.
Pierman. Apparition, The.
Pinsky. From the Childhood of Jesus.
Pound, E. Ballad of the Goodly Fere.
Powell, C. Nativity.

Powers, Arthur. Bag Lady's Body in the Financial District, A.
Prigov. Entry into Jerusalem.
Prudentius. Ye clouds and darkness, hosts of night.
Quarles. Christ and Our Selves.
 I saw him dead; I saw his Body fall.
 Upon the Day of Our Saviour's Nativity.
Quarles, J. At Home.
Ralegh, S. On the Card[e]s, and Dice.
Ransom, J. Armageddon.
Ray, H. Prayer: "O Christ, who in Gethsemane."
Richardson, J. J-O-Y.
Rilke. John 11:30–44; Now Jesus had not yet come into the village.
 John 20:11–18; But Mary stood weeping outside the tomb.
 John 2:1–12; On the third day there was a marriage.
 Mary at Peace with the Risen Lord.
 Matthew 26:17–29.
 Matthew 27:57–61; When it was evening, there came a rich man.
 Olive Garden, The.
 On the Marriage at Cana.
 Pietà.
Robinson, E. Calvary.
 Christmas Sonnet, A.
Rodgers, C. Mama's God.
Rodgers, W. It was a lovely night.
Rolle of Hampole. Cantus Amoris 2.
 Prayer to Jesus 1.
 Song of the Passion, A.
Rossetti, C. Better Resurrection, A.
 Bruised Reed Shall He Not Break, A.
 Christmas Eve.
 If Only.
 Long Barren.
 Lord, Grant Us Calm.
 Three Enemies, The.
Rossetti, D. Virgin and Child, by Hans Memmeling, A; in the Academy of Bruges.
Rossetti, W. M. Jesus Wept.
Rothenberg, J. Visions of Jesus.
Rugo. Pietà: "What she holds is the unimaginable."
Rukeyser, M. Holy Family.
 Traditional Tune.
Ryman. Nunc Puer Nobis Natus Est.
 Ther is a chielde, a heuenly childe.
Saint Patrick. St Patrick's Breastplate.
 Saint Patrick's Breastplate; or, The Deer's Cry.
Sandburg, C. Early Lynching.
Sandys, G. Hymn Written at the Holy Sepulchre in Jerusalem.
Sassoon, S. Christ and the Soldier.
Savitz, M. Stations of the Crux.
Schlegel. Be Still, My Soul.
Sedulius Scottus. Battle is joined on the open plain.
Sexton. Jesus Asleep.
 Jesus Dies.
 Jesus Suckles.
 Jesus Unborn.
Shaw, L. It is as if infancy were the whole of incarnation.
 Onlookers.
Sheperd. Who hath not knowne or herd.
Shomer. Falling for Jesus.
Smart, C. Crucifixion of Our Blessed Lord.
 Nativity of Our Lord and Saviour Jesus Christ, The.
Smith, R. Teresa.
Smith, S. Airy Christ, The.
 Christmas.
 Was He Married?
Smither. Mission Impossible.
Southwell. Burning Babe, The.
 Child[e] My Choice [or Choyse], A.
 Christ[e]'s Childhood[e].
 New Heaven, New War[re].
 New Prince, New Pomp[e].
Spenser, E. Sonnet 68: "Most glorious Lord of Life that on this day."
Staff. Portrait.

Steele, P. Cana.
Stone, S. Church's One Foundation, The.
Tadic. Jesus.
Tasso. Drearie trumpet blew a dreadfull blast, The.
Tate, N. While Shepherds Watched [Their Flocks by Night].
Taylor, E. Christ's Reply.
 Meditation. Joh. 15.5. Without me yee can do nothing.
 My Metaphors are but dull Tacklings tag'd.
 Reflexion, The.
 View, all ye eyes above, this sight which flings.
Tennyson, A. Ring Out, Wild Bells.
 Strong Son of God, immortal Love.
 Sweet after showers, ambrosial air.
Thomas Aquinas. Thee we adore, O hidden Saviour, thee.
Thomas, D. This Bread I Break.
Thomas, R. S. Pietà.
Thompson, C. Empty Tomb, The.
Thompson, F. Hound of Heaven, The.
Thompson, P. Death and Resurrection.
Toomer. Gum.
 Nora.
Traherne. Hymn upon St. Bartholomew's Day, An.
 Wonder.
Trapnell, A. O he is a rest that requires.
Tsvetayeva [or Tsvetaeva]. Bethlehem.
 Magdalene.
Turner, C. Dream, A.
Tynan Hinkson, K. Sheep and Lambs.
Unamuno. This Spanish Christ that hasn't lived.
Unknown. A! Sone, tak hede to me whos sone thou wast.
 Bitter Withy, The.
 Child this Day is Born, A.
 Children Do Linger.
 Christ the Apple-Tree.
 Christ was the Word that spake it.
 Deep Spring.
 Don't Be Weary, Traveller.
 Down to the Mire.
 Farewell, this world! I take my leve for ever.
 For Thy Sake Let the World Call Me Fool.
 Give Me Jesus.
 Go in the Wilderness.
 Good Christian men, rejoice.
 Guest, The.
 Hail, thou once despised Jesus.
 Hand by Hand We Shall Us Take.
 Harrowing, The.
 His Son's / A Jew.
 Hypocrite and the Concubine, The.
 I passed thurgh a gardyn grene.
 I pray you, be mery and synge with me.
 I Sing of a Maiden.
 I Wish I Been Dere.
 In Slumber Late.
 Jesu Christ, my Leman Swete.
 Just Now.
 Lo, How a Rose E'er Blooming.
 Lo, how a rose is growing.
 Lord, Remember Me.
 Man Be Merie as Bryd on Berie.
 Mervell nothyng, Joseph, that Mary be with chyld.
 No Man Can Hinder Me.
 Nowel, el, el, el, el!
 Nowell Sing We.
 O Come, All Ye Faithful.
 O come, O come, Emmanuel.
 Petition to Father and Son and Holy Ghost, A.
 Rock O' My Soul.
 Rose That Bore Jesu, The.
 See! Here, My Heart.
 Sodeynly affrayed, half wakyng, half slepyng.
 Steal Away to Jesus.
 That mayden mylde hir childe dide kepe.
 Ther bloweth a cold wynd to-day, to-day.
 There Is a Balm in Gilead.
 To-morrow shall be my dancing day.
 We Will March Through the Valley.
 Were You There When They Crucified My Lord?

 Were you there when they crucified my Lord?
 Whan I thenke on the rode.
 When morning gilds the skies.
 Whoso saw on rode.
 Wounds, as Wells of Life, The.
Vallejo. Black Messengers, The.
Vaughan, H. H. Scriptures.
 Incarnation and Passion, The.
 Lamp[e], The.
 Midnight.
 Peace.
 And do they so?
 Search, The.
 Shepherds [or Shepheards], The.
Verlaine. Parsifal.
 Voice of Pride: shout of blaring trumpets.
Verstegan [or Verstegen]. Lullaby: "Upon my lap my sovereign sits."
Very. Cross, The ("I must go on, till in my tearful line.").
 Garden, The.
 New Birth, The.
 Serpent, The.
 Son, The.
Villa, E. It is world of the back hune wone it is.
Vogelweide. Now My Life Has Gained Some Meaning.
Waters, M. Christ at the Apollo, 1962.
Watkyns. Gardener, The.
 Upon Christ's Nativity or Christmas.
Wesley, C. Catholic Love.
 Hark, how all the welkin rings! Glory to the King of Kings.
 Rejoice! The Lord is King.
White, D. Epistle of Love and of Consolation unto Israel, An.
Whitman, W. To Him That Was Crucified.
Whittier. Dedication: "I would the gift I offer here."
 Over-Heart, The.
 Pardon, Lord, the lips that dare.
Wickham. To a Crucifix.
Wilbur, R. Matthew 8, 28 ff.
 Matthew 8:28–34; And when he came to the other side.
Wilde, O. Ave Maria Gratia Plena.
 E Tenebris.
 Santa Decca.
Williams, Stephanie. Maid of Need, A.
Williams, William. Christian Pilgrim's Hymn.
Williams, William Carlos. Gift, The.
Winslow, P. God on a Bike.
Wordsworth, W. Hymn: "Blest are the moments, doubly blest."
Wright, James. Saint Judas.
Wright, Judith. Eli, Eli.
Wu Li. Singing of the Source of Holy Church.
 Tune: "Happily Flitting Oriole".
Yeats. I am Judas.
 Matthew 28:16–20; Now the eleven disciples went to Galilee.
 Stick of Incense, A.
Yi Sang. Two People : 1.
 Two People : 2.
Young, E. Submarine Jaunt, A.
Zinzendorf. Jesus, thy blood and righteousness.
Zucker, R. Post card (central park).
See also **Infant Jesus; Savior; Son of Man, The**

Jewelry
Alvi, M. Presents from My Aunts in Pakistan.
Bamber, J. Broken Necklace.
Forrest, G. Baubles, Bangles, and Beads.
Herrick. Seest thou those diamonds which she wears.
Hong Yunsuk. Discourse on an Ornament.
Howe, J. Lost Jewel, The.
Milton. Sabrina Fair.
Mirabai [or Mira Bai]. Coffer with the Poisonous Snake, The.
Montague, J. Locket, The.
Pope, A. Sol through white curtains shot a tim'rous ray.
Rakosi. Amulet.
Robin, L. Diamonds Are a Girl's Best Friend.
Teasdale. Jewels.
Trinidad. Moonstones.

Tuglik. Tuglik's Song.
Unknown. As the thread of my breath.
   Bracelets on my arms, jewelry around my neck.
   Do not hold me too closely in your arms.
   I used to have bracelets, I do not wear them now.
   Jewels wherever we look.
   My lover is the ornament around my neck. They wear.
Vagura. Love Poem, A.
Wakoski. Ring, The.
Wright, R. Baubles, Bangles, and Beads.
See also **Rings**

Jewish, Hebrew, and Yiddish Poetry
Bass, F. I am a Jew.
Ginsberg, A. Your last night in the darkness of the Bronx—I phonecalled—thru hospital to secret police.
Kunert. Theatrum Mundi.
Rosenfeld, M. Memorial to Triangle Fire Victims.

Jezebel
Brown, E. Jezebel to the Eunuchs.
Higgins, F. Song for the Clatter-Bones.
Morgan, Elin Llwyd. Contemporary Jezebel, The.

Jigsaw Puzzles
Boe, D. Jigsaw Puzzle.
Oppen. Solution.

Joan of Arc
Hemans. Joan of Arc, in Rheims.
Lowell, M. Rouen, Place de la Pucelle.
McCarriston. Coursier de Jeanne d'Arc, Le.
Péret. Joan of Arc.
Zubick, K. Evolution of Appetite.

Job (Bible)
Ashbery, J. Cæsura.
Bejerano, M. In a slick, black bodysuit Job stood before me.
   It has all begun with still waters.
   Job: I was cast onto a new life cycle.
Bible, *O.T.* Chapter 2 (Fragment).
   Chapter 42.
Glazova, A. Grant of death, The.
Kaufman, S. Job's Wife.
Macpherson, J. Beauty of Job's Daughters, The.
Pacheco, J. Job 18, 2.
Pagis, D. Homily.
Sewell, E. Job.
Shelton, R. Job the Father.
Sylvester, J. Job's Epitaph.
Unknown. Then Job spoke and cursed his day and chanted and said.

Jockeys
Hayward, D. To the Man Saying "Come on Seis" at Hollywood Park.
Higgins, F. Old Jockey, The.
See also **Horse Racing**

Jogging and Joggers
Ali, A. Jogger on Riverside Drive, 5:00 A.M., The.
Stafford, W. Run before Dawn.
See also **Running and Runners**

Johannesburg, South Africa
Brooks, G. Near-Johannesburg Boy, The.
Kuzwayo, E. Choice, The.
Serote. City Johannesburg.
Smith, P. Meanwhile, in Rwanda.

John of Austria
Chesterton. Lepanto.

John Paul II, Pope
Sanders, B. For What It's Worth.

John, Saint
Powell, D. A. When He Comes He Is Neither Sun Nor Shade: a China Doll.
Wheelwright. Bread-Word Giver.
Wylie. Peter and John.

John the Baptist, Saint
Beasley. What Did You Come to See.
Constable, H. To St John Baptist.
Drummond, W. For the Baptiste.
Rilke. 4. Mary's Visit with Elizabeth.
Smart, C. Nativity of St. John the Baptist, The.
Unknown. John, John, of the Holy Order.

Very. John.

Johnson, Lionel
Yeats. In Memory of Major Robert Gregory.

Johnson, Lyndon Baines
Duncan, R. Up Rising.
Friedlander, B. L. B. J. Tapes, The.
Huffstickler. Johnson City, Texas.

Johnson, Samuel
Jenyns. Doctor Johnson.
"Pindar.". Town Eclogue, A.
Synge. To the Oaks of Glencree.

Johnston, James Hugo
Johnson, M. James Hugo Johnston.

Jokes
Bacharach, D. New Joke, The.
Bennett, L. Dry-Foot Bwoy.
Dumdum. To My Mother.
Gilbert, W. Family Fool, The.
Li Po. To Send to Tu Fu as a Joke.
Pinsky. Impossible to Tell.
Unknown. My lover cannot take a joke.

Jonah (Bible)
Bancquart. Portrait of Jonah with woman.
Drayton. Song of Jonah in the Whale's Belly, The.
Jarrell, R. Jonah.
Melville, H. Ribs and Terrors, The.
Merriam, E. Wonderful Whale, The.
Owen, G. Jonah and the Whale.
Shapiro, D. In a Blind Garden.
Speyer. To a Song of Sappho Discovered in Egypt.
Unknown. Jonah and the Whale.

Jonathan (Bible)
Bible, *O.T.* David's Lament.

Jones, John Paul
Unknown. Yankee Man-of-War, The.

Jonson, Ben
Carew, T. To Ben Jonson.
Herrick. His Prayer to Ben Jonson.
   My Ben.
   Ode for Him [*or* Ben Jonson], An.
   Upon Ben Jo[h]nson.
Howell, J. Upon the Poet of His Time, Ben Jonson: His Honoured Friend and Father.
Kizer, C. Not Writing Poems about Children.
Randolph, T. Answer to Master [*or* Mr.] Ben Jonson's Ode, to Persuade Him Not to Leave the Stage, An.
   Gratulatory to Mr. Ben Johnson for His Adopting of Him to Be His Son, A.
Waller, E. Upon Ben Johnson [*or* Jonson].
Wilson, E. Nursery Vignette.

Joplin, Janis
Matthews, W. Penalty for Bigamy Is Two Wives, The.
Phillips, R. Death of Janis Joplin, The.
Speakes. Mama Loves Janis Joplin.

Jordan, Michael
McManus, J. Commercials exaggerate.
Troupe. Forty-one Seconds on a Sunday in June, in Salt Lake City, Utah.

Joseph (Bible, *O.T.*)
George, D. Asenath.
Herbert, G. Joseph's Coat.
Hubert. Joseph in Carcere.
Nemerov. September, the First Day of School.
Reznikoff. Israel II.
Sylvester, J. But, fair Iëmpsar (wife of Potiphar).

Joseph (Chief Joseph)
Niatum. Tribute to Chief Joseph, A.

Joshua (Bible)
Hugo, V. Sound, sound forever, trumpet-calls of thought!
Kennedy, X. Joshua.
Ostriker. Story of Joshua.
Roux, S. Sunrise.
Unknown. Battles of Joshua.
   Joshua Fit de Battle of Jericho [*or* ob Jerico].

Journalism and Journalists
Black, S. To a War Correspondent.
Cernuda. To Larra with Some Violets.
Forché. Memory of Elena, The.

Heaney, S. Whatever You Say Say Nothing.
Kipling, R. Journalists.
Mathews, C. Journalist, The.
McFadden, R. For the Record.
Moorer. Southern Press, The.
Ofeimun. Beyond Fear.
Sandburg, C. Buttons.
Smith, P. Meanwhile, in Rwanda.
Wolfe, H. British Journalist, The.
See also **Magazines; Newspapers**

Journeys
Bador, B. Odyssey.
Basho. Sick on a journey.
Bishop, M. Ah, To Be In.
Bly, R. Pitzeem and the Mare.
Cavafy. Ithaca.
Ch'u Yüan. On Encountering Trouble.
García Lorca. Song of the Rider ("Córdoba. / Distant and alone.").
Grosjean, Jean. Trial Desert.
Harryman. Next.
Hesse. Evil Time.
Jaccottet. Clouded Skies.
Kyger. Unexpectedly, from the outside.
Li Po. Hard Is the Journey.
Løvgreen, G. Life's Dovey Junctions.
Meddeb, Abdelwahab. On Forgotten Tracks.
Norton, O. Bound.
Okolo, M. Suspended Elegy, A.
Paljor, N. Robert Frost and I.
"Perse." Song: "I have halted my horse by the tree of the doves."
Prichard, C. Bargain, The.
Ray, D. Journey with Basho, A.
Rossetti, D. 73: The Choice ("Think thou and act; to-morrow thou shalt die").
Schubert, D. Peter and Mother.
Seminole Oral Tradition. Song for the Dying.
Spivack, K. Scroll, The.
Ts'ao Chih. Emotion.
Warsh. Inside Long Treks.
White, L. World as I Found It, The.
Wise, N. To Papaji.
Yu Hsin. Running Into Snow While Journeying Through the Suburbs.

Joy
Adesuyi, N. Rains.
   Springs.
Al-Ghuzzi. Quatrains for Joy.
Bachmann. Kind of Loss, A.
Bell, M. We Have Known.
Blake, W. Eternity.
   Infant Joy.
Bonnefoy. All, the Nothing, The.
Brome. Epithalamy.
Brown, G. Old Women, The.
Browning, R. Now.
Bunin. Flowers, and tall-stalked grasses, and a bee.
Buson. Autumn evening.
Butler, S. Love.
Campo, C. At Times I Say: Let's Try to Be Joyous.
Carruth, H. Alive.
Centolella. Joy.
Ceravolo. Happiness in the Trees.
   White Fish in Reeds.
Chalkhill. Coridon's Song.
Chang Yang-hao. Ch'ü Yüan's "sorrow".
Chang Yü. Merchant's Joy, The.
Chasin. Joy Sonnet in a Random Universe.
Chŏng Kŭgin. In Praise of Spring.
Coleridge, M. Solo.
Crews, J. Rejoice.
Cullen, C. From Life to Love.
Cummings, E. E. If everything happens that can't be done.
   You Shall Above All Things Be Glad and Young.
Dacre, C. Kiss, The: "Greatest bliss, The."
Dalton, R. Ars Poetica.
Davies, W. H. Best Friend, The.
   Joy and Pleasure.
Dawe, B. Going.
Dawe, G. Solstice.
De Angelis. Reasons for the Beginning.

Denby. Trastevere: A Dedication.
Dickey, J. In the Marble Quarry.
Dickinson, E. I Can Wade Grief.
Donne. Ecstasy, The.
Drummond de Andrade. Diminutive.
Dunbar, P. Little Brown Baby.
Emerson, R. Water: "Water understands / Civilization well, The."
Etter. Great Northern.
Field. To Christina Rossetti.
Gallup. Pretty Beads.
Gandlevsky, S. Oh, how the lilacs are this May! Bulging-large bunches fell.
Glück, L. Nativity Poem.
Godolphin. Thou Joy of my Life.
Greenberg, U. I thirst for water; wine is my need no longer.
Gregory, A. What Have I Gained?
Griffiths, B. South Song.
Guidacci. Before Our Encounter.
Gundy, J. Ancient Themes: The Night.
Ha-Levi, J. Summer.
Harms. Joy Addict, The.
Hernández, M. To Smile with the Joyful Sadness of the Olive Tree.
Herzberg. Morning.
Hierro, José. Fe de vida.
Hikmet. Fifth Letter.
Hillman, B. Adult Joy.
Hoagland, T. Grammar.
Hongo. Stomping with Pettit on the Battenkill.
Hopkins, G. Hurrahing in Harvest.
Howe, F. First Chance Twice.
Hulme, T. Embankment, The (The fantasia of a fallen gentleman on a cold, bitter night).
Inuit Oral Tradition. Utitia'q's Song.
Ishikawa Takuboku. Tanka: "Accidentally / having broken a teacup."
Jong, E. Testamant (Or, Homage to Walt Whitman).
Jonson, B. To Sir Henry Cary.
Joseph, A. Learning to Laugh.
Jourdan, Pierre-Albert. Prayer: "Let innocence remain."
Keats. Fancy.
Keble. Rainbow, The.
Killigrew, A. Farewell to Worldly Joys, A.
Levertov. Ache of Marriage, The.
Matins.
Triple Feature.
Lewis, S. I'm Sitting on Top of the World.
Li Po. Drinking Alone in the Moonlight.
Lu Chi. Summoning the Recluse.
MacKay, I. Meeting, The.
Majorino. Doing.
Martial. Just half our three score years and ten.
McCord, D. Blessed Lord, What It Is to Be Young.
McFadden, D. 6. Tortured by Kahlil Gibran.
Miles, S. Plumbers.
Milton. L'Allegro.
To the Lord General Cromwell.
Mistral, G. Lady Spring.
Morse, G. He kneels on the rumpled bed.
Nabbes. Song: "What a dainty life the milkmaid leads!"
Nashe [or Nash]. Spring, the Sweet Spring.
Nasrin. Eve Oh Eve.
Nguyễn Chí Thiện. Travel with Grief— Goodbye to Joy.
Ni Ghallchóir, C. Spark of Joy, The.
Owenson. Joy.
Parish. Sweet Lorraine.
Peele. Write write yow Croniclers of Tyme and Fame.
Phillips, C. Reach, The.
Po Chü-i. Chrysanthemums in the Eastern Garden, The.
Porter, C. At Long Last Love.
I Get a Kick Out of You.
Pyungyang Ungee. Reply to a Poem by Donglim.
"Rachel." [or "Rahel."]. Tiny joys, joys like a lizard's tail.
Ray, H. Shadow and Sunrise.
Reverdy. On the Threshold.

Rexford. Joy: "It's joy to be up in the morning when the dew's on the grass and clover."
Robin, L. Hooray for Love.
Roethke. All the Earth, All the Air.
Rossetti, C. Birthday, A.
Rukeyser, M. Reading Time : 1 Minute 26 Seconds.
Rumi. Say Yes Quickly.
Tonight with wine being poured.
Salzman, E. Grandmother.
Sarton, M. Small Joys.
Scott, G. All Our Joy Is Enough.
Seferis. Interlude of Joy.
Sexton. Welcome Morning.
Sherburne. Weeping and Kissing.
Shushtarī, A. My beloved has visited me and my moments have become sweet. My beloved listened to me.
Sidney. Sonnet 69: "O joy, too high for my low style to show."
Smith, S. Word, The.
Spenser, E. Epithalamion: "Ye learned sisters which have oftentimes."
Prothalamion.
Sri Sri. Man walks on the bridge and gives away the change in his, A.
Steele, T. Eros.
Stone, J. Gaudeamus Igitur: A Valediction.
Strode. Opposite to Melancholy.
Swift, J. Satirical Elegy on the Death of a Late Famous General, A.
Swirszczynska [or Swir]. Thank You, My Fate.
Tarkos, Christophe. 67 Words with One Vowel and One Consonant.
Teasdale. Answer, The.
Tiruvalluvar. Gift of Children, The.
Tolson, M. Victor Garibaldi.
Trần Thái-Tông, King. To the Monk Dúc Son at Thanh-phong Monastery.
Tsanev, Ivan. Fine Day.
Tzara. Waking.
Unknown. Come and be a flower on my chest.
Harper's Song for Inherkhawy, The.
In al this world nis a murier lyf.
Jun-zi yang-yang: The Gudeman's Come Hame (scoticè).
King Emanuel.
O Shout Away.
Vancrevel. About Time ("This silence at the sea's edge, so late in the afternoon.").
Veinberg, J. Last Shot.
Warren, R. Was It One of the Long Hunters of Kentucky who Discovered Boone at Sunset?
Watson, R. Of the Earth, Earthy.
Watts, M. Vision.
Webster, P. Jump for Joy.
Whitman, W. I Saw in Louisiana a Live-Oak Growing.
Wicks, S. Joy.
Wilbur, R. Hamlen Brook.
Wilde, L. Corinne's Last Love-Song.
Wordsworth, W. I Wandered Lonely as a Cloud.
Wright, J. Blessing, A: "Just off the highway to Rochester, Minnesota."
Wroth. Sonnet 38: "What pleasure can a bannish'd creature have."
Yi I. Where is the fourth bend?
Young, J. I'm Sitting on Top of the World.
Yüan Mei. Miscellaneous Feelings in the Sui Garden.

Joyce, James
Durcan. Bloomsday Murders, 16 June 1997, The.
Fox, Skip. Economics of Metonymy ("Balancing as metal, its sound, the metal in its sound.").
MacDiarmid, H. We must look at the harebell as if.
Mueller, L. Not Only the Eskimos.

Judaism and Jews
Abse. Footnote Extended, A.
Abu Ishaq al-Ilbin. O say to all of the inhāja, the full moons of the time, and the lions of the thicket.
Alkalay-Gut. So we begin to plan.
Amichai, Y. Biblical Meditations.

Course of a Life, The.
Jewish Time Bomb, The.
Jews in the Land of Israel.
National Thoughts.
Song of Lies on Sabbath Eve, A.
Antin. Real Estate.
Auden. Luke 23:26–38; And as they led him away.
Luke 23:26–38; And as they led him away.
Refugee Blues.
Baumel. Let Me In.
Samuel.
To the Parents of a Childhood Friend, a Suicide.
Baytelman, S. My Name is Shlomit.
Becker, R. Crypto-Jews, The.
Grief.
On the Eve of the Warsaw Uprising.
Spiritual Morning.
Yom Kippur, Taos, New Mexico.
Behar, R. Jewish Cemetery in Guanabacoa, The.
Survivals.
Bell, M. Book of the Dead Man #58, The.
Extermination of the Jews, The.
Getting Lost in Nazi Germany.
Israeli Navy, The.
Sound of the Resurrected Dead Man's Footsteps (#2).
Bibb. Wandering Jew, The.
Bobrowski. Elderblossom.
Borges. Spinoza.
Boss, L. At the Nuclear Rally.
Budy. Ellis Island, September 1907.
Celan. Death Fugue.
Death Fugue, A.
Deathfugue.
Fugue of Death.
Shibboleth.
Zurich, at the Stork.
Zürich, the Stork Inn.
Chess, R. Growing Up in a Jewish Neighborhood.
No Music.
Two and One.
Yiddish Poets in America.
Daiches, J. Jewish Cemetery, Frankfurt.
Daumal. Matthew 27:11–24; Now Jesus stood before.
Davie, D. Pilate.
Davison, P. Birthright, The.
Dead Sea, The.
Delphi.
Gift of Tongues, The.
Erlich, S. Garden of Shanah.
Ettinger, E. Excerpts from the Sabbath Dream Book.
Micrographic Manuscript, Miniature (1).
Ewer. Chosen People, The.
Falk. Home for Winter.
Sabbath Morning.
Shulamit in Her Dreams.
Ficowski. Assumption of Miriam from the Street in the Winter of 1942, The.
Both Your Mothers.
Execution of Memory, The.
Girl of Six from the Ghetto Begging in Smolna Street in 1942, A.
Fingueret, M. Eve in Eden.
My Father.
Tovu-Vavohu.
Finkelstein, C. Not Responsible.
Florsheim. Jewish Singles Event, The.
Futuransky, L. More Chagall than Chagall.
Garlick, R. Heiress, The.
Gelbtrunk, A. God said to Abraham.
Gerhardt, I. G. M. Rejected Gift, The.
Gershon. Experiments with God.
Race.
Ginsberg, A. Visiting Father and Friends.
Yiddishe Kopf.
Glaser, M. Magnificat!
Preparations for Seder.
Goetsch, D. Nobody's Hell.
Goldbarth. Gallery.
Shoyn Fergéssin: "I've Forgotten" in Yiddish.
Steerage.

World Above Suffering, A.
Goldensohn, B. Arch of Titus.
Gray, A. Why Your Grandfather Stopped
  Playing the Viola.
Greenberg, B. Man in the Moon, The.
Greenberg, U. I have never been at the top of
  wind-played Olympus.
  Ones Living by Their Virtue Say, The.
  Poem of Blessing.
Guri, H. Heritage.
Hacker, M. Boy, The.
  Graffiti from the Gare Saint-Manqué.
Hamburger, M. Treblinka.
Harris, R. Riding Over Belmore Park.
Hecht, A. More Light! More Light!
Hershon. Minnesota Farmers Blame Bad Crop
  on Jews.
Hill, A. Between Worlds.
Hirsch, E. Ancient Signs.
  My Grandfather's Poems.
Hollander, J. At the New Year.
  Letter to Jorge Luis Borges: Apropos of the
    Golem.
  Song at the End of a Meal.
Howe, F. White Lines.
Jacob, M. Yellow Star Again, The.
Jarrell, R. Jews at Haifa.
Kalina, R. I Am of the Tribe of Yehuda.
  Ritual.
  Testimonies.
Kalinski, E. 1936–1986.
Kamenetz. History of the Invisible.
  Missing Jew, The.
  This Is the Map.
  Why Ten Men?
Kamenszain. Eliahu.
  Torah Braids.
Klein, A. Autobiographical.
  Heirloom.
  Still Small Voice, The.
Klepfisz. Fradel Schtok.
  My Mother's Sabbath Days.
  These words are dedicated to those who died.
Klugman, E. She Who Listens.
Klugman, S. God's Body.
Knut. Woman from the Book of Genesis, A.
Kolmar. Judith.
Kramer, L. Shoemaker's Wife, The.
Kumin, M. Chain, The.
  In the Absence of Bliss.
  Living Alone with Jesus.
Lazarus, E. Crowing of the Red Cock, The.
  In Exile.
Levine, P. Old Testament, The.
Lifshin. Being Jewish in a Small Town.
  Yahrtzeit Light, The.
Limburg, J. Seder Night with My Ancestors.
Logghe. Her First Jew.
  Insomnia Litany.
Longfellow, H. Jewish Cemetery at Newport,
  The.
Lourie. Jewish.
MacDonald, C. And Cause His Countenance to
  Shine upon You: Corpus Christi, Texas.
Mak. Farewell to Russia.
Meltzer, D. Tell Them I'm Struggling to Sing
  with Angels.
  Tishah B'Ov / 1952.
  Who's the Jew.
Melville, H. Concerning Hebrews.
Merrill, J. Correct but cautious, that first night,
  we asked.
Mezey. To Levine on the Day of Atonement.
  Wandering Jew, The.
Moore, T. Weep, Children of Israel.
Moraes, D. Rendezvous.
Morris, Matt. Sham Jew.
Mulligan. Shylock.
Muñiz Huberman. Cabalists, The.
  Manuscript.
  Obsession.
  Sanctuary.
Murphy, M. Common Ground.
Nemerov. Debate with the Rabbi.
Obenzinger. This Passover or the Next I Will
  Never Be in Jerusalem.

Osherow. Song for the Music in the Warsaw
    Ghetto.
  To Eva.
  Yiddish Muses, The.
Ostriker. Bride, The.
  Eighth and the Thirteenth, The.
  If your mother is a Jew, you are a Jew.
  Meditation in Seven Days, A.
  Meditation in Seven Days, A.
  Opinion of Hagar, The.
Ozick. Origins, Divergences.
  When That with Tragic Rapture Moses Stood.
  Wonder-Teacher, The.
  Yom Kippur, 5726.
Paley, G. Some days I am lonesome I want to
  talk to my mother.
  Warning, A.
Parnell, T. From the black beach and broad
  expanse of sea.
Pastan. At the Jewish Museum.
  Name, A.
  Old Photograph Album.
  Passover.
  Short History of Judaic Thought in the
    Twentieth Century, A.
Pelletiere, M. Under Her Crib.
Piercy. At the New Moon: Rosh Hodesh.
  Candle in a Glass, A.
  Growing Up Haunted.
  Maggid.
Pinchas-Cohen. Her, Me, and Yochanan.
  Journey of a Doe.
  Yearning of Karakashian, The.
Pinsky. Avenue.
  Impossible to Tell.
  In Berkeley.
  Night Game, The.
  Poem about People.
  Poem with Refrains.
Plath. Daddy.
Plotnick, H. M. Jewish.
Press, K. Ancestors.
Quarles. Meditatio Septima.
Rakosi. Israel.
  Sandalwood Comes to My Mind.
  Services.
Ravikovitch, D. Blood Heifer.
Replansky. Six Million, The.
Reznikoff. Highway I was walking on, The.
  Joshua at Shechem.
  Kaddish.
  Luzzato.
  When the Second World War began.
Rich, A. At the Jewish New Year.
  Food Packages: 1947.
  Yom Kippur 1984.
Richman, L. Rue de Rosiers: To My Brother
  Fred.
Rosen, Ellen A. Out in the Cold.
Rosenberg, I. Jew, The.
Rosenberg, L. Edith B——and her mother on a
  Sunday afternoon.
Rothenberg, J. At the Castle.
  Cokboy.
  Connoisseur of Jews, The.
  In the Dark Word, Khurbn.
  Nokh Aushvits (After Auschwitz).
  Structural Study of Myth, The.
Rudman, M. What about that girl in first grade?
  The one who hopped up on her desk.
Rukeyser, M. Akiba.
  To be a Jew in the Twentieth Century.
Sachs, N. Chorus of the Dead.
  O the Chimneys.
Sadeh, P. At Nightfall, 1/27/91.
Sadoff. Nazis.
Sapgir. Psalm 137.
Schaeffer. May Levine.
  Yahrzeit.
Schultz, P. Bar Mitzvah, The.
  For My Father.
  For the Wandering Jews.
Schulzová, E. Evening in Terezin, An.
Scliar-Cabral. Fire and Embers.
  Sephirot.
Seiler. Digging in the Streets of Gold.

Selman, R. Descent.
  For the Field.
  Work Song.
Shapiro, A. Basement, The.
  Christmas Story, A.
  Mezuzah.
Shapiro, H. News, The.
Shapiro, K. Alphabet, The.
  151st Psalm, The.
Shapiro, M. To Jerusalem, 1990.
Sherman, J. For Mordecai Richler's Shalinsky
  Who Said "A Jew Is An Idea".
Shomer. Falling for Jesus.
  Freestyle, on the First of Tishri.
  From the Wailing Wall.
  Refusing the Call.
  Shards.
Shore. High Holy Days.
Simpson, L. Story About Chicken Soup, A.
Sivan, A. To Wither Like Weeds in an Easterly
  Wind.
Sklarew. After Theresienstadt.
  At three-thirty in the morning in America.
  On Muranowska Street.
  Three-Course Meal for the New Year, A.
Slonimski. Elegy: "No more, no more Jewish
  townships in Poland."
Smith, S. Songe d'Athalie.
Solomon, M. Comment on My Host, A.
Sommer, J. Mengele Shitting.
Spacks. Assimilation, The.
Spender, S. History and Reality.
Steinbergh. Religion.
Stern, G. Behaving Like a Jew.
  Dancing, The.
  Self-Portrait.
  Shirt Poem, The.
Swinburne. On the Russian Persecution of the
  Jews.
Szymborska, W. Still.
Teofilov, Ivan. Ortamezar—The Jewish Quarter.
Timrod. La Belle Juive.
Tsvetayeva [or Tsvetaeva]. Like a thick horse's
  mane.
Unknown. His Son's / A Jew.
  You and I.
Utkin. Tale of Red-Haired Motele, Mister
  Inspector, Rabbi Isaiah and Commissar Blokh,
  The.
Volach, Y. Tefillin.
Warren, R. Max Jacob at Saint Benoît.
Weisz, O. Sefarad.
Wiesel. Behold, God of Abraham, God of
  mercy.
Wilkie, B. Intuition, An.
Williams, C. K. Spit.
  Vessel, The.
Wilner, E. Miriam's Song.
  When Asked to Lie Down on the Altar.
"Zelda.". Place of Fire, A.
Zelenina, G. Shma Yisrael (Hear, O Israel).
Zolotow. Enemies.
Zukofsky, L. Fifth Movement: Autobiography.
  Song for the Year's End, A.

Judas Iscariot

De la Mare. Ballad of Christmas, A.
Grotz, J. Kiss of Judas.
Hecht, A. Handicap.
Herbert, Z. Hakeldama.
  Matthew 27:3–10; When Judas, his betrayer,
    saw.
Kossman. John 13:21–30; When Jesus had thus
  said, he was troubled.
  Judas' Reproach.
Malouf. Judas Touch, The.
Marks, Corey. Portrait of a Child.
Mason, R. Judas Iscariot.
Miller, V. Judas.
Nemerov. Historical Judas, The.
Pasternak, B. Garden of Gethsemane, The.
  Matthew 26:47–56; While he was still speaking,
    Judas came.
Roux, S. Sunrise.
Sitwell, O. Judas and the Profiteer.
Spender, S. Judas Iscariot.
Vinokurov. Mother of Judas, The.

Wright, J.   Saint Judas.
Yeats.   I am Judas.
Yi Yônju.   Clinic in a Dangerous Season 8, A.

Judges
Bible, *O.T.*   Psalm 58: "Judges, who rule the
   world by laws."
Carroll, L.   Mouse's Tale, The.
Cooley, N.   Mary Warren's Sampler.
Davie, D.   Pilate.
Dylan.   Lonesome Death of Hattie Carroll, The.
Espada.   Tires Stacked in the Hallways of
   Civilization.
Gilyard, K.   Letter.
Hauge.   Big Scales, The.
Hölderlin.   In the Days of Socrates.
Kees.   After the Trial.
Kipling, R.   Gallio's Song.
Kyger.   News bulletin from Keith Lampe.
Masters, E.   Justice Arnett.
McCarriston.   To Judge Faolain, Dead Long
   Enough: A Summons.
Roethke.   Matthew 7:1–2; "Judge not, that you
   be not".
Sáenz.   Angel.
Simmonds, Kevin.   White Man and the Judge,
   A.
Tkhorzhevskaya, V.   He wouldn't sign the death
   warrant.

Judgment
Adams, J.   Wants of Man, The.
Cowper, W.   Lines Written During a Period of
   Insanity.
Crane, S.   In Heaven, / Some little blades of
   grass.
Davis, O.   Small Number, A.
Derricotte.   After a Reading at a Black College.
Di Prima.   Death Sunyata Chant: A Rite for
   Passing Over.
Dickinson, E.   This Is My Letter to the World.
Galvin, J.   Station (4).
Han-shan.   I live in a little country village.
Heaney, S.   Haw Lantern, The.
   Stone Verdict, The.
Hirshfield, J.   To Judgement: An Assay.
Holway, J.   Throbbings.
Housman.   Laws of God, the Laws of Man, The.
Hugo, V.   Trumpet of Judgement, The.
Jarrell, R.   Variations.
Kipling, R.   Hour of the Angel, The.
Lear, E.   Limerick: "There was an Old Man of
   Whitehaven."
Peck, J.   Metal Denser Than, and Liquid, A.
Ransom, J.   Armageddon.
Sappho.   May winds and sorrows.
Senryū, K.   Yoshiwara.
Shakespeare, W.   Sonnet 121: "Tis better to be
   vile than vile esteemed."
Shelley, P.   As in that trance of wondrous
   thought I lay.
Su Tung-p'o.   Reading the Poetry of Meng
   Chiao: Two Poems.
Taylor, E.   Meditation 22 (First Series).
Trungpa, Chogyam.   His parents are having tea.
Unknown.   Little Black Train Is A-Comin'.
Warren-Moore.   For Etheridge Knight.
Wilner, E.   Judgment.
Wright, J.   At the Executed Murderer's Grave.

Judgment Day
Byron, G.   Vision of Judgment, The.
Cowley, A.   Resurrection, The.
Cruz Varela.   Kaleidoscope.
Faiz.   So Bring the Order for My Execution.
Farewell.   Quaerè.
Fletcher, P.   Against a Rich Man Despising
   Poverty.
Hart, K.   Last Day, The.
Herbert, G.   Death: "Death, thou wast once an
   uncouth hideous thing."
Herrick.   Gods Providence.
   Upon Himselfe Being Buried.
Hill, G.   Requiem for the Plantagenet Kings.
   They bespoke doomsday and they meant it by.
Johnson, J.   Judgment Day, The.
Khayr, A.   For men and women soon the day
   draws near.
Kipling, R.   Last Chantey, The.

Macaulay, T.   Dies IrÆ.
Metodiev, Ivan.   Sometimes: "Sometimes God
   resembles a kitten."
Nicholson, N.   Carol for the Last Christmas Eve.
Rosenberg, I.   One Lost, The.
Stickney, T.   And, the last day being come, Man
   stood alone.
Swift, J.   Day of Judgement, The.
Taylor, E.   Meditation 22 (First Series).
Unknown.   Day of Judgment, The.
   Heaven Bells, The.
   I Know Moon-Rise [*or* Moonrise].
   Muspilli.
   Pointless Pride of Man, The.
Vaughan, H.   Day of Judgement.
Watts, I.   How Doth the Little Busy Bee.
Whittier.   Abraham Davenport.
Wigglesworth.   Day of Doom, The: Verses 208–
   224.
Yeats.   Second Coming, The.
See also **Apocalypse; Armageddon; End of the
World**

Judith (Apocrypha)
Bibb.   Judith.
Cahun, C.   Sadistic Judith.
Feaver.   Judith.
Hyneman, R.   No. 5, Judith.
Lope de Vega.   Judith.
Menken.   Judith.
Ransom, J.   Judith of Bethulia.
Stanton, M.   Judith Recalls Holofernes.

Juggling and Jugglers
Morgan, E.   Cinquevalli.
Unknown.   Jolly Jugger, The.
Wilbur, R.   Juggler.

Julius Caesar
Murphey, John Collin.   Re-stringing 100 Year
   Old Wire.
Ursachi, Mihai.   Monologue, A.
See also **Caesar, Julius**

July
Bogan, L.   July Dawn.
Burke, J.   Sleigh Ride in July.
Busceti, G.   Suddenly on a day in July.
Clare, J.   July: "Loud is the Summer's busy
   song."
De Angelis.   July Has Come for the Dead.
Galina, M.   What, in July's honey heat, do you
   weep for, poor goy.
Gray-Kontar, D.   July.
Herrera y Reissig.   July.
Posey, A.   July.
Ray, H.   July.
Sanchez, S.   July.
Trommer, R.   Sonnet for July.

Jumping
Fisher, R.   Supposed Dancer, The.
King, R.   H E L P.
Knott.   Advice from the Experts.
Smith, S.   Harold's Leap.

June
Aridjis.   Rain is Falling, The.
Bei Dao.   June: "Wind at the ear says *June*."
Burns, R.   Red, Red Rose, A.
De Angelis.   Towards the Mind.
Dickinson, E.   I'm sorry for the Dead—Today.
Fordham.   June.
Hammerstein.   June Is Bustin' Out All Over.
Hanlo.   New Verses for June 7, 1951.
Kelly, R.   In June.
Larkin, P.   Cut Grass.
Lawrence, D. H.   Andraitx—Pomegranate
   Flowers.
Lowell, J.   Prelude to Part the First.
Mew.   June, 1915.
Nash, O.   Here Usually Comes the Bride.
Ray, H.   June.
Scott, D.   Night in June, A.
Sze.   June Ghazal.
Wilkinson, A.   In June and Gentle Oven.

Jungles
Brown, D.   When I Am 19 I Was a Medic.
Buzbee.   Sunday, Tarzan in His Hammock.
Hilliard, B.   Civilization (Bongo, Bongo,
   Bongo).

"K.".   Jungle Night.
Kipling, R.   Morning Song in the Jungle.
   Mowgli's Song Against People.
Lewis, A.   Grey monkeys gibber, ignorant and
   wise.
   Jungle, The.
Murray, L.   Louvres.
Nazareno, C.   Bohol's Tarsier Population.
Neruda.   Some Beasts.
Nguyễn Chí Thiện.   Jungle Night, A.
Ondaatje.   Henri Rousseau and Friends.
Scurfield, G.   Bitter Mangoes, The.
Shiraishi.   Wild Pigs of Kalimantan, The.
Smith, S.   Jungle Husband, The.
Wright, J.   Rainforest.

Juniper Trees
Behn, A.   On a Juniper-Tree, Cut Down to Make
   Busks.
Evans, A.   Juniper.
Heaney, S.   Sloe Gin.

Junk and Junkyards
Bolt, T.   I crossed.
Dickey, J.   Cherrylog Road.
Disch.   Garage Sale as a Spiritual Exercise, The.
Goldsmith, K.   One pair ridiculous gorilla
   slippers; 3 pairs of cheap shit sunglasses.
Kessler, R.   Elm Tree on Lafayette Street, The.
Merwin.   Drunk in the Furnace, The.
Reznikoff.   Among the heaps of brick and
   plaster lies.
Wilbur, R.   Junk.
Williamson, G.   Junkyard.

Jupiter (god)
Marlowe.   What is't, sweet wag, I should deny
   thy youth?
Ovid.   Europa and Jove.
   Io and Jove.
Wroth.   Sonnet 3: "Juno still jealous[e] of her
   husband Jove."

Jupiter (planet)
Sargent, E.   Planet Jupiter, The.

Justice
Algarin.   And in the U.S.A.
Austin, A.   Jameson's Ride.
Ba.   Seen to be Done.
Barker, G.   O Pearl and Breasted World.
Bible, *O.T.*   Psalm 58: "Do ye, o congregation."
   Psalm 58: "Judges, who rule the world by
   laws."
   Psalm 58. Si Vere Utique.
   Psalm 92. Bonum Est Confiteri.
Bowen, C.   Rain It Raineth, The.
Brown, J. *et al.*   Say It Loud—I'm Black and
   I'm Proud.
Burns, R.   Holy Willie's Prayer.
Cardenal.   Unrighteous Mammon (Luke 16:9).
Carson, A.   God's Justice.
Carson, C.   Judgement.
Castillo, O.   Before the Scales, Tomorrow.
Castro, R.   Justice of Men! I Go in Search of
   You.
Chapman, G.   Justice.
Coleridge, S.   Pitt.
Dante Alighieri.   Middle of life's journey; I,
   The.
Davies, W. H.   Inquest, The.
De Angelis.   July Has Come for the Dead.
Eady.   How I Got Born.
Eich.   Seminar for Backward Pupils.
Emerson, R.   Astræa.
Fearing.   Escape.
Fuertes.   Unknown Also Attracts Cowards, The.
Gelinas, D.   Dream of the Just, The.
   Sueño de los justos, El.
Goldberg, B.   Nights in the Constellation of the
   Tree Stepping from its Robe.
Gonzalez, R.   For the Other World.
Haavikko.   Before you ask for justice. Make
   sure.
Hall, D.   Small Fig Tree, A.
Hauge.   Big Scales, The.
Hughes, L.   Justice.
Jonson, B.   On Lieutenant Shift.
Kelber, M.   Pledge of Allegiance to the Family
   of Earth, A.

Khalifa, I.　No Need to Discourage Dreams.
Kinsella, T.　Another September.
Kinzie.　Sun and Moon.
Kipling, R.　Gallio's Song.
Klappert.　Court of Divine Justice, The.
Košek, M.　It All Depends on How You Look at It.
Lawrence, D. H.　When Wilt Thou Teach the People?
Levi, P.　Shemà.
Linden, M.　All We Ask Is Justice.
Lux.　Tarantulas on the Lifebuoy.
Masters, E.　Carl Hamblin.
Merwin.　Moths, The.
Ofeimun.　Judgement Day.
Ogundipe-Leslie.　On Reading an Archeological Article.
Quarles.　Luke 6.25.
Reznikoff.　Day of Atonement.
Roethke.　Matthew 7:1–2; "Judge not, that you be not".
Seferis.　Argonautica.
Shakespeare, W.　Fortune is Bardolph's foe, and frowns on him.
Simonides.　Distinguishes the fair and the shameful.
　It is hard to become a truly good.
Tellegen.　If Just For Once.
Unknown.　Fortune's Legacy.
　Lady of the Morning, The.
　Youth.
Vando.　Knife.
Various authors.　Because the govenment burdened the people.
　Many slandered him.
Volkow.　Arcana 8: Justice.
　Arcano 8: La Justicia.
Wallace-Crabbe.　Tribunal, The.
Whittier.　Cities of the Plain, The.
　Slave-Ships, The.
Wilner, E.　Judgment.
Wolff, Rebecca.　Criminal Justice System.

See also **Injustice**

Justification
Catullus.　To Aurelius and Furius.
Emerson, R.　Compensation ("Why should I keep holiday.").
Page, G.　Jerry's Plains, 1848.
Rich, A.　Women.
Shakespeare, W.　Sonnet 121: "Tis better to be vile than vile esteemed."
Unknown.　Among the yeomen's sons on my estate.
　Hebe and Ganymede.
　Sometimes I sauntered from my lone abode.
　Thou ermined judge, pull off that sable cap!
　Tree we plant will, when its boughs are grown, The.
　Wise Rejoice with Ganymede, The.
　Women as women, me had never charmed.

Juvenile Delinquency
Addonizio.　Broken Sonnets.
Brooks, G.　We Real Cool.
Hamer.　Charlene-N-Booker 4Ever.
Neely, L.　Rhonda, Age 15, Emergency Room.

K

Kabbala
Muñiz Huberman.　Cabalists, The.

See also **Cabala**

Kabul, Afghanistan
Unknown.　Go and fight in Kabul, my love.
　Tears are streaming down my face.

Kaczynski, Ted
Clapp, J.　Kaczynski.

Kafka, Franz
Hirsch, E.　Milena Jesenká.
Holub.　Jewish Cemetery at Olsany, Kafka's Grave, April, Sunny Weather, The.

Kahlo, Frida
Alexander, E.　Painting / (Frida Kahlo).
Dove, R.　Sonnet in Primary Colors.

Fanailova, E.　Frida's Album (*Frida Kahlo's Album*).
Guevara, M.　Make-Up.
Hand, M.　Tattooed Girl.
Hill, J.　Dream of Frida, A.
Rawson, J.　Self-portraits by Frida Kahlo.
Ruefle.　Rising Bodies.

Kalamazoo, Michigan
Gordon, M.　I've Got a Gal in Kalamazoo.
Kerlikowske.　Acceptance Speech.
Lindsay, V.　Kalamazoo.

Kālī
Basu Rāy, S.　Three Kalis appeared in Daksinesvar.
Bhāndārī, S.　Ma, You are Brahmani in the world of Brahma.
Bhattācārya, K.　Bee of my mind, The.
　Crazy Mind.
　Ever-blissful Kali.
　From now on.
　How can that black woman be so beautiful?
　How will You rescue me, Tara?
　Is my black Mother Syama really black?
　Kali / Is everything You do misleading?
　Kali! / Today in the dark grove.
　Kali, what family are You from?
　Kali, you have removed all my difficulties.
　Mother / You're always finding ways to amuse Yourself.
　Other than Your two red feet, Syama.
　So, forgetful Mahadeva.
　Tara, Mother / Lift me out by the hair.
　Tell me, Syama.
　Unperturbed at the battle.
　What's the fault of the poor mind?
　Who can describe the waves of Mother Syama's world?
　Who is this enchantress.
　Withered tree doesn't blossom, The.
Bhattācārya, M.　Ma, are you really dead?
　Oh Ma Kali, for a long time now.
　There's a huge hullabaloo in my lotus heart.
　What shall I say to You, Sankari?
　Your behavior proves how stingy You are, Ma.
Cakrabartī, N.　Can you claim to win.
Cakrabartī, M.　Ma, if You wore a Benarasi sari.
Dāsdatta, R.　Because You love cremation grounds.
Deb, A.　I started a fire with Kali's name.
Debī, T.　Tara, this is why I call upon You.
Dīnrām.　From the time of the womb.
　I've given up wanting.
　Ma, I've drunk Your poisoned nectar.
　Out of love for You.
Gupta, I.　I got some news from Kailasa!
Islām, N.　Oh hey, All-Destroyer.
　Syama Mother's lap a-climbing.
　Syama wakes on the cremation grounds.
　Talk to me, *javas*, talk to me.
　Wake up, Syama, wake up, Syama!
Māhtābcānd, M.　Who is this, all alone? Whose woman is She.
Mandal, B.　I'm not a child any more, Syama.
Mukhopādhyāy, K.　Am I afraid of the tenth day?
　Is there any treasure like the Mother's name?
Mukhopādhyāy, N.　Use your mental eye.
Mukhopādhyāy, R.　Why should I sit alone, eyes closed.
Nandī Majumdār, R.　Mind, I'm talking to you.
Nandī, R.　I understand now, Tara, I understand.
Pātunī, N.　Ma, Hara's Beloved, Tara.
Rāy, D.　It's no one else's fault, Syama Ma.
　Wake up, wake up, Mother!
　Who is this black.
Rāy, K.　Tara, You are Cintamayi, Full of Thought.
Rāy, M. R.　Give me food.
　Moon flashes in Her blessed face, The.
Rāy, N.　Everything is Your wish, Tara.
Rāy, R.　Who is this.
Rāy, T.　Wait a moment, Death.
Sāheb, A.　Victory to Yogendra's Wife, Great Illusion!
Sen, R.　At last I have a way to understand.

　Brother / This world.
　Death, get out of here!
　Her face / Is a spotless moon.
　Hey, it's not wine I drink.
　Hey! Who is She, dark as clouds.
　I have learned.
　It's not Siva.
　Kali, Ma.
　Kulakundalini, Goddess Full of Brahman, Tara.
　Let me tell You a thing or two, Tara.
　Ma, You're inside me.
　Meditate on Kali! Why be anxious?
　Mind, don't be duped by others' sneers.
　Mind, why this separation from the Mother's feet?
　Mind, you're still not rid of your illusions.
　Mother, make *me* Your treasurer.
　My Mind, my helmsman.
　Oh Kali Full of Brahman!
　Oh Mind, you don't know how to farm.
　Oh my Mind, worship Kali.
　Oh my Mind! You're just spinning.
　So, Mind / You've decided to go on pilgrimage?
　Supreme Savior of Sinners.
　Tara, what more are You planning?
　This is a fine mess.
　This time I've realized the essence.
　This time, Kali.
　Tongue, call out.
　Wait a minute, Death.
　What a joke!
　What's the fault of the poor mind?
　Who can understand Kali?
　Who is that Syama woman.
　World-Mother's police chief, The.
　World's a shoreless ocean, The.

Kangaroos
Field, B.　Kangaroo, The.
Gray, R.　Dusk, The.
Hull, C.　Flying Kangaroos.
Kumin, M.　Nurture.
Rodenko.　Bombing.
Salter.　Kangaroo.

Kansas City, Kansas and Missouri
Dahlberg.　Kansas City West Bottoms.

Kansas (state)
Bynner.　Haskell.
Costello, R.　Battle hymn.
David, M.　Sunflower.
Dunn, J.　Kansas.
　Ode to Governor Capper, An.
Etter.　Riding the Rock Island Through Kansas.
Gunn, T.　Small Plane in Kansas.
Justice, D.　Crossing Kansas by Train.
Lechlitner.　Kansas Boy.
Levis.　Edward Hopper, "Hotel Room," 1931.
Ondaatje.　7 or 8 Things I Know About Her—A Stolen Biography.
Stafford, W.　At Fourth and Main in Liberal, Kansas, 1932.
　Ceremony.
　Rescued Year, The.
Unknown.　Kansas 1.
Vogt, B.　Uncle with Landscape—Kansas, 1954.

Karate
Plumly.　Karate.

Kashmir
Muske, C.　Blue Kashmir, '74.

Katharine of Aragón, Queen of England
Bibb.　Catharine of Arragon.

Katmandu, Nepal
Justice, D.　Here in Katmandu.

Katydids
Lowell, A.　Katydids.

Kayaks
Griffin, T.　Observation.
Villanueva, A.　Peace #3.

Keaton, Buster
O'Grady, J.　Buster's Last Hand.

Keats, John
Baker, T.　armillaria mellea.
Barbour, D.　I know now I always wanted to write, to.
Brown, L.　Green Arbor, A.
Cistulli.　42.24.

Clare, J.   To the Memory of John Keats.
Cullen, C.   To John Keats, Poet, at Springtime [or Spring Time].
"Ern Malley.".   Colloquy with John Keats.
Graham, J.   Scirocco.
Harrison, T.   Kumquat for John Keats, A.
Hood, T.   False Poets and True.
Hunt, L.   To John Keats.
Keats.   There Was a Naughty Boy.
Kinnell.   Oatmeal.
Kublanovsky [or Kublanovskii].   In Memory of John Keats.
Levis.   Those Graves in Rome.
Muske, C.   Our Kitty.
Nichol.   Little song, A.
Owen, W.   To My Friend (With an Identity Disc).
Parker, D.   Lives and Times of John Keats, Percy Bysshe Shelley, and George Gordon Noel, Lord Byron, The.
Plumly.   Reading with the Poets.
Rukeyser, M.   Homage to Literature.
Shelley, P.   Adonais; An Elegy on the Death of John Keats.
One remains, the many change and pass, The.
Skirrow.   Ode on a Grecian Urn Summarized.
Snorri Hjartarson.   House in Rome.
Stainer.   Wound-dresser's Dream, The.

Kees, Weldon
Chin.   Leaving San Francisco.

Keller, Helen
Smith, George Jay.   When Helen Keller Spoke.

Kennedy, John Fitzgerald
Alexie.   November 22, 1983.
Brown, D.   Where I Was.
Burford, W.   Spell, The: "You can almost see him, looking as if well."
Ellis, T.   Zapruder.
Frost, R.   For John F. Kennedy; His Inauguration.
Graham, J.   Fission.
Herd.   Pink Rose Rings, The.
Livingston, M.   Arthur Thinks on Kennedy.
Myles, E.   American Poem, An.
Onassis, Jacqueline Kennedy.   Meanwhile in Massachusetts.
Pastan.   Remembering Frost at Kennedy's Inauguration.
Reed, I.   Nov 22, 1988.
Shuford.   Visit, The.
Whitbread.   November 25, 1963.

Kennedy, Robert Francis
Justice, D.   Assassination, The.
Sanders, E.   Flower from Robert Kennedy's Grave, A.

Kensington Gardens, London
Spark.   Kensington Gardens.
Unknown.   Poor Adam and Eve were from Eden turned out.

Kent, England
Gray, T.   On Lord Holland's Seat near Margate, Kent.
Randell.   Digging up weeds by the little hedge.
Rochester, J.   Tunbridge Wells.
Wright, K.   How the Wild South East Was Lost.

Kentucky
Ager, M.   Louisville Lou (The Vampin' Lady).
Berry, W.   First time I remember waking up.
Bolton, J.   American Tragedy.
In Memory of the Boys of Dexter, Kentucky.
Dietz, H.   Blue Grass.
Foster, S.   My Old Kentucky Home.
Kumin, M.   Living Alone with Jesus.
Loncar, M.   Kentucky.
Manning, Maurice.   First.
Tate, A.   Swimmers, The.
Warren, R.   In Italian They Call the Bird Civetta.
Was It One of the Long Hunters of Kentucky who Discovered Boone at Sunset?
Williams, W.   To Elsie.
Yellen, J.   Louisville Lou (The Vampin' Lady).

Kerouac, Jack
Coolidge, C.   On the Road.
Ginsberg, A.   Sunflower Sutra.

Sweet Levinsky.
Herrera.   Future Martyr of Supersonic Waves.
Kerouac.   Hymn.
Lea, S.   Green Room, The.
McClure, M.   For Jack Kerouac.
McNiece, R.   Kerouac, we knock.
Letter Left On the Porch of the Kerouac House.

Kesey, Ken
Ginsberg, A.   First Party at Ken Kesey's with Hell's Angels.

Kew Gardens, London
Noyes, A.   Barrel-Organ, The.
Barrel-Organ, The.

Key West, Florida
Lea, S.   Green Room, The.
Moore, H.   Window at Key West, A.
Stevens, W.   Farewell to Florida.
Idea of Order at Key West, The.
Two Figures in Dense Violet Night.

Keys
Bishop, E.   One Art.
Clarke, C.   Vicki and Daphne.
Forbes, C.   Home.
Garcia, R.   Story of Keys, The.
Jones, R.   Key, The.
Liang Xiaobin.   China, I've Lost My Key.
Milosz, O.   La Berline Arrêtée Dans la Nuit.
Ormond.   Key, The.
Robertson, R.   Wedding the Locksmith's Daughter.
Scupham.   Key, The.
Spaziani.   Role Reversal.
Stein, G.   Key to Closet.
Waldrep, G. C.   Hotel d'Avignon.

Kharma
Kim Sŭnghŭi.   Female Buddha.

Kidnapping and Kidnappers
Barnes, J.   For Roland, Presumed Taken.
Bejerano, M.   Interlude.
Eady.   How I Got Born.
Erdrich.   Captivity.
Kinsella, J.   Bright Cigar-Shaped Object Hovers Over Mount Pleasant, A.
Ovid.   Proserpine and Dis.
Philpot, T.   Road Trip as Clues, A.
Reed, I.   Beware: Do Not Read This Poem.
Simic.   I Was Stolen by the Gypsies.
Ts'ai Yen.   Poem of Sorrow.

Kierkegaard, Søren
Kizer, C.   Erotic Philosophers, The.

Kilcash, Ireland
Unknown.   Kilcash.

Killing and Killers
Ai.   Deserter, The.
Baraka, I.   Incident.
Bendall, F.   Outposts.
Bickerstaffe.   What a charming thing's a battle!
Brock, E.   Five Ways to Kill a Man.
Bryll.   Ballad of the Bayonet, A.
Causley.   On Being Asked to Write a School Hymn.
Charles, J. B.   Polish Girl Standing on a Chair, A.
Claus.   Tollund Man.
Crane, S.   Man feared that he might find an assassin, A.
Youth in apparel that glittered, A.
Darwish, M.   Sirhan Drinks His Coffee in the Cafeteria.
Steps in the Night.
Douglas, K.   How to Kill.
Eochaidh, E.   How to kill a living thing.
Forbes, C.   Killer Blues.
Fortini.   Perhaps the Time of Blood.
Fried, E.   Measures Taken, The.
Frost, C.   To Kill a Deer.
Guest, B.   Geese Blood.
Hammial.   Sadie.
Harding, R.   Brother is a Star.
Hodgins.   Shooting the Dogs.
Huchel.   Winter Billet.
Hughes, T.   Esther's Tomcat.
Hawk Roosting.
That Moment.
Ibycus.   And I killed the Molione boys.

Issa.   All the time I pray to Buddha.
Jensma.   Fear freedom.
Kandel.   First They Slaughtered the Angels.
Kelly, B.   Orchard, The.
Song: "Listen: there was a goat's head hanging by ropes in a tree."
Kelly, Erren Geraud.   7-30-96.
Koch, K.   To World War Two.
Kooser.   Shooting a Farmhouse.
Layton.   Cain.
Lenski, H.   Near the Mill.
Livingston, M.   Arthur Thinks on Kennedy.
Logue, C.   Fate's sister, fortune, favours those.
See how that royal fights.
Lowell, R.   Women, Children, Babies, Cows, Cats.
Lumsden, R.   Mercy.
Madgett.   Last Happy Day, The.
Mahon.   As It Should Be.
McFadden, D.   17. The Inchworm.
Millay, E.   Not to Be Spattered by His Blood.
Montale.   Elegy of Our Times.
O'Daly, M.   On Killing a Tax Collector.
Owen, Gerallt Lloyd.   Cilmeri.
Owen, W.   Strange Meeting.
Paz.   And the banquet, the exile, the first crime.
Petrova, A.   Tarantino's languor and dreaming back.
Press, K.   This, too.
Rāy, D.   Who is this black.
Rozhdestvensky [or Rozhdestvenskii].   They Killed the Lad.
Satyanarayana, V.   Your Chariot.
Seferis.   Memory 1.
Senryū, K.   That Tsugunobu.
Sidney.   Sonnet 48: "Soul's joy, bend not those morning stars from me."
Simic.   Psalm: "You've been a long time making up your mind."
Stanley, T.   Dr. Jack.
Todd, M.   To Kill Stray Dogs.
Tu Fu [or Du Fu].   Drawing a bow you must draw a strong one.
Unknown.   Arjuna, his war flag a rampant monkey.
Edward [or Edward, Edward].
Taking of Life Brings Serious Thoughts, The.
Voznesensky [or Voznesenskii].   Old Song.
Warren, R.   Dream He Never Knew the End of, The.
Whalen, P.   Regalia in Immediate Demand!
Wunderlich, M.   Predictions about a Black Car.

Kimonos
Eimers.   Another Kimono.
Issa.   Asked how old he was.
Merrill, J.   Kimono, The.

Kindness
Adler, L.   You: "When afternoon."
Belloc.   Frog, The.
Boroditskaya, M.   So much gentleness from unknown men.
Bryant, T.   Stranger.
Buchanan, G.   Lewis Mumford.
Davies, W. H.   Best Friend, The.
Forbes, Jack.   Something Nice.
Gershwin, I.   Oh, Lady, Be Good!
Glück, L.   Gratitude.
Gordon, M.   Love Thy Neighbor.
Hale, S.   Mary's Lamb [or Mary and Her Lamb].
Hemans.   Stranger's Heart, The.
Hoagland, T.   Oh Mercy.
Jacobs, B.   Friendly Skies.
Kaufman, S.   Bread and Water.
Kramer, L.   Shoemaker's Wife, The.
Langford.   Speak Gently.
Lawrence, D. H.   English Are So Nice!, The.
Leighton, Taigen Dan.   Giving Buddha to all beings is giving to oneself.
Martínez, V.   Human Universe, The.
Nye, N.   Kindness: "Before you know what kindness really is."
Oquendo de Amat, C.   Poem of the Sea and of Her.
Plath.   Kindness.
Ramsay, A.   Lover's Logic.

Stanard, C.   Baseball.
Thompson, P.   Kindly Deed, A.
Tiruvalluvar.   Kindness and Generosity.
Tucker, M.   Kindness.
Unknown.   Somebody's Mother.
Various authors.   Kind and selfless to his
   brothers.
Walders, D.   Kindness of Abishag, The.
Wayne, J.   By Accident.
Wright, J.   Sappho.
Young, J.   Was That the Human Thing to Do?
Zukofsky, L.   In that this happening.

King, B. B.
Lockett.   Oaktown CA.
Weems, M.   B.B. Blues.

King Kong
Ondaatje.   King Kong Meets Wallace Stevens.
Trowbridge, W.   Kong Breaks a Leg at the
   William Morris Agency.

King Lear
Howe, S.   WHITE FOOLSCAP / Book of
   Cordelia.
Keats.   On Sitting Down to Read *King Lear*
   Once Again.
Storace.   King Lear Bewildered.
Williams, W.   Lear.
Woloch, C.   Ottava Rima: Lear.

King, Martin Luther, Jr
Addison, L.   After MLK: the marksman marked
   leftover kill.
Barrax.   King: April 4, 1968.
Cornish, S.   Death of Dr. King.
Fisher, A. *et al.*   Martin Luther King.
Fort, C.   For Martin Luther King.
Hairston.   Alabama Bus.
Harper, M.   Martin's Blues.
   Studs.
Hernandez, D.   Martin and My Father.
Holmes, D.   Time for Guns, A.
LaMon, J.   Sammy Davis, Jr.
Madhubuti.   Assassination.
Sanchez, S.   Morning Song and Evening Walk.
Weatherly, T.   Canto 7: First Thesis.

King, William Lyon Mackenzie
Scott, F.   W. L. M. K.

Kingfishers
Alcman.   No longer, O honeytongued,
   holyvoiced maidens.
Ch'ien Ch'i.   Kingfisher with Fish in Beak.
Clampitt.   Kingfisher, The.
Davies, W. H.   Kingfisher, The.
Fenton, J.   Kingfisher's Boxing Gloves, The.
Fox, Skip.   Sic transit ("Kingfisher in highest
   cypress green.").
Heath-Stubbs.   Kingfisher, The.
Hopkins, G.   As Kingfishers Catch Fire.
Ibycus.   On its highest leaves.
Lloyd, J.   Kingfisher, The.
Olson, C.   Kingfishers, The.
Simonides.   As whenever.

Kings
Addison, L.   All the things of which there are
   none.
Aiyejina.   Dialogue, The.
Allingham, W.   Swing Song, A.
Anyte [*or* Anytes].   This Manes alive once was
   a slave; now dead.
Aragon.   Richard II Forty.
Baudelaire.   Spleen LXXVII.
Belloc.   Henry King, Who Chewed Bits of
   String, and Was Early Cut Off in Dreadful
   Agonies.
Bishop, E.   Twelfth Morning; or What You Will.
Blanco.   Three States and Three Kingdoms.
   Tres estados y los tres reinos, Los.
Browning, R.   Solomon and Balkis.
Buchanan, G.   To Henry Darnley, King of Scots.
Byron, G.   Harp the Monarch Minstrel Swept,
   The.
   To Belshazzar.
Cannell.   King, The.
Causley.   Figgie Hobbin.
Ch'ungdam, Master.   Statesmanship.
Davies, W. H.   Sluggard, The.
De Vere, E.   Poem: "Were I a king, I could

command content."
Denham.   Cooper's Hill.
Dickinson, E.   Belshazzar had a Letter.
   I met a King this afternoon!
Donne.   Anniversary [*or* Anniversarie], The.
Dowriche, A.   So him at first *De Nance
   commanded was to kill;*.
DuBois, W.   Song of the Smoke, The.
Edson, R.   Windows of the Castle, The.
Fairfax of Cameron.   On the Fatal Day January
   30, 1648.
Feilding, F.   One the Morening the King was
   Taken Ill my Dreame of Him.
Ferrell, M.   King with His Queen, The.
Field.   Fifty Quatrains.
   Will You Crucify Your King?
Fiskin.   Magi, The.
Gilbert, W.   There Lived a King.
Goethe.   King in Thule, The.
Greene, R.   Shepherd's Wife's Song, The.
Hébert, A.   Tomb of the Kings, The.
Herbert, Z.   Return of the Proconsul, The.
Herrick.   Difference Betwixt King and Subjects,
   The.
   Ill Government.
   King and No King, A.
   Power in the People, The.
Heyen.   King's Men, The.
Hill, G.   Requiem for the Plantagenet Kings.
Homer.   Gardens of Alcinous, The.
   Priam and Achilles.
Hope, A.   Pleasure of Princes, The.
Ibn ʿAmmār, A.   Pass round the glass for the
   breeze has arisen and the stars have slackened
   the reins of night travel.
Ibn Hamdīs, A.   Fortune that is wont to stumble
   often brought you honor, and a time in which
   you succored us has done you wrong, A.
Ibn Zumruk, M.   Question the horizon adorned
   by the bright stars, for I have entrusted a
   description of my condition to it.
Ibycus.   They destroyed the famous and wealthy.
Ko Ŭn.   Slice of Moon, A.
Lampman.   King's Sabbath, The.
Landor, W.   Georges, The.
Lawrence, D. H.   Snake.
Li Ho.   King of Ch'in Drinks Wine, The.
Li Po.   Song for the Falling Kingdom.
Lovelace, R.   To Lucasta, from Prison.
Mahon.   Last of the Fire Kings, The.
Mansour, J.   From an ass to an analyst and back.
Marlowe.   And ride in triumph through
   Persepolis?
Milne, A.   King's Breakfast, The.
Milosz, O.   King Don Luis.
Montgomerie, W.   Flodden.
Moore, M.   Steeple-Jack, The.
More, S.   De Principe Bono et Malo.
   Quis Optimus Reipublicae Status.
Munro, N.   Heather, The.
Nordhaus.   Aunt Lily and Frederick the Great.
Ojaide.   Where Everybody is King.
Philips, K.   On the 3 of September, 1651.
Pobo, K.   Stormy Lear.
Pope, A.   Epigram Engraved on the Collar of a
   Dog Given [*or* Which I Gave] to His Royal
   Highness.
Porter, P.   Soliloquy at Potsdam.
Quarles.   On Saul and David.
Rochester, J.   Satire on Charles II, A.
Rolleston.   Grave of Rury, The.
Rossetti, C.   After Communion.
Ruhani, G.   Gaffer Speaks.
Shelley, P.   England in 1819.
   Ozymandias.
Sidney.   Sonnet 75: "Of all the kings that ever
   here did reign."
Stafford, W.   Story That Could Be True, A.
Stesichoros.   They flung many quinces toward
   the chariot.
Stevenson, R.   Happy Thought.
Taha, A.   Wall of Genesis, The.
Tennyson, A.   Love is and was my Lord and
   King.
Thackeray.   King of Brentford's Testament *abr,
   The.*

Unknown.   Chen-gong: King's Serfs.
   Forever Martial.
   Fort of Rathangan, The.
   Great hand King Wu.
   Guest, The.
   King and Hermit.
   Muiveyo Cow, The.
   Qwhen Alexander our kynge was dede.
   Sir Patrick Spens [*or* Spence].
   Sky is a dark bowl, the stars die and fall, The.
   Song of the Gong and Chimes.
   Summer Sunday.
   You all by yourself fulfilled.
Various authors.   Anxious only to fulfill the
   royal clause.
   Because robbers poisoned the people.
   Because the govenment burdened the people.
   Brothers rebelled against one another, The.
   Even though they were rebellious.
   He did not boast of his natural gifts.
   He had many to help him.
   He opened the four borders.
   He was consistent from beginning to end.
   Heaven gave him courage and wisdom.
   His arrow was huge beyond compare.
   Kind and selfless to his brothers.
   Korea's six dragons flew in the sky.
   Though he was busy with war.
   Upon receiving an old scholar.
Veinberg, J.   Next to Tut.
Vietnamese Oral Tradition.   Harmony in the
   Kingdom.
   Testing the Confucian Ideal.
Wither.   If by mischance the people in the street.
Yeats.   Madness of King Goll, The.

Kingston, Jamaica
Espinet, R.   Merchant of Death.

Kipling, Rudyard
Carryl, G.   Ballad: "As I was walkin' the jungle
   round, a-killin' of tigers an' time."
O'Hara, F.   Captains Courageous.
Stephen, J.   To R. K.

Kisses
Adcock, F.   Kissing.
Addonizio.   First Kiss: "Afterwards you had that
   drunk, drugged look."
Alexander, E.   Zodiac.
Anacreon.   Elegy 2.
Angus.   Mary's Song.
Asclepiades.   We were having fun, that devil
   Hermione and I.
Bécquer, G.   Gentle Breeze with a Whispered
   Cry, The.
Bell, M.   What They Do to You in Distant
   Places.
Beveridge.   Dining Out.
Bevington, L.   With the Tide: A Cry of
   Weakness.
Blok.   Visitor.
Bouwers.   Final Signs, The.
Brinks, Dave.   Halo Factory, The.
Brown, L.   Impulse to Call & Spring Upon, The.
Browning, E.   Romance of the Swan's Nest,
   The.
   To George Sand: A Desire.
Browning, R.   Song: "Moth's kiss, first, The!".
Budenz.   Poeta Fui.
Burns, R.   Ae Fond Kiss.
Carnevali.   Kiss.
Catullus.   Carmen 5.
   Lesbia.
   To Juventius.
Cavalli.   To simulate the burning of the heart.
Ceravolo.   Spring in This World of Poor Mutts.
Cisneros, S.   14 de julio.
Cummings, E. E.   Thy fingers make early
   flowers of.
Dacre, C.   Kiss, The: "Greatest bliss, The."
David, M.   Sinner Kissed an Angel, A.
Davies, I.   Angry Summer 28, The.
Delmore, E.   Marmalade.
DeSylva, B. G.   Do It Again.
Diggs, L.   Fullness.
Dove, R.   Adolescence—1.
Drayton.   Since there's no help, come let us kiss
   and part.

Dunbar, P. Negro Love Song, A.
Dunn, S. Each from Different Heights.
Factor, J. Rubyfruit.
Faiz. Day Death Comes, The.
Field. Already to mine eyelids' shore.
Field, Miranda. Scold's Mask.
Fleming, P. How He Should Like to Be Kissed.
Fletcher, J. Take, Oh, Take Those Lips Away.
Gannon, K. Reciprocity.
Gerov, Alexander. Courtesy.
Gershwin, I. How Long Has This Been Going On?
Gibbons, S. Truce, The.
Goldberg, B. Twentieth Century Children (5): Blood-Kissing.
Gordon, I. Prelude to a Kiss.
Griffiths, J. Two Are Embracing.
Grotz, J. Kiss of Judas.
Hamer. Berkeley, Late Spring.
Hammerstein. I Cain't Say No.
Hayes, T. Elegant Tongue, The.
Herrick. To Electra ("I dare not ask a kiss[e].").
  Upon Jack and Jill: Epigram.
Hoover, P. Kiss, The: "She had imagined the kiss."
Howe, M. Kiss, The.
Hunt, L. Rondeau: "Jenny kissed [or kiss'd] me when we met."
Jackson, L. Take Hands.
Jonson, B. Begging Another, on Colour of Mending the Former.
  To the Same [Celia].
Kerrigan, T. Elvis Kissed Me.
Khoury, N. Death Is Your Salvation.
King, H. Boy's Answer to the Blackmoor, The.
Kitahara Hakushū. Kiss.
Kunitz, S. Game, The.
Kuzmin. Ah, those lips, kissed by so many. Nine delightful birthmarks.
Labé. Kiss me again, and kiss me still, and kiss.
Lassell. Kissing Ramén.
Lawrence, D. H. Kisses in the Train. Lightning.
Le Gallienne. Beauty Accurst.
Ledwidge. Spring Love.
Lee, M. Kiss, A.
Lenier. Finale.
Linder. First Kiss.
Locklin. Learning to See Crooked.
Loesser. My Darling, My Darling.
López Colomé, P. Death of the Kiss. Muerte del beso, La.
Loynaz, D. M. Time.
Lyly, J. Cupid and My Campaspe Played.
Lysaght, E. Kitty of Coleraine.
Macdonald, G. Sweet Peril.
Magidson, H. Continental (You Kiss While You're Dancing), The.
Majorino. Kisses.
Martial. Breath of balm from foreign branches pressed, The.
  Irresolute the down upon your cheek. They smell of Corycian saffron, of a.
Marvin, C. House, Garden, Madness.
McDaniel, J. Archipelago of Kisses, The.
McNiece, R. Memorizing your face.
Meleager. Night Alone, The.
Melo, M. Red Lipstick on a Straw.
Millay, E. Sonnet 43: "What lips my lips have kissed, and where, and why."
Mills, I. Prelude to a Kiss.
Moore, T. Did Not.
  Kiss, The.
Morris, T. Prelude to a Kiss.
Muske, C. Former Love, a Lover of Form, A.
Musset. Poet, The.
Nathan, L. Bladder Song.
Nesbit, E. Kiss, The.
Nims, J. Watching the Planes Come In at La Guardia.
O'Hara, F. Lebanon.
Orléans, C. Balade.
  Roundel: "Take, take this cosse, atonys, atonys, my hert!"
Ormsby, F. L'Orangerie.
Ovid. Elegy 1.5: "In summer's heat[e] and mid-

time of the day."
Paley, G. Here.
Parra, N. Letters to an Unknown Woman.
Paulus [or Paulos] Silentiarius. Come, give me kisses, Rhodope.
Petronius Arbiter. Doing, a filthy pleasure is, and short.
Plato. Kiss, The.
Popova, O. Curve of your lips, The.
Porter, C. Old-Fashioned Garden.
Powell, D. A. Triptych.
Prados, E. Song of Taking Leave.
Ríos, A. Teodoro Luna's Two Kisses.
Roethke. She.
Rossetti, D. 49: Willowwood ("I sat with Love upon a woodside well").
Rossiter. Nostalgia.
Rudaki. Came to me— / Who?
Rufinus. Kiss from Her, A.
Rux, C. H. Shunning an Imperative.
Samyn, A. Art of Kissing, The.
Scafidi, S. Prayer for a Marriage.
Secundus, J. Kisses, The.
Seibles, T. First Kiss: "Her mouth."
Shakespeare, W. If I profane with my unworthiest hand.
  Take, O Take Those Lips Away.
Shapcott, J. Muse.
Shelley, P. Love's Philosophy.
Shoneyin, T. Bedside Wreaths.
Shuttle. Passion.
Sidney. Sonnet 74: "I never drank of Aganippe well."
  Sonnet 81: "O kiss, which dost those ruddy gems impart."
Smith, J. Gimme a Little Kiss (Will Ya, Huh?).
Sŏ Chŏngju. Kilimanjaro Sunrise.
Spenser, E. Sonnet 64: "Coming [or Comming] to kiss[e] her lips [or lyps], such grace I found."
Stein, G. Kiss my lips. She did.
Strode. Kisses.
  Riddle: On a Kiss, A.
Surprice, L. Little Love Kiss.
Synge. With One Long Kiss.
Tanikawa, S. Kiss.
Teasdale. Look, The.
Thomas, L. Excitation.
Toomer. Her Lips Are Copper Wire.
Tranter. Burden of noise, of infections, A.
  Wild infusion fire, love and death.
Tsvetaeva [or Tsvetaeva]. To Kiss a Forehead Is to Erase Worry.
Tucker, M. Kiss, A.
Turk, R. Gimme a Little Kiss (Will Ya, Huh?).
Unknown. Black Hair.
  Brush the dark bangs on my forehead aside, kiss my beauty mark.
  First take me in your arms and hold me tight.
  I will gladly give you my mouth.
  Kiss me in the moon's sparkling glow.
  Learn how to consume my mouth!
  May God let him be invited to our home!
  My lover wants me to kiss him in the foliage of the blackberry bush.
  My mouth is yours, devour it and be not afraid.
  My whole mouth, all of it, is yours.
  Put your lips on my mouth.
  Put your mouth on mine.
  Unless you are mad with love for me.
  When you come to our house, my love, the "little horror" grows angry.
Villaurrutia. They and I.
Volkman. When kiss spells contradiction it spills an ocean of open clothes.
Walker, A. Kiss, The.
Waniek. Canticle for Abba Jacob, A.
Warner, S. After He Had Gone.
Watts, M. Vision.
Wharton, E. Mortal Lease, The: V.
Whitman, W. Behold This Swarthy Face.
Williamson, G. Visiting Couple Kissing and Halved Onion.
Wilson, C. Kiss her that she don't know how.
Wolff, Rebecca. Press Play.
Wyatt. Lover Showeth How He Is Forsaken of

Such as He Sometime Enjoyed, The.
Zetter, S. Misdemeanor.
Zukofsky, L. Two Dedications: Tibor Serly.

Kitchens
Baggott, J. Kitchens: 1959.
Branch, A. Monk in the Kitchen, The.
Brooks, G. Mrs. Small.
Carson, A. Kitchen.
Cook, W. Still-Life with Woodstove.
Davis, T. Boppin' is Safer than Grindin'.
Dooley, Twain. Kitchen: "Everywhere I go it's the same old thing."
Dove, R. Sunday Greens.
Giovanni. Wrong Kitchen, The.
Groarke, V. Imperial Measure.
Harjo, J. Perhaps the World Ends Here.
Jewsbury. My heart's in the kitchen, my heart is not here.
Joseph, A. Kitchen.
Kamienska. Saint Martha.
Khoury-Gata. She Used to Throw Her Old Crockery.
Merrill, J. Midnight Snack, The.
Mistral, G. Martha and Mary.
Morales, A. Kitchens.
Mun Chônghui. Little Kitchen Song, A.
Okamoto. Tanka: "Having let flow."
Peate, I. Museum Piece.
Salaam. Everywhere You Eat.
Silano, M. Such a Way to Go.
Talvikki, A. For Want.
Wright, C. State of Preservation.

Kites (ornithology)
Blok. Kite, The.
Issa. Kites shriek / Together—.
Lloyd, J. Thoughts of Boyhood.

Kites (toys)
Buson. Apprentice's day off.
  Paper kite, A.
Cohen, L. Kite Is a Victim, A.
Gilbert, C. Kite-Flying.
Issa. That gorgeous kite.
Judson, J. Whitman Again.
Kizer, C. Dangerous Games.
McCabe, B. Kite.
O'Keeffe. Kite, The.
Ōkuma Kotomichi. Kite, The.
Robertson, R. Affair of Kites.
Rosser, J. First Empathy.
Strand. Kite, The.
Sulchinskaya, O. Kite, The.
Swenson, M. Goodbye, Goldeneye.
Thompson, D. P. Laurel Street, 1950.
Williamson, G. Kites at the Washington Monument.

Kittens
Hood, T. Choosing Their Names.
López Colomé, P. Cachorros, Los.
  Cubs, The.
Lopez, L. Tomás.
MacCaig. Byre.
Metodiev, Ivan. Sometimes: "Sometimes God resembles a kitten."
Mother Goose. As I was going to St. Ives.
Twichell. Aisle of Dogs.
Williams, W. Mujer.
Yesenin [or Essenin]. For My Sister Shura.

Klee, Paul
Gould, R. Amateur Drummer.
Nemerov. Painter Dreaming in the Scholar's House, The.

Knees
Burns, R. Memory.
Buson. Shortcut, A.
Kuznetsova, I. Seagull shrilly in my head, A.

Knife-Grinding and Knife-Grinders
Canning, G. *et al.* Friend of Humanity and the Knife Grinder, The.
Whitman, W. Sparkles from the Wheel.

Knight, Etheridge
Boyd, M. Epitaph for Etheridge Knight.
Medina, T. Don't Say Goodnight to Etheridge Knight.
Steptoe. For Etheridge Knight.

Knighthood and Knights
Ahern, T.   Rubber Knight, The.
Antar [or Antara].   Black Night, The.
Askew, A.   Ballad Which Anne Askew[e] Made
   and Sang When She Was in Newgate, The.
Browning, R.   Childe Roland to the Dark Tower
   Came.
Butler, S.   When civil fury [or dudgeon] first
   grew high.
Chaucer.   Wife of Bath's Tale, The.
Ch'ungdam, Master.   Ode to Knight Kip'a.
Guiney.   Wild Ride, The.
Hawes, S.   True Knight [or True Knighthood],
   The.
Herbert, Z.   Passion of Our Lord painted by an
   anonymous hand from the Circle of Rhenish
   Masters, The.
Herebert.   Who is This that Cometh from
   Edom?
Heyen.   King's Men, The.
Hogg, J.   Charlie is my Darling.
Ingelow.   Winding-up Time.
Keats.   Belle Dame sans Merci, La [A Ballad].
Malveisin, W.   Fergus attempts to make off with
   the Sheild of Dunottar.
Mayer, G.   Ballad: "Knight went down to the
   river's rim, A."
Melville, H.   Medallion, The.
Morris, W.   Haystack in the Floods, The.
Poe.   Eldorado.
Procter, A.   Legend of Provence, A.
Ryan, G.   Epilogue: "His money-making
   properties come back like a beach."
Scott, S.   Along the bridge Lord Marmion rode.
   Lochinvar.
Smith, S.   Blue from Heaven, The.
Spenser, E.   Book 3, Canto 11.
   Lo I the man, whose muse whilome did maske.
Taylor, J.   Squire's Pew, The.
Unknown.   Cid Enters Burgos, The.
   I wende to deeth, knight stith in stour.
   Since the siege and the assault upon Troy were
   finished.
   Three Ravens, The.
Winters, Y.   Sir Gawaine and the Green Knight.
Yu Hsin.   Knights Errant.

Knights of Pythias
Kipling, R.   New Knighthood, The.
Linden, M.   For the Good of the Pythian Order.

Knitting and Knitters
Fisher, Diane G.   After the Miscarriage.
Forbes, D.   Forecast.
Fuertes.   Climbing.
Radoev, Ivan.   Sweater, The.
Shinkichi Takahashi.   Stitches.
Tucker, M.   Knitting.

Knives
Adamson.   Gutting the Salmon.
Annucci, Marilyn.   Wrecked World.
Bass, E.   Why People Murder.
Boruch.   Simple Machines.
Cabral de Melo Neto.   Knife All Blade, A.
   Like a bullet.
Chông Hwajin.   Knife Gets Bigger, A.
Dumdum.   To My Mother.
García Lorca.   Quarrel, The.
Gibson, W.   Luck.
Goldbarth.   Life Is Happy.
Hampton.   Women who Speak with Steak
   Knives.
Hume, C.   Birthday.
Khlebnikov, V.   Burning Field, The.
Masaoka Shiki.   Little knife, The.
McBride, M.   Knife-Thrower's Wife, The.
McKay, D.   Setting the Table.
Mirabai [or Mira Bai].   I was going to the river
   for water.
Moore, M.   Those Various Scalpels.
O'Daly, M.   Shaving of Murdoch, The.
Pak Sôwôn.   Obsession: "Knife on the fruit dish,
   The."
Radnóti.   Angel of Dread, The.
Robeson, E.   Memorium.
Sharp, S.   In the Tradition of Bobbitt.
Shinkichi Takahashi.   Lap Dog.
Sioux Oral Tradition.   Give me my knife.

Swenson, M.   Bleeding.
Symons, A.   Nerves.
Taksa, M.   Granite Jaw.
Walwicz.   Big Tease.
   Little Red Riding Hood.
   Tattoo, The.
Wilkinson, J.   Sideshow.
   Torn Ones, The.

Knowledge
Adamson.   Dreaming Up Mother.
Aleixandre.   In Front of the Mirror.
Ammons.   Ballad: "I want to know the unity in
   all things and the difference."
Archilochus.   Fox knows many things, The.
Aridjis.   Poem, The.
Atwood.   Procedures for Underground.
Baraka, I.   New World, The.
Berry, W.   At a Country Funeral.
Bhatt, S.   What Is Worth Knowing?
Bishop, E.   At the Fishhouses.
Blake, W.   All Religions Are One.
Bogan, L.   Knowledge.
Brett, L.   Leaving You.
Bringhurst.   Parśvanatha.
Bronk.   Ignorant Lust After Knowledge, The.
Caldwell, A.   I Know That You Know.
Caraion.   Ultimate Argument.
Carrera Andrade.   Perfect Life, The.
Castellanos.   Other, The.
Cavendish, M.   Of Many Worlds in This World.
Celan.   Zurich, at the Stork.
Chapman, G.   Learning ("So Learned Men in
   Controversies Spend").
Clare, J.   I Feel I Am.
Clough.   Questioning Spirit, The.
Cope, W.   Two Cures for Love.
Couani.   Obvious, The.
Cowley, A.   Tree of Knowledge, The.
Crane, S.   I met a seer.
Creeley.   Way, The.
Crompton.   Epigram LXVII: Time, the
   Interpreter.
Cruz, S.   I Entered Where I Did Not Know.
Cummings, E. E.   You Shall Above All Things
   Be Glad and Young.
Daive.   Lost in contemplation.
Darío, R.   Eheu!
Davies, S.   I know my soul hath power to know
   all things.
Davison, P.   Star Watcher, The.
Dickinson, E.   To know just how He suffered—
   would be dear.
Dillard, A.   Observations and Experiments.
   Sign of Your Father, The.
Ehrhart.   Way Light Bends, The.
Emerson, R.   Limits.
Feng Chih.   Sonnet: "We often pass a night
   warm and intimate."
Frost, R.   For Once, Then, Something.
   From Plane to Plane.
   Revelation.
Gamalinda, E.   Light Falls Obliquely.
George, S.   Do Not Ponder Too Much.
Gertsyk, A.   Silent, draped in the garments of
   sacrifice.
Ginsberg, A.   Psalm III: "To God: to illuminate
   all men. Beginning with Skid Road."
Gonzáles Martínez.   Last Journey.
Gorostiza, J.   Filled with myself, walled up in
   my skin.
Greville, F.   Mind of man is this world's true
   dimension, The.
Guiney.   In the Reading-Room of the Brtish
   Museum.
Habington.   Nox Nocti Indicat Scientiam.
Hamhur Kiwha.   Because of Certain Things.
Han-shan.   My home was at Cold Mountain
   from the start.
Harryman.   Knowledge ("Knowledge was being
   processed. It was in the argument machine.").
Hayâlî.   They do not know how to search for the
   World-Adorner.
Herbert, G.   Pearl, The. Matth. 13:45.
Hernández Cruz.   Perlas.
Hoffenstein.   You go to high school, even
   college.

Howe, F.   Catholic.
Hughes, T.   Man Seeking Experience Enquires
   His Way of a Drop of Water, The.
Issa.   Mother I never knew.
   Not knowing.
Jabès.   Desert, The.
Jamie, K.   Queen of Sheba, The.
Keats.   But there are.
Kekova.   Everything has come true. The
   punishment fits the crime.
Kenjeev.   You envied the flying birds and
   stones.
Kennedy, X.   Hummingbird.
Kerouac.   Orlanda Blues: 24th Chorus.
Killeen, G.   At the Black Edge.
Kirsanov.   New Heart, The.
Ko Un.   Asking the Way.
Koller.   Sitting Alone One Cold June Night
   Before an Empty Whiskey Bottle a Coffee Pot
   & an Oil Stove with a Window through which
   I Watched the Flames.
Kuzmin.   Were you apprenticed to a fortune
   teller?
Lal Ded [or Lalla].   I searched for my Self.
Lawrence, D. H.   You.
Lee, L.   Tearing the Page.
Lee, P.   I Don't Know Enough About You.
Lejeune, Claire.   Illiterate.
Levertov.   Contraband.
Levine, P.   On My Own.
Lugones.   Gray Waves.
March, A.   Much as a man who takes delight in
   dreaming.
Martynova, O.   What does the river know of its
   own bed.
Maybe, E.   Umbilical Cord.
McSweeney, Joyelle.   Wind Domes, The.
Mercer, J.   How Little We Know.
Michelangelo Buonarroti.   You know that I
   know, my lord, that you know.
Montgomerie, A.   Royall Palice of the Heichest
   Hewin, The.
Moore, M.   To a Snail.
Moore, R.   Mind's Disguise, The.
   Still without Life.
Murray, J.   Here We Stand Before the Temporal
   World.
   There Has Been More Than Beginning and End
   to Face.
Mutis.   Sonata.
Nathan, L.   Hole.
Nelson, M.   Drifter.
Nemerov.   Boy with Book of Knowledge.
Nims, J.   Knowledge of God.
"Novalis.".   When geometric diagrams and
   digits.
Oppen.   Image of the Engine.
   Knowledge not of sorrow, you were, The.
Parker, A.   No Fool, the God of Salt.
Parker, D.   Ballade at Thirty-Five.
Pinsky.   Serpent Knowledge.
Po Chü-i.   Laozi.
   Philosophers: Lao-Tzu, The.
Poe.   Al Aaraaf.
Pope, A.   Paragon of Animals, The.
Pound, E.   Great Digest of Confucius, The.
   Tree, The.
Quarles.   I wish a greater knowledge, then
   t'attaine.
Ramke, B.   Astronomer Works Nights: A
   Parable of Science, The.
Rege, S.   Old Leaves from the Chinese Earth.
Reznikoff.   Epilogue: "Blessed / in the light of
   the sun at the sight of the world."
Rhodes, M.   How Fast.
Rich, A.   To the Days.
Risset, Jacqueline.   M. S. 1544.
Ritsos.   Naked Face.
Romo-Carmona, M.   Crows.
Rosemurgy, C.   Angel Finally Admits What She
   Knows to Lou Binkler of Bethany, Missouri,
   An.
Rumi.   Two Kinds of Intelligence.
Rux, C. H.   Pledge of Allegiance.
Sabines.   I Do Not Know It for Sure.
St. John, D.   I Know.

Salaam. Always Know.
Senryū, K. Whole town, The.
Sexton. Black Art, The.
Shelley, P. Sonnet: Lift Not the Painted Veil.
Sorescu, M. Perseverance.
Stafford, W. Near.
Stein, G. On Her Way.
Stevens, W. It feels good as it is without the
  giant.
Straus, M. Log of Pi, The.
Szymborska, W. Once we knew the world well.
Taylor, B. Night the Second: All or Nothing.
Tennyson, A. To —. With the Following Poem.
Thomas, E. Some Eyes Condemn.
Thomas, R. S. Here.
Thoreau. Men say they know many things.
Torres Bodet. Living.
Twichell. All of It, The.
Unknown. A B C D.
  Death of Old Men, The.
  I Was Born Almost Ten Thousand Years Ago.
Very. Eye and Ear, The.
Vietnamese Oral Tradition. Husband and Wife.
  Whisky Lovers.
Villa, E. Lend me a battle of unavoidable
  suggestions.
  Ugly season of putrifying buzzards, An.
Viray, M. Two Strangers, The.
Ward, D. Approximately.
Washington, N. Woman's Intuition, A.
Welch, L. Step out onto the planet.
Williams, C. K. Doves.
Yang Hsün-chi. Inscribed on the Doors of My
  Bookshelves.
Yeryomin. Polyhedral kernels of wisdom.

Knox, George L.
Bibb. Lines to the Hon. George L. Knox.
Muir, E. Scotland 1941.

Knoxville, Tennessee
Giovanni. Knoxville, Tennessee.

Koran
El Janabi, A. Ink.

Korea and Koreans
Chu Yün-ming. Fan from Korea, A.
Corn. Kimchee in Worchester (Mass.).
Hwang Jiwoo. Variety Show, 1984.
Ko Chŏnghŭi. Let's Open the Dam: "Let's open
  the dam."
Ko Ŭn. Chrysanthemums.
Korean Oral Tradition. Song of Entertaining the
  Holy One.
Mura. Once near the Border.
Oguma Hideo. Long, Long Autumn Nights.
Pak Illo. Lament on the Water.
  Song of Peace.
Pak Mogwŏl [*or* Mokwŏl]. Hanbok.
Sŏ Chŏngju. Autumn, 1949: At the "Flower"
  Tea Room.
  In the Old Capital.
  Such a Land.
Unknown. Ari-rang Ari-rang A-ra-ri-yo.
  Some loves are soft, others are rough.
Yi Sanghwa. Will Spring Return to Stolen
  Fields?

Korean War
Berrigan, T. I Remember.
Biespiel, D. Lilacs.
Carruth, H. On a Certain Engagement South of
  Seoul.
Childress, W. Trying to Remember People I
  Never Really Knew.
Hinojosa, Rolando. Eighth Army at the
  Chongchon, The.
  Jacob Mosqueda Wrestles with the Angels.
  January-May 1951 Slaughter, The.
  Rest Due and Taken.
Kim, M. Under Flag.
Kim, Suji Kwock. Chasm, The.
  Flight.
  Fragments of the Forgotten War.
McGrath, T. Ode for the American Dead in
  Korea.
Meredith, W. Korean Woman Seated by a Wall,
  A.
Pak Inhwan. Sleepless Night, A.

Towards a New Resolve.
Saner. Flag Memoir.
Wilson, K. Circle, The.
  Memory of a Victory.
  Waterfront Bars.

Koresh, David
Glancy. Battery.

Krakow [*or* Cracow], Poland
Norwid, C. Those Who Love.

Kreisler, Fritz
Stern, G. Fritz.

Krishna
Mirabai [*or* Mira Bai]. Clouds, The.
  Faithfulness.
  Heat of Midnight Tears, The.
  His Hair.
  Music, The.
  Where Did You Go?
  Why Mira Can't Go Back to Her Old House.
Sastri, D. In Search of Krishna.
Satyanarayana, V. Song of Krishna.
Savithri, M. Black and White.

Ku Klux Klan
Baraka, I. Wise 5.
Hayden, R. Night, Death, Mississippi.
Howard Jr., W. Cross Burning Black.
Kay, J. Twelve Bar Bessie.
Komunyakaa, Y. Knights of the White Camellia
  and Deacons of Defense.
Newman, R. Salem, Indiana, 1983.
St. John, P. Lynching and Burning.
Taylor, Cecil. Scroll No. 1.
Taylor, Charles S. Poem to Ma Ferguson.

Kubla Khan
Coleridge, S. Kubla Khan: or, A Vision in a
  Dream.
Smith, S. Thoughts about the Person from
  Porlock.

Kurdistan and Kurds
Bekes Jr. Love: "There is many a country."
Goran. Lover's Song, A.
Griffiths, J. There Are Limits to Brotherly
  Love.
Herdi, A. God's Freedom Lovers.
Hilmi, F. Political Parties.
Peshew, A. Fratricide.
Samawi, A. Mountain of Dreams.
  Neighing of the Fingers.
  Suns in the Night of the Massacre.

Kyoto, Japan
Basho. Even in Kyoto.
  Even in Kyoto.
  Southern Kyoto.
Buson. Day slow in going, A.
Enright, D. Kyoto Garden, A.

L

La Coruna, Spain.
See Coruña, La, Spain
Labor and Laborers
Adair, V. H. Blueberry City.
Afrika, T. Queue.
Aiken, C. Road, The.
Alegría. Documentary.
Allbery. Assembler.
Alvarez, J. Woman's Work.
Anstett. Shift.
Arnold, B. No Tool or Rope or Pail.
Arundel, H. Adam.
Babcock, M. Be Strong.
Baca. So Mexicans Are Taking Jobs from
  Americans.
  Work We Hate and Dreams We Love.
Baillie, J. Hay making.
Baraka, I. Poem Some People Will Have to
  Understand, A.
Basho. All the field hands.
  Culture's beginnings.
  Singing, planting rice.
  This ruined temple.
Beatty, J. Pittsburgh Poem.
Beatty, P. That's Not in My Job Description.

Beecher, J. Altogether Singing.
  Report to the Stockholders.
Bersohn. Dignity of Labor, The.
Bevington, L. Morning.
Boden, F. As I Came Home from Labour.
Boileau-Despéaux. Epistle to My Gardener.
Brown, G. Taxman.
Brown, S. Call Boy.
  Southern Road.
Bunting. What the Chairman Told Tom.
Bush, D. Drainlayer.
Buson. That handsaw marks time.
  With the noon conch blown.
Bye. Blessing.
Cafagña, M. Hawthorne Metal, Detroit, 1939.
Campbell, R. Serf, The.
Campbell, S. Chairmaker, The.
Carpenter, M. One day I went to London.
Cary, A. To Solitude.
Celaya, G. Poetry Is a Weapon Loaded with the
  Future.
Césaire, A. In Memory of a Black Union
  Leader.
Chamberlain, B. Islandman.
Ch'en Lin. Song: "I watered my horse at the
  Long Wall caves."
Chevremont. Symphony of the Hammers.
Chipasula. Those Rainy Mornings.
Chock. Working Construction.
Ciardi, J. All about Boys and Girls.
Clover, J. El periférico, or Sleep.
Coleridge, S. Work without Hope.
Collier, M. Womans Labour, an epistle, The.
Conyus. Six Ten Sixty-Nine.
Cook, E. Song for the Workers, A.
Crozier, A. Driftwood and Seacoal.
Cullen, C. For a Lady I Know.
Day, L. Reject Jell-O.
de Folgar. Monday.
DuBois, W. Song of the Smoke, The.
Elliott, E. Child, Is Thy Father Dead?
Ellis, T. Atomic Bride.
Enzensberger, H. Vanished Work.
Figueroa, J. Jelly Bean Policy, The.
Fisher, J. Back on the Job.
Flecknoe. Ant, The.
Frost, R. Mowing.
  Out, Out—.
  Tuft of Flowers, The.
  Wood-Pile, The.
Fuller, H. Day Labor.
Galanskov. It shames one to look.
García, D. Orchard of Figs in the Fall, An.
García, J. I Ain't Going to Hurry No More.
Gladding. Fisherman's Wife, The.
Glück, L. School Children, The.
Goethe. Nature and Art.
González Prada, M. Forced Labour.
Goodison. Birth Stone.
Gould, A. Demolisher.
Hall, D. X.
Han-shan. Graceful handsome youth, A.
Han Yü. Leaves fall turning turning to the
  ground.
Harper, M. Camp Story.
Hawaiian Oral Tradition. Five O'Clock
  Whistle, The.
  Hana-Hana: Working.
  My Mother Dear.
  Stripping Leaves from Sugarcane.
Hayden, R. Those Winter Sundays.
Hayzler, K. At the Machine.
Heaney, S. Sunlight.
  When all the others were away at Mass.
Hill, G. Ovid in the Third Reich.
Hill, J. Preacher and the Slave, The.
Hood, T. Song of the Shirt, The.
Hopkins, G. God's Grandeur.
Hove. Country Life.
  You Will Forget.
Hsi-tseng Tsiang. Shantung.
Hutchinson, L. Verses Written by Mrs.
  Hutchinson.
Ingelow. Little babe, while burns the west.
Iolo Goch. Labourer, The.
Ishikawa Takuboku. Tanka: "I work."

Issa. My noontime nap.
People working fields.
Jacinto, A. Letter from a Contract Worker.
Johnson, M. What's de Use ob Wukin in de Summer Time at All.
Johnson, S. Paraphrase.
Johnston, E. Lines to Ellen, the Factory Girl. Working Man, The.
Jones, E. Song of the Lower Classes, The.
Jordan, J. If You Saw a Negro Lady.
Kelly, B. Leaving, The.
Kendall, M. Underground.
King, B. Pessimist, The.
Kinsella, J. Wild Radishes.
Komunyakaa, Y. Work.
Konishi Raizan. For rice-planting women.
Kurtz. Call, The.
Larkin, P. Aubade: "I work all day, and get half-drunk at night."
Toads.
Toads Revisited.
Lawrence, D. H. Morning Work.
Leapor. Sacrifice: An Epistle to Celia, The.
Lee, D. Tuesday Morning, Loading Pigs.
Levine, P. You Can Have It.
Lin Pu. Locust Wood Mallet for Papermaking, A.
Liu Cheng. Poem without a Category.
Livingstone, D. Dust: "Bundle in the gutter had its skull, The."
Longfellow, H. Psalm of Life, A.
Village Blacksmith, The.
MacLean, S. Highland Woman, A.
MacLeish. Burying Ground by the Ties.
Magdeburg, Mechthild von. True love in every moment praises God.
Markham, E. Man with the Hoe, The.
Martineau, J. Viejo.
Masefield. Consecration, A.
Mayakovsky [or Maiakovskii]. Good Attitude to Horses, A.
Merriam, E. Lazy Thought, A.
Meynell, A. Girl on the Land, The.
Monro, H. Man Carrying Bale.
Moore, L. From the Field.
Moraga. Half-Breed.
Morejón. Havana Harbor.
Morris, M. For Consciousness.
Mphande. Why the Old Woman Limps.
Nichols, G. Waterpot.
Orton, B. Beekeeper.
Ou-yang Hsiu. Reading the Poems of an Absent Friend.
Pak Nohae. Wind to the Stones, The.
Pfeiffer, E. Peace to the odalisque, whose morning glory.
Pickard, T. What Maks Makems.
Piercy. To Be of Use.
Pinsky. Shirt.
Pollarolo, G. Grocer's Dream, The.
Pomerantz, A. Chandeliers.
Rabi'a al-Adawiyya. I am fully qualified to work as a doorkeeper, and for this reason.
Racin, K. Tobacco Pickers.
Randall, D. George.
Rash, R. July, 1949.
Ravikovitch, D. Unusual Autumn, An.
Reznikoff. Girls outshout the machines, The.
Her work was to count linings.
She who worked patiently.
Shopgirls leave their work, The.
1. The Sinking.
Testimony.
Rich, A. Here is a map of our country.
Riley, J. Raggedy Man, The.
Rivard. Torque.
Rodgers, C. It Is Deep.
Roscoe, W. To the Harvest Moon.
Rukeyser, M. Absalom.
Alloy.
George Robinson: Blues.
Sadoff. February: Pemaquid Point.
Samaras, N. Translation.
Sandburg, C. Chicago.
Onion Days.
Shange. Tango.

Shapiro, D. House (Blown Apart).
Shelley, P. Song to the Men of England.
Shen Yüeh. Returning to My Garden Home: In Respectful Response to the Master of Hua-yang.
Shurin. Material's Daughter.
Simonides. Human strength.
Skipsey. Get Up!
Smith, C. To Dependence.
Snyder, G. Hay for the Horses.
Soto. Elements of San Joaquin, The.
Spenser, E. Penelope for her Ulisses sake.
Steele, T. Timothy.
Stephens, P. Signalmen, The.
Steptoe. O' Yes.
Stevenson, R. To A Gardener.
Stickney, T. Requiescam.
Six O'Clock.
Suárez. Worker Dies, A.
Swift, J. Description of the Morning, A.
Swingler. Acres of Power.
Synge. On an Island.
Sze. Moon Is a Diamond, The.
Tagami. Song of Pajaro.
Tayo-jo. People, more people.
Teitelboim, D. Jim the Janitor Is Dead.
Thomas, L. Twelve Gates.
Thomas, R. S. Sir Gelli Meurig.
Thomson, W. Contract Mucker, The.
Tindal. Cry of the Oppressed, The.
Toomer. Reapers.
Torres, A. Small Miracle, A.
Tranströmer. Outskirts.
Tretheway, E. Green Cadillac.
Trethewey, N. Drapery Factory, Gulfport, Mississippi, 1956.
Troupe. River Town Packin House Blues.
Tsvetayeva [or Tsvetaeva]. I Bless the Daily Labor.
I bless the everyday labor.
Unamuno. Throw Yourself Like Seed.
Unknown. Another Little Boy.
Corrido of the Uprooted Ones.
Gao-yang: In His Lambskin Coat.
Ground-Thumping Song.
John Henry.
Plucking the Rushes.
Poor Paddy Works on the Railway.
Tamping Ties.
Then why did I have to make.
Van Dyke. Work.
Vertreace, M. Arc Welder.
Vilariño. Like that man who kicks off his shoes.
Wachtel. Coriolis Effect, The.
Waniek. Balance.
Warner, S. Epitaph: "John Bird, a laborer, lies here."
Watts, I. How Doth the Little Busy Bee.
Whipple, L. My Dad.
Whitman, W. I Hear America Singing.
Wilson, K. Powerhouse, The.
Wise, W. When I Grow Up.
Wither. Husbandman, The.
Spade and the Wreath, The.
Yang Shih-ch'i. On the Hall of Precious Virtue.
Yeats. Adam's Curse.
Yorke. Our Gardener here, James Phillips see.
Yuan Mei. Writing What I've Seen.
Zenmaro. Tanka: "In sullen silence."
Zolynas. Zen of Housework, The.

Labor Day
Glück, L. Labor Day.

Labor Unions
Beecher, J. We Want More Say.
Cleghorn. Comrade Jesus.
Craig, David. Peter pumped Dorothy's hand.
Hahn, K. Everest.
Hill, J. Preacher and the Slave, The.
There Is Power in a Union.
Ridge, L. Stone Face.
Sandburg, C. Teamster's Farewell, A.
Unknown. Uprising of the 20,000, The.
See also **Strikes and Strikers**

Laboratories
Rodgers, Gordon. Laboratory, The.

Labrador, Canada
Crummey, Michael. What's Lost.

Labyrinths
Borges. Labyrinth, The.
Fritz, Walter Helmut (b. 1929). Labyrinth.
Gioia. Maze Without a Minotaur.
Muir, E. Labyrinth, The.
Torres Bodet. Labyrinth.
Volkow. Historia del laberinto, La.
Story of the Labyrinth, The.
Wroth. Sonnet 1: "In this strang[e] labyrinth [or labourinth] how shall I turn[e]?"

Ladybirds
Clare, J. Clock-A-Clay.
Mother Goose. Ladybird, Ladybird fly away home.
Rossetti, C. I caught a little ladybird.
Unknown. Ladybird.

Lafayette, Marie Joseph, Marquis de
Coleridge, S. La Fayette.

Lake District, England
Hemans. Remembrance of Grasmere, A.

Lakes and Ponds
Alexander, P. 1. Ipswich.
Amalrik. Lake Baskunchak.
Basho. Old pond:/ frog-jump-in.
Beachy-Quick, Dan. Echo and A.
Beddoes. Lake, A.
Bendall, M. Fete on the Lake.
Blunden. Midnight Skaters, The.
Buson. Miles of frost / On the lake.
Byron, G. Sonnet to Lake Leman.
Cavalli. Outside nothing's really changed.
Cherry, K. How to Wait.
Ching An. Beating the Heat at Jade Lake.
Clark, T. Lake, The.
You (III).
Coleridge, M. Lady of Trees, The.
Cross, D. Can't Oh.
Cuadra, P. Horses in the Lake.
Dewdney. Depth Sounding, Lake Windermere.
Durrell. Vega.
Eberhart, R. Loon Call, A.
Eimers. Night Without Stars, A.
Endrezze. Birdwatching at Fan Lake.
Frost, R. Spring Pools.
Gioia. Country Wife, The.
Glück, L. Pond, The.
Goll, I. In Age-Old Lakes.
Salt Lake, The.
Graham, W. Loch Thom.
Groarke, V. Islands.
Rainbearers.
Guest, B. Twilight Polka Dots.
Henry, B. Moraine Lake.
Howell, C. He Writes to the Soul.
Hsieh T'iao. Viewing the Three Lakes.
Hume, C. Lies Concerning Speed.
Justice, D. Nostalgia of the Lakefronts.
Kauffman, J. Round Lake.
Kelly, B. Leaving, The.
Lal Ded [or Lalla]. At the end of a crazy-moon night.
Lamartine. Lake, The.
Lake, The.
Lane, P. Lake Murry.
Lenski, H. Day turns to evening on the lake.
Levertov. Quest, The.
Lickbarrow, I. On Esthwaite Water.
Liu Ch'ang-ch'ing. On Seeing Wang Leave for the South.
Liu Yu Hsi. Gazing on Lake Dongting.
MacCaig. Small Lochs.
Maeng Sasŏng. Four Seasons by the Rivers and Lakes.
Major, C. Swallow the Lake.
Meng Hao Jan. Lake of the Ten Thousand Mountains, The.
Meyer, C. Blackshadow Chestnut.
Millay, E. Armenonville.
Milosz, C. House in Krasnogruda.
Morejón. I Never Saw Great Lakes.
Morrissey, S. On Waitakere Dam.
Newman, A. Architecture of the Wings, The.
O'Brien, G. Lake, The.

Paz. Lake.
Pei Di. Lake Yi.
Plath. Crossing the Water.
Poe. Lake: To———, The.
Pritchard, N. Paysagesque.
Ras. Childhood.
Saner. Rain Near Heart Lake.
Scammell, W. Inventions.
Scott, F. Lakeshore.
Seward. Lake, The; Or, Modern Improvement
　in Landscape.
Simms, C. Lochside silverschistsand disturbed-
　to-black-below distributed.
Stein, G. Custard.
Stickney, T. In the Past.
　Lakeward.
Su Tung-p'o. Little stream used to cross my
　land, A.
Supervielle. Missing France.
Unamuno. Beside Christ's Lake in Aldehuela
　de Yeltes, on a Night with a Full Moon.
Voznesensky [or Voznesenskii]. Call of the
　Lake, The.
Wang Ch'ang-ling. Autumn Evening on the
　Great Lake.
Wang Wei. At Lake Yi.
　Lake Yi.
Wen T'ing-yün. Near the Lizhou Ferry.
West, K. By Water Divined.
Wilbur, R. Marginalia.
Wright, D. Lakes, The.
Wright, J. Lake in Central Park, The.
Wylie. Atavism.
Young, D. Poem for Adlai Stevenson and
　Yellow Jackets.

Lamb, Charles
Coleridge, S. This Lime-Tree Bower My Prison.
Lamb, C. In My Own Album.

Lambs
Blake, W. Lamb, The.
Brock-Broido. Carrowmore.
Doolittle, Hilda. Now my right hand.
Eberhart, R. For a Lamb.
Gregg. Lamb, The.
Hale, S. Mary's Lamb [or Mary and Her
　Lamb].
Hughes, T. February 17th.
　Orf.
Jones, B. March Lambs.
Jones, D. On Seeing a Dead Lamb.
Krasicki, I. Lamb and the Wolves, The.
Larkin, P. First Sight.
Lope de Vega. Sonnet 188.
MacCaig. Gone Are the Days.
Marie de France. Wolf and the Lamb, The.
Marquis. Aesop Revised by Archy.
Mew. Fame.
Parry, R. Spring: "After the bitter weather."
Phaedrus. Wolf and the Lamb, The.
Revell, D. Tooms 4.
Roberson, E. Blue Horses.
Rossetti, C. Frisky Lamb, A.
Steven, K. Lamb.
Tekeyan. Sacred Wrath.
Unknown. Little Lamb, A.

Lament
Aneirin. Gorcheanu: The Three Laments.
Bobrowski. Pruzzian Elegy.
Brome. Riddle, The: "No more, no more."
Carew, T. Elegy upon the Death of the Dean of
　[St.] Paul's, Dr. John Donne, An.
Denney. Song: "No use to aim that sextant
　now."
Drayton. To His Coy Love, A Canzonet.
King, H. Exequy, The.
Neruda. Ode with a Lament.
Oodgeroo of the tribe Noonuccal. Dawn Wail
　for the Dead.
Rowe, E. Expostulation, The.
Shaughnessy, B. Epithalament.
Sidney. Sonnet 33: "I might, unhappy word, O
　me, I might."
Surrey. Epitaph for [or on] Thomas Clere.
Trask, H. Chant of Lamentation.
Unknown. How doth the city sit solitary that
　was full of people.

I have been brought into darkness.
　Scribes have cast the blame, The.

Lampreys
Diaper. Lamprey, glowing with uncommon
　fires, The.
Gay, J. To a Young Lady, with Some Lampreys.
See also **Eels**

Lamps and Lamplighting
Farley, P. Lamp, The.
Gekkutsu-Sei. I set down the emerald lamp.
Haskins, L. Dearborn North Apartments
　Chicago, Illinois.
Jacobsen, R. Gaslight.
Pomerantz, A. Chandeliers.
Rakosi. Objectivist Lamp.
Stevenson, R. Lamplighter, The.
Suzuki, M. Swiftly walking away.

Lancashire, England
Carew, T. To Saxham.

Lancelot du Lac
Creeley. Bresson's Movies.
Henley, W. E. At Queensferry.
Hunt, L. One day,—'twas on a summer
　afternoon.
Paulo and Francesca.

Landlords and Landladies
Atwood. Landlady, The.
Bunner, H. Behold the Deeds!
Espada. Imagine the Angels of Bread.
Herbert, G. Redemption.
Hughes, L. Ballad of the Landlord.
　Madam and the Rent Man.
Page, P. Landlady, The.
Soyinka. Telephone Conversation.
Swenson, K. Landlady in Bangkok, The.
Unknown. Big rats! Big rats!

Landor, Walter Savage
Parker, D. Walter Savage Landor.

Landscape
Apollinaire. Windows.
Ashbery, J. Nut Castle.
　Path to the White Moon, The.
Atwood. Autobiography: "First thing I can
　remember is a blue line, The. This was on the
　left."
Baker, K. Austin.
Barker, G. Morning in Norfolk.
Bawer. View from an Airplane at Night, over
　California, The.
Bécquer, G. Gentle Breeze with a Whispered
　Cry, The.
　Invisible Atoms of the Air, The.
Boston, B. Savage, Our Fathers, The.
Cabral de Melo Neto. Landscape of the
　Capibaribe River.
Cairns, Scott. In the General Area of North
　Texas.
Cendrars. Aleutian Islands.
Chaloner. Vista Vert.
Chan Fang-sheng. Sailing Back to the Capital.
Chang Chiu-ling. I close my door and trace the
　transformations of nature.
Chang K'o-chiu. Tune: "Merriment Before the
　Palace Hall".
　Tune: "Traveler Welcoming the Immortal".
Clare, J. Mist in the Meadows.
　Old pond full of flags and fenced around, The.
Cowper, W. Landscape Described, A.
Cross, D. Office Depot parking lot.
Dauthendey, Max (1867-1918). Inside the
　Bouquet.
De León, L. Tranquil Night.
De Roux, Paul. Day's Labor, The.
Deguy. O Great Apposition of the World.
Denney. Mathematician's Dream, The.
Desnos. Never Anyone but You.
Di Prima. Tassajara, 1969.
Divakaruni. Indigo.
Drake, J. Bronx.
Dunn, D. Land Love.
　Landscape with One Figure.
Dupin. When It Is Impossible.
Dyer, J. Now, I gain the Mountain's Brow.
Eliot, T. S. New Hampshire.
　Rannoch, by Glencoe.

Virginia.
Elytis, O. Origin of Landscape or the End of
　Mercy, The.
Evans, A. Martian Landscape.
Fumi Saito. As a landscape in the far distance.
Garioch. Wire, The.
Gascoyne. Snow in Europe.
Getsi. Woman Hanging from Lightpole, Illinois
　Route 136.
Gilman, C. California Colors: A Song.
Ginsberg, A. Wales Visitation.
Givens, Bettye Hammer. West Texas.
Goll, I. Journey into Misery.
Gould, J. Easter Sunday.
Grover, Dorys Crow. Ranch on the Limpia,
　The.
Gruffydd, P. Slate Quay: Felinheli.
Hall, H. Palmer. Ghost Lights.
Herrera y Reissig. July.
Hewitt, J. Ram's Horn, The.
Higginson, E. Dawn.
　Dawn on the Willamette.
　Opal Sea, The.
Hoggard, James. November: "Shimmering
　spreads of golden fire."
Hsieh Ling-yün. Night: Setting out from Shih-
　Kuan Pavilion.
　Scene from South Hill to North Hill Passing the
　Lake.
Hsieh T'iao. Roaming the East Field.
　Viewing the Three Lakes.
Ignatova, E. I have encountered a valley, in
　ragged bast matting.
Jiménez, J. Countryside Sleeps, Trembling, The.
Johnson, E. Joe.
Kafka. In the Evening's Gentle Sunshine.
Kavanagh, P. Come Dance with Kitty Stobling.
Knight, R. Landscape, The.
Knutson, G. Moon Fishing.
Kruit, J. Landscape.
K'ung Chih-kuei. Trip on Mount T'ai-P'ing.
Kuzmina-Karavayeva. Long-Barrow Princess 2.
Lam Thi My Da. Garden Fragrance.
Langgässer, E. Daphne.
Lanier, S. From the Flats.
Li Ho. Cold in the North (After Yueh-Fu).
　High the Mount of Wu.
　On and On: An Ancient Song (Yueh-Fu).
Li Po. Ascend the Phoenix Terrace.
　Barbarian pass is filled with windblown sand,
　The.
　Crossing Ching-Men to See a Friend Off.
　Listening to the Lute Played by Monk Chun
　from Shu.
　On Visiting Taoist Recluse of Tai-Tien-Shan and
　Not Finding Him.
　River Song.
　Taking Leave of a Friend.
　To See a Friend Off to Shu.
　Tune: "Beautiful Barbarians".
Liu Tsung-yüan. Morning Walk in Autumn to
　South Valley Passing an Abandoned Village.
　River Snow.
Lope de Vega. May Song.
Lu Chih. Tune: "Drunk in the East Wind".
Lugones. Indulgence.
MacDonald, A. Month of plants and of honey.
Machado Ruiz. Denuded Is the Earth.
　There, in the High Part.
　Who Placed, Amidst the Tracts of Ash.
MacLean, S. Kinloch Ainort.
Marsman. Landscape.
Marvell. Upon Appleton House [To My Lord
　Fairfax].
　Upon the Hill and Grove at Bilbrough.
Mathews, H. Lateral Disregard.
Mathias, R. Brechfa Chapel.
　Porth Cwyfan.
McMorris, M. Aphrodite of Economy.
McMurtry, Larry. For Erwin Smith, Cowboy
　Photographer.
McNulty, T. Bodhidharma Crossing the
　Graywolf River on a Ry-Krisp.
Mead, P. Cinema Point.
Melville, H. Attic Landscape, The.
　Enviable Isles, The.

Inscription, The: "While yet Rolfe's foot in stirrup stood."
Mendelssohn, Anna. Franked.
Meng Hao Jan. Stayover at Chien-Teh River.
Montale. Where the Tennis Court Was.
Murphey, John Collin. Lake Austin Diorama.
Muso Soseki. Beyond the World.
Temple of Eternal Light.
Myers, J. We Go Away at Home.
Nazareno, C. Cortes Swamp, The.
Neruda. Forgive me if my eyes see.
From the explosion to the iron split.
I did not touch your night, or your air, or dawn.
Men grow with all that grows.
Pardon me, if when I want.
North, C. Landscape and Chardin.
O'Daly, B. Whale in the Web, The.
O'odham. No. 84. I Am Going to See the Land.
Ou-yang Hsiu. Pear Leaves Redden, Cicada's Song is Done, The.
Padilla. Fountain, a House of Stone, A.
Landscapes.
Paz. Lake.
Native Stone.
Penrose, V. At My Windows.
Pow. Favourite Stretch of Disused Railway, A.
Robertson, Lexie Dean. Texas Memoranda.
Rouweler. Landscape.
Rukeyser, M. Homage to Literature.
Samyn, M. Trompe L'Oeil in Winter.
Sandburg, C. Nocturne in a Deserted Brickyard.
Sarton, M. December Moon.
Schelling. Commentary.
Seward. Lake, The; Or, Modern Improvement in Landscape.
Simms, C. Grey Wagtail on the Tyne.
Sinclair, I. Serious of Photographs, A.
Solórzano, L. Zacoalco o paisaje.
Zacoalco or Landscape.
Soto. After Tonight.
Spender, S. Mask.
Stéfan, Jude. Herrings and Birch Trees.
Stow. Singing Bones, The.
Teasdale. Day's Ending.
Thomas, E. I never saw that land before.
Tu Fu [or Du Fu]. Climbing on the Double Ninth Day.
Wu-Chueh.
Tu Shen-yen. Harmonizing a Spring Poem by Premier Lu of Chin-Ling.
Unknown. Tchirek Song (Northern Yueh-Fu).
Valéry. Oarsman, The.
Vallejo. It was Sunday in the fair ears of my burro.
Van Duyn. View, A.
Van Ostaijen. Landscape.
Wang Chih-huan. Ascend the Heron Tower.
Wang Wan. Stayover at Pei-Ku-Shan.
Wang Wei. After Source of the Peach Blossom Stream.
Autumn Dusk at a Mountain Lodge.
Mount Chung-Nan.
Passing the Temple of Teeming Fragrance.
Villa at the Foot of Mount Chungnan.
Wang Yung. River Song, The.
Wells, C. Pastoral in Posters, A.
White, K. McTaggart.
Williamson, G. Italics, Mine.
Up in the Air.
Wilson, S. Picture on the Purple Wall, the.
Wordsworth, W. Was it for this.
Xuan Quynh. Summer: "It's the season of birdsong."
Yao Sui. Tune: "Full Court of Fragrance".

Landscapes
Albrecht, A. Elkhorn Slough.
Alterman, N. Moon.
Auden. In Praise of Limestone.
Bachmann. Firstborn Land, The.
Bei Dao. Landscape Over Zero.
Birney. From the Hazel Bough.
Brownstein. Against the Grain.
Carper, Thomas. Aerial Photograph, An.
Cary, A. Katrina on the Porch.
Chang Chiu-ling. Climbing a Tall Building on an Autumn Evening: I Gaze to Where the

South River Touches the Shixing Road.
Chia Tao. Abode of the Unplanned Effect.
Farewell to T'ien Cho on Retreat on Hua Mountain.
Watching the Late Day Clear after Snowfall.
Ching An. At Lushan Temple.
On a Painting.
Cook, Geoffrey. Watermarks.
Craven, Sherry. Chalk Draw Ranch.
Crummey, Michael. Painting the Islands.
Dalchev, A. Snow: "Over strip-raked iron rooves."
Darwish, M. We Walk Towards a Land.
Dawe, Tom. Abandoned Outport.
De Kok. At this resort.
Di Prima. In This Landscape.
Dyer, J. Grongar Hill.
Ehrhart. Cycling the Rosental.
Eluard, P. et al. I've Told You.
Fagin, L. Landscape.
Fichman. Secrets of the Landscape, The.
Fischer, N. Tuesday, 17 April.
Follain. Landscapes They Walk Through, The.
Fulton, A. Little Heart to Heart with the Horizon, A.
Gerbasi, V. Hallucinatory Sunset, with Sons.
Gioia. Rough Country.
Graves, R. Lost Acres.
Guillory, D. Retinal burn of warm November light.
Han-shan Te-ch'ing. Flat Lake cold penetrates water-lily clothes.
Flat Lake's autumn water merges with the winter sky.
Resting at my open window I gaze out at mountains.
Hanzlicek, C. Sierra Noon.
Helwig. Sudden risk of birds, A.
Hemans. To a Distant Scene.
Hilberry. Body and Mind.
Hine. Point Grey.
Hirshfield, J. Recalling a Sung Dynasty Landscape.
Hồ Xuân Huong. Country Scene.
Hsieh Ling-yün. Here where I live.
Hwang Tonggyu. Happy Letter, A.
Wind Burial 3.
Ilton, Phil. No Goalies.
József, A. Dead Landscape.
Jungkwan Ilson. Returning to Dupawon.
Kenyon, J. Noiseless Wheel, The.
Kurtz. Andalusian Landscape.
Lamantia. There Are Many Pathways to the Garden.
Li Po. Ancient Airs.
On Hsin-P'ing Tower.
On Phoenix Tower in Chin-Ling.
Lowell, A. St. Louis.
Mariani. Mountain View with Figures.
Variations on a Theme by Justice.
Mathews, H. Ledge, The.
McDonald, W. Starting a Pasture.
Meek, Sandra. Windowseat.
Melville, H. Enviable Isles, The.
Pontoosuce.
Minulescu, I. Mechanical-landscape-poem.
Montague, J. Lost Tradition, A.
Windharp.
Moulds, J. Renoir's Bathers.
Murray, L. Craze Field, The.
Muske, C. Coming Over Coldwater.
Neufeldt, L. Yarrow.
Nichol. Landscape: 1.
Oliveira, D. San Joaquin.
Ostriker. Minor Van Gogh (He Speaks), A.
Pao Chao. Dalei Riverbank.
Paz. Landscape.
Peaux, A. Cold Landscape.
Reed, P. Container of Stars.
Reznikoff. Out of the hills the trees bulge.
Rohrer, J. Stopping by Fields on a Snowy Afternoon.
Scammell, W. Inventions.
Schneeman, G. Landscape.
Scollard. Ballads of the Wheel.
Sherman, M. Towards Sunset at Camino Cielo.

Smith, C. To the South Downs.
Smith, K. Again with Music.
Snyder, G. Walking through Myoshin-Ji.
Stickney, T. Mt. Lykaion.
Requiescam.
Strode. On Westwall Downes [or On Westwell Downs].
Su Tung-p'o. Red Cliff, The.
Sulchinskaya, O. Crimea.
Sze. Before Sunrise.
Thomas, R. S. Welsh Landscape.
Tomlinson, C. Saving the Appearances.
Second Song.
Zipangu.
Trần Thái-Tông, King. To the Monk Đúc Son at Thanh-phong Monastery.
Tretheway. Resurrection at West Lake.
Tu Fu [or Du Fu]. Clear after Rain ("Long after rainfall, Sorceress Hills grow dark.").
Landscape: "Clear autumn opens endlessly away."
Thatch House.
Verlaine. Brussels: Simple Frescos 1.
Brussels: Simple Frescos 2.
Vogt, B. Uncle with Landscape—Kansas, 1954.
Voltskaya, T. Low clouds, the shreds of dry grass, The.
Wang An-shih. Hui-chu Temple, Mount K'un.
Wang Chih-huan. Hooded Crane Tower.
View from Heron Tower.
Wang Ts'an. Climbing the Tower.
Wang Wei. Bird and Waterfall Music.
Bird-Cry Creek.
Crossing the Yellow River.
Poor dwelling near valley mouth.
Wayman. Long Beach Suite.
Williams, S. Town less, A.
Wordsworth, W. Lines Composed a Few Miles above Tintern Abbey on Revisiting the Banks of the Wye During a Tour, July 13, 1798.
Wright, C. Aubade: "Over Govino Bay, looking up from the water's edge, the landscape resembles nothing so much as the hills above Genova."
Wright, J. Night After Bushfire.
Wynne, F. Nocturne: "Long day was bright, The."
Yi I. Where is the third bend?
Yi Illo. On the River on a Spring Day.
Yi Kyubo. Leaves of the mountain pear are red, The.
Yi Sang. Poem No. 7.
Yi Yuksa. Thatched House.
Yost, C. Descano, California.
Young, G. It's Sunday, October ninth, and the earth here is barren after harvest.
Zawacki, Andrew. Velocity Among the Ruins of Angel Republic.

Landslides
Engels, J. Landslide.

Language
Abad, G. Light in One's Blood, The.
Acosta. Dangereux avril.
Adamo. Roches Moutonnees.
Adams, F. To a Thesaurus.
Agard, J. Listen Mr Oxford Don.
Albert-Birot. Balalaïka.
Bluesky.
Albiach. Hermitage Road, The.
"Theatre".
Ali, A. Ghazal: "Only language of loss left in the world is Arabic, The."
In Arabic.
Allen, P. Zen Americana.
Alvarez, J. Bilingual Sestina.
Andrews, B. Appetizers'.
DDD.
Gestalt Me Out!
Impatient Heart, The.
Methodology.
West West.
While.
Antin. Real Estate.
Apollinaire. Monday rue Christine.
To Linda.
Arensberg. Arithmetical Progression of the Verb

"To Be".
Ing.
Armantrout. As We're Told.
Up to Speed.
Arteaga, Alfred. Corrido Blanco.
Ashbery, J. All Messages Have Been Played.
Life As a Book That Has Been Put Down.
Limited Liability.
Pantoum.
Paradoxes and Oxymorons.
Soonest Mended.
Aubert, A. Opposite of Green, The.
Auden. Their Lonely Betters.
Ball, H. Complete Sound-Poems of Hugo Ball, The.
Flight out of Time.
Bandeira. Evocation of Recife.
Baraka, I. Heavy, The.
Wise 3.
Barkan, S. Italian Masons.
Barnett, A. Turbulence and Tongue.
Baron Supervielle, Silvia. Here Time.
Barot, R. Riffing.
Bateman, M. Decline of Gaelic, The.
Beachy-Quick, Dan. Halt (Naïve).
Belieu. My Field Guide.
Bell, M. These Green-Going-to-Yellow.
To No One in Particular.
Bendall, M. Book of Style, The.
Benson, S. Beethoven's Sixth Symphony.
Berger, D. Language Pile, The.
Bergvall, C. Hungry Form.
Berkson, B. Rebecca Cutlet.
Bernes, J. Desiderata on a Desert Island.
Outside You Cannot Breathe.
Sonnet with Lock and Key.
Bernstein, C. Age of Correggio and the Carracci, The.
Frequently unasked questions.
Have Pen, Will Travel.
Let's Just Say.
Our new / service orientation.
Wait.
Why we ask you not to touch.
Berrigan, T. Mud on the first day (night, rather.
Bible, O.T. And the whole earth was of one language, and of one speech.
Bienek. Resistance.
Bishop, M. Flowers of Rhetoric.
Naughty Preposition, The.
Bitsui, Sherwin. Northern Sun, The.
Bleakney, J. Fairytale Land of Um, The.
Bobrowski. Dead Language.
Boland, E. Anna Liffey.
Borges. Poem Written in a Copy of Beowulf.
Bosselaar. English Flavors.
Bowen, E. Youth of the Language, The.
Breeze. Dubbed Out.
Breytenbach. Struggle for the Taal, The.
Brossard, Nicole. I Want to Revise This Sequence.
Broumas, O. Artemis.
If I Yes.
Brown, L. Shiny jewel eye.
Bryan, S. BE-.
Budde, R. Bodiless.
Gag.
Lesion.
Stitch.
Tattoo.
Burgess, Leslie. Prostitute's Notebook, The.
Burn. For the Common Market.
Cabri, L. Salon, Salon.
Cage. Lecture on Nothing.
Campert. Message About the Times.
Sign of the Times.
Campion, T. Think'st thou to seduce me then.
Carruth, H. No Matter What, After All, and That Beautiful Word So.
Of Distress Being Humiliated by the Classical Chinese Poets.
Carson, A. Short Talk on the Truth to Be Had From Dreams.
Casey, M. Learning.
Castro, M. Blew It.
Celan. Language Mesh.

Speak You Too.
Césaire, A. New Year.
Chaloner. Emblem.
Vista Vert.
Waste.
Chapman, G. And, for our tongue, that still is so empayr'd.
Cheek. Rollercoaster.
Ch'en Tzu-ang. I dwell in seclusion and observe the creative process.
Chiasson, H. Apollo at Aberdeen.
Christie, J. Neutrino (means little one).
Clark, C. Border Affair, A.
Clifton, L. I am accused of tending to the past.
Cobbing. Bird Bee.
Hymn to the Sacred Mushroom.
Cocteau. Cape of Good Hope, The.
Coffey. Prayers, The.
Coleman, W. Essay on Language.
ISM, The.
Collobert. I Time of What.
III: "As if dead the buried text."
Conoley, G. Beckon.
Coolidge, C. On Induction of the Hand.
On the Road.
Ounce code orange.
Cope, W. Uncertainty of the Poet, The.
Corcoran. In the Red Book.
Corn. Contemporary Culture and the Letter "K".
Cortez, J. Phraseology.
Coviello, M. This hour is made of iron grates where the underground.
Creeley. Language, The.
Cross, E. Palabras.
Words.
Crouch, S. Blackie Thinks of His Brothers.
Crozier, A. Loopy Dupes.
Cuadra, A. Brief Letter to Donald Walsh (in memoriam).
Cullen, Y. This.
Curbelo. Between Language and Desire.
Curtis, T. We Can Say That.
Daniel, G. My Mother Tongue.
Darragh. Footnote at "Figure of Speech".
Lattice at/of (Com)pare (Dis)pair.
Lattice at "Split".
"Legion" to "Lent" for "R".
"Luteous" to "Lymph" for "F".
Sis Boom Ba.
Throwing Out at / of (Com)pare (Dis)pair, A.
Volcanic tuff.
Daumal. Poetry and Thought.
Davidson, M. Century of Hands.
Et in Leucadia Ego.
Davie, D. With the Grain.
Davies, A. New Sentience, The.
Thirty East Forty-Second Street.
Davis, O. Unbosoming, The.
Day, J. From Momentary Work, A Wrench.
Moving Object.
de Fréine, C. Mother tongue.
De la Mare. Antiques.
De León, L. O Courtesy, O Harborage Most Sweet.
Deltoro, A. Cartografía.
Cartography.
Deniz, G. Authoritarian School and How a Respectable Literary Genre Was Born, The.
Escuela autoritaria y cómo nació un respetable género de literatura, La.
Desnos. Hour Farther.
Like.
Like.
When children slap their father's face.
DiPalma. Annotations Tropes and Lacunae of the Itoku Master.
Bed, The.
Motion of the Cypher.
We Forego Mimicry.
Djanikian. How I Learned English.
Domin. Exile.
Donnelly, T. Twenty-seven Props for a Production of Eine Lebenszeit.
Dove, R. Poem in Which I Refuse Contemplation.

Drysdale, A. Language Difficulty.
Dubie. Pendulum, The.
Duhig, I. From the Irish.
Duo Duo. None.
Dupin. I Am Forbidden.
When It Is Impossible.
Eady. Sherbet.
Edwards, K. De—um majorettes.
Good Science.
Lexically.
Unconsciously.
Eidenier, Elon G. Failure of Language, The.
Eigner. Temporary Language, A.
Ellis, T. Hush Yo Mouf.
Sir Nose D'VoidofFunk.
Elmslie, K. Stage Duo.
Emerson, J. White Flowers.
Equi. In a Monotonous Dream.
Eskimo Oral Tradition. Magic Words.
Espada. Community College Revises Its Curriculum in Response to Changing Demographics, The.
Ferguson, G. Silent as Roses.
Finch, P. How Callum Innes Paints.
Marks the English Left on the Map.
Reds in the Bed.
Scaring Hens.
Fink, Robert A. For Micha's Mother, Who Signs.
Finlay, I. Garden Poem.
Fisher, A. African Boog.
Birdland.
Diary Theme, The.
Ditchley Portrait, The.
Machynlleth.
Murder One.
Progressions of Spacetime: I.
Rims of Distinction: I.
Stepping Out: 2.
Stepping Out: I.
Fisher, R. He paints words with the past.
Fordham. Saxon Legend of Language, The.
Forrest-Thomson. Lemon and Rosemary.
Fortini. Italy 1942.
Foster, T. Grammar of Waking, A.
France, L. Body Language.
North and South.
Francis, R. Hogwash.
Freer, U. Baseline pressure.
Fragmento.
TM.
Frénaud. Words of the Poem, The.
Fuller, H. Comic.
Galvin, J. Post-Modernism.
Gardiner, S. No Title.
Garelli, Jacques. Excess of Poetry.
Gershwin, I. Let's Call the Whole Thing Off.
Gilbert, J. It Is Clear Why the Angels Come No More.
Malvolio in San Francisco.
Perspective He Would Mutter Going to Bed.
Gillan. Public School No. 18: Paterson, New Jersey.
Giovanni. Poem (for Langston Hughes), A.
Giussani, S. Vegetable Calendar.
Glancy. First Reader Santee Training School, 1873, The.
Glatstein, J. To a Friend Who Wouldn't Bother to Strain His Noodleboard Because Even So It Is Hard to Go Hunting When Your Rifle Is Blunt and Love Is Soft as an Old Blanket.
Glazer, M. Purpose of Design Is to Make the Whole Greater Than the Sum of Its Parts, The.
Glück, L. Illuminations.
Goldberg, B. Say.
Goldsworthy. After Babel.
Goodyear, Dana. Umbra.
Graham, J. Breakdancing.
For One Must Want / To Shut the Other's Gaze.
Underneath (1).
Underneath (3).
Grangaud, Michelle. Isidore Ducasse comte de Lautréamont.
Graves, R. Cool Web, The.
In Broken Images.
Tilth.

Griffin, T.   Closed Discussion about the Future.
Imitation.
Observation.
Griffiths, B.   Shepherd's Calendar cont'd.
Griffiths, J.   Errata.
Lost and Found.
Guest, B.   Advance of the Grizzly, The.
Red Dye.
Words: "Simple contact with a wooden spoon
and the word, The."
You Can Discover.
Guevara, M.   Doña Josefina Counsels Doña
Concepción Before Entering Sears.
Guillén, N.   Don't Know No English.
Sensemayá.
Hacker, M.   Squares and Courtyards.
Hadas, R.   Three Silences.
Hall, D.   Peaches.
Hamby, B.   Six, Sex, Say.
Hamill, S.   Gift of Tongues, The.
Hamod, S.   Leaves.
Hannan, M.   Drive.
Hardy, T.   Liddell and Scott.
Harrison, T.   Classics Society.
On Not Being Milton.
Them & [uz].
Harryman.   Allegory.
That Can Not Be Taken Away From It.
Hartman, J.   Baroque Excess of Pig Latin and.
Hartnett.   Pity the Man Who English Lacks.
Hass, R.   Interrupted Meditation.
Meditation at Lagunitas.
Hayes, T.   Talk.
Hearle, K.   Politics of Memory, The.
Helle, A.   Poem for Natalia Ginzburg.
Hemensley.   Sulking in the Seventies.
Herbert, G.   Son[ne], The.
Herrera.   Hallucinogenic Bullfighter.
Hershon.   Calls from the Outside World.
Hillman, B.   Geology, A.
Hine.   Tabula Rasa?
Hocquard.   Three Moral Tales.
Holmes, O.   Aestivation [an Unpublished Poem,
by My Late Latin Tutor].
Holthaus, G.   Unexpected Manna.
Hoover, P.   Desire.
Hovanessian, D.   Two Voices.
Howe, S.   In its first dumb form.
Rückenfigur.
Huelsenbeck, R. *et al.*   L'amiral cherche une
maison à louer.
Hume, C.   Lies Concerning Speed.
True and Obscure Definitions of *Fly*, Domestic
and Otherwise.
Hutchinson, P.   Frost is All Over, The.
Inman, P.   Centered.
Colloam.
Field dodd.
Subtracted Words.
XX.
Ishkhan.   Armenian Language Is the Home of
the Armenian, The.
Jabès.   Desert, The.
Notebook, Two.
Jackson, L.   World and I, The.
Jacobsen, J.   Monosyllable, The.
Jandl, E.   Chanson.
Dilection.
Jerry.   Mabrak.
Joe, R.   Plawej ans L'nui'site'w (Partridge and
Indian-Speaking Priest).
Johnson, D.   Bilingual Means Having Two
Tongues.
Jones, R.   Obsolescence of *Thou*, The.
Jonson, B.   Fit of Rhyme against Rhyme, A.
Joseph, A.   On Being Told I Don't Speak Like a
Black Person.
Traitor.
Joyce, J.   Bronze by gold heard the hoofirons,
steelyringing.
Kaneko.   Bailey Gatzert: The First Grade, 1945.
Kay, J.   Old Tongue.
Keelan, C.   My Twentieth Century.
Kelly, R.   Ode to Language.
Sermon on Language.
Khlebnikov, V.   Zangezi: R, K, L, G—.

Kim Chôngnan.   Women's Language.
Kinsella, J.   Visitant Eclogue.
Kirchwey.   Oracular Degeneration.
Koch, K.   Permanently.
Kruchyonykh [*or* Kruchionykh *or* Kruchenykh].
Declaration of the Word as Such.
Pomade.
Kuzmin.   Not for nothing did we read the
theologians.
Lahey, Joy.   Buckles.
Lane, P.   Pissaro's Tomb.
Lange, A.   Perugia.
Larsen, W.   Learning the War.
Laurencin, M.   Tiger, The.
Lauterbach.   In the Museum of the Word (Henri
Matisse).
Novelist Speaks, The.
Lee, James R.   Stranger at Home.
Lee, L.   Persimmons.
Leftwich, Jim.   Eleusis.
Lehrer.   Wernher von Braun.
Leonard, T.   This is thi.
Lerner, A.   Rain in Spain, The.
Levertov.   Caedmon.
O Taste and See.
Lewis, G.   Beginning to Forget.
Interview with the Poet.
Interview with the Poet.
Language's Will and Testament, The.
Poet's Confession, A.
Lim-Wilson.   Alphabet Soup.
Upon Overhearing Tagalog.
Liu Yu Hsi.   Looking at My Knife-Hilt, a Song.
Lloyd, Paul.   Michelle Granguad Creating
Anagrams.
Lloyd, Rosemary.   Michelle Granguad Creating
Anagrams.
Loesser.   Murder, He Says.
Longfellow, H.   Picture-Writing.
López Mills, T.   Dead Weight of the Land, The.
Peso muerto de la tierra, El.
Lopez, T.   Dauntless the slug-horn to my lips I
set.
Lorde.   Coal.
Loy.   Gertrude Stein.
Lum.   Going Home.
Lumelli, A.   Candid Camera.
Lux.   Language Animal, The.
Solo Native.
Mac Lochlainn, G.   Second Tongue.
Mac Low.   Almost Casanova Electricity.
Lack of Balance but not Fatal, A.
7th Light Poem: For John Cage—17 June 1962.
MacCaig.   No Consolation.
MacDiarmid, H.   Caledonian Antisyzygy, The.
MacKenzie, R.   Like Pornography.
Square.
Mackey, N.   Alphabet of Ahtt.
MacNeacail.   Gaelic is alive.
MacSweeney.   Far Cliff Babylon.
Flame Ode.
Ode Long Kesh.
Ode: "Urals post-master, this is your."
Mahapatra, J.   Sanskrit.
Mahon.   Tractatus.
Maiden.   Assonance.
Major, D.   Nommo: how we come to speak.
Mandel, T.   Realism.
Marennikova, K.   I, Mariya, burn your fingers.
Markotić, N.   Try book-ending punctuation
vouchers.
Martin, Camille.   Mawkish me.
To abcs and from rimbaud.
Martin, Charles.   E. S. L.
Speech Against Stone.
Mateo.   There Is No Word for Sex in Taglog.
Mattawa.   Echo and Elixir 2.
Mayor, C.   Winter Night.
McCaffery.   Can there be a collision between
picture and application?
Little Hans.
McCallum, S.   Calypso.
In My Other Life.
McDonald, E.   Widdershins.
McGrath, T.   Language of the Dead, The.
McHugh, H.   Language Lesson 1976.

McLain, P.   Connor in the Wind and Rain with
His Coat on.
McMorris, M.   Aphrodite of Economy.
Near Speech, The.
Some Days in the City.
McOrlan.   Horse butcher, The.
Mead, J.   Sometimes the Mind.
Melo, M.   Scrambled Eggs and Garlic Pork.
Unlearning English.
Meredith, W.   Effort at Speech.
Rhode Island.
Merrill, J.   Lost in Translation.
Merwin.   After the Alphabets.
Last One, The.
Learning a Dead Language.
Losing a Language.
Michaels, A.   Language is the house with
lamplight in its windows.
Michaels, D.   Returning from Italy.
Midge, T.   Written in Blood.
Mills, B.   Ballad: Of Motion.
Milne, D.   And out of dominion.
Milosz, C.   Esse.
My Faithful Mother Tongue.
Readings.
Monk, G.   AC.
CS.
La Tormenta.
Montague, J.   Grafted Tongue, A.
Montale.   Don't ask us for the word to frame.
Mora.   Elena.
Morales.   I Am the Reasonable One.
I Recognize You.
Morgan, E.   Sir James Murray.
Morgan, R.   Jutaculla Rock.
Morley, D.   Jerusalem.
Mueller, L.   When I Am Asked.
Mullen, H.   Bilingual Instructions.
Denigration.
Present Tense.
Mutis.   Sonata.
Myrddin ap Dafydd.   Language Is Only Words,
A.
Nabokov.   On Translating "Eugene Onegin".
Nash, O.   Very Like a Whale.
What's in a Name? Some Letter I Always
Forget.
Nekrasov, V.   I repeat.
Nepote, M.   Image of the Fish.
Imagen del Pez.
Neruda.   I come to speak through your dead
mouth.
Ni Dhomhnaill.   Language Issue, The.
Language Issue, The.
Niccolai.   Careful that these *Frisbees*.
Nichol.   Scraptures: 7th Sequence.
St. Anzas VI.
St. Anzas IX.
Nickerson.   At Auke Bay the whales dance.
Noël, Bernard.   Portrait.
Noguere.   Scribes, The.
Norman, L.   SpaNglisH.
Odio, E.   Prologue to a Time That Is Not Itself.
Oliver, D.   "u", "je", "r", "r", "im", "a",
"finally".
Olson, C.   Moon Is the Number 18, The.
These Days: "Whatever you have to say, leave."
Oppen.   Building of the Skyscraper, The.
Emotions are engaged, The.
O'Sullivan, M.   Giant Yellow.
Hill Figures.
Lesson from the Cockerel.
Narrative Charm for Ibbotroyd.
2nd Lesson from the Cockerel.
Pacheco, J.   Job 18, 2.
Palmer, M.   All those words we once used for
things but have now discarded in order to
come to know things.
Eighth Sky.
Fifth Prose.
Recursus.
Sun ("Write this. We have burned all their
villages.").
Patchen.   Moon, Sun, Sleep, Birds, Live.
Pau-Llosa.   Hollow, The.
Paz.   Between What I See and What I Say.

Pembroke, M. To the Thrice-Sacred Queen Elizabeth.
Peppermint, Heidi. Real Toads.
Perelman. Broken Mirror, The.
Chronic Meanings.
Here 2.
Let's Say.
Seduced by Analogy.
Things.
Peri Rossi. Tired of women.
Philips, K. On the Welsh Language.
Phillips, D. From Arena.
I Held the Vein, But Death.
On Entries Emptiness.
Pinchas-Cohen. Her, Me, and Yochanan.
My English Teacher.
Ping. Syntax.
Pinsky. Ode to Meaning.
Plath. Incommunicado.
Magi.
Plumpp. Turf Song.
Portnoy, M. Of of Titmouse.
Posey, A. Ode to Sequoyah.
Powell, D. A. House Face.
Prévert. Dunce, The.
Pritchard, N. Metagnomy.
Prunty, Randy. Trigger D'evolution.
Radden, V. When You Talk That Talk.
Radiguet. Poem: "Horizon line."
Ragan, J. Standing at Pasternak's Table, Peredelkino.
Randall, M. I Want the Words Back.
Past Is, The.
Rankine. Testimonial.
Raworth. Dark Senses.
That More Simple Natural Time Tone Distortion.
Reedy, C. Doll Museum, The.
Retallack, J. Here's Looking at You Francis Bacon.
Not a Cage.
Western CIV, 4 and 5.
Reznikoff. Highway I was walking on, The.
How difficult for me is Hebrew.
Riley, D. Disintegrate Me.
Lure, 1963.
Rimbaud, A. Voyelles.
Riordan, M. Word from the Loki, A.
Ríos, A. Language of Great-Aunts, The.
Nani.
Roberson, E. It must be that in the midst.
Rodefer. Inscription.
Roffé. Landscape of return is drawn, A.
Rothenberg, J. Aleph Poem.
Rouse, A. Spunk Talking.
Rumi. Answers from the Elements.
Rumsey, Tessa. Never Mororcco.
Russell, N. Message of the Rain, The.
Sabina. 13th Horse Song of Frank Mitchell, The.
Sachs, Carly. Story, The.
Sáenz. Between Worlds.
Salazar. Piñon Nuts.
Salter. Summer 1983.
Samaras, N. Translation.
Sandburg, C. Languages.
Little Girl, Be Careful What You Say.
Precious Moments.
Primer Lesson.
Scalise, G. Amiti´ Amoureuse.
Man comes last: he's got to.
Schevill. Whitman Stock-Taking, Cataloguing.
Schwitters. Third movement.
Scully, M. Variations.
Seyburn, P. Alphabetizer Speaks, The.
Shapcott, J. Motherland.
Shapiro, K. Dirty Word, The.
Sheppard, R. Empty Diary 1990.
Sherry, J. Lepidoptery.
What should be the title of a king. Too, how also to include. What happened when.
Shin Kyŏngnim. Baby, The.
Sholl. Good News/Bad News.
Silliman. Lucky my ears 'pop' at the hilltop.
Not this. / What then?
Silva, C. Tea at the Magdalene.

Simic. Errata.
Simms, C. Lochside silverschistsand disturbed-to-black-below distributed.
Simpson, N. Sentencing.
Sinclair, I. Snow Lip.
World's Oldest Comedian Is Dead.
Sisson. Usk, The.
Skinner, J. Fetch.
Slavitt. Tryma.
Smelcer. My Indian Grandmother Speaks to Animals.
Smith, I. Shall Gaelic Die?
Smith, Tracy K. Spring: "Let's not talk."
Spahr, J. Localism or t/here.
Spicer, J. Duet for a Chair and a Table.
Thing Language.
Sriramulu, D. Other Tongue, The.
Stein, G. Act so that there is no use in a centre.
Cloth, A.
Frightful Release, A.
Light in the moon the only light is on Sunday, A.
Mounted Umbrella, A.
Picasso.
Purse, A.
Sacred Emily.
Stevens, W. On [or Of] the Manner of Addressing Clouds.
Sze. Do Not Speak Keresan to a Mescalero Apache.
Szporluk. Eohippus.
Holy Ghost.
Taggart, J. Body and Soul: Poem for Two Readers.
Monk.
Tarkos, Christophe. 67 Words with One Vowel and One Consonant.
Tennyson, A. I sometimes hold it half a sin.
Thomas, G. Welsh-speaking Welsh, The.
Thomas, L. Electricity of Blossoms.
Great Love Duets.
Thompson, P. Erato.
Tipton. I Want to Speak With the Blood that Lies Down.
Tomlinson, C. Las Trampas U.S.A.
Tornero, A. Arden la torcida, entre mis ojos, y la jerarquía intermedia de una imagen esta tarde.
Tranströmer. From March 1979.
Tranter. Hang up a yellow shirt—you cause joy.
Triplett, P. Story for the Mother Tongue.
Turnbull. Residues: Thronging the Heart.
There Are Words.
Twichell. Animal Languages.
Tzara. Dada Manifesto on Feeble and Bitter Love.
Great Lament of my Obscurity Three, The.
Maison Aragon.
Ullman. Living Near the Plaza of Thieves.
Unknown. Aborigine Sound Poem.
Bald Mountain Zaum-Poems.
I passed thurgh a gardyn grene.
Justice to Scotland.
Magic Words.
Valdés, Gina. English con Salsa.
Valentine, J. Waiting.
Vallejo. And What If after So Many Words.
Trilce.
Vando. Commonwealth, Common Poverty.
Velichansky, A. Flame's speech is confused, The. The muttering of the water is hollow.
Vicuña. Fables of the Beginning and Remains of the Origin.
Villa, D. What counts in any action.
Villa, E. Lend me a battle of unavoidable suggestions.
Trees were moving.
Ugly season of putrifying buzzards, An.
Voeten. Sun On My Hand, The ("Sun lights my hand writing, The.").
Sun On My Hand, The ("Writing with the sun on my hand.").
Volach, Y. Hebrew.
Volkman. Sonnet: "As the dream a consciousness adored."
Sonnet: "Never got, and never thought, and

yet."
Sonnet: "Nothing was ever what it claimed to be."
Von Freytag-Loringhoven. Appalling Heart.
Klink—Hratzvenga (Deathwail).
Voznesensky [or Voznesenskii]. Dogalypse.
Wah. Father / Mother Haibun #16.
Walcott. Codicil.
Waldrop, R. To explore the nature of rain I opened the door because inside the workings of language clear vision is impossible.
Wallace-Crabbe. Life of Ideas, The.
Ward, Geoff. Trapped Wind.
Warn. Word Between the World and God, The.
Warren-Moore. For Etheridge Knight.
Warren, R. Brotherhood in Pain.
Watten. Statistics.
Weaver, A. Luxembourg Garden.
Weiss, R. Conference, A.
Weiss, T. Conference, A.
Welish. Macbeth in Battle.
Scalpel in Hand.
Wellman, M. Of Power, Money, Cheese, Real Estate, Conboberation, Hoohah.
Williams, H. Old Tongue, The.
Williams, W. There's force to this cold sun, makes beard stubble stand shinily.
Williamson, G. Dark Days, The.
Waterfall.
Wilson, E. Miniature Dialogue.
Winter, M. Dux Bellorum.
Wohlfeld. That Which Is Fugitive, That Which Is Medicinally Sweet or Alterable to Gold, That Which Is Substantiated by Unscientific Means.
Wolfli. Nostalgic Song for My Beloved.
Woods, V. Meaning of a Word, The.
Wordsworth, D. Loving and Liking [Irregular Verses Addressed to A Child].
Worley, D. Las Flores para una Niña Negra.
Tongues in My Mouth.
Wright, C. Chickamauga.
Looking Outside the Cabin Window, I Remember a Line by Li Po.
Wright, J. Meta-A and the A of Absolutes.
Zephaniah. Speak.
Zukofsky, L. I's (pronounced *Eyes*).

Lanterns
Brown, S. Long Track Blues.
Buson. Lighting the lantern.
Chao Meng-fu. To a Pyrotechnist.
Frost, R. Draft Horse, The.
Heaney, S. Haw Lantern, The.
Martinson. March Evening.
Ward, D. My Brothers Make a Lantern.

Laocoön
Virgil [or Vergil]. By destiny compell'd, and in despair.
Then indeed into all our fluttering hearts.

Larches
Char. To Friend-Tree of Counted Days.

Larkin, Philip
Lehman. June 11.
Murray, L. Corniche.

Larks
Beranová, J. Mother's Mark.
Blind. On a Forsaken Lark's Nest.
Burns, R. Address to the Woodlark.
Earley, T. Lark.
Ferguson, S. Lark in the Clear Air, The.
Graves, R. Love Without Hope.
Hardy, T. Shelley's Skylark.
Henley, W. E. Margaritae Sororis.
Hopkins, G. Caged Skylark, The.
Sea and the Skylark, The.
Issa. My old village lies.
Neill. Lark.
Rosenberg, I. Returning, We Hear the Larks.
Shakespeare, W. Hark, hark! the lark at heaven's gate sings.
Shelley, P. To a Skylark.
Sŏ Chŏngju. Cuckoo and Skylark.
Unknown. Lark, The.
Lark, The.
Warren, R. Death of Time.

See also **Meadowlarks; Skylarks**

Las Vegas, Nevada
Darr. Flight as a Way of Life.
Fanning, R. Middle Age, The: "Between TV and computer screens."
Lederer, K. In Las Vegas.

Last Judgment
Borges. Matthew XXV:30.
Cornish, S. Something Terrible Something.
Hinsey, E. Update on the Last Judgment.
Howard, R. Giovanni da Fiesole on the Sublime.
Lindsay, J. Sudden Discords in the Trumpets of Overdelayed Last Judgement, 1956.
Shelley, P. England in 1819.

Last Rites
Scott, F. Last Rites.
See also **Extreme Unction**

Last Supper
Prévert. Last Supper, The.
Rilke. Matthew 26:17–29.
Southwell. Of the Blessed Sacrament of the Altar [*or* Aulter] ("In paschall feast, the end of a[u]ncient rite.").

Latin
Cummings, E. E. Noster, The.
Fox, Skip. Sic transit gloria mundi.
Hecht, A. Mysteries of Caesar, The.
Mathews, H. Sense of Responsibility, The.
Sanguineti. So it takes very little indeed: a brasserie.
Stallings. Dead Language Lesson.

Latin America and Latin Americans
Alexander, E. Ode.
Borges. Mythical Founding of Buenos Aires, The.
Cofer, J. What the Gypsy Said to Her Children.
Darío, R. Swans, The.
Espada. Alabanza: In Praise of Local 100.
For the Jim Crow Mexican Restaurant in Cambridge, Massachusetts, Where My Cousin Esteban was Forbidden to Wait Tables Because He Wears Dreadlocks.
La tormenta.
Moon Shatters on Alabama Avenue, The.
Prisoners of Saint Lawrence, The.
Tires Stacked in the Hallways of Civilization.
Toque de queda: Curfew in Lawrence.
Water, White Cotton, and the Rich Man.
Gaspar de Alba. Making Tortillas.
Hagedorn, J. Latin Music in New York.
Hernández Cruz. Side 12.
Hernandez, D. Armitage Street.
Istarú, A. From where you have come.
Jones, R. After Work.
Lars. Recollection of Gabriela Mistral.
Machado Ruiz. Crime Was in Granada, The.
Menes, O. Raspa.
Morales, A. South.
Morales. Africa.
Neruda. Amor America (1400).
Norris, M. Tortillas.
Otero, B. Written in Rain.
Parra, V. At the Center of Injustice.
Rodriguez, L. Fire.
Spear, R. Good Men.
Storni. Words to My Mother.
Wiethüchter. Without Histories.

Latin Poetry
Stallings. Dead Language Lesson.

Laughter
Al-Harizi. Lightning, The.
Allnutt, G. Sarah's Laughter.
Alvi, M. Laughing Moon, The.
Aridjis. Decomposition with Laughter.
Bataille, Georges. I Dreamed of Touching.
Berlin. You're Laughing at Me.
Blake, W. When the Green Woods Laugh.
Browning, R. Memorabilia.
Cairns, Scott. Coming Forth.
Charara, H. Holy Water.
Ch'in Kuan. Along the Grand Canal.
Chŏng Yagyong. Laughing at Myself.
Colonna, S. He spins about (laughing) then shows.

Corso. Zizi's Lament.
Creeley. Wicker Basket, A.
Davies, W. H. Visitor, The.
Day Lewis. Two Songs.
Désiré, J. Philosophy, A.
Dunbar, P. We Wear the Mask.
Dupin. He Breathes before Writing.
Eliot, T. S. Hysteria.
Fermini, I. Moments that hands without a vine...laughter.
Foix. When I Sleep, Then I See Clearly.
Foster, A. Nest of Hats, A.
Gershwin, I. They All Laughed.
Gilbert-Lecomte. Son of the Bone Speaks, The.
Gladding. Locust Shell.
Graham, J. Soul Says.
Grimké, A. Fragment.
Haavikko. Don't smile. So you won't become a Buddha.
Hadewijch. Love's Maturity.
Hernández, M. Lullabies of the Onion.
Lullaby of the Onion.
Hikmet. On Living.
Hughes, L. Railroad Avenue.
Johnson, G. I Want to Die While You Love Me.
Joseph, A. Learning to Laugh.
Keats. Why Did I Laugh Tonight?
Khlebnikov, V. Incantation by Laughter.
Kim Sŭnghŭi. Soaring.
Kinnell. Crying.
Kishu. Once the goal's reached.
Lanier, S. Laughter in the Senate.
Le Brun, Annie. Festivals.
Masefield. Laugh and Be Merry.
Matveyeva [*or* Matveieva]. Ginger-Haired Girl, The.
McCarthy, J. I'm Gonna Laugh You Right Out of My Life.
McKay, D. Laugh, The.
Milán, E. I let myself be led because I let loose. Me dejo guiar porque he dejado ir.
Nikonova, R. Earth is burning, The.
Nisker, Wes "Scoop.". No tears and no fears.
Page, P. Young Girls.
Prunty. Reading Before We Read, Horoscope and Weather.
Ríos, A. Teodoro Luna's Two Kisses.
Ritsos. One Skit, Then Another.
Roberts, L. Men's Talk.
Rumi. Like the rose I am laughing with all my body, not only with.
Sanchez, S. Haiku.
Sandburg, C. Bundles.
Schwartz, D. Sarah.
Sŏ Chŏngju. At a Wine House near Taegu.
Sondheim. Comedy Tonight.
Sornberger. When She Laughs.
Soudijn. Cleaning.
Régime.
Stroffolino. Love as Fear of Love in Laughter.
Swirszczynska [*or* Swir]. Sea and the Man, The.
Thomas, E. Some Eyes Condemn.
Tolson, M. Dark Laughter.
Tu Shan-fu. Tune: "Shua Hai-erh" Country Cousin at the Theater.
Villaurrutia. They and I.
Wagoner, D. Loons Mating.
Wright, R. In the falling snow.
See also **Mirth**

Laughton, Charles
Brecht, B. Letter to the Actor Charles Laughton concerning the Work on the Play "The Life of Galileo".

Laundry and Laundering
Barbauld. Washing-Day.
Barrax. Domestic Tranquility.
Brown, G. Mother, The: "On Monday she stood at the wooden wash-tub."
Chavez, L. Clean Sheets.
Davis, J. Time Bum.
Dobson, R. Folding the Sheets.
Dryansky, A. Size of a Bed Sheet, The.
Elmslie, K. Duo-Tang.
Fisher, Diane G. Sweet Hour.
Fordham. Washerwoman, The.

Fusselman, A. Journal.
Gallagher, T. I Stop Writing the Poem.
Grennan. Few Last Lines of Laundry, A.
Gustafson, R. Of Green Steps and Laundry.
Hartman, J. Lost. children have been known to.
Hughes, L. Song to a Negro Wash-woman, A.
Kang Ŭn'gyo. Woman Hanging Laundry.
Kauffman, J. Mennonite Farm Wife.
Kendrick, D. Alone for a Week.
Kennedy, Sarah. Maid.
Kinsella, T. Laundress, The.
Kutchins, L. Clothesline.
Merrill, J. Mad Scene, The.
Morikawa Kyoroku. Summer airing / On one pole.
Moss, T. Fisher Street.
Nelson, M. Washboard Wizard.
Niedecker. Clothesline post is set, The.
Young girl to marry.
North, C. Hospital.
Nowlan. Red Wool Shirt, The.
Pinchas-Cohen. Yearning of Karakashian, The.
Poetker-Thiessen, A. She tries to tell him.
Rankine. Eden.
Rees-Jones. Service Wash.
Ritchie. Sorting Laundry.
Robbins, R. Women of Lockerbie, The.
Rohrer, M. Precision German Craftsmanship.
Sandburg, C. Washerwoman.
Senryū, K. Laundryman, The.
Simpson, A. White, Mauve, Yellow.
Stone, R. In an Iridescent Time.
Summerfield. Washday Battles.
Swirszczynska [*or* Swir]. I Wash the Shirt.
Woman Writer Does Laundry, A.
Villani, L. Watching the Mayan Women.
Weatherford, C. Tar Baby on the Soapbox, The.
Wen Yi-tuo [*or* Wen I-to]. Laundry Song, The.
Wilbur, R. Love Calls Us to the Things of This World.
Williams, W. Young Laundryman, A.

Laurels
Bogan, L. Several Voices Out of a Cloud.
Kemble. Sonnet: "Thou poisonous laurel leaf, that in the soil."
Milton. Lycidas.
Ovid. Apollo and Daphne.
Suckling, S. Wits, The; A Session[s] of the Poets.
Thornton, R. Cherry Laurel, The.
Westmorland. Occasioned by Seeing a Walk of Bay Trees.
Winchilsea. Circuit of Apollo, The.
Wright, J. Portugal Laurel, The.

Lavender
Goodman, P. I planned to have a border of lavender.

Lavinia
Kirk, Kathleen. Lavinia.

Law and Lawyers
Auden. Law like Love.
Baer. Prosecutor.
Borges. Conjectural Poem.
Brinks, Dave. Tao Sequence, The.
Butler, S. Law, The.
Carroll, L. Mouse's Tale, The.
Carter, S. Passing of Arthur, The.
Clarke, A. Penal Law.
Davis, L. Mown Lawn, A.
Donne. Satire 5.
Empson. Legal Fiction.
Frazier, John Alexander, Jr. Deposed.
Galanskov. Murder.
Gilbert, W. When I, Good Friends, Was Called to the Bar.
Greenlaw, L. Love from a Foreign City.
Greville, F. Chorus Primus of Bashaws or Cadis.
Hardy, J. Objection Overruled.
Herbert, Z. Trial, The.
Trial, The.
Housman. Laws of God, the Laws of Man, The.
Hugo, V. Jeanne was holed up (pitch darkness; bread and water).
Kelly, R. Life of Intimate Fleeing, A.
Landor, W. Case at Sessions, A.

Macha, F.   Corruption.
Medina, T.   After the Verdict.
Moorer.   Injustice of the Courts.
 Legal Mouse, A.
O'Grady, J.   Anonymous Wedding Photo.
Prejsnar, Mark.   Government and Binding.
Quarles.   On God's Law.
Rossi, T.   Law.
Rumens.   Marriage.
Simpson, L.   Working late.
Sundiata.   Notes from the Defense of Colin
 Ferguson.
Thackeray.   Damages, Two Hundred Pounds.
Tsvetaeva [or Tsvetaeva].   I bless the everyday
 labor.
Unknown.   Among the yeomen's sons on my
 estate.
 Lawyers.
 Statesmen, in your exalted station know.

Lawes, Henry
Milton.   To Mr. H. Lawes On His Airs.
Philips, K.   To Mr. Henry Lawes.

Lawns
Davis, L.   Mown Lawn, A.
Dickinson, E.   Presentiment—is that long
 Shadow—on the lawn.
Empson.   Rolling the Lawn.
Lili'u-o-ka-lani.   Lawn Sprinkler, The.
Lux.   Man into Whose Yard You Should Not Hit
 Your Ball, The.
Ramsay, A.   Polwart on the Green.
Ruefle.   In the Bitter Country.
Smith, M.   Watering the New Lawn.
Warren, R.   Sitting on Farm Lawn on Sunday
 Afternoon.

Lawrence, D. H. (David Herbert)
Baraka, I.   Poem for Speculative Hipsters, A.
Hoagland, T.   Lawrence.
Lowenfels.   Among the Luminals.
O'Hara, F.   Poem: "I don't know as I get what
 D.H. Lawrence is driving at."
Warburton, N.   Snake on D. H. Lawrence, The.
Williams, W.   Elegy for D.H. Lawrence, An.

Lawrence, Edward
Milton.   To Mr. Lawrence.

Lawrence, T. E. (Thomas Edward)
MacEwen, G.   Apologies.
 Damascus.

Lazarus (Bible)
Baxter, J.   Lazarus.
Bensko.   Bones of Lazarus.
Browning, R.   Epistle Containing the Strange
 Medical Experience of Karshish, the Arab
 Physician, An.
Cairns, Scott.   Translation of Raimundo Luz,
 The: My Incredulity.
Carson, A.   Lazarus.
 Lazarus Standup: Shooting Script.
Chesterton.   Convert, The.
Colman, H.   On Lazarus Raised From Death.
Duffy, C.   Mrs Lazarus.
Feinstein, E.   Lazarus' Sister.
Frost, R.   Luke 16:19–26; "There was a rich
 man".
Jeffers, H.   Mary, Don't You Weep.
Koertge.   Lazarus.
Lewis, G.   There are great advantages to having
 been dead.
Nemes Nagy.   Lazarus.
Parra, N.   Anti-Lazarus, The.
Procter, A.   Homeless.
Rilke.   John 11:30–44; Now Jesus had not yet
 come to the village.
Sanguineti.   And now a few questions to end
 with.
Unknown.   I Want to Die Like-A Lazarus Die.
Wingfield.   Waking.

Laziness
Ali Hsiying.   Lazy Cloud's Nest 1.
Arodin, S.   Lazy River.
Barbour, D.   Mañana (Is Soon Enough for Me).
Carmichael, H.   Lazy River.
Cherry, K.   On Watching a Young Man Play
 Tennis.
Ch'i-chi.   Admonishing a Younger Teacher.

Cucchi, M.   Hibernation.
Cutler, Y.   Not-a.
De Coninck, H.   Ballad of Indolence.
Herrick.   Ass[e], The.
Hoskyns [or Hoskins].   Epitaph, An: On a Man
 for Doing Nothing.
Latouche, J.   Lazy Afternoon.
Lee, D.   Lazy.
Lee, P.   Mañana (Is Soon Enough for Me).
Mirville, E.   All the tongues are wagging.
Monnier, Pascalle.   Summer ("These are the first
 fine days.").
Muso Soseki.   Thanks Sent to Taihei Osho.
Nash, O.   Introspective Reflection.
Neruda.   Ode to Laziness.
Po Chü-i.   Lazy Man's Song.
 Lazy Man's Song.
Porter, C.   Laziest Gal in Town, The.
Prior.   Epitaph, An: "Interr'd [or Interred]
 beneath this marble stone."
Razaf, A.   My Handy Man Ain't Handy No
 More.
Ridland.   Lazy Man's Haiku, The.
Roethke.   Sloth, The.
Sidgwick, H.   Strenuous Life, The.
Tafolla.   San Antonio.
Unknown.   Get Up, Get Up.
 Good Scholars Make Bad Husbands.
 Lazy Man, The.
 Little horror does nothing—does not make love,
 does not make war, The.
Wang Ji.   Farmers.
Watts, I.   Sluggard, The.
Wells, A.   By Proxy.
Young, E.   Languid lady next appears in state,
 The.

Leadership
Brookes, J.   Officers and Gentlemen Down
 Under.
Brooks, G.   Song of Winnie.
Buchanan, G.   To Henry Darnley, King of Scots.
Crosby, E.   Military Creed, The.
Csoori.   My Masters.
Dryden, J.   Crown Prince of Dullness, The.
Edelman, M.   I Care and I'm Willing to Serve.
Homer.   Sarpedon's Speech to Glaucus.
Kavanagh, P.   Elegy for Jim Larkin.
Kipling, R.   Servant When He Reigneth, A.
Lê Thánh–tông.   Stick and Hat.
Leonard, T.   Feed Ma Lamz.
Lindsay, V.   Abraham Lincoln Walks at
 Midnight.
MacKay, C.   Clear the Way.
Markham, E.   Lincoln, the Man of the People.
Moses, G.   Poem for Trish, A.
Nguyen, Hoa.   Unorthodox and impractical one
 not led.
Rich, A.   Late summers, early autumns, you can
 see something that binds.
Robinson, E.   Master, The.
Rumi.   Lame Goat, The.
Shabtai, Aharon.   Sharon Resembles a Person.
Shakespeare, W.   They tax our policy and call it
 cowardice.
Stein, C.   Provisional Measures.
Taylor, B.   Night the Second: All or Nothing.
Tennant, E.   A Bas la Gloire!
Unknown.   Satire.
Various authors.   Anxious only to fulfill the
 royal clause.
 Millennium ago, A.
Whitman, W.   Thought ("Of obedience, faith,
 adhesiveness.").
Zaragoza Clubs.   My heart tells me.

Leander
Marlowe.   "O Hero, Hero!" thus he cried full
 oft.
See also **Hero and Leander**

Leap Year
Johnson, M.   Leap Yeah Party, De.
Palmer, M.   Untitled (February 2000).

Lear, Edward
Auden.   Edward Lear.
Cornett, S.   Lear Expands His Last Words to
 Cordelia.

Lear, E.   How Pleasant to Know Mr. Lear.

Lear, King
Clifton, C.   Lear Drives His Rambler across
 Laurel Mountain.
Lauinger, A.   Cordeilla.
 Leir.
Raymund, J.   Ordeal of Love, The.
Schulman.   First Nights.
Skloot.   Role of a Lifetime, The.
Wright, D.   Lines on Retirement, after Reading
 Lear.
See also **King Lear**

Learning
Abbot, E.   Awakening.
Atwood.   You Begin.
Babstock, Ken.   First Lesson in Unpopular
 Mechanics.
Berkeley, G.   On the Prospect of Planting Arts
 and Learning in America.
Bilgere, G.   Like Riding a Bicycle.
Buson.   From outside a hedge, a hen calls her
 chicks.
Centolella.   Joy.
Chung-ch'ang T'ung.   Speaking My Mind.
Cowley, A.   Against Fruition.
Denham.   Preface to *The Progress of Learning.*
Divakaruni.   Yuba City School.
Egatz, R.   Into First.
Garry, F.   Professor's Wife, The.
Glück, L.   Illuminations.
Graves, R.   Plea to Boys and Girls, A.
Held, George.   Learning to Ride My Bike.
Juan Chi.   Learning.
Kendrick, D.   Sophie, Climbing the Stairs.
Lal Ded [or Lalla].   To learn the scriptures is
 easy.
Lisella.   Song of the Third Generation.
Lorde.   Black Mother Woman.
Murphy, Timothy.   Mentor.
Mutis.   Sonata.
Nurkse.   August Horizon.
Pilling.   Specimen.
Pound, E.   Great Digest of Confucius, The.
Reder, C.   Lesson, The: "Stand next to your
 bike, like that."
Rudman, M.   There was only one problem—the
 steepness of the hill.
Senryū, K.   Each time footsteps.
 Learning and a ladder.
Shelley, P.   To a Skylark.
Snyder, G.   Axe Handles.
Sorrentino.   Razzmatazz.
Szymborska, W.   Two Apes of Brueghel, The.
Tiruvalluvar.   Learning.
Unknown.   Epitaph for Cu Chuimne.
 Learn how to consume my mouth!
Vázquez Montalbán, M.   In Memoriam ("I
 learned / the interminable list.").
Waugh, Arthur.   Ballade of the Devout Husband,
 The.
Whitman, W.   Beginning My Studies.

Leaves
Aiken, C.   Prelude XIX: "Watch long enough,
 and you will see the leaf."
 Room, The.
Ammons.   Above the Fray Is Only Thin Air.
Barnes, W.   Leaves a-Vallen.
Basho.   Pine mushroom.
Bell, M.   Dew at the Edge of a Leaf.
 Further Pulsations.
Binyon.   Now is the time for the burning of the
 leaves.
 Unreturning Spring, The.
Bukowski.   Tragedy of the leaves, The.
Buson.   Blown from the west.
 Field of mustard, A.
 Green leaves.
 Not a leaf stirring.
 Wind in the west / Fallen leaves.
Chin.   Autumn Leaves.
Chungji.   On Autumn.
Crapsey.   November Night.
Cullen, C.   Leaves.
Cummings, E. E.   L(a.
Dana, R.   Figures, The.
Davies, W. H.   Leaves.

Desnos. There once was a leaf.
Fargas. Out of Time.
Feldman, A. Contemporary American Poetry.
Field. Leaves.
  Lo, my loved is dying, and the call.
Frost, R. Leaf-Treader, A.
Gamalinda, E. Opposite of Nostalgia, The.
Greppi, C. Like a handful of leaves.
Herbert, W. Smirr.
Hiestand, E. Witch-Hazel Wood, The.
Hirshfield, J. Ars Poetica.
Howe, F. You float inside your water.
Irwin, M. Autumnal.
Johnson, L. Church of a Dream, The.
Kassid, A. Leaves.
Keble. November.
Kikaku. Leaf / Of the yam.
  Riding the wide leaf.
  Single yam leaf, A.
Larkin, P. Trees, The: "Trees are coming into leaf, The."
Lindtová, A. Campfire.
MacLeish. Old Men in the Leaf Smoke, The.
Niedecker. Paul / when the leaves.
Nikonova, R. Six charred leaves drift.
Po Chü-i. Cranes, The.
Prévert. Song of the snails on their way to a funeral.
Pritchard, N. Landscape with Nymphs and Satyrs.
Ransetsu. Single leaf falls, A.
Rexroth, K. Buddha took some Autumn leaves.
Robertson, R. Fall: "Leaves are falling, falling from trees, The."
Robinson, Edwin Arlington. Pity of the Leaves, The.
Robinson, Elizabeth. New Language, The.
Rossetti, C. Caterpillar, The.
  Who Has Seen the Wind?
Saroyan. Leaf, A / left.
Seferis. Poplar Leaf, The.
Seward. Behold that tree, in Autumn's dim decay.
Shelley, P. Ode to the West Wind.
"Shu Ting.". Maple Leaf.
Sone no Yoshitada. Lower leaves of the trees, The.
Sontrop. Acorn Speaks, The.
Stephens, J. Wind, The.
Stevens, W. Course of a Particular, The.
Tan Taigi. Fallen leaves / Raking.
Taneda Santoka. Waiting for what?
Thompson, C. Autumn Leaves.
Tranströmer. Darkening leaves, The.
Unknown. Words "I love you," The.
Very. Autumn Leaves.
  Sumach Leaves, The.
Vroomkoning. Returning.
  Together Again ("I behold her there.").
Wilbur, R. Alatus.
  October Maples, Portland.
Winters, Y. Fall of Leaves, The.
Wu of Han [*or* Wu Ti *or* Ou-ty *or* Liu Ch'e *or* Liu Ch'u]. Liu Ch'e.
See also **Autumn**

Lebanon and Lebanese
Abinader, E. Letters from Home.
Buffoni, F. Partitions.
Charara, H. Holy Water.
Joseph, L. Sand Nigger.
Liban, A. At a Time Like This.
Melville, H. Guide and Guard.
Nawwab, M. Bridge of Old Wonders.
Scollard. As I Came Down from Lebanon.

Leda
Clifton, L. Leda 3.
Darío, R. Leda.
Doolittle, Hilda. Leda.
Gogarty. Leda and the Swan.
Meinke. Helen.
Millay, E. I Dreamed I Moved among the Elysian Fields.
Sappho. They say that once Leda found.
Watkins, V. Music of Colours: The Blossom Scattered.
Yeats. Leda and the Swan.

Lee, Robert Edward
Davidson, D. Lee in the Mountains.
Howe, J. Robert E. Lee.
Ryan, A. Sword of Robert Lee, The.
Thompson, J. Lee to the Rear.

Leeds, England
Dyer, J. Leeds for Pleasure.
Harrison, T. On Not Being Milton.

Legacies and Legatees
Hölty. Legacy.
Jensma. Spanner in the what? works.
March, S. Legacy.

Legs
Basho. Clear water.
Burroughs, W. My Legs Señor.
Cho-yong. Song: "I carouse all night."
Eady. April.
Harington [*or* Harrington]. Ambiguity.
Herrera. Weaning of Furniture-Nutrition.
Herrick. Her Legs.
  To Dianeme ("Show [*or* Shew] me thy feet; show [*or* shew] me thy legs, thy thighs.").
Luca, Gherasim. My Folly of Being.
Mead, J. Paradise Consists of Forty-Nine Rotating Spheres.
Mother Goose. Two Legs Sat Upon Three Legs.
Neruda. Ritual of My Legs.
Ormond. Lament for a Leg.
Radoev, Ivan. Parable of the Poet's Reward.
Rehm, Pam. Thus I Find My Legs.
Seibles, T. Who.
Taylor, J. Epigram: "Fair Beatrice tucks her coat up somewhat high."
Terrazas. To a Pair of Legs.
Whitman, W. Runner, The.
Williams, W. Portrait of a Lady.

Leisure
Adcock, F. Three-Toed Sloth, The.
Ali Hsiying. Lazy Cloud's Nest 2.
Benlowes. Pleasures of Retirement, The.
Blanco, R. Letter to El Flaco on His Birthday.
Ch'ien T'ao. On Reading the Seas and Mountains Classic.
Chŏng Kügin. In Praise of Spring.
Chungji. Leisurely Enjoyment.
Clare, J. Nutting.
  Woodland Seat, A.
Coward. Poor Little Rich Girl.
Davies, W. H. Leisure.
Doubleday, T. No walk today;—November's breathings toss.
Drieu la Rochelle. Tennis.
Frishberg, D. Peel Me a Grape.
Góngora y Argote. Roistering I'll Chaff.
Hanson, M. To Fancy.
Hightower, J. On Reading the Seas and Mountains Classic.
Hood, T. Written in the Workhouse.
Jensma. Confidentially Yours.
Jewett, S. At Home from Church.
Jungkwan Haean. Various Songs of Leisure.
Liu Chih. Tune: "Sheep on the Mountain Slope".
Martial. Happy Life, A.
  Were lives of ease, dear Namesake, ours.
  While unquiet, *Juvenal*, you haunt.
McCarthy, J. Riviera, The.
McGinley. Evening Musicale.
  Village Spa.
Melville, H. Cypriote, The.
Moore, T. Fancy.
Nabbes. Song: "What a dainty life the milkmaid leads!"
Ou-yang Hsiu. Reading the Poems of an Absent Friend.
Pyungyang Ungee. Mountain Life.
Quiller-Couch. Harbour of Fowey, The.
Radcliffe, A. Sun-Rise: Sonnet, A.
Revett. Ode: Hastening His Friend into the Country.
Richman, L. To Valenton: Impressions circa 1947.
Ronald of Orkney, Saint. Attributes of a Gentleman, The.
Rossetti, C. Reflection.
Seward. When Life's realities the Soul perceives.
Shi Chong. Longing to Return: A Lament.
Sondheim. Ladies Who Lunch, The.
Stickney, T. In Ampezzo ("In days of summer let me go.").
Stroud, J. Homage: Summer/Winter, Shay Creek.
Su Tung-p'o. Tune: "Fragrance Fills the Courtyard".
  Tune: "Partridge Sky".
Tu Fu [*or* Du Fu]. Unemployed and lazy, I wander around the village.
Unknown. Work's end.
Vaughan, H. Since last we met, thou and thy horse, my dear.
Webster, A. Poor little diary, with its simple thoughts.
Westmorland. To Retiredness.
Wright, J. Lying in a Hammock at William Duffy's Farm in Pine Island, Minnesota.
Yü Hsüan-chi. Living in the Summer Mountains.

Lemmings
Beer, P. Lemmings.

Lemons
Cowley, A. Written in Juice of Lem[m]on.
Hadas, R. Lair, The.
Hannaham, D. If There's No Sugar.
Hernández, M. You Threw Me a Lemon.
Michiura, M. Suddenly.
Montale. In the Greenhouse.
Neruda. Ode to the Lemon.
No Ch'ŏnmyŏng. Lemon for Me, A.

Lenin, Vladimir Ilyich
MacDiarmid, H. Second Hymn to Lenin.
  Skeleton of the Future, The.
Muldoon, P. Salvador.
Orlovsky. Dream May 18, 1958.
Paulin. Impossible Pictures, The.
Tsanev, Stefan. Rehearsal for a Parade.
Van Winckel, N. Avant-Garde, The.
Wellesley. So I came down the steps to Lenin.

Leningrad, Russia
Inber. Teeth are bared, the mouth drawn tight, the face, The.
Nekrasov, V. Somehow I really want to go.
See also **Saint Petersburg** [*formerly* Leningrad], Russia

Lennon, John
Allen, P. Teaching Poetry at Votech High, Santa Fe, the Week John Lennon Was Shot.
Spellman, A. Did John's Music Kill Him?
Waters, M. Demonstration: Women's House of Detention, 1965.

Lent
Herrick. To Keep a True Lent.

Lent Magdalene
Rodgers, W. Lent.

Lentils
Pereira, P. Pot of Red Lentils, A.
Wayne, J. Cleaning Indian Dahl.
Zehrd [*or* Zahrad]. Woman Cleaning Lentils, The.

Leonardo da Vinci
Dowden, E. Leonardo's "Mona Lisa".
Field. La Gioconda; Leonardo Da Vinci, The Louvre.
Shelley, P. On the Medusa of Leonardo da Vinci in the Florentine Gallery.
Someck, R. Testifying to Beauty.

Leopards
Borges. Inferno 1, 32.
Ch'u Yüan. After Ch'u Yuan.
Dickinson, E. Civilization—spurns—the Leopard!
Kafka. Leopards in the Temple.
Kariara. Leopard Lives in a Muu Tree, A.
Roberts, C. Leopard, The.
Unknown. Careful!
White, G. Leopard in Eden, The.

Leopold III, King of the Belgians
Berryman. Moon and the Night and the Men, The.

Lepanto, Battle of (1571)
Chesterton. Lepanto.
Leprosy and Lepers
Bertrand. Lepers.
Bodel, J. Les Congés du Lépreux.
Citino. Francis Meets a Leper.
Pau-Llosa. Paredón.
Sŏ Chŏngju. Leper.
Swinburne. Leper, The.
Young, G. Damien.
Lesbians
Anacreon. Tossing a crimson ball.
B., L. After School Commute with My Girl.
Brand, D. Then it is this simple. I felt the
 unordinary romance of.
Broumas, O. Amazon Twins.
 Beauty and the Beast.
 Caritas.
 Rapunzel.
Burke, C. Lizzie.
Chrystos. I Bought a New Red.
 I Suck.
 You Know I Like to Be.
Clarke, C. Passing.
 Poet's Death, A.
 Vicki and Daphne.
Costello, R. When My Sister Was Fifteen.
Crown, K. Necklace: Rich Pink Corona Round
 a Flashing Yellow Heart.
Cyril. Just Because I Am.
Dunbar-Nelson. You! Inez!
Equi. Lesbian Corn.
Evans, A. Something More Obvious.
Feaver. Hemingway's Hat.
Forché. Kalaloch.
Gates, B. Cathy.
 Homeless.
 Triptych.
Goodman, M. February Ice Years.
 Lullabye for a Butch.
 New Comers.
 Open Poem.
Gordon, R. Adolescence.
Hacker, M. Boy, The.
Healy, E. Changing the Oil.
 Changing What We Mean.
Hope, M. Sacrifice.
Larkin, J. Risks.
Leon, R. Have you not heard the gossip and the
 rumour going around.
Leto. Anna Magnani at the Castro.
Liu, T. Strange Fruit.
Lorde. On a Night of the Full Moon.
Lowell, A. Vicarious.
McGuckian. Vanessa's Bower.
Myles, E. American Poem, An.
 Sleepless.
Obejas, A. Dancing in Paradise.
 Public Place (After Olga Broumas), The.
Pickering, R. Untitled: "First thought in my
 head waking up was, oh no."
Pratt, M. Crime Against Nature.
Rebolledo. Sapho's Kiss.
Sappho. I simply wish to die.
Schwartz, R. L. Possible.
Selman, R. Exodus.
 21 East 10th, 2BR, WBF, EIK.
Smukler. Days Inn.
 Home in Three Days. Don't Wash.
 Marry.
 Sign.
 Trash.
Sprackland, Jean. Ringlet, The.
Wolverton, T. Black Slip.
 In China.

See also **Homosexuality and Homosexuals**
Lesbos, Greece
Anacreon. Tossing a crimson ball.
Millay, E. Evening on Lesbos.
Sappho. Superior, as a singer from Lesbos to
 those of other lands.
Lethargy
Gershwin, I. Bidin' My Time.
Palés Matos. Pueblo.
Ransom, W. Pastime Café.

Lethe River
Conoley, G. New.
Holub. Teaching About Disease.
Letters
Aafjes. Last Letter, The.
Aiken, J. Do It Yourself.
Alegría. Letter to an Exile.
Ali, A. Country Without a Post Office, The.
 Stationery.
Amichai, Y. Letter.
Antokolsky. We are not always dependent on
 memory.
Apollinaire. Post Card.
Aridjis. Letter from Mexico.
Ashbery, J. Rain.
 Thoughts of a Young Girl.
Atwood. Postcard.
Auden. Letter, The.
Barber, M. Conclusion of a Letter to the Rev.
 Mr. C———, The.
Barresi. Late Summer News.
Behn, A. To Damon. To Inquire of Him if He
 Cou'd Tell Me by the Style, Who Writ Me a
 Copy of Verses that Came to Me in an
 Unknown Hand.
Bell, M. How I Got the Word.
Bensley. One's Correspondence.
Berggolts [*or* Bergholts]. Blockade Swallow,
 The.
Berry, J. Lucy's Letter.
Bishop, E. Letter to N.Y.
Bly, R. Driving to Town Late to Mail a Letter.
Bradstreet, A. Another.
 Another.
Campo, C. Now I Want All My Letters White
 Again.
Carson, A. He She We They You You.
Chavez, L. Clean Sheets.
Chernoff. Dead Letter Office, The.
Cisneros, A. Paris Cinquième.
Clare, J. Soldier, The.
Clark, T. You (III).
Clover, J. Institute for Social Change, The.
Cofer, J. Correspondence.
Comfort, A. Letter to an American Visitor.
Coolidge, C. Listene / secting.
Copus, J. Miss Havisham's Letter.
Coulette. Correspondence.
Cowley, A. Written in Juice of Lem[m]on.
Crane, H. My Grandmother's Love Letters.
Daryush. Still-Life.
DeFrees. Still Life: "After your letter arrived I
 left the oven on."
Desnos. Letter to Youki.
Dooley, M. Letters from Yorkshire.
Dove, R. Poem in Which I Refuse
 Contemplation.
Dransfield. Self-analysis.
Fainlight, R. Handbag.
Fried, E. Chain Mail.
Gallagher, T. Unanswered Letter.
García Lorca. Poet Asks His Love to Write to
 Him, The.
Gibb. Letter to Russel Barron.
Gilyard, K. Letter.
Graham, H. Waste.
Graves, R. Not at Home.
Greenberg, A. Letters from Camp.
Greenlaw, L. Five O'Clock Opera.
Gregory, H. Postman's Bell Is Answered
 Everywhere, The.
Hadas, R. Lair, The.
Hall, Daniel. Love-Letter-Burning.
Hall, Donald. Eleanor's Letters.
 Letter after a Year.
Hardy, T. Wife in London, A.
Heard, J. Love Letters.
Hernández, M. Letter: "Pigeon-house of letters,
 The."
Hubbard, S. Letter.
Hughes, L. Little Old Letter.
Hume, C. Various Readings of an Illegible
 Postcard.
Hyecho. Loneliness of a Wayfarer, The.
Isharaza, G. Grand Get Together, The.
Jacinto, A. Letter from a Contract Worker.

Letter From a Contract Worker.
Jarrell, R. Burning the Letters.
Kinnell. Correspondence School Instructor Says
 Goodbye to His Poetry Students, The.
Klein, M. Letters from the Front.
Koch, K. Railway Stationery, The.
 To Marina.
Kramer, L. Love Letters.
Krapf. Civil War Veteran from Indiana Recalls
 Visiting with Walt Whitman in a Washington
 Hospital, A.
Kreitman, N. Glossy Mail.
Kruit, J. Giving Way.
Kumin, M. Your laugh, your scarves, the gloss
 of your makeup.
Kunitz, S. Night Letter.
Landon. Lines Written Under a Picture of a Girl
 Burning a Love-Letter.
Leapor. Epistle of Deborah Dough, The.
Lenski, H. Light, my light, who commanded,
 'Disappear!
Leong, R. Aerogramme 1–5: Los Angeles.
Li Po. Remembering Our Excursion in the Past.
Li Shang-yin. Night Rains: A Letter to Go
 North.
Livesay, D. Children's Letters, The.
Lorde. Learning to Write.
Lowell, A. Letter, The.
Machado Ruiz. Form your letters slowly and
 well.
MacIntyre, S. Letters from the Concertina File
 1939–1940.
Madhubuti. Poem Looking for a Reader, A.
Maiden. New.
Marcus, M. Letter, The.
Marshall-Stoneking. Picture Postcard.
Mathews, A. Letter Following.
Mathias, R. Sir Gelli to R.S.
Mattawa. Letter to Ibrahim.
Maxwell, G. Poem to Mr Thomas and Mr Frost.
McGinnis, M. Letter to My Mother.
Mercer, J. P.S. I Love You.
Meredith, W. Illiterate, The.
 Love Letter from an Impossible Land.
Merrill, J. Body [*or* B o d y].
Merwin. Postcards from the Maginot Line.
Meynell, A. Letter from a Girl to Her Own Old
 Age, A.
Moore, M. Bowls.
Mun Chŏnghui. Letter, The.
Mura. Letters from Poston Relocation Camp
 (1942–45).
Nash, O. What's in a Name? Some Letter I
 Always Forget.
Neruda. Letter to Miguel Otero Silva, in
 Caracas.
 When I was writing my love poems, which
 sprouted from me.
Nickelson, C. Three men.
No Hyangnim. Autumn Letter.
Noël, Bernard. Portrait.
North, C. Postcard Element in Winter, The.
Nurkse. Letter to Ko.
O'Rourke, D. Letter From My Father, A.
O'Brien, F. Soldier's Letter, A.
Odio, E. Letter to Carlos Pellicer.
Oliver, D. "u", "je", "r", "r", "im", "a",
 "finally".
Orban, O. Letter, The.
Parra, N. Letters to an Unknown Woman.
Patterson, G. Letter from Home.
Plotkin, C. Greetings from My Shtetl (A Letter
 from Poland).
Po Chü-i. Letter, The.
Praed. Talented Man, The.
Press, K. Man with incomplete words on his
 roof, The.
Pulido, A. Dibuja una letra.
 Traces a letter.
Radnóti. Letter to My Wife.
 Picture Postcards.
Ransom, J. Parting, without a Sequel.
Rexroth, K. Night without end. Loneliness.
Rich, A. Letters in the Family.
Riddell, E. Letter, The.
Roberson, E. Four Lines of a Black Love Letter

between Teachers.
Sandburg, C. Bilbea.
Scott, D. Letters from Baron Von Hügel to a Niece.
Scott, J. Typing the Letters.
Senryū, K. Another letter?
Sexton. Some Foreign Letters.
Sharma, P. Dear ———.
Smith, S. Emily Writes Such a Good Letter. Jungle Husband, The.
Sorrentino. Oranges Returned, The.
Sosnora. Letter, A.
Spencer, B. Passed On.
Storni. Lyrical Letter to the Other Woman.
Street, D. Love Letters of the Dead.
Sutphen, J. Not for Burning.
Tidjani-Cissé. Home News.
Tranströmer. To Friends Behind a Frontier.
Tsaloumas. Note.
Tucker, M. Love-letter, A.
Tuqan, F. Face Lost in the Wilderness.
Unknown. I've lost my rifle and bayonet.
Unknown, fr. Terezin Concentration Camp. Letter to Daddy, A.
Valentine, J. Drinker's Wife Writes Back, The.
Van Duyn. Letters from a Father.
Vitiello. Letter to a Cretan Flute-Maker.
Walcott. Letter from Brooklyn, A.
Waldman, A. De Carlo Lots, The.
Warren, R. You Sort Old Letters.
Wei Ying-wu. Autumn Night: A Letter Sent to Ch'iu.
Whitman, W. Come Up from the Fields Father.
Wickham. Letter to a Boy at School.
Wicks, S. Protected Species.
Williams, G. Letters from a New England Negro.
Williamson, E. Belvedere Marittimo.
Yi Illo. On the River on a Spring Day.
Young Bear. Emily Dickinson, Bismarck and the Roadrunner's Inquiry.
Young, J. I'm Gonna Sit Right Down and Write Myself a Letter.
Yüan Chên. Letter Smuggled in a Fish.
See also **Mail and Mailmen**

Leukemia
Graham-Pole, J. Venipuncture.
Hall, D. Last Days.

Levees
Mullen, H. Malecón, El.
Powell, D. A. Mule-drawn Scraper Packed this Earth, A: Levees.

Leviathan
Levertov. Ache of Marriage, The.
Merwin. Leviathan.

Li Po
Dumdum. Li Pos of the Polis.
Harrison, J. Word Drunk.
Kim Ch'ŏnt'aek. Having given my clothes to a boy.
Phillips, C. Undressing for Li Po.
Tu Fu [*or* Du Fu]. Dreaming of Li Po ("Death at least gives separation repose.").
Dreaming of Li Po ("Parted by death, we'd strangle on our tears.").
Poem for Mr. Li in Early Spring.
Spring Day: Thinking of Li Po.
Thinking of Li Po.
To Li Po ("Floating cloud follows the sun, The.").
To Li Po on a Spring Day ("Po, the unrivalled poet.").
To Li Po on a Spring Day ("There's no poet quite like you, Li Po.").
To Li Po on a Winter Day.
To Li Po ("When the cold wind visits you from the corners of the earth.").

Liars
Buffoni, F. And those level fingernails of theirs.
Clarke, George Elliott. Prelude: "Shelley's a garden."
Crane, S. With eye and with gesture.
Eady. How I Got Born.
Hudgins. Homage to the Fox.
Jordan, J. Wasted.

Spellman, A. Beautiful day, The V.
See also **Lies and Lying**

Liberace
Drake, N. Man in the White Suit, The.
Holden, J. Liberace.

Liberalism and Liberals
Browning, R. Lost Leader, The.
Hummer, T. Ideal, The.
Jackson, R. Lonely Affair, A.

Liberia
Tolson, M. Ti.

Liberty
Al-Bayati, A. To TS Eliot.
Batista Felix, H. Coumbite.
Brontë, E. Prisoner, The. A Fragment.
Désiré, L. Dream: "Last night in sleep."
Gurnis, P. Body of Liberties, The.
Large, J. Snowcone Vendor.
Mirville, E. Liberty.
Odell. Song for A Fishing Party.
Paine, R. Adams and Liberty.
Paine, T. Liberty Tree.
Robinson, M. To Liberty.
Vaynshteyn [*or* Weinstein]. But when one stops to think back a moment.
Whitman, W. Europe the 72nd and 73rd Years of These States.
See also **Freedom**

Liberty Bell
Bible, *O.T.* Inscription on the Liberty Bell.
Unknown. Independence Bell—July 4, 1776.

Liberty, Statue of
Ai Ch'ing. Chilean Cigarette Pack, The.
Bierce. To the Bartholdi Statue.
Dove, R. Lady Freedom Among Us.
Haraway. Midnight Vigil.
Lazarus, E. New Colossus, The.

Libraries and Librarians
Borges. Other Tiger, The.
Brown, S. Chapter One. Marginalia.
Brownlow. James Clarence Mangan in Trinity College Library.
Collins, B. Tomes.
Dillard, R. Ghosts in the Stacks.
Earle, J. Saturday in the '20s, A.
Ellis, T. View of the Library of Congress from Paul Laurence Dunbar High School.
Hedrington, William. Bicycling Away from the Library.
Jarrell, R. Girl in a Library, A.
Le Gallienne. Library in a Garden, A.
Lockwood. Bookshop in Winter.
MacNeice. British Museum Reading Room, The.
Neidhardt, Frances E. Street Flower in Big D.
Roscoe, W. On Being Forced to Part with his Library for the Benefit of his Creditors.
Steele, T. Library, The.
Strand. Eating Poetry.
Tripp. Twilight in the Library.
Ward, T. On Being Kicked Out of the Harold Washington Library Center for Napping on the Floor.
Weiss, T. Fire at Alexandria, The.
Williams, C. K. Critic, The.
Yosef, H. In the Library.
Zu-Bolton. Dudley Randall.

Libya
Mattawa. History of My Face.

Lice
Basho. Fleas, lice. My summer robes.
Burns, R. To a Louse [On Seeing One on a Lady's Bonnet at Church].
Issa. Changing clothes / But not.
Mansour, J. Storm Sketches a Silver Margin, The.
Mei Yao Ch'en. Lice, The.
Shih-hou Pointed Out to Me That from Ancient Times There Had Never Been a Poem on the Subject of Lice.
Rimbaud, A. Lice-Seekers.
Rosenberg, I. Louse Hunting.

Lies and Lying
Amichai, Y. Song of Lies on Sabbath Eve, A.
Auden. Their Lonely Betters.
Ausonius. I am that Dido which thou here do'st see.
Belle, F. Exceptions.
Brown, S. I Was a Phony Baloney! Schadenfreude.
Carbó, N. Civilizing the Filipino.
Catullus. Unto no body my woman saith she had rather a wife be [*or* bee].
Chernoff. How Lies Grow.
Clarke, C. What Goes Around Comes Around, or The Proof is in the Pudding.
Clough. Yes, I have lied, and so must walk my way.
Coleridge, M. Insincere Wish Addressed to a Beggar, An.
True to myself am I, and false to all.
Collins, M. Lies.
Donaldson, W. Little White Lies.
Donne. Lame Beggar, A.
Dunbar, P. We Wear the Mask.
Edwards, D. Things, As They Are.
"Ephelia." To J. G.
Equi. Autobiographical Poem.
Evans, D. In the Vices.
Forché. Taking Off My Clothes.
Freed, A. I've Got a Feelin' You're Foolin'.
Friedman, B. Scottsboro.
Fuhrman, J. Here, I Say.
Gilbert, S. Ladies' Home Journal, The.
Glatt. One Night With a Stranger at 30.
Goldberg, B. Once a Shoot of Heaven.
Harrison, J. Our Other Sister.
Heller, R. Minister has all his notes in place, The.
Highfill, M. Rebis.
Housman. Purple William or The Liar's Doom.
Hudgins. Repentance.
Jones, P. If I Were Rita Hayworth.
Joyce, J. Though I thy Mithridates were.
Juana Inés de la Cruz. On Her Portrait.
Kay, J. Stincher, The.
Kim Sangyong. Love Is False.
Kipling, R. Common Form. Dead Statesman, A.
Laing, K. I Am the Freshly Dead Husband.
Lawrence, D. H. I Am in a Novel.
MacEwen, G. Tall Tales.
Mack, C. He's a Cousin of Mine.
Marie de France. Wolf and the Sow, The.
Martial. You lie and I concur. You "give".
Masaoka Shiki. Autumn wind / Gods, Buddha.
Maxwell, G. Rumplestiltskin.
Mitchell, A. To Whom It May Concern (Tell Me Lies about Vietnam?).
Moore, J. Poet is Scornful, The.
Nash, O. Golly, How Truth Will Out.
Nesbit, E. Appeal.
Nicholas, T. Caernarfon Circus, 1969.
Ofeimun. Beyond Fear. Poet Lied, The.
Owen, E. Epitaph: On the Near-Death Experience.
Parker, D. Comment. Social Note. Unfortunate Coincidence.
Parra, N. Sentences.
Paterson, D. White Lie, The.
Pessoa. Autopsychography.
Pilkington, L. Song, A: "Lying is an occupation."
Pope, J. Word of Encouragement, A.
Ralegh, S. Lie, The.
Raymund, J. Ordeal of Love, The.
Rich, A. Cartographies of Silence.
Robinson, E. How Annandale Went Out. Uncle Ananias.
Rumi. Twelve Lies, The.
Rux, C. H. Pledge of Allegiance.
Shakespeare, W. Sonnet 138: "When my love swear[e]s that she is made of truth."
Silverstein, S. Sick.
Stafford, W. Right Time, The.
Steiger. Ancient Custom, An.

Stesichoros. This story is not true.
Stone, J. Confabulation.
Tate, J. Book of Lies, The.
Taylor, J. Epigram: "There chanced to meet together in an inn."
Trethewey, N. White Lies.
Unknown. Heriger and the False Prophet.
If this were a world.
Satire.
Van hee. December.
Van Winckel, N. Basket with Blue Ox.
Weatherford, C. Tar Baby on the Soapbox, The.
Wilbur, R. Lying.
Woods, V. Song of Lies, A.
Zurita, R. 6.

Life

Acosta. Museum Piece (ca. Now).
Adams, L. But Alive.
Addonizio. Conversation in Woodside.
Agustini. Life.
Aiken, C. Things, The.
Aizenberg, M. Who of those who step into the stream.
Aldrich, T. Lycidas.
Alegría. Accounting.
Documentary.
Savoir Faire.
Summing Up.
Allestry. What art thou, love? Whence are those charms.
Amichai, Y. Course of a Life, The.
Ammons. Cut the Grass.
Easter Morning.
Anania. Fall, The.
Angelou, M. Life Doesn't Frighten Me.
Aridjis. Wounded Self-Portrait, A.
Arnold, M. To Marguerite—Continued.
Written in Butler's Sermons.
Ashbery, J. Improvement, The.
Awoonor. Something has happened to me.
Babu, S. Sound of Silence, The.
Bachmann. Kind of Loss, A.
Bacon, F. Life of Man, The.
Bahâyî, Sheyhülislâm. Oh cry, what are you doing, disturbing.
Bancquart. Curriculum vitae.
Epitaph.
Baraka, I. Minute of Consciousness, The.
Barbauld. Life.
Barker, D. Make Your Mark.
Basho. Life in this world.
This road.
Beaumont, J. Cheat, The.
Beaver. Angels' Weather.
Becker, R. Life Forms.
Beckett, S. Je suis ce cours de sable qui glisse.
My way is in the sand flowing.
Que ferais-je sans ce monde sans visage sans questions.
What would I do without this world faceless incurious.
Bécquer, G. Nameless Spirit.
Beedome. Question and Answer, The.
Bek, T. Oh life, long as an epic.
Bell, M. Man May Change, A.
Belloc. World's a Stage, The.
Berkson, B. Melting Milk.
Berrigan, T. Last Poem.
Berry, W. Sycamore, The.
Berryman. Sympathy, A Welcome, A.
Betsugen. All night long I think of life's labyrinth.
Bevington, L. Afternoon.
Bibbins, M. Now the sea moves up the lawn for him as those nearby view his life passing before their eyes.
Bible, *O.T.* To Everything There Is a Season.
Blackburn, P. Park Poem.
Blake, W. Sick Rose, The.
Blunden. Report on Experience.
Boncho. Piled for burning/ Brushwood.
Bonnefoy. Words of Evening, The.
Borson. Rain.
Brandi. Yagul.
Braschi. Final Manuscript.
Brass. There Isn't Any Death.

Breytenbach. Exile, Representative.
There Is Life.
Bromige. He thought it humanity's lot for ever to be persuading a huge rock up a mountainside.
Bronk. Life Supports.
Metonymy as an Approach to a Real World.
Brooks, G. Sadie and Maud.
Second Sermon on the Warpland, The.
Vacant Lot, The.
Brown, L. Life Is Just a Bowl of Cherries.
Brown, S. Odyssey of Big Boy.
Browning, R. Pisgah-Sights. I.
Pisgah-Sights. II.
Rabbi Ben Ezra.
Buchanan, G. Jill's Death.
Buckley, C. Concerning Paradise.
Buddingh'. Some Biographical Data.
Bukowski. Crucifix in a Deathhand.
Burkard. Breathless Storm.
Cami, B. You Stand.
Campbell, D. Here, under Pear-trees.
Campbell, J. Mors et Vita.
Carroll, J. Heroin.
Carruth, H. Wreck of the Circus Train, The.
Carver, R. Late Fragment.
Cary, A. Contradiction.
Castro, R. Ailing Woman Felt Her Forces Ebb, The.
Celaya, G. Meaning of Soup, The.
Ceni, A. Fragment.
Ceravolo. New Realism.
Cernuda. Nocturnal, you sword-fight.
You were a tender desire, an insinuating cloud.
Char. Every Life.
Cheng Hsieh. Song of Surfing on the Bore.
Chimombo. Death Song, A.
Chiyojo. From the mind.
Clark, T. As I walked out early.
Clary. When my heart asked for a way free, it was led into this lightless room.
Clifton, L. Cutting greens.
December.
Clover, J. Feral Floats the Form in Heaven and of Light.
Cohan. If I'm Going to Die I'm going to Have Some Fun.
I'm Mighty Glad I'm Living and That's All.
Life's a Funny Proposition after All.
Coleridge, S. Epitaph: "Stop, Christian passer-by!—Stop, child of God."
Collobert. III: "As if dead the buried text."
Corpus. Blkfeen-jungal.
Couani. Never-Dead, The.
Creeley. Bresson's Movies.
Song: "What's in the body you've forgotten."
Crenner, Jim. Out-of-Body Experience.
Cronin, A. Elegy for the Nightbound.
Trembling with engines, gulping oil, the river.
Cruz e Sousa. Antiphony.
Cullen, C. For One Who Gayly Sowed His Oats.
From Life to Love.
Cummings, E. E. Anyone lived in a pretty how town.
If everything happens that can't be done.
My father moved through dooms of love.
Out of midsummer's blazing most not night.
Cunningham, J. For a Woman with Child.
Life flows to death as rivers to the sea.
Daive. Woman measures, A.
Dalton, R. Ars Poetica.
Dante Alighieri. Middle of life's journey; I, The.
Davies, W. H. Leisure.
de Folgar. Panorama 2.
De Kok. Text of necessity.
De la Mare. Last Chapter, The.
"Dhoomil.". City, Evening, and an Old Man: Me, The.
Di Prima. Short Note on the Sparseness of the Language.
Dickinson, E. Between the form of Life and Life.
I am alive—I guess.
That it will never come again.

This Is My Letter to the World.
Water, is taught by thirst.
Word is dead, A.
DiPalma. When Torrid Rhymes with Forehead.
Dobyns. His life was the practice of forming a single.
No Map.
Dooley, Twain. Kitchen: "Everywhere I go it's the same old thing."
Doolittle, Hilda. White World.
Dove, R. Charm, The.
Fish in the Stone, The.
This Life.
Dowson. Vitae Summa Brevis Spem Nos Vetat Incohare Longam.
Drake, N. Foley Artist, The.
Drummond de Andrade. Dead in Frock Coats, THe.
Motionless Faces.
Residue.
Drummond, W. Madrigal: "This life, which seems so fair."
Dunbar, P. Common Things.
Duncan, R. After a Long Illness.
Dylan. Desolation Row.
Ebb, F. Cabaret.
Eberhart, R. Hard Structure of the World, The.
Worldly Failure.
Eichner, Maura. Eat bread. Drink wine. Try to sing the song.
Eigner. Live /, Bird Which.
Temporary Language, A.
Ekelof. If You Ask Me.
Elfyn, Menna. Couplings.
Eliot, T. S. Dry Salvages, The.
Eluard, P. *et al.* Shared Nights.
Emerson, R. Blight.
Climacteric.
Day's Ration, The.
Nominalist and Realist.
"Ern Malley.". Palinode.
Petit Testament.
Sybilline.
Young Prince of Tyre.
Faiz. When Autumn Came.
You Tell Us What to Do.
Fenton, J. Skip, The.
Ferlinghetti, L. River Still To Be Found, A.
25.
World is a beautiful place, The.
World is a beautiful place, The.
Field, E. Lower East Side: The George Bernstein Story.
New Cycle, A.
Field. It was deep April, and the morn.
Life Plastic.
Fisher, J. Gooseflesh.
Life, A.
Fisher, R. Toyland.
Florit, E. Present Evening, The.
Follain. Buying.
Francis, R. Hound, The.
Freneau. What is this Death, ye deep read sophists, say?
Fritz, Walter Helmut (b. 1929). Fiasco, The.
Frost, R. Master Speed, The.
On the Heart's Beginning to Cloud the Mind.
Road Not Taken, The.
Stopping by Woods on a Snowy Evening.
Fulton, A. A.M.: The Hopeful Monster.
Fumi Saito. As a landscape in the far distance.
Ganev, Nedelcho. Soul, The: "Flame is full, The."
Gay, J. My Own Epitaph.
Gershwin, I. One Life to Live.
Gervitz, G. Life is nothing but time.
Gezelle. Ego Flos.
Ghalib, M. Don't Skimp with Me Today.
Gilbert, W. To the Terrestrial Globe.
Gioia. Maze Without a Minotaur.
Giorno. Life Is a Killer.
Giovanni. Life I Led, The.
Glück, L. New Life, The.
Godfrey. In Front of a Large Number of People.
Goedicke. Meaning of Life, The.
Goethe. Ecstatic Longing.

Goldbarth. Life Is Happy.
González Prada, M. Living and Dying.
Gonzalez, R. Without Villages.
Gorenko, A. Death covers up nakedness.
Graham, A. Is life.
Life and death.
Grahn. Grand Grand Mother is returning.
Graves, R. To Evoke Posterity.
Greshoff, J. I Greet You.
Guiducci. Delivery.
Gumilyov [or Gumiliov or Gumilev]. Pre-Memory.
Gürpınar, Melisa. Like a Stranger.
Haavikko. Look, life has been constructed this way to make sure.
Habington. Cogitabo Pro Peccato Meo.
Hadas, R. Sentimental Education.
Hadewijch II. Tighten.
Hafiz, K [or Hafez]. Five Days Remaining, The (75).
Hagedorn, J. Smokey's Getting Old.
Something about You.
Hahn, O. Man.
Hamadani. Quatrain.
Hammond, W. On the Same [Death of My Dear Brother, Mr. H.S., Drowned]: The Boat.
Hannon. Beneath Cold Mountain.
Hardy, T. Placid Man's Epitaph, A.
Harjo, J. Remember.
Harris, Ken. Directions to the Maze.
Harry, J. Poem Films Itself, The.
Harryman. My Story.
Havergal. Just When Thou Wilt.
Hayden, R. Whipping, The.
Heaney, S. Casting and Gathering.
Heighton, S. Blackjack.
Heissenbüttel. Simple sentences.
Hejinian. Moment yellow, just as four years later when, A.
Moment yellow, just as four years later, when my father returned home from the war, A.
Henley, W. E. Madam Life's A Piece in Bloom.
To Robert Louis Stevenson.
Herbert, G. Life.
Herbert, Z. Elegy of Fortinbras.
Hernández, M. To Smile with the Joyful Sadness of the Olive Tree.
Herrick. Four[e] Things Make Us Happy Here.
Hierro, José. Fe de vida.
Hikmet. Fifth Letter.
On Living.
Since I Was Thrown Inside.
Hillman, B. Every Life.
Hillyer. As One Who Bears beneath His Neighbor's Roof.
Hirshfield, J. It Was Like This : You Were Happy.
Story, A.
Hogan, L. Return: Buffalo.
Holland, J. Sleep.
Three Tests for Darwin Duke.
Holub. Suffering.
Hongo. Pier, The.
Hoover, P. Family Romance.
Hopkins, G. Thou Art Indeed Just, Lord.
Hoskyns [or Hoskins]. Epitaph, An: On a Man for Doing Nothing.
Housman. Be still, my soul, be still; the arms you bear are brittle.
From far, from eve and morning.
Immortal Part, The.
Is my team ploughing.
Terence, this is stupid stuff.
Howard, R. Among the Missing.
Hughes, L. Mother to Son.
Hughes, T. Moon-Hops.
October Salmon[, An].
Hutchinson, L. Verses Written by Mrs. Hutchinson.
Hutchinson, P. Be Born a Saint.
Hwang Insuk. I'm Surplus.
Ichigen. Joshu exclaimed, "Dog's no Buddha".
Ingelow. Little babe, while burns the west.
Story, A.
Issa. First cicada / Life is.
Jaccottet. Letter of the 26th June.

Jackson, H. Danger.
Jacob, M. I thought he was bankrupt.
Jamie, K. Way we live, The.
Jarrell, R. Country Life, A.
Well Water.
Jeffers, R. Animals.
Ante Mortem.
Purse-Seine, The.
Jiménez, J. Dawn brings with it, The.
Oceans.
Jones, R. Beginning, A.
Jonson, B. To William Roe ("When Nature bids us leave to live, 'tis late.").
József, A. Seventh, The.
To Sit, to Stand, to Kill, to Die.
Juan Chi. Mujin Flowers Blossom on the Rolling Graves, The.
Juarroz. Bottom of things is neither life nor death, The.
Life Draws a Tree.
Somewhere There's a Man.
Kabir. I Cherish That Love.
Kanchev, Nikolai. Seventh Heaven Can Be Seen at First Glance.
Kaufman, S. Emperor of China, The.
Keats. Ode to a Nightingale.
Kekova. Already, no more suffering, no.
Kenyon, J. Happiness.
Kerouac. 113th Chorus.
211th Chorus.
Two Hundred and Twenty-Eighth Chorus.
Killigrew, A. On Death.
Kim Sŭnghŭi. Life Within an Egg.
Kindman, S. Fight and Play.
King, H. Sic Vita.
Kipling, R. Envoi: "There's a whisper down the field where the year has shot her yield."
Klein, M. Guardian Life.
Klink, J. And Having Lost Track.
Koch, K. One Train May Hide Another.
Koehler, T. As Long As I Live.
I've Got the World on a String.
Koethe. Songs of the Valley.
Koordada, M. You Can't Escape Your Life Record.
Ku K'uang. Hard Traveling.
Laing, K. Godhorse.
Huge Car with the Sad Voice, The.
Lake, P. Crime and Punishment.
Lal Ded [or Lalla]. This world.
Lamantia. Romantic Movement, The.
Landon. Lines of Life.
Secrets.
Small Miseries.
Stern Truth.
Lanier, S. Nirvâna.
Larbaud. Images.
Larkin, P. Afternoons.
Days.
Layton. Street Funeral.
Lazer, Hank. Teshuva: heading south.
Lea, S. Insomnia: The Distances.
Lear, E. O dear! How disgusting is life!
Lefevre, A. Halftime.
Levertov. Living.
O Taste and See.
Levine, P. Genius: "Two old dancing shoes my grandfather."
I Caught a Glimpse.
Rain Downriver.
Salami.
Sweet Will.
28.
Levy, A. Epitaph: "This is the end of him, here he lies."
Lewis, H. Life's Morning.
Li Po. Best of Life Is But, The.
Li Shang-yin. Where is it, the sad lyre which follows the quick flute?
LittleDog, Pat. Cowgirl.
Longfellow, H. Nature.
Psalm of Life, A.
Village Blacksmith, The.
Lowell, R. Book of Wisdom, The.
Lowry, M. Wild Cherry, The.
Lum. Riding the North Point Ferry.

Mac Low. 1st Dance—Making Things New—6 February 1964.
Machado Ruiz. Between living and dreaming.
If it's good to live.
Parables, I.
MacNeice. Prayer Before Birth.
MacSweeney. Seared to the echo.
Malroux. Octet Before Winter.
Mansei, S. Our Life in This World.
Mansour, J. Anti-mnemonic self-vaccination.
Tinfoil.
March, A. Much as a man who takes delight in dreaming.
Out scouting for sound counsels? How to prosper?
Marks, S. To the Ocean.
Martial. Pre-eminent among scholars.
Martinaitis, M. Kukutis's Song.
Masters, E. Jennie McGrew.
Lucinda Matlock.
Starved Rock.
Mathews, A. Caedmon.
Mayfield, C. Oh, It's You Again.
McAuley, J. Gnostic Prelude.
Released on Parole.
McClure, M. Mad Sonnet: Grace.
McPherson, S. Wings and Seeds: For My Birth Mother.
Melville, H. To———: "Ah, wherefore, lonely, to and fro."
Menicanti. Biographical News.
I Don't Know.
If.
Menken. Infelix.
Messerli. NARRATOR: Suddenly someone wakes me. Still half-asleep, I see standing in front.
Mezey. Reaching the Horizon.
Michaelis. Brilliantly Philosophising.
Miller, L. Let's fill in the form: date of birth.
Montale. Murder's not my forte.
Mörike [or Möricke]. Remember It, My Soul.
Mother Goose. Solomon Grundy.
Mueller, L. Curriculum Vitae.
Mumon Gensen. Life: a cloud crossing the peak.
Murray, L. People are eating dinner in that country north of Legge's Lake, The.
Muske, C. Applause.
Nadir, M. My Bas-Sheva.
Naito Joso. These branches.
Nash, O. Round About.
Nathan, L. Bladder Song.
Nemerov. Intimations.
Life, A.
Life Cycle of Common Man.
Nemes Nagy. Lazarus.
Neruda. Past.
Sexual Water.
Walking Around.
Walking Around.
Nerval. Golden Sayings.
Nervo. Ecstasy.
Neto. Grieved Lands, The.
Nezahualcoyotl. Be Indomitable, O My Heart.
Can It Be True That One Lives on Earth?
Ní Chuilleanáin. Pygmalion's Image.
Ni Dhomhnaill. Aubade: "It's all the same to morning what it dawns on."
Nichol. St. Anzas VI.
North, C. Elizabethan and Nova Scotian Music.
Few Facts about Me, A.
Leap Year.
Nortje. Newcombe at the Croydon Gallery.
Norwid, C. Those Who Love.
O'Driscoll, D. Life.
Ofeimun. Poet Lied, The.
Ogata Kenzon. Retrospective.
O'Grady, D. Purpose.
O'Hara, F. In Favor of One's Time.
In Memory of My Feelings.
Steps.
Ohnishi, T. Blossoms in the Wind.
Okigbo. Hurrah for Thunder.
Oliver, M. Going to Walden.
In Blackwater Woods.
Singapore.

Summer Day, The.
When Death Comes.
O'Loughlin. Posthumous.
Olson, C. Chain of memory is resurrection I am a vain man, The.
Omar, I. Not Quiet.
Ondaatje. Light.
Oness, C. Of All There Is.
Ormsby, F. Landscape with Figures.
Osgood, K. Driving Home the Cows.
Ovid. Elegy 1.15: "Envy, why carp'st [or carpest] thou my time is spent so ill."
Pack, R. Bounty.
Watchers.
Padilla. Man on the Edge.
Palladas [or Pallades]. Whose baggage from land to land is despair.
Parker, D. Coda: "There's little in taking or giving."
Résumé.
Parra, N. Anti-Lazarus, The.
Piano Solo.
Parra, V. Here's to Life.
I Thank Life for So Many Gifts.
Song for a Seed.
Pastan. Baseball.
Pasternak, B. Snow Is Falling.
Paz. Pause.
Response and Reconciliation.
Perillo, L. Dangerous Life.
Piatt, S. In Her Prison.
Piercy. Seven of Pentacles, The.
Pinsky. Jersey Rain.
Pitcher, O. Pale Blue Casket, The.
Po Chü-i. Climbing the Ling-ying Terrace and Looking North.
Golden Bells.
Realizing the Futility of Life.
Poe. Dreams: "Oh! That my young life were a lasting dream!"
Porter, P. Consumer's Report, A.
Pound, E. And the Days Are Not Full Enough.
Prior. Human Life.
Procter, A. Three Evenings in a Life.
Raboni, G. Hospital Interiors.
Radnóti. Clouded Sky.
Raine, K. Good Friday.
Ralegh, S. What Is Our Life?
Ransom, J. Here Lies a Lady.
Ray, H. Life.
Life's Boundary.
Reese, L. Tears.
To Life.
Reznikoff. I like this secret walking.
Rich, A. Burning Oneself Out.
Living Memory.
Tattered Kaddish.
Richardson, J. Vectors: Forty-five Aphorisms and Ten-second Essays.
Richez, Valérie-Catherine. Little Soul.
Rilke. I Find You, Lord, All Things and In All.
Swan, The ("This clumsy living that moves lumbering.").
Robin, L. Easy Living.
Robinson, A. Art and Life.
Robinson, E. Man against the Sky, The.
Rocha. Poem of Return.
Rodriguez, J. About this Woman.
Roethke. Judge Not.
Walk in Late Summer, A.
Roland Holst. Night Visit.
Rolle, S. Keeping Watch.
Rossetti, C. Birthday, A.
Cobwebs.
From the Antique.
Heaviness May Endure for a Night, But Joy Cometh in the Morning.
Life's Parallels, A.
Sappho.
Uphill [or Up-Hill].
World, The.
Roubaud. In This Tree.
Rouse, A. Birthday, A.
Rowe, E. Expostulation, The.
Rumens. Star Whisper.
Rumi. In this river the heart is like a ruined

waterwheel; in whichever direction it turns, there is water before it.
Ryan, T. Lunar Eclipse.
Ryokan. Faint trickle of.
Saenz, J. Let your permanency under the brilliance of the stars be long.
St. John, D. No Heaven.
St. John, P. Carnival.
Salaam. Spice of Life, The.
Til Death Do Us Part.
Sanchez, S. For Sweet Honey in the Rock.
Sandburg, C. Blue Island Intersection.
Broken-Face Gargoyles.
Chicago.
Early Copper.
Happiness.
Mag.
Onion Days.
People, Yes, The.
People, yes, the people, The.
Right to Grief, The.
Southern Pacific.
Teamster's Farewell, A.
Sarajlić, I. If I had died that Friday in Paris.
Scalapino. Flush / a Play.
Schnackenberg. Darwin in 1881.
Schultz, P. I'm Not Complaining.
Schwartz, R. L. Oh God, Fuck Me.
Seferis. Old Man on the River Bank, An.
Sexton. Courage.
Room of My Life, The.
Shakespeare, W. Seven Ages of Man, The.
Song: "When that I was and a little tiny boy."
Tomorrow, and Tomorrow, and Tomorrow.
Shange. I Live in Music.
Shapiro, D. Archaic Torsos.
Shelley, P. Sonnet: Lift Not the Painted Veil.
Sherwood, G. Love and Life.
Shinkichi Takahashi. Sheep.
"Shu Ting.". Assembly Line.
Shwarts [or Shvarts]. Elegies on the Cardinal Points.
Simic. Poem: "Every morning I forget how it is."
Sirr. Collector's Marginalia, The.
Skovron. Election Eve, with Cat.
Slessor. Fixed Ideas.
Last Trams.
Smith, C. Pressed by the Moon, Mute Arbitress of Tides.
Smith, M. Stopping to Take Notes.
Smith, S. Dream of Comparison, A.
Snodgrass. After Experience Taught Me.
April Inventory.
Spaziani. Present, The.
Spender, S. Sonnet: "You were born; must die; were loved; must love".
Stafford, W. Gift, The.
Stanley, T. Pythagoric Letter, The.
Stern, G. Dear waves, what will you do for me this year?
Lucky Life.
Royal Manor Road.
Stevens, W. Seventy Years Later.
Stowe. Only a Year.
Strand. Here: "Sun that silvers all the buildings here, The."
Story of Our Lives, The.
Stroud, J. Homage to Life: Jules Supervielle.
Suckling, S. Song: "I prithee spare me, gentle boy."
Supervielle. Return to Paris.
Swinburne. Before the Beginning of Years.
Swirszczynska [or Swir]. Poetry Reading.
Synková, A. I've met enough people.
Tears.
Taylor, A. Fitzroy.
Taylor, B. Goblet, The.
Taylor, H. Flying Change, The.
Tennyson, A. I know that this was Life—the track.
Teofilov, Ivan. Shared Existence.
Thomas, D. Force That through the Green Fuse Drives the Flower, The.
If I Were Tickled by the Rub of Love.
This Bread I Break.

Twenty-four Years.
Thomas, L. Magnetic Charms.
Thomas, R. S. Bright Field, The.
Lore.
Thomson, J. Part 2: "Because he seemed to walk with an intent."
Thoreau. I Am a Parcel of Vain Strivings Tied.
Life in us is like the water in the river, The.
My life has been the poem I would have writ.
Tilak, D. Night It Rained Life, The.
Toomer. Gods Are Here, The.
It is Everywhere.
Torres Bodet. Living.
Summary.
Torres, E. Lipsticktion.
Tranter. Enzensberger at 'Exiles'.
Tsaloumas. Falcon Drinking.
Tu Fu [or Du Fu]. By the Winding River.
Tucker, M. Life.
Mysteries of Life.
Unknown. Deor.
Inscription in Osmington Church, Dorset.
Loom of Time, The.
Nobody Knows the Trouble I've Had.
Only One Life.
Prayer of a Woman in Charge of Berry Picking in Knights Inlet.
Valley of Dry Bones, The.
What Care I Though the World Reprove.
Valek. Beating the Drum in Reverse.
Valentine, J. Letter: "Hornet holds on to the curtain, winter, The."
Trust Me.
Vallejo. Black heralds, The.
Down to the Dregs.
Our Daily Bread.
Van Doren. Good Appetite.
Van Duyn. Sonnet for Minimalists.
Van Hanh. Body of Man, The.
Van Peenen, H. Insulin Receptor.
Vaughan, H. Pursuit[e], The.
Vian, Boris. What for Do I Live Then.
Vicioso. Survival 1.
Viidikas. Future.
Vilariño. How to shrug off.
Lifelong farewell.
There is no hope.
What Was Life.
Vinokurov. Has the time come to draw up the accounts?
Virgil [or Vergil]. Death Plucks My Ear.
Waldman, A. Up Thru the Years.
Wallace-Crabbe. And the World was Calm.
Sonnet IV.
Watson, R. Of the Earth, Earthy.
Wearne. Elise.
Terri.
Webb, F. Clouds.
Webster, A. That some day death who has us all for jest.
Welch, L. Small Sentence to Drive Yourself Sane.
Wellman, M. Having Led a Charmed Life, He Had to be Hanged Twice.
Of Power, Money, Cheese, Real Estate, Conboberation, Hoohah.
Wenderoth, J. My Life: "Somehow it got into my room."
Wharton, E. Life.
White, D. Epistle of Love and of Consolation unto Israel, An.
Whitman, W. Beat! Beat! Drums!
Great Are the Myths.
I am of old and young, of the foolish as much as the wise.
Miracles.
When I Read the Book.
Wiethüchter. At This Juncture.
Movement.
Wilbur, R. Leaving.
Star System, The.
Trolling for Blues.
World Without Objects Is a Sensible Emptiness, A.
Williams, C. K. Shade, The.
Williams, W. Love Song: "Sweep the house

  clean."
  Pastoral: "Little sparrows, The."
Winter, M. Long Distance.
Wordsworth, D. Thoughts on my sick-bed.
Wordsworth, W. World Is Too Much with Us,
  The.
Wotton, S. De Morte.
Wright, C. Laguna Blues.
Wright, D. Funeral Oration, A.
Wright, James. Angel, The.
  Honey.
  Horse, The.
  Northern Pike.
  Secret Gratitude, A.
  Trying to Pray.
Wright, Judith. Song: "O where does the dancer
  dance."
Yamanoé [or Yamanoué] no Okura. Lament for
  the Evanescence of Life, A.
Yeats. Gyres, The.
  Meru.
  Wild Old Wicked Man, The.
Yi Kyŏngnim. Oh Life.
Young, A. Detroit 1958.
  From Bowling Green.
  How Stars Start.
  How the Rainbow Works.
  Myself When I Am Real.
Young, G. Our Life in California.
Young, J. Life Is a Song, Let's Sing It Together.
Zach, N. Be Careful.
Zaid. Furious Clarity, A.
Zhenkai. Accomplices.
Zucker, R. In Your Version of Heaven I am
  Younger.

Lifeguards
Dickey, J. Lifeguard, The.
Klein, M. Tides, The.
Meitner, E. All the Pools in Queens.

Light
Achterberg. Instrument.
Adams, Joan. Yellow Is Me, But All the Same
  Are We.
Adams, L. Light at Equinox.
Afrika, T. Nightrider.
Agustini. To Death, from the Genie of My
  Poetry.
Ali, A. Purse-Seiner *Atlantis*, The.
Allnutt, G. Notes on living inside the lightbulb.
Ammons. City Limits, The.
Andreus. Empty Room, The.
  Empty Room, The.
Angeles, C. Light Invested.
Ap Hywel, Elin. Understanding the Light.
Ash, J. Poor Boy: Portrait of a Painting.
Ashbery, J. Hod Carrier, The.
  Of the Light.
Bachmann. Paris.
Barber, D. Small Hours.
Basho. Awake at night.
  On the way to the outhouse.
Bawer. View from an Airplane at Night, over
  California, The.
Beranová, J. Williamsbridge.
Bernard, A. See It Does Rise.
Biespiel, D. There Were No Deer in the
  Thicket.
Bingen, Hildegard von. Alleluia-verse for the
  Virgin.
  Antiphon for the Angels.
  Song to the Creator.
Blake, W. To Morning.
Blanco. Set Theory.
  Teoría de conjuntos.
  Teoría de la luz.
  Theory of Light.
Bogan, L. Evening-Star.
Boland, E. Self-Portrait on a Summer Evening.
Bolton, J. Lights at Newport Beach, The.
Boruch. Light.
Bourdillon. Night Has a Thousand Eyes, The.
Bronk. Where It Ends.
Brown Rosellen. I want to understand light
  years.
Browning, E. Best Thing in the World, The.
Bruce, D. Sonnet 4.

Bu-er. Cut brambles long enough.
Buckley, C. Inverse Square Law of the
  Propagation of Light, The.
Buson. Happy traveler / Mosquito wick.
  Light of the moon.
  Lights are going out, The.
Byron, G. Darkness.
Cardenal. Lights.
Carew, T. Beautiful Mistress, A.
Celan. You be like you, ever.
Ceravolo. New Realism.
Ch'u Yüan. In the beginning of old.
Clover, J. El periférico, or Sleep.
Cohen, L. Twelve O'Clock Chant.
Coleridge, M. Fire, the lamp, and I, were alone
  together, The.
  In Disprayse of the Moon.
Colonna, V. I see in my mind, surrounding
  God.
Cook, E. Song of the Rushlight.
Cortes, F. Poem Composed During a Brownout.
Cowley, A. Hymn to Light.
Creeley. Kitchen.
  World, The.
Crouch, S. Like a Blessing.
De Angelis. There's a Hand that Nails Down.
DeFrees. Beetle Light.
Delaunay, S. Zenith.
Dickinson, E. Light exists in Spring, A.
  Poets light but Lamps, The.
  There's a certain Slant of light.
Donne. Nocturnal[l] upon Saint Lucy's [or S.
  Lucy's or S. Lucies] Day, Being the Shortest
  Day, A.
Dorantes, D. En la profunda cueva.
  In the deep cave.
Dumdum. Some Die of Light.
Duo Duo. None.
Earle, J. Visiting Light.
Eguren. Girls of the Light, The.
Eichner, Maura. Message from Inland.
Ferguson, G. Winter Sunflowers.
Field. They Shall Look on Him.
Fletcher, P. Ocean of Light.
Freeman, Jessica. Up Tchoupitoulas Nom de
  Guerre.
Gamalinda, E. Light Falls Obliquely.
García Lorca. Song Wants to Be Light, The.
Garrett, E. Airborne.
George, D. I'm Beginning to See the Light.
Gerlach, E. Turn and Turn About.
Gezelle. Ego Flos.
Giussani, S. Abel and Abel.
Glück, L. White Rose, The.
Goldberg, B. Nights with the Star-Ladle Over
  the House.
Goodison. Always Homing Now Soul Toward
  Light.
Gore-Booth. Vision of Niamh, The.
Graham, J. San Sepolcro.
Greiffenberg. On the Ineffable Inspiration of the
  Holy Spirit.
Gu Cheng. Generation, A.
Guest, B. Wild Gardens Overlooked by Night
  Lights.
Gunn, T. Map of the City, A.
Harjo, J. White Bear.
Harvey, M. One Filament against the
  Firmament.
Haskins, L. Dearborn North Apartments
  Chicago, Illinois.
Hatubou, S. Night 1.
Heaney, S. Sunlight.
Hecht, A. Illumination.
Hemans. Illuminated City, The.
Henderson, D. Lock City.
Hickey, E. For Richer, For Poorer.
Hinsey, E. Art of Measuring Light, The.
Howe, M. Certain Light, A.
Hudgins. Beneath Searchlights.
  What Light Destroys.
Huerta, D. Light from Parallel Worlds.
  Luz de los mundos paralelos.
Hume, C. Truth about Northern Lights, The.
Ibáñez, S. Island in the Light.
Issa. Autumn evening.

  Even considered.
  Lost in bamboo.
Izumi. Way I must enter, The.
Jabès. Beginning of the Book, The.
Jaccottet. Distances.
  I Rise with an Effort.
  Serenity.
Japicx, G. Lovelight.
Jones, D. In a Beautiful Glass.
Jones, M. Old Light, The.
Joubert. Brilliant Sky.
Juarroz. Lamp lit, A.
Kikaku. May he who brings / Flowers tonight.
Kooser. Happy Birthday, A.
  Late Lights in Minnesota.
Kosugi, T. Manodharma with Mr. Y.
Krynicki. I Can't Help You.
Kunitz, S. Round, The.
  When the Light Falls.
LaFemina. White Dwarf.
Langille. Sadness of Windows, The.
Lao Tzu. Boundless shaping Power, A.
Lawrence, D. H. Let There Be Light!
Lea, S. Telescope.
Levine, P. Belief.
Lewis, G. One day, feeling hungry.
Love, B. Bryan Ferry.
Lumelli, A. They could be reservoirs for water.
Mac Low. 59th Light Poem: for La Monte
  Young and Marian Zazeela—6 November
  1982.
MacCaig. Likenesses.
MacDiarmid, H. Milk-Wort and Bog Cotton.
MacNeice. Star-Gazer.
Mallarmé. Fine suicide fled victoriously, The.
Mansour, J. Desire as Light as a Shuttle.
Marsman. Polderland.
Martinez, D. Nocturnes: "He closed the deal on
  the night. A real."
Marvell. Mower to the Glowworms [or Glow-
  Worms or Glo-Worms], The.
McCabe, C. Light & Love.
McGrath, T. Reading by Mechanic Light.
Meinke. Unnatural Light.
Melville, H. In the Desert.
Michaels, A. Language is the house with
  lamplight in its windows.
Millay, E. First Fig.
Milton. Hail, Holy Light[!].
  On His Blindness.
Montale. Little Testament.
Moore, L. Homeplace, The.
Morley, C. Air Street.
Muso Soseki. Beyond Light.
  Don't ask suspiciously.
Myles, E. School of Fish.
Nelson, G. Shelving Fixtures.
Nelson, M. Brightness.
Nichol. St. Anzas VI.
Nijhoff. Light.
  Light, The.
  Musician, The.
Novakovich. Shadow.
O'Reilly, C. Brief History of Light, A.
Ōshima Ryōta. On rainy leaves / Glow.
Pasternak, B. Storm, an Endless Instant.
Patacara. When they plow their fields.
Paz. Native Stone.
Peterson, J. Stand Still.
Phillips, C. Clearing, The.
Piper, P. Christmas Eve, 2003.
Powell, Dannye Romine. Woman Who Allowed
  Light to Have Its Way with Her, The.
Prabhu. For the Lord of Caves.
Praxilla. Fairest thing I leave behind is sunlight,
  The.
Probyn. More than They that Watch for the
  Morning.
"Rachel." [or "Rahel."]. Barn, The.
Ramsdell, H. Bright Receding.
Rankine. Quotidian, The.
Rich, A. Insusceptibles, The.
  Integrity.
Ríos, A. Physics of Sudden Light, A.
Ritsos. His Lamp Near Daybreak.
Roberts, K. Plastic Cup, The.

Lighthouses _(continued)_

Roethke. Light Listened.
  To Have the Whole Air!
Romo-Carmona, M. Daylight.
Roubaud. Light, for Example.
Rumi. Light You Give Off, The.
St. John, D. In the Sulphur Garden.
St. John, P. Biological Light.
Samyn, M. Poem with Light on Its Shoulder.
Sarton, M. Light Left On, A.
Scalise, G. Dora Markus and Her Actors.
Schuyler, J. Shimmer.
Scovell. Light the Fire.
Seigen-yuiin. How vast karma.
Senghor. Pearls.
Shelley, P. As in that trance of wondrous
  thought I lay.
  One remains, the many change and pass, The.
Shwarts [or Shvarts]. My heart's cloth I shall
  spread before the Savior's feet.
Simms, C. Pallid Harrier.
Sitwell. Aubade: "Jane, Jane, / Tall as a crane."
Snyder, G. How Poetry Comes to Me.
Soto. Tale of Sunlight, The.
Spahr, J. Story goes like this: the light, The.
Stanley, T. Glowworm, The.
Stoutenburg. Midnight Saving Time.
Suian. Traceless, no more need to hide.
Symonds. Lux Est Umbra Dei.
Tabb. Tenebrae.
Tan Taigi. In the boat / Crescent moon's light.
Tanikawa, S. Stone and Light.
Thomas, D. Light Breaks Where No Sun
  Shines.
Thomas, L. Electricity of Blossoms.
Tomlinson, C. Above the Rio Grande.
Touré, A. O Lord of Light! A Mystic Sage
  Returns to Realms of Eternity!
Towle. Painting the Eaves.
Ungaretti. Where the Light.
Unknown. Alba, With a Refrain from the
  Provençal.
Van Ostaijen. Landscape.
  Souvenir.
Waldrop, R. At the Sea.
Walker, D. Daylight.
Wang Wei. Deer Enclosure.
Wat. Facing Bonnard.
Webb, F. Port Phillip Night.
Welch, L. Difficulty Along the Way.
White, J. To Night.
Wilbur, R. Star System, The.
Williams, T. My Love Was Light.
Williamson, A. Light's Reading, The.
Witt, S. Thermal Signatures ("I sing a place
  called Newborn.").
Wordsworth, W. Our birth is but a sleep and a
  forgetting.
Wright, C. Appalachian Book of the Dead 3,
  The.
Wright, J. Beginning.
  To the Evening Star: Central Minnesota.
Wroth. Sonnet 22: "Like to the Indians,
  scorched with the sun[ne]."
Wylie. Incantation: "White well, A."
  O Virtuous Light.
Yeryomin. Street lamp. Something missing.
  Drugstore.
Young, A. Written in Bracing, Gray L.A.
  Rainlight.

Lighthouses

Albrecht, A. Passing Piedras Blancas.
Bailey, A. Isosceles Lighthouse, The.
Bishop, E. Seascape.
Ceravolo. Lighthouse.
Clampitt. Baroque Sunburst, A.
Cullen, Y. To the Lighthouse.
Diego, G. Your Eyes Are Always Open.
Groarke, V. Shale.
Hirshfield, J. Lighthouse.
Jackson, H. My Lighthouses.
Knighton, R. Ballad of Echolocation, The.
Martinson. Lighthouse Keeper.
Mistral, G. Pious One, The.
Morshen. At the Lighthouse.
Quagliano. Edward Hopper's "Lighthouse at
  Two Lights".

Sadoff. February: Pemaquid Point.
Wilbur, R. Beacon, The.

Lightning

Al-Braikan, M. World of Lightning, A.
Al-Harizi. Lightning, The.
Basho. How admirable!
  How marvelous the man is.
  Lightning.
  Lightning flash.
Buson. Around the small house.
  Lightning flash—,A.
Bynner. Lightning.
Chernoff. Man Struck Twenty Times by
  Lightning, The.
Davis, J. He Is Lightning.
Dickinson, E. Lightning is a yellow Fork, The.
Espada. Owl and the Lightning, The.
Fargnoli, Patricia. Lightning Spreads Out across
  the Water.
Follain. Women Say, The: 'It Looks Like Rain'.
Grabill. Lightning, The.
Greiffenberg. On the Ineffable Inspiration of the
  Holy Spirit.
Issa. Dry riverbed, A.
Kinzie. Bolt, The.
Lal Ded [or Lalla]. On the way to God the
  difficulties.
Lawrence, D. H. Lightning.
  Storm in the Black Forest.
Long, H. Lightning.
MacDiarmid, H. Two Memories.
Macdonald, G. Baby-Sermon, A.
Martin, C. Reflections after a Dry Spell.
Martinez, D. Bad Alchemy.
Moss, H. Summer Thunder, The.
Schelling. High Up the Thunder Gods,
  Downstairs the Hunger.
Stevenson, R. Last night we had a thunderstorm
  in style.
Unknown. Songs of Spirits.

Lightning Bugs

Forrester, S. Just within my reach the lightning
  bug turns off.
Unknown. Bugs.
See also **Fireflies**

Lilacs

Biespiel, D. Lilacs.
Daugherty, B. Lilac.
Harjo, J. Santa Fe.
Kim Ch'unsu [or Chun-soo]. Lilac Petals.
Lowell, A. Lilacs.
Miliauskaite. These are Lilacs.
Shannon, J. Lilac.
Sinclair, S. Lilacs.
Solie, Karen. Lilacs.
Stern, G. Lilacs for Ginsberg.
Wilbur, R. Lilacs, The.

Lilies

Beddoes. Crocodile, A.
Bible, _O.T._ I Am the Rose of Sharon.
Black, D. Water-Lily, The.
Bleakney, J. Be Careful of the Lilies!
Bui-Burton. My Love is Like a Lily.
Coolbrith. Mariposa Lily, The.
Funkhouser. Lilies.
Glück, L. White Lilies, The.
Goldberg, B. Lilies at Night.
Gregory, H. Chinese Garden, The.
Guest, B. Red Lilies.
Keats. Belle Dame sans Merci, La [A Ballad].
Kreymborg. Tiger Lily.
Legaré. To a Lily.
Merrill, C. Day Lilies: Instructions and an
  Elegy.
Oliver, M. Lilies.
Robinson, A. Pallor.
Sexton. From the Garden.
Smart, C. On a Bed of Guernsey Lilies.
Tennyson, A. Come into the Garden, Maud.
  Now Sleeps the Crimson Petal.
Unknown. Lily Events.
Weslowski. Year I Found, The.
Whalen, P. Elizabethan Phrase, The.

Lilies of the Valley

Silkin. Lilies of the Valley.

Lilith

Benton, S. Lilith.
Bialik. Summer Night.
Fabian, C. Liturgy for Lilith.
Norris, K. Lilith and the Doctor.
Parnell, P. Medusa and Perseus III: Lilith.
Rossetti, D. 78: Body's Beauty.
Wechsler, E. Lilith, Adam's First Companion.

Limbo

Levy, A. Ballad of Religion and Marriage, A.
Pasternak, B. Moochkap.
Poe. Al Aaraaf.

Limestone

Auden. In Praise of Limestone.

Lincoln, Abraham

Berger, D. Lincoln Bedroom, The.
Bryant, W. Death of Lincoln, The.
Fletcher, J. Lincoln.
Hughes, L. Lincoln Monument: Washington.
Kennedy, X. Loneliness of Lincoln, The.
Knoepfle. Bath.
Lindsay, V. Abraham Lincoln Walks at
  Midnight.
Markham, E. Lincoln, the Man of the People.
Masters, E. Anne Rutledge.
Meigs, M. Abraham Lincoln.
Melville, H. Martyr, The.
Ray, H. Lincoln.
Robinson, E. Master, The.
Sandburg, C. Cool Tombs.
  Long Shadow of Lincoln: A Litany, The.
Schwartz, D. Lincoln.
Sorby. Land of Lincoln.
Tate, J. Diagnosis, The.
Thompson, M. Lincoln's Grave.
Whitman, W. Hush'd be the Camps To-Day.
  O Captain! My Captain!
  When Lilacs Last in the Dooryard Bloom'd.

Lincolnshire, England

Ingelow. High Tide on the Coast of
  Lincolnshire, 1571, The.

Lindbergh, Charles Augustus

Deutsch. Flight, The: "Earthen shadow lay on
  men's endeavor, An."

Linden Trees

Unknown. Under the Linden Tree.
Vogelweide. Under the linden.
  Under the Lindentree.

Linen

Longley, M. Linen Industry, The.

Linnets

Bridges, R. I Heard a Linnet Courting.
Brontë, E. Song: "Linnet in the rocky dells,
  The."
Webster, A. Since first my little one lay on my
  breast.

Lions

Azzawi, F. Lion and the Apostle, The.
Belev. Zoo.
Belloc. Jim Who Ran Away from His Nurse,
  and Was Eaten by a Lion.
  Lion, The.
Bialik. Do not.
Blake, W. Little Girl Found, The.
Byron, G. When the lion was young.
Carruth, H. Wreck of the Circus Train, The.
Daigu. Who dares approach the lion's.
Dubie. Buffalo Clouds over the Maestro Hoon.
  Elegy for Wright & Hugo.
Duncan, R. What of the structure of Rime? I
  said.
Edgar, M. Lion and Albert, The.
Ginsberg, A. Lion for Real, The.
Heywood, J. Egles byrde hath spred his wings,
  The.
Housman. African Lion, The.
Howell, C. Blessing's Precision.
Ilkov, Ani. Peony and a Lion, A.
Jacobsen, J. Bush.
Jarrell, R. Night with Lions, A.
Levy, A. Captivity.
MacLeish. End of the World, The.
McClure, M. For Zenshin Ryufu Philip Whalen.
Merry. Some Terrify Lions [or Anna Matilda].
Nash, O. Lion, The.

Patchen. Lions of fire, The.
Sackville-West. Greater Cats, The.
Seale, J. Big Bend: Lion Warning.
Smith, S. Sunt Leones.
Wheelwright. Lion.
Xuanjue. Roar of the Lion.

Lips
Carew, T. Lips and Eyes.
Cernuda. For Two Voices.
Chapman, G. Bridal Song: "O come, soft rest of cares, come Night."
Coffman. Girl/Spit.
de Gillies, G. De Puerorum osculis.
Dowson. Non Sum Qualis Eram Bonae sub Regno Cynarae.
González Prada, M. Your Lily Eyes Said Yes.
Herrick. Cherry-ripe [or Cherrie-ripe].
Larsen, L. Lips.
MacMuireadach. Farewell for ever to last night.
Morris, T. Prelude to a Kiss.
Morungen, H. Wound of Love, The.
Noble, R. Touch of Your Lips, The.
O'Hara, F. Lebanon.
Shakespeare, W. Sonnet 128: "How oft, when thou, my music, music play'st."
Take, O Take Those Lips Away.
Simon, L. Bernice Got Next to Isis.
Toomer. Evening Song.
Her Lips Are Copper Wire.
Wolverton, T. Tubes.

Lisbon, Portugal
Atkins, R. Lisbon.
Voltaire. Woeful mankind, born to a woeful earth!

Listening and Listeners
Ackerman, D. We Are Listening.
Allen, D. Time to Hear Ourselves Think.
Angeles, C. Words.
Auden. Turn off the wireless; we are tired.
Barresi. Back-Up Singer, The.
Bringhurst. Song of Ptahhotep, The.
Carman, B. Eavesdropper, The.
Castro, R. Bells, The.
Curnow. Out of Sleep.
De la Mare. Dove, The.
Dickinson, A. Cryo.
Emerson, J. Architecture (2).
Frankau, R. Thoughts While Broadcasting.
Gascoyne. Nightwatchers, The.
Gilbert, J. Prospero Listens to the Night.
Graham, D. Wireless, The.
Grimké, A. Rosabel.
Hamilton, S. Species of Audibles.
Isherwood. Turn off the wireless; we are tired.
Issa. Old dog bends his head listening, The.
Jackson, M. L. How to Listen.
Jenkins, Joyce. Piano Man.
Kanik. I Am Listening to Istanbul.
Lampman. Frogs, The.
Lauterbach. After Mahler.
Levertov. Aware.
Levison, B. Eighth Symphony Interruptus.
McHugh, H. Or Else.
Melançon, Robert. Beginning of Summer.
Merwin. Hearing.
Morejón. Richard Brought His Flute.
Okigbo. I am standing above the noontide.
Olsen, W. Frost's Last Lecture: A Tape: His Audience—1963.
Paz. As One Listens to the Rain.
Riesco. So You Would Listen to Me.
Rohrer, M. Last Look at the Mutineers, A.
Sachs, N. How Long Have We Forgotten How to Listen!
Storey, E. Wireless Aerial, The.
Synková, A. To Olga.
Szirtes. Short Wave.
Tomlinson, C. Word in Edgeways, A.
Trommer, R. If You Listen.
Unknown. What the Listener Thinks.
Wayne, J. Eavesdropper, The.
Wellman, M. Endowed fiction of a mouse ear.
Whitman, W. I Heard You Solemn-Sweet Pipes of the Organ.
Wilcox, E. In the Night.
Wonham, J. Emergency Services.

Zavatsky. Live at the Village Vanguard.
Zukofsky, L. In Arizona.

Literature
Berryman. Professor's Song, A.
Camlan. Literature and Action.
Castellanos. Meditation on the Threshold.
Ch'ien T'ao. On Reading the Seas and Mountains Classic.
Connolly, C. It was late last night when my lord came home.
Cook, William. Endangered Species.
Deniz, A. Authoritarian School and How a Respectable Literary Genre Was Born, The.
Escuela autoritaria y cómo nació un respetable género de literatura, La.
Derricotte. Passing.
Dylan. Desolation Row.
Guest, B. Hungry Knight, The.
Han-shan. Reading won't save us from death.
Hattersley, G. *On the Buses* with Dostoyevsky.
Hightower, J. On Reading the Seas and Mountains Classic.
Hill, G. Bibliographers, The.
Hirshfield, J. In Praise of Coldness.
Jacob, M. Rue Ravignan, The.
Leonard, T. 100 Differences Between Poetry and Prose.
Lewis, G. Oxford Booklicker.
Lopez, T. Path Marked with Breadcrumbs, A.
Studies in Classic American Literature.
Lu Chi. Rhymeprose on Literature.
Merry. Elegy Written after Reading the "Sorrows of Werter".
Mueller, L. American Literature.
Another Version.
Nelson, S. Anti-Foucault Poem, The.
Parker, D. Pig's-Eye View of Literature, A.
Ransom, J. Survey of Literature.
Reed, I. Badman of the Guest Professor.
Rukeyser, M. Homage to Literature.
St. John, P. Studying.
Smith, S. Souvenir de Monsieur Poop.
Unknown. Among the yeomen's sons on my estate.
Waller, E. Of English Verse.
Weingarten. Inquisition, The: A Romance.
Williams, W. Question and Answer.
Yépez, H. Juan Martínez, Juan Nadie, Juan Todos.
Juan Martínez, Juan Nobody, Juan All.
See also **Authorship and Authors; Criticism and Critics**

Lithuania
Martinaitis, M. Kukutis's Fruitless Bread.
Kukutis's Swallow's Hymn.
Kukutis's Trip on the Samogitian Highway.
Milosz, C. In Szetejnie.
With Her.
Pelletiere, M. Under Her Crib.

Little Bighorn, Battle of (1876)
Whitman, W. From Far Dakota's Cañons (June 25, 1876).

Little, Malcolm.
See **Malcolm X (Malcolm Little)**

Little Red Riding Hood
Bolton, G. Little Red Riding Hood and the Wolf.
Duffy, C. Little Red-Cap.
Zucker, R. What I Want You to See Is She When Not Here As in Now.

Lizards
Alegría. Toward the Jurassic Age.
Alipiev, V. Warmth, The.
Bethune, L. Today Tutu Is Beating the Same Burru As Me.
Grennan. Lizards in Sardinia.
Jarnot, L. Swamp Formalism.
Kinnell. Gray Heron, The.
Kreitman, N. Lizard.
Lamartine. Lizard, The.
Lawrence, A. Goanna.
Montale. If the green lizard darts.
Morley, H. Lizard, The.
Pender. Lizard, The.
Robinson, R. Jarrangulli.

Roethke. Lizard, The ("Time to Tickle a Lizard, The.").
Wish for a Young Wife.
Rogers, P. Justification of the Horned Lizard.
Stafford, W. At the Bomb Testing Site.

Llamas
Arnold, D. Song to the Alpaca.
Donegan, P. Check Up.

Lobsters
Carroll, L. Alice's Recitation.
Lobster Quadrille, A.
Gallup. Pretty Beads.
Hoffman, D. Lobsterpot Labyrinths.
Lieberman, L. Lobsters in the Brain Coral.
Lowell, R. Water.
MacDonald, C. Lobster, The.
Muldoon, P. Something Else.
Rakosi. Lobster, The.
Saroyan. Lobstee.
Sexton. Lobster.
Snodgrass. Lobsters in the Window.

Loch Ness
MacEwen, G. Death of the Loch Ness Monster, The.

Locker Rooms
Arnold, C. Locker Room Etiquette.

Locomotives
Cranch. Locomotive, The.
Jones, B. Engine Driver.
MacLeish. Pastoral.
Whitman, W. O the engineer's joys! to go with a locomotive!
Wilcox, E. Engine, The.
Yamaguchi Seishi. Up to summer grass.
See also **Trains; Railroads**

Locusts
Ipadeola, T. Companions.
Kinzie. Canicula.
Mengham, Rod. Another Name for the Cassiterides.
Unknown. Locusts a-wing, multiply.

Logging and Lumberjacks
Chŏng Ch'ŏl. Why does that pine tree stand.
Clare, J. Look backward on the days of yore.
Clausen. White in the Woods.
Frost, R. In winter in the woods alone.
Gurney, I. Felling a Tree.
Kinnell. Man Splitting Wood in the Daybreak, The.
Morris, G. Woodman, Spare That Tree.
Nguyen, Hoa. Kerouac Creek Work Tune.
Reading, P. Salopian.
Rosen, M. This Morning.
Snyder, G. Getting in the Wood.
Wagoner, D. Elegy for a Forest Clear-Cut by the Weyerhaeuser Company.
To a Farmer Who Hung Five Hawks on His Barbed Wire.
Yi Kyubo. Loom importunes, The.

London, England
Adcock, F. Immigrant.
Bancks. Description of London, A.
Barot, R. Three Amoretti.
Bateman, E. Cockney's Garden, The.
Belloc. Ballade of Hell and of Mrs. Roebeck.
Blackburn, T. Now Light Congeals.
Blake, W. Fields from Islington to Marybone, The.
London.
London: "I wander through [or thro'] each chartered [or charter'd] street."
Brecht, B. Contemplating Hell.
Bridges, R. London Snow.
Carpenter, M. One day I went to London.
Clampitt. Hairline Fracture, A.
Colman, G. London Rurality.
Cope, W. Not only marble, but the plastic toys.
Coward. London Pride.
Creeley. In London.
Cronin, A. Responsibilities.
Disch. Convalescing in London.
Dischell. Yellow Slicker, The.
Dooley, M. Mind the Gap.
Douglas, L. Impression de Nuit; London.
Dressel. Intercity, Swansea-London.

Dryden, J. Yet London, empress of the northern clime.
Dunbar, W. To [or In Honour of] the City of London.
"Eliot.". In a London Drawingroom.
Eliot, T. S. 3. The Fire Sermon.
Fisher, A. Birdland.
Ford, S. Hail, glorious day; mayst thou be writ in gold.
French, W. Mountains of Mourne, The.
Gershwin, I. Foggy Day (in London Town), A.
Ginsberg, A. Studying the Signs.
Griffiths, B. Fragment 1: "Adventure."
Guilpin. What more variety of pleasures can.
Guiney. Lights of London, The.
  Sunday Chimes in the City.
W. H.
Herrick. His Return to London.
Holloway, J. London, Greater London (After *Satire III*).
Housman. Eight O'Clock.
Hunt, L. To Hampstead ("Winter has reached thee once again at last.").
King, J. Intercity Dub.
Levy, A. London in July.
  London Plane-Tree, A.
  London Poets.
  Straw in the Street.
Lindsay, M. 'Tis Sixty Years Since.
MacNeice. London Rain.
  September has come and I wake.
  Streets of Laredo, The.
  Whit Monday.
Mallarmé. Pipe, The.
Maschwitz, E. Nightingale Sang in Berkeley Square, A.
Matthews, M. By a Ways.
McCabe, C. Postcard from London, A.
McOrlan. Produce from the colonies.
Meynell, A. November Blue.
Monk, G. South Bound: Facing North.
Morton, J. Spring in London.
Mother Goose. London Bridge.
Motteux. Song, A: "Slaves to London, I'll deceive you."
Nortje. Cosmos in London.
Noyes, A. Barrel-Organ, The.
Oldham, J. London.
Phillips, E. Ties.
Pope, A. Farewell to London in the Year 1715, A.
Robinson, M. London's Summer Morning.
St. John, D. Swan at Sheffield Park, The.
Satyamurti. Ghost Stations.
Shelley, P. Hell is a city much like London.
Spender, S. Rejoice in the Abyss.
Spires. Sunday Afternoon at Fulham Palace.
Stroud, J. Directions.
Suckling, S. Ballad[e] [upon a Wedding], A.
Swift, J. Description of a City Shower, A.
Thomas, D. Refusal to Mourn the Death, by Fire, of a Child in London, A.
Thomas, R. S. Welshman at St. James' Park, A.
Unknown. Cries of London, The.
  London Bells.
  London Lickpenny.
  Oranges and lemons, say the bells of St. Clement's.
Vaughan, H. Rhapsody, A.
  Town believes thee lost, and didst thou see, The.
Ward, E. South Sea Ballad, A.
Whitney, I. Aucthour Maketh Her Wyll and Testament, The.
  Manner of Her Will and What She Left to London and to All Those in It, at Her Departing, The.
Wilde, O. Impression du Matin.
  Symphony in Yellow.
Wilson, S. Room in Bloomsbury, A.
Wordsworth, W. As the black storm upon the mountain top.
  Composed upon Westminster Bridge, September 3, 1802.
  London 1802 ("Milton! thou shouldst be living at this hour.").

Loneliness
Abrahams, L. Privacy.
Afrika, T. Fist, The.
Aiken, J. John's Song.
Akera Kanko. Under a ragged loincloth.
Allnutt, G. Silk Light of Advent, The.
Amir, D. Nightingale of Uncle Yair, The.
Andreus. Empty Room, The.
  Empty Room, The.
Angel. Nothing That Is, The.
Apollinaire. Farewell, The.
  Pretty Redhead, The.
Arends, J. I Have.
Arnold, M. To Marguerite—Continued.
Auden. Minnelied.
  Miranda.
Avidan, D. Life of a Dead Dog.
Aytoun [or Ayton], R. Valediction.
Barnes, W. Lwonesomeness.
  Wife a-Lost, The.
Basheva. Morning: "Where was I last night? In whose arms?"
Basho. Autumn deepening.
  Loneliness.
  Lonely silence.
  On New Year's Day.
  Warmly wrapped.
  Wild sea, A.
  You could turn this way.
  Your song caresses.
Becker, R. Near Sheridan.
Beckett, S. Roundelay: "On all that strand."
Bécquer, G. Great Waves Breaking with a Roar.
  To See the Hours of Fever.
Behn, A. Verses Design'd by Mrs. A. Behn to be Sent to a Fair Lady.
Berkson, B. Fixture, A.
Berlin. What'll I Do?
  You Can't Get a Man with a Gun.
Berrigan, T. Living with Chris.
Berryman. He Resigns.
  I'm scared a lonely. Never see my son.
  Sometimes the night echoes to prideless wailing.
Betjeman. House of Rest.
Bibbins, M. Mud.
Blaga. Psalm.
Bly, R. Snowbanks North of the House.
Borson. After a Death.
Boutens. Lonely Night.
Brodsky, J. To Urania.
Brontë, A. Captive Dove, The.
Brontë, C. Again I find myself alone.
  Lonely Lady, The.
Brooks, G. Preacher: Ruminates behind the Sermon, The.
Brown, E. Tragic Hero.
Brown, K. Lonely Women.
Bukowski. Way it is now, The.
Burke, J. Good Time Charlie.
Burke, S. Black Coffee.
Buson. Autumn evening.
  Old post town, two or three houses.
Byron, G. Juan's Puberty.
Cahn, S. I'll Walk Alone.
Carruth, H. Time, Place, and Parenthood.
Celaya, G. Life One Leads, The.
Chen Zi'ang. Song on Youzhou Terrace.
Chih-Wen, S. On Old Zhang's Pine Tree.
Chin. Composed Near the Bay Bridge (after a wild party).
Ching An. Moored at Maple Bridge.
Chittendon. Ennui.
Cho Chihun. Waiting.
Ch'oe Ch'iwŏn. On a Rainy Autumn Night.
Chŏng Chiyong. Windowpane I.
Chŏng Ch'ŏl. Boys have gone out to gather bracken.
Chou Pang-yen. Tune: "Prince Lan-Ling".
Chu Shu-chen. Sorrow: "White moon gleams through scudding, The."
  Spring Joy.
Cisneros, A. Hampton Court.
Clare, J. Shepherd Boy, The.
  Song: "I peeled bits of straw and I got switches too."
Clarke, G. Am I Blue?

Cole, Maude E. Prairie Friend.
Coleridge, H. She Was a Queen.
Coleridge, S. Old Man's Sigh, The. A Sonnet.
Collins, B. Embrace.
Comden, B. Lonely Town.
Cope, W. Lonely Hearts.
Crane, H. Meticulous, past midnight in clear rime.
Crane, S. I explain the silvered passing of a ship at night.
Crapsey. Lonely Death, The.
Creamer, H. If I Could Be with You.
Creeley. Door, The: "It is hard going to the door."
  Whip, The.
Csoori. For the Seventh Day.
  Thin, Black Band, A.
Cummings, E. E. L(a.
  Wind has blown the rain away and blown, A.
Dalton, A. Almost Bird.
Darío, R. Sonatina.
Dauer. Mammals.
Davis, B. I'm Nobody's Baby.
De la Mare. Old Men, The.
Delmore, E. Difference, The.
des Forêts Louis-René. It Is High Time.
Deutsch. Solitude.
Dickinson, E. Loneliness One dare not sound, The.
  Shade upon the mind there passes, A.
  There is another Loneliness.
  We don't [or dont] cry—Tim and I.
Dixon, M. Would You Like to Take a Walk?
Dove, R. Breathing, the Endless News, The.
Ekelof. Moon, The.
Elliott, E. My Only Friends.
Emerson, R. Thine Eyes Still Shined.
Engvick, W. Who Can I Turn To?
Evance, S. To Melancholy.
Fan Chung-yen. Tune: "Walk on the Imperial Street".
Field. Life Plastic.
Field, R. Skyscrapers.
Fields, D. Blue Again.
Filkova, Fedya. Vulnerability.
Forman, R. Someone.
Fox, Skip. Another.
Freeman, J. Hounds, The.
Frost, R. Acquainted with the Night.
  Bereft.
  Desert Places.
  Hill Wife, The.
  Impulse, The.
  Most of It, The.
  Oft-Repeated Dream, The.
García Lorca. Amparo.
  Ballad of One Doomed to Die.
Garland, H. Plowing: A Memory.
George, D. It's Kind of Lonesome Out Tonight.
Gershwin, I. But Not for Me.
Gibbons, R. We Say.
Gizzi. Lonely Tylenol.
Goeckel, L. Short Hand.
Goodman, P. It was good when you were here.
Gorostiza, J. Who Will Buy Me an Orange?
Green, A. Lonely Town.
Green, G. Portuguese in Mergui, The.
Greenwell, D. Scherzo, A.
Gregory, A. Donal[l] Oge [or Og]: Grief of a Girl's Heart.
Hammerstein. Why Was I Born?
Hantoosh, G. Take Me, Loneliness.
Hardy, T. Bereft.
  Nobody Comes.
Harms. After Yes.
  My Own Little Piece of Hollywood.
Hart, L. Dancing on the Ceiling.
  It Never Entered My Mind.
  Nobody's Heart.
  Ship Without a Sail, A.
Hartnett. Death of an Irishwoman.
Heine, H. Pine Is Standing Lonely, A.
Hemans. Arabella Stuart.
  Stranger in Louisiana, The.
Hong Yunsuk. My Sea Has One Island.
Hope, M. INRI.

Horovitz, F. Women.
Hovey. At Sea.
Hsi-chün. Lost Horizon.
Hsieh Ling-yün. All Around My New House at Stone Gate.
Climbing Stone Drum Mountain.
I Follow the Jinzhu Torrent.
On Climbing Stone Drum Mountain, Near Shangshu.
What I Saw When I Had Crossed the Lake.
Hughes, L. Bound No'th Blues.
Hope ("Sometimes when I'm lonely.").
Miss Blues'es Child.
Hwang Chini. Ah, what have I done?
Hynes, M. Self-Sufficient Blues.
Ilagha, N. Adam's Cry.
Im Che. In a mound where the grass grows long.
Issa. Flowering plum, A.
For your fleas too.
Issahakian. For you fleas too.
Izumi. Lying here alone.
On nights when hail / falls noisily.
Jackson, L. Take Hands.
Jacobsen, R. Express Train.
Jarrell, R. Game at Salzburg, A.
Island, The.
Jennings, K. Couples.
Jewett, S. Widows' House, The.
Jones, R. White Towels.
Jordan, N. When A Woman Gets Blue.
Juan Chi. My steps lead me to a junction of three roads.
Justice, D. Poem To Be Read at 3 a.m.
Kafka. In the Evening's Gentle Sunshine.
Kahn, G. Love Me or Leave Me.
Kamienska. Annunciation.
Kantaris. Not-loving.
Kaputikyan, S. In the Sevan Mountains.
Kerouac. Mexican Loneliness.
Khlebnikov, V. I Went Out.
Lonely Masquerader.
Kim Chôngnan. Rain: "From which heaven did you return."
Women's Words—Yellow-Green Leaves and Low Sun.
Kim Koengp'il. My Way.
Kim Sowôl. Road Away, The.
Road, The.
Kim Suyông. Lonely Journey, A.
Kim Yŏngnang. Someone Who Knows My Heart.
Klink, J. Sea by Dusk.
Knight, E. Poem to Galway Kinnell, A.
Ko Chônghûi. Letter Written With the Left Hand, A.
People of the Earth 8.
Koehler, T. Stormy Weather (Keeps Rainin' All the Time).
When the Sun Comes Out.
Komunyakaa, Y. Heart's Graveyard Shift, The.
Never Land.
When Loneliness Is a Man.
Kool, M. Different.
Kyerang. Under a shower of pear blossoms.
Lamb, C. Was it Some Sweet Device of Faery Land.
Landesman. Spring Can Really Hang You Up the Most.
Larbaud. Gift of Oneself, The.
Lasker-Schüler. O God.
Li Ch'ing-chao. Butterflies Love Flowers.
Fading Plum Blossoms.
Li Ho. Life at the Capital.
Song: Green Water, Singing Girl.
Li Po. Crows at Dusk.
Lonely Wife, The.
Solitary Carouse on a Day in Spring, A.
Tune: "Beautiful Barbarians".
Verses: "Clean is the autumn wind."
Li Shang-yin. Alone by the Autumn River.
Spring Rain.
Li Yu [or Li Hou-Chu]. To the Tune: Beautiful Lady Yu.
Lihn. Six Poems of Loneliness.
Linden, M. Lonely World.

Lleshanaku, L. Still Life: "Here in a summer full of dust."
Loesser. I Don't Want to Walk Without You.
Spring Will Be a Little Late This Year.
Lowell, A. Letter, The.
Madonna of the Evening Flowers.
Lowry, M. Delirium in Vera Cruz.
Lu Chi. She Thinks of Her Beloved.
Machado Ruiz. Summer's Night, A.
There, in the High Part.
MacNeice. Autobiography.
Nostalgia.
MacSweeney. Pearl Alone.
Madgett. Plea for My Heart's Sake.
Mahon. Achill.
Mamalatan. What She Said.
Martelli, J. Mal'Occhio.
Masters, E. Lost Orchard, The.
Matthews, W. Cheap Seats, the Cincinnati Gardens, Professional Basketball, 1959.
Good Company.
Maude. Entanglement.
McElroy, C. In My Mother's Room.
McIlroy, L. Good-Bye, Valentine.
McMichael. Cat came / sleepily from a thick shrub and stopped and shook its head, A.
Mead, J. Concerning That Prayer I Cannot Make.
Merwin. Departure's Girl-Friend.
Second Psalm: The Signals.
Miller, J. American Odalisque.
Mistral, G. Ballad: "He went by with another."
Mitchell, E. Alice Uglier.
Miyoshi Toyoichiro. Shadow 1.
Monro, H. Solitude.
Montague, J. Locket, The.
Wild Dog Rose, The.
Morgan, R. Working in the Rain.
Nasir. Loneliness.
Natsume Soseki. It comes to my shoulder.
Neruda. Body of a Woman.
Forgive me if my eyes see.
Norworth. Shine On, Harvest Moon.
Nye, N. Rider, The.
Oliver, M. Lilies.
Ouwens. Some Tears.
Paek Sŏk. On the White Wall.
Pak Chaesam. In sunlight suffused.
Pak Inhwan. Rocking Horse and the Lady, The.
Pak Tujin. Sun.
Tobong Mountain.
Pao Hsien. Written on the Wall at Master Wei Feng's.
Parker, D. Bric-à-Brac.
Patchen. Lonesome Boy Blues.
Pearlman. Endings.
Pei Di. Deer Enclosure, The.
Petri. By an Unknown Poet from Eastern Europe, 1955.
Petronius Arbiter. Man in the Middle of the Street.
Phillips, R. Instrument of Choice.
Pilinszky, J. Fable: "Once upon a time / there was a lonely wolf."
Pinchas-Cohen. Her, Me, and Yochanan.
Po Chü-i. Cold Night.
Invitation to Hsiao Ch'u-shih.
Winter Night ("Those I love scattered away, poor.").
Poe. Alone.
Pollarolo, G. They All Think.
Porter, C. Down in the Depths.
Pound, E. Δωρια.
Prévert. Breakfast.
Prince, F. T. False Bay.
Quevedo y Villegas. Birds Are in the Air at Ease.
Raab, L. Being a Monster.
Randall, Deborah. Nightwatchman.
Randall, Dudley. Old Witherington.
Randall, M. Nushu.
Redding, E. End of a Love Affair, The.
Revell, D. Last.
Rexroth, K. Every morning, I.
Half in a dream.
Night without end. Loneliness.

Once I shone afar like a.
Rich, A. On this earth, in this life, as I read your story, you're lonely.
Rain on the West Side Highway.
Soledad. = f. Solitude, loneliness, homesickness; lonely retreat.
Robin, L. No Love, No Nothin'.
Robinson, E. Mr Flood's Party.
Robson, J. Blues for the Lonely*.
Rodgers, C. Not About Poems.
Roland Holst. Beggar Love.
Rose, B. Would You Like to Take a Walk?
Rossetti, C. At Home.
Chilly Night, A.
Sappho.
Rumsey, Tessa. More Important Than the Design of Cities Will Be the Design of Their Decay.
Russell, B. Don't Get Around Much Anymore.
Ryan, G. Elegy for 6 So Far.
Sabines. Entresol.
Lovers, The.
Sadi [or Saadi or Sa'di]. Last night without sight of you my brain was ablaze.
Sadoff. February: Pemaquid Point.
Salaam. 5 Minutes, Mr. Salaam.
Salinas, L. Sometimes Mysteriously.
Sansom, A. Prince.
Santly, L. I'm Nobody's Baby.
Sappho. Moon and the Pleiades have set, The.
Moon Has Set, The.
Moon has set, The.
Pleiades disappear, The.
Sarton, M. Fruit of Loneliness.
Seshadri. Lifeline.
Shakespeare, W. Sonnet 29: "When, in disgrace with fortune and men's eyes."
Shelley, P. Sonnet: Political Greatness.
Shepherd, R. Who Owns the Night and Lease Stars.
Smith, C. Religious Art.
Solie, Karen. Meeting Walter Benjamin.
Soto. After Tonight.
Stafford, W. Widow.
Stanley, G. Tell the Truth.
Stanton, M. Voice for the Sirens, A.
Stickney, T. Mnemosyne.
Storni. Lost Caress, The.
Strayhorn, B. Lonely Coed, A.
Lush Life.
Stroud, J. Comice.
Su Tung-p'o. Tune: "Always Having Fun".
Tune: "River Town".
Verses: "I am old, sick and lonely."
Sung Fang-hu. Traveler's Life, A.
Swan, E. When Your Lover Has Gone.
Swirszczynska [or Swir]. Very Sad Conversation at Night, A.
Sy, T. Stone Walls.
Symonenko, V. Lonely.
Tanikawa, S. Twenty Billion Light Years of Loneliness.
Taylor, B. On the Headland.
Tayson, R. Phone Sex.
Teasdale. Spring Night.
Tennyson, A. Mariana.
Tobin, D. Deep Shit.
Ts'ao Chih. Woe Indeed!
Tu Fu [or Du Fu]. Facing the Snow ("Northern snows invade the city.").
I Stand Alone.
Loneliness.
Lovely Lady.
Night Thoughts While Traveling.
Seven Songs Written while Living at T'ung-ku in 759.
Wasteland—Gazing Far Away.
Turk, R. Are You Lonesome Tonight?
Tzu Yeh. All Night.
Busy in the Spring.
Unknown. Ari-rang Ari-rang A-ra-ri-yo.
Faint moon in a heavy frost, The.
Grass by the River-Bank, The.
Green, green riverside grass.
I Know Where I'm Going.
I raise my brush to write a poem to tell my dear

wife.
Long night: unable to sleep.
My loved one is far away.
Night so.
Night Without End.
Song of an Old Maid.
Tatar Songs.
Threading Frost.
Through the front gate.
Tune: Eternal Longing.
Unspent.
Water the Horses at a Breach in the Great Wall.
Watering Horses at a Long Wall Hole.
Where is my husband now?
Why could you not come? For what reason.
Valente, J.   Evening Before, The.
Valentine, S.   How to Thank God for Your Loneliness.
Vallejo.   Agape.
Dead Idyll.
Van de Woestijne.   Oars Heavy with Seaweed, The.
Van Duyn.   Open Letter from a Constant Reader.
Vando.   In the Dark Backward.
Vietnamese Oral Tradition.   From *So* Mountain.
Wang Fan-chih.   Drinking Alone.
Wang Po-ch'eng.   Song of Parting.
Wang Shih-chieng.   After Snow, Longing for Elder Brother Hsi-ch'iao.
Wang Wei.   Deer Enclosure, The.
Return to Wang River.
Webster, A.   Circe.
Webster, P.   Black Coffee.
Wei Ying-wu.   Autumn Night: A Letter Sent to Ch'iu.
Weigl.   On the Anniversary of Her Grace.
Weil, J.   Ben Hur.
Wen T'ing-yün.   Embers of Incense.
She Sighs on Her Jade Lute.
Wheelock, C.   Divorcee.
Whitman, W.   As If a Phantom Caress'd Me.
I Saw in Louisiana a Live-Oak Growing.
Live Oak, with Moss.
This Moment Yearning and Thoughtful.
When I Peruse the Conquer'd Fame.
Wilbur, R.   Mayflies.
Williamson, G.   Italics, Mine.
Wither.   Sonnet: "I that erstwhile the world's sweet air did draw."
Sonnet: "I wandered out a while agone."
Wong, T.   Loneliness.
Wordsworth, W.   I Wandered Lonely as a Cloud.
Wright, F.   Loneliness.
Wright, James.   Northern Pike.
Speak.
Wright, Jay.   Lake in Central Park, The.
Wright, Judith.   Half-Caste Girl.
Wunderlich, M.   East Seventh Street.
Yakamochi.   [These] meetings in dreams.
Yellen, J.   Glad Rag Doll.
Yi Saek.   Rough clouds gather around the valley.
Yi Yuksa.   Twilight.
Young, K.   Soundtrack.
Yu Xuanji.   Vanishing Spring Moves to Regret.
Yun Tongju.   His Last Words.
Poem That Came Easily, A.
Zapruder, M.   School Street.
Zhang Hua.   Emotion.
See also Isolation; Absence; Separation
Long Island, New York
Bell, M.   Eastern Long Island.
Ferlinghetti, L.   Poem for Old Walt.
Lazarus, E.   Long Island Sound.
Moss, H.   Long Island Night, The.
Sahl.   Charter Flight into the Past, A.
Schuyler, J.   Can I Tempt You to a Pond Walk?
Swenson, M.   Written While Riding the Long Island Rail Road.
Wheelock, J.   Afternoon: Amagansett Beach.
Whitman, W.   As I Ebb'd with the Ocean of Life.
Wodehouse.   Bungalow in Quogue.
Longfellow, Henry Wadsworth
Adams, F.   If.

Betjeman.   Longfellow's Visit to Venice.
Hightower, S.   Tontine.
Lowell, J.   Poe and Longfellow.
Ray, H.   Longfellow.
Longing
Abu-l-Hasan Ibn Al-Qabturnuh.   In Battle.
Adamson, H.   Where Are You?
Addison, J.   Rosamond's Song.
Adler, L.   Smike.
Afrika, T.   To God.
Aist [or Eist], Dietmar von.   Yonder on the linden tree there sang a merry little bird.
Akenside.   Complaint, The.
Albrecht, A.   Anacapa.
Aled, Sion.   Tracks of Longing.
Alford, H.   You and I.
Alvarez, J.   On a Hill Above Your House.
Amir, D.   I Have Longings for My Dead.
Anacreon.   Lad, glancing like a virgin.
Anawrok.   Each Time.
Anderson, M.   It Never Was You.
Archilochus.   If only I might touch Neobule's hand.
Argentarius.   I can't bear to watch your hips.
Arnold, M.   Longing.
Ashbery, J.   Business Personals.
Song: "Song tells us of our old way of living, The."
Walkways, The.
Ato Tobira.   Only one fleeting.
Aygi, G.   Dream: Queue for Paraffin.
Baca.   Book 3: La Guerra; Poem Thirteen.
Bailey, A.   Rivière du Loup.
Banchs, E.   Mumbling.
Barnes, K.   Night Light.
Barnes, W.   Wind at the Door, The.
Barnfield [or Barnefield].   Sweet Corrall lips, where Nature's treasure lies.
Barot, R.   Three Amoretti.
Barry, C.   Finding.
Basho.   Give your longing to wound.
Smell of autumn / Heart longs.
Bathurst, B.   To Marthe.
Bayly.   Something to Love.
Beatrice [or Beatritz or Beatriz], Countess de Die [or Dia].   Lover's Prize, A.
Beck, Art.   Castro Street.
Bécquer, G.   I Am Ardent, I Am Brunette.
Behn, A.   Song. Love Arm'd [or Armed].
Verses Design'd by Mrs. A. Behn to be Sent to a Fair Lady.
Behrle.   White Album.
Bektaş, Cengiz.   Now: "I long for my voice that found you."
Berkeley, S.   Parting, The.
Berlin.   Remember.
Supper Time.
What'll I Do?
Bernard [or Bernart] de Ventadour [or Ventadorn].   Joy! a heart so overflowing.
When—presto—turf and trees are green.
Berrigan, T.   To gentle, pleasant strains.
Bibbins, M.   Slutty.
Blind.   Haunted Streets.
Bloem, J. C.   Honeysuckle.
Sunday.
Boker.   Sonnet 280: "Ah, lute, how well I know each tone of thee."
Boland, E.   In Her Own Image.
Bowering, G.   If I did complain, who among my friends.
Bowles, W.   Languid, and sad, and slow.
Brathwaite, E.   Naima.
Trane.
Brent, E.   Angel Eyes.
Brontë, E.   F. de Samara to A. G. A.
Shall Earth no more inspire thee.
Brooks, G.   To Be in Love.
Brooks, S.   Some of These Days.
Broumas, O.   Song / for Sanna.
Brown, L.   That Old Feeling.
Bryan, M.   To———: "O thou unknown disturber of my rest."
Burke, S.   Black Coffee.
Burns, R.   Mary Morison.
My Heart's in the Highlands.

Bynner.   Sigh, A.
Byron, G.   To Thyrza.
Cahn, S.   Guess I'll Hang My Tears Out to Dry.
Calpurnius Siculus.   Eclogue 3.
Campo.   My Voice.
Carew, T.   Divine Mistress, A.
To My Mistress[e] in My Absence.
Carmichael, H.   I Get Along Without You Very Well.
Carpenter, E.   To a Stranger.
Carter, J.   Adagio at Twilight.
Castillo, S.   At the Havana Hilton.
Catullus.   Lesbia's sparrow!
Cavafy.   In Despair.
Ceccoli.   Oh, and yet I see that I will return to you anyway, and throw myself at your feet and cry a lot over my sins, until my crime will be pardoned.
Sir, I have remained so overcome, that I can no longer suffer your attacks.
Celan.   Shot Forth.
Centamputan.   What She Said.
Cervantes.   A un Desconocido.
Isla Mujeres.
Chalfi, R.   Night Hair.
Chambers, G.   If Only for One Night.
Chen Zi'ang.   Just now in wild, free mood I yearn.
Chin, J.   Bergamot.
Chivers.   Lily Adair.
Cho Wen-chun.   Lament: "Hills are white with snow, The."
Chŏng Ch'ŏl.   Continued Song of Longing.
Juice of bitter herbs has, The.
Song of Longing.
Clare, J.   I Am.
Clarke, C.   Vicki and Daphne.
Clifton, L.   Climbing.
Coleridge, H.   Night.
Coleridge, M.   Wasted.
Coleridge, S.   Love: "All thoughts, all passions, all delights."
Collin, J.   Layman's Lament, The.
Cometas.   Phyllis, loving Demophoon.
Cooke, R.   Captive.
Cookshaw, M.   In the Spring of No Letters.
Coolbrith.   Longing.
Cooley, N.   Good Friday, Alice Liddell.
Cortes, F.   Dolce Far Niente.
Cory, W.   Desiderato.
Craik.   Douglas, Douglas, Tender and True.
Creamer, H.   If I Could Be with You.
Creeley.   Away.
In a Boat Shed.
Messengers, The.
Cruz, C.   Ariadne, waiting.
Cruz, S.   Spiritual Canticle, The.
Csoori.   For the Seventh Day.
Cummings, E. E.   Always before your voice my soul.
Curbelo.   Drinking Song.
Daniel, A.   Firm desire which enters, The.
Dante Alighieri.   Sestina: Of the Lady Pietra degli Scrovigni.
Darío, R.   I Seek a Form.
Nocturne.
DeLange, E.   Darn That Dream.
Solitude.
DeNiord, C.   There Is an Error at the Heart of Desire.
Dickinson, E.   I many times thought Peace had come.
Success is counted sweetest.
Donovan, K.   Yearn On.
Dooley, M.   Mansize.
Drummond, W.   Sonnet: "How many times night's silent queene her face."
Dunbar, P.   Longing.
Dylan.   Boots of Spanish Leather.
Eich.   Salt.
Elburg.   Wanting To.
Eliot, T. S.   Love Song of J. Alfred Prufrock, The.
Elizabeth I.   On Monsieur's Departure.
Emerson, R.   To Rhea.
Eyton, F.   Body and Soul.

Faber, F. Dream of Blue Eyes, A.
Faiz. Before You Came.
Field. Unbosoming.
Flynn, N. Emptying Town.
Forché. Morning Baking, The.
Foster, S. Jeanie with the Light Brown Hair.
Fulton, A. Little Heart to Heart with the Horizon, A.
Gallagher, T. Coming Home.
García Lorca. Gacela of Unforeseen Love.
Little Ballad of the Three Rivers.
Sleepwalkers' Ballad.
Sleepwalking Ballad, The.
Garcilaso de la Vega. Nemoroso.
Oh, to my sobs, Galatea, you are harder than a stone.
Gardinier. To Peace.
George, K. Six Minutes Writing.
Georgiev, Marin. Native Soil.
Georgiou, E. Space Between, The.
Gershon. Uphold Me.
Gershwin, I. Man That Got Away, The.
Someone to Watch over Me.
Ghalib, M. Freely in Hidden Fire.
Ghazal 34.
Ginsberg, A. Further Proposal, A.
Transcription of Organ Music.
Glück, L. Penelope's Song.
Glück, R. Odd to close my eyes during the day and open them at night.
This image is alive with my longing for you.
Goethe. Diary, The.
Holy Longing, The.
Hunter's Song at Nightfall, The.
Sonnet: "To work away in art's traditional measure."
Goodman, P. It was good when you were here.
Gordon, M. There's a Lull in My Life.
Gould, J. Earthquake Weather.
Greenberg, U. Song to Heaven.
Guillén, J. River.
Guinicelli. Canzone: Of the Gentle Heart.
Gundy, J. Old Water.
Rain.
Gunn, T. Autobiography.
Gurney, I. First March.
Haavikko. Look, life has been constructed this way to make sure.
Hahn, O. No Place Is Here or There.
Hammerstein. Lover, Come Back to Me!
Why Was I Born?
Han Yong'un [or Yongwun]. Artist, The.
Ferryboat and the Traveler.
Inverse Proportion.
Harbach, O. Smoke Gets in Your Eyes.
Harburg. It's Only a Paper Moon.
Hardy, T. Voice, The.
Hart, L. He Was Too Good to Me.
It Never Entered My Mind.
Hartman, J. [She Unties the Straps of Her Corselette Fire].
Harwood, L. Rain Journal: London: June '65.
Hass, R. Pact, A.
Hausen, F. Help! How Minne has deserted me.
Hayden, R. Ballad of Sue Ellen Westerfield, The.
Herbert, G. Longing.
Herman, J. If He Walked into My Life.
Herrera y Reissig. Heraldic Decoration.
Hewett, D. In Moncur Street.
Heyman, E. Body and Soul.
I Cover the Waterfront.
Hicok. Absence: "There are men and women huddled in rooms tonight."
Hill, M. Abomination.
Hilliard, B. In the Wee Small Hours of the Morning.
Hirshfield, J. Of Gravity and Angels.
Hogan, L. Crossings.
Hope, M. INRI.
Horace. Late Night Ode.
Hostetler, A. Priestess of Love.
Housman. Because I liked you better.
Far in a western brookland.
He would not stay for me; and who can wonder?

When the lad for longing sighs.
Hovanessian, D. Exiles.
Howells, W. Forlorn.
Hsieh T'iao. Complaint Near the Jade Stairs.
Complaint of the Jade Staircase.
I Sit in My Lofty Study.
Hsü Kan. Wife's Thoughts, The.
Hsü Tsai-ssu. On Love.
Hsueh Chao-yun. To the Tune: In the Hills.
Huang T'ing-chien. Tune: "A Thousand Autumns".
Hughes, H. At the Teahouse, 7 am.
Hughes, L. Deferred.
Miss Blues'es Child.
Subway Face.
Summer Night.
Hwang Chini. I will break the back.
I Will Cut Out the Middle Watch.
Hwang Tonggyu. Happy Letter, A.
Ibn Quzman, A. To a Beauty, White, Pure, and Constant.
Im Che. In a mound where the grass grows long.
Imr el [or ul] Kais. Ode of Imr El-Qais, The.
Ingelow. Divided.
Iosifova, Ekaterina. Cloud, The: "It's darker and cooler."
Iskrenko. How To Live Through This Night (A Dream).
Issa. I wish she were here.
Izumi. Lying down alone.
Tangled Hair.
Jaewol Kyunghun. Longing for a Man Faraway.
Jarnot, L. Ye White Antarctic Birds.
Jenkins, A. Barcelona.
Jiménez, J. Fleeting Return.
Johnson, J. Phyllis.
Johnston, C. I know thee not, bright creature, ne'er shall know.
Jones, R. Blasphemy, A.
Jong, E. Parable of the Four-Poster.
Joseph, A. Pure Pop.
Joseph, J. Inland sea, The.
Juana Inés de la Cruz. Describes Rationally the Irrational Effects of Love.
Verses Expressing the Feelings of a Lover.
Kahn, G. I'll See You in My Dreams.
I'm Through with Love.
Toot, Toot, Tootsie! (Good-bye).
Kalidasa. Even the man who is happy.
Kallatanar. What She Said.
Kasa. As one hears the cry.
Kasdorf. Riding Bike with No Hands.
Kaufman, S. Notes to my Daughters.
Keats. Day Is Gone and All Its Sweets Are Gone, The.
I Cry Your Mercy, Pity, Love—Ay, Love!
Kemble. Cover me with your everlasting arms.
Kim Sangyong. Love is a deceit.
Kinnell. Sheffield Ghazal 4: Driving West.
Klyuyev [or Kliuev or Klyuev]. Can I Tell You My Love with a Portrait.
Ko Chônghûi. Letter Written With the Left Hand, A.
Koehler, T. Stormy Weather (Keeps Rainin' All the Time).
Tess's Torch Song (I Had a Man).
Kumin, M. Bangkok Gang, The.
Seeing the Bones.
Kuzmin. People see gardens and houses.
When it was I first encountered you.
Kynaston. To Cynthia.
Landor, W. Rose Aylmer.
Lane, P. Garden Temple, The.
Lang, A. Romance.
Lasker-Schüler. Only for You.
Lassell. Kissing Ramén.
Lawrence, J. Linda.
Leonard, W. Indian Summer.
Lerner, A. Come Back to Me.
Lewis, A. Dawn on the East Coast.
In Hospital: Poona (1).
Song (On Seeing Dead Bodies Floating Off the Cape).
Li Chih-yi. Tune: "The Diviner".
Li Ch'ing-chao. Plum Blossoms.

To the Tune: Drunk in Flower Shadows.
To the Tune: Lips Painted Red.
Li Ho. Lament for a Courtesan.
Li Po. Autumn Lines.
Blue Water.
Longing for Someone.
O-mei Mountain Moon.
River Merchant's Wife, The; A Letter.
Song of Ch'ang-kan.
To Tu Fu from Shantung.
Li Shang-yin. Bite back passion. Spring now sets.
Li Tung-yang. On a Painting of Fish Being Caught, A Song.
Liang Te-sheng. Sent to My Fourth Son, Shao-Wu (to the Tune "Southern Countryside").
Lilburn, Tim. How To Be Here?
Lilley. You Have to Strike Back.
Liu, T. Ariel Singing.
Liu Tsung-yüan. From the City-Tower of Liuzhou To My Four Fellow-Officials at Zhang, Ding, Feng, and Lian Districts.
Liu Yung. Song: "It's the wine, this ache, this longing."
Song to the Tune "Ting Feng Po".
Tune: "Eight Beats of a Kan-chou Song".
Lo Pin-Wang. Mooring by Jiangzhen in the Evening.
On the Cicada: In Prison.
Lodge, T. Shepherd's Sorrow, Being Disdained in Love, The.
Loesser. I Don't Want to Walk Without You.
Sand in My Shoes.
Loncar, M. Picasso Shag.
Lope de Vega. Sonnet 188.
Sonnet 61.
Splendidly-shining darkness.
Lorde. Burning the Water Hyacinth.
Louise, E. Footprints.
Lowell, A. Lover, A.
Spring Longing.
Vernal Equinox.
Vicarious.
Lu Yu. Tune: "Hairpin Phoenix".
MacDiarmid, H. Wheesht, Wheesht.
Yet Ha'e I Silence Left.
MacKay, I. Meeting, The.
Mackenzie, K. Shall Then Another.
MacNeacail. Tonight You Being From Me.
Madan. Abelard to Eloisa.
Maguire, S. Divorce Referendum, The.
Mandela. I Waited for You Last Night.
Mansour, A. There Is Music Going Down the Stairs.
Martí. I Dream Awake.
Masters, E. Emily Sparks.
Reuben Pantier.
Matthews, W. Mood Indigo.
Maurus. To Grimold, Abbot of St. Gall.
May, D. Thoughts from a Bar Stool.
Mayakovsky [or Maiakovskii]. Cloud in Trousers, A.
McGrath, T. Epitaph: "Again, traveller, you have come a long way led by that star."
Medrano, F. Sonnet 41.
Meleager. Epigram: "At 12 o'clock in the afternoon."
Melville, H. John Marr.
Mercer, J. I Thought About You.
My Shining Hour.
Meredith, G. Love in the Valley.
Merwin. Vixen.
Mesmer, S. Lonely Tylenol.
Michelangelo Buonarroti. I see in your beautiful face, my lord.
Soul tries a thousand remedies in vain, The.
Violent burning for prodigious beauty, A.
Mills, I. Solitude.
Mirabai [or Mira Bai]. All I Was Doing Was Breathing.
Where Did You Go?
Mistral, G. Ballad: "He was strolling with another woman."
Mitchell, S. Of Earthly Love.
Montale. Black and white, The.
Here is the sign: it trembles.

I had almost lost.
Moraes, D.   Snow on a Mountain.
Mörike [or Möricke].   Beauty Rohtraut.
Murillo.   Angel in the Deluge.
Myŏngok.   They say dream visits.
Nairne.   Will Ye No Come Back Again?
Neruda.   Leaning into the Afternoons.
Poem 20.
Ni Dhomhnaill.   Marvellous Grass.
"Novalis.".   Longing for Death.
Nuccoli.   Since I abandoned and tied my soul to
   your sweet appearance and manners oh Sir,
   guide and light of my life, will I ever see you
   before I die?
   You have the light of my life, in your clear and
   pleasing face, and don't see me.
Nŭngun.   Waiting for My Love.
Nyunai, J.   Hour of Life, An.
Ojibwa Oral Tradition.   Loon upon the Lake,
   The.
Olds, S.   Monarchs.
Olson, C.   As the Dead Prey upon Us.
Ono no Komachi.   Although my feet.
   When longing for you.
Otomo no Sakanoé, L.   Though in my heart.
   Till the rough-gem moon.
Oyake.   Hidden in the clouds.
Padel, R.   Tell Me About It.
Paek Sŏk.   Natasha, the White Donkey, and I.
Paiute Oral Tradition.   Like always / like
   forever.
Pak Hyogwan.   If my lovesick dream.
   She came to my dream.
Pak Tujin.   Tobong Mountain.
Papaionnou.   Nights Without Hope (Rebetiko
   Song).
Parish.   Star Dust.
Parker, D.   On Being a Woman.
Paulin.   Lyric Afterwards, A.
Perk.   Iris.
Petrarch.   Loose to the wind her golden tresses
   streamed.
   Love's Fidelity.
   She used to let her golden hair fly free.
   When Simon received the high idea which, for
   my sake, put his.
Pfeiffer, E.   Nathaniel to Ruth.
Phillips, C.   Undressing for Li Po.
Piatt, S.   In Her Prison.
Piercy.   Raisin Pumpernickel.
Pizarnik.   Existing.
Po Chü-i.   Hangzhou.
Jiangnan.
Poe.   To One in Paradise.
Pommy-Vega.   [Ah certainty of love in the
   hand].
   [Here before the sunrise blue and in this
   solitude].
Porter, C.   In the Still of the Night.
   Night and Day.
   What Is This Thing Called Love?
   Where Is the Life That Late I Led?
Pound, E.   Papyrus.
   Speech for Psyche in the Golden Book of
   Apuleius.
Rabinowitz.   Of Joy Illimited: Polyphonic
   Soundings: Shore to Ship.
"Rachel." [or "Rahel."].   At the Window.
Rao, A.   Longing, A.
Razaf, A.   Memories of You.
Rees-Jones.   Service Wash.
Rexroth, K.   Coming.
   Every morning, I.
   Fires / Burn in my heart.
   I am sad this morning.
   I pass the day tense, day-.
   I waited all night.
   I wish I could be.
   If I thought I could get away.
   It is the time when.
   Two flowers in a letter.
   Void Only.
Rich, A.   Loser, The.
   Paula Becker to Clara Westhoff.
   Since we're not young, weeks have to do time.
Riddell, E.   Letter, The.

Robin, L.   No Love, No Nothin'.
Robinson, E.   Luke Havergal.
Robinson, M.   Laments the Volatility of Phaon.
   Previous to her Interview with Phaon.
Rohrer, M.   Gliding Toward the Lamps.
Rolfe, E.   First Love.
Rollings.   Light Years and the Love Lost in the
   Oleanders.
Rome, H.   Wish You Were Here.
Romo-Carmona, M.   Daylight.
Roripaugh, L.   Peony Lover.
Rose, B.   It's Only a Paper Moon.
Rose, J.   Marisel.
Ross, W.   Another Song.
Rossetti, C.   Youth gone, and beauty gone if
   ever there.
Rossetti, D.   Blessed Damozel, The.
4: Lovesight.
97: A Superscription.
50: Willowwood ("And now Love sang: but his
   was such a song").
49: Willowwood ("I sat with Love upon a
   woodside well").
51: Willowwood ("O ye, all ye that walk in
   Willowwood").
52: Willowwood ("So sang he: and as meeting
   rose and rose").
Rumi.   Captain Who Walks on His Deck, The.
   Human shape is a ghost, The.
   Strange Business.
   That moon which the sky never saw.
Russell, H.   Don't Get Around Much Anymore.
Sabines.   Entresol.
St. John, D.   Opal Trees, The.
Salinas, P.   On Dry Land.
Sánchez Peláez.   Portrait of the Beautiful
   Unknown Woman.
Sappho.   My Atthis, although our dear
   Anaktoria.
   On the throne of many hues, Immortal
   Aphrodite.
   Sweet mother, I cannot weave.
Sastri, D.   Palanquin, The.
Scamell, B.   Diaries.
Scève, M.   Dizains, Les.
Segal, J.   I Keep Going Back to Joe's.
   Wind in the Willow.
Seibles, T.   4AM.
Shakespeare, W.   All swoln with chasing, down
   Adonis sits.
Sonnet 20: "Woman's face with nature's own[e]
   hand painted, A."
Sonnet 27: "Weary with toil, I haste me to my
   bed."
Sonnet 57: "Being your slave, what should I
   do[e] but tend."
Sonnet 61: "Is it thy will thy image should keep
   open."
Shaughnessy, B.   Rise.
Shen Yüeh.   Spring: "Willows tangle like silk
   threads."
Sheppard, R.   Empty Diary 1905.
Shi Chong.   Longing to Return: A Lament.
Shokushi.   O cord of life!
Sidney.   Sonnet 89: "Now that of absence the
   most irksome night."
Smith, C.   Stanzas: "Ah! think'st thou, Laura,
   then, that wealth."
Smith, P.   Meeting Up with the Picaro.
Snyder, G.   Four Poems for Robin.
Sŏ Chŏngju.   Blue Days.
Sŏ Kyŏngdŏk.   My mind is foolish.
Sour, R.   Body and Soul.
Spenser, E.   By vew of her he ginneth to revive.
Stanton, M.   Sorrow and Rapture.
   Voice for the Sirens, A.
Steinberg, D.   Purple is the Color of Longing.
Stevens, W.   Bouquet of Belle Scavoir.
Stevenson, R.   To Mrs. Will H. Low.
Stickney, T.   As a sad man, when evenings
   grayer grow.
Strand.   It is a dreadful cry that rises up.
   Late Hour, The.
Surrey.   Seafarer, The.
Tagore.   Song That I Came to Sing, The.
Teasdale.   At Night.

Flight, The.
Tennyson, A.   Thy spirit ere our fatal loss.
Thaxter.   Alone.
Thicknesse.   Siena.
Thomas, L.   Cameo in Sudden Light.
Tibullus.   Cross the Aegean Without Me, Then,
   Messalla.
Tkachenko.   Dynamo Stadium, 1980.
   Engraving, An.
Trakl.   Elis.
Troup, B.   Baby, Baby All the Time.
Tso Ssu.   Summoning the Recluse.
Tuckerman, F.   Series 2, Sonnet 21.
Tŭgo [or Tŭgogok].   Ode to Knight Chukchi.
Turell, J.   You Beauteous Dames.
Tzu Yeh.   Busy in the Spring.
   End to Spring, An ("Your leaving brought an
   end to spring.").
   Illusions.
   So soon. Today, love, we.
   Song: "Longing, I watch out the open window."
Ujević, T.   Green branch with a sadness of
   yellow fruit.
Ulacia, M.   Tenochtitlán Blues.
Ullman.   Memo.
U'ng Binh.   At the Exiled King's River Pavilion.
Unknown.   Am I to go on.
   As the thread of my breath.
   Body's Speech, The.
   Go, litel bille, and do me recomaunde.
   God, let me be with him if only for a moment.
   Hiraeth.
   I have lived anxious and hurt.
   I loathe them, I loathe them.
   If I were but a bird.
   If it is but sleep.
   In the Shadows of the Wu-t'ung Tree.
   Jinny.
   Lament for Prince Chagoo.
   Lass A-Laundering.
   Lone Buck.
   Love Me Little, Love Me Long.
   Love, Why Don't You Come.
   Mulberry up the Lane.
   Romance of Love.
   Sad Song.
   Sigh, O thin sigh, through.
   So it is because.
   So soon. Today, love, we.
   Song of P'yŏngyang.
   Song of P'yŏngyang without Refrain.
   Tune: Eternal Longing.
   Watering Horses at a Long Wall Hole.
   Western Wind.
   When on a cold day with deep snow.
   Why could you not come? For what reason.
   Winter.
   Wulf and Eadwacer: A Woman's Lament.
   You intend, it seems.
   You were still waving, beloved.
   Zhong-feng: Wild and Windy.
Unknown, fr. Terezin Concentration Camp.
   Dusk.
   Homesick.
Vallejo.   Dead Idyll.
   In that corner where we slept together.
Van Ostaijen.   Landscape.
Vietnamese Oral Tradition.   Looking Out in All
   Directions.
   Pole at the Village Pagoda, The.
Villon.   Ballade to End With, A.
Virgil [or Vergil].   Eclogue 2: The Lament of
   Corydon for His Faithless Alexis.
   Priests, prophets, helpless. She's beside herself.
Vogel, D.   Silently you stand before me.
Volkman.   Shrewd star, who crudes our naming:
   you should be flame.
   We did things more dulcet, more marionette.
Wakoski.   Imagining Point Dume.
   Reading *Bonjour, Tristesse* at the Florence
   Crittenden Home for Unwed Mothers.
Walton, E.   In Recompense.
Wang Ji.   View of the Wilds.
Wang Kuo-wei.   Tune: "Rouged Lips".
Webster, A.   There's one I miss. A little
   questioning maid.

Webster, P.   Black Coffee.
Wei Chuang.   Tune: "Thinking of the Imperial Capital".
White, H.   Sonnet: "Give me a cottage on some Cambrian wild."
Whitman, W.   I Heard You Solemn-Sweet Pipes of the Organ.
O You Whom I Often and Silently Come.
Out of the Cradle Endlessly Rocking.
This is the meal pleasantly set . . . this is the meat and drink for natural hunger.
To a Stranger.
Whitmore, S.   Gamelia.
Wickham.   Divorce.
Wilbur, R.   Ballade for the Duke of Orléans.
Wilde, O.   Wasted Days.
Williams, C. K.   Gas Station, The.
Williams, S.   Sub Umbra Floreo.
Willis, N.   Confessional, The.
Winslow, P.   O god of spring forgive me.
Witt, S.   Michael Masse.
Wordsworth, W.   With Ships the sea was sprinkled far and nigh.
Wright, C.   As Our Bodies Rise, Our Names Turn into Light.
Wright, J.   Love Song in Absence.
Wroth.   Sonnet 3: "Ye[t]t is ther hope: Then Love but[t] play thy part."
Sonnet 37: "Night, welcome art thou to my mind destrest [or distressed]."
Wunderlich, M.   From a Vacant House.
Yao K'uan.   To an Ancient Tune.
Yen Shu.   Tune: "Spring in the Jade House".
Yesenin [or Essenin].   Yesterday's rain.
Yi Myŏnghan.   If the path of my dreams.
Young, J.   I'm Gonna Sit Right Down and Write Myself a Letter.
Yü Hsüan-chi.   Spring Thoughts Sent to Tzu-an.
Yüan Chĕn.   Letter Smuggled in a Fish.
Zaid.   Song of Pursuit.
Zhang Shuai.   Pining.
Zurita, R.   Splendor in the Wind.

Longing for Death

Dorgan, T.   Death Will Come.
Fuertes.   Scrawny Women, The.
Gerov, Alexander.   Eternity: "She's neither ugly nor fearful."
Eye to Eye.
Matter.
Ghalib, M.   My Spiritual State.
González, A.   Least Corpse, The.
Hodgson, R.   Moor, The.
Hopes.   Planxty Irwin.
Howe, M.   Dream, The.
Hudgins.   As a Child in the Temple.
Hughes, L.   Song for a Suicide.
Jiménez, J.   I Shall Run through the Shadow.
Kim Chŏngnan.   Sea at Twenty-Four, The.
Kocot, N.   I Am Like a Desert Owl, an Owl Among the Ruins.
Otero, B.   Cloister of the Shades, The.
Prados, E.   Song: "Bridge of my solitude."
Ristovic.   Essential, The.
Rossetti, D.   66: The Heart of the Night.
Shakespeare, W.   I have liv'd long enough: my way of life.
Skyrm, P.   Book 2: White Rose.
Stevenson, A.   Vertigo.
Stewart, S.   Seasons, The.
Stoyanova, Danila.   They say I don't love life.
Strand.   2002.
Tu Fu [or Du Fu].   Flying from Trouble.
Unknown.   Archangel Open the Door.
Brother, Guide Me Home.
Give Up the World.
Gold Band, The.
Golden Altar, The.
I Want to Die Like-A Lazarus Die.
I Want to Go Home.
I Want To Join the Band.
Jacob's Ladder.
Lord, Remember Me.
My Father, How Long!
Wake Up, Jacob.

Longshoremen

Heaney, S.   Docker.

Loons

Eberhart, R.   Loon Call, A.
Harper, M.   Loon, The.
Ojibwa Oral Tradition.   Loon upon the Lake, The.

Los Angeles, California

Ai.   Riot Act, April 29, 1992.
Alexander, E.   Stravinsky in L.A.
Beatty, P.   Stall Me Out.
Bernes, J.   South Central: Notes toward a Shooting Script.
Brecht, B.   Contemplating Hell.
Brunt, Nick Van.   Los Angeles.
Coleman, W.   Prisoner of Los Angeles (2).
Where I Live.
Gioia.   Los Angeles after the Rain.
Harjo, J.   Path to the Milky Way Leads Through Los Angeles, The.
Harms.   Los Angeles.
Los Angeles, The Angels.
Healy, E.   Artemis in Echo Park.
Two Centuries in One Day.
Hongo.   Yellow Light.
Jarrell, R.   Thinking of the Lost World.
Lassell.   Sunset Stripping: Visiting L.A.
Lem.   Office Hour.
Leong, R.   Aerogramme 1–5: Los Angeles.
Levis.   Oldest Living Thing in L.A., The.
Norte, M.   Angel.
Rivers, C.   Watts.
Rodriguez, L.   Always Running.
Meeting the Animal in Washington Square Park.
We Never Stopped Crossing Borders.
Snyder, G.   Night Song of the Los Angeles Basin.
Uyematsu.   Ten Million Flames of Los Angeles, The.
To All Us Sansei Who Wanted to Be Westside.
Waugh, E.   They told me, Francis Hinsley, they told me you were hung.

See also Hollywood, California

Loss

Abelard.   More than a brother to me, Jonathan.
Agosin.   When she showed me her photograph.
Aiken, C.   Senlin, walking before us in the sunlight.
Aini, L.   In Their House.
Akhmatova, A.   I wrung my hands under my dark veil.
Ali, A.   Ghazal: "Only language of loss left in the world is Arabic, The."
Snow on the Desert.
Alkalay-Gut.   Transportation.
Allen, D.   Lost Love.
Anderson, W.   I'm Naebody Noo.
Andrade, O.   Frontier.
Andrews, N.   Satori.
Anstett.   Worry.
Antin.   Definitions for Mendy.
Antipater of Sidon.   Never again, Orpheus.
Apollinaire.   Fete.
Archilochus.   Some Thracian exults in an excellent shield.
Aridjis.   Epitaph for a Poet.
Arnold, M.   Forsaken Merman, The.
Asekoff, L.   Invisible Hand.
Ashbery, J.   Lost and Found and Lost Again.
Aytoun [or Ayton], R.   Sonnet: On The Loss Of His Mistress.
Bachmann.   Kind of Loss, A.
Barnett, A.   Music of the Spheres.
Baumel.   Snow-Day.
Bayly.   Oh, No! We Never Mention Her.
Bécquer, G.   Black Swallows Will Return, The.
Bedregal.   Pointless Journey.
Beer, P.   Lost Woman, The.
Behlen, Charles.   Widow Zebach.
Bell, M.   To Dorothy.
Benét, S.   Love Came By From the Riversmoke.
Berryman.   Ball Poem, The.
Sonnet 115: "As usual I'm up before the sun."
Bevington, L.   Am I to Lose You?
Bibbins, M.   All but Lost.
Bidart.   If I Could Mourn Like a Mourning Dove.
Biespiel, D.   Tower.

Bishop, E.   One Art.
Blind.   Haunted Streets.
Boland, E.   What We Lost.
Borges.   Possession of Yesterday.
Bracho, C.   Sediment of Lukewarm and Radiant Rain.
Brandi.   In What Disappears.
Browning, E.   Year's Spinning, A.
Browning, R.   Any Wife to Any Husband.
Lost Leader, The.
Lost Mistress, The.
Waring.
Youth and Art.
Bukowski.   Last song, The.
Burns, R.   Ae Fond Kiss.
Man Was Made to Mourn, a Dirge.
Byron, G.   One Struggle More, and I Am Free.
Caddel.   For Tom.
Canning, J.   Indian Gone!, The.
Cardenal.   For me to lose you and for you to lose me, we both lose.
Carew, T.   Deposition from Love, A.
Carson, A.   Well there are many ways of being held prisoner.
Cavafy.   In Despair.
Chang Yen.   Tune: "Pure Serene Music".
Chernoff.   Lost and Found.
Chin, J.   Ex-Boyfriends Named Michael.
Chou Pang-yen.   Peach Blossom Stream.
Christine de Pisan.   Alone in Martyrdom.
Clanchy, K.   We Have Some Urgent Messages.
Claudel, P.   October.
Clifton, L.   To Ms. Ann.
Cofer, J.   Fever.
Coleridge, H.   She Was a Queen.
Coleridge, S.   It is an ancient Mariner.
Song: "Sunny shaft did I behold, A."
Collins, B.   Lines Composed Over Three Thousand Miles From Tintern Abbey.
Cooper, J.   Long, Disconsolate Lines.
Copus, J.   Sea-Polyp, The.
Crane, H.   Sad Indian, The.
Stark Major.
Voyages.
Creeley.   Parade.
To And.
Crunk, T.   Leaving.
Csoori.   My Masters.
Postponed Nightmare.
Somebody Consoles Me with a Poem.
Cullen, C.   Wind Bloweth Where It Listeth, The.
Cummings, E. E.   In heavenly realms of hellas dwelt.
Noster, The.
Curbelo.   Drinking Song.
Darley.   Song: "Sweet in her green dell the flower of beauty slumbers."
To Helene.
De la Mare.   Fare Well.
Deane, S.   Fording the River.
Denney.   Mathematician's Dream, The.
Song: "No use to aim that sextant now."
Dermée.   Poem: "I play tennis with the shells."
Dickey, J.   Leap, The.
Dickey, W.   Shortest Day, The.
Dickinson, E.   Except the Heaven had come so near.
Her sweet Weight on my Heart at Night.
I never lost as much but twice.
Loss of something ever felt I, A.
Donne.   Broken Heart, The.
Computation, The.
Doolittle, H.   Fragment 40: "Keep love and he wings."
Dorcey.   Night.
Dove, R.   "Blown Apart By Loss . . .".
Draycott.   Night Tree, The.
Drummond, W.   To His Lute.
Dylan.   Boots of Spanish Leather.
Eliot, T. S.   Fire Sermon, The.
Hollow Men, The.
Journey of the Magi.
Emerson, R.   Give All to Love.
Threnody: "South-wind brings, The."
"Ephelia.".   First Farewell to J.G.
Fagan.   Desire.

Farrar, J. Song for a Forgotten Shrine to Pan.
Fenton, J. Skip, The.
Wind: "This is the wind, the wind in a field of corn."
Fermini, I. You I know is losing you, The.
Forché. Skin Canoes.
Gallagher, T. Coming Home.
Even Now You Are Leaving.
Gamalinda, E. Lament Beginning w/a Line after Cavafy.
Garrett, E. Anatomy of Departure.
Garrigue. After Reading "The Country of the Pointed Firs".
Gaspar, Lorand. Flute Player.
Gerhardt, I. G. M. Remembrance Day.
Gertsyk, A. Silent, draped in the garments of sacrifice.
Gil de Biedma, J. Prince of Aquitania, in His Torn-down Tower, The.
Ginsberg, A. Elegy for Neal Cassady.
Godfrey. Where the Weather Suits My Clothes.
Gorostiza, J. Elegy: "Alone, with harsh marine aloneness."
Gotera. Manong Chito Tells Manong Ben about His Dream over Breakfast at the Manilatown Cafe.
Graham, J. What the End Is For.
Graves, R. Lost Love.
Gregerson. Safe.
Griffin, S. Our Mother Talks about Metaphor.
Grin, B. My Shtetl on the Dnestr.
Groarke, V. Riverbed, The.
Grotz, J. Wolf, The.
Guest, B. Nostalgia of the Infinite.
Guiterman. Little Lost Pup.
Gumilyov [or Gumiliov or Gumilev]. Streetcar That Lost Its Way, The.
Gunn, T. Autobiography.
Hacker, M. Autumn 1980.
Halperin. Two Lines from Paul Celan.
Hamer. Berkeley, Late Spring.
Harbach, O. Smoke Gets in Your Eyes.
Harington [or Harrington]. Astolfo flies by Chariot to the Moon, where he collects Orlando's lost wits.
Harms. From Now On.
Harper, M. Drowning of the Facts of a Life, The.
Hass, R. Bookbuying in the Tenderloin.
Meditation at Lagunitas.
Hayden, R. Road in Kentucky, A.
Hemans. Lost Pleiad, The.
Herrera, F. Sonnet 43.
Herrera y Reissig. Sadistic Love.
Herrick. Upon the Loss[e] of His Mistresses.
Vine, The.
Herzberg. Loss.
Hochman. Manhattan Pastures.
Sphinxes.
Hongo. Hilo: First Night Back.
Horace. Old Malediction, An.
Housman. Yon Far Country.
Howe, J. Lost Jewel, The.
My Last Dance.
Hsiao Kang. I Play My Zither.
Hsin Ch'i-chi. Tune: "The Bodhisattva's Golden Headdress".
Hughes, L. Homecoming.
Hugo, V. At Villequier.
Bridge, The.
Im Hwa. Again at the Crossroads.
Ingelow. Dappled sky, a world of meadows, A.
Ivanov, V. Winter Sonnets, The.
Jabès. Sunland.
Jaccottet. Clouded Skies.
Jackson, L. Summary for Alastor.
Jarrell, R. Second Air Force.
Truth, The.
Juan Chi. My steps lead me to a junction of three roads.
Katz, J. Falling.
King, Harriet Hamilton. Summer Lost.
King, Henry, Bishop of Chichester. Change, The.
Forfeiture, The.
Kipling, R. For to Admire.

Mesopotamia.
Kirsch, S. Wintery Music.
Kizer, C. For Sappho/After Sappho.
Klappert. In Memory of H. F.
Knight, E. Feeling Fucked/Up Up.
Knott. Christmas at the Orphanage.
Koch, K. To Marina.
Kochanowski, J. Where Is That Gate for Grief.
Kramer, L. Strong Winds Below the Canyons.
Kumin, M. How It Is.
Kupriyanov [or Kuprianov]. For a long time he tried to survive.
Lamb, C. Hester.
Old Familiar Faces, The.
Landor, W. Alas! 'Tis Very Sad to Hear.
Rose Aylmer.
Larcom. They Said.
Larkin, P. No Road.
So through that unripe day you bore your head.
Lear, E. Calico Pie.
Lee, L. Eating Alone.
Levy, A. On the Threshold.
Levy, E. It Is Still Early.
Lewis, A. Song (On Seeing Dead Bodies Floating Off the Cape).
Lewis, S. Five Foot Two, Eyes of Blue (Has Anybody Seen My girl?).
Li Ch'ing-chao. Long Melancholy Tune, A.
Tune: "Airing Inmost Feelings".
Tune: "Joy of Eternal Union".
Li Yü. Silently I ascend the western pavilion.
Tune: "Joy of Encounter".
Liu Shih. Tune: "Dreaming of Southland" Thinking of Someone.
Liu, T. Ariel Singing.
Poem: "Late butterflies gliding through the air."
Lloyd, C. Oh, she was almost speechless! nor could hold.
Lomax, M. July.
Longfellow, H. Cross of Snow, The.
Lowell, A. Patterns.
Lum. Urban Love Songs.
Lysohorsky. 22.6.1941.
Macaulay, T. Jacobite's Epitaph, A.
Marshall, J. Gift, A.
Martinaitis, M. Zuveliskes's Women Mourn Over Kukutis.
Masaoka Shiki. Chilly nights.
Mataka. Next Door.
Mattawa. Before.
McCosker. Tinnitus.
McGrath, T. After Tomasito's Departure.
End of the Line, The.
Meister. In That Place Was Another House.
Meleager. Love's night and a lamp.
Meynell, A. Maternity.
Mihalic. Elegy: "From the old settlements only the writings."
Millay, E. If I should learn, in some quite casual way.
Sonnet 43: "What lips my lips have kissed, and where, and why."
Miller, C. In celebration of surviving.
Milosz, C. On Pilgrimage.
Milton. Mulciber.
Mistral, G. Autumn.
Molina, E. Scream is a Kind of Coffin, The.
Montale. You know this: I must lose you again and cannot.
Moore, J. To Love That Well.
Moore, T. Journey Onwards, The.
Oft In the Stilly Night.
Morgan, R. Damn You, Lady.
Mura. To H.N.
Neruda. Final.
Past.
Poem.
Nilsson, H. On Inheriting Departure.
NorthSun. Moving Camp Too Far.
Oden. Testament of Loss.
Oliver, M. In Blackwater Woods.
Olson, C. Pacific Lament.
Orr, G. Sweater, The.
Pacheco, J. Boundaries.
Pack, R. Mountain Ash without Cedar Waxwings.

Pao Ling-hui. Added to a Letter Sent to a Traveler.
Parra, V. Song for a Seed.
Peacocke. At the Entrance.
Petrarch. Ye vales and woods! fair scenes of happier hours.
Philips, K. To the Queen of Inconstancy, Regina Collier, in Antwerp.
Phillips, C. Luna Moth.
Pickthall, M. Lost Friend, The.
Pinchas-Cohen. Remembering Our Fathers.
Pinkerton, H. For an End.
Pizarnik. Speaking Your Name.
Poe. Dream within a Dream, A.
Sleeper, The.
To One in Paradise.
Valley of Unrest, The.
Poliziano. What song will ever be so sorrowful.
Popa. Be Seeing You.
Portal. Attitude.
Porter, A. Four Poems in One.
Powell, D. A. Thicknesses of victor decreased: blanket->sheet->floss. Until no material would do, the.
Prince, F. T. For Fugitives.
Prys-Jones. Wife of Carcassone, The.
Raboni, G. For C., Who Died of Childbirth at the Age of One Year and Eleven Months.
Ransom, J. Dead Boy.
Reese, L. Rachel.
Renunciation.
Reid, C. Stones and Bones.
Rexroth, K. Half in a dream.
In the park a crow awakes.
Now the fireflies of our youth.
This flesh you have loved.
Rich, A. Loser, The.
Richard I, Coeur de Lion. Ja Nul Homs Pris Ne Ira a Raison.
Roberts, E. Old Love in Song, An.
Robinson, M. Phaon Forsakes Her.
Roethke. Visitant, The.
Roscoe, W. On Being Forced to Part with his Library for the Benefit of his Creditors.
Rossetti, C. Cousin Kate.
Echo.
Youth gone, and beauty gone if ever there.
Ruden, S. Stubble Burning, The.
Rukeyser, M. Waiting for Icarus.
Rumi. Come, come, for the rosebower has blossomed; come, come, for the beloved has arrived.
Ryan, G. Too Bad.
Ryan, M. Talking About Things.
Sabines. Entresol.
Salaam. Our World Is Less Full Now That Mr. Fuller Is Gone.
Samaras, N. Aubade: Macedonia.
Samson, J. Hypothetical.
Sanchez, S. Father and Daughter.
Sanguineti. At the offset it was calculated.
Sappho. That one seems to me to be like the gods, the man whosoever sits facing you and listens nearby to your sweet speech an desirable laughter.
Sassoon, S. Lamentations.
Saunders, R. Empty Glen, The.
Sawadsri, S. If You Come Close to Me.
Seed. Sofia.
Seward. Invocation, To the Genius of Slumber Written Oct. 1787.
Sexton. Ballad of the Lonely Masturbator, The.
Shakespeare, W. Sonnet 42: "That thou hast her, it is not all my grief[e]."
Sonnet 49: "Against that time, if ever that time come."
Sonnet 86: "Was it the proud full sail[e] of his great verse."
Sonnet 87: "Farewell! thou art too dear[e] for my possessing."
Sonnet 90: "Then hate me when thou wilt; if ever, now."
Sonnet 134: "So now I have confess'd that he is thine."
Shapiro, K. Leg, The.
Shen Yüeh. Seeing the Beloved in a Dream.

Sheridan, R. Lines by a Lady on the Loss of her Trunk.
Sidney. Sonnet 18: "With what sharp checks I in myself am shent."
Ye Goat-herd Gods.
Sigourney. Advertisement of a Lost Day.
Simmons, J. Long Way After Ronsard, A.
Simms, W. Lost Pleiad, The.
Smallpiece, A. M. Veil's removed, the gaudy, flimsy veil, The.
Smith, I. Clearances, The.
Smith, P. Building Nicole's Mama.
Sorrentino. Good Night!
Soupault. Song for Ghosts and for Those Now Gone.
Soyinka. He escape the lynch days. He survives.
Staff. Kingdom.
Stanley, T. Love Deposed.
Strickland, A. Forsaken, The.
Su Tung-p'o. Tune: "Always Having Fun".
Tune: "River Town".
Sundiata. Open Heart.
Swirszczynska [or Swir]. He Is Gone.
Sze. Before Completion.
String Diamond, The.
Tennyson, A. I envy not in any moods.
I held it truth, with him who sings.
O [or Oh] that 'twere possible.
Thomas, E. Return, The.
Thomas, L. Instructions for Your New Osiris.
Thoreau. Brother where dost thou dwell?
Tighe. Poor, fond deluded heart! wilt thou again.
Trinidad. Moonstones.
Tu Fu [or Du Fu]. Draft Board at Shih-hao, The.
Recruiting Officer of Shih-hao.
Tymnes. Maltese Dog, A.
Stone says that it covers here the white dog, The.
Unknown. Adieu, the years are a broken song.
Chant from the Iroquois Book of Rites.
I was drowsy, but my heart was awake. Listen!
Now goth sonne under wode,—.
On the Slope of Hua Mountain.
Synge we alle and seye we thus.
TEHKARIHHOKEN! / Continue to listen!
Your Thwarts in Pieces, Your Mooring Rope Cut.
Vázquez Montalbán, M. Summer and Smoke.
Voigt. House.
Volkman. Evening.
Wakoski. Ring of Irony, The.
Wang Ch'ang-ling. Silent at Her Window.
Wang Ts'an. Seven Sorrows.
Waniek. Mama I Remember.
Warren, R. Song: "Yellow coverlet, A."
Whitman, W. O Captain! My Captain!
Out of the Cradle Endlessly Rocking.
When Lilacs Last in the Dooryard Bloom'd.
Yonnondio.
Whittier. Farewell, The: "Gone, gone,—sold and gone."
Wilcox, E. Friendship After Love.
Wilde, O. Hélas!
Requiescat.
Williams, B. Night Flute, The.
Williams, C. K. Loss.
Williams, P. Passing Through.
Williams, W. Hemmed-in Males.
These.
Wilson, S. Home: After a Poem by Frost.
Wordsworth, W. Complaint, A.
She Dwelt among the Untrodden Ways.
Surprised by Joy.
Written in London, September, 1802.
Wright, F. Alcohol.
Flight.
Wroth. Sonnet 25: "Poor[e] eyes be[e] blind, the light behold no[e] more."
Wu of Han [or Wu Ti or Ou-ty or Liu Ch'e or Liu Ch'u]. Li Furen.
Wycherley, L. Cat's Cradle.
Yearsley. To———: "Lo! dreary Winter, howling o'er the waste."

Yeats. Lover Mourns for the Loss of Love, The.
Yosef, H. In the Library.
Young, J. Five Foot Two, Eyes of Blue (Has Anybody Seen My girl?).
You're Gonna Lose Your Gal.
Young, K. Letters from the North Star.
Zarco. My Worst Fear.
Zenmaro. Tanka: "No news of him."
Zisquit. Because passion is the absence we speak.
There is always a sound.
Word before the Last about Loss, A.

Lot (Bible)
Cowley, A. Lot's Wife.
Helwig. Lot.
Hope, A. Lot and His Daughters I.
Lot and His Daughters II.
Lesley, G. Behold, how Sodom swaggers in its Pride.

Lotus
Boryu. Cloud above lotus / It too.
Brebner, D. 1. The Golden Lotus.
Bu-er. Cut brambles long enough.
Buson. White lotus.
Chǒng Ch'ǒl. Dash of rain upon, A.
Let forty thousand pecks of pearls.
Dankyo-Myorin. Coming, I clench my hands.
Hsüeh T'ao [or Xue Tao]. Lotus-Gathering Boat.
Ishikawa Takuboku. Tanka: "Like a white lotus."
Issa. What a world / Where lotus flowers.
Kambala. KYE HO! Wonderful!
Lal Ded [or Lalla]. Coursing in emptiness.
Sǒ Chǒngju. Like a Wind from Lotus Blossoms.
Thompson, P. At the Nu'uanu Reservoir Pool.
Tokuo. Town's aflame with summer heat, The.
Tzu Yeh. Lotus Lover, The.
Unknown. Fragrance of the lotus, The.
Wen T'ing-yün. To the Tune: Southern Song.

Louis, Joe
Hernton, C. Ballad of the Life and Times of Joe Louis, A.

Louisiana (state)
As-Sabah. Jubilee.
Berkson, B. Obvious Tradition, The.
Coleman, W. Chuck Man.
De Forest. In Louisiana.
Hemans. Stranger in Louisiana, The.
Lane, P. Port Townsend Poems.
Smith, D. Black Silhouettes of Shrimpers.
Louisiana Sea of Faith, The.
Whitman, W. I Saw in Louisiana a Live-Oak Growing.

Love
Abu Sa'id. I Asked My Love.
Agee. Permit Me Voyage.
Akhmatova, A. Poem: "Twenty-first, The. Night. Monday."
Allen, Alfred. Love and the Years.
Allen, Annette. This River.
Amadiume. Union, The.
Anacreon. Again Love struck me like a smith with a giant.
Dice of Love are, The.
Ashbery, J. Meaningful Love.
Ball, A. Jazz.
Barker, S. There was not loveliness nor fortune there.
Basho. She cat, The.
Beltrán, Carmen Celia. Dried Flowers.
Berggolts [or Bergholts]. Don't turn around, don't look back.
Blumenthal, M. Disappointments of Childhood, The.
Bogardus. Narcissus to Echo.
Bradford, Perry. Crazy Blues.
Breton, A. Free Union.
On the Road to San Romano.
Bridges, R. Awake, My Heart, to Be Loved.
Muse and Poet.
Broda, Martine. I Wanted to Tell You.
Bryan, A. Peg O' My Heart.
Butler, S. Love.

Campbell, R. Sisters, The.
Campo, C. Ah that the Tiger.
Love, Today My Lip.
Catullus. Odi et Amo.
Char. Mortal Partner, The.
Cisneros, S. I Am on My Way to Oklahoma to Bury the Man I Nearly Left My Husband For.
Clanchy, K. Recognition.
Clare, J. Winter Winds Cold and Blea.
Clementelli. Circle and Obsession of Walls.
Your Hands, My Love.
Cobbold, E. Reproach.
Colonna, S. But what an idea she'd gotten into her head.
Cook, C. It's Just As Well About Heather.
Cope, W. Orange, The.
Coulehan, J. Lovesickness: A Medieval Text.
Craven, Sherry. Garden City Diner: Loving Back.
Croly. Domestic Love.
Cross, D. Cinema Yosemite.
Deguy. Who What.
Dickey, W. Plot, The.
Dillon, G. Hours of the Day, The.
Duncan, R. Morning Letter, A.
Eluard, P. et al. Earth Is Blue like an Orange, The.
Loving.
She Exists.
France, L. Mess With It.
Fritz. Love Poem (2): "Because you turn."
Gander, F. Deflection Toward the Relative Minor.
Garrett, E. Love's Parallel.
Ghalib, M. Ghazal 21.
Ghazal 34.
Gladding. Worsted Heather.
Glück, L. Seven Ages, The.
Goll, I. On the five thousandth evening of our love.
Gomez. My Chakabuku Mama: A Comic Tale.
Greenlaw, L. Earliest Known Representation of a Storm in Western Art, The.
Love from a Foreign City.
Guidacci, Margherita. First to feast is love, The.
On the scraps of love the fever feasts.
Guiducci, Armanda. Brevity of Embraces.
In Emily's Manner.
Perhaps One Day There Will Be Ways.
Under an Impure Star.
Upon Closing the Book.
Guinicelli. Love and Nobility.
Gumilyov [or Gumiliov or Gumilev]. Baby Elephant, A.
Hahn, S. Incontinence.
Hanh et al. Reverence is the nature of my love.
Hannah, S. Where is Talcott Parsons Now?
Hanzlicek, C. Egg.
Hejinian. Constantly I write this happily.
Henry, P. Love Birds.
Hiestand, E. Day Lily and the Fox, The.
Hochman. Manhattan Pastures.
Hollander, J. Carmen Ancillae.
Hoover, P. Theoretical People.
Howe, F. Doubt.
Hunt, L. One day,—'twas on a summer afternoon.
Issa. Having slept, the cat gets up.
Jackson, R. Poem That Was Once Called "Desperate" But Is Now Striving to Become the Perfect Love Poem.
Jarnot, L. Brooklyn Anchorage.
Jonson, B. Song: To Celia ("Drink to me only with thine eyes.").
Karp. Harm.
Kaufman, S. Emperor of China, The.
King, H. Exequy, The.
Kinsella, T. Je t'adore.
Kirsanov. I Am White, Darling.
Kupriyanov [or Kuprianov]. For a long time he tried to survive.
Lahey, Joy. Cotton and Gladiolas.
Lamar. Carmelita.
Landon. Bonds of Affection.
Lehman. Prophet's Lantern, The.
Li Po. To Meng Hao-jan.

Loy. Love Songs to Joannes.
Luschei, G. Pozo Basket, The.
Luterman, A. Justice of the Peace, The.
MacDonogh. She Walked Unaware.
MacInnes, Mairi. I Object, said the Object.
Mandelstam [or Mandelshtam]. I Hate the Light.
McCabe, C. Light & Love.
Menicanti. I Don't Know.
  If.
  Love Says.
Meredith, W. Traveling Boy.
Moore, T. Venetian Air.
Morabito, F. I've never been in love enough.
  No he amado bastante.
Motherwell. Jeanie Morrison.
Mueller, L. Love Like Salt.
Murray, G. On Being Disabled by Light at Dawn in the Wilderness.
Nichol. Blues.
Nims, J. Young Ionia, The.
Noguchi, Yonejiro (Yone). Lines: "Sun I worship, The."
Nossis. Nothing is sweeter than love, all other riches.
O'Reilly, M. House Call to a Man with Parkinson's Disease, A.
  Potter.
Osgood, F. Lines: "Oh, ye who in those Houses hold."
  Wraith of the Rose, The.
Oswald, A. Ballad of a Shadow.
Peacock, M. My God, Why Are You Crying?
Péret. Fountain.
  Hello.
Piercy. Morning Love Song.
Pollok. Happiness.
"Rachel." [or "Rahel."]. Love was late in coming, and coming.
Rago. 4. Terror and Love as Fugitives.
Reid, D. Between Aphorisms.
Renk, Charlotte. Mistletoe Kills.
Riley, D. Shantung.
Riley, P. 1134. 39.
Rimbaud, A. Romance.
Rossetti, C. I wish I could remember the [or that] first day.
Rothman, D. Shape of Water Most Like Love, The.
Roux, S. Sunrise.
Rumi. Love you alone have been with us.
  That moon which the sky never saw.
Samaras, N. Aubade: Macedonia.
Sappho. Love shook my senses.
Shapiro, K. V-Letter.
Shen Yüeh. Seeing the Beloved in a Dream.
Shillaber, B. Picture, A.
Shinder. One Secret That Has Carried, The.
Simpson, L. Ed.
Steiger. They will not ask us: have you sinned?
Stowe. Only a Year.
Tanaquil. Very Young Man Speaks, A.
Taylor, J. My Mother.
Tengour, H. Secret in Broad Daylight.
Tvardovsky [or Tvardovskii]. Poem: "Blue snow is turning black, The."
Unknown. All too soon, I fear.
  Cautiously bubbles that spring water.
  Lament: "Cheek by cheek on our pillow[s]."
  Please, Sir Second-born.
  Singing Maid, The.
  Some loves are soft, others are rough.
  Words "I love you," The.
Unknown, fr. Terezin Concentration Camp.
  Forgotten.
  Letter to Daddy, The.
Vallejo. Poem to Be Read and Sung ("I know there is someone.").
Vietnamese Oral Tradition. Bare Rocks and Stars.
  Coins of Van-Lich.
  Difficulties at Love.
  King Star, The.
  Love Lament.
  Pole at the Village Pagoda, The.
  Replies.

Walders, D. Anniversary.
Ward, Geoff. Trapped Wind.
White, D. Epistle of Love and of Consolation unto Israel, An.
Wiese, B. Going Home Madly.
Wilkinson, J. Rest of It, The.
Winters, Y. Alas, that I should be.
  To My Infant Daughter.
Wojahn. Inside, The.
Yesenin [or Essenin]. Do You Not Love Me.
Young, D. Sources of the Delaware.
See also **Affection; Companionship and Companions; Courtship; Dating; Desire; Erotic Love; Lust**

Love Poetry
Belieu. Love Poem: "There are too many similes for bed."
Cassells. Bargain, The.
Collins, B. Litany: "You are the bread and the knife."
Jackson, R. Poem That Was Once Called "Desperate" But Is Now Striving to Become the Perfect Love Poem.

Love Triangles
Larsen, W. Surrender.
Paschen. Voir Dire.
Vazirani, R. It's Me, I'm Not Home.

Lovebirds
Hippolyte. Revo Lyric.
Shapcott, J. Lovebirds.
Tomlinson, C. In the Borghese Gardens.
Wang Ho-ch'ing. Tune: "Po Pu-tuan" Fat Couple.

Lovers
Achebe. Love Cycle.
Addonizio. Prayer: "Sometimes, when we're lying after love."
Adebajo, K. Moonlight on the Lake.
Agosin. Your Hands.
Ahmed Dâi. Torture of the beloved is no punishment, The.
Aiken, C. All the Radios.
Aksal, S. Love Poem: "First line of this poem, The."
Aktan, F. Letter, The: "Few broken things linger in my palm, A."
Al-Bayati, A. Three Ruba'iyat.
al-Sayyab, B. Love Me.
Aleixandre. It's Raining.
Ali, A. Farewell: "At a certain point I lost track of you."
Allen, F. Foreign Relations.
Andrew, G. Evidently, She Says.
Angel. Vigil, The.
Ap Hywel, Elin. Useful.
Aprin Çor Tigin. My darling, / Best of all.
Aragon. Embrace, The.
Artaud. Love with No Letup.
Aşar, M. Sami. Weekly Agenda of Love.
Bang, M. Night Falling Fast.
Baqi. Sparks from my heart rise.
Baraka, I. Like Rousseau.
Bardwell. How my true love and I lay without touching.
Benedikt. Moralist of Bananas, The.
Berger, M. Empty Chairs.
Berk, İ. Never Did I See Such Loves Nor Such Separations.
Berkson, B. Wake Up (Call).
Berrigan, T. In Bed with Joan & Alex.
Blasing, R. Refuge.
Boland, E. Daphne with Her Thighs in Bark.
Bosquet, A. Lovers, The: "I said: "Your Christian name?"."
Bowers, E. Living Together.
Boyle, K. Monody to the Sound of Zithers.
Brebner, D. 1. The Golden Lotus.
Brouwer, J. Hamartia Symbolized by the Stray. Spots, The.
Brown, L. Respond to Me.
Bruce, G. Love in Age.
Buchanan, O. Term, The.
Buson. I've learned how.
Caleshu, A. After the Word Love Was Spoken. Collaboration: A Day at the Beach.

Cansever, Edip. Eyes: "It seems nothing can provoke."
Carman, B. Eavesdropper, The.
  Northern Vigil, A.
Carruth, H. Swept.
Catullus. My Sweetest Lesbia.
Cavanagh, E. Return to Avondale.
Cavé, S. Permit.
Citino. Situation No. 7: The Poison Lover.
Clare, J. Song: "Sad was the day when my Willie did leave me."
Clarke, George Elliott. Wisdom of Shelley, The.
Clinton, Robert. Modulation.
Cogswell, Fred. Water and the Rock, The.
Cooley. Poem on the First Day of Spring.
Cope, W. My Lover.
Cott, J. He Dreams What Is Going On Inside His Head.
  Natural Functions.
Crase. Covenant.
Cutler, Y. Shir Asheydim Ansher.
Daglarca. Leaf: "Your gaze stays awake in the night."
  You say / Stars.
Datcher, M. Soul gestures in spring.
Day Lewis. Jig.
  Song: "Come, live with me and be my love."
de Fréine, C. Chattels.
Dede, Esrâr. In the ruins, in the tavern.
Diego, G. Your Eyes Are Always Open.
Donnelly, T. Purgatory Chasm.
Drummond de Andrade. Ballad of Love through the Ages.
Edwards, Sonia. Between Two Lovers.
El-Shawwaf, H. Half a Lemon, Half a Cigarette, and Half a Desire to Have It Off.
Emre. Burning, burning, I drift and tread.
  Dear Friend, let me plunge into the sea of love.
  Go and let it be known to all lovers.
  Now hear this, lovers, my friends.
Fanthorpe. Atlas.
Fernández Retamar, Roberto. Man and a Woman, A.
Forbes, C. Plea, The.
Fuzuli. If my heart were a wild bird, it would nest.
Gardiner, S. Identity Crisis.
Ginsberg, A. At 4:00 a.m. the two.
Glaser, E. And in the Afternoons I Botanized.
Glazer, M. Sonnet: "Invisible in vernal pools." Wherein space is constructed that matter may reside in.
Goran. Lover's Song, A.
Gordon, R. Nights in Siuna.
Gorges. Tell me my harte how wilte thow doe.
Grainger, J. Bryan and Pereene.
Grant, C. Wishing You.
Greenberg, A. Nostalgia, Cheryl, Is the Best Heroin.
Greenlaw, L. Tryst.
Griffin, G. Gille Machree.
Grotz, J. Not Body.
Guillén, J. River.
Guiney. When on the Marge of Evening.
Gundy, J. Ancient Themes: The Night.
Hajjaj, N. Laila's Face.
Hanim, L. Drink all you want in the rose-garden. Who cares what they say!
  Get on with the festivities—let them say what they will.
Hanim, N. Tell Me Again.
Hantoosh, G. Love in the Time of Cholera. Poems for Rasmia.
Hardie, K. Hunter Home from the Hill, The.
Harwood, L. Rain Journal: London: June '65.
Hass, R. Feast, The.
  Misery and Splendor.
Henderson, D. Downtown-Boy Uptown.
Herbert, Z. Silk of a Soul.
Herd. Shadowed by your father.
Higgins, F. By the Field of the Crab-Trees.
  Roving Lover, The.
Hikmet. All the things I've written about us are untrue.
  I Shut My Eyes Tight.
  My Lady's Eyes Are Hazel.

Poems of Nine to Ten P.M.
Prison to Prison.
Snow closed the road.
Hill, S. I Know I Ought to Love You.
Hjern, K. To My Love.
Hoffenstein. Let us build a little house.
Hofmann, M. Ancient Evenings.
Hofmannsthal. Two, The.
Hopes. Invalid of Park Street, The.
Houlihan, J. H. Antecessor.
Hristov, Boris. At Night: "Our tree's shadow is green at night."
Hsiao Yen [*or* Emperor Wu of Liang]. Border Guard, A.
Huerta, D. Neblina veraniega.
Summer Mist.
Hummer, T. Courtly Love.
Hunt, L. Lover's Exchange.
Paulo and Francesca.
Hunter, C. Two Thousand and Two.
Hutchinson, P. Into Their True Gentleness.
Ilkov, Ani. Scene, A.
İnal, Gülseli. Love and the Forest.
Isharaza, G. Grand Get Together, The.
Ishikawa. For Her Lover.
Janess, D. Night, Hornby Island.
Jarnot, L. New Life, The.
Jenkins, A. Road Less Travelled, The.
Jernigan, Marla. Glorious.
Put together how it will.
Johnson, Peter. Enigma of the Stigma, or Vice Versa.
Johnston, D. Pyramus & Thisbe.
Jones, R. Loft, The.
Jong, E. Climbing You.
Ka, R. To My Beloved.
Kadir, A. On Bald Mountain.
Kanik. People Will Talk.
KaracaoǦlan. With its tender flakes, snow flutters about.
Kay, J. Dance of the Cherry Blossom.
What was it you said again there by the river.
Keith, Sally. Subtraction Song.
Kennelly. Raglan Lane.
Kimbrell, J. Letters to a Vanishing Fiancée.
Klink, J. Mariana Trench.
Kocot, N. Bicycle Poem.
Komunyakaa, Y. Ignis Fatuus.
Krysl. Warscape, with Lovers.
Lami'i Çelebi. Yesterday I saw that sun-faced beauty.
Lavut, E. About Love.
Ledwidge. Meeting, The: "She'll meet me with the gate thrown wide."
Li Ch'ing-chao. Written by Chance.
Li'aibi, S. Butterfly frozen in stone, A.
Liu Yu Hsi. Parrot Island.
Red Blossoms.
Lockward, D. Vegetable Love.
Machado Ruiz. Tell Me If You Remember, Love.
MacIntyre, T. On Sweet Killen Hill.
Markham, M. We Folded the Hours and Set Them in the Rain.
Marlatt, D. Small print.
Matthews, W. Misgivings.
McDaniel, J. Hunting for Cherubs.
McFadden, D. 8. Afternoon Bus to Toronto.
Meinke. Blow, Blow, Thou Winter Wind.
Menefee, S. September 30.
Meyer, B. Lovers' Sestina, The.
Mitchell, N. Leaving, The.
Montes de Oca, Marco Antonio. Fusion of Shadows, A.
Moore, T. Away with this Pouting.
Moroz, R. There's a cinnamon tree that grows on the Moon.
Morris, T. Lovers Total Recall.
Muhibbi. No end to this separation, no limit to this cruel pain.
Till the day I die, I shall never leave her beauty's sun.
Mullen, Kate. Thin-Legged Lover.
Murphey, John Collin. Texas Boomer.
Nadir, M. In Pencil.
Na'ili [*or* Yeni-Zada Mustafa Efendi]. My tears

became desire that illuminates.
Nasir, A. Moment of Love, A.
Nathan, L. Making a Love Poem.
Nedim. Delicacy was drawn out like the finest wire.
Nef'i. That black drunken eye has become a tavern.
Those who painted my portrait painted me.
Nejati. Heart is pleased when black down covers, The.
Spiraling, the sparks.
Neshâtî. We are desire hidden in the love-crazed call.
Nev'î. We don't need the cup of pleasure.
Ni Dhomhnaill. I Cannot Lie Here Anymore.
Nisâyî. We are the Mejnûn of our age, we dwell in the wilderness.
Nortje. Episodes with unusables.
Norton, C. Faithless Knight, The.
Nowlan. Canadian Love Song.
O'Callaghan, C. 10 The Salmon.
O'Connor, F. Exile: "What happier fortune can one find."
Olds, S. This Hour.
O'Siadhail. Between.
Ostriker. Army of Lovers, An.
O'Sullivan, L. Therapist, The.
Ozer. For Many Years.
Page, P. Cross.
Parker, A. Eclipse, The: "Having never been to a drive-in movie."
Parnell, T. Song: "When thy beauty appears."
Paterson, D. Imperial.
Wreck, The.
Peeradina, S. Song of Surrender.
Peirce. Riddles: "He opens her. She can't have him."
Pennar, Meirion. Lovers: "As a blind man."
Pérez Conde, P. Flor de oro.
Flower of Gold.
Ta te/ak'etik yorail ya x-ajk'otajik.
Tiempo de bailar los árboles.
Time for Trees to Dance.
Xnich k'anal tak'in.
Philpot, T. It Was a Boy.
Pilinszky, J. Definition of Your Attraction.
Relationship.
Prados, E. Like a Naked Light.
Song of Taking Leave.
Pryputniewicz, Tania. Dragonfly.
Raàm-Lachish, C. In the Night.
Rabkin, S. Wheels.
Radden, V. When You Talk That Talk.
Ramsdell, H. Good Sheep.
Rees-Jones. What It's Like To Be Alive.
Reeve, F. Voices: "When I hear my lover singing, I sing, too."
Reich, A. Siren of Love, A.
Reid, A. Figures on the Frieze, The.
Revânî. What do you say about that cypress body that hunts the heart?
Riordan, M. Southpaw.
Rosenstock, G. Search, The: "Where are the poems I promised."
Ruefle. Letter, The.
Perfect Reader.
Rumi. At one time when life was real, your soul was one with my soul.
Come, come, you will never find a friend like me.
Listen to the reed-flute telling its tales.
This is such a day: the sun is dazzling twice as before.
Rumsey, Tessa. Man-Torpedo-Boat.
Salaam. Moment of the First Day, The.
Salinas, P. Set Her Far from Me, Mirror.
Sanchez, S. Answer to yo / question / of am I not yo / woman / even if you went on shit again.
Sanger, R. 3: Who Was That? I Ask.
Santos, S. Talking Cure, The.
Saraç, Tahsin. To an Immortal Solitude Where We Now Pitch Our Stately Tent.
Schiff, H. Eye Poem.
Scott, W. We Are So Fond of One Another, Because Our Ailments Are the Same.

Senior. Tropic Love.
Şeyh Galib. To me, love is the flame.
Shafiq, H. Mountain, The.
Shimazaki Toson. Fox's Trick, The.
Silano, M. Sausage Parade, The.
Simic. Devils, The.
Simon, L. Measuring Apollo.
Skelton, J. With Lullay, Lullay, Like a Child.
Smith, Tracy K. Spring: "Let's not talk."
Solie, Karen. More Fun In The New World.
Spicer, J. Book of Music, A.
Stanley, T. Love Deposed.
Suhl. Kh'hob dikh lib.
Surprice, L. Little Love Kiss.
Sutphen, J. Problem Was, The.
Thomas, L. Even-Tempered Girl Holds Her Breath, An.
Townsend, A. Modern Love.
Tranströmer. At Funchal.
Tretheway. Reading the Signs.
Ts'ao Chih. Round the tall towers blow many mournful winds.
Twomey, M. Exchanges in Italy.
Tynan Hinkson, K. Dead-Tryst, The.
Unknown. All my hotheaded lovers will be pleased with me.
Already the accursed rooster and his sad departure song.
At midnight the memory of you is the only visitor.
At midnight when the world's at rest.
Be happy, my love, I shall take charge of our cares.
Come back to me, riddled with holes from a dark rifle's bullets.
Come, my love, let me embrace you.
Come onto my pathway one more time.
First take me in your arms and hold me tight.
Go and fight in Kabul, my love.
Go away then, my friend, and travel well!
God, please let my youth go up in smoke!
God, you may render me blind today!
Had I known the time of separation was to come.
Have you with your white beard no shame?
Hold me tight and very close to you.
Hold me tightly in your arms.
How did you come here beneath the full moon.
Hurry up, my love, and quickly rise to the assault.
I disgraced myself in my lover's eyes.
I used to have bracelets, I do not wear them now.
If you truly love me, my love, go off and liberate our land!
In battle today my lover turned his back to the enemy.
In the dark night that keeps us apart.
Jiang Zhong-zi: Hep-Cat Chung.
Juan-er: Curl-Grass.
Last night I had a dream.
Last night I had a dream that has come true.
Last night you were sleeping in my arms.
Leave the service of your master and be my loyal follower.
May God prohibit you from any pleasure as you travel.
My beloved, my sun, rise above the horizon and obliterate my nights of exile.
My courage fails me when I grasp my water jar.
My love, swear that you will come to me.
My lover cannot take a joke.
My lover is the ornament around my neck.
My lover prefers well mannered garden flowers.
My lover wants to keep my tongue inside his mouth.
My pants, the hue of fire, are slipping down my thighs.
Never shall I take an old man as a lover.
No longer will I draw water from the spring at dusk.
Of my bosom I have made a bed.
Oh damned rooster, I would like to strangle you!
Oh lute that I would like to see demolished!
Oh memory of my beloved, you are my one true

lover!

Oh my love beyond the mountains, gaze at the moon.

Oh rooster, wait a little with your song!

Oh springtime! The pomegranate trees are blooming.

One is dying of desire to see me if only for a moment.

Others dress up in their new clothes for the feast, The.

Pick the flowers by the handful.

Reed Flowers Turn White.

Silk-spread Blackbird.

To chain me down he takes charge of the chains.

To my lover I want to sacrifice it all.

What else can he do but behave like a hero.

Why do you come to me so seldom?

You have consumed my mouth but are not satisfied.

You wretch who did not come last evening!

Untermeyer, L.   Truce.

Vander Ven, Tom.   Sea Washes Sand Scours Sea.

Verlaine.   la Promenade, A.

Webb, P.   Second Hand, The.

Wei Chuang.   Hidden Tears.

Weiser, Karen.   How can the day arrest.

Wen T'ing-yün.   In Her Moonlit Chamber.

White, M.   Foursomes.

Wickham.   Tired Woman, The.

Williams, C.   Sugar.

Williams, S.   Sub Umbra Floreo.

Wright, C.   Prayer: "Bless my life—its inks."

Wright, J.   Young Good Man, The.

Yaqoob, J.   Only Choice, The.

Resurrections of Layla Al-Attar, The.

Yi Hyangji.   Joy of Love, The.

Youn, Monica.   Venice, Unaccompanied.

Yu Xuanji.   Divided by the Han River.

Spring Passion.

Zhang Shuai.   Pining.

Staring.

Zimmer.   Crazy with Love.

Lowell, James Russell

Lowell, J.   [James Russell] Lowell.

Lowell, Robert

Bishop, E.   North Haven.

Meredith, W.   Last Things.

Pygge.   *Robert Lowell's Notebook.*

Voznesensky [*or* Voznesenskii].   Monologue with Commentary.

Lowry, Malcolm

Lowry, M.   Epitaph: "Malcolm Lowry."

Loyalty

Agustini.   Intruder, The.

Berlin.   Always.

Bhattācārya, K.   From now on.

Boland, E.   Ready for Flight.

Burns, R.   O[h] Wert Thou in the Cauld Blast.

Red, Red Rose, A.

Byron, G.   Abdiel.

Caldwell, A.   I Know That You Know.

Camerarius, P.   Faithfullest Beast, The.

Cassells.   Beautiful Signor.

Catullus.   Carmen: 11.

Chinese Oral Tradition.   Transformation Text on the Boy Shun's Extreme Filial Piety.

Chŏng Mongju.   Though this frame should die and die.

Cisneros, A.   To a Dead Lady.

Comden, B.   Thanks a Lot, but No Thanks.

Crosby, F.   I Am Thine, O Lord.

Cruz, S.   One Dismal Night.

Garcilaso de la Vega.   One Moment My Hope Rises Up On Wings.

Your Face Is Written in My Soul.

Gaskill, C.   Prisoner of Love.

Green, A.   Thanks a Lot, but No Thanks.

Guevara, M.   To Christ Crucified.

Haavikko.   Bowmen, The.

Hardy, T.   Broken Appointment, A.

Hewitt, J.   If I had given you that love and care.

Holiner, M.   You Can't Stop Me from Lovin' You.

Howitt, M.   Tobias's Dog.

Hyneman, R.   No. 5, Judith.

Ignatova, E.   Summer Garden, The.

Kahn, G.   No, No, Nora.

Kemble.   On an Irish Retriever.

Kipling, R.   Gunga Din.

Korean Oral Tradition.   Abandoned Princess, The.

Li Po.   South-Folk in Cold Country.

López Velarde.   My Heart, Faithful.

Lovelace, R.   To Lucasta, from Prison.

Malloch, D.   Manly Love.

Martial.   Trusty Lydia, The.

You lie and I concur. You "give".

Mary Stuart.   For him also I powrit out mony teiris.

Melville, H.   Enthusiast, The.

Moller, V.   Faithfullest Beast, The.

Montgomerie, A.   Sonet: "Thocht Polibus, pisander, and with them."

Morris, L.   To the Tormentors.

Mugrón, Abbot of Iona.   Christ's Cross.

Nairne.   Will Ye No Come Back Again?

Ovid.   Friend, henceforth to be reckoned the foremost among my comrades.

You who are reading this work without malice, may you.

Peele.   His Golden Lock[e]s [Time Hath to Silver Turned].

Petrarch.   Oh! place me where the burning noon.

Porter, C.   Always True to You in My Fashion.

My Heart Belongs to Daddy.

Pratt, S.   Blind Man's Dog, The.

Prior.   Home-Loving Dog, The.

Robin, L.   Prisoner of Love.

Scott, S.   Poor Yarrow.

"Shu Ting.".   Brother, I Am Here.

Sidney.   Sonnet 54: "Because I breathe not love to every one."

Smith, C.   Stanzas: "Ah! think'st thou, Laura, then, that wealth."

Somervile [*or* Somerville].   All-Accomplished Rover.

Song.   Youngest Daughter, The.

Song Sun.   I discuss with my heart.

Southey, R.   Roderick's Faithful Theron.

Spencer, W.   Beth Gelert.

Ts'en Shen.   On the West Tower in Guozhou.

Turberville.   Love Me, Love My Dog.

Unknown.   Friend of Man, The.

Story of Kepa Falekaono, The.

Three Things Come Without Seeking.

We Fought South of the City Wall.

Various authors.   Brothers rebelled against one another, The.

He had many to help him.

Vietnamese Oral Tradition.   Phoenixes and Sparrows.

Wilder, A.   I'll Be Around.

Wodehouse.   You Never Knew About Me.

Yellen, J.   Mamma Goes Where Papa Goes.

Luanda, Angola

Neto.   Kinaxixi.

Lucifer

Cairns, Scott.   Lucifer's Epistle to the Fallen.

Luck

Adair, T.   Everything Happens to Me.

Benn.   This Is Bad.

Berry, D.   After Finding a One Hundred Dollar Bill.

Blane, R.   Ev'ry Time.

Bottoms.   Horseshoes.

Broumas, O.   If I Yes.

Bryan, C.   Contentment: "Strung along back elm."

Cassity.   Why Fortune Is the Empress of the World.

Comden, B.   Lucky to Be Me.

David, M.   I'm Just a Lucky So-and-So.

Fried, E.   Chain Mail.

Gaskill, C.   I Can't Believe That You're in Love with Me.

Gogarty.   Good Luck.

Googe.   Of Money.

Green, A.   Lucky to Be Me.

Heine, H.   Good Luck and Bad.

Herrick.   Coming of Good Luck, The.

Hewitt, J.   Local Poet, A.

Hughes, L.   Bad Luck Card.

Issa.   In my hidden house.

What good luck!

Komunyakaa, Y.   Thanks.

Lewis, J.   Holding the Holy Card.

Loesser.   Luck, Be a Lady.

Martin, H.   Ev'ry Time.

McDonald, C.   Nightfishing.

Meddemmen, J. G.   L.R.D.G.

Merrill, B.   People.

Merwin.   To Luck.

Milán, E.   Eficaz la pata de conejo, el no estar.

Rabbit-foot effectiveness, nonentity of.

Phillips, C.   Luck.

Pollarolo, G.   They All Think.

Pulido, A.   Mujer, Una / se persigna.

Woman, A / makes the sign of the cross.

Razaf, A.   You're Lucky to Me.

Rossetti, C.   Queen of Hearts, The.

Sakaki.   If you have time to chatter.

Shepherd, R.   Motive.

Sosnora.   Where are our horses.

Stein, G.   Much Later.

Stern, G.   Dear waves, what will you do for me this year?

Lucky Life.

Straus, M.   Luck.

Taylor, H.   Hayfork, The.

Turk, R.   Ain't That the Way It Goes?

Unknown.   Brush the dark bangs on my forehead aside, kiss my beauty mark.

Wong, J.   Good Luck Gold.

Wyatt.   He is not de[a]d that sometime [*or* somtyme] hath a fall.

See also **Chance; Fate; Fortune**

Lucknow, India

Whittier.   Pipes at Lucknow, The.

Lucretius

Leonard, W.   That once the gentle mind of my dead wife.

Luddites

Harrison, T.   On Not Being Milton.

Lullabies

Auden.   Lullaby: "Lay your sleeping head, my love."

Barber, D.   Nocturne.

Blake, W.   Cradle Song, A: "Sweet dreams form a shade."

Breytenbach.   Lullaby.

Causley.   Mary's Song.

Cox, P.   Mouse's Lullaby, The.

Dekker, T. *et al.*   Golden Slumbers.

Dubin, A.   Lullaby of Broadway.

Field, E.   Wynken, Blynken, and Nod.

Fordham.   Serenade: "Sleep, love sleep."

Gascoigne.   Lullaby [*or* Lullabie] of a Lover, The.

Goldbarth.   Sciences Sing a Lullabye, The.

Herrick.   Upon a Child.

Hood, T.   Serenade, A (Fragment): "Lullaby, O, lullaby!"

Jacobsen, J.   Primer, The.

Kurtz.   Spanish Lullaby.

Lee, M.   Child, You New Man.

McGinn, M.   Coorie Doon.

Mistral, G.   Night.

Mother Goose.   Bye, baby bunting.

Hush-a-bye, baby, on the tree-top.

Ni Dhomhnaill.   Shannon Estuary 1988.

Peacock, M.   Lullaby: "Big as a down duvet the night."

Prelutsky.   Mother Goblin's Lullaby.

Springer, E.   Freedom Child—Tilla's Lullaby.

Teitelboim, Z.   War Lullaby.

Tennyson, A.   Sweet and Low.

Unknown.   Lullabies, 2:174.

Lullaby of Donald Gorm, by his Nurse.

Lullaby: "On the moon's round cay."

Lullaby: "Someone would like to have you for her child."

Sleep-song.

Virgin's Lullaby, The.

Vazirani, R.   Lullaby: "I would not sing you to sleep."

Verstegan [or Verstegen]. Lullaby: "Upon my lap my sovereign sits."
Vietnamese Oral Tradition. Lullaby: "Little one, go to sleep. Sleep soundly."
Weiss, G. Lullaby of Birdland.

Lumumba, Patrice
Gelman. Epochs.
Patterson, R. Lumumba Blues.

Lunch
Bachner. Little Mouse, The.
Basho. Farmer's roadside, The.
Berrigan, T. Waterloo Sunset.
Bogen, L. I Eat Lunch with a Schizophrenic.
Burris. On Living with a Fat Woman in Heaven.
Cadwallender, K. Baz and the Freedom of the Press.
Charach, R. Question of Vitamins, A.
Ginsberg, A. Bricklayer's Lunch Hour, The.
Irwin, M. Woolworth's.
Košek, M. Little Mouse, The.
Leonidov, Rumen. Mouths of the people eating their lunch, The.
Löwy, H. Little Mouse, The.
Nye, N. Lunch in Nablus City Park.
O'Hara, F. Step Away from Them, A.
Padgett, R. Waterloo Sunset.
Sondheim. Ladies Who Lunch, The.

Lungs
Bush, D. Pneumoconiosis.
Norgate, S. Water on the Moon.
Yi Yŏnju. Our Old Home.

Lungworms
Fuller, R. Autobiography of a Lungworm.

Lust
Addaeus. When you meet a young boy, be direct.
Antipater of Sidon. This is Anacreon's grave. Here lie.
Archpoet. Never yet could I endure.
Auden. Love Feast, The.
Mad to be had, to be felt and smelled. My lips. Minnelied.
Automedon. Turkish. Belly-dancer. Sexy tricks.
Baker, K. Texas Cowboy.
Baraka, I. Like Rousseau.
New World, The.
Barnstone, T. *et al.* Trying to Sleep on My Father's Couch and Staring at the Fractured Plaster, I Recall.
Barot, R. Portishead Suite.
Baudelaire. Sed non satiata.
Behn, A. To Alexis in Answer to His Poem Against Fruition. Ode.
Belli, C. Down with the Money-Exchange.
Benn. Subway Train.
Betjeman. Late-Flowering Lust.
Birney. From the Hazel Bough.
Blake, W. Visions of the Daughters of Albion.
Boswell, M. Girls of the Rodeo.
Brownjohn. Looking at Her.
Brutus. Simple lust is all my woe, A.
Cain, Justin. My Required Tool.
Cavafy. Comes to Rest.
Chapman, G. Of her removed and soul-infused regard.
Cook, C. 8 O'Clock Defeat, Approximately.
Cope, J. Copula.
Cott, J. Natural Functions.
Crowley, A. Ballad of Passive Paederasty, A. Dedicace.
Go into the Highways and Hedges, And Compel Them to Come In.
Cummings, E. E. God pity me whom (god distinctly has).
Desportes. Conquest [or His Lady's Might].
DeSylva, B. G. Do It Again.
Dickinson, E. Wild Nights—Wild Nights!
Drayton. To His Coy Love, A Canzonet.
Drummond, W. For a Lady's Summons of Non-Entry.
Dubie. Obscure, The.
Dunn, S. Cohabiting.
Eggleton. Bouquet of Dead Flowers.
Emanuel, L. Of Your Father's Indiscretions and

the Train to California.
Outside Room Six.
Etherege. Song: "If she be not as kind as fair."
Feaver. River God, the.
Fisher, J. Six Part Lust Story.
France, L. In Kind.
New York Spring.
García Lorca. Unfaithful Wife, The.
Garnett, R. Dealing Scraps.
Georgiou, E. Intimate Mixture.
Talkin' Trash.
Gloeggler, T. Foreplay.
Goethe. Diary, The.
Goff, C. I Feel Unattractive during Mating Season.
Goodman, M. New Comers.
Graham, W. Letter VI.
Graves, R. Blue-Fly, The.
Down, Wanton, Down!
Gregg. Precision, The.
Griffin, P. To His Importunate Mistress.
Hatton, R. Epithalamium: "Hymen hath together tied."
Herrick. Vine, The.
Vision, The ("Sitting alone (as one forsook).").
Holan. Meeting in a Lift.
Holway, J. Throbbings.
Horace. Ode 2.8: "If for all the promises you regard so lightly."
Housman. When I watch the living meet.
Huang T'ing-chien. Tune: "A Thousand Autumns".
Ibn Quzman, A. My life is spent in dissipation and wantonness!
Iskrenko. Sex—A Five-Minute Briefing.
James, C. Bring Me the Sweat of Gabriela Sabatini.
Jennings, E. Thinking of Love.
Jernigan, Marla. Past Qualm of Hours.
Johnson, L. Dark Angel, The.
Jonson, B. On Groin.
Katrovas. Doggerel for the Great Czech Phallometer.
Kaufman, S. Emperor of China, The.
Komunyakaa, Y. Seven Deadly Sins.
Kurt, K. GYN-astics.
Levertov. Mutes, The.
Loy. Love Songs to Joannes.
MacNeice. Libertine, The.
Manrique, J. Tarzan.
Marlowe. "O Hero, Hero!" thus he cried full oft.
Martial. Breath of balm from foreign branches pressed, The.
Let every prudish reader use his feet.
My taste in women, Flaccus? Give me one.
Out of the house or be the wife I want.
Meleager. Epigram: "At 12 o'clock in the afternoon."
Melville, H. After the Pleasure Party [Lines Traced under an Image of Amor Threatening].
Michelangelo Buonarroti. Like dry wood in a burning fire.
Miles, S. Hares, The.
Millay, E. I too beneath your moon, almighty Sex.
Miller, V. Dirge in Jazz Time.
Milova, T. Tomato.
Murphy, Jack E. I Dreamt of Lasca.
Myles, E. Sleepless.
Nelson, M. Balance.
Norris, K. New Year's Eve in Bismarck, North Dakota.
Norse. I Would Not Recommend Love.
O'Hara, F. Poem: "I don't know as I get what D.H. Lawrence is driving at."
Olds, S. Greed and Aggression.
Sex without Love.
Orton, B. Love Poem.
Ovid. Elegy 1.5: "In summer's heat[e] and mid-time of the day."
Parker, D. Little Old Lady in Lavender Silk, The.
Pearlberg, G. G. Dog Star.
Sailor.
Penna. Found—my little angel.

Petronius Arbiter. Coition's brief, a nasty cheat.
Doing, a filthy pleasure is, and short.
Piercy. Moonburn.
Pitter. But for Lust.
Popova, O. Curve of your lips, The.
Porter, P. Now it's in all the novels, what's pornography to do?
Ramanujan. Pleasure.
Ramsdell, H. Moveable Figures.
Rees, Elizabeth. Rockstar Poet.
Rich, A. Two Songs.
Rimbaud, A. Our Assholes Are Different.
Robinson, E. John Evereldown.
Rochester, J. Ramble in St. James's Park, A.
Romond, E. Lady Macbeth, Afterward.
Rosenberg, L. Married Love.
Sadi [or Saadi or Sa'di]. O I repented, wore my pious cloak.
San Juan. End of the Affair, The.
Sanchez, S. Poem for My Father, A.
Sappho. Equal to the Gods.
What country woman bewitches your mind.
Senryū, K. Another letter?
There'll soon be.
Shakespeare, W. Sonnet 129: "Expense [or Expence] of spirit in a waste of shame, The [or Th']."
Sonnet 151: "Love is too young to know what conscience is."
Shepherd, R. Eros in His Striped Blue Shirt.
That Man.
Sidney. Fourth Song: "Only joy, now here you are."
Simpson, L. Summer Storm.
Southerne, T. Song: "Pursuing beauty, men descry."
Spenser, E. And in the midst of all, a fountaine stood.
Stallworthy, J. Source, The.
Stevenson, A. Sous-Entendu.
Strato [or Straton]. To start with, grapple your opponent 'round.
Twelve-year-old looks fetching in his prime, A.
Suckling, S. Upon My Lady Carlisle's Walking in Hampton Court Garden.
Swinburne. Aholibah.
Swirszczynska [or Swir]. Bitch, A.
Sylvester, J. Arrowhead Christian Center and No-Smoking Luncheonette.
Taylor, J. Epigram: "Lusty wench as nimble as an eel, A."
Teitelboim, D. Men.
Unknown. Midnight already and you are still not here.
Nine Times a Night.
Oh springtime of unquenched desires.
Verlaine. Balanide 2.
He's an awkward bedfellow and I love to keep.
Mille e tre.
Villiers. Cabin-Boy, The.
Volkman. May: "In May's gaud gown and ruby reckoning."
Walsh, W. *et al.* Imperfect Enjoyment, The.
Waniek. Balance.
Webb, P. Tall Tale, A; or, A Moral Song.
Whitman, W. I Am He That Aches with Love.
Native Moments.
Spontaneous Me.
Wilbur, R. Loves of the Puppets.
Williams, W. For What It's Worth.
Wither. Epigram: "Women, as some men say, unconstant be."
Wyatt. So unwarely was never no man caught [or cawght].

See also **Erotic Love; Sex**

Lutes
Al-Harizi. Lute, The.
Buson. Spring passing.
Campion, T. When to Her Lute Corinna [or Corrina] Sings.
Drummond, W. To His Lute.
Ibn Arfa' Ra'suh. Singing Lute, The.
Landon. Sappho's Song.
Li Ho. Magic Strings.
Li Shang-yin. Patterned Lute, The.
Pao Ling-hui. In the Key of Farewell.

Segalen. Faithful Betrayal.
Unknown. Oh lute that I would like to see demolished!
Wyatt. Blame Not My Lute.
  My Lute, Awake!

Luther, Martin
Buchanan, G. Pope from penance purgatorial, The.
Lahey, Joy. .22.
Melville, H. Epilogue: "If Luther's day expand to Darwin's year."
Steele, T. Wartburg, 1521–22, The.

Lynching
Allan, L. Strange Fruit.
Brown, S. He Was a Man.
Césaire, A. Lynch 1.
Cutler, Y. Neckst.
Derricotte. Note on my Son's Face, A.
Dunbar, P. Haunted Oak, The.
Emanuel, J. Emmett Till.
Estess. Mack Charles Parker Lynching, The.
Graham, R. Lynching for Skip James, A.
Hamer. Lesson.
Harjo, J. Strange Fruit.
Hayden, R. Night, Death, Mississippi.
Hughes, L. Bitter River, The.
  Blue Bayou.
  Silhouette.
  Song for a Dark Girl.
Lee, M. Negro on the Subway.
Lorde. Afterimages.
McKay, C. Lynching, The.
Moorer. Eutawville Lynching, The.
  Lynching.
  Retribution.
Moss, T. Lynching, The.
Murray, P. For Mack C. Parker.
Newman, R. Salem, Indiana, 1983.
Pratt, M. Red String.
Ridge, L. Morning Ride.
Rontsh, Y. Done a Good Job.
St. John, P. Lynching and Burning.
Skeeter. Western Trail Cook, 1880.
Tate, A. Swimmers, The.
Toomer. Portrait in Georgia.
Touré, A. Frontier of Rage, The.
Wright, R. Between the World and Me.

Lynx
Heyen. Fur.
Unknown. Magic Song.

Lyonnesse, Cornwall
Hardy, T. When I Set Out for Lyonnesse.

Lysergic Acid (LSD)
Ginsberg, A. Wales Visitation.
Tada. Universe of the Rose.

M

Macbeth
Holub. Teaching About Disease.
Lomax, M. Gruoch.
MacLeod, A. Shakespeare No More.
Upton, L. Ditch, The.

Macbeth, Lady
Romond, E. Lady Macbeth, Afterward.

Machiavelli, Niccolò
Sansom, A. Prince.

Machines
Ammons. Needs.
"Antler.". Machines waited for me, The.
Ap Hywel, Elin. Thing.
Benét, S. Nightmare Number Three.
Boruch. Simple Machines.
Brecht, B. General, your tank is a powerful machine.
Collins, B. Centrifuge, The.
Donaghy, M. Machines.
Eberhart, R. There are many intricate pieces of workmanship.
Frost, R. Egg and the Machine, The.
Harryman. Knowledge ("Knowledge was being processed. It was in the argument machine.").
Hayzler, K. Machine, The.

Isfoel. Tractor, The.
Jones, Nesta Wyn. Scream!
Kenney. Sawmill.
Kim Sŭnghŭi. Floating Metonymy 2.
Kyger. It's been a long time.
Loerke, Oskar (1884–1941). Envoi: "Must it be so? Should foreignness begin."
Mathews, H. Ring, The.
McOrlan. Weighing-machine, The.
Moore, M. To a Steam Roller.
Mueller, I. Night Shift at the Fruit Cannery.
O'Donoghue, M. She-Machines, The.
Oppen. Image of the Engine.
Pinsky. Haunted Ruin, The.
Rapoport, A. Strike.
Reed, H. Naming of Parts.
Snyder, G. Removing the Plate of the Pump on the Hydraulic System of the Backhoe.
Stein, G. Long Dress, A.
Tomlinson, C. Crane, The.
Untermeyer, L. Portrait of a Machine.
Voss, F. Termination.
Voznesensky [*or* Voznesenskii]. Beatnik's Monologue, The.
Wellman, M. All the way clear to Aliquippa.
Wilcox, E. Engine, The.
Wordsworth, W. Steamboats, Viaducts, and Railways.
Young, D. Four About Heavy Machinery.

Machismo
Norse. I'm Not a Man.
White, H. Men There Were Then, The.

MacLeish, Archibald
Sandburg, C. On a Flimmering Floom You Shall Ride.

MacNeice, Louis
Auden. Cave of Making, The.
MacNeice. Autobiography.
Mahon. In Carrowdore Churchyard.
Muldoon, P. Wystan.

Mad Song (genre)
Carroll, L. Mad Gardener's Song, The.
De la Mare. Song of the Mad Prince, The.
Herrick. Mad Maid's Song, The.
Unknown. Tom o' Bedlam's Song.

Madness
Anacreon. Dice of Love are, The.
Antin. List of the Delusions of the Insane / What They Are Afraid Of, A.
Anwar, C. At the Mosque.
Atwood. Progressive Insanities of a Pioneer.
Baraka, I. Preface to a Twenty Volume Suicide Note.
Berry, W. Mad Farmer Revolution, The.
  Meditation in the Spring Rain.
Blake, W. Mad Song.
  To Flaxman.
Brass. I Have This Vision of Madness.
Breeze. Riddym Ravings (The Mad Woman's Poem).
Bryan, M. Here, said my guide.
Buddy. Callin Buddy / Bolden.
Bukowski. Drooling Madness at St. Liz.
Butler, C. E. Letter to the Survivors.
Carkesse. His Rule of Behaviour: If You Are Civil, I Am Sober.
  On the Doctors' Telling Him that till He Left off Making Verses He Was Not Fit to be Discharged.
Carroll, L. Mad Gardener's Song, The.
Carson, C. Asylum.
Chasin. Getting the News.
Chen Zi'ang. Just now in wild, free mood I yearn.
Clare, J. I Am.
Colonna, S. He spins about (laughing) then shows.
Constantine, D. New Year Behind the Asylum.
Cook, F. Becalmed in the Tropics.
Crapsey. Madness.
De la Mare. Motley.
Dickinson, E. First Day's Night had come, The.
  I think I was enchanted.
  Much Madness is divinest Sense.
DiPalma. Pink Maniac, A.

Dobyns. Tenderly.
Donaldson, W. You're Driving Me Crazy (What Did I Do?).
Dowson. To One in Bedlam.
Drayton. As other men, so I myself do muse.
Duncan, R. In Blood's Domaine.
Eady. My Mother, If She Had Won Free Dance Lessons.
Engvick, W. Crazy in the Heart.
Fermini, I. You I know is losing you, The.
Fortini. Poetry of Roses, The.
Ginsberg, A. Howl.
Guest, B. Sassafras.
Hadewijch. Madness of Love, The.
Hall, L. Ophelia's Rant before She's Heavy with Drink.
Herrick. Mad Maid's Song, The.
Hicok. Whither Thou Goest.
Hill, G. Mad are predators, The. Too often lately they harbour.
Hoccleve [*or* Occleve]. Hoccleve Remembers His Madness.
Howard, R. Nikolaus Mardruz to his Master Ferdinand, Count of Tyrol, 1565.
Hwang Jiwoo. Mirror 2.
Irving, M. Marching Still.
Jeffers, R. Cassandra.
Johnson, L. Five Nights of Bleeding.
Johnson, T. Until He Comes.
Jones, P. Song: "I have so little sorrow."
Justice, D. Counting the Mad.
  On a Painting by Patient B of the Independence State Hospital for the Insane.
Kaufman, B. Would You Wear My Eyes?
Kavanagh, P. Come Dance with Kitty Stobling.
Kenyon, J. Travel: After a Death.
Kunitz, S. Reflection by a Mailbox.
Lewis, S. Five Foot Two, Eyes of Blue (Has Anybody Seen My girl?).
Livingston, M. Why?
Mahon. As It Should Be.
Martial. Nasica raped the doctor's pretty lad.
McCarthy, Lee. Running Loose around the Castle.
McDonald, N. Hatters, The.
Melville, H. Berg, The.
Merry. Madness.
Mew. Ken.
Mikha'il, M. Crazy Satan.
Millay, E. Siege.
Mirabai [*or* Mira Bai]. O friends, I am mad.
  Song of the flute, O sister, is madness, The.
Ni Tsan. Inscribed on a Painting by Myself.
Nichol. Monotones.
O'Lahsen, M. Dead Erect, The.
Opie. To a Maniac.
Owen, W. Mental Cases.
Padgett, R. First Drift.
Parra, N. Pilgrim, The.
Poe. Conqueror Worm, The.
Pogson, P. In Dreams.
Purdy, A. Madwoman on the Train, The.
Roethke. In a Dark Time.
Rukeyser, M. Rational Man.
Russell, B. Crazy She Calls Me.
St. John, D. Dolls.
  Iris.
Scalise, G. There have never been men crazier than these.
Seneca. Medea's Frenzy.
Sexton. Noon Walk on the Asylum Lawn.
Shakespeare, W. Sonnet 147: "My love is as a fe[a]ver, longing still."
Shange. Elegance in the Extreme.
Shapcott, J. Mad Cow Tries to Write the Good Poem, The.
Shin Kyŏngnim. Legend.
Sitwell, D. Madwoman in the Park, The.
Smith, C. On Being Cautioned against Walking on an Headland Overlooking the Sea, Because It Was Frequented by a Lunatic.
  Supposed To Be Written by Werter.
Stein, G. White Hunter, A.
Stickney, T. Age in Youth.
  Pity.
Strong, L. Mad Woman of Punnet's Town, The.

Symons, A. Nerves.
Taylor, A. Maniac's Song, The.
Tennant, E. Mad Soldier, The.
Tighe. Wine, I Say! I'll Drink to Madness!
Tu Fu [or Du Fu]. Madman, The.
Tucker, M. Crazed.
Turner, F. 110 Degrees in Dallas.
Unknown. Fowls [or Foweles or Fowles] in the Frith.
  Loving Mad Tom.
  Tom o' Bedlam's Song.
Vallejo. Babble.
Wang Chiu-ssu. This crazy man has escaped the world.
Weaver, A. Appaloosa, The.
Weiner, H. Little Books / 137 / Silence Mar 22 79.
  Little Books 137 Silence Mar 22 79.
Weiners. Poem for the Insane, A.
Wilbur, R. What is the opposite of nuts?
Williams, T. Beanstalk Country, The.
Williams, W. To Elsie.
Wilson, S. Mad Man.
Wylie. Nebuchadnezzar.
Yeats. Crazy Jane Talks with the Bishop.
Young, J. Five Foot Two, Eyes of Blue (Has Anybody Seen My girl?).
Youngblom, T. Ophelia Speaks.
"Zelda.". Crippled beggar who lives, The.
See also **Mental Illness**

Madonna [Singer]
Rosen, Corie. Madonna for the Damned—a 1980s Heroine.

Madonnas
Rafferty, P. In the Madonna Dell' Orto.
Varela. Madonna.

Madrid, Spain
Garlick, R. Capitals.
Hughes, L. Madrid [—1937].
Neruda. I'm Explaining a Few Things.
O'Hara, F. Madrid.
Paz. Madrid, 1937, / in the Plaza del Angel the women.

Magazines
Aiken, J. Do It Yourself.
Cadwallender, K. Baz and the Freedom of the Press.
Gilbert, S. Ladies' Home Journal, The.
Gioia. My Confessional Sestina.
Herd. Gia.
Jackson, R. One More Once.
Kim Suyŏng. Journal *Encounter*, The.
Wendt. Lady on the Cover of *Family Circle*, The.
Wilbur, R. Playboy.
See also **Journalism and Journalists; Newspapers**

Maggots
al-Sa'igh, Y. Thread.
Chŏng Hwajin. Dance: "Billions of maggots are being sucked into a whirlpool."
Komunyakaa, Y. Ode to the Maggot.

Magi
Baranczak, S. Three Magi, The.
Davis, D. Christmas Poem, A.
Dickey, J. Magus, The.
Eliot, T. S. Journey of the Magi.
  Matthew 2:1–12; Now when Jesus was born.
Fiskin. Magi, The.
Glück, L. Magi, The.
Godolphin. Hymn: "Lord, when the wise men came from far[r]."
Guthrie, R. Magi, The.
Hawker. Mystic Magi, The.
Heine, H. Wise Men Ask the Children the Way, The.
Hopkins, J. We Three Kings of Orient Are.
Kunitz, S. He.
Longfellow, H. Three Kings, The.
Merwin. Carol of the Three Kings.
Pilling. Adoration of the Magi, The.
Plath. Magi.
Ralegh, S. On the Card[e]s, and Dice.
Rilke. Three Holy Kings, The.
Tsvetayeva [or Tsvetaeva]. Bethlehem.
Wanley. Royal[l] Presents.

Williams, C. Kings Came Riding.
Williams, W. Adoration of the Kings, The. Gift, The.
Yeats. Magi, The.

Magic
Ashbery, J. Of the Light.
Baldwin, Sandy. Heralds of the hurricane.
Baraka, I. Ka 'Ba.
Cahn, S. It's Magic.
Cherokee Oral Tradition. Formula to Secure Love.
Cooley, N. Mary Warren's Sampler.
  Mother: Dorcas Good, The.
Daumal. Poetry and Thought.
Degentesh. 5-Year-Old Girls Encountered.
Dickinson, E. I think I was enchanted.
Eskimo Oral Tradition. Magic Words.
Evasco, M. Dancing a Spell.
Forman, R. We Are the Young Magicians.
Frost, R. Marriage: "First, it was the common magic."
Gibson, W. Music Stole In.
Harburg. We're Off to See the Wizard (The Wonderful Wizard of Oz).
Henderson-Holmes. Goodhousekeeping #17.
Hernandez, F. Autograph.
Holub. Žito the Magician.
Huidobro. Sailor.
Hutchinson, P. Bright after Dark.
Jacobs, H. It is not Just.
Jenkins, L. Walking through a Wall.
Keats. Belle Dame sans Merci, La [A Ballad].
Khosravani. There are four kinds of men who'll get no fee from me.
Leggott, M. Omphalos.
Li Ho. Song of the Magic Strings.
Li Shang-yin. Ch'ang-O.
Lumsden, R. Vanishing.
Luschei, G. Magic: "You went by my house."
Mandel, E. Houdini.
McElroy, C. This Is the Poem I Never Meant to Write.
Mercer, J. That Old Black Magic.
Miliauskaite. In the Damp Places.
Muir, E. Merlin.
Narautjarri, S. Witch Doctor's Magic Flight, The.
Nelson, M. 56 Westervelt.
Pastior, O. Abracadabra.
Pérez Estrada, R. My Uncle the Levitator.
Raine, K. Spell of Creation.
Reed, I. Black Cock, The.
Rowlands, D. Sawing His Wife in Half.
Shakespeare, W. Magic.
Silva, C. Magical Devices.
Sleigh. Lamentation on Ur.
Spell Spoken by Suppliant to Helios for Protection.
Stanton, M. Conjurer, The.
Tibullus. Fill up my glass again! The anodyne.
Unknown. First Nowell, The.
  Imploration for Clear Weather.
  Incantation Songs of the Klamath Lake People.
  Incantations of Modoc Conjurers.
  Magic Formula.
  Magic Song.
  Magic Words.
  Medicine Songs.
  Sixth Song of the Holy Young Men.
  Spell, A.
  Spell against Predatory Animals.
  Spell against Twisting an Ankle.
  Wizard's Chant, The.
Waldrop, K. Chances of Magic, The.
Wickham. Cherry-Blossom Wand, The.
Wohlfeld. That Which Is Fugitive, That Which Is Medicinally Sweet or Alterable to Gold, That Which Is Substantiated by Unscientific Means.
Ziedonis. At Maruža's.

Magnetism
Benedetti, M. Magnet, The.
Dooley, M. Explaining Magnetism.
O'Reilly, C. Augury.

Magnolias
Brown, L. Magnolia.

Coffman. Likely.
DeSylva, B. G. Magnolia.
Henderson, R. Magnolia.
Hovanessian, D. On Commonwealth Avenue and Brattle Street.
Humphrey, D. April in Houston.
Li Ch'ing-chao. To the Tune: Magnolia Blossoms.
Pei Di. Bank of the Magnolias, The.
Ruark. Hybrid Magnolias in Late April.
Varon, Lee. Pink magnolias, the punishment.
Wang Wei. Bank of the Magnolias, The.
Wicks, S. Moderato.
Williams, S. Summer mornings we.

Magpies
Glover, D. Magpies, The.
Grünbein, D. Alba.
Hanzlicek, C. On the Road Home.
Parker, A. Magpie.
Tranströmer. Black-and-white magpie.
Unknown. Magpies.
  Tune: Magpie on the Branch.
Vicinelli. I Met the Thieving Miss Magpie.
Wilson, T. Magpies in Picardy.
Winters, Y. Hunter, The.

Magritte, René
Sorby. Man without a Middle, The.

Mail and Mailmen
Ali, A. I read them, letters of lovers, the mad ones.
Barresi. Late Summer News.
Gibson, W. Advice to Travelers.
Janeczko. Mail King.
Jarrell, R. Hope ("Week is dealt out like a hand, The.").
Jenkins, L. Appointed Rounds.
Kennedy, X. Epitaph for a Postal Clerk.
Kirsch, S. Mail.
Kunitz, S. Reflection by a Mailbox.
Matthews, W. Mail Order Catalogs.
McNiece, R. Low gray skies over.
Merwin. Postcards from the Maginot Line.
Nash, O. What's in a Name? Some Letter I Always Forget.
Paterson, A. Travelling Post Office, The.
Pilling. Encounter at the Post Office Counter.
Tucker, M. Mail Has Come, The.
Unknown. Omagh Post Office Rhyme.
Venkatarao, K. Letter, A: "Mail runner carries the bag of mail, The."
Whitman, W. Orange Buds by Mail from Florida.
Williams, W. To Greet a Letter-Carrier.
See also **Letters**

Maine (state)
Armstrong, Tammy. Presque Isle, Maine.
Bailey, A. La Route Jackman.
Clampitt. Baroque Sunburst, A.
Eberhart, R. Chart Indent.
Lowell, R. Skunk Hour.
  Water.
Matthews, W. Rented House in Maine, The.
Oppen. Penobscot.
Quagliano. Edward Hopper's "Lighthouse at Two Lights".
Toomer. Merl.
Van Duyn. Moose in the Morning, Northern Maine.

Malaga, Spain
Hutchinson, P. Málaga.

Malawi
Chipasula. Love Poem for My Country, A.
Mapanje. On His Royal Blindness Paramount Chief Kwangala.

Malcolm X (Malcolm Little)
Baraka, I. Poem for Black Hearts, A.
Baraka, R. I Remember Malcolm.
Barrax. For Malcolm: After Mecca.
Brooks, G. Malcolm X.
Clifton, L. Malcolm.
Davis, T. Aria from X.
Harris, P. Next Malcolm Poem, The.
Hayden, R. El-Hajj Malik El-Shabazz.
Madhubuti. Malcolm Spoke / Who Listened?
  Possibiliites: Remembering Malcolm X.

Patterson, G.   BLS.
Walker, M.   For Malcolm X.
Warr, M.   Malcolm Is 'Bout More Than Wearing a Cap.
Whitlow.   Poem for the Children.

Mallards
Barnard, M.   Solitary, The.
Dupree, E.   At Present I Am Working as a Security Guard.

Malls
Hedin, R.   Old Liberators, The.
Scrimgeour, J.   Lines Started Outside Filene's Basement.
Watkins, William Jon.   Mall, The.
See also **Shopping Malls**

Malta
Blanco, R.   We're Not Going to Malta.
Forbes, J.   Malta.

Man, Primitive
Cuadra, P.   Birth of the Sun, The.
Day, C.   Yesterday explorers found.
Heaney, S.   Tollund Man, The.
See also **Cavemen**

Manatees
Duhamel.   Why, on a Bad Day, I Can Relate to the Manatee.

Manchuria
Hsi-tseng Tsiang.   Shantung.

Mandalay, Burma
Kipling, R.   Mandalay.

Mandela, Nelson
Al-Haidari, B.   Dialogue of the Colours.
Brook, D.   April 27, 1994.
Brooks, G.   Winnie Mandela, she.
Hoagland, E.   Fired Up!!
Holman, B.   1990.
Smith, P.   Finding His Fist.
Soyinka.   "No!" He Said.

Manet, Edouard
Atwood.   Manet's Olympia.

Mangan, James Clarence
Brownlow.   James Clarence Mangan in Trinity College Library.

Mangoes
Adisa.   Cultural Trip, A.
  Ethiopia Unda a Jamaican Mango Tree.
Bethune, L.   Today Tutu Is Beating the Same Burru As Me.
Blanco, P.   Mango's Core, The.
Cabico, R.   Mango Poem.
Damas.   No One Remembers.
Gotera.   First Mango.
Hernández Cruz.   Problems With Hurricanes.
Preston, R.   Dream of Mango.
Unknown.   Mango.
Waniek.   Canticle for Abba Jacob, A.
Warren, R.   Mango on the Mango Tree, The.

Manhattan
Berlin.   Manhattan Madness.
Byrne, Edward.   Early Evening.
Dubin, A.   She's a Latin from Manhattan.
Friedman, E.   Heading for Manhattan by Train.
Harburg.   Moon About Town.
Hochman.   Manhattan Pastures.
Jarnot, L.   Ye White Antarctic Birds.
Porter, C.   Down in the Depths.
Razaf, A.   Tan Manhattan.
Reznikoff.   [Winter Sketches V].
Schulman.   New Netherland, 1654.
See also **New York City**

Manitoba, Canada
Crawford, I.   Camp of Souls, The.
Purdy, A.   Wilderness Gothic.

Mannequins
Coon, M.   Trade Show.
Epstein, D.   Mannequins.
Light, K.   Safe-T-Man.

Manners
Barber, M.   To Novella, on Her Saying Deridingly, that a Lady of Great Merit, and Fine Address, Was Bred in the Old Way. An Epigram.
Brown, E.   Beauty and the Prince Formerly Known as Beast.

Brownjohn.   Sonnet of a Gentleman.
Carryl, G.   Embarrassing Episode of Little Miss Muffet, The.
Issa.   Leaping for the river, the frog.
Lee, P.   That's My Style.
McKay, D.   Setting the Table.
Nash, O.   Long Time No See, 'Bye Now.
Quintana.   Poem for Pancho Gonzales.
See also **Etiquette**

Man-of-War Birds
Whitman, W.   To the Man-of-War Bird.

Mantegna, Andrea
Rossetti, D.   For "An Allegorical Dance of Women" by Andrea Mantegna.

Mantis
Dalton, A.   Praying-Mantis, The.
See also **Praying Mantis**

Mantle, Mickey
Fairchild.   Body and Soul.
Heyen.   Mantle.
Miller, E.   Players.

Mao Tse-tung
Friedman, E.   Mao & Matisse.

Maple Sugar and Maple Syrup
Hall, D.   Maple Syrup.

Maple Trees
Chenette, S.   Ritual.
Espada.   All the People Who Are Now Red Trees.
Finch, P.   Acer.
Warren, R.   In Moonlight, Somewhere, They Are Singing.
Wilbur, R.   October Maples, Portland.

Maps
Alexander, E.   Ode.
Anderson, D.   Executive Geochrone.
Applewhite.   Map of Simplicities, A.
Ashbery, J.   Rivers and Mountains.
Bishop, E.   Map, The.
Blanco.   Mapas.
  Maps.
Blaser.   Suddenly.
Bogan, L.   Cartography.
Byrne, Edward.   Envying the Art of the Cartographer.
Caddy, C.   Three-Inch Reflector.
Calvino.   Eudoxia.
Carroll, L.   Fit the Second: The Bellman's Speech.
Carson, C.   Turn Again.
Couani.   Map of the World, The.
Davies, Lynn.   In the Beginning.
Deniz, G.   Map.
  Mapa.
Elfyn, Menna.   Pins.
Garlick, R.   Map Reading.
Guernsey, B.   Maps.
Guidacci.   Map of the Winter Sky, The.
Gunn, T.   Map of the City, A.
Hamer.   Because We Need Good Maps.
Hammial.   Jane.
Hardie, K.   We Change the Map.
Hendry, J.   Constant North, The.
Herd.   Missing.
Hinsey, E.   *Planisféria*, Map of the World, Lisbon, 1554.
Hogan, L.   Map.
Holmes, J.   Map of My Country.
Kumin, M.   Magellan Street, 1974.
Le Pan.   Incident, An.
Lewis, G.   Mapmaker's Song, The.
Morabito, F.   Mapas, Los / se hacen los domingos.
  Maps are drawn / on Sundays.
Morejón.   Requiem for the Left Hand.
Mullen, H.   Roadmap.
Nemerov.   Low-Level Cross-Country.
Oden.   Private Letter to Brazil, A.
Owen, L.   Chart Showing Rain, Winds, Isothermal Lines and Ocean Currents.
Pack, R.   Fathering the Map.
Rose, R.   Sestina of the Geographic Tongue.
Sorescu, M.   Map.
Soto.   Map, The.
Tranter.   Alphabet Murders, The.

Waugh, A.   Old Road Map, The.

Marathon, Battle of (490)
Graves, R.   Persian Version, The.

Marathon (race)
Cassells.   Marathon.
Ward, J.   Marathon.
Wilbur, R.   Running.

Marble
Dickey, J.   In the Marble Quarry.
Page, P.   Water and Marble.
Robeson, E.   Memorium.

Marbles
Albert-Birot.   Who is that blond child laughing as he runs after his colored marbles?

March
Bishop, E.   End of March, The.
Booth, P.   March Again.
Chamberlain, K.   Riding the Lion, Riding the Lamb.
Coatsworth.   March.
Dickinson, E.   Dear March, Come in.
Dragomoschenko.   March Elegy.
Engels, J.   In March.
Iosifova, Ekaterina.   March: "I'm going to your fair."
Lewis, J.   Garden Note II, March.
Ray, H.   March.
Reese, L.   Mid-March.
Stevens, W.   Not Ideas about the Thing but the Thing Itself.
Trommer, R.   March.
Wordsworth, W.   To My Sister.
  Written in March [While Resting on the Bridge at the Foot of Brother's Water].

Marching and Marches
Afrika, T.   Dancing in my city.
Belitt.   Spool, The.
Borawski.   Some of Us Wear Pink Triangles.
Darío, R.   Triumphal March.
Dillon, G.   Marching Song.
Eliot, T. S.   Triumphal March.
Emerson, R.   Days.
Fearing.   Old Story.
Ferlinghetti, L.   Green Street Mortuary Marching Band, The.
Gurney, I.   First March.
  Towards Lillers.
Italicus.   Memories of past struggles were expelled by fear.
Košek, M.   It All Depends on How You Look at It.
Mackintosh, E.   Cha Till Maccruimein (Departure of the 4th Camerons).
Owen, W.   Dulce et Decorum Est.
Radnóti.   Forced March.
  Forced March ("He is a fool who, collapsed on the ground, gets up and walks on.").
Ruefle.   March, The.
Rykard, R.   Whole two weeks after The Million Man March; and still, if you'd ask me, this is all I could say about it, A.
Ts'ao Ts'ao.   Song on Enduring the Cold.
Unknown.   Drill's the Thing.
  Over the Hills and Far Away, or, The Recruiting Officer.
  Refugee Song, A.
  War Lament: "Every plant is burnt yellow."
  We Will March Through the Valley.
  What grass not yellowed?
Unknown, fr. Terezin Concentration Camp.
  Closed Town, The.
Wilson, T.   Magpies in Picardy.
See also **Parades**

Marcus Aurelius
Keelan, C.   Instead of Reading Marcus Aurelius.

Margaret, Saint
Constable, H.   To Saint Margaret.

Marigolds
Buchanan, G.   To Henry Darnley, King of Scots.
Reese, L.   Fog.
Williams, W.   Negro Woman, A.
Wither.   Marigold, The.

Marijuana
Adisa.   Ethiopia Unda a Jamaican Mango Tree.
Breeze.   Playing the Messiah.

Degentesh. Seeds.
Gilmore, B. Hazing (for tony new and albee).
Hughes, L. Gauge.
Jackson, M. L. Blunts.
O'Hara, F. Poem: "Green things are flowers too."
Rakosi. Discoveries, Trade Names, Genitals, and Ancient Instruments.
Rosen, K. Of Marilyn, and Marijuana.
Savitz, M. Massive Stoner.
Twichell. Marijuana.

Mariners
Coleridge, S. I fear thee, ancient Mariner! It is an ancient Mariner.
Rime of the Ancient Mariner (1817 version).
Southey, C. Mariner's Hymn.
See also **Sailing and Sailors**

Marines
Adams, Cyd. Pete's Poem.
Aragon, F. Century, The.
D'Aguiar, F. Sound Bite.
Espada. Ezequiel.

Markets
Al-Aziz, M. Fall, The.
Brabazon. Victoria Market.
Brown, G. Hamnavoe Market.
Clarke, George Elliott. Haligonian Market Cry.
Dumas, H. Knees of a Natural Man.
Forbes, C. Potlicker Blues.
Glück, L. Baskets.
Goodison. Kenscoff.
Hall, D. Ox Cart Man.
Komunyakaa, Y. Hanoi Market, The.
Lima, M. Marketwoman of Luanda.
Maurice. Victoria Markets Recollected in Tranquility, The.
McPherson, S. Three from the Market.
Mirabai [*or* Mira Bai]. It's True I Went to the Market.
Nurkse. Letter to Ko.
Okantah. Market day.
Po Chü-i. Flower Market, The.
Reese, L. Lavender Woman, The.
Rothenberg, J. At Tsukiji Market Tokyo.
St. John, P. Pearle's Poem.
Shabtai, Aharon. Basel Square.
Shin Kyŏngnim. Market's Closing.
Simon, L. Hattie Went to Market.
Taylor, H. Bargain at Half the Price, A.
Ungria, R. Commerce and the Man.
Unknown. Cries of London, The.
Linstead Market.
Van Vliet. Old Champagne Glass.
Weatherford, C. Charleston Baskets.

Markiewicz, Constance Georgine, Countess
Yeats. In Memory of Eva Gore-Booth and Con Markievicz.

Marlborough, John Churchill, 1st Duke of
Addison, J. Poem to His Grace the Duke of Marlborough, A.
Southey, R. Battle of Blenheim, The.
Swift, J. Satirical Elegy on the Death of a Late Famous General, A.

Marley, Bob
Agard, J. For Bob Marley.
Berry, J. Sounds of a Dreamer.
Cooper, A. Stepping to da Muse/Sic.
D'Aguiar, F. Dread.
Gilbert, C. Chosen to Be Water.
Hippolyte. So Jah Sey.
Manley, R. Bob Marley's Dead.
Matthews, W. Elegy for Bob Marley, An.
McNeill, A. Bob Marley New King of the Music.
Philp, G. One Song.

Marmalade
Delmore, E. Marmalade.
Edson, R. Dr. Nigel Bruce Watson Counting.

Marriage
Adcock, F. Wife to Husband.
Ai. Anniversary, The.
Twenty-Year Marriage.
Aig-Imoukhuede. One Wife for One Man.
Akhmadulina. Bride, The.
Alexander, P. Marriage of Sorts, A.

Alvi, M. Backgrounds.
Carrying My Wife.
Fish.
Man Impregnated.
Amichai, Y. Pity, A. We Were Such a Good Invention.
Ancient Sumerian Oral Tradition. Bridegroom, dear to my heart.
Anderson, D. Nightly News, The.
Apparao, G. Gold.
Ashbery, J. Decoy.
Atwood. Habitation.
Aytoun [*or* Ayton], R. Posy, A: "Dear love, I am resolved with thee to live."
Balderston. Anne Steele.
Ball, J. And This Is So.
Barber, M. Conclusion of a Letter to the Rev. Mr. C——, The.
Barker, S. There was not loveliness nor fortune there.
Bateman, E. It's a Great Big Shame.
Beer, P. Faithful Wife, The.
Berry, W. Country of Marriage, The.
In Rain.
Marriage.
Berryman. Canto Amor.
89. Op. Posth. No. 12.
Bhattācārya, A. Get up, get up, Mountain: no more sleep for you!
Biespiel, D. White Roses.
Blake, W. Hail Matrimony, made of Love!
London: "I wander through [*or* thro'] each chartered [*or* charter'd] street."
Blamire. O Donald! Ye Are Just the Man.
Bloch, C. Discipline of Marriage, The.
Blumenthal, M. Marriage, A.
Blunden. Forefathers.
Borisova, M. It's not when they leave.
Bradstreet, A. To My Dear and Loving Husband.
Brodsky, J. Six Years Later.
Brontë, E. Day Dream, A.
Brooke, R. Sonnet Reversed.
Brooks, G. Bronzeville Mother Loiters in Mississippi, A. Meanwhile, a Mississippi Mother Burns Bacon.
Kitchenette building.
To Be in Love.
Brother Yao. Science of Forgetting, The.
Brown, L. My epithalamion.
Brown, S. Feminine Intuition.
Marriage.
Browning, E. Aurora Leigh.
Year's Spinning, A.
Browning, R. Any Wife to Any Husband.
Love in a Life.
My Last Duchess.
Bruce, D. Sonnet 4.
Buchanan, G. Song for Straphangers.
Budy. First Night in the New House.
Burns, R. John Anderson, My Jo ("John Anderson my jo, John / When we were first acquent.").
Burr, A. Lynmouth Widow, A.
Cahn, S. Love and Marriage.
Carey, H. Sally in Our Alley.
Cary, A. Bridal Veil, The.
Cary, P. Dorothy's Dower.
Shakespearian Readings.
Cassells. These Are Not Brushstrokes.
Castellanos. Parable of the Unfaithful Wife.
Cavafy. Che Fece. . .Il Gran Rifiuto.
Cave. Elegy on a Maiden Name, An.
Chapman, G. Bridal Song: "O come, soft rest of cares, come Night."
So her close beauties further blaze her fame.
Chatterton. There Lackethe Somethynge Style.
Chaucer. Alysoun.
Experience, though noon auctoritee.
Franklin's Tale, The.
Wife of Bath's Prologue, The.
Ch'en Lin. Horses at a Breach in the Great Wall.
Cherry, K. Bride of Quietness, The.
Cho Wen-chun. Poet's Wife, A.
Chudleigh. To the Ladies.

Chuo Wen-chün. Song of White Hair, A.
Cisneros, S. Rafaela Who Drinks Coconut & Papaya Juice on Tuesdays.
Clanchy, K. For a Wedding.
Clarke, G. Overheard in County Sligo.
Clifton, H. Id.
Clover, J. Map Room, The.
Coleridge, M. Marriage.
Corn. Marriage in the Nineties, A.
Corso. Marriage.
Song: "Oh, dear! Oh, me! Oh, my!"
Cox, M. Barbells of the Gods, The.
Crabbe, G. Marriage Ring, The.
Procrastination.
Crashaw. Epitaph Upon Husband and Wife Who Died and Were Buried Together, An.
Creeley. Ballad of the Despairing Husband. Marriage, A.
Naughty Boy.
Crews, J. Declaration at Forty.
Crozier, L. So This Is Love.
Cruz, S. Christmas Ballad.
Cullen, C. Wind Bloweth Where It Listeth, The.
Cummings, E. E. If there are any heavens my mother will (all by herself) have.
Cunningham, J. I married in my youth a wife. To My Wife.
Cushman, S. Make the Bed.
Dalton, Mary. Marriage, The.
Dangel. After Forty Years of Marriage, She Tries a New Recipe for Hamburger Hot Dish.
Davies, I. Angry Summer 28, The.
Davis, W. Sleep of the Insomniac, The.
Day, C. Who Drags the Fiery Artist Down?
Day, L. Reject Jell-O.
Derricotte. Promise, The.
Di Prima. Poem in Praise of My Husband (Taos).
Dickinson, E. Her sweet Weight on my Heart at Night.
Rearrange a "Wife's" affection!
She Rose to His Requirement—Dropt.
Title divine—is mine!
Wife—at Daybreak I shall be, A.
Divakaruni. Brides Come to Yuba City, The.
Domanski. Banns.
Donne. Antiquary.
Epithalamion, or Marriage Song on the Lady Elizabeth and Count Palatine Being Married on St. Valentine's Day, An.
Flea, The.
Dove, R. Beauty and the Beast.
Taking in Wash.
Drayton. By night within my bed, I roamed here and there.
Dryden, J. Why should a foolish marriage vow.
Dubin, A. Remember Me?
Dufferin and Clandeboye. Charming Woman, The.
Mother's Lament, The.
Dugan, A. Love Song: I and Thou.
Duhamel. Art.
How Much Is This Poem Going to Cost Me?
Sex with a Famous Poet.
Yes.
Duke, R. To Caelia.
Dunn, D. Land Love.
Durcan. Difficulty That Is Marriage, The.
Divorce Referendum, Ireland, 1986, The.
Edson, R. Automobile, The.
Crumble-Knees, The.
Edwards, Sonia. Empty Place, An.
Egerton, S. Emulation, The.
On My Wedding Day.
"Eliot.". Armgart, to many minds the first success.
English, W. Cashel of Munster.
"Ephelia.". To J.G. on the News of His Marriage.
Ezekiel. When the female railway clerk.
Factor, J. Scotch and Soda.
Ferlinghetti, L. In Golden Gate Park that day.
Field. I love you with my life.
So jealous of your beauty.
Fleming, R. Long Walk Home, The.
Fletcher, J. River[-]God's Song, The.

Florsheim. Jewish Singles Event, The.
Foot, E. Lord Arnold delicately sought to name.
Foppa. Woman.
Forbes, Jack. Something Nice.
Fordham. Marriage.
Foster, A. Field.
Frost, Richard. Marriage: "First, it was the common magic."
Frost, Robert. Hill Wife, The.
  Home Burial.
Fulton, A. My Second Marriage to My First Husband.
Garrett, E. Grandfather's Mint.
Gerstler. Marriage.
Ghos, G. Who said / If you took the name All-Destroyer.
Gioia. Summer Storm.
Gippius. Wedding Ring, The.
Gladding. Fisherman's Wife, The.
  Worsted Heather.
Glück, L. Edge, The.
  From the Suburbs.
  Horse.
Goldbarth. Arguing Bartusiak.
Goldsmith, O. Double Transformation, The.
Gomez, M. Chocolate Confessions.
Gotera. First Mango.
Graves, R. Henry and Mary.
  Slice of Wedding Cake, A.
Greenhalgh, C. My Funny Valentine.
  Of Love, Death and the Sea-Squirt.
Griffiths, S. Mines in Sepia Tint, The.
Groarke, V. Glasshouse, The.
Gylys, B. Family Reunion—Aunt Vern's Two Cents.
Hacker, M. Eight Days in April.
Hamby, B. Beriberi.
Harington, J. Husband to Wife.
  Wife to Husband.
Harms. Soon.
  Tomorrow, We'll Dance in America.
Harnick. (I'll Marry) the Very Next Man.
Harper, M. Elvin's Blues.
Hass, R. Forty Something.
Hatton, R. Epithalamium: "Hymen hath together tied."
Hawaiian Oral Tradition. If we can get married.
Hayes, T. Nothing.
  Ohio River Region.
Hayley. To Mrs. Hayley, On her Voyage to America. 1784.
Haynes, C. Any Wife or Husband.
Heaney, S. Summer Home.
Hearson. Nomenclaturik.
Heine, H. Young Man Loves a Maiden, A.
Hershenson. Husbands and Wives.
Hesketh. Dilemma.
Hewett, D. This Version of Love.
Hill, S. Being a Wife.
Hồ Xuân Hương. Condition of Women, The.
Hoagland, T. Candlelight.
Homer. Ulysses Reunited with Penelope.
Hope, A. Advice to Young Ladies.
Hopkins, G. Epithalamion: "Hark, hearer, hear what I do; lend a thought now, make believe."
Hovanessian, D. Mixed Marriage.
Howard, R. 1915: A Pre-Raphaelite Ending, London.
Hughes, T. Her Husband.
Hurd, B. My Son's Wedding, My Daughter's.
Ingelow. Long White Seam, The.
  Seven Time Six. Giving in Marriage.
  Seven Times Three. Love.
Ismail. Suggestion, A.
Istarú, A. Crescent moon, A.
Jabeen, M. Ideal Wife.
Jackson, R. Jamal's Lamentation.
Jacob, M. In the Hill Country.
Jarman, M. Butterflies under Persimmon.
Jarrell, R. Man Meets a Woman in the Street, A.
Jennings, E. One Flesh.
Johnson, M. F. Widow's Remarriage, The.
Jonson, B. On Giles and Joan.
Justice, D. But That Is Another Story.

Kabir. My First Marriage.
Kahn, G. Makin' Whoopee.
  Okay, Toots.
  Yes, Sir! That's My Baby.
Kalia, M. After Eight Years of Marriage.
Kasdorf. Eve's Striptease.
Kasischke. Dinner.
Katrovas. Rehab.
Kelly, B. Young Wife's Lament.
Kipling, R. Sergeant's Weddin', The.
Kizer, C. Afternoon Happiness.
Korean Oral Tradition. Chŏngsŏn Arirang.
  Wretched Married Life (Folk Song from Koch'ang).
Kuan Tao Shěng. Married Love.
Kumin, M. Long Marriage, The.
Kunitz, S. Route Six.
  Touch Me.
Lamb, A. Bird in a Gilded Cage, A.
Lamb, A. She Said / He Said.
Landon. Enchanted Island, The.
  Marriage Vow, The.
Larkin, P. Whitsun Weddings, The.
Lawrence, D. H. Wedding Morn.
  Young Wife, A.
Lear, E. Owl and the Pussy-Cat [or Pussycat], The.
Ledwidge. Wife of Llew, The.
Leithauser. Old Bachelor Brother.
Levertov. About Marriage.
  Ache of Marriage, The.
  Wedding-Ring.
Levy, A. Ballad of Religion and Marriage, A.
Lewis, M. Alonzo the Brave and the Fair Imogine.
Lewis, S. I'm Sitting on Top of the World.
Li Po. Ballad of Long Bank, The.
  Ch'ang-Kan Village Song.
  River Merchant's Wife, The; A Letter.
  Song of Ch'ang-kan.
Lihn. Memories of Marriage.
Linden, M. Marriage Vow.
Lindsay, L. Auld Robin Gray.
Liu Chi-hsün. Lament.
Loesser. Adelaide's Lament.
  Make a Miracle.
Logghe. Mixed Marriage.
  Something Like Marriage.
Lowell, A. Decade, [A].
Lowell, R. Flaw, The.
  Man And Wife.
  To Speak of Woe That Is in Marriage.
Loy. Effectual Marriage, The.
M–rt–n. Humble Wish, The.
MacDiarmid, H. O Wha's the Bride?
MacIntyre, S. Letters from the Concertina File 1939–1940.
MacSweeney. Ode Long Kesh.
Madhubuti. Union of Two, The.
Magrelli. Side by side after the meal.
Makuck. Story of Sound.
Marston, P. Speechless: Upon the Marriage of Two Deaf and Dumb Persons.
Martial. Bearded Callistratus wedded rugged Afer.
  For rank, descent and title famed.
  Out of the house or be the wife I want.
Martos. Casti Connubi.
Masters, E. Margaret Fuller Slack.
  Margaret Fuller Slack.
Mathews, A. Spectrum.
  Two Months Married.
Matthews, W. Good Company.
McCarthy, T. Toast.
McClanahan, R. Burial: "Like a sister who borrows."
McFadden, R. Epithalamium: "So you are married, girl. It makes me sad."
McGinley. Midcentury Love Letter.
McGough, R. 40— Love.
McKinney, I. Visiting My Gravesite: Talbott Churchyard, West Virginia.
Mei Sheng. Beautiful Toilet, The.
Mei Yao Ch'en. Marrying Again.
Merrill, J. My Father's Irish Setters.
Merriman [or Merryman]. Unmarried Clergy,

The.
Messer, S. Marriage Proposal.
  Some women marry houses.
Metras, G. Anniversary.
Metz, R. Father of the Bride.
Mew. Farmer's Bride, The.
Mhac an tSaoi. Finit.
Miller, E. Rebecca.
Minton, Helena. Building the Compost.
Mirikitani. Soul Food.
Momaday. Four Notions of Love and Marriage.
Montagu, L. Epistle from Mrs. Yonge to Her Husband.
  On the Death of Mrs. Bowes.
Montague, J. Herbert Street Revisited.
  Refrain.
Moolten, D. Voyeur.
Moore, M. Marriage.
Moss, H. Ménage à Trois.
Moulds, J. Late Summer Litany.
Moulsworth, M. Memorandum of Martha Moulsworth, Widow, The.
Mugo, M. G. Wife of the Husband.
Muir, E. Combat, The.
  Song: "Why should your face so please me."
Mura. Grandfather and Grandmother in Love.
Murphy, M. Villa Fidelia.
Murray, J. Epithalamium, An.
Muske, C. Epith.
Myers, J. Perfect Recall.
  Training Horses.
Naden. Love Versus Learning.
  Pessimist's Vision, The.
Nash, O. Song of Songs, The.
  Song to Be Sung by the Father of Infant Female Children.
  Word to Husbands, A.
Nasrin. Happy Marriage.
Nesbit, E. Goose-Girl, The.
Nguyễn Khuyến. To the Singing Girl Named Luu.
Niedecker. I married.
  Young girl to marry.
Nilsson, H. We Are Easily Reduced.
Norton, C. Laura was lightsome, gay, and free from guile.
O'Hehir, D. Questions and Answers.
Olds, S. I Go Back to May 1937.
  Wedding Vow, The.
Ormond. In September.
Ostriker. In the Twenty-Fifth Year of Marriage, It Goes On.
Parra, V. Attention Young Bachelors.
Parson-Nesbitt. Strange Country.
Paschen. Between the Acts.
  12 East Scott Street.
Pastan. 25th Anniversary.
Patmore, C. 'Twas When the Spousal Time of May.
Peacock, M. Wheel, The.
Peele. Song: "Whenas [or When as] the Rye [or Rie] reach to the chin."
Pelizzon, V. Clever and Poor.
Penrose, V. May—1941.
Peseroff. Hardness Scale, The.
Petersen, P. Groom of the Animal-Bride.
Pfeiffer, E. So the river—yes, the river; I have come to that at last.
Philips, K. Answer to Another Persuading a Lady to Marriage, An.
  Married State, A.
Phillips, Jayne Anne. Night in Gracie's Face.
Philpot, T. How to Live in the Elegy.
Piercy. Battle of Wills Disguised, A.
Pilkington, L. Fair and Softly goes far or, The Wary Physician.
  Wish, By a Young Lady, The.
Plath. Applicant, The.
Po Chü-i. Yin-yo laps in the reeds, my guest departs.
Pollarolo, G. At Breakfast.
  Good Marriage, A.
Porter, C. Where Is the Life That Late I Led?
Porter, P. Talking to You Afterwards.
Probyn. Kyrielle.
  Mésalliance, A.

Quinn, J. Strand of Hair, A.
Ramanujan. Love Poem for a Wife, 2.
  Routine Day Sonnet.
Ramsey, J. Tally Stick, The.
Rexroth, K. Andrée Rexroth ("Now once more
  gray mottled buckeye branches.").
Reznikoff. She sat by the window opening into
  the airshaft.
Rich, A. Marriage in the Sixties, A.
  Snapshots of a Daughter-in-Law.
Riley, P. E Questa Vita Un Lampo.
Rilke. John 2:1–12; On the third day there was
  a marriage.
  On the Marriage at Cana.
Robinson, Edwin Arlington. Eros Turannos.
Robinson, Elizabeth. Shatter.
Rogers, S. Ginevra.
Rolls. Bamboo.
Rome, H. Ring on the Finger.
Rosenberg, L. Married Love.
Rossetti, C. Bride Song.
  Cousin Kate.
  Maude Clare.
Rossetti, D. 91: Lost on Both Sides.
Rowe, E. Chapter II.
Rumens. Before these Wars.
  Double Bed.
  Marriage.
St. John, P. Ocean of the Streams of Story.
Sallah, T. No Argument Tonight.
Sandburg, C. Mag.
Sansom, A. Romance.
Sappho. Happy bridegroom, the marriage that
  you prayed for.
  There a bowl of ambrosia.
  There is no other girl, bridegroom, like this.
Savage, M. Letter to Miss E. B. on Marriage.
Scafidi, S. Prayer for a Marriage.
Schreiber, R. To Be Held.
Schulman. Psalm for an Anniversary.
Schwartz, P. Snapshots of the Chameleon
  Woman.
Scott, S. Lochinvar.
  Proud Maisie.
Sedley. Marriage and Money.
  See! Hymen comes; how his torch blazes!
Seward. To a Young Lady, Purposing to Marry
  a Man of Immoral Character in the Hope of his
  Reformation.
Sexton, A. Man and Wife.
Sexton, M. Marriage Patois.
Shakespeare, W. Sonnet 15: "When I consider
  every thing that grows."
  Sonnet 116: "Let me not to the marriage of true
  minds."
Shelton, R. Promises.
Sherry, J. Pay Cash Only.
Sidney. Epithalamium: "Let mother Earth".
Simmons, J. After Eden.
  Honeymoon, The.
Simpson, L. Ed.
  Man Who Married Magdalene, The.
Sims. Garden Song, A.
Smith, C. To the Countess of A—. Written on
  the Anniversary of Her Marriage.
Smith, M. Springtime at Twilight.
Smith, S. He Told His Life Story to Mrs.
  Courtly.
  I Remember.
  Lady "Rogue" Singleton.
  Major Macroo.
Smukler. Marry.
Spender, S. Polar Exploration.
Spenser, E. Epithalamion: "Ye learned sisters
  which have oftentimes."
  Prothalamion.
Stafford, W. Once in the 40s.
Stephens, J. Red-haired Man's Wife, The.
Stern, G. Modern Love.
Stesichoros. Since Tyndareos.
Stevenson, A. Daughter's difficulties as a wife,
  A: Mrs Ruben Chandler to her mother in New
  Orleans.
  Marriage, The.
Stoddard, E. Wife Speaks, The.
Storace. Archaeology of Divorce, The.

Wedding Song.
Strand. Courtship.
  Marriage, The.
Strong, L. Brewer's Man, The.
Su, A. Wedding Gifts.
Su Wu. Drafted.
Swift, J. Phyllis [or Phillis] [or Progress of
  Love, The].
Swift, T. Homage To Charlotte Rampling.
Swiontkowski, G. Old Moon With Her Youth In
  Her Arms.
Synge. On an Island.
Taylor, B. Proposal.
Taylor, E. Upon Wedlock and Death of
  Children.
Tennyson, A. Lord of Burleigh, The.
  Northern Farmer: New Style.
  Ocean-Spoil Alive, O!
  Today the grave is bright for me.
Thomas, L. Souvenir of the Manassah Ball.
Thomas, R. S. Marriage, A.
Tranter. Moonshine Sonata.
Tupper, M. Marriage Market, The.
Uflyand [or Ufliand]. Now, at last, even
  Nikifor's a suitor.
Ullman. Why There Are Children.
Unknown. Bo-zhou: Like a Lonely Bark.
  Bridegroom, beloved of my heart.
  Cautiously bubbles that spring water.
  Cherished Daughter, The.
  Cruel people, who see how an old man leads me
    to his bed.
  East Gate, The.
  Fate brought me as husband a child I must raise.
  Frail, frail, lone-growing bamboo.
  Get Up and Bar the Door.
  God send euerie Preist ane wyfe.
  Good and Better.
  Good Scholars Make Bad Husbands.
  Green, green riverside grass.
  Gu-feng: The Valley Wind.
  How do you cut an ax-handle?
  Humble Petition of a Beautiful Young Lady,
    The.
  In the vale of resteles mynde.
  Inanna spoke.
  It takes a very stupid dolt.
  Kuan-kuan, the ospreys.
  Long Time Back, A.
  Newly Wed Girl, The.
  No Balls at All.
  Our Little Sister is Worried.
  Peacock Southeast Flew, A.
  Railroad Man for Me, A.
  Shady Grove.
  So Long and Still No Mate.
  Song of a Marriageable Girl.
  Southeast the Peacock Flies.
  Sukey [or Suky], you shall be my wife.
  Swallow flies away, The.
  That peachtree so frail.
  Toishan Song, A.
  Too Late for a Husband.
  Zhong-feng: Wild and Windy.
Updike. Newlyweds, The.
Valentine, J. Bride's Hours, A.
Vaughan, H. Isaac's Marriage.
Vazirani, R. Mrs. Biswas of Maryland on the
  Phone.
Verga, Angelo. My Wife's Therapist.
Vietnamese Oral Tradition. Bare Rocks and
  Stars.
  Concubine, The.
  Girl with the Binh Tien Hairdo, The.
  Impossible Tasks.
Viorst. Honeymoon is Over, The.
Waldman, A. Marriage: "Marriage marriage is
  like you say everything everything in stereo
  stereo fall fall on the bed bed at dawn dawn
  because you work work all night."
Walker, F. X. Wishbone.
Ward, E. Dialogue between a Squeamish
  Cotting Mechanic and His Sluttish Wife, in the
  Kitchen.
Webb, C. Marrying.
Weinblatt, J. Marriage Song for Many Voices.

Weingarten. Inquisition, The: A Romance.
Welish. Macbeth in Battle.
Wharton, E. Last Giustiniani, The.
White, Brenda Black. Country Boy, City Girl.
Wickham. Marriage, The.
  Meditation at Kew.
  Nervous Prostration.
  Slighted Lady, The.
Wilcox, E. Way of It, The.
Williams, M. Love and How It Becomes
  Important in Our Day to Day Lives.
  Love Poem with Toast.
Williams, W. Marriage.
Winchilsea. Letter to Daphnis, A.
  Unequal Fetters, The.
Winters, Y. Marriage, The.
Wojahn. Inside, The.
Wong, N. Ironing.
Wordsworth, W. Thorn, The.
Yang Fang. Joy of Union, The.
Yau. Domestic Bliss.
Yeats. Collarbone [or Collar-Bone] of a Hare,
  The.
Yevtushenko [or Evtushenko]. Siberian Wooing.
Yi Hyangji. Joy of Love, The.
Yi Sang. I Wed a Toy Bride.
Young, E. Love of Fame, the Universal Passion.
Young, J. I'm Sitting on Top of the World.
Zamora, D. Loyal Housewife.
Zolynas. Living with Others.
Zucker, R. Avoid.
See also **Monogamy and Monogamists;**
  Polyandry; Wedding Songs; Weddings
Mars (god)
Aeschylus. For Ares, gold-exchanger for the
  dead.
Anyte [or Anytes]. Damis erected this mound
  for his dead steadfast.
Brecht, B. God of War, The.
Chaucer. On t'other side there stood destruction
  bare.
  Temple of Mars, The.
Hadas, R. Mars and Venus.
Korinna [or Corinna]. Over you, Hermes fights.
Longley, M. Sulpicia.
Mars (planet)
Berrigan, T. Bean Spasms.
Evans, A. Martian Landscape.
Marshes
Albrecht, A. Elkhorn Slough.
Bromige. Choice.
Clarke, A. Flower-Quiet in the Rush-Strewn
  Sheiling.
Doty, M. 1. Jade.
Gregerson. Waterborne.
Johnson, E. Marshlands.
Kusano Shimpei. Birthday Party.
Lanier, S. Marshes of Glynn, The.
Niedecker. Paean to Place.
  River-marsh-drowse.
Wyrebek, M. Example, An.
Marsyas
Herbert, Z. Apollo and Marsyas.
Roberts, S. Marsyas.
Strand. When after a long silence one picks up
  the pen.
Martha's Vineyard, Massachusetts
Wright, F. Walking to Martha's Vineyard.
Martial Arts
Hudgins. Air, The.
Martins
Jenkins, M. Martins.
Martyrs
al-Sa'igh, Y. Wake Up, Yousif.
Aytoun, W. Morning dawned full darkly, The.
Bedregal. Martyrdom.
Behn, A. Thousand Martyrs I Have Made, A.
Borges. John 1:14 (1964).
Brooks, G. Music for Martyrs.
Cairns, Scott. Martyr, The.
Christine de Pisan. Alone in Martyrdom.
Citino. Ignatius, Bishop and Martyr.
Crashaw. Love, thou art absolute sole lord.
  To the Infant Martyrs.
  Upon the Infant Martyrs.

Dickinson, E. Martyr Poets—did not tell, The.
Duncan, L. Festive Tolls.
Fisher, A. *et al.* Martin Luther King.
Florit, E. Martyrdom of Saint Sebastian, The.
Fouché, F. What Did They Think They Did?
Frost, C. Consent.
Hajjaj, N. Hungry Orange, A.
Hecht, A. More Light! More Light!
Herrick. Dirge of Jephthah's Daughter, The.
Jamie, K. Mrs McKellar, Her Martyrdom.
Johnson, L. Te Martyrum Candidatus.
Kizer, C. Race Relations.
Klassen, S. Artist and Medium.
Lamb, C. Salome.
Lamb, M. Salome.
Lowell, R. Colloquy in Black Rock.
MacNeice. Springboard, The.
Martinez, D. Pain.
Milton. On the Late Massacre [*or* Massacher] in Piedmont [*or* Piemont].
Montrose. On Himself, upon Hearing What Was His Sentence.
Pelizzon, V. Late Apostasy, A.
Quarles. Of St Stephen.
Randall, B. Be He Ezra Pound, Kennedy, or King.
Rontsh, Y. Rosa Luxemburg.
Rukeyser, M. Akiba.
Sepamla. I Remember Sharpeville.
Smith, S. Sunt Leones.
Stanley, T. On S. John the Baptist.
Suckling, S. Upon Stephen Stoned.
Tagami. Tobera.
Unknown. Martyr is like lightning that glitters and is then snuffed out, A.
  On our native soil, the martyr's drops of blood.
Vaughan, H. Incarnation and Passion, The.
Villon. Ballade to End With, A.
Voznesensky [*or* Voznesenskii]. Call of the Lake, The.
Weiners. With Meaning.
Welch, L. Basic Con, The.
Wilde, L. Who Will Show Us Any Good?
Williams, W. After the Mute Centuries.
  Bibelforscher, Die.
Yaqoob, J. Resurrections of Layla Al-Attar, The.

Marvell, Andrew
De Vries, P. To His Importunate Mistress.
MacLeish. You, Andrew Marvell.
Webb, P. Marvell's Garden.

Marx, Karl
Cisneros, A. Karl Marx Died 1883 Aged 65.
Connolly, C. M is for Marx.
Harrison, T. Red Lights of Plenty, The.
Soutar. To Karl Marx.
Wayman. Wayman in Love.

Mary Magdalene
Channing. Murillo's Magdalen.
Clarke, C. Palm Leaf of Mary Magdalene.
Cofer, J. Las Magdalenas.
Coleman, James. Vipers, Flies, and Women of the Cloth.
Coleridge, H. "Multum Dilexit".
Constable, H. To Saint Mary Magdalen.
Crashaw. Saint Mary Magdalene or The Weeper.
  Weeper, The.
Elliott, E. Three Marys at Castle Howard, in 1812 and 1837, The.
Erdrich. Mary Magdalene.
Hecht, A. Man Who Married Magdalene, The.
Herbert, G. Mary [*or* Marie] Magdalene.
Hudgins. Mary Magdalene's Left Foot.
Hughes, T. Matthew 27:45–56; Now from the sixth hour there was darkness.
Jeffers, H. I am your courtier.
Kingsley, H. Magdalene at Michael's gate.
Levy, A. Magdalen.
Lewis, S. Mary Magdalen.
Mew. "Find rest in Him!" One knows the parsons' tags.
Milosz, C. Matthew 28:1–6; Now after the sabbath.
Pasternak, B. Magdalene (I).
Pastior, O. O Magdalen!

Peck, J. Monologue of the Magdalene.
Rilke. John 20:11–18; But Mary stood weeping outside the tomb.
  Mary at Peace with the Risen Lord.
  Matthew 27:57–61; When it was evening, there came a rich man.
Rossetti, W. M. Jesus Wept.
Southwell. Marie [*or* Mary] Magdalens Complaint at Christs Death.
Spofford. Magdalen.
Tsvetayeva [*or* Tsvetaeva]. Magdalene.
Mary Queen of Scots
Brodsky, J. In my declining years, in a land beyond the ocean.
  Mary, the Scots are sots in any case.
  Part of the field, A. Trumpets sound and two men enter.
  That which ripped an amazed scream.
  Will a mouth that's muttered its goodbyes.
  With a simple, truly unrebellious pen.
Elizabeth I. Doubt of Future Foes.
Field. Tragic Mary Queen of Scots, The.
Hamilton, S. Farewell to France.
Harington [*or* Harrington]. Tragicall Epigram, A.
Scobie, S. Queen Mary, She's My Friend.
Mary, the Virgin
Abercrombie. Mary and the Bramble.
Alabaster, W. To the Blessed Virgin.
Appleman, P. Mary.
  Matthew 1:18–25: Now the birth of Jesus Christ took place.
Brecht, B. Luke 2:8–20; And in that region there were shepherds.
  Mary.
Brooke, R. Mary and Gabriel.
Brooks, G. Penitent Considers Another Coming of Mary, A.
Castellanos. Nazareth.
Clifton, L. Anna Speaks of the Childhood of Mary Her Daughter.
  Astrologer Predicts at Mary's Birth, The.
  Island Mary.
  Mary.
  Mary's Dream.
Coleridge, M. Our Lady.
Constable, H. To Our Blessed Lady.
Coverdale. Song of the Virgin Mary, The.
Craig, David. In the morning, when the sun.
Crashaw. Luke 11: Blessed Be the Paps Which Thou Hast Sucked.
  Tear[e], The.
Curzon, D. Tour of Ein Kerem, A.
Dante Alighieri. Virgin Mary, daughter of your Son.
Davis, D. Christmas Poem, A.
Dickey, J. Magus, The.
Eichner, Maura. From a Woman's Life.
Glück, L. Luke 2:1–7; In those days a decree went out from Caesar Augustus.
Gryphius. To the Virgin Mary.
Herbert, G. Anagram.
Herrick. Observation ("Virgin-Mother stood at distance (there), The.").
Hill, G. Love is at odds. Your beauty has gone out.
Jammes. Five Sorrowful Mysteries, The.
Kamienska. Luke 10:38–42; Now as they went on their way.
Kipling, R. Sons of Martha, The.
L'Engle. O Simplicitas.
Levi, P. Annunciation.
Lope de Vega. At Dawn the Virgin Is Born.
  Little Carol of the Virgin, A.
  Where Are You Going, Maiden.
Miller, M. Calvary Way.
Mistral, G. Martha and Mary.
Mitchell, S. Vermeer.
Muir, E. Annunciation, The.
No Hyegyông. Song of Mary.
O'Curry, E. Litany to Our Lady.
O'Donoghue, B. Apparition, The.
Pasternak, B. Christmas Star, The.
Powell, D. A. My Lot to Spin the Purple: that the Tabernacle Should Be Made.
Richter, J. Madonna del Parto: Our Lady of

Birth-Giving.
Rilke. John 11:30–44; Now Jesus had not yet come to the village.
  Luke 1:39–56: In those days Mary arose.
  Mary's Visitation.
Robinson, E. Gift of God, The.
Rugo. Pietà: "What she holds is the unimaginable."
Sexton. Jesus Suckles.
Smith, S. Dream of Comparison, A.
Starkey, D. Annunciation, The: "Surely God thought this would be a moment."
Thomas, R. S. Mother and Child.
Unknown. As I me rod this endre day.
  Hymn to the Virgin.
  I Sing of a Maiden.
  Litany to Our Lady.
  Marie moder, wel thee be!
  Mary's Dream.
  Our Lady's Song.
  Rose That Bore Jesu, The.
  Seven Virgins, The.
  Virgin Mary, The.
Vaughan, H. Knot, The.
Verstegan [*or* Verstegen]. Lullaby: "Upon my lap my sovereign sits."
Yeats. Mother of God, The.
Zucker, R. Sacristy.
Maryland (state)
Clifton, L. Slave Cabin, Sotterly Plantation, Maryland, 1989.
Cook, E. Sot-Weed Factor, The.
Dame. On the Road to Damascus, Maryland.
Randall, J. My Maryland.
Smith, D. Cumberland Station.
Masefield, John
Muldoon, P. Wystan.
Untermeyer, L. John Masefield Relates the Story of Tom, Tom, the Piper's Son.
Masks
Adkins, G. Children in Armour.
Brecht, B. Mask of Evil, The.
Browning, E. Mask, The.
Djoko Damono, S. Mask.
Dunbar, P. We Wear the Mask.
Gibran. Madman (Prologue), The.
Gregorio, R. Clown, The.
Jackson, L. Mask, The.
Jennings, E. Fear, A.
Kikaku. Sacred night / Through masks.
Kim Ch'unsu [*or* Chun-soo]. Masks.
Komunyakaa, Y. Untitled Blues; After a Photograph by Yevgeni Yevtushenko.
Landon. Mask of Gaiety, The.
Levertov. People at Night.
Lim, S. Lost Name Woman.
Meredith, W. Two Masks Unearthed in Bulgaria.
Milán, E. Do you care to remedy the faces of the gods? Make white.
  One's alone in this: making masks.
  ¿Quieres curar las caras de los dioses? Haz máscaras.
  Uno está solo frente a esto: haciendo máscaras.
Prejsnar, Mark. Assuage Bane.
Probyn. Masquerading.
Rafferty, P. After Carnival.
Reich, A. Siren of Love, A.
Ristovic. Essential, The.
Rukeyser, M. Poem as Mask, The.
Seiferle, R. Face in the Depths of the Desert, The.
  Gift, The: "I was wrong when I compared the mask of my own face."
Senghor. Prayer to the Masks.
Shelley, P. As I lay asleep in Italy.
Spenser, E. Book 3, Canto 12.
Taylor, J. Instructions to Her Next Husband.
Thomas, D. O Make Me a Mask.
Toufic, J. Emperor's New Costume, Or the Case of the Missing Mask, The.
Unknown. Song of Ch'ŏyong.
Williams, H. Last Poem.
Woodward, G. Murderer is a Cow, The.
Zimmer. Zimmer in Grade School.

Masochism
Ginsberg, A.   Please Master.
Gwynn, R.   Iago to His Torturers.
Hernton, C.   Long Blues, The.
Volach, Y.   Tefillin.
Wunderlich, M.   Trick, The.

Mass Media
Ai.   Paparazzi, The.
Cleary, B.   New Rock n Roll, The.
Greenhalgh, C.   Night I Met Marilyn, The.
Hardy, J.   Objection Overruled.
Hattersley, G.   *On the Buses* with Dostoyevsky.
   Singing.
Herd.   I stopped the car and stepped out onto
   gravel.
   Marilyn Climbs Out of the Pool.
Hill, G.   Age of mass consent: go global with
   her.
Pomeroy, R.   Gay Love and the Movies.
Rouse, A.   Lilies of the Field.

Massachusetts (state)
Bishop, E.   In the Waiting Room.
Comer, Carrie St. George.   Shelburne Falls.
Eberhart, R.   On a Squirrel Crossing the Road in
   Autumn, in New England.
Eliot, T. S.   Cape Ann.
Emerson, R.   Concord Hymn.
Longfellow, H.   Rhyme of Sir Christopher, The.
Lowell, R.   For the Union Dead.
Nichols, Travis.   Wild is the Wind.
Plath.   Point Shirley.
Terry, L.   Bars Fight [August 28, 1746].
Tompson.   On a Fortification at Boston Begun
   by Women [American edition].
Weaver, A.   Easy Living.
Whittier.   Massachusetts to Virginia.
   Snow-Bound [or Snow-Bound] [A Winter Idyl].
Wilbur, R.   Running.

Massacre of the Innocents
Hanzlik.   Clap Your Hands for Herod.
Hartwig.   Matthew 2:16–18; Then Herod, when
   he saw.
   Who Says.
Hope, A.   Massacre of the Innocents.
Lowell, R.   Holy Innocents, The.

Massacres
Ai.   Rwanda.
Alexie.   Texas Chainsaw Massacre.
Anderson, D.   Infantry Assault.
Bird, G.   Women Fell like Beautiful Horses,
   The.
Breytenbach.   Lullaby.
Brook, D.   Poem Wrapped Around Quotation
   from Samantha Power.
Darwish, M.   I am the witness of the massacre.
   Psalm 2.
Fenton, J.   Tiananmen.
Forché.   Ourselves or Nothing.
Hugo, V.   Night of the Fourth: A Recollection,
   The.
Levertov.   Day the Audience Walked Out on
   Me, and Why, The.
Love, M.   Trying to Sleep After Studying Color
   Photos of Goma.
Mapanje.   After Wiriyamu Village Massacre by
   Portuguese.
Meinke.   Anthills.
Milton.   On the Late Massacre [or Massacher]
   in Piedmont [or Piemont].
Samawi, A.   Mountain of Dreams.
   Suns in the Night of the Massacre.
Shelley, P.   As I lay asleep in Italy.
Sherrill, S.   Katyn Forest.
Simić, G.   Sorrow of Sarajevo, The.
Tester, V.   Santa Rita Massacre, 1837.
Wojahn.   Assassination of Robert Goulet as
   Performed by Elvis Presley: Memphis, 1968,
   The.

Masts
Campbell, R.   Choosing a Mast.

Materialism
Mattawa.   Growing Up with a Sears Catalog in
   Benghazi, Libya.
McClure, M.   Song: "I Work with the shape."
Mullen, H.   Souvenir from Anywhere.

Pak Sôwôn.   Small Wooden Vessel, A.
Pomerantz, A.   Sonnet and Duet for Flapper and
   Poet.
Rohrer, M.   My Government.

Maternity
Aini, L.   Empress of Imagined Fertility, The.
Ferguson, G.   Inhaling His Hair.
Jeffers, R.   Haunted Country.
Mistral, G.   Song.
Swirszczynska [or Swir].   Maternity.

Mathematics and Mathematicians
Arensberg.   Axiom.
   Theorem.
Blanco.   Teorí de Fractales.
Chitwood, Michael.   Division.
Clover, J.   Ceriserie.
Collins, M.   Lines: "Draw a line. Write a line.
   There."
Cornish, M.   Numbers: "I like the generosity of
   numbers."
Dove, R.   Flash Cards.
Essinger, C.   You Are Right.
Grumman, Bob.   Mathemaku No. 17.
Gundy, J.   For the New York City Poet Who
   Informed Me that Few People Live This Way.
Holub.   Žito the Magician.
Kendall, M.   Pure Hypothesis, A.
Kochanowski, J.   To a Mathematician.
Kovner, A.   To Myself.
Millay, E.   Euclid Alone Has Looked on Beauty
   Bare.
Mori.   Barbie Says Math is Hard.
Norris, K.   Naming the Living God.
Paris, T.   First Proof.
Rooney-Céspedes, A.   Twice the Man.
Rosenberg, L.   Introduction to Methods of
   Mathematical Physics.
Segade, G.   Theory of Fractals.
Welish.   Wild Sleeve.
Wilson, S.   Recreational Mathematics.
See also **Arithmetic**

Matisse, Henri
Boruch.   Interior with a Violin.
Friedman, E.   Mao & Matisse.
Glen, D.   Twa Warlds.
Hannan, M.   Life Model.
Johnson, T.   Matisse, Cut Outs.
Martinez, D.   Matisse: Blue Nude, 1952.
Pilling.   You and You, In the Pink.
Sanders, E.   Cutting Prow, The.
Snodgrass.   Matisse: "The Red Studio".
Toledo, N.   Na hermila limón.

Maturity
Chubb, R.   Song of My Soul.
Clampitt.   Imago.
Clark, P.   My Life with Horses.
Dodge, M.   Taking Time to Grow.
Gilmore, B.   Revolution.
Heaney, S.   Fosterling.
Hecht, A.   To Fortuna Parvulorum.
Hill, G.   Guardians, The.
   Holy Thursday.
Hoggard, James.   Eye of the Tornado.
Jacobsen, J.   Primer, The.
Kipling, R.   If.
Lamb, C.   To Louisa M[artin], Whom I Used to
   Call "Monkey".
Lerner, A.   I'm Glad I'm Not Young Any More.
Martial.   You rocked my cradle, Charidemus,
   once.
Martinez, D.   Cultivation of Orchids, The.
McFadden, D.   12. Shantideva.
Mun Chônghui.   For the Sake of Man.
Newbolt.   Clifton Chapel.
Parker, D.   Indian Summer.
Pasolini.   Part of a Letter to the Codignola Boy.
Rudaki.   All the teeth ever I had are worn down
   and fallen out.
Shakespeare, W.   Sonnet 102: "My love is
   strengthened, though more weak in seeming."
Shelton, R.   Promises.
Shepherd, R.   White Days.
Smith, S.   To Carry the Child.
Stafford, W.   Growing Up.
Steptoe.   Coming Ashore.

Unknown.   Girl's Song, A.
Waller, E.   Budd, The.
Wordsworth, W.   My Heart Leaps Up [When I
   Behold].

Mausoleums
MacDiarmid, H.   Skeleton of the Future, The.
Segalen.   Funerary Edict.
See also **Cemeteries; Graves; Monuments; Tombs**

Maximilian (emperor of Mexico)
de Gonz´les, Merced J.   Mexico Will Be Free.

May
Barnes, W.   Shellbrook.
Basho.   Hollyhocks, The.
Breton, N.   Phillida and Coridon.
Browning, R.   Home-Thoughts, from Abroad.
Buchanan, G.   May Morning.
Buson.   May rains.
Dafydd [or David] ap Gwilym.   Duw gwyddiad
   mai da y gweddai.
De la Mare.   There Blooms No Bud in May.
Dekker, T. et al.   O, the Month of May.
Hardy, T.   Afterwards.
Hass, R.   Late Spring.
Herrick.   Corinna's Going a-Maying.
Hirshfield, J.   Rain in May.
Hovell-Thurlow.   May.
Jacobsen, J.   Hourglass.
Kinoshita Mokutarō.   Gold Leaf Brandy.
Ko Chônghûi.   Prague Spring 8.
Koehler, T.   I've Got the World on a String.
Lanier, S.   Song for "The Jacquerie".
Larkin, P.   Trees, The: "Trees are coming into
   leaf, The."
Linden, M.   May.
Lope de Vega.   May Song.
Lowell, J.   May is a pious fraud of the almanac.
MacDonald, A.   Month of plants and of honey.
Neilson, J.   May.
Patmore, C.   'Twas When the Spousal Time of
   May.
Penrose, V.   May—1941.
Pritchard, N.   Springtime.
Ray, H.   May.
   May's Invocation after a Tardy Spring.
Rossetti, C.   May: "I cannot tell you how it
   was."
Spenser, E.   May.
Synge.   Masque of May, The.
Tolson, M.   Victor Garibaldi.
Unknown.   Fisherman's Rhyme.
   May in the Green-Wood.
   Now Is the Month of Maying.
   On May-day, when the lark began to rise.
Volkman.   May: "In May's gaud gown and ruby
   reckoning."
Watson, S.   Ode in May.
West, J.   To May.
Williams, T.   May: "Mortality shrinks back—
   because."
Williams, W.   Bird Song.
   Locust Tree in Flower, The.
   Tulip Bed, The.

May Day
Ewer.   May Day, 1917.
Herrick.   May-Pole, The.
Livingstone, D.   May Day.
Unknown.   In Praise of May.

Maya
Chilam Balam.   Flight of the Itzás.
Hill, S.   Elegy for the Bee-god.

Mayflower (ship)
Morgenstern, Felicia L.   Soul Roots.

McCarthy, Joseph
Ai.   Blue Suede Shoes.
Brook, D.   Pink Diapers.
Hughes, L.   Un-American Investigators.

McPherson, James Birdseye
Melville, H.   Dirge for McPherson, A.

Meadowlarks
Hanzlicek, C.   Moment.

Meadows
Abbott, W.   Aspen Meadows.
Bergland, B.   Up Yonder in the Meadow of
   Children.
Bryant, W.   When breezes are soft and skies are

fair.
Clare, J. Mist in the Meadows.
Duncan, R. Often I Am Permitted to Return to a Meadow.
Engels, J. Meadow.
Gilbert, S. Afternoon Walk: The Sea Ranch.
Gray, A. Music in the Meadow.
Gumilyov [or Gumiliov or Gumilev]. Childhood.
Hawkey, C. *Frälein,* can you.
Herrick. To Meadows [or Meddowes].
Ingelow. Dappled sky, a world of meadows, A. Divided.
Jandl, E. Summer Song, A.
Johnson, K. Meadow, The.
Kim Sowŏl. Golden Meadow, The.
Lezama Lima. Dark Meadow Invites Me, A.
Orr, G. Meadow in Spring.
Pagis, D. Art of Reduction, The.
Roethke. Meadow Mouse, The.
Stewart, S. Meadow, The.
See also **Fields and Pastures**
Meat
Bowman, C. 1-800-HOT-RIBS.
Chase, K. Venison.
Coward. Any Part of Piggy.
Follain. Black Meat.
Harper, M. Breaded Meat, Breaded Hands.
Herrick. Grace for a Child.
Jewsbury. My heart's in the kitchen, my heart is not here.
Komunyakaa, Y. Smokehouse, The.
Levine, P. Salami.
Lux. One Meat Ball.
Masterson, R. Making Love in the Meat Locker.
Melville, H. Maldive Shark, The.
Messer, S. Rendered Dog.
Monro, H. Cat's Meat.
Sioux Oral Tradition. Give me my knife.
Unknown. I want the robes, the skins of the game animals, the meat of the game animals. Bring them to me. Let us enjoy ourselves.
Waldman, A. Skin / Meat / BONES.
Watson, C. Knickerbocker Knockabout.
Wilbur, R. Rillons, Rillettes.
Young, K. Everywhere Is out of Town.
Mechanics
Armitage, S. Very Simply Topping Up the Brake Fluid.
Burke, C. Motor Oil Queen.
Jones, R. One of the Citizens.
McIlroy, L. How to Change a Flat.
Unknown. On Rainy Days.
Medals
Gilboa, A. And My Brother Was Silent.
Medea
Flaccus, G. Book 7.
Novak, H. Letter to Medea.
Ovid. Before the Moone should cirlcewise close both hir hornes in one.
Seneca. Medea's Frenzy.
Van Walleghen. In the Chariot Drawn by Dragons.
Wakoski. Reading *Bonjour, Tristesse* at the Florence Crittenden Home for Unwed Mothers.
Webster, A. Dead is he? Yes, our stranger guest said dead.
Medical and Sickness Poetry
McCord, D. Convalescence.
Medicine
Abse. Stethoscope, The.
Akhmadulina. Chills.
Alexander, E. Aspirin.
Belloc. On Hygiene.
Bierds, L. Pasteur on the Rue Vauquelin.
Blue Cloud. To-ta Ti-om.
Browning, R. Epistle Containing the Strange Medical Experience of Karshish, the Arab Physician, An.
Campo. Towards Curing AIDS. What the Body Told.
Charach, R. Evidence on Film, The. Labour and Delivery. MRI.

Coulehan, J. Anatomy Lesson. Dynamizer and the Oscilloclast, The. Lovesickness: A Medieval Text. Rule of Thirds, The.
D'Aguiar, F. Obeah Mama Dot.
Delgado, J. Recommitted.
Di Michele, A. Solstice / Surgery.
Dyer, E. Painting the Nude.
Foy, J. Autopsy.
Giscombe, C. 1962 At the Edge of Town.
Graham-Pole, J. Pain, The. Venipuncture.
Hoagland, T. Medicine: "Black hair of my Chinese doctor, The."
Holan. During an Illness.
Holub. Distant Howling.
Homer. This said, divine Talthybius he call'd, and bad him haste.
Huang E. Pearl-teardrops roll and gather.
Hufana, A. From the Raw.
Jones, A. Tap.
Joseph, A. Chalazion.
Kolodny, S. Tsuneko—Psychiatric Medications Clinic.
Lieberman, M. Prediction.
Logau. Best Medecines, The.
Longfellow, H. Day Is Done, The.
Martinez, D. Remedios.
Matthews, W. Dire Cure.
Mei Ch'eng. Seven Stimuli.
Moolten, D. Bio 7.
Mosquera, A. Tamoxifen.
Pasternak, B. At dusk you appear, a school-girl still.
Powell, D. A. In the course of travel: strychnine every few hours. some italian art. Sleek mechanical dart: the syringe noses into the blue vein marking the target of me.
Ridler. Corneal Graft.
Riley, D. I Take Two of These Tablets Tonight and in the Morning Go on Living.
Rosario, M. Curing.
Rowe, V. MRI of a Poet's Brain. Youth.
Shafer, A. Monday Morning.
Smith, R. Halcion.
Stone, J. Gaudeamus Igitur: A Valediction. He Makes a House Call.
Straus, M. Neuroanatomy Summer. Scarlet Crown.
Su, A. Antidepressant.
Tatarunis, P. I Have Two Sons and the One I Love Best Is Robert.
Unknown. Charm of the Nine Healing Herbs. Magic Formula. Poem of Medicine Puns.
Van Peenen, H. Insulin Receptor.
Walwicz. Daredevil.
Wang Shih-chieng. Medicine.
Woods, D. Prescription.
Wright, J. Therapy.
Wunderlich, M. Simplify Your Combination Therapy.
See also **Hospitals; Illness; Nurses; Doctors**
Mediocrity
Boroditskaya, M. Sound Letter.
Ch'i-chi. Quietly Discussing My Thoughts with the Collator of Texts Ts'ui.
Ezekiel. Company I Keep, The.
Yi Kyubo. Burning My Manuscripts.
Meditation
Bailey, Peter. Practice.
Baudelaire. Owls.
Berry, W. Meditation in the Spring Rain.
Bhattācārya, K. Stay within yourself, Mind.
Bly, R. Six Winter Privacy Poems.
Brown, Fleda. Elvis Decides to Become a Monk.
Brutus. Under House Arrest.
Cedering, S. Regarding Music.
Chang Chiu-ling. I close my door and trace the transformations of nature.
Ch'en Tzu-ang. I dwell in seclusion and observe the creative process.
Ching An. On the Spot Where Shih-chia Tzu Sits in Meditation.

Cohen, L. I Have Not Lingered in European Monasteries.
Coleridge, S. Frost at Midnight [1829 version].
Coote, G. Tenzo's Song.
Crozier, A. Loopy Dupes.
Cullen, Lisa. Reasons to Meditate.
Daegam Tanyon. At Munsoo Temple.
Darío, R. Eheu!
De Vere, E. SITTING alone upon my thought, in melancholy mood.
Deniz, G. Meditar. Meditate.
Dyer, J. Grongar Hill.
Fischer, N. Sesshin Poem.
Forrester, S. Meditation hall.
Frumkin. Falling into Meditation.
Gibson, M. Strange Altars.
Hamburger, M. Garden, Wilderness.
Han-shan Te-ch'ing. Deep among ten thousand peaks I sit alone cross-legged. Through a few splinters of.
Harris, D. Meditations 1: "For the beginning and the end."
Hejinian. Beginner, The.
Heyen. Tie, The.
Hsi Chou. Early Spring at the Capital, Sent to the Honorable Kuan.
Hughes, H. At the Teahouse, 7 am. Invitation to the Cricket.
Jacob, M. Visitation.
Juana Inés de la Cruz. Oh World, Why Do You Thus Pursue Me?
Kane, J. Reasons for Loving the Harmonica.
Kerouac. Buddha. How to Meditate.
Kyger. News bulletin from Keith Lampe.
Lojowski, M. In the Cage of Doves.
Mahadevi. So long as this breath fills your nostrils.
Mookam Choinul. Living at Eunjok Hermitage.
Mukhopādhyāy, K. Is there any treasure like the Mother's name?
Muso Soseki. Among rocks and valleys. Buddha's Satori. Curtain of cloud hangs, A. Mugoku Osho's Snow Poem. Old Man Advancing. Very high this mountain. With compassionate hands.
Nag Hammadi Library. Sent from the Power.
Naong. Hyunsonja Asks for an Enlightenment Song.
Nara Singde. Tune: "Sand of Silk-Washing Brook" In Memoriam.
Nguyen, Hoa. Sitting there nearly translucent You'll end up.
No Hyegyŏng. Miscellaneous Bouquet.
Nordbrandt. Old Man in Meditation.
Padilla. Discourse on Method, The.
Paljor, N. I woke up early.
Pierpoint, K. Going Swimmingly.
Ponsot. Analogue.
Pou Kuksa. Yo Hermitage.
Price, V. Balancing Zero.
Ramke, B. Revealing Oneself to a Woman.
Reizan. Myriad differences resolved by sitting, all doors opened, The.
Rexroth, K. Empty Mirror.
Richter, H. Self in Variation, The: Scenes From Meditation.
Riley, J. Summer Seeming.
Riley, P. Another damp Sunday morning up and walk over.
Ronci, Seido R. Becoming a Buddha. Old Monks Drinking.
Rumi. Walking with Others.
St. John, D. Meditation: "Quiet now, sorrow; relax. Calm down, fear."
Scully, M. Variations.
Sekioku-Seikyo. This body won't pollute.
Sen, R. Meditate on Kali! Why be anxious? Mind, why this separation from the Mother's feet? Tell me. This time I've realized the essence. Tongue, call out.

Steele, T.   Wartburg, 1521–22, The.
Stuart, D.   Rumination.
Sumangalamata.   At last free.
Tan Taigi.   Zazen / Fat mosquitoes.
Trigilio.   Sitting, Wedding Morning.
Unknown.   Buddhist Ruminations.
Very.   Columbine, The.
Waldman, A.   Recalling Former Travels.
Wang Wei.   Passing the Temple of Teeming
   Fragrance.
   Visiting Hsiang-Chi Monastery.
Warren, R.   Fear and Trembling.
Whalen, P.   Silence in the middle of traffic.
Wild, R.   In a melancholly studdy.
Williamson, A.   Light's Reading, The.
Wordsworth, W.   Most Sweet It Is with
   Unuplifted Eyes.
Wyatt.   Prologue: "Love, to give law unto his
   subject hearts."
Xuanjing.   Meditating at midnight.

Mediterranean Sea
Daglarca.   You say / Stars.
Jacob, M.   In Honor of the Sardana and the
   Tenora.
Lawrence, D. H.   Middle of the World.
McCarthy, J.   Riviera, The.
Santayana.   Ode 5: "Of thee the Northman by
   his beachèd galley."
Tate, A.   Mediterranean, The.

Medusa
Bogan, L.   Medusa.
Clampitt.   Athena.
   Medusa.
Hayden, R.   Perseus.
Parnell, P.   Apotheosis of Medusa.
Sarton, M.   Muse as Medusa, The.
Shelley, P.   On the Medusa of Leonardo da
   Vinci in the Florentine Gallery.
Tallie, M.   Medusa.
Turner, A.   Medusa: "Ageing woman combs her
   hair, The."
Weatherly, T.   Gandhabba #5.
Wilner, E.   Her Body Is Private.
Zaturenska.   Head of Medusa.

Melancholy
al-Rahim, A.   My Heart.
Algarin.   Infections.
Bowles, W.   To the River Cherwell.
Brooks, G.   Crazy Woman, The.
Burton, R.   Authors [*or* Author's] Abstract of
   Melancholy, The.
Byrom.   My Spirit Longeth for Thee.
Cavendish, M.   Discourse of Melancholy, A.
Cervantes.   Levee: Letter to No One, The.
Coleridge, S.   Dejection: An Ode.
   Letter to Sara Hutchinson.
   This Lime-Tree Bower My Prison.
Cranch.   Pines and the Sea, The.
Darío, R.   Melancholy.
Deane, J.   On a Dark Night.
Evance, S.   To a Violet.
   To Melancholy.
   To the Clouds.
   Written at Netley Abbey.
   Written in a Ruinous Abbey.
Field.   She is Singing to Thee, *Domine!*.
Fletcher, J.   Melancholy.
Ghalib, M.   Ghazal 12.
Hays, M.   Ah! let not hope fallacious, airy, wild.
Hemans.   Indian Woman's Death-Song, The.
   Second Sight.
Herrick.   His Litany to the Holy Spirit.
Hughes, L.   Neighbor.
   Weary Blues, The.
Hwang Jiwoo.   Melancholy.
Kavanagh, P.   Wet Evening in April.
Keats.   Ode on Melancholy.
Keller, D.   Melancholy.
Lenski, H.   Day turns to evening on the lake.
Li Yü.   Tune: "Joy of Encounter".
Manrique, J.   Barcelona Days.
Middleton, T.   Melancholy.
Milton.   Il Penseroso.
Molinari.   Little Ode to Melancholy.
Montagu, L.   Receipt to Cure the Vapours, A.
Morris, M.   Valley Prince.

Neruda.   Melancholy in the Families.
   Melancholy inside Families.
Ochiai Naobumi.   Song of the Faithful Daughter
   Shiragiku.
Pao Chao.   Imitating the Old Poems.
Penna.   Life...is remembering waking up.
Radcliffe, A.   Night ("O'er the dim breast of
   ocean's wave.").
Rossetti, C.   At Home.
   If Only.
Ruefle.   Melancholiacs, The.
Russell, T.   Dear Babe, whose meaning by fond
   looks expressed.
Sargant, J. A.   How gladly would I lay my
   aching head.
Shelley, P.   Stanzas Written in Dejection, Near
   Naples [*or* —December 1818, near Naples].
Sidney.   Sonnet 99: "When far-spent night
   persuades each mortal eye."
Smith, C.   To Melancholy. Written on the Banks
   of the Arun, October 1785.
   To the South Downs.
   Written in October.
   Written on the Sea Shore.—October, 1784.
Smith, S.   Away, Melancholy.
Steiger.   Dull rattle of shutters being lowered,
   The.
Stickney, T.   Melancholy year is dead with rain,
   The.
Strand.   Philosopher's Conquest, The.
Swinburne.   Itylus.
Szécsi.   Only with Radiance.
T'ao Ch'ien [*or* T'ao Yuan-ming].   Written on
   the Ninth Day of the Ninth Month of the Year
   Yi-you.
Thomas, E.   Return, The.
Tighe.   Can I look back, and view with tranquil
   eye.
   When glowing Phoebus quits the weeping earth.
   Written at Scarborough.
Todhunter.   Song: "Bring from the craggy
   haunts of birch and pine."
Tuckerman, F.   Series 3, Sonnet 10.
Unknown.   On Melancholy.
   Summer: "She has done with silkworms and the
   fieldwork."
   Through the front gate.
   What Care I Though the World Reprove.
Vallejo.   Intensity and Height.
Vietnamese Oral Tradition.   Evening.
Wakoski.   Blue Monday.
Wang Kuo-wei.   Tune: "Sand of Silk-Washing
   Brook" ("Faded hibiscus and its leaves.").
Wordsworth, W.   I Wandered Lonely as a Cloud.
   World Is Too Much with Us, The.
Yearsley.   Soliloquy: "What folly to complain."

See also **Blues (mood); Dejection**

Melons
Adair, V. H.   Ants on the Melon.
Basho.   Coolness of melons.
   Don't imitate me.
   Melon / In morning dew.
   Wet with morning dew.
Issa.   In a dream.
   They don't notice.
Kaya Shirao.   Moonlit night / By melon flowers.
Kinsella, J.   Pig Melons.
Lau, A.   Bittermelon.
Mei Yao Ch'en.   Melon Girl.
Oswald, A.   Melon Grower, The.
Ransetsu.   All by itself.
   Melon / How well.
Tan Taigi.   In the melon-patch / Thief, fox.

Melville, Herman
Aiken, C.   Herman Melville.
Crane, H.   At Melville's Tomb.
Elmslie, K.   Japanese City.
Horan.   Prometheus.
Koch, K.   You Were Wearing.
Lopez, T.   Studies in Classic American
   Literature.
Martin, C.   Satyr, Cunnilinguent: To Herman
   Melville.
Muir, E.   Scotland 1941.
Rich, A.   Seven Skins.

Memento Mori
Buson.   Sudden chill, A / In our room my dead
   wife's.
Neruda.   Almería.
Quevedo y Villegas.   Sonnet: Death Warnings.

Mementos and Keepsakes
Alexander, E.   At the Beach.
Beatty, A.   Geography.
Bierds, L.   Memento of the Hours.
Chenette, S.   Ritual.
Curbelo.   Photograph from Berlin.
Follain.   Should the Schoolboy Pull.
Goodman, M.   Poems from a Country House.
Jenkins, L.   Place for Everything, A.
Kuznetsova, I.   For a centenary.
Levine, P.   Return, The: "All afternoon my
   father drove the country roads."
Madgett.   Packrat.
McClatchy.   What They Left Behind.
Miller, M.   Gift from Kenya.
Molloy, D.   Grandma's Zoo.
Motion, A.   Lines, The: "November, and the
   Sunday twilight fallen."
Rowlands, D.   Little Boots, The.
St. John, D.   Zuni Ring.
Sexton.   Room of My Life, The.
Trethewey, N.   History Lesson.
Ward, T.   Poem Without a Freight Train or a
   Pocket Watch.
Warner, V.   Clearing Out.
Weatherford, C.   Queen Ijo's Blues.
Woods, V.   History Set, The.

Memling, Hans
Mathias, R.   Memling.

Memorial Day
Anania.   Memorial Day.
Collins, W.   How Sleep the Brave.
Finch, F.   Blue and the Gray, The.
Heard, J.   Decoration Day.
Thompson, C.   Memorial Day.
Young, E.   One to destroy, is murder by the law.

Memories
Agosin.   Dance, The.
   Memorial.
   Questions.
   When she showed me her photograph.
Aiken, C.   At a Concert of Music.
Aini, L.   Liquidation.
   Shower.
Akhmatova, A.   Pavlovsk.
Al-Haidari, B.   So That We Do Not Forget.
Alabaú.   Sister.
Alberti.   Going Back Through Color.
Aleixandre.   It's Raining.
Alipiev, Petar.   Old Man: "On his tired memory
   a splendid."
Amichai, Y.   Savage Memories.
Anderson, D.   Itinerary.
Aridjis.   Self-Portrait at Eleven on a Train.
Atwood.   Autobiography: "First thing I can
   remember is a blue line, The. This was on the
   left."
   Fainting.
   Making Poison.
Back, R.   After Eden.
Balakian, P.   After the Survivors Are Gone.
Bandeira.   Evocation of Recife.
Barford, W.   Sorting Things Out.
Barkova, A.   Few Autobiographical Facts, A.
Barnes, J.   Skipping.
Barney, W.   Long Gone to Texas.
Barresi.   Late Summer News.
Basheva.   N. N.
Battin, Wendy (b. 1953).   Mondrian's Forest.
Baudelaire.   Spleen LXXVI.
Bauer, G.   Oldies But Goodies.
Beatty, A.   Memorization.
Berggolts [*or* Bergholts].   To My Sister.
   Wish, A.
Bergman, A.   Way We Were, The.
Bergman, M.   Way We Were, The.
Berrigan, T.   I Remember.
Bidart.   Yoke, The.
Bierds, L.   Memento of the Hours.
Bilgere, G.   Madeleine, A.
Bilhana.   Even now.

Bly, R.   When My Dead Father Called.
Brainard, J.   I Remember.
   I remember biting on a little piece of flesh
      inside my mouth until a very sweet sort of
      pain came.
   I remember the first time I got a letter that said
      "After Five Days Return To" on the envelope.
Brewster, E.   Where I Come From.
Brines, F.   Having Sunk His Chin in His Hand.
Brown, E.   When I recall you—as I often do.
Brown, S.   Let Them Call It Jazz.
Bunting.   Riding silk, adrift at noon.
Burke, C.   Lizzie.
Cabalquinto.   Depths of Fields.
Calderón, T.   Affairs of Memory.
Cardenal.   León.
Carmi, T.   Memorial Day, 1969.
Carver, R.   Old Days, The.
Castillo, S.   En el Sol de Mi Barrio.
   Letter to Yeni on Peering into Her Life.
Cernuda.   I don't want to return a sad spirit.
   Impression of Exile.
Cheney-Coker.   Childhood.
Ch'i-chi.   Year Keng-Wu, Night of the Fifteenth,
   Facing the Moon, The.
Ch'in Kuan.   Song: "Pleading eyebrows,
   intoxicating eyes!"
Ch'oe Sûngja.   House of Memories.
Christie.   Belongings.
Clampitt.   Whippoorwill in the Woods, A.
Collins, B.   Forgetfulness.
Conway, J.   Marlo Thomas in Seven Parts and
   Epilogue.
   Modern English.
Cooley.   Poem on My Birthday.
Coslow, S.   My Old Flame.
Cunningham, J.   In a few days now when two
   memories meet.
Curtis, T.   Pembrokeshire Buzzards.
   Soup.
Dalton, R.   Looking for Trouble.
Davies, L.   Cape Enrage.
Davis, C.   Smoke We Make Pictures Of, The.
Davis, S.   Friends Beyond.
Day, J.   Picket before Bull Run, The.
DeCarteret, M.   Town Clerk, The.
Deltoro, A.   Almohadas.
   Pillows.
Ditzanny, R.   My Hand is Extended for the
   Peace of the Galilee.
Dooley, M.   Dancing at Oakmead Road.
   What Every Woman Should Carry.
Doolittle, H.   So I would rather drown,
   remembering.
Dorsett, T.   Survivor, The.
Duff, V.   Letters from an Exile.
Ebb, F.   Happy Time, The.
Edmond, L.   Anniversary.
Eich.   Viareggio.
Escandor, V.   Summer Nostalgia.
Espada.   Prisoners of Saint Lawrence, The.
Faiz.   Any Lover to Any Beloved.
Fein, Richard.   To Walt Whitman.
Feinstein, S.   Blues for Zoot.
Frost, R.   First Haircut.
Fuhrman, J.   Here, I Say.
Gandlevsky, S.   Dear God, allow me to recall
   my works.
García Lorca.   1910.
Geiger.   Dry Spell of Faith, A.
   Soundtracks.
Gervitz, G.   We docked at noon in the port of
   Veracruz. We wore our Russian furs.
Gibson, W.   Golden Room, The.
Gil de Biedma, J.   In Mournful Praise and
   Memory of the French Song.
Glück, L.   Balcony, The.
   Fantasy, A.
   Vita Nova.
Goldberg, B.   Retro Lullaby.
   Wren.
Goodman, M.   Cobwebs.
Gordon, M.   Serenade in Blue.
   There Will Never Be Another You.
Granados, J.   Espectros.
   Specters.

Grinshpan, Y.   To My Shtetl Years.
Grünbein, D.   Alba.
Hacker, M.   Squares and Courtyards.
Hagedorn, J.   Souvenirs.
Hahn, K.   Older Child, The.
Hajjaj, N.   Honey Fig.
Hamill, S.   Rising.
Hanighen, B.   'Round Midnight.
Hardy, T.   Church Romance, A.
Harer, K.   Lucky 7.
Harryman.   Next.
Hegland, Jean.   Crone I Will Become, The.
Herbert, W.   Praise of Italian Chip-Shops.
Hernández, M.   Each Time I Pass.
Herrera.   Atavistic: Traces after the Rain.
Hicok.   Memory: "I hated the Road Runner."
Hikmet.   Poems of Nine to Ten P.M.
Holland, W.   Journal of the Plague Years, A.
Hollander, J.   Under Cancer.
Howe, M.   What the Living Do.
Ibn Shuhayd, A.   When I observed that life had
   turned away its head and I became assured
   beyond doubt that death would seize me.
Ikeda, P.   Wood.
Ishikawa Jōzan.   Gardening Chrysanthemums, I
   Think of [T'ao] Yüan-Ming.
Ishikawa Takuboku.   Give me / the creeps.
Jeffers, H.   Eyes of Soon Children.
Jernigan, Marla.   This is Still Life.
Jin.   Judgement.
Joe, R.   Old Stories.
Johnston, P.   I'll Remember April.
Jones, G.   Where All Were Good to Me, God
   Knows.
Jones, R.   Failed Memory Exercise.
Kasa.   I shall think of you.
   Look at this keepsake.
Kaufman, S.   Emperor of China, The.
Kees.   1926.
Kessler, S.   Marty's Mother.
Kinsella, T.   Thinking of Mr D.
Kizer, C.   For Jan as the End Draws Near.
   Promising Author.
Knut.   Walking along the Sea of Galilee.
Koestenbaum, W.   Tea Dance.
Komunyakaa, Y.   Ignis Fatuus.
Krohn, Lita Hunter.   Recollections.
Kumin, M.   Your laugh, your scarves, the gloss
   of your makeup.
Kushner, A.   Memoirs.
Lassell.   Brady Street, San Francisco.
Lea, S.   Green Room, The.
Lee, L.   Pillow.
Leopardi.   To Sylvia.
Levertov.   Another Revenant.
Li Ch'ing-chao.   Written by Chance.
Li Po.   Her Presence Was a Roomful of Flowers.
   Remembering Our Excursion in the Past.
Lihn.   Memories of Marriage.
Limburg, J.   Return, The.
Lindtová, A.   Campfire.
Lloyd, C.   On the Death of Priscilla Farmer.
Lopez, L.   Only Now I Realize.
López Velarde.   Baleful Return.
Luu Trong Lu.   Autumn End.
MacDonald, Hugh.   Shingle Flies.
Machado Ruiz.   Portrait ("My childhood is
   memories of a patio in Seville.").
   Recuerdo Infantil.
   Tell Me If You Remember, Love.
Manrique, J.   My Night with Frederico García
   Lorca (As Told by Edouard Roditi).
Mansour, J.   Remember.
Mao Tse-tung [or Mao Zedong].   I stand alone
   in the cold autumn.
Martien, J.   Late 20th Century: Spring.
Martinaitis, M.   Kukutis's Lament under the
   Heavens.
Maschwitz, E.   These Foolish Things (Remind
   Me of You).
Masters, E.   Webster Ford.
McCallum, S.   What Lies Beneath.
McClatchy.   First Steps.
   1946, 1957.
   1971.
   Spirit sets about its task, but slowly, The.

Medina, P.   Exile, The.
Meireles.   Sketch.
Meng Hao Jan.   Night Mooring on the Jiande
   River, A.
Menicanti.   Biographical News.
   What's Left of You.
Mif.   Terezin.
Miller, J.   These Green Paths.
Moffett.   Reaching Around.
Montague, J.   Cage, The.
Montale.   Where the Tennis Court Was.
Moolten, D.   Voyeur.
Motherwell.   Jeanie Morrison.
Mphande.   Walking the Plateau.
Myles, E.   No Rewriting.
Nelson, M.   Cover Photograph.
Nemes Nagy.   Earth Remembers, The.
Neruda.   I remember you as you were that
   ultimate autumn.
Nesbit, E.   Gray Folk, The.
Norton, C.   Recollections: "Do you remember
   all the sunny places."
Notley.   Where Leftover Misery Goes.
Nutter, G.   Air War, The.
Obejas, A.   Dancing in Paradise.
Odio, E.   Memory of My Private Childhood.
Ogiwara Seisensui.   I suck at.
Oliveira, D.   Summer.
Pacheco, J.   From Some Time to This Place.
Palmer, M.   This Time.
Pasternak, B.   At dusk you appear, a school-girl
   still.
Pavlova.   Life calls us, and we go, massing our
   courage.
Paz.   Was it I making plans / for the summer—
   and for all the summers.
Penna.   Life . . . is remembering waking up.
Peterson, R.   Now and Then.
Phillips, J.   Night in Gracie's Face.
Pinchas-Cohen.   Remembering Our Fathers.
Pizarnik.   Poem for My Father.
Po Chü-i.   Dreaming of Long Ago.
   River Flute.
Prunty.   Ballad of the Several Past.
Raye, D.   I'll Remember April.
Razaf, A.   Memories of You.
Rein.   Return, The.
Rexroth, K.   Asagumori.
   Proust's Madeleine.
Richman, L.   Rue de Rosiers: To My Brother
   Fred.
Riley, J.   Old Sweetheart of Mine, An.
Robertson, R.   Aberdeen.
Rosales.   Evocation to Record a Music Box.
Rossiter.   Nostalgia.
Rostopchina.   Unfinished Sewing, The.
Rowe, E.   Parthenea, an Elegy.
Rux, C. H.   Asphalt Musings.
Ryokan.   Breeze is fresh, The.
Sachs, Carly.   Story, The.
Sáenz.   Between Worlds.
St. John, D.   I will tell you. Maybe.
Samaras, N.   After the Children Have Gone to
   Bed.
Sarah, R.   Courtney, Mentioned in Passing,
   Years After.
Savageau.   Trees.
Scarbrough, G.   Sunday Shopping.
Seto, T.   Jihad.
Sherman, M.   San Buenaventura.
Shoukry, G.   Good Man Talking to Himself, A.
"Shu Ting.".   Brother, I Am Here.
Silex, E.   Departure.
Simpson, A.   Waking.
Slessor.   Wild Grapes.
Smith, K.   Writing in Prison.
Snyder, G.   Aging Poet, on a Reading Trip to
   Dayton, Visits the Air Force Museum and
   Discovers There a Plane He Once Flew, The.
Solie, Karen.   To Have and Have Not.
Sondheim.   Remember?
Spaziani.   Present, The.
   Prison, The.
Stafford, W.   Wind from a Wing, A.
Stanley, G.   13/1/78.
Stern, G.   Suzanne.

Stone, R.   Resonance.
Stryk, L.   Black Bean Soup.
Su Tung-p'o.   Tune: "River Town".
Sze.   Apache Plume.
Tanikawa, S.   Nero.
Tate, J.   Manna.
Taylor, C. B.   Forever Arima.
  Plenty Time Pass Fast, Fas Dey So.
Teasdale.   Jewels.
Teillier, J.   Bridge in the South.
Thomas, C.   Anyone can.
Todd, M.   Post Scriptum.
Trethewey, N.   History Lesson.
Trigilio.   Body is Fragile, The.
Trinidad.   For Joe Brainard.
Triplett, P.   Portraits at the Epicenter.
Turner, J.   Plan, The.
U'ng Bình.   At the Exiled King's River Pavilion.
Unknown.   At midnight the memory of you is
  the only visitor.
  Between his hands.
  I Think Over Again My Small Adventures.
  Now that the fragrance.
  Oh memory of my beloved, you are my one true
    lover!
  Old Folks' Room, The.
  Old Maid's Reverie, An.
  Thinking of Lady Yang at Midnight.
  To an Ancient Tune.
  You: "Back from being."
Vazirani, R.   Mrs. Biswas Goes Through a Photo
  Album.
Velter André.   My Wife I Sing.
Verlaine.   Exchange of Feelings.
Vertinsky [*or* Vertinskii].   I remember the night.
Vietnamese Oral Tradition.   Saigon River, The.
Vinokurov.   I don't remember him.
Wah.   Father / Mother Haibun #3.
Walker, D.   Daylight.
Wang Wei.   In Retirement at Zhongnan.
Webster, A.   Where Home Was.
Wei Chuang.   To the Tune: Beautiful Barbarian.
Westheimer, David.   At the Movies.
Williams, J.   River Walk.
Williams, S.   Town less, A.
Williamson, G.   Group Photo with Winter Trees.
Wordsworth, W.   Mind Debarred, A.
  Old Man by the Brook, The.
Wrigley, R.   American Manhood.
Xiang Xiu.   Recalling Old Times.
Yeats.   Cold Heaven, The.
Yesenin [*or* Essenin].   Blue Mist.
  For My Sister Shura.
Yonathan, N.   Dust of Poems, The.
Young, P.   Photograph, 1958.
Yüan Chĕn.   Nearly a Sky Half Clear, Not Yet
  Half Light.
  Remembering.
Zuiderent.   Along the River.

Memory

Abbott, D.   All Day at Work.
Abse.   New Diary, A.
Ai.   Back in the World.
Akhmatova, A.   Don't Frighten Me.
  Instead of a Preface.
  Sentence, The.
Aldrich, T.   Memory.
Alegría.   From the Bridge.
Alexander, M.   Memory.
Alexander the Wild.   When We Were Children.
Ali, A.   Cracked Portraits.
  Farewell: "At a certain point I lost track of
    you."
  Postcard from Kashmir.
  Return to Harmony 3.
Allingham, W.   Four Ducks on a Pond.
Amichai, Y.   Anniversaries of War.
  Little Ruth.
Anguita, E.   Real Moment, The.
Antin.   Real Estate.
Apollinaire.   Voyager, The.
Aragon.   Lilacs and the Roses, The.
Ash, J.   Memories of Italy (Broken Sestina).
Ashbery, J.   Other Tradition, The.
  Rain.
Atwood.   Dufferin, Simcoe, Grey (4).

Four Small Elegies.
Auden.   On This Island.
  Question, The.
  Taller To-day.
Balaban.   News Update.
Bamber, J.   Broken Necklace.
Baraka, I.   In Memory of Radio.
Basho.   Weathered skeleton, A.
Baudelaire.   Harmony of Evening, The.
  Head of Hair.
Beatty, A.   Geography.
Becker, R.   Selective Memory.
Beeson, Colleen.   Minnie Henderson.
Bejerano, M.   I Made a New Memory for You.
Bell, M.   Further Pulsations.
Belloc.   Tarantella.
Berggolts [*or* Bergholts].   My insatiable memory
  is like.
Berlin.   Remember.
Bernheim, Erica.   I Love How Your Eyes Close
  Every Time You Kiss Me.
Bernstein, C.   Memories.
Berrigan, A.   Short History of Autumn, A.
Berrigan, T.   Last Poem.
Berry, W.   At a Country Funeral.
  Meditation in the Spring Rain.
Betham-Edwards.   To a Llangollen Rose, the
  Day after It Had Been Given by Miss
  Ponsonby.
Biespiel, D.   Tower.
Binyon.   They went with songs to the battle,
  they were young.
  Winter Sunrise.
Blake, W.   Song: "Memory, hither come."
Bloem, J. C.   Sunday.
Blood, B.   Late.
Blunden.   Behind the Line.
  1916 Seen from 1921.
Boland, E.   Black Lace Fan My Mother Gave
  Me, The.
  I Remember.
Bonset.   Remembering the Night Fountains.
Borges.   Limits.
  Limits (or Good-byes).
Borowski.   Sun of Auschwitz, The.
Boston, B.   Savage, Our Fathers, The.
Bowles, W.   To the River Wenbeck.
Brathwaite, E.   Ancestors.
Brett, L.   I Keep Forgetting.
Brodsky, J.   I Sit by the Window.
Bromige.   Logical Positivist, The.
Brontë, E.   All hushed and still within the house.
  Aye there it is! It wakes tonight.
  Remembrance: "Cold in the earth—and the deep
    snow piled above thee!"
  What winter floods, what showers of spring.
Brooks, G.   Bean Eaters, The.
Brooks, W.   Pilate Remembers.
Browning, E.   L.E.L.'s Last Question.
Browning, R.   Memorabilia.
Buchwald.   As Soon As It's Here It's Gone But
  So What.
Buckley, V.   Man, a Woman, A.
Bukowski.   Eulogy to a hell of a dame.
Buscani.   Miss Mary Mack.
Busceti, G.   Exhausted Inconsistency Floats
  Here, An.
Buson.   Mourning for Hokuju Rosen.
  Remembering how.
Byron, C.   Minding You.
Byron, G.   If Sometimes in the Haunts of Men.
  Remember Thee! Remember Thee!
  Stanzas for Music ("There's not a joy the world
    can give like that it takes away.").
Calverley.   Flight.
Campana.   Autumn Garden.
Campo.   Lost Plaza Is Everywhere, The.
Canning, G. *et al.*   Rogero's Song.
Carifi, Roberto.   Things don't forget.
Carmona.   Storing Memories.
Carruth, H.   Bearer, The.
Cassian.   Part of a Bird.
Castillo, S.   Almendares.
  Apagón, El.
Cataldi.   Advice.
Causley.   Armistice Day.

Eden Rock.
Cavafy.   Comes to Rest.
  Return.
  Their Beginning.
Cavalli.   How pointless this straining.
  When suddenly, you're hit with good health.
Ceni, A.   Key and the Tree, The.
Césaire, A.   In Memory of a Black Union
  Leader.
Ch'en Yü-yi.   Tune: "Immortal at the
  Riverbank".
Chesterton.   Donkey, The.
Chinnov.   Gust of memory stirs faded letters, A.
Chipasula.   Tramp.
Cisneros, S.   Good Hot Dogs.
Clare, J.   To the Memory of John Keats.
Clark, L.   Singing in the Streets.
Clements, S.   Susans.
Clifton, L.   Why some people be mad at me
  sometimes.
Cluysenaar.   Knife reduces a polished oval, The.
Cofer, J.   Dream of Birth, The.
Coleman, W.   Cousin Mary.
Coleridge, M.   Not Yet.
  Only a little shall we speak of thee.
  To Memory.
Collins, B.   Lines Lost among Trees.
Colonna, S.   So it tries to reach her inside her
  mind.
Comer, Carrie St. George.   Arbor.
Conoley, G.   New.
Cook, E.   To the Late William Jerdan.
Coolidge, C.   Album—A Runthru.
Copus, J.   Back Seat of My Mother's Car, The.
  Clothes, The.
Cory, W.   Desiderato.
  Deteriora.
  Heraclitus.
  Parting.
Coultas, B.   Weather Report.
Crane, H.   Emblems of Conduct.
  Repose of Rivers.
Creeley.   Away.
  Company, The.
  Echo ("Brutish recall.").
  For My Mother: Genevieve Jules Creeley.
  House, The ("Mas-Soñer / Restaurat—Any.").
  In London.
  Memory Gardens.
  Something.
Crews, J.   In the Rubble.
Cronin, J.   Naval Base (Part III), The.
Crozier, A.   Heifer, The.
Dacey, P.   Musica.
Dacre, C.   Power of Love, The.
Dalton, R.   Memory.
Darr.   At Sixteen.
Darwish, M.   Guests on the Sea.
Davie, D.   Time Passing, Beloved.
Davis, O.   Thirty Years Rising.
De Burine, C.   But When I Have.
De Coninck, H.   If Only.
De la Mare.   Fare Well.
  Old Men, The.
  Winter ("Green Mistletoe! / Oh, I remember
    now.").
Deane, S.   Brethren, The.
Dermée.   Poem: "Is it a plane in the sky."
Deutsch.   Memory.
Dewdney.   Memory Table 1, The.
Di Prima.   Backyard.
  Notes on the Art of Memory.
Dickey, W.   Memoranda.
Dickinson, E.   Heart! We [*or* Heart, we] will
  forget him!
  No Passenger was known to flee.
  Pain Has an Element of Blank.
Dietz, H.   Something to Remember You By.
DiPalma.   Memory's Wedge.
  Wrong Side of the Door, The.
Djanikian.   When I First Saw Snow.
Dobyns.   How To Like It.
  Tenderly.
Dodd, E.   Touched.
Dooley, M.   At Les Deux Magots.
  Does It Go Like this?

Heat.
History.
Mansize.
Doolittle, H. Helen.
Lethe.
So you have swept me back.
Dorcey. Night.
Doty, M. Days of 1981.
Dove, R. Charm, The.
Dusting.
Fifth Grade Autobiography.
In the Old Neighborhood.
Wingfoot Lake.
Dowson. Non Sum Qualis Eram Bonae sub
  Regno Cynarae.
Spleen.
Drayton. *Satyr* O never ask how I came to this
  place.
Drummond de Andrade. In the Middle of the
  Road.
Residue.
Dubin, A. Remember Me?
Duffy, C. In Your Mind.
Duncan, R. Tribal Memories.
Dunn, D. Kaleidoscope, The.
Dylan. Boots of Spanish Leather.
Eliot, T. S. Burnt Norton.
La Figlia Che Piange.
Rhapsody on a Windy Night.
Ellis, T. T.A.P.O.A.F.O.M.
Emanuel, L. Elsewhere.
Emerson, R. Memory.
Past, The.
Thine Eyes Still Shined.
English, T. Ben Bolt.
Equi. Date With Robbe-Grillet, A.
Estes, A. Serenade.
Evans, G. Eye Blade.
Revelation in the Mother Lode.
Fainlight, R. Handbag.
Fanshawe, C. When Last We Parted.
Fay, J. Santorini Daughter.
Felipe, L. Biography, Poetry, Destiny.
Ferdowsi, A. I've worked, I've worked so hard;
  reading, reading.
Ficke. Opus 118.
Ficowski. Execution of Memory, The.
Field. I sing thee with the stock-dove's throat.
Fitzpatrick, K. Highland, 1955.
Flint, R. August from My Desk.
Fogarty, L. By Accident, Blinked.
Forché. Elegy.
Forhan, C. Taste of Wild Cherry, The.
Forman, R. Kin.
Frere. Rogero's Song.
Frost, R. Directive.
Garcia, R. Elite Syncopations.
Nobody Here But Us.
Gardinier. Ghost of Santo Domingo, The.
Garland, H. Plowing: A Memory.
Garrett, E. Vista.
Gerhardt, I. G. M. Remembrance Day.
Remembrance Day.
Gershwin, I. They Can't Take That Away from
  Me.
Gerstler. Unforeseen, The.
Gervitz, G. And what were you searching for,
  in that dream?
Can you hear me? Under my name I am.
I listen through underground walls like prisoners
  signaling.
Nothing you tell me nothing.
She detaches herself from her shadow. She is an
  old woman and still beautiful.
She is crying.
Gilbert, C. Pushing.
Gilbert, J. Perspective He Would Mutter Going
  to Bed.
Gillan. In Memory We Are Walking.
Ginsberg, A. Kaddish.
No Way Back to the Past.
O mother / what have I left out.
On Neal's Ashes.
To Aunt Rose.
Gioia. Cruising with the Beach Boys.
Giovanni. Nikki-Rosa.

Giussani, S. Vegetable Calendar.
Glück, L. First Memory.
Pond, The.
Godfrey. Our Lady.
Goldberg, J. Luba 1.
Luba 3.
Luba 2.
Gonzalez, R. There.
Gordon, I. Unforgettable.
Gordon, J. Love.
Graham, J. Covenant.
Graves, R. Plea to Boys and Girls, A.
Recalling War.
Greacen. Carnival at the River.
Father and Son.
Gregg. Clapping, The.
Past Perfect.
Grenier. Has Faded in Part But Magnificent
  Also Late for RC / Mirrors.
Griffin, G. Song: "Place in thy memory, dearest,
  A."
Grimké, A. Butterflies.
Groarke, V. History of My Father's House, The.
Grosholz. Last of the Courtyard, The.
On the Ferry, Toward Patras.
Remembering the Ardèche.
Guest, H. Wales Re-visited.
Gumilyov [*or* Gumiliov *or* Gumilev]. Pre-
  Memory.
Gunn, T. Autobiography.
Death's Door.
Gurney, I. To His Love.
Hadas, R. Humble Herb is Rival to Prozac.
Sunday Afternoon.
Hall, D. Old Pilot, The.
Porcelain Couple, The.
Hamod, S. After the Funeral of Assam Hamady.
Hannah, S. Your Street Again.
Hardy, T. After a Journey.
Afterwards.
Ah, Are You Digging on My Grave?
One We Knew.
Shut Out That Moon.
Thoughts of Phena.
To Lizbie Browne.
Voice, The.
Harjo, J. Remember.
Skeleton of Winter.
Harms. As Always.
My Androgynous Years.
Harris, D. What we have lost.
Harryman. My Story.
Hass, R. Meditation at Lagunitas.
Pornographer, The.
Hayden, R. Ballad of Sue Ellen Westerfield,
  The.
Those Winter Sundays.
Whipping, The.
Heaney, S. Anahorish.
Summer of Lost Rachel, The.
When all the others were away at Mass.
Hecht, A. Hill, A.
Hejinian. Moment yellow, just as four years
  later when, A.
Herd. Pink Rose Rings, The.
Hesketh. Love's Advocate.
Hicok. Alzheimer's.
Hikmet. Things I Didn't Know I Loved.
Hine. Côte de Liesse.
Letting Go.
Hirsch, E. My Father's Back.
Hirshfield, J. Each Step.
Ho Hsun. Singing-Girls in the Brazen Bird.
Hochman. Hairbrush, The.
Hogan, L. New Apartment.
Holan. Reminiscence.
Holland, J. Having read up on the subject.
Hollander, J. Forget How to Remember How to
  Forget.
Hollo. Godlike.
Hongo. Hilo: First Night Back.
O-Bon: Dance for the Dead.
Hood, T. I Remember, I Remember.
Time, Hope, and Memory.
Howard, R. After 65.
1915: A Pre-Raphaelite Ending, London.

Howe, F. Doubt.
Hudgins. Around the Campfire.
Hughes, L. Blues at Dawn.
Hugo, R. Flying, Reflying, Farming.
Freaks at Spurgin Road Field, The.
White Center.
Hunt, L. Rondeau: "Jenny kissed [*or* kiss'd] me
  when we met."
Irby. Heredom.
Iskander. Blind Man, The.
Issa. My dear old village.
Jacob, M. Little Poem.
Jarman, M. Cavafy in Redondo.
Jarrell, R. Burning the Letters.
Dead Wingman, The.
Face, The.
Player Piano, The.
Jiménez, J. Remembrance Is Moving, A.
Johnston, M. Sea-Cucumber, The.
Jones, S. Illusions.
Joseph, A. Junior High Dance.
Justice, D. Invitation to a Ghost.
Men at Forty.
On the Death of Friends in Childhood.
Sonatina in Yellow.
Kaminsky, Ilya. Maestro.
Kaufman, B. Trip, Dharma Trip, Sangha Trip,
  The.
Kay, J. Even the Trees.
Stincher, The.
Keesing. Reverie of a Mum.
Kefala. Freedom Fighter.
Keith, Sally. Mechanics.
Kemble. Farewell to Italy.
Petition, A.
To Mrs. Norton.
Whene'er I recollect the happy time.
Kenney. Sailing.
Keyes, S. Elegy: "April again, and it is a year
  again."
Kgositsile. For Art Blakey and the Jazz
  Messengers.
Khodasevich. Automobile, The.
Ki no Tsurayuki. Out in the marsh reeds.
King, H. Exequy, The.
Kinnell. To William Carlos Williams.
When I come back to my father's house.
Kipling, R. Shock.
Kirsch, S. Pictures.
Knight, E. Poem of Attrition, A.
Koch, K. Circus, The ("I remember when I
  wrote The Circus.").
Energy in Sweden.
To Marina.
With Janice.
Komunyakaa, Y. Report from the Skull's
  Diorama.
When Loneliness Is a Man.
Kovaleva, I. I can still make you out.
Kruit, J. Post Heads.
Kumin, M. Envelope, The.
How It Is.
Nuns of Childhood, The: Two Views.
Kunitz, S. Abduction, The.
Kuzmin. Leaving my house in the morning.
When it was I first encountered you.
Lamb, C. Old Familiar Faces, The.
Landon. Lines Written Under a Picture of a Girl
  Burning a Love-Letter.
Song: "Farewell!—and never think of me."
Landor, W. Memory.
Rose Aylmer.
Lanier, E. Description of Cooke-ham [*or*
  Cookham], The.
Larkin, P. I Remember, I Remember.
So through that unripe day you bore your head.
Whatever Happened?
Lauterbach. Here and There ("Today I wake
  having swung, naked, in London.").
Laux, D. China.
Lawrence, D. H. Argonauts, The.
Hymn to Priapus.
Piano.
Southern Night.
Lea, S. At the Flyfisher's Shack.
Telescope.

Lee, J. My Father's Country.
Lee, L. I Ask My Mother to Sing.
Mnemonic.
Lehmann, G. What's that bird, Mr Long?
Lerner, A. I Remember It Well.
Leslie, E. Among My Souvenirs.
Levertov. Hymn, The.
Intrusion.
Note to Olga (1966), A.
Time Past, A.
Woman Meets an Old Lover, A.
Levine, P. Genius: "Two old dancing shoes my grandfather."
Levy, A. Old House, The.
Lewis, A. Post-Script: for Gweno.
Lewis, J. Patrick. Stories.
Lewis, Janet. Grandmother Remembers, A.
Li Ch'ing-chao. Tune: Spring at Wu Ling.
Li Po. Exile's Letter.
Li Shang-yin. Inlaid Lute, The.
Li Yü. Tune: "Memories of the South".
Tune: "Sand Washed by Waves".
Tune: "The Beauty of Yü".
Lim, S. Father from Asia.
Limonov. As if a quiet branch drew a line.
Lincoln, A. My Childhood-Home I See Again.
Lindsay, V. Eagle That Is Forgotten, The.
Lingafelter, A. Grandmothers, The.
Lisboa. Beyond the Image.
Lisnyanskaya [or Lisnianskaia]. Between hope and failure.
Liu Yung. Tune: "Eight Beats of a Kan-chou Song".
Livesay, D. Green Rain.
Lochhead, L. Grim Sisters, The.
Lodge, G. On an Æolian Harp.
Loftis, N. Ruth.
Longfellow, H. Fire of Drift-Wood, The.
Golden Mile-Stone, The.
My Lost Youth.
Longley, M. Ash Keys.
Remembering Carrigskeewaun.
Lopez, L. Images of San Luis.
López Mills, T. And Never Did.
Y nunca quise.
Lorde. Movement Song.
Lowell, J. Remembered Music.
Lowell, R. For Sheridan.
Lu Yu. Night Thoughts.
Lummis, Suzanne. Letter to My Assailant.
Lumsden, R. Then.
Lyons, S. Remembering.
MacDiarmid, H. Crystals like Blood.
Eemis-Stane, The.
Macgoye. August the First: The Shadow. Patel Speaks.
Mackintosh, E. In Memoriam, Private D. Sutherland.
MacLeish. Return.
Sentiments for a Dedication.
MacNeacail. Proper Schooling, A.
MacNeice. Soap Suds.
Madhubuti. Killing Memory.
Mansour, J. Anti-mnemonic self-vaccination.
Mansour, M. Desert 1.
My Memory.
Mapanje. We Wondered about the Mellow Peaches.
Marsman. Memory of Holland.
Marston, P. Vain Wish, A.
Martinez, D. Nocturnes: "He closed the deal on the night. A real."
Martínez, V. Night of Fathers.
Reliquaries, The.
Marvell. Gallery, The.
Masaoka Shiki. Thing long forgotten.
Matson, C. Bedside.
Matthews, W. Housework.
Mayer, B. Birthday Sonnet for Grace.
McCarriston. Billy.
Castle in Lynn, A.
McDaniel, J. Logic in the House of Sawed-Off Telescopes.
McDonald, W. Hauling Over Wolf Creek Pass in Winter.
McFadden, R. Contemplations of Mary.

Stringer's Field.
McGinley. 5:32, The.
McKay, C. Jasmine.
Tropics in New York, The.
McKean. After Listening to Jack Teagarden . . .
McPherson, S. Helen Todd: My Birthname.
Mei Yao Ch'en. Dream at Night, A.
Melville, H. Stonewall Jackson.
Menken. Memory, A.
Mercer, J. I Remember You.
Merrill, J. Broken Home, The.
David's Night in Veliès.
Days of 1964.
Days of 1935.
Midnight Snack, The.
Urban Convalescence, An.
Merwin. Poem, The: "Coming late, as always."
Meynell, A. Renouncement.
Mhlophe. Sometimes When It Rains.
Michaelis. I Was About Three Years of Age.
Millay, E. Cameo, The.
Only until this cigarette is ended.
Sonnet 2: "Time does not bring relief; you all have lied."
Sonnet 43: "What lips my lips have kissed, and where, and why."
Mitchell, S. Dead, The: "At night the dead come down to the river to drink."
Montemayor, C. Cytherea.
Moore, T. Echo ("At the mid hour of night, when stars are weeping, I fly.").
Journey Onwards, The.
No—Leave My Heart to Rest.
Oft In the Stilly Night.
Mora. Depression Days.
Gentle Communion.
Moritz [or Morits]. Fisherman, The.
Morris, G. Woodman, Spare That Tree.
Moss, H. Elegy for My Sister.
Moultrie. Forget Thee?
Mueller, L. Concert, The.
Muir, E. Animals, The.
Muldoon, P. History.
Soap-Pig, The.
Mura. Colors of Desire, The.
To H.N.
Nara Singde. Tune: "Sand of Silk-Washing Brook" In Memoriam.
Nemerov. Blue Suburban.
Models.
Snow Globe, The.
Neruda. Births.
Poem.
Sonnet 4.
Nerval. Fantasy.
To J—Y Colonna.
Nezval. Walker in Prague.
Nichol. Some Nets.
Niu Hsi-chi. Where the mist has torn.
Noguchi, R. Not Surfing Some Days.
North, M. Poems to My Father.
Nortje. Cosmos in London.
Notley. Beginning with a Stain.
California Girlhood, A.
O'Reilly, M. House Call to a Man with Parkinson's Disease, A.
Oandasan. Grandmothers Land.
O'Hara, F. Animals.
In Favor of One's Time.
In Memory of My Feelings.
Okolo, M. Still Burn.
Oliver, M. Picking Blueberries, Austerlitz, New York, 1957.
O'Loughlin. Posthumous.
Olson, C. At Yorktown.
Chain of memory is resurrection I am a vain man, The.
My memory is.
Thing Was Moving, The.
Ondaatje. Burning Hills.
Oppen. Forms of Love, The.
O'Reilly, C. Augury.
Orton, B. Beekeeper.
Sea Monkeys, The.
Ou-yang Chiung. Offering Congratulations to the Enlightened Reign.

Owen, W. To My Friend (With an Identity Disc).
Unreturning, The.
Pack, R. Thrasher in the Willow by the Lake, The.
Page, G. Late Night Radio.
Paley, G. People in My Family.
Paris, T. Memory Span of a Goldfish Is Three Seconds, The.
Parish. Star Dust.
Partnoy, A. To El Mingo (with Whom I Share Eva Victoria and Anahi Paz).
Pasternak, B. Courage.
Fresco Come to Life.
Mary Magdalene (I).
Paulin. In the Lost Province.
Paulinus of Nola. To Ausonius.
Peacock, T. Love and Age.
Penrose, V. Rain Finding Once More, The.
Pessoa. When in the widening circle of rebirth.
Peters, L. Home Coming.
Petri. Christmas 1956.
Gratitude.
Phillips, C. Abundance.
Africa Says.
Pilinszky, J. Passion of Ravensbrück.
Pinsky. Questions, The: "What about the people who came to my father's office."
Woman, A.
Planché. Self-Evident.
Po Chü-i. Dreaming that I Went with Li and Yu to Visit Yuan Zhen.
Tune: "Memories of the South".
Poe. To F——.
Porter, C. Begin the Beguine.
Old-Fashioned Garden.
Prévert. Barbara.
Prince, F. T. Babiaantje, The.
Probyn. Song Out of Season, A.
Prufer, K. For the Dead.
Pryde, A. Have We Had Easter Yet?
Pulido, A. Gets in / the damp.
Se mete / la humedad.
Pushkin, A. I Loved You.
Quevedo y Villegas. Love Beyond Death.
Raine, C. Onion, Memory, The.
Rainger, R. Thanks for the Memory.
Ramanujan. Breaded Fish.
Ramsey, J. Tally Stick, The.
Ransom, J. Antique Harvesters.
Equilibrists, The.
Rao, S. Memories: "My name is Lila."
Rayl, J. Spring Storm.
Reese, L. Lavender Woman, The.
Reverdy. Road.
Rexroth, K. Signature of All Things, The.
Reyes, A. Scarcely.
Rich, A. Dreamwood.
Grandmothers.
Living Memory.
Mathilde in Normandy.
What homage will be paid to a beauty built to last.
Riley, D. Misremembered Lyric, A.
Riley, J. As one who cons at evening o'er an album, all alone.
Robbins, Z. December 12th.
Roberts, L. My Father's Whistle.
Roberts, N. Max Factor Pink.
Robertson, R. Fugue for Phantoms.
Robin, L. Thanks for the Memory.
Robinson, A. Dead Friend, The.
Stornelli and Strambotti.
Valley, The.
Robinson, E. Calverly's.
Souvenir.
Rodriguez, L. Heavy Blue Veins.
Roethke. Dream, The.
Premonition, The.
Rolfe, E. First Love.
Romano, R. Bucket, The.
Rose, J. Marisel.
Rospigliosi. Leavetaking.
Rossetti, C. Echo.
From Sunset to Star Rise.
I wish I could remember the [or that] first day.

Remember [Me].
Song: "She sat and sang alway."
Rossetti, D. Sudden Light.
  50: Willowwood ("And now Love sang: but his was such a song").
  51: Willowwood ("O ye, all ye that walk in Willowwood").
  52: Willowwood ("So sang he: and as meeting rose and rose").
Rózewicz. Return, The.
Rudaki. All the teeth ever I had are worn down and fallen out.
Rukeyser, M. Woman as Market.
Rungano. Mother.
Rux, C. H. Asylum of Gestures.
Ryan, M. This Is a Poem for the Dead.
St. John, D. Desire: "There is a small wrought-iron balcony."
  Guitar.
  Quote Me Wrong Again and I'll Slit the Throat of Your Pet Iguana.
  Twin memory, we all seek it.
Salinas, R. Trip Through the Mind Jail, A.
Samyn, M. Poem with Light on Its Shoulder.
Sandburg, C. Haze.
Sansom, A. World is everything, The.
Sassoon, S. Aftermath.
Scalapino. Flush / a Play.
  Thin silver disc moon shredded at the bottom edge is.
Scalise, G. Amiti´ Amoureuse.
Scannell. Apple-raid, The.
Schilpp, M. Under the Scorpion's Heart.
Schnackenberg. Darwin in 1881.
Schwartz, R. L. Why I Forgive My Younger Self Her Transgressions.
Scott, J. Plato's Dog.
Scovell. Sandy Yard, The.
Seferis. Last Stop.
  Memory 1.
Selvinsky [or Sel'vinskii]. I Saw It!
Senghor. Porte Dorée.
Serote. Ofay-watcher looks back.
Sewell, L. Denied, The.
Sexton. Boat, The.
  Fury of Overshoes, The.
  I Remember.
Shakespeare, W. Sonnet 30: "When to the sessions of sweet silent thought."
  Sonnet 55: "Not marble, nor the g[u]ilded monuments."
  Sonnet 77: "Thy glass will show thee how thy beauties wear."
Shange. Where the Heart Is.
Shelley, P. To —: "Music, when soft voices die."
Shen Yüeh. Seeing the Beloved in a Dream.
Shinkichi Takahashi. Sea of Oblivion.
"Shu Ting.". Bits of Reminiscence.
  Maple Leaf.
Shwarts [or Shvarts]. Memorial Candle.
Silko. Where Mountain Lion Lay [or Laid] Down with Deer.
Sillitoe. Synagogue in Prague.
Simic. Empire of Dreams.
  Wall, A.
Simmons, J. Archæologist, The.
Sissman. Bruisingly cradled in a Harvard chair.
Skinner, J. Fetch.
Smith, C. *I* once was happy, when while yet a child.
Smith, I. Clearances, The.
Smith, P. Building Nicole's Mama.
Snodgrass. Mementos, 1.
Snyder, G. Autumn Morning in Shokoku-ji, An.
  For Lew Welch in a Snowfall.
  Four Poems for Robin.
  Working on the '58 Willys Pickup.
Sobin, G. On the Nature of the Iconic.
Solari, R. Currents.
Song. Out of Our Hands.
  Wind in the Trees, The.
Sorrentino. Good Night!
Sosnora. Letter, A.
Soto. Braly Street.
  Not Knowing.

Street.
  Who Will Know Us?
Soupault. Route.
Spaziani. Memory's Usefulness.
Speakes. Heartbreak Hotel Piano-Bar.
Spender, S. To T.A.R.H.
Spenser, E. By vew of her he ginneth to revive.
Srinivas, T. Chasing Memory.
Stanard, C. Baseball.
Steptoe. Sweet Brown Rice and Red Bones.
Stern, G. Dancing, The.
  Faces I Love, The.
Stevens, W. Anglais Mort à Florence.
  Clear Day and No Memories, A.
Stevenson, R. Blows the Wind Today.
Stickney, T. In the Past.
  Mnemosyne.
  Pity.
Stokesbury. Evening's End.
Strand. Pot Roast.
  Where Are the Waters of Childhood?
Strasser, J. Memory Lapse.
Su Tung-p'o. Tune: "Water Mode Song".
Suárez, V. Rice Comes to El Volcán.
Surrey. Prison in Windsor Castle.
Swinburne. Before the Mirror.
Symons, A. White Heliotrope.
Sze. Before Completion.
Szymborska, W. Laughter.
  Memory At Last.
Tabb. Echoes.
  Mid-Day Moon, The.
Talvikki, A. Afterwards: Caliban.
  Along the road, the bright painted crosses.
  At night, coolness like water lapping.
  Before first light, we would open the nets.
  Halley's Comet crossed the jungle sky.
  Teatro Amazonas, remnant, the.
  Waking, months after I leave the jungle.
Tapahonso. I Am Singing Now.
Taylor, A. Clearing Away.
Teare, Brian. Detail from "Set for a Southern Gothic".
Teasdale. Water-Lilies.
Tekeyan. Forgetting.
Tengour, H. In the Country of the Dead.
Tennyson, A. As when with downcast eyes we muse and brood.
  In the Valley of Cauteretz.
  Now, sometimes in my sorrow shut.
  O [or Oh] that 'twere possible.
  Tears, Idle Tears.
  Unwatched, the garden bough shall sway.
Thomas, E. Celandine.
  In Memoriam (Easter, 1915).
Tighe. Can I look back, and view with tranquil eye.
  When glowing Phoebus quits the weeping earth.
  Written at Scarborough.
Townsend, A. Mardi Gras Premortem.
Trethewey, N. Cameo.
Trinidad. Double Trouble.
Triplett, P. Spectral Dues.
Tripp. In Memory of Idris Davies.
Trowbridge, J. Recollections of "Lalla Rookh".
Tsvetayeva [or Tsvetaeva]. To Kiss a Forehead Is to Erase Worry.
Tu Fu [or Du Fu]. At the Sky's End, Thinking of Li Po.
  Night in a Room by the River.
  Winter Dawn.
Tucker, M. We Met.
Tuckerman, F. Series 2, Sonnet 16.
  Series 3, Sonnet 5.
Tuéni. In the Lebanese Mountains.
Tuqan, F. Face Lost in the Wilderness.
Twichell. Let's Talk.
Ulacia, M. Stone at the Bottom, The.
Unknown. Do You Remember That Night.
  Do You Remember That Night?
  Psalm 137.
  That Mountain Far Away.
  Wanderer, The.
Unknown, fr. Terezin Concentration Camp.
  Birdsong.
  Forgotten.

Valentine, J. Lines in Dejection.
Van de Woestijne. Fever Tune.
Van Duyn. Stream, The.
Van Vliet. City, The.
  Party.
Vaughan, H. They Are All Gone into the World of Light!
Velichansky, A. Memory of the past grows paler with each day.
Villon. Ballade: "Tell me where, in what country, where."
Vivar. Love is Round.
Voigt. Claiming Kin.
Voznesensky [or Voznesenskii]. I Am Goya.
  Why.
Walcott. Glory Trumpeter, The.
  Letter from Brooklyn, A.
  Village Life, A.
Walden, G. Misguided Angels.
Waldrop, R. Unaccountable Lapses.
Walker, J. Studying Physics with My Daughter.
Waniek. House on Moscow Street, The.
Waring, B. Reprieve on the Stoop.
Warner, S. Green Valley, The.
Warren, R. In Italian They Call the Bird *Civetta.*
Warsh. Suicide Rates, The.
Weaver, A. Easy Living.
Wei Chuang. Tune: "The Bodhisattva Foreigner".
Weigl. Her Life Runs Like a Red Silk Flag.
  Sailing to Bien Hoa.
Weiner, H. Remembered Sequel.
Weiss, T. Ten Little Rembrandts.
Welch, L. Tattoo.
Whalen, P. Slop Barrel, The.
White, E. Chairs in Snow.
Whitman, W. As Toilsome I Wander'd Virginia's Woods.
  Glimpse, A.
  My Picture-Gallery.
  Old Man's Thought of School, An.
  Once I Pass'd through a Populous City.
  Out of the Cradle Endlessly Rocking.
Whittier. Burning Drift-Wood.
  Snow-Bound [or Snow-Bound] [A Winter Idyl].
  Telling the Bees.
  To My Old Schoolmaster.
Wieners. Two Years Later.
Wiesel. Never Shall I Forget.
Wilbur, R. Finished Man, A.
  Mind-Reader, The.
  Pardon, The.
  Piazza di Spagna, Early Morning.
Wilder, A. Did You Ever Cross Over to Sneden's.
Williams, C. K. Blades.
  Repression.
  Still Life.
Williams, H. To the Strawberry.
Williams, S. California Light.
Williams, W. Paterson, Book V: The River of Heaven.
  To a Dog Injured in the Street.
Williamson, G. Drawing Hands.
Willis, N. Confessional, The.
Wingfield. Winter.
Winner, S. Listen to the Mocking Bird.
Witt, S. Americana.
  Michael Masse.
Woessner. Jungle Music.
Wojahn. Satin Doll.
Wong, N. Mama, Come Back.
Wordsworth, D. Thoughts on my sick-bed.
Wordsworth, W. Complaint, A.
  I Wandered Lonely as a Cloud.
  Surprised by Joy.
Wright, C. D. Kings' Daughters, Home for Unwed Mothers, 1948.
Wright, Charles. Gate City Breakdown.
  Homage to Paul Cézanne.
  Other Side of the River, The.
  Virginia Reel.
Wright, D. To the Gods the Shades Flavinus of the Cavalry Regiment.
Wright, James. On a Phrase from Southern

Ohio.
Wright, Jay. Albuquerque Graveyard, The.
Wu Wen-ying. Tune: "Sand of Silk-Washing
  Brook" A Reminiscence.
Wyatt. Lover Showeth How He Is Forsaken of
  Such as He Sometime Enjoyed, The.
  Steadfastness.
Yau. Cenotaph.
  Postcard from Trakl.
  Radiant Silhouette III.
Yeats. Circus Animals' Desertion, The.
  Tower, The.
  When You Are Old.
Yesenin [or Essenin]. Golden Grove, The.
Yevtushenko [or Evtushenko]. I am.
Young, K. Preserving, The.
Yusuf, S. Attention.
  Hamra Night.
Zamora, D. Downpour.
Zucker, R. Not Knowing Nijinsky or Diaghilev.
Zych. Auschwitz, 1987.

Memphis, Tennessee
Brown, S. Memphis Blues.
Handy, W. Beale Street Blues.
Llwyd, Iwan. Automobiles.
Seay. Audubon Drive, Memphis.
Tarpley. Feel Free.

Men
Agosin. Most Unbelievable Part, The.
Ai. Before You Leave.
Algarin. Trampling.
Andreus. For Some Future Day.
Andrews, N. Philosophical Inquiry into the
  Nature of the Human Cock, A.
Arp. Man, The. The Woman.
Arrillaga. Rosa/Filf.
Ash, J. Memories of Italy (Broken Sestina).
Atwood. Men with the heads of eagles.
  This story was told to me by another traveller.
Avidan, D. Six Local Poems.
Barlow, G. Place Where He Arose, The.
Basho. By the old temple.
Behn, A. To Alexis in Answer to His Poem
  Against Fruition.
  To Alexis in Answer to His Poem Against
    Fruition. Ode.
Benn. Before a Cornfield.
Berlin. You Can't Get a Man with a Gun.
Bernstein, M. Manly Sports.
Blane, R. Occasional Man, An.
Bogan, L. Men Loved Wholly Beyond Wisdom.
Borson. Talk.
Branch, A. I say that words are men and when
  we spell.
Butts, A. Belle Isle Men, The.
Campo, C. Canon 4.
Campo. For J. W.
Castellanos. You Are Not Poetry.
Celaya, G. Life One Leads, The.
Césaire, A. On the Islands of All Winds.
Cisneros, S. Man in My Bed Like Cracker
  Crumbs, A.
Clarke, C. Passing.
Clifton, L. Leda 3.
Coon, M. Trade Show.
Cope, W. Bloody Men.
  Rondeau Redoublé.
Crouch, S. Chops Are Flyin.
Dacey, P. Four Men in a Car.
Dacre, C. Similie.
Di Cicco. Male Rage Poem.
Ditlevsen. Eternal Three, The.
Dixon, M. Getting Your Rocks Off.
Duncan, R. Torso, The / Passages 18.
Dunn, S. Man Who Closed Shop, The.
Eberhart, R. Gnat on My Paper.
Edson, R. Feeding the Dog.
Éluard, P. Mirror of a Moment, The.
"Ephelia.". In the Person of a Lady, to Bajazet,
  Her Unconstant Gallant.
Essinger, C. You Are Right.
Evans, R. Femininity.
Ezekiel. I met a man once.
Fingueret, M. Leviticus (Chapter 7, Verse 2-5).
Foley, M. Brothers and Sisters.
Fordham. Coming Woman, The.

Gallagher, T. Black Silk.
Gilbert, C. Beginning by Value.
Gilmore, M. Eve-Song.
Glück, L. Labor Day.
  Palais des Arts.
Green, M. Finished Poem.
Greenhalgh, C. Man in the Valley of Women,
  A.
Greville, F. Mind of man is this world's true
  dimension, The.
Gunn, T. Innocence.
Hamby, B. St. Clare's Underwear.
Hands, E. Favourite Swain, The.
Hannaham, D. To a Flasher.
Harryman. Male, The.
Hayes, T. At Pegasus.
Hecht, A. Feast of Stephen, The.
Hernández Cruz. Slick.
Higgins, R. Did-You-Come-Yets of the Western
  World, The.
Hill, S. Please Can I Have a Man.
Hughes, T. Salem.
Irtenev. At the Pavelets radial-line station.
Issa. Autumn evening.
  Vanity of men, The.
Iverem, E. Daddy's Friends.
Jackson, B. Tired as I Can Be.
Johnston, E. Lines: To a Young Gentleman of
  Surpassing Beauty.
  Working Man, The.
Jonson, B. Another Lady's Exception, Present
  at the Hearing.
  Her Man Described by Her Own[e] Dictamen.
Juana Inés de la Cruz. Verses Against the
  Inconsequence of Men's Taste and Strictures.
Justice, D. Men at Forty.
Kim Kwang-kyu. Sketch of a Fetish.
Kipling, R. If.
Koertge. All Suffering Comes from Attachment.
Korteweg. Sed Non Frustra.
Lawrence, D. H. How Beastly the Bourgeois Is.
Lear, E. There Was an Old Man With a Beard.
Lerner, A. Hymn to Him, A.
Levertov. Abel's Bride.
  Mutes, The.
Limburg, J. Inner Bloke.
Livesay, D. Other.
Livingston, J. Femininity.
Lowry, M. Eye-Opener.
Madgett. Black Woman.
Malloch, D. Manly Love.
Mansour, J. Men's Vices.
Martin, H. Occasional Man, An.
Martinez, D. Cultivation of Orchids, The.
  Room itself, The. The women. The absence of
  women.
Mataka. Next Door.
McCarriston. Hotel Nights with My Mother.
Molloy, S. Grands Seigneurs, Les.
Moore, M. To an Intra-Mural Rat.
Moulds, J. Renoir's Bathers.
Muldoon, P. Why Brownlee Left.
Mullen, Kate. Thin-Legged Lover.
Murray, J. Men and Women Have Meaning
  Only as Man and Woman.
Naden. Love's Mirror.
Nasrin. At the Back of Progress . . . .
Nathan, L. Body Count.
Neruda. Walking Around.
Nolla. Thoughts on Innocence.
Norris, K. Emperor Has No Clothes!, The.
Norse. I'm Not a Man.
Nowlan. Rites of Manhood, The.
O'Donnell, D. Young Men of Blackburn, The.
Olds, S. Early Images of Heaven.
Orr, G. Who'd Want to Be a Man?
Otomo no Sakanoé. Were you a string of beads.
Padilla. Man on the Edge.
Parker, D. Chant for Dark Hours.
  Experience.
  General Review of the Sex Situation.
  Men.
  Song of One of the Girls.
Parker, M. Whither away good neighbour.
Parra, V. Attention Young Bachelors.
Peppermint, Heidi. Real Toads.

Pietri. 9th Untitled Poem.
Pitchford. Surgery.
Pollard, C. And Another Bloody Thing.
Pollarolo, G. Good Marriage, A.
Prescod. Women Are Different.
Probyn. Tête-à-Tête.
Rainey. See, See Rider.
Rich, A. From a Survivor.
  Phenomenology of Anger, The.
  Trying to Talk with a Man.
Roberson, E. Eclipse.
  True We Are Two Grown Men.
Roberts, L. Men's Talk.
Robinson, M. Modern Male Fashions.
Rochester, J. Satire [or Satyre or Satyr] against
  [Reason and] Mankind, A.
Rouse, A. Spunk Talking.
Rupchev, Georgi. Attraction.
Ryan, G. If I Had a Gun.
Rykard, R. Whole two weeks after The Million
  Man March; and still, if you'd ask me, this is
  all I could say about it, A.
Sabines. I Do Not Know It for Sure.
Sanchez, S. Prelude to Nothing.
Scalise, G. Man comes last: he's got to.
  There have never been men crazier than these.
Schuyler, J. Royals.
Seidel. Men and Women.
Shakespeare, W. Balthasar's Song.
Sharp, S. In the Tradition of Bobbitt.
Shepherd, R. Three A.M. Eternal.
Simmons, J. Influence of Natural Objects, The.
Smith, P. So Motown taught me all about men.
  Men worshipped.
Sri Sri. Man walks on the bridge and gives
  away the change in his, A.
Stevenson, R. Looking Forward.
Suckling, S. Constant Lover, A [or The].
Szymborska, W. Born of Woman.
Taggard. Everyday Alchemy.
Taylor, B. Goblet, The.
Teitelboim, D. Men.
Tennyson, A. We leave the well-beloved place.
Thomas, E. Forsaken Wife, The.
Tomlinson, C. Word in Edgeways, A.
Towers, T. Mission Poem.
Troupe. Reflections on Growing Older.
Unknown. Men Only Pretend.
  Visitors.
  Woman's Love.
Vallejo. Anger that Breaks a Man Down into
  Boys, The.
Van Winckel, N. Watching the Men Walk.
Vaughan, R. Men Together.
Vega. Brothers Loving Brothers.
Voss, F. Inspection, The.
Wallace, R. In a Pig's Eye.
West, K. On Track.
Whitman, W. I knew a man, a common farmer,
  the father of five sons.
  I Sing the Body Electric.
Whittemore, R. For the Life of Him and Her.
Wilder, A. Trouble Is a Man.
Wilkes, J. Then, say not Man's imperfect,
  Heaven in fault.
Williams, C. K. It Is This Way with Men.
Williams, S. She Had Known Brothers.
Williams, T. Nintendo.
Williams, W. Hemmed-in Males.
  Marriage.
Wodehouse. Bill.
  Bill (Original Version).
  It's a Hard, Hard World for a Man.
Wright, C. Everything Good Between Men and
  Women.
Yeats. Men Improve with the Years.
Zenmaro. Tanka: "All the young men I know."
Zukofsky, L. For you I have emptied the
  meaning.

Menageries
Tzara. Lion Tamer Remembers, The.
See also **Zoos**

Mennonites
Baehr, A. I Am Dancing with My Mennonite
  Father.
Brandt, D. Nonresistance, or love Mennonite

style.
Gundy, J.   How to Write the New Mennonite
  Poem.
Hostetler, S.   Not of This World.
Woman with the Screw in Her Mouth Speaks,
  The.
Klassen, S.   Russian Fables.
Rohrer, J.   Hotel.
Wright, D.   New Mennonite Replies to Julia
  Kasdorf, A.

Menopause
Clifton, L.   To my last period.
Cook, W.   Seth Bingham.
Mansour, J.   Woman Kneeling in the Sorry Jelly,
  A.
Romo-Carmona, M.   Signs.
Vicioso.   Wo/men.

Menstruation
Adams, Cyd.   Azaleas and Dogwoods.
Barrington, J.   Blood.
Clifton, L.   Wishes for Sons.
Donovan, K.   Underneath Our Skirts.
Dove, R.   After Reading *Mickey in the Night
  Kitchen* for the Third Time Before Bed.
Dunmore.   Safe period.
Feaver.   Women's Blood.
Glazer, J.   Point of No Return.
Goralik, L.   Every few weeks I see there is an
  empty chair in our local nursery.
Millay, E.   Menses.
Olds, S.   Eggs.
Woman in Heat Wiping Herself, A.
Pak Sôwôn.   Menstrual Irregularities.
Piercy.   Watch, The.
Porzecanski.   Every Month.
Radden, V.   Blood.
Shange.   We Need a God Who Bleeds Now.
Trethewey, N.   Drapery Factory, Gulfport,
  Mississippi, 1956.

Mental Illness
Alexie.   Theology.
Atkins, R.   While Waiting for a Friend to Come
  to Visit a Friend in a Mental Hospital.
Behn, R.   Origin.
Betjeman.   Huxley Hall.
Bogan, L.   Evening in the Sanitarium.
Bogen, L.   I Eat Lunch with a Schizophrenic.
Bryan, M.   Maniac, The (2).
Campo.   Asylum.
Citino.   Analysis, The.
Cowper, W.   Shrubbery, The.
Davis, C.   Out of Work, Out of Touch, Out of
  Sorts.
Delgado, J.   Recommitted.
  Visiting Father.
Dobyns.   Frenchie.
  Spiritual Chickens.
Dubie.   Dementia.
Fallon, P.   Himself.
Ferré.   You Have Lost, They Tell Me, Your
  Reason.
Field.   Sullenness.
Ginsberg, A.   Kaddish.
  O mother / what have I left out.
Goodison.   For Don Drummond.
Haines, J.   On a Certain Field in Auvers.
Hecht, A.   Third Avenue in Sunlight.
Herbert, Z.   Rain, The.
Holmes, J.   Depressive Episode.
Jennings, E.   Mental Hospital Sitting-Room, A.
Johnson, H.   Berlioz in the Madhouse.
Justice, D.   Counting the Mad.
Kenyon, J.   Depression in Winter.
Knight, E.   Hard Rock Returns to Prison from
  the Hospital for the Criminal Insane.
Kolodny, S.   Tsuneko—Psychiatric Medications
  Clinic.
Levy, A.   Cross-Road Epitaph, A.
Lowell, R.   Skunk Hour.
  Waking in the Blue.
Maiden.   Anorexia.
Mew.   Ken.
  On the Asylum Road.
Miller, J.   Crazed Woman, The.
Moolten, D.   Madame Butterfly.
Murray, G.   American Cheese.

North, C.   Note to Tony Towle (After WS), A.
Okamoto.   Tanka: "Ten years ago."
Opie.   To a Maniac.
Owen, W.   Mental Cases.
Page, P.   Schizophrenic.
Plath.   Tulips.
Pollarolo, G.   Man Went to See the Doltons, A.
Rector.   David's Rumor.
Rhodes, M.   Why She Hurries Out, Then Home.
Ritchie, E.   Electroconvulsive Therapy.
Sexton.   Music Swims Back to Me.
  You, Doctor Martin.
Silva, C.   Magical Devices.
Smith, S.   Away, Melancholy.
Strickland, A.   Maniac, The.
Tipping.   When You're Feeling Kind of
  Bonkers.
Unknown.   Limerick.
Weinstein, N.   Ethiopian Apocalypse of Don,
  The.
See also **Madness; Psychiatry and Psychiatrists**

Mental Retardation
Dodd, E.   Touched.
Johnson, M. F.   Idiot Girl, The.
Murray, L.   Dog Fox Field.
Nowlan.   He Sits Down on the Floor of a School
  for the Retarded.
Seale, J.   Playing the Flute for the TMR Class.
See also **Down's Syndrome**

Mephistopheles
Marlowe.   Had I as many souls as there be stars.
See also **Satan**

Mercenaries
Housman.   Epitaph on an Army of Mercenaries.
Jonson, B.   To Captain Hungry.
MacDiarmid, H.   Another Epitaph on an Army
  of Mercenaries.
Sagan.   Yojimbo.
Unknown.   No money yet, why then let's terrify
  with swords.

Merchants
Ammuvanar.   They Shout Out the Price of Salt.
Artmann.   Tea Merchant, The.
Bertrand.   Tulip Merchant, The.
Brown, A.   Old Neighborhood, The.
Chang Yü.   Merchant's Joy, The.
Dickinson, E.   I asked no other thing.
Espinet, R.   Merchant of Death.
Jamie.   Flower-sellers, Budapest.
Kroetsch.   Ledger, The.
Lu Yu.   Merchant's Joy, The.
Reznikoff.   Millinery District ("Clouds, piled in
  rows like merchandise, The.").
Millinery District ("Many fair hours have been
  buried here.").
Shin Kyŏngnim.   On a Winter's Night.
Toledo, N.   Cielo Min.
  Guibá xti min.
Unknown.   Song of Ch'ŏngŭp.
See also **Business and Businessmen; Clerks**

Mercury (god)
Anyte [*or* Anytes].   I, Hermes, stand here by the
  windy tree-lined.
Komunyakaa, Y.   Slam, Dunk, & Hook.
Korinna [*or* Corinna].   Kouretes hid the
  goddess's, The.
  Over you, Hermes fights.
Lawrence, D. H.   Maximus.
Palladas [*or* Pallades].   Where the Three Roads
  Meet.
Rilke.   Orpheus, Eurydice, Hermes.
Sappho.   There a bowl of ambrosia.
Unknown.   Stealing of Apollo's Cattle, The.

Mercury (planet)
Morgan, E.   First Men on Mercury, The.
Oswald, A.   Excursion to the Planet Mercury.

Mercy
Amichai, Y.   God Has Mercy on Kindergarten
  Children.
  God Has Pity on Kindergarten Children.
Bejerano, M.   Oh spare me, spare me.
Bhattācārya, K.   Kali, you have removed all my
  difficulties.
  What's the fault of the poor mind?
Bible, *O.T.*   Gods boundles bownties gods

promise ever abyding.
  Psalm 57. Miserere Mei Deus.
Bishop, E.   Fish, The.
Campert, J.   Eighteen Dead, The.
Chippewa Oral Tradition.   Song of the Captive
  Sioux Woman.
Dīnrām.   O Baba! Look at this Cadak tree.
Donne.   If poisonous [*or* poysonous] mineral[l]s,
  and if that tree.
Elytis, O.   Origin of Landscape or the End of
  Mercy, The.
García Lorca.   Ah secret voice of dark love! Ah
  bleating without wool! Ah wound! Ah prick of
  gall, sunken camellia!
Han Yü.   Humanity.
Hardy, T.   Often When Warring.
Herbert, G.   Discipline.
Herrick.   To Heaven.
Hopes.   Mercy on me Spirit.
Issa.   Don't kill that poor fly!
Klassen, S.   Act of Mercy.
Levertov.   On the dream sidewalk.
Levine, P.   Angel Butcher.
Love, C.   Modern Love Poem, A.
Lumsden, R.   Mercy.
Mitchell, S.   Luke 10:25–37; And behold, a
  lawyer.
Nahman [*or* Nachman] of Bratzlav.   From "The
  Torah of the Void".
Pavlova, V.   This is the way a row of official
  tulips.
Phillips, C.   Singing.
Ralegh, S.   Passionate Man['] Pilgrimage, The.
Reznikoff.   Day of Atonement.
Rossetti, C.   Before the Beginning.
Shakespeare, W.   How yet resolves the
  Governor of the town?
  Then must the Jew be mercifull.
Sidney.   Sonnet 40: "As good to write as for to
  lie and groan."
Södergran.   Question.
Southey, R.   Ship, The.
Tuckerman, F.   Rhotruda.
Unknown.   Epitaph: "My friend, judge not me."
  Mercy.
  Prayer of a Woman in Charge of Berry Picking
    in Knights Inlet.
  You and I.
Upton, L.   Quality of Mercy, The.
Various authors.   Because he loved men and
  sought their welfare.
Wheatley, P.   On Being Brought from Africa to
  America.
Whittier.   Robin, The.
Wordsworth, W.   Gravestone upon the Floor in
  the Cloisters of Worcester Cathedral, A.

Merlin
Chubb, T.   Merlin.
Deniz, G.   Merlin.
  Merlín.
Emerson, R.   Merlin.
Hill, G.   Merlin.
Norris, L.   Merlin and the Snake's Egg.

Mermaids and Mermen
Abdul-Salaam, A.   Mermaid, The.
Calverley.   In the Gloaming.
Crapsey.   Laurel in the Berkshires.
Cynewulf.   Nature of the Siren, The.
Darley.   Mermaidens' Vesper-Hymn, The.
De la Mare.   Sam.
Goethe.   Fisherman, The.
Goodison.   On Becoming a Mermaid.
Hedyla.   Either cockleshells from the Erythraian
  reef as gifts.
Hughes, L.   Catch.
Knight, S.   Mermaid Tank, The.
MacLeish.   Return.
McCullagh, J.   Mermaid's Song.
Mullen, H.   Mermaid of Palmares.
Nash, O.   Mermaid, The.
Neruda.   Fable of the Mermaid and the Drunks.
Reid, C.   Mermaids Explained.
Spires.   Comb and the Mirror, The.
Tennyson, A.   Merman, The.
Toledo, N.   Na Aurea.
Young, I.   Mermaid Knows, A.

Merrimac (ship)
Longfellow, H.   Cumberland, The.
Mitchell, S.   How the Cumberland Went Down.

Merriment
Herrick.   Ceremonies for Christmas[se].
Houlihan, J.   H. Antecessor.
McGinley.   City Christmas.
Tu Mu.   Take the Bottle, and Ascend.

Merry-Go-Rounds
Hughes, L.   Merry-Go-Round.
Mandel, E.   City Park Merry-Go-Round.
Morozov, S.   Poem about the Blue Horse.
Rilke.   Merry-go-round, The.

Merwin, W. S. (William Stanley)
Ali, A.   Of Fire.

Messengers
Browning, R.   How They Brought the Good
   News from Ghent to Aix.
Doolittle, H.   Hermes of the Ways.
Frost, R.   Bearer of Evil Tidings, The.
Glück, L.   Messengers.
Gunn, T.   Messenger, The.
Harvey, M.   Festival of Giovedo Grasso, The.
Kalidasa.   High on the Mount of Rama a yaksha
   dwelt, who for.
Kallatanar.   What She Said.
Lawrence, D. H.   Maximus.
Mitchell, S.   Annunciation, The.
Nemes Nagy.   Like One Who.
Olson, C.   Sun / right in my eye.
"Rachel." [or "Rahel."].   Messenger came in the
   night, The.
Seiferle, R.   Mythology of Heavenly
   Messengers, The.
Shakespeare, W.   My liege, I did deny no
   prisoners.
Sioux Oral Tradition.   Whole world is coming,
   The.
Unknown.   Breeze, you who blow from the
   mountainside where my lover fights.
   Now mountains are separating us.
Williams, W.   Bibelforscher, Die.

Messiah
Al-Bayati, A.   Nine Ruba'iyat.
Arapaho Oral Tradition.   He! When I met him
   approaching.
Bell, J.   Zombie Sunday (Had We but World
   Enough and Time).
Gascoyne.   Rex Mundi.
Hughes, T.   Gog.
Pope, A.   Messiah [a Sacred Eclogue, in
   Imitation of Virgil's Pollio].
Sioux Oral Tradition.   Father says so—*E'yayo!*,
   The.
   Whole world is coming, The.
Voznesensky [or Voznesenskii].   December
   Pastures.
Waldman, A.   Letter S.
Yeats.   Matthew 24:15–31.
   Second Coming, The.

Metals
Cox, M.   Treasure: "Ax heads and sledges,
   musket balls and elixir bottles."
Kinsella, J.   Akbar.
Mathews, H.   Relics, The.
Moore, M.   Odor of a Metal Is Not Strong, The.
Morley, D.   Metal-work.
Morrissey, S.   Jo Gravis in His Metal Garden.
Musa, Y.   Zinc.
Page, P.   Metal and the Flower, The.
Scovell.   Workers in Metal.

Metamorphosis
Miller, A.   Forever Afternoon.

Metaphor
Armitage, S.   Not the Furniture Game.
Baraka, A.   X.
Collins, B.   Death of Allegory, The.
   Litany: "You are the bread and the knife."
Davie, D.   With the Grain.
De Angelis.   Every Metaphor.
Dove, R.   History: "Everything's a metaphor,
   some wise."
France, L.   Body Language.
Gilbert, S.   Against Poetry.
Hollander, J.   What the Lovers in the Old Songs

Thought.
Kinsella, J.   Archetypal Chillies.
Levchev, Vladimir.   Four Seekers of the Great
   Metaphor.
Lowell, A.   Meeting-House Hill.
Luzi.   Postscriptum.
MacCaig.   No Choice.
Marvell.   Definition of Love, The.
Milán, E.   Marionetas son metáforas perfectas,
   Las.
   Riddle me what marionettes are.
Musa, Y.   There Is a Dead Poet Alive.
Nash, O.   Very Like a Whale.
Nyhart.   Vow.
Pastan.   Baseball.
   Overture.
Plath.   Metaphors.
Rilke.   Gazelle, The.
Sidney.   Sonnet 9: "Queen Virtue's court, which
   some call Stella's face."
Stevens, W.   Motive for Metaphor, The.
Thomas, D.   If I Were Tickled by the Rub of
   Love.
Tranter.   Great Artist Reconsiders the Homeric
   Simile, The.
Vallejo.   Conflict Between the Eyes and the
   Gaze, The.
Whalen, P.   Take dandelions first salad.
Williams, W.   Sort of a Song, A.
Williamson, G.   Dark Days, The.

See also **Symbols**

Metaphysics
Barbauld.   To Mr. S. T. Coleridge.
Herbert, Z.   Georg Heym—The Almost
   Metaphysical Adventure.
Lloyd, C.   Metaphysical Sonnet.
MacNeice.   London Rain.
McPherson, S.   Some Metaphysics of Junior
   Wells.
Muso Soseki.   Curtain of cloud hangs, A.
   Green mountains.
   No End Point.
   Old Man of Few Words.
Stevens, W.   Curtains in the House of the
   Metaphysician, The.
Tomlinson, C.   In Defence of Metaphysics.
Tranter.   Hang up a yellow shirt—you cause joy.
Wright, C.   California Dreaming.
Young, D.   Four About Metaphysics.

Meteors and Meteorites
Hirshfield, J.   That Falling.
Huntington, W.   Cold Meteorite, The.
Mayo, C.   Meteor.
Mulkey, R.   Blind-Sided.
Salazar.   Meteor Showers—Yosemite.
Schevill, Margaret Erwin.   Desert Center.
Shinkichi Takahashi.   Urn.
Szporluk.   Meteor.
Thomas, E.   Shooting Star, A.
Yungch'ŏn, Master.   Song of the Comet.

Methodism
Su, A.   I Can't Become a Buddhist.
Wesley, C.   My God! I know, I feel thee mine.

Mexican War
Acosta.   For Maximino Palomo.
Baca.   Mi Tío Baca el Poeta de Socorro.
Holley, Mary Austin.   Plea of Texas, The.
Houston, Margaret Moffette Lea.   To My
   Husband—December 1844.
Houston, Sam.   Texian Call to Arms.
Lamar.   San Jacinto.
Lind, Michael.   Now Crockett said, "You
   gentlemen are free".
Lowell, J.   Letter, A ("Thrash away, you'll hev
   to rattle").
Newton, Violette.   Witness, Susanna Dickinson,
   The.
Whittier.   Angels of Buena Vista, The.
Zaragoza Clubs.   My heart tells me.
   When the French, to their shame.

Mexico
Acosta.   Dangereux avril.
   Fragile soy.
Aridjis.   Letter from Mexico.
Ashbery, J.   Instruction Manual, The.

Baca.   So Mexicans Are Taking Jobs from
   Americans.
Birney.   Irapuato.
Bobyshev.   Trotsky in Mexico.
Bonazzi, Robert.   Changing Borders.
Brewer, G.   Mountains.
Burlingame.   After Bird Watching near the
   Mexican Border.
Campo.   El Día de los Muertos.
Cisneros, S.   You Bring Out the Mexican in Me.
Cortez, Sarah.   Attempt to Locate.
Crane, H.   Purgatorio.
Cumpian.   No Deposit Returns.
de Gonzáles, Merced J.   Mexico Will Be Free.
De Villagrá.   Canto 1.
Gilbert, J.   Elephant Hunt in Guadalajara.
Gonzales, R.   Head of Pancho Villa, The.
   Paso del Norte.
Gonzalez, R.   Still Life with Endings.
González, R.   You and the Tijuana Mule.
Herrera.   Dream of Christopher Columbus, The.
   Mexican World Mural / 5 x 25.
   Resurrection of the Flesh, The.
Huerta, E.   Declaration of Hate.
Johnson, D.   Dust of Mexico, The.
Juana Inés de la Cruz.   In Acknowledgment of
   the Praises of European Writers.
Kerouac.   Mexican Loneliness.
Lawrence, D. H.   Living Quetzalcoatl, The.
LittleDog, Pat.   Crossing the river to juárez.
López Velarde.   Baleful Return.
   Provincial Sundays.
McClure, M.   Reading Frank O'Hara in a
   Mexican Rainstorm.
McKendrick, J.   Shortened History in Pictures,
   A.
Miller, J.   Defense of the Alamo, The.
Mullen, H.   Viejas Locas.
Oppen.   Resort.
Pacheco, J.   High Treason.
Paz.   Hymn Among the Ruins.
Pellicer, C.   Wishes.
Ramírez, J.   Corazón mecánico.
   Ficción y las Cosas, La.
   Mechanical Heart.
   Of Fiction and Things.
   Tepozán.
Reed, I.   El Paso Monologue.
Reyes, A.   Tarahumara Herbs.
Ríos, A.   At Kino Viejo, Mexico.
Soto.   Graciela.
Stevens, W.   Sea Surface Full of Clouds.
Thomas, R.   Ensenada Wedding.
Torre, M.   How to Look at Mexican Highways.
Torres Bodet.   My Country.
Ulacia, M.   Tenochtitlán Blues.
Unknown.   Corrido of "Gregorio Cortez".
   Corrido of the Uprooted Ones.
   Deported.
   Discrimination.
   Kansas 1.
   Registration of 1918.
Van Duyn.   Into Mexico.
Villanueva, T.   Serving of Water, The.
Welch, L.   In Answer to a Question From P. W.
Wheeler, S.   In Juarez.
Williams, W.   Desert Music, The.
Wong, N.   On Plaza Garibaldi.
Wright, J.   Minneapolis Poem, The.
Yépez, H.   En la Calle Coahuila.
   Juan Martínez, Juan Nadie, Juan Todos.
   Juan Martínez, Juan Nobody, Juan All.
   Life of a Cucapá Woman, The.
   On Coahuila Street.
   Vida de una mujer cucapá, La.

Mexico City
Twichell.   Aisle of Dogs.

Mice
Bachner.   Little Mouse, The.
Baker, M.   In the pocket.
Bennett, R.   Witch of Willowby Wood, The.
Blight.   Death of a Whale.
Bodecker.   Cats and Dogs.
Brown, M.   Little Black Bug.
Brown, S.   Marriage.
Buffoni, F.   To be soldiers together and allies.

Burns, R.   To a Mouse; On Turning Her up in Her Nest, with the Plough, November, 1785.
Callimachus.   Mousetrap, The.
Carroll, L.   Mouse's Tale, The.
Chaucer.   Lat take a cat, and fostre him [or hym] wel[l] with milk.
Ciardi, J.   I Wouldn't.
Clare, J.   Clock-A-Clay.
  Mouse's Nest.
Coatsworth.   Mouse, The.
Cook, E.   Mouse and the Cake, The.
Cowley, A.   Country-Mouse, The.
Cox, P.   Mouse's Lullaby, The.
Cummings, E. E.   Me Up at Does.
Delmore, E.   Is It Not Strange?
Dixon, M.   Place, Places.
Erb, E.   Inedible.
Feinstein, S.   Summerhouse Piano.
Fisher, A.   Mouse Dinner.
Flynn, N.   Bag of Mice.
Fyleman.   (Mice).
Gerov, Alexander.   Mice.
Graves, R.   One Hard Look.
Gray, S.   On a Cat Aging.
Gunn, T.   Last Days at Teddington.
Issa.   In my house / Mice and fireflies.
  Spring rain.
Jarnot, L.   My Terrorist Notebook.
Kay, J.   Virus².
Kim Hyesun.   Mice.
Kinsella, J.   Chess Piece Cornered.
Košek, M.   Little Mouse, The.
Kupriyanov [or Kuprianov].   Everything gets forgotten.
La Fontaine.   Young mouse, poor, no experience, A.
Löwy, H.   Little Mouse, The.
Mitchell, L.   House of the Mouse, The.
Moore, M.   Camellia Sabina.
Moorer.   Legal Mouse, A.
Mother Goose.   Three blind mice, see how they run!
Nikonova, R.   Along the thread of veins.
Nims, J.   Mouse, The.
Norris, L.   Mice in the Hay.
Pitcher, O.   Formula for tragedy.
Remizov, Alexei.   Mouse, The.
Roethke.   Meadow Mouse, The.
Rossetti, C.   City Mouse and the Garden Mouse, The.
  City Mouse and the Garden Mouse, The.
Rothman, D.   Resurrection of a Mouse.
Serraillier.   Anne and the Field-Mouse.
Simic.   We Were So Poor.
Sosnora.   Owl and the Mouse, The.
Stevens, W.   Dance of the Macabre Mice.
Stroud, W.   Rustler.
Tsaloumas.   Old Friend.
Tu Fu [or Du Fu].   Travelling Northward.
Unknown.   Mouse in Her Room, A.
Unknown, formerly at. to Homer.   Ascend my shoulders, firmly keep thy seat.
Wellman, M.   Endowed fiction of a mouse ear.
Williams, W.   Mujer.
Yusuf, S.   Mouse, The.

Michael, Saint
Constable, H.   To St. Michael the Archangel.
Rossetti, C.   St. Michael and all Angels.

Michaelmas
Forrest-Thomson.   Michaelmas.
Nicholson, N.   Michaelmas.

Michelangelo Buonarroti
Allston.   On a Falling Group in the Last Judgement of Michael Angelo, in the Cappella Sistina.
  On Michael Angelo.
Browning, R.   "Moses" of Michael Angelo, The.
Cafagña, M.   Hawthorne Metal, Detroit, 1939.
McIlroy, L.   Good-Bye, Valentine.

Michigan (state)
Joseph, L.   Do What You Can.
Levine, P.   Drum: *Leo's Tool & Die, 1950.*
  Rain Downriver.

Microbes
Auden.   New Year Greeting, A.

Goedicke.   Imprint of Microscopic Life Found in Arctic Stones.

Microcosm
Bradstreet, A.   Contemplations.
Daumal.   I Speak in All Ages.
Dowden, E.   Two Infinities.
Frost, R.   Design.
Guevara, M.   Miniaturist, The.
Hughes, F.   Bird.
Kikaku.   Leaf / Of the yam.
Muso Soseki.   Chick feed is what I eat.
Pastan.   Egg.
Shinkichi Takahashi.   Gods.
Whitman, W.   I believe a leaf of grass is no less than the journey-work of the stars.

Microscopes
Bierds, L.   Van Leeuwenhoek: 1675.
Chin, J.   Undetectable.
Dickinson, E.   Faith is a fine invention.
Holub.   In the Miscroscope.
Thomas, G.   Microscope.

Midas
Kizer, C.   Ungrateful Garden, The.
Moss, H.   King Midas.
Pastan.   Obligation to Be Happy, The.
"Pindar.".   Epigram: "Midas, they say, possessed the art of old."

Middle Age
Adcock, F.   Kissing.
Beer, P.   Middle Age.
Clifton, L.   Thirty-Eighth Year, The.
Cooley.   Language of Departure.
Crews, J.   Declaration at Forty.
Desnos.   Mid-way.
Donne.   Autumnal[l], The.
Enzensberger, H.   At Thirty-Three.
Hall, D.   To a Waterfowl.
Hardie, K.   What's Left.
Hjern, K.   On the Growth of Hair in Middle Age.
Jarrell, R.   Next Day.
Justice, D.   Men at Forty.
Kunitz, S.   End of Summer.
Le Guin.   At the Party.
Logghe.   From *Rice.*
Longfellow, H.   Mezzo Cammin.
MacLeish.   Dover Beach—a Note to That Poem.
MacNeice.   Libertine, The.
Matthews, W.   Good Company.
McDonald, W.   Middle Years, The.
McGough, R.   40— Love.
Millar, J.   Midlife.
Mun Chônghui.   Song of a Middle-Aged Woman.
Pak Chaesam.   Looking at Winter Trees.
Parker, D.   Ballade at Thirty-Five.
Porter, P.   Sex and the Over Forties.
Preil, N.   Night. And I am drinking smoky black tea from China.
Rexroth, K.   Delia Rexroth ("Under your illkempt yellow roses.").
  Now the fireflies of our youth.
Rich, A.   Middle-Aged, The.
Różewicz.   In the Middle of Life.
Rukeyser, M.   Rondel: "Now that I am fifty-six."
Salerno.   Poetry is the Art of Not Succeeding.
Salinas, L.   Middle Age.
Simpson, L.   Middleaged Man, The.
Smith, C.   Thirty-eight: Addressed to Mrs H—y.
Thompson, D. P.   Dancing in Menopause.
  Laurel Street, 1950.
Tranströmer.   Black Postcards.
Tucker, M.   First Grey Hair, The.
Webb, C.   At Summer's End.
Yevtushenko [or Evtushenko].   At Forty.
Young, A.   Fifty-Fifty.

Middle Ages
Auden.   Ode to the Medieval Poets.
Browning, R.   Grammarian's Funeral, A.
Dubie.   Annual of the Dark Physics, An.
Hill, G.   Requiem for the Plantagenet Kings.

Middle East, The
Hillman, B.   Cheap Gas.
Nortje.   Nasser is dead.

Zayyad.   Here We Will Stay.

Middlesex, England
Betjeman.   Slough.

Midgets
Satyamurti.   Broken Moon.

Midnight
al-Rahim, A.   Wailing.
Atkins, R.   At Night Keep Still.
Basho.   Awakened at midnight.
  I would like to use.
  Midnight frost.
Bevington, L.   Midnight.
Breton, A.   In the Eyes of the Gods.
Brown, G.   Haddock Fishermen.
Buson.   Sound of a saw.
Crosby, F.   Thoughts in Midnight Hours.
de Fréine, C.   Bubbles.
Devi.   No Break.
Donne.   Nocturnal[l] upon Saint Lucy's [or S. Lucy's or S. Lucies] Day, Being the Shortest Day, A.
Fletcher, J.   Slowly along the lamp-emblazoned street.
Grossman, A.   Enough Rain for Agnes Walquist.
Hanighen, B.   'Round Midnight.
Huidobro.   Midnight.
Hull, L.   Midnight Reports.
Izumi.   Watching the moon.
Johnston, P.   Round About Midnight, Opus #6.
Kaufman, B.   Round About Midnight.
Kolodinsky, A.   Midnight.
Lane, P.   Midnight Song.
Lewis, S.   Street of Dreams.
Masaoka Shiki.   Midnight sound / Leap up.
Patumanãr.   What She Said.
Po Chü-i.   Night in the Palace with Ch'ien Hui.
Stoutenburg.   Midnight Saving Time.
Su Tung-p'o.   Lyrics to the Tune "Fairy Grotto".
Unknown.   Autumn.
  Thinking of Lady Yang at Midnight.
Watson, R.   Midnight Harvest, A.
Whitman, W.   Clear Midnight, A.
Wilson, E.   Past Midnight.
Xuanjing.   Meditating at midnight.

Midsummer
Christopher.   Midsummer.
Fletcher, J.   Iridescent vibrations of midsummer light, The.
Hardy, T.   On a Midsummer Eve.
Leiter, Deborah.   Midsummer's Eve.

Midwives
Macari, A.   New York, 1927.

Mignonettes
Lawrence, D. H.   Red Geranium and Godly Mignonette.

Migraine
Clarke, G.   Migraine.

Migrant Workers
Delgado, J.   Awakened in a Field.
  Campesinos.
García, D.   Tísica.
González, R.   Penny Men.
Hawaiian Oral Tradition.   Contract is over and yet, The.
  I hate hole hole work.
  If we can get married.
  In the rush at pau hana.
  Laborers keep on coming, The.
  Should I return to Japan?
  With one woven basket.
Janzen, J.   August Nights.
Levis.   Photograph: Migrant Worker, Parlier, California, 1967.
McDaniel, W.   Ruby Red's Migrant Camp.
Oliveira, D.   Little Travel Story, A.
Rozga, M.   To California Where Rhymes Fail.
Spear, R.   Good Men.
  Nest for Everyone, A.
Zepeda, R.   Wreckers, The.
See also **Farmworkers**

Migration
Brodsky, J.   September came on Tuesday.
Bryant, W.   To a Waterfowl.
Caleshu, A.   Collaboration: Migration Patterns.
Cody, James.   Whooping Crane.

Crummey, Michael. Capelin Scull.
Dameron, Chip. Banding near the South Texas
  Coast, Late April.
Doty, M. Migratory.
Dove, R. Event, The.
  Straw Hat.
Eich. End of a Summer, The.
Freneau. On the Emigration to America [and
  Peopling the Western Country].
Grennan. On a 3 1/2 Oz. Lesser Yellowlegs,
  Departed Boston August 28, Shot Martinique
  September 3.
Hoagland, T. Migration.
Hope, A. Death of the Bird, The.
Horan. Soft Swimmer, Winter Swan.
Hughes, L. Good Morning.
Johnson, D. Migration.
Mattawa. History of My Face.
Savitz, M. To the Horizon.
Weaver, A. Brooklyn.

Milan, Italy
Levine, P. And the Trains Go On.
Quasimodo. Milan, August 1943.
Seidel. Racine.

Militarism
Amadiume. We Have Even Lost our Tongues!
Belli, G. Nicaragua Water Fire.
Hardy, T. Channel Firing.

Military Conscription
Ewer. Only Way, The.
Forché. Selective Service.
Loesser. They're Either Too Young or Too Old.
Logue, C. Song of the Dead Soldier, The.
Murray, C. Dockens afore his Peers.
Pak Mogwŏl [or Mokwŏl]. Today.
Pak Nohae. Road to Corruption, The.
Sassoon, S. Conscripts.
Wei Chuang. Against Conscription.

Military Justice
Kipling, R. Cells.
  Danny Deever.

Military Life
Allen, E. In the Defences.
Butler, C. E. Rifle Range: Louisiana.
Dalby, L. MacArthur High School.
Matthews, W. Poetry Reading at West Point, A.
McKay, D. 3. The Base.
Mikhail, D. Non-Military Statements.
Morris, J. Man and Boy.
Pak Nohae. Road to Corruption, The.
Porter, P. Soliloquy at Potsdam.
Queneau. Reinforcements [1].
Rome, H. Military Life, The.
See also **Army Life**

Military Officers
Asim, J. 1st Lt. Vernon J. Baker: Hero on the
  Hill.
  Staff Sgt. Edward A. Carter, Jr.: There and
  Back.
Bejerano, M. States of War.
Mackintosh, E. In Memoriam, Private D.
  Sutherland.
Pak Illo. Lament on the Water.
Prévert. Quartier Libre.
Sassoon, S. Base Details.
Unknown. Lay of the Lash, The.

Milk and Milking
Bancquart. Return of Ulysses.
Boland, E. Night Feed.
Chaucer. Lat take a cat, and fostre him [or
  hym] wel[l] with milk.
Corso. Mad Yak, The.
Frost, R. Cow in Apple Time, The.
Heaney, S. Churning Day.
Herrick. Fresh Cheese and Cream.
Khoury, N. People of Figs.
Maguire, S. Spilt Milk.
Monro, H. Milk for the Cat.
Montague, J. Drink of Milk, A.
Nash, O. Cow, The.
Pai, S. Milkstone.
Plumpp. I wonder.
Riordan, M. Milk.
Ruefle. Execution Poster, The.
Santos, S. Dairy Cows of Maria Cristina Cortes.

Shwarts [*or* Shvarts]. Remembrance of Strange
  Hospitality.
Taylor, E. Meditation 150 (Second Series).
Ziedonis. At Maruža's.

Milkmaids
Pfeiffer, E. Sonsy Milkmaid, The.

Milkmen
Gardner, I. Milkman, The.
Raye, D. Milkman, Keep Those Bottles Quiet!
Someck, R. Till When Will We Sleep after the
  Whore.

Milkweed
Kasdorf. Streak, The.
Wright, J. Milkweed.

Milky Way, The
Basho. Sea grows rough, The.
  Wild sea, A.
Li Po. Viewing the Waterfall at Mount Lu.
Li'aibi, S. Soul of a pebble on top of the
  mountain.
Masaoka Shiki. Dew, clinging / To potato field.
Muso Soseki. At the Nachi Kannon Hall.
Wei Ying-wu. Milky Way.
Wintu Oral Tradition. You and I Shall Go.

Millay, Edna St. Vincent
Adams, F. If.
Untermeyer, L. Edna St. Vincent Millay
  Exhorts Little Boy Blue.

Millennium
Beer, P. Millennium.
Brock-Broido. Domestic Mysticism.
Ferlinghetti, L. Millennium Cities.
Kyger. Once Again Another Century Ahead.
Mares, E. Millennium.
McInnis, C. 2G (Another Millennium Poem).
Pawlak. Official Versions.
Pierce, T. Twenty-First Century, Farewell.
Pollard, C. On the first of January.
Shapiro, H. Bus Ride.
Smith, D. 2000.
Whittier. Astræa.
Yeats. Second Coming, The.

Millet, Jean François
Markham, E. Man with the Hoe, The.

Million Man March
Keller, B. One Million Men Marching 2.

Mills and Millers
Chaucer. Miller's [*or* Milleres] Tale, The.
Foster, A. Wythop Mill.
Kalar, J. Papermill.
Komunyakaa, Y. Gristmill.
Lenski, H. Near the Mill.
Markus, P. Black Light.
Nelson, M. Molino.
Rendall, R. Horse-Mill, The.
Robinson, E. Mill, The.
Rumi. Mill, the Stone, and the Water, The.
Wainwright, J. 1815.

Milton, John
Auden. John Milton.
Beer, P. John Milton and My Father.
Blake, W. Preface: "And did those feet in
  ancient time."
Deane, S. Reading *Paradise Lost* in Protestant
  Ulster 1984.
Devaney, T. Sonnet: "You know all those
  sonnets the ones where I said, I love you,
  well."
Dryden, J. Lines Printed under the Engraved
  Portrait of Milton [In Tonson's Folio of the
  "Paradise Lost"].
Lazarus, E. City Visions.
Longfellow, H. Milton.
Marvell. On Mr Milton's "Paradise Lost".
Muir, E. Milton.
Myles, E. December 9th.
Ray, H. Milton.
Snyder, G. Milton by Firelight.
Tabb. Milton.
Wordsworth, W. London 1802 ("Milton! thou
  shouldst be living at this hour.").

Mind
Bang, M. Louise in Love.
Basho. Weathered bones.
Bhattācārya, K. Crazy Mind.

Bhattācārya, M. Look at all these waves.
Black, S. Asylum.
Chazal, M. Logic.
Chifu. No mind, no Buddhas, no live beings.
Chŏng Ch'ŏl. Dash of rain upon, A.
Clark, T. Bun.
Colonna, S. So it tries to reach her inside her
  mind.
Daglarca. Beauty and Mind.
Davies, W. H. Mind's Liberty, The.
De Angelis. Main Idea, The.
  Towards the Mind.
Dogen. Coming, going, the waterfowl.
Dragomoschenko. Instructing Clarity in a
  Confusion.
Genko. Unaware of illusion or enlightenment.
Gerov, Alexander. Urban Tree.
Giussani, S. Clothes Without the Monk, The.
  Towards a Beginning.
Graham, A. Hands and feet.
Greenberg, U. Song of the Great Mind.
Guchu. Men without rank, excrement spatulas.
Han-shan Te-ch'ing. Through a few splinters of.
Hancock, Butch. My Mind's Got a Mind of Its
  Own.
Hochman. Hairbrush, The.
Hope, A. Wandering Islands, The.
Ilkov, Ani. Peony and a Lion, A.
Jungkwan Haean. Various Songs of Leisure.
Karasumaru-Mitsuhiro. Beware of gnawing the
  ideogram of nothingness.
Kyger. Watching TV.
Lodge, T. Minde through thee divines on
  endlesse things, The.
MacEwen, G. Dark Pines under Water.
Mead, J. Sometimes the Mind.
Moore, R. Still without Life.
Mueller, J. Portrait of My Father as the Boy of
  Winander.
Muso Soseki. Many times the mountains have
  turned from green to yellow.
  Mugoku Osho's Snow Poem.
Nandī, R. Mind, let's go to an estate that's
  decent.
Padgett, R. Bun.
Pasternak, B. Storm, an Endless Instant.
Pollitt. Mind-Body Problem.
Roethke. In a Dark Time.
Ryushu Shutaku. Mind set free in the Dharma-
  realm.
Scalise, G. Dora Markus and Her Actors.
Sen, R. My Mind, my helmsman.
  Oh Mind, you don't know how to farm.
  Oh my Mind! You're just spinning.
  Tell me.
Seng-ts'an. Believing Mind, The.
Shishin-Goshin. Talking: seven steps, eight
  falls.
Shozan. No mind, no Buddha.
Shunryu Suzuki. Beginner's Mind.
Skloot. Role of a Lifetime, The.
Soen. On Visiting Shorin Temple, Where
  Bodhidharma Once Lived.
Song Ikp'il. To the Moon.
Staveley, B. Speak Again.
Stevens, W. Of Mere Being.
  Snow Man, The.
Stevenson, A. Vertigo.
Sze. Network, The.
Taneda Santoka. Somewhere / inside my head.
Tanzan. Madness, the way they gallop off to
  foreign shores!
Tekkan. No mind, no Buddha, no being.
Tlingit Oral Tradition. Carrying My Mind
  Around.
Twichell. Paper River, The.
Venkatarao, K. You on My Mind.
Volach, Y. I Have a Stage in My Head.
Wylie. This Corruptible.
See also **Intellect and Intellectuals**

Minerals
Coolidge, C. Dalliance with Salt Sides, A.
Dupin. Mineral Kingdom.
Hemans. Epitaph on Mr W—.
Jones, R. Strata.
MacDiarmid, H. Crystals like Blood.

Timoner, J. Earliest Crows in Mineral.
See also **Mining and Miners; Metals**

Minerva
Fletcher, G. I saw, sweet Licia, when the spider ran.
Hood, T. To Minerva.
Ovid. I have (may I always keep!) blonde Minerva's protection: my vessel.
Toledo, N. Temple.
Templo.
Yudu.
See also **Athena**

Mingus, Charles
Komunyakaa, Y. Copacetic Mingus.
Matthews, W. Mingus at The Showplace.
Oliphant. Denton.

Mining and Miners
Bierds, L. Desire.
Davies, I. There are countless tons of rock above his head.
Gibson, W. White Dust, The.
Grinshpan, Y. Miner's Family, The.
Heyen. Canary.
Huddle. Almost Going.
Holes Commence Falling.
Johnson, D. Poem: "There was something I can't bring myself."
Larkin, P. Explosion, The.
McGinn, M. Coorie Doon.
McKinney, I. Deep Mining.
Twilight in West Virginia: Six O'Clock Mine Report.
Menai. Where shall the eyes a darkness find.
Miljkovic. Miners.
More, H. Patient Joe; or, The Newcastle Collier.
Morgan, R. Mica Country.
Owen, W. Miners.
Page, P. Photos of a Salt Mine.
Reibetanz, J. Head and Torso of the Minotaur.
Sassoon, S. Case for the Miners, The.
Snyder, G. Milton by Firelight.
Tachibana Akemi. Walking Around Watching the Miners Digging.
Unknown. Clementine.
Curse on Mine-Owners, A.
Untermeyer, L. Caliban in the Coal Mines.
Ward, B. Twenty Million Buckets.
Watkins, V. Collier, The.
Williams, M. Redundant Miners.
Wrigley, R. Sinking of Clay City, The.
See also **Coal Mining and Coal Miners; Gold Mining and Gold Miners**

Ministers
Heller, R. Minister has all his notes in place, The.
Hughes, L. Madam and the Minister.
Stevenson, A. Minister.
Wheatley, P. To the Rev. Dr. Thomas Amory on Reading His Sermons on Daily Devotion.
Young, D. Last Lauch.
See also **Clergy**

Mink
Derricotte. Minks, The.
Hannan, M. Coming Down from Derry Hill.

Minnesota (state)
Etter. Great Northern.
Feela. Cut.
Kooser. Late Lights in Minnesota.
Redmond, J. Bemidji.
Ryan, R. Winter in Minneapolis.
Wanek. Duluth, Minnesota.
Wright, J. Blessing, A: "Just off the highway to Rochester, Minnesota."
Lying in a Hammock at William Duffy's Farm in Pine Island, Minnesota.
Minneapolis Poem, The.

Minotaur
Gioia. Maze Without a Minotaur.
Howell, C. Christian Science Minotaur, The.
Powell, D. A. Minotaur at Supper, The: Spare the Noritake and the Spade.
Reibetanz, J. Head and Torso of the Minotaur.
Wright, F. Depiction of Childhood.

Minstrels
Dransfield. Minstrel.
Hughes, L. Minstrel Man.
Lydgate. O thow Minstral that cannest so note and pipe.
Moore, T. Minstrel Boy, The.
Scott, S. Breathes there the [*or* a] Man with soul so dead.
Minstrel, The.
Stanley, T. Imperialism—The Dancing Do Not Die.

Miracles
Aiken, C. Miracles.
Appleman, P. Mary.
Archilochus. Nothing is unexpected or sworn impossible.
Awoonor. This Earth, My Brother.
Bishop, E. Miracle for Breakfast, A.
Cortázar. Very Real Story, A.
Creeley. Kore.
De Los Santos, M. Milagros Mourns the Queen of Scat.
De Viau. Ode: "Raven croaks before me, A."
Donne. Relic, The.
Drayton. Sonnet 35: Some, misbelieving and profane.
Field. Maidenhair.
Ginsberg, A. Galilee Shore.
Herrick. Widow's Tears [*or* Widdowes Teares]: or, Dirge of Dorcas, The.
Kowit. Trick, A.
Lux. Wife Hits Moose.
Masters, E. Business Reverses.
McGough, R. Poem With a Limp.
Merton. Cana.
Milosz, C. Mark 5:21–43; And when Jesus had crossed.
Muske, C. Miracles.
Ni Dhomhnaill. Deep-Freeze.
Pasternak, B. Evil Days, The.
Miracle, The.
Peacock, M. Little Miracle.
Plath. Black Rook in Rainy Weather.
Rilke. Just as the Winged Energy of Delight.
Rumi. Two Kinds of Miracles.
Smart, C. Crucifixion of Our Blessed Lord.
Smith, G. Penitential Cries of Jupiter Hammond, The.
Sobin, G. What the Music Wants.
Steptoe. In Black Churches.
Tate, J. Manna.
Torres, A. Small Miracle, A.
Unknown. No Man Can Hinder Me.
Vaughan, H. Religion.
Wen Yi-tuo [*or* Wen I-to]. Miracle.
Whitman, W. Miracles.
Wilbur, R. Matthew 8:28–34; And when he came to the other side.

Mirages
Kassabova, K. Mirages.
Tranströmer. November sun, The.

Miranda
Kirk, Kathleen. Miranda.

Miró, Joan
Alvi, M. I Would Like to be a Dot in a Painting by Miró.

Mirrors
Abse. Footnote Extended, A.
Aiken, C. Dear Uncle Stranger.
Ajanta. Me on the Wall.
Ali, A. Rooms Are Never Finished.
Ammons. Reflective.
Aridjis. Self-Portrait at Thirteen Years of Age.
Arvio, S. Mirrors.
Atwood. Tricks With Mirrors.
Auden. Miranda.
Bächler, W. Revolt in the Mirror, A.
Barnfield [*or* Barnefield]. Sighing, and sadly sitting by my Love.
Basho. Holy mirror, The.
Polished and polished.
Bogan, L. Man Alone.
Bracho, C. Sobre él discurren con suavidad.
Upon It They Gently Reflect.
Browning, R. Love in a Life.

Caddy, C. Three-Inch Reflector.
Carroll, L. Welcome Queen Alice.
Chernoff. Vanity, Wisconsin.
Ch'ôn Yanghûi. Every Morning in the Mirror.
Coleridge, M. Other Side of a Mirror, The.
Cortázar. Behavior of Mirrors on Easter Island, The.
Cronin, J. Motho Ke Motho Ka Batho Babang (A Person Is a Person Because of Other People).
Curbelo. Bedtime Stories.
Dafydd [*or* David] ap Gwilym. Mirror, The.
DeCarteret, M. Town Clerk, The.
Follain. Mirror, A.
Garrigue. Cracked Looking Glass.
Goldberg, L. From My Mother's Home.
Graham, J. Underneath (7).
Graves, R. Face in the Mirror, The.
Foreboding, The.
Pier-Glass, The.
Hauge. Looking at an Old Mirror.
Hemans. Mirror in the Deserted Hall, The.
Hemphill. Family Jewels.
Housman. Look not in my eyes, for fear.
Hsü Ling. Maid's Thanks for a Mirror, A.
Hwang Jiwoo. Mirror 1.
Ikuo-Myotan. Seventy-two years I've hung.
Jabès. Mirror and Scarf.
Jackson, L. With the Face.
Jinkag Haesim. Facing the Shadow.
Kim Hyesun. Remembering the Day I Gave Birth to a Daughter.
Kipling, R. Looking Glass, The.
Kornblith, M. Mirrors.
Kowit. Cosmetics Do No Good.
In the Morning.
La Fontaine. Man and His Image, The.
Levertov. Seeing for a Moment.
Li Ch'ing-chao. Hopelessness.
Lisnyanskaya [*or* Lisnianskaia]. Whenever I looked in the mirror.
Lochhead, L. Hickie, The.
Lowry, M. Delirium in Vera Cruz.
Mahadevi. When the body becomes Your mirror.
Majorino. Mirrored.
Meireles. Portrait.
Mok, J. Winter Mirror.
Morgan, R. Rearview Mirror.
Nasrallah, I. Outside my image in the frame.
Nawaz, G. Riddle.
Nicholson, N. From a Boat at Coniston.
No Hyegyông. Triangle, Comb.
Triangle, Mirror.
Noguere. Whirling Round the Sun.
Oates. Insomnia.
Pasha, Koja Râgıb. Dark thought is revealed in the twists and curves.
Pasternak, B. Mirror, The.
Piatt, S. Witch in the Glass, The.
Plath. Mirror.
Pope, A. Sol through white curtains shot a tim'rous ray.
Prior. Lady Who Offers Her Looking-Glass to Venus, The.
Probyn. Model, The.
Rakosi. Lord, What is Man?
Reed, I. Beware: Do Not Read This Poem.
Rexroth, K. Empty Mirror.
Ritsos. Morning.
Rojas. Bed with Mirrors.
Rosales. Loosening Water.
Rupchev, Georgi. Reversal of Worlds.
Salinas, P. Set Her Far from Me, Mirror.
Shakespeare, W. Sonnet 3: "Look in thy glass, and tell the face thou viewest."
Shepherd, R. Narcissus Learning the Words to This Song.
Shiomi, M. Mirror.
Simic. Miracle Glass Co.
Mirrors at 4 A.M.
Stone is a mirror which works poorly, The.
Stanford, A. Double Mirror.
Stoddard, E. Before the Mirror.
Suian. Traceless, no more need to hide.
Swinburne. Before the Mirror.

Tillema, M. So Soon ("So soon, so tired.").
So Soon ("So soon—so without tomorrow.").
Torres Bodet. Labyrinth.
Traherne. Shadows in the Water.
Tree-Leaf Woman. Who speaks the sound of an echo?
Troupe. Sense of Coolness, A.
Twichell. Cat and Mirror.
Ulacia, M. En un baño de vapor.
In the Steam Bath.
Wakoski. Imagining Point Dume.
Webster, A. By the Looking-Glass.
Wetzsteon. Late Show, The.
Whitman, W. Eidólons.
Hand-Mirror, A.
Williams, W. Mists Over the River.
Yi Sang. Mirror.
Poem No. 15.
Yusuf, S. Poetry: "Who broke these mirrors."
Zagajewski. Auto Mirror.
Zamora, D. Hand Mirror.

Mirth
Bateman, M. O Bonnie Man, Lovely Man.
Bowles, W. Languid, and sad, and slow.
Herrick. Hock-Cart, or Harvest Home, The.
To Live Merrily, and To Trust to Good Verses.
Hunt, L. To the Grasshopper and the Cricket.
Lowry, M. Strange Type.
Milton. To Cyriack Skinner.
Rodriguez, J. Eskimo occasion.
See also **Laughter; Merriment**

Misanthropy
Goethe. Three Stanzas.
Shakespeare, W. Misanthropos.
Wylie. Eagle and the Mole, The.

Miscarriages
Bierds, L. Stillness, the Dancing, The.
Clanchy, K. Miscarriage, Midwinter.
Clancy, J. Miscarriage.
Duran, J. Miscarriage.
Fisher, Diane G. After the Miscarriage.
Hecht, A. Vow, The.
Morrissey, S. Stitches.
Townsend, A. First Death.

Mischief
Aleshire. Fingers in the Bread.
Brown, L. I Want to Be Bad.
DeSylva, B. G. I Want to Be Bad.
Graves, R. Nobody.
Henderson, R. I Want to Be Bad.
Hood, T. Parental Ode to My Son, A.
Swenson, K. Ice-Cream Sandwich, The.
Unknown. Mr Nobody.
Williams, M. First Kill.

Misers
Leiris, Michel. Miserly.

Misfortune
Adair, T. Everything Happens to Me.
Ahmed Arif. Your Love Never Left.
Alexandru. End of the War, The.
Archilochus. Be Bold! That's One Way.
May he lose his way on the cold sea.
Barbour, D. Mañana (Is Soon Enough for Me).
Beckett, S. Ooftish.
Benn. This Is Bad.
Bhartrihari. Bald-Headed Man, A.
Blandiana. Covered with Dew.
Blane, R. Ev'ry Time.
Burns, R. Man Was Made to Mourn, a Dirge.
To a Mouse; On Turning Her up in Her Nest, with the Plough, November, 1785.
Camões [*or* Camõens *or* Camoëns], L. Sonnet: My Errors My Loves My Unlucky Star.
Comden, B. All of My Life.
You Mustn't Feel Discouraged.
Cowper, W. Shrubbery, The.
Dickinson, E. One need not be a Chamber—to be Haunted.
Elizabeth I. Ah silly pug wert thou so sore afraid.
Gascoigne. I set aside to tell the restless toil.
Graves, R. All Except Hannibal.
Green, A. All of My Life.
You Mustn't Feel Discouraged.
Harris, R. Call, The.

Harte, B. Mrs. Judge Jenkins[; Being the Only Genuine Sequel to "Maud Muller"].
Hernández, M. Final Sonnet.
Hikmet. Rubai.
Koehler, T. Ill Wind.
Lanier, S. Revenge of Hamish, The.
Lee, P. Mañana (Is Soon Enough for Me).
Lindsay, L. Auld Robin Gray.
Martial. Ted's studio burnt down, with all his poems.
Martin, H. Ev'ry Time.
Masters, E. Indignation Jones.
McKay, C. Castaways, The.
Nixon-Roulet, M. Highroller.
Notley. Where Leftover Misery Goes.
Petrarch. Ever mine [*or* myn] hap[pe] is slack and slo[w] in coming [*or* commyng].
Piatt, S. Giving Back the Flower.
Ralegh, S. Fortune Hath Taken Away.
Shakespeare, W. Sonnet 29: "When, in disgrace with fortune and men's eyes."
Sia, B. Enemy.
Stickney, T. Six O'Clock.
T'ao Ch'ien [*or* T'ao Yuan-ming]. Lament: "Ways of heaven are mysterious, The."
Miscellaneous Poem.
Towers, T. Three Observations on Belief.
Unknown. Malediction.
Southern Blues.
Stackalee.
Wordsworth, W. Thorn, The.
Wotton, S. Upon the Sudden Restraint of the Earl[e] of Somerset, Then Falling from Favor [*or* Favour].
Wroth. Sonnet 38: "What pleasure can a bannish'd creature have."
Wyatt. Lover Showeth How He Is Forsaken of Such as He Sometime Enjoyed, The.
Yi Kyubo. Thoughts on Eyes Growing Dim: Presented to Chŏn Iji.

Misogyny
Algarin. Trampling.
Askhari. Circular Fate.
Bradford, E. Equality.
Clare, J. Song: "I peeled bits of straw and I got switches too."
Goodwin, Eli. Untitled: "Number 1 bus jerks to a stop at Mass. Ave., The."
Pollitt. Onion.
Rich, A. From an Old House in America.
Rochester, J. Song: "Love a woman? You're [*or* Y'are] an ass."
Swift, J. Gentle Echo on Woman, A.
Yi Kyŏngnim. Korean Women.

Missionaries
Breytenbach. Dung-beetle.
Chitwood, Michael. After the Missionaries.
Dhompa, T. Sun Storm.
Heber. From Greenland's Icy Mountains.
Johnson, H. Magalu.
Linden, M. Missionary, The.
Moorer. Africa.
Morgan, E. Columba's Song.
Reito. Ox bridle tossed, vows taken.
Sims. Told to the Missionary.
Townsend, A. After the End.

Mississippi River
Applewhite. On the Mississippi.
Clifton, L. Mississippi river empties into the gulf.
Crane, H. River, The.
Fox, Skip. Most Notoriously Absent North American Bird in Her Face, The.
Garland, H. On the Mississippi.
Gehrke, S. Near the Mississippi.
Hammerstein. Ol' Man River.
Hayden, R. Night, Death, Mississippi.
Mattawa. Road from Biloxi, The.
Ransom, J. Antique Harvesters.
Redmond. River of Bones and Flesh and Blood.
Shange. Where the Mississippi meets the Amazon.
Steptoe. Mississippi Blues.
Ward, J. I Have Felt the Gulf: Mississippi.

Mississippi (state)
Allen, J. Mud Wit.

Allen, S. Apple Trees in Sussex, The.
Anderson, J. 13th Letter, The.
Brooks, G. Bronzeville Mother Loiters in Mississippi, A. Meanwhile, a Mississippi Mother Burns Bacon.
Cornish, S. Mississippi on the Doorstep.
Dove, R. Mississippi.
Dumas, H. Son of Msippi.
Eberhart, R. La Crosse at Ninety Miles an Hour.
Hayden, R. Night, Death, Mississippi.
Hughes, L. Bitter River, The.
Bound No'th Blues.
Kimbrell, J. Salvation.
Knight, E. Once on a Night in the Delta: A Report From Hell.
Poem for Myself (Or Blues for a Mississippi Black Boy), A.
Miller, E. Mississippi.
Sundiata. Making Poems; on the road in Minneapolis.
Trethewey, N. Miscegenation.
Troupe. Eye Change Dreams.
Walker, M. Jackson, Mississippi.
Ward, J. Mississippi: Bell Zone 1.

Missouri (state)
Barnes, J. Sunday Dreamer's Guide to Yarrow, Missouri, A.
Gallagher, T. 3 A.M. Kitchen: My Father Talking.
Knight, E. Poem to Galway Kinnell, A.
Ryan, M. When I Was Conceived.
Sterling, A. Meet Me in St. Louis, Louis.

Mist
Basho. It's spring, all right.
Bishop, E. Cape Breton.
Bridges, R. Garden in September, The.
Buson. Village with a thousand eaves.
Clare, J. Mist in the Meadows.
Hokushi. Sailboats in line.
Jaccottet. Daybreak.
Kaya Shirao. Mountain mist / Torches dropped.
Keats. To Autumn: "Season of mists and mellow fruitfulness!"
Kikaku. Shrine gate / Through morning mist.
Kitahara Hakushū. Summer Mist, A.
Naito Joso. About the grave / Waves of spring mist.
Sampu. Moving / Deep into mist.
Suian. Traceless, no more need to hide.
Watson, R. Children of the Mist.
See also **Fog**

Mistletoe
Tucker, M. Mistletoe.

Mistresses
Amadiume. Mistress of My Own Being.
Baudelaire. Soup and the Clouds, The.
Chinese Oral Tradition. Scroll 1: "From the Three Emperors and Five Kings down to Hsia, Shang, and Chou."
De Vries, P. To His Importunate Mistress.
Donne. On His Mistress [*or* Mistris].
Herrick. Upon the Loss[e] of His Mistresses.
Hsü Ling. Bagatelle.
Marvell. To His Coy Mistress.
Montague, J. Deer Park.
Nelson, M. Ballad of Aunt Geneva, The.
Nguyễn Gia Thiều. You were a fool, Old Man of the Moon.
Orléans, C. Roundel: "Take, take this cosse, atonys, atonys, my hert!"
Pan Chieh-yû. Song of Regret.
Pao Chao. Ballad in Imitation of "The Prince of Huainan".
P'Bitek. Woman with Whom I Share My Husband, A.
Picasso. Her Great Thighs.
Rilke. Flamingos, The.
Rimbaud, A. Bottom.
Shakespeare, W. O[h] Mistress Mine.
Sonnet 130: "My mistress' eyes are nothing like the sun."
Smith, S. Infelice.
Suckling, S. Sonnet: "O[h]! for some honest lover's ghost."

Unknown. All Seasons in One.
Marrying Maiden, The.
My Mistress.
My mistress in a hive of bees.
Yi Chŏngbo. When the owl hoots.

Misunderstanding
Amichai, Y. What is it? An airplane at dawn.
No.
Baird, M. Do Not Make Things Too Easy.
Murray, L. Hearing Impairment.
Rich, A. Trying to Talk with a Man.
Unknown. Since First I Saw Your Face.

Mites
Frost, R. Considerable Speck, A.

Mithridates the Great
Emerson, R. Mithridates.

Mittens
Allen, M. Mitten Song, The.
See also **Gloves**

Moas
Curnow. Skeleton of the Great Moa in the
Canterbury Museum, Christchurch, The.

Mobile Bay, Battle of (1864)
Brownell, H. Bay Fight, The.
Meredith, W. Farragut, Farragut.

Mobility
Jordan, J. Roman Poem Number Nine.

Mockingbirds
Bukowski. Mockingbird, The.
Drake, J. Mocking-Bird, The.
Estes, A. Serenade.
Fordham. To the Mock-Bird.
Hayden, R. Mourning Poem for the Queen of
Sunday.
Heard, J. My Mocking Bird.
House, Boyce. Mocking-bird, A.
Hovey. Mocking-Bird, The.
Jarrell, R. Mockingbird, The.
Lanier, S. Mocking Bird, The.
Moore, M. Bird-witted.
Unknown. Mocking-Bird's Song, The.
Van Duyn. Mockingbird Month.
Wilde, R. To the Mocking-Bird.
Winner, S. Listen to the Mocking Bird.

Models
Cabico, R. Antonio Banderas in His Underwear.
Calvino. Fedora.
Dailey. Rio.
Hannan, M. Life Model.
Herd. Gia.
Malanga. 3 Poems for Benedetta Barzini.
Moore, H. Girl in a Fur-Trimmed Dress.
Nye, N. Morning Paper, Society Page.
Probyn. Model, The.
Rossetti, C. In An Artist's Studio.
Shapiro, K. Editing *Poetry*.
Wearne. Division of O'Dowd, The.
Terri.
Wendt. Lady on the Cover of *Family Circle*,
The.

Moderation
Anacreon. Come, boy, bring us.
Armstrong, J. Rustic Interior.
Cullen, C. Song in Spite of Myself.
Kirby, D. Moderation Kills (Excusez-Moi, je
Suis Sick as a Dog).
Lao Tzu. Best be done before the last degree.
Li Mi-an. Half-and-Half Song, The.
Martial. My carefree Namesake, this the art.
Thompson, F. Counsel of Moderation, A.
Tu Fu [*or* Du Fu]. Drawing a bow you must
draw a strong one.
Yuan Mei. Writing What I've Seen.

Modern Man
Adams, L. Kids!
Adonis [*or* Adunis]. Mirror for the Twentieth
Century, A.
Ai. Testimony of J. Robert Oppenheimer, The.
Allen, P. Kopis'taya.
Ama Ata Aidoo. Gynae One.
Amichai, Y. Flock of Sheep Near the Airport,
A.
Apollinaire. Zone.
Armitage, S. Killing Time #2.

"Arudra.". Death of Man.
Ashbery, J. Cæsura.
Auden. Unknown Citizen, The.
Baraka, I. Political Poem.
Benn. Quaternary.
Berry, W. Purification, A.
Bidart. Another Life.
Bond, E. How We See.
Borges. Juan Lopez and John Ward.
Bronk. At Tikal.
Burliuk *et al.* Slap in the Face of Public Taste,
A.
Cairns, Scott. Translation of Raimundo Luz,
The: My Amusing Despair.
Castro, R. Glowworm Scatters Flashes, A.
Cendrars. Newspaper.
Césaire, A. Lay of the Rover.
Since Akkad, Since Elam, Since Sumer.
Chedid, A. Man-today.
Cohan. Twentieth-Century Love.
Coke, A. Change, The.
Cortez, J. What's Happening.
Cummings, E. E. Boys i mean are not refined,
The.
Plato told.
Day, J. Man's Natural Infirmity.
Doolittle, H. Yet we, the latter-day twice-born.
Duncan, A. Shield of Perseus, The.
Dunmore. Glad of These Times.
Dylan. Quinn the Eskimo.
Ebb, F. Nowadays.
Eliot, T. S. Love Song of J. Alfred Prufrock,
The.
Preludes: "Winter evening settles down, The."
Waste Land, The.
Enright, D. Remembrance Sunday.
Enzensberger, H. For the Primer of Senior
High.
"Ern Malley.". Documentary Film.
Fearing. Dirge: "1-2-3 was the number he
played but today the number came 3-2-1."
Feaver. Way We Live, The.
Ferlinghetti, L. In Goya's greatest scenes we
seem to see.
Lost Parents.
Forbes, C. Blue Monday.
French, J. Pity the Bastards.
Fuller, R. Sonnet: "Crumbled rock of London is
dripping under, The."
Gilbert, A. Relative Heat Index.
Ginsberg, A. Change, The: *Kyoto-Tokyo
Express.*
Grim Skeleton.
Howl.
Sunflower Sutra.
Goetz. Pianist looks like an airline pilot who's
afraid to land, The.
Goldbarth. Reality Organization.
Goldberg, B. Twentieth Century Children.
Goodtimes. Jojopan.
Grass. Afterwards.
Gwynn, R. Among Philistines.
Harjo, J. Post-colonial Tale, A.
Harrison, J. Geo-Bestiary #X.
Hart, L. Zip.
Hass, R. Now Winter Nights.
Hofmannsthal. Twilight of the Outward Life.
Hogan, L. Skin.
Holloway, J. London, Greater London (After
Satire III).
Holm, B. Icelandic Language, The.
Holz. In the Thiergarten, on a bench, I'm sitting
and smoking.
Hupfeld, H. As Time Goes By.
Ilio, D. Children of the Atomic Age.
Ismaili. Lagos.
Jacobsen, R. Green Light.
Silence Afterwards, The.
Jandl, E. At the Delicatessen Shop.
Jones, R. James Dean.
Joseph, L. Do What You Can.
Some Sort of Chronicler I Am.
Kaschnitz. Hiroshima.
Kinnell. Sheffield Ghazal 4: Driving West.
Kipling, R. New Knighthood, The.
Kleinzahler. Case in Point, A.

Korican, L. City Goddess.
Krolow. Robinson.
Kunitz, S. Night Letter.
Lamantia. Voice of Earth Mediums.
Levine, P. Drum: *Leo's Tool & Die, 1950.*
Loesser. Make a Miracle.
Lopez, T. Studies in Classic American
Literature.
Lowell, R. For the Union Dead.
Loy. Apology of Genius.
MacCaig. Gone Are the Days.
MacNeice. Close and slow, summer is ending in
Hampshire.
Shelley and jazz and lieder and love and hymn-
tunes.
McDonald, P. Cash Positive.
Mendelssohn, Anna. Strictly personal.
Mercer, J. I'm Old-Fashioned.
Merrill, J. Clearing the Title.
Urban Convalescence, An.
Merwin. Shore, The.
Michaux. Future.
Milne, D. And out of dominion.
Sweet shift go slow go.
Milosz, C. Preparation.
Monro, H. Every Thing.
Motsapi, S. Djeni.
Mphande. Pain.
Nagnamuni. Wooden Horse.
Nash, O. I'm a Stranger Here Myself.
Nathan, L. At the Well.
Nelson, M. Wish Fulfillment.
Nemerov. Life Cycle of Common Man.
O'Driscoll, D. Life.
Olson, C. In Cold Hell, in Thicket.
Poem 143.
Oppen. And Their Winter and Night in
Disguise.
Anniversary Poem.
But So as by Fire.
Impossible Poem, The.
Now in the helicopters the casual will.
Overton, R. Psychic Killed by Train.
Parnell, P. Apotheosis of Medusa.
Parra, N. Vices of the Modern World.
Patterson, R. Forerunner.
Paz. Solo for Two Voices.
Porter, C. Anything Goes.
Portnoy, M. Dinogon.
Hints at Distance.
Instant Control.
Pound, E. Tea-rose tea-gown, etc., The.
Prynne. Did you light furtive aggregate late-
flow samples.
Reis, P. Ancient Ones, The.
Rich, A. Ghazal.
Riley, P. 147. 67.
Rimbaud, A. City.
Rodefer. My mind to me mangles iron. An error
is mirror to the truth.
Pretext.
Ryan, G. Epilogue: "His money-making
properties come back like a beach."
Global Rewards Redemption Centre, The.
Pure and Applied.
Sharma, P. Transit.
Shepherd, R. Self-Portrait in the New World
Order.
Shindo, R. Puddle.
Simpson, L. Quiet Desperation.
Souster. Words Before a Statue of Champlain.
Steele, T. Wartburg, 1521–22, The.
Stern, A. Europa.
Stevens, W. Mozart, 1935.
Of Modern Poetry.
Sze. Great White Shark, The.
Torres, E. Gigabyte Me—How Much RAM in
Your Summer of Love?
Lipsticktion.
Tranter. Un-American Women, The.
Updike. Dea ex Machina.
On the Inclusion of Miniature Dinosaurs in
Breakfast Cereal Boxes.
Vitale, M. You Oh Even.
Von Freytag-Loringhoven. Dozen Cocktails—
Please, A.

Wagoner, D.   Silence of the Stars, The.
Ward, Geoff.   Trapped Wind.
Warren, R.   To a Face in a Crowd.
Wellman, M.   Lost from an airy.
Whitman, W.   One's-Self I Sing.
   Years of the Modern.
Whittemore, R.   Psalm: "Lord feeds some of His
   prisoners better than others, The."
Wilkie, B.   Modern Western History.
Wilkinson, J.   Torn Ones, The.
Williams, C. K.   Spit.
Wright, C.   Stone Canyon Nocturne.
Yeats.   Second Coming, The.
Zukofsky, L.   First Movement: "And out of olde
   bokes, in good feith".

Modesty
Berlin.   Little Things in Life, The.
Bialik.   If you found my heart's scroll in the
   dust.
Chaucer.   Ballade: "Hide, Absalom, thy gilte
   tresses clear."
Chŏng Ch'ŏl.   Juice of bitter herbs has, The.
Lowell, J.   Sonnet: "Amid these fragments of
   heroic days."
Martial.   Out of an Epigram of Martial.
   To His Book[e].
Smart, C.   Nail in the Grass, The.
Various authors.   He battled against the king's
   enemy.
Waller, E.   Song: "Go[e], lovely rose."

Moles
Alterman, N.   Mole, The.
Blunden.   Mole Catcher.
Cox, M.   Moles, The.
De la Mare.   All but Blind.
D'Haen.   Mole, The.
Faigao, B.   Kundiman.
Frost, C.   Sexual Jealousy.
Rossetti, C.   Handy Mole who plied no shovel,
   A.
Smith, D.   Moles in Spring.
Unknown.   Burrowing Yankees.
Wylie.   Eagle and the Mole, The.
Young, A.   Dead Mole, A.

Mona Lisa
Blackwell, Holley.   Message No. 44.
Dowden, E.   Leonardo's "Mona Lisa".
Evans, R.   Mona Lisa.
Field.   La Gioconda; Leonardo Da Vinci, The
   Louvre.
Grimké, A.   Mona Lisa, A.
Livingston, J.   Mona Lisa.
Martin, Angela.   Viewing Mona Lisa.
Pater.   Mona Lisa.
Roberts, N.   Mona Lisa Tea Towel, The.
Wharton, E.   Mona Lisa.

Monaghan.
See County Monaghan, Ireland

Monarchy
McKendrick, J.   Shortened History in Pictures,
   A.
Unknown.   Blind musicians, the blind musicians,
   The.
   Common people are very weary, The.
   Extensive the lands flanking that southern
   mountain.
   Towering is that southern mountain.

Monasteries
Alexander, W.   Let us recall the illusion.
Arnold, M.   Stanzas from the Grande
   Chartreuse.
Chia Tao.   Spending the Night at a Mountain
   Temple.
Daio.   I have had a companion on the road.
Davidkov, Ivan.   Monastery.
Hui Ch'ung.   Given to Wen Chao.
Li Po.   Written on a Wall at Hsiu-Ching
   Monastery in Wu-Ch'ang.
Ma Chih-yüan.   Evening Bells near a Temple.
Mei Yao Ch'en.   Solitary Falcon above the
   Buddha Hall of the Monastery of Universal
   Purity, A.
Muso Soseki.   Pure Sound Pavilion of the
   Riverside Temple, The.
Norris, K.   Mysteries of The Incarnation: "She

   Said Yeah".
Po Chü-i.   At Flowering-Brightness Monastery
   in Yung-Ch'ung District.
Rein.   Monastery.
Ssu-k'ung Shu.   Oxhead Temple.
Su Tung-p'o.   At Gold Hill Monastery.
Suzuki, M.   Monastery gate.
Trần Thái-Tông, King.   To the Monk Dúc Son at
   Thanh-phong Monastery.
Tu Fu [or Du Fu].   Leaving Ch'in-chou.
   Visiting the Monastery at Lung-men.
Twichell.   Pine.
   Rain in Ivy.
Unknown.   Pangur Bán.
Wang An-shih.   Hui-chu Temple, Mount K'un.
Wang Wei.   At the Hermitage of Master Fu.
   Twilight Comes.
   Visiting Hsiang-Chi Monastery.
Wang Yang-ming.   Magic City Monastery.
Yi Illo.   Written on the Wall of Ch'ŏnsu
   Monastery.
See also **Monks**

Monday
Giovanni.   Monday.
Hughes, L.   Blue Monday.
McNiece, R.   Ordinary, The.
Wakoski.   Blue Monday.

Mondrian, Piet
Battin, W.   Mondrian's Forest.

Monet, Claude
Ferlinghetti, L.   Monet's Lilies Shuddering.
Georgiou, E.   From Where I Stand.
Hayden, R.   Monet's "Waterlilies".
Hollander, J.   Effet de Neige.
Mueller, L.   Monet Refuses the Operation.
Welch, L.   Claude Monet's Water Landscapes.

Money
Armour.   Money.
Bécquer, G.   It Goes Against My Interest to
   Confess It.
Bedford.   Munition Wages.
Belli, C.   Down with the Money-Exchange.
Belloc.   Fatigue.
Berry, J.   Fantasy of an African Boy.
Bock, J.   Little Tin Box.
Brown, K.   Money As Water.
Brownstein.   Jet Set Melodrama.
Burke, J.   Pennies from Heaven.
Cardenal.   Luke 16:1–9; He also said to the
   disciples.
   Unrighteous Mammon (Luke 16:9).
Carroll, L.   White Knight's Song, The.
Cary, P.   Dorothy's Dower.
Cecil.   Some Terms in Real Estate Defined.
Celaya, G.   Great Moments.
Clough.   Spectator ab Extra.
Cohan.   When a Fellow's on the Level with a
   Girl That's on the Square.
Connor, T.   She Was One of the Early Birds.
Coultas, B.   Capitalist Projections.
Cox, J.   Nobody Knows You When You're
   Down and Out.
Crane, S.   Impact of a dollar upon the heart,
   The.
Cronin, A.   Elegy for the Nightbound.
Curnow.   You Get What You Pay For.
Davies, W. H.   Money.
De Vries, P.   To His Importunate Mistress.
Duffy, C.   Making Money.
Dumas, H.   America.
Feirstein.   Mark Stern.
Fisher, J.   Pearls.
Forbes, J.   Love Poem.
Goldberg, B.   Money.
Googe.   Of Money.
Haavikko.   Precisely the way you divide your
   small change between two.
Hardy, T.   By Her Aunt's Grave.
Hart, L.   I've Got Five Dollars.
Hatton, J.   Christmas Bills.
Herd.   Big Girls.
Hoagland, T.   America.
Hughes, L.   Little Lyric (*Of Great Importance*).
Hume, C.   Arctic Sun.
Hupfeld, H.   Are You Makin' Any Money?

Issa.   Five yen each / A cup of tea.
Johnson, F.   Minister, The.
Jonson, B.   On Lieutenant Shift.
Kalagoe, C.   This johnny / is Mr Strong from
   Strongtown.
Kshetrayya.   Courtesan to a Young Customer, A.
Lamb, A.   Bird in a Gilded Cage, A.
Larkin, P.   Money.
Lewis, S.   I'm Sitting on Top of the World.
Li Po.   Hard Is the Journey.
Liptsin, S.   Going Up.
Llwyd, I.   Dust Truck Blues.
Lowell, R.   Skunk Hour.
MacSweeney.   Totem Banking.
Martial.   You gave Bithynicus thousands yearly;
   still.
   You sold a slave just yesterday.
   You've told me, Maro.
Masters, E.   Sexsmith the Dentist.
Meynell, A.   To 'A Certain Rich Man'.
Mills, D.   Chembank Card.
Nakano Shigeharu.   Rate of Exchange, The.
Nemerov.   Money.
   Ultima Ratio Reagan.
North, C.   Elizabethan and Nova Scotian Music.
North, M.   Account, An.
Notley.   Destroy.
Pak Nohae.   How Much Is This One?
Perelman.   Money.
Prévert.   At the Florist's.
Quevedo y Villegas.   Mighty Lord Is Money, A.
Razaf, A.   I'd Give a Dollar for a Dime.
Rome, H.   Money Song, The.
Ryan, G.   Epilogue: "His money-making
   properties come back like a beach."
Ryan, K.   Poetry Is a Kind of Money.
Rybicki, J.   Brother Ben.
Sarangapani.   Madam to a Young Courtesan,
   The.
Sedley.   Marriage and Money.
Smith, W.   American Primitive.
Soto.   How Things Work.
Spender, S.   Ultima Ratio Regum.
Strange.   Hunger.
Swift, J.   To Their Excellencies the Lords
   Justices of Ireland, the Humble Petition of
   Frances Harris, Who Must Starve, and Die a
   Maid if It Miscarries.
Tennyson, A.   Northern Farmer: New Style.
Thomas, L.   Argent, L'.
   Clear Channel.
Tu Fu [or Du Fu].   By the Winding River.
Tu Mo.   Mandarins Got Their Raise, The.
Unknown.   Crows on City Walls.
   Hush, little baby, don't say a word.
   Mode of France, The.
   Money, Money.
   My horse / thickens.
   No money yet, why then let's terrify with
   swords.
   Penny.
   Sons and grandsons are dearest to one's heart.
Vazirani, R.   E-Mail.
Ward, Geoff.   What's Wrong.
Warren, H.   Gold Digger's Song (We're in the
   Money), The.
Wilbur, R.   Finished Man, A.
Williams, C. K.   Money.
Williamson, G.   Annual Returns.
Young, J.   I'm Sitting on Top of the World.
Zephaniah.   De Rich Getting Rich.

Mongolia
Barkova, A.   Tatar Anguish.
Natsagdorzh, D.   My Country.
Unknown.   Death of Yesugei, The.
   Last Battle and Death of Chingis Khan, The.
   Temujin Becomes Chingis Khan.

Monk, Thelonius
Baraka, I.   Monk's World.
Jensma.   Letter to Thelonius.
Komunyakaa, Y.   Elegy for Thelonious.
March, S.   Monk's Misterioso.
Neal, Gaston.   Monk.
Powell, N.   Coda: Thelonius Monk, d. 17
   February 1982.
Weaver, A.   Thelonius.

Monkeys
al-Braikan, M. Monkey's Journey, The.
Basho. Winter showers.
  Year after year.
  You've heard monkeys crying.
Bracho, C. Fish of Fleeting Skin.
  Peces de piel fugaz.
Brownstein. Monkey Blues.
Daio. I have had a companion on the road.
Espada. Do Not Put Dead Monkeys in the
  Freezer.
Frost, R. At Woodward's Gardens.
Gay, J. Two Monkeys, The.
Houellebecq, Michel. In the Limpid Air.
Huddle. Snow Monkey Argues with God, The.
Khodasevich. Monkey.
Kreymborg. Tree, The.
Lamb, C. To Louisa M[artin], Whom I Used to
  Call "Monkey".
Li Po. Autumn Cove.
Lux. To Help the Monkey Cross the River.
McElroy, C. End of Civilization as We Know
  It, The.
Mole, J. Musical Monkey, The.
Moore, M. Monkeys, The.
Rice, S. Monkey Hill.
Sholl. Monkey House.
Stein, G. Dog, A.
Swenson, M. Motherhood.
Tranter. Tell me we will drink water, and drink
  to me.
Unknown. Makeme.
  Monkey knows, The.
  My dugout flibbles.
Wang An-shih. Bald Mountain.
Weelkes. Madrigal: "Ay me, alas, heigh ho,
  heigh ho!"
Weigl. Monkey.
Weöres. Monkeyland.
Zhiyuan, S. In Praise of Ch'an Master Wang
  You Who Cares for the Bonnet Monkeys
  around His Mountain Studio.

Monks
Abbott, K. What she thought was.
Baggok Choneung. Sending off My Fellow
  Monk Hae.
Basho. Monk sips morning tea, A.
  Water-drawing rites.
  Whore and monk, we sleep.
Berrigan, D. Assembled sirs. The courtesies
  afforded us by the Dali Lama.
Browning, R. Grammarian's Funeral, A.
  Soliloquy of the Spanish Cloister.
Buhyu Sunsoo. To a Monk.
Bun-Etsu. Sixty-five years.
Buson. In a bitter wind.
Chia Tao. Farewell to Monk Chih-Hsing.
Chien Chang. Sent to Zen Master Yun-Shui.
Chimi Sucho. To a Monk Asking About Zen.
Chungji. In My Leisure.
  Parody.
Craig, David. Young Monk (Denver).
Daegak Euchon. At Chonymyung Temple.
Deanovich. My Favorite Monk Is.
Dowson. Carthusians.
Heaney, S. Annals say: when the monks of
  Clonmacnoise, The.
Hemingway. Earnest Liberal's Lament, The.
Hirshfield, J. Heart's Counting Knows Only
  One, The.
  Monk Stood Beside a Wheelbarrow, The.
Hsü Wei. Buddhist Monk Cut and Burned His
  Own Flesh to Make The Rains Stop—A Man
  From His Native Place Asked Me to Write a
  Poem to Send to Him, A.
Hueung Powoo. Taking Pleasure in Myself.
Jinkag Haesim. Facing the Shadow.
Jungkwan Haean. Ridiculing the Monk Who
  Builds a Stupa.
Jungkwan Ilson. To an Old, Deaf, and Blind
  Monk.
Kaschnitz. Hiroshima.
Kinsella, T. Monk, The.
Kitahara Hakushū. Completely blind.
Manan. Unfettered at last, a traveling monk.
Masaoka Shiki. Imagine / The monk took off.

Meyerhoff, J. Million times, A.
Montague, J. Footnote on Monasticism, A:
  Dingle Peninsula.
Muso Soseki. For the Death of a Monk.
  To the Emperor's Messenger.
Naong. Song of the Pure Land.
O'Daly, M. Shaving of Murdoch, The.
Pou Kuksa. Yo Hermitage.
Rakosi. Menage, The.
Ramanujan. Pleasure.
Reito. Ox bridle tossed, vows taken.
Shinkichi Takahashi. Burning Oneself to Death.
Smith, R. Illumination.
Sōsan, Great Master. In Praise of the Portrait of
  My Former Master.
Tung Chieh-yüan. Chapter 2: "Stopping before
  the steps, the young monk gushed."
Unknown. Monk that slept here must, after all,
  have been a man, The.
  Ode to Yangji.
  Pangur Bán.
  Story of How the Monk Tripiṭaka of the Great
    Country of T'ang Brought back the Sūtras,
    The.
Wang Wei. Climbing to the Monastery of
  Perception.
  Meal for the Monks, A.
Waniek. Letter to a Benedictine Monk.
Wen Chao. Farewell to Master Yu Chao.
Wonhyo, Great Master. To Master Monk
  Nangjee.
Yi Kyubo. Moon in the Well, The.
Yüan Mei. Motto.
Zagajewski. Quick Poem, A.
See also **Clergy; Monasteries**

Monmouth, Battle of (1778)
Richards, L. Molly Pitcher.

Monmouth, James Scott, Duke of
Behn, A. Silvio's Complaint: A Song, to a Fine
  Scotch Tune.
Dryden, J. Absalom and Achitophel.
  In pious times ere [or e'r] priest-craft did begin.

Monogamy and Monogamists
Aig-Imoukhuede. One Wife for One Man.
Donne. Confined Love.

Monotony
Bell, M. Senilio Passes, Singing.
Disch. Bookmark, A.
Hacker, M. Villanelle: Late Summer.
MacNeice. Nature Morte.
Roethke. Monotony Song, The.
Tardieu Jean. Seine in Paris, The.
Tkachenko. Like Thousands of Others.

Monroe, James
Mac Low. 1817.

Monroe, Marilyn
Alexie. November 22, 1983.
Berrigan, T. Sonnet LIX: "In Joe Brainard's
  collage its white arrow."
Cardenal. Prayer for Marilyn Monroe.
Grahn. I Have Come to Claim Marilyn
  Monroe's Body.
Greenhalgh, C. Night I Met Marilyn, The.
Herd. Marilyn Climbs Out of the Pool.
Komunyakaa, Y. Hanoi Market, The.
Olds, S. Death of Marilyn Monroe, The.
Romero, L. Marilyn Monroe Indian.
Rosen, K. Of Marilyn, and Marijuana.

Monsters
Adcock, F. Bogyman.
Berry, W. Enemies.
Carroll, L. Jabberwocky.
Cranch. Locomotive, The.
Dalton, A. Kitchen Beast.
De Los Santos, M. Wiglaf.
Deanovich. Zombie Jet.
Dickey, J. Sheep Child, The.
Éluard, P. Dawn Dissolves the Monsters.
  Meetings.
Erdrich. Windigo.
Fletcher, P. Say Muses, say; who now in those
  rich fields.
Forhan, C. Without Presumptions.
Graves, R. Hide and Seek.
Hamby, B. St. Clare's Underwear.

Heath-Stubbs. Vision of Beasts, A.
Homer. Ulysses Insults over the Cyclops.
Iroquois Oral Tradition. Dancing Speech of O-
  No'-Sa, The.
Jaimes Freyre. Night-time.
Knight, S. In Case of Monsters.
Komunyakaa, Y. Never Land.
Lee, D. I Eat Kids Yum Yum!
Legaré. Tallulah.
MacEwen, G. Death of the Loch Ness Monster,
  The.
Mitchell, K. Monster, The.
Morisseau-Leroy, F. Zombies.
Nguyễn Chí Thiện. Model Children of the
  Regime, The.
Pepler. Concerning Dragons.
Popa. Song of the Tower of Skulls.
Powell, J. Doxology.
Raab, L. Sudden Appearance of a Monster at a
  Window.
Robinson, K. Pontoon.
Ruddock, G. Double-decker.
Silverstein, S. Slithergadee, The.
Tadic. Dogs Gambol.
Tennyson, A. Kraken, The.
Unknown. FROM Beowulf.
  Hrothgar Answered.
  Introduction: History and Praise of the Danes;
    Account of Grendel's Attacks on Heorot.
  Then down the brave man lay with his bolster.
Wang Yen-Shou. Nightmare, The.
See also **Demons**

Mont Blanc
Coleridge, S. Hymn before Sunrise, in the Vale
  of Chamouni.
Kinsella, J. Bluff Knoll Sublimity.
Shelley, P. Mont Blanc.

Montale, Eugenio
Muldoon, P. Eugenio Montale: The Eel.

Montana (state)
Chester, L. Search to get lost in a great big
  coat, The.
Cunningham, J. Montana Pastoral.
Davenport, S. Up from the Wreck Conjuring
  Montana Sonnet.
Hugo, R. Degrees of Gray in Philipsburg.
  Driving Montana.
  Lady in Kicking Horse Reservoir, The.
  Letter to Goldbarth from Big Fork.
  Letter to Haislip from Hot Springs.
  Letter to Oberg from Pony.
  Map of Montana in Italy, A.
Ward, Whitney. Montana's Biggest Weekend.
Welch, J. Christmas Comes to Moccasin Flat.
  Harlem, Montana.
Wright, C. Looking Outside the Cabin Window,
  I Remember a Line by Li Po.

Monterrey, Mexico
Reyes, A. Monterrey Sun.

Months
Andrade, E. Friend is sometimes desert, A.
Bodecker. One Year.
Coleridge, S. Garden Year, The.
Hesiod. Beware of the month Lenaion, bad
  days.
Longfellow, H. Poet's Calendar, The.

Montreal, Quebec
Klein, A. Montreal.

Monuments
Bishop, E. Monument, The.
Blaser. Image-Nation 23 (imago-mundi).
Cairns, Scott. Regarding the Monument.
Cullen, Y. Memorial: "There had to be a way of
  making a building talk."
Denney. Building the Dam.
Elfyn, Menna. May in My Lai.
Emerson, R. Concord Hymn.
Hacker, M. Verlaine.
Hemans. Effigies, The.
Horace. Ode 3.30: This Monument Will Outlast
  (Exegi monumentum aere perennius).
Hughes, L. Lincoln Monument: Washington.
Johnstone, P. High Wood.
Kennedy, X. Loneliness of Lincoln, The.
Khodasevich. Monument, A.

Komunyakaa, Y.   Facing It.
Lowell, R.   For the Union Dead.
Martial.   Traveller on the Flaminian Way.
Melville, H.   Inscription: "To them who crossed the flood."
Mew.   Cenotaph, The.
Muso Soseki.   Turtle Head Stupa.
Ormond.   Ancient Monuments.
Page, G.   Smalltown Memorials.
Philipott.   To Sir Henry Newton, upon His Re-edifying the Church of Charleton in Kent.
Philips, K.   Wiston Vault.
Press, K.   Statues.
Shakespeare, W.   Sonnet 55: "Not marble, nor the g[u]ilded monuments."
Stafford, W.   At the Robert Frost Memorial.
Stevens, W.   Dance of the Macabre Mice.

Moods
Ashbery, J.   Crazy Weather.
Aytoun [or Ayton], R.   Answer, The.
 Upon His Unconstant Mistress.
Caesar.   Sometimes I'm Happy.
Denby.   Climate, The.
Donne.   Oh, to vex me, contraries [or contraryes] meet in one.
Drinkwater.   Reciprocity.
Fields, D.   I'm in the Mood for Love.
Hirshfield, J.   It Was Like This : You Were Happy.
Murray, L.   Sprawl is the quality.
Volkman.   Sonnet: "Tilt the placeless waver of this moving."

Moon
Adams, Cyd.   Longview, Texas.
Adams, L.   Moon and Spectator, The.
Adebajo, K.   Moonlight on the Lake.
Aisenberg, N.   Woman in the Moon, The.
Akhmadulina.   Lunatics.
al-Mala'ika, N.   Song for the Moon.
Aldington.   Evening.
Aleixandre.   Man Doesn't Exist.
Alexander, E.   Apollo.
Allen, P.   Meditations on the Moon.
Alvi, M.   Laughing Moon, The.
Amor, P.   CXLII.
Armantrout.   View.
Ato Tobira.   Only one fleeting.
Auden.   Moon Landing.
 This Lunar Beauty.
Basheva.   It Was War.
Basho.   All the field hands.
 All this foolishness.
 Among moon gazers.
 Autumn moon / Tide foams.
 Autumnal full moon.
 Calm moon, A.
 Cats making love.
 Cloud peaks.
 Clouds come and go, The.
 Clouds, The.
 Cuckoo cries, A.
 Dozing on horseback / smoke from tea-fires.
 Felling a tree.
 Field of cotton, A.
 Group of them, A.
 Harvest moon.
 It's fall and a full moon.
 It's not like anything.
 Jars of octopus, The.
 Moonlight slanting.
 This bright harvest moon.
 Very brief.
 Winter garden.
Behn, H.   Circles.
Běkes.   Oh, Moon.
Bell, M.   White Clover.
Berg, S.   On This Side of the River.
Berryman.   Moon and the Night and the Men, The.
Bertrand.   Moonlight.
Bishop, E.   Insomnia.
 Man-Moth, The.
Black, S.   Blank Abandon of Beds, The.
Blackburn, J.   Moonlight in Vermont.
Bogan, L.   July Dawn.
Bradley, Leo.   Sub Umbra.

Brecht, B.   Alabama Song.
Brooks, B.   Moon in the Mirror.
Burke, J.   Moonlight Becomes You.
Buson.   Avoiding fishnet.
 Bat flits, A.
 By flowering pear.
 By moonlight.
 Calligraphy of geese.
 Darting here and there.
 Escaped the nets.
 Field of bright mustard.
 Field of bright mustard.
 Happy traveler / Mosquito wick.
 Harvest moon.
 Head pillowed on arm.
 In pale moonlight.
 Light of the moon.
 Listening to the moon.
 Listening to the moon.
 Miles of frost / On the lake.
 Moon in midsky, high.
 My arm for a pillow.
 Plum scent / Haloing.
 Short night, The.
 Such a moon.
 Tears.
 With a woman friend.
Bye.   Effendi.
Bynner.   Moon, The.
Byron, G.   So We'll Go No More A-Roving.
Campo.   Asylum.
Ceni, A.   With What Courage.
Ch'i-chi.   Year Keng-Wu, Night of the Fifteenth, Facing the Moon, The.
Chikako.   On this summer night.
Chiyojo.   Grazing.
Ch'ŏn Yanghûi.   Crescent Moon.
Chu Yohan.   To Catch the Moon.
Clarke, George Elliott.   Hymn for Portia White.
Coleridge, M.   In Dispraise of the Moon.
 Witches' Wood, The.
Coleridge, S.   To the Autumnal Moon.
Crapsey.   Moon-Shadows.
 Niagara.
Creeley.   Form of Women, A.
Crowe, T.   Winter Moon Haiku.
Cynewulf.   Sun and Moon.
Daive.   Space instead.
Dao.   Moon Festival.
Davies, W. H.   Moon, The.
Davis, K.   Searching for Mooncakes.
De Cristoforo, Violet Kazue.   Tenth Wedding Anniversary (July 3, 1994): Tsuki Oboro Totsugishi Yoru No Sora Datta.
De la Mare.   Silver.
De la Selva.   Deliverance.
Deutsch.   To the Moon, 1969.
Dickey, J.   2: The Moon Ground.
Dickinson, E.   I watched the Moon around the House.
 Moon is distant from the Sea, The.
 Moon upon her fluent Route, The.
Dodge, M.   Moon Came Late, The.
Donaghy, M.   Present, The.
Donovan, K.   Moon.
Doolittle, H.   Moonrise.
Duncan, R.   Chords Passages 14.
 Moon, The.
Eguren.   Peregrin, Wandering Hunter of Faces.
Ekelof.   Moon, The.
Empson.   To an Old Lady.
Erdrich.   Leonard Refuses to Atone.
Ermakova, I.   Gethsemane: "Moon swims to the fore in the pale heavens, The."
Evans, R.   No Moon at All.
Faiz.   Vista.
Farley, P.   Diary Moon.
Field.   Penetration.
Frost, R.   Freedom of the Moon, The.
 Moon Compasses.
Fujiwara no Teika.   After his tryst.
Gallagher, T.   Heart-Mirror.
Gangemi, K.   Notes on a Moonwatcher.
Gannon, K.   Moonlight Cocktail.
García Lorca.   Moon Sails Out, The.
Gifford, F.   Moon Folly.

Ginsberg, A.   Moon in the dewdrop is the real moon, The.
Glück, L.   Mock Orange.
Goethe.   To the Moon.
Goyette, Susan.   Moon on Friday Night, The.
Greenberg, Aluin.   Man in the Moon, The.
Greenberg, Arielle.   Afterward, There Will Be a Hallway.
Grenier.   Autumn Moon Rising.
Guillén, N.   Moon.
Gumilyov [or Gumiliov or Gumilev].   Moon at Sea.
Hamill, S.   After a Winter of Grieving.
 Reading Seferis.
Hamilton, N.   How High the Moon.
Harburg.   Moon About Town.
 Old Devil Moon.
Hardy, T.   Shut Out That Moon.
Harington [or Harrington].   Astolfo flies by Chariot to the Moon, where he collects Orlando's lost wits.
Hart, L.   Blue Moon.
Hayden, R.   Full Moon.
Herd.   Coronach.
Hernández Cruz.   Milagrosa, La.
Ho Hsun.   Watching the New Moon, I Compose These Verses to Show to My Fellow-Travelers, Stranded with Me.
Hoitsu.   Buddha / Cherry flowers.
Hopkins, G.   Moonrise.
Howard, B.   Fly Me to the Moon (In Other Words).
Hsiao Yen [or Emperor Wu of Liang].   Border Guard, A.
Hughes, L.   Winter Moon.
Hughes, T.   Full Moon and Little Frieda.
 Moon-Hops.
Issa.   Autumn moon.
 Brilliant moon.
 Crescent moon.
 Evening moon.
 Face of the spring moon.
 Full moon.
 Here in Shinano.
 I wish she were here.
 In this mountain village.
 Like misty moonlight.
 Lost in bamboo.
 Moon and the flowers, The.
 Moon, plum blossoms.
 Moon tonight, The.
 She's put the child to sleep.
 Tonight you too / Are rushed.
 Under the evening moon.
 Under this bright moon.
 Vanity of men, The.
 Washing the saucepans.
 With this rising bath-mist.
Istarú, A.   Moon became mired on our bed, The.
Izumi.   Although the wind.
 I cannot say.
 Watching the moon.
 Way I must enter, The.
 You told me it was / because of me.
Jacob, M.   Moon Poem.
Jacobs, J.   Nearing Long Moons.
Jacobsen, R.   Moon and Apple.
Jiménez, J.   Full Moon.
 Moon, The.
Jinkag Haesim.   For the Great Zen Master Sagum.
Jones, A. M.   To the Moon.
Jonker, I.   Dog.
Jonson, B.   Hymn[e] to Cynthia.
Jordan, J.   Mendocino Memory.
Kawai Suimei.   Snowflame.
Kaya Shirao.   Moonlit night / By melon flowers.
Keats.   Bright Star.
Keita, N.   Cycles.
Keithley.   Small Moon on the Shoulder of New York.
Kennedy, L.   Moonburn.
Kerouac.   Moon had, The.
Keyes, S.   Moon is a poor woman, The.
Kikaku.   Full autumn moon / On the straw mat.
 May he who brings / Flowers tonight.

Over the long road.
Kim Namjo. Moonlit Night.
Kim Sujang. Moonlight shines on the lotus pond.
Kim Yŏngnang. Intoxicating Moonlight.
King, H. Moonlight Ride, A.
Kingsolver. Remember the Moon Survives.
Kitahara Hakushū. Moon god's light, The.
Ko Ŭn. Slice of Moon, A.
Kojijū. On the Spirit of the Heart as Moon-Disk.
Komrij. Park of the Dead.
Kuan Hsiu. Three or four young sylph women.
Kunitz, S. Flight of Apollo, The.
Kupriyanov [or Kuprianov]. Everything gets forgotten.
Kyger. Joanne.
Laforgue. Clair de Lune.
Lawrence, D. H. Aware.
Southern Night.
White Blossom, A.
Leopardi. Remembering Leopardi's Moon.
Levertov. Scraps of moon.
Song for Ishtar.
Lewis, G. One day, feeling hungry.
Li Ho. Song: Dragons at Midnight.
Li Po. Calm Night Thought.
Drinking Alone in the Moonlight.
Drinking Alone with the Moon.
Night Thoughts.
Quiet Night Thought.
Quiet Night Thoughts.
Still Night Thoughts.
Thoughts in Night Quiet.
Li'aibi, S. My days pass with the beads of the rosary.
Liu Yu Hsi. Gazing on Lake Dongting.
Llwyd, Alan. Moons of Llŷn, The.
Longfellow, H. Harvest Moon, The.
Lowell, A. Dissonance.
Moon Haze.
Wind and Silver.
Loy. Lunar Baedeker.
Lugones. White Solitude.
Macdonald, G. Wind and the Moon, The.
MacKenzie, R. Blue Sky in Morning.
MacLeish. Voyage to the Moon ("Wanderer in our skies.").
Madden, E. By the Light of the Silvery Moon.
Mann, D. No Moon at All.
Mariani. Moonrise as Abstraction.
Marsman. Paradise Regained.
Polderland.
Masahide. Barn's burnt down.
When bird passes on.
Masaoka Shiki. Imagine / The monk took off.
McCarthy, E. Ending.
McGrath, T. Guiffre's Nightmusic.
Mei Yao Ch'en. Crescent Moon, The.
Meng Hao Jan. Night Mooring on the Jiande River, A.
Mercer, J. Moon River.
Metodiev, Ivan. These Things from Words.
Michie. Arizona Nature Myth.
Miliauskaite. On Winter Nights.
Miller, L. When the Moon Isn't Shining.
Milnes. Lady Moon.
Moore, L. Haiku.
Moore, R. Personal Atlas.
Moore, T. Young May Moon, The.
Morley, H. Parents.
Moroz, R. There's a cinnamon tree that grows on the Moon.
Mueller, L. Farewell, a Welcome, A.
Mukai Kyorai. Returning from a funeral.
Muso Soseki. Bridge Where the Moon Crosses, The.
Moon Tree Cliff.
Reply to Bukko Zenji's Poem at Seiken-ji.
Naden. Moonlight and Gas.
Nanei. Splitting the void in half.
Narihira. Regretting the Past.
Nealon, Mary Jane. Moon Landing, 1969.
Nekrasov, V. And I Speak of Cosmic Things.
Nemerov. Goose Fish, The.
Nezval. Moon over Prague.

Nichol. Monotones.
Nishikawa, Etsudo. Round, round, more round than the moon.
Norgate, S. Water on the Moon.
Norworth. Shine On, Harvest Moon.
Nutter, G. II:II.
Ogiwara Seisensui. It walks the sky, cloudless.
Olson, C. Moon Is the Number 18, The.
Ormsby, E. Jaham Sings of the Fear of the Moon.
Osundare. Frantic as a prentice poet.
Madding moon, A.
Moon is an exile, The.
Otomo no Sakanoé, L. Till the rough-gem moon.
Oyake. Hidden in the clouds.
Pathabhi. Moon in China Bazaar.
Pavese. August Moon.
Piercy. Moon Is Always Female, The.
Plath. Moon and the Yew Tree, The.
Plomer. To the Moon and Back.
Po Chü-i. Starting Early from the Ch'u-ch'ĕng Inn.
Porter, D. P. M. T.
Purdy, J. From rivers, and from the earth itself.
Raboni, G. Moon.
Radnóti. Clouded Sky.
Ray, H. Vision of Moonlight, A.
Reese, L. One Night.
Rendra. Moon's Bed, the Bride's Bed, The.
Reyes, A. To-and-Fro of Saint Theresa.
Rich, A. Amends.
Rickword. Moon-talk.
Ritsos. Naked, astride an elephant.
New moon, The.
Rivas, J. Marea roja.
Red Tide.
Roberts, K. Darkness Was Upon the Face of the Deep.
Robinson, M. Her Address to the Moon.
Roland Holst. Night Visit.
Roscoe, W. To the Harvest Moon.
Roseliep. EVA Psalm.
Ross, G. At the Threshold of the Moon.
Rossetti, D. Match with the Moon, A.
Rukeyser, M. Nevertheless the Moon.
Rumi. Thief in the Night, A.
Ryokan. Wait for the moonlight.
Saiokuken Socho. Moon this evening, The.
Salaam. Quarter Moon Rise.
Saleh. Beach, Later.
Sentry.
Sandburg, C. Auctioneer.
Moist Moon People.
Nocturne in a Deserted Brickyard.
Sanpu. First cherry blossoms.
Sappho. Evening Star who gathers everything.
Full moon was rising, The.
Moon Has Set, The.
Pleiades disappear, The.
Stars around the fair moon, The.
Stars around the luminous moon—how soon they.
Satyamurti. Broken Moon.
Schelling. March Crescent Moon Song.
Shakespeare, W. How sweet the moonlight sleeps upon this bank!
Moonlight.
Shelley, P. To the Moon.
Shiki. Full moon ringed, The.
Shinkichi Takahashi. Moon.
Moon and Hare.
Shockley, E. Shall become as.
Shumyatsher, E. Earth Dream.
Sidney. Sonnet 31: "With how sad steps, O Moon[e], thou climb'st the skies."
Silano, M. Moon, The.
Silva, C. Moon's Cadaver, The.
Simms, W. New Moon, The.
Simpson, L. Working late.
Sin Hŭm. Don't laugh if my roof beams.
Smith, C. To the Moon.
Written September 1791, During a Remarkable Thunder Storm, in which the Moon Was Perfectly Clear, While the Tempest Gathered in Various Directions Near the Earth.

Soen. Calm, activity—each has its use. At times.
Song Ikp'il. To the Moon.
Sorrentino. Magic Composer.
Steele, T. Joseph.
Stevens, W. Lunar Paraphrase.
Stevenson, R. Mile an' a Bittock, A.
Moon, The.
Storni. Words to My Mother.
Strand. Prediction, The.
Subbarao, N. He Didn't Come Back.
Suessdorf, K. Moonlight in Vermont.
Summers, P. If keir hardie was the man on the moon.
Supervielle. Missing France.
Sute-Jo, Lady Den. Are there / Short-cuts in the sky.
Sutskever [or Sutzkever]. Honey of a Wild Bee.
Swenson, M. First Walk on the Moon.
Tagami Kikusha. Only the moon.
Takuan. Though night after night.
Tan Taigi. In the boat / Crescent moon's light.
Teasdale. Moon's Ending.
Tolkien. Man in the Moon Stayed up To Late, The.
Toomer. Beehive.
Trakl. Evening, The: "With the ghostly shapes of dead heroes."
Trouillot, L. Clay Pot Broken, A.
Tu Fu [or Du Fu]. Full Moon ("Above the tower—a lone, twice-sized moon.").
I Pass the Night at General Headquarters.
Moon Festival.
Moonlit Night ("In Fuzhou, far away, my wife is watching.").
Moonlit Night ("Tonight, moon over Fu-chou.").
New Moon.
Night Thoughts While Travelling ("Light breeze rustles the reeds, A.").
Tuqan, F. After Twenty Years.
Unknown. All Other Love Is Like the Moon.
Here in my garden.
How far from enough.
I See the Moon.
Kiss me in the moon's sparkling glow.
Moon Eclipse Exorcism.
Moon, round moon, moon that shines.
Moon, The.
New Moon, The.
One son of God, The.
While I asked myself.
Verlaine. Moonlight.
White Moonglow, The.
Walafrid Strabo. To His Friend in Absence.
Wang Kuo-wei. Tune: "Sand of Silk-Washing Brook" ("Hazy mountain temple hides away behind the setting sun, A.").
Wang Wei. Bamboo Lane House.
Bamboo-Midst Cottage.
Sitting in mystic bamboo grove, back unseen.
Warren, R. In Moonlight, Somewhere, They Are Singing.
White, A. Moon Daughters.
Wiese, B. Going Home Madly.
Williams, H. To the Moon.
Williams, L. Crater.
Williams, W. Rigamarole.
Wilson, R. Envoi: "Sun in the mouth of the day."
Winters, Y. Moonlight Alert.
To the Moon.
Wordsworth, W. "With how sad steps, O Moon, thou climb'st the sky".
Wright, C. Appalachian Book of the Dead 3, The.
Wright, J. Beginning.
Secret Gratitude, A.
Wright, J. Train Journey.
Xuanjue. One Moon Seen, The.
Ye Zi. All night I could not sleep.
Yeats. Cat and the Moon, The.
Sorrow of Love, The [1892 Version].
Yi Kyubo. Evening on the Mountain: Song to the Moon in the Well.
Moon in the Well, The.
Yi Yŏng. Who sliced the crescent moon so

small.
Yüan Hung-tao.   Slowly, Slowly Poem, The.
Yun Sŏndo.   Small but floating high.
Zhang Ruoxu.   Spring, River, Flowers, Moon, Night.

Moonflowers
Masaoka Shiki.   Midnight sound / Leap up.

Moonrises
Jiménez, J.   Song: "Setting sun left my heart, The."
Lojowski, M.   Horizon.

Moonshiners
Adams, Cyd.   River Road.
De la Mare.   Moonshine.
Wheatley, D.   Moonshine.

Moore, Marianne
Bishop, E.   Invitation to Miss Marianne Moore.
Niedecker.   If I Were a Bird.

Moore, Thomas
Trowbridge, J.   Recollections of "Lalla Rookh".

Moors (geography)
Blicher, S.   My birthplace is the brown heather-land.
Buson.   Crossing the autumn moor.
Channing.   Barren Moors, The.
Coleridge, M.   Master and Guest.
Dickinson, E.   I never saw a Moor.
Eliot, T. S.   Rannoch, by Glencoe.
Fell, A.   Rannoch Moor.
Garioch.   Wire, The.
Hodgson, R.   Moor, The.
Hughes, T.   Telegraph Wires.
Thomas, R. S.   Moor, The.
   Moorland.
Unknown.   Hidden-in-winter.

Moors (people)
Camões [or Camõens or Camoëns], L.   With glad reception our Commander meets.
Flecker, J.   War Song of the Saracens.
Hughes, L.   Letter from Spain.
Watson, R.   Moor Girl's Well, The.

Moose
Bierds, L.   Ritual for the Dead, Lake Sakami, Quebec, 1980.
Bishop, E.   Moose, The.
Dugan, A.   On the Elk, Unwitnessed.
Duncan, R.   Poetry, a Natural Thing.
Harrison, J.   Adirondack Moosehead.
Henry, B.   Across the River.
Lassaw-Paljor, Denise.   For a Moose.
Lux.   Wife Hits Moose.
Nowlan.   Bull Moose, The.
Van Duyn.   Moose in the Morning, Northern Maine.
Wanek.   Duluth, Minnesota.

Morality Plays
Campo.   Towards Curing AIDS.

Morisot, Berthe
Waldman, A.   Berthe Morisot.

Mormons
Healy, E.   Moroni on the Mormon Temple / Angel on the Wall.

Morning
Achterberg.   Instrument.
Aiken, C.   Morning Song.
Ammons.   Easter Morning.
   Improvisation for the Stately Dwelling, An.
Anderson, J.   Waking Up Twice.
Angeles, C.   Light Invested.
Assultani, F.   Morning.
Atwood.   Morning in the Burned House.
Auden.   Lauds.
Baillie, J.   Winter's Day, A.
Baraka, I.   Song Form.
Bartlett, L.   Successions, The.
Basho.   Coolness of melons.
   Melon / In morning dew.
   Monk sips morning tea, A.
   Snowy morning, a.
Belloc.   Early Morning, The.
Berlin.   Oh! How I Hate to Get Up in the Morning.
Bible, *O.T.*   Glory Glory / Psalm 19.
Blagg, T.   In Bed this Morning.

Blake, W.   Morning.
   To Morning.
Bly, R.   Waking from Sleep.
Bogan, L.   Morning.
Bonnefoy.   Task of Hope, The.
Brontë, E.   Stars.
Browning, R.   Pippa's Song.
Burns, R.   Up in the Morning Early.
Buson.   Dewy morn / These saucepans.
   Morning breeze.
   Village with a thousand eaves.
Carver, R.   At Least.
   Happiness.
   This Morning.
Cassian.   Morning Exercises.
Chazal, M.   Bicycle rolls on the road, A.
Chia Tao.   Morning Travel.
Chin.   Aubade: "Waking is this easy."
Clare, J.   God Looks on Nature With a Glorious Eye.
Collins, B.   Morning: "Why do we bother with the rest of the day."
   Tuesday, June 4, 1991.
Cotton, C.   Morning Quatrains, The.
Couzyn.   Morning.
Crabbe, G.   Bright Morning, A.
Cullen, Y.   Not a Letter.
Davenant [or D'Avenant].   City Morning, The.
Davis, W.   Spider.
Dawe, B.   Morning Becomes Electric.
Dawson, M.   Late for Breakfast.
Donne.   Break of Day.
   Sun Rising, The.
Drummond, W.   Invocation: "Pheobus, arise! / And paint the sable skies."
Eliot, T. S.   Morning at the Window.
Emperor Ch'ien-wen of Liang.   Getting Up in Winter.
Esposito, Nancy.   Doing Good.
Field, R.   Summer Morning, A.
Finch, B.   Written in a Winter's Morning.
Fodeba, K.   And it's morning.
Forrester, S.   Morning light.
Freed, A.   Good Morning.
Fulton, A.   A.M.: The Hopeful Monster.
Gascoigne.   Gascoigne's Good-Morrow.
Ginsberg, A.   We Rise on Sun Beams and Fall in the Night.
Grenier.   Sunday Morning.
Hammerstein.   Oh, What a Beautiful Mornin'!
Hartnett.   Last Vision of Eoghan Rua Ó Súilleabháin, The.
Hay, G.   Hind of Morning, The.
Heard, J.   Matin Hymn.
   Morn.
Herlin.   Morning space.
Herrera y Reissig.   Grey Dawn.
Herrick.   Matins [or Mattens], or Morning Prayer.
Herzberg.   Morning.
Hollander, J.   By the Sound.
   Edward Hopper's Seven A.M.
   Morning in the Islands.
Housman.   Reveille.
Hughes, L.   Blues at Dawn.
Hughes, T.   Horses, The.
Huidobro.   Morning.
Issa.   New Year's morning.
   Nightingale's song / this morning.
   Red morning sky.
Jaimes Freyre.   Dawn, The.
Jarrell, R.   Nestus Gurley.
Jones, T.   Bird on a Jaunt.
Kahn, G.   Carolina in the Morning.
Keithley.   First Morning.
Kenney.   Aubade: "Cold snap. Five o'clock."
Kikaku.   Shrine gate / Through morning mist.
Kunitz, S.   Round, The.
Kuskin.   I Woke Up This Morning.
Kyle, C. J.   Fire in Early Morning.
Lasker-Schüler.   And Look for God.
Laurencin, M.   Present, The.
Lawrence, D. H.   Morning Work.
Layton.   Aubade, An.
Lee, L.   Early in the Morning.
Levertov.   Matins.

Lewis, J.   Remembered Morning.
Livingstone, D.   Lake Morning in Autumn.
   Morning, A.
Longfellow, H.   Daybreak.
Lowell, R.   Waking Early Sunday Morning.
Lowry, M.   Eye-Opener.
MacKenzie, R.   Blue Sky in Morning.
MacNeice.   Morning Sun.
   Sunday Morning: "Down the road someone is practising scales."
Mahon.   Everything Is Going to Be All Right.
Malroux.   Every morning.
Marzán.   Sunday Morning in Old San Juan.
McCarthy, J.   Cloudy Morning.
Meng Hao Jan.   Spring Morning, A.
Meredith, W.   Poem about Morning.
Merwin.   Rain Travel.
Mihalic.   Morning Roar of the City, The.
Miller, V.   Morning Person.
Minhinnick.   Sunday Morning.
Mistral, G.   Morning.
Morabito, F.   Piazza Gimma.
Morotskaya, S.   Morning sleep / it's sweeter than your palms.
Muldoon, P.   Avenue, The.
Murray, P.   Introit.
Nameroff, R.   California Dreaming.
Ni Dhomhnaill.   Aubade: "It's all the same to morning what it dawns on."
Ogiwara Seisensui.   Morning with a baby crying with all its might.
O'Hara, F.   Getting Up Ahead of Someone (Sun).
Okantah.   African Morning.
Oliver, M.   Morning Poem.
   Waking on a Summer Morning.
Olson, C.   Variations Done for Gerald Van De Wiele.
Padilla.   Daily Habits.
Pavese.   Grappa in September.
   Morning Star.
Penn, R. E.   Morning Songs.
Percival.   Morning among the Hills.
Petri.   Morning Coffee.
Piercy.   Morning Love Song.
Pinsky.   First Early Mornings Together.
Plath.   Sheep in Fog.
Pleynet.   In the Daylight.
Powell, D. A.   Who won't praise green. Each minute to caress each minute blade of spring. Green slice us open.
Previn, D.   Morning After, The.
Rakosi.   Good Morning.
   Lying in Bed on a Summer Morning.
Rashad, J.   Morning After, The.
Richardson, K.   Aubade: "Geese flew by as you entered me, The."
Rimbaud, A.   Lovely Morning Thought.
Ritsos.   Morning.
Roberts, E.   Disconsolate Morning.
Roethke.   Carnations.
Ronsard.   Time To Be Up, Marie, Young Sleepyhead.
Sanchez, S.   Haiku.
Sandburg, C.   Halsted Street Car.
Saner.   Morning Snowfield.
Schwartz, D.   In the Naked Bed, in Plato's Cave.
Scott-Heron.   I Think I'll Call It Morning.
Seward.   Sonnet Written from an Eastern Apartment in the Bishop's Palace at Lichfield, Which Commands a View of Stowe Valley.
Sexton.   Welcome Morning.
Shakespeare, W.   Hark, hark! the lark at heaven's gate sings.
   Sonnet 33: "Full many a glorious morning have I seen[e]."
Simic.   Mirrors at 4 A.M.
   Summer Morning.
Simpson, L.   Early in the Morning.
Southerland.   Recitation.
Stevenson, R.   Winter Time [or Winter-Time].
Strand.   A.M.
   Morning, Noon and Night.
Stryk, L.   Enough.
Supervielle.   Early in the morning.

Swift, J.   Description of the Morning, A.
Tantan.   Morning frost / Mount Fuji.
Tati-Loutard.   Early.
Thaxter.   Chanticleer.
Thomas, E.   Glory, The.
Thoreau.   Guido's Aurora.
Thurman.   Zebra.
Torres, E.   Elbow in Dumberland, An.
Ungaretti.   Morning.
Unknown.   Already the accursed rooster and his sad departure song.
  Morning Ride.
  Morning's sun.
  Oh rooster, wait a little with your song!
  Sister, Awake!
Valente, J.   Morning: "Naked morning, the day's transparent."
Vallejo.   Our Daily Bread.
Vaughan, H.   Morning-Watch, The.
Very.   Clouded Morning, The ("Morning comes, and thickening clouds prevail, The.").
  Fair Morning, The.
  Morning Watch, The.
Viray, M.   Saturday Morning, A.
Wang Po.   Departing from Yiyang in the Early Morning.
Wang Wei.   Morning.
Wesley, C.   Morning Hymn.
Whitehead, C.   Daybreak.
  Morning Thesis.
Wilbur, R.   Late Aubade, A.
  Love Calls Us to the Things of This World.
  Summer Morning, A.
Wilde, O.   Impression du Matin.
Williams, W.   January Morning.
Wordsworth, W.   Composed upon Westminster Bridge, September 3, 1802.
Wright, C.   California Spring.
Wright, F.   Morning.
Yin Luoth.   Phnom Penh Morning.
Yusuf, S.   Good Morning, Fakhani.

Morning Glories
Basho.   Morning glories, The.
  Morning glory also, The.
  Sad beauty?
Chiyojo.   In the well-bucket / A morning glory.
  Morning glory!, The.
  Since morning glories.
Issa.   Morning glories, yes.
  My hut / Thatched.
Kakei.   Morning glory / So pure.
Kikaku.   I begin each day.
Koufman, Stefanie.   Violins tickling.
Whitman, S.   Morning-Glory, The.
Wilner, E.   Conversation with a Japanese Student.

Morocco
Burke, J.   Road to Morocco, The.
Cavalli.   Moroccans with the carpets, The.
Mendes, M.   Graffito in Meknès.
Rumsey, Tessa.   Never Mororcco.
Synková, A.   To Olga.
Ulacia, M.   Arabian Knight.
  En el Ritz de Meknés.
  In the Ritz at Meknes.

Morris, William
Ruefle.   Furthermore.

Mortality
Abbey, L.   Broken Silence.
Abercrombie.   Mary and the Bramble.
Adcock, F.   For Andrew.
Adler, L.   Last Day, The.
  On the Night of the Day the Worlds Ends.
Ågren, G.   Death's Secret.
Aiken, C.   Letter from the Grass, A.
  Prelude I: "Winter for a moment takes the mind; the snow."
  Prelude II: "Two coffees in the Español, the last."
  Tetélestai.
Ainsworth, H.   Fire in My Meditation Burned.
Aisenberg, N.   Leaving Eden.
Aizenberg, M.   Look what's come to light.
Ajanta.   Dateline Hyderabad.
Akinlolu, S.   Can't You See?
Aleixandre.   Body and the Soul, The.

Allen, A.   Love and the Years.
Althaus, Keith.   Little Elegy.
Alvarez, J.   Sonnet 1: "Everything that happens to me these days."
Amichai, Y.   All the Generations Before Me.
  Man in His Life, A.
  Savage Memories.
Ammons.   In Memoriam Mae Noblitt.
  In View of the Fact.
  This Black Rich Country.
Anacreon.   Already my temples are grey.
Aridjis.   Letter from Mexico.
Auden.   Lullaby: "Lay your sleeping head, my love."
Ball, A.   Attempt, An.
Bandeira.   Interview.
Barbauld.   Life.
Basho.   Buddha's death-day / Old hands.
  How marvelous the man is.
  Journey's end / Still alive.
  Sick on a journey.
  This road.
  Tomb, bend / To autum wind—.
Baudelaire.   Autumn Song.
  Spleen LXXV.
Beaumont, Jeanne Marie.   After: "All long labors, whether for hunger, for duty, for."
Beausoleil, B.   This Gate.
Bécquer, G.   To See the Hours of Fever.
Bek, T.   I breathed my fill—and then breathed out.
Bell, M.   Book of the Dead Man #1, The.
Berlin, E.   Sea World.
Berrigan, D.   You Finish It: I Can't.
Berrigan, T.   Last Poem.
Bibbins, M.   Counting.
Blackhawk, Terry.   Dawn of the Navajo Woman, The.
Blake, W.   London.
  To Tirzah.
Bly, R.   August Rain.
  Empty Place, An.
  Kneeling Down to Look [*or* Peer] into a Culvert.
Boker.   Blood, blood! The lines of every printed sheet.
  Sonnet 25: "Leaden eyelids of wan twilight close, The."
Bonnefoy.   Book, for Growing Old, The.
  Well, The.
Borges.   Enigmas, The.
  Limits (or Good-byes).
  Witness, The.
Bosselaar.   Listener of Bats.
Bousoño, C.   How Am I To Tell You.
  Three Poems on Death.
Bradstreet, A.   Before the Birth of One of Her Children.
Brines, F.   Ashes in Oxford.
Brock-Broido.   Radiating Naïveté.
Brooke, R.   Second Best.
Brown, K.   Return of the Prodigals.
Brown, S.   Thoughts of Death.
Bruce, D.   Plunder.
  Prognosis.
Buchan, J.   Fisher Jamie.
Buckley, C.   Star Apocrypha.
Budbill.   First Green of Spring, The.
  Tomorrow: "Tomorrow / we are."
Bunting.   You idiot! What makes you think decay will.
Burns, R.   To a Mountain Daisy [On Turning One Down, with the Plough, in April—1786].
Buson.   Short nap / Waking.
Byron, G.   Manfred.
Cairns, Scott.   Coming Forth.
Carew, T.   Song[, A]: "Ask[e] me no more where Jove bestow[e]s."
Case, David.   Fear No More.
Cavendish, M.   Dissert, A.
Celan.   When you lie.
Celaya, G.   Poetry Is a Weapon Loaded with the Future.
  Theory of Silences.
Char.   Mortal Partner, The.
Chase, K.   Before She Died.

Ch'oe Sûngja.   Untitled 2.
  While Watching Sunset.
Chŏng Ch'ŏl.   Let's drink a cup of wine; let's drink another!
Chu Yohan.   Life, Death.
Cisneros, A.   Spider Hangs Too Far from the Ground, The.
Citino.   Christina the Astonishing: Virgin.
  Last Rites.
Clarke, George Elliott.   Lear Of Whylah Falls.
Clifton, L.   1994.
Close, J.   Mentem Mortalia Tangunt.
Colman, H.   On Mortality.
Comer, Carrie St. George.   Shelburne Falls.
Cooley.   Brother Body.
Corob, T.   Either Way.
Cory, W.   Mimnermus in Church.
Coulehan, J.   Azalea Poem, The.
Craig, David.   Apprentice Eats Glass, The.
Crawford, R.   Downtown Sunday.
Creeley.   Be of Good Cheer.
  Oh my god—you.
Crosby, F.   We Are Going.
Cullen, C.   Leaves.
  Nothing Endures.
Cunningham, J.   All in Due Time.
  Epitaph for Anyone, An.
  Epitaph for Someone or Other.
Darío, R.   Doom.
  Fatality.
Davies, J.   Today / there came a breeze thin as the needle of a syringe.
Dawes, K.   Black Heart.
Delmore, E.   Difference, The.
Desnos.   Midway.
Dickinson, E.   Exultation is the going.
  "Heavenly Father"—take to thee.
  Somehow myself survived the Night.
  'Tis not that Dying hurts us so.
  Visitor in Marl, A.
  Wounded Deer Leaps Highest, A.
Disch.   Convalescing in London.
Dobyns.   His life was the practice of forming a single.
Donne.   Anniversary [*or* Anniversarie], The.
  Farewell to Love.
  Song: "Sweetest love, I do not go[e]."
  When that rich soul[e] which to her heaven is gone.
Douglas, K.   Simplify Me When I'm Dead.
Dowson.   Vitae Summa Brevis Spem Nos Vetat Incohare Longam.
Drake, N.   Very Rich Hours, The.
Dudley, E.   Pathologist.
Dunbar, W.   Lament for the Makaris [*or* Makars *or* Makers].
Dunn, S.   Sweetness.
Duran, J.   Time Zones.
Edson, R.   Rule and Its Exception, The.
Elfyn, Menna.   Driver.
Eliot, T. S.   Whispers of Immortality.
Elliot, A.   Latitudes of Home, The.
Emerson, J.   White Flowers.
Emerson, R.   Hamatreya.
  Hamatreya.
Emre.   Whole universe is full of God, The.
Ewart.   14-Year-Old Convalescent Cat in the Winter, A.
Faverey.   If the opening were forever.
  Train scarcely slackens speed, The.
Feinfeld, D.   Carmelita.
Flanner.   Noon on Alameda Street.
Forbes, J.   Death, an Ode.
Ford, Katie.   Colosseum.
Francia, L.   Is there There in dying.
Fried, D.   Story Having to Do with Walt Whitman, A.
Fuertes.   Climbing.
García Lorca.   Malaguena.
Garcilaso de la Vega.   Rough Are the Roads.
  Song 3: "Surrounded by the gentle sound."
Garrett, G.   Pastoral: "Ghosts of summer learn, The."
Gerov, Alexander.   Problem, A.
Ghalib, M.   When the Day Comes.
Gilgun, J.   Zen Frost.

Glück, L. Earthly Love.
Garden, The: "One sound. Then the hiss and whir."
Triumph of Achilles, The.
Goedicke. American Exercises.
For Walt Whitman.
Goldberg, L. Not for a long time now has anyone waited for me.
Góngora y Argote. Allegory of the Brevity of Things Human.
Goodman, P. Little Ode.
Gorenko, A. Flowers live faster than rotting of cherries.
Graham-Pole, J. Candor.
Graham, R. Without Shadow.
Gray, T. Elegy Written in a Country Churchyard.
Greig, A. Orkeny / This Life.
Gudzenko. Before the Attack.
Gumilyov [or Gumiliov or Gumilev]. Childhood.
Gürpınar, Melisa. Like a Stranger.
Gwynn, R. Anacreontic.
Release.
Hahn, O. Gladioli by the Sea.
Hahn, S. Her Purse, at the Winter Solstice.
Hall, D. Footnote.
Hall, J. Job. I.
Hamer. Different Strokes Bar, San Francisco, The.
Hamill, S. Orchid Flower, The.
Han Yü. Humanity.
Haviaras, Stratis. Stone-Throw.
Hawes, S. Epitaph of Graunde [or La Graunde] Amoure, The.
Healey, S. As Western Culture Declined Without Its Knowing.
Heaney, S. Dog Was Crying Tonight in Wicklow Also, A.
Hemans. Remembrance of Nature.
Voice of Spring, The.
Hemphill. Cordon Negro.
Henderson, H. Flyting o' Life and Daith, The.
Herbert, G. Church Monuments.
Employment.
Mortification.
Time.
Virtue [or Vertue].
Herbert, Z. Remembering My Father.
Herrick. To Daffodils.
Upon the Troublesome Times.
Hidalgo, J. Flowers Under the Dead.
It's Always Waiting.
You Came Down.
You Have to Go Down.
Hierro, José. Requiem ("Manuel del Río, born.").
Hodgson, R. After.
Holmes, J. Mediterranean Cooking for Two.
Hopes. If the flowers could ask me.
Hopkins, G. Spring and Fall [To a Young Child].
Horace. Bring Roses and Cardamom (2.3).
Houlihan, J. Biological Imperative.
Housman. Be still, my soul, be still; the arms you bear are brittle.
From far, from eve and morning.
I hoed and trenched and weeded.
They Say My Verse Is Sad: No Wonder.
With rue my heart is laden.
Hovald, I. Stele for Lenz.
Hristov, Boris. Dandelion Bone.
Hughes, F. Kookaburra.
Hughes, T. October Salmon[, An].
Walt.
Hwang Insuk. I'm Surplus.
Imbriglio, C. Emily.
Issa. As I grow older.
Insects.
Outliving / Them all, all.
Ivanov, G. Old man shuffles to the fish market, The.
Jaccottet. Don't worry.
Right at the end of night.
Jackson, L. Starved.
Jeffers, R. Age in Prospect.

Jiménez, J. Definitve Journey, The.
Jones, I. Alley Games 6/The Ascension.
Jordan, A. Beggar's Song.
Juana Inés de la Cruz. On Her Portrait.
Justice, D. Men at Forty.
Psalm and Lament.
Variations on a Text by Vallejo.
Kabir. Eternity.
Hopeful Spiritual Athlete, The.
Kaplinski, J. Death does not come from outside.
Kaufman, B. Awe.
Keats. Ode on a Grecian Urn.
Ode to a Nightingale.
When I Have Fears [That I May Cease to Be].
Why Did I Laugh Tonight?
Kekova. Having submitted your petition for dismissal.
Kenjeev. And a fool, and a smart one, a miser.
Khalvati. Needlework.
Khomin, I. They met at the Tagansky subway station.
Kim Chôngnan. Between May and June.
Kim Hyesun. Women: "Did I write that I'll endure this."
Kim Kwanguk. Have you seen a person.
Kim, Suji Kwock. Occupation.
Kincaid, Jamaica. Letter from Home, The.
King, H. Sic Vita.
Kinzie. Lunar Frost.
Kleinschmidt. Giorni.
Klink, J. And Having Lost Track.
Ko Ûn. Crossing Rice Fields at Nightfall.
Impermanence.
Kocbek. Earth, I Get Everything From You.
Koch, K. To Old Age.
Kramer, L. Brilliant Windows.
Images of the San Francisco Disaster.
Kuhar, M. On the death of philip whalen.
Kumin, M. Envelope, The.
Our Ground Time Here Will Be Brief.
Thinking of Death and Dogfood.
Kurtz. Andalusian Landscape.
Lansdown. Behind the Veil.
Larkin, P. Aubade: "I work all day, and get half-drunk at night."
Laux, D. Prayer: "Sweet Jesus, let her save you, let her take."
Levchev. Dénouement.
Lewis, A. Sentry, The.
To a Comrade in Arms.
Lewis, Emyr. Once-in-a-Lifetime, Never-to-Be-Repeated, A.
Lewis, G. Second time the comet swung by, The.
Thousands arrive when a bird's about to fly.
Li Po. Old Dust.
Remembering Ancient Days in Yueh.
Xiangyang Song.
Lieberman, M. Regret.
Lihn. Old Man's Monologue with Death, The.
Lisnyanskaya [or Lisnianskaia]. Wind blows and makes the light tremble, The.
Locklin. Stranger, The.
Lodge, G. Strong saturation of sea! O widely flown.
Longfellow, H. Mezzo Cammin.
Lowell, A. New Heavens for Old.
Lumsden, R. Mercy.
Machado Ruiz. Clock Struck Twelve Times, The.
To die. . .To fall like a drop.
MacNeice. Sunlight on the Garden, The.
Madonick, M. Settled In.
Maio, Samuel. In Memoriam: "On this coast where they once arrived destined."
Major, C. Education by Degrees.
Malroux. In October.
Manrique, J. Barcelona Days.
Markham, E. Leaf from the Devil's Jest-Book, A.
Marks, Corey. Portrait of a Child.
Three Bridges.
Martial. Why is it modern poets are ignored.
Marvell. Picture of Little T. C. in a Prospect of Flowers, The.
Masefield. Passing Strange, The.

McAuley, J. Gnostic Prelude.
In a Late Hour.
McFadden, D. Shouting Your Name Down the Well.
McKinnon. Arrhythmia.
McLaughlin-Carruth, J. Black Irish Blues.
Meddeb, Abdelwahab. I Take the Path.
Melville, H. Epilogue: "If Luther's day expand to Darwin's year."
Pontoosuce.
Tom Deadlight.
Meng Chiao. Despair.
Meredith, G. Dirge in Woods.
Mersaal, E. Too Many Times.
Merwin. For the Anniversary of My Death.
Milán, E. I let myself be led because I let loose.
Me dejo guiar porque he dejado ir.
Millay, E. First Fig.
Poet and His Book, The.
When you, that at this moment are to me.
Milosz, C. Encounter.
Mistake, A.
Milosz, O. Bridge, The.
Mistral, G. Final Tree.
Let Him Not Grow Up.
Mitchell, S. Of Earthly Love.
Molina, E. To Vahine (Painted by Gaugin).
Mukand, J. First Payment.
Muso Soseki. From My Hut in Miura.
Na Hûidôk. That Place Isn't Far.
Nadir, M. Afterwards: "Earth will flame and glow, The."
Out of the Depths.
Third, A.
Naito Joso. About the grave / Waves of spring mist.
Nasir, A. Trilogy of the Man in Black.
Neruda. Dead Woman.
Only Death.
Nezahualcoyotl. I, Nezahualcóyotl ask it.
Niedecker. Death of my poor father, The.
Nisker, W. No tears and no fears.
No Hyegyông. Face: "Suddenly below my ankles."
Norris, K. Desert Run Scenario.
Olds, S. Exact Moment of His Death, The.
Oldys. On a Fly Drinking out of [or from] His Cup.
Oliver, M. In Blackwater Woods.
When Death Comes.
Oppen. Image of the Engine.
Population.
Orr, G. Best.
Osherow. Dust on the Mantel: Sonnet.
Otero, B. Chap. 10 Book 2.
Eternal, The.
Something Like A.
Outram, R. Round of Life.
Owen, Gerallt Lloyd. Cilmeri.
Owen, W. A Terre.
Anthem for Doomed Youth.
Exposure.
Send-Off, The.
Pagis, D. Sominex.
Winter's End.
Pak Mogwôl [or Mokwôl]. Eternity of Pure Color.
Pao Chao. Ballad in Imitation of "The Prince of Huainan".
Parry, R. Mortality.
Pastan. After Minor Surgery.
Death's Blue-Eyed Girl.
Early Afterlife, An.
Erosion.
Pasternak, B. Indian Summer.
Mary Magdalene (I).
Patterson, G. I Used to Go to Church.
Paz. And the banquet, the exile, the first crime.
Pessoa. When in the widening circle of rebirth.
Phillips, C. In the blood, Winnowing.
Kill, The.
Luck.
Pleasure.
Words of Love.
Pietri. Intermission from Sunday.
Pinsky. ABC.

Pizarnik. Awakening, The.
Poe. Eldorado.
Popa. In the Ashtray.
Porter, A. Five Wishes.
　Oaks and Squirrels.
Pound, E. And the Days Are Not Full Enough.
Preil, G. Night. And I am drinking smoky black tea from China.
Proctor, T. Respice Finem.
Propertius. When Thou Must Home.
Quevedo y Villegas. Everything Is Swept Away by the Brief Year.
　I Gaze Upon My Country's Walls.
　Now Great and Awesome in My Heart.
Radoev, Ivan. Sweater, The.
Ramke, B. Paul Verlaine at the Grave of Lucien Létinois.
Ransom, J. Piazza Piece.
Ratushinskaya [or Ratushinskaia]. Try to Cover Your Shivering Shoulders.
Rexroth, K. Some day in six inches of.
Reyes, C. Bridges: "My first bridge was a log— a slippery one across a muddy creek."
Reynolds, M. This World.
Reznikoff. Heart and Clock.
Ritsos. Marpessa's Choice.
Robertson, Lisa. Tuesday.
Robinson, E. Pity of the Leaves, The.
Rojas. Chapter and Verse.
Ronci, Seido R. Diamond Cutter.
Rosales. Loosening Water.
Root, The.
Rosenberg, I. I Am the Blood.
Rossetti, D. 71: The Choice ("Eat thou and drink; to-morrow thou shalt die").
　101: The One Hope.
Ruefle. From Here to Eternity.
　March, The.
Rupchev, Georgi. Ceremony.
Ryan, K. Death by Fruit.
Sachs, N. Mouth Sucking in Death.
Sackville-West. Greater Cats, The.
St. John, D. Elegy: "It's true such reckless grace should never die."
Salaam. Name the Oldest Member of Your Family.
Salinas, P. Deaths ("First thing I forgot was your voice, The.").
　Not in Marble Palaces.
Santayana. Echo.
Saroyan. Ex- / track.
Sayigh, M. Lament: "Those we love die like birds."
Schwartz, R. L. Edgewater Park.
Serrano, P. Vértigo.
Shakespeare, W. Dirge for Fidele.
　Sonnet 19: "Devouring Time, blunt thou the lion's [or Lyons] paw[e]s."
　Sonnet 65: "Since brass, nor stone, nor earth, nor boundless sea."
Shapiro, D. Lord I Sleep and I Sleep.
Shapiro, H. Nights: "Drunk and weeping. It's another."
Shapiro, K. Cut Flower, A.
Shaw, R. Shut In.
Shelley, P. Conclusion.
Shinkichi Takahashi. Moon.
Simonides. Human strength.
　Who, trusting his mind, could praise the man of Lindos, Kleoboulos.
Simpson, L. Early in the Morning.
Singer, B. Poem About Death, A.
Sisson. In Flood.
　Tristia.
Skelton, J. Upon a Dead Man's Head.
Slutsky [or Slutskii]. My old men are dying.
Smith, J. Philodendron Named Joan, A.
　What I Learned From the Movies.
Smith, L. Calligraphy of Birds.
Spender, S. One More New Botched Beginning.
Spires. Cemetery Reef.
　Glass-Bottom Boat.
Steiger. Until the sun sinks into a green.
Stein, K. In the Kingdom of Perpetual Repair.
Stesichoros. Across from glorious Erytheia.
Stevens, W. Clear Day and No Memories, A.

Peter Quince at the Clavier.
Postcard from the Volcano, A.
Stickney, T. Athenian Garden, An.
　Be still. The Hanging Gardens were a dream.
Stone, R. For My Dead Red-Haired Mother.
Strand. 2032.
Straus, M. What I Heard on the Radio Today.
Suárez. Workwoman's Death, A.
Subbarao, N. My Love.
Sze. Before Completion.
　String Diamond, The.
Szymborska, W. Contribution to Statistics, A.
T'aego, National Preceptor. On a Deathbed.
Taggard. To the Powers of Desolation.
Tagore. Last Poems 13.
Tahmiscic. You're Not a Man If You Don't Die.
Tanikawa, S. Dusk.
T'ao Ch'ien [or T'ao Yuan-ming]. Drinking Alone in the Rainy Season.
　Substance, Shadow, and Spirit ("Heaven and Earth endure and do not perish.").
Tate, A. Non Omnis Moriar.
Tate, J. Diagnosis, The.
Taylor, E. This Year's Drive to Appomattox.
Teitelboim, D. Jim the Janitor Is Dead.
Tennyson, A. Tithonus.
Terán, V. Biluxe.
　It's Over.
　Se acabó.
Thomas, C. Bullet, A / slams.
Thomas, G. Last Things, The.
Tilak, D. Police Report.
Tomlinson, C. After a Death.
Trakl. Descent and Defeat.
　Mourning: "Dark eagles, sleep and death, The."
Trethewey, N. Native Guard.
Trowbridge, W. Curtain Call.
Tsanev, Stefan. Old woman leans against the pine tree, The.
Tu Fu [or Du Fu]. Traveler's Pavilion.
　West of my hut, I grow mulberry.
Unknown. Airman, The.
　Captive's Song.
　Clothes.
　Dew on the Shallot.
　I Shall Not Pass This Way Again.
　If the hour has not rung, death will not be coming.
　Last Survivor's Speech, The.
　Lonesome Valley.
　My beloved, come and sit a moment close to me.
　No Road Back.
　Oh Earth! The dues that you exact weigh far too much.
　Only One Life.
　Qiyuge.
　Quickly, my love, I want to offer you my mouth!
　Steal Away to Jesus.
　What Yo' Gwine to [or t'] Do When Yo' [or de] Lamp Burn Down?
Vallejo. Black Stone Lying on a White Stone.
　Good Sense.
　Need to Die, The.
　Today I like life much less.
Vanshenkin. Sunset fades, and from the little hill, The.
Vaughan, H. Death.
　Joy of My Life! While Left Me Here.
　Quickness.
Verlaine. Beauty of women, their weakness, those pale hands.
Vertreace, M. Caged Stone.
Vinokurov. Has the time come to draw up the accounts?
Vogel, D. There Is a Last, Solitary Coach.
Volkman. I believe there is a song that is stranger than wind, that sips the scald from the telling, toss, toss.
Wagoner, D. Curtains.
Walcott. Tomorrow, Tomorrow.
Wang the Zealot. Ghosts Clap Hands.
Warren, R. Acquaintance with Time in Early Autumn.
　After the Dinner Party.

Watson, E. Natural.
Watts, I. Mr. Mead, Mr. Bates, and Mr. Gouge [or An Elegy on Mr. Thomas Gouge].
Webster, J. Burial, The.
Wenderoth, J. Narrative Poem.
Wharton, E. Autumn Sunset, An.
　Experience.
　Life.
Whitman, W. This Compost.
　To Think of Time.
Whitney, I. Aucthour Maketh Her Wyll and Testament, The.
Wilbur, R. Lilacs, The.
　To His Skeleton.
Wilder, R. Baby, The.
Wilkinson, J. Funk Qualms.
Williams, M. Some Lines Finished Just Before Dawn at the Bedside of a Dying Student It Has Snowed All Night.
Williams, T. May: "Mortality shrinks back— because."
Winchilsea. Spleen, The: A Pindaric Poem.
Witt, S. Americana.
Wolff, Rebecca. Lamb, Willow: An Arch Dolefulness Has Taken Me This Far.
Wolfli. And now: And now: here begins Our Voyage, hunters and naturalists of indefatigable enthusiasm.
Woods, D. Waiting.
Wordsworth, W. Extempore Effusion upon the Death of James Hogg.
Trosachs, The.
Wright, C. Quotations.
Wrigley, R. Skull of a Snowshoe Hare, The.
Wunderlich, M. Peonies.
Wylie. This Corruptible.
Yesenin [or Essenin]. All Too Soon.
　I Regret Nothing.
　Sleigh, The.
Yi Yônju. Holiday Inside an Incubator.
Young, A. Mountains of California: Part 2, The.
Young, David. After My Death.
Young, Dean. Colophon.
Yuan Mei. Last Poem: Goodbye to My Garden.
Zenmaro. Evidence.
Zukofsky, L. No it was no dream of coming death.

Morticians
　Ai. Mortician's Twelve-year-old Son, The.
　Dubie. Parish.
　Mirville, E. In the land of Haiti.
See also **Undertakers**

Moscow, Russia
　Fleming, P. To the Great City of Moscow, as He Was Leaving June 25, 1636.
　Garlick, R. Capitals.
　Iofe, Y. Thing or Two about Childhood, A.
　Lermontov. Borodino.
　Okudzhava. To me, Muscovites are sweethearts out of old stories.
　Prigov. It's better not to live in Moscow.
　Rein. Moscow Station, The.
　Secret Agent, A.
　Shwarts [or Shvarts]. Elegies on the Cardinal Points.
　Tsvetayeva [or Tsvetaeva]. Cupolas flame, in Moscow where I live.
　Tonight—I am alone in the night.

Moses
　Agosin. Miriam.
　Aleixandre. Old Man Is Like Moses, The.
　Allen, S. Harriet Tubman aka Moses.
　Bible, O.T. Psalm 114: "When Isr'el, freed from Pharoh's hand."
　De Luca, G. Streams in the Desert.
　Dickinson, E. It always felt to me—a wrong.
　Dickinson, P. Moses and the Princess.
　"Eliot.". Death of Moses, The.
　Glück, L. Day Without Night.
　Harper, F. Oh never on that mountain.
　Hart, S. Sundays.
　Hope, A. Luke 24:36–49; As they were saying this, Jesus.
　Moran, M. Pharao's Daughter.
　Naden. Moonlight and Gas.
　Nemerov. John 3:1–15; Now there was a man.

Ni Dhomhnaill.　Language Issue, The.
Sagay-Lights, V.　If Harriet Tubman Were Alive Today.
Unknown.　Come Along, Moses.
Go Down, Moses.
Let God's Saints Come In.
Railroad Section Leader's Song.
Very.　Moses in Infancy.
Wilner, E.　Epitaph: "Young then, / we were bored already."
Wither.　First Song of Moses, The.

Mosques
Bracho, C.　En esta oscura mezquita tibia.
In This Warm Dark Mosque.

Mosquitoes
Basho.　Searching storehouse eaves.
Buson.　At the ancient well.
"Ern Malley.".　Culture as Exhibit.
Issa.　All the time I pray to Buddha.
As we grow old / What triumph.
At prayer / Bead-swinging.
Clouds of mosquitoes / It would be bare.
Mosquito at my ear.
Poor quarter, A.
This stupid world.
What good luck!
Kikaku.　In the Emperor's bed.
Kinzie.　Among mosquitoes.
Lawrence, D. H.　Mosquito Knows, The.
Mosquito, The.
Leithauser.　Mosquito, A.
Lindsay, V.　Little Turtle, The.
Masaoka Shiki.　Swatting mosquitoes.
Murray, L.　Forests and State Forests, all down off the steeper country; mosquitoes are always living in there.
Naong.　Mosquito.
Ozaki Hosai.　Splendid breasts.
Pagis, D.　Mosquito, The.
Tan Taigi.　Zazen / Fat mosquitoes.

Moss
Blind.　Entangled.
Boruch.　Moss Burning.
Irby.　January 1965, Looking on.
Roethke.　Moss-Gathering.
Wordsworth, W.　Thorn, The.

Motels
Culbert, Steven Tye.　Van Horn.
Grosholz.　Outer Banks, The.
Hiestand, E.　Moon Winx Motel.
Hummer, T.　Mechanics.
Jacob, M.　In Search of the Traitor.
Klein, M.　Tides, The.
Knight, S.　Surf Motel, The.
Mörling, M.　In a Motel Room at Dawn.
Nelson, M.　Motel Story.
Pape.　In the Bluemist Motel.
Snodgrass.　Leaving the Motel.
Solie, Karen.　More Fun In The New World.
Yuson.　Dead Center.
See also **Hotels**

Mother Goose
Jacobsen, J.　Primer, The.

Mother Nature
Hawkey, C.　*Fräulein*, can you.
Unknown.　I ask all blessings.

Mothers
Abse.　X-Ray.
Abu Khalid.　Mother's Inheritance.
Two Little Girls.
"Ada.".　Slave Girl's Farewell, The.
Adams, A.　To My Mother.
Adamson.　Dreaming Up Mother.
My House.
Addonizio.　Gravity.
Adelman, P.　My Exorcist Mother.
Adisa.　Things No One Told Me.
Aguero, Kathleen.　Working Mother.
Aguilar-Cariño.　Dinakdakan.
Agustini.　Another Race.
Vision.
Akhmatova, A.　Requiem.
Allen, E.　Rock Me to Sleep[, Mother].
Allingham, W.　In Snow.
Alvarez, J.　Naming the Fabrics.

Wallpaper.
Amichai, Y.　My Mother Once Told Me.
My Son.
Angela, F.　Old Stone Age.
Anhalt, D.　That Jewish Crusader.
Anyte [*or* Anytes].　Often keening on her daughter's tomb, Kleina.
Ap Hywel, Elin.　In My Mother's House.
Appleman, P.　Birthday Card to My Mother.
Apuleius, L.　I who am Nature, mother of all.
Arcana, J.　Great with Child.
Aridjis.　To Emerge from a Woman Is to Become Separate.
Armantrout.　Incidence.
Arrillaga.　Mariana II.
Asekoff, L.　Will.
Assultani, F.　My Mother, in memoriam.
Ausländer, R.　My Nightingale.
Baggett.　Barely Eight.
Baillie, J.　Mother to Her Waking Infant, A.
Bandeira.　Interview.
Barber, D.　Nocturne.
Barber, M.　Written for My Son, and Spoken by Him at His First Putting on Breeches.
Baring, A.　Song, The: "Beehive source."
Barker, G.　O Pearl and Breasted World.
Sonnet to My Mother.
Basu, R.　How are you faring, Uma.
I had a good dream last night.
Bat-Miriam.　Precious stones that my mother.
Bateman, M.　Picture of My Mother.
Baumel.　Snow-Day.
Baxter, J.　Homecoming, The.
Bayly.　We Met.
Beer, P.　Lost Woman, The.
Belieu.　Another Poem for Mothers.
Belli, G.　Birth.
Bellman.　Fredman's Epistle No. 23.
Ben-Lev, D.　Broken Helix.
Bensley.　Single Parent.
Berezan, J.　Hail Mother full of grace power is with thee.
Berg, S.　Prayer: "Nobody understands so let the Rabbi."
Berger, J.　Between Worlds.
Berland, D.　Blazon.
Berman, C.　Poem for the Shechina.
Bernstein, C.　Cup of Coffee, The.
Berry, W.　To My Mother.
Bhāndārī, S.　Menaka says, Hey listen, Mountain King.
Bhattācārya, K.　Consulting the omens.
From her autumn-lotus mouth.
Here, Queen of the Mountains.
How could you have forgotten her.
Jaya, tell him that Uma will not be sent.
Kali, you have removed all my difficulties.
My Gauri / You've come home!
My Uma has come!
Tell me, Syama.
Tell me / What can I do?
Turn back, Uma.
Bialosky, J.　After father died.
Bingxin.　Paper Boat—Sent to Mother.
Springwater, part 105.
Birney.　Gray Woods Exploding, The.
Blind.　Motherhood.
Noonday Rest.
Boland, E.　Blossom, The.
Born, A.　End of the Row.
Bourne, Lesley-Anne.　Boy I Never Met, The.
Boyle, K.　Mothers: "In the still of night."
Bradstreet, A.　Before the Birth of One of Her Children.
Epitaph on my Dear and Ever Honored Mother Mrs. Dorothy Dudley.
In Reference to Her Children, 23 June, 1659 [*or* 1659].
To My Dear Children.
Brandt, D.　Great dark rush of mothering, The.
My mother found herself one late summer.
Breeze.　Natural High.
Bremer, C.　Crack, The.
Grieta, La.
Brett, L.　Leaving You.
Brion, R.　Love Song: "One long and humid

afternoon."
Brooks, G.　Children of the poor, The (1).
Jessie Mitchell's Mother.
Mrs. Small.
Brown, G.　Mother, The: "On Monday she stood at the wooden wash-tub."
Browning, E.　Mother and Poet.
Brunk, J.　Where My Mother Cries.
Bryner.　Desert Flowers.
Budbill.　What I Heard at the Discount Department Store.
Burnshaw.　House in St. Petersburg.
Busia, A.　Liberation.
Buson.　Long, long ago.
Cabico, R.　Mango Poem.
Campbell, D.　Mothers and Daughters.
Campbell, R.　Zulu Girl, The.
Campbell, S.　Constant Welcome, The.
Campion, T.　Fain Would I Wed.
Candī, A.　Bring Tara quickly, Mountain.
Cardona-Hine.　Acquaintances.
Carrera Andrade.　Second Life of My Mother.
Carroll.　In the Shakespeare Garden at Northwestern University.
Carson, A.　God's Mother.
Short Talk on Walking Backwards.
Castro, R.　Mild Was the Air.
Causley.　What Has Happened to Lulu?
Cavafy.　Supplication.
Celan.　Aspen Tree.
Cerenio.　My Mother.
Chase, N.　Music Mother.
Chipasula, S.　I'm My Own Mother, Now.
Chippewa Oral Tradition.　Sioux Woman Defends Her Children, The.
Cisneros, S.　Muddy Kid Comes Home.
Clanchy, K.　Stance.
Clementelli.　Moviola.
Clements, S.　Reservation, The.
Clifton, L.　Admonitions.
Death of thelma sayles, The.
Fury.
Here is another bone to pick with you.
I was born with twelve fingers.
My Mama Moved among the Days.
Thirty-Eighth Year, The.
Clinton, M.　Eviction.
Clive.　Mother, The.
Clurman, D.　Berkeley Marina at Dusk, The.
Cluysenaar.　Knife reduces a polished oval, The.
Cofer, J.　Counting.
Fever.
Unspoken.
Coleman, W.　American Sonnet (10).
Coles, R.　Goddam Street, The.
Collins, B.　Tomes.
Collymore.　Ballad of an Old Woman.
Colum, P.　Interior.
Cooley.　Poem on My Birthday.
Cooper, J.　My Mother in Three Acts.
Cornford, F.　Sick Queen, The.
Cornish, S.　Harriet Tubman.
Corso.　Sea Chanty.
Couzyn.　Transformation.
Cowper, W.　On the Receipt of My Mother's Picture out of Norfolk, the Gift of My Cousin Ann Bodham.
Creeley.　For My Mother: Genevieve Jules Creeley.
Memory Gardens.
Mother's Voice.
Cross, E.　Kali.
Cruz, C.　Persephone.
Persephone 2.
Csoori.　Visitor's Memories, The.
Dancing Bear, J. P.　Caliban.
De Kok.　My mother's house hold.
de Portalatin.　Second Elegy.
Dean, D. K.　Back to Back.
Stitches.
DeFrees.　Letter to an Absent Son.
Derricotte.　Christmas Eve: My Mother Dressing.
Note on my Son's Face, A.
Dickey, J.　Buckdancer's Choice.
Dickey, R.　Mulatto Lullaby.

Dobyns. Tomatoes.
Dodson, O. Black Mother Praying.
Donovan, K. Grooming.
Dorn, E. On the Debt My Mother Owed to Sears Roebuck.
Dove, R. After Reading *Mickey in the Night Kitchen* for the Third Time Before Bed.
Mother Love.
Poem in Which I Refuse Contemplation.
Doyle, S. This Shade.
Dromgoole. Old Ladies.
Drummond de Andrade. Infancy.
Dudis, Ellen Kirvin. Riding Their Bikes.
Dufferin and Clandeboye. Mother's Lament, The.
Dumas, H. Afro-American.
Dumdum. To My Mother.
Duncan, R. My Mother Would Be a Falconress.
Dunn, S. Routine Things Around the House, The.
That Saturday Without a Car.
Eady. My Mother is a God Fearing Woman.
Eclipse. Cicada.
Edson, R. Windows of the Castle, The.
Ellis, T. Making Ends Meet.
Elon, Florence. In the New World.
Elsschot. Mother.
Emmott, K. Who Looks after Your Kids?
Espinet, R. Merchant of Death.
Ezekiel. Night of the Scorpion.
Fainlight, R. Handbag.
Falcón, J. Indian Locks.
Fay, J. Santorini Daughter.
Feinstein, E. Mother Love.
Feldman, I. Dream, The.
Ferebee, Gideon. For My Mother Magnetic Poetry Series.
Ferré. Message.
Ficowski. Both Your Mothers.
Filkova, Fedya. Frost: "Hospital garden on Sunday, A."
Fingueret, M. Leviticus (Chapter 7, Verse 2-5).
Finney, N. Lobengula: Having a son at 38.
Fisher, A. On Mother's Day.
Fishman, L. Diagnosis: My Mother's Breast.
Floyd-Miller, C. She kneels at the wailing wall.
Flynn, N. Cartoon Physics, Part 2.
Fragment (Found Inside My Mother).
Foppa. Nocturne.
Wound.
Fordham. Mother's Recall.
To My Mother.
Foster, A. Gap, The.
Foster, S. Conant. Boycycle, The.
France, P. Death.
Gallagher, K. Distances.
Gallagher, T. Coming Home.
García, D. Green Corn Season.
Garcia, R. Elite Syncopations.
Mi Mamá, the Playgirl.
Gardinier. Letter to My Mother.
Garrett, E. Airborne.
Vista.
Gates, E. My Mother's Hands.
Gehrke, S. Mouth to Mouth.
Gex-Breaux, Q. Memory Waves.
Gezelle. Little Mother.
Gillan. Waiting for the Results of a Pregnancy Test.
Gilman, C. Mother's Charge, The.
Ginsberg, A. Kaddish.
O mother / what have I left out.
Giovanni. Mothers.
Glatt. Amanda.
What We Did After My Mother's Mastectomy.
Gloria. Whisper, The.
Glück, L. Lullaby: "My mother's an expert at one thing."
School Children, The.
Godfrey. My Mother, Life.
González, R. Marías, Old Indian Mothers.
Goodison. Birth Stone.
I Am Becoming My Mother.
Goodman, M. Cobwebs.
Goodtimes. Learning to Smile.
Gorbanevskaya. Drought, malevolent

stepmother.
Gottlieb, A. Meditation on the Feminine Nature of Shekinah, A.
Goyette, Susan. Peonies, The.
Graham-Pole, J. Leaving Mother, 1954.
Graham, W. Conscript Goes, The.
Graves, R. Frosty Night, A.
Gray-Kontar, D. Cuz' mama played jazz.
Greenlaw, L. Love from a Foreign City.
Griffin, S. Our Mother.
Grimald. From A Funeral Song, Upon the Decease of Annes His Mother.
I, in your frutefull woomb conceyved, born was.
Grindrod, C. Searching.
Grosholz. Eden.
Grossman, A. Runner, The.
Guevara, M. Reader of This Page.
Guidacci. Crazy Mother, The.
Gywnn, R. S. At Rose's Range.
Hacker, M. Autumn 1980.
Nearly a Valediction.
No better lost than any other woman.
Hadas, R. Three Silences.
Hahn, K. Sewing Without Mother: A Zuihitsu.
Hai-Jew, S. Kinged.
Hall, D. Porcelain Couple, The.
Hardie, K. Young Woman Stands on the Edge of Her Life, The.
Harechavi. Already Night, Already Day.
Harper, Cynthia. Día de Los Muerto.
Harper, F. Slave Mother, The.
Slave Mother, The: A Tale of the Ohio.
Harris, D. For My Mother.
Harryman. Mothering.
Harvor, Elisabeth. Four O'Clock, New Year's Morning, New River Beach.
Hashimoto, S. Mirror of Matsuyama, The.
Hayden, R. Whipping, The.
Hayes, T. Blue Terrance, The.
Heaney, S. When all the others were away at Mass.
Heard, J. Mother.
Herbert, G. Ah Mater, quo te deplorem fonte?
Dolores.
Hinckley, P. New Our Father, The.
Hirschhorn, N. Number Our Days.
Hixon, L. My blissful Mother exists fully through every creature!
Who can keep a blazing fire tied in a cotton cloth?
Hoagland, T. Lucky.
Hodges, Janice W. Annuals and Perennials.
Hogg, J. Wife of Crowle, The.
Holan. Mother.
Holland, J. Pulse.
Three Tests for Darwin Duke.
Hope, M. Our Mothers.
Hostetler, A. Female Ancestor.
Painting with My Daughter.
Houlihan, J. Matter.
Hove. Country Life.
Hristov, Boris. My Mother's Wedding.
Hughes, L. Cross.
Letter ("Dear Mama, / Time I pay rent and get my food.").
Mother to Son.
Hughes, T. Revenge Fable.
Hugo, V. Grandmother, The.
Ignatow, D. Kaddish.
Ingelow. Seven Time Six. Giving in Marriage.
Ironbiter, S. Song to the Mother of the World.
Ishikawa Takuboku. Tanka: "Just for fun."
Islām, N. Let's be girls, Ma.
Issa. Its mother on guard.
Mother I never knew.
Mother, I weep.
Nursing her child.
Iverem, E. Murmur.
Jackson, A. Peacock of Motherhood, The.
Jackson, R. 1973.
Jarrell, R. Bats.
Death of the Ball Turret Gunner, The.
Lost Children, The.
Jeffers, H. Another Easter Poem.
Jĕn Jui. Midnight.
Johnson, G. Motherhood.

Johnston, E. Mother's Love, A.
Jones, R. What effect has your new son had on your writing life?
Joseph, A. Domestic Humiliation.
Kitchen.
Kakkai Patiniyar Naccellaiyar. Many Said.
Karade, B. Yemoja.
Kasdorf. What I Learned from My Mother.
Kasischke. Pall.
Kaufman, S. Apples.
Mothers, Daughters.
Notes to my Daughters.
Kavanagh, P. In Memory of My Mother.
Kay, J. Telling Part, The.
Waiting Lists, The.
Kazantzis. Midwife.
Keeshig-Tobias. Mother with Child.
Keesing. Reverie of a Mum.
Kelly, B. Arguments of Everlasting.
Kendrick, D. Sidney, Looking for her Mother.
Kennedy, X. Mother's Nerves.
Kerim. Mother.
Kerouac. One Hundred and Forty-Ninth Chorus.
Kessler, S. Marty's Mother.
Kgositsile. To Mother.
Khalvati. Knocking on the door.
Khoury, N. People of Pomegranates.
Kim Hyesun. Memories of the Day I Gave Birth to a Daughter.
Remembering the Day I Gave Birth to a Daughter.
Women.
Kim Namjo. For Baby.
Kim Sŭnghŭi. Between Saint and Witch.
Love Song for the Belly Button 1.
Mother's Feet.
Kipling, R. Nativity, A.
Unknown Female Corpse.
Kizer, C. Intruder, The.
Klein, M. Scenes for an Elegy.
Ko Chŏnghŭi. People of the Earth 8.
Prague Spring 6.
Komunyakaa, Y. Boys in Dresses.
My Father's Love Letters [or Loveletters].
Korinna [or Corinna]. Wishing to take her son.
Kramer, L. On Shutting the Door.
Krechel. To Mainz!
Krysl. Persephone, to Demeter.
Kumin, M. Envelope, The.
Nurture.
Seeing the Bones.
Lake, P. Blue Jay.
Lamb, C. Gipsy's Malison, The.
Landon. Dying Child, The.
Landor, W. Mother, I Cannot Mind My Wheel.
Larkin, J. Beatings.
Cold River.
Legacy.
Larsen, L. Lips.
Laux, D. Nurse, The.
Layton. Keine Lazarovitch, 1870-1959.
Le Guin. Child on the Shore, The.
Lee, L. Eternal Son, The.
I Ask My Mother to Sing.
Levertov. Arctic Spring.
Death in Mexico.
Levine, P. On the Birth of Good and Evil During the Long Winter of '28.
Soloing.
Levison, B. Eighth Symphony Interruptus.
Levitt, Peter. Mother, you were born.
Lewis, M. My Mother.
Lewis, S. Rock-a-Bye Your Baby with a Dixie Melody.
Lezama Lima. Call of the Desirous.
Lifshin. Curling on the Bottom of My Mother's Bed.
I Remember Haifa Being Lovely But.
Lim, S. Starlight Haven.
Lisick, B. Empress of Sighs ("Mom says getting to the new home is a snap.").
Liu, T. Mama.
Livingston, M. Working with Mother.
Llewellyn-Williams. Making Babies.
Lochhead, L. Sorting Through.

Loftin, E.   April '68.
Lomax, M.   Amor Diving.
   July.
Lorde.   Black Mother Woman.
   From the House of Yemanjá.
   Hanging Fire.
   Now That I Am Forever with Child.
Lowell, R.   Sailing Home from Rapallo.
Lubomirski, K.   Mother.
Macgoye.   August the First; Court Martial. The
   Mother Speaks.
Macha, F.   Artist and a Wailing Mother, An.
MacIntyre, S.   Christmas Present for My
   Mother.
Madgett.   Offspring.
   Reluctant Light.
Madhubuti.   Mothers.
Maguire, S.   Invisible Mender, The.
Majorino.   Kisses.
Makeda (Queen of Sheba).   Wisdom is / sweeter
   than honey.
Marie de France.   Wolf and the Sow, The.
Martínez, V.   Children of the Disappeared.
Masefield.   C. L. M.
McAdams, J.   Leaving the Old Gods.
McCallum, S.   Jamaica, October 18, 1972.
McElroy, C.   In My Mother's Room.
   Ruth.
McFadden, D.   12. Shantideva.
McGinley.   Adversary, The.
McGinnis, M.   Letter to My Mother.
McKay, C.   My Mother.
McPherson, S.   Wings and Seeds: For My Birth
   Mother.
Mead, J.   Third Stair, Seventh Stair, Landing.
Mehren, S.   Mother, We Were a Heavy Burden.
Meynell, A.   Cradle-Song at Twilight.
   Girl on the Land, The.
   Maternity.
   Modern Mother, The.
Mezey.   My Mother.
Miles, J.   Belief.
   Conception: "Death did not come to my
   mother."
Millay, E.   Courage that my mother had, The.
Miller, E.   My Father's Girlfriend.
Miller, J.   Bravest battle that ever was fought,
   The.
Milne, A.   Disobedience.
Milosz, C.   With Her.
Min, N. M.   My Mother Has Forgotten My
   Name.
Mistral, G.   Close to Me.
   My Mother.
   Rocking.
   Woman, A.
Mitchell, E.   Mother, Dear Mother.
Moir, L.   Handnotes.
Molloy, D.   Looking for Mother.
Molodovsky [or Molodowsky].   Mother, A:
   "Mother in the green sweater walks and walks
   along the street, The."
Monsour.   Sweeping.
Montague, J.   Flowering Absence, A ("How can
   one make an absence flower.").
   Locket, The.
Moon, Susan.   Unintended.
Moore, L.   Praisesong: From Son to Mother.
Moraga.   For the Color of My Mother.
   Half-Breed.
Morejón.   Mother.
Morgan, Robert.   Code, The.
Morgan, Robin.   As it was in the beginning.
Mori.   Speaking Through White: For My
   Mother.
Morris, A.   Worry All the Time.
Mugo, M. G.   Where are those Songs?
Muir, E.   Childhood.
Muldoon, P.   Ma.
Mullen, H.   Eyes in the Back of Her Head.
   Momma Sayings.
Murphy, M.   Contact Sheet.
Muske, C.   August, Los Angeles, Lullaby.
   Wyndmere, Windemere.
Mutén, B.   Queen Hera.
Napier, F.   I Do Not Want the Ceiling of the

Sistine Chapel.
Natzler, C.   There.
Nelson, H.   With My Mother, Missing the Train.
Nelson, M.   Cover Photograph.
Nesbit, E.   Song: "Oh, baby, baby, baby dear."
Nichols, G.   Praise Song for My Mother.
   Wha Me Mudder Do.
Nijhoff.   At a Grave.
Nimmo, D.   Exorcism.
   My Father's Shadow.
Nirmala, K.   Birds Love the Net.
Noel-Scott.   Hansel and Gretel.
Norris, K.   Persephone.
   Prayer to Eve, A.
Norton, C.   Mother's Heart, The.
Notley.   Incidentals in the Day World.
   Three Strolls.
Nowlan.   Mother and Son.
Nyhart.   Vow.
Obejas, A.   Lifes.
   Sunday.
Odio, E.   Memory of My Private Childhood.
Ofeimun.   Naming Day, A.
Ogilvy.   Natal Address to My Child, March 19th
   1844, A.
O'Hara, F.   Ave Maria.
O'Keefe, E.   Chords.
Olds, S.   Her List.
   Mother, The.
   New Mother.
   Quake Theory.
   Try-Outs, The.
   Young Mothers 1.
Ono.   Mother of the Universe.
Ormsby, F.   Winter Offerings.
Orr, G.   City of Salt, The.
Osborne, J.   Naming of Flowers, The.
Ostriker.   Shekhinah as mute, The.
O'Sullivan, L.   Cord, The.
Owen, M.   Topography.
Pak Chaesam.   Road Back, The.
Paley, G.   Some days I am lonesome I want to
   talk to my mother.
Palmer, Debbra.   Wade's Hoggers.
Parnell, P.   Medusa and Perseus III: Lilith.
Paschen.   12 East Scott Street.
Pasolini.   Prayer to My Mother.
Pastan.   Marks.
   Self-Portrait.
   To a Daughter Leaving Home.
Paterson, E.   Griselda.
Pawlak.   After Burying Her Son, A Mother
   Speaks.
Peacock, M.   Dogged Persistence.
Perdomo, W.   Unemployed Mami.
Perillo, L.   Sweaters, The.
Peseroff.   Raptor in the Kitchen.
Petit, P.   My Mother's Clothes.
   My Mother's Skin.
Piatt, S.   This World.
Piñero.   On The Day They Buried My Mother.
Pinsky.   Poem with Refrains.
Plath.   Disquieting Muses, The.
   Morning Song: "Love set you going like a fat
   gold watch."
   Parliament Hill Fields.
Plath, Z.   Cooking Lesson.
Poe.   To My Mother.
Pogson, P.   Fifteen.
Prado, A.   Murmur.
Pratt, M.   Poem for My Sons.
Preston, R.   Mama.
Pryde, A.   I'll See You Down the Lane.
Quayle, L.   Woman Who Drank Us Up, The.
Rai San'yo.   Escorting My Mother Home: A
   Short Song for the Road.
Raine, E.   Heirloom.
Ramírez, J.   Topografía.
   Topography.
Randall, M.   Nushu.
Rash, R.   July, 1949.
Ray, H.   To My Mother.
Redmond, G.   Mama's Magic.
Reese, L.   War Memory, A.
Rexroth, K.   Delia Rexroth ("California rolls
   into.").

Delia Rexroth ("Under your illkempt yellow
   roses.").
Reznikoff.   She who worked patiently.
Rice, N.   Mother's Room.
Ridl.   Video Mama.
Riley, D.   Affections Must Not.
Ríos, A.   Nani.
Rivas, J.   Río 1.
   River 1.
Robertson, R.   Waves: "I have swum too far."
Rock, D.   Changing.
   Mother.
Rodgers, C.   It Is Deep.
Rodríguez, A.   Extracted.
Rodriguez, L.   Speaking with Hands.
Romero, L.   My Mother Didn't Learn.
Roripaugh, L.   Pearls.
Rossetti, C.   Chilly Night, A.
Rukeyser, M.   Night Feeding.
Rumsey, Tessa.   Assembling My Shepherd.
Rungano.   Labour.
   Mother.
Sachs, N.   Already Embraced by the Arm of
   Heavenly Solace.
   Dead Child Speaks, A.
Sackett, F.   Another Kind of Skin.
Sāheb, A.   Victory to Yogendra's Wife, Great
   Illusion!
St. John, P.   Pearle's Poem.
Saitō Mokichi.   From far off I have brought
   medicines, she watches me because I am her
   son.
Salaam, K.   N.
Salter.   What Do Women Want?
Sanders, E.   Leaves of Heaven, The.
Sappho.   Evening Star who gathers everything.
   It's no use.
Sarton, M.   August Third.
Savageau.   At the Powwow.
Schechter.   What Were You Patching?
Schulman.   Home Movie.
Schultz, P.   Stories.
Scott, D.   Onondaga Madonna, The.
Scott, Mary.   At the Crossroads.
Scott, W.   My Mother.
Seaton, M.   Blonde Ambition.
Sen, R.   Brother / This world.
   Her face / Is a spotless moon.
   How wonderful! Look what.
   I'll die of mental anguish.
Serote.   Three mothers, The.
Shinder.   Changing: "Your unmistakable breasts,
   plain, finely wrinkled."
Shinkichi Takahashi.   Mother and I.
Sholl.   Good News/Bad News.
   You Figure It Out.
Shomer.   My Mother's Body.
Shorter.   Mother, The.
Shumaker.   Waitress's Kid, The.
Siddal.   At Last.
Simic.   My Mother was a Braid.
   Spoons with Realistic Dead Flies on Them.
Simon, L.   Kali.
Sims, H.   Left Rites.
Smith, P.   Biting Back.
Smith, S.   Human Affection.
   Mother, among the Dustbins.
   Mother Love.
Snodgrass.   Mother, The: "She stands in the
   dead center like a star."
Sō Chōngju.   Grandmother's Verandah.
Song.   Mother of Us All.
   Youngest Daughter, The.
Sorby.   Synchronized Swimming.
Speakes.   Mama Loves Janis Joplin.
Stafford, W.   Our Kind.
Stead, C.   Between.
Stesichoros.   Don't pile cruel cares upon those
   griefs.
Stevenson, A.   Mother, The.
   When the Camel Is Dust it Goes Through the
   Needle's Eye.
Stoddard, E.   One Morn I Left Him in His Bed.
Stone, R.   For My Dead Red-Haired Mother.
Storni.   Words to My Mother.
Strand.   Pot Roast.

Strickland, A. Infant, The.
Suárez. Another Poem to My Mother.
  Now That I Have Grown Up, Mother.
Sullivan, B. Hair.
Sutton, V. Housekeeping.
Swenson, M. Motherhood.
Swirszczynska [or Swir]. Conversation Through
  the Door, A.
Szporluk. Meteor.
Szymborska, W. Born of Woman.
Tanikawa, S. River.
Tatarunis, P. I Have Two Sons and the One I
  Love Best Is Robert.
Tate, A. Mother and Son.
Tate, J. Distance from Loved Ones.
Taylor, E. Woman as Artist.
Taylor, J. My Mother.
Thomas, R. S. Mother and Child.
Thompson, D. P. Laurel Street, 1950.
Thrilling. Mother.
Thwaite, A. Throes.
Tighe. Sonnet Addressed to My Mother.
Titherage. And Her Mother Came Too.
Townsend, Alison. Hospital Corners.
Townsend, Ann. Eighteenth-Century Medical
  Illustration: The Infant in its Little Room.
Trethewey, N. Hot Comb.
  Limen.
Tsvetkov. Like a ruddy child you fall asleep in
  september.
Tucker, M. My Mother's Voice.
Tuqan, F. Behind Bars, Sel.
Tur-Malka, A. Mirror of the Battle.
Turnbull. Transmutation ("Every evening a
  mother makes up another episode of the same
  story for her son.").
Unknown. Cherished Daughter, The.
  Holy Goddess Tellus.
  Homage to Tara Our Mother.
  Hou Ji (Lord Millet), Progenitor of Zhou.
  I beg you, beg you, mother.
  I Sing of a Maiden.
  Maternal Love.
  Mother's Song.
  Mother's Song, The.
  Somebody's Mother.
  Wife of Usher's Well, The.
Unknown, fr. Terezin Concentration Camp.
  Letter to Daddy, A.
Untermeyer, J. Autumn.
Vacietis. Goodbye to a Spaceman.
Valerie, J. Astrology?
Vallejo. Good Sense.
  Right Meaning, The.
Van Duyn. Stream, The.
Van hee. December.
Vando. My Mother Cunning, Yet Innocent.
Vazirani, R. Daughter-Mother-Maya-Seeta.
  Mrs. Biswas of Maryland on the Phone.
Vecchione, P. Sugarmother's Daughter Dreams.
Vertreace, M. Caged Stone.
Vietnamese Oral Tradition. Arranged Marriage,
  The.
  Red Cloth, The.
Villanueva, A. From the Healing Dark.
  Planet Earth Speaks, The.
Vinokurov. Mother of Judas, The.
Voigt. Claiming Kin.
  For My Mother.
Voisine, C. Blue Hat.
Vold, J. Thor Heyerdahl's Mother.
Wah. Father / Mother Haibun #11.
  Father / Mother Haibun #12.
  Father / Mother Haibun #17.
Wallace, W. Hand That Rocks the Cradle Is the
  Hand That Rules the World, The.
Waniek. Bali Hai Calls Mama.
  Mama I Remember.
Warner, S. Road 1940.
Warren, R. Only Poem, The.
  Revelation.
  Tale of Time.
  There's a Grandfather's Clock in the Hall.
  Wet Hair: If Now His Mother Should Come.
Watson, E. Natural.
Webster, A. Her father lessons me I at times am

hard.
  Little child she, half defiant came, A.
  Love's Mourner.
  Since first my little one lay on my breast.
  That she is beautiful is not delight.
Weiners. My Mother.
White, G. Queen Gertrude's Soliloquy.
Whitman, W. Now what my mother told me
  one day as we sat at dinner together.
Wieners. My Mother.
Williams, C. K. My Mother's Lips.
Williams, C. For the White Lady Holding Me.
Williams, K. I Watched.
Williams, L. Interruption of Flight.
Williams, P. Libation.
Williams, Sharron K. Letter to a Black Woman.
Williams, Sherley Anne. California Light.
Williams, W. Young Woman at a Window.
Wilner, E. As soft and as pink as a nursery.
Wilson, F. Bathing My Mother.
Wilson, K. Arrival of My Mother, The.
Winters, A. Chair by the Window, The.
  Night Light.
Wiseman. April Elegy (Sam Selvon d.1994).
Wong, N. Dreams in Harrison Railroad Park.
  Ma, my heart must be made of rice straw.
  Mama, Come Back.
Wood, D. Christmas Fare.
Wordsworth, W. Affliction of Margaret, The.
Worley, N. Sandra.
Wren, A. Surrogate Mothers.
Wright, F. Flight.
  Wedding, The.
Yamada. Night before Good-Bye, The.
Yeats. Song of the Old Mother, The.
Yesenin [or Essenin]. Letter to My Mother.
Yi Hyangji. Song of a Balloon in Search of Her
  Mom's balloon.
Yi Sang. Face.
Young, I. Mermaid Knows, A.
Young, J. Rock-a-Bye Your Baby with a Dixie
  Melody.
Yun Tongju. One Night I Count the Stars.
Zamora, D. Mother's Day.
Zamora-Linmark. Election Day.
Zanzotto. From a New Height.
Zepeda, O. Bury Me with a Band.
Zucker, R. Diary (Underworld).

Mother's Day
  Elam, P. Mother's Day at McDonald's.

Mothers-in-Law
  Ciardi, J. Censorship.
  Snyder, G. Coffee, Markets, Blossoms.
  Unknown. Mother-in-law, do not stamp.
  Unexpected Pleasure, An.

Moths
  Ali, A. Purse-Seiner *Atlantis*, The.
  Bartlett, J. From a Paris Hotel Room.
  Ceravolo. Dusk: "Before the dusk grows
    deeper."
  Clampitt. Whippoorwill in the Woods, A.
  Collins, B. Japan.
  Crapsey. Warning, The.
  Ginsberg, A. White sun up behind pines.
  Issa. How *much.*
    This moth saw brightness.
  Kasischke. Visibility of Spirits, The.
  Krynicki. I Can't Help You.
  Leithauser. Haunted, The.
  Mandela. I Waited for You Last Night.
  Ni Dhomhnaill. Labasheedy (The Silken Bed).
  Leaba Shíoda.
  Peseroff. Stray Moth, Asleep.
  Phillips, C. Luna Moth.
  Ponge. Candle, The.
  Richard, M. C. Snow: "White moths in crazy
    mobs."
  Romero, L. When She Opens the Door.
  Snodgrass. Lying Awake.
  Wellman, M. Moth house is taking over, Sir
    Footfall.
  Williams, W. Prelude to Winter.
  Zagajewski. Moths.

Motion
  Ammons. Cascadilla Falls.
  Basho. Still old pond, The.

Brewster, E. Moving Image, The.
Campert. Avignon.
Cavalli. In that small dark fever of every
  reawakening.
Creeley. To And.
Crozier, A. Loopy Dupes.
Garcia, R. Brief Entanglements.
Garrett, E. Contrary Motion.
Greenwald, T. I Hear a Step.
Gunn, T. On the Move.
Herbert, Z. Georg Heym—The Almost
  Metaphysical Adventure.
Juarroz. Any movement kills something.
Kloos, W. Evening.
Korteweg. Entirely You.
Levertov. Wavering.
Loseff [/or Losev]. Petrograd Side, The.
Lovelace, R. Gratiana Dancing [or Dauncing]
  and [or &] Singing.
MacCaig. Sleeping Compartment.
Mills, B. Ballad: Of Motion.
Mörling, M. For the Woman with the Radio.
Petrovykh, M. Air Is Motionless with Heat,
  The.
Shakespeare, W. How sweet the moonlight
  sleeps upon this bank!
Tanikawa, S. Landscape with Yellow Birds.
Tarn. Retreat toward the Spring.
Vicinelli. Crossing the River.
Volkman. I won't go in today, I'll stay out
  today.
  Now I promise the shriek that the pressure of
    days, the pressure of days will be weapon.
Wunderlich, M. One Explanation of Beauty.
Yi Sang. Motion.

Motorcycles and Motorcycling
  Aguilar, L. Memo, Who Loved Motorcycles.
  Babstock, Ken. What We Didn't Tell the Medic.
  Daniels, J. Wheels: "My brother kept."
  Gunn, T. On the Move.
  Unsettled Motorcyclist's Vision of His Death,
    The.
  Jordan, J. Speculations on the Present through
    the Prism of the Past.
  Llwyd, Iwan. Harley Davidson.
  Locklin. Leader of the Pack, The.
  Moolten, D. Motorcycle Ward.
  Pierpoint, K. Combustion Engine.
  Simon, L. Kali.
  Stafford, W. Fifteen.
  Tate, J. Motorcyclists, The.
  Van Duyn. What the Motorcycle Said.
  Walker, A. Kiss, The.
  Williams, L. Interruption of Flight.

Mottoes
  Matthews, J. Inverse Proportions.
  Mullen, H. Bumber to Bumper.

Mount Fuji
  Buson. Only Mount Fuji.
  Kusano Shimpei. Mount Fuji [1943].

Mount Olivet
  Kaufman, S. Mount of Olives, The.
  Khoury, N. People of Olives.

Mount Saint Helens, Washington
  Rose. Loo-wit.

Mount Sinai
  Avidan, D. Settlement.
  Bible, O.T. Psalm 114: "When Isr'el, freed from
    Pharoh's hand."

Mount Tamalpais
  Oppen. Impossible Poem, The.
  Rexroth, K. Mt. Tamalpais.

Mountain Climbing
  Chŏng Chiyong. Paengnokdam: White Deer
    Lake.
  Dupin. Even If the Mountain.
  Francis, R. Rock Climbers, The.
  Han-shan. Way to Cold Mountain, The.
  Hsieh Ling-yün. Climbing Stone Drum
    Mountain.
  I Follow the Jinzhu Torrent.
  On Cimbing Mount Green Crag in Yongjia.
  On Climbing Stone Drum Mountain, Near
    Shangshu.
  On Climbing the Highest Peak of Stone Gate.

Huntington, W.   From Green Mountain.
Jinkag Haesim.   Mountain Excursion.
Justice, D.   Here in Katmandu.
Kawano, Y.   Climbing the mountain pass.
Kinnell.   Flower Herding on Mount Monadnock.
Kinsella, J.   Bluff Knoll Sublimity.
MacCaig.   Climbing Suilven.
Muso Soseki.   Moon Mountain.
  Patriarch Peaks.
  Strange Peak.
O'Connor, M.   Kuan-Yin Shan: Mother-of-
  Mercy Mountain.
Rich, A.   Phantasia for Elvira Shatayev.
Su Tung-p'o.   Climbing Yun-lung Mountain.
Tu Fu [or Du Fu].   Summit, The.
Unknown.   When on a cold day with deep snow.
Welch, L.   December 1972: First Winter
  Ascension of the Sass Maor.
Yi Yuksa.   Summit, The.

Mountain Lions
Galvin, B.   Cougar.
Goldensohn, B.   Mountain Lion.
Lawrence, D. H.   Mountain Lion.

Mountain Men
Glassman, Bernard Tetsugen.   Ascending the
  Mountain.

Mountains
Adonis [or Adunis].   Song of a Man in the
  Dark.
Ammons.   Close-up.
  Mountain Talk.
Annand.   Mountain Pule.
Back, R.   You ask.
Baggok Choneung.   Leaving the Mountain.
Basho.   Autumn wind / Blasting the stones.
  Coolness.
  Misty rain.
  Ploughing the land.
  Traveling this high.
  With plum blossom scent.
Blackburn, P.   Net of Place, The.
Brecht, B.   Three Fragments.
Brewer, G.   Mountains.
Bringhurst.   Under the sunrise the mountains.
Burn.   Welsh Love Letter.
Burns, R.   My Heart's in the Highlands.
Buson.   Mountains of Yoshino / Shedding petals.
  They swallow clouds.
Chang K'o-chiu.   At Waterfall Temple.
Chang Yang-hao.   T'ung Pass.
Chappell, F.   Remembering Wind Mountain at
  Sunset.
Chia Tao.   At I-Chou, Climbing the Tower of
  Lung-Hsing Temple to View the High Northern
  Mountains.
  Farewell to T'ien Cho on Retreat on Hua
  Mountain.
  Passing by a Mountain Village at Dusk.
Chiao-jan.   Cold Mountain.
Chimi Sucho.   Mountain Life.
Ching An.   Third Time Wandering to Cloud
  Sluice Peak.
Ch'ŏn Yanghŭi.   Mountain Stroll.
Ch'u Ch'uang I.   Mountain Spring, A.
Chungji.   Hermit's Life, A.
Cohn, J.   Jemez Mountains Meditation.
Corcoran.   Music of the Altai Mountains.
Davies, P.   When I Was a Boy.
Dickinson, E.   Sweet Mountains—Ye tell Me no
  lie.
Donegan, P.   Half-Open.
Duggan, L.   Five. One.
  One. One.
Emrys James, D.   Pwllderi.
Freneau.   Towering Alps, the haughty Appenine,
  The.
Gregg.   Night Music.
Grossman, A.   Enough Rain for Agnes Walquist.
Haavikko.   Bowmen, The.
Hakuyo.   Over the peak spreading clouds.
Hall, D.   Mount Kearsarge.
Han-shan.   Cold Mountain has many hidden
  wonders.
  In the Mountains.
Han-shan Te-ch'ing.   Mountains stand unmoving
  just the way they are, The.

My long white hair is framed by green
  mountains.
  Through a few splinters of.
Hannon.   Beneath Cold Mountain.
  Beyond Freedom.
  Real Estate.
Hardi, C.   Escape Journey, 1988.
Harrison, J.   Geo-Bestiary #X.
Hemans.   Rock of Cader Idris, The.
Henry, B.   Moraine Lake.
Hernández Cruz.   Mountain Building.
Hernández, M.   Tomb of the Imagination.
Hikmet.   About Mount Uludağ.
Holmes, O.   Nearing the Snow-Line.
Hsieh Ling-yün.   On Climbing the Highest Peak
  of Stone Gate Mountain.
  On My Way from South Mountain to North
  Mountain, I Glance at the Scenery from the
  Lake.
  Poem on Stone House Mountain, A.
Hueng Guobin.   Mountain Life.
Hueung Powoo.   Climbing Enlightenment
  Mountain.
  Spring on the Mountain.
Hulü Chin.   Song of the Tölös.
Issa.   Autumn wind / Mountain's shadow.
  Before this autumn wind.
  Climb Mount Fuji.
  Cuckoo sings, The.
  Distant mountains, The.
  Evening clears, The.
  In this mountain village.
  Mountain cuckoo, The.
  O summer snail.
  Pheasant cries, The.
  Reflected / In the dragonfly's eye—.
Jaewol Kyunghun.   Strangeness of Mountains
  after Rain, The.
Jomei.   Written After Climbing Kaguyama to
  Survey the Land.
Kagawa Kageki.   Looking back upon.
Kal, Jan.   Mont Ventoux.
Kaputikyan, S.   In the Sevan Mountains.
Kaya Shirao.   Mountain mist / Torches dropped.
Keble.   Malvern at a Distance.
Kiko.   Mount Sumeru—my fist!
Ko Un.   Walking Down a Mountain.
Kuan Hsiu.   Written in the Mountains.
K'ung Chih-kuei.   Wandering Round Mount
  Taiping.
Landor, W.   Separation.
Levertov.   Witness.
Li Po.   Birds have Vanished, The.
  Climbing Xie Tiao's North Tower at Xuan in
  Autumn.
  Conversation among the Mountains.
  Conversations in the Mountains.
  Farewell Dinner for My Uncle Li Yun, the
  Collator, at Xie Tiao's Tower in Xuan
  Prefecture.
  In the Mountains on a Summer Day.
  Lu Mountain Song For the Palace Censor
  Empty-Boat Lu, A.
  Mountain Dialogue.
  My Trip in a Dream to the Lady of Heaven
  Mountain A Farewell to Several Gentlemen
  of Eastern Lu.
  Summit Temple, The.
  To Tan Ch'iu.
  Zazen on Ching-t'ing Mountain.
Logghe.   Marriage of Heaven and Hell in
  Española.
Lux.   From the High Ground.
Mackey, N.   Glenn on Monk's Mountain.
Mayfield, C.   In a Glazed-Over World.
Melville, H.   Guide and Guard.
Meng Hao Jan.   Returning at Night to Lumen
  Mountain.
  Seeking out Master Chan on Incense Mountain.
Miyazawa Kenji.   Snow on Saddle Mountain,
  The.
Monroe, H.   In High Places.
Mphahlele.   Homeward Bound.
Munom-Ekai.   Thunderbolt—eyes wide, A.
Muso Soseki.   Abiding Mountain.
  Another Summit.

East Peak.
  Flat Mountain.
  Gem Mountain.
  Heaven Peak.
  Joy Mountain.
  Laughing Mountain.
  Lover of Mountains.
  Magnificent Peak.
  Moon Mountain.
  Mourning for the Layman Named Cloud Peak.
  Old Mountain.
  Patriarch Peaks.
  Poem on Dry Mountain (A Zen Garden).
  Snow.
  Strange Peak.
  Very high this mountain.
Nara Singde.   Tune: "Butterflies Lingering over
  Flowers".
Nishikawa, Etsudo.   Round, round, more round
  than the moon.
Niu Hsi-chi.   Spring Mountains.
O'Connor, M.   Overnight at a Buddhist
  Mountain Temple.
Ortiz.   Look to the Mountain.
Papago.   There was a mountain, over its black
  roots [the deer].
Paz.   Lake.
Peate, I.   Roncesvalles.
Pei Di.   Deer Enclosure, The.
  Magnolia Enclosure, The.
Po Chü-i.   Dream of Mountaineering, A.
Pou Kuksa.   Cloudy Mountain.
Pyungyang Ungee.   Mountain Life.
Radcliffe, A.   Storied Sonnet.
Rafferty, P.   Off the Beaten Track.
Rakan-Keinan.   Today Rakan, riding an iron
  horse.
Ransford, Tessa.   Viewpoint.
Rexroth, K.   Wheel Revolves, The.
Ridge, J.   Mount Shasta: "Behold the dread Mt.
  Shasta, where it stands."
Robinson, E.   Vickery's Mountain.
Roubaud.   Ice In.
Rukeyser, M.   Summer, the Sacramento.
Saner.   Autumn Aspens: Cumbres Pass.
  Waking at the Middle of Nowhere.
Santos Chocano.   Volcanoes, The.
Segovia, F.   It Isn't Gentleness.
  No es la suavidad.
Shafiq, H.   Mountain, The.
Shockley, E.   Shall become as.
Smith, B.   Black Mountain Blues.
Snyder, G.   Meeting the Mountains.
Soyinka.   Around Us, Dawning.
Spicer, J.   Phonemics.
Stafford, W.   Silver Star.
Stevens, W.   Poem That Took the Place of a
  Mountain, The.
Suk Mumyong.   After Getting Drunk in a
  Hermitage on Chiri Mountain.
Sun Ch'o.   Wandering on Mount Tiantai.
Sung Yu.   Gao Tang Rhapsody, The.
Takushitsu.   Breeze strokes the water of the
  spring, A.
Taneda Santoka.   Deeper I go, The.
  Mountain's stillness, The.
T'ao Hung Ching.   Poem Written in Answer to
  His Majesty's Question: "What Is There in the
  Mountains?".
Teasdale.   Lines.
Tomlinson, C.   Above the Rio Grande.
Tozan-Gyoso.   Way's not for the blind.
Tu Fu [or Du Fu].   Looking at Mount T'ai.
  Written on the Wall at Zhang's Hermitage.
Tu Mu.   Mountain Walk, A.
Unknown.   Grass on the Mountain, The.
  Invocation To Dsilyi N'Eyani.
  One of the Awl Songs.
Vietnamese Oral Tradition.   From So Mountain.
Voltaire.   Mountain Mountainous in Parturition,
  A.
Voznesensky [or Voznesenskii].   In the
  Mountains.
Wang An-shih.   Bald Mountain.
  On Chung Mountain.
Wang Chih-huan.   Hooded Crane Tower.

Wang Shih-chieng. Ch'ai-kuan Mountain Pass.
Wang Wei. Alighting from my horse to drink with you.
  Cold Mountain, The.
  Deer Camp.
  Deer Enclosure, The.
  Deer Park.
  Magnolia Enclosure, The.
  Mount Zhongnan.
  On the Mountain.
Whalen, P. Sourdough Mountain Lookout.
Wilcox, E. Attraction.
Wilcox, F. Nine Flower Mountain.
Williams, M. Heading for the Heights.
Winged Serpent. Two Rain Songs (Papago).
Wonhyo, Great Master. To Master Monk Nangjee.
Wordsworth, W. Farewell, A: "Farewell thou little Nook of mountain-ground."
  When the third summer freed us from restraint.
Young, Al. Mountains of California: Part 1, The.
Young, Andrew. Suilven.
Yu Ch'an. Looking at Stone Drum Mountain.
Yuan Mei. On the Road to T'ien-t'ai.
Zurita, R. March of the Cordilleras, The.

See also **Hills and Mountains**

Mourning and Mourners
Abbott, W. Funeral, The: "I see, under the canopy of death."
Abelard. More than a brother to me, Jonathan.
Adair, V. H. Last Marriage, A.
Addonizio. What the Dead Fear.
Akhmatova, A. In Memory of M. B.
Alarcon, F. Las calles lloran / Streets Are Crying.
Ali, A. Ghazal: "What will suffice for a true-love knot? Even the rain?"
Alterman, N. Mole, The.
Amichai, Y. My Father's Memorial Day.
Anderson-Thompkins. To Love a Stranger.
Aneirin. Lord of Gododdin will be praised in song, A.
  When a crowd of cares.
Antokolsky. You share your mourning with all Moscow. There.
Anyte [*or* Anytes]. I mourn maiden Antibia: desiring her, many.
  Often keening on her daughter's tomb, Kleina.
  Youth buried you, Captain; as sons for their mother, The.
Ap Hywel, Elin. In My Mother's House.
Aragon, F. Tricycles.
Arp. Kaspar Is Dead.
Auden. Song: "Stop all the clocks, cut off the telephone."
Ayhan, E. Epitafio.
Ayukawa Nobuo. Sister, I'm Sorry.
Baggett. Rachel: *Crown of Thorns.*
Bandele, A. After diana died.
Barker, W. Trying To.
Bateman, M. After the Funeral.
Beckman, J. Lament for the Death of a Bullfighter.
Behn, A. On the Death of the Late Earl of Rochester.
Benson, J. Columbarium.
Bibb. In Memory of Arthur Clement Williams.
Bion. Lament for Adonis.
Bleakney, J. In Memoriam: "If it's over, *let it be over.*"
Blind. Mourning Women.
Bloomfield. Trouncer, the Foxes Foe.
Bowles, W. On the Death of William Linley, esq.
Bradstreet, A. Epitaph on my Dear and Ever Honored Mother Mrs. Dorothy Dudley.
  In Memory of My Dear Grandchild Anne Bradstreet Who Deceased June 20, 1669, Being Three Years and Seven Months Old.
  In Memory of My Dear Grandchild Elizabeth Bradstreet Who Deceased August, 1665, Being a Year and Half Old.
  On My Dear Grandchild Simon Bradstreet, [Who Died on 16TH November, 1669, Being But A Month And One Day Old].

To the Memory of My Dear and Ever Honored Father Thomas Dudley Esq. Who Deceased July 31, 1653, and of His Age 77.
Brontë, A. Penitent, The.
Brontë, C. On the Death of Anne Brontë.
  On the Death of Emily Jane Brontë.
Browning, E. Grief.
Bryan, S. Beyond Recall.
Buchan, J. Alastair Buchan (1917).
Burns, R. Man Was Made to Mourn, a Dirge.
Buson. Mourning for Hokuju Rosen.
  You left in the morning. In the evening, my heart in a thousand shards.
Bykova, Z. Potatoes in flower.
Byron, G. If Sometimes in the Haunts of Men.
  One Struggle More, and I Am Free.
Callimachus. Epigram.
  News of Your Death.
  Someone told me, Heracleitus.
Carew, T. Ask Me No More.
  Elegy upon the Death of the Dean of [St.] Paul's, Dr. John Donne, An.
Carrera Andrade. Second Life of My Mother.
Catullus. By strangers' coasts and waters, many days at sea.
Chang Chi. Elegy: "We carved our names."
Ch'in Kuan. Farewell Song.
Ching An. At Hu-k'ou, Mourning for Kao Po-tsu.
Chivers. Avalon.
  Miss Adair.
Chông Hwajin. Sewing Box, The.
Christine de Pisan. Alone in Martyrdom.
Chu Yohan. Fireworks.
Cofer, J. Cultivator.
Coleman, W. Having Lost My Son, I Confront the Wreckage.
Coleridge, M. Mistaken.
Cooper, J. Faithful, The.
  Long, Disconsolate Lines.
Corcadail, A. I. O rosary that recalled my tear.
Cornish, S. Death of Dr. King.
Crane, S. Behold, the grave of a wicked man.
Davies, J. Black Thorn, The.
Davison, P. Under the Roof of Memory.
Della Cruscans. Moods 2.
Dickey, W. Shortest Day, The.
Dickinson, E. Bustle in a House, The.
  Last Night that She Lived, The.
Donne. Valediction, A: Forbidding Mourning.
Douglas, L. Dead Poet, The.
Drummond, W. Sextain: "Sith gone is my delight and only pleasure."
Edmond, L. Presences.
Elfyn, Menna. Passing On.
"Eliza.". To My Husband.
Erinna. Girls / Brides / Tortoise.
Erskine, T. Deserted Died.
Espada. Ghazal for Open Hands.
  Moon Shatters on Alabama Avenue, The.
Espinet, R. Merchant of Death.
Field. Beloved, My Glory in Thee is Not Ceased.
Finch, F. Blue and the Gray, The.
Ford, F. This is Charing Cross.
French, Nora May. Mourner, The: "Because my love has wave and foam for speech."
Frost, R. Home Burial.
Gallagher, T. Wake.
  Widow in Red Shoes.
  Yes.
García Lorca. Absence of the Soul.
  Ah secret voice of dark love! Ah bleating without wool! Ah wound! Ah prick of gall, sunken camellia!
  Elegy for Joan the Mad One.
Garcilaso de la Vega. O waters running pure and crystal clear.
Gardinier. Two Girls.
Garrett, G. Rugby Road.
Gillan. In New Jersey Once.
Ginsberg, A. Kaddish.
Gorostiza, J. Elegy: "Alone, with harsh marine aloneness."
Graves, R. When I'm Killed.
Gray, T. Elegy Written in a Country

Churchyard.
  Sonnet [on the Death of Mr. Richard West].
Groarke, V. Folderol.
Gurney, I. To His Love.
Hall, D. Letter with No Address.
  Porcelain Couple, The.
Hanzlicek, C. Feeding Frenzies.
Hardy, T. Caged Goldfinch, The.
Harjo, J. Mourning Song.
Harper, M. Drowning of the Facts of a Life, The.
Hayden, R. Mourning Poem for the Queen of Sunday.
Hemans. Edith; a Tale of the Woods.
Herd. Coronach.
Herrick. Mad Maid's Song, The.
  To His Dying Brother, Master William Herrick.
Hewitt, J. Local Poet, A.
Heyen. Stadium, The.
Hicok. Goodbye in the Shape of a Knot.
Hirsch, E. In Memoriam Paul Celan.
Hirshfield, J. Dead Do Not Want Us Dead, The.
Homer. Achilles' Dream.
  Achilles' Lament and the Funeral of Patroclus.
  So mourn'd Pelides his late loss, so weighty were his moans.
Hongo. Pier, The.
Hooks. Woman's Mourning Song, The.
Howard, A. Elegy on the Death of Her Husband.
Howe, F. Then I'll bear the torch and the needle.
Hughes, L. As Befits a Man.
  Night Funeral in Harlem.
  Wake.
Hughes, T. Day He Died, The.
Hugo, R. Elegy: "I expected him to look dead in the casket."
Hugo, V. Tomorrow, when the meadows grow.
Ibáñez, S. You, for My Meditation.
Ignatow, D. Kaddish.
Issa. On the Death of the Poet's Daughter Sato.
Jeffers, R. May-June, 1940.
Jennings, E. After a Time.
Jiménez, J. Vigil.
Johnson, J. Go Down Death (A Funeral Sermon).
Johnston, E. Nelly's Lament for the Pirnhouse Cat.
Jonson, B. On My First Son.
Joyner, C. They Do Not Have to Nest in Your Hair: A Tribute to Ron Brown.
Kakinomoto no Hitomaro. Mourning Princess Asuka.
Kao Ch'i. Written on Seeing the Flowers, and Remembering My Daughter.
Kaufman, S. After.
Kemble. On an Irish Retriever.
Khayr, A. His absence is the knife that cuts your throat?
  If I've been dead for twenty years or so.
Khazak, Y. Wake.
Kim Sowŏl. Cuckoo, The.
King, H. Exequy, The.
Klyuyev [*or* Kliuev *or* Klyuev]. Can I Tell You My Love with a Portrait.
Komunyakaa, Y. Facing It.
Kuan P'an-p'an. Mourning.
Kumin, M. How It Is.
Kunene. Elegy for My Friend E. Galo.
Lamartine. Autumn.
Landon. Stanzas on the Death of Mrs Hemans.
Landor, W. Rose Aylmer.
Larkin, J. Cold River.
Lawrence, D. H. Sorrow.
Le Ngoc Hiep. I Am Sad.
Leivick, H. Lament at Night.
Leonard, H. Lost Friend, A.
Leonard, W. That once the gentle mind of my dead wife.
Levertov. Olga Poems.
Li Ch'ing-chao. Spring at Wu Ling.
  To the Tune: Happiness Approaches.
Li K'ai-hsien. Thanking Doctor Jen.
Li Po. In Memory of Ho Chi-chen.
Lifshin. Night Robert Frost Died, The.

Lilburn, Tim. Contemplation Is Mourning.

Limburg, J. Return, The.

Limonov. For whisper and orchestra.

Lisboa. Elegy: "At first the dead."

Lochhead, L. Sorting Through.

Machado Ruiz. Breeze Tells Me, Loved One, The.

MacNeice. Canto XX: "To Wales once more, though not on holiday now."

Mallock. Questions: "Where are you now, little wandering."

Mandiela, A. Mih Feel It.

Martí. I want, in the shade of a wing.

Martial. Aulus, my girlfriend's in a dreadful plight.

Fronto, Father, Flaccilla, Mother, extend.

Pre-eminent among scholars.

Trusty Lydia, The.

Mary Stuart. For him also I powrit out mony teiris.

Maude. Entanglement.

McCabe, C. In Memory of My Mother.

McHugh, H. Form.

Mei Yao Ch'en. Sorrow.

Meng Chiao. Invariably pure and austere, poets mostly.

Mew. May, 1915.

Millay, E. Elegy: "Let them bury your big eyes."

Miller, H. Kaddish.

Milosz, C. With Her.

Milton. Lycidas.

Monette. Half Life.

Monroe, H. Farewell, A: "Good-bye!—no [or nay] do not grieve that it is over."

Morgan, E. Glass, The.

Motion, A. Lines, The: "November, and the Sunday twilight fallen."

Na Ceapaich, S. Alasdair of Glengarry.

Narovchatov. In Those Years.

Nonnus. But Dionysos had no healing physic for his comrade fallen, of dancing he thought no more.

Where Carpos wandered and died, I will fall headlong.

O'Rahilly. Lament for Tadhg Cronin's Children.

Orr, G. Gathering the Bones Together.

Lament: "I thought of you."

Padel, R. Tell Me About It.

Padgett, R. Wonderful Things.

Page, P. About Death.

Pak Inhwan. Towards a New Resolve.

Palés Matos. Elegy for the Duke of Marmalade.

P'an Yüeh. In Mourning for His Dead Wife.

Paterson, D. Eyes, The.

Paul, C. Georgina.

Pawlak. After Burying Her Son, A Mother Speaks.

Petronius Arbiter. However, Eumolpus, our champion in time of trouble and the author of the present harmony.

Phaedrus. Widow and the Soldier or: The Measure of a Woman's Inconstancy and Lust, The.

Pinsky. Impossible to Tell.

Poem with Refrains.

Raine, K. Heroes.

Ransom, J. Agitato Ma Non Troppo.

Reese, L. Death's Guerdon.

Rein. Nanny Tanya.

Rexroth, K. Andrée Rexroth ("Now once more gray mottled buckeye branches.").

Andrée Rexroth ("Years have gone, The. It is spring.").

Rich, A. Valediction Forbidding Mourning, A.

Rimington, J. God of the Flies.

Robinson, A. Stornelli and Strambotti.

Robinson, E. Reuben Bright.

Roethke. Elegy for Jane.

Rossetti, C. After Death.

Remember [Me].

Song: "When I am dead, my dearest."

Why did baby die. . .?

Ruan Yu. Driving My Chariot Through the Northern Suburbs Gate.

Ruark. Postscript to an Elegy.

Santos, S. Still Life with Minnows.

Sappho. Delicate Adonis is dying, Kytheria— what should we do?

In the house of those who serve the Muses, a dirge.

Scott, S. Jock of Hazeldean.

Scott, W. My Mother.

Seneca. Trojan Women.

Sexton. Truth the Dead Know, The.

Shakespeare, W. Sonnet 71: "No longer mourn for me when I am dead."

Shelley, P. Adonais; An Elegy on the Death of John Keats.

Sia, B. Howl.

Silva, J. Nocturne: "One night / One night full of perfumes, music of wings and murmurs."

Simonides. They wept for the violet-wreathed [lady's].

Smith, C. Metamorphosis.

Spady, S. Tending Flowers.

Spenser, E. First was Fancy, like a lovely boy, The.

StacyLynn. Lookin Good.

Statius. In Memory of His Father.

Strand. New Year, The.

Su Tung-p'o. Remembering My Wife.

Suermondt, Tim. Missing Supper.

Swift, J. Here shift the scene, to represent.

T'ang Hsien-tsu. On the Day of Washing the Buddha in the Year Ting-wei (1607), I Dreamed That My Late Son Shih-ch'ü Was Holding a Book, and Appeared To Be Quite Happy. He Said That He Had Earned His Chin-shih Degree in the Underworld. After We Sighed and La.

T'ao Ch'ien [or T'ao Yuan-ming]. Elegy for Myself.

Three Dirges: Written in Imitation of an Ancient Funeral Song.

Tennyson, A. Dark house, by which once more I stand.

Fair ship, that from the Italian shore.

I held it truth, with him who sings.

I sometimes hold it half a sin.

Rizpah.

Tears of the widower, when he sees.

Theocritus. Adonis.

Thoreau. Sympathy.

Tsvetayeva [or Tsvetaeva]. They thought: Human!

Tu Fu [or Du Fu]. Lament for Ch'en T'ao.

Tur-Malka, A. Memorial Service.

Unknown. Chant from the Iroquois Book of Rites.

Close by the shore, the shore.

I beg you, beg you, mother.

Lament for the Death of Guillén Peraza.

Lament of Gilgamesh for Enkidu, The.

My Boy Willie.

My friends, which of these two to choose?

On Some Elegies on a Lap-Dog.

Songs from the Great Feast to the Dead.

TEHKARIHHOKEN! / Continue to listen!

Unquiet Grave, The.

Wife of Usher's Well, The.

With the first light of the early morning dawning.

You all by yourself fulfilled.

Valentine, J. She Would Long.

Van Duyn. Stream, The.

Vaughan, H. Joy of My Life! While Left Me Here.

Silence and Stealth of Day[e]s!

Wang Wei. Mourning for Yin Yao.

Weeping for Ying Yao.

Warren, R. Tale of Time.

Whitman, W. And I saw askant the armies.

Hush'd be the Camps To-Day.

Vigil Strange I Kept on the Field One Night.

When Lilacs Last in the Dooryard Bloom'd.

Wieseltier, M. Again a Drab Khaki Light is Coming Down.

Wilbur, R. To an American Poet Just Dead.

Winchilsea. *Bolder Youth*, grown of capable arms, A.

Wŏlmyŏng. Requiem for the Dead Sister.

Wordsworth, W. Surprised by Joy.

Wright, J. Angel, The.

Yamanoé [or Yamanoué] no Okura. Longing for His Son, Furuhi.

Yi Kyubo. Grieving for My Little Girl.

Yüan Chĕn. Elegy: "O loveliest daughter of Hsieh."

"Zelda.". How Much a Word Could Help.

See also **Funerals; Grief**

Mouths

Al-Qasim. General's Property, The.

Beath, M. Put a Stone in Your Mouth.

Buson. Sparrow singing.

Chubb, R. Song of My Soul.

Creeley. Language, The.

Crowley, A. Go into the Highways and Hedges, And Compel Them to Come In.

Domin. Exile.

Foust, G. On the Evening of a Wedding.

Góngora y Argote. Sonnet 82.

Hadewijch II. If I desire something, I know it not.

Hamilton, S. Species of Audibles.

Leonidov, Rumen. Mouths of the people eating their lunch, The.

López Colomé, P. Death of the Kiss.

Muerte del beso, La.

Markham, M. Orange Tree Glistens, The.

Mattson, N. Her Other Language.

Nye, N. Shapes of Mouths at Parties, The.

Ricardo. Orchid.

Ricketts, W. Scout.

Robinson, E. Meshes.

Solon. Love of Boys, The.

Swenson, M. Cardinal Ideograms.

Tate, G. Tonguing.

Unknown. My mouth is yours, devour it and be not afraid.

Movies

Allen, P. Judy.

Ashbery, J. Forties Flick.

Interesting People of Newfoundland.

Azzawi, F. Film in a railway station, A.

Baker, D. Pulp Fiction.

Bentley, N. Cecil B. De Mille.

Berkson, B. Bicycle Thief, The.

Berrigan, T. Sonnet LIX: "In Joe Brainard's collage its white arrow."

Berry, W. Vacation, The.

Brinks, Dave. Any Blue Movie.

Carson, A. Lazarus Standup: Shooting Script.

Creeley. Bresson's Movies.

Cross, D. Cinema Yosemite.

Trilogy.

Cummings, E. E. O pr / gress verily thou art m.

Day Lewis. Newsreel.

Ellis, T. Slow Fade to Black.

Elmslie, K. Shirley Temple Surrounded by Lions.

Feela. Cut.

Field, E. Curse of the Cat Woman.

Garrigue. Movie Actors Scribbling Letters Very Fast in Crucial Scenes.

Gizzi. Fables of Critique.

Last Cigar.

Graham, J. Dream of the Unified Field, The.

Gwynn, R. Drive-In, The.

Hayden, R. Double Feature.

Hershon. Cowboy and the Farmer Should Be Friends, The.

Joseph, A. On Viewing Two Different Date Rape Movies.

Kim Sŭnghŭi. Horror Movie.

Koertge. Sidekicks.

Kunitz, S. Magic Curtain, The.

Levertov. Triple Feature.

Watching "Dark Circle".

Magrelli. I sit, in treatment, at the movies, devoted.

Martin, D. If We Were in a Gregg Araki Movie.

Messer, S. Look.

Mueller, L. Possessive Case, The.

Muldoon, P. Weepies, The.

O'Brien, G. Techniques of Mass Persuasion.

O'Hara, F. Ave Maria.

To the Film Industry in Crisis.

Olin. Para-Olympic Legacy, The.
Parker, A. Eclipse, The: "Having never been to a drive-in movie."
Petrova, A. Tarantino's languor and dreaming back.
Pinsky. Samba.
Salter. Home Movies: A Sort of Ode.
Sanders, James. Poem with Referees.
Saroyan. Film Noir.
Simic. Cameo Appearance.
Smith, B. Song of the Ransom of the Dark.
Smith, J. What I Learned From the Movies.
Soupault. Movie-house.
Stroud, J. Documentary.
Taylor, H. After a Movie.
Turner, J. TV Movie.
Turner, W. Full Supporting Programme.
Villanueva, T. Serving of Water, The.
Waldman, A. Culture Drift.
Ward, D. Re-Verse.
Wilbur, R. Prisoner of Zenda, The.
Wilson, R. Old Movies.
Worley, D. Las Flores para una Niña Negra.
Yi Kyŏngnim. Anam Street 2—Outside the Cinema.
Zagajewski. Watching Shoah in a Hotel Room in America.

Moving and Movers
Aizenberg, M. So where is that guy who left us piles.
Bottoms. In a U-Haul North of Damascus.
Brown, F. Last of England, The.
Byron, C. Shipping the Pictures from Belfast.
Campbell, D. Duchesses.
Crucefix. Air-Waves.
Divakaruni. Restroom.
Dunn, D. Removal from Terry Street, A.
Gunn, T. Last Days at Teddington.
Hamod, S. So we move now.
Kamienska. Those Who Carry.
Kay, J. Pounding Rain.
Mark, Sabrina Orah. Babies, The.
Matthews, T. Private But Sulphurous.
McGuckian. Little House, Big House.
Paulin. Peacetime.
Polley, J. Moving House.
Ramsey, Martha. Moving Out.
Realuyo. Sojourners, The.
Shapiro, K. October 1.
Smith, D. Cumberland Station.
Tu Fu [or Du Fu]. Departing from Ch'in-chou.

Mowing and Mowers
Ammons. Needs.
Dybek. Mowing.
Frost, C. Refusal.
Frost, R. Mowing.
Tuft of Flowers, The.
Lawrence, D. H. Youth Mowing, A.
Lewis, L. May Mowing Clover.
Marvell. Damon the Mower.
Mower Against Gardens, The.
Mower to the Glowworms [or Glow-Worms or Glo-Worms], The.
Mower's Song, The.
Thomas, E. Haymaking.
Toomer. Reapers.

Mozambique
Sousa, N. Let My People Go.

Mozart, Wolfgang Amadeus
Bachhuber, D. Mozart in a Classroom of Children.
Bandeira. Mozart in Heaven.
Berger, B. To Answer Your Question.
Foerster. Mozart's Death.
Hooper, P. Listening to Mozart at Meadow Brook.
Kaddour, Hédi. Variations.
Meynell, A. To Silence.
Okudzhava. Departure.
Rossini, C. Valediction.
Stanton, M. Ode to Mozart.
Stevens, W. Mozart, 1935.
Watson, R. Die Zauberflöte.
Wendt. Singing the Mozart Requiem.
Whitman, R. Hearing a Mozart Duo at 36,000 Feet.

Mud
Allen, J. Mud Wit.
Basho. Coolness of melons.
Wet with morning dew.
Bibbins, M. Mud.
Boncho. Nightingale / My clogs.
Brown, S. Riverbank Blues.
Buson. Wading through it.
Cisneros, S. Muddy Kid Comes Home.
Cummings, E. E. In Just.
Heaney, S. Mud Vision, The.
Hillman, B. Formation of Soils, The.
Kalamaras, G. Mud.
Kambala. KYE HO! Wonderful!
Kasischke. Fatima.
Knight, E. Poem for Myself (Or Blues for a Mississippi Black Boy), A.
Lihn. Mud.
Otten, W. J. Mud-Flat.
Todd, M. Mud Season.

Muffins
Torres, E. How Long Does the Curator Dance For?

Muffs
Lovelace, R. Her Muffe.
See also **Gloves; Mittens**

Muhammad
Al-Bayati, A. Elegy to Aisha, An.
Writing on Aisha's Tomb.
Rumi. Deliberation.

Mulberry Trees
Gilbert, J. Explicating the Twilight.

Mules
Ammons. Silver.
González, R. You and the Tijuana Mule.
Lezama Lima. Rhapsody for the Mule.
Machado Ruiz. Water Wheel, The ("Afternoon arrived, The.").
Muldoon, P. Mules.
Plumpp. Another Mule.
Vallejo. Mule Drivers, The.

Mummies
Claus. Tollund Man, The.
Field. Mummy Invokes His Soul, The.
Gardner, I. In the Museum.
Gould, H. Child's Address to the Kentucky Mummy, The.
Heaney, S. Punishment.
Marquis. Archy Interviews a Pharoah.
Parra, N. Mummies.
Speyer. To a Song of Sappho Discovered in Egypt.
Veinberg, J. Next to Tut.
Wilkie, B. Mummification and Space Travel.
Observations of Egyptian Artifacts.

Munch, Edvard
Llwyd, Alan. Scream, The: Edvard Munch (1893).
Mahon. Girls on the Bridge.
Van Haren, E. Stepping Out With Edvard Munch ("When from the other world you.").
Stepping Out With Edvard Munch ("When from the virile grave.").
Weiners. Poem for museum goers, A.

Murasaki Shikibu
Guest, B. Wild Gardens Overlooked by Night Lights.

Murder and Murderers
Ai. Good Shepherd, The: Atlanta, 1981.
Kid, The.
Aisenberg, N. Leaving Eden.
Akhmatova, A. Fear turns objects over in the darkness.
Allen, J. For Michael Griffith, Murdered Dec. 21, 1986, Howard Beach, NY.
Baer. Prosecutor.
Bandele, A. Prayer for the Living, A.
Bartók-Baratta, E. Men Who Killed My Brother, The.
Belli, C. Unknown Voice, An.
Berry, W. Morning's News, The.

Blake, W. Fair Elenor.
Bloem, R. Amsterdam Chronicle.
Bolger. I drifted into sleep.
Borges. Conjectural Poem.
Brathwaite, E. Stone: "When the stone fall that morning out of the johncrow sky."
Brooks, G. Bronzeville Mother Loiters in Mississippi, A. Meanwhile, a Mississippi Mother Burns Bacon.
Brown, S. Southern Cop.
Browning, R. Do you see this square old yellow Book, I toss.
Laboratory, The (Ancien Régime).
Porphyria's Lover.
Candelaria. Killers.
Carew, T. Another [On the Duke of Buckingham].
Cary, A. Sea-Side Cave, The.
Charara, H. On the Murder of an Ice Cream Man.
Clarke, George Elliott. Student's Tale, The.
Coleridge, M. Fire, the lamp, and I, were alone together, The.
Collier, M. 2212 West Flower Street.
Cook, C. It's Just As Well About Heather.
Culbert, Steven Tye. Hoodoo Scott Cooley Scalps John Wohrle.
Davies, W. H. Inquest, The.
Davis, C. How Can I Turn Off This Engine Now?
Murderer, The.
Davis, Cortney. What Man Might Kill.
de Portalatin. Black Autumn.
Derricotte. Minks, The.
On the Turning Up of Unidentified Black Female Corpses.
Domina, L. Pharoah's Army Got Drowned.
Dylan. Lonesome Death of Hattie Carroll, The.
Eady. Birthing.
Elagin. Amnesty.
My murderer is no thief.
Espada. Ezequiel.
Majeski Plays the Saxophone.
Moon Shatters on Alabama Avenue, The.
Felltham [or Feltham]. On the Duke of Buckingham, Slain by Felton, the 23rd August, 1628.
Ferré. Opprobium.
Fisher, A. Murder One.
Forché. Memory of Elena, The.
Galanskov. Murder.
Galvin, P. With My Little Red Knife.
García Lorca. Death of Antoñito el Camborio.
Quarrel.
Glazier, L. On TV.
Graham, Taylor. Pieces of Henry.
Graves, R. Nobody.
Grealy, L. Murder.
Grinshpan, Y. In Any Case.
Gunn, T. Victim, The.
Hamilton, M. Midnight in Mississippi.
Harnick. Ballad of the Shape of Things, The.
Harper, M. Fireplace, The.
Hart, L. To Keep My Love Alive.
Hartwig. Matthew 2:16–18; Then Herod, when he saw.
Hass, R. Forty Something.
Heaney, S. I had come to the edge of the water.
Hedderman, R. First Player's Monologue, The.
Herbert, Z. Return of the Proconsul, The.
Hershon. Woman Strangles, A.
Heyen. Blue.
Hongo. Legend, The.
Hood, T. Dream of Eugene Aram [the Murderer], The.
Housman. Farewell to barn and stack and tree.
Fragment of a Greek Tragedy.
Huerta, D. Baraja.
Deck of Cards.
Jarrell, R. Eighth Air Force.
Joans, T. .38, The.
Jones, H. Emine and Hamide.
Jordan, Judy. Through These Halls.
Jordan, June. Test of Atlanta 1979, The.
Kaufman, S. Accuser, The.
Kees. Crime Club.

Kennedy, X. Loose Woman.
Kim Chôngnan. Woman I Carelessly Killed, The.
Knott. Two Vietnam Poems: (1966).
Komunyakaa, Y. Fragging.
Livingstone, D. Dust: "Bundle in the gutter had its skull, The."
Loesser. Murder, He Says.
Mabuza. Death to the Gold Mine!
MacGregor, Mrs., of Glenstrae. Lament for MacGregor of Glenstrae.
Machado Ruiz. Crime Was in Granada, The.
Mandiela, A. Mih Feel It.
Martínez, V. Children of the Disappeared.
Masefield. No man takes the farm.
Masters, E. Oscar Hummel.
Merwin. Last One, The.
Meynell, A. Parentage.
Miller, E. You Send Me: Bertha Franklin, December 11, 1964.
Min, N. M. Deep in the Pit.
Mirosevich, T. Hygiene.
Montale. Murder's not my forte.
Mörling, M. Three-Card Monte.
Morris, W. Haystack in the Floods, The.
Morrison, B. Ower t'ills o Bingley.
Nawaz, S. Initiation, The.
Newbolt. He Fell among Thieves.
Orban, O. Chile.
Padilla. Question for the Frankfurt School, A.
Page, G. Premeditations.
Palladas [or Pallades]. Murderer and Sarapis, The.
Patchen. From My High Love.
Philips, K. Upon the Double Murther of King Charles I.
Phillips, R. After the Fact: To Ted Bundy.
Plath. Daddy.
Porter, C. Miss Otis Regrets.
Powell, D. A. Darling can you kill me: with your mickeymouse pillows.
Quintana. Teddy.
Raboni, G. Alibi of a Dead Man.
Rainey. See, See Rider.
Ranaldo, L. HIS:STORY.
Killed.
Refugee, A.
Reading, P. Life is too black as he paints it and "Reading's nastiness sometimes".
Reznikoff. 3. The Immigrants.
Roberson, E. Any moment (12/4/69 4:30 A.M. chicago).
Romond, E. Lady Macbeth, Afterward.
St. John, P. Benign Neglect / [West Point,] Mississippi, 1970.
Salaam. Threnody: "What's your story Atlanta/America?"
Saltus. Two loves found refuge in my happy heart.
Sapgir. Psalm 1.
Schwartz, D. For the One Who Would Take Man's Life in His Hands.
Seidel. Dune Road, Southampton.
Service. Fulmars.
Shooting of Dan McGrew, The.
Shabtai, Aharon. Rosh HaShanah.
Shakespeare, W. Ill blows the wind that profits nobody.
It is the cause, it is the cause, my soul [or (my soule)].
Vaulting Ambition.
Shelley, P. As I lay asleep in Italy.
Sidney. Sonnet 20: "Fly, fly, my friends."
Silesky. Prime Time.
Simmons, J. Claudy.
Stephens, J. Wind, The.
Stillman, M. Two Princes, The.
Sundiata. Notes from the Defense of Colin Ferguson.
Symonds. Midnight at Baiae.
Taksa, M. Granite Jaw.
Tapahonso. Pay Up or Else.
Taylor, H. Landscape with Tractor.
Taylor, M. Well-Bred Woman, A.
Thomas, L. Blues Variations.
Trench, H. Jean Richepin's Song.

Unknown. Bonny Earl of Murray, The [Version from Tea-Table Miscellany].
Dowie Dens of Yarrow, The [Version from Blackwood's Magazine].
Feltons Epitaph.
Frankie and Albert.
Frankie and Johnny [or Johnnie or Albert].
Little horror will not die of his own fever, The.
Lord Randal[l].
Now for that slawnders sake.
Stackalee.
Story of Kepa Falekaono, The.
Van Ostaijen. Murderers, The.
Vando. Knife.
Lydia's Phantasmagoria.
Vaughan, H. Abel's Blood.
Vaynshteyn [or Weinstein]. Negro Dies, A.
Vliet. Penny Ballad of Elvious Ricks.
Walker, A. Revolutionary Petunias.
Warren-Moore. For Paula Cooper.
Warren, R. Ballad of Billie Potts, The.
Crime.
Webb, C. Meat Michelangelo.
Wilde, O. Ballad of Reading Gaol, The.
There is no chapel on the day.
Williams, C. K. Fragment: "This time the hold up man didn't know a video-sound camera hidden up in a corner."
Winter, M. As If I Knew.
Wolf, M. Lucky Smile.
Woodward, G. Murderer is a Cow, The.
Wright, J. At the Executed Murderer's Grave.
Secret Gratitude, A.
Wright, R. Between the World and Me.
Young, E. One to destroy, is murder by the law.

Murfreesboro, Battle of (1862–63)
Tate, A. Battle of Murfreesboro.

Muses
Akhmatova, A. Muse, The.
Solitude.
Alcman. Love, again sweetly streaming down.
Andrade, M. Inspiration.
Archilochus. I am a servant of the War Lord.
Barbauld. To Mr. S. T. Coleridge.
Washing-Day.
Blake, W. To the Muses.
Bradstreet, A. Prologue, The: "To sing of wars, of captain[e]s, and of kings."
Brodsky, J. To Urania.
Callimachus. Prologue to the Aetia.
Chapman, G. Muses that fame's loose feathers beautify.
Cowley, A. Muse, The.
Creeley. Door, The: "It is hard going to the door."
Dana, M. Real Comfort.
Daniels, K. Prayer to the Muse of Ordinary Life.
De Mello Breyner. Muse.
Deniz, G. Musa.
Muse.
Drayton. March strongly forth, my Muse, whilst yet the temperate air.
Ode Written in the Peak[e], An.
Du Bellay. Las, Où Est Maintenant Ce Mespris de Fortune.
Dunn, S. Blind Date with the Muse.
Eich. Marketplace.
Éluard, P. Lady Love.
Equi. Bouquet of Objects, A.
France, L. My Muse, the Whore.
Glück, L. Poem: "In the early evening, as now, a man is bending."
Goodman, P. Woman eternal my muse, lean toward me.
Grainger, J. Call to the Muse.
Gray, T. Progress of Poesy, The.
Herrick. Departure of the Good Daemon, The.
His Winding-Sheet.
Hood, T. First Attempt in Rhyme, A.
Horace. Let's Do This Poem (1.26).
Ilkov, Ani. Muses.
Jewsbury. Farewell to the Muse, A.
Jonson, B. To Lucy, Countess of Bedford, with Mr. Donne's Satires.
Killigrew, A. On the Soft and Gentle Motions

of Eudora.
Upon the Saying That My Verses Were Made by Another.
Kinzie. Muse of Satire, The.
Korinna [or Corinna]. Kouretes hid the goddess's, The.
Terpsichore [told] me.
Thespia, bearing a beautiful race, stranger-loving, Muse-beloved.
Leapor. On Winter.
Sacrifice: An Epistle to Celia, The.
Levertov. Illustration, The [—a Footnote].
To the Muse.
Long, R. Muse Is Gone, The.
Martial. Ted's studio burnt down, with all his poems.
Matthews, W. Telegram from the Muse, A.
Montale. My Muse.
Musset. Muse, The.
Poet, The.
Nossis. Stranger, if you sail to the land of lovely dances, Mitylene.
When you've laughed out loud and said a friendly.
O'Reilly, C. To the Muse.
Ovid. Elegy 3.1: "Old wood stands uncut, of long years' space, An."
Parnok, S. I shall not lie to find a lurid rhyme.
Pastan. Muse.
"Philo-Philippa.". To the Excellent Orinda.
Puttenham. O mightye Muse.
Ray, H. Invocation to the Muse.
Richardson, J. Parnassus Rising.
Robinson, A. To My Muse.
Rouse, A. Virginian Arcady.
Rowe, E. Forgo the charming Muses! No, in spite.
Rowlands. Prologue: "Under the shadow of the gloomy night."
Sappho. In the house of those who serve the Muses, a dirge.
Seiferle, R. Muse.
Shakespeare, W. Sonnet 78: "So oft have I invok'd thee for my muse."
Sonnet 100: "Where art thou, Muse, that thou forget'st so long."
Shoman, K. Cords.
Sidney. Sonnet 1: "Loving in truth, and fain[e] in verse my love to show."
Sonnet 3: "Let dainty wits cry on the sisters nine."
Sonnet 6: "Some lovers speak, when they their Muses entertain."
Skelton, J. Garden of the Muses: Iopas' Song, The.
Smith, C. Partial Muse, has from my earliest hours, The.
To Mr. Hayley, on Receiving Some Elegant Lines from Him.
Stephens, J. Whisperer, The.
Thoreau. Inspiration ("Whate'er we leave to God, God does.").
Unknown. Elegy upon the Death of Mrs. A. Behn, the Incomparable Astrea, An.
Urdang. Muse Is Always the Other Woman, The.
Urusova, E. O Muses! I beseech you, fire my heart with song.
Virgil [or Vergil]. Arms, and the Man I sing, who, forc'd by Fate.
Walcott. Camps hold [or held] their distance—[of] brown chestnuts and grey smoke, The.
Upstate.
Watkins, V. Demands of the Muse.
Whalen, P. Complaint: To the Muse.
Wheatley, P. To Maecenas.
Wheelwright. Week End Bid II.
Whitman, W. Muse in the New World, The.
Wilner, E. Muse, The.
Wither. *Sun* hath run his course through all the Signes, The.
Wroth. Sonnet 9: "My muse now hap[p]y, lay thy self to rest."

Museums
Acosta. Museum Piece (ca. Now).
Adcock, F. Leaving the Tate.

Alexander, E.   Josephine Baker Museum, The.
Allston.   On the Luxembourg Gallery.
Bang, M.   Crossed-Over, Fiend-Snitched, X-ed Out.
Boland, E.   Dolls Museum in Dublin, The.
Cliff.   History of Costume, A.
Di Prima.   American Indian Art: Form and Tradition.
Digges.   Seersucker Suit.
Dobyns.   Nouns of Assemblage.
Duggan, L.   Town on the Ten Dollar Note, The.
Empson.   Homage to the British Museum.
Erb, E.   Banat Museum.
Fox, S.   Miss Pimberton Of.
Fuller, R.   Coptic Socks.
Gardner, I.   In the Museum.
Gilbert, C.   African Sculpture.
Gioia.   Guide to the Other Gallery.
Griffiths, J.   Two Are Embracing.
Harryman.   Master Mind, The.
Harvey, Y.   Museum Cashier, The.
Herbert, J.   Dossers at the Imperial War Museum.
Hinz-Penner, R.   Opening in Santa Fe, The.
Hollander, J.   No Foundation.
Horovitz, F.   Visit to the British Museum.
Imbriglio, C.   Museum.
Ismail.   Van Gogh's Ear.
Jamie, K.   Arraheids.
Kim Hyesun.   National Museum Hallway.
MacNeice.   Museums.
Nemes Nagy.   Walk at the Museum, A.
Pai, S.   Gathering at the Orchid Pavilion, The.
Pastan.   At the Jewish Museum.
 At the Train Museum.
Peate, I.   Museum Piece.
Perillo, L.   Ghost Shirt, The.
Philpot, T.   How to Live in the Elegy.
Plath.   Morning Song: "Love set you going like a fat gold watch."
Reedy, C.   Doll Museum, The.
Szymborska, W.   Museum, The.
 Pietà.
Thorpe, M.   Open-Air Museum.
Walker, D.   Astronomy.
Weiners.   Poem for museum goers, A.
Wilbur, R.   Museum Piece.

Mushrooms
Basho.   Pine mushroom.
Clark, M.   Mushrooms.
Cobbing.   Hymn to the Sacred Mushroom.
Gilonis, H.   Orange Birch Bolete (Leccinum versipelle).
Ishikawa Jōzan.   Eating Roasted *Matsutake* Mushrooms.
Jacob, M.   Moon Poem.
MacInnes, Mairi.   Mass.
Mahon.   Disused Shed in Co. Wexford, A.
Merwin.   Field Mushrooms.
Milosz, C.   Goddess, A.
Muldoon, P.   Gathering Mushrooms.
Plath.   Mushrooms.
Shinkichi Takahashi.   Mushroom.
Todd, R.   Of Moulds and Mushrooms.
Torrance.   Acrospirical Meanderings in a Tongue of the Time.
 It Is Difficult to Exaggerate the Importance of Mushrooms as Food.
Young, A.   Fairy Ring, The.
Young, G.   Eating Wild Mushrooms.
Zondberg, O.   To die. And be born as an inspector of playgrounds for tiny tots.

Music and Musicians
Adams, L.   Magnificat in Little.
Adisa.   Count Ossie.
Ai.   Archangel.
 Man with the Saxophone, The.
Al-Harizi.   Lute, The.
al-Sa'igh, Y.   Tune, The.
Alexander, E.   Farewell to You.
Alexander, R.   For Years My Father.
Algarin.   Prologue.
Allen, E.   Street Music.
Allen, S.   I Say, Mr. A.
Andrade, E.   Music.
Andrews, L.   Time Signature.

Annand.   Mavis.
Anton, S.   Phantasmagoria.
Anyte [*or* Anytes].   Why, rustic Pan, sitting in the lone shady wood.
Applewhite.   Road Down Home.
Ashanti.   Just Another Gig.
Ashbery, J.   Syringa.
Atkins, R.   Dark Area.
Aubert, A.   Bessie.
Bachhuber, D.   Mozart in a Classroom of Children.
Baker, H.   Of Walter White's Father in the Rain.
 Tobacco Warehouse Blues.
Baker, T.   Armillaria Mellea.
Bandeira.   Mozart in Heaven.
Baraka, I.   All is One for Monk.
 Am/Trak.
 In the Funk World.
Barber, D.   Little Overture.
Barlow, G.   In My Father's House.
Baron, S.   Tom-Tom Talk.
Barrax.   Singer, The.
Barresi.   Venice Beach: Brief Song.
Basho.   There is the old pond!
Bauer, G.   Oldies But Goodies.
 She Calms the Savage Beast with Her Aubade.
 So You Want to Hear the Blues.
Bennett, K.   99.9 FM Radio Nostalgia.
Berger, B.   Salad Days.
 Stout Brahms.
 To Answer Your Question.
Berkson, B.   Variation.
Berlin.   Alexander's Ragtime Band.
 Pretty Girl Is Like a Melody, A.
Berrigan, T.   Sonnet I: "His piercing pince-nez. Some dim frieze."
Bishop, E.   Sonnet: "I am in need of music that would flow."
Blake, W.   Piping Down the Valleys Wild.
Blessing.   Elegy for Elvis.
Bly, R.   Listening to the Köln Concert.
Bobyshev.   Return.
Bogan, L.   M., Singing.
 Musician.
 Sub Contra.
Boker.   Sonnet 280: "Ah, lute, how well I know each tone of thee."
Bonset.   X-Rays.
Bopp, R.   I wake up.
Borden, M.   Morning Chamber Orchestra Near Piney Crick, Wyoming, 7 A.M., The.
Boroditskaya, M.   Poor composer.
Bottoms.   Homage to Lester Flatt.
Bowers, N.   On the Elvis Mailing List.
Bowles, W.   On the Death of William Linley, esq.
Brathwaite, E.   Naima.
 Trane.
Breeze.   Dubbed Out.
 Eena Mi Corner.
Brett, L.   La Pathétique.
Brock, V.   All the Stars Are Foxfire.
 I Stopped in Tupelo, Elvis.
 Sphinx.
Brooks, G.   First Fight. Then Fiddle.
 Piano after War.
 Third Sermon on the Warpland, The.
Brooks, S.   (That's the Way) Dixieland Started Jazz.
Brown, Sterling Allen.   Ma Rainey.
 When de Saints Go Ma'chin' Home.
Brown, Stewart.   Let Them Call It Jazz.
Brown, T.   Preparation.
Browning, E.   Musical Instrument, A.
Browning, R.   Abt Vogler.
 Toccata of Galuppi's, A.
Buchwald.   As Soon As It's Here It's Gone But So What.
Buckley, C.   Nostalgia.
 Playing for Time.
Bunina.   From the Seashore.
Burns, R.   Red, Red Rose, A.
Buson.   Walking on dishes.
Butts, A.   Massenet.
Bye.   Car Music.
 Frank's Song.

 Not Tyrants.
Bynner.   Lovers: "From somewhere over the houses, through the silence."
Byron, G.   Stanzas for Music ("There be none of Beauty's daughters.").
Cage.   25 Mesostics Re and Not Re Mark Tobey.
Campion, T.   Rose-cheeked Laura[, Come].
 When to Her Lute Corinna [*or* Corrina] Sings.
Carleton, Bob.   Ja Da.
Carroll, K.   Domino Theory (or Snoop Dogg rules the world), The.
Carruth, H.   High above themselves. Above everything, flux, ooze.
Carson, A.   Homo Ludens.
Castro, M.   Blew It.
Cawein.   Music.
Cecil.   Richard's Blues.
Cedering, S.   Regarding Music.
 Variations for the Piano.
Ceravolo.   Celebration.
Césaire, A.   Batouque.
Chambers, G.   Meditations on Stevie.
 Waxing Poetic on Marvin.
Chapman, L.   Stevie Wonder.
Chase, K.   What You Can't See.
Chase, N.   Music Mother.
Chaucer.   Miller's [*or* Milleres] Tale, The.
Ch'eng-kung Sui.   Rhapsody on Whistling.
Cherry, K.   Raiment We Put On, The.
Ch'i-chi.   On an Autumn Evening Listening to Reverend Yeh Play the Ch'in.
Chmielarz.   They Come Humming.
Chuang Tzu.   Breath of Nature, The.
Chunghur Hyujung.   On Hearing the Sound of a Komunko While Passing a Mansion.
Church, R.   Earphones.
Clampitt.   Syrinx.
Cleary, B.   New Rock n Roll, The.
Clover, J.   Ceriserie.
Coffman.   Courage, or One of Gene Horner's Fiddles.
Cohan.   I Want to Hear a Yankee Doodle Tune.
Cole, T.   Lines Suggested by Hearing Music on the Boston Common at Night.
Coleridge, M.   Day-dream, A.
 Impromptu.
 To a Piano.
Coleridge, S.   Aeolian [*or* Eolian] Harp, The.
Coles, R.   New Jersey Boys.
Collins, K.   Trio.
Collobert.   For Which the Sun.
Congreve, W.   Music.
Cook, E.   To My Lyre.
Coolbrith.   Lines.
Cooper, J.   Wanda's Blues.
Corcoran.   Music of the Altai Mountains.
Corey, S.   Preparing to Live Among the Old.
Corn.   Conch from Sicily, A.
Cornford, F.   Guitarist Tunes Up, The.
Cornish, S.   His Fingers Seem to Sing.
Cortez, J.   I See Chano Pozo.
 Into This Time.
Cox, N.   Singing Alone.
Cranch.   Music.
Crane, H.   Black Tambourine.
 Broken Tower, The.
Crashaw.   Music[k]'s Duel[l].
Cristall.   Morning. Rosamonde.
 Ode on Truth: Addressed to George Dyer.
 Song. Tune, The Heavy Hours: "Balmy comforts that are fled, The."
Crockett-Smith, D.   Hell Hound Blues.
Crouch, S.   Revelation, The.
 Up on the Spoon.
Cullen, C.   Night Rain.
Cummings, E. E.   God pity me whom (god distinctly has).
Cushing, J.   Autumn Leaves.
 Every Time We Say Goodbye.
 Lover Man.
Dacey, P.   Drummer, The.
 Musica.
 Musician, The.
Damas.   Hiccups.
Dancing Bear, J. P.   Caliban.

Dao. Untitled: "Trumpet like a sharp plow, A."
Darío, R. It Was a Gentle Air.
Tropic Afternoon.
Davenant [or D'Avenant]. Lark Now Leaves His Watery [or Wat'ry] Nest.
Davies, S. Orchestra; or, A Poem[e] of Da[u]ncing.
Speach of Love persuading men to learn Dancing, The.
Davis, F. Jazz Band.
Davis, T. C. T. at the Five Spot.
Rogue and Jar: 4/27/77.
Zoom (The Commodores).
Dawes, K. Black Heart.
Some Tentative Definitions 1.
Trickster 1 (for Winston Rodney).
Trickster 2 (for Lee "Scratch" Perry).
De León, L. Ode to Francisco Salinas.
Denby. Aaron.
Dèr Mouw. Audible Still.
Derricotte. Black Boys Play the Classics.
Blackbottom.
Di Prima. I Ching.
On Sitting Down to Write, I Decide Instead to Go to Fred Herko's Concert.
Dickinson, E. Better—than Music! For I—who heard it.
He fumbles at your Soul.
I would not paint—a picture.
Trees like Tassels—hit—and swung, The.
Dietz, H. You and the Night and the Music.
Digges. Rough Music.
Disch. Concise History of Music, A.
Dittberner-Jax. Blues for Aunt Ruth.
Dobyns. Loud Music.
Utopian Melodies.
Doolittle, H. New sensation, A.
Dove, R. Canary.
Event, The.
Hully Gully.
Listen to the Sound of My Horn.
Musician Talks about "Process," The.
Straw Hat.
Drummond, W. To His Lute.
Dryden, J. Alexander's Feast; or, The Power of Music [or Musique].
Song for St Cecilia's Day, 1687, A.
Duffy, C. Prayer: "Some days, although we cannot pray, a prayer."
Dugan, A. Poem for Elliot Carter on His 90th Birthday.
Dunbar, P. When Malindy Sings.
Duncan, R. Bending the Bow.
Passages 37.
Presence of the Dance / The Resolution of the Music, The.
What of the structure of Rime? I said.
Duran, J. Mr Teller the Piano Teacher.
Durcan. Death by Heroin of Sid Vicious, The.
In Memory: The Miami Showband—Massacred 31 July 1975.
Eady. Chuck Berry.
Hank Mobley's.
Ebb, F. Cabaret.
Ekelof. Like Ankle-Rings, This Music.
Eliot, T. S. When lovely woman stoops to folly and.
Elledge. Household Gods.
Ellis, T. Atomic Bride.
Practice.
Practice: For Derek Walcott.
Sir Nose D'VoidofFunk.
Tambourine Tommy.
Tapes.
Emerson, J. Architecture (2).
Emerson, R. Merlin I.
Saadi.
Enright, D. Apocalypse.
Espada. Dándole la mano a Mongo.
Latin Night at the Pawnshop.
Majeski Plays the Saxophone.
Shaking Hands with Mongo.
Espaillat. Metrics.
Esteves. In the Beginning.
Evans, M. Boss Communication.
Fabio. For Louis Armstrong, A Ju-Ju.

Tribute to Duke.
Fairley, B. Bach Fugue.
Feinstein, S. Blues for Zoot.
Blues Villanelle for Sonny Criss.
Christmas Eve.
Singapore, July 4th.
Sonnets for Stan Gage (1945–1992).
Finnell. Over *Voice of America*.
Firer. 1956, The Year My Sister, Using Her Ill Health Once Again, Blackmailed My Parents into an Accordion.
Saxophone Julie.
Fisher, R. Thing About Joe Sullivan, The.
Fitzpatrick, K. Highland, 1955.
Fleckenstein, M. Getting Even.
Fletcher, J. *et al.* Music.
Flynn, L. By My Skin.
Foerster. Mozart's Death.
Ford, W. Of Miles Davis.
Foreman, Paul. Huddie Ledbetter.
Forrest, G. Strange Music.
Frost, R. Never Again Would Birds' Song Be The Same.
Fuller, M. Sistrum.
Gaines, R. Kill the dj.
Garioch. I Was Fair Beat.
Gay, J. I rage, I melt, I burn.
Gerstler. Dear Boy George.
Ghigna. Lesson of Night, A.
Gibb. Letter to Russel Barron.
Gibson, W. Music Stole In.
Gilbert, C. Time with Stevie Wonder in It.
Gilonis, H. Song 9.
Gioia. Lives of the Great Composers.
Giovanni. Genie in the Jar, The.
Monday.
Giussani, S. Clothes Without the Monk, The.
Gizzi. Ding Repair.
Goedicke. Interior Music, The.
Wind of Our Going: Adagio Ma Non Troppo.
Goldberg, B. He Said Discipline Is the Highest Form of Love.
Gonzalez, R. Some Sixties.
Goodison. For Don Drummond.
Göransson. Last Instrument, The.
Gordon, G. Gas.
Tercios del Muerte.
Gordon, M. Serenade in Blue.
Gould, R. Amateur Drummer.
Graham, W. Johann Joachim Quantz's Five Lessons.
Gray, A. Music in the Meadow.
Why Your Grandfather Stopped Playing the Viola.
Gray-Kontar, D. Breath.
Cuz' mama played jazz.
Greenberg, A. Berlin Series.
Greppi, C. Subtle erratic vocation, A.
Grosholz. Last of the Courtyard, The.
Grunke, A. Learning to Live with the Piano.
Guest, B. Dissonance Royal Traveller.
Guillén, N. Wake for Papa Montero.
Guiney. At a Symphony.
Gunn, T. Elvis Presley.
Victim, The.
Hagedorn, J. Latin Music in New York.
Hammerstein. Sound of Music, The.
Hanley, J. Zing! Went the Strings of My Heart.
Harer, K. Lucky 7.
Harjo, J. Bird.
Healing Animal.
We Encounter Nat King Cole as We Invent the Future.
Harms. My Own Little Piece of Hollywood.
Harper, M. Alone.
Bandstand.
Dear John, Dear Coltrane.
Elvin's Blues.
For Bud.
Here Where Coltrane Is.
If You Don't Force It.
Narrative of the Life and Times of John Coltrane: Played by Himself, A.
Hart, J. Only Applebaum Can Make a Tree.
Harvey, S. Mighty Tropicale Orchestra, The.
Harwood, G. Nightfall.

Simple Story, A.
Haskins, L. Prodigy, The.
To Play Pianissimo.
Heard, J. Music.
Heithaus. What a Little Moonlight Can Do.
Henderson, D. Elvin Jones Gretsch Freak.
Lee Morgan.
Heng Chao. Listening to Master Yu Chao Play the Lute.
Herbert, G. Church-Music[k].
Herbert, Z. Apollo and Marsyas.
Drawer.
Hernández Cruz. Ironing Goatskin.
Latin and Soul for Joe Bataan.
Loíza Aldea.
Side 20.
Hernandez, D. Rooftop Piper.
Hernandez, F. De cómo Robert Schumann fue vencido por los demonios.
On How Robert Schumann Was Defeated by Demons.
Herrera. Iowa Blues Bar Spiritual.
Herrick. To Music, to Becalm His Fever.
Heyward, D. Jasbo Brown.
Hirsch, E. Art Pepper.
Hirshfield, J. Music Like Water, The.
Hodgson, R. Song of Honor [or Honour], The.
Holm, B. Blizzard.
Playing the Goldberg Variations on Sunday Morning.
Scott Joplin.
Whale Breathing: Bartlett Cove, Alaska.
Hooper, P. Listening to Mozart at Meadow Brook.
Howard, H. Soulgroovin Ditty #7.
Hsiao Yen [or Emperor Wu of Liang]. Flute, The.
Hsüeh T'ao [or Xue Tao]. Listening to a Monk Play the Reed Pipes.
Wind.
Huddle. Music.
Ooly Pop a Cow.
Hudgins. Around the Campfire.
Versification of a Passage from Penthouse.
Hughes, L. Be-Bop Boys.
Boogie: 1 a.m.
Daybreak in Alabama.
Dream Boogie: Variation.
Easy Boogie.
Jam Session.
Juke Box Love Song.
Neon Signs.
Note on Commercial Theatre.
Testimonial.
To Midnight Nan at Leroy's.
Trumpet Player.
Weary Blues, The.
Hugo, R. My Buddy.
Hull, L. Lost Fugue for Chet.
Hummer, T. Poem in the Shape of a Saxophone.
Hupfeld, H. When Yuba Plays the Rumba on the Tuba.
Hutchinson, P. True Story Ending in False Hope, A.
Ibn Sharaf. Satire.
Ignatova, E. Italian Marcello, you breathe a much sweeter air.
Illyés, G. While the Record Plays.
Inada. Great Bassist, The.
Inez. Listening to Dvorak's Serenade in E.
Ingram-Roberts, A. Poem 2 (for Duckie Simpson of Black Uhuru).
Isaacs, A. Mi Negrito.
Issa. Blossoms at night.
Holes in the wall, The.
Jackson, A. Billie in Silk.
Make/n My Music.
Ohnedaruth.
Jackson, Reuben. Lady's Way.
Love # 49: "This is how I felt."
63rd and broadway.
Thelonious.
Jackson, Richard. Shadows.
Jacob, M. In Honor of the Sardana and the Tenora.
Jacobs, H. And sometimes i hear this song in

my head.
Jacobsen, R. Age of the Great Symphonies, The.
Jarman, M. Supremes, The.
Jarvenpa, D. Polka.
Jauss. After the End of the World.
  Last Solo: Charlie Parker, Hotel Stanhope, March 12, 1955.
Jeffers, L. How High the Moon.
Jensma. Letter to Thelonius.
Jewett, S. At Home from Church.
Jewsbury. Farewell to the Muse, A.
Jiménez, J. I wish that all my poems.
  Music: "Music— / a naked woman."
Johnson, H. Berlioz in the Madhouse.
  Fringe-Area Reception.
Johnson, J. Music for the Cows.
Johnson, L. Five Nights of Bleeding.
  Reggae Sounds.
Jones, P. Birth of Rhythm and Blues, The.
Jordan, J. October 23, 1983.
Josefowitz, N. Music.
Joseph, A. Fourth Supreme, The.
  My Father's Heroes ("He gloried in the feats.").
  Pure Pop.
  Wedding Party.
Justice, D. Mrs. Snow.
  Variations for Two Pianos.
Kabir. Music without Strings, The.
Kaddour, Hédi. Variations.
Kane, J. Reasons for Loving the Harmonica.
Kaufman, B. Battle Report.
Keats. 'How Many Bards Gild the Lapses of Time!'.
Keble. Happiness.
Keene, J. After C (3): Tayloriana.
Keita, N. Rapid Transit.
Kenjeev. Gone is the sound of my favorite misfortune, which even yesterday.
Kgositsile. For Art Blakey and the Jazz Messengers.
Khodasevich. Music.
Kim Yŏng. Snowflakes flutter—butterflies chase flowers.
King, J. Intercity Dub.
Kinsella, T. Harmonies.
Kitahara Hakushū. Ailing child, An.
Kizer, C. Muse of Water, A.
Kleinschmidt. Cooking to Music.
  Orchestrion.
Knight, E. As You Leave Me.
Koehler, T. Spreadin' Rhythm Around.
Koethe. Songs of the Valley.
Komunyakaa, Y. Copacetic Mingus.
  Elegy for Thelonious.
  Euphony.
  February in Sydney.
  Villon/Leadbelly.
Kresh. Musical Saw.
Kumin, M. Bangkok Gang, The.
Kuo P'o. Kingfishers sport among orchids and begonias.
Kuzmin. At the Party.
Kyger. It's been a long time.
Laforgue. Mystery of the Three Horns, The.
Lagrone. I Heard the Byrd.
Lanier, S. To Beethoven.
Lawrence, D. H. Piano.
Levertov. For Those Whom the Gods Love Less.
Levine, P. Soloing.
Levis. Decrescendo.
Lewis, J. Time and Music.
Li Ho. Lute Player, The.
Li Po. Hearing the Flute in the City of Loyang in a Spring Night.
  Listening to a Monk from Shu Playing the Lute.
  Listening to the Lute Played by Monk Chun from Shu.
Li Shang-yin. Inlaid Lute, The.
Lindsay, V. Jazz of This Hotel, The.
Lodeizen. Ode: In a Few Hours.
Loesser. I Hear Music.
Loftin, E. Scabible.
Long, D. Black Love Black Hope.
Long, J. Music's Wife.

Longfellow, H. Spirit of Poetry, The.
Longley, M. Words for Jazz Perhaps.
Lowe, J. Club House.
Lowell, A. Music.
Lux. Night above the Town.
Mac Low. Pieces O'six—XXIV.
Mackinnon, R. Bruckner.
MacNeice. Bagpipe Music.
Macpherson, H. Looking for 78's in the 40's.
Madgett. Plea for My Heart's Sake.
Madhubuti. Knocking Donkey Fleas off a Poet from the Southside of Chi.
  Sun House.
Madigan. Curtis Fuller.
  Stereo Time with Booker Little.
Magidson, H. Music, Maestro, Please!
Malachi. Psalm of Silk.
Mallarmé. Saint.
Mapanje. On African Writing.
March, S. Legacy.
  Monk's Misterioso.
Marshall, J. Gift, A.
Marston, P. Love's Music.
Martin, H. Miss Rosie Mae Watches Elvis Presley on The Ed Sullivan Show.
Martinez, D. Moto Perpetuo.
  Standard Time: Novena for My Father.
Masters, E. In Memory of Bryan Lathrop.
Matthews, W. Accompanist, The.
  Bud Powell, Paris, 1959.
  Buddy Bolden Cylinder, The.
  Mingus at The Showplace.
  Unrelenting Flood.
Max, L. Equal Temperament.
  Pedagogy.
McAuliffe, J. Effects.
McClure, M. For Monk.
  Jazz at the Intergalactic Nightclub.
McDonald, W. Songs We Fought For, The.
McGinley. Evening Musicale.
McGrath, B. Concert Choir.
McGrath, C. Jeffrey Lee Pierce.
McGrath, T. Guiffre's Nightmusic.
  Song: Miss Penelope Burgess, Balling the Jack.
McKean. After Listening to Jack Teagarden . . .
  .
McLaughlin-Carruth, J. Black Irish Blues.
McManus, J. Two Songs for Hendrix.
McNeill, A. For the D.
McPherson, S. Some Metaphysics of Junior Wells.
  Suspension: Junior Wells on a Small Stage in a Converted Barn.
Meeks, B. Is Culcha Weapon?
Meltzer, D. 17:II:82.
Meredith, G. Phoebus with Admetus.
Merrill, B. Music That Makes Me Dance.
Merrill, J. Victor Dog, The.
Mew. Forest Road, The.
Millay, E. On Hearing a Symphony of Beethoven.
Milova, T. Sometimes, not often, it's true.
Milton. At a Solemn Music[k].
  To Mr. H. Lawes On His Airs.
Minhinnick. Sax.
Mirabai [or Mira Bai]. Song of the flute, O sister, is madness, The.
Mitchell, A. From Rich Uneasy America to My Friend Christopher Logue.
Moerman. Louis Armstrong.
Montale. My Muse.
Moore, L. Bluesman's Blues, A.
Moore, M. Mind Is an Enchanting Thing, The.
Moore, T. Harp That Once through Tara's Halls, The.
Mor. Coming of John, The.
Morejón. Richard Brought His Flute.
Morgan, R. Music of the Spheres.
Mörling, M. For the Woman with the Radio.
Morris, M. Valley Prince.
Moskowitz, F. Bird Lives.
Moss, T. Landscape with Saxophonist.
Mueller, L. Concert, The.
  Possessive Case, The.
  Romantics: Johannes Brahms and Clara Schumann.

What the Dog Perhaps Hears.
Muench, S. Elegy for the Unsaid.
Mullen, H. Music for Homemade Instruments.
Muratori. Re-Emergence of the Trombone, The.
Murray, L. Powerline Incarnation, The.
Mutis. Sonata.
Nathan, L. Quartet.
Neal, L. Lady's Days.
Nelson, H. Peepers.
Nerval. Fantasy.
Niccolai. Careful that these *Frisbees*.
Nijhoff. Musician, The.
Noguere. Barney Bigard.
Noyes, A. Barrel-Organ, The.
Nurske, D. Involuntary Music.
Oates. Waiting on Elvis, 1956.
O'Brien, L. Diabolus in Musica.
O'Hara, F. Day Lady Died, The.
  Radio.
Okantah. Afreeka Brass.
  Southern Road.
Okara. Piano and Drums.
Okudzhava. Departure.
  How the young flutist smiles.
O'Meally. Make Music with Your Life.
O'Shaughnessy, A. Ode: "We are the music-makers."
Osterhaus, J. New York Minute.
Ostriker. Eighth and the Thirteenth, The.
Overton, R. Blues in "C".
Owen, W. Music.
Padgett, R. Blue Bananas.
Pagis, D. Europe, Late.
Pak P'aengnyŏn. Upon Listening to the Flute.
Palmer, M. Man Undergoes Pain Sitting at a Piana, A.
  Untitled (February 2000).
Paman. On Christmas Day to My Heart.
Pao Chao. To you, fine wine in gold cup.
Pastan. Orpheus.
  Overture.
Patterson, R. Hopping Toad Blues.
Peabody, J. After Music.
Pederson, C. Summer Recital.
Pedretti, Erica. Here.
Perry, S. Fugue.
  Orpheus.
  Toadfish.
Philips, K. To Mr. Henry Lawes.
Phillips, R. Persistence of Memory, the Failure of Poetry, The.
Pierpont, J. In what rich harmony, what polished lays.
Pilling. Webern.
Pinsky. Hearts, The.
Pitter. Military Harpist, The.
Plumpp. Be-Bop.
  Ornate with Smoke.
Po Chü-i. River Flute.
  Song of the P'i-P'a.
  Yin-yo laps in the reeds, my guest departs.
Poe. Israfel.
Pordage. To Lucia Playing on Her Lute, Another.
Porter, C. Begin the Beguine.
Porter, P. It's there, somewhere in the Platonic cold store.
Powell, D. A. Sonnet: "Morsels of my lifework: the story of a professional party hostess."
  Tall and thin and young and lovely the michael with kaposi's sarcoma *goes walking.*
Powell, K. Genius Child.
Powell, N. Coda: Thelonius Monk, d. 17 February 1982.
Preston, R. Chicago Blues.
  Deep-Sea Bathing (Inna Reggae Dancehall).
Prior. Ode, An: "Merchant, to secure his treasure, The."
Procter, A. Lost Chord, A.
Quinn, J. Go through and down the steps.
Quintana. Teddy.
Raboni, G. Madrigal.
Raine, C. For Hans Keller.
Rakosi. Instructions to the Player.
Randall, D. Langston Blues.
Ravikovitch, D. Sound of Birds at Noon, The.

Ray, H.   Perfect Orchestra, The.
Two Musicians, The.
Räy, M. N.   You've enchanted the world.
Razaf, A.   I'd Give a Dollar for a Dime.
Redmond.   Ballad of Black/Essence.
Dance Bodies #1.
Distance.
Reid, A.   Lesson in Music, A.
Rich, A.   At a Bach Concert.
Ninth Symphony of Beethoven Understood at
Last as a Sexual Message, The.
Richardson, L.   Poet Sings His Painting, The.
Riley, D.   Lyric: "Stammering it fights to get."
Riley, T.   Low End, The.
Rilke.   On Music.
Rivard.   Baby Vallejo.
Rivers, C.   Underground.
Roberson, E.   It must be that in the midst.
Roberts, E.   Orpheus.
Roberts, I.   My Father's Whistle.
Robinson, A.   Search for Apollo, A.
Robinson, E.   L'Envoi.
Robson, J.   Blues for the Lonely*.
Rodriguez, L.   Rainfall Piano.
Roland Holst.   Being.
Rollings.   In Your Own Sweet Time.
Root, W.   Sonnet 20: Remembering, from a Nazi
Prison, a Teacher Years Before.
Ross, L.   James Brown.
Roston.   Program Notes.
Roubaud.   Everywhere the.
Rukeyser, M.   Bunk Johnson Blowing.
Night-Music.
Rumi.   Music Master.
Rupchev, Georgi.   Still Life: "Cello on the bed,
A."
Rux, C. H.   Suite Repose.
Rylander, E.   Dancing on Beethoven's Birthday.
Midnight Rocker, Tiananmen Square, May 27,
1989.
Salaam.   Always Know.
Secondline Send Off.
Sama, B.   Song, The.
Sanchez, S.   To Anita.
Sandburg, C.   Jazz Fantasia.
Sanguineti.   To the mini-skirted customs official
who with sibyl-dove eyes.
Sappho.   Come, divine lyre, speak to me.
Schoerke, Meg.   Practice.
Schuyler, J.   Greetings from the Chateau.
Man in Blue, A.
Schwartz, R. L.   Flamenco Guitar.
Seale, J.   Playing the Flute for the TMR Class.
Sedakova.   Grasshopper and the Cricket, The.
Seibles, T.   Manic: A Conversation with Jimi
Hendrix.
Serros, M.   Mr. BOOM BOOM Man.
Sexton.   Music Swims Back to Me.
Shakespeare, W.   How sweet the moonlight
sleeps upon this bank!
If Music be the food of love, play on.
Sonnet 128: "How oft, when thou, my music,
music play'st."
Shange.   I Live in Music.
Sheehan, M.   My Father's Singing.
Sheldon, G.   Blames, for Rane and Diane.
Shelley, P.   Hymn of Pan.
Ode to the West Wind.
To —: "Music, when soft voices die."
Shepherd, R.   Difficult Music, The.
Lucky One, The.
Sherrill, J.   Woodstock.
Shiomi, M.   Event for Late Afternoon.
Shirley, A.   Hours Musicians Keep, The.
Sholl.   Don't Explain.
Shunoku.   After the spring song, "Vast
emptiness, no holiness,".
Shwarts [or Shvarts].   Elegy on an X-ray Photo
of My Skull.
Simic.   Crepuscule with Nellie.
Simmons, J.   Didn't He Ramble.
Sin Sukchu.   Upon Listening to the Flute.
Skelton, J.   Than, if this noble kyng.
Skloot.   Music Appreciation.
Twilight Time.
Slessor.   Full Orchestra.

Smith, P.   What It's Like to Be a Black Girl (For
Those of You Who Aren't).
Sneeden.   Coltrane and My Father.
Sobin, G.   What the Music Wants.
Sol, A.   Conductor, The.
Solonche.   Chopin Preludes, Opus 28.
Someck, R.   Blues for Elliot Sharp.
Sŏng [or Sung] Sammun.   Upon Listening to the
Flute.
Soniat.   Harp/Desire.
Speakes.   Heartbreak Hotel Piano-Bar.
Spellman, A.   Did John's Music Kill Him?
John Coltrane: An Impartial Review.
Spicer, J.   Orfeo.
Ssu-k'ung Shu.   In Illness, Dismissing My
Singing Girl.
Stanard, C.   Rap Is.
Stanton, M.   Ode to Mozart.
Stern, G.   Bela.
Fritz.
Romania, Romania.
Stevens, W.   Anglais Mort à Florence.
Mozart, 1935.
Peter Quince at the Clavier.
Stevenson, A.   Musician's Widow.
Stevenson, R.   Song of a Traveller, The.
Stewart, B.   August Town.
Stillman, A.   Jukebox Saturday Night.
Stokesbury.   Evening's End.
Straus, M.   What I Heard on the Radio Today.
Strode.   In Commendation of Music.
On a Gentlewoman that Sung and Played upon a
Lute.
Stroud, J.   Hacedor.
Homage: Doo-Wop.
Sweeney, M.   Appointment, The.
Sweet, B.   "New World" Interview.
Sylvester, J.   Variable.
Taylor, H.   Elevator Music.
Teasdale.   Lines.
Thomas, L.   Excitation.
Historiography.
Onion Bucket.
Thomas, R. S.   Pavane.
Thompson, J.   Music in Camp.
T'Hooft.   Worn-Out Pop Song, A.
Thoreau.   Music.
Thorne, T.   Whatever Happened to Conway
Twitty?
Tiger.   Lovepoem Writing Me.
Tolson, M.   Mu.
Touré, A.   O Lord of Light! A Mystic Sage
Returns to Realms of Eternity!
Trammell, Robert.   Nightclub, A: on the
Jacksboro Highway.
Tranströmer.   Schubertiana.
Trinidad.   Meet the Supremes.
Tu Fu [or Du Fu].   Song for a Young General.
Unknown.   Blind Musicians, The.
Blind musicians, the blind musicians, The.
Ling-tai: He Measured Out His Spirit Tower.
Updike.   Player Piano.
Vando.   Swallows of Salangan.
Verlaine.   Art of Poetry, The ("You must have
music first of all.").
Piano kissed by a slender hand, The.
Vigil, A.   That's the Way, Uh Huh, Uh Huh, I
Liked It.
Vinz.   Blues, The.
Vliet.   Goodnight sweet prince.
Volkman.   Evening.
Voznesensky [or Voznesenskii].   War Ballad.
Wagoner, D.   Chorus: "That rain-strewn night in
the woods, the chorus, chorus."
Silence of the Stars, The.
Wah.   Music At The Heart Of Thinking 22.
Wakoski.   Valentine for Ben Franklin Who
Drives a Truck in California, A.
Wallenstein.   Blues 1.
Blues 2.
Walton, A.   Dissidence.
Wang Chien.   Round Fan.
Wang Wei.   Bamboo Lane House.
Bamboo-Midst Cottage.
Sitting in mystic bamboo grove, back unseen.
Waters, M.   Christ at the Apollo, 1962.

"Night in the Tropics" (1858-59?).
Weems, M.   Return to Temptation.
Weinstein, N.   Drummond's Lover Sings the
Blues.
Ethiopian Apocalypse of Don, The.
Garvey's Head as Value.
Migration of Drummond's Organs (After
Death), The.
Welburn.   Ben Webster: "Did You Call Her
Today?".
Gonsalves.
Wenderoth, J.   Billy's Famous Lounge.
Westheimer, David.   At the Movies.
Wheelwright.   Would You Think?
Whitman, R.   Hearing a Mozart Duo at 36,000
Feet.
Whitman, T.   Hunger and Imagination.
Whitman, W.   Italian Music in Dakota.
Proud Music of the Storm.
Wilde, O.   Hélas!
Wilkes, K.   Dolce.
Williams, B.   Night Flute, The.
Williams, W.   Dance, The: "In Brueghel's great
picture, The Kermess."
Shoot It Jimmy!
Willson, M.   Seventy Six Trombones.
Winder.   Lesson.
On Fourteen Maple Street.
Unaccompanied Suite.
Woessner.   Jungle Music.
Wojahn.   Assassination of John Lennon as
Depicted by the Madame Tussaud Wax
Museum, Niagara Falls, Ontario, 1987, The.
At Graceland with a Six Year Old, 1985.
Buddy Holly Watching *Rebel Without a Cause*,
Lubbock, Texas, 1956.
Colorizing: Turner Broadcasting Enterprises,
Computer Graphics Division, Burbank,
California, 1987.
Custom Job: Hank Williams, Jr., and the Death
Car, 1958.
Elvis Moving a Small Cloud: The Desert Near
Las Vegas, 1976.
Fab Four Tour Deutschland: Hamburg, 1961.
Francis Ford Coppola and Anthropologist
Interpreter Teaching Gartewienna Tribesmen
to Sing "Light My Fire," Philippine Jungle,
1978.
Homage: Light from the Hall.
John Berryman Listening to Robert Johnson's
"King of the Delta Blues," January 1972.
Matins: James Brown and His Famous Flames
Tour the South, 1958.
"Mystery Train" Janis Joplin Leaves Port Arthur
for Points West, 1964.
Nixon Names Elvis Honorary Federal Narcotics
Agent at Oval Office Ceremony, 1973.
Tattoo, Corazon: Ritchie Valens, 1959.
Trashmen Shaking Hands with Hubert
Humphrey at the Opening of Apache Plaza
Shopping Center, Suburban Minneapolis,
August 1963, The.
Woody Guthrie Visited by Bob Dylan: Brooklyn
State Hospital, New York, 1961.
Wolfli.   Nostalgic Song for My Beloved.
Wong, N.   On Plaza Garibaldi.
Wordsworth, W.   Mutability.
Wormser.   It's a Party (1959).
Soul Music.
Wren, A.   Harmony.
Wright, D.   Beethoven's Romance in G.
Wright, D.   Musician, The.
Wright, James.   Art of the Fugue, The: A Prayer.
Wright, Jay.   What is Beautiful.
Wright, R.   Strange Music.
Wu Wen-ying.   Tune: "Rouged Lips" Rain Just
Over on the Night of the Lantern Preview.
Yearsley.   Rural Lyre, The.
Yeats.   Fiddler of Dooney, The.
Madness of King Goll, The.
Yi I.   Where is the eighth bend?
Yi Kae.   Upon Listening to the Flute.
Yi Sŏkhyŏng.   Upon Listening to the Flute.
Young, A.   Dance of the Infidels.
From Bowling Green.
Jazz as Was.

Lester Leaps In.
Ravel: Bolero.
Studio Up Over In Your Ear.
Young, Andy.   Foxfire.
Young, K.   Eddie Priest's Barbershop and Notary.
Everywhere Is out of Town.
Yun Sŏndo.   At My Study.
Zabolotsky [or Zabolotskii].   Warning.
Zagajewski.   Electric Elegy.
Quick Poem, A.
Zarco.   Saxophonetyx.
Zaturenska.   Woman at the Piano.
Zavatsky.   Live at the Village Vanguard.
Zeiger, D.   Mostly Mozart at Planting Fields Arboretum.
Zeppa, M.   Aleatory.
Zimmer.   But Bird.
Duke Ellington Dream, The.
Sitting with Lester Young.
Zolynas.   Love in the Classroom.
Zukofsky, L.   Non Ti Fidar.
Two Dedications: Tibor Serly.
See also **Blues (music); Gospel Music**

Music Festivals
Hutchinson, P.   Fleadh Cheoil.
Sherrill, J.   Woodstock.
Whitman, A.   Lute of Afric's Tribe, The.

Music Halls
Ellis, T.   Tapes.
Rukeyser, M.   Paper Anniversary.

Music Lessons
Barrax.   Pittsburgh, 1948, The Music Teacher.
Duran, J.   Mr Teller the Piano Teacher.
Justice, D.   Pupil, The.
Mullen, H.   Music for Homemade Instruments.
Oles.   To a Daughter at Fourteen Forsaking the Violin.
Ratzlaff, K.   Group Portrait with Ukuleles.
Wallace, R.   At the St. Louis Institute of Music.

Musical Instruments
Hayes, T.   Clarinet.
Hsiao Kang.   I Play My Zither.
Hurbak Myungjo.   Sitting Alone.
Kosugi, T.   Organic Music.
Mackinnon, R.   Bruckner.
McKay, D.   Early Instruments.
Moore, L.   Black Soldier, A.
Nathan, L.   Quartet.
Nickel, B.   For Peter, My Cousin.
Phillips, R.   Instrument of Choice.
Plumpp.   History, Hollers, and Horn.
Sagay-Lights, V.   Savannah Brass.
Wier.   Chance Encounter with a Wounded Man Playing a Theremin.
Wright, C.   Secret Life of Musical Instruments, The.
Zolynas.   Pastorale for Spring.

Musk Oxen
Lynes, Jeanette.   Muskoxen.

Muslims and Islam
Abu Ishaq al-Ilbin.   O say to all of the inhāja, the full moons of the time, and the lions of the thicket.
al-Mala'ika, N.   Hijrah [Migration] to God, The.
Anwar, C.   Heaven.
Dharker.   Purdah, 1.
Hamod, S.   After the Funeral of Assam Hamady.
Hunt, L.   Abou Ben Adhem.
Krause, K.   Eid Al-Fitr.
Mathias, J.   Bogomil in Languedoc.
Melville, H.   By the Jordan.
Mohiuddin, K.   Birthmark.
Muhammad, T.   Extremes Ain't My Thing As Salaam Alaikum.
Penn, R. E.   Morning Songs.
Pinsky.   In Berkeley.
Qasmi.   Thought.
Rudaki.   Prayer.
Satyamurti.   Striking Distance.
Shapiro, H.   News, The.
Tati-Loutard.   Early.
Unknown.   Let the mullah raise his prayer to the dawn.
My lover is Hindu and I am a Muslim.

Noble, enduring, ever-renewed peace do I attribute exclusively to his highness, the best of Caliphs, A.
Whittier.   Palm-Tree, The.

Mussels
McDonald, C.   Fresh Mussels.

Mustaches
Mark, Sabrina Orah.   Mustache, The.

Mutability
Apollinaire.   Voyager, The.
Windows.
Zone.
Chang Chiu-ling.   I close my door and trace the transformations of nature.
Ch'en Tzu-ang.   I dwell in the forest nursing a long illness.
Men in the market pride themselves on their knowledge and craft, The.
De Burine, Claude.   But When I Have.
Donne.   His Picture.
Dunbar, W.   Of[f] Lentren in the first mornyng [or morning].
Field, R.   Some People.
Fisher, R.   To origin, which is another patch of sun.
Forbes, D.   Recension Day.
Harms.   Joy Addict, The.
Hewett, D.   Sunset flames over the city, The.
Housman.   On Wenlock Edge the wood's in trouble.
Levy, A.   London Poets.
Mackenzie, K.   Children Go, The.
Marteau.   I Consent That Everything Vanishes.
Radiguet.   Handless Clock.
Ralegh, S.   Thus now I leave my love in fortunes {bandes / bandes}.
Shakespeare, W.   O[h] Mistress Mine.
Sonnet 15: "When I consider every thing that grows."
Sonnet 64: "When I have seen by Time's fell hand defac'd [or defaced]."
Sonnet 116: "Let me not to the marriage of true minds."
Taylor, J.   Squire's Pew, The.
Volkman.   We did things more dulcet, more marionette.

Muteness
García Lorca.   Little Mute Boy, The.
Gertsyk, A.   Silent, draped in the garments of sacrifice.
Hirsch, E.   Song: "This is a song for the speechless."
Lear, E.   Limerick: "There was a Young Lady of Parma."
Marston, P.   Speechless: Upon the Marriage of Two Deaf and Dumb Persons.
Reznikoff.   Idiot, The.
Samaras, N.   Mute Prophets.

Mutiny
Beeching, J.   Gaudy Camp Follower, The.
Belloc.   Maxim Gun, The.
Kocan.   Mutineer's Ballad, The.
Rohrer, M.   Last Look at the Mutineers, A.

Mystery
Akhmatova, A.   Poem: "Twenty-first, The. Night. Monday."
Al-Bayati, A.   Secret of Fire.
al-Saygh, S.   Mysterious.
Arnold, M.   Written in Butler's Sermons.
Assultani, F.   That Thing.
Behn, A.   To Damon. To Inquire of Him if He Cou'd Tell Me by the Style, Who Writ Me a Copy of Verses that Came to Me in an Unknown Hand.
Bejerano, M.   In a slick, black bodysuit Job stood before me.
Benedetti, M.   Magnet, The.
Berry, W.   To the Unseeable Animal.
Bhattācārya, K.   Is my black Mother Syama really black?
Cairns, Scott.   Prospect of the Interior.
Carter, C.   Parts of a Mystery.
Chang Yü.   Pavilion for Listening to Fragrance, The.
Cole, T.   I Saw a Cave of Sable Depth Profound.

Colonna, S.   Disconnections.
Cruz, S.   I Know Full Well the Water's Flowing Power.
Cullen, C.   Yet Do I Marvel.
Dickinson, E.   Some things that fly there be.
Doolittle, H.   Mysteries, The.
Doyle, B.   Forensics.
Eberhart, R.   Loon Call, A.
Ewart.   Owl Writes a Detective Story, The.
Fanshawe, C.   Enigma.
Field.   Embalmment.
Gonzáles Martínez.   Like Sister and Brother.
Gorey.   Limerick: "From Number Nine, Penwiper Mews."
Gorostiza, J.   Fireflies.
Hafiz, K [or Hafez].   Cries We Make, The (64).
Hamhur Kiwha.   Because of Certain Things.
Hannon.   Beneath Cold Mountain.
Subterranean.
Temporary Heart.
Hemans.   Spirit's Mysteries, The.
Hsin Ch'i-chi.   Tune: "The Dark Clouds of Ch'u" Visiting the Rainy Crag Alone.
James, P.   Can This Be Love?
Koch, K.   To You: "I love you as a sheriff searches for a walnut."
Lampadius.   As a symbol.
Landon.   Power of Words, The.
Lao Tzu.   Ways that can be walked are not the eternal Way, The.
Lion-Face.   KYE HO! Wonderful!
MacDiarmid, H.   Light and Shadow.
Magrelli.   Things have an admirable life.
Martynova, O.   What does the river know of its own bed.
Milán, E.   I let myself be led because I let loose. Me dejo guiar porque he dejado ir.
Mitchell, R.   It.
Mo Shih-lung.   To the Monk Wu-hsia on the Occasion of His Editing the Lotus Sutra.
Muldoon, P.   Why Brownlee Left.
Muso Soseki.   Dry Tree.
Nielsen, K.   Self Portrait as Nancy Drew, Girl Sleuth.
Paz.   Mystery.
Phillips, C.   Words of Love.
Prado, A.   Siesta.
Pugh.   What If This Road.
Reese, L.   Mystery.
Rich, A.   Diving into the Wreck.
Richards, T.   Challenge to the Reader, A.
Rumi.   Inside water, a waterwheel turns.
Russell, G.   Secret, The.
Ryan, T.   Lunar Eclipse.
Santos Chocano.   Who Knows?
Sarton, M.   Light Left On, A.
Sen, R.   Who can understand Kali?
Shelley, P.   Sonnet: Lift Not the Painted Veil.
Smith, E.   God in the darkness, God beyond our knowing.
Stever, E.   Her Back to Me.
Symonds.   Midnight at Baiae.
Unknown.   More than the color.
Van Duyn.   In Bed with a Book.
Vietnamese Oral Tradition.   Woman's Heart, A.
Vinokurov.   All Grows Old.
Whitman, W.   There is that in me—I do not know what it is—but I know it is in me.
Winter, M.   Elegy: "There is a question."
Wright, C.   Chinese Journal.
Yeats.   Magi, The.

Mysticism
Artaud.   Civil Status.
Benton, S.   Second Coming, The.
Brock-Broido.   Domestic Mysticism.
Carey, T.   Zohar.
Cohen, L.   I Have Not Lingered in European Monasteries.
de Fierro.   Oblivion.
Oracle.
Emre.   Burning, burning, I drift and tread.
Dear Friend, let me plunge into the sea of love.
Go and let it be known to all lovers.
I love you beyond the depths of my own soul.
Love is minister to us, our flock is the inmost soul.

Now hear this, lovers, my friends.
Fingueret, M.   Tovu-Vavohu.
Frost, R.   Witch of Coös, The.
Goethe.   Mystical Chorus.
Hafiz, K [or Hafez].   Stain of the Sea, The (414).
Han-shan.   My place is on Cold Mountain.
Hernández Cruz.   Discovery.
For the Far-Out Experimental Writer.
Physics of Ochun, The.
Hill, S.   Questioning Mr Bonnet.
Hopes.   Witch the lakemen call her, this wind.
Lawrence, D. H.   Mystic.
Li Po.   Suite in the Ch'ing-p'ing Mode, A.
Li Shang-yin.   Master Chia.
Li Te-yü.   To Patriarch Sun at Hua-yang Grotto.
Machado Ruiz.   Come sing with me in chorus: it's nothing, all we know.
Meredith, W.   Bachelor.
Muñiz Huberman.   Ablution.
Cabalists, The.
Manuscript.
Sanctuary.
Neruda.   Flag, The.
Olds, S.   Ecstasy.
Robinson, R.   Jarrangulli.
Rumi.   Answers from the Elements.
Daylight, full of small dancing particles.
Do you think I know what I'm doing?
Drunkards, The.
Ecstatic Love Is an Ocean.
Edge of the Roof, The.
For years, copying other people, I tried to know myself.
I, you, he, she, we.
Like This.
Music Master.
Out beyond ideas of wrongdoing and rightdoing.
Quietness.
Thief in the Night, A.
Twelve Lies, The.
Silva, C.   Magical Devices.
Toledo, N.   Na tacha.
Touré, A.   O Lord of Light! A Mystic Sage Returns to Realms of Eternity!
Ungar.   Groundhog Day.
Unknown.   Spirit Song.
Wang Shih-chieng.   Ch'ai-kuan Mountain Pass.
Whitman, W.   When I Heard the Learn'd Astronomer.
Wu Yun.   Apotheosis.
Young Bear.   Emily Dickinson, Bismarck and the Roadrunner's Inquiry.

Mythology

Aborigine Oral Tradition.   Mapooram.
Platypus, The.
Star-Tribes, The.
Two Sisters, The.
Agoos, J.   To Atlas in the Attic.
al-Mala'ika, N.   Myths.
Alcaeus [or Alkaios].   Come! Put by Pelops' Isle.
Come tip a few with me.
Alegría.   Letter to an Exile.
Anacreon.   Weaving a garland long ago.
Annensky.   Capitol, The.
Antipater of Thessalonica.   Priapus, seeing Cimon's rigid rod.
Apuleius, L.   I who am Nature, mother of all.
Atwood.   Daphne and Laura and So Forth.
Auden.   Atlantis.
Behn, A.   Paraphrase on Oenone to Paris, A.
Benton, S.   Lilith.
Second Coming, The.
Berry, W.   Mad Farmer Revolution, The.
Blake, W.   Book of Urizen [or First Book of Urizen], The.
Boland, E.   Listen. This is the Noise of Myth.
Brown, E.   What Song the Syrens Sang.
Budapest.   Medea speaks: / This is God, children, listen up well. The.
Cacciatore, E.   Third Warning Sign: An Endless Surprise.
Campo.   My Voice.
Carbó, N.   I Found Orpheus Levitating.
Carew, T.   Song[, A]: "Ask[e] me no more

where Jove bestow[e]s."
Castillero, S.   Chimera.
Quimera.
Castillo, S.   Cuba.
Caulfield.   In My Labyrinth (The Minotaur's Game).
You All Know the Story of the Two Lovers.
Cavafy.   Ithaka.
Chapman, G.   So her close beauties further blaze her fame.
Chia Yi.   Owl, The.
Ch'u Yüan.   Heavenly Questions.
Citino.   Letter from the Shaman: The Tribe with No Myth.
Clampitt.   Athena.
Dodona: Asked of the Oracle.
Cofer, J.   How to Get a Baby.
Coleridge, M.   Alcestis to Admetus.
Cooley, N.   Undine.
Copus, J.   Topsell's Beasts.
Corn.   To Hermes.
Cott, J.   Isis (Lady of Petals).
Crane, H.   Atlantis.
Darío, R.   It Was a Gentle Air.
Leda.
Seashell, The.
Swan, The.
Darley.   Rebellion of the Waters, The.
Davidson, M.   Troth.
Davie, D.   Fountain of Cyanë, The.
Davies, I.   Hywel and Blodwen.
Deanovich.   American Avalon.
Donovan, K.   Entering the Mare.
Doolittle, H.   Evil was active in the land.
Holy Satyr.
Lais.
Splintered the crystal of identity.
Dunbar, P.   Black Samson of Brandywine.
Duncan, R.   Fire, The.
Duncombe, S.   To Aspasia.
Eguren.   Peregrin, Wandering Hunter of Faces.
Eliot, T. S.   Mr. Apollinax.
Sweeney among the Nightingales.
Erinna.   Girls / Brides / Tortoise.
I'm the tomb of Baukis, a bride; passing the deeply lamented.
Fabian, C.   Liturgy for Lilith.
Prayer of Dedication.
Qadesha (Sacred Whore).
Faverey.   Bit by Bit.
Fay, J.   Mother of Andromeda, The.
Ferré.   Opprobium.
Field.   Climbing the hill a coil of snakes.
Prometheus fashioned man.
'Sing to us Sappho!' cried the crowd.
Why should I praise thee, blissful Aphrodite?
Flaccus, G.   Book 7.
Forché.   Ancapagari.
Fulton, A.   Give: A Sequence Reimagining Daphne & Apollo.
Gewanter, D.   Xenia: Stranger/Guest.
Gifford, H.   In the Praise of Music.
Glück, L.   Hyacinth.
Mythic Fragment.
Golding, A.   . . . This Damsell was not famous for the place.
Góngora y Argote.   Come Hymen come, for here to thee we bring.
Dedication: to the Count of Niebla.
Polyphemus' Love Song.
Greenlaw, L.   Clownfish.
Gregg.   Singers Change, the Music Goes On, The.
Guest, B.   Farewell Stairway, The.
Halsey, A.   His acre. His arbour.
Saracen SAS or Assasseen called Nasir claims on HTV, A.
32s. 6d. for the chattels of Robert Hod, fugitive, Michaelmas 1230 at York.
Weakened by loss of blood Robin's last act was to slash his sword.
Hardie, K.   Things That Are Lost.
Hardy, J.   Computer Aided Design: Creation.
Harrigan, S.   Pecos Bill in Decline.
Heaney, S.   Dog Was Crying Tonight in Wicklow Also, A.

Hecht, A.   Goliardic Song.
Herbert, Z.   Envoy of Mr. Cogito, The.
Hernández Cruz.   Islandis.
Hildebrandt, Z.   Persephone.
Hill, G.   Orpheus and Eurydice.
Homer.   Dardanus...was son of Zeus the Lord of the clouds.
Now Here of the Golden Throne, looking out from where she stood on the summit of Olympus, was quick to observe two things.
Housman.   Crossing Alone the Nighted Ferry.
Howe, S.   Revisionist work in.
Huchel.   Under the naked hoe of the moon.
Ibycus.   And I killed the Molione boys.
They destroyed the famous and wealthy.
Jaimes Freyre.   Eternal Farewell.
Jones, A. M.   To Echo.
Jones, S.   New World.
Jones, W.   Hymn to Su'rya, A.
Keats.   Fall of Hyperion, The; A Dream.
Kizer, C.   Fearful Women.
Kocot, N.   I Am Like a Desert Owl, an Owl Among the Ruins.
Korean Oral Tradition.   Song of Entertaining the Holy One.
Korican, L.   Her Story.
Korinna [or Corinna].   Are you, happy man, grandson of Kronos.
Kouretes hid the goddess's, The.
Of your daughters: Zeus, Father.
Krysl.   Persephone, to Demeter.
Lanier, S.   To Richard Wagner.
Lawrence, D. H.   Argonauts, The.
Leggott, M.   Songs of Good Hope, The.
Li Ch'ing-chao.   Tune: "Fisherman's Pride".
Lim-Wilson.   Beginning of Things, The.
Llewellyn-Williams.   Two Rivers.
Llwyd, R.   Beaumaris Bay.
Longfellow, H.   Galaxy, The.
Lucretius.   Gods, by right of Nature, must possess, The.
Malenis, L.   Hopeless Eveningsong.
Mandelstam [or Mandelshtam].   Lightheartedly Take from the Palms of My Hands.
On Stony Pierian Spurs.
Marlowe.   By this Leander being near the land.
"O Hero, Hero!" thus he cried full oft.
Martial.   Read of Thyestes, Oedipus, dark suns.
Who deem epigrams mere trifles.
Masters, E.   Webster Ford.
Mathews, H.   Comatas.
Mathias, R.   Laus Deo.
McCallum, S.   Calypso.
Mei Ch'eng.   Seven Stimuli.
Monaghan.   Persephone's Journey.
Venus of Laussel.
Montague, J.   Old Mythologies.
Moore, M.   Charity Overcoming Envy.
Moritz [or Morits].   Between Scylla and Charybdis.
Morton, T.   Poem, The: "Rise Oedipus, and if thou canst unfold."
Mutén, B.   Demeter's Blessing.
Hesperides, The.
Queen Hera.
Queen Medusa.
Ngunaitponi.   Song of Hungarrda, The.
Nichols, G.   Long-Man.
Nolla.   Reencounter with the Goddess.
Nonnus.   Dionysus and Ampelos.
Norris, K.   Persephone.
Ortiz.   Creation.
Ovid.   Apollo and Hyacinthus.
Arethusa Saved.
Rape of Lucrece, The.
Zeus and Ganymede.
Pao Chao.   Magic Cinnabar.
Parnell, P.   Apotheosis of Medusa.
Medusa and Perseus III: Lilith.
Pastan.   Orpheus.
Patterson, G.   Lament.
Perry, S.   Orpheus.
Petri.   Electra.
Pfeiffer, E.   Klytemnestra.
Studies from the Antique.
"Philo-Philippa.".   To the Excellent Orinda.

Philpot, T. Road Trip as Clues, A.
Plath. Death of Myth-making, The.
Porter, C. They Couldn't Compare to You.
Powell, D. A. Minotaur at Supper, The: Spare the Noritake and the Spode.
Praxilla. Learning from the tale of Admetos, my friend, love the brave.
Pugh. Coming into Their Own.
Reed, H. Philoctetes.
Richter, H. Beginning.
Robinson, M. Describes her Bark.
  Previous to her Interview with Phaon.
  Sappho's Prayer to Venus.
  To the Muses.
Rodgers, W. Home Thoughts from Abroad.
Rossetti, D. For Spring, by Sandro Botticelli, in the Accademia of Florence.
Rothenberg, J. Structural Study of Myth, The.
Rukeyser, M. In the Underworld.
Santayana. On an Unfinished Statue.
Sonnet 48: "Of Helen's brothers, one was born to die."
Sappho. Prayer to my lady of Paphos.
  Queen Hera, may your [graceful form].
Savitz, M. Massive Stoner.
Seferis. Argonautica.
  Memory 1.
Seneca. This said, she twirled the thread on an ugly spool.
Shelley, P. Prometheus Unbound.
Simonides. Danae and Perseus.
Smith, John. How Could They.
Smith, R. Halcion.
Spenser, E. First was Fancy, like a lovely boy, The.
  Penelope for her *Ulisses* sake.
  There now he lives in everlasting joy.
Stainer. Xochiquetzal.
Stanton, M. Voice for the Sirens, A.
Starhawk. Demeter's Song.
Statius. Book 10.
Stesichoros. Across from glorious Erytheia.
Stickney, T. Be still. The Hanging Gardens were a dream.
Storni. To Eros.
Stratanovsky. Herostratos and Herostratos.
Sung Yu. Wind, The.
Symonds. Midnight at Baiae.
Tada. Odyssey or "On Absence," The.
Taylor, B. Hylas.
Tennyson, A. Tithonus.
Triplett, P. Manora.
Tu Fu [or Du Fu]. At the Sky's End, Thinking of Li Po.
Unknown. Coming of Enkidu, The.
  Death of Enkidu, The.
  Hymn to Nut.
  Lament of Gilgamesh for Enkidu, The.
  Let the first syllable of PEnelope be followed by the first of DIdo, the first of CAnus by that of REmus.
  Lofty trees of the south, The.
  May Isis heal me.
  See there, that tree is a digging stick.
  Song of the Rising Sun Dance.
  Songs of Spirits.
  We Have Chosen a Timely Day.
Van Winckel, N. Basket with Blue Ox.
Vettese. Scottish Mythology.
Volkman. Sonnet: "Sky we bear on our shoulders, heaven-height, The."
Waddington, M. Ulysses Embroidered.
Walcott. Ajax, / lion-coloured stallion from Sealey's stable.
Watkins, V. Music of Colours: The Blossom Scattered.
Weatherly, T. Gandhabba #5.
Whitmore, S. Gamelia.
  Lenaia.
Whittier. Robin, The.
Wilbur, R. Lying.
Wilde, O. Santa Decca.
Wohlfeld. Sea.
Woolagoodjah. Lalai (Dreamtime).
Yeats. Leda and the Swan.
Yi Chehyŏn. Long ago in Silla, Venerable Ch'ŏyong.
Yün-k'an Tzu. Out of chaos.
Zaid. Circe.
Zanzotto. Eclogue 4: "Shell-bursting births, comas, and the mute."

N

Nagasaki, Japan
Clifton, L. 1. at nagasaki.
Dixon, M. Nagasaki.
Dougherty, E. Why I Think About Hiroshima and Nagasaki.
Griswold, J. Origami.
Kinnell. Fundamental Project of Technology, The.
Strickland. Shadow.
Wilner, E. Conversation with a Japanese Student.

Nakedness
Addonizio. Alone in Your House.
Amadiume. Creation.
Ap Hywel, Elin. Disarmed.
Arnold, C. Locker Room Etiquette.
Bible, *O.T.* Psalm 139. Domine, Probasti.
Browning, R. Rhyme for a Child Viewing a Naked Venus in a Painting [of "The Judgement of Paris"].
Chubb, R. Transfiguration.
Clanchy, K. One Night When We Paused Half-way.
Copus, J. Masaccio's *Expulsion from Paradise*.
Crummey, Michael. Naked Man, The.
Cunningham, J. Epitaph for Someone or Other.
Dauer. Mammals.
Donne. To His Mistress Going to Bed.
Ducal, C. Duke and I 2, The.
Essbaum, J. Post-Communion Striptease.
Everson, W. Stone Face Falls.
Frost, C. Undressing, The.
Gaitán Durán. They Unite Naked.
Giussani, S. Body Politic.
Greppi, C. If it had been possible.
Ismail. You: "You're mine."
Issa. Naked.
Jiménez, J. Full Moon.
Kennelly. Restoration, A.
Kolodinsky, A. Midnight.
Li Po. Summer Days in the Mountains.
Mahadevi. On Her Decision to Stop Wearing Clothes.
Mansour, M. My Memory.
Muske, C. Our Kitty.
Neruda. Hero, The.
Nolens, L. Tributary.
Norris, K. Throne of Grace, The.
Okamoto. Tanka: "Stark naked."
Olds, S. Lifting, The.
Oppen. Morality Play, A: Preface.
Paulus [or Paulos] Silentiarius. Take off your clothes, my love!
Peacock, M. Lullaby: "Big as a down duvet the night."
Pearse, P. Naked I Saw You.
Phillips, C. Undressing for Li Po.
Ping. Syntax.
Reynolds, C. Worst of it, The.
Rock, D. Changing.
Shannon, A. JoNelle.
Shomer. My Mother's Body.
Spenser, E. And in the midst of all, a fountaine stood.
Trommer, R. Sonnet for July.
Warren, R. Birth of Love.
Wilner, E. Her Body Is Private.
Zamora, D. Vision of Your Body.

Names
Aichinger. In Which Names.
Alakoye. Eshu.
Alvarez, J. Bilingual Sestina.
Ashbery, J. Just Walking Around.
  Myrtle.
Auden. My First Name, Wystan.
Baraka, R. I Remember Malcolm.
Barolini. Having the Wrong Name for Mr. Wright.
Baytelman, S. My Name is Shlomit.
Belieu. My Field Guide.
Belloc. Frog, The.
Benét, S. American Names.
Bentley, E. Wynkyn de Worde.
Berman, D. Community College in the Rain.
Berrigan, D. My Name.
Betham-Edwards. In a Letter to A.R.C. on Her Wishing to Be Called Anna.
Blake, W. Infant Joy.
Borges. Golem, The.
Boston, B. Apiary.
Brooks, G. Kojo: I Am A Black.
  Primer for Blacks.
Browning, E. To George Sand: A Recognition.
Browning, R. Names, The.
Budy. Ellis Island, September 1907.
Cardenal. From those theaters, Claudia, from those feasts.
Carruth, H. Fantastic Names of Jazz, The.
Catacalos. Swallow Wings.
Cave. Elegy on a Maiden Name, An.
Cernuda. If Man Could Name.
Cherry, K. History.
  Raiment We Put On, The.
Chin, J. Ex-Boyfriends Named Michael.
Chin. How I Got That Name.
Cisneros, S. Muddy Kid Comes Home.
  You Called Me *Corazón*.
Clements, S. Susans.
Clifton, L. Light / on my mother's tongue.
Cohan. Mary's a Grand Old Name.
Cole, W. Mutual Problem.
Coleman, James. Black Women with Jewish Names.
Collins, B. Names, The.
Coolidge, C. Dalliance with Salt Sides, A.
Cope, W. Names: "She was Eliza for a few weeks."
Corey, S. Tempest, The.
Crouch, S. Riding Across John Lee's Finger.
Davies, A. Personality syndrome, The.
Dickinson, E. I'm ceded—I've stopped being Theirs.
Disch. Vowels of Another Language, The.
Donnelly, S. Eve Names the Animals.
Dove, R. Dusting.
Dugan, A. Nomenclature.
Eliot, T. S. Naming of Cats, The.
Espada. Beloved Spic.
Farawell, M. Everything I Need to Know I Learned in Kindergarten.
Fingueret, M. 86 Pasteur Corner.
Foix. I Arrived in that Town, Everyone Greeted Me and I Recognized no One. When I Was Going to Read My Verses, the Devil, Hidden Behind a Tree, Called Out to Me Sarcastically and Filled My Hands with Newspaper Clippings.
Frishberg, D. Van Lingle Mungo.
García, D. Other Marías.
  Squaring the Names.
Gardiner, S. No Title.
Gillan. Arturo.
Gotera. Madarika.
Goyette, Susan. True Names of Birds, The.
Graves, R. My Name and I.
Guillén, N. My Last Name.
Gunn, T. Pope's Carnations Knew Him.
Hadewijch. Love has seven names.
Hamod, S. Dying with the Wrong Name.
Han-shan. Storied cliffs were the fortune I cast.
Harris, D. Water from the Well.
Hayden, R. Mystery Boy Looks for Kin in Nashville.
  Names.
Hernández Cruz. Slick.
Hernandez, F. Autograph.
Hill, G. Pet-name, a common name, A. Best-selling brand, curt.
Hollander, J. Adam's Task.
Holthaus, G. Unexpected Manna.
Hood, T. Choosing Their Names.
Howe, S. Rückenfigur.

Hughes, L. Madam and the Census Man.
Hugo, Lynne. Small Power.
Ilkov, Ani. Evaporations.
Imbriglio, C. In Nomine.
Inez. Lake Song.
Ivanov, G. On the boundary of snow and melting.
Jackson, R. Jamal's Lamentation.
Jacob, M. Rue Ravignan, The.
Jiménez, J. Name Drawn from the Names, The.
Jordan, A. N-e-m-e-s-i-s Blues.
Kim Namjo. For Baby.
Komunyakaa, Y. Audacity of the Lower Gods.
Kumin, M. Riddle of Noah, The.
Laird, N. Layered, The.
Lamb, C. Family Name, The.
Landor, W. Well I Remember How You Smiled.
Lao Tzu. Way as "Way" bespoke is no true lasting way; The.
Lauture, D. Strokes of an Adult's Pencil.
Lee, L. Out of Hiding.
Leto. Mary Morelle Show, The.
Levertov. I Learned That Her Name Was Proverb.
Lim-Wilson. Explaining the Origin of My Name.
Limburg, J. Barton in the Beans.
Locker-Lampson. My Life Is a———.
Logghe. Insomnia Litany.
Mack, C. That's Why They Call Me "Shine".
Mackey, N. Ghede Poem.
Majaj. Recognized Futures.
Maxwell, G. Rumplestiltskin.
McDonald, R. Hollow Thesaurus, The.
McGrath, C. Delphos, Ohio.
  Florida.
McGuckian. Captain Lavender.
  Mantilla.
McLagan, Elizabeth. Reading the Names.
Miller, E. Mississippi.
Min, N. M. My Mother Has Forgotten My Name.
Morgan, D. Registering the Little One.
Moss, H. Geography: a Song.
Mueller, L. Naming the Animals.
Mullen, H. Momma Sayings.
Nash, O. What's in a Name? Some Letter I Always Forget.
Nekrasov, V. What kind of Pushkin am I.
Neruda. Too Many Names.
Nhat Hanh. Please Call Me by My True Names.
Nowlan. Word, The: "Though I have the gift of tongues."
O'Loughlin. Cuchulainn.
Oppen. Myth of the Blaze.
Orlen. Onomastics and the Falling Snow.
Palmer, M. O you in that little bark.
Parker, D. Art of the Nickname, The.
Partnoy, A. To *El Mingo* (with Whom I Share Eva Victoria and Anahi Paz).
Pastan. Name, A.
Patchen. Empty Dwelling Places.
Patten, B. How the New Teacher Got Her Nickname.
Paz. Shrine.
  Wind and Water and Stone.
Preston, K. Lapsus Linguae.
Prigov. Dialogue No. 5.
Quasimodo. To the Fifteen of Piazzale Loreto.
Ransford, Tessa. Viewpoint.
Ratcliff, C. So Gallantly Streaming: To the Poet.
Reed, H. Naming of Parts.
Repetto. 6th Grade—Our Lady of Pompeii.
Rodriguez, L. My Name's Not Rodriguez.
Rome, H. Call Me Mister.
Rose. Naming Power.
Rosen, M. Humpty Dumpty.
Salazar. Taking It Back.
Salinas, P. Deaths ("First thing I forgot was your voice, The.").
Saloy, M. "N" Word, The.
Sigourney. Indian Names.
Siken, Richard. Saying Your Names.
Silva, C. Tea at the Magdalene.
Simon, L. Nellie Gives into Blanche.

Simpson, A. Name, Many Names, A.
Simpson, L. Riverside Drive.
Smith, J. Philodendron Named Joan, A.
Spenser, E. Sonnet 75: "One day I wrote her name upon the strand."
Steele, T. Timothy.
Stefanile. How I Changed My Name, Felice.
Stevenson, R. Ticonderoga: A Legend of the West Highlands.
Strange. Barbershop Ritual.
Straus, M. Scarlet Crown.
Strejilevich. When They Robbed Me of My Name.
Szymborska, W. Still.
Taylor, J. Epigram, A Supposed Construction.
Tranströmer. Signatures.
Trethewey, N. Miscegenation.
Troup, B. Baby, Baby All the Time.
Tsvetayeva [*or* Tsvetaeva]. Your name—a bird on my hand.
Unknown. Angel of Death, The.
Updike. I Missed His Book, but I Read His Name.
Vettese. Scottish Names.
Wagner, M. Miss Clement's Second Grade.
Wakoski. For Whitman.
Wallace-Crabbe. Life of Ideas, The.
Webb, C. Biblical Also-Rans.
  Identifying with the Buddha.
Weinberger, E. Changs.
Whitman, W. What Am I After All.
Wilbur, R. Rillons, Rillettes.
Wilcox, E. Woman.
Williams, S. You Were Never Miss Brown to Me.
Winchilsea. Adam Posed.
Wolverton, T. Tubes.
Wong, N. It's in the Blood.
Wright, C. As Our Bodies Rise, Our Names Turn into Light.
Wright, J. Minneapolis Poem, The.
Wright, J. Boleros #21.
Zurita, R. Sparkling Beaches, The.
See also **Place Names**

Nantucket, Massachusetts
Lowell, R. Quaker Graveyard in Nantucket, The.
Teasdale. Wisdom.
  Wood Song.
Williams, W. Nantucket.

Naples, Italy
Ash, J. Ungrateful Citizens, The.
Hugo, R. Napoli Again.

Napoleon I
Barlow, J. Advice to a Raven in Russia [December, 1812].
Browning, R. Incident of the French Camp.
Byron, G. Napoleon's Farewell.
De la Mare. Napoleon.
Dubie. Apocrypha of Jacques Derrida, The.
Ford, F. For the white-limbed heroes of Hellas ride by upon their horses.
Heine, H. Grenadiers, The.
Holub. Napoleon.
Hugo, V. It was snowing. For the first time, conquered.
  Waterloo! Waterloo! Waterloo! dismal plain!
Kipling, R. St. Helena Lullaby, A.
Plath. Swarm, The.
Shelley, P. Feelings of a Republican on the Fall of Bonaparte.
Thackeray. Napoleon.
Unknown. Boney.
  This is a message to those who live here not to worry excessively.
  To Buonaparte.
Wodehouse. Napoleon.
Wordsworth, W. 1801.
  October, 1803 ("When, looking on the present face of things.").

Napoleon III
Hugo, V. Conscience.
  Night of the Fourth: A Recollection, The.
  Set Him Apart!
  That Night.

Rimbaud, A. Poster of Our Dazzling Victory at Saarbrucken, A.
Napoleonic Wars
Barlow, J. Advice to a Raven in Russia [December, 1812].
Browning, R. Incident of the French Camp.
Byron, G. There Was a Sound of Revelry by Night.
Hugo, V. After the Battle.
  It was snowing. For the first time, conquered. Russia 1812.
Lermontov. Borodino.
Mickiewicz. Year 1812, The.
Wordsworth, W. November, 1806.
  To the Men of Kent (October, 1803).
Narcissism and Narcissists
Housman. Look not in my eyes, for fear.
Mayer, G. Narcissus.
Zamora, D. Hand Mirror.
Narcissus (botany)
White, E. Window Ledge in the Atom Age.
Narcissus (mythology)
Chappell, F. Narcissus and Echo.
Glazer, M. Echo to Narcissus.
Housman. Look not in my eyes, for fear.
Mayer, G. Narcissus.
Ovid. So, when she saw Narcissus wandering through the lonely countryside, Echo fell in love with him, and followed secretly in his steps.
Narcotics
Groves. Heroine.
Heine, H. Death and Morphine.
Katz, J. Falling.
Shuster, D. Mellow on Morphine.
See also **Drug Addiction**
Nasturtiums
Spencer, A. Lines to a Nasturtium.
National Anthems
Key. Star-Spangled Banner, The.
McManus, J. Two Songs for Hendrix.
Praitis, I. Anthems.
Nationalism
Andrade, O. Babbling.
Bachmann. Every Day.
Belli, G. Nicaragua Water Fire.
Bhattācārya, M. Come, brothers, everyone together.
Bidgood. Dragon.
Bobyshev. Return.
Buuck, D. Geopolitical, The.
Chedid, A. Future and the Ancestor, The.
Dennis, C. World History.
Gandlevsky, S. Is it time to change the record? But I'm dreaming again.
Glaser, I. Last Good War—and Afterward, The.
Hofer, J. Of Deaths, Days, Futures, Nations ("On the corner of plato and national army a man early.").
Holmes, O. International Ode.
Huerta, E. Declaration of Hate.
Im Hwa. Again at the Crossroads.
Jabès. Sunland.
Ko Ŭn. Chrysanthemums.
Lazarus, E. How Long?
Lim, S. Learning to Love America.
Martí. Two Countries.
Martinaitis, M. Kukutis's Trip on the Samogitian Highway.
Neruda. Pardon me, if when I want.
Ortiz. On late-night television, two U.S. scientists talk about why the U.S.
Pacheco, J. High Treason.
Padilla. Landscapes.
Pegram, A. Deliverance.
Ratushinskaya [*or* Ratushinskaia]. For the cry from the well of "mama!".
Sandburg, C. Old Timers.
Thelwall. Vanity of National Grandeur, The.
Thomas, F. Behind the Nationalist's Flag.
Thomas, R. S. Reservoirs.
Torres Bodet. My Country.
Veiga. Wind of Liberty.
Vicioso. Haiti.

Native Americans

Adler, F.   Voices Are Coming Up, The.
Alexie.   After the Trial of Hamlet, Chicago.
 Airplane.
 At Navajo Monument Valley Tribal School
  (from the Photograph by Skeet Mcauley).
 Capital Punishment.
 Crazy Horse Speaks.
 Crow Testament.
 Defending Walt Whitman.
 Evolution.
 Exaggeration of Despair, The.
 Father and Farther.
 How to Write the Great American Indian Novel.
 Indian Boy Love Song (#2).
 November 22, 1983.
 Powwow at the End of the World, The.
 Sonnet: Tattoo Tears.
 Texas Chainsaw Massacre.
 Tourists.
 Translated from the American.
 Vision (2).
 Why We Play Basketball.
Algarin.   Taos Pueblo Indians: 700 strong
  according to Bobby's last census.
Ali, A.   Snow on the Desert.
Allen, P.   Taku Skanskan.
Andrade, O.   Portuguese Mistake.
Armstrong, J.   I Study Rocks.
Baehr, A.   I Will Not Pretend.
Ballowe, J.   Starved Rock.
Beach, L.   2 Months Rent Due and 1 Bag of
  Rice.
Big Boy, M.   I Will Bring You Twin Grays.
Bitsui, Sherwin.   Chrysalis.
 Northern Sun, The.
Blaeser.   Rituals, Yours—and Mine.
Blue Cloud.   Crazy Horse Monument.
 Turtle.
 Yellowjacket.
Brant, B.   Stillborn Night.
Breton, A.   Go For Broke.
Bruchac.   Birdfoot's Grampa.
 Wahsah Zeh (War Dance)—As Long as the
  Grass.
Bryant, W.   Disinterred Warrior, The.
 Indian at the Burial-Place [or Burying-Place] of
  His Fathers, An.
 Indian Story, An.
Burgess, H.   Rational.
Burlingame.   Walking Past the Dugout of Felix
  McKittrick.
Bynner.   Haskell.
Caldwell, K.   Moonlight.
Canning, J.   Indian Gone!, The.
Cardiff.   Grey Woman.
 It has something to do with final words.
Castillo, A.   Toltec, The.
Cawein.   Dead Cities.
Chrystos.   As I Leave You.
 I Bring You Greetings: How.
 Old Indian Granny, The.
 Real Indian Leans Against, The.
 Soap Bubbles.
 Today Was a Bad Day Like TB.
Clements, S.   Deer Cloud.
 Matinee.
 Reservation, The.
Cochran, J.   To Keep the Spirits.
Cody, James.   Heart of Texas, The.
Coke, A.   Change, The.
Cole, Maude E.   Over Texas Hills.
Consuegra, D.   You and I.
Cook-Lynn.   Grandfather at the Indian Health
  Clinic.
Coolbrith.   Captive of the White City, The.
Crane, H.   Sad Indian, The.
Crosby, F.   Mandan Chief, The.
Crowell, N.   Texas Trails.
Cuthand, B.   Dancing with Rex.
 She Ties Her Bandanna.
Cutler, B.   February 12, 1865.
Dauenhauer.   How To Make Good Baked
  Salmon from the River.
Davenport, S.   Up from the Wreck Conjuring
  Montana Sonnet.

Davis, W.   Texas: Sesquicentennial.
de Aerenlund, C.   Cuando el tecolote canta, el
  Indio muere.
Di Prima.   American Indian Art: Form and
  Tradition.
 Brief Wyoming Meditation.
Dove, R.   Taking in Wash.
Duhig, I.   Fundamentals.
Dumas, H.   Concentration Camp Blues.
Duncan [Too-qua-stee], D.   Dead Nation, The.
Dunn, C.   Margaret/Haskell Indian School.
Erdrich, H.   Hopi Prophet Chooses a Pop.
Erdrich.   Captivity.
 Dear John Wayne.
 Family Reunion.
 Fooling God.
 Indian Boarding School: The Runaways.
 Sacraments, The.
Espada.   Thanksgiving.
Evans, B.   K-Doe Codas.
Eyen, J.   New Dream, A (Wuski A-Baw-Tan).
Falcón, J.   Burial Clothes.
 Indian Locks.
Fife, C.   Dear Webster.
Finch, A.   Native American Birds, The.
Fisher, L.   Child of the Sun.
Forché.   Ancapagari.
Fordham.   Cherokee, The.
Freneau.   Indian Burying Ground, The.
 On the Civilization of the Western Aboriginal
  Country.
George, P.   Battle Won Is Lost.
Gilbert, C.   Sorrow Since Sitting Bull, A.
Gilfillan, M.   Horseshoe.
Giovanni.   Walking Down Park.
Glancy.   First Reader Santee Training School,
  1873, The.
 Great Indian Father in the Subway.
 Hides.
Goll, I.   Lackawanna Elegy.
González Prada, M.   Inca's Arrows, The.
 Mitayo, The.
González, R.   Marías, Old Indian Mothers.
Gould, J.   Coyotismo.
Green, R.   Coosaponakeesa (Mary Mathews
  Musgrove Bosomsworth), Leader of the
  Creeks, 1700–1783.
Grieves, C.   Connuche.
 Indian Car.
Haines, J.   Train Stops at Healy Fork, The.
Halfe, L.   Pāhkahkos.
Hall, D.   New Mexico.
Halleck, F.   Red Jacket.
Harjo, J.   Autobiography.
 Deer Dancer.
 Insomnia and the Seven Steps to Grace.
 Woman Hanging from the Thirteenth Floor
  Window, The.
Harrigan, S.   Papalote Creek.
Harte, B.   Truthful James to the Editor.
Hemans.   American Forest Girl, The.
 Indian Woman's Death-Song, The.
Herández-Ávila.   Presente.
Hershon.   Light and Dark, East and West.
Hill, R.   To Rose.
 Waning August Moon.
Hogan, L.   New Apartment.
 Skin.
 Truth Is, The.
Hollander, J.   State of Nature, A.
Howe, S.   Gabion / Parapet.
Hugo, R.   Letter to Hill from St. Ignatius.
 Map of Montana in Italy, A.
Inada.   15. The Legend of the Full Moon over
  Amache.
Iroquois Oral Tradition.   Dancing Speech of O-
  No'-Sa, The.
 Tree of the Great Peace, The.
Jeffers, R.   Inquisitors, The.
 New Mexican Mountain.
Joe, R.   Expect Nothing Else from Me.
 Old Stories.
 Plawej ans L'nui'site'w (Partridge and Indian-
  Speaking Priest).
Jussawalla, F.   Indian.
Keeshig-Tobias.   I Grew Up.

Klein, A.   Indian Reservation: Caughnawaga.
Knoepfle.   Confluence.
Landon.   She Sat Alone beside Her Hearth.
Lane, P.   Winter 40: "She is a northern woman,
  barely more."
Le Sueur.   Behold This and Always Love It.
Lee, A.   Confession.
Lewis, J.   Indians in the Woods, The.
Lindsay, V.   Ghosts of the Buffaloes, The.
Livingston, M.   First Thanksgiving.
Logghe.   Her First Jew.
Longfellow, H.   By the shores of Gitche[e]
  Gumee.
 Hiawatha: The White Man's Foot.
Louis, A.   Nevada Red Blues.
 Something About Being an Indian.
 That Great Wingless Bird.
MacLeish.   Wildwest.
Major, C.   Lost in the Desert.
Manyarrows.   Lakota Sister/Cherokee Mother.
 See No Indian, Hear No Indian.
Martinez, D.   Blessing Poem.
 Song: "I dreamed my voice was an Anasazi
  pot."
Masters, E.   Starved Rock.
Mattawa.   Road from Biloxi, The.
McGlashan, J.   Island of Women, The.
McGrath, T.   You Can Start the Poetry Now, Or:
  News from Crazy Horse.
Midge, T.   Written in Blood.
Million, D.   Housing Poem, The.
Miranda, Deborah A.   Stories I Tell My
  Daughter.
Moore, L.   Indian Girl.
Mottram.   Zuni Dancers.
Napier, A.   Tulum Saw the Coming.
Naranjo-Morse.   Gia's Song.
 Tradition and Change.
Neihardt.   Summer turned.
Neruda.   Amor America (1400).
 I did not touch your night, or your air, or dawn.
Nezhukumatathil, A.   Tallahassee.
Niedecker.   War.
Noel, L.   Understanding Each Other.
NorthSun.   Moving Camp Too Far.
Nystrom.   Regardless of the Final Score.
O'Grady, D.   Great Horse Fair, The.
Ortiz.   At the Salvation Army.
 Creation.
 Earth and Rain, the Plants & Sun.
 Juanita, Wife of Manuelito.
 State's Claim That It Seeks in No Way to
  Deprive Indians of Their Rightful Share of
  Water, The.
 Travels in the South.
 Upstate.
Paiute Oral Tradition.   Like always / like
  forever.
Pape.   Indian Ruins Along Rio de Flag.
Paschen.   Two Standards.
Penn, M.   Calling Up the Spirit of the Lost
  Child.
Perillo, L.   Ghost Shirt, The.
Plato.   Natives of America, The.
Pope, A.   Lo, the poor Indian! whose untutor'd
  mind.
Posey, A.   Hotgun on the Death of Yadeka
  Harjo.
 Ode to Sequoyah.
Purdy, A.   Remains of an Indian Village.
Red Hawk.   2 Ways of Crossing the Creek.
Rendon.   You See This Body.
Reposa, Carol Coffee.   Hill County Rest Home.
Revard.   Parading with the Veterans of Foreign
  Wars.
Reyes, A.   Tarahumara Herbs.
Ridge, J.   Stolen White Girl, The.
Riordan, M.   Some Sporting Motifs.
Rivers, J.   Illinois: At Night, Black Hawk's
  Statue Broods.
Rodriguez, L.   My Name's Not Rodriguez.
Romero, L.   If Marilyn Monroe.
 Marilyn Monroe Indian.
Rose.   Endangered Roots of a Person.
 For the White Poets Who Would Be Indian.
 Long Division; a Tribal History.

Naayawva Taawi.
Ta Tiopa Maza Win / Iron Door Woman.
Rothenberg, J. Cokboy.
Salaam. Flying over America.
Sandburg, C. Circles.
Early Copper.
Santos Chocano. Who Knows?
Savageau. At the Powwow.
Like the Trails of Ndakinna.
Looking for Indians.
To Human Skin.
Schoolcraft. My Brother, my brother.
Otagamiad.
Scott, D. At Gull Lake; August, 1810.
Forsaken, The.
On the Way to the Mission.
Onondaga Madonna, The.
Watkwenies.
Sigourney. Indian Names.
Indian's Welcome to the Pilgrim Fathers, The.
Silko. In Cold Storm Light.
It Was a Long Time Before.
Long Time Ago.
When Sun Came to Riverwoman.
Sirr. Understanding Canada.
Smelcer. My Indian Grandmother Speaks to Animals.
Smith, P. Jemez Pueblo: December 26.
Smoker, M. Another Attempt at Rescue.
Letter to David James Duncan, February 16, 2003.
Snodgrass. Powwow.
Stafford, W. Indian Cave Jerry Ramsey Found, The.
Vacation.
Sweet, D. My Mother and I Had a Discussion One Day.
Sze. Do Not Speak Keresan to a Mescalero Apache.
Tallmountain. Indian Blood.
Tapahonso. Pay Up or Else.
What Danger We Court.
Taylor, R. Dakota: October, 1822, Hunkpapa Warrior.
Terry, L. Bars Fight [August 28, 1746].
Tester, V. First Horses, 1519.
Santa Rita Massacre, 1837.
Tohe. She Was Telling It This Way.
Toya, D. Hunter's Dance in Early Fall.
Trask, H. Sisters.
Tremblay, G. Urban Indians, Pioneer Square, Seattle.
Turcotte, M. Battlefield.
Indian Things.
Reflection.
Unknown. American Indian, The.
Dead on the War Path.
From the South.
I Will Arise with My Tomahawk.
Prayer of a Warrior (Assiniboine).
Song for a Fallen Warrior.
Song of Bekotsidi, The.
Taking of Life Brings Serious Thoughts, The.
War Song.
Warpath Song.
Very. Indian's Retort, The.
Warton, J. Dying Indian, The.
Welch, J. Christmas Comes to Moccasin Flat.
Harlem, Montana.
Man from Washington, The.
Plea to Those Who Matter.
Whitman, W. Now what my mother told me one day as we sat at dinner together.
Osceola.
Yonnondio.
Whittier. Metacom.
Willerton, Chris. Battle of Adobe Walls.
Wilson, R. Dry Rivers—Arizona.
Winnebago Oral Tradition. Felix White Sr.'s Introduction to Wakjankaga.
Woody. Girlfriends, The.
She-Who-Watches . . . The Names are Prayer.
Yépez, H. Del estilo de vida "poco común" de los indios cucapá citados por R. W. Haly Hardy, teniente Británico explorando el Golfo de California.

Life of a Cucapá Woman, The.
On the "Unusual" Lifestyle of the Cucapá Indians as Recorded by R. W. Hardy, British Lieutenant, While Exploring the Gulf of California.
Vida de una mujer cucapá, La.
Young Bear. Drive to Lone Ranger, A.
From the Spotted Night.
Song Taught to Joseph, The.
Zuni Oral Tradition. Dismissal of the Koyemshi.
Following their road of exit, they stooped over and came out.
House Blessing.
Indeed, the enemy.
Perhaps if we are lucky.
Sayatasha's Night Chant.

Nativity, The
Appleman, P. Matthew 1:18–25: Now the birth of Jesus Christ took place.
Chesterton. Joseph.
Coatsworth. Barn, The.
Coleridge, S. Christmas Carol, A: "Shepherds went their hasty way, The."
Craig, David. Hewn Hands.
Crashaw. In the Holy Nativity of Our Lord God.
Donne. Nativity [*or* Nativitie].
Glück. Nativity Poem.
Gryphius. To the Virgin Mary.
Hall, D. Carol, A.
Hall, J. For Christmas Day.
Heath-Stubbs. For the Nativity.
Hill, G. Picture of a Nativity.
Hughes, L. Shepherd's Song at Christmas.
Jonson, B. Carol.
Lee, L. Nativity.
Mendes, M. Christmas 1961.
Milton. On the Morning of Christ's Nativity.
Mohr, J. Silent Night.
Murray, L. Animal Nativity.
Nims, J. Christmas.
Pestel [*or* Pestell]. Psalm for Christmas Day.
Rilke. Three Holy Kings, The.
Rooney-Céspedes, A. Nativity.
Smart, C. Nativity of Our Lord and Saviour Jesus Christ, The.
Southwell. New Prince, New Pomp[e].
Thomas, G. Nativity Play, The.
Vaughan, H. Nativity, The.
Williams, W. Adoration of the Kings, The.
See also **Christmas**

Naturalists
Bentley, E. "Dinner-time?" said Gilbert White.
Heaney, S. Death of a Naturalist.
Seale, J. To a Late Local Environmentalist.

Nature
Ackerman, D. Beija-Flor.
Adams, L. Rounds and Garlands Done, The.
Addison, J. Ode: "Spacious firmament on high, The."
Addonizio. Alone in Your House.
Aguilar, M. Poem from Sierra Madre.
Akhmatova, A. Alone.
Alcman. All asleep: mountain peaks and chasms.
Fragment 58: Night and Sleep.
Alexander, C. All Things Bright and Beautiful.
Alexander, E. Washington Etude.
Alexander, P. Lightfall.
Marriage of Sorts, A.
Allen, H. In the Forest.
Ama Ata Aidoo. Gynae One.
Ammons. Arc Inside and Out, The.
Cut the Grass.
Gravelly Run.
Hymn: "I know if I find you I will have to leave the earth."
Motion's Holdings.
Strolls.
Terrain.
Widespread Implications.
Andrews, B. West West.
Angira. Symphony from the Balcony.
Apuleius, L. I who am Nature, mother of all.
Armstrong, J. I Study Rocks.

Arnold, M. In Harmony with Nature.
Ashbery, J. Rivers and Mountains.
These Lacustrine Cities.
Atwood. Landcrab II.
Auden. Fall of Rome, The.
Balaban. Daddy Out Hitch-Hiking at 3:30 A.M.
Heading Out West.
Bampfylde. Written at a Farm.
Basho. Banana tree, The.
From every direction.
How reluctantly.
How wild the sea is.
Lead my pony.
Morning glories, The.
Nothing in the cry.
This first fallen snow.
Warbler sings, The.
Whore and monk, we sleep.
With a warbler for.
Baudelaire. Correspondences.
Giantess, The.
Becker, R. Life Forms.
Bécquer, G. Nameless Spirit.
Bedregal. Poppies.
Bei Dao. Accomplices.
Belev. Lake.
Bell, M. Self and the Mulberry, The.
To Be.
Ben-Lev, D. Sensualist Speaks on Faith, A.
Bensko. Butterfly Net, The.
Benton, S. Second Coming, The.
Berk, İ. Never Did I See Such Loves Nor Such Separations.
Berrigan, A. Mercy Flight.
Berry, W. Enriching the Earth.
He goes free of the earth.
Independence Day.
Man Born to Farming, The.
1985 I.
Peace. Let men, who cannot be brothers.
Peace of Wild Things, The.
Bertolino. See Willow.
Bevington, L. Morning.
Bible, Apocrypha. Steel Usurps the Forests; Silence Dethrones Dialogue.
Biespiel, D. There Were No Deer in the Thicket.
Bingen, Hildegard von. I am the one whose praise.
Birney. From the Hazel Bough.
Bishop, E. Brazil, January 1, 1502.
Cold Spring, A.
North Haven.
Song for the Rainy Season.
Blake, E. J. Within and Without.
Blind. Red Sunsets, 1883, The.
Bloem, J. C. Dapper Street.
Place of Fire.
Bobrowski. Latvian Autumn, The.
Boccaccio. Two Dreams, The.
Bogan, L. Night: "Cold remote islands, The."
Boiardo. Canto de li Augei di Frunda in Frunda, Il.
Bolt, T. Glimpse of Terrain.
I crossed.
Meditation in Loudoun County.
Booth, P. How to See Deer.
Within.
Borden, W. Morning Chamber Orchestra Near Piney Crick, Wyoming, 7 A.M., The.
Borisova, M. Dry birch tree stood, The.
Borowski. Sun of Auschwitz, The.
Bowles, W. Languid, and sad, and slow.
To the River Wenbeck.
Bowman, C. Demographics.
Boyse. Triumphs of Nature, The.
Bracho, C. From Their Eyes Adorned With Vitreous Sands.
Braithwaite. City Garden, A.
Brannon, J. Evolution on 38th Street.
Breytenbach. There Is Life.
Bringhurst. Under the sunrise the mountains.
Brontë, E. Shall Earth no more inspire thee.
Stanzas: "Often rebuked, yet always back returning."
Tell me, tell me, smiling child.

Why do I hate that lone green dell?
Brooke, R.   Hill, The.
Brown, L.   Best Things in Life Are Free, The.
Brown, P.   Leaving.
Browne, W.   Happyer those times were, when the Flaxen clew.
Browning, R.   Pippa's Song.
Brownstein.   Oracle night / the porch is frozen.
Bruchac.   Birdfoot's Grampa.
  Prayer: "Let my words."
  Spring Peepers.
Bryant, W.   Fountain, The.
  Oh [or O] Fairest of the Rural Maids.
  Thanatopsis.
Buckmaster.   Wilpena Pound.
Bunina.   From the Seashore.
Burns, R.   My Heart's in the Highlands.
  To a Mouse; On Turning Her up in Her Nest, with the Plough, November, 1785.
Busia, A.   Mawu of the Waters.
Buson.   Listening to the moon.
Byron, G.   Cornelian, The.
  Lake Leman.
Caldwell, K.   Moonlight.
Camlan.   Education in Wales.
Campbell, D.   Man in the Honeysuckle, The.
Campion, T.   I Care Not for These Ladies.
Carew, T.   Spring, The: "Now that the Winter's gone, the earth hath lost."
Carman, B.   Vestigia.
Carroll, J.   Styro.
  Withdrawal Letter.
Carver, R.   This Morning.
Cary, A.   Contradiction.
Castellanos.   Destiny.
Castro, R.   Atmosphere Is Incandescent, The.
  Candescent Lies the Air.
  Feet of Spring Are on the Stair, The.
  Glowworm Scatters Flashes, A.
  They Say that the Plants Do Not Speak.
Causley.   I Am the Song.
Cavendish, M.   Dialogue betwixt Man, and Nature, A.
  Dissert, A.
  Landscape, A.
  Posset for Nature's Breakfast, A.
Césaire, A.   Day and Night.
  Do Not Have Pity.
  Sun Serpent.
Chang Chi.   Maple Bridge Night Mooring.
Chang Chiu-ling.   I close my door and trace the transformations of nature.
Channing.   Then spoke the Spirit of the Earth.
Chazal, M.   Bicycle rolls on the road, A.
Chedid, A.   Imagine.
Ch'en Tzu-ang.   I dwell in the forest nursing a long illness.
Ch'in Kuan.   Tune: "Happiness Approaches".
  Tune: "Sand of Silk-Washing Brook".
  Tune: "Spring in the Painted Hall".
Chipasula.   Double Song.
Cho Chihun.   As I Play the Flute.
Chŏng Ch'ŏl.   Little Odes on Mount Star.
Christopher.   Midsummer.
Chuang Tzu.   Breath of Nature, The.
  Man Is Born in Tao.
Chubb, R.   Song of My Soul.
  Transfiguration.
Clare, J.   God Looks on Nature With a Glorious Eye.
  July: "Loud is the Summer's busy song."
  Last of April, The.
  Maple Tree, The.
  Nutting.
  Shadows.
  Shepherd's Tree, The.
  To an Angry Bee.
  Winter.
  Woodland Seat, A.
  Wren, The.
  Wryneck's Nest, The.
Clark, T.   Our boat touches the bank.
  Sit for a while on a stone.
Clarke, G.   1.5.
Clementelli.   I'd Like to Try Telling You of Spring.

Clerk.   Country Seat, The.
Clifton, L.   Earth Is a Living Thing, The.
Coatsworth.   Swift Things Are Beautiful.
Cobbing.   Bird Bee.
Cogswell, Fred.   Beach at Noon, The.
Cole, T.   Painter, A.
Coleridge, H.   All nature ministers to Hope. The snow.
Coleridge, M.   No Newspapers.
Coleridge, S. T.   Frost at Midnight [1798 version].
  Frost at Midnight [1829 version].
  This Lime-Tree Bower My Prison.
  To Nature.
  Work without Hope.
Coleridge, S.   Garden Year, The.
Collins, M.   Warmer.
Cooke, R.   Captive.
  R. W. Emerson.
Coolbrith.   Longing.
Cooper, W.   Pollen.
Cordeiro, James.   Monsoon Song.
Corn.   Water: City Wildlife and Greenery.
Cotton, C.   Chatsworth.
Couzyn.   Spell for Birth.
Cowper, W.   Just when our drawing-rooms begin to blaze.
  Landscape Described, A.
Craig, David.   Francis Helps a Brother Who Is in Sin.
  John Says Mass on All Souls' Day.
Cranch.   Correspondences.
Creeley.   Messengers, The.
Cristall.   Holbain.
  Noon. Lysander.
  Ode, An: "Almighty Power! who rul'st this world of storms!"
  Song on Leaving the Country Early in the Spring.
  Written in Devonshire, Near the Dart.
Croly.   Domestic Love.
Cronin, A.   Trembling with engines, gulping oil, the river.
Cruickshank, H.   Ponnage Pool, The.
Crunk, T.   Reunion.
  Visiting the Site of One of the First Churches My Grandfather Pastored.
Cummings, E. E.   I Thank You God.
  O sweet spontaneous.
  Wherelings whenlings / (daughters of if but offspring of hopefear).
Curtis, T.   Spirit of the Place, The.
Dahlberg.   February Ground.
Daio.   I have had a companion on the road.
Darío, R.   It Was a Gentle Air.
  Springtime.
  Tropical Afternoon.
Darwin.   Kew.
Davidson, L.   America.
Davis, W.   Snow.
de Burgos.   Sea and You, The.
de Fierro.   Grain of Sand.
De la Mare.   All That's Past.
De León, L.   Life Withdrawn, The.
DeSylva, B. G.   Best Things in Life Are Free, The.
Dewdney.   August a haze amniotic our dream aether and lens of distance. Tree sentinels in.
  She is liquid darkness occult with desire.
Di Piero.   Why not violate sense and say.
Dickinson, E.   Bring me the sunset in a cup.
  Earth has many keys, The.
  Further in Summer than the Birds.
  I had been hungry, all the Years.
  I Taste a Liquor Never Brewed.
  Nature—sometimes sears a Sapling.
  Sky is low—the Clouds are mean, The.
  Snake, The.
  This Is My Letter to the World.
  Trees like Tassels—hit—and swung, The.
Dillard, A.   Thanksgiving—Christmas 3.
DiPrima, C.   Her Eyes a Thousand Times Over.
Dodd, E.   Dieback.
Domanski.   Banns.
Doolittle, H.   Are these ashes in my hand.
  Moon in Your Hands, The.

White World.
Douskey.   Dog Days and Delta Nights.
Dovaston, J. F. M.   Streamlet! methinks thy lot resembles mine.
Dove, R.   Fish in the Stone, The.
Dowden, E.   Two Infinities.
Drake, J.   Bronx.
Drinkwater.   Reciprocity.
Drummond, W.   Book, The.
Duck.   On Richmond Park.
Dudek.   At Lac en Coeur.
Dufault.   Burden.
Duffy, C.   Plainsong.
Duggan, L.   Five. One.
  One. One.
Dunn, C.   Margaret/Haskell Indian School.
Dunn, D.   Gardeners.
Dunn, S.   Landscape at the End of the Century.
Dupin.   From a thread in space, endless and unbroken. Without unravelling.
Dybek.   Benediction.
  Mowing.
Dyer, J.   Grongar Hill.
Dyer, S.   Lowest trees have top[p]s, the ant[e] her gall, The.
Eberhart, R.   Centennial For Whitman.
  Hard Structure of the World, The.
  On a Squirrel Crossing the Road in Autumn, in New England.
  Spider, The.
Eguren.   Peregrin, Wandering Hunter of Faces.
Eich.   End of a Summer, The.
Eichner, Maura.   Back Porch Fundamentalist.
Eigner.   Environs.
Elman.   October Observed, Hudson Falls, New York in Bill's Back Yard.
Éluard, P.   Nature Was Caught in the Nets of Your Life.
Elytis, O.   Origin of Landscape or the End of Mercy, The.
  Sun the First.
Emerson, R.   Awed I behold once more.
  Blight.
  Circles.
  Dear Brother, Would You Know the Life.
  Each and All.
  Experience.
  Musketaquid.
  Nature [1836].
  Nature [1844].
  Problem, The.
  Song of Nature.
  Waldeinsamkeit.
  Xenophanes.
Everson, W.   Stone Face Falls.
Fagan.   Weather They Were Written In, The.
Fallon, P.   Spring Song.
Farid-uddin Attar.   Invocation to the Conference of the Birds.
Fenollosa, M.   Miyoko San.
Fenton, J.   Kingfisher's Boxing Gloves, The.
Ferril.   Something Starting Over.
Ficke.   Sonnet: "There are strange shadows fostered of the moon."
Finch, B.   Written in a Shrubbery Towards the Decline of Autumn.
  Written in a Winter's Morning.
Finch, P.   Man in the Fields.
Fletcher, J.   Blue Symphony.
  Green Symphony.
Forché.   Ancapagari.
  Kalaloch.
  Skin Canoes.
Foster, A.   Union.
Foy, J.   Autopsy.
Freisinger.   Walt Whitman at Timber Creek.
Freneau.   On the Religion of Nature.
  On the Uniformity and Perfection of Nature.
Frost, C.   Sin: "Tree bore the efflorescence of October apples, The."
Frost, R.   Design.
  Directive.
  Lucretius versus the Lake Poets.
Fuller, M.   Sistrum.
Galvin, B.   Bullfrog.
Galvin, J.   Nature, Beside Herself.

García Lorca.   Questions: "Parliament of grasshoppers is in the field, A."
Gardelle, C.   Air.
Rain.
Garren, Christine.   Figure and Ground.
Gensei.   Distant View from a Grass Hill.
Evening View from Grass Hill.
Georgiev, Marin.   Native Soil.
Gibson, M.   One Body.
Gidlow.   Creed for Free Women, A.
Giles, J.   Leasowes: Or, A Poetical Description of the Late Mr. Shenstone's Rural Retirement, The.
Gillan.   In New Jersey Once.
Ginsberg, A.   Easter Sunday.
Wales Visitation.
Gioia.   Los Angeles after the Rain.
Gladding.   Worsted Heather.
Glazer, J.   Final Disposition.
Goethe.   May Song.
Meeting, the Departure, The.
Nature and Art.
Goetsch, D.   Smell and Envy.
Goldbarth.   Life Is Happy.
Goodtimes.   Jojopan.
Graves, R.   Love Story, A.
Return of the Goddess [Artemis].
She Tells Her Love While Half Asleep.
To Juan at the Winter Solstice.
Gray, A.   Music in the Meadow.
Greenwell, D.   Scherzo, A.
Gregg.   Dark Thing Inside the Day, A.
Flower No More Than Itself, A.
Precision, The.
Grennan.   Facts of Life, Ballymoney.
Shoreline After Storm.
Sunday Morning Through Binoculars.
Greville, F.   Chorus Sacerdotum.
Griffith, L.   Office Window.
Grigson.   Landscape Gardeners, The.
Gudo.   It's not nature that upholds utility.
Guest, B.   Nebraska.
Sassafras.
Guidacci.   Tiny dew reinvigorates the tiny grass, The.
Guillén, J.   Nature Alive.
Guiney.   Down Stream.
Gunn, T.   Last Man, The.
Habington.   To Castara, upon an Embrace.
Hadas, R.   Easter Afternoon.
Haines, J.   Roadside Weeds.
Yeti.
Haley, M.   Tropicalia.
Han-shan.   Cold Mountain Path, The.
People ask the way to Cold Mountain.
Someone sits in a mountain gorge.
Storied cliffs were the fortune I cast.
Han-shan Te-ch'ing.   I let mind and body go and gained a life of freedom.
Hardy, T.   Nature's Questioning.
Harris, R.   Literary Excellence.
Harry, J.   Walking, when the Lake of the Air is Blue with Spring.
Hart-Smith.   Nullarbor.
Harter.   Tulip.
Hartnett.   For My Grandmother, Bridget Halpin.
Hartwig.   Above Us.
Harvey, James Clarence.   At Eventide.
Harwood, G.   Carnal Knowledge 2.
Clair de Lune.
Hass, R.   After I Seized the Pentagon.
Letter to a Poet.
Measure.
Healy, R.   Primula veris.
Heaney, S.   Anahorish.
Heine, H.   Pine Is Standing Lonely, A.
Hejinian.   Nights.
Hemans.   Indian Woman's Death-Song, The.
Meeting of the Bards, The. Written for an Eisteddford, or Meeting of Welsh Bards, Held in London, 22 May 1822.
Remembrance of Nature.
Henderson, R.   Best Things in Life Are Free, The.
Hernández Cruz.   Poem: "Your head it waves outside."

Herrera y Reissig.   Grey Dawn.
Herrick.   Art above Nature, to Julia.
To Find[e] God.
Hesketh.   Death of a Gardener.
Hewitt, J.   Because I Paced My Thought.
Ram's Horn, The.
Substance and Shadow.
Heynen.   I Think That I Shall Never See.
Hikmet.   Letters from a Man in Solitary.
Things I Didn't Know I Loved.
Hildebrandt, Z.   In Hecate's Garden.
Hill, M.   Abomination.
Ruth.
Hill, R.   To Rose.
Waning August Moon.
Hine.   Northwest Passages.
Hinsey, E.   On the Uncountable Nature of Things.
Hofmannsthal.   Traveller's Song.
Hogan, L.   Bear Fat.
Map.
Hogg, J.   Kilmeny.
Hölderlin.   Half of Life, The.
Halflife.
Pleasant to wander.
Hollander, J.   Old-Fashioned Song, An.
Variations on a Fragment by Trumbull Stickney.
Hollander, V.   Rosh Chodesh Tisheri.
Holloway, G.   Indian Rope Trick.
Holm, B.   Blizzard.
Holmes, O.   Living Temple, The.
Hood, T.   I Remember, I Remember.
Hooper, P.   Listening to Mozart at Meadow Brook.
Hopes.   And Job from his mountain sees.
Under the Drumlin.
Hopkins, G.   Epithalamion: "Hark, hearer, hear what I do; lend a thought now, make believe."
God's Grandeur.
Inversnaid.
Pied Beauty.
That Nature Is a Heraclitean Fire and of the Comfort of the Resurrection.
Howe, S.   Elegiac western Imagination.
Hsiao Kang.   Pheasant on His Morning Flight, A.
Hsieh Ling-yün.   Crossing the Mountain, I Follow the Chin-chu River.
From Chin-Chu Creek, Past the Ridge, Along the Stream.
On Climbing the Highest Peak of Stone Gate Mountain.
On My Way from South Mountain to North Mountain, I Glance at the Scenery from the Lake.
On Spending Some Time at the Bai'an Pavilion.
Visiting Pai-an Pavilion.
What I Saw When I Had Crossed the Lake.
Hsieh T'iao.   To Hsuan-Ch'eng, Past Hsin-Lin-P'u, Toward Pan-Ch'iao.
Hsin Ch'i-chi.   Tune: "The Dark Clouds of Ch'u" Visiting the Rainy Crag Alone.
Hsu Hsuan.   Lu-lung Village, Autumn.
Hsüeh T'ao [or Xue Tao].   Crabapple Brook.
Lotus-Gathering Boat.
Wind.
Hudgins.   Consider.
Persistence of Nature in Our Lives, The.
Hughes, T.   Gog.
October Robin, An.
Roe-Deer.
Thrushes.
Huidobro.   New Song.
Hunt, L.   To Hampstead ("Sweet upland, to whose walks, with fond repair.").
Ibáñez, S.   You, for My Meditation.
Ignatova, E.   I have encountered a valley, in ragged bast matting.
Ikkyu Sojun.   After ten years in the red-light district.
Ten years of whorehouse joy I'm alone now in the mountains.
Irwin, M.   Give.
Issa.   New Year's Day.
Jackson, H.   My House Not Made with Hands.
Jacob, M.   In Honor of the Sardana and the

Tenora.
Jacobs, J.   Nearing Long Moons.
Snakeroot.
Jacobsen, J.   Hourglass.
Jacobsen, R.   Green Light.
Jaimes Freyre.   Sad Voices, The.
Jakushitsu.   Refreshing, the wind against the waterfall.
Jandl, E.   At the Delicatessen Shop.
Jeffers, R.   Boats in a Fog.
Noon.
Place for No Story, The.
Jewett, S.   At Home from Church.
Jiménez, J.   Countryside Sleeps, Trembling, The.
Definitve Journey, The.
Yes, If I Could Only Smash.
Jinkag Haesim.   Sitting and Teaching at Night.
Johnson, M. F.   Second Evening.
Johnston, E.   Address to Nature on its Cruelty, An.
Juan Chi.   Hibiscus grows lushly on the grave mounds, The.
Lucent dew congeals into frost, The.
Juana Inés de la Cruz.   Verses Expressing the Feelings of a Lover.
Katz, J.   Taxonomy.
Kavanagh, P.   Canal Bank Walk.
Kearney, M.   Nature Poetry.
Keats.   In [a] Drear-nighted December.
To Some Ladies.
Keelan, C.   End is an Animal, The.
Keithley.   Small Moon on the Shoulder of New York.
Kekova.   Sky is covered with stars, like a body with sores, The.
Keller, D.   Melancholy.
Kelly, B.   To the Lost Child.
Kemble.   Sonnet: "If there were any power in human love."
Kenjeev.   You envied the flying birds and stones.
Kennedy, X.   Landscapes with Set-Screws.
Khlebnikov, V.   Four Poems.
Hey...y! Uh...hm!, covered with sweat.
Kim Yŏng.   Snowflakes flutter—butterflies chase flowers.
Kinnell.   Under the Williamsburg Bridge.
Kinzie.   Want, predation, sleep.
Klappert.   In Memory of H. F.
Klugman, S.   God's Body.
Knight, R.   Landscape, The.
Kooser.   Interchange.
Kopland.   Thanks to the Things.
Koster, E. B.   Shoal of Silver Angelfish, A.
Kruchyonykh [or Kruchionykh or Kruchenykh].   Sahara to America, The.
Kuo P'o.   Kingfishers sport among orchids and begonias.
Poem on the Wandering Immortal.
Kupriyanov [or Kuprianov].   Lesson in Natural History, A.
Kwŏn P'il.   Alone at Night.
Kyle, C. J.   Argument, The.
Season of Locking-In, The.
Lady of the Assembly.   Assembly of Ladies, The.
Lamantia.   Voice of Earth Mediums.
Lamartine.   Lake, The.
Valley, The.
Lamb, C.   O! I Could Laugh to Hear the Midnight Wind.
Landor, W.   I Strove With None.
Lange, A.   Sonnet for the Season.
Lanier, E.   Yet you (great lady) mistress of that place.
Lanier, S.   To Bayard Taylor.
Lanyer.   Yet you (great lady) mistress of that place.
Lao Tzu.   Valley spirit never dies, The.
Lars.   Sketch of the Frontier Woman.
Lasker-Schüler.   Only for You.
Lauterbach.   Stones (Istanbul, Robert Smithson).
Lawrence, D. H.   Elemental.
Self-Protection.
Wild Common, The.
Lazarus, E.   South, The.

Le Sueur. Behold This and Always Love It.
Leapor. On Winter.
Leithauser. In a Japanese Moss Garden.
Leopardi. Infinite, The.
Levertov. Gathered at the River.
Living.
Reminder, The.
Lewis, J. For the Father of Sandro Gulotta.
Reader, The.
Li Ho. Chang'gu: A Poem Written on the
Twenty-Seventh Day of the Fifth Month.
Grave of Little Su, The.
Ravine on a Cold Evening.
Li Po. My sword at my waist, I climb a high
tower.
Poem by the Bridge at Ten-shin.
Poem Composed at the Command of the
Emperor.
Rhymeprose on the Sword Gallery.
Li Shang-yin. Without Title (2).
Lindley, D. Cromwell: The Last Portrait.
Liu Pang. Song of the Great Wind.
Liu, T. Poem: "Late butterflies gliding through
the air."
Liu Yu Hsi. Tune: "Memories of the South".
Llwyd, R. Beaumaris Bay.
Lo Pin-Wang. Mooring by Jiangzhen in the
Evening.
On the Cicada: In Prison.
Lodge, G. Pastoral: "Slopes of the sun and vine,
and thou dark stream."
Long, H. Cobweb.
Longfellow, H. Aftermath.
By the shores of Gitche[e] Gumee.
Nature.
Snow-Flakes.
Spirit of Poetry, The.
Longley, M. Ash Keys.
Frozen Rain.
Lönnrot. It is my desire, it is my wish.
Lopez, L. Abiquiu.
Lorde. Echo.
Lothamer. October Falls in Black and White.
Loynaz, D. M. Snow.
Lu Chi. Summoning the Recluse.
Lucretius. Darling of Gods and Men, beneath
the gliding stars.
Lugones. Indulgence.
Rain Psalm.
Lydgate. Complaint of the Black Knight, The.
MacCaig. Basking Shark.
Feeding Ducks.
MacDonald, A. Month of plants and of honey.
Machado Ruiz. Who Placed, Amidst the Tracts
of Ash.
Mackey, N. Kiche Manitou.
MacNeice. Evening in Connecticut.
House on a Cliff.
Western Landscape.
Madge. Solar Creation.
Mao Tse-tung [or Mao Zedong]. Glitter of a
northern kingdom.
Mapanje. Visiting Zomba Plateau.
Marlowe. Passionate Shepherd to His Love,
The.
Marsman. Memory of Holland.
Martí. Opposite of Ornate and Rhetorical
Poetry, The.
Martinaitis, M. Kukutis's Swallow's Hymn.
Silly Spring.
Unhappy Kukutis in the Potato Patch.
Martinson. Creation Night.
Marvell. Mower Against Gardens, The.
Masaoka Shiki. Glass door.
Mashinskaya, I. Newspapers on the Plateau.
Mason, W. Alcander's Flower Garden.
Some Early Gardenists.
Mazur. Common, The.
McDonald, W. Hauling Over Wolf Creek Pass
in Winter.
McGrath, C. First Trimester, The.
Florida.
McGrath, T. Return, The.
McKay, D. 3. The Base.
McPherson, S. Wings and Seeds: For My Birth
Mother.

Mead, P. Melbourne or the Bush.
Meireles. Sketch.
Melville, H. Attic Landscape, The.
Haglets, The.
Little Good Fellows, The.
Malvern Hill.
Pontoosuce.
Meng Hao Jan. Passing Seven-League Rapids.
Seeking out Master Chan on Incense Mountain.
Meredith, G. Dirge in Woods.
Love in the Valley.
Merrick, A. Hartwell Gardens.
Merrill, J. Syrinx.
Messerli. Scared Cows.
This That and Then.
Mew. In the Fields.
Millay, E. God's World.
Journey: "Ah, could I lay me down in this long
grass."
Miller, J. Rise of the Afternoon is a Wide
Glory, The.
Milosz, C. Slow River.
Minhinnick. Sap.
Mistral, G. Empty Walnut, The.
Pious One, The.
Mitchell, A. Nature Poem.
Mitchell, R. North.
Mitford. Forget-Me-Not, The.
Mole, J. Musical Monkey, The.
Molinari. Ode to a Long Sorrow.
Momaday. Headwaters.
Montale. Eel, The.
Sit the noon out, pale and lost in thought.
"Monty Python.". All Things dull and Ugly.
Morgan, R. Shadow Valley.
Morgenstern. Blueprint for Disaster.
Morley, H. Curve of the Water.
Moro, C. Battle at the Edge of the Falls.
Morris, S. Here in these fretted caverns whence
the sea.
Salt sprays deluge it, wild waves buffet it,
hurricanes rave.
Morris, W. Love Is Enough.
Moss, H. New Hampshire.
Moxon. Loud midnight-soothing melancholy
bird.
Mphande. Wood-Cutter, The.
Murphy, P. Manifesto.
Murray, P. Returning Spring.
Muso Soseki. Incomparable-Verse Valley.
My thatched hut.
On the blue waves.
Nashe [or Nash]. Spring, the Sweet Spring.
Neckar, Ninon. On the Road.
Nelson, H. Peepers.
Nelson, J. If You Knew September.
Nemerov. Dependencies, The.
Holding the Mirror Up to Nature.
Salt Garden, The.
Neruda. Dead Gallop.
From the explosion to the iron split.
Introduction: My Themes.
Sonnet 4.
Nesbit, E. Great Industrial Centre, A.
Newman, A. Darwin's Unfinished Notes to
Emma.
Fall under. To succumb to; come under an
influence or power.
Newman, J. Elements, The.
Nezval. Trap Door.
Ní Chuilleanáin. Pygmalion's Image.
Niatum. Rufous Hummingbird.
Stones Speak of an Earthless Sky.
Nicholson, N. Five Minutes.
Niedecker. Element Mother, The.
Paean to Place.
War.
Nietzsche. Against the Laws.
Nijhoff. At a Grave.
Norris, L. Stone and Fern.
North, C. Note to Tony Towle (After WS), A.
North, M. Pinder.
Shap.
Oakes-Smith, E. 'Tis the summer prime, when
the noiseless air.
Oden. Review from Staten Island.

Olds, S. Ecstasy.
Oliver, M. Design.
In Blackwater Woods.
Landscape.
Skunk Cabbage.
Snapshots.
Some Questions You Might Ask.
Wild Geese: "You do not have to be good."
Wings.
Opie. Ode to Borrowdale in Cumberland.
On the Approach of Autumn.
To Winter.
Oquendo de Amat, C. Poem of the Sea and of
Her.
Ormsby, F. Soldier Bathing.
Ortiz. Earth and Rain, the Plants & Sun.
Vision Shadows.
Ossip, K. Nature of Things, The.
O'Sullivan, M. Giant Yellow.
Hill Figures.
Osundare. Excursion.
Goree.
Our Earth Will Not Die.
We called the statue.
Who Says That Drought Was Here?
Ou-yang Hsiu. Old Fisherman.
Pear Leaves Redden, Cicada's Song is Done,
The.
Ovid. Golden Age, The.
Owen, W. From My Diary, July 1914.
Pacheco, J. On the Fragile Labyrinth.
Pack, R. It Would Have Been Enough.
Mountain Ash without Cedar Waxwings.
Parker, A. Alchemy.
Patchen. Deer and the Snake, The.
Like a Mourningless Child.
Pastoral: "Dove walks with sticky feet, The."
Paz. Pause.
Wind and Water and Stone.
Peacocke. Remembrance.
Peck, J. Woods Burial.
Peele. Song: "Whenas [or When as] the Rye [or
Rie] reach to the chin."
Peirce. Riddles: "He opens her. She can't have
him."
Perry, S. Toadfish.
Peterson, J. Stand Still.
Petrarch. Sonnet: "When she walks by here."
Pfeiffer, E. If we be fools of chance, indeed,
and tend.
O Nature! thou whom I have thought to love.
To a Moth that Drinketh of the Ripe October.
Philips, K. To Mr. Henry Lawes.
Philpot, T. Wildlife.
Piatt, S. In A Queen's Domain.
Pickard, T. Bush Telegram.
Piercy. Development, The.
Postcard from the Garden.
Pierpont, J. In what rich harmony, what
polished lays.
Po Chü-i. Planting Flowers on the Eastern
Embankment.
Tune: "Memories of the South".
Poe. Stanzas: "How often we forget all time,
when lone."
Valley of Unrest, The.
Ponge. Prairie, The.
Popa. Burning Shewolf.
Pope, A. Epistle to Lord Burlington.
Intended for Sir Isaac Newton.
Of all the causes which conspire to blind.
Porta. Traveler.
Porteous. I Envy the Cracked, Black Basalt.
Porter, P. Australian Garden, An.
Quevedo y Villegas. Happy and Contented in
Your Hut.
Radcliffe, A. Sonnet: "Now the bat circles on
the breeze of eve."
To the Bat.
Ragan, J. Standing at Pasternak's Table,
Peredelkino.
Raine, K. Angelus.
Good Friday.
Heirloom.
Ramsey, J. Comet and Treefrog.
Randell. And if my light should.

Hedge breaks out in bud, The.
Walking towards the village.
Rankin, J. Old Circles.
Raworth. Out of a Sudden.
Ray, H. At Nature's Shrine.
Instability.
Nature's Minor Chords.
Nature's Uplifting.
Reed, H. Naming of Parts.
Reese, L. Crows.
Revard. Christmas Shopping.
October, Isle of Skye.
Reverdy. Air: "Forgetting."
Rexford. Joy: "It's joy to be up in the morning
when the dew's on the grass and clover."
Rexroth, K. Floating.
On Flower Wreath Hill.
Reyes, A. Tarahumara Herbs.
Reznikoff. Grove of small trees, branches thick
with berries, A.
Riley, J. Travel Notes.
Rilke. I Find You.
I Find You, Lord, All Things and In All.
I Have Faith.
Just as The Watchman.
Roberson, E. Blue Horses.
Roberts, E. Disconsolate Morning.
Roberts, S. Autochthon.
Robinson, E. Poem for Max Nordau, A.
Torrent, The.
Roethke. Far Field, The.
Field of Light, A.
Minimal, The.
Otto.
Rose, The.
Shape of the Fire, The.
Thing, The.
Visitant, The.
Walk in Late Summer, A.
Rogers, P. Before the Beginning: Maybe God
and a Silk Flower Concubine Perhaps.
Into the Light.
Kingdom of Heaven, The.
Opus from Space.
Rohrer, M. Hunger of the Lemur, The.
Rossetti, C. Cobwebs.
Frisky Lamb, A.
Who Has Seen the Wind?
Rossi, T. System.
Rothman, D. One of the Lords of Life.
Rumi. In this river the heart is like a ruined
waterwheel; in whichever direction it turns,
there is water before it.
Ryan, R. Lake of the Woods, The.
Sachs, N. Someone Will Take The Ball.
World, Do Not Ask Those Snatched from Death.
Sackville-West. Land, The.
Sadoff. Against Whitman.
Saïd, A. And We Were Born.
St. John, P. Carnival.
Saner. This Grizzly.
Savageau. All Night She Dreams.
Trees.
Scarbrough, G. Eastward in Eastanalle.
Schuyler, J. Father or Son.
Schwartz, L. Leaves.
Scott, S. Proud Maisie.
Sedakova. Grasshopper and the Cricket, The.
Seed. This Curious Involvement, a Dominant
Species.
Seidman. Making of Color, The.
Seward. By Derwent's Rapid Stream.
Eyam.
Shakespeare, W. Sonnet 98: "From you have I
been absent in the spring."
Shapiro, D. Commentary Text Commentary
Text Commentary Text.
Shapiro, K. Travelogue for Exiles.
Shauqi. Andalusian Exile, An.
Shaw, A. Bird Nests.
Small Pleasures.
Shelley, P. Love's Philosophy.
Mont Blanc.
To a Skylark.
To Jane: The Invitation.
Shen Chou. Written on a Landscape Painting in

an Album.
Shen Yüeh. Listening to Gibbons at Rock-Pool
Creek.
Shepherd, R. Another Version of an Ocean.
Shillaber, B. Sagamore, The.
"Shu Ting.". Gifts.
Shumaker. Ajo Lily.
Siegel, J. How the Tortoise Knew It Was Her
Time.
Silko. When Sun Came to Riverwoman.
Simms, C. Grey Wagtail on the Tyne.
Pallid Harrier.
Sirr. Collector's Marginalia, The.
Skinner, J. City Out of the Boy, The.
Skloot. Closer to Home.
Slessor. South Country.
Smart, C. On a Bed of Guernsey Lilies.
Smelcer. Bonanza Creek.
Smith, C. Early worshipper at Nature's shrine,
An.
I once was happy, when while yet a child.
To the South Downs.
Walk by the Water, A.
Written at Bignor Park in Sussex, in August,
1799.
Smith, Douglas Burnet. Walk After Rain.
Smith, I. Contrasts.
Smith, S. Away, Melancholy.
Lady "Rogue" Singleton.
Pretty.
Smollett. To Leven Water.
Snyder, G. Burning Island.
Gaia.
Milton by Firelight.
Night Song of the Los Angeles Basin.
Old Woman Nature.
Piute Creek.
Södergran. Homecoming.
"There is no one . . .".
Sŏng Hon. Mountain is silent, The.
Song Sun. Ten Years It Took.
Soto. Elements of San Joaquin, The.
Southwell. Vale of Tear[e]s, A.
Spenser, E. Then since within this wide great
Universe.
Stafford, W. How to Regain Your Soul.
Stainer. Seals, The.
Standing. Mouvance.
Stevens, W. Anecdote of the Jar.
Room on a Garden, A.
Stewart, P. Estes' Backyard, The.
Stickney, T. Athenian Garden, An.
In Ampezzo ("Only once more and not again—
the larches.").
Lakeward.
Storni. Camp Fire.
World is Bitter, The.
Su Tung-p'o. On a Painting by Wang the Clerk
of Yen Ling.
Tune: "Butterflies Lingering over Flowers".
Tune: "Calming Windswept Waves".
Tune: "Partridge Sky".
Suárez, V. Florida, La.
Sun Ch'o. Orchid Pavilion.
Swann, B. Old Song of the Musk Ox People.
Swann, R. EFT.
Sylvester, J. Cunning Painter, that with curious
care, The.
Synge. Prelude: "Still south I went and west
and south again."
Sze. Apache Plume.
Before Completion.
Great White Shark, The.
String Diamond, The.
Szporluk. Axiom of Maria.
Szymborska, W. View with a Grain of Sand.
Taggard. Bounding Line.
Fructus.
Hymn to Yellow.
Thirst.
Talvikki, A. Along the road, the bright painted
crosses.
At night, coolness like water lapping.
Before first light, we would open the nets.
Halley's Comet crossed the jungle sky.
Teatro Amazonas, remnant, The.

Waking, months after I leave the jungle.
T'ao Ch'ien [or T'ao Yuan-ming]. Returning to
Fields and Gardens (1) ("When I was young, I
did not fit in.").
T'ao Hung Ching. Poem Written in Answer to
His Majesty's Question: "What Is There in the
Mountains?".
Taylor, A. Earth.
Teasdale. There Will Come Soft Rains.
Tennyson, A. Check every outflash, every ruder
sally.
Flower in the Crannied Wall.
That which we dare invoke to bless.
Thy voice is on the rolling air.
Today the grave is bright for me.
Wish, that of the living whole, The.
Witch-elms that counterchange the floor.
Thomas, D. This Bread I Break.
Thomas, R. S. Line from St. David's, A.
Thoreau. Low-anchored cloud.
Poet's Delay, The.
Winter and Spring Scene, A.
Thorne, T. High Country.
Tighe. Written at the Eagle's Nest, Killarney.
July 26, 1800.
Written in Autumn.
Todd, M. Game Trail, The.
Todd, R. Of Moulds and Mushrooms.
Todhunter. Moment, A.
Tomlinson, C. John Maydew or The Allotment.
Toomer. Nullo.
Storm Ending.
Torrance. Acrospirical Meanderings in a
Tongue of the Time.
It Is Difficult to Exaggerate the Importance of
Mushrooms as Food.
Trask, H. Sisters.
Trommer, R. March.
Ts'ao Ts'ao. Variant on the Songs of the East
and West Gates.
View of the Blue Sea.
Tso Ssu. Summoning the Recluse.
Tu Fu [or Du Fu]. At the Sky's End, Thinking
of Li Po.
Clear After Rain ("Autumn, cloud blades on the
horizon.").
Six Choruses.
South Wind.
Standing Alone.
Sunset ("Sunset glitters on the beads.").
Wu-Chuen.
Tuckerman, F. How Oft in Schoolboy Days.
Series 2, Sonnet 18.
Series 2, Sonnet 30.
Series 3, Sonnet 4.
Turner, C. Prisoner, The.
Ungar. Groundhog Day.
Ungaretti. You Were Broken.
Unknown. Holy Goddess Tellus.
Incantations of Modoc Conjurers.
May the wind blows sweetness.
Mayden in the moor lay—.
New View of Sunday Cycling, A.
Richmond Gardens: A Poem.
Rise and Progress of the Present Taste in
Planning Parks, Pleasure Grounds, Gardens,
etc, The.
Song of Blodeuwedd, The.
Song to the Trees and Streams.
Songs and Chants.
Southern Paiute Poetry.
Sumer Is Icumen [or Ycomen] In.
WHEN, lo, by break of morning.
Wild Man Comes to the Monastery, The.
Van Duyn. View, A.
Vaughan, H. Love and Discipline.
Regeneration.
Verlaine. Moonlight.
White Moonglow, The.
Verwey, A. North-Sea, The.
Very. Nature ("Bubbling brook doth leap when
I come by, The.").
Silent, The.
Song, The.
Villa, E. Natus de Muliere, Brevi Vivens.
Voigt. Nocturne.

Volkman. There comes a time to rusticate the numbers. The way the birds, jug.

Wagoner, D. Chorus: "That rain-strewn night in the woods, the chorus, chorus."

Five Dawn Skies in November.

Making Camp ("When their eyes opened, it was more than morning.").

Making Camp ("You've found the place in time—no permanent shade.").

Source, The.

Waller, E. On St. James's Park, as Lately Improved by His Majesty.

Wang Chih-huan. Climbing the Stork Pavilion.

Wang Fan-chih. I have a couple acres of land.

Wang Hsi-chih. Orchid Pavilion.

Wang Shih-chieng. Pure Sound Pavilion.

Wang Wei. Bird-Singing Stream.

Climbing Pien-chueh Temple.

Deer Enclosure.

Deer Park.

Four Examples from the Poems of River Wang Deer Enclosure.

Hsin-I Village.

Passing Hidden Fragrance Temple.

Spring Night at Bamboo Pavillion, Presenting a Poem to Subprefect Qian about His Staying for Good in Blue Field Mountains.

Warton, T. While summer-suns o'er the gay prospect played.

Wat. From "Songs of a Wanderer".

Watkins, V. Music of Colours—White Blossom.

Replica, The.

Watts, I. Flying Fowl, and Creeping Things, Praise Ye the Lord.

Wei Ying-wu. East of the Town.

Weismiller. Vermont: Spring Rains.

Wellman, M. Mad Wolf in Lunar Web, Mad Crow on the Beach.

Two hollow eyes follow a cat's crie.

Wen T'ing-yün. News So Seldom Comes.

Tune: "Beautiful Barbarians".

Wen Yi-tuo [or Wen I-to]. Dead Water.

Werfel. Lasting Things, The.

West, J. To May.

Westmorland. To Sir John Wentworth, Upon His Curiosities and Courteous Entertainment at Summerly in Lovingland.

Wheelwright. Would You Think?

Whitehead, W. On the Late Improvements at Nuneham, the Seat of the Earl of Harcourt.

Whitman, T. Hunger and Imagination.

Whitman, W. Give Me the Splendid Silent Sun.

Italian Music in Dakota.

Proud Music of the Storm.

Spontaneous Me.

To a President.

When I Heard At The Close Of The Day.

World below the Brine, The.

Whittier. Over-Heart, The.

Prelude: "Along the roadside, like the flowers of gold."

River Path, The.

Wilbur, R. Ceremony.

Hamlen Brook.

Mined Country.

Wall in the Woods, A: Cummington.

Wilcox, C. Sultry noon, not in the summer's prime, A.

Wilcox, E. Attraction.

Wilkinson, A. Nature Be Damned.

Williams, H. Blest Poesy! Oh sent to calm.

Sonnet to Twilight.

Williams, J. In Duffryn Woods.

Pastoral: "You see that forest on the height?"

Williams, W. Raleigh Was Right.

Wilson, Ramona. Dry Rivers—Arizona.

Wilson, Robley. Sparrow Hills.

Winchilsea. Nocturnal Reverie, A.

Winkler Prins. Shower.

Winters, Y. Barnyard, The.

Magpie's Shadow, The.

Two Songs of Advent.

Wintu Oral Tradition. Six Dream Songs.

Witt, S. Waterfowl Descending.

Wohlfeld. Sea.

Wolfe, C. Song: "Oh say not that my heart is

cold."

Wordsworth, D. Floating Island at Hawkshead.

Loving and Liking [Irregular Verses Addressed to A Child].

Peaceful Our Valley, Fair and Green.

Thoughts on my sick-bed.

Wordsworth, W. American Tradition.

As the black storm upon the mountain top.

Child of the clouds! remote from every taint.

Conclusion: "But here no cannon thunders to the gale."

Expostulation and Reply.

Farewell, A: "Farewell thou little Nook of mountain-ground."

Flowers.

How shall I paint thee?—Be this naked stone.

Lines Composed a Few Miles above Tintern Abbey on Revisiting the Banks of the Wye During a Tour, July 13, 1798.

Lines Written in Early Spring.

London Images.

Methinks 'twere no unprecedented feat.

No record tells of lance opposed to lance.

Not hurled precipitous from steep to steep.

O mountain Stream! the Shepherd and his Cot.

Ode: Intimations of Immortality from Recollections of Early Childhood.

On the Projected Kendal and Windermere Railway.

Open Prospect.

Plain of Donnerdale, The.

Resting-Place, The.

Return.

Return, Content! for fondly I pursued.

Same Subject, The.

Sole listener, Duddon! to the breeze that played.

Stepping-Stones, The.

Tables Turned, The.

Take, cradled Nursling of the mountains, take.

Thorn, The.

Three Years She Grew [in Sun and Shower].

Tradition.

Tributary Stream.

Trosachs, The.

What aspect bore the Man who roved or fled.

When the third summer freed us from restraint.

Whence that low voice?—A whisper from the heart.

World Is Too Much with Us, The.

Written in London, September, 1802.

Written in March [While Resting on the Bridge at the Foot of Brother's Water].

Wotton, S. On a Bank [or Banck] as I Sat[e] [a-]Fishing; a Description of the Spring.

Wright, C. California Spring.

Chinese Journal.

December Journal.

Disjecta Membra.

Night Journal.

Self-Portrait.

Stone Canyon Nocturne.

Wright, D. Caleb Barnes.

Lakes, The.

Those Walks We Took.

Winter at Gurnard's Head.

Wright, J. Depressed by a Book of Bad Poetry, I Walk toward an Unused Pasture and Invite the Insects to Join Me.

Horse, A.

Wright, J. At Cooloolah.

Rainforest.

Wu Wen-ying. Tune: "Sand of Silk-Washing Brook" A Reminiscence.

Wunderlich, M. Anchorage, The.

Wylie. Wild Peaches.

Yeats. Coole Park, 1929.

Her Anxiety.

Lake-Isle of Innisfree, The.

Sorrow of Love, The [1927 Version].

Yesenin [or Essenin]. Golden Grove, The.

Young, Al. Mountains of California: Part 2, The.

Young, Andy. In Anguish, the Heart Finally Prays.

Young, K. Degrees.

Young, M. J. On an Early Spring.

Yu Chien-wu. Spring Day.

Yüan Chüeh. Shipboard Song.

Yun Sŏndo. How many friends have I? Count them.

Zabolotsky [or Zabolotskii]. Snakes.

Yesterday Reflecting Upon Death.

Zanzotto. Eva, forma futuri.

If It Were Not.

Zawacki, A. Credo.

Zeiger, D. Mostly Mozart at Planting Fields Arboretum.

Zukofsky, L. Xenophanes.

Nature of Love

Adams, F. Lines Where Beauty Lingers.

Arvio, S. Love: "It was not to them I wanted to speak."

Drayton. Like an Adventurous Seafarer Am I.

Fahy, F. Little Mary Cassidy.

Mayer, B. Sonnet: "Love is a babe as you know and when you."

Motsapi, S. Enia.

Savage-Armstrong, G. Wee Lassie's First Luve, The.

Williams, W. Rain: "As the rain falls."

Nautilus (mollusk)

Ashbery, J. Franchises in Flux.

Holmes, O. Chambered Nautilus, The.

Moore, M. Paper Nautilus, The.

Navajo, The

Blackhawk, Terry. Dawn of the Navajo Woman, The.

Pape. Storm Pattern.

Naval Battles

Campbell, T. Battle of the Baltic.

Day, J. North Sea.

Defoe, D. Word's gone out, and now they spread the main, The.

Donne. Burnt Ship, A.

Dryden, J. Now van to van the foremost squadrons meet.

Our fleet divides, and straight the Dutch appear.

Hemans. Casabianca.

Kenney. Battle of Valcour Island, The.

Longfellow, H. Cumberland, The.

Marvell. For Santacruze the glad fleet takes her way.

Melville, H. *Temeraire*, The.

Utilitarian View of the Monitor's Fight, A.

Mitchell, S. How the Cumberland Went Down.

Pak Illo. Lament on the Water.

Sackville, C. Song Written at Sea in the First Dutch War (1665), the Night before an Engagement.

Smith, C. Sea View, The.

Thwaites. On either side the *Jervis Bay* the convoy was dipping.

Whitman, W. Would you hear of an old-time [or old-fashioned] sea fight?

Navels

Elfyn, Menna. Belly Button Song.

Navy, Great Britain

Campbell, T. Ye Mariners of England.

Dryden, J. English Fleet Goes Out, The.

Our fleet divides, and straight the Dutch appear.

Garrick. Heart of Oak.

Marvell. For Santacruze the glad fleet takes her way.

Navy Life

Burns, R. Silver Tassie, The.

Dove, R. Passage, The.

Ross, A. Destroyers in the Arctic.

Navy, United States

Brownell, H. Bay Fight, The.

Haines, J. Mothball Fleet: Benicia, California.

Holmes, O. Old Ironsides.

Meredith, W. Farragut, Farragut.

Romtvedt. Black Beauty, A Praise.

Wilson, K. Circle, The.

Nazis

Abse. Footnote Extended, A.

Asim, J. 1st Lt. Vernon J. Baker: Hero on the Hill.

Bell, M. Getting Lost in Nazi Germany.

Sounds of the Resurrected Dead Man's Footsteps (#1).

Sound of the Resurrected Dead Man's Footsteps (#2).
Bobrowski. Kaunas 1941.
Brecht, B. 1940.
  War Has Been Given a Bad Name.
  What Did the Nazi Send His Wife?
Bringhurst. For the Bones of Josef Mengele, Disinterred June 1985.
Char. Leaves of Hypnos No. 128.
Dobyns. Confession.
Éluard, P. Nazi Song.
Fearing. AD.
Ficowski. Pawiak 1943.
Frumkin. Bad Dream and the Friend.
George, S. Antichrist, The.
Hamburger, M. Between the Lines.
Hecht, A. More Light! More Light!
Heyen. Blue.
  Riddle: "From Belsen a crate of gold teeth."
Hill, G. Christmas Trees.
  Ovid in the Third Reich.
Klepfisz. Death Camp.
MacLean, S. Death Valley.
Marcinkevičius, J. Prelude to 'Blood and Ash'.
Niemoller. First They Came for the Jews.
Peck, J. Metal Denser Than, and Liquid, A.
Plath. Daddy.
  Lady Lazarus.
Pratt, E. From Stone to Steel.
Sadoff. Nazis.
Schiff, Robyn. Chanel N° 5.
Snodgrass. Albert Speer.
  Hermann Fegelein.
Stone, R. In the Next Galaxy.
Troupe. Signals and Demarcations.
Unger, B. Photo Taken in Winter, 1944.
Vaynper, Z. Word: "So many bright words covered."
Williams, C. K. Spit.

Nebraska (state)
Belieu. Radio Nebraska.
Eiseley. Prairie Spring.
Guest, B. Nebraska.
McPherson, S. Pornography, Nebraska.
Sandburg, C. Limited.
  Sunset from Omaha Hotel Window.
Whalen, P. Off. . . / over / that way.

Nebuchadnezzar
Disch. Hooray for Hollywood.
Wylie. Nebuchadnezzar.

Necrophilia
Dudley, E. Pathologist.
Duffy, C. Havisham.
See also **Corpses**

Need
Ammons. Needs.
Angel. Breaking the Rock Down.
Bart, L. As Long As He Needs Me.
Berry, W. Wild Geese, The.
Brown, L. It All Depends on You.
Brutus. Let not this plunder be misconstrued.
Bunting. Thrush in the syringa sings, A.
Burns, R. Grace at Kirkudbright.
Cataldi. It's Easy.
Ceravolo. Spring in This World of Poor Mutts.
Creeley. For W. C. W ("Rhyme is after, The.").
DeSylva, B. G. It All Depends on You.
DJ Renegade. Thursday Poem.
Evans, R. To Each His Own.
Harburg. Necessity.
Heard, J. Thine Own.
Henderson, R. It All Depends on You.
Livingston, J. To Each His Own.
Loesser. Somebody, Somewhere.
Majorino. Say--So I'll Say.
Mayakovsky [*or* Maiakovskii]. Listen!
McBride, M. Knife-Thrower's Wife, The.
Merrill, B. People.
Meynell, A. Modern Mother, The.
Nye, N. Famous.
Olson, C. Telesphere, The.
Orton, B. Sea Monkeys, The.
Pinsky. Samurai Song.
Pritchard, N. WE NEED—please read this and see if you.

Sabines. Lovers, The.
Shepherd, R. Another Version of an Ocean.
Talvikki, A. For Want.
Tsvetayeva [*or* Tsvetaeva]. You, Walking Past Me.
Udeozo, O. Slave Boat.
Unknown. I have walked to the very ends of the earth.
Volkman. I won't go in today, I'll stay out today.
Welish. Detained by Rest.
Winter, M. Long Distance.
Young, A. Dance of the Infidels.
See also **Poverty**

Needles
Clarke, C. Stuck.
Cole, H. 40 Days and 40 Nights.
Elfyn, Menna. Pins.
Hahn, K. Pine.
Kamienska. Matthew 19:16–24; And behold, one came up to him.
  Things of This World.
Lear, E. Limerick: "There was an old Lady of Winchelsea."
Mother Goose. Old Mother Twitchett had [*or* has] but one eye.
Pan Chao. Needle and Thread.
Perillo, L. Needles.
Unknown. Thread the Needle.
Zhao. Needle and Thread.

Needlework
Terranova. Needlework.

Nefertiti
Unknown. Queen Nefertiti.

Neglect
Alegría. Grandmother, The.
Claman, E. Show Biz Parties.
Crabbe, G. Delay has Danger.
  Three weeks had past, and Richard rambles now.
Dubie. Trakl.
Landon. Song: "My heart is like the failing hearth."
Li Po. Barbarian pass is filled with windblown sand, The.
Mahon. Disused Shed in Co. Wexford, A.
Martelli, J. Mal'Occhio.
Thompson, D. P. Sister Lakin and Lally.
Tu Fu [*or* Du Fu]. In Seclusion.
Tzu Yeh. Admonition.
Unknown. We cannot tell now.
Wilbur, R. Shame.
Yi Talch'ung. Neglected Wife, The.

Neighborhoods
Jarnot, L. New Life, The.
Lux. Neighborhood of Make-Believe, The.
Martin, Gail. Lemons.
Mayfield, C. When I Moved into the Neighborhood.
Meitner, E. Gentrification.

Neighbors
Abbott, K. Our honest neighbor's rolled.
Anstett. Worry.
Basho. Deep autumn.
  It's late fall.
Brown Rosellen. I have a neighbor.
  Storm high.
Charara, H. My Father Breaks the Neighbor's Nose.
Crabbe, G. Invitation to the Waltz.
Deltoro, A. Neighbors.
  Vecinos.
Deniz, G. Superior.
Eady. My Mother, If She Had Won Free Dance Lessons.
Elledge. Their Hats Is Always White.
Erdrich, H. Future Debris.
Frost, R. Mending Wall.
Geiger. Disproportionate.
Gex-Breaux, Q. Wisdom Is.
Goldberg, B. Once a Shoot of Heaven.
Gordon, M. Love Thy Neighbor.
Gregerman, D. Lullaby.
Gunn, T. All Do Not All Things Well.
Harms. Dogtown.

Heaney, S. Other Side, The.
Heywood, J. Quiet Neighbour, A.
Hill, J. Economics of Gererosity, The.
Jamie, K. Way we live, The.
Khodasevich. Music.
Khomin, I. Dike, a flower bed, a bare linden tree, A.
Kirby, D. Search for Baby Combover, The.
Ku Sang. Spring Chrysanthemums.
Lawrence, D. H. Love Thy Neighbour.
Lea, S. Feud, The.
Lochhead, L. Grim Sisters, The.
Maroon, B. Neighbor.
Millay, E. Portrait by a Neighbor.
Moulds, J. Late Summer Litany.
Osterhaus, J. New York Minute.
Pape. Minotaur Next Door, The.
Pinsky. Street, The.
Prunty. Downtown Bus, The.
Rein. Monastery.
Richman, L. Rue de Rosiers: To My Brother Fred.
Roberts, K. How Late Desire Looks.
Rodgers, C. Slave Ritual.
Smith, A. Roslyn Malamud the Coup.
Torres, E. Elbow in Dumberland, An.
Tu Fu [*or* Du Fu]. Guest, A.
Vinz. Wall between Us, The.
Waters, C. Singer, The.
Williams, W. Exercise No. 2.
Williamson, G. Group Photo with Winter Trees.
  Neighboring Storms.
Young, A. Studio Up Over In Your Ear.

Nelson, Horatio Nelson, Viscount
Campbell, T. Battle of the Baltic.
Graves, R. 1805.
Hardy, T. Certain sort of bravery, A.
  What are you thinking, that you speak no word?
Melville, H. *Temeraire*, The.

Nepal
Justice, D. Here in Katmandu.

Neptune (god)
Campion, T. Hymn in Praise of Neptune, A.
Homer. Neptune Goes to the Greeks.
Korinna [*or* Corinna]. Are you, happy man, grandson of Kronos.
Marlowe. Amorous Leander, beautiful and young.
  "O Hero, Hero!" thus he cried full oft.
Spires. Comb and the Mirror, The.

Nero
Herrick. Cruelties.
Seneca. This said, she twirled the thread on an ugly spool.

Neruda, Pablo
Figueroa, J. Pablo Neruda.
Hass, R. Elegy Residence on Earth.
Lim, S. In California with Neruda.
Page, P. Planet Earth.
Williams, W. Tribute to Neruda the Poet Collector of Seashells.

Nerval, Gérard de
Muldoon, P. Something Else.

Nerve Gas
Rawling. Gas Drill.

Nests
Basho. Crow's / Abandoned nest.
Clare, J. Birds' Nest.
Dalton, A. Nest.
Moldaw. Nest, The.
Ruefle. Wasps' Nest.
Spear, R. Nest for Everyone, A.
Unknown. Que-chao.
Unknown, fr. Terezin Concentration Camp. Birdsong.
Yosef, H. Reflections on a Dove.
See also **Birds' Nests**

Netherlands
Cary, P. Leak in the Dike, The.
Marvell. Character of Holland, The.

Nettles
Bowen, E. Nettles in May.
Thomas, E. Tall Nettles.
Unknown. Nettle.

Nevada (state)
Anderson, W.　There's Not a Friend like the Lowly Jesus.
Hass, R.　Tahoe in August.
Levi, J.　Tuscarora.
Louis, A.　Nevada Red Blues.
Roggeman.　Archaeological Find.
Stafford, W.　Vacation.

New England
Betjeman.　Longfellow's Visit to Venice.
Clifton, L.　Driving through new england.
De la Selva.　Deliverance.
Dobyns.　Dancing in Vacationland.
Dubie.　New England, Springtime.
Fink, Robert A.　Abilene, TX: We Pull Out For New England.
Lowell, A.　Lilacs.
St. Louis.
Major, C.　Not This—This Here!
McGinley.　New England Pilgrimage.
Myles, E.　New England Wind.
Nemerov.　For Robert Frost, in the Autumn, in Vermont.
Oppen.　Product.
Rakosi.　Origins.
Revell, D.　Memory of New England, The.
Robinson, E.　New England.
Snydal, L.　Frost.
Tagliabue.　March Blizzard.
Thoreau.　On Ponkawtasset, since, we took our way.
Weismiller.　Hemlocks in Autumn.
Wheatley, P.　America.
Farewell[l] to America, A. To Mrs. S. W.
Wheelwright.　Come Over and Help Us; a Rhapsody.
Williams, S.　Letters from a New England Negro.

New Hampshire (state)
Borawski.　Power of One.
Brown Rosellen.　I want to understand light years.
Eliot, T. S.　New Hampshire.
Hinsey, E.　Art of Measuring Light, The.
Kinnell.　Flower Herding on Mount Monadnock.
Matthews, W.　On the Porch at the Frost Place, Franconia, NH.
McKay, C.　Spring in New Hampshire.
Moss, H.　New Hampshire.
O'Hara, F.　Raspberry Sweater, A.
Rakosi.　Founding of New Hampshire, The.

New Jersey (state)
Ammons.　Corsons Inlet.
Baraka, I.　Contract. (For The Destruction and Rebuilding of Paterson), A.
Berger, D.　Dinner in the Sun.
Coles, R.　New Jersey Boys.
De Vries, R.　On Alabama Ave., Paterson, NJ, 1954.
Dodd, E.　Dieback.
Enzensberger, H.　In Memory of William Carlos Williams.
Gillan.　In New Jersey Once.
Hull, L.　Midnight Reports.
Jackson, R.　63rd and broadway.
Kennedy, X.　In a Prominent Bar in Secaucus [One Day].
Kleinzahler.　Snow in North Jersey.
Oppen.　Undertaking in New Jersey, The.
Pinsky.　At Pleasure Bay.
Jersey Rain.
Long Branch Song, A.
Whitman, W.　Patrolling Barnegat.
Williams, W.　Preface: "Rigor of beauty is the quest. But how will you find beauty when it is locked."

New Mexico (state)
Ai.　Chance.
Bartlett, M.　What We Say in New Mexico.
Hall, D.　New Mexico.
Harjo, J.　Insomnia and the Seven Steps to Grace.
Ivey, M.　Golden, New Mexico.
Jeffers, R.　New Mexican Mountain.
Logghe.　Something Like Marriage.
Lopez, L.　To a Coal Miner in Madrid, New

Mexico.
MacNaughton.　New Mex Hip.
McGinnis, M.　New Mexico Time.
Quintana.　At the New Mexico Viet Nam Veterans Memorial.
Smith, C.　Religious Art.
Smith, P.　San Luis, New Mexico.
Snyder, G.　I Went Into the Maverick Bar.
Sze.　Do Not Speak Keresan to a Mescalero Apache.
Tomlinson, C.　Matachines, The.
Santa Fe Railroad, The.
Wilson, K.　Arrival of My Mother, The.
Still Life: "Three old New Mexican men."
Wright, J.　Boleros #21.

New Orleans, Louisiana
Adamo.　New Orleans.
Bly, R.　Day We Visited New Orleans, The.
Brinks, Dave.　Proscenium Moon.
Citino.　Walt Whitman in New Orleans, 1848.
Creamer, H.　Way Down Yonder in New Orleans.
Evans, Brett.　K-Doe Codas.
Freeman, Jessica.　November 1st.
Harjo, J.　New Orleans.
Komunyakaa, Y.　Untitled Blues; After a Photograph by Yevgeni Yevtushenko.
Larkin, P.　For Sidney Bechet.
Salaam.　I Just Heard John Buffington Died.
Smith, D.　New Orleans Engagement.
Steptoe.　Mississippi Blues.

New Testament
Fogdall, Kristin.　Demas, in Love with This Present World.

New Year
Algarin.　Happy New Year.
Avison.　New Year's Poem.
Baranczak, S.　Three Magi, The.
Basho.　In the mountain village.
On New Year's Day.
Brathwaite, E.　New Year Letter.
Buson.　New Year's first poem.
Spring Wind on the Riverbank at Kema.
Césaire, A.　New Year.
Ching An.　To Show You All, on the First Morning of the Year.
Chu Ŭisik.　Boy stops outside my window, A.
Clare, J.　Old Year, The.
Constantine, D.　New Year Behind the Asylum.
Davenant [or D'Avenant].　For the Lady Olivia Porter; a Present upon a New Year's Day.
Drayton.　To the New Year.
Fordham.　Passing of the Old Year.
Greenlaw, L.　New Year's Eve.
Grimes, A.　Alice's Cat, New Year's Eve 1990.
Guest, B.　Outside of This, That Is.
Hardy, T.　New Year's Eve.
Hwang Insuk.　New Year's Card, A.
Inahata Teiko.　As if happiness.
Issa.　New year arrived, The.
New Year's Day.
New Year's morning.
Kao Ch'i.　Silkworm Song of Torchlit Fields.
Larkin, P.　New Year.
Levine, P.　New Year's Eve, in Hospital.
Linden, M.　Last Day of the Year; or, New Year's Eve, The.
New Year's Morning; or, the First Day of the Year.
Lowell, R.　New Year's Day.
Muske, C.　Crack the Whip.
Naito Joso.　Gruel heaped / In a perfect bowl.
Nantembo.　On New Year's Day.
Nims, J.　New Year's Eve, 1938.
Okigbo.　On the New Year.
Othman, A.　This Year.
Patchen.　At the New Year.
Piercy.　On New Year's Day.
Rich, A.　At the Jewish New Year.
Sanguineti.　Wind shoves my New Year's Day sun in my face, The.
Sanpu.　First cherry blossoms.
Sarton, M.　Small Joys.
Shakhova.　Autobiographical Response from a Provincial Wasteland (in Reply to a New Year's Greeting Sent with a Bouquet).

Shore.　High Holy Days.
Shuford.　Celebration.
Smart, C.　New Year.
Strand.　New Year, The.
Swenson, M.　Last Day.
Tate, N.　Ode upon the New Year.
Thompson, P.　Old Year, The.
To the New Year.
Tolson, M.　Festus Conrad.
Trần Tế Xu'o'ng.　New Year's Season and Its Poetasters, The.
Tu Fu [or Du Fu].　New Year's Eve at the Home of Tu Wei.
Unknown.　Hey, ey, hey, ey / Make we myrie as we may.
Wetzsteon.　Poem for a New Year.
Wilbur, R.　Year's End.
Williamson, G.　New Year's: A Short Pantoum.
Wright, C.　Reading Lao Tzu Again in the New Year.
Yang Wen-li.　New Year's Eve.
Yi Kyubo.　Composed Playfully on New Year's Day.
Yomono Akara.　Season greeter, The.
Yoneda, Karl.　New Year's Day came quietly and left silently.
New Year's Day on Angel Island.

New York City
Alexander, M.　News of the World.
Algarin.　Dante Park.
Ali, A.　Lenox Hill.
Andrew, G.　Rolls-Royce Dreams.
Applewhite.　Prayer for My Son.
Ashbery, J.　Chapter 2, Book 35.
Holding Mode, A.
Barot, R.　Portishead Suite.
Three Amoretti.
Becker, R.　Subject / Matter.
Bell, M.　These Green-Going-to-Yellow.
Benét, S.　Metropolitan Nightmare.
Berlin.　Puttin' on the Ritz (Revised Version).
Slumming on Park Avenue.
Berrigan, A.　Mercy Flight.
Selected Poses.
Short History of Autumn, A.
Berrigan, T.　American Express.
Bean Spasms.
For You.
Personal Poem # 7.
Sonnet XXX: "Into the closed air of the slow."
Whitman in Black.
Bishop, E.　Invitation to Miss Marianne Moore.
Letter to N.Y.
Blake, J.　Sidewalks of New York, The.
Blevins, S.　New York.
Brainard, J.　I remember living on the Lower East Side.
Brecht, B.　Late Lamented Fame of the Giant City of New York.
Brown, A.　Old Neighborhood, The.
Brown, L.　Shiny jewel eye.
Brutus.　Off to Philadelphia in the Morning.
Burke, J.　Road to Morocco, The.
Carrington, H.　Lament: "While my city gently sleeps."
Carruth, H.　Day very solid February 12th, 1944, A.
Memory.
Castro, M.　New York City.
Clampitt.　Times Square Water Music.
Clark, T.　Sonnet: "Five a.m. on East Fourteenth I'm out to eat."
Clifton, H.　Euclid Avenue.
Cohan.　Give My Regards to Broadway.
Comden, B.　New York, New York.
Cooley, N.　Diane Arbus, New York.
Cording.　Peregrine Falcon, New York City.
Corn.　*Navidad*, St. Nicholas Ave.
Photographs of Old New York.
Coultas, B.　Third Farming Poem.
Crane, H.　Tunnel, The.
Crase.　Elegy for New York, The.
Cummings, E. E.　I was sitting in mcsoreley's.
outside it was New York and beauti- / fully snowing.
Degentesh.　Seeds.

Delgado, Alvin.   When I Was a Kid in Nueva York.
Denby.   City Without Smoke.
  Climate, The.
  Mykonos.
  New York Face, A.
  New York, smog-dim under August.
  Northern Boulevard.
  Out of Bronx subway June forest.
  Snoring in New York: An Elegy.
  Summer: "I stroll on Madison in expensive clothes, sour."
Doty, M.   Lilacs in NYC.
Dubin, A.   Forty-second Street.
Duke, V.   Autumn in New York.
Duran, J.   Time Zones.
Eiseley.   And as for Man.
Johnson, E.   Chelsea.
Esteves.   South Bronx Testimonial.
Farber.   Manhattan Lullaby.
Fearing.   Ballad of the Salvation Army.
  Death and Transfiguration of Fourteenth Street.
Feirstein.   Mark Stern.
  Mark Stern Wakes Up.
Ferlinghetti, L.   And Pablo Neruda / that Chilean omnivore of poetry.
  Retired Ballerinas, Central Park West.
Field, E.   New Yorkers.
  Oh, the Gingkos.
Field, R.   Manhattan Lullaby.
Fried, P.   Early, Late.
Friedman, E.   Heading for Manhattan by Train.
García Lorca.   New York.
  Ode to Walt Whitman ("Along the East River and the Bronx.").
Garcia, R.   Diver for the NYPD Talks to His Girlfriend, A.
Gardinier.   To Peace.
Garrison, D.   Worked Late on a Tuesday Night.
Ginsberg, A.   'Back on Times Square, Dreaming of Times Square'.
  Charnel Ground, The.
  Manhattan May Day Midnight.
  Mugging.
  My Sad Self.
  Velocity of Money.
Giovanni.   Walking Down Park.
Green, A.   New York, New York.
Greenberg, S.   East River's Charm.
Grue.   Dogs of New York, The.
Hacker, M.   Elysian Fields.
Hadas, R.   Riverside Park.
  Sunday Afternoon.
  Tangerine Orchids.
Hahn, K.   Boerum Hill Tanka.
Harris, D.   On the uptown lexington avenue express: Martin Luther King Day 1995.
Hart, L.   Manhattan.
Henderson, D.   African Burial Ground called Tribeca, The.
Hernández Cruz.   Poem: "Greater cities are, The."
  Side 32.
Holland, W.   Christopher Street 1979.
Hopkins, L.   Flash.
Houston, Margaret Bell.   Song from the Traffic.
Hughes, L.   Advertisement for the Waldorf-Astoria.
  Good Morning.
  Pennsylvania Station.
  Projection.
  Subway Face.
Jackson, R.   63rd and broadway.
  Smile.
Jiménez, J.   Author's Club.
Johnson, H.   Bottled [New York].
Johnson, J.   My City.
Johnston, P.   Dewey Square, 1956.
  Lexington Avenue Express.
Jones, R.   After Work.
Jordan, J.   Directions for Carrying Explosive Nuclear Wastes through Metropolitan New York.
Joseph, L.   Some Sort of Chronicler I Am.
Kasdorf.   Green Market, New York.
Kaufman, B.   East Fifth Street (N.Y.).

Kearney, M.   Nature Poetry.
Kees.   Aspects of Robinson.
Kerouac.   Hymn.
Kinnell.   Under the Williamsburg Bridge.
Kirchwey.   Nocturne, Morningside Heights.
Koehler, T.   Spreadin' Rhythm Around.
Laughlin, J.   Above the City.
Levin, D.   Cinema Verité.
Lodge, G.   Lower New York.
Lowell, R.   Inauguration Day: January 1953.
Loy.   On Third Avenue.
Lummis, Suzanne.   Shangri-la.
M-1.   Police State.
McDaniel, J.   Leonard.
McKay, C.   Dawn in New York.
Merrill, J.   Urban Convalescence, An.
Merwin.   St. Vincent's.
Mesmer, S.   Lonely Tylenol.
Morales, A.   Old Countries.
Myles, E.   Flowers.
  Milk.
  No Rewriting.
Newton, B.   Owed to New York.
Oden.   Private Letter to Brazil, A.
  Review from Staten Island.
O'Hara, F.   How to Get There.
  Rhapsody.
  Step Away from Them, A.
  Steps.
Olds, S.   Summer Solstice, New York City.
Olin.   "Colors" starring Patti, Grandma, & me at twenty-five.
  Larry Kept Saying Primo Levi Was an Accident.
  Vanishing Point.
Oppen.   Emotions are engaged, The.
  For the people of that flow.
Orlovsky.   Poems from Subway to Work.
Overton, R.   Two Stories.
Pastan.   At the Jewish Museum.
Patterson, G.   Autobiography of a Black Man.
Piccione.   Watching Ants Play Soccer in Central Park.
Pietri.   Old Buildings, The.
  Traffic Misdirector.
Piñero.   Lower East Side Poem, A.
  This Is Not the Place Where I was Born.
Pinsky.   Samba.
Pomerantz, A.   New York.
Ponsot.   Rockefeller the Center.
Postell, T.   Gertrude Stein Rides the Town Down El.
  I Want a Solid Piece of Sunlight and a Yardstick to Measure it With.
Redmond.   New York Seizures.
Reed, J.   I have watched the summer day come up from the top of a pier of the Williamsburgh Bridge.
Ricard, R.   Party Crash.
Rich, A.   Upper Broadway.
Ridge, L.   Morning Ride.
  Phyllis.
Robin, L.   Little Girl from Little Rock.
Rodriguez, J.   New York Sonnet.
Rome, H.   Who Knows?
Rosenblatt, S.   Visiting New York.
Rukeyser, M.   Seventh Avenue.
Rushin.   Word Problems.
Sapia.   Grandmother, a Caribbean Indian, Described by My Father.
Schiff, H.   Eye Poem.
Schuyler, J.   Dining Out with Doug and Frank.
Senghor.   To New York.
Sheeler, J.   This Old Man.
Short, Spencer.   Romanticism.
Shumyatsher, E.   My New York Street Sings.
Simic.   St. Thomas Aquinas.
Simpson, L.   Riverside Drive.
  Summer Morning.
Stern, G.   96 Vandam.
Sticman.   Police State.
Sundiata.   Blink Your Eyes.
Taylor, C. B.   Plenty Time Pass Fast, Fas Dey So.
  Round Irving High School.
Thomas, L.   Great Love Duets.
Toomer.   Skyline.

Towle.   Immaterial Nocturnes: Hudson and Worth.
Troupe.   Eye Change Dreams.
Urdang.   Returning to the Port of Authority: A Picaresque.
Villemaire, Y.   Quartz and Mica.
Walcott.   Blues: "Those five or six young guys."
  Village Life, A.
Waldman, A.   Giant Night.
Weaver, A.   Providence Journal V: Israel of Puerto Rico.
Whitman, W.   City of Orgies.
  Crossing Brooklyn Ferry.
  Give Me the Splendid Silent Sun.
  Mannahatta.
Wieners.   Morgana La Fay.
Wiese, B.   Going Home Madly.
Willis, N.   City Lyrics.
Wright, J.   End of an Ethnic Dream, The.
Wunderlich, M.   East Seventh Street.
  Given in Person Only.
Young, A.   Dance of the Infidels.
See also **Broadway, New York City; Bronx, The, New York City; Brooklyn, New York City; Harlem, New York City; Queens, New York City; Rockefeller Center, New York City**

New York Poetry
Duncan, R.   At the Poetry Conference: Berkeley After the New York Style.
Elmslie, K.   Bare Bones.
Fox, Skip.   In Referring to What Does Not Exist.
Jarnot, L.   Poem Beginning with a Line by Frank Lima.
Olin.   Warner Bros. Newest Thriller *Valentine*.

New York (state)
Allen, W.   Erie Canal, The.
Foerster.   Playland.
Harper, M.   Grandfather.
Hecht, A.   Sestina d'Inverno.
Hollander, J.   State of Nature, A.
Keithley.   Small Moon on the Shoulder of New York.
Plumly.   Dusk Coming on outside ———, New York.
Unknown.   E-ri-e, The.
Walcott.   Upstate.
Wilbur, R.   Sleepless at Crown Point.
Williams, W.   Rapid Transit.

New Zealand
Baxter, J.   Bay, The.
  East Coast Journey.
  New Zealand.
Curnow.   Landfall in Unknown Seas.
  Unhistoric Story, The.

Newark, New Jersey
Baraka, I.   New Ark Space.
Braunstein, Evan.   Newark.

Newfoundland, Canada
Ashbery, J.   Interesting People of Newfoundland.
Hayman, R.   To a Worthy Friend, Who Often Objects the Coldness of the Winter in Newfound-Land.
  To All Those Worthy Women, Who Have Any Desire to Live in Newfound-Land.

Newman, John Henry, Cardinal
Rossetti, C.   Cardinal Newman.

News
Berry, W.   Morning's News, The.
Bloem, R.   Amsterdam Chronicle.
Campert.   Stroll to Parfondeval, A.
Catacalos.   Letter to a Brother in Exile.
Citino.   Whole Wheat, Decaf Black, a Morbid Curiosity.
Friedlaender.   Progress: "There was a time when peace at evening."
Graham, W.   What's the News?
Greenlaw, L.   Five O'Clock Opera.
Hamilton, I.   Newscast, The.
Hölderlin.   Descriptive Poetry.
Hovanessian, D.   Exiles.
Jackson, B.   Shooting, Killing, Drug Busts, Cover-Ups, Fuck-Ups, Lighter Sides, Weather, and Sports.

Jordan, J.   Through These Halls.
Kushner, A.   Don't bother about the news!
Leapor.   Epistle of Deborah Dough, The.
Leonard, T.   This is thi.
Lochhead, L.   Interference Song.
Lucas, J.   Nes From Nowhere.
Mahon.   Morning Radio.
May, J.   On the Air.
Menicanti.   Biographical News.
Moritz [or Morits].   Eternally to be waiting for
  bloody news.
Mullen, H.   Headlines.
Nobleman, B.   Tabloid News.
Olin.   Tom Brokaw.
Razaf, A.   Guess Who's in Town? (Nobody but
  That Gal of Mine).
Reading, P.   Life is too black as he paints it and
  "Reading's nastiness sometimes".
  These are the days of the horrible headlines.
Roberson, E.   News continued release.
Rosen, M.   Here is the News.
Sabgir, G.   Radio Gibberish.
Salter.   Chernobyl.
Southwick.   Star Is Born in the Eagle Nebula, A.
Unknown.   News, The.
Wen T'ing-yün.   News So Seldom Comes.
Zagajewski.   Electric Elegy.

Newspapers

Atwood.   It Is Dangerous to Read Newspapers.
Beatty, P.   New York Newsday: Truth, Justice
  and Vomit.
Benedikt.   Editing *The Gazette of the Infinite.*
Breton, A.   Mystery Corset, The.
Coleridge, M.   No Newspapers.
Crane, S.   Newspaper is a collection of half-
  injustices, A.
de Folgar.   Protest.
Dobson, R.   Country Press.
Dodge, M.   Note.
Eady.   Jack Johnson Does the Eagle Rock.
Eliot, T. S.   *Boston Evening Transcript,* The.
Espada.   Fidel in Ohio.
Gelinas, D.   Dream of the Just, The.
  Sueño de los justos, El.
Holub.   Brief Reflection on Brief Reflections.
Hovanessian, D.   Exiles.
Ishikawa Takuboku.   Old newspaper!, An.
Jarrell, R.   Nestus Gurley.
Lehman.   Towards the Vanishing Point.
Lewis, Emyr.   Mad Magnet of a Wild Wind.
Mackie, A.   Newsboy.
Masters, E.   Carl Hamblin.
  Editor Whedon.
Moise *et al.*   Newspaper, The.
Moore, J.   Poet is Scornful, The.
Moorer.   Southern Press, The.
Niedecker.   Cricket-song.
Paulin.   Personal Column.
Plomer.   Headline History.
Prunty.   Reading Before We Read, Horoscope
  and Weather.
Quinn, J.   High and Dry.
St. John, D.   Quote Me Wrong Again and I'll
  Slit the Throat of Your Pet Iguana.
Sharaf, M.   Behind the House.
Sheeler, J.   This Old Man.
Southwick.   Star Is Born in the Eagle Nebula, A.
Thomas, E.   Cries of the Newsboy.
Whittier.   Tent on the Beach: [The Dreamer].
Wilbur, R.   After the Last Bulletins.
Wolfe, H.   British Journalist, The.
Yourcenar, Marguerite.   Daily Papers.
Zephaniah.   Sun, The.

See also **Journalism and Journalists; Magazines**

Newton, Sir Isaac

Blake, W.   Mock On, Mock On, Voltaire,
  Rousseau.
Jarrell, R.   Emancipators, The.
Pilinszky, J.   Homage to Issac Newton.
Pope, A.   Intended for Sir Isaac Newton.
Soloukhin.   Apple, The.
Unknown.   Sir Isaac Newton.

Nez Percé

Bird, G.   Women Fell like Beautiful Horses,
  The.

Niagara Falls

Alexander, P.   Sight.
Bishop, M.   Public Aid for Niagara Falls.
Crapsey.   Niagara.
Drake, J.   Niagara.
Dubin, A.   Shuffle Off to Buffalo.
Dugan, A.   Niagara Falls.
Gaspar de Alba.   4: The Niagara River Speaks
  Three Languages.
Neal, J.   Battle comes again, The. The charging
  host.
  There's a fierce gray Bird, with a bending beak.

Nicaragua

Cardenal.   León.
  Lights.
  Mosquito Kingdom.
Darío, R.   Far Away and Long Ago.
Espada.   Jeep Driver, The.
Moramarco, F.   Volunteer's Fairy Tale, A.
Zamora, D.   Report on the Protest in Front of
  the United States Embassy by the Pino Grande
  Movement, A.

Nice, France

Koch, K.   Ville de Nice, La.

Nietzsche, Friedrich

Hass, R.   Supple Wreath of Myrtle, A.
Jones, R.   One of the Citizens.
Salamun.   Words.

Nigeria and Nigerians

Acholonu.   Nigeria in the Year 1999.
Adesuyi, N.   New Testament, The.
Adewale, T.   Olayimika.
Agali, A.   Boeing.
Akinlolu, S.   Can't You See?
Clark Bekederemo.   Epilogue to Casualties.
Ifowodo, O.   Homeland.
Ismaili.   Lagos.
Kalu, U.   Extended Relations (1).
Kay, J.   Pride.
Ogundipe-Leslie.   Nigeria of the Seventies.
Ojaide.   Launching Our Community
  Developement Fund.
Okantah.   African Morning.
Raji Oyelade, R.   Cyclone.
Southerland.   Blue Clay.
  Night in Nigeria.
Soyinka.   Ikeja, Friday, Four O'Clock.
Zakama, K.   Call of the Fulani Maid.
  My Generation.

Night

Abinader, E.   On a Summer Night.
Adair, T.   Night We Called It a Day, The.
Afrika, T.   Nightrider.
Agosin.   Night.
Ahmet Hasim.   Moonstruck Storks.
Aichinger.   Correspondence.
Aiken, C.   All the Radios.
Alcman.   Fragment 58: Night and Sleep.
Aldrich, T.   Lycidas.
Aleixandre.   Closed.
Allen, F.   Sodium Light.
Alterman, N.   Summer Night.
Ammons.   Above the Fray Is Only Thin Air.
Andrade, M.   Nocturne.
Angel.   Veils of Prayer.
Arturo, A.   Song of the Silent Night.
Asekoff, L.   Starwork.
Ashbery, J.   Morning Jitters.
Atkins, R.   Night and a Distant Church.
Auden.   Summer Night, A.
Aytoun [or Ayton], R.   Upon Mr Thomas
  Murrays Fall.
Azzawi, F.   Unknown man, The.
Bachmann.   Invocation of the Great Bear.
  Paris.
Baehr, A.   Ritual.
Bairagi.   Who Is Awake in the Dead of Night?
Balingit, J.   Quiet Evening, Home Away.
Baraka, I.   World Is Full of Remarkable Things,
  The.
Barbauld.   Summer Evening's Meditation, A.
  'Tis now the hour.
Barer, M.   On Such a Night As This.
Barnes, W.   Winter Night, A.
Basheva.   Fifth Floor.

Basho.   Awake at night.
  Clouds come and go, The.
  Cold night: the wild duck.
  Cool fall night, A.
  Cool it is, and still.
  Fall of night.
  Harvest moon.
  Lovely spring night, A.
  Many nights on the road.
  This bright harvest moon.
  Very brief.
Baxter, J.   Buried Stream, The.
Beachy-Quick, Dan.   Nightbook.
Beddoes.   To Night.
Bedregal.   Night, I Know All About You.
  Nocturne of Hope.
Belieu.   Legend of the Albino Farm.
  Nocturne: My Sister Life.
Benét, W.   Night.
Bennett, G.   Street Lamps in Early Spring.
Beranová, J.   Williamsbridge.
Bibbins, M.   Sinking.
Bible, *O.T.*   Song: "At night on my bed I longed
  for."
Bishop, E.   Man-Moth, The.
Blake, W.   Night.
Blok.   Night: A Street.
Bly, R.   Two Ramages for Old Masters.
Bodenheim.   Interlude.
Bogan, L.   Night: "Cold remote islands, The."
Bonset.   Remembering the Night Fountains.
Bopp, R.   I wake up.
Borowski.   Night over Birkenau.
Bourdillon.   Night Has a Thousand Eyes, The.
Boutens.   Lonely Night.
Bowers, M.   Answer.
Bowles, W.   Written at Bamborough Castle.
Bracho, C.   Desde esta luz.
  From This Light.
Bradbury, R.   Switch on the Night.
Brecht, B.   First Psalm (Posthumous).
Bridie, J.   West End Perk, The.
Bristol.   Night.
Brontë, A.   Night.
Brontë, C.   'What does she dream of'.
Brooke, R.   Second Best.
Browning, R.   Meeting at Night.
Brummer, N.   Why Is This Night Different from
  All Other Nights?
Brutus.   At Night.
  Nightsong: City.
Bryan, M.   To———: "O timeless guest!—so
  soon returned art thou."
Buchsbaum, J.   Slowly, Slowly, Horses.
Bukowski.   Not Much Singing.
Buson.   Amid white plum blossoms.
  In the white plum blossoms.
  Night deepens.
  Short night, The.
  That handsaw marks time.
  With a runny nose.
Byron, G.   She Walks In Beauty.
  So We'll Go No More A-Roving.
  Stars are forth, the moon above the tops, The.
Caldwell, E.   Love Poem: "Olfactory paradise."
Campion, T.   Now Winter Nights Enlarge.
Cane.   Hymn to Night.
Carman, B.   Northern Vigil, A.
Carrington, H.   Lament: "While my city gently
  sleeps."
Carson, A.   Longing, a Documentary.
Cawein.   Orgie.
Celan.   Little night.
Ceni, A.   Atrium.
Césaire, A.   Different Horizon.
Chalfi, R.   Night Hair.
Chang Chi.   Night at Anchor by Maple Bridge.
  Night-Mooring at Maple Bridge.
  Night-Mooring near Maple Bridge, A.
Chang Yüeh.   Hearing Bells at Night in the
  Mountains.
Chazal, M.   Bicycle rolls on the road, A.
Ch'i-chi.   Not Sleeping.
Chikako.   On this summer night.
Chin, J.   Night.
Ching An.   Night Sitting.

Chipasula. Dusk.
Ch'oe Ch'ung. In the Night.
Ch'oe Sŭngja. Night Owl.
Ch'ŏn Kŭm. Night draws near in a mountain village.
Clark, T. Sonnet: "Five a.m. on East Fourteenth I'm out to eat."
Coleridge, H. Night.
Coleridge, M. Doubt.
Coolidge, C. Darkling Thrums.
Cope, W. At 3 A.M.
Cortes, F. Poem Composed During a Brownout.
Coulette. Night Thoughts: "Your kind of night, David, your kind of night."
Crane, H. In Shadow.
Crane, S. I explain the silvered passing of a ship at night.
Crawford, I. Dark Stag, The.
Creeley. Somewhere.
Song: "What I took in my hand."
Crevel, R. Nighttime.
Cristall. Song: "Both gloomy and dark was the shadowy night."
Song of Arla, Written During Her Enthusiasm, A.
Written When the Mind Was Oppressed.
Cronin, A. Elegy for the Nightbound.
Crosby, F. Thoughts in Midnight Hours.
Crowe, T. Pond in the Woods, A.
Cruz, S. Dark Night.
Dark Night, The.
One Dismal Night.
Cullen, C. Night Rain.
Cummings, E. E. Hours rise up putting off stars and it is, The.
Curbelo. Last Call.
Curnow. Continuum.
Cushman, S. Make the Bed.
Daglarca. Leaf: "Your gaze stays awake in the night."
Sultan of the Animals Is the Night, The.
Darío, R. Nocturne.
Darwish, M. Steps in the Night.
Davies, W. Nightfall.
Davies, W. H. Hour of Magic, The.
Day Lewis. Winter Night.
de Folgar. Nocturnal.
de Jesús. Curfew.
De la Mare. Birthnight: To F, The.
Silver.
De Mello Breyner. Night and the House.
Deane, S. Power Cut.
Denham, J. Night Haul.
Desnos. Sleep Spaces.
St Merri district, The.
Dickinson, E. Aurora.
First Day's Night had come, The.
Good Morning—Midnight.
When Night is almost done.
Wild Nights—Wild Nights!
Dietz, H. You and the Night and the Music.
Dodd, W. Of Rain and Air.
Donovan, K. Wild Night, A.
Doolittle, H. Evening.
Dove, R. Nigger Song: An Odyssey.
Dransfield. Endsight.
Drinkwater. Moonlit Apples.
Drummond de Andrade. Elegy: "I've won (lost) my day."
Drummond, W. Madrigal: "Unhappie [or Unhappy] Light."
Dunbar, P. Night.
Dunn, D. From the Night-Window.
Duo Duo. Night.
Eady. Seduction.
Edmond, L. 3 A.M.
Edwards, K. About this time streetlamps flicker up like.
Night falls on single vision zombies everywhere.
Eguren. Peregrin, Wandering Hunter of Faces.
Eigner. For Sleep.
Ekelof. If You Ask Me.
Eliot, T. S. Rhapsody on a Windy Night.
Eluard, P. et al. She Exists.
Elytis, O. Even when they destroy you it will

still be beautiful.
"Ern Malley.". Night Piece.
Espada. Transient Hotel Sky at the Hour of Sleep.
Estes, A. Nocturne.
Factor, J. Song Beside a Sippy Cup.
Farber. Manhattan Lullaby.
Taking Turns.
Farjeon, E. Good Night.
Night Will Never Stay, The.
Fermini, I. You I know is losing you, The.
Field. Nightfall.
Field, R. Manhattan Lullaby.
Fishman, L. V's Farmhouse.
Fontanella. In The Nighttime Someone.
Fox, S. In the Evening.
Francis, R. Night Train.
Freneau. Nor look'd I back, till to a far off wood.
Frost, Richard. Night Person, The.
Frost, Robert. Acquainted with the Night.
Two Tramps in Mud Time.
Furberg, J. Nightspell.
Galvin, B. Inside Job, An.
García Lorca. City That Does Not Sleep.
Night of Sleepless Love.
Second Anniversary.
Sleepwalkers' Ballad.
Sleepwalking Ballad, The.
Gardinier. Blues.
Gascoyne. Nightwatchers, The.
Gerov, Alexander. Accra.
Ghalib, M. Ghazal 15.
Ginsberg, A. Last Night in Calcutta.
Gioia. Country Wife, The.
In Chandler Country.
Giussani, S. Body Politic.
Glück, L. Pond, The.
Godfrey. What It Takes.
Goethe. Meeting, the Departure, The.
Goldberg, B. Nights with the Star-Ladle Over the House.
González, A. Without Warning.
Gonzalez, N. Wanderer in the Night of the World, A.
Goodison. Always Homing Now Soul Toward Light.
Goodman, P. It was good when you were here.
Gould, A. Observed Observer, The.
Graves, R. Frosty Night, A.
Grimké, A. Beso, El.
Groarke, V. Tonight of Yesterday.
Gu Cheng. Generation, A.
Guidacci. Before Our Encounter.
Spring.
Guillén, J. Without Lights.
Gunn, T. Night Piece, The: "Fog drifts slowly down the hill, The."
Gyatso, T. I sought my lover at twilight.
Hagiwara Sakutaro. Spring Night.
Haines, J. If the Owl Calls Again.
Hardy, T. Shut Out That Moon.
Harms. Los Angeles, the Angels.
Hartnett. Moonsnow '77.
Harvor, Elisabeth. Four O'Clock, New Year's Morning, New River Beach.
Heard, J. Night.
Heine, H. Night Thoughts.
Hejinian. Nights.
Hemans. Night-Blooming Flowers.
Hernandez, D. Rooftop Piper.
Herrick. Dream[e]s.
Night-Piece, to Julia, The.
To Daisies, Not to Shut So Soon[e].
Heym. Clearer Now the Days Are Passing.
Hicok. Busy Days of My Nights, The.
Hidalgo, J. Shore of Night.
Hinsey, E. Art of Measuring Light, The.
Hirshfield, J. At Night.
Half-sleeping, / my body pulls toward yours.
Invocation: "This August night, raccoons."
Hŏ Nansŏrhŏn. For My Brother Hagok.
Hofmannsthal. Do You See the Town?
Hongo. Yellow Light.
Horace. Late Night Ode.
Horovitz, F. Night-Piece.

Houston, D. Night Out, A.
Huerta, E. Men of Dawn, The.
Hughes, L. Summer Night.
Hughes, T. Thought-Fox, The.
Hugo, V. Djinns, The.
Hulme, T. Autumn.
Hwang Chini. I Will Cut Out the Middle Watch.
Ibarbourou. Rainy Night.
Iio Sogi. Night frost / Pulsing wings.
Iosifova, Ekaterina. At My Doorstep.
Ishikawa Takuboku. Tanka: "Sorrow / its outlines blurred."
Issa. Blossoms at night.
For you too, my fleas.
For your fleas too.
Night is so long, The.
Short night / Scarlet flower.
Summer night.
With this rising bath-mist.
Issahakian. For you fleas too.
Jaccottet. In the Steps of the Moon.
Letter of the 26th June.
Right at the end of night.
Jaimes Freyre. Night-time.
Jarman, M. Psalm: The New Day.
Jeffers, R. Night.
Jiménez, J. Countryside Sleeps, Trembling, The.
Street Is Waiting for the Night, The.
Jobim, A. Quiet Nights of Quiet Stars (Corcovado).
Johnston, P. Round About Midnight, Opus #6.
Jones, A. M. To the Moon.
József, A. Freight Trains.
Kagami Shiko. Night snow / Neighbor's cock.
Kahal, I. Night Is Young and You're So Beautiful, The.
Kannan. What Her Girl Friend Said to Him.
Kaya Shirao. Moonlit night / By melon flowers.
Kekova. With much effort, I glimpse in the darkness and rubbish.
Kelly, B. Leaving, The.
Kenney. Apples on Champlain.
Keplinger, D. Inside: George Gaines at Graterford Prison, 1981.
Khalvati. On Reading Rumi.
Kim Namjo. Evening Primrose.
Kingsolver. Remember the Moon Survives.
Kinnell. How Many Nights.
Kipling, R. Morning Song in the Jungle.
Kirchwey. Nocturne, Morningside Heights.
Kitahara Hakushū. Ailing child, An.
Knight, S. In Case of Monsters.
Kolmar. Judith.
Komrij. Park of the Dead.
Komunyakaa, Y. When Loneliness Is a Man.
Kooser. Late Lights in Minnesota.
Kumin, M. Sound of Night, The.
Kuzma. Night Things.
Kwŏn Homun. Nights After Rain When the Moon.
Kwŏn P'il. Alone at Night.
Lal Ded [or Lalla]. On the way to God the difficulties.
Lamartine. Infinite in the Skies, The.
Lanier, S. Song for "The Jacquerie".
Larkin, P. Sad Steps.
Laux, D. Smoke.
Lawrence, D. H. Southern Night.
Leivick, H. Lament at Night.
Levertov. Eye Mask.
Levin, P. Night Coach.
Levine, P. Simple Truth, The.
Lewis, A. Sentry, The.
Lezama Lima. Fragments of the Night, The.
Li Po. Jade-Staircase Grievance.
Verses: "Clean is the autumn wind."
Li Shang-yin. Ch'ang-O.
Night Rains: A Letter to Go North.
Without Title (1).
Li Yü. Tune: "The Crow's Nocturnal Cry".
River Rolling Eastward, The.
Li'aibi, S. My days pass with the beads of the rosary.
Linden, M. Silent Night, The.
Livingston, M. Night, The.

Lochhead, L. Noises in the Dark.
Longfellow, H. Day Is Done, The.
  Hymn to the Night.
  Night.
Lope de Vega. Where Are You Going, Maiden.
Lowell, A. Night Clouds.
Lowell, R. Night Sweat.
Loy. Three Moments in Paris.
Lu Lun. Grass rustle through dim woods.
Lugones. Indulgence.
  White Solitude.
MacDiarmid, H. Eemis-Stane, The.
Machado Ruiz. Song: "Now the moon is
  rising."
  Summer Night.
MacLeish. You, Andrew Marvell.
MacMuireadach. Farewell for ever to last night.
Mallarmé. Gift of the Poem.
  When the shade threatened with the fatal decree.
Mandelstam [or Mandelshtam]. I Was Washing
  Outside in the Darkness.
  O Lord, Help Me to Live Through This Night.
Marchant, F. Screen Porch.
Margulies, S. Relentlessly Lovelorn, the Non-
  Sleeper Whispers and Re-Whispers a Magic
  Charm Against His Wound's Roar.
Marlowe. Now ore the sea from her old Love
  comes she.
Martí. Two Countries.
Martínez de Navarrete. Separation from Clorila,
  The.
Martinez, D. Nocturnes: "He closed the deal on
  the night. A real."
Martínez, V. Nocturne: "To the interior, limbs
  folded."
Martynova, O. Night unwraps the true stuff of
  the world.
Marvell. Mower to the Glowworms [or Glow-
  Worms or Glo-Worms], The.
Mastin. Flying.
McAuley, J. Nocturne.
McClellan. September Night, A.
McCombs, J. Love Poem, Later.
McCord, D. This Is My Rock.
McDonald, C. Nightfishing.
McDonald, W. War in Bosnia, The.
McGrath, T. Guiffre's Nightmusic.
  Nocturne Militaire.
  Reading by Mechanic Light.
McMaster, R. Back Steps Lookout.
  Clockface.
McOrlan. Battery woman.
Mead, P. There.
Meleager. Night Alone, The.
Meng Hao Jan. Night on the Great River.
  Returning at Night to Lumen Mountain.
Merriam, E. Lullaby "Purple".
Merwin. Carol: "On vague hills the prophet
  bird."
Meynell, A. At Night.
Mezey. Owl.
Mihalic. Drinking Spree Beneath the Open Sky.
Miliauskaite. On Winter Nights.
Millay, E. Night is my sister, and how deep in
  love.
  Winter Night.
Miller, C. Night in San Francisco.
Miller, J. Four times during the night.
Miller, L. When the Moon Isn't Shining.
Milton. Il Penseroso.
Mistral, G. Night.
Mohr, J. Silent Night.
Momaday. Colors of Night, The.
Montale. Day and Night.
  Little Testament.
Montgomerie, A. Night Is Near [or Neir] Gone,
  The.
Moore, T. Echo ("At the mid hour of night,
  when stars are weeping, I fly.").
  Oft In the Stilly Night.
Morley, D. Air Street.
Moxon. Loud midnight-soothing melancholy
  bird.
Murphy, M. Villa Fidelia.
Na Hûidôk. There's Such an Evening.
Nelson, H. Peepers.

Neruda. If Each Day Falls.
  Poem 20.
Neumann, S. Winter Night.
Nguyễn Chí Thiện. Jungle Night, A.
Niedecker. Subliminal.
Oliver, D. Little Night, A.
Oliver, M. Design.
  Poem 12.
  White Night.
Ono no Komachi. Autumn nights, it seems.
  When longing for you.
  Yielding to a love.
O'odham. Songs for the Four Parts of the
  Night.
Oppen. Animula.
Orten. Last Poem, The.
Osherow. Villanelle for the Middle of the Night.
Osundare. Frantic as a prentice poet.
Pao Chao. Ballad: A Song in the Night.
Papaionnou. Nights Without Hope (Rebetiko
  Song).
Parker, A. Vandals, Horses.
Peacock, M. Of Night.
Pizarnik. Ashes.
  Deaf Lantern.
Po Chü-i. Rain.
  Sitting at Night.
  Village Snow, Sitting at Night.
  Winter Night.
Pope, A. Reign of Chaos, The.
  Yet, yet a moment, one dim ray of light.
Porta. Dialogue with Herz.
Porter, C. In the Still of the Night.
Posey, A. Nightfall.
Pound, E. Night Litany.
Price, C. Night Fishing.
Pushkin, A. Demons.
  Lines Written at Night During Insomnia.
Radcliffe, A. Night ("Now Ev'ning fades! her
  pensive step retires.").
  Night ("O'er the dim breast of ocean's wave.").
Rampolekeng. Wet Pain . . . Tread with Care.
Randell. Our hands crushed.
Rankine. Quotidian, The.
Reese, L. Nocturne: "Topple the house down,
  wind."
  One Night.
Reverdy. Nocturne: "Street is pure black and
  there are no seasonal traces, The."
  On the Threshold.
  Post.
Rexroth, K. Another Spring.
  Two flowers in a letter.
Reyes, C. Arizona Nocturne.
Reznikoff. House-wreckers, The.
  Still much to read, but too late.
Rilke. Last Evening, The.
Rimbaud, A. Decidedly we are out of the
  world. No longer any sound.
Roberts, K. Night Tumbles into Town by Rail.
Robinson, E. John Evereldown.
Rodgers, W. Stormy Night.
Roland Holst. Night Visit.
  Time, Please.
Rontsh, Y. Ballad of the Night.
Rosales. Growing Toward the Earth.
Rose, B. Night Is Young and You're So
  Beautiful, The.
Rossetti, C. From Sunset to Star Rise.
Rossetti, D. 66: The Heart of the Night.
Rukeyser, M. et al. My night awake.
Rumens. Jarrow.
Rumi. Inside water, a waterwheel turns.
  Night and Sleep.
  Night comes so people can sleep like fish.
  Thief in the Night, A.
  This night there are no limits to what may be
  given.
Rybicki, J. For Daniel Beels, Third Generation
  Bricklayer.
Ryokan. Late at night, listening to the winter
  rain.
Sachs, N. If the Prophets Broke in.
  Sleepwalker, The.
  You.
St. John, D. Lucifer in Starlight.

Salaam. All Nite Long.
  Our Natures Rise.
  Quarter Moon Rise.
Salinas, L. Nights in Fresno.
Salom. Walking at Night.
Samawi, S. Quartets of Inner Whispering.
Sandburg, C. Nocturne in a Deserted Brickyard.
  Window.
Sanguineti. Like a disk, a trembling coin
  spinning on its own diameter.
Sappho. Moon Has Set, The.
  Pleiades disappear, The.
Sassoon, S. Falling Asleep.
Satchell. Velvet Blanket.
Schultz, R. She Speaks to Her Husband,
  Asleep.
Scott, D. Night in June, A.
Scott, S. Melrose Abbey.
Seibles, T. 4AM.
Senghor. Before Night Comes.
  I Am Alone.
  Nocturne (I Accompanied You).
Serote. Night-time.
Sexton. Starry Night, The.
Shapiro, A. Cold Wood.
Sharp, S. Good Nights.
Shelley, P. To Jane: The keen stars were
  twinkling.
  To Night.
Shen Yüeh. Listening to Gibbons at Rock-Pool
  Creek.
Shepherd, R. Who Owns the Night and Lease
  Stars.
Sherwin, J. Nightpiece.
Shreve, S. Landing.
"Shunzei's Daughter.". Brought by the breeze.
Sidney. Sonnet 99: "When far-spent night
  persuades each mortal eye."
Sidney, R. Songe 17: "Sun is set, and masked
  night, The."
Silva, J. Nocturne: "One night / One night full
  of perfumes, music of wings and murmurs."
Simic. Night Picnic.
  Something, The.
Simon, M. Night.
Simpson, L. After Midnight.
Sitwell. Madwoman in the Park, The.
Slessor. Choker's Lane.
Smith, C. To Night.
  To the Moon.
Snyder, G. Night Song of the Los Angeles
  Basin.
Somoza, J. Late Light.
Soto. Soup, The.
Soupault. Condemned.
Soyinka. Night: "Your hand is heavy, Night,
  upon my brow."
Spark. Elementary.
Spencer, B. Night-Time: Starting to Write.
Stevens, W. Domination of Black.
  Girl in a Nightgown.
  Reality Is an Activity of the Most August
  Imagination.
  Two Figures in Dense Violet Night.
  Valley Candle.
Stevenson, A. Sonnet: "If it be night . . . ".
Stevenson, R. Bed in Summer.
  Moon, The.
Stever, E. Her Back to Me.
Strand. Late Hour, The.
  Morning, Noon and Night.
Strange. Night Work.
Swann, B. Walking at Night.
Swinburne. Garden of Proserpine, The.
Szymborska, W. Four in the Morning.
Taylor, J. Fairies' Song, The.
  Star, The.
Teasdale. August Night.
  Night.
Teillier, J. In the Secret House of Night.
Thomas, E. Out in the Dark.
Thompon, E. My Study.
Thompson, P. Winter Night, A.
Thomson, J. Night. Summer Meteors. A Comet.
Torres, E. Summertime Late Show.
Trakl. Decline.

Downfall.
Evening, The.
Grodek ("At evening the woods of autumn are full of the sound.").
Grodek ("In the evening the autumn woods ring.").
Revelation and Decline.
Romance to Night, A.
Summer: "At evening the complaint of the cuckoo."
Tranströmer.   Homewards.
Start of a Late Autumn Novel.
Track.
Trench, H.   She Comes Not When Noon Is on the Roses.
Tsang.   Street Angel, The.
Tsvetaeva [or Tsvetaeva].   Black as an iris, as an iris sucking up the.
Tu Fu [or Du Fu].   Autumn Night.
Brimmed Whole.
Chaos of mountains upon mountains, A.
Coming Home Late at Night.
Midnight.
New Moon.
Night feast at the Tsos.
Night Feast, Zuo Family Village.
Night in a Room by the River.
Night Thoughts While Travelling ("Light breeze rustles the reeds, A.").
Night Up in the Tower.
Passing the Night.
Restless Night. ("Cool of bamboo invades my room, The.").
Restless Night ("As bamboo chill drifts into the bedroom.").
Restless Night in Camp, A.
Spring Vigil in the Imperial Chancellery.
Summer Night.
Traveler at Night Writes His Thoughts, A.
Travelling Northward.
Tu Mu.   Mooring at River Ch'in-Huai.
Unsent.
Tzu Yeh.   It is night again.
Ungaretti.   Watch.
Unknown.   Author of this is Ossian, The.
Dum Diana Vitrea.
Girl and Her Companion, The.
Here in my garden.
How far from enough.
Hymn to Night.
In the dark night that keeps us apart.
In the Night.
In Time.
Moon shines on valley.
Mother's Song.
Night after night, I do not.
Night so.
Night so.
Night Was Growing Cold, The.
Oh Lord! Once again your long and dismal night is here.
Orchid Door, The.
Prayer to the Gods of the Night.
Were I to send word.
Yourself and Myself.
Unknown, fr. Terezin Concentration Camp.
Night in the Ghetto.
Untermeyer, L.   Robber, The.
Van den Bergh.   Nocturn: "Moon rows burning, The."
Vancrevel.   About Time ("At dusk the silence by the sea.").
About Time ("This silence at the sea's edge, so late in the afternoon.").
Vasileva, E.   She's calling God, she wants to ask Him.
Vaughan, H.   Night, The.
Very.   Morning Watch, The.
Night.
Villaurrutia.   Nocturne.
Nocturne of the Statue.
Nocturne: The Eternal.
Virgil [or Vergil].   Night-Piece, The.
Vogel, D.   How Can I See You, Love.
On autumn nights.
Volkman.   I was watching for it, everytime

watching, for the neck that was.
Wagoner, D.   Chorus: "That rain-strewn night in the woods, the chorus, chorus."
Wakoski.   Remembering the Pacific.
Walcott.   Nights in the Gardens of Port of Spain.
Wang Kuo-wei.   Tune: "Rouged Lips".
Tune: "Sand of Silk-Washing Brook" ("Hazy mountain temple hides away behind the setting sun, A.").
Wang Po.   Parting by Moonlight in a River Pavilion.
Wang Wei.   Autumn Mountain Evening.
Bird and Waterfall Music.
Bird-Cry Creek.
Bird-Singing Stream.
Ward, T.   Dark Underfoot.
Warner, G.   Midnight percussion.
Warren, R.   Birth of Love.
Night Walking.
Waters, M.   "Night in the Tropics" (1858-59?).
Weatherly, T.   P.W.T.
Webb, F.   Hospital Night.
Port Phillip Night.
Wei Chuang.   Candle Dies, A.
Wei Ying-wu.   Autumn Night Message: To Qiu.
Weiners.   Acts of Youth, The.
Welch, L.   Empress Herself Served Tea to Su Tung-Po, The.
Wen T'ing-yün.   Embers of Incense.
To the Tune: The Water Clock.
White, J.   To Night.
Whitman, W.   I wander all night in my vision.
On the Beach at Night.
Wicks, S.   Night Toad.
Wilbur, R.   After the Last Bulletins.
Sonnet: "Winter deepening, the hay all in, The."
Wilcox, E.   In the Night.
Williams, B.   Night Flute, The.
Williams, H.   To the Moon.
Williams, W.   Good Night.
Goodnight, A.
Rigamarole.
Wilson, K.   Dusk in My Backyard.
Winchilsea.   Nocturnal Reverie, A.
Wordsworth, W.   I watch, and long have watched, with calm regret.
Wright, C. D.   Elements of Night.
Wright, Charles.   Clear Night.
Nightletter.
Wright, F.   Lines Written in the Dark Illegible Next Day.
Wright, J.   Camphor Laurel.
Wrigley, R.   American Manhood.
Wroth.   Sonnet 1: "When night's black mantle could most darknes[s] prove."
Sonnet 19: "Come darkest night, be[e]coming sorrow best."
Sonnet 37: "Night, welcome art thou to my mind destrest [or distressed]."
Wynne, F.   Nocturne: "Long day was bright, The."
Ye Zi.   All night I could not sleep.
Yi Sanghûi.   I Ask in Late Evening.
Van Gogh.
Yolen.   Shepherd's Night Count.
Yu Xuanji.   Vanishing Spring Moves to Regret.
Zabolotsky [or Zabolotskii].   Nocturnal Garden.
Signs of the Zodiac are fading, The.
Zukofsky, L.   Ferry.
See also **Evening**

Nightclubs
Allen, F.   Way Back Then.
Barresi.   Nine of Clubs, Cleveland, Ohio.
Berke.   Dancing to the Track Singers at the Nightclub.
Davis, F.   Jazz Band.
Elmslie, K.   Amazon Club.
Gilbert, J.   Elephant Hunt in Guadalajara.
Hayes, T.   At Pegasus.
Hughes, L.   College Formal: Renaissance Casino.
Jazz Band in a Parisian Cabaret.
Jazzonia.
Neon Signs.
Saturday Night.
To Midnight Nan at Leroy's.

Iozia, J.   Last Night at the Flamingo.
McClure, M.   Jazz at the Intergalactic Nightclub.
Pollard, C.   I enjoy dancing.
On the first of January.
Tolson, M.   Mu.
Weaver, A.   Left Bank Jazz Society, The.
Wheeler, S.   In Juarez.
White, J.   Oshi.
Zimmer.   Romance.

Nightgowns
Stevens, W.   Disillusionment of Ten O'Clock.

Nightingales
Arnold, M.   Philomela.
Ausländer, R.   My Nightingale.
Barney, W.   Mr. Bloomer's Birds.
Barnfield [or Barnefield].   Philomel.
Blind.   Russian Student's Tale, The.
Boncho.   Nightingale / My clogs.
Borges.   To the Nightingale.
Bowen, E.   Nightingale, The.
Bridges, R.   Nightingales.
Cook, E.   Lines / Suggested by the Song of a Nightingale.
Drummond, W.   To a Nightingale.
Henley, W. E.   Blackbird, The.
Issa.   Don't fly off, nightingale.
Five yen each / A cup of tea.
Flowering plum, A.
Nightingale's song / this morning.
Keats.   Ode to a Nightingale.
Khoury-Gata.   She Used to Throw Her Old Crockery.
Lindsay, V.   Chinese Nightingale, The.
Marvell.   Mower to the Glowworms [or Glow-Worms or Glo-Worms], The.
Masaoka Shiki.   Aged nightingale / How sweet.
Maschwitz, E.   Nightingale Sang in Berkeley Square, A.
Monro, H.   Nightingale near the House, The.
Moxon.   Loud midnight-soothing melancholy bird.
Randolph, T.   On the Death of a Nightingale.
Ransom, J.   Philomela.
Rossetti, C.   Pain or Joy.
Shelley, P.   There the voluptuous nightingales.
Sidney.   Nightingale, The.
Smith, C.   On the Departure of the Nightingale.
To a Nightingale.
Takai Kito.   Nightingale / Rarely seen.
Unknown.   Alba ("When the nightingale to his mate").
Webb, H.   Nightingales, The.
Williams, W.   Chinese Nightingale.
Winchilsea.   To the Nightingale.

Nightmares
Abdul Karim.   Nightmare 1.
Nightmare 3.
al-Sa'igh, Y.   Intermittent.
Bampfylde.   On a Frightful Dream.
Belev.   Dream: "When the trees began to calcify, and the birds to coalesce with the branches."
Cisneros, S.   Poet Reflects On Her Solitary Fate, The.
D'Aguiar, F.   Airy Hall Nightmare.
Deltoro, A.   Anestesia.
Douglas, L.   To Sleep.
Frumkin.   Bad Dream and the Friend.
Harper, M.   Nightmare Begins Responsibility.
Heym.   Why Do You Come, White Moths.
Hudgins.   Mostly My Nightmares Are Dull.
Huerta, D.   Pathological Beings.
Seres patológicos.
Hughes, L.   Nightmare Boogie.
Jeffers, R.   Apology for Bad Dreams.
Kang Ûn'gyo.   Sound 8.
Kim Chiha.   No One.
Kim Sünghûi.   Horror Movie.
Lasheen, M.   Nightmares Fit to Arouse Misgivings.
Light, K.   My Worst Nightmare.
Loynaz, D. M.   I have slept and I awaken . . . Or I haven't awakened.
MacNeice.   Bad Dream.
Morisseau-Leroy, F.   Shooshoon.
Myers, B.   Dream Prison.
Raji Oyelade, R.   Cyclone.

Salganicoff. Nightmare.
Samaras, N. First Nightmare Waking.
Sarton, M. Tortured, The.
Stoyanova, Danila. Sea woke up, The.
Tatarunis, P. Before the Brain Surgery.
Tayson, R. Nightsweats.
Thomas, C. Bullet, A / slams.
Vando. In the Crevices of Night.
Wang Yen-Shou. Nightmare, The.
Warren, R. Original Sin [: A Short Story].
Wiseman. Triolets for Ken.
See also **Dreams and Dreaming**

Nihilism
Aiken, C. Prelude I: "Winter for a moment
takes the mind; the snow."
Ch'oe Sûngja. My Phone Rings Endlessly.
Lowell, R. Nihilist as Hero, The.
Mayakovsky [*or* Maiakovskii]. Cloud in
Trousers, A.
McNeil, R. It Just Doesn't Matter.
Murphy, K. Eighties Meditation.
Nemes Nagy. Shapelessness, The.
Nikolic, G. Under the Ninth Sky.
Ray, D. Automat.
Rochester, J. Upon Nothing.
Seneca. After Death Nothing Is.

Nijinsky, Vaslav
Hahn, S. Nijinksy's Dog.
Seferis. Nijinski.
Tyler, P. Nijinsky.

Nike
Allen, H. Wingless Victory, The.
Bryll. Nike.
Ilagha, N. Nike.

Nile (river)
Carroll, L. Crocodile, The.
Hunt, L. Nile, The.
López Mills, T. Advertisement.
Anuncio.
Love, C. Modern Love Poem, A.
Swift, J. Dogs of Nile, The.
Touré, A. Dawnsong!
Unknown. Voice of the Swallow, Flittering,
Calls to Me, The.

1950s
Elledge. Man I Love and I Have a Typical
Evening the Night Richard M. Nixon Dies,
The.
Koethe. From the Porch.

1960s
Baraka, I. Courageousness.
Barresi. Vacation, 1969.
Brown, S. No, No Nostalgia!
Burris. Very True Confessions.
Clinton, M. I Wanna Be Black.
DeFoe, M. Forgetting the Sixties.
García. Barrio Beateo.
Goldbarth. Counterfeit Earth!, The.
Gonzalez, R. Some Sixties.
Komunyakaa, Y. How I See Things.
La Loca. Why I Choose Black Men for My
Lovers.
Llwyd, Iwan. El Buen Samaritano keeps
reappearing.
Loftin, E. April '68.
Long, R. What's So Funny 'bout Peace, Love
and Understanding.
Machan. In 1969.
Murphy, K. Eighties Meditation.
Piercy. Learning Experience.
Poniewaz. Why Young Men Wore Their Hair
Long in the Sixties.
Soto. Dizzy Girls in the Sixties.
Heaven.
TV in Black and White.
Trinidad. Meet the Supremes.
Van Duyn. Christmas Card, After the
Assassinations, A.
What the Motorcycle Said.

Niobe
Ray, H. Niobe.

Nirvana
Andrews, N. Nirvana: "After you left me, I was
so lonely and sad, I became but an apparition,
a ghost of who I had been."

Baekoon Kyunghan. Untitled: "I've traveled
eight thousand miles."
Basho. Behind Ise Shrine.
Daegak Euchon. Riding a Horse in the Rain.
Hakuin. How lacking in permanence the minds
of the sentient.
Issa. Buddha's Nirvana / Beyond flowers.
Jinkag Haesim. At the Zendo.
Laughlin, J. What Is Hoped For.
Muso Soseki. For the Death of a Monk.
Pendell, D. Amra: The Neuropharmacology of
Nirvana.
Rexroth, K. It Is a German Honeymoon.
Sabok. At My Mother's Funeral.
Soyo Taeneung. Deathbed Song.
Sun Ch'o. Wandering on Mount Tiantai.
Wang Wei. Climbing Pien-chueh Temple.
Wonhyo, Great Master. Enlightenment Song.

Nixon, Richard Milhous
Balaban. April 30, 1975.
Di Prima. Brief Wyoming Meditation.
Quinn, J. Backgrounds.
Whalen, P. Regalia in Immediate Demand!
Woddis. Final Curtain.

Noah
Adonis [*or* Adunis]. New Noah, The.
Beer, P. Flood, The.
Cassells. From the Theater of Wine.
Daniells. Noah.
Deniz, G. Arca.
Ark.
Drayton. Hundred years the Ark in the building
was, A.
Duncan, R. Ballad of Mrs. Noah, The.
Gelinas, E. Jardín de madera.
Wood Garden.
Heath-Stubbs. History of the Flood, The.
Kingfisher, The.
Kendall, M. Vision of Noah, The.
Lewis, C. Late Passenger, The.
MacDiarmid, H. Parley of Beasts.
McGough, R. Noah's Ark.
Merwin. Noah's Raven.
Ombres. Ballad of Noah's Daughter.
Pau-Llosa. Noah.
Unknown. Noye, to me thou arte full able.
Wilbur, R. Still, Citizen Sparrow.

Nobility
Basho. How very noble!
Campion, T. What Fair[e] Pomp[e].
Cohan. Harrigan.
Guinicelli. Love and Nobility.
Hughes, Daniel. Too Noble.
Ibn Bājja. Trail the edge of your robe wherever
it pleases, and add more drunkenness to your
intoxication.
Lanier, E. Description of Cooke-ham [*or*
Cookham], The.
Lanyer. Description of Cooke-ham [*or*
Cookham], The.
Metwalli, M. This Is How the Magician
Produces a Dove out of the Hat.
Montague, J. Dowager.
Muso Soseki. From the beginning.
Osgood, F. Wraith of the Rose, The.
Unknown. That Shady Crab.

Noises
Albert-Birot. Balalaïka.
Allen, F. Sound Waves.
Atkins, R. At Night Keep Still.
Ball, H. Flight out of Time.
Clary. Another hot afternoon upstairs after
school.
Dacey, P. Squeak.
Densmore. Sky Will Resound, The.
Dunbar, P. When Malindy Sings.
Eigner. It Sounded.
Ellis, T. Practice.
Sir Nose D'VoidofFunk.
Francia, L. In Gurgle Veritas.
Graham, D. Varied Carol, The.
Gullar. Noise.
Hart, L. Johnny One-Note.
Hattersley, G. *On the Buses* with Dostoyevsky.
Herzberg. Seagulls.
Hugo, V. Open Windows.

Inada. Clearing.
Inez. Courtyard Noises from the North, Twenty-
fourth Precinct.
Lisnyanskaya [*or* Lisnianskaia]. Quiet days and
quiet evenings.
Lochhead, L. Noises in the Dark.
Marinetti. Landscape Heard, A.
McAuley, J. Dialogue.
McElroy, C. Illusion.
Morgan, E. Loch Ness Monster's Song, The.
Osherow. Villanelle for the Middle of the Night.
Raye, D. Milkman, Keep Those Bottles Quiet!
Roberts, L. Another Spring on Olmstead Street.
Stephens, J. In the Night.
Sundiata. Ear Training.
Unknown. Bald Mountain Zaum-Poems.
Yang Wan-li. Cold Sparrows.
Zukofsky, L. When the crickets.

Nomads
Dos Passos. Crimson Tent.

Noon
Bachmann. Early Noon.
Blind. Noonday Rest.
Clampitt. Meridian.
Clare, J. Noon.
Corbett, W. Cold Lunch.
Delaunay, S. Zenith.
Dickinson, E. It's like the Light.
Ferril. Noon.
Issa. Noon.
Jeffers, R. Noon.
Kuzmin. At noon I must have been conceived.
Li Shang-yin. High Noon.
Meynell, A. Study, A.
Montale. Sit the noon out, pale and lost in
thought.
O'Sullivan, L. Earth.
Strand. Morning, Noon and Night.
Xuanjing. Meditating at midnight.
Yi Sang. Noon—A Certain.

Normandy, Invasion of (1944)
Heaney, S. Testimony.
Henderson, H. Ballad of the D-Day Dodgers.
St. John, D. Six/Nine/Forty-Four.
Simpson, L. Carentan O Carentan.

Norse Mythology
Trakl. Grodek (Second Version).
Youn, Monica. Naglfar.

North Carolina (state)
Ammons. Alligator Holes Down Along About
Old Dock.
Applewhite. Village After Sunset, The.
Crawley, W. Bud.
Glück, L. Cottonmouth Country.
Mahon. Globe in [North] Carolina, The.
Rukeyser, M. Outer Banks, The.

North Dakota (state)
Bly, R. Scandal, The.
Flint, R. August from My Desk.
Wright, J. Poem Written under an Archway in a
Discontinued Railroad Station, Fargo, North
Dakota, A.

North Pole
Goedicke. Imprint of Microscopic Life Found
in Arctic Stones.
Jarrell, R. 90 North.

North Star
Mitchison. To a Fisherman with the Present of a
Knife.
Psaila, K. Polestar.

North, The
Alexander, E. Letter: Blues.
Crouch, S. Blackie Thinks of His Brothers.
Momaday. Winter Holding off the Coast of
North America.

North Wind
Kingsley, C. Ode to the Northeast Wind.
Unknown. Bei-feng: Cold Is the North Wind.

Northern Ireland
Bentley, N. Londonderry Air, The.
Cleary, B. Sealink.
Slouch.
Coles, R. Christmas, Belfast.
Grattan, P. Signs of an Organised Hand.
Heaney, S. Anahorish.

Casualty.
Funeral Rites.
Strand at Lough Beg, The.
Ulster Twilight, An.
Whatever You Say Say Nothing.
Killeen, G.   My Father's Angels.
Mac Lochlainn, G.   Rite of Passage.
MacNeice.   Carrickfergus.
Mahon.   Ecclesiastes.
Montague, J.   Cave.
   Last Journey.
   Lost Tradition, A.
Muldoon, P.   More a Man Has the More a Man
   Wants, The.
Paulin.   Settlers.
Pugh.   King Billy on the Walls.
Unknown.   Omagh Post Office Rhyme.

Northumberland, England
Halleck, F.   Alnwick Castle.
Lomax, M.   Kith.
Simms, C.   First English Wildcat, The.

Norway
Anderson, J.   Going to Norway.
Gregerson.   Norway.
Schnackenberg.   Returning North.

Noses
Bierce.   Nose.
Charara, H.   My Father Breaks the Neighbor's
   Nose.
Chin, D.   Sterling Williams' Nosebleed.
Dufferin and Clandeboye.   Mother's Lament,
   The.
Edson, R.   Elephant Tears.
Fagin, L.   Hello Again.
Issa.   From the end of the nose.
Lear, E.   Dong with a Luminous Nose, The.
Makusho, Layman.   Loving old priceless things.
Onitsura.   Plum blossoms / One's nose.
Quevedo y Villegas.   On a Chaplain's Nose.
   To a Nose.
Smith, I.   Nose, The.
Stone, R.   Nose, The.
Williams, W.   Smell.

Nostalgia
Adams, Cyd.   Longview, Texas.
Adams, L.   Once Upon a Time.
   Those Were the Days.
Adamson, H.   It's Been So Long.
Adcock, B.   Photograph of the Courthouse
   Square, 1950s.
Aridjis.   Self-Portrait in the Doorway.
Arturo, A.   Madrigal 3.
Atwood.   Before the War.
Ayukawa Nobuo.   Last I Heard, The.
Baca.   Book 3: La Guerra; Poem Thirteen.
   Book 5: Rebirth; Poem Twenty-Eight.
Barnstone, T. *et al.*   Trying to Sleep on My
   Father's Couch and Staring at the Fractured
   Plaster, I Recall.
Barot, R.   Reading Plato.
Bart, L.   Fings Ain't Wot They Used t'Be.
Baton, M.   Childhood in the Country, A.
Bauer, G.   Oldies But Goodies.
   On Seeing a '57 Chevy Cruising 16th and O.
Behlen, Charles.   Windy Day/Slayton, Texas.
Berger, B.   Waterfall: "Creek's easy purr, The."
Berlin.   White Christmas.
Berman, D.   Classic Water.
Bernstein, C.   When My Grandmother Said
   "Pussy."
Bibbins, M.   All but Lost.
Bishop, J.   Past and Present.
Blanco, R.   Elegant Endings.
   Silver Sands, The.
Bloze.   Beneath the Stars.
Boss, L.   At the Nuclear Rally.
Bowers, N.   On the Elvis Mailing List.
Breton, N.   Olden Love-making.
Brody.   Family Album, A.
Brown, S.   No, No Nostalgia!
Buckley, C.   Nostalgia.
Burnside, J.   Anstruther.
Carnevale.   Walking by the Cliffside Dyeworks.
Ćatić, M.   Nostalgia: "Way. . .way back. . .nine
   hills away."
Cavalieri.   First, The.

Charara, H.   My Father Breaks the Neighbor's
   Nose.
Chen Zi'ang.   Meditation on the Past at White
   Emperor City.
Ch'oe Sŭngja.   Do You Remember Ch'ŏongp'a
   Street?
   Voice, A: "Voice hidden in midair, The."
Christie.   Belongings.
Clanchy, K.   Timetable.
Clare, Eli.   This Familiarity.
Coleman, James.   Vipers, Flies, and Women of
   the Cloth.
Collins, B.   Nostalgia.
Cook, E.   Song of the Modern Time.
Coolbrith.   Retrospect: "Breath of balm—of
   orange bloom!, A."
Cooley, N.   Diane Arbus, New York.
Cortéz, L.   I Remember: "I remember
   kindergarten."
Coslow, S.   My Old Flame.
Crozier, L.   Packing for the Future: Instructions.
Curnow.   Country School.
Cuthbert, J.   Memories of St. George's Caye.
Davie, D.   Remembering the 'Thirties.
Davies, B.   Blue.
Davies, Grahame.   Liverpool.
Dawe, G.   Likelihood of Snow, The/ The
   Danger of Fire.
De Cristoforo, Violet Kazue.   Tenth Wedding
   Anniversary (July 3, 1994): Tsuki Oboro
   Totsugishi Yoru No Sora Datta.
DeFoe, M.   Dream Lover.
DeSylva, B. G.   California, Here I Come.
Doolittle, H.   Blue-geese, white-geese, you may
   say.
Drake, E.   It Was a Very Good Year.
   Just for Today.
Duffy, C.   Close.
Durcan.   Around the Corner from Francis
   Bacon.
Eady.   Nature Poem.
   Too Young to Know.
Ebb, F.   Class.
   Happy Time, The.
Eliot, T. S.   Marina.
Fanthorpe.   Mother-in-law.
Feinstein, S.   Singapore, July 4th.
Fiacc.   First Movement.
Fink, Robert A.   Certified Public Accountant
   recalls the Early 1950s, The.
Fitz-Simon, E.   Woods of Kylinoe, The: Song of
   the Irish Emigrant in North America.
Fried, E.   Invitation to Forget.
Frost, R.   Range-finding.
García.   Barrio Beateo.
García Lorca.   Song of the Cuban Blacks.
Georgiev, Marin.   Native Soil.
Gillies, V.   We Meet Again.
Gilmore, M.   Saturday Tub, The.
Ginsberg, A.   After Yeats.
Glaser, M.   Changing Address Books.
   English-Speaking Persons Will Find
   Translations.
Glenday, J.   Empire of Lights, The.
Glück, L.   Nostos.
Goldberg, B.   Bedtime Story.
Grey, C.   Hallelujah!
Hall, D.   Maple Syrup.
Hamod, S.   Leaves.
Harbach, O.   Yesterdays.
Harburg.   Last Night When We Were Young.
Hardy, T.   After a Journey.
   Lines to a Movement in Mozart's E-Flat
   Symphony.
   Places.
Harnick.   Sunrise, Sunset.
Harper, M.   Camp Story.
Harwood, G.   At Mornington.
Heissenbüttel.   Homesick.
Herbert, Z.   In a City.
Hernandez, D.   Armitage Street.
Hernández, M.   Each Time I Pass.
Hierro, José.   Accelerando.
Hill, J.   Grist for Grace.
Hirsch, E.   Days of 1968.
Holmes, D.   Nostalgia.

Hovald, I.   Stele for Lenz.
Howells, W.   November.
Hugo, R.   Places and Ways to Live.
Huws, Meirion MacIntyre.   Coat.
Issa.   My old home.
Jarnot, L.   What In Fire Did I, Firelover, Starter
   of Fires, Love?
Jarrell, R.   Player Piano, The.
Jenkins, A.   Chopsticks.
Jolson, A.   California, Here I Come.
Jones, R.   Failed Memory Exercise.
   Sweep.
Joseph, A.   Soul Train.
   Wedding Party.
Joyce, J.   Tutto è Sciolto.
Justice, D.   Nostalgia of the Lakefronts.
Kahn, G.   Love Me or Leave Me.
Kil Chae.   I return on horseback.
Killeen, G.   Rewind.
Kim Kwanguk.   Bamboo stick, the sight of you.
Kim Namjo.   Moonlit Night.
Kimbrell, J.   Salvation.
Kipling, R.   King, The.
Kleinzahler.   Hamburger.
Knight, S.   Big Parade, The.
Koch, K.   To My Twenties.
Koethe.   From the Porch.
Kuan Hsiu.   Song of the Palace of Ch'en.
Kumin, M.   For My Great-Grandfather: A
   Message Long Overdue.
   Height of the Season, The.
Lamb, C.   Old Familiar Faces, The.
Landon.   To My Brother: "Do you recall the
   fancies of many years ago."
Larkin, J.   Co-alcoholic.
Lawrence, D. H.   Piano.
Lehman.   January 20.
Leslie, E.   Among My Souvenirs.
Levis.   Picking Grapes in an Abandoned
   Vineyard.
   Widening Spell of the Leaves, The.
Lewis, A.   All Day It Has Rained.
   Mountain over Aberdare, The.
Li Po.   Ages have passed since the stately Odes
   flourished.
   Thinking of East Mountain ("It's forever since I
   faced East Mountain.").
Lihn.   Old Man's Monologue with Death, The.
Lim, S.   Black and White.
Lin, D.   Nostalgia: "O, fruitful district Corozal!"
Lloyd, C.   My pleasant home! where erst when
   sad and faint.
Llwyd, Iwan.   El Buen Samaritano keeps
   reappearing.
Longfellow, H.   My Lost Youth.
Longley, M.   Pattern, The.
Lumsden, R.   ITMA.
MacBeth [*or* Macbeth].   Shotts.
MacNeice.   Nostalgia.
Mahon.   Old Snaps, The.
Maio, Samuel.   Love Song: "New pier is
   concrete, the streets are paved, The."
Mallarmé.   Pipe, The.
Mayfield, C.   Thinking of a Friend.
McDonald, P.   Pleasures of the Imagination.
   Sunday in Great Tew.
McElroy, C.   From Homegrown: An Asian-
   American Anthology of Writers.
McFadden, R.   First Letter to an Irish Novelist.
   My Mother's Young Sister.
McGuckian.   Little House, Big House.
Melville, H.   Aeolian Harp, The.
   Archipelago, The.
   Temeraire, The.
Meng Hao Jan.   Night on the Great River.
   Written for Old Friends in Yang-Jou City While
   Spending the Night on the Tung-Lu River.
Merrill, J.   Days of 1994.
Mesmer, S.   What Becomes Us.
Milosz, O.   King Don Luis.
Mitsui.   Because of My Father's Job.
Montague, J.   Hearth Song.
   Herbert Street Revisited.
Mura.   To H.N.
Nathaniel, Isabel.   Elegy at Mustang Island.
   Galveston.

Neruda. Final.
Niccolai. "What's that?" the boy asks his mother, pointing to the flag.
Nims, J. Tennis Trophy.
No Ch'ŏnmyŏng. Nostalgia.
Road.
Noguchi, Yonejiro (Yone). In Japan Beyond.
Nye, N. Boy Removes All Traces from His Room, The.
Okita. Nice Thing About Counting Stars, The.
Orban, O. Blade of Grass, A.
Ortiz, D. Ladders.
Ortiz. My Mother and My Sisters.
Parish. Deep Purple.
Patchen. Street Corner College.
Peacock, T. In the days of old.
Penna. When I don't feel well, I wander among.
Peterson, J. Cody. La Jolla. In 3 Acts.
Petrov, V. Cry from Childhood, A.
Piatt, S. Hundred Years Ago, A.
Pierce, T. Twenty-First Century, Farewell.
Popa. Little Box, The.
Pound, E. Hugh Selwyn Mauberley.
Preil, G. Brief Note from Jerusalem, A.
Randall, M. Borders.
Ras. Childhood.
Reed, I. Reactionary Poet, The.
Rekdal, Paisley. Americana.
Reposa, Carol Coffee. At Fort Clark. Hempstead, 1923.
Rexroth, K. How long, long ago.
Once again I hear.
Reynolds, R. Surplus.
Rich, A. Living Memory.
Riley, J. Days Gone By, The.
Rilke. Childhood.
Robin, L. Hallelujah!
Robinson, E. Calverly's.
Miniver Cheevy.
Roethke. Otto.
Rosales. Evocation to Record a Music Box.
Rossiter. Nostalgia.
Rozhdestvensky [or Rozhdestvenskii]. Nostalgia.
Runciman, L. Robert Frost.
Sacré, J. Little Boy, I'm Not Sure Anymore, A.
Salaam. Moment of the First Day, The.
Schultz, P. Stories.
Schuyler, J. Can I Tempt You to a Pond Walk?
Scott, P. Dying In.
Shin Kyŏngnim. Road, The.
Simmons, J. One of the Boys.
Stephano Remembers.
Smith, C. Written in Farm Wood, South Downs, in May 1784.
Smith, D. Tire Hangs in the Woods, The.
Snodgrass. Mementos, 1.
Sŏ Chŏngju. New Year's Prayer: 1976.
Sokol, J. Robert Frost's Books, Ripton, Vermont, 1980.
Song. Father and Daughter.
Spender, S. I Think Continually of Those Who Were Truly Great.
Stanford, A. I Thought Back and.
Stevens, C. J. New Blue Bike, A.
Stevenson, R. Home no more home to me, whither must I wander?
Stewart, J. On Speed, or How We Murdered Nostalgia.
Stickney, T. Quiet after the rain of morning.
Sullivan, Mary Louise. Unearth.
Swift, T. Tenant Of Wildfeld Hall, The.
T'ao Ch'ien [or T'ao Yuan-ming]. After Kuo Chu-Pu's Poems.
Taylor, H. Flying Change, The.
Tennyson, A. Break, Break, Break.
Tears, Idle Tears.
Terán, V. En la palma de mi mano.
In the Palm of My Hand.
Ndaani' batanaya'.
Thể Lũ'. Green Nostalgia.
Thomas, E. I never saw that land before.
Thomas, L. Back in the Day.
Thompson, P. Shape of Things, The.
Two Photographs.
Tornero, A. Lisos al extremo cuando voltearon

diurnos.
Smooth in the extreme when they turned around diurnal.
Townsend, A. Mardi Gras Premortem.
Trakl. Song of the Western Countries.
Trinidad. Meet the Supremes.
Movin' with Nancy.
Tsanev, Stefan. Nostalgia, or a Painful Return to Memories.
Turner, C. Hence with your jeerings, petulant and low.
Valentine, J. Night Lake.
Vaughan, H. Retreat[e], The.
Villanueva, T. Haciendo Apenas la Recolección.
Wah. Father / Mother Haibun #4.
Warton, T. Sonnet: To the River Lodon.
Weaver, A. Blind Solo.
Weems, M. Yesterday.
Westendorf. I'll Take You Home Again, Kathleen.
Whitbread. November 25, 1963.
White, H. Men There Were Then, The.
Whitman, W. Old Man's Thought of School, An.
Williams, C. K. Dress, The.
Sanctity, The.
Still Life.
Williams, W. Raleigh Was Right.
Williamson, A. Childhood Around 1950, A.
Wodehouse. Tulip Time in Sing Sing.
Wong, N. Dreams in Harrison Railroad Park.
Woodworth, S. Old Oaken Bucket, The.
Wright, C. Homage to Claude Lorrain.
Other Side of the River, The.
Poet Grows Older, The.
Wright, J. Sisters, The.
Wu Wen-ying. Tune: "Rouged Lips" Rain Just Over on the Night of the Lantern Preview.
Xue Di. Nostalgia.
Yi Hyangji. What Did You Do Yesterday?
Yi Sanghûi. Morning Stroll, A.
Organizing a Drawer.
Yi Yuksa. Small Park, A.
Yup. Things I Miss, The.
Zand, R. Hot House.
Zimmer. Another Place.

Nothingness
Alféri, Pierre. When Nothing Entices Nothing.
Amichai, Y. Like Our Bodies' Imprint.
Artaud. Nerve Meter, The.
Bang, M. Eye Like a Strange Balloon Mounts Toward Infinity, The.
Beck, T. Sonnet to Nothing.
Beckett, S. Something There.
Benn. Fragments.
Bevington, L. Midnight.
Breytenbach. Padmapani.
Cage. Lecture on Nothing.
Celan. Psalm: "No one kneads us again out of earth and clay."
Chang Yüeh. Hearing Bells at Night in the Mountains.
Clifton, L. 1. at nagasaki.
Coolidge, C. Saturday Night.
Daito. To slice through Buddhas, Patriarchs.
De Angelis. Main Idea, The.
DiPalma. Bed, The.
Ekelof. Like Ankle-Rings, This Music.
Fletcher, P. To Thomalin.
Getsudo. I moved across the Dharma-nature.
Gevirtz, S. Hyphen's Hyphen.
Gido. Inscription over His Door.
Gilbert-Lecomte. Preface or The Drama of Absence in an Eternal Heart.
Glück, L. Moonless Night.
Glück, R. Famous monk dropped to this knees before a giant image and cried, A.
Hadewijch II. Tighten.
Hakuin. You no sooner attain the great void.
Han Wo. Letter to a Zen Master.
Hayes, T. Nothing.
Hernton, C. Being Exit in the World.
Hood, T. No!
Ikkyu Sojun. Form in Void.
Void in Form.
Jabès. Notebook, Two.

Juarroz. Bell is full of wind, The.
Every word is a doubt.
Kanzan-Shigyo. Where is the dragon's cave?
Karasumaru-Mitsuhiro. Beware of gnawing the ideogram of nothingness.
Keats. When I Have Fears [That I May Cease to Be].
Kloos, W. Trees, Late in the Season.
Kokai. Taking hold, one's astray in nothingness.
Kukoku. Riding backwards this wooden horse.
Kyurin-Eki. Eighty-three years—at last.
Lao Tzu. Thirty spokes converge on a single hub.
Lejeune, Claire. Illiterate.
Li Po. Inscription on an Old Tomb at Guangling.
Lochhead, D. Nothing: "Now, this beginning."
MacLeish. End of the World, The.
Mandelstam [or Mandelshtam]. [Last Poems]. O how much I would like—.
McClure, M. Unchanged.
Milán, E. ¿Cuál coro?
He sends word for them not to be in His place.
I believe in nothing, I collaborate, I assist.
Manda decir que no estén en Su lugar.
What chorus?
Yo no creo nada, yo colaboro, ayudo.
Murray, L. Quality of Sprawl, The.
Muso Soseki. Vainly I dug for a perfect sky.
Nanei. Splitting the void in half.
Nensho. Only genuine awakening results in that.
Niedecker. What horror to awake at night.
Padgett, R. Nothing in That Drawer.
Paquin, Ethan. Hearing Music Through Dark Trees.
Parra, N. Resounding Zero, A.
Pasolini. Presence, The.
Piatt, S. If I Had Made the World.
Rakan-Keinan. Today Rakan, riding an iron horse.
Ramanujan. Salamanders.
Rexroth, K. Void Only.
Robinson, E. Man against the Sky, The.
Rodgers, W. Neither Here nor There.
Roethke. Duet.
Ryushu Shutaku. For all these years, my certain Zen.
Sahagún, C. Story Begins Here, The.
Saisho. On Joshu's Nothingness.
Sekishitsu-Soei. Fifty-three years / This clumsy ox has managed.
Slonimski. Elegy: "No more, no more Jewish townships in Poland."
Smith, S. Dream of Comparison, A.
Stevens, W. Clear Day and No Memories, A.
Snow Man, The.
Stramm. Urdeath.
T'aego, National Preceptor. Nothingness.
Tekkan. No mind, no Buddha, no being.
Tessho. Finally out of reach.
Villa, D. In the end.
Whitman, W. Hast Never Come to Thee an Hour.
Woljo Toan. Deathbed Song.
Wright, C. Sitting Outside at the End of Autumn.
Xuanjue. Let Them Mock!
Yoketsu. Nothing longed for.
Zekkai Chushin. Void has collapsed upon the earth, The.
Zych. Auschwitz, 1987.
See also **Nihilism**

Notre Dame Cathedral
Mandelstam [or Mandelshtam]. Notre Dame.
Notre Dame.
Takamura Kotaro. Cathedral in the Thrashing Rain.

Nova Scotia, Canada
Bishop, E. First Death in Nova Scotia.
Poem: "About the size of an old-style dollar bill."
Carman, B. Low Tide on Grand Pré.
Lochhead, D. Winter Lanscape—Halifax.

Novels
Alexie. How to Write the Great American

Indian Novel.
Berman, D.   Democratic Vistas.
Campbell, R.   On Some South African Novelists.
Cope, W.   Exchange of Letters.
Datcher, M.   Soul gestures in spring.
Jones, R.   Novel, The.
Joyce, J.   Blurb for *Anna Livia Plurabelle*, A.
Moramarco, F.   Novel.
Mueller, L.   Possessive Case, The.
Nemerov.   Style.
Norwid, C.   Recipe for a Warsaw Novel.

Novelty
Lejeune, Claire.   Death, I Speak of It.
Olson, C.   Celestial Evening, October 1967.

November
Bancquart.   I Walk in the Solitude of Books.
Bryant, W.   November.
Coleridge, H.   November.
Crapsey.   November Night.
Doubleday, T.   No walk today;—November's breathings toss.
Frost, R.   My November Guest.
Honig, E.   November through a Giant Copper Beech.
Hood, T.   No!
Howells, W.   November.
Jeffers, R.   November Surf.
Kelly, B.   To the Lost Child.
Levine, A.   Four November 9ths.
Morgan, E.   Birthday, The: "I'm driving tonight into November."
Ray, H.   November.
Ruefle.   American Dream, An.
   Melancholiacs, The.
Sterling, G.   Last Days, The: "Russet leaves of the sycamore, The."
Tomlinson, C.   Saving the Appearances.
Toomer.   November Cotton Flower.
Ts'en Shen.   Song for General Zhao.
Whitman, S.   November Landscape, A.

Nuclear Accidents
Bhatt, S.   Wine from Bordeaux.
Canan.   Radioactive.
Chadwick, J.   Eight-Legged Colt, Chernobyl.
Lewis, G.   Chernobyl Icon.
Meinke.   Atomic Pantoum.
Metras, G.   Utilities Advertisement in the Wake of Three Mile Island.
Moore, H.   Spuyten Duyvil.
Nobles, E.   Nuclear Winter.
Romtvedt.   Kiev, the Ukraine, Nuclear Accident.
Salter.   Chernobyl.
Stainer.   Sarcophagus.
   Xochiquetzal.
Tranter.   Glow-boys.
Wojahn.   Workmen Photographed inside the Reactor.

See also **Radiation and Radiation Sickness**

Nuclear Energy
Bass, E.   They're Family Men.
Bruchac.   Wahsah Zeh (War Dance)—As Long as the Grass.
de Fréine, C.   Inside.
Ginsberg, A.   Plutonian Ode.
Griffin, S.   Prayer for Continuation.
Hillard, J.   Message, The.
Jordan, J.   Directions for Carrying Explosive Nuclear Wastes through Metropolitan New York.
Metras, G.   Utilities Advertisement in the Wake of Three Mile Island.
Morgan, R.   Uranium.
Sanchez, S.   Reflections After the June 12th March for Disarmament.
Shinkichi Takahashi.   Explosion.
Stainer.   Sarcophagus.
Williams, C. K.   Tar.

Nuclear Tests
Ai.   Chance.
Heyen.   N.
La Morticella.   Liturgy for Trinity, A.
Louis, A.   Nevada Red Blues.
Rich, A.   Trying to Talk with a Man.
Stafford, W.   At the Bomb Testing Site.

Trentham, E.   Hurricane Season.
Vasquez, R.   Early Morning Test Light over Nevada, 1955.
Zimmer.   But Bird.

Nuclear War
Ai.   Testimony of J. Robert Oppenheimer, The.
Antler.   Bringing Zeus to His Knees.
Bensley.   War Games.
Bold, A.   As if a few odd bombs were bouncing around.
Buckley, C.   Why I'm in Favor of a Nuclear Freeze.
Canan.   Radioactive.
Cherry, K.   Prayer for a Future Beyond Ideology and War.
Clifton, L.   1. at nagasaki.
Cooper, Allan.   To an Unborn Child.
Dickey, W.   Armageddon.
Ehrhart.   Way Light Bends, The.
Figueroa, J.   Confessions from the Last Cloud.
Goedicke.   Shadow.
Grabill.   Lightning, The.
Griffin, S.   Prayer for Continuation.
Harris, J.   Dream of the Hair Burning Smell.
Hoffman, D.   Seals in Penobscot Bay, The.
Holmes, D.   We Have Never Seen the Sky Light Up.
Huchel.   Psalm: "That from the seed of men."
Hudgins.   Late Spring in the Nuclear Age.
Kay, J.   Waiting Lists, The.
Keenan, T.   After the Neutron.
Kinnell.   Fundamental Project of Technology, The.
Kizer, C.   Election Day, 1984.
   Twelve O'Clock.
Kumin, M.   How to Survive Nuclear War.
Laux, D.   Garden, The.
Levertov.   Age of Terror.
Lowell, R.   Fall 1961.
MacBeth [*or* Macbeth].   Crab-Apple Crisis, The.
Martin, C.   Terminal Colloquy.
McGrath, T.   Nuclear Winter.
   War Resisters' Song.
Mitchell, A.   Fifteen Million Plastic Bags.
Moore, H.   Spuyten Duyvil.
Niedecker.   Radio talk this morning, The.
Olds, S.   When.
Oresick.   In this third year of Reagan, my 27th year.
Porter, P.   Your Attention Please.
Ray, J.   Rose Bay Willow Herb.
Romtvedt.   Eating Dinner at My Sister's.
Sankichi, T.   Flames.
Simon, M.   Tale Before the End of the World.
Snyder, G.   Strategic Air Command.
   Vapor Trails.
Spires.   Sunday Afternoon at Fulham Palace.
Strand.   When the Vacation Is Over for Good.
Sumrall.   Silence at the End of the World.
Vilariño.   Maybe Then.
Wilbur, R.   Advice to a Prophet.
Williams, B.   Srategies for Survival.
Wisenberg, S.   May 28, 1945.
Wright, C.   On the Eve of Our Mutually Assured Destruction.
Yourcenar, Marguerite.   Daily Papers.
Zimmer.   Because of Duties, Zimmer Had Forgotten the Forest.

See also **Atomic Bomb; Radiation and Radiation Sickness**

Nuclear Winter
Cherry, K.   Prayer for a Future Beyond Ideology and War.
McGrath, T.   Nuclear Winter.
Nobles, E.   Nuclear Winter.
Samaras, N.   Nuclear Winter.

Nudity and Nudists
Bataille, Georges.   I Dreamed of Touching.
Berger, J.   Gun, The.
Buson.   With no underrobes.
Campbell, R.   Sisters, The.
Cavafy.   Days of 1908.
Damas.   Through the Half-Opened Window.
Drieu la Rochelle.   Tennis.
Dunn, S.   Cohabiting.
Feldman, I.   Se Aprovechan.

Graves, R.   Naked and the Nude, The.
Jones, R.   Nudes.
Kennedy, X.   Nude Descending a Staircase.
Kirby, D.   To a French Structuralist.
Lal Ded [*or* Lalla].   Soul, like the moon, The.
Lawrence, D. H.   Innocent England.
McDowell.   Where and What You Are.
Moulds, J.   Renoir's Bathers.
Mueller, L.   Nude by Edward Hopper, A.
Noguchi, R.   Turn of Privacy, The.
Olds, S.   Once.
Phillips, C.   Luncheon on the Grass.
Pritchard, N.   Springtime.
Ryan, K.   Chemise.
Saje, N.   Male in the Women's Locker Room, A.
Stafford, W.   Adults Only.
Sutherland, Fraser.   On the Beach One Day.
Wagoner, D.   Walt Whitman Bathing.
Wilbur, R.   Playboy.

Numbers
Alcosser.   My Number.
Branch, A.   I used to think . . . number was fixed and still.
Conoley, G.   New.
Coolidge, C.   At the Poem.
Cornish, M.   Numbers: "I like the generosity of numbers."
Dillard, A.   God: "Numbers from one to ten, however, are called."
Gioia.   Counting the Children.
Hamby, B.   Six, Sex, Say.
Haxton.   Interval of Five Tones Being the Dominant, An.
József, A.   Seventh, The.
Kalina, R.   To Anne Frank.
Khlebnikov, V.   Numbers: R, K, L, G—.
Leigh, C.   I've Got Your Number.
Niccolai.   Careful that these *Frisbees*.
Palmer, M.   Sonnet: "Now I see them sitting me before a mirror."
Péret.   My Final Agonies.
Reed, I.   Loup Garou Means Change Into.
Rothenberg, J.   Numerology.
Smith, D.   2000.
Soto.   Teaching Numbers.
Stein, G.   Kneeling.
Swenson, M.   Cardinal Ideograms.
Volkman.   There comes a time to rusticate the numbers. The way the birds, jug.
Wah.   Music At The Heart Of Thinking 54.
Wheatley, D.   Numerology.

Nuns
Brownjohn.   In a Convent Garden.
Chaucer.   Prioresse, A.
Cho Chihun.   Nun's Dance, The.
Clarke, A.   Martha Blake at Fifty-one.
Cofer, J.   Purpose of Nuns, The.
Davidson, J.   Ballad of a Nun, A.
Dennis, C.   St. Francis and the Nun.
Di Prima.   To the Unnamed Buddhist Nun Who Burned Herself to Death on the Night of June 3, 1966.
Durcan.   Sister Agnes Writes to Her Beloved Mother.
Freeman, Jessica.   Garden District Soubrette.
Hopkins, G.   Heaven-Haven.
   Wreck of the Deutschland, The.
Jennings, E.   Mental Hospital Sitting-Room, A.
Jones, B.   Portrait of a Nun.
Kizer, C.   Election Day, 1984.
Klein, A.   For the Sisters of the Hôtel Dieu.
Korean Oral Tradition.   Wretched Married Life (Folk Song from Koch'ang).
Kumin, M.   Nuns of Childhood, The: Two Views.
Lluellyn [*or* Lluelyn].   Epithalamium: To Mistress M. A.
Milton.   Sonnet 9: "Ladie [*or* Lady], that in the prime of earliest youth."
Mo Shih-lung.   Saying Good-bye to a Singing Girl Who Has Decided to Become a Nun.
Ormond.   To a Nun.
Palazzeschi.   Nuns Go Walking.
Parry-Williams.   From a Travel Diary.
Procter, A.   Legend of Provence, A.

Rohrer, M.   Short History of Illumination, A.
Senryū, K.   As he smiles.
Shakhova.   Autobiographical Response from a
   Provincial Wasteland (in Reply to a New
   Year's Greeting Sent with a Bouquet).
Shomer.   Falling for Jesus.
Teasdale.   Effigy of a Nun.
Unknown.   Bleeding Nun, The.
   God send euerie Preist ane wyfe.
Wilcox, F.   Nine Flower Mountain.
Wronsky, G.   Be a child forever.
Yasui.   Asking the Second Nun.

Nuremberg, Germany
Cunard.   To Eat To-day.
Slessor.   Nuremberg.

Nursery Rhymes
Cyril.   Children's Games.
Kennedy, X.   Help!
Mother Goose.   Three blind mice, see how they
   run!
Otiono, T.   Rainsong.
Unknown.   Old Mother Hubbard.
   Ride a cock-horse to Banbury Cross.
   Sam, Sam, the butcher man.
   See-saw, Margery Daw.
   Sukey [*or* Suky], you shall be my wife.

Nurses
Betjeman.   Death in Leamington.
Blake, W.   Nurse's Song ("When the voices of
   children are heard on the green.").
Centolella.   Woman of Three Minds, The.
Darling, J.   Nurses.
Eigner.   How It Comes About.
Fagg, M.   Mrs Nightingale.
Fenton, J.   Red Light District Nurse, The.
Fuller, J.   Red Light District Nurse, The.
Jeffers, H.   To Keep from Shouting Something.
Kendrick, D.   Inpatient.
Kipling, R.   Nurses, The.
Laux, D.   Nurse, The.
Levertov.   Malice of Innocence, The.
Locker-Lampson.   Terrible Infant, A.
Longfellow, H.   Santa Filomena.
Moorer.   Negro Heroines.
Mueller, J.   Year.
Po Chü-i.   Remembering Golden Bells.
Jones, R.   Nurse, The.
Roethke.   Frau Bauman, Frau Schmidt, and Frau
   Schwartze.
Ryan, T.   Enough.
Schneider, M.   Bath: "Kindness, an Irish lilt in
   her voice."
Scott, F.   Last Rites.
Shuster, D.   Mellow on Morphine.
Unknown.   Hospital Duties.
   Sweet Polly Oliver.
Waring, B.   Baby Random.
Whitman, W.   Bearing the bandages, water and
   sponge.
   Wound-Dresser, The.
Yau.   Late Night Movies I.

Nursing Homes
Bourne, Lesley-Anne.   Boy I Never Met, The.
Chase, N.   My Mother, Listening to Flowers.
Craig, David.   Nursing Home, 3rd Shift.
Garcia, R.   Nobody Here But Us.
Gardiner, S.   Cactus.
Potter, Carol.   White Hotel.

Nurturing
Agustini.   Life.
Aubert, A.   Baobab.
Coles, R.   Goddam Street, The.
Flynn, N.   Workers (attendants).
Gex-Breaux, Q.   Padded Steps/Sister Song (a
   litany).
Giovanni.   Always There Are the Children.
Katrovas.   Rehab.
Kumin, M.   Nurture.
Mistral, G.   Rocking.
Perrier, Anne.   All Earth's Things.
Price, V.   Artemis: "Bear mother, supple."
Shiphrah, T.   Grandma.
Suárez.   Now That I Have Grown Up, Mother.
Whitman, W.   Roots and Leaves Themselves
   Alone.

Winbush-David, W.   African Sunrunner.

Nymphs
Anyte [*or* Anytes].   Lone Theudotos placed this
   gift beneath the mountain.
Barnes, B.   Sestine 4.
Black, S.   Personals.
Calvino.   Armilla.
Darwin.   Fine Figure of a Nymph.
Doolittle, H.   Oread.
Herrick.   To the Water Nymphs, Drinking at the
   Fountain.
Mallarmé.   Afternoon of a Faun, The.
   Favn in the Afternoon, A.
Marvell.   Nymph Complaining for the Death of
   Her Faun [*or* Fawn], The.
Moiro.   Tree nymphs, daughters of River,
   ambrosial.
More, H.   Inscription in a Beautiful Retreat
   Called Fairy Bower.
Pastorius.   Penance, A.
Piccolo.   Veneris Venefica Agrestis.
Prior.   Question, to Lisetta, The.
Pritchard, N.   Landscape with Nymphs and
   Satyrs.
Radcliffe, A.   Song of a Spirit.
Seward.   Speech of the Nymph.
Smith, C.   To the Naiad of the Arun.
Van den Bergh.   Nocturn: "Moon rows burning,
   The."
Warton, T.   On Bathing.
Wilbur, R.   Ceremony.
Winchilsea.   Adam Posed.
Wroth.   Sonnet 3: "Juno still jealous[e] of her
   husband Jove."

O

Oak Trees
Basho.   Oak tree, The.
   That great blue oak.
Ceravolo.   Drunken Winter.
Drayton.   Then Frome (a nobler flood) the
   Muses doth implore.
Houston, Margaret Bell.   Old Oak Speaks, The.
Hudgins.   Young Oaks, The.
Kushner, A.   Oak, The.
Kyurin-Eki.   Eighty-three years—at last.
Lanier, E.   Now let me come unto that stately
   tree.
Lanyer.   Now let me come unto that stately tree.
Locker-Lampson.   Old Oak Tree at Hatfield
   Broadoak, The.
Pinkerton, H.   Nature Note: The California
   Poison Oak.
Ransom, J.   Parting, without a Sequel.
Reid-Marr, David Tokuyu.   Live Oak.
Roberson, E.   Sonnet.
Robertson, R.   New Gravity.
Shannon, A.   Wet Oak.
Synge.   To the Oaks of Glencree.
Warren, R.   Bearded Oaks.
Whitman, W.   I Saw in Louisiana a Live-Oak
   Growing.
   Live Oak, with Moss.
Williams, G.   Oak Tree.

Oases
Anyte [*or* Anytes].   I, Hermes, have been set up.
   Stranger, below the boulder rest your spent
   limbs.
Cameron, N.   Green, Green Is El Aghir.
See also **Deserts**

Obedience
Chernoff.   Miss Congeniality.
Cooley.   Poem on the First Day of School.

Obesity
Ansen.   Fatness.
Ap Glyn, Ifor.   I'm the Guy with the Gut.
Eliot, T. S.   Bustopher Jones: The Cat About
   Town.
Erdrich, H.   Fat in America.
Nichols, G.   Invitation.
   Thoughts drifting through the fat black woman's
   head while having a full bubble bath.
Palmer, Debbra.   Wade's Hoggers.

Queneau.   Reinforcements [2].
Raye, D.   Mister Five by Five.
Schneiders, J.   Weight.
Wright, James.   Old Bud.
Wright, John.   Walking the Dog.
Yolen.   Fat Is Not a Fairy Tale.

Obituaries
Hierro, José.   Requiem ("Manuel del Río,
   born.").
Holman, M.   Mr. Z.
Mattawa.   I Was Buried in Janzoor.

Oblivion
Amichai, Y.   Like Our Bodies' Imprint.
Apollinaire.   Stanzas Against Forgetting.
Bobrowski.   Elderblossom.
Borges.   Everness.
   Ewigkeit.
Brooks, G.   When you have forgotten Sunday:
   the love story.
Catullus.   Carmen 5.
Davenant [*or* D'Avenant].   Lover and
   Philosopher.
Dıranas, A.   Oblivion: "Twilight hours are
   always gruff and gory."
Dowson.   Dregs.
Eberhart, R.   On a Squirrel Crossing the Road in
   Autumn, in New England.
Hannon.   Real Estate.
Hughes, L.   Shame on You.
Ivask, Y.   Shall we forget the shiver.
Kang Ŭn'gyo.   Sleet.
Lawrence, D. H.   Tabernacle.
MacDiarmid, H.   Eemis-Stane, The.
Mallarmé.   With her pure nails offering their
   onyx high.
Oliver, M.   Little Owl Who Lives in the
   Orchard.
Pilinszky, J.   Passion of Ravensbrück.
Preil, G.   Words of Oblivion and Peace.
Ritsos.   Underneath Oblivion.
Shinkichi Takahashi.   Sea of Oblivion.
Sisson.   Un-Red Deer, The.
Soupault.   Condemned.
Szymborska, W.   End and Beginning.
   End and the Beginning, The.
Taneda Santoka.   Nothing left of the house.

Obscenity
Gogarty.   On First Looking into Krafft-Ebing's
   Psychopathosexualis [*or* Psychopathia
   Sexualis].
Hirschman, J.   Tremor, The.
Hoagland, T.   Dickhead.
Lawrence, D. H.   Broadcasting to the G.B.P.
   Innocent England.
Unknown.   Army Dance, The.
   Generals Ride in Cars.
   I ask you to witness, Priapus.
   Oh! Fucking Halkirk.
   Twats in the Ops Room.
See also **Pornography**

Obscurity
Barkova, A.   Few Autobiographical Facts, A.
Cooley.   For Jude the Obscure.
De Vere, E.   Poem: "Were I a king, I could
   command content."
Gioia.   Guide to the Other Gallery.
Goldsmith, K.   One pair ridiculous gorilla
   slippers; 3 pairs of cheap shit sunglasses.
Kizer, C.   To an Unknown Poet.
Sappho.   When you die you'll lie dead, no
   memory of you.
Shwarts [*or* Shvarts].   Sale of a Historian's
   Library.
Simonides.   There is a tale.
Williamson, G.   Counterfeiter, The.

Observatories
Eady.   View from the Roof, Waverly Place.
Keyes, S.   Greenwich Observatory.
See also **Astronomy and Astronomers**

Obsessions
Adam, H.   I Love My Love.
Agustini.   Ineffable, The.
Al-Bayati, A.   Shiraz Moon.
Bernard [*or* Bernart] de Ventadour [*or*
   Ventadorn].   When—presto—turf and trees

are green.
Berryman. Canto Amor.
Brown, E. Tell me I'm beautiful, and bring me flowers.
Byron, G. Last Words on Greece.
Chinese Oral Tradition. Scroll 1: "From the Three Emperors and Five Kings down to Hsia, Shang, and Chou."
Clarke, G. Marged.
Clementelli. Circle and Obsession of Walls.
Coleridge, S. Recollections of Love.
Dalton, A. In Love.
Desnos. Obsession.
Dett. Conjured.
Dietz, H. I See Your Face Before Me.
Estep, M. I Have to Go Now.
Gay, J. Molly Mog [or The Fair Maid of the Inn].
Gilsdorf, E. Walk, The.
Habila, H. After the Obsession.
Ibn Hazm al-Andalusi. I love you with a love that knows no waning, whereas some of men's loves are midday mirages.
Katrovas. Black English.
Lamb, M. Helen.
Lewis, G. Interview with the Poet.
MacCaig. Small Lochs.
MacSweeney. Totem Banking.
Meyer, T. Merchant's Daughter.
Montale. In the Greenhouse.
Moore, T. Thee, Thee, Only Thee.
Muñiz Huberman. Obsession.
Nash, O. Curl Up and Diet.
Oswald, A. Melon Grower, The.
Pak Sŏwŏn. Obsession: "Knife on the fruit dish, The."
Sondheim. Losing My Mind.
Unknown. Either I want you on my bosom always.
Van Walleghen. Crabapples.
Wroth. Sonnet 23: "When every one to pleasing pastime hies."
Yi Kyubo. Poetry: A Chronic Disease.
Zaid. Circe.
Zaturenska. White Dress, The.

Obsolescence
Dunn, D. Ballad of the Two Left Hands.

Occult, The
Gregg. Flower No More Than Itself, A.
Reid, A. Spell for Sleeping, A.

Occupations
Fitzpatrick, R. Fine Occupation, A.
Kopland. Ontology.
Meitner, E. Job: "My mother sold life insurance."
Nolens, L. Origins.
Parker, D. Pour Prendre Congé.
Portugal, Anne. Every Shack.
Solonche. Worse.

Ocean
Ammons. Spit.
Balakian, P. Ocean.
Barrow, Raymond. There is a Mystic Splendour.
Berlin. How Deep Is the Ocean? (How High Is the Sky?).
Bly, R. On the Oregon Coast.
Clampitt. Marine Surface, Low Overcast.
Cornwall. Address to the Ocean.
Crane, S. I explain the silvered passing of a ship at night.
Curry, N. St Kilda.
Darío, R. Seashell, The.
Tropical Afternoon.
Dimitrova. Blind woman was more intimate with it, The.
Dunn, S. Because You Mentioned the Spiritual Life.
Emerson, R. Sea-Shore.
Francia, L. Secret in the Roar, The.
Frost, R. West-Running Brook.
Fuller, H. To a Tropic Reef.
Góngora y Argote. Dedication: to the Count of Niebla.
Harmon. Concrete Seascape.
Hawthorne, N. Ocean, The.
Hood, T. To the Ocean.

Hooper, V. Reading, A.
Issa. Mother I never knew.
Jabeen, M. Physical Geography.
Jeffers, R. Continent's End.
Evening Ebb.
Kiko. Mount Sumeru—my fist!
Kirsanov. Suddenly.
Langille. Scanning an Afternoon in Winter.
Maar, Dora. If the Touching Memory.
Mackey, N. Phantom Light of All Our Day, The.
Martinson. Sea Wind, The.
Marvell. Bermudas.
Noguchi, M. Not Surfing Some Days.
Oliver, M. At the Shore.
Onassis, Jacqueline Kennedy. Sea Joy.
Oppen. Confession.
Taste, The.
Percival. Coral Grove, The.
Pfeiffer, E. Mid-Ocean.
Pilling. Cast Away.
Procter, A. Address to the Ocean.
Ray, H. Ocean Musing, An.
Reddy, Srikanth. Hotel Lullaby.
Schmitz. Abbott's Lagoon.
Sedakova. Female Figure.
Shwarts [or Shvarts]. Parrot at Sea, A.
Stern, G. Dear waves, what will you do for me this year?
Lucky Life.
Stoutenburg. Before We Drown.
Stuart, D. Figure on the Edge.
Subbarao, N. Is This All!
Tardieu Jean. Fly and the Ocean, The.
Torres, E. Vase of the Universe, The.
Tuckerman, F. Series 3, Sonnet 6.
Van de Woestijne. Oars Heavy with Seaweed, The.
Vivien. Ransom, The.
Wilson, Emily. Relict.
Wyrebek, M. Recovery.
Young, E. Who sings the source.
Zandvakili, K. No Trespassing (Private Beach).

See also **Sea**

October
Alexander, M. October Journey.
Berkson, B. October: "It's odd to have a separate month. It."
Bonnefoy. Words of Evening, The.
Brodsky, J. October Tune.
Bronk. Where It Ends.
Campo, C. Indian Summer.
White Summer Clothes are Folded Away, The.
Carman, B. Vagabond Song, A.
Clarke, George Elliott. 1.5.
Dunbar-Nelson. Snow in October.
Elman. October Observed, Hudson Falls, New York in Bill's Back Yard.
Fordham. October.
Gamalinda, E. Opposite of Nostalgia, The.
Hayden, R. October.
Hayne, P. October.
Herlin. Sky has recovered, The.
Hopes. October: "It's nuthatch on the box elder outside the window."
Jaccottet. Clouded Skies.
Jackson, H. October.
October's Bright Blue Weather.
Klyuyev [or Kliuev or Klyuev]. October, A Copper-Crawed Cock.
Kudimova. Pleated strata of air, The.
Levertov. October.
Linden, M. October Is Here.
Loden. Miss October.
Malroux. In October.
Nurkse. October Marriage.
O'Hara, F. How to Get There.
Piersanti. When Slow October Changes Color.
Ray, H. October.
Rice, D. Taproots.
Rilke. Day in October.
Smith, D. Fieldswirl, October.
Snyder, G. Late October Camping in the Sawtooths.
Soniat. Last Warm Day, A.
Suhl. My October Song.

Thomas, D. Especially When the October Wind.
Poem in October.
Thomas, E. October.
Tranströmer. Sketch in October.

Octopuses
Basho. Jars of octopus, The.
Octopuses caught in floating pots.
Clark, P. Elvis the Performing Octopus.
Hilton, A. Octopus.
Holmes, J. Mediterranean Cooking for Two.
Mandelstam [or Mandelshtam]. Lamarck.
Merrill, J. Octopus, The.
Moore, M. Octopus, An.
O'Reilly, C. Octopus.

Odin
Furberg, J. Blōdmōnath.

Odysseus
Alegría. Letter to an Exile.
Cavafy. Ithaca.
Collier, M. Argos.
Dorgan, T. Choice, The: "I watched Odysseus go on board the flagship."
Dunn, S. Odysseus's Secret.
Ermakova, I. Lullaby for Odysseus.
Ermoshina, G. Autumn your bellringing, the apple of bright weeping.
Homer. Odysseus and Argus.
Odysseus and the Swineherd.
Ratushinskaya [or Ratushinskaia]. Penelope, the screaming is all over.
Rexroth, K. Homer in Basic.
Ryan, G. Achilleus to Odysseus.
Stesichoros. Helen suddenly saw a divine omen.

See also **Ulysses**

Oedipus
Borges. Oedipus and the Riddle.
Deniz, G. Edipo al cubo.
Oedipus to the Third Power.
Dryden, J. When Athens all the Graecian state did guide.
Kunitz, S. Approach to Thebes, The.
Ray, H. Antigone and Oedipus.
Rukeyser, M. Myth.
Sophocles. Colonus' Praise.
Oedipus the King.
Statius. Book 10.

Offa, King of Mercia
Hill, G. Coins handsome as Nero's; of good substance and.
He adored the desk, its brown-oak inlaid with ebony.
King of the perennial holly-groves, the riven sandstone.
Mad are predators, The. Too often lately they harbour.
Not strangeness, but strange likeness. Obstinate.
'Now when King Offa was alive and dead', they were.
Pet-name, a common name, A. Best-selling brand, curt.
Princes of Mercia were badger and raven, The. Thrall.
So much for the elves' wergild, the true governance.

Office Workers
Dawe, B. Beatitudes.
Foster, S. Conant. From Out the Heated City.
Hope, M. Only Days.
Hummell, A. Saraband.
Newburn, L. Office Geraniums.
O'Driscoll, D. Lads, The.
Page, P. Stenographers, The.
Paris, T. Reception.
Roethke. Dolor.
Storm, T. At the Desk.

See also **Clerks; Secretaries**

Ogres
Graves, R. Ogres and Pygmies.
Singer, B. Local Ogres Are Against Me Here, The.

See also **Monsters; Trolls**

O'Hara, Frank
Berrigan, T. Sonnet LV: "Grace to be born and live as variously as possible."

Brainard, J.   I Remember.
Corn.   Kimchee in Worchester (Mass.).
Duncan, R.   At the Poetry Conference: Berkeley After the New York Style.
Fox, Skip.   In Referring to What Does Not Exist.
Ginsberg, A.   City Midnight Junk Strains.
Koch, K.   Circus, The ("I remember when I wrote The Circus.").
O'Hara, F.   Day Lady Died, The.
Palmer, M.   Notes for Echo Lake 3.

Ohio River
Alexander, P.   Sight.
Emmett.   Boatman's Dance.
Harper, F.   Slave Mother, The: A Tale of the Ohio.
McNiece, R.   *Kudzu* has crossed.
Ransom, J.   Antique Harvesters.

Ohio (state)
Allbery.   Produce.
Giscombe, C.   Home Avenue.
Harper, M.   Double Elegy.
Hayes, T.   Ohio River Region.
Hudgins.   Flamingos Have Arrived in Ashtabula.
Lewis, W.   To the People of a Small Town in Ohio, Who As I Approach Them on the Street, Are Afraid That This Black Man Is Going to Do Them Harm.
Pollitt.   Poet of Our Climate, A.
Weigl.   Oh, Atonement.
Woolson.   One.
Wright, J.   At the Executed Murderer's Grave.
Autumn Begins in Martins Ferry, Ohio.
In Response to a Rumor that the Oldest Whorehouse in Wheeling, West Virginia, Has Been Condemned.
Old WPA Swimming Pool in Martins Ferry, Ohio, The.
Sumac in Ohio, The.
Yamada.   Cincinnati.

Oil
Basho.   Awake at night.
Dickson, J.   Fossil Fuel.
Fried, E.   Marvel Mystery Oil.
Ginsberg, A.   Who Runs America?
Jones, R.   News of the Cranes.
Khoury, N.   People of Olives.
North, C.   Year of the Olive Oil, The.
Schreiber, R.   Public Stammer, The.
Thurman.   Oil Slick.
Waterhouse, A.   Speaking About My Cracked Sump.

Oil Industry
Barney, W.   Wide-Eyed.
Benevento, Joe.   Yankees in East Texas.
Ginsberg, A.   Who Runs America?
Hillman, B.   Cheap Gas.
House, Boyce.   Justice in Old Ranger.
Jones, R.   Photo of a Rotary Crew, Sour Lake Oilfield, 1904.
Lee, D.   This all happened before.
Robertson, Lexie Dean.   Pioneer: The Vignette of an Oil-Field.
Ross, Grace.   Oil Well Fire.

O'Keeffe, Georgia
Clampitt.   Fog.
Hinz-Penner, R.   Flowers: "I have not missed the irony of this magnetism, my being."
Opening in Santa Fe, The.
Hirsch, E.   Evening Star.
Kumin, M.   Calling, A.

Okinawa, Japan
Hawaiian Oral Tradition.   Hana-Hana: Working. My Mother Dear.

Oklahoma City Bombing (1995)
Lightfoot, T.   In Oklahoma.

Oklahoma (state)
Harjo, J.   Autobiography.
He Told Me His Name Was Sitting Bull.
Hayes, T.   Postcard from Okemah, A.
Lightfoot, T.   In Oklahoma.
Stevens, W.   Life Is Motion.

Old Age
Abse.   Millie's Date.

Acholonu.   Going Home.
Adair, V. H.   Last Marriage, A.
Agosin.   *Mi Estomago* / My Belly.
Al-Haidari, B.   Old Age: "Another winter."
Why Didn't They Apologize. . .?
Aleixandre.   Old Man and the Sun, The.
Old Man Is Like Moses, The.
Alipiev, Petar.   Old Man: "On his tired memory a splendid."
Ammons.   All's All.
Anacreon.   Already my temples are grey.
Tossing a crimson ball.
Arnold, M.   Growing Old.
Atwood.   Daguerreotype Taken in Old Age.
Basho.   How pitiful!
Now I see her face.
Some of them with staves.
Visting the graves.
Baudelaire.   Seven Old Men, The.
Beckett, S.   Song: "Age is when to a man."
Belieu.   How the Elderly Drive.
Berrigan, D.   Prague: Old Woman in the Street.
Berry, W.   I stand at the cistern in front of the old barn.
Betjeman.   Late-Flowering Lust.
Binyon.   Statues, The.
Blackburn, P.   Phone Call to Rutherford.
Blake, W.   In a Myrtle [or Mirtle] Shade.
Infant Sorrow.
Blunden.   Almswomen.
Bly, R.   Prayer for My Father.
Bogan, L.   Crows, The.
Bonnefoy.   Voice, A.
Booth, P.   Sixty-Six.
Borges.   In Praise of Darkness.
Bowles, W.   Grown Old Together.
Bradley, G.   E Pur Si Muove.
Bradstreet, A.   Old Age.
Brand, D.   Blues Spiritual for Mammy Prater.
Breytenbach.   Struggle for the Taal, The.
Brontë, E.   Love and Friendship.
Brooks, G.   Bean Eaters, The.
To An Old Black Woman, Homeless and Indistinct.
Brown, G.   Old Women, The.
Brown, S.   Legend: "Old black man was stood on the block, The."
Browning, R.   Dîs Aliter Visum; or, Le Byron de Nos Jours.
Rabbi Ben Ezra.
Bruce, C.   Eastern Shore.
Buckholts, Claudia.   Old Woman Reclining.
Bukowski.   3 Old Men at Separate Tables.
Buson.   My old man's ears.
Old man, The.
Springs passed.
Byron, C.   Minding You.
Campbell, J.   Old Woman, The.
Cardiff.   Grey Woman.
Carroll, L.   Father William.
White Knight's Song, The.
Carruth, H.   Saturday at the Border.
Castellanos.   Hecuba's Testament.
Cernuda.   Remorse Dressed Up as Night.
Ch'en Meng-chia.   Old White Russian, An.
Chasin.   City Pigeons.
Chédid Andrée.   Looking at Childhood.
Ch'i-chi.   Autumn Evening: To Send to my Nieces and Nephews.
Delighted That the Monk Ch'ien-chou Has Come a Long Way to Visit Me.
Speaking My Mind.
Ch'ien T'ao.   Blaming Sons.
Clare, J.   Frolicsome Old Dog, The.
Clive.   Old Age.
Cofer, J.   Old Women.
Coleridge, H.   Long Time a Child.
Coleridge, S.   Youth and Age.
Constantine, D.   Hoist, The.
Cope, W.   Names: "She was Eliza for a few weeks."
Corbett, E.   Three Wise Old Women.
Corey, S.   Preparing to Live Among the Old.
Cornford, F.   Childhood.
Creeley.   Self-Portrait.
Dao.   In Memory.

Davies, T.   Bailiff, The.
De Kok.   Leavetaking.
De la Mare.   All That's Past.
Last Chapter, The.
Nod.
Old Men, The.
Old Susan.
Delmore, E.   Difference, The.
Denby.   Old age, lookit, it's stupid, a big fart.
Donne.   Canonization, The.
Donovan, K.   Old Women's Summer.
Doolittle, H.   In Time of Gold.
You come late.
Dorsett, T.   Survivor, The.
Dransfield.   Pioneer Lane.
Dromgoole.   Old Ladies.
Dubie.   Dementia.
Duran, J.   Great Grandfathers.
Eijkelboom.   As Old As Then.
Eliot, T. S.   Gerontion.
Lines for an Old Man.
Emerson, R.   Terminus ("It is time to be old.").
Empson.   To an Old Lady.
Everwine.   Gray Poem.
Ewart.   Yorkshiremen in Pub Gardens.
Fairchild.   Old Men Playing Basketball.
Felltham [or Feltham].   To Phryne.
Ferdowsi, A.   I've worked, I've worked so hard; reading, reading.
Firdowsi.   When the sword of sixty comes nigh his head.
Foley, M.   *Sois sage, ô ma doleur* . . . I don't.
Follain.   Eclogue: "In the closed house."
Francis, R.   On a Theme by Frost.
Frost, R.   Old Man's Winter Night, An.
Provide, Provide.
Fu.   Don't, Don't.
Garcia, R.   Nobody Here But Us.
Gates, E.   My Mother's Hands.
Ghalib, M.   Ghazal 13: "Where are your woo-trysts and your heart-wreches now, Ghalib?"
Gilsdorf, E.   Walk, The.
Ginsberg, A.   Not Dead Yet.
Gloria.   Aleng Maria.
Gomes, A.   Martyred Tamarind, The.
Googe.   To Doctor Bale.
Graves, R.   Grotesques.
Grenfell, J.   Stately as a Galleon.
Grosholz.   Old Fisherman, The.
Gruffydd, O.   Old, old/ To live on, wretched to behold.
Guevara, M.   Long Distance.
Guiducci.   I Look at You So Old.
Guiney.   Open, Time.
Gumilyov [or Gumiliov or Gumilev].
Fragments 1920–1921.
Han-shan Te-ch'ing.   I let mind and body go and gained a life of freedom.
My body is like deadwood my thoughts are like ashes.
Hardy, T.   He Never Expected Much.
I Look into My Glass.
Near Lanivet, 1872.
Harrigan, S.   Pecos Bill in Decline.
Harris, D.   For My Father.
Harteis.   Tempus Fugit.
Hartnett.   Person as Dreamer: We Talk about the Future, The.
Sonnet: "I saw magic on a green country road."
Heaney, S.   Follower.
Hecht, A.   Sarabande on Attaining the Age of Seventy-Seven.
Hegland, J.   Crone I Will Become, The.
Henry, J.   Very Old Man.
Herbert, G.   Forerunners, The.
Herd.   Big Girls.
Herrick.   On Himself[e] ("Here down my wearied [or wearyed] limbs I'll [or Ile] lay.").
On Himself[e] ("I will no longer kiss.").
To Perilla.
Hewitt, J.   Local Poet, A.
Higgins, B.   Strange Beasts.
Higgins, F.   Old Jockey, The.
Hine.   After the Solstice.
Ho Ch'e Ch'ang.   Homecoming: "I was a boy when I left home."

Return, The.
Hoagland, T. Lucky.
Hodgson, R. Moor, The.
Holloway, G. Old Man.
Holmes, O. Last Leaf, The.
Poet Grows Old, The.
Hong Yunsuk. Discourse on an Ornament.
Hopkins, G. Leaden Echo and the Golden Echo, The.
Horace. To a Randy Old Woman.
Howard, R. After 65.
Howe, F. First Chance Twice.
Hutchinson, P. Flames.
Iofe, Y. Thing or Two about Childhood, A.
Irving, M. Marching Still.
Jacobsen, R. Memories of Horses.
Old Age.
Old Women, The.
Jamie, K. Den of the Old Men.
Jarrell, R. Face, The.
Jeffers, R. Age in Prospect.
Deer Lay Down Their Bones, The.
Fawn's Foster-Mother.
Promise of Peace.
Jenkins, N. Yr Iaith.
Jennings, E. One Flesh.
Johnson, F. Aunt Hannah Jackson.
Johnson, G. When You and I Were Young, Maggie.
Jones, D. Old Woman, An.
Joseph, J. Warning.
Juan Chi. In the Shadow of Death.
Juana Inés de la Cruz. Perpetual Infirmity of Hope.
Justice, D. Grandfathers, The [or After a Line by John Peale Bishop].
Winter Ode to the Old Men of Lummus Park, Miami, Florida, A.
Keary E. Old Age: "Such a wizened creature."
Kenyon, J. In the Nursing Home.
Kerouac. In my medicine cabinet.
Kingsley, C. Young and Old.
Kinsella, T. Tear.
Kipling, R. Old Men, The.
Kizer, C. Thrall.
Kleinzahler. Hamburger.
Koch, K. To Old Age.
Kooser. Happy Birthday, A.
In the Basement of the Goodwill Store.
Very Old, The.
Ku Sang. Wings.
Kuan Han-ch'ing. To the Tune "A Spray of Flowers" (Not Giving In to Old Age).
Kunitz, S. Touch Me.
Laing, K. Senior Lady Sells Garden Eggs.
Lamb, C. Old Familiar Faces, The.
Landor, W. Age.
Alas! 'Tis Very Sad to Hear.
I Strove With None.
Lazić, R. I'll Be a Wicked Old Woman.
Lea, S. Wrong Way Will Haunt You, The.
Lear, E. There was an Old Man who forgot.
Li Ch'ing-chao. To the Tune "Clear Peace Happiness".
To the Tune: Eternal Joy.
Linden, M. Life's Golden Sunset.
Prospect of the Future, The.
Lingche. In Reply to Wei Dan.
Lisnyanskaya [or Lisnianskaia]. Jealousy: "I look out of the window at the retreating back."
Two carousing hawk moths, their wings like nervous silk.
Loesser. They're Either Too Young or Too Old.
Loftin, E. Weeksville Women.
Longfellow, H. Nature.
Longley, M. Flowering, A.
Lowell, A. Lady, A.
Lowell, R. Grandparents.
Lu Chih. Seventy Years Are Few.
Lu Yu. Stone on the Hilltop, The.
Written in a Carefree Mood.
Lux. So You Put the Dog to Sleep.
Ly Ngoc Kieu. Birth, old age.
Lynes, Jeanette. Brave.
Mabuza. Tired Lizi Tired.
MacDiarmid, H. Wheesht, Wheesht.

Machado Ruiz. Daydreams Have Endlessly Turning Paths.
Madgett. Old Women, The.
Mahon. Refusal to Mourn, A.
Mandelstam [or Mandelshtam]. Valley Bleeds with Roman Rust, The.
Mangan, J. Twenty Golden Years Ago.
Mapanje. These Too Are Our Elders.
Marquis. Mehitabel's Song.
Marshall-Stoneking. Passage.
Masefield. On Growing Old.
Matthews, T. Cowboy Film.
Matthews, W. Grandmother, Dead at 99 Years and 10 Months.
Matveyeva [or Matveieva]. Eggplants Have Pins and Needles, The.
McDowell, Garrett. Blooming in the Valley, A.
McElroy, C. At 102, Romance Comes Once a Year.
Merrill, B. Staying Young.
Mew. À Quoi Bon Dire.
Meynell, A. Letter from a Girl to Her Own Old Age, A.
Michaux. Jetty, The.
Millay, E. Oh, my belovèd, have you thought of this.
Mitchell, A. Dog Called Elderly, A.
Mitchell, E. Alice Uglier.
Montague, J. Dowager.
Like Dolmens Round My Childhood.
Wild Dog Rose, The.
Moolten, D. Voyeur.
Moore, R. On Coming to Nothing.
Moore, Robert John. Skin You Wore, The.
Morabito, F. Elefantes nacen viejos, Los.
Elephants are born old.
Morgan, E. At Eighty.
Morris-Jones. Old Age.
Mphande. Why the Old Woman Limps.
Muso Soseki. Free Old Man.
Old Man Advancing.
Old Man in Retirement.
Old Man To-The-Point.
Nadir, M. Old Woman, The.
Napier, F. I Have Taken the Suits and Shoes to Oxfam.
Nash, O. Portrait of the Artist as a Prematurely Old Man.
Nasir, A. Poem Looking in a Mirror, A.
Nemerov. Brief Journey West, The.
Nesbit, E. Things That Matter, The.
Niatum. Apology.
Nicholson, N. Halley's Comet.
Nowlan. Weakness.
O'Hehir, D. Bedside.
Olds, S. Space Heater, The.
Oles. One Page in The American Heritage Dictionary.
Oppen. Confession.
Ortiz. Yuusthiwa.
Owen, W. Parable of the Old Men and the Young, The.
Pagis, D. Winter's End.
Pak Mogwŏl [or Mokwŏl]. Hanbok.
Paley, G. Here.
People in My Family.
Parker, D. Little Old Lady in Lavender Silk, The.
Pastan. Ethics.
Pavlova. Crone, The.
Peele. His Golden Lock[e]s [Time Hath to Silver Turned].
Petit, P. Strait-Jackets, The.
Platt, F. Coincidentally.
Po Chü-i. Looking in the Lake.
Realizing the Futility of Life.
Wind Sickness Strikes.
Pope, W. Old Man's Wish, The.
Posey, A. Hotgun on the Death of Yadeka Harjo.
Prado, A. Easter.
Serenade.
Prunty. Elderly Lady Crossing on Green.
Pryde, A. Have We Had Easter Yet?
Pugh. Shoni Onions.
Queneau. Reinforcements [1].

Reinforcements [2].
Rakosi. Old Lovers.
Unswerving Marine.
Raleigh, W. Wishes of an Elderly Man[, Wished at a Garden Party, June 1914].
Randall, D. George.
Rands. Cat of Cats, The.
Ransom, J. Captain Carpenter.
Piazza Piece.
Rector. My Grandfather Always Promised Us.
Reed, H. Chard Whitlow.
Reese, L. Old Belle, An.
Reid, C. What the Uneducated Old Woman Told Me.
Reznikoff. Showing a torn sleeve, with stiff and shaking fingers the old man.
Rich, A. One Life.
Riley, J. Old Swimmin'-Hole, The.
Ríos, A. Man Who Became Old, The.
Robinson, E. Mr Flood's Party.
Rochester, J. Song of a Young Lady to Her Ancient Lover, A.
Ronsard. When you are old, at evening candle-lit.
Rowe, V. Youth.
Rudaki. All the teeth ever I had are worn down and fallen out.
Ruefle. Public Garden with a Weeping Tree.
Russell, N. Message of the Rain, The.
Salaam. Name the Oldest Member of Your Family.
Sallah, T. Elders Are Gods, The.
Sappho. You / Put success in the mouth.
Satyamurti. Day Trip.
Scott, W. Garland for Advancing Years, A.
Senryū, K. Sitting Idly.
Shakespeare, W. Sonnet 73: "That time of year thou may'st in me behold."
Shamlu, A. Somber Song.
Simic. Northern Exposure.
Old Couple.
Sitwell. Poet Laments the Coming of Old Age, The.
Slutsky [or Slutskii]. My old men are dying.
Smith, I. Old Woman.
Old Woman, The.
Smith, K. Old Women and Love.
Smith, S. He Told His Life Story to Mrs. Courtly.
Snodgrass. April Inventory.
Sŏ Chŏngju. At a Wine House near Taegu.
Sŏng Hon. Mountain is silent, The.
Song Sun. I discuss with my heart.
Southey, R. Old Man's Comforts and How He Gained Them, The.
Remembrance.
Steele, T. In the King's Rooms.
Stickney, T. Requiescam.
Storni. Encounter.
Strand. Old Man Leaves Party.
Strong, L. Old Dan'l.
Zeke.
Su Tung-p'o. Verses: "I am old, sick and lonely."
Suarez, V. Duende.
Surrey. Laid in My Quiet Bed.
Swift, J. Satirical Elegy on the Death of a Late Famous General, a.
Swirszczynska [or Swir]. Greatest Love, The.
Second Madrigal, The.
She Does Not Remember.
Sze. Moon is a Diamond, The.
Talbot, N. Ballad of Old Women & of How They Are Constrained To Simulate Youth In Order To Avoid Shocking the Young.
Tannahill. Eild.
T'ao Ch'ien [or T'ao Yuan-ming]. Drinking Alone in the Rainy Season.
Teasdale. I Shall Live To Be Old.
Long Hill, The.
Tennyson, A. Tithonus.
Ulysses.
We leave the well-beloved place.
Thomas, D. Do Not Go Gentle into That Good Night.
Thomas, R. S. Lore.

Thompson, P. Old Freedman, The.
Thwaite, A. Throes.
Troupe. Old Black Ladies Standing on Bus Stop Corners #2.
Old People Speak of Death, The.
Ts'ui Hao. Yellow Crane Tower.
Tu Fu [or Du Fu]. By Yangtze and Han.
Departing from Ch'in-chou.
Drinking with Elder Cheng the Eighth at Crooked River.
Facing the Snow ("Weeping over battle, many new ghosts.").
Flying from Trouble.
Madman, The.
Poem for Mr. Li in Early Spring.
Presented to Wei Ba, Gentleman in Retirement.
Seven Songs Written while Living at T'ung-ku in 759.
Taking Leave of Two Officials.
To Abbot Min the Compassionate.
Traveler's Pavilion.
Walking Alone by the Riverbank Seeking Flowers.
Tyutchev. Last Love.
U T'ak. Sticks in one hand.
Wind that melted the spring hills, The.
Unknown. At Fifteen I Went to War.
Before my back was bent I was eloquent.
Death of Old Men, The.
Hag of Beare, The.
Have you with your white beard no shame?
Never shall I take an old man as a lover.
Old Folks' Room, The.
Old-Saxon Fragment.
Somebody's Mother.
Song of an Old Gray Wolf.
Will You Love Me When I'm Old?
Young once / and dreaming.
Youth and Age.
Van Duyn. Falling in Love at Sixty-Five.
Letters from a Father.
Stream, The.
Vaux. Aged Lover Renounceth Love, The.
Velichansky, A. Infant is white, like down, The.
And the youth dark-complexioned, like shingle.
Venaille, Franck. Now They Tell Me.
Vinokurov. All Grows Old.
Volkman. May: "In May's gaud gown and ruby reckoning."
Vroomkoning. Returning.
Together Again ("You get these thoughts in melancholy Autumn.").
Waddington, M. Old Women of Toronto.
Walcott. Glory Trumpeter, The.
Letter from Brooklyn, A.
Oak inns creak in their joints as light declines, The.
Waller, E. Of the Last Verses in the Book.
Seas are quiet when the winds give o'er, The.
Wang Wei. Reply to a Magistrate.
Ward, F. Who.
Weiss, T. Pair of Shoes, A.
Whitman, W. Hours Continuing Long.
Thanks in Old Age.
To Old Age.
Wilkinson, A. On a Bench in a Park.
Williams, W. For What It's Worth.
Last Words of My English Grandmother, The.
To a Poor Old Woman.
To an Old Jaundiced Woman.
To Waken an Old Lady.
Wilson, S. It's Never Too Late to Fall in Love.
Winters, Y. Dream Vision, A.
Winthrop, Jeanette I. Couple Having Breakfast in the Deli, The.
Woloch, C. Ottava Rima: Lear.
Wordsworth, W. Animal Tranquillity and Decay.
Fountain, The.
Old Man by the Brook, The.
Old Man Travelling [Animal Tranquillity and Decay, a Sketch].
Simon Lee, the Old Huntsman; with an incident in which he was concerned.
Wright, F. Circle Drawn in Water.

Wright, J. Poem Written under an Archway in a Discontinued Railroad Station, Fargo, North Dakota, A.
Wright, K. Here Come Two Very Old Men.
Yeats. Acre of Grass, An.
Apparitions, The.
Coming of Wisdom with Time, The.
Lamentation of the Old Pensioner, The (1890 version).
Lamentation of the Old Pensioner, The (1925 version).
Prayer for Old Age, A.
Sailing to Byzantium.
Scholars, The.
Spur, The.
Tower, The.
When You Are Old.
Wild Old Wicked Man, The.
Yevtushenko [or Evtushenko]. Saints of Jazz.
Yezzi, David. Woman Holding a Fox.
Yi Hwang. Twelve Songs of Tosan.
Yi Kyubo. Composed Playfully on New Year's Day.
Poetry: A Chronic Disease.
Young, G. Night Call.
Yüan Mei. Growing Old (1).
Yuan Mei. Old and Traveling.
See also **Pensions and Pensioners; Retirement and Retirees**
"Old Ironsides".
See **Constitution (ship)**
Old Testament
Osherow. 9 (Looking through the Window: Psalm 121).
Olive Trees and Olives
Brosman. Olives.
Hedin, R. At the Olive Grove of the Resistance.
Hemans. Olive Tree, The.
Housman. Olive, The.
Khoury, N. People of Olives.
North, C. Year of the Olive Oil, The.
Robinson, A. Tuscan Olives.
Spencer, B. Olive Trees.
Wilbur, R. Grasse: The Olive Trees.
Olympics
Bacchylides. Ode 6: "Lachon has brought home the bacon."
Fagg, M. Golden Road to Barcelona: 1992, The.
Pindar. Water is preeminent and gold, like a fire.
Tkachenko. Dynamo Stadium, 1980.
Omar Khayyám
Lowell, J. In a Copy of Omar Khayyám.
Omens
Aworinde. If a Suite in Praise of the Yoruba Oracle.
Boruch. Omens.
Breytenbach. Firewing.
Brownstein. Oracle night / the porch is frozen.
Burr, A. Lynmouth Widow, A.
Cervantes. Body as Braille, The.
Chia Yi. Owl, The.
Year was tan-wo, it was the fourth month, summer's first, The.
Davis, K. Miracle.
Dobyns. Where We Are.
"Ern Malley.". Sybilline.
Graves, R. On Portents.
Spoils.
Hristov, Boris. Sign from Heaven, A.
Jacob, M. War.
Kanchev, Nikolai. Miracle.
Kunitz, S. Day of Foreboding.
Longfellow, H. Hiawatha: The White Man's Foot.
Mann, R. Fiduciary.
McKendrick, J. Ancient History.
Melville, H. Portent, The.
Phillips, C. Custom.
Poe. Raven, The.
Schnackenberg. Signs.
Segovia, F. Premonición.
Premonition.
Stevenson, R. Ticonderoga: A Legend of the

West Highlands.
Trakl. Dream of Evil (First Version).
Trethewey, N. Genus Narcissus.
Unknown. Chi-chi (Already across the stream).
I have braided my hair but it has come undone.
Marrying Maiden, The.
My pants, the hue of fire, are slipping down my thighs.
Omens.
Omens on the Road to Burgos.
Prophetic Powers.
See the great vultures.
Wei-chi (Not yet across the stream).
Vegin, P. Explanation of a Sign.
Virgil [or Vergil]. Who dares deny the burning truth of the sun?
Omnipotence
Bhattācārya, K. Ever-blissful Kali.
Heford, Will. That God Made.
Murray, P. Canticle of the Void, The.
Rāy, N. Everything is Your wish, Tara.
Rilke. I Find You.
Ryan, K. Blandeur.
Sakaki. Let's Eat Stars.
Scupham. Nondescript, The.
Sylvester, J. Father, The.
Unknown. You and I.
Williams, M. Why God Permits Evil: For Answers to This Question of Interest to Many Write Bible Answers, Dept. E-7.
Omniscience
Brother Yao. Born.
Harris, J. Beneath the Pole of Proud Raven.
Shepherd, R. Also Love You.
Unknown. God Knows Why.
Onassis, Jacqueline Kennedy
Bowman, C. Jackie in Cambodia.
Herd. Pink Rose Rings, The.
Merrill, J. Neo-Classic.
Onions
Blount, R. Song to Onions.
Crozier, L. Onions.
Duffy, C. Valentine: "Not a red rose or a satin heart."
Flanders, J. Planting Onions.
Francis, R. Onion Fields.
Goodison. I Am Becoming My Mother.
Hernández, M. Lullabies of the Onion.
Lullaby of the Onion.
Ishikawa Takuboku. Tanka: "As if in water."
Kim, Suji Kwock. Monologue for an Onion.
Matthews, W. Onions.
Neruda. Oda a la Cebolla.
Ode to the Onion.
Nye, N. Traveling Onion, The.
Piercy. Bite into the Onion.
Raine, C. Onion, Memory, The.
Unknown. Onion.
Wilbur, R. Shallot, A.
Williamson, G. Visiting Couple Kissing and Halved Onion.
Ontario, Canada
Klein, A. Winter Night: Mount Royal.
Ondaatje. Burning Hills.
Purdy, A. Country North of Belleville, The.
Wilderness Gothic.
Ontario, Lake
Ray, H. Thought of Lake Ontario, A.
Opera
Anwar, C. Ordinary Song, An.
Booth, P. Public Broadcast.
Calder, A. October Opera for Kate.
Colquitt. Duet.
Downie. O Mary.
Duran, J. For the Woman Who Dressed Up to Listen to Gigli on the Radio.
"Eliot.". Armgart, to many minds the first success.
Field, E. Callas.
Lawrence, D. H. After the Opera.
Levy, N. Carmen.
Rigoletto.
Tannhauser.
Moolten, D. Madame Butterfly.
Wheelwright. Lion.

Ophelia
Ausländer, R.   In the Color of Sleep.
Bécquer, G.   As the Breeze that Cools the
  Blood.
Burns, E.   Ophelia: "Always the daughter."
Dierking, K.   Delacroix's Version.
Eidenier, Elon G.   Failure of Language, The.
Friman.   Ophelia.
Greenway, W.   Ophelia Writes Home.
Hall, L.   Ophelia's Rant before She's Heavy
  with Drink.
Hedderman, R.   Ophelia.
Herd.   Ophelia's Confession.
Horsley, K.   Poem to Ophelia.
Imbriglio, C.   I Loved Ophelia.
Joseph, A.   Not Ophelia.
Kaschock, Kirsten.   As Birds in Rain.
Külebi, C.   Lost Love: "She keeps singing a
  song."
Kunert.   Theatrum Mundi.
Lynch, K.   Ophelia in Utah.
McCarthy, Lee.   Running Loose around the
  Castle.
Montgomery, Judith H.   Ophelia, in Winter.
Pilling.   Ophelia.
Shepherd, R.   Snowdrops and Summer
  Snowflakes, Drooping.
Stillman, M.   Ophelia.
Terris, S.   Ophelia.
Van Cleave, R.   Ophelia on a Graveled Garden
  Walk in Purgatory.
Watkins, V.   Ophelia.
Youngblom, T.   Ophelia Speaks.

Opium
Coleridge, S.   Kubla Khan: or, A Vision in a
  Dream.
Crapsey.   Languor After Pain.
Doubleday, T.   Poppies, that scattered o'er this
  arid plain.
Hamilton, S.   Poppy, The.
Lowell, M.   Opium Fantasy, An.
Seward.   To the Poppy.
Sǒ Chǒngju.   Midday.
Tucker, M.   Evanishings.
  Opium-Eater, The.
Unknown.   Face haggard turning yellow and
  puffy.

Opossums
Levis.   Oldest Living Thing in L.A., The.
Unknown.   Carmen Possum.

Oppen, George
Rodefer.   Brief To Butterick.

Oppenheimer, J. Robert
Ai.   Testimony of J. Robert Oppenheimer, The.

Opportunity
Agosin.   Dance, The.
Browning, R.   Dîs Aliter Visum; or, Le Byron
  de Nos Jours.
  Youth and Art.
Cofer, J.   Seizing the Day.
Davis, J.   You Turn Around.
Doty, M.   Michael's Dream.
  New Dog.
Góngora y Argote.   O Noble and Most High in
  Beauty, Thou.
González Prada, M.   Treasures and Glories of
  Life, The.
Graham, H.   Opportunity.
Harburg.   When I'm Not Near the Girl I Love.
Hardy, T.   Midnight on the Great Western.
Hoagland, T.   Ecology.
Ibarbourou.   Hour, The.
Jackson, H.   Opportunity.
Jackson, M.   Gifts.
Mutis.   East Song.
Nervo.   Cowardice.
Rossi, T.   Possibility.
Schwartz, R. L.   Edgewater Park.
  Possible.
Sill.   Opportunity.
Sosnora.   There it all was: the gaslamp,
  drugstore.
Tsvetaeva [*or* Tsvetaeva].   Staircase.

Opposites
Berry, W.   Third Possibility, A.

Blake, W.   Marriage of Heaven and Hell, The.
Borges.   Labyrinth, The.
Bracho, C.   Allure of Forms, The.
  Deleite de las formas, El.
Castellanos.   Other, The.
Ch'u Yüan.   In the beginning of old.
Edson, R.   Antimatter.
Emerson, R.   Brahma.
Graves, R.   In Broken Images.
Han Yong'un [*or* Yongwun].   Inverse
  Proportion.
Kipling, R.   Bonfires, The.
Kozameh, A.   Presence. Opposites. Absence.
  Forces exercising pressure against.
Lao Tzu.   Whenever all the world declares fair
  "fair".
Martinaitis, M.   Kukutis Describes His Hut.
Melville, H.   Art: "In placid hours well-pleased
  we dream."
Pavlova, V.   This is the way a row of official
  tulips.
Prados, E.   Song: "Bridge of my solitude."
Ruefle.   Topophilia.
Volkman.   If it be event, I go towards and not
  back. I go tower, not floor.
Whitman, W.   I have heard what the talkers
  were talking, the talk of the beginning and the
  end.
Wilbur, R.   What is the opposite of nuts?
Young, K.   Negative.

Oppression
Acam-Oturu.   Arise to the Day's Toil.
"Ada.".   Slave, The.
Aiyejina.   When the Monuments.
Alexie.   Vision (2).
Allen, L.   Rub a Dub Style inna Regent Park.
Ama Ata Aidoo.   Gynae One.
Amadiume.   Nok Lady in Terracotta.
  Oya Now.
  We Have Even Lost our Tongues!
Anzaldúa.   Horse.
Ashbery, J.   Holding Mode, A.
Auden.   They are and suffer; that is all they do.
  Yes, we are going to suffer, now; the sky.
Awoonor.   First Circle, The.
Azuah, U.   Forbidden.
Baca.   Oppression.
Baraka, I.   I Am.
Belli, C.   Segregation #1.
Belli, G.   Nicaragua Water Fire.
Benedetti, M.   With Your Permission.
Bly, R.   Romans Angry about the Inner World.
Brecht, B.   In Dark Times.
  World's One Hope, The.
Breytenbach.   Firewing.
  Struggle for the Taal, The.
Bryce, Colette.   Word, The.
Cervantes.   Poem for the Young White Man
  Who Asked Me How I, An Intelligent, Well-
  Read Person Could Believe in the War
  Between Races.
Chamberlayne, W.   Bad Landlord, The.
Cheney-Coker.   Analysis.
  Peasants.
  Poet Among Those Who Are Also Poets.
Chudleigh.   To the Ladies.
  Unhappy they, who by their duty led.
Clifton, L.   Why some people be mad at me
  sometimes.
Crane, H.   Black Tambourine.
Crockett-Smith, D.   Homestead, USA.
Dao.   Answer.
De Kok.   Our Sharpeville.
  Small passing.
Dove, R.   Parsley.
Duncan [Too-qua-stee], DeWitt Clinton.   Dead
  Nation, The.
El-Hadi, S.   Tired Man, The.
Espada.   Green and Red, Verde y Rojo.
Espirito Santo.   Grandma Mariana.
Gardinier.   Admirals (Columbus).
Gelman.   History.
Gomes, A.   Martyred Tamarind, The.
Gwala.   Beyond fences.
Hagedorn, J.   Song of Bullets, The.
Harrison, T.   Earthen Lot, The.

Hawaiian Oral Tradition.   Hana-Hana: Working.
Hawoldar.   You Have Touched My Skin.
Heine, H.   Silesian Weavers, The.
Herbert, Z.   Power of Taste, The.
  What I Saw.
Heywood, J.   Wilt thou use turners craft still? ye
  by my truth.
Horne, N.   Note to My Liberal Feminist Sister,
  A.
Hsi-tseng Tsiang.   Shantung.
Hubert.   Joseph in Carcere.
Hughes, L.   Bitter River, The.
  Black Clown, The.
  Brass Spittoons.
  Freedom Train.
  Harlem ("What happens to a dream deferred?").
  I, Too.
  Let America Be America Again.
  Share-Croppers.
  Uncle Tom ("Within— / The beaten pride.").
Hugo, R.   On Hearing a New Escalation.
Ibarbourou.   Woman.
Ignatow, D.   For Medgar Evers.
Im Hwa.   My Brother and the Brazier.
Inada.   Projected Scenario of a Performance to
  Be Given Before the UN.
Ismaili.   Lagos.
  Queue.
  Yet Still.
Ivanov, Binyo.   Man, A.
Jara, V.   Estadio Chile.
Jastrun, T.   Polish Knot, The.
Kalina, R.   Testimonies.
Kim Chiha.   In Burning Thirst.
  Story of a Sound, The.
  Well.
Klassen, S.   Russian Fables.
Konie, G.   In the Fist of Your Hatred.
Laing, K.   Tatale Swine.
Lara, A.   Nights.
Lee, K.   On South Africa.
Levin, D.   Marvelous Father.
Lima, M.   Shoeshine Boy.
Lisnyanskaya [*or* Lisnianskaia].   Whenever I
  looked in the mirror.
Lom.   Lament for the State of the Country, A.
Lorde.   Black Unicorn, The.
Loynaz, D. M.   I have slept and I awaken . . .
  Or I haven't awakened.
Lysohorsky.   Ballad of Jan Palach, Student and
  Heretic.
Macgoye.   August the First: The Watchman
  Speaks.
  Muffled Cry, A.
Madhubuti.   B Network, The.
  Killing Memory.
Mahon.   Disused Shed in Co. Wexford, A.
Mandel, T.   Say Ja.
Mandela.   I Have Tried Hard.
Mandelstam [*or* Mandelshtam].   I Was Washing
  Outside in the Darkness.
Mandiela, A.   Speshal Rikwes.
Manyarrows.   See No Indian, Hear No Indian.
Markham, E.   Man with the Hoe, The.
Martinaitis, M.   Kukutis's Fruitless Bread.
Mayakovsky [*or* Maiakovskii].   Last Statement.
M'Baye d'Erneville.   Labane.
McKay, C.   Birds of Prey.
Miller, J.   Woman I Know, The.
Milne, A.   Bad Sir Brian Botany.
Moraga.   For the Color of My Mother.
Morrissey, S.   Clocks.
Moss, T.   Lessons from a Mirror.
Motsapi, S.   Brotha saul (furtha meditashuns).
  Shak-shak.
Nelson, M.   Chopin.
Niemoller.   First They Came for the Jews.
Nolla.   Thoughts on Innocence.
Ofeimun.   Handle for the Flutist, A.
  New Brooms, The.
Olson, C.   Kingfishers, The.
Opoku-Agyemang.   King Tut in America.
Parra, V.   At the Center of Injustice.
  Because the Poor Have Nothing.
Pegram, A.   I Will Still Sing.
  Mr. White Discoverer.

Towards Abraham's Bosom.
Pietri. Old Buildings, The.
Po Chü-i. Red Cuckatoo, The.
Pound, E. Commission.
Pratt, M. Crime Against Nature.
Putnam. Words of an Old Woman.
Quinonez, N. My Shattered Sister.
Raboni, G. Alibi of a Dead Man.
Rahim, J. Felling of a Tree, The.
Raji Oyelade, R. Cyclone.
Ratushinskaya [or Ratushinskaia]. For the cry
 from the well of "mama!".
Rich, A. Burning of Paper instead of Children,
 The.
 Culture and Anarchy.
 For Ethel Rosenberg.
 From an Old House in America.
 Memory says: Want to do right? Don't count on
 me.
 No one's fated or doomed to love anyone.
Riesco. Burdens.
Ritsos. Missing, The.
Rose. For the Angry White Student Who
 Wanted to Know.
Rushin. Black Back-Ups, The.
Santos Chocano. Who Knows?
Schneider, I. History of the Caesars, A.
Segalen. Faithful Betrayal.
Seneca. Chorus.
Sepamla. I Remember Sharpeville.
Sepúlveda-Pulvirenti. From Now Until Chile.
 September 11, 1973.
Shannon, A. JoNelle.
Shapiro, K. University.
Shin Tongyŏp. Back when we were children.
Sigourney. To the First Slave Ship.
Silva, L. Island and Europe, The.
Sousa, N. Call.
 Our Voice.
Soyinka. Apologia (Nkomati).
Stein, G. Piece fo Coffee, A.
Szöcs, G. Commentary on an Old Review.
Teschke, H. Documentary Film.
Thelwall. Vanity of National Grandeur, The.
Tindal. Cry of the Oppressed, The.
Tolson, M. Dark Symphony.
Troupe. Boomerang: A Blatantly Political
 Poem.
Unger, B. Observance.
Unknown. My parents are old; my family is
 poor.
 Noble, enduring, ever-renewed peace do I
 attribute exclusively to his highness, the best
 of Caliphs, A.
Vicioso. Haiti.
 Perspectives.
Vivar. Femmemasochism.
Walker, A. Women.
Walker, M. For My People.
Wiethüchter. Without Histories.
Wilcox, E. Burdened.
Wilner, E. Found in the Free Library.
Woo, D. Great Helmsman, The.
Yeats. Fascination of What's Difficult, The.
Yi Sang. Publications Law.
Young, A. Poem for Players, A.
Zakama, K. My Generation.
Zulu, P. You are Mad: and I Mean It!

See also Apartheid; Dehumanization; Sexism;
 Slavery and Slaves; Tyranny

Optimism
Adams, L. Put on a Happy Face.
Adcock, F. For Andrew.
Alexander, C. All Things Bright and Beautiful.
Bairagi. Give Me Confidence.
Balamani Amma. To My Daughter.
Barbour, D. It's a Good Day.
Bartlett, B. Basement Tale, A.
Brown, L. Sunny Side Up.
Browning, R. Pippa's Song.
Case, D. Fear No More.
Chŏng Yagyong. Laughing at Myself.
Citino. Cleveland, Angels, Ogres, Trolls.
Clough. Say Not the Struggle Nought Availeth.
Connolly, G. New House.
Creeley. Invitation, The.

DeSylva, B. G. Look for the Silver Lining.
 Sunny Side Up.
Elfyn, M. Some Kind of Thanks.
Eliscu, E. Great Day.
Fields, D. I'm Livin' in a Great Big Way.
 It's All Yours.
Gershwin, I. Sunny Disposish.
 Things Are Looking Up.
Hammerstein. Many a New Day.
 Oh, What a Beautiful Mornin'!
Hardy, T. When the clouds' swoln bosoms echo
 back the shouts of the many and strong.
Hauge. It Is That Dream.
Henderson, R. Sunny Side Up.
Hernández, M. To Smile with the Joyful
 Sadness of the Olive Tree.
Howe, F. She put her hand.
Inada. Ness.
Jackson, L. Toward the Corner.
Keller, B. Keep a Good Thought.
Koehler, T. When the Sun Comes Out.
Lee, P. It's a Good Day.
Leigh, C. Hey, Look Me Over.
Mahon. Everything Is Going to Be All Right.
McNair. Big Cars.
Mercer, J. Accentuate the Positive.
Nash, O. Sweet Bye and Bye.
O'Hara, F. Lines to a Depressed Friend.
Ortiz. Juanita, Wife of Manuelito.
Parker, D. Comment.
Reid, A. Scotland: "It was a day peculiar to this
 piece of the planet."
Rolfe, E. First Love.
Rose, B. Great Day.
Rukeyser, M. Yes.
Saijo, A. Bodhisattva Vows.
Scott-Heron. I Think I'll Call It Morning.
Smith, S. Away, Melancholy.
Sondheim. Everything's Coming Up Roses.
Unknown. Brian O'Linn.
Volkman. Sonnet: "Never got, and never
 thought, and yet."
Yellen, J. Happy Days Are Here Again.
Zukofsky, L. In Arizona.

Oracles
Clampitt. Dodona: Asked of the Oracle.
de Fierro. Oracle.
Dugan, A. Last Statement for a Last Oracle.
Hooper, V. Reading, A.
Jackson, L. Unthronged Oracle, The.
Korinna [or Corinna]. Of your daughters: Zeus,
 Father.
McCallum, S. What the Oracle Said.
Walden, G. Oracle.

Orange (color)
Bhatt, S. Looking Through a French
 Photographer's Portrayal of Rajasthan with
 Extensive Use of Orange Filters.
MacBeth [or Macbeth]. Orange Poem, The.
O'Hara, F. Why I Am Not a Painter.

Orange Trees and Oranges
Amadiume. Creation.
Apollinaire. Windows.
Cope, W. Orange, The.
Cunningham, P. Aubade: "Man is squeezing
 oranges in my kitchen, A."
Eluard, P. et al. Earth Is Blue like an Orange,
 The.
García Lorca. Song of the Sterile Orange Tree.
Gorostiza, J. Who Will Buy Me an Orange?
Hajjaj, N. Hungry Orange, A.
Jacobs, J. Two Varieties of the Bitter Orange.
Lima, M. Marketwoman of Luanda.
Nelson, J. Never Eat Oranges!
Okigbo. Dark waters of the beginning.
Pelizzon, V. Wedding Day, The.
Ruefle. Kiss of the Sun.
 Peeling the Orange.
Sitwell, S. Red-Gold Rain, The.
Soto. Oranges.
Tipton. There Are Rivers of Oranges.
Unknown. Now that the fragrance.

Oratory
Antin. David ross called up from syracuse and
 wanted to know if.
Garioch. Did Ye See Me?

Kizer, C. Oration, The.

Orchards
Barnes, W. My Orcha'd in Lindèn Lea.
Doolittle, H. Orchard.
Eliot, T. S. New Hampshire.
Frost, F. Deserted Orchard.
Harvey, M. Image Cast by a Body Intercepting
 Light.
Jaccottet. Fruit.
Johnson, R. William Stukeley made his own
 Stonehenge.
Kelly, B. Orchard, The.
Kenney. Plume.
Kinzie. Orchard dying, The.
Machej. Orchards in July.
Margolis, G. On the Way to the Sitter's.
Masters, E. Lost Orchard, The.
Ni Ghallchóir, C. In the Garden of Apples.
Oliver, M. Through Ruddy Orchards.
Pak Chaesam. In sunlight suffused.
Paz. Grove, The.
Sandburg, C. Wind Song.
Sappho. Come to me from Krete to this holy.
Snodgrass. Old Apple Trees.
Spear, R. Nest for Everyone, A.
Stevenson, A. In the Orchard.
Twichell. Snow in Condoland.
Tynan Hinkson, K. Of an Orchard.
Williams, W. Wild Orchard.

Orchids
Beachy-Quick, Dan. Botany.
Carson, A. Short Talk on Orchids.
Doolittle, H. At Baia.
Hadas, R. Tangerine Orchids.
Hamill, S. Orchid Flower, The.
Mitchell, S. Orchid and Rock.
Ricardo. Orchid.
Roethke. Orchids.

Order
Ammons. Corsons Inlet.
Baraka, I. How People Do.
Bejerano, M. From morning slumber a stir a
 shift a spinning motion of tossing.
Bellen, Martine. Cucina.
Bible, O.T. To Everything There Is a Season.
Bonar. Precedence.
Crane, S. Once there came a man.
Creeley. Window, The.
Eberhart, R. Hard Structure of the World, The.
Fortini. Perhaps the Time of Blood.
Francis of Assisi. Cantica: Our Lord Christ: Of
 Order.
Herbert, Z. Georg Heym—The Almost
 Metaphysical Adventure.
Kim Sŭnghŭi. Institutions.
Kosugi, T. Anima 1.
Kruit, J. Post Heads.
Laux, D. Reetika Arranges My Closet.
Lowell, A. Patterns.
Meredith, G. Lucifer in Starlight.
Neruda. Still, I am here.
Pope, A. Awake, my St. John! leave all meaner
 things.
Rogers, P. Origin of Order, The.
Seyburn, P. Alphabetizer Speaks, The.
Stevens, W. Anecdote of the Jar.
 Connoisseur of Chaos.
 Idea of Order at Key West, The.
 Room on a Garden, A.
Tennyson, A. Love is and was my Lord and
 King.
Vivar. Order and the Days, The.
Wordsworth, W. As the black storm upon the
 mountain top.

Oregon (state)
Beath, M. Oregon Inlet.
Broumas, O. Oregon Landscape with Lost
 Lover.
Kaufman, B. Oregon.
Kinnell. On the Oregon Coast.

Orestes (mythology)
Moxley, Jennifer. Stem of the Tree of Orestes.

Organs and Organists
Heard, J. New Organ, The.
Lewis, D. Lost Chord, The.

Lieberman, L.   Organist's Black Carnation, The.
Loerke, O.   Down There.
Purser, J.   Love Poem: "No nightfall in June."
   Organist Confesses to His Mirror, The.

Orient
Fletcher, J.   Over the roof-tops race the shadows
   of clouds.
Ginsberg, A.   After Yeats.
Starbuck, G.   Said ("J. Alfred Prufrock to.").
Taylor, B.   To a Persian Boy in the Bazaar at
   Smyrna.

Origami
Williamson, G.   Origami.

Original Sin
Balaban.   Atomic Ghost.
Chaucer.   Nun's Priest's [or Nonne Preestes]
   Tale, The.
Dickinson, E.   "Heavenly Father"—take to thee.
Donne.   If poisonous [or poysonous] mineral[l]s,
   and if that tree.
Howe, M.   Part of Eve's Discussion.
Nash, O.   Ha! Original Sin!
Someck, R.   Sign of the Bite, The.
Unknown.   Adam Lay Ybounden [or I-
   bounden].
Vaughan, H.   Corruption.
Very.   Garden, The.
Warren, R.   Original Sin [: A Short Story].
Youmans, Greg.   Pear's Complaint.

Orioles
Dickinson, E.   One of the ones that Midas
   touched.
Dunbar, P.   Summer in the South.
Issa.   Noon.
Lowell, R.   Fall 1961.
Tu Fu [or Du Fu].   Yellow Orioles.
Vietnamese Oral Tradition.   Husband and Wife.
Webster, P.   Baltimore Oriole.

Orion (constellation)
Dings, Fred.   Redwing Blackbirds.
Rich, A.   Orion.
Turner, C.   Orion.

Orion (mythology)
Korinna [or Corinna].   Are you, happy man,
   grandson of Kronos.
   Mighty Orion conquered.
   Terpsichore [told] me.

Orkney Islands
Blair, H.   Bloody Orkneys, The.

Orphans
Blind.   Beautiful Beeshareen Boy, The.
Brontë, C.   Orphan Child, The.
Cervantes.   Refugee Ship.
Ch'oe Sŭngja.   From Early On I Was.
Davis, G.   Orphan, The.
de Fréine, C.   Skills.
Ellis, T.   Atomic Bride.
Ficowski.   Both Your Mothers.
Fink, Robert A.   Aunt May.
Goralik, L.   Here I am, looking at you, my
   orphan. Your thick scarf. Your cold cigarette.
Kikaku.   On Buddha's birthday.
Kim Hyesun.   Ripe Apple.
Knott.   Christmas at the Orphanage.
Levine, P.   On My Own.
Linden, M.   Orphan Girl, An.
Lysohorsky.   22.6.1941.
Martínez, V.   Traveler.
Masters, E.   Constance Hately.
Metodiev, Ivan.   These Things from Words.
Murphy, P.   New Boy, The.
Nye, N.   At Mother Teresa's.
Riley, J.   Little Orphant Annie.
Ros.   Little Belgian Orphan, A.
Rossetti, C.   Iniquity of the Fathers upon the
   Children, The.
Ruan Yu.   Driving My Chariot Through the
   Northern Suburbs Gate.
Shin Tongyŏp.   Scene 8.
Sigourney.   Suttee, The.
Unknown.   Babes in the Wood, The.
   Ballad of the Orphan Boy, The.
Verlaine.   Peaceful eyes my only wealth.

Orpheus
Antipater of Sidon.   Never again, Orpheus.

Ausländer, R.   In the Color of Sleep.
Bancquart.   Counterfable of Orpheus.
Carbó, N.   I Found Orpheus Levitating.
Chénier.   When the Euxine goddess with
   astonished eyes.
Graham, J.   Orpheus and Eurydice.
   What the End Is For.
Gunn, T.   For the Late R. F.
Henryson.   Syne nethir-mare he went quhare
   Pluto was.
Hill, G.   Orpheus and Eurydice.
Howell, C.   New Orpheus, The.
Kinsella, J.   Orpheus.
Klink, J.   Orpheus. Eurydice. Hermes.
Kochanowski, J.   Where Is That Gate for Grief.
Levertov.   Tree Telling of Orpheus, A.
Ovid.   Death of Orpheus, The.
Pastan.   Orpheus.
Perry, S.   Orpheus.
Phillips, C.   Rest of Love, The.
Poliziano.   What song will ever be so sorrowful.
Rich, A.   I Dream I'm the Death of Orpheus.
Rilke.   Orpheus, Eurydice, Hermes.
Rukeyser, M.   Poem as Mask, The.
Seneca.   Deaths of Orphues and Hercules, The.
Simonides.   Countless birds.
Sinclair, S.   Orpheus Meets Eurydice in the
   Underworld.
Spenser, E.   Epithalamion: "Ye learned sisters
   which have oftentimes."
Spicer, J.   Orfeo.
Strand.   Orpheus Alone.
Vicinelli.   Crossing the River.
Winchilsea.   Answer, The [To Pope's
   Impromptu].

Osiris
Duncan, R.   What I Saw.

Oslo, Norway
Griffin, T.   I Have Folded This Letter in Ten
   Places.

Ospreys
Peaux, A.   Old Houses on the Quays.
Snyder, G.   No Shadow.
Unknown.   Kuan-kuan, the ospreys.
Wheelock, J.   Fish-Hawk, The.

Ostriches
Moore, M.   He "Digesteth Harde Yron".
Morgan, Elin Llwyd.   Your Ostrich Nature.
Nwankwo.   Poem: "In sand."

Oswald, Lee Harvey
Burford, W.   Spell, The: "You can almost see
   him, looking as if well."
O'Callaghan, C.   5 The Bull.
Spears, Rebecca.   Marina's Daughters, 1964.

Othello
Bishop, J.   Speaking of Poetry.
Lindsay, V.   Colloquial Reply, A: To Any
   Newsboy.
Ward, B. J.   Daily Grind.

Ottawa, Ontario
Kleinzahler.   Spleen.

Otterburn, Battle of (1388)
Unknown.   [Battle of Otterburn, The] [Version
   from Minstrelsy of the Scottish Border].

Otters
Grennan.   One Morning: "Looking for
   distinctive stones, I found the dead otter."
Hartnett.   Wounded Otter, The.
Heaney, S.   Otter, The.
Hughes, T.   Otter, An.
Mac Low.   Giant Otters.
   Giant Philosophical Otters.
McMichael.   Lutra, the Fisher.
Thurston, H.   River Otters at Play.

Ouija Boards
Merrill, J.   Voices from the Other World.
   Zero hour. Waiting yet again.

Outlaws
Darley.   Free-booter, The.
Gonzales, R.   Head of Pancho Villa, The.
Montgomery, W.   Outlaws.
Parker, Bonnie.   Story of Bonnie and Clyde,
   The.
Ross, Claire Ottenstein.   Judge, The.
Shuford.   Sam Bass.

See also **Crime and Criminals**
Ovenbirds
Frost, R.   Oven Bird, The.

Overpopulation
Kenney.   Millenary.

Ovid (Publius Ovidius Naso)
Ficowski.   Ovid Twice Exiled.
Gardelle, C.   Peaceful Sunday.
Guest, Paul.   Intrusion of Ovid, The.
Haavikko.   Take heart, Ovid. No sentence.
Hill, G.   Ovid in the Third Reich.
Howe, S.   Revisionist work in.
Ignatova, E.   To Ovid.
Jones, D.   Summer Is a Poem by Ovid.
Leon, E.   On the Second Tristia of Ovid.
Prior.   Written in an Ovid.
Ransom, J.   Philomela.
Walcott.   Hotel Normandie Pool, The.

Owen, Wilfred
Downie.   For Wilfred Owen.

Owls
al-Rahim, A.   Wailing.
Alexander, P.   Mt. Auburn Owl.
Baudelaire.   Owls.
Bishop, E.   Song for the Rainy Season.
Carroll, L.   Alice's Recitation.
Chia Yi.   Owl, The.
   Year was tan-wo, it was the fourth month,
   summer's first, The.
Ch'oe Sŭngja.   Night Owl.
De la Mare.   Owl, The.
Densmore.   No. 72. Brown Owls.
Duncan, R.   Sentinels, The.
Espada.   Owl and the Lightning, The.
Ewart.   Owl Writes a Detective Story, The.
Frost, R.   Questioning Faces.
Haines, J.   If the Owl Calls Again.
Hollander, J.   Owl.
Howe, S.   Revisionist work in.
Hughes, R.   Glaucopis.
Issa.   O owl!
   Owls are calling / "Come, come".
   Pigeon Makes His Request, The.
Lear, E.   Children of the Owl and the Pussy-Cat,
   The.
   Owl and the Pussy-Cat [or Pussycat], The.
   There Was an Old Man With a Beard.
MacBeth [or Macbeth].   Owl.
Mezey.   Owl.
Middleton, C.   Wooden Dog.
Miranda, Deborah A.   Stories I Tell My
   Daughter.
Montgomery, Vaida Stewart.   Funeral.
Mora.   Bruja: Witch.
Moss, T.   Owl In Daytime, The.
Nguyen, Hoa.   Dark.
Niedecker.   Monster owl, A.
Norris, L.   Barn Owl.
Oliver, M.   Little Owl Who Lives in the
   Orchard.
O'odham.   No. 72. Brown Owls.
   No. 75. They Come Hooting.
   Songs for the Four Parts of the Night.
Oswald, A.   Owl Village.
Paquin, Ethan.   Hearing Music Through Dark
   Trees.
Peaux, A.   Old Houses on the Quays.
Plath.   Owl.
Russell, T.   To the Owl.
Schuyler, J.   Korean Mums.
Smith, D.   Sea Owl.
Sŏ Chŏngju.   Owl.
Sosnora.   Footsteps of an Owl and His Lament,
   The.
   Owl and the Mouse, The.
Spireng, M.   Snowy Owl.
Stafford, W.   Owls at the Shakespeare Festival.
Thomas, E.   Owl, The.
Thomas, R. S.   Ancients of the World, The.
   Still.
Tu Fu [or Du Fu].   Travelling Northward.
Unknown.   Limerick.
   Song of the Owl.
   Sweet Suffolk Owl.
Warren, R.   In Italian They Call the Bird

Civetta.
Owl, The.
Wells, N.   Owl Wives.
Wilbur, R.   Barred Owl, A.
Winchilsea.   Nocturnal Reverie, A.
Witt, S.   Thermal Signatures ("There is nothing
  to remember but flight. The owl's eyes
  spoke.").
Wyrebek, M.   Night Owl.
Young, G.   Four Poems.
Zimmer.   What I Know About Owls.

Oxen
Darío, R.   Far Away and Long Ago.
Davis, D.   Christmas Poem, A.
Drummond de Andrade.   Boi Vě os Homens,
  Um.
  Ox Looks at Man, An.
Dyer, J.   My Ox Duke.
Edson, R.   Ox, The.
Hardy, T.   Oxen, The.
Jiménez, J.   Lumber Wagons, The.
  Oxcarts Are Now on Their Way, The.
Monroe, H.   Meeting, The.
Muso Soseki.   Ox Turned Loose.
Simpson, L.   White Oxen.
Sutskever [*or* Sutzkever].   Death of an Ox, The.
Unknown.   Ox.
Van Winckel, N.   Basket with Blue Ox.

Oxford, England
Arnold, M.   Scholar Gypsy, The.
Auden.   Oxford.
Hopkins, G.   Duns Scotus's Oxford.
MacNeice.   I ought to be glad.
Ransom, J.   Philomela.
Russell, T.   To Oxford.

Oxford University
Bartlett, E.   Stretchmarks.
Moore, T.   Scene from a Play, Acted at Oxford,
  Called "Matriculation".

Oysters
Carroll, L.   Walrus and the Carpenter, The.
Drummond, W.   Comparison of His Thoughts to
  Pearls.
Ercilla, M.   Oysters and Zarzuelas.
Heaney, S.   Oysters.
Howard, R.   Oystering.
  Wildflowers.
Ponge.   Oyster, The.
Porter, C.   Tale of the Oyster, The.
Swift, J.   Oysters.
See also **Clams and Clamming; Shells**

Ozark Mountains
Blackwell, Holley.   Message No. 32.

P

Pacific Ocean
Curnow.   Pacific 1945-1995.
Fitzgerald, R.   Pacific.
Frost, R.   Once by the Pacific.
Gunn, T.   Discovery of the Pacific, The.
Harms.   Elegy as Evening, as Exodus.
Jeffers, R.   Eye, The.
Loewinsohn.   Siv, With Ocean (Pacific).
McGrath, T.   Remembering That Island.
Miller, J.   By the Pacific Ocean.
Silko.   Prayer to the Pacific.
Stevens, W.   Sea Surface Full of Clouds.
Unknown.   Loud waves up and down.
Wakoski.   Remembering the Pacific.
Whitman, W.   Facing West from California's
  Shores.
Winters, Y.   On Teaching the Young.
  Slow Pacific Swell, The.
Wright, C.   Looking West from Laguna Beach at
  Night.

Pacifism and Pacifists
Belloc.   Pacifist, The.
Crosby, E.   I am a great inventor, did you but
  know it.
  Military Creed, The.
Ezekiel.   Patriot, The.
Homer.   Goddess intervenes between Achilles
  and Agamemnon, The.

Housman.   Oh stay at home, my lad, and
  plough.
Kasdorf.   Mennonites.
Lowell, R.   After the Surprising Conversions.
  Memories of West Street and Lepke.
Millay, E.   Conscientious Objector.
Newbolt.   Non-Combatant, The.
Palmer, R. F.   Conchie, The.
Shapiro, K.   Conscientious Objector, The.
Stafford, W.   At the Un-National Monument
  along the Canadian Border.
Unknown.   Hymn: "O God of Hosts, thine Ear
  incline."
Whittier.   Brown of Ossawatomie.

See also **Conscientious Objectors**

Paganism and Pagans
Borges.   Witness, The.
Field.   Fellowship.
Klyuyev [*or* Kliuev *or* Klyuev].   Conversational
  Melody, A Good Verse, A.
Parker, D.   Flaw in Paganism, The.
Parry, R.   Pagan.
Sidney.   Ye Goat-herd Gods.
Wordsworth, W.   World Is Too Much with Us,
  The.
Ziedonis.   At Maruža's.

Pain
Adamson.   Passing Through Experiences.
Aeschylus.   God, whose law it is that he who
  learns must suffer.
Aini, L.   Empress of Imagined Fertility, The.
Aldrich, T.   Lycidas.
Amichai, Y.   Ibn Gabirol.
Archilochus.   No townsman, Perikles, will
  blame us for groaning.
Arends, J.   I.
Armantrout.   Winter.
Baraka, I.   Agony, An. As Now.
Basho.   Come, see / real flowers.
Benson, L.   P Word Poem, The.
Berger, D.   Language Pile, The.
Berry, W.   Way of Pain, The.
Bierds, L.   Phantom Pain.
Breytenbach.   Breyten Prays for Himself.
Broumas, O.   Beauty and the Beast.
Brown, T.   Pain.
Brutus.   Let not this plunder be misconstrued.
Bryant, W.   Mutation.
Carew, T.   To My Inconstant Mistress [*or*
  Mistris].
Carson, C.   Knee, The.
Cassian.   Ghost.
Ceni, B.   Key and the Tree, The.
Ceravolo.   Autumn-Time, Wind and the Planet
  Pluto.
  Conception.
Cernuda.   Shadow, The.
Chernoff.   Toothache.
Chipasula.   Talking of Sharp Things.
Ch'ŏn Yanghŭi.   To Single Women.
Coleridge, S.   Dejection: An Ode.
Colonna, S.   Disconnections.
Cooper, D.   10 Dead Friends.
Couzyn.   Pain, The.
Coward.   Never Again.
Crapsey.   Languor After Pain.
  Release.
Creeley.   Flower, The: "I think I grow tensions."
Cristall.   Written When the Mind Was
  Oppressed.
Cruz e Sousa.   Acrobat of Pain.
Csoori.   Postponed Nightmare.
Cullen, C.   Song in Spite of Myself.
Dalton, R.   Ars Poetica.
Darío, R.   Doom.
Derricotte.   Furious Boy, The.
Di Prima.   For H. D.
Dickinson, E.   After great pain a formal feeling
  comes.
  Final Inch, The.
  I Can Wade Grief.
  Morning after Woe, The.
  Nearness to Tremendousness, A.
  Pain Has an Element of Blank.
  Pain—expands the Time.
  There is a pain—so utter.

'Tis not that Dying hurts us so.
  Wounded Deer Leaps Highest, A.
Duhamel.   I'm Dealing with My Pain.
Eirian, S.   Pain, The.
Empson.   Villanelle: "It is the pain, it is the
  pain, endures."
"Ephelia.".   To J. G.
Ferguson, G.   Puritan against the Wind.
Fermini, I.   Detouring through the rooms were
  men and fumes.
First unexpected pain is beautiful, The.
Flynn, L.   Brinkwomanship.
Foppa.   Wound.
Fortini.   Italy 1942.
Galanskov.   I am in pain.
García Lorca.   Night of Sleepless Love.
  Poet Speaks the Truth, The.
Gardinier.   Democracy.
Gascoyne.   Ecce Homo.
Ghalib, M.   My Destiny.
Glück, L.   First Memory.
Gonzáles Martínez.   Pain.
Goodman, P.   In the Jury Room, in Pain.
Graham-Pole, J.   Pain, The.
Grahn.   Ella, in a Square Apron, Along
  Highway 80.
Greenwell, D.   Broken Chain, The.
Grosholz.   Back Trouble.
Gunn, T.   Innocence.
  Man With Night Sweats, The.
  Painkillers.
Hadewijch.   Cult of Love, The.
Hans.   Hurt.
Harryman.   The. Corner. Of.
Hartnett.   I Have Exhausted the Delighted
  Range.
Haslam, M.   30 55.
Hayden, R.   Road in Kentucky, A.
  Whipping, The.
Herrera y Reissig.   Sadistic Love.
Hongo.   O-Bon: Dance for the Dead.
Howe, F.   First Chance Twice.
  Very pain it came first.
Hsü Wei.   Buddhist Monk Cut and Burned His
  Own Flesh to Make the Rains Stop—A Man
  From His Native Place Asked Me to Write a
  Poem to Send to Him, A.
Hughes, F.   Different Voice, The.
Hughes, T.   God, A.
Ishikawa Takuboku.   Like being.
Jaccottet.   With Effort, I Sit up and Look
  Outside.
  Wound seen from afar.
Jarrell, R.   Field Hospital, A.
  90 North.
Johnson, L.   Reggae Sounds.
Kaufman, S.   Security.
Keats.   Ode to a Nightingale.
Kerouac.   Orizaba Blues: 64th Chorus.
Khoury, N.   People of Figs.
Kim Sŭnghŭi.   Roses and Thorns.
Kinsella, J.   Archetypal Chillies.
Kocot, N.   Ordinary Evening, An.
Labé.   Bright Venus, Who Across the Heavens
  Stray.
Larcom.   They Said.
Levertov.   Ache of Marriage, The.
Levy, A.   Cambridge in the Long.
  Oh, Is It Love?
Li Shang-yin.   Bite back passion. Spring now
  sets.
Li Yu [*or* Li Hou-Chu].   Immeasurable Pain.
Limburg, J.   Queen of Swords, The.
Lovelace, R.   To Lucasta.
MacCaig.   Of You.
Macgoye.   August the First; Court Martial. The
  Mother Speaks.
Martinez, D.   Pain.
McDaniel, J.   Disasterology.
McDonald, C.   Cheers.
McGough, R.   Poem With a Limp.
Meddeb, Abdelwahab.   On Forgotten Tracks.
Merry.   Adieu and Recall to Love, The.
Mew.   In Nunhead Cemetery.
Meynell, V.   Sympathy.
Millay, E.   And must I then, indeed, Pain, live

with you.
Mirabai [or Mira Bai].   O friends, I am mad.
Moss, H.   Wars, The.
Murray, L.   Cotton Flannelette.
Nelson, M.   Shiner.
 Wish.
Nijhoff.   Dancer.
Nishiyama Soin.   Cherry blossoms / dizzying.
Noguchi, R.   From Rooftops, Kenji Takezo
 Throws Himself.
Nolens, L.   Saint Vitus's Dance in October 10.
O'Donnell, C.   Process.
 Security.
Oppian [of Corycus].   Loves of the Tortoise,
 The.
Owen, W.   Greater Love.
 Hospital Barge at Cérisy.
Palmer, M.   Man Undergoes Pain Sitting at a
 Piano, A.
Parham, M.   Other People's Pain.
Picasso.   Her Great Thighs.
Piercy.   When a Friend Dies.
Pogson, P.   Apples.
Pound, E.   Long Wind, the Dawn Wind.
Procter, A.   Lost Chord, A.
Raboni, G.   For C., Who Died of Childbirth at
 the Age of One Year and Eleven Months.
"Rachel." [or "Rahel."].   Love was late in
 coming, and coming.
Ramanujan.   Pleasure.
Raz, H.   Teaching, Hurt.
Rhodes, M.   Small Pain, A.
Rich, A.   Dear Adrienne, / I feel signified by
 pain.
 Splittings.
 That conversation we were always on the edge.
Robinson, M.   Her Confirmed Despair.
Rochester, J.   Song: "Oh gentle Venus, ease a
 tarse."
Ros.   End of "Pain", The.
Rossetti, C.   Chilly Night, A.
 Introspective.
 Many in aftertimes will say of you.
Roy, L.   Triple Overtime.
Rozhdestvensky [or Rozhdestvenskii].   They
 Killed the Lad.
Russell, G.   Pain.
Sarton, M.   Tortured, The.
Scamell, B.   Party, The.
 Stranger to a Small Child.
Seferis.   Narration.
Seibert.   Casey Jones.
Sidney.   Sonnet 1: "Loving in truth, and fain[e]
 in verse my love to show."
 Sonnet 14: "Alas, have I not pain enough, my
 friend."
 Sonnet 16: "In nature apt to like when I did
 see."
Smith, K.   Essential Serbo-Coat.
 Here.
Snodgrass.   Flat One, A.
Soyinka.   Fado Singer.
Spenser, E.   Sonnet 26: "Sweet is the rose, but
 grows upon a brere."
Stein, G.   Orange in.
Stryk, L.   Enough.
Suckling, S.   Love's Offence.
 Song: "I prithee spare me, gentle boy."
Sutherland, Fraser.   Undergoing: Jewish General
 Hospital, Montreal 6:35 a.m.
Szporluk.   Triage.
Tarn.   First Zen Abbess of America, The.
 Hearing about the Virtual Destruction of Pain.
Taylor, J.   Remedy for Backache.
Thomas, G.   Greetings.
Thompson, C.   After-Glow of Pain, The.
Townsend, A.   Bicycle Racers, The.
Unknown.   As in thee resteth my joye and
 comfort.
 As the thread of my breath.
 My / wide eyes watch.
 O'er the Crossing.
 Streamers of farewell.
Vallejo.   I Am Going to Speak of Hope.
 I Am Going to Talk About Hope.
Vietnamese Oral Tradition.   Body Is Pain, The.

Vilariño.   There is no hope.
Vlasova, E.   I see / your hands in my
 nightmares.
Walcott.   Fist, The.
Wang, Y.   My Pain.
Wayne, J.   By Accident.
Wetzsteon.   Surgical Moves.
 Three Songs.
 Urban Gallery.
White, E.   Village Revisited.
Whitman, W.   I Sit and Look Out.
Wilbur, R.   Another Voice.
Wilcox, E.   Solitude.
Wilkinson, J.   Oiled Sweater.
Williams, C. K.   Alzheimer's: The Wife.
Williams, M.   Thinking about Bill, Dead of
 AIDS.
Wordsworth, W.   Complaint, A.
Wroth.   Sonnet 6: "My pain[e], still smothered
 [or smother'd] in my grieved bre[a]st."
Wunderlich, M.   From a Vacant House.
Wyatt.   Sighs are my food, drink are my tears.
Wyrebek, M.   Recovery.
Young, A.   Detroit 1958.

Paine, Thomas
Freneau.   On Mr. Paine's Rights of Man.

Painting and Painters
Agran, R.   Wearing Dad's White Shirt
 Backwards.
Ai.   Back in the World.
Alberti.   Blue.
 Giotto.
Alexander, E.   Painting / (Frida Kahlo).
Ash, J.   Poor Boy: Portrait of a Painting.
Ashbery, J.   Painter, The.
Auden.   Musée des Beaux Arts.
Ausonius.   Echo.
Baxter, C.   Diptych: Jesus and the Stone.
Benn.   Before a Cornfield.
Berkson, B.   Out There.
Berryman.   Winter Landscape.
Bishop, E.   Poem: "About the size of an old-
 style dollar bill."
Bishop, J.   Recollection, A.
Bloch, C.   What a Poet Does.
Boland, E.   From the Painting "Back from
 Market" by Chardin.
 I Remember.
 Self-Portrait on a Summer Evening.
Bonds, D.   Life of the Body, The.
Boruch.   Light.
Brandi.   After Li Ch'ing-Chao.
Browning, R.   Andrea del Sarto.
 Fra Lippo Lippi.
Bryant, W.   To Cole, the Painter, Departing for
 Europe.
Byron, C.   Shipping the Pictures from Belfast.
Cage.   25 Mesostics Re and Not Re Mark
 Tobey.
Carpenter, W.   Evening Wind.
 Night Shadows.
Carter, A. B.   Cobb's Barns.
Carver, R.   Bonnard's Nudes.
Cary, A.   Katrina on the Porch.
Cassells.   These Are Not Brushstrokes.
Cendrars.   Newspaper.
Chang Pi.   Butterfly.
Channing.   Murillo's Magdalen.
Char.   Mortal Partner, The.
Chen Huan.   Presented to the Taoist Paragon
 Mao.
Clark, T. J.   Landscape with a Calm.
Clarke, A.   Early Unfinished Sketch.
Cole, H.   Folly.
Conquest.   Rokeby Venus, The.
Coolidge, C.   Jerome in His Study.
Copus, J.   Masaccio's Expulsion from Paradise.
Corso.   Rembrandt—Self Portrait.
Craig, David.   Christ Bearing the Cross by El
 Greco.
Cranch.   My Old Palette.
Crane, H.   Sunday Morning Apples.
Crashaw.   Flaming Heart, The.
Cronin, A.   Lines for a Painter.
Cross, D.   Ceci n'est pas une pipe.
Cullar, Carol.   12,000 Years Is Not Too Long.

Curbelo.   Bedtime Stories.
 Dreaming Horse.
Curdy.   On a Painting by a Member of the
 Northwest Visionary School.
Curtis, T.   Portrait of the Painter Hans Theo
 Richter and His Wife Gisela in Dresden, 1933.
Cutts, S.   On parquet.
Denby.   Alex Katz Paints His North Window.
Deutsch.   Poem, The: "Painter of Dante's awful
 ferry-ride, The."
Dickinson, E.   I would not paint—a picture.
Dierking, K.   Delacroix's Version.
Dove, R.   Agosta the Winged Man and Rasha
 the Black Dove.
Drake, J.   National Painting, The.
Duhamel.   Art.
Dunn, S.   Impediment.
Dyer, E.   Painting the Nude.
Elton, W.   Hopper: In the Cafe.
Erinna.   Delicate hands fashioned this portrait:
 good Prometheus.
Felipe, L.   Caption for "The Child from
 Vallecas" by Velázquez.
Fenollosa, M.   Miyoko San.
Ferry.   Cythera.
Fichman.   Secrets of the Landscape, The.
Field.   La Gioconda; Leonardo Da Vinci, The
 Louvre.
 L'indifférent.
 Portrait, A.
Finch, P.   How Callum Innes Paints.
Flanders, J.   Cloud Painter.
Foreman, Paul.   Impressionist.
Fox, Skip.   In Referring to What Does Not
 Exist.
Gaspar, Lorand.   Late Minoan I: (Ewers of
 Hagia Triada).
Georgiou, E.   From Where I Stand.
Gilder, R.   Hour in a Studio, An.
Gillespie, N.   Seated in a Chinese Painting, He
 Speaks.
Giscombe, C.   Bro Duncanson.
Gonzáles Martínez.   Nectar of Ápan, The.
Graham, D.   Dogs in Dutch Paintings, The.
Graham, J.   At Luca Signorelli's Resurrection of
 the Body.
Greenberg, S.   Conduct.
Greger.   Man on the Bed, The.
Guest, B.   Roses.
 Wild Gardens Overlooked by Night Lights.
Guevara, M.   Easter Revolt Painted on a
 Tablespoon, The.
 Long Woman Bathing, The.
 Make-Up.
Gunn, T.   In Santa Maria del Popolo.
Halleck, F. et al.   National Painting [or
 Paintings], The.
Harryman.   Master Mind, The.
Harvey, M.   Nude on a Horsehair Sofa by the
 Sea.
Hearne, V.   Gauguin's White Horse.
Hecht, A.   At the Frick.
 Death the Painter.
Herbert, Z.   Painter.
Herrera.   Yellow Room, The.
Hilberry, Jane.   Crazy Jane Goes to Painting
 Class.
Hine.   Here is another poem in a picture.
Hirsch, E.   Edward Hopper and the House by
 the Railroad.
 Magic Mirror, The.
Hirschman, J.   Painting, The.
Hirshfield, J.   Painting.
Hollander, J.   Edward Hopper's Seven A.M.
 Sunday A.M. Not in Manhattan.
Holub.   How to Paint a Perfect Christmas.
Hostetler, A.   Painting with My Daughter.
Howard, R.   Giovanni da Fiesole on the
 Sublime.
Huang T'ing-chien.   To Go with Shih K'o's
 Painting of an Old Man Tasting Vinegar.
Hughes, T.   To Paint a Water Lily.
Hugo, R.   Milltown Union Bar, The.
Jacob, M.   In Honor of the Sardana and the
 Tenora.
Jennings, E.   Christ Seen by Flemish Painters.

Johnson, J.   Before a Painting.
Johnston, M.   Sea-Cucumber, The.
Jones, B.   Vermeer's Paint.
Jonson, B.   Picture of the Body, The.
Justice, D.   Anonymous Drawing.
On a Painting by Patient B of the Independence
   State Hospital for the Insane.
Kates.   No Altarpiece.
Kenny, M.   Still-Life.
Kim Ch'unsu [or Chun-soo].   Snow over
   Chagall's Village.
Kopland.   Breughel's Winter.
Kumin, M.   Calling, A.
Lahey, Joy.   Cotton and Gladiolas.
Lawrence, D. H.   Innocent England.
Levertov.   For Those Whom the Gods Love
   Less.
Life of Art, The.
   Salvator Mundi: Via Crucis.
Levitt, Peter.   Four hundred hairs of a brush.
Li Po.   In Praise of a Gold and Silver Painted
   Scene of the Buddha Manifestation in the Pure
   Land of the West, with a Preface.
Llwyd, Alan.   Scream, The: Edvard Munch
   (1893).
Longley, M.   Man Lying on a Wall.
Lothamer.   Be a Painter.
Love, B.   Bryan Ferry.
Lovelace, R.   To My Worthy Friend Mr. Peter
   Lely [or Lilly].
Lowell, R.   Epilogue: "Those blessèd structures,
   plot and rhyme."
Ludvigson.   Inventing My Parents.
Mariani.   Mountain View with Figures.
Markham, E.   Man with the Hoe, The.
Markham, M.   After Aesop.
Marks, Corey.   Portrait of a Child.
Marvell.   After two sittings, now our Lady State.
Mathias, R.   Memling.
McClatchy.   Capriccio of Roman Ruins and
   Sculpture with Figures, A.
McGuckian.   Sitting, The.
Melville, H.   Bench of Boors, The.
   Fruit and Flower Painter.
Mezey.   Evening Wind.
Mitchell, S.   Vermeer.
Monroe, H.   Rubens.
Montague, J.   Woodtown Manor.
Mooney, M.   Painting the Angel.
Moore, H.   Girl in a Fur-Trimmed Dress.
Morejón.   Tree of Earthly Delights.
Mueller, L.   American Literature.
   Monet Refuses the Operation.
   Nude by Edward Hopper, A.
Nelson, M.   Prayer of Miss Budd, The.
Nemerov.   Painter Dreaming in the Scholar's
   House, The.
   Vermeer.
Niatum.   In the Labyrinth of Elements.
Nossis.   Kallo dedicated her portrait in the house
   of golden.
   This portrait captures Thaumareta's form—it
   renders.
Noyes, S.   Dream Painter, The.
Oates.   Edward Hopper's Nighthawks, 1942.
O'Hara, F.   Having a Coke with You.
   Why I Am Not a Painter.
Ono.   Painting to be Constructed in Your Head.
   Painting To Hammer a Nail.
Opie.   To Mr. Opie, on His Having Painted for
   Me the Picture of Mrs Twis.
Ormond.   Certain Questions for Monsieur
   Renoir.
Ostriker.   Minor Van Gogh (He Speaks), A.
Padgett, R.   High Heels.
   Joe Brainard's Painting "Bingo".
Pagis, D.   Art of Reduction, The.
Palmer, M.   O you in that little bark.
Pastan.   Ethics.
Petrarch.   When Simon received the high idea
   which, for my sake, put his.
Picasso.   9.1.59: II.
   9.1.59: VI.
Pinkerton, H.   On Vermeer's *Young Woman with
   a Water Jug* (1658) in the Metropolitan
   Museum.

Pound, E.   Of Jacopo del Sellaio.
Quagliano.   Edward Hopper's "Lighthouse at
   Two Lights".
Raab, L.   After Edward Hopper.
Ray, D.   Automat.
   Midnight Diner by Edward Hopper, A.
Revell, D.   Fauviste.
Rilke.   Flamingos, The.
Rodriguez, J.   Nu-plastik Fanfare Red.
Rossetti, C.   In An Artist's Studio.
Rossetti, D.   For "An Allegorical Dance of
   Women" by Andrea Mantegna.
For Spring, by Sandro Botticelli, in the
   Accademia of Florence.
For 'The Wine of Circe' by Edward Burne
   Jones.
Marriage of St Katharine, by the same, A; in the
   Hospital of St John at Bruges.
Venetian Pastoral, by Giorgone, in the Louvre,
   A ("Water, for anguish of the solstice:—
   nay.").
Virgin and Child, by Hans Memmeling, A; in
   the Academy of Bruges.
Rowlands.   Epigram 29: "Gentlewoman of the
   dealing trade, A."
Rudolf.   Edward Hopper.
Rukeyser, M.   Birth of Venus, The.
   Painters.
Ryan, K.   Death by Fruit.
Salmon, A.   Painting.
Salter.   Young Girl Peeling Apples.
Sanders, E.   Cutting Prow, The.
Sanger, Peter.   Escalade (Paul-Émile Borduas,
   1905-1960).
Schulman.   American Solitude.
Scott, J.   Helen Paints a Room (1984).
Sexton.   Starry Night, The.
Shapiro, K.   Dome of Sunday, The [or A].
Singleton, G.   Defensive Driving.
Smith, V.   At an Exhibition of Historical
   Paintings, Hobart.
Snodgrass.   Matisse: "The Red Studio".
Snyder, M.   Painting, The.
Song.   Beauty and Sadness.
   Immaculate Lives.
Standing.   Hopper's Women.
Stanton, J.   Finger Paintings.
Stevenson, A.   Painting It In.
Stickney, T.   In Ampezzo ("In days of summer
   let me go.").
   On Sandro's Flora.
Stone, J.   Early Sunday Morning.
Stone, R.   Cabbage, The.
Su Tung-p'o.   On a Painting by Wang the Clerk
   of Yen Ling.
   When Yü-k'o painted bamboo.
Swenson, M.   Painting the Gate.
Swift, J.   Advice to a Dog Painter.
Szymborska, W.   Women of Rubens, The.
Tanahashi, K.   Can five hundred paintings be
   created in one stroke?
   Does the brush paint, or does the ink? Or does
   the paper.
Tardieu Jean.   Cézanne.
Thomas, R. S.   View from the Window, The.
Tomlinson, C.   Cézanne at Aix.
   Farewell to Van Gogh.
   Paring the Apple.
Townsend, A.   Rouge.
Trethewey, N.   Bellocq's Ophelia.
Tu Fu [or Du Fu].   Hawk in a Painting, A.
   Homage to the Painter General Ts'ao.
Verlaine.   Brussels: Simple Frescos 1.
   Brussels: Simple Frescos 2.
Very.   Sumach Leaves, The.
Vietnamese Oral Tradition.   Painting, The.
Violi.   Hazards of Imagery, The.
   Index.
Wade, S.   Gas.
Walcott.   Gauguin.
Waldrep, G. C.   Miracles of St. Sebasatian, The.
Wat.   Facing Bonnard.
Weigl.   Painting on a T'ang Dynasty Water
   Vessel.
Wieners.   Poem for Painters, A.
Welch, L.   Claude Monet's Water Landscapes.

In Cézanne's studio, we're dappled with joy.
Wharton, E.   Two Backgrounds.
Wheatley, P.   To S. M., a Young African Painter.
White, E.   I Paint What I See.
White, K.   McTaggart.
Whitman, W.   Death's Valley.
Wilbur, R.   Museum Piece.
Wilde, O.   Impression du Matin.
Williams, W.   Adoration of the Kings, The.
   Dance, The: "In Brueghel's great picture, The
   Kermess."
   Hunters in the Snow, The.
   Parable of the Blind, The.
Williamson, A.   Light's Reading, The.
Wilson, S.   Picture on the Purple Wall, The.
Wordsworth, W.   Elegiac Stanzas: Suggested by
   a Picture of Peele Castle, in a Storm, Painted
   by Sir George Beaumont.
Wunderlich, M.   Thirst.
Wyatt.   In Spayn.
Wylie.   Castilian.
Yellen.   Nighthawks.
Yi Yuksa.   Thatched House.
Young, G.   Miracle, The.

Pakistan
Allen, F.   When the Car Gave Up the Ghost.
Merrill, J.   Tomorrows.

Palaces
Kuan Hsiu.   Palace halls loomed high, encaged
   in purple vapor.
Li Yu [or Li Hou-Chu].   Past, The.
Po Chü-i.   Wu.
Trakl.   In Hellbrunn.
Yang Hsiung.   Sweet Springs Palace, The.

Paleontology and Paleontologists
Bierds, L.   Altamira: What She Remembered.
Harte, B.   Society upon the Stanislaus, The.
Lee, E.   Forests and Caverns.
Warfield.   Forests and Caverns.

See also **Dinosaurs; Evolution; Extinction; Fossils**

Palestine
Ali, A.   Land.
Alkalay-Gut.   Think of the children in Baghdad.
Brandt, D.   There are no words in me for Gaza,
   for what i saw.
Byron, G.   On Jordan's Bank.
Charara, H.   Hamza Aweiwi, a Shoemaker in
   Hebron.
Dao.   Ramallah.
Darwish, M.   Psalm 2.
   Ramallah—January, 2002.
   Sirhan Drinks His Coffee in the Cafeteria.
Hajjaj, N.   In the Burning Wood.
Kaufman, S.   Security.
Khoury, N.   People of Olives.
Knut.   Walking along the Sea of Galilee.
Lindsay, V.   John Brown.
Muhawi, I.   Bad Moon Rising.
Nadal, L.   Warrior Womb.
Nawwab, M.   Bridge of Old Wonders.
Ravikovitch, D.   You Can't Kill a Baby Twice.
Samaras, N.   Notes in Jerusalem.
Shapiro, M.   To Jerusalem, 1990.
Tuqan, F.   Gone Are Those We Love.
X, M.   Palestine.
Yosef, H.   Reflections on a Dove.
Yusuf, S.   Trees of Ithaca, The.

See also **Israel**

Palm Sunday
Chesterton.   Donkey, The.
Clampitt.   Palm Sunday.
Mayer, B.   Palm Sunday Maple Syrup Poem.

Palm Trees
Agard, J.   Palm Tree King.
Crane, H.   Royal Palm.
Cuney.   No Images.
Del Valle, S.   Political Life of Palm Trees, The.
Hemans.   Palm-Tree, The.
Melville, H.   Rolfe and the Palm.
Raab, E.   Serenade for Two Poplars, A.
Stevens, W.   Of Mere Being.
Unknown.   Sea-palms.
   Truth: "Breast / nursery."
Whittier.   Palm-Tree, The.

Pan (god)
Anyte [or Anytes]. Lone Theudotos placed this gift beneath the mountain.
Why, rustic Pan, sitting in the lone shady wood.
Browning, E. Flush or Faunus.
Musical Instrument, A.
Byron, G. Aristomenes.
Cornwall. Sonnet; A Still Place.
Emerson, R. Patient Pan, The.
Farrar, J. Song for a Forgotten Shrine to Pan.
Fletcher, J. Hymn to Pan.
Kyger. Pan as the Son of Penelope.
Lyly, J. Pan's Syrinx.
Robinson, A. Valley, The.
Shelley, P. Hymn of Pan.
Van den Bergh. Nocturn: "Moon rows burning, The."
Wilmer, S. Mess Boy, The.
Panama
Sylvain, P. Panama.
Unknown. Golden Island, The; or, the Darian Song.
Pancakes
Agran, R. Cakes Continue to Rise.
Rossetti, C. Mix a Pancake.
Pandas
Revell, D. Tooms 4.
Pandora
Jean-Gilles, M. Circumcising Pandora.
Pansies
Binyon. Harebell and Pansy.
Pantheism and Pantheists
Aminado. Our Sunday Rest.
Bryant, W. Thanatopsis.
Kavanagh, P. One, The.
Naden. Pantheist's Song of Immortality, The.
Ortiz. Creation.
Swinburne. Higher Pantheism in a Nutshell, The.
Tennyson, A. Higher Pantheism, The.
Wordsworth, W. It Is a Beauteous Evening.
Panthers
Carroll, L. Alice's Recitation.
Faverey. Seldom has a panther's leap.
Nash, O. Panther, The.
Rilke. Panther, The.
Whitmore, S. Lenaia.
Papacy
Housman. Pope, The.
Wilde, O. Easter Day.
See also **Catholicism and Catholics**
Paperweights
Schnackenberg. Paperweight, The.
Parachuting and Parachutists
Burke, M. Former WWII Paratrooper Dreams of Suicide, 1977, A.
Guest, B. Parachutes, My Love, Could Carry Us Higher.
Motion, A. Letter, The: "If I remember right, his first letter."
Unknown. Tatton Parachute Training School.
Vinokurov. When the Parachute Does Not Open.
See also **Sky Diving and Sky Divers**
Parades
Berlin. Easter Parade.
Cocteau. Fairy Scene.
Darío, R. Triumphal March.
Eliot, T. S. Triumphal March.
Harte, B. Second Review of the Grand Army, A.
Herman, J. Before the Parade Passes By.
Jacobik, G. Under the Sign of Walt Whitman.
Knight, S. Big Parade, The.
Merrill, B. Don't Rain on My Parade.
Nasir. Parade.
Ochester. Thanksgiving.
Revard. Parading with the Veterans of Foreign Wars.
Rimbaud, A. Ruts.
Sassoon, S. Suicide in the Trenches.
Tsanev, Stefan. Rehearsal for a Parade.
Whitman, W. Boston Ballad, A.
Willson, M. Seventy Six Trombones.

See also **Marching and Marches**
Paradise
Alegría. Ars Poetica.
Cernuda. Lover Digresses, The.
Forrest, G. Stranger in Paradise.
Guidacci. It Is like a Shortness of Breath.
Hafiz, K [or Hafez]. On the Way to the Garden (77).
Herbert, G. Paradise.
Issa. Closer, closer / to paradise—.
Jacob, M. Egg, An.
Johnson, L. Red Wind, The.
Kaplinski, J. To eat a pie and to have it.
Kaschnitz. Poem, A: "Poem made of words, A."
Kipling, R. Envoi, L'.
Laux, D. If This Is Paradise.
Levertov. Contraband.
Marsman. Paradise Regained.
Martinson. Once I Came to Paradise.
Mead, J. Paradise Consists of Forty-Nine Rotating Spheres.
Mikha'il, M. Don't Despair.
Milton. Prospect of Eden, The.
Muir, E. Milton.
Rattenbury, A. Rain Falls on Utopia Too.
Reznikoff. As I Was Wandering with My Unhappy Thoughts.
Rivas, J. Season of Paradise, A.
Temporada de Paraíso, Una.
Rumi. When the heart bursts into flame.
Sappho. Come to me from Krete to this holy.
Scliar-Cabral. Sephirot.
Shirley, J. Garden, The.
Stewart, S. Apple.
Unknown. Build a House in Paradise.
Very. Nature ("Bubbling brook doth leap when I come by, The.").
Wright, R. Stranger in Paradise.
Yoketsu. Nothing longed for.
See also **Heaven**
Paradise Lost
Marvell. On Mr Milton's "Paradise Lost".
Muir, E. Milton.
See also **Milton, John**
Paradoxes
Ashbery, J. Paradoxes and Oxymorons.
Buffoni, F. And those level fingernails of theirs.
Cain, Justin. My Required Tool.
Devaney, T. American Pragmatist Fell in Love, The.
Dunn, S. Happiness.
Gallagher, T. Not There.
Hart, L. I Wish I Were in Love Again.
Hewison. Limerick: "Said an erudite sinologue: 'How'."
Koethe. Moore's Paradox.
Loy. There is no Life or Death.
Lumelli, A. There are no pacts.
Muñoz, C. Lockerbie.
Quevedo y Villegas. Amorous Sonnet Defining Love.
Saarikoski. I lived in a ruin called The Lion.
Sidney. Sonnet 6: "Some lovers speak, when they their Muses entertain."
Villon. I Die of Thirst While at the Fountain Side.
Parakeets
Karp. Harm.
Stevens, W. Bird with the Coppery, Keen Claws, The.
Paralysis
Hicok. Sudden Movements.
Michaux. Slices of Knowledge.
Mörling, M. For the Woman with the Radio.
Paranoia
Bogen, L. I Eat Lunch with a Schizophrenic.
Butts, A. Poe Story, A.
Charara, H. Thinking American.
Colby, T. Boy and the Girl, The.
Creeley. Dishonest Mailmen, The.
Fox, Skip. Perhaps the rain on the roof is some hyper-phrenetic code from Shadowland.
Musgrave. I Am Not a Conspiracy Everything Is Not Paranoid the Drug Enforcement

Administration Is Not Everywhere.
Nielsen, D. Paranoid Egotist, A.
Nolens, L. Paranoia.
Sexton. Noon Walk on the Asylum Lawn.
Spicer, J. Conspiracy: "Violin which is following me, A."
Strand. Tunnel, The.
Tranter. Hang up a yellow shirt—you cause joy.
Wolff, Rebecca. Sybil.
Pardons and Pardoners
Chaucer. Pardoner's Prologue, The.
Vallejo. Our Daily Bread.
Parental Love
Amichai, Y. My Child Blossoms Sadly.
Asim, J. Baby's Breath.
Belev. Love: "What do you scrawl."
Bottoms. Daughter's Fever, A.
Cardona-Hine. Trumpet Voluntary in Praise of My Four Children.
Cornett, S. Lear Expands His Last Words to Cordelia.
Daniels, J. Falling Bricks.
De Kok. My mother's house hold.
Eskimo Oral Tradition. Magic Words to Cure a Sick Child.
Fennelly. Latching On, Falling Off.
Friesen, P. Pa poem 4: naked and nailed.
Griffin, S. Two, Hers and Mine.
Harjo, J. Rainy Dawn.
Harrison, J. Arrival: "I will consider my son William."
Hawoldar. To My Little Girl.
Houlihan, J. And Everywhere Offering Human Sound.
Ibn az-Zaqqāq, A. My two friends, the love of one's two sons is not heresy, so surely you will both establish my innocence concerning the matter.
Jones, R. Freight, The.
Son.
What effect has your new son had on your writing life?
Moore, L. Praisesong: From Son to Mother.
Mun Chônghui. To My Son.
Nurkse. Birth Room, The.
O'Daly, W. Naturalist, A.
Porter, A. For My Son Johnny.
Romero, L. My Mother Didn't Learn.
Seiferle, R. Face in the Depths of the Desert, The.
Gift, The: "I was wrong when I compared the mask of my own face."
Spady, S. Push-Pull of This Love, The.
Swenson, K. Mother and Son.
Sze. Murmur, The.
Thermos, The.
Wah. Father / Mother Haibun #11.
Walders, D. Kindness of Abishag, The.
Wilder, R. Baby, The.
Parenthood
Adams, L. Kids!
Baca. Thirteen.
Berry, W. Way of Pain, The.
Coleridge, S. Sonnet to a Friend Who Asked How I Felt When the Nurse First Presented My Infant to Me.
Dove, R. Daystar.
Duhig, I. First Second, The.
Emmott, K. Who Looks after Your Kids?
Hadas, R. Red Hat, The.
Hammerstein. Soliloquy.
Harnick. Sunrise, Sunset.
Harwood, G. In the Park.
Hecht, A. Adam.
Herbert, W. Baby Poem Industry Poem, The.
Hô Xuân Huong. Condition of Women, The.
Hood, T. Parental Ode to My Son, Aged Three Years and Five Months, A.
Housman. Fragment of an English Opera.
Jonson, B. On My First Daughter.
Kim Namjo. For Baby.
Kinnell. After Making Love We Hear Footsteps.
Kizer, C. Children.
Parents' Pantoum.
Kooser. At the End of the Weekend.

Kumin, M.　Bangkok Gang, The.
　Family Reunion.
Lorde.　What My Child Learns of the Sea.
Madgett.　Offspring.
McGinley.　Velvet Hand, The.
McLain, P.　Connor in the Wind and Rain with
　His Coat on.
Meredith, W.　Parents.
Miedzyrzecki.　Penguins.
Orr, G.　Father's Song.
Osgood, F.　Ellen Learning to Walk.
Pak Mogwŏl [or Mokwŏl].　Family.
Plath.　Morning Song: "Love set you going like
　a fat gold watch."
Ridler.　For a Child Expected.
Salzman, E.　Double Crossing.
Shakespeare, W.　Sonnet 2: "When forty winters
　shall besiege thy brow."
Smith, D.　August, on the Rented Farm.
Stafford, W.　For a Lost Child.
Su Tung-p'o.　On the Birth of His Son.
Taylor, E.　Upon Wedlock and Death of
　Children.
Thompson, S.　Living at the Frost Place.
Tiruvalluvar.　Gift of Children, The.
Todd, R.　Personal History; for My Son.
Traherne.　Rapture, The.
Unknown.　Maternal Love.
Walker, J.　Studying Physics with My Daughter.
Weaver, A.　Improvisation for Piano.
Wilson, E.　Lakeside.
Yeats.　Prayer for My Daughter, A.

Parents

Ali, A.　Dream of Glass Bangles, A.
　Houses.
Amir, D.　What Seeps In.
Bartlett, E.　God Is Dead—Nietzche.
Basu, R.　I had a good dream last night.
Behn, R.　Ancient New Parents.
　Still Life: "There is a train, no, there are train."
Belli, C.　Father, Mother.
　My Parents, Know It Well.
Berger, B.　Without.
Berryman.　Sympathy, a Welcome, A.
Bhattācārya, K.　Hara came and made off with
　my Gauri.
　Hey, Hara, Ganges-Holder.
　You ask me, Queen, time after time.
Blake, W.　Infant Sorrow.
Bloch, C.　Discipline of Marriage, The.
Bly, R.　For My Son Noah, Ten Years Old.
Boyle, K.　What Parents Do Not Yet Know.
Brooks, G.　Jamal; Nineteen Cows In a Slow
　Line Walking.
Brummer, N.　That Rank Bed.
Byron, C.　Shipping the Pictures from Belfast.
Carson, A.　Short Talk on Reading.
Casterton, J.　One Flesh.
Causley.　Eden Rock.
Ciardi, J.　Sometimes Even Parents Win.
Cisneros, S.　My Wicked Wicked Ways.
Claman, E.　Show Biz Parties.
Collins, B.　No Time.
Cook, E.　Written at the Couch of a Dying
　Parent.
Coolidge, C.　Album—A Runthru.
Cornford, F.　Ode on the Whole Duty Of
　Parents.
Cornwall.　To My Child.
Cummings, E. E.　If there are any heavens my
　mother will (all by herself) have.
Curbelo.　Photograph of My Parents.
Davies, H.　Beachy Head.
Davies, J.　Bafflement.
Edson, R.　Fall, The: "There was a man who
　found two leaves and came indoors holding
　them out saying to his parents that he was a
　tree."
Elliot, A.　Latitudes of Home, The.
Ellis, T.　Kiss in the Dark, A.
Ferlinghetti, L.　Lost Parents.
　#2.
Gbadamosi.　Reading, The.
Gershon.　I Was Not There.
Ghos, G.　You're home, Uma! Stay here.
Glück, R.　Invaders from Mars.

Golding, N.　Wardrobes.
Graves, R.　Parent to Children.
Grosholz.　Eden.
Gruffydd, W.　Gwladys Rhys.
Gwynn, R.　Drive-In, The.
Hall, D.　Goggles and Helmet.
　My Son, My Executioner.
Hamod, S.　Leaves.
Holmes, D.　Nostalgia.
Hongo.　Hongo Store 29 Miles Volcano Hilo,
　Hawaii, The.
Issa.　Bedbugs, The.
Janzen, J.　How They Loved.
Jarman, Geraint.　Dad and Me.
Jarrell, R.　Player Piano, The.
Joshu, K.　Whenever I hear.
Kalia, J.　After Eight Years of Marriage.
Kapos, M.　Pulse, The.
Kearney, M.　Goodnight, Goodbye.
Kinnell.　Lackawanna.
Komunyakaa, Y.　My Father's Love Letters [or
　Loveletters].
Kornblith, M.　Parents.
Krayer, S.　My Mother Dressed for the
　Wedding.
Kunitz, S.　Quinnapoxet.
Larkin, P.　This Be The Verse.
Lawrence, P.　Hit Men, The.
Lee, D.　Billy Batter.
Levis.　Cry, The: "Then, everything slept."
Ludvigson.　Inventing My Parents.
Martinez, D.　Need.
McAuley, J.　Because.
McCarthy, T.　Mr. Nabokov's Memory.
McLaughlin-Carruth, J.　Parents They Would
　Be, The.
Merrill, J.　Broken Home, The.
　Childlessness.
Merwin.　Lament for the Makers.
Mesmer, S.　My Life in Yonago.
Meynell, A.　Parentage.
Michelson, J.　Rings.
Mirikitani.　Suicide Note.
Mitchelson, T.　Circa.
Morley, H.　Parents.
Morrissey, S.　Genetics.
Moses, G.　Black Banana House.
Moss, T.　One for All Newborns.
Muldoon, P.　Mixed Marriage, The.
Nash, O.　Parent, The.
Newman, A.　**Fall back.** To give ground; recede;
　retreat.
Nossis.　Melinna herself is re-created: notice the
　face.
Nowlan.　Warren Pryor.
O'Hehir, D.　Bedside.
Olds, S.　I Go Back to May 1937.
O'Reilly, C.　Possession.
Palis, Y.　Floor, The.
Polley, J.　Smoke.
Rosenberg, L.　Offspring, The.
　Which One Is the Grown-up? Haiku.
Rosenblatt, S.　Mom and Dad Getting Older.
Rossetti, C.　Why did baby die. . .?
Rumens.　Before these Wars.
Salaam.　Sharing is Hereditary.
Satyamurti.　Where Are You?
Schneider, M.　Photograph, The.
Seiler.　Digging in the Streets of Gold.
Shapiro, A.　Cold Wood.
Shimabukuro, Mira Chieko.　After the
　Separation, Dad Takes Me to the Dance for the
　Dead.
Simic.　Book Full of Pictures, A.
Simpson, L.　My Father in the Night
　Commanding No.
Sleigh.　In the Park.
Stafford, W.　Story That Could Be True, A.
　Vocation.
Steffler, J.　Hollis Street Square, Halifax.
Sund.　Two Poems for the Good Given.
Triplett, P.　Next to Last Prayer.
Trungpa, Chogyam.　His parents are having tea.
Turcotte, M.　Indian Things.
Ullman.　Why There Are Children.
Unknown.　Limerick.

My country wasn't sold, it was stolen.
Van Duyn.　Relationships.
Vasquez, R.　For Jose Mercado Vasquez and
　Frances Roman Vasquez.
Vietnamese Oral Tradition.　Lullaby: "Little one,
　go to sleep. Sleep soundly."
Wah.　Father / Mother Haibun #2.
　Father / Mother Haibun #3.
　Father / Mother Haibun #14.
Wakayama Bokusui.　Sight of my father and
　mother, The.
Walker, F. X.　Wishbone.
Wallace, R.　Facts of Life, The.
Watson, E.　Battered Toddler, Page B6.
Whalen, P.　"Never Apologize; Never Explain".
Williams, K.　Momma in Red.
Zinnemann-Hope.　Taking Tea with My Father
　and Mother.

Paris, France

Apollinaire.　Monday rue Christine.
　Zone.
Aragon.　Embrace, The.
　Waltz of the Twenty-Year-Olds, The.
Bancquart.　Town.
　Vanished, The.
Baudelaire.　Swan, The.
Belieu.　At St. Sulpice.
Bishop, E.　Paris, 7 A.M.
Boyle, K.　Complaint for M and M, A.
Cendrars.　Contrasts.
　Prose of the Trans-Siberian and Little Jean of
　France.
　Prose of the Trans-Siberian and of Little Jeanne
　of France, The.
Cisneros, A.　Paris Cinquième.
Clover, J.　Ceriserie.
Cranch.　In the Palais Royal Garden.
Desnos.　Night Watchman of Pont-au-Change,
　The.
　St Merri district, The.
Dove, R.　Bistro Styx, The.
　Island Women of Paris, The.
Fenton, J.　In Paris with You.
Frishberg, D.　Another Song About Paris.
Garlick, R.　Capitals.
Gordon, M.　Mam'selle.
Greger.　Notre Dame, Sainte Chapelle, Sacré
　Coeur by foot—.
Hammerstein.　Last Time I Saw Paris, The.
Harburg.　April in Paris.
Hinsey, E.　Art of Measuring Light, The.
Hochman.　Sphinxes.
Hughes, L.　Cubes.
　Jazz Band in a Parisian Cabaret.
Huidobro.　Blind.
　Eiffel Tower.
　Morning.
Kahal, I.　I'll Be Seeing You.
Leland, C.　Breitmann in Paris.
Lerner, A.　Paris Is Paris Again.
Lewis, S.　How 'Ya Gonna Keep 'Em Down on
　the Farm? (After They've Seen Paree).
Maar, Dora.　These Tall Constructions.
Malroux.　Octet Before Winter.
Maschwitz, E.　Paris Is Not the Same.
Masters, E.　Reuben Pantier.
Mathews, H.　Dream-Work, The.
　Ring, The.
McOrlan.　Accessories shop, The.
　Produce from the colonies.
Millay, E.　Armenonville.
Miller, J.　In Père La Chaise.
Milosz, C.　Bypassing Rue Descartes.
　Esse.
Osofisan.　Paris Latin Quarter.
Piatt, S.　Palace-Burner, The.
Porter, C.　You Don't Know Paree.
Pound, E.　In a Station of the Metro.
Prévert.　August Bank Holiday.
Ransom, J.　Amphibious Crocodile.
Rapin.　Of Gardens.
Senghor.　In Memoriam.
Soupault.　Horizon.
Supervielle.　Return to Paris.
Thackeray.　Ballad of Bouillabaisse, The.
Tzara.　For Robert Desnos.

Vallejo. Black Stone on a White Stone.
Three hundred womanly states of the Eiffel Tower are frozen, The.
Voigt. Gobelins.
Weiss, T. Ten Little Rembrandts.
Wilbur, R. Place Pigalle.
Young, A. Dance of the Infidels.
One Snapshot I Couldn't Take in France, The.
Young, J. How 'Ya Gonna Keep 'Em Down on the Farm? (After They've Seen Paree).

Paris [Mythology]
Doolittle, H. I am not nor mean to be.

Parker, Charlie
Ashanti. Just Another Gig.
Barlow, G. Mingus Speaks: Found Poems.
Brathwaite, E. Blues.
Brown, A. Assassination of Charlie Parker, The.
Cherry, J. Bird.
Crouch, S. Up on the Spoon.
Finnell. Over Voice of America.
France, L. Blues for Bird.
Harjo, J. Bird.
Harper, M. Brother John.
Hull, L. Ornithology.
Jackson, R. Shadows.
Jauss. Last Solo: Charlie Parker, Hotel Stanhope, March 12, 1955.
Kaufman, B. Walking Parker Home.
Lagrone. I Heard the Byrd.
Levis. Whitman.
May, K. Valentine's Day.
Mitchell, A. Goodbye.
Moskowitz, F. Bird Lives.
Reed, I. Poetry Makes Rhythm in Philosophy.
Thomas, L. Historiography.
Zimmer. But Bird.

Parks
Algarin. Dante Park.
Avison. Ramsden.
Bachner. Yes, That's the Way Things Are.
Bland, P. Notes for the Park Keeper.
Campert. Silver Talk.
Costanzo. Washington Park.
Cross, D. Sterling Park.
Crow, C. City Park.
Davies, W. H. Hill-Side Park, The.
Davison, P. From the Outland.
Deming, A. Tilden Park.
Duck. On Richmond Park.
Ellingham, L. Tompkins Sq. Branches With Snowy Arms.
Foerster. Bronx Park.
Ghigna. Park Elms.
Gibbons, R. Affect of Elms, The.
Hadas, R. Riverside Park.
Hare, P. Deceit in the Park.
Ingram, A. Castle Howard, the Seat of the Rt. Hon. Charles, Earl of Carlisle.
Jones, P. In the Park.
Kirby, D. To a French Structuralist.
Košek, M. Yes, That's the Way Things Are.
Langhorne. Studley Park.
Lewis, G. Sunday Park.
Livingston, M. Envoi: Washington Square Park.
Lowell, R. Public Garden, The.
Löwy, H. Yes, That's the Way Things Are.
MacLaine, Brent. North Shore Park.
Mandel, E. City Park Merry-Go-Round.
McAuliffe, J. Calm, The.
Millay, E. Armenonville.
Miyazawa Kenji. Some Views Concerning the Proposed Site of a National Park.
Mueller, J. Peninsula.
Murphy, M. Park mole.
Nedim. Song: "Come, let's grant joy to this heart of ours that founders in distress."
Nemes Nagy. Four-Light Window, A.
Nye, N. Lunch in Nablus City Park.
Pasternak, B. Hamlet.
Pearlberg, G.G. Loop-the-Loop in Prospect Park (1905).
Pedretti, Erica. Heimgarten.
Piccione. Watching Ants Play Soccer in Central Park.
Shepherd, R. Eros in His Striped Blue Shirt.
Provisional.

Sontrop. Park, A.
Sosnora. Crow.
Stevens, W. Vacancy in the Park.
Thomas, D. Hunchback in the Park, The.
Thomas, R. S. Welshman at St. James' Park, A.
Turner, W. Magic.
Unknown. Rise and Progress of the Present Taste in Planning Parks, Pleasure Grounds, Gardens, etc, The.
Waller, E. On St. James's Park, as Lately Improved by His Majesty.
Westmorland. To Sir John Wentworth, Upon His Curiosities and Courteous Entertainment at Summerly in Lovingland.
Wyrebek, M. Recovery.
Yeryomin. Helioptér of a skyscraper hotel.
Yi Yuksa. Small Park, A.

Parks, Rosa
Dove, R. Rosa.

Parliament, Great Britain
Carey [or Cary]. Fig for the Lower House, A.
Carpenter, M. One day I went to London.
Milton. On the New Forcers of Conscience Under the Long Parliament.
Unknown. Character of a Roundhead, The.
Vaughan, H. Charnel-house, The.
Young, E. Ye Nations, Tremble! Parliament has Met.

Parma, Italy
Lear, E. Limerick: "There was a Young Lady of Parma."

Parodies
Borges. From an Apocryphal Gospel.
Bynner. Opus 17.
Opus 2.
Carroll, L. Crocodile, The.
Father William.
White Knight's Song, The.
Cope, W. Not only marble, but the plastic toys. Reading Scheme.
De Vries, P. To His Importunate Mistress.
Duhig, I. Fred.
Evans, D. Song of Racquetball.
Ficke. Opus 118.
Opus 131.
Herbert, W. To a Mousse.
Koch, K. Variations on a Theme by William Carlos Williams.
Overton, R. Fire and Ice by Robert Frost: an early draft.
Rawls, Alex. H. S. Mauberley (Life and Contacts) Part 1 by Ezra Pound.
Marriage of Heaven and Hell by William Blake, The.
Song of Myself by Walt Whitman.
Sanders, James. From the Mark Prejsnar Playbook.
Shen Manyuan. Parody of the Other Woman.
Trinidad. Of Mere Plastic.
Unknown. Pilot's Psalm, The.
Zukofsky, L. First Movement: "And out of olde bokes, in good feith".

Parrots
Doty, M. Letter to Walt Whitman.
Dove, R. Parsley.
Gibson, W. Parrot, The.
Hill, S. Parrots.
Hsüeh T'ao [or Xue Tao]. Parrot Parted from Her Cage.
Lisboa. Echo.
Mac Lochlainn, G. Irish-speaking Mynah, The.
Nye, N. Lost Parrot, The.
Padgett, R. Poem for El Lissitzky.
Shwarts [or Shvarts]. Parrot at Sea, A.
Sitwell, S. "Psittachus Eois Imitatrix Ales ab Indis".
Skelton, J. Parrot's Soliloquy.
Unknown. Next Morning.
Webb, C. Invaders from South of the Border Imperil Native Population.
Wright, K. Sergeant Brown's Parrot.

Parsifal
Verlaine. Parsifal.

See also **Arthurian Legend**

Parthenon
Bolton, J. Parthenon at Nashville, The.
Davidson, D. On a Replica of the Parthenon.
Keats. On Seeing the Elgin Marbles.
Melville, H. Parthenon, The.

Parties
Abu Nuwas. Party's Over, The.
Armstrong, Tammy. Mother's Winter Guests.
Arnold, C. Disembodied Voices of Women, The.
Party She Outdid Herself, The.
Auden. Love Feast, The.
Avison. Party, The.
Bensley. One's Correspondence.
Berlin. Pack Up Your Sins and Go to the Devil.
Top Hat, White Tie, and Tails.
Betjeman. False Security.
Bibbins, M. Slutty.
Bottke, A. How to Approach Your Lover's Wife.
Brown, L. Don't Bring Lulu.
Brown, P. I Remember Dexedrine. 1970.
Carson, C. Céilí.
Ceravolo. Celebration.
Chin. Composed Near the Bay Bridge (after a wild party).
Claman, E. Show Biz Parties.
Comden, B. Party's Over, The.
Couto. Tea Party.
Coward. I've Been to a Marvelous Party.
Davidson, M. Bad Modernism.
Deanovich. American Avalon.
Drayton. Since there's no help, come let us kiss and part.
Eady. Song.
Earle, J. Tea Party, The.
Eliot, T. S. Mr. Apollinax.
Elmslie, K. Amazon Club.
Ezekiel. Goodbye Party for Miss Pushpa T. S.
Finkel. Party, The.
Gilbert, C. Now.
Ginsberg, A. First Party at Ken Kesey's with Hell's Angels.
Green, A. Party's Over, The.
Hernton, C. Poem: "And I went up to that chandeliered place."
Howe, J. Outside the Party.
Hupfeld, H. Let's Put Out the Lights and Go to Sleep.
Isharaza, G. Grand Get Together, The.
Jackson, M. L. Block Party.
Jacobsen, J. Birthday Party, The.
Johnson, a. Joint is Jumpin', The.
Johnson, J. Joint is Jumpin', The.
Kasischke. Grace.
Hostess.
Kefala. Party, The.
Kendrick, D. 26th Person, The.
Kuskin. Rose on My Cake, The.
Kuzmin. At the Party.
Leland, C. Hans Breitmann's Party [or Barty].
Li Ho. King Ch'in Drinks Wine.
Li Po. River Song.
March, J. Gang was there when midnight came, The.
McGinley. Office Party.
Mitchell, R. To Walt Whitman on America's Birthday.
Nikolayeva [or Nikolaeva]. Party on Women's Day, A.
Nye, N. Art of Disappearing, The.
O'Hara, F. For Grace, after a Party.
Olds, S. One Girl at the Boys Party, The.
Pafunda, Danielle. RSVP.
Phillips, C. Cotillion.
Piatt, S. Child's Party, A.
Pitcher, O. Remark, The.
Po Chü-i. After Getting Drunk, Becoming Sober in the Night.
Prasad, V. Empty.
Razaf, A. Joint is Jumpin', The.
Read, H. Garden Party.
Rose, B. Don't Bring Lulu.
Rosen, M. Eddie and the Birthday.
Scamell, B. Party, The.
Shepherd, R. Three A.M. Eternal.

Tafolla. Aquí.
Tranströmer. Below Freezing.
Tranter. Un-American Women, The.
Tu Fu [*or* Du Fu]. Night feast at the Tsos.
Unknown. Distressed: single cane, I return.
  Ling-tai: He Measured Out His Spirit Tower.
Waniek. Sleepless Nights.
Warren, R. After the Dinner Party.
Whittemore, R. For the Life of Him and Her.
Wilbur, R. Leaving.
Wood, V. Saturday Night.
Zimunya. Kisimiso.

Parting
Adair, T. Night We Called It a Day, The.
Alley, R. Canary Man and You, The.
Allingham, W. Winding Banks of Erne, The[:
  Or, The Emigrant's Adieu to His Birthplace].
Amichai, Y. Letter.
  Quick And Bitter.
Apollinaire. Cavalier's Farewell, The.
Asaf, Özdemir. Lavinia.
Auden. Aubade: "At break of dawn."
Bachmann. Songs from an Island.
Baker, Carol. Your Going.
Banchs, E. Mumbling.
Bendall, M. After Estrangement.
Berkeley, S. Parting, The.
Berlin. When the Midnight Choo-Choo Leaves
  for Alabam'.
Berryman. Parting as Descent.
Bhāndārī, S. Menaka says, Hey listen,
  Mountain King.
Bhattācārya, K. Jaya, tell him that Uma will not
  be sent.
  Turn back, Uma.
Boker. Sonnet 24: "Farewell once more,—and
  yet again farewell!"
Bolton, J. Parthenon at Nashville, The.
Bowes-Lyon. Feather, The.
Bradstreet, A. Before the Birth of One of Her
  Children.
Brontë, E. F. de Samara to A. G. A.
Brooke, R. Chilterns, The.
Brooks, S. Some of These Days.
Broumas, O. Song / for Sanna.
Brown, P. Leaving.
Browning, R. Parting at Morning.
Burgoyne, J. Dashing White Sergeant, The.
Burns, R. Ae Fond Kiss.
  Red, Red Rose, A.
  Silver Tassie, The.
Bykova, Z. At the Stop.
Byron, G. Fare Thee Well.
  Lines to Mr Hodgson.
  When We Two Parted.
Camões [*or* Camöes *or* Camoëns], L. Sonnet:
  That Sad and Joyful Dawn.
Campbell, J. Good Night, Sweetheart.
Carew, T. To My Mistress[e] in My Absence.
Castillo, S. Apagón, El.
Cavalli. Before when you left you would
  always forget.
Chia Tao. At Ni-Yang Inn.
  Farewell to Monk Chih-Hsing.
  Memento on the Departure of a Friend, from
    Yeh, Last Day of the Second Moon.
  Winter Night Farewell.
Chin, J. Why He Had to Go.
Chŏng Chisang. Parting.
Clarke, G. Am I Blue?
Cohan. So Long, Mary.
Comden, B. Some Other Time.
Conley, L. Cottage for Sale, A.
Connelly, R. Good Night, Sweetheart.
Constantine, D. You Are Distant, You Are
  Already Leaving.
Cooper, W. Leaving the Country.
Cornford, F. Parting in Wartime.
Cory, W. Parting.
  Preparation.
Coward. I'll See You Again.
  Never Again.
  Sail Away.
Creamer, H. After You've Gone.
Cummings, E. E. Goodby Betty,don't remember
  me.

Dante Alighieri. And now, with the reflected
  lights that glow.
Dao. Leaving Home.
De Kok. Stay here.
Delgado, J. When You Leave.
Densmore. My Love Has Departed.
Di Prima. Travel Poem.
Dickinson, E. My life closed twice before its
  close.
  'Tis customary as we part.
Dietz, H. Something to Remember You By.
Divakaruni. Leaving Yuba City.
Donne. Song: "Sweetest love, I do not go[e]."
  Valediction, A: Forbidding Mourning.
Dowson. O Mors! Quam Amara Est Memoria
  Tua Homini Pacem Habenti In Substantiis
  Suis.
Drayton. As Love And I.
  Farewell to Whitefoot.
  Since there's no help, come let us kiss and part.
Dufferin and Clandeboye. Lament of the Irish
  Emigrant.
Duo Duo. At Parting.
Dylan. Boots of Spanish Leather.
Elizabeth I. On Monsieur's Departure.
Ewing, J. Gifts.
Ezekiel. Goodbye Party for Miss Pushpa T. S.
Faiz. Before You Came.
Fanshawe, C. When Last We Parted.
Feaver. Coat.
Field. Second Thoughts.
Flower. At Parting: "False love, since thou and
  I must sever."
Flynn, N. Emptying Town.
Forrest, G. It's a Blue World.
Freed, A. Good Morning.
Fuller, J. Wild Raspberries.
Gershwin, I. Man That Got Away, The.
  They Can't Take That Away from Me.
Gibb, B. Vigil.
Glück, L. Departure.
  Letters, The.
González, A. City.
  Whatever You Want.
González Prada, M. Forced Labour.
Gorbanevskaya. Sukhanovo.
Gordon, M. There Will Never Be Another You.
Green, A. Some Other Time.
Gu Cheng. Seven Days.
Guidacci. Spring.
Haavikko. Days become years. Years.
Hacker, M. Conclusion: "Did you love well
  what very soon you left?"
Hammerstein. Lover, Come Back to Me!
Han Yong'un [*or* Yongwun]. Your Silence.
Hardy, T. Going, The.
Harper, F. Slave Auction, The.
Hart, L. He Was Too Good to Me.
Hass, R. Bashō, A Departure.
Hayden, R. Ballad of Sue Ellen Westerfield,
  The.
  Road in Kentucky, A.
Heard, J. Parting Kiss, The.
  Parting, The.
Hefer, H. We Left Slowly.
Hemans. Madeline, A Domestic Tale.
  Parting Song, A.
Henry VIII, King of England. To His Lady.
Herrick. To His Dying Brother, Master William
  Herrick.
Hine. Letting Go.
Homer. To this, great hector said.
Housman. Shake hands, we shall never be
  friends, all's over.
Hovey. At Sea.
Hsi Chou. Farewell to Wei Feng, Going to Far-
  South Mountain.
Hsieh T'iao. Prince Went Wandering, A.
Huidobro. Express.
Hwang Chini. Taking Leave of Minister So
  Seyang.
Ibn Shuhayd, A. I observe certain eyes gazing
  steadily at me as if speckled snakes [issuing
  from them] were attacking me from both sides.
Im Hwa. Pier of Yokohama under the Umbrella,
  The.

Irby. Sequence.
Ishikawa Takuboku. Like being.
Islām, N. Don't go back, Ma, don't go back,
  Mother.
Issa. Don't weep, insects / Lovers, stars,
  themselves.
Jenkins, A. Road Less Travelled, The.
Jiménez, J. Fleeting Return.
Jones, G. Esyllt.
Kahal, I. I'll Be Seeing You.
Kahn, G. Guilty.
  I'm Through with Love.
  Toot, Toot, Tootsie! (Good-bye).
Kalmar *et al.* Who's Sorry Now?
Kapovich, K. Parting makes simple sense.
Keats. On Leaving Some Friends at an Early
  Hour.
Kemble. Parting.
Killeen, G. Tristia.
Kim Chiha. Road to Seoul, The.
Kim Sowŏl. Azaleas.
Kim Yŏngnang. Selections from "Quatrains".
King, H. Exequy, The.
Knight, E. As You Leave Me.
Koehler, T. Don't Worry 'Bout Me.
  Sing, My Heart.
Laine, F. We'll Be Together Again.
Laleau. Hot Ports.
Lawrence, D. H. Butterfly.
  Winter's Tale, A.
Lerner, A. If Ever I Would Leave You.
Levertov. Invocation: "Silent, about-to-be-
  parted-from house."
  September 1961.
Lewis, A. Christmas Holiday.
  Goodbye.
  Post-Script: for Gweno.
Lewis, S. For All We Know.
  Just Friends.
Li Cunxu, E. Deep Peach Glades.
Li Po. In a Village by the River.
  On Hsin-P'ing Tower.
  On Yellow-Crane Tower, Farewell to Meng
    Hao-Jan Who's Leaving for Yang-Chou.
  Parting.
  River Merchant's Wife, The; A Letter.
  Saying Good-bye in a Ch'in-ling Wineshop.
  Saying Good-bye to Meng Hao-jan at Yellow
    Crane Pavilion.
  Taking Leave of a Friend.
  To Wang Lun.
Li Shang-yin. Chance to Meet Is Difficult, The.
Li Yü. To the Tune "Meeting Happiness".
Liu Ch'ang-ch'ing. On Seeing Wang Leave for
  the South.
Liu Yung. Cicada Song.
  Song: "After the eating, the drinking, the
    singing."
Loesser. Sand in My Shoes.
Lope de Vega. If You Leave at Daybreak.
  Sonnet 61.
Lorde. Movement Song.
Lovelace, R. To Lucasta, [on] Going beyond
  the Seas.
  To Lucasta, [on] Going to the War[re]s.
Lowell, A. Taxi, The.
Majumdār, H. Jaya / Don't wake up Hara's
  wife.
Mandelstam [*or* Mandelshtam]. Tristia.
Mangan, J. Lover's Farewell, The.
'Marnia. Accoutrement.
Martinez, D. Carp.
Maxton. On Failing to Translate.
McFadden, D. 8. Afternoon Bus to Toronto.
McGrath, Carmelita. How to Leave an Island.
McGrath, T. Fresco: Departure for an
  Imperialist War.
McNiece, R. Memorizing your face.
Meng Hao Jan. Taking Leave of Wang Wei.
Merrill, J. Renewal, A.
Mew. À Quoi Bon Dire.
  Sea Love.
Milton. Adam and Eve led out of Paradise.
Mistral, G. Absence.
Mitsui. Destination: Tule Lake Relocation
  Center, May 20, 1942.

Montale. Long goodbyes, the whistles in the dark, The.
You know, I must leave you again and I can't.
Moore, T. Fire-Worshippers, The.
Morrissey, S. Hazel Goodwin Morrissey Brown.
Muldoon, P. Avenue, The.
Something of a Departure.
Myles, E. Sadness of Leaving, The.
Nairne. Will Ye No Come Back Again?
Nashe [or Nash]. Adieu, Farewell, Earth's Bliss[e].
Nazario, A. Melt me.
Neiburg, A. It's the Talk of the Town.
Nesbit, E. At Parting.
Ni Dhomhnaill. I Cannot Lie Here Anymore.
Niu Hsi-chi. Spring Mountains.
Where the mist has torn.
Noble, R. Good Night, Sweetheart.
Nutter, G. II:II.
O'Connor, F. Exile: "What happier fortune can one find."
Oliver, M. Journey, The.
O'Neill, R. I Made a House of Houselessness.
Oppen. Anniversary Poem.
Ovid. Nagging reminders: the black ghost-melancholy vision.
Pak Mogwŏl [or Mokwŏl]. Today.
Pastan. To a Daughter Leaving Home.
Patmore, C. Farewell, A.
Philips, K. Lucasia, Rosania and Orinda Parting at a Fountain, July 1663.
Orinda to Lucasia Parting, October, 1661, at London.
To Mrs M. A. at Parting.
Phillips, C. Africa Says.
Piatt, J. Taking the Night-Train.
Pinkney, E. On Parting.
Po Chü-i. Letter, The.
Porter, C. Ev'ry Time We Say Good-bye.
Just One of Those Things.
Potter, Carol. In the Upstairs Window.
Pound, E. Long Wind, the Dawn Wind.
Praxilla. Fairest thing I leave behind is sunlight, The.
Probyn. Rondelet: "Which way he went?"
Procter, A. Woman's Last Word, A.
"Rachel." [or "Rahel."]. He too will soon go away.
Ralegh, S. Fortune Hath Taken Away.
Randall, D. Ballygrand Widow.
Redding, E. End of a Love Affair, The.
Rexroth, K. As the wheel follows the hoof.
Rich, A. Valediction Forbidding Mourning, A.
Rilke. Last Evening, The.
Rimbaud, A. Departure.
Robinson, E. John Gorham.
Unforgiven, The.
Rochester, J. Upon [His] Leaving His Mistress.
Rodriguez, J. In-flight Note.
Rosenblatt, S. Leaving Home.
Ruby, H. Who's Sorry Now?
Rupchev, G. Still Life: "Cello on the bed, A."
Rybicki, J. In Directions.
Sappho. I simply wish to die.
Scève, M. Dizains, Les.
Scott, A. Hence, heart, with her that must depart.
Scupham. Key, The.
Shakespeare, W. Sonnet 87: "Farewell! thou art too dear[e] for my possessing."
Sharah. Parting Roundel.
Sidney. Eleventh Song: "Who is it that this dark[e] night."
Silex, E. Departure.
Smith, L. Following the Road.
Snyder, G. Saying Farewell at the Monastery After Hearing the Old Master Lecture on "Return to the Source".
Song Sun. Do not grieve, little birds.
Sŏngjong, King of Chosŏn. Stay: / will you go? Must you go?
Stein, G. Let Us Describe.
Stern, G. Waving Good-Bye.
Stevens, W. Farewell to Florida.
Stickney, T. Autumn's done; they have the golden corn in, The.

Departure, The.
Strobel. Encounter.
Subbarao, N. He Didn't Come Back.
Swenson, M. Feel Me.
Swinburne. Leave-taking, A.
Swirszczynska [or Swir]. Very Sad Conversation at Night, A.
Symes, M. It's the Talk of the Town.
Tallmountain. There Is No Word for Goodbye.
Teasdale. Gift, The.
Thompson, P. Adown the Heights of Ages.
Tregian. Imprisoned Recusant Writes to His Wife, An.
Trenet, C. I Wish You Love (Que Reste-t-il de Nos Amours?).
Ts'ao Chih. Round the tall towers blow many mournful winds.
Tucker, M. Adieu.
Tuckerman, F. Series 2, Sonnet 21.
Turk, R. Are You Lonesome Tonight?
Tzu Yeh. So soon. Today, love, we.
Unknown. En un Vergier Soiz Folha D'Albespi.
Horse neighs, wants to gallop, A.
Love Song: "Like pain of fire runs down my body my love to you, my dear!"
On His Mistress Going from Home [Song].
Parting turns to fire.
Queen wept but thought: It is not appropriate to show such grief, The.
Shi-shu: Rats.
So Long and Still No Mate.
Which is worse.
Yesterday Morning.
Vallejo. In That Corner Where We Slept Together.
Van Vliet. City, The.
Coastline, The.
Valediction—To My Father.
Vasalis. Sotto Voce.
Vietnamese Oral Tradition. Love Lament.
Tiny Bird, A.
Vilariño. No More.
Virgil [or Vergil]. Passion of the Queen, The.
Walker, A. Even as I Hold You.
Wang Ch'ang-ling. Parting with Hsin Chien at Hibiscus Tavern.
Wang Po. Departing from Yiyang in the Early Morning.
Parting by Moonlight in a River Pavilion.
Wang Wei. At Parting.
Farewell.
Goodbye to Meng Haoran.
Parting.
Seeing Someone Off.
So Farwell. and If for Ever, Still for Ever Fare Ye Well.
To See a Friend Off.
Warner, S. After He Had Gone.
Webster, A. Passing Away.
Weller. Ngungalari.
Wen Chao. Farewell to Master Yu Chao.
Wen T'ing-yün. To a Friend Bound East.
Whitman, W. After the Supper and Talk.
Good-Bye, My Fancy!
Once I Pass'd through a Populous City.
What Think You I Take My Pen in Hand?
Whittier. Godspeed.
Whur. And So Home.
Wilbur, R. Leaving.
Williams, S. If He Let Us Go Now.
Wingfield. Winter.
Winters, Y. At the San Francisco Airport.
Wolfe, C. To Mary.
Woods, H. We Just Couldn't Say Good-bye.
Woods, V. After the American Wake.
Wright, R. It's a Blue World.
Wroth. Song 4: "Sweetest love return[e] again[e]."
Wu Wei-yeh. Broken Lampstand, The.
Wyatt. Lover's Appeal, The.
Yi Kae. Candle burns in the room, The.
Yi Myŏnghan. With tears I cling to your sleeves.
Young, J. I'm Gonna Sit Right Down and Write

Myself a Letter.
Zach, N. Against Parting.
Partridges
Wang Chien. Willow.
Pasadena, California
Healy, E. City Beneath the City, The.
Winters, Y. On a View of Pasadena from the Hills.
Pasolini, Pier Paolo
Glück, R. Pasolini.
Passion
Abbott, K. Illusion Collector, Age 37, The.
Abrahams, L. Out of illness.
Ackerman, J. First Night.
Addison, J. Rosamond's Song.
Addonizio. Stolen Moments.
Aguilar-Cariño. For the Lover.
Agustini. Another Race.
Akhmatova, A. Visitor, The.
Apollinaire. Pretty Redhead, The.
Archilochus. Such passion for love coiled in my heart.
Arnold, M. Growing Old.
Auden. That night when joy began.
Aygi, G. Dream: Flight of a Dragonfly.
Balce, N. Pizza and Pretense.
Ball, J. And This Is So.
Barker, J. To Her Lover's Complaint.
Barnes, J. Passion at Forty.
Beaumont, S. Description of Love, A.
Beaumont, J. Love's Mystery.
Behn, A. Disappointment, The.
On a Juniper-Tree, Cut Down to Make Busks.
Song: On Her Loving Two Equally.
Berryman. Astronomies and slangs to find you, dear.
Bilhana. Even now.
Binyon. Nothing Is Enough.
Bogan, L. Knowledge.
Borges. Houses like Angels.
Breton, N. Let mee thinke no more on thee.
Brodsky, J. Six Years Later.
Brontë, E. Shall Earth no more inspire thee.
Brooks, G. To Be in Love.
Broumas, O. Beauty and the Beast.
Brown, S. Schadenfreude.
Byron, G. Last Words on Greece.
Campion, T. Fire, fire, fire!
I Care Not for These Ladies.
Carbó, N. Votive Candles.
Carew, T. Mediocrity in Love Rejected.
Prayer to the Wind, A.
Rapture, A.
Cartwright, W. Falsehood.
Catullus. De Amore Suo.
He Seems to Me Almost a God.
Ipsithilla, my pet, my favorite dish.
Caulfield. For Albert, the Terrible.
Cavafy. Comes to Rest.
One Night.
Chapman, G. But dwell in darkness, for your god is blind.
Clark, P. Excitement.
Cofer, J. Life of an Echo, The.
Coleridge, H. Is love a fancy, or a feeling? No.
Cooke, R. Semele.
Cortez, J. So Long.
Cowley, A. Michal her modest flames sought to conceal.
Crabbe, G. Marriage Ring, The.
Crane, H. River, The.
Creeley. Marriage, A.
Cullen, C. Nothing Endures.
Song in Spite of Myself.
Cunningham, J. Aged Lover Discourses in the Flat Style, The.
Daniel, A. Resolute Desire That Enters, The.
Davie, D. Jacob's Ladder.
Devaney, T. American Pragmatist Fell in Love, The.
D'Haen. Epiphany.
Donne. Canonization, The.
Doolittle, H. Fragment 113: "Not honey, / not the plunder of the bee."
Doty, M. Tiara.
Drayton. To the Reader of These Sonnets.

Dunbar, P.   Passion and Love.
Duncan, R.   Among My Friends.
  I Am a Most Fleshly Man.
"Eliot.".   *from* Chapter 46.
"Ephelia.".   To One That Asked Me Why I
  Loved J.G G.
Finch, P.   We Are in the Fields.
Flatman.   Appeal to Cats in the Business of
  Love, An.
Fleming, P.   Concerning Himself.
Foley, H.   Touch Wood.
Garcia-Camarillo, C.   Dream 8.
García, D.   Other Marías.
García Lorca.   Elegy for Joan the Mad One.
Garrigue.   Movie Actors Scribbling Letters Very
  Fast in Crucial Scenes.
Gelman.   Eyes.
Gershwin, I.   There's Magic in the Air.
Gilbert, J.   Great Fires, The.
Gillies, V.   Look-Alike, The.
Ginsberg, A.   Green Automobile, The.
Goethe.   Meeting, the Departure, The.
  To Charlotte von Stein.
Gregg.   Adult.
  Official Love Story.
Guarini.   Shepherd Thirsis longed to die, The.
Hahn, O.   With Passion without Compassion.
Harwood, L.   Czech Dream.
Heard, J.   Slumbering Passion.
Herbert, E.   Ditty: "If you refuse me once, and
  think again."
Hernández Cruz.   Scarlet Skirt.
Hernández, M.   You Threw Me a Lemon.
Hicok.   Over Coffee.
Hoover, P.   Kiss, The: "She had imagined the
  kiss."
Huang O [*or* Huang Ho].   To the Tune "A
  Floating Cloud Crosses Enchanted Mountain".
Hudgins.   Heat Lightning in a Time of Drought.
Huiyin, L.   Do Not Throw Away.
Ibarbourou.   Hour, The.
  Wild Root.
Ibn Sahl al-Isrāīlī, I.   Does the fawn of al-imā
  know that he has kindled the heart of a lover in
  which he dwelt.
Ibycus.   In the Spring the quince and the.
Iqbal.   Make Your Radiant Twining Curls.
Issa.   Give me a homeland.
Jabeen, M.   Author's Consent.
Jewsbury.   To My Own Heart.
Jiménez, J.   To the bridge of love.
Jones, J.   Watching the Wheat.
Jonson, B.   Fair friend, 'tis true, your beauties
  move.
Joyce, J.   Flood.
Kabir.   To Be a Slave of Intensity.
Keats.   But there are.
Labé.   Sonnet 17: "I flee the city, temples, and
  each place."
Laux, D.   Prayer: "Sweet Jesus, let her save you,
  let her take."
Lawrence, D. H.   History.
  Kisses in the Train.
  Lightning.
Lefroy.   Palaestral Study, A.
Lenier.   Finale.
Levy, A.   Oh, Is It Love?
Li Ho.   Melancholic.
Lim-Wilson.   Beginning of Things, The.
Lindley, D.   Cryptogram, The.
Lleshanaku, L.   Electrolytes.
Lloyd, C.   Whether thou smile or frown, thou
  beauteous face.
Lumsden, R.   Prayer to Be with Mercurial
  Women.
MacSweeney.   Wreckage is the only Answer.
Mallarmé.   Afternoon of a Faun, The.
  Favn in the Afternoon, A.
Mallet, D.   On an Amorous Old Man.
Marlowe.   Passionate Shepherd to His Love,
  The.
Marston, P.   Love's Music.
  Speechless: Upon the Marriage of Two Deaf and
  Dumb Persons.
Melville, H.   Fruit and Flower Painter.
Merrill, J.   Days of 1964.

Michaels, A.   Passionate World, The.
Michelangelo Buonarroti.   Flee, lovers, from
  Love, flee from his fire.
  Like dry wood in a burning fire.
Mirabai [*or* Mira Bai].   O friends, I am mad.
Mistral, G.   Rose, The.
Morgan, F.   Winter Poem.
Moronelli da Fiorenza.   Canzonetta: A Bitter
  Song to His Lady.
Morungen, H.   Alas, shall I not see again.
Mun Chônghui.   Storm, The: "Isn't there a
  man."
Nabi.   At the gathering of joy, the wine cup.
Naden.   Sister of Mercy, The.
Na'ili [*or* Yeni-Zada Mustafa Efendi].   Since the
  thunderbolt of disaster set our.
Nazario, A.   Melt me.
Neruda.   My love, if I die and you don't.
O'Hara, F.   Blocks.
Ovid.   Elegy 1.4: "Thy husband to a banquet
  goes with me."
  Elegy 1.5: "In summer's heat[e] and mid-time
  of the day."
  Elegy 2.1: "I, Ovid, poet of my wantonness."
Owen, M.   For Emily (Dickinson).
Paz.   Better the crime, / the suicides of lovers,
  the incest committed.
  Crystal willow, a poplar of water, A.
Philodemus.   You Cry, Whine, Peer Strangely at
  Me.
Pilinszky, J.   Passion of Ravensbrück.
Poe.   Eulalie—A Song.
  Romance.
Poliziano.   To Giovan Battista Buoninsegni.
Porter, C.   Miss Otis Regrets.
Prado, A.   Pelican, The.
Propertius.   When Thou Must Home.
Ransom, J.   Good Ships.
  Spiel of [the] Three Mountebanks.
Revell, D.   How Passion Comes to Matter.
Rexroth, K.   Fires / Burn in my heart.
  I scream as you bite.
  On the bridges.
  Scorched with love, the cicada.
  Your tongue thrums and moves.
Rich, A.   Paula Becker to Clara Westhoff.
  Since we're not young, weeks have to do time.
  Sleeping, turning in turn like planets.
Rilke.   Spanish Dancer.
Robinson, M.   Bower of Pleasure, The.
  Canzonet.
  Contemns its Power.
  Describes the Characteristics of Love.
  Her Passion Increases.
  Laura to Petrarch.
  Previous to her Interview with Phaon.
  Sappho Discovers her Passion.
  Sappho Rejects Hope.
  She Endeavors to Fascinate Him.
  Tyranny of Love, The.
Rochester, J.   Platonic Lady, The.
Rojas.   What Do We Love When We Love?
Rosenberg, L.   Married Love.
Rossetti, C.   Bed of Forget-Me-Nots, A.
Rowe, E.   To Cleone.
Rumi.   Let the lover be disgraceful, crazy.
  Someone Digging in the Ground.
  When I am with you, we stay up all night.
  When I have you, the passions of love make me
  stay awake.
Salaam.   Spice of Life, The.
Sansom, M.   To My Heavenly Charmer.
Sappho.   You / Put success in the mouth.
Scalise, D.   Passion circles round our body, A.
Schwartz, R. L.   Flamenco Guitar.
Senryū, K.   How long it seems.
Shakespeare, W.   Sonnet 15: "When I consider
  every thing that grows."
  Sonnet 116: "Let me not to the marriage of true
  minds."
Shcherbina.   Eros Poesis.
Shelley, P.   Lines: "When the lamp is shattered
  [*or* shatter'd]."
  Love's Philosophy.
Shirley, J.   Lover that Durst Not Speak to His
  M[istress], A.

Shokushi.   Guide me on my way.
"Shu Ting.".   Singing Flower, The.
Smith, C.   Supposed To Be Written by Werter.
Stirling, S.   Echo, An.
Story, W.   Cleopatra.
Stover, D.   Fire/Water Blues.
Swinburne.   Anactoria.
  Sonnet for a Picture.
Symonds.   In years of old.
  What Cannot Be.
Talley, N.   Vegetables make love above the
  tenors.
Taylor, B.   Love Returned.
  Paean to the Dawn, A.
Tennyson, A.   Dear friend, far off, my lost
  desire.
  Thy voice is on the rolling air.
Thompson, P.   At the Nu'uanu Reservoir Pool.
Tibullus.   Fill up my glass again! The anodyne.
Turner, C.   Kiss of Betrothal, The.
Ungo Kiyo.   Whirled by the three passions,
  one's eyes go blind.
Unknown.   Either I want you on my bosom
  always.
  For wele or wo I wyl not flee.
  Girl's Song.
  Here's a jolly couple! Oh the jolly jolly cuple!
  Hidden-in-winter.
  I was drowsy, but my heart was awake. Listen!
  If I might offer.
  Mulberry up the Lane.
  My love, come quickly and appease him.
  My love, come quickly to subdue it.
  Prayer yo Hymen.
  Rooster is already announcing dawn, The.
  When I am dead and thou wouldst try.
  Would you be a man in fashion?
Virgil [*or* Vergil].   Priests, prophets, helpless.
  She's beside herself.
Wheeler, J.   Falstaff's Dream.
Whitman, S.   To ———: "Vainly my heart had
  with thy sorceries striven."
Whitman, W.   Native Moments.
  Once I Pass'd through a Populous City.
Wilde, O.   Hélas!
  Silentium Amoris.
Wilkes, K.   Dolce.
Witt, S.   Everlasting Quail.
Wolff, R.   Flame On.
Wordsworth, W.   Strange Fits of Passion Have I
  Known.
Wright, C.   Peace Corps Volunteer Comes
  Home, The.
Wroth.   Sonnet 1: "When night's black mantle
  could most darknes[s] prove."
  Sonnet 3: "Ye[t]t is ther hope: Then Love but[t]
  play thy part."
  Sonnet 21: "When last I saw thee, I did not[t]
  thee see."
  Sonnet 48: "How like a fire doth love increase
  in me[e]."
Wyatt.   Lover Showeth How He Is Forsaken of
  Such as He Sometime Enjoyed, The.
Yang Fang.   Joy of Union, The.
Yang Shen.   To the Tune "Moon Over West
  River".
Zisquit.   Because passion is the absence we
  speak.
  Because passion is the silence we share.

Passivity
Levertov.   Goodbye to Tolerance.
Rupchev, G.   Bewilderment.
Wilbur, R.   Shame.

Passover
Foster, J.   Seder.
Heyen.   Passover: the Injections.
Klein, A.   Still Small Voice, The.
Kollar.   Late Arrivals.
Limburg, J.   Seder Night with My Ancestors.
Pastan.   Passover.
Rilke.   Matthew 26:17–29.
Shabtai, A.   I Love Passover.

Past
Acquah.   They're Tearing Up the Old
  Graveyard.
Addonizio.   At Moss Beach.

Young, K. Field Trip.
Yüan Chieh. After the Raiders Have Gone: To Clerks and Officials.
Zukofsky, L. As to How Much.
  I Sent Thee Late.

Pasternak, Boris
Davies, G. Death in Venice.
Kushner, A. To B. P.

Pastoral Verse
Bampfylde. Written at a Farm.
Barnfield [or Barnefield]. But if thou wilt not pittie my complaint.
  Daphnis to Ganymede.
  Oh would to God he would but pitty mee.
  Scarce had the morning starre hid from the light.
  When will my May come, that I may embrace thee?
Basho. Farmer's roadside, The.
Blackwell, H. August 2000.
Calpurnius Siculus. Eclogue 1.
  Eclogue 2.
  Eclogue 3.
  Eclogue 4.
  Eclogue 5.
  Eclogue 6.
  Eclogue 7.
Campbell, C. When midst the summer-roses the warm bees.
Chaloner. Emblem.
Chang Yang-hao. Ch'ü Yüan's "sorrow".
Ch'iao Lai. Tune: "Partridge Sky" I Rejoice to Meet a Friend Visting at My Rustic Study.
Ch'ien T'ao. On Reading the Seas and Mountains Classic.
Clare, J. Pastoral Poesy.
  Rural Scenes.
  Wren, The.
  Wryneck's Nest, The.
Clerk. Country Seat, The.
Deutsch. Urban Pastoral.
Forrest-Thomson. Not Pastoral Enough.
Garcilaso de la Vega. Oh, to my sobs, Galatea, you are harder than a stone.
Gay, J. Birth of the Squire; an Eclogue, The.
  I rage, I melt, I burn.
Hightower, J. On Reading the Seas and Mountains Classic.
Hsin Ch'i-chi. Tune: "Partridge Sky" At Po-shan Monastery.
  Tune: "Partridge Sky" For a Friend.
Hulü Chin. Song of the Tölös.
Hunt, L. To Hampstead ("Sweet upland, to whose walks, with fond repair.").
James, J. Idyl: "Tiny fish."
Johnson, J. Unmarked Stop in Front of Westmond General Store, Westmond, Idaho.
Kinsella, J. Rabbiters: A Pastoral, The.
Knox, J. Pastoral with Internet Porn.
Longfellow, H. This is the forest primeval. The murmuring pines and the hemlocks.
Mallarmé. Afternoon of a Faun, The.
Marlowe. Passionate Shepherd to His Love, The.
McCaffery. Some Versions of Pastoral.
Milton. L'Allegro.
  Lycidas.
Mitford. Forget-Me-Not, The.
Montale. Ecologue.
Nelligan, E. Watteau, a Dream.
North, C. Pastoral, The: "Now the body is the body's flower."
Pratt, S. Cottage Pictures.
Ralegh, S. Nymph's [or Nimphs] Reply to the [Passionate] Shepherd [or Sheepheard], The.
Reverdy. Air: "Forgetting."
Roscoe, W. To the Harvest Moon.
Sidney. My Sheep Are Thoughts.
  Ye Goat-herd Gods.
Spenser, E. Aprill.
  October.
Tennyson, A. Now, sometimes in my sorrow shut.
Theocritus. Idyll 1: "Whisper of the wind in, The."
Tu Shan-fu. Tune: "Shua Hai-erh" Country Cousin at the Theater.

Virgil [or Vergil]. Eclogue 2: The Lament of Corydon for His Faithless Alexis.
Walcott. Camps hold [or held] their distance—[of] brown chestnuts and grey smoke, The.
Wang Fan-chih. I have a couple acres of land.
Wordsworth, W. O mountain Stream! the Shepherd and his Cot.
  Open Prospect.
Wylie. Spring Pastoral.

Paterson, New Jersey
Williams, W. Episode 17.
  Preface: "Rigor of beauty is the quest. But how will you find beauty when it is locked."
  Preface: "To make a start."

Paths
Alexander, P. Crossing.
Ammons. Gravelly Run.
Aygi, G. Two Epilogues: "Cleanness of the path."
Baggok Choneung. Sending off My Fellow Monk Hae.
Bakusui. Returning / By an unused path—violets.
Bapiraju, A. Steps.
Bass, F. Garden, The.
Bat-Miriam. Sound of the waves in the silence, The.
Berry, W. In Rain.
Bradstreet, A. There is a path no vulture's eye hath seen.
Bromige. Choice.
Budde, R. Gag.
Buson. Dandelions blooming in fives and threes.
  Road becomes three, The.
Campert. Stroll to Parfondeval, A.
Crane, S. Wayfarer / Perceiving the pathway to truth, The.
Dimitrova. Grass.
Fisher, C. Those Who Make Paths.
Gonzalez, N. I Made Myself a Path.
Gregorio, R. Marginal Way.
Gurevitch. Line of a Poem.
Hafiz, K [or Hafez]. Where is my ruined life, and where the fame.
Hughes, R. Walking Road, The.
Jones, G. Common Path, The.
Jungkwan Ilson. On My Way Back to Kojokdae.
Ko Chônghûi. Sisters, Now We Are the Path and the Light.
Machado Ruiz. Walker, It Is Your Footsteps.
Mirabai [or Mira Bai]. O friends on this Path.
Moore, L. Homeplace, The.
Muso Soseki. Spring Cliff.
  Suzan Osho's Visit.
Ofeimun. Let Them Choose Paths.
Pritchard, N. Narrow Path, The.
Rexroth, K. Asagumori.
Roberts, K. Postcard from the Coast.
Rossetti, C. Amor Mundi.
Ryokan. Faint trickle of.
Schuyler, J. Along Overgrown Paths.
Snyder, G. Riprap.
Stillborn, Myra. Trail, The.
Sund. Considering Poverty and Homelessness.
Todd, M. Game Trail, The.
Unknown. Come onto my pathway one more time.
Vanshenkin. Path, The.
Wang Wei. Way to the Temple, The.
Whittier. River Path, The.
Wordsworth, W. Simplon Pass, The.

Patience
Barbauld. To the Poor.
Blumenthal, M. Deep Ecology.
Boyle, K. Ode to a Maintenance Man and His Family.
Brooks, G. My Dreams, My Works, Must Wait Till After Hell.
Carey, H. Sally in Our Alley.
Carver, R. Waiting.
Chŏng Hyŏnjong. Are You a Star?
Cucchi, M. I wouldn't know what it's like to be a pawn.
Ezekiel. Poet, Lover, Birdwatcher.

Fields, J. Jolly Fat Widows, The.
Graves, R. Carol of Patience.
  Not at Home.
Hardy, T. Waiting Both.
Harechavi. And It Is Still That Way.
Herrick. To Fortune.
Hewitt, J. How have I served you? I have let you waste.
Hopkins, G. My Own Heart Let Me More Have Pity On.
Jennings, E. Delay.
Khalvati. Stone of Patience.
Olds, S. New Mother.
Procter, A. Strive, Wait, and Pray.
Rossetti, C. Study (A Soul), A.
Ryan, K. Patience.
Sidney. Sonnet 56: "Fie, school of Patience, fie; your lesson is."
Tekeyan. Sacred Wrath.
Thompson, C. His Answer.
Unknown. Lord, Make Me More Patient.
Walker, F. X. Sweet Bread.
Webb, P. Patience: "Patience is the wideness of the night."
Woods, D. Waiting.
Yeats. Down by the Salley Gardens.
Young, M. J. To Time.

Patients
Abrahams, L. Privacy.
Abse. Doctor, The.
Akhmadulina. Chills.
Bejerano, M. I Made a New Memory for You.
Borthwick, P. Ward Mouth.
Campo. John Doe.
Coulehan, J. I'm Gonna Slap Those Doctors.
  Man with a Hole in His Face, The.
Darling, J. My Old Friend Hospital.
Dennis, C. St. Francis and the Nun.
Fanthorpe. Children Imagining a Hospital.
Feinfeld, D. Carmelita.
Galich. Hospital Gypsy Song.
Getsi. Washing Your Hair.
Ginsberg, A. Chief of Medicine, The.
  Line Drive.
Gittins, C. There Are Things I Must Realise You Can No Longer Do.
Higgins, B. Strange Beasts.
Hirsch, E. Two Suffering Men.
Lamb, H. Intensive Care.
Mukand, J. First Payment.
  Lullaby.
Platt, F. Coincidentally.
Routh, J. Pale.
Rowe, V. Time Heals All Wounds—But One.
Sabgir, G. Radio Gibberish.
Satyamurti. In-Patient.
  Knowing Our Place.
  Out-Patients.
Shafer, A. Gurney Tears.
Shapiro, H. 6/20/97.
Stone, J. Confabulation.
  Gaudeamus Igitur: A Valediction.
Straus, M. Log of Pi, The.
Sutherland, Fraser. Undergoing: Jewish General Hospital, Montreal 6:35 a.m.
Thwaite, A. Freedom.
Vogel, D. Waiting-rooms.
Wardle, S. Flight: "Mother blackbird I've been feeding, The."
Woods, D. Waiting.
Wright, J. Therapy.
  Walking the Dog.
Yun Tongju. Hospital.

Patriarchy
Piercy. Barbie Doll.
Plath. Lady Lazarus.
Rich, A. Cartographies of Silence.
  From a Survivor.
  No one's fated or doomed to love anyone.
  Paula Becker to Clara Westhoff.
  Your small hands, precisely equal to my own.

Patrick, Saint
Patrick, S. St Patrick's Breastplate.
  Saint Patrick's Breastplate; or, The Deer's Cry.

Patriotic Songs
Bates, K. America the Beautiful.

Cohan. I Want to Hear a Yankee Doodle Tune.
If Washington Should Come to Life.
Over There.
Dickinson, J. Liberty Song, The.
Garrick. Heart of Oak.
Gershwin, I. Of Thee I Sing.
'Strike Up the Band.
Howe, J. Battle Hymn [or Battle-Hymn] of the Republic, The.
Key. Star-Spangled Banner, The.
Randall, J. My Maryland.
Smith, S. America.
Stephens, P. God Shed His Grace.
Timrod. Carmen Triumphale.
Unknown. Alphabet.
Battle Cry of Freedom, The.
Burrowing Yankees.
Irishman's Epistle to the Officers and Troops at Boston, The.
Public Spirit of the Women, The.
Refugee Song, A.
Van Dyke. America for Me.

Patriotism and Patriots
Alvi, M. Sari, The.
Arana, Milton. Birth of a Nation.
Atwood. Thoughts from Underground.
Ausländer, R. Motherland.
Baker, D. Patriotics.
Betjeman. In Westminster Abbey.
Brome. New-Courtier, The.
Saints' Encouragement, The.
Brooke, R. Soldier, The: "If I should die, think only this of me."
Camlan. Lady Charlotte Guest.
Carberry. It takes a mighty fire.
Cayetano, E. Roy. Drums of My Fathers.
Cheney-Coker. On Being a Poet in Sierra Leone.
Chipasula. Going Back Patiently.
Manifesto on Ars Poetica.
My Friendly People.
Talking of Sharp Things.
Cohan. Yankee Doodle Boy, The.
Cook, E. Entry of the Marines [or The Red Cross of England].
Cummings, E. E. Come, gaze with me upon this dome.
Next to of course god america i.
Cunningham, A. Hame, Hame, Hame.
Darwish, M. In This Land.
Davies, E. Will no young British bard, on rhyme intent.
Dawe, G. Names.
Emerson, R. In an Age of Fops and Toys.
Espada. Year I Was Diagnosed with a Sacrilegious Heart, The.
Evans, E. Whatever clime we travel or explore.
Faber, Reginal. Forward to Nationhood.
Gilman, C. Matriatism.
Glaser, I. Last Good War—and Afterward, The.
Greenberg, U. Poem of Blessing.
Splendor from the Splendid.
Heine, H. Grenadiers, The.
Hemans. Palm Tree, The.
Hewitt, J. Scar, The.
Hoagland, T. My Country.
Housman. New Mistress, The.
Howe, J. Battle Hymn [or Battle-Hymn] of the Republic, The.
Hsin Ch'i-chi. Tune: "The Bodhisattva's Golden Headdress".
Jones, J. Glyndwr's War Song.
Keats. Happy Is England! I Could Be Content.
Kickham. Slievenamon.
Kipling, R. Recessional.
Lanier, S. To Richard Wagner.
Larkin, P. MCMXIV.
Lazarus, E. New Colossus, The.
MacNeice. Western Landscape.
Major, C. Media on War: or, the Square Root of Vietnam.
Masters, E. Harry Williams.
Moore, T. Harp That Once through Tara's Halls, The.
Pro Patria Mori.
Moorer. Loyalty to the Flag.

Mullen, H. Land of the Discount Price, Home of the Brand Name.
Newbolt. Clifton Chapel.
Ofeimun. Prologue: "I have come down."
Ogundipe-Leslie. Song at the African Middle Class.
Omer, H. Word from the Gray Soldiers.
Owen, W. Dulce et Decorum Est.
Parks, R. Dawn of Freedom.
Peck, R. Four of July.
Ramirez, L. Yet to Come.
Rich, A. One night on Monterey Bay the death-freeze of the century.
Sassoon, S. Fight to a Finish.
Scott of Amwell. Ode: "I hate that drum's discordant sound."
Scott, S. Breathes there the [or a] Man with soul so dead.
Selman, S. Community School.
Shabtai, Aharon. Nostalgia.
Shoman, K. 321738.
Stewart, F. Black Winter.
Stow. My Wish for My Land.
Thomas, E. This Is No Case of Petty Right or Wrong.
Towle. Prospects.
Ts'ao Chih. White Horses.
Turner, C. Great Britain Through the Ice: Or, Premature Patriotism.
Unknown. Our Flag.
We mean to thrash these Prussian Pups.
Van Dyke. America for Me.
Whitman, W. Beat! Beat! Drums!
Boston Ballad, A.
I Hear America Singing.
Whittier. Barbara Frietchie.
Wilbur, R. Patriots' Day.
Wordsworth, W. Composed by the Sea-Side, near Calais, August, 1802.
I Travelled among Unknown Men.
Young, E. With a Yo, Ho, Ho.

Patrons
Bunina. Though poverty's no stain.
Daniel, S. To the Right Honorable, the Lady Mary, Countess of Pembroke.
Dugan, A. American Variation on How Rilke Loved a Princess and Got to Stay in Her Castle.
Ibn Arfa' Ra'suh. Singing Lute, The.
Jonson, B. To Lucy, Countess of Bedford, with Mr. Donne's Satires.
Kovur Kilar. We Hope For Patrons.
Prince, F.T. Epistle to a Patron, An.
Smith, C. To the Earl of Egremont.

Paul, Saint
Constable, H. To St. Peter and St. Paul.
Corbet [or Corbett]. Distracted Puritan, The.
Dobson, R. Eutychus.
Kipling, R. At His Execution.
Gallio's Song.
Merton. St. Paul.
Muldoon, P. Third Epistle to Timothy.
Waters, M. Conversion of Saint Paul, The.
Wesley, C. He Shook off the Beast.
Wither. Conversion of S. Paul, The.

Pawnbrokers and Pawnshops
Alexie. Evolution.
Johnston, E. Last Sark, The.
Ward, T. Poem Without a Freight Train or a Pocket Watch.
Yi Kyubo. How I Felt Pawning My Coat: Shown to Ch'oe Chongbon.
Chu Hsiang. Pawnshop, The.
Espada. Latin Night at the Pawnshop.

Peace
Agustini. In Fields of Sleepdreaming.
Aldrich, T. Lycidas.
Alkalay-Gut. Public Outcry.
Allen, E. In the Defences.
Amichai, Y. My Child Smells of Peace.
Two Songs of Peace.
Two Songs of Peace.
Wildling Peace.
Auden. Taller To-day.
Baingana, D. Song to Come, The.
Balaban. April 30, 1975.

Bat-Tzion, Ellla. Peace.
Berry, W. Peace of Wild Things, The.
Bible, *O.T.* But in the last days it shall come to pass.
Bierce. Year's "Casualties", A.
Bly, R. After Long Busyness.
Brooke, R. Peace.
Bryant, W. After a Tempest.
Autumn Woods.
Buchanan, G. War-and-Peace.
Budbill. Sixth of January, The.
Byron, G. She Walks In Beauty.
Cairncross, A. Munich.
Calpurnius Siculus. Eclogue 1.
Campbell, T. Soldier's Dream, The.
Campo. Begging for Change in Winter.
Ch'ang Chien. Buddhist Retreat Behind Broken-Mountain Temple, A.
Chapman, G. Learning ("So Learned Men in Controversies Spend").
Peace of Death, The.
Chiao-jan. Playful Poem.
Ch'iu Wei. Seeking a Hermit on West Mountain and Not Finding Him.
Clifton, L. Let There Be New Flowering.
Cohn, J. On Non-Violence & Observation.
Collins, W. Ode to Evening.
Cooke, R. Arachne.
Crane, H. Enrich My Resignation.
Cummings, E. E. All nearness pauses, while a star can grow.
De la Mare. Ghost, The ("Peace in thy hands / Peace in thine eyes.").
Dixon, R. To Peace.
Doolittle, H. Or is it a great tide that covers the rock-pool.
Take me home.
Trance.
Drummond de Andrade. Motionless Faces.
Du Tù' Lè. What I Leave to My Son.
Dunbar, P. Ere Sleep Comes Down to Soothe the Weary Eyes.
Eliot, T. S. Song for Simeon, A.
Enzensberger, H. For the Grave of a Peace-Loving Man.
Ferlinghetti, L. History of the Airplane.
Fordham. Ode to Peace.
Francis of Assisi. Prayer of St. Francis of Assisi for Peace.
Fugai. Only the Zen-man knows tranquillity.
Gardelle, C. Peaceful Sunday.
Gilman, C. Matriatism.
Greville, F. What is the cause, why states, that war and win.
Gurney, I. After War.
Han-shan. Settled at Cold Mountain.
Hardy, T. Christmas Ghost-Story, A.
Harper, M. Peace Plan: Meditation on the 9 Stages of "Peacemaking" as Tribute to Senator Claiborne Pell: 1997.
Hass, R. Measure.
Hefer, H. Other Days, The.
Herbert, G. L'Envoy.
Peace.
Herbert, Z. To Marcus Aurelius.
Hill, G. Pastoral, A: "Mobile, immaculate and austere."
Hoffman, D. Riddle, A.
Holmes, O. Prologue.
Housman. Isle of Portland, The.
Hsieh Ling-yün. Visiting Pai-an Pavilion.
Written on the Lake While Returning to Stone Cliff Hermitage.
Iroquois Oral Tradition. Tree of the Great Peace, The.
Katagiri, Dainin. Peaceful Life.
Kaufman, B. Private Sadness.
Knevet. Vote, The.
Koeppel, M. Meditation: "Sorrow is to be discarded."
Kuzma. Peace, So That.
Landor, W. Foreign Ruler, A.
I Strove With None.
Lao Tzu. Let there be a small state with few people.
Larkin, P. Coming.

Lawrence, D. H.   Pax.
Lee, J.   Firebell for Peace.
Lisnyanskaya [or Lisnianskaia].   Like the earth turning, I creak, and dream.
Longfellow, H.   Arsenal at Springfield, The.
Longinovic.   Glorious Ruins.
Longley, M.   Ceasefire.
Lopez, L.   Images of San Luis.
Majorino.   Say--So I'll Say.
Marsman.   Landscape.
Meredith, W.   On Falling Asleep by Firelight.
Millay, E.   I Forgot for a Moment.
Moore, M.   In Distrust of Merits.
Muldoon, P.   Truce.
Muso Soseki.   Lamenting the Civil War.
Nemerov.   Easter: "Even this suburb has overcome Death."
   Song of Degrees, A.
Neruda.   Keeping Quiet.
Pak Illo.   Song of Peace.
Patchen.   Pastoral: "Dove walks with sticky feet, The."
Po Chü-i.   Ease.
Polet.   Self-Repeating Poem.
   Zelfrepeterend gedicht.
Pound, E.   Canto 117 et seq., Notes for.
Preil, G.   Words of Oblivion and Peace.
Radnóti.   Peace, Horror.
Ralin, Radoi.   Man Who Didn't Sign, The.
Ransom, J.   Spiel of [the] Three Mountebanks.
Rilke.   12. The Quiet Mary Knew with the Risen Christ.
Rodney.   Bardo of War and Peace.
Rothman, D.   One of the Lords of Life.
Ryushu Shutaku.   For all these years, my certain Zen.
Sahagún, C.   In the Beginning.
Sanchez, S.   Reflections After the June 12th March for Disarmament.
Sandburg, C.   A. E. F.
   For You.
Sappho.   Come to me from Krete to this holy.
Seaton, M.   Fiddleheads.
Shabtai, Aharon.   Sharon Resembles a Person.
Shaler, N.   Merry Truce, The.
Sophocles.   Colonus' Praise.
Southerland.   Two Fishing Villages.
Southwell.   Content and Ri[t]ch[e].
Stafford, W.   At the Un-National Monument along the Canadian Border.
Stein, K.   Upon Finding a Black Woman's Door Sprayed with Swastikas, I Tell Her This Story of Hands.
Steinbergh.   Give Peace a Chance.
Taggard.   Everyday Alchemy.
Thompson, F.   Non Pax—Expectatio.
Thoreau.   When with pale cheek and sunken eye I sang.
Tibullus.   Peace.
Tighe.   Written at Killarney. July 29, 1800.
Timrod.   Christmas.
   Retirement.
Tranströmer.   Allegro.
Ts'ao Ts'ao.   Drinking Song.
Tu Fu [or Du Fu].   Early Rising.
   Evening after Rain.
Unknown.   Deep River.
   Hierusalem.
   Hymn: "O God of Hosts, thine Ear incline."
   Peace, Rain, Plenty.
   Song of the Gong and Chimes.
   Translation of "Pax Bello Potior".
   Will You Go?
Various authors.   He opened the four borders.
Vaughan, H.   Night, The.
   Peace.
Vietnamese Oral Tradition.   Harmony in the Kingdom.
   Red Cloth, The.
Villanueva, A.   Peace #3.
Vinkenoog.   ((((((Hollanditis)))))).
Walcott.   Season of Phantasmal Peace, The.
Wallis, S.   Prayer for Peace, A.
Wang Wei.   Chi River Gardens and Fields.
   Visiting the Mountain Hermitage of a Monk at Gan-hua Monastery.

Watkyns.   Peace and War.
Whitman, W.   Base of All Metaphysics, The.
   Reconciliation.
Whittier.   Battle Autumn of 1862, The.
Wilde, O.   E Tenebris.
Winters, Y.   Before Disaster.
Wither.   Sun hath run his course through all the Signes, The.
Wroth.   Sonnet 2: "Is to leave all, and take the thread of love."
Yeats.   Michael Robartes Bids His Beloved Be at Peace.
Yi Kyubo.   Village mill echoes, The.
Yüan Chieh.   After the Raiders Have Gone: To Clerks and Officials.

Peach Trees and Peaches
Abse.   Peachstone.
Clarke, G.   Everything Is Peaches Down in Georgia.
Fox, S.   Peaches.
Graves, R.   Blue-Fly, The.
Hall, D.   Peaches.
Kuan Hsiu.   Palace halls loomed high, encaged in purple vapor.
Larsen, L.   Peach.
Lee, L.   From Blossoms.
   Weight of Sweetness, The.
Lewis, J.   Garden Note I, Los Altos.
Li Cunxu, E.   Deep Peach Glades.
Li Po.   Late Bloomer at the Front of My Garden.
Muldoon, P.   Peaches.
Oomen, A.   Peaches: "In the only moment of ecstasy I have."
Phillips, C.   Aubade: Some Peaches, After Storm.
Stern, G.   Peaches.
Unknown.   At the wind that blew last night.
   Shi-you chang-chu: In the Lowlands.
Wang Wei.   Song of Peach Tree Spring.
Warren, R.   Riddle in the Garden.
Wylie.   Wild Peaches.

Peacocks
Bobyshev.   White Peacock, The.
Carryl, G.   Patrician Peacocks and the Overweening Jay, The.
Heyrick.   On a Peacock.
Hopkins, G.   Peacock's Eye, The.
Jamme, Franck André.   Life of a Beetle, The.
Merrill, J.   Peacock, The.
Mishol, A.   Estate.
Morejón.   Disillusion for RubéDarío.
Nietzsche.   Notes.
O'Callaghan, C.   1 The Peacock.
Roux, S.   Aviary, The.
Scarbrough, G.   Han-Shan Fashions a Myth.
Stevens, W.   Domination of Black.
Wagoner, D.   Peacock Display.

Pear Trees and Pears
Brebner, D.   1. The Golden Lotus.
Curtis, T.   Neighbour's Pear Tree.
Doolittle, H.   Orchard.
   Pear Tree.
Kiyooka, R.   Pear Tree Pomes.
Kuan Hsiu.   Three or four young sylph women.
Lux.   View From a Porch.
Millay, E.   Pear Tree, The.
Nye, N.   Last Day of August, The.
Page, P.   Deaf-Mute in the Pear Tree.
Parnok, S.   Childhood memory: those pears, A.
Po Chü-i.   At the End of Spring.
Stevens, W.   Study of Two Pears.
Stewart, S.   Pear.
Talvikki, A.   Flemish Beauty.
Unknown.   Don't Chop That Pear Tree.
   Silvery red shirt is half covered with dust, The.
Youmans, Greg.   Pear's Complaint.

Pearl Diving
Yüan Chên.   Song of the Pearl-Fishers, The.

Pearl Harbor
Jeffers, R.   Pearl Harbor.
Miles, J.   Dec. 7, 1941.

Pearls
Al-Aziz, M.   We Asked.
Bernstein, C.   Caught.

Daumal.   I Speak in All Ages.
Dickinson, E.   Her breast is fit for pearls.
   'Tis little I— could care for Pearls.
Drummond, W.   Comparison of His Thoughts to Pearls.
Duffy, C.   Warming Her Pearls.
Hernández Cruz.   Perlas.
Holmes, O.   Chambered Nautilus, The.
Howe, J.   Lost Jewel, The.
Huang E.   Pearl-teardrops roll and gather.
Marshall, Susan.   Chicago.
Pak Sôwôn.   Midnight Caller, The.
Ponge.   Oyster, The.
Roripaugh, L.   Pearls.
Senghor.   Pearls.
Shakespeare, W.   Full Fathom Five.
Thomas, E.   Deep-Sea Pearl, The.
Thompson, P.   Precious Pearl, The.
Unknown.   Perle, plesaunte to prynces paye.
Wang Chien.   South, The.
Wilde, L.   Poet's Destiny, The.
Yüan Chên.   Song of the Pearl-Fishers, The.

Peas
Jones, H.   On a Fine Crop of Peas Being Spoiled by a Storm.
Kingston, M.   Spring Harvest of Snow Peas.
Kumin, M.   In the Pea Patch.
Unknown.   Peas.

Peasants
Auden.   Epilogue: "'O where are you going?' said reader to rider".
Bolton, J.   Fin de Siècle.
Campbell, J.   I Am the Mountainy Singer.
Chandra.   Peasants Waiting for Rain.
Clare, J.   Peasant Poet, The.
Hemans.   Peasant Girl of the Rhone, The.
Issa.   Her row veering off.
Kharms.   Optical Illusion, An.
Lewis, A.   Peasants, The.
Lindsay, J.   Voice of the Wheat, The.
Po Chü-i.   Lodging with the Old Man of the Stream.
Russell, G.   Exiles.
Sappho.   What country woman bewitches your mind.
Uflyand [or Ufliand].   Peasant, The.
Unknown.   Big rats! Big rats!
   Cutty Wren, The.

Pedantry and Pedants
Coultas, B.   Lecture #1.
Edwards, T.   On the Edition of Mr. Pope's Works with a Commentary and Notes.
Nash, O.   Purist, The.
Pope, A.   Now crowds on crowds around the goddess press.
Whitman, W.   When I Heard the Learn'd Astronomer.
See also **Scholarship and Scholars**

Peddling and Peddlers
Bennett, L.   South Parade Peddler.
Dowland.   Fine Knacks for Ladies.
Follain.   Marshmallow Man, The.
Kang Ûn'gyo.   Woman.
Mew.   Pedlar, The.
Richards, L.   Old Joe Jones.
Shakespeare, W.   Autolycus as Peddler.
Su Tung-p'o.   Walk in the Country, A.
Swift, J.   Oysters.
Unknown.   Chapmen.
   Cries of London, The.
   People, kind people, please buy my powder and rouge.
Vietnamese Oral Tradition.   Venturing Out.

Pedestrians
Collins, B.   Man Listening to Disc.
Jiji, Dobashi.   My Bicycle Bell.
Kennedy, X.   Close Call.
McGinley.   J's the Jumping Jay-Walker.
Pedretti, Erica.   Here.
Torre, M.   How to Look at Mexican Highways.

Peeping Toms
Gioia.   Voyeur, The.
Sallaska, S.   To Raise the Blind on Purpose.
See also **Voyeurism and Voyeurs**

Pelicans
Jeffers, R. Pelicans.
Le Guin. Riding on the Coast Starlight.
Lear, E. Pelican Chorus, The.
Prado, A. Pelican, The.
Wright, J. Pelicans.

Penelope (mythology)
Cofer, J. Learning to Walk Alone.
Doolittle, H. At Ithaca.
Glück, L. Penelope's Song.
  Quiet Evening.
Harrison, J. Penelope.
Homer. Odyssey, The.
  Ulysses Reunited with Penelope.
Jackson, A. Spinster Song: African-American
  Woman Guild.
Kyger. Pan as the Son of Penelope.
Millay, E. Ancient Gesture, An.
Montgomerie, A. Sonet: "Thocht Polibus,
  pisander, and with them."
Moore, Robert John. Room with a view.
Parker, D. Penelope.
Ratushinskaya [or Ratushinskaia]. Penelope, the
  screaming is all over.
Spenser, E. *Penelope* for her *Ulisses* sake.
Stesichoros. Helen suddenly saw a divine omen.
Stevens, W. World as Meditation, The.
Unknown. Let the first syllable of PEnelope be
  followed by the first of DIdo, the first of
  CAnus by that of REmus.
Waddington, M. Ulysses Embroidered.

Penguins
Hughes, F. Birds.
Jarnot, L. Ye White Antarctic Birds.
Tsanev, Stefan. Penguins.
Wright, J. Against Surrealism.

Peninsular War (1808–14)
Wolfe, C. Burial of Sir John Moore, The.

Pennsylvania (state)
Djanikian. How I Learned English.
Stern, G. Dancing, The.

Pens
Abbott, K. Drop my new pen.
Hilton, D. In Praise of Bic Pens.
Pinsky. Jar of Pens.
Wah. Father / Mother Haibun #4.

Pensions and Pensioners
Pak Nohae. How Much Is This One?
See also **Old Age; Retirement and Retirees**

Pentecost
Achterberg. Pentecost.
Caedmon. Caedmon's Hymn.
Collins, M. Pentecost.
Lewis, G. Pentecost.
MacSweeney. Wreckage is the only Answer.
Shuttle. Angel.
Young, Andy. Vodou Headwashing Ceremony.

Peonies
Basho. Bee, A.
  How reluctantly.
Buson. Cut the peony.
  Heavy cart rumbles by, A.
  Peonies scattering.
  People visiting all day.
  Short night, The.
  When a heavy cart.
Firer. Peonies: "Young girls walk by looking
  like wedding, The."
Ilkov, Ani. Peony and a Lion, A.
Kenyon, J. Peonies at Dusk.
Kim Yŏngnang. Until Peonies Bloom.
Lowell, A. Afterglow.
Martinson. Peonies.
Masaoka Shiki. Haiku: "I think I'll die."
Van Duyn. Sonnet for Minimalists.
Wunderlich, M. Peonies.
Yu Xuanji. Selling Wilted Peonies.

Peppers
Baca. Green Chile.
King, R. H E L P.
Sinclair, S. Red Pepper.
Willard, N. How to Stuff a Pepper.

Perception
Adamo. New Orleans.
Adcock, F. Dreaming.

Ammons. Corsons Inlet.
Baudelaire. Which One Is Genuine?
Beckett, S. Something There.
Bernlef. Disconcerting Object.
Bogan, L. Late.
Brooks, G. To Be in Love.
Cavendish, M. Dialogue betwixt the Body and
  the Mind, A.
Ceravolo. Drunken Winter.
  Heart Feels the Water.
  White Fish in Reeds.
Creeley. For Love.
Curbelo. If You Need a Reason.
Davis, W. In a Room.
De Coninck, H. Your Sweaters.
De Cristoforo, Violet Kazue. Stockade prisoners
  on hunger strike: Nani Mo Mite Inai Kokoro
  No Hi Ga Tsuzuki Kogen Natsu Takenawa.
De la Mare. All but Blind.
Deguy. O Great Apposition of the World.
Dickinson, E. I heard a Fly buzz—when I died.
  Much Madness is divinest Sense.
  Perception of an object costs.
  Tint I cannot take—is best, The.
Donnelly, T. New Intelligence, The.
Doolittle, H. Moon in Your Hands, The.
Drake, N. Man in the White Suit, The.
Eberhart, R. Blunting, The.
Eliot, T. S. Rhapsody on a Windy Night.
Emerson, R. Astræa.
  Illusions.
  Memory.
Fenton, J. This Octopus Exploits Women.
Fox, S. Almagest, Last Letter to Zakarias.
Fuhrman, J. Watching Trains.
Gascoyne. Yves Tanguy.
Ghalib, M. Ghazal 5.
Ginsberg, A. Land O'Lakes, Wisconsin:
  Vajrayana Seminary.
  Terms in Which I Think of Reality, The.
Guillén, J. Happy Armchair.
Han-shan. Try and Make It.
Harte, B. What the Bullet Sang.
Hollander, J. Morning in the Islands.
Jackson, L. Prisms.
Jarrell, R. Orient Express, The.
Jones, S. Illusions.
Kabir. How Much Is Not True.
  Knowing Nothing Shuts the Iron Gates.
Kipling, R. Conundrum of the Workshops, The.
  Looking Glass, The.
  We and They.
Knott. Feeding the Sun.
Lahey, Joy. Cattails Along Red River.
  Habitat Photo.
Levertov. Seeing for a Moment.
  Witness.
MacDiarmid, H. We must look at the harebell
  as if.
Majorino. Doing.
Mansour, J. I Opened Your Head.
Martin, Camille. Repo winter.
  Solfège parasite.
Milosz, C. Who?
Moffitt. To Look at Any Thing.
Moore, R. Mind's Disguise, The.
Murray, L. Equanimity.
Muso Soseki. Beyond the World.
Neri, G. Case of the Same Name, A.
Niccolai. "What's that?" the boy asks his
  mother, pointing to the flag.
Nooteboom. Basho 3.
North, C. Detail.
  Landscape and Chardin.
Pasman. Black Hairs, The.
Paz. Between Going and Staying.
  Certainty.
  Here.
Piercy. In the men's room(s).
Ragosta, R. Capitalization of "Clue", The.
Raine, K. Angelus.
Rakosi. Figures in an Ancient Ink.
Ransom, J. Painted Head.
Reed, H. Judging Distances.
Rilke. Panther, The.
Rodney. Bardo of Perception.

Rolfe, E. Casualty.
Rossetti, D. Woodspurge, The.
Rouweler. Landscape.
Rumsey, Tessa. Never Mororcco.
Sanguineti. Like a disk, a trembling coin
  spinning on its own diameter.
Scalise, G. Amiti′ Amoureuse.
Schuyler, J. Freely Espousing.
Scovell. Space Between, The.
Shaughnessy, B. You Love, You Wonder.
Shinkichi Takahashi. Afterimages.
  Position of the Sparrow, The.
  Stitches.
Smith, S. Not Waving but Drowning.
Stafford, W. Near.
Stevens, W. Anglais Mort à Florence.
  Bantams in Pine-Woods.
  Course of a Particular, The.
  Idea of Order at Key West, The.
  Motive for Metaphor, The.
  Poems of Our Climate, The.
  Reality Is an Activity of the Most August
    Imagination.
  Sea Surface Full of Clouds.
  Snow Man, The.
  Study of Two Pears.
  Thinking of a Relation between the Images of
    Metaphors.
  Thirteen Ways of Looking at a Blackbird.
Strand. Keeping Things Whole.
Swenson, M. In Love Made Visible.
Sze. Apache Plume.
  Before Completion.
  Great White Shark, The.
  Ice Floe.
  In Your Honor.
  Network, The.
  Parallax.
  String Diamond, The.
Szymborska, W. View with a Grain of Sand.
Tardieu Jean. Céanne.
Vitale, M. Joy Island.
Walcott. Map of Europe, A.
Ward, T. Tacit.
Warr, M. Brain on Ice.
Whitbread. Whomp and Moonshiver.
Whitman, W. Of the Terrible Doubt of
  Appearances.
Williams, W. New Clouds, The.
  Short Poem.
Willson, M. Till There Was You.
Wiman, C. Hearing Loss.
Winter, M. Ascent, The.
Young, A. How the Rainbow Works.
Zanzotto. Existing Psychically.

Percy, Sir Henry
Unknown. [Battle of Otterburn, The] [Version
  from Minstrelsy of the Scottish Border].

Perfection
Abercrombie. Epitaph: "Sir, you should notice
  me: I am the Man."
Berrigan, E. History of the Human Body, The.
Bhartrihari. While His Body's Vigor Is Whole.
Buffoni, F. De Pisis--Piacenza Papers.
Caesar. What a Perfect Combination.
Crooker. Barbie and Ken Maximize Their
  Options.
Finch, A. Intellect of Woman, The.
Glatstein, J. Matthew 5:38–48; "You have heard
  that it was said, 'An eye'".
Gogarty. Perfection.
Harnick. Matchmaker.
Heaney, S. Pitchfork, The.
Herbert, Z. Pebble, The.
Herrick. His Request to Julia.
Hill, S. Please Can I Have a Man.
Hughes, T. Bride and Groom Lie Hidden for
  Three Days.
Iijima Koichi. Imperfect Poetry and
  Meaningless Poetry.
Kalmar *et al.* What a Perfect Combination.
Kim Sünghŭi. Between Saint and Witch.
Lu Chi. Riding Crop, The.
Lux. Perfect God, The.
McClure, M. Unchanged.
Norris, L. Eden.

Perfumes
Olson, C.   As the Dead Prey upon Us.
Porter, P.   It's there, somewhere in the Platonic
    cold store.
Rafferty, C.   Story of the Man Whose Tastes
    Were Too Refined.
Ruby, H.   What a Perfect Combination.
Stevens, W.   Asides on the Oboe.
Vitale, M.   Three Written Poems, Unconnected.
Wellman, M.   So perfectly done and yet.
Wilkes, J.   Then, say not Man's imperfect,
    Heaven in fault.
Wright, J.   Birds.

Perfumes
Chang Wu-chien.   Vase of Perfume, The.
Chin, J.   Bergamot.
Dickinson, E.   Essential oils—are wrung.
Donne.   Perfume, The.
Granados, J.   Perfumist, The.
    Perfumista, La.
Jiménez, J.   I Took Off Petal After Petal.
Mackenzie, K.   Ginger-flowers.
Symons, A.   White Heliotrope.
Unknown.   Fragrance Comes from the Scent I
    Wear, The.
    Fragrance is due to perfumes.

Pericles
Shepherd, R.   Pericles, Prince of Tyre: A
    Commentary.

Perplexity
Eady.   Sherbet.

Persecution
Auden.   Refugee Blues.
Ballowe, J.   Starved Rock.
Bell, M.   Book of the Dead Man #58, The.
Benét, R. et al.   Cotton Mather.
Benét, S.   Cotton Mather.
Bienek.   Exodus.
Bobrowski.   Elderblossom.
Breytenbach.   Out There.
Brutus.   Robben Island Sequence.
Carroll, L.   Long Tale, A.
    Mouse's Tale, The.
Celan.   Shibboleth.
Cheney-Coker.   Outsider, The.
Darwish, M.   He Embraces His Murderer.
Elagin.   My murderer is no thief.
Fried, E.   What Happens.
Frost, C.   Consent.
Gander, F.   Deflection Toward the Relative
    Minor.
Glaser, M.   Magnificat!
Housman.   Oh who is that young sinner with the
    handcuffs on his wrists?
Klassen, S.   Repenting.
Kumin, M.   In the Absence of Bliss.
Longfellow, H.   Jewish Cemetery at Newport,
    The.
Macgoye.   August the First: The Watchman
    Speaks.
Mackay, J.   Nameless Love, The.
Madhubuti.   Killing Memory.
Masters, E.   A. D. Blood.
Merwin.   Night of the Shirts, The.
Montale.   Prisoner's Dream, The.
Nartsissov, B.   Marated Bastilled age, A.
Nasrin.   At the Back of Progress.
Niemoller.   First They Came for the Jews.
Pagis, D.   Last Ones, The.
Pavlov, Konstantin.   Wonderful in Poetry, or a
    Victim of Goldfish, The.
Pelletiere, M.   Under Her Crib.
Pickard, T.   Devil's Destroying Angel Exploded,
    The.
Sadeh, P.   At Nightfall, 1/27/91.
Strejilevich.   When They Robbed Me of My
    Name.
Swinburne.   On the Russian Persecution of the
    Jews.
Winner, R.   Segregated Railway Diner—1946.

Persephone
Boland, E.   Pomegranate, The.
Creeley.   Kore.
Cruz, C.   Persephone.
    Persephone 2.
Daumal.   Persephone That Is to Say Double

Issue.
Dove, R.   Demeter, Waiting.
    Persephone Underground.
Finkelstein, C.   Persephone's Notes.
Hildebrandt, Z.   Persephone.
Hope, A.   Return of Persephone, The.
Krysl.   Persephone, to Demeter.
Lawrence, D. H.   Bavarian Gentians.
MacLeod, A.   Persephone's Daughter.
Monaghan.   Persephone's Journey.
Muske, C.   Wish Foundation, The.
Norris, K.   Persephone.
O'Reilly, C.   Proserpine.
Ovid.   Persephone ate seven pomegranate seeds.
    So What? I'll tell you what.
    Proserpine and Dis.
Swinburne.   Garden of Proserpine, The.
    Hymn to Proserpine.
Vinal.   To Persephone.
Wicks, S.   Persephone.
Zucker, R.   Diary (Underworld).

Perseus
Hayden, R.   Perseus.
Levy, A.   Reminiscence, A.
Parnell, P.   Apotheosis of Medusa.
Simonides.   Danae and Perseus.
    When in the skillfully welded chest.
Zaturenska.   Head of Medusa.

Perseverance
Baca.   Oppression.
Bousoño, C.   Cost of Truth, The.
Brodsky, J.   May 24, 1980.
Cadiot, Oliver.   Why I Became a Saint.
Castillo, R.   Distances.
Celaya, G.   Great Moments.
Clanchy, K.   Slattern.
Clark, T.   As the Human Village Prepares for Its
    Fate.
    Like Musical Instruments.
Clough.   Say Not the Struggle Nought Availeth.
Cottle.   Ratiocinative.
Creeley.   Marriage, A.
    Oh No.
Dao.   End or a Beginning, An.
Disch.   Entropic Villanelle.
Dunn, S.   Competition.
Eliot, T. S.   Little Gidding.
Garrigue.   Bad Times Song.
Hauge.   I Stand Here, Do You Understand.
Herbert, G.   Employment.
    Pilgrimage, The.
Hernández, M.   I Have Plenty of Heart.
Hewitt, J.   Colony, The.
Holden, J.   Liberace.
Hopkins, G.   Carrion Comfort.
Hughes, L.   Mother to Son.
    Still Here.
Jackson, H.   My Lighthouses.
Jarrell, R.   Knight, Death, and the Devil, The.
Jefferys [or Jeffries].   We Have Lived and
    Loved Together.
Kando.   It's as if our heads were on fire, the
    way.
Kipling, R.   Old Men, The.
Kocot, N.   Civilization Day.
Koestenbaum, W.   Gaudy Slave Trader.
Longfellow, H.   Excelsior.
    Psalm of Life, A.
Moore, M.   Nevertheless.
Newbolt.   Vitaï Lampada.
Palmer, T.   Try, Try Again.
Piercy.   To Be of Use.
Prior.   In Imitation of Anacreon.
Sandburg, C.   Upstream.
Sargent, E.   Rockall.
Shakespeare, W.   Great lords, wise men ne'er sit
    and wail their loss.
Smith, L.   In Muddy Waters.
Song.   Out of Our Hands.
Sorescu, M.   Perseverance.
T'ao Ch'ien [or T'ao Yuan-ming].   Fire, Sixth
    Month, 408.
Tennyson, A.   Ulysses.
Unknown.   Hold Out to the End.
    Hunting for the Lord.
    My Body Rock 'Long Fever.

Not Weary Yet.
    O Brothers, Don't Get Weary.
Warren, R.   To a Face in a Crowd.
Whitman, W.   Noiseless Patient Spider, A.
Williams, W.   Pink Locust, The.
Wylie.   Let No Charitable Hope.

Persia
Bandeira.   Off to Pasárgada.
Khalvati.   Amanuensis.
    Persian Miniature, A.
Taylor, B.   To a Persian Boy in the Bazaar at
    Smyrna.
See also **Iran and Iranians**

Persian Gulf War
al-Saygh, S.   Schwartzkopf's Copters.
Alkalay-Gut.   Instead of his leash.
    So we begin to plan.
    Some people terrified for their lives cut.
    Think of the children in Baghdad.
    Tonight we wait for the alarm.
    Unable to move.
Anyidoho.   Desert Storm.
Derksen, J.   Interface.
Jacobson, D.   Night Vision of the Gulf War.
Juma'h, J.   Thus my brother.
Kizer, C.   On a Line from Valéry.
Levertov.   In California During the Gulf War.
Lomax, M.   Gulf.
Mahdi, S.   War Diaries.
Mayer, B.   Maple Syrup Sonnet ("Syrup's up
    again.").
McManus, J.   Two Songs for Hendrix.
Moore, L.   Letter from Kuwait.
Myrddin ap Dafydd.   War Cabinet, The.
Nurkse.   Liberators.
    Swiftness With Which Those Cities Fell, The.
Pawlak.   Ace.
Rutsala.   Sunday Morning Walk.
Wachtel.   Two Quarters, Two Nickels, and the
    Jacket of the One Album He Ever Recorded—
    America Welcomes Home the Desert Sax—Are
    in the Open Felt-Lined Case On the Platform
    of the Astor Place Subway Station: Gulf War 1.
Wilner, E.   Operations: Desert Shield, Desert
    Storm.

Persian Wars (500 B.C.–449 B.C.)
Graves, R.   Persian Version, The.
Hope, A.   Inscription for a War.
Simonides.   For the Spartan Dead at
    Thermopylai (480 B.C.).
    Greek Dead at Thermopylae, The.
    On the Spartan Dead at Thermopylae.

Persians
Graves, R.   Persian Version, The.

Persimmon Trees
Basho.   This old village.
Jarman, M.   Butterflies under Persimmon.
Masaoka Shiki.   Evening bell / Persimmons pelt.
Nelson, M.   Wish.
Stroud, J.   Oh Yes.

Peru
Belli, C.   Father, Mother.
    Segregation #1.
Bryant, W.   Damsel of Peru, The.
Coolidge, C.   Peru Eye, the Heart of the Lamp.
Duran, J.   Time Zones.
González Prada, M.   Inca's Arrows, The.
    Mitayo, The.
Neruda.   Then up the ladder of the earth I
    climbed.
Santos Chocano.   Manifesto, A.
Vallejo.   It was Sunday in the fair ears of my
    burro.
    Telluric and Magnetic.
Wright, C.   Sierra Walk.

Pessimism
Auden.   Epilogue: "'O where are you going?'
    said reader to rider".
Bartlett, B.   Basement Tale, A.
Belloc.   Is there any reward?
Carruth, H.   On Being Asked to Write a Poem
    Against the War in Vietnam.
Comden, B.   You Mustn't Feel Discouraged.
Creeley.   Turn, The.
Durcan.   Honeymoon Postcard.

Green, A. You Mustn't Feel Discouraged.
Hardy, T. Epitaph on a Pessimist.
Hoffenstein. You buy yourself a new suit of clothes.
King, B. Pessimist, The.
Knox, R. To a Pessimist.
Lowell, R. Waking Early Sunday Morning.
Naden. Pessimist's Vision, The.
Parker, D. Prophetic Soul.
   Symptom Recital.
Reid, A. Scotland: "It was a day peculiar to this piece of the planet."
Rich, A. Ghost of a Chance.
Shepherd, R. Provisional.
Snodgrass. Diplomacy: The Father.

Pesticides
Cooper, W. Pollen.
Dupree, E. At Present I Am Working as a Security Guard.
Kumin, M. Woodchucks.

Peter Pan
Holmes, E. Fathers, The: "Something's familiar about that villain."

Peter, Saint
Browning, E. Meaning of the Look, The.
Constable, H. To St. Peter and St. Paul.
Hardy, T. In the Servants' Quarters.
Levertov. St. Peter and the Angel.
Lumbreras, E. Keys of the Saint.
   Llaves de santo.
Ni Ghallichóir, C. Dream of the White-headed Boy, A.
Rossetti, C. St. Peter ("St. Peter once: "Lord, dost Thou wash my feet?".").
Unknown. Full and True Account of a Dreaded Fire, that Lately Broke out in the Pope's Breeches, A.
   When in My Pilgrimage.
Wylie. Peter and John.

Peter the Great
Pushkin, A. Tale of St. Petersburg, A.

Peterloo Massacre (1819)
Bamford. Touch Him!
Shelley, P. Song to the Men of England.

Petrarch (Francesco Petrarca)
Cobbold, E. Reproach.
Eich. Lauras.
Hill, G. Vergine bella.
Robinson, M. Laura to Petrarch.
Russell, T. Sonnet to Valclusa.
Shepherd, R. Refrain.
Sidney P. Sonnet 15: "You that do search for every purling spring."

Petrels
Murphy, R. Stormpetrel.
Whitman, W. To the Man-of-War Bird.

Pets
Anyte [*or* Anytes]. For the cricket (nightingale of the field) and oak.
Barrington, P. I Had a Hippopotamus.
Bone, K. Catlike.
Brown, Polly. This Is for Megan.
Byron, G. Watch-Dog's Honest Bark, The.
Calverley. Disaster.
Clark, T. Lake, The.
Collins, B. Dharma.
Cornford, F. Child's Dream, A.
Cowper, W. Epitaph on a Hare.
Creeley. If You.
Hale, S. Mary's Lamb [*or* Mary and Her Lamb].
Herrick. Upon His Spaniel[l] Tracie [*or* Tracy].
Hughes, T. Roger the Dog.
Jordan, J. July 4, 1984: For Buck.
Kherdian. Dogs on a leash.
King, Julie. Giving the House Away.
Kumin, M. Retrieval System, The.
Lummis, Suzanne. Fish I Remember.
MacCaig. Praise of a Collie.
Mitford. Fleet Marmion.
Olds, S. Forty-one, Alone, No Gerbil.
Orton, B. Sea Monkeys, The.
Ransom, J. Janet Waking.
Roethke. Meadow Mouse, The.
Sarton, M. Death and the Turtle.

Schelling. Run My Hand Under.
Smart, C. My Cat Jeoffry.
Snyder, G. Nansen.
Svoboda. Death Stayed.
Tanikawa, S. Nero.
Thesen. Animals.
Weaver, A. Dogs, The.
Wilbur, R. Marché aux Oiseaux.
Williams, C. K. My Fly.
Williams, M. Animals.

Peyote
Reyes, A. Tarahumara Herbs.

Phaeton
Levy, A. Ballade of an Omnibus.
Longfellow, H. Galaxy, The.

Phantoms
Bang, M. Louise in Love.
Cho Chihun. Apparition.
Hunt, L. Fish, the Man, and the Spirit, The.
Jacob, M. Translated from the German or the Bosnian.
Robertson, R. Fugue for Phantoms.

Pheasants
Hart-Smith. Golden Pheasant.
Issa. Pheasant cries, The.
Kikaku. Scratching.
North, M. Pheasant Plucker's Son, The.
Rexroth, K. On the mountain.
Unknown. Song of the Pheasant.
Yaba. Here there pheasants.
Yamei. Spring plain / Gulped.

Philadelphia, Pennsylvania
Alexander, E. Overture: Watermelon City.
Baraka, I. Pause of Joe, The.
Brutus. Off to Philadelphia in the Morning.
Dove, R. Musician Talks about "Process," The.
Guiterman. Philadelphia.
Jeffers, H. Philly in the Light.
Kemble. To the Wissahiccon.
Sanchez, S. Elegy (for MOVE and Philadelphia).
   Philadelphia: Spring, 1985.
Weaver, A. Black Man's Sonata, A.
Williams, K. Snapshot: West Philly.

Philanthropy and Philanthropists
Anderson, M. Closed Mill.
Hollander, J. No Foundation.
Kendall, M. Philanthropist and the Jelly-fish, The.
See also **Charity**

Philippines
Carbó, N. In Tagalog Ibon Means Bird.
   When the Grain Is Golden and the Wind Is Chilly, Then It Is the Time to Harvest.
Igloria, L. Lost Photograph.
Kipling, R. White Man's Burden, The.
Lim-Wilson. Explaining the Origin of My Name.
   Upon Overhearing Tagalog.
Moody, W. On a Soldier Fallen in the Philippines.
Remoto. Rain.
Wojahn. Francis Ford Coppola and Anthropologist Interpreter Teaching Gartewienna Tribesmen to Sing "Light My Fire," Philippine Jungle, 1978.
See also **Filipinos**

Philistines
Pound, E. Les Millwin.

Phillips, Wendell
Ray, H. Wendell Phillips.

Philomela
Arnold, M. Philomela.
Ransom, J. Philomela.
Sidney P. Nightingale, The.

Philosophy and Philosophers
al-Mala'ika, N. Myths.
Anderson, C. Platonic Love.
Ashbery, J. My Philosophy of Life.
Baraka, I. Balboa, the Entertainer.
Barker, J. Invitation to my Friends at Cambridge, An.
Bartlett, E. God Is Dead—Nietzsche.
Berrigan, A. Advice to a Young Philosopher.

Black, S. Lust.
Blake, W. Mock On, Mock On, Voltaire, Rousseau.
Bromige. Logical Positivist, The.
Brydges. No more by cold philosophy confined.
Budbill. Three Goals, The.
Byron, G. To be or not to be! That is the question.
Carson, A. Homo Ludens.
Carson, C. Irish for No, The.
Cendrars. My Dance.
Chazal, M. Logic.
Conn. First Light: "Near Nunnerie, where Daer and Potrail meet."
Cowley, A. To the Royal Society: "Philosophy the great and only Heir."
Dacre, C. Female Philosopher, The.
Duhamel. Buddhist Barbie.
Emerson, R. Humble-Bee, The.
Francis, R. Waxwings.
Galina, M. Ghazal: "For the sake of a Turkish woman from Shiraz, consumed in the deadly fumes."
García Lorca. Questions: "Parliament of grasshoppers is in the field, A."
Gascoigne. Gascoigne's Woodmanship.
Greger. Man on the Bed, The.
Guest, B. Eating Chocolate Ice Cream: Reading Mayakovsky.
Healy, R. Mutability Checkers.
Holub. Immanuel Kant.
Johnson, J. Inside Out.
Jones, R. One of the Citizens.
Kenyon, J. Happiness.
Kizer, C. Erotic Philosophers, The.
Krolow. Fear.
Kuan Chung. Inner Workings.
Kyger. Descartes and the Splendor of *a Real Drama of* Everyday Life. In Six Parts.
Larkin, P. Days.
Lefroy. Idler Listening to Socrates Discussing Philosophy with His Boy-Friends, An.
Leftwich, Jim. Eleusis.
Levy, A. Philosophy.
Mahon. Consolations of Philosophy.
   Tractatus.
Manifold. Makhno's Philosophers.
Mason, W. Some Early gardenists.
Mayakovsky [*or* Maiakovskii]. Cloud in Trousers, A.
Melville, H. Fragments of a Lost Gnostic Poem of the Twelfth [*or* 12th] Century.
Michaelis. Brilliantly Philosophising.
Moxley, Jennifer. Soleil Cou Coupé.
North, C. Philosophical Songs.
Ostriker. I Brood about Some Concepts, for Example.
Padgett, R. Ladies and Gentlemen in Outer Space.
Padilla. Question for the Frankfurt School, A.
Palmer, M. Autobiography: "All clocks are clouds."
Parker, A. Days like Prose.
Po Chü-i. Philosophers: Lao-Tzu, The.
Prismanova. Lomonosov.
Radoev, Ivan. Ballad for Dialectical Materialism.
Ramsdell, H. If It Is True What Is Said of the Work.
Reito. Ox bridle tossed, vows taken.
Rexroth, K. Vitamins and Roughage.
Rodefer. Stewed and Fraught with Birds.
Rumi. Little by little, wean yourself.
Smith, S. On the Death of a German Philosopher.
Steele, T. Chanson Philosophique.
Stevens, W. Homunculus et La Belle Etoile.
   To an Old Philosopher in Rome.
Stevenson, A. Ballad for Apothecaries, A.
Tomlinson, C. In Defence of Metaphysics.
Unknown. Among the yeomen's sons on my estate.
Vallejo. In the Moment.
Man Walks By with a Loaf of Bread on His Shoulder, A.
Viray, M. Saturday Morning, A.

Weigl. Why I Hate Theory.
Whitman, W. Base of All Metaphysics, The.
Zabolotsky [or Zabolotskii]. Poem about Rain.
Zukofsky, L. [Dedication].

Phoebus Apollo
"Philo-Philippa.". To the Excellent Orinda.

See also **Apollo**

Phoenix
Carew, T. Song[, A]: "Ask[e] me no more where Jove bestow[e]s."
Cynewulf. When stars are hid in the western wave, dimmed at dawn.
Darley. O blest unfabled incense tree.
Doolittle, H. Amen.
Greiffenberg. I look.
Kinnell. Another Night in the Ruins.
Klinger, A. Transformation.
Mallarmé. With her pure nails offering their onyx high.
Manley, R. Bob Marley's Dead.
Merrill, J. About the Phoenix.
Ngo Chi Lan. Autumn.
Shakespeare, W. Phoenix and the Turtle, The.
Smith, A. News of the Phoenix.
Tsugen Jakurei. Not a mote in the light above.
Tu Fu [or Du Fu]. Song of the Vermeil Phoenix.
Vietnamese Oral Tradition. Phoenixes and Sparrows.
Wilbur, R. Cottage Street, 1953.
Yi Hyangji. Phoenix, The.

Photocopying
Safie, D. Meditation by the Xerox Machine.

Photography and Photographers
Abbey, L. Broken Silence.
Acorn. Ballad of the Pink-Brown Fence, The.
Ai. Paparazzi, The.
Alegría. Documentary.
Ali, A. Postcard from Kashmir.
Amir, D. What Seeps In.
Amis, K. Mightier than the Pen.
Ashbery, J. City Afternoon.
Atwood. Daguerreotype Taken in Old Age. This Is a Photograph of Me.
Berger, B. Photo Safari.
Berkson, B. Breath.
Bernstein, C. Caught.
Bhatt, S. Looking Through a French Photographer's Portrayal of Rajasthan with Extensive Use of Orange Filters.
Bierds, L. Vespertilio.
Brand, D. Blues Spiritual for Mammy Prater.
Brodsky, J. Polar Explorer, A.
Brody. Family Album, A.
Brown, L. If I Had a Talking Picture of You.
Byrd, Bobby. Gabachos in the Photograph, The.
Byrne, Edward. Envying the Art of the Cartographer.
Byron, C. Shipping the Pictures from Belfast.
Cabico, R. Antonio Banderas in His Underwear.
Cassells. Courtesy, A Trenchant Grace, A.
Castillo, S. Primos.
Charach, R. Evidence on Film, The.
Chernoff. Lost and Found.
Clifton, L. Photograph.
Clinton, M. History as Trash.
Conway, J. Weight Belt.
Cooley, N. Diane Arbus, New York.
Coolidge, C. Album—A Runthru.
Corn. Photographs of Old New York.
Cortes, F. Palace of Fine Arts in San Francisco, The.
Couzyn. You Have Shown Me a Strange Image, and We Are Strange Prisoners.
Cranch. Photograph, The.
Curbelo. Photograph from Berlin. Photograph of My Parents.
Curtis, T. Land Army Photographs.
Daniels, K. War Photograph.
DeSylva, B. G. If I Had a Talking Picture of You.
Dickey, W. Arrival of the Titanic, The.
Drummond de Andrade. Dead in Frock Coats, The.
Duffy, C. War Photographer.

Dunn, D. St Kilda's Parliament: 1879–1979.
Durcan. Irish Hierarchy Bans Colour Photography.
Ellis, T. Shooting Back.
Etter. Well You Needn't.
Ferry. Photographs from a Book: Six Poems.
Figueroa, J. Puerto Rico Made in Japan.
Fuller, R. Middle of a War, The.
Gander, F. Sinister.
Garcia-Camarillo, C. Dream 8. Family Photographs.
Gatina, D. My eyes are.
Greenhalgh, C. Big No-No, The.
Groarke, V. Family Photograph, The.
Grotz, J. Self-Portrait as a Drowned Man.
Gullar. Poster.
Hai-Jew, S. Three Gypsies.
Harper, M. Three O'Clock Love Song.
Henderson, R. If I Had a Talking Picture of You.
Herd. We are sailing on a charming bay.
Heyen. Tie, The.
Hoover, P. Family Romance.
Hughes, T. Six Young Men.
Igloria, L. Lost Photograph.
Jamie, K. Child with Pillar Box and Bin Bags.
Johnson, K. High Altitude Photo of Hiroshima (Circa 1944).
Karr. History of Photography, A.
Kinzie. Sound Waves.
Kirsch, S. Pictures.
Komunyakaa, Y. Untitled Blues; After a Photograph by Yevgeni Yevtushenko.
Kramer, L. Images of the San Francisco Disaster.
Kuo. Then they are young and on vacation, their camera.
Larkin, P. Lines on a Young Lady's Photograph Album. Whatever Happened?
Lassell. Three Poems.
Levertov. In Thai Binh (Peace) Province.
Levis. Sensationalism. Widening Spell of the Leaves, The.
Lim, S. Black and White.
Llwyd, Iwan. Old Photograph, An.
Lowe, J. Between Acts.
Lowell, R. Epilogue: "Those blessèd structures, plot and rhyme."
Lum. Picture of my Mother's Family, A.
Madgett. Last Happy Day, The.
Mahon. Old Snaps, The.
Masterson, R. Bunch of Pictures Back from the Drugstore, A: The Four Good Ones.
Mathews, H. Ledge, The.
Matthews, W. Photo of the Author with a Favorite Pig.
McElroy, C. From Homegrown: An Asian-American Anthology of Writers.
McKendrick, J. Shortened History in Pictures, A.
McMurtry, Larry. For Erwin Smith, Cowboy Photographer.
Merrill, J. David's Night in Veliès.
Mueller, J. Peninsula.
Murphy, M. Contact Sheet.
Obejas, A. Lifes.
O'Grady, J. Anonymous Wedding Photo.
Oppen. Civil war photo. From a Photograph.
Ormsby, F. War Photographers, The.
Pagis, D. Ein Leben. Ein Leben.
Palmer, M. I killed a bee on the Street of Scissors.
Pastan. At the Jewish Museum. Old Photograph Album.
Peseroff. Hardness Scale, The.
Phillips, L. My Son Shows Me a Photograph of Michael Jordan Performing a Slam Dunk.
Pinkerton, H. On Dorothea Lange's Photograph "Migrant Mother" (1936).
Ray, D. Eskimo Girl, The.
Rich, A. Modotti.
Rivard. Summons.
St. John, D. Grandfather's Cap, My.

Saitō Sanki. Photographed / face by face. Photographed— / prisoners of war shout commands.
Sapgir. From an Album.
Schneider, M. Photograph, The.
Schwartz, D. Poem: "You, my photographer, you, most aware."
Seay. Audubon Drive, Memphis.
Shepherd, R. What Cannot Be Kept.
Stafford, W. Archival Print, An.
Stevenson, A. Who's Joking with the Photographer?
Sundiata. Making Poems; on the road in Minneapolis.
Sutter. Hoarfrost and Fog.
Sze. Negative, The.
Thompson, P. Two Photographs.
Toledo, N. Bandaa sti bianni. Shadow That Draws the Light, The. Sombra que dibuja la luz, La.
Tomlinson, C. Snapshot.
Trethewey, N. Bellocq's Ophelia. (Self) Portrait. Vignette.
Triplett, P. Portraits at the Epicenter. Studies in Desire.
Tsaloumas. Old Snapshot.
Tucker, M. Family Portraits.
Tufariello, C. In Glass.
Updike. Snapshots.
Vazirani, R. Mrs. Biswas Goes Through a Photo Album.
Vertreace, M. Black Tulips.
Vicioso. Survival 2.
Wakoski. Photos, The.
Wallace, R. Makings of Happiness, The.
Warren, R. In Creve Coeur, Missouri.
Warsh. Suicide Rates, The.
Wenderoth, J. Disfortune.
Whalen, P. Upon the Poet's Photograph.
Whittemore, R. Mother's Past.
Wilbur, R. Looking into History.
Wilder, A. Photographs.
Wojahn. Wartime Photos of My Father.
Wright, C. Negatives.
Wright, K. Victorian Family Photograph.
Yau. Cenotaph.
Zavatsky. Walker Evans in Bridgeport.

See also **Cameras**

Physicians
Campo. Medical Student Learns Love and Death, A.
Masters, E. Doctor Meyers.
Unknown, fr. Terezin Concentration Camp. Pain Strikes Sparks on Me, the Pain of Terezin.
Warren, R. Pursuit.

See also **Doctors**

Physics and Physicists
Blanco. Quantum Theory. Teoría cuántica. Teoría de la luz. Theory of Light.
Brown Rosellen. I want to understand light years.
Buckley, C. Inverse Square Law of the Propagation of Light, The.
Clewell. Vegetarian Physics.
Flynn, N. Cartoon Physics, Part 1.
Kendall, M. Ether Insatiable.
Rosenberg, L. Introduction to Methods of Mathematical Physics.
Seaton, M. Tagging.
Wilson, A. Antlia the Air Pump. Particle Limericks.

Pianists and Pianos
Baker, T. Armillaria Mellea.
Barney, W. Mr. Watts and the Whirlwind.
Boruch. Piano Tuning.
Cedering, S. Variations for the Piano.
Chmielarz. They Come Humming.
Coleridge, M. To a Piano.
Cox, M. Sonata.
Duran, J. Mr Teller the Piano Teacher.
Fairchild. Dumka, The. Machinist, Teaching His Daughter to Play the

Piano, The.
Feinstein, S.   Summerhouse Piano.
Fraser, K.   One is whole. One is not.
Frost, R.   Investment, The.
Gilonis, H.   Song 9.
Grunke, A.   Learning to Live with the Piano.
Haskins, L.   Prodigy, The.
Hernandez, F.   De cómo Robert Schumann fue
  vencido por los demonios.
  On How Robert Schumann Was Defeated by
  Demons.
Jenkins, Joyce.   Piano Man.
Jordan, J.   October 23, 1983.
Justice, D.   Pupil, The.
  Variations for Two Pianos.
Kamienska.   Those Who Carry.
Lasker-Schüler.   My Blue Piano.
  My Blue Piano.
Lawrence, D. H.   Piano.
  Piano, The.
Llywelyn-Williams.   On a Visit.
Madgett.   Echoes.
Manguso, S.   Piano, The: "I try to imagine the
  lid closing but it won't."
Max, L.   Equal Temperament.
Neal, Gaston.   Monk.
Nurske, D.   Involuntary Music.
Palmer, M.   Man Undergoes Pain Sitting at a
  Piano, A.
Shapiro, K.   Piano Tuner's Wife, The.
Solonche.   Chopin Preludes, Opus 28.
Speakes.   Heartbreak Hotel Piano-Bar.
Stevens, W.   Mozart, 1935.
Tranströmer.   Allegro.
Unknown, fr. Terezin Concentration Camp.
  Concert in the Old School Garret.
Updike.   Player Piano.
Verlaine.   Piano kissed by a slender hand, The.
Vlasova, E.   On an old grand piano.
Voznesensky [*or* Voznesenskii].   War Ballad.
Waters, M.   "Night in the Tropics" (1858-59?).
Weaver, A.   Thelonius.
Weissbort.   Mourning.
Wilkinson, J.   Impatient Man Kills with his
  Piano-playing, The.
Winder.   On Fourteen Maple Street.
Wright, C.   Tours.

Picasso, Pablo
Aragon.   Embrace, The.
Cassells.   These Are Not Brushstrokes.
Cummings, E. E.   Picasso / you give us Things.
Guest, B.   On the Verge of the Path.
Jacob, M.   In Honor of the Sardana and the
  Tenora.
Kaufman, B.   Picasso's Balcony.
Morgan, Elin Llwyd.   Schizo de Picasso.
Norse.   Picasso Visits Braque.
Salmon, A.   Painting.
Scalapino.   Picasso and Anarchism.
Stein, G.   If I Told Him: A Completed Portrait
  of Picasso.
  Picasso.
Stewart, J.   On Seeing Man with a Guitar at the
  Moma.

Pickles
Myers, J.   Experts, The.

Picnics and Barbecues
Abbott, W.   Aspen Meadows.
Adamson.   My Tenth Birthday.
Causley.   Eden Rock.
Colby, T.   Labor Day Picnic Poem.
de Fréine, C.   Bubbles.
Elmslie, K.   Picnic.
Fagin, L.   Occasional Poem.
Gizzi.   New Picnic Time.
Hirshfield, J.   Picnic.
Logan, J.   Picnic, The: "It is the picnic with
  Ruth in the spring."
Mayfield, C.   Oh, It's You Again.
Muldoon, P.   Truce.
Murray, L.   Barbecues smoke is rising at
  Legge's Camp; it is steaming into the midday
  air.
Roethke.   Thing, The.
Sulchinskaya, O.   Wind paces on the lower
  branch, The.

Tagami.   Mussel Rock/Lowtide—Santa Cruz,
  California 1959.
Tanikawa, S.   Picnic to the Earth.
T'ao Ch'ien [*or* T'ao Yuan-ming].   Picnic by the
  Xie River, A.
Warren, R.   Renoir.
Weaver, A.   Picnic, an Homage to Civil Rights,
  The.
Wong, N.   Picnic.

Pierrot
Laforgue.   Pierrot Says.
Pritchard, N.   From Where the Blues?

Pies
DJ Renegade.   Thursday Poem.

Piety
Bible, *N.T.*   Luke 7; She Began To Wash His
  Feet with Teares and Wipe Them with the
  Haires of Her Head.
Chinese Oral Tradition.   Transformation Text on
  the Boy Shun's Extreme Filial Piety.
Donne.   Hymn[e] to Christ, at the Author's Last
  Going into Germany, A.
  Oh, to vex me, contraries [*or* contraryes] meet
  in one.
Esrefoğlu.   O My God Do Not Part Me from
  Thee.
Gippius.   Incantation.
Herrick.   Chewing [of] the Cud, The.
  His Offering, with the Rest, at the Sepulcher.
  To Keep a True Lent.
Kabir.   Ascetic Dyes His Robes, The.
Khosravani.   There are four kinds of men who'll
  get no fee from me.
Kyunyŏ, Great Master.   I will at once follow the
  vows.
  When the realm of living runs out.
  Would that all my good deeds.
Mistral, G.   Pious One, The.
Wright, J.   Meta-A and the A of Absolutes.
Yun Tongju.   Foreward.

Pigeons
Angel.   Evolving Similarities.
Bishop, E.   Paris, 7 A.M.
Buson.   Behavior of the pigeon, The.
Dubie.   Sky Harbor.
Farjeon, E.   Mrs. Peck-Pigeon.
Fell, A.   Pigeons: "Pigeons / Are tossing."
Heyen.   Derailment.
  Pigeons, The.
Issa.   O owl!
Kherdian.   Hawthorne berries, The.
  Wind rips through the.
MacCaig.   Wild Oats.
McGinley.   Trinity Place.
Merwin.   Fly.
O'Callaghan, C.   Pigeons.
Rossetti, C.   On the Wing.
Schwartz, R. L.   Can Pigeons Be Heroes?
Seth.   Pigeons.
Shinkichi Takahashi.   Peach Blossom and
  Pigeon (painting by Kiso).
Sia, B.   Enemy.
Stein, G.   Pigeons on the grass alas.
Tobin, D.   Pigeons.
Unknown.   Doodle durdle.
  Song of the Pigeon.
Wormser.   Pigeons.
Wright, J.   Lament for Passenger Pigeons.

Pigs
Artaud.   All Writing Is Garbage.
Benson, G.   Cat and the Pig, The.
Blunden.   Poor Man's Pig, The.
Corso.   Song: "Oh, dear! Oh, me! Oh, my!"
Dubie.   Obscure, The.
Duffy, C.   Circe.
Edson, R.   Performance at Hog Theater, A.
Espada.   Cada Puerco Tiene Su Sábado.
Evans, D.   Pig Killing Day.
Fanning, R.   Oink as Taunt.
Garlick, R.   Still Life.
Gay, J.   Wild Boar and the Ram, The.
Glück, R.   Circe's Power.
Gunn, T.   Moly.
Hall, D.   Eating the Pig.
Hughes, T.   View of a Pig.

Humphreys, E.   Apple Tree and a Pig, An.
Keplinger, D.   Distance Between Zero and One,
  The.
Kinnell.   Saint Francis and the Sow.
La Fontaine.   Pig, Goat, Sheep.
Lee, D.   For Jan, with Love.
  Jan's Birthday.
  Tuesday Morning, Loading Pigs.
Leslie, S.   Muckish Mountain (The Pig's Back).
Levertov.   Watching "Dark Circle".
Levine, P.   Animals Are Passing from Our
  Lives.
Like, J.   James Dean and the Pig.
Marie de France.   Wolf and the Sow, The.
Martinaitis, M.   Kukutis's Sermon to the Pigs.
Matthews, W.   Photo of the Author with a
  Favorite Pig.
McDonald, W.   Hauling Over Wolf Creek Pass
  in Winter.
McKay, C.   If We Must Die.
Mishol, A.   Estate.
Mother Goose.   This Little Pig Went to Market.
Murray, L.   Pigs.
Padgett, R.   Detach, Invading.
Rosser, J.   First Empathy.
Rossetti, C.   If a pig wore a wig.
Seshadri.   Wolf Soup.
Shiraishi.   Wild Pigs of Kalimantan, The.
Siegel, R.   Hog Heaven.
Smith, D.   Pulling a Pig's Tail.
Unknown.   Judged by the Company One Keeps.
  Pig, The.
  Riddle: "As I went down that yella bank."
Wallace, R.   In a Pig's Eye.
Watson, C.   Knickerbocker Knockabout.
Wesley, S.   Freeborn Pindaric never does refuse.
Wilbur, R.   Matthew 8, 28 ff.
  Matthew 8:28–34; And when he came to the
  other side.
Yi Hyangji.   Ringing in My Ears.

Pike (fish)
Hughes, T.   Pike.
Lowell, A.   Pike, The.

Pilgrimages and Pilgrims
Bradstreet, A.   As Weary Pilgrim, Now at Rest.
Bunyan.   Pilgrim Song, The.
Chaucer.   General Prologue, The.
  Miller's [*or* Milleres] Tale, The.
Clive.   Old Age.
Freeman, Jessica.   Bayou Arabic Argot.
Gelbtrunk, A.   God said to Abraham.
Gomez, M.   Lost Daughter.
Graves, R.   Travel[l]er's Curse after
  Misdirection[, The].
Gumilyov [*or* Gumiliov *or* Gumilev].   First
  Canzone.
Hall, D.   Woolworth's.
Hardy, T.   Hap.
Hemans.   Landing of the Pilgrim Fathers [in
  New England], The.
Herbert, G.   Pilgrimage, The.
Kabir.   Thirsty Fish, The.
Krylova, E.   Pilgrims, The.
Liu Ch'ang-ch'ing.   Climbing in Autumn for a
  View from the Temple on the Terrace of
  General Wu.
  On Parting with the Buddhist Pilgrim Ling-
  Ch'ê.
Melville, H.   Hostel, The.
  Medallion, The.
Milosz, C.   On Pilgrimage.
Reznikoff.   Luzzato.
Rossetti, C.   Uphill [*or* Up-Hill].
Seiken-Chiju.   Twenty years a pilgrim.
Sen, R.   So, Mind / You've decided to go on
  pilgrimage?
Senghor.   Song of the Initiate.
Shakespeare, W.   If I profane with my
  unworthiest hand.
Sutskever [*or* Sutzkever].   1980.
Vaughan, H.   Pilgrimage, The.

Pilgrims, The
Emerson, R.   Boston Hymn.
Hemans.   Landing of the Pilgrim Fathers [in
  New England], The.
McDaniel, J.   Bad Pilgrim Room, The.

Pilots
Apollinaire. Zone.
  Zone.
Doolittle, H. R.A.F.
Gwynn, R. Randolph Field, 1938.
Hall, D. Man in the Dead Machine, The.
Jarrell, R. Pilot from the Carrier, A.
Kipling, R. R.A.F. (Aged Eighteen).
Kushner, A. Airman, The.
Matthews, W. Black Box.
Meredith, W. Navy Field.
Pack, R. Black Hole, The.
Pawlak. Ace.
Receveur. Cobra Pilot.
Rukeyser, M. Ceiling Unlimited.
Sandburg, C. To Beachey, 1912.
Shapcott, J. Phrase Book.
Stafford, W. At the Grave of My Brother:
  Bomber Pilot.
Tate, J. Lost Pilot, The.
Twichell. Immortal Pilots, The.
Waniek. Freeman Field.
  Porter.
  Star-Fix.
  Tuskegee Airfield.
See also **Air Warfare**

Pimps
Hughes, L. Sliver of Sermon.
  What?

Pindar
Duncan, R. Poem Beginning with a Line by
  Pindar, A.
Korinna [*or* Corinna]. I blame even clear-
  voiced.

Pine Trees
Bachmann. Invocation of the Great Bear.
Basho. Coolness.
Bugeja, M. Conifer King, The.
Cherry, K. Pines Without Peer, The.
Ch'i-chi. Little Pines.
Chih-Wen, S. On Old Zhang's Pine Tree.
Chŏng Ch'ŏl. Snow falling in the pine forest.
  Why does that pine tree stand.
De Cristoforo, Violet Kazue. Dooshi Sorou
  Soshite Matsu No Me Futori Shoka No Sora.
De Mello Breyner. Beach.
Doolittle, H. Oread.
Gensler. Bowl with Pine Cones.
Ginsberg, A. Against red bark trunk.
  White sun up behind pines.
Hahn, K. Pine.
Hakutsu. O pine-tree standing.
Hamhur Kiwha. Pine Bark Bread.
Inada. Forest Family.
Issa. Not yet become a Buddha.
Jamie, K. Pipistrelles.
Levertov. Calvary Path, A.
MacEwen, G. Dark Pines under Water.
Monroe, B. In the Pines.
Muldoon, P. Yggdrasill.
Muso Soseki. Cave of the Thousand Pines.
Nemes Nagy. Pinetree.
No Ch'ŏnmyŏng. Road.
Noguchi, Yonejiro (Yone). I Hear You Call,
  Pine Tree.
  In Japan Beyond.
Pagis, D. Conversation.
Plath. Black Pine Tree in an Orange Light.
Po Chü-i. Song of the pines.
Reps, Paul. Pine needling.
Rice, D. Remains.
Seferis. It's Time for Me to Go.
Smith, D. Pine Cones.
Sŏng [*or* Sung] Sammun. Were you to ask me
  what I'd wish to be.
Swanger. Knob Pines.
Tomlinson, C. Pines at Hakone, The.
Tranströmer. Gaunt tousled pine-trees.
Unknown. All too soon, I fear.
  Chickcharnies.
Uyematsu. Lone Pine.
Vietnamese Oral Tradition. Tao.
Warren, R. Return, The: An Elegy.
Yi I. Where is the fourth bend?
Yu Chao. Pine Whisk, The.
Yun Sŏndo. Flowers bloom when it is warm.

Zanzotto. Epiphany.
Zisquit. There is always a sound.

Pioneers
Atwood. Progressive Insanities of a Pioneer.
Benét, R. *et al.* Western Wagons.
Benét, S. Ballad of William Sycamore, The.
  Western Wagons.
Bowering, G. Grandfather.
Cary, P. Homes for All.
Clampitt. Imago.
Crosby, F. On Hearing a Description of a
  Prairie.
Dallas, R. Photographs of Pioneer Women.
Davidson, D. Descending Chestnut Ridge.
Davis, M. Going Out and Coming In.
Emerson, R. Forerunners.
Fisher, A. *et al.* Pioneers.
Fisher, L. Pioneers.
Freneau. On the Civilization of the Western
  Aboriginal Country.
Johnson, E. Joe.
Kroetsch. Ledger, The.
Longfellow, H. Hiawatha: The White Man's
  Foot.
Parkes, B. Lilian's Second Letter.
Pfeiffer, E. Lost Light, The.
Piatt, J. Farther.
Rich, A. Face to Face.
  From an Old House in America.
Ridge, J. And shall we view these miracles and
  more.
Sanchez, S. Right On: White America.
Sigourney. Western Emigrant, The.
Smith, W. Tempest, The.
Unknown. State of Arkansas, The.
Wenthe, William. White Settlement.

Pipers
Blake, W. Piping Down the Valleys Wild.
Browning, R. Pied Piper of Hamelin, The.
Mallarmé. Afternoon of a Faun, The.
  Favn in the Afternoon, A.

Piracy and Pirates
Babb, Stanley E. Portrait of a Pirate.
Cowley, A. Cheer Up, My Mates.
Ewing, B. Stealth-pirates of Cyberia.
Masefield. Captain Stratton's Fancy.
Meigs, M. Pirate Don Durk of Dowdee, The.
Pessoa. Ah, pirates, pirates, pirates!
Püsküllüoğlu. Old Pirate in These Waters, An.
Stevenson, R. Pirate Ditty.
  Pirate Story.

Pitcher, Molly
Richards, L. Molly Pitcher.

Pitt, William
Coleridge, S. Pitt.

Pittsburgh, Pennsylvania
Anderson, M. Closed Mill.
  Invention of Pittsburgh, The.
Beecher, J. We Want More Say.
Gilbert, J. Searching for Pittsburgh.
Stern, G. Dancing, The.

Pity
Agustini. Public Prayer.
Alegría. Have Pity.
Altizer. Sonnet 2: "My own heart let me have.
  More pity on."
Apollinaire. Pretty Redhead, The.
Arapaho Oral Tradition. Father, have pity on
  me.
Arnold, C. Extravagance of Zoos, The.
Barrax. Pittsburgh, 1948, the Music Teacher.
Bourne, W. Heart's Fine Gold, The.
Chaucer. Pardoner's Introduction, The.
Chippewa Oral Tradition. Song of the Captive
  Sioux Woman.
Coleridge, S. Love: "All thoughts, all passions,
  all delights."
  To a Young Ass.
Dengina, S. Russia.
Fuertes. Plastic Virgin.
Hewitt, J. How have I served you? I have let
  you waste.
Holub. Napoleon.
Hopkins, G. My Own Heart Let Me More Have
  Pity On.

Howard, R. Man Who Beat Up Homosexuals
  Reported to Have AIDS Virus.
Howe, F. From a donkey, excuse me, one
  lesson is given.
Howitt, M. Cry of the Animals, The.
Hyde, D. Will You Be as Hard?
Jaccottet. I Rise with an Effort.
Keats. I Cry Your Mercy, Pity, Love—Ay,
  Love!
Li Ho. At Ch'ang-ku, Reading: To Show to My
  Man Pa.
Mansfield, K. Man with the Wooden Leg, The.
Mayer, B. Generic Elbows.
Millay, E. Pity me not because the light of day.
Pafunda, Danielle. RSVP.
Prunty. Elderly Lady Crossing on Green.
Rossetti, C. After Death.
Schuyler, J. Self-Pity Is a Kind of Lying, Too.
Shakespeare, W. Sonnet 111: "O, for my sake
  do you with Fortune chide."
Sidney P. Sonnet 45: "Stella oft sees the very
  face of woe."
Su Tung-p'o. Lament of the Farm Wife of Wu.
Ukon. Me.
Unknown. Foxes move in pairs.
  Some Valiant Solider.
  Summer Song.
Villon. Ballade of the Men Who Were Hanged.
Wright, J. At the Executed Murderer's Grave.

Pizza
Kildibekova, M. Pizza's a populous island.
Silano, M. Sweet Red Peppers, Sun-Drieds, the
  Hearts of Artichokes.

Place Names
Addison, M. Names.
Benét, S. American Names.
Kearney, M. After Barranquillo, before Belize.
Limburg, J. Barton in the Beans.
Merton. Place Names.
Pedretti, Erica. It's Snowing in Plouda.
Sigourney. Indian Names.

Plagiarism and Plagiarists
Unknown. To a Living Author: "Your comedy
  I've read, my friend."

Plague
Greenlaw, L. Earliest Known Representation of
  a Storm in Western Art, The.
Kees. Coming of the Plague, The.
Lux. Plague Victims Catapulted Over Walls
  Into Besieged City.
Melville, H. In the Desert.
Nashe [*or* Nash]. Adieu, Farewell, Earth's
  Bliss[e].
Starbuck, G. Prognosis.
Toomer. November Cotton Flower.

Plains
Gundy, J. Where I Grew Up.
Todd, M. Son et Lumière.
Verlaine. Endless sameness.
Yamei. Spring plain / Gulped.
See also **Prairies**

Planets
Goldstein, L. Firmament on High.
Kendall, M. Ether Insatiable.
MacCaig. Stars and Planets.
MacDiarmid, H. Bonnie Broukit Bairn, The.
Welch, L. Step out onto the planet.
Winters, A. Night Light.

Plantations
Cornish, S. In Mr. Turner's Fields.
Elliott, G. Poem About Myself.
Foster, S. Old Folks at Home.
Jacinto, A. Monangamba Estate.

Plants
Alegría. I Am Root.
Beaver. Day 20.
Bell, M. Introduction to My Anthology, An.
Buson. I went down the bank to pick fragrant
  plants.
  Only the shoots.
Calil, A. Blouse of Felt.
Ch'u Yüan. On Encountering Trouble.
Citino. Sea of Kansas, Ohio Tundra, Time Still
  Running Out, The.
Clampitt. Sun Underfoot Among the Sundews,

The.
Cross, E.   Banyan.
Darwin.   Caryo's sweet smile DIANTHUS proud admires.
Fair Chunda smiles amid the burning waste.
On DOVE'S green brink the fair TREMELLA stood.
Weak with nice sense, the chaste MIMOSA stands.
Where cool'd by rills and curtain'd round by woods.
Faverey.   Its only riddle: *how*.
Greenberg, A.   Wintering Over at the End of the Century.
Grobman, M.   In mass graves the bodies of plants.
Guidacci.   Anniversary with Agave Plants.
Harvey, M.   In Defense of Our Overgrown Garden.
Hopes.   Glacier's Daughters, The.
Humphrey, D.   No Immunity.
Ibarbourou.   Wild Root.
Issa.   Cuckoo's crying / Nothing special to do.
From burweed / Such a butterfly.
Let's take / The duckweed way.
Jones, Einir.   Cockles.
Jones, Tudur Dylan.   Gardening.
Kendall, M.   Education's Martyr.
Kim Chôngnan.   Leafy Plant of Wisdom, A.
Levine, P.   Later Still.
Liu, T.   Brooklyn Botanic Garden, The.
Lowery, Janet.   Houston Heights.
Madgett.   Woman with Flower.
Mayer, B.   Aeschyleans, The.
McNiece, M.   *Kudzu* has crossed.
Moore, M.   Nevertheless.
Nelson, M.   Subway in March, 5:45 P.M.
Nicholas, J.   Bush, The.
Nichols, G.   Sugar Cane.
Ondaatje.   Agatha Christie Books By the Window, The.
Pack, R.   Bounty.
Penrose, V.   At My Windows.
Phillips, C.   Reach, The.
Pound, E.   Vitex in swamp ground.
Radnóti.   Root ("Through the root power flashes unseen.").
Roethke.   Cuttings.
Cuttings (later) ("This urge, wrestle, resurrection of dry sticks.").
Moss-Gathering.
Root Cellar.
Shepherd, R.   Snowdrops and Summer Snowflakes, Drooping.
Smart, C.   Nail in the Grass, The.
Solórzano, L.   Herbario.
Herbarium.
Stevenson, R.   To A Gardener.
Taggard.   Fructus.
Taylor, A.   Clearing Away.
Thoreau.   I Am a Parcel of Vain Strivings Tied.
Thorpe, M.   Presence and Process.
Townsend, A.   Purple Loosestrife.
Tu Mu.   Plantains.
Unknown.   Green beyond green, the grass along the river.
Parts of a Thornbush, The.
Plantain.
Planting Initiation Song.
Plucking The Rushes.
Welch, L.   Springtime in the Rockies, Lichen.
Whitman, W.   Roots and Leaves Themselves Alone.
Wilbur, R.   Seed Leaves.
Williams, W.   It Is a Small Plant.
Wormser.   It's a Party (1959).
Yates, D.   Century Plant.

Plath, Sylvia
Alexander, E.   Female seer will burn upon this pyre, The.
Hughes, T.   Daffodils.
Mason, D.   Winter, 1963.
Otiono, T.   Moon Dance (Listen Sylvia).
Sexton.   Sylvia's Death.
Stevens, Meic.   Sylvia.
Wilbur, R.   Cottage Street, 1953.

Plato
Orr, G.   Available Now: Archaic Torsos of Both Sexes.
Sidney P.   Sonnet 21: "Your words my friend (right healthful caustics) blame."
Unknown.   Spirit of Plato.
Platonic Love
Anderson, C.   Platonic Love.
Atwood-Fukuda.   Wreck of the *Platonic*, The.
Ballagas.   Of Another Fashion.
Butler, S.   She was too kind, wooed too persistently.
Cartwright, W.   No Platonic [*or* Platonique] Love.
Ceravolo.   Lighthouse.
Cooper, D.   Dreamt Up.
Cowley, A.   Platonic[k] Love.
Donne.   Air[e] and Angels.
Ecstasy, The.
Hadewijch.   Love has seven names.
Herbert, E.   Platonic Love.
Hine.   Lines on a Platonic Friendship.
Ivanov, Binyo.   Wind Is Coming and I Love You, The.
József, A.   Attila József.
Maurus.   To Grimold, Abbot of St. Gall.
Michelangelo Buonarroti.   Violent burning for prodigious beauty, A.
North, D.   Platonic.
Norton, C.   Mother's Heart, The.
Paulinus of Nola.   To Ausonius.
Philips, K.   To My Excellent Lucasia, On Our Friendship.
Rowe, E.   Platonic Love.
St. John, D.   My Friend.
Tennyson, A.   Dear friend, far off, my lost desire.
Fair ship, that from the Italian shore.
I held it truth, with him who sings.
I know that this was Life—the track.
Love is and was my Lord and King.
Now, sometimes in my sorrow shut.
So careful of the type? but no.
Tears of the widower, when he sees.
Thy spirit ere our fatal loss.
Thy voice is on the rolling air.
Varchi.   What part of my holiest and most beautiful feelings.
Platypuses
Aborigine Oral Tradition.   Platypus, The.
Barrington, P.   I Had a Duck-billed Platypus.
Play
Adams, A.   Cooking.
Adams, S.   Sliding.
Aldis, D.   Kick a Little Stone.
Allen, P.   Judy.
Ammons.   Pet Panther.
Ashbery, J.   Paradoxes and Oxymorons.
Benson, G.   Play No Ball.
Benson, S.   Beaten Track, The.
Berger, B.   Waterfall: "Creek's easy purr, The."
Blake, W.   Nurse's Song ("When the voices of children are heard on the green.").
Bryce, Colette.   Every Winged Fowl of the Air.
Cavanagh, E.   Return to Avondale.
Charles, D.   Getting Dirty.
Ciardi, J.   All about Boys and Girls.
What Johnny Told Me.
Dalton, A.   How to Disappear.
Davies, W.   To W.S.—On his Wonderful Toys.
Davis, C.   Nod.
Greenberg, A.   Analogies.
Gunn, T.   Aquarium, The.
Harrison, G.   Playground, The.
Harryman.   Knowledge ("White fuzz in the air froze on a screen. Baby danced the cancan.").
Magic (or Rousseau).
Hartwig.   Above Us.
Hoberman.   Let's Dress Up.
Hudgins.   One Threw a Dirt Clod and It Ran.
Hughes, L.   Piggy-back.
Jamie, K.   Mother-May-I.
Johns.   Invitation.
Kaucher, Jennifer Hill.   Reading *Othello* and Watching a Girl Skip Rope.
Kennedy, X.   Little Elegy.

Kinsella, J.   Fall, The.
Kunitz, S.   Testing-Tree, The.
Lee, D.   Dickery Dean.
Lihn.   Dark Room, The.
Livingston, M.   Lemonade Stand.
Millay, E.   From a Very Little Sphinx.
Moore, L.   Sometimes.
Mother Goose.   Dance to your [*or* thee] daddy.
Piatt, S.   Palace-Burner, The.
Rodenko.   February Sun.
Rossetti, C.   Frisky Lamb, A.
I caught a little ladybird.
Rózewicz.   Transformations.
Russell, G.   Frolic.
Scannell.   Hide and Seek.
Schwartz, D.   I Am Cherry Alive.
Smith, W.   Around My Room.
Soto.   Behind Grandma's House.
Spender, S.   Abrupt and charming mover.
Stafford, W.   At the Playground.
Stein, G.   Identity A Poem.
Stern, G.   Suzanne.
Stevenson, R.   At the Seaside [*or* Sea-Side].
Block City.
Gardener, The.
Land of Counterpane, The.
Land of Story-Books, The.
Pirate Story.
Swing, The.
Swenson, M.   Centaur, The.
Tranter.   Debbie and Co.
Turner, A.   Red-Dress Girl.
Unknown.   Draw a pail of water.
See-saw, Margery Daw.
Tae titly.
Vallejo.   To My Brother Miguel.
Verlaine.   Femme et Chatte.
Woman and Cat.
Watson, R.   White Lady, The.
Wordsworth, W.   Kitten at Play, The.
Wright, J.   Camphor Laurel.
Playmates
Jaques, F.   There Once Was a Puffin.
Landon.   To My Brother: "Do you recall the fancies of many years ago."
Stevenson, R.   Gardener, The.
My Shadow.
Yeats.   To a Squirrel at Kyle-Na-No.
Plays and Playwrights
Applewhite.   On the Mississippi.
Berman, D.   April 13, 1865.
Corey, S.   Understanding *King Lear*.
Donnelly, T.   Twenty-seven Props for a Production of *Eine Lebenszeit*.
Fathy, S.   For Heiner Muller: Poem 1.
Gwynn, R.   Horatio's Philosophy.
Shakespearean Sonnet.
Hedderman, R.   First Player's Monologue, The.
Hudgins.   Adoration of the Magi, The.
Jonson, B.   Prologue: "Ends of all, who for the scene do write, The."
Moore, H.   To Janet, on Galileo.
Peterson, J.   As If.
Raab, L.   Revised Versions, The.
Sanford, C.   Rachel's Recovery (Fucking with the Angels).
Shepherd, R.   Pericles, Prince of Tyre: A Commentary.
Pleasure
Anacreon.   Epicure, The.
Andrews, N.   Zen 101.
Auden.   Mad to be had, to be felt and smelled.
My lips.
Bass, E.   God and the G-Spot.
Baudelaire.   Invitation au Voyage, L'.
Invitation to the Voyage.
Berrigan, T.   Many Happy Returns.
Broumas, O.   Choir, The.
Tryst.
Browning, E.   Best Thing in the World, The.
Bunan.   When you're both alive and dead.
Buson.   Utter aloneness—.
Cavafy.   In the Street.
Coleridge, S.   Kubla Khan: or, A Vision in a Dream.
Collins, W.   Ode to Evening.

Constantine, D.   Pleasure.
Cornish, W.   Pleasure It Is.
Cott, J.   Enjoyment Body.
Coward.   Poor Little Rich Girl.
Crozier, L.   Poem for Sigmund.
Daniel, S.   Are They Shadows [That We See]?
Davidson, D.   Redivivus.
Davies, W. H.   Best Friend, The.
  Joy and Pleasure.
de Fierro.   Hidden Pleasure.
Dickinson, E.   Heart asks Pleasure—first, The.
  I Taste a Liquor Never Brewed.
Doubleday, T.   No walk today;—November's
  breathings toss.
Drayton.   And thus like slaves we sell our soules
  to sinne.
Drieu la Rochelle.   Tennis.
Dunn, S.   From the Manifesto of the Selfish.
Duran, J.   Mere Pleasure of Flying, The.
Durcan.   Martha's Wall.
Ekelof.   Hangman.
Feldman, A.   Contemporary American Poetry.
Fraire.   Minute the sun comes out, The.
Godfrey.   So Let's Look at It Another Way.
Goldsmith, O.   Entry of the Villagers.
Gorbanevskaya.   Hurry, take pleasure in the
  oblique caress of rain while the sun shines.
Hacker, M.   Canzone: "Consider the three
  functions of the tongue."
Hall, D.   Digging.
Hamill, S.   Orchid Flower, The.
Hanson, M.   To Fancy.
Hass, R.   Now Winter Nights.
Herbert, E.   You well-compacted groves, whose
  light and shade.
Herrick.   On Himself[e] ("I fear[e] no Earthly
  Powers.").
Holt, R.   Pleasure of Feeling Inside Your Body,
  The.
Issa.   Just to say the word.
Johnson, S.   Short Song of Congratulation, A
  [or To a Young Heir].
Joseph, A.   Learning to Laugh.
  Pleasure.
Juan Chi.   Weird Dances.
Ka, R.   To My Beloved.
Lazić, R.   Pleasures.
Levertov.   Pleasures.
Loden.   Far In.
Lu Chi.   Satisfaction, The.
Marvell.   Dialogue Between the Resolved Soul
  and Created Pleasure, A.
Massimi.   On Happiness.
McFadden, D.   6. Tortured by Kahlil Gibran.
Mikha'il, M.   Talk.
Milton.   L'Allegro.
Moore, T.   Fancy.
Onassis, Jacqueline Kennedy.   Thoughts.
Poliziano.   Love Song for Chrysokomos
  (Goldenlocks).
  To Giovan Battista Buoninsegni.
Pongnim, Prince.   What amuses you in the
  sound.
Porter, C.   I Get a Kick Out of You.
Pound, E.   Immorality, An.
Pratt, M.   Done.
"Rachel." [or "Rahel."].   At the Window.
Radcliffe, A.   Sun-Rise: Sonnet, A.
  To the Visions of Fancy.
Ramanujan.   Pleasure.
Robinson, M.   Bower of Pleasure, The.
  Rejects the Influence of Reason.
Rossetti, C.   Goblin Market.
Ryushu Shutaku.   For all these years, my certain
  Zen.
Schwartz, D.   Pleasure.
Schwartz, R. L.   Edgewater Park.
Seward.   When Life's realities the Soul
  perceives.
Shaw, A.   Small Pleasures.
Shinkichi Takahashi.   Mushroom.
Shuttle.   Old Man, The.
Simonides.   Without pleasure.
Southwell.   Man's Civil[l] War[re].
Spenser, E.   Sonnet 26: "Sweet is the rose, but
  grows upon a brere."

Staple, W.   Shen Tao.
Stein, G.   Why Do You Feel Differently.
Strode.   Justification.
Tachibana Akemi.   Pleasure is / when you rarely
  cook.
Talfourd.   'Tis a Little Thing.
Tana, P.   You Bring Me Back.
Thelwall.   Anacreontic.
Theognis.   Man who doesn't love boys and
  single-foot horses and dogs, his heart will
  never know pleasure, The.
Unknown.   I'm sixty, this autumn.
  I've returned to Hong Kong from America.
  Things That Stand One's Hair on End.
Vroman.   Wrinkling Together.
Wroth.   Sonnet 11: "Unprofitably pleasing, and
  unsound."
Yang Wei-chen.   Mating.
Yi Chŏngbo.   Memory, A.
Young, D.   Pleasure.
Zukofsky, L.   Cocktails / and signs of.

Pleiades
Hemans.   Lost Pleiad, The.
Pawnee Oral Tradition.   Song of the Pleiades.
Stevenson, A.   Sonnet: "If it be night . . . ".
Whitman, W.   On the Beach at Night.
Williams, W.   Moon, the dried weeds, The.

Plisetskaya, Maya
Voznesensky [or Voznesenskii].   Chorus of
  Nymphs, A.
  Portrait of Plisetskaya.

Plowing and Plowmen
Brown, G.   Ballad of John Barleycorn, the
  Ploughman, and the Furrow, The.
Carruth, H.   Woodcut on the Cover of Robert
  Frost's *Complete Poems*, The.
Cho Chonsŏng.   Boy, bring my morning
  porridge.
Colum, P.   Plower, The.
Everson, W.   Winter Ploughing.
Heaney, S.   Follower.
Holmes, O.   Ploughman, The.
Hopkins, G.   Harry Ploughman.
Housman.   When smoke stood up from Ludlow.
Hughes, T.   Hawk in the Rain, The.
Kavanagh, P.   To the Man after the Harrow.
Khlebnikov, V.   Hey...y! Uh...hm!, covered with
  sweat.
Langland, W.   Plowing of Piers's Half-acre, The.
Muldoon, P.   Winter Wheat.
Quarles.   On the Ploughman [or Plough-Man].
Simpson, L.   Summer Storm.
Thomas, E.   As the Team's Head-Brass.
Unknown.   Riddle: "My snout chews the field
  like a prow."

Plum Trees and Plums
Basho.   Crow's / Abandoned nest.
  In the plum blossom scent.
  Longing for the plum blossoms.
  Searching storehouse eaves.
  With plum blossom scent.
Biespiel, D.   Under a Blossoming Plum Tree.
Buson.   Amid white plum blossoms.
  Darting here and there.
  Fallen red blossoms.
  Green plum.
  Plum blossoms scent.
  Plum scent / Haloing.
  Plums in blossom.
  Song of the Yodo River.
  Two plum trees, The.
  White plum blossoms.
  White plum blossoms.
Chasin.   Word *Plum,* The.
Ch'i-chi.   Early Plum Blossoms.
Corbett, W.   Wickson Plums.
Dooley, M.   At Les Deux Magots.
Gogarty.   Plum Tree by the House, The.
Han-shan Te-ch'ing.   Clouds release the hillsides
  and wake the scenes of spring.
Hoin.   On the rocky slope, blossoming.
Issa.   Blossoming plum!
  Flowering plum, A.
  January.
  Not very anxious.
  Village named Little-Plum-Tree, A.

  When plum / Blooms—.
Kinsella, J.   Plumburst.
Kyoriku.   Scent of plum blossoms.
Li Ch'ing-chao.   Fading Plum Blossoms.
Lu Mei-Po.   Snow and the Plum, The—1.
  Snow and the Plum, The—2.
McClure, M.   For Jack Kerouac.
Miles, J.   Conservancies.
Mirabai [or Mira Bai].   Wild woman of the
  forests, The.
Mother Goose.   Little Jack Horner/ Sat in a
  corner.
Onitsura.   Plum blossoms / One's nose.
  To finally know.
Orrick.   Wild Plum.
Ransetsu.   On the old plum tree.
Ríos, A.   Man Then Suddenly Stops Moving, A.
Snyder, G.   Plum Blossom Poem, The.
Sontag, K.   Plum Crazy.
Tan Taigi.   "Don't touch!" my host cried.
Toomer.   Song of the Son.
Unknown.   Here in my garden.
  More than the color.
Wang Wei.   You Come from My Village.
Whalen, P.   Dharmakaya.
Williams, W.   This Is Just to Say.
  To a Poor Old Woman.

Plumbing and Plumbers
Cortázar.   Loss and Recovery of the Hair, The.
Dove, R.   Genie's Prayer Under the Kitchen
  Sink.
Glazer, M.   All That in the Voice I Have
  Adopted for This Lie.
Koch, K.   Mending Sump.
Miles, S.   Plumbers.

Plunder and Plundering
Brecht, B.   What Did the Nazi Send His Wife?
Ewart.   Personal Footnote, A.
Harrison, T.   Cycles of Donji Vakuf.
Hewitt, J.   Colony, The.
Heym.   Demons of the Cities, The.
Marlowe.   Now fetch me out the Turkish
  concubines.
Spencer, B.   Invaders, The.

Plutonium
Bruchac.   Wahsah Zeh (War Dance)—As Long
  as the Grass.
de Fréine, C.   Inside.
Ginsberg, A.   Plutonian Ode.
Griswold, J.   Origami.

Plymouth, England
Spender, S.   Air Raid Across the Bay at
  Plymouth.

Poaching and Poachers
Hahn, K.   Rockhopper, The.

Pocahontas
Bibb.   Capt. Smith and Pocahontas.
Ochester.   Pocahontas.
Sandburg, C.   Cool Tombs.

Poe, Edgar Allan
Butts, A.   Poe Story, A.
Christopher.   Walt Whitman at the Reburial of
  Poe.
Hirshfield, J.   Poe: An Assay (1).
Jiménez, J.   Poe's House.
Koch, K.   You Were Wearing.
Longfellow, H.   Couplet: February 24, 1847.
Lowell, J.   Poe and Longfellow.
Loy.   Poe.
Mallarmé.   Tomb of Edgar Allan Poe, The.
  Tomb of Edgar Poe, The.
Smith, S.   After-Thought, The.
Spicer, J.   Improvisations on a Sentence by Poe.
Very.   Forevermore.
Whitman, S.   If thy sad heart, pining for human
  love.
  On our lone pathway bloomed no earthly hopes.
  Raven, The.
  To ———: "Vainly my heart had with thy
  sorceries striven."
Winch.   Mysteries.

Poetic Meter
Cope, W.   Emily Dickinson.
Longfellow, H.   Couplet: February 24, 1847.
  Peradventure of old, some bard in Ionian

Islands.
Verlaine. Art of Poetry, The ("Let's hear the music first and foremost.").

Poetry and Poets
Abrahams, L. At revolution's end.
Out of illness.
Adams, F. Us Poets.
Adamson. O to be in the news again—now as fashion runs.
Southern skua, The.
Adnan. Maïakovsky.
Aiyejina. Dialogue, The.
Akhmadulina. Coffee Imp, The.
Akhmatova, A. Sister, I have come to take your place.
Solitude.
Aksal, S. Love Poem: "First line of this poem, The."
al-Mala'ika, N. To Poetry.
Alarcon, F. Los árboles son poetas / Trees Are Poets.
Albert-Birot. Who is that blond child laughing as he runs after his colored marbles?
Alberti. Coming Back of an Assassinated Poet, The.
Alcman. Love, again sweetly streaming down.
Alegría. Ars Poetica.
Aleixandre. Who I Write For.
Alexander, A. For Raftery.
Algarin. Christmas Eve: Nuyorican Café.
Happy New Year.
Talking.
Ali Hsiying. Lazy Cloud's Nest 1.
Alkalay-Gut. Public Outcry.
Allen, D. Poet at Eighteen, The.
Allen, P. Teaching Poetry at Votech High, Santa Fe, the Week John Lennon Was Shot.
Alvarez, J. On Not Shoplifting Louise Bogan's *The Blue Estuaries.*
Amichai, Y. Ibn Gabirol.
Ammons. Anxiety's Prosody.
Conserving the Magnitude of Uselessness.
Anacreon. Fragment 17.
Anderson-Thompkins. Epitaph for Willie or Little Black Poet with No Future.
Andrade, O. Frontier.
Andrews, N. Poets on Poets.
Antin. Real Estate.
Antiphanes. Strange race of critics, A.
"Anvari.". Composing.
Arends, J. I.
Arghezi. Testament.
Aridjis. Borders, Cages and Walls.
Poem, The.
Self-Portrait at Age Ten.
Armand. Another Poetics.
Poem with Skin.
Armantrout. Manufacturing.
Armitage, S. Dead Sea Poems, The.
Zoom!
Arnold, M. Poet, The.
Artaud. Revolt Against Poetry.
Arturo, A. Madrigal 3.
Ashbery, J. All Messages Have Been Played.
Paradoxes and Oxymorons.
What Is Poetry.
Auden. Jumbled in the Common Box.
Ode to the Medieval Poets.
Truest Poetry Is the Most Feigning, The [or, Ars Poetica for Hard Times].
Avison. Butterfly Bones; or, Sonnet against Sonnets.
Azzawi, F. Poet, The.
Baca. Book 1: As Life Was; Poem Two.
Balaban. Anna Akhmatova Spends the Night on Miami Beach.
Georgi Borisov in Paris.
Poetry Reading at the Varna Ruins.
Bandeira. Poetics.
Bandele, A. 1980–1990: A Poet's Personal Review.
Baraka, I. A, B, C's, The.
Balboa, the Entertainer.
Baraka, R. American Poetry.
Baranczak, S. December 14, 1979: A Poetry Reading.

February 8, 1980: And No One Has Warned Me.
Baratier, D. Fall of Because, The.
Barbour, D. I know now I always wanted to write, to.
Barkan, S. I Have not Woven My Poems.
Barker, G. To Whom Else.
Barskova, P. Evening at Tsarskoe Selo.
Poet has passed away, The. Or rather, snuffed.
Basheva. Fifth Floor.
Basho. Each year it is but a peck of rice.
Sick on a journey.
Singing, planting rice.
Baudelaire. Albatross, The.
Beachy-Quick, Dan. Afterword.
Prologue: "Editor, / Here are the lines my mind fathomed."
Beatty, P. Stall Me Out.
Beaulieu, D. Pronoun Woven.
Beckman, J. Final poem for the gently sifting public begins on the streets.
Bécquer, G. It Goes Against My Interest to Confess It.
Begley, T. Photovoltaic.
Sappho's Gymnasium ("Outside memory worship never dies.").
Behn, A. To Damon. To Inquire of Him if He Cou'd Tell Me by the Style, Who Writ Me a Copy of Verses that Came to Me in an Unknown Hand.
BehramoḠlu, Ataol. All Over Again.
Bejerano, M. I Made a New Memory for You.
Oh spare me, spare me.
Bekes Jr. Separation.
Belev. Tale: "Children's poet's own child is dying, A."
Belieu. I Can't Write a Poem about Class Rage.
Bell, Martin. Whitman's Grass.
Bell, Marvin. Instructions to Be Left Behind.
Introduction to My Anthology, An.
Sound of the Resurrected Dead Man's Footsteps (#2).
Bellen, Martine. Cucina.
Benedetti, M. With Your Permission.
Benson, L. Asante.
Berger, M. Constrained Response.
Bergvall, C. Hungry Form.
Bernstein, C. Autonomy Is Jeopardy.
Dysraphism.
Freud's Butcher.
Klupzy Girl, The.
Of Time and the Line.
Our new / service orientation.
Solidarity Is the Name We Give to What We Cannot Hold.
Berrigan, A. Drugged and Hooded into a Prose Poem.
Sabotage.
Berryman. 3. To William Meredith.
Bevington, H. Ballade of Poetic Material.
Bhairavayya. Raped Poem.
Bibbins, M. Whitman on the Beach.
Bierce. Elegy: "Cur foretells the knell of parting day, The."
Bishop, J. Speaking of Poetry.
Black, S. Rilke's Letter from Rome.
Blaisdell, G. To a Poet (the Pearl).
Blanco. Metamorfosis de la silla.
Metamorphosis of a Chair.
Bloch, C. What a Poet Does.
Bly, R. Day We Visited New Orleans, The.
Gaiety of Form, The.
On the Oregon Coast.
Bobrowski. Trakl.
Boncho. Each year it is but a peck of rice.
Bond, E. First World War Poets.
Borges. Ars Poetica: "To look at the river made of time and water."
Conjectural Poem.
Other Tiger, The.
Other Tiger, The.
Poem of the Gifts.
Boroditskaya, M. Poor composer.
Bottoms. Sierra Bear.
Bracho, C. Allure of Forms, The.
Deleite de las formas, El.

Bradley, Dickie. Souls of Poets, The.
Bradstreet, A. I am obnoxious to each carping tongue.
In Honour of that High and Mighty Princess Queen Elizabeth of Happy Memory.
Prologue, The: "To sing of wars, of captain[e]s, and of kings."
Brathwaite, E. Stone: "When the stone fall that morning out of the johncrow sky."
Braxton, C. Bluesman.
Brecht, B. On Reading a Recent Greek Poet.
Brehm, J. At the Poetry Reading.
Breton, A. On the Road to San Romano.
On the Road to San Romano.
Breton, N. Let mee thinke no more on thee.
Breytenbach. Constipation.
Bridges, R. To Francis Jammes.
Bringhurst. These Poems, She Said.
Broda, Martine. I Wanted to Tell You.
Brodsky, J. With a simple, truly unrebellious pen.
Bromige. Eastward Ho! A Succession.
Brossa, J. Note.
Broughton, T. Shall I Compare Thee?
Broumas, O. Artemis.
Photovoltaic.
Sappho's Gymnasium ("Outside memory worship never dies.").
Brown, C. What Her Absence Means.
Brown, L. My epithalamion.
Browning, E. Fifth Book.
Mother and Poet.
Browning, R. How It Strikes a Contemporary.
Brownstein. Stepping Out.
Bryan, J. I've Looked Everywhere.
Bryan, S. Lunch with Girl Scouts.
Bryant, W. Poet, The.
Bryce, Colette. Line: "You were drawn in the voice of my mother."
Buckley, V. Teaching German Literature.
Buffoni, F. On Poetry.
Bukowski. Comments upon my last book of poesy.
Not So Good Night in the San Pedro of the World, A.
Poetry readings.
Bunina. Conversation between Me and the Women.
Burkard. Meditation Brought About by George Bogin's Translation of Jules Supervielle's Poem "The Sea".
2 Poems on the Same Theme.
Burn. In Japan.
Burns, R. While briers an' woodbines budding green.
Bursk. Does Poetry Matter?
Busceti, G. Dissonances.
Buson. End of spring, The.
New Year's first poem.
Passing spring, The.
Bynner. Idols.
Byrd, Bobby. Breaking and Entering: A Very Short Novel in Verse.
Byron, G. English Bards and Scotch Reviewers.
Oh! Southey! Southey! cease thy varied song!
Cabalquinto. Ordinance, The.
Cabico, R. In Bed with James Tate.
Cabral de Melo Neto. To Carlos Drummond de Andrade.
Cady. After Hearing Heterosexual Poets in October 1974: What It Seems Like To Write a Male Homosexual Love Poem Now.
Callimachus. Prologue to the Aetia.
Campbell, R. Volunteer's Reply to the Poet, The.
Campert. Futile Poem, A.
Campo. For J. W.
Carbó, N. I Found Orpheus Levitating.
Cardenal. From those theaters, Claudia, from those feasts.
I offer these verses to you, Claudia, because you are their mistress.
Carew, T. Elegy upon the Death of the Dean of [St.] Paul's, Dr. John Donne, An.
Carey, H. Namby-Pamby. A Panegyric on the New Versification, Address'd to A———

P———, Esq. ("All ye poets of the age.").
Carper, Thomas. Oh Keep the Poet Hence.
Carrington, H. Lament: "While my city gently sleeps."
Carroll, L. Poeta Fit, Non Nascitur.
Carroll, P. Ode to the Angels Who Move Perpetually toward the Dayspring of Their Youth.
Carruth, H. At Seventy-Five: Rereading an Old Book.
California: "To come again into the place of revolutionary."
Impossible Indispensability of the Ars Poetica, The.
Last Poem in the World, The.
Saturday at the Border.
Sonnet: "To see a woman long oppressed by fear."
Sonnet: "You rose from our embrace and the small light spread."
Carson, A. Essay on What I Think about Most.
Stanzas, Sexes, Seductions.
Cartelli, Mary Anne. Water.
Carver, D. Poet, The.
Castellanos. Palm Tree, A.
Poetry Is Not You.
You Are Not Poetry.
Catullus. To Aurelius and Furius.
Cavafy. Passing Through.
Their Beginning.
When They Come Alive.
Cavendish, M. Poet[r]ess's Hasty Resolution, The.
Celaya, G. Great Moments.
Poetry Is a Weapon Loaded with the Future.
Cendrars. Contrasts.
Hammock.
Cepollaro, B. Requiem in C.
Cervantes. First Beating.
On the Poet Coming of Age.
Chaloner. Thicket of Time.
Chan Fang-sheng. Sailing Back to the Capital.
Chao Meng-fu. Admonition to Myself, An.
Chapman, G. For words want art and art wants words to praise her.
Muses that fame's loose feathers beautify.
Char. Argument.
Chédid Andrée. Trials of the Poet.
Cherry, K. On Watching a Young Man Play Tennis.
Ch'i-chi. Sent to a Poetry Friend.
Speaking My Mind.
Chiasson, D. Elephant, The.
My Ravine.
Stealing from Your Mother.
Chin. Leaving San Francisco.
Ching An. Dusk of Autumn: Writing What My Heart Embraces.
Facing Snow and Writing What My Heart Embraces.
Laughing at Myself 1.
Third Time Wandering to Cloud Sluice Peak.
Chipasula. Manifesto on Ars Poetica.
Cho Wen-chun. Poet's Wife, A.
Chŏng Hyŏnjong. Are You a Star?
Christie, J. Vernal Conifer Seance.
Chubb, R. Song of My Soul.
Clampitt. Cure at Porlock, A.
Imago.
Clanchy, K. Spell.
War Poetry.
Clare, J. To the Memory of John Keats.
Clark, T. Free Speech.
Lake, The.
Clarke, C. Poet's Death, A.
Clarke, George Elliott. 1.5.
Cleary, B. New Rock n Roll, The.
Clerk. Country Seat, The.
Clewell. Accomplice, The.
Clifton, L. Driving through new england.
Fury.
My Dream About the Poet.
When i stand around among poets.
Close, J. Haloes, Not Hats [or A Vision of the Gods].
Cocteau. Cape of Good Hope, The.

Codrescu. Paper on Humor.
Coleridge, S. Homeric Hexameter, The.
Metrical Feet.
Collins, B. Introduction to Poetry.
Japan.
Lines Composed Over Three Thousand Miles From Tintern Abbey.
Sonnet: "All we need is fourteen lines, well, thirteen now."
Taking Off Emily Dickinson's Clothes.
Workshop.
Colquitt. Poetry and Post, Texas.
Conn. Stolen Light.
Constantine, D. Pleasure.
Cooley. History of Poetry, The.
Coolidge, C. Ashbery Explains.
At the Poem.
Note, A.
Cooper, D. Poem for George Miles.
Cope, W. Emily Dickinson.
Not only marble, but the plastic toys.
Uncertainty of the Poet, The.
Waste Land Limericks.
Corcoran. In the Red Book.
Corn. Long-Distance Call to Gregg, Who Lived with AIDS as Long as He Could.
Marriage in the Nineties, A.
Cortez, J. For the Poets.
Opening Act.
Cory, W. Desiderato.
Cottle, J. Virtue Protests [or Epistle to Lord Byron].
Cottle, Katherine. My Poetess' Eyes.
Cowley, A. Muse, The.
Cowley, H. Off Duty [or To Della Crusca].
Creeley. Dishonest Mailmen, The.
Cross, D. Can't Oh.
Cross, E. Epifanía.
Epiphany: "Sometimes you show yourself."
Crouch, A. L. Mirabeau B. Lamar.
Cruz e Sousa. Antiphony.
Cruz Varela. Love Song for Difficult Times.
Csoori. Somebody Consoles Me with a Poem.
Cuadra, P. Manuscript in a Bottle.
Cullen, C. For Hazel Hall, American Poet.
Yet Do I Marvel.
Cummings, E. E. Little joe gould has lost his teeth and doesn't know where.
Since feeling is first.
Cunningham, J. For My Contemporaries.
Cunningham, P. Hats.
D'Aguiar, F. Langston.
Daiches. Notes for a History of Poetry.
Daie-Soko. Life's as we / Find it—death too.
Dailey. Poetry fro Dummies.
Dalton, R. Ars Poetica.
Dana, M. Real Comfort.
Dancing Bear, J. P. Iago, the Poet.
Daniel, S. Poet and Critic.
To the Right Honorable, the Lady Mary, Countess of Pembroke.
Dante Alighieri. But tell me if the man whom I see here.
But with regard to me, I'll satisfy.
Natural thirst that never can be quenched.
Dao. Landscape Over Zero.
Darío, R. I Seek a Form.
Melancholy.
Spring.
Springtime.
Swan, The.
Davie, D. In the Stopping Train.
Davies, E. Will no young British bard, on rhyme intent.
Dawe, Tom. If Sonnets Were in Fashion.
de Burgos. I Have Lost A Verse.
To Julia de Burgos.
De Coninck, H. Your Sweaters.
de Folgar. Protest.
Delaunay, S. Greetings, Blaise Cendrars.
Desnos. Ars Poetica.
Like.
Deutsch. Poem, The: "Painter of Dante's awful ferry-ride, the."
Dharker. Minority.
Di Prima. To Philip Whalen, 1999.

Dickinson, E. I dwell in Possibility.
I reckon—when I count at all.
They shut me up in Prose.
Dickson, J. Poemectomy.
Diego, G. Julio Campal ("We were walking to your funeral, eleven friends.").
Dimitrova. Ars Poetica: "Write each of your poems."
DiPalma. Prerogative of Lieder, The.
Disch. Poems: "I think that I shall never read."
Dissanayake. Freedom.
DJ Renegade. Adventures of Grandmaster Flash, The.
Dodge, M. Note.
Doherty, T. Raven's Revenge.
Dovaston, J. F. M. There are who say the sonnet's meted maze.
Downie. Some Poetry.
Drayton. To the Reader of These Sonnets.
What spirit can lift you up, to that immortall praise.
Drummond de Andrade. Elegy: "I've won (lost) my day."
Drummond, W. Sextain: "With elegies, sad songs, and mourning lays."
Dubie. Ars Poetica: A Stone Soup.
Dudek. At Lac en Coeur.
Duffy, C. Little Red-Cap.
Dugan, A. American Variation on How Rilke Loved a Princess and Got to Stay in Her Castle.
Duhamel. How Much Is This Poem Going to Cost Me?
Sex with a Famous Poet.
Duhig, I. Fred.
Margin Prayer from an Ancient Psalter.
No Derry slubberdegullion with college airs.
Dumdum. Li Pos of the Polis.
Dunbar, W. Lament for the Makaris [or Makars or Makers].
Duncan, R. At the Poetry Conference: Berkeley After the New York Style.
Poetry, a Natural Thing.
Structure of Rime XVIII.
Structure of Rime XXIII.
Dunn, D. Envoi: "Why did I bring you to this Hull."
Duo Duo. Handicraft—After Marina Tsvetaeva.
Eberhart, R. Immortal Picture, The.
Worldly Failure.
Edwards, K. Provisionally.
Eich. Inventory.
Lauras.
Eigner. In Imitation.
Elburg. Nothing of All That.
Elliott, E. Powers of the Sonnet.
Ellis, T. T.A.P.O.A.F.O.M.
Elmslie, K. Bare Bones.
Elytis, O. As Endymion.
Whatever I was able to acquire in my life by way of acts visible to all, that is, to win my own transparency, I owe to a kind of special courage Poetry gave me: to be wind for the kite and kite for the wind, even when the sky is missing.
Emanuel, L. Homage to Sharon Stone.
Politics of Narrative, The: Why I Am a Poet.
Emerson, R. Merlin.
Motto to "The Poet".
Poet.
Empson. Missing Dates.
Enzensberger, H. For the Primer of Senior High.
"Ern Malley.". Sonnets for the Novachord.
Etter. Green-Eyed Boy after Reading Whitman and Sandburg.
Ezekiel. Company I Keep, The.
Poet, Lover, Birdwatcher.
Ezrokhi, Z. Day at Home, A.
Repetition.
Faber, F. Sonnet-writing. To F. W. F.
Fagin, L. Hello Again.
Fanning, R. Baudelaire's Ablutions.
Fathy, S. For Heiner Muller: Poem 1.
Feinstein, E. Infidelities.
Feldman, A. Contemporary American Poetry.

Felipe, L.   Biography, Poetry, Destiny.
I am no one: a man.
I Am Not the Great Diver.
Let the Poet Come.
Ferlinghetti, L.   And Pablo Neruda / that
Chilean omnivore of poetry.
Fermini, I.   Waiting for sleep at the air roots.
Field.   It was deep April, and the morn.
'Sing to us Sappho!' cried the crowd.
Figueroa, J.   Pablo Neruda.
Poet Pedro Pietri.
Fink, Robert A.   Atmosphere for Poetry in
Abilene, The.
For Micha's Mother, Who Signs.
Fiorentino, J.   Prairie Long Poem.
Fischer, N.   Favorable Prospects.
Poetry's a Way Not a Subject.
Fisher, A.   Ditchley Portrait, The.
Fitzpatrick, R.   Fine Occupation, A.
Forbes, J.   Monkey's Pride.
Forman, R.   This Poem.
Forrest-Thomson.   Not Pastoral Enough.
Francis, R.   Catch.
Frénaud.   Words of the Poem, The.
Freneau.   To a New England Poet.
Fried, Elliot.   Why I Want to Be the Next Poet
Laureate.
Fried, Erich.   Logos.
Friesen, P.   Anna.
Frost, R.   In a Poem.
Frym.   Only two know the meaning of us.
Fuller, M.   Lines Written in Boston on a
Beautiful Autumnal Day.
Fullerton.   Poetry.
Fulton, A.   Wonder Bread.
Gallagher, T.   I Stop Writing the Poem.
Galvin, J.   Art Class.
Ganev, Nedelcho.   Matter.
Garelli, Jacques.   Excess of Poetry.
Garrett, E.   Reprieve, The.
Garrett, G.   Envoy: "Little poem, the two of us
know too much."
Georgiou, E.   Space Between, The.
Gil de Biedma, J.   Art of Poetry, The.
Gilbert, J.   Malvolio in San Francisco.
Gilbert, S.   Against Poetry.
Retrun of the Muse, The.
Ginsberg, A.   City Midnight Junk Strains.
Grim Skeleton.
Last Night in Calcutta.
Written in My Dream by W. C. Williams.
Gioia.   Next Poem, The.
Giovanni.   Poem (for Langston Hughes), A.
Poetry: "Poetry is motion graceful."
Gladstone, W. E.   To a Rejected Sonnet.
Goedicke.   For Walt Whitman.
Wind of Our Going: Adagio Ma Non Troppo.
Goethe.   Sonnet: "To work away in art's
traditional measure."
Goetsch, D.   Smell and Envy.
Goldberg, B.   Nights in the Constellation of the
Tree Stepping from its Robe.
Goldberg, L.   That poem I didn't write.
Gomez, M.   Solo Palabras.
Goodman, M.   Open Poem.
Goodman, P.   Now only praise makes me cry.
Sentences After *Defence of Poetry.*
Gorostiza, J.   Elegy: "Alone, with harsh marine
aloneness."
Fireflies.
Gosse.   Sestina: "In fair Provence, the land of
lute and rose."
Grennan.   Detail.
Grin, B.   Dead Chrysanthemums.
Guest, B.   Confession of My Images.
Valorous Vine.
Gullar.   In the Body.
Noise.
Oswald Dead.
Gumilyov [or Gumiliov or Gumilev].
Fragments 1920–1921.
Gundy, J.   For the New York City Poet Who
Informed me that Few People Live This Way.
How to Write the New Mennonite Poem.
Gunn, T.   For the Late R. F.
Gurevitch.   Line of a Poem.

Gutiérrez Nájera.   Non Omnis Moriar.
Gwynn, R.   Approaching a Significant Birthday,
He Peruses The Norton Anthology of Poetry.
Haavikko.   Tyrant inspires small poems, The.
Hacker, M.   Ballad of Ladies Lost and Found.
Elegy for a Soldier.
Feeling and Form.
Hahn, K.   These Current Events.
Hahn, S.   Confession.
Halperin.   Two Lines from Paul Celan.
Hamer.   Berkeley, Late Spring.
Hamill, S.   Another Duffer.
Each word carefully.
New York Poem, The.
Reading Seferis.
Rising.
To Hayden Carruth on His Eightieth Birthday.
True Illumination Is Habitude.
Han-shan.   One Budding-Talent Wang.
Whoever has Cold Mountain's poems.
Whoever reads my poems.
Han Yong'un [or Yongwun].   To the Readers.
Upon Reading Tagore's "The Gardener".
Hanson, M.   Occasioned by Reading Mrs. M.
Robinson's Poems.
To Mrs. Charlotte Smith.
Hantoosh, G.   Glass of Ancient Wine, A.
Happiest Man in the World, The.
Harms.   Soon.
Harris, W.   Grandfather Poem, A.
Harrison, J.   Geo-Bestiary #X.
I am four years older than you but scarcely an
unwobbling.
I don't have any medals. I feel their lack.
I wanted to feel exalted so I picked up.
It would surely be known for years after as the
day I shot.
Lustra. Officially the cold comes from
Manitoba.
Rabbit is born, The.
What if I own more paper clips than I'll ever
use in this.
Word Drunk.
Harrison, T.   Heartless Art, The.
Heredity.
Harry, J.   Poem Films Itself, The.
Hart, S.   Sundays.
Harvey, M.   Thermae.
Harwood, L.   Poem for Writers, A.
Hass, R.   Churchyard.
Envy of Other People's Poems.
Interrupted Meditation.
Letter to a Poet.
Hattersley, G.   Frank O'Hara Five, Geoffrey
Chaucer Nil.
Hauge.   Leaf Huts and Snow Houses.
Healy, E.   From Los Angeles Looking South.
Heaney, S.   Fosterling.
Hejinian.   No form at all—it's impossible to
imagine its being.
Hemans.   Corinna at the Capitol.
Thought from an Italian Poet.
Hemensley.   Look! she said you can see.
My poem's in the oven where it.
Place was famed for, The.
Poem by John Thorpe, A.
Henderson, H.   Prologue: "Obliterating face and
hands."
Herbert, G.   Jordan (1).
Jordan (2).
Quidditie [or Quiddity], The.
Sonnet: "My God, where is that ancient heat
towards Thee."
Herbert, W.   Baby Poem Industry Poem, The.
Herbert, Z.   Biology Teacher.
Five Men.
Georg Heym—The Almost Metaphysical
Adventure.
Hernández Cruz.   Anonymous.
Side 32.
Herrick.   His Prayer for Absolution.
Ode for Him [or Ben Jonson], An.
To Live Merrily, and To Trust to Good Verses.
Hierro, José.   Poem Without Music.
Highfill, M.   Marginalization of Poetry, The.
Hill, G.   Vergine bella.

Hillman, B.   Little Furnace.
Hinz-Penner, R.   Once, in Santa Fe.
Hirshfield, J.   Letter to Hugo from Later.
Reading Chinese Poetry before Dawn.
Hisle, Janeya K.   And All the Sisters Said.
Hồ Xuân Huong.   Country Scene.
Hogan, L.   Heartland.
Hokushi.   Writing / Rubbing it out—.
Holan.   Night with Hamlet, A.
Holland, J.   Having read up on the subject.
Pulse.
Wavelength.
Hollander, J.   By Heart.
Some Walks With You.
What the Lovers in the Old Songs Thought.
Holman, B.   Death of Poetry, The.
Performance Poem.
Holmes, O.   At the "Atlantic" Dinner, December
15, 1874.
Poesy.
Poet Grows Old, The.
Holthaus, G.   Writing the Poem.
Hood, T.   Literary Reminiscences.
Sonnet to a Sonnet.
Horace.   Anger Poem, The (1.16).
Exegi Monumentum.
Let's Do This Poem (1.26).
Howe, F.   Doubt.
Howe, S.   Plain chair or two back.
Hristov, Boris.   Window, The: "I stand on tiptoe
to reach the window that's open a crack."
Hsin Ch'i-chi.   Tune: "Picking Mulberry Seeds"
Written on a Wall en route to Po-shan.
Hu Shih.   Dream and Poetry.
Huang T'ing-chien.   Tune: "Courtyard Full of
Fragrance, The".
Huchel.   Garden of Theophrastus, The.
Hughes, F.   Birds.
Huidobro.   Ars Poetica.
Poetry Is a Heavenly Crime.
Hulme, T.   Embankment, The (The fantasia of a
fallen gentleman on a cold, bitter night).
Hummer, T.   Poem in the Shape of a Saxophone.
Hwang Jiwoo.   Memo on Composition.
Hyde, E.   About Poems.
Ibáñez, S.   Empty Page, The.
Ibarra, Filomena.   In Ancient Rome There
Stood.
Ibycus.   They destroyed the famous and wealthy.
Iijima Koichi.   Imperfect Poetry and
Meaningless Poetry.
Ilkov, Ani.   Green and Gold.
Ram.
Irby.   [Record].
Ishikawa Takuboku.   He sees me.
Ivanov, G.   Not so long ago, the world was
complete.
Ivory, H.   Note to the reader: this is not a poem.
Jabeen, M.   Author's Consent.
Jaccottet.   Don't worry.
Jackson, L.   Poet: A Lying Word.
Jacob, M.   Spanish Generosity.
Jamie, K.   Meadowsweet.
Jaramillo Agudelo, D.   Some Day.
Jarmain.   These Poems.
Jarman, Geraint.   Wood, The.
Jeffers, H.   Instructions for Academic Poets
Who Talk to God.
Jennings, E.   About These Things.
Jennings, K.   Couples.
Jiménez, J.   At First She Came to Me Pure.
Author's Club.
I wish that all my poems.
Johns.   Salon de Vers.
Johnston, M.   In Memoriam.
Jonas, S.   Book V.
Ear Injured by Hearing Things, An.
Lens.
Little Magic, A.
What you can see.
Jones, R. Gerallt.   For Ewan McLachlan.
To Derek Walcott.
Jones, Richard.   Comment on this: in the real
scheme of things, poetry is marginal.
Poet's Heart, The.
Jones, Rodney.   End of Communism, The.

Jones, S.   Ann Griffiths.

Jones, T. Harri.   Mr Jones as the Transported Poet.

Jones, Thomas James.   Dylan.

Jonson, B.   Epistle Answering to One That Asked to Be Sealed of the Tribe of Ben, An.

Fit of Rhyme against Rhyme, A.

Sonnet to the Noble Lady, the Lady Mary Wroth, A.

To John Donne ("Who shall doubt, Donne, where [or whe'er] I a poet be[e].").

To the Memory of My Beloved, the Author Mr [or Master] William Shakespeare: And What He Hath Left Us.

Jooris.   Village, A.

What Does One Do.

Jordan, B.   This Poem.

Jordan, J.   Something Like a Sonnet for Phillis Miracle Wheatley.

Joseph, A.   Shame of the Writers' Conference.

Juarroz.   Somewhere There's a Man.

Tenth.9.

Justice, D.   About My Poems.

In Memory of the Unknown Poet, Robert Boardman Vaughn.

Pantoum of the Great Depression.

Juvenal.   Satire 1.

Kaliba, L.   Bebop Trumpet.

Kamanda, K.   Poet's Poem, The.

Kamienska.   Prayer That Will Be Answered, A.

Kang Ŭn'gyo.   It Speaks.

Poem's Visit, A.

Kao Ch'i.   Song of the Man of Green Hill, The.

Kaplan, A.   Hey.

Kaplinski, J.   Once I got a postcard from the Fiji Islands.

Poetry is Verdant.

To eat a pie and to have it.

Kapovich, K.   Green One over There, The.

Kaschnitz.   Poem, A: "Poem made of words, A."

Kasdorf.   Poetry in America.

Kaufman, B.   "Michaelangelo" the Elder.

Terror Is More Certain, A.

Kaufman, S.   By the Rivers.

Daily Ritual.

Poem in November.

Keita, N.   Dedicated to the domestics.

Kekova.   Already, no more suffering, no.

Kenjeev.   Gone is the sound of my favorite misfortune, which even yesterday.

Kennedy, X.   Poets.

Kerouac.   To Edward Dahlberg.

Khlebnikov, V.   To Everyone.

Khoury, N.   Death Is Your Salvation.

Kim Chiha.   Core.

Kim Chŏngnan.   Poetry: "Many entrances. Open. Everywhere. But reaching nowhere. Wandering."

King, I.   If Ye Hivni.

Kinnell.   For Robert Frost.

Oatmeal.

Kinsella, J.   Bluff Knoll Sublimity.

Rust Eclogues, The: Radnoti, Poetry, and the Strains of Appropriation.

Kizer, C.   Afternoon Happiness.

Ashes, The.

For Sappho/After Sappho.

Ingathering.

Not Writing Poems about Children.

Singing Aloud.

To an Unknown Poet.

Klappert.   To Whom.

Klee.   Poem: "I stand in full armor."

Klein, M.   Scenes for an Elegy.

Kloos, W.   Self-Transformation.

Klyuyev [or Kliuev or Klyuev].   Can I Tell You My Love with a Portrait.

Fourth Rome, The.

Knight, E.   Haiku: "Eastern guard tower."

To Make a Poem in Prison.

Knoepfle.   Late Winter in Menard County.

Ko Ŭn.   Chrysanthemums.

Kocbek.   I Haven't Done Playing With Words.

Koch, K.   Stones of Time, The.

To My Old Poems.

To Old Age.

To World War Two.

Koertge.   My Students.

Koethe.   North Point North.

To an Audience.

Kohler.   Vessel.

Kombem.   Another Moment.

Komrij.   Poet, The.

Kooser.   Rabbit is born, The.

Korinna [or Corinna].   I blame even clear-voiced.

Terpsichore [told] me.

Kosen.   Blind horse trotting up an icy ledge, A.

Kowit.   I Attend a Poetry Reading.

Kruchyonykh [or Kruchionykh or Kruchenykh].   Pomade.

Krukowski, D.   Minor Poets, The.

Kshemendra.   Poet should learn with his eyes, A.

Kuan Hsiu.   Written in the Mountains.

Kuhar, M.   All holyroadz home.

Kumin, M.   Calling, A.

Final Poem, The.

Kunitz, S.   Three Small Parables for My Poet Friends.

Kuusisto, Stephen.   Erasing Stars.

Kuzma.   Poetry: "Old forms are like birdhouses that, The."

Kwŏn P'il.   Leaves fall with rain in these vacant mountains.

Kyger.   Duncan's class met last night and more talk.

L'Abbé, Sonnet.   Freestyle (Why They Don't Like Rap).

Labrador, Sean Manzano.   Dark Continent, The.

Laird, N.   Poetry: "It's a bit like looking through the big window."

Lake, P.   Introduction to Poetry.

Landon.   Felicia Hemans.

Poet's Lot, The.

Landor, W.   Ianthe.

Lane, M. Travis.   Poem Upon the Forcible Entry by Cat into a Poem Originally Upon Trilliums.

Large, J.   Snowcone Vendor.

Lars.   Recollection of Gabriela Mistral.

Laughlin, J.   I Know How Every Poet.

Poets.

Then and Now.

Lauterbach.   Mimetic.

Laux, D.   Finding What's Lost.

Garden, The.

Layton.   Birth of Tragedy, The.

Le Guin.   For CALYX.

Leapor.   Mira's Will.

Lee, C.   Proem: "Bad Verse I sing, and since 'twere best, I deem."

Lee, D.   Loading a Boar.

Leonard, T.   100 Differences Between Poetry and Prose.

Levchev.   Rooftops.

Levertov.   Cancion: "When I am the sky."

Goodbye to Tolerance.

Illustrious Ancestors.

Poet and Person.

Williams: An Essay.

Levin, D.   Ars Poetica (the idea).

Ars Poetica: "This hush, my pollen—the ordinary grace in the buds."

Glass Heart.

Levine, P.   Genius: "Two old dancing shoes my grandfather."

I Sing the Body Electric.

Poem of Chalk, The.

Levis.   Poem You Asked For, The.

Lewis, G.   Oxford Booklicker.

Poet's Confession, A.

Ritual.

Li Po.   About Tu Fu.

For Du Fu.

Night Morring at Cow's Creek: I Think of the Old Man.

River Song.

To See Secretary Shu-Yun Off at the Hsieh T'iao Tower at Hsuan-Ch'eng.

Liban, A.   At a Time Like This.

Lima, J.   Distribution of Poetry.

Lin Pu.   Locust Wood Mallet for Papermaking, A.

Livingstone, D.   Waste land at Station 14, The.

Lockward, D.   My Husband Discovers Poetry.

Loftis, N.   Changes—Eight.

Logue, C.   To My Fellow Artists.

Longfellow, H.   Broken Oar, The.

Milton.

Longley, M.   Waterfall, The.

Lope de Vega.   Sonnet All of a Sudden, A.

López-Adorno, P.   Throbs for the Instructress.

Lopez, T.   In Memory.

Loseff [or Losev].   Conversation with a New York Poet.

I know—the Mongol yoke, the years of famine.

Lourie.   Letters to the Dead: Denise Levertov.

Lovelace, R.   On Sanazar's being honoured with six hundred Duckets by the Clarissimi of Venice, for composing an Elegiack Hexastick of The City. A Satyre.

Lowell, J.   Alcott.

Channing and Thoreau.

Philothea (Lydia Child).

Phoebus.

Science and Poetry.

Lowell, R.   Epilogue: "Those blessèd structures, plot and rhyme."

Lu Chi.   Rhymeprose on Literature.

Lu Mei-Po.   Snow and the Plum, The—1.

Snow and the Plum, The—2.

Lumbreras, E.   ¿Hacia Donde?

Where To?

Lux.   Walt Whitman's Brain Dropped on Laboratory Floor.

Luzi.   Postscriptum.

Mac Lochlainn, G.   Second Tongue.

MacDiarmid, H.   British Leftish Poetry, 1930–40.

Machado Ruiz.   Denuded Is the Earth.

I Have Never Wanted Fame.

Poem: "Naked is the earth."

Portrait.

Water Wheel, The.

Water Wheel, The ("Afternoon arrived, The.").

What the poet is searching for.

MacLeish.   Ars Poetica: "Poem should be palpable and mute, A."

Madhubuti.   Killing Memory.

Major, C.   Purchase, The.

Malé.   And Here are the Poets in Their Sad Portraits.

Greek Metamorphosis.

Poet's Biography.

Mallarmé.   Toast.

Tomb.

Tomb of Charles Baudelaire, The.

Tomb of Edgar Allan Poe, The.

Tomb of Edgar Poe, The.

Mandiela, A.   Mih Feel It.

Manhire.   On Originality.

Manigat, M.   Morisseau-Leroy.

Manrique, J.   Baudelaire's Spleen.

My Night with Frederico García Lorca (As Told by Edouard Roditi).

Mansour, A.   We Must Be Assured That a Fine Poet Will Be Born, Even after Fifteen Years.

Mapanje.   On Being Asked to Write a Poem for 1979.

Marinetti.   Correction of proofs + desires in speed.

We had stayed up all night, my friends and I, under hanging mosque lamps.

Markotić, N.   No such thing as a prose poem.

Seven blind curves.

Martí.   I am an honest man.

Opposite of Ornate and Rhetorical Poetry, The.

Martial.   Cornelius sighs . . . the lines I write.

He scanned me closely, Rufus, just as.

Here he is whom you read and clamor for.

Issa's Portrait.

Ligurra's fearful I'll contrive.

Read of *Thyestes*, *Oedipus*, dark suns.

Slipshod writing, premature publication.

Ted's studio burnt down, with all his poems.

Who deem epigrams mere trifles.

Why is it modern books are little read.

Why is it modern poets are ignored.
You often say my work is coarse. It's true.
Martinez, D.   Pain.
Marvell.   On Mr Milton's "Paradise Lost".
Mason, D.   Whit for Whitman, A.
Winter, 1963.
Masters, E.   Minerva Jones.
Petit, the Poet.
Matthews, M.   Language.
Matthews, W.   Poetry Reading at West Point, A.
Telegram from the Muse, A.
Matveyeva [or Matveieva].   Re-Conversion.
Maulpoix, Jean-Michel.   Giving Birth, The.
Maxwell, G.   Poem Recalls the Poet, The.
Poem to Mr Thomas and Mr Frost.
Mayakovsky [or Maiakovskii].   Cloud in Trousers, A.
My most respected / comrades of posterity!
Screaming My Head Off.
Mayer, B.   Generic Elbows.
Incorporation of Sophia's Cereal, The.
Palm Sunday Maple Syrup Poem.
Turning Prose into Poetry.
"Mbala.".   History of Dub Poetry, The.
McClatchy.   Bishop Reading.
McGrath, T.   You Can Start the Poetry Now, Or: News from Crazy Horse.
McHugh, H.   What He Thought.
McMorris, M.   Time Once Again.
McNeil, R.   Mirrors in the Room.
Meckel, C.   Speaking of the Poem.
Medina, T.   Don't Say Goodnight to Etheridge Knight.
Poem for Teacup Mantlepiece Poets Palpitating Poot Booty Plagiarists Imprisoned in Ivy League White Supremacist Mental Biological Warfare Labs.
Mei Yao Ch'en.   Necessities.
Meltzer, D.   For Jack Spicer.
Mendelssohn Anna.   Photrum.
Meng Chiao.   Despair.
Meredith, W.   American Living Room, The: A Tract.
In Memory of Robert Frost.
Merkureva, V.   Grandmother of Russian Poetry: A Self-Portrait, The.
Merwin.   Berryman.
Lament for the Makers.
On the Subject of Poetry.
Poem, The: "Coming late, as always."
Messerli.   From Hear to Air.
Millay, E.   To Elinor Wylie ("Oh, she was beautiful in every part!").
Miller, E.   Incantation: "Let all poems speak and address themselves."
Miller, J.   Poetry: "Invited onto the grounds of the god."
Miller, L.   Light cross of lonely strolls, The.
Milligan, Bryce.   San Antonio Nights.
Milosz, C.   Dedication: "You whom I could not save."
In Szetejnie.
Poetic State, A.
Reading the Japanese Poet Issa (1762–1826).
Report.
You Who Wronged.
Milton.   To Mr. H. Lawes On His Airs.
Miranda.   Second-Born Son: Lines for Walt Whitman Composed on Nantucket Island.
Mishol, A.   Sacred Cow of Hardship, The.
Mistral, G.   Flower of Air, The.
Mitchell, E.   This Poem.
Mooney, M.   Anna Akhmatova's Funeral.
Moore, M.   Critics and Connoisseurs.
Past Is the Present, The.
Poetry [1921 version]: "I, too, dislike it: there are things that are important beyond all this fiddle."
Poetry [1925 Version].
Poetry [1967 Version].
Morales, A.   Other Heritage, The.
Sugar Poem.
Morejón.   Disillusion for RubéDarío.
Love, Attributed City.
Morgan, E.   Opening the Cage.
Moritz [or Morits].   Between Scylla and

Charybdis.
Morotskaya, S.   Screams and hair come out.
Morrissey, S.   Wound Man, The.
Morshen.   Storm, A.
Moss, S.   Exchange of Hats, An.
Mouré.   Morphine, Or The Cutting Stone.
Moustaki, N.   How to Write a Poem after September 11th.
Mueller, L.   Possessive Case, The.
Muench, S.   Elegy for the Unsaid.
Mukai Kyorai.   Each year it is but a peck of rice.
Mullen, H.   Fancy Cortex.
Unacknowledged Legislator.
Murray, L.   Poetry and Religion.
Musa, Y.   There Is a Dead Poet Alive.
Musgrave.   Hidden Meaning.
Muske, C.   Our Kitty.
Stage and Screen, 1989.
Muso Soseki.   Incomparable-Verse Valley.
Musset.   Muse, The.
Poet, The.
Poet, The.
Myles, E.   Merk.
Nabokov.   On Translating "Eugene Onegin".
Nadir, M.   Out of the Depths.
Selfwriting.
Na'ili [or Yeni-Zada Mustafa Efendi].   We are the snake hidden in the staff.
Nakano Shigeharu.   Paul Claudel.
Nash, O.   Very Like a Whale.
Nasir, A.   Poem Looking in a Mirror, A.
Poet's Fate, A.
Natsume Soseki.   Not a Christian, not a Buddhist, not a Confucian either.
Nazario, A.   Kevin and Nicole.
Nekrasov, V.   What kind of Pushkin am I.
Nelson, M.   Misunderstanding, A.
Nemerov.   Because You Asked about the Line between Prose and Poetry.
Neruda.   Ambassador, The.
From My Notebook.
Ode to César Vallejo.
Poem 20.
Poetry.
Sweetness, Always.
Tonight I Can Write the Saddest Lines.
When I was writing my love poems, which sprouted from me.
Newton, Violette.   Texas Poetry.
Nguyễn Trãi.   Bamboo Hut, The.
Nichol.   Some Nets.
Niedecker.   Cricket-song.
If I Were a Bird.
Nikolayeva [or Nikolaeva].   Once I used to study languages dead for millenia.
Nolens, L.   Paranoia.
Nooteboom.   Basho 1.
Basho 2.
Basho 3.
Basho 4.
Basho ("Old man among the reeds mistrust of the poet.").
Basho ("Oude man tussen het riet achterdocht van de dichter.").
North, C.   Words from Robert W. Service.
Nortje.   Asseverations.
Sonnet two: "I have drunk up nights and spent the days."
Nossis.   Stranger, if you sail to the land of lovely dances, Mytilene.
Notley.   Where Leftover Misery Goes.
Nowlan.   Exchange of Gifts, An.
O'Brien, S.   Welcome, Major Poet!
Odio, E.   Letter to Carlos Pellicer.
O'Donoghue, M.   Stylist, The.
O'Hara, F.   Short History of Bill Berkson, A.
Okudzhava.   Save us, the poets, save us, we have but.
Older.   Two Worlds.
Oliver, D.   Little Night, A.
"u", "je", "r", "r", "im", "a", "finally".
Walnut and Lily.
Ondaatje.   Oh Rilke, I want to sit down calm like you.
Oppen.   And Their Winter and Night in

Disguise.
Boy's Room.
Gold on Oak Leaves.
In Memoriam Charles Reznikoff.
Orozco.   Olga Orozco.
Orr, G.   Some Part of the Lyric.
Sweater, The.
Orten.   Last Poem, The.
Osterhaus, J.   Gambier.
Otero, B.   Censored.
Last Judgement.
Written in Rain.
Otiono, T.   Moon Dance (Listen Sylvia).
Otten, W. J.   Poet Dives, The.
Ou-yang Hsiu.   Reading the Poems of an Absent Friend.
Ovid.   And now my work is done: no wrath of Jove.
Death of Orpheus, The.
Elegy 2.1: "I, Ovid, poet of my wantonness."
Every letter you've read in this whole book was written.
Friend of the arts and artists, scholar, generous patron.
If you're one who keeps a bust made in my likeness.
Little book—no, I don't begrudge you—you're off to the City.
Padgett, R.   Blue Bananas.
First Drift.
Joe Brainard's Painting "Bingo".
Talking to Vladimir Mayakovsky.
Padilla.   Promise, The.
Pak Mogwŏl [or Mokwŏl].   Bare Wind, A.
Pak Tujin.   Book of Poems.
Palmer, M.   Notes for Echo Lake 3.
Palmer, R.   Sterling Brown.
Pankey.   Unstrung Lyre, The.
Parker, A.   After the Poem Who Knows.
Another Poem about the Vandals.
Cruelty, the Vandals Say.
Practicing Their Diffidence, the Vandals.
Vandals, The.
Vandals Dying, The.
Parker, D.   Bric-à-Brac.
D. G. Rossetti.
Fighting Words.
Pig's-Eye View of Literature, A.
Pour Prendre Congé.
Parnok, S.   Childhood memory: those pears, A.
I shall not lie to find a lurid rhyme.
Parra, N.   Letters from the Poet Who Sleeps in a Chair.
Roller Coaster.
Roller Coaster.
Seven Voluntary Labors and One Seditious Act.
Parry, R.   Propaganda of the Poet, The.
Passerat.   Sonnet Addressed to Henry III on the Death of Thulène, the King's Fool.
Pastan.   Ars Poetica.
Patchen.   Moon, Sun, Sleep, Birds, Live.
Paterson, D.   Poetry: "In the same way that the mindless diamond keeps."
Paulin.   Where Art Is a Midwife.
Pavlov, Konstantin.   Wonderful in Poetry, or a Victim of Goldfish, The.
Pavlova, V.   On the way to you.
Paz.   Between What I See and What I Say.
Peacock, M.   Desire.
Pellicer, C.   To Poetry.
Penna.   Always boys in my poems!
My poetry will not be.
Perelman.   Marginalization of Poetry, The.
Pérez Conde, P.   Ak'a ta majtanal te lotil.
Give Away the Lie.
Regala la mentira.
Persius.   Satire 1: "Who's going to read that?"
Pessoa.   Autopsychography.
"Startling Reality of Things," The.
Pham Tien Duat.   To Return to the Urges Unconscious of their Beginnings.
Phillips, C.   Passing.
Undressing for Li Po.
"Philo-Philippa.".   To the Excellent Orinda.
Pickard, T.   My Pen.
Pietri.   1st Untitled Poem.

10th Untitled Poem.
Title of This Poem Was Lost, The.
Traffic Misdirector.
Piñero. La Bodega Sold Dreams.
Lower East Side Poem, A.
Pinsky. If You Could Write One Great Poem, What Would You Want It to Be About?
Impossible to Tell.
Piombino. Pyramids, The.
Pizarnik. Fragments to Overcome Silence.
Po Chü-i. Long Lines Sent to Ling Hu-Ch'u before He Comes to Visit My Tumbledown Home.
Old, and a Fever.
On Hearing Someone Sing a Poem by Yuan Zhen.
Reading Yuan Chen on a Boat.
Poe. Stanzas.
Pollitt. Poet of Our Climate, A.
Pomerantz, A. Sonnet and Duet for Flapper and Poet.
Ponge. Blackberries.
Blackberries.
Rhetoric.
Pope, A. But most by numbers judge a poet's song.
Popova, O. What's left for me to say? God.
Porter, P. It's there, somewhere in the Platonic cold store.
Pound, E. Further Instructions.
Ité.
Papyrus.
Shades of Callimachus, Coan ghosts of Philetas.
Tenzone.
Powell, D. A. Sonnet: "Morsels of my lifework: the story of a professional party hostess."
Prado, A. Fluency.
In Portuguese.
Siesta.
Pratt, S. Cottage Pictures.
Preil, G. Rain Poem.
Tired Hunter, The.
Radiguet. Poem: "Horizon line."
Radnóti. In Hiding.
Raftery [or Raifteiri]. I Am Raftery [or Raferty].
Mary Hynes.
Ragan, J. Huckster at Noontime.
Rajendra, C. My Message.
Rakosi. In the First Circle of Limbo.
Ramke, B. Enter Celia, with a Writing.
Famous Poems of the Past Explained.
Ranaldo, L. Refugee, A.
Randall, D. Poet Is Not a Jukebox, A.
Randall, M. Poetry Became.
Ratcliff, C. So Gallantly Streaming: To the Poet.
Ratushinskaya [or Ratushinskaia]. Like Mandelstam's swallow.
Ratzlaff, K. My Students against the Cemetery Pines.
Ravikovitch, D. Real Love Isn't What It Seems.
Surely You Remember.
Reddy, Srikanth. Scarecrow Eclogue.
Reeves, J. W.
Remoto. Exile.
Rexroth, K. August 22, 1939.
Reynolds, Elinor Wyn. Night I Won the Crown in the National Eisteddfod of My Dreams, The.
Ricard, R. Oh.
Rich, A. I Am in Danger—Sir.
I know you are reading this poem.
In a Classroom.
Late Ghazal.
Richardson, J. First Lady Challenges a Loa-as-Poem.
Riley, D. Flip, Flop.
Rimbaud, A. Drunken Boat.
Drunken Boat, The.
Hearing the thunder of the intransitive weirs.
Risset, Jacqueline. Love of Poetry.
Ritchie. How to Write a Villanelle.
Ritsos. Meaning of Simplicity, The.
Rivera, L. Disdirected, The.
Roberts, C. Poor Zelda.
Robinson, M. Poet's Garret, The.

[Sonnet] Conclusive.
Sonnet Introductory.
Robles. Ryokan the Crazy Snow Poet.
Rodas. Poems from the Erotic Left.
Rodefer. Brief To Butterick.
Rodney. Bardo of Writing.
Rodriguez, J. How to Be a Street Poet.
Roethke. To an Anthologist.
Rogow, J. Symmetron: You and Brother Will.
Rojas. And to Be Born Is Here an Unnameable Feast.
Rosenstock, G. Search, The: "Where are the poems I promised."
Rosidi, A. Only in Poetry.
Ross, L. Requiescat.
Requiescat.
Ross, W. Another Song.
Rouse, A. Memo to Auden.
Virginian Arcady.
Rowe, V. MRI of a Poet's Brain.
Rózewicz. Questions about Poetry since Auschwitz.
Rubin, L. Houses of Emily Dickinson, The.
Rukeyser, M. Sixth Night: Waking, The.
Rukeyser, M. et al. My night awake.
Russell, T. To Boccaccio.
Ryan, K. Poetry Is a Kind of Money.
Ryokan. How admirable—the fine gentleman.
Who says my poems are poems?
St. John, P. Ars Poetica: "At the edge of the forest."
Saint-Natus, C. Poet, The: "Voice of the drum slowly unravels, The."
Sakaki. Top Ten of American Poetry.
Salaam. Call of the Wild, The.
Salerno. Poetry is the Art of Not Succeeding.
Salinas, L. For Larry Levis in Memory.
Sall, A. Letter to a Roving Poet.
Sanchez, S. To P. J. (2 Yrs Old Who Sed Write a Poem for Me in Portland, Oregon).
Sanfield. I like my poems short.
Santos Chocano. Manifesto, A.
Sappho. Come, divine lyre, speak to me.
When you die you'll lie dead, no memory of you.
Sassoon, S. Limitations.
Sastri, C. Born for Poetry.
Scammell, W. Poem for a Younger Son.
Scarbrough, G. Han-Shan Fashions a Myth.
Scheele. Prose Poem, The.
Schelling. Tyger Tyger.
Schjeldahl. Reading, The.
Younger Poet, A.
Schnackenberg. Then Gabriel sent down a dream that I stood.
Schorn, B. Entering Poetic Blindspots.
Schwartz, D. Sonnet on Famous and Familiar Sonnets and Experiences.
Scott, J. Helen Paints a Room (1984).
Scott, William. Early Aspirations.
Scott, Winfield. Uses of Poetry.
Sedakova. Fifth Stanzas. De Arte Poetica.
Grasshopper and the Cricket, The.
In Memory of a Poet.
Seiferle, R. Muse.
Poetic Voice.
Sengai Gibon. On Basho's "Frog".
Service. Inspiration.
Seward. To Mr. Henry Cary, On the Publication of his Sonnets.
Shakespeare, W. Lunatic, the Lover, and the Poet, The.
Sonnet 54: "O[h] how much more doth beauty beauteous seem."
Sonnet 55: "Not marble, nor the g[u]ilded monuments."
Sonnet 80: "O, how I faint when I of you do write."
Shakhova. Autobiographical Response from a Provincial Wasteland (in Reply to a New Year's Greeting Sent with a Bouquet).
Shamlu, A. Poetry That Is Life.
Shapiro, D. Old Poems.
Shapiro, K. Bourgeois poet closes the door of his study and lights his pipe, The.
Shats, E. Sleep soundly, dear poet.

Shcherbina. Eros Poesis.
Shea, James. Haiku: "Upon Kissing You after You Vomited."
Shiraishi. Seven Cats Are Happy, The.
Shockley, E. N-word, The.
Shoman, K. Cords.
Shwarts [or Shvarts]. Imitation of Boileau.
Sidney P. Sonnet 1: "Loving in truth, and fain[e] in verse my love to show."
Sonnet 15: "You that do search for every purling spring."
Sonnet 74: "I never drank of Aganippe well."
What Length of Verse?
Sigourney. Poetry.
Sikong Tu. Twenty-Four Modes of Poetry.
Simpson, L. American Poetry.
Variations on a Poem by Reznikoff.
Simpson, R. All Friends Together.
Sinclair, I. Serious of Photographs, A.
Skelton, J. Garden of the Muses: Iopas' Song, The.
Than, if this noble kyng.
Slutsky [or Slutskii]. Coppers.
Smith, C. Santa Monica.
Smith, D. Spring Poem, The.
Smith, I. Poem of Lewis.
Smith, R. On Poems.
Smith, Tracy K. History.
Smith, W. Robert Frost: The Road Taken.
Smoker, M. Another Attempt at Rescue.
Snyder, G. As for Poets.
Axe Handles.
How Poetry Comes to Me.
What You Should Know to Be a Poet.
Sŏ Chŏngju. Autumn, 1949: At the "Flower" Tea Room.
Someck, R. Ice Cream.
Song. Poet in the House, A.
Sorrentino. Handbook of Versification.
Sosnora. Supreme Hour, The.
Spacks. Poetry Bug, The.
Spenser, E. October.
Spicer, J. Thing Language.
Sri Sri. Call of Poetry.
Stanford, A. 365 Poems.
Starkey, D. Poet Is Like a Church, The.
Status. In Memory of His Father.
Stefans, Brian Kim. They're Putting a New Door In.
Stevens, W. High-Toned Old Christian Woman, A.
Of Modern Poetry.
Planet on the Table, The.
Poem That Took the Place of a Mountain, The.
Poetry Is a Destructive Force.
Poetry is the subject of the poem.
Soldier, there is a war between the mind.
Ultimate Poem Is Abstract, The.
Stewart, B. Words Is Not Enough.
Stone, J. Getting to Sleep in New Jersey.
Stone, R. Always on the Train.
Poems: "When you come back to me."
Storni. To My Lady of Poetry.
Strand. I am sure you would find it misty here.
Idea, The.
In Memory of Joseph Brodsky.
Strato [or Straton]. Begin with Zeus, Aratus said; but, Muse.
In years to come, I ask, be kind.
Stroud, J. Homage to Life: Jules Supervielle.
Homage to the Word-Hoard.
Stryk, L. Dawn.
Oeuvre.
Su Tung-p'o. On a Painting by Wang the Clerk of Yen Ling.
Thoughts in Exile.
Suárez. Poem, The: "If you start to write a poem."
Sutphen, J. Problem Was, The.
Swirszczynska [or Swir]. Poetry Reading.
Synge. On an Anniversary.
Szymborska, W. In Praise of My Sister.
Words ("La Pologne? La Pologne? It's awfully cold there, isn't it? she asked.").
Taggard. All Around the Town.
To Mr. Maunder Maunder, Professional Poet.

Tanahashi, Kazuaki. One-line poem? Why not one-word poem?

Taneda Santoka. Heaven / doesn't kill me.

Tate, J. Dream On.

  Miss Cho Composes in the Cafeteria.

  Poem to Some of my Recent Poems.

  There's a Certain Point Each Evening.

Taylor, E. Envoy: "Better than any of you, poems."

Tennyson, A. Deep in the night I woke: she, near me, held.

  I sometimes hold it half a sin.

Tennyson, F. Poetical Happiness.

Theocritus. Epitaph: Justice.

Thomas, D. In My Craft or Sullen Art.

Thomas, L. Another Poem in English.

Thomas, R. S. Taliesin 1952.

Thoreau. My life has been the poem I would have writ.

  Poet's Delay, The.

Tobin, D. For Christine at the Frost Farm.

Tolson, M. Nu.

Tomlinson, C. Yamadera.

Torregian. After Mayakovsky.

Torres, A. Kettle Rooted to the Void.

Torres, E. Poetry Detective.

Towle. Night.

Trần Tế Xu'o'ng. New Year's Season and Its Poetasters, The.

Tranströmer. April and Silence.

  Morning Bird Songs.

Tranter. Alphabet Murders, The.

Tripp. Last at Lucy's, The.

Tsanev, Stefan. When a Poet is Born.

Tsvetayeva [or Tsvetaeva]. Like a thick horse's mane.

  Opened my veins—unhaltable.

  Verses: "Written so long ago, I didn't even."

Tu Fu [or Du Fu]. Dreaming of Li Po ("Death separation: sobs hard to swallow.").

  River Pavilion.

  Spring Day: Thinking of Li Po.

  T'ao Ch'ien withdrew from all the world.

  Thoughts on a Night Journey.

  Thoughts, Traveling at Night.

  To Pi Ssu Yao.

Turcotte, M. Indian Things.

Tureski, L. Song, The: "It's the tone, not the harp."

Turnbull. There Are Words.

Turner, C. No trace is left upon the vulgar mind.

Ungria, R. Commerce and the Man.

  Sui Veneris/The Poet of No Return.

Unknown. Bailiff, why your useless plaints about.

  I crossed the deep sea.

  Limerick: "Well, it's partly the shape of the thing."

  Poet Dreamt of Heaven, The.

  Why do these prudes fear Prakrit poetry.

Urusova, E. O Muses! I beseech you, fire my heart with song.

Valente, J. With Plain Words.

Valentine, J. Elegy for Jane Kenyon (2).

Vallejo. Man Walks By with a Loaf of Bread on His Shoulder, A.

Van Doren. First Poem, The.

Van hee. December.

Vando. Commonwealth, Common Poverty.

Vazirani, R. Dedicated to You.

Verlaine. Art of Poetry, The ("Let's hear the music first and foremost.").

  Art of Poetry, The ("You must have music first of all.").

Vicinelli. Crossing the River.

Vietnamese Oral Tradition. Pole at the Village Pagoda, The.

Villaurrutia. Poetry.

Voltaire. Mountain Mountainous in Parturition, A.

Voltskaya, T. Rhyme is a woman, trying on clothes.

Voznesensky [or Voznesenskii]. Mayakovsky in Paris.

Vroman. Regeneration.

Wagner, S. Second Language.

Wagoner, D. Trying to Make Music.

Wah. Father / Mother Haibun #9.

  Music At The Heart Of Thinking 42.

Walcott, B. Much of Your Poetry Is Beautiful.

Waller, K. On the Road to Homer Noble Farm.

Walsh, C. Matter / of fact.

Waltner-Toews, D. Coyotes at Eyebrow Lake, Saskatchewan.

Wang Wei. Bamboo Grove.

Waniek. Emily Dickinson's Defunct.

Warn. Word Between the World and God, The.

Warren, R. Only Poem, The.

Warsh. Free Speech.

  Suicide Rates, The.

Watts-Dunton. Sonnet's Voice, The.

Webb, P. Marvell's Garden.

Wei Ying-wu. Autumn Night Message: To Qiu.

Weinstock, D. You Don't Want to Hear a Poem, Do You?

Weiss, T. After All.

Welch, L. Whenever I Make a New Poem.

Welish. Detained by Rest.

  Textile 9.

  Textile 11.

Welt. I stopped writing poetry.

Wershler-Henry, D. Ten Out of Ten, or, Why Poetry Criticism Sucks in 2003.

Weslowski. Pablo.

Wetzsteon. Poem for a New Year.

  Rival, A.

Whalen, P. International Date Line, Monday/ Monday 27:XI:67.

Wheatley, P. To Maecenas.

Wheelwright. Poem by David McCord, A.

Whitman, W. I am the poet of the Body and I am the poet of the Soul.

  I celebrate myself, and sing myself.

  No Labor-Saving Machine.

  Not Heaving from My Ribb'd Breast Only.

  Out of the Cradle Endlessly Rocking.

  Scented Herbage of My Breast.

  Trickle Drops.

Wickham. Egoist, The.

Wieners. To H.

  With Meaning.

Wilkinson, A. Lens.

Williams, G. After Reading *Poems to Einhir*.

Williams, J. On Reading Aloud My Early Poems.

Williams, W. Coronal, A.

  Some fools once were listening to a poet reading his poem.

Williamson, G. Italics, Mine.

Wilner, E. Ars Poetica: "They wanted from us."

  Theory and Practice in Poetry.

Wilson, S. Contemporary Poet, A.

Winch. Diagnosis.

Wither. Sun hath run his course through all the Signes, The.

Wordsworth, W. Glad Preamble, The.

  Scorn Not the Sonnet [Critic, You Have Frowned].

Wright, C. D. And it Came to Pass.

  Morning Star.

  What Keeps.

Wright, Charles. Cicada Blue.

  In Praise of Han Shan.

  Yard Work.

Wright, J. Brevity.

Wrigley, R. Letter to a Young Poet.

Wylie. Sonnet: "You are the faintest freckles on the hide."

Yadoyano [or Yadoya] Meshimori. When it comes to poets.

Yahya Beg. Poetry holds the written veil across its face, shyly.

Yang Chu-Yuan. Early Spring East of Town.

Yang Wan-li. Don't Read Books!

  Written on a Cold Evening.

Yaqoob, J. Only Choice, The.

Yeats. Adam's Curse.

  When You Are Old.

Yenser, S. Harmonie du Soir.

Yevtushenko [or Evtushenko]. Streetcar Named Poetry, A.

Yi I. Where is the fifth bend?

Yi Kyubo. On Poetry.

  Poetry: A Chronic Disease.

Yonathan, N. Dust of Poems, The.

Young, D. White Crane.

Young, K. Langston Hughes.

Young Bear. Emily Dickinson, Bismarck and the Roadrunner's Inquiry.

Yüan Hao-wen. I know my foolishness, a mere ant trying to shake a tree.

  With Chang Hung-lüeh, Court Attendant, Discussing Literature.

Yun Tongju. Poem That Came Easily, A.

Yuson. World Poetry Circuit.

Yusuf, S. How L'Akhdar Ben Youssef Wrote His Last Poem.

Zabolotsky [or Zabolotskii]. Warning.

  Yesterday Reflecting Upon Death.

Zamora-Linmark. Day 1: Portrait of the Artist, Small-kid Time.

Zarco. Manila Paper.

Zephaniah. According to my Mood.

Zukofsky, L. Anew 20.

  [Dedication].

Poetry: Study and Teaching

Bell, M. First Poem: "Bulletin board flutters with a flair, The."

Davies, Mererid Puw. Poet on 'Poets on Poets', A: And Other Poems.

Gu Cheng. Solar Flare.

Juan Chi. Confucianist is versed in the Six Arts, The.

Kingsolver. Beating Time.

Kingston, M. Idea!: Four-word poems!

Li Po. Ages have passed since the stately Odes flourished.

  To Send to Tu Fu as a Joke.

Matthews, W. Inspiration: "Rumpled, torpid, bored, too tasteful to rhyme."

Parra, N. Note on the Lessons of Antipoetry.

Pizarnik. Foundation Stone.

Reznikoff. My grandfather, dead long before I was born.

Smith, P. Great Pat Smith American Dreampoem, The.

Yen Shu. Tune: "Sand of Silk-Washing Brook".

Pogroms

Abu Ishaq al-Ilbin. O say to all of the inhāja, the full moons of the time, and the lions of the thicket.

Boroditskaya, M. Christmas Eve.

Hoornik. Pogrom.

Utkin. Tale of Red-Haired Motele, Mister Inspector, Rabbi Isaiah and Commissar Blokh, The.

See also **Massacres**

Poison

Apollinaire. Meadow Saffron.

Atwood. Making Poison.

Berrigan, T. Mid-Friday morn, 10 o'clock, I go to India.

Coleridge, M. Poison Flower, The.

Crockett-Smith, D. Hell Hound Blues.

Empson. Missing Dates.

Enzensberger, H. Poison, The.

Góngora y Argote. Sonnet 82.

Heine, H. Envenomed are my songs.

Herbert, Z. Return of the Proconsul, The.

Heyen. Poison.

Higgins, R. Power of Prayer, The.

Ivanov, G. Oh, how fastidious you once were.

Kim Chôngnan. Woman I Carelessly Killed, The.

Kizer, C. On a Line from Valéry.

Notley. Where Leftover Misery Goes.

Padel, R. Yew Berries.

Pinkerton, H. Nature Note: The California Poison Oak.

Stewart, S. Apple.

Unknown. Death of Yesugei, The.

  Lord Randal[l].

Upton, L. Scroll.

Poker

Montgomery, Vaida Stewart. Cattle Brands.

Nance. Frontier Mystery.

Rexroth, K.   Proust's Madeleine.

Poland
Baranczak, S.   December 14, 1979: A Poetry Reading.
Borowski.   Project: Flag.
  Two Countries.
Charles, J. B.   Polish Girl Standing on a Chair, A.
Ettinger, E.   Micrographic Manuscript, Miniature (2).
Goldbarth.   Recipe.
Herbert, Z.   Report from the Besieged City.
Jastrun, T.   Polish Knot, The.
Milosz, C.   Dedication: "You whom I could not save."
  My Faithful Mother Tongue.
  With Her.
Norwid, C.   But Just to See.
Pawlikowska-Jasnorzewska, M.   Polish Colours.
Quinn, J.   Linger, tag, let go.
Reznikoff.   When the Second World War began.
Slonimski.   Elegy: "No more, no more Jewish townships in Poland."
Swirszczynska [or Swir].   Conversation Through the Door, A.
Szymborska, W.   Words ("La Pologne? La Pologne? It's awfully cold there, isn't it? she asked.").
Wat.   Imagerie d'Epinal.
Zagajewski.   To Go to Lvov.
  Watching Shoah in a Hotel Room in America.

Police and Police Stations
Ai.   Endangered Species.
Baraka, R.   Five-0.
Baranczak, S.   Three Magi, The.
Bennett, L.   South Parade Peddler.
Betjeman.   Arrest of Oscar Wilde at the Cadogan Hotel, The.
Brown, S.   Southern Cop.
Chesterton.   Christmas Carol, A: "God rest you merry gentlemen."
Clewell.   Poem for the Man Who Said Shit.
Clifton, L.   Powell (officer charged with the beating of rodney king).
Cortez, J.   Give me the Red on the Black of the Bullet (for Claude Reece Jr.).
  Rape.
Cortez, Sarah.   Interlude: "I watch a handsome young female."
Davis, F.   Sam Jackson.
Domina, L.   Pharoah's Army Got Drowned.
Eady.   False Arrest.
Espada.   Community College Revises Its Curriculum in Response to Changing Demographics, The.
Fogarty, L.   Remember Something Like This.
Garcia, R.   Diver for the NYPD Talks to His Girlfriend, A.
Garioch.   Fair Cop, A.
George, B.   In this day and age.
Ginsberg, A.   Kral Majales.
Hahn, K.   Mortal Remains.
Heaney, S.   Constable Calls, A.
Heyen.   King's Men, The.
Jackson, B.   Riot at Winchell's.
Jackson, M. L.   Pest.
Jacob, M.   Horrible Today, The.
Jones, J.   Drugs.
Kelly, Erren Geraud.   7-30-96.
Kharms.   Event on the Street, An.
Laing, K.   Tatale Swine.
Lehman.   First Offense.
Leonard, T.   Before the 1820 rising in the West of Scotland a network of.
  Evidence, The.
Lytton, E.   Sordid Scene.
McGough, R.   P.C. Plod versus the Dale St. Dog Strangler.
Mora.   La Migra.
Muske, C.   Field Trip.
Nasir.   Parade.
Parker, D.   Sand.
Pawlak.   Protective and Defensive Devices.
Perillo, L.   Skin: "Back then it seemed that wherever a girl took off her clothes the police would find her."

Press, K.   Rotten fish.
  This is not a riot policeman.
Randall, D.   Idiot, The.
Reverdy.   That.
Rodriguez, L.   To the Police Officer Who Refused to Sit in the Same Room as My Son because He's a "Gang Banger".
Sadoff.   Civil Rights.
Sanchez, S.   Philadelphia: Spring, 1985.
Sen, R.   World-Mother's police chief, The.
Sheeler, J.   This Old Man.
Shy, S.   Bringing My Son to the Police Station to Be Fingerprinted.
Sondheim.   Gee, Officer Krupke.
Sutton, V.   While Watching *Cops* I Think of You.
Takei, Sojin.   While the MP's wait.
Taylor, M.   Well-Bred Woman, A.
Wieners.   Poem for vipers, A.
Williamson, G.   Appalachian Trees Encircled by Police Tape.
Wright, K.   Sergeant Brown's Parrot.

Police Brutality
Agüeros.   Psalm for Amadou Diallo.
Cherry, J.   Amadou.
Dufflar, C.   Amadou Diallo from Guinea to the Bronx Dead on Arrival.
Graham, J.   Hiding Place, The.
Jabeen, M.   Live Walls.
Johnson, L.   Sonny's Lettah.
Moore, M.   Another Scream.
Parra, N.   To Make a Long Story Short.
Pawlak.   Protective and Defensive Devices.
Press, K.   This is not a riot policeman.

Police States
Akhmatova, A.   Requiem: "No foreign sky protected me."
  Requiem: "No, not under the vault of alien skies."
Baranczak, S.   December 14, 1979: A Poetry Reading.
  February 8, 1980: And No One Has Warned Me.
Bobrowski.   Report.
Brutus.   Somehow We Survive.
  Sounds Begin Again, The.
Chimsoro.   Curfew Breakers, The.
Chipasula.   Love Poem for My Country, A.
de Jesús.   Curfew.
Gwala.   From the Outside.
Hecht, A.   More Light! More Light!
M-1.   Police State.
Muir, E.   Interrogation, The.
Ofeimun.   Handle for the Flutist, A.
Ratushinskaya [or Ratushinskaia].   But Only Not to think.
Serge.   Dialectic.
Sticman.   Police State.

Political Parties
Fried, E.   Retrospect.
Lourie.   Portrait in Rhythm and Blues.
Mohammad, K. Silem.   Mars Needs Terrorists.
Newman, H.   Testimonial.
Scharpenberg, Margot (b. 1924).   Field of Red Tulips.

Political Poetry
MacDiarmid, H.   British Leftish Poetry, 1930–40.

Politics and Politicians
Abrahams, L.   At revolution's end.
Agosin.   Disappeared Woman V.
Ai.   Blue Suede Shoes.
  Self Defense.
Alegría.   Toward the Jurassic Age.
Allen, S.   View from the Corner.
Andrade, O.   Election.
Angira.   Obbligato from a Public Gallery.
Aspden, B.   News of the Changes.
Auden.   Statesmen.
Balakian, P.   End of the Reagan Era, The.
Baldwin, Sandy.   Basic system code.
Baraka, I.   Clay.
Behn, A.   Cabal at Nickey Nackeys, The.
Belloc.   Epitaph on the Politician Himself.
  On a General Election.

This, the last ornament among the peers.
Benét, S.   Congressmen Came Out To See Bull Run.
Bierce.   Safety-Clutch.
  Statesmen, The.
Boadiba.   Madam President.
Borawski.   Some of Us Wear Pink Triangles.
Broumas, O.   Artemis.
Brutus.   Their Behaviour.
Burnett, W.   My Shadow.
Cabico, R.   Check One.
Cardenal.   For Those Dead, Our Dead.
  Psalm 5: "Give ear to my words, O Lord."
Carruth, H.   Republicans? We've got a few. In fact.
Cervantes.   Poem for the Young White Man Who Asked Me How I, An Intelligent, Well-Read Person Could Believe in the War Between Races.
Chasin.   Getting the News.
Chesterton.   Elegy in a Country Churchyard.
Chipasula.   Going Back Patiently.
Clark Bekedermo.   Casualties, The.
Cohan.   If Washington Should Come to Life.
Corrie.   Rebel Tam.
Cowper, W.   Great princes have great playthings. Some have played.
Cummings, E. E.   Next to of course god america i.
  Politician, A.
  Salesman, A.
  Way to hump a cow is not, The.
Dailey.   S'what Up.
Davie, D.   Barnsley and District.
Davies, B.   Berne.
Davies, I.   Angry Summer, The ("From Abertillery and Aberdare.").
Dodge, M.   Mayor of Scuttleton, The.
Dunn, S.   To a Terrorist.
Durcan.   Divorce Referendum, Ireland, 1986, The.
  Irish Hierarchy Bans Colour Photography.
Earley, T.   Rebel's Progress.
Ekelof.   Monologue with Its Wife.
Elliott, E.   Fatal Birth, The.
Espada.   All the People Who Are Now Red Trees.
  Cockroaches of Liberation.
Ezenwa-Ohaeto.   I Wan Bi President.
Ferguson, S.   Lament for the Death of Thomas Davis.
Finkel.   Party, The.
Friedman, E.   Cultivation.
Galich.   Goldminers' Waltz, The.
Gamalinda, E.   La Naval De Manila: Selim Sot as a Modern Political Observer.
Gil de Biedma, J.   In the Forties.
Gilbert, W.   Gilbertian Cats.
Ginsberg, A.   America: "America I've given you all and now I'm nothing."
  Kral Majales.
Glück, R.   Pasolini.
Gowar.   Rat Trap.
Hanson, M.   How proudly Man usurps the power to reign.
Harjo, J.   Wolf Warrior.
Harper, F.   Aunt Chloe's Politics.
Hass, R.   After I Seized the Pentagon.
Helle, A.   Poem for Natalia Ginzburg.
Hilmi, F.   Political Parties.
Hippolyte.   Revo Lyric.
Hollo.   Dream of Instant Total Representation, The.
Hone.   Political House that Jack Built, The.
  This is THE MAN—all shaven and shorn.
Hove.   Child's Parliment.
Hsiao Kang.   Pheasant on His Morning Flight, A.
Hughes, L.   Un-American Investigators.
Hugo, V.   That Night.
Hwang Jiwoo.   Variety Show, 1984.
Ismaili.   Bajji.
Ivanov, G.   Oh, how fastidious you once were. Should I tell of all the absolute fools.
Jacob, M.   Rooster and the Pearl, The.
Jeffers, R.   Sinverguenza.

Stars Go Over the Lonely Ocean, The.
Joans, T.   Skip The Byuppie.
Johnson, L.   Mi Revalueshanary Fren.
Jones, M.   Election Reflection.
Jonson, B.   To the Same [Robert, Earl of Salisbury] [Upon the Accension of the Treasurership to Him].
Jordan, J.   Poem About My Rights.
Kearney, L.   Man with His Kids on a Table, The.
Khlebnikov, V.   Trumpet, Shout, Carry!
Kim Suyŏng.   Emerging from the Old Palace One Day.
Ha . . . No Shadows.
Kinsella, J.   Bright Cigar-Shaped Object Hovers Over Mount Pleasant, A.
Kipling, R.   Dead Statesman, A.
Klein, A.   Political Meeting.
Kleinzahler.   Spleen.
Krivulin.   And the silver age, unattainable.
Kyger.   Deeply Immoral Arrogant and Ignorant.
Laing, K.   Same Corpse, The.
Lanier, S.   Laughter in the Senate.
Lao Tzu.   Let there be a small state with few people.
Lee, D.   1838.
Leland, C.   There's a liddle fact of hishdory vitch few hafe oondershtand.
Leonard, T.   Before the 1820 rising in the West of Scotland a network of.
Li Po.   Third month in T'ientsin, The.
Li Shang-yin.   Master Chia.
Lindley, D.   Marxist to Liberals, A.
Lindsay, V.   Bryan, Bryan, Bryan, Bryan.
Why I Voted the Socialist Ticket.
Logue, C.   I Shall Vote Labour.
Lourie.   Portrait in Rhythm and Blues.
Lowell, J.   Boss, The.
Macartney.   Kyrielle: Party Politics.
Margolis, G.   Town Meeting.
Maxton.   Urgent Letter, An.
McClure, M.   Senate Hearings.
McDonald, C.   Asdrubral Jiménez.
Milosz, C.   You Who Wronged.
Miyazawa Kenji.   Politicians, The.
Moore, T.   Tory Pledges.
Morisseau-Leroy, F.   Down with All Candidates.
Nogueras, L.   Poem, A.
Notley.   State of the Union.
Nurkse.   Olmos.
Ojaide.   Launching Our Community Developement Fund.
Okigbo.   Elegy for Alto.
Parra, N.   Discourse of the Good Thief, The.
Petty.   Great Poll-Tax Victory of '88, The.
Philips, K.   To Antenor.
"Pindar.".   Epigram: "Midas, they say, possessed the art of old."
Po Chü-i.   Iranian Whirling Girls.
Potts.   Comrade Laugher.
Praed.   Chancery Morals.
Prior.   Fable, A: "In Æsop's tales an honest wretch we find."
Quinn, J.   Backgrounds.
You meet them at mid-afternoon receptions.
Ravikovitch, D.   Unusual Autumn, An.
Rich, A.   History.
Rodas.   Poems from the Erotic Left.
Rome, H.   Doing the Reactionary.
Sackville, C.   My Opinion.
Sanguineti.   I defended Genet on the subject of terror in London.
I tell you it was a hard punch to my brain.
To the mini-skirted customs official who with sibyl-dove eyes.
Schreiber, R.   Public Stammer, The.
Scott, F.   W. L. M. K.
Shakespeare, W.   Go bind thou up young dangling apricots.
Sidney, P.   Sonnet 30: "Whether the Turkish new moon minded be."
Smith-Soto, M.   How It Happened.
Sŏ Chŏngju.   Autumn, 1949: At the "Flower" Tea Room.
Sosnora.   Supreme Hour, The.
Spahr, J.   January 28, 2003.

Swift, J.   Character of Sir Robert Walpole, The.
Taylor, C.   Scroll No. 2.
Teschke, H.   Documentary Film.
Thelwall.   To Ancestry.
Vanity of National Grandeur, The.
Unknown.   Age of War, The.
Eccho, An.
Make quiet, so quiet, your awesome bearing.
Old-Saxon Fragment.
Withered, withered, by the wind's omen.
Villa, D.   It is.
Waniek.   Alderman.
Watkyns.   Common People, The.
Watts, I.   Mr. Mead, Mr. Bates, and Mr. Gouge [or An Elegy on Mr. Thomas Gouge].
Wheelwright.   Anathema. Maranatha!
Whitman, W.   Thought ("Of obedience, faith, adhesiveness.").
To a President.
Wilner, E.   Found in the Free Library.
Woddis.   Doctor, The.
I Shall Vote Centre.
Wright, D.   Cockermouth.
Wright, J.   Eisenhower's Visit to Franco, 1959.
Yeats.   Politics.
Yüan Chĕn.   Iranian Whirling Girls.
Zenmaro.   Tanka: "Work on the impossible."

Pollock, Jackson
Hirsch, E.   Magic Mirror, The.
Johnson, Harold L.   At the Jackson Pollock Retrospective in L.A.
Martinez, D.   Moto Perpetuo.
McClure, M.   Ode to Jackson Pollock.
McGinley.   Squeeze Play.

Pollution
Adesuyi, N.   New Testament, The.
Aliesan.   There is no real edge to anything.
Baker, D.   Works and Days.
Benevento, Joe.   Yankees in East Texas.
Bennett, R.   Smoke Animals.
Chaloner.   Unnamed.
Citino.   Sea of Kansas, Ohio Tundra, Time Still Running Out, The.
Cronin, A.   Trembling with engines, gulping oil, the river.
Dupree, E.   At Present I Am Working as a Security Guard.
Eliot, T. S.   3. The Fire Sermon.
Feld, Andrew.   Boxers, The.
Gay, Garry.   Hole in the ozone.
Ginsberg, A.   Homework.
Hoffmann, R.   Bering Bridge, The.
Howard, B.   River's Answer, The.
Johnson, A.   Oil on Troubled Waters.
Kendall, M.   Underground.
Kizer, C.   On a Line from Valéry.
Major, C.   Water USA.
Marshall, J.   Wing and Prayer.
Meredith, W.   Country Stars.
Nuriddin, J. M.   Children of the Future.
Oles.   Radioactive Ball, The.
Ortiz.   Vision Shadows.
Reed, I.   El Paso Monologue.
Reznikoff.   They have built red factories along Lake Michigan.
Roy, T.   Nowadays.
Seward.   Scene of superfluous grace, and wasted bloom.
Spacks.   Malediction.
Welch, L.   Sausalito Trash Prayer.
See also **Conservation; Ecology and Ecologists**

Polo
Various authors.   It was a polo match played by royal order.

Polo, Marco
Tomlinson, C.   Epilogue: "This advanced frontier."

Polyandry
Aig-Imoukhuede.   One Wife for One Man.
See also **Marriage; Monogamy and Monogamists**

Pomegranates
Boland, E.   Pomegranate, The.
Delgado, J.   Winter Fruit.
Elytis, O.   Mad Pomegranate Tree, The.
Hildebrandt, Z.   Persephone.

Hirshfield, J.   Pomegranates.
Janzen, J.   Pomegranate.
Khoury, N.   People of Pomegranates.
Lawrence, D. H.   Andraitx—Pomegranate Flowers.
Lejeune, Claire.   Death, I Speak of It.
Soloukhin.   How to Drink the Sun.
Unknown.   Pick a pomegranate.

Pompeii, Italy
Goldbarth.   Counterfeit Earth!, The.
Hemans.   Image in Lava, The.
Ray, H.   Listening Nydia.
Scupham.   Pompeii: Plaster Casts.

Ponds
Basho.   Ancient silent pond.
Harvest moon.
Old pond / Leap-splash.
Old pond, The.
Old pond, The.
Old pond—frogs jumped in—sound of water.
Old-time pond, from off whose shadowed depth, An.
Still old pond, The.
There is the old pond!
Brouwer, J.   Conservatory Pond, Central Park, New York, New York.
Buson.   Straw sandal half sunk.
Clare, J.   Old pond full of flags and fenced around, The.
Holley, M.   Dancer, The.
Issa.   Its mother on guard.
New Year's morning.
Kinnell.   Vapor Trail Reflected in the Frog Pond.
Kuan Hsiu.   Nacreous land had no dust, The.
Lea, S.   Fish Pond, The [1993] ("Not full of fish—that's imprecise—but full.").
Malouf.   For Two Children.
Menicanti.   If.
Merriam, E.   Summer's End.
Mills, R.   Water Lilies.
Morris, M.   Pond, The.
Muso Soseki.   Hui-neng's Pond.
Naong.   Playing at Jeoksun Pond on a Moonlit Night.
Paloff, B.   On Transportation.
Schuyler, J.   Can I Tempt You to a Pond Walk?
Serrano, P.   Pool.
Poza.
Shinkichi Takahashi.   Near Shinobazu Pond.
Sorescu, M.   Pond.
Swift, J.   Steelhead in the Whitehorse Rearing Pond.
Tomlinson, C.   Shugakuin Garden.
Tu Mu.   Basin Pond.
Unknown.   Deep in the Forest.
Voigt.   Stone Pond.
Wright, C.   Ponds, in Love.
See also **Lakes and Ponds**

Ponies
Basho.   Lead my pony.
Guiterman.   Three Ponies.
Harte, B.   Tale of a Pony, The.
Harvey, M.   Crowds Cheered as Gloom Galloped Away, The.
Martinaitis, M.   Pony in Kukutis's Ear, A.
Wright, J.   Blessing, A: "Just off the highway to Rochester, Minnesota."

Pontius Pilate
Daumal.   Jesus Before Pilate.
Davie, D.   Pilate.

Pony Express
Crowell, N.   Texas Trails.
Dobyns.   Pony Express.

Pool (game)
Baker, D.   8-Ball at the Twilite.
Brooks, G.   We Real Cool.
Carruth, H.   Capper Kaplinski at the North Side Cue Club.
Haug.   Pool is a Godless Sport.
Jackson, R.   Eight Ball.

Pope, Alexander
Edwards, T.   On the Edition of Mr. Pope's Works with a Commentary and Notes.
Gay, J.   Mr. Pope's Welcome from Greece.
Montagu, L.   Epitaph: "Here lies John Hughes

and Sarah Drew."
  When God created thee, one would believe.
Tate, A.   Mr. Pope.
Unknown.   On the Death of Mr. Pope.
Winchilsea.   Answer, The [To Pope's
  Impromptu].

Popes
Healy, E.   Pope at 7:00 P.M., The.
Olds, S.   Pope's Penis, The.
Tate, J.   How the Pope is Chosen.

Poplar Trees
Cowper, W.   Poplar Field, The.
De Roux, Paul.   Cold Again, The.
Doolittle, H.   Mid-day.
Egemo.   Silver Poplar at Sunrise.
Hopkins, G.   Binsey Poplars (Felled 1879).
Raab, E.   Serenade for Two Poplars, A.
Sedakova.   Female Figure.
See also **Aspen Trees**

Poppies
Aygi, G.   Poppies of This Year.
Bellinger, A. R.   Bright as a single poppy in a
  field.
Coolbrith.   Copa de Oro (The California Poppy).
Curry, N.   Poppy Heads.
Doolittle, H.   Sea Poppies.
Doubleday, T.   Poppies, that scattered o'er this
  arid plain.
Foster, A.   Field.
Glück, L.   Red Poppy, The.
Hamilton, S.   Poppy, The.
Harrison, D.   Formula for Blue Blues Babies.
Hokushi.   Writing / Rubbing it out—.
Hooson, I.   Red Poppy, The.
Janevski.   Silence.
Jones, Nesta Wyn.   Poppies.
Plath.   Poppies in October.
Press, K.   She brought home poppies.
St. John, D.   Black Poppy (At the Temple).
Seward.   To the Poppy.
Sŏ Chŏngju.   Midday.
Stephens, J.   In the Poppy Field.
Unamuno.   Black Heart.
Warner, S.   Drawing You, Heavy With Sleep.

Porcupines
Amor, P.   CXXX.
Finlay, I.   Gift: "How silly and how dear, how
  very dear."
Kinnell.   Porcupine, The.
Welch, J.   Day after Chasing Porcupines.

Pornography
Anderson, J.   Ode to Pornography.
Andrews, N.   Zen 101.
Cadwallender, K.   Baz and the Freedom of the
  Press.
Campbell, S.   Legacy.
Cooper, D.   Being Aware.
  No God.
Davis, C.   Pietà.
Hall, D.   X.
Hass, R.   Pornographer, The.
Knox, J.   Pastoral with Internet Porn.
MacKenzie, R.   Like Pornography.
Nemerov.   Reading Pornography in Old Age.
Penna.   Found—my little angel.
Pitt-Kethley.   God made the sex-shop keeper.
Porter, P.   Now it's in all the novels, what's
  pornography to do?
Shaw, A.   Pornography.
Trinidad.   As one young guy screwed another
  young guy.
Wallace, R.   Thirteen.
Wojahn.   My Father's Pornography.
See also **Obscenity**

Porter, Cole
Bentley, N.   On Lady A———.
Coward.   Let's Do It.

Porters
Razaf, A.   Porter's Love Song to a
  Chambermaid, A.

Portia
Kirk, Kathleen.   Portia.

Portland, Maine
Longfellow, H.   My Lost Youth.

Portraits
Ashbery, J.   Self-Portrait in a Convex Mirror.
Bandeira.   Portrait.
Blood, B.   Stop!—Gaze thro' this hushed
  gallery! The air.
Boland, E.   Self-Portrait on a Summer Evening.
Browning, E.   On a Portrait of Wordsworth by
  B. R. Haydon.
Browning, R.   My Last Duchess.
Coleman, A.   Portraiture.
Cowper, W.   On the Receipt of My Mother's
  Picture out of Norfolk, the Gift of My Cousin
  Ann Bodham.
  On the Receipt of My Mother's Picture out of
  Norfolk [the Gift of My Cousin Ann
  Bodham].
Cruz, C.   Self Portrait in Horse Hair Wig.
De la Mare.   Portrait, A.
Donne.   His Picture.
Edwards, T.   Sonnet on a Family Picture.
Eliot, T. S.   Lines for Cuscuscaraway and Mirza
  Murad Ali Beg.
Erinna.   Delicate hands fashioned this portrait:
  good Prometheus.
Fanthorpe.   Portraits of Tudor Statesmen.
Foppa.   First Portrait of My Son.
Gogarty.   Portrait with Background.
Graham, M.   Matthew Brady Speaks of
  Whitman.
Graves, R.   Face in the Mirror, The.
Halleck, F.   Red Jacket.
Hồ Xuân Huong.   On a Portrait of Two
  Beauties.
Howard, R.   Nadar.
Howells, W.   Royal Portraits, The.
Issa.   Even considered.
Jonson, B.   Picture of the Body, The.
Juana Inés de la Cruz.   On Her Portrait.
  On Her Portrait.
Klyuyev [or Kliuev or Klyuev].   Can I Tell You
  My Love with a Portrait.
Kowit.   Whitman Portrait, A.
Leapor.   On Winter.
Lezama Lima.   Portrait of José Cemí.
Machado Ruiz.   Portrait.
Malé.   And Here are the Poets in Their Sad
  Portraits.
Mariani.   Shadow Portrait.
Martial.   Epigram: Likeness, The.
  This was the young Camonus; this his face.
Massey.   Dead Boy's Portrait and His Dog, The.
Mays, M.   #4, In Red.
McPherson, S.   Six Movements for Portraits of
  Erzulie.
Meireles.   Portrait.
Melville, H.   Formerly a Slave.
Molina, E.   To Vahine (Painted by Gaugin).
Moody, W.   Faded Pictures.
Morejón.   Angela Dominguez, Ever Present.
North, M.   Portrait in a Brass Gong.
Nossis.   Even from a distance, this picture is
  known.
  Kallo dedicated her portrait in the house of
  golden.
  This portrait captures Thaumareta's form—it
  renders.
Po Chü-i.   On a Portrait of the Poet.
Ramanujan.   Self-Portrait.
Rossetti, C.   In An Artist's Studio.
Rowlands.   Epigram 29: "Gentlewoman of the
  dealing trade, A."
St. John, D.   Portrait: "There is in his daughter's
  gaze."
Sánchez Peláez.   Portrait of the Beautiful
  Unknown Woman.
Sawyer, A.   Lines, / Written on Seeing My
  Husband's Picture, painted when he was
  young: "Those are the features, those the
  smiles."
Seiffert.   Cubist Portrait.
Shiomi, M.   Portrait Piece.
Sōsan, Great Master.   In Praise of the Portrait of
  My Former Master.
Tate, A.   Sonnet: To a Portrait of Hart Crane.
Teillier, J.   Portrait of My Father, Militant
  Communist.

Trethewey, N.   Vignette.
Vietnamese Oral Tradition.   Painting, The.
Wetzsteon.   Dinner at Le Caprice.
Wylie.   Castilian.
  Self-portrait.
See also **Painting and Painters; Photography and
Photographers**

Ports
Anwar, C.   Light Leaving a Small Harbour.
Laleau.   Hot Ports.
Lane, P.   Port Townsend Poems.
Masefield.   Port of Holy Peter.
See also **Harbors and Ports**

Portugal and the Portuguese
Andrade, O.   Portuguese Mistake.
Johnson, J.   Saudades.
Lear, E.   Limerick: "There was a young lady of
  Portugal."
Mapanje.   After Wiriyamu Village Massacre by
  Portuguese.
Prado, A.   In Portuguese.
Wyatt.   In Spayn.

Poseidon

Posterity
Bécquer, G.   To See the Hours of Fever.
Byron, G.   Last Words on Greece.
Emerson, R.   Limits.
Enright, D.   Posterity.
Herrick.   Upon His Verses.
Laughlin, J.   My Ambition.
MacLeish.   Epistle to Be Left in the Earth.
  Sentiments for a Dedication.
Padilla.   Legacies.
Prismanova.   Brontë Sisters, The.
Ramke, B.   Paul Verlaine at the Grave of Lucien
  Létinois.
Sappho.   I say someone in another time will
  remember us.
Shapiro, K.   Manhole Covers.
Shwarts [or Shvarts].   Sale of a Historian's
  Library.
Snyder, G.   For the Children.
Thomas, R. S.   Gifts.
Whitman, W.   Full of Life Now.
  No Labor-Saving Machine.
Young, A.   Fifty-Fifty.

Postmen
Molloy, D.   Postman's Knock.
Sage, C.   Retired Postman Recalls the Old
  Route, A.
Sholl.   Postmaster's Children, The.
See also **Mail and Mailmen**

Potatoes
Bly, R.   Potato, A.
Bryan, T.   Planting Potatoes during Chernobyl.
Buson.   Harvest moon.
Curtis, L.   Potato, The.
Donnell.   Potatoes.
France, L.   Chip City.
Heaney, S.   Digging.
Hogan, L.   Potatoes.
Hugo, R.   Way a Ghost Dissolves, The.
Hwang, Cynthia.   Potato Manifesto, The.
Irwin, T.   Potato-Digger's Song, The.
Kavanagh, P.   Fields were bleached white, The.
  Spraying the Potatoes.
Komunyakaa, Y.   Banking Potatoes.
Lindley, D.   Potato Blight.
Macari, A.   After the Rain.
Martinaitis, M.   Unhappy Kukutis in the Potato
  Patch.
Michaelis.   Brilliantly Philosophising.
Mitchell, A.   Giving Potatoes.
Mueller, L.   Hope.
Saarikoski.   Potato Thief.
Shinkichi Takahashi.   Sweet Potato.
Unknown.   Bugs.
  Riddle: "Riddle a riddle as I suppose, A."

Potomac River
Aldrich, T.   By the Potomac.
Beers, E.   All Quiet Along the Potomac.
Hovey.   Evening on the Potomac.

Pottery and Potters
Bell, M.   Drawn by Stones, by Earth, by Things
  That Have Been in the Fire.

Donovan, K. Potter's House, The.
Field. Life Plastic.
Forbes, C. Potter's Wheel, The.
Hollander, J. Mad Potter, The.
Hufana, A. Contemporary.
Hugo, V. Broken Vase, The.
Komunyakaa, Y. Back Then.
Masaoka Shiki. Thing long forgotten.
Miller, A. Song of the Wheel.
Miller, E. What the Women Told Me.
Mistral, G. Earthen Jugs.
Mullen, L. Alba.
Naranjo-Morse. Tradition and Change.
Vidya. Fate Is a Cruel and Proficient Potter.

Pound, Ezra
Berryman. Cage, The.
Bukowski. Drooling Madness at St. Liz.
Bunting. On the Fly-Leaf of Pound's Cantos.
Eichner, Maura. Imagist at Coney Island.
Holub. Brief Reflection on Brief Reflections.
  Meeting Ezra Pound.
Larkin, T. Cho-Fu-Sa.
Levertov. September 1961.
López Mills, T. Ending by Pound, An.
  Final de Pound, Un.
Lopez, T. Studies in Classic American
  Literature.
Lowell, R. Ezra Pound.
MacLeish. Epistle to the Rapalloan.
Morton, J. Another Canto.
Nichols, R. Talking of Ezra Pound and long-
  dead pantos.
Pilling. Dear Ez.
Rawls, Alex. H. S. Mauberley (Life and
  Contacts) Part 1 by Ezra Pound.
Ruark. Robert Frost to Ezra Pound's Daughter
  from His Deathbed.
Scott, J. Typing the Letters.
Snyder, G. Axe Handles.
Starbuck, G. Said ("J. Alfred Prufrock to.").

Poussin, Nicolas
Clark, T. J. Landscape with a Calm.

Poverty
Addonizio. Broken Sonnets.
Agüeros. Psalm for Distribution.
  Psalm for the Next Millennium.
Aizenberg, M. So where is that guy who left us
  piles.
Alexie. After the Trial of Hamlet, Chicago.
Andrade, E. Penniless Lovers.
Ashbery, J. Street Musicians.
Awoonor. Agosu if you go tell them.
Baraka, I. Short Speech to My Friends.
Barbauld. To the Poor.
Basho. Come out to view.
Beach, L. 2 Months Rent Due and 1 Bag of
  Rice.
Beecher, J. Appalachian Landscape.
Belli, C. Father, Mother.
  Segregation #1.
Berlin. I Got the Sun in the Morning.
Bernstein, C. Our new / service orientation.
Bishop, E. Miracle for Breakfast, A.
  Pink Dog.
Blackman, P. Sometimes all night I kept vigil
  with men stripped of their flesh.
Blake, W. Holy Thursday [1].
  Holy Thursday [2].
  London.
  London: "I wander through [or thro'] each
  chartered [or charter'd] street."
Blane, R. I Never Felt Better.
Bolton, J. American Tragedy.
Borges. Matthew 25:14–30; "For it will be as
  when a man".
Brand, D. Thirsty.
Brandt, D. There are no words in me for Gaza,
  for what i saw.
Brecht, B. Concerning the Infanticide, Marie
  Farrar.
  From a German War Primer.
Brooks, G. Bean Eaters, The.
  Lovers of the Poor, The.
  Novelle; My Grandmother Is Waiting For Me
  To Come Home.
  Tinsel Marie; The Coora Flower.

To An Old Black Woman, Homeless and
  Indistinct.
Bunina. Though poverty's no stain.
Burns, R. For A' That and A' That ["Is there,
  for honest poverty"].
Buson. Priestly poverty—.
  That handsaw marks time.
Butterfield, F. G. For Services Rendered.
Carbó, N. Votive Candles.
  When the Grain Is Golden and the Wind Is
  Chilly, Then It Is the Time to Harvest.
Cassells. Courtesy, A Trenchant Grace, A.
Castera, G. Zilch Movement.
Célestin-Mégie, E. I'm Writing a Poem.
Cervantes. To We Who Were Saved by the
  Stars.
Chavez, L. After the Prom.
Cheney-Coker. Peasants.
  Poet Among Those Who Are Also Poets.
Ch'i-chi. Old Farmer, The.
Clanchy, K. Foreign.
Clare, J. My Mary.
Clarke, A. Envy of Poor Lovers, The.
Clarke, G. Second Hand Rose.
Clifton, L. Good Times.
Coleman, W. Aunt Jessie.
  Where I Live.
Coleridge, M. Insincere Wish Addressed to a
  Beggar, An.
Coles, R. Goddam Street, The.
Constantine, D. Door, The.
Cook, C. Will Run Like Rabbits for Food.
Cope, W. Variation on Belloc's "Fatigue".
Cortez, J. Global Inequalities.
Costanzo. Everything You Own.
Cowley, M. Winter Tenement.
Crabbe, G. Baileys, The.
  Peter Grimes.
  Village Life.
D'Aguiar, F. Dreadtalk.
Darling, J. Poverty.
Davidson, J. Thirty Bob a Week.
Davidson, M. Framing.
Davies, I. Angry Summer, The ("Mrs. Evans
  fach, you want butter again.").
Davis, G. Children in the Arbor.
Day Lewis. Carol, A.
  Song: "Come, live with me and be my love."
Dekker, T. et al. Happy Heart, The.
Dharker. Namesake.
Dickinson, E. None can experience stint.
Dixon, M. Great Big Bunch of You, A.
  River, Stay 'Way from My Door.
Dobyns. Dancing in Vacationland.
Du Bellay. To walk with sober step, to raise the
  eyebrow.
Dunbar, P. Common Things.
  Companion's Progress, A.
Eady. How to Do.
Edson, R. Good Son Jim.
Egan, R. Ain't We Got Fun.
Elliott, E. Child, Is Thy Father Dead?
Ellis, T. Making Ends Meet.
Ellis, Zoila. Luwani Dangriga.
Emerson, R. Chartist's Complaint, The.
English, W. Cashel of Munster.
Espino, A. Sweet Pale Girl.
Espirito Santo. Far from the Beach.
Ferry. Guest Ellen at the Supper for Street
  People, The.
Fields, D. I Can't Give You Anything but Love.
Fletcher, P. Against a Rich Man Despising
  Poverty.
Forman, R. We Are the Young Magicians.
Fraser, G. Lean Street.
Gamalinda, E. Lament Beginning w/a Line after
  Cavafy.
García, D. Tísica.
Garrett, E. Miser.
Garrett, J. Luck's Shining Child.
George, D. I Ain't Got Nothin' But the Blues.
Gershwin, I. I Got Plenty o' Nuthin'.
Gil de Biedma, J. Sad Night of October 1959.
Gilbert, C. Time with Stevie Wonder in It.
Giovanni. Nikki-Rosa.
Gomez, M. Making It.

Solo Palabras.
Gray, A. Why Your Grandfather Stopped
  Playing the Viola.
Grimké, A. Fragment.
Haavikko. Woman raises her garment, rain,
  wind, darkness rise, The.
Hacker, M. Elysian Fields.
Hadewijch. Love has subjugated me.
Hahn, K. Everest.
  These Current Events.
Han-shan. Cold Mountain Poem No. 158.
  They laugh at me hey farm boy.
Hardy, T. Reminder, The.
Heine, H. Silesian Weavers, The.
Hernandez, D. Workers.
Hershon. Unless You Are a Horse.
Herzog, A. God Bless the Child.
Hewitt, J. Irishman in Coventry, An.
Higgins, R. Some People.
Ho Ching-ming. Ballad of the Government
  Granary Clerk.
Hŏ Nansŏrhŏn. Poor Woman.
Hoagland, E. Big Zeb Johnson.
Holan. Snow.
Holcroft. Gaffer Gray.
Holiday. God Bless the Child.
Hood, T. Song of the Shirt, The.
Hove. Other Syllabus, The.
  You Will Forget.
Hughes, L. Advertisement for the Waldorf-
  Astoria.
  Ballad of the Man Who's Gone.
  Come to the Waldorf-Astoria.
  Letter ("Dear Mama, / Time I pay rent and get
  my food.").
  Madam and the Rent Man.
  Necessity.
  Visitors to the Black Belt.
Hummer, T. Mechanics.
Im Yŏngjo. Textbook.
Innocent, C. Poor Man's Life, The.
Ishikawa Takuboku. Tanka: "I work."
Issa. Poor quarter, A.
Johnson, S. Poverty in London.
Johnston, E. Last Sark, The.
Jones, R. End of Communism, The.
Jonson, B. To Alchemists.
József, A. Encouraging.
Kahn, G. Ain't We Got Fun.
Katz, M. Hungerdance, The.
Kenjeev. You envied the flying birds and
  stones.
Khlebnikov, V. Burning Field, The.
Khoury, N. People of Olives.
Kim Chiha. Story of a Sound, The.
Kizer, C. To an Unknown Poet.
Kooser. In the Basement of the Goodwill Store.
Kovur Kilar. We Hope For Patrons.
Kyger. Empty Shrine Buddha, The.
Lamb, M. Two Boys, The.
Landon. Dying Child, The.
  Poor, The.
Lawson, H. When Your Pants Begin to Go.
Lax. Alley Violinist.
Lee, W. Aunt Martha.
Lewis, A. Karanje Village.
Li Tung-yang. On a Painting of Fish Being
  Caught, a Song.
Lihn. Torture Chamber.
Lindsay, V. Buddha.
Liptsin, S. Going Up.
Liu Yu Hsi. Blacktail Row.
Longley, M. Ghetto.
Lourie. Song Embodying What I've Learned in
  Thirty-Five Years.
Lovelace, R. Grasshopper, The [To My Noble
  Friend Mr Charles Cotton: Ode].
Lyndsay [or Lindsay], D. Complaynt [or
  Compleynt or Complaint] of the Comoun [or
  Common] Weill of Scotland, The.
MacDiarmid, H. Glass of Pure Water, The.
Macgoye. Freedom Song, A.
MacLean, S. Calvary: "My eye is not on
  Calvary."
Madgett. Simple.
Mandelstam [or Mandelshtam]. Where Can I

Hide in January.
Mansour, J.   Seated on her bed legs spread open.
Martin, H.   I Never Felt Better.
Martinez, D.   Temporary Losses.
Mattes, L.   On the Street Corner.
Matthews, M.   Language.
McCarthy, T.   Claud Cockburn.
Mei Yao Ch'en.   Lice, The.
  Shih-hou Pointed Out to Me That from Ancient
    Times There Had Never Been a Poem on the
    Subject of Lice.
Meredith, W.   Korean Woman Seated by a Wall,
  A.
Meynell, A.   Lady Poverty, The.
Mhlophe.   Sometimes When It Rains.
Milligan, S.   Christmas 1970.
Mistral, G.   House, The.
Montague, J.   Locket, The.
Morejón.   Mother.
Morgan, R.   Mica Country.
Morton, "Jelly Roll.".   Mamie's Blues.
Murray, L.   Tin Wash Dish, The.
Neto.   Saturday in the Sand-Slums.
Nguyễn Trãi.   Bamboo Hut, The.
  Plough and a Spade, A.
North, M.   Ordnance Survey in the Northern
  Counties.
Osgood, F.   Wraith of the Rose, The.
Oswald, A.   Pilchard-Curing Song, The.
Otero, B.   Censored.
Owen, M.   Topography.
Pak Chaesam.   Road Back, The.
Parra, V.   At the Center of Injustice.
  Because the Poor Have Nothing.
Peacock, T.   Rich and Poor; or, Saint and Sinner.
Pelizzon, V.   Clever and Poor.
Perdomo, W.   Unemployed Mami.
Peters, L.   I am asking about the way ahead.
Pollarolo, G.   Man Went to See the Doltons, A.
Porter, P.   And No Help Came.
Powell, K.   For Aunt Cathy.
Press, K.   Dispossessed words.
Prévert.   August Bank Holiday.
Prodromos.   To the Emperor.
Ralin, Radoi.   Man Who Didn't Sign, The.
Ravenscroft, T.   Sing we now merily.
Rein.   Monastery.
Reisen, A.   Household of Eight.
Rexroth, K.   Bad Old Days, The.
Roberson, E.   Poor Houses, The.
Robinson, A.   Scape-Goat, The.
Robinson, E.   Poor Relation, The.
Rodriguez, L.   Rant, Rave and Ricochet.
Roland Holst.   Quatrain: "We're snug as a bug
  in a heated house."
Rutsala.   Shame.
Salkey.   Dry River Bed.
Sargant, J. A.   'Lo, on her dying couch, the
  sufferer lies.
Seaton, M.   Fear of Shoplifting.
Seferis.   Days of April '43.
Shakespeare, W.   Sonnet 125: "Were't aught to
  me I bore the canopy."
Shange.   About Atlanta.
Sheppard, R.   Empty Diary 1936.
Sheridan, R.   Thou Canst Not Boast of Fortune's
  Store.
Shih Shu.   After Shih-te ("My ragged cloak is
  streaked with mountain shadows.").
Shin Kyŏngnim.   They.
Sholl.   Late Psalm.
Sia, B.   Open Letter to the Entertainment
  Industry, An.
Simic.   Austerities.
  We Were So Poor.
Smith, C.   Female Exile, The.
Smith, K.   1984 Tour of Britain, The.
Sŏ Chŏngju.   Autumn, 1949: At the "Flower"
  Tea Room.
Soto.   Envying the Children of San Francisco.
Sousa, N.   Poem of a Distant Childhood.
Spender, S.   Elementary School Classroom in a
  Slum, An.
Stephens, J.   To the Four Courts, Please.
Stratanovsky.   Leningrad stairwell, A.
Su Tung-p'o.   Lament of the Farm Wife of Wu.

Sund.   Considering Poverty and Homelessness.
Sung Yu.   Wind, The.
Swift, J.   Phyllis [or Phillis] [or Progress of
  Love, The].
Synge.   Patch-Shaneen.
  Winter.
T'ao Ch'ien [or T'ao Yuan-ming].   Thinking of
  Impoverished Ancients.
Taylor, R.   Princess of Scotland, The.
Teiga.   In the poor man's house.
Thomas, R. S.   Other.
Tree.   Pity the Slain that Laid Away Their Lives.
Tremblay, G.   Urban Indians, Pioneer Square,
  Seattle.
Tsaloumas.   Consolation.
Tsvetayeva [or Tsvetaeva].   If the Soul was Born
  with Pinions.
  Staircase.
Tu Fu [or Du Fu].   Empty Purse.
  Empty Purse, The.
  Guest Arrives, A ("North of my lodge, south of
    my lodge, spring rivers all.").
  Hundred Worries, A.
  Journey North, The.
  Long hoe, long hoe, handle of white wood.
  Second Letter to My Nephew Wulang.
  Sent to the Magistrate of P'eng-chou.
  To Pi Ssu Yao.
Tucker, M.   Christmas Eve, South, 1865.
  Men swell the current,—many of them wear.
Unknown.   Brian O'Linn.
  East Gate, The.
  Foxes move in pairs.
  Poor Girl's Meditation, The.
  Poverty Knock.
Valente, J.   Morning: "Naked morning, the day's
  transparent."
Vallejo.   Anger.
  Man Walks By with a Loaf of Bread on His
    Shoulder, A.
Veiga.   Wind of Liberty.
Vicioso.   Perspectives.
Vietnamese Oral Tradition.   Concubine, The.
Walcott.   Laventille.
Walton, A.   Gwendolyn Brooks.
Wang Chiu-ssu.   Ballad of Selling a Child.
Waniek.   Sacrament of Poverty, The.
Wayne, J.   Cleaning Indian Dahl.
Weiners.   Children of the Working Class.
Whitlow.   Rockin' A Man, Stone Blind.
Williams, P.   Trails.
Williams, W.   Pastoral: "When I was younger."
  Poor, The ("It's the anarchy of poverty.").
  Proletarian Portrait.
  To a Poor Old Woman.
Wood, S.   Hollow.
Wordsworth, W.   Alice Fell; or, Poverty.
Wright, R.   On winter mornings.
Wu Chia-chi.   Grain-Barge Wife, The.
Wunderlich, M.   East Seventh Street.
Yang Shih-ch'i.   On the Hall of Precious Virtue.
Yi Kyubo.   How I Felt Pawning My Coat:
  Shown to Ch'oe Chongbon.
Yu Mongin.   Poor Woman, A.
Yüan Mei.   Growing Old (2).
Zenmaro.   Tanka: "All the young men I know."
Zhiyuan, S.   Living in Poverty.
Zimmer.   Example, The.
See also Need
Power
Adcock, F.   Below Loughrigg.
Adisa.   Women at the Crossroad / (May Elegba
  Forever Guard the Right Doors).
Anyte [or Anytes].   This Manes alive once was
  a slave; now dead.
Atwood.   Procedures for Underground.
Auden.   Epitaph on a Tyrant.
Baraka, I.   Hymn for Lanie Poo.
  Short Speech to My Friends.
  Wise 5.
Beachy-Quick, Dan.   Botany.
Belloc.   Maxim Gun, The.
Berry, W.   Dark with power.
Bible, O.T.   Gods boundles bownties gods
  promise ever abyding.
Bingen, Hildegard von.   Song to the Creator.

Black Elk.   Everything the Power of the World
  Does is Done in a Circle.
Blake, W.   Tyger, The.
Brome.   Riddle, The: "No more, no more."
Brutus.   Their Behaviour.
Busia, A.   Liberation.
Canan.   Inanna's Chant.
  Oh Kali.
  Radioactive.
Cardenal.   I offer these verses to you, Claudia,
  because you are their mistress.
Cataldi.   Advice.
Cernuda.   You were a tender desire, an
  insinuating cloud.
Chuang Tzu.   Need to Win, The.
Chudleigh.   To the Ladies.
Cortez, J.   Pray for the Lovers.
Curry, N.   Poppy Heads.
de Fierro.   Only You.
Dickinson, E.   I Can Wade Grief.
  One crown that no one seeks.
Dimitrova.   Ars Poetica.
Ducal, C.   Duke and I 2, The.
Edson, R.   Windows of the Castle, The.
Enheduanna.   From The Hymn to Inanna.
Ewart.   To the Virgins, to Make the Most of
  Time.
Fabian, C.   Liturgy for Lilith.
Galvin, J.   Little Dantesque.
Ginsberg, A.   Please Master.
Glover, S.   Power of the Soul.
Gogarty.   Tell Me Now.
Greiffenberg.   On the Ineffable Inspiration of the
  Holy Spirit.
Hacker, M.   Rune of the Finland Woman.
Han-shan.   Reading won't save us from death.
Harechavi.   Already Night, Already Day.
Harper, M.   Song: I Want a Witness.
Herrick.   On Himself[e] ("I fear[e] no Earthly
  Powers.").
  Shame, No Statist.
Hollo.   Italics.
Imbriglio, C.   Block Island Ferry.
Ironbiter, S.   Song to the Mother of the World.
Jeffers, L.   When I Know the Power of my
  Black Hand.
Juan Chi.   Last Rays of the Sun.
Kearney, L.   Man with His Kids on a Table,
  The.
Kemble.   Sonnet: "If there were any power in
  human love."
Knox, E.   Director, The.
Laing, K.   Steps.
Landon.   Power of Words, The.
Lê Thánh-tông.   Stick and Hat.
Lucretius.   Darling of Gods and Men, beneath
  the gliding stars.
Malé.   Women Don't Die on the Front Lines.
Mistral, G.   I Love, Love.
Moore, H.   Spuyten Duyvil.
Nag Hammadi Library.   Sent from the Power.
Nezahualcoyotl.   Our Lord.
Nolla.   Manifest, The.
Ono.   Mother of the Universe.
Oppen.   Power, the Enchanted World.
Parker, A.   No Fool, the God of Salt.
Patterson, O.   Autobiography of a Black Man.
Perelman.   Here 2.
Pollarolo, G.   Good Marriage, A.
Prado, A.   Heart's Desire.
Public Enemy.   Party for your Right to Fight.
Quevedo y Villegas.   Mighty Lord Is Money, A.
Ransom, J.   Judith of Bethulia.
Rāy, M. R.   Moon flashes in Her blessed face,
  The.
Robinson, E.   Richard Cory.
Sanchez, S.   Song No. 2: "I say. all you young
  girls waiting to live."
Simon, L.   Kali.
Simonides.   Without pleasure.
Simpson, M.   Millet's The Gleaners.
Spenser, E.   Who lists to see, what ever nature,
  arte.
Stanton, M.   Conjurer, The.
Strange.   Acts of Power.
Swingler.   Acres of Power.

Thomas, D.   Hand That Signed the Paper, The.
Thomas, L.   Cameo in Sudden Light.
Ts'ao Ts'ao.   Graveyard Song.
Unknown.   Hoatchunk' Narwoanar, or
    Winnebago War Song.
   Holy Goddess Tellus.
   Little Things.
   Proud Queen of the Earth Gods, Supreme
    Among the Heaven Gods.
   This Is the Trouble of the World.
   Warsong of the Kwakiutl.
Vallejo.   Black Heralds, The.
Waldrop, K.   Wandering Curves.
Walker, M.   For My People.
Weatherford, C.   Ladies of Dimbaza, The.
Weitsman, Sojun Mel.   Mondo.
Whitman, W.   I think I could turn and live with
    animals, they are so placid and self-contained.
Wilbur, R.   She.
Williams, W.   At the Ball Game.
Wise, S.   Testimony.
Wordsworth, W.   Child of the clouds! remote
    from every taint.
Wroth.   Sonnet 7: "Love leave to urge, thou
    know'st thou hast the hand."
Zen Center Sangha.   Mondo.
Zukofsky, L.   Ferry.

**Prague, Czech Republic [*formerly*
   Czechoslovakia]**
Bachner.   Man Proposes, God Disposes.
Celan.   In Prague.
Ginsberg, A.   Kral Majales.
Gorbanevskaya.   That time I did not save
    Warsaw, nor Prague later.
Košek, M.   Man Proposes, God Disposes.
Kuppner.   Architecture is when the sun shines
    on a facade daily.
   Old Guide-Book to Prague, An.
Löwy, H.   Man Proposes, God Disposes.
Lysohorsky.   Ballad of Jan Palach, Student and
    Heretic.
Nezval.   City With Towers.
   Lilac by the Museum on St. Wenceslas Square,
    The.
   Moon over Prague.
   Prague in the Midday Sun.
   Walker in Prague.
Sillitoe.   Synagogue in Prague.

Prairie Dogs
Gordon, Roxy.   Living Life as a Living Target.
Navajo Oral Tradition.   Coyote, Skunk, and the
    Prairie Dogs.

Prairies
Bryant, W.   Prairies, The.
   These are the gardens of the Desert, these.
Cather, W.   Macon Prairie.
   Prairie Spring.
Chippewa Oral Tradition.   Song of Spring, A.
Crosby, F.   Let Me Die on the Prairie.
   On Hearing a Description of a Prairie.
Dickinson, E.   To make a prairie it takes a
    clover and one bee.
Elizabeth, M.   Way of Words, The.
Guest, B.   Prairie Houses.
Hill, C.   Little Towns of Texas, The.
Montgomery, W.   Death Rode a Pinto Pony.
Peterson, R.   Midwest Town.
Ponge.   Prairie, The.
Reiter, T.   Rights of Way.
Russell, David Riley.   State Fair.
Sandburg, C.   Haze.
Sorby.   Gossip.
Taylor, C.   Winterdirge.
Whitman, W.   Prairie-Grass Dividing, The.

Praise
Bacchylides.   Ode 6: "Lachon has brought home
    the bacon."
Bachmann.   Paean to the Sun, A.
Breton, A.   Free Union.
Breton, N.   Oh That My Heart Could Hit Upon
    a Strain.
Bynner.   More Lovely than Antiquity.
Caedmon.   Caedmon's Hymn.
Cardona-Hine.   Trumpet Voluntary in Praise of
    My Four Children.
Clarke, George Elliott.   To Selah.

Dillard, A.   You go down the hall.
Durcan.   She Mends an Ancient Wireless.
Guerra, T.   Canto Twenty-Four: "Cunt is a
    spiderweb, The."
Hāzim al-Qarṭājannī.   Dawn for you is night and
    darkness is light;[now] the girls of enjoyable
    company shy away, contrary to the days of
    youth.
Hopkinson, F.   Toast to Washington, A.
Hudgins.   Homage to the Fox.
   Isaiah ate the blood-red ember.
Ibn 'Ammār, A.   Pass round the glass for the
    breeze has arisen and the stars have slackened
    the reins of night travel.
Ibn Zumruk, M.   Question the horizon adorned
    by the bright stars, for I have entrusted a
    description of my condition to it.
Ishikawa Takuboku.   Old newspaper!, An.
   Once in a while.
Kolsson, K.   I have nine principal talents.
Li Po.   Night Morring at Cow's Creek: I Think
    of the Old Man.
Merrill, C.   Love Poem: "Your silver hair, a
    galaxy."
Muske, C.   Ovation.
Péret.   Wink.
Picasso.   Her Great Thighs.
Piercy.   Cast Off, The.
Pindar.   Water is preeminent and gold, like a
    fire.
Rilke.   To praise is the whole thing! A man who
    can praise.
Sundiata.   Shout Out.
Taylor, C.B.   Like a Dog.
Unknown.   Praise, Member.
   Qi-yu [Translations].
   Your hair is like a panther's shadow.
Veinberg, J.   Last Shot.
Wen T'ing-yün.   Gold Glimmers and Fades.
Wesley, C.   My God! I know, I feel thee mine.

Prayer
Adams, H.   Prayer to the Virgin of Chartres.
Aitken, R.   Gathas.
Alakoye.   Eshu.
Alberti.   Giotto.
Ali, A.   Rooms Are Never Finished.
Allen, J.   Prayer to Eshbu-Elegba.
Amichai, Y.   Psalm: "Psalm on the day, A."
Angel.   Veils of Prayer.
Appleman, P.   O Karma, Dharma, pudding and
    pie.
Applewhite.   Prayer for My Son.
Arghezi.   Psalm.
Ashbery, J.   Painter, The.
Ashur-Nasir-Pal.   Hymn to Ishtar.
Awoonor.   This Earth, My Brother.
Baca.   Book 5: Rebirth; Twenty-Nine.
Bandele, A.   Prayer for the Living, A.
Barrax.   In the Restaurant.
Barry, M.   Hymn of Freedom.
Basho.   On Buddha's deathday.
   Summer mountains.
Beeching, H.   Prayers.
Beedome.   Petition, The.
Begay.   Mother's Lace.
Berrigan, D.   Prayer: "I left Cornell / with half a
    wit; six mismated socks."
Berry, W.   Purification, A.
Betjeman.   In Westminster Abbey.
Bialik.   If you found my heart's scroll in the
    dust.
Bible, *O.T.*   Psalm 142. Voce mea ad Dominum.
Bienek.   Resistance.
Bly, R.   Prayer for My Father.
Bradstreet, A.   [Here Follows Some] Verses
    upon the Burning of Our House [July 10th,
    1666. Copied Out of a Loose Paper].
Brew.   Plea for Mercy, A.
Breytenbach.   Breyten Prays for Himself.
   First Prayer for the Hottentotsgod.
Brontë, E.   Old Stoic, The.
Brooks, G.   Religion.
Browne, E.   When I Am Dead.
Brutus.   Prayer: "O let me soar on steadfast
    wing."
Burns, R.   Holy Willie's Prayer.

Buson.   In a bitter wind.
Cairns, Scott.   More Earnest Prayer of Christ,
    The.
Campo, C.   Ah that the Tiger.
Cardenal.   Prayer for Marilyn Monroe.
   Psalm 5: "Give ear to my words, O Lord."
Carroll, K.   DC Nocturne.
Carruth, H.   At Seventy-Five: Rereading an Old
    Book.
Catacalos.   Casa, La.
Cavafy.   Supplication.
Cavendish, M.   Common Fate of Books, The.
Celan.   Into the Foghorn.
   Tenebrae.
Char.   Unbending Prayer.
Chesterton.   Prayer in Darkness, A.
Clare, J.   Lord, Hear My Prayer.
Clare of Assisi.   Blessing Attributed to Saint
    Clare, The.
Clifton, L.   Slaveship[s].
Cofer, J.   Counting.
Coffey.   Prayers, The.
Coleridge, H.   Jesus Praying.
   Prayer.
Congreve, W.   Pious Selinda [*or* Celinda].
Cook, E.   Our Father.
Cortes.   Great Prayer.
Cortez, J.   Pray for the Lovers.
Crashaw.   C[h]aritas Nimia; or, The Dear[e]
    Bargain.
   Song: "Lord, when the sense of Thy sweet
    grace."
   Two Went Up into the Temple To Pray.
Crouch, S.   Revelation, The.
Cummings, E. E.   Noster, The.
Cuney.   Death Bed, The.
Davenant [*or* D'Avenant].   Praise and Prayer.
Davis, C.   God's Cutt-Off TV Screen's
    Vanishing Mirror Seems an Unshared Point.
Day, J.   Prayer: "Grant that no Hobgoblins fright
    me."
De la Mare.   Motley.
de Portalatin.   Humble Litany.
De Vere, S.   Right Use of Prayer, The.
Delgado, J.   Flora's Plea to Mary.
Desnos.   Hour Farther.
Dickinson, E.   At least—to pray—is left—is left.
   My period had come for Prayer.
   Of Course—I prayed.
   Prayer is the little implement.
Dillard, A.   You go down the hall.
Dimitrova.   Blind woman was more intimate
    with it, The.
Dodson, O.   Black Mother Praying.
Donne.   Hymn[e] to God the Father, A.
Duffy, C.   Prayer: "Some days, although we
    cannot pray, a prayer."
Eliot, T. S.   Song for Simeon, A.
Faiz.   Tyrant, The.
Falk.   Morning *Minyan.*
Farid-uddin Attar.   Invocation to the Conference
    of the Birds.
Feinstein, E.   Prayer.
Fink, Robert A.   Drought: Sure Signs in Merkle,
    Texas.
Flanner.   Prayer: "With Him who sets the lily on
    the stem."
Floyd-Miller, C.   She kneels at the wailing wall.
Francis of Assisi.   Prayer of St. Francis of Assisi
    for Peace.
Fuertes.   Prayer: "You are here on earth, our
    Father."
Gardiner, S.   Colorado Desert Night.
Garren, Christine.   Figure and Ground.
Garrett, E.   Lost Property.
Gascoigne.   Gascoigne's [*or* Gascoygnes] Good-
    Night.
Gervitz, G.   And what were you searching for,
    in that dream?
Gioia.   Litany, The.
   Prayer: "Echo of the clocktower, footstep."
Gloria.   Aleng Maria.
Glück, L.   Matins: "Unreachable father, when
    we were first."
Goffette, Guy.   Max Jacob.
Gomez, M.   Troubled Awakening.

Goodman, P.   Little Prayers.
Gottlieb, L.   Greeting Shekinah.
Gregg.   Flower No More Than Itself, A.
Gudding, Gabriel.   One Petition Lofted into the Ginkgos.
Hall, D.   Grace, A.
Matthew 21:18–22; In the morning.
Harjo, J.   Eagle Poem.
Harmsen van Beek.   Introduction to a Prayer.
Harvey, A.   Prayer to the Divine Mother, A.
Hayati.   Is this darkness the night of Power, or the black falling of your hair?
Heaney, S.   Poor Women in a City Church.
Heard, J.   Unuttered Prayer.
Hemans.   Evening Prayer, at a Girls' School.
Mountain Sanctuaries.
Olive Tree, The.
Herbert, G.   Denial[l].
Praise (2).
Prayer (1): "Prayer the Church's banquet, Angels' age."
Temper (1), The.
Wreath, A.
Herrick.   Evensong.
Grace for a Child.
His Litany to the Holy Spirit.
His Prayer for Absolution.
Matins [or Mattens], or Morning Prayer.
Thanksgiving to God for His House, A.
To God: an Anthem, Sung in the Chapel at White-Hall, Before the King.
To God ("Come to me God; but do not come.").
Heynen.   Boys Go to Ask a Neighbor for Some Apples, The.
Hinckley, P.   New Our Father, The.
Hogan, L.   Prayer for Men and Children.
Howe, F.   Edge of the dome is slipping, The.
Hudgins.   Loose Change.
Praying Drunk.
Huerta, D.   Oración del 21 de agosto.
Prayer for August 21.
Hugo, V.   Bridge, The.
Hŭimyŏng.   Hymn to the Thousand-Eyed Sound Observer.
Hunter, A. et al.   Down-Hearted Blues.
Issa.   All the time I pray to Buddha.
At prayer / Bead-swinging.
Fat priest, The.
Flies in the temple, The.
Jacob, V.   Tam i' the Kirk.
Johnson, G.   Suppliant, The.
Jones, D.   Queen of the differentiated sites, administratrix of the.
Jonson, B.   To Heaven.
Kamenszain.   Eliahu.
Kamienska.   Prayer That Will Be Answered, A.
Kaminsky, Ilya.   Author's Prayer.
Kan, T.   Prayer for a Good Death, A.
Keats.   Fragment of an Ode to Maia Written on May Day, 1818.
Keble.   Hezekiah's Display.
Samuel's Prayer.
Kees.   Small Prayer.
Khalvati.   Amanuensis.
Killigrew, A.   Upon the Saying That My Verses Were Made by Another.
Kipling, R.   Rabbi's Song, The.
Recessional.
Kishkan, T.   Spell for a Daughter.
Klugman, E.   She Who Listens.
Ko Chŏnghŭi.   Our Baby is a Living Prayer.
Koeppel, M.   Begin with the Heron and the Bat.
Kremer.   Epiphany.
Kwangdŏk.   Prayer to Amitāyus.
Lambert, R.   Prayer: "Bones in your foot that were shattered, The."
Landon.   Girl at Her Devotions, A.
Larkin, P.   Faith Healing.
Lasker-Schüler.   And Look for God.
Lawrence, D. H.   Hands of God, The.
Matthew 6:7–15; "And in praying do not heap up empty".
Lea, S.   Do not trust in these deceptive words.
Still dark when we file like children out on the turf.
Levin, P.   Third Day, The.

Levitt, Peter.   Though she is deaf.
Lewis, C.   Prayer: "Master, they say that when I seem."
Lewis, S.   Prayer at the End.
López Mills, T.   Dead Weight of the Land, The.
Peso muerto de la tierra, El.
Lugones.   Rain Psalm.
Lyte.   Abide With Me.
Machado Ruiz.   Rainbow at Night.
MacNeice.   Prayer Before Birth.
Mandelstam [or Mandelshtam].   O Lord, Help Me to Live Through This Night.
Your image, tormenting and elusive.
McFerrin, B.   23rd Psalm, The: "Lord is my Shepherd, I have all I need, The."
McGough, R.   Prayer to Saint Grobianus.
Mead, J.   Concerning That Prayer I Cannot Make.
Merton.   Evening Prayer.
Mew.   Old Shepherd's Prayer.
Miller, H.   Kaddish.
Miller, V.   Without Ceremony.
Milosz, C.   On Angels.
Mistral, G.   House, The.
Miyazawa Kenji.   Dawn: "Rolling snow turned peach-color."
Montague, J.   Footnote on Monasticism, A: Dingle Peninsula.
Moore, M.   Cumae.
Morabito, F.   I've forgotten the words.
Yo que he olvidado las palabras.
More, S.   Prayer, A.
Mulock, D.   Labor and Rest.
Murray, P.   Introit.
Navajo Oral Tradition.   Prayer of First Dancers.
Nawaz, G.   Riddle.
Nervo.   Gift, The.
Newman, J.   Pillar of the Cloud, The.
Nicholson, N.   For Hokey and Henrietta.
Norris, K.   Prayer to Eve, A.
Nye, N.   Small Vases from Hebron, The.
Okara.   One Night at Victoria Beach.
Okigbo.   Overture.
Ono.   Mother of the Universe.
Orr, G.   Dark Prayer.
Orten.   Last Poem, The.
Ortiz.   Bend in the River.
O'Sullivan, L.   Prayer, The.
Ovid.   You gods of sea and sky—what's left me now but prayer?
Owen, J.   Hour of Fear.
Pak Mogwŏl [or Mokwŏl].   Prayer in Four Verses.
Parra, V.   Why Is It This Way, Almighty God?
Pasolini.   Prayer to My Mother.
Pavlova, V.   This is the way a row of official tulips.
Peele.   Bethsabe's Song.
Pizarnik.   Awakening, The.
Pope, A.   Universal Prayer, The [Deo Opt. Max.].
Pound, E.   Sandalphon.
Prado, A.   Fluency.
Preston, R.   Ten Seconds.
Prior.   Letter to the Honourable Lady Margaret Cavendish Holles-Harley, A.
Quarles.   Booke of Common Pray'r excels the rest, The.
Rakosi.   Services.
Ralegh, S.   Authours Epitaph, Made by Himself, The.
Ray, H.   Evening Prayer.
Prayer: "O Christ, who in Gethsemane."
Réda, Jacques.   Amen.
Reichard, W.   Cloud Game, The.
Rilke.   I Have Faith.
Rimbaud, A.   In Tsegihi.
Robbins, Z.   October 7th.
Robinson, M.   Sappho's Prayer to Venus.
Rolle, S.   Hands in the Motion of Prayer.
Rudaki.   Prayer.
Rumi.   Like the rose I am laughing with all my body, not only with.
Sachs, N.   Rushing at Times Like Flames.
St. John, P.   Sunday.
Sapgir.   Psalm 1.

Psalm 137.
Sappho.   Prayer to my lady of Paphos.
Queen Hera, may your [graceful form].
Schuyler, J.   Our Father.
Seminole Oral Tradition.   Song for Bringing a Child into the World.
Serge.   Hands.
Sharp, S.   How to Build a Prayer.
Sherwin, J.   To Whom it may concern.
Sill.   Fool's Prayer, The.
Simmons, J.   Rogation Day: Portrush.
Smart, C.   Hymn 2. Hope.
Spender, S.   Rejoice in the Abyss.
Stevenson, R.   Epitaph: "Angler rose, he took his rod, The."
Last night we had a thunderstorm in style.
Subido, T.   Paganly.
Sylvester, J.   Father, The.
Tadic.   Antipsalm.
Taylor, E.   Dull. Dull indeed! What shall it e'er be thus?
Huswifery.
Taylor, H.   Goodbye to the Old Friends.
Tekeyan.   Prayer on the Threshold of Tomorrow.
Tennyson, A.   Prayer: "Pray for my soul. More things are wrought by prayer."
Thomas, D.   Conversation of Prayer, The.
Thomas, R. S.   Empty Church, The.
To be alive then.
Thompson, C.   Out of the Deep.
Thompson, P.   Old Saint's Prayer, The.
Thomson, D.   Lewis.
Thoreau.   Light-winged smoke, Icarian bird.
Tilak, D.   Prayer, A: "God / save this country."
Tsvetayeva [or Tsvetaeva].   White Low Sun, A.
Tuckerman, F.   Sonnets: "Starry flower, the flower-like stars that fade, The."
Twichell.   My Listener.
Ungar.   Common Prayer.
Unknown.   Beguines who hear these words.
Corpus Inscriptionum Latinarum 14.3565.
God Got Plenty o' Room.
Good Old Way, The.
Have oon god in worshipe.
How come alle ye that ben i-broght.
I passed thurgh a gardyn grene.
Invocation to the U' wannami.
Limerick.
Lord, Remember Me!
Ne hath my soule but fyr and yse.
On hire is al my lyf ylong.
Poet's Prayer, The.
Pray All de Member.
Pray On.
Prayer of a Woman in Charge of Berry Picking in Knights Inlet.
Prayer to the Sockeye Salmon.
Psalm 137.
Queen wept but thought: It is not appropriate to show such grief, The.
Rain Song of the Quer'ränna Chai' än, A.
Rain Song of the Shu'-wi Chai' än (Snake Society), A.
Sith al that in this world hath ben in rerum natura.
Towering is that southern mountain.
Whan I thenke on the rode.
Whan I thenke thynges three.
Van Duyn.   Gardener to His God, The.
Vasileva, E.   She's calling God, she wants to ask Him.
Verlaine.   Voice of Pride: shout of blaring trumpets.
Very.   My Meat and Drink.
Prayer of Jabez, The.
Prayer, The ("Wilt Thou not visit me?").
Waring, A.   My Times Are in Thy Hand.
Watts, I.   Man Frail, and God Eternal.
Webb, C.   Faith.
Wesley, C.   None is like Jeshuron's God.
Whitman, W.   Prayer of Columbus.
Whittier.   Dedication: "I would the gift I offer here."
Wilde, O.   E Tenebris.
Wither.   Prayer of Hezekiah, The.
Prayer of Nehemiah, The.

Wright, J.   Art of the Fugue, The: A Prayer. Trying to Pray.

Wyatt.   Prologue: "Love, to give law unto his subject hearts."

Yeats.   Mohini Chatterjee.
   Prayer for My Daughter, A.
   Prayer for My Son, A.

Young, Andy.   In Anguish, the Heart Finally Prays.

Zagajewski.   Flame, A.

Zakaria Youssef, M.   Sadder Man, The.

Praying Mantis

Zach, N.   King Solomon's Camel.

Zukofsky, L.   "Mantis".

Preaching and Preachers

Arnold, M.   Progress.

Benedikt.   Moralist of Bananas, The.

Berryman.   Carpenter's Son, The.

Clough.   Across the Sea, Along the Shore.

Dickinson, E.   He fumbles at your Soul.

Dobson, R.   Eutychus.

Goldsmith, O.   Near yonder copse, where once the garden smiled.

Harris, D.   On the uptown lexington avenue express: Martin Luther King Day 1995.

Hill, J.   Preacher and the Slave, The.

Hudgins.   At the Piano.

Kipling, R.   At His Execution.

McGinley.   Theology of Jonathan Edwards, The.

Melville, H.   Rose Window.

Moorer.   Southern Pulpit, The.

Nichol.   Easter Pome.

Roethke.   Judge Not.

Thomson, J.   Paraphrase of the Latter part of the Sixth Chapter of St. Matthew, A.

Tolson, M.   Old Pettigrew.

Unknown.   Vicar of Bray, The.

Warren, R.   Amazing Grace in the Back Country.

See also **Clergy**

Precocity

Ellis, T.   Practice.

Predators

Adamson.   Southern skua, The.

Ginsberg, A.   Who Eats Who?

Hanzlicek, C.   Feeding Frenzies.

Hill, G.   Re-birth of Venus, The.

Kang Ǔn'gyo.   Spider: "What I throw out to the world."

Knox, J.   Son of The House of a Thousand Chandeliers.

McKay, C.   Birds of Prey.

Melville, H.   Maldive Shark, The.

Owen, W.   Arms and the Boy.

Rossetti, C.   Handy Mole who plied no shovel, A.

Taylor, E.   Upon a Spider Catching a Fly.

Unknown.   Spell against Predatory Animals.

Wang Yü-ch'eng.   Song of the Crow Pecking at My Scarred Donkey.

Wilson, E.   Lakeside.

Yezzi, David.   Woman Holding a Fox.

Predestination

Hardy, T.   Subalterns, The.

Herrick.   Predestination.

Hughes, T.   Whether you say it, think it, know it.

Moore, M.   Book of How, The.

Nemerov.   Western Approaches, The.

Storm, Hester G.   Bop for Laotzu.

Pregnancy

Aini, L.   Empress of Imagined Fertility, The.

Alvi, M.   Man Impregnated.

Andriescu, Radu.   Apple, The.

Baraka, I.   For Hettie.

Barbauld.   To a Little Invisible Being Who Is Expected Soon to Become Visible.

Barresi.   In Waking Words.

Bhatt, S.   White Asparagus.

Boss, L.   Sitting in the Doctor's Office the Next Day.

Brereton, J.   Unborn.

Brown, T.   Between Our Folding Lips.

Bruce, D.   Sonnet 2: "Deep in her seventh month, my sister dozes."

Two Couples.

Carroll, K.   Truth About Karen, The.

Ceravolo.   Pregnant, I Come.

Clive.   Mother, The.

Cofer, J.   How to Get a Baby.

Conoley, G.   As in the Small Gaps Between Minutes.

Cooley.   Poem on My Birthday.

Crane, H.   Stark Major.

Cunningham, J.   For a Woman with Child.

Curzon, D.   Tour of Ein Kerem, A.

Daniels, K.   Women's Room in Pennsylvania Station, The.

Davis, Cortney.   It Is August 24th.

Dooley, M.   Freight.

Dove, R.   History: "Everything's a metaphor, some wise."
   Weathering Out.

Dunmore.   Scan at 8 Weeks.

Durcan.   Sister Agnes Writes to Her Beloved Mother.

Edmond, L.   Tempo.

Ennis.   Alice of Daphne, 1799.

Erdrich.   Birth.

Ferguson, G.   Scan.

Fleming, R.   For All Unwed Mothers.

Foppa.   Woman.

Fusselman, A.   Ticker.

García, A.   Clog of Her Body, The.
   Green Corn Season.

Gillan.   Waiting for the Results of a Pregnancy Test.

Grennan.   Conjunctions.

Gunn, T.   Baby Song.

Hikmet.   Evening Walk, The.

Houlihan, J.   Infant Spouse, The.

Jeffers, H.   Another Easter Poem.

Jones, B.   Portrait of a Pregnant Woman.
   Pregnant Woman.

Jonker, I.   Pregnant Woman.

Kanik.   Erol Güney's Cat.

Khoury, N.   People of Pomegranates.

Kinzie.   Sound Waves.

Lawrence, D. H.   Youth Mowing, A.

Livingstone, D.   Wheels.

Lorde.   Now That I Am Forever with Child.

Lux.   Upon Seeing an Ultrasound Photo of an Unborn Child.

Macphee, K.   Ultrasound at 13 Weeks.

Mahon.   Ford Manor.
   Unborn Child, An.

Major, C.   On Trying to Imagine the Kiwi Pregnant.

Makeda (Queen of Sheba).   I fell.

Maksimovic.   For the Barren Woman.

Mardi, Jas.   Perseverance.

Masters, E.   Amanda Barker.

Mayer, B.   We've Solved the Problem.

McAdams, J.   Leaving the Old Gods.

McGrath, C.   Delphos, Ohio.

McPherson, S.   Pregnancy.

Mikhail, D.   Urgent Call, An.

Morris, A.   Imani's Song.

Morrissey, S.   Stitches.

Moss, T.   Crystals.

Muldoon, P.   Birth, The.
   Sonogram, The.

Murphy, M.   Occasions.

Myers, J.   Gift, The.

No Hyegyông.   Song of Mary.

Olds, S.   First Birth.
   May 1968.

Ondaatje.   Dates.

O'Sullivan, L.   Journey, The.
   When We Were Good.

Pak Sôwôn.   Menstrual Irregularities.

Phelps, D.   Ordinary Country Girl, An.

Plath.   Metaphors.

Qunta, C.   Know, The.

Rakosi.   L'Chayim.

Ramsay, A.   Jenny Nettles.

Randell.   Its this familiar black line from the tops.

Ras.   Pregnant Poets Swim Lake Tarleton, New Hampshire.

Realuyo.   La Querida.

Redel, V.   Ninth Month.

Reynolds, R.   Peridot.

Richter, J.   Madonna del Parto: Our Lady of Birth-Giving.

Rilke.   4. Mary's Visit with Elizabeth.
   Mary's Visitation.

Roberts, K.   Cantata, 8: "Early March, trickle and rush of ice melt in mountains."

Rungano.   Labour.

Shange.   Oh, I'm 10 Months Pregnant.

Shinkichi Takahashi.   Raw Fish and Vegetables.

Spaziani.   Ultrasound.

Stainer.   Ringing Chamber, The.

Starodubtseva, N.   Roundabouts stolidly turn.

Swenson, M.   Motherhood.

Swirszczynska [*or* Swir].   Three Bodies.

Taggard.   With Child.

Unknown.   Jenny Nettles.
   Waly, Waly [Love Be Bonny].

Vasquez, R.   Early Morning Test Light over Nevada, 1955.

Vivar.   Delivery.

Volkman.   Pregnant Lady Playing Tennis, The.

Ward, T.   At Twenty-Three Weeks She Can No Longer See Anything South of Her Belly.

Wickham.   After Annunciation.

Wright, J.   Woman to Child.
   Woman to Man.

Zucker, R.   In Your Version of Heaven I am Younger.
   What I Want You to See Is She When Not Here As in Now.

Prehistoric Man

Lasheen, M.   Nearly Three Million Years Ago.

See also **Cavemen; Man, Primitive**

Prejudice

Atkins, R.   Late Bus (After a Series of Hold-Ups).

Baca.   So Mexicans Are Taking Jobs from Americans.

Baraka, I.   Agony, An. As Now.

Boss, L.   When You Are Grown, Amanda Rose.

Brown, S.   Children's Children.

Campo.   Towards Curing AIDS.

Cassells.   Soul Make a Path Through Shouting.

Chinn.   Skin Color from the Sun.

Derricotte.   After a Reading at a Black College.
   Family Secrets.
   Weakness, The.

Divakaruni.   Founding of Yuba City, The.
   Yuba City School.

Domina, L.   Pharoah's Army Got Drowned.

Eady.   Sherbet.

Espada.   Beloved Spic.
   Toque de queda: Curfew in Lawrence.

Fanthorpe.   You Will Be Hearing from Us Shortly.

Galich.   Hospital Gypsy Song.

Gillan.   In Memory We Are Walking.
   Public School No. 18: Paterson, New Jersey.

Henderson-Holmes.   Battle, Over and Over Again, The.

Hewitt, J.   From the Tibetan.

Kipling, R.   Tommy.

Kramer, L.   Shoemaker's Wife, The.

Levine, P.   Old Testament, The.

Lewis, W.   To the People of a Small Town in Ohio, Who As I Approach Them on the Street, Are Afraid That This Black Man Is Going to Do Them Harm.

Mak.   Farewell to Russia.

McElroy, C.   Foul Line—1987.

Moorer.   Prejudice.

Mura.   Argument: on 1942, An.
   Grandfather-in-law.

Ostriker.   Lamenting the Inevitable.

Plotnick, H. M.   Jewish.

Reed, I.   Jacket Notes.

Rivers, C.   Watts.

Roberts, N.   Nigger and Some Poofters, A.

Rodriguez, L.   We Never Stopped Crossing Borders.

Saint.   Heart and Soul.

Saunders, R.   Lawd, Dese Colored Chillum.

Scannell.   Popular Mythologies.

Smart, C.   Insular Prejudice.

Steptoe.   Such a Boat of Land.
Viscusi.   Autobiography.
See also **Racial Prejudice; Racism and Racists; Sexism**
Presbyterianism and Presbyterians
Dryden, J.   Presbyterians, The.
Milton.   On the New Forcers of Conscience Under the Long Parliament.
Paulin.   Presbyterian Study.
Presence
Coote, G.   Tenzo's Song.
Creeley.   Edges.
   Like They Say.
Davies, A.   This evening / Is the only evening.
Goralik, L.   Here I am, looking at you, my orphan. Your thick scarf. Your cold cigarette.
Hahn, O.   No Place Is Here or There.
Herrick.   Gods Presence ("God's evident, and may be said to be.").
Jiménez, J.   Lamb Was Bleating Softly, The.
Levertov.   Wings, The.
McDaniel, W.   Asking Favors.
Mueller, L.   Hope.
Natzler, C.   There.
Olson, E.   Presence, The.
Oswald, A.   Mountains.
Poetker-Thiessen, A.   My kingdom is of this world.
Prigov.   It's better not to live in Moscow.
Radnóti.   Serbian Postcard 1.
Twichell.   Next and Last.
Unknown.   Because We're Here.
Voltskaya, T.   God is the first snow. He is a leaf, a mosquito.
Whitman, W.   Not Heaving from My Ribb'd Breast Only.
Young, A.   Blues Don't Change, The.
Presents
Abu Madi.   Holiday Present.
Alexandru.   End of the War, The.
Alvi, M.   Presents from My Aunts in Pakistan.
Harryman.   Baby. (For B and T).
Kyger.   Never talk ahead.
Laurencin, M.   Present, The.
Yu Hsin.   Offered in Thanks for a Present of Wine and a Goose.
See also **Gifts and Giving**
Presidency, The, United States
Boylan, G.   Dames of Washington.
Hitchman-Britton, O.   Road to the Presidency.
Hollander, J.   Historical Reflections.
Kendrick, D.   Solo: The Good Blues.
Lindsay, V.   Bryan, Bryan, Bryan, Bryan.
McClure, M.   Souls.
Moorer.   Presidents, The.
Shot, D.   Executive Privilege.
Steptoe.   Election Time.
Tate, J.   Bounden Duty.
Taylor, H.   Speech.
Van Winckel, N.   Let Me Remind You You Are Still under Oath.
Whitman, W.   To the States, To Identify the 16th, 17th, or 18th Presidentiad.
Williams, M.   Of History and Hope.
Presley, Elvis
Ai.   Resurrection of Elvis Presley, The.
Baraka, I.   In the Funk World.
Blessing.   Elegy for Elvis.
Bogen, D.   All Shook Up.
Bowers, N.   Conversions.
   On the Elvis Mailing List.
Brock, V.   I Stopped in Tupelo, Elvis.
   Mary's Dream.
   Sphinx.
Brown, Fleda.   Elvis Decides to Become a Monk.
Bukowski.   Elvis Lives.
Clifton, L.   Them and Us.
Cornish, S.   Elvis.
   My Father's House.
Driskell, M.   Talismans.
Eady.   Young Elvis.
Elledge.   Their Hats Is Always White.
Fulton, A.   About Face.
   Elvis from the Waist Up.

New Release, A.
   Some Cool.
Gilmore, B.   Elvis.
Gunn, T.   Elvis Presley.
   Painkillers.
Hudgins.   Versification of a Passage from Penthouse.
Huff, S.   First Time I Heard Elvis, The.
Jackson, F.   Death of Gladys Presley, The.
   Elvis Acts as His Own Pallbearer.
   Elvis at the End of History.
   Elvis Goes to the Army.
   Elvis Reads The Wild Swans at Coole.
   Elvis Sings Gospel.
   I Visit the Twenty-four Coin-op Church of Elvis.
   Women Who Love Elvis All Their Lives, The.
Kerrigan, T.   Elvis Kissed Me.
Koncel, M.   Come Back, Elvis, Come Back to Holyoke.
McMahon, L.   Elvis for the Ages, An.
Nameroff, R.   Elvis Presley.
Oates.   Waiting on Elvis, 1956.
Ray, D.   Brides of Elvis, The.
   Sunday Morning.
Sadler, L.   Why God Chose Robert Frost Over Elvis.
Seay.   Audubon Drive, Memphis.
Stokes, T.   Elvis Elevator, The.
Stuart, D.   Fishing with Elvis.
Swartwout.   I Wannabe Your Queen.
Vélez, E.   Elvis P. and Emma B.
Wakoski.   Blue Suede Shoes.
Wojahn.   Assassination of Robert Goulet as Performed by Elvis Presley: Memphis, 1968, The.
   At Graceland with a Six Year Old, 1985.
   Elvis Moving a Small Cloud: The Desert Near Las Vegas, 1976.
   Nixon Names Elvis Honorary Federal Narcotics Agent at Oval Office Ceremony, 1973.
   Pharaoh's Palace.
   W. C. W. Watching Presley's Second Appearance on The Ed Sullivan Show: Mercy Hospital, Newark, 1956.
Presumption
Cummings, E. E.   Space being(don't forget to remember)Curved.
Pretension
Campion, T.   Heart's Music.
Chaucer.   Man of Law's Epilogue, The.
Delgado, J.   When You Leave.
Donne.   Satire 4.
Eliot, T. S.   Conversation Galante.
   Portrait of a Lady.
Frishberg, D.   I'm Hip.
Gilbert, W.   Bunthorne's Song.
Herbert, G.   Jordan (2).
Jiménez, J.   Author's Club.
Jonson, B.   On English Monsieur.
Nash, O.   Just How Low Can a Highbrow Go When a Highbrow Lowers His Brow?
   "Pindar.".   Town Eclogue, A.
Pound, E.   Portrait d'une Femme.
Sanger, R.   3: Who Was That? I Ask.
Shapiro, K.   University.
Tranter.   Having Completed My Fortieth Year.
Pride
Arana, Milton.   Birth of a Nation.
Barber, M.   To Novella, on Her Saying Deridingly, that a Lady of Great Merit, and Fine Address, Was Bred in the Old Way. An Epigram.
Barber, W.   Explanation.
Bécquer, G.   Into Her Eyes a Tear Crept.
Bennett, G.   To a Dark Girl.
Booth, Kwan.   Untitled One.
Breeze.   Natural High.
Brooks, G.   Kojo: I Am A Black.
   Primer for Blacks.
Brown, J. *et al.*   Say It Loud—I'm Black and I'm Proud.
Brown, S.   Sporting Beasley.
   To Sallie, Walking.
Burgoyne, J.   Dashing White Sergeant, The.
Buson.   New Year's first poem.

Ceravolo.   Wild Provoke of the Endurance Sky.
Clifton, L.   Listen Children.
Cohan.   Harrigan.
Coleridge, M.   Pride.
Cortez, Sarah.   Attempt to Locate.
Cotter, J.   Is It Because I Am Black?
Coward.   London Pride.
Cunningham, J.   In a few days now when two memories meet.
Dove, R.   Sunday Greens.
Elytis, O.   I was late in understanding the meaning of humility.
Enright, D.   Flowers.
Gillan.   Growing Up Italian.
Gonzales, R.   Praise the Tortilla, Praise the Menudo, Praise the Chorizo.
Hanson, M.   How proudly Man usurps the power to reign.
Herbert, G.   Church Monuments.
   Flower, The.
   Vanity [*or* Vanitie] (1).
Herrick.   To Dianeme ("Sweet, be not proud of those two eyes.").
Hope, A.   Paradise Saved.
Hyde, E.   Super High.
Inp'yŏng, Prince.   Don't mock a pine.
Issa.   Mountain cuckoo, The.
Jeffers, R.   Rock and Hawk.
Jones, I.   Haiku for My Brothers.
Kay, J.   Pride.
Kim Sujang.   Standing in your lofty tower.
Knott.   Two Vietnam Poems: (1966).
Kolsson, K.   I have nine principal talents.
Komunyakaa, Y.   Pride.
   Seven Deadly Sins.
Kooser.   Myrtle.
Kramer, L.   Non-Emigrant, The.
Landon.   Mask of Gaiety, The.
Landor, W.   Proud word you never spoke, but you will speak.
Leigh, R.   Greatness in Little.
Levine, P.   Animals Are Passing from Our Lives.
Li Shang-yin.   Boasting of My Son.
Lisnyanskaya [*or* Lisnianskaia].   Whenever I looked in the mirror.
Longfellow, H.   Rhyme of Sir Christopher, The.
Lorde.   Naturally.
Lowell, J.   Contrast, A.
Lowery, Janet.   Texas Splendor.
Magdeburg, Mechthild von.   God's Absence.
McKay, C.   If We Must Die.
McOrlan.   Hairdresser's, The.
Meredith, G.   Lucifer in Starlight.
Nye, N.   Mind of Squash, The.
Owen, W.   Parable of the Old Men and the Young, The.
Parker, D.   Fighting Words.
Pope, A.   Of all the causes which conspire to blind.
Price, V.   Pride: "It becomes your soul: that sucking, itch that."
Qunta, C.   Know, The.
Reverdy.   Fires Smouldering Under Winter.
Rukeyser, M.   Bubble of Air.
Sandburg, C.   Primer Lesson.
Scott, S.   Proud Maisie.
Shelley, P.   Ozymandias.
Sherwood, G.   Satire against Reason and Mankind, A.
Sidney, P.   Sonnet 27: "Because I oft, in dark abstracted guise."
   Sonnet 31: "With how sad steps, O Moon[e], thou climb'st the skies."
   Sonnet 53: "In martial sports I had my cunning tried."
Stafford, W.   Our Kind.
Suárez.   Worker Dies, A.
Thomas, E.   Forsaken Wife, The.
Torres Bodet.   My Country.
Unknown.   Come back to me, riddled with holes from a dark rifle's bullets.
   Girl, don't be so haughty.
   Pointless Pride of Man, The.
   Tamping Ties.
   Wa-Sissica, the War Song.

Verlaine. Humble life of dull and easy work, The.
Villalongo. In the Good Old U. S. A.
Weiner, E. When My Poem Appeared.
Whitman, W. Woman Waits for Me, A.
Whittier. Cities of the Plain, The.
  Forgiveness.
Wilmer, S. Mess Boy, The.
Yi T'aek. O roc, don't ridicule the small black birds.

Priests
Andrade, O. Hierofant.
Berrigan, D. In Memoriam (2): "Young priest, dead suddenly, A."
  We Will Now Hear the Word of God from Each of Our Beloved Chaplains.
Burroughs, W. My Legs Señor.
Busceti, G. One Hundred Eighty.
Buson. Nobly, the great priest.
  Priestly poverty—.
Foley, Jack. Eli, Eli.
González Prada, M. Pope.
Issa. Fat priest, The.
Jinkag Haesim. Upon Entering the Priesthood: A Warning.
Joe, R. Plawej ans L'nui'site'w (Partridge and Indian-Speaking Priest).
Kreitman, N. In Torrett, Minorca.
Magrelli. Things have an admirable life.
Muso Soseki. For a Monk Going West.
  For Sho the New Head Priest of Erin-ji.
  For Tetsu the New Head Priest of Erin-ji.
Naong. Haesunja Asks for an Enlightenment Song.
Riordan, M. Holy Land, The.
  Lines to His New Instructress.
Ríos, A. Death of Anselmo Luna, The.
Scott, F. Last Rites.
Silesky. Kingdom, The.
Tafolla. Mission San José.
Unknown. Full and True Account of a Dreaded Fire, that Lately Broke out in the Pope's Breeches, A.
  God send euerie Preist ane wyfe.
Young, G. Damien.
See also **Clergy**

Primroses
Biespiel, D. Lilacs.
Buson. Evening primrose.
Clare, J. Primrose, The.
Cranch. Evening Primrose, The.
Davies, W. H. Days Too Short.
Herrick. Primrose, The.
Kim Namjo. Evening Primrose.
Shaw, A. Crepuscule.
Wordsworth, W. Primrose of the Rock, The.

Princes and Princesses
Aiken, J. Palace Cook's Tale.
Aneirin. Lord of Gododdin will be praised in song, A.
  When a crowd of cares.
Aytoun [*or* Ayton], R. On the Prince's Death, to the King.
Bandele, A. After diana died.
Bevington, H. Princess and the Pea, The.
Bopp, R. Begins here, the ciphered forest.
Boychuk. Fairy Tale, A.
Daniel, S. Theare be great Prince, such as will tell you howe.
Darío, R. Sonatina.
  Sonatina.
  Story for Margarita.
Gil de Biedma, J. Prince of Aquitania, in His Torn-down Tower, The.
Gorges. Written upon the Death of the Most Noble Prince Henrie.
Gwyer, J. At evening too the dazzled light.
Kakinomoto no Hitomaro. Mourning Princess Asuka.
Korean Oral Tradition. Abandoned Princess, The.
Kuzmina-Karavayeva. Long-Barrow Princess 2.
Landon. Princess Victoria, The.
Lili'u-o-ka-lani. Sanoe ("Where can you be, Sanoe?").
Limonov. It is good in May, in marvelous wet

May, to be the chairman of the All-Russian Extraordinary Committee in the city of Odessa.
Machan. Hazel Tells LaVerne.
Mei Sheng. Seven Exhortations to Rise, The.
Mitchell, S. From the Journals of the Frog Prince.
Moore, T. Duke Is the Lad [to Frighten a Lass], The.
More, S. Good Princes and Bad.
Mörike [*or* Möricke]. Beauty Rohtraut.
Mu, King of Paekche. Song of Sŏdong.
Postnikova, O. Archangel Cathedral.
Sidney, P. Since wailing is a bud of causeful sorrow.
Sitwell, D. King of China's Daughter, The.
Spark. We Were Not Expecting the Prince To-day.
Unknown. Cleared by its flowing, dip the flood water up.
  Lament for Prince Chagoo.
  Now we have heard stories of high valor.
  Qi-yu [Translations].
Volkow. Historia del laberinto, La.
  Story of the Labyrinth, The.
Watson, R. Enchanted Princess, An.
Wieseltier, M. Military Call-up.

Printing and Printers
Adams, F. Composed in the Composing Room.
Cranch. Printing-Press, The.
Delanty. Compositor, The.
Di Prima. To Philip Whalen, 1999.
Dobson, R. Country Press.
Espada. Who Burns for the Perfection of Paper.
Fogel, A. Printer's Error, The.
Hughes, L. Madam's Calling Cards.
McGough, R. Italic.
Wodehouse. Printer's Error.

Prisoners of War
Darwish, M. Ramallah—January, 2002.
Davico, O. Cell, The.
Dickey, J. Performance, The.
Freneau. Two hulks on Hudson's stormy bosom lie.
Jarmain. Prisoners of War.
Jarrell, R. Prisoners.
Juma'h, J. Thus my brother.
Kaufman, S. Bread and Water.
Komunyakaa, Y. Prisoners.
Lee, J. German Prisoners.
Merton. Dark Morning, The.
Morgan, R. Road from Elmira, The.
Mura. Blueness of the Day, The.
Richard I, Coeur de Lion. Ja Nul Homs Pris Ne Ira a Raison.
Ruefle. Letter, The.
Saitō Sanki. Photographed / face by face.
  Photographed— / prisoners of war shout commands.
Wojahn. Wartime Photos of My Father.

Prisons and Prisoners
Adamson. O to be in the news again—now as fashion runs.
  Passing Through Experiences.
Addonizio. Chicken.
Akhmatova, A. Dedication.
  Requiem.
  Requiem: "No, not under the vault of alien skies."
Al-Haidari, B. Death in Four Voices.
Alexie. Capital Punishment.
Algarin. And in the U.S.A.
Ali, M. Condition.
Alterman, N. Time and the Response, The.
Amrane. You Called to Me, Prison Windows.
Anton, S. Prisoner's Song, A.
Awoonor. They Shall Know.
Azzawi, F. Political Prisoner.
Baca. Cloudy Day.
  How We Carry Ourselves.
  I Applied for the Board.
  Immigrants in Our Own Land.
  It Started.
  Like an Animal.
Batraville, D. Paper 33.
Berrigan, D. Rehabilitative Report: We Can Still Laugh.

Berryman. Dream Song 45.
Blake, W. Crystal Cabinet, The.
  How Sweet I Roamed [*or* Roam'd] from Field to Field.
Borowski. Project: Flag.
Brontë, E. Prisoner, The. A Fragment.
  Still let my tyrants know, I am not doomed to wear.
Brown, S. Southern Road.
Brutus. At Night.
  Endurance.
  On the Island.
  Somehow We Survive.
  Sounds Begin Again, The.
  Under House Arrest.
Bursk. Does Poetry Matter?
Byron, G. Prisoner of Chillon, The.
  Sonnet on Chillon.
Cafagña, M. Lithium.
Canning, G. *et al.* Rogero's Song.
Carkesse. On the Doctors' Telling Him that till He Left off Making Verses He Was Not Fit to be Discharged.
Carmichael, H. Hong Kong Blues.
Centolella. Woman of Three Minds, The.
Cernuda. Invisible wall, The.
Clare, J. I Feel I Am.
Clark, T. Going to Jail.
Cobbett. Elegy in Newgate.
Conyus. Upon Leaving the Parole Board Hearing.
Cook, E. Song of the Imprisoned Bird.
Coolbrith. Captive of the White City, The.
Cory, W. Parting.
Dalton, R. My Neighbor.
Darwish, M. Earth Poem.
  Prison.
  Prison.
  Sirhan Drinks His Coffee in the Cafeteria.
Dawe, B. On the Death of Ronald Ryan.
De León, L. On Leaving Prison.
Derieva, R. Beyond Siberia again Siberia.
Desnos. Letter to Youki.
Dickinson, E. I never hear the word "escape".
  Mine—by the Right of the White Election!
  Of Paul and Silas it is said.
  Prison gets to be a friend, A.
Dobyns. Exile.
Donne. Oh my black[e] soul[e]! now thou art summoned.
Douglas, K. Prisoner, The.
Duemer. Theory of Tragedy.
Dunbar, P. Sympathy: "I know what the caged bird feels, alas!"
Eich. Inventory.
  Inventory.
Elizabeth I. Written with a Diamond On Her Window at Woodstock.
Éluard, P. To Her of Whom They Dream.
Espada. Prisoners of Saint Lawrence, The.
Faiz. Fragrant Hands.
  Prison Daybreak, A.
  Prison Evening, A.
Fearing. Escape.
Ferrell, M. Stories from the Tower.
Fitzgerald, R. Wind at Your Door, The.
Frazier, John Alexander, Jr. Visiting Hours.
Frere. Rogero's Song.
Fuller, H. Comic.
García Lorca. Arrest of Antoñito el Camborio.
  Death of Antoñito el Camborio.
Gaskill, C. Prisoner of Love.
Genet. Man Condemned to Death, The.
Gilyard, K. Letter.
Giovanni. Train Rides.
Giovannitti. Walker, The.
Gonzales, R. Prison, San Elizario, Texas, The.
Gorbanevskaya. I will not be able to explain why.
Graves, R. Love Without Hope.
Gunn, T. In the Tank.
  Tamer and Hawk.
Gurney, I. To God.
Hamburger, M. Between the Lines.
Hampton, Jr, F. Trouble I've Seen, The.
HaNagid. Prison, The.

Harris, W.   We Live in a Cage.
Hawoldar.   I Have Gone into My Prison Cell.
Henderson, D.   Alvin Cash/Keep on Dancin'.
Hernández, M.   Tomb of the Imagination.
Hicok.   Memory: "I hated the Road Runner."
Higgerson, R.   Utah Jazz, The.
Hikmet.   About Mount Uludağ.
 Evening Walk, The.
 Letters from a Man in Solitary.
 Letters from Chankiri Prison.
 Poems from Prison.
 Poems of Nine to Ten P.M.
 Prison to Prison.
 Since I Was Thrown Inside.
Ho Chi Minh.   Two Prison Poems.
Hoilette, A.   Blooming Death. . .Blossoms.
House, Boyce.   Justice in Old Ranger.
Housman.   Oh who is that young sinner with the
 handcuffs on his wrists?
Howe, F.   Scattered Light.
 White Lines.
Hughes, T.   Jaguar, The.
Hugo, R.   In Your Dream after Falling in Love.
 Letter to Birch from Deer Lodge.
Hwang Tonggyu.   One Flower and Another
 Flower.
Ifowodo, O.   Abundance of Grey, An.
Im Yŏngjo.   Matches.
Irish Oral Tradition.   Convict of Clonmel, The.
Jacob, M.   In Search of the Traitor.
Jarrell, R.   O My Name It Is Sam Hall.
 Prisoners.
Jastrun, T.   Hat.
Johnson, G.   Heart of a Woman, The.
Johnson, M.   Visit to the Cities of Cheese, A.
Jones, D.   Dartmoor.
Jones, H.   New Southern Exposure.
Jordan, J.   Poem Against the State (Of Things):
 1975.
Keats.   Written on the Day That Mr. Leigh Hunt
 Left Prison.
Keplinger, D.   Inside: George Gaines at
 Graterford Prison, 1981.
Kim Chiha.   Story of a Sound, The.
Kinzie.   Ringing Words.
Kipling, R.   Cells.
 Half-Ballad of Waterval.
Knight, E.   Eastern guard tower.
 For Freckle-Faced Gerald.
 Haiku: "Eastern guard tower."
 Hard Rock Returns to Prison from the Hospital
 for the Criminal Insane.
 He Sees Through Stone.
 Idea of Ancestry, The.
 To Make a Poem in Prison.
 Warden Said to Me the Other Day, The.
 WASP Woman Visits a Black Junkie in Prison,
 A.
Kocbek.   Longing for Jail, A.
Koestenbaum, P.   Sonnet 37: "I'd decided I
 initiate most."
Kudimova.   Prison, *zona*, the camps, Taldái-
 Kustanái, and the low road.
Kunze, R.   Hymn To a Woman Under
 Interrogation.
Lenski, H.   There broke into my cell last night.
Lo Pin-Wang.   On the Cicada: In Prison.
Loftis, N.   Changes—One.
Lovelace, R.   To Althea, from Prison.
 To Lucasta, from Prison.
Lowell, R.   After the Surprising Conversions.
 Memories of West Street and Lepke.
Luterman, A.   Another Vigil at San Quentin.
Lysohorsky.   At a Sunlit Window.
MacNamara, F.   Convict's Tour to Hell, A.
Madan.   Abelard to Eloisa.
Mandelstam [*or* Mandelshtam].   You Took
 Away All the Oceans and All the Room.
Maroon, B.   Fire Keeper.
Mary Stuart.   My lord and my God, I have
 hoped in Thee.
Matthews, W.   Old Folsom Prison.
McAuley, J.   Released on Parole.
McNeill, A.   Ode to Brother Joe.
Messerli.   Closure.
Mikhail, D.   Prisoner, The.

Montale.   Prisoner's Dream, The.
Morant, H.   Last Rhyme and Testament of Tony
 Lumpkin.
Morrill, D.   Man who melts a plastic garbage
 bag, The.
Morris, W.   In Prison.
Mpina.   Reborn.
Myers, B.   Dream Prison.
Neruda.   Poet's Obligation.
 Poet's Obligation, The.
Nguyễn Chí Thiện.   Jungle Night, A.
 Model Children of the Regime, The.
 Party holds you down and you lie still, The.
 This Land's No Joy.
Nicholas, T.   To a Sparrow.
Niyazi, S.   Thinker Between The Bronze Shield
 And The Human Flesh, The.
No Ch'ŏnmyŏng.   Spring of the Steel Bar
 Window.
Nortje.   Letter from Pretoria Central Prison.
Novikov, N.   In our world it's unusual.
Orléans, C.   Ballade: "I was in blossom when I
 was a child."
Padilla.   Man on the Edge.
 Self-Portrait of the Other.
Pape.   In the Bluemist Motel.
Parks, R.   Song of Freedom, A.
Parry, R.   J S L.
Pau-Llosa.   Paredón.
Paulin.   Surveillances.
Pavese.   Words from Confinement.
Peterson, R.   San Quentin 1968.
Petri.   To Be Said Over and Over Again.
Piatt, S.   In Her Prison.
Pilinszky, J.   Passion of Ravensbrück.
 Passion of Ravensbrück, The.
Po Chü-i.   Red Cuckatoo, The.
Pommy-Vega.   For Boats Only.
Ratushinskaya [*or* Ratushinskaia].   I Will Live
 and Survive.
Reese, D.   Ol' Hannah.
Rilke.   Panther, The.
 Panther, The.
Robin, L.   Prisoner of Love.
Rossetti, C.   Verse II.
Rukeyser, M.   Columbus.
Salazar.   Cricket at Central California Women's
 Facility.
Sandburg, C.   Teamster's Farewell, A.
Simic.   Much Dwindled, Starker Annotator, A.
Smith, K.   Writing in Prison.
Smith, R.   Softball at Julia Tutwiler Prison.
Smith, S.   Commuted Sentence, The.
Spender, S.   Prisoners, The.
Spenser, E.   Sonnet 73: 'Being my self captived
 here'.
Spicer, J.   Song of a Prisoner.
Sprackland, Jean.   Translating Birdsong.
Stafford, K.   Inside the Fence: Tule Lake
 Internment Camp.
Stafford, W.   Message from the Wanderer, A.
Surrey.   Prison in Windsor Castle.
 Prisoned in Windsor, He Recounteth His
 Pleasure There Passed.
Sweeney, M.   Box, The.
Sylvain, P.   Palace of Mourners, A.
Tennyson, A.   I envy not in any moods.
Tester, V.   Broken Glass.
Tranströmer.   November: "When the hangman's
 bored he turns dangerous."
Tregian.   Imprisoned Recusant Writes to His
 Wife, An.
Tu Fu [*or* Du Fu].   Spring View.
Tucker, M.   Soldier Boy's Dream, The.
Tuqan, F.   Behind Bars, Sel.
Turner, C.   Prisoner, The.
Unknown.   Convicts' Rum Song.
 Down in the Valley.
 Female Transport, The.
 For one month I was imprisoned; my slippers
 never moved forward.
 I raise my brush to write a poem to tell my dear
 wife.
 I went east to Asia; I went west to Europe.
 It was four days before the Chongyang Festival.
 Jock o' the Side [Version from Poetical

 Museum; Albyn's Anthology 2].
Kinmont Willie.
 Silvery red shirt is half covered with dust, The.
 Song of the Breaking of the Willow.
 This is a message to those who live here not to
 worry excessively.
 This place is called an island of immortals.
 Today is the last day of winter.
 Young children do not yet know worry, The.
Vaysman, N.   Anne Pauker.
Verlaine.   In Prison.
Walker, F. X.   Crooked Afro.
Walker, R.   Solitary Confinement.
Warren-Moore.   Dannemora Contraband.
 For Paula Cooper.
Warsh.   Going to Jail.
Watts-Dunton.   Coleridge.
Whalen, P.   Pet Shop.
Wilde, O.   Ballad of Reading Gaol, The.
 For oak and elm have pleasant leaves.
 He does not sit with silent men.
 There is no chapel on the day.
Wither.   If by mischance the people in the street.
Wodehouse.   Tulip Time in Sing Sing.
Woods, V.   Asylum is Water, The.
Wordsworth, W.   Sonnet: "Nuns fret not at their
 convent's narrow room."
Wright, J.   Old Prison, The.
Yi Sang.   Publications Law.
Yoneda, Karl.   New Year's Day came quietly
 and left silently.
Young, A.   Conjugal Visits.
Zabolotsky [*or* Zabolotskii].   Face of a Horse,
 The.
 Snakes.

Privacy
Abrahams, L.   Privacy.
 Thresholds of tolerance.
Aizenberg, M.   Not in the chimney, but in the
 gas-pipes.
Bone, K.   Corners.
Broumas, O.   Privacy.
Coleridge, M.   No Newspapers.
Dickinson, E.   I'm Nobody! Who are you?
Dunn, S.   Corners.
 Secret Life, A.
Ellis, T.   Kiss in the Dark, A.
Gardner, I.   Milkman, The.
González, A.   Inventory of Places Propitious for
 Love.
Greenhalgh, C.   Night I Met Marilyn, The.
 Of Love, Death and the Sea-Squirt.
Harris, W.   We Live in a Cage.
Harryman.   Privacy.
Laing, R.   Sonnet 16: "Now all our guests have
 come and gone away."
Pedretti, Erica.   No, That Can't Be.
Ross, Martin.   Body Cavity.
Sidney, P.   Sonnet 54: "Because I breathe not
 love to every one."
Wilner, E.   Her Body Is Private.
Wright, C.   Privacy.
See also **Solitude**

Prizefighting and Prizefighters
Trethewey, N.   Amateur Night.

Procrastination
Barbour, D.   Mañana (Is Soon Enough for Me).
Ceravolo.   Wind Is Blowing West, The.
Crabbe, G.   Delay Has Danger.
Jackson, L.   Postponement of Self.
Justice, D.   Self-Portrait as Still Life.
Lee, P.   Mañana (Is Soon Enough for Me).
Martial.   Procrastination.
 You say, *Postumus*, you'll live tomorrow.
Milosz, C.   Preparation.
Thoreau.   Poet's Delay, The.

Prodigal Son
Bishop, E.   Prodigal, The.
Bunin.   Flowers, and tall-stalked grasses, and a
 bee.
Cynan.   It was all go with the jazz-band and all
 go with the dance.
Eichner, Maura.   Father, The.
Goldberg, L.   Prodigal Son, The.
Kipling, R.   Prodigal Son, The.

Martinez, D. Prodigal Son Considers a Diplomatic Career, The.
Merwin. "Prodigal Son," The.
Muñiz Huberman. Prodigal Daughter.
Powell, D. A. My Riches I Have Squandered. Spread with Honey.
Rilke. Departure of the Prodigal Son*, The.
Luke 15:11–19; And he said, "There was a man".
Robinson, E. Luke 15:20–32; And he arose and came.
Prodigal Son, The.
Tsvetayeva [or Tsvetaeva]. And, Not Crying in Vain.

Prodigality
Dante Alighieri. Natural thirst that never can be quenched.
Juan Chi. In My Youth.
Kabysh, I. Whenever the prodigal son returns home.
Meredith, G. He cancelled the ravaging Plague.
Moore, M. Americans in 1933–4–5–6–7–8–, Etc.

Progress
"Arudra.". Death of Man.
Atwood. Is / Not.
Auden. Moon Landing.
Berry, W. Against the War in Vietnam.
Manifesto: The Mad Farmer Liberation Front.
Callimachus. Would that there had never been swift ships!
Cohan. If Washington Should Come to Life.
Nothing New Beneath the Sun.
Cummings, E. E. O pr / gress verily thou art m.
Pity This Busy Monster,Manunkind.
Daugherty, J. Pack train, stage coach, pony express, climb over the mountain passes.
Davidson, L. America.
Enzensberger, H. Poison, The.
Fanning, R. Middle Age, The: "Between TV and computer screens."
Fenton, J. Kingfisher's Boxing Gloves, The.
Gunn, T. Considering the Snail.
Halliday, M. Population.
Hardy, T. Christmas: 1924.
Heaney, S. From the Canton of Expectation.
Mud Vision, The.
Hoffenstein. Progress.
Holub. Helping Hand, A.
Hugo, R. Letter to Oberg from Pony.
Lauture, D. Our Destiny.
Lecky. Decline of Love, The.
Linden, M. To the Wheel of Progress.
Nash, O. No Wonder Our Fathers Died.
Oppen. Bicycles and the Apex, The.
Building of the Skyscraper, The.
Phillips, D. If It's Only Rhythm.
Praed. Chaunts of the Brazen Head, The. II.
Rukeyser, M. Book of the Dead, The.
Sandburg, C. Four Preludes on Playthings of the Wind.
Southwick. Earthly Light.
Spender, S. Not Palaces.
Szymborska, W. Century's Decline, The.
Tsaloumas. Progressive Man's Indignation, A.

Proletariat
Galanskov. Last Platform, The.
Helfrich, Karen. Influencing Factors.
Im Hwa. My Brother and the Brazier.
Pier of Yokohama under the Umbrella, The.
Khlebnikov, V. Burning Field, The.
Shwarts [or Shvarts]. Dump, The.
Tkachenko. Battle.
See also **Bourgeoisie**

Prometheus
Byron, G. Prometheus.
Dyer, S. Prometheus, when first from heaven high.
Field. Prometheus fashioned man.
Horan. Prometheus.
Shelley, P. Prometheus Unbound.
Swift, J. Prometheus: "As, when the squire and tinker, Wood."
Tomlinson, C. Prometheus.

Promiscuity
Berkson, B. Strawberry Blond.
Brown, K. Lonely Women.
Cunningham, J. Epigram: "You ask me how Contempt you claims to sleep."
Hughes, L. Ballad of the Girl Whose Name Is Mud.
Jouve. More and More Woman.
O Cham. Turkish Bakery, The.
Parker, D. Little Old Lady in Lavender Silk, The.
Rochester, J. Mock Song, The.
Signior Dildo.

Promises
Anderson, M. Lost in the Stars.
Anderson-Thompkins. brken promises.
Anthony, M. Ugly Heart, The.
Beausoleil, B. Wearing.
Cader. Promise, A.
Campbell, J. If I Had You.
Connelly, R. If I Had You.
Di Prima. For Suzuki Roshi.
Donne. On His Mistress [or Mistris].
Dugan, M. Coolun, The.
Herrick. Rainbow; or Curious Covenant, The.
To His Conscience.
Howe, M. Promise, The: "In the dream I had when he came back, not sick."
Hurd, B. My Son's Wedding, My Daughter's.
Irish Oral Tradition. O Donall Oge : The Grief of a Girl's Heart.
Italicus. At the city's heart stood the shrine to Dido's ghost.
Jones, R. Key, The.
Jonson, B. Urging Her of a Promise.
Koehler, T. As Long As I Live.
Lochhead, L. Promises.
Olds, S. Wedding Vow, The.
Padilla. Promise, The.
Rehm, Pam. Vow 2.
Robinson, E. Vickery's Mountain.
Rossetti, C. Promises like Pie-Crust.
Segovia, F. Promesa.
Promise.
Smart, C. To the Rev. Mr. Powell.
Spenser, E. Sonnet 65: "Doubt which ye misdeeme, fayre love, is vaine, The."
Subbarao, R. Chained.
Swift, J. Twelve Articles.
Unknown. Frail, frail, lone-growing bamboo.
If this were a world.
Lament: "Cheek by cheek on our pillow[s]."
Over the Pillow.
Wyatt. What should I say.

Proms
Chavez, L. After the Prom.
Witte, Francine. Prom.

Propaganda
Day Lewis. Where Are the War Poets?
Galanskov. Last Platform, The.
Herbert, Z. Transformations of Livy.
Osman, J. Dropping Leaflets.
Shaku Chōkū. Tanka: "Imagining / the grassy ground not shown."

Propertius, Sextus
Propertius. Ghost, The.

Property
Agali, A. Sister: "House, A. A car. Sweet things. Gold."
Belli, C. Segregation #1.
Coolbrith. Ownership.
Davis, C. Belongings.
Dickinson, E. I am afraid to own a Body.
Durcan. Tullynoe: Tête-à-Tête in the Parish Priest's Parlour.
Eich. Inventory.
Inventory.
Felipe, L. Farm Is Yours, The.
Fuertes. Things.
Garioch. Property.
Hanzlicek, C. What I Want Is.
Ismail. You: "You're mine."
Kamienska. Things of This World.
Lope de Vega. Sonnet 188.
MacCaig. Chauvinist.

Marlatt, D. Ghost.
Miles, J. Ride.
Norris, J. My Estate.
North, M. Ordnance Survey in the Northern Counties.
Padilla. Fountain, a House of Stone, A.
Patterson, R. No Jive.
Philips, A. Salute to Property.
Ragain. Hungry Ghost Surrenders His Tackle Box, A.
Sin Hŭm. Don't laugh if my roof beams.
Soto. Ode to the Yard Sale.
Unknown. Home on the Range.
My lover wants to keep my tongue inside his mouth.
Pick the flowers by the handful.
Warton, T. Of George, and Property.
Whitman, W. I think I could turn and live with animals, they are so placid and self-contained.
Wickham. Soul's Liberty.

Prophecy and Prophets
Akhmatova, A. Dream, A.
Anderson, W. There's Not a Friend like the Lowly Jesus.
Baratier, D. Estrella's Prophecies #47.
Barkova, A. Few Autobiographical Facts, A.
Blake, W. Merlins Prophecy.
Chagy. Haggai.
Chizhova. Cassandra.
Cowley, A. 34. Chapter of the Prophet Isaiah, The.
Dawes, K. Trickster 1 (for Winston Rodney).
El Janabi, A. Ink.
Eliot, T. S. Luke 2:21–40; And at the end of eight days, when he was circumcised.
Gay, J. Birth of the Squire; an Eclogue, The.
George, S. Antichrist, The.
Graves, R. Christmas Robin, The.
Hall, D. Prophecy.
Hemans. Second Sight.
Hernández Cruz. Keeping Track of the Serpents.
Italicus. At the city's heart stood the shrine to Dido's ghost.
Ivanov, G. On the boundary of snow and melting.
Jeffers, H. Ezekiel Saw de Wheel.
Johnson, L. Mystic and Cavalier.
Korinna [or Corinna]. Of your daughters: Zeus, Father.
Lehman. Prophet's Lantern, The.
Levertov. Man Wearing Bird.
Lope de Vega. They slew by night.
Malachi. Psalm of Silk.
Manley, R. Bob Marley's Dead.
McCallum, S. What the Oracle Said.
McGrath, T. End of the World, The.
Napier, A. Tulum Saw the Coming.
Pavlova. Crone, The.
Pinsky. Hearts, The.
Poe. Stanzas.
Robinson, M. Foresees her Death.
Sachs, N. If the Prophets Broke in.
Your Eyes, O My Beloved.
Samaras, N. Mute Prophets.
Seaton, M. Nostradamus Predicts the Destruction of Chicago.
Shakespeare, W. Sonnet 106: "When in the chronicle of wasted time."
Skelton, J. Than, if this noble kyng.
Spender, S. Pylons, The.
Tennyson, A. Babylon.
Tindal. Birth Wail, The.
Unknown. Ezekiel Saw de [or the] Wheel.
Heriger and the False Prophet.
Prophetic Powers.
Vallejo. Black Stone on a White Stone.
Virgil [or Vergil]. Fourth Ecologue: Pollio, The.
Volkman. Sonnet: "What is this witness, the watching ages."
Weatherford, C. From the Mouth of the Gxara.
Whitman, W. Song of the Answerer.
Wilbur, R. Advice to a Prophet.
Yeats. Matthew 24:15–31.
See also **Oracles**

Prose
Mayer, B.   Turning Prose into Poetry.
Nemerov.   Because You Asked about the Line
   between Prose and Poetry.
Welt.   I stopped writing poetry.
Proserpina [*or* Proserpine]
Ovid.   Ceres and Proserpina.
See also **Persephone**
Prospero
Dancing Bear, J. P.   Heart-Shaped Island, A.
Stillman, M.   Prospero.
Prostitution and Prostitutes
Ai.   Everything: Eloy, Arizona, 1956.
Anderson, D.   Purification.
Anwar, C.   Heaven.
Asclepiades.   Here Lies Archeanassa.
Barresi.   Class Dress.
Basho.   Staying at an inn.
   Under the same roof.
   Whore and monk, we sleep.
Beeching, J.   Gaudy Camp Follower, The.
Bell, E.   Help is a Discotheque.
Blind.   Russian Student's Tale, The.
Breton, A.   Man and a Woman Absolutely
   White, A.
   Man and Woman Absolutely White, A.
Brook, D.   Why I Am a Whore.
Brooks, G.   Coora Flower, The.
Broumas, O.   Etymology.
Burgess, Leslie.   Prostitute's Notebook, The.
Chin, J.   Cocksucker's Blues.
Ch'u Kuang-hsi.   Streets of Ch'ang-an.
Clarke, A.   Young Woman of Beare, The.
Clifton, H.   Id.
   Monsoon Girl.
Cofer, J.   Las Magdalenas.
Coleman, H.   OK Corral East: Brothers in the
   Nam.
Cooper, D.   Being Aware.
Cotton, C.   Epitaph on M. H., An.
Crawford, R.   Love Song of Tommo Frogley.
Cross, D.   Painted Ladies, The.
Cullen, C.   For Daughters of Magdalen.
Dōyaku Sensei, Master Artery.   To Master
   Groggy, From Afar.
Dowson.   Non Sum Qualis Eram Bonae sub
   Regno Cynarae.
Dunqul.   Corner.
Erdrich.   Lady in the Pink Mustang, The.
France, L.   My Muse, the Whore.
Gonzales, R.   Paso del Norte.
Hardy, T.   Ruined Maid, The.
Hass, R.   Bookbuying in the Tenderloin.
Henley, W. E.   Madam Life's A Piece in Bloom.
Howard, R.   My Last Hustler.
Howard Jr., W.   Paralyzed.
Hughes, L.   Sliver of Sermon.
Issa.   Prostitute's shack, The.
Jackson, M. L.   Euphoria.
Jana Bai.   Cast off all shame.
Jenkins, A.   Street Life.
Kakei.   In a rice field.
Kendrick, D.   Solo: The Good Blues.
Kim Chiha.   Road to Seoul, The.
Kirstein.   Snatch.
Knight, E.   As You Leave Me.
Knox, J.   Cruising for Prostitutes.
Ko Chŏnghûi.   Prague Spring 6.
Komunyakaa, Y.   Tu Do Street.
Kshetrayya.   Courtesan to a Young Customer, A.
Kuan Han-ch'ing.   In the Southern Mode, to the
   Tune "A Sprig of Flowers" The Refusal to Get
   Old.
Lovelace, R.   La Bella Bona-Roba.
Lukata, B.   Ashy Gal.
Mapanje.   Cheerful Girls at Smiller's Bar, 1971,
   The.
   Messages.
Mapun, D.   O Myland Woman.
Maraini.   Plaza de Mayo.
Martineau, J.   Hooker.
McGrath, T.   Song: Miss Penelope Burgess,
   Balling the Jack.
McKay, C.   Midnight Woman to the Bobby, A.
McOrlan.   Wood merchant's parlour, The.
Nashe [*or* Nash].   Choise of valentines, The.

Nokhem, Y.   Hounds Howl at the Moon.
Okereke, C.   Starlette.
Pearlberg, G.G.   Loop-the-Loop in Prospect
   Park (1905).
Plomer.   French Lisette: A Ballad of Maida
   Vale.
Porter, C.   Love for Sale.
Powell, D. A.   [Coda & discography].
Purdy, J.   Do You Wonder Why I Am Sleepy.
Ramsay, A.   Lucky Spence's Last Advice.
Ridge, L.   Phyllis.
Robertson, Lexie Dean.   Pioneer: The Vignette
   of an Oil-Field.
Rodgers, W.   Net, The.
Rouse, A.   Lilies of the Field.
Sandburg, C.   Harrison Street Court.
Senryū, K.   Even her smile.
   When the night falls.
Simmons, J.   Cavalier Lyric.
Simpson, L.   Bower of Roses, A.
   Man Who Married Magdalene, The.
Sŏ Chŏngju.   At a Wine House near Taegu.
Swift, J.   Beautiful Young Nymph Going to Bed,
   A.
Taylor, J.   Epigram: "Look how yon lecher's
   legs are worn away."
   Me thinks I heare some Cavillers object.
Tran, B.   Women Next Door, The.
Trethewey, N.   Bellocq's Ophelia.
   Countess P———'s Advice for New Girls.
   Photograph of a Bawd Drinking Raleigh Rye.
Unknown.   Green mansion is a place of filth and
   shame, A.
   In the early hours of the next morning dawning.
   Shari Wag El Burka.
   Thus feverish fancies floated in my brain.
Villon.   Ballad of Villon and Fat Madge, The.
   I love and serve my lady with a will.
Vollmer.   On Reporting the Murder of a Young
   Prostitute.
Walker, M.   Whores.
Weigl.   Way of Tet, The.
Whitman, W.   To a Common Prostitute.
Wilbur, R.   Place Pigalle.
Wilde, O.   Harlot's House, The.
   Impression du Matin.
Williams, C. K.   Gas Station, The.
Wright, J.   In Response to a Rumor that the
   Oldest Whorehouse in Wheeling, West
   Virginia, Has Been Condemned.
Protestantism and Protestants
Coles, R.   Christmas, Belfast.
Donne.   Show me dear[e] Christ, thy spouse, so
   bright and clear[e].
Herbert, G.   British Church, The.
Hill, G.   Christmas Trees.
Morrissey, S.   Thoughts in a Black Taxi.
Ormsby, F.   Spot the Ball.
Proust, Marcel
Disch.   Bookmark, A.
Jarrell, R.   Man Meets a Woman in the Street,
   A.
Provence, France
Gosse.   Sestina: "In fair Provence, the land of
   lute and rose."
Procter, A.   Legend of Provence, A.
Wilbur, R.   Grasse: The Olive Trees.
Williams, W.   To Ford Madox Ford in Heaven.
Providence
Herrick.   Gods Providence.
Wheatley, P.   Thoughts on the Works of
   Providence.
Providence, Rhode Island
Weaver, A.   Providence Journal V: Israel of
   Puerto Rico.
Psyche (mythology)
Duncan, R.   Poem Beginning with a Line by
   Pindar, A.
Espaillat.   Psyche Revised.
Goldberg, B.   Hound and Leper.
Greger.   Psyche and Eros in Florida.
Keats.   Ode to Psyche.
Mandelstam [*or* Mandelshtam].   When Psyche,
   Who Is Life, Descends Among the Shades.
Pound, E.   Speech for Psyche in the Golden

   Book of Apuleius.
Tighe.   Glimpse of Love, A.
Willis, N.   Psyche, Before the Tribunal of
   Venus.
Psychiatry and Psychiatrists
Bogan, L.   Psychiatrist's Song.
Clements, S.   Deer Cloud.
Coles, R.   On Dutch's Death.
Ezekiel.   Family.
Kolodny, S.   Tsuneko—Psychiatric Medications
   Clinic.
Lister, R.   Mind Reborn in Streatham Common,
   A.
Pinsky.   Their Speech, Compared with Wisdom
   and Poetry.
Rector.   David's Rumor.
Ritchie, E.   Electroconvulsive Therapy.
Verga, Angelo.   My Wife's Therapist.
Yi Kyŏngnim.   Korean Women.
See also **Mental Illness**
Psychoanalysis and Psychoanalysts
Berryman.   Group.
Cleary, B.   Chicken & Sex.
Coles, R.   On Dutch's Death.
Durrell.   Ballad of the Oedipus Complex.
Everhard.   Curing Homosexuality.
Jenkins, P.   Six Small Fires.
Kay, J.   Maw Broon Visits a Therapist.
McClatchy.   1971.
McGrath, C.   At the Freud Hilton.
Wilner, E.   Muse, The.
Fox, Skip.   Economics of Metonymy
   ("Balancing as metal, its sound, the metal in its
   sound.").
Hajjaj, N.   Psychotherapy.
Jonas, S.   Muddle, A.
Santos, S.   Talking Cure, The.
Waterhouse, A.   Speaking About My Cracked
   Sump.
Puberty
Baggett.   Barely Eight.
Byron, G.   Juan's Puberty.
Hampton.   In Andrea's Garden.
Hope, M.   Bare Floors.
   Sixth Grade.
Joseph, A.   Adolescence.
Mitchell, A.   Puppy Called Puberty, A.
Olds, S.   Photograph of the Girl.
Tati-Loutard.   Man-Myth: Puberty.
Tayson, R.   First Sex.
Unknown.   Song for a Young Girl's Puberty
   Ceremony.
Wrigley, R.   Prophecy, The.
Publishing and Publishers
Byron, G.   To Mr. Murray.
Carroll, L.   Poeta Fit, Non Nascitur.
Hecht, A.   From the Grove Press.
Koch, K.   Supposing that one walks out into the
   air.
Larkin, P.   Limerick: "There was an old fellow
   of Kaber."
   Limerick: "There was an old fellow of Kaber."
Le Guin.   For CALYX.
Morton, J.   Someone Asked the Publisher.
Wells, C.   Of Modern Books.
Pudding
Iglesias, H.   Thursday Afternoon: Life Is Sweet.
Puddles
Frost, R.   Spring Pools.
Puerto Ricans
Algarin.   El Jibarito Moderno.
   Happy New Year.
   Prologue.
   Taos Pueblo Indians: 700 strong according to
   Bobby's last census.
   Wire Tap.
Coralin, J.   Rosa's Beauty.
Espada.   David Leaves the Saints for Paterson.
   My Native Costume.
   Spanish of Our Out-Loud Dreams, The.
   Tony Went to the Bodega but He Didn't Buy
   Anything.
Esteves.   Celebration of Home Birth: November
   15th, 1981, A.
   For Lolita Lebron.

Here.
In the Beginning.
Lil' Pito.
Take the Hearts of Children.
Figueroa, J. Boricua.
Murdered Luggage.
Poet Pedro Pietri.
Gomez, M. Making It.
Solo Palabras.
To the Latin Lover I Left at the Candy Store.
Hernández Cruz. Anonymous.
Borinkins in Hawaii.
Discovery.
Energy.
If Chickens Could Talk.
Ironing Goatskin.
Latin and Soul for Joe Bataan.
Loíza Aldea.
Man Who Came to the Last Floor, The.
Mountain Building.
Physics of Ochun, The.
Poem: "Greater cities are, The."
Poem: "Your head it waves outside."
Side 18.
Side 21.
Tale of Bananas, A.
Two Guitars.
You Gotta Have Your Tips on Fire.
Lloréns [or Lorens] Torres. Ugly Duckling,
   The.
Morales, A. Ending Poem.
Immigrants.
Kitchens.
1930.
Other Heritage, The.
Puertoricanness.
Sugar Poem.
Tita's Poem.
Morales, R. Dinner, The.
Ending Poem.
Getting Out Alive.
I Am the Reasonable One.
I Recognize You.
Perdomo, W. Nigger-Reecan Blues.
Unemployed Mami.
Pietri. Intermission from Monday.
Traffic Misdirector.
Piñero. La Bodega Sold Dreams.
Lower East Side Poem, A.
This Is Not the Place Where I was Born.
Winch. Six Families of Puerto Ricans.

Puerto Rico
Carruth, H. In filthy Puerto Rico lives a bird
   with no.
Espada. Coca-Cola and Coco Frío.
Cockroaches of Liberation.
Figueroa, J. Boricua.
Puerto Rico Made in Japan.
Hernández Cruz. New/Aguas Buenas/Jersey.
Puerta Rica.
Marzán. Sunday Morning in Old San Juan.
McDonald, W. Middle Years, The.
Mistral, G. Caribbean Sea.
Morales, A. Child's Christmas in Puerto Rico,
   A.
Pau-Llosa. Paredón.
Sondheim. America.
Weaver, A. Providence Journal V: Israel of
   Puerto Rico.

Pumas
Galvin, B. Cougar.

Pumpkins
Apache Oral Tradition. Corn Ceremony.
Goodison. From the Garden of the Women
   Once Fallen.
Lilburn, Tim. Pumpkins.
Nye, N. What Brings Us Out.

Punctuation
Gorbanevskaya. Epiphanies, / and commas,
   commas.
Markotić, N. Repeat the capitalism of narrative.
Seven blind curves.
Stewart, S. Lost Rules of Usage.
Violi. Appeal to the Grammarians.

Punishment
Berggolts [or Bergholts]. My insatiable memory
   is like.
Bible, *O.T.* Psalm 58. Si Vere Utique.
Burns, R. Holy Willie's Prayer.
Erdrich. Indian Boarding School: The
   Runaways.
Garcia, R. Zapato, El.
Graham, H. L'Enfant Glacé.
Haavikko. Take heart, Ovid. No sentence.
Hajjaj, N. Mr. Dheeb Al-Rifa'i.
Hayden, R. Whipping, The.
Heaney, S. Punishment.
Hernández, M. For Pulling the Feathers from
   Icy Archangels.
Herrick. Gods Providence.
Persecutions Purifie.
Hsüeh T'ao [or Xue Tao]. Parrot Parted from
   Her Cage.
Issa. I envy.
It once happened.
Leonard, T. Four of the Belt.
Leonidov, Rumen. Misery.
Lesley, G. Behold, how Sodom swaggers in its
   Pride.
Leto. For Talking.
Loynaz, D. M. XXX.
McDaniel, J. Bad Pilgrim Room, The.
Merwin. Lament for the Makers.
Mitchell, A. Dumb Insolence.
Myrddyn (Merlin). Yscolan.
Olds, S. Unjustly Punished Child.
Palladas [or Pallades]. Murderer and Sarapis,
   The.
Patchen. Lions of fire, The.
Patmore, C. Toys, The.
Raffalovich, M. A. World Well Lost 18, The.
Reynolds, O. Hazel.
Reznikoff. Testimony: The United States
   (1901–1910) Recitative/The South.
Ross, C. Jack.
Sharpless. Low Church.
Ulku, A. History.
Unknown. Bitter Withy, The.
Deserter, The.
Having left behind its cutting.
Lay of the Lash, The.
Let the first syllable of PEnelope be followed by
   the first of DIdo, the first of CAnus by that of
   REmus.
To a Traitor.
What business, this? What reason should we
   give.
Warren, R. Wet Hair: If Now His Mother
   Should Come.
Webster, A. Little child she, half defiant came,
   A.
Wilde, O. Ballad of Reading Gaol, The.
Wright, J. Song for the Middle of the Night, A.
Yosano Akiko. Let men pay for their.

Punks
Goldsmith, K. One pair ridiculous gorilla
   slippers; 3 pairs of cheap shit sunglasses.
Loncar, M. Peoria.
Lumsden, R. ITMA.
Sicoli. All Shook Up.
Stone, A. Rocket to Russia.

Puns
Goodyear, Dana. Umbra.
Ingoldsby, T. Lines Left at Mr Theodore Hook's
   House in June, 1834.
McDaniel, J. Play It Again, Salmonella.
Portnoy, M. Roget, Papier, Schism!
Shakespeare, W. Sonnet 135: "Whoever [or
   Who ever] hath her wish, thou hast thy Will."
Torres, E. Gigabyte Me—How Much RAM in
   Your Summer of Love?
Unknown. Poem of Medicine Puns.
Zukofsky, L. I's (pronounced *Eyes*).

Puppets and Puppeteers
Boruch. Book of Hand Shadows, The.
Fuhrman, J. Here, I Say.
Holub. Funeral, The.
Teaching About Disease.
March, S. Thousand Marionettes, A.
Milán, E. Riddle me what marionettes are.

Revell, D. Tooms 4.
Robinson, E. Snow: "Purpose of the blanket,
   The."
Sabry, M. Marionette.
Verlaine. Weird as Puppets.
Wilde, O. Harlot's House, The.
Zawacki, Andrew. Ventriloquy.

Puppies
Collins, M. Tory, a Puppy.
Ingelow. Pups and the Fish, The.
McGrath, G. Noticing a man unable.
Püsküllüoğlu. Old Pirate in These Waters, An.
Riordan, M. Holy Land, The.

Purgatory
Dante Alighieri. And now, with the reflected
   lights that glow.
But with regard to me, I'll satisfy.
To course across more kindly waters now.
Schwartz, L. Proverbs from Purgatory.
Van Cleave, R. Ophelia on a Graveled Garden
   Walk in Purgatory.

Puritanism and Puritans
Butler, S. When civil fury [or dudgeon] first
   grew high.
Corbet [or Corbett]. Distracted Puritan, The.
Equi. Puritans.
Longfellow, H. Rhyme of Sir Christopher, The.
Lowell, R. After the Surprising Conversions.
Maule. To Cotton Mather, from a Quaker.
Quarles. On Those That Deserve It.
Shapiro, K. Puritan, The.
Unknown. Zealous Puritan, The.
Wylie. Puritan Sonnet.
Baker, D. Puritan Way of Death, The.

Purity
Barker, J. To Her Lover's Complaint.
Blunt, W. As To His Choice of Her.
Bowers, N. Flight: "River slops under the
   bridge, The."
Chavez, L. Clean Sheets.
Coe, C. Possibility.
Debravo, J. Beds of Purification.
Drayton. Sonnet 35: Some, misbelieving and
   profane.
Ekelof. Ayíasma.
Gilbert, W. Bunthorne's Song.
Hafiz, K [or Hafez]. Stain of the Sea, The
   (414).
Herbert, G. Superliminare.
Herrick. Persecutions Purifie.
Hogg, J. Thirteenth Bard's Song, The.
Johnson, J. Unmarked Stop in Front of
   Westmond General Store, Westmond, Idaho.
Kakei. Morning glory / So pure.
Kim Chôngnan. Veronica, a Double Life.
Lamb, C. Timid grace sits trembling in her eye,
   A.
Levine, P. Genius: "Two old dancing shoes my
   grandfather."
Lindsay, V. General William Booth Enters into
   Heaven.
Lovelace, R. Her Muffe.
MacNeice. Individualist Speaks, The.
Mei Yao Ch'en. On the Death of a New Born
   Child.
Millay, E. Love is not all: it is not meat nor
   drink.
Peralta Family Oral Tradition. O Blanca Virgen.
Plumly. Wight.
Prado, A. Stained Glass Window.
Robinson, M. Temple of Chastity, The.
Roscoe, W. Camellia, The.
Sahagún, C. In the Beginning.
Schwartz, C. Hands: "Hands were purified in
   fire."
Shcherbina. Stepmother, The.
Sidney, P. Sonnet 72: "Desire, though thou my
   old companion art."
Storni. You Want Me White ("You want me
   pure.").
Sy, T. Cup of Clear Water, A.
Takushitsu. Breeze strokes the water of the
   spring, A.
Traherne. Instruction, The.
Varchi. What part of my holiest and most
   beautiful feelings.

Watson, R.   Ruined Altar, A.
Winkler Prins.   Shower.
Wroth.   Sonnet 3: "His flames ar[e] joy[e]s, his bands true lovers' might."
Yahya Efendi, Sheyhülislâm.   Let the hypocrites practice their way.
Young, A.   Art of Benny Carter, The.

Pursuit
Aktan, F.   Pia.
Castro, R.   I Know Not What I Seek Eternally.
Crane, S.   I saw a man pursuing the horizon.
Ignatow, D.   Bagel, The.
Jandl, E.   Romance, A.
Kim Sünghŭi.   Horror Movie.
Livingstone, D.   Traffic interlude: Descent from the Tower.
Merwin.   Animals, The.
Pietri.   Intermission from Thursday.
Rankin, J.   Man is following me, A.
Reese, L.   Mystery.
Rodríguez, A.   Apple.
Silverstein, S.   Slithergadee, The.
Teitelboim, D.   Men.
Unknown.   Allansford Pursuit, The.
Zaid.   Song of Pursuit.

Pushers
Gunn, T.   Street Song.
See also **Drug Addiction**

Pushkin, Aleksandr Sergeyevich
Nabokov.   On Translating "Eugene Onegin".
Nekrasov, V.   What kind of Pushkin am I.
Quintane, Nathalie.   My Pushkin.
Zabolotsky [*or* Zabolotskii].   Yesterday Reflecting Upon Death.

Pygmalion
Gorbanevskaya.   Savage cold of Russian winters, The.
Marston, J.   *Pigmalion,* whose hie love-hating minde.
Ovid.   Pygmalion.

Pygmies
Bogen, L.   Pygmy Headhunters and Killer Apes, My Lover and Me.
Graves, R.   Ogres and Pygmies.
Limonov.   Fantastic!

Pym, John
Drummond, W.   On Pym.

Pyramids
Baudelaire.   Spleen LXXVI.
Giovanni.   Ego Tripping (There May Be a Reason Why).
Greville, F.   Peace is the next in order, first in end.
Hecht, J.   On the Strength of All Conviction and the Stamina of Love.
Henry, B.   Pyramid, The.
MacEwen, G.   Inside the Great Pyramid.
Mendes, M.   Everything happens / In an Egypt of aerial corridors.
Wenderoth, J.   As Hour and Year Collapsed.

Pyramus and Thisbe
Johnston, D.   Pyramus & Thisbe.

Pyromania and Pyromaniacs
Cooley, N.   Arson.
Prunty.   Pyromaniac, The.

Q

Quail
Smith, W.   Quail in Autumn.
Trowbridge, J.   Idyl of Harvest Time, An.

Quakers
Halpine.   Quakerdom (The Formal Call).
Irish Oral Tradition.   John McGoldrick's Trial for the Quaker's Daughter.
Maule.   To Cotton Mather, from a Quaker.
Taylor, H.   Goodbye to the Old Friends.
Toomer.   Our Growing Day.
See also **Friends, Society of**

Quarrels
Blaser.   Suddenly.
Fauset.   Words! Words!
Frost, R.   From Plane to Plane.

García Lorca.   Quarrel.
Gonzalez, N.   How the Heart Aches.
Harte, B.   Society upon the Stanislaus, The.
Heard, J.   Quarrel, The.
Hughes, L.   Early Evening Quarrel.
Johnson, T.   12 second poem.
Justice, D.   But That Is Another Story.
Kharms.   Beginning of a Beautiful Day (A Symphony), The.
Kunitz, S.   Quarrel, The.
Mayakovsky [*or* Maiakovskii].   Past One O'Clock . . . .
Muldoon, P.   Sushi.
Padilla.   Song of the Juggler.
Philips, K.   On the 3 of September, 1651.
Phillips, S.   Apparition, The.
Piatt, S.   Her Word of Reproach.
Prior.   To a Lady: She Refusing to Continue a Dispute with Me.
Salom.   Walking at Night.
Shakespeare, W.   Sonnet 40: "Take all my loves, my Love, yea, take them all."
   Sonnet 120: "That you were once unkind, befriends me now."
Thompson, P.   After the Quarrel.
   Domestic Storm, A.
Unknown.   Cats of Kilkenny, The.
   Jolly Pinder of Wakefield, The.
   When I started wanting.
Warsh.   Static, The.
Yi Sang.   Poem No. 3.
See also **Anger**

Quarries
Dickey, J.   In the Marble Quarry.
Nicholson, N.   Rockferns.
Rukeyser, M.   Sand-Quarry with Moving Figures.
Salkey.   Clearsightedness.
Toledo, N.   Cadidi Laaga Lua.
   Revelación.
   Revelation.
Williams, T.   Quarry.

Quebec City, Canada
Ray, H.   Quebec.

Quebec (province), Canada
Klein, A.   Indian Reservation: Caughnawaga.
   Rocking Chair, The.

Queen Anne's Lace
Souster.   Queen Anne's Lace.
Williams, W.   Queen Anne's Lace.

Queens
Akhmadulina.   Queen, A.
Angus.   Alas! Poor Queen.
Carroll, L.   Welcome Queen Alice.
Cavendish, M.   Courting the Faerie Queen.
   Pastime of the Queen of Fairies, The.
Coleridge, M.   Regina.
Davenant [*or* D'Avenant].   To the Queen[e], Entertain[e]d at Night by the Countess[e] of Anglesey.
Drayton.   Queen Katherine to Owen Tudor.
Duffy, C.   Queen Herod.
Graves, R.   Queen Mother to New Queen.
Hoagland, E.   Fired Up!!
Housman.   1887.
Jamie, K.   Queen of Sheba, The.
Lanier, E.   To the Queen's Most Excellent Majesty.
Lawson, H.   English Queen, The.
Levin, P.   Lost Bee, The.
Lomax, M.   Gruoch.
Meitner, E.   All the Pools in Queens.
Narcisse, P.   Singing Queen, Where Are You?
Pfeiffer, E.   Lost Light, The.
Ralegh, S.   Sir Walter Ralegh to the Queen.
Sappho.   Queen Hera, may your [graceful form].
Scott, A.   Welcum, illustrat Ladye, and oure Quene!
Synge.   Queens.
Unknown.   Queen Nefertiti.
   Queen, Queen, Caroline.
Wotton, S.   On His Mistress [*or* Mistris], the Queen of Bohemia.

Queens, New York City
Llwyd, Iwan.   Far Rockaway.

Parker, D.   When Mark Deloach Ruled the World.
Shapiro, H.   Bus Ride.

Questions
Agosin.   Questions.
al-Sa'igh, Y.   Final Question, The.
Albiach.   Hermitage Road, The.
Auden.   Question, The.
Bandeira.   Interview.
Beckett, S.   Que ferais-je sans ce monde sans visage sans questions.
   What would I do without this world faceless incurious.
Bernheimer.   20 Questions.
Bousoño, C.   Door, The.
Brown, L.   My Uncruel April, My Totally Equal Unfortold April Unfolded.
Cavendish, M.   Discourse of Beasts, A.
Collins, B.   Centrifuge, The.
Coulette.   Postscript: "There are some questions one should know by heart."
Darío, R.   Unhappy He.
De la Mare.   Last Chapter, The.
DiPalma.   Prerogative of Lieder, The.
Donegan, P.   Something Happened.
Dunbar, P.   Mystery, The.
Duncan, R.   Among My Friends.
Dunn, D.   Sundial, The.
Edwards, K.   Provisionally.
Eigner.   In Imitation.
Ekelof.   Questionnaire.
Emerson, R.   Sphinx, The.
Etherege.   To a Lady Asking Him How Long He Would Love Her.
Forrester, S.   Only one flower.
Fox, Skip.   Sic transit ("Neither does the world answer but.").
Freeman, Jessica.   Up Tchoupitoulas Nom de Guerre.
Georgiou, E.   Week in the Life of the Ethnically Indeterminate, A.
Ghalib, M.   Questions: "Since nothing actually exists except You."
Gier, J.   Examining the I.
Gorostiza, J.   Fireflies.
Guevara, M.   Abuelo, Answers and Questions.
Hanzlicek, C.   Egg.
Hoffenstein.   Progress.
Hume, C.   Comprehension Questions.
Johnson, T.   Until He Comes.
Kees.   What the Spider Heard.
Maclean, A.   Question and Answer.
Mapanje.   Another Fools' Day Touches Down: Shush.
Marennikova, K.   Mother, squatting hurts.
Melville, H.   Spirit Appeared to Me, A.
Mikhail, D.   America: "Please don't ask me, America."
Muir, E.   Interrogation, The.
Neruda.   And what did the rubies say.
   And when light was forged.
   How did the grapes come to know.
   Who works harder on earth.
Owen, W.   Maundy Thursday.
Padilla.   Question for the Frankfurt School, A.
Piatt, S.   Answering A Child.
Robinson, E.   Two Men.
Sandburg, C.   Haze.
Santayana.   Cape Cod.
Sidney, P.   Sonnet 31: "With how sad steps, O Moon[e], thou climb'st the skies."
Sorrentino.   Oranges Returned, The.
Stefanile.   Answering Robert Frost.
Stein, G.   Long Dress, A.
Straus, M.   Log of Pi, The.
Tagore.   Last Poems 13.
Unknown.   Examination Question.
   Shall I Die?
   Will You Love Me When I'm Old?
   Words of the All-Wise, The.
Von Freytag-Loringhoven.   Is It?
Walker, A.   Reassurance.
Wallace-Crabbe.   Binary.
Wang Wei.   Farewell.
Weingarten.   Inquisition, The: A Romance.
Wheelwright.   Cross Questions.

Whitman, W. To the States.
Williams, C. K. Question, The.
Wright, J. Annihilation's Trio: Three Irrational Sonnets Begging the Question of Being and Act.
Xenophanes. War Memories.
Yi Sanghûi. I Ask in Late Evening.

Quests
Anderson, M. It Never Was You.
Browning, R. Childe Roland to the Dark Tower Came.
Cruz, S. Not Without Hope Pulsing My Breast.
Dickinson, E. Each Life Converges to some Centre.
Ehrhart. Finding My Old Battalion Command Post.
Eliot, T. S. Waste Land, The.
Gardinier. To Peace.
Graves, R. White Goddess, The.
Guiney. Wild Ride, The.
Hollo. Journey, 1966.
Kim Sünghûi. Song of Children in the Land of Ice Who Love the Sun.
Leiber *et al.* Searchin'.
Lewis, S. Five Foot Two, Eyes of Blue (Has Anybody Seen My Girl?).
Melville, H. Of Mortmain.
Onassis, Jacqueline Kennedy. Meanwhile in Massachusetts.
Poe. Eldorado.
Russell, G. Desire.
Spenser, E. Lo I the man, whose muse whilome did maske.
Stoller. Searchin'.
Thoreau. I am bound, I am bound, for a distant shore.
Unknown. Loving Mad Tom.
Warren, R. Pursuit.
Whitman, W. I celebrate myself, and sing myself.
I know I have the best of time and space, and was never measured and will never be measured.
Song of Myself.
Young, J. Five Foot Two, Eyes of Blue (Has Anybody Seen My Girl?).
Zuni Oral Tradition. Following their road of exit, they stooped over and came out.

Quilts and Quilting
Baggett. Rachel: *Crown of Thorns.*
Rachel: *Queen Charlotte's Crown.*
Bruce, D. Sonnet 4.
Buson. Cover my head.
Clarke, George Elliott. Quilt.
Clifton, L. Quilting.
Divakaruni. Quilt, The.
Kikaku. Summer airing / Trying on a quilt.
Lowe, J. Between Acts.
McFee. Cold Quilt.
McPherson, S. Quilt of Rights.
Ormond. Design for a Quilt.
Pau-Llosa. Quilt Complex.
Peirce. Quilts.
Rich, A. Aunt Jennifer's Tigers.
Townsend, A. First Quilt.
Ward, J. Comfort-Maker.
Wilson, C. History of the Quilt That Heaved Life into Stars Patched, Circled, Stitched and Square.
Wohlfeld. Quilt.

Quince Trees and Quinces
Donhauser, M. Quince, The.
Ni Dhomhnaill. As for the Quince.
As for the Quince.
Unknown. Cai-fan: Pluck the Quince.
Stesichoros. They flung many quinces toward the chariot.

Quotidian
Artmann. Blacksmith's Shop, The.
Ashbery, J. Problem of Anxiety, The.
Bell, M. Book of the Dead Man #87, The.
Brainard, J. Aug. 29, 1967.
Celaya, G. Life One Leads, The.
Meaning of Today.
Clarke, G. Overheard in County Sligo.
Daniels, K. Prayer to the Muse of Ordinary

Life.
Fargue. Fragrance of Night, A.
Flint, R. Seasonal, 1991.
Foster, A. Starting School.
Jarrell, R. Well Water.
Johnson, D. Incognito Lounge, The.
Jourdan, Pierre-Albert. Prayer: "Let innocence remain."
Kincaid, Jamaica. Letter from Home, The.
Kreymborg. To W. C. W. M. D.
Lewis, A. Mountain over Aberdare, The.
Michaelis. Brilliantly Philosophising.
Montale. Story of Every Day, The.
Niccolai. "What's that?" the boy asks his mother, pointing to the flag.
Rafferty, P. Personal.
Reece, Spencer. Clerk's Tale, The.
Reverdy. In the Fields or on the Hill.
Ritsos. Our Land.
Roubaud. Meditation of 8/5/85.
Rupchev, Georgi. Ceremony.
Schuyler, J. Red Brick and Brown Stone.
Stern, G. December 1, 1994.
Thesen. Broken Cup, The.
Van de Woestijne. Oars Heavy with Seaweed, The.
Villa, E. Natus de Muliere, Brevi Vivens.

R

Rabbis
Bloch, C. White Petticoats.
Borges. Golem, The.
Glazova, A. Grant of death, The.
Kalina, R. Cabalistic Rabbis, The.
Kumin, M. In the Absence of Bliss.
Longfellow, H. Spanish Jew's Tale: The Legend of Rabbi Ben Levi, The.
Nemerov. Debate with the Rabbi.
Pinchas-Cohen. Her, Me, and Yochanan.

Rabbits
Carrera Andrade. Perfect Life, The.
Cassian. Rabbit, The.
Clare, J. Hares at Play.
Coatsworth. Song of the Rabbits Outside the Tavern, The.
Collier, M. Real-Life Drama, A.
Galina, M. I said to him—Just don't throw me into that briar patch.
Johnson, J. Brer Rabbit, You's de Cutes' of 'Em All.
Kinsella, J. Rabbiters: A Pastoral, The.
Larkin, P. Myxomatosis.
Legiardi-Laura, Roland. Trickster Rabbit.
McWhirter. Era of Easy Meat at Locarno, An.
Milosz, C. Encounter.
Mitchison. House of the Hare, The.
Moore, L. Again.
Skrzynecki. Hunting Rabbits.
Stevens, W. Rabbit Is King of the Ghosts, A.
Toomer. Nullo.
Unknown. Railroad Section Leader's Song.
Varon, Lee. Pink magnolias, the punishment.
See also **Hares**

Raccoons
Davis, K. Animal Zen.
Hirshfield, J. Invocation: "This August night, raccoons."
Vail, Alice Ewing. Coons in the Corn.

Rachel (Bible)
Burns, R. Patriarch, The.
Celan. Near, in the aorta's arch.

Rachmaninov, Sergei
O'Hara, F. On Rachmaninoff's Birthday #158.

Racial Prejudice
Agard, J. Half-caste.
Palm Tree King.
Allen, S. Moment Please, A.
Awoonor. American Memory of Africa, An.
Baraka, I. Poem for Willie Best, A.
Bennett, L. Pass fi White.
Blake, W. Little Black Boy, The.
Brand, D. No Language Is Neutral.
Brooks, G. Bronzeville Woman in a Red Hat.

Riot.
Rites for Cousin Vit, The.
Brown, S. Legend: "Old black man was stood on the block, The."
Old Lem.
Slim Greer.
Southern Cop.
Browning, E. Runaway Slave at Pilgrim's Point, The.
Bynner. Defeat.
Cataldi. Advice.
Cervantes. Poem for the Young White Man Who Asked Me How I, An Intelligent, Well-Read Person Could Believe in the War Between Races.
Clarke, T. Will They Always Remember.
Cofer, J. What the Gypsy Said to Her Children.
Cullen, C. For a Lady I Know.
Incident.
Tableau.
Uncle Jim.
Cyril. Children's Games.
Jump Black Honey Jump Black.
Damas. S.O.S.
Durham. Justiniano Lamé Has Been Killed.
Eady. Wrong Street, The.
Ellis, T. Slow Fade to Black.
Gomez, M. To the Latin Lover I Left at the Candy Store.
Harper, M. American History.
Grandfather.
Hemphill. Cordon Negro.
Family Jewels.
Hughes, L. Beaumont to Detroit: 1943.
Bitter River, The.
Brass Spittoons.
Children's Rhymes ("By what sends.").
Cross.
Dinner Guest: Me.
Dream Boogie.
I, Too.
Visitors to the Black Belt.
Inada. Projected Scenario of a Performance to Be Given Before the UN.
Jacobs, B. Black on Black.
Jex, Z. What Colour's a Man.
Johnson, G. Prejudice.
Jones, I. Echoes of the Murder of Emmett Till.
Jordan, J. Poem About My Rights.
What Would I Do White?
Kelen. Rabbit Shoeshine.
Kizer, C. Race Relations.
Lorde. Power.
MacDiarmid, H. With the Herring Fishers.
Mack, C. That's Why They Call Me "Shine".
Mandela. I Saw as a Child.
Marinho, T. Colour.
Marson. Kinky Hair Blues.
Martial. Since you, Charmenion, come from Corinth.
McElroy, C. Foul Line—1987.
McKay, C. Midnight Woman to the Bobby, A.
White House, The.
Miller, E. Boys of Summer, The.
Moss, T. Interpretation of a Poem by Frost.
Nelson, M. Washboard Wizard.
Nickelson, C. Charleston, South Carolina.
Ortiz. Creation.
Rodgers, C. Walk Like Freedom.
Sandburg, C. Circles.
Sapgir. Psalm 137.
Shannon, A. Integration.
Simmonds, Kevin. White Man and the Judge, A.
Smith, A. Roslyn Malamud the Coup.
Soyinka. Telephone Conversation.
Stanard, C. Wrong Color.
Sundiata. Blink Your Eyes.
Trejo. Cloud Unfolding, The.
Trethewey, N. Drapery Factory, Gulfport, Mississippi, 1956.
Native Guard.
Unknown. Just for a while.
Kansas 1.
Run, Nigger, Run!
Walcott. Blues: "Those five or six young guys."

Gulf, The.
Walker, M. Now.
Walters, W. Meridian Hill Terrace.
Waniek. Freeman Field.
Weaver, A. Poets, The.
Welch, J. Harlem, Montana.
Williams, C. K. Racists.
Wong, N. When I Was Growing Up.
Young, A. Poem for Players, A.
Young, K. Negative.

See also **Apartheid; Racism and Racists**

Racing and Racers

Cameron, N. Unfinished Race, The.
Cantor, Michael. Tour de France.
Cloves, Jeff. For Fausto Coppi (1916–60) et
  Tous les Copains de la Bicyclette.
Dubie. Death of the Race Car Driver, The.
Galef. Bicycle Race in *Beowulf*, The.
Montale. Buffalo.
Townsend, A. Bicycle Racers, The.

See also **Horse Racing; Track Athletics**

Racism and Racists

Abrahams, L. Our way of life.
"Ada.". Appeal to Women, An.
Agüeros. Psalm for the Next Millennium.
Ai. Endangered Species.
  Self Defense.
Alexander, E. Affirmative Action Blues (1993).
  Boston Year.
  Ladders.
  Venus Hottentot, The.
Alexie. On the Amtrak from Boston to New
  York City.
Allan, L. Strange Fruit.
Allen, J. For Michael Griffith, Murdered Dec.
  21, 1986, Howard Beach, NY.
  Mud Wit.
Allen, S. Lingering Doubt, The.
  Moment Please, A.
Allison, O. Billy.
Amadiume. Nok Lady in Terracotta.
Anderson, W. There's Not a Friend like the
  Lowly Jesus.
Angelou, M. Miss Scarlet, Mr. Rhett and other
  Latter-Day Saints.
As-Sabah. Transition #2.
Askhari. Circular Fate.
  REcreation.
Aubert, A. Opposite of Green, The.
Ballard, B. Hate Crime.
Baraka, I. Hymn for Lanie Poo.
  Nation Is Like Ouselves, The.
  Wise 5.
Barkan, S. Negro Song.
Beatty, P. That's Not in My Job Description.
Bennett, L. No Lickle Twang.
Benson, L. P Word Poem, The.
Blake, W. Little Black Boy, The.
Booth, P. Stations.
Boss, L. When You Are Grown, Amanda Rose.
Brooks, G. Bronzeville Mother Loiters in
  Mississippi, A. Meanwhile, a Mississippi
  Mother Burns Bacon.
  Bronzeville Woman in a Red Hat.
  Negro Hero.
  White Troops Had Their Orders but the Negroes
  Looked Like Men.
Broumas, O. Pealing, The.
Brown, Cecil. Integrating the Strawberry
  Swimming Pool in 1998.
Brown, S. Bitter Fruit of the Tree.
  He Was a Man.
  Slim in Atlanta.
  Strong Men.
Brutus. Off to Philadelphia in the Morning.
Cabañas, S. It's Called Kings.
Cabico, R. Gameboy.
Carbó, N. Civilizing the Filipino.
Carroll, K. Laughin at cha.
  Something easy for Ultra Black nationalists.
  Upper Marlboro.
Celaya, G. After a Native Poem from the
  Solomon Islands that Begins: "Your Shameful
  Parts Are the White Man's Gramophone".
Cerenio. 23 October 1992.
Cervantes. Poem for the Young White Man

Who Asked Me How I, An Intelligent, Well-
  Read Person Could Believe in the War
  Between Races.
  Poema para los Californios Muertos.
Charara, H. More Than We Dared.
Chinn. Not Translation, Not Poetry.
  Skin Color from the Sun.
Chrystos. I Bring You Greetings: How.
  Old Indian Granny, The.
Clifton, L. Still.
Clinton, M. Plan of the Klan.
Consuegra, D. You and I.
Cornish, S. His Fingers Seem to Sing.
Cortez, J. Give me the Red on the Black of the
  Bullet (for Claude Reece Jr.).
  Rape.
Cullen, C. Incident.
  Uncle Jim.
D'Aguiar, F. Langston.
Daniels, J. Time, Temperature.
Daniels, K. Bus Ride.
Davidson, D. Sequel of Appomattox.
Davis, F. Christ is a Dixie Nigger.
  Sam Jackson.
De Kok. Small passing.
de Portalatin. Black Autumn.
Derricotte. Note on my Son's Face, A.
  On the Turning Up of Unidentified Black
  Female Corpses.
  Passing.
Divakaruni. Founding of Yuba City, The.
Dove, R. Great Palaces of Versailles, The.
Dunbar, P. Harriet Beecher Stowe.
Eady. False Arrest.
  Sherbet.
  Song.
  Song: "*Nigger-Lover* is a song, spat out."
  Thrift.
  William Carlos Williams.
Espada. Beloved Spic.
  Other Names, The.
Factor, J. Mother to Son.
Fay, S. Back in My Day.
Flores, J. Last Visit to Chestnut Middle School.
Forbes, C. Poet's Shuffle, The.
Friedman, B. Scottsboro.
Gilyard, K. Letter.
Giovanni. Train Rides.
Glancy. First Reader Santee Training School,
  1873, The.
Gray-Kontar, D. Not no socialism/communism
  classical, but some power to the people jazz.
Griffin, S. I Like to Think of Harriet Tubman.
Grinshpan, Y. Grand Central by Night.
Guevara, M. Doña Josefina Counsels Doña
  Concepción Before Entering Sears.
Hairston. Alabama Bus.
Hamer. Lesson.
  Line Up.
Hamilton, M. Midnight in Mississippi.
Harjo, J. Strange Fruit.
Harper, M. American History.
  Nightmare Begins Responsibility.
Harris, D. On the uptown lexington avenue
  express: Martin Luther King Day 1995.
Harris, R. Usual Suspects, The.
Harte, B. Plain Language from Truthful James.
  Truthful James to the Editor.
Hayden, R. [American Journal].
  Frederick Douglass.
  Monet's "Waterlilies".
  Mystery Boy Looks for Kin in Nashville.
Hayes, T. Talk.
Heard, J. Black Sampson, The.
Hemphill. Cordon Negro.
  Family Jewels.
Henderson-Holmes. To Hell and Back, with
  Cake.
Hershon. Light and Dark, East and West.
Hoilette, A. Blooming Death. . .Blossoms.
Holman, M. Mr. Z.
Hottel, J. Shikata ga nai.
Hughes, L. Ballad of the Landlord.
  Black Clown, The.
  Blue Bayou.
  Brass Spittoons.

  Comment on Curb.
  Freedom Train.
  Good Morning.
  Harlem ("What happens to a dream deferred?").
  Jim Crow Car.
  Merry-Go-Round.
  Mulatto.
  Note on Commercial Theatre.
  Same in Blues.
  Silhouette.
  Tell Me.
  Uncle Tom ("Within— / The beaten pride.").
Hunter, K. I worked on race at the factory.
Ignatow, D. Harold.
Iman. Love Your Enemy.
Iverem, E. Keeper.
Jackson, A. Miz Rosa Rides the Bus.
Jackson, B. In Exchange for Forty Acres.
Jackson, R. Lonely Affair, A.
Jacobs, B. After the 200th White Person Locks
  Her Car Door at Me.
Jemeni. America Eats Its Young.
Johnson, J. Color Sergeant, The.
  O Southland!
Johnson, L. Mi Revalueshanary Fren.
  Sonny's Lettah.
Jordan, J. Poem Against the State (Of Things):
  1975.
Joseph, A. In the Bookstore.
  Numbers: "My father taught me to measure."
Joseph, L. Sand Nigger.
Kalinski, E. Teacher of Defeated Hebrew
  Language.
Kay, J. Twelve Bar Bessie.
Khalique, H. In London.
Kizer, C. Race Relations.
Knight, E. Hard Rock Returns to Prison from
  the Hospital for the Criminal Insane.
  Once on a Night in the Delta: A Report From
  Hell.
Komunyakaa, Y. Salt.
  Tu Do Street.
  Untitled Blues; After a Photograph by Yevgeni
  Yevtushenko.
Lansana, Q. Woolworth's Poem, The.
Lara, A. Nights.
Lee, M. Negro on the Subway.
Leonard, T. Evidence, The.
Levertov. Day the Audience Walked Out on
  Me, and Why, The.
Long, R. Conspiracy, The.
Lorde. Afterimages.
  For the Record.
M-1. Police State.
Macgoye. Letter to a Friend.
Madgett. Race Question, The.
Madhubuti. Don't Cry, Scream.
  My Brothers.
Major, C. News Story.
  Paragraph from English Speaking World.
Manyarrows. See No Indian, Hear No Indian.
Mathews, E. K. Indian, The.
McElroy, C. Ghost-Who-Walks, The.
McKay, C. Lynching, The.
  White City, The.
  White House, The.
Medina, T. After the Verdict.
  Big House Revisited, The.
Midge, T. Written in Blood.
Miko, C. Mississippi Girls, Plaited.
Mills, D. And Now Yu.
Morales. I Am the Reasonable One.
Moss, T. Reconsideration of the Blackbird, A.
Mullen, H. Denigration.
  Father (Part 1).
  We Are Not Responsible.
Mura. Argument: on 1942, An.
Nelson, M. Minor Miracle.
Newman, R. Salem, Indiana, 1983.
Norris, M. Tortillas.
Osofisan. Paris Latin Quarter.
Parkerson. Statistic.
Pegram, A. I Will Still Sing.
  Mr. White Discoverer.
  Towards Abraham's Bosom.
Phi, T. Asian Am Anthem, An.

Powell, K.   Don't Feel No Way.
Pratt, M.   Red String.
Preston, R.   Champion Chant.
   Ten Seconds.
Quintana.   Good Nigger.
Randall, D.   Idiot, The.
Randall, J.   When Something Happens.
Rankine.   New Windows.
Redmond.   Love Necessitates.
Reed, I.   Jacket Notes.
   Railroad Bill, A Conjure Man.
Richardson, J.   My Man Caliban!
Ridge, L.   Morning Ride.
Rivers, C.   Watts.
Roberson, E.   American culture is the pot.
Rodriguez, L.   To the Police Officer Who
   Refused to Sit in the Same Room as My Son
   because He's a "Gang Banger".
Rontsh, Y.   Scottsboro.
Rose, P.   Wind Debates Asian Immigration, The.
Ross, L.   Indecent Exposure (A True Story).
Rushin.   Black Back-Ups, The.
Salaam.   I Live in the Mouth of History.
Samwell.   Negro Boy, The.
Sanchez, S.   Poem for July 4, 1994.
   Right On: White America.
Seibles, T.   Manic: A Conversation with Jimi
   Hendrix.
Shapiro, K.   University.
Shepherd, R.   Difficult Music, The.
Shockley, E.   N-word, The.
Silva, L.   Emigrant's Son, The.
Skeeter.   Midwest, Midcentury.
Smith, P.   Blonde White Women.
Spencer, A.   White Things.
Stein, K.   Upon Finding a Black Woman's Door
   Sprayed with Swastikas, I Tell Her This Story
   of Hands.
Steptoe.   Window Shopping.
Sticman.   Police State.
Tait, G.   U.S.A. Court of No Appeal, The.
Taylor, C.   Scroll No. 1.
Thompson, C.   Uncle Rube on the Race
   Problem.
   Uncle Rube to the Young People.
Toomer.   People.
   Portrait in Georgia.
Travis, N.   Sunbathing.
Unknown.   Barren grassland, A.
   Discrimination.
   Some push us around, some curse us.
Uyematsu.   December 7 Always Brings
   Christmas Early.
Van Jordan, A.   If I Write a Poem.
Vando.   Knife.
Vaynper, Z.   Whiteness.
Vaynshteyn [*or* Weinstein].   Negro Dies, A.
Villalongo.   In the Good Old U. S. A.
Wade-Gayles.   Inquisition.
Walcott.   Blues: "Those five or six young guys."
   Glory Trumpeter, The.
Walker, M.   For My People.
   Since 1619.
Waniek.   Alderman.
   Ballad of Aunt Geneva, The.
   Diverne's Waltz.
Warren, R.   Pondy Woods.
Wayman.   Hating Jews.
Weaver, A.   Borders.
   Picnic, an Homage to Civil Rights, The.
Welch, J.   Harlem, Montana.
Wieners.   Poem for Cocksuckers, A.
Wiler, J.   Bensonhurst.
Williams, C.   In Search of Aunt Jemima.
Wilson, T.   And the Saga Continues.
Winner, R.   Segregated Railway Diner—1946.
Wright, J.   On a Phrase from Southern Ohio.
Wright, R.   Between the World and Me.
Young, K.   Field Trip.
   No Offense.
Zephaniah.   Sun, The.
Zulu, P.   You are Mad: and I Mean It!
See also **Racial Prejudice**

Radiation and Radiation Sickness
Bruchac.   Wahsah Zeh (War Dance)—As Long
   as the Grass.

de Fréine, C.   Inside.
Gibson, M.   Radiation.
Johnson, K.   Trilobytes.
McGrath, T.   War Resisters' Song.
Robinson, Matt.   Winter's affection, A;
   radiomimetic.
Seaton, M.   Nostradamus Predicts the
   Destruction of Chicago.
Shinkichi Takahashi.   Explosion.
Sirota, L.   Radiophobia.
Stainer.   Sarcophagus.
Tatarunis, P.   Chest X-Ray.
Thiele, C.   Radiation Victim.
Witherup.   Mervyn Clyde Witherup.
Wojahn.   Workmen Photographed inside the
   Reactor.
See also **Nuclear Accidents; Nuclear War**

Radio
Aragon.   Hilversum, Kalundborg, Brno, the loud
   world over.
Auden.   Turn off the wireless.
   Turn off the wireless; we are tired.
Baraka, I.   In Memory of Radio.
Bennett, C.   Drowned Radio, The.
Bennett, K.   99.9 FM Radio Nostalgia.
Booth, P.   Public Broadcast.
Brecht, B.   To My Little Radio.
Breeze.   Eena Mi Corner.
Brownjohn.   September 1939.
Butler, C. E.   Letter to the Survivors.
Church, R.   Earphones.
Clarke, G.   On Air.
Davis, S.   Friends Beyond.
Dunn, A.   Radio.
Duran, J.   For the Woman Who Dressed Up to
   Listen to Gigli on the Radio.
Eady.   Radio.
Farjeon, E.   F is for Forecast.
Fogarty, L.   No Grudge.
Frankau, R.   Thoughts While Broadcasting.
Friedlaender.   Progress: "There was a time when
   peace at evening."
Gascoyne.   Nightwatchers, The.
Geiger.   Soundtracks.
Goldbarth.   Talk Show, The.
Graham, D.   Wireless, The.
Greenlaw, L.   Five O'Clock Opera.
Heaney, S.   Dogger, Rockall, Malin, Irish Sea.
Hill, G.   Age of mass consent: go global with
   her.
Isherwood.   Turn off the wireless.
   Turn off the wireless; we are tired.
Jarnot, L.   Poem Beginning with a Line by
   Frank Lima.
Jordan, A.   Public Radio Plays Eddie Harris.
Llewellyn-Williams.   Short Wave.
Loerke, O.   Down There.
Lopez, L.   Only Now I Realize.
Mahon.   Morning Radio.
May, J.   On the Air.
McFee.   First Radio.
Monroe, H.   Radio.
Noyes, A.   Dane Tree, The.
O'Hara, F.   Radio.
Page, G.   Late Night Radio.
Porter, P.   Radio Caliban.
Priory, J.   Emma and the Radio.
Roberts, M.   Wireless.
Sabgir, G.   Radio Gibberish.
Seyburn, P.   You and Them.
Shanahan, D.   Morning Radio.
Spicer, J.   Sporting Life.
Stern, G.   December 1, 1994.
Storey, E.   Wireless Aerial, The.
Straus, M.   What I Heard on the Radio Today.
Swift, T.   My Radios.
Szirtes.   Short Wave.
Taylor, H.   Speech.
Thorne, T.   Whatever Happened to Conway
   Twitty?
Trinidad.   Monday, Monday.
Unknown.   News, The.
   What the Listener Thinks.
   Wireless at Night.
Wah.   Father / Mother Haibun #15.
Waltham, B.   Radio 3.

Waters, M.   Burden Lifters, The.
Western Brothers.   Connected with County, and
   landed estates.
Wheelwright.   Poem by David McCord, A.
Wojahn.   Homage: Light from the Hall.
Wonham, J.   Emergency Services.
Zagajewski.   Electric Elegy.

Radishes
Bailey, Peter.   Don't be saddish.
Basho.   When the winter chrysanthemums go.
Bodecker.   Radish.
Issa.   Man pulling radishes, The.

Ragworts
Stevenson, A.   Ragwort.

Railroad Wrecks
Carruth, H.   Wreck of the Circus Train, The.
Davies, Lynn.   On the Train.
George, D.   Wreck of the Old 97.
Hedin, R.   Wreck of the Great Northern, The.
Hummer, T.   Train Wreck, 1890: My
   Grandmother Lies Down with the Dead.
Moore, J.   Ashtabula Disaster, The.
Nims, J.   Trainwrecked Soldiers.

Railroads
Ashbery, J.   Melodic Trains.
Baker, T.   Railway Boom, 1845, The.
Betjeman.   Metropolitan Railway, The.
Booth, P.   Stations.
Broonzy.   Southern Blues, The.
Brown, S.   Call Boy.
   Long Track Blues.
   Southern Road.
Buckley, C.   Train in the Desert—1916.
Christensen, Paul.   Summer Nights.
Collier, M.   North Corridor.
Conyus.   Six Ten Sixty-Nine.
Cooper, J.   Wanda's Blues.
Cornford, F.   Parting in Wartime.
Cornish, S.   Love Song of a Red Cap.
Cranch.   Locomotive, The.
Crane, H.   River, The.
Craveirinha.   3D.
Delmore Brothers.   Wabash Cannonball, The.
Dooley, M.   Explaining Magnetism.
Eiseley.   And as for Man.
Ezekiel.   When the female railway clerk.
Francis, R.   Night Train.
Frost, R.   On the Heart's Beginning to Cloud the
   Mind.
Galvin, B.   For a Daughter Gone Away.
Gibbons, R.   American Trains.
Ginsberg, A.   In back of the real.
   Sunflower Sutra.
Gioia.   In Cheever Country.
Glück, L.   Departure.
Greenberg, A.   Freight Train, Freight Train.
Hall, D.   Sister on the Tracks, A.
Hanzlicek, C.   Last Trains, The.
Holland, J.   Loco.
Hope, A.   Observation Car.
Hudgins.   Southern Crescent Was on time, The.
Hughes, L.   Homesick Blues.
Jefferson, B.   Easy Rider Blues.
Justice, D.   Train.
Koch, K.   Railway Stationery, The.
Lattimore.   Note on the L and N.
Lowe, L.   Sea Shells.
MacLeish.   Burying Ground by the Ties.
   Pastoral.
McGonagall.   Beautiful new railway bridge of
   the Silvery Tay.
   Beautiful Railway Bridge of the Silvery Tay!
Merwin.   Wheels of the Trains, The.
Monroe, B.   In the Pines.
Neihardt.   Summer turned.
Nemerov.   Low-Level Cross-Country.
Niedecker.   Get a load.
Nims, J.   Freight.
O'odham.   No. 80. Song of a Spirit.
Parini.   Coal Train.
Peacocke.   Railway Allotments.
Plumly.   For Esther.
Pow.   Favourite Stretch of Disused Railway, A.
Pratt, E.   Road itself was like a stream that men,
   The.
Reed, I.   Railroad Bill, A Conjure Man.

Railway Stations (cont.)

Roethke. Night Journey.
Sandburg, C. Southern Pacific.
Seibert. Casey Jones.
Shapiro, K. Terminal.
Sissman. Big Rock-Candy Mountain, The.
Slessor. Last Trams.
Soto. Who Will Know Us?
Swenson, M. Written While Riding the Long
    Island Rail Road.
Tomlinson, C. Santa Fe Railroad, The.
Unknown. Beulah Railway, The.
I Been Working on the Railroad.
John Henry.
Poor Paddy Works on the Railway.
Railroad Blues, The.
Railroad Cars Are Coming, The.
Railroad Man for Me, A.
Railroad Section Leader's Song.
Tamping Ties.
Working on the Railway.
Van Doren. Dream of Trains, A.
Warren, R. He Was Formidable.
Whitman, W. To a Locomotive in Winter.
Wilbur, R. In the Smoking-Car.
Wojahn. "Mystery Train" Janis Joplin Leaves
    Port Arthur for Points West, 1964.
Wordsworth, W. On the Projected Kendal and
    Windermere Railway.
Wright, J. Poem Written under an Archway in a
    Discontinued Railroad Station, Fargo, North
    Dakota, A.
See also **Trains; Locomotives**

Railway Stations
Azzawi, F. Film in a Railway Station, A.
Bierds, L. White Bears: Tolstoy at Astapovo.
Fontanella. Victoria Station.
Hughes, L. Pennsylvania Station.
Rein. Moscow Station, The.
Shinkichi Takahashi. Railroad Station.
Smith, D. Cumberland Station.
Stone, R. Winter: "Ten o'clock train to New
    York, The."
Thomas, E. Adlestrop.
Wharton, E. Terminus.
Wright, J. Poem Written under an Archway in a
    Discontinued Railroad Station, Fargo, North
    Dakota, A.

Railway Travel
Ashbery, J. Leaving the Atocha Station.
Bly, R. In a Train.
Davie, D. In the Stopping Train.
Garlick, R. Poetry of Motion, The.
Handy, W. Yellow Dog Blues.
Jarrell, R. Orient Express, The.
Montague, J. Last Journey.
Mukhopādhyāy, K. Ma, the mail train is leaving
    now.
Pastan. Last Train, The.
Piatt, J. Taking the Night-Train.
Prunty. Ballad of the Several Past.
Sansom, A. From the Moment I Picked Up
    Your Book.
Senghor. All Day Long.
Shinkichi Takahashi. Railroad Station.
Stafford, W. Vacation.
Stevenson, R. From a Railway Carriage.
Tomlinson, C. Yamadera.
Wilbur, R. In the Smoking-Car.
Zagajewski. At Daybreak.

Rain
Abbott, W. First Rain.
Acholonu. Dissidents, The.
Adcock, F. Unexpected Visit.
Aiken, C. And in the Hanging Gardens.
Al-Rihani. It Was All for Him.
Aleixandre. It's Raining.
Ali, A. Ghazal: "What will suffice for a true-
    love knot? Even the rain?"
Amichai, Y. Rain on the Battlefield.
Aridjis. Rain is Falling, The.
Atkins, R. Irritable Songs.
    Spyrytual.
Baker, D. More Rain.
Barot, R. Eight Elegies.
Basheva. Fast train, The? The express?
Basho. Banana tree, The.

Chilling autumn rains.
Cold rain starting, A.
Crane's legs, The.
First winter rain.
Gathering.
Have the summer rains.
Hollyhocks, The.
I'm a wanderer.
June rain / hollyhocks turning.
Kisagata.
Long rains, The.
Misty rain.
On the cow shed.
Spring rain.
Winter rain.
Winter showers.
Batraville, D. Paper 33.
Baudelaire. Spleen LXXV.
Benét, S. Rain after a Vaudeville Show.
Berlin. Isn't This a Lovely Day (To Be Caught
    in the Rain?).
Bernstein, C. Frequently unasked questions.
Berrigan, T. Go fly a kite he writes.
Berry, W. In Rain.
Bishop, E. Rain Towards Morning.
    Sestina: "September rain falls on the house."
Bluger, M. Leafsmoke.
Bly, R. August Rain.
Bodecker. Small Rains.
Bontemps. Return, The.
Borson. Rain.
Bowen, C. Rain It Raineth, The.
Brecht, B. When Evil-Doing Comes Like
    Falling Rain.
Breytenbach. Threat of the Sick.
Brock-Broido. Carrowmore.
Buckley, C. Rain/Light.
Burkard. I have a silence in the rain.
    Weather.
Burke, J. Here's That Rainy Day.
    Pennies from Heaven.
Burt, S. Sudden Rain in the Green Mountains,
    A.
Buson. Along the roadside.
Bamboo hat, straw coat—.
Camellia tips, The.
Deer in rain / Three cries.
Early summer rain.
Evening cloudburst—, An.
Ferry departs, The.
In seasonal rain.
In the summer rain.
Light winter rain.
Lightning flash—,A.
Lights are going out, The.
Long hard journey, A.
May rains.
My old man's ears.
Rain falls on the grass.
Rainy season, The.
Shortcut, A.
Sweet springtime showers.
Winter rain on moss.
Cairns, Scott. Our Lost Angels.
Carrera Andrade. Transfiguration of the Rain.
Cavalli. Rain brings me back, The.
Ceravolo. Rain: "Rain is not surrounded by
    sleep like a drum."
Chiang Chieh. To the Tune "The Fair Maid of
    Yu."
Chippewa Oral Tradition. Song of the Crows.
Chŏng Chiyong. Rain.
Chŏng Ch'ŏl. Let forty thousand pecks of
    pearls.
Chu Yohan. Sound of Rain, The.
Clare, J. Sudden Shower.
Clark, P. Walk in the Rain.
Clark, T. You (I).
Claudel, P. Sadness of Water, The.
Clifton, H. Monsoon Girl.
Collins, M. Warmer.
Cranch. Autumn Rain, The.
Creeley. Rain, The: "All night the sound had."
Cross, E. Mandap.
    Mandap.
    Monsoon.

Monzón.
Cross, T. Complected.
Cullen, C. Night Rain.
Cummings, E. E. Now comes the good rain
    farmers pray for(and).
Daegak Euchon. Riding a Horse in the Rain.
D'Aquino, A. Naranja de luz abierta, La.
    Opened Orange of Light, The.
DeSylva, B. G. April Showers.
Dickinson, E. Like Rain it sounded till it
    curved.
Didsbury, P. Shorter Life, The.
Dischell. Yellow Slicker, The.
Dodd, W. Of Rain and Air.
Doolittle, H. I go where I love and where I am
    loved.
Dove, R. Dog Days, Jerusalem.
    Wiederkehr.
Dubin, A. September in the Rain.
Dubrava. Miraculous Marriage of Zarife
    Dominquez.
Duggan, L. South Coast Haiku.
Eady. Drizzle.
Eichner, Maura. Woman is Waiting for a Bus,
    A.
Eigner. If You Weep, I Think That.
Elliot, A. Northern Morning, A.
Elmslie, S. Forecast: Nadja.
Emerson, Claudia. Flood: "This had happened
    before: rain that began."
Esteves. It Is Raining Today.
Evans, A. Under Cover.
Evans, M. Rain.
Field. Lo, my loved is dying, and the call.
Foix. When I Sleep, Then I See Clearly.
Forrester, S. Summer afternoon.
    Temple bell ringing.
Freed, A. Singin' in the Rain.
Gallagher, T. Sudden Journey.
Gardinet, C. Wet Dream.
Gilbert, C. Chosen to Be Water.
Gioia. Los Angeles after the Rain.
Gizzi. It Was Raining in Delft.
Glück, L. Time: "There was too much, always,
    then too little."
Gorbanevskaya. Hurry, take pleasure in the
    oblique caress of rain while the sun shines.
Grin, B. Rain: "Little ears of corn are parched,
    The."
Groarke, V. Rainbearers.
Gu Cheng. Feel of the Wind, The.
Gundy, J. Rain.
Gurney, I. Soaking, The.
Gyodai. Slowly / Over cedars.
Hall, D. Pluvia.
Hanu. Some said the northern window was
    bright.
Hardie, K. Rain in April.
    She Replies to Carmel's Letter.
Hardy, T. Rain on a Grave.
    Weathers [*or* Weather].
Harjo, J. Rainy Dawn.
Harrington, Jonathan. Rain of Bicycles, A.
Hass, R. Spring Rain.
Heaney, S. Summer of Lost Rachel, The.
Hejinian. It is the writer's object.
Herbert, W. Black Wet, The.
Hernández Cruz. Thursday.
Herzberg. Loss.
Heyen. Passover: the Injections.
Hillman, B. Formation of Soils, The.
Hirshfield, J. Half-sleeping, / my body pulls
    toward yours.
    Rain in May.
Houlihan, J. Squall Line.
Hovanessian, D. On Commonwealth Avenue
    and Brattle Street.
Hsü Wei. Buddhist Monk Cut and Burned His
    Own Flesh to Make The Rains Stop—A Man
    From His Native Place Asked Me to Write a
    Poem to Send to Him, A.
Hubbell, L. W. Birth-Hour.
Hughes, L. April Rain Song.
    In Time of Silver Rain.
Hughes, T. Hawk in the Rain, The.
    Heptonstall.

Hume, C. Miraculous Panoptic Precipitations.
Ibarbourou. Rainy Night.
Iio Sogi. Life in this world.
Ilkov, Ani. Evaporations.
Iosifova, Ekaterina. March: "I'm going to your fair."
Ishikawa. For Her Lover.
Issa. In spring rain.
In the beggar's tin.
Naked.
Nightingale's song / this morning.
O owl!
Sheet of rain, A.
Spring rain.
Jackson, A. Hitch-Haiku.
Jacobs, H. It is not Just.
Johnson, J. View Café, The.
Jones, R. Front Window, The.
Jones, T. Thursday.
Kanchev, Nikolai. Feeling.
Kang Ûn'gyo. Rise, Grass.
Kay, J. Pounding Rain.
Keeler, C. Drouth, The.
Kenyon, J. August Rain, after Haying.
Kerouac. Birds singing.
Kgositsile. Gods Wrote, The.
Kikaku. Leaf / Of the yam.
Kim Chôngnan. Rain: "From which heaven did you return."
Kim Sangyong. Listlessly I hear the rain.
Kimball, H. Angel of the Rain.
Kooser. At the Office Early.
Kuan Han-ch'ing. Tune: "Vast Virtue".
Kwŏn Homun. Nights After Rain When the Moon.
Lane, P. Rain Ditch.
Larkin, J. Housework.
Larkin, P. Card-Players, The.
Whitsun Weddings, The.
Laughlin, J. Then and Now.
Lerner, A. Rain in Spain, The.
Levine, P. Rain Downriver.
Levitt, Peter. Within each petal.
Lewis, A. All Day It Has Rained.
Li Ho. Days of Rain.
Li Hsun. To the Tune: The Wine Spring: "Eternal autumn rain—evening sounds."
Li Shang-yin. Spring Rain.
Lili'u-o-ka-lani. Ka Waiapo Lani.
Lima, F. Lime.
Liu Yin. Miscellaneous Poem on Rural Life.
Liu Yung. Tune: "Bells in the Rain".
Livesay, D. Green Rain.
Longfellow, H. Rain in Summer.
Lowell, A. Shower, A.
Lugones. Gray Waves.
Rain Psalm.
Lumbreras, E. Reunión de violonchelos.
Reunion of Cellos.
Macari, A. After the Rain.
MacDiarmid, H. Cloudburst and Soaring Moon.
Macdonald, G. Sweet Peril.
Maclean, A. After Culloden.
MacLeish. Memorial Rain.
MacNeice. London Rain.
Mahadevi. It was like a stream.
Markham, M. Rock in the Garden Allows People In, The.
We Folded the Hours and Set Them in the Rain.
Marsman. Polderland.
Masaoka Shiki. Sudden rain / Rows of horses.
Summer sky / Clear after rain.
Maxton. On Failing to Translate.
McAuley, J. Wet Day.
McCarthy, G. Hooded Legion, The.
McCord, D. Summer Shower.
McCorkle. Infidelities.
McDuffie, C. Finally the Rain.
Meng Hao Jan. Spring Dawn.
Merriam, E. Weather.
Merrill, B. Don't Rain on My Parade.
Merrill, J. Childlessness.
Merwin. Rain Travel.
Metodiev, Ivan. Sonnet-Mantra of the Crickets.
Mhlophe. Sometimes When It Rains.
Milán, E. Now that we're nothing, for example.

Ya que no somos nada, por ejemplo.
Millar, J. Poem for a New Girlfriend.
Mitchell, K. Night Rain.
Mokusetsu. Long summer rains / Barley's tasteless.
Moore, L. Tanka.
Morgan, R. Working in the Rain.
Morris, W. Haystack in the Floods, The.
Mother Goose. Rain, rain, go to Spain.
Motsapi, S. Kulu.
Myles, E. New England Wind.
Na Hûidôk. Cold Rain Comes, A.
Naong. Rain During Drought.
Natsume Soseki. Is it showering?
Newman, A. Architecture of the Wings, The.
Nhat Hanh. Existence.
Nishiwaki Junzaburo. Rain.
Nordbrandt. China Observed Through Greek Rain in Turkish Coffee.
O'Connor, M. Sakura.
O'Brien, S. After Laforgue.
O'Callaghan, C. History of Rain, The.
Ogundipe-Leslie. Rain at Noon-time.
Oliver, M. Rain: "All afternoon it rained, then."
Otiono, T. Rainsong.
Otsu. For You.
Paek Sŏk. Mountain Rain.
Page, P. After Rain.
Stories of Snow.
Parker, A. Lullaby: "Sleep and rain, two gangsters."
Pasternak, B. Sultry Night, A.
Paz. As One Listens to the Rain.
Reliefs.
Relieves.
Pei Di. Stream at the House of the Luans, The.
Penrose, V. Rain Finding Once More, The.
Pessoa. Inside, the church lights up today's rain.
Petri. Night Song of the Personal Shadow.
Philpot, T. Rain My Wife, The.
Pinsky. Jersey Rain.
Round.
Piper, E. Big Swimming.
Po Chü-i. Evening Rain.
Rain.
Ponge. Rain.
Rain: "Rain falling in the courtyard where I watch adopts three manners, each distinct, The."
Prévert. Barbara.
Barbara.
Radner, Rebecca. I Want to Write like a Postcard.
Randell. Temperament is related to physique.
Rankin, J. Old Circles.
Rattenbury, A. Rain Falls on Utopia Too.
Ray, H. Voices of the Rain.
Read, T. Summer Shower, The.
Remoto. Rain.
Reznikoff. Free Verse.
My work done, I lean on the window-sill.
Rainy Season.
[Winter Sketches IV].
Riggs, L. Santo Domingo Corn Dance.
Rilke. Before Summer Rain.
Rivas, J. Don de resbalar.
Knack for Slipping Away, A.
Robinson, A. Song: "Oh for the wings of a dove."
Robinson, R. Jarrangulli.
Romtvedt. Kiev, the Ukraine, Nuclear Accident.
Roubaud. It Is Raining.
Ruden, S. Letter.
Ruefle. Evangelical.
Rain Effect.
Russell, N. Message of the Rain, The.
Sandburg, C. People know what the land knows, The.
Saner. Rain Near Heart Lake.
Sanfield. Walking in the rain.
Savoie. Reading Whitman's Democratic Vistas.
Scamell, B. More Rain.
Schoolcraft. To Sisters on a Walk in the Garden, after a Shower.
Sedakova. Rain: "It's raining, / and still people say there's no God!"

Shakespeare, W. Song: "When that I was and a little tiny boy."
We are but warriors for the working-day.
Shelley, P. Cloud, The.
Shepherd, R. West Willow.
Where When Was.
Shinkichi Takahashi. Mother and I.
Rain.
Sky.
Shuttle. Taxing the Rain.
Sodo. Sudden shower / Cooling lava.
Soyinka. I Think It Rains.
Stanley-Wrench. Storm, The.
Steinberg, J. Rain at Night.
Stevenson, R. Rain.
Stickney, T. Melancholy year is dead with rain, The.
Stock, N. First Time I Robbed Tiffany's, The.
Stoyanova, Danila. Three mares.
Su Tung-p'o. At the Temple of Kuan Yin in the Rain.
Black Clouds—Spilled Ink.
Rain in the Aspens.
Tune: "Calming Windswept Waves".
Suarez, V. Aguacero.
Supervielle. Rain and the Tyrants.
Swift, J. Description of a City Shower, A.
Synková, A. Tears.
Tanikawa, S. Rain Please Fall.
T'ao Ch'ien [or T'ao Yuan-ming]. To-Em-Mei's "The Unmoving Cloud".
Teasdale. Moods.
Thomas, E. It Rains.
Rain: "Rain, midnight rain, nothing but the wild rain."
Tu Fu [or Du Fu]. After Rain.
Clear After Rain ("Autumn, cloud blades on the horizon.").
Evening Shower in Spring, An.
Good Rain: A Night in Spring.
In Praise of Rain.
Kindly Rain, The.
Spring Night, Happy Rain.
Tu Mu. Plantains.
Tynan Hinkson, K. Blind Country.
Ullman. Rain.
Unknown. Being helpless.
Doctor Foster went to Gloucester.
Drop by Drop.
Mocking-Bird's Song, The.
No More Rain Fall for Wet You.
Peace, Rain, Plenty.
Rain Song of the Quer'ränna Chai' än, A.
Riddle: "Round the house and round the house / and there lies a black glove in the window."
Song for the Sun That Disappeared behind the Rainclouds.
Water pouring from clouds.
Upton, L. Somewhere So Lush.
Window Seat at the Paradise.
Vallejo. Down to the Dregs.
Van Winckel, N. As is His Wont.
Vanshenkin. Rain.
Verlaine. Falling tears in my heart.
Like city's rain, my heart.
Tears Fall in My Heart.
Very. Hath the Rain a Father?
Latter Rain, The ("Latter rain, it falls in anxious haste, The.").
Winter Rain, The.
Vogel, D. With gentle fingers.
Wanek. After Us.
Wang Wei. After Long Rain.
Rill of the House of the Luans.
Second Song for the Worship of the Goddess at Yu Mountain: "Bidding the Goddess Farewell".
Stream at the House of the Luans, The.
Warren, R. Holly and Hickory.
Vermont Ballad: Change of Season.
Warsh. Suicide Rates, The.
Watson, M. Sestina Halted in a Rain Delay.
Watson, R. Ballad of the Were-Wolf, A.
Watta. Cloud Rains.
Welish. Crossing Disappearing behind Them.
Wen T'ing-yün. In the South Courtyard.

Wenderoth, J.   Death.
Weöres.   Rain.
Whitmore, S.   Gamelia.
Wicks, S.   Rain Dance.
Wieners.   Invitation au Voyage 2.
Williams, W.   Rain: "As the rain falls."
   Red Wheelbarrow, The.
Williamson, G.   Belvedere Marittimo.
Wiman, C.   In Lakeview Cemetery.
Winged Serpent.   Two Rain Songs (Papago).
Winkler Prins.   Shower.
Wodehouse.   Till the Clouds Roll By.
Wordsworth, W.   Written in March [While
   Resting on the Bridge at the Foot of Brother's
   Water].
Wright, C.   Until words turn to moss.
Wright, R.   Waking from a nap.
Yang Shih-ch'i.   Night Rain: A Wall
   Collapses—Sent To My Neighbors.
Yang Wan-li.   Night Rain at Luster Gap.
Yeryomin.   Seamstress stitches on a sewing
   machine, The.
Yesenin [or Essenin].   Yesterday's rain.
Yi Illo.   Night Rain on the Rivers Hsiao and
   Hsiang.
Zabolotsky [or Zabolotskii].   Poem about Rain.

Rainbows
Begum, S.   Qaus-e Qazah.
Birney.   Bushed.
Coslow, S.   (Up on Top of a Rainbow) Sweepin'
   the Clouds Away.
Davies, W. H.   Great Time, A.
Dunbar, P.   Place Where the Rainbow Ends,
   The.
Harburg.   Over the Rainbow.
Herrick.   Rainbow; or Curious Covenant, The.
Keble.   Rainbow, The.
Laraque, P.   Rainbow.
MacDiarmid, H.   Watergaw, The.
Machado Ruiz.   Clouds Ripped Open.
McCarthy, J.   I'm Always Chasing Rainbows.
Salaam.   New Orleans Rainbow.
Stickney, T.   I hear a river thro' the valley
   wander.
Strong, L.   Door, The.
Turner, C.   Drowned Spaniel, The.
East or West?
Unknown.   If there be a rainbow in the eve.
   Rainbow i'th'morning.
   Song for the Sun That Disappeared behind the
   Rainclouds.
Wah.   Father / Mother Haibun #5.
Wordsworth, W.   My Heart Leaps Up [When I
   Behold].
Wright, J.   Legend.

Rainey, Gertrude ("Ma")
Brown, S.   Ma Rainey.
Okantah.   Southern Road.

Ralegh, Sir Walter
Elizabeth I.   Ah silly pug wert thou so sore
   afraid.

Ramadan
Krause, K.   Eid Al-Fitr.

Rameses II, King of Egypt
Shelley, P.   Ozymandias.
Unknown.   In the Days of Old Rameses.

Rams
Maclean, A.   Rams.
See also **Sheep**

Ranches
Garcia-Camarillo, C.   Rancho.
Hartog, D.   Oasis.
Miller, J.   Which Religion Vouchsafes.
Shomer.   First Sunset at Outler's Ranch.
Todd, M.   Rigby.
Unknown.   Corrido of "Gregorio Cortez".

Rape
Acholonu.   Other Forms of Slaughter.
Adamson.   Rimbaud Having a Bath.
Ai.   Sleeping Beauty.
Alcaeus [or Alkaios].   Having done most
   shameful, unjust things.
Alcosser.   Warrior's Tale, A.
Alexander, E.   Kevin of the N.E. Crew.
Anderson-Thompkins.   Interlude.

Baer.   Prosecutor.
Barker, G.   O Golden Fleece.
Belieu.   Man Who Tried to Rape You, The.
Berger, J.   Gun, The.
Bhairavayya.   Raped Poem.
Blackwell, Holley.   Another.
Bottoms.   Night Strategies.
Bryant, W.   Indian Story, An.
Ch'ŏyong.   Song of Ch'ŏyong.
Clinton, M.   Black Rape.
Cortez, J.   Rape.
Craighead, L.   Wo/man's Voice Must Be Heard,
   A.
Davie, D.   Fountain of Cyanë, The.
Derricotte.   On the Turning Up of Unidentified
   Black Female Corpses.
Desnos.   Ars Poetica.
Disch.   Rapist's Villanelle, The.
Donne.   Apparition, The.
   Batter my heart, three-personed [or three
   person'd] God; for you.
Duhamel.   Four Hours.
Field, E.   Bride of Frankenstein, The.
Frazier, John Alexander, Jr.   Deposed.
Gahan, Carmel.   Asking for it.
García Lorca.   Thamar and Amnon ("Moon
   turns in the sky, The.").
Gerstler.   Unexpected Adventure, An.
González, R.   Rapist: A Romance.
Griffin, S.   To the Far Corners of Fractured
   Worlds.
Hardy, J.   Objection Overruled.
Hogue.   Monique.
Howe, M.   Sixth Grade.
Irby.   Sequence.
Jordan, J.   Poem About My Rights.
Joseph, A.   On Viewing Two Different Date
   Rape Movies.
Khali, S.   Walking On: A Declaration of
   Wholeness.
Knutson, G.   Moon Fishing.
Larkin, P.   Deceptions.
Levertov.   Scraps of moon.
Limonov.   Fantastic!
Lummis, Suzanne.   Letter to My Assailant.
Martial.   Nasica raped the doctor's pretty lad.
McCarriston.   Castle in Lynn, A.
Menes, O.   Sodomy.
Moss, T.   Goodness and the Salt of the Earth.
Nasrin.   At the Back of Progress . . . .
Neely, L.   Rhonda, Age 15, Emergency Room.
Olinka, S.   Chinese Man in Smyrna, A.
Ovid.   Apollo and Daphne.
   Io and Jove.
   Rape of Lucrece, The.
Pope, A.   "Restore the lock!" she cries; and all
   around.
Reading, P.   Life is too black as he paints it and
   "Reading's nastiness sometimes".
Reznikoff.   3. The Immigrants.
Robbins, Z.   December 12th.
Rungano.   Woman, The.
Schreiber, R.   They Kill Us.
Seaton, M.   Story of Stonewall, A.
Shange.   It's Not so Good to be Born a Girl/
   Sometimes.
Sharp, S.   In the Tradition of Bobbitt.
Szporluk.   Libido.
Teschke, H.   Minutes of Hasiba, The.
Trinidad.   He said his name was Nick; later I
   learned.
Unknown.   Having left behind its cutting.
   Under the Linden Tree.
   What business, this? What reason should we
   give.
Walsh, W. et al.   Imperfect Enjoyment, The.
Waniek.   Chosen.
Yeats.   Leda and the Swan.
Young, D.   Ballant o' the Laird's Bath, The.

Raphael [Archangel]
Goethe.   Chorus of the Archangels, The.
Wright, J.   Boleros #31.

Raphael [Painter]
Allston.   On the Group of the Three Angels
   Before the Tent of Abraham, by Raffaelle, in
   the Vatican.

Ray, H.   Raphael.

Raspberries
Dienstfrey, Patricia.   Let the Raspberry Jam in
   the Crystal Jar Stand for It.

Rastafarianism
Adisa.   Ethiopia Unda a Jamaican Mango Tree.
Agard, J.   For Bob Marley.
Brathwaite, E.   Wings of a Dove.
Dawes, K.   Black Heart.
Goodison.   Jah Music.
   Upon a Quarter Million.
Hippolyte.   Antonette's Boogie.
   Jah Son / Another Way.
   Reggae Cat (for Boston Jack).
Ingram-Roberts, A.   Poem 2 (for Duckie
   Simpson of Black Uhuru).
Jerry.   Mabrak.
Malachi.   Psalm of Silk.
McNeill, A.   Ode to Brother Joe.
   Saint Ras.
Morris, M.   Rasta Reggae.
Preston, R.   Champion Chant.
   Italist Chant.
Scott, D.   Dreadwalk.
Weinstein, N.   Garvey's Head as Value.

Rationalism and Rationalists
Blake, W.   Mock On, Mock On, Voltaire,
   Rousseau.
Burkard.   Summer after Last, The.
Hejinian.   Presences that constitute life do so by
   entering life, The.
Poe.   Sonnet—To Science.
See also **Intellect and Intellectuals; Reason**

Rats
Atwood.   Rat Song.
Browning, R.   Pied Piper of Hamelin, The.
Buson.   Light winter rain.
   Walking on dishes.
Carruth, H.   Little Citizen, Little Survivor.
Cook, W.   Still-Life with Woodstove.
Davies, W. H.   Rat, The.
Frénaud.   Words of the Poem, The.
Gilbert, J.   Explicating the Twilight.
Gowar.   Rat Trap.
Han-shan.   Cold Mountain Poem No. 158.
Jones, D.   You can hear the silence of it.
Kim Hyesun.   In the Night.
Lear, E.   Limerick: "There was an Old Man who
   supposed."
Logue, C.   Rat, O Rat.
Mei Yao Ch'en.   Offering for the Cat, An.
   Sharing Lodging with Hsieh Shih-hou.
Mew.   Trees Are Down, The.
Moore, M.   To an Intra-Mural Rat.
Nguyen Binh Khiem.   Hated Rats, The.
Ondaatje.   Rat Jelly.
Rohrer, M.   My Government.
Smith, S.   Pretty.
Toomer.   Reapers.
Torres, E.   Bio-Rodent-Oriole.
Unknown.   Boss Rat.
   Rat, The.
   Sans Equity and sans Poise.
   Shi-shu: Rats.
Vietnamese Oral Tradition.   Cat, The.
Wu Wei-yeh.   Broken Lampstand, The.
Yi Kyubo.   Mad Rout of the Rat, The.

Rattlesnakes
Hoggard, James.   Oil Field Road off Clyte
   Escarpment.
McDonald, W.   Hawks in a Bitter Blizzard.
Montgomery, Vaida Stewart.   To the
   Rattlesnake.
Stodghill, Pat.   Rattlesnake Roundup.
Warren, R.   Rattlesnake Country.

Ravel, Maurice
Young, A.   Ravel: Bolero.

Ravens
Alexander, P.   Crossing.
Barlow, J.   Advice to a Raven in Russia
   [December, 1812].
Borisov.   Ravens.
Carryl, G.   Sycophantic Fox and the Gullible
   Raven, The.
Coleridge, S.   Raven, The.

Dana, R. Dying Raven, The.
Doherty, T. Raven's Revenge.
Everson, W. These Are the Ravens.
McNiece, R. Wet sand raven tracks.
Merwin. Noah's Raven.
Meyerhoff, J. Three Ravens.
Poe. Raven, The.
Sosnora. Where are our horses.
Unknown. Three Ravens, The.
Twa Corbies, The.
Wellman, M. Evil Raven, have paper pity upon those.

Reading and Readers
Alarcon, F. X in My Name, The.
Aleixandre. Who I Write For.
Antin. Private Occasion in a Public Place, A.
Aridjis. Self-Portrait at Six Years of Age.
Armand. Another Poetics.
Braille for Left Hand.
Bell, M. Whitman's Grass.
Berg, S. Prayer: "Nobody understands so let the Rabbi."
Bernstein, C. Why we ask you not to touch.
Berry, D. On Reading Poems to a Senior Class at South High.
Blumenthal, M. Accountant, The.
Bly, R. Warning to the Reader.
Boland, E. Oral Tradition, The.
Borges. Poem of the Gifts.
Branch, A. In the Beginning Was the Word.
Brown Rosellen. I have a neighbor.
Brownell, H. Suspiria Noctis.
Burkard. Cloud of Dusk, A.
Buson. By flowering pear.
Caballero-Robb, M. Memoranda for Rosario.
Cardenal. I offer these verses to you, Claudia, because you are their mistress.
Carroll, L. Poeta Fit, Non Nascitur.
Carson, A. Short Talk on Reading.
Cernuda. Boy Behind a Window.
Cherry, K. Reading, Dreaming, Hiding.
Cisneros, A. Paris Cinquième.
Clanchy, K. Spell.
Collier, M. Argos.
Collins, B. First Reader.
Marginalia.
Cooke, R. Schemhammphorasch.
Corn. Reading *Pericles* in New London.
Cunningham, J. Coffee.
Dao. Reading: "Taste the unnecessary tears."
Davis, O. Sweet Reader, Flanneled and Tulled.
De la Mare. Old Susan.
Deltoro, A. Libro de Segunda Mano.
Secondhand Book.
Dickinson, E. There is No Frigate Like a Book.
Dove, R. First Book, The.
Dubie. Of Politics, & Art.
Earle, J. Saturday in the '20s, A.
Ermakova, I. Toward morning around seven.
Ferdowsi, A. I've worked, I've worked so hard; reading, reading.
Forbes, C. Poet's Shuffle, The.
Reading Walt Whitman.
Fried, D. Story Having to Do with Walt Whitman, A.
Gibson, M. Reading in Bed.
Glancy. First Reader Santee Training School, 1873, The.
Gotera. Dance of the Letters.
Grapes, J. Listen.
Guevara, M. Reader of This Page.
Guiducci. Readings.
Upon Closing the Book.
Gullar. Noise.
Han-shan. Reading won't save us from death.
Han Yong'un [*or* Yongwun]. To the Readers.
Harper, F. Learning to Read.
Herrick. To the Sour[e] Reader.
Hicok. Active Reader, The.
Hughes, T. Platform One.
Hume, C. Various Readings of an Illegible Postcard.
Hunt, L. Paulo and Francesca.
Issa. Fat priest, The.
Jackson, L. Troubles of a Book, The.
Jonson, B. To the Reader ("Pray thee, take care,

that tak'st my book[e] in hand.").
Joseph, A. Reading Room.
Kan Chazan. Reading a Book on a Winter Night.
Keats. On First Looking into Chapman's Homer.
On Sitting Down to Read *King Lear* Once Again.
Kemble. Lines.
Kendrick, D. Sophie, Climbing the Stairs.
Kooser. Selecting a Reader.
Krysl. Carpe Diem: Time Piece.
Kuusisto, S. Night Seasons.
Larkin, P. Fiction and the Reading Public.
Study of Reading Habits, A.
Laughlin, J. Inn at Kirchstetten, The.
Lejeune, Claire. Illiterate.
So Where.
Leonard, T. Fathers and Sons.
Lisella. Song of the Third Generation.
Liu, T. Reading Whitman in a Toilet Stall.
Longfellow, H. Day Is Done, The.
MacCaig. Chauvinist.
Madhubuti. Poem Looking for a Reader, A.
Markotić, N. Repeat the capitalism of narrative.
Martial. Let every prudish reader use his feet.
Read of *Thyestes, Oedipus,* dark suns.
To His Book[e].
McGrath, T. Reading by Mechanic Light.
You Can Start the Poetry Now, Or: News from Crazy Horse.
McIlroy, L. Siesta.
Meinke. Robert Frost in Warsaw.
Menicanti. To the Readers Who Write to Me.
Milosz, C. Readings.
Moore, M. Poetry [1921 version]: "I, too, dislike it: there are things that are important beyond all this fiddle."
Mullen, H. Fancy Cortex.
Murphy, R. Reading Lesson, The.
Mutis. Word, A.
Nelson, M. Chopin.
Nishiwaki Junzaburo. Man Who Reads Homer, A.
Orr, G. Insomnia Song.
Pagis, D. Story, The.
Parkes, B. To Elizabeth Barrett Browning.
Pellicer, C. To Poetry.
Po Chü-i. Reading Yuan Chen on a Boat.
Procter, A. My Journal.
Rexroth, K. Homer in Basic.
Rich, A. Diving into the Wreck.
Novel, The.
Richards, T. Challenge to the Reader, A.
Ritsos. Myopic Child, A.
Sanguineti. What you're reading (if you're reading me) are the effects.
Sansom, A. From the Moment I Picked Up Your Book.
Savoie. Reading Whitman's *Democratic Vistas.*
Schilpp, M. Non Sequitur.
Shapiro, D. Book of Glass, A.
Smith, C. Should the lone Wanderer, fainting on his way.
Spaziani. To the Readers.
Stevens, W. House Was Quiet and the World Was Calm, The.
Large Red Man Reading.
Phosphor Reading by His Own Light.
Reader, The.
Strand. Reading in Place.
Stroud, J. Homage: Summer/Winter, Shay Creek.
Su Tung-p'o. Reading the Poetry of Meng Chiao: Two Poems.
Tate, J. There's a Certain Point Each Evening.
Tu Fu [*or* Du Fu]. On the Spur of the Moment.
Van Duyn. In Bed with a Book.
Velichansky, A. Trunks of birches, like scrolls.
Waller, E. Of the Last Verses in the Book.
Warn. After Reading the Book of Splendor.
Wells, C. Of Modern Books.
Problem, A.
Whitman, W. Whoever You Are Holding Me Now in Hand.
Williams, C. K. Reading: The Bus.

Williams, J. On Reading Aloud My Early Poems.
Yeats. When You Are Old.
Young, K. Central Standard Time.
Reagan, Ronald W.
Kizer, C. Election Day, 1984.
Mikolowski, K. Witness, The.
Real Estate
Cecil. Some Terms in Real Estate Defined.
Tretheway. Homesteading.
Reality
Adcock, F. Dreaming.
Albiach. Theatre.
Ammons. Corsons Inlet.
Andrews, B. Rich little circle south.
Baekoon Kyunghan. Mountain Life.
Baraka, I. Poem for Deep Thinkers, A.
Beasley. Red Reed.
Bell, M. Book of the Dead Man #33, The.
Bely [*or* Belyi]. By-street was bathed in sun, The.
Benson, S. As sincerely as possible.
Blue Book 18 Pages 1–4.
Berkson, B. Melting Milk.
Bernstein, C. Whose Language.
Berrigan, A. Anti-Preening Poem.
Berrigan, T. Mid-Friday morn, 10 o'clock, I go to India.
Bingxin. Myriad Stars, Part 132.
Blackwell, Holley. Message No. 69.
Borges. Other Tiger, The.
Bronk. Corals and Shells.
Way, The.
Brooks, G. Kitchenette building.
Brutus. Sand Wet and Cool, The.
Budy. First Night in the New House.
Burliuk *et al.* Slap in the Face of Public Taste, A.
Busceti, G. Eight Phases of Contemplation.
Child, A. Motive for Mayhem, A.
Surplus.
Chu Úisik. What is life, I ponder.
Clark, T. Society.
Collobert. III: "As if dead the buried text."
Couani. What a Man, What a Moon.
Cross, D. Ceci n'est pas une pipe.
Cummings, E. E. My sweet old etcetera.
Daniel, S. Are They Shadows [That We See]?
Davis, W. On Lookout: Guadalupe River Ranch.
Denby. Aaron.
DiPalma. Each Moment is Surrounded.
Empire Smoke, Forgeries, Salient and The Ritz.
Poem: "In danger of which."
Sheaf Mark.
Donnelly, T. New Intelligence, The.
Drake, N. Foley Artist, The.
Man in the White Suit, The.
Driscoll, Frances. Real Life.
Drummond de Andrade. Residue.
Duchamp. 1914 Box, The.
World in Yellow, A.
Duncan, R. Close.
What of the structure of Rime? I said.
Dupin. At Instants I Thought.
Durcan. In Memory: The Miami Showband— Massacred 31 July 1975.
Equi. Date With Robbe-Grillet, A.
Evans, M. World I See, The.
Fanthorpe. Atlas.
Fenton, J. Skip, The.
Fumi Saito. Lit up.
Genko. Unaware of illusion or enlightenment.
Ginsberg, A. Change, The: *Kyoto-Tokyo Express.*
Gizzi. Tout les Matins du Monde.
Glück, L. Celestial Music.
Winged Horse, The.
Gross, P. Mappa Mundi.
Grumman, Bob. Reality.
Guest, B. Eating Chocolate Ice Cream: Reading Mayakovsky.
Emphasis Falls on Reality, An.
Words: "Simple contact with a wooden spoon and the word, The."
Han-shan Te-ch'ing. Hard cold rain a forest of

wind, A.
Harburg.   It's Only a Paper Moon.
Harris, Allison.   Nothing Much.
Harryman.   Realism.
Hejinian.   Nights.
Hinsey, E.   On the Uncountable Nature of
  Things.
Ikkyu Sojun.   My Real Dwelling.
Inada.   Ness.
Iosifova, Ekaterina.   Beneath Winter's Roof.
Jabès.   Mirror and Scarf.
Jarrell, R.   Märchen, The.
Jeffers, R.   Boats in a Fog.
Jones, R.   Front Window, The.
Kassabova, K.   Mirages.
Kerouac.   113th Chorus.
Kim Sŭnghŭi.   Floating Metonymy 5.
Kruchyonykh [or Kruchionykh or Kruchenykh].
  Sahara to America, The.
Lahey, Joy.   Habitat Photo.
Lalic.   Places We Love.
Lawrence, D. H.   Red Geranium and Godly
  Mignonette.
Levertov.   Seeing for a Moment.
Levitt, Peter.   No life but this one.
Mahon.   Tractatus.
Mandel, T.   Realism.
Mansour, J.   From an ass to an analyst and back.
Marinetti.   They are Coming.
  We had stayed up all night, my friends and I,
    under hanging mosque lamps.
Markham, E.   After Reading Shakspere.
Mayakovsky [or Maiakovskii].   Screaming My
  Head Off.
Mayer, B.   Earthworker's God is Healed, The.
McClure, M.   Hymn to Saint Geryon.
McDaniel, J.   Obvious, The.
McDonald, R.   Hollow Thesaurus, The.
Mikhail, D.   Urgent Call, An.
Millay, E.   Love is not all: it is not meat nor
  drink.
Molina, P.   Events Like Palaces.
Mullen, H.   Anthropic Principle, The.
Naden.   Love's Mirror.
Neruda.   Too Many Names.
North, C.   Pastoral, The: "Now the body is the
  body's flower."
Olson, C.   Moon Is the Number 18, The.
Ondaatje.   Gentleman Compares His Virtue to a
  Piece of Jade, A.
Ono no Komachi.   Although my feet.
Orozco.   Reality and Desire.
Orpingalik.   Alcheringa Definitions.
Palmer, M.   Eighth Sky.
  Untitled (February 2000).
Paz.   Certainty.
Perelman.   Things.
Péret.   On All Fours.
Pessoa.   "Startling Reality of Things," The.
Picabia.   Eunuch Unique.
Pinsky.   Hearts, The.
Piombino.   My Lady Carries Stones.
Prado, A.   Grace.
Prassinos.   Conversation, A.
Ray, D.   Midnight Diner by Edward Hopper, A.
Restifo, Elaine.   Jealousy: "I've watched a
  young woman fondling three strands of her
  own hair."
Rexroth, K.   Grammar of cause, The.
Rimbaud, A.   Bottom.
Rivera-Garza, C.   Tercer Mundo.
  Third World.
Rolfe, E.   Paris—Christmas 1938.
Rose, B.   It's Only a Paper Moon.
Rossetti, D.   Sea-Limits, The.
Saisho.   On Joshu's Nothingness.
Salinas, P.   Do You Hear How They Beg for
  Realities?
Schuyler, J.   Letter to a Friend: Who Is Nancy
  Daum?
Schwitters.   Murder Machine 43.
Seshadri.   Disappearances, The.
Sherry, J.   Radiant.
Shinkichi Takahashi.   Position of the Sparrow,
  The.
  Stitches.

Shrine Priestess of Ise.   My mind is dazzled.
Snyder, G.   Milton by Firelight.
Sodo.   Question clear, the answer deep, The.
Soupault.   Comrade.
Sri Sri.   Bitter Poem, A.
  Really?
  Vedantist, The.
Stadler.   Saying, The.
Stainer.   Quanta.
Steele, T.   Chanson Philosophique.
Stevens, W.   Course of a Particular, The.
  Indigo Glass in the Grass, The.
  Man on the Dump, The.
  Motive for Metaphor, The.
  Not Ideas about the Thing but the Thing Itself.
  Of Mere Being.
  Plain Sense of Things, The.
  Poems of Our Climate, The.
  Sunday Morning.
Strand.   Keeping Things Whole.
Sze.   Apache Plume.
  Axolotl.
  Before Completion.
  Network, The.
  String Diamond, The.
Szymborska, W.   View with a Grain of Sand.
Tate, J.   Descent, The.
Taylor, C.   Choir.
Templeton, F.   Act II - Crossing At the Tracks.
Thomas, L.   Argent, L'.
Tomlinson, C.   Song: "To enter the real."
Troupe.   Gray Day in January in La Jolla.
Tzara.   Dance of the Greased Women, The.
  Metal Coughdrops.
Unknown.   Pawnee War-Song.
  Truth: "Breast / nursery."
Van Duyn.   Causes.
Vâsıf, Enderunlu.   Gazelles have bound their
  hearts, The.
Von Freytag-Loringhoven.   Affectionate.
Waldrop, R.   Feverish Propositions.
Ward, D.   Tables in Pictures.
Welch, L.   Small Sentence to Drive Yourself
  Sane.
Welish.   Casting Sequences.
  Detained by Rest.
  If I Blindfold You.
  Scalpel in Hand.
Wenderoth, J.   Moon River.
White, E.   Village Revisited.
Whitman, W.   I Am the Poet.
  That Shadow My Likeness.
Williams, Gerwyn.   Final Curtain.
Wright, C. D.   Lake Echo, Dear.
Wright, Charles.   Reading Lao Tzu Again in the
  New Year.
Yauch, Adam.   Update, The.
Yeats.   Meru.

Reaping and Reapers
Berry, W.   Mad Farmer Revolution, The.
Bontemps.   Black Man Talks of Reaping, A.
Dowson.   Last Word, A.
Hood, T.   Ruth.
Toomer.   Harvest Song.
  Reapers.
Unknown.   Pick ferns, pick ferns.
Wilde, O.   Wasted Days.
Wordsworth, W.   Solitary Reaper, The.

Reason
Barnfield [or Barnefield].   Sporting at fancie,
  setting light by love.
Bevington, L.   Afternoon.
Blake, W.   Marriage of Heaven and Hell, The.
  Mock On, Mock On, Voltaire, Rousseau.
Brontë, C.   Reason.
Cavendish, M.   Discourse of Beasts, A.
Cole, H.   White Spine.
Dennis, C.   To Reason.
Dickinson, E.   I reason, Earth is short.
Donne.   If poisonous [or poysonous] mineral[l]s,
  and if that tree.
Dove, R.   Geometry.
Dryden, J.   Dim, as the borrow'd beams of
  moon and stars.
Eluard, P. et al.   Shared Nights.
Follen, E.   Lines on Nonsense.

Forhan, C.   Big Jigsaw.
Golffing.   Higher Empiricism, The.
Heinemann, M.   For R. J. C. (Summer, 1936).
Jaccottet.   Reason.
Juana Inés de la Cruz.   Describes Rationally the
  Irrational Effects of Love.
Kendall, M.   Lower Life, The.
Langland, W.   Dreamer Meets Conscience and
  Reason.
  Thus I awoke, God knows, when I lived in
    Cornhill.
Levertov.   Contraband.
  Quest, The.
Matthews, W.   Psychopathology of Everyday
  Life, The.
Miles, J.   Reason: "Said, Pull her up a bit will
  you, Mac, I want to unload there."
Milosz, C.   Incantation.
Olson, C.   Poem 143.
Owenson.   Fragment 3.
Plath.   Death of Myth-making, The.
Pope, A.   On a Certain Lady at Court.
Robinson, M.   Canzonet.
  Invokes Reason.
  Rejects the Influence of Reason.
Rochester, J.   Were I (who to my cost already
  am).
Rukeyser, M.   Rational Man.
Sherwood, G.   Satire against Reason and
  Mankind, A.
Sidney, P.   Sonnet 5: "It is most true that eyes
  are formed to serve."
  Sonnet 10: "Reason, in faith thou art well
    served, that still."
  Sonnet 18: "With what sharp checks I in myself
    am shent."
  Sonnet 71: "Who will in fairest book of Nature
    know."
Sitwell, D.   Heart and Mind.
Smith, C.   Written near a Port on a Dark
  Evening.
Stead, C.   Between.
Suckling, S.   Barley-Break , A.
Tollet.   On Loving Once and Loving Often.
Whitman, W.   When I Heard the Learn'd
  Astronomer.
Zenmaro.   Tanka: "Nothing / but reason."
Zukofsky, L.   Anew 21.
See also **Intellect and Intellectuals; Rationalism
and Rationalists**

Rebellions and Rebels
Akhmadulina.   Chills.
Arrillaga.   Dream.
Benedetti, M.   We All Conspire.
Berry, W.   Manifesto: The Mad Farmer
  Liberation Front.
  To My Mother.
Blanchard, Mary Loving.   Bloodlines.
Brathwaite, E.   New World A-Comin'.
Breeze.   Red Rebel Song.
Brome.   On Sir G. B. His Defeat.
  Satire on the Rebellion, A.
Browning, R.   Italian in England, The.
  Through the Metidja to Abd-el-Kadr.
Cheek.   Rollercoaster.
Corrie.   Rebel Tam.
Coviello, M.   This hour is made of iron grates
  where the underground.
Cummings, E. E.   Boys i mean are not refined,
  The.
D'Aguiar, F.   Mama Dot Warns Against an
  Easter Rising.
Darwish, M.   On Wishes.
De Kok.   Our Sharpeville.
Dharker.   They'll say, "She must be from
  another country".
Drummond, W.   Against the King.
  If of the dead save good nought should be said.
Dunbar, P.   Conquerors, The: The Black Troops
  in Cuba.
Ekevall, K.   Telling Myself.
Emerson, R.   Uriel.
Farr, R.   At general Electric, where they eat
  their/young.
Guevara, M.   Easter Revolt Painted on a
  Tablespoon, The.

Guiducci. I Look at You So Old.
Heaney, S. At Toomebridge.
 Requiem for the Croppies.
Helle, A. Poem for Natalia Ginzburg.
Hoagland, E. Fired Up!!
Holloway, S. Old Sam.
Hugo, V. Jeanne was holed up (pitch darkness; bread and water).
Johnson, L. Five Nights of Bleeding.
Kalina, R. Testimonies.
Keller, D. Joining the Circus.
Kipling, R. Pict Song, A.
Korzhavin. We can string words on a line.
Lane, P. Children.
Leonard, T. Before the 1820 rising in the West of Scotland a network of.
Lindsay, V. Factory Windows Are Always Broken.
Lindsay, V. Voice of the Wheat, The.
Martin, Steve. Cows in Trouble.
Mihalic. Under the Microscope.
Milton. March of the Rebel Angels.
 On the Detraction Which Followed upon My Writing Certain Treatises ("I did but prompt the age to quit their [or thir] clogs.").
Mure. O Heavens! O Earth! heer I must pause a space.
Nelson, M. Ballad of Aunt Geneva, The.
Obejas, A. Sunday.
Palis, Y. Waking Up.
Pegram, A. Deliverance.
 I Will Still Sing.
"Pindar.". Hymn to the Guilotine.
Po Chü-i. Song of Lasting Regret, The.
Pope, A. Epistle to Dr. Arbuthnot.
Preston, R. Lift Every Fist and Swing.
Randolph, I. Rebel, The.
Reynolds, S. F. Whipping, The.
Rich, A. Phenomenology of Anger, The.
Rylander, E. Midnight Rocker, Tiananmen Square, May 27, 1989.
Sepúlveda-Pulvirenti. September 11, 1973.
Slutsky [or Slutskii]. Law, which each citizen knows well.
Sousa, N. Call.
 Our Voice.
Taha, A. Anwar Kamel Celebrates Le Quatorze Juillet.
Touré, A. Ab*original* Elegy: The Once and Future Queen.
Tu Fu [or Du Fu]. Lovely Lady.
Unknown. Humble Petition of the British Jacobins to their Brethren of France, The.
 Little horror, take your rifle and kill me now.
 Upon Arch-bishop Laud, Prisoner in the Tower. 1641.
Whitman, W. We Two Boys Together Clinging.
Worpole, K. Sleeper.
Zulu, P. You are Mad: and I Mean It!
See also **Revolution and Revolutionaries**

Rebirth
Ai. More.
Alegría. Desire.
Amichai, Y. Four Resurrections in the Valley of the Ghosts.
Awoonor. This Earth, My Brother.
Bachmann. Settlement.
 Songs from an Island.
Beaver. More than 9 Lives.
Bensko. Bones of Lazarus.
Berrigan, D. In Memoriam (2): "Young priest, dead suddenly, A."
Bevington, L. Midnight.
Bontemps. My Heart has Known its Winter.
Bousoño, C. There's a Miracle Going On in the Ashes.
Brodsky, J. Elegy: "About a year has passed. I've returned to the place of battle."
Césaire, A. In Order to Speak.
Collins, A. Song.
Confucius. Great Digest, The.
Cullen, C. For My Grandmother.
Cummings, E. E. I Thank You God.
 When God Lets My Body Be.
Daumal. Persephone That Is to Say Double Issue.

Drayton. Since there's no help, come let us kiss and part.
Ferlinghetti, L. I am waiting for my case to come up.
Flores, M. Whenever something dies.
Frost, R. Onset, The.
Glück, L. Cottonmouth Country.
 Fantasy, A.
Grimké, A. At April.
Hardy, T. For Life I Had Never Cared Greatly.
Herbert, Z. Remembering My Father.
Hoagland, T. Benevolence.
Holan. Resurrection.
Hudgins. Flag of Honeysuckle, A.
Hughes, L. In Time of Silver Rain.
Iqbal. Poem: "Are you Alive, Dead or DeadAlive?"
József, A. Seventh, The.
Kalina, R. Testimonies.
Kanemitsu-Kogun. My hands released at last, the cliff soars.
Kinnell. Saint Francis and the Sow.
Kwangdŏk. Prayer to Amitāyus.
Levine, P. Belief.
Lewis, G. There are great advantages to having been dead.
Lynch, K. Ophelia in Utah.
Mabuza. Death to the Gold Mine!
Mahapatra, J. Sanskrit.
Mandelstam [or Mandelshtam]. Mounds of Human Heads.
 Mounds of Human Heads Are Wandering into the Distance.
Martin, C. Easter Sunday, 1985.
McGrath, Carmelita. Let Us Go and Find a Place of Worship.
McKay, C. Baptism.
Millay, E. Renascence.
Mitchell, S. Havana Birth.
Murray, J. Lullaby: "Sleep, little architect. It is your mother's wish."
Nichols, G. Epilogue: "I have crossed an ocean."
Osundare. I Sing of Change.
Popa. Burning Shewolf.
Rossetti, C. Caterpillar, The.
 Shut Out.
Sanchez, S. Part Four: Rebirth.
Sen, R. Black clouds have risen in my sky.
 I came to this world.
Simic. Past-Lives Therapy.
Szymborska, W. Theater Impressions.
Tabb. Evolution.
Taylor, J. As Gold is better that's in fire tride.
Tekeyan. Dream.
 Prayer on the Threshold of Tomorrow.
Tennyson, A. Today the grave is bright for me.
Thomas, D. I Have Longed to Move Away.
Vallejo. Masses.
Vaughan, H. Ascension Hymn.
 I Walked [or Walkt or Walk'd] the Other Day to Spend My Hour.
Wilbur, R. Alatus.
 April 5, 1974.
 Lilacs, The.
Williams, W. Spring and All.
Zagajewski. When Death Came.
See also **Renewal; Regeneration**

Rebuilding
Kanchev, Nikolai. Feeling.
Szymborska, W. End and the Beginning, The.
Turpin, Mark. Box, The.

Recipes
Follon, C. Love Rats.
Harris, Ken. Old Poetess Makes a Child, The.
Norwid, C. Recipe for a Warsaw Novel.
Suárez, V. Donatilia's Unrequited Love Remedy.
Umpierre, L. Only the Hand That Stirs Knows What's in the Pot.

Recognition
Berry, W. Wild Rose, The.
Byrne, Elena Karina. In Particular.
Clanchy, K. Recognition.
Cornford, F. Avenue, The.
Feng Chih. Sonnet: "We often pass a night

warm and intimate."
Guest, B. Nostalgia of the Infinite.
Guidacci. Crazy Mother, The.
Homer. Laertes.
Housman. Look not in my eyes, for fear.
József, A. Dog, The.
Kuppner. Architecture is when the sun shines on a facade daily.
Levertov. People at Night.
MacNeice. Elegy for Minor Poets.
Mutis. Amen.
Ramsdell, H. Nearly Circle.
Ransom, J. Jack's Letter.

Reconciliation
Aiken, C. Quarrel, The.
Amaru. Lying in Bed.
Baehr, A. Ritual.
Chaucer. Pardoner's Tale, The.
Chin, J. Ex-Boyfriends Named Michael.
Coles, R. Christmas, Belfast.
Copus, J. Miss Havisham's Letter.
Heard, J. Sunshine after Cloud.
Homer. Achilles and Priam.
Kenneally, B. Reconciliation: "Do not torment me, woman."
Marcus, J. Delaying Relevance.
Marlowe. He's gone, and for his absence thus I mourn.
Melville, H. America.
Press, K. Welcome.
Ransom, J. Armageddon.
Shakespeare, W. Sonnet 119: "What potions have I drunk of Siren tears."
Williamson, G. Neighboring Storms.

Reconstruction, United States
Lanier, S. Laughter in the Senate.
Thompson, M. Lincoln's Grave.
Tucker, M. Men swell the current,—many of them wear.

Record Players
Gray-Kontar, D. Cuz' mama played jazz.
Jackson, R. Love # 49: "This is how I felt."
Macpherson, H. Looking for 78's in the 40's.
Morejón. Richard Brought His Flute.
Razaf, A. I'd Give a Dollar for a Dime.
Trethewey, N. Secular.
Wallace, R. Sound Systems.
White, L. Soundtrack.

Red (color)
Chippewa Oral Tradition. Arrow Song.
Crawford, I. Camp of Souls, The.
Dixon, M. Lady in Red, The.
Donne. Oh my black[e] soul[e]! now thou art summoned.
Espada. Green and Red, Verde y Rojo.
Field, E. Red.
Finch, P. Reds in the Bed.
Guest, B. Red Dye.
Hernández Cruz. Scarlet Skirt.
Hughes, L. When Sue Wears Red.
Issa. Dragonfly, The.
 Red morning sky.
Jones, Nesta Wyn. Poppies.
Larsen, L. Red.
MacDiarmid, H. Why I Choose Red.
Mays, M. #4, In Red.
O'Grady, J. Poem for the Womb.
Parker, D. Red Dress, The.
Rodriguez, J. Nu-plastik Fanfare Red.
Rybicki, J. This Sun.
Stein, G. Box, A.
 Red Hat, A.
Townsend, A. Rouge.
Wetzsteon. Surgical Moves.

Red Jacket (Seneca Chief)
Halleck, F. Red Jacket.

Red Sea
Benton, S. Lilith.

Redding, Otis
Mitcham. On the Otis Redding Bridge.

Redemption
Auden. Ballad of Barnaby, The.
Beaumont, J. Garden, The.
Benbow. Larson Arson.
Campion, T. Author of light, revive my dying

spright.
Seek the Lord.
View Mee, Lord.
Cruz e Sousa.　Good Friday.
Davis, W.　Snow.
Donne.　Batter my heart, three-personed [*or* three person'd] God; for you.
Good Friday [*or* Goodfriday], 1613. Riding Westward.
Oh my black[e] soul[e]! now thou art summoned.
Foerster.　Tantum Ergo.
Herbert, G.　Pulley, The.
Redemption.
Sion.
World, The.
Hopkins, G.　God's Grandeur.
Keene, J.　God Lovingly Counterattacks.
Machado Ruiz.　Young Spain, A.
Mahon.　Globe in [North] Carolina, The.
Merton.　Cana.
Meynell, A.　Beyond Knowledge.
I Am the Way.
Milton.　Thus began / Outrage from lifeless things; but Discord first.
Moxley, Jennifer.　Stem of the Tree of Orestes.
Murray, P.　Redemption.
Pinchas-Cohen.　Journey of a Doe.
Pitter.　Task, The.
Ralegh, S.　Passionate Man['']s Pilgrimage, The.
Riley, P.　Elf Shots.
Robinson, E.　Children of the Night, The.
Smart, C.　Hymn to the Supreme Being.
Spenser, E.　Sonnet 68: "Most glorious Lord of Life that on this day."
Thomas, D.　There Was a Saviour.
Thompson, F.　Hound of Heaven, The.
Unknown.　Blow Your Trumpet, Gabriel.
Nobody Knows the Trouble I've Had.
Sequence for the First Sunday in Advent.
Sinner Won't Die No More.
Turn, Sinner, Turn O!
What Yo' Gwine to [*or* t'] Do When Yo' [*or* de] Lamp Burn Down?
You Must Be Pure and Holy.
Vaughan, H.　Regeneration.
Very.　I Was Sick and in Prison.
Vietnamese Oral Tradition.　Ship of Redemption.
Wesley, C.　Free Grace.
Wicks, S.　On Re-recording Mozart.
Wilbur, R.　Proof, The.
Wilde, O.　E Tenebris.

Redwood Trees
Hemschemeyer.　O Mother My Giant Redwood.

Reeds
Beasley.　Red Reed.
Rumi.　Listen to the reed-flute telling its tales.
Seferis.　Memory 1.
Unknown.　After spring has come.

Refinement
Cofer, J.　Women Who Love Angels.
Lovelace, R.　Song: "Strive not, vain Lover, to be fine."

Reflections
Atwood.　Tricks With Mirrors.
Behn, A.　Angellica's Lament.
Belev.　Train.
Boyarskikh, E.　Person is reflected by the whirlpool, not the face, A.
Bracho, C.　Sobre él discurren con suavidad.
Upon It They Gently Reflect.
Burns, R.　Of A' the Airts [the Wind Can Blaw].
Carruth, H.　Soft Time of the Year, The.
Choeui Eusoon.　Autumn Thought.
Davis, O.　Small Number, A.
Dovaston, J. F. M.　Streamlet! methinks thy lot resembles mine.
Elytis, O.　Anniversary.
Ferlinghetti, L.　21.
Fisken, Thomas Scott.　Window Box.
Frost, R.　For Once, Then, Something.
Giovanni.　Walking Down Park.
Graves, R.　Foreboding, The.
Griffiths, S.　Getting It Wrong, Again.
Gumilyov [*or* Gumiliov *or* Gumilev].　Porcelain

Pavilion, The.
Han-shan Te-ch'ing.　Deep among ten thousand peaks I sit alone cross-legged.
Ho Hsun.　Watching the New Moon, I Compose These Verses to Show to My Fellow-Travelers, Stranded with Me.
Issa.　Reflected / In the dragonfly's eye—.
Jarrell, R.　Game at Salzburg, A.
Jinkag Haesim.　By the Water.
Knott.　Shorts / Excerpts.
Komunyakaa, Y.　Facing It.
Kooser.　In the Basement of the Goodwill Store.
Li Po.　Mirror Lake's waters are moon-clear.
Lindtová, A.　Campfire.
Lisnyanskaya [*or* Lisnianskaia].　Triptych of Reflection.
Lochhead, L.　Hickie, The.
Lovelace, R.　Song: "Strive not, vain Lover, to be fine."
MacEwen, G.　Dark Pines under Water.
MacNeice.　Perdita.
Magdeburg, Mechthild von.　How the Soul Speaks to God.
McGuire, Jerry.　Not A Ton Notation.
Moss, T.　Lessons from a Mirror.
Muso Soseki.　Pure Sound Pavilion of the Riverside Temple, The.
Naito Joso.　How green— / Flowering slopes.
Ovid.　So, when she saw Narcissus wandering through the lonely countryside, Echo fell in love with him, and followed secretly in his steps.
Pack, R.　Thrasher in the Willow by the Lake, The.
Palmer, M.　This Time.
Pei Di.　Lake Yi.
Rexroth, K.　Signature of All Things, The.
Rich, A.　One Life.
Richez, Valérie-Catherine.　Little Soul.
Rodriguez, L.　Reflection on El Train Glass.
Rosenberg, I.　Mirror, The.
Rowe, E.　Reflection, The.
Rumi.　If you're not going to sleep.
Rupchev, Georgi.　Reversal of Worlds.
Saimaro.　Mirrored by stream / Swallow darts—.
Salinas, P.　Set Her Far from Me, Mirror.
Sŏ Chŏngju.　Grandmother's Verandah.
Spivack, K.　Scroll, The.
Stoddart, G.　Night We Stole a Full-Lenght Mirror, The.
Tennyson, A.　As when with downcast eyes we muse and brood.
Thomas, R. S.　Via Negativa.
Tu Mu.　Basin Pond.
Villa, D.　Blades and slime, the limits, The.
Wang Wei.　Lake Yi.
Wright, K.　Other Side of the Mountain, The.
Wunderlich, M.　Continent's Edge.
Xuanjue.　Heart's Mirror Clear.
Yi Kyubo.　Moon in the Well, The.
Yu Chien-wu.　On the Third Day I Wait on the Emperor at a Banquet and Describe the Reflection of the Candles in the Serpentine.
Yujŏng.　Sitting at Night at an Old Inn in Silla.
Yun Tongju.　Self-portrait.

Refrigerators
Sinclair, S.　Refrigerator, The.

Refugees
Auden.　Refugee Blues.
Barrax.　Pittsburgh, 1948, The Music Teacher.
Breytenbach.　Exile, Representative.
Browning, R.　Italian in England, The.
Char.　On the Bell Frieze of a Roman Church.
Davidson, D.　Refugees.
Dhompa, T.　Autonomy of the Mind.
Sun Storm.
Dickinson, E.　These Strangers, In a Foreign World.
Ferebee, Gideon.　Refugee.
Fogarty, L.　Remember Something Like This.
Grade.　Refugees.
Hajjaj, N.　Honey Fig.
Harper, M.　Camp Story.
Jarrell, R.　Refugees, The.
Kirstein.　DP's.
Komunyakaa, Y.　Boat People.

Lazarus, E.　New Colossus, The.
Press, K.　Hope for refugees.
Rollings.　For Dear Life.
Salganicoff.　Girl Refugee, The.
Schiff, H.　When It Happened.
Seferis.　Last Stop.
Shapcott, T.　Shadow of War, 1941.
Spender, S.　History and Reality.
Sylvain, P.　Refugees.
Tu Fu [*or* Du Fu].　P'eng-ya Road.
P'eng-Ya Song.
Song of Pengya.
Yosef, H.　Jaffa, July 1948.
Yusuf, S.　Mouse, The.

Regeneration
Althaus, Keith.　Little Elegy.
Berry, W.　Slip, The.
Sycamore, The.
Clifton, L.　To my Friend, Jerina.
Hopkins, G.　God's Grandeur.
Montale.　Eel, The.
Pound, E.　Return, The.
Shapiro, K.　Leg, The.
Vaughan, H.　Regeneration.
Vroman.　Regeneration.
Whitman, W.　Child said *What is the grass?* fetching it to me with full hands, A.
See also **Rebirth; Renewal**

Reggae
Adisa.　Count Ossie.
Allen, L.　Riddim an' Hardtimes.
Rub a Dub Style inna Regent Park.
Bethel, M.　Reggae Prophecy.
Breeze.　Dubbed Out.
Eena Mi Corner.
D'Aguiar, F.　Now the Two Are One.
Dawes, K.　Black Heart.
Some Tentative Definitions 1.
Some Tentative Definitions 11.
Trickster 1 (for Winston Rodney).
Trickster 2 (for Lee "Scratch" Perry).
Trickster 4 (for Sister Patra).
Goodison.　Jah Music.
Upon a Quarter Million.
Hippolyte.　Antonette's Boogie.
Ingram-Roberts, A.　Poem 2 (for Duckie Simpson of Black Uhuru).
Johnson, L.　Reggae Sounds.
King, J.　Intercity Dub.
Malachi.　Psalm of Silk.
"Mbala.".　History of Dub Poetry, The.
Morris, M.　Rasta Reggae.
Philp, G.　Dance Hall.
Dance Hall: Version.
Heirlooms.
One Song.
Preston, R.　Music.
Richardson, L.　Poet Sings His Painting, The.
Sing, D.　Baap-Nemesthe Reggae Song.
Steede, V.　Reggae.
Wojahn.　Rajah in Babylon.
Young, C.　Night-Mullins River.

Regret
Adamson, H.　It's Been So Long.
Ade.　R-E-M-O-R-S-E.
Akhmatova, A.　I wrung my hands under my dark veil.
Basho.　From deep within.
Bécquer, G.　Into Her Eyes a Tear Crept.
They Closed Her Eyes.
Berryman.　Snow Line.
Bibbins, M.　Bluebeard.
Bone, K.　What Might Have Been.
Brooks, G.　Mother, The.
Brooks, S.　Some of These Days.
Brown Rosellen.　Fry says a word.
Burke, J.　Here's That Rainy Day.
Burns, R.　To a Mouse; On Turning Her up in Her Nest, with the Plough, November, 1785.
Butler, C. E.　Letter to the Survivors.
Bykova, Z.　Close of day.
Cambridge, A.　Virgin Martyr, The.
Ch'i-chi.　Thinking of a Monk of Flower Summit on Mount T'ien-t'ai.
Chiasson, D.　Poem Beginning with a Line from Frost.

Chŏng Chiyong.　Star.
Coleridge, M.　Mistaken.
Comden, B.　If You Hadn't—But You Did.
Congreve, W.　False Though She Be.
Coviello, M.　Self-Portrait.
Creamer, H.　After You've Gone.
Cunningham, J.　Moral Poem, A.
Dennis, C.　Tune-Up.
Dooley, M.　What Every Woman Should Carry.
Doolittle, H.　So you have swept me back.
Dransfield.　Portrait of the Artist as an Old Man.
Drayton.　Satyr O never ask how I came to this place.
Dunbar, P.　Debt, The.
Dunmore.　Three Ways of Recovering a Body.
Dunn, D.　Envoi: "Why did I bring you to this Hull."
Ehrhart.　Beautiful Wreckage.
Eliot, T. S.　Love Song of J. Alfred Prufrock, The.
Elizabeth I.　When I Was Fair and Young.
Enzensberger, H.　Short History of the Bourgeoisie.
Fenton, J.　Mistake, The.
Skip, The.
Ficowski.　I Did Not Manage To Save.
Field.　Ebbtide at Sundown.
Foley, M.　On the Waterfront.
Fried, D.　She Didn't Mean to Do It.
Story Having to Do with Walt Whitman, A.
García Lorca.　Sonnet of Sweet Weeping.
Gilbert, J.　It Is Clear Why the Angels Come No More.
Green, A.　If You Hadn't—But You Did.
Gregory, A.　What Have I Gained?
Grimké, A.　Eyes of My Regret, The.
Hacker, M.　Boy, The.
Harte, B.　Mrs. Judge Jenkins[; Being the Only Genuine Sequel to "Maud Muller"].
Hayden, R.　Ballad of Sue Ellen Westerfield, The.
Herman, J.　If He Walked into My Life.
Hewitt, J.　Search, The.
Hicok.　Man of the House.
Holan.　She Asked You.
Hollo.　Godlike.
Hope, L.　I Shall Forget.
Housman.　When the bells justle in the tower.
Hughes, L.　Po' Boy Blues.
Hull, L.　Midnight Reports.
Jackson, H.　Opportunity.
Johnstone, R.　Fruit of Knowledge, The.
Various instants I'm not with you.
Keller, D.　Man Who Knew the Words to "Louie, Louie", The.
Khlebnikov, V.　To Everyone.
Kim Yŏngnang.　At the Sight of Water.
Selections from "Quatrains".
Koch, K.　To Marina.
Koethe.　North Point North.
Kool, M.　Different.
Kunitz, S.　Quarrel, The.
Kuzmina-Karavayeva.　Long-Barrow Princess 2.
Landon.　Gifts Misused.
Lassell.　Brady Street, San Francisco.
Li Po.　Springtime South of the Yangtze.
Li Shang-yin.　Ch'ang-O.
Li Yü.　Tune: "Joy of Encounter".
Tune: "Memories of the South".
Tune: "New Bounty of Royalty".
Tune: "Pure Serene Music".
Tune: "Sand Washed by Waves".
Tune: "Sand Washed by Waves".
Past, The.
Lieberman, M.　Regret.
Liu Yung.　Song: "After the eating, the drinking, the singing."
Song to the Tune "Ting Feng Po".
Longley, M.　Water-burn.
Luschei, G.　Highway.
Malanova, M.　Among the men some carved-bone dice are thrown.
Merrill, J.　Renewal, A.
Merwin.　Home for Thanksgiving.
Mills, I.　Sophisticated Lady.
Moronelli da Fiorenza.　Canzonetta: A Bitter

Song to His Lady.
Nelson, M.　Minor Miracle.
Nims, J.　Young Ionia, The.
Otogami.　In the blackberry.
Owen, W.　A Terre.
Strange Meeting.
Padilla.　Legacies.
Parish.　Sophisticated Lady.
Patmore, C.　Toys, The.
Patterson, G.　Lament.
Phillips, C.　Pleasure.
Pittman, Al.　Echo of the Ax, The.
Poe.　Bridal Ballad.
Pollard, C.　Breakfast Poem.
Pollitt.　Mind-Body Problem.
Porter, C.　Miss Otis Regrets.
Where Is the Life That Late I Led?
Ransom, J.　Parting, without a Sequel.
Rees, Elizabeth.　Rockstar Poet.
Rees-Jones.　And Please Do Not Presume.
Reid, A.　Manse, The.
Roberts, K.　How Late Desire Looks.
Robinson, E.　Miniver Cheevy.
Rodríguez, C.　Petty Time.
Rodriguez, L.　Victory, Victoria, My Beautiful Whisper.
Rossetti, D.　97: A Superscription.
Scott, W.　Continuity of Life.
Seibles, T.　Friend and Beloved.
Shaughnessy, B.　Me in Paradise.
Sidney.　Sonnet 33: "I might, unhappy word, O me, I might."
Solie, Karen.　More Fun In The New World.
Spires.　Apology.
Steptoe.　To the Father of Me.
Supervielle.　Regretting the Earth.
Tennyson, A.　We leave the well-beloved place.
Thoreau.　Sympathy.
Timrod.　Cotton Boll, The.
Tsaloumas.　Old Snapshot.
Tu Fu [or Du Fu].　Climbing on the Double Ninth Day.
Song of T'ung-ku.
Tu Mu.　Too Late.
Unknown.　Now goth sonne under wode,—.
Vaughan, H.　Retreat[e], The.
Vietnamese Oral Tradition.　Coins of Van-Lich.
Wang Ch'ang-ling.　Complaint from a Lady's Chamber.
Ward, T.　On Being Kicked Out of the Harold Washington Library Center for Napping on the Floor.
Whittier.　Maud Muller.
Williams, H.　Prayer.
Wright, J.　Regret for a Spider Web.
Yeats.　Down by the Salley Gardens.
Men Improve with the Years.
Yen Shu.　Tune: "Spring in the Jade House".
Yesenin [or Essenin].　I Regret Nothing.
Yu Xuanji.　Vanishing Spring Moves to Regret.
Zimmer.　Another Place.

Reims, France
Hemans.　Joan of Arc, in Rheims.

Reincarnation
Ausländer, R.　My Nightingale.
Belli, C.　Father, Mother.
Bishop, M.　We Have Been Here Before.
Brown, S.　Interview with an Alchemist in the New Age.
Gilbert, S.　November 26, 1992: Thanksgiving at the Sea Ranch, Contemplating Metempsychosis.
Hardy, T.　Transformations.
Hass, R.　To Phil Dow, in Oregon.
Hristov, Boris.　Dandelion Bone.
Kerouac.　Poem: "I could become a great grinning host."
Poem: "I demand that the human race."
Kim Kwangsŏp.　Having Died.
Kim Sowŏl.　Cuckoo, The.
Levine, P.　Fox, The.
Mahon.　Lives.
Marquis.　Expression is the need of my soul.
Meynell, A.　Song of Derivations, A.
Mirabai [or Mira Bai].　It's True I Went to the Market.

Odarchenko.　Path I'm following, The.
Pessoa.　When in the widening circle of rebirth.
Pinsky.　At Pleasure Bay.
Rossetti, D.　Sudden Light.
Rumi.　Tell Me, What Have I Lost?
Sanfield.　Concern.
Scupham.　Nondescript, The.
Smith, J.　Honeybee upon the Tundra.
Tate, J.　Promotion, The.
Vietnamese Oral Tradition.　Tao.
Watson, R.　Nirvana.

Reindeer
Moore, C.　Visit from St Nicholas, A.

Rejection
Ahmed Pasha.　Ask about my wailing from the prayers.
Alegría.　Letter to an Exile.
Angus.　Doors of Sleep, The.
Mary's Song.
Anthony, M.　So suddenly.
Ugly Heart, The.
Anyidoho.　Murmuring.
Aytoun [or Ayton], R.　Answer, The.
Rejection, The.
Upon His Unconstant Mistress.
Barrington, P.　Take Me in Your Arms, Miss Moneypenny-Wilson.
Beckett, S.　Cascando.
Bécquer, G.　Sighs Are Air, and Go to the Air.
Bickerstaffe.　Expostulation, An.
Blind.　Many Will Love You.
Borowski.　Farewell to Maria.
Buson.　Through snow / Lights of homes.
Calbert.　Like.
Campion, T.　Shall I Come, Sweet Love.
Carew, T.　Spring, The: "Now that the Winter's gone, the earth hath lost."
To My Inconstant Mistress [or Mistris].
Catullus.　To Juventius.
Cavalli.　To simulate the burning of the heart.
Ceccoli.　Sir, I have remained so overcome, that I can no longer suffer your attacks.
Coslow, S.　True Blue Lou.
Darley.　To Helene.
Dixon, S.　Request of Alexis, The.
Donne.　Damp[e], The.
Love's Deity [or Deitie].
Dryden, J.　Disdain Punished.
"Eliot.".　How Lisa Loved the King.
"Ephelia.".　To J.G. on the News of His Marriage.
To My Rival.
Fell, A.　And Again.
Field.　Sweeter Far than the Harp, More Gold than Gold.
Gershwin, I.　I Can't Get Started.
Gladstone, W. E.　To a Rejected Sonnet.
Glück, L.　Hesitate to Call.
Hai-Jew, S.　Kinged.
Heine, H.　Young Man Loves a Maiden, A.
Hemans.　Properzia Rossi.
Herbert, G.　Denial[l].
Hope, A.　Meditation on a Bone.
Housman.　He would not stay for me; and who can wonder?
Howe, J.　Outside the Party.
Huddle.　Vermont.
James, C.　Book of My Enemy Has Been Remaindered, The.
Jonson, B.　Song. To Celia ("Drink to me only with thine eyes.").
Joyce, J.　Post Ulixem Scriptum.
Juana Inés de la Cruz.　World! why do you hound me?
Kizer, C.　Bitch.
Klappert.　Court of Divine Justice, The.
Lamb, C.　Timid grace sits trembling in her eye, A.
Landon.　Girl at Her Devotions, A.
Landor, W.　Maid's Lament, The.
Lisnyanskaya [or Lisnianskaia].　To be thought an outcast in my beloved country.
Livingston, M.　Angry Valentine, An.
Lovelace, R.　To Lucasta.
Lowell, A.　Carrefour.
'Marnia.　I Want to Love You Very Much.

Meinke. Love Poem 1990.
Merrill, S. Ballade of the Outcasts.
Meynell, A. Renouncement.
Millay, E. Love me no more, now let the god depart.
Nejati. Those tulip-cheeked ones—what they dared do in the garden!
O'Hara, F. Meditations in an Emergency.
Okudzhava. Ah, Nadya, Nadyenka.
Ono no Komachi. Diver does not abandon, A.
Pan Chieh-yû. Song of Regret.
Perillo, L. Sweaters, The.
Pollard, C. Breakfast Poem.
Popova, O. Among black trees.
Pound, E. To Kalon.
Powell, K. Love/a Many Splintered Thing.
Ralegh, S. Nymph's [or Nimphs] Reply to the [Passionate] Shepherd [or Sheepheard], The.
Richardson, M. Sonnet: "I still shall smile and go my careless way."
Robin, L. True Blue Lou.
Robinson, M. Contemns Philosophy.
Describes the Fascinations of Love.
Laments her Early Misfortunes.
Sappho's Address to the Stars.
Suspects his Constancy.
To Phaon ("Can'st thou forget, O! Idol of my soul!").
To Phaon ("Oh! I could toil for thee o'er burning plains.").
To Phaon ("Why art thou changed? O Phaon! tell me why?").
Rochester, E. Song: "Nothing ades to Loves fond fire."
Rossetti, C. No, Thank You, John.
Rowe, E. Reply to Mr.———, The.
Rumsey, Tessa. Man-Torpedo-Boat.
Sadi [or Saadi or Sa'di]. If you should say to me Don't mention love.
San Juan. End of the Affair, The.
Sappho. Kypris, / May she find you very bitter.
Scott, A. Return thee, heart.
Seward. Farewell, false Friend!—our scenes of kindness close!
Shelley, P. To—: "One word is too often profaned."
Sidney, P. Eighth Song: "In a grove most rich of shade."
Ninth Song: "Go, my flock, go get you hence."
Sonnet 31: "With how sad steps, O Moon[e], thou climb'st the skies."
Smith, S. Lady "Rogue" Singleton.
Pad, Pad.
Starkey, D. Scrabble.
Stirling, S. Echo, An.
Strickland, A. Maniac, The.
Swinburne. Leave-taking, A.
Tennyson, A. Locksley Hall.
Theocritus. Idyll 20: Neteheard [or Neatherd].
Thomas, D. Not from This Anger.
Tsvetayeva [or Tsvetaeva]. I didn't want this, not.
Unknown. Cold Fountain, Cold Fountain.
Mulberry up the Lane.
Singing Maid, The.
Soft wind of the vale.
Three Things Come Without Seeking.
Virgil [or Vergil]. Eclogue 2: The Lament of Corydon for His Faithless Alexis.
Whitman, W. Sometimes with One I Love.
Wroth. Sonnet 14: "Except my hart which you beestow'd before."
Wyatt. Farewell, love, and all thy law[e]s forever [or for ever].
Zucker, R. Not Knowing Nijinsky or Diaghilev.

Relatives
Brathwaite, E. Ancestors.
Cempulappeyanirar. What He Said.
Ehrenburg [or Erenburg]. Our Grandsons Will Be Astonished.
Kumin, M. For My Great-Grandfather: A Message Long Overdue.
Ormond. My Dusty Kinsfolk.
Robinson, E. Poor Relation, The.

Relativity
Auden. Law like Love.

Cummings, E. E. Space being(don't forget to remember)Curved.
Howell, C. Bride of Long Division, The.
MacNeice. What is Truth? Says Pilate.
Szymborska, W. View with a Grain of Sand.

Relief
Crapsey. Release.
Divakaruni. Alley of Flowers, The.
Foster, S. Conant. To Flight.
Hoffenstein. I'm Fond of Doctors.
Kouchag, N. I Was Suffering Exile.
Kunitz, S. Long Boat, The.
Sewell, L. Release.
Shinkichi Takahashi. Spinning Dharma Wheel.
Tu Fu [or Du Fu]. Hearing of Imperial Forces Retaking Ho-Nan and Ho-Pei.
In Praise of Rain.
Vilariño. If I Died Tonight.

Religion
Abad, G. Holy Order.
'Abd al-Hayy. Ode of Signs.
Abse. Stethoscope, The.
Alexie. Theology.
Amichai, Y. Course of a Life, The.
Andrade, M. Sunday.
Andrade, O. Hierofant.
Apollinaire. Zone.
Zone.
Appleman, P. O Karma, Dharma, pudding and pie.
Atkins, R. Lisbon.
Awoonor. Weaver Bird, The.
Balingit, J. Quiet Evening, Home Away.
Barnstone, A. First Amendment.
Baudelaire. Fuses I and II.
Benét, R. et al. Cotton Mather.
Benét, S. Cotton Mather.
Bentley, E. "No, sir," said General Sherman.
Berg, S. Prayer: "Nobody understands so let the Rabbi."
Berry, W. Meditation in the Spring Rain.
Bible, O.T. Stanzas Imitated From Psalm 119.
Bidgood. Banquet.
Blackwell, Holley. Another.
Blake, W. All Religions Are One.
Garden of Love, The.
Lacedemonian Instruction.
Mock On, Mock On, Voltaire, Rousseau.
There Is No Natural Religion.
Blaser. Even on Sunday.
Borges. From an Apocryphal Gospel.
Braithwaite. Rye Bread.
Buchanan, G. Pope from penance purgatorial, The.
Burns, R. Holy Fair, The.
Butler, S. For his religion it was fit.
Byron, G. Spirit Pass'd Before Me, A.
Caballero-Robb, M. Dear Rosario.
Cacciatore, E. Second Warning Sign: the Game Heats Up.
Caldwell, R. Bible Buckle, The.
Carbó, N. Votive Candles.
Carson, A. My Religion.
Castro, R. Glowworm Scatters Flashes, A.
Chasin. Strength.
Ch'eng-kung Sui. Rhapsody on Whistling.
Chesterton. Antichrist, or the Reunion of Christendom; an Ode.
Chia Yi. Owl, The.
Coleman, James. Black Women with Jewish Names.
Coles, R. Christmas, Belfast.
Cook, C. Will Run Like Rabbits for Food.
Cooley, N. John Winthrop, "Reasons to be Considered for...the Intended Plantation in New England," 1629.
Creeley. After Lorca.
Dana, R. Radiance.
Darío, R. Nicaraguan Triptych.
de Folgar. Irreverent Epistle to Jesus Christ.
Dharker. Name of god, The.
Namesake.
Postcards from God (1).
Di Prima. I Fail as a Dharma Teacher.
Dickinson, E. I'm ceded—I've stopped being Theirs.

Some keep the Sabbath going to Church.
There's a certain Slant of light.
'Tis little I— could care for Pearls.
Disch. Ballade of the New God.
Donne. Canonization, The.
Satire 3 [Religion].
To the Countess of Bedford ("Madam, / Reason is our soul's left hand, Faith her right.").
Doolittle, H. Evil was active in the land.
Now my right hand.
Splintered the crystal of identity.
Dryden, J. Dim, as the borrow'd beams of moon and stars.
Duhig, I. Fundamentals.
Dunbar, P. Spiritual, A.
Dunn, S. Religion.
Eliot, T. S. Hippopotamus, The.
Song for Simeon, A.
Emerson, R. Problem, The.
Emre. Love is minister to us, our flock is the inmost soul.
Erdrich. Fooling God.
Ewer. Only Way, The.
Fallon, P. Herd, The.
Fischer, N. Violence of Oneness, The.
Foster, A. God and the Holy Stones.
Gelbtrunk, A. All Illusion Is a Form of Hope.
Glaser, M. Magnificat!
Grey, C. Hallelujah!
Hahn, K. Glass Bracelets, The.
Han-shan. His mind is as high as a mountain.
Han Yü. Girl of Mount Hua, The.
Hardy, T. Christmas: 1924.
Dream Question, A.
Respectable Burgher, The.
Harington [or Harrington]. Groome of the Chambers religion in King Henry the eights time, A.
Hayden, R. Those Winter Sundays.
Helle, A. Poem for Natalia Ginzburg.
Herbert, G. Religion stands on tip-toe in our land.
Hernández Cruz. Keeping Track of the Serpents.
Hershon. Woman Strangles, A.
Heyen. Stadium, The.
Hill, G. Vergine bella.
Hill, J. Preacher and the Slave, The.
Hirsch, E. Simone Weil: In Assisi.
Hope, A. Advice to Young Ladies.
Hopkins, G. Wreck of the Deutschland, The.
Housman. Laws of God, the Laws of Man, The.
Hudgins. Southern Crescent Was on time, The.
Hughes, L. Goodbye Christ.
Madam and the Minister.
Mystery.
Huxley, A. Burning Wheel, The.
Ingoldsby, T. Jackdaw of Rheims, The.
Iskander. Gegard.
Johnson, F. Minister, The.
Johnson, L. Church of a Dream, The.
Jones, D. In the middle silences of this night's course the blackthorn.
Kaufman, B. Oregon.
Khlebnikov, V. Hey...y! Uh...hm!, covered with sweat.
One Book, The.
Kinsella, J. Visitant Eclogue.
Kizer, C. Dixit Insipiens.
Klassen, S. Repenting.
Knott. Funny Poem.
Kumin, M. In the Park.
Living Alone with Jesus.
Larkin, P. Church Going.
High Windows.
Water.
Laux, D. Children's Train, The.
Levertov. Flickering Mind.
Lima, J. Stranger, Stranger.
Logan, W. Valentine for Matthew Arnold, A.
Louise, E. Jesus' Song.
Lyon, G. Foot-Washing, The.
MacDiarmid, H. Two Memories.
MacLean, S. Highland Woman, A.
MacSweeney. Far Cliff Babylon.
Malé. Creed.

Mapanje. From Florrie Abraham Witness, December 1972.
Marsman. Polderland.
Mathews, A. Caedmon.
McGinley. Day After Sunday, The.
  How to Start a War.
Melville, H. Fragments of a Lost Gnostic Poem of the Twelfth [or 12th] Century.
Mesmer, S. My Life in Yonago.
Mew. Ken.
Millay, E. Make Bright the Arrows.
Miller, J. Which Religion Vouchsafes.
Milton. On the Late Massacre [or Massacher] in Piedmont [or Piemont].
Montague, J. Woodtown Manor.
Moorer. Southern Pulpit, The.
Muldoon, P. Our Lady of Ardboe.
Mullen, H. Dance She Does, The.
Murray, J. There Has Been More Than Beginning and End to Face.
Murray, L. Poetry and Religion.
  Say-but-the-Word Centurion Attempts a Summary, The.
Nandĩ, R. I understand now, Tara, I understand.
Nash, O. Seven Spiritual Ages of Mrs. Marmaduke Moore, The.
Nemerov. Boom!
Nervo. Sorrow Vanquished.
Nye, N. Man Who Makes Brooms, The.
Otero, B. Far Away.
Parra, V. Because the Poor Have Nothing.
Pasolini. Redefining "Orthodoxy".
Pau-Llosa. Hollow, The.
Pinsky. Avenue.
Plato. Advice to Young Ladies.
Pollard, V. Heavens Cherubim High Horsed or The Meeting of the Two Sevens (May 1977).
Pollarolo, G. Foretold Futures.
Reading, P. This is unclean: to eat turbots on Tuesdays.
Reed, I. I Am a Cowboy in the Boat of Ra.
Robin, L. Hallelujah!
Robinson, A. Sibyl, The.
Rodgers, C. Mama's God.
Rukeyser, M. Gates, The.
St. John, P. Sunday.
Sanger, R. Lines in the Sand.
Sassoon, S. They.
Scott, F. Brébeuf and His Brethren.
Sen, R. This time I've realized the essence.
Senghor. Totem.
Sexton. With Mercy for the Greedy.
Shelley, P. Prometheus Unbound.
Sheperd. Who hath not knowne or herd.
Sidney, P. Leave Me O Love.
Silva, C. Who Will Throw the First Stone?
Skelton, J. Over this the foresayd lay.
Skyrm, P. Book 2: White Rose.
Sosnora. Supreme Hour, The.
Spender, S. Landscape near an Aerodrome, The.
Stead, W. T. Now that war is in the air, e'en the parson in his lair.
Stevens, W. Gray Stones and Gray Pigeons.
  High-Toned Old Christian Woman, A.
  Sunday Morning.
Stevenson, R. Epitaph: "Angler rose, he took his rod, The."
Stone, S. Church's One Foundation, The.
Swinburne. Higher Pantheism in a Nutshell, The.
Tabb. Sisters, The.
Taylor, E. View, all ye eyes above, this sight which flings.
Thomas, R. S. Calling, The.
  Llanrhaeadr Ym Mochnant.
Thompson, F. Hound of Heaven, The.
Thribb. In Memoriam Krishna Menon.
Tornero, A. Cempasúchil, copal—en la parte alta de librero bajo—libamen, oblación.
  Cempasúchil, copal—on the top part of the low bookcase—libation, offering.
Touré, A. JuJu.
Traherne. Apostacy, The.
Travis, N. Church Ladies.
Unknown. Among the yeomen's sons on my

estate.
  Farewell, this world! I take my leve for ever.
  Have oon god in worshipe.
  I'm Going Home.
  Inscription at Mount Vernon.
  Now thise foweles syngen and maken her blisse.
  Old [or Ould] Orange Flute, The.
  Old-Time Religion.
  Seven Songs and Song Pictures.
  This Is the Trouble of the World.
  Upon Arch-bishop Laud, Prisoner in the Tower. 1641.
  Vicar of Bray, The.
  Wizard's Chant, The.
Valente, J. Elegy That Was Never Finished, An.
Various authors. Because his bright nature.
Vaughan, H. Nativity, The.
  Religion.
Villa, E. It is world of the back hune wone it is.
Voigt. Woman Who Weeps.
Waldrep, G. C. Hotel d'Avignon.
Waller, E. Upon His Majesty's [or Majesties] Repairing of Paul's.
Weaver, A. Water Song.
Whitehead, C. Marian Hymn.
Whittier. Worship.
Wilbur, R. Matthew 8, 28 ff.
Wild, R. In a melancholly studdy.
Witt, S. Ikonostasis. The Sound of the Sea Filling a Faraway Room.
Wolfe, H. Gray Squirrel, The.
Wright, J. Sketch for an Aesthetic Project.
  Wednesday Night Prayer Meeting.
See also **Faith**

Religious Life
Arnold, M. Dover Beach.
Betjeman. Huxley Hall.
  Undenominational.
Bunyan. Pilgrim Song, The.
Campbell, R. Mass at Dawn.
Cofer, J. Saint Rose of Lima.
Crane, H. Emblems of Conduct.
Dickinson, E. Ourselves we do inter with sweet derision.
Elizabeth, Queen of Bohemia. Verses by the Princess Elizabeth, Given to Lord Harington, of Exton, Her Preceptor.
Erdrich. Sacraments, The.
Fenton, J. Kingfisher's Boxing Gloves, The.
Gascoigne. From depth of dole wherein my soul doth dwell.
Gerstler. Unforeseen, The.
Gruffydd, W. Gwladys Rhys.
Habington. Cupio Dissolvi.
Hall, J. Song of Esechia, The.
Harvey, C. Church Festivals.
Herbert, G. Affliction (1).
  Holy [or H.] Communion, The ("Not in rich furniture, or fine array.").
  Invitation, The.
Herrick. Thanksgiving to God for His House, A.
Hopkins, G. I Wake and Feel the Fell of Dark, Not Day.
  Let me be to Thee as the circling bird.
  To Seem the Stranger.
Jewell, Terri L. Sistah Flo.
Jonson, B. To Heaven.
Kasdorf. First TV in a Mennonite Family.
  Mennonites.
Mathews, A. Caedmon.
Melville, H. Pillow, The.
Nemerov. Boom!
Owen, M. African Sunday.
Quarles. Galatians 6.14.
  Matthew 9.12.
Southwell. Content and Ri[t]ch[e].
Taylor, E. Dull. Dull indeed! What shall it e'er be thus?
Huswifery.
  Meditation. Heb. 13.10. We[e] have an Altar.
Toplady. Rock of Ages.
Unknown. Almost Over.
Vaughan, H. Disorder and Frailty.
  Jacob's Pillow, and Pillar.
  Stone, The.

Very. Created, The.
Whittier. Ezekiel.
Winchilsea. Some Reflections.
Wright, D. New Mennonite Replies to Julia Kasdorf, A.
See also **Clergy; Convents; Monasteries; Monks; Nuns; Rabbis**

Religious Wars
Brodsky, J. Part of the field, A. Trumpets sound and two men enter.
Jonson, B. Epistle to a Friend, to Persuade Him to the Wars, An.
Paulin. Desertmartin.
Yūsuf III. My friend go gently, for Time is as you know it to be, since there is no avoiding an easy life in spite of the present trace of hardship.

Rembrandt, Harmenszoon van Rijn
Allston. On Rembrant; Occasioned by His Picture of Jacob's Dream.
Corso. Rembrandt—Self Portrait.
Pastan. Ethics.
Walcott. Polish Rider, The.
Young, G. Miracle, The.

Remorse
Benét, W. Brazen Tongue.
Brontë, E. Come, walk with me.
Burns, R. Prayer, in the Prospect of Death, A.
Cernuda. Remorse Dressed Up as Night.
Dickinson, E. Remorse—is Memory—awake.
Donne. Hymn[e] to God the Father, A.
Garrett, E. History Goes to Work.
Grimké, A. Beso, El.
Hood, T. Dream of Eugene Aram [the Murderer], The.
Johnstone, R. Fruit of Knowledge, The.
Kinzie. Sun and Moon.
Lawrence, D. H. Piano.
Macdonald, G. Prayer, A: "When I look back upon my life nigh spent."
O'Donnell, C. Resolution.
Tichborne [or Tichbourne]. Tichborne's Elegy.
Waugh, E. They told me, Francis Hinsley, they told me you were hung.

Renaissance
Browning, R. Fra Lippo Lippi.
Cole, H. Folly.
Collins, B. Death of Allegory, The.
Follain. Red Apple, The.
Hill, G. Humanist, The.
  Pre-Raphaelite Notebook, A.

Renewal
Abad, G. Jeepney.
Adler, L. Plaisir.
Anderson, J. Re-member Us.
"Antler.". Ungag our souls!! Unstrangle our souls!! Unsmother our souls!!
Arapaho Oral Tradition. Songs of the Arapaho.
Arnold, M. To the Hungarian Nation.
Berry, W. Anniversary, An.
Blanco, R. How It Begins / How It Ends.
Bulich, V. From My Diary, 3.
Ch'u Ch'uang I. Evening in the Garden, Clear after Rain.
Cohen, L. You Have the Lovers.
Cornford, A. And it came to pass just as they had foretold.
Creeley. House, The ("Mas-Soñer / Restaurat— Any.").
Cummings, E. E. Spring is like a perhaps hand.
Dafydd [or David] ap Gwilym. Duw gwyddiad mai da y gweddai.
Dove, R. Turning Thirty, I Contemplate Students Bicycling Home.
Dupin. Begin Like Tearing.
Edwards, D. Birthday: "I have fallen to the ground."
Hill, G. Veni Coronaberis.
Hirsch, E. And So It Begins Again.
Holley, M. Tree of Life, The.
Hopes. And Job from his mountain sees.
Jeffers, R. Shiva.
Jiménez, J. Love.
Kenyon, J. Pardon.
Kunitz, S. Round, The.

Machado Ruiz.　On the Bare Roadway.
Merrill, J.　Renewal, A.
Merwin.　Before a Departure in Spring.
Mistral, G.　Empty Walnut, The.
Mugo, M. G.　Look How Rich We are Together.
Muso Soseki.　Old Hut.
Olson, C.　Chain of memory is resurrection I am
　a vain man, The.
Painter, F. V. N.　Pastoral, A: "Sun looks o'er
　the mountain fair, The."
Pao Chao.　Do you not see the riverside grass.
Paz.　Crystal willow, a poplar of water, A.
　Face I can see to see my face, A.
　Solo for Two Voices.
Prados, E.　Song of Taking Leave.
Rafferty, P.　Back End.
Rossetti, C.　First Spring Day, The.
Shakespeare, W.　Sonnet 56: "Sweet love, renew
　thy force; be it not said."
　Sonnet 108: "What's in the brain[e] that in[c]k
　may character."
Shakhova.　Autobiographical Response from a
　Provincial Wasteland (in Reply to a New
　Year's Greeting Sent with a Bouquet).
Sioux Oral Tradition.　Songs of the Sioux.
Smith, S.　New Age, The.
Southwell.　Times [*or* Tymes] Go[e] By
　Turn[e]s.
Storni.　You Want Me White ("You want me
　pure.").
Szymborska, W.　End and Beginning.
　End and the Beginning, The.
　Reality Demands.
Thoreau.　Music.
Unknown.　In Praise of May.
　Songs of the Kiowa.
　Songs of the Paiute.
Verwey, A.　Beautiful World, The.
Vietnamese Oral Tradition.　Ke-Mo Village Girl.
Whalen, P.　Saturday.
Whitehead, C.　Daybreak.
Williams, W.　Paterson: The Falls.
Wordsworth, W.　I watch, and long have
　watched, with calm regret.
See also **Rebirth; Regeneration**

Renoir, Pierre Auguste
Bowering, G.　Swing, The.
Moulds, J.　Renoir's Bathers.
Ormond.　Certain Questions for Monsieur
　Renoir.
Warren, R.　Renoir.

Repentance
Allen, R.　See! How the Nations Rage Together.
Berkeley, S.　Mass is Over, The.
Birnbaum, M.　Visiting Jesus.
Campion, T.　Awake, Awake! [Thou Heavy
　Sprite].
Davis, O.　Six Apologies, Lord.
Dickinson, E.　Renunciation—is a piercing
　Virtue.
Donne.　At the round earth's imagined [*or*
　imagin'd] corners, blow.
Goodwin, Eli.　Confession: "I held your sins
　against you for so long."
Herbert, G.　Discipline.
　Mary [*or* Marie] Magdalene.
　Sin's Round.
Hopes.　Mercy on me Spirit.
Jonson, B.　Hymn[e] to God the Father, A.
Kyunyŏ, Great Master.　I have committed errors.
Milton.　On His Blindness.
Osherow.　Yom Kippur Sonnet, with a Line from
　Lamentations.
Oxenham.　So Little and So Much.
Rossetti, C.　Convent Threshold, The.
Russell, G.　Reconciliation.
Ryman.　Have mynde how I mankynde have
　take.
Toplady.　Rock of Ages.
Unknown.　Every Hour in the Day.

Repression
Bekri, Tahar.　Return to Tunisia.
Bishop, E.　Sonnet: "Caught—the bubble."
Chŏng Hyŏnjong.　Like Leaving an Umbrella
　Somewhere.
Cullen, C.　Timid Lover.

Frost, R.　Home Burial.
Ginsberg, A.　Kral Majales.
Hughes, L.　Dream Boogie.
Kim Suyŏng.　Emerging from the Old Palace
　One Day.
Kleiser.　Most Vital Thing in Life, The.
Lim-Wilson.　Ringmaster's Wife.
Milton.　On His Blindness.
Osgood, F.　Ah! Woman Still.
Racin, K.　Tobacco Pickers.
Shapiro, K.　Buick.
Sheppard, R.　Empty Diary 1954.
Symonds.　What Cannot Be.
Unknown.　Issei's history.
　Women as women, me had never charmed.
Wilde, O.　Wasted Days.
Williams, C. K.　Repression.

Reproach
Carroll, L.　Duchess's Lullaby, The.
Chaucer.　Chaucer's Wordes unto Adam, his
　Owne Scriveyn.
Fuzuli.　Pointed reproach of the enemy, The.
Li Po.　Jewel Stairs' Grievance, The.
MacLeish.　You Also, Gaius Valerius Catullus.
Parker, A.　Days like Prose.
Valerie, J.　On Apologies.

Reptiles
Couzyn.　Spell to Protect Our Love.
Dorantes, D.　Iguana láctea.
　Lacteal iguana.
Kendall, M.　Ballad of the Ichthyosaurus.
Nystrom.　Insomnia.
Santos Chocano.　Dream of the Caiman, The.
Young, K.　Clyde Peeling's Reptiland in
　Allenwood, Pennsylvania.

Reputation
Catullus.　To Aurelius and Furius.
Clarke, A.　Young Woman of Beare, The.
Graves, R.　1805.
Harburg.　We're Off to See the Wizard (The
　Wonderful Wizard of Oz).
Hughes, L.　Ballad of the Girl Whose Name Is
　Mud.
Jonson, B.　To the Memory of My Beloved, the
　Author Mr [*or* Master] William Shakespeare:
　And What He Hath Left Us.
Lady Ise.　Because we suspected / the pillow
　would say "I know".
Massimi.　Advice to Paulinus.
Otomo no Sakanoé, L.　Though in my heart.
Pacheco, J.　Enquiry Concerning the Bat, An.
Pound, E.　Further Instructions.
Robinson, E.　Flammonde.
Shakespeare, W.　Sonnet 111: "O, for my sake
　do you with Fortune chide."
Unknown.　God, please rescue just that one!

Rescues
Anstett.　Man Saves Own Life.
Berlin.　I Got Lost in His Arms.
Chinese Oral Tradition.　Transformation Text on
　Mahāmaudgalyāyana Rescuing His Mother
　from the Underworld.
Fanthorpe.　Not My Best Side.
Ficowski.　I Did Not Manage To Save.
Grotz, J.　Wolf, The.
Hemans.　American Forest Girl, The.
Hudgins.　In the Well.
Lepson, Ruth.　They Were Gliding.
Levertov.　Re-Rooting.
Lim, G.　Animal Liberation.
Mary Stuart.　My lord and my God, I have
　hoped in Thee.
Oles.　For the Drunk.
Phillips, C.　Erasure.
Ransom, J.　Lady Lost.
Schiff, Robyn.　Woodpecker Finch.
Stone, J.　He Makes a House Call.
Sutskever [*or* Sutzkever].　1980.
Tagore.　Break Open the Door.
Tate, J.　Rescue.
Unknown.　God, please rescue just that one!
Vietnamese Oral Tradition.　Testing the
　Confucian Ideal.

Reservations, Native American
Alexie.　Tourists.

Algarin.　Taos Pueblo Indians: 700 strong
　according to Bobby's last census.
Klein, A.　Indian Reservation: Caughnawaga.
Lopez, B.　Desert Reservation.
McKinnon, K.　Crossing: "Have we always been
　close to."
Smith, P.　Some Reservation Valentines.
Smoker, M.　Letter to David James Duncan,
　February 16, 2003.
Warrior.　Reginald Pugh, The Man Who Came
　from the Army.

Reservoirs
Mathias, R.　Flooded Valley, The.

Resistance
Adler, R.　Whatever Lola Wants (Lola Gets).
Aridjis.　Decomposition with Laughter.
Azuah, U.　Forbidden.
Campion, T.　Sweet, exclude me[e] not, nor be
　divided.
Darío, R.　To Roosevelt.
Desnos.　Night Watchman of Pont-au-Change,
　The.
DeSylva, B. G.　Do It Again.
Fuertes.　Climbing.
Herbert, Z.　Pebble, The.
Ivanov, G.　Oh, how fastidious you once were.
Koestenbaum, W.　Gaudy Slave Trader.
La Fontaine.　Pig, Goat, Sheep.
Mandiela, A.　Speshal Rikwes.
Mercer, J.　Something's Gotta Give.
Meynell, A.　Renouncement.
Pearse, P.　Naked I Saw You.
Philp, G.　Dance Hall.
Rich, A.　Mark of Resistance, A.
Ross, J.　Whatever Lola Wants (Lola Gets).
Stewart, B.　August Town.
Unknown.　Issei's history.
　Thy Heart.
　What else can you do but fight?
Valerie, J.　Lesson on Braces.
Vázquez Montalbán, M.　Summer and Smoke.
Williams, Stephanie.　Coarse rigors.

Respectability
Catacalos.　Katakalos.
Eberhart, R.　New England Bachelor, A.
Frere.　And certainly they say, for fine behaving.
Frost, R.　Considerable Speck, A.
Holmes, O.　At the "Atlantic" Dinner, December
　15, 1874.
Taylor, J.　Gods *Houses*, almost like *Troyes
　Ilion,*.

Responsibility
Alkalay-Gut.　Public Outcry.
　Transportation.
Brooks, G.　Kitchenette building.
Browning, E.　Curse for a Nation, A.
Cahn, S.　Call Me Irresponsible.
Clewell.　Poem for the Man Who Said Shit.
Gil de Biedma, J.　Art of Poetry, The.
Giovanni.　December of My Springs, The.
Griffin, T.　Closed Discussion about the Future.
Heyen.　Riddle: "From Belsen a crate of gold
　teeth."
Joseph, J.　Warning.
Kipling, R.　Refined Man, The.
Knox, J.　Bright Light of Responsibility, The.
McDaniel, J.　Uncle Eggplant.
Merwin.　Ballad of John Cable and Three
　Gentlemen.
　Yesterday: "My friend says I was not a good
　son."
Millar, J.　Midlife.
Nolens, L.　Tributary.
Peacock, M.　Good Girl.
Ramsay, A.　Jenny Nettles.
Rich, A.　For the Record.
Stafford, W.　With Kit, Age 7, at the Beach.
Straus.　All-Purpose Apology Poem.
Unknown.　God send euerie Preist ane wyfe.
　Jenny Nettles.
Vietnamese Oral Tradition.　Cat, The.
Wright, C.　Self-Portrait.

Rest
Alexander, P.　Scherzo.
Anyte [*or* Anytes].　Stranger, below the boulder

rest your spent limbs.
Basho. Exhausted, I sought.
  Taking coolness.
Blind. Noonday Rest.
Clare, J. Woodland Seat, A.
Frost, R. Acceptance.
Gascoigne. Lullaby [or Lullabie] of a Lover,
  The.
Goethe. Wanderer's Night Song.
Gorbanevskaya. We live—sometimes.
Han-shan Te-ch'ing. In Jetavana Park I found a
  place to rest.
Hartnett. Prayer for Sleep, A.
Heifetz-Tussman. Keep Me.
Herbert, G. Pulley, The.
Howe, J. House of Rest, The.
Ivanov, Binyo. One Can Rest.
Keats. To One Who Has Been Long in City
  Pent.
Kloos, W. Evening.
Levine, P. Sleepless Night, A.
Liu Cheng. Poem without a Category.
Lovelace, R. Ant, The.
Ma Chih-yüan. Tune: "Song of Clear River".
Mackenzie, K. Door swung open . . . , The.
Mansour, J. Storm Sketches a Silver Margin,
  The.
Mipham, Sakyong. Snow Fell Twice, the Sun
  Always Shone.
Mother Goose. Forehead, Eyes, Cheeks, Nose,
  Mouth, and Chin.
Nesbit, E. Song: "Oh, baby, baby, baby dear."
Pavlova. Life calls us, and we go, massing our
  courage.
Po Chü-i. Ease.
Poe. For Annie.
Ravikovitch, D. Unusual Autumn, An.
Ross, A. Mess Deck.
Rossetti, C. Cardinal Newman.
  Rest.
  Sleeping at Last.
  Uphill [or Up-Hill].
Seneca. Climb at court for me that will.
Sidney, P. Sonnet 39: "Come Sleep! O sleep the
  certain knot of peace."
Smith, C. Pressed by the Moon, Mute Arbitress
  of Tides.
Strand. I am sure you would find it misty here.
Strobel. Pastoral: "This is a place of ease."
Teitelboim, D. Threesome.
Timrod. Retirement.
Unknown. Orchid Door, The.
Si-mu: Request for Furlough.
Westphalen, E. You Came to Rest.
Whitman, W. Evening Lull, An.
Wilbur, R. Sonnet: "Winter deepening, the hay
  all in, The."
Wyrebek, M. Recovery.
Yeats. Michael Robartes Bids His Beloved Be
  at Peace.

Restaurants
Bejerano, M. Noon. 12:45 already.
Betjeman. Huxley Hall.
Cartwright, K. ALL-YOU-CAN-EAT / catfish
  houses.
Corn. Kimchee in Worchester (Mass.).
Cummings, E. E. Item.
Derricotte. On Stopping Late in the Afternoon
  for Steamed Dumplings.
Espada. For the Jim Crow Mexican Restaurant
  in Cambridge, Massachusetts, Where My
  Cousin Esteban was Forbidden to Wait Tables
  Because He Wears Dreadlocks.
Evasco, M. Baked Oysters Rockefeller.
Ferrari, M. Ristorante San Marco, The.
Gardinier. At Work.
Humphreys, E. On the Guincho.
Kingston, M. Restaurant.
Kirkpatrick. Class.
Light, K. 2. San Francisco.
Limonov. Japanese restaurant is good in
  autumn—in dank weather—the hot napkins,
  the warm sake, The.
Lowell, A. Thompson's Lunch Room—Grand
  Central Station.
McElroy, C. Foul Line—1987.

Parker, A. Practicing Their Diffidence, the
  Vandals.
Pettit. Vanna White's Bread Pudding.
Ransom, W. Pastime Café.
St. Germain, S. Cajun.
Saltman. Hunger, A.
Schuyler, J. Dining Out with Doug and Frank.
Segal, J. I Keep Going Back to Joe's.
Simic. Partial Explanation, The.
Spanel, Ann. Pez Dorado.
Tammaro. 'Mericn Fst Fd.
Unknown. I Had But Fifty Cents.
Urdang. At Frank 'n' Helen's.
Violi. Appeal to the Grammarians.
Wetzsteon. Dinner at Le Caprice.
Williams, W. Brilliant Sad Sun.
Young, D. Pleasure.

Restlessness
Alexander, M. Memory.
  People of Unrest.
Baxter, J. Homecoming, The.
Cárdenas, B. Sonido Ink(quieto).
Cawthorn. Wit was a strange unlucky child.
Chu Shu-chen. Plaint.
Cristall. Before Twilight. Eyezion.
Davis, O. Panic of Birds, The.
Derricotte. Invisible Dreams.
Donegan, P. Something Happened.
Fagin, L. Women.
Gwala. One small boy longs for summer.
Jungkwan Ilson. Revisiting Kumkang Pavilion.
Lane, P. Spring.
Levy, A. March Day in London, A.
Longfellow, H. Seaweed.
Milán, E. No hay porqué, hay órdenes de canto.
  There is no wherefore, there is a command of
  song.
Prince, F.T. Babiaantje, The.
Pulido, A. Girl, A / leans on the railing.
Rivas, J. Marea roja.
  Red Tide.
Robinson, A. Darwinism.
Rodriguez, A. Sonido Ink(quieto).
Spaziani. Crossroads, The.
Tu Fu [or Du Fu]. Restless Night.

Restraint
Bunting. Now that sea's over that island.
Cavendish, M. Claspe, The.
Drummond de Andrade. Looking for Poetry.
Glück, L. Palais des Arts.
Hill, G. Masque of Blackness, The.
Kizer, C. Bitch.
McKay, C. White City, The.
Philips, K. Answer to Another Persuading a
  Lady to Marriage, An.
Reese, L. Reserve.
Sadi [or Saadi or Sa'di]. If you should say to
  me Don't mention love.
Sansom, A. Confinement.
Teillier, J. No Sign of Life.
Unknown. Please, Sir Second-born.

Resurrection, The
Bell, M. Sounds of the Resurrected Dead Man's
  Footsteps (#3).
Bryce, Colette. Word, The.
Burns, R. Jesus Speaks to the Church at
  Eastertime.
Coverdale. Of the Resurrection.
Cowley, A. Resurrection, The.
Crabbe, G. Resurrection.
Donne. Resurrection, Imperfect.
Doolittle, H. In resurrection, there is confusion.
  Yet resurrection is a sense of direction.
Dunbar, W. Done is a battell [or battle] on the
  dragon blak [or black].
Haviaras, Stratis. Easter Feast.
Herbert, G. Dawning, The.
  Easter ("Rise heart; thy Lord is risen. Sing his
  praise.").
Hopkins, G. That Nature Is a Heraclitean Fire
  and of the Comfort of the Resurrection.
Jennings, E. Resurrection, The.
Kaschnitz. Not Courageous.
Levertov. Ikon: The Harrowing of Hell.
Levin, P. Third Day, The.
Milosz, C. Lecture 5.

Matthew 28:1–6; Now after the sabbath.
Murray, L. Easter 1984.
  Say-but-the-Word Centurion Attempts a
  Summary, The.
Norris, K. Emperor Has No Clothes!, The.
Pankey. Luke: 24:13–32; That very day two of
  them.
Powell, D. A. Ice Hadn't Cracked, The. Stingy
  Ground: Frozen with its Hoard of Bulbs.
Rilke. John 20:11–18; But Mary stood weeping
  outside the tomb.
  12. The Quiet Mary Knew with the Risen
  Christ.
Rossetti, C. Better Resurrection, A.
Spenser, E. Sonnet 68: "Most glorious Lord of
  Life that on this day."
Thompson, C. Empty Tomb, The.
Unknown. Christ Triumphant.
  Happy Morning.
  Resurrection Morn, The.
  Steal Away to Jesus.
Wanley. Resurrection, The.
Wordsworth, W. Composed in One of the
  Valleys of Westmoreland, on Easter Sunday.

Retirement and Retirees
Babb, Stanley E. Portrait of a Pirate.
Buckley, C. 20 Years of Grant Applications and
  State College Jobs.
Cistulli. 47.57.
Copus, J. Cricketer's Retirement Day, The.
Edson, R. Retirement of the Elephant, The.
Heyen. Where.
Jacobsen, J. Hourglass.
Jamie, K. God Almighty the First Garden
  Made.
Kessler, M. Secret Love.
Kyger. Retirement: "Unfamiliar warble 9 times
  more, An."
Leonard, T. Opting for Early Retirement.
Lisick, B. Empress of Sighs ("Mom and Dad
  have abandoned the family home and retired to
  Palm.").
Marvell. Garden, The.
  Upon the Hill and Grove at Bilbrough.
Muso Soseki. Mourning for the Layman Named
  Cloud Peak.
Ní Chuilleanáin. Swineherd.
Reed, I. White Hope.
Rouse, A. Her Retirement.
Song Sun. I discuss with my heart.
Towle. Postmodern Maturity.
Van Jordan, A. My Father's Retirement.
Wang Wei. In Reply to Vice-Magistrate Chang.
  In Retirement at Zhongnan.
Wright, D. Lines on Retirement, after Reading
  Lear.
Yeats. Lamentation of the Old Pensioner, The
  (1890 version).
Yüan Chên. Retirement.
See also **Old Age**

Retribution
Archilochus. Buffeted by the waves.
Eberhart, R. Fury of Aerial Bombardment, The.
Jeffers, R. Home.
Jones, I. Revolutionary Vision, The.
Longley, M. Butchers, The.
Sappho. May winds and sorrows.
Sassoon, S. Blighters.
Unknown. God, burn the houses down.

Reunions
Arnold, C. Why I Skip My High School
  Reunions.
Benét, S. Love Came By From the Riversmoke.
Blake, W. Little Boy Found, The.
Burns, R. Auld Lang Syne.
Castellanos. Return.
Ch'iao Lai. Tune: "Partridge Sky" I Rejoice to
  Meet a Friend Visting at My Rustic Study.
Cortez, Sarah. Reunion.
Crunk, T. Reunion.
Devlin, D. Renewal by Her Element.
Dickinson, E. Return, The.
Donne. Valediction, A: Forbidding Mourning.
Hardy, T. Minute before Meeting, The.
Hughes. Lover's Return.
Ingelow. Long White Seam, The.

Ivanov, G.   Quarter century of exile has passed, A.
Jones, T.   Back?
Kizer, C.   Semele Recycled.
Kumin, M.   Family Reunion.
Levertov.   Woman Meets an Old Lover, A.
Livingston, M.   Coming from Kansas.
McGrath, T.   Celebration: "How wonderful, Tomasito!"
Mew.   Again.
Montague, J.   All Legendary Obstacles.
   At Last.
   Silver Flask, The ("Sweet, though short, our.").
Moore, L.   Haiku.
Novello, I.   We'll Gather Lilacs.
Oliphant.   Too talented to give a hot damn.
Owen, W.   Unreturning, The.
Porter, C.   Get Out of Town.
Ratushinskaya [or Ratushinskaia].   Penelope, the screaming is all over.
Rich, A.   Face to Face.
Rossetti, C.   Birthday, A.
Rukeyser, M.   More of a Corpse Than a Woman.
Steiger.   Not an epilogue, but everything coming to an end.
T'ao Ch'ien [or T'ao Yuan-ming].   Return, The.
Tu Fu [or Du Fu].   For the Recluse Wei Pa.
   Presented to Wei Ba, Gentleman in Retirement.
   Return, The.
   To Wei Pa, a Retired Scholar.
   Visit.
Unknown.   My love is coming! I take dinner early.
Watkins, V.   Returning to Goleufryn.
Wright, C.   Reunion.
Yi Chehyŏn.   Magpie chatters in a flowering bough by the hedge, A.

Revelation (Bible)
Bard, W. E.   Seventh Seal, The.
Blake, W.   Mental Traveller, The.
Braxton, C.   Apocalypse.
George, S.   Antichrist, The.
Herrick.   To God ("Do with me, God! as Thou didst deal with John.").
Lima, J.   Trumpets, The.
Lowry, R.   Beautiful River.
Spenser, E.   Sonnet 12: "I saw an ugly beast come from the sea."
   Sonnet 13: "I saw a woman sitting on a beast."
   Sonnet 14: "Then might I see upon a white horse set."
   Sonnet 15: "I saw new Earth, new Heaven, said Saint John."
Trapnell, A.   Therefore John read how that thou wouldst.
Unknown.   There's a Meeting Here To-Night.

Revelry
Cho Chonsŏng.   Boy, lead a cow to the northern village.
Hemans.   Revellers, The.
Jarvenpa, D.   Polka.
Ou-yang Hsiu.   Tune: "Gathering Mulberry Leaves".
Parker, A.   Another Poem about the Vandals.
P'i Jih-hsiu.   Impromptu on a Hangover.
Townsend, A.   Mardi Gras Premortem.
Trethewey, N.   Photograph of a Bawd Drinking Raleigh Rye.
Unknown.   Hey, ey, hey, ey / Make we myrie as we may.
   Man in the World Lodging.
   Tune: Eternal Longing.
Vaughan, H.   Since last we met, thou and thy horse, my dear.

Revenge
Amichai, Y.   Ideal Woman, An.
Belli, G.   Revenge 1.
Brontë, A.   Song.
Bryant, W.   Indian Story, An.
Cahun, C.   Sadistic Judith.
Campo.   Allegory.
Carew, T.   To My Inconstant Mistress [or Mistris].
Ch'oe Sŭngja.   House of Memories.
Congreve, W.   False Though She Be.

Damas.   On Sale.
Davenant [or D'Avenant].   'Tis, in good truth, a most wonderful thing.
Dickinson, E.   Mine Enemy is growing old.
Donne.   Apparition, The.
Fielding.   Revenge.
Gay, J.   Wild Boar and the Ram, The.
Gbadamosi.   Sango's son came down to the river.
Heine, H.   Revenge—?
Herrick.   Revenge.
Holden, J.   Liberace.
Homer.   Achilles with wild fury in his heart.
Hughes, T.   Revenge Fable.
Johnston, C.   Spirit of evil, with which the earth is rife.
Kalmar et al.   Who's Sorry Now?
Khlebnikov, V.   To Everyone.
Komunyakaa, Y.   Fragging.
Kuzmina-Karavayeva.   Long-Barrow Princess 2.
Landon.   Revenge.
Lanier, S.   Revenge of Hamish, The.
Lea, S.   Feud, The.
Loden.   Revenge, Like Habanero Peppers.
Loftis, N.   Brief Encounter.
MacGregor, Mrs., of Glenstrae.   Lament for MacGregor of Glenstrae.
Marlowe.   Here is the form of Gaveston's exile.
McKay, D.   1. The Man from Nod.
Mejía Godoy, L.   Revenge.
Melville, H.   Martyr, The.
Merson.   Spaniard That Blighted My Life, The.
Merwin.   Last One, The.
Millay, E.   Oh, Oh, you will be sorry for that word!
Milton.   Deliverer, The.
   On the Late Massacre [or Massacher] in Piedmont [or Piemont].
Moxley, Jennifer.   Stem of the Tree of Orestes.
Nawaz, S.   Initiation, The.
Nervo.   Revenge.
Pagis, D.   Autobiography.
   Autobiography.
Parker, D.   Frustration.
Petersen, M.   What I Would Do.
Petit, P.   Fish Daughter, The.
Petri.   Electra.
Plath.   Lady Lazarus.
Powers, Arthur.   Iago.
Rao, K.   We Should Remember.
Rattray, D.   They Don't Have to Have That Look.
Robin, L.   Little Girl from Little Rock.
Rosser, J.   Parable of the Cheek.
Ruby, H.   Who's Sorry Now?
Sadhu Binning.   Revenge: "Hands on the steering wheel."
Samaras, N.   Elegy for a Professor.
Shaw, C.   Search, The.
Sorescu, M.   Don Juan (After He'd Consumed Tons of Lipstick).
Stesichoros.   Since Tyndareos.
Stock, N.   What I Said.
Teasdale.   I Shall Not Care.
Tucker, M.   Revenge.
Unknown.   Death of Parcy Reed, The [Version from Richardsons' Borderers' Table Book].
   Fair and Scornful.
   Hrothgar Answered.
   I Will Arise with My Tomahawk.
   If the land of the Flowery Flag is occupied by us in turn.
   Leaving behind my writing brush and.
   Low building with three beams merely shelters the body, The.
   Prayer of a Warrior (Assiniboine).
Vando.   Lydia's Phantasmagoria.
Walker, M.   Kissie Lee.
Webb, C.   Prayer for the Man Who Mugged My Father, 72.
Webb, C.   Revenge.
Xue Di.   Interplay.

Revere, Paul
Livingston, M.   Paul Revere Speaks.
Longfellow, H.   Paul Revere's Ride [The Landlord's Tale].

Revivalism and Revivalists
Crown, K.   Holy Ghost Flies into Second Baptist on Airline Highway in Baton Rouge, The.
Marson.   Gettin[g] de Spirit.
Nowlan.   Daughter of Zion.
Warren, R.   Amazing Grace in the Back Country.
Young, K.   Revival.
See also **Evangelism and Evangelists; Religion**

Revolution and Revolutionaries
Ackland.   Communist Poem, 1935.
Adnan.   Maïakovsky.
Aguilar, M.   Poem from Sierra Madre.
Akao, A.   Zombies Arise.
al-Mala'ika, N.   Jamilah and Us.
"Antler.".   Ungag our souls!! Unstrangle our souls!! Unsmother our souls!!
Anyidoho.   Elegy for the Revolution.
Auden.   Epilogue: "'O where are you going?' said reader to rider".
Baraka, I.   Cuba Libre.
   New Reality Is Better Than a New Movie!, A.
   Short Speech to My Friends.
   When We'll Worship Jesus.
Berberova.   To Shakespeare.
Bienek.   Resistance.
Bomani, M.   Roots.
Borges.   Page to Commemorate Colonel Suárez, Victor at Junín, A.
Brown, S.   Old Woman Remembers, An.
Browning, E.   Part II.
Buchanan, G.   Speaker in the Square, A.
Burns, R.   Scots Wha Hae.
Cardenal.   Lights.
Carson, C.   Hamlet.
Castera, G.   I Have a Comrade.
Cisneros, S.   I Am So in Love I Grow a New Hymen.
   Loose Women.
Dalton, R.   From a Revolutionary to J. L. Borges.
   Petty Bourgeoisie, The.
Day Lewis.   You That Love England.
Di Prima.   April Fool Birthday Poem for Grandpa.
   Revolutionary Letter #1.
Đỗ Tấn Xuân.   Twenty Years.
Duff, V.   Letters from an Exile.
Duo Duo.   When the People Stand Up out of the Hard Cheese.
Ehrenburg [or Erenburg].   Our Grandsons Will Be Astonished.
Enzensberger, H.   Old Revolution.
Espada.   Jeep Driver, The.
Ewer.   Gentlemen.
Faiz.   Don't Ask Me for That Love Again.
Fiacc.   British Connection, The.
Frost, R.   Semi-Revolution, A.
Garcia, R.   Elite Syncopations.
Gelman.   Eyes.
Ginsberg, A.   Vow, A.
Gordon, R.   Nights in Siuna.
Gray-Kontar, D.   July.
Guevara, E.   Song to Fidel.
Gullar.   Sweet Talk.
   There Are Many Traps in the World.
Hahn, K.   Everest.
Harper, M.   Song: I Want a Witness.
Hawoldar.   In the Fist of Your Hatred.
Hedin, R.   At the Olive Grove of the Resistance.
Herbert, Z.   Transformations of Livy.
Herrera.   Mexican World Mural / 5 x 25.
   Poetry of America, The.
Hippolyte.   Revo Lyric.
Hobday, C.   Thirty Years On.
Hughes, L.   Letter to the Academy.
Ilio, D.   Prokosch in Tehran, 1978.
Jabeen, M.   Live Walls.
Jackson, R.   Lonely Affair, A.
Jensma.   In memoriam Ben Zwane.
Jigerkhwen.   I am the Voice.
Johnson, L.   Mi Revalueshanary Fren.
Johnston, G.   Blood Is the Argument.
Jones, I.   Revolutionary Vision, The.
Jones, Llion.   Illusions.

Jordan, J.   Poem Against the State (Of Things): 1975.
Katz, E.   In Praise of the Seattle Coalition.
Khlebnikov, V.   Iranian Song.
Knight, E.   On the Yard.
Kriapur (Kristianto Agus Purnomo).   Men on Fire.
Kushner, A.   Memoirs.
Lamantia.   Voice of Earth Mediums.
Laraque, P.   Mardi Gras.
  Poem for You, A.
Lawrence, D. H.   Fight! O My Young Men.
  O! Start a Revolution.
Lihn.   Revolution.
Limonov.   And it's the summer civil war. Fantastic!
  It is good in May, in marvelous wet May, to be the chairman of the All-Russian Extraordinary Committee in the city of Odessa.
  Japanese restaurant is good in autumn—in dank weather—the hot napkins, the warm sake, The.
"Lucebert.".   I Reel Off.
Macaulay, T.   Radical War Song, A.
Machado Ruiz.   Meditation for this Day.
Mao Tse-tung [or Mao Zedong].   Return to Shaoshan.
Maroon, B.   Fire Keeper.
Mataka.   Ornithology.
Maunick.   Seven Sides and Seven Syllables.
McFadden, R.   First Letter to an Irish Novelist.
Morales.   My Revolution.
Morisseau-Leroy, F.   Sometimes I'm Not Myself.
Moro, C.   Balcony.
Muldoon, P.   Lunch with Pancho Villa.
Musa, Y.   Imagine a Revolution.
  Where Are They?
Nathan, L.   Coup.
Okigbo.   Elegy for Slit-Drum.
Okudzhava.   To me, Muscovites are sweethearts out of old stories.
Padilla.   Discourse on Method, The.
Parkes, B.   Lilian's Second Letter.
Pasolini.   Redefining "Orthodoxy".
Perdomo, W.   Revolutionary.
Petri.   Christmas 1956.
Pope, A.   Epistle to Dr. Arbuthnot.
Powell, K.   Mental Terrorism.
Reddy, S.   We Write.
Reed, I.   Reactionary Poet, The.
Senghor.   In Memoriam.
Serge.   Dialectic.
Simidor, D.   Slippery Ground.
Slutsky [or Slutskii].   Law, which each citizen knows well.
Sykes, B.   Cycle.
Taha, A.   Anwar Kamel Celebrates Le Quatorze Juillet.
Tsanev, Ivan.   Koprivshtitsa.
Tsanev, Stefan.   Rehearsal for a Parade.
Unknown.   Cutty Wren, The.
  Diggers' Song, The.
  Ode to a Jacobin.
Upton, C.   When I was very young.
Waldman, A.   How the Sestina (Yawn) Works.
Walker, M.   For My People.
Williams, C.   Revolutionary Thoughts.
Wright, C.   Post-Revolutionary Letter.
Yevtushenko [or Evtushenko].   John Reed's Monologue.
Yusuf, S.   Good Morning, Fakhani.
See also **Rebellions and Rebels**

Revolutionary War, American
Cooke, R.   Hospital Soliloquy, A.
Freneau.   New York Tory, to His Friend in Philadelphia, A.
Hopkinson, F.   Toast to Washington, A.
Lowell, J.   Old Joe is gone, who saw hot Percy goad.
Pierpont, J.   Warren's Address at Bunker Hill [or to the American Soldiers].
Trumbull, J.   Town-Meeting, A.M., The.
Unknown.   Alphabet.
  Burrowing Yankees.
  Irishman's Epistle to the Officers and Troops at Boston, The.
  King's Own Regulars, The [And Their Triumphs Over the Irregulars].
  Public Spirit of the Women, The.
  Refugee Song, A.
  Yankee Doodle.
See also **American Revolution**

Rewards
Benjamin, P.   Press On.
Berrigan, A.   Advice to a Young Philosopher.
Campo, C.   At Times I Say: Let's Try to Be Joyous.
Unknown.   My whole mouth, all of it, is yours.
  No More Rain Fall for Wet You.

Rexroth, Kenneth
Ferlinghetti, L.   At Kenneth Rexroth's.

Reynolds, Sir Joshua
Goldsmith, O.   Sir Joshua Reynolds.

Reznikoff, Charles
Niedecker.   If I Were a Bird.
Oppen.   In Memoriam Charles Reznikoff.

Rhine (river), Germany
Coleridge, S.   Cologne.
Crockett-Smith, D.   Rhinemaiden.
Stadler.   On Crossing the Rhine Bridge at Cologne by Night.

Rhinoceroses
Nash, O.   Rhinoceros, The.

Rhode Island (state)
Burt, S.   Ocean State.
Dietz, H.   Rhode Island Is Famous for You.
Meredith, W.   Rhode Island.

Rhythm
Allen, L.   Riddim an' Hardtimes.
Breeze.   Dubbed Out.
Caesar.   Crazy Rhythm.
Césaire, A.   Batouque.
D'Aguiar, F.   Now the Two Are One.
Fisher, A.   Stepping Out: 2.
  Stepping Out: I.
Gershwin, I.   Fascinating Rhythm.
Kahn, G.   All God's Chillun Got Rhythm.
Koehler, T.   Spreadin' Rhythm Around.
Mistral, G.   Rocking.
Reed, I.   Poetry Makes Rhythm in Philosophy.
Roberson, E.   It must be that in the midst.

Ribbons
Aisenberg, N.   Woman in the Moon, The.
Carew, T.   Upon a Ribbon [or Ribband].
Herrick.   Bracelet to Julia, The.

Rice
Basho.   Beginnings of poetry.
  By the old temple.
  Culture's beginnings.
  Culture's beginnings.
  From the city: news.
  Peasant's child, The.
  Planting rice seedlings.
  Singing, planting rice.
  Through frozen rice fields.
  Whole field of.
  Wrapping the rice cakes.
Buson.   Listening to the moon.
  With the noon conch blown.
Forrester, S.   Monk's bowl.
Issa.   In the thicket's shade.
  That pretty girl.
Ko Ŭn.   Crossing Rice Fields at Nightfall.
Komunyakaa, Y.   Buried Light.
Konishi Raizan.   For rice-planting women.
Menes, O.   Raspa.
Mukai Kyorai.   After the green storm / True color.
Oliver, M.   Rice.
Po Chü-i.   Climbing the Ling-ying Terrace and Looking North.
Ransetsu.   Fly, dare take / The rice grain.
Strange.   Offering.
Su Tung-p'o.   I planted rice before Spring Festival.
Unknown.   Song of the Pestle.
Valentine, J.   Bit of Rice, A.
Yayu.   Transplanting rice / He pisses.

Richard III, King of England
Stillman, M.   Two Princes, The.

Riches
Adams, F.   Rich Man, The.
Apparao, G.   Gold.
Michaux.   Jetty, The.
See also **Wealth**

Riddles
Angwin, R.   I offer you four things.
Beeson, J.   Bald head with the fringe, The.
Bennett, C.   I live alone where echoes roost.
Berry, J.   I am cuddle-shaped and freckled.
Bewick, E.   Black my beginning.
Bishop, P.   Like the tides I rise and fall.
Bletsoe, E.   Weird stuff this.
Borges.   Oedipus and the Riddle.
Born, A.   I chuck their chins.
Brading, T.   Punt gliding under a chain of smiles, A.
Brownjohn.   Your fingers fully awake, it.
Cameron, N.   I have no substance and no form.
Charles, T.   I saw a great building with many storeys piled high.
Clarke, G.   All afternoon I hope.
Condee.   Mrs. Charles Sanders Peirce, or The Solution to the Universe.
Constantine, D.   What we reminded you of you are already forgetting.
Cook, J.   For being unfaithful though ever true.
Cotton, J.   We are a crystal zoo.
Crossley-Holland.   They're marked men. Their park is like an open prison.
Crucefix.   There is a whole world involved in me.
Cynewulf.   Sun and Moon.
  Swan, The.
Dale, P.   I start with a straight back and two points.
Dickinson, E.   Riddle we can guess, The.
  Snake, The.
Duran, J.   When I lean down to stir the bathwater.
Eglinton, E.   Alive, I flourish.
Fairfax, J.   My emblem is an arrow.
Fanshawe, C.   Riddle, A: "'Twas in heaven pronounced, and 'twas muttered in hell."
Fanthorpe.   Door, A.
Feaver.   Without you, I prefer the nights.
Fell, F.   Gifted with vision the snowman would see.
Fontana, J.   Ask many women and they'll claim no knowledge, but some.
Frémon, Jean.   Autumn: "Shogun, always on the lookout for ways to increase his glory, The."
Garfitt, R.   Rarest of the esculents, its distribution.
Garrett, E.   I am the difficult silk that slides from your grasp.
Gillilan, P.   You lie with me nightly. In bathrooms I'm there.
Goodland, G.   More powerful than the government.
Greenwell, B.   When my stomach bulges, I hurl wild whoops.
Guest, H.   No fragrance yet the fold.
Hadfield, C.   My skin shimmers with all the colours.
Hannah, S.   Narrow for love that must be fitted in.
Harpur, J.   I work in the evening, alone and in silence.
Hart, D.   Hair on your body, The.
Hart, H.   Riddle: "Rooted in fresh earth, I am a bush of flies."
Hawkhead, J.   I am a glider on time's thermals.
Hawkhead, P.   I am the swift scribble.
Hayden, R.   Sphinx.
Hegley.   I'm skulking by the scandal and the handle on the door.
Henry, M.   Though starlings imitate me.
Henson, S.   Grab the beast by the horns.
Herbert, B.   I do not have a body.
Hill, S.   Who's that knocking on my ring, says the chin.
Hoffman, D.   Riddle, A.
Houston, L.   I can lift gravity's stern glower.

Invocation to the U′ wannami.
Prayer upon Cutting down the Sacred Tree.
Throw me a quince.
We Have Chosen a Timely Day.
Very. My Meat and Drink.
Villa, D. In the end.
Volach, Y. Tefillin.
Yeats. Collarbone [or Collar-Bone] of a Hare, The.
Zuni Oral Tradition. Sayatasha's Night Chant.

Rivalry
Adam, H. Pre-Teen Trot.
Barnfield [or Barnefield]. Beauty and majesty are fallen at odds.
Behn, A. To My Lady Morland at Tunbrige [or Tunbridge].
Carew, T. To My Rival.
"Ephelia.". To My Rival.
Erb, E. Bickering.
Frost, R. Fifteen: "Late that summer my girlfriend's boyfriend."
Korinna [or Corinna]. Over you, Hermes fights.
Marlowe. Ah, wicked King! Accursed Gaveston!
My father is deceas'd. Come, Gaveston.
Paschen. Voir Dire.
Sappho. To me it seems.
Shakespeare, W. Sonnet 80: "O, how I faint when I of you do write."
Unknown. God, please let my youth go up in smoke!
Wetzsteon. Rival, A.
See also **Competition**

Rivera, Diego
Nance. Rio Grande Hills.
Shiki. In the winter river.
White, E. I Paint What I See.

Rivers
Abrahams, L. Thoughts on Johannesburg's centenary.
Adams, L. River in the Meadows, The.
Adonis [or Adunis]. Tree of Fire.
Aguilar-Cariño. Gabi.
Aitchison. Dipper Territory.
al-Mala'ika, N. Lover River, The.
Alberti. Going Up the Rivers.
Alcosser. Approaching August.
Aldrich, T. By the Potomac.
Allen, A. This River.
Applewhite. Water from the Lamp Bottle.
Aridjis. Rivers.
Arodin, S. Lazy River.
Ashbery, J. Myrtle.
Aytoun [or Ayton], R. Sonnet: On the River Tweed.
Baker, D. Mercy.
Bansode. Woman.
Basho. Gathering.
  Gathering the rains.
  Pouring the hot day.
  This hot day swept away.
Batraville, D. Paper 18.
Belloc. Evenlode, The.
Berry, W. Slip, The.
Bertolino. Snail River.
Bevington, L. With the Tide: A Cry of Weakness.
Bishop, E. One Art.
Bopp, R. Begins here, the ciphered forest.
Borges. Ars Poetica: "To look at the river made of time and water."
Bowers, N. Flight: "River slops under the bridge, The."
Bowles, W. To the River Cherwell.
To the River Itchin, near Winton.
To the River Wenbeck.
Broumas, O. Oregon Landscape with Lost Lover.
Brown, S. Riverbank Blues.
Bryant, W. Green River.
Night Journey of a River, The.
Buson. Crossing.
  Early summer rain.
  Flowers offered to the Buddha.
  In seasonal rain.
  Petals fall, The.

Short night, The.
Short night, The.
Spring Wind on the Riverbank at Kema.
Cabral de Melo Neto. Landscape of the Capibaribe River.
Campion, T. Fire, fire, fire, fire!
Carman, B. Low Tide on Grand Pré.
Carmichael, H. Lazy River.
Carson, A. Longing, a Documentary.
Carver, R. River, The: "I waded, deepening, into the dark water."
Woman Bathing.
Caston, A. Gathering at the River.
Ceravolo. Spring of Work Storm.
Chamberlain, K. Stepping in the Same River.
Chan Fang-sheng. Sailing into the South Lake.
Chao Shan-ch'ing. Autumn on the Riverbank.
Chenette, S. Ritual.
Chia Tao. Late in the Day, Gazing Out from a River Pavilion.
Ch'u Yüan. Yellow River's Earl, The.
Clark, T. Sonnet: "Five a.m. on East Fourteenth I'm out to eat."
Clive. Mosel, The.
Cohen, L. Suzanne [Takes You Down].
Coleridge, S. Sonnet to the River Otter.
Crane, H. Repose of Rivers.
River, The.
Creeley. River wandering down.
  When it comes.
Cruickshank, H. Ponnage Pool, The.
Curry, N. Mute Swans.
da Silva. Along the Banks of the Charles.
Deane, S. Fording the River.
Dickey, J. Inside the River.
Dixon, M. River, Stay 'Way from My Door.
Dovaston, J. F. M. Streamlet! methinks thy lot resembles mine.
Dove, R. Event, The.
Dowson. Spleen.
Eberhart, R. La Crosse at Ninety Miles an Hour.
Eichner, Maura. Dream Songs Concluded.
Eliot, T. S. Dry Salvages, The.
Virginia.
Emerson, R. Musketaquid.
Two Rivers.
Erdrich. I Was Sleeping Where the Black Oaks Move.
Faiz. You Tell Us What to Do.
Farjeon, E. Tide in the River, The.
Ferlinghetti, L. River Still To Be Found, A.
Fishman, C. Whapmagoostui.
Fisk, M. Red River.
Fletcher, J. River[-]God's Song, The.
Foerster. Bronx Park.
Fordham. Maiden and River.
Foreman, Paul. Brazos de Dios.
Foster, S. Old Folks at Home.
Fujita, Jun. Chicago River.
García Lorca. Little Ballad of the Three Rivers.
My Little Girl Went to the Sea.
Garcia, R. Diver for the NYPD Talks to His Girlfriend, A.
Gehrke, S. Near the Mississippi.
Georgiev, Marin. Riverbend.
Goll, I. Last River, The.
Gonzalez, R. At the Rio Grande Near the End of the Century.
Goodison. Wedding in Hanover.
Greenberg, S. East River's Charm.
Gregerson. Waterborne.
Groarke, V. Riverbed, The.
Guillén, J. River.
Guiney. Down Stream.
Reason for Silence, A.
Hacker, M. Going Back to the River.
Hay, J. Jim Bludso of the Prairie Belle.
Heaney, S. Broagh.
New Song, A.
Heard, J. To Clements' Ferry.
Hemans. Indian Woman's Death-Song, The.
Henley, W. E. At Queensferry.
Herrick. To Dean-bourn, a Rude River in Devon, by Which Sometimes He Lived.
Hill, M. Ruth.

Hoggard, James. Anniversary Trip.
Hollander, J. Variations on a Fragment by Trumbull Stickney.
Holmes, O. Two Streams, The.
Homer. Then Achilles.
Homfray. Thoughts on Happiness.
Howard, B. River Song.
River's Answer, The.
Hsieh Ling-yün. I Follow the Jinzhu Torrent.
Hughes, L. Bitter River, The.
Negro Speaks of Rivers, The.
Suicide's Note.
Hughes, T. River.
Hugo, R. Reflen Now, The.
Skykomish River Running.
Hulü Chin. Song of the Tölös.
Hunt, L. Nile, The.
Hwang Chini. Mountains are steadfast.
Ifan, W. Vale of My Youth, The.
Iosifova, Ekaterina. Nightfall: "Shadows dart, the wind has risen."
Ismail. Seen from an Island in Godavari.
Issa. Dry riverbed, A.
From the bough.
Noon.
O flea! whatever you do.
Spring rain.
Washing the saucepans.
Ivanova, S. Subterranean River Poem.
Jeffers, H. Tuscaloosa: Riversong.
Johnson, E. Wave-Won.
Johnson, W. River Meditation.
Jordan, J. Sandbar at Moore's Creek.
Kavanagh, P. Consider the Grass Growing.
Kees. River Song.
Keller, D. Melancholy.
Kemble. To the Wissahiccon.
Kendrick, D. Drowned River, The.
Khlebnikov, V. One Book, The.
Kim Yŏngnang. Endless River Flows, An.
Kinsella, T. Nuchal, a Fragment.
Tao and Unfitness at Inistiogue on the River Nore.
Knoepfle. Confluence.
Late Winter in Menard County.
Ko Ǔn. Beside the Evening River.
Kunitz, S. King of the River.
Lampman. Morning on the Lièvre.
Lane, P. I walk to the river in deep snow. The ice is thick.
Lanier, S. Song of the Chattahoochee.
Larkin, J. Cold River.
Larkin, T. Cho-Fu-Sa.
Lassell. Three Poems.
Levertov. Eros at Temple Stream.
Li Chih-yi. Tune: "The Diviner".
Lope de Vega. Seguidillas of the Guadalquivir River.
Lorde. Burning the Water Hyacinth.
Lowry, R. Beautiful River.
Loynaz, D. M. Calm, The.
Embrace.
Futile Flight, Futile Fugue.
Lu Yu. Blue Rapids.
Lux. Can Tie Shoes but Won't.
To Help the Monkey Cross the River.
Lyons, S. Loving Along Western Rivers.
Ma Chih-yüan. Tune: "Song of Clear River".
MacLeish. What Any Lover Learns.
Maeng Sasŏng. Four Seasons by the Rivers and Lakes.
Mandelstam [or Mandelshtam]. In This Cool Transparent Spring.
Mao Tse-tung [or Mao Zedong]. Glitter of a northern kingdom.
I stand alone in the cold autumn.
Marks, Corey. Three Bridges.
Martinson. On the Congo.
Mei Yao Ch'en. I Remember the Blue River.
Meng Hao Jan. From a Mooring on the Tonglu to a Friend in Yangzhou.
Mercer, J. Moon River.
Metodiev, Ivan. River: "River, River."
Meynell, A. Watershed, The.
Miljkovic. Agon.
Minhinnick. Sap.

Morgan, R.   Shadow Valley.
Morgenstern.   Blueprint for Disaster.
Muhammad ibn Ghalib al-Rusafi.   Blue River.
Murray, P.   Conquest.
Musgrave.   At Nootka Sound.
Muso Soseki.   Pure Sound Pavilion of the
  Riverside Temple, The.
Nara Singde.   Tune: "Butterflies Lingering over
  Flowers".
Nasrin.   Border.
Nemerov.   "Good-bye," said the river, "I'm
  going downstream.".
Ni Dhomhnaill.   Language Issue, The.
Niedecker.   River-marsh-drowse.
Nurkse.   August Horizon.
O'Brien, C.   River, The: "Poor Mick was
  trotting on to the town."
O'Callaghan, C.   River at Night.
Ortiz.   Bend in the River.
Otomo no Sakanoé, L.   Don't you cut the brush.
  Where the plovers cry.
Pape.   Indian Ruins Along Rio de Flag.
Pasternak, B.   As With Them.
Pfeiffer, E.   So the river—yes, the river; I have
  come to that at last.
Posey, A.   Song of the Oktahutchee.
Raymond, M.   Crossing the River.
Redmond.   River of Bones and Flesh and Blood.
Rilke.   Tombs of the Hetaerae.
  Tombs of the Hetaerae.
Rimbaud, A.   Blackcurrant River.
Rivas, J.   Río 1.
  River 1.
Robinson, M.   Canzonet.
Roethke.   Meditation at Oyster River.
  Meditation at Oyster River.
Rondin, Leslie.   Heraclitus.
Rosenberg, L.   Susquehanna.
Rühmkorf, P.   Formerly, When We Still Parted
  the Big Rivers.
Sahagún, C.   River: "They named this stretch of
  river Postwar."
Saitō Mokichi.   I was standing there.
Salaam.   Sunrise on the River.
Sampley.   South Rim: Big Bend National Park.
Sarton, M.   After a Train Journey.
Schmitz.   Monstrous Pictures of Whales.
Scovell.   River Steamer, The.
Servasius.   Rivers level granite mountains.
Shillaber, B.   Picture, A.
Simms, W.   By the Swanannoa.
Sitwell, S.   River God, The.
Smith, C.   To the River Arun ("Be the proud
  Thames of trade the busy mart!").
  To the River Arun ("On thy wild banks, by
  frequent torrents worn.").
  Walk by the Water, A.
Smith, S.   River God, The.
Snyder, G.   Raven's Beak River at the End.
Southerland.   Night in Nigeria.
Spear, R.   River Song.
Stafford, W.   Ask Me.
  At Cove on the Crooked River.
  Ceremony.
Stevens, W.   River of Rivers in Connecticut,
  The.
Stevenson, R.   Where Go the Boats?
Stickney, T.   I hear a river thro' the valley
  wander.
Su Tung-p'o.   At Gold Hill Monastery.
  Lyrics to the Tune "The Charms of Niennu": At
  the Red Cliff I Ponder Over Antiquity.
  Tune: "Charming Nien-Nu".
  Tune: "Immortal by the River".
Synge.   'Mergency Man, The.
Tafolla.   This River Here.
Tana, P.   River, The.
Tanikawa, S.   River.
Tomlinson, C.   Heron.
Tu Fu [or Du Fu].   Brimming Water.
  Déjeuner sur l'herbe.
  Heavenly River.
  River Jade-Gray.
  Walking Alone by the Riverbank Seeking
  Flowers.
Tu Mu.   Mooring at River Ch'in-Huai.

U'ng Bình.   At the Exiled King's River Pavilion.
Ungaretti.   Rivers, The.
Unknown.   Chen and Wei are brimming, The.
  I leap into the river, the current doesn't carry me
  away.
  Oshun, the River Goddess.
  Pao-you ku-ye: Bitter Blade.
  South of the Yangtze.
  Tweed and Till.
  Wide, Ho? / A reed will cross its flow.
Van Winckel, N.   Nicholas by the River.
Venkatarao, K.   Home: "Like sapphire and
  terracotta mingling in the Ganga."
Vicinelli.   Crossing the River.
Vietnamese Oral Tradition.   Autumn: "Autumn
  rains blow."
  Saigon River, The.
Wakoski.   Canoer, The.
Wang Chiu-ssu.   Floating, floating, the river
  waters.
Wang Wei.   After Source of the Peach Blossom
  Stream.
  Floating on the River Han.
  Sailing Down the Han.
Wang Yung.   River Song, The.
Ward, D.   Hunting in Twilight.
Warner, S.   Drawing You, Heavy With Sleep.
Warton, T.   Sonnet: To the River Lodon.
Wat.   By a great, swift water.
  Joke, A.
Watson, R.   Children of the Mist.
Weigl.   River Journal.
Wenderoth, J.   Detailed History of the Western
  World.
Whitman, W.   Crossing Brooklyn Ferry.
Whitten, Martha E.   Beautiful in Death.
Whittier.   River Path, The.
Williams, W.   January Morning.
  Mists Over the River.
Wilson, K.   River Girl.
Woolson.   Detroit River.
Wordsworth, W.   Composed upon Westminster
  Bridge, September 3, 1802.
  Conclusion: "But here no cannon thunders to
  the gale."
  Flowers.
  How shall I paint thee?—Be this naked stone.
  Hymn for the Boatmen, as They Approach the
  Rapids under the Castle of Heidelberg.
  KIRK of ULPHA to the pilgrim's eye, The.
  Methinks 'twere no unprecedented feat.
  Not hurled precipitous from steep to steep.
  O mountain Stream! the Shepherd and his Cot.
  Open Prospect.
  Plain of Donnerdale, The.
  Return, Content! for fondly I pursued.
  Same Subject, The.
  Sole listener, Duddon! to the breeze that played.
  Stepping-Stones, The.
  Take, cradled Nursling of the mountains, take.
  Tributary Stream.
  What aspect bore the Man who roved or fled.
  Whence that low voice?—A whisper from the
  heart.
  Who swerves from innocence, who makes
  divorce.
Wright, C.   Looking Outside the Cabin Window,
  I Remember a Line by Li Po.
Wright, J.   Eli, Eli.
  River Bend.
Yamaguchi Seishi.   Summer river, The.
Yen Chen.   On the Willow Bank.
Yi Illo.   Night Rain on the Rivers Hsiao and
  Hsiang.
Yi Jung.   River Darkens on an Autumn Night,
  The.
Young, C.   Night-Mullins River.
Young, D.   Sources of the Delaware.
Young, Seth.   All says a glass doorknow
  Parabola ghost.
Yu Ch'an.   Third Day of the Third Month at the
  Meandering River, The.
Zagajewski.   On Swimming.
Zhang Ruoxu.   Spring, River, Flowers, Moon,
  Night.
Zukofsky, L.   Not much more than being.

See also **Brooks and Streams**
Roads
Aiken, C.   Road, The.
Al-Haidari, B.   Premature Elegy.
al-Rahim, A.   Road, The.
Alexander, P.   2. Plum Island.
Allen, Alma Stacey.   Road Trip.
Allnutt, G.   Road Home, The.
Armand.   Word to the Wise, A.
Aygi, G.   Two Epilogues: "Cleanness of the
  path."
Basho.   As for the hibiscus.
  Blowing stones.
  It's fall and dusk.
  Many nights on the road.
  This road.
  Tired.
Blackburn, P.   El Camino Verde.
Bolt, T.   Glimpse of Terrain.
Buckley, V.   Origins.
Buson.   Along the roadside.
Cervantes.   Como lo Siento.
  Freeway 280.
Césaire, A.   Since Akkad, Since Elam, Since
  Sumer.
Chang Yang-hao.   T'ung Pass.
Chazal, M.   Bicycle rolls on the road, A.
Chesterton.   Rolling English Road, The.
Chitwood, Michael.   Hard Surface Road.
Curnow.   On the Road to Erewhon.
Dauenhauer, R.   Driving in a Snowstorm, King
  Salmon to Naknek.
Davies, Lynn.   In the Beginning.
Dickinson, E.   Little Road—not made of Man,
  A.
Dransfield.   Minstrel.
Drummond de Andrade.   In the Middle of the
  Road.
  In the Middle of the Road.
Fox, Skip.   I cannot observe myself unobserved.
Frost, R.   Road Not Taken, The.
García Lorca.   Little Infinite Poem.
Garcilaso de la Vega.   Rough Are the Roads.
Goodison.   Road of the Dread, The.
Gray, R.   Flames and Dangling Wire.
Greene, Jonathan.   Ruts.
Grin, B.   On Roads.
Grunberger, A.   Old Road, The.
Hamill, S.   After a Winter of Grieving.
Han-shan.   People ask about Cold Mountain
  Way.
Harburg.   We're Off to See the Wizard (The
  Wonderful Wizard of Oz).
Hardy, T.   Roman Road, The.
Healy, E.   Artemis in Echo Park.
  Moon on the Porch.
Herbert, W.   Slow Animals Crossing.
Huchel.   Roads.
Hughes, L.   Bound No'th Blues.
  Florida Road Workers.
Hugo, R.   Letter to Gale from Ovando.
Hwang Tonggyu.   When I See a Wheel.
Ishikawa Takuboku.   Tanka: "On the roadside."
Jacobsen, R.   Country Roads.
  Road's End.
Jamie, K.   Hill-track, The.
Johnson, D.   Road-Kill.
Johnson, J.   View Café, The.
Kavanagh, P.   Inniskeen Road: July Evening.
Kim Sowŏl.   Road, The.
King, H.   Moonlight Ride, A.
Kipling, R.   Way Through The Woods, The.
Kuhar, M.   All holyroadz home.
Larkin, P.   No Road.
Leggott, M.   Thoroughfares await them.
Leigh, C.   Rules of the Road, The.
Li Ho.   Country Road, A.
Li Po.   Leave-taking Near Shoku.
  Road to Shu Is Hard, The.
Lux.   Black Road Over Which Green Trees
  Grow.
Machado Ruiz.   I go on dreaming.
  On the Bare Roadway.
Marsman.   Polderland.
Mew.   On the Asylum Road.
Morgan, E.   Itinerary.

Nash, O.   Song of the Open Road.
Noyes, S.   Wolf's Road, The.
Perkins, S.   Common Road, The.
Pinsky.   Jersey Rain.
Po Chü-i.   Chancelor's Gravel-Drive, The.
Pugh.   What If This Road.
Reverdy.   Road.
Serote.   Long road, The.
Shin Kyŏngnim.   Road, The.
Slessor.   Last Trams.
Song.   Beauty and Sadness.
Spaziani.   Crossroads, The.
Tekeyan.   Forgetting.
Thomas, E.   Roads.
Tretheway.   Green Cadillac.
Wright, J.   Brother and Sisters.
See also **Streets**

Robbers
Darley.   Free-booter, The.
Hattersley, G.   Remembering Dennis's Eyes.
Jarman, M.   Unholy Sonnet ("This boy listening
    eagerly to his friend.").
Montgomery, Vaida Stewart.   Cattle Brands.
Rivard.   For Michaela.
Stock, N.   First Time I Robbed Tiffany's, The.
Turner, W.   Robber, The.
See also **Crime and Criminals**

Robert I [*or* Robert the Bruce], King of Scotland
Burns, R.   Scots Wha Hae.

Robeson, Paul
Alexander, E.   Robeson at Rutgers.
Johnston, P.   To paul robeson, opus no. 3.

Robespierre, Maximilien Marie Isidore
Scalapino.   Slaves' Outside Evening or Evening,
    Pal Mal Comic.

Robin Hood
Halsey, A.   His acre. His arbour.
    Saracen SAS or Assasseen called Nasir claims
    on HTV, A.
    32s. 6d. for the chattels of Robert Hod, fugitive,
    Michaelmas 1230 at York.
    Weakened by loss of blood Robin's last act was
    to slash his sword.
Peacock, T.   Robin Hood and the Grey Friars.
Unknown.   Jolly Pinder of Wakefield, The.
    Lythe and listin, gentilmen.
    Robin Hood and Allen [*or* Allin] -a-Dale.
    Robin Hood and the Monk.

Robins
Coccimiglio.   St. Francis Speaks to Me at a
    Young Age.
Daniel, G.   Robin, The.
Dickinson, E.   Come show thy Durham Breast.
Fagan.   Weather They Were Written In, The.
Karim, F.   Robin (The bird that was devoured by
    the cat in the garden of the house).
Khoury-Gata.   Autumn Preceded Summer.
Kunitz, S.   Robin Redbreast.
Lee, D.   You Too Lie down.
Melville, H.   Little Good Fellows, The.
Meynell, A.   October Redbreast, The.
Mother Goose.   Who Killed Cock Robin.
Rye.   Redbreast, The.
Salter.   Robin's Nest, A.
Scott, S.   Proud Maisie.
Webster, J.   Call for the Robin-Redbreast and
    the Wren.
Whittier.   Robin, The.
Woods, H.   When the Red, Red Robin Comes
    Bob, Bob, Bobbin' Along.
Yolen.   First Robin.

Robinson Crusoe
Bishop, E.   Crusoe in England.
Drummond de Andrade.   Infancy.
Jarrell, R.   Island, The.
Kafka.   Robinson Crusoe.
Krolow.   Robinson.
Oppen.   We are pressed, pressed on each other.
Walcott.   Crusoe's Island.

Robinson, Jackie
Miller, E.   Boys of Summer, The.

Robots
Christie, J.   Solvent.
Cistulli.   47.57.
Wallace-Crabbe.   Opener.

Rochester, John Wilmot, 2d Earl of
Behn, A.   On the Death of the Late Earl of
    Rochester.
Wharton, A.   Elegy on the Earl of Rochester.

Rock and Roll
Balakian, P.   Rock 'n Roll.
Berke.   Fifties Rock Party, 1985.
Coles, R.   New Jersey Boys.
DeFoe, M.   Forgetting the Sixties.
Eady.   Chuck Berry.
Elledge.   Duckling, Swan.
    Strangers: An Essay.
Gilbert, C.   Enclosure.
Goldbarth.   People Are Dropping Out of Our
    Lives.
Hirsch, E.   Days of 1968.
Keller, D.   Man Who Knew the Words to
    "Louie, Louie", The.
Lowery, Janet.   Texas Splendor.
Machan.   In 1969.
Mueller, L.   Deaf Dancing to Rock, The.
Murray, D.   Incomplete History of Rock Music
    in the Hebrides, An.
Nameroff, R.   Elvis Presley.
Pietri.   First Rock and Roll Song of 1970, The.
Rivard.   Cures.
Rosemurgy, C.   Mostly Mick Jagger.
Seay.   Johnny B. Goode.
Shirley, A.   Hours Musicians Keep, The.
Silliman.   When that april with his sure as soot
    the draft of March has pierced it to the root.
Skloot.   Everly Brothers, The.
    Year the Space Age Was Born, The.
Smith, B.   How Garnett Mims and the
    Enchanters Came into Your Life.
Stein, K.   First Performance of the Rock 'n Roll
    Band *Puce Exit.*
Stillpoint, H.   Form a Band, Goddammit.
Wallace, R.   Sound Systems.
Webb, C.   Ooh My Soul.
Woessner.   Jungle Music.
Wojahn.   Buddy Holly.
    Necromancy: The Last Days of Brian Jones,
    1968.
    Song of the Burning.
Wormser.   Fans.
Wrigley, R.   Prophecy, The.

Rockefeller Center, New York City
Cardenal.   Room 5600.
White, E.   I Paint What I See.

Rockets
Brathwaite, E.   New Year Letter.
Johnson, R.   Reverse Engineering.
Magee, W.   Giant Rocket.
Penoyer, Ron.   Countdown.
Probyn.   As the Flower of the Grass.
Shinkichi Takahashi.   Moon and Hare.
See also **Space and Space Travel**

Rocking Chairs
Carmichael, H.   Rockin' Chair.
Klein, A.   Rocking Chair, The.

Rocks
Abercrombie.   Stream's Song, The.
Bye.   Prescott Slur, The.
Cogswell, Fred.   Water and the Rock, The.
Dickey, J.   2: The Moon Ground.
Enzensberger, H.   Finnish Tango.
Field, E.   Open Sesame.
Kerouac.   Bath Tub Thought.
Lear, E.   Limerick: "There was an Old Man on
    some rocks."
Mitchell, S.   Orchid and Rock.
Ponge.   Slate.
Salkey.   Clearsightedness.
Tomlinson, C.   Above the Rio Grande.
See also **Stones and Rocks**

Rockwell, Norman
Baggott, J.   Mary Rockwell, 1950.

Rocky Mountains
Higginson, E.   Moonrise in the Rockies.
Vanek, Mary.   Homing Instinct.

Rodeos
Boswell, M.   Girls of the Rodeo.
Swenson, M.   Bronco Busting, Event #1.
Ward, Whitney.   Montana's Biggest Weekend.

Rodin, Auguste
Greer, J.   Rodin's "Gates of Hell".
Rilke.   Panther, The.
Stickney, T.   On Rodin's "L'Illusion, Sœur
    d'Icare".

Roethke, Theodore
Niatum.   Lines for Roethke Twenty Years after
    His Death.

Roland
MacLeish.   Too-Late Born, The.
Tsvetayeva [*or* Tsvetaeva].   Horn of Roland,
    The.
Unknown.   Charles the King, our Emperor, the
    great.
    In wrath and grief away the Paynims fly.
    Marsilion sees his people's martyrdom.
    Now Roland feels that he is at death's door.
    Oliver's climbed upon a hilly crest.
    Roncevalles.
    They arm themselves with Saracen hauberks.

Roller Skating and Roller Skaters
Livingston, M.   74th Street.

Roller-Coasters
Parra, N.   Roller Coaster.

Roman Empire
Appleman, P.   Peace with Honor.
Hofmann, M.   Lament for Crassus.
Housman.   On Wenlock Edge the wood's in
    trouble.
Hudgins.   In Alesia.
Moxley, Jennifer.   Easter Lesson, The.
Tsanev, Ivan.   Archaeological Site, An.

Romantic Love
Ada, Ahmet.   I Love You So.
Adams, F.   Us Poets.
Addison, J.   King Henry's Song.
Agali, A.   Sister: "House, A. A car. Sweet
    things. Gold."
Aiken, C.   At a Concert of Music.
Akhmatova, A.   In the Evening ("Music rang
    out in the garden, The.").
Al-Bayati, A.   Love Under the Rain.
    Shiraz Moon.
al-Sa'igh, Y.   Final Question, The.
Allingham, W.   Lovely Mary Donnelly.
Apparao, G.   Gold.
Auden.   Some say that love's a little boy.
Barot, R.   Reading Plato.
Baxter, J.   My Love Late Walking.
Beachy-Quick, Dan.   Unworn.
BehramoĞlu, Ataol.   All Over Again.
Belloc.   Love and Honour.
Bendall, M.   Book of Style, The.
Bleakney, J.   Summer love was ever thus.
Bousoño, C.   How Am I To Tell You.
Brautigan.   It's Raining in Love.
Broughton, T.   Shall I Compare Thee?
Browning, E.   Snoblesse Oblige.
Cankoçak, Gülten Akın.   Not the Fear of
    Shivering.
Comer, Carrie St. George.   Arbor.
Copus, J.   Love, Like Water.
Cott, J.   Natural Functions.
Craig, M.   Love Poem: "Flowers upon your lips
    and hands."
Cristall.   Before Twilight. Eyezion.
    Morning. Rosamonde.
Crumpacker, C.   Trans-Relational Love Poem.
Daglarca.   Beauty and Mind.
    Beyond: "Whenever I love a woman."
Dante Alighieri.   Great Canzon, The.
Donnelly, T.   New Intelligence, The.
Doolittle, H.   Antistrophe.
    Strophe.
Drayton.   Love, in a humour, played the
    prodigal.
    Owen Tudor to Queen Katherine.
    Queen Katherine to Owen Tudor.
Eady.   I'm a Fool to Love You.
Hull, E.   What Is Love?
Fagin, L.   Love: "Everything is out today."
Ferlinghetti, L.   #2.
Finch, R.   Egg-and-Dart.
France, L.   If Love Was Jazz.
Frumkin.   Surreal Love Life.

Galina, M. Ghazal: "For the sake of a Turkish woman from Shiraz, consumed in the deadly fumes."
Gilbert, J. Great Fires, The.
Gosse. Revelation.
Hafiz, K [or Hafez]. Night and Dawn.
Halman. Love Tomorrow.
Hartman, J. Baroque Excess of Pig Latin and.
Hikmet. Kneeling, I'm staring at the soil.
Hirshfield, J. Knowing Nothing.
Hoagland, T. Candlelight.
Hopes. Don't think the stars and moon are all.
Hsiao Kang. Spiders' Spun Threads.
Ipadeola, T. Companions.
Kanik. Did I Fall in Love?
Keith, Sally. Orphean Song.
Külebi, C. Lost Love: "She keeps singing a song."
Once Upon a Time: "Every morning you used to play hooky."
Lecky. Decline of Love, The.
Li Po. Her Presence Was a Roomful of Flowers.
Li Shang-yin. Walls of Emerald, The.
Logan, W. Song: "Her nose is like a satellite."
MacDermott, M. Girl of the Red Mouth.
MacGuigan, B. Contentment: "Why am I."
MacMuireadach. Farewell to Last Night.
Mark, Sabrina Orah. Mustache, The.
McFadden, D. 4. Love's Two Hemispheres.
McNally, L. Lass of Richmond Hill, The.
Merry. Tiff, The [or The Interview].
Meyer, B. Diet, The.
Meyer, K. Liadan and Curithir.
Michaels, A. Passionate World, The.
Millay, E. Sonnet: "Women have loved before as I love now."
Moore, T. Love Thee, Dearest? Love Thee?
Muske, C. Heroine.
Nasir, A. Moment of Love, A.
Newman, A. **Fall for.** *Informal.* 1. To become infatuated with; fall suddenly in love with. 2. To be tricked or deceived by; be taken in by.
Ni Ghallchóir, C. Escape.
Nurkse. Letter to Ko.
O'Brien, F. Soldier's Letter, A.
O'Grady, D. Love War, The.
Orban, O. Blade of Grass, A.
O'Siadhail. Welcome.
Page, P. Water and Marble.
P'an Yüeh. Homeward.
Paschen. Voir Dire.
Paterson, D. Poetry: "In the same way that the mindless diamond keeps."
Piercy. On Guard.
Pietri, P. January Hangover.
Pope, D. Getting Through.
Quasimodo. Only if Love Should Pierce You.
Raab, L. Revised Versions, The.
Reece, Spencer. Autumn Song.
Rumi. Love is the water of eternal life, cures every woe.
Saba, Z. Love Poem: "When you think of me."
Sait Faik. Now's the Time for Love.
Salkeld. That Corner.
Sanchez, S. Ballad: "Forgive me if i laugh."
Sastri, D. Palanquin, The.
Savitz, M. Sweetness.
Schevill. Love Song in Summer's Furnace Heat.
Serrano, P. Flying.
Vuelo.
Şeyh Galib. My darling with the rosy face—at one glance.
Sheridan, R. Thou Canst Not Boast of Fortune's Store.
Siken, Richard. Saying Your Names.
Sılay, C. You Will Come to Me.
Sissle, N. I'm Just Wild About Harry.
Smith, S. Like This (2).
Spahr, J. Localism or t/here.
Synge. Wish, A: "May one sorrow every day."
Szporluk. Elsewhere.
Terán, V. Duda.
Indecision.
Lu ti nagana.
Seis variaciones acerca del amor.
Six Variations on Love.

Xhoopa' diidxa' rui' xiinga guendaranaxhii.
Thomas, L. Argent, L'.
Tolson, N. Bullet Hole Man.
Townsend, A. Modern Love.
Tu Mu. Old Love.
Udeozo, O. Tomato.
Unamuno. Beside Christ's Lake in Aldehuela de Yeltes, on a Night with a Full Moon.
Unknown. Come, oh love's great sorrow!
If you did not know how to love.
My beloved, I have nothing to offer you.
My heart said this to me: "I have no role to play".
My love, capture me, embrace me!
My soul yearns for you.
Other girls are starting with new loves, The.
People tell me.
Put your mouth on mine.
What Is the Matter With Me?
Untermeyer, L. Victor, The.
Volkman. Well, You Needn't.
Volková, B. I am not an Amazon—a warrior.
Winter, M. Ascent, The.
That Is the Way.
Yi Yônju. Clinic in a Dangerous Season 1, A.

Romanticism and Romantics
Bryan, J. I've Looked Everywhere.
Clark, P. Zoo.
Cope, W. Triolet.
Dermée. Coffee grinder.
Fox, Skip. Sic transit gloria mundi.
Gifford, W. Lo, Della Crusca! In his closet pent.
Keelan, C. Romanticism.
Mueller, L. Romantics: Johannes Brahms and Clara Schumann.
Muir, E. Scotland 1941.
North, C. Dawn, The: "TO BE / Immortal."
Pastan. Bess.
Robinson, E. Miniver Cheevy.
Short, Spencer. Romanticism.
Stevenson, R. Song of a Traveller, The.

Rome, Italy
Auden. Roman Wall Blues.
Bell, M. True Story, A.
Belli, G. Bosses of Rome, The.
Boethius. Lib. 2. Metrum 5.
Brodsky, J. Roman Elegies.
Browning, R. Two in the Campagna.
Calpurnius Siculus. Eclogue 7.
Casson, C. To the South: "Journey to Italy began in your youth, The."
Cavafy. Waiting for the Barbarians.
Waiting for the Barbarians.
Cawein. Rome.
DiPalma. Hadrian's Lane.
Du Bellay. Antiquitez de Rome.
Rome.
Rome.
Dyer, J. Ruins of Rome, The.
Garlick, R. Capitals.
Herbert, Z. Return of the Proconsul, The.
To Marcus Aurelius.
Holland, J. Laocöon! thou great embodiment.
Italicus. Furiously along the banks stormed Hannibal.
Jonson, B. To Sir Henry Savile [upon His Translation of Tacitus].
Juvenal. Northward beyond the Lapps to the world's end, the frozen.
Kaufman, B. Solitary thoughts on death and other illegal mysteries carried off.
Kipling, R. Pict Song, A.
Song to Mithras, A.
Koch, K. To the Roman Forum.
Kunitz, S. Thief, The.
Kuzmin. Antinous.
Leigh, C. When in Rome (I Do As the Romans Do).
Levis. Those Graves in Rome.
Mandelstam [or Mandelshtam]. Like Grumbling Roman Plebs.
Valley Bleeds with Roman Rust, The.
Martial. Ad Quintilianum.
Bearded Callistratus wedded rugged Afer.

Marvell. Flecknoe, an English Priest at Rome.
Masefield. Night on the Downland.
McClatchy. Capriccio of Roman Ruins and Sculpture with Figures, A.
Melinno. Hail, Roma, daughter of Ares.
Melville, H. Arch, The.
Mengham, Rod. Another Name for the Cassiterides.
Milton. Rome.
"Panormitanus.". Rome.
Pasolini. Roman Evening.
Persius. Satire 1: "Who's going to read that?"
Philips, K. On the Welsh Language.
Pound, E. Shades of Callimachus, Coan ghosts of Philetas.
Prufer, K. Rise of Rome, The.
Quevedo y Villegas. To Rome Entombed in Her Ruins.
Redhill, M. Haiku Monument for Washington, D.C.
St. John, D. Last Night with Rafaella.
Lucifer in Starlight.
Sisson. Carmen Saeculare.
Spenser, E. Ruines of Time, The.
Who lists to see, what ever nature, arte.
Statius. Thanksgiving to the Emperor Augustus Germanicus Domitianus.
Stevens, W. To an Old Philosopher in Rome.
Tomlinson, C. In the Borghese Gardens.
Virgil [or Vergil]. Arms, and the Man I sing, who, forc'd by Fate.
Prologue.
Who dares deny the burning truth of the sun?
Wilbur, R. Baroque Wall-Fountain in the Villa Sciarra, A.
Piazza di Spagna, Early Morning.

Romeo and Juliet
Garza, D. Act One.
Hall, H. Palmer. Romeo Is Dead.
Hart, L. This Can't Be Love.
Khalvati. Persian Miniature, A.
Lockward, D. On First Reading *Romeo and Juliet.*
Runyan, Tania. Teaching Shakespeare.
Santos, S. Romeo and Juliet.
Spacks. Film Version, The.

Roofing and Roofers
Bye. Blessing.
Dunn, D. On Roofs of Terry Street.
Grennan. Men Roofing.
Kimbrell, J. Rooftop.
Levchev. Rooftops.
Press, K. Man with incomplete words on his roof, The.
Rumi. Edge of the Roof, The.
Tu Fu [or Du Fu]. My Thatched Roof Is Ruined by the Autumn Wind.
Williams, C. K. Tar.
Williams, W. Fine Work with Pitch and Copper.
Zepeda, R. Philosophical Emancipation, The.

Rooks
Field. Nests in Elms.
Hodgson, R. Late, Last Rook, The.
Moritz [or Morits]. Crow.
Plath. Black Rook in Rainy Weather.
Rimbaud, A. Rooks, The.
Sosnora. Crow.

Roosevelt, Franklin Delano
Hollander, J. Danish Wit.
Rome, H. F.D.R. Jones.

Roosevelt, Theodore
Darío, R. To Roosevelt.
Espada. Bully.
Hall, D. T. R.
Lindsay, V. In Which Roosevelt Is Compared to Saul.

Roosters
Anyte [or Anytes]. No longer, as before, plying with whirring wings.
Bishop, E. Roosters.
Cabral de Melo Neto. Tecendo a manhã.
Weaving the Morning.
Chaucer. Nun's Priest's [or Nonne Preestes] Tale, The.
Garrett, E. Grandfather's Mint.

Ibn Billita. Rooster, The.
Kushner, A. Rooster, The.
Liu Cheng. Cockfight.
Matveyeva [*or* Matveieva]. Eggplants Have Pins and Needles, The.
Ogiwara Seisensui. Morning with a baby crying with all its might.
Polkowski. I Don't Know That Man.
Rossetti, C. "Kookoorookoo! kookoorookoo!" / Crows the cock before the morn.
Sedley. On a Cock at Rochester.
Smith, S. Cock-a-Doo.
Ssu-ma Hsiang-ju. Cock-Phoenix, Hen-Phoenix.
Stevens, W. Bantams in Pine-Woods.
Tate, J. Rooster.
Unknown. I Have a Gentle Cock [*or* Gentil Cok].
   Of flying birds and beasts that craw.
   Oh damned rooster, I would like to strangle you!
   Rooster is already announcing dawn, The.
Yang Shih-ch'i. On the Hall of Precious Virtue.
Yi Chehyŏn. I carve a small rooster from wood.
See also **Chickens**

Rope
Bryce, Colette. Full Indian Rope Trick, The.
Clifton, L. Climbing.
Kennedy, X. Little Elegy.
Komunyakaa, Y. How I See Things.
Longfellow, H. Ropewalk, The.

Rosary
Basho. Buddha's death-day / Old hands.
Cofer, J. Counting.
Corcadail, A. I. O rosary that recalled my tear.

Rosenberg, Julius and Ethel
Faiz. We Who Were Executed.
Rich, A. For Ethel Rosenberg.
Rosen, Ellen A. Out in the Cold.
Schiff, Robyn. Chanel Nº 5.
Werner, Judith. Ethel Rosenberg and Me.

Roses
Al-Qasim. General's Property, The.
Apollinaire. Fete.
Aygi, G. Rose of Silence.
Bachmann. In the Storm of Roses.
Bass, F. Garden, The.
Behn, R. On Giving My Father a Book About Roses.
Betham-Edwards. To a Llangollen Rose, the Day after It Had Been Given by Miss Ponsonby.
Bible, *O.T.* I Am the Rose of Sharon.
Biespiel, D. White Roses.
Bishop, E. Vague Poem.
Blake, W. My Pretty Rose-Tree.
   Sick Rose, The.
Blunden. One among the Roses.
Brontë, E. Love and Friendship.
Broome. Rose-Bud, The.
Browning, R. Women and Roses.
Burns, R. Banks o' Doon, The ("Ye banks and braes o' bonie [*or* bonnie] Doon.").
   Banks o' Doon, The ("Ye flowery banks o' bon[n]ie Doon.").
   Red, Red Rose, A.
Campbell, C. When midst the summer-roses the warm bees.
Castro, R. I in My Bed of Thistles.
Celan. Psalm: "No one kneads us again out of earth and clay."
Cherry, K. Rose, The.
Chippewa Oral Tradition. Love-Charm Song.
Clare, J. Love's Emblem.
Coleridge, M. Gifts.
Cooke, R. Che Sara Sara.
Cortázar. Therapies.
Desnos. If, like winds.
Dickinson, E. Essential oils—are wrung.
   Go not too near a House of Rose.
Doolittle, H. Garden.
   Sea Rose.
Doty, M. 2. Beach Roses.
Drown, D. Rose by the Wayside, The.
Dunbar, P. Summer in the South.
Eliot, T. S. Little Gidding.

Ferguson, G. Silent as Roses.
   Winter Rose, The.
Field. Goad, The.
   Sweet-Briar in Rose.
   Your Rose is Dead.
Fortini. Poetry of Roses, The.
Frost, R. Rose Family, The.
Fuertes. Love Turns You into a Rosebush.
García Lorca. Casida of the Rose.
Godfrey. Show Me a Rose.
Goethe. Rosebud in the Heather.
Grimké, A. Rosabel.
Guest, B. Roses.
Habington. To Roses in the Bosom[e] of Castara.
Herman, J. I Won't Send Roses.
Herrick. Funeral[l] Rites of the Rose, The.
   How Roses Came Red ("Roses at first were white.").
   How Roses Came Red ("'Tis said, as Cupid danced [*or* danc't] among.").
   Meditation for His Mistress[e], A.
Hodgson, R. Mystery, The.
Ignatova, E. Then there was the rose I fell in love with.
Issa. Faint yellow rose, A.
Keats. To a Friend Who Sent Me Some Roses.
Keller, G. Now Have I Fed and Eaten Up the Rose.
Kemble. Parting.
Kim Sŭnghŭi. Roses and Thorns.
LaFemina. Her Rose Tattoo.
Lawrence, D. H. Gloire de Dijon.
Lehmann, G. Roses.
Levertov. Gypsy's Window, The.
MacDiarmid, H. Little White Rose, The.
Maclaren. Island Rose.
McElroy, C. To Welcome a Changeling.
Meinke. Sonnet on the Death of the Man Who Invented Plastic Roses.
Melville, H. Rosary Beads.
   Rose Farmer, The.
Mistral, G. Rose, The.
   Rose, The.
Montague, J. Wild Dog Rose, The.
Motsapi, S. Roses for the folks we know, A.
Naden. Pantheist's Song of Immortality, The.
Nedîm. Take Yourself to the Rose-Garden.
Nervo. Revenge.
North, C. Little Cape Cod Landscape.
Okamoto. Tanka: "As I gaze upon."
O'Reilly, J. White Rose, A.
Parker, D. One Perfect Rose.
Peabody, J. Far-Off Rose, A.
Pessoa. I the roses love in the gardens of Adonis.
Probyn. Kyrielle.
Quevedo y Villegas. Rosebush, Less Presumption.
Roethke. Rose, The.
Ronsard. Corinna In Vendome.
   Roses.
Rossetti, C. Summer Is Ended.
Scovell. Space Between, The.
Seferis. Mathios Paskalis among the Roses.
Shats, E. Rose, A / a / shameless.
Skelton, J. Laud and Praise Made For Our Sovereign Lord the King.
Sodo. Late spring / Paling rose.
Sondheim. Everything's Coming Up Roses.
Stern, G. Roses: "There was a rose called Guy de Maupassant."
Swenson, M. Couple, A.
Tada. Universe of the Rose.
Tkhorzhevskaya, V. Wild Rose.
Unknown. All Night by the Rose.
   Lo, How a Rose E'er Blooming.
   Of a Rose, a Lovely Rose.
   Of a rose, a lovely rose.
Very. Wild Rose of Plymouth, The.
Vilariño. What Was Life.
Villaurrutia. Rose Nocturnal.
Waller, E. Budd, The.
   Song: "Go[e], lovely rose."
Whur. Morning arose, and its beauties were beaming, The.

Wilbur, R. Beautiful Changes, The.
Williams, S. Youth and Maidenhood.
Williams, W. Act, The.
   Poem: "Rose fades, The."
   Rose, The ("Rose is obsolete, The.").
   To Flossie.
Wood, S. Four Roses.
Wright, C. Until words turn to moss.
Yeats. Secret Rose, The.
   To the Rose upon the Rood of Time.
Young, D. Only One of My Deaths.

Rosh Hashanah
Abrahams, L. Spring report.
Pinchas-Cohen. Remembering Our Fathers.
Shabtai, Aharon. Rosh HaShanah.

Rossetti, Christina Georgina
Alvi, M. Country at My Shoulder, The.

Rossetti, Dante Gabriel
Carper, Thomas. Oh Keep the Poet Hence.
Nichol. Little song, A.

Rothko, Mark
Cross, D. Rothko.
Muirhead, Eric. Reflection on the Paintings of Mark Rothko's Chapel, A.

Rousseau, Henri
Ondaatje. Henri Rousseau and Friends.

Rousseau, Jean Jacques
Abish, Walter. What Else (*Part 2*).
Blake, W. Mock On, Mock On, Voltaire, Rousseau.
Harryman. Magic (or Rousseau).
Reid, C. Whole School of Bourgeois Primitives, A.

Rowing and Rowers
Acorn. Squall, The.
Chen Zi'ang. Entering Quiao Gorge and Anju Creek.
Eberhart, R. Loon Call, A.
Faverey. Bit by Bit.
Homer. Now all day long until the sun went down.
ibn Hariq, A. Galley Oars.
Jamie, K. Crossing the Loch.
Jerome, W. Row, Row, Row.
Leslie, K. Sonnet: "Silver herring throbbed thick in my seine, The."
MacDonald, A. Incitement for Rowing to Sailing-place.
Mansei, S. Our Life in This World.
Strand. Morning, A.
Valéry. Oarsman, The.
Wenderoth, J. Detailed History of the Western World.

Royal Society
Cowley, A. To the Royal Society: "Philosophy the great and only Heir."

Royalty
Ap Hywel, Elin. History.
Belloc. Imitation.
Bradstreet, A. Here sleeps the Queen, this is the royall bed.
Cibber. Let there be light!
Coleridge, H. To a Lofty Beauty, from Her Poor Kinsman.
Crowley, A. Dedicace.
Daniel, G. Landscape, The.
De' Medici. (To the Virgin).
Denham. Cooper's Hill.
Dickinson, E. Mine—by the Right of the White Election!
Drayton. Owen Tudor to Queen Katherine.
Dryden, J. Crown Prince of Dullness, The.
Graves, R. Henry and Mary.
Greville. For as the harmony which sense admires.
Guiterman. Routine.
Hamilton, S. Farewell to France.
Heaney, S. First Kingdom, The.
Holloway, G. Ford Castle: The Borders.
Howells, W. Royal Portraits, The.
Hsi-chün. Lost Horizon.
Jacob, M. Spanish Generosity.
Kao Shih. Ruined Terrace, The.
Kikaku. In the Emperor's bed.
Kitasono Katsue. Vin du Masque.

Landor, W.   Georges, The.
Rose Aylmer.
Li Po.   Intoxication of Love.
Sy-che and the King.
Lomax, M.   Gruoch.
Marlowe.   My father is deceas'd. Come,
Gaveston.
Marquis.   Archy Interviews a Pharoah.
Montague, J.   Deer Park.
Pao Chao.   Magic Cinnabar.
Po Chü-i.   Iranian Whirling Girls.
Song of Lasting Regret, The.
Rimbaud, A.   Royalty.
Robertson, J.   Royalty.
Russell, G.   Tragedy.
Smith, S.   Lord Barrenstock.
Ssu-ma Hsiang-ju.   Sir Fantasy.
Sung Yu.   Wind, The.
T'ao Hung Ching.   Poem Written in Answer to
His Majesty's Question: "What Is There in the
Mountains?".
Terranova.   Needlework.
Thackeray.   King of Brentford's Testament, The
[abr.].
Unknown.   Praise Song for the Oba of Benin.
Song of the Viet Boatman.
Wilner, E.   Epitaph: "Young then, / we were
bored already."
Yüan Chěn.   Iranian Whirling Girls.
See also Kings; Princes and Princesses; Queens
Rubens, Peter Paul
Allston.   Rubens.
Monroe, H.   Rubens.
Szymborska, W.   Women of Rubens, The.
Rugs and Carpets
Cavalli.   Moroccans with the carpets, The.
Guevara, M.   Magic Carpet, The.
Longley, M.   Amish Rug, An.
Ruins
Adams, S.   Hill Fort, Caerleon.
Alberti.   Angels of the Ruins, The.
Homecoming of Love Amongst Illustrious
Ruins.
Aragon.   Poem to Shout in the Ruins.
Aridjis.   Self-Portrait in the Doorway.
Balaban.   Poetry Reading at the Varna Ruins.
Baraka, I.   A, B, C's, The.
Basho.   This ruined temple.
Berryman.   Dream Song 45.
Binyon.   House That Was, The.
Brodsky, J.   Elegy: "About a year has passed.
I've returned to the place of battle."
Bromige.   Edible World, The.
Brooks, C.   Lines: Composed at the Old
Temples of Maralipoor.
Browning, R.   Love among the Ruins.
Bruce, C.   Orchard in the Woods.
Carson, C.   Clerance.
Cavafy.   City, The.
Coleridge, S.   On a Ruined House in a Romantic
Country.
Cummings, E. E.   Ponder, darling, these busted
statues.
Dafydd [or David] ap Gwilym.   Ruin, The.
Davies, I.   Gwalia Deserta XXII.
Deguy.   When the wind.
DiPalma.   Hadrian's Lane.
Dove, R.   Sightseeing.
Drummond, W.   Content and Resolute.
Du Bellay.   Rome.
Éluard, P.   November 1936.
Evance, S.   Written in a Ruinous Abbey.
Forrester, S.   Temple ruin.
Garrett, G.   Crows at Paestum.
Góngora y Argote.   Ruins of Time, The.
Gorenko, A.   There the folk museum alone lies
in its embers.
Gregg.   Lamb, The.
Groarke, V.   Way It Goes, The.
Han-shan.   Wrecked Town, The.
Hantoosh, G.   Celebration.
Herlin.   Echo of fireplace, An.
Hinsey, E.   Roman Arbor, The.
Hood, T.   Silence.
Hope, A.   Beware of Ruins.
Howells, W.   Empty House, The.

Hsi Chou.   Broken Tablets.
Huchel.   Rome.
Izumi.   Although the wind.
Kanchev, Nikolai.   Feeling.
Kao Shih.   Ruined Terrace, The.
Koch, K.   To the Roman Forum.
Kuan Hsiu.   Song of the Palace of Ch'en.
Landon.   Fountain's Abbey.
Levertov.   Fragrance of Life, Odor of Death.
Li Yü [or Li Hou-Chu].   One Dream.
Long, H.   New Music, A.
Lu Yu.   Mural, Ch'ien-ming Temple.
McClatchy.   Capriccio of Roman Ruins and
Sculpture with Figures, A.
Pleasure of Ruins, The.
McKay, D.   3. The Base.
Melville, H.   Ravaged Villa, The.
Michaux.   My Statues.
Neruda.   Stone upon stone, and man, where was
he?
Then up the ladder of the earth I climbed.
Ojaide.   Verdict of Stone, A.
Pao Chao.   Desolate City, The: A Rhapsody.
Ruined City, The.
Pape.   Indian Ruins Along Rio de Flag.
Paz.   Hymn Among the Ruins.
Purdy, A.   Remains of an Indian Village.
Quasimodo.   Anno Domini MCMXLVII.
Quevedo y Villegas.   I Gaze Upon My
Country's Walls.
To Rome Entombed in Her Ruins.
Robinson, E.   House on the Hill, The.
St. John, D.   Black Poppy (At the Temple).
Samaras, N.   Farasa.
Scott, S.   Melrose Abbey.
Shelley, P.   Ozymandias.
Smith, H.   Ozymandias.
Spenser, E.   Who lists to see, what ever nature,
arte.
Taylor, H.   Hughesville Scythe, The.
Tennyson, A.   So sang the gallant glorious
chronicle.
Thomas, E.   Tale, A [Revised Version].
Tu Fu [or Du Fu].   Jade Flower Palace ("Stream
swirls, The. The wind moans in.").
Jade Flower Palace ("Where the stream winds
pine winds linger.").
Tu Mu.   Spring South of the River.
Unknown.   At Fifteen I Joined the Army.
Last Oracle from Delphi.
Ruin, The.
Ruin, The.
Vaughan, H.   They Are All Gone into the World
of Light!
Voigt.   House.
Walcott.   Ruins of a Great House.
Warren, R.   Well House, The.
Waterhouse, A.   Now the City Has Fallen.
Webb, H.   Abbey Cwmhir.
Wen T'ing-yün.   Passing a Ruined Palace.
Weston, M.   Primitive Place.
Wheatley, D.   Along a Cliff.
Rukeyser, Muriel
Cooper, J.   Hotel de Dream.
Marshall-Stoneking.   On the Death of Muriel
Rukeyser.
Rich, A.   Catch if you can your country's
moment, begin.
Rum
Hernández Cruz.   Perlas.
Masefield.   Captain Stratton's Fancy.
Unknown.   Convicts' Rum Song.
Rumor
Berlin.   They Say It's Wonderful.
De Tabley.   Sonnet: "Record is nothing, and the
hero great."
Hume, C.   Explanation.
Issa.   Cries of wild geese.
Kasa.   As one hears the cry.
Lady Ise.   Pillows know, they say.
Leon, R.   Have you not heard the gossip and the
rumour going around.
Otomo no Sakanoé.   Though in my heart.
Sevelingen, Meinloh von.   Woe Then to the
Gossips.
Unknown.   Just because of you.

Qing-ying: Buzz Buzz, the Blue Flies.
Wright, C.   Virginia Reel.
Wright, K.   My Version.
See also Fame; Gossip and Gossips; Reputation
Running and Runners
Bell, M.   Slow.
What They Do to You in Distant Places.
Cameron, N.   Unfinished Race, The.
Carpenter, W.   Ghosts.
Cyril.   Jump Black Honey Jump Black.
Galvin, B.   Running.
Grimké, A.   Black Runner, The.
Grossman, A.   Runner, The.
Housman.   To an Athlete Dying Young.
Kelly, R.   Life of Intimate Fleeing, A.
Levin, D.   Field.
MacCaig.   Ringed Plover by a Water's Edge.
Mann, R.   Elegy for the Hurdler.
Nicarchus of Alexandria.   Mighty Runner, A.
Piercy.   Morning Athletes.
Pulido, A.   Meanwhile / a young man.
Mientras / un hombre joven.
Rayburn, Mary Kathleen.   Hurdler Explains Her
Reasons, A.
Roach.   At Guaracara Park.
Seyburn, P.   Good Water.
Sorescu, M.   Start.
Sorley.   Song of the Ungirt Runners, The.
Spenser, E.   Sonnet 80.
Stafford, W.   Run before Dawn.
Welch, J.   Harlem, Montana.
Whitman, W.   Runner, The.
Wilbur, R.   Running.
Williams, W.   Moon, the dried weeds, The.
Young, P.   Three Point Five Nine.
Ruskin, John
Mitchell, E.   Thoughts After Ruskin.
Randall, D.   Blue Dome, The.
Haymakers.
His Favourite Seat.
Russell, Lucy, Countess of Bedford
Jonson, B.   On Lucy, Countess of Bedford.
To Lucy, Countess of Bedford, with Mr.
Donne's Satires.
Russia
Akhmadulina.   Lines Written During a Sleepless
Night in Tbilisi.
Akhmatova, A.   Introduction.
Northern Elegies.
Our Own Land.
When in the throes of suicide.
Barkova, A.   Tatar Anguish.
Barlow, J.   Advice to a Raven in Russia
[December, 1812].
Berberova.   To Shakespeare.
Berryman.   Soviet Union, The.
Blok.   Kite, The.
On the Plain of Kulikovo.
Bolton, J.   Fin de Siècle.
Brodsky, J.   In my declining years, in a land
beyond the ocean.
To Urania.
Will a mouth that's muttered its goodbyes.
Bunina.   Though poverty's no stain.
Cendrars.   Back then I was still young.
Dengina, S.   Russia.
Dragomoschenko.   March Elegy.
Ehrenburg [or Erenburg].   Our Grandsons Will
Be Astonished.
Fraser, G.   Rostov.
Gandlevsky, S.   Dear God, allow me to recall
my works.
Is it time to change the record? But I'm
dreaming again.
Oh, how the lilacs are this May! Bulging-large
bunches fell.
There's our street, let's say.
Gorbanevskaya.   Hurry, take pleasure in the
oblique caress of rain while the sun shines.
Greenlaw, L.   World Where News Travelled
Slowly, A.
Hejinian.   No form at all—it's impossible to
imagine its being.
Herbert, W.   Three Year Ode, A.
Hugo, V.   It was snowing. For the first time,

conquered.
Ignatow, D. 1905.
Ivanov, G. Not so long ago, the world was complete.
Kharms. Symphony No. 2.
Khlebnikov, V. Lonely Masquerader.
Me and Russia.
Russia, I give you my divine.
To Everyone.
Khodasevich. Monument, A.
Khomin, I. Dike, a flower bed, a bare linden tree, A.
Klyuyev [or Kliuev or Klyuev]. Conversational Melody, a Good Verse, A.
Fourth Rome, The.
Mother Sabbath.
Krivulin. Idea of Russia, The.
Southwest.
Kublanovsky [or Kublanovskii]. Armor of the Petrograd oak is rusty, but, The.
In Memory of John Keats.
Kushner, A. Memoirs.
Kuzmin, D. Our hairdresser friend.
Kuzmina-Karavayeva. Ruth.
Larbaud. Images.
Lermontov. Borodino.
Limonov. It is good in May, in marvelous wet May, to be the chairman of the All-Russian Extraordinary Committee in the city of Odessa.
López Mills, T. And Never Did.
Y nunca quise.
Loseff [or Losev]. Conversation with a New York Poet.
I know—the Mongol yoke, the years of famine.
Petrograd Side, The.
Mak. Farewell to Russia.
Mandelstam [or Mandelshtam]. I Was Washing Outside in the Darkness.
Leningrad.
Leningrad.
Stalin Epigram, The.
Mayakovsky [or Maiakovskii]. Last Statement.
Merkureva, V. Grandmother of Russian Poetry: A Self-Portrait, The.
Moritz [or Morits]. Between Scylla and Charybdis.
Morozov, S. Poem about the Blue Horse.
Narovchatov. In Those Years.
Nikolayeva [or Nikolaeva]. Daughter.
Here, everything gets eaten: drippings, marinade.
Party on Women's Day, A.
Seven Beginnings.
Olds, S. Photograph of the Girl.
Ostriker. Eighth and the Thirteenth, The.
Pasternak, B. Fresco Come to Life.
Pinsky. Countries and Explanations.
Pushkin, A. Ode on the Hills of Georgia.
Ratushinskaya [or Ratushinskaia]. For the cry from the well of "mama!".
Like Mandelstam's swallow.
Reed, I. El Paso Monologue.
Rein. Return, The.
Salter. Chernobyl.
Seaton, M. Wings.
Shelvakh, A. Veterans.
Shwarts [or Shvarts]. Sale of a Historian's Library.
Tkachenko. Dynamo Stadium, 1980.
Tkhorzhevskaya, V. Wild Rose.
Tsvetayeva [or Tsvetaeva]. In my melodious city cupolas burn.
Turberville. To Spencer.
Turgeniev, I. Sphinx, The.
Uflyand [or Ufliand]. Peasant, The.
Unknown. And in the mountains of Kiev, Sviatoslav.
Harry Pollit Was a Bolshie.
Urusova, E. O Muses! I beseech you, fire my heart with song.
Utkin. Tale of Red-Haired Motele, Mister Inspector, Rabbi Isaiah and Commissar Blokh, The.
Vegin, P. "Moscow" Pool.
Voloshin. Holy Russia.
Voznesensky [or Voznesenskii]. Chorus of

Nymphs, A.
Vyazemsky, P. Russian God, The.
Wheelwright. Anathema. Maranatha!
Yeryomin. Faceted grains of wisdom.
Yesenin [or Essenin]. Field Upon Field Upon Field.
Yevtushenko [or Evtushenko]. Babii Yar.
Fear (Extracts).
Hundred miles from the capital city of hope, A.
Zukofsky, L. Fifth Movement: Autobiography.

Russian Revolution
Cendrars. Prose of the Trans-Siberian and of Little Jeanne of France, The.
Ehrenburg [or Erenburg]. Our Grandsons Will Be Astonished.
Fried, Michael. Next Bend in the Road, The.
Gumilyov [or Gumiliov or Gumilev]. Worker, The ("Grizzly squab comrade, A.").
Kharms. Symphony No. 2.
Khlebnikov, V. Burning Field, The.
Limonov. For whisper and orchestra.
Manifold. Makhno's Philosophers.
Mayakovsky [or Maiakovskii]. My most respected / comrades of posterity!
Nartsissov, B. Marated Bastilled age, A.
Selvinsky [or Sel'vinskii]. I Saw It!
Serge. Dialectic.
Uflyand [or Ufliand]. Now, at last, even Nikifor's a suitor.

Russians, The
Akhmatova, A. Our Own Land.
Bly, R. Russian, The.
Ch'en Meng-chia. Old White Russian, An.
Gershwin, I. Tchaikowsky (And Other Russians).
Hunt, G. Dogs of war are loose and the rugged russian bear, The.
Ivanova, O. To Russian Women.
Kabysh, I. Making Jam in July.
Khlebnikov, V. Me and Russia.
Lodeizen. Its Pliancy.
Loseff [or Losev]. I know—the Mongol yoke, the years of famine.
Malanova, M. Morning: "Main thing is not to oversleep, so as later not to have to run for dear life, The."
Pinsky. Countries and Explanations.
Pushkin, A. Tale of St. Petersburg, A.
Ratushinskaya [or Ratushinskaia]. Thus you lived your life without regret.
Unger, B. Observance.
Yeryomin. Polyhedral kernels of wisdom.

Ruth (Bible)
Hood, T. Ruth.
Hugo, V. Boaz Asleep.
Kamenszain. Return 2.

Ruth, George Herman ("Babe")
Kelly, Timothy. Babe Ruth Pointing.

Rwanda
Ai. Rwanda.
Burleson, D. Democracy.
Love, M. Trying to Sleep After Studying Color Photos of Goma.

S

Sabbath
Aminado. Our Sunday Rest.
Dickinson, E. Some keep the Sabbath going to Church.
Ettinger, E. Excerpts from the Sabbath Dream Book.
Herrick. Sabbaths.
Klyuyev [or Kliuev or Klyuev]. Mother Sabbath.
MacNeice. Sunday Morning: "Down the road someone is practising scales."
Mangan, G. Kirkintilloch Revisited.
Unknown. Sabbath Has No End.
Vaughan, H. Son-Days [dayes].
See also **Sunday**

Sacco-Vanzetti Case
Grin, B. Sacco and Vanzetti.
Millay, E. Justice Denied in Massachusetts.

Rexroth, K. August 22, 1939.

Sachs, Nelly
Celan. Zurich, at the Stork.

Sacrifice
Ai. I Have Got to Stop Loving You. So I Have Killed My Black Goat.
Alcman. But often on the mountain peaks when.
Alon, E. Always in Anguish.
Angelou, M. Many and More.
Bedient, C. When the Gods Put on Meter.
ben Yoseph, R. On the Readiness for Sacrifice.
Bremer, C. Festival of Izcalli or Eighteenth Month.
Fiesta de izcalli o décimo octavo mes.
Bunina. Though poverty's no stain.
Byron, G. Jephtha's Daughter.
Ch'en Lin. Horses at a Breach in the Great Wall.
Chin. Turtle Soup.
Ching An. Laughing at Myself 2.
Chipasula. Those Rainy Mornings.
Coleridge, S. To Nature.
Colman, H. On the Inscription Over the Head of Christ on the Cross.
Davenport, R. Sacrifice, A.
de Portalatin. Second Elegy.
Eldan, A. When You Grow Up.
Emerson, R. Give All to Love.
To Rhea.
Ephraim ben Jacob. Sacrifice of Isaac, The.
Everson, W. Passion Week.
Gogarty. Marcus Curtius.
Hefer, H. Young Dead Soldiers, The.
Herrick. Ass[e], The.
Good Friday: Rex Tragicus, or, Christ Going to His Cross[e].
Hymne to Love, An.
Hill, B. Glory of Love, The.
Homer. And then went down to the ship.
Ulysses Invokes the Dead.
Hope, M. Sacrifice.
Horace. Poem for Artemis (3.22).
Housman. If it chance your eye offend you.
Hudgins. Gift, The: "They hung the lambs and cut their white throats. Blood."
Hughes, F. In the Shadow of Fire.
Hughes, T. God, A.
Jeffers, R. But I Am Growing Old and Indolent.
Kipling, R. Convoy Escort.
Knott. Feeding the Sun.
Kolmar. Sacrifice, The.
Kremer. Choice, Inanna and the Galla.
Lorde. 125th Street and Abomey.
Marinho, T. Ear of a Goat, The.
Masters, E. Constance Hately.
Mathews, A. Caedmon.
Mathews, H. Invitation to a Sabbath.
McGrath, T. Offering.
Mendelssohn Anna. Wrong Room, The.
Mphande. Why the Old Woman Limps.
Myles, E. Merk.
Nisâyî. We are the Mejnûn of our age, we dwell in the wilderness.
Noll. Abraham's Madness.
Owen, W. To Eros.
Parra, N. Who are my friends / the sick / the weak / the poor in spirit.
Pollarolo, G. At Breakfast.
Rein. Secret Agent, A.
Roberson, E. Ideas Gray Suits Bowler Hats Baal.
Rontsh, Y. Rosa Luxemburg.
Shakhova. Autobiographical Response from a Provincial Wasteland (in Reply to a New Year's Greeting Sent with a Bouquet).
Shinkichi Takahashi. Canna.
Smart, C. Hymn 1. Faith.
Sobin, G. On the Nature of the Iconic.
Stern, G. Stepping Out of Poetry.
Symonds. In years of old.
Taggard. To One Loved Wholllly Within Wisdom.
Taylor, E. Meditation. Numb. 28.4.9. One Lamb shalt thou offer in the Morning, and the other at Even. And on the Sabbath day two Lambs

etc.
Tennyson, A. Charge of the Light Brigade, The.
Tur-Malka, A. Heralds of New Jerusalem.
Unknown. Cai-bin: I Pluck the Grass.
  Shootingway Ceremony Prayer.
  Story of Kepa Falekaono, The.
  To my lover I want to sacrifice it all.
  Twelfth Song of the Holy Young Men.
  We Have Chosen a Timely Day.
Wilner, E. Sarah's Choice.
Wylie. Felo de Se.
Yang Hsiung. Sweet Springs Palace, The.
Yi Yŏnju. Taking a Watermelon as a Paradigm.
Zafrir, Y. Forced March in Summer.
Zisquit. After Years of Feasting and No
  Sacrifice.

Sacrilege
Whittier. Official Piety.

Sade, Donatien Alphonse François, Marquis de
Breton, A. Marquis de Sade, The.
Simic. Eastern European Cooking.

Sadism and Sadists
Arp. Great Unrestrained Sadist, The.
Cahun, C. Sadistic Judith.
Chin, J. Why a Boy.
Derricotte. Boy at the Paterson Falls.
Volach, Y. Tefillin.

Sadness
al-Sa'igh, Y. Supper.
Alterman, N. Moon.
Arnold, M. Isolation: To Marguerite.
Atwood. Sad Child, A.
Ballagas. Of Another Fashion.
Banchs, E. Mumbling.
Baraka, I. Invention of Comics, The.
Basho. Autumn deepening.
  Cormorant fishing / How stirring.
  Exciting at first.
  Not this human sadness.
  Sad beauty?
  Sad nodes.
Bass, F. Illness.
Becker, R. Sad Sestina.
Beckford, W. Elegiac Sonnet to a Mopstick.
Bêkes. Oh, Moon.
Bly, R. Night Abraham Called to the Stars, The.
Bogan, L. Didactic Piece.
Bowles, W. Languid, and sad, and slow.
Bridges, R. Weep Not To-Day.
Brown, E. Tragic Hero.
Burns, R. Address to the Woodlark.
Buson. Sweet springtime showers.
Campana. Window, The.
Carranza, E. Azure Because of You.
Carruth, H. Cows at Night, The.
Castro, R. Black Mood.
  I Was Born at Birth of Blossoms.
Cernuda. I don't want to return a sad spirit.
Chia Tao. At Ni-Yang Inn.
Ch'in Kuan. Tune: "Perfumed Garden".
  Tune: "Spring in the Painted Hall".
Chipasula. Because the Wind Remembers.
Coleridge, M. Awake.
  Sadness.
Creeley. Air: "The Love of a Woman".
Crozier, A. Humiliation in Its Disguises.
Curbelo. Tonight I Can Almost Hear the
  Singing.
Daniel, G. It Makes Me Sad.
De Los Santos, M. Wiglaf.
Dobyns. No Moment Past This One.
Donne. Song: "Sweetest love, I do not go[e]."
Dunn, S. Sadness.
Elam, P. Mother's Day at McDonald's.
Elytis, O. Aegean Melancholy.
Fan Chung-yen. Tune: "Sumuche Dancers".
Garrett, E. Tyranny of Choice.
Ginsberg, A. My Sad Self.
Gundy, J. Ancient Themes: The Night.
Hafiz, K [or Hafez]. Sitting in the Grief House
  (250).
Hagiwara Sakutaro. So Terrifyingly
  Melancholy.
Hanighen, B. 'Round Midnight.
Hanim, N. Tell Me Again.
Hanson, M. To Fancy.

Harms. Joy Addict, The.
Hart, L. Glad to Be Unhappy.
Harvey, M. Crowds Cheered as Gloom
  Galloped Away, The.
Hemans. Despondency and Aspiration.
Hô Sugyông. When I Think About the Past.
Holmes, O. Illustration of a Picture.
Housman. They Say My Verse Is Sad: No
  Wonder.
Hove. Lost Bird.
  Red Hills of Home.
Howells, W. November.
Hughes, L. Miss Blues'es Child.
Ishikawa Takuboku. Spoonful of Cocoa, A.
Jaimes Freyre. Sad Voices, The.
James, J. Sister Midnight.
Jiménez, J. Dawn brings with it, The.
  Dawn Outside the City Walls.
Juan Chi. Sleepless at Midnight.
Kang Ûn'gyo. Azalea.
Karim, F. Crumbled Paper for Future Poems.
Kaufman, B. Private Sadness.
Kenyon, J. Pharaoh.
Killeen, G. Tristia.
Knott. Two Vietnam Poems: (1966).
Landesman. Ballad of the Sad Young Men, The.
Larkin, P. Home Is So Sad.
Le Ngoc Hiep. I Am Sad.
Levin, J. Ars Poetica: "This hush, my pollen—
  the ordinary grace in the buds."
Li Ch'ing-chao. Banana Trees.
Li Ho. Song: Dragons at Midnight.
Li Po. City of Choan, The.
Li Yu [or Li Hou-Chu]. Flowered Woods, The.
  Nightlong I Wander.
Lihn. Farewell.
Lisnyanskaya [or Lisnianskaia]. To be thought
  an outcast in my beloved country.
Liu Yung. Lament: "Late autumn, a brief
  shower."
Loncar, M. Picasso Shag.
Longfellow, H. Day Is Done, The.
Lugones. Gray Waves.
Machado Ruiz. I Have Walked Down Many
  Roads.
  In the Fields.
MacNeice. And Love Hung Still.
Mahon. Dejection [Ode].
Mapun, D. O Myland Woman.
March, A. As someone on his back for months
  of illness.
McHugh, H. Form.
Milton. Il Penseroso.
Moore, T. Oft In the Stilly Night.
Nasrin. Another Life.
Neruda. Tonight I Can Write the Saddest Lines.
Norton, G. My Melancholy Baby.
O Riordain. Switch.
O'odham. Sadly I was treated, sadly I was
  treated.
Palmer, M. Song of the Round Man.
Paulin. Ulster Unionist Walks the Streets of
  London, An.
Penna. When I don't feel well, I wander among.
Piatt, S. Sad Spring-Song.
Portugal, Anne. Seen from Over Here ("Seen
  from over here.").
Powell, D. A. How his body stood against a
  thicket. rich in hardwood gentry: ponderous
  and gloomy.
Ramsdell, H. Nearly Circle.
Ray, H. Broken Heart.
  Shadow and Sunrise.
Rexroth, K. I am sad this morning.
Robinson, M. Phaon Forsakes Her.
Roethke. Dolor.
Rossetti, C. At Home.
  Why did baby die. . .?
Saba, U. Winter Noon.
Sadi [or Saadi or Sa'di]. This I write, mix ink
  with tears.
Sappho. Honestly I'd as soon be dead!
Shakespeare, W. Sonnet 20: "Woman's face
  with nature's own[e] hand painted, A."
Shaku Chōkū. Tanka: "Somewhere around."
Shange. She waz sullen.

Sharma, P. Performance Test.
Siken, Richard. Boot Theory.
Smith, B. Empty Bed Blues.
Smith, C. By the Same. To Solitude.
  To a Nightingale.
  To Hope.
Su Tung-p'o. Mid-Autumn Moon.
Suarez, V. Duende.
Supervielle. Some day shall I be.
Tanikawa, S. Sadness.
  Zoo.
Townsend, A. They Call You Moody.
Trakl. De Profundis.
Tu Fu [or Du Fu]. Seven Songs Written while
  Living at T'ung-ku in 759.
Tu Mu. Old Love.
Unamuno. Snowfall Is So Silent, The.
  Throw Yourself Like Seed.
Unknown. For wele or wo I wyl not flee.
  Sad Song.
  Sad Song.
  Today is the last day of winter.
  With eyes filled with tears.
Valentine, J. In the Burning Air.
Van de Woestijne. Fever Tune.
Vasalis. Sotto Voce.
Verlaine. Sadness, the languor of the human
  body, The.
Vietnamese Oral Tradition. From *So* Mountain.
  Love Lament.
  Red Cloth, The.
  Tao.
Vogel, D. With gentle fingers.
Wang Chien. Round Fan.
Wen T'ien-hsiang. Chin-ling Post Station.
Whalen, P. Waiting for Claude.
Wild, R. In a melancholly studdy.
Williams, H. To the Moon.
Williams, W. Sadness of the Sea, The.
Wright, J. Portugal Laurel, The.
Yeats. To the Rose upon the Rood of Time.
Yesenin [or Essenin]. Golden Birch Grove's,
  The.
  Winds, Winds, Winds.
Young, A. Detroit 1958.
Zukofsky, L. As to How Much.

Sailing and Sailors
Achterberg. Departure.
Adamson. Sibyl.
Alberti. If My Voice Dies While on Land.
Alcaeus [or Alkaios]. Come! Put by Pelops'
  Isle.
  Come to me, leaving the Peloponnesos.
  I don't understand the conflict of the winds.
Alfonso X. Scorpions, The.
Antipater of Sidon. Priapos of the Harbor.
Antiphilus [or Antiphilos]. On the Death of the
  Ferryman, Glaucus.
Anyte [or Anytes]. This is Kypris' place; it ever
  pleases her.
Archilochus. May he lose his way on the cold
  sea.
Bailey, A. Isosceles Lighthouse, The.
  Unreturning, The: "Blue is my sky peter."
Bell, M. Hole in the Sea, The.
Belli, G. Brief Lessons in Eroticism 1.
Bishop, E. Imaginary Iceberg, The.
  Unbeliever, The.
Bontemps. Nocturne of the Wharves.
Boyle, K. To a Seaman Dead on Land.
Brown, L. Respond to Me.
Brown, T. Land, Ho!
Bruce, C. Eastern Shore.
Buchanan, R. Wanderers, The.
Buckley, C. Catechism of the Sea.
Byron, G. Lines to Mr Hodgson.
Camões [or Camõens or Camoëns], L. On a
  Shipmate, Pero Moniz, Dying at Sea.
  With glad reception our Commander meets.
Campbell, R. Choosing a Mast.
Campbell, T. Ye Mariners of England.
Carroll, L. Fit the Second: The Bellman's
  Speech.
  Hunting of the Snark, The.
Cavafy. Supplication.
Clough. Qua Cursum Ventus.

Cofer, J.   Drowned Sailor, The.
Coleridge, S.   Rime of the Ancient Mariner, The (1798 version).
Coolbrith.   Sailed.
Corbett, E.   Three Wise Old Women.
Coward.   Sail Away.
Crane, S.   I explain the silvered passing of a ship at night.
Crummey, Michael.   Painting the Islands.
Cuadra, P.   Evening Star, The.
   Manuscript in a Bottle.
Cunningham, A.   Sea-Song, A.
Curnow.   Landfall in Unknown Seas.
Davies, W. H.   Sheep.
Dawe, G.   Seamen's Mission.
Day Lewis.   Conflict, The.
De la Mare.   Silver Penny, The.
Dickinson, E.   Exultation is the going.
   Wild Nights—Wild Nights!
Donne.   Calm[e], The.
   Hymn[e] to Christ, at the Author's Last Going into Germany, A.
   Storm[e], The.
Doolittle, H.   Shrine, The.
Drayton.   To the Virginian Voyage.
Drummond, W.   Sonnet: "Slide soft, fair forth, and make a crystal plain."
Elburg.   Nothing of All That.
Eliot, T. S.   4. Death by Water.
Erinna.   Escort fish, Pompilos, sending sailors a fair sailing.
Farley, P.   Lamp, The.
Fields, J.   Alarmed Skipper, The.
   Ballad of the Tempest.
Finlay, I.   Evening—Sail.
Fletcher, J.   Clipper-Ships.
Foot, E.   Captain scans the ruffled zone, The.
Garrick.   Heart of Oak.
Gibson, W.   Luck.
Gilbert, W.   Captain Reece.
   Yarn of the *Nancy Bell*, The.
Grimké, A.   Little Grey Dreams.
Grumman, Bob.   Mathemaku No. 17.
Ha-Levi, J.   Greetings ladies, kith and kin.
Hammial.   Sadie.
Harvey, S.   Mighty Tropicale Orchestra, The.
Hatubou, S.   Night 9.
Hewitt, G.   Sailor, The.
Heym.   Seafarers.
Hill, G.   Guardians, The.
Hirsch, E.   Tristan Tzara.
Holden, M.   Seaman, 1941.
Homer.   And then went down to the ship.
   Odyssey, The.
Hovey.   Sea Gypsy, The.
Huchel.   Aristeas 2.
Hughes, L.   Sailor.
Huidobro.   Sailor.
Irish Oral Tradition.   Irish Sailor, The.
Jones, D.   Ship's master: / before him, in the waist and before it.
Kenney.   Sailing.
Kipling, R.   Last Chantey, The.
   Nurses, The.
Knighton, R.   Ballad of Echolocation, The.
Landon.   To My Brother: "Do you recall the fancies of many years ago."
Lear, E.   Jumblies, The.
   Limerick: "There was a young lady of Portugal."
   Owl and the Pussy-Cat [or Pussycat], The.
Lewis, A.   Song (On Seeing Dead Bodies Floating Off the Cape).
Li Ch'ing-chao.   Fisherman's Honor, The.
Lightfoot.   Wreck of the Edmund Fitzgerald, The.
Llywelyn-Williams.   When I Was a Boy.
Longfellow, H.   Broken Oar, The.
   Tide Rises, the Tide Falls, The.
   Wreck of the Hesperus, The.
MacCaig.   Basking Shark.
Mallarmé.   Sea Breeze.
   Toast.
   Toast.
Manifold.   Fife Tune.
Martinson.   On the Congo.

Marvell.   Bermudas.
Masefield.   Cargoes.
   Port of Many Ships.
   Rounding the Horn.
   Sea Fever.
   Valediction, A (Liverpool Docks).
Mayer, B.   Port, The.
   Sea: "It's he, it's sea. the sea is continuous; a continuous body."
Meade, G.   Schrimshaw Sailor, The.
Melville, H.   Billy in the Darbies.
   Haglets, The.
   Island, The.
   John Marr.
   To Ned.
   Tom Deadlight.
Meredith, G.   Camelus Saltat: Continued.
Merwin.   Odysseus.
Michaels, A.   Passionate World, The.
Miller, J.   Columbus: "Behind him lay the gray Azores."
Miller, V.   How Far?
Mooney, M.   Salting the Brae.
Moschus.   Ocean, The.
Moss, H.   Tourists.
Murphy, R.   Sailing to an Island.
Muso Soseki.   By the sea.
Nash, O.   Columbus.
O'Hara, F.   To the Harbormaster.
Oppen.   Mast / Inaudibly soars; bole-like, tapering, The.
   Three wide / Funnels raked aft, and the masts slanted, The.
Ovid.   Dipped now in Ocean, the She-Bear's stellar guardian.
   Every letter you've read in this whole book was written.
   I have (may I always keep!) blonde Minerva's protection: my vessel.
   You gods of sea and sky—what's left me now but prayer?
Pearlberg, G.G.   Sailor.
Penna.   Life...is remembering waking up.
Petrarch.   Galley.
   My ship laden with forgetfulness passes through a harsh sea, at.
Pickthall, M.   Ebb Tide.
Pratt, E.   Lee-Shore, The.
Probyn.   Barcarolle.
Prys.   Poem to Show the Trouble That Befell Him When He Was at Sea, A.
Rakosi.   Fluteplayers from Finmarken.
   Unswerving Marine.
Ray, H.   Boat Song.
Reznikoff.   Four sailors on the bus, dressed in blue denim shirts.
Rivas, J.   Thalassa.
   Thalassa.
Roberts, C.   Let Go of It.
Rosemurgy, C.   Hard Put.
Ross, A.   Destroyers in the Arctic.
Rupchev, Georgi.   Attraction.
Salinas, P.   On Dry Land.
Schjeldahl.   Ocean Liner.
Seferis.   Bottle in the Sea.
Shostakovskaya, I.   Sailor sailor got ashore.
Slamnig, I.   Sailor, A.
Smith, C.   Beachy Head.
Smith, I.   Exiles, The.
Snyder, G.   Ship in Yokohama, The.
Southey, C.   Mariner's Hymn.
Southey, R.   Ship, The.
Spaziani.   It is Said by Some Sailors, the Old.
Spence, L.   Prows O' Reekie, The.
Stevenson, R.   Christmas at Sea.
Surrey.   Seafarer, The.
Sze.   Network, The.
Tate, A.   Mediterranean, The.
Tennyson, A.   Crossing the Bar.
   Fair ship, that from the Italian shore.
   Sweet and Low.
Thomas, P.   Lascars, The.
Tucker, M.   Hugging the Shore.
Turner, C.   Buoy-Bell, The.
Unknown.   Battle of Brunanburh.
   Bran at the Island of Women.

   Close by the shore, the shore.
   Every Bullet Has Its Billet.
   My Boy Willie.
   Old Ship of Zion, The [North Carolina version].
   Sail, O Believer.
   Sailor Boy's Song.
   Seafarer, The.
   Seafarer, The.
   Sir Patrick Spens [or Spence].
   Skye Boat Song.
Vaysman, N.   Sail me.
Walcott.   He yawned and watched the lilac horns of his island.
Warren, R.   Masts at Dawn.
Wei Ying-wu.   Mooring at Twilight in Yuyi District.
Westmorland.   In Praise of Fidelia.
Whitman, W.   Old Salt Kossabone.
   Ship Starting, The.
   Song for All Seas, All Ships.
Whittier.   Slave-Ships, The.
Williams, W.   Yachts, The.
Wilmer, S.   Mess Boy, The.
Wyatt.   Sonnet: "My Galley Charged".
Yang Wan-li.   Sailing Through the Gorges.
Yüan Chĕn.   Dreaming of My Wife.

St. Agnes' Eve
Keats.   Eve of St. Agnes, The.
Tennyson, A.   St. Agnes' Eve.
St. Crispin's Day
Shakespeare, W.   O! that we now had here.
St. David's Day
Huws, Meirion MacIntyre.   Conscience.
Unknown.   In Honour of St. David's Day.
St. James's Park, London
Rochester, J.   Ramble in St. James's Park, A.
Waller, E.   On St. James's Park, as Lately Improved by His Majesty.
Saint Joseph
Rilke.   5. The Suspicions of Joseph.
Saint Lawrence (river), Canada
Ray, H.   On the rapids of the St. Lawrence.
St. Louis, Missouri
Hicok.   Arch of Sanctification, The.
Lowell, A.   St. Louis.
Russell, B.   You Came a Long Way from St. Louis.
Sterling, A.   Meet Me in St. Louis, Louis.
Saint Lucia (island nation)
Walcott.   Ajax, / lion-coloured stallion from Sealey's stable.
Saint Peter's Church, Rome
Denby.   Ciampino: Envoi.
Wilde, O.   Easter Day.
Saint Petersburg [formerly Leningrad], Russia
Akhmatova, A.   Introduction.
   Requiem: "No foreign sky protected me."
Berggolts [or Bergholts].   Blockade Swallow, The.
Burnshaw.   House in St. Petersburg.
Hejinian.   No form at all—it's impossible to imagine its being.
Ivanov, G.   Quarter century of exile has passed, A.
Kublanovsky [or Kublanovskii].   Armor of the Petrograd oak is rusty, but, The.
Loseff [or Losev].   Petrograd Side, The.
Mandelstam [or Mandelshtam].   Leningrad.
   Leningrad.
   O Lord, Help Me to Live Through This Night.
Olds, S.   Leningrad Cemetery, Winter of 1941.
Pushkin, A.   Tale of St. Petersburg, A.
Stratanovsky.   Leningrad stairwell, A.
Saint Stephen
Dickinson, P.   St. Stephen's Day.
Nichols, K.   Feast of Stephen, The.
Sawyer, R.   Feast o' Saint [or St.] Stephen, The.
Suckling, S.   Upon Stephen Stoned.
Unknown.   Good King Wenceslas.
St. Stephen's Day
Unknown.   Virgin's Lullaby, The.
Saint Thomas
Hill, G.   Canticle for Good Friday.
Smart, C.   St. Thomas.

Saints

Azzawi, F. Lion and the Apostle, The.
Baffo, G. Sonnet: "My meditation turns to thinking."
Bingen, Hildegard von. Hymn to St. Maximinus, A.
Bobrowski. Novgorod: Coming of the Saints.
Cadiot, Oliver. Why I Became a Saint.
Citino. Agatha.
 Christina the Astonishing: Virgin.
 Francis Meets a Leper.
 Ignatius, Bishop and Martyr.
Clarke, A. Martha Blake at Fifty-one.
 St Christopher.
Coolidge, C. Jerome in His Study.
Cowper, W. Light Shining out of Darkness.
Crashaw. Flaming Heart, The.
 Love, thou art absolute sole lord.
 O sweet incendiary! shew here thy art.
Curry, N. In a Calendar of Saints.
Derricotte. Weakness, The.
Dickinson, E. I Taste a Liquor Never Brewed.
Donne. Canonization, The.
 Relic, The.
Dove, R. On Veronica.
Erdrich. Saint Clare.
Fallon, P. Holy Well.
Florit, E. Martyrdom of Saint Sebastian, The.
Frost, C. Consent.
Greenberg, A. Saints.
Gregerson. Saint's Logic.
Hamby, B. St. Clare's Underwear.
Herrera. Future Martyr of Supersonic Waves.
Johnson, L. Church of a Dream, The.
Kamienska. Saint Martha.
Kavanagh, P. Sanctity.
Kendall, M. Legend of the Crossing-Sweeper.
Kim Sŭnghŭi. Between Saint and Witch.
Lewis, J. Holding the Holy Card.
Mallarmé. Saint.
 Saint.
McGrath, T. On the Head of a Pin.
Merwin. St. Vincent's.
Mew. Madeleine in Church.
Muso Soseki. Tiger Valley.
Ormond. To a Nun.
Pelizzon, V. Late Apostasy, A.
Ragan, J. St. Jacob's Church of the Hanging Hand.
Rossetti, C. Hark! the Alleluias of the great salvation.
Rossetti, D. Marriage of St Katharine, by the same, A; in the Hospital of St John at Bruges.
Shakespeare, W. If I profane with my unworthiest hand.
Shoichi. All-meaning circle, The.
Thomas, R. S. Line from St. David's, A.
 Llanrhaeadr Ym Mochnant.
Tsvetayeva [or Tsvetaeva]. You're going by, west of the sun.
Unknown. Death of Saint Marinus, The.
 Epigram: "Says a Reverend Priest to a less Rev'rend friend."
 Feilire of Adamnan, The.
 John, John, of the Holy Order.
 Let God's Saints Come In.
 When the Saints Go Marchin' [or Marching] In.
Whitehead, C. Marian Hymn.
Williams, L. Saints.
Yevtushenko [or Evtushenko]. Saints of Jazz.

Salads

Basho. Teeth sensitive to the sand.
Berger, B. Salad Days.
Breckenridge. Cooking Catalogue.
Locklin. Iceberg Theory, The.
Rühmkorf, P. Formerly, When We Still Parted the Big Rivers.
Smith, S. Salad, A.
Wells, C. Universal Favorite, The.

Salamanders

DeFoe, M. Red Salamander—Video Store Parking Lot.
Ramanujan. Salamanders.

Sales Clerks

Senryū, K. Whatever he says.
See also **Clerks**

Salesmen

Cavalli. Moroccans with the carpets, The.
Cummings, E. E. Salesman, A.
Daniels, J. Hoagie Scam, The.
Goyette, Susan. Mythology of Cures, The.
Grosholz. Life of a Salesman.
Martinez, D. Cole Porter.
Ochester. Working at the Wholesale Curtain Showroom.
Padgett, R. Poem for El Lissitzky.
Seyburn, P. Persuasion.

Salmon

Adamson. Gutting the Salmon.
Basho. Dried salmon.
 Snowy morning, A.
Graham, J. Salmon.
Hughes, T. October Salmon[, An].
 That Morning.
Mitchison. Dick and Colin at the Salmon Nets.
Niatum. Salmon, The.
Swift, J. Wild Salmon: Stillaguamish Tribal Hatchery.
Unknown. Prayer to the Sockeye Salmon.

Salome

Lamb, C. Salome.
Lamb, M. Salome.

Salt

Ammuvanar. They Shout Out the Price of Salt.
Barlow, G. Salt.
Brown, H. Salting of Snow, A.
Di Prima. For H.D.
Eich. Salt.
Georges, D. Another Ode to Salt.
Goll, I. Salt Lake, The.
Holst-Warhaft. Matthew 5:13; You are the salt of the earth.
 Old Men of Athens, The.
Ikeda, P. Salt.
Merrill, J. Upward Look, An.
Moss, T. Goodness and the Salt of the Earth.
Mueller, J. Bonneville.
Mueller, L. Love Like Salt.
Neruda. Ode to Salt.
 Ode to Salt.
Page, P. Photos of a Salt Mine.
Phillips, C. Reach, The.
Quintana. Poem for Salt.
Stern, G. On the Island.
Wang An-shih. Confiscating Salt.

Salvation

Abrahams, L. Song for the new order.
Awoonor. Weaver Bird, The.
Bhattācārya, K. How will You rescue me, Tara? Other than Your two red feet, Syama.
Borson. Save Us From.
Bradstreet, A. As Weary Pilgrim, Now at Rest.
Cairns, Scott. Salvation.
Chipasula, S. Your Name is Gift.
Citino. Sea of Kansas, Ohio Tundra, Time Still Running Out, The.
Clarkson. Behold, the King of glory now is come.
Dalton, A. Nest.
Dana, R. Husband's and Wife's Grave, The.
Donne. At the round earth's imagined [or imagin'd] corners, blow.
 Batter my heart, three-personed [or three person'd] God; for you.
 I am a little world made cunningly.
 Oh my black[e] soul[e]! now thou art summoned.
 This is my play's [or playes] last scene, here heavens appoint.
Eichner, Maura. Eat bread. Drink wine. Try to sing the song.
Eliot, T. S. Hippopotamus, The.
 Song for Simeon, A.
Éluard, P. Unknown, She Was My Favorite Shape.
Ewer. Only Way, The.
Farewell. Privy-Love for My Landlady.
Ferguson, G. Winter Rose, The.
Graves, R. Song: Lift-Boy.
Hecht, A. Prospects.
Herbert, G. Bunch of Grapes, The.
 Call, The.
 Dialogue, A.
 Divinity.
 Easter Wings.
 Holdfast, The.
 Love Unknown.
 Peace.
 Redemption.
Herrick. To His Saviour.
Hogan, L. Return: Buffalo.
Hopkins, G. Myself unholy, from myself unholy.
Hughes, L. Madam and the Minister.
Islām, N. Wherever are the lowly, the suffering, and the poor.
Jaufré Rudel. Love Song.
Jauss. Quotations for a Winter Evening.
Jonson, B. Hymn[e] on the Nativity [or Nativitie] of My Saviour, A.
Lansdown. Behind the Veil.
Laux, D. Prayer: "Sweet Jesus, let her save you, let her take."
Lindsay, V. General William Booth Enters into Heaven.
Mahon. Spring Vacation, The.
Mandela. Saviour.
Milosz, C. Dedication: "You whom I could not save."
Mitchell, S. Good Samaritan et Al, The.
Muske, C. Fault, The.
Muso Soseki. No Gain.
 With compassionate hands.
Okudzhava. Save us, the poets, save us, we have but.
Oliver, M. In Blackwater Woods.
Ponge. Rhetoric.
Ralegh, W. Authours Epitaph, Made by Himself, The.
Rāy, M. R. Give me food.
Sen, R. Supreme Savior of Sinners.
 World's a shoreless ocean, The.
Senghor. Suddenly Startled.
Shwarts [or Shvarts]. My heart's cloth I shall spread before the Savior's feet.
Smith, R. Teresa.
Tate, A. Cross, The.
Unknown. Nobody Knows the Trouble I've Had.
 Ther bloweth a cold wynd to-day, to-day.
Very. Forevermore.
 Garden, The.
Wesley, C. Come on, my partners in distress.
 None is like Jeshuron's God.
Whittier. Over-Heart, The.

Salvation Army

Fearing. Ballad of the Salvation Army.
Robinson, E. Karma.

Samson

Crashaw. Samson to His Delilah.
Graves, R. Angry Samson.
Gwynn, R. Among Philistines.
Heard, J. Black Sampson, The.
Ipadeola, T. Companions.
Levi, P. Delilah.
 Samson.
Longfellow, H. Warning, The.
Milton. But peace, I must not quarrel with the will.
 But what is strength without a double share.
 Deliverer, The.
Pino, José Manuel del. Doré V.

San Francisco, California

Ackerman, D. San Francisco Sunrise.
Alarcon, F. Blues del SIDA / AIDS Blues.
Berrigan, A. Short History of Autumn, A.
Chin. Leaving San Francisco.
Corso. Ode to Coit Tower.
Cortes, F. Dolce Far Niente.
Cross, D. Big words.
Di Prima. Letter to Jeanne (at Tassajara).
Ferlinghetti, L. Green Street Mortuary Marching Band, The.
 Starting from San Francisco.
Gilbert, J. Malvolio in San Francisco.
Ginsberg, A. Sunflower Sutra.
Gunn, T. San Francisco Streets.
Harper, M. Three O'Clock Love Song.

Hass, R. Bookbuying in the Tenderloin.
Hayes, T. Midnight: "You call."
Hirschman, J. Tremor, The.
Lassell. Sunset Stripping: Visiting L.A.
Light, K. 2. San Francisco.
Marcus, M. Picnic on the Bay Bridge.
Miller, C. Night in San Francisco.
Pearlberg, G.G. Dog Star.
Rich, A. Catch if you can your country's moment, begin.
Rukeyser, M. Bunk Johnson Blowing.
Snodgrass. Returned to Frisco, 1946.
Snyder, G. Night Herons.
Things to Do Around San Francisco.
Soto. Envying the Children of San Francisco.
Villanueva, A. They Didn't Get Me.
Voznesensky [or Voznesenskii]. Monologue with Commentary.
Weatherly, T. P.W.T.
Welch, L. Sausalito Trash Prayer.

Sancho Panza
Borges. Soldier of Urbina, A.

Sanctuaries
Ammons. Triphammer Bridge.
Chŏng Ch'ŏl. Little Odes on Mount Star.
Cofer, J. Purpose of Nuns, The.
Dobyns. Exile.
Han Yong'un [or Yongwun]. Come to Me.
Hattersley, G. On the Buses with Dostoyevsky.
Hemans. Mountain Sanctuaries.
Issa. Young sparrows.
Ivask, Y. Emily Dickinson.
Liu, T. Wellfleet.
Lugones. Slow Delight.
Meng Hao Jan. Lake of the Ten Thousand Mountains, The.
Montague, J. Cave.
Muso Soseki. At Whole-World-In-View-Hut.
Thanks for Daisen Osho's Visit.
Parker, D. Sanctuary.
Rolle, S. Birds' Refuge, The.
Yi I. Nine Songs of Mount Ko.

Sand
Bursk. Tearing Up the Tracks.
Cook, E. Building upon the Sand.
Creeley. All That Is Lovely in Men.
de Fierro. Grain of Sand.
Eberhart, R. Ceremony by the Sea, A.
Frost, R. Neither Out Far Nor In Deep.
Gascoyne. Yves Tanguy.
Hartnett. Quicksand.
Ishikawa Takuboku. Never forget.
Jarmain. Sand.
Kinzie. In air hard as sand.
Kistler, W. Kyoto 1—Kinkaku-ji.
Landor, W. Well I Remember How You Smiled.
Loesser. Sand in My Shoes.
Longfellow, H. Sand of the Desert in an Hour-Glass.
Tide Rises, the Tide Falls, The.
Milán, E. I let myself be led because I let loose.
Me dejo guiar porque he dejado ir.
Millay, E. Second Fig.
Mitchell, A. Speck Speaks, A.
Nwankwo. Poem: "In sand."
Osterhaus, J. New York Minute.
Pagis, D. Snake.
Po Chü-i. One anchorage of sand appears as another dissolves away.
Rohrer, M. Starfish Waving to Me from the Sand.
Spenser, E. Sonnet 75: "One day I wrote her name upon the strand."
Staff. Foundations.
Stevenson, R. At the Seaside [or Sea-Side].
Stuart, D. Desolation: "At the top of the dune."
Thomas, D. We Lying by Seasand.
Young, A. Culbin Sands.

"Sand, George" (Amandine Aurore Lucie Dupin, Baronne Dudevant)
Browning, E. To George Sand: A Desire.
To George Sand: A Recognition.
Parker, D. George Sand.

Sandpipers
Bishop, E. Sandpiper.

Santa Claus
Aubert, A. December 1982/Detroit.
Deniz, G. Christmas.
Navidades.
Gillespie, H. Santa Claus Is Comin' to Town.
Martinson. Santa Claus: "Each year when the trees turn white."
Mikhail, D. Santa Claus.
Moore, C. Visit from St Nicholas, A.
Powell, D. A. When you touch down upon this earth. little reindeers.
Webb, C. Death of Santa Claus, The.
Whalen, P. Damachi.

Santayana, George
Stevens, W. To an Old Philosopher in Rome.

Sappho
Baker, H. Sappho's Leap.
Begley, T. Sappho's Gymnasium ("For healthy cells please remember.").
Sappho's Gymnasium ("Outside memory worship never dies.").
Broumas, O. Sappho's Gymnasium ("For healthy cells please remember.").
Sappho's Gymnasium ("Outside memory worship never dies.").
Brown, R. Sappho's Reply.
Dacre, C. Sappho; or, The Resolve.
Doolittle, H. Fragment 113: "Not honey, / not the plunder of the bee."
Fragment 68: "I envy you your chance of death."
Field. Atthis, my darling, thou did'st stray.
'Sing to us Sappho!' cried the crowd.
Why should I praise thee, blissful Aphrodite?
Gomez de Avellaneda. Imitating an Ode by Sappho.
Hemans. Last Song of Sappho, The.
Higginson, E. Dream of Sappho, A.
Kizer, C. For Sappho/After Sappho.
Landon. Sappho's Song.
Lowell, A. Sisters, The.
Mandelstam [or Mandelshtam]. On Stony Pierian Spurs.
Norton, C. Picture of Sappho, The.
Nossis. Stranger, if you sail to the land of lovely dances, Mitylene.
Oakes-Smith, E. Ode to Sappho.
"Philo-Philippa.". To the Excellent Orinda.
Pound, E. Papyrus.
Preston, M. Erinna's Spinning.
Robinson, M. Sappho Discovers her Passion.
Sappho's Address to the Stars.
Sappho's Prayer to Venus.
Rossetti, C. Sappho.
Sappho. Sapphics.
Speyer. To a Song of Sappho Discovered in Egypt.
Wright, J. Sappho.

Sarah (Bible)
Allnutt, G. Sarah's Laughter.
Nemerov. Nicodemus.
Schwartz, D. Sarah.
Wilner, E. Sarah's Choice.

Sarajevo, Bosnia and Herzegovina
Grubb, D. Windows of Sarajevo, The.
Harrison, T. Bright Lights of Sarajevo, The.
Hugo, R. Yards of Sarajevo, The.
Oktenberg, A. It was an open-air market.
Sarajlić, I. Luck in Sarajevo.
Simić, G. Sorrow of Sarajevo, The.

Saratoga, New York
Berkson, B. Sheer Strips.

Sarto, Andrea del
Browning, R. Andrea del Sarto.

Sashimi and Sushi
Muldoon, P. Sushi.
Sze. In Your Honor.

Satan
Auden. From "The Prolific and the Devourer".
Bejerano, M. It has all begun with still waters.
Belloc. On Lady Poltagrue, A Public Peril.
Blake, W. Book of Urizen [or First Book of Urizen], The.
Memorable Fancy, A.
Bloom, V. Sun-a-shine, Rain-a-fall.

Burns, R. Address to the Deil.
Causley. Infant Song.
Chesterton. Aristocrat, The.
Coleridge, M. Devil's Funeral, The.
Coleridge, S. Devil's Thoughts, The.
Cullen, C. For a Mouthy Woman.
Dickinson, E. Snake, The.
Goldbarth. Closer.
Gowar. Rat Trap.
Herbert, Z. Devil, A.
Hill, G. Bibliographers, The.
Hope, A. Möbius Strip-Tease.
Johnson, L. Dark Angel, The.
Kipling, R. Conundrum of the Workshops, The.
Komunyakaa, Y. Devil's Workshop, The.
Lawrence, D. H. Root of Our Evil, The.
Meredith, G. Lucifer in Starlight.
Mikha'il, M. Crazy Satan.
Talk.
Milton. As when of old some orator renowed.
He sat; and in the assembly next upstood.
Now had th' Almighty Father from above.
Other way Satan went down, Th'.
Prospect of Eden, The.
Satan's Journey.
Serpent Finds Eve Alone, The.
Sin and Death.
Moore, T. Copy of an Intercepted Despatch from His Excellency Don Strepitoso Diabolo.
Olds, S. Satan Says.
Pagis, D. Homily.
Parra, N. Lord's Prayer.
Rich, A. Lucifer in the Train.
Rossetti, C. Three Enemies, The.
Rossetti, D. 90: Retro me, Sathana!
Salaam. 5 Minutes, Mr. Salaam.
Snyder, G. Milton by Firelight.
Southey, R. Devil, The.
Devil's Thoughts, The.
Tolson, M. Old Pettigrew.
Unknown. Come Go With Me.
Demon Lover, The.
Devil in Texas, The.
Hold Your Light.
I an' Satan Had a Race.
I Know When I'm Going Home.
Satan's Camp a-Fire.
Wait, Mr. Mackright.
With huntis vp, with huntis vp.
Very. Serpent, The.
Wylie. Knight Fallen on Evil Days, The.
See also **Devil**

Satie, Erik
Merrill, J. Angel.

Satire and Satirists
Bogardus. Narcissus to Echo.
Donne. Satire 3 [Religion].
Juvenal. Satire 1.
Satire 10.
Satire 6.
Kinzie. Muse of Satire, The.
Klappert. To Whom.
Moore, E. To the Right Hon. Henry Pelham.
Persius. Satire 1: "Who's going to read that?"
Satire 5: "From the earliest poets, the fashion stands."
Satire 6: "Has Sabine winter brought you to your fireside."
Wang Ho-ch'ing. Tune: "Tsui-chung T'ien" To the Giant Butterfly.

Satiric Verse
Brome. Satire on the Rebellion, A.
Carroll, L. Duchess's Lullaby, The.
Father William.
Mad Hatter's Song, The.
Cope, W. Cherry blossom, The.
Mitchell, A. Nothingmas Day.
Quarles. Booke of *Common Pray'r* excels the rest, The.
Stéfan, Jude. Butcher's Meat by Loti.
Emma Zola at Wimbledon Let's Say.
See also **Satire and Satirists**

Saturday
Ceravolo. I Like to Collapse.
Leopardi. Saturday Night in the Village.

Mullen, H. Saturday Afternoon, When Chores Are Done.
Rouse, A. Sunday Morning.
Thompson, D. P. Blues at 1.
Trethewey, N. Collection Day.
Viray, M. Saturday Morning, A.
See also **Sabbath**

Saul (Bible)
Bible, *O.T.* David's Lament.
Byron, G. Song of Saul before His Last Battle.
Levine, P. Death of Saul, The.
Lindsay, V. In Which Roosevelt Is Compared to Saul.
Merton. St. Paul.
Quarles. On Saul and David.
Wither. Conversion of S. Paul, The.

Sausages
Silano, M. Sausage Parade, The.

Savannah, Georgia
Bates, C. Hard-Hearted Hannah (The Vamp of Savannah).
Bigelow, B. Hard-Hearted Hannah (The Vamp of Savannah).
Yellen, J. Hard-Hearted Hannah (The Vamp of Savannah).

Savior
Chandar, M. Child Is Born, A.
Citino. Sister Mary Appassionata Lectures the Folklore Class: Doctrines of the Strawberry.
Dillard, A. Sign of Your Father, The.
Doddridge, P. Hark! the glad sound! the Savior comes.
Erdrich. Savior, The.
Hill, G. On the sixth day, as I rode.
Keble. Christmas Day: "What sudden blaze of song."
Murray, L. Say-but-the-Word Centurion Attempts a Summary, The.

Sawmills and Sawyers
Arp. Cities Have Been Cut Off at the Feet, The.
Minhinnick. Boathouse, The.

Scarecrows
Basho. I would like to use.
Brownjohn. In a Convent Garden.
Buson. In the drained fields.
Owner of the field, The.
De la Mare. Scarecrow, The.
Gay, Garry. Slowly. . . / The Scarecrow.
Issa. Cricket.
Don't know about the people.
Where.
Kawai Chigetsu [*or*Chigetsu-Ni]. Chirping / Grasshopper.
Kirkup. Scarecrows.
Mahon. Going Home.
Reddy, Srikanth. Scarecrow Eclogue.
Simic. Scarecrow, The.
Thomson, D. Scarecrow.
Wilbur, R. Sonnet: "Winter deepening, the hay all in, The."

Scheherazade
Allnutt, G. Scheherazade.
Hudgins. Telling, The.
St. John, P. Ocean of the Streams of Story.

Schiele, Egon
Hannan, M. Life Model.

Schoenberg, Arnold
Heissenbüttel. Fragment 3: "All horizons are round."

Scholarship and Scholars
Arnold, M. Scholar Gypsy, The.
Barkova, A. Few Autobiographical Facts, A.
Belloc. Lines to a Don.
Bentley, E. "Dinner-time?" said Gilbert White.
Bertrand. Tulip Merchant, The.
Browning, R. Grammarian's Funeral, A.
Buckley, C. 20 Years of Grant Applications and State College Jobs.
Cunningham, J. Homer was poor. His scholars live at ease.
This Humanist whom no beliefs constrained.
Davis, F. Giles Johnson, Ph.D.
Eady. Paradiso.
Eliot, T. S. Mr. Apollinax.
Foley, M. Lucky Eugene.

Han-shan. Graceful handsome youth, A.
Huerta, D. Baroque Cell, A.
Celda barroca, Una.
Kuzmin. Not for nothing did we read the theologians.
Kwŏn Homun. Nature makes clear the windy air.
Laughlin, J. My Ambition.
Lewis, Emyr. Drivel.
Lu Yu. Merchant's Joy, The.
Matthews, T. Happy Arabia.
McCord, D. Baccalaureate.
Nguyễn Văn Lạc. Shrimps.
Pao Chao. Scholar Recruit, The.
Portnoy, M. Roget, Papier, Schism!
Ranaldo, L. Refugee, A.
Reid, C. Perversion, A.
Salzman, E. Double Dactyls.
Senryū, K. Learning and a ladder.
Seshadri. Scholar, The.
Stevens, W. On [*or* Of] the Manner of Addressing Clouds.
Stevenson, A. Ballad for Apothecaries, A.
Unknown. Good Scholars Make Bad Husbands.
Scholar and the Cat, The.
Various authors. He did not boast of his natural gifts.
His nature being one with Heaven.
Though he was busy with war.
Upon receiving an old scholar.
Yeats. Scholars, The.
Yi I. Mount Ko's nine-bend pool.
Where is the fifth bend?
See also **Pedantry and Pedants; Students; Teaching and Teachers**

School and Schools
Algarin. Meeting Gaylen's 5th Grade Class.
Amis, K. Ever-Fixed Mark, An.
"Antler.". Raising My Hand.
Aridjis. Self-Portrait at Six Years of Age.
Arnold, C. Why I Skip My High School Reunions.
Berry, D. On Reading Poems to a Senior Class at South High.
Bibb. Class Song of '91.
Bibbins, M. Geometry Class.
Blake, W. School-Boy, The.
Bottoms. Desk, The.
Brooks, G. Tinsel Marie; The Coora Flower.
We Real Cool.
Burt, L. Melissa Quits School.
Bynner. Haskell.
Caesar, V. In 5th Grade.
Canning, G. *et al.* Rogero's Song.
Carbó, N. Civilizing the Filipino.
Carson, C. Slate Street School.
Cassells. Soul Make a Path Through Shouting.
Chavez, L. After the Prom.
Christie. Belongings.
Clanchy, K. Timetable.
Colquitt. Honor Card.
Cooley. Poem on the First Day of School.
Cooper, J. Wanda's Blues.
Cortéz, L. I Remember: "I remember kindergarten."
Cott, J. He Dreams What Is Going On Inside His Head.
Cramer. For the Bullies of West Morris High.
Curnow. Country School.
De la Mare. Scholars.
Deane, S. Brethren, The.
Delgado, J. Letters from School, The.
Deniz, G. Authoritarian School and How a Respectable Literary Genre Was Born, The.
Escuela autoritaria y cómo nació un respetable género de literatura, La.
Derricotte. High School.
In an Urban School.
Divakaruni. Yuba City School.
Djanikian. In the Elementary School Choir.
Dove, R. Flash Cards.
Dubie. Of Politics, & Art.
Duhamel. Ego.
Dunn, D. Glasgow Schoolboys, Running Backwards.
Durham. Columbus Day.

Farawell, M. Everything I Need to Know I Learned in Kindergarten.
Fay, S. Back in My Day.
Follain. School and Nature.
Foster, A. Starting School.
Frere. Rogero's Song.
Glancy. First Reader Santee Training School, 1873, The.
Glück, L. School Children, The.
Goetsch, D. Nobody's Hell.
Guevara, M. Once When I Was in the Eighth Grade.
Hale, S. Mary's Lamb [*or* Mary and Her Lamb].
Hall, D. X.
Harrison, G. Playground, The.
Hassaan, Y. I Considered Myself.
Hemans. Evening Prayer, at a Girls' School.
Henderson-Holmes. Battle, Over and Over Again, The.
Hernández Cruz. Three Days/out of Franklin.
Hope, M. Sixth Grade.
Hughes, J. Dog Day Lesson.
Jordan, J. Through These Halls.
Kaneko. Bailey Gatzert: The First Grade, 1945.
Kingsolver. Beating Time.
Koch, K. Schoolyard in April.
Komunyakaa, Y. White Port and Lemon Juice.
Kuan Kuan. Autobiography of a Sloppy Sluggard.
Lane, P. On Being Head of the English Department.
Lawrence, D. H. Last Lesson of the Afternoon.
Leto. For Talking.
Levine, P. On My Own.
Lifshin. Being Jewish in a Small Town.
Loftis, N. Fights After School.
Lorde. Hanging Fire.
Lumsden, R. Show and Tell.
MacNeice. I ought to be glad.
Madgett. Images.
Major, C. I Was Looking for the University.
Masters, E. In Memory of Bryan Lathrop.
Mathews, H. Sense of Responsibility, The.
McPherson, S. Helen Todd: My Birthname.
Miller, E. Night Before the First Day of School, The.
Milligan, S. Bad Report—Good Manners.
Moore, M. Student, The.
Moorer. Negro Schools, The.
Tree of Knowledge, The.
Morse, B. Day on the Planet, A.
Muldoon, P. Anseo.
O'Grady, D. This introspective exile here today.
Partridge, D. Hostage.
Piercy. Learning Experience.
Porter, B. First Time Going to School All by Myself.
Portnoy, M. Voucher.
Prufer, K. Pause, Pause.
Rector. First Grade.
Reiter, T. Class Bully.
Rich, A. In a Classroom.
Memory lifts her smoky mirror: 1943.
School Among the Ruins, The.
Ríos, A. Domingo Limón.
Roberts, David Thomas. Tiff Belt Parley.
Roberts, L. Assignment, The.
Rosenberg, L. They Are Planning to Cancel the School Milk Program to Fund a Tax Cut for the Middle Class.
Ruefle. Hand, The: "Teacher asks a question, The."
St. John, P. Reading a Story to My Child.
Sanchez, S. Norma.
Selman, S. Community School.
Shaw, D. Retrospection.
Silverstein, S. Sick.
Smith, B. How Garnett Mims and the Enchanters Came into Your Life.
Soto. Saturday at the Canal.
Spender, S. Elementary School Classroom in a Slum, An.
Svoboda. Report from High School.
Swift, J. Description of the Morning, A.
Thompson, P. Examination, The.

Lines to an Old School-House.
Truitt, S. Old World Monkeys.
Unknown. Country School, The.
Valerie, J. On Apologies.
Venn, G. Poem Against the First Grade.
Wagner, M. Miss Clement's Second Grade.
Warren, R. School Lesson Based on Word of Tragic Death of Entire Gillum Family.
Wayman. Did I Miss Anything?
Weaver, A. Poets, The.
Whitman, W. Old Man's Thought of School, An.
Whittemore, R. High School Band, The.
Whittier. To My Old Schoolmaster.
Williamson, G. Drawing Hands.
  Walter Parmer.
Wren, A. Day at School, A.
Yeats. Among School Children.
Zamora-Linmark. Day 1: Portrait of the Artist, Small-kid Time.
Zarzyski. Hurley High.
Zimmer. Zimmer in Grade School.
  Zimmer's Head Thudding against the Blackboard.
See also **Colleges and Universities**

Schoolmasters
Basheva. N. N.
Ko Un. Headmaster Abe.
See also **Teaching and Teachers**

Schopenhauer, Arthur
Adams, F. Ballade of Schopenhauer's Philosophy.

Schubert, Franz
Tranströmer. Schubertiana.
Welish. Textile 11.

Schumann, Robert
Hernandez, F. De cómo Robert Schumann fue vencido por los demonios.
  On How Robert Schumann Was Defeated by Demons.

Science and Scientists
Ai. Testimony of J. Robert Oppenheimer, The.
Alexander, E. Venus Hottentot, The.
Barbauld. To Mr. S. T. Coleridge.
Brontë, C. Reason.
Citino. Sister Mary Appassionata Lectures the Science Class: Fossils, Physics, Apple, Heart.
Cummings, E. E. Pity This Busy Monster,Manunkind.
  Space being(don't forget to remember)Curved.
Davies, S. Science.
Duhamel. Ego.
Edson, R. Counting Sheep.
Espada. Do Not Put Dead Monkeys in the Freezer.
Fenton, J. Kingfisher's Boxing Gloves, The.
Fox, S. Almagest, Last Letter to Zakarias.
Fuhrman, J. Evidence.
Gewanter, D. Divorce and Mr. Circe.
Goldbarth. Sciences Sing a Lullabye, The.
Harte, B. Society upon the Stanislaus, The.
Hernández Cruz. Keeping Track of the Serpents.
  Physics of Ochun, The.
Hicok. Absence: "There are men and women huddled in rooms tonight."
Holub. Brief Reflection on Accuracy.
  Suffering.
Hope, A. On an Engraving by Casserius.
Jarrell, R. Emancipators, The.
Katz, J. Taxonomy.
Kizer, C. Twelve O'Clock.
Kumin, M. Heaven as Anus.
Lawrence, D. H. Self-Protection.
Lehrer. Wernher von Braun.
Lindsay, V. Horrid Voice of Science, The.
Lowell, J. Science and Poetry.
MacDiarmid, H. Poetry and Science.
Magrelli. If you melt some lead.
Merrill, J. Laboratory Poem.
Morris, T. Apology to Pangea.
Naden. Scientific Wooing.
Nash, O. Purist, The.
Nemerov. Intimations.
Norris, K. Naming the Living God.

O'Driscoll, D. Experimental Animals.
Ortiz. On late-night television, two U.S. scientists talk about why the U.S.
Peskett. Bottles in the Zoological Museum.
Poe. Sonnet—To Science.
Pope, A. Intended for Sir Isaac Newton.
Ramke, B. Astronomer Works Nights: A Parable of Science, The.
Rukeyser, M. Gyroscope, The.
Sadi [*or* Saadi *or* Sa'di]. When once the soul is ready to depart, sir.
Sherry, P. Fermi Lab: Sisyphus of Quarks.
Solie, Karen. Science and the Single Girl.
Tate, J. Teaching the Ape to Write Poems.
Updike. V. B. Nimble, V. B. Quick.
Wilkie, B. Very Fine Lines.

Science Fiction
Amis, K. Science Fiction.
Baldwin, Sandy. Heralds of the hurricane.
Collins, B. Man in Space.
Goldbarth. Meop.
Revard. Discovery of the New World.
Stanton, M. Space.

Scorn
Aleshire. Double, The.
Anacreon. Not / But near another you have a timid.
Cristall. Morning. Rosamonde.
Donne. Apparition, The.
Glück, L. Horse.
Hahn, O. Good Night Dear.
Hölderlin. No Pardon.
Joyce, J. Bahnhofstrasse.
Marlowe. Nephew, I must to Scotland. Thou stay'st here.
Nezahualcoyotl. Our Lord.
Ovid. So, when she saw Narcissus wandering through the lonely countryside, Echo fell in love with him, and followed secretly in his steps.
Philips, K. To the Queen of Inconstancy, Regina Collier, in Antwerp.
Robinson, E. Miniver Cheevy.
Sidney, P. Sonnet 31: "With how sad steps, O Moon[e], thou climb'st the skies."
Tennyson, A. How thought you that this thing could captivate?
Theocritus. Idyll 20: Neteheard [*or* Neatherd].
Unknown. Fair and Scornful.
  Little horror does nothing—does not make love, does not make war, The.
Wilde, L. Désillusion.

Scorpions
Alfonso X. Scorpions, The.
Ezekiel. Night of the Scorpion.
Gerov, Alexander. Accra.
Plomer. Scorpion, The.
Saitō Sanki. Machine gun, A.
Smith, S. Scorpion.

Scotland
Adams, J. There's Nae Luck about the House.
Anderson, W. I'm Naebody Noo.
Aneirin. Lord of Gododdin will be praised in song, A.
  When a crowd of cares.
Angus. Blue Jacket, The.
  Doors of Sleep, The.
Aytoun, W. Morning dawned full darkly, The.
Bernstein, M. Manly Sports.
Bowles, W. At a Village in Scotland.
Brodsky, J. In my declining years, in a land beyond the ocean.
Brown, G. Kirkyard.
Buchan, T. Scotland the Wee.
Burns, R. Cotter's Saturday Night [Inscribed to Robert Aiken [*or* R. A****], Esq.], The.
  Halloween.
  Scotch Drink.
  Scots Wha Hae.
  Such a Parcel of Rogues in a Nation.
  Tam o' Shanter; A Tale.
  To a Haggis.
Burnside, J. Dundee.
Cameron, N. Meeting My Former Self.
Campbell, T. Lord Ullin's Daughter.
  To the Evening Star.

Wizard.
Clark, T. Some Details of Hebridean House Construction.
Corcadail, A. I. O rosary that recalled my tear.
Crawford, R. Result, The.
Cunningham, A. Thistle's Grown aboon the Rose, The.
Davidson, J. Contraption,—that's the bizarre, proper slang.
  Northern Suburb, A.
  Thirty Bob a Week.
Dunn, D. Land Love.
  Landscape with One Figure.
  St Kilda's Parliament: 1879–1979.
Fordham. Highland Mary.
Fraser, G. Home Town Elegy.
Gilfillan, R. Exile's Song, The.
Graham, H. Cockney of the North, The.
Graham, W. Loch Thom.
Gray, S. Scotland.
Greig, A. Orkney / This Life.
Hamilton, J. Oor Location.
Hay, G. Bizerta.
Herbert, W. Socialist Manifesto for East Balgillo, The.
Hogg, J. Charlie is my Darling.
  Thirteenth Bard's Song, The.
Hugo, R. Langaig.
Jamie, K. Arraheids.
  Crossing the Loch.
  Mr and Mrs Scotland Are Dead.
  Queen of Sheba, The.
  St Bride's.
Johnston, A. To Robert Baron.
Johnston, E. Last Sark, The.
  Working Man, The.
Keats. There Was a Naughty Boy.
Leonard, T. Before the 1820 rising in the West of Scotland a network of.
  Jist Ti Let Yi No.
Lochhead, L. Something I'm Not.
Lom. Lament for the State of the Country, A.
Lomax, M. Kith.
Lyndsay [*or* Lindsay], D. Complaynt [*or* Compleynt *or* Complaint] of the Comoun [*or* Common] Weill of Scotland, The.
MacCaig. Return to Scalpay.
  Small Lochs.
MacDiarmid, H. In the Pantry.
  Language that but sparely floo'ers, The.
  Little White Rose, The.
  Scotland Small?
  We must look at the harebell as if.
MacDonald, A. Month of plants and of honey.
Macdonald, G. Song.
MacGregor, Mrs., of Glenstrae. Lament for MacGregor of Glenstrae.
MacIntyre, D. To the Air of a Pibroch.
Mackinnon, R. Scotland: "Green-coated elms stand placidly around."
MacLean, S. Calvary: "My eye is not on Calvary."
  Hallaig.
  Kinloch Ainort.
Macleod, M. Blue Song.
MacNeice. Bagpipe Music.
Mangan, G. Glasgow 1956.
McDonald, E. Widdershins.
McMillan, H. Leaving Scotland by Train.
Mitchison. Scottish Renaissance in Glasgow, The: 1935.
Morgan, E. Loch Ness Monster's Song, The.
Muir, E. Childhood.
  Scotland 1941.
  Scotland's Winter.
Munro, N. Hey, Jock, Are Ye Glad Ye 'Listed?
Mure. O Heavens! O Earth! heer I must pause a space.
Na Ceapaich, S. Alasdair of Glengarry.
Nairne. Heiress, The.
NicNèill, S. For Eric Blair.
O'Donnell, D. Young Men of Blackburn, The.
Paterson, D. Chartres of Gowrie, The.
Pfeiffer, E. Among the Hebrides.
Ramsay, A. Jenny Nettles.
Reid, A. Scotland: "It was a day peculiar to this

piece of the planet."
Retallack, J. Biographia Literaria.
Robertson, R. Aberdeen.
Ronald of Orkney, Saint. Attributes of a
  Gentleman, The.
Ross, W. Another Song.
Scott, A. Welcum, illustrat Ladye, and oure
  Quene!
Scott, S. Breathes there the [or a] Man with
  soul so dead.
  Hellvellyn.
  Lochinvar.
  Melrose Abbey.
Sempill, F. Maggie Lauder.
Shakespeare, W. What bloody man is that? He
  can report.
Skirving. Johnnie Cope.
Smith, I. Clearances, The.
  Contrasts.
  Exiles, The.
  Gaelic Stories.
  Listen.
  Shall Gaelic Die?
Smith, S. Grace of God and the Meth-Drinker,
  The.
  War in Fife, The.
Smith, W. Glenaradale.
Soutar. Tryst [or Trysting Place], The.
Southey, R. Inchcape Rock, The.
Tannahill. Eild.
  Tap-Room, The.
Taylor, R. Princess of Scotland, The.
Tennant, W. Sang First.
Thomson, D. Herring Girls, The.
Todd, R. About Scotland, &C.
Tomlinson, C. Mr. Brodsky.
Unknown. Author of this is Ossian, The.
  Jenny Nettles.
  Justice to Scotland.
  Mary Hamilton.
  Mary [or Marie] Hamilton [Version from
    Motherwell's Manuscript].
  Qwhen Alexander our kynge was dede.
  Sir Patrick Spens [or Spence].
  Tam Lin.
  Tayis Bank.
Vettese. Scottish Mythology.
  Scottish Names.
Young, A. Wet Day, A.

Scots, The
Burns, R. Cotter's Saturday Night [Inscribed to
  Robert Aiken [or R. A****], Esq.], The.
  Scotch Drink.
  Scots Wha Hae.
  Such a Parcel of Rogues in a Nation.
  To a Haggis.
Cleveland, J. Nature herself doth Scotchmen
  beasts confess.
  Rebel Scot, The.
Crawford, R. Alba Einstein.
  Saltcoats Structuralists, The.
Duffy, C. In Your Mind.
Fergusson. To the Principal and Professors of
  the University of St Andrews, on their Superb
  Treat to Dr Samuel Johnson.
Herbert, W. Coco-de-Mer.
  King and Queen of Dumfriesshire, The.
Kay, J. English Cousin Comes to Scotland.
Leonard, T. Fathers and Sons.
  This is thi.
MacNeacail. Gaelic is alive.
Macrae, J. Sleep Softly.
Morgan, E. Sir James Murray.
Muir, E. Scotland 1941.
Scott, A. Scotched.
Smith, I. Listen.
Stevenson, R. Ticonderoga: A Legend of the
  West Highlands.
Unknown. Battle of Inverlochy, The.
  Sir Patrick Spens [or Spence].

Scott, Sir Walter
Smith, I. At the Scott Exhibition, Edinburgh
  Festival.

Scottish Borders
Elliot, J. Flowers of the Forest, The.

Scott, S. Dreary Change, The.
  Lochinvar.
Tremayne. North of Berwick.

Scottish Highlands
Burns, R. My Heart's in the Highlands.
Stevenson, R. In the highlands, in the country
  places.

Scottsboro Case
Cutler, Y. Neckst.
Friedman, B. Scottsboro.
Rontsh, Y. Done a Good Job.
  Scottsboro.

Screams
Bashir, S. Her Scream Has Been Stolen.
Creeley. Turn, The.
Ezekiel. Song to be Shouted Out.
Freneau. O'er a dark field I held my dubious
  way.
Hill, S. I Know I Ought to Love You.
Lisboa. Echo.
Mihalic. Screams in the Dark.
Smith, P. Finding His Fist.
Unknown, fr. Terezin Concentration Camp.
  Closed Town, The.

Scribes
Chaucer. Chaucer's Wordes unto Adam, his
  Owne Scriveyn.
Ettinger, E. Micrographic Manuscript,
  Miniature (1).
See also **Secretaries**

Sculpture and Sculptors
Agoos, J. To Atlas in the Attic.
Brouwer, J. Conjurer's Honor.
Browning, E. Hiram Powers' "Greek Slave".
Byron, G. Or view the Lord of the unerring
  bow.
Cawein. Mnemosyne.
Cherry, K. Bride of Quietness, The.
Coleridge, M. On a Bas-relief of Pelops and
  Hippodameia.
Darío, R. Victory of Samothrace, The.
Doty, M. Days of 1981.
Elliott, E. Criticism.
Fuller, M. Flaxman.
Gilbert, C. African Sculpture.
Gower, J. Pygmaleon.
Hall, D. Dusting.
Higginson, E. Statue, The.
Hinsey, E. Roman Arbor, The.
Hirshfield, J. Earthly Beauty, An.
Hummell, A. Sculpture Garden.
Jarrell, R. Bronze David of Donatello, The.
Keats. On Seeing the Elgin Marbles.
Leconte de Lisle, C. Venus de Milo.
Mathews, C. Sculptor, The.
Meinke. Helen.
Michelangelo Buonarroti. My lady, how comes
  it about—what all can see.
  "Night" in the Medici Chapel.
Middleton, C. Anasphere: Le torse antique.
Moore, M. No Swan So Fine.
Oppenheim, M. Dream in Barcelona.
Ovid. Pygmalion.
Padel, R. Icicles Round a Tree in
  Dumfriesshire.
Ray, H. Sculptor's Vision, The.
  Tireless Sculptor, The.
Rilke. Birth of the Smile, The.
Rogers, S. To the Fragment of a Statue of
  Hercules, Commonly Called the Torso.
Sadoleto. Poem of Jacobus Sadoletus on the
  Statue of Laocoon, The.
Santayana. Before a Statue of Achilles.
Scollard. Bit of Marble, A.
Shockley, E. My last modernist poem, #2 (or,
  mugshot).
Stickney, T. On Rodin's "L'Illusion, Sœur
  d'Icare".
Teasdale. Effigy of a Nun.
Volkow. Arcana 4: The Emperor.
  Arcano 4: El Emperador.
Walker, T. Owl.
Wolfe, H. Tulip.
Yeats. Statues, The.

Sea
Acholonu. Water Woman.
Ackland. Since the first toss of gale that blew.
Adam, H. Song for a Sea Tower.
Aiken, C. Sea Holly.
Akhmatova, A. Land not mine, still, A.
Al-Aziz, M. We Asked.
Alberti. Amparo.
  Angel of Sand, The.
Ammons. So I Said I Am Ezra.
Amor, P. CXXXIV.
Angira. Old Wharf Canto.
Anyte [or Anytes]. This is Kypris' place; it ever
  pleases her.
Apollinaire. Listen to the sea.
Arnold, M. Dover Beach.
  To Marguerite—Continued.
Ashbery, J. Painter, The.
Atkins, R. Lakefront, Cleveland.
Auden. On This Island.
Awoonor. Sea Eats the Land at Home, The.
Bancquart. Portrait of Jonah with Woman.
  Sea.
  Woman asleep.
Bansode. Woman.
Barrax. There Was A Song.
Basho. Autumnal full moon.
  Early fall.
  How wild the sea is.
  Sea darkening, The.
  Sea grows dark, The.
  Sea grows rough, The.
  Seas slowly darken.
  Still alive.
  Wild sea, A.
Baxter, J. East Coast Journey.
Bei Dao. August Sleepwalker, The.
Beaver. Angels' Weather.
Beckett, S. Dieppe.
  Dieppe.
Beer, P. Jane Austen.
Bell, M. Hole in the Sea, The.
Belli, G. Brief Lessons in Eroticism 1.
Benttinen, T. Maritime Pastoral.
Berkson, B. Non Dimenticar.
Betjeman. East Anglian Bathe.
Bishop, E. At the Fishhouses.
  Map, The.
  Seascape.
  Song: "Summer is over upon the sea."
  Twelfth Morning; or What You Will.
Blackmur. Seas Incarnadine.
Blight. Down from the Country.
  Landfall, The.
Borges. Sea, The.
Brooks, C. Lines: Composed at the Old
  Temples of Maralipoor.
Browning, R. Meeting at Night.
  Parting at Morning.
Brownstein. War.
Brutus. At Night.
Bunina. From the Seashore.
Bunting. I am agog for foam. Tumultuous
  come.
Busia, A. Mawu of the Waters.
Buson. Field of mustard, A.
  Spring sea rising, The.
Bynner. Wave, The.
Cabral de Melo Neto. Canefield and the Sea,
  The.
  Daily Space.
Camões [or Camõens or Camoëns], L. On a
  Shipmate, Pero Moniz, Dying at Sea.
Campo. My Voice.
Carroll, L. Lobster Quadrille, A.
Cary, A. Katrina on the Porch.
Catherine of Siena. We were enclosed.
Cavendish, M. Sea Similized to Meadows and
  Pastures, The: the Mariners, to Shepherds: the
  Mast, to a May-Pole: the Fish, to Beasts.
Cendrars. Fish Cove.
Césaire, A. Bucolic.
  On the Islands of All Winds.
Chin. Repulse Bay.
Chivers. Wind, The.
Chŏng Chiyong. Sea 6.

Chunghur Hyujung. While Sleeping at the Southern Sea.
Clampitt. Beach Glass.
Clarke, George Elliott. Hymn for Portia White.
Clifton, L. Lost baby poem, The.
Coleridge, S. I fear thee, ancient Mariner!
Cooley, N. Undine.
Cooley, P. Secret, The.
Copus, J. Cricketer's Retirement Day, The.
Corn. Naskeag.
Cornwall. Address to the Ocean.
Corso. Sea Chanty.
Cowper, W. Light Shining out of Darkness.
Cox, M. Sonata.
Crane, H. And Bees of Paradise.
  At Melville's Tomb.
  Ave Maria.
  Voyages.
Crane, S. Man adrift on a slim spar, A.
Cristall. Song: "Both gloomy and dark was the shadowy night."
Cronin, J. Naval Base (Part III), The.
Cummings, E. E. How many moments must(amazing each).
  Maggie and milly and molly and may.
Curnow. You Will Know When You Get There.
Daive. Lost in contemplation.
Dalton, Mary. Water Man, The.
Darley. Hurry me Nymphs! O, hurry me.
  Rebellion of the Waters, The.
Darwish, M. Guests on the Sea.
Davidson, L. Charnel Ship, The.
Davison, P. Equinox 1980.
Dawes, K. Trickster 4 (for Sister Patra).
de Burgos. Sea and You, The.
  Seawall.
De Mello Breyner. Day of Sea.
  Inscription.
Desnos. Obsession.
Dickey, J. At Darien Bridge.
Dickinson, E. By the Sea.
  Wild Nights—Wild Nights!
Donnelly, T. Purgatory Chasm.
Doolittle, H. Blue-geese, white-geese, you may say.
  Hermes of the Ways.
  Or is it a great tide that covers the rock-pool.
  Oread.
Dove, R. Fish in the Stone, The.
Drinan. Men on the Rocks, The.
Du Maurier. Music.
Dugan, A. Plague of Dead Sharks.
Duncan, R. Achilles' Song.
Eberhart, R. Chart Indent.
Éluard, P. Deaf and Blind, The.
Elytis, O. Anniversary.
Emerson, R. Sea-Shore.
Fanning, M. Consolation: "I wend to the sea."
Fenton, J. This Octopus Exploits Women.
Ferguson, G. Swimming Pool Ghost, The.
Fermini, I. It descends rapidly under the twistable vine in the sky.
  That bound and tied they fled.
Fisher, C. Severn Bore.
Foot, E. Disaster at Sea.
Forbes, C. Dark Mirror.
  Home.
Fowler, W. Upon this firthe, as on the sees of love.
Francis, R. Onion Fields.
Fraser, S. Looking Out to Sea Again on the Uptown Express.
Frost, R. Neither Out Far Nor In Deep.
  Once by the Pacific.
Gallagher, T. Sea Inside the Sea.
Gibson, W. Prelude: "As one, at midnight wakened by the call."
Gilder, R. On the Bay.
Giussani, S. Hot and Cold.
Googe. Coming Homeward out of Spain.
Graham, J. Complex Mechanism of the Break, The.
Graham, W. Night's Fall.
Greenberg, U. Song of My People-Forest, People-Sea.
Griffiths, B. Dolphins.

Grosholz. Old Fisherman, The.
Guiterman. Sea-Chill.
Ha-Levi, J. Greetings ladies, kith and kin.
Hadas, R. House Beside the Sea, The.
Hahn, O. Gladioli by the Sea.
Haida. Song for Smooth Waters.
Hardy, T. Beeny Cliff.
Hartmann, S. Cyanogen Seas Are Surging.
Harwood, G. Clair de Lune.
Hawthorne, N. Ocean, The.
Heaney, S. Visible sea at a distance from the shore, The.
Hemans. Written on the Sea-Shore.
Herbert, J. Irish Scullery Maid, The.
Herrera. Weaning of Furniture-Nutrition.
  When He Believed Himself to Be a Young Girl Lifting the Skin of the Water.
Heym. Seafarers.
Higginson, E. Opal Sea, The.
Hill, G. Wreaths.
Hillman, B. Formation of Soils, The.
Hirschman, J. Headlands.
Hoban. Old Man Ocean.
Hollander, J. Morning in the Islands.
Hooper, V. Reading, A.
Houlihan, J. Hydrangeas.
Hughes, L. Sea Calm.
Hughes, T. Relic.
Hugo, R. Note from Capri to Richard Ryan on the Adriatic Floor.
  Salt Water Story.
Iorwerth, D. Sea.
Issa. Mother, I weep.
  These sea slugs.
Istarú, A. From where you have come.
James, J. Bye Bye Blackbird.
Jamie, K. Bosegran.
Jarman, M. Cavafy in Redondo.
Jeffers, R. Evening Ebb.
  Eye, The.
  November Surf.
  Ocean's Tribute, The.
  Place for No Story, The.
Jiménez, J. Sea Is Enormous, The.
Johnstone, R. Robot Camera.
Jones, Rodney. News of the Cranes.
Jones, Roland. Foam.
Joyce, J. On the Beach at Fontana.
Kadima-Nzuji. Incantations of the Sea: Moando Coast.
Kassid, A. Seer, The.
Kaufman, B. Celebrated White-Cap Spelling Bee, The.
Keats. On the Sea.
Kees. If this Room is Our World.
Kelley, E. At the Center, Creator Hourglass.
Kennelly. Island, The.
Khlebnikov, V. One Book, The.
Khoury, N. Death Is Your Salvation.
Kim Chôngnan. Sea at Twenty-Four, The.
Kimball, H. In Reverie.
Kipling, R. Dykes, The.
  Last Chantey, The.
Klink, J. Sea by Dusk.
Klyuyev [or Kliuev or Klyuev]. Sky Lies Blue—Like a Sea, The.
Kruit, J. House By the Sea.
Lady Ise. Flower of waves, A.
Laing, K. One Hundred Lines for the Coast.
Lal Ded [or Lalla]. I drag a boat over the ocean.
Landon. Sappho's Song.
Lanier, S. Marsh Song—At Sunset.
Larkin, P. Absences.
Lawrence, D. H. Butterfly.
  Whales Weep Not!
Le Guin. Child on the Shore, The.
Lear, E. Jumblies, The.
Levine, P. New Year's Eve, in Hospital.
  Sea We Read About, The.
Li Po. Ancient Air.
Lodge, G. Strong saturation of sea! O widely flown.
  Tuckanuck.
Longfellow, H. Broken Oar, The.
  Seaweed.

Sound of the Sea, The.
Tide Rises, the Tide Falls, The.
Longley, M. Freeze-Up.
Lorde. What My Child Learns of the Sea.
Lowell, A. Shore Grass.
Lowell, R. Water.
Lowry, M. Wild Cherry, The.
Loynaz, D. M. Sea Surrounded.
Lummis, Suzanne. Sea Chanty.
Lux. Marine Snow at Mid-Depths and Down.
Machado Ruiz. Lord, You Have Ripped Away.
  Mankind owns four things.
  Moldering Hulk, The.
  People Possess Four Things.
  Summer's Night, A.
Mackey, N. Dream Thief.
  Phantom Light of All Our Day, The.
MacLeish. Return.
MacNeice. Thalassa.
Madani. Here I am Once More.
Maio, Samuel. Love Song: "New pier is concrete, the streets are paved, The."
Mallarmé. Sea Breeze.
Mandelstam [or Mandelshtam]. Insomnia.
  Insomnia. Homer. Taut Sails.
  Sleeplessness. Homer. The sails tight.
Mansour, J. Beyond the breakers.
Markham, E. Sea, The.
Marsman. Paradise Regained.
Marvell. Bermudas.
Masefield. Sea Fever.
  Wanderer's Song, A.
Mattawa. Road from Biloxi, The.
Matveyeva [or Matveieva]. Ginger-Haired Girl, The.
Mayer, B. Boats.
  Sea: "It's he, it's sea. the sea is continuous; a continuous body."
McCabe, C. End of January, The.
McDonald, E. Itherness.
Melville, H. Maldive Shark, The.
  Pebbles.
  Song from Mardi.
Messerli. Going to Sea.
Mew. Sea Love.
Michaux. Jetty, The.
Mickiewicz. Storm, The.
Miljkovic. Sea Without Poets.
Millay, E. Burial.
  Hearing Your Words, and Not a Word Among Them.
  Inland.
  Ragged Island.
Miller, J. At Our Golden Gate.
Minhinnick. Surfers.
Mirabai [or Mira Bai]. O friend, understand: the body.
Moore, L. Until I Saw the Sea.
Moore, M. Fish, The: "Wade / through black jade."
  Grave, A.
  Jellyfish, A.
Morejón. Havana Harbor.
  To a Boy.
Morgan, E. Sea, The.
Morrison, L. Surf.
Moschus. Ocean, The.
Mother Goose. Three wise men of Gotham.
Mu Hua. Sea, The.
Muldoon, P. Briefcase, The.
Murford. Storm and Calm: Sent from Embden to M. Edw. Ma. and M. Tho. Ly, The.
Muso Soseki. By the sea.
Nash, O. Beginner's Guide to the Ocean, A.
Nemerov. Salt Garden, The.
Neruda. Different Ship, A.
  Enigmas: "You've asked me what the lobster is weaving there with his golden feet?"
  Poet's Obligation.
Nicholson, N. Sea to the West.
Nickerson. At Auke Bay the whales dance.
Nietzsche. Notes.
No Hyangnim. Ap'ae Island 1—Diving Women.
  Dream: "Sea was in front of me, The."
Noguere. Barney Bigard.

O'Hara, F. Elegy: "Salt water. and faces dying."
  Sonnet: "Blueness of the hour, The."
Okara. One Night at Victoria Beach.
Oppen. Animula.
  Gold on Oak Leaves.
  Party on Shipboard.
  Silver as / The needle's eye.
O'Sullivan, V. By the Sea-Wall.
Oswald, A. Sea Sonnet.
Pacheco, J. Song to Be Written on a Wave.
Padilla. Sometimes I plunge into the ocean . . . .
Paterson, D. St Brides: Sea-Mail.
Peacocke. We're Staying at the Castlemount,
  Western Esplanade.
Percival. Coral Grove, The.
Petrarch. Galley, The.
Phylip, S. Seagull, The.
Pittman, Al. Lupines.
Plath. Blackberrying.
  Point Shirley.
Poe. Annabel Lee.
  City in the Sea, The.
  To Helen ("Helen, thy beauty is to me.").
  To One in Paradise.
Pogson, P. Deep.
Portal. Thirst for the Sea.
Press, K. Bird.
Pritchard, N. Burnt Sienna.
Probyn. Barcarolle.
Procter, A. Address to the Ocean.
Prunty. Offset, The.
Pulido, A. Dibuja una letra.
  Traces a letter.
Radcliffe, A. Sea-View, A.
Raine, K. Moment, The.
Rankin, J. Sea and Other Stories, The.
  Sea-bundle.
Reeves, J. Sea, The.
Rich, A. Insusceptibles, The.
Richter, H. Surfaces.
Rimbaud, A. Drunken Boat.
  Drunken Boat, The.
  Seascape.
Rivas, J. Marea roja.
  Red Tide.
Rodríguez, C. Foam.
Roethke. Rose, The.
Roland Holst. Being.
Rossetti, C. By the Sea.
  Horses of the Sea, The.
  What Are Heavy?
  Wind Has Such a Rainy Sound, The.
Rossetti, D. Sea-Limits, The.
Ruefle. Search Party.
Rukeyser, M. Outer Banks, The.
  Summer, the Sacramento.
Rumann, Son of Colman. Storm at Sea.
Saïd, A. My Woman's Transparence.
St. John, P. Song.
  Sunday.
Saleh. Beach, Later.
  December Nap.
Salinas, L. Sea Song.
Samaras, N. Crossing the Strait.
Sandburg, C. Adelaide Crapsey.
  Be Ready.
  Bones.
Scammell, W. St Bees in Winter.
Schick. Last summer.
Schuyler, J. Crystal Lithium, The.
Seferis. Bottle in the Sea.
  Stratis the Sailor by the Dead Sea.
Shinkichi Takahashi. Sea of Oblivion.
Shokushi. Guide me on my way.
Silko. Prayer to the Pacific.
Silverstein, S. Slithergadee, The.
Simic. Hundred-Year-Old China Doll's Head,
  The.
Sisson. In Flood.
Skelton, R. Night Piece.
Smith, C. Pressed by the Moon, Mute Arbitress
  of Tides.
  Sea View, The.
  Written on the Sea Shore.—October, 1784.
Smith, I. You Are at the Bottom of My Mind.
Smith, J. Sea Marke.

Smith, S. Kenless Strand, The.
Smither. Sea Question, The.
Spaziani. It is Said by Some Sailors, the Old.
Spender, S. Seascape.
Spicer, J. Phonemics.
Stainer. Seals, The.
Stephens, J. Main-Deep, The.
  Shell, The.
Stevens, W. Farewell to Florida.
  Idea of Order at Key West, The.
  Paltry Nude Starts on a Spring Voyage, The.
  Sea Surface Full of Clouds.
Stevenson, R. At the Seaside [or Sea-Side].
Stickney, T. At Sainte-Marguerite.
Storni. Me at the Bottom of the Sea.
  Sorrow.
  Words to My Mother.
Stoyanova, Danila. Sea woke up, The.
Street, S. Shipping Forecast, Donegal.
Supervielle. Like an ox.
Swann, B. Land at the World's End, The.
Swenson, M. Fire Island.
  Staring at the Sea on the Day of the Death of
    Another.
  Stone Gullets.
  Waking from a Nap on the Beach.
  Wave and the Dune, The.
Swift, T. Influence of Anxiety at the Seaside
  with Tea, The.
Swinburne. I Will Go Back to the Great Sweet
  Mother.
Swirszczynska [or Swir]. Sea and the Man,
  The.
Takamura Kotaro. Whale Spouting.
Taylor, B. On the Headland.
  On the Sea.
Teasdale. After Love.
  On the Dunes.
Tennyson, A. Break, Break, Break.
  Calm is the morn without a sound.
  Crossing the Bar.
  Kraken, The.
  Sweet and Low.
Thaxter. Imprisoned.
Thomas, E. Deep-Sea Pearl, The.
Thomson, D. Lewis.
Ts'ao Ts'ao. View of the Blue Sea.
Tucker, M. Beautiful Sea, The.
Ulacia, M. En la playa.
  On the Beach.
Unknown. Battle of Brunanburh.
  Bran at the Island of Women.
  Forest Trees of the Sea.
  North-East.
  Sea.
  Seafarer, The.
  Sir Patrick Spens [or Spence].
  Song of Blodeuwedd, The.
Untermeyer, J. High Tide.
Uvavnuk. Shaman Song.
Vancrevel. About Time ("At dusk the silence by
  the sea.").
  About Time ("This silence at the sea's edge, so
    late in the afternoon.").
Vázquez Montalbán, M. Yramín and the Sea.
Verlaine. Beams.
Verwey, A. North-Sea, The.
Villaurrutia. Nocturnal Sea.
Waddington, M. Sea Bells.
Walcott. Missing the Sea.
  Sea Is History, The.
Waldrop, R. At the Sea.
Warner, S. Since the first toss of gale that blew.
Watson, R. Midnight Harvest, A.
Watts-Dunton. Sonnet's Voice, The.
Webb, F. End of the Picnic.
Webster, A. Enigma No. 6.
Whitman, W. After the Sea-Ship.
  As I Ebb'd with the Ocean of Life.
  Facing West from California's Shores.
  Had I the Choice.
  Out of the Cradle Endlessly Rocking.
  Patrolling Barnegat.
  Ship Starting, The.
  Song for All Seas, All Ships.
  To the Man-of-War Bird.

  World below the Brine, The.
  You sea! I resign myself to you also—I guess
    what you mean.
Wilbur, R. Beacon, The.
Williams, W. Flowers by the Sea ("When over
  the flowery, sharp pasture's.").
  Sadness of the Sea, The.
  Yachts, The.
Winters, Y. Fable, The.
Witt, S. Ikonostasis. The Sound of the Sea
  Filling a Faraway Room.
Wohlfeld. Sea.
Woods, V. Asylum is Water, The.
Wordsworth, W. It Is a Beauteous Evening.
Wyatt. Sonnet: "My Galley Charged".
Yi Yônju. Grandmother's Sea.
Young, I. Mermaid Knows, A.
Zinger, G. Strategy.
Zukofsky, L. It's hard to see but think of a sea.
See also **Sailing and Sailors**
Sea Chanteys
Fletcher, J. Clipper-Ships.
Sea Creatures
Darwin. Ae Fond Kiss, and Then.
Fenton, J. This Octopus Exploits Women.
Frost, C. Chimera.
Glazova, A. Venice: "Enormous clock at the
  sandy mansion, An."
Gyodai. Inching / From dark to dark—.
Knight, S. Surf Motel, The.
Moore, M. Fish, The: "Wade / through black
  jade."
  Sea Unicorns and Land Unicorns.
Neruda. Enigmas: "You've asked me what the
  lobster is weaving there with his golden feet?"
Tennyson, A. Kraken, The.
Thurston, H. Dragging Bottom.
Vivien. Rançon, La.
Williams, T. Foam.
Williams, W. Sea-Elephant, The.
Sea Gulls
Bonnefoy. Task of Hope, The.
Herzberg. Seagulls.
Jones, G. Dafydd's Seagull and the West Wind.
McCabe, B. Seagull.
Menicanti. Seagulls.
Nadir, M. My Bas-Sheva.
Nash, O. Sea-Gull and the Ea-Gull, The.
Watson, R. Midnight Harvest, A.
Williams, T. Foam.
See also **Gulls**
Sea Monsters and Sea Serpents
Berezovchuk, L. Calm rocks to sleep in your
  usual place.
Morgan, E. Loch Ness Monster's Song, The.
Tennyson, A. Kraken, The.
Sea Poetry
Day, C. Once As Thoth Beside The Sea.
Sea Shells
Basho. Between the waves.
Chivers. Shell, The.
Coolbrith. Sea-Shell, The.
Darío, R. Seashell, The.
Doolittle, H. There is a spell, for instance.
Lowe, L. Sea Shells.
See also **Shells**
Sea Voyages
"Ada.". Slave Girl's Farewell, The.
Booth, P. Navigation.
Carryl, C. Walloping Window-Blind, The.
Chinese Oral Tradition. Song of the Wife of a
  Gold Mountain Man.
Coolbrith. Sailed.
Drayton. Like an Adventurous Seafarer Am I.
Dryden, J. By viewing nature, nature's
  handmaid, art.
Greene, Richard. Crossing the Straits.
Maggs, Randall. Night Crossing in Ice.
Melville, H. Call me Ishmael.
Nortje. Night ferry.
Swift, J. Holyhead. September 25, 1727.
Sze. Network, The.
Unknown. Family treasures.
  Loud waves up and down.
See also **Voyages**

Seacoasts
Addonizio.   At Moss Beach.
Adesuyi, N.   New Testament, The.
Albrecht, A.   Below White Cliffs.
   Passing Piedras Blancas.
Ammons.   Corsons Inlet.
Bishop, E.   Little Exercise.
Bruce, C.   Early Morning Landing.
Coolbrith.   Sea-Shell, The.
Craig, M.   Love Poem: "Flowers upon your lips
   and hands."
Darío, R.   Tropic Afternoon.
Devlin, D.   Wishes for Her.
Doolittle, H.   Shrine, The.
Hartley, M.   Lapping of waters / thick, upon
   razorblade.
Hopkins, G.   Sea and the Skylark, The.
Keats.   To Ailsa Rock.
Momaday.   Winter Holding off the Coast of
   North America.
Muso Soseki.   Chick feed is what I eat.
   Reply to Bukko Zenji's Poem at Seiken-ji.
Pinsky.   Woman, A.
Schuyler, J.   Crystal Lithium, The.
Stevens, W.   Fabliau of Florida.
Thomas, D.   Author's Prologue.
Tomlinson, C.   Fiascherino.
See also **Beaches; Shores**

Seafaring and Seafarers
Bontemps.   Nocturne of the Wharves.
Camões [or Camõens or Camoëns], L.   Feats of
   Arms, and famed heroick Host, The.
Doolittle, H.   Shrine, The.
Heaney, S.   Dogger, Rockall, Malin, Irish Sea.
Homer.   And then went down to the ship.
Hughes, L.   Water-Front Streets.
Jackson, L.   There Is No Land Yet.
Jamie, K.   Rooms.
Longfellow, H.   Wreck of the Hesperus, The.
Masefield.   Sea Fever.
Mason, F. C.   Sunken Sailor.
Miller, J.   Columbus: "Behind him lay the gray
   Azores."
Poe.   To Helen ("Helen, thy beauty is to me.").
Rimbaud, A.   Drunken Boat.
   Drunken Boat, The.
Simpson, L.   To the Western World.
Stainer.   Sighting the Slave Ship.
   Wound-dresser's Dream, The.
Unknown.   Seafarer, The.
   What Shall We Do for the Striking Seamen?
See also **Sailing and Sailors**

Seals
Bly, R.   Dead Seal [near McClure's Beach], The.
Chamberlain, B.   Seal Cave.
Delanty.   Williams Was Wrong.
Eberhart, R.   Seals, Terns, Time.
Hartman, J.   Petition Hecate at the seal.
Hoffman, D.   Seals in Penobscot Bay, The.
Murphy, R.   Seals at High Island.
Sexton, T.   Seal Island.
Stainer.   Seals, The.

Seamstresses
Gippius.   Seamstress, The.
Hö Nansŏrhŏn.   Poor Woman.
Toledo, N.   Casa de Olga, La.
   Liidxi na Olga.
   Olga's House.
Yeryomin.   Seamstress stitches on a sewing
   machine, The.

Seashores
Albrecht, A.   Passing Piedras Blancas.
Bailey, J.   Ceasefire.
Baker, T.   Le passage (Morbihan).
Banks, Jr., T. H.   Tempest.
Benttinen, T.   Maritime Pastoral.
Berkson, B.   Non Dimenticar.
Bold, A.   Shore.
Boyd, M.   Sea Spray.
Brown, G.   Hamnavoe.
Burnside, J.   History.
Cogswell, Fred.   Beach at Noon, The.
Curbelo.   Tourism in the Late 20th Century.
Davies, Lynn.   Cape Enrage.
Delanty.   Williams Was Wrong.

Durcan.   Martha's Wall.
Forché.   Kalaloch.
Gladding.   Fisherman's Wife, The.
Gregerson.   Cranes on the Seashore.
Harwood, L.   Seaside, The.
Heaney, S.   Deserted harbour stillness. Every
   stone.
Hillman, B.   Foghorn, A.
Hoffman, D.   Lobsterpot Labyrinths.
Hollander, J.   Late August on the Lido.
James, S.   How I'll Live Then.
Jones, B.   South Shore (Aberystwyth), The.
Jones, G.   Morning.
Klappert.   In Memory of H. F.
Martínez, V.   Reliquaries, The.
Mathias, R.   Porth Cwyfan.
McCabe, C.   End of January, The.
   Jastrzebia Góra.
McGrath, T.   Half Measures.
Meredith, W.   June: Dutch Harbor.
Merwin.   Migrants by Night.
Moore, R.   Shipwreck: "Watching, watching
   from the shore."
Morris, S.   Here in these fretted caverns whence
   the sea.
Musgrave.   Equinox.
O'Grady, Thomas.   Some Days, Paradise.
Rivas, J.   Season of Paradise, A.
   Temporada de Paraíso, Una.
Roberts, S.   Tantramar Revisited, The.
Seward.   On the damp margin of the sea-beat
   shore.
Shepherd, R.   Another Version of an Ocean.
Shostakovskaya, I.   Sailor sailor got ashore.
Unknown.   Kadavu.
Warsh.   Moving through Air.
Wheatley, D.   Along a Cliff.
Wunderlich, M.   Anchorage, The.
See also **Shores; Beaches**

Seasickness
Heine, H.   Sea-Sickness.
Martinson.   Letter from a Cattleboat.

Seasons
Anderson, M.   September Song.
Bang, M.   Like a Fire in a Fire.
Basho.   Autumn approaches.
   I'm a wanderer.
   In the withering gusts.
Bergman, A.   Summer Me, Winter Me.
Bergman, M.   Summer Me, Winter Me.
Bishop, E.   Song for the Rainy Season.
Blake, W.   Earth's Answer.
Boccaccio.   Two Dreams, The.
Bogan, L.   After the Persian.
   Zone.
Booth, P.   Seasons.
Brock-Broido.   Domestic Mysticism.
Brontë, E.   Song: "Fall, leaves, fall; die, flowers,
   away;"
Bryant, W.   Winter Piece, A.
Caddel.   Against Numerology.
Cambridge, G.   Fallen Maple Leaves.
Castro, R.   Ailing Woman Felt Her Forces Ebb,
   The.
   Atmosphere Is Incandescent, The.
   Candescent Is the Air.
   Feeling Her End Would Come with Summer's
   End.
Chang Yü.   Pavilion for Listening to Fragrance,
   The.
Chiasson, H.   And the Season Advances.
Ch'in Kuan.   Tune: "Spring in the Painted Hall".
Chippewa Oral Tradition.   Song of Spring, A.
Chiu Tsz-yung.   Lament for Fortune's Frailty, A.
Clare, J.   Last of April, The.
   Shadows.
   Winter.
Coleridge, S.   Garden Year, The.
Collins, W.   Ode to Evening.
Coolbrith.   My Cloth of Gold.
Cope, J.   Winter Sky.
Cornwall.   Address to the Ocean.
Cowper, W.   Winter Walk at Noon, The.
Cristall.   Song: "Through springtime walks, with
   flowers perfumed."
Cullen, C.   Leaves.

Dickinson, E.   As imperceptibly as Grief.
   It was a quiet way—.
Dixon, Z.   Season of Beginning and End.
Donne.   Love's Growth.
   Nocturnal[l] upon Saint Lucy's [or S. Lucy's or
   S. Lucies] Day, Being the Shortest Day, A.
Doubleday, T.   No walk today;—November's
   breathings toss.
Eberhart, R.   Spider, The.
Emerson, J.   Lighthouse, The.
Evance, S.   To Melancholy.
   Written in Ill Health at the Close of Spring.
Fanthorpe.   Waiting Room.
Finch, B.   Written in a Shrubbery Towards the
   Decline of Autumn.
   Written in a Winter's Morning.
Flint, R.   Seasonal, 1991.
Frost, R.   Oven Bird, The.
Fujiwara no Teika.   Weary wild geese who
   came.
George, F.   Wilderness.
Goodison.   Quartet of Daffodils, A.
Greiffenberg.   On the Fruit-Providing Autumn
   Season.
Hadewijch.   Love's Constancy.
Hall, D.   Winter's asperity mollifies.
Halpern, D.   Annuals.
Han Yü.   When white dew descends on the
   hundred grasses.
Harpur, J.   Young Man of Galway's Lament,
   The.
Hartmann, S.   Tanka.
Hemans.   Hour of Death, The.
Hennen.   Life of a Day, The.
Hesketh.   Death of a Gardener.
Hine.   Sapphics.
Hoagland, T.   Change, The.
Hölderlin.   Halflife.
   To the Fates.
Horace.   Ode 4.7: "Snows dissolving, grass
   returns to meadow."
   Ode 4.7 To L. Manlius Torquatus.
   Solvitur Acris Hiems.
Housman.   Night Is Freezing Fast, The.
Hove.   Lost Bird.
   Migratory Bird.
Hunter, A.   Winter.
Ignatova, E.   Summer Garden, The.
Israeli, H.   Sway.
Jiménez, J.   Love.
Kakei.   In the withering gusts.
Kawamura Yoichi.   On the Sand Dune.
Keats.   To Autumn: "Season of mists and
   mellow fruitfulness!"
Kenney.   In April.
Khoury-Gata.   Autumn Preceded Summer.
Kim Chŏngnan.   Between May and June.
Leader, M.   Madrigal: "How the tenor warbles
   in April!"
Lerner, A.   If Ever I Would Leave You.
Levine, P.   Later Still.
Lewis, W.   To the People of a Small Town in
   Ohio, Who As I Approach Them on the Street,
   Are Afraid That This Black Man Is Going to
   Do Them Harm.
Li Ch'ing-chao.   Tune: Spring at Wu Ling.
Li Po.   Wine.
Li Shang-yin.   Alone by the Autumn River.
Li Yü.   Tune: "Joy of Encounter".
Llwyd, M.   Excuse, The.
Loesser.   Spring Will Be a Little Late This Year.
Lorde.   What My Child Learns of the Sea.
Lovelace, R.   Grasshopper, The [To My Noble
   Friend Mr Charles Cotton: Ode].
Lu Yu.   Stone on the Hilltop, The.
Maeng Sasŏng.   Four Seasons by the Rivers and
   Lakes.
Magee, W.   British Garden, A.
Martinaitis, M.   Kukutis's Swallow's Hymn.
   Unhappy Kukutis in the Potato Patch.
McAuley, J.   Keep the Season.
Melville, H.   Little Good Fellows, The.
   Pontoosuce.
Molinari.   Little Ode to Melancholy.
   Ode to a Long Sorrow.
Morris, W.   Summer Dawn.

Motion, A.   Mythology.
Neri, G.   Seasons.
New, W.   Acoustics.
Nicholls, J.   Season Song.
Nicholson, N.   For Hokey and Henrietta.
Opie.   On the Approach of Autumn.
  To Winter.
O'Siadhail.   Welcome.
Ovid.   Ceres and Proserpina.
Piercy.   Snow, Snow.
Pope, A.   Garden, The.
Praed.   Good Night to the Season.
Pratt, E.   Come Not the Seasons Here.
Procter, A.   Address to the Ocean.
Reeves, J.   Sea, The.
Rimbaud, A.   O Saisons, O Châteaux.
  O seasons, o châteaux.
Robinson, E.   New Language, The.
Rossetti, C.   Autumn Violets.
  Fly Away, Fly Away.
  I wish I could remember the [or that] first day.
  If Only.
  Under Willows.
Rossetti, D.   83: Barren Spring.
Scamell, B.   More Rain.
Seward.   To Time Past.
Shakespeare, W.   Holla, Approach.
  Songs for the Seasons: A Distant Collaboration.
  Sonnet 97: "How like a winter hath my absence been[e]."
  Sonnet 98: "From you have I been absent in the spring."
  Spring.
Shelley, P.   Ode to the West Wind.
Smith, C.   Composed During a Walk on the Downs, in November 1787.
Smith, J.   Sea Marke.
Soupault.   One Two or Three.
Stevenson, R.   Autumn Fires.
Stewart, S.   Seasons, The.
Stillman, M.   Songs for the Seasons: A Distant Collaboration.
Tate, A.   Seasons of the Soul.
Thomson, J.   Evening and Night.
  Hymn on the Seasons, A.
Thoreau.   Pray to what earth does this sweet cold belong.
Tighe.   1802.
  Written in Autumn.
Unknown.   All Seasons in One.
  Feilire of Adamnan, The.
  Ode to the Seasons.
  Season Song.
  Whan the nyghtengale syngeth the wodes waxen grene.
Vaughan, H.   Love and Discipline.
Villa, D.   Then if I think about it.
Volkman.   Sonnet: "This ellipse, slip between seasons."
Ward, J.   Comfort-Maker.
Warren, R.   Vermont Ballad: Change of Season.
  Was It One of the Long Hunters of Kentucky who Discovered Boone at Sunset?
Warton, T.   On Bathing.
  While summer-suns o'er the gay prospect played.
West, J.   To May.
Wilbur, R.   April 5, 1974.
Willis, N.   New Year, The.
Wordsworth, W.   Lines Composed a Few Miles above Tintern Abbey on Revisiting the Banks of the Wye During a Tour, July 13, 1798.
Wright, D.   Caleb Barnes.
  Juxtapositions.
Wright, J.   Love in the Weather's Bells.
Yang Mu.   Let the Wind Recite.
Yasui.   In the withering gusts.
Yearsley.   To———: "Lo! dreary Winter, howling o'er the waste."
Young, M. J.   On an Early Spring.

Seattle, Washington
Bowering, G.   Kingdome 1974, The.
Fanning, A.   Space Needle, The.
Grabill.   Dream of the Closeness of Venus, A.
Guiterman.   Seattle.

Seaweed
Bly, R.   Looking into a Tide Pool.
Dauenhauer.   Kelp.
Longfellow, H.   Seaweed.
Melville, H.   Tuft of Kelp, The.
Ono no Komachi.   Doesn't he realize / that I am not / like the swaying kelp.
Takai Kito.   Seaweed / Between rocks—.
Unknown.   Am I to go on.
  If it is but sleep.

Sebastian, Saint
Waldrep, G. C.   Miracles of St. Sebasatian, The.

Seclusion
Basho.   Winter seclusion—.
Buhyu Sunsoo.   Reply to a Poem by Songgyedang.
Ch'ien T'ao.   Poems After Drinking Wine.
Darío, R.   Sonatina.
De León, L.   On Leaving Prison.
Donne.   Satire 1 [A London Street].
Hayden, R.   Soledad.
Hsi Chou.   Early Spring at the Capital, Sent to the Honorable Kuan.
Hsieh Ling-yün.   All Around My New House at Stone Gate.
  Poem on Stone House Mountain, A.
Kim Koengp'il.   My Way.
Levertov.   Closed World, The.
Lu Chi.   Summoning the Recluse.
Mahon.   Woods, The.
Meng Hao Jan.   Passing Seven-League Rapids.
Muso Soseki.   Cloud Mountain.
  Dragon-Gate House.
  From My Hut in Miura.
  Loud thunder.
  Suzan Osho's Visit.
Myŏngok.   Snow falls on the mountain village.
Pao Hsien.   Autumn Path.
Prigov.   It's better not to live in Moscow.
Pyŏn Wŏngyu.   To a Friend.
Rich, A.   I Am in Danger—Sir.
Tso Ssu.   Summoning the Recluse.
Tu Fu [or Du Fu].   Evening after Rain.
  Homestead.
  In Seclusion.
  Madman, The.
Wang Fan-chih.   Reclusive.
Wordsworth, W.   Experiment that Failed, An.
Yi I.   Where is the second bend?
Yüan Chěn.   Retirement.
Zhidun.   Song of My Mountain Dwelling.

Second Coming
Unknown.   King shall come when morning dawns, The.
Yeats.   Second Coming, The.

See also **Millennium**

Second World War.
Blanding Henriette de Saussure.   Aftermath (1945).
Bottoms.   Sunday Dinner, A.

See also **World War II**

Secrecy and Secrets
Adler, R.   Hernando's Hideaway.
Akhmatova, A.   Land not mine, still, A.
Armand.   Braille for Left Hand.
Balce, N.   Pizza and Pretense.
Blaeser.   Certificate of Live Birth.
Blake, W.   Love's Secret.
Bomani, M.   Voudou Mama.
Bonitto-Burwell, T.   Leaving Winston-Salem.
Brandt, D.   Little one, black angel.
Brontë, A.   Fragment, A: "Maiden, thou wert thoughtless once."
Browning, R.   Meeting at Night.
Brutus.   Postscripts 2.
Burns, R.   Whistle, and I'll Come to You, My Lad.
Byron, G.   When We Two Parted.
Carroll, K.   Truth About Karen, The.
Catullus.   Carmen 5.
Cepollaro, B.   Requiem in C.
Citino.   Invention of Secrecy, The.
Clanchy, K.   Mitigation.
Clifton, L.   Listen Children.
Coleman, H.   Poem for a "Divorced" Daughter.

Crapsey.   Song: "I make my shroud but no one knows."
Cruz, C.   How to Catch a Ghost in a Jar.
Cruz, S.   One Dismal Night.
Daniels, K.   Women's Room in Pennsylvania Station, The.
Dauer.   William.
Davis, T.   Desire 1.
De la Mare.   Portrait, A.
Donne.   Perfume, The.
  Undertaking, The.
Doolittle, H.   In no wise is the pillar-of-fire.
  We have had too much consecration.
Dove, R.   Adolescence—1.
Dunbar, P.   We Wear the Mask.
Dunn, S.   Secret Life, A.
Elledge.   Triptych.
Emerson, R.   Sphinx, The.
Fichman.   Secrets of the Landscape, The.
Field.   Palimpsest, A.
Flynn, N.   Fragment (Found Inside My Mother).
Francia, L.   Secret in the Roar, The.
García, D.   Green Corn Season.
Garrett, E.   Moules à la Marinière.
Gershon.   At a Reception.
Gioia.   Unsaid.
Grapes, J.   My Rodeo.
Harburg.   If This Isn't Love.
Hātim Ibn Sa'īd.   Sun drew near to a full moon: wine and a drinking companion!, A.
Hernández Cruz.   Going Uptown to Visit Miriam.
Hill, G.   Turtle Dove, The.
Ho Thien.   Green Beret.
Homer.   "Here," said the Cloud-gatherer Zeus, "that is a journey you may well postpone.
Hsi Chou.   Sent to Huai Ku.
Huidobro.   Quiet Spaces.
Kasa.   Have I let my love.
Knight, E.   He Sees Through Stone.
La Fontaine.   Shrimp and Her Daughter, The.
Landon.   Secrets.
Lawrence, J.   What's Your Story, Morning Glory.
Levertov.   Secret, The.
Levy, A.   At a Dinner Party.
Lindley, D.   Cryptogram, The.
López Velarde.   Purple Spot, The.
MacEwen, G.   Open Secrets.
Machan.   No, Superman Was Not the Only One.
MacMuireadach.   Farewell for ever to last night.
Masters, E.   Serepta Mason.
Mistral, G.   One Word.
Muldoon, P.   Hedgehog.
Myles, E.   American Poem, An.
Nervo.   Revenge.
Nesbit, E.   Things That Matter, The.
Noguere.   Secret, The.
Okigbo.   Bright / with the armpit-dazzle of a lioness.
Otomo no Sakanoé.   Don't you cut the brush.
Paulus [or Paulos] Silentiarius.   Come, give me kisses, Rhodope.
Philodemus.   Make the Bedlamp Tipsy with Oil.
Plath, Z.   Cooking Lesson.
Pogson, P.   Sleeper.
Rein.   Secret Agent, A.
Rexroth, K.   Oh the anguish of these secret meetings.
Rilke.   Mary at Peace with the Risen Lord.
Ritsos.   Evening Walk.
Rodgers, C.   Poem No. 1.
Romano, R.   Bucket, The.
Rosen, K.   Along the Charles.
Ross, J.   Hernando's Hideaway.
Rossetti, C.   Winter: My Secret.
Sachdev.   Well, The.
Sachs, N.   Butterfly.
Schilpp, M.   Devotions in Confidence.
Shepherd, R.   Motive.
"Shunzei's Daughter.".   Burning in Secret.
Simic.   At the Cookout.
Stein, G.   Key to Closet.
T'ao Ch'ien [or T'ao Yuan-ming].   Peach-Blossom Spring ("Ch'in's First Emperor ravaged the sense.").

Teare, Brian. Trick Noir.
Teasdale. Those Who Love.
Teillier, J. In the Secret House of Night.
Tindal. Birth Wail, The.
Tsvetayeva [*or* Tsvetaeva]. Gold that was my hair has turned, The.
Staircase.
Umpierre, L. Only the Hand That Stirs Knows What's in the Pot.
Unknown. All too soon, I fear.
Come, my beloved, come quickly and be close to me!
Do not hold me too closely in your arms.
Do not look at me.
How did you come here beneath the full moon.
In secret I burn, in secret I weep.
My courage fails me when I grasp my water jar.
Qiang-you-ci: Off the Wall.
Were I to send word.
When you come to our house, my love, the "little horror" grows angry.
Yourself and Myself.
Velichansky, A. Flame's speech is confused, The. The muttering of the water is hollow.
Villaurrutia. Los Angeles Nocturne.
Violi. Harold and Imogene.
Vogelweide. Under the linden.
Webster, P. Secret Love.
What's Your Story, Morning Glory.
Whitney, I. I. W. To her unconstant Lover.
Wilner, E. Secret Garden, The.
Wyatt. Lover Showeth How He Is Forsaken of Such as He Sometime Enjoyed, The.
Yeats. Secret Rose, The.

Secretaries
Bryden, Diana Fitzgerald. Age and the Secretary.
Clinic Day.
Page, P. Stenographers, The.
Piercy. Secretary Chant, The.
Rouse, A. Her Retirement.
See also **Scribes**

Sectarianism
Davies, I. Capel Calvin.
Ferlinghetti, L. Buddha in the Woodpile, A.
Heaney, S. Casualty.
Whatever You Say Say Nothing.
Montague, J. Cave.

Secularism and Secularists
Keelan, C. Secularist, The.
Wilkie, B. Modern Western History.

Security
Brutus. Postscripts 2.
Colum, P. Old Woman of the Roads, The.
Cross, E. Balancing Act.
Equilibrismo.
Cullen, C. For a Poet.
Frost, R. Provide, Provide.
Grosholz. Eden.
Gunn, T. Hug, The.
Hardy, J. Wet Feet.
Kaufman, S. Security.
Levertov. Christmas 1944.
Levi, P. Shemà.
Lezama Lima. Ah, That You Escape.
Light, K. Safe-T-Man.
Locklin. Do you remember the scene in *The Godfather* where James Caan says, "Now make sure that the gun gets stashed in the rest room—I don't want my kid brother walking out of there with nothing but his dick in his hand"?
Lyte. Abide With Me.
McGinley. Velvet Hand, The.
McGrath, T. Poem: "When I carry my little son in the cold."
Parini. After the Terror.
Pastan. Who Is It Accuses Us?
Tonks. Story of a Hotel Room.
Ulku, A. Lullaby: "You are safe / You are lying in a hammock."
Unknown. Psalm 23: "Lord to me [*or* mee] a shepherd is, The."
Voznesensky [*or* Voznesenskii]. Dead Still.
Winch. Social Security.

Seduction
Agard, J. English Girl Eats Her First Mango.
Anacreon. Fragment 17.
Archilochus. I said, "Be mine.".
Behn, A. Disappointment, The.
Song: "I led my Silvia to a grove."
Belev. Lake.
Campbell, J. Sighle of the Lovespot.
Campion, T. Sweet, exclude me[e] not, nor be divided.
Think'st thou to seduce me then.
Thrice Toss[e] These Oaken Ashes in the Air [*or* Ayre].
Carroll, K. Short Poem.
Catullus. To Aurelius.
Cockburn, C. Vain Advice, The.
Coleridge, M. Moment, A.
Crowley, A. Dedicace.
Dermée. Silver Clasps.
These apples.
Donne. Flea, The.
Garrison, D. Worked Late on a Tuesday Night.
Gershon. At a Reception.
Gilmore, M. Eve-Song.
Glaukos. Where once you could win over grasping boys.
Hanu. Why should you freeze to sleep?
Harbach, O. She Didn't Say "Yes".
Hardy, T. Dark-Eyed Gentleman, The.
Herrick. Art above Nature, to Julia.
Delight in Disorder.
Upon Julia's Clothes.
Homer. "Here," said the Cloud-gatherer Zeus, "that is a journey you may well postpone.
Now Here of the Golden Throne, looking out from where she stood on the summit of Olympus, was quick to observe two things.
Huang O [*or* Huang Ho]. To the Tune "A Floating Cloud Crosses Enchanted Mountain".
Hulse, M. Concentrating.
Jacob, M. Rooster and the Pearl, The.
Jarman, M. Cavafy in Redondo.
Jonson, B. Song. To Celia ("Come my Celia, let us prove.").
Kuan Han-ch'ing. In the Southern Mode, to the Tune "A Sprig of Flowers" The Refusal to Get Old.
Kuzmin. At the Party.
Landon. Proud Ladye, The.
Levi, P. Delilah.
Li Yen-nien. Song, A: "In the north there is a lovely woman."
Loesser. Baby, It's Cold Outside.
Longley, M. Sulpicia.
Lorde. On a Night of the Full Moon.
Lowell, A. Carrefour.
Lumsden, R. Tricks for the Barmaid.
Luschei, G. Magic: "You went by my house."
Marlowe. By this Leander being near the land. What is't, sweet wag, I should deny thy youth?
Marvell. Fair Singer, The.
McDaniel, J. D.
Michaux. Simplicity.
Mullen, H. Pretty Piece of Tail.
Nesbit, E. Villeggiature.
Orton, B. Love Poem.
Ou-yang Hsiu. Tune: "Drunk in Fairyland".
Petronius Arbiter. However, Eumolpus, our champion in time of trouble and the author of the present harmony.
Po Chü-i. Iranian Whirling Girls.
Porter, C. Let's Do It, Let's Fall in Love.
Prado, A. Serenade.
Purdy, J. Do You Wonder Why I Am Sleepy.
Raffalovich, M. A. Rose Leaves When the Rose Is Dead.
Ransom, J. Judith of Bethulia.
Robinson, M. Phaon Awakes.
She Endeavors to Fascinate Him.
To the Eolian Harp.
Rohrer, M. Brooklyn Bridge.
Seyburn, P. Persuasion.
Shaw, A. Rear Window.
Sheppard, R. Empty Diary 1905.
Sirowitz, H. Lending Out Books.
Sondheim. Remember?

Ssu-ma Hsiang-ju. Beautiful Person, The.
Cock-Phoenix, Hen-Phoenix.
Strato [*or* Straton]. I loathe a boy who won't be hugged and kissed.
To start with, grapple your opponent 'round.
Tallie, M. Medusa.
Tu Shan-fu. Tune: "Shua Hai-erh" Country Cousin at the Theater.
Unknown. Come close to me, my love.
Green, green riverside grass.
If I stare at you with such great insistence.
In the wilds, a dead doe.
Intoxicated just because I smiled at you.
Large-headed beauty, head so alluring, The.
My perfume!
On the offering mound, a dead roe.
Pleasant Songs of the Sweetheart Who Meets You in the Fields.
So plentiful, the babes-in-a-pot.
Song of Crede, Daughter of Guare, The.
Sun sinks low, The. I.
Throw me a quince.
Waly, Waly [Love Be Bonny].
When I started wanting.
Ye-you si-jun: Lies a Dead Deer.
Webb, M. Why?
Witt, S. Everlasting Quail.
Wormser. Single Urge, The.
Wray, C. Private Thoughts.
Wyatt. Lover Showeth How He Is Forsaken of Such as He Sometime Enjoyed, The.
Yüan Chĕn. Iranian Whirling Girls.

Seeds
Addison, L. All the things of which there are none.
Buckmaster. Seed.
Cruz, C. Persephone 2.
Curzon, D. Instructions to a Seed.
Finch, A. Sapphics for Patience.
Graham, J. Of Forced Sightes and Trusty Ferefulness.
Haines, J. Sun on Your Shoulder, The.
Heaney, S. Seed Cutters, The.
Hofer, J. Tactics ("Licit tremendous unjust oxidized fancified notions tremulously.").
Housman. I hoed and trenched and weeded.
Ismail. Poetry: "Beautiful woman, A."
Jacobsen, R. Sunflower.
Sunflower.
Kavanagh, P. To the Man after the Harrow.
Mitchell, S. Matthew 13:1–9; That same day Jesus.
Parable of the Sower, The.
Molodovsky [*or* Molodowsky]. Prayers: I.
Mun Chônghui. Single Blossom, A.
Nemerov. Cabinet of Seeds Displayed, A.
Pack, R. Bounty.
Pasolini. Day of My Death, The.
Patacara. When they plow their fields.
Rakosi. Avocado Pit, The.
Ramanujan. Foundlings in the Yukon.
Reiter, T. Rights of Way.
Richter, J. Everywhere the Earth Is Opening.
Rumi. Wished-For Song, A.
Schelling. Below Fourth of July Mine.
Huerfano Valley Seed Songs.
Shcherbina. Still-Life.
Stein, G. Custard.
Thomas, D. After the Funeral.
Vaughan, H. Seed Growing Secretly, The.
Wagoner, D. Nuthatch.
Wilbur, R. Seed Leaves.
Wright, D. Addison Street.

Seine (river), France
Apollinaire. Mirabeau Bridge.
Tardieu Jean. Seine in Paris, The.

Self
Abrahams, L. Dry self-portrait.
Adamson. Home, The Spare Room, The.
Addison, L. I by you put on.
Alegría. From the Bridge.
I Am Root.
Alexander, E. Painting / (Frida Kahlo).
Alvarez, J. Sonnet 42: "Sometimes the words are so close I am."
Alvi, M. I Would Like to be a Dot in a Painting

by Miró.
Ammons.   So I Said I Am Ezra.
Arends, J.   I.
I Have.
Artaud.   Revolt Against Poetry.
Ashbery, J.   Evening in the Country.
Paradoxes and Oxymorons.
These Lacustrine Cities.
Atwood.   More and More.
Auden.   Lullaby, A: "Din of work is subdued,
The."
Prime.
Prologue at Sixty.
Baca.   Like an Animal.
Baraka, I.   Agony, An. As Now.
Funk Lore.
Poem Some People Will Have to Understand, A.
Barbauld.   Life.
Barresi.   Prodigal Daughter, The.
Baudelaire.   Fuses I and II.
Beasley.   This is the finger of God.
Beckman, J.   Final poem for the gently sifting
public begins on the streets.
Behn, R.   On Giving My Father a Book About
Roses.
Origin.
Bell, M.   Self and the Mulberry, The.
Berrigan, T.   Last Poem.
Bidart.   Self-Portrait [1969].
Blackburn, P.   At the Well.
Blake, W.   Little Fly.
Blaser.   Universe is Part of Ourselves, The.
Blight.   Down from the Country.
Bogan, L.   Man Alone.
Bonitaz Nuño.   Smoke.
Borges.   Borges and Myself.
Everything and Nothing.
Boruch.   All Those People.
Brandt, D.   My mother found herself one late
summer.
Brodsky, J.   I Sit by the Window.
Bronk.   Plainest Narrative, The.
Brontë, E.   Stanzas: "Often rebuked, yet always
back returning."
Brooks, G.   My dreams, my works must wait till
after hell.
Browning, R.   House.
Buson.   Head pillowed on arm.
Cao Bá Quát.   On Reading The Book of Odes.
Cataldi.   13 November 1983.
Cavalli.   I remember little of myself.
Who ever again will be able to say.
Ceravolo.   Grow.
Cervantes.   Freeway 280.
Césaire, A.   Lagoonal Calendar.
Citino.   Situation No. 9: The Corposant.
Clark, T.   Sit for a while on a stone.
Cohen, Lynne.   Body Doubled.
Cole, H.   Original Face.
Coleman, W.   Wanda Why Aren't You Dead.
Coleridge, S.   Phantom.
Conoley, G.   Sky Drank In, The.
Cooley.   Brother Body.
Coolidge, C.   Glance in White Space.
Copus, J.   Sea-Polyp, The.
Coviello, M.   Self-Portrait.
Crane, S.   In the desert.
Creeley.   Edge, The ("Long over whatever
edge.").
Form of Women, A.
Oh my god—you.
Self-Portrait.
Cronin, J.   Motho Ke Motho Ka Batho Babang
(A Person Is a Person Because of Other
People).
Cruz, C.   How to Catch a Ghost in a Jar.
Cuadra, A.   In Brief.
Cummings, E. E.   Maggie and milly and molly
and may.
Curtis, T.   Spirit of the Place, The.
Daive.   I rise from the depths.
D'Almeida, F.   By Forty-Sixth.
Dao.   Answer.
Darwish, M.   Identity Card.
Words.
Davidson, M.   Dream Dream, The.

Davies, A.   Personality syndrome, The.
Davis, O.   If You Are Asked.
Davis, T.   Desire 1.
Day, J.   Moving Object.
De la Mare.   Things: "Things are the mind's
mute looking-glass."
Dickey, R.   Leaving Eden.
Dickinson, E.   Aurora.
I am alive—I guess.
Me from Myself—to banish.
Disch.   Agreement of Predicate Pronouns, The.
Donnelly, T.   Birdsong from Inside the Egg.
Doolittle, H.   Yet we, the latter-day twice-born.
Dransfield.   Self-analysis.
Drayton.   You not alone, when you are still
alone.
Drummond de Andrade.   Seven-Sided Poem.
Duncan, R.   Close.
Roots and Branches.
Songs of an Other.
Eberhart, R.   Gnat on My Paper.
Elfyn, Menna.   Burning Multitude, The.
Eliot, T. S.   Little Gidding.
Elizabeth I.   On Monsieur's Departure.
Elmslie, K.   Squatter in the Foreground.
Fagin, L.   Twelve Poems.
Fein, Richard.   To Walt Whitman.
Ferrell, M.   Geburt des Monicakinds.
Fingueret, M.   Second Portrait.
Ford, Katie.   Hands of the Body Without the
Body, and Nothing to Hold, The.
Gallagher, T.   Black Silk.
Sudden Journey.
Gardiner, S.   Second Person.
Gelbtrunk, A.   Empty House, The.
George, F.   Sudden Tug of the Familiar, The.
Gibson, W.   Advice to Travelers.
Giussani, S.   Hot and Cold.
Glazer, M.   Box.
González, A.   Before I Could Call Myself Ángel
González.
Gonzalez, R.   Calling the White Donkey.
Grapes, J.   I Like My Own Poems.
Green, M.   Epistle to Mr. Cuthbert Jackson, An.
Greenberg, U.   I thirst for water; wine is my
need no longer.
Greenlaw, L.   Electricity.
Greenwell, D.   Scherzo, A.
Griffiths, S.   Getting It Wrong, Again.
Grotz, J.   Self-Portrait as a Drowned Man.
Gumilyov [or Gumiliov or Gumilev].   Pre-
Memory.
Guri, H.   Like Beirut.
Ha Jin.   Past, The.
Habington.   Cogitabo Pro Peccato Meo.
Hadewijch II.   All things.
If I desire something, I know it not.
Hall, J.   Proverb, XXX.
Halliday, M.   Sax's and Selves.
Hardy, J.   Difference, The.
Harryman.   Magic (or Rousseau).
My Story.
Hayden, R.   Names.
Hejinian.   Moment yellow, just as four years
later when, A.
Solitude flared out, The.
Herbert, G.   Jordan (2).
Herrick.   On Himself[e] ("Lost to the world; lost
to my selfe [or myself]; alone.").
Hierro, José.   Any Afternoon.
Hilberry, Jane.   Crazy Jane Goes to Painting
Class.
Hirsch, E.   Self-Portrait.
Holub.   Immanuel Kant.
Hopkins, G.   Candle Indoors, The.
I Wake and Feel the Fell of Dark, Not Day.
My Own Heart Let Me More Have Pity On.
Housman.   Oh, when I was in love with you.
Howard, R.   After 65.
Howell, C.   Bride of Long Division, The.
Hsin Ch'i-chi.   Tune: "Partridge Sky" At Po-
shan Monastery.
Hughes, F.   Bird.
Laszlo.
Hughes, T.   Man Seeking Experience Enquires
His Way of a Drop of Water, The.

Huidobro.   Canto I (excerpt).
Hume, C.   Million Futures of Late, A.
Truth about Northern Lights, The.
Ivanov, Binyo.   Man, A.
Izumi.   Watching the moon.
Jackson, L.   Dimensions.
One Self.
Postponement of Self.
Reasons of Each, The.
Jacobs, H.   On extending the olive branch to my
own self.
Jarrell, R.   Face, The.
Woman at the Washington Zoo, The.
Jiménez, J.   I Am Not I.
Jones, E.   Study in Blue.
Jordan, J.   Toward a Personal Semantics.
József, A.   Attila József.
Attila József.
Juarroz.   Prompting of my shadow, The.
Kay, J.   Somebody Else.
Keats.   Ode on Indolence.
Kiko.   Mount Sumeru—my fist!
Kimbrell, J.   Empty House.
Kinzie.   Heat-heavy creatures.
Klee.   Poem: "Big animals: despondent / at
table: unsated, The."
Kloos, W.   Sonnet.
Knight, E.   Welcome Back, Mr. Knight: Love of
My Life.
Knott.   Death: "Going to sleep, I cross my hands
on my chest."
Sonnet: "Way the world is not, The."
Koch, K.   Alive for an Instant.
Girl and Baby Florist Sidewalk Pram Nineteen
Seventy Something.
Kocot, N.   I Am Like a Desert Owl, an Owl
Among the Ruins.
Kopland.   Ontology.
Kossman.   Backward Sound.
Krechel.   Early November.
Kuan Han-ch'ing.   To the Tune "A Spray of
Flowers" (Not Giving In to Old Age).
Kunina, Y.   Inconsistent Self-Portrait.
Lal Ded [or Lalla].   Coursing in emptiness.
I searched for my Self.
Larkin, P.   Counting.
Lawrence, D. H.   Eloi, Eloi, Lama Sabachthani?
I Am in a Novel.
Wild Common, The.
Leapor.   Epistle of Deborah Dough, The.
Mira's Will.
Lee, L.   Night Mirror.
Lehman.   November 19.
Levertov.   After "Mindwalk".
In Mind.
Levine, M.   Work Song.
Levine, P.   Baby Villon.
Never Before.
Lewis, G.   One day, feeling hungry.
Limburg, J.   Inner Bloke.
Lindley, D.   Cryptogram, The.
Locklin.   Stranger, The.
Loftin, E.   Barefoot Necklace.
Lothamer.   Allen.
Lowell, R.   Reading Myself.
Lumelli, A.   You first, shift your attention (that
is, if you withdraw).
Lumsden, R.   Man I Could Have Been, The.
Luzi.   Reflective life separates us from the
sources of reflection.
Machado Ruiz.   Portrait.
Portrait ("My childhood is memories of a patio
in Seville.").
Mackowski, Joanie.   Self-Portrait, Double
Exposed.
MacNeice.   Once-in-Passing, The.
Macpherson, J.   Lost Soul, A.
Magdeburg, Mechthild von.   Desert Has Many
Teachings, The.
How the Soul Speaks to God.
Malroux.   Every morning.
Mandela.   I Have Tried Hard.
Martinez, D.   Kinescope.
Mathias, R.   Testament.
Mattawa.   I Was Buried in Janzoor.
McAdams, J.   Leaving the Old Gods.

McCarthy, T.   Mr. Nabokov's Memory.
McClure, M.   Hymn to Saint Geryon.
McDaniel, J.   Lineage.
McHugh, H.   ID.
Mendelssohn Anna.   Strictly personal.
  Myself.
Merrill, J.   Self-Portrait in Tyvek(TM)
  Windbreaker.
  Syrinx.
Merwin.   One of the Lives.
  Whoever You Are.
Milán, E.   Ahora que no hay yo, vamos al yo
  general.
  Now that there's no self, let's proceed to the
  general self.
Mishol, A.   Estate.
Mo Shih-lung.   Saying Good-bye to a Singing
  Girl Who Has Decided to Become a Nun.
Mouré.   Toxicity.
Mueller, L.   What Is Left to Say.
Mullen, L.   Applications of.
  White Paintings V.
Nathan, L.   Hole.
Nemerov.   Salt Garden, The.
Neruda.   Ode to the Cat.
  Poetry.
  We Are Many.
Neshâtî.   We are desire hidden in the love-
  crazed call.
Nolens, L.   Address.
Nye, N.   Whole Self, The.
O'Callaghan, C.   Anon.
O'Driscoll, D.   You.
O'Hara, F.   To the Harbormaster.
Okamoto.   Tanka: "Ten years ago."
Olds, S.   Nurse Whitman.
Oliver, M.   Journey, The.
Olson, C.   As the Dead Prey upon Us.
Padgett, R.   Famous Flames.
Page, P.   Selves, The.
Pagis, D.   Snake.
Palmer, M.   Autobiography: "All clocks are
  clouds."
  Word is coming up on the screen, give me a
  moment, I.
Pasolini.   Part of a Letter to the Codignola Boy.
  Presence, The.
Pasternak, B.   To Be Famous Isn't Decent.
Patterson, G.   Autobiography of a Black Man.
Paz.   Crystal willow, a poplar of water, A.
  Face I can see to see my face, A.
  Small Variation.
Peacock, M.   Spell, The.
Penna.   Pitiless war of love I fought, A.
Phillips, C.   Somewhere Holy.
Philpot, T.   Constellations of Self, The.
Piatt, S.   Doubt, A.
Piercy.   Moonburn.
Plath.   In Plaster.
  Nick and the Candlestick.
Plumly.   Wight.
Popa.   Dream of the Quartz Pebble, The.
Porta.   To become a tree.
Pound, E.   De Aegypto.
Prévert.   I'm the Way I Am.
Quarles.   I wish a greater knowledge, then
  t'attaine.
Queneau.   That Don't Scare Me.
Rakosi.   Lord, What is Man?
Ramanujan.   Elements of Composition.
  Self-Portrait.
Ray, H.   Self-Mastery.
Rees-Jones.   I Know Exactly the Sort of Woman
  I'd Like to Fall in Love With.
Reese, L.   Renunciation.
  To Life.
Rich, A.   Delta.
  Integrity.
  Rain on the West Side Highway.
  Trying to Talk with a Man.
  Upper Broadway.
Riley, D.   Flip, Flop.
Rilke.   Self-Portrait.
Robinson, K.   Intent to consider.
Rodgers, C.   Group Therapy.

Rossetti, C.   Verse II.
  Verse III.
Rossetti, D.   98: He and I.
Roy, L.   Ride, The.
Rukeyser, M.   Then I Saw What the Calling
  Was.
Ryan, M.   Your Own Image.
Sadoff.   Against Whitman.
Sahagún, C.   Photograph of a Boy.
St. John, P.   Carnival.
Schultz, P.   I'm Not Complaining.
Schwartz, D.   Heavy Bear Who Goes with Me,
  The.
  Self Unsatisfied Runs Everywhere, The.
Senghor.   Kaya-Magan, The.
Sereni.   First Year.
Serrano, P.   Acotamiento.
  Boundary.
  Rosario.
  Rosary.
Sexton.   Ballad of the Lonely Masturbator, The.
Shaughnessy, B.   Panopticon.
Shelley, P.   Sonnet: Political Greatness.
Shinkichi Takahashi.   Let's Live Cheerfully.
  Wood in Sound, A.
Simic.   Charles Simic.
  Inner Man, The.
  My Shoes.
  Past-Lives Therapy.
Slessor.   To Myself.
Smith, Tracy K.   Self-Portrait as the Letter Y.
Soupault.   Life-Saving Medal.
Souza.   De Souza Prabhu.
Stepanchev.   Seven Horizons.
Stern, G.   Diary.
Stétié, Salah.   Garden of the One, The.
Stevens, W.   Anglais Mort à Florence.
  Man on the Dump, The.
  Poems of Our Climate, The.
Strand.   In Memory of Joseph Brodsky.
  My Life by Somebody Else.
  Night, The Porch, The.
  To Himself.
Su, A.   I Can't Become a Buddhist.
Supervielle.   Traveller, traveller.
Swenson, M.   Stripping and Putting On.
Swirszczynska [or Swir].   I Talk to My Body.
Tada.   Poetry Calendar, A.
Tate, J.   Shadowboxing.
Taylor, E.   Meditation. Heb. 13.10. We[e] have
  an Altar.
Templeton, F.   Act II - Crossing At the Tracks.
Thomas, E.   Lights Out.
Thoreau.   I Am a Parcel of Vain Strivings Tied.
Tillema, M.   So Soon ("So soon, so tired.").
  So Soon ("So soon—so without tomorrow.").
Trethewey, N.   (Self) Portrait.
Twichell.   Cat and Mirror.
  Hunger for Something.
Unknown.   Invocation for Storing Corn.
Urdang.   Portrait.
Vallejo.   Today I like life much less.
Volach, Y.   When You Come Sleep with Me.
Wade, J.   Runnin.
Wakoski.   My Trouble.
Walcott.   Hotel Normandie Pool, The.
  Love after Love.
Wallace-Crabbe.   Abhorring a Vacuum.
Wang An-shih.   Had I been an ox or horse.
Warsh.   Before I Was Born.
Watten.   Isolate and.
Weigl.   Self-Portrait at Fifty-Three.
Whitman, W.   Are You the New Person Drawn
  toward Me?
  As I Lay with My Head in Your Lap Camerado.
  By that Long Scan of Waves.
  Child said What is the grass? fetching it to me
  with full hands, A.
  Hand-Mirror, A.
  Here the Frailest Leaves of Me.
  Houses and rooms are full of perfumes, the
  shelves are crowded with perfumes.
  I believe a leaf of grass is no less than the
  journey-work of the stars.
  I believe in you my soul, the other I am must
  not abase itself to you.

  I celebrate myself, and sing myself.
  I know I have the best of time and space, and
  was never measured and will never be
  measured.
  I Saw in Louisiana a Live-Oak Growing.
  One's-Self I Sing.
  Past and present wilt—I have filled them,
  emptied them, The.
  Song of Myself.
  That Shadow My Likeness.
  There is that in me—I do not know what it is—
  but I know it is in me.
  To be in any form, what is that?
  Trippers and askers surround me.
  Twenty-eight young men bathe by the shore.
  Who goes there? hankering, gross, mystical,
  nude.
  Who Learns My Lesson Complete.
  Woman Waits for Me, A.
Wilbur, R.   Leaving.
Williams, C. K.   Shade, The.
Williams, W.   Danse Russe.
Winchilsea.   On Myself.
Wright, C.   Self-Portrait ("Charles on the
  Trevisan, night bridge.").
Wright, D.   On Himself.
Wright, K.   Other Side of the Mountain, The.
Yeats.   Dialogue of Self and Soul, A.
Yi Sang.   Mirror.
Yosano Akiko.   In the First Person.
Zabolotsky [or Zabolotskii].   All That My Soul
  Possessed.
Zanzotto.   Existing Psychically.
Zawacki, Andrew.   One of me stuttered and one.
  Vertigo.

Self-Deceit
Bruchac.   Prayer: "Let my words."
Buchsbaum, Julianne.   Thrillsville.
Chandar, M.   Birth Postponed, A.
Coleridge, S.   On a Discovery Made Too Late.
Crane, S.   I saw a man pursuing the horizon.
Dalton, A.   In Love.
Dunn, S.   Grudges.
Hahne, M.   Lies We Tell Ourselves.
Imara, L.   Diogenes.
Jacobs, B.   Black on Black.
Lawrence, J.   Foolin' Myself.
Loftis, N.   Changes—Five.
Malroux.   Every Breath.
Montalvan, J.   Self-Deceaver, The.
Moxley, Jennifer.   Soleil Cou Coupé.
Parker, D.   Story.
Rich, A.   Power.
Scliar-Cabral.   Deceiving Words.
Smith, S.   Infelice.
Snodgrass.   Locked House, A.
Stratanovsky.   Terrorist, The.
Teasdale.   Effigy of a Nun.
Whittier.   Changeling, The.
  Haschish, The.

Self-Doubt
Aiken, C.   Dear Uncle Stranger.
Baron Supervielle, Silvia.   Here Time.
Bly, R.   Anger Against Children.
Campos, Á.   Tobacco Shop, The.
Ch'oe Sûngja.   For the Second Time in Thirty-
  Three Years.
Cistulli.   34.57.
Finlay, I.   Finlay's House (in Rousay).
Glück, L.   Mutable Earth.
Goll, I.   On the five thousandth evening of our
  love.
Herbert, G.   Love (3): "Love bade me welcome:
  yet my soul drew back."
Hô Sugyông.   No Return.
Hwang Insuk.   New Year's Card, A.
Jacob, M.   Shady Soul.
Jeffers, R.   Love the Wild Swan.
Joseph, A.   Shame of the Writers' Conference.
Lahey, Joy.   Cattails Along Red River.
Levin, S.   With Your Mother in a Café.
Lope de Vega.   Lachrimae Amantis.
Milosz, C.   Temptation.
No Hyegyông.   Peace on Earth.
  Triangle, Comb.
Nortje.   All hungers pass away.

Self-Hatred

Olson, C.   Maximus, to Himself.
Pearlman.   Endings.
Porta.   Age of unhappiness has arrived, or is it, The.
Rich, A.   Dialogue.
Shakespeare, W.   Sonnet 46: "Mine eye and heart are at a mortal war."
Sonnet 76: "Why is my verse so barren of new pride?"
Simon, L.   Measuring Apollo.
Skloot.   Frost.
Spark.   Elementary.
Stern, G.   I Hate My Moaning.
Symonds.   What Cannot Be.
Szymborska, W.   In Praise of Self-Deprecation.
Tallmountain.   Indian Blood.
Timoner, J.   Push the Feathered Glory.
Valéry.   Seaside Cemetery, The.
Walcott.   Codicil.
Wingfield.   Where is the lumber-room of what was important?
Wright, C.   Laguna Blues.
Wylie.   Malediction upon Myself.
Yi Sang.   Poem No. 15.

Self-Hatred

Aguero, Kathleen.   Looking for Another Version.
Belieu.   Against Writing about Children.
Goldberg, B.   My Husband's Bride.
Marcus, M.   Forgiveness.
Norris, M.   Tortillas.
Otero, B.   Chap. 10 Book 2.
Sabines.   I Love You at Ten in the Morning.
Serrano, P.   Beacon.
Hacho.
Woloch, C.   Blink.

Selfishness

Ammons.   Coming Right Up.
"Anvari.".   Take What He GIves You.
Bierce.   Egotist.
Blake, W.   Clod & the Pebble, The.
Bunina.   Conversation between Me and the Women.
Cary, P.   Legend of the Northland, A.
Cook, E.   Mouse and the Cake, The.
Cutler, Y.   Not-a.
Dancer.   Variety, The.
Dickinson, E.   Mine—by the Right of the White Election!
Dunn, S.   From the Manifesto of the Selfish.
Fox, Sarah.   Interruption.
Han-shan.   Unfortunate human disorder, The.
Hughes, L.   Preference.
Komunyakaa, Y.   Seven Deadly Sins.
Lawrence, D. H.   Intimates.
North, C.   Few Facts about Me, A.
Shakespeare, W.   Sonnet 62: "Sin[ne] of self[e]-love possesseth all mine eye [or eie]."
Solie, Karen.   Emergency Response.
Steiger.   Nobody waits at the foot of the stairs any more.
Unknown.   Song of a Foolish Wife.
Wesley, C.   On Worldly Prelates.

Self-Knowledge

Agustini.   Break, The.
Sweet Reliquaries, The.
Aiken, C.   Dear Uncle Stranger.
Amadiume.   Mistress of My Own Being.
Ammons.   Reflective.
So I Said I Am Ezra.
Somers Point.
Anderson, S.   American Spring Song.
Ap Glyn, Ifor.   I'm the Guy with the Gut.
Aridjis.   Self-Portrait at Age Ten.
Armstrong, Tim.   Knowledge.
Arrillaga.   Like Raquel.
Ashbery, J.   Late Echo.
Poem of Unrest, A.
Behn, A.   Angellica's Lament.
Berg, S.   Don't Forget.
Berkson, B.   Russian New Year.
Berrigan, A.   Bloodletting.
Berry, J.   One.
Binyon.   For Mercy, Courage, Kindness, Mirth.
Blaisdell, G.   Omoide no Tsukimi.
Bukowski.   Trouble with spain.

Burnside, J.   Unwittingly.
Calderón, T.   State of Seige.
Chedid, A.   Movement.
Stepping Aside.
Clark, T.   In a strange game I saw myself.
Conn.   Under the Ice.
Cummings, E. E.   Maggie and milly and molly and may.
de Fierro.   Only You.
de Folgar.   Panorama 2.
Derricotte.   Blackbottom.
Dharker.   Honour Killing.
Di Prima.   Loba as Eve.
Dillard, A.   In the deeps are the violence and terror of which psychology has warned us.
Donegan, P.   Tonight / while shampooing my hair.
Drinan.   Measures.
Duncan, R.   After a Long Illness.
Dunn, S.   In the House.
Éluard, P.   Mirror of a Moment, The.
She Is Always Unwilling to Understand.
Eskimo Oral Tradition.   Song: "And I thought over again."
Fenton, J.   Ideal, The.
Gangopadhyay.   From Athens to Cairo.
Gibran.   Madman (Prologue), The.
Goodman, P.   Dreams Are the Royal Road to the Unconscious.
Graham, J.   Guardian Angel of Self-Knowledge, The.
Hadewijch II.   You who want.
Hafiz, K [or Hafez].   Come pass me the cup quickly and hand it on.
Harjo, J.   Autobiography.
I Give You Back.
Harris, V.   Dare to Be Different.
Havel, V.   It Is I Who Must Begin.
Hodges, Janice W.   Control.
Hogan, L.   Truth Is, The.
Hughes, L.   Theme for English B.
Hughes, T.   Wodwo.
Hussein, H.   I Can Talk to Them.
Izumi.   Watching the moon.
Jarman, J.   What we all.
Jordan, J.   Poem About My Rights.
Juarroz.   There Are Points of Silence Circling the Heart.
Kassabova, K.   Someone else's life.
Kenyon, J.   Here.
Knott.   At the Crossroads.
Kolsson, K.   I have nine principal talents.
Kunitz, S.   King of the River.
Larkin, P.   Reasons for Attendance.
Lihn.   Mud.
MacCaig.   Summer Farm.
Macpherson, J.   Lost Soul, A.
Manyarrows.   Today We Will Not Be Invisible Nor Silent.
Martin, Camille.   Learning to talk over and over.
McFadden, D.   13. The Worst of People.
McGinley.   View from a Suburban Window.
McGrath, T.   You Taught Me.
McHugh, H.   Ghazal of the Better-Unbegun.
ID.
Michaels, Jesse.   Knowledge.
Mirabai [or Mira Bai].   All I Was Doing Was Breathing.
Montale.   What you knew of me.
Moolten, D.   Madame Butterfly.
Muso Soseki.   Time for a walk.
Nawaz, G.   Riddle.
Nilsson, H.   My Least Skirtable Deficiency.
No Hyegyông.   Happy Walk.
Nolla.   Manifest, The.
Nye, N.   Whole Self, The.
Olson, C.   In Cold Hell, in Thicket.
Newly Discovered "Homeric" Hymn, A.
Oppen.   Confession.
Orr, G.   Hand, The: "Brightness Falls from the Air".
Owen, W.   Show, The.
Parra, N.   Something Like That.
Paz.   Was it I making plans / for the summer— and for all the summers.
Peabody, J.   After Music.

Petrovykh, M.   Air Is Motionless with Heat, The.
Po Chü-i.   On a Portrait of the Poet.
Portal.   Attitude.
Prassinos.   Apostle Qualities.
Qunta, C.   Know, The.
Raffalovich, M. A.   Sonnet 120.
Ragosta, R.   Capitalization of "Clue", The.
Ransom, J.   Amphibious Crocodile.
Reilly, P.   Imagine a woman who honors the face of the Goddess in her own changing face.
Repetto.   6th Grade—Our Lady of Pompeii.
Rich, A.   Diving into the Wreck.
Every peak is a crater. This is the law of volcanoes.
Rilke.   I Am Too Alone in the World.
Roethke.   Open House.
Rumi.   For years, copying other people, I tried to know myself.
Human shape is a ghost, The.
We take long trips.
Wise teacher tell me.
Russell, P.   Be Careful When You Go Looking for a Madonna Cuz You Just Might Find a Woman.
Sachs, N.   World, Do Not Ask Those Snatched from Death.
Saïd, A.   Paths of Light.
Sawadsri, S.   If You Come Close to Me.
Schjeldahl.   Release.
Seferis.   Epiphany, 1937.
Shakespeare, W.   Sonnet 121: "Tis better to be vile than vile esteemed."
Sharp, S.   How to Build a Prayer.
Shauqi.   Andalusian Exile, An.
Shoukry, G.   Personal Portrait, A.
Smith, C.   Partial Muse, has from my earliest hours, The.
Sŏ Chŏngju.   Self-portrait ("Father was a serf.").
Soyinka.   Dragonfly at My Windowpane.
Stafford, W.   Story That Could Be True, A.
Stern, G.   For Song.
Strand.   Night, the Porch, The.
Suárez.   Like the Magic Glow of Paradise.
Poem for Mankind and Its Hope.
Supervielle.   Poet, A.
Tillinghast, R.   Table.
Timrod.   Dreams.
Tremblay, G.   Surviving.
Turk, R.   I Don't Know Why (I Just Do).
Turnbull.   Transmutation ("It was as if she couldn't know herself. Only other persons could do that.").
Twichell.   Passing Clouds.
Saint Animal.
Soul in Space.
Unknown.   Among the yeomen's sons on my estate.
Sometimes I sauntered from my lone abode.
Toltecs were wise, The.
Tree we plant will, when its boughs are grown, The.
Very.   Lost, The ("Fairest day that ever yet has shone, The.").
Villalongo.   In the Good Old U. S. A.
Volach, Y.   Life You Have, The.
Whitman, W.   Preface to *Leaves of Grass* [1855].
This is the meal pleasantly set . . . this is the meat and drink for natural hunger.
Wiethüchter.   At This Juncture.
Wright, C.   California Dreaming.
Chinese Journal.
Gate City Breakdown.
Self-Portrait.
Wylie.   Let No Charitable Hope.
Malediction upon Myself.
Yesenin [or Essenin].   Sergei Yesenin.
Young, A.   Fifty-Fifty.
Zamora, D.   Lineage.
Mother's Day.
Zanzotto.   That's How We Are.

Self-Pity

Bellman.   Fredman's Epistle No. 23.
Cahn, S.   I Should Care.
Catullus.   What for?

Cunningham, J. Aged Lover Discourses in the Flat Style, The.
Felipe, L. I am no one: a man.
Hodgins. Self-Pity.
Izumi. Being a person.
Jiménez, J. Daybreak.
Kaddour, Hédi. Bus Driver, The.
Mesmer, S. What Becomes Us.
Ossip, K. Nature of Things, The.
Schuyler, J. Self-Pity Is a Kind of Lying, Too.
Sharma, P. Performance Test.
Tichborne [or Tichbourne]. Tichborne's Elegy.
Unknown. Sometimes I Go about Pitying Myself.
   Song of the Thunders.
Werfel. Man is Dumb, A.
Westmorland. Shamed by the Creature.
Wright, K. All Purpose Country and Western Self Pity Song, The.
Wroth. Sonnet 42: "If ever love had force in huma[i]ne bre[a]st?"
Wylie. Malediction upon Myself.
Yun Tongju. Self-portrait.

Self-Reliance
Agustini. Break, The.
Bandele, A. Subtle art of breathing, The.
Baraka, I. Young Soul.
Brontë, E. Stanzas: "Often rebuked, yet always back returning."
Bukowski. Nobody but you.
Calderón, T. State of Seige.
Carroll, K. Something easy for Ultra Black nationalists.
Ceravolo. Data.
Chipasula, S. I'm My Own Mother, Now.
Clifton, L. She Lived.
Cofer, J. What the Gypsy Said to Her Children.
Collins, M. Re:composition.
Conkling, G. I Will Not Give Thee All My Heart.
Corman. Learn to live.
Cunningham, N. Giving.
Dove, R. Canary.
Feldman, A. This Fog.
Gex-Breaux, Q. Padded Steps/Sister Song (a litany).
Henley, W. E. Invictus.
Housman. Laws of God, the Laws of Man, The.
Hughes, L. Madam's Past History.
Iosifova, Ekaterina. Nightfall: "Shadows dart, the wind has risen."
Kain, G. Cocaine Mad-Scream Article #33 LoveSong.
Kaprow, Allan. Suppose you telephone your own answering.
Klyuyev [or Kliuev or Klyuev]. Fourth Rome, The.
'Marnia. I Must be Able to Protect You.
Miles, J. In the town where every man is king.
Mora. La Migra.
Nielsen, D. My Philosophy.
Oppen. Myself I Sing.
Parker, D. Neither Blood Nor Bowed.
Pinsky. Samurai Song.
Prado, A. Time.
Reed, I. Sky Diving.
Rich, A. Dark lintels, the blue and foreign stones, The.
Rohrer, M. My Government.
Rose. Naayawva Taawi.
Saïd, A. Paths of Light.
Samawi, S. Solo for the Lone Intuition, A.
Singleton, Giovanni. For my 27th birthday: a poem longer than 10 lines in which pronouns appear.
StacyLynn. Dirt.
Stumbrs. Song at a Late Hour.
Tranströmer. At Funchal.
Whyte, D. Working Together.

Self-Restraint
Housman. Because I liked you better.
Kharms. Incidents.
Lefroy. Palaestral Study, A.
Razaf, A. Ain't Misbehavin'.
   Keepin' Out of Mischief Now.
Washington, N. Nearness of You, The.

Yosano Akiko. From Paris on a Postcard.
Young, K. Soundtrack.

Self-Righteousness
Burns, R. Holy Willie's Prayer.
Lourie. Theological.
Wylie. Malediction upon Myself.
Young, E. Runcible Thought, A.

Semele
Kizer, C. Semele Recycled.

Senegal
Dixon, M. Tour Guide: La Maison des Esclaves.
Hughes, L. Cubes.
Norton, O. Senegal Sestina.
Senghor. All Day Long.
   Camp 1940.

Senility
Denby. Sant' Angelo d'Ischia.
Hicok. Alzheimer's.
Moore, R. On Coming to Nothing.
Paulin. Anastasia McLaughlin.
Prévert. Quartier Libre.
Renk, Charlotte. Past Perm and Glitz.
Suntsova, E. City of summer you inhabit a fluff-light city of little claws.
Tatarunis, P. I Have Two Sons and the One I Love Best Is Robert.
Villani, L. Watching the Mayan Women.

Senses
Apollinaire. Bonds.
Archilochus. Such passion for love coiled in my heart.
Baudelaire. Correspondences.
   Correspondences.
Belev. Woman: "Weeds loom."
Buson. Listening to the moon.
Byrne, Elena Karina. In Particular.
Cary, A. In Bonds.
Cassian. Temptation.
Cavalli. Outside nothing's really changed.
   This time I won't permit the blue.
   When suddenly, you're hit with good health.
Ceravolo. Drunken Winter.
   Grow.
May: "I am lost. / I had swum before."
Chazal, M. Plastic Sense (1947 version).
   Plastic Sense (1948 version).
Clegg, D. Five Senses.
Collobert. I Time of What.
Coolidge, C. Disturbing the Sallies Forth.
Davidson, M. Redivivus.
Davidson, M. Feeling Type and His Friends, The.
De Coninck, H. Ballad of Indolence.
Dickinson, E. I heard a Fly buzz—when I died.
   Light exists in Spring, A.
Doolittle, H. New sensation, A.
Dorantes, D. Meter todas las manos en el agua.
   To put all hands into the water.
Eady. April.
Engle, P. Look! The air shudders when you breathe it in.
Garrett, E. Ribes rubrum.
Griffin, J. Venerating Senses Save Us.
Hamilton, S. Species of Audibles.
Harris, Allison. Nothing Much.
Hébert, A. Earth at Its Origin.
Jungkwan Ilson. To an Old, Deaf, and Blind Monk.
Kendall, M. Philanthropist and the Jelly-fish, The.
Kopland. Ontology.
Lane, P. Lyric: I Am Looking at Music.
Lazarus, E. Evening.
Levchev, Vladimir. Blue Pond at Berkovitsa.
Michelangelo Buonarroti. From sweet weeping to a painful smile.
Naong. Lonely Hermitage.
Nichols, G. Black.
   White.
O'Reilly, C. Lecture Upon the Bat, A.
Padel, R. On the Line.
Peacock, M. Desire.
Penna. Shadowless sun on male bodies.
Rafferty, P. 66°7' N/22°17' W.

Sanchez, S. Under a Soprano Sky.
Sappho. Love shook my senses.
Schuyler, J. Freely Espousing.
Shakespeare, W. Sonnet 141: "In faith, I do[e] not love thee with mine eyes."
Spaziani. Memory's Usefulness.
Stevens, W. Thinking of a Relation between the Images of Metaphors.
Thomas, D. When All My Five and Country Senses See.
Tsogyel. Listen.
Van Ostaijen. Souvenir.
Verlaine. Muted Tones.
   Spleen.
Very. Eye and Ear, The.
Villa, D. What counts in any action.
Watson, E. First Sight: "Blind woman—who by some miracle can, A."
Woods, V. Fourth World, The.
Young, C. Proximity.
Zondberg, O. Variety of animals, said Khlebnikov, The.
Zukofsky, L. When the crickets.

Sensitivity
Ayewanu, S. Man with a Hat, A.
Campbell, J. Try a Little Tenderness.
Colonna, S. But your imagining was wrong.
Connelly, R. Try a Little Tenderness.
Langworthy, C. Why I Look at Girls.
Levertov. O Taste and See.
Owen, W. Insensibility.
Woods, H. Try a Little Tenderness.

Sensuality
Africa-Bolasco. Sauna 2.
Agosin. Language.
Aguilar-Cariño. For the Lover.
   Gabi.
Agustini. Marble Beads.
   Swan, The.
Akiwumi, V. Unconditionals #3.
Ancient Sumerian Oral Tradition. Word they had spoken, The.
Andrade, M. Nocturne.
Archilochus. She delighted to hold a slip of myrtle.
Balce, N. Pizza and Pretense.
Bandeira. Spiritual Wedding.
Baudelaire. Correspondences.
   Head of Hair.
   Snake that Dances, The.
Baudri of Bourgueil. Your Appearance is Pleasing.
Behn, A. Dream, The.
Ben-Lev, D. Sensualist Speaks on Faith, A.
Bethel, M. Reggae Prophecy.
Bhartrihari. Bearing the lustre of a full moon.
Broumas, O. Amazon Twins.
   Caritas.
   Oregon Landscape with Lost Lover.
   Sometimes, as a Child.
Carmona. Storing Memories.
Carpenter, E. Summer Heat.
Cummings, E. E. Since feeling is first.
Dawes, K. Some Tentative Definitions 7.
Drieu la Rochelle. Roundness.
Georgiou, E. Intimate Mixture.
Gregg. Official Love Story.
Hacker, M. Canzone: "Consider the three functions of the tongue."
Harryman. Privacy.
Harwood, G. Carnal Knowledge 2.
Hass, R. Now Winter Nights.
Hébert, A. Earth at Its Origin.
Herbert, E. You well-compacted groves, whose light and shade.
Hilary. To an English Boy: "Hail, fair youth, who seeks no bribe."
Hine. Under the Hill.
Hopkins, G. Epithalamion: "Hark, hearer, hear what I do; lend a thought now, make believe."
Hughes, T. Bride and Groom Lie Hidden for Three Days.
Istarú, A. Crescent moon, A.
   Then / an awakened citron.
   Your penis rolls to the dream.
Keats. Sudden a thought came like a full-blown

rose.
Khalvati. On Reading Rumi.
Laux, D. Laundromat, The.
Lefroy. Idler Listening to Socrates Discussing Philosophy with His Boy-Friends, An.
Levertov. Eros at Temple Stream.
Lili'u-o-ka-lani. Sanoe.
Lim-Wilson. Beginning of Things, The.
Martínez, V. New World, The.
Merwin. West Wall.
Mirabai [or Mira Bai]. All I Was Doing Was Breathing.
Don't Go, Don't Go.
Why Mira Can't Go Back to Her Old House.
Montemayor, C. Cytherea.
Morejón. To a Boy.
Neruda. I did not touch your night, or your air, or dawn.
I love the handful of the earth you are.
Nicholas, A. Strange / that we wake.
Nolla. Erotic Suite.
Olds, S. Ecstasy.
Pennar, Meirion. Lovers: "As a blind man."
Pindar. Ode on Theoxenos.
Pound, E. Alba.
Immorality, An.
Prado, A. In Portuguese.
Pelican, The.
Prassinos. Loving Poem.
Rexroth, K. Aspen Meadows.
Coming.
Floating.
I cannot forget.
Spring is early this year.
Rhianos. To Theodorus et al.
Rich, A. Floating Poem, Unnumbered, The.
Rohrer, J. Gearshift Poem, The.
Rollings. Dirty Dreams and God Smiling.
Rupchev, Georgi. Attraction.
Sabines. Entresol.
Lovers, The.
"Shunzei's Daughter.". Brought by the breeze.
Simic. My Beloved.
Steele, N. Diminutive.
Stillpoint, H. This I Whisper.
Tremblay, G. Surviving.
Ungria, R. Sui Veneris/The Poet of No Return.
Unknown. Jewels wherever we look.
More than the color.
Rare sight, a woman lost in the trance.
She likes it, the conjugal act.
Spring Song from "Tzu-Yeh" Songs of the Four Seasons.
Why do these prudes fear Prakrit poetry.
Unknown, fr. Sumerian cuneiform. Word they had spoken, The.
Vallejo. I'm thinking of your sex.
Verlaine. It's languor and ecstasy.
Virgil [or Vergil]. Eclogue 2: The Lament of Corydon for His Faithless Alexis.
Wakoski. Belly Dancer.
Whitman, W. From Pent-up Aching Rivers.
To the Garden the World.
Twenty-eight young men bathe by the shore.
Walt Whitman, a kosmos, of Manhattan the son.
Yi Chehyŏn. At a wash place by the stream under a drooping willow.
Yüan Chĕn. Oriole.
White Dress.

Seoul, Korea

Kim Chiha. Road to Seoul, The.
Story of a Sound, The.
Kim Hyesun. Daybreak in Seoul.
Saturday Night, Arriving in Seoul.
Yi Hyangji. Leaving Home.

Separation

Adams, J. There's Nae Luck about the House.
Aguero, Kathleen. Looking for Another Version.
Ahmed Dâi. Torture of the beloved is no punishment, The.
Ai. Back in the World.
Akhmatova, A. Don't Frighten Me.
Requiem.
Aktan, F. Letter, The: "Few broken things linger in my palm, A."

Alarcon, F. Border.
Frontera.
Frontera / Border.
Alkalay-Gut. Transportation.
Amichai, Y. Quick And Bitter.
Arnold, M. Forsaken Merman, The.
Isolation: To Marguerite.
Aşar, M. Sami. Weekly Agenda of Love.
Ashbery, J. Rivers and Mountains.
Atwood. Postcard.
Aytoun [or Ayton], R. Valediction.
Baraka, I. Agony, An. As Now.
Basu, R. How are you faring, Uma.
Beckett, S. Cascando.
Beer, P. Faithful Wife, The.
Berk, İ. Never Did I See Such Loves Nor Such Separations.
Berryman. He Resigns.
Bhattācārya, K. Hey, Hara, Ganges-Holder.
Bible, O.T. I am come into my garden, my sister, my spouse.
Black, S. Rilke's Letter from Rome.
To a War Correspondent.
Blue Cloud. Old man's lazy, The.
Boland, E. Ready for Flight.
Bomani, N. 1/Vacant.
Borisova, M. It's not when they leave.
Bourne, Lesley-Anne. She Sends Him a Postcard of the Sea.
Bradstreet, A. Another.
Brodsky, J. Will a mouth that's muttered its goodbyes.
Browning, R. Last Ride Together, The.
Waring.
Brownstein. Last Spell Cast, The.
Bryan, M. To My Brother ("O, thou art far away from me—dear boy!").
To My Brother ("Oh transient sorrows, light as morning dews.").
To My Brother ("Once in our customed walk a wounded bird.").
Burns, R. Highland Mary.
Red, Red Rose, A.
Silver Tassie, The.
Buson. I go.
Byron, G. Epistle to Augusta.
Fare Thee Well.
Juan and Haidee [from Cantos 2-4].
When We Two Parted.
Campbell, J. Sighle of the Lovespot.
Carruth, H. Swept.
Cary, P. Jacob.
Cassian. Sand.
Castillo, S. Primos.
Chalfi, R. Reading the I Ching.
Chang, D. Foreign Ways.
Ch'i-chi. Autumn Evening: To Send to my Nieces and Nephews.
Chia Tao. Thinking of Retired Scholar Wu on the River.
Chinese Oral Tradition. How Liu Chih-yüan Bade San-niang Good-bye and Joined the Army in T'ai-yüan.
Cho Chihun. Falling Petals.
Waiting.
Chŏng Sŏ. Regret.
Chu Shu-chen. Spring Joy.
Spring Night.
Clare, J. Ballad: "Mary, fate lent me a moment of pleasure."
Cofer, J. What the Gypsy Said to Her Children.
Cogswell, Fred. Beach at Noon, The.
Cohen, M. Evensong.
Cole, T. Lago Maggiore.
Colum, P. She Moved through the Fair.
Copus, J. Back Seat of My Mother's Car, The.
Cornford, F. Parting in Wartime.
Cory, D. Miss You.
Creedon. Litany.
Creeley. America.
Ballad of the Despairing Husband.
Feeling, A.
Cunningham, J. Jack and Jill.
Cussrooee. My Grief on the Sea.
Davies, Lynn. When You Can't Leave Me Anymore.

Dede, Esrâr. You left, but don't forget, my heart.
Devi. Distance.
Dickinson, E. We miss Her, not because We see.
Dixon, M. Place, Places.
Donne. Computation, The.
His Picture.
Valediction, A: Forbidding Mourning.
Drayton. O breake my hart quoth he, O breake and dye.
Since there's no help, come let us kiss and part.
Duncan, R. Passage over Water.
Eliot, T. S. Portrait of a Lady.
Elliot, J. Flowers of the Forest, The.
Elytis, O. Aegean Melancholy.
Emerson, R. Unity.
Fearing. Love, 20c the First Quarter Mile.
Ferlinghetti, L. In Golden Gate Park that day.
Third World Calling.
Fevrî. Arrow of your glance pierces my wounded, The.
Field. After Soufrière.
Forché. As Children Together.
Fowler, W. Upon this firthe, as on the sees of love.
Fu Hsüan. Pity Me!
Gallagher, T. Kidnap[p]er.
García. I Ain't Going to Hurry No More.
García Lorca. Poet Asks His Love About the Enchanted City of Cuenca, The.
Garnett, R. Dealing Scraps.
Garrett, E. Anatomy of Departure.
Love's Parallel.
George, K. Six Minutes Writing.
Glück, L. Hesitate to Call.
Horse.
Gorostiza, J. Who Will Buy Me an Orange?
Gould, J. Tanana Valley.
Green, G. Portuguese in Mergui, The.
Greville, F. I, with whose colors [or colours] Myra dressed [or dress'd or drest] her head.
Griffin, T. I Have Folded This Letter in Ten Places.
Guest, B. Santa Fe Trail.
Guevara, M. Long Distance.
Hacker, M. Going Back to the River.
If we talk, we're too tired to make love; if we.
Rondeau after a Transatlantic Telephone Call.
Villanelle: "Every day our bodies separate."
Hadas, R. Red Hat, The.
Hannah, S. Your Street Again.
Hardy, T. At Castle Boterel.
Walk, The.
Harms. From Now On.
Harnik, R. Your Socks.
Harpur, J. Young Man of Galway's Lament, The.
Harris, M. Trial Separation.
Harwood, L. Rain Journal: London: June '65.
Heaney, S. Westering.
Hemans. Arabella Stuart.
Henry VIII, King of England. To His Lady.
Hernández, M. Letter: "Pigeon-house of letters, The."
Hewett, D. You Gave Me Hyacinths First a Year Ago.
Hikmet. Poems from Prison.
Snow closed the road.
Hine. Apart from You.
Hooper, P. At the Terminal.
Hopes. Holy Innocents.
Housman. Because I liked you better.
He would not stay for me; and who can wonder?
Hsi-chün. Lost Horizon.
Hsiao Yen [or Emperor Wu of Liang]. Border Guard, A.
Hsieh T'iao. Autumn Night, An.
Hsü Kan. Wife's Thoughts, The.
Hughes, L. Letter ("Dear Mama, / Time I pay rent and get my food.").
Poem [2]: "I loved my friend."
So Long.
Hull, L. Midnight Reports.
Hwang Chini. Ah, what have I done?

Ibn Shuhayd, A.   There is no one in the abandoned encampment to inform us of the beloved ones, so from whom will we seek information about their condition?

Ibn Zaydūn, A.   Morning hour of mutual separation has replaced that of mutual proximity and the moment of our mutual separation from the sweetness of our proximity has come, The.

Ingelow.   Dappled sky, a world of meadows, A.

Jacinto, A.   Letter from a Contract Worker.

Jackson, L.   City Seems, A.

Jarman, M.   Supremes, The.

Jewett, S.   Letter, A.

Jiménez, J.   Sea Is Enormous, The.

Johnson, J.   Sence You Went Away.

Jones, R.   Times Like This.

Kadir, A.   On Bald Mountain.

Katrovas.   Black English.
Sky.

Kaufman, S.   Notes to my Daughters.

Kendrick, D.   Alone for a Week.

Kennelly.   Raglan Lane.

Kickham.   Slievenamon.

Killeen, G.   Tristia.

Kim Sowŏl.   Road Away, The.

Kimbrell, J.   Letters to a Vanishing Fiancée.

Kinnell.   Vow, The.

Kizer, C.   Race Relations.
Semele Recycled.

K'o Chun.   Springtime South of the Yangtze.

Komunyakaa, Y.   My Father's Love Letters [or Loveletters].

Kumin, M.   Seeing the Bones.

Kupriyanov [or Kuprianov].   For a long time he tried to survive.

Kyerang.   Under a shower of pear blossoms.

Landor, W.   Separation.

Lasker-Schüler.   O God.

Levertov.   Divorcing.
In California During the Gulf War.
Poem Unwritten, The.

Li Chih-yi.   Tune: "The Diviner".

Li Ch'ing-chao.   Plum Blossoms.
Sorrow of Departure.
Tune: "On the Trail of Sweet Incense".
Written on the Seventh Day of the Seventh Month.

Li Hsun.   To the Tune: The Wine Spring: "Rain falls on fallen flowers."

Li Po.   Ballad of Long Bank, The.
Ch'ang-Kan Village Song.
Letter, A: "My love, / When you were here there was."
Lonely Wife, The.
Long Banister Lane.
Longing for Someone.
Rhymeprose on the Sword Gallery.
River Merchant's Wife, The; A Letter.
Separation on the River Kiang.
Song of Ch'ang-kan.
To a Friend.
To Send Far Away.

Li Shang-yin.   Without Title (2).

Li Yü.   Tune: "Pure Serene Music".
Silent and Alone.

Lilley.   You Have to Strike Back.

Liu Shih.   Tune: "Dreaming of Southland"
Thinking of Someone.

Liu Yung.   Tune: "Bells Ringing in the Rain".

Llewellyn, K.   Finished.

Lloyd, C.   Erst when I wandered far from those I loved.
Oh, she was almost speechless! nor could hold.

Lomax, M.   Gulf.
Kith.

Lovelace, R.   To Lucasta, [on] Going beyond the Seas.
To Lucasta, [on] Going to the War[re]s.

Lover.   What Will You Do, Love?

MacNeice.   And Love Hung Still.

Mahon.   Globe in [North] Carolina, The.

Mak.   Farewell to Russia.

Mandelstam [or Mandelshtam].   Because I Let Go Your Hands.
Tristia.

Mao Wen-hsi.   Drunk Among the Flowers.
I Mustn't Ask.

Marlowe.   He's gone, and for his absence thus I mourn.

Martínez de Navarrete.   Separation from Clorila, The.

Marvell.   Definition of Love, The.

Mastin.   From the Telephone.

Maurus.   To Grimold, Abbot of St. Gall.

McClanahan, R.   Burial: "Like a sister who borrows."

McGinley.   Midcentury Love Letter.

Menicanti.   Love Says.

Merwin.   Rain Travel.
Separation.
When You Go Away.

Mew.   In Nunhead Cemetery.

Meyer, K.   Liadan and Curithir.

Meynell, A.   Thoughts in Separation.

Miedzyrzecki.   29-77-02.

Montague, J.   Point, The.
Refrain.

Montale.   Personae Separatae.

Moore, T.   Journey Onwards, The.

Morgan, R.   Damn You, Lady.

Motsapi, S.   Brotha saul.

Mudrooroo Narogin.   Hide and Seek.

Mura.   Letters from Poston Relocation Camp (1942–45).

Muso Soseki.   Reply to Gen'no Osho's Poem.

Nabi.   When we watch the spinning of the sky.

Nejati.   Those glances rain down arrows on the country.

Neruda.   My love, if I die and you don't.

Neshâtî.   You're gone—I'm alone in the company.

Nilsson, H.   On Inheriting Departure.

Nuccoli.   Since I abandoned and tied my soul to your sweet appearance and manners oh Sir, guide and light of my life, will I ever see you before I die?
You have the light of my life, in your clear and pleasing face, and don't see me.

Okita.   Notes for a Poem on Being Asian American.

Olds, S.   On The Subway.

Olson, C.   Boats' lights in the dawn going so swiftly the, The.
Newly Discovered "Homeric" Hymn, A.

Olstein, L.   We Still Have Basketball, Sara.

Ome Shushiki.   Frost of separation / Father, child.

Padel, R.   On the Line.
Tell Me About It.

Pak Chaesam.   In sunlight suffused.
Night at Tongbak Temple.

Pak Inhwan.   Fortnight.

P'an Yüeh.   Homeward.

Pao Ling-hui.   Added to a Letter Sent to a Traveler.

Parker, D.   On Being a Woman.

Paschen.   Between the Acts.
12 East Scott Street.

Passerat.   Villanelle: "I've lost her now, my turtle-dove."

Philips, K.   Lucasia, Rosania and Orinda Parting at a Fountain, July 1663.
Orinda to Lucasia.

Plath.   Parliament Hill Fields.

Po Chü-i.   Autumn Thoughts, Sent Far Away.

Pope, A.   Epistle to Miss [or Miss Teresa] Blount, on Her Leaving the Town after the Coronation.

Preseren, F.   Where?

Press, K.   Heart's Hunger.

Prince, F.T.   For Fugitives.

Raàm-Lachish, C.   In the Night.

Radnóti.   Letter to My Wife.

Ransom, J.   Jack's Letter.
Spectral Lovers.

Reed, H.   Judging Distances.

Reverdy.   Adieu.

Rexroth, K.   If I thought I could get away.

Reznikoff.   Though our thoughts often, we ourselves.

Rich, A.   Rain on the West Side Highway.

Splittings.

Ridler.   At Parting.
Before Sleep.

Robinson, M.   Bids Farewell to Lesbos.
Determines to Follow Phaon.
Phaon Forsakes Her.
Reproaches Phaon.

Rodriguez, L.   Always Running.

Rohrer, J.   Stopping by Fields on a Snowy Afternoon.

Romero, L.   If Marilyn Monroe.

Rossetti, C.   Aloof.
Come back to me, who wait and watch for you.
Many in aftertimes will say of you.
Remember [Me].

Rossetti, D.   Blessed Damozel, The.
Insomnia.

Rozhdestvensky [or Rozhdestvenskii].
Nostalgia.

Rukeyser, M.   Meeting, The.

Rumi.   When I have you, the passions of love make me stay awake.

Sadi [or Saadi or Sa'di].   He glanced at me one day—but then his mean.

Safie, D.   Danger, Men in Trees.

St. John, D.   Homage to Robert Johnson.

Salinas, P.   I Don't See You, Yet I Know.

Samaras, N.   Aubade: Macedonia.
Translation.

Sappho.   Some say an army of horsemen, others.

Seneca.   Britannia, free from foes and foreign kings.

Seward.   Farewell, false Friend!—our scenes of kindness close!

Şeyh Galib.   To me, love is the flame.

Shakespeare, W.   O[h] Mistress Mine.
Sonnet 36: "Let me confess[e] that we two must be twain[e]."
Sonnet 57: "Being your slave, what should I do[e] but tend."
Sonnet 61: "Is it thy will thy image should keep open."
Sonnet 97: "How like a winter hath my absence been[e]."
Sonnet 98: "From you have I been absent in the spring."
Sonnet 99: "Forward violet thus did I chide, The."

Shapiro, K.   V-Letter.

Shen Yüeh.   Green, Green Riverside Grass.

Shimabukuro, Mira Chieko.   After the Separation, Dad Takes Me to the Dance for the Dead.

Sholl.   Dawn.
Outside the Depot.

Shoneyin, T.   Quiver of Questions, A.

Sidney, P.   Sonnet 87: "When I was forced from Stella ever dear."
Sonnet 89: "Now that of absence the most irksome night."

Silva, J.   Nocturne: "One night / One night full of perfumes, music of wings and murmurs."

Snodgrass.   Locked House, A.

Solie, Karen.   More Fun In The New World.

Stern, G.   Waving Good-Bye.

Strand.   Marriage, The.

Strong, L.   Brewer's Man, The.

Su Tung-p'o.   Mid-Autumn Moon.

Su Wu.   Drafted.

Synge.   With One Long Kiss.

Tallmountain.   Brother Wolverine.

Tarn.   Heart Stumbles in Darkness, The.

Tennyson, A.   Thy spirit ere our fatal loss.

Thicknesse.   Siena.

Thompson, P.   Adown the Heights of Ages.

Ts'ao Chih.   In the northwest there is a Weaving-maid.

Tsvetayeva [or Tsvetaeva].   Cupolas flame, in Moscow where I live.

Tu Fu [or Du Fu].   All day, all night, I worry.
Dreaming of Li Po ("Death at least gives separation repose.").
Dreaming of Li Po ("Parted by death, we'd strangle on our tears.").
I have a sister, little sister, living in Zhongli.
I have brothers, younger brothers in a place far

away.
Moonlit Night ("In Fuzhou, far away, my wife is watching.").
Moonlit Night ("This same moon hangs over Fu-chou.").
Seven Songs Written while Living at T'ung-ku in 759.
Spring View.
They Say You're Staying in a Mountain Temple.
Thinking of My Little Boy.
To My Younger Brother.
Word from My Brothers.
Tuckerman, F.   Series 2, Sonnet 21.
Turner, C.   Kiss of Betrothal, The.
Ujević, T.   Green branch with a sadness of yellow fruit.
Unknown.   Already the accursed rooster and his sad departure song.
Autumn: "Autumn wind sweeps in through the windows, The."
Breaking a Willow-Branch.
Bright Moon, The.
Cai-ge [Translations].
Cao-chong: Hopper-Grass.
Faint moon in a heavy frost, The.
Far Away.
For wele or wo I wyl not flee.
Going on always on and on.
Had I known the time of separation was to come.
Hold me tight and very close to you.
Juan-er: Curl-Grass.
Last night you were sleeping in my arms.
Life-Parting.
May God prohibit you from any pleasure as you travel.
My Husband, Before Leaving.
Now mountains are separating us.
Of my bosom I have made a bed.
Oh damned rooster, I would like to strangle you!
Oh my love beyond the mountains, gaze at the moon.
Ru-fen: Along Yew's Banks.
So soon. Today, love, we.
Suliko.
Threading Frost.
To G.
Together We Know Happiness.
Western Wind.
Why could you not come? For what reason.
Wulf and Eadwacer: A Woman's Lament.
Yesterday Morning.
You: "Back from being."
Zi-jin: The Student's Blue Collar or Lapel.
Vasalis.   Sotto Voce.
Vaughan, H.   Retreat[e], The.
Vehbî, Sünbülzâde.   Oh east wind, come, what news from that garden.
Vertinsky [*or* Vertinskii].   I remember the night.
Vietnamese Oral Tradition.   Colonial Troops Transport, The.
Homesick Bride, The.
Painting, The.
Voigt.   At the Movie: Virginia, 1956.
Volkman.   Daffodils.
Sonnet: "Lease of my leaving, heartfelt lack, what does."
Voznesensky [*or* Voznesenskii].   For a Portrait of Annette Vallon.
Walafrid Strabo.   To His Friend in Absence.
Wang Chien.   Willow.
Wang Po-ch'eng.   Song of Parting.
Wang Shih-chieng.   After Snow, Longing for Elder Brother Hsi-ch'iao.
Waniek.   Star-Fix.
Webster, A.   There's one I miss. A little questioning maid.
Wei Chuang.   I Remember.
Wei Ying-wu.   Milky Way.
Whitman, R.   Laughing Gas.
Whitman, W.   Good-Bye, My Fancy!
Hours Continuing Long.
Williams, B.   Night Flute, The.
Williams, H.   Song, A: "No riches from his scanty store."

Willis, N.   Confessional, The.
Winchilsea.   Letter to Daphnis, A.
Winner, R.   Segregated Railway Diner—1946.
Winters, Y.   At the San Francisco Airport.
Wordsworth, W.   Complaint, A.
Tradition of Oker Hill in Darley Dale, Derbyshire, A.
Wroth.   Sonnet 21: "When last I saw thee, I did not[t] thee see."
Yan Yanzhi.   Pure Wife, A.
Yen Shu.   Tune: "Spring in the Jade House".
Yesenin [*or* Essenin].   Letter to My Mother.
Yi Chehyŏn.   Magpie chatters in a flowering bough by the hedge, A.
Yosano Akiko.   Channel Boat, The.
What shall I wear to sleep in alone?
Young, K.   Letters from the North Star.
Yüan Chĕn.   Dreaming of My Wife.
Remembering.
When We Are Apart.
Yun Tongju.   One Night I Count the Stars.
Zanzotto.   How Long.
Zhang Hua.   Emotion.
Zhang Shuai.   Pining.
Staring.
Zisquit.   Word before the Last about Loss, A.
Zolynas.   Love in the Classroom.

See also **Absence; Isolation; Loneliness**

September
Bridges, R.   Garden in September, The.
Brodsky, J.   September came on Tuesday.
Coleridge, M.   September.
Dubin, A.   September in the Rain.
Greenaway.   Three Little Girls.
Gutteridge.   In September 1939.
Hausman.   September City.
Housman.   Tell Me Not Here [It Needs Not Saying].
Jackson, H.   September [Days Are Here].
Kasischke.   My Heart.
Kinnell.   Blackberry Eating.
Kinsella, T.   Another September.
Lawrence, D. H.   Bavarian Gentians.
MacNeice.   September has come and I wake.
Nelson, J.   If You Knew September.
O'Donoghue, M.   Go-Summer.
Ormond.   In September.
Ouwens.   Farmer, The.
Parry-Williams.   Two Poems.
Pastan.   September.
Ray, H.   September.
Roethke.   Carnations.
Seibles, T.   4AM.
Taylor, J.   Libra, September.
Webb, P.   Ten white blooms on the sundeck.

September 11th, 2001
Beeson, M.   Flight.
Bidart.   Curse.
Brook, D.   Poem Wrapped Around Quotation from Samantha Power.
Brown, A.   Ash Wednesday, 2002.
Old Neighborhood, The.
Cortez, J.   I Am New York City 2.
Di Prima.   Notes Toward a Poem of Revolution.
Drummond, R.   As Zeus.
Dunn, S.   Grudges.
Espada.   Alabanza: In Praise of Local 100.
Ferlinghetti, L.   History of the Airplane.
Fischer, N.   Violence of Oneness, The.
Fuhrman, J.   Return to Normalcy.
Garrison, D.   I Saw You Walking.
Hadas, R.   Tangerine Orchids.
Hahn, K.   Boerum Hill Tanka.
Mortal Remains.
Hamill, S.   New York Poem, The.
Hirshfield, J.   Dead Do Not Want Us Dead, The.
Hoagland, E.   From Ground Zero.
Howe, F.   9-11-01.
Inez.   September Morning.
Jones, P.   All Saints Day, 2001.
Joris, P.   9/11/01.
Katz, E.   When the Skyline Crumbles.
Kinnell.   When the Towers Fell.
Kushner, E.   Friends.
In the Hairy Arms of Whitman.
Kwa, Lydia.   You must exist. Writing this book

depends on it. It has occurred to.
Lehman.   9/14/01.
9/15/01.
Lima, F.   Good Morning America.
Mass, R.   No Surprises.
Menefee, S.   September 30.
Moustaki, N.   How to Write a Poem after September 11th.
Murray, G.   Statue, The.
Murray, J.   Survivors—Found.
Nurkse.   October Marriage.
Parini.   After the Terror.
Pawlak.   All the News—September 23, 2001.
Official Versions.
Peacock, M.   Land of the Shí, The.
Reed, P.   September 11.
September 18.
Reibetanz, D.   Norgberto Hernandez— Photographed Falling September Eleventh.
Rothenberg, M.   Apocalyptic Yearnings.
Seidman.   New York: "I read over my lines."
Shepherd, R.   Objects in Mirror Are Closer Than They Appear.
Shipley, V.   Birdsong for September 11, 2001.
Spahr, J.   January 28, 2003.
Stenhouse, S.   Circling.
Stock, N.   What I Said.
Towle.   Prospects.
Trinidad.   Adam and Eve on the Hollywood Tread Mill.
Witt, S.   Thermal Signatures ("There is nothing to remember but flight. The owl's eyes spoke.").

Serbia
Ritterbusch.   Thousand Cranes, A.
Smith, K.   Essential Serbo-Coat.
Spera, G.   Balkan.

Serbians, The
Satyamurti.   Striking Distance.

Serenity
Carruth, H.   Forty-Five.
Cetina, G.   Madrigal: Eyes of Clear Serenity.
Chia Tao.   Abode of the Unplanned Effect.
Han-shan.   Like a Drifting Boat.
Hayden, R.   Monet's "Waterlilies".
Hutchinson, P.   Into Their True Gentleness.
Kim Chŏngnan.   Women's Language.
Kipling, R.   If.
Kunitz, S.   Long Boat, The.
Ortiz.   Serenity in Stones, The.
Simic.   Summer Morning.
Tan Taigi.   Beyond serenity / Gray kites.
Tosui Unkei.   Content with chipped bowl and tattered robe.
Verlaine.   Uneven rows of hedges.
Wigglesworth.   Still was the night, serene and bright.
Zukofsky, L.   Not much more than being.

Sermons
Andrews, N.   Notes for a Sermon on the Mount.
Borges.   Matthew 5:1–12; Seeing the crowds, he went up on the mountain.
Carnevali.
Han Yong'un [*or* Yongwun].   Master's Sermon, The.
Hughes, R.   Sermon, The.
Shiki.   Just when the sermon.
Wheatley, P.   To the Rev. Dr. Thomas Amory on Reading His Sermons on Daily Devotion.
Young, K.   Wake.

Servants
Archilochus.   I am a servant of the War Lord.
Borges.   Matthew 25:14–30; "For it will be as when a man".
Brooks, G.   Bronzeville Woman in a Red Hat.
Brown, S.   Scotty Has His Say.
Butlin.   Advertisement for a Scottish Servant.
Cardenal.   Luke 16:1–9; He also said to the disciples.
Clare, J.   My Mary.
Cuney.   No Images.
De [*or* Du] Guillet.   But if he came straight for me.
Dransfield.   War of the Roses, The.
Duffy, C.   Warming Her Pearls.

Eliot, T. S.   Aunt Helen.
Evans, M.   When in Rome.
Harington [or Harrington].   Ambiguity.
Henson, S.   Heron, The.
Herbert, J.   Irish Scullery Maid, The.
Herrick.   Upon Prue [or Prew], His Maid.
Howe, F.   Scattered Light.
Hughes, L.   Madam and Her Madam.
Kipling, R.   Servant When He Reigneth, A.
Krivulin.   Glory to caesar! and glory to God in
   the highest!
Kunitz, S.   Magic Curtain, The.
MacSweeney.   Pearl Alone.
Partridge, E.   Vuillard Interior.
Rilke.   Luke 15:11–19; And he said, "There was
   a man".
Ríos, A.   Nani.
Senryū, K.   For a housemaid.
Sigourney.   Erin's Daughter.
Slessor.   Full Orchestra.
Sŏ Chŏngju.   Floor in Goethe's House, The.
Ssu-k'ung Shu.   In Illness, Dismissing My
   Singing Girl.
Stokesbury.   Reynaldo in Paris.
Swift, J.   Mary the Cook-Maid's Letter to Dr.
   Sheridan.
   To Their Excellencies the Lords Justices of
   Ireland, the Humble Petition of Frances
   Harris, Who Must Starve, and Die a Maid if
   It Miscarries.
Trethewey, N.   Domestic Work, 1937.
Turner, F.   On the Pains of Translating Miklós
   Radnóti.
Unknown.   My Sodger Laddie.
Vazirani, R.   Dream of the Evil Servant.
Vietnamese Oral Tradition.   Concubine, The.
Wickham.   Butler and the Gentleman, The.
Wilbur, R.   Summer Morning, A.
Williams, S.   Letters from a New England
   Negro.
Yuson.   Andy Warhol Speaks to His Two
   Filipino Maids.

Service Stations.
See Gasoline Stations

Sestina (form)
Alvarez, J.   Bilingual Sestina.
Anderson, P.   Sestina in Time of Winter.
Ashbery, J.   Farm Implements and Rutabagas in
   a Landscape.
Barnes, B.   Sestina: "Then first with locks
   dishevelled and bare."
Bishop, E.   Miracle for Breakfast, A.
   Sestina: "September rain falls on the house."
Cummins, J.   Sestina: "He wanted to tell her the
   weekend idea was 'neat'."
France, L.   Blues for Bird.
Gioia.   My Confessional Sestina.
Gosse.   Sestina: "In fair Provence, the land of
   lute and rose."
Hecht, A.   Book of Yolek, The.
   Sestina d'Inverno.
Justice, D.   Here in Katmandu.
Kipling, R.   Sestina of the Tramp-Royal.
McCabe, C.   Postcard from London, A.
Muldoon, P.   Misfits, The.
Nims, J.   Tide Turning.
Porter, F.   Island in the Evening, The.
Pound, E.   Sestina: Altaforte.
Ridland.   Blue Plate Tea Room: Sestina, The.
Ríos, A.   Nani.
Sidney, P.   Sestina: "Farewell, O Sun".
Swinburne.   Sestina: "I saw my soul at rest upon
   a day."
Waldman, A.   How the Sestina (Yawn) Works.
Wojahn.   Floating Houses.

Seven Deadly Sins
Dunbar, W.   Dance of the Sevin Deidly Synnis
   [or Seven Deadly Sins], The.

Severn River, England
Tennyson, A.   Danube to the Severn gave, The.

Seville, Spain
Lope de Vega.   Seguidillas of the Guadalquivir
   River.
Torre, M.   Driven by a Strange Desire.

Sewall, Samuel
Hecht, A.   Samuel Sewall.
Seward, William H.
Harrison, J.   Ghazal 39: "If you laid out all the
   limbs from the Civil War hospital."
Sewers
Carter, S.   Paean.
Schiff, Robyn.   House of Dior.
Sewing
Aalfs, J.   Sewing the Torn Sleeve.
Alvarez, J.   Naming the Fabrics.
Ap Hywel, Elin.   Stitching.
Bell, A.   This is my work so.
Bly, R.   Yellow Dot, The.
Boruch.   Sewing.
Chŏng Hwajin.   Sewing Box, The.
Connolly, G.   Mother, a Young Wife Leans to
   Sew.
De Kok.   Mending.
Dean, D. K.   Stitches.
Denham, Joe.   Mending.
Donovan, K.   Stitching.
Dunbar-Nelson.   I Sit and Sew.
Ford, Katie.   Nocturne: "I can see the whole
   city, lights edging the harbor like yellow pins
   in uneven."
Gippius.   Seamstress, The.
Gray, F.   With cheerful mind we yield to men.
Groarke, V.   Indoors.
Hall, H.   Instruction.
   Listening Macaws, The.
   Seams.
Han Yong'un [or Yongwun].   Embroidery's
   Secret, The.
Hayzler, K.   Machine, The.
Joseph, A.   Plenty.
Khalvati.   Needlework.
Kurtz.   Call, The.
Lilley.   Sewing Lesson, The.
MacLeod, Sue.   When night meets thread and
   needle and lies down among the bedclothes.
Maguire, S.   Invisible Mender, The.
Pan Chao.   Needle and Thread.
Peirce.   Quilts.
Pelham.   When i was young.
Powell, D. A.   My Father and Me Making
   Dresses: Together.
Ramke, B.   According to Ovid.
Rostopchina.   Unfinished Sewing, The.
Sagan.   Winter burn.
Taylor, E.   Huswifery.
Van Ostaijen.   Ode to Singer.
Ward, J.   Comfort-Maker.
Zhao.   Needle and Thread.
See also **Seamstresses; Tailoring and Tailors**
Sex
Adcock, F.   Against Coupling.
   Happy Ending.
   Prelude: "Is it the long dry grass that is so
   erotic."
Addaeus.   When you meet a young boy, be
   direct.
Addonizio.   Prayer: "Sometimes, when we're
   lying after love."
   Theodicy.
Adisa.   Discover Me.
Ai.   Before You Leave.
   New Crops for a Free Man.
   Twenty-Year Marriage.
   Why Can't I Leave You?
Akhmatova, A.   1915.
Alexander, P.   Well-Known Elizabethan Double
   Entendre, A.
Algarin.   Rosa.
Amichai, Y.   Quick And Bitter.
Ammons.   Their Sex Life.
Ancient Sumerian Oral Tradition.   Bridegroom,
   dear to my heart.
   Word they had spoken, The.
Anderson, C.   Platonic Love.
Andrade, E.   Fable.
   Music.
Andrews, N.   Zen 101.
Anthony, M.   So suddenly.
   You cared whether I died or not.

Antipater of Thessalonica.   Priapus, seeing
   Cimon's rigid rod.
Archilochus.   Fireworks on the Grass.
   Hold back completely.
   I said, "Be mine.".
Argentarius.   Her perfect naked breast.
   I can't bear to watch your hips.
Arnold, C.   Disembodied Voices of Women,
   The.
Arvio, S.   Mirrors.
Asclepiades.   We were having fun, that devil
   Hermione and I.
Auden.   Aubade: "At break of dawn."
   Glad.
   Mad to be had, to be felt and smelled. My lips.
   Minnelied.
Automedon.   Turkish. Belly-dancer. Sexy tricks.
Babu, S.   Sex Everywhere.
Baffo, G.   Sonnet: "My meditation turns to
   thinking."
Baker, D.   Pulp Fiction.
   Sex.
Barber, W.   Gay Poet, The.
Barker, G.   O Golden Fleece.
Barrax.   Adagio.
Barrows, A.   Pleasures of the Flesh.
Basheva.   Morning: "Where was I last night? In
   whose arms?"
Basho.   Cat's wife, A.
Bass, E.   God and the G-Spot.
   To Praise.
Baudelaire.   Sed non satiata.
Behn, A.   Disappointment, The.
Belev.   Woman: "Weeds loom."
   Zoo.
Bellman.   Fredman's Epistle No. 23.
Beresford.   Courtship, The.
Berger, J.   Getting to Know Her.
Berk, İ.   Poem: "Yellow, Loveliest, enters my
   city."
Berlin.   You'd Be Surprised.
Berrigan, T.   In Bed with Joan & Alex.
   Poem upon the page is as massive as, The.
Bhattācārya, K.   Unperturbed at the battle.
Bhattācārya, M.   There's a huge hullabaloo in
   my lotus heart.
Bibbins, M.   Slutty.
Bible, O.T.   I am come into my garden, my
   sister, my spouse.
Biespiel, D.   Tower.
Bishop, E.   Exchanging Hats.
   Vague Poem.
Blake, W.   Sick Rose, The.
   Visions of the Daughters of Albion.
Boland, E.   Daphne with Her Thighs in Bark.
Bond, S.   Tuesday Night Affair.
Bowman, C.   Demographics.
Brecht, S.   Here then is the life-giving activity
   given to every man: the sexual / act,
   vivificator.
Bromige.   Logical Positivist, The.
Brossard, Nicole.   I Want to Revise This
   Sequence.
   Typhoon Thrum.
Broumas, O.   Caritas.
   Choir, The.
   For Every Heart.
   Tryst.
   With the clear.
Brouwer, J.   Development: "I learned to fuck
   one summer in a burgeoning subdivision."
Brown, E.   Probably the most human thing I do.
   Tragic Hero.
Buchanan, S.   Alone in Belize.
Buchman, Ruth.   Short Story.
Budy.   First Books.
Burke, C.   Motor Oil Queen.
Burns, R.   Fornicator. A New Song, The.
   I Once Was a Maid.
   Patriarch, The.
   Wat ye what my Minnie did.
Cable, G.   Criole Candjo.
Caesar.   What a Perfect Combination.
Campbell, S.   Legacy.
Carbone, L.   Flight from the Marriage Bed.
Carew, T.   Rapture, A.

Carruth, H.   Alive.
Capper Kaplinski at the North Side Cue Club.
Carson, A.   Stanzas, Sexes, Seductions.
Cartwright, W.   No Platonic [or Platonique]
Love.
Catullus.   Ipsithilla, my pet, my favorite dish.
Just now I found a young boy.
To Aurelius.
Cavafy.   In Despair.
In the Street.
One Night.
Their Beginning.
Celan.   When you lie.
Cendrars.   Great Fetishes, The.
Ceravolo.   Pregnant, I Come.
Cervantes.   On the Poet Coming of Age.
Chavez, L.   After the Prom.
Child, A.   Squeeze.
Chin, J.   Why He Had to Go.
Chiyojo.   Whether astringent.
Chrystos.   I Bought a New Red.
I Suck.
You Know I Like to Be.
Chu Shu-chen.   Spring Joy.
Chubb, R.   Song of My Soul.
Ciardi, J.   Censorship.
Citino.   Sister Mary Appassionata Lectures the
Bible Study Class: Homage to Onan.
Claman, E.   Show Biz Parties.
Clark, T.   What I've Learned in My Travels.
Clarke, A.   Strolling one day, beyond the
Kalends, on Mount Cyllene.
Cleary, B.   Chicken & Sex.
Clifton, H.   Monsoon Girl.
Cofer, J.   How to Get a Baby.
Life of an Echo, The.
Cohen, L.   You Have the Lovers.
Coleman, W.   African Sleeping Sickness.
Breast Examination.
Congreve, W.   Pious Selinda [or Celinda].
Constantine, D.   As our bloods separate.
Conway, J.   Hangover.
Modern English.
Cornish, S.   Generations 1.
Cortez, J.   So Long.
Cott, J.   Enjoyment Body.
Coultas, B.   Dr. Wasserman.
Crowley, A.   Ballad of Passive Paederasty, A.
Dedicace.
Go into the Highways and Hedges, And Compel
Them to Come In.
Rondels.
Crozier, L.   Poem for Sigmund.
Cruz, C.   Traveling Gospel.
Cullen, C.   Sacrament.
Cummings, E. E.   I like my body when it is with
your.
May i feel said he.
She being Brand.
Cummins, J.   Sestina: "He wanted to tell her the
weekend idea was "neat"."
Cunningham, J.   Epitaph for Someone or Other.
History of Ideas.
Lip.
Dacey, P.   Squeak.
Dailey.   Thong.
Dali.   Great Masturbator, The.
Dalton, R.   Memory.
D'Aquino, A.   Amoroso.
Amorous.
Daumal.   Persephone That Is to Say Double
Issue.
Davidkov, Ivan.   Returning from the Fair.
Davidman.   Night-Piece.
Davie, D.   Jacob's Ladder.
Davies, S.   Faith (wench) I cannot court thy
sprightly eyes.
Davis, C.   Pietà.
Davis, W.   Spider.
Dawes, K.   Some Tentative Definitions 7.
De [or Du] Guillet.   But if he came straight for
me.
Delgado, J.   Two Timer.
Deutsch.   Solitude.
D'Haen.   Epiphany.
Dickey, J.   Sheep Child, The.

Djogo.   Wooden Handle, The.
Doty, M.   Days of 1981.
Doubiago, S.   How to Make Love to a Man.
Dove, R.   Adolescence—2.
Dowson.   Non Sum Qualis Eram Bonae sub
Regno Cynarae.
Drayton.   To His Coy Love, A Canzonet.
Duffy, C.   Oppenheim's Cup and Saucer.
Duhamel.   Kinky.
Duncan, R.   I Am a Most Fleshly Man.
Dunmore.   Safe period.
Three Ways of Recovering a Body.
Dunn, S.   After Making Love.
Man Who Closed Shop, The.
Durcan.   My Belovèd Compares Herself to a
Pint of Stout.
Edson, R.   Conjugal.
Eirian, S.   Englishwoman, An.
Elliott, A.   Angel.
Here Today.
Love Poem, The.
Ellis, T.   Kiss in the Dark, A.
Elmslie, K.   One Night Stand.
Ennis.   Alice of Daphne, 1799.
"Ern Malley.".   Boult to Marina.
Estep, M.   I Have to Go Now.
Evans, R.   Femininity.
Fanning, R.   In the Barn.
Farley, C.   Grand Canyon.
Feierstein, R.   Sex: "You can sense, after a slow
apprenticeship."
Fell, A.   And Again.
Fields, D.   Fine Romance, A.
Fisher, J.   Six Part Lust Story.
Flanders, M.   Have Some Madeira, M'dear?
Flatman.   Appeal to Cats in the Business of
Love, An.
Foley, M.   Middle Manager in Paradise, The.
Follain.   Hardware Store.
Forché.   Taking Off My Clothes.
Fox, Sarah.   Interruption.
Fox, Skip.   Economics of Metonymy: sic transit.
France, L.   Body Language.
Eater of Wives, The.
In Kind.
My Muse, the Whore.
Freeman, J.   Fifteen.
Fusselman, A.   Puffy Jacket.
Gallagher, T.   Sea Inside the Sea.
García Lorca.   Faithless Wife, The.
Unfaithful Wife, The.
Unfaithful Wife, The.
Gardinier.   Where Blind Sorrow Is Taught to
See.
Garshman, B.   Keys.
Genet.   Man Condemned to Death, The.
Gerstler.   BZZZZZZZ.
Ginsberg, A.   Change, The: Kyoto-Tokyo
Express.
Howl.
On Neal's Ashes.
Please Master.
Sphincter.
This Form of Life Needs Sex.
Giorno.   Pornographic Poem.
Glatt.   One Night With a Stranger at 30.
Gloeggler, T.   Foreplay.
Glück, L.   Edge, The.
Labor Day.
Mock Orange.
Song of Obstacles.
Wound, The.
Godfrey.   Bath.
Goethe.   Here my garden is growing, the flowers
of Eros I tend here.
Gogarty.   On First Looking into Krafft-Ebing's
Psychopathosexualis [or Psychopathia
Sexualis].
Goldberg, B.   Torture Boy at the Easter Confest,
Repentance Creek.
Goldberg, N.   Two Iowa Farmers.
Goodman, M.   February Ice Years.
New Comers.
Gorham.   White Tiger Leaps, The.
Green, M.   Finished Poem.
Greenhalgh, C.   Big No-No, The.

My Funny Valentine.
Griffin, P.   To His Importunate Mistress.
Groarke, V.   Shale.
Hacker, M.   Wagers.
Hahn, K.   Artist's Daughter, The.
Hahne, M.   Lies We Tell Ourselves.
Halliday, M.   Population.
Hammial.   Jane.
Handy, W.   Yellow Dog Blues.
Hannan, M.   Seq.
Hardy, J.   Difference, The.
Harper, M.   Elvin's Blues.
Harris, D.   What we have lost.
Harris, J.   Balance.
Harvey, Y.   Sex.
Hass, R.   Privilege of Being.
Hecht, A.   End of the Weekend, The.
Heffernan, M.   Message, The.
Heine, H.   My zenith was luckily happier than
my night.
Words, Words, Words, and Nothing Doing.
Hejinian.   Solitude flared out, The.
Yesterday I saw the sun.
Hemphill.   Where Seed Falls.
Higgins, R.   Did-You-Come-Yets of the Western
World, The.
Hill, S.   Small Hotel, A.
Hô Sugyông.   Train Leaving.
Holan.   Meeting in a Lift.
Holland, W.   Christopher Street 1979.
Hope, A.   Fafnir.
Imperial Adam.
Lingam and the Yoni, The.
Lot and His Daughters I.
Hope, M.   Bare Floors.
Only Days.
Horace.   To a Randy Old Woman.
Horovitz, F.   Night-Piece.
Howe, F.   Once on a summer night.
Huang O [or Huang Ho].   Farewell to a
Southern Melody, A.
Hudgins.   Versification of a Passage from
Penthouse.
Huelsenbeck, R.   "We Hardly".
Huerta, D.   Thirteen Propositions against Trivial
Love.
Trece intenciones contra el amor trivial.
Hughes, T.   Bride and Groom Lie Hidden for
Three Days.
Ibn Kamal.   How an Old Man Can Regain His
Youth Through Sexual Potency.
Iskrenko.   Sex—A Five-Minute Briefing.
Istarú, A.   Crescent moon, A.
Then / an awakened citron.
Your penis rolls to the dream.
Jacobik, G.   Sphere, The: "Their first time, they
were wonderfully tender."
Jamie, K.   Hill-track, The.
Jayadeva.   Song of Krishna: The Fourth Song,
Sung with Raga "Ramakari".
Jenkins, A.   Barcelona.
Johnson, G.   I Want to Die While You Love Me.
Jones, Rae.   Shakti.
Jones, Rodney.   Carpe Diem: "Though pretty, it
rarely worked, lining seduction."
Jong, E.   Colder.
Juvenal.   Satire 6.
Kahn, G.   Makin' Whoopee.
Kalmar et al.   What a Perfect Combination.
Kantaris.   Airing the Chapel.
Kasdorf.   Body Remembers, The.
Kasischke.   Fatima.
Pall.
Kassabova, K.   And they were both right.
Kay, J.   Close Shave.
Kemp, A.   100 Times.
Kennelly.   Love-Cry.
Kenney.   In April.
Kim Suyông.   Sex.
Kinnell.   After Making Love We Hear
Footsteps.
Last Gods.
Rapture.
Waking, The.
Kizer, C.   Copulating Gods, The.
Klappert.   Court of Divine Justice, The.

Klein, M.   Scenes for an Elegy.
Koestenbaum, P.   Sonnet 37: "I'd decided I initiate most."
Kombem.   Another Moment.
Komunyakaa, Y.   Sunday Afternoons.
Kshetrayya.   Courtesan to Her Lover, A.
Kumin, M.   In the Pea Patch.
Kunert.   Venice Lost.
Kurt, K.   GYN-astics.
Labrador, Sean Manzano.   Dark Continent, The.
Larkin, J.   Risks.
Laughlin, J.   O Best of All Nights, Return and Return Again.
Laux, D.   China.
2 am.
Lawrence, D. H.   Love On the Farm.
Lederer, K.   Dream of Mimesis, A.
Lee, W.   Sex Has a Way.
Leon, R.   Have you not heard the gossip and the rumour going around.
Levertov.   Ache of Marriage, The.
Poem Unwritten, The.
To the Snake.
Lim-Wilson.   Beginning of Things, The.
Liu, T.   Ikon.
Livingston, J.   Femininity.
Llwyd, Alan.   Bull of Bryncelyn, The.
Lochhead, L.   Dreaming Frankenstein.
Loesser.   Take Back Your Mink.
Loftis, N.   Brief Encounter.
Lomax, M.   Gruoch.
Lovelace, R.   On Sanazar's being honoured with six hundred Duckets by the Clarissimi of Venice, for composing an Elegiack Hexastick of The City. A Satyre.
To Amarantha, That She Would Dishevel[l] Her Hair[e].
Lowry, M.   Volcano is Dark, The.
Lowther, John.   Asleeping: a kind of rendezvous.
Loy.   Love Songs to Joannes.
Luca, Gherasim.   End of the World, The: To Embody.
Lukata, B.   Interpretations.
Lumbreras, E.   Reunión de violonchelos.
Reunion of Cellos.
Lumsden, R.   Then.
Lyons, S.   Loving Along Western Rivers.
Mackenzie, K.   Fool, The.
Ginger-flowers.
Searchlights.
MacLeish.   You Also, Gaius Valerius Catullus.
MacNeice.   And Love Hung Still.
MacSweeney.   Cute Petite.
Major, C.   Inside Diameter.
On Trying to Imagine the Kiwi Pregnant.
Mansour, J.   I Want to Sleep with You.
Mardi, Jas.   Perseverance.
Marlis, S.   Snack.
Marlowe.   Men of wealthy Sestos, every year, The.
Martial.   Artemidorus sold his land to buy a boy.
Cornelius sighs . . . the lines I write.
Gaurus, you have a fault for which.
Lydia is as wide and slack.
Nasica raped the doctor's pretty lad.
Out of the house or be the wife I want.
People have the oddest kinks.
When you say, "Quick, I'm going to come,".
Your slave boy's cock is aching, Naevolus.
Martin, C.   Satyr, Cunnilinguent: To Herman Melville.
Victoria's Secret.
Martinson.   Creation Night.
Massimi.   Advice to Paulinus.
Masters, E.   Margaret Fuller Slack.
Margaret Fuller Slack.
Mataka.   Can We Talk?
Licorice.
Matanov, I.   Still I See in Front of Me.
Mateo.   There Is No Word for Sex in Taglog.
Matthews, W.   Accompanist, The.
Max, L.   Stone Fruit.
Mayer, B.   First Turn to Me.
McCarriston.   Castle in Lynn, A.
McGuckian.   Captain Lavender.

McHugh, H.   Coming.
McLain, P.   Willing.
McNair.   What Became.
McNaughton.   Balls.
Meinke.   Helen.
Meleager.   Hot day. Dying of thirst. Slake myself.
To Diodorus, Dorotheus, Callicrates et al.
Mesmer, S.   Lonely Tylenol.
My Life in Yonago.
Metwalli, M.   This Is How the Magician Produces a Dove out of the Hat.
Michaux.   Simplicity.
Millay, E.   I, Being Born A Woman [And Distressed].
Miller, E.   She Is Flat on Her Back.
Mohammad, K. Silem.   Mars Needs Terrorists.
Molloy, D.   First Blood.
Monnier, Pascalle.   Summer ("Good, it's hot.").
Montagu, L.   Between Your Sheets.
Receipt to Cure the Vapours, A.
Moore, H.   First Time: 1950.
Green Place, A.
Moore, T.   Did Not.
Morgenstern, Felicia L.   Ride Me Baby, Ride Me.
Morrissey, S.   And Forgive Us Our Trespasses.
Moulds, J.   When Bad Angels Love Women.
Muldoon, P.   History.
Mullen, H.   Kamasutra Sutra.
Pretty Piece of Tail.
Mullen, L.   Series of Failures So That I'm Sick of the Word, A.
Murphy, P.   Sequence: "Standing in her basement."
Murray, J.   Epithalamium, An.
Muske, C.   Our Kitty.
Nagai, M.   Histories of Bodies.
Nashe [or Nash].   Choise of valentines, The.
Nazario, A.   Melt me.
Neely, L.   Eight Ways of Looking at Pussy.
Neruda.   Nuptial Material.
Sexual Water.
Nguyễn Khuyến.   To the Singing Girl Named Luu.
Nicholas, A.   Strange / that we wake.
Nichols, G.   Come up and see me sometime.
Configurations.
Nolla.   Erotic Suite.
Nordbrandt.   Sailing.
Notley.   Destroy.
Ntiru.   Listen—listen.
Obejas, A.   Dancing in Paradise.
O'Grady, J.   Poem for the Womb.
O'Hara, F.   Ave Maria.
Cornkind.
Mary Desti's Ass.
Olds, S.   Ecstasy.
It.
Knowing, The.
Last Night.
Moment the Two Worlds Meet, The.
Monarchs.
Necking.
New Mother.
Sex without Love.
Sisters of Sexual Treasure, The.
True Love.
Wellspring, The.
Olin.   Blue Collar Holiday.
No Matter What Sign You Are.
Para-Olympic Legacy, The.
Ondaatje.   Cinnamon Peeler, The.
Oppian [of Corycus].   Loves of the Eel [or Fishes], The.
O'Sullivan, L.   When We Were Good.
Ovid.   Elegy 1.5: "In summer's heat[e] and mid-time of the day."
She'd looks, she'd style.
Padgett, R.   First Drift.
Tell Us, Josephine.
Palladas [or Pallades].   Having Slept with a Man.
Parker, Dominique.   Foxfire.
Parker, Dorothy.   General Review of the Sex Situation.

Parker, P.   For Willyce.
Pasolini.   Sex, Consolation for Misery.
Patchen.   Figure Motioned with Its Mangled Hand Toward the Wall Behind It, The.
Paulus [or Paulos] Silentiarius.   Take off your clothes, my love!
Tantalos.
Pavlova, V.   Armpits smell of linden blossom.
Paz.   Madrid, 1937, / in the Plaza del Angel the women.
Was it I making plans / for the summer—and for all the summers.
Peacock, M.   Have You Ever Faked an Orgasm?
Lullaby: "Big as a down duvet the night."
My God, Why Are You Crying?
Return, The.
Surge, The.
Perrine.   Limerick: "Sex-life her husband dreamed of, The."
Peskett.   Window Dressing.
Petri.   Gratitude.
Petronius Arbiter.   Coition's brief, a nasty cheat.
Doing, a filthy pleasure is, and short.
Good God, What a Night That Was.
Phaedrus.   Widow and the Soldier or: The Measure of a Woman's Inconstancy and Lust, The.
Phillips, C.   Kill, The.
Phillips, D.   Five.
Philodemus.   Demo and Thermion Both Slay Me.
Make the Bedlamp Tipsy with Oil.
Picabia.   Spermal Chimney.
Piercy.   Crabs.
Implications of One Plus One.
It Arrives Suddenly and Carries Us Off As Usual.
Pilkington, L.   Fair and Softly goes far or, The Wary Physician.
Polito.   Overheard in the Love Hotel.
Pollard, C.   Heavy-Petting Zoo, The.
I enjoy dancing.
Porter, C.   They Couldn't Compare to You.
Too Darn Hot.
Porter, P.   Now it's in all the novels, what's pornography to do?
Sex and the Over Forties.
Pound, E.   Temperaments, The.
Pratt, M.   Done.
Propertius.   Night's best of all. Night brings delight.
Radden, V.   Blood.
Sex.
Ramírez, J.   Corazón mecánico.
Mechanical Heart.
Randall, D.   Ballygrand Widow.
Rattenbury, A.   War Memoir, A.
Razaf, A.   My Man o' War.
Rebolledo.   Sapho's Kiss.
Redel, V.   Singing to Tony Bennett's Cock.
Redmond.   My Tongue Paints a Path.
Rees-Jones.   What It's Like To Be Alive.
Reid, D.   Between Aphorisms.
Rekdal, Paisley.   Crash of rhinos, A.
Rexroth, K.   As I came from the.
Floating.
I cannot forget.
I hold your head tight between.
I scream as you bite.
Lying in the meadow, open to you.
Making love with you.
Sottoportico San Zaccaria.
You wake me.
Your tongue thrums and moves.
Reynolds, O.   Bestiary.
Eous.
Rich, A.   My mouth hovers across your breasts.
That "old last act"! / And yet sometimes.
Two Songs.
Two Songs.
Rickword.   Moon-talk.
Rimbaud, A.   Obscur et froncé.
Our Assholes Are Different.
Riordan, M.   Lines to His New Instructress.
Roberts, L.   Problem, The.
Rochester, J.   Mock Song, The.

Ramble in St. James's Park, A.
Signior Dildo.
Song: "By all love's soft, yet mighty powers."
Song of a Young Lady to Her Ancient Lover, A.
Song: "Oh gentle Venus, ease a tarse."
Roethke. Four for Sir John Davies.
 Mistake, The.
Rohrer, M. After the Wedding Party.
Rojas. Bed with Mirrors.
Rosemurgy, C. Hard Put.
Rothenberg, J. Song of Quavering, A.
Roubaud. Light, for Example.
Rouse, A. Lilies of the Field.
 Spunk Talking.
 Uni-Gym, The.
Ruby, H. What a Perfect Combination.
Ruefle. Merengue.
Rukeyser, M. Rondel: "Now that I am fifty-six."
Rumens. Double Bed.
Ryan, G. In the Purple Bar.
Ryan, M. This Is a Poem for the Dead.
Ryan, T. Bite.
Sabines. 4: The Animals.
Sabry, M. Harem, The.
St. John, D. My Friend.
Salzman, E. Alex, Tiffany, Meg.
Sanchez, S. Haiku.
 Prelude to Nothing.
Sanders, T. Temporary Insanity.
Sappho. But as my friend, take to a younger bed.
 Night / Virgins.
Sarangapani. Madam to a Young Courtesan, The.
Scammell, W. Act, The.
Schjeldahl. David's Sister.
Schneiders, J. Weight.
Schwartz, R. L. Oh God, Fuck Me.
Schwerner. Tablet V.
Scott, J. Changing Room.
Segovia, F. Ánimo vegetal.
 Vegetal Animus.
Selman, R. Exodus.
Sen, R. Oh my Mind! You're just spinning.
 Who is that Syama woman.
Senryū, K. How long it seems.
 Young master, The.
Seth. Unclaimed.
Sexton. Ballad of the Lonely Masturbator, The.
 From the Garden.
 Us.
Shapcott, J. Muse.
Shapiro, K. First Time, The.
Sherrill, J. Woodstock.
Shinder. One Secret That Has Carried, The.
Shinkichi Takahashi. Little Sunlight, A.
Sholl. Midnight Vapor Light Breakdown.
Shurin. City of Men.
 Forward or Back.
Shuttle. Old Man, The.
 Passion.
Simic. Breasts.
Simmons, J. Honeymoon, The.
 Rogation Day: Portrush.
Simon, M. Blue Movies.
Sirowitz, H. Equality.
Slessor. Sleep.
Smile. Nothing Happened.
Smith, A. Giving Thanks.
Smith, D. Allegheny Happiness.
Smith, P. Dylan, Two Days.
Smith, S. Conviction (iv).
Smukler. Days Inn.
 Trash.
Sŏ Chŏngju. Midday.
Solari, R. Currents.
Solie, Karen. To Have and Have Not.
Sondheim. I Never Do Anything Twice (Madam's Song).
Soutar. Tryst [or Trysting Place], The.
Spivack, K. Love U.S.A.
Stainer. Honeycomb, The.
Steinman. Farmhand lay all hidden, A.
Stoddart, G. Blindfold, The.
Storni. To Eros.

Strato [or Straton]. Boys' members, Diodorus, come in three.
Don't hitch your dear little cunt against that wall.
Fitness expert. Big gym-man.
In the bed are two, submissive.
Yesterday in the bath Diodes' penis.
Your rosy-fingered prick that used to charm.
Sutton, V. While Watching Cops I Think of You.
Swenson, M. Riding the "A".
Swirszczynska [or Swir]. Bitch, A.
Tana, P. Marvelous Beast.
Tanikawa, S. Porno-Bach.
Tate, J. Chaste Stranger, The.
 Coming Down Cleveland Avenue.
Taylor, J. Epigram: "Lusty wench as nimble as an eel, A."
 Virgo, August.
Tayson, R. Phone Sex.
Teare, Brian. Detail from "Set for a Southern Gothic".
 Set for a Southern Gothic.
 Trick Noir.
Terán, V. Huadxí que ziyaba.
 It Was Early Evening.
 Tarde caía, La.
Theocritus. Idyll 27: Daphnis.
Thurston, H. River Otters at Play.
Tolliver, I. Hardest Part About Love, The.
Tolson, M. Lena Lovelace.
Tonks. Story of a Hotel Room.
Torres, E. Of My Nipple Ring Halos.
Trocchi, A. For John Donne: Master Metaphysical.
Tzu Yeh. It is night again.
 Song: "Winter skies are cold and low."
Ulacia, M. En el Ritz de Meknés.
 In the Ritz at Meknes.
Ullman. Memo.
Ungria, R. Sui Veneris/The Poet of No Return.
Unknown. Advice to a Young Man.
 Bridegroom, beloved of my heart.
 Butcher of Abbeville, The.
 Chalcan Female Song.
 Cosmology.
 First take me into your arms and hold me close.
 Full and True Account of a Dreaded Fire, that Lately Broke out in the Pope's Breeches, A.
 Girl's Song.
 I married an emancipated woman.
 I Sometimes Think.
 I will gladly give you my mouth.
 I'm sixty, this autumn.
 Lady T-rc----l's Ring.
 Let the first syllable of PEnelope be followed by the first of DIdo, the first of CAnus by that of REmus.
 Maid's Complaint for Want of a Dil Doul, The.
 Newly Wed Girl, The.
 Next Morning.
 No Balls at All.
 Oh my God! Once again you send me the dark night.
 One Writing against His Prick.
 Prayer to Hymen.
 Romans, I appeal to you.
 Sea-palms.
 She likes it, the conjugal act.
 Stretched out I want to take him into me.
 Substituted Poem of Laureate Quynh, The.
 This knave came in where he knew she'd be.
 To the Tune "The Drunken Young Lord".
 What Really Goes on in the College of Cardinals.
 What's that in which good housewives take delight.
 When I start my fast driving.
 White-haired, but wanton still.
 Wild Dreams, The.
 Wise Rejoice with Ganymede, The.
 Ye-you man-cao: Mid the Bind-Grass.
Unknown, fr. Egyptian hieroglyphics. Is there anything sweeter than this hour?
Unknown, fr. Sumerian cuneiform. Word they had spoken, The.

Valente, J. Evening Before, The.
Vallejo. I'm thinking of your sex.
 In that corner where we slept together.
 Trilce.
Verlaine. Balanide 2.
 He's an awkward bedfellow and I love to keep.
 Mille e tre.
 On the Grass.
 Sonnet to the Asshole.
Vidya. On Makeshift Bedding.
Vietnamese Oral Tradition. Across the Field of the Old Corporal.
Villiers. Cabin-Boy, The.
Villon. Ballad of Villon and Fat Madge, The.
 I love and serve my lady with a will.
Virgil [or Vergil]. Sky rumbles. Gathers. Rain.
Vogelweide. Under the linden.
Volach, Y. Hebrew.
 Tefillin.
Vroomkoning. Returning.
 Together Again ("I behold her there.").
 Together Again ("You get these thoughts in melancholy Autumn.").
Wagoner, D. Loons Mating.
Wakoski. Reading Bonjour, Tristesse at the Florence Crittenden Home for Unwed Mothers.
Wallace, R. Facts of Life, The.
Walwicz. Wonderful.
Warren, R. You Sort Old Letters.
Warsh. What I've Learned in My Travels.
Waters, M. Making Love at the Frost Place.
Wayman. Wayman in Love.
Weaver, A. Lines: "I feel your legs touching."
 Message on Cape Cod, The.
 Sin, 1969.
Wharton, E. Terminus.
Whitman, R. Bubba Esther, 1888.
Whitman, W. Blind loving wrestling touch! Sheathed hooded sharptoothed touch!
 Dalliance of the Eagles, The.
 From Pent-up Aching Rivers.
 I believe in you my soul, the other I am must not abase itself to you.
 This is the female form.
 Woman Waits for Me, A.
Wickham. Fired Pot, The.
Wicks, S. Rain Dance.
Wieners. Acceptance.
 Act #2.
 Doll.
 Loneliness, The.
 Long Nook.
 Suck, The.
 To H.
 What Happened?
Wilbur, R. Late Aubade, A.
Wilkes, J. Awake my Fanny! leave all meaner things.
 Pleased to the last, she likes the luscious food.
 Then, say not Man's imperfect, Heaven in fault.
Williams, H. Saturday Morning.
Williams, P. In the Dark.
Wilmer, S. Mess Boy, The.
Wilson, S. Recreational Mathematics.
Wood, V. Saturday Night.
Wright, K. Underneath the Archers or What's All This about Walter's Willy?
Wunderlich, M. Given in Person Only.
 Trick, The.
Yang Wei-chen. Mating.
Yates, D. Sex.
Yellen, J. Glad Rag Doll.
Yi Chŏngbo. Memory, A.
Young, A. Conjugal Visits.
Zwicky. Jack Frost.

See also **Erotic Love; Homosexuality and Homosexuals**

Sexism
Barbauld. Rights of Woman, The.
Bradstreet, A. I am obnoxious to each carping tongue.
Browne, F. Australian Emigrant, The.
Browning, E. Lord Walter's Wife.
Bunina. Conversation between Me and the Women.
Chudleigh. To the Ladies.

Coleridge, M. Clever Woman, A.
Collins, B. Man in Space.
Egerton, S. Emulation, The.
Erdrich. Fooling God.
Fife, C. Dear Webster.
Goodwin, Eli. Untitled: "Number 1 bus jerks to a stop at Mass. Ave., The."
Han-shan. Raise girls but not too many.
Harper, F. Double Standard, A.
Hawoldar. You Have Touched My Skin.
Hồ Xuân Huong. Condition of Women, The.
Holland, J. Baize Queens.
Hope, A. Advice to Young Ladies.
Huxley, A. Second Philosopher's Song.
Ibarbourou. Woman.
Jackson, L. Divestment of Beauty.
Jiles. Paper Matches.
Jordan, J. Poem About My Rights.
Kendall, M. Woman's Future.
Kizer, C. Erotic Philosophers, The.
  Fearful Women.
Millay, E. I, Being Born A Woman [And Distressed].
Mitchison. Dick and Colin at the Salmon Nets.
Noel, L. Understanding Each Other.
Nolla. Greek History.
Piercy. Barbie Doll.
  Moon Is Always Female, The.
Rahim, J. Felling of a Tree, The.
Rich, A. Snapshots of a Daughter-in-Law.
Shange. It's Not so Good to be Born a Girl/ Sometimes.
Song. Lost Sister ("In China, / even the peasants.").
Wakoski. Poet Recognizing the Echo of the Voice, A.
Wickham. Affinity, The.
Winchilsea. Introduction, The: "Did I, my lines intend for public[k] view."
Zephaniah. Sun, The.

Sexton, Anne
Dugan, A. Drunken Memories of Anne Sexton.

Sexual Abuse
Addonizio. From Then to Now.
Anderson, A. Suicide Year, The.
Barnett, R. Anorexic, The.
Bernstein, C. Profaning the Dead.
Bevington, L. One More Bruised Heart!
Brandt, D. Nonresistance, or love Mennonite style.
Chin, J. Why a Boy.
Clifton, L. Shapeshifter Poems.
  To my Friend, Jerina.
Dove, A. Crab.
Foley, Jack. Eli, Eli.
France, L. What I Know Now.
Frost, R. Subverted Flower, The.
Gregerson. For the Taking.
Hahn, K. Glass Bracelets, The.
Howe, M. How Many Times.
  Mother, The.
Larkin, J. Origins.
Lee, A. Confession.
Macphee, K. No fairy story.
McCarriston. Castle in Lynn, A.
Oktavi. At Five.
Olds, S. My Father Speaks to Me from the Dead.
Sholl. Postmaster's Children, The.
Strange. Crazy Girl, The.
Tolliver, I. Hardest Part About Love, The.
Unknown. Romans, I appeal to you.

Sexual Exploitation
Cooper, D. Being Aware.
García, D. Clog of Her Body, The.
Hannaham, D. To a Flasher.
Hughes, L. Mulatto.
Love, M. Objects of Desire.
Maroon, B. Nude Woman Spotted in Cappuccino Cup.
Unknown. Under the Linden Tree.

Sexuality
Adcock, F. Against Coupling.
Addonizio. What Do Women Want?
Agustini. Vision.
Amadiume. Bloody Masculinity.

Arnold, C. XX.
Asclepiades. Dorkion, sweet little tomboy.
Ayres, R. Corporeal.
Baca. Thirteen.
Barnett, R. Anorexic, The.
Barot, R. Three Amoretti.
Belieu. Rondeau at the Train Stop.
Bibbins, M. All but Lost.
Brainard, J. I Remember.
Breton, A. Free Union.
Broumas, O. Rapunzel.
Buchanan, G. Theatrical Venus.
Bukowski. Sexpot.
Cacciatore, E. Where do I stand and where do you? Seems like.
Campbell, S. Legacy.
Carbó, N. In Tagalog Ibon Means Bird.
Casey, M. LZ Gator Body Collector, The.
Cavafy. Passing Through.
Cavalli. I don't have any seed to cast about the world.
Chaucer. Experience, though noon auctoritee.
Cisneros, S. Black Lace Bra Kind of Woman.
Claman, E. Show Biz Parties.
Conoley, G. Beauty and the Beast.
Cullar, Carol. Heat.
de Aerenlund, C. Cuando el tecolote canta, el Indio muere.
De Coninck, H. Ballad of Indolence.
Dickinson, E. Wild Nights—Wild Nights!
Dobyns. Allegorical Matters.
Donne. To His Mistress Going to Bed.
Douglas, L. Two Loves.
Dove, R. After Reading *Mickey in the Night Kitchen* for the Third Time Before Bed.
Duhamel. Barbie's Molester.
Eliot, T. S. Whispers of Immortality.
Ellis, T. Atomic Bride.
  On Display.
Emanuel, L. Outside Room Six.
Erdrich. Mary Magdalene.
Ewart. Semantic Limerick According to Dr. Johnson's Dictionary (Edition of 1765), The.
  Semantic Limerick According to the Shorter Oxford English Dictionary (1933), The.
Fabian, C. Liturgy for Lilith.
  Qadesha (Sacred Whore).
Fanning, R. In the Barn.
Farewell. Quaerè.
Fêng Mêng-lung. Feeling the Itch.
  Fooling Mom.
  My Old Man's Small.
  No Old Lady.
  Smart.
Ferlinghetti, L. Dark Portrait, A.
Fox, S. Grandmother.
Fu Hsüan. Pity Me!
Garrett, Edward. Bachelors, The.
Garrett, Elizabeth. Womanhood, The.
Gilonis, H. Song for Annie.
Ginsberg, A. Green Automobile, The.
  This Form of Life Needs Sex.
Gloeggler, T. Fowler Street.
Gogarty. On First Looking into Krafft-Ebing's *Psychopathosexualis* [or Psychopathia Sexualis].
González, A. Inventory of Places Propitious for Love.
Graves, R. Cry Faugh!
Greenhalgh, C. Man in the Valley of Women, A.
Hacker, M. If we talk, we're too tired to make love; if we.
Hamilton, M. While Communing with a Tree Near My Home.
Higgerson, R. Utah Jazz, The.
Holloway, G. Lovers, The.
Hoover, P. Baseball.
Hope, A. Flower Poem.
Howe, M. Practicing.
Hsüeh T'ao [or Xue Tao]. Lotus-Gathering Boat.
Huang T'ing-chien. Tune: "A Thousand Autumns".
Hughes, L. Desire.
  Jazzonia.

To Midnight Nan at Leroy's.
Hwang Insuk. All Dreams Are Sexual.
Ibarbourou. Wild Root.
Issa. Now we are leaving.
Jordan, A. Black Drag Queen.
Joseph, A. Pure Pop.
Kariara. Leopard Lives in a Muu Tree, A.
Kasdorf. Eve's Striptease.
Katz, J. Falling.
Kearney, M. First Blow-Job.
Kizer, C. Erotic Philosophers, The.
Komunyakaa, Y. Thorn Merchant's Mistress, The.
Kuan Han-ch'ing. In the Southern Mode, to the Tune "A Sprig of Flowers" The Refusal to Get Old.
Larkin, P. Annus Mirabilis.
Laurencin, M. Present, The.
Lavender, Bill. Note to Skip on Max and Maxine, A.
Levertov. Mutes, The.
Li Ch'ing-chao. Tune: "Rouged Lips".
Li Po. Suite in the Ch'ing-p'ing Mode, A.
Lima, F. Hand, The.
Liu, T. Echoes.
  Mama.
  Size of It, The.
Mabuza. Love Song, A: "It was good."
MacKenzie, R. Category Mistakes in Biochemistry.
Malanga. 3 Poems for Benedetta Barzini.
McElroy, C. In My Mother's Room.
McFadden, R. Contemplations of Mary.
McGuire, Jerry. Feeling Rosemary.
Melville, H. After the Pleasure Party [Lines Traced under an Image of Amor Threatening].
Myers, J. Perfect Recall.
Nameroff, R. Elvis Presley.
Neruda. Single Gentleman.
  Youth: "Odor like an acid sword made, An."
Olds, S. Connoisseuse of Slugs, The.
Orlen. Androgyny.
Ovid. Iphis and Ianthe.
Pafunda, Danielle. Saltbox Brothel.
Pasolini. Civil Song.
  Lines from the Testament.
  Southern Dawn.
Paz. Better the crime, / the suicides of lovers, the incest committed.
  I travel your body as I would travel the world.
Perillo, L. Skin: "Back then it seemed that wherever a girl took off her clothes the police would find her."
Porter, C. I'm a Gigolo.
Prado, A. Stained Glass Window.
Putnam. Romeo and Juliet.
Raworth. Future Models May Have Infra-Red Sensors.
Rich, A. Dialogue.
  History.
Riley, P. E Questa Vita Un Lampo.
Rimbaud, A. Cheated Heart.
Robinson, M. Bower of Pleasure, The.
Rosselli. Sex violent as an object (whitened quarry of marble).
Rukeyser, M. Along History.
St. John, D. Quote Me Wrong Again and I'll Slit the Throat of Your Pet Iguana.
Schoenberger. Epithalamion.
Schwartz, R. L. AIDS Education, Seventh Grade.
Segovia, F. Promesa.
  Promise.
Shange. One.
Shaw, A. Pornography.
Shepherd, R. West Willow.
Sheppard, R. Empty Diary 1954.
  Empty Diary 1968.
  Empty Diary 1987.
Shinder. New Year: "Let me dive to the bottom of the hotel pool."
Simms, C. First English Wildcat, The.
Simon, M. Boy Crazy.
Simpson, M. Homo Erectus, Cerne Abbas.
Smith, B. Young Woman's Blues.
Smith, P. Dream of Rimbaud.

Soto.   Trees that Change Our Lives.
Strand.   In Celebration.
Szporluk.   Axiom of Maria.
Tejani, B.   Lines for a Hindi Poet.
Townsend, A.   Night Watch in the Laboratory.
Tripp.   Caroline Street, Cardiff.
Unknown.   Chaste Maiden, shining scarlet, The.
  Hebe and Ganymede.
  Morning's sun.
  Night after night, I do not.
  Tree we plant will, when its boughs are grown,
  The.
  Women as women, me had never charmed.
  Zeus as an eagle came to Ganymede.
Voss, F.   Inspection, The.
Wagner, Catherine.   Lover.
Walden, G.   Misguided Angels.
Waldman, A.   *Sexy Things*.
Weaver, A.   Michele.
Whitman, W.   As Adam Early in the Morning.
  Behold This Swarthy Face.
  From Pent-up Aching Rivers.
  Spontaneous Me.
  To the Garden the World.
  Walt Whitman, a kosmos, of Manhattan the son.
Wilbur, R.   Catch, The.
Williams, C. K.   Love: Beginnnings.
Wunderlich, M.   Chapel of the Miraculous
  Medal.
Zilahy, P.   Dictators.

Shadows
Aesop.   Dog and the Shadow, The.
Alterman, N.   Shadow, The.
Angelou, M.   Life Doesn't Frighten Me.
Atkins, R.   Dark Area.
Barnes, W.   Hill-Shade, The.
Basho.   Bucket of azaleas, A.
  Ploughing the land.
  Through frozen rice fields.
  Winter sun, The.
  Wintry day / On my horse.
Bierds, L.   Seconds, The.
Binyon.   Winter Sunrise.
Blanco.   Set Theory.
  Teoría de conjuntos.
Bornholdt, J.   Instructions for How to Get
  Ahead of Yourself While the Light Still Shines.
Boruch.   Book of Hand Shadows, The.
Bosselaar.   Listener of Bats.
Butts, A.   Skin.
Campion, T.   Follow Thy Fair Sun[ne]
  [Unhappy Shadow].
Carpenter, W.   Night Shadows.
Celan.   Speak You Too.
Ceravolo.   Dangers of the Journey to the Happy
  Land.
Clifton, L.   Death of Crazy Horse, The.
Coleridge, M.   Shadow.
Corey, S.   Complicated Shadows.
Crane, H.   At Melville's Tomb.
  Garden Abstract.
Crapsey.   Moon-Shadows.
Cuney.   Death Bed, The.
Daniel, S.   Are They Shadows [That We See]?
De' Medici.   To the Virgin.
Donne.   Lecture upon the Shadow, A.
Dove, R.   Dusting.
Duchamp.   Cast Shadows.
Eady.   Seduction.
Empson.   Legal Fiction.
Field.   Beloved, My Glory in Thee is Not
  Ceased.
Forrester, S.   Winter afternoon.
Galassi.   Argument.
García Lorca.   Song of the Barren Orange Tree.
Ginsberg, A.   Against red bark trunk.
Glück, L.   Hawk's Shadow.
Greenlaw, L.   Shape of Things, The.
Grimké, A.   Tenebris.
Guillén, J.   Shadows, The.
Haewŏn.   Song for My Own Shadow.
Harvey, M.   Image Cast by a Body Intercepting
  Light.
Hayden, R.   Broken Dark, The.
Herrera y Reissig.   Sorrowful Shadow, The.
Hewitt, J.   Substance and Shadow.

Hierro, José.   Wherever you are, and how.
Hodges, Janice W.   Control.
Hollander, J.   Sunday A.M. Not in Manhattan.
  Swan and Shadow.
Howe, S.   He plodded away through drifts of
  ice.
Hubbell, P.   Shadows.
Iosifova, Ekaterina.   At My Doorstep.
Issa.   Autumn wind / Mountain's shadow.
Jaccottet.   Serenity.
  These wood-shadows.
Jinkag Haesim.   Facing the Shadow.
  For the Great Zen Master Sagum.
Johnson, G.   Escape.
Johnston, E.   Mother's Love, A.
Jones, Einir.   Shadows of Trees on the Lawn,
  January.
Juarroz.   Prompting of my shadow, The.
Kang Ŭn'gyo.   Rotation 1.
Kassiane.   Troparion.
Kassid, A.   What the Shadow Said in the
  Presence of the Poem.
Kikaku.   Full autumn moon / On the straw mat.
Kilbride, Jerry.   Jumping rope.
Kim Pyŏngyŏn.   Song for My Shadow, A.
Kovner, A.   What's Not in the Heart.
Landon.   Farewell, The.
Lehman.   Prophet's Lantern, The.
Levertov.   Scenes from the Life of the
  Peppertrees.
Levin, P.   Shadow Returns, The.
Li Po.   Drinking Alone with the Moon.
Long, H.   Day and Night.
  In the Dark World.
Madhubuti.   After Her Man Had Left Her for
  the Sixth Time That Year (An Uncommon
  Occurrence).
Mahapatra, J.   Shadows: "Shadows can never
  open their mouths."
Maiden.   Climbing.
Martinez, D.   Nocturnes: "He closed the deal on
  the night. A real."
Masaoka Shiki.   Indian summer / Dragonfly
  shadows seldom.
McNiece, R.   My shadow in waves.
Merwin.   Last One, The.
Muir, E.   Then.
Novakovich.   Shadow.
Oswald, A.   Ballad of a Shadow.
Piatt, J.   My Shadow's Stature.
Pinkerton, H.   On Dorothea Lange's Photograph
  "Migrant Mother" (1936).
Popa.   Adventure of the Quartz Pebble, The.
Press, K.   Bird.
Salinas, P.   And if the Shadows Weren't.
Shurin.   Blue Shade.
Silva, J.   Nocturne: "One night / One night full
  of perfumes, music of wings and murmurs."
Sirota, L.   Your Glance Will Trip on My
  Shadow.
Snyder, G.   No Shadow.
Stevens, W.   Rabbit Is King of the Ghosts, A.
Stevenson, R.   My Shadow.
Stewart, S.   Zero.
Strickland.   Shadow.
Symonds.   Lux Est Umbra Dei.
T'ao Ch'ien [or T'ao Yuan-ming].   Substance,
  Shadow, and Spirit ("Earth and heaven endure
  forever.").
Tate, J.   Shadowboxing.
Tranströmer.   Borne by the darkness.
Troupe.   Sense of Coolness, A.
Unknown.   Because of this love.
  Water Bug and the Shadows, The.
Viktor, A.   Shadows: "Black-blue shadows on
  red-brown bricks."
Villa, D.   It is.
Villaurrutia.   Nocturne.
Volkow.   Arcana 8: Justice.
  Arcano 8: La Justicia.
  Washerwoman, The.
Walcott.   Season of Phantasmal Peace, The.
Wilde, O.   Harlot's House, The.
Williamson, G.   Up in the Air.
Winters, Y.   Shadow's Song, The.
Woods, V.   House, The.

Yau.   Radiant Silhouette I.
Yi Kyŏngnim.   Anam Street 1.
Zanzotto.   How Long.
Zukofsky, L.   Anew 21.

Shaftesbury, Anthony Ashley Cooper, 1st Earl of
Dryden, J.   Absalom and Achitophel.
  In pious times ere [or e'r] priest-craft did begin.
  Of these the false Achitophel was first.
  Shaftesbury.

Shakers (First Church of The Millennium)
Unknown.   Walk Softly.

Shakespeare, William
Adams, Sylvia.   Shakespeare's Eyebrows.
Arnold, M.   Shakespeare: "Others abide our
  question. Thou art free."
Bell, M.   Shakespeare's Wages.
Berberova.   To Shakespeare.
Bogan, L.   To an Artist, to Take Heart.
Bogardus.   Narcissus to Echo.
Browning, R.   Names, The.
Cole, W.   William Shakespeare.
Corey, S.   Understanding *King Lear.*
  Whatever Light.
Corn.   Reading *Pericles* in New London.
Duffy, C.   Anne Hathaway.
Eliot, T. S.   2. A Game of Chess.
Emerson, R.   Shakspeare.
Field.   It was deep April, and the morn.
Gwynn, R.   Shakespearean Sonnet.
Highfill, M.   Sea Breeze.
Holland, H.   Upon the Lines and Life of the
  Famous Scenic Poet, Master William
  Shakespeare.
Jonson, B.   To the Memory of My Beloved, the
  Author Mr [or Master] William Shakespeare:
  And What He Hath Left Us.
Keats.   On Sitting Down to Read *King Lear*
  Once Again.
Kemble.   To Shakspeare.
Koertge.   My Students.
Lanier, S.   Marsh Song—At Sunset.
Lawrence, D. H.   When I Read Shakespeare.
Leiter, Deborah.   Midsummer's Eve.
Like, J.   Postmodern: A Definition.
MacLeod, A.   Shakespeare No More.
Marquis.   Archy Confesses.
Melville, H.   Coming Storm, The.
Milton.   On Shakespear[e].
Peterson, J.   As If.
Porter, C.   Brush Up Your Shakespeare.
Raab, L.   Revised Versions, The.
Ray, H.   Shakespeare.
Riach, A.   Antenor.
Robinson, E.   Ben Jonson Entertains a Man
  from Stratford.
Rogow, J.   Symmetron: You and Brother Will.
Schwartz, D.   Dogs Are Shakespearean,
  Children Are Strangers.
Simmons, J.   Stephano Remembers.
Spacks.   Film Version, The.
Ward, BJ.   Shakespeare as a Waiter.

Shamanism and Shamans
Guevara, M.   Tuesday Shaman.
Hufana, A.   From the Raw.
Korean Oral Tradition.   Abandoned Princess,
  The.
  Song of Entertaining the Holy One.
Rivas, J.   Río 1.
  River 1.
Uvavnuk.   Shaman Song.

Shame
Aleshire.   Double, The.
Bentley, E.   When their lordships asked Bacon.
Bhattācārya, M.   What shall I say to You,
  Sankari?
Byron, G.   When We Two Parted.
Cofer, J.   They Never Grew Old.
Dafydd [or David] ap Gwilym.   Rattle Bag, The.
Dharker.   Purdah, 1.
Donne.   Flea, The.
  Triple Fool, The.
Dunn, S.   Shame Place, The.
  With No Experience in Such Matters.
Duo Duo.   In England.
Galanskov.   It shames one to look.

Gloria.　Assimilation.
Goldsmith, O.　When Lovely Woman Stoops to Folly.
Grotz, J.　First Glasses.
Han Yong'un [or Yongwun].　To the Readers.
Herrick.　Shame, No Statist.
Jana Bai.　Cast off all shame.
Jenkins, P.　Six Small Fires.
Khoury, N.　People of Fire.
Ku Sang.　Shame.
Levertov.　In California During the Gulf War.
Limonov.　As if a quiet branch drew a line.
MacBeth [or Macbeth].　Worst Fear, The.
Macgoye.　Letter to a Friend.
MacKay, C.　Only a Thought.
Martinaitis, M.　Pony in Kukutis's Ear, A.
Merwin.　Avoiding News by the River.
　Spiders I Have Known.
Mora.　Cortez's Horse.
Owen, Gerallt Lloyd.　Shame of Llanfaes, The.
Pegram, A.　Mr. White Discoverer.
Petrarch.　You who hear in scattered rhymes the sound of those sighs with.
Polkowski.　I Don't Know That Man.
Rosemurgy, C.　Hard Put.
Rumi.　Answers from the Elements.
Rutsala.　Shame.
Sadi [or Saadi or Sa'di].　Prayers: "My shoes are mulberry with dew."
Salganicoff.　Shame.
Sappho.　I wish to say something to you, but shame.
Seneca.　Stand [or Stond] who so list upon the slipper top[pe].
Shakespeare, W.　Sonnet 72: "O, lest the world should task you to recite."
　Sonnet 129: "Expense [or Expence] of spirit in a waste of shame, The [or Th']."
Shenstone.　Chase of Jessy, The.
Shoha.　Shameful / Dead grass.
Sleigh.　Shame: "If only I'd known then what I was reaching for."
Smukler.　Sign.
Sono-Jo, Lady.　Shameful / These clothes.
Storni.　Encounter.
Suk Mumyong.　After Getting Drunk in a Hermitage on Chiri Mountain.
Ts'en Shen.　On the West Tower in Guozhou.
Unknown.　Dust for you, but never my mouth again.
　In battle today my lover turned his back to the enemy.
　My beloved! If you turn your back upon the enemy, do not come home again!
　Qiang-you-ci: Off the Wall.
Viscusi.　Autobiography.
Voznesensky [or Voznesenskii].　Poem: "From us, like appendicitis."
Wilbur, R.　Shame.
Zdanys.　Angels of Wine, The.
Zukofsky, L.　In that this happening.

Shamrocks
Cherry, A.　Green Little Shamrock of Ireland, The.

Shannon (river), Ireland
Kennelly.　Swimmer, The.
Ni Dhomhnaill.　Race, The.

Sharecroppers
Hughes, L.　Share-Croppers.

Sharks
Carroll, L.　Alice's Recitation.
Dugan, A.　Plague of Dead Sharks.
Grainger, J.　Bryan and Pereene.
Gunn, T.　Cannibal.
MacCaig.　Basking Shark.
Melville, H.　Maldive Shark, The.
Pinsky.　Want Bone, The.
Pratt, E.　Shark, The.
Sze.　Great White Shark, The.
Willard, N.　Sand Shark.

Shaving
Anzai Hitoshi.　New Blade.
Blanco, R.　Shaving.
Cartwright, K.　In / dreams / diving deeper / than my disbelief.

Fisher, J.　Life, A.
Houle, A.　I Learned about Being Tough from a Stetson Ad.
Kay, J.　Close Shave.
Kishu.　Once the goal's reached.
Korteweg.　Sed Non Frustra.
O'Daly, M.　Shaving of Murdoch, The.
Unknown.　Burma-Shave Roadside Signs.

Shaw, Robert Gould
Dunbar, P.　Robert Gould Shaw.
Lowell, J.　Memoriae Positum R. G. Shaw.
Lowell, R.　For the Union Dead.
Moody, W.　Ode in Time of Hesitation, An.
Ray, H.　Robert G. Shaw.

Sheep
Baca.　Mantanza to Welcome Spring.
Blake, W.　Answer to the Parson, An.
　Shepherd, The.
Bonnefoy.　Top of the World, The.
Brown, H.　Counting Sheep.
Calpurnius Siculus.　Eclogue 5.
Clarke, G.　Ram.
Davies, W. H.　Sheep.
Degenaar.　Irish Sheep, The.
Djogo.　Black Sheep, The.
Dyer, J.　Pastoral ("In cold stiff soils the bleaters oft complain.").
　Pastoral ("Wild rove the flocks, no burdening fleece they bear.").
Gay, J.　Wild Boar and the Ram, The.
Hardie, K.　Sheep Fair Day.
Helwig.　Sudden risk of birds, A.
Heyen.　Witness.
Hughes, T.　Crib Goch.
Ignatova, E.　To Ovid.
Jones, T.　Thursday.
Kelly, R.　Tune.
La Fontaine.　Pig, Goat, Sheep.
Mandelstam [or Mandelshtam].　Like Grumbling Roman Plebs.
Meynell, A.　Shepherdess, The.
Mother Goose.　Baa, baa, black sheep, have you any wool?
　Little Bo-Peep.
O'Donoghue, M.　Bova.
Ontjes, Linden.　Kepler Considers the Dimensions of a Sheep.
Ramsdell, H.　Good Sheep.
Rossetti, C.　Blessed that flock safe penned in Paradise.
Sappho.　Evening Star who gathers everything.
Scott, D.　Flanking Sheep in Mosedale.
Shapcott, J.　Lies.
Shenstone.　Home Industries First: The Song of Colin, a Discerning Shepherd, Lamenting the State of the Woollen Manufactory.
Shinkichi Takahashi.　Sheep.
Shiraishi.　Afternoon of the Sheep, The.
　Donkey Speculates, The.
Sidney, P.　My Sheep Are Thoughts.
Snyder, M.　Choreograph of the Robed Sheep.
Unknown.　Shearing, The.
　Sky is strewn with stars, The.
Voigt.　Trust, The.
Yalden.　Treacherous Towser.

See also Lambs

Sheepshearing and Sheepshearers
Calpurnius Siculus.　Eclogue 5.
Unknown.　Banks of the Condamine, The.

Sheets
Chavez, L.　Clean Sheets.
Coultas, B.　Dr. Wasserman.
Follain.　Women Say, The: 'It Looks Like Rain'.
Martínez, V.　Into the Next One.
Simpson, A.　White, Mauve, Yellow.
Townsend, A.　Hospital Corners.
Warren-Moore.　All-Night Issue, The.

Shelley, Mary Wollstonecraft
Niedecker.　Who Was Mary Shelley?
　Who was Mary Shelley?

Shelley, Percy Bysshe
Browning, R.　Memorabilia.
Claus.　Ten Ways of Looking at P.B. Shelley.
　Tien manieren om P.B. Shelley te zien.
Corso.　I Held a Shelley Manuscript.

Hardy, T.　Shelley's Skylark.
Hood, T.　False Poets and True.
Hunt, L.　To Percy Shelley.
　To the Same.
McIntyre.　We have scarcely time to tell thee.
Monroe.　To W. S. M.
Nichol.　Little song, A.
Niedecker.　Who Was Mary Shelley?
Parker, D.　Lives and Times of John Keats, Percy Bysshe Shelley, and George Gordon Noel, Lord Byron, The.
Simic.　Shelley.

Shells
Basho.　Along the shore.
　Fall going.
Bynner.　But for these apertures.
Corn.　Conch from Sicily, A.
Darío, R.　Seashell.
Field.　Onycha.
Hartley, M.　Wingaersheek Beach.
Herbert, Z.　Conch.
Holmes, O.　Chambered Nautilus, The.
Lovelace, R.　Snail [or Snayl], The.
Martinez, D.　Altruism.
McDonald, E.　Itherness.
Moore, M.　Paper Nautilus, The.
Pak Sôwôn.　Midnight Caller, The.
Raboni, G.　Moon.
Ray, H.　Enchanted Shell, The.
Scott, G.　Frutta di Mare.
Shinkichi Takahashi.　Shell.
Stephens, J.　Shell, The.
Stickney, T.　On Some Shells Found Inland.
Unknown.　Shootingway Ceremony Prayer.
Williams, W.　Tribute to Neruda the Poet Collector of Seashells.
Wordsworth, W.　I have seen / A curious child, who dwelt upon a tract.

See also Snails; Clams and Clamming; Oysters

Shellshock
Bottoms.　Sunday Dinner, A.
Ivanov, Binyo.　One Can Rest.
Owen, W.　Conscious.
　Dulce et Decorum Est.
　Mental Cases.
Simpson, L.　Old Soldier.

Shelter
Basho.　Exhausted, / time to find a lodging.
Davies, W. H.　Elements, The.
Han-shan Te-ch'ing.　Solitary winter lantern casts a feeble shadow, A.
Peacock, M.　Land of the Shí, The.
Schelling.　Below Fourth of July Mine.

Shenandoah River and Shenandoah Valley
Melville, H.　Portent, The.
Ticknor.　Virginians of the Valley, The.

Shepherds and Shepherdesses
Arnold, M.　Scholar Gipsy, The.
Barnfield [or Barnefield].　But if thou wilt not pittie my complaint.
　Daphnis to Ganymede.
　Oh would to God he would but pitty mee.
　Scarce had the morning starre hid from the light.
　When will my May come, that I may embrace thee?
Behn, A.　Disappointment, The.
Blake, W.　Shepherd, The.
Bonnefoy.　Book, for Growing Old, The.
Breton, N.　Merry Country Lad, The.
　Olden Love-making.
Cavalcanti.　Encounter, An.
Clare, J.　Shepherd Boy, The.
Countryman, L.　Going to God with the Shepherds.
Crashaw.　In the Holy Nativity of Our Lord God.
Cruz, S.　Shepherd, Young and Mournful, Grieves Alone, A.
D'Annunzio.　I pastori (The Shepherds).
Davis, D.　Christmas Poem, A.
De la Mare.　Nod.
Dodge, M.　Shepherd John.
Drayton.　Roundelay Between Two Shepherds, A.
Drummond, W.　All Changeth.

Dupin. Even If the Mountain.
"Ephelia.". On a Bashful Shepherd.
Espada. Ezequiel.
Fitts. Ya Se Van Los Pastores.
Florián, M. Pastora.
Greene, R. Description of the Shepherd and His Wife, The.
   Shepherd's Wife's Song, The.
Griffiths, B. Shepherd's Calendar.
Guarini. Shepherd Thirsis longed to die, The.
Hands, E. Perplexity: A Poem.
Herrera y Reissig. Return, The.
Hogg, J. When the Kye Comes Hame.
Hughes, L. Shepherd's Song at Christmas.
Hugo, V. Shepherds and Flocks.
Ignatova, E. To Ovid.
Kirkup. Shepherd's Tale, The.
Landor, W. Alciphron and Leucippe.
Lodge, T. Shepherd's Sorrow, Being Disdained in Love, The.
Lope de Vega. Shepherd Who With Your Tender Calls.
   Strange Shepherd, Set My Bellwether Free.
MacNeice. Nuts in May.
Marlowe. Passionate Shepherd to His Love, The.
Mew. Old Shepherd's Prayer.
Meynell, A. Shepherdess, The.
Molloy, D. Pascual the Shepherd.
Mother Goose. Little Bo-Peep.
Nicholson, N. Shepherds' Carol.
Nishiwaki Junzaburo. Shepherd in Capri.
Passerat. Song: "Shephard loveth thow me vell?"
"Pindar.". Old Friends.
Ralegh, W. Nymph's [or Nimphs] Reply to the [Passionate] Shepherd [or Sheepheard], The.
Rifat. Flute, The.
Sidney, P. My Sheep Are Thoughts.
   Ye Goat-herd Gods.
Smith, C. Blessed is yon shepherd on the turf reclined.
Spenser, E. Aprill.
   May.
Stafford, W. Shepherd.
Tate, N. While Shepherds Watched [Their Flocks by Night].
Theocritus. Idyll 1: "Whisper of the wind in, The."
Thiele, C. Tom Farley.
Unknown. Gray She-Wolf, The.
   Inanna spoke.
   Red sky at night, A.
   Sheepheards Description of Love, The.
Vaughan, H. Shepherds [or Shepheards], The.
Virgil [or Vergil]. Eclogue 2: The Lament of Corydon for His Faithless Alexis.
Yeats. Song of the Happy Shepherd, The.

Sheridan, Philip Henry
Melville, H. Sheridan at Cedar Creek.
Read, T. Sheridan's Ride.

Sherman, William Tecumseh, Union general
Bentley, E. "No, sir," said General Sherman.
Melville, H. Iris.
Work. Marching through Georgia.

Shields
Archilochus. Some Saian sports my splendid shield.
   Some Thracian exults in an excellent shield.
Cagnone, N. Book Three: On Preparation.
Homer. Shield of Achilles, The.
Nossis. Shields Bruttians threw from their doomed shoulders.
Shostakovskaya, I. Boy bears a gray shield, The.
Unknown. Riddle, A.
   Riddles.
Virgil [or Vergil]. Shield of Aeneas, The.

Shiloh, Battle of (1862)
Hill, G. Shiloh Church, 1862: Twenty-Three Thousand.
Melville, H. Shiloh (A Requiem).

Ships and Shipbuilding
Agustini. Miraculous Ship, The.
Alcaeus [or Alkaios]. Come to me, leaving the

Peloponnesos.
Ali, A. Purse-Seiner *Atlantis*, The.
Armstrong, Tammy. Boat Builder.
Bei, Dao. Evening Scene, An.
Bishop, E. Casabianca.
   Song: "Summer is over upon the sea."
Blight. Into the Ark.
Bontemps. Nocturne of the Wharves.
Booth, P. Navigation.
Bridges, R. Passer-by, A.
Brooks, S. Middle Passage.
Buson. Korean ship, The.
Callimachus. Would that there had never been swift ships!
Carver, R. At Least.
Causley. HMS *Glory*.
Cavendish, M. Sea Similized to Meadows and Pastures, The: the Mariners, to Shepherds: the Mast, to a May-Pole: the Fish, to Beasts.
Cendrars. Frisco-City.
Cervantes. Refugee Ship.
Clare, S. On the Good Ship Lollipop.
Clifton, L. Slaveship[s].
Clough. Qua Cursum Ventus.
Coleridge, S. It is an ancient Mariner.
Corbière. Old Roscoff.
Corcoran. In the Red Book.
Crane, S. I explain the silvered passing of a ship at night.
Davidson, L. Charnel Ship, The.
Dawe, G. Question of Covenants, A.
Dickinson, E. There is No Frigate Like a Book.
Dryden, J. By viewing nature, nature's handmaid, art.
Dunbar, P. Ships That Pass in the Night.
Dunn, D. Ships.
Flecker, J. Old Ships, The.
Fowler, W. Upon this firthe, as on the sees of love.
French, T. Ghost Ship.
Freneau. Rude, from the wide extended Chesapeke.
   Two hulks on Hudson's stormy bosom lie.
Gershwin, I. My Ship.
Góngora y Argote. On the Armada That Battled Against England.
Griffiths, B. Ship, The.
Grimké, A. Little Grey Dreams.
Haines, J. Mothball Fleet: Benicia, California.
Hart, L. Ship Without a Sail, A.
Hass, R. Feast, The.
Heaney, S. Annals say: when the monks of Clonmacnoise, The.
Hendry, J. Ship, The.
Holmes, O. Chambered Nautilus, The.
Jackson, H. Emigravit.
Jiménez, J. Ship, Solid and Black, The.
Johnson, B. Storm: "Edges of slave ships are narrow and difficult for footing, The."
Kahn, G. When My Ship Comes In.
Kipling, R. Derelict, The.
King, The.
Ko Changsu. Ocean Liner.
Lawrence, D. H. Argonauts, The.
   Ship of Death, The ("Now it is autumn and the falling fruit.").
Lear, E. Jumblies, The.
Longfellow, H. And as he laboured, his mind ran o'er.
   Building of the Ship, The.
Lope de Vega. Seguidillas of the Guadalquivir River.
   Today Delight's Fair Ship.
Lorde. Fishing the White Water.
MacAdams. Pockets of Haze.
Machado Ruiz. Moldering Hulk, The.
Masefield. Cargoes.
   Sea Fever.
Mayer, B. Poem: "I am beginning to alter."
   Port, The.
McGrath, C. Shrimp Boats, Biloxi.
Meade, G. Schrimshaw Sailor, The.
Melville, H. Berg, The.
   Man-of-War Hawk, The.
Temeraire, The.
Montejo, E. Marina.

Mother Goose. I saw a ship a-sailing.
   Three wise men of Gotham.
Neruda. Different Ship, A.
Ní Chuilleanáin. Second Voyage, The.
Nicholls, J. Mary Celeste.
Niedecker. My Life by Water.
O'Brien, S. HMS Glasshouse.
Oppen. Bolt / In the frame.
   Confession.
   Taste, The.
Ovid. I have (may I always keep!) blonde Minerva's protection; my vessel.
Pak Illo. Lament on the Water.
Pickard, T. What Maks Makems.
Prado, A. Pelican, The.
Putnam. Ship of State and Grandpa.
Rakosi. Unswerving Marine.
Ransom, J. Good Ships.
Rose, D. Figurehead.
Saitō Mokichi. At daybreak.
Snyder, G. Ship in Yokohama, The.
Southey, R. Ship, The.
Stevens, W. Farewell to Florida.
Stevenson, R. Rain.
   Where Go the Boats?
Supervielle. Like an ox.
Thomas, R. S. Navigation.
Toledo, N. Na hermila limón.
Tranströmer. Syros.
Unknown. Blow, Boys, Blow [or Blow, Bullies, Blow].
   My little ship, three-masted.
   Old Ship of Zion, The [Maryland version].
Volkman. Shipwreck Poem.
Whitman, W. Aboard at a Ship's Helm.
   After the Sea-Ship.
   Dismantled Ship, The.
   Patrolling Barnegat.
   Ship Starting, The.
   Song for All Seas, All Ships.
   Would you hear of an old-time [or old-fashioned] sea fight?
Whittier. To a Cape Ann Schooner.
Wordsworth, W. Where lies the Land to which yon Ship must go?
   With Ships the sea was sprinkled far and nigh.
Yosano Akiko. Sakai Harbor.
Youn, Monica. Naglfar.

See also **Boats and Boating; Freighters; Tugboats; Yachts**

Shipwrecks
Baranda, M. Epistle of the Shipwreck.
   Epistola del náufrago.
Bhattācārya, M. Look at all these waves.
Byron, G. But to our tale: the Donna Inez sent.
   Shipwreck, The.
Clark, T. Time.
Corbière. Old Roscoff.
Cowper, W. Castaway, The.
Damas. Wind, The: "Wide sea—black night—I woke up lovesick."
Dickinson, E. Glee—The great storm is over.
Fordham. Shipwreck.
   Tribute to a Lost Steamer.
Fowler, W. Ship-broken Men Whom Stormy Seas Sore Toss.
Gibbs, Robert J. Manes P. Aground Off Fort Dufferin, The.
Góngora y Argote. It was the flowery season of the year.
Gu Cheng. Ark.
Hardy, T. Convergence of the Twain, The.
Hemans. Wreck, The.
Hewitt, G. Sailor, The.
Hope, A. Wandering Islands, The.
Hopkins, G. Wreck of the Deutschland, The.
Horace. Ode 4.7: "Snow dissolv'd no more is seen, The."
Hughes, T. I can understand the haggard eyes.
Lee-Hamilton. Sunken Gold.
Lightfoot. Wreck of the Edmund Fitzgerald, The.
Long, J. Bermuda Triangle.
Longfellow, H. Wreck of the Hesperus, The.
Marks, Corey. After the Shipwreck.
McGrath, T. Offering.

Melville, H. Aeolian Harp, The.
  Berg, The.
  Haglets, The.
Menken. Ship That Went Down, The.
Mickiewicz. Storm, The.
Moore, R. Shipwreck: "Watching, watching
  from the shore."
Nathaniel, Isabel. Coast of Texas, The.
Oppen. Obsessed, bewildered / By the
  shipwreck.
Ostriker. After the Shipwreck.
Ragosta, R. At the Coast.
Reese, L. Indian Summer.
Reznikoff. If the ship you are traveling on is
  wrecked.
  1. The Sinking.
Rich, A. Diving into the Wreck.
Rivas, J. Thalassa.
  Thalassa.
Rossetti, D. White Ship, The.
Saijo, A. Bodhisattva Vows.
Schjeldahl. Ocean Liner.
Schwartz, D. Poem: "You, my photographer,
  you, most aware."
Shakespeare, W. Full Fathom Five.
Shwarts [or Shvarts]. Parrot at Sea, A.
Southey, R. Inchcape Rock, The.
Spaziani. It is Said by Some Sailors, the Old.
Supervielle. Poet, A.
Tan Taigi. Thunder / Voices of drowned.
Unknown. Sir Patrick Spens [or Spence].
Valéry. Crusoe.
Vietnamese Oral Tradition. Testing the
  Confucian Ideal.
Volkman. Shipwreck Poem.
Waller, E. Upon His Majesty's [or Majesties]
  Repairing of Paul's.
Watson, R. Midnight Harvest, A.
Whitman, W. To the Man-of-War Bird.
Whittier. Skipper Ireson's Ride.

Shirts
Agran, R. Wearing Dad's White Shirt
  Backwards.
Johnston, E. Last Sark, The.
Merwin. Good-Bye Shirts, The.
  Night of the Shirts, The.
Perillo, L. Ghost Shirt, The.
Pinsky. Shirt.
Sandburg, C. Shirt ("My shirt is a token and
  symbol.").
Shapcott, T. Blue Paisley Shirt, The.
Townsend, A. Shirt Collar, The.
Vietnamese Oral Tradition. Ke-Mo Village Girl.
Whitney, Louise Grassi. Beautiful Eyes.
Winter, M. Dux Bellorum.

Shiva
Bairagi. Give Me Confidence.
Basu, R. How are you faring, Uma.
Bhattācārya, K. From her autumn-lotus mouth.
  Go, my Lord of the Mountains.
  Hara came and made off with my Gauri.
  Hey, Hara, Ganges-Holder.
  Hey, Mountain King, Gauri is sulking.
  Kali! / Today in the dark grove.
  Kali, what family are You from?
  Queen asks, The.
  So, forgetful Mahadeva.
  Unperturbed at the battle.
  What happened? / The ninth night is over.
  Who is this enchantress.
  You ask me, Queen, time after time.
Bhattācārya, M. There's a huge hullabaloo in
  my lotus heart.
Cakrabarttī, M. Ma, if You wore a Benarasi
  sari.
Candī, A. Bring Tara quickly, Mountain.
Cross, E. Shakti.
  Shakti.
Dās, R. Now I'll see whether Siva.
Dāsdatta, R. Because You love cremation
  grounds.
Debī, T. Tara, this is why I call upon You.
Dīnrām. Renunciation's agonies.
Ghos, G. I plaster myself with ashes.
  Who said / If you took the name All-Destroyer.
  You're home, Uma! Stay here.

Gupta, I. I got some news from Kailasa!
Islām, N. Wake up, Syama, wake up, Syama!
Jeffers, R. Shiva.
Mahadevi. I do not call it his sign.
  It was like a stream.
  Vein of sapphires, A.
  When I am hungry.
  When the body becomes Your mirror.
Māhtābcānd, M. Who is this, all alone? Whose
  woman is She.
Meenakshi. If Hot Flowers Come to the Street.
Rāy, D. Wake up, wake up, Mother!
Rāy, M. R. Give me food.
Rāy, R. Who is this.
Rāy, T. Wait a moment, Death.
Sen, R. Her face / Is a spotless moon.
  It's not Siva.
  It's silly to hope for Father's wealth.
  Kali, Ma.
  Kulakundalini, Goddess Full of Brahman, Tara.
  Love Her, Mind.
  Meditate on Kali! Why be anxious?
  Mother, make me Your treasurer.
  Oh Kali Full of Brahman!
  Oh my Mind! You're just spinning.
  So, Mind / You've decided to go on pilgrimage?
  What a joke!
  What's the fault of the poor mind?
  Who can understand Kali?
  Who is that Syama woman.

Shoemakers
Dunbar, W. Amendis [or Amends] to the
  Telyouris [or Tailors] and Sowtaris [or Soutaris
  or Soutars or Shoemakers].

Shoes
Agüeros. Psalm for Distribution.
Ai. Riot Act, April 29, 1992.
Barer, M. Very Soft Shoes.
Bendall, M. Need for Shoes, The.
Bernstein, C. Loose Shoes.
Buson. Sleeping late.
  Straw sandal half sunk.
Charara, H. Hamza Aweiwi, a Shoemaker in
  Hebron.
Dallerès, J. Museum.
Dubie. Last Poem, Snow Tree.
Edson, R. Wounded Breakfast, The.
Finkelstein, C. Casus Belli.
Gallagher, T. Monologue at the Chinook Bar
  and Grill.
  Widow in Red Shoes.
Garcia, R. Zapato, El.
Guillén, J. Death of a Pair of Shoes.
Haskins, L. Shoes, The.
Hawoldar. To My Little Girl.
Jess, T. Father's Shoes.
Jones, B. South Shore (Aberystwyth), The.
Kay, J. Shoes of Dead Comrades, The.
Kerouac. Bottoms of my shoes, The.
Kramer, L. Shoemaker's Wife, The.
Lear, E. Limerick: "There was an old man of
  Thermopylae."
  Limerick: "There was an old man of Toulouse."
  O dear! How disgusting is life!
Lee, W. Simple Like That.
Leggott, M. Dark torch.
Lima, M. Shoeshine Boy.
Lleshanaku, L. Still Life: "Here in a summer
  full of dust."
Lowell, A. Red Slippers.
Masaoka Shiki. Chilly nights.
  Heath grass / Sandals.
Merwin. Dachau Shoe, The.
Miles, J. Sale.
Morgan, M. Red High-heeled Shoes.
Nyhart. Shoes, The.
Ormond. At His Father's Grave.
Pak Mogwŏl [or Mokwŏl]. Family.
Petri. To Be Said Over and Over Again.
Sappho. Many-colored sandal, A.
Sexton. Fury of Overshoes, The.
Simic. My Shoes.
Sutskever [or Sutzkever]. Cartload of Shoes, A.
Sutter. Shoe Shop.
Swirszczynska [or Swir]. White Wedding
  Slippers.

Unknown. Limerick: "There was an archdeacon
  who said."
  Limerick: "There was an old man of [or from]
  Peru / Who dreamt [or dreamed] he was
  eating his shoe."
  My Darlings' Shoes.
Weaver, A. Sub Shop Girl.
Weiss, T. Pair of Shoes, A.
Wolfe, F. Choosing Shoes.
Wylie. Velvet Shoes.
Zonas. Charon.

See also **Galoshes**

Shoplifting and Shoplifters
Alvarez, J. On Not Shoplifting Louise Bogan's
  The Blue Estuaries.
Dauer. Philip the Store Policeman.
Dougherty. Long Coats with Deep Pockets.
Seaton, M. Fear of Shoplifting.
Stanton, M. Shoplifters.
Wormser. Shoplifting.

Shopping and Shops
Aini, L. Liquidation.
Arp. Dragon Carries the Inscription
  "Kunigundula" and Is Led on a Leash, The.
Ashbery, J. How to Continue.
Atkins, R. New Storefront.
Aygi, G. Dream: Queue for Paraffin.
Bialoszewski. Ballad of Going Down to the
  Store, A.
Bourne, Lesley-Anne. Out of the Blizzard.
Carson, C. Dresden.
Clarke, G. Second Hand Rose.
Clover, J. Alas, That Is the Name of Our Town;
  I Have Been Concealing It All This Time.
Dauer. Philip the Store Policeman.
Derricotte. 1994 Inventory.
Desnos. St Merri district, The.
Disch. Rapist's Villanelle, The.
Dixon, M. I Found a Million Dollar Baby (In a
  Five and Ten Cent Store).
Elledge. Man I Love and I Shop at Jewel, The.
Evans, A. Old Yellow Shop, The.
Field, R. General Store.
Follain. Buying.
  Shops.
Friman. Diapers for My Father.
Griffiths, B. Fragment 18: "Met Noel at
  Cheshire Street."
Guevara, M. Doña Josefina Counsels Doña
  Concepción Before Entering Sears.
Helfand, J. Girl in the Boy's Dressing Room,
  The.
Hongo. Winnings.
Jennings, E. My Grandmother.
Johnson, J. Unmarked Stop in Front of
  Westmond General Store, Westmond, Idaho.
Joseph, A. In the Bookstore.
Kooser. In the Basement of the Goodwill Store.
Longley, M. Greengrocer, The.
MacNeice. Christmas Shopping.
Matthews, W. Mail Order Catalogs.
McIlroy, L. Siesta.
McOrlan. Accessories shop, The.
  Hairdresser's, The.
Murray, G. Shopping for Midnight.
Naranjo-Morse. Tradition and Change.
Peacock, M. How I Had to Act.
Pierson, J. Thrift Shop Ladies.
Piñero. La Bodega Sold Dreams.
Ponge. Three Shops, The.
Revard. Christmas Shopping.
Rome, H. Chain Store Daisy.
Rose, B. I Found a Million Dollar Baby (In a
  Five and Ten Cent Store).
Rosenblatt, S. Procession, The.
Soto. Ode to the Yard Sale.
Suárez, V. Song for the Sugar Cane.
Thompson, C. Christmas Rush, The.
Tolson, M. African China.
Trowbridge, W. What We Could Do.
Unknown. Unspent.
Voznesensky [or Voznesenskii]. Chorus of
  Nymphs, A.
Watkins, William Jon. Mall, The.

Shopping Malls
Disch. Garage Sale as a Spiritual Exercise, The.

Gilmore, B.   Bow to Allah.

Shores
Addonizio.   China Camp, California.
Ammons.   So I Said I Am Ezra.
Barnard, M.   Shoreline.
Barrington, J.   Villanelle VI.
Basho.   Along the shore.
Baxter, J.   Bay, The.
Bentley, N.   Iron Man of the Hoh.
Bergman, A.   To Eugene P. Loveman.
Berryman.   Henry's Understanding.
Bishop, E.   Little Exercise.
Blamire.   O Bid Me Not to Wander.
Blight.   Landfall, The.
Bowles, P.   Extract.
Browning, R.   Meeting at Night.
Carroll, L.   Lobster Quadrille, A.
Catullus.   Accept, O Priapus, the moister.
Collins, M.   Winter in Brighton.
Cranch.   Pines and the Sea, The.
Croly.   Aestuary, An.
Darío, R.   Seashell, The.
  Symphony in Gray Major.
  Tropical Afternoon.
Denham, Joe.   Shoreline, The.
Du Shenyan.   Written at Jumble-Rock Mountain
  by the South Sea.
Duggan, L.   Five. One.
  One. One.
Eliot, T. S.   Cape Ann.
Emerson, R.   Sea-Shore.
Frost, R.   Once by the Pacific.
Grosholz.   Outer Banks, The.
Guillén, N.   Bars.
Hadas, R.   Sentimental Education.
Haines, J.   Nocturnal.
Harwood, G.   Clair de Lune.
Heaney, S.   Postscript.
Joyce, J.   On the Beach at Fontana.
Lewis, G.   Flaggy Shore, The.
Lewis, J.   At Carmel Highlands.
Liu, T.   Wellfleet.
Longfellow, H.   By the shores of Gitche[e]
  Gumee.
Ma Chih-yüan.   Tune: "Winds of Falling
  Plums".
MacCaig.   Notations of Ten Summer Minutes.
MacLean, S.   Shores.
Millay, E.   I shall go back.
Miller, J.   By the Pacific Ocean.
Momaday.   Winter Holding off the Coast of
  North America.
Moss, H.   Shorelines.
Neruda.   Introduction: My Themes.
Nickerson.   At Auke Bay the whales dance.
Nims, J.   Tide Turning.
O'Daly, B.   Whale in the Web, The.
O'Loughlin.   Bunkers, The.
Oppen.   Edge of the ocean, The.
Rea, T.   Lugs Benedict on the Coast, 1934.
Rimbaud, A.   Promontory.
  Seascape.
Roethke.   Meditation at Oyster River.
  Meditation at Oyster River.
  Rose, The.
Rose, P.   Anglo-Saxon Comedy.
Seed.   During War, the Timeless Air.
Silliman.   Revolving door.
Smith, C.   On Being Cautioned against Walking
  on an Headland Overlooking the Sea, Because
  It Was Frequented by a Lunatic.
  Written near a Port on a Dark Evening.
  Written on the Sea Shore.—October, 1784.
Smith, S.   Kenless Strand, The.
Snyder, G.   Wild Edge, The.
Södergran.   Forest Lake.
Stevenson, R.   At the Seaside [or Sea-Side].
Storni.   Sorrow.
Thomas, D.   We Lying by Seasand.
Tu Fu [or Du Fu].   Midnight.
  Sun Rises from Water.
Unknown.   Close by the shore, the shore.
Warn.   After Reading the Book of Splendor.
Webb, F.   End of the Picnic.
Whitman, W.   As I Ebb'd with the Ocean of
  Life.

Patrolling Barnegat.
Whittier.   Burning Drift-Wood.
Zukofsky, L.   Ferry.
See also **Beaches**

Show Business
Berlin.   There's No Business Like Show
  Business.
Claman, E.   Show Biz Parties.
Coward.   Why Must the Show Go On?
March, J.   Queenie was a blonde, and her age
  stood still.
Porter, C.   Anything Goes.
Thribb.   In Memoriam Larry Parnes ("Mr Parnes
  Shillings and Pence").
See also **Acting and Actors; Movies; Theater and
  Theaters**

Shrimp
Glazer, M.   Sonnet: "Invisible in vernal pools."
La Fontaine.   Shrimp and Her Daughter, The.
Smith, D.   Black Silhouettes of Shrimpers.

Shrines
Di Prima.   Pine shadow falls on the tent wall,
  The.
Doolittle, H.   Invisible, indivisible Spirit.
Italicus.   At the city's heart stood the shrine to
  Dido's ghost.
Mipham, Sakyong.   Snow Fell Twice, the Sun
  Always Shone.
Muso Soseki.   Hall of the Guardian God.
Nossis.   O Honored Hera, who often descending
  from heaven.
Sanchez, S.   Haiku: "Your voice unwrapping."
Snow, C.   Tour: "Near a shrine in Japan he'd
  swept the path."
Teasdale.   Shrine, The.
Tomlinson, C.   Pines at Hakone, The.
Ts'ai Yung.   Stele for Wang Ziqiao.
Vietnamese Oral Tradition.   Phoenixes and
  Sparrows.
Yüan Mei.   On the Way to Pa-ling.
See also **Mausoleums; Monuments**

Shropshire, England
Housman.   On Wenlock Edge the wood's in
  trouble.

Shrouds
Brown, G.   Shroud.
Crapsey.   Song: "I make my shroud but no one
  knows."
De la Mare.   Snow.
Donne.   Funeral[l], The.
Flynn, L.   Miracle of F6/18, The.
Mackey, N.   Sound and Cerement.
Morikawa Kyoroku.   Summer airing / On one
  pole.

Shylock
Mulligan.   Shylock.

Shyness
Clarke, George Elliott.   Monologue for Selah
  Bringing Spring to Whylah Falls.
Deltoro, A.   Shy Ones, The.
  Tímidos, Los.
Hassaan, Y.   I Considered Myself.
Horace.   Ode 1.23: To Chloë.
L'Abbé, Sonnet.   Shyness, the delay to say, The.
Wright, N.   Acrophobia.

Siberia
Akhmadulina.   Recollections of Siberia.
Bienek.   Vorkuta.
Cendrars.   Prose of the Trans-Siberian and of
  Little Jeanne of France, The.
Derieva, R.   Beyond Siberia again Siberia.
Hurley, M.   Country of Origin.
Mangan, J.   Siberia.
Marshall, J.   In the Shadow of the Poisoned
  Wind.

Siblings
Allnutt, G.   Silk Light of Advent, The.
Ayukawa Nobuo.   Sister, I'm Sorry.
Barnes, W.   Sister Gone.
Erb, E.   Bickering.
Howe, M.   Promise, The: "In the dream I had
  when he came back, not sick."
McDonald, W.   Crossing the Road.
Muir, E.   Mary Stuart.

Wojtyla.   Sister.

Sibyl
Hopkins, G.   Spelt from Sibyl's Leaves.
Levis.   Elegy with a Thimbleful of Water in the
  Cage.

Sicily
Henderson, H.   51st Highland Division's
  Farewell to Sicily, The.
Lawrence, D. H.   Bare Almond-Trees.
Radcliffe, A.   Scene on the Northern Shore of
  Sicily.
Sea-View, A.
Robinson, M.   Reaches Sicily.
Simic.   Old World, The.

Sickness
Andreus.   Empty Room, The.
  Empty Room, The.
Arnold, C.   My Love Is Sick.
Basho.   Cold night: the wild duck.
  Sick on a journey.
  Sick on a journey / Over parched fields.
  Sick on my journey.
  Sickly.
  Withering winds.
Blamire.   O Bid Me Not to Wander.
Breytenbach.   Threat of the Sick.
Buson.   Brushing flies.
  Sick man passing.
Ch'i-chi.   Start of Autumn: Hearing a Cicada
  While Sick in Bed.
Chia Tao.   Sick Cicada, A.
Chunghur Hyujung.   Thought on My Sickness,
  A.
Clementelli.   Moviola.
Constable, H.   Uncivil sickness, hast thou no
  regard.
Cornford, F.   Sick Queen, The.
Darling, J.   How to Behave with the Ill.
De Coninck, H.   If Only.
Diaz-Duque.   Why Don't I?
Doty, M.   Brilliance.
du Perron.   Sick Man, The.
Glück, L.   Time: "There was too much, always,
  then too little."
Hannah, S.   Symptoms.
Hannan, M.   Tom Passey's Child.
Hardie, K.   She Replies to Carmel's Letter.
Hughes, L.   Lover's Return.
Ignatow, D.   Sunday at the State Hospital.
Kay, J.   Dance of the Cherry Blossom.
Kees.   Small Prayer.
Keita, N.   Back road.
Masaoka Shiki.   Glass door.
Mei Ch'eng.   Seven Stimuli.
Montale.   Frost on the windowpanes; the sick.
Mura.   Hibakusha's Letter (1955), The.
Petit, P.   During the Eclipse.
Richter, J.   Nothing but Bad News.
Shen Yüeh.   Harmonizing with a Poem by Left
  Assistant Yu Kao-chih Requesting Sick Leave.
Smallpiece, A. M.   Written in Ill Health.
Stone, R.   In the Next Galaxy.
Thwaite, A.   Throes.
Townsend, A.   Institutional Blue.
Unknown.   Death of Enkidu, The.
  Unspent.
Unknown, fr. Terezin Concentration Camp.
  Theresienstadt's Hospital.
Van de Woestijne.   Fever Tune.
Waldman, A.   Sick.
Wildman, E.   Cure, The.
Wotton, S.   Hymn to My God in a Night of My
  Late Sickness[e], A.
Wunderlich, M.   Simplify Your Combination
  Therapy.
Yi Kyŏngnim.   Certain Sickness, Deep Love.
See also **Illness**

Siddons, Mrs. Sarah
Coleridge, S.   Mrs. Siddons.

Sidney, Sir Philip
Herbert, E.   Epitaph on Sir Philip Sidney Lying
  in St Paul's without a Monument, to be
  Fastned upon the Church Door.
Jonson, B.   To Elizabeth, Countess of Rutland.
  To Penshurst.

Wilson, E.   Scène de Boudoir.

Siena, Italy
Moss, S.   Postcard to Walt Whitman from Siena.

Sierra Leone
Cheney-Coker.   On Being a Poet in Sierra Leone.

Sierra Nevada Mountains
Levine, P.   Sierra Kid.
Miller, J.   Sierras.
Rexroth, K.   Blues: "Tops of the higher peaks, The."
Young, A.   In the Sierras.

Siestas
Catullus.   Ipsithilla, my pet, my favorite dish.
Cofer, J.   Hour of the Siesta, The.
Coward.   Mad Dogs and Englishmen.
Darío, R.   Symphony in Gray Major.
Herrera y Reissig.   Siesta.
Horst, C.   Siesta.
McIlroy, L.   Siesta.
Prado, A.   Siesta.

Sight
Ashbery, J.   Hod Carrier, The.
Berkson, B.   All You Want.
Borges.   In Praise of Darkness.
Burkard.   Cloud of Dusk, A.
Chang, E.   Near-Sightedness.
Clegg, D.   Five Senses.
Creeley.   Window, The.
Dupin.   I Am Forbidden.
Ghalib, M.   Don't Skimp with Me Today.
Gibson, W.   Sight.
Graham, J.   Philosopher's Stone.
Grotz, J.   First Glasses.
Gundy, J.   Inquiry into Gifts, or the Indigo Bunting.
Harris, Ken.   A in I as was Blackening Read (Mandala).
Harvey, M.   Translation.
Hejinian.   This conscious attempt to see is producing sensations of.
Jernigan, Marla.   Kind of Ransom.
Koeppel, M.   Begin with the Heron and the Bat.
Kuzmin.   People see gardens and houses.
Lauterbach.   After Mahler.
Lowell, R.   Eye and Tooth.
Milosz, C.   Esse.
Murray, W.   On Being Disabled by Light at Dawn in the Wilderness.
Muso Soseki.   Beyond Light.
  It.
Ridler.   Corneal Graft.
Rilke.   Entrance.
Schmitz.   Because the Eye Is a Flower Whose Root is the Hand.
Sze.   Acanthus.
Taylor, E.   Meditation 16 (First Series).
Traherne.   Preparative, The.
Vietnamese Oral Tradition.   Looking Out in All Directions.
Zukofsky, L.   In Arizona.

Sign Language
Jones, B.   Conversation of the Deaf, The.
Lloyd, M.   Simplest and the Hardest, The.
Pinsky.   If You Could Write One Great Poem, What Would You Want It to Be About?
Smukler.   Sign.

Signorelli, Luca
Graham, J.   At Luca Signorelli's Resurrection of the Body.
Kimbrell, J.   True Descenders.

Silence
Abrahams, L.   Winter report.
Agustini.   Night Came in the Drowsy Living Room, The.
Alegría.   Silence.
Alterman, N.   First Smile.
Andrade, E.   Silence.
Aygi, G.   Rose of Silence.
Basho.   But for a woodpecker.
  Forbidden to speak.
  Lonely silence.
Beckett, S.   Music of Indifference.
  Musique de l'indifférence.
Bevington, L.   With the Tide: A Cry of

Weakness.
Bible, *O.T.*   But God is Silent / Psalm 114.
Bloem, J. C.   Sunday.
Bogan, L.   Train Tune.
Bonnefoy.   Snow, The.
Boroditskaya, M.   Now I am a fan of silence.
Boutens.   Lonely Night.
Brecht, B.   When Evil-Doing Comes Like Falling Rain.
Brecht, S.   Silence.
  Silence, 2.
Brett, L.   La Pathétique.
Browning, E.   Substitution.
Budbill.   Sixth of January, The.
Buson.   It cried three times.
Bynner.   Sigh, A.
Byron, G.   When We Two Parted.
Cadiot, Oliver.   Psst!
Cage.   Lecture on Nothing.
Campert.   Message About the Times.
  Sign of the Times.
Campo, C.   Love, Today My Lip.
Carruth, H.   Forty-Five.
Castillo, O.   Apolitical Intellectuals.
Celan.   Alchemical.
  Language Mesh.
Celaya, G.   Theory of Silences.
Chinnov.   Black bird on a black and snowy branch, A.
Clampitt.   Silence, A.
Cofer, J.   Fever.
Crapsey.   Triad.
Creeley.   Kitchen.
Cruz Varela.   Invocation.
Darío, R.   Nocturne.
Day Lewis.   Two Songs.
De la Mare.   Autumn.
  Listeners, The.
Dickinson, E.   Still—Volcano—Life, A.
Dizhur.   Silence.
Dowson.   O Mors! Quam Amara Est Memoria Tua Homini Pacem Habenti In Substantiis Suis.
Drummond de Andrade.   Looking for Poetry.
Duncan, R.   Sentinels, The.
Dunn, D.   Modern Love.
Dunn, S.   After the Argument.
  Secret Life, A.
Ebb, F.   Quiet Thing, A.
Emerson, R.   Merops.
Everwine.   Distance.
Faiz.   When Autumn Came.
Ferguson, G.   Silent as Roses.
Fiallo, F.   Silence of Eyes, A.
Ficowski.   Girl of Six from the Ghetto Begging in Smolna Street in 1942, A.
Field.   Onycha.
Filkova, Fedya.   Under a Wing.
Fulton, R.   Forecast for a Quiet Night.
Galich.   Goldminers' Waltz, The.
Gervitz, G.   Silence is a task that will last all her life. It continues.
Gilbert, J.   To See if Something Comes Next.
Gilmore, B.   Gas Station Attendant.
Glück, L.   Horse.
  Quiet Evening.
Gomringer, E.   Untitled Concrete Poem.
Graham, J.   In/Silence.
Graves, R.   Nobody.
Gregg.   What Is Kept.
Grotz, J.   Not Body.
Guiney.   Reason for Silence, A.
Gurney, I.   Silent One, The.
Hadas, R.   Three Silences.
Han Yong'un [*or* Yongwun].   Your Silence.
Han-shan Te-ch'ing.   Fire pit is cold the stone bed like ice, The.
Hannan, M.   Tom Passey's Child.
Harwood, G.   Andante.
Haskins, L.   To Play Pianissimo.
Herlin.   Light brush of dawn, A.
Holland, J.   Wavelength.
Holub.   Silence.
Hood, T.   Silence.
Hostetler, S.   Not of This World.
Huidobro.   Midnight.

  Quiet Spaces.
Imara, L.   Diogenes.
Inada.   Keep Quiet.
Iosifova, Ekaterina.   If the Silence Should Suddenly Return.
Issa.   Noon.
  Under my house.
Jacobsen, R.   Silence Afterwards, The.
Janevski.   Silence.
Jiménez, J.   Immense Hour.
  Ship, Solid and Black, The.
Johnson, L.   Precept of Silence, The.
Jordan, J.   Winter.
Jourdan, Pierre-Albert.   Speak.
Juarroz.   There Are Points of Silence Circling the Heart.
Kang Ŭn'gyo.   Love's Way.
Karpowicz.   Silence.
King, H.   Silence: A Sonnet.
Kinnell.   That Silent Evening.
Kinzie.   Canicula.
Kloefkorn.   Why the Stone Remains Silent.
Knott.   Sonnet: "Way the world is not, The."
Komunyakaa, Y.   In the Background of Silence.
Kosugi, T.   Micro 1.
Kovner, A.   What's Not in the Heart.
Kruit, J.   Birds Leaving.
Lane, P.   Wind Thoughts.
Larkin, P.   Myxomatosis.
  Talking in Bed.
Lee, L.   Out of Hiding.
Levertov.   What Were They Like?
Levi, P.   Voices.
Levine, P.   Waking in March.
Li Po.   Inscribed at Summit Temple.
Longfellow, H.   Curfew.
Lumsden, R.   Then.
MacDiarmid, H.   Yet Ha'e I Silence Left.
MacMuireadach.   Farewell to Last Night.
Magrelli.   I prefer to come from silence to talk.
  Wood of my thoughts is on fire, The.
Majorino.   Hints.
Mallarmé.   Saint.
Marston, P.   Speechless: Upon the Marriage of Two Deaf and Dumb Persons.
Martin, C.   Speech Against Stone.
Masaoka Shiki.   Such silence / Snow tracing wings.
Masters, E.   Silence.
McDaniel, J.   Quiet World, The.
McNiece, R.   Bare birch mountainside.
Merritt, C.   Lullaby: "Say to me: out there are only streets, and cars."
  Mute Swan, The.
Merwin.   "Prodigal Son," The.
  Utterance.
Metodiev, Ivan.   Sonnet-Mantra of the Crickets.
Meyerhoff, J.   Snow.
Meynell, A.   To Silence.
  To the Beloved.
Montag, T.   May 25, 2001 (1).
Moore, L.   Eternal Landscape, The.
Moore, M.   Silence.
Moore, T.   Harp That Once through Tara's Halls, The.
Morabito, F.   I do not wish, in spite of all.
  No quiero, pese a todo.
Mun Chŏnghui.   Stare, The.
Muso Soseki.   Hut in Harmony.
  No-Word Hut.
Neruda.   Poem 15.
Novikov, N.   In our world it's unusual.
Onitsura.   True obedience.
Ory, Carlos Edmundo de.   Silence: "No one's here I'm alone with the violin of silence."
Ouwens.   Farmer, The.
Owen, Gilberto.   Interior.
Ozaki Hosai.   All day long.
Padilla.   In Trying Times.
Pavese.   Poetics.
Pilinszky, J.   On the Wall of a KZ-Lager.
  Passion of Ravensbrück.
  Passion of Ravensbrück, The.
  Relationship.
Pilling.   She Lies Silent.
Piombino.   Frozen Witness, The.

Pitcher, O.　Dust of Silence.
Pizarnik.　Poem for the Father.
Silences.
Po Chü-i.　Laozi.
Philosophers: Lao-Tzu, The.
To a Talkative Guest.
Poe.　Sonnet—Silence.
Prados, E.　Like a Naked Light.
Pritchard, N.　Cloak, The.
"Rachel." [or "Rahel."].　In my great loneliness.
Rahman, S.　Strike, The.
Rapoport, A.　Strike.
Reverdy.　Nocturne: "Street is pure black and there are no seasonal traces, The."
Rich, A.　Cartographies of Silence.
That conversation we were always on the edge.
Riley, J.　Silence.
Ritsos.　Distant, The.
Requiem on Poros.
Rodríguez, A.　Extracted.
Rosenberg, L.　Silence of Women, The.
Rossetti, C.　Aloof.
Introspective.
Youth gone, and beauty gone if ever there.
Rossetti, D.　19: Silent Noon.
Rouweler.　Silent Time.
Różewicz.　Voice, A.
Rumens.　Star Whisper.
Rumi.　Quietness.
Rux, C. H.　Suite Repose.
Sadi [or Saadi or Sa'di].　Prayers: "My shoes are mulberry with dew."
Saitō Mokichi.　Is this what.
Sassoon, S.　Elected Silence.
Scott, D.　Skiddaw House.
Segovia, F.　Claridad del silencio.
Clarity of Silence.
Sepamla.　Silence: 2.
Shiomi, M.　Music For Two Players 2.
Shishin-Goshin.　Talking: seven steps, eight falls.
Simic.　Dismantling the Silence.
Simpson, L.　Silent Piano, The.
Slauerhoff.　Within My Life.
Smith, P.　Finding His Fist.
Smith, Tracy K.　Spring: "Let's not talk."
Snyder, G.　Without.
Southerland.　Recitation.
Steven, K.　Long Silence, The.
Stevenson, R.　Gardener, The.
Stickney, T.　In the Past.
Suckling, S.　Song: "Why so pale and wan, fond lover?"
Szymborska, W.　Unexpected Meeting.
Taneda Santoka.　Mountain's stillness, The.
Tarn.　Retreat toward the Spring.
Teasdale.　Night Song at Amalfi.
Those Who Love.
Thomas, L.　Onion Bucket.
Thomas, R. S.　Via Negativa.
Tkhorzhevskaya, V.　Silence: "This is addressed to you—A century later."
Trakl.　Summer: "At evening the complaint of the cuckoo."
Tu Fu [or Du Fu].　Dawn Over the Mountains.
Turnbull.　Takings.
Turner, W.　Silence.
Tyutchev.　Silentium.
Unamuno.　How Quiet under the Earth.
It Is Night, in My Study.
Unknown.　Get Up and Bar the Door.
Raid of the Reidswire, The.
Vancrevel.　About Time ("At dusk the silence by the sea.").
About Time ("This silence at the sea's edge, so late in the afternoon.").
Velichansky, A.　Kalmyk poppies, horde of pan-Mongol tulips.
Very.　Silent, The.
Villaurrutia.　Nocturne.
Vogel, D.　Waiting-rooms.
Wang Ch'ang-ling.　Silent at Her Window.
Wang Wei.　To Magistrate Zhang.
Warren-Moore.　All-Night Issue, The.
Whitman, W.　When I Heard the Learn'd Astronomer.

Wicks, S.　On Re-recording Mozart.
Wilde, O.　Silentium Amoris.
Williams, W.　Silence.
Winters, Y.　One Ran Before.
Wojahn.　Distance.
Wright, J.　Sparrows in a Hillside Drift.
Wroth.　Sonnet 37: "Night, welcome art thou to my mind destrest [or distressed]."
Wylie.　Velvet Shoes.
Yeats.　After Long Silence.
Long-Legged Fly.
Yi Chinmyŏng.　Pure Talk.
Zenmaro.　Tanka: "In sullen silence."
Zinger, L.　I'm speaking to make you silent.
Zisquit.　Because passion is the absence we speak.
Because passion is the silence we share.

Silk
Allnutt, G.　Silk Light of Advent, The.
Hall, H.　Made of Crêpe de Chine.
Herrick.　Upon Julia's Clothes.
Horovitz, F.　Loving You.
Martínez, V.　Tesoro.
Pan Chao.　Needle and Thread.
Pound, E.　Garden, The: "Like a skein of loose silk blown against a wall."
Remoto.　Black Silk Pajamas.
Salzman, E.　Sexual Love.
Shange.　Elegance in the Extreme.
Zhao.　Needle and Thread.

Silkworms
Basho.　Long rains, The.
Doolittle, H.　We have had too much consecration.
Okamoto.　Tanka: "Innately reserved."
Stainer.　This Atomising of Things.
Unknown.　Ballad of the Mulberry Road, A.

Silver
Bialosky, J.　Silver.
Buson.　Short night, The.
Campert.　Silver Talk.
De la Mare.　Silver.
Herbert, Z.　Hakeldama.

Similes
Foerster.　Failure of Similes, The.
Reznikoff.　Similes.
Vâsıf, Enderunlu.　Gazelles have bound their hearts, The.
See also **Metaphor**

Simplicity
Ali, Taha Muhammad.　Abd El-Hadi Fights a Superpower.
Applewhite.　Map of Simplicities, A.
Basho.　Give your longing to wound.
Boethius.　Lib. 2. Metrum 5.
Brown, S.　Feminine Intuition.
Budbill.　Irrelevant and Useless.
Cavendish, M.　Claspe, The.
Chungji.　Mountain Life.
Coleridge, S.　To Simplicity.
Collins, W.　Ode to Simplicity.
Crowe, T.　Occam's Razor.
Daegak Euchon.　At Hongbub Temple.
Davies, W. H.　Sluggard, The.
Dubin, A.　Cup of Coffee, a Sandwich, and You.
Emerson, R.　Poet.
Evans, T.　Keep It Simple.
Ghalib, M.　Clay Cup, The.
Herbert, G.　Wreath, A.
Hoffenstein.　Your little hands.
Holm, B.　Icelandic Language, The.
Hostetler, S.　Instructions.
Hsieh Ling-yün.　On Spending Some Time at the Bai'an Pavilion.
Visiting Pai-an Pavilion.
Jiménez, J.　At First She Came to Me Pure.
Jonson, B.　Sweet Neglect, The.
Kendall, M.　Lay of the Trilobite.
Liu Tsung-yüan.　Reading Buddhist Classics with Chao at His Temple in the Early Morning.
Livingston, J.　Keep It Simple.
Lux.　Amiel's Leg.
Mahon.　Mayo Tao, The.
Mok, J.　Winter Mirror.
Nance.　State Song.

Pastan.　Weather.
Pellicer, C.　Wishes.
Quevedo y Villegas.　Happy and Contented in Your Hut.
Raboni, G.　Madrigal.
Ransom, J.　Captain Carpenter.
Red Hawk.　2 Ways of Crossing the Creek.
Ritsos.　Meaning of Simplicity, The.
Rose, B.　Cup of Coffee, a Sandwich, and You.
Ruby, H.　Give Me the Simple Life.
Sidney, P.　Sonnet 28: "You that with allegory's curious frame."
T'ao Ch'ien [or T'ao Yuan-ming].　Elegy for Myself.
Peach-Blossom Spring ("Ch'in's First Emperor ravaged the sense.").
Tsvetayeva [or Tsvetaeva].　I am happy to live correctly and simply.
Unknown.　Mauberes, The.
Vinokurov.　Has the time come to draw up the accounts?
Wellman, M.　Most simple things repel.
Wilbur, R.　Baroque Wall-Fountain in the Villa Sciarra, A.
Wright, J.　Birds.
Xuanjian.　Zen Sermon.

Sin
Addonizio.　Theodicy.
Baudelaire.　To the Reader.
To the Reader.
Belli, G.　Greed.
What Might Have Been.
Berry, W.　Purification, A.
Betjeman.　Huxley Hall.
Bible, N.T.　John 3; But Men Loved Darknesse Rather than Light.
Bible, O.T.　Psalm 58: "Do ye, o congregation."
Psalm 57. Miserere Mei Deus.
Bingen, Hildegard von.　Antiphon for the Holy Spirit.
Blake, W.　Was Jesus Chaste? or did he.
Bradstreet, A.　Flesh and the Spirit, The.
Brown, L.　Call for Vertical Integration in the Eye of the Storm, A.
Buffoni, F.　De Pisis--Piacenza Papers.
Byron, G.　Prayer of Nature, The.
Cairns, Scott.　Recuperation of Sin, A.
Campion, T.　View Mee, Lord.
Cano, Luis.　I Light My Lamp.
Castro, R.　Justice of Men! I Go in Search of You.
Chaucer.　Pardoner's Tale, The.
Citino.　Situation No. 7: The Poison Lover.
Clough.　Here am I yet, another twelvemonth spent.
Coleridge, H.　Sonnet 27.
Congreve, W.　Pious Selinda [or Celinda].
Copus, J.　Masaccio's Expulsion from Paradise.
Coverdale.　Let Go the Whore of Babylon.
Crane, S.　Black riders came from the sea.
Crashaw.　But Men loved Darkness[e] Rather Than [or Then] Light.
Cullen, C.　For Daughters of Magdalen.
Darío, R.　Fount, The.
David, M.　Sinner Kissed an Angel, A.
De Coninck, H.　Ballad of Indolence.
Donne.　Flea, The.
I am a little world made cunningly.
Spit in my face ye [or you] Jew[e]s, and pierce my side.
Drayton.　And thus like slaves we sell our soules to sinne.
To My Noble Friend Master William Browne: Of the Evil Time.
Dunbar, P.　Distinction.
Erdrich.　Leonard Refuses to Atone.
Gautier.　Carmen.
Gorey.　Limerick: "To his club-footed child said Lord Stipple."
Gwynn, R.　Snow White and the Seven Deadly Sins.
Hatun.　At one glance.
Herbert, G.　Agony [or Agonie], The.
Love (3): "Love bade me welcome: yet my soul drew back."
Sin (1).

Sin's Round.
Herrick.   To God: an Anthem, Sung in the
   Chapel at White-Hall, Before the King.
To His Conscience.
Hine.   Destruction of Sodom, The.
Hopkins, G.   Myself unholy, from myself
   unholy.
Howe, F.   Little Wrongs.
Hughes, L.   Madam and the Minister.
Hummer, T.   Antichrist in Arkansas, The.
Issa.   Winter lull / No talents.
Jeffers, R.   Original Sin.
Jones, D.   Sin.
Jones, R.   Letters from the Earth.
Jonson, B.   Hymn[e] to God the Father, A.
Of Life and Death.
Song. To Celia ("Come my Celia, let us
   prove.").
Kocan.   AIDS, Among Other Things.
Komunyakaa, Y.   Seven Deadly Sins.
Kuzmin.   Not for nothing did we read the
   theologians.
Lanier, E.   Now Pontius Pilate is to judge the
   cause.
Our Mother *Eve,* who tasted of the Tree.
Larkin, P.   High Windows.
Lesley, G.   Behold, how Sodom swaggers in its
   Pride.
Lindsay, V.   Unpardonable Sin, The.
Locke, A.   Sin and Despair Have So Possess'd
   My Heart.
So Foul Is Sin and Loathsome in Thy Sight.
MacKay, C.   Only a Thought.
Martinaitis, M.   Kukutis's Sinful Spirit.
Marvell.   Coronet, The.
Mower Against Gardens, The.
Masters, E.   Mrs. Meyers.
Michelangelo Buonarroti.   I live in sin, and
   dying to myself I live.
Mikha'il, M.   You Have Your Calamity And I
   Have Mine.
Milton.   No more of talk where God or Angel
   Guest.
Mookam Choinul.   Bath, A.
Moore, T.   Did Not.
Nash, O.   Ha! Original Sin!
Inter-Office Memorandum.
Portrait of the Artist as a Prematurely Old Man.
Nemerov.   Historical Judas, The.
Ni Ghallchóir, C.   Dream of the White-headed
   Boy, A.
Otero, B.   Far Away.
Last Judgement.
Pasternak, B.   Mary Magdalene (I).
Penna.   Shadowless sun on male bodies.
Philips, K.   To the Queen of Inconstancy,
   Regina Collier, in Antwerp.
Price, V.   Pride: "It becomes your soul: that
   sucking, itch that."
Quarles.   On Dinah.
What is the *World?* A great *Exchange* of ware.
Rafferty, P.   Passage.
Richardson, J.   J-O-Y.
Rilke.   Luke 15:11–19; And he said, "There was
   a man".
Robinson, A.   Scape-Goat, The.
Robinson, E.   Children of the Night, The.
Luke 15:20–32; And he arose and came.
Tavern, The.
Rodgers, W.   Lent.
Rossetti, C.   Amor Mundi.
World, The.
Ryman.   Have mynde how I mankynde have
   take.
Sandburg, C.   Washerwoman.
Sanger, R.   Lines in the Sand.
Scamell, B.   Sin.
Scott, F.   Sting of Death, The.
Service.   Woman and the Angel, The.
Shakespeare, W.   Sonnet 35: "No more be[e]
   grieved [*or* greev'd] at that which thou hast
   done."
Sonnet 94: "They that have power [*or* pow'r *or*
   powre] to hurt[e], and will do[e] none."
Sonnet 119: "What potions have I drunk of
   Siren tears."

Sidney, P.   Sonnet 14: "Alas, have I not pain
   enough, my friend."
Simic.   Scarecrow, The.
Southwell.   Man's Civil[l] War[re].
Spenser, E.   Bower of Bliss, The.
Stanley, T.   Ode XV.
Steiger.   They will not ask us: have you sinned?
Tate, A.   Ah, Christ, I love you rings to the wild
   sky.
Taylor, E.   Meditation 42 (First Series).
State, a state, oh! dungeon state indeed, A.
Tendo-Nyojo.   Sixty-six years.
Trench, R.   Lord, Many Times.
Unknown.   Adam Lay Ybounden [*or* I-
   bounden].
Full and True Account of a Dreaded Fire, that
   Lately Broke out in the Pope's Breeches, A.
God, is this then a sin?
Gospel Train, The.
In *Bath* a wanton wife did dwell.
Seven Sins, The.
Sin-Sick Soul, The.
Sith al that in this world hath ben in rerum
   natura.
Turn, Sinner, Turn O!
Wel, who shal thise hornes blowe.
You Must Be Pure and Holy.
Vaughan, H.   Corruption.
Verlaine.   Voice of Pride: shout of blaring
   trumpets.
Very.   Serpent, The.
Walcott.   Crusoe's Island.
Warren, R.   Original Sin [: A Short Story].
Wilde, O.   E Tenebris.
For oak and elm have pleasant leaves.
Yeryomin.   House over the garden is a bouquet
   of evening windows, The.
Yosano Akiko.   Let men pay for their.

See also **Original Sin; Seven Deadly Sins**

Singing and Singers
Aizenberg, M.   Not in the chimney, but in the
   gas-pipes.
Akhmatova, A.   Such Days as These.
al-Sayyab, B.   Singer Has Aged, The.
Alféri, Pierre.   Choirist.
Anacreon.   Fragment 17.
Andal.   O you who guard over.
Auden.   As I Walked Out One Evening.
Barber, D.   Nocturne.
Barrax.   Singer, The.
Barresi.   Back-Up Singer, The.
Basho.   Even in Kyoto.
Even these long days.
Moor / Point my horse.
Singing, planting rice.
Skylark.
Batraville, D.   Paper 18.
Bauer, G.   She Calms the Savage Beast with Her
   Aubade.
Bayly.   I'm Saddest When I Sing.
Beecher, J.   Altogether Singing.
Berke.   Dancing to the Track Singers at the
   Nightclub.
Berlin.   Let Me Sing and I'm Happy.
Bernard, A.   Praise Psalm of the City-Dweller.
Bertrand.   Mason, The.
Blake, W.   When the Green Woods Laugh.
Blanvillain, J.   (All of a Sudden) My Heart
   Sings.
Bogan, L.   M., Singing.
Bonnefoy.   To the Voice of Kathleen Ferrier.
Bottoms.   Homage to Lester Flatt.
Brooks, G.   Kitchenette building.
Browning, E.   I heard last night a little child go
   singing.
Bunting.   Autobiography, An.
Burns, R.   Of A' the Airts [the Wind Can Blaw].
Buson.   Such a moon.
Calpurnius Siculus.   Eclogue 1.
Eclogue 2.
Eclogue 3.
Eclogue 4.
Eclogue 6.
Campbell, J.   I Am the Mountainy Singer.
Campion, T.   Rose-cheeked Laura[, Come].
Chasin.   Joy Sonnet in a Random Universe.

Chesterton.   Christmas Carol, A: "God rest you
   merry gentlemen."
Chipasula.   Singing Drum, The.
Clarke, G.   Rag Time Cowboy Joe.
Cohan.   Down by the Erie Canal.
Cook, E.   On Seeing a Bird-Catcher.
Song of the Imprisoned Bird.
Cortez, J.   Grinding Vibrato.
Coward.   I'll See You Again.
Cox, N.   Singing Alone.
Crane, S.   There was a man with tongue of
   wood.
Creeley.   Air: "The Love of a Woman".
Cullen, C.   Colored Blues Singer.
Damacion, K.   Canciones.
Davies, W. H.   Jenny Wren.
Songs of Joy.
Davis, T.   Zoom (The Commodores).
Dawes, K.   Trickster 4 (for Sister Patra).
Day Lewis.   Conflict, The.
De Vere, A.   Song: "Slanting both hands against
   her forehead."
Di Prima.   For the Dead Lecturer.
Dickey, J.   Buckdancer's Choice.
Dickinson, E.   Hope is the thing with feathers.
I shall keep singing!
Dixon, M.   Bye Bye Blackbird.
Dove, R.   Canary.
Dowden, E.   Singer, The.
Du Bellay.   Given all my worries over each
   day's trivia.
Dubie.   Aubade of the Singer and Saboteur,
   Marie Triste: 1941.
Dunbar, P.   Sympathy: "I know what the caged
   bird feels, alas!"
When Malindy Sings.
Eady.   Young Elvis.
"Eliot.".   Armgart, to many minds the first
   success.
Emerson, R.   Saadi.
Esteves.   Some People Are about Jam.
Etter.   Singing in the Toyota.
Evans, M.   And the Old Women Gathered.
Evasco, M.   Dancing a Spell.
Fane, V.   Siren, The.
Field, E.   Callas.
Field, M.   Fellowship.
Fifty Quatrains.
I sing thee with the stock-dove's throat.
She is Singing to Thee, *Domine!*.
Freed, A.   Singin' in the Rain.
Frost, R.   Aim Was Song, The.
Oven Bird, The.
Galloway, T.   Whiffenpoof Song.
García Lorca.   Portrait of Silverio Franconetti.
Gex-Breaux, Q.   Jazz Rain.
Memory Waves.
Gibbons, O.   Silver Swan, The.
Gilbert, C.   Enclosure.
Giscombe, C.   Ballad Values (2).
Goldbarth.   People Are Dropping Out of Our
   Lives.
Gorbanevskaya.   This is sung at dawn.
Gordon, M.   I, Yi, Yi, Yi, Yi (I Like You Very
   Much).
Graham, D.   Jesus Never Sleeps.
Graves, R.   Love Without Hope.
Gregg.   Singers Change, the Music Goes On,
   The.
Grotz, J.   Last Living Castrato, The.
Guevara, M.   Buddy Holly Poem, The.
Hamer.   Allegiance.
Harris, P.   Some Songs Women Sing.
Harris, W.   Practical Concerns.
Harryman.   Baby. N. Baseball. Song.
Hart, L.   Johnny One-Note.
Hattersley, G.   Singing.
Hayes, T.   Mute Trout.
Hemans.   Corinna at the Capitol.
To a Wandering Female Singer.
Henderson, D.   Song of Devotion to the Forest.
Henley, W. E.   Margaritae Sorori.
Henson, L.   I Am Singing the Cold Rain.
Herrick.   Upon Julia's Voice.
Hirsch, E.   Song: "This is a song for the
   speechless."

Hô Sugyông. Weeping Singer, A.
Hollander, J. By Heart.
Holm, B. Blizzard.
Hughes, L. Songs.
　To Midnight Nan at Leroy's.
　Weary Blues, The.
Hugo, R. Langaig.
Hugo, V. Be Like the Bird.
Huidobro. Blind.
Hutchison, J. Joni Mitchell.
Issa. Cuckoo sings / To me, to the mountain.
　Even with insects.
　Insects on a bough.
　Skylarks singing / The farmer.
Jackson, A. Billie in Silk.
Jackson, R. Lady's Way.
Janzen, J. Learning to Sing in Parts.
Jeffers, L. Nina Simone.
Jenkins, N. Land of Song.
Johnson, Jaqueline. Phyllis.
Johnson, James W. Lift Every [or Ev'ry] Voice and Sing.
　O Black and Unknown Bards.
Johnson, R. Beam 7.
Joseph, A. On Sidewalks, on Streetcorners, as Girls.
Keats. Ode to a Nightingale.
Kenjeev. Gone is the sound of my favorite misfortune, which even yesterday.
Kim Sujang. Moonlight shines on the lotus pond.
Kinnell. Last Songs.
Koehler, T. Sing, My Heart.
Koethe. Songs of the Valley.
Korinna [or Corinna]. Terpsichore [told] me.
Laux, D. Singing Back the World.
Lawrence, D. H. Piano.
Leader, M. Madrigal: "How the tenor warbles in April!"
Lee, L. I Ask My Mother to Sing.
　You Must Sing.
Levis. Decrescendo.
Lewis, S. Rock-a-Bye Your Baby with a Dixie Melody.
Li K'ai-hsien. On the Cold Food Festival, Entertaining at the Southern Estate—the Guests Were Li Chiu-ho, Ma Nan-yeh, Wei Tung-kao, Li Hu-ch'uan, Huang K'ung-ts'un, Li Lung-t'ang, and Hu Hu-shan.
Li Po. There was a sojourner in Ying who intoned "White Snows".
Liu, T. Vox Angelica.
Livesay, D. Uninvited, The.
Loden. Tumbling Dice.
López Mills, T. Mi voz fiel como la sombra.
　My Voice Faithful as a Shadow.
Lorde. Day They Eulogized Mahalia, The.
Love, B. Bryan Ferry.
MacDiarmid, H. Empty Vessel.
MacLellan. Sang.
Magdeburg, Mechthild von. I cannot dance, O Lord.
Marion, G. Ladies Who Sing with a Band, The.
Marvell. Fair Singer, The.
Matthews, W. Old Folsom Prison.
　Penalty for Bigamy Is Two Wives, The.
McCord, D. Blessed Lord, What It Is to Be Young.
McGrath, B. Concert Choir.
McPherson, S. Ability to Make a Face Like a Spider While Singing Blues: Junior Wells, The.
Miller, V. Dirge in Jazz Time.
Minnigerode. Whiffenpoof Song.
Mistral, G. Song.
Mitcham. On the Otis Redding Bridge.
Mkangelwa. Women Sing, The.
Moore, L. Bluesman's Blues, A.
Moore, T. Echo ("At the mid hour of night, when stars are weeping, I fly.").
Morley, T. Sing We and Chant It.
Morris, W. Apology, An.
Mugo, M. G. Where are those Songs?
Murray, L. Gaelic Long Tunes, The.
Narcisse, P. Singing Queen, Where Are You?
Neal, L. Lady's Days.
Nelson, H. Peepers.

O'Hara, F. Day Lady Died, The.
Olds, S. Try-Outs, The.
O'Reilly, C. Duets.
O'Shaughnessy, A. Ode: "We are the music-makers."
Ou-yang Hsiu. East Wind.
Padgett, R. Flower's Escape.
Parkes, B. For Adelaide.
Pasternak, B. To Love.
Perry, S. Toadfish.
"Perse." Song: "I have halted my horse by the tree of the doves."
Phelps, D. Ordinary Country Girl, An.
Philodemus. Xanthippe, singing at her lyre.
Pinsky. At Pleasure Bay.
　Uncreation, The.
Pizarnik. Poem for the Father.
Po Chü-i. Madly Singing in the Mountains.
　On Hearing Someone Sing a Poem by Yuan Zhen.
Pomeroy, G. Whiffenpoof Song.
Porter, C. It's De-Lovely.
　Red, Hot and Blue.
Ratzlaff, K. Gospel.
Ravenscroft, T. Sing we now merily.
Redel, V. Singing to Tony Bennett's Cock.
Reeve, F. Voices: "When I hear my lover singing, I sing, too."
Robinson, A. Personality.
　Search for Apollo, A.
Rohrer, M. Short History of Illumination, A.
Rome, H. (All of a Sudden) My Heart Sings.
Rose. Throat Song: The Whirling Earth.
Rosen, Corie. Madonna for the Damned—a 1980s Heroine.
Ross, L. James Brown.
Rossetti, C. Birthday, A.
Rushin. Black Back-Ups, The.
Sandburg, C. Splinter.
Sappho. I will now sing this beautifully.
　Mika / But I will not allow you.
　Since yes you [were] once a child.
　Superior, as a singer from Lesbos to those of other lands.
Sassoon, S. Everyone Sang.
Sharshar, S. Singer, The.
Sheehan, M. My Father's Singing.
Shelley, P. To Jane: The keen stars were twinkling.
Shirley, A. Hours Musicians Keep, The.
Shumyatsher, E. My New York Street Sings.
Sin Hŭm. Person who made a song, The.
Skelton, J. Garden of the Muses: Iopas' Song, The.
Skloot. Everly Brothers, The.
Smith, I. Two Girls Singing.
Soen. Calm, activity—each has its use. At times.
Soloukhin. For the Tree to Sing...
Sousa, N. Let My People Go.
Speakes. Patsy Cline.
Spires. Apology.
　Interrogations of the Sparrow.
Stanley, T. Celia Singing.
Stephens, P. God Shed His Grace.
Stevens, W. Idea of Order at Key West, The.
Sub-ok. Spring at Yesan Station.
Tagore. Song That I Came to Sing, The.
Theocritus. Idyll 1: "Whisper of the wind in, The."
Thomas, D. In My Craft or Sullen Art.
Thomas, L. Song: "You asked me to sing."
Thompson, D. P. Blues at 1.
Trinidad. Answer Song.
Tu Fu [or Du Fu]. Coming Home Late at Night.
Turgeniev, I. Skulls, The.
Unknown. I beg you, beg you, mother.
　Spoils of Annwn, The.
　This song explodes.
Unknown, fr. Terezin Concentration Camp.
　Birdsong.
Van Vliet. Courtyard, The.
Very. Song, The.
Vessup, A. Mighty Blood, The.
Vietnamese Oral Tradition. Singer with a Bad Voice, The.

Wagner, S. A Cappella.
Wagoner, D. Chorus: "That rain-strewn night in the woods, the chorus, chorus."
　Singing Lesson, The.
Wakoski. Singer, The.
Walker, M. Since 1619.
Waniek. Source of the Singing, The.
Washington, N. Give Me a Heart to Sing To.
Waters, C. Singer, The.
Weatherford, C. Queen Ijo's Blues.
Welish. Textile 11.
Wendt. Singing the Mozart Requiem.
Wetzsteon. Witness.
White, J. Oshi.
Whitman, T. Hunger and Imagination.
Whitman, W. Chanting the Square Deific.
　I Hear America Singing.
　To a Certain Cantatrice.
Williams, C. K. Singing, The.
Williams, Stephanie. Drunkard Promise, A.
Williams, W. Late Singer, The.
Wojahn. Buddy Holly.
　Song of the Burning.
Woods, H. Side by Side.
Wordsworth, W. Solitary Reaper, The.
Wright, J. Homecoming Singer, The.
Wyatt. My Lute, Awake!
Yi Kyubo. Sung Impromptu.
Yosano Akiko. Temple bell, The.
Young, J. Rock-a-Bye Your Baby with a Dixie Melody.

Single Women
Ch'ŏn Yanghûi. To Single Women.
Mun Chônghui. For the Sake of Man Again.

Sioux, The
Chippewa Oral Tradition. Sioux Woman Defends Her Children, The.
　Sioux Women Gather Up Their Wounded, The.
　Song of the Captive Sioux Woman.
Taylor, R. Dakota: October, 1822, Hunkpapa Warrior.

Sirens (mythology)
Atwood. Siren Song.
Brown, E. What Song the Syrens Sang.
Browne, W. Sirens' Song, The.
Cynewulf. Nature of the Siren, The.
Daniel, S. Ulysses and the Siren [or Syren].
Darley. Mermaidens' Vesper-Hymn, The.
Day Lewis. Nearing Again the Legendary Isle.
Fane, V. Siren, The.
Hass, R. Envy of Other People's Poems.
Hedyla. Either cockleshells from the Erythraian reef as gifts.
Kafka. Sirens, The.
Killigrew, A. Farewell to Worldly Joys, A.
Manifold. Sirens, The.
McLain, P. Beauty, That Lying Bitch.
Milton. At a Solemn Music[k].
Reid, C. Mermaids Explained.
Storni. Siren, The.

Sirens (warning devices)
Robeson, E. Counsel of Birds, The.
Winters, Y. Moonlight Alert.

Sisters
Acorn. Ballad of the Pink-Brown Fence, The.
Agosin. Miriam.
Agustini. Miraculous Ship, The.
Akhmatova, A. Sister, I have come to take your place.
Alabaú. Sister.
Aldis, D. Little.
Aleshire. Double, The.
Anderson, L. Red Hot.
Andrew, G. Hurricane Sisters Work Regardless, The.
　O That Summer.
Angus. Blue Jacket, The.
Armstrong, Tammy. Wood Stove Sunday.
Bacharach, D. New Joke, The.
Berggolts [or Bergholts]. To My Sister.
Bogan, L. Sleeping Fury, The.
Bourne, Lesley-Anne. Out of the Blizzard.
Bradley, Dickie. Sista.
Browning, E. Bertha in the Lane.
Bruce, D. Sonnet 2: "Deep in her seventh

month, my sister dozes."
Bryan, M.　To My Brother ("Oh transient sorrows, light as morning dews.").
To My Brother ("Once in our customed walk a wounded bird.").
Burkard.　Your Sister Life.
Byron, G.　Epistle to Augusta.
Campbell, R.　Sisters, The.
Carroll, L.　Brother and Sister.
Causley.　What Has Happened to Lulu?
Clifton, L.　To Ms. Ann.
Collins, K.　Sisters.
Costello, R.　When My Sister Was Fifteen.
Cotton, C.　Resolution in Four Sonnets, of a Poetical Question Put to Me by a Friend, Concerning Four Rural Sisters.
Duhamel.　Ugly Step Sister, The.
Feinstein, E.　Lazarus' Sister.
Firer.　1956, The Year My Sister, Using Her Ill Health Once Again, Blackmailed My Parents into an Accordion.
Galvin, J.　Station (1).
Station (2).
Glück, L.　Descending Figure.
Gonzáles Martínez.　Like Sister and Brother.
Hardie, K.　Young Woman Stands on the Edge of Her Life, The.
Harrison, J.　Our Other Sister.
Im Hwa.　My Brother and the Brazier.
Jones, S.　Another Lazarus.
Kamienska.　Saint Martha.
Kim Sowŏl.　Cuckoo, The.
Lamb, C.　If From My Lips Some Angry Accents Fell.
Lili'u-o-ka-lani.　Sanoe ("Where can you be, Sanoe?").
Lochhead, L.　Grim Sisters, The.
Poem for My Sister.
MacLeod, Sue.　When night meets thread and needle and lies down among the bedclothes.
McGuckian.　Sitting, The.
Millay, E.　Night is my sister, and how deep in love.
Moore, O.　Eulogy for Sister.
Mullen, H.　Kirstenography.
Nelson, M.　I Decide Not to Have Children.
No Hyegyông.　Children on Top of the Hill.
Olds, S.　Elder Sister, The.
Indictment of Senior Officers.
Sisters of Sexual Treasure, The.
Remoto.　Images of John (1967–92).
Rich, A.　Women.
Rossetti, C.　Noble Sisters.
Sachs, N.　O Sister.
Saloy, M.　This Poem Is for You, My Sister.
Schoolcraft.　To Sisters on a Walk in the Garden, after a Shower.
Seward.　On a Lock of Miss Sarah Seward's Hair Who Died in her Twentieth Year.
Sherman, C.　Roots.
Song.　Lost Sister ("In China.").
Soto.　Blanco.
Szymborska, W.　In Praise of My Sister.
Taggard.　Weed, The.
Traig, Jannifer.　For My Sister.
Tu Fu [or Du Fu].　I have a sister, little sister, living in Zhongli.
Unknown.　Brotherless Sisters.
Down to the Mire.
Our Little Sister is Worried.
West, K.　To My Twin Sister Who Died at Birth.
Wilner, E.　Epitaph: "Young then, / we were bored already."
Wŏlmyŏng.　Requiem for the Dead Sister.
Wright, J.　Sisters, The.

Sisyphus
Alcaeus [or Alkaios].　Drink...with me, Melanippos. Why (think that).
Blind.　Scarabaeus Sisyphus.
Glück, L.　Mountain, The.
Yaqoob, J.　Only Choice, The.

Sitting Bull (Sioux Chief)
Arapaho Oral Tradition.　When I Met Him Approaching.

Sitwell, Dame Edith
Coward.　Contours.

Size
Barer, M.　Shall We Join the Ladies?
Bell, M.　Who I am is a short person with small feet.
Berlin.　How Deep Is the Ocean? (How High Is the Sky?).
Blanco.　Teorí de Fractales.
Callimachus.　Prologue to the Aetia.
Carmi, T.　Short Song.
Cohn, J.　Jemez Mountains Meditation.
Edson, R.　Cottage in the Wood, A.
Ettinger, E.　Micrographic Manuscript, Miniature (1).
Micrographic Manuscript, Miniature (2).
Haavikko.　I always bow down deep before a small tree and a great tyrant.
Karr.　Hubris.
Martial.　Lydia is as wide and slack.
Quevedo y Villegas.　On a Chaplain's Nose.
Radoev, Ivan.　Tiny Man, The.
Ruiz, J.　Charms of Small Women.
Sappho.　Doorkeeper has feet seven fathoms long, The.
Scève, M.　Every Wide and Long Expanse of Sea.
Segade, G.　Theory of Fractals.
Voiture.　You Know Where You Did Despise.
Wodehouse.　Napoleon.

Skateboarding and Skateboarders
Gunn, T.　Skateboard.
Morrison, L.　Sidewalk Racer Or, On the Skateboard, The.
See also **Roller Skating and Roller Skaters**

Skating and Skaters
Berssenbrugge.　Swan, The.
Blunden.　Midnight Skaters, The.
Conn.　Under the Ice.
Fletcher, J.　Skaters, The.
Knibbe, H.　Skater, The.
Livingston, M.　74th Street.
Lynch, T.　Skating with Heather Grace.
Mueller, J.　Bonneville.
Muske, C.　Crack the Whip.
Roberts, S.　Skater, The.
Wyrebek, M.　Trendelenburg Position.
See also **Roller Skating and Roller Skaters; Skateboarding and Skateboarders**

Skeletons
Alexie.　Evolution.
Basho.　Weathered skeleton, A.
Deanovich.　My Favorite Monk Is.
Ferguson, G.　Grey Kirk in the Mearns.
Foley, Jack.　Skeleton's Defense of Carnality, The.
Garner, P.　Lucy, Lucie.
Guidacci.　First to feast is love, The. On the scraps of love the fever feasts.
Harper, Cynthia.　Día de Los Muerto.
Herd.　Hyperion's Bones.
Houlihan, J.　H. Antecessor.
Longfellow, H.　Skeleton in Armor [or Armour], The.
Lovelace, R.　La Bella Bona-Roba.
Poetker-Thiessen, A.　Fallen Women.
Schmitz.　Monstrous Pictures of Whales.
Shorter.　Skeleton in the Cupboard, The.
Toledo, N.　Dxiibi Guidxa.
Espanto tonto.
Silly Ghost.
Wilbur, R.　To His Skeleton.
See also **Bones**

Skepticism
Appleman, P.　O Karma, Dharma, pudding and pie.
Inez.　Skeptic, The.
Johnson, M. F.　Invocation to the Spirit Said to Haunt Wroxall Down.
Kshetrayya.　Wife to a Friend, A.
See also **Doubt**

Skiing and Skiers
Page, P.　T-Bar.
Trungpa, Chogyam.　Skiing in a red and blue outfit.

Skin
Armand.　Poem with Skin.
Askhari.　Colorstruck.
Blaser.　Cups #5.
Brooks, S.　Sweet molasses.
Brown Rosellen.　This is no baby skin—.
Butts, A.　Skin.
Chandidas.　Why Tell Me What to Do?
Dransfield.　Epiderm.
Dugan, A.　Prison Song.
Eimers.　Night Without Stars, A.
Giscombe, C.　Light, Bright, Etc.
Grahn.　Fortunately the skins.
Hunter, K.　I worked on race at the factory.
Kay, J.　Chapter 7: Black Bottom.
Kwa, Lydia.　You must exist. Writing this book depends on it. It has occurred to.
Leslie, E.　T'ain't No Sin to Dance Around in Your Bones.
Loden.　Far In.
Lope de Vega.　White Was I.
Lorde.　Hanging Fire.
McClatchy.　Tattoos.
Morgan, R.　Code, The.
Mudrooroo Narogin.　Song Thirty-Four.
O'Reilly, C.　Thin.
Orlowsky, D.　To Our Cosmeticians.
Padel, R.　Skin.
Perdomo, W.　Nigger-Reecan Blues.
Perillo, L.　Skin: "Back then it seemed that wherever a girl took off her clothes the police would find her."
Petit, P.　My Mother's Skin.
Porter, C.　I've Got You Under My Skin.
Ranaldo, L.　No Deal.
Roberson, E.　Poll.
Spahr, J.　December 1, 2002.
Strong, G.　Modern Hiawatha, The.
Sute-Jo, Lady Den.　Woman.
Tafolla.　Mission San José.
Thomas, L.　Subway Witnesses, The.
Tillema, M.　So Soon ("So soon, so tired.").
So Soon ("So soon—so without tomorrow.").
Velichansky, A.　Infant is white, like down, The. And the youth dark-complexioned, like shingle.
Verlaine.　Without Guile.
Vroman.　Wrinkling Together.
Waldman, A.　Skin / Meat / BONES.
Welish.　Skin.
Wright, J.　Skins.
Wyrebek, M.　Trendelenburg Position.
Yost, C.　Lai with Sounds of Skin.

Skulls
Bancquart.　Baroque.
Bell, M.　Sound of the Resurrected Dead Man's Footsteps (#2).
Brand, D.　Canto 1: "Ashes head to toes."
Bye.　On the Rails.
Donegan, P.　Tonight / while shampooing my hair.
Gonzales, R.　Head of Pancho Villa, The.
Kates.　Nothing in Art.
MacDiarmid, H.　Perfect.
Minnis, Chelsey.　Skull Ring, The.
Nye, N.　Morning Paper, Society Page.
Popa.　Song of the Tower of Skulls.
Scott, W.　U.S. Sailor with the Japanese Skull, The.
Turgeniev, I.　Skulls, The.
Weismiller.　Skull.
Wrigley, R.　Skull of a Snowshoe Hare, The.
Yates, D.　Washing the Cow's Skull.

Skunks
Heaney, S.　Skunk, The.
Lowell, R.　Skunk Hour.
Miles, J.　Bureau 2.
Navajo Oral Tradition.　Coyote, Skunk, and the Prairie Dogs.

Sky
Addison, J.　Ode: "Spacious firmament on high, The."
Ahmet Hasim.　Moonstruck Storks.
Alexander, E.　Ode.
Ash, J.　Sky My Husband, The.
Ashbery, J.　Variant.
Asim, J.　Memory of Wings.
Auden.　Summer Night, A.

Back, R. You ask.
Basho. To the capital / Snow-clouds forming.
Berlin. Blue Skies.
Bevington, L. Measurements.
Bobrowski. Deserted Village.
 Place of Fire.
Bonnefoy. Top of the World, The.
Buson. Calligraphy of geese.
Byron, G. She Walks In Beauty.
Carroll, J. Love Rockets.
Carroll, L. Mad Hatter's Song, The.
Char. Tree Frog, The.
Conoley, G. Sky Drank In, The.
Cope, J. Winter Sky.
Crane, H. To the Cloud Juggler.
Daive. Space instead.
 Under the wind.
Dao. Night Sky.
Dauer. Falling.
De León, L. Tranquil Night.
De Mello Breyner. Day of Sea.
Densmore. Sky Will Resound, The.
Dickinson, E. Aurora.
 Lightly stepped a yellow star.
Dove, R. Teach Us to Number Our Days.
Duran, J. Mere Pleasure of Flying, The.
Eigner. Back to it.
 In Imitation.
Éluard, P. *et al.* She Exists.
Flanders, J. Cloud Painter.
Gilbert, C. Directions, The.
Grumman, Bob. Mathemaku for Beethoven.
Han Yong'un [*or* Yongwun]. I Cannot Know.
Hass, R. Elm.
Henderson, D. Horizon Blues.
Herlin. Morning space.
 Red round sun, The.
 Sky has recovered, The.
Hoffmann, R. Bering Bridge, The.
Holub. On the Origin of the Contrary.
Howe, F. Scattered Light.
Issa. From now on.
 New year arrived, The.
 Red morning sky.
 Worldly sky / From now on.
Ivask, Y. Shall we forget the shiver.
Joubert. Brilliant Sky.
Kaplinski, J. We started home, my son and I.
Kassabova, K. Preparation for the Big
 Emptiness.
Keble. Malvern at a Distance.
Khodasevich. Music.
Khoury-Gata. She Used to Throw Her Old
 Crockery.
Kinnell. Daybreak: "On the tidal mud, just
 before sunset."
Kizer, C. On a Line from Valéry.
Klyuyev [*or* Kliuev *or* Klyuev]. Sky Lies
 Blue—Like a Sea, The.
Latouche, J. Cabin in the Sky.
Levertov. Clouds.
Li Ch'ing-chao. "Fisherman's Honor," The.
Lima, J. Words of Departure.
Lion-Face. KYE HO! Wonderful!
Loynaz, D. M. Cloud, The.
Lumbreras, E. Cielo, El.
 Cielo, El / puede venirse abajo esta mañana.
 Sky, The.
 Sky, The / could collapse this morning.
MacKenzie, R. Blue Sky in Morning.
Mallarmé. When the shade threatened with the
 fatal decree.
Mansour, J. Beyond the breakers.
Masaoka Shiki. Summer sky / Clear after rain.
Mead, J. Incomplete Scenario Involving What
 the Voice Said.
Meredith, W. Airman's Virtue.
Merrill, J. Downward Look, A.
 Upward Look, An.
Miller, L. Heavens are playing with the earth,
 The.
Mills, R. Water Lilies.
Miyazawa Kenji. Spring & Asura.
Mokusetsu. Long summer rains / Barley's
 tasteless.
Muso Soseki. For years I dug in the earth.

Nemes Nagy. Between.
 Four-Light Window, A.
Neruda. I love the handful of the earth you are.
Nichol. Monotones.
Popa. Burning Shewolf.
Posey, A. Nightfall.
Radnóti. Clouded Sky.
Ray, H. Sky Picture.
Redmond, J. Charlie and Joe.
Roberts, E. Sky, The.
Robinson, K. Nursery Rhyme.
Ryuzan. Clear in the blue, the moon!
Saiokuken Socho. Moon this evening, The.
Sandburg, C. Be Ready.
 People, Yes, The.
Shaku Chōkū. Vultures—in the Midst of War.
Shapiro, D. Commentary Text Commentary
 Text Commentary Text.
Shiki. Full moon ringed, The.
Shin Tongyŏp. Scene 9.
Shokaku. High wind, cold moon.
Simic. My Mother was a Braid.
 Night Picnic.
Sŏ Chŏngju. Winter Sky.
Somoza, J. Late Light.
Stafford, W. Sky.
Stevenson, R. Swing, The.
Storni. Siren, The.
 White Claw, The.
Sute-Jo, Lady Den. Are there / Short-cuts in the
 sky.
Swenson, M. Fire Island.
Taylor, J. Star, The.
Tewa Oral Tradition. Song of the Sky Loom.
Thomson, J. Part 17: "How the moon triumphs
 through the endless nights!"
Traherne. To the Same Purpos[e].
Tu Fu [*or* Du Fu]. Heavenly River.
Turner, F. Spring Evening.
Unknown. Eagle Above Us, The.
 Looking through the window.
 Red sky at night, A.
 Spirit Song.
Volkman. Sonnet: "Sky we bear on our
 shoulders, heaven-height, The."
Ward, T. Dark Underfoot.
Weigl. Sky in Daduza Township, A.
Welish. Within This Book, Called Marguerite.
Wellman, M. Blue sky in a human face.
Whitman, W. On the Beach at Night.
 On the Beach at Night Alone.
Williams, W. Desolate Field, The.
Wonhyo, Great Master. Axe without a Handle.
Yau. Engines of Gloom and Affection.
Yin Luoth. Phnom Penh Morning.
Zhenkai. Collection, The.

See also **Constellations; Stars**

Sky Diving and Sky Divers
Merrill, C. Erosion.
Reed, I. Sky Diving.

See also **Parachuting and Parachutists**

Skye, Isle of, Scotland
Revard. October, Isle of Skye.
Unknown. Skye Boat Song.

Skylarks
Basho. Even these long days.
 Midfield.
 Skylark.
Clare, J. Sky Lark, The.
Issa. Even on the smallest islands.
 Skylarks singing / The farmer.
 When the wild turnip.
Mercer, J. Skylark.
Shiki. Skylark school, The.
Sora. Skylark / Soaring—her young.
Yayu. One sneeze / Skylark's.

See also **Larks**

Skyscrapers
Black, S. Skyscrapers.
Corso. Ode to Coit Tower.
Field, R. Skyscrapers.
Hodgeon, G. In Conference.
Laughlin, J. Above the City.
Oppen. Building of the Skyscraper, The.
 So spoke of the existence of things.

Ramsey, L. That Which Hovers.
Sandburg, C. Prayers of Steel.
 Skyscraper.
Schmitz. Climbing Sears Tower.
Unknown. 2 Termite Skyscrapers.
Yolen. Sky Scrape / City Scape.

Slander
Bertrans de Born. Protestation.
Bhartrihari. Apathy Is Ascribed to the Modest
 Man.
Ellis, T. Sir Nose D'VoidofFunk.
Shakespeare, W. Sonnet 70: "That thou art
 blam'd shall not be thy defect."
 Sonnet 140: "Be wise as thou art cruel; do not
 press."
Various authors. Many slandered him.
Yeats. He Thinks of Those Who Have Spoken
 Evil of His Beloved.

Slaughter of the Innocents
Ruffin. Burying.

See also **Massacre of the Innocents**

Slaughterhouses
Alexander, M. Chicago.
Heaney, S. Testimony.
Keplinger, D. Distance Between Zero and One,
 The.
Lawrence, A. Goanna.
Masterson, R. Making Love in the Meat
 Locker.
McNair. Killing the Animals.
Stéfan, Jude. Butcher's Meat by Loti.
Troupe. River Town Packin House Blues.
Yi Hyangji. Ringing in My Ears.

Slavery and Slaves
"Ada.". Slave Girl's Farewell, The.
 Slave, The.
Adisa. No, Women Don't Cry.
Al-Bayati, A. Transformations of Aisha:
 Aisha's Birth and Death in the Magical Rituals
 Inscribed in Cuneiform on the Nineveh
 Tablets.
Alexander, E. Passage.
Allen, S. Apple Trees in Sussex, The.
Anyte [*or* Anytes]. This Manes alive once was
 a slave; now dead.
Askhari. Isalutu.
Azzawi, F. Song of the Slave Girl, The.
Baraka, I. Biography.
 Wise 5.
 Y The Link Will Not Always Be "Missing" #40.
Barlow, J. Columbiad, The.
Beecher, J. Altogether Singing.
Benét, S. Invocation: "American muse, whose
 strong and diverse heart."
 John Brown's Prayer.
Bennett, G. To a Dark Girl.
Bierce. Hesitating Veteran, The.
Bland, J. Carry Me Back to Old Virginny.
Boyd, M. Epitaph for Etheridge Knight.
Bradley, Dickie. Sista.
Brathwaite, E. New World A-Comin'.
Brooks, S. Middle Passage.
Brown, S. Bitter Fruit of the Tree.
 Master and Man.
 Memo: For the Race Orators.
 Old King Cotton.
 Strong Men.
Browning, E. Hiram Powers' "Greek Slave".
 Runaway Slave at Pilgrim's Point, The.
Brutus. There Was a Time When the Only
 Worth.
Bryant, W. African Chief, The.
 Death of Slavery, The.
Cable, G. Dirge of St. Malo, The.
 English muskets went bim! bim!, The.
Campbell, R. Serf, The.
Carey, H. Sally in Our Alley.
Cary, P. Harvest Gathering.
Clifton, L. At the cemetery, walnut grove
 plantation, south carolina, 1989.
 Slave Cabin, Sotterly Plantation, Maryland,
 1989.
 Slaveship[s].
Cowper, W. Negro's Complaint, The.
 Sweet Meat Has Sour Sauce.

Crouch, S. Chops Are Flyin.
Cumberbatch, L. I Swear to You, That Ship
  Never Sunk in Middle-Passage!
D'Aguiar, F. Langston.
  Mama Dot.
  Mama Dot Warns Against an Easter Rising.
Davidson, D. Sequel of Appomattox.
Davis, M. Cry of a People.
de Burgos. Ay, Ay, Ay of the Kinky-Haired
  Negress.
De [or Du] Guillet. But if he came straight for
  me.
Derricotte. 1994 Inventory.
Diop, D. Vultures, The.
Dixon, M. Tour Guide: La Maison des
  Esclaves.
Dove, R. Adolescence—1.
  Belinda's Petition.
  House Slave, The.
DuBois, W. My Country 'Tis of Thee.
Dunbar, P. Ante-Bellum Sermon, An.
  Sympathy: "I know what the caged bird feels,
  alas!"
Emerson, R. Boston Hymn.
Espirito Santo. Grandma Mariana.
Esteves. From Fanon.
Evans, M. Speak the Truth to the People.
Follen, E. Children in Slavery.
  For the Fourth of July.
Forbes, C. Gone.
Freneau. To Sir Toby.
Garrett, G. Old Slavemarket: St. Augustine, Fla.
Gelman. History.
González Prada, M. Mitayo, The.
Grainger, J. Advice to Slave-Owners.
  Book 4.
Greenwell, D. Broken Chain, The.
Griffin, S. I Like to Think of Harriet Tubman.
Guillén, N. My Last Name.
Harper, F. Bible Defence of Slavery.
  Bury Me in a Free Land.
  Deliverance, The.
  Eliza Harris.
  Learning to Read.
  Lines: "At the Portals of the Future."
  Slave Auction, The.
  Slave Mother, The.
  Slave Mother, The: A Tale of the Ohio.
Harper, M. American History.
  Makin' Jump Shots.
Hayden, R. Frederick Douglass.
  Middle Passage.
  Runagate Runagate.
Hayretî. We are not slaves of Süleymân, nor the
  captives.
Heard, J. Black Sampson, The.
  To Clements' Ferry.
Hoagland, E. Gorée.
Horton, G. On Hearing of the Intention of a
  Gentleman to Purchase the Poet's Freedom.
  On Liberty and Slavery.
Hughes, L. American Heartbreak.
  Aunt Sue's Stories.
Iman. Love Your Enemy.
Jackson, B. In Exchange for Forty Acres.
Jackson, G. Alice.
  Fugitive Slaves.
  1619. Virginia.
Jeffers, H. Ellen Craft.
Jeffers, L. Nina Simone.
Jensma. Cry Me a River.
Johnson, B. Storm: "Edges of slave ships are
  narrow and difficult for footing, The."
Jordan, J. Something Like a Sonnet for Phillis
  Miracle Wheatley.
  Speculations on the Present through the Prism of
  the Past.
Kay, J. Even the Trees.
  Finger.
Kendrick, D. Sadie Snuffs a Candle.
  Sidney, Looking for her Mother.
  Sophie, Climbing the Stairs.
Kgositsile. To Mother.
Koestenbaum, W. Gaudy Slave Trader.
Komunyakaa, Y. Back Then.
  Family Tree.

Kuzmin. Were I a general of olden times.
"Leadbelly.". Take this Hammer.
Lickbarrow, I. On the Slave-Trade.
Lima, J. That Black Girl Fulô.
Longfellow, H. Slave in the Dismal Swamp,
  The.
  Slave's Dream, The.
  Warning, The.
  Witnesses, The.
Lorde. Between Ourselves.
Lourie. Three Recent Trips to the Golden Past:
  East Village, Clarksdale Mississippi, Athens.
Martial. Ad Quintilianum.
  Artemidorus sold his land to buy a boy.
  You rocked my cradle, Charidemus, once.
  You sold a slave just yesterday.
  Your slave boy's cock is aching, Naevolus.
Martinson. On the Congo.
Mattawa. Road from Biloxi, The.
Matthews, W. By a Ways.
Maunick. Seven Sides and Seven Syllables.
McLoughland. Whippoorwill Calls, The.
McManus, K. 450 Years of Selective Memory
  (Smile).
Melville, H. Formerly a Slave.
  Meditation, A.
  Misgivings.
Miller, E. Tomorrow.
Mohammad, K. Silem. Mars Needs Terrorists.
Moorer. Emancipation Day.
  Must Be Freed.
  Peonage System, The.
More, H. No; they have heads to think, and
  hearts to feel.
  Slavery.
  Strange power of song! the strain that warms the
  heart.
Morris, M. Rasta Reggae.
Morris, W. No Master, High or Low!
Nesbit, E. Wife of All Ages, The.
Neto. Grieved Lands, The.
Nichols, G. Out of Africa.
Opie. Negro Boy's Tale, The.
Patterson, R. Black Power.
Piatt, S. Child's Party, A.
Pierpont, J. Fugitive Slave's Apostrophe to the
  North Star, The.
Plumpp. Remembered.
  Turf Song.
Pommy-Vega. For Boats Only.
Randall, D. Southern Road, The.
Reynolds, S. F. Whipping, The.
Robinson, E. Sonnet: "Master and the slave go
  hand in hand, The."
Rodriguez, L. My Name's Not Rodriguez.
Rogers, E. In 'Fifty Congress Passed a Bill.
Sabry, M. Harem, The.
Sanchez, S. Reflections After the June 12th
  March for Disarmament.
Scalapino. Slaves' Outside Evening or Evening,
  Pal Mal Comic.
Schwartz, D. Winter Twilight, Glowing Black
  and Gold, The.
Seibles, T. Douglass, a Last Letter.
Seneca. Trojan Women.
Sigourney. To the First Slave Ship.
Simmons, S. All the shoes are shined and the
  cotton is picked.
Simpson, J. Grieve not, my wife—grieve not
  for me.
Skeeter. California, 1852.
Smith, D. To Isle of Wight.
Smith, G. Penitential Cries of Jupiter
  Hammond, The.
Smith, S. Was It Not Curious?
Sousa, N. Our Voice.
Southey, R. Did then the bold slave rear at last
  the sword.
  Hold your mad hands! for ever on your plain.
  Oh he is worn with toil! the big drops run.
  'Tis night; the mercenary tyrants sleep.
  Why dost thou beat thy breast and rend thine
  hair.
Spaulding-Convy, A. Why Women Become
  Water.
Stainer. Sighting the Slave Ship.

Stokes, G. Blue Texarkana.
Taylor, C. Scroll No. 2.
Thompson, P. Address to Ethiopia.
  Favorite Slave's Story, The.
  Fugitive, The.
  Husband's Return, The.
  My Father's Story.
  Prayer, A: "Oh, Lord! I lift my heart."
Tindal. Cry of the Oppressed, The.
Tolson, M. Dark Symphony.
Toomer. Song of the Son.
Trethewey, N. Native Guard.
Udeozo, O. Slave Boat.
Unknown. Away Down in Sunbury.
  Go Down, Moses.
  Harriet Tubman.
  Johnny come down de hollow.
  Let My People Go.
  No More Auction Block.
  Steal Away to Jesus.
  There's a Meeting Here To-Night.
  What else can you do but fight?
Van Jordan, A. Question: "What up, brother?
  the white teen with dreadlocks."
  Very. Slavery.
Walker, M. Delta.
  Since 1619.
Wang Chiu-ssu. Ballad of Selling a Child.
Waniek. Chosen.
Watley, M. 100 Million.
Weatherford, C. Charleston Baskets.
Wheatley, P. On Being Brought from Africa to
  America.
  To the Right Honourable William, Earl of
  Dartmouth.
Whitfield. America.
Whitman, A. Lute of Afric's Tribe, The.
Whitman, W. Runaway slave came to my house
  and stopt outside, The.
Whittier. Christian Slave, The.
  Farewell, The: "Gone, gone,—sold and gone."
  For Righteousness' Sake.
  Haschish, The.
  Ichabod[!].
  Massachusetts to Virginia.
  Official Piety.
  Slave-Ships, The.
  Song of Slaves in the Desert.
Williams, H. Poem on the Bill Lately Passed
  for Regulating the Slave-Trade, A.
Wright, J. Sketch for an Aesthetic Project.

Sleds
Houlihan, J. All the Cold Mechanicals.
Johnson, J. Midnight Run.
Patchen. Great-Sledmakers, The.
Reznikoff. It had long been dark, though still an
  hour before supper-time.
See also **Sleighs**

Sleep
Adams, L. Moon and Spectator, The.
Ajanta. Sleep: "Nobody nowhere they've all
  gone home."
Akhmadulina. Lines Written During a Sleepless
  Night in Tbilisi.
Al-Harizi. Lightning, The.
Alberti. Soldiers Sleep, The.
Alcman. All asleep: mountain peaks and
  chasms.
  Fragment 58: Night and Sleep.
Alden, J. Sleepy Time Gal.
Alexie. Reservation Love Song.
Ali Hsiying. Lazy Cloud's Nest 2.
Andrews, C. Morn's Recompense.
Aragon, F. Earplugs.
Armstrong, J. On Feather Beds.
Atwood. Variation on the Word Sleep.
Auden. Lullaby, A: "Din of work is subdued,
  The."
Ausländer, R. In the Color of Sleep.
Awoonor. Song of War.
  Songs of Sorrow.
Aygi, G. Going to Sleep in Childhood.
Balaban. At 4:00 A.M. Asleep.
Basho. All the field hands.
  Cold night: the wild duck.
  Dozing on horseback / smoke from tea-fires.

Kisagata.
Staying at an inn.
Bécquer, G. I Lay Awake, Wandering in that Limbo.
Belieu. Sleeping Man Must Be Awakened to Be Killed, A.
Bell, M. Last Thing I Say, The.
Berlin. Oh! How I Hate to Get Up in the Morning.
Berryman. Henry by Night.
Bibbins, M. Counting.
Bible, O.T. Song: "Come, my beloved."
Song: "I was asleep but my heart stayed awake."
Bidart. Yoke, The.
Bishop, E. Insomnia.
Sleeping on the Ceiling.
Unbeliever, The.
Blake, W. Cradle Song, A: "Sweet dreams form a shade."
Little Girl Found, The.
Blind. Noonday Rest.
Bly, R. Afternoon Sleep.
Defeated.
Waking from Sleep.
Bogan, L. Tears in Sleep.
Breton, A. Vigilance.
Brontë, C. Is this my tomb, this humble stone.
Brontë, E. Song: "Linnet in the rocky dells, The."
Brown, H. Counting Sheep.
Browning, E. Sleep, The.
Bryden, Diana Fitzgerald. Sleepers Awake.
Buson. Butterfly.
Clinging to the bell.
Home for three days.
Listening to the plovers.
Short nap / Waking.
Sleeping late.
Byrd. Song: "Let not the sluggish sleep."
Byron, G. Alas, they were so young, so beautiful.
Carroll, K. DC Nocturne.
Carryl, C. Sleepy Giant, The.
Carver, R. Quiet Nights.
Cavalli. In that small dark fever of every reawakening.
Cavé, S. Permit.
Celan. All those sleep shapes.
Chikako. On this summer night.
Chin, J. Night.
Chivers. To Isa Sleeping.
Ch'oe Sŭngja. Instead of a Dream.
Christie. Overture.
Chungji. Waking from a Nap.
Clark, T. "Before Dawn..".
Codrescu. Work.
Cofer, J. Hour of the Siesta, The.
Coleridge, M. But in That Sleep of Death What Dreams May Come?
Hush.
Coleridge, S. Pains of Sleep, The.
Cooley. Psalm before Sleep.
Sleep of Beasts, The.
Cornford, F. At Night.
Couzyn. Morning.
Cuddihy. This Body.
Cullen, C. Night Rain.
de Burgos. Poem of My Sleeping Sorrow.
De Kok. This thing we learn from others.
De la Mare. Nod.
Sleeper, The ("As Ann came in one summer's day.").
de Vries, H. My Brother.
Denby. Snoring in New York: An Elegy.
Denham. Song, A: "Morpheus, the humble god, that dwells."
Diego, G. Sleeplessness.
Dodge, M. Early to Bed.
Donne. Song: "Sweetest love, I do not go[e]."
Dougherty. Double Helix.
Douglas, L. To Sleep.
Dowson. Spleen.
Drummond, W. Sleep, Silence' Child.
Dufault. First Night, A.
Dunbar, P. Ere Sleep Comes Down to Soothe

the Weary Eyes.
Duncan, R. Sleep is a Deep and Many Voiced Flood.
Eady. Insomnia.
Egan, R. Sleepy Time Gal.
Eigner. For Sleep.
Ekelof. Moon, The.
Hull, E. Sleep-Song of Grainne over Dermuid, The.
Ellis, R. Hour of Sleep, The.
Éluard, P. To Her of Whom They Dream.
Elytis, O. As Endymion.
Erdrich. I Was Sleeping Where the Black Oaks Move.
Everwine. Just Before Sleep.
Farjeon, E. Good Night.
Fermini, I. Waiting for sleep at the air roots.
Field, E. Sugar-Plum Tree, The.
Wynken, Blynken, and Nod.
Field, M. And on My Eyes Dark Sleep by Night.
Finch, A. For Grizzel McNaught (1709–1792).
Foix. When I Sleep, Then I See Clearly.
Foppa. Nocturne.
Forbes, C. Dark Mirror.
Picture of a Man.
Fournier, R. Encounter.
Francis, R. While I Slept.
Frost, Richard. Night Person, The.
Frost, Robert. Stopping by Woods on a Snowy Evening.
Fusselman, A. Sleeper.
García Lorca. Ghazal of the Dark Death.
Garland, H. Boyish sleep.
Garrett, E. Mimesis.
Gerlach, E. Turn and Turn About.
Ghalib, M. Ghazal 15.
Ginsberg, A. At 4:00 a.m. the two.
Glück, L. New Life, The.
Goethe. To Belinda.
Goll, I. Your Sleep.
Grass. Music for Brass.
Graves, R. She Tells Her Love While Half Asleep.
Greenberg, U. Hour is tired as if it were time for bed, The.
Griffin, B. Care-Charmer Sleep.
Groarke, V. Tonight of Yesterday.
Guillén, J. I Want to Sleep.
Gumilyov [or Gumiliov or Gumilev]. Pre-Memory.
Gunn, T. Hug, The.
Night Piece, The: "Fog drifts slowly down the hill, The."
Touch.
Hadas, R. Mars and Venus.
Haines, Anne. Catching the Scent.
Hall, H. Light Sleep.
Harryman. That Can Not Be Taken Away From It.
Hartnett. Prayer for Sleep, A.
Hauge. Dream, The: "Let us slip into."
Heine, H. Ah, Death is Like the Long Cool Night.
Hernández, M. Humming Eyelashes.
Herrick. To Daisies, Not to Shut So Soon[e].
Upon a Child.
Hill, M. Sleep.
Holland, J. Sleep.
Hood, T. Good Night.
Serenade, A (Fragment): "Lullaby, O, lullaby!"
Housman. When the Eye of Day Is Shut.
Hughes, L. Morning After.
Hughes, T. Roger the Dog.
Hupfeld, H. Let's Put Out the Lights and Go to Sleep.
Inuit Oral Tradition. Utitia'q's Song.
Issa. After a long nap.
Borrowing my house / From insects.
Flopped on the fan.
His sleeping form.
My noontime nap.
Napped half the day.
People working fields.
She's put the child to sleep.
Snail gets up.

Istarú, A. From where you have come.
Ives, G. With Whom, then, should I Sleep?
Jackson, B. Shooting, Killing, Drug Busts, Cover-Ups, Fuck-Ups, Lighter Sides, Weather, and Sports.
Johnson, M. Old Dog.
Joyce, J. I hear an army charging upon the land.
Juana Inés de la Cruz. Because my Lord was born to suffer.
Kabir. Why Arrange the Pillows.
Kannan. What Her Girl Friend Said to Him.
Keats. To Sleep.
Kees. If this Room is Our World.
Kendrick, D. Jenny in Sleep.
Kennedy, X. One Winter Night in August.
Kenyon, J. Often.
Kinsella, T. Endymion.
Kinzie. Want, predation, sleep.
Kipling, R. Sleepy Sentinel, The.
Kirsch, M. Sleep's Underside.
Knott. Death: "Going to sleep, I cross my hands on my chest."
Kocbek. Dialectics.
Kocot, N. Bicycle Poem.
Kollan Alici. What Her Friend Said.
Kolodinsky, A. Midnight.
Korinna [or Corinna]. Are you sleeping endlessly? You never did before, Korinna.
Krohn, Lita Hunter. Recollections.
Kunitz, S. Science of the Night, The.
Labé. Bright Venus, Who Across the Heavens Stray.
Lady Ise. Because we suspected / the pillow would say "I know".
Lauterbach. Boy Sleeping.
Leader, M. Her Door.
Lear, E. Limerick: "There was an Old Man who supposed."
Lee, D. Coming of Teddy Bears, The.
You Too Lie down.
Lee, W. Sex Has a Way.
Leivaditis, Tasos. Eternal Dialogue.
Levis. Cry, The: "Then, everything slept."
Li Ch'ing-chao. Tune: "Dream Song".
Li Po. Abandon.
Livesay, D. Going to Sleep.
Loesser. Two Sleepy People.
Logghe. Insomnia Litany.
Lowther, John. Asleeping: a kind of rendezvous.
Loy. One O'Clock at Night.
Loynaz, D. M. I have slept and I awaken . . . Or I haven't awakened.
MacNeice. Cradle Song: "Clock's untiring fingers wind the wool of darkness, The."
Cradle Song: "Sleep, my darling, sleep."
Magrelli. Before the last curve of the day.
Mansour, J. Auditory Hallucinations.
I Saw You through My Closed Eye.
Martí. I Dream Awake.
Marvin, C. Alba: Aberdeen.
Masaoka Shiki. Amid a jumble of.
Masefield. Sea Fever.
Maxton. Elegies.
Mayer, B. Sonnet: "Beauty of songs your absence I should not show."
McDaniel, J. Following Her to Sleep.
McKay, D. Waking At The Mouth Of The Willow River.
Melville, H. Bench of Boors, The.
Meng Hao Jan. Spring Dawn.
Spring Dawn ("Spring sleep, not yet awake to dawn.").
Springtime Sleep.
Meredith, W. On Falling Asleep by Firelight.
Merrill, J. About the Phoenix.
Merwin. Weight of Sleep, The.
Mew. Not for That City.
Michelangelo Buonarroti. "Night" in the Medici Chapel.
Mihalic. Morning Roar of the City, The.
Miller, W. Willie Winkie.
Mirabai [or Mira Bai]. O friends, I am mad.
Mistral, G. Close to Me.
Night.
Mok, J. Winter Mirror II.

Mole, J. Trick, The.
Monsour. Dream of Dying, A.
Montejo, E. Marina.
Moore, L. Again.
Moore, M. Peter.
Moore, T. Oft In the Stilly Night.
Morley, C. Plumpuppets, The.
Morotskaya, S. Morning sleep / it's sweeter than your palms.
Mukai Kyorai. Even in my town / Now, I sleep.
Murray, J. Lullaby: "Sleep, little architect. It is your mother's wish."
Na Hûidôk. Five A.M.
Nara Singde. Tune: "As If in a Dream".
Niedecker. Subliminal.
Oates. Insomnia.
Oliver, M. Sleeping in the Forest.
  White Night.
Ondaatje. For you I have slept.
Parker, A. Lullaby: "Sleep and rain, two gangsters."
Paschen. Litany.
Pastan. At the Train Museum.
Patumanâr. What She Said.
Pinkney, E. Serenade: "Look out upon the stars, my love."
Piombino. My Lady Carries Stones.
Po Chü-i. After Getting Drunk, Becoming Sober in the Night.
  Dreaming of Yuan Zhen.
  Last Poem.
Popa. Yawn of Yawns, The.
Prados, E. Something Remembered.
Price, R. On, Off, Over.
Prigov. Imagine this: a mighty giant asleep.
Propertius. Ariadne Lay, Theseus' Ship Sailing Away.
Pushkin, A. Lines Written at Night During Insomnia.
Queyras, S. Tonight the Sky Is My Begging Bowl.
Radnóti. Anxiously Autumn Arrives.
Ransom, J. Janet Waking.
Ravenscroft, T. Belmans Song, A.
Raye, D. Milkman, Keep Those Bottles Quiet!
Reid, A. Spell for Sleeping, A.
Reverdy. Behind Eyelids.
Rhodes, M. For Her Children.
  How Fast.
Rimbaud, A. Common Nocturne.
Roberts, E. Evening Song.
Robinson, E. For Karen.
Rochester, J. Song: "Absent from thee, I languish still."
Rodney. Bardo of Sleep and Dream.
Roethke. Root Cellar.
  Waking, The ("I wake to sleep, and take my waking slow.").
Ronsard. Time To Be Up, Marie, Young Sleepyhead.
Rossetti, D. 6a: Nuptial Sleep.
Ruefle. Before Bed.
Rumi. Caring for My Lover.
  Night and Sleep.
  Night comes so people can sleep like fish.
Samson, J. Liminal Highway.
Sandburg, C. Wind Song.
Sappho. May you sleep on the breast of a tender companion.
Sassoon, S. Falling Asleep.
Schley, J. Cradle Song: "Reapers and sowers, gleaners and drovers."
Schultz, R. She Speaks to Her Husband, Asleep.
Schwartz, D. O Child, Do Not Fear the Dark and Sleep's Dark Possession.
Seeger, A. I Have a Rendezvous with Death.
Segovia, F. Ahí Donde Duermes.
  Chrysalis.
  Crisálida.
  There Where You Sleep.
Seward. Invocation, To the Genius of Slumber Written Oct. 1787.
Shakespeare, W. How many thousand of my poorest subjects.
Shapcott, J. My Life Asleep.

Sharma, P. Principles, When I Felt Them.
Shelley, P. Poet wandering on, through Araby, The.
Shrine Priestess of Ise. My mind is dazzled.
Sidney, P. Second Song: "Have I caught my heav'nly jewel."
  Sonnet 39: "Come Sleep! O sleep the certain knot of peace."
Slauerhoff. Within My Life.
Smith, C. To Sleep.
Smith, M. Asleep in the City.
Sŏng [or Sung] Sammun. White Banners.
Soupault. You Who Sleep.
Statius. To Sleep.
Stevenson, A. Marriage, The.
Stevenson, R. Bed in Summer.
Stillman, M. Lullaby for Suzanne.
Stoddard, C. Old Monterey.
Swenson, M. Waking from a Nap on the Beach.
Swinburne. Garden of Proserpine, The.
  Love And Sleep.
Tan Taigi. Swellfish eaten / He chants nembutsu.
Taneda Santoka. Sleep on the ground.
Tayson, R. Nightsweats.
Tennyson, A. Deep in the night I woke: she, near me, held.
  Sweet and Low.
Thomas, E. Lights Out.
Tobin, D. At the Egyptian Exhibit.
Toomer. Evening Song.
Tornes, Beth. Sleep.
Torres, E. Summertime Late Show.
Trakl. Sleep (Second Version).
Tranter. Moment of Waking, The.
Tsvetayeva [or Tsvetaeva]. To Kiss a Forehead Is to Erase Worry.
  Who sleeps at night? No one is sleeping.
Tsvetkov. Like a ruddy child you fall asleep in september.
Tu Fu [or Du Fu]. Daytime Dream.
Unknown. As night succeeds night.
  By your side I am beautiful with my mouth extended and my open arms.
  God, provide the "little horror" with an eternal sleep!
  Grania's Song to Diarmuid.
  If it is but sleep.
  If you sleep you will have nothing but dust.
  Last night you were sleeping in my arms.
  Long night: unable to sleep.
  Lullabies; 2:174.
  Mother's Song.
  Oh for the love of God, sleep, don't let it come to this!
  Weep [or Weepe] You No More [Sad Fountains].
  While I asked myself.
Upton, L. Bedtime Story.
Valentine, J. Sleep Drops Its Nets.
Very. Morning Watch, The.
Villa, D. Sometimes, Doctor, I awake.
Virgil [or Vergil]. Sleep of Palinurus, The.
Voigt. Exile.
Voznesensky [or Voznesenskii]. Dead Still.
Waldman, A. Death is all things we see awake.
Wang Yen-Show. Nightmare, The.
Warner, S. Drawing You, Heavy With Sleep.
Warren-Moore. All-Night Issue, The.
Warren, R. Lullaby: Moonlight Lingers.
Warton, T. Come, gentle sleep, death's image though thou art.
Watson, R. Nirvana.
Webb, F. Gunner, The.
  Port Phillip Night.
Wei Ying-wu. Mooring at Twilight in Yuyi District.
Wen T'ing-yün. Brilliant Moon, A.
Wheelwright. Week End Bid II.
Whitlow. Book of Routh.
Whitman, W. I wander all night in my vision.
  Sleepers, The.
  Sleepers, The.
Wilbur, R. After the Last Bulletins.
  Beasts.
  In the Smoking-Car.

  Walking to Sleep.
Williams, W. Death the Barber.
  Goodnight, A.
Winter, M. Dux Bellorum.
Winters, A. Night Light.
Winters, Y. Sleep.
Wintu Oral Tradition. Sleep.
Wordsworth, W. Slumber Did My Spirit Seal, A.
Wright, J. Old Bud.
Wrigley, R. Milkflowers.
Yang Wan-li. Moored for the Night at the Lan-chi Riverside Courier Station.
Ye Zi. All night I could not sleep.
Yeats. Lullaby: "Beloved, may your sleep be sound."
Yosano Akiko. Channel Boat, The.
  What shall I wear to sleep in alone?
Young, M. J. To Dreams.
Zabolotsky [or Zabolotskii]. Snakes.
Zanzotto. Subnarcosis.
Zukofsky, L. When the crickets.

Sleeping Beauty
Hope, A. Parabola.
Jarrell, R. Sleeping Beauty, The: Variation of the Prince.
Sexton. Briar Rose (Sleeping Beauty).
Unknown. Fair rosa.

Sleepwalking and Sleepwalkers
Dybek. Sleepwalking Soho.
Enzensberger, H. Old Revolution.
See also **Somnambulism and Somnambulists**

Sleet
Kang Ún'gyo. Sleet.
  Sleet.
MacCaig. Sleet.

Sleighs
Burke, J. Sleigh Ride in July.
Yesenin [or Essenin]. Sleigh, The.

Slides
Anderson, A. Licking Wounds.
Einzig et al. Slide Show, The.

Sligo.
See **County Sligo, Ireland**

Sloth
Komunyakaa, Y. Seven Deadly Sins.
Price, V. Sloth.
Roethke. Sloth, The.
Sandburg, C. Galoots.
Watts, I. Sluggard, The.

Sloths
Adcock, F. Three-Toed Sloth, The.
Roethke. Sloth, The.

Slugs
Basho. Still alive.
Birney. Slug in Woods.
Ferguson, G. Slugs.
Gyodai. Inching / From dark to dark—.
Issa. These sea slugs.
Olds, S. Connoisseuse of Slugs, The.
Ransetsu. Large slug slides, A.
  Traveling / old armor.
Redgrove, P. Negotium Perambulans.
Siegel, R. Slug.
Willard, N. Speckled Hen's Morning Song to Biddy Early, The.
See also **Snails**

Slums
Brooks, G. Lovers of the Poor, The.
Daryush. You should at times go out.
Davies, W. H. Rat, The.
Dove, R. Teach Us to Number Our Days.
González, A. Summer in Slumville.
Neto. Saturday in the Sand-Slums.
Oppen. Bicycles and the Apex, The.
Pasolini. Southern Dawn.
Spender, S. Elementary School Classroom in a Slum, An.
Walcott. Laventille.

Smallness
Chuang Tzu. Man: "Consider: if we measured the Four Oceans."
Goedicke. For Walt Whitman.
Hirsch, E. Whitman Leaves the Boardwalk.

Smallpox
Unknown. Little Things.
Things the Smaller the Better.
Waniek. Dusting.

Smallpox
Jones, M. After the Small Pox.
Jonson, B. Epigram, An. To the Small-Pox.
Montagu, L. Saturday: The Small-Pox.
Muldoon, P. Meeting the British.

Smart, Christopher
Cope, W. My Lover.
Gilbert, J. Explicating the Twilight.
Hirsch, E. Wild Gratitude.
Shaw, S. Christopher Smart.

Smells
As-Sabah. I'll Never Know No Sunday in This
Weekday Room.
Basho. As the sound fades.
I don't know.
Bilgere, G. Madeleine, A.
Bishop, E. Prodigal, The.
Bloem, J. C. Honeysuckle.
Bremer, C. Metro Taxqueña.
Metro Taxqueña.
Brewster, E. Where I Come From.
Buson. In pale moonlight.
Plum blossoms scent.
Plum scent / Haloing.
Chang Yü. Pavilion for Listening to Fragrance,
The.
Chin, J. Bergamot.
Clegg, D. Five Senses.
Coleridge, S. Cologne.
Dao. Smells.
Deltoro, A. Almohadas.
Pillows.
Dickinson, E. Essential oils—are wrung.
Donne. Perfume, The.
Eskimo Oral Tradition. Love Song: "I cannot
bear it, I cannot bear it at all."
Fainlight, R. Handbag.
Field. Onycha.
Forhan, C. My Gospel Is.
Goetsch, D. First Time Reading Freud.
Goodman, M. February Ice Years.
Hammerstein. Mister Snow.
Hecht, A. Sarabande on Attaining the Age of
Seventy-Seven.
Herrick. To the Most Fair and Lovely Mistress
Anne Soame, Now Lady Abdie.
Iofe, Y. Thing or Two about Childhood, A.
Kitahara Hakushū. My senses are stirred.
Levertov. Laying the Dust.
Martial. They smell of *Corycian* saffron, of a.
Masaoka Shiki. Heath grass / Sandals.
McCorkle. Infidelities.
McGuckian. Orchid House, The.
McKay, C. Jasmine.
Michelangelo Buonarroti. Very dear though it
was I have bought you.
Michiura, M. Suddenly.
Moore, M. Odor of a Metal Is Not Strong, The.
Muso Soseki. Fragrance of the Udumbara, The.
Olds, S. His Smell.
Probyn. Changes.
Rexroth, K. Spring is early this year.
Salaam. Our Natures Rise.
Shapcott, J. Rosa Odorata.
"Shunzei's Daughter.". Brought by the breeze.
Stevenson, A. Himalayan Balsam.
Supervielle. Sphere.
Swift, J. Lady's Dressing Room, The.
Tarn. Great Odor of Summer, The.
Taylor, E. Meditation. Can. 1.3. Thy Good
Ointment.
Thomas, E. Digging.
Unknown. More than the color.
Now that the fragrance.
Others dress up in their new clothes for the
feast, The.
Vietnamese Oral Tradition. Saigon River, The.
Williams, W. Smell.
Wright, C. Relics.

Smiles
Adams, L. Put on a Happy Face.
Barlow, G. Nook.
Blake, W. Smile, The.

Coffman. Girl/Spit.
Coleridge, M. True to myself am I, and false to
all.
Creeley. Oh No.
Dickinson, E. They might not need me—yet
they might.
Dunbar, P. Made to Order Smile, The.
We Wear the Mask.
Field. La Gioconda; Leonardo Da Vinci, The
Louvre.
Figueroa, J. Homemade Smiles.
Freed, A. Singin' in the Rain.
Graves, R. One Hard Look.
Haavikko. Don't smile. So you won't become a
Buddha.
Hardy, T. Neutral Tones.
Herford. Smile of the Goat, The.
Smile of the Walrus, The.
Landesman. Say "Cheese!".
Leslie, E. Kansas City Kitty.
Rodgers, C. Poem No. 1.
Roggeman. Fata Morgana in Flanders.
Shange. You are Sucha Fool.
Shiomi, M. Disappearing Music for Face.
Unknown. Do not look at me.
Warren-Moore. Dannemora Contraband.
Wilner, E. All the Wide Grin of Him.

Smith, Bessie
Aubert, A. Bessie.
Bessie Smith's Funeral.
Baker, H. Of Walter White's Father in the Rain.
Harper, M. Last Affair: Bessie's Blues Song.
Hayden, R. Homage to the Empress of the
Blues.
Kay, J. Twelve Bar Bessie.
McElroy, C. Mae West Chats It Up with Bessie
Smith.
Ondaatje. Bessie Smith at Roy Thomson Hall.
Vinz. Blues, The.

Smith, John (1580–1631)
Bibb. Capt. Smith and Pocahontas.

Smoke
Basho. Dozing on horseback / smoke from tea-
fires.
Bennett, R. Smoke Animals.
Bodenheim. Death.
Borowski. Farewell to Maria.
Ceravolo. Data.
DuBois, W. Song of the Smoke, The.
Forché. Elegy.
Harbach, O. Smoke Gets in Your Eyes.
Henderson, D. Blackman in the Desecrated
Synagogue—Living in the Last Days.
Hill, G. September Song.
Issa. Over paddies / At its foot.
Jaccottet. Serenity.
Komunyakaa, Y. Smokehouse, The.
Laux, D. Smoke.
Lee, L. Interrogation, The.
Levine, P. Smoke.
Nicholson, N. On the Closing of Millom
Ironworks.
Ono. Smoke Painting.
Riley, P. 171. 115.
Sachs, N. O the Chimneys.
Shinkichi Takahashi. Downy Hair.
"Shunzei's Daughter.". Burning in Secret.
Simic. My Mother was a Braid.
Thoreau. Light-winged smoke, Icarian bird.
Tranter. Backyard.
Twichell. Hunger for Something.
Unknown. Riddle: "Chip chip cherry."
Ya'oz-kest. Smoke Rose.
Yi Yŏng. Who sliced the crescent moon so
small.
Young, K. Song of Smoke.

Smoking and Smokers
Aridjis. Self-Portrait at Age Sixteen.
Aytoun [or Ayton], R. Upone Tabacco.
Campo. Lost in the Hospital.
Copeland, J. Ed.
Dizhur. Silence.
Dunbar, P. Companion's Progress, A.
Ewart. Yorkshiremen in Pub Gardens.
Finney, Janice. Lightning and Thunder.
Ford, Katie. Nocturne: "I can see the whole

city, lights edging the harbor like yellow pins
in uneven."
Glaser, E. Smoking.
Hicok. Radical Neck.
Holz. In the Thiergarten, on a bench, I'm sitting
and smoking.
Kessler, S. Cigarette Case.
Lingafelter, A. Candy Poem, The.
Mallarmé. Pipe, The.
Mersaal, E. Portrait, A.
Myers, J. Perfect Recall.
Nelligan, E. Roundel to My Pipe.
Pearlberg, G.G. Marianne Faithfull's Cigarette.
Penna. Found—my little angel.
Rakha, Y. Dust Storm, The.
Robinson, E. Meshes.
Seferis. Mathios Paskalis among the Roses.
Stanley, G. Fewer.
Straus, M. Luck.
Thribb. Lines on the Award "Pipe Man of the
Year" to Magnus Magnusson.
Vigil, A. At the Stop Light, the Braided Blond
Man.
Wallace, R. Smoking.

Smuggling and Smugglers
Musgrave. I Am Not a Conspiracy Everything
Is Not Paranoid The Drug Enforcement
Administration Is Not Everywhere.
O'Connor, M. On the Road to Denver in a Coat
and Tie, I Think of My Old Friend Master Red
Pine and the Example He Inspires.

Snails
Adcock, F. For a Five-Year-Old.
Bishop, E. Giant Snail.
Bourne, V. Snail, The.
Buson. That snail.
Carroll, L. Lobster Quadrille, A.
Deschamps, E. Ballade 1.
Faverey. Extremely slowly the snail.
Gunn, T. Considering the Snail.
Issa. Climb Mount Fuji.
O summer snail.
Red morning sky.
Snail gets up.
Snail gets up, The.
Under the evening moon.
Issahakian. Climb Mount Fuji.
Under the evening moon.
Lovelace, R. Snail [or Snayl], The.
Maar, Dora. If the Touching Memory.
Montague, J. Small Secrets.
Moore, M. To a Snail.
Murray, L. Mollusc.
Prévert. Song of the snails on their way to a
funeral.
Sarton, M. Eine Kleine Snailmusik.
Taylor, J. Natural Woman.
Thompson, P. Snail's Lesson, The.
See also **Shells; Slugs**

Snakebites
Anyte [or Anytes]. You, too, perished by a bush
with tangled roots.
Rivas, J. Río 1.
River 1.

Snakes
Abse. Snake.
Acholonu. Water Woman.
Amor, P. CXXXIV.
Arp. Snakebread.
Beddoes. Lake, A.
Bell, M. Old Trembling, An.
Belloc. Viper, The.
Bethune, L. Today Tutu Is Beating the Same
Burru As Me.
Braxton, J. Conversion.
Brown, K. Song for Serpents, A.
Bynner. Snake Dance.
Ceni, A. With What Courage.
Césaire, A. Sun Serpent.
Collier, M. Snake, The.
Crozier, L. Fear Of Snakes.
D'Aquino, A. Brief Viper.
Vibora breve.
Dickey, J. Poisoned Man, The.
Dickinson, E. In Winter in my Room.

Snake, The.
Dumas, H.   Island within Island.
England, A.   Art of the Snake Story, The.
Field.   Dying Viper, A.
Frost, C.   St. Louis Zoo, The.
Ghiselin.   Rattler, Alert.
Gonzales, R.   Three Snakes, Strawberry Canyon, Berkeley.
Guillén, N.   Sensemayá.
Harper, M.   Alice.
Hernández Cruz.   Keeping Track of the Serpents.
Herrick.   Silken Snake, The.
Hughes, T.   Cleopatra to the Asp.
ibn Hariq, A.   Galley Oars.
Ko Chônghúi.   What Is History? 1.
Kunitz, S.   Snakes of September, The.
Lawrence, D. H.   Snake.
Levertov.   Closed World, The.
To the Snake.
Mackenzie, K.   Snake, The.
Marvell.   Coronet, The.
Merrill, C.   Erosion.
Milton.   Other way Satan went down, Th'.
To whom thus also th' Angel last repli'd.
Mirabai [or Mira Bai].   Coffer with the Poisonous Snake, The.
Momaday.   Pit Viper.
Morgan, E.   Siesta of a Hungarian Snake.
Nash, O.   Experiment Degustatory.
Nystrom.   Insomnia.
O'Hara, F.   In Memory of My Feelings.
Oliver, L.   Horned Snake, The.
Padel, R.   On the Venom Farm.
Pagis, D.   Snake.
Palmer, V.   Snake, The.
Parnell, P.   Apotheosis of Medusa.
Patchen.   Deer and the Snake, The.
Petit, P.   Snake Dress, The.
Pinsky.   Serpent Knowledge.
Plath.   Medallion.
Ramanujan.   Snakes.
Rankin, J.   Forever the Snake.
Roethke.   Serpent, The.
Rohrer, M.   Winged Snake Found on a Path.
Sadoleto.   Poem of Jacobus Sadoletus on the Statue of Laocoon, The.
Sappho.   With his venom.
Sen, R.   My Mind.
Sen, S.   Love.
Shinkichi Takahashi.   Four Divine Animals.
Sô Chôngju.   Flower-Patterned Snake.
Stewart, S.   Apple.
Tadic.   Laocoon/Serpent.
Tarn.   Before the Snake.
Tsaloumas.   Grudge, The.
Unknown.   Long ago there was a mighty snake, and beings evil to men.
Origin of the Snake, The.
Springfield Mountain.
Van Doren.   Where I Saw the Snake.
Waller, E.   To a Fair Lady Playing with a Snake.
Walwicz.   Tattoo, The.
Warburton, N.   Snake on D. H. Lawrence, The.
Wee, R.   Hoop Snake.
Williams, W.   Sort of a Song, A.
Wright, J.   Killer, The.
Wunderlich, M.   Voluntary Servitude.
Zabolotsky [or Zabolotskii].   Poem about Rain.
Snakes.
Ziedonis.   At Maruža's.

Sneezing
Carroll, L.   Duchess's Lullaby, The.
Kaya Shirao.   Moonlit night / By melon flowers.
Marcus, M.   My Father's Hobby.
Unknown.   Sneezing.
Yayu.   One sneeze / Skylark's.

Snobbery and Snobs
Bentley, N.   Londonderry Air, The.
Berlin.   Slumming on Park Avenue.
Bossidy.   Boston.
Canning, G. et al.   Friend of Humanity and the Knife Grinder, The.
Hannah, S.   Postcard from a Travel Snob.
Hughes, L.   Low to High.
Stephen, J.   On a Rhine Steamer.

Various authors.   On the Hon. George Nathaniel Curzon, Commoner of Balliol.
Young, A.   One Snapshot I Couldn't Take in France, The.

See also **Social Class**

Snoring
Chin, D.   Sleeping Father.
Hughes, L.   Morning After.
Khalid, A.   Relic, A.
Nash, O.   Arthur.

Snow
Adonis [or Adunis].   Passage, The.
Aichinger.   Glimpse from the Past.
Akhmadulina.   Snow Maiden, The.
Albert-Birot.   City is free of sin, The.
Aldington.   Faun Sees Snow for the First Time, The.
Alexander, P.   Crossing.
Ali, A.   Snow on the Desert.
Ammons.   White Echo.
Baillie, J.   Winter's Day, A.
Baker, D.   Envoi: Waking After Snow.
Barclay, A.   Winter.
Basho.   Crossing half the sky.
First snow.
Holy mirror, The.
Let's go.
Sea darkening, The.
This first fallen snow.
To the capital / Snow-clouds forming.
Baumel.   Snow-Day.
Becker, R.   Subject of Our Lives, The.
Behlen, Charles.   Two Ice Storms.
Berlin.   White Christmas.
Berman, D.   Snow: "Walking through a field with my little brother Seth."
Bernard, A.   Snowfall.
Berrigan, T.   For You.
Où sont les neiges des neiges?
Bielski.   Intruder.
Bishop, J.   Aliens.
Blake, W.   Soft Snow.
Blind.   Winter Landscape, A.
Bly, R.   Looking at New-Fallen Snow from a Train.
Six Winter Privacy Poems.
Bobrowski.   Invocation: "High on, above the lake, the mute Nowgorod."
Bond, A.   After Snow-Mobiling.
Bonnefoy.   All, the Nothing, The.
De Natura Rerum.
Snow, The.
Summer Again.
Bridges, R.   London Snow.
Brontë, A.   Song.
Brooks, G.   Cynthia in the Snow.
Brown, H.   Salting of Snow, A.
Brown, L.   Winter Sonnet.
Buson.   Straw sandal half sunk.
Tethered horse, A.
Buxton.   Putting the World to Bed.
Cahn, S.   Let It Snow! Let It Snow! Let It Snow!
Carson, C.   Slate Street School.
Ching An.   Written on the Painting "Cold River Snow".
Chinnov.   Black bird on a black and snowy branch, A.
Chiyojo.   Were it not for / Cries in snow.
Chŏng Chiyong.   Spring Snow.
Chŏng Ch'ŏl.   Snow falling in the pine forest.
Ciardi, J.   First Snow on an Airfield.
Clanchy, K.   Miscarriage, Midwinter.
Clarke, George Elliott.   Blank Sonnet.
Coatsworth.   On a Night of Snow.
Coe, C.   Possibility.
Collins, B.   Shoveling Snow with Buddha.
Snow Day.
Collins, M.   Epiphany.
Crapsey.   Snow.
Triad.
Creeley.   To And.
Crooker.   Grating Parmesan.
Crow, S.   Revival.
Cummings, E. E.   I was sitting in mcsoreley's. outside it was New York and beauti- / fully

snowing.
Daive.   Nomad, A.
Dalchev, A.   Snow: "Over strip-raked iron rooves."
Dauenhauer, R.   Driving in a Snowstorm, King Salmon to Naknek.
Davidson, J.   Snow: "Who affirms that crystals are alive?"
Davies, B.   Snow in Wrexham.
Davies, Lynn.   When You Can't Leave Me Anymore.
Davis, W.   Snow.
Day Lewis.   Snowfall on a College Garden.
De la Mare.   Snow.
There Blooms No Bud in May.
Winter ("Clouded with snow / The cold winds blow.").
Winter ("Green Mistletoe! / Oh, I remember now.").
Dickey, J.   Snow on a Southern State.
Dickinson, E.   Snow, The.
Dillon, G.   Snow.
Djanikian.   When I First Saw Snow.
Dodd, E.   Lyric: "It doesn't matter / whether / a tree falls."
Domanski.   Child of the Earth.
Doolittle, H.   Birds in Snow.
Dougherty.   Cocoons.
Dubie.   Last Poem, Snow Tree.
Dufault.   First Night, A.
Dunbar-Nelson.   Snow in October.
Dybek.   Stain.
Ellingham, L.   Tompkins Sq. Branches With Snowy Arms.
Emerson, R.   Snow-Storm [or Snowstorm], The.
Erdrich, H.   Quiet Earth, The.
Espada.   Prisoners of Saint Lawrence, The.
Etsujin.   First snow / Head clear.
Ficowski.   Assumption of Miriam from the Street in the Winter of 1942, The.
Field.   Cyclamens.
Finkel.   Metaphysic of Snow.
Fordham.   Snow Storm, The.
Snowdrop, The.
Forrester, S.   Melting into pure water the snow buddha.
France, P.   Death.
Francis, R.   Slow.
Frost, R.   Desert Places.
Dust of Snow.
Onset, The.
Patch of Old Snow, A.
Stopping by Woods on a Snowy Evening.
Storm Fear.
García Lorca.   Little Infinite Poem.
Gascoyne.   Rex Mundi.
Snow in Europe.
Gay, Garry.   New snow.
Gillespie, N.   Blessing of Snow, The.
Glazer, M.   Wherein space is constructed that matter may reside in.
Gorbanevskaya.   Hold out a handful of snow.
Graham, J.   San Sepolcro.
Graves, R.   She Tells Her Love While Half Asleep.
Guillén, J.   Snow: "White is lying on top of the green, The."
Hall, D.   Snow, The: "Snow is in the oak."
Han-shan Te-ch'ing.   Snow covers earth and sky everything is new.
Hardy, T.   Light Snow-Fall after Frost, A.
Snow in the Suburbs.
Hartnett.   Moonsnow '77.
Hass, R.   Our Lady of the Snows.
Hikmet.   Cucumber, The.
Hirsch, E.   First Snowfall: Intimations.
Holan.   Snow.
Housman.   Eight O'Clock.
Loveliest of trees, the cherry now.
Howe, S.   He plodded away through drifts of ice.
Humphries, R.   Dafydd ap Gwilym Resents the Winter.
Issa.   Delicious Looking!
Gratitude for gifts.
Here.

Just beyond the gate.
Just by being / I'm here.
Pissing in the snow.
Shinano.
Snow is melting, The.
This, I guess, is.
Writing shit about new snow.
Italicus.   Memories of past struggles were expelled by fear.
Ivanov, Binyo.   Tale That's Not a Tale, A.
Ivey, M.   Preparing for Snow.
Jacob, M.   War.
Jinkag Haesim.   By the Water.
Johnson, K.   Meadow, The.
Juarroz.   To die, but far away.
Justice, D.   Absences.
Kagami Shiko.   Night snow / Neighbor's cock. Small fish-boats / After what.
Kawai Suimei.   Snowflame.
Keller, D.   After the First Snow.
Kenjeev.   And a fool, and a smart one, a miser.
Kikaku.   O Great Buddha.
Kim Hyesun.   Driving During a Shower. Mice.
Kim Suyŏng.   Snow.
Kleinzahler.   Snow in North Jersey.
Konishi Raizan.   Green, green, green / Herbs splash.
Kuzma.   Ice Skating.
Laird, N.   Evening forecast for the region, The.
Levine, P.   Snow: "Today the snow is drifting."
Lingche.   Spending the Night at East Forest Temple.
Liu Ch'ang-ch'ing.   Snow on Lotus Mountain.
Liu Tsung-yüan.   River-Snow.
Loden.   My Test Market.
Longfellow, H.   Cross of Snow, The. Excelsior.
Fragment: December 18, 1847.
Snow-Flakes.
Lowell, A.   Falling Snow.
Lowell, J.   First Snowfall [or Snow-Fall], The. First Snow-fall, The.
Loynaz, D. M.   Snow.
Lu Lun.   Black moon geese fly high.
Lu Mei-Po.   Snow and the Plum, The—1. Snow and the Plum, The—2.
Lux.   Marine Snow at Mid-Depths and Down.
Mackinnon, R.   After the Snow.
MacLeish.   Snowflake Which Is Now and Hence Forever, The.
MacNeice.   Snow.
Macphee, K.   Night before the last day of January, The.
Mahon.   Snow Party, The.
Mallarmé.   Virginal, vibrant, and beautiful dawn, The.
Masaoka Shiki.   I keep asking. Such silence / Snow tracing wings.
Matthews, W.   Grief.
Mayer, B.   End of Human Reign on Bashan Hill, The.
Generic Elbows.
McClatchy.   Old Song Ended, An.
McGough, R.   Snow Poem.
Mechain, G.   Snowfall, The.
Meyerhoff, J.   Snow.
Middleton, David.   Embertide in Advent.
Mikhail, D.   Snow Storm.
Millay, E.   Buck in the Snow, The.
Milne, A.   More It Snows, The.
Miyazawa Kenji.   Dawn: "Rolling snow turned peach-color."
Monk, M.   Fire Us with Ice, Burn Us with Snow.
Mooney, M.   Footballers in the Snow.
Morley, D.   White, White.
Moss, H.   New Hampshire.
Mueller, J.   Betrayed by KC.
Mueller, L.   Not Only the Eskimos.
Mullen, L.   Stopping By.
Mun Chônghui.   Seeing Snow.
Murray, J.   Once in a Lifetime, Snow.
Muso Soseki.   Reply to Suzan Osho's Snow Poem.
Snow.

Nash, O.   Winter Morning.
Nemerov.   Because You Asked about the Line between Prose and Poetry.
Niedecker.   Element Mother, The.
Nims, J.   Not / above / a juggler's.
No Hyangnim.   Country Where Snow Has Not Yet Fallen, A.
Pack, R.   Her Black Hair.
Paek Sŏk.   Natasha, the White Donkey, and I.
Page, P.   Stories of Snow.
Paljor, N.   Cars stuck in the snow.
Palmer, M.   Letter 5.
Pasternak, B.   Snow Is Falling.
Winter Night: "Snow, snow over the whole land."
Peacocke.   Late Snow.
Peaux, A.   Cold Landscape.
Pedretti, Erica.   It's Snowing in Plouda.
Piercy.   Snow, Snow.
Pizarnik.   Suspicion.
Po Chü-i.   Passing Tianmen Street in Chang'an and Seeing a Distant View of Zhongnan Mountains.
Village Snow, Sitting at Night.
Preil, G.   Little Research in Snow, A.
Prufer, K.   Car Has Fallen from a Bridge, A.
Quintana.   Poem for Salt.
Rakosi.   January of a Gnat, The.
Ray, H.   Snow Song.
Reverdy.   Breath.
Rothman, D.   Let It Snow.
Ryuichi.   Invisible Tree.
Samawi, S.   Dream of a Snow Flower, The.
Saner.   Morning Snowfield.
Sanpu.   First cherry blossoms.
Sarton, M.   December Moon.
Schuyler, J.   White City, A.
Shenstone.   Lines Written on a Window at The Leasowes.
Simon, M.   Snow.
Smrek, J.   December: "God gave a sign—and the."
Snodgrass.   One. now another. one.
Sokan.   Cold, yes / But don't test.
Southwell.   Burning Babe, The.
Stafford, W.   Holding the Sky.
Near.
Stanley, T.   Snow-Ball, The.
Stephens, J.   Hangman.
Stevens, W.   Annual Gaiety.
Snow Man, The.
Stewart, S.   Forms of Forts.
Stroud, J.   Manna.
Su Tung-p'o.   Terrace in the Snow, The.
Tagliabue.   March Blizzard.
Tantan.   On the rock / Waves can't reach.
Tate, J.   Coming Down Cleveland Avenue.
Thomas, E.   Snow.
Thaw.
Thompson, F.   To a Snowflake.
Thompson, P.   Snow-Flakes, The.
Tomlinson, C.   Second Song.
Snow Signs.
Trommer, R.   If You Listen.
Tuckerman, F.   Rhotruda.
Twichell.   Snow in Condoland.
Unamuno.   Snowfall Is So Silent, The.
Unknown.   Bitter Cold.
Riddle: "Round the house and round the house / and there lies a white glove in the window."
Riddle: "White bird featherless."
Warren, R.   Snow Day.
Wells, J.   Fool's Errand.
White, E.   Chairs in Snow.
Wilbur, R.   First Snow in Alsace.
Willard, N.   Angels in Winter.
Willerton, Chris.   Winter at the Intersection.
Williams, C. K.   Snow: II.
Williams, G.   City Under Snow.
Williams, M.   Listen.
Williamson, G.   New Year's: A Short Pantoum.
Wojahn.   Photo of My Father in a Snowbound Train.
Riding the Empire Builder, 1948.
Wordsworth, W.   Lucy Gray.
Wright, J.   Sparrows in a Hillside Drift.

Wright, R.   In the falling snow.
Wrigley, R.   Ashtray in the Snow.
Wylie.   Velvet Shoes.
Yi Chehyŏn.   After the Snow in the Mountains.
Yi Chinmyŏng.   Snow: "It snowed comfortably. No, that's not it. In the beginning, it snowed violently."
Young Bear.   From the Spotted Night.
Yu Hsin.   Running Into Snow While Journeying Through the Suburbs.
Zimmer.   Lester Tells of Wanda and the Big Snow.
Zucker, R.   Kind of Catastrophe, A.
Zukofsky, L.   As to How Much.
(Ryokan's scroll).
See also **Snowflakes; Snowmen**
Snow White
Bennett, B.   True Story of Snow White, The.
Kirsch, S.   Already the Air Smells of Snow.
Koertge.   Seven Dwarfs, Each on His Deathbed, Remember Snow White, The.
Sexton.   Snow White and the Seven Dwarfs.
Snowdrops
Evans, M.   Snowdrops.
Fordham.   Snowdrop, The.
Hughes, T.   Snowdrop.
MacBeth [or Macbeth].   Snowdrops.
Snowflakes
Bly, R.   Watering the Horse.
Bodecker.   First Snowflake.
Cha.   Morcels: Between the Lines.
Dickinson, E.   Snow flakes / I counted till they danced so.
Hashin.   No sky and no earth at all.
Lau, A.   Wintermelon.
Merrill, J.   Processional.
Muso Soseki.   Mugoku Osho's Snow Poem. Snow Garden.
Snow Valley.
Nemerov.   Snowflakes.
Nims, J.   Not / above / a juggler's.
Orlen.   Onomastics and the Falling Snow.
Sansom, C.   Snowflakes.
Strand.   Piece of the Storm, A.
See also **Snow**
Snowmen
Bodecker.   Snowman Sniffles.
Gay, Garry.   Slowly. . . / The Scarecrow.
McGough, R.   Snowman in a field.
Pagis, D.   Winter's End.
Wilbur, R.   Boy at the Window.
Soap
Im Yŏngjo.   Soap.
Lear, E.   Limerick: "There was an old person of Bow."
MacNeice.   Soap Suds.
Muldoon, P.   Soap-Pig, The.
Peacocke.   Soap.
Stern, G.   Soap.
Weatherford, C.   Tar Baby on the Soapbox, The.
Young, K.   Boiling, The.
Sobriety
Blane, R.   That Face.
Carver, R.   Gravy.
Goff, C.   First Sober Morning, The.
Hô Sugyŏng.   Sober, Remaining.
Martin, H.   That Face.
Morris, T.   Just Say No Blues.
Soccer
McCabe, C.   Summer in Killowen.
Merrill, C.   Boy Juggling a Soccer Ball, A.
Mooney, M.   Footballers in the Snow.
Norris, L.   Ballad of Billy Rose, The.
Piccione.   Watching Ants Play Soccer in Central Park.
Rouse, A.   England Nil.
Sáenz.   Between Worlds.
Social Class
Adewale, T.   Explorer of Aromas.
Akinlolu, S.   Can't You See?
Anti-Jabobins, The.   Canto First.
Auden.   Capital, The.
Barkova, A.   Tatar Anguish.
Barresi.   Class Dress.
Bayly.   Novel of High Life, A.

Belieu. I Can't Write a Poem about Class Rage.
Belloc. Lord Heygate.
Bentley, N. Londonderry Air, The.
Berkson, B. Stains of Stalin.
Berlin. Top Hat, White Tie, and Tails.
Bersohn. Dignity of Labor, The.
Betjeman. False Security.
Breedlove, N. Black and Divided or Chittlins and Caviar.
Breeze. Wife of Bath Speaks in Brixton Market.
Brooks, G. Beverly Hills, Chicago.
Buddingh'. Ode to the Bicycle.
Burke, J. Ain't It a Shame About Mame.
Canning, G. *et al.* Friend of Humanity and the Knife Grinder, The.
Canning, G. *et al.* Canto First.
Cawein. On Reading the Life of Haroun Er Reshid.
Chang K'o-chiu. Tune: "Merriment Before the Palace Hall".
Chang Yang-hao. Tune: "Sheep on the Mountain Slope".
Chimombo. Of Promises and Prophecy.
Clare, J. My Mary.
Cleyre, V. Out of the Darkness.
Codrescu. Circle Jerk.
Cook, W. Still-Life with Woodstove.
Cornwall. Leveller, The.
Coslow, S. (I'm In Love With) The Honorable Mr. So and So.
Coward. Stately Homes of England, The.
Crabbe, G. Baileys, The.
Creeley. After Lorca.
Cullen, C. For a Lady I Know.
Cummings, E. E. Come,gaze with me upon this dome.
Little joe gould has lost his teeth and doesn't know where.
Dalton, R. Petty Bourgeoisie, The.
Davies, Grahame. Red.
Dickinson, E. Pedigree of Honey, The.
Doyle, R. E. Ma Ramon.
Duhamel. Art.
Ebb, F. Class.
Enzensberger, H. Middle Class Blues.
Short History of the Bourgeoisie.
Ewer. Gentlemen.
Fenton, J. This Octopus Exploits Women.
Field, E. Lower East Side: The George Bernstein Story.
Fuller, H. Day Labor.
Hamill, G. Limerick: "If you're aristocratic, said Nietzsche."
Hands, E. Poem on the Supposition of the Book Having Been Published and Read, A.
Hannah, S. Where is Talcott Parsons Now?
Hargreaves, W. Burlington Bertie from Bow.
Harris, J. Don't Cheapen Yourself.
Harrison, T. Earthen Lot, The.
Hart, L. Lady Is a Tramp, The.
Hernandez, D. Pigeons.
Heynen. Clean People, The.
Hill, G. He adored the desk, its brown-oak inlaid with ebony.
Hirsch, E. Two Suffering Men.
Hughes, L. High to Low.
Low to High.
Innocent, C. Poor Man's Life, The.
Jones, E. Song of the Lower Classes, The.
King, I. If Ye Hivni.
Kinsella, J. Bright Cigar-Shaped Object Hovers Over Mount Pleasant, A.
Kirkpatrick. Class.
Knight, E. WASP Woman Visits a Black Junkie in Prison, A.
Knott. Funny Poem.
Komunyakaa, Y. Salt.
Kumar, A. Primary Lessons in Political Economy.
Lapierre, B. Tomorrow's Hope.
Lawrence, D. H. O! Start a Revolution.
Li Po. Third month in T'ientsin, The.
Liu Chih. Tune: "Sheep on the Mountain Slope".
Liu Yu Hsi. Raven Robe Lane.
Lux. Swimming Pool, The.

Marquis. Mehitabel's Song.
Martial. For rank, descent and title famed.
Masefield. Consecration, A.
Medina, T. Poem for Teacup Mantlepiece Poets Palpitating Poot Booty Plagiarists Imprisoned in Ivy League White Supremacist Mental Biological Warfare Labs.
Melville, H. Rose Farmer, The.
Meredith, W. American Living Room, The: A Tract.
Mullen, H. Mantra for a Classless Society, or Mr. Roget's Neighborhood.
Murray, L. Sprawl is the quality.
Nash, O. Song of Songs, The.
Nekrasov, V. So who of us.
Ni Dhomhnaill. As for the Quince.
Ogundipe-Leslie. Song at the African Middle Class.
Parra, V. Because the Poor Have Nothing.
Pelegrin, A. Trailer Trash.
Pollarolo, G. While My Father.
Porter, C. Tale of the Oyster, The.
Pound, E. Garden, The: "Like a skein of loose silk blown against a wall."
Portrait d'une Femme.
Praed. Arrivals at a Watering-Place.
Good Night to the Season.
Ralin, Radoi. Seduced and Abandoned.
Rattenbury, A. War Memoir, A.
Rimbaud, A. Bad Blood.
Rosenberg, I. Dawn Behind Night.
Rosenberg, L. They Are Planning to Cancel the School Milk Program to Fund a Tax Cut for the Middle Class.
Rushin. Word Problems.
Rutsala. Shame.
Sahagún, C. Life in the Provinces.
Selman, R. 21 East 10th, 2BR, WBF, EIK.
Shepherd, R. Three A.M. Eternal.
Sholl. Late Psalm.
Sondheim. Ladies Who Lunch, The.
Sosnora. Supreme Hour, The.
Spark. Evelyn Cavallo.
Stickney, T. Six O'Clock.
Strong, L. Old Woman, Outside the Abbey Theater, An.
Thompson, D. P. Intelligence Quotients.
Torregian. After Mayakovsky.
Tsvetayeva [*or* Tsvetaeva]. Staircase.
Unknown. How cut haft for an axe?
One Little Boy.
Seafarer, The.
Vicar of Bray, The.
With a mere glance at the fur coat.
Verlaine. Mille e tre.
Vicioso. Perspectives.
Wachtel. On Class and Desire.
Workingman's Wife: *Who She Is, Who She Is Not, What She Buys—And Why.*
Wang Fan-chih. Poem: "When the rich pass proudly by."
Wang Wei. Peerless Lady, The.
Wells, C. Problem, A.
Whitman, W. Native Moments.
Song for Occupations, A.
Whittier. Maud Muller.
Wickham. Butler and the Gentleman, The.
Wilcox, E. No Classes!
Williams, H. Like Father.
Zagajewski. Fire: "Probably I am an ordinary middle-class."

Social Protest
Afrika, T. Hit squad.
Alexie. On the Amtrak from Boston to New York City.
Anderson, J. American Flag.
Anhalt, D. That Jewish Crusader.
Baca. Immigrants in Our Own Land.
Bly, R. After the Industrial Revolution, All Things Happen at Once.
Brandi. Preparing the Nets at New Stuyahok.
Breton, A. War.
Brome. Leveller's Rant, The.
Brooks, G. First Fight. Then Fiddle.
Lovers of the Poor, The.
Cambridge, A. Fashion.

Castillo, O. Distances.
Clough. Latest Decalogue, The.
Conquest. Bagpipes at the Biltmore.
Cornish, S. Brother of the Streets.
Davidson, J. Thirty Bob a Week.
Davie, D. Barnsley and District.
Dove, R. Rosa.
Dylan. Lonesome Death of Hattie Carroll, The.
Emerson, R. Ode, Inscribed to W. H. Channing.
Enzensberger, H. Song for Those Who Know.
Espada. All the People Who Are Now Red Trees.
Cockroaches of Liberation.
Year I Was Diagnosed with a Sacrilegious Heart, The.
Forché. Ourselves or Nothing.
Fort, C. For Martin Luther King.
Francia, L. In Gurgle Veritas.
Gilbert, C. Theory of Curve.
Ginsberg, A. America: "America I've given you all and now I'm nothing."
Howl.
Gurney, I. Strange Hells.
Gwala. Getting off the ride.
Hairston. Alabama Bus.
Harrison, T. V.
Henderson-Holmes. "C" ing in Colors: Blue.
Hirsch, E. Song: "This is a song for the speechless."
Hood, T. Song of the Shirt, The.
Hughes, L. Advertisement for the Waldorf-Astoria.
Beaumont to Detroit: 1943.
Black Clown, The.
Freedom Train.
Goodbye Christ.
I, Too.
Let America Be America Again.
Hwang Jiwoo. Variety Show, 1984.
Ignatow, D. All Quiet.
Kizer, C. Race Relations.
Komunyakaa, Y. How I See Things.
Knights of the White Camellia and Deacons of Defense.
2527th Birthday of the Buddha.
Lawrence, D. H. How Beastly the Bourgeois Is.
Levertov. At 6 a.m. the ominous zooming, war-sound, of helicopters breaks into our sleep.
At the Justice Department November 15, 1969.
Day the Audience Walked Out on Me, and Why, The.
Protesting at the Nuclear Test Site.
Lowell, R. After the Surprising Conversions.
March 2, The.
Memories of West Street and Lepke.
"Lu Hsün.". Call to Arms.
Lyndsay [*or* Lindsay], D. Complaynt [*or* Compleynt *or* Complaint] of the Comoun [*or* Common] Weill of Scotland, The.
MacSweeney. Far Cliff Babylon.
Flame Ode.
Ode: "Urals post-master, this is your."
Shells Her Auburn Hair Did Show, The.
Madhubuti. Killing Memory.
Mapanje. On Being Asked to Write a Poem for 1979.
McDonald, Joe. I-Feel-Like-I'm Fixin'-To-Die Rag.
McElroy, C. Foul Line—1987.
McKain. Opening Day.
McKay, C. If We Must Die.
Mikolowski, K. Witness, The.
Millay, E. Apostrophe to Man.
Moorer. Jim Crow Cars.
Mottram. Elegy 11: Ford.
Mudrooroo Narogin. Peaches and Cream.
Mueller, L. Triage.
Mulford. Nevrazumitelny.
Nye, N. Rebellion against the North Side.
O'Brien, S. Cousin Coat.
Otero, B. Censored.
Pak Nohae. Wind to the Stones, The.
Peacock, T. Rich and Poor; or, Saint and Sinner.
Perdomo, W. Revolutionary.
Picasso. Bottle of Suze, A.
Pickard, T. Devil's Destroying Angel Exploded,

The.
 My Pen.
Piercy. Low Road, The.
Poniewaz. Why Young Men Wore Their Hair
 Long in the Sixties.
Randall, D. Ballad of Birmingham.
Ratushinskaya [or Ratushinskaia]. I Had a
 Strange Dream.
Raworth. Future Models May Have Infra-Red
 Sensors.
Raymond, V. People, No, The.
Rexroth, K. August 22, 1939.
 Bad Old Days, The.
Rich, A. Burning of Paper instead of Children,
 The.
Rukeyser, M. Rational Man.
Rykard, R. Whole two weeks after The Million
 Man March; and still, if you'd ask me, this is
 all I could say about it, A.
Sadoff. Civil Rights.
Scott, P. Dying In.
Seeger, P. Where Have All the Flowers Gone?
Sepamla. Measure for Measure.
Shelley, P. Song to the Men of England.
Sheppard, R. Empty Diary 1968.
Starbuck, G. Of Late.
Strasser, J. Protest at Los Alamos, August 2000.
Troupe. Boomerang: A Blatantly Political
 Poem.
Unknown. Beautiful Nahid rose up and in her
 clear voice cried, The.
 Diggers' Song, The.
 I Don't Want to Be a Soldier.
 Soup Kitchen Song.
 Thou ermined judge, pull off that sable cap!
 Uprising of the 20,000, The.
Waldman, A. Dispersal of It.
Walker, M. For My People.
 Street Demonstration.
Wayman. Picketing Supermarkets.
Weaver, A. Picnic, an Homage to Civil Rights,
 The.
Whittier. Astræa.
Wordsworth, W. On the Projected Kendal and
 Windermere Railway.
Wormser. Soul Music.
Wright, D. Protest Poem, A.
Yao Chen. Ballad on the Investigation of a
 Disaster.
Zamora, D. Report on the Protest in Front of
 the United States Embassy by the Pino Grande
 Movement, A.

Social Reform
Afrika, T. Dancing in my city.
Kasdorf. Poetry in America.
Machado Ruiz. For Don Francisco Giner de
 Los Ríos.
Mendelssohn Anna. Britain 1967.
Otero, B. Written in Rain.
Unknown. Ode to a Jacobin.
Ward, Geoff. What's Wrong.

Social Work and Social Workers
Addonizio. Broken Sonnets.
Millar, J. Midlife.

Socialism
Conquest. Progress.
Duff, V. Letters from an Exile.
Herbert, W. Socialist Manifesto for East
 Balgillo, The.
Hughes, L. Come to the Waldorf-Astoria.
Ishikawa Takuboku. After Endless Discussions.
Kay, J. Shoes of Dead Comrades, The.
Kodama Kagai. Setting Sun, The.
Lindsay, V. Why I Voted the Socialist Ticket.
Mitchison. To Some Young Communists from
 an Older Socialist.
Wardman, G. Revisionism.
Yevtushenko [or Evtushenko]. John Reed's
 Monologue.
Young, A. And It Shall Come.

Socrates
Duemer. Theory of Tragedy.
Johnson, Peter. Socrates.
Lefroy. Idler Listening to Socrates Discussing
 Philosophy with His Boy-Friends, An.
Levchev, Vladimir. Athens.

Sodom
Duncan, R. This Place Rumord to Have Been
 Sodom.
Lesley, G. Behold, how Sodom swaggers in its
 Pride.
Whittier. Cities of the Plain, The.

Softball
Hugo, R. Missoula Softball Tournament.
Smith, R. Softball at Julia Tutwiler Prison.

Solace
Arlen, H. One for My Baby (And One More for
 the Road).
Bowles, W. To the River Cherwell.
Carver, R. Window, The.
Chapman, G. For words want art and art wants
 words to praise her.
Churchyard. That humor now, declines for age
 drawes on.
Dunn, S. Guardian Angel, The.
Eliscu, E. Without a Song.
Hammerstein. My Favorite Things.
Harris, W. Samantha Is My Negro Cat.
Hawoldar. You.
Herrick. To the Willow-Tree.
Hölderlin. Patmos.
Hopkins, G. No Worst, There Is None. Pitched
 Past Pitch of Grief.
Kruit, J. Post Heads.
Lamartine. Valley, The.
Magidson, H. Music, Maestro, Please!
Mercer, J. One for My Baby (And One More
 for the Road).
Montagu, L. Receipt to Cure the Vapours, A.
Rose, B. Without a Song.
Surrey. Prison in Windsor Castle.
Winchilsea. Nocturnal Reverie, A.

Soldiers
Adcock, B. Kaiser's Burnout.
Adkins, G. Arthur.
Aeschylus. If I were to tell of our labours, our
 hard lodging.
Al-Qasim. Sons of War.
Alberti. Soldiers Sleep, The.
Albizzi. Prolonged Sonnet: When the Troops
 were Returning from Milan.
Alegría. Nocturnal Visits.
Alterman, N. Around the Campfire.
 Silver Platter, The.
 Time and the Response, The.
Amichai, Y. God Has Mercy on Kindergarten
 Children.
 Rain on the Battlefield.
 Two Poems about the First Battles.
Askew, A. Ballad Which Anne Askew[e] Made
 and Sang When She Was in Newgate, The.
Asquith. Volunteer, The.
Auden. O What Is That Sound [Which So
 Thrills the Ear].
 Roman Wall Blues.
 Taller To-day.
Ausländer, R. So That No Light Would Remain
 to Love Us.
Avidan, D. Settlement.
Bachri. Soldiers.
Balaban. Guard at the Binh Thuy Bridge, The.
Baqi. Your rebellious glance lines up the
 cavalry.
Basho. Summer grasses.
 Summer grasses / All that remains.
 Ungraciously, under.
Baton, M. Unspeakable Wounds of War, The.
Bayly. Soldier's Tear, The.
Bell, M. Uniform, The.
Bertrand. Mason, The.
Bierce. Corporal.
Bierds, L. Van Leeuwenhoek: 1675.
Blanco, P. Soldiers.
Blunden. Two Voices.
Bly, R. Russian, The.
Boker. Dirge for a Soldier.
 Oh! craven, craven! while my brothers fall.
Bond, E. First World War Poets.
Borges. Soldier of Urbina, A.
Bottoms. Sunday Dinner, A.
Brecht, B. General, your tank is a powerful
 machine.

Brooke, R. Soldier, The: "If I should die, think
 only this of me."
Brooks, G. Gay Chaps at the Bar.
 My Dreams, My Works, Must Wait Till After
 Hell.
 Still Do I Keep My Look, My Identity.
Brown, D. When I Am 19 I Was a Medic.
Browning, E. Forced Recruit, The.
Bryce, Colette. Break.
Buffoni, F. To be soldiers together and allies.
Bunno [Wen Wang or King Wen]. Song of the
 Bowmen of Shu [1954].
Burgoyne, J. Dashing White Sergeant, The.
Burns, R. I Once Was a Maid.
Butterfield, F. G. For Services Rendered.
Byron, G. There Was a Sound of Revelry by
 Night.
Cameron, N. Forgive Me, Sire.
Campbell, R. Volunteer's Reply to the Poet,
 The.
Campbell, T. Soldier's Dream, The.
Carman, B. Buie Annajohn.
Casey, M. On What the Army Does with
 Heads.
Castillo, S. Contra, The.
Causley. Song of the Dying Gunner A.A.1.
Cecil. Apology.
Chin Ho. Ballad of the Maiden of Lan-ling.
Clare, J. Returned Soldier, The.
 Song: "Sad was the day when my Willie did
 leave me."
Coleman, H. OK Corral East: Brothers in the
 Nam.
Collins, W. How Sleep the Brave.
Cortez, Sarah. Attempt to Locate.
Cowley, M. Danny.
Crane, S. War Is Kind.
Curtis, T. Eighth Dream, The.
Cynan. Monastir.
Dalton, R. Soldier's Rest.
Davenant [or D'Avenant]. Soldier Going to the
 Field, The.
Derieva, R. Theory of Recruiting.
Ditzanny, R. My Hand is Extended for the
 Peace of the Galilee.
Djabali. For My Torturer, Lieutenant D.
Donne. Canonization, The.
Douglas, K. Aristocrats.
 Vergissmeinnicht.
Dove, R. Alfonzo Prepares to Go Over the Top.
Doyle, S. Private of the Buffs; or, The British
 Soldier in China.
Dubie. Anagram Born of Madness at
 Czernowitz, 12 November 1920.
Duchamp. Deferment.
Dugan, A. Portrait from the Infantry.
 Self-Exhortation on Military Themes.
 Stentor and Mourning.
Duhig, I. Chocolate Soldier.
Dunbar, P. Black Samson of Brandywine.
 Colored Soldiers, The.
 When Dey 'Listed Colored Soldiers.
Dunn, D. War Blinded.
Duo Duo. When the People Stand Up out of the
 Hard Cheese.
Duran, J. Spanish Peasant Boy.
Eliot, T. S. Triumphal March.
Elliot, J. Flowers of the Forest, The.
Elliott, E. Battle Song.
Elytis, O. March toward the Front, The.
Emerson, R. [In an Age of Fops and Toys].
 Voluntaries.
Enquist, A. December Offensive.
Evans, G. Horse on a Fence.
Eytan Eytan. Wind Grinds, The.
Farrow, S. Civil War, The.
Feldman, I. Se Aprovechan.
Fiacc. Enemy Encounter.
Fitzgerald, R. Amphibians.
Flecker, J. War Song of the Saracens.
Fletcher, J. Rebel, A.
Foley, M. Sword is a cold bride. Yuk!, The.
Ford, F. That Exploit of Yours.
Ford Lena, Guilbert. Keep the Home Fires
 Burning (Till the Boys Come Home).
Frankau. Deserter, The.

Freneau. American Soldier, The.
Jeffery, or, the Soldier's Progress.
Frost, R. Not to Keep.
Garrick. Heart of Oak.
Gascoigne. Soldiers, behold, and captains, mark
  it well.
Gibson, W. Breakfast.
Gifford, H. For Soldiers.
Gilbert, W. I Am the Very Model [or Pattern] of
  a Modern Major-General.
Gilmore, P. When Johnny Comes Marching
  Home.
Graves, R. Sergeant-Major Money.
Greenberg, U. Poem of Blessing.
  Splendor from the Splendid.
Grenfell, J. Into Battle.
Grimke, C. Gathering of the Grand Army, The.
Guernsey, B. Maps.
Guest, E. Things that Make a Soldier Great,
  The.
Gunn, T. Innocence.
Guri, H. Like Beirut.
  On a Stone Pillow.
  Prayer: "Bestow a blessing on the young men,
    because the time has come."
Gurney, I. Bach and the Sentry.
  Bohemians, The.
  First Time In.
  La Gorgue.
  Mangel-Bury, The.
  Towards Lillers.
Gwynn, R. Body Bags.
Hardy, T. Colonel's Soliloquy, The.
  Drummer Hodge.
  Man He Killed, The.
  Men Who March Away.
  Often When Warring.
  Subalterns, The.
Harjo, J. No.
Hart, K. Story, The.
Hayden, R. Dream, The.
Heaney, S. Toome Road, The.
Hefer, H. Sappers, The.
  We Left Slowly.
Hemingway. Champs d'Honneur.
  Riparto d'Assalto.
Hood, R. Faithless Nelly Gray.
Hopkins, G. Soldier, The.
Horgan. Tintype of a Private in the Fifteenth
  Georgia Infantry.
Housman. Deserter, The.
  Epitaph: "Here dead lie we because we did not
    choose."
  Epitaph on an Army of Mercenaries.
  Grenadier.
  Lancer.
  Oh stay at home, my lad, and plough.
  Soldier from the Wars Returning.
Huddle. Vermont.
Hudgins. Serenades in Virginia.
  Soldier on the Marsh, A.
Hughes, L. Casualty.
Hughes, T. Six Young Men.
Hugo, R. Where We Crashed.
Inada. 6. The Legend of the Great Escape.
  10. The Legend of the Magic Marbles.
Irby. Heredom.
Jacob, M. War.
Jarmain. Embarkation, 1942.
Jarrell, R. Description of Some Confederate
  Soldiers, A.
  Eighth Air Force.
  O My Name It Is Sam Hall.
  Prisoners.
Johnson, Harold L. Names of Summer, The: A
  War Memory.
Jones, D. And to Private Ball it came as if a
  rigid beam of great weight.
  This Dai adjusts his slipping shoulder-straps.
Jones, T. Thirty soldiers, exhausted and grim-
  faced.
Katz, M. Into a Dead Zone.
Kennedy, B. Bad Luck to This Marching.
Kharms. Death of the Wild Warrior.
Kim, Suji Kwock. Occupation.
Kinnell. Vapor Trail Reflected in the Frog Pond.

Kipling, R. Absent-Minded Beggar, The.
  Arithmetic on the Frontier.
  Ballad of East and West, The.
  Boots.
  Bridge-Guard in the Karroo.
  Brown Bess.
  Cells.
  Cholera Camp.
  Danny Deever.
  Fuzzy-Wuzzy.
  Gentlemen-Rankers.
  Gunga Din.
  Recessional.
  Return, The.
  Screw-Guns.
  Shillin' a Day.
  Song to Mithras, A.
  Tommy.
  When first under fire an' you're wishful to duck.
  Widow at Windsor, The.
Kirstein. Foresight.
  P.O.E.
  Rank.
  Snatch.
Koch, K. To World War Two.
Krapf. Civil War Veteran from Indiana Recalls
  Visiting with Walt Whitman in a Washington
  Hospital, A.
Kunitz, S. Careless Love.
Kushner, A. Picture, A.
Kuzmin. Antinous.
Lamar. Carmelita.
Larkin, P. Homage to a Government.
  MCMXIV.
Lawrence, D. H. Tommies in the Train.
Lee, M. Kiss, A.
Lenski, H. Near the Mill.
Levchev. Front Line.
Lewis, A. All Day It Has Rained.
  Dawn on the East Coast.
  Infantry.
  Peasants, The.
  Sentry, The.
  To a Comrade in Arms.
  Unknown Soldier, The.
Li Ho. Under the Walls of Ping City.
Lleshanaku, L. Self-Defense.
Longfellow, H. Killed at the Ford.
Lovelace, R. To a Lady with Child that Asked
  [or Ask'd] an Old Shirt.
  To Lucasta, [on] Going to the War[re]s.
MacDiarmid, H. Another Epitaph on an Army
  of Mercenaries.
  Under the Greenwood Tree.
Mackintosh, E. Cha Till Maccruimein
  (Departure of the 4th Camerons).
  In Memoriam, Private D. Sutherland.
MacLean, S. Heroes.
MacLeish. Memorial Rain.
Manifold. Fife Tune.
Mansfield, K. Man with the Wooden Leg, The.
Mar, Y. Anonymous Squad, An.
  Between Sickle and Sword.
Masefield. To-morrow.
Masters, E. Many Soldiers.
Mayer, B. Aeschyleans, The.
McCarthy, G. Hooded Legion, The.
McCrae, J. In Flanders Fields.
McGrath, T. Blues for Warren.
  Go Ask the Dead.
  Nocturne Militaire.
  Ode for the American Dead in Korea.
Mehmedinović, Semezdin. Hero.
Melville, H. Ball's Bluff.
  March into Virginia, The.
Mikhail, D. Urgent Call, An.
Miller, E. Bringing Back the Draft.
  What the Women Told Me.
Milton. When the Assault Was Intended to the
  City.
Moody, W. Harmonics.
  On a Soldier Fallen in the Philippines.
Moolten, D. Brandy Station, Virginia.
Moore, L. Black Soldier, A.
Muldoon, P. Narrow Road to the Deep North,
  The.

Truce.
Munro, N. Hey, Jock, Are Ye Glad Ye 'Listed?
Mura. Natives, The.
Murray, L. Drugs of War, The.
  Lament for the Country Soldiers.
Nemerov. Fable of the War, A.
  Grand Central, with Soldiers, in Early Morning.
Nims, J. Trainwrecked Soldiers.
Norton, C. Bingen on the Rhine.
Nye, N. Jerusalem.
Ofek, U. Hagomel.
Okudzhava. Once there was a soldier boy.
Olds, S. Nurse Whitman.
O'Loughlin. Elegy for the Unknown Soldier.
Omer, H. Squad in the Land, A.
  Word from the Gray Soldiers.
Orwell. Italian soldier shook my hand, The.
Otero, B. Something Like A.
Owen, J. Hour of Fear.
Owen, W. A Terre.
  Anthem for Doomed Youth.
  Apologia Pro Poemate Meo.
  Arms and the Boy.
  At a Calvary near the Ancre.
  Disabled.
  Dulce et Decorum Est.
  Exposure.
  Futility.
  Insensibility.
  Mental Cases.
  Send-Off, The.
  Show, The.
  Strange Meeting.
Padel, R. Trial.
Pagis, D. Twenty Years in the Wadi.
Pak Nohae. Road to Corruption, The.
Pao Chao. Going Out Through the North Gate
  of Chi.
  Rough Road, A.
  Scholar Recruit, The.
Parker, M. Maunding Soldier; or, The Fruits of
  Warre Is Beggery, The.
Patchen. Body Beside the Ties, The.
Peacock, T. War Song of Dinas Vawr, The.
Piatt, S. Army of Occupation.
Pickering [or Pikerying]. Haltersick's Song.
Pierpont, J. Warren's Address at Bunker Hill
  [or to the American Soldiers].
Piontek. In the Woods.
Pope, J. Beau Ideal, The.
Prévert. Familial.
Prince, F.T. Soldiers Bathing.
Raàm-Lachish, C. In the Night.
Ravikovitch, D. You Can't Kill a Baby Twice.
Rawson, J. Border, The ("Leaping from the
  eucalyptus branch, the wild desert pigs.").
Read, H. Happy Warrior, The.
  To a Conscript of 1940.
Reed, H. Judging Distances.
  Naming of Parts.
Reynolds, O. Hazel.
Reznikoff. Romance.
Rickword. Soldier Addresses his Body, The.
Rilke. Last Evening, The.
Rimbaud, A. Cheated Heart.
Robinson, E. Field of Glory, The.
Rosenberg, I. Break of Day in the Trenches.
  Louse Hunting.
  Soldier: Twentieth Century.
  Troop ship, The.
Ross, A. Mess Deck.
Rottman. Porter on the Trail, A.
Sabry, M. Troy.
Sakhltkhutsishvili, U. Soldiers: "Crossing the
  mountains."
Sandburg, C. Among the Red Guns.
  Buttons.
  Old Timers.
Sarig, Y. Return: "Not thirsting for battle."
Sarton, M. Navigator: "This lazy prince of
  tennis balls and lutes."
Sassoon, S. Aftermath.
  Attack.
  Base Details.
  Christ and the Soldier.
  Does It Matter?

Dreamers.
Dug-Out, The.
Everyone Sang.
General, The.
Glory of Women.
Repression of War Experience.
Suicide in the Trenches.
"They".
Working Party, A.
Scannell.   Great War, The.
Scott of Amwell.   Ode: "I hate that drum's
  discordant sound."
Seeger, P.   Where Have All the Flowers Gone?
Senghor.   Taga for Mbaye Dyôb.
Service.   Pot of Tea, A.
Shakespeare, W.   We are but warriors for the
  working-day.
Shapiro, K.   Homecoming: "Lost in the vastness
  of the void Pacific."
Troop Train.
Shemer, N.   On Silver Wings.
Shephard, S.   Four and Twenty Soldiers.
Short, J.   Leave in Mid-Winter.
Shostakovskaya, I.   Today I'm a proper king's
  daughter.
Simpson, L.   Battle, The.
Bower of Roses, A.
Runner, The.
Slutsky [or Slutskii].   My Friends.
Smith, W.   Epithalamium in Olive Drab.
Snodgrass.   Ten Days Leave.
Sorley.   All the hills and vales along.
Soyinka.   Civilian and Soldier.
Spender, S.   Two Armies.
Stephen, J.   Malines.
Stevens, W.   Death of a Soldier, The.
Soldier, there is a war between the mind.
Stevenson, R.   Ticonderoga: A Legend of the
  West Highlands.
Stryk, L.   Pit, The.
Sniper.
Suckling, S.   Soldier, A.
Surrey.   Epitaph for [or on] Thomas Clere.
Swingler.   Day the War Ended, The.
Swirszczynska [or Swir].   Conversation Through
  the Door, A.
He Was Lucky.
Taggard.   To the Veterans of the Abraham
  Lincoln Brigade.
Tennant, E.   Mad Soldier, The.
Tennyson, A.   Charge of the Light Brigade, The.
Riflemen Form.
Teschke, H.   Minutes of Hasiba, The.
Thomas, E.   Owl, The.
Private, A.
Tears.
Thompson, M.   Address by an Ex-Confederate
  Soldier to the Grand Army of the Republic,
  An.
Ticknor.   Little Giffen.
Tilden.   Song of Braddock's Men, The.
Tilley, H.   Democracy, my grannie's foot!
Trapnell, N.   Lament of a Desert Rat.
Ts'ao Chih.   Tumbleweed that leaves its root
  and stock, The.
White Horses.
Tsvetayeva [or Tsvetaeva].   White Low Sun, A.
Tu Fu [or Du Fu].   Ballad of the Army Carts.
Conscription, The.
Pressgang at Shihao Village, The.
Pressgang, The.
Recruiting Officer of Shih-hao.
Song of the War Wagons.
Tucker, M.   Soldier Boy's Dream, The.
Ungaretti.   Soldiers.
Unknown.   Ballad of Mulan, The.
Ballad of Mulan, The.
Breaking a Willow-Branch.
Breeze, you who blow from the mountainside
  where my lover fights.
British Grenadiers, The.
Cai-wei: We Pick Ferns, We Pick Ferns.
Cao-chong: Hopper-Grass.
Enlisted Today.
I Don't Want to Be a Soldier.
Johnny, I Hardly Knew Ye.

King's Own Regulars, The [And Their Triumphs
  Over the Irregulars].
Little Jock Elliot.
Message from your distant lover is the smell of
  gunpowder, The.
My Sodger Laddie.
No Balls at All.
Over the Hills and Far Away, or, The Recruiting
  Officer.
Soldier stood at the pearly gate.
Soldiers.
Soldier's Song.
Sweet Polly Oliver.
Wanderer, The.
War Lament: "Every plant is burnt yellow."
Zhi-hu: Young Soldier Thinks of Home.
Unknown, fr. Terezin Concentration Camp.
Closed Town, The.
Various authors.   He battled against the king's
  enemy.
Wishing to entrust him with a great task.
Zealous to deliver the suffering people.
Verlaine.   Asleep in the Valley.
Vietnamese Oral Tradition.   Outpost Soldier,
  The.
Voznesensky [or Voznesenskii].   Old Song.
Wang Han.   Song of Liang-chou.
Wang Wei.   Army Ballad.
Webb, C.   Killing the Animals.
Weigl.   Hand to Hand.
Weismiller.   To the Woman in Bond Street
  Station.
Whitman, W.   Army Corps on the March, An.
Artilleryman's Vision, The.
As Toilsome I Wander'd Virginia's Woods.
Ashes of Soldiers.
By the Bivouac's Fitful Flame.
Cavalry Crossing a Ford.
Hush'd be the Camps To-Day.
March in the Ranks Hard-Prest, and the Road
  Unknown, A.
O Tan-Faced Prairie-Boy.
Sight in Camp [in the Daybreak Gray and Dim],
  A.
Spirit Whose Work Is Done.
Vigil Strange I Kept on the Field One Night.
Wound-Dresser, The.
Wieseltier, M.   Military Call-up.
Wilbur, R.   Place Pigalle.
Winchilsea.   Trail All Your Pikes.
Woodhouse, P.   I see a Soldiers service is forgot.
Wright, J.   Speak.
Yeats.   Irish Airman Foresees His Death, An.
Road at My Door, The.
Yi Sunsin.   In the Chinhae Camp.
Yonathan, N.   Friends: "Joseph is without doubt
  rent in pieces an evil beast hath devoured
  him."
Young, S.   Epitaph for a Concord Boy.
Zafrir, Y.   Forced March in Summer.
Zenmaro.   Tanka: "No news of him."
See also **War**

Solipsism
Cranch.   Pines and the Sea, The.
Housman.   I Counsel You Beware.
'Marnia.   Accoutrement.
I Must be Able to Protect You.
I Want to Love You Very Much.
Plath.   Soliloquy of the Solipsist.

Solitude
Ai.   Man with the Saxophone, The.
Aiken, C.   Solitaire.
Akhmatova, A.   Alone.
Solitude.
Alberti.   Song: "I want to sing: to be a flower."
Amadiume.   Mistress of My Own Being.
Amichai, Y.   Flock of Sheep Near the Airport,
  A.
My Mother Once Told Me.
Apollinaire.   Mirabeau Bridge.
Arends, J.   I Have.
Arnold, M.   To Marguerite—Continued.
Auden.   Lauds.
Awoonor.   Songs of Sorrow.
Basho.   Winter solitude.
Baudelaire.   Autumn Lament.

Bedregal.   Gestures From My Window.
Martyrdom.
Belieu.   Rondeau at the Train Stop.
Bell, M.   Nature: "Hand that tries to shake a
  hand, A."
Berry, W.   Stay Home.
Berryman.   Huffy Henry hid the day.
When by me in the dusk my child sits down.
Bly, R.   After Long Busyness.
Driving to Town Late to Mail a Letter.
Six Winter Privacy Poems.
Boland, E.   Woman in Kitchen.
Bone, K.   Corners.
Bosnick, Eli.   Larger Loneliness, A.
Bowles, W.   At a Village in Scotland.
Brontë, A.   Captive Dove, The.
Brontë, C.   Again I find myself alone.
Obscure and little seen my way.
Brontë, E.   I am the only being whose doom.
Little while, a little while, A.
To Imagination.
Bukowski.   Tragedy of the leaves, The.
Busceti, G.   Eight Phases of Contemplation.
Buson.   Goodbye. I will go.
I go out alone.
Utter aloneness—.
With a runny nose.
Byron, G.   Lake Leman.
Caesar.   Tea for Two.
Caldwell, A.   Left All Alone Again Blues.
Carmona.   Stretched Out in Solitude.
Carruth, H.   Alive.
Cary, A.   Contradiction.
To Solitude.
Ch'en Tzu-ang.   I dwell in the forest nursing a
  long illness.
Ch'ien T'ao.   Poems After Drinking Wine.
Choeui Eusoon.   Arriving at Yongmun Temple.
Chunbong Manwoo.   On the Mountain.
Chungji.   In My Leisure.
Cisneros, S.   Poet Reflects On Her Solitary Fate,
  The.
Citino.   Christina the Astonishing: Virgin.
Clare, J.   I Am.
Song: "I peeled bits of straw and I got switches
  too."
Cofer, J.   Life of an Echo, The.
Cohen, M.   Evensong.
Colby, T.   Captain's Log.
Coleridge, M.   Solo.
Coleridge, S.   I fear thee, ancient Mariner!
Cox, N.   Singing Alone.
Crabbe, G.   Alas! for Peter not an helping Hand.
Creeley.   Flower, The: "I think I grow tensions."
Crozier, A.   Humiliation in Its Disguises.
Cruz Varela.   Invocation.
Cuddihy.   Solitude.
Cummings, E. E.   No Thanks, No. 70.
Daegak Euchon.   At Hongbub Temple.
Studying in the Temple.
Daive.   Woman measures, A.
Dauer.   William.
de Burgos.   Poem Arrested at Daybreak.
De León, L.   Life Withdrawn, The.
DeCarteret, M.   Town Clerk, The.
DeLange, E.   Solitude.
Desbordes-Valmore.   My Room.
Dickey, J.   One, The.
Dickinson, E.   This Is My Letter to the World.
Dietz, H.   Alone Together.
Dizhur.   Here is an island. Here is a house on
  stilts.
Dodd, E.   Like Memory, Caverns.
Dooley, M.   Up on the Roof.
Dove, R.   Daystar.
Weathering Out.
Duffy, C.   Plainsong.
War Photographer.
Duncan, R.   Passage over Water.
Dunn, S.   Corners.
Eggen, Arnljot.   He Called Her His Willow.
Elytis, O.   Anniversary.
Evans, Aled Lewis.   Alone.
Fan Chung-yen.   Tune: "Sumuche Dancers".
Field.   Eros.
Onycha.

Foix. Sonnet: "Alone, in mourning, wearing an archaic black gown."
Frost, R. Acquainted with the Night.
Desert Places.
Good Hours.
Most of It, The.
Gallagher, T. On Your Own.
Gilliams, M. Tristitia Ante.
Glassman, Bernard Tetsugen. Ascending the Mountain.
Goll, I. Journey into Misery.
Gomez, M. Looking Deep.
Góngora y Argote. It was the flowery season of the year.
González, A. Inventory of Places Propitious for Love.
Graham, W. Malcolm Mooney's Land.
Gregerman, D. Lullaby.
Silent Globe.
Gregorio, R. Solitude Dinner.
Hacker, M. Going Back to the River.
Han-shan. Cold Mountain Path, The.
I've lived at Cold Mountain—how many autumns.
Rough and Dark.
Someone sits in a mountain gorge.
Han-shan Te-ch'ing. Shade of noble trees spreads in all directions, The.
Hanzlicek, C. On the Road Home.
Hayden, R. Road in Kentucky, A.
Hejinian. Solitude flared out, The.
Herrick. Upon the Loss[e] of His Mistresses.
Hewitt, J. Father's Death, A.
Hirsch, E. Edward Hopper and the House by the Railroad.
Hitchcock. Solitaire.
Hopkins, G. Heaven-Haven.
Horovitz, F. Rain—Birdoswald.
Hristov, Boris. Solitary Man.
Hsieh Ling-yün. Replying to a Poem from My Cousin Huilian.
Hsü Pen. To a Hermit in the Mountains.
Hughes, T. Thought-Fox, The.
Hugo, R. Living Alone.
Salt Water Story.
Hurbak Myungjo. Sitting Alone.
Ikkyu Sojun. After ten years in the red-light district.
Ten years of whorehouse joy I'm alone now in the mountains.
Inada. 4. The Legend of Lost Boy.
Iosifova, Ekaterina. Cloud, The: "It's darker and cooler."
Issa. I wish she were here.
Jackson, H. Solitude.
Jarrell, R. 90 North.
Jeffers, R. Compensation.
Jensma. In solitary.
Jones, R. White Towels.
Joyce, J. I hear an army charging upon the land.
Juana Inés de la Cruz. Oh World, Why Do You Thus Pursue Me?
Juarroz. Emptiness of the day, The.
Kavanagh, P. Inniskeen Road: July Evening.
Keats. Bright Star.
O Solitude! If I Must With Thee Dwell.
Kemble. Cover me with your everlasting arms.
Keplinger, D. Inside: George Gaines at Graterford Prison, 1981.
Kim Koengp'il. My Way.
Kim Sujang. In my quiet grass hut.
Kipling, R. For to Admire.
Kowit. Snapshot.
Kruit, J. House By the Sea.
Way of the Water, The.
Kwa, Lydia. You must exist. Writing this book depends on it. It has occurred to.
Laâbi Abdellatif. Tomorrow Will Be the Same Day.
Lamantia. High.
Lampman. In November: "Hills and leafless forests slowly yield, The."
Lane, P. Garden Temple, The.
Larkin, P. Reasons for Attendance.
Lee, L. Eating Alone.
Leonard, W. Indian Summer.

Levchev. Cronies.
Levertov. Losing Track.
Woman Alone, A.
Li Po. Drinking Alone in the Moonlight.
Drinking Alone with the Moon.
Retreat of Hsieh Kung, The.
Zazen on Ching-t'ing Mountain.
Li Shang-yin. East wind sighs, the fine rains come, The.
Li Yü. To the Tune "Meeting Happiness".
Tune: "Beating Silk Floss".
Tune: "Joy of Encounter".
Tune: "The Crow's Nocturnal Cry".
Liu Ch'ang-ch'ing. Sent to the Taoist of Dragon Mountain, Hsu Fa-leng.
Liu Tsung-yüan. Morning Walk in Autumn to South Valley Passing an Abandoned Village.
Liu Yung. Tune: "Eight Beats of a Kan-chou Song".
Livesay, D. On Looking into Henry Moore.
Longfellow, H. Broken Oar, The.
Lorde. Hanging Fire.
Lowell, A. Solitaire.
Loynaz, D. M. XXX.
"Lu Hsün.". Hesitation.
Lu Yu. Lazy.
Lugones. White Solitude.
Machado Ruiz. In my solitude.
Macphee, K. IVF.
Madhubuti. Loneliness, A.
Magrelli. Like ground that's been walked over, it echoes.
Mahapatra, J. Monsoon Day Fable, A.
Majorino. My Flesh in its Sweat.
March, A. Not so with me as with the little page.
Martinez, D. Years of Solitude.
Marvell. Garden, The.
McGinnis, M. Sending Men Back to the Sea.
McGrath, T. Ordonnance.
Return, The.
McMichael. Cat came / sleepily from a thick shrub and stopped and shook its head, A.
Miller, J. Bird dressed as solitude and tears.
Mills, B. Ballad: Of Motion.
Mills, I. Solitude.
Milton. Il Penseroso.
Mistral, G. Ballad: "He was strolling with another woman."
Mollineux. Solitude.
Mother Goose. Little Jumping Joan.
Mudrooroo Narogin. Hide and Seek.
Muso Soseki. All on my own I'm happy.
Don't ask suspiciously.
In this small hut.
On the Wall of Cloud-Friend Hut.
Pine Shade.
Na Hûidôk. There's Such an Evening.
Nasir. Loneliness.
Neruda. Taste.
Nguyen Binh Khiem. Worried.
Nienhauser, W. H. Sent to the Taoist of Dragon Mountain, Hsu Fa-leng.
No Ch'ŏnmyŏng. Nameless Woman, A.
No Hyangnim. Black Hole.
Nolens, L. Tributary.
Norton, C. To My Books.
Nye, N. Art of Disappearing, The.
O'Hara, F. Autobiographia Literaria.
Poem: "Eager note on my door said "Call me", The."
Ojibwa Oral Tradition. Loon upon the Lake, The.
Oodgeroo of the tribe Noonuccal. Last of His Tribe.
Orozco. There Are No Doors.
Ozaki Hosai. In coughing too.
Padilla. Self-Portrait of the Other.
Pak Mogwŏl [or Mokwŏl]. April.
Parker, D. Sanctuary.
Pasolini. Lines from the Testament.
Paz. After: "After chopping off all the arms that reached out to me."
Pei Di. Hermitage of the Bamboos, The.
Penna. When I don't feel well, I wander among.
Petri. To S.V.

Pickthall, M. Quiet.
Pilinszky, J. Passion of Ravensbrück.
Passion of Ravensbrück, The.
Pinkerton, H. On Vermeer's *Young Woman with a Water Jug* (1658) in the Metropolitan Museum.
Pitter. Old, Childless, Husbandless.
Po Chü-i. Long Lines Sent to Ling Hu-Ch'u before He Comes to Visit My Tumbledown Home.
Madly Singing in the Mountains.
Poe. Alone.
Pollarolo, G. They All Think.
Pommy-Vega. Here before the sunrise blue and in this solitude.
Pope, A. Ode on Solitude.
Prados, E. Song: "Bridge of my solitude."
Prasad, V. First Blood.
Prince, F.T. False Bay.
Ravikovitch, D. Surely You Remember.
Reddy, Srikanth. Evening with Stars.
Revell, D. Memory of New England, The.
Reverdy. Fires Smoulderning Under Winter.
Rexroth, K. On Flower Wreath Hill.
Riley, P. Another damp Sunday morning up and walk over.
Rilke. Day in October.
Entrance.
I Am Too Alone in the World.
Ritsos. Afternoon.
Robinson, A. Personality.
Robinson, E. Aaron Stark.
Rosser, J. Message: Bottle #32.
Rossetti, C. Autumn ("I dwell alone—I dwell alone, alone.").
L. E. L.
Verse II.
Salinas, L. Sea Song.
Samawi, S. Solo for the Lone Intuition, A.
Sanfield. Birthday Poem.
Santayana. Cape Cod.
Saraç, Tahsin. To an Immortal Solitude Where We Now Pitch Our Stately Tent.
Sarton, M. Glass of Water, A: "Here is a glass of water from my well."
Sassoon, S. Elected Silence.
Schulman. American Solitude.
Scliar-Cabral. Deceiving Words.
Seferis. Word for Summer, A.
Senghor. I Am Alone.
Senryū, K. His wife away from home.
Laying a fart.
Serge. Hands.
Seward. On the damp margin of the sea-beat shore.
Seek not, my Lesbia, the sequestered dale.
Shakespeare, W. Sonnet 29: "When, in disgrace with fortune and men's eyes."
Sharma, P. Poorly Matched.
Shelley, P. Sonnet: Political Greatness.
Shinkichi Takahashi. Camel.
Sidney. Delight of Solitariness, The.
Silva, J. Nocturne: "One night / One night full of perfumes, music of wings and murmurs."
Simic. My Noiseless Entourage.
Solitude.
Simmons, J. Pleasant Joys of Brotherhood, The.
West Strand Visions.
Simpson, L. After Midnight.
Sisson. Tristia.
Smith, C. By the Same. To Solitude.
Snodgrass. Song: "Sweet beast, I have gone prowling."
Snyder, G. Mid-August at Sourdough Mountain Lookout.
Solari, R. Truro.
Sŏng Hon. By Chance.
Mountain is silent, The.
Song Sun. I have spent ten years.
Soyinka. Hunchback of Dugbe, The.
Stevenson, A. Willow Song.
Stickney, T. In Ampezzo ("In days of summer let me go.").
Stone, J. Getting to Sleep in New Jersey.
Stoutenburg. Midnight Saving Time.
Strand. Garden, The.

Morning, A.
Old Man Leaves Party.
Sulchinskaya, O. Wind paces on the lower branch, The.
Swift, T. Ballad Of The Solitary Diner.
Sykes, B. One Day.
Symonds. Midnight at Baiae.
Synge. Prelude: "Still south I went and west and south again."
Synková, A. I'd Like to Go Alone.
Tagami Kikusha. Only the moon.
Taneda Santoka. Came along / a mountain path.
T'ao Ch'ien [or T'ao Yuan-ming]. To-Em-Mei's "The Unmoving Cloud".
Tate, J. Stray Animals.
Teasdale. Open Windows.
Over the Roofs.
Solitary, The.
Tennyson, A. Palace of Art, The.
Thomas, D. Hunchback in the Park, The.
Thomas, E. Rain: "Rain, midnight rain, nothing but the wild rain."
Tighe. Can I look back, and view with tranquil eye.
Written at Scarborough.
Towle. Seasonal Ramble.
Tranströmer. Alone.
Solitude.
Tsang. Street Angel, The.
Tu Fu [or Du Fu]. Autumn Night.
Shady, Shady.
Standing Alone.
Tuckerman, F. Series 3, Sonnet 10.
Turner, A. Red Flower.
Tweedy, Jeff. Prayer #3: "I have pondered."
Unamuno. It Is Night, in My Study.
Unknown. Hold me tightly in your arms.
Seafarer, The.
Venaille, Franck. Now They Tell Me.
Very. I Was Sick and in Prison.
Vogel, D. How Can I See You, Love.
Voznesensky [or Voznesenskii]. Two Poems.
Walcott. Letter from Brooklyn, A.
Winding Up.
Wang An-shih. Spring Evening on Pan Mountain.
Wang Wei. At a House in the Bamboo Grove.
Deep in the Mountain Wilderness.
Hermitage of the Bamboos, The.
Wellman, M. Silvery tells no sphere to go and.
Wen T'ing-yün. Brilliant Moon, A.
Wessling, Suki. Angry.
Whitman, W. I Saw in Louisiana a Live-Oak Growing.
Whyte, D. Sweet Darkness.
Wilcox, E. Solitude.
Wilde, R. Lament of the Captive, The.
Williams, W. Danse Russe.
Winchilsea. Give me, O indulgent fate!
Wither. Sonnet: "I that erstwhile the world's sweet air did draw."
Wordsworth, W. Solitary Reaper, The.
Wright, C. Sitting at Night on the Front Porch.
Wright, James. Two Postures beside a Fire.
Wright, Jay. Lake in Central Park, The.
Wunderlich, M. Aubade: "All day I've been searching for omens, flimsy as they are, and the cat."
Wylie. Eagle and the Mole, The.
Yeats. Apparitions, The.
Lake-Isle of Innisfree, The.
Yen Shu. Tune: "Sand of Silk-Washing Brook".
Yi I. Where is the ninth bend?
Yi Yônju. Clinic in a Dangerous Season 7, A.
Yosano Akiko. Spring Thaw.
Yun Sŏndo. At My Study.
Zanzotto. Distance.

Solomon (Bible)
Bible, *O.T.* Song: "I am dark, daughters of Jerusalem."
Browning, R. Solomon and Balkis.
Cassells. New Song of Solomon.
Herbert, G. Sion.
Moore, M. O To Be A Dragon.
Naden. Solomon Redivivus, 1886.
Rakosi. Sandalwood Comes to My Mind.

Scott, G. What Was Solomon's Mind?
Surrey. I, Solomon, David's son, King of Jerusalem.
Yeats. On Woman.
Solomon and the Witch.

Somerset, England
Coleridge, S. This Lime-Tree Bower My Prison.

Somnambulism and Somnambulists
García Lorca. Somnambulist Ballad.
Hirsch, E. For the Sleepwalkers.

Son of Man, The
Carson, A. God's Mother.
Fitzgerald, J. Great Little One.
Unknown. O come, thou Wisdom from on high.
See also **Infant Jesus; Jesus Christ; Savior**

Songwriters and songs
Achterberg. Instrument.
Trinity.
Alvarez, J. Redwing Sonnets.
Amir, D. Nightingale of Uncle Yair, The.
Andal. We rose before dawn.
Anderson, S. Evening Song.
Andreus. Song: "All roocoogirls."
Annand. Mavis.
Ashbery, J. Hotel Lautréamont.
Baraka, I. Alba.
Barrax. There Was A Song.
Basho. Cicada shell, A.
Culture's beginnings.
Culture's beginnings.
Midfield.
Singing, flying, singing.
Ungraciously, under.
What voice.
Winter garden.
Your song caresses.
Bateman, M. O Bonnie Man, Lovely Man.
Beddoes. And what's your tune?
Berlin. Let Me Sing and I'm Happy.
Song Is Ended (But the Melody Lingers On), The.
Bible, *O.T.* Psalm 100.
Bishop, E. Sonnet: "I am in need of music that would flow."
Brecht, B. Three Fragments.
Buffoni, F. Song of Diamond Eyes, The.
Burkard. My Aunt and the Sun.
Buson. With the noon conch blown.
Calverley. Ballad: "Auld wife sat at her ivied door, The."
Campbell, R. Choosing a Mast.
Campo. My Voice.
Carmi, T. Short Song.
Castro, R. As I Composed This Little Book.
Celan. Thread suns.
Ceravolo. Sunset.
Ch'in Kuan. Along the Grand Canal.
Churchyard. That humor now, declines for age drawes on.
Cleary, B. Boys' Own.
Conway, J. Modern English.
Crane, S. Once, I knew a fine song.
Cristall. Song: "Come, let us dance and sing."
Song: "Eve descends with radiant streaks, The."
Song: "Tossed midst life's terrific storms."
Song: "Wandering in the still of eve."
To a Lady on the Rise of Morn.
Darwish, M. Earth Poem.
Psalm 2.
De Mello Breyner. Muse.
DeFoe, M. Aviary.
Dream Lover.
Densmore. No. 73. In the Blue Night.
Dickey, J. Buckdancer's Choice.
Donne. Triple Fool, The.
Dooley, M. Does It Go Like this?
Dowson. Dregs.
Dunbar, P. Compensation.
Eliscu, E. Without a Song.
Evans, Mayme. Song for a Baby on Padre Island.
Field. 'Sing to us Sappho!' cried the crowd.
Folade Mondisa Speaks. Tonal Embryology.
García Lorca. Song Wants to Be Light, The.
Garrigue. Song in Sligo.

Geiger. Soundtracks.
Gerhardt, I. G. M. Remembrance Day.
Gershwin, I. Blah, Blah, Blah.
Gil de Biedma, J. In Mournful Praise and Memory of the French Song.
Gioia. Cruising with the Beach Boys.
Goldbarth. Seriema Song.
Graham, J. Of Forced Sightes and Trusty Ferefulness.
Grahame, K. Duck's Ditty.
Song of Mr Toad, The.
Gregg. Dark Thing Inside the Day, A.
Gregory. Christmas Lullaby for a New-Born Child.
Hall, H. Maker of Songs.
Hammerstein. Song Is You, The.
Harris, Ken. Call and Response.
Harris, P. Some Songs Women Sing.
Hart, L. With a Song in My Heart.
Hattersley, G. Singing.
Heine, H. Ah, Death is Like the Long Cool Night.
Hejinian. Mask of Anger, A.
Henley, W. E. I am the feast-maker.
Hölderlin. Brevity.
Holmes, O. Prologue.
Hooks. Woman's Mourning Song, The.
Hovanessian, D. Inside Green Eyes, Black Eyes.
Howe, J. Battle Hymn [or Battle-Hymn] of the Republic, The.
Hsüeh T'ao [or Xue Tao]. Cicadas.
Hughes, L. Songs.
Hugo, R. My Buddy.
Inuit Oral Tradition. Utitia'q's Song.
Issa. Cuckoo singing.
Cuckoo sings, The.
Don't fly off, nightingale.
From the bough.
In the thicket's shade.
My noontime nap.
Nightingale's song / this morning.
Noon.
Old dog listens, The.
Old dog, The.
Village named Little-Plum-Tree, A.
Jaccottet. Wishes.
Jackson, A. Ohnedaruth.
Jayadeva. Song of Krishna: The Fourth Song, Sung with Raga "Ramakari".
Johnson, J. Lift Every [or Ev'ry] Voice and Sing.
Keats. On the Grasshopper and [the] Cricket.
Kelly, B. Song: "Listen: there was a goat's head hanging by ropes in a tree."
Kenyon, J. Insomnia at the Solstice.
Koehler, T. Happy As the Day Is Long.
I Gotta Right to Sing the Blues.
Koethe. Songs of the Valley.
Konishi Raizan. For rice-planting women.
Kreymborg. Improvisation.
Kurtz. No Pasarán.
Larkin, P. Love Songs in Age.
Lee, L. I Ask My Mother to Sing.
Levy, A. First Extra, The.
Li Po. Spring Night in Luoyang—Hearing a Flute.
Liu, T. Ikon.
Long, N. Now the BBC once wrote to me and said 'Dear Norman Long'.
Longfellow, H. Day Is Done, The.
Lönnrot. It is my desire, it is my wish.
Luca, Gherasim. My Folly of Being.
Lux. One Meat Ball.
Mackey, N. Sound and Cerement.
Martinaitis, M. Kukutis in the Reich's Guard House.
Kukutis's Song.
Martinez, D. Song: "I dreamed my voice was an Anasazi pot."
Mayes, J. Descant.
McDonald, W. All the Old Songs.
McKay, C. Negro Spiritual.
Meynell, A. To Silence.
Montale. Lemon Trees, The.
Lemon Trees, The.

Moore, L.   Song Poem, The.
Moss, H.   Persistence of Song, The.
Mugo, M. G.   Where are those Songs?
Murray, C.   Charon's Song.
Nakano Shigeharu.   Song: "You, Don't sing."
Nameroff, R.   California Dreaming.
Nesbit, E.   To Vera, Who Asked a Song.
Norris, L.   His Father, Singing.
O'odham.   No. 73. In the Blue Night.
Orpingalik.   Songs are Thoughts, Sung Out with the Breath.
Orr, G.   Insomnia Song.
Ortiz.   Look to the Mountain.
Padilla.   Song of the Juggler.
Pak Tujin.   Song in a Graveyard.
Pao Chao.   Ballad: A Song in the Night.
Goblet of Wine, A.
Splash water on level ground.
Pao Ling-hui.   In the Key of Farewell.
Parish.   Star Dust.
Piatt, S.   Sad Spring-Song.
Powell, D. A.   Coda & discography.
Who won't praise green. Each minute to caress each minute blade of spring. Green slice us open.
Probyn.   Song Out of Season, A.
Rafferty, P.   Personal.
Rakosi.   Sandalwood Comes to My Mind.
Riley, D.   Misremembered Lyric, A.
Riley, J.   Nonsense Rhyme, A.
Rivard.   Cures.
Roberts, E.   Old Love in Song, An.
Roethke.   Light Listened.
Roland Holst.   I Who Was Born.
Rose, B.   Without a Song.
Rossetti, D.   50: Willowwood ("And now Love sang: but his was such a song").
Rothenberg, J.   Song of Quavering, A.
Rumi.   Wished-For Song, A.
Sappho.   Mika / But I will not allow you.
Shakespeare, W.   Pray you fetch him hither.
Shelley, P.   To a Skylark.
Shiki.   Skylark school, The.
Sidney.   First Song: "Doubt you to whom my Muse these notes intendeth [or entendeth]."
Snodgrass.   Song: "Sweet beast, I have gone prowling."
Snyder, G.   Night Song of the Los Angeles Basin.
Stern, G.   For Song.
Suckling, S.   Ballad[e] [upon a Wedding], A.
Taggard.   Hymn to Yellow.
Takai Kito.   Barley-reaping song / Smith's hammer.
Teasdale.   Little While, A.
Tennyson, A.   Dying Swan, The.
Theognis.   Captive.
Todd, M.   Wire Song.
Toomer.   Song of the Son.
Torneol.   Lady's Farewell, The.
Trakl.   Elis.
Trinidad.   Monday, Monday.
Tu Fu [or Du Fu].   Long hoe, long hoe, handle of white wood.
Unknown.   Dead Man Asks for a Song, The.
I Came from Under the Earth.
Love Me Little, Love Me Long.
Van Doren.   So Simple.
Van Duyn.   Mockingbird Month.
Van Ostaijen.   Song of the Alpine Hunter.
Verlaine.   Autumn Song ("With long sobs.").
Voigt.   Song and Story.
Walker, M.   For My People.
Watson, R.   Die Zauberflöte.
Serenade: "Who is it sings the gypsies' song to-night."
Weaver, A.   Sub Shop Girl.
Welburn.   Gonsalves.
Whitman, W.   Chanting the Square Deific.
Out of the Cradle Endlessly Rocking.
Whittier.   Tent on the Beach: [The Dreamer].
Wickham.   Song-Maker, A.
Wilbur, R.   Plain Song for Comadre, A.
Williams, Stephanie.   Drunkard Promise, A.
Duchess of Dogs.
Williams, W.   Botticellian Trees, The.

Wise, S.   Closure Opening Its Trap.
Wizlaw von Rügen.   Only Love.
Wodehouse.   Land Where the Good Songs Go, The.
Wolff, Rebecca.   Press Play.
Wong, N.   Grandmothers' Song.
Wright, D.   Musician, The.
Yeats.   Coat, A.
Yi Chehyŏn.   Contemporary Folk Songs.
Young, J.   Life Is a Song, Let's Sing It Together.
Young, K.   Errata.
Zarin.   Song: "My heart, my dove, my snail, my sail, my."
Zimmer.   Romance.
Zukofsky, L.   Anew 10.
To my wash-stand.
Two Dedications: Tibor Serly.

Sonnets
Bernes, J.   Sonnet with Lock and Key.
Bowles, W.   At a Village in Scotland.
Brodsky, J.   With a simple, truly unrebellious pen.
Burns, R.   Sonnet upon Sonnets, A.
Chasin.   Joy Sonnet in a Random Universe.
Collins, B.   Sonnet: "All we need is fourteen lines, well, thirteen now."
Devaney, T.   Sonnet: "You know all those sonnets the ones where I said, I love you, well."
Donne.   Canonization, The.
Dovaston, J. F. M.   There are who say the sonnet's meted maze.
Dutton, P.   So'net 3.
Elliott, E.   Powers of the Sonnet.
Faber, F.   Sonnet-writing. To F. W. F.
Gilder, R.   Sonnet, The.
Gladstone, W. E.   To a Rejected Sonnet.
Goethe.   Sonnet: "To work away in art's traditional measure."
Hood, T.   Sonnet to a Sonnet.
Keats.   If by Dull Rhymes Our English Must Be Chained.
Koestenbaum, P.   Sonnet 37: "I'd decided I initiate most."
Lee-Hamilton.   What the Sonnet Is.
Lope de Vega.   Sonnet All of a Sudden, A.
Sonnet Right off the Bat.
Morgan, E.   Opening the Cage.
Rossetti, D.   Sonnet is a moment's monument, A.
Symonds.   Sonnet (III), The.
Teare, Brian.   Dead House Sonnet.
Watts-Dunton.   Sonnet's Voice, The.
Wilcox, E.   Sonnet, The.
Wordsworth, W.   Scorn Not the Sonnet [Critic, You Have Frowned].
Sonnet: "Nuns fret not at their convent's narrow room."

Sons
Al-Bayati, A.   Two Poems for My Son, Ali.
Amichai, Y.   My father fought their war four years or so.
My Son.
Antokolsky.   We are not always dependent on memory.
You must dig in black ashes a long time.
You share your mourning with all Moscow. There.
Applewhite.   Prayer for My Son.
Armitage, S.   Kid.
Arnold, M.   Then Sohrab with his sword smote Rustum's helm.
Arrillaga.   Rosa/Filí.
Baraka, I.   Wise 3.
Barber, M.   Written for My Son, and Spoken by Him at His First Putting on Breeches.
Bateman, M.   Thank You, My Little Son.
Berryman.   Sympathy, A Welcome, A.
Bly, R.   My Father at 85.
Prodigal Son, The.
Bowers, E.   Prince, The.
Brodsky, J.   Odysseus to Telemachus.
Callimachus.   Here Philip the father buried.
Carlson, D.   Russ Joy Little League.
Carrera Andrade.   Second Life of My Mother.
Ch'ien T'ao.   Blaming Sons.

Clarke, T.   For Babies Unborn.
Clifton, L.   Admonitions.
Donor.
Wishes for Sons.
Comfort, A.   Notes for My Son.
Cooley.   Fathers and Sons.
Corbet [or Corbett].   To His Son [or Sonne], Vincent Corbet[t].
Davidson, D.   Randall, My Son.
Day Lewis.   Walking Away.
DeFrees.   Letter to an Absent Son.
Dickey, J.   Bee, The.
Dickey, R.   Mulatto Lullaby.
Duhig, I.   First Second, The.
Duncan, R.   My Mother Would Be a Falconress.
Eldan, A.   When You Grow Up.
Fearing.   Any Man's Advice to His Son.
Feinstein, E.   At Seven a Son.
Finney, N.   Lobengula: Having a son at 38.
Fitzgerald, R.   Figlio Maggiore.
Foppa.   First Portrait of My Son.
Wound.
Fordham.   Sonnet to My First Born.
Galvin, J.   Shadow-Casting.
García Lorca.   Rundown Church (Ballad of the First World War).
Geier.   On Your Twenty-First Birthday.
Glück, L.   Mirror Image.
Goethe.   Erl-King.
Erl-King, The.
Goralik, L.   Every few weeks I see there is an empty chair in our local nursery.
Gregory, H.   For You, My Son.
Ha Thi Thao.   Our Son's Profession.
Hall, D.   My Son, My Executioner.
Heaney, S.   When all the others were away at Mass.
Hegley.   Dreaming My Dad.
Henry, J.   Son's a poor, wretched, unfortunate creature, The.
Hernández Cruz.   Ruskie's Boy.
Hernández, M.   Lullaby of the Onion.
Hershon.   Sentimental Moment or Why Did the Baguette Cross the Road?
Higgins, R.   Almost Communication.
Hippolyte.   So Jah Sey.
Hirschhorn, N.   Number Our Days.
Hogg, J.   Wife of Crowle, The.
Holub.   End of the World, The.
Hood, T.   Parental Ode to My Son, A.
Hristov, Boris.   My Mother's Wedding.
Hughes, L.   Letter ("Dear Mama, / Time I pay rent and get my food.").
Mother to Son.
Mulatto.
Hughes, T.   Revenge Fable.
Humphreys, E.   From Father to Son.
Ignatow, D.   Rightful One, The.
Time Comes When You Are Facing Him, The.
Issa.   Why did the wild pink break?
Jackson, A.   Peacock of Motherhood, The.
Jess, T.   Letter to an Unconceived Son.
Jonson, B.   On My First Son.
Kakkai Patiniyar Naccellaiyar.   Many Said.
Kaplinski, J.   We started home, my son and I.
Khalvati.   Blue Moon.
Khodasevich.   Dactyls.
Khurshid-Banu.   To My Son, Abbas.
Kinnell.   After Making Love We Hear Footsteps.
Kipling, R.   Son, A.
Sons of Martha, The.
Komunyakaa, Y.   *Bui Doi*, Dust of Life.
Kooser.   At the End of the Weekend.
Korinna [or Corinna].   Wishing to take her son.
Kunitz, S.   Father and Son.
Lancaster, John.   Yellow Bike, The.
Lassell.   Going to Europe.
Lea, S.   Paternity.
Lee, L.   Eternal Son, The.
Weight of Sweetness, The.
Leivick, H.   Lament at Night.
Levertov.   Son, The.
Levine, P.   Every Blessed Day.
Starlight.
Lezama Lima.   Call of the Desirous.

Li Shang-yin. Boasting of My Son.
Liang Te-sheng. Sent to My Fourth Son, Shao-Wu (to the Tune "Southern Countryside").
Linden, M. Wayward Son, The.
Long, H. For Tony, Embarking in Spring.
McCarriston. Kitchen Terrarium.
McDonald, W. War in Bosnia, The.
McGrath, T. Poem: "My little son comes running with open arms!"
Poem: "My little son, laughing, singing...."
Poem: "When I carry my little son in the cold."
McLagan, Elizabeth. At Twelve.
Meinke. This is a poem to my son Peter.
Merwin. Yesterday: "My friend says I was not a good son."
Meynell, A. Father of Women, A [Ad Sororem E. B.].
Unto Us a Son Is Given.
Milne, A. Disobedience.
Mistral, G. Night.
Montague, J. At Last.
Moon, Susan. Unintended.
Mooney, M. Painting the Angel.
Mun Chônghui. To My Son.
Myers, J. Visitation Rites.
Newbolt. Clifton Chapel.
Nichols, R. Beginning when I was six I became my father's accomplice.
Nizami Arudi. Calling the Doctor (1000 A.D.).
North, M. Pheasant Plucker's Son, The.
Nowlan. Mother and Son.
Only When My Heart Freezes.
O'Brien, L. Diabolus in Musica.
Olds, S. Mother, The.
Ortiz. What I Tell Him.
Penna. Lady on Streetcar.
Phillips, L. My Son Shows Me a Photograph of Michael Jordan Performing a Slam Dunk.
Piñero. On The Day They Buried My Mother.
Reid, A. Daedalus.
Rich, A. Jerusalem.
Rilke. Luke 15:11–19; And he said, "There was a man".
Rodriguez, L. To the Police Officer Who Refused to Sit in the Same Room as My Son because He's a "Gang Banger".
Ryan, M. This Is a Poem for the Dead.
St. John, P. Reading a Story to My Child.
Scammell, W. Poem for a Younger Son.
Senryū, K. Official's little son, The.
Shafer, A. Monday Morning.
Shakespeare, W. Ill blows the wind that profits nobody.
Shapiro, D. To My Son.
Shelton, R. Letter to a Dead Father.
Simic. Spoons with Realistic Dead Flies on Them.
Simon, L. Kali.
Skloot. Hook.
Smith, C. Essential Story, The.
Smith, D. August, on the Rented Farm.
Smith, S. Correspondence between Mr. Harrison in Newcastle and Mr. Sholto Peach Harrison in Hull.
Stallworthy, J. Almond Tree, The.
Stein, K. It Didn't Begin with Horned Owls Hooting at Noon.
Stevens, W. John Smith and His Son, John Smith.
Stone, J. Bass, The.
Su Tung-p'o. On the Birth of His Son.
T'ang Hsien-tsu. My son, you loved telling the story of Prince Nata.
On the Day of Washing the Buddha in the Year Ting-wei (1607), I Dreamed That My Late Son Shih-ch'ü Was Holding a Book, and Appeared To Be Quite Happy. He Said That He Had Earned His Chin-shih Degree in the Underworld.
T'ao Ch'ien [or T'ao Yuan-ming]. Putting the Blame on His Sons.
Scolding My Sons.
Tatarunis, P. I Have Two Sons and the One I Love Best Is Robert.
Tate, A. Mother and Son.
Tate, J. Distance from Loved Ones.

Taylor, C.B. Round Irving High School.
Taylor, E. Few Days in the South in February, A.
Thwaite, A. Throes.
Torrence. Son, The.
Troupe. Gray Day in January in La Jolla.
Tu Fu [or Du Fu]. Thinking of My Little Boy.
Unknown. Dad is busy.
Enlisted Today.
Somebody's Mother.
Such Is the Grief of the Grey-Haired Man.
Wife of Usher's Well, The.
Vallejo. Good Sense.
Right Meaning, The.
Vando. Father's Day.
Voisine, Connie. Blue Hat.
Wah. Father / Mother Haibun #12.
Wallace, R. Friday Night Fights, The.
Warren, R. Lullaby: Moonlight Lingers.
Night Walking.
Only Poem, The.
Whitman, W. Dirge for Two Veterans.
Vigil Strange I Kept on the Field One Night.
Williams, C. K. Heart, The.
Williams, L. Interruption of Flight.
Wordsworth, W. Affliction of Margaret, The.
Wright, F. Wedding, The.
Wright, J. Two Postures beside a Fire.
Youth.
Yamanoé [or Yamanoué] no Okura. Longing for His Son, Furuhi.
Yeats. Prayer for My Son, A.
Yi Sang. Face.
Poem No. 2.
Young, G. Miracle, The.
Zamora-Linmark. Election Day.
Zweig, P. Father.

Sophocles
Akhmatova, A. Death of Sophocles, The.
Arnold, M. Dover Beach.
To a Friend.

Sorcery and Sorcerers
Glück, L. Circe's Power.
Harburg. We're Off to See the Wizard (The Wonderful Wizard of Oz).
Simic. Modern Sorcery.

Sorrow
Abse. Origin of Music, The.
Adonis [or Adunis]. Song of a Man in the Dark.
Agalí, A. Boeing.
Alexander, M. People of Unrest.
Alley, R. Dissecting Uncle Sorrow.
Amichai, Y. Is all this sorrow? I don't know.
Psalm: "Psalm on the day, A."
Quick and Bitter.
Apollinaire. Fete.
Ashbery, J. Variant.
Awoonor. First Circle, The.
Songs of Sorrow.
Ballagas. Nocturne and Elegy.
Basho. Delight, then sorrow.
This dark autumn.
Bayly. I'm Saddest When I Sing.
Beckett, S. Enueg 2.
Beedome. Question and Answer, The.
Berryman. Sometimes the night echoes to prideless wailing.
Bialik. My Soul Sinks.
Blaga. Psalm.
Blake, W. Infant Sorrow.
On Another's Sorrow.
Bowering, G. If I did complain, who among my friends.
Boyle, K. Mothers: "In the still of night."
Brines, F. Grief: "With eyes happy."
Brodsky, J. To Urania.
Brontë, E. I am the only being whose doom.
Spellbound.
Brown, L. (Here Am I) Broken Hearted.
Browning, E. Cry of the Children, The.
Mask, The.
My Heart and I.
Year's Spinning, A.
Brutus. They Hanged Him, I Said Dismissively.
Bunno [Wen Wang or King Wen]. Song of the

Bowmen of Shu [1915].
Burns, R. Ae Fond Kiss.
Banks o' Doon, The ("Ye banks and braes o' bonie [or bonnie] Doon.").
Banks o' Doon, The ("Ye flowery banks o' bon[n]ie Doon.").
Despondency, an Ode.
Man Was Made to Mourn, a Dirge.
Red, Red Rose, A.
Buson. You left in the morning. In the evening, my heart in a thousand shards.
Byron, G. By the Rivers of Babylon We Sat Down and Wept.
Oh! Weep for Those.
Campbell, T. Lines Written on Visiting a Scene in Argyleshire.
Campion, T. When to Her Lute Corinna [or Corrina] Sings.
Carew, T. Epitaph on the Lady Mary Villiers ("Lady Mary Villiers lies, The.").
To Celia, upon Love's Ubiquity.
Carman, B. World Voice, The.
Cary, A. Window Just Over the Street, The.
Castellanos. Hecuba's Testament.
Chang Chiu-ling. I close my door and trace the transformations of nature.
Chao Luan-luan. Willow Eyebrows.
Chinnov. Black bird on a black and snowy branch, A.
Cho Wen-chun. Lament: "Hills are white with snow, The."
Chŏng Chiyong. Spring Snow.
Clampitt. Procession at Candlemas, A.
Clifton, L. Sorrow Song.
Coleridge, S. On a Discovery Made Too Late.
Cook, E. Written at the Couch of a Dying Parent.
Cowper, W. Shrubbery, The.
Craig, David. Litany: "Mother of Sorrow."
Creamer, H. After You've Gone.
Cruickshank, H. Sae Lang Has Sorrow.
Cummings, E. E. Always before your voice my soul.
de Burgos. Poem of My Sleeping Sorrow.
De la Mare. Dove, The.
Ghost, The ("Who knocks? I, who was beautiful.").
Delmore, E. Such Sweet Sorrow.
Di Prima. For H.D.
Dickinson, E. One need not be a Chamber—to be Haunted.
Dobie, K. Aberfan.
Dodge, M. Someone in the Garden.
Dodson, O. Sorrow Is the Only Faithful One.
d'Oettingen. Outcries.
Donaldson, W. Little White Lies.
You're Driving Me Crazy (What Did I Do?).
Dowson. O Mors! Quam Amara Est Memoria Tua Homini Pacem Habenti In Substantiis Suis.
Spleen.
Drummond de Andrade. Dead in Frock Coats, The.
Dunbar, P. We Wear the Mask.
Duncan, R. Among My Friends.
Ebb, F. My Coloring Book.
El-Hadi, S. Tired Man, The.
Elliot, J. Flowers of the Forest, The.
Faiz. We Who Were Executed.
Feng Yen-ssu. Cloud That Drifted, The.
Field. Picture, A.
Fraser, G. Lament: "In a dismal air; a light of breaking summer."
Freed, A. I Cried for You.
Frost, R. My November Guest.
Fuertes. Painted Windows.
Fuller, M. Meditations.
Garcilaso de la Vega. Oh, to my sobs, Galatea, you are harder than a stone.
Gardinier. Where Blind Sorrow Is Taught to See.
Glück, L. Elms.
Goese, M. I slowly crack my joints to ready and steady myself. Sharpen my mind on.
Gordon, M. There's a Lull in My Life.
Gorham. Princess Parade.

Graves, R.   Lost Love.
Green, D. R.   Names and sorrows.
Greenwald, R.   Half-Life of Sorrow, The.
Griffith, L.   Exile: Welsh Service from Daventry.
Günther.   Departure Aria.
Hacker, M.   Conclusion: "Did you love well what very soon you left?"
Hamill, S.   What the Water Knows.
Hammond, W.   To the Same [My Dear Sister, Mrs S.]: The Tears.
Hantoosh, G.   Happiest Man in the World, The.
Hardy, T.   Going, The.
Herbert, G.   Joseph's Coat.
Herman, J.   Time Heals Everything.
Hernández, M.   Your Heart?—It Is a Frozen Orange.
Herrera, F.   Sonnet 32.
Herrera y Reissig.   Sorrowful Shadow, The.
Herrick.   Bad Season Makes the Poet Sad, The.
On Himself[e] ("I fear[e] no Earthly Powers.").
To the Willow-Tree.
Homer.   Laertes.
Howe, F.   Doubt.
Howells, W.   Forlorn.
Hsieh T'iao.   Roaming the East Field.
Hsin Ch'i-chi.   To an Old Tune.
Tune: "Picking Mulberry Seeds" Written on a Wall en route to Po-shan.
Huidobro.   New Song.
Hwang Insuk.   Sorrow Wakes Me.
Im Che.   Woman's Sorrow, A.
Ingelow.   Story, A.
Ishikawa Takuboku.   Tanka: "As if in water."
Tanka: "Like a white lotus."
Tanka: "Sorrow / its outlines blurred."
Issa.   Mother, I weep.
Izumi.   So forlorn am I.
Jordan, J.   Sandbar at Moore's Creek.
Winter.
Joyce, J.   I hear an army charging upon the land.
Kahn, G.   One I Love (Belongs to Someone Else), The.
Tomorrow Is Another Day.
Kalmar et al.   Who's Sorry Now?
Katz, J.   Falling.
Kaufman, B.   I Have Folded My Sorrows.
Keats.   O Thou Whose Face Hath Felt the Winter's Wind.
Ode to a Nightingale.
Kemble.   Impromptu.
Khoury, N.   Death Is Your Salvation.
Kim Yǒngnang.   Until Peonies Bloom.
Kipling, R.   Harp Song of the Dane Women.
Klink, J.   Porch in Snow.
Koehler, T.   Ill Wind.
Stormy Weather (Keeps Rainin' All the Time).
Tess's Torch Song (I Had a Man).
Komunyakaa, Y.   When Loneliness Is a Man.
Kuan Han-ch'ing.   Tune: "Vast Virtue".
Kublanovsky [or Kublanovskii].   Armor of the Petrograd oak is rusty, but, The.
Labé.   Bright Venus, Who Across the Heavens Stray.
Landon.   Child Screening a Dove from a Hawk, A.
Small Miseries.
Lanier, S.   Raven Days, The.
Lawrence, D. H.   Sorrow.
Levine, P.   Red Dust.
Li Ching.   Sorrow for Spring.
Li Ch'ing-chao.   Long Melancholy Tune, A.
To the Tune: Eternal Joy.
To the Tune "You Move in Fragrance".
Tune: "On the Trail of Sweet Incense".
Tune: Spring at Wu Ling.
Li Po.   Moon over the Mountain Pass, The.
My sword at my waist, I climb a high tower.
Seeing Off a Friend.
To See Secretary Shu-Yun Off at the Hsieh T'iao Tower at Hsuan-Ch'eng.
Li Shang-yin.   Alone by the Autumn River.
For ever hard to meet, and as hard to part.
From the Heights.
Without Title.
Li Yü.   Bella Donna Iu.
Silent and Alone.

To the Tune "Meeting Happiness".
Tune: "Sand Washed by Waves".
Tune: "Sand Washed by Waves".
Tune: "The Beauty of Yü".
Liu Yung.   Tune: "Bells Ringing in the Rain".
Tune: "Eight Beats of a Kan-chou Song".
Lloyd, C.   Erst when I wandered far from those I loved.
Longfellow, H.   Bridge, The.
Ma Chih-yüan.   Love Song: "Clouds circle the moon."
Macari, A.   Counting the Years.
Machado Ruiz.   Deep Song.
MacKay, C.   Only a Thought.
Magrelli.   Especially in weeping.
Mallarmé.   Sea Breeze.
Martial.   Just half our three score years and ten.
Martínez de Navarrete.   Separation from Clorila, The.
Martínez, V.   Night of Fathers.
McCarthy, T.   Mr. Nabokov's Memory.
McKay, C.   Negro Spiritual.
Mei Yao Ch'en.   Sorrow.
Melville, E.   Upon one day as I did mourn full sore.
Mikha'il, M.   You Have Your Calamity And I Have Mine.
Millay, E.   Sorrow.
Milton.   Lycidas.
Molinari.   Ode to a Long Sorrow.
Moore, T.   Oft In the Stilly Night.
Morisseau-Leroy, F.   Sometimes I'm Not Myself.
Morungen, H.   I believe there is no one alive who weeps for my sorrow.
Neruda.   Poem 20.
Nervo.   Sorrow Vanquished.
Nilsson, H.   On Inheriting Departure.
Ofeimun.   How Can I Sing.
O'Hara, F.   Aus Einem April.
Orléans, C.   Las! Mort Qui T'a Fait Si Hardie.
Ovid.   Nagging reminders: the black ghost-melancholy vision.
Pao Chao.   Splash water on level ground.
Parker, D.   Anecdote: "So silent I when Love was by."
Autumn Valentine.
Perk.   Iris.
Petrarch.   Soote Season, The.
You who hear in scattered rhymes the sound of those sighs with.
Philips, K.   Lucasia, Rosania and Orinda Parting at a Fountain, July 1663.
Po Chü-i.   Song of Everlasting Sorrow.
Poe.   Bridal Ballad.
Haunted Palace, The.
Valley of Unrest, The.
Porter, C.   Down in the Depths.
Ev'ry Time We Say Good-bye.
Powell, D. A.   Thicknesses of victor decreased: blanket->sheet->floss. Until no material would do, The.
Pyungyang Ungee.   Reply to a Poem by Donglim.
Radnóti.   Letter to My Wife.
Ralegh.   Butt stay my thoughts, make end, geve fortune way.
Ramsdell, H.   In repetition, minor violences grew more blunt and less precise.
Rankine.   Elsewhere, Things Tend.
Reese, L.   Rachel.
Rexroth, K.   As the wheel follows the hoof.
Delia Rexroth ("Under your illkempt yellow roses.").
Ridler.   At Parting.
Robinson, A.   Stornelli and Strambotti.
Robinson, E.   Walt Whitman: "Master-songs are ended, and the man, The."
Robinson, M.   Bids Farewell to Lesbos.
Contemns Philosophy.
Describes the Fascinations of Love.
Determines to Follow Phaon.
Her Confirmed Despair.
Her Last Appeal to Phaon.
Laments her Early Misfortunes.
Reproaches Phaon.

Sappho's Address to the Stars.
Sappho's Conjectures.
To a Sigh.
To Phaon ("Can'st thou forget, O! Idol of my soul!").
To Phaon ("Oh! I could toil for thee o'er burning plains.").
To the Muses.
Roscoe, W.   On Being Forced to Part with his Library for the Benefit of his Creditors.
Rossetti, C.   Remember [Me].
Shut Out.
Ruby, H.   Who's Sorry Now?
Rumi.   Come, come, for the rosebower has blossomed; come, come, for the beloved has arrived.
Sahagún, C.   River: "They named this stretch of river Postwar."
Sappho.   May winds and sorrows.
Sassoon, S.   Lamentations.
Scott, L.   Ettrick.
Seward.   Sonnet 31.
Sewell, L.   Release.
Shelley, P.   To—: "One word is too often profaned."
Shin Tongyǒp.   Scene 9.
Siddal.   Dead Love.
Sidney.   Sonnet 108: "When sorrow (using mine own fire's might)."
Sidney, R.   Sonnet 25: "Yow that take pleasure in yowr cruelty."
Sin Hǔm.   Person who made a song, The.
Rain came overnight, A.
Smedley, M.   Sorrowful Sea-Gull, The.
Smith, C.   On the Departure of the Nightingale.
Sorescu, M.   With a Green Scarf.
Sosnora.   Where are our horses.
Southwell.   Vale of Tear[e]s, A.
Soyinka.   I Think It Rains.
Spenser, E.   Iambicum Trimetrum.
Ye wastefull woodes bear witness of my woe.
Stern, G.   Behaving Like a Jew.
Stickney, T.   Here in the North I chase an old despair.
Storni.   Sorrow.
Su Tung-p'o.   Tune: "River Town".
Swinburne.   Anactoria.
Synge.   Wish, A: "May one sorrow every day."
Tapahonso.   Old Salt Woman.
Tennyson, A.   I envy not in any moods.
Thoreau.   Brother where dost thou dwell?
Tighe.   Poor, fond deluded heart! wilt thou again.
Townsend, A.   First Death.
Ts'ai Yen.   Poem of Sorrow.
Ts'ao Chih.   Emotion.
Tu Fu [or Du Fu].   Ballad of the Army Wagons, The.
Evening near Serpent River.
Facing the Snow ("New ghosts weep over lost battles.").
Facing the Snow ("Weeping over battle, many new ghosts.").
I Stand Alone.
Jade Flower Palace ("Where the stream winds pine winds linger.").
Leaving Ch'in-chou.
Loneliness.
Recruiting Officer of Shih-hao.
Song of T'ung-ku.
Tuckerman, F.   Coralie.
Tuqan, F.   Face Lost in the Wilderness.
Turk, R.   Are You Lonesome Tonight?
Turner, C.   Bliss of Heaven, Maria, shall be thine, The.
Unknown.   Be happy, my love, I shall take charge of our cares.
Fowls in the Frith.
Fowls [or Foweles or Fowles] in the Frith.
I may wel sike for grevous is my peyne.
I Saw My Lady Weep.
Lü-yi: Green Robe.
Perle, plesaunte to prynces paye.
Pine boat a-shift.
Song of Green Mountain.
Tatar Songs.

Thinking of Lady Yang at Midnight.
 Together We Know Happiness.
Valente, J.   Elegy That Was Never Finished, An.
Van de Woestijne.   Fever Tune.
Van Vliet.   Coastline, The.
Verlaine.   Tears Fall in My Heart.
Vietnamese Oral Tradition.   Bare Rocks and
 Stars.
 Colonial Troops Transport, The.
Villon.   Complaint of the Fair Armoress [*or*
 Armouress], The.
Voigt.   House.
Volkman.   Daffodils.
 No noise subtracts it. It won't leave, or scatter
 jokes or fathoms, no tiny failing.
Wang Ch'ang-ling.   Silent at Her Window.
Wang Ts'an.   Seven Sorrows.
Warton, T.   Ode on the Passion.
Wei Chuang.   Moon Dips Low, The.
Whitman, S.   Past, The.
 Raven, The.
Whitman, W.   Hours Continuing Long.
 I Sit and Look Out.
 O Captain! My Captain!
 When Lilacs Last in the Dooryard Bloom'd.
Wilcox, E.   Way of It, The.
Williams, H.   To the Strawberry.
Williams, W.   Waiting.
 Widow's Lament in Springtime, The.
Wolfe, C.   To Mary.
Wordsworth, W.   Her cottage, then a cheerful
 object, wore.
Wright, C.   Him.
Wroth.   Song 2: "All night I weep[e], all day I
 cry, Ay me[e]."
 Sonnet 9: "Be[e] you all pleased [*or* pleas'd]?
 your pleasures grieve not[t] me[e]."
 Sonnet 11: "You endless torments that my rest
 opress."
Wyatt.   Divers[e] [*or* Dyvers] doth[e] use, as I
 have heard and kno[w].
Wylie.   Desolation Is a Delicate Thing.
Yi Illo.   Night Rain on the Rivers Hsiao and
 Hsiang.
Yi Myŏnghan.   Morning star has set, The. A
 lark.
Zukofsky, L.   In that this happening.
See also **Funerals; Grief; Mourning and
 Mourners**

Soul
Abse.   In the Theatre.
 Souls.
Achterberg.   Instrument.
Addison, J.   Soul, The.
Agustini.   Sweet Reliquaries, The.
al-Rahim, A.   Wailing.
Alberti.   Eviction.
Aldana.   Sonnet 12: "Which is the reason my
 Damon that although."
Aleixandre.   Body and the Soul, The.
Ammons.   Terrain.
Aygi, G.   People Are a Temple, The.
 Rose of Silence.
Baca.   Book 1: As Life Was; Poem Two.
Baraka, I.   Invention of Comics, The.
 Young Soul.
Barbauld.   Call, The.
Basheva.   Not long ago a whole sun.
Basho.   Dried salmon.
Beasley.   This is the finger of God.
Bei Dao.   Evening Scene, An.
Bejerano, M.   States of War.
Bernstein, C.   From Lines of Swinburne.
Bevington, L.   'Egoisme à Deux'.
 Wrestling.
Blake, W.   Introduction: "Hear the voice of the
 Bard!"
Blumenthal, M.   Man Lost by a River, A.
Boadiba.   Autozobop.
Boutens.   Lonely Night.
Boyle, D. M.   Curtain, The.
Bradley, Dickie.   Souls of Poets, The.
Bradstreet, A.   There is a path no vulture's eye
 hath seen.
Braithwaite.   Rye Bread.
Brock-Broido.   Soul Keeping Company.

Brontë, E.   No Coward Soul is Mine.
Brown, Laura Soul.   Oh! Mercy Mercy Me! A
 Family Gathers to Marvin Gaye.
Browning, E.   Fifth Book.
Brownstein.   Last Spell Cast, The.
Cabral de Melo Neto.   Education by Stone.
 Emptiness of Man, The.
Camões [*or* Camoëns *or* Camoëns], L.   Sonnet:
 That Sad and Joyful Dawn.
Campion, T.   Rose-cheeked Laura[, Come].
Campo, C.   At Times I Say: Let's Try to Be
 Joyous.
 Devout like a Branch.
Cavendish, M.   Dialogue betwixt Man, and
 Nature, A.
 Dialogue betwixt the Body and the Mind, A.
Celan.   Language Mesh.
Ch'u Yüan.   Summons of the Soul, The.
Chudakov.   When the cry goes up.
Cohen, L.   Suzanne [Takes You Down].
Coleridge, H.   Sonnet 27.
Coleridge, M.   Friends—With a Difference.
 Wilderspin.
Cowley, A.   Platonic[k] Love.
Crashaw.   Upon the Book and Picture of the
 Seraphical Saint Teresa.
Cummings, E. E.   Cambridge ladies who live in
 furnished souls, The.
Dacre, K.   Kiss, The: "Greatest bliss, The."
Davenant [*or* D'Avenant].   There, when they
 thought they saw in well sought Books.
Davies, J.   Intellectual Powers of the Soul, The.
DeNiord, C.   Soul as a Body, The.
Di Piero.   Near Damascus.
Dickinson, E.   Choice.
 Dare you see a Soul *at the White Heat?*.
 Death is a Dialogue between.
 Difference between Despair, The.
 Faith—is the Pierless Bridge.
 Go slow, my soul, to feed thyself.
 He fumbles at your Soul.
 Hope is the thing with feathers.
 No Rack can torture me.
 Props assist the House, The.
 Single Screw of Flesh, A.
 Soul has Bandaged moments, The.
 Soul selects her own Society, The.
 Soul that hath a Guest, The.
 Soul's distinct connection, The.
 Spirit lasts, but in what mode, The.
Diego, G.   I Stripped Your Soul Down.
Dobell, S.   Liberty to M. le Diplomate.
Dolben.   One night I dreamt that in a gleaming
 hall.
Dolin, S.   My Soul's Wardrobe.
Donne.   Air[e] and Angels.
 Ecstasy, The.
 Funeral[l], The.
 Resurrection, Imperfect.
 Valediction, A: Forbidding Mourning.
 What if this present were the world's last night?
Doty, M.   Michael's Dream.
Douglas, L.   Green River, The.
Dove, R.   History: "Everything's a metaphor,
 some wise."
Drummond de Andrade.   Elegy: "I've won (lost)
 my day."
Dunbar, P.   Ere Sleep Comes Down to Soothe
 the Weary Eyes.
Eberhart, R.   Worldly Failure.
El Janabi, A.   Against Ibn Arabi.
"Eliot.".   *from* Chapter 46.
Emerson, R.   World-Soul, The.
Empson.   This Last Pain.
Espaillat.   Metrics.
Ettinger, E.   Micrographic Manuscript,
 Miniature (2).
Eyton, F.   Body and Soul.
Ferguson, G.   Puritan against the Wind.
Ferguson, S.   Lark in the Clear Air, The.
Field.   Mummy Invokes His Soul, The.
Follain.   Face the Animal.
Fox, Skip.   Sic transit ("Thus does the sun.").
Freneau.   Too nearly join'd to sickness, toils,
 and pains.
Fullerton.   Poetry.

Ganev, Nedelcho.   Matter.
Garcilaso de la Vega.   Sonnet 5.
Garrett, E.   History Goes to Work.
Glenday, J.   Concerning the Atoms of the Soul.
Glück, L.   Day Without Night.
 New Life, The.
Goldberg, B.   Lilies at Night.
Goodison.   Always Homing Now Soul Toward
 Light.
Graham, J.   Soul Says.
Greer, J.   Rodin's "Gates of Hell".
Grosholz.   Back Trouble.
Guidacci.   Madame X.
Guillén, J.   I Want to Sleep.
Haavikko.   Soul against the state, The.
Hadrian.   Adriani Morientis ad Animam Suam.
 Emperor Hadrian on his Soul.
Halpern, D.   Her Body.
Hayati.   Before there was a trace of this world
 of men.
 Is this darkness the night of Power, or the black
 falling of your hair?
Hedin, R.   Transcanadian.
Hemans.   Indian Woman's Death-Song, The.
Henley, W. E.   Invictus.
Herbert, G.   Virtue [*or* Vertue].
Heyman, E.   Body and Soul.
Hill, G.   Let mind be more precious than soul; it
 will not.
Hirsch, E.   Poor Angels.
Holmes, O.   Chambered Nautilus, The.
 Tartarus.
Hopkins, G.   Caged Skylark, The.
Housman.   Be still, my soul, be still; the arms
 you bear are brittle.
Howe, J.   Soul-Hunter, The.
Howe, S.   He plodded away through drifts of
 ice.
Howell, C.   He Writes to the Soul.
Hwang Insuk.   When He Said "Soul".
Ignatova, E.   To Ovid.
Ilkov, Ani.   Of Stone.
Izumi.   So forlorn am I.
Jacobsen, R.   Crust on Fresh Snow.
Jiménez, J.   Dawn Outside the City Walls.
 I Am Not I.
 I Took Off Petal After Petal.
 Night Piece.
 Road: "They are all asleep, below."
Jones, M.   After the Small Pox.
Joseph, M.   Riddle, A: Of the Soul.
József, A.   Attila József.
 Attila József.
Kabir.   Guest Is Inside, The.
 Thirsty Fish, The.
Kanchev, Nikolai.   Smile, A.
Kendrick, D.   Note to the Ophthalmologist.
Kleinzahler.   Where Souls Go.
Kloos, W.   Sonnet.
Kochanowski, J.   Where Is That Gate for Grief.
Kowit.   What Chord Did She Pluck.
Krivulin.   Idea of Russia, The.
Krukowski, D.   Intellectual Life, The.
Lal Ded [*or* Lalla].   I drag a boat over the
 ocean.
 Soul, like the moon, The.
Lanier, S.   To Beethoven.
Larminie.   Consolation: "Yes, let us speak, with
 lips confirming."
Lauture, D.   Zaps of Zombifying Powder.
Lawrence, D. H.   Healing.
Levertov.   Eye Mask.
 Weeping Woman.
Levis.   Elegy with a Chimneysweep Falling
 Inside It.
Levy, A.   Twilight.
Li Yu [*or* Li Hou-Chu].   Immeasurable Pain.
Lindsay, C.   To My Own Face.
Longfellow, H.   Psalm of Life, A.
 Sound of the Sea, The.
Lope de Vega.   Sonnet 61.
Lovelace, R.   To Althea, from Prison.
Lowell, J.   Sonnet: "Amid these fragments of
 heroic days."
Machado Ruiz.   But look in your mirror for the
 other one.

Is My Soul Asleep?
It Doesn't Matter Now.
Look for your other half.
Wind, One Brilliant Day, The.
Mackenzie, K.   Snake, The.
Two Trinities.
MacLeish.   What the Serpent Said to Adam.
Magdeburg, Mechthild von.   God Speaks to the Soul.
How God Comes to the Soul.
Majorino.   Scene-Script.
Marvell.   Dialogue Between The Resolved Soul and Created Pleasure, A.
Dialogue between the Soul and [the] Body, A.
Gallery, The.
On a Drop of Dew.
Masefield.   Sea Change.
McClure, M.   Souls.
McGrath, C.   Wheatfield Under Clouded Sky.
McGrath, T.   Revisionist Poem—Octavio Paz.
McHugh, H.   Animal Song.
Mew.   Forest Road, The.
Here Lies a Prisoner.
Mikha'il, M.   Beggar, The.
Mistral, G.   Intimate.
Molina, E.   Way It Must Be, The.
Monkhouse.   Any Soul to Any Body.
Moore, M.   What Are Years?
Nijhoff.   Light.
Light, The.
Oliver, M.   Some Questions You Might Ask.
Olson, C.   Chain of memory is resurrection I am a vain man, The.
Oppen.   Animula.
Orlen.   Onomastics and the Falling Snow.
Oswald, A.   Owl Village.
Prayer: "Here I work in the hollow of God's hand."
Othman, A.   Dual Call, The.
Owen, W.   Show, The.
Pasolini.   Presence, The.
Pasternak, B.   Mirror, The.
Patterson, R.   Harlem Suite.
No Jive.
Peck, J.   Metal Denser Than, and Liquid, A.
Peeradina, S.   Testament.
Penna.   Shadowless sun on male bodies.
Philips, K.   L'Amitié: To Mrs M Awbrey.
To My Excellent Lucasia, On Our Friendship.
Piatt, S.   Shapes of a Soul.
Poe.   Sonnet—Silence.
To One in Paradise.
Ulalume [or Ulalume—a Ballad].
Quevedo y Villegas.   From the White Day to Take Me.
Love Constant Beyond Death.
Love Constant Beyond Death.
Raine, K.   Instrument, The.
Ralegh, S.   Lie, The.
Rankin, J.   Tale.
Ray, H.   Soul's Courts, The.
Roberts, L.   Window of Our Soul.
Robinson, A.   Oasis, An.
Rochester, J.   Mistress, The: A Song.
Roethke.   Her Reticence.
In a Dark Time.
Rossetti, C.   Introspective.
Pause, A.
Study (A Soul), A.
Rossetti, D.   77: Soul's Beauty.
Rowe, E.   Reflection, The.
Rumi.   Daylight, full of small dancing particles.
When the heart bursts into flame.
Sachs, N.   Rushing at Times like Flames.
Sadi [or Saadi or Sa'di].   When once the soul is ready to depart, sir.
Salaam.   5 Minutes, Mr. Salaam.
St. Louis Cemetery Crypt.
Salinas, P.   So Transparent Your Soul.
Sandburg, C.   Under a Hat Rim.
Sappho.   Their souls became cold.
Seferis.   Argonautica.
Shakespeare, W.   Sonnet 74: "But be contented: when that fell arrest."
Sonnet 146: "Poor[e] soul[e], the centre [or center] of my sinful[l] earth."

Shapiro, A.   Soul.
Sheykhi.   Your sun-face is a mirror of the soul.
Shokushi.   O cord of life!
Siddal.   Lust of the Eyes, The.
Simic.   Old World, The.
Simpson, J. C.   Oh! if thou lov'st me, love me not so well!
Smith, S.   Lord Barrenstock.
Scorpion.
Sorescu, M.   Map.
Sour, R.   Body and Soul.
Spenser, E.   Sonnet 79: "Men call you fair [or fayre], and you do[e] credit it."
Sonnet 81: "Fair [or Fayre] is my love, when her fair [or fayre] golden heares."
Sulchinskaya, O.   Kite, The.
Supervielle.   Early in the morning.
Traveller, traveller.
Swenson, M.   In Love Made Visible.
Swinburne.   Lake of Gaube, The.
Sestina: "I saw my soul at rest upon a day."
Swirszczynska [or Swir].   Troubles with the Soul at Morning Calisthenics.
Synková, A.   I've met enough people.
Szymborska, W.   Few Words on the Soul, A.
Taylor, E.   Here is a Mudwall tent, whose Matters are.
Meditation 8 (First Series).
Meditation 16 (First Series).
Teasdale.   Broken Field, The.
Tennyson, A.   How pure at heart and sound in head.
Thomas, D.   Turning of the Year, The.
Toomer.   Nora.
Traherne.   Demonstration, The.
Preparative, The.
Tsvetayeva [or Tsvetaeva].   If the Soul was Born with Pinions.
You're going by, west of the sun.
Tuqan, F.   I Found It.
Unknown.   Call of the Soul, The.
I Know Moon-Rise [or Moonrise].
Lyke-Wake Dirge, The [or A].
Not Weary Yet.
Sin-Sick Soul, The.
Songs of the Sacred Mysteries.
Soul's Desire, The.
Uvavnuk.   Shaman Song.
Valentine, J.   Annunciation: "I saw my soul become flesh breaking open."
Vallejo.   In the Moment.
Vaughan, H.   Peace.
Verwey, A.   Soul and Love, The.
Vigil, A.   Hogarcito de La Madrugada, El.
Voigt.   For My Mother.
Waldrop, K.   Lawn of Excluded Middle.
Waller, E.   Of the Last Verses in the Book.
Ward, F.   Who.
Wheatley, P.   On Being Brought from Africa to America.
Whitman, W.   Clear Midnight, A.
I believe in you my soul, the other I am must not abase itself to you.
I celebrate myself, and sing myself.
Last Invocation, The.
Noiseless Patient Spider, A.
Not Heaving from My Ribb'd Breast Only.
Wilbur, R.   Love Calls Us to the Things of This World.
Wilcox, E.   Nothing New.
Wilde, O.   Hélas!
Winchilsea.   Nocturnal Reverie, A.
On Myself.
Wintu Oral Tradition.   Dandelion Puffs.
Wylie.   Self-portrait.
This Corruptible.
Yeats.   Dialogue of Self and Soul, A.
Zanzotto.   Campèa.

Soul Mates
Aldington.   Possession.
Brother Yao.   Passing Through This House.
Longenbach.   Orphic Night.
Winthrop, Jeanette I.   Couple Having Breakfast in the Deli, The.

Sound
Alexander, E.   Stravinsky in L.A.

Apollinaire.   Cantor.
Basho.   Ancient silent pond.
As the sound fades.
Awake at night.
Heard, not seen.
Old pond / Leap-splash.
Old pond, The.
Old pond, The.
Old pond—frogs jumped in—sound of water.
Old-time pond, from off whose shadowed depth, An.
Petal shower, A.
Still old pond, The.
Temple bell stops, The.
Beckett, S.   Roundelay: "On all that strand."
Bertolino.   Baying, The.
Biespiel, D.   After the Wedding.
Brecht, S.   Silence, 2.
Buson.   Coolness.
Crossing the autumn moor.
Lightning flash—, A.
Listening to the moon.
My old man's ears.
Old well.
Sound of a bell.
Thwack of an ax, The.
Cage.   There is no.
Cavalli.   In that small dark fever of every reawakening.
When I listen for the sound of.
Cherry, K.   Pines Without Peer, The.
Chiang Chieh.   To the Tune "The Fair Maid of Yu".
Church, R.   Earphones.
Clampitt.   Syrinx.
Clary.   Another hot afternoon upstairs after school.
Coleridge, M.   To a Piano.
Coolidge, C.   Bee Elk.
Darkling Thrums.
One of Essence's Entrances.
Ounce code orange.
Soda Gong.
There Is a Caterpillar That Makes a Very Complicated Hammock.
Copus, J.   Forgiveness.
Coviello, M.   Self-Portrait.
Curnow.   Out of Sleep.
Darragh.   Pie in the Sky: Part 2.
Deanovich.   Zombie Jet.
Densmore.   Sound Is Fading Away, The.
Dèr Mouw.   Audible Still.
Dickinson, E.   Wind, The.
DiPalma.   Rebus Tact.
Drake, N.   Foley Artist, The.
Felltham [or Feltham].   Upon a Rare Voice.
Francis, R.   Sound I Listened For, The.
Freneau.   And from the woods the late resounding note.
Garland, H.   In August.
Gerhardt, I. G. M.   Remembrance Day.
Remembrance Day.
Graham, D.   Varied Carol, The.
Gregory, H.   Cage of Voices, The.
Haines, J.   Nocturnal.
Hannan, M.   Making Conversation.
Harris, Ken.   Bough Well Bounds The Vowel Bounds Well, A.
Holland, J.   Wavelength.
Hollander, J.   By the Sound.
Huidobro.   New Song.
Hwang Insuk.   Walk, A.
Jackson, L.   Footfalling.
Jones, A.   World, The.
Justice, D.   Insomnia of Tremayne, The.
Kaufman, B.   Crootey Songo.
Kenyon, J.   Noiseless Wheel, The.
Kikaku.   Shrine gate / Through morning mist.
Killeen, G.   Wishes.
Kirsch, M.   Sleep's Underside.
Kollan Alici.   What Her Friend Said.
Kumin, M.   Bangkok Gang, The.
Sound of Night, The.
L'Abbé, Sonnet.   Shyness, the delay to say, The.
Lane, P.   Lyric: I Am Looking at Music.
Lindsay, M.   Hurlygush.

Longfellow, H.   Spirit of Poetry, The.
Lumsden, R.   Then.
Lux.   Unlike, for Example, the Sound of a Riptooth Saw.
MacCaig.   Blue Tit on a String of Peanuts.
Majorino.   Say--So I'll Say.
Masaoka Shiki.   Midnight sound / Leap up.
Mayer, B.   Index.
  Laura Cashdollars.
  Steps.
McCosker.   Tinnitus.
McDonald, E.   Itherness.
McGuckian.   Mantilla.
McGuire, Jerry.   Plate Pieces.
Merritt, C.   Lullaby: "Say to me: out there are only streets, and cars."
Meyerhoff, J.   Resounding echo of the buddha's words, The.
Montague, J.   Hearth Song.
  Windharp.
Mörling, M.   For F. M. Who Did Not Get Killed Yesterday on 57th Street.
Nye, N.   What Brings Us Out.
O'Brien, M.   Poem: "Little bones of."
Preston, R.   Chicago Blues.
Pritchard, N.   Gyre's Galax.
Rea, T.   Lugs Benedict on the Coast, 1934.
Romo-Carmona, M.   Crows.
Rossetti, C.   Wind Has Such a Rainy Sound, The.
Salaam.   SOUND is ProFound Sense.
Sanfield.   Poem for Those of You Who Are Sometimes Troubled by Barking Dogs and Low Flying Jets, A.
Shange.   I Live in Music.
Shen Yüeh.   Listening to Gibbons at Rock-Pool Creek.
Shinkichi Takahashi.   Wood in Sound, A.
Smith, L.   Into Still Air.
Stanton, M.   In Ignorant Cadence.
Stevens, W.   Autumn Refrain.
  Pleasures of Merely Circulating, The.
Sundiata.   Ear Training.
Tabb.   Whisper.
Tomlinson, C.   In the Studio.
Tremblay, G.   Not Sense.
Tureski, L.   Song, The: "It's the tone, not the harp."
Unknown.   Treeback.
Velichansky, A.   Policeman does not blow his whistle, The.
Vitale, M.   Loop, Fleck, Sound and So On.
Volkman.   No noise subtracts it. It won't leave, or scatter jokes or fathoms, no tiny failing.
Warner, G.   Midnight percussion.
Wen Chao.   Hearing the Gibbons Call in Pa Gorge.
Whitman, W.   Proud Music of the Storm.
Wills, J.   One Day We'll Be Able to Talk to the Dead.
Wright, J.   Depressed by a Book of Bad Poetry, I Walk toward an Unused Pasture and Invite the Insects to Join Me.
Yang Wan-li.   Night Rain at Luster Gap.
Zisquit.   There is always a sound.
Zukofsky, L.   Two Dedications: Tibor Serly.

Soup
Ap Hywel, Elin.   Song about Soup, A.
Basho.   From all these trees.
Baudelaire.   Soup and the Clouds, The.
Breckenridge.   Cooking Catalogue.
Bruce, G.   Soup and Sherry.
Caesar.   Animal Crackers in My Soup.
Carroll, L.   Song of the Mock Turtle, The.
Celaya, G.   Meaning of Soup, The.
Crawford, R.   Scotch Broth.
Curtis, T.   Soup.
Goldbarth.   Recipe.
Hernández Cruz.   If Chickens Could Talk.
Koehler, T.   Animal Crackers in My Soup.
Lau, A.   Morning reflections over the miso soup.
Penn, P.   Soup, The: "On the day of your scan, I make a soup."
Rhodes, M.   All the Soups.
Sandburg, C.   Soup.
Schneider, M.   Soup and Slavery.

Stein, G.   Orange in.
Vroman.   Thin Wire.
Young, K.   Boiling, The.
  Campbell's Black Bean Soup.

Sousa, John Philip
Cohan.   I Want to Hear a Yankee Doodle Tune.
Ruefle.   March, The.

South Africa
Breytenbach.   Dar es-Salaam: Harbour of Peace.
  Firewing.
  Journey.
Brook, D.   April 27, 1994.
  Message to Mary Ferrari in Jo'Burg.
Brooks, G.   Music for Martyrs.
  Song of Winnie.
Brutus.   On the Island.
  Robben Island Sequence.
Campbell, R.   Attend my fable if your ears be clean.
  On Some South African Novelists.
Cronin, J.   Naval Base (Part III), The.
Hoagland, E.   Fired Up!!
Jensma.   In memoriam Ben Zwane.
Jordan, J.   Poem About My Rights.
Kizer, C.   Race Relations.
Lee, K.   On South Africa.
Mabuza.   Death to the Gold Mine!
Mphahlele.   Poem, A: "What is there that we can do or say."
Nortje.   Letter from Pretoria Central Prison.
  Soliloquy: South Africa.
Press, K.   Causality and Chance in Love.
Ruden, S.   Beggar Outside Cape Town Station, A.
Sepamla.   I Remember Sharpeville.
  Measure for Measure.
  Odyssey, The.
  Silence: 2.
Weatherford, C.   From the Mouth of the Gxara.
Weigl.   Sky in Daduza Township, The.

South America
Campo.   Lost Plaza Is Everywhere, The.
Guevara, M.   After the Colombian Earthquake.
Kirby, D.   I Think I Am Going to Call My Wife Paraguay.
Kowit.   Trick, A.
Mercer, J.   Tangerine.
Rome, H.   South America, Take It Away!
Talvikki, A.   Along the road, the bright painted crosses.
  At night, coolness like water lapping.
  Before first light, we would open the nets.
  Halley's Comet crossed the jungle sky.
  Teatro Amazonas, remnant, The.
  Waking, months after I leave the jungle.
Wright, C.   Wander Luís.

South Carolina (state)
Coogler.   Alas! Carolina!
Jefferson, B.   Long Distance Moan.
Kahn, G.   Carolina in the Morning.
Lewis, S.   Dinah.
Moorer.   Crum Appointment, The.
Nickelson, C.   Charleston, South Carolina.
Simms, W.   Ode: "Do ye quail but to hear, Carolinians."
Timrod.   Carolina.
  Charleston.
  Ode: "Sleep sweetly in your humble graves."
Young, J.   Dinah.

South Sea Islands
Unknown.   First Coconut Tree, The.

South, The, United States
Alexander, E.   Letter: Blues.
Allan, L.   Strange Fruit.
Allison, O.   Billy.
Angelou, M.   Miss Scarlet, Mr. Rhett and other Latter-Day Saints.
Applewhite.   Southland Drive-In.
  Water from the Lamp Bottle.
Bontemps.   Southern Mansion.
Brooks, S.   (That's the Way) Dixieland Started Jazz.
Brown, Lee Ann.   Call for Vertical Integration in the Eye of the Storm, A.
Brown, Lew.   Birth of the Blues, The.

Caesar.   Is It True What They Say About Dixie?
Cartwright, K.   ALL-YOU-CAN-EAT / catfish houses.
Cendrars.   South.
Crouch, S.   Blackie Thinks of His Brothers.
Davis, M.   Cry of a People.
DeSylva, B. G.   Birth of the Blues, The.
Dickey, J.   Snow on a Southern State.
Emmett.   Dixie [or Dixie's Land].
Foster, S.   Oh! Susanna.
Giscombe, C.   1978, Remembering 1962.
  Recent Past, The.
Harris, D.   Landscapes.
Hayden, R.   Runagate Runagate.
Henderson, R.   Birth of the Blues, The.
Herman, J.   Mame.
Hiestand, E.   Moon Winx Motel.
Hudgins.   At the Piano.
  Chinaberry Trees, The.
  Southern Literature.
Hughes, L.   Bitter River, The.
  Blue Bayou.
  Christ in Alabama.
  Merry-Go-Round.
  Mulatto.
  Po' Boy Blues.
  Silhouette.
  Song for a Dark Girl.
Jeffers, H.   Eatonton Tableaux.
  Philly in the Light.
  Tuscaloosa: Riversong.
Johnson, J.   O Southland!
Jones, R.   Small Lower-Middle-Class White Southern Male.
Kelly, Erren Geraud.   7-30-96.
Komunyakaa, Y.   Gristmill.
Kumin, M.   Chain, The.
Lazarus, E.   South, The.
Lazer, Hank.   8 / (in transit).
Lerner, S.   Is It True What They Say About Dixie?
Lewis, S.   Rock-a-Bye Your Baby with a Dixie Melody.
Lorde.   Afterimages.
McGrath, C.   Shrimp Boats, Biloxi.
Melville, H.   Iris.
Mercer, J.   Blues in the Night.
Myers, J.   We Go Away at Home.
Powell, K.   Southern Birth.
Pratt, M.   Red String.
Preston, M.   Hymn to the National Flag.
Randall, D.   Southern Road, The.
Randolph, I.   Rebel, The.
Reese, L.   Old Belle, An.
Rome, H.   Don't Wanna Write About the South.
Sadoff.   Civil Rights.
Shockley, E.   Cause i'm from dixie too.
Smith, D.   To Isle of Wight.
Thompson, M.   To the South.
Toomer.   Georgia Dusk.
  Reapers.
Unknown.   Confederate Memorial Day.
  Southern Blues.
Van Jordan, A.   Question: "What up, brother? the white teen with dreadlocks."
Walcott.   Arkansas Testament, The.
Walker, M.   Childhood.
  Delta.
  Southern Song.
Weaver, A.   Borders.
  Easy Living.
Webster, P.   Jump for Joy.
Wood, S.   Hollow.
Wright, J.   Invitation to Madison County, An.
Young, Andy.   Foxfire.
Young, J.   Rock-a-Bye Your Baby with a Dixie Melody.
Young, K.   East Jesus.
Young, Seth.   All says a glass doorknow Parabola ghost.

South Wind
Nishiwaki Junzaburo.   Rain.
O'Brien, C.   River, The: "Poor Mick was trotting on to the town."

Southern Cross, The (constellation)
Melville, H.   Southern Cross.

Southey, Robert
Byron, G. Dedication: "Bob Southey! You're a poet—poet-laureate."
Carroll, L. Father William.

Soviet Union
Draycott. Night Driving.
Ginsberg, A. Not Dead Yet.
Gorbanevskaya. That time I did not save Warsaw, nor Prague later.
Iofe, Y. Olsanski Cemetery, The.
Thing or Two about Childhood, A.
Khlebnikov, V. Trumpet, Shout, Carry!
Mengham, Rod. To the Soviet Embalmers.
Rein. Breakfast on the Balcony.
Sosnora. Owl and the Mouse, The.
See also **Russia**

Soweto, South Africa
Kuzwayo, E. Choice, The.
Mandela. There's an Unknown River in Soweto.
Smith, P. Woman Who Died in Line, The.
Soyinka. Funeral Sermon, Soweto.
We wish only to bury our dead. Shorn.

Space and Space Travel
Adams, Cyd. Longview, Texas.
Apollinaire. Always.
Auden. Moon Landing.
Azzawi, F. Leave the earth behind you!
Black, S. Blank Abandon of Beds, The.
Brouwer, J. Space Memorabilia Auction, Superior Stamp and Coin, Beverly Hills, California.
Bruchac. Let the Midnight Special.
Buchan, T. Everlasting Astronauts, The.
Buckley, C. Inverse Square Law of the Propagation of Light, The.
Burke, J. Swinging on a Star.
Dabney. Earth's Bondman.
Di Michele, A. Archipelago (Interra Diocesan).
Eberhart, R. Dam Neck, Virginia.
Erdrich, H. Future Debris.
Fox, Skip. Sic Transit ("We who were alive, held you in arms, welcomed you to table, to.").
Gautier. Unknown Shores.
George, W. Armstrong and Aldrin on the Moon.
Goldstein, L. Firmament on High.
Guest, B. Homage.
Hans. Fueled.
Harvey, Y. Museum Cashier, The.
Henniker-Heaton. Post Early for Space.
Heyen. Steadying, The.
Kendall, M. Ether Insatiable.
Kunitz, S. Flight of Apollo, The.
Laux, D. Each Sound.
Lewis, G. Drew trips over his shadow by the pool.
Last suppers, I fancy, are always wide-screen.
There are great advantages to having been dead.
Thousands arrive when a bird's about to fly.
Magee, W. Giant Rocket.
How to Reach the Sun . . . on a Piece of Paper.
Mallarmé. When the shade threatened with the fatal decree.
Martinez, D. Bad Alchemy.
Momaday. Walk on the Moon.
Morgan, E. First Men on Mercury, The.
Morshen. In superstitious panic.
Nealon, Mary Jane. Moon Landing, 1969.
Nemerov. Witnessing the Launch of the Shuttle *Atlantis*.
Novikov, N. In our world it's unusual.
Ortiz. On late-night television, two U.S. scientists talk about why the U.S.
Perillo, L. Destruction of the Mir, The.
Plomer. To the Moon and Back.
Robeson, E. Answers, The.
Rutherford, Brett. Viking.
Seaton, M. Wings.
Sharah. Package for Another World.
Shinkichi Takahashi. Braggart Duck.
Skloot. Year the Space Age Was Born, The.
Smith, P. Annie Pearl Smith Discovers Moonlight.
Södergran. On Foot I Had to Walk Through the Solar Systems.
Stafford, W. Dog Asleep.

Swenson, M. First Walk on the Moon.
Thomas, L. Flash Point.
Thomas, R. Repairing the Hubble Telescope.
Tomlinson, C. Ararat.
Updike. Open Letter to Voyager II, An.
Vacietis. Goodbye to a Spaceman.
Wilkie, B. Mummification and Space Travel.
Williams, W. Heel and Toe to the End.
World Contracted to a Recognizable Image, The.
Winter, M. Space Parable.
Wintu Oral Tradition. You and I Shall Go.

Spain
Alberti. To the Sun of the War.
Arnold, C. Your friend's arriving on the bus.
Barker, G. O Hero Akimbo on the Mountains of To-morrow.
Belloc. Tarantella.
Bergman, A. To Eugene P. Loveman.
Caesar. Spanish Jake.
Cernuda. Impression of Exile.
To Larra with Some Violets.
Dacey, P. Musica.
Darwish, M. On Our Last Evening on This Land.
Ettinger, E. Micrographic Manuscript, Miniature (1).
Fritz, Walter Helmut (b. 1929). Columbus.
García Lorca. Little Ballad of the Three Rivers.
Gil de Biedma, J. In Mournful Praise and Memory of the French Song.
In the Forties.
Sad Night of October 1959.
Hughes, T. You Hated Spain.
Jacob, M. Spanish Generosity.
Jeffers, R. Sinverguenza.
Lawless, E. In Spain.
Lerner, A. Rain in Spain, The.
Lerner, S. Spanish Jake.
Levine, P. On the Murder of Lieutenant José del Castillo by the Falangist Bravo Martinez, July 12, 1936.
Salami.
Machado Ruiz. For Don Francisco Giner de Los Ríos.
Here's another Spaniard! Welcome!
Meditation for this Day.
On the Banks of the Duero.
Rainbow at Night.
Song: "Now the moon is rising."
Today's Meditation.
Young Spain, A.
MacNeice. And I remember Spain.
Marlowe. This said, the restles generall through the darke.
Millay, E. Say that We Saw Spain Die.
Neruda. Almería.
I Explain a Few Things.
O'Hara, F. Madrid.
Plath. Alicante Lullaby.
Prados, E. When It Was Spring.
Quevedo y Villegas. I'll not be silent, though you put your finger.
Rexroth, K. Requiem for the Spanish Dead.
Rolfe, E. City of Anguish.
Rundī, A. Everything declines after reaching perfection, therefore let no man be beguiled by the sweetness of a pleasant life.
Salazar. Taking It Back.
Vallejo. Spain, Take This Cup from Me.
Wright, James. Eisenhower's Visit to Franco, 1959.
Wright, Jay. Madrid.
Young, A. Ravel: Bolero.

Spanish-American War
Johnson, J. Color Sergeant, The.
Kipling, R. White Man's Burden, The.
Moody, W. Ode in Time of Hesitation, An.
On a Soldier Fallen in the Philippines.

Spanish Armada
Góngora y Argote. On the Armada That Battled Against England.

Spanish Civil War
Celan. Shibboleth.
Duran, J. Pyrenees, The.
Spanish Peasant Boy.

Hernández, M. Sitting on Top of Corpses.
Morrissey, S. Wound Man, The.
Paz. Madrid, 1937, / in the Plaza del Angel the women.
Rickword. To the Wife of a Non-interventionist Statesman (March 1938).
See also **Civil War, Spain**

Spanish Succession, War of the
Addison, J. Poem to His Grace the Duke of Marlborough, A.
Defoe, D. Word's gone out, and now they spread the main, The.
Southey, R. Battle of Blenheim, The.
See also **Blenheim, Battle of (1704)**

Spankings
Hayden, R. Whipping, The.

Sparrows
al-Rahim, A. My Heart.
Barney, W. Rufous-Crowned Sparrow Seen Loitering below Possum Kingdom Dam.
Basho. Good house.
Berry, W. Sparrow.
Buckley, C. Sparrows: "Like the poor, they are with us always."
Buson. Evening cloudburst—, An.
Sparrow singing.
Sudden shower.
Collier, M. Brave Sparrow.
Collin, Bernard. Perpetual *Look* Physics: 17/5.
Dunn, D. France: "Dozen sparrows scuttled on the frost, A."
Dunn, S. With No Experience in Such Matters.
Frater, H. Wee Cock Sparra, The.
Gibbons, R. Sparrow.
Hecht, A. House Sparrows.
Inagaki Chikai. Butterflies.
Issa. Be respectful / Sparrows.
Come and.
Hey, sparrow!
Little sparrows.
No doubt about it.
Young sparrows.
Johnston, B. Did You Ever Hear an English Sparrow Sing?
Kherdian. Hawthorne berries, The.
Kikaku. Sprinkle water wide / For the sparrow.
Kim, Suji Kwock. On Sparrows.
Macrae, D. Wee Cock Sparra, The.
Mamalatan. What She Said.
Martin, C. His Eye Is on the Sparrow.
Muske, C. Love Song: "Love comes hungry to anyone's hand."
Nemerov. Because You Asked about the Line between Prose and Poetry.
Nomura Akitari. Butterflies.
Oliver, M. Look and See.
Ostroff. Sparrows at the Airport, The.
Rodríguez, C. Sparrow.
Sadoff. I Join the Sparrows.
Shinkichi Takahashi. Eternity.
Flight of the Sparrow.
Four Divine Animals.
Near Shinobazu Pond.
Position of the Sparrow, The.
Sparrow and Bird-Net Building.
Sparrow in Withered Field.
Skelton, J. Pla ce bo.
Spires. Apology.
Interrogations of the Sparrow.
Stern, G. Red Bird.
Trejo. Some Sparrows.
Vietnamese Oral Tradition. Phoenixes and Sparrows.
Williams, W. Breakfast.
Pastoral: "Little sparrows, The."
To a Sparrow.
Winters, Y. Dream Vision, A.
Wright, J. Sparrows in a Hillside Drift.
Yang Wan-li. Cold Sparrows.
Yenser, S. Another Lo-Cal Elegy.

Sparta, Greece
Dugan, A. Self-Exhortation on Military Themes.
Simonides. For the Spartan Dead at Thermopylai (480 B.C.).

On the Spartan Dead at Thermopylae.
Thermopylae.

Spas
Rochester, J. Tunbridge Wells.

Speaking in Tongues
Erdrich. New Vows.
Hamill, S. Gift of Tongues, The.
Sriramulu, D. Other Tongue, The.

Speech
Abrahams, L. Don't say it.
Angeles, C. Words.
Armand. Poem with Skin.
Arteaga, Alfred. Corrido Blanco.
Barlow, G. Nook.
Beachy-Quick, Dan. Echo and A.
Bernstein, C. Let's Just Say.
Bogan, L. Henceforth, from the Mind.
Bringhurst. Song of Ptahhotep, The.
Brock-Broido. One Thousand Days, The.
Brooks, S. Grandma Talk.
Carroll, L. Fit the Second: The Bellman's
Speech.
Carruth, H. Sonnet: "Well, she told me I had an
aura. "What?" I said."
Castro, R. They Say that the Plants Do Not
Speak.
Celan. Speak You Too.
Clare, Eli. Learning to Speak.
Clough. It is most curious to see what a power
a few calm words.
Darío, R. Unhappy He.
Davis, O. New Philosophy of Composition, or,
How to Ignore the Non-Reasoning Creature
Capable of *Speeech* Perched Outside Your
Bathroom Window, A.
de Fierro. Speak to Me.
Dhompa, T. How Thubten Sang His Songs.
Dodge, M. Way To Do It, The.
Eich. Marketplace.
Emerson, R. Merops.
Ferguson, G. Silent as Roses.
Follain. Speech Alone.
Friesen, P. Pa poem 1: firstborn.
Ginsberg, A. Stroke.
Graves, R. Cool Web, The.
Hannan, M. Making Conversation.
Harburg. I Like the Likes of You.
What Is There to Say?
Harrison, T. Earthen Lot, The.
Heaney, S. Roof it again. Batten down. Dig in.
Hölderlin. But speech.
Hyppolite, M. Speech.
Jackson, L. O Vocables of Love.
Johnson, D. Bilingual Means Having Two
Tongues.
Joseph, A. On Being Told I Don't Speak Like a
Black Person.
Kirby, D. Dear Derrida.
Kloefkorn. Why the Stone Remains Silent.
Kuznetsova, I. Speech is a stream.
Larsen, W. Learning the War.
Lehman. Alternative to Speech, An.
Lux. Language Animal, The.
MacLeish. Speech to a Crowd.
Magrelli. I prefer to come from silence to talk.
Matthews, W. Men at My Father's Funeral.
Moir, L. Handnotes.
Montale. Don't ask us for the word to frame.
Ours is group solitude.
Mueller, L. Triage.
Nibenegenesabe. Quiet Until the Thaw.
Ortiz. Speaking.
Palmer, M. Said the Speaker.
Quevedo y Villegas. I'll not be silent, though
you put your finger.
Razaf, A. S'posin'.
Reddy, Srikanth. Corruption.
Reznikoff. Girls outshout the machines, The.
Riley, J. Smitten Purist, The.
Rukeyser, M. Effort at Speech between Two
People.
Sandburg, C. Languages.
Sappho. When anger spreads in the breast.
Slessor. Full Orchestra.
Solórzano, L. Mute Poem.
Poema mudo.

Speech Poem.
Stevens, W. On [*or* Of] the Manner of
Addressing Clouds.
Two Figures in Dense Violet Night.
Stickney, T. And, the last day being come, Man
stood alone.
Swiggart, Katherine. Exhaled, The.
Tana, P. No.
Tipton. I Want to Speak With the Blood that
Lies Down.
Tornero, A. Cosas que se tocan sonidos
materiales surcaron.
Things touching each other sounds materials
furrowed.
Vitale, M. Patois.
Walsh, Agnes. Time That Passes, The.
Whitmore, S. Bird, The.
Williams, C. K. My Mother's Lips.
Youngblom, T. Ophelia Speaks.
See also **Screams; Talk**

Speed
Alexander, P. Bicycle Sprint.
Brown, James. Lesson, The: "Cleaned, lubed
and wiped."
Coatsworth. Swift Things Are Beautiful.
Cohan. Twentieth-Century Love.
Crunk, T. Reunion.
Daugherty, J. Pack train, stage coach, pony
express, climb over the mountain passes.
Dryden, C. Scorcher's Farewell to His Steed,
The.
Frost, R. Master Speed, The.
Gizzi. Tout les Matins du Monde.
Kandinsky [*or* Kandinskii]. Chalk and Soot.
Knibbe, H. Skater, The.
Larkin, T. With Cheerful Speed.
MacCaig. Ringed Plover by a Water's Edge.
McDaniel, J. Disasterology.
Nye, N. Rider, The.
Rukeyser, M. *et al.* Believe that we bloom upon
this stalk of time.
Strange, E. Scorcher, The.
Unknown. Piao-you-mei: Like Falling Fruit.
Railroad Man for Me, A.
Untermeyer, L. Down-hill on a Bicycle.

Spelling
Bierce. Orthography.
Coolidge, C. Listene / secting.
Guest, B. Fit Für Gaing Farth.
Lee, L. Persimmons.
Nash, O. What's in a Name? Some Letter I
Always Forget.

Spenser, Edmund ("Colin Clout")
Bentley, R. How vigilant was Spenser.
Ralegh. Vision upon This Concei[p]t of the
Faerie [*or* Faery] Queen[e], A.

Sphinx
Auden. Sphinx, The.
Baudelaire. Spleen LXXVI.
Black, S. Lust.
Borges. Oedipus and the Riddle.
Emerson, R. Sphinx, The.
Gilbert, C. Questions about the Sphinx.
Hayden, R. Sphinx.
Rukeyser, M. Myth.
Turgeniev, I. Sphinx, The.
Wilde, O. Fin-de-Siècle Cat.

Spider Webs
Barber, D. Little Overture.
Calvino. Octavia.
Carver, R. Cobweb, The.
Cooke, R. Arachne.
Eberhart, R. Spider, The.
Kees. What the Spider Heard.
Llwyd, Iwan. Spider.
Mead, J. Paradise Consists of Forty-Nine
Rotating Spheres.
Merwin. Encampment at Morning, An.
Miles, J. Fields of Learning.
Murray, L. On Removing Spiderweb.
Noguchi, Yonejiro (Yone). Like a cobweb hung
upon the tree.
Simic. Devils, The.
Smith, C. To the Insect of the Gossamer.
Unamuno. On Reading Jules Renard's Diary.

Whitman, W. Noiseless Patient Spider, A.

Spiders
Basho. Spider, if you had a voice.
What voice.
Bunting. Riding silk, adrift at noon.
Cavendish, M. Common Fate of Books, The.
Cisneros, A. Spider Hangs Too Far from the
Ground, The.
Cooke, R. Arachne.
Cucchi, M. I wouldn't know what it's like to be
a pawn.
Davis, W. Spider.
Dickinson, E. Spider sewed at Night, A.
DJ Renegade. Fireflies in a Jar.
Eberhart, R. Spider, The.
Empson. Arachne.
Faverey. What it is all about.
Fletcher, G. I saw, sweet Licia, when the spider
ran.
Frost, R. Design.
In White.
Giussani, S. Aridness of Air, The.
Golding, A. This Damsell was not famous for
the place.
Graham, J. Geese, The.
Hackett, J. Up close, at the place.
Hajjaj, N. Laila's Face.
Hopes. On the Feast of Saint John the
Evangelist.
Horan. Little City.
Howitt, M. Spider and the Fly, The.
Issa. Don't worry, spiders.
Jackson, A. Transformable Prophecy.
Jackson, L. Elegy in a Spider's Web.
Kang Ŭn'gyo. Spider: "What I throw out to the
world."
Lau, A. Wintermelon.
Llwyd, Iwan. Spider.
Lowell, R. Mr. Edwards and the Spider.
Marchant, F. Screen Porch.
McPherson, S. Ability to Make a Face Like a
Spider While Singing Blues: Junior Wells, The.
Merwin. Broken, The.
Encampment at Morning, An.
Spiders I Have Known.
Muldoon, P. Spider: "How you like these
threads, said white spider."
Richards, M. Christmas Spider, The.
Rivera, D. Dinner Together.
Russell, T. To the Spider.
Sarton, M. Love: "Fragile as a spider's web."
Spenser, E. Sonnet 71: "I joy to see how in
your drawen work."
Stern, G. Spider: "How you like these threads,
said white spider."
Swift, J. Spider.
Sze. Earthstar.
Taylor, E. Upon a Spider Catching a Fly.
Triplett, P. Spider of Doubt.
Vallejo. Spider, The.
White, E. Natural History.
Whitman, W. Noiseless Patient Spider, A.
Wright, J. Regret for a Spider Web.
Zimmer. Brain of the Spider, The.

Spies
Handy, J. Mata Hari Blues or Why I Will Never
Be a Spy.
Unknown. God, provide the "little horror" with
an eternal sleep!
See also **Spying and Spies**

Spinning and Spinners
Alterman, N. Spinner, The.
Graves, A. Irish Spinning-Wheel, The.
Powell, D. A. My Lot to Spin the Purple: that
the Tabernacle Should Be Made.
Preston, M. Erinna's Spinning.
Seneca. This said, she twirled the thread on an
ugly spool.
Unknown. Factory Workers' Song.
Maiden, The.
You might easy know a doffer.
Valéry. Spinner, The.
Volkman. Sonnet: "Now you nerve. Flurred,
avid as the raw."
Waller, J. Spinning-Wheel, The.

Spinoza, Baruch
Borges. Baruch Spinoza.
Spinoza.
Herbert, Z. Mr. Cogito Tells about the
Temptation of Spinoza.
Zukofsky, L. First Movement: "And out of olde
bokes, in good feith".

Spinsters
Auden. Miss Gee.
Chudleigh. To the Ladies.
Couto. Lizzie.
Duffy, C. Havisham.
Harrison, S. Catharine Plouffe.
Jackson, A. Spinster Song: African-American
Woman Guild.
Kasdorf. Leftover Blessings.
Lochhead, L. Grim Sisters, The.
Montague, J. Wild Dog Rose, The.
Parra, N. Tunnel, The.
Pitter. Old, Childless, Husbandless.
Plath. Spinster.
Unknown. Song of an Old Maid.

Spirits
Bottoms. Recording the Spirit Voices.
Chang Heng. Bones of Zhuangzi, The.
Du Shenyan. Written at Jumble-Rock Mountain
by the South Sea.
Goodwin, Sister Elizabeth Hope. Centennial
Year for the Spirits.
Johnson, R. Me and the Devil Blues.
Kasischke. Visibility of Spirits, The.
Lilley, Gary. Meetin the Conjure Woman.
McClure, M. Song: "I work with the shape."
O'odham. No. 81. We Will Join Them.
No. 86. The Waters of the Spirits.
Shannon, A. Returning the Water.
Steptoe. Spookism.
Strange. Night Work.
Unknown. Paddle-song.
Wintu Oral Tradition. There Above.

Spiritualism and Spiritualists
Bandeira. Spiritual Wedding.
Brontë, E. I'm happiest when most away.
Browning, E. Sleep, The.
Dunn, S. Because You Mentioned the Spiritual
Life.
Ellis, T. Being There.
Hernández Cruz. Spirits.
Mapanje. These Too Are Our Elders.
Visiting Zomba Plateau.
Martinaitis, M. Kukutis's Sinful Spirit.
Mirabai [*or* Mira Bai]. All I Was Doing Was
Breathing.
O'odham. No. 79. Yonder Lies the Spirit Land.
Ryan, G. Global Rewards Redemption Centre,
The.
Smith, S. Mrs Simpkins.

Spirituals
Johnson, J. O Black and Unknown Bards.
Notley. Where Leftover Misery Goes.
Sousa, N. Let My People Go.
Unknown. Go Down, Moses.

Spittoons
Hughes, L. Brass Spittoons.

Spoons
Boruch. Simple Machines.
McKay, D. Setting the Table.

Sports
Alexander, E. Today's News.
Betjeman. Subaltern's Love-Song, A.
Calder, A. Curling: Old Murrayfield Ice Rink.
Cherry, K. On Watching a Young Man Play
Tennis.
Drieu la Rochelle. Tennis.
Guillén, N. Small Ode to a Black Cuban Boxer.
Holland, J. Baize Queens.
Jonson, B. To Sir Henry Goodyere.
Kumin, M. 400-Meter Freestyle.
Liu Cheng. Cockfight.
Margolis, G. Lacrosse.
Noguchi, R. Breath He Holds, The.
Turn of Privacy, The.
Pushkin, A. On the Statue of a Player at Svaika.
Riordan, M. Some Sporting Motifs.
Scott, D. Playing for England.

Sidney. Sonnet 53: "In martial sports I had my
cunning tried."
Tkachenko. Dynamo Stadium, 1980.
Townsend, A. Bicycle Racers, The.
Tranter. Some sports are odious, but.
Weaver, A. Poets, The.
Webb, H. Vive Le Sport.
Williams, J. River Walk.
Wright, J. Mad Fight Song for William S.
Carpenter, 1966, A.
Wrigley, A. Owdham Footbo'.
See also **Athletics and Athletes; Games**

Spring
Abrahams, L. Spring report.
Allingham, W. In a Spring Grove.
Amichai, Y. Lips of the dead once
thoughtlessly.
Ammons. Spring Coming.
Anderson, S. American Spring Song.
Antipater of Sidon. Priapos of the Harbor.
Ashbery, J. Spring Day.
Barbauld. Ode to Spring.
Bartlett, M. Spring in Placitas.
Basho. Awe inspiring!
Crane's legs, The.
First day of spring.
In the plum blossom scent.
It's spring, all right.
Lovely spring night, A.
Spring!
Spring going.
Spring going.
Spring / gradually taking form.
Spring rain.
Spring we don't see, The.
Village where they ring, A.
Village without bells, A.
Bennett, G. Street Lamps in Early Spring.
Berry, W. Purification, A.
Bertrans de Born. Sirventes.
Bibb. Early Spring.
Bishop, E. Cold Spring, A.
Blake, W. Echoing [*or* Ecchoing] Green, The.
Spring.
To Spring.
When the Green Woods Laugh.
Blane, R. Spring Isn't Everything.
Bloem, J. C. After Liberation.
Blue Cloud. Spring Equinox.
Bonnefoy. All, the Nothing, The.
Bontemps. My Heart Has Known its Winter.
Bottomley. Eager Spring.
Boye. That profound waiting time.
Brown, S. After Winter.
Browne, S. Signs of Spring.
Browning, R. Home-Thoughts, from Abroad.
Pippa's Song.
Brummer, N. Why Is This Night Different from
All Other Nights?
Bryant, W. Yellow Violet, The.
Buchanan, G. May Morning.
Bulich, V. From My Diary, 3.
Burns, R. O Were My Love Yon Lilac[k] Fair.
Buson. End of spring, The.
End of spring, The.
In the white plum blossoms.
Lighting one candle.
Lights are going out, The.
Long, long ago.
Mad girl, The.
Moored boat, A.
No bridge.
Passing spring, The.
Riding.
Spring passing.
Spring rain! And as yet.
Spring sea rising, The.
Spring Wind on the Riverbank at Kema.
Sweet springtime showers.
These lazy spring days.
Wading through it.
Willow leaves fallen, The.
With no underrobes.
Campbell, R. Georgian Spring.
Carew, T. Spring, The: "Now that the Winter's
gone, the earth hath lost."

Carmona. Another Day.
Castro, R. Feet of Spring Are on the Stair, The.
Cather, W. Prairie Spring.
Cawein. Purple Valleys, The.
Ceravolo. Spring in This World of Poor Mutts.
Warmth.
Césaire, A. Lynch 1.
Chang Yen. Tune: "Pure Serene Music".
Ch'i-chi. Song of the Spring Wind.
Ch'iao Chi. Love Song: "Orioles and orioles."
Chien Chang. Given to Master Ch'ing-lun of
Hsia Mountain.
Ch'in Kuan. From a Dream.
Tune: "Happiness Approaches".
Ching An. On the Road: A Spring Day at Ling-
Feng.
Cho Chihun. Spring Day.
Chŏng Chiyong. Spring Snow.
Chŏng Hyŏnjong. Greenly the Earth.
Chŏng Kŭgin. In Praise of Spring.
Chu Shu-chen. Spring Joy.
Clare, J. Last of April, The.
Primrose, The.
Clementelli. I'd Like to Try Telling You of
Spring.
Clifton, L. Spring Song.
Coatsworth. March.
Cofer, J. Spring.
What We Feared.
Coleridge, S. Answer to a Child's Question.
Collins, A. Song.
Conyus. Upon Leaving the Parole Board
Hearing.
Cooley. Poem on the First Day of Spring.
Vespers: "Now it is evening, the light rushes to
fall."
Cowley, A. Spring, The: "Though you be
absent here, I needs must say."
Cristall. Song: "Through springtime walks, with
flowers perfumed."
Song on Leaving the Country Early in the
Spring.
To a Lady on the Rise of Morn.
Verses Written in the Spring.
Cullen, C. To John Keats, Poet, at Springtime
[*or* Spring Time].
Cummings, E. E. Greedy the people, The.
In Just.
O sweet spontaneous.
Spring is like a perhaps hand.
Spring omnipotent goddess thou dost.
Dafydd [*or* David] ap Gwilym. Duw gwyddiad
mai da y gweddai.
Darío, R. Spring.
Springtime.
Davies, W. H. Days Too Short.
Davis, O. In the Clear Long After.
Demy, J. You Must Believe in Spring.
Dennis, C. Spring: "All the truth you'll ever be
able to cull."
Dickinson, E. Before you thought of Spring.
Dear March, Come in.
I dreaded that first Robin, so.
Letter to Bee.
Light exists in Spring, A.
Little Madness in the Spring, A.
Dings, Fred. Redwing Blackbirds.
Dobell, S. Chanted Calendar, A.
Donne. Love's Growth.
Dove, R. Rusks.
Turning Thirty, I Contemplate Students
Bicycling Home.
Eberhart, R. This Fevers Me.
Elliott, E. Spring.
Emanuel, L. Technology of Spring, The.
Emerson, R. Musketaquid.
Ennis. Drink of Spring, A.
Evance, S. Written in Ill Health at the Close of
Spring.
Ewer. May Day, 1917.
Fallon, P. Spring Song.
Fel-Yelin, S. Breath of Spring.
Field. Goad, The.
Finkelstein, C. Persephone's Notes.
Frost, R. Prayer in Spring, A.
Spring Pools.

García Lorca.   Spring Song.
Gertsyk, A.   Spring.
Gilsdorf, E.   Away from Us.
Ginsberg, A.   Easter Sunday.
Giovanni.   Springtime.
Glück, L.   Matins: "Sun shines; by the mailbox, leaves, The."
Grigson.   In the Spring Garden.
Grimké, A.   At April.
Guidacci.   Spring.
Guiney.   Garden Chidings.
Hagiwara Sakutaro.   Spring Night.
Hall, D.   Winter's asperity mollifies.
Hammerstein.   It Might As Well Be Spring.
Younger Than Springtime.
Han-shan Te-ch'ing.   Clouds release the hillsides and wake the scenes of spring.
Spring has come again the snow has finally stopped.
Harburg.   April in Paris.
Springtime Cometh, The.
Harry, J.   Walking, when the Lake of the Air is Blue with Spring.
Hart, L.   Spring Is Here.
Harte, B.   California Madrigal.
Hass, R.   Spring Rain.
Hawker.   Are They Not All Ministering Spirits?
Healey, S.   Where Spring Is.
Hemans.   Voice of Spring, The.
Herrick.   To Daffodils.
Heyman, E.   Ho Hum.
I Wanna Be Loved.
Hine.   Sapphics.
Hölderlin.   Spring.
Holtby, W.   Man Who Hated the Spring, The.
Hope, A.   Return of Persephone, The.
Hopkins, G.   Spring and Fall [To a Young Child].
Spring: "Nothing is so beautiful as Spring."
Horace.   Ode 4.7: "Snows dissolving, grass returns to meadow."
Solvitur Acris Hiems.
Housman.   Loveliest of trees, the cherry now.
Oh see how thick the goldcup flowers.
Howells, W.   Earliest Spring.
Hsi Chou.   Early Spring at the Capital, Sent to the Honorable Kuan.
Hsin Ch'i-chi.   Tune: "Partridge Sky" For a Friend.
Hu Chih-yu.   Love Song: "Lazy flowers brew honey for the bees."
Huang T'ing-chien.   Tune: "Ch'ing-P'ing Song".
Tune: "Courtyard Full of Fragrance, The".
Hudgins.   Late Spring in the Nuclear Age.
Hughes, L.   In Time of Silver Rain.
Hughes, T.   Swifts.
Hwansung Jian.   Enjoying Spring.
Ibycus.   In Spring.
Iio Sogi.   Spring.
Ikkyu Sojun.   Form in Void.
Im Ŏngnyŏng.   To a Friend.
Irwin, M.   Five Panels.
Issa.   As the great old trees.
Face of the spring moon.
In spring rain.
Melting snow.
My spring is just this.
O owl!
Pigeon Makes His Request, The.
Spring day, The.
Spring rain.
This year on, forever.
Thus spring begins: old.
With this rising bath-mist.
Jacobsen, J.   Blue-Eyed Exterminator, The.
Hourglass.
James I, King of Scotland.   Spring Song of the Birds.
Jarnot, L.   Specific Incendiaries of Springtime, The.
Jiménez, J.   Yellow Spring.
Jones, B.   Spring at Nant Dywelan.
Kasdorf.   Green Market, New York.
Keats.   After Dark Vapours Have Oppressed Our Plains.
Kell.   Spring Night.

Kenney.   In April.
Keyes, S.   Early Spring.
Ki no Tsurayuki.   Hue is as rich, The.
On a spring hillside.
Kim Sowŏl.   Golden Meadow, The.
King, H.   Summer Lost.
Ko Un.   Great Springtime.
Ku Sang.   Spring Chrysanthemums.
Landesman.   Spring Can Really Hang You Up the Most.
Lane, P.   Spring.
Larkin, P.   Coming.
First Sight.
Spring.
Lawrence, D. H.   Enkindled Spring, The.
Spring Morning.
Ledwidge.   Spring Love.
Lenski, H.   Lightly a slight shadow floats on the March snows.
Levine, P.   Sleepless Night, A.
Li Ching.   Sorrow for Spring.
Li Ch'ing-chao.   End to Spring, An.
On Spring.
Tune: Spring at Wu Ling.
Tune: "The Charm of a Maiden Singer;" Spring Thoughts.
Li Po.   Awakening from Drunkenness on a Spring Day.
Conversations in the Mountains.
Poem Composed at the Command of the Emperor.
Solitary Carouse on a Day in Spring, A.
Spring Song: "Young lass, A."
Spring Thoughts.
Li Shang-yin.   Spring Rain.
Li Yü [or Li Hou-Chu].   Shaken, They Cling Again.
Lisnyanskaya [or Lisnianskaia].   Two carousing hawk moths, their wings like nervous silk.
Liu Yu Hsi.   Tune: "Memories of the South".
Liu Yung.   Song to the Tune "Ting Feng Po".
Llwyd, M.   Excuse, The.
Spring, The.
Locke, M.   Sonnet: "I hate the Spring in parti-coloured vest."
Long, H.   New Music, A.
Longley, M.   Freeze-Up.
Lowell, A.   Vernal Equinox.
Lowell, J.   May is a pious fraud of the almanac.
Lu Yu.   Idleness.
Lazy.
Lyly, J.   Trico's Song.
Machado Ruiz.   Primavera.
Rose of Fire.
Spring Has Come.
Maeng Sasŏng.   Spring comes to rivers and lakes.
Mahon.   Spring Vacation, The.
Majer.   Spring.
Man Giac.   Rebirth.
Mandelstam [or Mandelshtam].   In This Cool Transparent Spring.
On Stony Pierian Spurs.
Martinaitis, M.   Silly Spring.
Mayer, B.   Spring House.
Mayfield, C.   In a Glazed-Over World.
McDaniel, W.   First Spring in California, 1936.
McGough, R.   Fight of the Year, The.
McGrath, C.   Spring Comes to Chicago.
McGrath, T.   Black Train, The.
McKay, C.   Spring in New Hampshire.
Meng Hao Jan.   In spring you sleep and never know when the morn comes.
Spring Dawn.
Spring Dawn ("Spring sleep, not yet awake to dawn.").
Spring Dreams.
Spring Morning, A.
Springtime Sleep.
Merwin.   Before a Departure in Spring.
Mew.   I so liked Spring last year.
May, 1915.
Millay, E.   Spring: "To what purpose, April, do you return again?"
Milosz, C.   Slow River.
Mistral, G.   Lady Spring.

Miyazawa Kenji.   Spring and the Ashura.
Mnookin.   Signs.
Moore, L.   Haiku.
Moorer.   Easter; or, Spring-Time.
Morales.   Spring Fever.
Morton, J.   Spring in London.
Murray, P.   Returning Spring.
Muske, C.   Jacaranda.
Muso Soseki.   House of Spring.
Plum Window.
Myles, E.   Flowers.
Naito Joso.   About the grave / Waves of spring mist.
Narihira.   Regretting the Past.
Nashe [or Nash].   Spring, the Sweet Spring.
Nesbit, E.   Child's Song in Spring.
Niedecker.   Swept snow, Li Po.
Noin.   Spring in a Mountain Village.
Norris, K.   Monastery Orchard in Early Spring, The.
Nukada, P.   Polite Debate, A.
O'Driscoll, D.   Lighting Up Time.
Olson, C.   Variations Done for Gerald Van De Wiele.
Osundare.   Eyeful Glances.
Ou-yang Hsiu.   Green Jade Plum Trees in Spring.
Tune: "Magnolia Flower".
Overbury.   Springtime It Brings On the Shearing, The.
Overton, R.   Blues in "C".
Pak Chaesam.   Spring's Path.
Parini.   Mizzle.
Parker, A.   Alchemy.
Peaux, A.   Spring Landscape.
Petrarch.   Soote Season, The.
Piatt, S.   Sad Spring-Song.
Piercy.   Snow, Snow.
Pietri.   First Day of Spring, The.
Po Chü-i.   At the End of Spring.
Flower Market, The.
Passing Tianmen Street in Chang'an and Seeing a Distant View of Zhongnan Mountains.
Tune: "Memories of the South".
Pommy-Vega.   [Ah certainty of love in the hand].
Pongnim, Prince.   What amuses you in the sound.
Powell, D. A.   Who won't praise green. Each minute to caress each minute blade of spring.
Green slice us open.
Prados, E.   When It Was Spring.
Pratt, E.   Come Not the Seasons Here.
Pritchard, N.   Springtime.
Ransetsu.   On the old plum tree.
Ray, H.   Coming of Spring, The.
Idyl of Spring, An.
Rayl, J.   Spring Storm.
Reese, L.   April in Town.
Day Before Spring, The.
Mid-March.
Reznikoff.   April.
Rilke.   Spring Has Returned.
Roberts, L.   Another Spring on Olmstead Street.
Rose, B.   I Wanna Be Loved.
Rossetti, C.   Amen.
First Spring Day, The.
L. E. L.
May: "I cannot tell you how it was."
What's in a Name?
Winter: My Secret.
Rossetti, D.   83: Barren Spring.
For Spring, by Sandro Botticelli, in the Accademia of Florence.
Rudaki.   Spring.
Ruden, S.   Letter.
Ryokan.   First Days of Spring.
Sadoff.   In the Bog behind My House.
Schilpp, M.   Triage.
Seeger, A.   I Have a Rendezvous with Death.
Seward.   On the fleet streams, the Sun, that late arose.
Sonnet Written from an Eastern Apartment in the Bishop's Palace at Lichfield, Which Commands a View of Stowe Valley.
Shakespeare, W.   Blossom, The.

Hark, hark! the lark at heaven's gate sings.
Holla, Approach.
Spring.
When Daffodils Begin to Peer.
Shelley, P. Cloud, The.
Question, The: "I dream'd that, as I wander'd by the way."
Shen Yüeh. I Climb High to Look at Spring.
Peach.
Spring: "Willows tangle like silk threads."
Shepherd, R. Where When Was.
White Days.
Sheykhi. It's the season of spring, let us be.
Shinkichi Takahashi. Spring.
Simic. Spring: "This is what I saw—old snow on the ground."
Simidor, D. Spring: "Spring afternoon, a lovely sky, bright sunshine, A."
Smart, C. On a Bed of Guernsey Lilies.
Smith, Charlie. Still Winter (Spring).
Smith, Charlotte. Sonnet Written at the Close of Spring [or Elegiac Sonnet].
To Spring.
Written in Farm Wood, South Downs, in May 1784.
Smith, D. Spring Poem, The.
Snyder, G. What Have I Learned.
Sodo. Late spring / Paling rose.
Song Sun. Do not grieve, little birds.
Spenser, E. Sonnet 70: "Fresh Spring the herald of love's [or loves] mighty king."
Steingesser. Spring Forward.
Stern, G. Modern Love.
Stickney, T. Age in Youth.
On Sandro's Flora.
Su Tung-p'o. Spring Scene.
Walk in the Country, A.
Swinburne. Vision of Spring in Winter, A.
When the Hounds of Spring.
Synge. On a Birthday.
Sze. Solstice Quipu.
Tai Shu-lun. Su Creek Pavilion.
Tate, A. Seasons of the Soul.
Tayo-jo. People, more people.
Teasdale. There Will Come Soft Rains.
Thomas, E. Thaw.
Thoreau. Winter and Spring Scene, A.
Tran Nhan-tong. Spring View.
Tranströmer. April and Silence.
Tsugen Jakurei. Not a mote in the light above.
Ts'ui Hao. Yellow Crane Tower.
Tu Fu [or Du Fu]. Another Spring ("White birds over the grey river.").
Quatrain: In Late Sun.
Good Rain: A Night in Spring.
River Jade-Gray.
Spring.
Spring Rain.
Sun Lengthens.
To the south there is a dragon living in a mountain pool.
Written on the Wall at Zhang's Hermitage.
Wu-Chueh.
Tu Shen-yen. Harmonizing a Spring Poem by Premier Lu of Chin-Ling.
Tucker, M. Spring.
Turner, F. Early Warning.
Spring Evening.
Tzu Yeh. Late Spring.
Ungar. Common Prayer.
Unknown. Aura Lee.
Greening Yang.
Hidden-in-winter.
It is springtime, here the leaves are sprouting on the trees.
Just because of you.
Levis Exsurgit Zephirus.
Loosed from Winter's prison.
Myrie a tyme I telle in May.
Now Is the Month of Maying.
Oh springtime of unquenched desires.
Oh springtime! The pomegranate trees are blooming.
Sadness in Spring.
Sound of my lover, The.
Spring: "Spring wind stirs my romantic heart,

The."
Spring Blossoms into Flower.
Spring in the Bronx.
Spring Overflows the Pavilion.
Spring Song from "Tzu-Yeh" Songs of the Four Seasons.
Sumer Is Icumen [or Ycomen] In.
Two Spring Charms.
Whan the nyghtengale syngeth the wodes waxen grene.
Vanhomrigh. Hail, Blushing Goddess, Beauteous Spring!
Vaughan, H. Unprofitablenes.
Very. Spirit, The.
Winter Rain, The.
Vicuña. Thirst.
Virgil [or Vergil]. Wave, The.
Volkman. Seasonal.
Wah. Father / Mother Haibun #18.
Wang, J. Tune: "The Charm of a Maiden Singer;" Spring Thoughts.
Wang Shih-chieng. Composed at the West Wall of Tsou-p'ing Three Days After the Festival of Pure Brightness.
Wang Wei. Birdsong Torrent.
Playfully Inscribed on a Large Boulder.
Song of Peach Tree Spring.
Warren, H. Spring Isn't Everything.
Wei Chuang. Tune: "Thinking of the Imperial Capital".
Wei Ying-wu. At Chuzhou on the Western Stream.
West, J. To May.
Wilbur, R. April 5, 1974.
Seed Leaves.
Wilde, O. Magdalen Walks.
William of Aquitaine. Spring Song.
Williams, C. K. Spring: another / joke.
Williams, W. Bird Song.
Late Singer, The.
Spring and All.
Spring Strains.
Winters, Y. Time and the Garden.
Wolfe, M. Thaw, The.
Wordsworth, W. Lines Written in Early Spring.
To My Sister.
Written in March [While Resting on the Bridge at the Foot of Brother's Water].
Wotton, S. On a Bank [or Banck] as I Sat[e] [a-]Fishing; a Description of the Spring.
Wright, C. April.
Wright, J. Child, The.
Yaba. Beginning / House repairs in.
Yang Chi. Five-Color.
Yang Wen-li. New Year's Eve.
Yen Shu. Tune: "Spring in the Jade House".
Tune: "Treading on Fragrant Grass".
Yi I. Where is the second bend?
Yi Inbok. Drumbeats.
Yi Jang'hi. Spring is a Cat, The.
Young, M. J. On an Early Spring.
Yu Chien-wu. Spring Day.
Zolynas. Pastorale for Spring.
Zwicky, Jan. You Must Believe in Spring.
Springs
Anyte [or Anytes]. Sit, everyone, under the luxuriant laurel.
Applewhite. Water from the Lamp Bottle.
Basho. From Hot Springs Mountain.
Bryant, W. Fountain, The.
Ch'u Ch'uang I. Mountain Spring, A.
Long, H. Our Spring Needs Shoveling.
Machej. Orchards in July.
Voigt. Spring, The.
Yi I. Where is the fourth bend?
Spying and Spies
Allen, F. Time for Blushing, A.
Auden. Secret Agent, The.
Bowers, E. Prince, The.
Delano, P. L. Sonnet for an SR-71.
Dunn, S. What They Wanted.
Homer. All silent stood; at last stood forth one dolon, that did dare.
Jonson, B. On Spies.
Kipling, R. Spies' March, The.
Kowit. Lurid Confessions.

Leonard, T. Before the 1820 rising in the West of Scotland a network of.
Miller, V. Light Reading.
Petri. Night Song of the Personal Shadow.
Schiff, Robyn. Chanel N° 5.
Spenser, E. And in the midst of all, a fountaine stood.
Unknown. After spring has come.
Ward, Geoff. Horace Belisha.
Squalor
Chénier. We live; we live in squalor. And so? It had to be.
Squash (botany)
Gallagher, T. Mixed.
Nye, N. Mind of Squash, The.
Squid
Basho. Squid seller's call, The.
Blumenthal, M. Squid.
Chin. Floral Apron, The.
Denham, Joe. Gutting.
Mandelstam [or Mandelshtam]. Lamarck.
Steffler, J. They All Save One Last Squirt.
Squires
Foot, E. Good Young Squire, The.
Squirrels
Alcosser. Golden-Mantled Ground Squirrel.
Buson. Flying squirrel, A.
Flying squirrel, A.
Carson, A. New Rule.
De Luca, C. Telling the Time.
Dove, R. Musician Talks about "Process," The.
Eberhart, R. On a Squirrel Crossing the Road in Autumn, in New England.
Emerson, R. Fable: "Mountain and the squirrel, The."
Gilbert, C. Glimpses.
Hoggard, James. Oil Field Road off Clyte Escarpment.
Kherdian. In the autumn-come-winter park.
Stern, G. I Remember Galileo.
Van Duyn. Sonnet for Minimalists.
Wolfe, H. Gray Squirrel, The.
Yeats. To a Squirrel at Kyle-Na-No.
Sri Lanka
Ondaatje. Heat of explosions, The.
House on a Red Cliff.
Letters & Other Worlds.
To be buried in times of war.
Stables
Hall, D. Carol, A.
Rawson, J. Map Burnt Through.
Wylie. Twelfth Night.
Stained Glass
Kelly, B. Imagining Their Own Hymns.
Mallarmé. Saint.
Prado, A. Stained Glass Window.
Worth, V. Door.
Stairs
Behn, R. Below the Cellar of the Yellow House There Is Another Set of Stairs.
DeSylva, B. G. Stairway to Paradise.
Dunn, S. Stairway, The.
Francis, A. Stairway to Paradise.
Greenlaw, L. Spirit of the Staircase, The.
Hughes, L. Mother to Son.
Levertov. Calvary Path, A.
Jacob's Ladder, The.
McDaniel, J. Modern Day Sisphus.
Slessor. Up in Mabel's Room.
Tsvetayeva [or Tsvetaeva]. Staircase.
Stalin, Joseph
Levis. Anastasia and Sandman.
Mandelstam [or Mandelshtam]. Stalin Epigram, The.
You Took Away All the Oceans and All the Room.
Prigov. Dialogue No. 5.
Ralin, Radoi. Ideological Tango.
"Sagittarius.". Stalin Moy Golubchik.
Stalingrad, Battle of (1942–43)
Nicholson, N. Stalingrad: 1942.
Stalking and Stalkers
Abbott, W. Quite Mercenary He Stalked Her.
Adler, F. Riding the Eye.

Gatina, D.   I'm being stalked by a bird.
McGrath, Carmelita.   Booman.
Mendelssohn, Anna.   Photrum.
Prufer, K.   Man in Miami, The.

Starfish
Cervantes.   Starfish.
Kinnell.   Daybreak: "On the tidal mud, just before sunset."
McHugh, H.   After You Left.
Ormsby, E.   Starfish.
Rohrer, M.   Starfish Waving to Me from the Sand.

Starlings
Hayden, R.   Plague of Starlings, A.
Heath-Stubbs.   Starling, The.
Kennelly.   Glimpse of Starlings, A.
Padel, R.   Starling, The.
Prichard, C.   Bargain, The.
Smith, L.   Calligraphy of Birds.
Teschke, H.   Massacre of the Innocents, The (after Brueghel).
Wilbur, R.   Writer, The.

Stars
Adams, L.   Fragmentary Stars.
Aiken, C.   Prelude LVII: "One star fell and another as we walked."
al-Rahim, A.   Poisonous Illusions.
Alcaeus [or Alkaios].   Wet your lungs with wine—the dogstar rises.
Aldrich, T.   Lycidas.
Ali, A.   Stars.
Althaus, Keith.   Little Elegy.
Anderson, M.   Lost in the Stars.
"Antler.".   Star-Struck Utopias of 2000.
Arp.   Around the Star's Throne.
Asekoff, L.   Starwork.
Ashbery, J.   Just Walking Around.
Auden.   More Loving One, The.
Barnes, J.   La Plata, Missouri: Clear November Night.
Basho.   Wild sea, A.
Beachy-Quick, Dan.   Stellar Elements.
Bêkes.   Bright Star.
Blake, W.   How Sweet I Roamed [or Roam'd] from Field to Field.
To the Evening Star.
Bleakney, J.   Black and White.
By Starlight on Narin Strand.
Bly, R.   Night Abraham Called to the Stars, The.
Bonnefoy.   Top of the World, The.
Well, The.
Boulus.   Entries for a Possible Poem.
Bourdillon.   Night Has a Thousand Eyes, The.
Brock, V.   All the Stars Are Foxfire.
Brontë, E.   Stars.
Bryant, W.   Hymn to the North Star.
Song of the Stars.
Buckley, C.   Inverse Square Law of the Propagation of Light, The.
Presocratic, Surfing, Breathing Cosmology Blues, The.
Star Apocrypha.
Burke, J.   Swinging on a Star.
Buson.   Not quite dark yet.
Byron, G.   She Walks In Beauty.
Campbell, T.   To the Evening Star.
Cavendish, M.   Of Stars.
Cawein.   Stars, The.
Cervantes.   To We Who Were Saved by the Stars.
Char.   Fighters.
Chivers.   Apollo.
Chŏng Chiyong.   Star.
Chŏng Hyŏnjong.   Are You a Star?
Conoley, G.   World, The: "It was just a gas station. It was not spectacular carnage."
Coslett.   Pole Star, The.
Craig, M.   Good Night, Star.
Crase.   Astropastoral.
Cumpian.   Estrellitas.
Daive.   Space instead.
Darley.   Fallen Star, The.
Davison, P.   Star Watcher, The.
De la Mare.   Birthnight: To F, The.
De Roux, Paul.   Cold Again, The.
DeLange, E.   Shake Down the Stars.

Desnos.   Three Stars.
Di Prima.   Notes on the Art of Memory.
Dickinson, E.   Moon upon her fluent Route, The.
Outer—from the Inner, The.
Donaghy, M.   Present, The.
Doolittle, H.   Or anywhere.
Sirius.
Stars wheel in purple, yours is not so rare.
Dove, R.   Planning the Perfect Evening.
Duncan, R.   Passages 37.
Eimers.   Night Without Stars, A.
Farber.   Taking Turns.
Ferril.   Jupiter at Beer Springs.
Field.   Constancy.
Fields, A.   Ephemeron.
Frost, R.   Canis Major.
Choose Something like a Star.
Come In.
Star in a Stoneboat, A.
Gallagher, T.   Mixed.
Gehrke, S.   Walking Fields at Night South of Hampton, Iowa.
Ghalib, M.   Ghazal 15.
Graves, R.   Star-Talk.
Greville, F.   You little stars that live in skies.
Gryphius.   To Himself.
Guest, B.   Homage.
Guidacci.   Map of the Winter Sky, The.
Guiducci.   Under an Impure Star.
Gunn, T.   My Sad Captains.
Guthrie, R.   Magi, The.
Haavikko.   It has been proposed that the stars should be removed from sight.
Habington.   Nox Nocti Indicat Scientiam.
Hardy, T.   Waiting Both.
Harte, B.   Relieving Guard.
Healy, R.   Size of This Universe, The.
Hemans.   Lost Pleiad, The.
Herbert, G.   Artillery [or Artillerie].
Hirsch, E.   In Spite of Everything, the Stars.
Hollander, J.   Great Bear, The.
Hopkins, G.   Starlight Night, The.
Hugo, R.   Elegy: "I expected him to look dead in the casket."
Hugo, V.   At the Window in the Dark.
Ibn Ezra, A.   My Stars.
Inada.   Concentration Constellation.
Issa.   Summer night.
Jaccottet.   Distances.
Jackson, A.   Moment.
Joe, R.   Passamaquoddy Song of the Stars.
Johnson, D.   Heavens, The.
Johnson, J.   Sence You Went Away.
Joyce, J.   Bahnhofstrasse.
Keats.   Bright Star.
Kinnell.   Daybreak: "On the tidal mud, just before sunset."
Kipling, R.   Astrologer's Song, An.
Klink, J.   Lodestar.
Shooting Star.
Kuusisto, Stephen.   Erasing Stars.
Lamartine.   Infinite in the Skies, The.
Lewis, G.   One day, feeling hungry.
Longfellow, H.   Galaxy, The.
Three Kings, The.
MacCaig.   Blue Tit on a String of Peanuts.
Stars and Planets.
MacLean, S.   Lìonmhorachd anns na speuran.
Tumultuous Plenty in the Heavens.
MacLeish.   Epistle to Be Left in the Earth.
MacNeice.   Star-Gazer.
Mallarmé.   With her pure nails offering their onyx high.
Mayakovsky [or Maiakovskii].   Listen.
Meredith, G.   Lucifer in Starlight.
Meredith, W.   Country Stars.
Merwin.   Glassy Sea.
Moore, T.   Love Thee, Dearest? Love Thee?
Morley, T.   You Black Bright Stars.
Morris-Jones.   North Star, The.
Murray, A.   Under the Stars.
Nijhoff.   New Stars, The.
Nisker, Wes "Scoop.".   I sit in wonder.
Noguchi, Yonejiro (Yone).   Are the fallen stars.
Okigbo.   Eyes Watch the Stars.

Parini.   Stars Falling.
Parish.   Stars Fell on Alabama.
Pawnee Oral Tradition.   Song of the Pleiades.
Piper, P.   Morning Star, The.
Plath.   Stars over the Dordogne.
Plato.   Aster.
Plutzik.   Cancer and Nova.
Popa.   Heaven's Ring.
Rabi'a al-Adawiyya.   O my Lord.
Ramke, B.   Difference Between Night and Day, The.
Revealing Oneself to a Woman.
Ray, H.   Star Song.
Reed, P.   Container of Stars.
Rexroth, K.   Heart of Herakles, The.
Rich, A.   Planetarium.
Robeson, E.   Answers, The.
Robinson, A.   Idea, The.
Unum est Necessarium.
Robinson, E.   Credo: "I cannot find my way."
Rohrer, M.   Hotel de L'Etoile.
Rose, R.   Sestina of the Geographic Tongue.
Rossetti, C.   Where Innocent Bright-Eyed Daisies Are.
Rumens.   Star Whisper.
Rumi.   Inside water, a waterwheel turns.
Sachs, N.   Chorus of the Stars.
Sakaki.   Let's Eat Stars.
Sandburg, C.   Stars.
Sappho.   Stars around the fair moon, The.
Stars around the luminous moon—how soon they.
Schilpp, M.   Triage.
Segovia, F.   Evening Star.
Lucero de la Tarde.
Shiki.   Full moon ringed, The.
Sidney.   Sonnet 48: "Soul's joy, bend not those morning stars from me."
Sigourney.   Stars, The.
Simms, W.   Lost Pleiad, The.
Simon, M.   Atomic Psalm.
Smith, I.   Tinily a star goes down.
Smith, R.   Halcion.
Snyder, G.   Waiting for a Ride.
Spaziani.   To the Readers.
Sterling, G.   Aldebaran at Dusk.
Stevens, W.   Homunculus et La Belle Etoile.
Stewart, S.   Dark the Star.
Stoddard, E.   Above the Tree.
Strand.   Black Maps.
Tait.   Contracting Universe, The.
Tanikawa, S.   Concerning a Girl.
Tarn.   Narrative of the Men and Women Who Became Stars.
Taylor, J.   Star, The.
Teasdale.   Falling Star, The.
Thomas, E.   Shooting Star, A.
Thomson, J.   Part 17: "How the moon triumphs through the endless nights!"
Thoreau.   On Ponkawtasset, since, we took our way.
Toomer.   Face.
Transt.   Track.
Tu Fu [or Du Fu].   Winter Dawn.
Tuckerman, F.   Series 2, Sonnet 17.
Series 2, Sonnet 23.
Sonnets: "Starry flower, the flower-like stars that fade, The."
Turner, C.   Orion.
Unknown.   Night Roof.
Song of the Stars, The.
Wishing Poem.
Valentine, J.   December 21st.
Vaughan, H.   Joy of My Life! While Left Me Here.
They Are All Gone into the World of Light!
Vietnamese Oral Tradition.   King Star, The.
Vitale, M.   I Read That It Was All a Chain.
Wagoner, D.   Silence of the Stars, The.
Whitman, W.   On the Beach at Night.
On the Beach at Night Alone.
When I Heard the Learn'd Astronomer.
Williams, W.   El Hombre.
Flight to the City.
Wordsworth, W.   I watch, and long have watched, with calm regret.

Wright, C. Morning Star.
Wright, J. To the Evening Star: Central Minnesota.
Yeats. Sorrow of Love, The [1892 Version].
Yosano Akiko. Star that once, A.
Young, A. How Stars Start.
Young, K. Letters from the North Star.
Yun Tongju. One Night I Count the Stars.
Zawacki, Andrew. Astrelegy.
See also **Astronomy and Astronomers**

Statistics
Brett, L. I Keep Forgetting.
Lumsden, R. Incident in a Filing Cupboard.
Szymborska, W. Contribution to Statistics, A.

Statues
Agustini. Marble Beads.
 Public Prayer.
 Wild for Love.
Alegría. Ars Poetica.
Allston. On the Statue of an Angel, by Bienaimé, in the Possession of J.S. Copley Greene, Esq.
Anyte [*or* Anytes]. I, Hermes, stand here by the windy tree-lined.
 This is Kypris' place; it ever pleases her.
Berryman. Boston Common.
Bogan, L. Statue and Birds.
Boker. Sonnet 165.
Brodsky, J. Mary, the Scots are sots in any case.
Campana. Autumn Garden.
Creeley. Figures, The.
Cross, E. Sri Nityananda Mandir (The Temple of Nityananda).
Davidson, D. Twilight on Union Street.
Druce. Apropos of Garden Statuary: A Disquisition upon a Minor Genre.
Fermini, I. Statue, The.
Fuertes. Plastic Virgin.
Gabrielian, N. Phoenician Statuette, A.
Gerhardt, I. G. M. Rejected Gift, The.
 Rejected Gift, The.
Gorbanevskaya. Savage cold of Russian winters, The.
Guest, B. Walking Buddha.
Hacker, M. Verlaine.
Herbert, W. Why the Elgin Marbles Must be Returned to Elgin.
Higginson, E. Statue, The.
Holub. Special Performance for Statues, A.
Imbriglio, C. Museum.
Johnson, L. By the Statue of King Charles [I] at Charing Cross.
Justice, D. Mrs. Snow.
Kaufman, S. Buddha of Sŏkkuram, The.
Lê Thánh–tông. Stone Dog, The.
Lieberman, L. God's Measurements.
Lloyd, C. Looking at a Portrait Sculpture of the Indian Holy Man, Asanga, (Japanese, Mujaku, Flowered about 350 C.E.—Stands in the Kofukuji Treasure Hall of Nara Japan.
Marston, J. *Pigmalion,* whose hie love-hating minde.
Mathews, C. Sculptor, The.
Michaux. My Statues.
Moiro. Tree nymphs, daughters of River, ambrosial.
Nemes Nagy. I Carried Statues.
Nossis. When we go to the temple, let's see Aphrodite's.
Orr, G. Available Now: Archaic Torsos of Both Sexes.
Padgett, R. Statue of a Libertine, The.
Phillips, C. Toys.
Piatt, J. To the Statue on the Capitol.
Piatt, S. Stone For A Statue.
Plath. Colossus, The.
Press, K. Statues.
Pushkin, A. On the Statue of a Player at Svaika.
Ray, H. Venus of Milo, The.
Reverdy. Heavier.
Ridge, L. Stone Face.
Rilke. Archaic Torso of Apollo.
 Archaic Torso of Apollo.
Rose, D. Figurehead.
Rossetti, C. Study (A Soul), A.
Ryan, G. Penserosa, La.

St. John, D. In the Sulphur Garden.
Santayana. Before a Statue of Achilles.
 On an Unfinished Statue.
Shelley, P. Ozymandias.
Souster. Words Before a Statue of Champlain.
Spenser, E. Britomart in the House of the Enchanter Busyrane.
Stevens, W. Dance of the Macabre Mice.
Thomas, D. Walking in Gardens.
Umpierre, L. Statue, The.
Unknown. Epigram: "Says a Reverend Priest to a less Rev'rend friend."
Van Winckel, N. Avant-Garde, The.
Villaurrutia. Nocturne of the Statue.
Volkow. Arcana 4: The Emperor.
 Arcano 4: El Emperador.
Watson, R. White Lady, The.
Wenderoth, J. As Hour and Year Collapsed.
Yeats. Statues, The.

Steak
Creeley. Naughty Boy.
Moore, L. Haiku.
Takamura Kotaro. Steak Platter, A.

Steam Baths
Ulacia, M. En un baño de vapor.
 In the Steam Bath.
See also **Baths and Bathing**

Steam Shovels
Malam. Steam Shovel.

Steamers
Scovell. River Steamer, The.
See also **Ships and Shipbuilding**

Steel
Beecher, J. Report to the Stockholders.
Conyus. Six Ten Sixty-Nine.
Mandelstam [*or* Mandelshtam]. In This Cool Transparent Spring.
Markus, P. Black Light.
Ralin, Radoi. Ideological Tango.
Sandburg, C. Prayers of Steel.
Wachtel. Coriolis Effect, The.
Wagoner, D. My Father's Garden.
See also **Iron**

Steeples
Moore, M. Steeple-Jack, The.
Pierpoint, K. Steeplejack.

Stein, Gertrude
Carson, A. Short Talk on Gertrude Stein About 9:30.
Loy. Gertrude Stein.
Muldoon, P. More a Man Has the More a Man Wants, The.
Postell, T. Gertrude Stein Rides the Town Down El.

Stepfathers and Stepmothers
Gorbanevskaya. Drought, malevolent stepmother.
Smith, S. Papa Love Baby.
Swirszczynska [*or* Swir]. Second Madrigal, The.
 She Does Not Remember.
Todd, M. Game Trail, The.
Wolverton, T. Dead Stepfather, The.

Stepmothers
Livingston, D. Stepmother.
Shcherbina. Stepmother, The.
See also **Stepfathers and Stepmothers**

Sterility
García Lorca. Song of the Sterile Orange Tree.

Sterne, Laurence
Muldoon, P. Yggdrasill.

Stevens, Wallace
Berryman. 219: So Long? Stevens.
Blanco, R. Tía Olivia Serves Wallace Stevens a Cuban Egg.
Grumman, Bob. Cryptographiku for Wallace Stevens.
Justice, D. After a Phrase Abandoned by Wallace Stevens.
Lim, S. I Defy You.
Niedecker. If I Were a Bird.
Ondaatje. Dates.
 King Kong Meets Wallace Stevens.
Ridland. Blue Plate Tea Room: Sestina, The.

Ruefle. Perfect Reader.

Stewards and Stewardesses
Dauer. Falling.
Jacobs, B. Friendly Skies.

Still Lifes
Justice, D. Self-Portrait as Still Life.
Kenny, M. Still-Life.
Rilke. Self-Portrait.
Ryan, K. Death by Fruit.
Shcherbina. Still-Life.
Tomlinson, C. Paring the Apple.
Welch, L. In Cézanne's studio, we're dappled with joy.

Stilts
Sale, Richard. Stilts and Other Vehicles.

Stockholm, Sweden
Van Vliet. Old Champagne Glass.

Stoicism
Brontë, E. Old Stoic, The.
Dickinson, E. It might be lonelier.
Keelan, C. Instead of Reading Marcus Aurelius.
Muldoon, P. Stoic, The.
Rossetti, C. Study (A Soul), A.

Stonecutting and Stonecutters
Hernández, M. Tomb of the Imagination.
Jeffers, R. To the Stone-Cutters.
Mooney, M. For Thoth.
Randell. Digging up weeds by the little hedge.

Stonehenge, England
Daniel, S. Stonehenge.
Johnson, R. William Stukeley made his own Stonehenge.
Rich, A. Dark lintels, the blue and foreign stones, The.

Stones and Rocks
Abrahams, L. Stone stood in her house, A.
Agosin. Seven Stones.
Aiken, C. Sea Holly.
al-Braikan, M. Meditations on a World of Stones.
Armand. Word to the Wise, A.
Barnes, J. Skipping.
Basho. Autumn wind / Blasting the stones.
 Blowing stones.
 Hailstones.
 Stillness.
Beachy-Quick, Dan. Stellar Elements.
Bidgood. Standing Stone.
Bielski. Token.
Blake, W. Clod & the Pebble, The.
Blunden. Survival, The.
Bracho, C. Piedra en la arena.
 Stone in the Sand.
Brathwaite, E. Stone: "When the stone fall that morning out of the johncrow sky."
Buson. Willow leaves fallen, The.
Cabral de Melo Neto. Education by Stone.
Cervantes. Archeology.
Corn. Naskeag.
Creeley. I Keep to Myself Such Measures.
Dante Alighieri. Great Canzon, The.
Dickinson, E. How happy is the little Stone.
 Soul selects her own Society, The.
Dixon, M. Getting Your Rocks Off.
Doolittle, H. Or is it a great tide that covers the rock-pool.
Dove, R. Fish in the Stone, The.
Drummond de Andrade. In the Middle of the Road.
 In the Middle of the Road.
Du Bouchet. Stone or Water.
Dufault. Burden.
Eberhart, R. La Crosse at Ninety Miles an Hour.
Forrester, S. Stone, A / i saved.
Foster, A. God and the Holy Stones.
Geiger. Disproportionate.
Goldberg, L. In the Jerusalem Hills.
Han Yü. Song of the Stone Drums.
Haviaras, Stratis. Stone-Throw.
Hemans. Epitaph on Mr W—.
Herbert, Z. Pebble, The.
Hudgins. One Threw a Dirt Clod and It Ran.
Hughes, F. Stonepicker.
James, S. How I'll Live Then.

Jeffers, R.   Rock and Hawk.
To the Stone-Cutters.
Johnson, R.   Beam 7.
Kaufman, S.   Stones.
Khalvati.   Stone of Patience.
Kirsanov.   I Am White, Darling.
Kloefkorn.   Why the Stone Remains Silent.
Knight, E.   He Sees Through Stone.
Korinna [or Corinna].   Kouretes hid the
goddess's, The.
Kuzwayo, E.   Choice, The.
Leonidov, Rumen.   Another Stone in the
Swamp.
Stone in the Swamp, A.
Levitt, Peter.   Measure, The.
Li Po.   Fall River Song.
MacDiarmid, H.   All is lithogenesis – or lochia.
Crystals like Blood.
Mahadevi.   Vein of sapphires, A.
Mandelstam [or Mandelshtam].   Ode on Slate,
The.
Martien, J.   Rocks Along the Coast, The.
Martínez, V.   Tesoro.
Masaoka Shiki.   Stone / On summer plain.
Masters, E.   Starved Rock.
Masterson, R.   She Called Them Stones.
McCarthy, T.   Phenomenology of Stones, The.
McCord, D.   This Is My Rock.
Millay, E.   Second Fig.
Molodovsky [or Molodowsky].   Prayers: I.
Montag, T.   July 6, 2001 (2).
Mouré.   8 Little Theatres of the Cornices.
Neruda.   Stone upon stone, and man, where was
he?
Nervo.   Revenge.
Ortiz.   Serenity in Stones, The.
Ovid.   Deucalion and Pyrrha, sole survivors of
the Flood, renew Creation by casting stones
behind them.
Pagis, D.   Twelve Faces of the Emerald.
Parry-Williams.   Conviction.
Paz.   Landscape.
Native Stone.
Wind and Water and Stone.
Peacock, M.   How I Come to You.
Piatt, S.   Stone For A Statue.
Pinchas-Cohen.   Journey of a Doe.
"Pindar.".   On a Stone Thrown at a Very Great
Man, But Which Missed him.
Piombino.   My Lady Carries Stones.
Popa.   Adventure of the Quartz Pebble, The.
Dream of the Quartz Pebble, The.
Porter, P.   What I Have Written I Have Written.
Pound, E.   Ts'ai Chi'h.
Pratt, E.   Come Not the Seasons Here.
Pritchard, N.   Cassandra and Friend.
Narrow Path, The.
Reeve, F.   Hope.
Reid, C.   Stones and Bones.
Robinson, E.   Salisbury Plain.
Rolle, S.   Blue Rock, The.
Shinkichi Takahashi.   Rocks.
Silva, C.   Who Will Throw the First Stone?
Simic.   Stone.
Stone is a mirror which works poorly, The.
Sŏ Chŏngju.   If I Became a Stone.
Sobin, G.   Eleven Rock Poems.
Tanikawa, S.   Stone and Light.
Tantan.   On the rock / Waves can't reach.
Tomlinson, C.   In Defence of Metaphysics.
Picture of J. T. in a Prospect of Stone, The.
Stone Speech.
Tranströmer.   Clearing, The.
Unknown.   Death of Saint Marinus, The.
Vaughan.   Stone, The.
Walcott.   Ruins of a Great House.
Ward, D.   Hunting in Twilight.
Williams, T.   Quarry.
Winters, Y.   Fable, The.
Yuasa Hangetsu.   Twelve Stones. Chapter 1:
Prologue.
Yun Sŏndo.   Why do flowers fade so soon.

Storms
Abbott, W.   First Rain.
Acorn.   Squall, The.
Aiken, C.   Hatteras Calling.

Alcaeus [or Alkaios].   I don't understand the
conflict of the winds.
Archilochus.   Glaukos, look: already the deep
sea is troubled.
Ashbery, J.   Morning Jitters.
Avison.   Butterfly, The.
Bachmann.   In the Storm of Roses.
Banks, Jr., T. H.   Tempest.
Barbauld.   Summer Evening's Meditation, A.
'Tis now the hour.
Basho.   Storm on Mount Asama!
Winter storm, The.
Beath, M.   Oregon Inlet.
Bécquer, G.   Great Waves Breaking with a Roar.
Berlin.   Let's Have Another Cup of Coffee.
Bishop, E.   Little Exercise.
Blaser.   Finder, The.
Blunden.   Eastern Tempest.
Boyle, K.   Summer: "Flying curved to the wind
shear-waters turn their bodies in the wave."
Bridges, R.   Low Barometer.
Storm is over, the land hushes to rest, The.
Brooks, G.   Michael Is Afraid of the Storm.
Brown Rosellen.   Storm high.
Bryant, W.   After a Tempest.
Burns, R.   Tam o' Shanter; A Tale.
Bush, D.   Sunday the Power Went Off, The.
Buson.   Toward Toba Palace.
Bynner.   All tempest.
Caldwell, E.   Love Poem: "Olfactory paradise."
Campbell, T.   Lord Ullin's Daughter.
Carver, R.   Window, The.
Chippewa Oral Tradition.   Approach of the
Storm, The.
Chŏng Hwajin.   Monsoon Season Opens
Children's Eyes.
Clampitt.   Meridian.
Clare, J.   Thunder mutters louder and more loud,
The.
Clark, T.   On the Beach.
Clarke, C.   Poet's Death, A.
Coleridge, S.   Storm, The.
Crane, H.   Eternity.
Davies, Lynn.   When Ships Sail Too Close.
Dawe, G.   Sheltering Places.
De la Mare.   Silver Penny, The.
Dickinson, E.   Glee—The great storm is over.
Storm.
These are the Nights that Beetles love.
Thunder-Storm, A.
Wind begun to knead the Grass, The.
Didsbury, P.   Hailstone, The.
Donne.   Storm[e], The.
Doolittle, H.   Storm.
Dubie.   Parish.
Peace of Lodi, The.
Dugan, M.   Coolun, The.
Durkin, Kevin.   American Pylons.
Emerson, R.   Snow-Storm [or Snowstorm], The.
Fickert.   Bad Weather at the Airport.
Fields, J.   Ballad of the Tempest.
Follain.   Women Say, The: 'It Looks Like Rain'.
Fordham.   Snow Storm, The.
Freneau.   Hurricane, The.
Frost, R.   Once by the Pacific.
Storm Fear.
Garland, H.   Boyish sleep.
Gerhardt, I. G. M.   Remembrance Day.
Remembrance Day.
Gioia.   Summer Storm.
Goldberg, B.   Money.
Graves, R.   Apple Island.
Greenberg, S.   Secrecy.
Grennan.   Shoreline After Storm.
Hadewijch.   Knowing Love in Herself.
Hall, D.   Mount Kearsarge Shines.
Hardy, T.   She Hears The Storm.
Hausman.   Appaloosa Hail Storm.
Holm, B.   Blizzard.
Hopkins, G.   Hailstorm in May.
Howe, J.   Wild Night, A.
Hughes, T.   Wind.
Jacob, M.   1914.
Jacobik, G.   Dust Storm.
Jaimes Freyre.   Night-time.
Jeffers, R.   Gale in April.

Johnson, M. F.   Thunder Storm.
Jones, H.   On a Fine Crop of Peas Being
Spoiled by a Storm.
Jones, R.   Storm, The.
Kay, J.   Pounding Rain.
Keithley.   Thunder Storm.
Kennelly.   Island, The.
Kipling, R.   Storm Cone, The.
Koehler, T.   Stormy Weather (Keeps Rainin' All
the Time).
Komunyakaa, Y.   After the Fall [of Saigon].
Monoon Season.
Kyger.   Caption for a Miniature.
Lake, P.   In Rough Weather.
Lawrence, D. H.   Lightning.
Storm in the Black Forest.
Lear, E.   Jumblies, The.
Lenski, H.   Moon's brightness turns a freezing
blue, The.
Lewis, J.   Garden Note I, Los Altos.
Lima, J.   Enormous Hand, The.
Liu Yin.   Miscellaneous Poem on Rural Life.
Lugones.   Rain Psalm.
MacEwen, G.   Eden, Eden.
Mansour, J.   Storm Sketches a Silver Margin,
The.
Masaoka Shiki.   Storm—chestnuts / Race along.
McAuliffe, J.   Calm, The.
McIlroy, L.   How to Change a Flat.
Melville, H.   Enviable Isles, The.
Misgivings.
Meng Hao Jan.   Spring Morning, A.
Mickiewicz.   Storm, The.
Mikhail, D.   Snow Storm.
Millay, E.   Hearing Your Words, and Not a
Word Among Them.
Mitchell, K.   Tree Stillness.
Mitchell, S.   Thunderstorm.
Monro, H.   City-Storm.
Montale.   Fan, The.
Storm, The.
Moody, W.   Bracelet of Grass, The.
Morgan, E.   Strawberries.
Morshen.   Storm, A.
Mukai Kyorai.   After the green storm / True
color.
Mun Chŏnghui.   Storm, The: "Isn't there a
man."
Murford.   Storm and Calm: Sent from Embden
to M. Edw. Ma. and M. Tho. Ly, The.
Nemerov.   Brainstorm.
Storm Windows.
Neri, G.   Case of the Same Name, A.
Nutter, G.   Pastoral: "We're passing the whole
summer, all of us."
Ovid.   Dipped now in Ocean, the She-Bear's
stellar guardian.
Every letter you've read in this whole book was
written.
You gods of sea and sky—what's left me now
but prayer?
Pak Sŏwôn.   Plantain.
Pasternak, B.   Storm, an Endless Instant.
Paterson, D.   Chartres of Gowrie, The.
Pinsky.   Round.
Polak, J.   Storm, The.
Pratt, E.   Lee-Shore, The.
Rayl, J.   Spring Storm.
Reese, L.   White Fury of the Spring, The.
Rexroth, K.   Sottoportico San Zaccaria.
Rich, A.   Storm Warnings.
Ridge, J.   Rainy Season in California, The.
Ridge, L.   Kerensky.
Rilke.   Man Watching, The.
Rumann, Son of Colman.   Storm at Sea.
Santos Chocano.   Indignation.
Scarbrough, G.   Storm, The.
Seferis.   Day was cloudy, The. No one could
come to a decision.
Sen, R.   Black clouds have risen in my sky.
Shiki.   Thunderstorm breaks up, The.
Shin Kyŏngnim.   They.
Silko.   In Cold Storm Light.
Simonides.   When in the skillfully welded chest.
Simpson, L.   Summer Storm.
Smith, B.   Backwater Blues.

Smith, C. Pressed by the Moon, Mute Arbitress of Tides.
Written September 1791, During a Remarkable Thunder Storm, in which the Moon Was Perfectly Clear, While the Tempest Gathered in Various Directions Near the Earth.
Smith, D. New Orleans Engagement.
Smith, W. Tempest, The.
Solari, R. Currents.
Southey, R. Ship, The.
Spaziani. It is Said by Some Sailors, the Old.
Stanley, G. Rupert Winds.
Steele, T. Waiting for the Storm.
Steinberg, J. All of a Summer.
Stevenson, R. Last night we had a thunderstorm in style.
Stryk, L. Winter Storm.
Su Tung-p'o. Black Clouds—Spilled Ink.
Takamura Kotaro. Cathedral in the Thrashing Rain.
Tannahill. Eild.
Thomson, J. For, see! where Winter comes, himself, confest.
Tindley, C. Stand by Me.
Todd, M. Son et Lumière.
Toomer. Storm Ending.
Unknown. Far off brough, A.
Feng-yu: Cold Wind, and the Rain.
Proud Queen of the Earth Gods, Supreme Among the Heaven Gods.
Threading Frost.
Thunder floats.
Zhong-feng: Wild and Windy.
Walker, J. Safe.
Ward, J. I Have Felt the Gulf: Mississippi.
Warn. Nuit Blanche, Une.
Warren, R. 1. Over Prairie.
Wheeler, Post. Rain Race, The.
White, M. Recurrence.
Whitman, W. Patrolling Barnegat.
Proud Music of the Storm.
Williams, G. Wild Night at Treweithan.
Williamson, G. Neighboring Storms.
Wordsworth, W. Lucy Gray.
Wright, C. Storm.
Wright, D. Lines on Retirement, after Reading Lear.
Yamamura Bochō. Dance.
Yeats. Mad as the Mist and Snow.
Yu Ŭngbu. Do you say the wind blew last night.
Zanzotto. Behold the Thin Green.
Zaturenska. Tempest, The.

See also Blizzards; Tornadoes; Hurricanes

Storytelling and Storytellers
Archilochus. Here is a fable men tell.
Armantrout. As We're Told.
Atwood. It's the story that counts.
Bei Dao. In Memory.
Blue Cloud. Turtle.
Brown, D. When I Am 19 I Was a Medic.
Carson, C. Cocktails.
Chappell, F. My Father's Hurricane.
Chaucer. Franklin's Prologue, The.
Pardoner's Introduction, The.
Coleridge, S. Love: "All thoughts, all passions, all delights."
Cooper, W. Leaving the Country.
Creeley. Bresson's Movies.
Cucchi, M. It's over now, the time for observation, for.
Darío, R. Story for Margarita.
Davie, D. Remembering the 'Thirties.
De la Mare. Martha.
Delgado, J. La Llorona.
Dickinson, E. Ended, ere it begun.
Disch. Hooray for Hollywood.
Dodge, M. Way To Do It, The.
Dunbar, P. Harriet Beecher Stowe.
Emanuel, L. Like God.
England, A. Art of the Snake Story, The.
Fermini, I. First unexpected pain is beautiful, The.
Fishman, L. Promiscuity.
Flynn, N. Cartoon Physics, Part 2.
Fogarty, L. Remember Something Like This.

Forman, R. Kin.
Francis, M. Sitting with My Uncle.
Galvin, J. Story of the End of the Story, The.
Gil de Biedma, J. Prince of Aquitania, in His Torn-down Tower, The.
Giscombe, C. Bro Duncanson.
1978, Remembering 1962.
Graham, W. Imagine a Forest.
Graves, R. Devil's Advice to Story-Tellers, The.
To Juan at the Winter Solstice.
Gregg. Singers Change, the Music Goes On, The.
Hamburger, M. Treblinka.
Harris, Ken. Vigil.
Hart, K. Story, The.
Hass, R. Faint Music.
Hudgins. Telling, The.
Hughes, L. Aunt Sue's Stories.
Ingelow. Story, A.
Jaccottet. Letter of the 26th June.
Jackson, G. 1691. Tituba of Salem.
Jones, R. Novel, The.
Justice, D. But That Is Another Story.
Kennelly. Story, The.
Kim, Kalehua Parrilla. Ka Hale / The Nurturing Place.
Korinna [or Corinna]. Terpsichore [told] me.
Longfellow, H. Prelude: The Wayside Inn.
López Mills, T. Carta.
Letter: "Endings always erase the traces of their plot."
Lott, B. Post Script.
Madhubuti. Union of Two, The.
Markham, E. Sea, The.
McElroy, C. Griots Who Know Brer Fox, The.
Under the Oak Table.
McGuire, Jerry. Gongula.
Mitchell, S. Good Samaritan et Al, The.
Montag, T. May 25, 2001 (1).
Ortiz. State's Claim That It Seeks in No Way to Deprive Indians of Their Rightful Share of Water, The.
"Pindar.". Town Eclogue, A.
Popa. Story of a story, The.
Reid, A. Spell for Sleeping, A.
Riley, J. Little Orphant Annie.
Rohrer, M. Childhood Stories.
Ruefle. Jewel, The.
Rumi. Minute I heard my first love story, The.
St. John, D. Gin.
St. John, P. We Are Going to Be Here Now.
Sandburg, C. They have yarns / Of a skyscraper so tall they had to put hinges.
Sastri, D. In Search of Krishna.
Schultz, P. Eight-Mile Bike Ride, The.
Sexton. Cinderella.
Shafiq, H. Destinies.
Shurin. Blue Shade.
Sidney. Sonnet 45: "Stella oft sees the very face of woe."
Simic. Hundred-Year-Old China Doll's Head, The.
Smith, C. Essential Story, The.
Smith, I. Gaelic Stories.
Smith, P. Jemez Pueblo: December 26.
Soupault. Twilight.
Spahr, J. Stories go like this: the light, The.
Stevenson, R. Land of Story-Books, The.
Stewart, P. Singing down the Breadfruit.
T'ang Hsien-tsu. My son, you loved telling the story of Prince Nata.
Thompson, E. Mythology.
Thomson, J. In the Room.
Turnbull. Transmutation ("Every evening a mother makes up another episode of the same story for her son.").
Unknown. Middle- and small-sized needles.
True storyteller is a, The.
Wah. Father / Mother Haibun #15.
Walcott. Man Who Loved Islands, The.
Waltner-Toews, D. Request from Tante Tina to the Mennonite Women's Missionary Society to Put Salman Rushdie on the Prayer List, A.
Waniek. Sleepless Nights.
Warren, R. Tell Me a Story.
Weinberger, E. Anecdotal Evidence.

Wilner, E. As soft and as pink as a nursery.
Wunderlich, M. Voluntary Servitude.
Stowe, Harriet Beecher
Dunbar, P. Harriet Beecher Stowe.
Parker, D. Harriet Beecher Stowe.
Ray, H. Greeting.
Strafford, Thomas Wentworth, 1st Earl of
Cleveland, J. Epitaph on the Earl of Strafford.
Strangers
Al-Rihani. It Was All for Him.
Anderson-Thompkins. To Love a Stranger.
Barnes, B. Something Cool.
Barrax. Strangers Like Us: Pittsburgh, Raleigh, 1945–1985.
Berkson, B. Roots.
Berryman. Dream Song 45.
Bialoszewski. Ballad of Going Down to the Store, A.
Boadiba. We Pass through a Foreigner's House.
Boroditskaya, M. So much gentleness from unknown men.
Buchanan, G. Conversations with Strangers.
Bunting. Orotava Road, The.
Carpenter, E. To a Stranger.
Carroll, L. Visitor, A.
Castillo, S. Monday Night at Pedro's.
Clifton, L. C. C. Rider.
Crane, H. Tunnel, The.
Deltoro, A. Contemporáneos. Contemporaries.
Disch. Vowels of Another Language, The.
Forrest, G. Stranger in Paradise.
Gallagher, T. Hug, The.
Gregerman, D. High Speed.
Hemans. Stranger's Heart, The.
Hewitt, J. Search, The.
Ho Ch'e Ch'ang. Return, The.
Hope, A. Inscription for a War.
Housman. Shades of Night, The.
Hughes, L. Madam and the Wrong Visitor.
Subway Face.
Issa. Under cherry trees / There are.
Knutson, G. Moon Fishing.
Kuppner. Architecture is when the sun shines on a facade daily.
Levertov. People at Night.
Levin, P. Meeting of Friends, A.
Lima, J. Stranger, Stranger.
Locklin. Stranger, The.
Lu Chao-lin. Old Idea of Choan by Rosoriu.
Mew. Again.
Mistral, G. Stranger, The.
Mitchell, N. Incognito.
Muir, E. Killing, The.
Patterson, G. Letter from Home.
Poloskey, M. Encounter.
Rakha, Y. Dust Storm, The.
Robinson, E. Flammonde.
Fleming Helphenstine.
Seth. Unclaimed.
Shange. Elegance in the Extreme.
Shepherd, R. Who Owns the Night and Lease Stars.
Strand. Night, The Porch, The.
Tadic. Nobody.
Thwaite, A. Great Foreign Writer Visits Age-Old Temple, Greeted by Venerable Abbess, 1955.
Unknown. Curse on a Closed Gate, A.
Vallejo. Finished the stranger, with whom, late.
Very. Strangers, The.
Yourself.
Vigil, A. At the Stop Light, the Braided Blond Man.
Viray, M. Two Strangers, The.
Wetzsteon. Drinks in the Town Square.
Whitman, W. This Moment Yearning and Thoughtful.
To a Stranger.
Wilbur, R. Caserta Garden.
Transit.
Wilson, S. Experiments in the Impersonal.
Woo, D. Habit.
Wood, E. Recognition.
Wright, R. Stranger in Paradise.
Yi Hyangji. Reply at an Unknown Place.

Strathclyde (region), Scotland
Smith, A.   Sing, Poet, 'tis a merry world.
Stravinsky, Igor
Alexander, E.   Stravinsky in L.A.
Strawberries
Alexander the Wild.   Strawberry Picking.
Atwood.   Strawberries: "Strawberries when I
   first remember them are not red but blue, The."
Citino.   Sister Mary Appassionata Lectures the
   Folklore Class: Doctrines of the Strawberry.
Dunmore.   Wild Strawberries.
Jackson, H.   My Strawberry.
Johnson, M.   Strawberry, The.
Kenny, M.   Wild Strawberry.
Logue, C.   Good Taste.
Merwin.   Strawberries.
Morgan, E.   Strawberries.
Swenson, M.   Strawberrying.
Taggard.   Millions of Strawberries.
Villa.   Now I Prize Yellow Strawberries.
Williams, H.   To the Strawberry.
Streams
Ammons.   Enfield Falls.
Angus.   Anemones.
Bryant, W.   When breezes are soft and skies are
   fair.
Choeui Eusoon.   On the Bank of a Stream by
   Taedun Temple.
Guillén, J.   Stream with Washerwomen.
Gundy, J.   Old Water.
Li Po.   Wandering Ch'ing-Ling Strea in Nan-
   Yang.
Louise, E.   Jesus' Song.
Pei Di.   Stream at the House of the Luans, The.
Pou Kuksa.   Stone Stream.
Walcott.   Streams.
Wang Ch'ang-ling.   At the Stream's Source in
   Spring: A Party.
Wang Wei.   Stream at the House of the Luans,
   The.
See also **Brooks and Streams**
Street People
Clark, T.   Prophet.
Jones, B.   Portrait of an Overpopulated Woman.
Kerouac.   Orizaba Blues: 64th Chorus.
Lilley, Gary.   Who Sez Thunderbirds Can't Fly.
Simic.   December: "It snows."
Sundiata.   Space. A Prose Poem Monologue.
See also **Homeless, The**
Street Performers
Ashbery, J.   Street Musicians.
Mole, J.   Musical Monkey, The.
Moore, L.   Haiku.
No Ch'ŏnmyŏng.   Performer, Male.
Streetcars
Auden.   Aubade: "At break of dawn."
Gumilyov [*or* Gumiliov *or* Gumilev].   Streetcar
   That Lost Its Way, The.
Hare, M.   Determinism.
Levine, P.   On the Birth of Good and Evil
   During the Long Winter of '28.
Sandburg, C.   Halsted Street Car.
Yevtushenko [*or* Evtushenko].   Streetcar Named
   Poetry, A.
See also **Trolleys**
Streetlights
Jacobsen, R.   Light Pole.
Streets
Allen, E.   Street Music.
Avison.   Rondeau Redoublé.
Bachmann.   Paris.
Bandeira.   Evocation of Recife.
Barrax.   Strangers Like Us: Pittsburgh, Raleigh,
   1945–1985.
Bell, M.   Street Fair: The Quartet.
Bialoszewski.   Ballad of Going Down to the
   Store, A.
Blok.   Night: A Street.
Bryant, W.   Crowded Street, The.
Cavafy.   In the Street.
Denby.   Silence at Night, The.
Desnos.   St Merri district, The.
Eady.   Wrong Street, The.
Faiz.   Vista.
Fargue.   Boulevard, The.

Feinstein, E.   Magic Apple Tree, The.
Flanner.   Noon on Alameda Street.
Foster, T.   Grammar of Waking, A.
González Prada, M.   To Be with the Dead.
Gunn, T.   San Francisco Streets.
Hannah, S.   Your Street Again.
Harris, W.   Samantha Is My Negro Cat.
Hernández Cruz.   Side 20.
Hogan, L.   Potholes.
Howe, J.   Street Yarn.
Hughes, L.   Railroad Avenue.
Im Hwa.   Again at the Crossroads.
Ingelow.   Winding-up Time.
Jiménez, J.   Street Is Waiting for the Night, The.
Lassell.   Brady Street, San Francisco.
Lerner, A.   On the Street Where You Live.
Levy, A.   Sequel to 'A Reminiscence," The.
   Straw in the Street.
Liu Yu Hsi.   Raven Robe Lane.
Machado Ruiz.   Her Street Is Dark.
Monro, H.   Cat's Meat.
Morejón.   Love, Attributed City.
Moss, T.   Fisher Street.
Nemes Nagy.   Proportions of the Street, The.
Nordbrandt.   Streets.
Nye, N.   New Year.
O'Hara, F.   Step Away from Them, A.
Paulin.   Desertmartin.
Paz.   Along Galeana Street.
   Here.
Pinsky.   Street, The.
Rybicki, J.   For Daniel Beels, Third Generation
   Bricklayer.
Salaam.   French Quarter Intimacies.
Salom.   Walking at Night.
Salter.   Rebirth of Venus, The.
Shapiro, K.   Manhole Covers.
Shwarts [*or* Shvarts].   What That Street Is
   Called.
Simpson, L.   After Midnight.
Slessor.   Choker's Lane.
   William Street.
Soto.   Street.
Strange.   Streetcorner Church.
Thomson, J.   Part 2: "Because he seemed to
   walk with an intent."
Villaurrutia.   Los Angeles Nocturne.
Welish.   Crossing Disappearing behind Them.
Wunderlich, M.   East Seventh Street.
See also **Roads**
Strength
Akers, E.   Bringing Our Sheaves with Us.
Arnold, M.   Growing Old.
Babcock, M.   Be Strong.
Bek, T.   Oh life, long as an epic.
Brooks, G.   Winnie Mandela, she.
Brown, S.   Strong Men.
Cervantes.   First Beating.
Chasin.   Strength.
De [*or* Du] Guillet.   But if he came straight for
   me.
Dunn, S.   That Saturday Without a Car.
"Eliot.".   *from* Chapter 46.
Emerson, R.   Compensation ("Wings of Time
   are black and white, The.").
Galindo.   Short Story, A.
Gallaher, C.   Deb at the Ham Slicer.
Gex-Breaux, Q.   Padded Steps/Sister Song (a
   litany).
Gilbert, C.   Beginning by Value.
Giovanni.   Crutches.
Grosholz.   Eden.
Hadewijch.   Love has subjugated me.
Hayes, T.   Goliath Poem.
Henley, W. E.   Invictus.
Hymans, D.   Passacaglia.
Ikeda, P.   Wild Iris.
Itaikkunrurkilar.   His Legs Strong and Lithe.
Jeffers, R.   Rock and Hawk.
Jennings, E.   Letter to Peter Levi, A.
Majorino.   Say--So I'll Say.
Mark, D.   Suzie Wong Doesn't Live Here.
Moore, M.   Peter.
Pfeiffer, E.   Lost Light, The.
Plath.   Mushrooms.
Ransom, J.   Agitato Ma Non Troppo.

Spiel of [the] Three Mountebanks.
Rich, A.   Phantasia for Elvira Shatayev.
   Power.
Rilke.   I Find You.
Robertson, J.   Royalty.
Rossetti, C.   Study (A Soul), A.
Sandburg, C.   Upstream.
Smart, C.   Strength.
Stratidakis, E.   Need for Armor, A.
Tennyson, A.   Mine be the strength of spirit
   fierce and free.
Unknown.   Song of the Peasants in the Time of
   Yao.
Very.   Mountain, The.
Whitney, H.   To a Woman.
Yeats.   Wild Old Wicked Man, The.
Zamora, D.   Mother's Day.
Strikes and Strikers
Davies, I.   Angry Summer, The ("Mrs. Evans
   fach, you want butter again.").
   Do You Remember 1926?
   What will you do with your shovel, Dai.
Dent, A.   Restricting Gate, The.
Espada.   Cockroaches of Liberation.
Graham, J.   Hiding Place, The.
Grin, B.   Strike of the Coal Miners.
Guiney.   Strikers in Hyde Park.
Ilio, D.   Prokosch in Tehran, 1978.
Johnson, D.   Poem: "There was something I
   can't bring myself."
Jordan, J.   For Beautiful Mary Brown: Chicago
   Rent Strike Leader.
Kurtz.   Call, The.
Lewis, Emyr.   Above us, where the clouds'.
MacDiarmid, H.   Ballad of the General Strike.
Millar, J.   Fiber Optics.
Rahman, S.   Strike, The.
Sassoon, S.   Case for the Miners, The.
Stein, K.   Benefit Picnic, Cigar Makers' Strike,
   August 1884.
Taggard.   At Last the Women are Moving.
Unknown.   Glorious Strike of the Builders, The.
   What Shall We Do for the Striking Seamen?
Ward, B.   Twenty Million Buckets.
String
Belloc.   Henry King, Who Chewed Bits of
   String, and Was Early Cut Off in Dreadful
   Agonies.
Brown, G.   Shroud.
Koehler, T.   I've Got the World on a String.
See also **Rope**
Striptease
Dubie.   Genesis Text for Larry Levis, Who Died
   Alone, A.
Durrell.   Strip-tease.
Dyer, E.   'Round Killar.
Elmslie, K.   Girl Machine.
Endrezze.   Stripper, The.
Lewis, G.   Strip-Tease.
Masterson, R.   Chinese Stripper.
St. John, D.   Swan at Sheffield Park, The.
Stafford, W.   Adults Only.
Toledo, N.   Agricola.
   Agrícola.
   Na Agrícola.
Van Clief-Stefanon, L.   Strip.
Voznesensky [*or* Voznesenskii].   Striptease.
See also **Burlesque**
Strokes
Ammons.   Parting.
Ginsberg, A.   Stroke.
McNair.   Visit, The: "We were at the camp, it
   must have been."
Shapiro, H.   6/20/97.
Stephens, P.   Hangman.
Voss, F.   Termination.
Wagoner, D.   Walt Whitman Bathing.
Young, G.   Night Call.
Stuart, Charles Edward (The Young Pretender)
Nairne.   Will Ye No Come Back Again?
Unknown.   Will He No Come Back Again?
Stuart, James Ewell Brown ("Jeb")
Preston, M.   Grave in Hollywood Cemetery,
   Richmond, A.
Thompson, J.   Obsequies of Stuart.

Students

Abse. Carnal Knowledge.
Allen, P. Teaching Poetry at Votech High, Santa Fe, the Week John Lennon Was Shot.
Anderson, Tenshin Reb. To My First Teacher.
Bartlett, E. God Is Dead—Nietzche.
Basho. Don't imitate me.
Blake, W. School-Boy, The.
Blankenburg, G. Mouse, The.
Blind. Russian Student's Tale, The.
Campo. Medical Student Learns Love and Death, A.
Clanchy, K. War Poetry.
Clarke, A. Straying Student, The.
Clarke, George Elliott. Student's Tale, The.
Collins, B. Marginalia.
Delgado, J. Letters from School, The.
Deniz, G. Auditor.
Oyente.
Dunn, D. Glasgow Schoolboys, Running Backwards.
Eady. Why Do So Few Blacks Study Creative Writing?
Espada. Year I Was Diagnosed with a Sacrilegious Heart, The.
Farawell, M. Everything I Need to Know I Learned in Kindergarten.
Flores, J. Last Visit to Chestnut Middle School.
Follain. Shops.
Gallagher, T. Sah Sin.
Germain, Carmen. Literature 100.
Giovanni. Alabama Poem.
Gorey. Limerick: "Some Harvard men, stalwart and hairy."
Heaney, S. Alphabets.
Hilton, A. Heathen Pass-ee, The.
Hostetler, A. Resisting Geometry.
Hughes, L. Theme for English B.
Kabir. Simple Purification, The.
Kinnell. Correspondence School Instructor Says Goodbye to His Poetry Students, The.
Koertge. My Students.
Kuan Chung. Duties of the Student.
Lem. Office Hour.
Lockward, D. On First Reading *Romeo and Juliet.*
Mac Lochlainn, G. Rite of Passage.
MacNeice. I ought to be glad.
Martin, C. E. S. L.
Moore, M. Student, The.
Moore, T. Scene from a Play, Acted at Oxford, Called "Matriculation".
Muso Soseki. Climbing Down the Snowy Mountain.
Old Hut.
Naden. Scientific Wooing.
Nelson, M. Prayer of Miss Budd, The.
Nemerov. September, the First Day of School.
Po Chü-i. After Reading Lao Tzu.
Prodromos. To the Emperor.
Ratzlaff, K. My Students against the Cemetery Pines.
Roethke. Elegy for Jane.
Rome, H. Chain Store Daisy.
St. John, P. Studying.
Snodgrass. Campus on the Hill, The.
Straus, M. Neuroanatomy Summer.
Unknown. Good Scholars Make Bad Husbands.
Student, The.
Zi-jin: The Student's Blue Collar or Lapel.
Wheatley, P. To the University of Cambridge, in New-England.
Whitman, W. To a Western Boy.
Wordsworth, W. Mind Debarred, A.
Yun Tongju. Poem That Came Easily, A.

Stupidity

Armour. Pachycephalosaurus.
Centolella. Small Acts.
Dryden, J. Mac Flecknoe [or, A Satire upon the True-Blue Protestant Poet T. S.].
Issa. Bath when you're born.
This stupid world.
Thus spring begins: old.
Powell, D. A. Nicholas the ridiculous: you will always be 27 and impossible. No more expectations.

Rekdal, Paisley. Stupid.
Smith, W. Plain Talk.
Wright, J. Presentation of Two Birds to My Son, A.

Stuttering and Stutterers

Brooks, F. Stuttering Lover, The.
Montague, J. Flowering Absence, A ("How can one make an absence flower.").
O'Hara, G. K-K-K-Katy.

Stuyvesant, Peter

Schulman. New Netherland, 1654.

Sublimity

Mahon. Antarctica.
Ryan, K. Bad Time for the Sublime, A.
Turner, F. Texas Eclogues.

Submarines

Henry, B. Submarine.
McKain. Opening Day.
Romtvedt. Black Beauty, A Praise.

Submission

Auden. Legend.
Bateman, E. It's a Great Big Shame.
Brandt, D. Nonresistance, or love Mennonite style.
Byron, G. Last Words on Greece.
Crosby, F. Blessed Assurance.
Cunningham, N. Giving.
Davies, M. Love Song: "There is a strong wall about me to protect me."
Dickey, J. Leap, The.
Donne. Why are we[e] by all creatures waited on?
Frost, R. Reluctance.
Gunn, T. In Santa Maria del Popolo.
Herrick. To Anthea, Who May Command Him Anything.
Kearney, M. First Blow-Job.
Killigrew, A. Pastoral Dialogue.
Kizer, C. Bitch.
M—rt—n. Humble Wish, The.
Michelangelo Buonarroti. Soul tries a thousand remedies in vain, The.
Why should I still pour out my intense desire.
Mitchison. My True Love Hath My Heart.
Murray, P. Conquest.
Nash, O. Tweedledee and Tweedledoom.
Nejati. Spiraling, the sparks.
Piercy. Friend, The.
Prince, F.T. Epistle to a Patron, An.
Reddy, Srikanth. Second Circle.
Rukeyser, M. Long Enough. Long Enough.
Rumi. Say Yes Quickly.
Rungano. Woman, The.
Teasdale. I Would Live in Your Love.
Tennyson, A. Love is and was my Lord and King.
Trefusis. Valentine, A.
Unknown. Send Him Back Hard By Your Lady's Small Window.
Thy Heart.
Vaughan, R. Insight into private affairs. . .raises certain barristers and magistrates to such great heights.
Welch, J. Plea to Those Who Matter.
Wickham. Slighted Lady, The.
Tired Woman, The.

Suburbs and Suburban Life

Aiken, C. Three Star Final.
Balaban. At 4:00 A.M. Asleep.
Bawer. Grand Central Station, 20 December 1987.
Betjeman. Slough.
Burt, S. Paysage Moralisé.
Christie. Dusk and the Wife.
Ciardi, J. Suburban.
Clover, J. Alas, That Is the Name of Our Town; I Have Been Concealing It All This Time.
Dailey. Dear Bubble.
S'what Up.
Davidson, J. Northern Suburb, A.
DeFoe, M. Aviary.
Derricotte. Blackbottom.
Eigner. Trees Green the Quiet Sun.
Elmslie, K. Marbled Chuckle in the Savannahs.
Ewart. Nursery Rhyme.

Firer. Saxophone Julie.
Gwynn, R. Classroom at the Mall, The.
Hardy, T. Snow in the Suburbs.
Harvey, M. Our Square of Lawn.
Iglesias, H. Feeding Frenzy.
Ignatow, D. Suburbia.
Jeffers, R. Carmel Point.
Kaplan, L. He takes me to see his mother. She lives in the.
Katz, J. Imperfect Is Our Paradise, The.
Kleinzahler. Lunatic of Lindley Meadow, The.
Kress, L. Backyards of America.
Kuhar, M. Suburban buddha, coffeehouse christ.
Lawrence, D. H. Suburbs on a Hazy Day.
Lomax, M. Other Woman, The.
Lopez, T. Dauntless the slug-horn to my lips I set.
McGinley. View from a Suburban Window.
McGrath, C. First Trimester, The.
Miles, J. Housewife.
Nilsson, H. How Came What Came Alas.
Noguchi, R. Really Long Ride, The.
Parker, A. Days like Prose.
Perry, S. Fugue.
Piercy. Development, The.
Prunty. Downtown Bus, The.
Riddell, E. Suburban Song.
Rouse, A. Springfield, Virginia.
Schuyler, J. Man in Blue, A.
Serote. Night-time.
Simpson, L. In the Suburbs.
Szporluk. Occupant of the Hose.
Taylor, H. Buildings and Grounds.
Thelwall. On the Rapid Extension of the Suburbs.
Thorpe, J. Man in a Semi-Detached House.
Tsvetayeva [or Tsvetaeva]. Like a thick horse's mane.
Volkman. Kiss Me Deadly.
Wendt. Starting from Scratch.
Wenthe, William. White Settlement.
Wilbur, R. To an American Poet Just Dead.
Williams, Stephanie. Coarse rigors.
Williamson, G. Nervous Systems.
Winder. On Fourteen Maple Street.

Subways

Agee. Rapid Transit.
Aiken, C. All Death, All Love.
As-Sabah. Transition #2.
Baraka, I. Clay.
Betjeman. Metropolitan Railway, The.
Charara, H. Here It Is.
Clampitt. Times Square Water Music.
Crane, H. Tunnel, The.
Denby. Out of Bronx subway June forest.
Subway, The.
Dunmore. To Virgil.
Esteves. South Bronx Testimonial.
Field, E. Graffiti.
Field, Miranda. Subway.
Friedman, E. Heading for Manhattan by Train.
Glancy. Great Indian Father in the Subway.
Harris, D. On the uptown lexington avenue express: Martin Luther King Day 1995.
Hernández Cruz. Going Uptown to Visit Miriam.
Hopkins, L. Subways Are People.
Hughes, L. Subway Face.
Jacobs, L. Subway Train, The.
Johnston, D. Lexington Avenue Express.
Jordan, J. All the World Moved.
Kaufman, B. Late Lamented Wind, Burned in Indignation, The.
Keita, N. Rapid Transit.
Kim Chôngnan. In the Subway—Getting Used to Ugliness 3.
McKay, C. Subway Wind.
Milosz, C. Esse.
Monk, G. South Bound: Facing North.
Montague, J. Cage, The.
Nelson, M. Subway in March, 5:45 P.M.
Notley. Woman came into "a car I rode" "about thirty-seven" "maybe", A.
O'Donoghue, M. This is Sunday.
Okudzhava. How the young flutist smiles.

Olds, S.   On The Subway.
Orlovsky.   Poems from Subway to Work.
Perillo, L.   Ghost Shirt, The.
Postell, T.   Gertrude Stein Rides the Town Down El.
Pound, E.   In a Station of the Metro.
Reznikoff.   If there is a scheme.
[Winter Sketches II: Subway].
Schwartz, D.   Tired and Unhappy, You Think of Houses.
Seaton, M.   Fear of Subways.
Sholl.   Good News/Bad News.
Swenson, M.   Riding the "A".
Walcott.   Village Life, A.
Warr, M.   Brain on Ice.
Weiners.   My Mother.
Wood, E.   Recognition.
Wunderlich, M.   East Seventh Street.

Success
Akst, H.   Straw Hat in the Rain.
Bolton, K.   In Ferrara.
Brown, L.   Straw Hat in the Rain.
Dickinson, E.   Success is counted sweetest.
We grow accustomed to the Dark.
Eady.   Success.
Ezekiel.   Case Study.
Forbes, J.   Death, an Ode.
Guest, E.   Don't Quit.
It Couldn't Be Done.
Hardy, T.   Ruined Maid, The.
Herrick.   Wassaile, The.
Jenkins, J. et al.   In Ferrara.
Kipling, R.   If.
Lanier, E.   To you I dedicate this work of grace.
Lazarus, E.   Success.
Martineau, J.   Life's Success.
Po Chü-i.   Yin-yo laps in the reeds, my guest departs.
Procter, A.   Envy.
Serchuk.   My Other Life.
Stafford, W.   Silver Star.
Stein, G.   There.
Strand.   Coming to This.
Whitman, W.   When I Heard At The Close Of The Day.
Yeats.   To a Friend Whose Work Has Come to Nothing.

Sudan
Clark Bekedermo.   New from Ethiopia and the Sudan, The.
Kipling, R.   Fuzzy-Wuzzy.

Sudden Death
Beckman, J.   Thirst of the crowd, The. We laid the surfer down.
Davidkov, Ivan.   Meteor.
Fargnoli, Patricia.   Lightning Spreads Out across the Water.
Kharms.   Incidents.
Lux.   Man Gets Off Work Early, A.
Rekdal, Paisley.   Stupid.
Turgeniev, I.   Insect, The.
Walker, J.   Flt #4372.
Whur.   Morning arose, and its beauties were beaming, The.
Unfortunate Gentleman, The.

Suez Canal
Nemerov.   Reflexions on the Seizure of the Suez, and on a Proposal to Line the Banks of That Canal with Billboard Advertisements.

Suffering
Addison, J.   King Henry's Song.
Aeschylus.   If I were to tell of our labours, our hard lodging.
Afterman.   Pietà.
Ahmed Pasha.   Ask about my wailing from the prayers.
Akhmatova, A.   Requiem.
al-Sa'igh, Y.   Final Question, The.
Alberti.   Millares 1965.
Alexander, M.   Memory.
Anwar, C.   Me.
Twilight at a Little Harbor.
Auden.   Musée des Beaux Arts.
Avianus.   Calf and the Ox, The.
Bahâyî, Sheyhülislâm.   Oh cry, what are you

doing, disturbing.
Baqi.   That tyrant, is she not persuaded by the tears.
Barkan, S.   Bring Me Your Woes.
Barot, R.   Many Are Called.
Berenguer.   Signs on the Table, The.
Berlin, E.   Sea World.
Berlin, I.   You're Just in Love.
Berrigan, D.   Prague: Old Woman in the Street.
Bevington, L.   One More Bruised Heart!
Bhattācārya, K.   From now on.
Bontemps.   My Heart Has Known its Winter.
Brecht, B.   Concerning the Infanticide, Marie Farrar.
Brontë, E.   Stars.
Brooks, G.   My Dreams, My Works, Must Wait Till After Hell.
Brown, S.   Let Them Call It Jazz.
Browning, E.   Convinced by Sorrow.
Bryan, J.   Bindweed.
Budbill.   What Issa Heard.
Bunina.   From the Seashore.
Castillo, O.   Before the Scales, Tomorrow.
Celan.   Tenebrae.
Ceravolo.   Indian Suffering.
Cetina, G.   In What Region, in What Part of the World.
Chipasula.   Because the Wind Remembers.
Manifesto on Ars Poetica.
Ritual Girl.
Talking of Sharp Things.
Clifton, L.   Cigarettes.
Coleman, W.   Notes on a Departure.
Constable, H.   Uncivil sickness, hast thou no regard.
Crabbe, G.   Peter Grimes.
Dach.   Lamentation during His Most Painful Illness.
Davie, D.   Across the Bay.
Davies, A.   New Sentience, The.
Davis, O.   If You Are Asked.
de Vries, H.   My Brother.
Dennis, C.   St. Francis and the Nun.
Dickinson, E.   After great pain a formal feeling comes.
For each ecstatic instant.
To know just how He suffered—would be dear.
Dorsett, T.   Survivor, The.
Douglas, K.   Desert Flowers.
Drayton.   Crier, The.
Dunbar, P.   Prayer, A: "O Lord, the hard-won miles."
We Wear the Mask.
Eich.   Huge Person, The.
Ekevall, K.   Telling Myself.
Emre.   Burning, burning, I drift and tread.
Eugenius Vulgarius.   Metrum Parhemiacum Tragicum.
Faiz.   Before You Came.
Felipe, L.   I Have Not Come to Sing.
Foley, Jack.   Prose for Two Voices.
Fox, A.   Why She Suffers.
Fuertes.   Scrawny Women, The.
Gallagher, T.   Not a Sparrow.
García Lorca.   City That Does Not Sleep.
Night of Sleepless Love.
Poet Asks His Love About the Enchanted City of Cuenca, The.
Poet Asks His Love to Write to Him, The.
Sonnet of Sweet Complaint.
Sonnet of Sweet Weeping.
Garcilaso de la Vega.   Sonnet 10: "Oh, sweet gifts brought forth for my misfortune."
Ghalib, M.   Ghazal 12.
Ghazal 21.
My Head and My Knees.
Gibson, M.   Summer Birds and Flowers (2).
Woman Resting on a Bundle of Kindling.
Ginsberg, A.   Change, The: Kyoto-Tokyo Express.
Glück, L.   Elms.
Poem: "In the early evening, as now, a man is bending."
Queen of Carthage, The.
Graham-Pole, J.   Pain, The.
Gryphius.   Epitaph for Mariana Gryphius, His

Brother Paul's Little Daughter.
Human Misery.
Guest, Paul.   Intrusion of Ovid, The.
Ha Thi Thao.   Our Son's Profession.
Hadewijch.   Knowing Love in Herself.
Hafiz, K [or Hafez].   Sitting in the Grief House (250).
Halliday, M.   Credentials.
Hamer.   Crossroads.
Hardy, T.   Hap.
Hausen, F.   Help! How Minne has deserted me.
Hawaiian Oral Tradition.   Stripping Leaves from Sugarcane.
Hayden, R.   Soledad.
Hayes, T.   Blue Terrance, The.
Heaney, S.   Human beings suffer.
Henry, B.   Across the River.
Herbert, G.   Dialogue, A.
Love Unknown.
Herbert, Z.   Mr. Cogito Meditates on Suffering.
Hernández, M.   I Have Plenty of Heart.
Sitting on Top of Corpses.
Herrera y Reissig.   Heraldic Decoration.
Herrick.   His Saviour['s] Words, Going to the Cross[e].
Heyen.   Grace.
Hirsch, E.   In the Midwest.
Hirschhorn, N.   Number Our Days.
Hölderlin.   Schicksalslied.
Hopes.   Don't think the stars and moon are all.
Horan.   Prometheus.
Howard, A.   Elegy on the Death of Her Husband.
Howe, F.   His legs were long and thin, his knees bent and feet crossed.
Hughes, L.   Minstrel Man.
Strange Hurt.
Hughes, T.   God, A.
Ibn Quzman, A.   To a Beauty, White, Pure, and Constant.
Inber.   Teeth are bared, the mouth drawn tight, the face, The.
Jackson, L.   Wind Suffers [of Blowing], The.
Jackson, R.   For a Long Time I Have Wanted to Write a Happy Poem.
Jiménez, J.   My Feet, So Deep in the Earth.
Johnson, J.   We To America.
Johnson, S.   Lines Contributed to Goldsmith's "The Traveller".
Jonson, B.   What He[e] Suffered.
József, A.   Dog, The.
Juana Inés de la Cruz.   Because my Lord was born to suffer.
Kaufman, B.   Would You Wear My Eyes?
Kaufman, S.   Job's Wife.
Keelan, C.   Embers.
Kendall, M.   Failures.
Kloefkorn.   Why the Stone Remains Silent.
Knevet.   Bottle, The.
Kocot, N.   Civilization Day.
Koehler, T.   Stop! You're Breakin' My Heart.
Koeppel, M.   Meditation: "Sorrow is to be discarded."
Korean Oral Tradition.   Wretched Married Life (Folk Song from Koch'ang).
Kosman, Admiel.   Something Hurt.
Kouchag, N.   I Was Suffering Exile.
Krukowski, D.   Minor Poets, The.
Labé.   Sonnet 17: "I flee the city, temples, and each place."
Lane, P.   Midnight Song.
Levy, A.   Epitaph: "This is the end of him, here he lies."
Felo de Se.
Minor Poet, A.
Li Yu [or Li Hou-Chu].   River Rolling Eastward, The.
Limonov.   As if a quiet branch drew a line.
Liu Chi-hsün.   Lament.
Lloyd, C.   Metaphysical Sonnet.
Longinovic.   Glorious Ruins.
López Velarde.   Purple Spot, The.
MacCaig.   Red and the Black, The.
MacEwen, G.   Child Dancing, The.
Macgoye.   Freedom Song, A.
MacLean, S.   Turmoil, The.

Mandal, B. I'm not a child any more, Syama.
Mansour, J. Seated on her bed legs spread open.
March, A. Out scouting for sound counsels? How to prosper?
Mayakovsky [or Maiakovskii]. Cloud in Trousers, A.
McNiece, R. Ordinary, The.
Melville, H. Armies of the Wilderness, The. Pebbles.
Meredith, W. Korean Woman Seated by a Wall, A.
Merwin. Chaff, The.
Mhlophe. Sometimes When It Rains.
Mif. Terezin.
Millay, E. Ancient Gesture, An. Pity me not because the light of day.
Montale. Many years, and one of them a little harder.
Mörling, M. Three-Card Monte.
Morungen, H. Wound of Love, The.
Mukand, J. First Payment.
Mura. Argument: On 1942, An.
Murray, L. Cotton Flannelette.
Musset. Muse, The. Poet, The.
Na'ili [or Yeni-Zada Mustafa Efendi]. Since the thunderbolt of disaster set our.
Nichol. From Catullus Poem LI.
Nikonova, R. Along the thread of veins.
Ojaide. Ward 6.
Olds, S. I Go Back to May 1937.
Ono no Komachi. When longing for you.
Orr, G. Some Part of the Lyric.
Parker, D. Pour Prendre Congé.
Pavese. Poetics.
Pavlich. Black Flower.
Plotkin, C. Greetings from My Shtetl (A Letter from Poland).
Quevedo y Villegas. Continues in the Same State of Feeling.
Ramsdell, H. Thank you for saying pathos instead of pathetic, keeping us the same size as before.
Ransom, J. Lady Lost. Necrological.
Rāy, K. Tara, You are Cintamayi, Full of Thought.
Reuental, Neidhart von. There is pain in my heart.
Rexroth, K. August 22, 1939.
Rich, A. For a Friend in Travail.
Rilke. O you lovers that are so gentle, step occasionally.
Rimbaud, A. Lice-Seekers.
Ritchie, E. Electroconvulsive Therapy.
Rodefer. Brief To Butterick.
Rollings. In Your Own Sweet Time.
Ronsard. Génèvres Hérissez, et Vous, Houx Espineux.
Rosselli. How many fields which like a sponge.
Rossetti, C. Sappho.
Rowe, V. Time Heals All Wounds—But One.
Rungano. Mother.
Samawi, A. Iraqi Sorrows.
Sappho. To me it seems.
Sargant, J. A. How gladly would I lay my aching head. 'Lo, on her dying couch, the sufferer lies.
Schelling. High Up the Thunder Gods, Downstairs the Hunger.
Sen, R. Let me tell You a thing or two, Tara.
Senghor. Nocturne (I Accompanied You).
Shafer, A. Gurney Tears.
Shcherbina. About Limits.
Shokushi. O cord of life!
"Shunzei's Daughter.". Burning in Secret.
Shwarts [or Shvarts]. My heart's cloth I shall spread before the Savior's feet.
Sidney. Sonnet 2: "Not at [the] first sight, nor with a dribbed shot." Sonnet 47: "What, have I thus betrayed my liberty?"
Smith, C. Sighing I see yon little troop at play.
Smith, L. Following the Road. In Muddy Waters.
Sŏ Chŏngju. Such a Land.

Spender, S. Epilogue to a Human Drama.
Stainer. Wound-dresser's Dream, The.
Stevens, W. This was the salty taste of glory.
Strabo, W. Elegy on Reichenau.
Tassis y Peralta. Love Is Not Will But Destiny.
Tennant, E. Mad Soldier, The.
Thomas, R. S. Island, The.
Trakl. Winter Night, A.
Trethewey, N. Hot Comb.
Tu Fu [or Du Fu]. Another Spring ("In all the country."). Ballad of the Army Carts. Spring View. Summit, A.
Tu Mo. Mandarins Got Their Raise, The.
Unknown. Bo-zhou: That Boat of Cypress Wood. Common people are very weary, The. Every Hour in the Day. Heaven Bell A-Ring. If I might offer. My Father, How Long! Poor Rosy. Then Job spoke and cursed his day and chanted and said. Trouble of the World, The. You intend, it seems. You Love Her.
Unknown, fr. Terezin Concentration Camp. Pain Strikes Sparks on Me, the Pain of Terezin.
Valente, J. Morning: "Naked morning, the day's transparent."
Vallejo. Black Cup, The. Black heralds, The. Black Messengers, The. Man Walks By with a Loaf of Bread on His Shoulder, A.
Various authors. Because the wolves wrought havoc.
Verlaine. Endless sameness.
Very. My People are destroyed for lack of Knowledge.—Hosea 4:6.
Vilariño. Like a dog howling endlessly. Maybe Then. No.
Villaurrutia. Nocturnal Sea. They and I.
Waldman, A. After-Life, The.
Wetzsteon. Witness.
Whalen, P. Pathogenesis.
Whitman, W. And I saw askant the armies.
Whittier. Christian Slave, The.
Wilde, L. Who Will Show Us Any Good?
Wilde, O. There is no chapel on the day.
Williams, C. K. Dog, The.
Williams, W. Complaint.
Wroth. Song: "[O]h] me[e], the time is [or has] come to part." Sonnet 6: "Ö[h] strive not[t] still to heap[e] disdain[e] on me[e]." Sonnet 39: "If I were giv'n to mirthe 'twowld [or 'twould] be more cross."
Wyatt. His Reward.
Yahya Beg. Poetry holds the written veil across its face, dryly.
Yeats. Fascination of What's Difficult, The.
Yesenin [or Essenin]. Winds, Winds, Winds.
Yi Kyŏngin. Song: "In the world are many roads I haven't walked, and I have pain."
Young, C. Infidelity.
Young, D. Frottage.
Zamora, D. Loyal Housewife.
Zimunya. Arrivants.
Zisquit. Word before the Last about Loss, A.

See also **Pain**

Suffolk, England
Crabbe, G. Alas! for Peter not an helping Hand.

Sugar
Clampitt. Hispaniola.
Farley, P. Treacle.
Grainger, J. Shame of France, The.
Morales, A. Sugar Poem.
Vecchone, P. Sugarmother's Daughter Dreams.
Wallenstein. Blues 1.
Williams, C. Sugar.

Sugar Cane
Ai. Cuba, 1962.
Bhatt, S. Shérdi.
Cabral de Melo Neto. Canefield and the Sea, The.
Clampitt. Hispaniola.
Cofer, J. Lesson of the Sugarcane, The.
Grainger, J. Book 4.
Hawaiian Oral Tradition. Contract is over and yet, The. Five O'Clock Whistle, The. I hate hole hole work. In the rush at pau hana. Laborers keep on coming, The.
Martínez, V. Traveler.
Suárez, V. Song for the Sugar Cane.

Suicide
Abse. Footnote Extended, A.
Aiken, C. Solitaire.
Alterman, N. Time and the Response, The.
Amir, D. Thoughts about Sari's Jump.
Anderson, A. Suicide Year, The.
Arends, J. I Have.
Ashbery, J. Illustration.
Atkins, R. Furious'd Garb.
Banning, L. Epitaph for a Scientist.
Barot, R. Eight Elegies.
Beasley. Witness.
Beer, P. Lemmings.
Bejerano, M. Noon. 12:45 already.
Belli, C. Father, Mother.
Berg, S. Nostalgia.
Berryman. Henry's Understanding. Of Suicide.
Bialosky, J. Adolescent Suicide, The.
Bidart. Sacrifice, The.
Birnbaum, M. Man Who Hanged Himself, The.
Boruch. Window, The.
Brecht, B. Epistle on Suicide.
Brett, L. My Mother's Friend.
Brontë, E. F. de Samara to A. G. A.
Brown, L. Sonnet Around Stephanie.
Bürger, G. Lass of Fair Wone, The.
Burke, M. Former WWII Paratrooper Dreams of Suicide, 1977, A.
Campo. Manuel.
Catullus. What for?
Chavez, L. In the Season of Suicides.
Chesterton. Ballade of Suicide, A.
Chikamatsu Monzaemon. Journey, The.
Chudakov. Suicide is a duel with yourself.
Clarke, G. Suicide on Pentwyn Bridge.
Coleman, W. Dog Suicide.
Collier, M. 2212 West Flower Street.
Cooley, N. Resurrection.
Cooper, D. 10 Dead Friends.
Cortázar. Lines of the Hand, The.
Couani. What a Man, What a Moon.
Crozier, L. Last Testaments.
Dacre, C. Power of Love, The.
Dawe, B. Family Man, The.
Denby. Climate, The.
Di Prima. To the Unnamed Buddhist Nun Who Burned Herself to Death on the Night of June 3, 1966.
Dickey, J. Leap, The.
Dickey, W. Death of John Berryman,The.
Dierking, K. Delacroix's Version.
Dobyns. Seeing Off a Friend.
Donze, R. Vermont Has a High Suicide Rate.
Drummond de Andrade. Don't Kill Yourself. Don't Kill Yourself.
Eichner, Maura. Dream Songs Concluded.
Feinstein, S. Blues Villanelle for Sonny Criss.
Flynn, N. Bag of Mice.
Friman. Ophelia.
Gates, B. Ron. Triptych.
Graves, R. Song: Lift-Boy.
Greenhalgh, C. Of Love, Death and the Sea-Squirt.
Gunn, T. Gas-poker, The.
Harjo, J. Drowning Horses. Woman Hanging from the Thirteenth Floor Window, The.
Hauge. Across the Swamp.

Hedderman, R.   Ophelia.
Heinemann, M.   Ringstead Mill.
Herd.   Shadowed by your father.
Hewett, D.   This Version of Love.
Heyen.   Frost Song.
Heym.   Umbra Vitae.
Hinz-Penner, R.   Crossing Over.
Holmes, J.   Depressive Episode.
Holzer, R.   Current "Now, Voyager" Fantasy.
Hood, T.   Bridge of Sighs, The.
   Faithless Nelly Gray.
Housman.   I Counsel You Beware.
   It nods and curtseys and recovers.
   Shot? so quick, so clean an ending?
Howe, F.   Doubt.
Hughes, L.   Song for a Suicide.
   Suicide's Note.
Hugo, R.   Death in the Aquarium.
Huxley, A.   Second Philosopher's Song.
Hwang Hyŏn.   On Killing Myself.
Ĭnce.   Wind, Ant, History.
Ivanov, G.   Oh, how fastidious you once were.
Johnson, Peter.   Accomplice.
Kaschock, Kirsten.   As Birds in Rain.
Katz, M.   Suicide: "As if a wood of oaks gave."
Kirby, D.   Half-Dead.
Knight, E.   Black Poet Leaps to His Death, A.
   For Black Poets Who Think of Suicide.
Knott.   Advice from the Experts.
   Ant Dodger.
   Shorts / Excerpts.
Kodama Kagai.   Suicide of an Unemployed
   Person, The.
Komunyakaa, Y.   2527th Birthday of the
   Buddha.
Krolow.   Free Fall.
Kumin, M.   How It Is.
Kunitz, S.   Portrait, The.
Kwa, Lydia.   You must exist. Writing this book
   depends on it. It has occurred to.
Laforgue.   Sunday Piece.
Landon.   She Sat Alone beside Her Hearth.
Levy, A.   Cross-Road Epitaph, A.
   Felo de Se.
   Minor Poet, A.
Lorde.   Between Ourselves.
Lowell, R.   After the Surprising Conversions.
Loy.   Jules Pascin.
Lynch, K.   Ophelia in Utah.
MacNeice.   Springboard, The.
   Suicide, The.
Mahon.   Antarctica.
Marcus, M.   Poem for Gonzales, California,
   The.
McNeil, R.   Mirrors in the Room.
Miller, E.   Mississippi.
Mirikitani.   Suicide Note.
Morris, M.   Valley Prince.
Nemerov.   To D———, Dead by Her Own
   Hand.
Noguchi, R.   Kenji Takezo Becomes Water.
Ochester.   Mary Mihalik.
Olds, S.   Summer Solstice, New York City.
Owen, W.   S.I.W.
Pagis, D.   Late Author: Snapshot in the Rain,
   The.
Pak Nohae.   How Much Is This One?
Parker, D.   Résumé.
Pfeiffer, E.   So the river—yes, the river; I have
   come to that at last.
Piercy.   My Rich Uncle, Whom I Only Met
   Three Times.
Pinsky.   At Pleasure Bay.
Plath.   Ariel.
   Edge.
   Lady Lazarus.
Press, K.   Dispossessed words.
Ranaldo, L.   HIS:STORY.
   Killed.
Reznikoff.   When the Second World War began.
Rich, A.   From a Survivor.
   Tattered Kaddish.
Ridl.   Coach in Effigy.
Ritsos.   Requiem on Poros.
Robinson, E.   Mill, The.
   Richard Cory.

Robinson, M.   Her Reflections on the Leucadian
   Rock Before She Perishes.
   Resolves to Take the Leap of Leucata.
Rodriguez, L.   Heavy Blue Veins.
Rose, J.   Suicide, The.
Rukeyser, M.   Double Dialogue: Homage to
   Robert Frost.
   Gates, The.
   Power of Suicide, The.
Rushin.   In Answer to the Question: Have You
   Ever Considered Suicide.
Sassoon, S.   Suicide in the Trenches.
Senryū, K.   Priest in charge, The.
Sexton.   Wanting to Die.
Shakespeare, W.   Hamlet's Soliloquy.
   Sonnet 66: "Tired [or Tyr'd or Tir'd] with all
      these, for restful[l] death I cry."
Shenstone.   Chase of Jessy, The.
Shinkichi Takahashi.   Burning Oneself to Death.
   Canna.
Sholl.   Girl Named Spring, A.
Silesky.   Screens.
Silex, E.   Elegy: "What remains of the suicide's
   voice is the last conversation."
Smith, C.   New Bride, The.
Smith, S.   Exeat.
Sora.   In the deutzia.
Sorescu, M.   Start.
Spender, S.   History and Reality.
Spenser, E.   Who travels [or trauels] by the
   wearie wandring way.
Starbuck, G.   Of Late.
Stephens, P.   Hangman.
Stevenson, R.   Celestial Surgeon, The.
Stillman, M.   Ophelia.
Surrey.   Sardanapalus.
Thomson, J.   In the Room.
Tsvetayeva [or Tsvetaeva].   I opened my veins.
   Unstoppably.
Tucker, S.   Boy Exploded on the Corner Today,
   A.
Ungaretti.   In Memoriam: "His name was /
   Mohammed Sceab."
Unknown.   If I might offer.
   Peacock Southeast Flew, A.
   To G.
Venaille, Franck.   Now They Tell Me.
Virgil [or Vergil].   Passion of the Queen, The.
Wakoski.   For Craig Who Leapt Off a Cliff in to
   Hummingbird Light.
Walsh, W.   Despairing Lover, The.
Ward, T.   In the Interest of Possibility.
Warren, R.   Confederate Veteran Tries to
   Explain the Event, A.
   You Sort Old Letters.
Wat.   Joke, A.
Wheelwright.   Fish Food.
Wright, James.   Minneapolis Poem, The.
Wright, Judith.   Precipice, The.
Wright, Lillian.   West Texas Suicide.
Wu Chia-chi.   Grain-Barge Wife, The.
Wylie.   Felo de Se.
Yesenin [or Essenin].   Esenin's Suicide Note.

Sumac
Very.   Sumach Leaves, The.
Wright, J.   Sumac in Ohio, The.

Summer
Abinader, E.   On a Summer Night.
Adams, L.   Country Summer.
Agran, R.   Door Thrown Open to Daisies.
Akimine.   Beloved person must I think, The.
Alexander, E.   Nineteen.
Alley, R.   Canary Man and You, The.
Alterman, N.   Summer Night.
Anderson, A.   Licking Wounds.
Andrews, N.   That Cold Summer.
Asch.   Summer.
Baillie, J.   Summer's Day, A.
Bampfylde.   On a Wet Summer.
Basho.   Fleas, lice.
   Have the summer rains.
   Hut of the Phantom Dwelling, The.
   It's not like anything.
   Jars of octopus, The.
   My summer robes.
   Octopuses caught in floating pots.

Summer grass.
Summer grasses.
Summer grasses grow, The.
Summer mountains.
Beissel, H.   Tanka: "Ice rain coats berries."
Benson, S.   Beaten Track, The.
Bialik.   Summer is dying in the purple and gold
   and russet.
Bishop, E.   Song: "Summer is over upon the
   sea."
Blake, W.   How Sweet I Roamed [or Roam'd]
   from Field to Field.
   School-Boy, The.
Bleakney, J.   Summer love was ever thus.
Bogan, L.   Dark Summer.
   Roman Fountain.
Bonnefoy.   Stone, A.
   Summer Again.
Bryant, W.   June.
   Midsummer.
   Summer Wind.
Bu-er.   Late Indian summer's.
Buchsbaum, Julianne.   In Squire Park with M.,
   Esquire.
Busceti, G.   Eight Phases of Contemplation.
Bush, D.   Summer 1984.
Buson.   Crossing.
   Early summer rain.
   In the summer rain.
   My old man's ears.
   Not a leaf stirring.
   Remembering how.
   Shortcut, A.
   Sick man passing.
Cahn, S.   Things We Did Last Summer, The.
Campbell, C.   When midst the summer-roses the
   warm bees.
Campo, C.   White Summer Clothes are Folded
   Away, The.
Carpenter, E.   Summer Heat.
Castro, R.   Feeling Her End Would Come with
   Summer's End.
Cavafy.   Comes to Rest.
Chiyojo.   Grazing.
Christensen, Paul.   Summer Nights.
Clampitt.   Meridian.
Clare, J.   Give Me the Gloomy Walk.
Clark, T.   You (III).
Comer, Carrie St. George.   Shelburne Falls.
Cordeiro, James.   Monsoon Song.
Cornish, S.   Generations 1.
Cristall.   Song: "Through springtime walks, with
   flowers perfumed."
Crowell, G.   Summer Nights in Texas.
Cummings, E. E.   Out of midsummer's blazing
   most not night.
De Cristoforo, Violet Kazue.   Dooshi Sorou
   Soshite Matsu No Me Futori Shoka No Sora.
   Orokashisa Tada Ni Natsu No Hi O Kurashi
   Mukou Castle Rock.
De la Mare.   Summer Evening.
Denby.   Northern Boulevard.
   Summer: "I stroll on Madison in expensive
   clothes, sour."
Dickinson, E.   As imperceptibly as Grief.
   Bee is not afraid of me, The.
   Consulting summer's clock.
   Further in Summer than the Birds.
   Indian Summer.
   Renunciation.
   So much Summer.
   Soft Sea washed around the House, A.
   Some one prepared this mighty show.
   'Twas here my summer paused.
Doolittle, H.   Blue-geese, white-geese, you may
   say.
Dunbar, P.   Song of Summer.
   Summer in the South.
   Summer's Night, A.
Dybek.   Summer Afternoon in Solon, Iowa.
Eliot, T. S.   New Hampshire.
Emrys James, D.   Pwllderi.
Escandor, V.   Summer Nostalgia.
Field, M.   O Wind, thou hast thy kingdom in the
   trees.
   Tiger-Lilies.

Unbosoming.
Field, R.   Summer Morning, A.
Flanner.   True Western Summer.
Forman, R.   Waitin on Summer.
Forrester, S.   Summer afternoon.
Garner.   Summer Solstice.
Gerhardt.   Go out in this dear summertide.
Gershwin, G.   Summertime.
Gibson, M.   Summer Birds and Flowers (2).
Gilbert, C.   Now.
Giovanni.   Knoxville, Tennessee.
González, A.   Summer in Slumville.
Gould, J.   Tanana Valley.
Graves, R.   Blue-Fly, The.
Gray-Kontar, D.   July.
Ha-Levi, J.   Summer.
Hadas, R.   Moments of Summer.
Harris, Ken.   Bough Well Bounds The Vowel
   Bounds Well, A.
Harwood, L.   Summer: "These hot afternoons
   "it's quite absurd" she whispered."
Hass, R.   Bashō, A Departure.
   Tahoe in August.
Heaney, S.   Summer Home.
   Summer of Lost Rachel, The.
Henderson-Holmes.   Friendly Town #1.
Henley, W. E.   Ballade Made in the Hot
   Weather.
Hirsch, E.   Summer Surprised Us.
Hölderlin.   Summer.
Hollander, J.   Late August on the Lido.
Hopkins, G.   Epithalamion: "Hark, hearer, hear
   what I do; lend a thought now, make believe."
Hunt, L.   One day,—'twas on a summer
   afternoon.
Ignatova, E.   Summer Garden, The.
Iremonger.   Clear View in Summer.
Issa.   O summer snail.
   She's put the child to sleep.
   Summer night.
Jackson, R.   Sunday Brunch.
Jensen, L.   To a Stranger (At the End of a
   Caboose).
Joseph, A.   Good Humor.
Kavanagh, P.   Consider the Grass Growing.
Kenyon, J.   Insomnia at the Solstice.
Kikaku.   Summer airing / Trying on a quilt.
King, H.   Summer Lost.
Kinsella, T.   Chrysalides.
Kunitz, S.   Touch Me.
Kuusisto, Stephen.   Summer at North Farm.
Lahey, Joy.   .22.
Lampman.   Heat.
Latouche, J.   Summer Is a-Comin' In.
Lazarus, E.   Long Island Sound.
Levy, A.   London in July.
Li Po.   In the Mountains on a Summer Day.
Llwyd, M.   Summer, The.
   What? summer now? divisions ring.
Lux.   There Were Some Summers.
MacCaig.   Notations of Ten Summer Minutes.
   So Many Summers.
   Summer Farm.
MacDonald, A.   Month of plants and of honey.
Macdonald, G.   Sweet Peril.
Machado Ruiz.   Summer Night.
   Tell Me If You Remember, Love.
Maeng Sasŏng.   Summer comes to rivers and
   lakes.
Magrelli.   In summer, like the theaters, I close
   up.
Mahapatra, J.   Summer Poem, A.
Malé.   For the Moment.
Marchant, F.   Screen Porch.
Marlatt, D.   Summer of the New Well.
Martinson.   Peonies.
Mathews, H.   Lateral Disregard.
Matthews, W.   On the Porch at the Frost Place,
   Franconia, NH.
McGrath, T.   Black Train, The.
McNair.   Visit, The: "We were at the camp, it
   must have been."
Melançon, Robert.   Beginning of Summer.
Meynell, A.   Summer in England, 1914.
Moore, L.   Indian Girl.
   Tanka.

Mori.   At Thirty.
Morris, W.   Summer Dawn.
Mpina.   Summer Fires of Mulanje Mountain.
Nashe [or Nash].   Fair Summer Droops.
Neruda.   Ode to Bicycles.
Nicholson, N.   For Hokey and Henrietta.
No Hyangnim.   Yard.
Noguchi, Yonejiro (Yone).   Lines: "Sun I
   worship, The."
O'Brien, J.   Revelation on a Summer Walk.
Oliveira, D.   Summer.
Oliver, M.   Waking on a Summer Morning.
Ovid.   Elegy 1.5: "In summer's heat[e] and mid-
   time of the day."
Owen, W.   From My Diary, July 1914.
Pederson, C.   Summer Recital.
Peele.   Song: "Whenas [or When as] the Rye [or
   Rie] reach to the chin."
Petrarch.   Soote Season, The.
Phillips, C.   Summer, A.
Pinsky.   Ralegh's Prizes.
Posey, A.   Midsummer.
Powell, J.   It Was Fever That Made the World.
Probyn.   Song Out of Season, A.
Qunanbaev, A.   Summer: "Summer climbs the
   mountains."
Rafferty, P.   Back End.
Ragain.   Don't Expect Anything.
Rakosi.   Lying in Bed on a Summer Morning.
Rexroth, K.   Heart of Herakles, The.
Ridlon.   That Was Summer.
Rimbaud, A.   Dawn.
Robinson, M.   London's Summer Morning.
Rossetti, C.   Fly Away, Fly Away.
   Summer Is Ended.
Rukeyser, M.   Summer, the Sacramento.
Rutsala.   Summer: "There is no breeze, sounds
   travel far in the dead air."
Saleh.   Summer.
Saner.   Sierra Cup.
Sarton, M.   Small Joys.
Schuyler, J.   Haze.
   Shimmer.
Schwartz, R. L.   Late Summer.
Seed.   'From Escomb, County Durham': July
   1990.
Sexton.   I Remember.
Shakespeare, W.   Sonnet 18: "Shall I compare
   thee to a summer's day?"
Shelley, P.   Summer and Winter.
Shields, R.   In the Good Old Summer Time.
Simmons, J.   For Imelda.
Skloot.   Flight: "Summer night is flying, The."
Smith, K.   On Sundays in Summer.
Södergran.   Forest Lake.
Sora.   Shaving my head.
Soutar.   Summer Is By.
Spark.   Kensington Gardens.
Steiger.   Until the sun sinks into a green.
Steven, K.   Edge.
Stevenson, A.   When the Camel Is Dust it Goes
   Through the Needle's Eye.
Strange.   Childhood.
Tarn.   Great Odor of Summer, The.
Tate, A.   Seasons of the Soul.
Teasdale.   August Night.
   Summer Night, Riverside.
Thomson, J.   Night. Summer Meteors. A Comet.
Tighe.   1802.
Tranströmer.   It's been a hard winter, but
   summer is here and the fields.
Tranter.   Backyard.
Tu Fu [or Du Fu].   South Wind.
   Summer Night.
Tuckerman, F.   Cricket, The.
Unknown.   Song of Summer.
   Sumer Is Icumen [or Ycomen] In.
   Summer.
   Summer Has Come.
   Summer Song.
   Summer Sunday.
Valentine, J.   Summer Was Not Long Enough,
   The.
Vanek, Mary.   Summer Begins Outside Dalhart,
   Texas.
Walcott.   Midsummer, Tobago.

Warren, R.   Fear and Trembling.
Wilbur, R.   Exeunt.
   Praise in Summer.
Williams, C. K.   Shade, The.
Williams, W.   At the Faucet of June.
   Botticellian Trees, The.
   It Is Still Warm Enough.
   Ivy Crown, The.
Wright, C.   Lake Echo, Dear.
Wrigley, R.   For the Last Summer.
Xuan Quynh.   Summer: "It's the season of
   birdsong."
Yi Chinmyông.   Record of a Certain Summer.
Young, D.   Poem for Adlai Stevenson and
   Yellow Jackets.
Young, K.   Preserving, The.
Yü Hsüan-chi.   Living in the Summer
   Mountains.
Zanzotto.   Campèa.

Sumner, Charles
Hightower, S.   Tontine.
Ray, H.   Charles Sumner.

Sun
Akhenaton [or Akhnaton].   Hymn to the Sun.
Akutagawa Ryunosuke.   Slime on the stones.
Al-Harizi.   Sun, The.
Alberti.   To the Sun of the War.
Aleixandre.   Old Man and the Sun, The.
Alexander, M.   People of Unrest.
Allen, P.   Weed.
Bacharach.   Poem for the Sefirot as a Wheel of
   Light, A.
Bachmann.   To the Sun.
Ball, H.   Sun, The.
Baraka, I.   I Investigate the Sun.
Barrow, Raymond.   Dawn is a Fisherman.
Basho.   Hollyhocks, The.
   June rain / hollyhocks turning.
   Winter sun, The.
   With plum blossom scent.
Bedregal.   Intact Pitcher.
Behn, H.   Circles.
Berlin.   I Got the Sun in the Morning.
Bialik.   Only a single ray, but suddenly.
Bibb.   Ode to the Sun.
Blake, W.   Ah, Sun-Flower [or Ah! Sun-
   Flower].
Blight.   Sun.
Bonds, D.   Life of the Body, The.
Borowski.   Sun of Auschwitz, The.
Brontë, A.   Home.
Brooks, G.   Boy Breaking Glass.
Brown, E.   Out.
Browning, R.   Parting at Morning.
Bryant, W.   When breezes are soft and skies are
   fair.
Burkard.   My Aunt and the Sun.
Buson.   Field of bright mustard.
   Field of bright mustard.
   Gleaning the rice field.
   No bridge.
Campion, T.   Follow Thy Fair Sun[ne]
   [Unhappy Shadow].
Catullus.   Sun May Set, The.
Celan.   Thread suns.
Ceravolo.   Invisible Autumn.
Césaire, A.   Sun Serpent.
Chazal, M.   Plastic Sense (1947 version).
Cho, P.   One Wintry Day.
Cho Sik.   Wearing hemp clothes in the coldest
   winter.
Chông Hwajin.   Sunlight Showers Down in
   Sheets.
Clampitt.   Sun Underfoot Among the Sundews,
   The.
Collobert.   For Which the Sun.
Collop.   Praise of a Yellow Skin, The, or An
   Elizabeth in Gold.
Colosi, David.   Sun with Issues.
Cook, E.   Thought, A [or Sunshine].
Creeley.   Anger.
Crosby, H.   Photoheliograph (For Lady A.).
Cuadra, P.   Birth of the Sun, The.
Cutts, S.   On parquet.
Cynewulf.   Sun and Moon.
D'Aquino, A.   Naranja de luz abierta, La.

Opened Orange of Light, The.
Sol abre los labios y nos dice, El.
Sun opens its lips and says to us, The.
Daryush. I saw the daughter of the sun.
Davison, P. Frozen Drought.
de Fierro. Heart of Time.
De la Mare. Christmas Eve.
Delaunay, S. Zenith.
Dickinson, E. Alter! When the Hills do—.
Daisy follows soft the Sun, The.
Sun and Fog Contested, The.
Yellow Man, Purple Man.
DiPalma. Fragment.
Donne. Resurrection, Imperfect.
Sun Rising, The.
Doolittle, H. Now my right hand.
Dove, R. Dusting.
Drinkwater. Sun, The.
Drummond, W. Invocation: "Pheobus, arise! /
And paint the sable skies."
Eguren. Girls of the Light, The.
Elytis, O. Sun the First.
Felipe, L. I Am Going Because the Ear of
Wheat and the Dawn Are Not Mine.
Fermini, I. First unexpected pain is beautiful,
The.
Field. Ebbtide at Sundown.
Fields, D. On the Sunny Side of the Street.
Fletcher, G. As when the cheerfull Sunne,
elamping wide.
Forrester, S. Backyard sun shower.
Sun on the windowsill.
Fraire. Minute the sun comes out, The.
Friedmann. Butterfly, The.
Gaffarel. Celestial Alphabet Event.
Gezelle. Ego Flos.
Gillespie, H. That Lucky Old Sun.
Goodwin, Eli. After an All Day Skirmish with
the Clouds.
Greenwell, D. Sun-Flower, The.
Gyodai. Slowly / Over cedars.
Harington [or Harrington]. Thus all that day,
they spent in divers talke.
Harrison, D. Yellow.
Hayati. Before there was a trace of this world
of men.
Henderson, D. Horizon Blues.
Lock City.
Hennen. Soaking Up Sun.
Herbert, G. Son[ne], The.
Herlin. Red round sun, The.
Sky has recovered, The.
Hernton, C. Mob, The.
Hidalgo, J. Sun of Death.
Hogan, L. Seeing through the Sun.
Hughes, T. Crow's Last Stand.
Huidobro. Morning.
Hume, C. Arctic Sun.
Ilkov, Ani. Scene, A.
Imbriglio, C. Aubade: "Dead woodchuck in the
dog's mouth drooped, The."
Ismail. Van Gogh's Ear.
Issa. Woodpecker, The.
Jackson, L. All Things.
Juan Chi. Ten Suns Rise in the East, The.
Kaufman, B. SUN IS A NEGRO, THE.
Kim Chŏngnan. Images: "Scene 1. Front angle,
dark sky, or the middle of the universe."
Kim Sŭnghŭi. Sun Mass.
Kinzie. In air hard as sand.
Knott. Feeding the Sun.
Koehler, T. When the Sun Comes Out.
Kuzmin. At noon I must have been conceived.
Leaving my house in the morning.
La Fontaine. Phoebus and Boreas.
Lane, P. Winter 9: "Each day the time grows
less, the hours."
Larkin, P. Solar.
Lehman. Prophet's Lantern, The.
Levis. Morning After My Death, The.
Lewis, J. Reader, The.
Li Po. Red sun comes out of the Eastern corner,
The.
Lindsay, V. Indian Summer Day on the Prairie,
An.
Llwyd, Iwan. Fingerprints.

Lope de Vega. White Was I.
MacLeish. Autumn.
You, Andrew Marvell.
MacNeice. Morning Sun.
Sunlight on the Garden, The.
Madge. Solar Creation.
Magee, W. How to Reach the Sun . . . on a
Piece of Paper.
Major, C. Lost in the Desert.
Marsman. Paradise Regained.
Martinaitis, M. Kukutis in the Reich's Guard
House.
Marvell. On a Drop of Dew.
Matveyeva [or Matveieva]. Ginger-Haired Girl,
The.
McGrath, Carmelita. Solar Eclipse, St. John's,
Newfoundland.
Michie. Arizona Nature Myth.
Miles, J. Forecast.
Montag, T. May 25, 2001 (1).
Morgan, E. Strawberries.
Muso Soseki. Snow.
Naong. Western Peak.
Nemerov. Blue Swallows, The.
Ngafua, Z. Nommo.
Niedecker. My friend tree.
O'Hara, F. True Account of Talking to the Sun
at Fire Island, A.
Olson, C. Sun / right in my eye.
Ortiz. Bend in the River.
Earth and Rain, the Plants & Sun.
Owen, W. Futility.
Patterson, R. Sundown Blues.
Paz. Mystery.
Philips, K. Answer to Another Persuading a
Lady to Marriage, An.
Ponge. Sun as a Spinning Top (I), The.
Popa. In the Ashtray.
Postell, T. I Want a Solid Piece of Sunlight and
a Yardstick to Measure it With.
Probyn. End of the Journey, The.
Purdy, J. From rivers, and from the earth itself.
Reese, D. Ol' Hannah.
Reyes, A. Monterrey Sun.
Reznikoff. If you cannot look at the sun.
Rodenko. February Sun.
Rossi, T. Law.
System.
Roy, L. Bread Man, The.
Ruefle. Topophilia.
Sanguineti. Wind shoves my New Year's Day
sun in my face, The.
Schierbeek. Sun, The: Day.
Seferis. Our Sun.
Senghor. Young Sun's Greeting, The.
Shakespeare, W. Sonnet 33: "Full many a
glorious morning have I seen[e]."
Sonnet 34: "Why didst thou promise such a
beauteous day."
Sidney. Sestina: "Farewell, O Sun".
Sidney, R. Songe 17: "Sun is set, and masked
night, The."
Sleigh. To the Sun.
Sorescu, M. With a Green Scarf.
Soupault. Twilight.
Stevens, W. Brave Man, The.
Not Ideas about the Thing but the Thing Itself.
Stevenson, R. Summer Sun.
Sze. June Ghazal.
Tarn. As If There Were Any Matter.
Thompson, F. Sun, The.
Trakl. Sun, The: "Each day the gold sun comes
over the hill."
Travis, M. Sunbathing.
Tsvetayeva [or Tsvetaeva]. White Low Sun, A.
Tu Fu [or Du Fu]. Sun Lengthens.
Turner, W. Sun, The.
Unamuno. On Reading Jules Renard's Diary.
Unknown. Before light became time.
One son of God, The.
Riddle: "Hickamore hackamore."
Song for the Sun That Disappeared behind the
Rainclouds.
Tatar Songs.
Unknown, fr. Terezin Concentration Camp. On a
Sunny Evening.

Vallejo. Conflict Between the Eyes and the
Gaze, The.
Vaughan, H. Cock-crowing.
Veenendaal. Sun-crossed.
Velter André. Other One, The.
Voeten. Sun On My Hand, The ("Sun lights my
hand writing, The.").
Sun On My Hand, The ("Writing with the sun
on my hand.").
Voss, F. Sun Worshiper.
Welish. Scalpel in Hand.
Whitman, W. Give Me the Splendid Silent Sun.
Wilbur, R. Black November Turkey, A.
Grasse: The Olive Trees.
Williams, W. Metric Figure ("There is a bird in
the poplars.").
Wilson, R. Envoi: "Sun in the mouth of the
day."
Worth, V. Sun.
Yavuz, Hilmi. Windy Windows.
Zukofsky, L. Anew 21.

Sunburn
Gay, Garry. Hole in the ozone.
Song. Sunworshippers.
Vollmer. Nursing the Sunburn.

Sunday
Aminado. Our Sunday Rest.
Andrade, M. Sunday.
Berkson, B. Sheer Strips.
Bloem, J. C. Sunday.
Brewer, G. Penance and the Work Week.
Brooks, G. Sunday Chicken.
Sundays of Satin-Legs Smith, The.
Bush, D. Sunday the Power Went Off, The.
Carrera Andrade. Sunday.
Deltoro, A. Domingo.
Sunday.
Denby. People on Sunday.
Gardelle, C. Peaceful Sunday.
Grenier. Sunday Morning.
Hayden, R. Mourning Poem for the Queen of
Sunday.
Those Winter Sundays.
Heard, J. Sabbath Bells.
Holm, B. Playing the Goldberg Variations on
Sunday Morning.
Hughes, L. Sunday by the Combination.
Jewett, S. At Home from Church.
Johnson, Harold L. Names of Summer, The: A
War Memory.
Kefala. Sunday Visit.
Lewis, G. Sunday Park.
Liu, T. Sunday.
López Velarde. Provincial Sundays.
Lucas, J. Good Sunday.
MacNeice. Sunday Morning: "Down the road
someone is practising scales."
McAuley, J. World on Sunday.
Minhinnick. Sunday Morning.
Morabito, F. Mapas, Los / se hacen los
domingos.
Maps are drawn / on Sundays.
Obejas, A. Sunday.
O'Donoghue, M. This is Sunday.
Rouse, A. Sunday Morning.
Scarbrough, G. Sunday Shopping.
Simic. Sunday Papers.
Smith, K. On Sundays in Summer.
Smith, M. Sunday Morning Services.
Soupault. Sunday.
Spivack, K. Sunday.
Trethewey, N. Domestic Work, 1937.
Troupe. In Jimmy's Garden.
Ungar. Common Prayer.
Unknown. Jine 'Em.
No More Rain Fall for Wet You.
Vaughan, H. Son-Days [dayes].
Wordsworth, C. O Day of Rest and Gladness.
Wright, F. Sunday Afternoon.
See also **Sabbath**

Sundews
Clampitt. Sun Underfoot Among the Sundews,
The.

Sundials
Crapsey. Sun-Dial, The.

Cunningham, J.   Motto for a Sun Dial.
Dobson, A.   Sundial, The.
Dunn, D.   Sundial, The.
Zaid.   Sundial.

Sunflowers
Blake, W.   Ah, Sun-Flower [*or* Ah! Sun-Flower].
David, M.   Sunflower.
Ferguson, G.   Winter Sunflowers.
Forrester, S.   End of summer.
Ginsberg, A.   Sunflower Sutra.
Greenwell, D.   Sun-Flower, The.
Jacobsen, R.   Sunflower.
Lilburn, Tim.   Sunflowers at Prime.
Montale.   Bring Me the Sunflower.
   Bring me the sunflower, I'll plant it here.
Rich, A.   Late summers, early autumns, you can see something that binds.
Slicer, D.   Sunflowers, Wyoming.
Winters, Y.   Wild Sunflower.

Sunrise
Ackerman, D.   San Francisco Sunrise.
Binyon.   Winter Sunrise.
Bogan, L.   July Dawn.
Booth, P.   Relations: Old Light / New Sun / Postmistress / Earth / 04421.
Bosselaar.   Listener of Bats.
Cecil.   Threnody for Sunrise ("Please, when you ask me in this dream.").
Chu Ŭisik.   Boy stops outside my window, A.
Crawford, I.   Dark Stag, The.
Daryush.   Still-Life.
Dickinson, E.   I'll tell you how the Sun rose.
   Sunrise runs for Both, The.
Donne.   Sun Rising, The.
Fenollosa.   Fuji at Sunrise.
Fox, Skip.   Sic transit ("Thus does the sun.").
Frost, C.   Sin: "Tree bore the efflorescence of October apples, The."
Graham, J.   Gulls.
Henry, J.   Another and another and another.
Housman.   Reveille.
Machado Ruiz.   Autumn Sunrise.
Pak Tujin.   Sun.
Radcliffe, A.   Sun-Rise: Sonnet, A.
Roux, S.   Sunrise.
Tu Fu [*or* Du Fu].   Sun Rises from Water.
Unknown.   Song of the Rising Sun Dance.
   Sunrise Sequence.
Wright, C.   Aubade: "Over Govino Bay, looking up from the water's edge, the landscape resembles nothing so much as the hills above Genova."
Yi Hyangji.   Sunrise: "Blood stolen from my body before dawn."
Yi I.   Where is the first bend?

Sunset
Adams, L.   Sundown.
Aled, Sion.   Sunset Over Llŷn.
Apache Oral Tradition.   Corn Ceremony.
Bierds, L.   Seconds, The.
Blind.   Red Sunsets, 1883, The.
Buson.   Having reddened the plum blossoms.
Cain, Edney.   Sunset Reverie.
Castera, G.   Blood.
Cecil.   Threnody for Sunset ("It's five o'clock. Someone's taped my name out.").
Chappell, F.   Remembering Wind Mountain at Sunset.
Ching An.   Over King Yu Mountain with a Friend.
Ch'oe Sŭngja.   While Watching Sunset.
Clampitt.   Baroque Sunburst, A.
Cope, J.   Sunset.
Cummings, E. E.   Who are you,little i.
Curnow.   You Will Know When You Get There.
Dickinson, E.   I'll tell you how the Sun rose.
   Presentiment—is that long Shadow—on the lawn.
Esteves.   Ahora.
Fisher, J.   Pearls.
Fordham.   Sunset.
Frost, R.   Acceptance.
Gerbasi, V.   Hallucinatory Sunset, with Sons.
Goodwin, Eli.   After an All Day Skirmish with the Clouds.

Graham, J.   Gulls.
Henry, J.   Another and another and another.
Herlin.   Red round sun, The.
Hodgson, R.   Late, Last Rook, The.
Hollander, J.   Under Cancer.
Hughes, L.   Blue Bayou.
Ingalls, J.   Gun Emplacement: Sundown.
Jeffers, R.   Ocean's Tribute, The.
Jiménez, J.   Song: "Setting sun left my heart, The."
   Sunset.
Johnson, J.   Sunset in the Tropics.
Kinnell.   Daybreak: "On the tidal mud, just before sunset."
Kodama Kagai.   Setting Sun, The.
Koeppel, M.   9 PM Summer.
Lamartine.   West, The.
Lane, P.   Lake Murry.
Lanier, S.   Marsh Song—At Sunset.
Lawrence, D. H.   In Trouble and Shame.
   Love On the Farm.
Li Shang-yin.   From the Heights.
Logghe.   Marriage of Heaven and Hell in Española.
Ma Chih-yüan.   Tune: "Heaven-Cleansed Sands".
   Tune: "Sky-Pure Sand".
Machado Ruiz.   In the Fields.
   Poem: "Naked is the earth."
Mahon.   Globe in [North] Carolina, The.
Meng Hao Jan.   Mooring on Chien-Te River.
Miller, L.   Man Who Is Out of Work Talks to His Son about the Sunset, The.
Morter, L.   Sunset on the River.
Motion, A.   Glass of Wine, A.
Nicholson, N.   Sea to the West.
Pei Di.   Hill of Huazi, The.
Pobo, K.   Grand Canyon.
Ray, H.   Afterglow, The.
   At Sunset.
   Sunset Picture.
Robinson, E.   Dark Hills, The.
Rossetti, D.   70: The Hill Summit.
Russell, G.   Great Breath, The.
Sandburg, C.   Flash Crimson.
   Hits and Runs.
   Sunset from Omaha Hotel Window.
   Sunsets.
Scott, S.   Dreary Change, The.
Sherman, M.   Towards Sunset at Camino Cielo.
Sidney.   Madrigal.
Stern, G.   On the Far Edge of Kilmer.
Stickney, T.   In Ampezzo ("In days of summer let me go.").
Tate, J.   Cages, The.
Teasdale.   Day's Ending.
Tennyson, A.   Crossing the Bar.
Tu Fu [*or* Du Fu].   Sunset ("How beautiful the river is in spring.").
   Sunset ("Sunset glitters on the beads.").
   Wasteland—Gazing Far Away.
Unknown.   Song of the Rising Sun Dance.
Valentine, J.   Sunset at Wellfleet.
Vanshenkin.   Sunset fades, and from the little hill, the.
Vasquez, R.   Pismo, 1959.
Volkow.   En el Valle de Zapata.
   Valley of Zapata, The.
Wang Ji.   View of the Wilds.
Wang Wei.   Hill of Huazi, The.
Watts, Enos D.   Longliner at Sunset.
Wharton, E.   Autumn Sunset, An.
Whitman, S.   November Landscape, A.
Whitman, W.   Prairie Sunset, A.
Yates, D.   Sunset Along U.S. Highway 90 Between Langtry and Sanderson.
Yi I.   Where is the ninth bend?

Superficiality
Duhamel.   Buddhist Barbie.

Superheroes
Armitage, S.   Kid.
Campo.   Superman Is Dead.
Clifton, L.   Note, Passed to Superman.
Keene, J.   Captain America at Home.
Koertge.   Dear Superman.
Machan.   No, Superman Was Not the Only One.

Powell, D. A.   My neck a toothsome feeding ground. vespered swarms had drunk of me before this new batman.

Superiority
Barer, M.   Beyond Compare.
Han-shan.   His mind is as high as a mountain.
Nekrasov, V.   So who of us.
Nemerov.   Walking the Dog.
Rodgers, C.   Walk Like Freedom.
Wilmer, S.   Mess Boy, The.
Wotton, S.   On His Mistress [*or* Mistris], the Queen of Bohemia.

Superman
Campo.   Superman Is Dead.
Clifton, L.   Note, Passed to Superman.
Koertge.   Dear Superman.
Machan.   No, Superman Was Not the Only One.
Moramarco, F.   Clark Kent, Naked.

Supermarkets
Brinkmann, R.   Self-Portrait in the Supermarket.
Brown, S.   Allegory of the Supermarket.
Eady.   How to Do.
Elledge.   Man I Love and I Shop at Jewel, The.
Enzensberger, H.   Portrait of a House Detective.
Gildner.   High-Class Bananas, The.
Ginsberg, A.   Supermarket in California, A.
Meinke.   Supermarket.
Mishol, A.   Shopping.
Nemerov.   Grace to Be Said at the Supermarket.
O'Donoghue, M.   This is Sunday.
Pape.   In Line at the Supermarket.
Wayman.   Picketing Supermarkets.

Supernatural
Bridges, R.   Low Barometer.
Burns, R.   Tam o' Shanter; A Tale.
Coleridge, S.   Rime of the Ancient Mariner, The (1798 version).
Collins, W.   Ode on the Poetical Character.
Cooke, P.   Orthone.
Davidson, J.   Ballad of Hell, A.
Hogg, J.   Kilmeny.
Keats.   Belle Dame sans Merci, La [A Ballad].
Longfellow, H.   Skeleton in Armor [*or* Armour], The.
Momaday.   Headwaters.
Nimmo, D.   Exorcism.
Poe.   City in the Sea, The.
   Raven, The.
   Ulalume [*or* Ulalume—a Ballad].
Service.   Cremation of Sam McGee, The.
Stanley, G.   Chinatown.
Strand.   Prediction, The.
Thompson, F.   Kingdom of God, The.
Traherne.   Shadows in the Water.
Unknown.   Tam Lin.
Wolfe, H.   Green Candles.
Yeats.   Leda and the Swan.

Superstition
Alvarez, J.   Sonnet 1: "Everything that happens to me these days."
Blunden.   Barn, The.
Burns, R.   Halloween.
   Holy Fair, The.
Diego, G.   On These Conditions.
Harries, E.   Bone Prison, The.
Holan.   Chicken, The.
Jackson, Y.   How to Make It.
Johnson, M.   Superstitions.
Jones, A. M.   To the Moon.
Kaschnitz.   Girl thinks if I can only manage, The.
Kinsella, J.   Visitant Eclogue.
Lamb, C.   Was it Some Sweet Device of Faery Land.
Le Brun, Annie.   Rituals.
Milosz, C.   On Angels.
Morshen.   In superstitious panic.
Pulido, A.   Mujer, Una / se persigna.
   Woman, A / makes the sign of the cross.
Southwick.   Magic Broom, The.
Thompson, C.   Johnny's Pet Superstition.
Troupe.   Conjuring Against Alien Spirits.
Unknown.   See a pin and pick it up.
Vegin, P.   Explanation of a Sign.
Winter, M.   Elegy: "There is a question."

Zabolotsky [or Zabolotskii].   Metamorphoses.

Supper
al-Sa'igh, Y.   Supper.
Berlin.   Supper Time.
Cervantes.   Interpretation of Dinner by the
    Uninvited Guest, An.
Dana, R.   A Capella.
Hood, T.   Public Dinner, A.
Hudgins.   Supper.
Kasischke.   Dinner.
Keller, D.   After Supper.
Serrano, P.   Prurito.
    Ticklish Moments.
Taylor, E.   Reflexion, The.
Townsend, A.   Dinner Guest, The.

Supplication
Atwood.   People come from all over to consult
    me, bringing their limbs.
Bhattācārya, K.   I know, I know, Mother.
    Tara, Mother / Lift me out by the hair.
    Tell me, Syama.
Ceccoli.   Oh, and yet I see that I will return to
    you anyway, and throw myself at your feet and
    cry a lot over my sins, until my crime will be
    pardoned.
Dāsdatta, R.   Because You love cremation
    grounds.
Debī, T.   Tara, this is why I call upon You.
Dīnrām.   I've given up wanting.
Gershon.   Uphold Me.
Herrick.   To His Ever-Loving God.
Islām, N.   Wake up, Syama, wake up, Syama!
Justice, D.   Invitation to a Ghost.
Kyunyŏ, Great Master.   Though all the buddhas.
    To the majestic assembly of buddhas.
Mulock, D.   Labor and Rest.
Nuccoli.   Your promises come to me always
    together with your betrayals, which you have
    more of than the fox.
Rāy, D.   It's no one else's fault, Syama Ma.
Rāy, K.   Tara, You are Cintamayi, Full of
    Thought.
Rāy, M. R.   Give me food.
Scully, M.   Variations.
Sen, R.   Mother, make *me* Your treasurer.
    Supreme Savior of Sinners.
    World's a shoreless ocean, The.
Unknown.   God, please rescue just that one!
    Hail, Mary.
    John, John, of the Holy Order.
    My beloved, my sun, rise above the horizon and
        obliterate my nights of exile.
    Some Valiant Solider.

Surfing and Surfers
Beckman, J.   Thirst of the crowd, The. We laid
    the surfer down.
Blaustein, N.   Water and Light.
Cheng Hsieh.   Song of Surfing on the Bore.
Gunn, T.   From the Wave.
Jarman, M.   Supremes, The.
Noguchi, R.   Not Surfing Some Days.
    Really Long Ride, The.
    Turn of Privacy, The.
Pape.   Storm Surf.

See also **Swimming and Swimmers**

Surgery
Abse.   In the Theatre.
Adams, Cyd.   Omens.
Becker, R.   Medical Science.
Bond, B.   Host.
Chisholm, A.   Contact.
Clifton, L.   Donor.
    Lumpectomy Eve.
    Poem to my uterus.
Cook, E.   Surgeon's Knife, The.
    There are hearts—stout hearts,—that own no
    fear.
Deltoro, A.   Anestesia.
    Anesthesia.
Dickinson, E.   Surgeons must be very careful.
Ditzanny, R.   Complicated and Innovative
    Orthopedic Surgery.
Elliot, A.   Latitudes of Home, The.
Gilyard, K.   Daughter, That Picture of You.
Gould, J.   Going Home.

Harper, M.   Deathwatch.
Hearle, K.   Lesson, The.
Henley, W. E.   Before.
Hughes, F.   Laszlo.
Joseph, A.   Chalazion.
Kees.   For H. V. (1901–1927).
Kitson, H.   Post-operative.
Knight, E.   Hard Rock Returns to Prison from
    the Hospital for the Criminal Insane.
Lux.   Commercial Leech Farming Today.
Minton, Helena.   Day Surgery Pre-Op.
Moore, M.   Those Various Scalpels.
Pastan.   After Minor Surgery.
Phillips, C.   Going Under.
Pitchford.   Surgery.
Platke, S.   Gut Catcher.
Ritch, O.   When I Woke, Everything Was the
    Same but Different.
Robertson, R.   Immoralist, The.
Roripaugh, L.   Hiroshima Maiden.
Rouse, A.   Anaesthetist, The.
Salisbury.   After Heart-Bypass Surgery, Another
    Ritual for Continuing Struggle.
Salter.   Half a Double Sonnet.
Shapcott, T.   Post Operative.
Stallworthy, J.   Letter from Berlin, A.
Tatarunis, P.   Before the Brain Surgery.
Townsend, A.   Touch Me Not.
Wallace, E.   War.
Wetzsteon.   Surgical Moves.
Wunderlich, M.   Suture.
Wyrebek, M.   Example, An.

See also **Hospitals; Medicine; Doctors**

Surprise
Berlin.   You'd Be Surprised.
Burke, J.   Welcome to My Dream.
Cairns, Scott.   Surprise.
Creeley.   Something.
    Warning, The.
Cronin, A.   Surprise.
Dickinson, E.   As if some little Arctic flower.
Graves, R.   Grotesques.
Jiménez, J.   Who Knows What Is Going On.
Knott.   Sonnet: "Way the world is not, The."
Mead, J.   Sometimes the Mind.
Meinke.   Poet, Trying to Surprise God, The.
Mulkey, R.   Blind-Sided.
Oquendo de Amat, C.   Poem of the Sea and of
    Her.
Rupchev, Georgi.   Bewilderment.
Schilpp, M.   Non Sequitur.
Unknown.   My lover was dozing on armfuls of
    flowers.
    Surprise, Surprise.
Wellman, M.   Blue sky in a human face.

Surrealism and Surrealists
Aragon.   Big Spectacular Play.
    Embrace, The.
Artaud.   Letter to André Breton.
Breton, A.   Mystery Corset, The.
    Three Excerpts.
Colby, T.   Labor Day Picnic Poem.
Diego, G.   On These Conditions.
Edwards, K.   Good Science.
    Lexically.
Éluard, P.   Lady Love.
    Earth Is Blue like an Orange, The.
Forrest-Thomson.   Richard II.
Frumkin.   Surreal Love Life.
Howard, R.   Job Interview, The.
Jacob, M.   Meeting.
Laurencin, M.   Tiger, The.
    Zebra, The.
Mengham, Rod.   Concession to Perpetuity No.
    166.
Muldoon, P.   Salvador.
Reverdy.   Is Ajar.
Senghor.   African Image Is Not An Image by
    Equation, The.
    Speech and Image: An African Tradition of the
    Surreal.
Tzara.   Cosmic Realities Vanilla Tobacco
    Wakings.
    Death of Guillaume Apollinaire, The.
Waldman, A.   Paul Eluard.
Wright, J.   Against Surrealism.

Survival
Abad, G.   Jeepney.
Agustini.   Life.
Alcosser.   Warrior's Tale, A.
Aliger.   I live / with a bullet in my heart.
Becker, R.   Crypto-Jews, The.
Behar, R.   Survivals.
Bek, T.   We've all got history on our hands.
Belli, G.   Blood of Others, The.
Berryman.   Huffy Henry hid the day.
Bobyshev.   Other World, The.
Boland, E.   Emigrant Irish, The.
Brecht, B.   I, the Survivor.
    To Those Born Later.
Brett, L.   My Mother's Friend.
Brooks, G.   To Black Women.
Carruth, H.   Little Citizen, Little Survivor.
Char.   Faction Du Muet.
Chedid, A.   For Survival.
Clark, T.   As the Human Village Prepares for Its
    Fate.
Clifton, L.   She Lived.
    Won't you celebrate with me.
Coleman, T.   Chicago on the Day Brother
    Increases His Chances of Reaching Age 21.
Denby.   Domestic Cat, A.
Donne.   Prohibition, The.
Dorsett, T.   Survivor, The.
Dugan, A.   Weeds as Partial Survivors.
Enzensberger, H.   Reprieve, The.
Fried, E.   Conversation with a Survivor.
Galich.   Goldminers' Waltz, The.
Garrigue.   Bad Times Song.
Gershon.   I Was Not There.
Gilbert, W.   Yarn of the *Nancy Bell*, The.
Guidacci.   Tiny dew reinvigorates the tiny grass,
    The.
Gunn, T.   In the Post Office.
Hacker, M.   Cancer Winter.
Hardy, T.   Heredity.
Harjo, J.   Anchorage.
Harris, R.   Riding Over Belmore Park.
Haviaras, Stratis.   Checkmark.
    Still Life.
Hemphill.   Better Days.
    Cordon Negro.
Herbert, Z.   Abandoned, The.
    Pebble, The.
Hirsch, E.   Song Against Natural Selection.
Kearney, M.   Nature Poetry.
Kinnell.   Bear, The.
Kumin, M.   How to Survive Nuclear War.
Kunitz, S.   Old Cracked Tune, An.
    Three Small Parables for My Poet Friends.
Kunze, R.   Aerial, The.
    Reply.
Kupriyanov [or Kuprianov].   For a long time he
    tried to survive.
Levi, P.   Survivor, The.
Lewis, J.   Stories.
Limburg, J.   Seder Night with My Ancestors.
Lleshanaku, L.   Self-Defense.
Logue, C.   Good Taste.
Malouf.   Judas Touch, The.
Martinaitis, M.   Zuveliskes's Women Mourn
    Over Kukutis.
Mathews, H.   Out of Bounds.
McGrath, T.   Nuclear Winter.
Mistral, G.   Caribbean Sea.
Montague, J.   Wild Dog Rose, The.
Montale.   Little Testament.
Muir, E.   Horses, The.
Muñiz Huberman.   Obsession.
Nemerov.   To My Least Favorite Reviewer.
O'Driscoll, D.   Life.
Ofek, U.   Hagomel.
Ogundipe-Leslie.   Tendril Love of Africa.
Oppen.   Myth of the Blaze.
Peele.   Write write yow Croniclers of Tyme and
    Fame.
Popa.   In the Village of My Forefathers.
Porteous.   I Envy the Cracked, Black Basalt.
Pound, E.   Rest, The.
Preston, R.   Champion Chant.
Ratushinskaya [or Ratushinskaia].   But Only
    Not to Think.

I Will Live and Survive.
Reynolds, C.   Worst of it, The.
Reznikoff.   Joshua at Shechem.
Roffé.   Wanted.
Rohrer, M.   We Never Should Have Stopped at Pussy Island.
Rózewicz.   Survivor, The.
Ryan, T.   Enough.
Schwartz, R. L.   When They Know.
Scupham.   Lesssons in Survival.
Simmons, J.   In the Wilderness.
Smith, C.   Still Winter (Spring).
Song.   Lost Sister ("In China, / even the peasants.").
Sousa, N.   Call.
Sutskever [or Sutzkever].   Between Chimneys.
Peasant Who Saw God, The.
Swirszczynska [or Swir].   Good Lord Saved Her, The.
We Survived Them.
Tallmountain.   Good Grease.
Tapahonso.   What Danger We Court.
Tu Fu [or Du Fu].   Ch'iang Village.
Turk, R.   I'll Get By (As Long As I Have You).
Vicioso.   Survival 1.
Survival 2.
Weigl.   What Saves Us.
Williams, C.   Negro Survival 101 or Poem for Tiger Woods and Other Multiethnic Other's.
Wright, C.   On the Eve of Our Mutually Assured Destruction.
Wright, C.   Survivalist.
Yana Oral Tradition.   Now then.
Young, G.   Night Call.
Young, K.   Casting.
Zach, N.   Be Careful.
Zolynas.   Way He'd Like It, The.

Susanna (Bible)
Crapsey.   Susanna and the Elders.
Dye, Jeffrey.   Copyright Renewal Under the Texaco Star.
Stevens, W.   Peter Quince at the Clavier.

Sussex, England
Belloc.   South Country, The.
West Sussex Drinking Song.

Sutter, John
Winters, Y.   John Sutter.

Swallows
Axelrod, D.   Guide to Urban Birds, A.
Bécquer, G.   Darkling Swallows Will Come Again, The.
Berggolts [or Bergholts].   Blockade Swallow, The.
Buson.   On these southern roads. Swallows / In eaves of mansions.
Char.   Swift, The.
Clare, J.   Sand Martin, The.
Coatsworth.   Swallows, The.
Collin, Bernard.   Perpetual Look Physics: 17/5.
Cowley, A.   Swallow, The.
Curry, N.   Swallows and Tortoises.
Euenus.   To a Swallow.
To the Swallow.
Finlay, I.   Cloud's Anchor, The.
Fletcher, J.   Skaters, The.
Issa.   From the Great Buddha's.
Montale.   Black and white, The.
Nemerov.   Blue Swallows, The.
Rossetti, C.   Fly Away, Fly Away.
Saimaro.   Mirrored by stream / Swallow darts—.
Sedakova.   Sant'Alessio, Roma.
Swinburne.   Itylus.
Tai Shu-lun.   Su Creek Pavilion.
Tu Fu [or Du Fu].   River swallows know my shack is humble.
Unknown.   Voice of the Swallow, Flittering, Calls to Me, The.
Yeats.   Coole Park, 1929.

Swamps
Budbill.   First Green of Spring, The.
Ceravolo.   Caught in the Swamp.
"Ern Malley.".   Culture as Exhibit.
Frost, R.   Wood-Pile, The.
Gray, R.   Flames and Dangling Wire.
Haskins, L.   Prayer for the Everglades.

Hauge.   Across the Swamp.
Heaney, S.   Bogland.
Jarnot, L.   Swamp Formalism.
Leonidov, Rumen.   Stone in the Swamp, A.
Menicanti.   If.
Moore, M.   I May, I Might, I Must.
Nazareno, C.   Cortes Swamp, The.
Pound, E.   Vitex in swamp ground.
Swenson, M.   Shu Swamp, Spring.
Unknown.   Ze-bi: By That Swamp's Shore.

Swans
Agustini.   Swan, The.
Arensberg.   Voyage à l'Infini.
Baudelaire.   Swan, The.
Swan, The.
Benedikt.   Editing The Gazette of the Infinite.
Berssenbrugge.   Swan, The.
Black, S.   Personals.
Bogan, L.   Winter Swan.
Browning, E.   Romance of the Swan's Nest, The.
Clifton, L.   Leda 3.
Curry, N.   Mute Swans.
Cynewulf.   Swan, The.
Darío, R.   Leda.
Swan, The.
Swans, The.
Doolittle, H.   Leda.
Durrell.   Swans.
Dyment.   Swans, The.
"Ern Malley.".   Sweet William.
Ewart.   Semantic Limerick According to the Shorter Oxford English Dictionary (1933), The.
Fogarty, L.   By Accident, Blinked.
George, S.   Do Not Ponder Too Much.
Have you his lovely image still in mind.
Gibbons, O.   Silver Swan, The.
Glück, L.   Palais des Arts.
Gogarty.   Leda and the Swan.
Gonzáles Martínez.   Wring the Swan's Neck.
Hernández Cruz.   Swans' Book, The.
Hollander, J.   Swan and Shadow.
Jeffers, R.   Love the Wild Swan.
Longley, M.   Swans Mating.
MacCaig.   Intruder in a Set Scene.
MacDiarmid, H.   Two Memories.
Macpherson, J.   Swan, The.
Mallarmé.   This virginal long-living lovely day. Virginal, vibrant, and beautiful dawn, The. Virginal, Vivid, Beautiful, Will This Be.
Merritt, C.   Mute Swan, The.
Millay, E.   Wild Swans.
Moore, M.   Critics and Connoisseurs.
No Swan So Fine.
Morgan, E.   Siesta of a Hungarian Snake.
Nutter, G.   Definition of Swan, The.
Oliver, M.   Swans on the River Ayr.
Pitter.   Swan Bathing, The.
Rexroth, K.   Poem: "As the full moon rises."
Rilke.   Swan, The.
Swan, The ("This clumsy living that moves lumbering.").
Rodgers, W.   Swan, The.
St. John, D.   Swan at Sheffield Park, The.
Schwartz, R. L.   Swan at Edgewater Park, The.
Sitwell, E.   Swans, The.
Spenser, E.   With that I saw two swans of goodly hue [or hew].
Spicer, J.   Transformations.
Tennyson, A.   Dying Swan, The.
Unknown.   Swan Sequence, The.
Wilner, E.   You, Failed Pronoun.
Wilson, E.   Lakeside.
Wingfield.   Back.
Yeats.   Among School Children.
Leda and the Swan.
Wild Swans at Coole, The.

Swansea, Wales
Hatton, J.   Swansea Bay.
Watkins, V.   Ode to Swansea.

Sweatshops
Altizer.   Sonnet 5: "No, I'll not, carrion, comfort you. Comfort."
Pinsky.   Shirt.
Reznikoff.   Shopgirls leave their work, The.

Sweden
DeCormier-Shekejian.   Grandmother.
Koch, K.   Energy in Sweden.
Stewart, F.   Black Winter.

Swift, Jonathan
Bogan, L.   Hypocrite Swift.
Montagu, L.   Reasons That Induced Dr. Swift to Write a Poem Called "The Lady's Dressing-Room", The.
Pope, A.   Happy Life of a Country Parson, The.
Sheridan, T.   Tom Punsibi's Letter to Dean Swift.
Swift, J.   Here shift the scene, to represent.
Verses on the Death of Dr. Swift, D.S.P.D, Occasioned by Reading a Maxim in Rochefoucauld.
Yeats.   Swift's Epitaph.

Swifts
Char.   Swift, The.
Jarman, M.   Chimney Swifts.
Jones, G.   Swifts.

Swimming and Swimmers
Agran, R.   Swimming with Seiger.
Avison.   Swimmer's Moment, The.
Booth, P.   First Lesson.
Bourne, Lesley-Anne.   Teaching My Husband to Swim.
Bright, S.   Riding the Currents.
Brown, Cecil.   Integrating the Strawberry Swimming Pool in 1998.
Buson.   How awkward it looks.
Byron, G.   Written After Swimming from Sestos to Abydos.
Caleshu, A.   Collaboration: Storming the Beaches.
Collins, B.   By a Swimming Pool Outside Siracusa.
Connolly, G.   Summer I Was Sixteen, The.
Dickey, J.   Lifeguard, The.
Dubie.   Ars Poetica: "It is almost polio season. The girls."
Dunbar, P.   Boy's Summer, A.
Duran, J.   Conversations with Louis.
Fargnoli, Patricia.   Lightning Spreads Out across the Water.
Ferguson, G.   Swimming Pool Ghost, The.
Francis, R.   Swimmer.
Gibbons, R.   Breath.
Greger.   Frog in the Swimming Pool, The.
Grunberger, A.   Swimming Upstream.
Hoggard, James.   Eye of the Tornado.
Hopkins, G.   Epithalamion: "Hark, hearer, hear what I do; lend a thought now, make believe."
Horst, C.   Swimming.
Kennelly.   Swimmer, The.
Klein, A.   Lone Bather.
Klein, M.   Tides, The.
Kumin, M.   400-Meter Freestyle.
Junior Life Saving.
Morning Swim.
To Swim, to Believe.
LaMon, J.   Sammy Davis, Jr.
Lane, P.   Rain Ditch.
Laughlin, J.   Deep Pool, The.
Levi, J.   Not Bad, Dad, Not Bad.
Levine, P.   Belle Isle, 1949.
Livingston, M.   Swimming Pool.
Lorde.   Question of Climate, A.
Lux.   Swimming Pool, The.
MacCaig.   Kingfisher.
Maguire, S.   Perfect Timing.
Mahon.   Swim in Co. Wicklow, A.
Marlowe.   Amorous Leander, beautiful and young.
Maxwell, G.   Helene and Heloise.
McElroy, C.   Learning to Swim at Forty-Five.
McNiece, R.   Skinny-Dipping the Ganges.
Melville, H.   Song from Mardi.
Merrill, J.   Swimming By Night.
Mitchell, K.   Night Rain.
Moore, Dinty.   What Surprises Him.
Mullen, L.   Catch, The.
Murphy, P.   Learning to Swim at Poverty Beach.
Noguchi, R.   Breath He Holds, The.
From Rooftops, Kenji Takezo Throws Himself.
I, the Neighbor Mr. Uskovich, Watch Every

Morning Kenji Takezo Hold His Breath.
O'Callaghan, C.   River at Night.
O'Donoghue, M.   Harmony in Blue.
Olds, S.   One Girl at the Boys Party, The.
Ondaatje.   Inner Tube.
Pierpoint, K.   Going Swimmingly.
Swim Right Up to Me.
Ras.   Pregnant Poets Swim Lake Tarleton, New
Hampshire.
Riley, J.   Old Swimmin'-Hole, The.
Rilke.   Swan, The.
Riordan, M.   Lines to His New Instructress.
Rowlands, D.   Archipelago.
Ryan, M.   First Exercise.
Satyamurti.   Day Trip.
Schulman.   Home Movie.
Scott, F.   Lakeshore.
Simic.   Bather, The.
Sorby.   Synchronized Swimming.
Tomlinson, C.   Swimming Chenango Lake.
Tranter.   Debbie and Co.
Triplett, P.   Winter Swim.
Unknown.   Prayer to the Sockeye Salmon.
Vegin, P.   "Moscow" Pool.
Walls, D.   Summer the Beatles Went Over
Seven Minutes on a Single, The.
Zagajewski.   On Swimming.
See also **Surfing and Surfers**

Swinburne, Algernon Charles
Cole, W.   Algernon Charles Swinburne.
Collins, M.   If.
Holtby, M.   Sister Swallow to Swinburne.

Swings
Allingham, W.   Swing Song, A.
Gay, Garry.   Bald tire.
Hwang O.   Swing, The.
Li K'ai-hsien.   Colorful frames are erected
beside the Yellow River, The.
On the Cold Food Festival, Entertaining at the
Southern Estate—the Guests Were Li Chiu-
ho, Ma Nan-yeh, Wei Tung-kao, Li Hu-
ch'uan, Huang K'ung-ts'un, Li Lung-t'ang,
and Hu Hu-shan.
Muske, C.   Our Kitty.
Smith, D.   Tire Hangs in the Woods, The.
Spady, S.   Push-Pull of This Love, The.
Stafford, W.   At the Playground.
Stevenson, R.   Swing, The.

Switzerland
Dickinson, E.   Our lives are Swiss.
Klopstock.   Lake of Zurich, The.
Merrill, J.   Country of a Thousand Years of
Peace, The.
Schiff, H.   German Frontier at Basel: 1942 and
1992, The.
Shelley, P.   Mont Blanc.
Tzara.   Zurich Chronicle February 1916.
Wordsworth, W.   Thought[s] of a Briton on the
Subjugation of Switzerland.

Swords
Ch'i-chi.   Song of the Old Sword.
Chŏnggam, Great Master.   At the Moment of
My Death.
Gonzalez, R.   José's Japanese Sword.
Henley, W. E.   I am the feast-maker.
Hill, G.   Clash of salutation. As keels thrust into
shingle.
Kipling, R.   Runes on Weland's Sword, The.
mac Lenini, C.   In Praise of a Sword Given Him
by His Prince.
Meng Chiao.   Risks.
Sill.   Opportunity.
Unknown.   End of Clonmacnois, The.
Wilde, O.   There is no chapel on the day.
Zuian.   Sky-piercing sword, gleaming cold.

Sycamore Trees
Falcón, J.   Sycamore.
White, L.   Station. He.She.You.Me.

Sydney, Australia
Beveridge.   In the Park.
Dransfield.   Flying.
Murray, L.   Flight from Manhattan, The.

Symbols
Aiken, C.   Prelude XIX: "Watch long enough,
and you will see the leaf."

Blaisdell, G.   After the Symbols.
Blanco.   Teorí de Fractales.
Borges.   Other Tiger, The.
Bremer, C.   No hay centros pero el círculo
existe.
There are no centers but the circle exists.
Budbill.   Three Goals, The.
Cervantes.   To We Who Were Saved by the
Stars.
Cook, William.   Endangered Species.
Doolittle, H.   Sheltered Garden.
Doty, M.   My Tattoo.
Ginsberg, A.   Is About.
Gonzalez, R.   Cabato.
Guillén, N.   Madrigal.
Harding, R.   Brother is a Star.
Hartman, J.   J unsubtle serif H or gemini a fish
or eternity in(terrupt)completed, A.
Herbert, G.   Church-Floor[e], The.
Herrick.   Primrose, The.
Jernigan, Marla.   Palm at the Entrance to the
Arm, A.
Ludvigson.   Not Swans.
Memmi, A.   Shot of sunlight, A.
Merrill, J.   Body [or B o d y].
Graffito.
Neri, G.   Inn of Angels, The.
Orozco.   To Make a Talisman.
Paulin.   Where Art Is a Midwife.
Piatt, J.   To the Statue on the Capitol.
Rouse, A.   Queynt.
Sandburg, C.   Shirt ("My shirt is a token and
symbol.").
Scalise, G.   Testing out the door-posts.
Segade, G.   Theory of Fractals.
Stevens, W.   Thirteen Ways of Looking at a
Blackbird.
Ward, T.   Tacit.
Williams, W.   Rose, The ("Rose is obsolete,
The.").
Wright, C.   Grace: "Its hair is a fine weed."
See also **Metaphor**

Sympathy
Ch'oe Sûngja.   For the Second Time in Thirty-
Three Years.
Cowley, H.   Well-Aimed Tear, The [or To Della
Crusca].
Czerkawska.   Thread.
Davie, D.   Rejoinder to a Critic.
Dobyns.   Frenchie.
Dunbar, P.   Passion and Love.
Ginsberg, A.   Chief of Medicine, The.
Hardy, T.   Often When Warring.
Hikmet.   Angina Pectoris.
Holmes, O.   3. Sympathies.
Hughes, F.   Laszlo.
Landon.   Poor, The.
Levine, P.   Angel Butcher.
Mayakovsky [or Maiakovskii].   Good Attitude
to Horses, A.
Meynell, V.   Sympathy.
Moorer.   Sympathy.
Pinsky.   Questions, The: "What about the people
who came to my father's office."
Revell, D.   What Can Stop This.
Rich, A.   I know you are reading this poem.
Sandburg, C.   Choose.
Sidney.   Sonnet 31: "With how sad steps, O
Moon[e], thou climb'st the skies."
Warren-Moore.   For Etheridge Knight.
Wilbur, R.   Another Voice.
Youssri, Z.   Why Are Seaman Always
Miserable?
Zabolotsky [or Zabolotskii].   All That My Soul
Possessed.

Synagogues
Jones, H.   Caught, April 2002—A Prayer for
Peace.
Lazarus, E.   In the Jewish Synagogue at
Newport.
Sillitoe.   Synagogue in Prague.

Synge, John Millington
Yeats.   Coole Park, 1929.
In Memory of Major Robert Gregory.

Syphilis
Sadiq, M.   Tuskegee Experiment.
Wilbur, R.   Pangloss's Song: A Comic-Opera
Lyric.
See also **Venereal Disease**

Syria
Brownstein.   Stepping Out.

T

Tadpoles
Brion, R.   One Morning Beside a Pond.
Kusano Shimpei.   4 Or 5 Tadpoles.

Tagore, Sir Rabindranath
Han Yong'un [or Yongwun].   Upon Reading
Tagore's "The Gardener".

Tailoring and Tailors
Dunbar, W.   Amendis [or Amends] to the
Telyouris [or Tailors] and Sowtaris [or Soutaris
or Soutars or Shoemakers].
Han Yong'un [or Yongwun].   Embroidery's
Secret, The.
Hŏ Nansŏrhŏn.   Poor Woman.
Shakespeare, W.   Thy gown? Why, ay. Come,
tailor, let us see't.
Zach, N.   Against Parting.

Taliban
Scalapino.   Flower, Pal Mal Comic Book.

Taliesin
Lewis, Emyr.   Taliesin.
Thomas, R. S.   Taliesin 1952.
Unknown.   I Am Taliesin. I Sing Perfect Metre.
Watkins, V.   Taliesin and the Mockers.

Talk
Algarin.   Talking.
Alvarez, J.   Redwing Sonnets.
Betjeman.   Reproof Deserved; or After the
Lecture.
Borson.   Talk.
Boruch.   All Those People.
Bynner.   Sigh, A.
Campert.   Silver Talk.
Davidson, M.   Et in Leucadia Ego.
Esteves.   Some People Are about Jam.
Georgiou, E.   Talkin' Trash.
Ginsberg, A.   Not a word! Not a word!
Green, M.   Sometimes I dress, with women sit.
Ha Jin.   Ways of Talking.
Hammerstein.   Happy Talk.
Hannan, M.   Drive.
Higgins, F.   By the Field of the Crab-Trees.
Jacinto, J.   Absence.
Mirville, E.   Talk, talk, talk. . .talk, talk, talk.
Mullen, H.   Blah-Blah.
Omar, I.   Not Quiet.
Pasternak, B.   Sultry Night, A.
Porter, C.   Let's Not Talk About Love.
Radden, V.   Our Second Night.
Robinson, K.   Ice Cube.
Shinkichi Takahashi.   Words: "I don't take your
words."
Shozan.   Guest gone / I stroke the brazier.
Taneda Santoka.   Came along / a mountain path.
Yi Chinmyông.   Pure Talk.
See also **Speech**

Tango
Enzensberger, H.   Old Revolution.

Tanguy, Yves
Gascoyne.   Yves Tanguy.

Tanks (vehicle)
Hagiwara Sakutaro.   Army, The.

Tannhäuser
Levy, N.   Tannhauser.

Taoism and Taoists
Brinks, Dave.   Tao Sequence, The.
Chen Huan.   Presented to the Taoist Paragon
Mao.
Chia Yi.   Owl, The.
Chunggwan, Great Master.   Upon Reading
Chuang Tzu.
Han-shan.   Yesterday I went to a cloud
observatory.
Han Yü.   Girl of Mount Hua, The.

Hsieh Ling-yün. Scene from South Hill to North Hill Passing the Lake.
Jungkwan Haean. On Reading Namwha Sutra.
Kuan Chung. Inner Workings.
Kuo P'o. Kingfishers sport among orchids and begonias.
Lao Tzu. Way and Its Power, The.
Li Po. On Visiting Taoist Recluse of Tai-Tien-Shan and Not Finding Him.
Li Te-yü. To Patriarch Sun at Hua-yang Grotto.
Liu Ch'ang-ch'ing. Sent to the Taoist of Dragon Mountain, Hsu Fa-leng.
While Visiting on the South Stream the Taoist Priest Chang.
Mahon. Mayo Tao, The.
Nienhauser, W. H. Sent to the Taoist of Dragon Mountain, Hsu Fa-leng.
Po Chü-i. After Reading Lao Tzu.
Sikong Tu. Twenty-Four Modes of Poetry.
T'ao Ch'ien [or T'ao Yuan-ming]. Drinking Alone in the Rainy Season.
Tu Fu [or Du Fu]. Six Choruses.
Vietnamese Oral Tradition. Tao. Whisky Lovers.
Wright, C. Reading Lao Tzu Again in the New Year.

Taos, New Mexico
Hughes, L. House in Taos, A.
Jeffers, R. New Mexican Mountain.

Tap Dancing
Herman, J. Tap Your Troubles Away.
Locklin. Tap Dancing Lessons.
Moore, L. Black Girl Tap Dancing.

Tapestries
Ap Hywel, Elin. Stitching.
Moore, M. Charity Overcoming Envy.
Rich, A. Aunt Jennifer's Tigers.
Santayana. On a Piece of Tapestry.
Simic. Tapestry.
Waddington, M. Ulysses Embroidered.

Tara, Ireland
Moore, T. Harp That Once through Tara's Halls, The.

Tarantulas
Lux. Tarantulas on the Lifebuoy.

Tasmania
Afterman. Van Diemen's Land.
Meredith, L. Tasmanian Scenes.
Porter, H. Hobart Town, Van Diemen's Land (11th June, 1837).
Rose. Truganinny.
Smith, V. Tasmania.
Unknown. Van Dieman's Land.

Taste
Bentley, J. Dead Mouth, High Weather, Mixture.
Clegg, D. Five Senses.
Crowley, A. Go into the Highways and Hedges, And Compel Them to Come In.
Dragomoschenko. Footnotes.
Garrett, E. Moules à la Marinière.
Góngora y Argote. Sonnet 82.
Hacker, M. Canzone: "Consider the three functions of the tongue."
Hall, D. Mangosteens.
Holst-Warhaft. Matthew 5:13; You are the salt of the earth.
Levertov. O Taste and See.
Mirabai [or Mira Bai]. Wild woman of the forests, The.
Mokusetsu. Long summer rains / Barley's tasteless.
Moore, O. Taste of Life Going On, The.
Nekrasov, V. And I Speak of Cosmic Things.
Salaam. Makes You Go Oohhh!
Su Tung-p'o. I planted rice before Spring Festival.
Supervielle. Return to Paris.

Tate, Allen
Davidson, D. Lines Written for Allen Tate on His Sixtieth Anniversary.

Tattoos (skin markings)
Addonizio. First Poem for You.
Alexie. Sonnet: Tattoo Tears.
Allen, P. Tattoo #47, "Happy Dragon".

Bartlett, J. When I Got My First Tattoo I Was.
Bottoms. Chinese Dragons.
Clarke, C. Make-Up.
Cullar, Carol. He's Crossed the River.
Doty, M. My Tattoo.
Dye, Jeffrey. Copyright Renewal Under the Texaco Star.
Feinfeld, D. Carmelita.
Finch, P. Tattoo, The.
Franklin, K. Tattooing the Motherline.
Harburg. Lydia, the Tattooed Lady.
Hayden, R. Tattooed Man, The.
Hughes, L. Sailor.
Jenkins, L. Confessional Poem.
Johnson, Peter. Tattoo.
LaFemina. Her Rose Tattoo.
McClatchy. Tattoos.
McPherson, S. Pornography, Nebraska.
Morris, T. Why I Wont Wear a Tatoo.
Mririda n'Ait Attik. Praise to the Tattoo Mistress.
Norton, O. Tattoo, or Henna.
St. John, D. Last Night with Rafaella.
Senryū, K. Tattoo of, A.
Unknown. Girl's Song.
Walwicz. Tattoo, The.

Taverns
Baker, D. 8-Ball at the Twilite.
Cavafy. Comes to Rest.
García Lorca. Malaguena.
Guillén, N. Bars.
Kirstein. Rank.
Robinson, E. Tavern, The.
Rumi. Who Says Words with My Mouth.
Stephens, J. Glass of Beer, A.
Vaughan, H. Rhapsody, A.

Taxes
Bierce. To the Bartholdi Statue.
Brown, G. Taxman.
Burns, R. De'il's [or Deil's] Awa wi' th' [or the] Exciseman, The.
Ch'i-chi. Old Farmer, The.
Elliott, E. Fatal Birth, The.
Guevara, M. Magic Carpet, The.
Lowell, J. Letter Six—The Pious Editors' Creed.
Maksimovic. Matthew 22:15–22; Then the Pharisees went and.
O'Daly, M. On Killing a Tax Collector.
Steptoe. O' Yes.

Taxidermy
Barnett, R. Taxidermist at the Zoo, The.
Follain. Taxidermist, A.
Mark, Sabrina Orah. Mustache, The.
Warren, R. Red-Tail Hawk and Pyre of Youth.
Yamaguchi Seishi. On a hook he hangs.

Taxis
Davis, J. Zoo, The.
Gunn, T. Night Taxi.
Hemphill. Family Jewels.
Henderson, H. Ballad of the Taxi Driver's Cap.
Lowell, A. Taxi, The.
MacNeice. Taxis, The.
Mattawa. Echo and Elixir 2.
Musgrave. Hidden Meaning.
Rouse, A. Narrows, The.
Slessor. All-night Taxi Stand, The.
Taylor, H. After a Movie.
Webb, F. Tip for Saturday, A.

Tchaikovsky, Peter Ilyich
Mayhall. Painkiller.

Tea
Artmann. Tea Merchant, The.
Basho. Monk sips morning tea, A.
Betjeman. Death in Leamington. How to Get On in Society.
Buson. Ten holy nights / Even tea.
Bynner. What though they conquer us?
Carroll, L. Welcome Queen Alice.
Ch'u Ch'uang I. Tea.
Earle, J. Tea Party, The.
Elliot, A. Northern Morning, A.
Flynn, L. Myth of Tea Boy, The.
Gorham. Princess Parade.
Han-shan Te-ch'ing. I wake up a novice and

ask him to make tea.
Issa. Five yen each / A cup of tea.
Jacobs, J. Two Varieties of the Bitter Orange.
Jones, B. Having Our Tea.
Kikaku. I begin each day.
Koestenbaum, W. Tea Dance.
Lear, E. There was an Old Man who forgot.
Monro, H. Milk for the Cat.
Odarchenko. Claudia Petrovna.
Prior-Pitt. Fitting.
Rilke. Going Blind.
Ritsos. Miniature.
Scafidi, S. Prayer for a Marriage.
Schippers. No, No, Nanette.
Scudder, A. Tea Making.
Service. Pot of Tea, A.
Swift, T. Influence of Anxiety at the Seaside with Tea, The.
Taylor, J. Recreation.
Trần Tế Xu'o'ng. Women.
Trungpa, Chogyam. His parents are having tea.
Uyematsu. Tea.
Welch, L. Empress Herself Served Tea to Su Tung-Po, The.
Zinnemann-Hope. Taking Tea with My Father and Mother.

See also **Teahouses**

Teaching and Teachers
Agran, R. Wearing Dad's White Shirt Backwards.
Algarin. Meeting Gaylen's 5th Grade Class.
Allen, P. Teaching Poetry at Votech High, Santa Fe, the Week John Lennon Was Shot.
Amorosi. Good Teacher, The.
Anderson, Tenshin Reb. To My First Teacher.
Anderton. Marking of Folders.
Bachhuber, D. Mozart in a Classroom of Children.
Baraka, I. Why Didnt He Tell Me the Whole Truth.
Barolini. Having the Wrong Name for Mr. Wright.
Beeson, Colleen. Minnie Henderson.
Berg, S. Writing Class.
Berger, B. To Answer Your Question.
Berryman. Professor's Song, A.
Black, D. Educators, The.
Blankenburg, G. Mouse, The.
Bly, R. Gratitude to Old Teachers.
Buddingh'. Some Biographical Data.
Buhyu Sunsoo. To a Monk.
Burkard. White City, A: "In the dream, N. is singing "a white city." A teacher he had is wearing a girdle."
Cahn, S. Teach Me Tonight.
Ch'i-chi. Admonishing a Younger Teacher.
Chikusen. He's part of all, yet all's transcended.
Chin. Floral Apron, The.
Collins, B. History Teacher, The.
Di Prima. Dokusan: Visit to Katagiri Roshi. I Fail as a Dharma Teacher. Poem on the Limits for My Writing Group: Atlantic Center for the Arts, New Smyrna Beach, Florida.
Dubie. Of Politics, & Art.
Duffy, C. Good Teachers, The.
Duran, J. Mr Teller the Piano Teacher.
Eady. Why Do So Few Blacks Study Creative Writing?
Ellis, Zoila. Luwani Dangriga.
Engman. Mushroom Clouds.
Feld, Andrew. On Fire.
Finney, N. Fishing Among the Learned.
Firer. Mrs. Post's 6th-Hour English Class.
Fitzgerald, R. Figlio Maggiore.
Foster, M. Recruiting Song.
Garioch. Elegy: "They are lang deid, folk that I used to ken."
Gilbert, C. And, Yes, Those Spiritual Matters.
Glass, Jesse. Lecturing on Walt Whitman and Emily Dickinson in China.
Glück, L. Mountain, The.
Grace, P. Butterflies.
Graham, W. Johann Joachim Quantz's Five Lessons.
Guevara, M. Once When I Was in the Eighth

Grade.

Hajjaj, N. Mr. Dheeb Al-Rifa'i.

Hall, D. For an Early Retirement.

Han-shan Te-ch'ing. I wake up a novice and ask him to make tea.

Hecht, A. Mysteries of Caesar, The.

Herbert, Z. Biology Teacher.

Herodas. Schoolmaster, The.

Heyen. Where.

Huddle. Miss Florence Jackson.

Hughes, T. Crow's First Lesson.

Hugo, R. Letter to Haislip from Hot Springs.

Izumi. In the Autumn, on Retreat at a Mountain Temple.

Janzen, J. Learning to Sing in Parts.

Jinkag Haesim. Fan.

Jonson, B. To William Camden.

Kamienska. Luke 10:38–42; Now as they went on their way.

Kaneko. Bailey Gatzert: The First Grade, 1945.

Kaplinski, J. Shunryu Suzuki.

Katagiri, Dainin. You are nearly as old as the number of years it has been since I came to America.

Kennedy, X. Hummingbird.

Kim Chŏngnan. In the Subway—Getting Used to Ugliness 3.

Kinnell. Correspondence School Instructor Says Goodbye to His Poetry Students, The.

Kinzie. Ringing Words.

Kizer, C. Reunion.

Kuan Chung. Duties of the Student.

Kyger. It's a great day. Last night I visited my old.

Lal Ded [or Lalla]. Soul, like the moon, The.

Li Qi. To Zhang Xu.

MacKie, A. Primary Teachers.

Macpherson, J. Some Ghosts and Some Ghouls.

Max, L. Pedagogy.

McCallum, S. Perfect Heart, The.

McCord, D. History of Education.

McElroy, C. Learning to Swim at Forty-Five.

McGrath, T. You Taught Me.

McLagan, Elizabeth. Reading the Names.

Mendelssohn Anna. On being reproached by saintly mediators for bad budgeting.

Meredith, C. Jets.

Montague, J. Flowering Absence, A ("How can one make an absence flower.").

Muso Soseki. Old Hut.

Nash, O. Purist, The.

Nooteboom. Basho 2.

O'Brien, S. In Residence: A Worst Case View.

Patten, B. How the New Teacher Got Her Nickname.

What Happened to Miss Frugle.

Pinchas-Cohen. My English Teacher.

Pope, A. Now crowds on crowds around the goddess press.

Raz, H. Teaching, Hurt.

Reagon. They Are All Falling around Me.

Roberson, E. Four Lines of a Black Love Letter between Teachers.

Robertson, J. George Buchanan in Old Age.

Roethke. Elegy for Jane.

Rosenthal, G. Ghetto Dokusan.

Runyan, Tania. Teaching Shakespeare.

Seale, J. Playing the Flute for the TMR Class.

Silano, M. In Henry Carlile's *Writing 213*.

Simmons, J. In the Wilderness.

Snodgrass. April Inventory.

Campus on the Hill, The.

Snyder, G. Axe Handles.

Song. Out of Our Hands.

Sotoba, Layman. Mountain—Buddha's body, The.

Stein, G. Teachers taught her, The.

Tafolla. At the Very Last Battle.

Traherne. That childish thoughts such joys inspire.

Tripp. Headmaster.

Tuckerman, F. And two I knew, an old man and a boy.

Twichell. Tutelage.

Unknown. Make yourself my father's follower.

Vaughan. When he did read how did we flock to hear.

Vázquez Montalbán, M. In Memoriam ("I learned / the interminable list.").

Wagner, M. Miss Clement's Second Grade.

Walker, T. Owl.

Weitsman, Sojun Mel. One third of my life has been spent in this practice and you.

Whitman, W. I am the teacher of athletes.

Whittier. To My Old Schoolmaster.

Williamson, G. Drawing Hands.

Winder. Lesson.

Zen Center Sangha. One third of my life has been spent in this practice and you.

Zolynas. Love in the Classroom.

See also **Scholarship and Scholars**

Teahouses

Buson. Old woman at the teahouse, The.

Willow, The.

Howe, F. As Like As Not.

See also **Tea**

Team Spirit

Hicok. Team Effort.

Holden, J. Saturday Afternoon, October.

Newbolt. Vitaï Lampada.

Tears

Alexie. Sonnet: Tattoo Tears.

Armand. Poem with Skin.

Ausländer, R. Well, The.

Basho. Spring going.

Belieu. Part of the Effect of the Public Scene Is to Importune the Passing Viewer.

Blunt, W. On Her Vanity.

Bogan, L. Tears in Sleep.

Brontë, C. What does she dream of.

Brooke, R. Hill, The.

Brown, S. Chillen Get Shoes.

Browning, E. Cry of the Children, The.

Flush or Faunus.

Buson. Tears.

Byron, G. Tear, The.

When We Two Parted.

Cabral de Melo Neto. Daily Space.

Cahn, S. Guess I'll Hang My Tears Out to Dry.

Castro, R. He Who Weeps Goes Not Alone.

Chang Pi. Butterfly.

Clarke, C. What Goes Around Comes Around, or The Proof is in the Pudding.

Claudel, P. Sadness of Water, The.

Coleridge, M. Solo.

Collier, M. Argos.

Coulehan, J. Anatomy Lesson.

Crane, H. To Emily Dickinson.

Crashaw. Tear[e], The.

Weeper, The.

Crozier, L. Excellence in the Small. Tears Frozen on Your Face.

De la Selva. Tropical Childhood.

Delmore, E. Such Sweet Sorrow.

Dickinson, E. Life's Trades.

Donne. Twickenham [or Twicknam] Garden.

Valediction, A: of Weeping.

Dumas, H. If I Were Earth.

Eigner. If You Weep, I Think That.

El-Hage, N. Overflow.

Ellis, Zoila. Catalyst.

Favery. She has let herself fall on her bed.

Ficowski. Girl of Six from the Ghetto Begging in Smolna Street in 1942, A.

Field, E. Journey, A.

Field, M. Already to mine eyelids' shore.

Fitts, Susan Love. Clearly Through My Tears.

Fitzhardinge, M. B. Louis.

Fletcher, P. Hymn: "Drop, drop, slow tears, and bathe those beauteous feet."

Freed, A. I Cried for You.

Glück, L. Moonless Night.

Trillium.

Guidacci. Spring.

Harbach, O. Smoke Gets in Your Eyes.

Harper, F. Slave Auction, The.

Herbert, Z. From the Technology of Tears.

Herrick. Seest thou those diamonds which she wears.

Ishikawa Takuboku. Never forget.

Issa. As I grow older.

Her row veering off.

Mother, I weep.

Jarrell, R. On the Railway Platform.

Jensma. Suspect under section a1 special.

Johnson, J. Sence You Went Away.

Jonson, B. Echo's [or Eccho's] Song.

Juana Inés de la Cruz. Pleaure Given by Suspicion with the Rhetoric of Crying, The.

This Evening When I Spoke to You.

Katz, M. To a Butterfly.

Kim Hyesun. Teardrop, A.

Kim Sŭnghŭi. Wailer.

Kinnell. Crying.

Labé. Bright Venus, Who Across the Heavens Stray.

Landor, W. Foreign Ruler, A.

Tears of the Dying.

Levertov. Weeping Woman.

Lindsay, V. Rain.

Liu, T. Echoes.

Marvell. Eyes and Tears.

Meynell, A. Maternity.

Miller, J. Bird dressed as solitude and tears.

Mirabai [or Mira Bai]. Heat of Midnight Tears, The.

Murray, L. Absolutely Ordinary Rainbow, An.

Musset. Poet, The.

Nathan, L. Toast.

Neruda. Dictators, The.

Walking Around.

November, Yehoshua. How a Place Becomes Holy.

Otero, B. About to Fall.

Ouwens. Some Tears.

Peacock, M. My God, Why Are You Crying?

Pfeiffer, E. Any Husband to Many a Wife.

Philodemus. You Cry, Whine, Peer Strangely at Me.

Po Chü-i. Dreaming of Yuan Zhen.

Letter, The.

Ponge. Water of Tears, The.

Prasad, V. Liberation.

Rãy, D. It's no one else's fault, Syama Ma.

Reese, L. Tears.

Ríos, A. They Said I Was a Crying Bride.

Rosales. Locked with a Tear.

Saleh, S. Tears: "There is a scream that binds my heart to."

Sanchez, S. Depression.

Sandburg, C. Bundles.

Seshadri. Lifeline.

Shafer, A. Gurney Tears.

Shen Yüeh. Peach.

Shiraishi. From the Precious Tears of the Donkey.

Smedley, M. Cavour.

Smith, S. Death Sentence, The.

Sorescu, M. Tear, The.

Southwell. Vale of Tear[e]s, A.

Spence, L. Capernaum.

Steinberg, J. All of a Summer.

Stickney, T. Athenian Garden, An.

Synková, A. Tears.

Tennyson, A. Tears, Idle Tears.

Thomas, D. Hand That Signed the Paper, The.

Unknown. Having not yet crossed the Yellow River, my heart is not at peace.

I Saw My Lady Weep.

Insects chirp outside the four walls, The.

Maxim Revised, A.

Warpath Song.

Weep [or Weepe] You No More [Sad Fountains].

Unknown, fr. Terezin Concentration Camp. Birdsong.

Verlaine. Falling tears in my heart.

Like city's rain, my heart.

Tears Fall in My Heart.

Voigt. Woman Who Weeps.

Wheelwright. Esprit d'Escalier.

Whitman, W. Tears.

Williamson, G. Visiting Couple Kissing and Halved Onion.

Wordsworth, W. Old Man by the Brook, The.

Yi Myŏnghan. With tears I cling to your sleeves.

Yi Sanghûi. Dance: "When I wait."
Yu Xuanji. Spring Passion.
Zenmaro. Tanka: "Nothing / but reason."
Zhang Shuai. Staring.

Technology and Technologists
Algarin. At the Electronic Frontier.
Armantrout. Manufacturing.
Bidart. For the Twentieth Century.
Blaeser. Dictionary for the New Century.
Blanco. Music in the Age of Iron.
Blumenthal, M. Over Ohio.
Borisova, M. Dry birch tree stood, The.
Citino. Principles of Scarcity, Doctrines of Growth.
Close, J. Beelah Viaduct, The.
Cornford, A. And it came to pass just as they had foretold.
Cummings, E. E. In heavenly realms of hellas dwelt.
Halliday, M. Population.
Huidobro. Eiffel Tower.
Jackson, F. Industrial Teflon Comes Into Domestic Use.
Kinnell. Fundamental Project of Technology, The.
Sheffield Ghazal 4: Driving West.
Martinson. Makers of Perpetuum Mobile, The.
Portnoy, M. Of of Titmouse.
Prynne. Did you light furtive aggregate late-flow samples.
Shinkichi Takahashi. Beach.
Torres, E. Gigabyte Me—How Much RAM in Your Summer of Love?

Teddy Bears
Kennedy, Jimmy. Teddy Bear's Picnic.

Teenagers
Alexander, E. Zodiac.
Aridjis. Self-Portrait at Age Sixteen.
Bialosky, J. Adolescent Suicide, The.
Brooks, G. We Real Cool.
Burt, L. Melissa Quits School.
Cherry, K. For Teen-Age Boys Murdered in Texas: The Refusal to Dramatize Bloodlust.
Cooper, D. Teen Idols.
Davis, T. Letter to My Mother, Sixteen Years after the Fact.
Dodd, E. Touched.
Dove, R. Adolescence—1.
Adolescence—2.
Adolescence—3.
Glatt. Talking About Boys.
Gross, P. I'm fat, look, *fat*.
Hirsch, E. Boy With a Headset.
Jarman, M. Ground Swell.
Johnson, J. Girl of Fifteen.
Kasischke. Bike Ride with Older Boys.
Fatima.
Lux. Swimming Pool, The.
McKean. After Listening to Jack Teagarden.
Mohammad, K. Silem. Mars Needs Terrorists.
Obadike, M. Fifteen.
Pollard, C. Heavy-Petting Zoo, The.
Potos. One Red-haired Summer, The.
Smith, P. Biting Back.
Sorby. Glossolalia.
Soto. Saturday at the Canal.
Stern, G. Samaritans.
Swiss. On a Stanza by Rilke.
Teofilov, Ivan. Teenagers.
Uyematsu. Deliberate.
Wheatley, D. Fourteen.

Teeth
Basho. Teeth sensitive to the sand.
Brown, S. Her lips disclosed to view.
Chao Meng-fu. Admonition to Myself, An.
Cofer, J. Lesson of the Teeth, The.
Dickey, W. Poet's Farewell to His Teeth, The.
Gyatso, T. White teeth smiling.
Han Yü. Losing a Tooth.
Poem on Losing One's Teeth.
Holub. Teeth.
Hopkins, L. This Tooth.
Issa. In my hidden house.
Kay, J. Crown and Country.
Teeth.
Kosugi, T. Manodharma with Mr. Y.

Lamb, C. First Tooth, The.
Lamb, M. First Tooth, The.
Larsen, L. Red.
Lau, A. Eating habits of the old man.
Lux. Little Tooth, A.
Melville, H. Maldive Shark, The.
Milligan, S. Teeth.
Mother Goose. Teeth and Gums.
Quevedo y Villegas. Toothpuller Who Wanted to Turn a Mouth into a Grinding Machine, The.
Unknown. My Last Tooth.
W., C. A. To have it out or not? that is the question.
See also **Dentistry and Dentists; Toothaches**

Tel Aviv, Israel
Goldberg, L. Tel Aviv 1935.

Telegrams
Howard, J. Hello! My Baby.
Kramer, L. Red Cross Telegram, The.

Telegraph
Grossmith, G. You Can't Make Love by Wireless.
Guerra, T. Canto Three.
Hughes, T. Telegraph Wires.
Murray, L. Morse.
Untermeyer, L. To a Vine-clad Telegraph Pole.
Very. First Atlantic Telegraph, The.
Wodehouse. You Can't Make Love by Wireless.

Telemachus
Brodsky, J. Odysseus to Telemachus.
Stesichoros. Helen suddenly saw a divine omen.

Telephones and Telephoning
Algarin. Wire Tap.
Bolton, K. Nonplussed.
Carver, R. Old Days, The.
Ch'oe Sûngja. My Phone Rings Endlessly.
Cisneros, S. You Called Me *Corazón*.
Corn. Long-Distance Call to Gregg, Who Lived with AIDS as Long as He Could.
Dorfman, A. Vocabulary.
Estep, M. I Have to Go Now.
García Lorca. Poet Speaks with Love by Telephone, The.
Ginsberg, A. I Am a Victim of Telephone.
Guevara, M. Long Distance.
Hacker, M. Rondeau after a Transatlantic Telephone Call.
Hannan, M. Tap.
Harrison, T. Long Distance II.
Hughes, T. Telegraph Wires.
Inez. Taking Calls in Freeport, NY.
Iskrenko. How To Live Through This Night (A Dream).
Kerouac. To Edward Dahlberg.
Kim Chôngnan. Phone Call From Immortality—From Agnes to Mr. Kundera, A.
Kim Sûnghûi. Floating Metonymy 2.
Martinson. Cable Ship, The.
Mastin. From the Telephone.
Mayer, G. 529 1983.
McCabe, V. People at the Pay Telephone, The.
Michaels, A. Once you called at midnight.
Millar, J. Fiber Optics.
Telephone Repairman.
Miller, J. Topos.
Muske, C. Call, The: "When I heard the voice on the telephone."
Nathan, L. Breathing Exercises.
Nemerov. Primer of the Daily Round, A.
O'Sullivan, L. Cord, The.
Palmer, O. Wasting Time.
Paris, T. Reception.
Porter, D. Lollies Noir.
Pugh, C. Rotary.
Richards, L. Eletelephony.
Rozhdestvensky [*or* Rozhdestvenskii]. In the Night.
Sandburg, C. Manual System.
Shiraishi. Donkey Speculates, The.
Smith, K. Message on the Machine.
Soyinka. Telephone Conversation.
Stein, K. World Without End.
Steinbergh. Burial.
Stroud, J. Hear That Phone Ringing? Sounds

Like a Long Distance Call.
Tayson, R. Phone Sex.
Toomer. Her Lips Are Copper Wire.
Vazirani, R. Mrs. Biswas of Maryland on the Phone.
Witte, Francine. When You Call Again.
Wong, T. Loneliness.

Telescopes
Bradley, G. At the Other End of the Telescope.
Scruton, J. In the Age of the Radio Telescope.
Thomas, R. Repairing the Hubble Telescope.

Television
Ahern, T. Popeye in the 19th Century.
Ahl, L. Defining Moment.
Alexander, E. Apollo.
Alvarez, J. How I Learned to Sweep.
Anderson, D. Nightly News, The.
Angira. Newscast.
Ben-Lev, D. Broken Helix.
Bruck. Pretty Soon.
Campo. X Files, The.
Carson, A. Lazarus.
TV is presocial, like Men.
Codrescu. Telyric.
Coleman, J. Soap.
Conway, J. Marlo Thomas in Seven Parts and Epilogue.
Cooper, D. David Cassidy Then.
Davies, J. Visitor's Book, 9, The.
Davis, J. Kids on Television Imagine Me, The.
Deanovich. Natalie gets discovered in her pit by an old, drunken transient.
Dlugos. Gilligan's Island.
Durcan. Going Home to Mayo, Winter, 1949.
Wife Who Smashed Television Gets Jail.
Enzensberger, H. War, Like.
Espy. My TV Came down with a Chill.
Francia, L. Video Victim.
Fusselman, A. Ticker.
Gunn, T. Death's Door.
Gwynn, R. Oprah Out of Control.
Harjo, J. Post-colonial Tale, A.
Harryman. The. Open. Box.
Hattersley, G. *On the Buses* with Dostoyevsky.
Ignatow, D. First on TV, A.
Jones, R. TV.
Joseph, A. Soul Train.
Kasdorf. First TV in a Mennonite Family.
Kelen. Gods Ash Their Cigarettes, The.
Klipschutz. Funicello at 50.
Kyger. Watching TV.
Leto. Mary Morelle Show, The.
Like, J. Postmodern: A Definition.
Lochhead, L. Interference Song.
Loftin, E. April '68.
Lopez, T. Dint.
Martin, H. Miss Rosie Mae Watches Elvis Presley on The Ed Sullivan Show.
McCarthy, J. Ending.
McGinley. Robin Hood.
McGrath, C. Xena, Warrior Princess.
Merriam, E. Tube Time.
Nemerov. Way of Life, A.
Olin. Tom Brokaw.
Pettit. Vanna White's Bread Pudding.
Reading, P. Dirty sex violence of TV.
Ridl. Video Mama.
Sallah, T. Television as God.
Samaras, N. After the Children Have Gone to Bed.
Shange. Different Love Poem / We Need a Change, A.
Silverstein, S. Jimmy Jet and His TV Set.
Soto. TV in Black and White.
Sutton, V. While Watching *Cops* I Think of You.
Turner, J. TV Movie.
Vando. Lydia's Phantasmagoria.
Waldman, A. How the Sestina (Yawn) Works.
Warr, M. TV Dinner.
Williams, Gerwyn. Final Curtain.
Wilson, R. Old Movies.
Wojahn. W. C. W. Watching Presley's Second Appearance on The Ed Sullivan Show: Mercy Hospital, Newark, 1956.
Zolotow. Enemies.

Temperance
Moore, J.   Anti-Bacchics 1.
   Anti-Bacchics 2.
Temples
Ch'ang Chien.   Buddhist Retreat Behind
   Broken-Mountain Temple, A.
Ch'i-chi.   After the Rebellion, Visiting West
   Mountain Temple.
   Thinking of a Monk of Flower Summit on
   Mount T'ien-t'ai.
Chia Tao.   Seeing Off the Monk Ts'ung-Ch'ih
   Returning to the Capital.
Ching An.   At Lushan Temple.
Cho Chihun.   Ancient Temple.
Ch'ôn Yanghûi.   Mountain Stroll.
Daegak Euchon.   At Chonymyung Temple.
   Reply to Sir Kukwon's "Sleeping in the Temple
   in Autumn".
Forrester, S.   Temple bell ringing.
Jinkag Haesim.   On the Death of the Most
   Reverend Priest.
Kalamaras, G.   You Keep Coming upon Your
   Breath at the Altar.
Kistler, W.   Kyoto 2—Ryoanji.
Maezumi, Taizan.   Untransmittable and moving
   eastward.
Ōkuma Kotomichi.   Vespers.
Pak Chaesam.   Night at Tongbak Temple.
Pak Mogwŏl [or Mokwŏl].   Blue Deer.
Reverdy.   Spirit Escapes, The.
Spires.   Celestial, The.
Toledo, N.   Temple.
   Templo.
   Yudu.
Unknown.   Cai-fan: Pluck the Quince.
Wenger, Michael.   Zen Corners.
Yi Tal.   Mountain Temple.
Zinger, G.   I'm speaking to make you silent.
Temptation
Agard, J.   English Girl Eats Her First Mango.
Amaru.   Much Too Close.
Auden.   From "The Prolific and the Devourer".
Aytoun [or Ayton], R.   To His Forsaken
   Mistress.
Beeching, J.   Gaudy Camp Follower, The.
Bhartrihari.   Bearing the lustre of a full moon.
Brooks, G.   Song in the Front Yard, A.
Brown, L.   After Sappho.
D'Aguiar, F.   Airy Hall Icongraphy.
Donne.   Thou hast made me, and shall thy
   work[e] decay?
Goethe.   Death of a Fly.
Hall, D.   Small Fig Tree, A.
Herbert, G.   Quip, The.
   Sin (1).
Herbert, Z.   Mr. Cogito Tells about the
   Temptation of Spinoza.
Holmes, O.   Living Temple, The.
Hughes, T.   Theology.
Juana Inés de la Cruz.   In Containing a Thought
   Satisfied with Chaste Love.
Komunyakaa, Y.   Work.
Kshetrayya.   Wife to a Friend, A.
MacLeish.   What the Serpent Said to Adam.
Mapanje.   We Wondered about the Mellow
   Peaches.
Marvell.   Dialogue Between The Resolved Soul
   and Created Pleasure, A.
Milosz, C.   Matthew 4:1–11; Then Jesus was led
   up by the spirit.
Milton.   As when of old some orator renowned.
   Tempter Disarmed, The.
   To whom thus also th' Angel last repli'd.
Morgan, Elin Llwyd.   Contemporary Jezebel,
   The.
Nasrin.   Eve Oh Eve.
Pak Sŏwôn.   To the Man Holding a Sickle.
Ransom, J.   Tall Girl, The.
Rossetti, C.   Goblin Market.
   World, The.
Rossetti, D.   90: Retro me, Sathana!
Service.   Woman and the Angel, The.
Shakespeare, W.   Sonnet 144: "Two loves I have
   of comfort and despair [or dispaire]."
Spenser, E.   Bower of Bliss, The.
Tsvetayeva [or Tsvetaeva].   Fatal Volume, The.

Tu Fu [or Du Fu].   Singing Girls (Written in
   Jest).
Unknown.   On to Glory.
   Wait, Mr. Mackright.
Verlaine.   Beauty of women, their weakness,
   those pale hands.
   Parsifal.
Wagoner, D.   Dead Letter From Out of Town.
Weigl.   Temptation.
Wodehouse.   It's a Hard, Hard World for a Man.
Young, C.   In the Wilderness.
Ten Commandments
Clough.   Latest Decalogue, The.
Rosenberg, I.   Jew, The.
Taylor, J.   10 Commandments, are the Law
   Divine.
Watts, I.   Law Given at Sinai, The.
Tennessee (state)
Bolton, J.   Parthenon at Nashville, The.
Davidson, D.   Descending Chestnut Ridge.
Gordon, M.   Chattanooga Choo-Choo.
Melville, H.   Shiloh (A Requiem).
Stevens, W.   Anecdote of the Jar.
Walton, A.   McDonald's, Scottsboro, April,
   1997.
Wright, J.   Homecoming Singer, The.
Tennis
Avison.   Tennis.
Cherry, K.   On Watching a Young Man Play
   Tennis.
Drieu la Rochelle.   Tennis.
Gilmore, B.   Coming to the Net (for Arthur
   Ashe).
Gunn, T.   For the Late R. F.
Heath-Stubbs.   Watching Tennis.
Higgins, F.   Tennis in the City.
Hoagland, T.   Change, The.
James, C.   Bring Me the Sweat of Gabriela
   Sabatini.
Kinnell.   On the Tennis Court at Night.
Lux.   Midnight Tennis Match, The.
Stéfan, Jude.   Emma Zola at Wimbledon Let's
   Say.
Volkman.   Pregnant Lady Playing Tennis, The.
Tennyson, Alfred Tennyson, 1st Baron
Andrews, T.   Cinema Vérité: The Death of
   Alfred, Lord Tennyson.
Bullett, G.   Footnote to Tennyson.
Heard, J.   Tennyson's Poems.
Hecht, A.   Still Life.
Layton.   Black Huntsmen, The.
Parker, D.   Alfred Lord Tennyson.
Tents
Dos Passos.   Crimson Tent.
Frost, R.   Silken Tent, The.
Kumin, M.   Despair.
Termites
Jackson, M. L.   Pest.
Nash, O.   Termite, The.
Unknown.   2 Termite Skyscrapers.
Terns
Eberhart, R.   Seals, Terns, Time.
Terror
Akhmatova, A.   Introduction.
   Requiem: "No foreign sky protected me."
   Requiem: "No, not under the vault of alien
   skies."
Beausoleil, B.   This Gate.
Galanskov.   I am in pain.
Gerov, Alexander.   Urban Tree.
González, A.   Without Warning.
Ingalls, J.   Apprehension.
   Vision of St. Michael and St. John, The.
Kaufman, B.   Terror Is More Certain, A.
Kinnell.   How Many Nights.
Lowell, R.   Fall 1961.
Musgrave.   Hidden Meaning.
Rago.   4. Terror and Love as Fugitives.
Rattray, D.   They Don't Have to Have That
   Look.
Ratushinskaya [or Ratushinskaia].   Try to Cover
   Your Shivering Shoulders.
Rolfe, E.   About Eyes.
Sachs, N.   Someone.
Serge.   Dialectic.

Trinidad.   Shower Scene in *Psycho*, The.
Unknown.   Introduction: History and Praise of
   the Danes; Account of Grendel's Attacks on
   Heorot.
Vazirani, R.   Lullaby: "I would not sing you to
   sleep."
Yeats.   Mother of God, The.
Terrorism and Terrorists
Ali, A.   Land.
Amichai, Y.   Diameter of the Bomb, The.
Berrigan, A.   Drugged and Hooded into a Prose
   Poem.
Brook, D.   Poem Wrapped Around Quotation
   from Samantha Power.
Carruth, H.   Essay on Death.
Dunn, S.   To a Terrorist.
Esteves.   For Lolita Lebron.
Fischer, N.   Violence of Oneness, The.
Heaney, S.   Two Lorries.
Hoagland, E.   How Could All That Have
   Happened Here?
Ishikawa Takuboku.   Spoonful of Cocoa, A.
Jarnot, L.   My Terrorist Notebook.
Jones, H.   Caught, April 2002—A Prayer for
   Peace.
Katz, E.   Weather Seems Different, The.
Kaufman, S.   After.
Lehman.   World Trade Center, The.
Mahon.   Afterlives.
McClatchy.   Jihad.
Merrill, J.   Casual Wear.
Michelson, P.   Enduring Witness, the Mosques
   of Kattankudi.
Mohammad, K. Silem.   Mars Needs Terrorists.
Ostriker.   Window, at the Moment of Flame,
   The.
Someck, R.   Transparent.
Stock, N.   What I Said.
Stratanovsky.   Terrorist, The.
Szymborska, W.   One Twenty Pub, The.
   Terrorist, He Watches, The.
   Terrorist Is Watching, A.
Wheatley, D.   Gasmask, The.
Wieseltier, M.   Military Call-up.
Yusuf, S.   Trees of Ithaca, The.
Texas (state)
Acosta.   Apparition (ca. 1896).
   Fragile soy.
Baker, K.   Austin.
   Nacogdoches Speaks.
Barney, W.   Long Gone to Texas.
Behlen, Charles.   My Grandfather's Hammer.
Benevento, Joe.   Yankees in East Texas.
Blanchard, Mary Loving.   Bloodlines.
   East Texas Blues.
Bonazzi, Robert.   Changing Borders.
   Houston's Adolescence.
Burlingame.   Late Winter in West Texas.
Bynner.   Defeat.
Cairns, Scott.   In the General Area of North
   Texas.
Catacalos.   Homesteaders.
   Katakalos.
Christensen, Paul.   Prolog.
Cody, James.   Heart of Texas, The.
Colquitt.   Duet.
   Poetry and Post, Texas.
Crouch, A. L.   Mirabeau B. Lamar.
Crowell, G.   Summer Nights in Texas.
   Texas Autumn.
Davis, W.   Overnight Winder: Texas.
   Texas: Sesquicentennial.
Desprez.   Lasca.
Ferlinghetti, L.   Buddha in the Woodpile, A.
Fink, Robert A.   Abilene, TX: We Pull Out For
   New England.
   Atmosphere for Poetry in Abilene, The.
   Aunt May.
Foreman, Paul.   Pecans.
Givens, Bettye Hammer.   Lonesome Texas.
   West Texas.
Gonzalez, R.   Prayer to the Boys of San
   Antonio.
Hill, C.   Little Towns of Texas, The.
Houston, Margaret Bell.   Old Oak Speaks, The.
   Song from the Traffic.

Houston, Sam. Texian Call to Arms.
Huffstickler. October 31, 1981.
Hummer, T. Plate Glass.
Johnson, R. Reverse Engineering.
Kimbrell, J. Slow Night on Texas Street, A.
Lowery, Janet. Texas Splendor.
Lynch, Peggy Zuleika. True Texan, A.
MacDonald, C. Kilgore Rangerette Whose Life
 Was Ruined, The.
Mares, E. Canyon, Texas Sestina.
Mazur. Bluebonnets.
McDonald, W. After the Rains of Saigon ("I put
 back the rifle on a steel rack.").
 All the Old Songs.
McMurtry, Larry. For Erwin Smith, Cowboy
 Photographer.
Miller, V. Whitewash of Houston.
Milligan, Bryce. Copano, 1834.
 Trusting steel.
Murphy, Jack E. I Dreamt of Lasca.
Nance. Cattle.
 State Song.
Newton, Violette. Texas Poetry.
Nye, N. Thinking About Cows at Ten O'Clock
 in the Morning, Abilene.
O'Daniel, Wilbert Lee. Beautiful Texas.
O'Dwyer, Caley. Texas.
Oliphant. Dallas.
Reposa, Carol Coffee. Dawn in El Paso.
 Hempstead, 1923.
Robertson, Lexie Dean. Aunt Gilly.
 Memorabilia.
 Texas Memoranda.
Rogers, D. Customs of the Country.
 Near the Rio Grand.
 Some Nights I Love Everybody in Texas.
Ruffin. Storm Cellar, The.
Russell, David Riley. State Fair.
Sáenz. Benjamín.
Sale, Richard. Stilts and Other Vehicles.
Sampley. South Rim: Big Bend National Park.
Shuford. Horse in My Yard, The.
Smith, James Gregory. Antonio López and
 Emily.
Spragins, Anna Word. Farewell to Texas.
Stodghill, Pat. August 1, 1966.
 Traitor.
Stokes, G. Blue Texarkana.
Tafolla. San Antonio.
 This River Here.
Taylor, C. Poem to Ma Ferguson.
Thomas, Larry D. Red Raging Waters, The.
Thomas, Lorenzo. Liquid City.
Turner, F. Early Warning.
Unknown. Corrido of "Gregorio Cortez".
 Devil in Texas, The.
 Midnight Special.
 Texas Corrido.
 Yellow Rose of Texas, The.
Villanueva, T. Haciendo Apenas la Recolección.
Ward, William Allen. Texas.
Willerton, Chris. Our Speaker This Morning.
 Winter at the Intersection.
Williams, W. Desert Music, The.
Wood, S. Four Roses.
Wright, C. Hardin County.
Yates, D. Sex.

Thackeray, William Makepeace
Andrews, T. Cinema Vérité: William
 Makepeace Thackeray Follows His Bliss.

Thailand
Triplett, P. Story for the Mother Tongue.

Thames (river), England
Blake, W. London: "I wander through [*or* thro']
 each chartered [*or* charter'd] street."
Denham. Here should my wonder dwell, and
 here my praise.
 Thames from Cooper's Hill, The.
Herrick. His Tears to Thamesis [*or* Thamasis].
Sidney. Sonnet 103: "O happy Thames, that
 didst my Stella bear."
Wilde, O. Symphony in Yellow.

Thankfulness
Aizenberg, M. Who of those who step into the
 stream.
Ap Hywel, Elin. Blue.

Burns, R. Grace at Kirkudbright.
Buson. Rocks rising from the rushing water.
Cairns, Scott. Imperative.
Carver, R. Late Fragment.
Durcan. Difficulty That Is Marriage, The.
Elfyn, Menna. Some Kind of Thanks.
Elvey, G. Come, Ye Thankful People, Come.
Ezekiel. Night of the Scorpion.
Florit, E. Present Evening, The.
Greenlaw, L. Shape of Things, The.
Gunn, T. Lines for a Book.
Hayden, R. Those Winter Sundays.
Hung Hung. Hymn to Hualien, A.
Komunyakaa, Y. Thanks.
Levertov. Midnight Gladness.
Lummis, Suzanne. Why Life Is Worth Living.
Lux. Poem in Thanks.
Marvell. Bermudas.
Mistral, G. My Mother.
Parra, V. Here's to Life.
 I Thank Life for So Many Gifts.
Prado, A. Grace.
Rein. Monastery.
Shakespeare, W. Sonnet 37: "As a decrepit
 father takes delight."
Unknown. Feng-nian: Good Year.
Waniek. Dusting.
Zagajewski. Try to Praise the Mutilated World.
See also **Gratitude**

Thanksgiving
Alford, H. Harvest Home.
Cummings, E. E. I Thank You God.
Elvey, G. Come, Ye Thankful People, Come.
Emerson, R. Grace.
Espada. Thanksgiving.
Herrick. Grace for a Child.
 Thanksgiving to God for His House, A.
Lassaw-Paljor, Denise. For a Moose.
Livingston, M. First Thanksgiving.
Moorer. Thanksgiving.
Philpot, T. Thanksgiving.
Procter, A. Thankfulness.
Snyder, G. Prayer for the Great Family.
Turner, N. First Thanksgiving of All.
Unknown. Thanksgivings, The.
 Truly now.

Thanksgiving Day
Child, L. Thanksgiving Day.
Dunbar, P. Signs of the Times.
Fisher, A. Thanksgiving Dinner.
Hammond, M. Thanksgiving.
Johnson, M. Day befo' Thanksgibin', De.
 Story of Lovers Leap, The.
Prelutsky. First Thanksgiving, The.

Thatcher, Margaret
Kazantzis. Thatcher, A.
Wardman, G. Revisionism.

Thaw and Thawing
Birnbaum, M. By the River.
Dove, R. Rusks.
Ransford, Tessa. First Thaw.
Wrigley, R. Ashtray in the Snow.

Theater and Theaters
Aragon. Big Spectacular Play.
Blunden. Concert Party: Busseboom.
Brecht, B. Friends, The.
Calpurnius Siculus. Eclogue 7.
Campert. Theatre.
 Theatre, The.
Cassells. From the Theater of Wine.
Chapman, G. Muses that fame's loose feathers
 beautify.
Cook, E. To Charlotte Cushman.
Coward. Why Must the Show Go On?
Dietz, H. That's Entertainment.
Donnelly, T. Twenty-seven Props for a
 Production of *Eine Lebenszeit.*
Dryden, J. Mac Flecknoe [or, A Satire upon the
 True-Blue Protestant Poet T. S.].
Dubin, A. Dames.
Ellis, T. Slow Fade to Black.
Fathy, S. For Heiner Muller: Poem 2.
Hecht, A. Peripeteia.
Herbert, Z. What I Saw.
Hochman. Cannon Hill.

Holub. Special Performance for Statues, A.
Hughes, L. Note on Commercial Theatre.
Jackson, R. Tee.
Johnson, S. Prologue Spoken by Mr[.] Garrick
 at the Opening of the Theatre in Drury Lane,
 1747.
Jonson, B. Ode to Himself, An ("Where dost
 [*or,* do'st] thou careless[e] lie.").
 To the Memory of My Beloved, the Author Mr
 [*or* Master] William Shakespeare: And What
 He Hath Left Us.
Kollar. Sunday Matinee.
Lumsden, R. Vanishing.
Marinetti. Futurism Wants to Transform the
 Variety Theater into a Theater of Amazement,
 Record-setting, and Body-madness.
Masters, E. Flossie Cabanis.
Muldoon, P. On.
Nossis. When you've laughed out loud and said
 a friendly.
O'Hara, F. Ave Maria.
Ritsos. One Skit, Then Another.
Roeske, P. In the Theatre.
Rothenberg, J. Realtheater Piece Two.
Sassoon, S. Blighters.
Scalise, G. Dora Markus and Her Actors.
Smith, J. Playhouse Musings.
Snyder, G. Feathered Robe, The.
Sondheim. Comedy Tonight.
Spenser, E. Sonnet 54: "Of this world's Theatre
 in which we stay."
Stern, G. Adler.
Stevens, W. Of Modern Poetry.
Strong, L. Old Woman, Outside the Abbey
 Theater, An.
Szymborska, W. Theater Impressions.
Taylor, J. As Gold is better that's in fire tride.
Trinidad. As one young guy screwed another
 young guy.
Tu Shan-fu. Tune: "Shua Hai-erh" Country
 Cousin at the Theater.
Untermeyer, L. End of the Comedy.
Volach, Y. I Have a Stage in My Head.
Weaver, A. Imitation of Life.
Wotton, S. De Morte.
Yeats. Fascination of What's Difficult, The.
See also **Show Business**

Theft
Alexie. I Would Steal Horses.
Chiasson, D. Stealing from Your Mother.
Duffy, C. Stealing.
Espada. Moon Shatters on Alabama Avenue,
 The.
Ginsberg, A. Thief Stole This Poem, A.
Guevara, M. Magic Carpet, The.
Jarman, M. Unholy Sonnet ("This boy listening
 eagerly to his friend.").
Ortiz. At the Salvation Army.
Stoddart, G. Night We Stole a Full-Length
 Mirror, The.
Unknown. Stealing of Apollo's Cattle, The.
 Village Burglar, The.
Volkman. Theft.
See also **Crime and Criminals; Thieves**

Theocritus
Wilde, O. Theocritus: A Villanelle.

Theology
Dickinson, E. He preached upon "Breadth" till
 it argued him narrow.
Hardy, T. Respectable Burgher, The.
Hughes, T. Crow's Theology.
Newman, R. Theology.
Wordsworth, W. World Is Too Much with Us,
 The.

Theresa, Saint, of Avila
Crashaw. Flaming Heart, The.
 Hymn to the Name and Hono[u]r of the
 Admirable Saint[e] Teresa, A.
 Love, thou art absolute sole lord.
 Upon the Book and Picture of the Seraphical
 Saint Teresa.
Wilbur, R. Teresa.

Thermopylae, Battle of (480 B.C.)
Simonides. For the Spartan Dead at
 Thermopylai (480 B.C.).

Greek Dead at Thermopylae, The.
On the Spartan Dead at Thermopylae.

Theseus
Muir, E.   Labyrinth, The.
Propertius.   Ariadne Lay, Theseus' Ship Sailing
    Away.
Reibetanz, J.   Head and Torso of the Minotaur.
See also **Minotaur**

Thieves
Al-Bayati, A.   Who Owns the Homeland?
Barnfield [*or* Barnefield].   Sporting at fancie,
    setting light by love.
Baxter, J.   I am dying now because I do not die.
    Thief and Samaritan.
    Wild Bees.
Berkson, B.   Bicycle Thief, The.
Bhattācārya, M.   You can't catch the thief,
    Mind.
Buson.   Such a moon.
Chaucer.   Rape of Chanticleer, The.
Daniels, J.   Hoagie Scam, The.
Drayton.   If he, from heaven that filched the
    living fire.
Fouad, I.   Truth: I Have Five Fingers on Each
    Hand!
Gander, F.   Mission Thief.
Guignard, L.   Homing In.
Gunn, T.   Idea of Trust, The.
Harington [*or* Harrington].   Of honest Theft. To
    my good friend Master Samuel Daniel.
Hicok.   Bond, The.
Horace.   Satire 1.8: "Once I was wood from a
    worthless old fig tree."
Issa.   They don't notice.
Jacobs, B.   Lost.
Kennedy, X.   Curse on a Thief, A.
Kunitz, S.   Thief, The.
Kuzmin.   Were I a general of olden times.
Lover.   Whistlin' Thief, The.
McGough, R.   Kleptomaniac, The.
Melville, H.   By the Jordan.
Mitchell, S.   Good Samaritan et Al, The.
Mitford.   To Tray—Stolen.
Prunty.   Note of Thanks, A.
Reznikoff.   Testimony: The United States
    (1901–1910) Recitative/The South.
Ridge, J.   Stolen White Girl, The.
Rothenberg, J.   Structural Study of Myth, The.
Rumi.   Thief in the Night, A.
Senryū, K.   Off to work.
Tan Taigi.   In the melon-patch / Thief, fox.
Taylor, H.   Hughesville Scythe, The.
Trigilio.   Five Verses for Shariputra Mugged
    Outside His Building.
Unknown.   Dick o' the Cow.
    Rookhope Ryde.
    Run, Nigger, Run!
    What business, this? What reason should we
    give.
Very.   Indian's Retort, The.
Yakusai, Layman.   Deafening peal, A.
See also **Crime and Criminals, Theft**

Thinness
Basho.   Girl cat / So thin.
    She cat, The.
Foley, Jack.   Skeleton's Defense of Carnality,
    The.
Han-shan Te-ch'ing.   Spring has come again the
    snow has finally stopped.
Issa.   Fleas in my hut.
    This stupid world.
Lorde.   Song for a Thin Sister.
Lover.   I'm Not Myself at All!
Nash, O.   Curl Up and Diet.
Shiseki.   My old thighs / How thin.

Thirst
Alcaeus [*or* Alkaios].   Wet your lungs with
    wine—the dogstar rises.
Arapaho Oral Tradition.   Father, have pity on
    me.
Baqi.   Fountain of my spirit thirsts for your
    ruby.
Busceti, G.   Suddenly on a day in July.
Cameron, N.   Green, Green Is El Aghir.
Castro, R.   Spring Does Not Flow Now, The.

Cook, E.   Becalmed in the Tropics.
Dickinson, E.   Let me not thirst with this Hock
    at my Lip.
Espada.   Water, White Cotton, and the Rich
    Man.
Greppi, C.   Rain of hollow malice, A.
Kim Chiha.   In Burning Thirst.
Kinzie.   Orchard dying, The.
Lili'u-o-ka-lani.   Lawn Sprinkler, The.
Lux.   Thirst of Turtles, The.
Machado Ruiz.   Good Thing Is, We Know, The.
    It is good knowing that glasses.
Mahadevi.   When I am hungry.
Meleager.   Hot day. Dying of thirst. Slake
    myself.
Muske, C.   Coming Over Coldwater.
Ronsard.   By looking too long on your perfect
    face.
Rumi.   We can't help being thirsty.
Vicuña.   Thirst.
Wilbur, R.   Ballade for the Duke of Orléans.
Wunderlich, M.   Thirst.
Yüan Chěn.   Pitcher, The.
See also **Hunger**

Thistles
Castro, R.   I in My Bed of Thistles.
Cunningham, A.   Thistle's Grown aboon the
    Rose, The.
Hughes, T.   Thistles.
MacDiarmid, H.   Language that but sparely
    floo'ers, The.
Scheele.   Thistle.
Shinkichi Takahashi.   Thistles.

Thomas, Dylan
Garlick, R.   Dylan Thomas at Tenby.
Jones, T.   Dylan.
Kingston, M.   Saturday April 8 Swansea, where
    Dylan Thomas was born on October 27th, the
    same day I was born.
Olin.   Larry Kept Saying Primo Levi Was an
    Accident.
Watkins, V.   Cwmrhydyceirw Elegiacs.

Thomas, Edward ("Edward Eastaway")
Gibson, W.   Golden Room, The.
Lewis, A.   All Day It Has Rained.
    To Edward Thomas.

Thomas the Rhymer (Thomas of Erceldoune)
Unknown.   Thomas the Rhymer.
    Thomas the Rhymer [*or* Rimer].

Thor
Smith, D.   Blowfish and Mudtoad.

Thoreau, Henry David
Clausen.   White in the Woods.
Liu, T.   Thoreau.
Lowell, J.   Channing and Thoreau.
McClure, M.   Thoreau's Eyes: Two Poems for
    Kazuaki Tanahashi.
Oliver, M.   Going to Walden.
Ray, H.   Thought at Walden, A.

Thought
Agustini.   Ineffable, The.
Aiken, C.   Prelude LVII: "One star fell and
    another as we walked."
Allen, D.   Time to Hear Ourselves Think.
Ammons.   Corsons Inlet.
Arnold, M.   Below the Surface-Stream.
Baraka, I.   Look for You Yesterday, Here You
    Come Today.
Beckman, J.   Don't be mad.
Bell, M.   Pulsations.
Bergman, A.   Windmills of Your Mind, The.
Bergman, M.   Windmills of Your Mind, The.
Bernes, J.   Outside You Cannot Breathe.
Berrigan, A.   Four Minute History of Getting It
    Together in Order to Be Fabulous, Briefly, A.
    Looking Up My Balance.
Berrigan, J.   Other Contexts.
Berssenbrugge.   Texas.
Blackwell, Holley.   SEEing yu.
Blake, W.   Little Fly.
Bogan, L.   Henceforth, from the Mind.
Brehm, J.   When My Car Broke Down.
Brownstein.   Pounds and Ounces.
Budbill.   This Shining Moment in the Now.
Byron, G.   If Sometimes in the Haunts of Men.

Carranza, E.   Azure Because of You.
Ch'ôn Yanghûi.   Millet Field in My Mind.
Codrescu.   Against Meaning.
Coleman, W.   ISM, The.
Coleridge, S.   Constancy to an Ideal Object.
Coolidge, C.   Crack, The.
    What is Thought but Won't Hold Still.
Coulette.   Night Thoughts: "Your kind of night,
    David, your kind of night."
Crabbe, G.   Three weeks had past, and Richard
    rambles now.
Creeley.   I Keep to Myself Such Measures.
    Long road of it all, The.
Daichi.   Thoughts arise endlessly.
Dana, R.   Chanting Cherubs, The [A Group by
    Greenough].
Davie, D.   Fountain, The.
    Gardens No Emblems.
Davies, S.   Cosmus hath more discoursing in his
    head.
De Angelis.   Towards the Mind.
Dickinson, E.   I felt a Cleaving in my Mind.
    One need not be a Chamber—to be Haunted.
DiPalma.   Rumor's Rooster.
Dragomoschenko.   Instructing Clarity in a
    Confusion.
Drayton.   To the Reader of These Sonnets.
Fermini, I.   First unexpected pain is beautiful,
    The.
Frost, R.   All Revelation.
    Bond and Free.
Gensei.   Distant View from a Grass Hill.
Gerov, Alexander.   Dandelion.
Ginsberg, A.   Moon in the dewdrop is the real
    moon, The.
Giussani, S.   Abel and Abel.
    Clothes Without the Monk, The.
Graham, J.   Exit Wound.
    Thinking.
Griffiths, B.   Fragment 11: "My latest thought
    brick for an abundant supply for home and
    clothes."
Gunn, T.   Lines for a Book.
Hall, D.   Poem, The: "It discovers by night."
Han Yü.   Leaves fall turning turning to the
    ground.
Han-shan Te-ch'ing.   Hundred thousand worlds
    are flowers in the sky, A.
Heine, H.   Night Thoughts.
Herford.   Smile of the Walrus, The.
Hernández Cruz.   Essay on William Carlos
    Williams, An.
Hewitt, J.   Because I Paced My Thought.
    I Write For.
Hierro, José.   Boy with the Empty Cage, The.
Holan.   Between.
Howard, R.   Stanzas in Bloomsbury.
"Hsiung Hung.".   Thinking of Someone.
Hughes, L.   Blues at Dawn.
Hughes, T.   Thought-Fox, The.
Hunt, L.   Nile, The.
Ibáñez, S.   You, for My Meditation.
Jackson, L.   Footfalling.
    Opening of Eyes.
Jiménez, J.   Black Thought, A.
    Who Knows What Is Going On.
    Yes, If I Could Only Smash.
Jonas, S.   Ear Injured by Hearing Things, An.
Juarroz.   Somewhere There's a Man.
Judson, J.   Whitman Again.
Kerouac.   211th Chorus.
Kloos, W.   Sonnet.
Lawrence, D. H.   Red Geranium and Godly
    Mignonette.
    Thought.
Lazarus, E.   Echoes.
Leopardi.   Antistrophe.
Lovelace, R.   Song: "Strive not, vain Lover, to
    be fine."
Lu Yu.   Night Thoughts.
Luzi.   Reflective life separates us from the
    sources of reflection.
MacDiarmid, H.   At My Father's Grave.
    Light and Shadow.
Mackey, N.   Shower of Secret Things, The.
Magrelli.   There are words that coast alongside

thought.
  Wood of my thoughts is on fire, The.
Majorino. Doing.
Manzan. One minute of sitting, one inch of
  Buddha.
Marcus, B. Justice.
Mathews, H. Histoire.
McNiece, R. Skinny-Dipping the Ganges.
Menicanti. What's Left of You.
Merrill, J. Dedication: "Hans, there are
  moments when the whole mind."
Moore, M. Mind Is an Enchanting Thing, The.
Mörling, M. In a Motel Room at Dawn.
Muldoon, P. Something Else.
Naong. Lonely Hermitage.
No Hyegyông. Miscellaneous Bouquet.
Noble, R. Very Thought of You, The.
North, C. Postcard Element in Winter, The.
O'Hara, F. Poem: "And tomorrow morning at 8
  o'clock in Springfield, Massachusetts."
Olson, C. Moon Is the Number 18, The.
Palmer, M. Thought, The.
  Voice and Address.
Ponsot. A La Une.
Porter, C. I Concentrate on You.
Qasmi. Thought.
Rankine. Short Narrative of Breasts and Wombs
  in Service of Plot Entitled, A.
Rexroth, K. You ask me what I thought about.
Reyes, A. Scarcely.
Rich, A. Ghost of a Chance.
Rodefer. My mind to me mangles iron. An error
  is mirror to the truth.
Rosselli. Actions in my brain: these verbs,
  whose celerity.
  Worthless as was her itinerary to fame.
  You might as well think one thing or another.
Ryan, G. Penserosa, La.
Safie, D. Meditation by the Xerox Machine.
Salzman, E. Sexual Love.
Sandburg, C. Bundles.
  Murmurings in a Field Hospital.
Sanguineti. I defended Genet on the subject of
  terror in London.
  Like a disk, a trembling coin spinning on its
  own diameter.
Shaughnessy, B. Your Name on It.
Sidney. My Sheep Are Thoughts.
Simic. Night Picnic.
  Something, The.
Smith, S. After-Thought, The.
  White Thought, The.
Stevens, W. Homunculus et La Belle Etoile.
  Of Mere Being.
Swinburne. Free Thought.
Toomer. People.
Tu Fu [or Du Fu]. Night Thoughts While
  Travelling ("Light breeze rustles the reeds,
  A.").
Tuckerman, F. Let me give something!—though
  my spring be done.
  Nor strange it is, to us who walk in bonds.
Unknown. On the Flightiness of Thought.
Venkatarao, K. You on My Mind.
Viray, M. Patio.
Vitale, M. Joy Island.
Vroman. Thin Wire.
Waldrop, K. Will to Will.
Ward, D. Shakeout.
Wells, C. Problem, A.
Whalen, P. End of the line, The.
Whitman, W. Aboard at a Ship's Helm.
  By the Bivouac's Fitful Flame.
Wilbur, R. Mind.
  Praise in Summer.
Williams, W. There is neither beginning nor end
  to the imagination.
  To the Shade of Po Chü-I.
Wordsworth, W. Those [or These] words were
  uttered as in [or in a] pensive mood.
Wright, C. Storm.
Yeats. Meru.
Zaid. Cloister.
Zukofsky, L. It's hard to see but think of a sea.

See also **Intellect and Intellectuals; Reason**

Three Mile Island, Pennsylvania
Metras, G. Utilities Advertisement in the Wake
  of Three Mile Island.
Williams, C. K. Tar.

Thrushes
Allen, F. Glenasmole.
Bunting. Thrush in the syringa sings, A.
Crapsey. To a Hermit Thrush.
Dowden, E. Singer, The.
Frost, R. Come In.
Hardy, T. Darkling Thrush, The.
  Reminder, The.
Hughes, T. Thrushes.
Mew. I so liked Spring last year.
Meynell, A. Thrush before Dawn, A.
Penrose, V. At My Windows.
Rossetti, C. Last Rites.
Watson, R. Die Zauberflöte.
Whitman-Raymond, Lee Miriam. Quickening.

Thumbs
Bergman, M. Sore Thumb.

Thunder
Ammons. Standing Light Up.
Bell, M. Book of the Dead Man (#13), The.
Chippewa Oral Tradition. Approach of the
  Storm, The.
Clare, J. Thunder mutters louder and more loud,
  The.
Dibdin, T. Origins of Naval Artillery.
Dickinson, E. Farthest Thunder that I heard,
  The.
Eady. My Mother is a God Fearing Woman.
Hume, C. Dialogue of Thunder.
Johnson, M. F. Thunder Storm.
Lawrence, D. H. Trees in the Garden.
Lowry, M. Volcano is Dark, The.
Macdonald, G. Baby-Sermon, A.
McAuley, J. One Tuesday in Summer.
Moss, H. Summer Thunder, The.
Munom-Ekai. Thunderbolt—eyes wide, A.
Muso Soseki. Don't ask suspiciously.
Okigbo. Come Thunder.
  Thunder Can Break.
Scott, J. Hatching Thunder.
Stevenson, R. Last night we had a thunderstorm
  in style.
Tan Taigi. Thunder / Voices of drowned.
Tennyson, A. Kraken, The.
Toomer. Storm Ending.
Unknown. Dream Song.
  First Song of the Thunder.
  Thunder floats.
  Twelfth Song of the Thunder.
  Winter's thunder.
Wright, C. Until words turn to moss.

Tiananmen Massacre (1989)
Fenton, J. Tiananmen.
Martinez, D. Hysteria.
Rylander, E. Midnight Rocker, Tiananmen
  Square, May 27, 1989.

Tiber River
Mayröcker. Ostia Will Receive You.

Tibet
Alexander, W. Let us recall the illusion.
Donegan, P. Check Up.
Paljor, N. Wish of my Amala, The.

Tides
Baldwin, A. Moons . . . tides.
Basho. Autumn moon / Tide foams.
  Autumnal full moon.
Bevington, L. With the Tide: A Cry of
  Weakness.
Buson. Spring sea rising, The.
Carman, B. Low Tide on Grand Pré.
Cheng Hsieh. Song of Surfing on the Bore.
Clampitt. Beach Glass.
Emerson, J. Apophatic.
Farjeon, E. Tide in the River, The.
Hill, G. Wreaths.
Ingelow. High Tide on the Coast of
  Lincolnshire, 1571, The.
Jackson, H. Tides.
Kingston, M. Saturday April 8 Swansea, where
  Dylan Thomas was born on October 27th, the
  same day I was born.

Knight, S. Surf Motel, The.
Longfellow, H. Tide Rises, the Tide Falls, The.
Mew. Sea Love.
Nash, O. Beginner's Guide to the Ocean, A.
Nims, J. Tide Turning.
Slessor. Five Bells.
Spenser, E. Sonnet 75: "One day I wrote her
  name upon the strand."
Szporluk. Duressor.
Takai Kito. Seaweed / Between rocks—.
Unknown. Wag ballock wag.

Tigers
Belloc. Tiger, The.
Blake, W. Tyger, The.
Borges. Dreamtigers.
  Other Tiger, The.
  Other Tiger, The.
Bunting. Fearful Symmetry.
Campo, C. Ah that the Tiger.
Deltoro, A. Eggs Laid by a Tiger.
  Huevos puestos por un tigre.
Goodison. On Becoming a Tiger.
Greppi, C. Boy's Afraid of the Live Tiger, The.
Hernández Cruz. Side 22.
Jackson, L. Tiger, The.
Livingstone, D. Traffic interlude: Descent from
  the Tower.
López Colomé, P. Cachorros, Los.
  Cubs, The.
Menicanti. Felines.
Mokusen. On Climbing the Mountain Where
  Buddha Trained.
Monkhouse. There Was a Young Lady of Niger.
Muso Soseki. Tiger Valley.
O'Hara, F. Chez Jane.
Oppen. Myth of the Blaze.
Raab, E. Folk Tune.
Rich, A. Aunt Jennifer's Tigers.
Sackville-West. Greater Cats, The.
Shinkichi Takahashi. Four Divine Animals.
Thê Lü'. Green Nostalgia.
Thomas, R. S. White Tiger, The.
Turner, W. India.
Unknown. There was a young lady of Riga.
Villa. Inviting a Tiger for the Weekend.
Wang Ch'ang-ling. Song by the Walls.
Wilkinson, A. Tigers Know from Birth.
Wojahn. Rajah in Babylon.

Tightropes and Tightrope Walkers
Dubie. Buffalo Clouds over the Maestro Hoon.
See also **Acrobatics and Acrobats**

Till, Emmett
Brooks, G. Last Quatrain of the Ballad of
  Emmett Till, The.
Emanuel, J. Emmett Till.
Jones, I. Echoes of the Murder of Emmett Till.
Lorde. Afterimages.
Nelson, M. Wreath for Emmett Till, A.

Time
Achterberg. Across the Jarbok.
Ackland. Clock Plods On, The.
Adams, J. To the Sun-Dial.
Adamson, H. Time on My Hands.
Agoos, J. To Atlas in the Attic.
Aiken, C. North Infinity Street.
  Prelude LVI: "Rimbaud and Verlaine, precious
  pair of poets."
Alberti. Angels of the Ruins, The.
Allen, A. Love and the Years.
Allen, E. Rock Me to Sleep[, Mother].
Allen, F. Modern Times.
  Visitant, The.
Allen, S. Moment Please, A.
Amichai, Y. Man in His Life, A.
Anderson, D. Executive Geochrone.
Anwar, C. Tuti's Ice Cream.
Apollinaire. Mirabeau Bridge.
  Zone.
Arghezi. Last Hour, The.
Armantrout. Up to Speed.
Armitage, S. Killing Time #2.
Ashbery, J. Soonest Mended.
  Wind thrashes the maple seed-pods, The.
Atwood. Beauharnois (1).
  Dufferin, Simcoe, Grey (4).

Four Small Elegies.
Auden. As I Walked Out One Evening.
 Fish in the Unruffled Lakes.
 If I Could Tell You.
 Jumbled in the Common Box.
Aygi, G. Poppies of This Year.
Baraka, I. Node.
Barba-Jacob. Song of the Fleeting Day.
Basho. Another year gone.
 First snow.
 Old-time pond, from off whose shadowed depth, An.
 Skylark.
 Village without bells, A.
 Year's end / All corners.
 Year's end / Still in straw hat.
Baudelaire. Clock, The.
 Clock, The.
 Get High.
Beaumont, J. Hourglass, The.
Beckett, S. Je suis ce cours de sable qui glisse.
 My way is in the sand flowing.
Bei Dao. Accomplices.
 Rose of Time, The.
Bek, T. If a song flies to me from the garden.
Bell, M. Mystery of Emily Dickinson, The.
Benét, R. et al. So we march into the present.
Benét, S. So we march into the present.
 Song of the Riders.
Bennett, J. In a Rose Garden.
Bentley, N. On Lady A———.
Berger, B. Ballad of the Bright Angel.
Berkson, B. Melting Milk.
Berry, W. Anniversary, An.
 Wheel, The.
Betsugen. All night long I think of life's labyrinth.
Bevington, L. Twilight.
Bible, O.T. To Everything There Is a Season.
Bishop, E. Paris, 7 A.M.
Bodecker. Garden Calendar.
Bogan, L. Come, Break with Time.
Boland, E. Anna Liffey.
Bontemps. To a Young Girl Leaving the Hill Country.
Borges. In Praise of Darkness.
 Labyrinth, The.
 Manuscript Found in a Book of Joseph Conrad.
Borson. Save Us From.
Borthwick, P. Forest.
Bowles, W. Time and Grief.
Bracho, C. Sobre él discurren con suavidad.
 Upon It They Gently Reflect.
Bradstreet, A. Contemplations.
Brass. There Isn't Any Death.
Brodsky, J. Lagoon.
Brontë, E. Tell me, tell me, smiling child.
Brooks, G. Marie Lucille.
Broughton, J. Aglow in Nowhere.
Brown, L. Green Arbor, A.
Bryant, W. Ages, The.
 Fountain, The.
 Rivulet, The.
Buckley, C. Playing for Time.
Buckley, V. Child is Revenant to the Man, The.
Buson. Long, slow days of spring, The.
 Short nap / Waking.
Bynner. Any other time would have done.
Byron, G. So We'll Go No More A-Roving.
 Stanzas for Music ("There's not a joy the world can give like that it takes away.").
Caraion. Ultimate Argument.
Cardenal. Like Empty Beer Cans.
Carrera Andrade. Clock, The.
Carroll, J. Heroin.
Carroll, P. In the Shakespeare Garden at Northwestern University.
Carruth, H. Testament.
Carson, A. Well there are many ways of being held prisoner.
Carver, R. Woman Bathing.
Castillo, S. En el Sol de Mi Barrio.
Castro, R. Hour After Hour, Day After Day.
Cavalli. How pointless this straining.
 I pretend to wait for you to enlarge the minutes.
 Now that the time seems all mine.

Celan. Corona.
 When you lie.
Cendrars. Hammock.
Cernuda. Lover Digresses, The.
Cetina, G. Happy Hours that Hurry Away.
Chan Fang-sheng. Sailing into the South Lake.
Chang K'o-chiu. Tune: "Unbroken".
Ch'en Yü-yi. Tune: "Immortal at the Riverbank".
Chen Zi'ang. Song on Youzhou Terrace.
Cherry, K. Waiting for the End of Time.
Chin. Year Passes in My Morning Teacup, The.
Chitwood, Michael. Hardened Arm, The.
Chŏng Ch'ŏl. Song of Longing.
Clare, J. To an Hour-Glass.
Clarke, G. On Air.
Clementelli. Bend of the gulf.
Colby, T. Captain's Log.
Cole, T. Dial, The.
Coleridge, H. All nature ministers to Hope. The snow.
Coleridge, S. Time, Real and Imaginary.
Collins, B. Nostalgia.
Comden, B. Just in Time.
 Some Other Time.
Cook, E. Song of the Modern Time.
Cope, W. Bloody Men.
Copus, J. Widower.
Cornford, F. Unbeseechable, The.
Cortes. Space Song.
Cranch. December.
 My Old Palette.
 Spirit of the Age, The.
Crane, H. My Grandmother's Love Letters.
Crapsey. Sun-Dial, The.
 Trapped.
Creeley. Again.
 Kitchen.
 Rescue, The.
 River wandering down.
 Time: "How long for the small yellow flowers."
Crompton. Epigram LXVII: Time, the Interpreter.
Cuadra, A. In Brief.
Cuddihy. This Body.
Cummings, E. E. Anyone lived in a pretty how town.
 Hours rise up putting off stars and it is, The.
 How many moments must(amazing each).
 If everything happens that can't be done.
 If(touched by love's own secret)we,like homing.
 Now is a ship / which captain am.
 Ponder, darling, these busted statues.
 Sonnet IV.
 Wherelings whenlings / (daughters of if but offspring of hopefear).
Cunningham, J. Coffee.
 Time heals not: it extends a sorrow's scope.
Daegak Euchon. At Hongbub Temple.
Daichi. Thoughts arise endlessly.
Davidson, M. Thinking the Alps.
Davie, D. Time Passing, Beloved.
Davies, D. At Branwen's Grave.
Davies, G. Time's Muteness.
Davies, W. H. Leisure.
Day Lewis. Poem for an Anniversary.
De Angelis. Every Metaphor.
 July Has Come for the Dead.
de Fierro. If Time Waits.
 Oblivion.
Degenaar. Irish Sheep, The.
Dekker, T. et al. Folly's Song.
Dennis, C. Defining Time.
Desnos. If, like winds.
 Midway.
Dickinson, E. Clock strikes one that just struck two, The.
 Great Streets of silence led away.
 They Say That Time Assuages.
 Too happy Time dissolves itself.
Disch. Convalescing in London.
Dobson, A. Sundial, The.
d'Oettingen. To Il y a.
Donaghy, M. Present, The.
Donne. Anniversary [or Anniversarie], The.
 Computation, The.

Dooley, M. Heat.
Doolittle, H. Antistrophe.
Dragomoschenko. Footnotes.
Dransfield. Visiting Hour (Repatriation Hospital).
Drayton. To My Noble Friend Master William Browne: Of the Evil Time.
Drummond de Andrade. Elegy: "I've won (lost) my day."
Du Bellay. Rome.
Duhig, I. I prayed to the ghost of Carrie.
Dunn, S. Each from Different Heights.
Dupin. At Instants I Thought.
Duran, J. Time Zones.
Eberhart, R. Garden God, The.
Ehret, T. Lost Body.
Elder daughter of Lady Otomo no Sakanoé, t. When we could have met.
Eliot, T. S. Burnt Norton.
 Little Gidding.
Elytis, O. As Endymion.
Emerson, R. Compensation ("Wings of Time are black and white, The.").
 Days.
 Past, The.
 Two Rivers.
Eriksen, Mariane Baggers. I dropped something. I picked it up.
Erlich, S. Garden of Shanah.
Fan Chung-yen. Tune: "Trimming the Silver Lamp".
Farrar, J. Song for a Forgotten Shrine to Pan.
Field. Palimpsest, A.
Finch, A. Reply From His Coy Mistress, A.
Fisher, J. It's February But.
Flecker, J. Stillness.
Florian. First.
Florit, E. Present Evening, The.
Follain. Should the Schoolboy Pull.
Forbes, D. Recension Day.
Francis, R. Coming and Going.
 Mouse Whose Name Is Time, The.
Frost, R. Nothing Gold Can Stay.
Galemire, J. Inventing Fables about the Stone.
Galvin, J. Two Horses and a Dog.
Garcia, R. Brief Entanglements.
Garrett, E. Unguentarium.
Garrett, G. For a Bitter Season.
Gekko-Sojo. How Zenists carry on.
George, F. Charioteer, The.
Gervitz, G. Life is nothing but time.
 She detaches herself from her shadow. She is an old woman and still beautiful.
Ginsberg, A. Caw caw caw crows shriek in the white sun over grave stones.
Gioia. Becoming a Redwood.
Giussani, S. Clothes Without the Monk, The.
 Towards a Beginning.
Gizzi. Fables of Critique.
Glück, L. Aubade: "World was very large, The. Then."
 Magi, The.
 Time: "There was too much, always, then too little."
Góngora y Argote. Deceiver Time.
 Whistling arrow flies less eagerly, The.
Gordon, M. Time on My Hands.
Gould, A. Observed Observer, The.
Graham, J. Exit Wound.
 Philosopher's Stone.
Graham, R. Without Shadow.
Graham, W. Lines on Roger Hilton's Watch.
Graves, R. Counting the Beats.
 Love Story, A.
Green, A. Just in Time.
 Some Other Time.
Greppi, C. Those quiet little feet in the reflected room.
Grünbein, Durs (b. 1962). Bad Luck with the Second Throw.
Gryphius. Not Mine the Years Time Took Away.
Guillevic. I Don't Speak.
Gullar. In the Body.
Gumilyov [or Gumiliov or Gumilev]. Pre-Memory.

Village.
  Was it I making plans / for the summer—and
    for all the summers.
Peacock, T. Love and Age.
Pearse, P. Wayfarer, The.
Peele. His Golden Lock[e]s [Time Hath to
  Silver Turned].
Pellicer, C. Studies.
Peskett. Star and Sea.
Phillips, D. Five.
  From Arena.
Piatt, S. Lesson in a Picture, A.
Pindar. Hyperboreans, The.
Piombino. Frozen Witness, The.
  Time Travel.
Poe. Coliseum, The.
Portal. Watch of Time.
Pound, E. Erat Hora.
  Silet.
Powell, D. A. Always Returning: Holidays and
  Burials. Not Every Week.
Prado, A. Time.
Preil, G. Eternal Present, The.
  From a Late Diary.
Pritchard, N. Cloak, The.
Pulido, A. And regardless / the heat.
  Y sin embargo.
Quarles. I saw him dead; I saw his Body fall.
  On the Life of Man.
Queneau. If You Imagine.
Quevedo y Villegas. Everything Is Swept Away
  by the Brief Year.
Raboni, G. Hospital Interiors.
Radiguet. Handless Clock.
Radnóti. Clouded Sky.
Raine, K. Moment, The.
Ralegh. Authours Epitaph, Made by Himself,
  The.
  Even Such Is Time.
  Nature, That Washed [or Washt] Her Hands in
    Milk[e].
  Nymph's [or Nimphs] Reply to the [Passionate]
    Shepherd [or Sheepheard], The.
Ramke, B. Famous Poems of the Past
  Explained.
Ranaldo, L. Five Weeks.
  Time Presses Me.
Randall, D. His Favourite Seat.
Randell. Tomorrow I shall.
Ransetsu. Traveling / old armor.
Reddy, Srikanth. Corruption.
  Second Circle.
Reed, H. Judging Distances.
Reeves, J. Slowly.
Rexroth, K. Another Spring.
  Wheel Revolves, The.
Reznikoff. Heart and Clock.
  Her work was to count linings.
Riley, J. Summer Seeming.
Risset, Jacqueline. M. S. 1544.
Robinson, E. Clerks, The.
  Three Quatrains.
Rodríguez, C. Petty Time.
Roland Holst. Time, Please.
Rossetti, C. Amen.
  Bride Song.
  Life's Parallels, A.
Rossetti, D. Sea-Limits, The.
Rothman, D. Whistling in January.
Rouweler. Silent Time.
Rukeyser, M. et al. Believe that we bloom upon
  this stalk of time.
Ryan, M. Shape for It, A.
Ryushu Shutaku. Mind set free in the Dharma-
  realm.
Saenz, J. Let your permanency under the
  brilliance of the stars be long.
St. John, D. Grandfather's Cap, My.
Saleh. December Nap.
Salinas, L. My Fifty-Plus Years Celebrate
  Spring.
Salinas, P. Not in Marble Palaces.
Salter. Sunday Skaters.
Sandburg, C. Four Preludes on Playthings of
  the Wind.
  Languages.

Limited.
  People, Yes, The.
  Sunset from Omaha Hotel Window.
Sansom, A. Confinement.
Sarton, M. Now I Become Myself.
Scott, D. Uncle Time.
Scovell. Past Time.
Seneca. Voracious Time, uprooting all,
  consumes it.
Serrano, P. Noria, La.
  Treadmill.
Servasius. Rivers level granite mountains.
Shakespeare, W. Motley's the Only Wear.
  Seven Ages of Man, The.
  Sonnet 12: "When I do count the clock that tells
    the time."
  Sonnet 15: "When I consider every thing that
    grows."
  Sonnet 19: "Devouring Time, blunt thou the
    lion's [or Lyons] paw[e]s."
  Sonnet 55: "Not marble, nor the g[u]ilded
    monuments."
  Sonnet 60: "Like as the waves make toward[s]
    the pebbled [or pibled] shore."
  Sonnet 64: "When I have seen by Time's fell
    hand defac'd [or defaced]."
  Sonnet 65: "Since brass, nor stone, nor earth,
    nor boundless sea."
  Sonnet 77: "Thy glass will show thee how thy
    beauties wear."
  Sonnet 106: "When in the chronicle of wasted
    time."
  Sonnet 116: "Let me not to the marriage of true
    minds."
  Sonnet 123: "No! Time, thou shalt not boast that
    I do change."
  Sonnet 124: "If [or Yf] my dear[e] love were
    but the child[e] of state."
  Sonnet 126: "O thou, my lovely boy, who in thy
    power."
Shaw, R. 4. Hourglass.
Shelley, P. Conclusion.
  Ozymandias.
Shinkichi Takahashi. Absence.
  Braggart Duck.
  Drizzle.
  Eternity.
  Flight of the Sparrow.
  Hand.
  Let's Live Cheerfully.
  Mother and I.
  Position of the Sparrow, The.
  Raw Fish and Vegetables.
  Sea of Oblivion.
  Sparrow and Bird-Net Building.
  Sparrow in Withered Field.
  Spring.
  Wood in Sound, A.
Sidney, R. Forsaken woods, trees with sharp
  storms oppressed.
Simic. Mirrors at 4 A.M.
Simpson, A. Möbius Strip.
Simpson, J. C. Oh! if thou lov'st me, love me
  not so well!
Slessor. Five Bells.
Smith, S. Grange, The.
Snyder, G. Four Poems for Robin.
  Milton by Firelight.
Södergran. There Is No One.
Sodo. Late spring / Paling rose.
Spaziani. Present, The.
Spender, S. Epilogue: "Time is a thing."
Spenser, E. Ruines of Time, The.
Stafford, W. Gift, The.
Steinberg, J. Till Evening.
Stern, G. I Hate My Moaning.
Stevenson, R. Nay, but I fancy somehow, year
  by year.
Stillman, M. Song: "Love is a green girl."
Su Tung-p'o. To a Traveler.
Suckling, S. Constant Lover, A [or The].
  Love's Clock.
Sundiata. Ear Training.
Sylvester, J. Father, The.
Synková, A. To Olga.
Szymborska, W. Prologue to a Comedy.

Taggard. Time Out: "We will put Time to sleep
  on that warm hill."
Tan Taigi. Barley's season / Dust mutes.
Tanikawa, S. Dusk.
  Growth.
Tardieu Jean. Days.
Taylor, C. Choir.
Taylor, C.B. Plenty Time Pass Fast, Fas Dey
  So.
Taylor, H. Flying Change, The.
Teasdale. Song: "Let it be forgotten, as a flower
  is forgotten."
ten Berge. Fortunes in knee breeches.
Tennyson, A. Break, Break, Break.
Thomas, D. Force That through the Green Fuse
  Drives the Flower, The.
Thomas, E. Gone, Gone Again.
Thomas, R. S. Centuries.
  Evening.
  Llanrhaeadr Ym Mochnant.
Thompson, P. Adown the Heights of Ages.
Tkachenko. Dynamo Stadium, 1980.
  Engraving, An.
Towle. Postmodern Maturity.
Townshend [or Townsend]. Dialogue betwixt
  Time and a Pilgrim[e], A.
Trakl. Descent and Defeat.
Tranströmer. For Mats and Laila.
Ts'ui Hao. Yellow Crane Tower.
Tu Fu [or Du Fu]. Dragon sleeps three winter
  months, A.
  Going to the Palace with a Friend at Dawn.
  Jade Flower Palace ("Stream swirls, The. The
    wind moans in.").
  Jade Flower Palace ("Where the stream winds
    pine winds linger.").
  Passing Mr. Sung's Old House.
  River Jade-Gray.
  Yen-chou City Wall Tower.
Turner, C. East or West?
Twichell. Next and Last.
Ulku, A. Spring Forward, Fall Back.
Ullman. Why There Are Children.
Unamuno. On Reading Jules Renard's Diary.
Unknown. Cai-ge [Translations].
  In Time.
  Last Survivor's Speech, The.
  Words "I love you," The.
Unknown, fr. Terezin Concentration Camp.
  Concert in the Old School Garret.
  Night in the Ghetto.
Vallejo. It was Sunday in the fair ears of my
  burro.
Van Duyn. Homework.
Vancrevel. About Time ("At dusk the silence by
  the sea.").
  About Time ("This silence at the sea's edge, so
    late in the afternoon.").
  Very. Lost, The ("Fairest day that ever yet has
    shone, The.").
Vicinelli. Crossing the River.
  When time--irreversible--begins to doze.
Vietnamese Oral Tradition. Replies.
Vilariño. Each Afternoon.
  Lifelong farewell.
Villa, D. In the end.
  It is.
Vitale, M. Loop, Fleck, Sound and So On.
Vivar. Love is Round.
Vogel, D. There Is a Last, Solitary Coach.
Volkman. Although the paths lead into the
  forest, we are bitter with the bodies of days
  that end too early.
  I won't go in today, I'll stay out today.
  Sonnet: "What is this witness, the watching
    ages."
Voznesensky [or Voznesenskii].
  Recommendation.
Waldman, A. Death is all things we see awake.
Walsh, C. Matter / of fact.
Waniek. House on Moscow Street, The.
Warner, S. Clock Plods On, The.
Warren, R. Acquaintance with Time in Early
  Autumn.
  Bearded Oaks.
  Death of Time.

There's a Grandfather's Clock in the Hall.
Wearne.   Go on, tell me the season is over.
Webb, P.   Second Hand, The.
Webster, A.   Faded.
Welish.   Within This Book, Called Marguerite.
Wellman, M.   Needle growing in ancient basalt.
Whitman, W.   Hours Continuing Long.
   I have heard what the talkers were talking, the talk of the beginning and the end.
   To Think of Time.
Wickham.   Envoi: "God, thou great symmetry."
Wilbur, R.   Year's End.
Williams, S.   Green Eyed Monsters of the Valley Dusk, The.
Willis, H.   Time's Whirligig, Or, The Blue-New-Made-Gentleman Mounted.
Wither.   *Sun* hath run his course through all the Signes, The.
Witt, S.   Americana.
Woods, D.   Waiting.
Wordsworth, W.   Mutability.
Wroth.   Sonnet 32: "How fast thou fliest, O Time, on loves swift wings."
Yeats.   Folly of Being Comforted, The.
   Gyres, The.
   Lamentation of the Old Pensioner, The (1890 version).
   Lamentation of the Old Pensioner, The (1925 version).
Yen Shu.   Song: "Old song with new words, An."
Yesenin [*or* Essenin].   Golden Birch Grove's, The.
Yi Hyangji.   Sea, The: "Ladies, why don't you lift a stone."
Yi Kyubo.   Loom importunes, The.
Young, A.   California Peninsula: El Camino Real.
Young, K.   Central Standard Time.
Young, M. J.   To Time.
Yuan Mei.   Last Poem: Goodbye to My Garden.
Zabolotsky [*or* Zabolotskii].   Nocturnal Garden.
Zaid.   Sundial.
Zapruder, M.   Ten Questions for Mona.
Zukofsky, L.   I Sent Thee Late.

Times Square [New York City]
Troupe.   Eye Change Dreams.

Tinkers
Dodge, M.   Tinker, Come Bring Your Solder.

Tinter Abbey
Wordsworth, W.   Lines Composed a Few Miles above Tintern Abbey on Revisiting the Banks of the Wye During a Tour, July 13, 1798.

Tintoretto
Follain.   Red Apple, The.

Tiresias
Basho.   Many, many things.
Clarke, A.   Strolling one day, beyond the Kalends, on Mount Cyllene.
Field.   Climbing the hill a coil of snakes.
Homer.   And then went down to the ship.

Titanic (ship)
Bynner.   Titanic, The.
Dickey, W.   Arrival of the Titanic, The.
Eady.   Jack Johnson Does the Eagle Rock.
Hardy, T.   Convergence of the Twain, The.
Kim Hyesun.   Titanic, Reincarnate, The.
Knight, E.   Dark Prophecy: I Sing of Shine.
Mikhail, D.   Jewel, The.
Slavitt.   Titanic.
Unknown.   *Titanic*, The.

Titian (Tiziano Vecellio)
Aretino.   If famous Apelles with his hand of art.

Titus (Roman emperor)
Pagis, D.   Mosquito, The.

Toads
Arreola, Juan José.   Toad, The.
Bringhurst.   Behind you: the owl, whose eyes.
Grahame, K.   Song of Mr Toad, The.
Grass.   Gasco.
Issa.   Toad! It looks like, The.
MacCaig.   Toad.
Maggs, Randall.   Tropical Toads.
Parker, A.   Cruelty, the Vandals Say.
Patterson, R.   Hopping Toad Blues.

Petrova, A.   In Juda desert.
Rossetti, C.   Hopping frog, hop here and be seen.
Shinkichi Takahashi.   Toad.
Soutar.   Philosophic Taed, The.
Tomlinson, C.   John Maydew or The Allotment.
Unknown.   Toad grabbed a fly in its mouth, A.
Wicks, S.   Night Toad.
Wilbur, R.   Death of a Toad, The.

Toasters
Smith, W.   Toaster, The.

Tobacco
Aytoun [*or* Ayton], R.   Upone Tabacco.
Berry, W.   First time I remember waking up.
Browne, I.   Blest leaf! whose aromatic gales dispense.
Cook, E.   Sot-Weed Factor, The.
Cotton, C.   On Tobacco.
Kauffman, J.   Working Tobacco.
Matherne, B.   La Fabrique de Tabac (Tobacco Harvest).
Melville, H.   Herba Santa.
Moore, L.   From the Field.
Overton, R.   Re: The Tobacco Institute.
Racin, K.   Tobacco Pickers.
Rimbaud, A.   Cheated Heart.
Rodefer.   Stewed and Fraught with Birds.
Unknown.   If the clouds come good, our tobacco will grow. We will be happy.
Wisdome.   Religious Use of [Taking] Tobacco, A.

Tobago.
See **Trinidad and Tobago**

Toes
Borges.   Toenails.
Edson, R.   Rule and Its Exception, The.
Halpern, D.   Her Body.
Unknown.   Hairy Toe, The.
Updike.   In Extremis.
See also **Feet**

Tokyo, Japan
Rothenberg, J.   At Tsukiji Market Tokyo.
Tanikawa, S.   Two Tokyos.

Toledo, Spain
Campbell, R.   Toledo.

Tolerance
Cook, E.   Live and Let Live.
Dunbar, P.   Accountability.
Hudgins.   Fire and St. Francis.
Marinho, T.   Colour.
Powell, D. A.   Nicholas the ridiculous: you will always be 27 and impossible. No more expectations.
Rosselli.   Negro blood flowing on his brown.

Tolstoy, Leo
Bierds, L.   White Bears: Tolstoy at Astapovo.

Tomatoes
Chase, N.   Plenty.
Milova, T.   Tomato.
Thomas, Yumi.   Love Poem to an Avocado from a Tomato.
Young, A.   Seeing Red.

Tombs
Anyte [*or* Anytes].   Instead of bridal bed and holy wedding songs.
Ashbery, J.   How Much Longer Will I Be Able to Inhabit the Divine Sepulcher.
Beer, P.   Ninny's Tomb.
Bloem, J. C.   Writing on a Tombstone.
Brontë, C.   Is this my tomb, this humble stone.
Coleridge, M.   To a Piano.
Daniel, S.   Stonehenge.
Dickinson, E.   Admirations—and Contempts—of time, The.
Erinna.   I'm the tomb of Baukis, a bride; passing the deeply lamented.
   Stele and my sirens and mournful urn.
Field.   Embalmment.
Góngora y Argote.   Ruins of Time, The.
Hébert, A.   Tomb of the Kings, The.
Hemans.   Queen of Prussia's Tomb, The.
Herbert, G.   Church Monuments.
Herrick.   His Winding-Sheet.
Issa.   When I go / Guard my tomb well.
Jacobsen, R.   Catacombs in San Callisto, The.

Jiménez, J.   Mariner's Ideal Epitaph.
Keats.   This Living Hand, Now Warm and Capable.
Kim Sowŏl.   Golden Meadow, The.
Larkin, P.   Arundel Tomb, An.
Mallarmé.   Fine suicide fled victoriously, The. Tomb.
   Tomb of Charles Baudelaire, The.
   Tomb of Edgar Allan Poe, The.
Martial.   De Cœnatione Micae.
Masaoka Shiki.   Among Saga's / Tall weeds.
Michelangelo Buonarroti.   My lady, how comes it about—what all can see.
Monsour.   Sweeping.
Morgan, E.   Shilpit dog fucks grimly by the close, A.
Ormond.   Design for a Tomb.
Philips, K.   Wiston Vault.
Plato.   Epitaph, An: "I am a drowned man's tomb. There is a farmer's."
Poe.   Annabel Lee.
Prior.   For My Own Monument.
Rochester, J.   Mistress, The: A Song.
Ros.   On Visiting Westminster Abbey.
Rossetti, C.   Last Rites.
Sandburg, C.   Cool Tombs.
Simonides.   Thermopylae.
Sleigh.   Augusto Jandolo: On Excavating an Etruscan Tomb.
Smith, C.   Pressed by the Moon, Mute Arbitress of Tides.
Sparrow, J.   Epitaph: "This stone, with not unpardonable pride."
Stevens, W.   Worms at Heaven's Gate, The.
Unknown.   Grave, The.
   My love, open my tomb and see.
   Spirit of Plato.
Wharton, E.   Tomb of Ilaria Giunigi, The.
Wordsworth, W.   Surprised by Joy.
Wyndham, W.   Shipwrecked Tippoo.
See also **Cemeteries; Graves; Monuments; Mausoleums**

Tongues
Agosin.   Language.
Anderson, A.   Licking Wounds.
Beath, M.   Put a Stone in Your Mouth.
Bosselaar.   English Flavors.
Chubb, R.   Song of My Soul.
Dove, R.   Adolescence—2.
Field, Miranda.   Scold's Mask.
Hacker, M.   Canzone: "Consider the three functions of the tongue."
Herbert, Z.   Tongue, The.
Lorde.   Echoes.
Mac Lochlainn, G.   Second Tongue.
Nepote, M.   To take up the word again.
   Tomar de nuevo la palabra.
Redmond.   My Tongue Paints a Path.
Rose, R.   Sestina of the Geographic Tongue.
Salaam.   Makes You Go Oohhh!
Tate, G.   Tonguing.
Unknown.   My lover wants to keep my tongue inside his mouth.
Warren-Moore.   Pink Poem.
Weiss, Lynne.   Other Tongues.
Wellman, M.   No tongue but bumbles, has.

Tools
Barber, D.   Spirit Level, The.
Heaney, S.   Pitchfork, The.
Hudgins.   Tools: An Ode.
Ormsby, F.   Under the Stairs.
Raymond, M.   June: "You can't hang a heavy mirror."
Tu Fu [*or* Du Fu].   Long hoe, long hoe, handle of white wood.
Van Peenen, H.   Will Campbell Displays His Craniotribe.

Toothaches
Chernoff.   Toothache.
See also **Teeth**

Torah, The
Ficowski.   Both Your Mothers.

Tornadoes
Barney, W.   Mr. Watts and the Whirlwind.
Fulton, A.   News of the Occluded Cyclone.

Jones, Daryl E. Going On.
Kerman, J. In Tornado Weather.
Levin, D. Wind.
McDonald, W. After the Random Tornado.
Moss, T. Tornados.
Revard. Swinging Low.
Spaziani. If it were a sea, this immense wind.

Tortillas
Gaspar de Alba. Making Tortillas.

Tortoises
Cairns, Scott. On Slow Learning.
Clarke, C. Tortoise and Badger.
Curry, N. Swallows and Tortoises.
Gabrielian, N. Tortoise.
Lawrence, D. H. Lui et Elle.
Tortoise Shell.
Tortoise-Shout.
Li Po. Snapshot, A.
Muso Soseki. Snow Valley.
Oppian [of Corycus]. Loves of the Tortoise, The.
Patten, B. Complacent Tortoise, The.
Shinkichi Takahashi. Four Divine Animals.
Siegel, J. How the Tortoise Knew It Was Her Time.

Torture
al-Mala'ika, N. Jamilah and Us.
Atwood. Footnote to the Amnesty Report on Torture.
Beer, P. Footbinding.
Berenguer. Signs on the Table, The.
Bly, R. Romans Angry about the Inner World.
Bolton, J. American Tragedy.
Cardenal. For Those Dead, Our Dead.
Carmona. Tenderness.
Craig, D. Latest News.
de Jesús. Curfew.
Djabali. For My Torturer, Lieutenant D.
Dorfman, A. Last Waltz in Santiago.
Drayton. To His Coy Love, A Canzonet.
Ekelof. Hangman.
Engle, P. Torture.
Espirito Santo. Where are the Men Chased Away by that Mad Wind?
Faiz. Prison Daybreak, A.
Forché. Return.
Gwynn, R. Iago to His Torturers.
Hamburger, M. Between the Lines.
Herbert, Z. What I Saw.
Hernández, M. Final Sonnet.
Hetherington, G. Man from Changi, The.
Hughes, J. Respect for Law and Order, A.
Ignatow, D. First on TV, A.
Levertov. On a Theme from Julian's Chapter 20.
Martinez, D. Pain.
McFadden, D. Shouting Your Name Down the Well.
Oden. Riven Quarry, The.
Plath. Hanging Man, The.
Ratushinskaya [or Ratushinskaia]. I Will Live and Survive.
Reznikoff. Entertainment.
Rózewicz. Voice, A.
Rukeyser, M. Rational Man.
Seto, T. Jihad.
Simic. Eastern European Cooking.
Tadic. Antipsalm.
Thwaite, A. Freedom.
Unknown, fr. Terezin Concentration Camp. Pain Strikes Sparks on Me, the Pain of Terezin.
Winkfield, T. Nature Study.
Wise, S. I Was Very Prolific.

Touch
Akiwumi, V. Unconditionals #3.
Anawrok. Each Time.
Archilochus. If only I might touch Neobule's hand.
Armand. Braille for Left Hand.
Bardwell. How my true love and I lay without touching.
Bracho, C. Misterios del tacto, Los.
Mysteries of Touch, The.
Broumas, O. Touched.
Cervantes. Body as Braille, The.
Clegg, D. Five Senses.

Doty, M. Michael's Dream.
New Dog.
Douglas, K. Prisoner, The.
Durand, M. Reading Postures 3.
Field, T. Compass Room, The: East.
Floyd-Miller, C. Taboo.
Gloria. Touch.
Glück, L. Song of Obstacles.
Gunn, T. Touch.
Han Yong'un [or Yongwun]. Your Touch.
Harris, Ken. Poem In Progress.
Horovitz, F. Do You Not Know that I Need to Touch You.
Hughes, F. Laszlo.
Jernigan, Marla. This is Still Life.
Who are you.
Kalendek, Julie. No part of the hand was hungry.
Kinzie. Glinting like water.
Lyons, S. Touching You Underwater.
Mew. Ne Me Tangito.
Miller, L. Triangle.
Moffett. Reaching Around.
O'Donoghue, M. Textures, The.
Pearlman. Staying in Touch.
Raine, K. Love-Poem: "Yours is the face that the earth turns to me."
Rossetti, C. I wish I could remember the [or that] first day.
Sono-Jo, Lady. How cool / forehead touched.
Swenson, M. Feel Me.
Tana, P. I Have Touched.
No.
Teitelboim, D. Your Arms.
Ullman. Memo.
Unknown. Gently slide your hand inside my sleeves.
Whitman, W. Blind loving wrestling touch! Sheathed hooded sharptoothed touch!
Is this then a touch? . . . quivering me to a new identity.
To be in any form, what is that?
Young, C. Proximity.
Zawinski, A. You Touch Me.

Toulouse-Lautrec, Henri de
Justice, D. Mule Team and Poster.
Olin. Blue Collar Holiday.

Tourism and Tourists
Adisa. Cultural Trip, A.
Algarin. Taos Pueblo Indians: 700 strong according to Bobby's last census.
Amichai, Y. Tourists.
Atwood. At the Tourist Centre in Boston.
Bromige. Edible World, The.
Castillo, S. Rincón.
Clanchy, K. Foreign.
Comden, B. New York, New York.
De Kok. This thing we learn from others.
Della Cruscans. Notice to Tourists.
Dixon, M. Nagasaki.
Dobyns. Dancing in Vacationland.
Dove, R. Sightseeing.
Dugan, A. Memorial Service for the Invasion Beach Where the Vacation in the Flesh Is Over.
Niagara Falls.
Duggan, L. Qantas Bags.
Figueroa, J. Puerto Rico Made in Japan.
Garrett, G. Old Slavemarket: St. Augustine, Fla.
Goldensohn, B. Arch of Titus.
González, R. You and the Tijuana Mule.
Green, A. New York, New York.
Grosholz. Outer Banks, The.
Hoagland, E. Gorée.
Jiménez, J. Walt Whitman: "But do you really want to see Whitman's house instead of Roosevelt's?"
Justice, D. Tourist from Syracuse, The.
Kistler, W. Kyoto 2—Ryoanji.
Krivulin. Crossing the keyboards of the palace.
Kunitz, S. Thief, The.
Kuppner. Architecture is when the sun shines on a facade daily.
Lewis, G. Pentecost.
Lindsay, V. Niagara.
Major, C. Purchase, The.

Melville, H. Attic Landscape, The.
Merrill, J. Casual Wear.
Moss, H. Tourists.
Owens, P. Croeso i Gymru.
Page, P. Permanent Tourists, The.
Phillips, C. You Are Here.
Porter, C. I've a Shooting Box in Scotland.
Katie Went to Haiti.
You Don't Know Paree.
Powers, Arthur. Historical Site.
Richie, E. Airports of the World.
Rose, P. Anglo-Saxon Comedy.
Salter. Kangaroo.
Seferis. Stratis the Sailor by the Dead Sea.
Sia, B. Things to Do in Holland.
Szymborska, W. Pietà.
Tibble. Trials of a Tourist.
Tsaloumas. Progressive Man's Indignation, A.
Walcott. Virgins, The.
Weaver, A. Message on Cape Cod, The.
Zagajewski. Auto Mirror.

Tournaments
Hemans. Corinna at the Capitol.

Toussaint L'Ouverture, François Dominique
Goodison. Kenscoff.
Ray, H. Toussaint L'Ouverture.
Wordsworth, W. To Toussaint L'Ouverture.

Towns
Adams, Cyd. Longview, Texas.
Akhmadulina. Chills.
Allen, E. In the Defences.
Amis, K. Aberdarcy: The Main Square.
Andrade, O. Hierofant.
Basho. Each year it is but a peck of rice.
Berggolts [or Bergholts]. Wish, A.
Boncho. Each year it is but a peck of rice.
Burnside, J. Out of Exile.
Cervantes. Poema para los Californios Muertos.
Collins, M. Winter in Brighton.
Corn. Kimchee in Worchester (Mass.).
Cummings, E. E. Anyone lived in a pretty how town.
Davies, J. Port Talbot.
Deerchild, R. This is a small northern town.
Dobson, A. In Town.
Dodge, M. Mayor of Scuttleton, The.
Dove, R. Small Town.
Eijkelboom. A Nos Glorieux Morts.
Town a Bird Sanctuary, The.
Fargue. In Yellow Towns.
Fraser, G. Home Town Elegy.
Harms. Dogtown.
Hill, C. Little Towns of Texas, The.
Hofmannsthal. Do You See the Town?
Kinsella, T. Tao and Unfitness at Inistiogue on the River Nore.
Knoepfle. Late Winter in Menard County.
Larkin, P. Here.
Laux, D. What Could Happen.
Lawrence, D. H. End of Another Home Holiday.
Whether or Not.
Lee, D. Benediction.
López Velarde. Baleful Return.
Provincial Sundays.
Lux. Grim Town in a Steep Valley.
Lynch, T. At the Opening of Oak Grove Cemetary Bridge.
Machado Ruiz. Plaza and the Flaming Orange Trees, The.
Song: "Now the moon is rising."
Markham, M. We Folded the Hours and Set Them in the Rain.
Marsman. Memory of Holland.
Miller, J. Which Religion Vouchsafes.
Milova, T. Sometimes, not often, it's true.
Moore, M. Steeple-Jack, The.
Mukai Kyorai. Each year it is but a peck of rice.
Neruda. I'm Explaining a Few Things.
Nye, N. Endurance of Poth, Texas, The.
Oppen. Undertaking in New Jersey, The.
Pagis, D. Souvenir, The.
Palés Matos. Pueblo.
Prigov. Imagine this: a mighty giant asleep.
Reese, L. April in Town.

Ríos, A.   Purpose of Altar Boys, The.
Rylant, C.   Living in Cheston.
Salinas, L.   Nights in Fresno.
Stafford, W.   Right Time, The.
Stanton, M.   Sorrow and Rapture.
Suckling, S.   Summons to Town, A.
Tomlinson, C.   Two Views of Two Ghost
   Towns.
Unknown.   Cypress on the Mound, The.
Wagoner, D.   Dead Letter From Out of Town.
Wallace, R.   State Poetry Day.
Ward, J.   Unusual View of the Town.
Wei Ying-wu.   East of the Town.
Whalen, P.   Off. . . / over / that way.
White, M.   Recurrence.
Wickham.   Fired Pot, The.
Wright, D.   Cockermouth.
Wright, K.   Unlikely Obbligato of
   Andersonstown.
Wrigley, R.   Sinking of Clay City, The.
Yost, C.   Descano, California.
Young, A.   Leaving Syracuse.
See also Cities; Villages

Toys
Abad, G.   Toys.
Browne, M.   His Toys.
Cerenio.   20 July 1994.
Cowper, W.   Great princes have great
   playthings. Some have played.
Davies, W.   To W.S.—On His Wonderful Toys.
De la Selva.   Tropical Childhood.
Dodge, M.   Wooden Horse, The.
Edson, R.   Toy-Maker, The.
Field, E.   Duel, The.
   Little Boy Blue.
Hardy, T.   New Toy, The.
Hoban.   Tin Frog, The.
Johnson, M.   Lost Teddy Bear, The.
Kendall, M.   In the Toy Shop.
Kinzie.   Boy.
McMahon, L.   Barbie's Ferrari.
Merritt, C.   Woman of Color.
Mole, J.   Jack-in-the-Box.
Montale.   Haul Your Paper Boats.
Nemerov.   Models.
   Snow Globe, The.
Okudzhava.   Once there was a soldier boy.
Patmore, C.   Toys, The.
Phillips, C.   Toys.
Pyle.   Toys Talk of the World, The.
Roubaud.   Everywhere the.
Rowlands, D.   Schutzstaffeln 45326.
Shapiro, K.   Terminal.
Stevenson, R.   Block City.
   Land of Counterpane, The.
   Song of a Traveller, The.
Tate, J.   How the Pope is Chosen.
Zarco.   Once upon a Seesaw with Charlie Chan.

Track Athletics
Evans, D.   Pole Vaulter.
Saroyan.   Ex- / track.
Sorescu, M.   Start.
Stanton, M.   Pole Vaulting.
Whitman, W.   Runner, The.

Tractors
Hughes, T.   Tractor.
Isfoel.   Tractor, The.
Unknown.   Drive a Tractor.

Tradition
Baraka, R.   In the Tradition Too.
Chaloner.   Thicket of Time.
Chinese Oral Tradition.   Song of the Wife of a
   Gold Mountain Man.
Cohan.   Nothing New Beneath the Sun.
Davies, J.   Bafflement.
Garcia, Edward H.   Chicana.
Gertler, P.   Right Thing, The.
Hewitt, J.   From the Tibetan.
Jabeen, M.   Ideal Wife.
Kamenszain.   Eliahu.
Kipling, R.   Land, The.
Lovelace, R.   To a Lady with Child that Asked
   [*or* Ask'd] an Old Shirt.
Mahon.   Last of the Fire Kings, The.
Martinson.   Makers of Perpetuum Mobile, The.

McElroy, C.   This Is the Poem I Never Meant to
   Write.
Montague, J.   Lost Tradition, A.
P'Bitek.   Woman with Whom I Share My
   Husband, The.
Rich, A.   At the Jewish New Year.
   Cartographies of Silence.
   Rules break like a thermometer, The.
Shakur, A.   Tradition, The.
Tu Fu [*or* Du Fu].   Autumn Wastes, The: 1 and
   2.
Young, K.   Boiling, The.

Trafalgar, Battle of (1805)
Hardy, T.   Night of Trafalgar, The.

Traffic
Baxter, C.   Purest Rage, The.
Castro, M.   New York City.
Harrison, J.   Swifts at Evening.
Jarnot, L.   Still Life.
Kharms.   Event on the Street, An.
Lewis, Emyr.   M4.
Lewis, G.   Flyover Elegies.
Mullen, H.   Bumper to Bumper.
Okantah.   Market day.
Pedretti, Erica.   Here.
Sandburg, C.   Blue Island Intersection.
Swenson, M.   Bison Crossing Near Mt.
   Rushmore.
Winters, Y.   Before Disaster.

Traffic Accidents
Coleman, W.   Dog Suicide.
Delgado, J.   Campesinos.
Kennedy, X.   Close Call.
Seaton, M.   Ice.
Sirowitz, H.   Slowing Down for Death.
See also **Automobile Accidents**

Traherne, Thomas
Hill, G.   So what is faith if it is not.
Wilbur, R.   World Without Objects Is a Sensible
   Emptiness, A.

Trains
Alexander, E.   Farewell to You.
Alexie.   On the Amtrak from Boston to New
   York City.
Anderson, S.   Evening Song.
Aridjis.   Self-Portrait at Eleven on a Train.
Ashbery, J.   Leaving the Atocha Station.
   Melodic Trains.
Barber, D.   Little Overture.
Belev.   Train.
Belieu.   Rondeau at the Train Stop.
Berlin.   When the Midnight Choo-Choo Leaves
   for Alabam'.
Berryman.   Traveller [*or* Traveler], The.
Bertolino.   Baying, The.
Biespiel, D.   White Roses.
Bly, R.   Looking at New-Fallen Snow from a
   Train.
Bogan, L.   Train Tune.
Booth, P.   Stations.
Brooks, G.   Jamal; Nineteen Cows In a Slow
   Line Walking.
Broonzy.   Southern Blues, The.
Brown, S.   Call Boy.
   Long Track Blues.
   Sister Lou.
Bruchac.   Let the Midnight Special.
Buckley, C.   Train in the Desert—1916.
Burnside, J.   Autobiography.
Bursk.   Tearing Up the Tracks.
Cendrars.   Prose of the Trans-Siberian and Little
   Jean of France.
   South.
Clark, T.   You (I).
Clarke, C.   Passing.
Clarke, T.   Will They Always Remember.
Collier, M.   North Corridor.
Conn.   Tremors.
Cranch.   Locomotive, The.
Crane, H.   River, The.
Dameron, Chip.   South Texas Boxcar Blues.
Dawe, B.   Renewal Notice.
Delmore Brothers.   Wabash Cannonball, The.
Devi.   Going out of Town.
Dobyns.   Freight Cars.

Dooley, M.   Mind the Gap.
Durcan.   Tullynoe: Tête-à-Tête in the Parish
   Priest's Parlour.
Eiseley.   And as for Man.
Empson.   Beautiful Train, The.
Étienne, Marie.   Nightmares.
Etter.   Great Northern.
   Riding the Rock Island Through Kansas.
Ferlinghetti, L.   Starting from San Francisco.
Field, E.   Journey, A.
Francis, R.   Night Train.
Frost, R.   On the Heart's Beginning to Cloud the
   Mind.
Fuhrman, J.   Watching Trains.
Fusselman, A.   Sleeper.
Gallagher, T.   Not There.
Galvin, B.   For a Daughter Gone Away.
George, D.   Wreck of the Old 97.
Gibbons, R.   American Trains.
Gioia.   In Cheever Country.
Giovanni.   Train Rides.
Giussani, S.   Towards a Beginning.
Gordon, M.   Chattanooga Choo-Choo.
Greenberg, A.   Freight Train, Freight Train.
Haines, J.   Train Stops at Healy Fork, The.
Hall, D.   Sister on the Tracks, A.
Hanzlicek, C.   Last Trains, The.
Hardy, T.   Midnight on the Great Western.
Hart-Smith.   Nullarbor.
Hawkesworth, P.   Meeting Place.
Hayden, R.   Runagate Runagate.
Hayes, T.   Boxcar.
Hedin, R.   Transcanadian.
   Wreck of the Great Northern, The.
Helfgott, S.   Trains, The.
Herlin.   Light brush of dawn, A.
Heyen.   Tie, The.
Hikmet.   Things I Didn't Know I Loved.
Hilberry.   Body and Mind.
Hô Sugyông.   Train Leaving.
Hoch, James.   Riding Backwards on a Train.
Holland, J.   Loco.
Hope, A.   Observation Car.
Hughes, L.   Freedom Train.
   Jim Crow Car.
Hughes, T.   Platform One.
Hugo, R.   Elegy: "I expected him to look dead
   in the casket."
   Yards of Sarajevo, The.
Jacob, M.   Invitation to a Voyage.
Jacobsen, R.   Express Train.
Jarrell, R.   On the Railway Platform.
   Orient Express, The.
Jefferson, B.   Easy Rider Blues.
Jensen, L.   To a Stranger (At the End of a
   Caboose).
József, A.   Freight Trains.
Justice, D.   Crossing Kansas by Train.
   Train.
Kaufman, B.   Novels from a Fragment in
   Progress.
Kendall, M.   Underground.
Kennelly.   Limerick Train, The.
Kinsley, R.   Walk Along the Old Tracks, A.
Kinnell.   Lackawanna.
Kooser.   City Limits.
Larbaud.   Ode: "Lend me your great sound,
   your fine smooth speed."
Larcom.   What the Train Ran Over.
Lattimore.   North Philadelphia, Trenton, and
   New York.
   Note on the L and N.
Laux, D.   Children's Train, The.
Lawrence, D. H.   Tommies in the Train.
Le Guin.   Riding on the Coast Starlight.
Levertov.   Don't You Hear that Whistle Blowin'.
Levin, P.   Night Coach.
Levine, P.   And the Trains Go On.
Lewis, Emyr.   Stale Spit is the Morning Train.
Machado Ruiz.   Rainbow at Night.
MacLeish.   Burying Ground by the Ties.
   Pastoral.
MacNeice.   Canto XX: "To Wales once more,
   though not on holiday now."
Manrique, J.   Baudelaire's Spleen.
McCabe, C.   Postcard from London, A.

McCord, D.   Song of the Train.
McGrath, T.   Black Train, The.
  End of the Line, The.
McMillan, H.   Leaving Scotland by Train.
Mercer, J.   On the Atchison, Topeka and the
  Santa Fe.
Merwin.   Wheels of the Trains, The.
Millay, E.   From a Train Window.
Miller, V.   How Far?
Mitchell, E.   Passenger Opposite, The.
Monk, G.   South Bound: Facing North.
Monroe, B.   In the Pines.
Moorer.   Jim Crow Cars.
Mueller, L.   Commuter.
Naranjo.   Part One: The Orders Begin.
Nash, O.   Unwinged Ones, The.
Nelson, H.   With My Mother, Missing the Train.
Nemerov.   Low-Level Cross-Country.
Nichols, R.   Beginning when I was six I became
  my father's accomplice.
Nims, J.   Freight.
Osherow.   Villanelle from a Sentence in a Poet's
  Brief Biography.
Parini.   Coal Train.
Pastan.   At the Train Museum.
  Last Train, The.
Pettit.   Self-Portrait Approaching Promontory,
  Utah.
Plath.   Getting There.
Plumly.   For Esther.
Powell, J.   Lines Written for a Friend on the
  Death of His Brother, Caused by a Railway
  Train Running Over Him Whilst He Was in a
  State of Inebriation.
Purdy, A.   Madwoman on the Train, The.
Randall, D.   Southern Road, The.
Randell.   O house, o sloping field, o poplar trees
  whose tall arms salute.
Ras.   My Train.
Rein.   Moscow Station, The.
Reiter, T.   Rights of Way.
Reverdy.   Departure.
Rich, A.   Lucifer in the Train.
Riley, P.   119. 3.
Roberson, E.   True We Are Two Grown Men.
Roberts, K.   Night Tumbles into Town by Rail.
Robin, L.   Beyond the Blue Horizon.
Roethke.   Night Journey.
Rohrer, M.   After the Wedding Party.
Rose, P.   Terminus.
Rosidi, A.   Only in Poetry.
Ross, L.   Indecent Exposure (A True Story).
St. John, D.   Iris.
Sandburg, C.   Limited.
  Southern Pacific.
  Window.
Sarton, M.   After a Train Journey.
Scamell, B.   From the Provinces.
Scammell, W.   Trains.
Seibert.   Casey Jones.
Shapiro, K.   Terminal.
Sissman.   Big Rock-Candy Mountain, The.
Smith, D.   Allegheny Happiness.
  Roundhouse Voices, The.
Soto.   Who Will Know Us?
Spender, S.   Express, The.
Stephens, P.   God Shed His Grace.
  Signalmen, The.
Sternlieb.   Right of Way.
Stevenson, R.   From a Railway Carriage.
Stone, R.   Always on the Train.
Sub-ok.   Spring at Yesan Station.
Sundiata.   Notes from the Defense of Colin
  Ferguson.
Swenson, M.   Riding the "A".
  Written While Riding the Long Island Rail
  Road.
Tate, J.   Manna.
Tranströmer.   Below Freezing.
  Track.
  Tracks.
Triplett, P.   Story for the Mother Tongue.
Tsanev, Ivan.   Express Train.
Tsvetayeva [or Tsvetaeva].   You, Walking Past
  Me.
Ulacia, M.   Conrail Wax Museum.

Conrail Wax Museum.
Unknown.   Gospel Train, The.
  I Been Working on the Railroad.
  Little Black Train Is A-Comin'.
  Poor Paddy Works on the Railway.
  Railroad Blues, The.
  Railroad Cars Are Coming, The.
  Song: The Railway Train.
  Texas Corrido.
  Train is A-Comin'.
Van Doren.   Dream of Trains, A.
Veenendaal.   On My Fourteenth Wedding
  Anniversary I Ride on Trains.
Verlaine.   Malines.
Warren, R.   He Was Formidable.
  I Can't Even Remember the Name.
Warsh.   Before I Was Born.
Weaver, A.   Afternoon Train.
Webb, F.   Laid Off.
West, K.   On Track.
Weston, M.   Departure.
White, E.   Commuter.
Whitman, W.   To a Locomotive in Winter.
Wilbur, R.   In the Smoking-Car.
Williams, Stephanie.   Drunkard Promise, A.
Williams, W.   Overture to a Dance of
  Locomotives.
Williamson, G.   Outbound.
Wojahn.   "Mystery Train" Janis Joplin Leaves
  Port Arthur for Points West, 1964.
  Photo of My Father in a Snowbound Train.
Woolson.   One.
  Other, The.
Wright, J.   Train Journey.
Wyrebek, M.   Example, An.
Young, D.   Project for Freight Trains, A.
Zagajewski.   At Daybreak.
See also **Railroads; Locomotives**

Traitors
Eastman, M.   To Genevieve Taggard Who
  Called Me Traitor in a Poem.
Joseph, A.   Traitor.
Unknown.   To a Traitor.
See also **Treason and Traitors**

Tramps
Anacreon.   Not / But near another you have a
  timid.
See also **Vagabonds**

Transcendence
Ammons.   He Held Radical Light.
Anbun.   Years keeping that in mind.
Armitage, S.   Tyre, The.
Berman, C.   Deep inside me at my core.
Bhattācārya, M.   Screening its face amongst
  lotus stalks.
Bunan.   Moon's the same old moon, The.
Chang, D.   On Being in the Midwest.
Chifu.   No mind, no Buddhas, no live beings.
Chŏng Ch'ŏl.   Milky rain on the green hills.
Coleridge, M.   Marriage.
Daito.   At last I've broken Unmon's barrier!
Dangai.   Earth, river, mountain.
Dankyo-Myorin.   Coming, I clench my hands.
Dickinson, E.   After great pain a formal feeling
  comes.
  There's a certain Slant of light.
Eian.   Joshu's "Oak in the courtyard".
Eichu.   My eyes eavesdrop on their lashes!
Emre.   I love you beyond the depths of my own
  soul.
Gasan.   Invaluable is the Soto Way.
Gesshu Soko.   Seven seas sucked up together,
  The.
Gido.   Inscription over His Door.
Ginsberg, A.   Kral Majales.
Gojusan.   Seamless.
Grosjean, Jean.   Ancestor, The.
Hoge.   How long the tree's been barren.
Hoin.   On the rocky slope, blossoming.
Hughes, L.   Dream Variation[s].
Jinzu.   In serving, serve.
Kaigen.   Old master held up fluff, The.
Kanzan-Shigyo.   Where is the dragon's cave?
Keppo.   Searching Him took.
Kishu.   Once the goal's reached.

Kuchu.   Joshu's word—Nothingness.
Kuzmin.   Were I a general of olden times.
Mallarmé.   Virginal, vibrant, and beautiful dawn,
  The.
Manan.   Unfettered at last, a traveling monk.
Michelangelo Buonarroti.   Violent burning for
  prodigious beauty, A.
Moan.   Clear, clear—clearest!
Monju-Shindo.   Joshu's "Oak in the courtyard".
Munom-Ekai.   Thunderbolt—eyes wide, A.
Muso Soseki.   Bamboo Garden.
  Buddha's Satori.
  Curtain of cloud hangs, A.
  For years I dug in the earth.
  Free Old Man.
  Gate of Universal Light, The.
  Moon Mountain.
  Temple of Eternal Light.
  Toki-no-Ge (Satori Poem).
  Vainly I dug for a perfect sky.
Nan-o-myo.   Not falling, not ignoring.
Nensho.   Only genuine awakening results in
  that.
Paz.   All is transformed and is sacred.
  Better the crime, / the suicides of lovers, the
  incest committed.
  Madrid, 1937, / in the Plaza del Angel the
  women.
  Was it I making plans / for the summer—and
  for all the summers.
Sabok.   At My Mother's Funeral.
Schwartz, H.   Recruiting Poster.
Seigen-yuiin.   How vast karma.
Seiken-Chiju.   Twenty years a pilgrim.
Sen, R.   Meditate on Kali! Why be anxious?
Shofu.   No dust speck anywhere.
Soan.   Sailing on Men River, I heard.
Soen.   Master Joshu and the dog.
Stevens, W.   Sunday Morning.
Tekkan.   No mind, no Buddha, no being.
Tessho.   Finally out of reach.
Unknown.   My country wasn't sold, it was
  stolen.
Wilde, O.   Hélas!
Yuishun.   Why, it's but the motion of eyes and
  brows!

Transformation
Agosin.   Seven Stones.
Ai.   Man with the Saxophone, The.
Alterman, N.   Householder Departs from the
  City, The.
Atwood.   Autobiography: "First thing I can
  remember is a blue line, The. This was on the
  left."
Beachy-Quick, Dan.   Psalm (Traherne).
  Stellar Elements.
Bedregal.   Night, I Know All About You.
Berman, C.   Deep inside me at my core.
Bhāndārī, S.   Ma, You are Brahmani in the
  world of Brahma.
Bhattācārya, K.   Is my black Mother Syama
  really black?
  Mother / You're always finding ways to amuse
  Yourself.
Bhattācārya, M.   Oh Ma Kali, for a long time
  now.
Blunden.   Survival, The.
Boland, E.   Woman Turns Herself into a Fish,
  The.
Brooks, A.   Here is the queen.
Buchanan, O.   Girls, The.
Cairns, Scott.   Regarding the Monument.
Canan.   Oh Kali.
Carrera Andrade.   Transfiguration of the Rain.
Cassian.   Temptation.
Chedid, A.   Movement.
Citino.   Sister Mary Appassionata Lectures the
  Folklore Class: Doctrines of the Strawberry.
Claus.   Woman 12, A.
Coleridge, H.   Prayer.
Couzyn.   Transformation.
de Fierro.   If Time Waits.
De la Tierra.   Butterflying.
Deerchild, E.   Snag.
Dickinson, E.   He touched me, so I live to know.
Duncan, R.   Something is taking place.

Eady. Thrift.
  Young Elvis.
Earle, J. Exits.
El-Shawwaf, H. Devil's Symbol, The.
Feinstein, E. Patience.
Field, E. Curse of the Cat Woman.
Gewanter, D. Divorce and Mr. Circe.
Gibran. Seven Stages, The.
Gladding. Locust Shell.
Glück, L. Moonless Night.
Goodison. On Becoming a Tiger.
Grass. Transformation.
Greenhalgh, C. Man in the Valley of Women, A.
Hall, D. Digging.
Hardy, T. Transformations.
Hart-Smith. Nullarbor.
Henson, L. I Am Singing the Cold Rain.
Hirsch, E. Paul Celan: A Grave and Mysterious Sentence.
Hollander, V. Rosh Chodesh Tisheri.
Ignatow, D. Cloud Creates, A.
  Time Comes When You Are Facing Him, The.
Issa. Now listen, you watermelons.
Jarman, M. Psalm: The New Day.
Kasdorf. Streak, The.
Khoury-Gata. Here there was once a country.
Klinger, A. Transformation.
Komunyakaa, Y. Never Land.
Kunitz, S. Layers, The.
Lal Ded [or Lalla]. I was passionate.
Levertov. Acolyte, The.
Lewis, G. Hedge, The.
Marvin, C. House, Garden, Madness.
Mayer, B. We've Solved the Problem.
"Mbala.". New Dub, A.
McGrath, T. Revisionist Poem—Octavio Paz.
Memmi, A. Shot of sunlight, A.
Merrill, J. Processional.
Merwin. Hope for Her.
Mirabai [or Mira Bai]. Coffer with the Poisonous Snake, The.
  It's True I Went to the Market.
Monaghan. Persephone's Journey.
Mugo, M. G. Look How Rich We are Together.
Nandi, R. I understand now, Tara, I understand.
Nonnus. But Dionysos had no healing physic for his comrade fallen, of dancing he thought no more.
Oliver, M. Spring Azures.
Orlen. Androgyny.
Ovid. Apollo and Hyacinthus.
  Iphis and Ianthe.
  Pygmalion.
Padgett, R. Symbols of Transformation.
Petersen, P. I Listen to Alice Walker on a Pocket Radio.
Phylip, S. Seagull, The.
Piper, P. Morning Star, The.
Pizarnik. I gave the surge of myself to the dawn.
Plath. Love Letter.
Rilke. Walk, A.
Rimbaud, A. Bottom.
Rojas. Chapter and Verse.
Rózewicz. Transformations.
Ruark. Hybrid Magnolias in Late April.
Rukeyser, M. Hostages, The.
Rumi. New Rule, The.
  We can't help being thirsty.
Savageau. All Night She Dreams.
Schelling. Commentary.
Schwartz, H. Recruiting Poster.
Seferis. Nijinski.
Sen, R. Kali, Ma.
  Ma, You're inside me.
  Oh Kali Full of Brahman!
  Who can understand Kali?
Shcherbina. Except for love everything.
Shelley, P. One remains, the many change and pass, The.
Shinkichi Takahashi. Fish.
Simic. Lives of Alchemists, The.
Sŏ Chŏngju. If I Became a Stone.
Spicer, J. Transformations.
Tanikawa, S. Request.

Tennyson, A. Thy spirit ere our fatal loss.
Tomlinson, C. Door, The.
  Prometheus.
Tontongi. Go There.
Unknown. Because of this love.
  My lover prefers sky-colored eyes.
Untermeyer, L. To a Vine-clad Telegraph Pole.
Vander Ven, Tom. Sea Washes Sand Scours Sea.
Villa, E. Trees were moving.
Warsh. Gout.
Whalen, P. Absolute / Reality, namely.
Wilbur, R. Beautiful Changes, The.
Woo, M. Under a Full Moon.

Transience
Anguita, E. Real Moment, The.
Apollinaire. Voyager, The.
Aridjis. Letter from Mexico.
Auden. As I Walked Out One Evening.
Banning, L. Romancero.
Basho. Tremble, oh my gravemound.
  With dewdrops dripping.
Bateman, M. Lightness.
Bécquer, G. Arrow Flying Past, An.
  Darkling Swallows Will Come Again, The.
Berlin. Song Is Ended (But the Melody Lingers On), The.
Bethell. Time.
Blok. Visitor.
Bobyshev. White Peacock, The.
Bolton, E. Palinode, A.
Boruch. Think of the Words.
Buchwald. As Soon As It's Here It's Gone But So What.
Budbill. Like Smoke from Our Campfire.
Bunting. Remember, imbeciles and wits.
Burkard. But Beautiful.
Buson. These lazy spring days.
Calderón de la Barca. Those Which Were Pomp and Delight.
Carew, T. Song[, A]: "Ask[e] me no more where Jove bestow[e]s."
Catullus. Sun May Set, The.
  Unto no body my woman saith she had rather a wife be [or bee].
Cetina, G. Happy Hours that Hurry Away.
Clare, J. Shadows.
Conway, J. Hangover.
Cory, W. Deteriora.
Cowley, A. Chronicle, The; a Ballad.
Creeley. Faces, The.
Dermée. Poem: "Is it a plane in the sky."
d'Oettingen. To Il y a.
Donne. Anniversary [or Anniversarie], The.
Doty, M. Michael's Dream.
Drayton. How Many Paltry, Foolish, Painted Things.
Eberhart, R. Groundhog, The.
Eigner. Back to it.
Elfyn, Menna. Welsh Ice.
Eliot, T. S. Burnt Norton.
  Dry Salvages, The.
Fogdall, Kristin. Demas, in Love with This Present World.
Follain. This Plant, So Exceptional.
Ford, Katie. Colosseum.
Freneau. Hills sink to plains, and man returns to dust.
  Vanity of Existence, The.
Frost, R. Nothing Gold Can Stay.
Fujiwara no Yasusue. Nothing Whatsoever.
Fuller, M. Let Me Gather from the Earth.
Goedicke. Meaning of Life, The.
Góngora y Argote. O Noble and Most High in Beauty, Thou.
González Prada, M. Treasures and Glories of Life, The.
Goodman, P. Ballade of the Moment After.
Graham, J. Prayer: "Over a dock railing, I watch the minnows, thousands, swirl."
Griffiths, J. Errata.
Guiterman. On the Vanity of Earthly Greatness.
Gustafson, R. Of Green Steps and Laundry.
Habington. Nox Nocti Indicat Scientiam.
  To the Moment Last Past: "O whither dost thou flye? Cannot my vow."

Hass, R. Late Spring.
Heaney, S. Blackberry-Picking.
Herbert, G. Virtue [or Vertue].
Herrick. Corinna's Going a-Maying.
  To Blossoms.
  To Daffodils [or Daffadills].
  To Dianeme ("Sweet, be not proud of those two eyes.").
Heyman, E. Easy Come, Easy Go.
Hill, G. Even now one is amazed.
Hillman, B. Every Life.
Hirshfield, J. Not-Yet.
Hồ Xuân Hương. Country Scene.
Hofmannsthal. On the Transitory.
Horace. Ode 4,7: "Snow dissolv'd no more is seen, The."
Houlihan, J. Matter.
Housman. Along the field as we came by.
Huang T'ing-chien. Tune: "Ch'ing-P'ing Song".
Iio Sogi. Life in this world.
Issa. Before I arrived.
  Brilliant moon.
  Like misty moonlight.
  Listen / All creeping things.
  Vanity of men, The.
  What's the lord's vast wealth.
Jeffers, R. To the Stone-Cutters.
Jiménez, J. Fleeting Return.
Jonson, B. It Is Not Growing Like a Tree.
Juan Chi. Learning.
  Mujin Flowers Blossom on the Rolling Graves, The.
  Ten Suns Rise in the East, The.
Kabir. Eternity.
Kenjeev. And a fool, and a smart one, a miser.
Kim Ch'unsu [or Chun-soo]. Riding a Mule.
King, H. Sic Vita.
Lamartine. Lake, The.
Landon. Dancing Girl, The.
Lederer, K. Sympathy and Envy.
Levertov. Living.
Levine, P. Sweet Will.
Lima, J. Words of Departure.
Lisnyanskaya [or Lisnianskaia]. Between hope and failure.
Long, H. New Music, A.
Longfellow, H. Elegiac Verse 12.
  Fragment: August 4, 1856.
Lowell, A. Falling Snow.
Machado Ruiz. All things die and all things live forever.
MacNeice. Sunlight on the Garden, The.
Magidson, H. Gone with the Wind.
Manrique, J. Baudelaire's Spleen.
Mansei, S. Our Life in This World.
Martí. Two Countries.
McGrath, T. Return, The.
McOrlan. Wood merchant's parlour, The.
Melville, H. Malvern Hill.
Milosz, C. House in Krasnogruda.
Molina, E. As the Great Days Flow.
Molinari. Little Ode to Melancholy.
Montagu, L. Lover, The; a Ballad.
Montague, J. Small Secrets.
Moore, T. No—Leave My Heart to Rest.
Nash, O. Speak Low.
Nashe [or Nash]. Adieu, Farewell, Earth's Bliss[e].
Newman, A. **Fall under.** To succumb to; come under an influence or power.
Nezahualcoyotl. Be Indomitable, O My Heart.
  Can It Be True That One Lives on Earth?
Norton, C. In the cold change, which time hath wrought on love.
Ohnishi, T. Blossoms in the Wind.
Pao Chao. Do you not see the riverside grass.
Pasolini. Lines from the Testament.
Peabody, J. Far-Off Rose, A.
Peacock, T. Love and Age.
Phillips, C. Kill, The.
Plato. Apple, The.
Po Chü-i. At the End of Spring.
Prufer, K. My Father Recounts a Story from His Youth.
Radiguet. Handless Clock.
  Map.

Ralegh.   Even Such Is Time.
Nymph's [or Nimphs] Reply to the [Passionate] Shepherd [or Sheepheard], The.
Ransom, J.   Blue Girls.
Ravikovitch, D.   Real Love Isn't What It Seems.
Rexroth, K.   Some day in six inches of.
This flesh you have loved.
Riley, J.   Summer Seeming.
Robinson, E.   Man against the Sky, The.
Rohrer, M.   Hunger of the Lemur, The.
Rossetti, C.   Bed of Forget-Me-Nots, A.
May: "I cannot tell you how it was."
Sandburg, C.   Flash Crimson.
Languages.
Sarton, M.   Silence Now, The.
Schwartz, R. L.   Edgewater Park.
Why I Forgive My Younger Self Her Transgressions.
Shakespeare, W.   Dirge for Fidele.
Epilogue: "Our revels now are ended. These our actors."
Sonnet 1: "From fairest creatures we desire increase."
Sonnet 3: "Look in thy glass, and tell the face thou viewest."
Sonnet 5: "Those hours that with gentle work did frame."
Sonnet 12: "When I do count the clock that tells the time."
Sonnet 18: "Shall I compare thee to a summer's day?"
Sonnet 19: "Devouring Time, blunt thou the lion's [or Lyons] paw[e]s."
Sharma, P.   Transit.
Shcherbina.   What's it you're howling, siren-telephone.
Shelley, P.   Hymn to Intellectual Beauty.
Ozymandias.
Sidney.   Leave Me O Love.
Sidney, R.   Songe 17: "Sun is set, and masked night, The."
Simonides.   All things come to one hideous Charybdis.
Being human, don't ever say what happens tomorrow.
Smith, C.   To the Insect of the Gossamer.
Smith, D.   New Orleans Engagement.
Smith, H.   Ozymandias.
Spenser, E.   Sonnet 79: "Men call you fair [or fayre], and you do[e] credit it."
Spires.   Mansion Beach.
Storm, T.   Woman's Ritornelle.
Suckling, S.   Constant Lover, A [or The].
Sung Tzu-hou.   Song: "On the Eastern Way at the city of Lo-yang."
Sze.   June Ghazal.
Taylor, C.B.   Plenty Time Pass Fast, Fas Dey So.
Teillier, J.   Bridge in the South.
Tennyson, A.   Break, Break, Break.
Tears, Idle Tears.
Thackeray.   Ballad of Bouillabaisse, The.
Tsanev, Ivan.   Archaelogical Site, An.
Ts'ao Chih.   In the south country there lives a lovely lady.
Tu Fu [or Du Fu].   Dragon Gate Gorge.
Turner, C.   East or West?
Unknown.   Come, my love, let me embrace you.
Despise the World.
Man in the World Lodging.
My beloved, come and sit a moment close to me.
Ruin, The.
Unknown, sometimes at. to Sir Walter Ralegh.
As You Came from the Holy Land [of Walsingham].
Van Hanh.   Body of Man, The.
Verlaine.   Exchange of Feelings.
Villon.   Ballade of the Ladies of Time Past.
Gone Ladies.
Viray, M.   Saturday Morning, A.
Waller, E.   Song: "Go[e], lovely rose."
Wang Wei.   After Source of the Peach Blossom Stream.
Warren, R.   Well House, The.
Washington, N.   Hundred Years from Today, A.

Whitman, W.   As If a Phantom Caress'd Me.
Wilbur, R.   Looking into History.
Transit.
Williams, T.   We Have Not Long to Love.
Wŏn Ch'ŏnsŏk.   Fortune determines rise and fall.
Wright, C.   Snow.
Wyatt.   Varium et Mutabile.
Yamanoé [or Yamanoué] no Okura.   Lament for the Evanescence of Life, A.
Young, J.   Hundred Years from Today, A.
See also Change
Translation and Translators
Barnstone, W.   Jiang Yuying, Famous Professor at Beijing University, Who Daringly Rendered into Chinese the First Complete Walt Whitman.
Castillo, S.   Contra, The.
Clarke, G.   Translation.
Elfyn, Menna.   Handkerchief Kiss.
Rice Papers.
Enzensberger, H.   Finnish Tango.
González Prada, M.   Who Translates a Poet Badly.
Hollander, J.   For "Fiddle-De-De".
Horst, C.   Interpreter.
Jandl, E.   Chanson.
Jonson, B.   To Clement Edmonds, on His Caesar's Commentaries Observed, and Translated.
To Sir Henry Savile [upon His Translation of Tacitus].
Keats.   On First Looking into Chapman's Homer.
Lesser.   Translation.
Lewis, G.   Interview with the Poet.
Mandelstam [or Mandelshtam].   Three Octets.
Matveyeva [or Matveieva].   Re-Conversion.
Merrill, J.   Lost in Translation.
Moore, H.   Poem for the End.
Nims, J.   Verse Translator.
Portnoy, M.   Of of Titmouse.
Preil, G.   Lesson in Translation, A.
Purdy, A.   On the Decipherment of "Linear B".
Rich, A.   Translations.
Samaras, N.   Translation.
Schelling.   High Up the Thunder Gods, Downstairs the Hunger.
Szymborska, W.   Words ("La Pologne? La Pologne? It's awfully cold there, isn't it? she asked.").
Tomlinson, C.   Las Trampas U.S.A.
Wilkinson, J.   Grace.
Transmutation
Petersen, P.   Groom of the Animal-Bride.
Simic.   Lives of Alchemists, The.
Transvestites
Doty, M.   Crêpe de Chine.
Jordan, A.   Black Drag Queen.
Makofske, Mary.   Viola, to Olivia.
Trapezes and Trapeze Artists
Koch, K.   Circus, The ("We will have to go away, said the girls in the circus.").
Morgan, E.   Cinquevalli.
Szporluk.   Trapeze.
Trapping and Trappers
Blunden.   Mole Catcher.
Cahn, S.   (Love Is) The Tender Trap.
Cook, E.   On Seeing a Bird-Catcher.
Gojusan.   Seamless.
Gullar.   There Are Many Traps in the World.
Harvey, M.   Abandoned Conversation with the Senses.
Hughes, F.   Different Voice, The.
Larkin, P.   Myxomatosis.
Le Pan.   Coureurs de Bois.
Snyder, G.   One Should Not Talk to a Skilled Hunter about What Is Forbidden by the Buddha.
Spenser, E.   Sonnet 37: "What guile [or guyle] is this, that those her golden tresses."
Unknown.   Pleasant Songs of the Sweetheart Who Meets You in the Fields.
Tu-zhi: Hares.
Wright, D.   Map of the Kingdom, A.

Trash
Adewale, T.   Explorer of Aromas.
Craighead, L.   Dancin' Our Lives Away.
Crews, J.   In the Rubble.
Ofeimun.   New Brooms, The.
Smukler.   Trash.
Stevens, W.   Man on the Dump, The.
See also Garbage and Garbage Men
Travel Poetry
Basho.   Exhausted, I sought.
Baudelaire.   Voyage, The.
Bolt, T.   Glimpse of Terrain.
Cendrars.   Hammock.
Cross, D.   Bus poems, The.
Crunk, T.   Leaving.
Davies, Grahame.   Rough Guide.
Flanagan, D. B.   Three Years from Sorrento.
Ho Ch'e Ch'ang.   Written Impromptu upon Returning to My Hometown.
Hsieh Ling-yün.   On Climbing the Highest Peak of Stone Gate Mountain.
On My Way from South Mountain to North Mountain, I Glance at the Scenery from the Lake.
Jones, D. Cyril.   Letters to a Kenyan Friend.
Li Po.   There was a sojourner in Ying who intoned "White Snows".
Meng Hao Jan.   Passing Seven-League Rapids.
Seeking out Master Chan on Incense Mountain.
Reverdy.   Road.
Rhys, K.   Interlude.
Robinson, M.   Describes her Bark.
Unknown.   Cautiously bubbles that spring water.
Wang Chih-huan.   Climbing the Stork Pavilion.
Wu Yun.   Apotheosis.
Traveling and Travelers
Abish, Walter.   What Else (Part 2).
Adair, T.   Let's Get Away from It All.
Adler, L.   Traveling Out, The.
Agoos, J.   Portinaio.
Alexander, E.   Passage.
Alexander, M.   October Journey.
Ali, M.   Flight.
Allen, F.   When the Car Gave Up the Ghost.
Allen, S.   Harriet Tubman aka Moses.
Amir, D.   I Have Longings for My Dead.
Anyte [or Anytes].   I, Hermes, stand here by the windy tree-lined.
Stranger, below the boulder rest your spent limbs.
Apollinaire.   Traveller, The.
Voyager, The.
Windows.
Zone.
Zone.
Arnold, C.   Your friend's arriving on the bus.
Arnold, M.   Scholar Gypsy, The.
Asekoff, L.   North Star.
Ashbery, J.   Melodic Trains.
My Philosophy of Life.
Wind thrashes the maple seed-pods, The.
Atwood.   Journey to the Interior.
Auden.   Legend.
Baker, T.   Le passage (Morbihan).
Pavane on Mr Wray's Locations, A.
Bandeira.   Off to Pasárgada.
Barras, J.   Peace.
Basho.   All along this road.
Along my journey.
Bucket of azaleas, A.
Crossing half the sky.
Exhausted, / time to find a lodging.
In the withering gusts.
In the withering gusts.
Journey's end / Still alive.
Long conversations.
Sick on a journey / Over parched fields.
Through frozen rice fields.
Tired.
Traveling this high.
Baudelaire.   Invitation au Voyage, L'.
Invitation to the Voyage.
Bécquer.   Arrow Flying Past, An.
Where Do I Come From?
Belieu.   At St. Sulpice.
Benn.   Bunch of Drifter Sons Hollered, A.

Berkson, B.   Traveler's Companion.
Berman, D.   From His Bed in the Capital City.
Berrigan, D.   Prayer: "I left Cornell / with half a wit; six mismated socks."
Berry, W.   Air and Fire.
Berryman.   Traveller [or Traveler], The.
Bishop, E.   Moose, The.
Over 2000 Illustrations and a Complete Concordance.
Questions of Travel.
Bishop, R.   Ah, To Be In.
Blanco, R.   We're Not Going to Malta.
Bobrowski.   East.
Bolton, K.   In Ferrara.
Bontemps.   Nocturne of the Wharves.
Branch, A.   Connecticut Road Song.
Breytenbach.   Asylum.
Journey.
Brion, R.   Love Song: "One long and humid afternoon."
Brock-Broido.   Carrowmore.
Browning, R.   Home-Thoughts, from the Sea.
Burnside, J.   Autobiography.
Buson.   Goodbye. I willgo.
Happy traveler / Mosquito wick.
I set out from my village three springs ago.
Long hard journey, A.
Moon in midsky, high.
Spring Breeze on the Kema Embankment.
Bynner.   Foreigner, A.
Byron, G.   Lines to Mr Hodgson.
Shipwreck, The.
Cabico, R.   Mango Poem.
Caldwell, A.   Left All Alone Again Blues.
Caleshu, A.   Collaboration: Between Countries.
Campert.   Avignon.
Campo.   Belonging.
Cardenal.   Lights.
Casson, C.   To the South: "Journey to Italy began in your youth, The."
Castro, R.   Spring Does Not Flow Now, The.
Cawein.   Uncalled.
Cedering, S.   Variations for the Piano.
Cendrars.   My Dance.
Prose of the Trans-Siberian and Little Jean of France.
South.
Chan Fang-sheng.   Sailing Back to the Capital.
Sailing into the South Lake.
Chang Chi.   Coming at Night to a Fisherman's Hut.
Chang K'o-chiu.   Tune: "Merriment Before the Palace Hall".
Tune: "Traveler Welcoming the Immortal".
Chang Yen.   Tune: "Pure Serene Music".
Chang Yü.   Merchant's Joy, The.
Chia Tao.   Farewell to Master Tan Returning to Min.
Morning Travel.
Passing by a Mountain Village at Dusk.
Spring Travel.
Child, L.   Thanksgiving Day.
Chimi Sucho.   Returning to Dongrae.
Ch'in Kuan.   Tune: "Perfumed Garden".
Chine-Jo, Lady.   Wild geese / Fellow travelers.
Ching An.   Over King Yu Mountain with a Friend.
Ch'u Yüan.   Ying from "The Nine Declarations".
Cistulli.   47.57.
Clare, J.   Winter.
Woodland Seat, A.
Cocteau.   Cape of Good Hope, The.
Cohen, L.   Suzanne [Takes You Down].
Cooley, N.   John Winthrop, "Reasons to be Considered for...the Intended Plantation in New England," 1629.
Coolidge, C.   On the Road.
Corcoran.   In the Red Book.
Cortázar.   Travel.
Cory, W.   Parting.
Coviello, M.   This hour is made of iron grates where the underground.
Crane, H.   River, The.
Cristall.   Holbain.
Crozier, L.   Packing for the Future: Instructions.

Cunningham, J.   Traveller, the highway my guide, A.
Daio.   I have had a companion on the road.
Dame.   On the Road to Damascus, Maryland.
Darwish, M.   We Travel Like Other People.
Davie, D.   Epistle. To Enrique Caracciolo Trejo.
Davies, Grahame.   Liverpool.
Davison, P.   Where the Sun Ends.
De la Mare.   Listeners, The.
Deane, S.   Return.
Denby.   Ciampino: Envoi.
Dennis, C.   Traveller, The.
Devi.   Going out of Town.
Dib, M.   To a Voyager.
Dickinson, E.   Caterpillar ("How soft a Caterpillar steps—.").
I watched the Moon around the House.
DiPalma.   Wrong Side of the Door, The.
Dixon, M.   Place, Places.
d'Oettingen.   Kilimanjaro.
Donne.   On His Mistress [or Mistris].
Song: "Sweetest love, I do not go[e]."
Dorn, E.   Geranium.
Drayton.   To the Virginian Voyage.
Dubie.   Poem: "Mule kicked out in the trees, A. An Early."
Duffy, C.   In Your Mind.
Edgar, C.   Cloud of Unknowing, The.
Eich.   Viareggio.
Eliot, T. S.   Journey of the Magi.
Erdrich.   Lady in the Pink Mustang, The.
Evans, E.   Whatever clime we travel or explore.
Fan Chung-yen.   Tune: "Sumuche Dancers".
Ferlinghetti, L.   Starting from San Francisco.
Field, Edward.   Journey, A.
Field, Eugene.   Wynken, Blynken, and Nod.
Figueroa, J.   Murdered Luggage.
Fisher, A.   African Boog.
Flynn, L.   Furthest Distances I've Travelled, The.
Forhan, C.   Taste of Wild Cherry, The.
Fraser, G.   Traveller Has Regrets, The.
Freeman, Jessica.   Bayou Arabic Argot.
Slate Roof Blues.
Freneau.   Rude, from the wide extended Chesapeake.
Fuller, J.   Wild Raspberries.
Galvin, J.   Indirective.
Gandlevsky, S.   Dear God, allow me to recall my works.
Garioch.   Property.
Gershwin, I.   Let's Take a Walk Around the Block.
Gillespie, H.   Breezin' Along with the Breeze.
Giussani, S.   Towards a Beginning.
Gizzi.   Tout les Matins du Monde.
Gloria.   Rizal's Ghost.
Glück, L.   Magi, The.
Goethe.   Diary, The.
Mignon.
Song of the Traveler at Evening.
Wanderer's Night Song.
Góngora y Argote.   Sonnet 103.
Gonzalez, N.   I Made Myself a Path.
Wanderer in the Night of the World, A.
Goodison.   Road of the Dread, The.
Granados, J.   Promised Land, The.
Tierra prometida, La.
Graves, R.   Cloak, The.
Travel[l]er's Curse after Misdirection[, The].
Gray, R.   Journey: the North Coast.
Greenlaw, L.   Galileo's Wife.
Griffin, T.   I Have Folded This Letter in Ten Places.
Grin, B.   On Roads.
Grosholz.   Life of a Salesman.
Gunn, T.   Discovery of the Pacific, The.
Gurney, I.   Song: "Only the wanderer."
Gustafsson, L.   Ballad of the Dogs.
Guthrie, R.   Magi, The.
Hadas, R.   Journey Out.
Hafiz, K [or Hafez].   Come pass me the cup quickly and hand it on.
Hagiwara Sakutaro.   On a Trip.
Hall, D.   Hermit with Landscape.
Han-shan.   Back at Cold Mountain.

Body Asking Shadow.
My place is on Cold Mountain.
People ask the way to Cold Mountain.
Pole your three winged galleons.
Hannah, S.   Postcard from a Travel Snob.
Hanu.   Some said the northern window was bright.
Harburg.   Let's Take a Walk Around the Block.
Harington [or Harrington].   Thus all that day, they spent in divers talke.
Harwood, L.   Czech Dream.
Hayley.   To Mrs. Hayley, On her Voyage to America. 1784.
Hecht, A.   Prospects.
Hedin, R.   Transcanadian.
Heng Chao.   Farewell to Vinaya Master Ts'ung, Traveling in the West.
Herrick.   Salutation.
Heym.   With the Ships of Passage.
Hiestand, E.   Moon Winx Motel.
Hikmet.   Things I Didn't Know I Loved.
Hirshfield, J.   Leaving the October Palace.
Hofmannsthal.   Traveller's Song.
Hood, T.   To the Ocean.
Hsieh Ling-yün.   From Chin-Chu Creek, Past the Ridge, Along the Stream.
Night: Setting out from Shih-Kuan Pavilion.
Hsieh T'iao.   To Hsuan-Ch'eng, Past Hsin-Lin-P'u, Toward Pan-Ch'iao.
Hsin Ch'i-chi.   Tune: "Partridge Sky" At Po-shan Monastery.
Tune: "Pure Serene Music" En Route to Po-shan.
Tune: "The Bodhisattva's Golden Headdress".
Huang T'ing-chien.   Tune: "Courtyard Full of Fragrance, The".
Huffstickler.   Travel Note.
Hughes, L.   Bound No'th Blues.
Hughes, T.   Platform One.
Hugo, R.   Driving Montana.
Montesano Unvisited.
Imr el [or ul] Kais.   Ode: "Weep, ah weep love's losing, love's with its dwelling-place."
Jackson, A.   Love of Travellers, The.
Jackson, H.   Emigravit.
Found Frozen.
Jackson, M. L.   Indian Song.
Jacob, M.   Invitation to a Voyage.
Jamie, K.   Way we live, The.
Jarrell, R.   On the Railway Platform.
Jefferson, B.   Long Distance Moan.
Jenkins, A.   Road Less Travelled, The.
Jenkins, J. et al.   In Ferrara.
Johnson, H.   Fringe-Area Reception.
Jones, R.   Novel, The.
Jones, T.   Cwmchwefri.
Jordan, J.   Roman Poem Number Nine.
Kakei.   In the withering gusts.
Kang [Grossjean], Ok-Ku [or Ok-Koo].   Were I a Flower.
Kassid, A.   Trilogy of Travel.
Katz, J.   Concerning the Islands Newly Discovered.
Keats.   There Was a Naughty Boy.
Kenyon, J.   Here.
Kikaku.   Over the long road.
Kim Ch'unsu [or Chun-soo].   Riding a Mule.
Kim Sowŏl.   Road, The.
Kipling, R.   Sestina of the Tramp-Royal.
Koch, K.   Ville de Nice, La.
Ku K'uang.   Hard Traveling.
Larbaud.   Images.
Larkin, P.   Arrivals, Departures.
Lattimore.   North Philadelphia, Trenton, and New York.
Lauterbach.   In the Museum of the Word (Henri Matisse).
Lear, E.   Jumblies, The.
Levine, P.   Travelling Music.
Levis.   Widening Spell of the Leaves, The.
Li Ch'ing-chao.   To the Tune: Partridge Sky.
Tune: "Fisherman's Pride".
Li Po.   Crossing Ching-Men to See a Friend Off.
Early Departure from White Emperor Fortress.
Lu Mountain Song For the Palace Censor Empty-Boat Lu, A.

My sword at my waist, I climb a high tower.
On Visiting a Taoist Master in the Daitian Mountains and Not Finding Him.
Parting.
Rhymeprose on the Sword Gallery.
Road to Shu Is Hard, The.
Taking Leave of a Friend.
To See a Friend Off to Shu.
To See Meng Hao-Jan Off to Yang-Chou.
To the Tune: Beautiful Barbarian.
Tune: "Beautiful Barbarians".
Li Yü. Tune: "Beauty Yu".
Liu Ch'ang-ch'ing. Rejoicing that the Zen Master Pao Has Arrived from Dragon Mountain.
Locklin. Where we are.
Loncar, M. There Goes the Bride.
Longfellow, H. Excelsior.
Tide Rises, the Tide Falls, The.
Lope de Vega. Today Delight's Fair Ship.
Lu Chao-lin. Old Idea of Choan by Rosoriu.
Lu Yu. At Ta-an I Got Sick from Wine and Had to Lay Over for Half a Day. Governor Wang Invited Me to His Place Again.
Blue Rapids.
I Had Occasion to Tell a Visitor about an Old Trip I Took.
Rain on the River [1956].
Rain on the River [1970].
Ma Chih-yüan. Tune: "Sky-Pure Sand".
MacCaig. Crossing the Border.
Machado Ruiz. I go on dreaming.
Rainbow at Night.
Tavern Guitar Playing a *Jota* Today.
Macrae, J. Sleep Softly.
Madhubuti. Poet: What Ever Happened to Luther?
Mallarmé. Sea Breeze.
Martial. Believe me, sir, I'd like to spend whole days.
Martinson. March Evening.
Masefield. Sea Fever.
Mathews, E. K. Indian, The.
McFarland. Memoir of the Cosmopolite Who Stayed Home.
McGinley. New England Pilgrimage.
McGrath, C. Delphos, Ohio.
Spring Comes to Chicago.
McGrath, T. Epitaph: "Again, traveller, you have come a long way led by that star."
From here it is necessary to ship all bodies east.
McGuckian. To a Cuckoo at Coolanlough.
McLain, P. Residue.
McNulty, T. Bodhidharma Crossing the Graywolf River on a Ry-Krisp.
Mei Yao Ch'en. I Remember the Blue River.
Menashe. 49th Birthday Trip (What Are You On?).
Meng Hao Jan. Returning by Night to Lu-Men.
Returning Home to Deer-Gate Mountain at Night.
Stayover at Chien-Teh River.
Merrill, J. Clearing the Title.
Merwin. Wheels of the Trains, The.
Michaels, D. Returning from Italy.
Mickiewicz. Ackermann Steppe, The.
Miller, E. Tomorrow.
Miller, J. American Odalisque.
Mills, B. Ballad: Of Motion.
Mitchell, E. Passenger Opposite, The.
Miyazawa Kenji. Morning of the Last Farewell, The.
Moore, H. Edward.
Poem for the End.
Morales, A. South.
Moramarco, F. Volunteer's Fairy Tale, A.
Moss, H. Tourists.
Mueller, L. Commuter.
Mukai Kyorai. Even in my town / Now, I sleep.
Muldoon, P. Making the Move.
Muso Soseki. At Gen's Embarkation for Yuan China.
At Iku's Embarkation for Yuan China.
At Kan's Embarkation for Yuan China.
Wandering.
Nara Singde. Tune: "Butterflies Lingering over

Flowers".
Nash, O. Unwinged Ones, The.
Nathan, L. United Flight 608.
Nemerov. Song of Degrees, A.
Neruda. Introduction: My Themes.
Nguyễn Chí Thiện. Travel with Grief— Goodbye to Joy.
Nichol. Ferry Me Across.
Nichols, G. Epilogue: "I have crossed an ocean."
Nooteboom. Basho 1.
Nortje. Native's letter.
Nye, N. Whole Self, The.
O'Hara, F. Mary Desti's Ass.
Okudzhava. Ah, Nadya, Nadyenka.
Departure.
Orléans, C. Lost.
Ortiz. San Diego Poem, A: January-February 1973.
Travelling.
Travels in the South.
Upstate.
Padgett, R. Statue of a Libertine, The.
Padilla. Nuclear Umbrella.
Pak Mogwŏl [*or* Mokwŏl]. Wayfarer, The.
Palladas [*or* Pallades]. Whose baggage from land to land is despair.
Pao Chao. Ascend Lu-Shan.
Pao Ling-hui. Poem Sent to a Traveler.
Parnell, P. Sile Na gCioch.
Parry-Williams. From a Travel Diary.
Pastan. Last Train, The.
Paterson, D. Trans-Siberian Express, The.
Paz. I travel your body as I would travel the world.
Peabody, J. After Music.
Pellicer, C. Studies.
Peskett. From Belfast to Suffolk.
Pfeiffer, E. Mid-Ocean.
Phillips, D. Hounds are either the work of wind, The.
Piombino. Time Travel.
Plath. Getting There.
Plumly. For Esther.
Po Chü-i. Dream of Mountaineering, A.
Sleeping on Horseback.
Starting Early from the Ch'u-ch'ěng Inn.
Popa. Journey.
St Sava's Journey.
Porta. Traveler.
Porter, C. I've a Shooting Box in Scotland.
Katie Went to Haiti.
Pound, E. Gypsy, The.
Powell, D. A. In the course of travel: strychnine every few hours. some italian art.
Price, L. Maidens of London's Brave Adventures, Or, a Boon Voyage Intended for the Sea, The.
Probyn. End of the Journey, The.
Purdy, A. Blue City, The.
Pushkin, A. Demons.
Radcliffe, A. Storied Sonnet.
Rafferty, P. Passage.
Remoto. Rain.
Reverdy. Departure.
Endless Journeys.
Riley, P. Another damp Sunday morning up and walk over.
119. 3.
Rimbaud, A. Departure.
Robin, L. Beyond the Blue Horizon.
Robinson, E. John Evereldown.
Robinson, M. Reaches Sicily.
Roethke. Night Journey.
Rosenblatt, S. Visiting New York.
Rossetti, C. Old-World Thicket, An.
Uphill [*or* Up-Hill].
Rossetti, D. Constant keeping-past of shaken trees.
Rosten. We came during those years.
Rukeyser, M. Ajanta.
Rumi. That Journeys Are Good.
Samaras, N. Aubade: Macedonia.
Sarah, R. Courtney, Mentioned in Passing, Years After.
Sarton, M. After a Train Journey.

Scammell, W. Inventions.
Scott, D. For Norman Nicholson.
Seale, J. Travel North: The Rules.
Shapcott, J. Phrase Book.
Shapiro, M. To Jerusalem, 1990.
Shelley, P. Ozymandias.
World's Wanderers, The.
Sigourney. Western Emigrant, The.
Smith, W. Robert Frost: The Road Taken.
Soen. On Visiting Shorin Temple, Where Bodhidharma Once Lived.
Soupault. Horizon.
Soyinka. Death in the Dawn.
Spence, L. Prows O' Reekie, The.
Stevenson, R. From a Railway Carriage.
Tropics vanish, and meseems that I, The.
Vagabond, The.
Stow. Landfall.
Su Tung-p'o. Tune: "Immortal by the River".
Sung Fang-hu. Traveler's Life, A.
Supervielle. Traveller, traveller.
Swenson, K. Landlady in Bangkok, The.
T'ao Ch'ien [*or* T'ao Yuan-ming]. Return, The.
Tate, J. Descent, The.
Taylor, A. Goethe and Brentano.
Teft. On a Friend's Taking a Journey.
ten Berge. Fortunes in knee breeches.
Trakl. Revelation and Decline.
Tranter. Moment of Waking, The.
Triplett, P. Story for the Mother Tongue.
Tripp. Diesel to Yesterday.
Troup, B. (Get Your Kicks On) Route 66!
Ts'ao Chih. Woe Indeed!
Ts'ao Ts'ao. Bitter Cold: A Song.
Tu Fu [*or* Du Fu]. At the Sky's End, Thinking of Li Po.
Chengtu.
Climbing on the Double Ninth Day.
Journey North.
Night Thoughts While Traveling.
To Wei Pa, a Retired Scholar.
Traveler, a traveler, Zimei his name, A.
Traveling at Night.
Yellow Orioles.
Tu Mu. Departing in Early Morning.
Easing My Heart.
Li Bo put it in a poem, this West-of-the-Waters Abbey.
Whirled ten years beyond all bounds.
Tu Shen-yen. Harmonizing a Spring Poem by Premier Lu of Chin-Ling.
Turnbull. And I Think it Yours.
Ungria, R. Carillonneur.
Unknown. Ballad of Mulan, The.
Don't Be Weary, Traveller.
Farewell Poem.
Going on always on and on.
Goodnight Irene.
Horse neighs, wants to gallop, A.
I passed thurgh a gardyn grene.
I went east to Asia; I went west to Europe.
My island spirit.
Old Song.
Sad Song.
Story of How the Monk Tripiṭaka of the Great Country of T'ang Brought back the Sūtras, The.
Thus feverish fancies floated in my brain.
Tune: Eternal Longing.
Tune: Eternal Longing.
Tune: Eternal Longing.
Water the Horses at a Breach in the Great Wall.
Vallejo. It was Sunday in the fair ears of my burro.
Van Duyn. Into Mexico.
Viidikas. Future.
Vogel, D. Silently you stand before me.
Volkman. Shipwreck Poem.
Waddington, M. Ulysses Embroidered.
Wakayama Bokusui. How many mountains.
Walcott. Fortunate Traveller, The.
Tomorrow, Tomorrow.
Walton, A. McDonald's, Scottsboro, April, 1997.
Wang Shih-chieng. Ch'ai-kuan Mountain Pass.
Wang Wan. Stayover at Pei-Ku-Shan.

Wang Wei. After Source of the Peach Blossom Stream.
  Arriving at Ba Gorge in the Morning.
  Floating on the River Han.
  Light rain is on the light dust.
  Melody of Wei City.
  Mission to the Frontier.
  Mount Chung-Nan.
  To See a Friend Off.
Warren, R. Dream He Never Knew the End of, The.
Weatherford, C. From Birmingham to Bristol in a Boxcar.
Weaver, A. My Father's Geography.
Weston, M. Departure.
Wetzsteon. Late Show, The.
Whalen, P. Hoist great blocks of language into place.
White, H. Winter Traveler, The.
Whitman, W. I take to the open road.
  Promise to California, A.
Whittier. To a Cape Ann Schooner.
Wicks, S. Clever Daughter, The.
Williams, H. To the White Bird of the Tropic.
Williams, J. In Duffryn Woods.
Wolverton, T. In China.
Woo, D. Expatriates.
Woolson. Other, The.
Wordsworth, W. I Travelled among Unknown Men.
  Most Sweet It Is with Unuplifted Eyes.
  Simplon Pass, The.
  Stepping Westward.
Wright, C. Peace Corps Volunteer Comes Home, The.
Wright, Jay. Sketch for an Aesthetic Project.
Wright, Judith. Train Journey.
Wunderlich, M. Anchorage, The.
Yasui. In the withering gusts.
  Who's that?
Yi Saek. Rough clouds gather around the valley.
Youn, Monica. Night Ferry to Naxos 2.
Young, A. Leaving Syracuse.
Young, K. Quivira City Limits.
Yu Hsin. Bidding Farewell to Secretary Chou.
Yüan Chüeh. Shipboard Song.
Yuan Mei. Old and Traveling.
  On the Road to T'ien-t'ai.
  On the Way to Pa-ling.
Zagajewski. To Go to Lvov.
Zaid. Mortal Practice.
Zuni Oral Tradition. Following their road of exit, they stooped over and came out.

Treason and Traitors
Burns, R. Such a Parcel of Rogues in a Nation.
De la Mare. Ballad of Christmas, A.
Elizabeth I. Doubt of Future Foes.
Hammial. Treason's Choice.
Harington [or Harrington]. Of Treason.
Layamon. Arthur's Dream.
Neruda. They Receive Instructions Against Chile.
Pacheco, J. High Treason.
Rich, A. For Ethel Rosenberg.

Treasures
Ap Hywel, Elin. Treasure.
Bell, M. True Story, A.
Cox, M. Treasure: "Ax heads and sledges, musket balls and elixir bottles."
Doolittle, H. In no wise is the pillar-of-fire.
Lee-Hamilton. Sunken Gold.
Mistral, G. Rose, The.

Treaties
MacNeice. Munich Agreement, The.
Pagis, D. Draft of a Reparations Agreement.
Thomas, D. Hand That Signed the Paper, The.

Tree of Life
Holley, M. Tree of Life, The.
Yamamura Bochō. Mandala.

Trees
Abley, M. Down.
Adamson. Elm Tree in Paddington, An.
Adcock, F. Trees.
Adisa. Rainbow, The.

Adonis [or Adunis]. Tree of Fire.
Al-Harizi. Sun, The.
Alarcon, F. Los árboles son poetas / Trees Are Poets.
Ammons. Ballad: "I want to know the unity in all things and the difference."
  Improvisation for Jerald Bullis, An.
Antler. Trees Seen Now.
Ashbery, J. Some Trees.
Assultani, F. Tree, A.
Atkins, R. Lines in Recollection.
Aubert, A. Baobab.
Azzawi, F. For Everyone His Own Tree.
Barrax. There Was A Song.
Bartlett, B. Afterlife of Trees, The.
Basho. Coolness.
  Crow, A.
  Felling a tree.
  From all these trees.
  Having planted a banana tree.
  I don't know.
  Moonlight slanting.
  Oak tree, The.
  Spring we don't see, The.
  Winter storm, The.
Bass, E. All the Trees.
Bei Dao. Stretch out your hands to me.
Belitt. Orange Tree, The.
Berrigan, T. Each tree stands alone in stillness.
Berry, W. Old Man Climbs a Tree, The.
  Sycamore, The.
Bhattācārya, K. Withered tree doesn't blossom, The.
Bingen, Hildegard von. Alleluia-verse for the Virgin.
Blake, W. In a Myrtle [or Mirtle] Shade.
Blasing, R. Refuge.
Bontemps. Blight.
Bosnick, Eli. Larger Loneliness, A.
Breton, A. More than Suspect.
Brion, R. If Fortune Smiles.
Brooks, G. Birth in a narrow room, The.
Brown, L. Green Arbor, A.
Bugeja, M. Conifer King, The.
Buson. Buying leeks.
  By moonlight.
  Cherry blossoms fallen.
  Dog barking, A.
  End of spring, The.
  Having reddened the plum blossoms.
  In the white plum blossoms.
  Mountain cuckoo, The.
  Petals fall, The.
  Two plum trees, The.
  Willow leaves fallen, The.
Campbell, D. Here, under Pear-trees.
Campo, C. Devout like a Branch.
Cariaga. Family Tree, The.
Carter, M. Bitter Wood.
Castellanos. Palm Tree, A.
Cendrars. Great Fetishes, The.
Ceni, A. Key and the Tree, The.
Ceravolo. Happiness in the Trees.
Chavarría, L. Lone Tree.
Cherry, K. Late Afternoon at the Arboretum.
Christie, J. Vernal Conifer Seance.
Clare, J. Fallen Elm, The.
  Maple Tree, The.
  Nutting.
  Shepherd's Tree, The.
Clark, T. Shadow extends the tree.
Coleman, A. Portraiture.
Coolbrith. My Cloth of Gold.
Copus, J. Pulling the Ivy.
Crapsey. Fragment.
Crawford, I. City Tree, The.
Creeley. Turn, The.
Cross, E. Baniano.
  Banyan.
Cucchi, M. Every season has its dead.
Davis, G. Children in the Arbor.
Davis, K. Green Noise of Ohio Hardwoods, The.
Davison, P. Cross Cut.
Dawe, B. Renewal Notice.
De la Mare. Three Cherry Trees, The.

  Two Gardens.
Delmore, E. Willow.
  Yew.
Deming, A. Tilden Park.
Dickey, J. One, The.
Dickinson, E. Tree in Winter.
Disch. Poems: "I think that I shall never read."
Dodd, E. Dieback.
  Lyric: "It doesn't matter / whether / a tree falls."
Doolittle, H. Amen.
Dove, R. Dusting.
  Horse and Tree.
Dubie. Last Poem, Snow Tree.
Dugan, A. On Trees.
Dumas, H. Root Song.
Dunbar, P. Haunted Oak, The.
Ellingham, L. Tompkins Sq. Branches With Snowy Arms.
Erdrich, H. Quiet Earth, The.
Everson, W. High Embrace, The.
  Passion Week.
Feinstein, E. Magic Apple Tree, The.
Field, E. Sugar-Plum Tree, The.
Field, M. Nests in Elms.
  O Wind, thou hast thy kingdom in the trees.
Fink, Robert A. Mesquite.
Finney, N. Uncles.
Fletcher, J. Trees, like great jade elephants, The.
Foster, A. Union.
Francis, R. As Easily As Trees.
  Broken View, A.
Frost, R. Birches.
  On a Tree Fallen Across the Road (To Hear Us Talk).
  Sound of Trees, The.
  Spring Pools.
  Tree at My Window.
Fulton, R. End of an Age, The.
Galanskov. Bird-cherry was my wife, The.
Galeano, J. Tree: "Man in love with a tree goes to live with him awhile before getting married, A."
Gallagher, T. Choices.
García Lorca. Song of the Barren Orange Tree.
  Sonnet of Sweet Complaint.
Garioch. Maple and the Pine, The.
Garrett, G. For a Bitter Season.
Gaspar. Tree, The.
Gehrke, S. Near the Mississippi.
George, F. Shagbark.
Ghigna. Park Elms.
Gilliams, M. Tristitia Ante.
Gioia. Planting a Sequoia.
Giovanni. Alabama Poem.
Godfrey. Unholy Spring.
Goll, I. I'd like to be nothing.
Gorham. Empress Receives the Head of a Taiping Rebel, The.
Graves, R. Hide and Seek.
Grimké, A. Tenebris.
Guiney. Planting the Poplar.
Gurney, I. Felling a Tree.
  Possessions.
Gyodai. Slowly / Over cedars.
Haavikko. Plant trees. Exactly against this tree.
Hagiwara Sakutaro. One Who's in Love with Love, The.
  So Terrifyingly Melancholy.
Hahn, S. Baobab Tree 1996, The.
Hall, D. Surface.
Hall, H. Things That Grow.
Halpern, D. Annuals.
Han Yü. Withered Tree, A.
Hardy, T. Tree and the Lady, The.
Harms. Sky.
Hass, R. Elm.
Haviaras, Stratis. Tree.
Heine, H. Pine Is Standing Lonely, A.
Herrick. To Blossoms.
Hirshfield, J. Tree.
Hoekstra. Cedar, The.
Honig, E. November through a Giant Copper Beech.
Hope, A. Australia.
Hopkins, G. Binsey Poplars (Felled 1879).

Hudgins. Tree.
Hwang Jiwoo. Out of the Winter-Tree Into the
  Spring-Tree.
Ikkyu Sojun. Form in Void.
Im Yŏngjo. Winter Tree.
Inada. Just Made It.
Iroquois Oral Tradition. Tree of the Great
  Peace, The.
Irwin, M. Tree, A.
Issa. As the great old trees.
  January.
  Not yet become a Buddha.
Jacobsen, R. Catacombs in San Callisto, The.
Jarman, Geraint. Wood, The.
Jiménez, J. Lumber Wagons, The.
Jones, Einir. Shadows of Trees on the Lawn,
  January.
Juarroz. Lamp lit, A.
Kang Ŭn'gyo. Woods: "Tree trembles, A."
Kariara. Leopard Lives in a Muu Tree, A.
Kenney. Sawmill.
Kilmer, J. Trees.
Kinnell. Perch, The.
Kirsch, S. Mail.
Kloos, W. Trees, Late in the Season.
Kollan Alici. What Her Friend Said.
Kreymborg. Tree, The.
Kunitz, S. War against the Trees, The.
Kushner, A. Cypress.
Larkin, P. Trees, The: "Trees are coming into
  leaf, The."
Lawrence, D. H. Trees in the Garden.
Levertov. Contraband.
  Gathered at the River.
  Re-Rooting.
  Tree Telling of Orpheus, A.
Levine, P. Sleepless Night, A.
Levy, A. London Plane-Tree, A.
Lewis, J. Garden Note I, Los Altos.
  Garden Note II, March.
Locker-Lampson. Old Oak Tree at Hatfield
  Broadoak, The.
Longley, M. Beech Tree, The.
Lorde. Ballad from Childhood.
Loynaz, D. M. Calm, The.
MacDiarmid, H. Sunny Gale.
  Under the Greenwood Tree.
MacLean, S. Hallaig.
Mahon. Going Home.
Mandelstam [or Mandelshtam]. Shy speechless
  sound, The.
McAuley, J. Tomb of Heracles, The.
McCollough, Aaron. Eros, Ethos, Economuos.
McCord, D. Every Time I Climb A Tree.
Melville, H. Time's Betrayal.
Metastasio. On thy grey bark, in witness of my
  flame.
Mew. Forest Road, The.
  Trees Are Down, The.
Millay, E. Counting-out Rhyme.
  Grow not too high, grow not too far from home.
Milosz, C. Goddess, A.
Mistral, G. Final Tree.
Miyazawa Kenji. Spring and the Ashura.
Moffitt. To Look at Any Thing.
Montag, T. May 9, 2001 (4).
Montale. Lemon Trees, The.
  Lemon Trees, The.
  Storm, The.
Moore, L. From the Field.
Morejón. Tree of Earthly Delights.
Moritz [or Morits]. My apple-tree, my willow.
Morris, G. Woodman, Spare That Tree.
Moss, H. Pruned Tree, The.
Muldoon, P. Wind and Tree.
Muso Soseki. Dry Tree.
  From the beginning.
  Moon Tree Cliff.
  Pine Shade.
Na Ceapaich, S. Alasdair of Glengarry.
Naimy, M. Hunger.
Nash, O. Song of the Open Road.
Nelson, J. If a Fish Fell in a Forest.
Nemerov. Learning by Doing.
  Learning the Trees.
Nemes Nagy. Trees.

Nesbit, E. Child's Song in Spring.
Neto. African Poem.
Niedecker. My friend tree.
Nielsen, D. My Philosophy.
Oliver, M. Black Walnut Tree, The.
Olson, C. Merce of Egypt.
Oppen. Building of the Skyscraper, The.
Ortiz. Speaking.
  What I Tell Him.
Ou-yang Hsiu. Green Jade Plum Trees in
  Spring.
Ovid. Myrrha and Cinyras.
Pak Chaesam. Looking at Winter Trees.
Parini. Some Compensation.
Parry-Williams. Barrenness.
Pastan. Hardwood.
Pasternak, B. Miracle, The.
Peake. Conceit.
Peaux, A. Spring Landscape.
Petrovykh, M. Air Is Motionless with Heat,
  The.
Philips, K. Upon the graving of her Name upon
  a Tree in Barnelmes Walks.
Plath. Polly's Tree.
  Words.
Po Chü-i. Planting Flowers on the Eastern
  Embankment.
Ponge. Trees That Come Undone within a
  Sphere of Fog.
Porta. Nearby creatures of the air.
  To become a tree.
Pound, E. Girl, A.
  Tree, The.
Prunty. Elbow Tree, The.
Rahim, J. Felling of a Tree, The.
Ramsdell, H. Bright Receding.
Randell. And if my light should.
  Walking towards the village.
Ransom, J. Dead Boy.
Reznikoff. April.
  Grove of small trees, branches thick with
  berries, A.
Rhodes, M. Disguised.
Rich, A. Trees, The.
Roberts, David Thomas. Toward Mena.
Robinson, E. New Language, The.
Rosemurgy, C. Love, with Trees and Lightning.
Rosen, K. Kildan Women, The.
Rossetti, C. Autumn ("I dwell alone—I dwell
  alone, alone.").
  Who Has Seen the Wind?
Roubaud. In This Tree.
Saigyō. In a tree standing.
Salaam. Round Midnight, Place de Congo.
Saner. Autumn Aspens: Cumbres Pass.
Savageau. All Night She Dreams.
  Trees.
Schuyler, J. Noon Office.
Scott, S. Flowers and Trees.
Sedakova. Female Figure.
Seferis. Poplar Leaf, The.
Shepherd, R. West Willow.
  What Cannot Be Kept.
Shillaber, B. Picture, A.
Shiomi, M. Passing Music for a Tree.
Shore. Sawdust.
Simic. Fear: "Fear passes from man to man."
Sirowitz, H. I Finally Managed to Speak to Her.
Sitwell. Tulip Tree.
Smith, D. Egret Tree, The.
Södergran. My Childhood Trees.
Soloukhin. For the Tree to Sing...
Sone no Yoshitada. Lower leaves of the trees,
  The.
Sontrop. Acorn Speaks, The.
Souster. Very Short Poem.
Stafford, W. British Columbia.
Stephens, J. Wind, The.
Stevenson, A. Hemlock at Sunset, A.
Stewart, S. These Trees in Particular.
Stoddard, E. Above the Tree.
Strand. Keeping Things Whole.
  Prediction, The.
Suárez, V. Song to the Banyan.
Suzuki, M. Swiftly walking away.
Sylvester, J. Palms.

Tagliabue. Bare Arms of Trees, The.
Thomas, E. Aspens.
Tornero, A. Arden la torcida, entre mis ojos, y
  la jerarquía intermedia de una imagen esta
  tarde.
  They blaze, between my eyes, the wick-twist
  and the intermediate hierarchy of an image
  this afternoon.
Turner, W. Music of a Tree, The.
Ungaretti. Soldiers.
Unknown. Christ the Apple-Tree.
  First Coconut Tree, The.
  Forest Trees of the Sea.
  Jiu-mu: South, Droops a Tree.
  Rain Song of the Shu'-wi Chai' än (Snake
  Society), A.
  Song to the Trees and Streams.
  Treeback.
  We love the daylight.
Various authors. Tree, whose roots are deep,
  The.
Voigt. Two Trees.
Wagoner, D. Nuthatch.
Wang Wei. In the Mountain.
Warren, R. Holly and Hickory.
Waters, M. First Lesson: Winter Trees.
Welish. Textile 9.
Whitman, W. I Saw in Louisiana a Live-Oak
  Growing.
Wilbur, R. Alatus.
  In Trackless Woods.
Williams, W. Locust Tree in Flower, The.
  To Waken an Old Lady.
  Young Sycamore.
Williamson, G. Annual Returns.
  Appalachian Trees Encircled by Police Tape.
Wiman, C. In Lakeview Cemetery.
Wordsworth, W. Nutting.
  Tradition of Oker Hill in Darley Dale,
  Derbyshire, A.
Wright, J. Camphor Laurel.
  Gum-trees Stripping.
Wylie. Golden Bough.
Yi Sang. Flowering Tree.
Zimmer. Because of Duties, Zimmer Had
  Forgotten the Forest.
Zukofsky, L. As to How Much.
  In Arizona.

Trench Warfare
Graves, R. It's a Queer Time.
Jones, D. So thus he sorrowed till it was day
  and heard the foules sing, then somewhat he
  was comforted.
Manning, F. Trenches, The.
Owen, W. Anthem for Doomed Youth.
  Exposure.
Rickword. Winter Warfare.
Rosenberg, I. Break of Day in the Trenches.
  Dead Man's Dump.
Sassoon, S. Aftermath.
  Attack.
  Counter-Attack.
  Dreamers.
  Dug-Out, The.
  Rear-Guard, The.
  Working Party, A.
Scannell. Great War, The.
Service. Only a Boche.
West, A. Night Patrol, The.

Tricksters
Adam, H. Song for a Sea Tower.
Clare, J. Teased Pet, The.
DeSylva, B. G. You're an Old Smoothie.
Galina, M. I said to him—Just don't throw me
  into that briar patch.
Jonson, B. Volpone.
McElroy, C. Circus of the City, The.
Navajo Oral Tradition. Coyote, Skunk, and the
  Prairie Dogs.
Winnebago Oral Tradition. Felix White Sr.'s
  Introduction to Wakjankaga.

Trilobites
Coolidge, C. Ounce code orange.
Kendall, M. Lay of the Trilobite.

Trinidad and Tobago
Walcott. Midsummer, Tobago.

Port of Spain.

Trinity, The
Achterberg. Trinity.
Field. Trinity.
Hardie, K. Avatar, The.
Herrick. To God ("God's undivided, One in Persons Three.").
Langland, W. Trinity, The.
Unknown. Early Irish Triads.
Sacred Trinity, The.

Triolet (form)
Cornford, F. To a Fat Lady Seen from the Train.

Tristram and Isolde
Binyon. Tristram's End.
Carson, A. Homo Ludens.
Cunningham, J. Within this mindless vault.
Howe, S. Rückenfigur.
Unknown. Trystan and Esyllt.
Wagner, R. Smile his lips, A.

Triviality
Bhatt, S. What Is Worth Knowing?
Donaghy, M. Shibboleth.
Huerta, D. Thirteen Propositions against Trivial Love.
Trece intenciones contra el amor trivial.
Morabito, F. I've never been in love enough.
No he amado bastante.
Strand. Black Maps.
Wilbur, R. What's Good for the Soul is Good for Sales.

Troilus and Cressida
Chaucer. Conclusion.
Double sorwe of Troilus to tellen, The.
Henryson. O ladyis fair of Troy and Grece, attend.

Trojan War
Aeschylus. For Ares, gold-exchanger for the dead.
If I were to tell of our labours, our hard lodging.
Alcaeus [*or* Alkaios]. And excited the heart of Argive.
Having done most shameful, unjust things.
Story goes, from evil, The.
Brecht, B. On Reading a Recent Greek Poet.
Bridges, T. Squabbling gods the fight forsake, The.
Dugan, A. Stentor and Mourning.
Homer. Achilles' Dream.
Achilles' Lament and the Funeral of Patroclus.
Achilles Over the Trench.
And then went down to the ship.
Apollo Defeats Patroclus.
Death of Hector, The.
Embassy to Achilles, The.
Hector Returns to Troy.
Night Piece: the Trojans outside Troy.
Odyssey, The.
Patroclus Fights and Dies.
Priam and Achilles.
Rage of Achilles, The.
Rude Mars had th' ordering of their spirits; of Greeks, the learned Maid.
So mourn'd Pelides his late loss, so weighty were his moans.
Then to th' extremest heat of fight he did his valour turn.
Through the host with this the goddess ran.
Thus Neptune rous'd these men.
Tide of Battle Turns, The.
Ibycus. They destroyed the famous and wealthy.
Logue, C. Battle swayed, The.
Fate's sister, fortune, favours those.
See how that royal fights.
Longley, M. Horses, The.
Marlowe. Grecian soldiers, tired with ten years' war.
Sadoleto. Poem of Jacobus Sadoletus on the Statue of Laocoon, The.
Seneca. Trojan Women.
Triem. Witness, The.
Valéry. Helen ("It is I, O Azure, come from the caves below.").
Virgil [*or* Vergil]. By destiny compell'd, and in despair.
Death of Priam, The.

Then indeed into all our fluttering hearts.
Walcott. Menelaus.
Yeats. Leda and the Swan.

Trolleys
Blane, R. Trolley Song, The.
Martien, J. Late 20th Century: Spring.
Martin, H. Trolley Song, The.
See also **Streetcars**

Trolls
Stanton, M. Drugstore Trolls.

Trotsky, Leon
Ai. Killing Floor.

Troubadours
Nolla. Troubadour Love.

Trout
Buson. Leaves some trout.
Carson, A. Short Talk on Trout.
Hugo, R. Skykomish River Running.
Montague, J. Trout, The.
Onitsura. Leaping trout sees, The.
Wilbur, R. Hamlen Brook.

Troy
Alcaeus [*or* Alkaios]. Story goes, from evil, The.
Gunn, T. Wound, The.
Muir, E. Troy.
Sabry, M. Troy.
Sappho. Queen Hera, may your [graceful form].
Seneca. Trojan Women.
Shepherd, R. Homeric Interim.
Man Named Troy, A.
Stesichoros. This story is not true.
Virgil [*or* Vergil]. How They Took the City.
See also **Trojan War**

Trucks and Truckers
Allen, D. Poet at Eighteen, The.
Cruz, C. Traveling Gospel.
Dyson, W. Trucker, The.
Francis, M. Sitting with My Uncle.
Fuhrman, J. Atlantis.
Greene, Jonathan. Ruts.
Heaney, S. Two Lorries.
Koehler, T. Truckin'.
Llwyd, Iwan. Dust Truck Blues.
Mayes, J. Pedaling Paranoia.
Nutter, G. Train Station Zoetrope.
Schonborg. Rumble, A.
Snyder, G. Why Log Truck Drivers Rise Earlier Than Students of Zen.
Stone, J. Truck, The.
Tomlinson, C. At Barstow.

Truman, Harry S.
Glancy. Harry S Truman Library, Independence, Missouri.
Ray, D. For Harry S Truman in Hell.
Wallace, R. Hell Mural, The: Panel I.

Trumpeters and Trumpets
Dryden, J. Song for St Cecilia's Day, 1687, A.
Trumpet's loud clangor, The.
Goodwin, Everett. John Birks Gillespie: An Appreciation and Reflection.
Grass. Music for Brass.
Hemans. Trumpet, The.
Hristov, Boris. Evening Trumpet.
Hugo, V. Trumpet of Judgement, The.
Jeffers, L. How High the Moon.
Larkin, P. Reasons for Attendance.
Lima, J. Trumpets, The.
McGinley. Women of Jericho, The.
Unknown. Blow Your Trumpet, Gabriel.
Sons d'un Cornet, Li.

Trust
Aksal, S. Love Poem: "First line of this poem, The."
Baird, M. Do Not Make Things Too Easy.
Barresi. How It Comes.
Bogan, L. Heard by a Girl.
Bricusse, L. Who Can I Turn To (When Nobody Needs Me?).
Clarke, C. Vicki and Daphne.
Creeley. For Friendship.
Darley. It Is Not Beauty I Demand.
Doolittle, H. Now let the cycle sweep us here and there.

Gunn, T. Idea of Trust, The.
Hewitt, J. Ram's Horn, The.
Horovitz, F. Do You Not Know that I Need to Touch You.
Johnson, J. Eclipse.
Khali, S. Walking On: A Declaration of Wholeness.
Lee, L. Gift, The: "To pull the metal splinter from my palm."
Mann, R. Fiduciary.
Newley, A. Who Can I Turn To (When Nobody Needs Me?).
Philips, K. Epitaph on her Son *H. P.* at St. Syth's Church [where her body also lies Interred].
Pritchard, N. Burnt Sienna.
Reese, L. Trust.
Rohrer, M. Credo: "I believe there is something else."
Southey, C. On Trust.
Spenser, E. Sonnet 65: "Doubt which ye misdeeme, fayre love, is vaine, The."
Steinberg, D. With you I begin.
Tennyson, A. O[h], yet we trust that somehow good.
Theresa [*or* Teresa]. Poem: "Nothing move thee."
Vando. Father's Day.
Vietnamese Oral Tradition. Difficulties at Love.
Whitney, I. Ye virgins that from Cupid's tents.
Yellen, J. Mamma Goes Where Papa Goes.
Zawacki, Andrew. From the Book of Divine Consolation.

Truth
Aiyejina. Dialogue, The.
Al-Aziz, M. Fall, The.
Ashbery, J. Rain Moving In.
Basho. Come out to view.
Berlin. Say It Isn't So.
Boland, E. Oral Tradition, The.
Borges. John 1:14; And the Word became flesh and dwelt among us.
Bousoño, C. Cost of Truth, The.
Brontë, E. Stanzas: "Often rebuked, yet always back returning."
Browning, E. Best Thing in the World, The.
Buhyu Sunsoo. To an Outstanding Elder.
Cacciatore, E. Third Warning Sign: An Endless Surprise.
Campo. What the Body Told.
Carew, T. Disdain Returned.
Cernuda. If Man Could Name.
Invisible wall, The.
You were a tender desire, an insinuating cloud.
Chiao-jan. I hide my heart and not my deeds.
Ch'ien T'ao. Poems After Drinking Wine.
Chipasula. Manifesto on Ars Poetica.
Clarke, C. What Goes Around Comes Around, or The Proof is in the Pudding.
Clough. With Whom Is No Variableness, Neither Shadow of Turning.
Coleridge, H. Is love a fancy, or a feeling? No.
Coleridge, M. Contents of an Ink-bottle, The.
Insincere Wish Addressed to a Beggar, An.
True to myself am I, and false to all.
Crane, S. Wayfarer / Perceiving the pathway to truth, The.
Cristall. Ode on Truth: Addressed to George Dyer.
Cunningham, P. Cats—A Retrospective.
Dickinson, E. I died for Beauty—but was scarce.
Opinion is a flitting thing.
Truth—is as old as God.
Donne. Satire 3 [Religion].
Dooley, M. Heat.
Dowden, E. Old Letters.
Dunn, S. What They Wanted.
Edwards, D. Things, As They Are.
Eichner, Maura. Dream Songs Concluded.
Eliot, T. S. Hippopotamus, The.
Emerson, R. Harp, The.
Uriel.
Evans, M. Speak the Truth to the People.
Faverey. In the Service of the Wheel.
Frost, R. Night Person, The.

Fuller, M.   One in All, The.
Gascoigne.   Gascoigne's Woodmanship.
Gekkutsu-Sei.   I set down the emerald lamp.
Gershwin, I.   It Ain't Necessarily So.
Gioia.   Insomnia.
Glück, L.   Day Without Night.
   Lamium.
Graham, J.   In/Silence.
Graves, R.   Pier-Glass, The.
Guchu.   Men without rank, excrement spatulas.
Gwala.   Children of Nonti, The.
Hakuyo.   Over the peak spreading clouds.
Harper, M.   Alice.
Hauge.   Don't Come to Me with the Entire
   Truth.
Heard, J.   Truth.
Herbert, G.   Jordan (1).
Hill, G.   Crack of a starting pistol. Jean Jaurès.
Holmes, O.   Our Limitations.
Holst-Warhaft.   John 1:1 and 14.
Howard, R.   Vocational Guidance, with Special
   Reference to the Annunciation of Simone
   Martini.
Hudgins.   Repentance.
Hughes, L.   Theme for English B.
Hume, C.   Explanation.
Jackson, L.   Helen's Burning.
Jeffers, R.   Advice to Pilgrims.
   Cassandra.
Kaigen.   Old master held up fluff, The.
Keats.   Ode on a Grecian Urn.
Kim Chiha.   Core.
   Truth.
Kinsella, T.   Another September.
Kipling, R.   Fabulists, The.
Krivulin.   Two in a Room.
Landon.   Stern Truth.
Langland, W.   Piers Plowman Shows the Way to
   Saint Truth.
Lanier, S.   To Beethoven.
Lawrence, D. H.   Elemental.
Levertov.   Goddess, The.
   Illustration, The.[—a Footnote].
Levine, P.   I Was Born in Lucerne.
   Poem of Flight, The.
   Simple Truth, The.
Lindley, D.   Cryptogram, The.
Liu Ch'ang-ch'ing.   While Visiting on the South
   Stream the Taoist Priest Chang.
Mac Low.   Pieces O'six—XVIII.
MacNeice.   What is Truth? Says Pilate.
Macpherson, J.   Well, The.
Makusho, Layman.   Loving old priceless things.
Markotić, N.   Verbatim begins with this decade's
   hit and miss.
Meinke.   Supermarket.
Melville, H.   Enthusiast, The.
Michaels, A.   Once you called at midnight.
Milán, E.   ¿Cuál coro?
   What chorus?
Moise et al.   Newspaper, The.
Moorer.   Duty, or Truth at Work.
   Truth Suppressed, The.
Mumon Gensen.   Life: a cloud crossing the
   peak.
Muso Soseki.   At Kan's Embarkation for Yuan
   China.
   Old Man To-The-Point.
   Truth Hall.
Nadir, M.   Afterwards: "Earth will flame and
   glow, The."
Nolens, L.   Paranoia.
Ofeimun.   How Can I Sing.
   Prologue: "I have come down."
Olson, C.   Kingfishers, The.
Ovid.   Golden Age, The.
Padgett, R.   Joe Brainard's Painting "Bingo".
Padilla.   In Trying Times.
Parkes, B.   To an Author who Loved Truth
   More than Fame.
Parnok, S.   I shall not lie to find a lurid rhyme.
Peacocke.   Remembrance.
Perelman.   Things.
Porchia, Antonio.   Voices (an Excerpt).
Quevedo y Villegas.   I'll not be silent, though
   you put your finger.

Ragain.   If You Cannot Find the Truth Right
   Where You Are, Where Do You Expect to Find
   It?
Ralegh, S.   Lie, The.
Ramke, B.   Astronomer Works Nights: A
   Parable of Science, The.
Rexroth, K.   Buddha took some Autumn leaves.
Rilke.   Entrance.
Rodgers, C.   Feminism.
Roethke.   Open House.
Rojas.   What Do We Love When We Love?
Rossetti, C.   Hark! the Alleluias of the great
   salvation.
   My Dream.
Rukeyser, M.   Ballad of Orange and Grape.
   Poem as Mask, The.
Russell, G.   Truth.
Rux, C. H.   Pledge of Allegiance.
Sabines.   If Someone Tells You It's Not for
   Sure.
Sanguineti.   To the mini-skirted customs official
   who with sibyl-dove eyes.
Sansom, A.   Voice.
Scalise, G.   There have never been men crazier
   than these.
Serote.   Her name Is 'Dooti'.
Sexton.   Truth the Dead Know, The.
Shakespeare, W.   Phoenix and the Turtle, The.
   Sonnet 54: "O[h] how much more doth beauty
   beauteous seem."
Shelley, P.   Sonnet: Lift Not the Painted Veil.
Siddal.   Dead Love.
Sidney.   Sonnet 1: "Loving in truth, and fain[e]
   in verse my love to show."
Smith, S.   Magna Est Veritas.
Spellman, A.   Truth You Carry Is Very Dark,
   The.
Spires.   Woman on the Dump, The.
Stanley, G.   27/10/76.
Stanton, M.   Ballad of the Magic Glasses.
Steiger.   Until the sun sinks into a green.
Stevenson, R.   Whole Duty of Children.
Swenson, M.   In Love Made Visible.
Tennyson, A.   Higher Pantheism, The.
Thomas, E.   Glory, The.
Tsvetayeva [or Tsvetaeva].   I know the truth—
   give up all other truths!
Unknown.   Drinking Wine.
   Prayer to the Gods of the Night.
   Truth: "Breast / nursery."
Van Dyke.   Reliance.
Vitale, M.   Truth Put It.
Wang Wei.   To Magistrate Zhang.
Warren, R.   Vision.
Whittier.   Brown of Ossawatomie.
Wilbur, R.   Lying.
Wyatt.   What should I say.
Yakusai, Layman.   Deafening peal, A.
Yeats.   Leaders of the Crowd, The.
   Song of the Happy Shepherd, The.
Young, J.   True Love.
Zabolotsky [or Zabolotskii].   Poem about Rain.

Truth, Sojourner
Fauset.   Oriflamme.
Upton, Elaine Maria.   Streetwalker Trying to
   Speak to Sojourner Truth, A.

Trysts
Aiken, C.   All the Radios.
Buchsbaum, Julianne.   Power Plant, The.
García Lorca.   Unfaithful Married Woman, The.
Greenlaw, L.   Tryst.
James, T.   Reasons.
Kay, J.   What was it you said again there by the
   river.
Lumsden, R.   Always.
   Older Woman, An.
Merry.   Some Terrify Lions [or Anna Matilda].
Riordan, M.   Southpaw.
Ulacia, M.   Hampstead Heath.
   Hampstead Heath.
Unknown.   At night the verandah is dark, the
   beds too numerous.
Chu-qi dong-men: At the Great Gate.
   Hurry up, my love, if you want to delight in me.
   Midnight already and you are still not here.
   My courage fails me when I grasp my water jar.

My love, swear that you will come to me.
   Sang-zhong: Hunting the Dodder.
   Why do you come to me so seldom?
   You wretch who did not come last evening!
Van Winckel, N.   Nicholas by the River.

Tu Fu
Kleinzahler.   Watching Dogwood Blossoms Fall
   in a Parking Lot Off Route 46.
Kwŏn P'il.   Upon Reading Tu Fu's Poetry.
Li Po.   For Du Fu.
O'Hara, F.   To John Ashbery.

Tuberculosis
Cofer, J.   They Never Grew Old.
García, D.   Tísica.
Straus, M.   What I Heard on the Radio Today.
Thompson, P.   Consumptive, The.
Williams, S.   Wishon Line, The.

Tubman, Harriet
Allen, S.   Harriet Tubman aka Moses.
Clifton, L.   Harriet.
Cornish, S.   Harriet Tubman.
Griffin, S.   I Like to Think of Harriet Tubman.
Hayden, R.   Runagate Runagate.
Holmes, D.   Tubman Strong.
Jacobs, H.   Growing into my name.
McLoughland.   Whippoorwill Calls, The.
Sagay-Lights, V.   If Harriet Tubman Were Alive
   Today.
Unknown.   Harriet Tubman.

Tugboats
Oppen.   On the water, solid.
   Tug against the river.
Pitcher, O.   Remark, The.
Tranströmer.   Sun disappears, The.

Tulip Trees
Sitwell, O.   Tulip Tree.

Tulips
Bertrand.   Tulip Merchant, The.
Filkova, Fedya.   Arrival: "Did you hear."
Halperin.   Tulips.
Herrick.   Meditation for His Mistress[e], A.
Nichol.   Easter Pome.
Plath.   Tulips.
Tillema, M.   Considering Tulips.
   Tulips.
Williams, W.   Tulip Bed, The.

Tumbleweeds
Ward, T.   In the Interest of Possibility.

Tunnels and Tunnelling
Reid, C.   In the Echoey Tunnel.

Turkey
Catacalos.   Katakalos.
Griffiths, J.   There Are Limits to Brotherly
   Love.
Hikmet.   Evening Walk, The.
   Things I Didn't Know I Loved.
Kanik.   I Am Listening to Istanbul.
Olinka, S.   Chinese Man in Smyrna, A.
Sze.   Acanthus.

Turkeys
Clare, J.   Turkeys.
Etter.   Stuffy Turkey.
Heaney, S.   Turkeys Observed.
Jacobik, G.   Turkeys in August.
Kelly, B.   Wild Turkeys; The Dignity of the
   Damned.
Mackenzie, K.   Table-Birds.
Wilbur, R.   Black November Turkey, A.
Zimmer.   Romance for the Wild Turkey, A.

Turner, Lana
O'Hara, F.   Poem: "Lana Turner has collapsed!"

Turner, Nat
Aubert, A.   Nat Turner in the Clearing.

Turnips
Nichol.   Turnips Are.
Thomas, E.   Swedes.
Thompson, J.   Turnip Field.

Turtles
al-Sa'igh, Y.   Turtle.
Blue Cloud.   Turtle.
Bly, R.   Turtle, A.
Bottoms.   Armored Hearts.
Bynner.   But for these apertures.
Carroll, L.   Lobster Quadrille, A.

Song of the Mock Turtle, The.
Chin.   Turtle Soup.
Chŏng Hwajin.   South Yard, The.
Harter.   Turtle Blessing.
Lee, D.   First Turtle.
Lindsay, V.   Little Turtle, The.
Lux.   Thirst of Turtles, The.
Marlis, S.   Risible.
Nash, O.   Turtle, The.
O'Connor, M.   Turtles Hatching.
Ryan, K.   Turtle: "Who would be a turtle who could help it?"
Santos, S.   Of Haloes & Saintly Aspects.
Sarton, M.   Death and the Turtle.
Shakespeare, W.   Phoenix and the Turtle, The.
Siegel, R.   Turtles.
Spahr, J.   Write like one walks.
Unknown.   Long ago there was a mighty snake, and beings evil to men.
Williams, W.   Turtle, The.
See also **Tortoises**
Tuscany
Poliziano, A.   Splendor and pride I celebrate.
Wright, J.   Journey, The.
"Twain, Mark" (Samuel Langhorne Clemens)
Padgett, R.   Second Why.
Twelfth Night
Helton.   Old Christmas Morning.
Twickenham, England
Donne.   Twickenham [*or* Twicknam] Garden.
Twilight
Adams, L.   Home-coming.
Angel.   Twilight.
Anwar, C.   Twilight at a Little Harbor.
Basho.   Plates and bowls.
Beckett, S.   Roundelay: "On all that strand."
Bevington, L.   Twilight.
Bialik.   At Twilight.
Bogan, L.   Short Summary.
Boker.   Sonnet 25: "Leaden eyelids of wan twilight close, The."
Boland, E.   Women, The.
Buson.   Utter aloneness—.
Carter, J.   Adagio at Twilight.
Ceravolo.   Dusk: "Before the dusk grows deeper."
Ch'en Yün.   Twilight.
Dickey, J.   Dusk of Horses, The.
González, A.   Death in the Afternoon.
Gray, R.   Dusk, The.
Grimké, A.   Dusk.
  Winter Twilight, A.
Guest, B.   Twilight Polka Dots.
Haines, J.   Evening Change.
Hirsch, E.   Man on a Fire Escape.
Hsiao Kang.   Soft Echoes.
Kang Ŭn'gyo.   Twilight Song.
Lawrence, D. H.   Twilight.
Longfellow, H.   Afternoon in February.
  Children's Hour, The.
López Velarde.   In the Dying Afternoon.
Lugones.   Slow Delight.
Martinson.   Dusk in the Country.
Mezey.   Twilight Under Pine Ridge.
Morshen.   In superstitious panic.
Niu Hsi-chi.   Where the mist has torn.
Owen, W.   Anthem for Doomed Youth.
Parish.   Deep Purple.
Pritchard, N.   Burnt Sienna.
Ritsos.   Not Even Mythology.
Robinson, E.   Dark Hills, The.
Russell, G.   By the Margin of the Great Deep.
Skloot.   Twilight Time.
Smith, C.   Written near a Port on a Dark Evening.
Sone no Yoshitada.   Lower leaves of the trees, The.
Soupault.   Twilight.
Tan Taigi.   Beyond serenity / Gray kites.
Toomer.   Georgia Dusk.
Tripp.   Twilight in the Library.
Tu Fu [*or* Du Fu].   Sunset ("Sunset glitters on the beads.").
Voznesensky [*or* Voznesenskii].   Edge, The.
Wang Wei.   Twilight Comes.

Whitman, W.   Hours Continuing Long.
Williams, H.   Sonnet to Twilight.
Wright, C.   California Twilight.
Yi Yuksa.   Twilight.
Young, A.   Who Am I in Twilight.
See also **Evening; Sunset**
Twins
Bartlett, B.   Basement Tale, A.
Baudelaire.   Seven Old Men, The.
Broumas, O.   Landscape with Next of Kin.
Cooley, N.   Resurrection.
Erdrich.   Christ's Twin.
Farish, H.   Newly Born Twins.
Graves, R.   Twins.
Ibycus.   And I killed the Molione boys.
Paino.   1965.
Shapiro, K.   Twins, The.
Swartwout.   Siamese Twins in Love.
U Sam Oeur.   Loss of My Twins, The.
Van Duyn.   Twins, The.
West, K.   To My Twin Sister Who Died at Birth.
Tyndale, William
Bowers, E.   From William Tyndale to John Frith.
Typewriters
Cendrars.   Letter.
Typing and Typists
Blumenthal, M.   Back from the Word-Processing Course, I Say to My Old Typewriter.
Page, P.   Typists.
Seiferle, R.   What We Need Words For.
Tyranny
Agüeros.   Psalm for the Damnation of Pig Pino Oink Ochet, Who Unlike His Victims Will Neither Die nor Disappear, Because He Was Never Human.
Al-Bayati, A.   Dragon, The.
Anene, L.   D-Hour.
Anton, S.   Prism, A: Wet With Wars.
Auden.   Epitaph on a Tyrant.
Bible, *O.T.*   Psalm 52. Quid Gloriaris?
Blake, W.   Grey Monk, The.
Cook, E.   Idiot-Born, The.
Egerton, S.   Emulation, The.
Faiz.   Prison Evening, A.
Gray, T.   Tophet.
Greville, F.   Chorus Sacerdotum.
Haavikko.   I always bow down deep before a small tree and a great tyrant.
  Precisely the way you divide your small change between two.
  Tyrant inspires small poems, The.
  When the tyrant is young. Everyone waits.
  When you go to the tyrant. Keep your head on a platter.
Hartwig.   Who Says.
Herrick.   Duty to Tyrants.
Jacobs, B.   Jeep Cherokee.
Jeffers, R.   Ave Caesar.
Jensma.   Chant of praise for the idi amin dada.
Johnson, L.   Mi Revalueshanary Fren.
Landor, W.   Foreign Ruler, A.
Maraini.   Plaza de Mayo.
Martin, C.   Easter Sunday, 1985.
Melville, H.   Timoleon.
Milosz, C.   You Who Wronged.
Mphahlele.   Poem, A: "What is there that we can do or say."
Neruda.   Dictators, The.
Ngoma.   Demockery.
Pilkington, L.   Wish, By a Young Lady, The.
Rosen, M.   Fighters For Life.
Saarikoski.   No, Quetzalcoatl, don't come back.
Shafiq, H.   Picture of a Tyrant.
Shelley, P.   Song to the Men of England.
Sitwell, O.   Shaking Hands with Murder.
Smith, S.   Christmas.
Supervielle.   Rain and the Tyrants.
Sylvain, P.   Army of Draculas.
Thelwall.   To Tyranny.
Thomas, D.   Hand That Signed the Paper, The.
Tranter.   Tell me we will drink water, and drink to me.
Unknown.   Humble Petition of the British Jacobins to their Brethren of France, The.

Trumpet of Liberty, The.

U

UFOs (Unidentified Flying Objects)
Chasin.   In Communication with a UFO.
Morgan, M.   Unidentified Flying Object on an Errand of Love.
See also **Flying Saucers**
U. S. S. R. (Union of Soviet Socialist Republics)
Astley, N.   East of Easter.
Herbert, W.   Three Year Ode, A.
Kaminsky, Ilya.   Dancing in Odessa.
Khlebnikov, V.   Trumpet, Shout, Carry!
Rein.   Breakfast on the Balcony.
Scammell, W.   Act, The.
Sosnora.   Owl and the Mouse, The.
See also **Soviet Union**
Ugliness
Browning, R.   And were I not, as a man may say, cautious.
Cook, E.   Song of the Ugly Maiden.
Drosinēs, G.   Wild Creeper.
González Prada, M.   Very Strong Stomach Has Mr. Luke, A.
Hoccleve [*or* Occleve].   Description of His Ugly Lady, A.
Jackson, L.   Mask, The.
Jeffers, R.   Carmel Point.
Jennings, E.   Ugly Child, The.
Mansour, J.   Vices of Men, The.
"Monty Python."   All Things Dull and Ugly.
Moss, T.   Owl In Daytime, The.
Ross, C.   John, Tom, and James.
Sanchez, S.   Song No. 3: "Cain't nobody tell me any different."
Shakespeare, W.   Sonnet 130: "My mistress' eyes are nothing like the sun."
Sidney.   What Length of Verse?
Soto.   Brown Girl, Blonde Okie.
Welch, L.   Chicago Poem.
Ukraine
Romtvedt.   Kiev, the Ukraine, Nuclear Accident.
Ulysses
Bancquart.   Return of Ulysses.
Brodsky, J.   Odysseus to Telemachus.
Cavafy.   Ithaka.
Daniel, S.   Ulysses and the Siren [*or* Syren].
Davies, P.   I Was with Ulysses.
Doolittle, H.   At Ithaca.
Flecker, J.   Old Ships, The.
Granados, J.   Minimal Ulysses.
  Mínimos Ulises.
Graves, R.   Ulysses.
Homer.   All silent stood; at last stood forth one dolon, that did dare.
  And then went down to the ship.
  Laertes.
  Odyssey, The.
  Suitors watch Ulysses string the bow, The.
  Ulysses Describes His Visit to the Underworld.
  Ulysses Insults over the Cyclops.
  Ulysses Invokes the Dead.
  Ulysses Reunited with Penelope.
  We bore down on the ship at sea's edge.
Kyger.   Maze, The.
Lang, A.   Odyssey, The.
Levine, Jeffrey.   Dawn, with Cardinals.
Longley, M.   Butchers, The.
McCallum, S.   Calypso.
Merwin.   Odysseus.
Montgomerie, A.   Sonet: "Thocht Polibus, pisander, and with them."
Muldoon, P.   Making the Move.
Ovid.   Friend, henceforth to be reckoned the foremost among my comrades.
Parker, D.   Penelope.
Pope, A.   Argus.
Queneau.   That Don't Scare Me.
Ramke, B.   Like Ulysses.
Saba, U.   Ulysses.
Stevens, W.   World as Meditation, The.
Tennyson, A.   Ulysses.
Venclova.   Canto Eleven.

Umā

Waddington, M.   Ulysses Embroidered.

Umā

Basu, R.   How are you faring, Uma.

I had a good dream last night.

Bhāndārī, S.   Ma, You are Brahmani in the world of Brahma.

Menaka says, Hey listen, Mountain King.

Bhattācārya, A.   Get up, get up, Mountain: no more sleep for you!

Bhattācārya, K.   Consulting the omens.

From her autumn-lotus mouth.

Go, my Lord of the Mountains.

Hara came and made off with my Gauri.

Here, Queen of the Mountains.

Hey, Hara, Ganges-Holder.

Hey, Mountain King, Gauri is sulking.

How could you have forgotten her.

Jaya, tell him that Uma will not be sent.

King of the Mountains is on his way to Hara's abode, The.

My Gauri / You've come home!

My Uma has come!

Tell me / What can I do?

Turn back, Uma.

What a dream I had last night!

What happened? / The ninth night is over.

You ask me, Queen, time after time.

Cakrabarttī, M.   Wherever there's a woman in any Bengali home.

Candī, A.   Bring Tara quickly, Mountain.

Dās, R.   Now I'll see whether Siva.

Dīnrām.   Ma, I've drunk Your poisoned nectar.

Ghos, G.   I plaster myself with ashes.

Who said / If you took the name All-Destroyer. You're home, Uma! Stay here.

Gupta, I.   I got some news from Kailasa!

Islām, N.   Don't go back, Ma, don't go back, Mother.

He who has seen my Mother.

Now there'll be a new mantra, Mother.

Wherever are the lowly, the suffering, and the poor.

Majumdār, H.   Jaya / Don't wake up Hara's wife.

Mukhopādhyāy, K.   Am I afraid of the tenth day?

Pātunī, N.   Ma, Hara's Beloved, Tara.

Rāy, R.   Mountain / Whose woman have you brought home to our mountain city?

Sāheb, A.   Victory to Yogendra's Wife, Great Illusion!

Sen, R.   Can someone / Called Daughter of a Stone.

How wonderful! Look what.

Love Her, Mind.

Mother, make *me* Your treasurer.

Unknown.   Get up, Mountain, get up!

Umbrellas

Cabral de Melo Neto.   To Carlos Drummond de Andrade.

Chŏng Hyŏnjong.   Like Leaving an Umbrella Somewhere.

Dickinson, E.   Bat, The.

Ginsberg, A.   Four skinheads stand.

Wright, R.   Haiku: "Just enough of rain."

Uncertainty

Ackerman, D.   We Are Listening.

Angel.   And the Grass Did Grow. Twilight.

Auden.   September 1, 1939.

Beachy-Quick, Dan.   Flag-Tree.

Beckett, S.   Enueg 2.

Bolton, K.   Nonplussed.

Bousoño, C.   Cost of Truth, The.

Burrell.   Chloe and Myra.

Cassian.   Orbits.

Corbin, A.   Love Me At Last.

Crist-Evans, C.   No Guarantee.

Cummins, J.   Sestina: "He wanted to tell her the weekend idea was "neat"

Davis, O.   If You Are Asked.

De la Mare.   Dear Sir.

Dickinson, E.   If you were coming in the Fall. Wonder—is not precisely Knowing.

Donne.   Satire 3 [Religion].

Doolittle, H.   Fragment 36 [*or* Thirty-Six]: "I

know not what to do."

Etherege.   To a Lady Asking Him How Long He Would Love Her.

Field.   Second Thoughts.

Foix.   I Arrived in that Town, Everyone Greeted Me and I Recognized No One. When I Was Going to Read My Verses, the Devil, Hidden Behind a Tree, Called Out to Me Sarcastically and Filled My Hands with Newspaper Clippings.

Ford, Katie.   Nocturne: "I can see the whole city, lights edging the harbor like yellow pins in uneven."

Frénaud.   Toast in Response.

Herzberg.   Loss.

Heyen.   Where.

Izumi.   From one darkness.

Jennings, K.   Just the Two of Us.

Kanchev, Nikolai.   Church: "I've come to kneel before you, while you're falling down."

Keith, Sally.   Orphean Song.

Lea, S.   Insomnia: The Distances.

Levy, E.   It Is Still Early.

Lowell, J.   In a Copy of Omar Khayyám.

Lumelli, A.   You first, shift your attention (that is, if you withdraw).

MacNeice.   Entirely.

Mark, Sabrina Orah.   Experiments Lasted Through the Winter, The.

Mattawa.   Echo and Elixir 1.

Melville, H.   Arch, The.

Merrill, J.   About the Phoenix.

Montale.   Bird-Shooting.

Muir, E.   In Love For Long.

North, C.   Leap Year.

O'Hara, F.   Cornkind.

Meditations in an Emergency.

Peacock, M.   Veil of If, The.

Powell, D. A.   What direction will you take when the universe collapses. you who when you go must go someplace.

Rekdal, Paisley.   Crash of Rhinos, A.

Ritsos.   End of Dodona II, The.

Shoneyin, T.   Quiver of Questions, A.

Simic.   Clouds Gathering.

Speght.   *Disswasion* hearing her assigne my helpe.

Strand.   Is it you standing among the olive trees.

Talvikki, A.   Origin Charm Against Uncertain Injuries.

Teasdale.   Flight, The.

Thomas, D.   Should Lanterns Shine.

Unknown.   I'm A-Trouble in de Mind.

Van Vliet.   Coastline, The.

Volkman.   Well, You Needn't.

Whitman, W.   As I Lay with My Head in Your Lap Camerado.

Whittier.   Song of Slaves in the Desert.

Wright, C.   Nightletter.

Uncle Tom

Hughes, L.   Uncle Tom ("Within— / The beaten pride.").

Uncle Tom's Cabin

Bibb.   Eliza in Uncle Tom's Cabin.

Uncles

Algarín.   Always Throw the First Punch.

Barlow, G.   Salt.

Bernlef.   Uncle Charles: A Home Movie.

Bernstein, C.   Profaning the Dead.

Brathwaite, E.   Ogun.

Brooke, R.   Sonnet: In Time of Revolt.

Brooks, G.   Merle; Uncle Seagram.

Carson, C.   Asylum.

Conn.   Todd.

Crawley, W.   Bud.

Cullen, C.   Uncle Jim.

Cummings, E. E.   Nobody loses all the time.

Dhompa, T.   Bardo.

Etter.   Well You Needn't.

Harrison, T.   Study.

Harryman.   Baby. (For B and T).

Inada.   10. The Legend of the Magic Marbles.

Jordan, J.   Through These Halls.

Kasdorf.   Uncle.

Knight, E.   My Uncle Is My Honor and a Guest in My House.

Lear, E.   Incidents in the Life of My Uncle Arly.

McDaniel, J.   Uncle Eggplant.

McDonald, E.   Uncle: "Sam was a family embarrassment."

Pérez Estrada, R.   My Uncle the Levitator.

Piercy.   My Rich Uncle, Whom I Only Met Three Times.

Rojas.   Coast, The.

Silook, Susie.   Uncle Good Intentions.

Smith, D.   Roundhouse Voices, The.

Vogt, B.   Uncle with Landscape—Kansas, 1954.

Walker, F. X.   Crooked Afro.

Wilson, A.   Pegasus the Winged Horse.

Unconditional Love

Adams, Sylvia.   Shakespeare's Eyebrows.

Bouvard.   Landscape: "Dimensions are dizzying; peaks, The."

Brunk, J.   On This Earth.

Cisneros, A.   Dedicatory (to My Wife).

Cox, M.   Garglers, The.

Edwards, Sonia.   Between Two Lovers.

Hannaham, D.   I Love You, Though You're Unemployed.

Hirsch, E.   Whitman Leaves the Boardwalk.

Hope, M.   Our Mothers.

Ibn Hazm al-Andalusi.   I love you with a love that knows no waning, whereas some of men's loves are midday mirages.

Lubasch, L.   Enough to Say.

Morgenstern, Felicia L.   Temple of Your Familiar.

Rochelle, T.   Feeding the Worms.

Şeyh Galib.   I won't abandon you, though you cause me.

Shaughnessy, B.   Me in Paradise.

Shelley, P.   To Harriet ("Whose is the love that, gleaming through the world.").

Tollet.   Winter Song.

Traig, Jannifer.   For My Sister.

Unknown.   Over the Pillow.

Van Doren.   My Brother Lives Too Far Away.

Vinograd.   In These Dark Times.

Yi Yŏnju.   Clinic in a Dangerous Season 8, A.

Underground Railroad

Hayden, R.   Runagate Runagate.

McLoughland.   Whippoorwill Calls, The.

Unknown.   Harriet Tubman.

Undertakers

Moss, T.   Owl In Daytime, The.

Undertaker's Daughter Feels Neglect, The.

Nash, O.   Tweedledee and Tweedledoom.

Paloff, B.   My Corpses.

Underwear

Cabico, R.   Antonio Banderas in His Underwear.

Elfyn, Menna.   Nothing but Curves.

Ferlinghetti, L.   Underwear.

Ford, Terri.   Panty Raid.

Friman.   Diapers for My Father.

Joseph, A.   Poem for the Purchase of a First Bra.

Mayer, B.   Maple Syrup Sonnet ("For over ten years now.").

Soto.   Chitchat with the Junior League Women.

Wolverton, T.   Black Slip.

Yosano Akiko.   Channel Boat, The.

What shall I wear to sleep in alone?

Unemployment

Afrika, T.   Queue.

Amir, D.   Nightingale of Uncle Yair, The.

Butterfield, F. G.   For Services Rendered.

Cavafy.   Days of 1908.

Days of 1908.

Davis, C.   Out of Work, Out of Touch, Out of Sorts.

Dugan, A.   Prayer: "God, I need a job because I need money."

Gil de Biedma, J.   Sad Night of October 1959.

Hannaham, D.   I Love You, Though You're Unemployed.

Harburg.   Brother, Can You Spare a Dime?

Higgins, R.   Some People.

Kalar, J.   Papermill.

Levine, P.   What Work Is.

McGinley.   Trinity Place.

Miller, L.   Man Who Is Out of Work Talks to

Poem Written in a Copy of *Beowulf*.
Browning, R.   Pisgah-Sights. I.
   Pisgah-Sights. II.
Buckley, C.   Concerning Paradise.
Chen Zi'ang.   Song on Youzhou Terrace.
Condee.   Mrs. Charles Sanders Peirce, or The
   Solution to the Universe.
Crane, S.   Man said to the universe, A.
Dickinson, E.   Bees.
Fischer, N.   Model of the Universe, A.
Follain.   Music of Spheres.
Galvin, J.   On Exploration.
Gerov, Alexander.   Urban Tree.
Healy, R.   Size of This Universe, The.
Jiménez, J.   Faster, Earth, Faster.
Kekova.   Space is arched like a sail.
Kelly, R.   Looking.
Li Po.   Inscription on an Old Tomb at
   Guangling.
MacLean, S.   Tumultuous Plenty in the
   Heavens.
Marteau.   I Consent That Everything Vanishes.
Meynell, A.   Christ in the Universe.
Mitchell, S.   Sense of Proportion, The.
Mookam Choinul.   Sitting Alone.
Morsztyn, Z.   Emblem 51.
Nahman [*or* Nachman] of Bratzlav.   From "The
   Torah of the Void".
Neruda.   Ode to the Lemon.
   Poetry.
Nims, J.   Understanding the Universe.
Olson, T.   Hypothesis.
Ono.   Mother of the Universe.
Pack, R.   Proton Decay.
Pope, A.   Awake, my St. John! leave all meaner
   things.
Reverdy.   Head Filled with Beauty, The.
Rogers, P.   Origin of Order, The.
Roux, S.   Aviary, The.
Rumi.   Little by little, wean yourself.
Scruton, J.   In the Age of the Radio Telescope.
Shinkichi Takahashi.   Braggart Duck.
   Clay Image.
   Destruction.
   Hand.
   Let's Live Cheerfully.
   Sparrow in Withered Field.
Simpson, L.   Physical Universe.
Tada.   Universe of the Rose.
Tait.   Contracting Universe, The.
Tanikawa, S.   Twenty Billion Light Years of
   Loneliness.
Torre, M.   Driven by a Strange Desire.
Towle.   North.
Traherne.   Eden.
Tuckerman, F.   Sonnet: "And so, as this great
   sphere (now turning slow)."
Unknown.   Cosmogony.
Von Reis, Siri.   Vast Problem Still Obscure.
Zolynas.   Same Air, The.

Universities
Jordan, A.   Orientation: Wittenberg University,
   1983.
MacSweeney.   Cute Petite.
Thomas, J.   His father did intend that Harry
   should.
See also **Colleges and Universities**

Unknown Soldier
Baxter, J.   Elegy for an Unknown Soldier.
Masters, E.   Unknown Soldiers.
Timrod.   Unknown Dead, The.

Unrequited Love
Ahmed Pasha.   Is there any heart not bleeding.
al-Sayyab, B.   Love Me.
Baqi.   That tyrant, is she not persuaded by the
   tears.
Bell, M.   Being in Love.
Calbert.   Like.
Cristall.   Evening. Gertrude.
De Vere, A.   Song: "Slanting both hands against
   her forehead."
Farquhar.   Song: "Come, fair one, be kind."
Flower.   Proud Lady, The.
Gilbert, S.   Retrun of the Muse, The.
Harvey, M.   Pity the Bathtub Its Forced
   Embrace of the Human Form.

Hedderman, R.   Ophelia.
Hô Sugyông.   Love in an Empty Lot.
Jarnot, L.   Still Life.
Landon.   She Sat Alone beside Her Hearth.
Millay, E.   I know I am but summer to your
   heart.
   Thursday.
NicNèill, S.   Steel Yourself.
O'Grady, D.   In the Greenwood.
Parker, D.   Story.
Pope, D.   Getting Through.
Rowe, E.   Reply to Mr.———, The.
Segalen.   Out of Respect.
Trench, H.   Jean Richepin's Song.
Unknown.   Desolate City, The.
   Look what your love has done to me.
   Ze-bi: By That Swamp's Shore.
Whitman, W.   Sometimes with One I Love.
Young, A.   She's My Love.

Unspoken Love
Buchsbaum, Julianne.   In Squire Park with M.,
   Esquire.
Hātim Ibn Sa'īd.   Sun drew near to a full moon:
   wine and a drinking companion!, A.
Makuck.   Story of Sound.
Seibles, T.   Friend and Beloved.
Steele, S.   Love-Sick Maid, The.
Thompson, P.   Shape of Things, The.
Unknown.   At the Beginning of Winter.
Zelenina, G.   With grown-up clever hands.

Unwed Mothers
Bürger, G.   Lass of Fair Wone, The.
English, W.   Cashel of Munster.
Shenstone.   Chase of Jessy, The.

Urania
Milton.   Invocation to Urania.

Urban Life
Alexander, M.   News of the World.
Allnutt, G.   About Benwell.
Apollinaire.   Windows.
Auden.   Capital, The.
Avison.   Rondeau Redoublé.
Barker, G.   Street Ballad.
Barot, R.   Eight Elegies.
Beckman, J.   Final poem for the gently sifting
   public begins on the streets.
Bodenheim.   Rear Porches of an Apartment
   Building, The.
Borson.   City Lights.
Buchsbaum, Julianne.   Phantoms of Utopia.
Byrne, Edward.   Early Evening.
Carrington, H.   Sting—a South Carolina Ave.
   Folk Tale.
Cernuda.   Cemetery in the City.
Chin.   Urban Love Poem.
Cole, Maude E.   Prairie Friend.
Coleman, W.   American Sonnet (46).
Crawford, I.   City Tree, The.
Dalchev, A.   Snow: "Over strip-raked iron
   rooves."
Deguy.   Ballad, The: "In those days, wasy of
   feinting and of tenderness."
Derricotte.   Whitman, Come Again to the Cities.
Di Prima.   In This Landscape.
Dos Passos.   Crimson Tent.
Eliot, T. S.   3. The Fire Sermon.
   Preludes: "Winter evening settles down, The."
Eluard, A. *et al*.   Diamond He Didn't Give You,
   The.
Fearing.   Aphrodite Metropolis (3).
Flint, J.   Metropolitan Metaphysics.
Fujita, Jun.   Chicago River.
   Michigan Boulevard.
Fuller, R.   Sonnet: "Crumbled rock of London is
   dripping under, The."
García Lorca.   While the Chinamen was crying
   on the roof.
Gerstler.   Slowly I Open My Eyes.
Ginsberg, A.   Charnel Ground, The.
   Manhattan May Day Midnight.
   Mugging.
Greenberg, Alvin.   City Life.
Greenberg, Arielle.   Berlin Series.
Greenlaw, L.   Zombies.
Guest, B.   Homage.
   If So, Tell Me [1999].

Guillén, J.   City Life.
Harrison, J.   Birds That Woke Us: an Urban
   Pastoral, The.
Henderson, D.   Lock City.
Hirsch, E.   Poor Angels.
Hofer, J.   Three ("Once upon a time there would
   be the bluest bitch of the pack.").
House, Boyce.   Beauty is Elsewhere.
Hunter, K.   No like place.
Jacob, M.   Rue Ravignan, The.
Jarman, J.   Non-cognitive aspects of the City.
Jones, Llion.   Illusions.
Kaplan, A.   Hey.
Kaplan, L.   I wait for him by the subway exit.
   It's night, the.
Kim Hyesun.   Saturday Night, Arriving in
   Seoul.
Komunyakaa, Y.   Urban Renewal.
Kuhar, M.   On the galloping cusp of the new
   now.
Lansana, Q.   For Gwendolyn Brooks.
Leggott, M.   Omphalos.
Levin, D.   Cinema Verité.
Lewis, Emyr.   Hayes, The.
Malroux.   Appointment in June.
Martynova, O.   Night unwraps the true stuff of
   the world.
McAuliffe, J.   North Brunswick Street Lullaby.
McElroy, C.   Circus of the City, The.
McFadden, D.   11. Spring in Toronto.
Mullen, H.   #6 Sepulveda.
   Wino Rhino.
Nortje.   Sonnet one: "Supremely individual,
   flamboyant, proud."
Obradović, B.   Intrusion, The.
Oliphant.   Dallas.
Pinsky.   City Dark, The.
   Samba.
Rakha, Y.   Dust Storm, The.
Ramsey, L.   That Which Hovers.
Redmond.   New York Seizures.
Reverdy.   Is Ajar.
Reznikoff.   As I Was Wandering with My
   Unhappy Thoughts.
   Still much to read, but too late.
Rimbaud, A.   City.
Rong Zi.   Flowers No Longer Fly in Our City.
Sanchez, S.   For Sweet Honey in the Rock.
Santos, S.   Romeo and Juliet.
Schreiber, R.   Somerville Saturday Night.
Seidman.   Demonstration.
Sepúlveda, O.   Three ("Once upon a time there
   would be the bluest bitch of the pack.").
   Tres ("Habría una vez la perra más azul de la
   manada.").
Shepherd, R.   Self-Portrait in the New World
   Order.
Simic.   Dream Avenue.
Smith, K.   Message on the Machine.
Steptoe.   Three Legged Chairs.
Thomas, L.   Great Love Duets.
   Liquid City.
Toomer.   Seventh Street.
Van Eeden, F.   City Evening.
Van Hoddis.   End of the World.
Vazirani, R.   It's Me, I'm Not Home.
Von Freytag-Loringhoven.   Appalling Heart.
Waugh, Arthur.   Town and Country.
Weaver, A.   Afternoon Train.
   Baby Boy.
Williams, C. K.   Reading: The Bus.
Yépez, H.   On Coahuila Street.

Uriel
Emerson, R.   Uriel.

Urns
Cullen, C.   Uncle Jim.
Olds, S.   His Ashes.
Shinkichi Takahashi.   Urn.

Ursa Major
Hollander, J.   Great Bear, The.
McHugh, H.   Night in a World, A.

Ursula, Saint
Williams, G.   Saint Ursula of Llangwyryfon.

Usury
Guillén, N.   Usurers, The.

Utah (state)
Frost, R.   On the Heart's Beginning to Cloud the Mind.
Stevenson, A.   Utah.

Utopia
Beerbohm, M.   In a Copy of More's (or Shaw's or Wells's or Plato's or Anybody's) Utopia.
Bobyshev.   Other World, The.
Coleridge, S.   Kubla Khan: or, A Vision in a Dream.
Pantisocracy.
Dobyns.   Utopian Melodies.
Gilbert, W.   Utopia Anglicized.
Hall, D.   Hermit with Landscape.
Hucks, J.   To Freedom.
T'ao Ch'ien [or T'ao Yuan-ming].   Peach Blossom Spring, The ("Ying clan disrupted Heaven's ordinance, The.").
Thelwall.   On the Rapid Extension of the Suburbs.
Unknown.   Big Rock Candy Mountains, The.
Wodehouse.   Land Where the Good Songs Go, The.

Vacation
Barresi.   Vacation, 1969.
Berry, W.   Vacation, The.
Bourne, Lesley-Anne.   She Sends Him a Postcard of the Sea.
Enzensberger, H.   Holiday, The.
Gannon, K.   Dreamer's Holiday, A.
Jackson, R.   Sunday Brunch.
Li Po.   To See Secretary Shu-Yun Off at the Hsieh T'iao Tower at Hsuan-Ch'eng.
Pietri.   Intermission from Monday.
Rossi, T.   Beach.
St. John, D.   From the Lake.
Stafford, W.   Vacation.

Vacuum Cleaners and Vacuum Cleaning
Conran.   Thirteen Ways of Looking at a Hoover.
Nemerov.   Vacuum, The.

Vagabonds
Cairns, Scott.   Exile: "Here *exactly*—a little elbow room. Here, in this margin of poor housing."
Carman, B.   Vagabond Song, A.
Catacalos.   One Man's Family.
Chia Tao.   While Traveling.
Colum, P.   Old Woman of the Roads, The.
Crane, H.   River, The.
Dawe, B.   Drifters.
Delmore Brothers.   Wabash Cannonball, The.
Dobyns.   Freight Cars.
Dyer, J.   House Beautiful, The.
Frost, R.   Two Tramps in Mud Time.
Hardy, T.   Trampwoman's Tragedy, A.
Higgins, F.   Roving Lover, The.
Hopes.   Jack Rhymer.
Hughes, L.   Vagabonds.
Huidobro.   Blind.
Kinnell.   Memory of Wilmington.
Kipling, R.   Sestina of the Tramp-Royal.
Lavut, E.   In the body of the town I'm a pupil.
Levine, P.   And the Trains Go On.
Lumbreras, E.   Good-for-nothings on a White Corner.
Vagos en una esquina blanca.
Masefield.   Wanderer's Song, A.
Mullen, H.   Wino Rhino.
Riley, J.   Raggedy Man, The.
Stevenson, R.   Vagabond, The.
Tate, J.   Vagabond, A.
Vays, S.   To Mani Leyb.

Valentine's Day
Donne.   Epithalamion, or Marriage Song on the Lady Elizabeth and Count Palatine Being Married on St. Valentine's Day, An.
Duffy, C.   Valentine: "Not a red rose or a satin heart."
Fagin, L.   Valentine's Day.
Hall, D.   Valentine.
Hart, L.   My Funny Valentine.
Hemingway.   Valentine.
Howard, R.   Landed: A Valentine.
Livingston, M.   Angry Valentine, An.
Lochhead, L.   I Wouldn't Thank You for a Valentine.
MacSweeney.   I Looked Down on a Child Today.
Shakespeare, W.   Song: "Tomorrow is saint valentine's day."
Sholl.   Postmaster's Children, The.
Smith, P.   Some Reservation Valentines.
Spicer, J.   Valentine, A.
Stein, G.   Very Valentine, A.
Thompson, P.   Valentine, A.

Valentino, Rudolph
Sapia.   Valentino's Hair.

Valkyries
Trakl.   Grodek (Second Version).

Vallejo, César
Crozier, L.   Excellence in the Small. Tears Frozen on Your Face.

Valleys
Azzawi, F.   Crossing the Valley.
Byron, G.   Lachin y Gair.
Harrison, J.   Collage for Richard Davis—Two Short Forms, A.
Jones, G.   Quiet Valley, The.
Koethe.   Sorrento Valley.
Lamartine.   Valley, The.
Lux.   Grim Town in a Steep Valley.
McDowell, Garrett.   Blooming in the Valley, A.
Mistral, G.   Song.
Muso Soseki.   Tiger Valley.
Peterson, J. Cody.   La Jolla. In 3 Acts.
Salinas, L.   My Fifty-Plus Years Celebrate Spring.
Sandburg, C.   Moist Moon People.
Thomas, E.   Combe, The.
Unknown.   In the valley where the stream leaps.
Veinberg, J.   Owl's Landscape, An.
Volkow.   En el Valle de Zapata.
Valley of Zapata, The.
Wang Wei.   Birdsong Valley.
Wheelock, J.   Earth, Take Me Back.
Williams, S.   Buildings of the, The.
Wilson, K.   People from the Valley, The.
Wordsworth, D.   Peaceful Our Valley, Fair and Green.
Young, Andy.   Foxfire.

Value
Brouwer, J.   Space Memorabilia Auction, Superior Stamp and Coin, Beverly Hills, California.
Coffman.   Cheerleaders.
Dickinson, E.   I took one Draught of Life.
Fisher, R.   Least, The.
George, D.   Tulip or Turnip.
Giscombe, C.   Bro Duncanson.
Hafiz, K [or Hafez].   Deciding Not to Go to India (147).
Five Days Remaining, The (75).
Hamhur Kiwha.   My Hobby on the Mountain.
Herman, J.   I Won't Send Roses.
Koehler, T.   Good for Nothin' Joe.
Lanier, S.   Clover.
Mayakovsky [or Maiakovskii].   Good Attitude to Horses, A.
Nathan, L.   Bladder Song.
So?
Rimbaud, A.   Sales.
Shakespeare, W.   Sonnet 52: "So am I as the rich, whose blessed key."
Skelton, J.   For though my rhyme be ragged.

Vampires
Azzawi, F.   Night with the Vampire, The.
Clark, T.   Year from Monday, A.
Guillén, N.   Usurers, The.
Kipling, R.   Vampire, The.
Lytton, E.   I found a corpse, with golden hair.
McDonald, R.   Incident in Transylvania.
Samaras, N.   After the Children Have Gone to Bed.
Schiff, Robyn.   Vampire Finch.
Shwarts [or Shvarts].   Remembrance of Strange Hospitality.
Smith, S.   Great Unaffected Vampires and the Moon.
Sylvain, P.   Army of Draculas.
Thomas, L.   Dracula.
Warsh.   Year from Monday, A.
Yi Sanghûi.   Dracula.

Van Buren, Martin
Mac Low.   1841 (I).
1837.

Van Doren, Mark
Hayden, R.   Ballad of Remembrance, A.

Van Gogh, Vincent
Assultani, F.   Van Gogh.
Breytenbach.   Constipation.
Haines, J.   On a Certain Field in Auvers.
Ismail.   Van Gogh's Ear.
Stryk, L.   Enough.
Tagliabue.   Moderation Is Not a Negation of Intensity, But Helps Avoid Monotony.
Tomlinson, C.   Farewell to Van Gogh.
Vertreace, M.   Black Tulips.
Yi Sanghûi.   Van Gogh.

Vancouver, British Columbia
Birney.   Vancouver Lights.
Fanning, R.   Parable of the Boy and the Polar Bear.
Morrissey, S.   There was Fire in Vancouver.
Purdy, A.   Madwoman on the Train, The.

Vandalism
Beaver.   Drummer, The.
Bottoms.   Desk, The.
Knight, S.   Double Writing.
Liu, T.   Strange Fruit.
Parker, A.   After the Poem Who Knows.
Another Poem about the Vandals.
Cruelty, the Vandals Say.
Practicing Their Diffidence, the Vandals.
Vandals Dying, The.
Vandals, The.

Vanity
Archilochus.   I don't like a tall general, swaggering.
Arnold, C.   Party She Outdid Herself, The.
Blunt, W.   On Her Vanity.
Bolton, E.   Palinode, A.
Bradstreet, A.   Flesh and the Spirit, The.
[Here Follows Some] Verses upon the Burning of Our House [July 10th, 1666. Copied Out of a Loose Paper].
Vanity of All Worldly Things, The.
Brown, E.   Beauty and the Prince Formerly Known as Beast.
Byron, G.   'All Is Vanity, Saith the Preacher'.
Carew, T.   Ingrateful[l] Beauty Threatened.
Chernoff.   Vanity, Wisconsin.
Coogler.   More Care for the Neck Than for the Intellect.
Crabbe, G.   Delay Has Danger.
Crosby, E.   Hail to the hero!
Cummings, E. E.   Cambridge ladies who live in furnished souls, The.
"Ephelia.".   To a Proud Beauty.
Freneau.   Vanity of Existence, The.
Graves, R.   Vain and Careless.
Gryphius.   All Is Vanity.
Guiterman.   On the Vanity of Earthly Greatness.
Gunn, T.   Lines for a Book.
Hall, J.   Even as the Wandering Traveler.
Herbert, G.   Vanity [or Vanitie] (1).
Hill, S.   My Sister's Jeans.
Howitt, M.   Spider and the Fly, The.
Issa.   Vanity of men, The.
La Fontaine.   Man and His Image, The.
Lawrence, D. H.   Intimates.
Snake.
Le Gallienne.   Beauty Accurst.
Leigh, H.   Lady and the Doctor, The.
Machado Ruiz.   Don't trace out your profile.
Narcissism / is an ugly fault.
Makah Oral Tradition.   Song of Repulse to a Vain Lover.
Mayer, G.   Narcissus.
Merrill, J.   Peacock, The.
Nash, O.   Evening Out, The.
Piercy.   Barbie Doll.
Prior.   Oft have I said, the praise of doing well.
Rodgers, C.   Feminism.
Rossetti, D.   71: The Choice ("Eat thou and drink; to-morrow thou shalt die").

101: The One Hope.
Scott, S.   Proud Maisie.
Sexton.   Snow White and the Seven Dwarfs.
Shakespeare, W.   Sonnet 1: "From fairest creatures we desire increase."
Smith, H.   Ozymandias.
Swift, J.   Lady's Dressing Room, The.
Tate, J.   Teaching the Ape to Write Poems.
Unknown.   How come alle ye that ben i-broght.
Restored Terrace is new and fresh, The.
Vanshenkin.   Sunset fades, and from the little hill, The.
Vaughan, H.   Vanity of Spirit.
Watts, I.   Man Frail, and God Eternal.
Wenderoth, J.   First Impression.
Wordsworth, W.   Column Intended by Buonaparte for a Triumphal Edifice in Milan, Now Lying by the Way-Side in the Simplon Pass, The.
See also **Pride**

Vashti
Harper, F.   Vashti.
Spencer, A.   Before the Feast of Shushan.

Vaudeville
Beatty, P.   Why That Abbott and Costello Vaudeville Mess Never Worked with Black People.
Howard, J.   Hello! My Baby.

Vaughan, Henry
Thomas, J.   His father did intend that Harry should.

Vegetables
Baca.   Green Chile.
Buson.   Buying leeks.
Clarke, George Elliott.   Haligonian Market Cry.
Clifton, L.   Cutting greens.
Craig, David.   Pentecost.
Dove, R.   Sunday Greens.
Florian.   Send My Spinach.
Forbes, C.   Potlicker Blues.
Ibn Sara.   Eggplant.
Issa.   When the wild turnip.
Lindley, D.   Curly Kale.
Fennel.
Lindsey, Kay.   Stringbeans.
Locklin.   Iceberg Theory, The.
Lockward, D.   Vegetable Love.
McAlmon.   For Instance.
Messerli.   Angry with China.
Mole, J.   Trick, The.
Nash, O.   Parsnip, The.
Ormsby, E.   Skunk Cabbage.
Prunty.   Vegetable Garden, The.
Segovia, F.   Ánimo vegetal.
Vegetal Animus.
Shange.   Different Love Poem / We Need a Change, A.
Stein, G.   Asparagus.
Talley, N.   Vegetables make love above the tenors.
Thomas, E.   Swedes.
Thomas, L.   Onion Bucket.
Thomas, Yumi.   Love Poem to an Avocado from a Tomato.
Unknown.   Do you carrot all for me?
Plantain.

Vegetarians
Clewell.   Vegetarian Physics.
Coccia, M.   We Are Not Vegetarians.
Devaney, T.   Sonnet: "You know all those sonnets the ones where I said, I love you, well."

Velázquez, Diego Rodríguez de Silva y
Conquest.   Rokeby Venus, The.
Felipe, L.   Caption for "The Child from Vallecas" by Velázquez.
Wylie.   Castilian.

Venereal Disease
Olin.   Stick-up.

Vengeance
Barnes, B.   Sestina: "Then first with locks dishevelled and bare."
Brathwaite, E.   Irae.
Brown, E.   Jezebel to the Eunuchs.
Carter, S.   Incident in Italy.

Cooperman, R.   Good-by and Keep Cold.
Cortez, J.   Rape.
Horne, R.   Beth Gelert.
Kelly, Erren Geraud.   7-30-96.
Kreyter, S.   Vengeance: "Once on a night of sparkling sin."
Ntiru.   Listen—listen.
Paulin.   Impossible Pictures, The.
Tennyson, A.   Hear Icenian, Catieuchlanian, hear Coritanian, Trinobant!
Unknown.   Dick o' the Cow.
Go first, my love, to avenge the martyrs' blood.
Whittier.   Cities of the Plain, The.
Yesenin [*or* Essenin].   Mysterious, Ancient World of Mine.

Venice, Italy
Betjeman.   Longfellow's Visit to Venice.
Brodsky, J.   Lagoon.
Browning, R.   Toccata of Galuppi's, A.
Byron, G.   I stood in Venice, on the Bridge of Sighs.
Christie.   Coming Off a Depression, She Prepares for Venice.
Dove, R.   Ta Ta Cha Cha.
Durrell.   Water-Colour of Venice, A.
Glazova, A.   Venice: "Enormous clock at the sandy mansion, An."
Howard, R.   Keeping.
Kunert.   Venice Lost.
Longfellow, H.   Venice.
Melville, H.   In a Bye-Canal.
Venice.
Moore, T.   Venetian Air.
Pound, E.   Night Litany.
Rexroth, K.   Sottoportico San Zaccaria.
Wilson, J.   Death in Venice.
Wordsworth, W.   On the Extinction of the Venetian Republic.

Venus (goddess)
Baudelaire.   Voyage to Cythera, A.
Voyage to Cythera, A.
Conquest.   Rokeby Venus, The.
Hadas, R.   Mars and Venus.
Herrick.   Wounded Cupid, The.
Hill, G.   Re-birth of Venus, The.
Lowell, A.   Venus Transiens.
Lucretius.   Darling of Gods and Men, beneath the gliding stars.
Montemayor, C.   Cytherea.
Outram, R.   Tourist Stricken at the Uffizi.
Ovid.   Venus and Adonis.
Prior.   Ode, An: "Merchant, to secure his treasure, The."
Rimbaud, A.   Lovely Morning Thought.
Robinson, M.   Sappho's Prayer to Venus.
Rossetti, C.   Venus's Looking-Glass.
Roux, S.   Aviary, The.
Rukeyser, M.   Birth of Venus, The.
Salter.   Rebirth of Venus, The.
Spenser, E.   Epithalamion: "Ye learned sisters which have oftentimes."
Strato [*or* Straton].   Yesterday in the bath Diodes' penis.
Unknown.   Wise Rejoice with Ganymede, The.
Urdang.   Birth of Venus.
Virgil [*or* Vergil].   In Heaven, Queen Juno saw. She's trapped.
Willis, N.   Psyche, Before the Tribunal of Venus.
Wroth.   Sonnet 9: "My muse now hap[p]ly, lay thy self to rest."
Young, I.   Visit to the Palace of Venus.
See also **Aphrodite**

Venus (planet)
Bleakney, J.   On Going Without Saying.
Bogan, L.   Evening-Star.
Fox, Skip.   Another.
Sic transit ("Neither does the world answer but.").
Grabill.   Dream of the Closeness of Venus, A.
Holmes, O.   Flaneur [*or* Flâneur], The.

Venus of Milo (statue)
Gilder, R.   Two Worlds.
Keller, G.   Venus de Milo.
Lazarus, E.   Venus of the Louvre.

Leconte de Lisle, C.   Venus de Milo.

Verdi, Giuseppe
Noyes, A.   Barrel-Organ, The.

Verlaine, Paul
Aiken, C.   Prelude LVI: "Rimbaud and Verlaine, precious pair of poets."
Hacker, M.   Verlaine.
Hovey.   Verlaine.
Mallarmé.   Tomb.
Ramke, B.   Paul Verlaine at the Grave of Lucien Létinois.
Robinson, E.   Verlaine.
Starbuck, G.   Boston.
Wheatley, D.   Verlaine Dying.

Vermeer, Johannes
Jones, B.   Vermeer's Paint.
Nemerov.   Vermeer.
Pinkerton, H.   On Vermeer's *Young Woman with a Water Jug* (1658) in the Metropolitan Museum.
Stainer.   Quanta.
Tranströmer.   Vermeer.

Vermont (state)
Blackburn, J.   Moonlight in Vermont.
Brainard, J.   Aug. 29, 1967.
Carruth, H.   Republicans? We've got a few. In fact.
Chiasson, D.   Vermont.
Corbett, W.   Vermont Apollinaire.
Donze, R.   Vermont Has a High Suicide Rate.
Frost, R.   Out, Out—.
Kinnell.   Angling, a Day.
Margolis, G.   Town Meeting.
Rich, A.   Living Memory.
Suessdorf, K.   Moonlight in Vermont.
Warren, R.   Vermont Ballad: Change of Season.
Weismiller.   Vermont: Spring Rains.

Verona, Italy
Claudian.   Old Man of Verona, The.
Reed, H.   Map of Verona, A.
Wright, C.   Homage to Claude Lorrain.

Versailles, France
Moore, M.   No Swan So Fine.
Rich, A.   Versailles.

Vesta
Ibarra, Filomena.   In Ancient Rome There Stood.

Veterans
Ai.   Back in the World.
I Can't Get Started.
Anderson, D.   Itinerary.
Bausch, V.   What They Wanted.
Benedict, E.   At Ease.
Bierce.   Hesitating Veteran, The.
Bowen, K.   Playing Basketball with the Viet Cong.
Bronk.   Memorial: "If we do not lift quickly the dead bodies from the beaches."
Brown, D.   When I Am 19 I Was a Medic.
Burke, M.   Former WWII Paratrooper Dreams of Suicide, 1977, A.
Colquitt.   Man in the VA Hospital, The.
Connolly, D.   Little Man, The.
Dugan, A.   Portrait from the Infantry.
Duhig, I.   Chocolate Soldier.
Fenton, J.   His wife nods, and a secret smile.
Freneau.   American Soldier, The.
Glazer, M.   Star-Spangled.
Gonzalez, R.   José's Japanese Sword.
Hall, D.   Man in the Dead Machine, The.
Hedin, R.   Old Liberators, The.
Herbert, Z.   Rain, The.
Hinojosa, Rolando.   Vale.
Hughes, T.   Walt.
Janeczko.   Mail King.
Jarrell, R.   Transient Barracks (1944).
Kilbride, Jerry.   Firecrackers.
Kinzie.   Summers of Vietnam.
Komunyakaa, Y.   Losses.
Report from the Skull's Diorama.
Lahey, A.   Post-War Procession.
Larsen, W.   Learning the War.
Macpherson, J.   They Return.
Major, C.   Vietnam.
McDonald, W.   After the Noise of Saigon ("If

where we hunt defines us.").
McGough, R.   Snipers.
McGrath, T.   Homecoming: "After the cries of gulls and the fogbound island."
Mura.   Blueness of the Day, The.
Nemerov.   Redeployment.
Oppen.   I cannot even now.
Ortiz.   8:50 AM Ft. Lyons VAH.
　Travelling.
Pak Inhwan.   Sleepless Night, A.
Péret.   Hymn of the Patriotic War Veterans.
Rattenbury, A.   War Memoir, A.
Revard.   Parading with the Veterans of Foreign Wars.
Romero, E.   *Nuestro* Marine.
Sandy.   Survivor, Walking.
Sassoon, S.   Does It Matter?
　Fight to a Finish.
　Memorial Tablet.
Shephard, S.   Homeless Vets.
Simpson, L.   Old Soldier.
Sitwell, O.   Next War, The.
Sivan, A.   Unpleasantness During a Memorial Service.
Snodgrass.   Returned to Frisco, 1946.
Taylor, C.   Our Texas Economy.
Thomas, C.   As / the.
Wachtel.   Two Quarters, Two Nickels, and the Jacket of the One Album He Ever Recorded—*America Welcomes Home the Desert Sax*—Are in the Open Felt-Lined Case On the Platform of the Astor Place Subway Station: Gulf War 1.
Waring, B.   Refuge at the One Step Down.
Warren, R.   Confederate Veteran Tries to Explain the Event, A.
Weigl.   On the Anniversary of Her Grace.
Williams, C. K.   From My Window.
Wormser.   By-Products.
Wrigley, R.   What My Father Believed.
Young Bear.   Wadasa Nakamoon, Vietnam Memorial.
See also **Soldiers**

Veterans Day
Tripp.   Armistice Day '77, Honiton.
See also **Armistice**

Veterinarians
Markell, Jennifer.   Veterinary Student, The.

Vice
Archpoet.   His Confession.
Bart, L.   Fings Ain't Wot They Used t'Be.
Baudelaire.   To the Reader.
　To the Reader.
Chapman, G.   To living virtues turns the deadly vices.
Evans, D.   In the Vices.
Juvenal.   Satire 1.
Kinnell.   Last Songs.
Latouche, J.   Maybe I Should Change My Ways.
Mansour, J.   Vices of Men, The.
Martial.   Gaurus, you have a fault for which. You are a stool pigeon and.
Massimi.   Advice to Paulinus.
Masters, E.   A. D. Blood.
Niedecker.   Museum man!, The.
Parker, D.   Observation.
Trần Tế Xu'o'ng.   Women.
Unknown.   Archpoet's Confession, The.
See also **Sin**

Vicksburg Campaign (1862–63)
Hayne, P.   Vicksburg.

Victoria, Queen of England
French, W.   Queen's After-Dinner Speech, The.
Housman.   1887.
Kipling, R.   Widow at Windsor, The.
Lawson, H.   English Queen, The.
Linden, M.   To the Queen of the British Government.
McGonagall.   All hail to the Empress of India, Great Britain's Queen.

Victory
Allen, H.   Wingless Victory, The.
Archilochus.   Heart, my heart churning with fathomless cares.
Behn, A.   Thousand Martyrs I Have Made, A.

Booth, P.   Public Broadcast.
Ciardi, J.   V-J Day.
Dickinson, E.   Success is counted sweetest.
　Triumph—may be of several kinds.
　Victory comes late.
Donne.   Death be not proud, though some have called thee.
Dupin.   Even If the Mountain.
Hardy, T.   Men Who March Away.
Harrison, T.   Cycles of Donji Vakuf.
Herrick.   To the King; Upon His Taking of Leicester.
Itaikkunrurkilar.   His Legs Strong and Lithe.
Jonson, B.   Her Triumph.
Landor, W.   Crimean Heroes, The.
Lermontov.   Borodino.
Li Po.   Remembering Ancient Days in Yueh.
Martial.   Rome, I am Scorpus, foremost in the race.
Marvell.   Fair Singer, The.
　For Santacruze the glad fleet takes her way.
　Horatian Ode upon Cromwell's Return from Ireland, An.
Miller, J.   At Our Golden Gate.
Pindar.   For Midas, the Man from Akragas First in the Flute Match.
　Olympia 11—For Agesidamus of the Westwind Locrians: Winner in the Boys' Boxing Match.
Pitter.   Victory Bonfire.
Pope, A.   Reign of Chaos, The.
Ransom, J.   Judith of Bethulia.
Reznikoff.   Te Deum.
Sedulius Scottus.   Battle is joined on the open plain.
Seneca.   Britannia, free from foes and foreign kings.
Sill.   Opportunity.
Treece.   Conquerors.
Unknown.   Joshua Fit de Battle of Jericho [*or ob* Jerico].
Whitman, W.   Old Salt Kossabone.
Yosano Tekkan.   Victory Arches.

Vietnam
Alexander, E.   Nineteen.
Alvarez, J.   How I Learned to Sweep.
Balaban.   April 30, 1975.
　Guard at the Binh Thuy Bridge, The.
　News Update.
　Thoughts Before Dawn.
Berry, W.   Against the War in Vietnam.
　Dark with power.
Bly, R.   Counting Small-Boned Bodies.
　Driving through Minnesota during the Hanoi Bombings.
Clifton, H.   Death of Thomas Merton.
Coleman, H.   OK Corral East: Brothers in the Nam.
Dawe, B.   Homecoming.
Duncan, R.   Up Rising.
Elfyn, Menna.   Rice Papers.
Evans, G.   Eye Blade.
　Revelation in the Mother Lode.
Fried, E.   What Things Are Called.
Ginsberg, A.   Vow, A.
Gwynn, R.   Body Bags.
Ha Thi Thao.   Our Son's Profession.
Huddle.   Vermont.
Knott.   Two Vietnam Poems: (1966).
Komunyakaa, Y.   Buried Light.
　Hanoi Market, The.
　Reed Boat, A.
Levertov.   Advent 1966.
　Fragrance of Life, Odor of Death.
　In Thai Binh (Peace) Province.
　Weeping Woman.
　What Were They Like?
McClure, M.   Song: "Platinum fur and brass revolver shine."
McDonald, W.   Children of Saigon, The.
　Christmas Bells, Saigon.
　Hauling Over Wolf Creek Pass in Winter.
　Last Still Days in a Bunker, The.
　Middle Years, The.
Mezey.   How Much Longer?
Mitchell, A.   To Whom It May Concern (Tell Me Lies about Vietnam).

Moore, L.   Winter 1967.
Mura.   Natives, The.
Nguyễn Chí Thiện.   Party holds you down and you lie still, The.
　This Land's No Joy.
Notley.   White Phosphorus.
Ormsby, F.   Home.
Paquet.   It Is Monsoon at Last.
Quintana.   Good Nigger.
Salkey.   Remember Haiti, Cuba, Vietnam.
U'ng Bình.   At the Exiled King's River Pavilion.
Vietnamese Oral Tradition.   Colonial Troops Transport, The.
　Looking Out in All Directions.
　Saigon River, The.
Vuong-Riddick, T.   My Beloved Is Dead in Vietnam.
Weigl.   Burning Shit at An Khe.
　Dialectical Materialism.
　Her Life Runs Like a Red Silk Flag.
　Him, on the Bicycle.
　Last Lie, The.
　Mines.
　Monkey.
　Sailing to Bien Hoa.
　Temple Near Quang Tri, Not on the Map.
　Way of Tet, The.
　Why Nothing Changes for Miss Ngo Thi Thanh.
Whalen, P.   Regalia in Immediate Demand!
Williams, C. K.   From My Window.
Young Bear.   Wadasa Nakamoon, Vietnam Memorial.

Vietnam War
Abbey, L.   Broken Silence.
Anderson, D.   Infantry Assault.
　Itinerary.
　Papasan.
　Purification.
Anderson, J.   American Flag.
Appleman, P.   Peace with Honor.
Balaban.   April 30, 1975.
Bausch, V.   What They Wanted.
Bly, R.   Driving West in 1970.
Bowen, K.   Playing Basketball with the Viet Cong.
Brown, D.   When I Am 19 I Was a Medic.
Carruth, H.   On Being Asked to Write a Poem Against the War in Vietnam.
Casey, M.   Bummer, A.
　Learning.
　LZ Gator Body Collector, The.
　On What the Army Does with Heads.
Chasin.   Strength.
Chu, B.   Mother's Pearls.
Cofer, J.   Anniversary.
Coleman, H.   OK Corral East: Brothers in the Nam.
Connolly, D.   Little Man, The.
DeFoe, M.   Forgetting the Sixties.
Ehrhart.   Beautiful Wreckage.
　How It All Comes Back.
Eirian, S.   Pain, The.
Elfyn, Menna.   May in My Lai.
Fink, Robert A.   At Our Backs.
Fried, E.   Naturalization.
Hamer.   Because We Need Good Maps.
　Lesson.
Hamilton, I.   Newscast, The.
Ho Thien.   Green Beret.
Huddle.   Ooly Pop a Cow.
　Vermont.
　Work.
Hugo, R.   On Hearing a New Escalation.
Ignatow, D.   All Quiet.
Kasdorf.   First TV in a Mennonite Family.
Kinnell.   Vapor Trail Reflected in the Frog Pond.
Kinsella, J.   Radnoti Quarantine: Razglednicas.
Komunyakaa, Y.   After the Fall [of Saigon].
　Ambush.
　Between Days.
　Boat People.
　Bui Doi, Dust of Life.
　Camouflaging the Chimera.
　Facing It.
　Fragging.
　Losses.

Missing in Action.
Monoon Season.
Prisoners.
Report from the Skull's Diorama.
Sappers.
Starlight Scope Myopia.
Thanks.
Toys in a Field.
Tu Do Street.
Tunnels.
2527th Birthday of the Buddha.
Water Buffalo.
We Never Know.
You and I Are Disappearing.
Kuzma.   Peace, So That.
Lam Thi My Da.   Garden Fragrance.
  Night Harvest.
Larsen, W.   Learning the War.
Levertov.   At 6 a.m. the ominous zooming, war-
  sound, of helicopters breaks into our sleep.
  Tenebrae.
  Weeping Woman.
Long, R.   Conspiracy, The.
Lowell, R.   March 1, The.
  March 2, The.
Major, C.   Media on War: or, the Square Root of
  Vietnam.
  Vietnam.
McDonald, Joe.   I-Feel-Like-I'm Fixin'-To-Die
  Rag.
McDonald, W.   After the Noise of Saigon ("If
  where we hunt defines us.").
  After the Rains of Saigon ("I put back the rifle
  on a steel rack.").
  Flying Dutchman, The.
McManus, J.   Two Songs for Hendrix.
Merwin.   Asians Dying, The.
Mitchell, A.   To Whom It May Concern (Tell
  Me Lies about Vietnam).
Moore, L.   Gifts.
Nye, J.   Dead Weight.
Oomen, A.   Peaches: "In the only moment of
  ecstasy I have."
Otero, B.   Something Like A.
Padel, R.   Trial.
Paley, G.   Two Villages.
Palmer, M.   Sun ("Write this. We have burned
  all their villages.").
Paquet.   Basket Case.
  It Is Monsoon at Last.
Ritterbusch.   Choppers.
Sandage, C.   Interview with a Combat
  Photographer.
Schuyler, J.   May, 1972.
Seibles, T.   Manic: A Conversation with Jimi
  Hendrix.
Siegel, Marcella.   Waiting Wife.
Starbuck, G.   Of Late.
Stein, K.   Night Shift, after Drinking Dinner,
  Container Corporation of America, 1972.
Thomas, C.   As / the.
Thomas, L.   Fit Music.
Tran, B.   Women Next Door, The.
Wadsworth, W.   Need for Attention, The.
Walden, G.   Misguided Angels.
Weigl.   Burning Shit at An Khe.
  Convoy.
  Last Lie, The.
  Self-Portrait at Fifty-Three.
Wojahn.   Assassination of Robert Goulet as
  Performed by Elvis Presley: Memphis, 1968,
  The.
  It's Only Rock and Roll but I Like It: The Fall
  of Saigon, 1975.
Zarzyski.   How Near Vietnam Came to Us.

Vietnam War Memorial
Bilgere, G.   At the Vietnam Memorial.
Chu, B.   Mother's Pearls.
Dacey, P.   Whitman: The Wall.
Komunyakaa, Y.   Facing It.
Quintana.   At the New Mexico Viet Nam
  Veterans Memorial.
Williams, Gerwyn.   Washington.
Young Bear.   Wadasa Nakamoon, Vietnam
  Memorial.

Vigilantes
  Estess.   Mack Charles Parker Lynching, The.
Vikings
  Feirstein.   Rune-Maker, The.
  Longfellow, H.   Skeleton in Armor [or Armour],
    The.
Vileness
  Hughes, L.   Bad Man.
Village Idiots
  Brown, S.   It Took a Village.
Villages
  Abdul-Salaam, A.   Village Near a Church, A.
  Alberti.   Song: "I want to sing: to be a flower."
  Applewhite.   Village After Sunset, The.
  Bartolomé, E.   Tattoos in the Water.
    Tatuajes en el Agua.
  Basho.   This old village.
  Benedetti, M.   We All Conspire.
  Blamire.   North Country Village, A.
  Brown, M.   Village Woman.
  Brown, S.   It Took a Village.
  Buson.   My village / Dragonflies.
    Night deepens.
    Short night, The.
    Urine-stained quilt, A.
    Village with a thousand eaves.
  Cho Chihun.   At Toriwpn.
  Davidkov, Ivan.   Villages Like Ghosts.
  Dove, R.   Sightseeing.
  Earle, J.   Village.
  Erb, E.   This and That.
  Fodeba, K.   And it's morning.
  Goldsmith, O.   Sweet was the sound, when oft
    at evening's close.
  Hood, T.   Our Village—by a Villager.
  Issa.   Bats flying.
    Don't know about the people.
    In this mountain village.
    My dear old village.
    My old village lies.
    Snow is melting, The.
    Village named Little-Plum-Tree, A.
  Jacobsen, R.   Express Train.
  Jooris.   Village, A.
  Leopardi.   Village Saturday, The.
  Lisnyanskaya [or Lisnianskaia].   To be thought
    an outcast in my beloved country.
  Longfellow, H.   Golden Mile-Stone, The.
    Preamble to a Tale of Acadie.
    Ropewalk, The.
    Village Blacksmith, The.
  López Velarde.   Provincial Sundays.
  Lu Chih.   Tune: "Drunk in the East Wind".
  Lux.   People of the Other Village, The.
  Marcinkevičius, J.   Prelude to 'Blood and Ash'.
  Molinari.   Poem of the Girl from Velázquez.
  Paz.   Village.
  Peterson, R.   Midwest Town.
  Rhys, K.   Interlude.
  Roland Holst.   Time, Please.
  Rowlands, D.   Village, The.
  Shin Tongyŏp.   Back when we were children.
  Smith, I.   Listen.
  Southerland.   Two Fishing Villages.
  Thomas, R. S.   Village, The.
  Tripp.   Eglwys Newydd.
  Tu Fu [or Du Fu].   In a Village by the River.
    Song of the War-Chariots (Yueh-Fu).
    Village by the River.
  Vietnamese Oral Tradition.   Leaving the Village.
  Wang Wei.   Poem: "You who come from my
    village."
  Yang Wan-li.   Watching a Village Festival.
  Yau.   Radiant Silhouette V.
  Yesenin [or Essenin].   Horn of doom is blaring!,
    The.
  Yevtushenko [or Evtushenko].   Hundred miles
    from the capital city of hope, A.
  Yi Kyubo.   Leaves of the mountain pear are red,
    The.
    Village mill echoes, The.
  Yi Yuksa.   Thatched House.
See also **Cities; Towns**
Villanelle (form)
  Abrahams, L.   Song for the new order.

  Auden.   If I Could Tell You.
  Bishop, E.   One Art.
  Carruth, H.   Saturday at the Border.
  Cope, W.   Lonely Hearts.
    Reading Scheme.
  Davidson, J.   Unknown, The.
  Dowson.   Villanelle of His Lady's Treasures.
    Villanelle of Marguerites.
  Empson.   Villanelle: "It is the pain, it is the
    pain, endures."
  Hacker, M.   Villanelle: Late Summer.
  Hugo, R.   Freaks at Spurgin Road Field, The.
  Justice, D.   In Memory of the Unknown Poet,
    Robert Boardman Vaughn.
    Villanelle at Sundown.
  Kumin, M.   Nuns of Childhood, The: Two
    Views.
  Orr, G.   Some Part of the Lyric.
  Osherow.   Villanelle for the Middle of the Night.
    Villanelle from a Sentence in a Poet's Brief
    Biography.
  Parini.   After the Terror.
  Passerat.   Villanelle: "I've lost her now, my
    turtle-dove."
  Plath.   Admonitions.
  Ritchie.   How to Write a Villanelle.
  Robinson, E.   Villanelle of Change.
  Roethke.   Waking, The ("I wake to sleep, and
    take my waking slow.").
  Salter.   Video Blues.
  Thomas, D.   Do Not Go Gentle into That Good
    Night.
  Vazirani, R.   It's Me, I'm Not Home.
  Waniek.   Daughters, 1900.
  Wilde, O.   Theocritus: A Villanelle.
  Yau.   Chinese Villanelle.
Villon, François
  Berrigan, A.   Sabotage.
  Komunyakaa, Y.   Villon/Leadbelly.
  Okudzhava.   François Villon.
Vilna, Poland
  Sutskever [or Sutzkever].   Cartload of Shoes, A.
Vinci, Leonardo da.
See **Leonardo da Vinci**
Vines
  Alexander, P.   Vines.
  Chiyojo.   From the mind.
  Greenway, W.   Vines, The.
  Joyce, J.   Flood.
  József, A.   Dead Landscape.
  Moiro.   Beneath Aphrodite's golden portico you
    now lie.
  Natsume Soseki.   Onto a charcoal kiln.
  Unknown.   Jiu-mu: South, Droops a Tree.
  Vidya.   And What of Those Arbors of Vines.
  Yi Chŏngbo.   May my love become an alder
    tree.
Vineyards
  Lewis, S.   Vineyard Place in My Care, A.
  Na Hûidôk.   Like the Vineyard.
Viola (Shakespeare)
  Kenny, Melanie.   Hungry as the Sea.
  Makofske, Mary.   Viola, to Olivia.
  Terrio, Chris.   Viola Recalls.
Violence
  Acholonu.   Other Forms of Slaughter.
  Addonizio.   Broken Sonnets.
  Agosin.   Most Unbelievable Part, The.
  Ai.   Endangered Species.
    Kid, The.
    Mother's Tale, The.
  Al-Haidari, B.   From Behind the Closed Door.
  al-Mala'ika, N.   Hijrah [Migration] to God, The.
  Alcosser.   Warrior's Tale, A.
  Alexie.   Texas Chainsaw Massacre.
  Aminado.   Our Sunday Rest.
  Anyidoho.   Elegy for the Revolution.
  Apollinaire.   Fete.
  Artaud.   Love with No Letup.
  Bador, B.   Curdled Skulls.
  Baker, D.   Patriotics.
    Pulp Fiction.
  Balaban.   April 30, 1975.
  Ballard, B.   Hate Crime.
  Baraka, I.   Poem Some People Will Have to

Understand, A.
Violence of the mind is the violence of god, The.
Barrax. King: April 4, 1968.
Bass, E. Bearing Witness.
Beaver. Drummer, The.
Bei Dao. Résumé.
Bekes Jr. Picture.
Belli, G. Nicaragua Water Fire.
Benedetti, M. With Your Permission.
Berger, J. Gun, The.
Bishop, W. Evidence of Death's Voodoo—Inside and Outside the "Gun As Art Exhibit". Violence.
Bobis, M. Driving to Katoomba.
Bök, Christian. Greek schemers seek egress *en ténèbres*, then enter the melee.
Brass. Only Silly Faggots Know.
Brendan-Brown, S. Dark Side of Dazzle, The.
Brewer, G. Essays on Excess and Escape.
Brutus. Robben Island Sequence.
Buchanan, O. Walk, The.
Bugeja, M. Littleton.
Bukowski. Me against the world.
Butler, S. Arms and the Man.
Byrd, B. Top Stories.
Cabico, R. Gameboy.
Cafagña, M. Lithium.
Campbell, R. In a Motel in Louisiana I Watch the Pirates And the OJ Simpson Freeway Chase at the Same Time.
Campo. Asylum.
My Childhood in Another Part of the World.
Carson, A. Grace That Comes by Violence, The.
Cavendish, M. Some with sharp swords, to tell O most accursed!
Charara, H. My Father Breaks the Neighbor's Nose.
On the Murder of an Ice Cream Man.
Chavez, L. Woman Who Raised Dogs, The.
Cheney-Coker. Poet Among Those Who Are Also Poets.
Chernoff. News, The.
Cherry, K. For Teen-Age Boys Murdered in Texas: The Refusal to Dramatize Bloodlust.
Chin, J. Why a Boy.
Chipasula. Because the Wind Remembers.
Dusk.
Talking of Sharp Things.
Christensen, Paul. Going Postal.
Cleary, B. Sealink.
Clifton, L. 4/30/92 for Rodney King.
Cohn, J. On Non-Violence & Observation.
Coleman, W. Brute Strength.
Collins, M. Rights.
Connolly, C. Something is going to go, baby.
Conoley, G. Violence, The.
Cooley, N. Arson.
Cooley, P. Incantation.
Craighead, L. Whole Truth So Help Me God—Also Known as the Gettin' Rid of Nigguz Business.
Crane, S. Black riders came from the sea.
Crawley, W. Bud.
Crow, M. Cityscape.
Dana, R. Here and Now.
Daniels, J. Hard-Boiled Egg.
Davis, C. Jojo's.
Davis, F. Sam Jackson.
Davis, O. Moorer Denies Holyfield in Twelve.
De Kok. Al Wat Kind Is.
Our Sharpeville.
Delgado, J. Flora's Plea to Mary.
Dengina, S. Russia.
Derricotte. Poem for My Father.
Dharker. Name of god, The.
Dickey, R. Father.
Doyle, S. Some Girls.
Drummond, W. Content and Resolute.
Ellis, T. Tapes.
Feirstein. Rune-Maker, The.
Gibbons, R. For My Daughter.
Glück, L. Edge, The.
Goldberg, B. Torture Boy at the Easter Confest, Repentance Creek.

Gonzalez, Ray. Prayer to the Boys of San Antonio.
González, Rigoberto. Perla at the Mexican Border Assembly Line of Dolls.
Greenberg, A. Nostalgia, Cheryl, Is the Best Heroin.
Gregg. Night Music.
Griffiths, S. Mines in Sepia Tint, The.
Hagedorn, J. Song of Bullets, The.
Harter. Turtle Blessing.
Haskins, L. Times.
Hattersley, G. New Mr Barnsley Something, The.
Remembering Dennis's Eyes.
Hayden, R. [American Journal].
Heaney, S. Whatever You Say Say Nothing.
Hecht, A. Third Avenue in Sunlight.
Herrera. Ten Still Lives.
Hicok. Bond, The.
Over Coffee.
Holden, J. Why We Bombed Haiphong.
Holmes, J. Green Tuxedo, The.
Hongo. Legend, The.
Hoornik. Pogrom.
Hoover, P. Night of the Hunter.
Howe, F. What We Learned.
Hudgins. Around the Campfire.
Hutchinson, P. Into Their True Gentleness.
Ingram-Roberts, A. Poem 2 (for Duckie Simpson of Black Uhuru).
Jackson, B. Riot at Winchell's.
Jackson, M. L. Don Pullen at the Zanzibar Blue Jazz Café [2006].
Jarman, M. Unholy Sonnet ("He loads his weapons, but the Lord God sees him.").
Jeffers, H. Philly in the Light.
Jeffers, R. Bloody Sire, The.
Jensma. I come.
Joans, T. .38, The.
Johns, L. Pink Triangles.
Johnson, L. Five Nights of Bleeding.
Johnson, Peter. Tattoo.
Jordan, J. Mid-Year Report: For Haruko.
Joseph, L. Sand Nigger.
Kay, J. Dressing Up.
Keplinger, D. Inside: George Gaines at Graterford Prison, 1981.
Kharms. Beginning of a Beautiful Day (A Symphony), The.
Kinsella, J. Pig Melons.
Radnoti Quarantine: Razglednicas.
Kloefkorn. News.
Knorr, J. Wreckage along the River, The.
Komunyakaa, Y. My Father's Love Letters [or Loveletters].
Konie, G. In the Fist of Your Hatred.
Lear, E. Limerick: "There was an old man who screamed out."
Levertov. Triple Feature.
Lilley. Sewing Lesson, The.
Lim, S. Pantoun for Chinese Women.
Liu, T. Against Nature.
Kindertotenlieder.
Poem.
López Colomé, P. Cachorros, Los.
Cubs, The.
Lorde. For the Record.
Lowery, J. Hate Crimes.
Mapanje. On Being Asked to Write a Poem for 1979.
Marennikova, K. My head is spinning to the right.
Martínez, V. Human Universe, The.
Mayer, B. Sonnet: Kamikaze: "Dawn and night of fighting, lovers like actual wars."
McCarriston. Castle in Lynn, A.
Hotel Nights with My Mother.
To Judge Faolain, Dead Long Enough: A Summons.
McClure, M. Black Dahlia.
McDaniel, J. Leonard.
McDonald, C. Asdrubral Jiménez.
McHugh, H. Fence, The.
Miliauskaite. Temporary City.
Mirsal. I Usually Look Around Me.
Molina, P. Your Anger.

Montagu, L. Epitaph: "Here lies John Hughes and Sarah Drew."
Montague, J. Cave.
Moore, H. First Time: 1950.
Moore, R. Dirge for the Living.
Morgan, R. Battery.
Morley, D. Answers on a Postcard.
Morrill, D. Man who melts a plastic garbage bag, The.
Moses, G. Black Banana House.
Mottram. Elegy 11: Ford.
Muir, E. Then.
Muske, C. Field Trip.
Nathan, L. Body Count.
Neto. Saturday in the Sand-Slums.
Niyazi, S. Thinker Between The Bronze Shield And The Human Flesh, The.
Norris, L. Ballad of Billy Rose, The.
Olsen, W. Blood.
Olson, C. Anecdotes of the Late War.
Orlen. Happy As I Am.
Ostriker. Window, at the Moment of Flame, The.
Parker, M. Whither away good neighbour.
Pasolini. Southern Dawn.
Peacock, M. Say You Love Me.
Those Paperweights with Snow Inside.
Phillips, R. Persistence of Memory, the Failure of Poetry, The.
Pound, E. Sestina: Altaforte.
Prejsnar, Mark. Ode to Toge.
Press, K. Tiresias Remembers.
Putnam. Words of an Old Woman.
Rao, K. We Should Remember.
Reading, P. Dirty sex violence of TV.
Redmond. Love Necessitates.
Regier, G. Of Violence.
Rich, A. For a Friend in Travail.
Your small hands, precisely equal to my own.
Rodgers, C. Slave Ritual.
Rodriguez, L. Rainfall Piano.
Rose, R. What the Japanese Perhaps Heard.
Rouse, A. England Nil.
Spunk Talking.
St. John, P. Violence of Pronoun, The.
Seaton, M. Tagging.
Sepúlveda-Pulvirenti. September 11, 1973.
Shapiro, K. Fly, The.
Sheppard, R. Empty Diary 1905.
Empty Diary 1987.
Sholl. Outside the Depot.
Sia, B. Claim to Fame.
Simon, L. Hattie Went to Market.
Sirowitz, H. Cookies for Peace.
Smith, R. This Is How It Comes.
Sologuren. Oh, Astonishing Love.
Stanford, A. Beating, The.
Storni. To Eros.
Sundiata. Notes from the Defense of Colin Ferguson.
Swirszczynska [or Swir]. He Was Lucky.
Szporluk. Duressor.
Libido.
Triage.
Terry, L. Bars Fight [August 28, 1746].
Torres, E. Vase of the Universe, The.
Tranströmer. Out in the Open.
Trowbridge, W. Stark Weather.
Unknown. Cats of Kilkenny, The.
Get Up and Bar the Door.
Vallejo. Black Riders, The.
Voznesensky [or Voznesenskii]. Someone Is Beating a Woman.
Walcott. Blues: "Those five or six young guys."
Weaver, A. Beginnings.
Missing Patriarch, The.
Webb, C. Killing the Animals.
Weigl. Last Lie, The.
Sky in Daduza Township, The.
Snowy Egret.
Whalen, P. International Date Line, Monday/ Monday 27:XI:67.
Wicks, S. Voice.
Wiethüchter. Without Histories.
Wilbur, R. Tywater.
Williams, W. At the Ball Game.

Mezzo Forte.
Wise, S.   50 Years in the Career of an Aspiring Thug.
Wright, C.   Wander Luís.
Yamada.   Club, The.
Young, K.   Clyde Peeling's Reptiland in Allenwood, Pennsylvania.
Youssri, Z.   Why Are Seaman Always Miserable?

Violets
Adair, T.   Violets for Your Furs.
al-Musawi, S.   Four Beats of the Heart.
Bakusui.   Returning / By an unused path—violets.
Basho.   Traveling this high.
Bryant, W.   Yellow Violet, The.
Cobbold, E.   On Some Violets Planted in My Garden by a Friend.
Doolittle, H.   Sea Violet.
Downie.   Some Poetry.
Dunbar-Nelson.   Sonnet: "I had no thought of violets of late."
Evance, S.   To a Violet.
Goethe.   Violet, The.
Herrick.   Meditation for His Mistress[e], A.
To Violets.
Issa.   Before I arrived.
Rossetti, C.   Autumn Violets.
Stanley, T.   On a Violet in Her Breast.
Taylor, J.   Violet, The.
Wright, R.   I cannot find it.

Violinists and Violins
Alexander, R.   For Years My Father.
Boruch.   Interior with a Violin.
Dryden, J.   Song for St Cecilia's Day, 1687, A.
Goldberg, B.   He Said Discipline Is the Highest Form of Love.
Hart, J.   Only Applebaum Can Make a Tree.
Kendrick, D.   For Gwendolyn Brooks: As I Civilize a Space.
Nickel, B.   Three Poems for Violin.
No Hyangnim.   Rooftop Violin.
Palmer, M.   I am an architect in Vienna.
Petit, P.   Self-Portrait as a Warao Violin.
Preil, G.   With Walter and Amati.
Shiomi, M.   Event for Late Afternoon.
Soloukhin.   For the Tree to Sing...
Wright, D.   Beethoven's Romance in G.

Virgil [or Vergil]
Creeley.   Heroes.
Dante Alighieri.   And now, with the reflected lights that glow.
Inferno.
Natural thirst that never can be quenched.
To course across more kindly waters now.
Dunmore.   To Virgil.
Longley, M.   Beech Tree, The.
López Mills, T.   Leyendo a Virgilio.
On Reading Virgil.
Tennyson, A.   To Virgil [or Vergil].
Virgil [or Vergil].   Fourth Ecologue: Pollio, The.

Virgin Islands
Walcott.   Virgins, The.

Virgin Mary
Delgado, J.   Flora's Plea to Mary.
Downie.   O Mary.
Elliott, E.   Three Marys at Castle Howard, in 1812 and 1837, The.
Fuertes.   Plastic Virgin.
Hemans.   Mary at the Feet of Christ.
Memorial of Mary, The.
Hill, G.   Vergine bella.
Howard, R.   Vocational Guidance, with Special Reference to the Annunciation of Simone Martini.
Jennings, E.   Annuciation, The.
Rilke.   1. The Birth of Mary.
2. Mary Presented at the Temple.
4. Mary's Visit with Elizabeth.
12. The Quiet Mary Knew with the Risen Christ.
Rossetti, D.   Virgin and Child, by Hans Memmeling, A; in the Academy of Bruges.
Ryman.   Sancta Maria, ora pro nobis.
Unknown.   A! Sone, tak hede to me whos sone

thou wast.
Child this Day is Born, A.
Lo, How a Rose E'er Blooming.
Mervell nothyng, Joseph, that Mary be with chyld.
Nowell Sing We.
Of a rose, a lovely rose.
On hire is al my lyf ylong.
Sodeynly affrayed, half wakyng, half slepyng.
That mayden mylde hir childe dide kepe.
Williams, W.   Adoration of the Kings, The.

See also **Mary, the Virgin**

Virginia (state)
Aldrich, T.   Fredericksburg.
Bland, J.   Carry Me Back to Old Virginny.
Brown, S.   Virginia Portrait.
Drayton.   To the Virginian Voyage.
Eady.   Sherbet.
Eliot, T. S.   Virginia.
Frost, R.   Gift Outright, The.
Jackson, G.   1619. Virginia.
Plumly.   Blossom.
Rouse, A.   Springfield, Virginia.
Rylant, C.   Living in Cheston.
Smith, D.   Leafless Trees, Chickahominy Swamp.
Night Traffic Near Winchester, Virginia.
On a Field Trip at Fredericksburg.
Ticknor.   Virginians of the Valley, The.
Weigl.   Snowy Egret.
Whitman, W.   As Toilsome I Wander'd Virginia's Woods.
Whittemore, R.   Farmhouse, The.
Whittier.   Farewell, The: "Gone, gone,—sold and gone."
Massachusetts to Virginia.
Wright, C.   Christmas East of the Blue Ridge.
Virginia Reel.

Virgins
Alcaeus [or Alkaios].   Story goes, from evil, The.
Anacreon.   Lad, glancing like a virgin.
Beaumont, J.   Whiteness, or Chastity.
Blake, W.   Merlins Prophecy.
Visions of the Daughters of Albion.
Blunt, W.   As To His Choice of Her.
Carew, T.   Maria Wentworth.
Cockburn, C.   Caution, The.
Cummings, E. E.   She being Brand.
Devi.   This World, Poor Thing.
Donne.   Flea, The.
Ewart.   To the Virgins, to Make the Most of Time.
Gelinas, D.   Miracle Country.
País de los milagros, El.
Goldsmith, O.   When Lovely Woman Stoops to Folly.
Goodison.   Wedding in Hanover.
Guiney.   Tarpeia.
Hartmann, S.   Cyanogen Seas Are Surging.
Heinowitz, C.   Five Men.
Hernández Cruz.   Milagrosa, La.
Herrick.   Dirge of Jephthah's Daughter, The.
To the Virgins, to Make Much of Time.
To Violets.
Herschberger.   Virgin, The.
Israeli, A.   Eulogy: "This should be a eulogy without words."
Jackson, L.   Virgin, The.
Keats.   Eve of St. Agnes, The.
Killigrew, A.   On a Picture Painted by Herself [or Her self], Representing Two Nymphs [or Nimphs] of Diana's, One in a Posture to Hunt, the other Bath[e]ing.
Lima, J.   Poem of Any Virgin.
Lluellyn [or Lluelyn].   Epithalamium: To Mistress M. A.
MacDiarmid, H.   O Wha's the Bride?
Massimi.   Love Song for Marcus, A.
Milton.   Chastity ("I Mean That Too, But Yet a Hidden Strength").
Moldaw.   Widening, The.
Montagu, L.   Lover, The; a Ballad.
Pavlova, V.   Juice.
Pérez Conde, P.   Ak'a ta majtanal te lotil.
Give Away the Lie.

Regala la mentira.
Philips, K.   Answer to Another Persuading a Lady to Marriage, An.
Philodemus.   Demo and Thermion Both Slay Me.
Prior.   True Maid, A.
Rutter, J.   Epithalamium: "Hymen, god of marriage bed."
St. John, D.   Coffee.
Sappho.   Bride: Virginity, virginity, where have you gone leaving me behind?
Do I still desire virginity?
Night / Virgins.
Raise high the roof.
To goldenhaired Phoibos whom Leto bore.
Shapiro, K.   First Time, The.
Stein, G.   Virgo Poem, The: Ouspensky Addresses a Congress of Virgoes.
Taylor, J.   Virgo, August.
Tayson, R.   First Sex.
Unknown.   LIKE to a ring without a finger.
Whitehead, C.   Marian Hymn.
Whitney, I.   Ye virgins that from Cupid's tents.
Wilkes, J.   Pleased to the last, she likes the luscious food.

Virtue
Barnfield [or Barnefield].   Beauty and majesty are fallen at odds.
Basho.   How very noble!
Behn, A.   Angellica's Lament.
Bhartrihari.   Apathy Is Ascribed to the Modest Man.
Browne, W.   Shall I tell you whom I love?
Campion, T.   Man of Life Upright, The.
Carew, T.   Divine Mistress, A.
In Praise of His Mistress.
Ingrateful[l] Beauty Threatened.
To My Rival.
Chapman, G.   Her look doth promise and her life assure.
Nor riches to the virtues of my love.
Of her removed and soul-infused regard.
So her close beauties further blaze her fame.
To living virtues turns the deadly vices.
Constable, H.   Of his Mistress, upon Occasion of her Walking in a Garden.
Deutsch.   Flight, The: "Earthen shadow lay on men's endeavor, An."
Donne.   Undertaking, The.
Dowriche, A.   So him at first *De Nance* commanded was to kill.
Drayton.   To My Noble Friend Master William Browne: Of the Evil Time.
Felltham [or Feltham].   On a Hopeful Youth.
Gershwin, I.   Oh, Lady, Be Good!
Gibran.   Seven Stages, The.
Gilman, C.   Christian Virtues.
Gilonis, H.   Answer to Herrick, An.
Goldsmith, O.   When Lovely Woman Stoops to Folly.
Gorostiza, J.   Elegy: "Alone, with harsh marine aloneness."
Herbert, G.   Virtue [or Vertue].
Herrick.   King and No King, A.
Hoffenstein.   You're a good girl; you're gray with virtue.
Hunt, L.   Abou Ben Adhem.
Jacob, M.   Rooster and the Pearl, The.
Jinkag Haesim.   Maxim for a Man of Virtue.
Jonson, B.   Elegy, An: "Though beauty be the mark of praise."
Epitaph on Elizabeth, L. H.
To Sir Henry Cary.
Kuzmin.   Not for nothing did we read the theologians.
Lamb, C.   To Dora W[ordsworth]; *On Being Asked By Her Father to Write in Her Album.*
Landor, W.   Rose Aylmer.
Lanier, E.   To you I dedicate this work of grace.
Martial.   Chrestus, your balls are depilated.
Massimi.   Advice to Paulinus.
Milton.   They err who think it glorious to subdue.
Moore, M.   Blessed Is the Man.
To a Snail.
Muso Soseki.   No Gain.

Ovid. Not so dear was Lyde to the Clarian poet, not so truly.
Parker, D. Observation.
Pembroke, M. To the Thrice-Sacred Queen Elizabeth.
Penna. Shadowless sun on male bodies.
Puttenham. Her Majestie resembled to the crowned piller. Ye must read upward.
Rowe, E. To Celinda.
Sidney. Sonnet 25: "Wisest scholar of the wight most wise, The."
Sonnet 31: "With how sad steps, O Moon[e], thou climb'st the skies."
Sonnet 52: "Strife is grown between Virtue and Love, A."
Sonnet 71: "Who will in fairest book of Nature know."
Smith, S. Exeat.
Sophocles. Colonus' Praise.
Spenser, E. Sonnet 79: "Men call you fair [or fayre], and you do[e] credit it."
Swift, J. To the Earl of Oxford, Late Lord Treasurer.
T'ao Ch'ien [or T'ao Yuan-ming]. Written on the First Day of the Fifth Month.
Taylor, H. Virtue alone can never die. but lives to.
Thoreau. Rumors from an Aeolian Harp.
Sympathy.
Ts'ao Chih. Goddess of the Luo, The.
Unknown. Perle, plesaunte to prynces paye.
That peachtree so frail.
Vijghen, Samira. Fallen.
Webster, A. Poor little diary, with its simple thoughts.
Wodehouse. It's a Hard, Hard World for a Man.
Wotton, S. Upon the Sudden Restraint of the Earl[e] of Somerset, Then Falling from Favor [or Favour].
Wyatt. Of the Courtier's Life.

Viruses
Ferguson, G. In Hospital-land.
Reed, I. I am not the walrus.
Wilkie, B. Virus, The.

Vishnu
Chalfi, R. Reading the I Ching.
Lewis, A. Karanje Village.
Mirabai [or Mira Bai]. All I Was Doing Was Breathing.
Ankle Bells.
Dark one, / how can I sleep?
Don't Go, Don't Go.
It's True I Went to the Market.
O friends, I am mad.
Rāy, D. Wake up, wake up, Mother!
Sama, B. Song, The.
Satyanarayana, V. Beginning, The.
Unknown. Between his hands.

Vision
Agustini. Vision.
Amichai, Y. Near the Wall of a House.
Andrade, M. Processions, The.
Arapaho Oral Tradition. He! When I met him approaching.
Armand. Braille for Left Hand.
Bitar. Happy Hour.
Bond, E. How We See.
Bui-Burton. Look at Me.
Byron, G. Love and Death.
Cassells. Marathon.
Ceravolo. Geological Hymn.
Chazal, M. Plastic Sense (1948 version).
Chubb, R. Transfiguration.
Clifton, L. 11/10 Again.
Copus, J. Art of Interpretation, The.
Crane, H. Wine Menagerie, The.
Crane, S. I met a seer.
Davie, D. Hill Field, The.
Dickinson, E. Mine—by the Right of the White Election!
Dooley, M. Fundoscopy.
Dunn, D. Sundial, The.
Edson, R. Optical Prodigal, The.
Edwards, K. This juxtaposition of events without.
Frost, R. Neither Out Far Nor In Deep.

Giussani, S. In the Distance.
Gunn, T. Unsettled Motorcyclist's Vision of His Death, The.
Hannon. Beyond Freedom.
Hartley, M. What Have We All—a Soliloquy of Essences.
Harvey, M. One Filament against the Firmament.
Heaney, S. His Dawn Vision.
Visible sea at a distance from the shore, The.
Hecht, A. Hill, A.
Henry, B. Discovery.
Hikmet. I Shut My Eyes Tight.
Hirsch, E. Man on a Fire Escape.
Hoekstra. Cedar, The.
Ibáñez, S. I Cannot.
Island in the Light.
Ingalls, J. Vision of St. Michael and St. John, The.
Issa. Mother I never knew.
Jarrell, R. Orient Express, The.
Jensma. Somewhere in the middle, Sunday.
Joubert. Brilliant Sky.
Juarroz. Look First at the Air and Its Black Element Which Never Stops.
Keble. Malvern at a Distance.
Kendrick, D. Note to the Ophthalmologist.
Kornblith, M. Mirrors.
Lauterbach. Mimetic.
Levertov. Uncertain Oneiromancy.
Li Po. My sword at my waist, I climb a high tower.
Lisboa. Beyond the Image.
Loftis, N. Delirium.
Longfellow, H. Galaxy, The.
Lowell, R. For Sheridan.
MacCaig. Instrument and Agent.
MacConglinne. Vision of MacConglinne, The.
Machado Ruiz. Breeze Tells Me, Loved One, The.
Eye You See Isn't, The.
Merrill, J. Octopus, The.
Morley, D. Exact Fares.
Muso Soseki. At Whole-World-In-View-Hut.
Myles, E. Eileen's Vision.
Nemerov. I Only Am Escaped Alone to Tell Thee.
Nicholson, N. From a Boat at Coniston.
Obejas, A. Public Place (After Olga Broumas), The.
Ortiz. Vision Shadows.
Paz. Lake.
Mystery.
P'Bitek. Eyeshop, The.
Prado, A. Pelican, The.
Rendall, R. Angle of Vision.
Reznikoff. Epilogue: "Blessed / in the light of the sun at the sight of the world."
Rilke. Panther, The.
Robinson, M. Visions Appear to Her in a Dream.
Rossetti, C. Later Life: A Double Sonnet of Sonnets.
Who Has Seen the Wind?
Ryan, T. Eclipse, Kenwick, 1974.
Trompe l'oeil.
Sachs, N. In the Evening Your Vision Widens.
Saenz, J. Let your permanency under the brilliance of the stars be long.
Salter. Half a Double Sonnet.
Saxe, J. Blind Men and the Elephant, The.
Shapiro, K. Dome of Sunday, The [or A].
Sorrentino. Handbook of Versification.
Spender, S. To T.A.R.H.
Stanton, M. Ballad of the Magic Glasses.
Storni. White Claw, The.
Strabo, W. Dearest, You Come Suddenly and Suddenly You Depart.
Thomas, E. Some Eyes Condemn.
Towle. Painting the Eaves.
Tu Fu [or Du Fu]. Looking at Mount T'ai-Shan.
Van Duyn. Vision Test, The.
Vietnamese Oral Tradition. Clear Skies, Still Sea.
Walcott. Hotel Normandie Pool, The.
Wang Chih-huan. Climbing the Stork Pavilion.

Warren, R. Vision.
Whalen, P. Off. . . / over / that way.
Wilbur, R. Beacon, The.
Wilkinson, A. Lens.
Wroth. Sonnet 21: "When last I saw thee, I did not[t] thee see."
Yi Kyubo. Thoughts on Eyes Growing Dim: Presented to Chŏn Iji.
Zaid. Cloister.
Mortal Practice.

Visions
Ayewanu, S. God's Voice.
Berry, Jake. In the clutch of blind embryo.
Brines, F. Grief: "With eyes happy."
Burkard. Cloud of Dusk, A.
Cairns, Scott. And Also from the Son.
Catling. Pittancer, The.
Dimitrova. Sunstroke.
Hatun. I opened my eyes from sleep, and suddenly.
Ilagha, N. Nora.
Jacob, M. Revelation, The.
Lami'i Çelebi. Yesterday I saw that sun-faced beauty.
Lopez, T. In Memory.
Moxley, Jennifer. Transom Over Death's Door, A.
Noël, Bernard. Angers.
Patterson, G. I Used to Go to Church.
Trakl. Dream of Evil (First Version).
Tynan Hinkson, K. I Wonder Why.
Whitman, W. Sleepers, The.
Sleepers, The.
Wilkinson, J. Grace.

Visiting and Visitors
Akhmatova, A. Guest, The.
Allen, F. Visitant, The.
"Alta.". Judy Comes to Visit.
Anderson, J. Going to Norway.
Beerbohm, M. Chorus of a Song That Might Have Been Written by Albert Chevalier.
Bourne, Lesley-Anne. Boy I Never Met, The.
Bryan, M. Here, said my guide.
Buson. I go out alone.
People visiting all day.
Chang Chi. Night-Mooring at Maple Bridge.
Chiao-jan. Playful Poem.
Ch'ien Ch'i. From My Study at the Mouth of the Valley: A Message to Censor Yang.
Child, L. Thanksgiving Day.
Cohen, J. Walt Whitman in Ohio.
Conn. Visiting Hour.
Csoori. Visitor's Memories, The.
De Kok. Visitor.
De la Mare. Some One.
Delgado, J. Visiting Father.
Dickinson, E. Infinite a sudden Guest, The.
Eich. Huge Person, The.
Fanthorpe. After Visiting Hours.
Unprofessionals, The.
Foot, E. Graceful Divine, A.
Frazier, John Alexander, Jr. Visiting Hours.
Gallagher, T. Sah Sin.
Hahn, O. Death Is Sitting at the Foot of My Bed.
Halpine. Quakerdom (The Formal Call).
Hamilton, I. Visit, The.
Herrick. Night-Piece, to Julia, The.
Hertz, D. Return, The.
Hsieh Ling-yün. Replying to a Poem from My Cousin Huilian.
Hughes, L. Madam and the Wrong Visitor.
Ibn Hazm al-Andalusi. Visit, The.
Jacinto, J. Visitation.
Jenkins, A. Visiting.
Kaplan, L. He takes me to see his mother. She lives in the.
Kelly, B. Visitation, The.
Kim Yŏng. Snowflakes flutter—butterflies chase flowers.
Lars. Recollection of Gabriela Mistral.
Levertov. Poet and Person.
Li Kuang-t'ien. Dead Turk, A.
Li Po. On Visiting Taoist Recluse of Tai-Tien-Shan and Not Finding Him.
Llywelyn-Williams. On a Visit.

Martial.   Believe me, sir, I'd like to spend whole days.
McGrath, T.   Probable Cause.
Meng Hao Jan.   In Passing an Old Friend's Farm.
Montale.   Visit to Fadin.
Mullen, L.   Stopping By.
Muso Soseki.   My thatched hut.
  Suzan Oshos's Visit to My West Mountain Hut.
  Tengan Osho's Visit to Erin-ji.
  Thanks Sent to Taihei Osho.
  To Kengai Osho of Engaku-ji.
  Visiting My Old Hut in Late Spring.
Nekrasov, V.   Somehow I really want to go.
O'Hara, F.   Poem: "Eager note on my door said "Call me", The."
Pei Di.   Path of the Ashtrees, The.
Po Chü-i.   Visiting the Recluse Cheng.
Rossetti, C.   Echo.
  Enrica, 1865.
Schnackenberg.   Returning North.
Sheridan, T.   Tom Punsibi's Letter to Dean Swift.
Tagore.   You Did Not Find Me.
Tellegen.   Visit, The.
Unknown.   Ten-Day Visitor, The.
Vilariño.   Visitor, A.
Wang Fan-chih.   Reclusive.
Wang Wei.   Path of the Ashtrees, The.
Young, A.   One West Coast.
Yüan Chiu-ts'ai.   Warm Invitation, A.
Yuson.   World Poetry Circuit.

Vitality
Sappho.   You / Put success in the mouth.
Su Tung-p'o.   Who Says a Painting Must Look Like Life?

Vocations
Craig, David.   Young Monk (Denver).
Fried, E.   Logos.
Othman, A.   Dual Call, The.
See also **Occupations**

Vodka
Shelvakh, A.   Veterans.
Someck, R.   Short history of vodka, A.

Voices
Aizenberg, M.   Not in the chimney, but in the gas-pipes.
Alberti.   If My Voice Dies While on Land.
Baron, S.   Tenebrae.
Basho.   Spider, if you had a voice.
  What voice.
Baudelaire.   Cracked Bell, The.
Baudri of Bourgueil.   Your Appearance is Pleasing.
Bektaş, Cengiz.   Now: "I long for my voice that found you."
Belli, C.   Unknown Voice, An.
Blake, W.   London: "I wander through [*or* thro'] each chartered [*or* charter'd] street."
Bogan, L.   Song for the Last Act.
Bottoms.   Recording the Spirit Voices.
Bringhurst.   Parable of the Voices.
Browning, R.   Meeting at Night.
Campo.   My Voice.
Castillo, S.   Letter to Yeni on Peering into Her Life.
Cemal Süreya.   8:10 Ferry, The.
Ch'oe Sŭngja.   Voice, A: "Voice hidden in midair, The."
Cooper, W.   Leaving the Country.
Creeley.   Messengers, The.
Cullen, Y.   For Letters.
Dauenhauer.   Voices.
Felipe, L.   Farm Is Yours, The.
  I am no one: a man.
Filkova, Fedya.   Under a Wing.
Finch, A.   Dickinson.
García, D.   Serpentine Voices.
García Lorca.   Ah secret voice of dark love! Ah bleating without wool! Ah wound! Ah prick of gall, sunken camellia!
  Boy Unable to Speak, The.
  Poet Speaks with Love by Telephone, The.
Griffiths, J.   Lost and Found.
Grotz, J.   Last Living Castrato, The.

Guillén, J.   River.
Hall, D.   White Apples.
Hart, L.   Johnny One-Note.
Hass, R.   Sonnet: "Man talking to his ex-wife on the phone, A."
Herrick.   Upon Julia's Voice.
Hovanessian, D.   Inside Green Eyes, Black Eyes.
Hugo, V.   Open Windows.
Hunter, C.   What the Voice Sees.
Hutchison, J.   Joni Mitchell.
Jaimes Freyre.   Sad Voices, The.
Jigerkhwen.   I am the Voice.
Johnson, J.   Lift Every [*or* Ev'ry] Voice and Sing.
Jones, Nesta Wyn.   Voices: "Yes, this is my voice."
Kawai Suimei.   Living Voice.
Komunyakaa, Y.   Twilight Seduction.
Levi, P.   Voices.
Levin, D.   Ars Poetica: "Six monarch butterfly cocoons."
Lisboa.   Echo.
López Colomé, P.   Dramatis Personae.
  Dramatis personae.
López Mills, T.   Mi voz fiel como la sombra.
  My Voice Faithful as a Shadow.
Lorde.   Echoes.
Majorino.   Say--So I'll Say.
McClure, M.   For Gary Snyder and Carole Koda.
McKay, D.   Sometimes a Voice 1.
Meynell, A.   To the Beloved.
Miller, J.   Topos.
Montale.   Dora Markus.
Monzón, R.   Opaque Copper.
Naden.   Sister of Mercy, The.
O'Reilly, C.   Duets.
Palés Matos.   Calling, The.
Pei Di.   Deer Enclosure, The.
Rankine.   Elsewhere, Things Tend.
Risset, Jacqueline.   Voice: "World put back on its."
Salaam.   French Quarter Intimacies.
Sanchez, S.   Haiku: "Your voice unwrapping." This is Not a Small Voice.
Sansom, A.   Voice.
Schubert, D.   Successful Summer, A.
Scott, D.   More Poem.
Shapiro, A.   Cold Wood.
Shelley, P.   To --: "Music, when soft voices die."
Simonides.   No leaf-shaking blast of winds.
Sobin, G.   What the Music Wants.
Southerland.   Recitation.
Stanton, M.   In Ignorant Cadence.
Stephen, J.   Sonnet, A: "Two voices are there: one is of the deep."
Suzuki, M.   Soft rain.
Tan Taigi.   Thunder / Voices of drowned.
Tennyson, A.   Break, Break, Break.
  Thy voice is on the rolling air.
Thomas, L.   Great Love Duets.
Unknown, fr. Terezin Concentration Camp.
  Birdsong 2.
Valentine, J.   Under Voice, The.
Verlaine.   Voice of Pride: shout of blaring trumpets.
Volach, Y.   Bird.
Wang Wei.   Deer Enclosure, The.
Wicks, S.   Voice.
Wordsworth, W.   Thought[s] of a Briton on the Subjugation of Switzerland.
Wright, J.   Speak.
See also **Screams; Speech; Talk**

Volcanoes
Bishop, E.   Crusoe in England.
Breton, A.   They Tell Me That Over There.
Chitwood, Michael.   After the Missionaries.
Day Lewis.   Poem for an Anniversary.
Dickinson, E.   Still--Volcano--Life, A.
  Volcanoes be in Sicily.
d'Oettingen.   Kilimanjaro.
Enzensberger, H.   Reprieve, The.
Hemans.   Image in Lava, The.
Hongo.   Eruption: Pu'u Ō'ō.

Hongo Store 29 Miles Volcano Hilo, Hawaii, The.
Hugo, V.   Inquisition, The.
Issa.   Over paddies / At its foot.
Kennedy, L.   I am in the most exquisite distress.
Kuznetsova, I.   Repairs are like the fall of Pompeii.
Lowry, M.   Volcano is Dark, The.
MacDonald, C.   Dangers of Looking Back, The.
Ray, H.   Listening Nydia.
Rich, A.   Every peak is a crater. This is the law of volcanoes.
Rose.   Loo-wit.
Santos Chocano.   Volcanoes, The.
Scupham.   Pompeii: Plaster Casts.
Sears, P.   Volcanic Ash.
Shinkichi Takahashi.   Afterimages.
Snyder, G.   Burning Island.
Sodo.   Sudden shower / Cooling lava.
Tayankannanar.   Overspread with Salty Soil.
Turner, W.   Romance.
Van Sertima.   Volcano.

Voltaire, François Marie Arouet de
Blake, W.   Mock On, Mock On, Voltaire, Rousseau.

Voodoo
Boadiba.   Autozobop.
Bomani, M.   Voudou Mama.
Cartwright, K.   Delta, The / Itch of cayenne.
Castro, A.   Hoodoo Whisper.
D'Aguiar, F.   Obeah Mama Dot.
Floyd-Miller, C.   Roots 2: the conjure woman replies.
Freeman, Jessica.   Garden District Soubrette.
Hernton, C.   Medicine Man.
Hyppolite, M.   Speech.
Waniek.   Women's Locker Room.
Young, Andy.   Vodou Headwashing Ceremony.

Voting and Voters
Balakian, P.   End of the Reagan Era, The.
Chudleigh.   To the Ladies.
Coolidge.   My Rights.
Cross, D.   Vote, The.
Dickinson, E.   Mine--by the Right of the White Election!
Gilman, C.   Anti-Suffragists, The.
Gwala.   Election pincers.
Harper, F.   Aunt Chloe's Politics.
  Deliverance, The.
Kizer, C.   Election Day, 1984.
Lindsay, V.   Bryan, Bryan, Bryan, Bryan.
  Why I Voted the Socialist Ticket.
Moorer.   Negro Ballot, The.
Nathan, L.   Election, The.
Pierpont, J.   Ballot, The.
Smith, P.   Woman Who Died in Line, The.
Unknown.   Vote for Lunn.
Zamora-Linmark.   Election Day.
See also **Campaigns, Political; Women's Suffrage**

Vowels
Bök, Christian.   Writing is inhibiting. Sighing, I sit, scribbling in ink.
Emerson, J.   Lighthouse, The.
L'Abbé, Sonnet.   Shyness, the delay to say, The.
Rimbaud, A.   Vowels.

Voyages
Alexander, P.   Well-Known Elizabethan Double Entendre, A.
Baudelaire.   Voyage, The.
  Voyaging.
Ch'in Kuan.   Tune: "Rouged Lips".
Crane, H.   Voyages.
Deltoro, A.   Viaje.
  Voyage.
Drayton.   To the Virginian Voyage.
Emerson, R.   Thine Eyes Still Shined.
Esteban, Claude.   Once Evening's Fallen.
Ferry.   Cythera.
  Embarkation for Cythera, The.
Glissant.   For Mycea.
Gould, A.   Ice.
Homer.   And then went down to the ship.
Jackson, H.   My Lighthouses.
Lewis, G.   Second time the comet swung by, The.

W

What is her vanishing point?
Lima, F.   Lime.
Moore, R.   Personal Atlas.
Sandburg, C.   You can go now yes go now. Go east or west, go north or.
Sexton.   Crossing the Atlantic.
Simic.   Arctic Voyager, An.
Stevenson, R.   Christmas at Sea.
Walcott.   Schooner Flight, The.
Waldrep, G. C.   O Canada!
White, K.   Brandan's Last Voyage.
Whittier.   Godspeed.
Wright, C.   Voyage, The: "At first I was overly cautious, procedure being all-important."

Voyageurs
Moore, T.   Canadian Boat Song, A.
Morrice, K.   Voyager.
Whitman, W.   Untold Want, The.

Voyeurism and Voyeurs
Castillo, S.   Voyeur.
Dove, R.   Small Town.
Eady.   View from the Roof, Waverly Place.
Field, Miranda.   Subway.
Gosse.   Revelation.
Heath, R.   Seeing Her Dancing.
Henry, B.   Skin: "Never mind the fantasy about the tweezers and the tongue."
Holloway, G.   Lovers, The.
Hristov, Boris.   Window, The: "I stand on tiptoe to reach the window that's open a crack."
Lawrence, D. H.   Gloire de Dijon.
Moolten, D.   Voyeur.
Saje, N.   Male in the Women's Locker Room, A.
Shapiro, K.   Dome of Sunday, The [or A].
Shaughnessy, B.   Panopticon.
Unknown.   You were hiding behind the door.
Waller, E.   Song: "Go[e], lovely rose."
Whalen, P.   Off. . . / over / that way.
Whitman, W.   Twenty-eight young men bathe by the shore.

Vulcan
Auden.   Shield of Achilles, The.
Homer.   Shield of Achilles, The.
Russell, T.   Sonnet: Suppos'd to Be Written at Lemnos.

Vulnerability
Ash, J.   Poor Boy: Portrait of a Painting.
Brouwer, J.   Aesthetics.
Creeley.   Something.
"Eliot.".   from Chapter 14.
Fuzuli.   If my heart were a wild bird, it would nest.
Green, B.   That's My Weakness Now.
Hayes, T.   Goliath Poem.
Huxley, A.   Armour.
McDowell.   Where and What You Are.
Peacock, M.   How I Come to You.
Randell.   She had the stance of a snowdrop.
Rich, A.   Storm Warnings.
Shapiro, K.   First Time, The.
Stept, S.   That's My Weakness Now.

Vultures
Atwood.   Vultures.
Belloc.   Vulture, The.
Bottoms.   Under the Vulture-Tree.
Diop, D.   Vultures, The.
Greger.   Prince of the Powers of the Air.
Griffin, S.   This Is Not Love's Offering.
Jeffers, R.   Vulture.
Jones, H.   Mannyelanong.
Kennedy, X.   Vulture.
Kim, Suji Kwock.   Chasm, The.
Muir, E.   Mythical Journey, The.
Page, G.   Elegist, The.
Shaku Chōkū.   Vultures—in the Midst of War.
Sterling, G.   Black Vulture, The.
Unknown.   See the great vultures.
Van Winckel, N.   Appetite, the Great Painting.
Wilbur, R.   Still, Citizen Sparrow.

See also **Buzzards**

Wagner, Richard
Darío, R.   Swan, The.
Duncan, R.   Structure of Rime XVIII.
Lanier, S.   To Richard Wagner.
Levy, N.   Tannhauser.

Wagon Trains
Chittenden.   Old Mackenzie Trail, The.
Guest, B.   Santa Fe Trail.
Nance.   Old Fort Griffin.

Wagtails
Clare, J.   Little Trotty Wagtail.

Wailing Wall, The
Hefer, H.   Paratroopers Are Weeping, The.

Waiters and Waitresses
Akhmadulina.   Queen, A.
Clarke, M.   Wail of the Waiter, The.
Cullen, C.   Atlantic City Waiter.
Eady.   Sherbet.
Gardinier.   At Work.
Grahn.   Ella, in a Square Apron, Along Highway 80.
Greenberg, A.   Saints.
Hull, L.   Night Waitress.
Johnson, M.   All-Night Diner, The.
Jones, R.   On the Bearing of Waitresses.
McCord, D.   Epitaph on a Waiter.
Mutis.   Sonata.
Oates.   Waiting on Elvis, 1956.
Quinn, J.   Go through and down the steps.
Shinder.   Waitress.
Stone, J.   Rosemary.
Veinberg, J.   To an Exeter City Cocktail Waitress.
Ward, BJ.   Shakespeare as a Waiter.
Waring, B.   Tip, The.

Waiting
Afrika, T.   Queue.
Aiken, C.   Three Star Final.
Angus.   Anemones.
Basheva.   Fast train, The? The express?
Bowers, E.   Living Together.
Carman, B.   Northern Vigil, A.
Cherry, K.   How to Wait.
Dalton, Mary.   Flirrup.
Donovan, K.   Wild Night, A.
Eichner, Maura.   Woman is Waiting for a Bus, A.
Fickert.   Bad Weather at the Airport.
Hahn, O.   Candlelight Dinner.
Iosifova, Ekaterina.   At My Doorstep.
Ishikawa.   For Her Lover.
Machado Ruiz.   Close to the Road.
Meng Hao Jan.   At the Mountain-Lodge of the Buddhist Priest Ye Waiting in Vain for My Friend Ding.
Mikhail, D.   Non-Military Statements.
Na Hûidôk.   For Five Minutes.
Norton, C.   Faithless Knight, The.
O'Connor, M.   Sakura.
Ochiai Naobumi.   Song of the Faithful Daughter Shiragiku.
Otsu.   For You.
Penn, P.   Soup, The: "On the day of your scan, I make a soup."
Taneda Santoka.   Waiting for what?
Thomas, R. S.   Kneeling.
Unknown.   Midnight already and you are still not here.
Oh my love beyond the mountains, gaze at the moon.
Why do you come to me so seldom?
You wretch who did not come last evening!
Van Cleave, R.   Confession #1.
Vasileva, E.   I wish I could look.
Vázquez Montalbán, M.   Yramín and the Sea.
Whalen, P.   False Senryū.
Waiting for Claude.
Wright, C.   Voyage, The: "At first I was overly cautious, procedure being all-important."

Waiting Rooms
Bishop, E.   In the Waiting Room.
Clampitt.   From a Clinic Waiting Room.
Darling, J.   Waiting Room in August, A.
Dove, R.   Vacation.
Fanthorpe.   Waiting Room.
France, L.   In the Waiting Room: "Consult your tongue like a weather forecast."
Nemerov.   Waiting Rooms.
Norgate, S.   Perfect example of a paralysed larynx, A.
Terranova.   Self-Examination.
Vogel, D.   Waiting-rooms.

Wakes
Gallagher, T.   Wake.
Rexroth, K.   Requiem for the Spanish Dead.
Unknown.   Finnegan's Wake.

Waking
Alberti.   Good Angel, The.
Andal.   O sister of wealth.
Atwood.   Up.
Azuah, U.   Frame of Fear.
Bador, B.   Essence.
Basho.   Awakened at midnight.
Berrigan, T.   In Bed with Joan & Alex.
Bly, R.   Waking from Sleep.
Cairns, Scott.   Another Song.
Carver, R.   At Least.
Catulus.   Waking Intuitively.
Clarke, A.   Flower-Quiet in the Rush-Strewn Sheiling.
Curnow.   Out of Sleep.
Daglarca.   Day Within a Day.
Dante Alighieri.   And now, with the reflected lights that glow.
Davenant [or D'Avenant].   O Thou That Sleep'st like Pig in Straw.
De Roux, Paul.   Day's Labor, The.
Dobyns.   Music One Looks Back On, The.
Donne.   Good-Morrow, The.
Emperor Ch'ien-wen of Liang.   Getting Up in Winter.
Field.   Love rises up some days.
Ford, M.   Long Man, The.
Fugai.   Only the Zen-man knows tranquillity.
Gascoigne.   Gascoigne's Good-Morrow.
Griffiths, B.   Fragment 4: "Little Jo wakes me up."
Gumilyov [or Gumiliov or Gumilev].   Pre-Memory.
Han-shan Te-ch'ing.   Bone-chilling snow on a thousand peaks.
Higginson, E.   Dawn.
Ingelow.   Winding-up Time.
Islām, N.   Wake up, Syama, wake up, Syama!
Jaewol Kyunghun.   Sleeping in Pulil Hermitage.
Joyce, J.   My dove, my beautiful one.
Kaplan, A.   Hey.
Keats.   Bright Star.
Kinnell.   Rapture.
Koeppel, M.   While the Wolf Walks the Edge of the Woods.
Lal Ded [or Lalla].   At the end of a crazy-moon night.
To learn the scriptures is easy.
Lee, L.   Early in the Morning.
Lowell, R.   Waking Early Sunday Morning.
Machado Ruiz.   If it's good to live.
Mackey, N.   Phantom Light of All Our Day, The.
MacNeice.   September has come and I wake.
Melançon, Robert.   Wakening.
Meredith, W.   Poem about Morning.
Merwin.   Rain Travel.
Meynell, A.   Study, A.
Morales, A.   Puertoricanness.
Nara Singde.   Tune: "As If in a Dream".
O'Hara, F.   Getting Up Ahead of Someone (Sun).
Othman, A.   Dual Call, The.
Pinsky.   First Early Mornings Together.
Pizarnik.   Awakening, The.
Quinn, J.   I wake early into.
Reed, H.   Door and the Window, The.
Rexroth, K.   Chilled through, I wake up.
Ritch, O.   When I Woke, Everything Was the Same but Different.
Roethke.   Waking, The ("I wake to sleep, and take my waking slow.").

Samson, J.   Hypothetical.

Shakespeare, W.   Hark, hark! the lark at heaven's gate sings.

"Shunzei's Daughter.".   Brought by the breeze.

Simic.   Poem: "Every morning I forget how it is."

Simpson, A.   Waking.

Sŏ Chŏngju.   Peony Afternoon.

Steele, T.   Joseph.

Subbarao, N.   You in My Dream.

Tennyson, A.   Now Sleeps the Crimson Petal.
Now Sleeps the Crimson Petal.

Thaxter.   Chanticleer.

Torres, E.   Elbow in Dumberland, An.

Unknown.   Get Up, Get Up.
Let the mullah raise his prayer to the dawn.

Waldman, A.   Gonna change my life.

Wei Chuang.   Moon Dips Low, The.

Wen T'ing-yün.   In the South Courtyard.

Wilbur, R.   Love Calls Us to the Things of This World.

Williams, W.   Spring and All.

Wingfield.   Waking.

Winslow, P.   Rise: "Marvellous how the house builds itself."

Wray, C.   Star, The.

Wright, J.   I Try to Waken and Greet the World Once Again.

Wyatt.   Lover Showeth How He Is Forsaken of Such as He Sometime Enjoyed, The.

Yüan Mei.   Growing Old (1).

Zisquit.   After Years of Feasting and No Sacrifice.

Walden Pond, Massachusetts

Channing.   Walden.

Oliver, M.   Going to Walden.

Thoreau.   Life in us is like the water in the river, The.

Wales

Adams, S.   Hill Fort, Caerleon.

Aspden, B.   News of the Changes.

Bidgood.   Dragon.

Camlan.   Education in Wales.

Clarke, G.   Taid's Grave.

Davies, D.   Carmarthenshire.

Davies, E.   Will no young British bard, on rhyme intent.

Davies, G.   Incomers.

Davies, I.   Angry Summer, The ("From Abertillery and Aberdare.").
Angry Summer, The ("Mrs. Evans fach, you want butter again.").
Gwalia Deserta XXII.
Hywel and Blodwen.

Davies, W. H.   Days That Have Been.

Dyment.   Derbyshire Born, Monmouth Is My Home.

Evans, Aled Lewis.   Alone.

Evans, E.   Whatever clime we travel or explore.

Finch, P.   Welsh Wordscape, A.

Garlick, R.   Dylan Thomas at Tenby.

Ginsberg, A.   Wales Visitation.

Graves, R.   Welsh Incident.

Gruffydd, P.   Slate Quay: Felinheli.

Guest, H.   Wales Re-visited.

Homfray.   Thoughts on Happiness.

Hooker, J.   Take a long view from Mynydd Bach.

Humphries, R.   Dafydd ap Gwilym Resents the Winter.

Jones, D.   Adrift.
Wales.

Jones, G.   Morning.

Jones, J.   Glyndwr's War Song.

Jones, T.   Cwmchwefri.

Jones, Tudur Dylan.   Great Glasshouse at the National Botanic Garden of Wales.

Lewis, E.   We Who Were Born.

Lewis, G.   Mapmaker's Song, The.

Lewis, S.   Vineyard Place in My Care, A.

Llewellyn-Williams.   Two Rivers.

Llwyd, R.   Beaumaris Bay.

Mathias, R.   Brechfa Chapel.
Laus Deo.
Porth Cwyfan.
Sir Gelli to R.S.

Morgan, J.   My Welsh Home.

Morgan, R.   Shadow Valley.

Morris, S.   Here in these fretted caverns whence the sea.
Salt sprays deluge it, wild waves buffet it, hurricanes rave.

Owen, Gerallt Lloyd.   Inheritance: "We had a country to keep."
Man on the Horizon, The.

Parry, R.   Wales 1937.

Parry-Williams.   This One.

Philips, K.   On the Welsh Language.

Phillips, D.   Maridunum.

Prichard.   What can you see in yonder bay.

Rhys, K.   Interlude.

Thomas, D.   Author's Prologue.
Fern Hill.

Thomas, J.   His father did intend that Harry should.

Thomas, R. S.   Ancients of the World, The.
Line from St. David's, A.
Reservoirs.
Welsh Hill Country, The.
Welsh History.
Welsh Landscape.

Thrale [*later* Mrs. Piozzi].   Winter in Wales, A.

Tripp.   Capital.
Diesel to Yesterday.
Welcome to Wales.

Walcott.   Streams.

Ward, J.   Unusual View of the Town.

Watkyns.   Golden Grove, Carmarthen.

Webb, H.   Cywydd o Fawl.
Epil y Filiast.
Nightingales, The.
Stone Face, The.

Williams, H.   To Dr Moore, in Answer to a Poetical Epistle Written by Him in Wales.

Williams, W.   Preseli.
Welsh and Wales.

See also **Welsh, The**

Walking and Walkers

Ammons.   Corsons Inlet.
Strolls.

Armand.   Word to the Wise, A.

Aua.   To Lighten Heavy Loads.

Auden.   As I Walked Out One Evening.

Barnes, D.   Walking-Mort, The.

Barnes, W.   Turnstile, The.

Basho.   Calm moon, A.
Harvest moon.
It's fall and a full moon.

Beckett, S.   Enueg 1.

Berlin.   Couple of Swells, A.

Bethune, L.   Harlem Freeze Frame.

Blake, W.   London: "I wander through [*or* thro'] each chartered [*or* charter'd] street."

Breeze.   Mother. . .Sister. . .Daughter.

Brown, L.   Winter Sonnet.

Bryant, W.   To a Waterfowl.

Buckley, C.   Playing for Time.

Buson.   Buying leeks.

Butcher.   Crow Is Walking.

Byron, G.   She Walks In Beauty.

Cahn, S.   I'll Walk Alone.

Campert.   Stroll to Parfondeval, A.

Carver, R.   Walk, A.

Cofer, J.   Learning to Walk Alone.

Coleridge, M.   Witch, The.

Collins, B.   Man Listening to Disc.

Cornish, S.   Generations 2.

Crane, H.   In Shadow.

Creeley.   I Know a Man.

Crowe, T.   Pond in the Woods, A.

Deltoro, A.   Viaje.
Voyage.

Densmore.   I Am Walking.

Dixon, M.   Would You Like to Take a Walk?

Ema Saikō.   Evening Stroll.

Engels, F.   Walking to Cootehill.

Fan Chung-yen.   Tune: "Walk on the Imperial Street".

Fields, D.   On the Sunny Side of the Street.

Frost, R.   Acquainted with the Night.
Good Hours.
Meeting and Passing.

Furber, D.   Lambeth Walk.

Gay, N.   Lambeth Walk.

Gehrke, S.   Walking Fields at Night South of Hampton, Iowa.

Gershwin, I.   Let's Take a Walk Around the Block.

Gilbert, S.   Afternoon Walk: The Sea Ranch.

Gillan.   In Memory We Are Walking.

Gilsdorf, E.   Walk, The.

Giovannitti.   Walker, The.

Griffiths, B.   Fragment 4: "Little Jo wakes me up."

Gurney, I.   If I Walked Straight Slap.

Hammerstein.   You'll Never Walk Alone.

Harburg.   Let's Take a Walk Around the Block.

Hardy, T.   Walk, The.

Hill, M.   Abomination.

Hollander, J.   Effet de Neige.

Hsieh T'iao.   Roaming the East Field.

Hsu Hsuan.   Lu-lung Village, Autumn.

Hunt, Irmgard.   Midday.

Jackson, L.   Footfalling.

Jordan, J.   Poem About My Rights.

Katrovas.   Sky.

Kavanagh, P.   Come Dance with Kitty Stobling.

Kenyon, J.   Walking Alone in Late WInter.

Kim Sŏnggi.   Shaking off the red dust.

Kleban, E.   One.

Knight, E.   Green Grass and Yellow Balloons.

Ko Chŏnghŭi.   On the Way to Ch'ŏngju.

Kosugi, T.   Theater Music.

La Fontaine.   Shrimp and Her Daughter, The.

Lane, M. Travis.   Portobello.

Layton.   Cold Green Element, The.

Lear, E.   Table and the Chair, The.

Leigh, C.   I Walk a Little Faster.

Levitt, Peter.   Walking the path.

Levy, A.   March Day in London, A.
To Vernon Lee.

Li K'ai-hsien.   Sent to the Master Physician, "Almond Orchard" Shih.

Liu Ch'ang-ch'ing.   While Visiting on the South Stream the Taoist Priest Chang.

Liu Tsung-yüan.   Morning Walk in Autumn to South Valley Passing an Abandoned Village.

Loesser.   I Don't Want to Walk Without You.

Machado Ruiz.   There, in the High Part.
Walker, It Is Your Footsteps.

Mangan, J.   O'Hussey's Ode to the Maguire.

Marsman.   Polderland.

Martinez, D.   Moto Perpetuo.

McGrath, C.   Spring Comes to Chicago.

Meredith, W.   Crossing Over.

Merwin.   Air: "Naturally it is night."

Millay, E.   Departure.

Miller, V.   How Far?

Nelson, M.   Molino.

Neruda.   Walking Around.

Nesbit, E.   Vies Manquées.

Nezval.   Trap Door.

No Hyegyŏng.   Happy Walk.

O'Brien, J.   Revelation on a Summer Walk.

Ortiz.   Yuusthiwa.

Osgood, F.   Ellen Learning to Walk.

Paz.   Here.

Pei Di.   Hill of the Hatchet-Leaved Bamboos.

Plumpp.   Poem: "Poems are not places."

Reznikoff.   I like this secret walking.

Rilke.   O you lovers that are so gentle, step occasionally.
Swan, The.

Robinson, A.   Tuscan Olives.
Venetian Nocturne.

Rose, B.   Would You Like to Take a Walk?

Rumi.   Keep walking, though there's no place to get to.

Sanchez, S.   To Anita.

Scammell, W.   Walk, The.

Schuyler, J.   Can I Tempt You to a Pond Walk?

Schwartz, D.   Heavy Bear Who Goes with Me, The.

Scott, S.   Proud Maisie.

Sexton.   Noon Walk on the Asylum Lawn.

Shin Kyŏngnim.   Road, The.

Simic.   Evening Walk.

Sleigh.   Field, The: "Once I left the room."

Spahr, J.   Write like one walks.
Strand.   Keeping Things Whole.
Szirtes.   My father carries me across a field.
Taneda Santoka.   Autumn wind.
Thomas, E.   Sun Used to Shine, The.
Thomson, J.   Part 2: "Because he seemed to walk with an intent."
Tranströmer.   Out in the Open.
Turk, R.   Walkin' My Baby Back Home.
Unknown.   Behind the Mountain.
   Millets in full rows.
   One of the Awl Songs.
Verlaine.   Beams.
Wakoski.   Hummingbird Light.
Wang Wei.   Hill of the Hatchet-Leaved Bamboos.
   Villa at the Foot of Mount Chungnan.
Ward, Geoff.   Distance Learning.
Warren, R.   Night Walking.
Warsh.   Inside Long Treks.
Wheatley, D.   Autumn, the Nightwalk, the City, the River.
Whitman, W.   Dalliance of the Eagles, The.
   Leaf for Hand in Hand, A.
Whittier.   Forgiveness.
Whur.   Unfortunate Gentleman, The.
Williams, W.   Poem: "As the cat."
Wordsworth, W.   I Wandered Lonely as a Cloud.
   Stepping Westward.
Wright, D.   Those Walks We Took.
Wylie.   Velvet Shoes.

Wall Street, New York City
Hernández Cruz.   Side 26.
Rukeyser, M.   Paper Anniversary.

Wallace, Sir William
Burns, R.   Scots Wha Hae.

Walls
Ali, A.   Rooms Are Never Finished.
Amichai, Y.   Near the Wall of a House.
Arghezi.   Flowers of Mildew.
Bremer, C.   Crack, The.
   Grieta, La.
Buson.   My village / Dragonflies.
Bynner.   Wall, The.
Clementelli.   Circle and Obsession of Walls.
Coleridge, M.   Gone.
   Impromptu.
Colonna, V.   I see in my mind, surrounding God.
Deguy.   Wall, The.
Eigner.   Wholes.
Frost, R.   Mending Wall.
Goetsch, D.   Walls, The.
Herbert, Z.   Wall, The.
Herlin.   Warmth of the wind-break wall, The.
Hernton, C.   Wall, The.
Ho Ching-ming.   Ballad of the Government Granary Clerk.
Jabeen, M.   Live Walls.
Johnston, D.   Pyramus & Thisbe.
Kaufman, S.   Emperor of China, The.
Kendrick, D.   We are the Writing on the Wall.
Kinzie.   Ringing Words.
Lumbreras, E.   Cielo, El / puede venirse abajo esta mañana.
   Sky, The / could collapse this morning.
Morabito, F.   I do not wish, in spite of all.
   No quiero, pese a todo.
Motion, A.   Wall, A.
Muir, E.   Then.
Muldoon, P.   Loaf, The.
Paek Sŏk.   On the White Wall.
Pau-Llosa.   Paredón.
Pere, V.   At the Wall.
Plumpp.   Another Mule.
Quevedo y Villegas.   I Gaze Upon My Country's Walls.
Robinson, A.   Personality.
Simic.   Wall, A.
Sornberger.   Wallpapering to Patsy Cline.
Spellman, A.   Twist, The.
Tennyson, A.   Flower in the Crannied Wall.
Splendour [*or*Splendor] Falls, The.
Tsaloumas.   Old Friend.
Unknown.   Meng Jiangnü at the Long Wall.
   Ruin, The.

Wang Shih-chieng.   Composed at the West Wall of Tsou-p'ing Three Days After the Festival of Pure Brightness.
Wilbur, R.   Caserta Garden.
Williams, W.   On Gay Wallpaper.
Wilson, S.   Picture on the Purple Wall, The.
See also **Fences**

Walnut Trees and Walnuts
Guillén, J.   Nature Alive.
Jastrzebska.   Cracking Walnuts.
Oliver, D.   Walnut and Lily.
Oliver, M.   Black Walnut Tree, The.

Walruses
Carroll, L.   Walrus and the Carpenter, The.
Corn.   Walrus Tusk from Alaska, A.
Herford.   Smile of the Walrus, The.
Nowlan.   In Praise of the Great Bull Walrus.

Walt Disney
Brouwer, J.   Conjurer's Honor.
McNiece, R.   Letter Left On the Porch of the Kerouac House.
Murray, C.   Mickey Mouse.
Ochester.   Pocahontas.
Reed, Tennessee.   Disney's Cinderella.
Wynne, R.   Revisionist History: Magic Kingdom.

Walton, Izaak
Cotton, C.   To My Dear and Most Worthy Friend, Mr. Isaac Walton.

Waltzes and Waltzing
Aragon.   Waltz of the Twenty-Year-Olds, The.
Haug.   Tennessee Waltz, The.
Leland, C.   Hans Breitmann's Party [*or* Barty].
Levy, A.   First Extra, The.
Roethke.   My Papa's Waltz.
Stroud, J.   Homage: Doo-Wop.
Wilde, O.   Harlot's House, The.
Wright, S.   Out of the Wailing.

Wanderlust
Auden.   Wanderer, The.
Baraka, I.   Legacy.
Basho.   I'm a wanderer.
Bejerano, M.   From morning slumber a stir a shift a spinning motion of tossing.
Brown, S.   Long Gone.
Burke, J.   My Heart Is a Hobo.
Carman, B.   Vagabond Song, A.
Chen Zi'ang.   Entering Quiao Gorge and Anju Creek.
   Meditation on the Past at White Emperor City.
Davidkov, Ivan.   Some Day.
Goethe.   Mignon.
Hovey.   Sea Gypsy, The.
Kipling, R.   Sestina of the Tramp-Royal.
Larkin, P.   Poetry of Departures.
Liu Yu Hsi.   Parrot Island.
Masefield.   Sea Fever.
   Wanderer's Song, A.
McCallum, S.   What the Oracle Said.
North, C.   Words from Robert W. Service.
Riddell, E.   Wakeful in the Township.
Roethke.   My Papa's Waltz.
Smith, S.   Lightly Bound.
   Wanderer, The.
Sŏ Chŏngju.   Wanderer's Bouquet.
Stickney, T.   Age in Youth.
Tennyson, A.   Ulysses.
Unknown.   Life-Parting.
   Man in the World Lodging.
   Walk on again walk on.
Wright, C.   Wander Luís.
Yeats.   Madness of King Goll, The.

Wanting
Averill.   Shoplifter Hands.
Hirshfield, J.   Cedary Fragrance, A.
Leifso, B.   What Do You Want?
Luterman, A.   On Not Flying to Hawaii.
Ruefle.   Intended, The.
Van Winckel, N.   As is His Wont.
Whitman, W.   Untold Want, The.

War
Aafjes.   Last Letter, The.
Abdul Karim.   Nightmare 3.
Abu-l-Hasan Ibn Al-Qabturnuh.   In Battle.
Abulafia, A.   Battle, The.

Acam-Oturu.   Agony . . . A Resurrection, An.
Acholonu.   Harvest of War.
Adonis [*or* Adunis].   Diary of Beirut Under Siege, 1982, The.
Akhmatova, A.   When in the throes of suicide.
al-Sa'igh, Y.   Iraqi Evening, An.
Alberti.   Warlike Angels, The.
Alcaeus [*or* Alkaios].   Having done most shameful, unjust things.
   Wretched me / I live a rustic live.
Aldrich, T.   Memory.
Alegría.   Toward the Jurassic Age.
Alexandru.   End of the War, The.
Allen, F.   Surveyor's Story, The.
Allen, R.   See! How the Nations Rage Together.
Alon, E.   If There Is a God.
Amichai, Y.   Anniversaries of War.
   Half of the people in the world.
   I have nothing to say about the war.
   My father fought their war four years or so.
   Thoughts came to him like long lines of freight, The.
   Two of Us Together, Each of Us Alone, The.
   What is it? An airplane at dawn. No.
Amis, K.   Last War, The.
Anderson, M.   Spitting in the Leaves.
Aneirin.   Lord of Gododdin will be praised in song, A.
   When a crowd of cares.
   Youth.
Angira.   Newscast.
Antar [*or* Antara].   Black Night, The.
Anton, S.   Prism, A: Wet With Wars.
   Wars 1.
Anyte [*or* Anytes].   Stand there, manslaying spear; no longer drip.
Apollinaire.   Cavalier's Farewell, The.
   Fete.
Appleman, P.   Peace with Honor.
Aragon.   Hilversum, Kalundborg, Brno, the loud world over.
Archilochus.   Heart, my heart churning with fathomless cares.
   I don't give a damn if some Thracian ape strut.
   You see that high crag.
Aristophanes.   How the Women Will Stop War.
Arnold, M.   Dover Beach.
Ashbery, J.   Rivers and Mountains.
Asim, J.   1st Lt. John R. Fox: Rain of Fire.
Atwood.   Before the War.
Auden.   Here war is harmless like a monument.
   Taller To-day.
Avidan, D.   Six Local Poems.
Awoonor.   At the Gates.
   Song of War.
   Songs of Sorrow.
Aytoun, W.   Sonnet to Britain.
Azzawi, F.   Every Morning The War Gets Up From Sleep.
Bachmann.   Every Day.
   Every Day.
   Every Day.
Balaban.   News Update.
   Thoughts Before Dawn.
   Words for My Daughter.
Baraka, R.   After-Word.
Barker, G.   O Hero Akimbo on the Mountains of To-morrow.
   Sonnet to My Mother.
Barks.   Becoming Milton.
Barlow, J.   Advice to a Raven in Russia [December, 1812].
Basheva.   It Was War.
Baton, M.   Unspeakable Wounds of War, The.
Bayliss.   Reported Missing.
Beers, E.   All Quiet Along the Potomac.
Bei Dao.   Postwar.
Bejerano, M.   States of War.
Benét, S.   1935.
Berberova.   To Shakespeare.
Berlin.   This Is the Army, Mr. Jones.
Berry, W.   Against the War in Vietnam.
Berryman.   Moon and the Night and the Men, The.
Bertrans de Born.   In Praise of War.
Bible, *O.T.*   David's Lament.

Psalm 84.
Bickerstaffe.   What a charming thing's a battle!
Binyon.   Unreturning Spring, The.
Bishop, J.   In the Dordogne.
Black, S.   To a War Correspondent.
Blok.   Kite, The.
  On the Plain of Kulikovo.
Blunden.   Behind the Line.
  Country God, A.
  1916 Seen from 1921.
  Report on Experience.
Bly, R.   Counting Small-Boned Bodies.
  Driving through Minnesota during the Hanoi
    Bombings.
  To President Bush at the Start of the Gulf War.
Boker.   Brave comrade, answer! When you
    joined the war.
Bond, E.   First World War Poets.
Bowers, E.   Stoic, The: For Laura Von Courten.
Braun, V.   Desert Storm.
Brecht, B.   Friends, The.
  From a German War Primer.
  General, your tank is a powerful machine.
  God of War, The.
  This Summer's Sky.
  To My Little Radio.
  War Has Been Given a Bad Name.
Breton, A.   More than Suspect.
  War.
Brodsky, J.   Elegy: "About a year has passed.
  I've returned to the place of battle."
Brooke, R.   Soldier, The: "If I should die, think
    only this of me."
Brooks, G.   First Fight. Then Fiddle.
  White Troops Had Their Orders but the Negroes
    Looked Like Men.
Brownstein.   War.
Brutus.   There Was a Time When the Only
  Worth.
Bryant, W.   Conjunction of Jupiter and Venus,
  The.
Buchanan, G.   War-and-Peace.
Burns, R.   Scots Wha Hae.
  Silver Tassie, The.
Butler, S.   Arms and the Man.
Byron, G.   By the Rivers of Babylon We Sat
    Down and Wept.
  Oh, thou eternal Homer! I have now.
  Song of Saul before His Last Battle.
Caleshu, A.   Collaboration: Storming the
  Beaches.
Campbell, T.   Hohenlinden.
  Wizard.
Carbó, N.   When the Grain Is Golden and the
    Wind Is Chilly, Then It Is the Time to Harvest.
Cardenal.   For Those Dead, Our Dead.
  Lights.
  Psalm 5: "Give ear to my words, O Lord."
Carruth, H.   On Being Asked to Write a Poem
    Against the War in Vietnam.
  Paragraph 36.
Carson, A.   TV is presocial, like Men.
Carson, C.   Cocktails.
  Hamlet.
  Mouth, The.
Carver, D.   Poet, The.
Causley.   Armistice Day.
  Song of the Dying Gunner A.A.1.
Cavendish, M.   Some with sharp swords, to tell
  O most accursed!
Cervantes.   Poem for the Young White Man
    Who Asked Me How I, An Intelligent, Well-
    Read Person Could Believe in the War
    Between Races.
Chang Yang-hao.   Tune: "Sheep on the
    Mountain Slope".
Chao Meng-fu.   To a Pyrotechnist.
Chapman, G.   Of her removed and soul-infused
  regard.
Ch'i-chi.   Stopping at Night at Hsiang-yin.
Chin Ho.   Ballad of the Maiden of Lan-ling.
Chipasula.   Tramp.
Chippewa Oral Tradition.   Sioux Woman
  Defends Her Children, The.
  Sioux Women Gather Up Their Wounded, The.
  Song of the Captive Sioux Woman.

Cho Chihun.   At Toriwpn.
Cisneros, A.   To a Dead Lady.
Clanchy, K.   War Poetry.
Clark Bekedermo.   Casualties, The.
  Epilogue to Casualties.
Clark, T.   Year from Monday, A.
Clarke, G.   Field-Mouse, The.
Clarke, T.   For Babies Unborn.
Cleveland, J.   How? 'Providence', and yet a
  Scottish crew?
  Rebel Scot, The.
Clifton, L.   Death of Crazy Horse, The.
Coleridge, S.   Fire, Famine, and Slaughter.
  Thankless too for peace.
Comfort, A.   Letter to an American Visitor.
Cortez, J.   Rape.
Crane, S.   Battle Hymn, The.
  Once there came a man.
  War Is Kind.
Crowe, W.   In evil hour, and with unhallow'd
  voice.
Csoori.   We Were Good, Good and Obedient.
Cummings, E. E.   My sweet old etcetera.
  Next to of course god america i.
Cunningham, A.   Hame, Hame, Hame.
Curnow.   Pacific 1945-1995.
Currey.   Burial Flags.
  Unseen Fire.
D'Aguiar, F.   Sound Bite.
Dalton, R.   Soldier's Rest.
Darío, R.   Triumphal March.
Davidson, J.   Battle.
Dawe, G.   Question of Covenants, A.
Day, J.   North Sea.
Day Lewis.   Almost Human.
  Where Are the War Poets?
De la Mare.   Motley.
Deane, S.   History Lessons.
Dizhur.   Silence.
Dorfman, A.   I Just Missed the Bus and I'll Be
  Late for Work.
Douglas, K.   Aristocrats.
  Enfidaville.
  Gallantry.
  How to Kill.
  Offensive, The.
  Vergissmeinnicht.
Dove, R.   Alfonzo Prepares to Go Over the Top.
Doyle, B.   War Is Over, The.
Doyle, S.   Some Girls.
Duffy, C.   War Photographer.
Dugan, A.   On an East Wind from the Wars.
Dunbar-Nelson.   I Sit and Sew.
Duncan, R.   Fire, The.
  Up Rising.
Duo Duo.   When the People Stand Up out of the
  Hard Cheese.
Eberhart, R.   Fury of Aerial Bombardment, The.
  There are many intricate pieces of
    workmanship.
Elliot, J.   Flowers of the Forest, The.
Elliott, E.   War.
Empson.   Just a Smack at Auden.
Engman.   Mushroom Clouds.
Enquist, A.   December Offensive.
Enzensberger, H.   Explaining the Declaration.
  War, Like.
Evans, G.   Eye Blade.
  Revelation in the Mother Lode.
Fenton, J.   Cambodia.
  Dead Soldiers.
  His wife nods, and a secret smile.
  In a Notebook.
  Staffordshire Murderer, A.
  Wind: "This is the wind, the wind in a field of
    corn."
Fiacc.   Enemy Encounter.
  Intimate Letter 1973.
  Soldiers.
Figueroa, J.   Homemade Smiles.
  Taino.
Fitzgerald, E.   War begets Poverty.
Flecker, J.   War Song of the Saracens.
Flint, R.   Seasonal, 1991.
Foley, M.   Ah no, ah no, they weren't all gross
  and slow.

Follain.   First Grade.
Fraser, G.   Lament: "In a dismal air; a light of
  breaking summer."
Freneau.   Two hulks on Hudson's stormy bosom
  lie.
Fuller, R.   Autumn 1942.
  In Africa.
García Lorca.   Rundown Church (Ballad of the
  First World War).
Garlick, R.   Heiress, The.
Gascoigne.   I set aside to tell the restless toil.
Gascoyne.   De Profundis.
  Snow in Europe.
  Uncertain Battle, The.
George, P.   Battle Won Is Lost.
Gibson, W.   In the Ambulance.
Gifford, H.   For Soldiers.
Gil de Biedma, J.   In Mournful Praise and
  Memory of the French Song.
Glaser, I.   Last Good War—and Afterward, The.
Gloria.   Milkfish.
Góngora y Argote.   Capture of Larache, The.
  On the Armada That Battled Against England.
Graham, M.   After the War; When Coltrane
  Only Wanted to Play Dance Tunes.
Graham, W.   What's the News?
Graves, R.   All Except Hannibal.
  Corporal Stare.
  Escape.
  It's a Queer Time.
  Recalling War.
  Spoils.
Greene, Richard.   Utopia.
Grenfell, J.   Into Battle.
Grennan.   Soul Music: The Derry Air.
Greville, F.   What is the cause, why states, that
  war and win.
Grimke, C.   Gathering of the Grand Army, The.
Grin, B.   My Shtetl on the Dnestr.
Groarke, V.   Imperial Measure.
Gryphius.   My Country Weeps.
Guest, B.   Otranto.
Guevara, E.   Song to Fidel.
Guiney.   Atoning Yesterday, The.
Gunn, T.   Last Man, The.
Gurney, I.   First Time In.
  Mangel-Bury, The.
  Silent One, The.
  Strange Hells.
Gwynn, R.   Body Bags.
Hahn, O.   Vision of Hiroshima.
Hall, D.   Sister on the Tracks, A.
HaNagid.   First War.
Hardy, T.   Channel Firing.
  In Time of "The Breaking of Nations".
  Man He Killed, The.
  Night of Trafalgar, The.
  Often When Warring.
  Something stands here to peril our advance.
Harjo, J.   No.
Harry, J.   Shot of War, A.
Haviaras, Stratis.   Still Life.
Hawthorne, N.   I Left My Low amd Humble
  Home.
Hay, G.   Bizerta.
Hayden, R.   Monet's "Waterlilies".
Heaney, S.   His Dawn Vision.
Hecht, A.   Dover Bitch, The.
  Still Life.
Hedd Wyn.   War.
Hefer, H.   Other Days, The.
Hejinian.   Moment yellow, just as four years
  later, when my father returned home from the
  war, A.
Heller, R.   Minister has all his notes in place,
  The.
Henderson, H.   Opening of an Offensive.
Heóghusa.   On Maguire's Winter Campaign.
  Winter Campaign, A.
Herbert, J.   Dossers at the Imperial War
  Museum.
Herbert, Z.   Abandoned, The.
  Rain, The.
  Report from the Besieged City.
  To Marcus Aurelius.
Hernández, M.   War.

Hinsey, E.   Approach of War, The.
Hogan, L.   Skin.
Holloway, G.   Ford Castle: The Borders.
Holmes, O.   Ploughman, The.
Holub.   Corporal Who Killed Archimedes, The.
Five Minutes after the Air Raid.
History Lesson, A.
Lesson, THe.
Housman.   Deserter, The.
Howe, J.   Battle Hymn [or Battle-Hymn] of the Republic, The.
Hsiao Kang.   Pheasant on His Morning Flight, A.
Hughes, T.   Out.
Hugo, R.   On Hearing a New Escalation.
Where We Crashed.
Hugo, V.   Night of the Fourth: A Recollection, The.
Hunt, G.   Dogs of war are loose and the rugged russian bear, The.
Hwang Jiwoo.   527.
Ibáñez, S.   Island in the Earth.
Ibn Shuhayd, A.   There is no one in the abandoned encampment to inform us of the beloved ones, so from whom will we seek information about their condition?
Ingalls, J.   Gun Emplacement: Sundown.
Itaikkunrurkilar.   His Legs Strong and Lithe.
Italicus.   Death comes in strange forms and contrasting images.
Furiously along the banks stormed Hannibal.
Give me Maeonian Homer's resonant tongue.
Horses which Titan when discharged for the night, The.
Ivanov, Binyo.   Bulletin.
One Can Rest.
Jackowska.   Proud Shore For Legends, A.
Jarmain.   These Poems.
Jarnot, L.   United States of America, The.
Jarrell, R.   Eighth Air Force.
Pilot from the Carrier, A.
Jeffers, R.   Bloody Sire, The.
Eye, The.
Jin.   Judgement.
Johnson, B.   Artifice of War, The.
Johnson, D.   Heavens, The.
Johnson, Harold L.   At the Jackson Pollock Retrospective in L.A.
Johnson, L.   Five Nights of Bleeding.
Jones, D.   And to Private Ball it came as if a rigid beam of great weight.
This Dai adjusts his slipping shoulder-straps.
Jones, H.   Weather.
Jones, J.   Glyndwr's War Song.
Jones, Nesta Wyn.   Shadows.
Jonson, B.   Wake, friend, from forth thy lethargy; the drum.
Jordan, J.   Mid-Year Report: For Haruko.
Kandel.   First They Slaughtered the Angels.
Kaufman, S.   Emperor of China, The.
Kearney, L.   Man with His Kids on a Table, The.
Kelly, B.   To the Lost Child.
Kennedy, B.   Bad Luck to This Marching.
Kennedy, X.   Joshua.
Kenney.   Battle of Valcour Island, The.
Kersch.   Soldier, A: His Prayer.
Keyes, S.   Europe's Prisoners.
Moon is a poor woman, The.
War Poet.
Kharms.   Death of the Wild Warrior.
Khlebnikov, V.   Hey...y! Uh...hm!, covered with sweat.
Suppose I Make a Timepiece of Humanity.
Khodasevich.   Monkey.
Killigrew, A.   Alexandreis.
Kipling, R.   Boots.
Common Form.
Fuzzy-Wuzzy.
Gunga Din.
Hymn before Action.
Storm Cone, The.
Kirstein.   P.O.E.
Kizer, C.   On a Line from Valéry.
Klein, M.   Letters from the Front.
Knott.   Two Vietnam Poems: (1966).

Koch, K.   To World War Two.
Krige.   Taking of the Koppie, The.
Krysl.   Warscape, with Lovers.
Kunitz, S.   Last Picnic, The.
Reflection by a Mailbox.
Kunze, R.   Hymn To a Woman Under Interrogation.
Kushner, A.   Picture, A.
Kyger.   Deeply Immoral Arrogant and Ignorant.
Landor, W.   To Arthur de Noé Walker.
Lao Tzu.   Weapons are the tools of violence.
Larkin, P.   Homage to a Government.
MCMXIV.
Lasker-Schüler.   My Blue Piano.
Lawrence, D. H.   Bombardment.
Song of a Man Who Has Come Through.
Lee, L.   Moment of War, A.
Leeflang.   1945.
Lenski, H.   Moon's brightness turns a freezing blue, The.
Near the Mill.
Levertov.   Advent 1966.
Christmas 1944.
In California During the Gulf War.
In Thai Binh (Peace) Province.
Life at War.
Levine, P.   And the Trains Go On.
Baby Villon.
Death of Saul, The.
Lewis, A.   All Day It Has Rained.
Autumn, 1939.
Christmas Holiday.
Easter at Christmas.
Goodbye.
Peasants, The.
Raiders' Dawn.
Lewis, Emyr.   Taliesin.
Li Po.   Barbarian pass is filled with windblown sand, The.
Fighting on the South Frontier.
Fighting South of the Wall.
Ku Feng (After the Style of Ancient Poems).
Lament of the Frontier Guard.
Old Style Poem.
Song of War, A.
War South of the Great Wall.
Li Shang-yin.   Hearing a Startled Bird During Stayover at Chin-Ch'ang Pavilion.
Liban, A.   At a Time Like This.
Lima, J.   Stranger, Stranger.
Lindsay, V.   Unpardonable Sin, The.
Lisboa.   Elegy: "At first the dead."
Livingstone, D.   Recondite war on women, The.
Longfellow, H.   Arsenal at Springfield, The.
Santa Filomena.
Longley, M.   All of These People.
Death of a Horse.
Ghetto.
Wounds.
Lope de Vega.   Judith.
López Mills, T.   Ending by Pound, An.
Final de Pound, Un.
Mi voz fiel como la sombra.
My Voice Faithful as a Shadow.
López Velarde.   Baleful Return.
Lovelace, R.   To Lucasta, [on] Going to the War[re]s.
Lowell, A.   In Time of War.
Patterns.
September, 1918.
Lux.   Plague Victims Catapulted Over Walls Into Besieged City.
Macaulay, T.   Battle of Naseby, The.
Macgoye.   Mathenge.
Machado Ruiz.   On the Banks of the Duero.
Mackey, N.   Phantom Light of All Our Day, The.
MacLeish.   Invocation to the Social Muse.
Too-Late Born, The.
MacNeice.   Carrickfergus.
Mahon.   Afterlives.
Malé.   Women Don't Die on the Front Lines.
Malouf.   Year of the Foxes, The.
Mandelstam [or Mandelshtam].   I Drink to the Asters of War.
Manifold.   Fife Tune.

Manning, F.   Leaves.
Mansour, J.   Regulation equipment.
Marlowe.   But now my boys, leave off, and list to me.
This said, the restles generall through the darke.
Martinez, D.   Discreet Prayer, A.
Marvell.   Horatian Ode upon Cromwell's Return from Ireland, An.
Mayakovsky [or Maiakovskii].   Last Page of the Civil War.
McCarthy, T.   Claud Cockburn.
Wisdom of AE, The.
McClure, M.   Madame Secretary.
Song: "Platinum fur and brass revolver shine."
McDaniel, W.   Realist of 1939–40, A.
McDonald, W.   Last Still Days in a Bunker, The.
Songs We Fought For, The.
McGinley.   How to Start a War.
Women of Jericho, The.
McGough, R.   Mother the Wardrobe Is Full of Infantrymen.
McGrath, T.   Fresco: Departure for an Imperialist War.
Nocturne Militaire.
Ordonnance.
Meddemmen, J. G.   L.R.D.G.
Melville, H.   Conflict of Convictions, The.
Utilitarian View of the Monitor's Fight, A.
Mendes, M.   Graffito in Meknès.
Mercer, J.   Jubilation T. Cornpone.
Meredith, W.   Navy Field.
Meynell, A.   Summer in England, 1914.
Michaelis.   I Was About Three Years of Age.
Miidhu.   War Dance.
Mikhail, D.   Jewel, The.
Santa Claus.
War Works Hard, The.
Millay, E.   Apostrophe to Man.
Milosz, C.   Preparation.
Milton.   He sat; and in the assembly next upstood.
On the Late Massacre [or Massacher] in Piedmont [or Piemont].
They err who think it glorious to subdue.
Mitchison.   Hartmanswillerkopf.
Montale.   Fan, The.
Far away, still I was with you.
Moore, M.   In Distrust of Merits.
To Military Progress.
Moore, R.   Dirge for the Living.
Morshen.   Storm, A.
Motsapi, S.   Sol/o.
Muhammad ibn Ghalib al-Rusafi.   Were you to go to the fire of the Guidance on the side of Mount Sinai, you could take all the knowledge and light you wish.
Muir, E.   Horses, The.
Scotland 1941.
Muldoon, P.   Brock.
Meeting the British.
Mure.   O Heavens! O Earth! heer I must pause a space.
Murray, L.   Drugs of War, The.
Immortal, An.
Muso Soseki.   For Myo's Departure for Anzen-ji.
Lamenting the Civil War.
Na Ceapaich, S.   Alasdair of Glengarry.
Naimy, M.   My Brother.
Nasir, A.   Trilogy of the Man in Black.
Nemerov.   Fable of the War, A.
Memory of the War, A.
Redeployment.
Ultima Ratio Reagan.
Neruda.   I Explain a Few Things.
I'm Explaining a Few Things.
Newbolt.   Vitaï Lampada.
Nguyen Binh Khiem.   Worried.
Niedecker.   War.
Nortje.   Autopsy.
Nasser is dead.
Nossis.   Shields Bruttians threw from their doomed shoulders.
Notley.   Back.
How the Dead Women May Operate from Negative Space.

Nutter, G. Air War, The.
Nye, N. Lunch in Nablus City Park.
O'Grady, D. Love War, The.
Okigbo. Elegy for Alto.
O'Loughlin. Bunkers, The.
Oppen. Survival: Infantry.
Ormsby, F. Apples, Normandy, 1944.
  Soldier Bathing.
  War Photographers, The.
Osgood, K. Driving Home the Cows.
Owen, W. A Terre.
  Apologia Pro Poemate Meo.
  Arms and the Boy.
  At a Calvary near the Ancre.
  Conscious.
  Disabled.
  Dulce et Decorum Est.
  Exposure.
  Futility.
  Insensibility.
  Mental Cases.
  Parable of the Old Men and the Young, The.
  S.I.W.
  Send-Off, The.
  Sentry, The.
  Show, The.
  Strange Meeting.
  We'd found an old Boche dug-out, and he knew.
Padilla. Song of the Juggler.
Pak Illo. Song of Peace.
Paley, G. People in My Family.
Palmer, M. I Do Not.
Pao Chao. Do you not see the young men off to war.
Paquet. It Is Monsoon at Last.
Paulin. Peacetime.
Pavlich. Black Flower.
Pawlak. All the News—September 23, 2001.
Peacock, T. War Song of Dinas Vawr, The.
Peake. Babe was born in the reign of George, A.
Pedro, J. Homecoming.
Penna. Pitiless war of love I fought, A.
Péret. Nungesser und Coli Sind Verreckt.
Pfeiffer, E. Fight at Rorke's Drift, The.
Picasso. Bottle of Suze, A.
Pinsky. Serpent Knowledge.
Pinter, H. American Football (A Reflection upon the Gulf War).
Platke, S. Gut Catcher.
Plotkin, C. Greetings from My Shtetl (A Letter from Poland).
Po Chü-i. Song of Lasting Regret, The.
Porzecanski. Every Month.
Potocki, W. Winter, Before the War.
Pound, E. Sestina: Altaforte.
Prévert. Barbara.
  Discourse on Peace, The.
  Familial.
Prince, F.T. Soldiers Bathing.
Radnóti. Postcard (Found on His body after He Was Killed by the Nazis).
Ralin, Radoi. Man Who Didn't Sign, The.
Read, H. My Company.
  To a Conscript of 1940.
Reed, H. Judging Distances.
  Naming of Parts.
  Unarmed Combat.
Revard. Parading with the Veterans of Foreign Wars.
Reverdy. Behind Eyelids.
Rexroth, K. Requiem for the Spanish Dead.
Reznikoff. I walked through the lonely marsh.
  Romance.
Rich, A. Eye, The.
  Memory lifts her smoky mirror: 1943.
  One night on Monterey Bay the death-freeze of the century.
  School Among the Ruins, The.
Rickword. Soldier Addresses his Body, The.
  Winter Warfare.
Ridler. At Parting.
Rimbaud, A. Rooks, The.
Robinson, E. Field of Glory, The.
Rocha. Guerilla Fighter.
Rodgers, W. Sing, Brothers, Sing!

Rodney. Bardo of War and Peace.
Rohrer, M. We Never Should Have Stopped at Pussy Island.
Rolls. Dog Fight.
Ros. Little Belgian Orphan, A.
Rosenberg, I. Break of Day in the Trenches.
  Louse Hunting.
Ross, A. En Route.
Rouse, A. Memo to Auden.
Rukeyser, M. Käthe Kollwitz.
  Poem: "I lived in the first century of world wars."
  Who in One Lifetime.
Rumsey, Tessa. Man-Torpedo-Boat.
Safie, D. Meditation by the Xerox Machine.
Sahagún, C. River: "They named this stretch of river Postwar."
"Saki.". Carol: "While shepherds watched their flocks by night."
Sandburg, C. Among the Red Guns.
  Bas-Relief.
  Buttons.
  Little girl saw her first troop parade and asked, "What are those?", The.
  Murmurings in a Field Hospital.
Sappho. Some say an army of horsemen, others.
  Some there are who say that the fairest thing seen.
Sarig, Y. Return: "Not thirsting for battle."
Sassoon, S. Aftermath.
  Attack.
  Does It Matter?
  Everyone Sang.
  General, The.
  Glory of Women.
  Repression of War Experience.
  "They".
Satyamurti. Striking Distance.
Scalapino. Pal Mal Comic, Or.
Scannell. Great War, The.
Schippers. No, No, Nanette.
Scott, S. Lochinvar.
Scott of Amwell. Ode: "I hate that drum's discordant sound."
Scurfield, G. Bitter Mangoes, The.
Sedulius Scottus. Battle is joined on the open plain.
Seeger, A. I Have a Rendezvous with Death.
Seeger, P. Where Have All the Flowers Gone?
Seferis. Euripides the Athenian.
Seifert. Candlestick, The.
Sen, R. Hey! Who is She, dark as clouds.
Seshadri. Sketch from the Campaign in the North, A.
Seto, T. Jihad.
Shabtai, Aharon. War.
Shakespeare, W. Henry V at the Siege of Harfleur.
  How yet resolves the Governor of the town?
  My liege, I did deny no prisoners.
  They tax our policy and call it cowardice.
Shaku Chōkū. Tanka: "Imagining / the grassy ground not shown."
  Vultures—in the Midst of War.
Shapiro, K. Conscientious Objector, The.
  Lord, I Have Seen Too Much.
  Scyros.
  Troop Train.
Sherwin, J. To Whom It May Concern.
Shinkichi Takahashi. Beach.
Shumyatsher, E. Toye-Voye.
Shuster, D. Mellow on Morphine.
Simic. Empire of Dreams.
Simmons, J. From the Irish.
Simonides. Because of these men's courage, no smoke rose.
Simpson, L. Battle, The.
  Early in the Morning.
  Memories of a Lost War.
  On the Ledge.
Sitwell, E. Lullaby: "Though the world has slipped and gone."
Sitwell, O. Next War, The.
Skirving. Johnnie Cope.
Smith, S. War in Fife, The.
Snodgrass. After Experience Taught Me.

Sorley. Hundred Thousand Million Mites, A.
  To Germany.
Soupault. You Who Sleep.
Soutar. Permanence of the Young Men, The.
Southerland. Two Fishing Villages.
Southey, R. Battle of Blenheim, The.
Southwell. New Heaven, New War[re].
Spender, S. Epilogue to a Human Drama.
  Two Armies.
Stafford, W. Men.
  Some Remarks When Richard Hugo Came.
  Wind from a Wing, A.
Stansbury, J. When Good Queen Elizabeth Governed the Realm.
Starbuck, G. Prognosis.
Stead, W. T. Now that war is in the air, e'en the parson in his lair.
Stevens, W. Dry Loaf.
Sylvester, J. War is the mistress of enormity.
Szymborska, W. End and Beginning.
  End and the Beginning, The.
  End and the Beginning, The.
  Reality Demands.
Taggard. Fructus.
Taha, A. Arabesque.
Tasso. Who first of Christian warriors now did chance.
Tate, A. Ode to Our Young Pro-consuls of the Air.
Taylor, A. Clearing Away.
Teitelboim, D. War Lullaby.
Tennyson, A. Splendour [orSplendor] Falls, The.
Thomas, C. Anyone can.
  Bullet, A / slams.
Thomas, D. Hand That Signed the Paper, The.
Thomas, E. As the Team's Head-Brass.
  Owl, The.
  This Is No Case of Petty Right or Wrong.
Thoreau. When with pale cheek and sunken eye I sang.
Tkachenko. Battle.
Trakl. Song of the Western Countries.
Troupe. Signals and Demarcations.
Ts'ao Ts'ao. Variant on the Songs of the East and West Gates.
Ts'en Shen. Song of the Running Horse River, A: Presented on Saying Farewell to the Army Going on Campaign to the West.
Tu Fu [or Du Fu]. Another Spring ("In all the country.").
  Ballad of the Army Carts.
  Ballad of the Army Wagons, The.
  Chaos of mountains upon mountains, A.
  Conscription, The.
  Facing the Snow ("New ghosts weep over lost battles.").
  Hearing of Imperial Forces Retaking Ho-Nan and Ho-Pei.
  Impromptu.
  Journey North, The.
  Lament for Ch'en T'ao.
  Moon Festival.
  Moonlit Night Thinking of My Brothers.
  Night Up in the Tower.
  Pressgang at Shihao Village, The.
  Pressgang, The.
  Restless Night in Camp, A.
  Second Letter to My Nephew Wulang.
  Song of the War-Carts.
  Song of the War-Chariots (Yueh-Fu).
  Spring Scene.
  Spring View.
  Spring View.
  Thatched Hut, The.
  Travelling Northward.
  Word from My Brothers.
Tueni, N. I think of the land and the wheat.
Ungaretti. Rivers, The.
Unknown. Age of War, The.
  Arjuna, his war flag a rampant monkey.
  Arjuna sat dejected.
  At Fifteen I Joined the Army.
  At Fifteen I Went to War.
  Ballad of Mulan, The.
  Battle of Brunanburh.

Between his hands.
Combat of Ferdia and Cúchulainn.
Courage shall grow keener, clearer the will.
Down by the Riverside.
Drill's the Thing.
Fighting, south of the ramparts.
Forever Martial.
Fort of Rathangan, The.
From the South: 2.
Gentlemen, for this day's work our chance has not been ill.
Graves the rain makes wet and sleek, The.
Great War Dance, The.
Ha-Kon-E-Crase, the Eagle Dance.
Hēr Æþoelstān cyning, eorla drihten.
He's to the War.
Hymn: "O God of Hosts, thine Ear incline."
Hymn to the Fallen.
I crossed the deep sea.
I wende to deeth, knight stith in stour.
Johnny, I Hardly Knew Ye.
Jun-zi yu-yi [Translations].
Last Battle and Death of Chingis Khan, The.
Mu-Lan.
Old Song.
Pick ferns, pick ferns.
Raid of the Reidswire, The.
Son, if you desert our war.
Song of the Lenape Warriors Going against the Enemy, The.
Spoils of Annwn, The.
There is smoke above the hawks in the hall of the king.
They Fought South of the Wall.
Translation of "Pax Bello Potior".
Wanderer, The.
War Dance.
War Lament: "Autumn flowers."
War Lament: "Every plant is burnt yellow."
War Songs.
War Songs.
War the Source of Riches.
Warsong of the Kwakiutl.
We mean to thrash these Prussian Pups.
What grass not yellowed?
Wulf and Eadwacer: A Woman's Lament.
Untermeyer, L.   End of the Comedy.
Uyematsu.   Same Month They Bombed Cambodia, The.
Various authors.   Because he loved men and sought their welfare.
Your four ancestors never enjoyed peace.
Veiga.   Wind of Liberty.
Velichansky, A.   In the evil time.
Viereck, P.   Kilroy.
Ripeness Is All.
Vilariño.   Maybe Then.
Vinkenoog.   ((((((Hollanditis))))))).
Violi.   House of Xerxes.
Voznesensky [*or* Voznesenskii].   I Am Goya.
War Ballad.
Wallace, E.   War.
Wallace, R.   Nightline: An Interview with the General.
Wang Ch'ang-ling.   Silent at Her Window.
Wang Wei.   Army Ballad.
Waring, B.   Refuge at the One Step Down.
Warner, S.   Become as little children.
Road 1940.
Warsh.   Year from Monday, A.
Watkyns.   Peace and War.
Watson, C.   Then the old fruit-and-vegetable economy dried up and blew away but self-defense gave us a way.
Weigl.   Burning Shit at An Khe.
Him, on the Bicycle.
Monkey.
Temptation.
Welish.   Macbeth in Battle.
Wen T'ien-hsiang.   Chin-ling Post Station.
West, A.   Night Patrol, The.
Whalen, P.   Regalia in Immediate Demand!
Whitman, W.   Beat! Beat! Drums!
Chants Democratic and Native Americans: 5.
Respondez!
Wicks, S.   Protected Species.

Wilbur, R.   Another Voice.
First Snow in Alsace.
Looking into History.
Mined Country.
Place Pigalle.
Williams, C. K.   Hearth, The.
Williams, W.   Illegitimate Things.
These.
Williamson, G.   Dark Days, The.
Wilner, E.   Conversation with a Japanese Student.
Winters, Y.   Summer Noon: 1941.
Wolfe, C.   Burial of Sir John Moore, The.
Woolson.   Yew.
Wordsworth, W.   No record tells of lance opposed to lance.
Wright, J.   Mad Fight Song for William S. Carpenter, 1966, A.
Wrigley, R.   What My Father Believed.
Yamada.   Night before Good-Bye, The.
Yeats.   Ancestral Houses.
Irish Airman Foresees His Death, An.
On Being Asked for a War Poem.
Road at My Door, The.
Yoshihara.   Air Raid.
Young, E.   One to destroy, is murder by the law.
Yourcenar, Marguerite.   Epitaph in Time of War.
Yusuf, S.   Hamra Night.
Zimunya.   Let It Be.

See also **Soldiers; War Casualties; War Dead**

War Casualties
Alcaeus [*or* Alkaios].   And excited the heart of Argive.
Anderson, D.   Nightly News, The.
Balaban.   For the Missing in Action.
Bierce.   Year's "Casualties", A.
Bly, R.   Driving through Minnesota during the Hanoi Bombings.
Byrd, Bobby.   Steak and Eggs.
Carson, C.   Bloody Hand.
Chirikure, C.   This Is Where We Laid Him to Rest.
Clifton, L.   Dear Jesse Helms.
Clough.   *Dulce* it is, and *decorum*, no doubt, for the country to fall, to.
Daniels, K.   War Photograph.
Ditzanny, R.   Brand Plucked from the Anti-tank Fire, A.
Complicated and Innovative Orthopedic Surgery.
Legging Behind.
My Hand is Extended for the Peace of the Galilee.
Piggy-back.
Doolittle, H.   R.A.F.
Dunn, D.   War Blinded.
Fenton, J.   Dead Soldiers.
Staffordshire Murderer, A.
Ferlinghetti, L.   Third World Calling.
Frost, R.   Not to Keep.
Garioch.   Wire, The.
Gogarty.   Conquest, The.
Graves, R.   Leveller, The.
Gurney, I.   Mangel-Bury, The.
Guthrie, W.   Blinding of Isaac Woodard, The.
Gutteridge.   Enemy Dead, The.
Henderson, H.   Ninth Elegy: Fort Capuzzo.
Hillyer.   Dead Man's Corner.
Hồ Xuân Hương.   General's Plaque, The.
Hood, T.   Faithless Nelly Gray.
Hughes, L.   Casualty.
Hugo, V.   Night of the Fourth: A Recollection, The.
Jarrell, R.   Field Hospital, A.
Jayyusi, S.   In the Casbah.
Jones, H.   Laments for the Afghan Women.
Keyes, S.   Europe's Prisoners.
Khazak, Y.   I saw you. / You were like scarred stones scattered on the green.
Kyong-Nim, S.   Yollim Kut Song.
Landor, W.   To Arthur de Noé Walker.
Logue, C.   Fate's sister, fortune, favours those.
See also that royal fights.
Longley, M.   Wounds.
Mackintosh, E.   Cha Till Maccruimein (Departure of the 4th Camerons).

Magrelli.   Each photographed face.
Matthews, H.   Women Are Not Gentlemen.
Muldoon, P.   Field Hospital, The.
Olebara, N.   Warrior's Lament, A.
Owen, W.   A Terre.
Conscious.
Disabled.
Dulce et Decorum Est.
Futility.
Mental Cases.
Sentry, The.
Plowman.   Dead Soldiers, The.
Plumly.   Blossom.
Rukeyser, M.   Leg in a Plaster Cast, A.
Sandburg, C.   Buttons.
Sassoon, S.   Does It Matter?
"They".
Searle, J.   Matthew the Bayman.
Service.   Only a Boche.
Simmons, J.   From the Irish.
Simpson, L.   Carentan O Carentan.
Sitwell, O.   Next War, The.
Sivan, A.   Concerning the Rehabilitation of the Disabled from the Wars of Israel.
Slutsky [*or* Slutskii].   Hospital, The.
Spera, G.   Balkan.
Taylor, E.   Welcome Eumenides.
Thomas, C.   Alone / with only.
Thomas, D.   Among Those Killed in the Dawn Raid Was a Man Aged a Hundred.
Tu Fu [*or* Du Fu].   Journey North.
Ungaretti.   Whole night, A.
Unknown.   Death Song.
Far Away.
Sure, a little bit of shrapnel fell from out the sky one day.
Upton, L.   Civilian Histories.
Various authors.   Seeing the bodies lying in heaps.
Verlaine.   Asleep in the Valley.
Vinokurov.   Eyes.
Waldinger, E.   Lidice.
Whitman, W.   Bearing the bandages, water and sponge.
March in the Ranks Hard-Prest, and the Road Unknown, A.
Vigil Strange I Kept on the Field One Night.
Wound-Dresser, The.
Williams, C. K.   From My Window.
Zach, N.   On the Desire to Be Precise.

See also **Soldiers; War Dead**

War Dead
Abse.   Cousin Sidney.
Adonis [*or* Adunis].   Diary of Beirut Under Siege, 1982, The.
Aiken, C.   Three Star Final.
Al-Qasim.   Sons of War.
Allison, D.   Funeral Oration, A.
Alon, E.   Always in Anguish.
Coffins.
In the Mount of Final Repose.
Leave-Taking ("Death in a war.").
Missing Out.
Amichai, Y.   From the Songs of the Land of Zion and Jerusalem.
Is all this sorrow? I don't know.
My father fought their war four years or so.
Seven Laments for the War-Dead.
Since Then.
We Have No Unknown Soldiers.
Apollinaire.   Stanzas Against Forgetting.
Arcos.   Dead, The.
Arundel, H.   Adam.
Asquith.   Volunteer, The.
Balaban.   After Our War.
Baxter, J.   Elegy for an Unknown Soldier.
Bell, M.   David Guest.
Reason for Refusal.
Betjeman.   In Memory of Basil, Marquess of Dufferin and Ava.
Bhatt, S.   Written After Hearing About the Soviet Invasion of Afghanistan.
Bierce.   To E. S. Salomon.
Bilgere, G.   At the Vietnam Memorial.
Binyon.   For the Fallen.
They went with songs to the battle, they were

young.
Bogan, L.   To My Brother: Killed: Hammont Wood: October, 1918.
Bronk.   Memorial: "If we do not lift quickly the dead bodies from the beaches."
Soldiers in Death.
Brooke, R.   Dead, The ("These hearts were woven of human joys and cares.").
Browning, E.   Forced Recruit, The.
Mother and Poet.
Browning, R.   Incident of the French Camp.
Carmi, T.   Memorial Day, 1969.
Military Funeral in the Heat of Day.
Causley.   At the British War Cemetery, Bayeux.
Cavendish, M.   Some with sharp swords, to tell O most accursed!
Chesterton.   English Graves, The.
Ch'u Yüan.   Nine Songs, The.
Ciardi, J.   Box Comes Home, A.
Elegy for a Cave Full of Bones.
Elegy Just in Case.
V-J Day.
Clifton, H.   Death of Thomas Merton.
Collins, W.   How Sleep the Brave.
Crane, S.   War Is Kind.
Crosland.   Slain.
Dawe, B.   Homecoming.
Day, J.   North Sea.
De Tabley.   Sonnet: "Record is nothing, and the hero great."
Dickey, J.   Hunting Civil War Relics at Nimblewill Creek.
Performance, The.
Dickinson, E.   It feels a shame to be Alive.
My Triumph lasted till the Drums.
Douglas, K.   Gallantry.
Vergissmeinnicht.
Dunbar, P.   Unsung Heroes, The.
Eberhart, R.   Ceremony by the Sea, A.
Emerson, R.   Concord Hymn.
Fairfax, J.   Forest of the Dead, The.
Feldman, I.   Se Aprovechan.
Finch, F.   Blue and the Gray, The.
Fitzgerald, R.   Amphibians.
Ford, F.   That Exploit of Yours.
Fried, E.   What Things Are Called.
García Lorca.   Rundown Church (Ballad of the First World War).
Gilboa, A.   And My Brother Was Silent.
Graves, R.   Devil's Advice to Story-Tellers, The.
Greenberg, U.   Memorial: "He who knew to serve as one of the oridnary soldiers."
Ones Living by Their Virtue Say, The.
Guri, H.   Behold, Our Bodies are Laid Out.
Death of the Man in the Field, The.
Ones Forgotten, The.
Gurney, I.   To His Love.
Gutteridge.   Enemy Dead, The.
Hardy, T.   Drummer Hodge.
I Looked Up from My Writing.
Man He Killed, The.
Wife in London, A.
Harnik, R.   Your Socks.
Harry, J.   Shot of War, A.
Harte, B.   Second Review of the Grand Army, A.
Heaney, S.   In Memoriam Francis Ledwidge.
Heard, J.   Decoration Day.
National Cemetery, Beaufort, South Carolina, The.
Hefer, H.   Parade of the Fallen.
Young Dead Soldiers, The.
Hemans.   Effigies, The.
Hemingway.   Champs d'Honneur.
Henderson, H.   First Elegy: End of a Campaign.
Hope, A.   Inscription for a War.
Housman.   Astronomy.
Epitaph: "Here dead lie we because we did not choose."
Epitaph on an Army of Mercenaries.
On the idle hill of summer.
Hughes, T.   Six Young Men.
Hugo, R.   Note from Capri to Richard Ryan on the Adriatic Floor.
Israeli, A.   Eulogy: "This should be a eulogy without words."

Jarrell, R.   Burning the Letters.
Dead Wingman, The.
Death of the Ball Turret Gunner, The.
Losses.
Protocols.
Second Air Force.
Jones, H.   Genuflection to Petty Officer First Class Leonette Masters.
Keyes, S.   Expected Guest, The.
Kipling, R.   Death-Bed, A.
Epitaphs of the War [1914–1918].
Gethsemane.
Hyaenas [or Hyenas], The.
Mesopotamia.
Knight, E.   Poem for Black Relocation Centers, A.
Koch, K.   Poem for My Twentieth Birthday.
Komunyakaa, Y.   Between Days.
Facing It.
Please.
We Never Know.
Lanier, S.   Dying Words of Stonewall Jackson, The.
Larkin, P.   MCMXIV.
Lasker-Schüler.   Georg Trakl.
Lewis, A.   Raiders' Dawn.
Unknown Soldier, The.
Longfellow, H.   Killed at the Ford.
Lowell, R.   For the Union Dead.
Holy Innocents, The.
MacDiarmid, H.   Another Epitaph on an Army of Mercenaries.
MacGill.   Matey.
Mackintosh, E.   In Memoriam, Private D. Sutherland.
MacLeish.   Memorial Rain.
Masaoka Shiki.   No one to busy.
Masters, E.   Unknown Soldiers.
Matthews, G.   For Edward Thomas Killed at Arras.
McCrae, J.   In Flanders Fields.
McGrath, T.   Ode for the American Dead in Korea.
Melville, H.   Inscription: "To them who crossed the flood."
Memorial on the Slain at Chickamauga.
Requiem[:] for Soldiers Lost in Ocean Transports, A: "When, after storms the woodlands rue."
Menashe.   Beachhead.
Mew.   Cenotaph, The.
Meynell, A.   Parentage.
Moody, W.   On a Soldier Fallen in the Philippines.
Moore, T.   Minstrel Boy, The.
Nabokov.   When he was small, when he would fall.
Nemerov.   War in the Air, The.
Nicholl, T.   His Friend's Last Battle.
Olds, S.   Leningrad Cemetery, Winter of 1941.
O'Loughlin.   Elegy for the Unknown Soldier.
Omer, H.   To the Memory of a Comrade.
Word from the Gray Soldiers.
Owen, W.   Anthem for Doomed Youth.
Dulce et Decorum Est.
Futility.
Greater Love.
Miners.
Send-Off, The.
Strange Meeting.
Page, G.   Smalltown Memorials.
Pagis, D.   Battle, The.
Evidence.
Parry, R.   On a Soldier Killed in the Great War.
Pasternak, B.   Courage.
Pauker, J.   Jethro Somes' Apostrophe to His Former Comrades.
Quasimodo.   To the Fifteen of Piazzale Loreto.
Randall, D.   Memorial Wreath.
Ransom, J.   Necrological.
Ravikovitch, D.   You Don't Kill Babies Twice.
Rickword.   Moonrise Over Battlefield.
Trench Poets.
Rosenberg, I.   Dead Man's Dump.
Rosenthal, G.   Only 20 Years Old.
Ryan, A.   Lines: "Gather the sacred dust."

St. John, D.   Six/Nine/Forty-Four.
Saitō Sanki.   Machine gun, A.
Machine gun soars, A.
Sandburg, C.   Grass.
Sassoon, S.   Base Details.
Death-Bed, The.
Hero, The.
On Passing the New Menin Gate.
To His Dead Body.
Shakespeare, W.   Sonnet 25: "Let those who are in favour with their stars."
Simmons, J.   From the Irish.
Simonides.   For the Spartan Dead at Thermopylai (480 B.C.).
Greek Dead at Thermopylae, The.
On the Spartan Dead at Thermopylae.
Simpson, L.   Arm in Arm.
Sivan, A.   To Wither Like Weeds in an Easterly Wind.
Slessor.   Beach Burial.
Slutsky [or Slutskii].   My Friends.
Smith, D.   On a Field Trip at Fredericksburg.
Snodgrass.   Flat One, A.
Someck, R.   Till When Will We Sleep after the Whore.
Sorley.   Sonnet, A: "When you see millions of the mouthless dead."
Spender, S.   Ultima Ratio Regum.
Street, D.   Love Letters of the Dead.
Stryk, L.   Pit, The.
Tabenkin, M.   Eulogy: "Bereavement revolves in our garden like a sword."
Tate, A.   Ode to the Confederate Dead.
Tate, J.   Lost Pilot, The.
Tennyson, A.   Charge of the Light Brigade, The.
Splendour [orSplendor] Falls, The.
Thackeray.   Due of the Dead, The.
Thomas, E.   As the Team's Head-Brass.
In Memoriam (Easter, 1915).
Private, A.
Thompson, J.   Burial of Latané, The.
Timrod.   Christmas.
Ode: "Sleep sweetly in your humble graves."
Trakl.   Grodek ("At evening the woods of autumn are full of the sound.").
Grodek ("In the evening the autumn woods ring.").
On the Eastern Front.
Ts'ao Ts'ao.   Graveyard Song.
Tur-Malka, A.   For the Fighters—A Lament.
Heralds of New Jerusalem.
Memorial Service.
Unknown.   Hymn to the Fallen.
Johnny, I Hardly Knew Ye.
May you perish on the field of honor, my beloved!
Song for a Fallen Warrior.
We Fought South of the City Wall.
Vallejo.   Mass.
Viereck, P.   Vale from Carthage.
Warren, R.   History among the Rocks.
Two Studies in Idealism: Short Survey of American and Human History.
Whitman, W.   And I saw askant the armies.
As Toilsome I Wander'd Virginia's Woods.
Ashes of Soldiers.
Come Up from the Fields Father.
Dirge for Two Veterans.
Reconciliation.
Sight in Camp [in the Daybreak Gray and Dim], A.
Vigil Strange I Kept on the Field One Night.
Wieseltier, M.   Again a Drab Khaki Light is Coming Down.
Wolfe, C.   Burial of Sir John Moore, The.
Yeats.   Irish Airman Foresees His Death, An.
Yonathan, N.   Dust of Poems, The.
Without the Boy.
Young, S.   Epitaph for a Concord Boy.
Zenmaro.   Evidence.
See also Soldiers
War in Afghanistan [2001]
Kearney, L.   Man with His Kids on a Table, The.
Lojowski, M.   On the Sixth Day of the War.
Raworth.   Ozymandias.

Scalapino. Flower, Pal Mal Comic Book.

War in Iraq
Dana, R. In Heaven.
Hoagland, T. Kind of Shadow That Calls Out Fate, The.

War of 1812
Cable, G. English muskets went bim! bim!, The.
Freneau. On the Conflagrations at Washington.
Key. Star-Spangled Banner, The.

Warblers
Basho. Warbler sings, The.
With a warbler for.
Buson. Winter warbler.
Issa. Village named Little-Plum-Tree, A.
Murasaki Shikibu. Warblers are today as long ago, The.
Shoha. When the bush warbler.

Warhol, Andy
Becker, J. In the Proximity of Andy Warhol.
Kinsella, J. Warhol at Wetlands.
Yuson. Andy Warhol Speaks to His Two Filipino Maids.

Warning
Carew, T. Deposition from Love, A.
Corwin, N. Grandmother Living in Fear of Free Verse.
Hall, D. Prophecy.
Hofer, J. Tactics ("Will not tolerate will expend offer known facts armed with knives.").
Issa. Cricket, be.
Little sparrows.
Ivanov, Binyo. Crickets, green-faced.
Kakinomoto no Hitomaro. May the men who are born.
Klyuyev [or Kliuev or Klyuev]. Conversational Melody, A Good Verse, A.
Michelangelo Buonarroti. Flee, lovers, from Love, flee from his fire.
Mitchell, E. This Poem.
Parra, N. Warnings.
Philips, K. Married State, A.
Plath. Admonitions.
Praxilla. Watch for a scorpion, my friend, under every stone.
Ralegh. Sir Walter Ra[u]le[i]gh to His Son[ne].
Ross, Martin. This Message Will Self-Destruct in Sixty Seconds.
Smith, S. Songe d'Athalie.
Sondheim. Everybody Says Don't.
Tsvetayeva [or Tsvetaeva]. Beware.
Turner, C. Buoy-Bell, The.
Unknown. Withered Fish, A.
Yao's Warning.
Waldman, A. Admonitions of the Boudoir.
Warren, R. Pondy Woods.
Riddle in the Garden.

Warren, Joseph
Pierpont, J. Warren's Address at Bunker Hill [or to the American Soldiers].

Warren, Robert Penn
Lawrence, A. Robert Penn Warren's Book.

Wars of the Roses
Pound, E. Tudor indeed is gone and every rose.

Warsaw Ghetto
Bobrowski. Report.
MacEwen, G. Child Dancing, The.
Milosz, C. Poor Christian Looks at the Ghetto, A.
Murphy, M. Common Ground.
Paterson, E. History Teacher in the Warsaw Ghetto Rising.
Slonimski. Elegy: "No more, no more Jewish townships in Poland."
Valentine, J. Forgiveness Dream, The: Man from the Warsaw Ghetto.

Warsaw, Poland
Ashbery, J. My Name Is Dimitri.
Flanders, J. House That Fear Built: Warsaw, 1943, The.
Gorbanevskaya. That time I did not save Warsaw, nor Prague later.
Meinke. Robert Frost in Warsaw.
Norwid, C. Recipe for a Warsaw Novel.
Voznesensky [or Voznesenskii]. New Year's

Letter in Warsaw, A.

Washing
Armstrong, J. On Washing.
Bishop, E. Under the Window: Ouro Prêto.
Bishop, P. Woman Washing.
Buson. Washing the hoe.
Fanning, R. Baudelaire's Ablutions.
Fisher, J. Camp.
Glazer, J. Point of No Return.
Issa. Washing the saucepans.
Kassiane. Troparion.
Khalid, A. Aïda.
Lapeyrère, J. Dishes, The.
Lyon, G. Foot-Washing, The.
Mother Goose. They That Wash on Monday.
Muñiz Huberman. Ablution.
Ozaki Hosai. When I wash the soles of my feet.
Rilke. Pietà.
Robinson, Matt. Move to liquid, A.
Shepherd, R. Hygiene.
Volkow. Washerwoman, The.

See also **Baths and Bathing**

Washing Machines
Holland, J. Spin-Cycle.

See also **Laundry and Laundering**

Washington, Booker Taliaferro
Johnson, M. To See Ol' Booker T.
Linden, M. Our Noble Booker T. Washington.
McLucas, L. Negotiation.
Moorer. Notable Dinner, A.
Randall, D. Booker T. and W. E. B.
Stafford, W. Monuments for a Friendly Girl at a Tenth Grade Party.

Washington, D.C.
Davis, C. Out of Work, Out of Touch, Out of Sorts.
Dove, R. Banneker.
Harrison, T. Red Lights of Plenty, The.
Hemphill. Family Jewels.
Heyen. Steadying, The.
Iverem, E. Keeper.
Redhill, M. Haiku Monument for Washington, D.C.
Rome, H. Money Song, The.
Snyder, G. It Pleases.
Tate, A. Aeneas at Washington.
Welch, J. Man from Washington, The.

Washington, George
Barlow, J. Advice to a Raven in Russia [December, 1812].
Cohan. If Washington Should Come to Life.
Hopkinson, F. Toast to Washington, A.
Mac Low. 1789.
Merriam, E. Which Washington?
Nash, O. Watchman, What of the First First Lady?
Unknown. Inscription at Mount Vernon.
Wheatley, P. To His Excellency General Washington.

Washington Square, New York City
Livingston, M. Envoi: Washington Square Park.
Pitcher, O. Washington Square: August Afternoon.
Rodriguez, L. Meeting the Animal in Washington Square Park.
Stanard, C. Washington Square Park and a Game of Chess.

Washington (state)
Bierds, L. Desire.
Hugo, R. White Center.
Snyder, G. Mid-August at Sourdough Mountain Lookout.

Wasps
Alley, R. Growing Days, The.
Basho. Spring rain.
Beachy-Quick, Dan. Botany.
Constantine, D. Wasps, The.
Fisher, A. Fair Exchange.
Jones, B. Wasp.
Kay, J. Virus².
Mandelstam [or Mandelshtam]. Eyesight of Wasps.
Muir, E. Late Wasp, The.
Paulin. Sting, The.
Prunty. Haying.

Ruefle. Wasps' Nest.
Taylor, E. Upon a Wasp Chilled [or Child] with Cold.
Wojahn. Poison, 1959.

Waste and Wastefulness
Macari, A. Even Love.
Matthews, W. Bear at the Dump, The.
McDaniel, M. Burned in the Test.
Shearin, F. Sinking, The.
Wickham. Envoi: "God, thou great symmetry."
Yi Sanghûi. Organizing a Drawer.

Watches
Allen, F. Modern Times.
Auden. Parable: "Watch upon my wrist, The."
Cornford, F. Watch, The.
Gallagher, T. Kidnap[p]er.
Graham, W. Lines on Roger Hilton's Watch.
Lewis, G. Watch, The.
Maguire, S. Perfect Timing.
McClatchy. Bishop Reading.
Simic. Watch Repair.
Smith, I. Tinily a star goes down.
Yi Sang. Motion.

See also **Clocks**

Water
Acholonu. Water Woman.
Adcock, F. Below Loughrigg.
Akutagawa Ryunosuke. Slime on the stones.
Allen, P. He Na Tye Woman.
Auden. In Praise of Limestone.
Awoonor. So the World Changes.
Bangaramma, C. Hibiscus on the Lake.
Bartolomé, E. Agua desdichada, El.
Ill-fated Water, The.
Tattoos in the Water.
Tatuajes en el Agua.
Basho. At the ancient pond.
Clear water.
Fishy smell, A.
Heard, not seen.
Old pond, The.
Old pond—frogs jumped in—sound of water.
Petal shower, A.
There is the old pond!
Water-drawing rites.
Beddoes. Song on the Water.
Bennett, C. Drowned Radio, The.
Betjeman. East Anglian Bathe.
Bishop, E. Under the Window: Ouro Prêto.
Blackwell, Holley. Message No. 57.
Bobrowski. In the Torrent.
Bonnefoy. Well, The.
Borges. Sea, The.
Brehm, J. Sea of Faith.
Brontë, C. Diving.
Brooks, G. Kitchenette building.
Brown, K. Money As Water.
Buson. Escaped the nets.
Evening wind.
Green leaves.
Misty grasses.
Night deepens.
Only the shoots.
Wading through it.
Washing the hoe.
Calvino. Armilla.
Cameron, N. Green, Green Is El Aghir.
Carrera Andrade. Transfiguration of the Rain.
Carroll, J. Blue Poles.
Ceravolo. Heart Feels the Water.
Césaire, A. Blank to Fill in on the Visa of Pollen.
Charara, H. Hamza Aweiwi, a Shoemaker in Hebron.
Holy Water.
Chiyojo. Morning glory!, The.
Since morning glories.
Chŏng Hwajin. Hidden Path, The.
Sunlight Showers Down in Sheets.
Water in a Gourd.
Clampitt. Marine Surface, Low Overcast.
Times Square Water Music.
Clark, P. Walk in the Rain.
Clary. Lightning. And the Mile Between.
Cogswell, Fred. Water and the Rock, The.
Coleridge, M. Lord of the winds, I cry to Thee.

Copus, J.   Love, Like Water.
Creeley.   Act of Love, The.
Croly.   Aestuary, An.
Cruz, S.   I Know Full Well the Water's Flowing Power.
Daive.   Lost in contemplation.
D'Aquino, A.   Brief Viper.
  Vibora breve.
Diego, G.   Perpetual Motion.
Domanski.   Drowning Water.
Doolittle, H.   Pool, The.
Doyle, B.   Error of the Hydrographers, An.
Du Bouchet.   Stone or Water.
Dubrava.   Miraculous Marriage of Zarife Dominquez.
Duhig, I.   I prayed to the ghost of Carrie.
Eberhart, R.   Garden God, The.
  Loon Call, A.
Ekelof.   Ayíasma.
Éluard, P.   Deaf and Blind, The.
Emerson, R.   Water: "Water understands / Civilization well, The."
Ennis.   Drink of Spring, A.
Finch, A.   Landing under Water, I See Roots.
Finlay, I.   Boat's Blueprint, The.
Frost, R.   West-Running Brook.
Gilbert, C.   Chosen to Be Water.
Giussani, S.   Aridness of Air, The.
Góngora y Argote.   Pride of the Fourth and Liquid Element.
Gorostiza, J.   Filled with myself, walled up in my skin.
Gregerson.   Waterborne.
Grennan.   Shoreline After Storm.
Greppi, C.   Like a handful of leaves.
Hadewijch.   Love's Constancy.
Hamill, S.   What the Water Knows.
Hannaham, D.   If There's No Sugar.
Hannan, M.   Lamper, The.
Haslam, M.   No Bloody Matter 43 42.
Heaney, S.   Drink of Water, A.
Helton.   Lonesome Water.
Herrick.   To the Water Nymphs, Drinking at the Fountain.
Highfill, M.   Rebis.
Hirshfield, J.   Music Like Water, The.
  To Drink.
Hogan, L.   Chambered Nautilus.
Holan.   During an Illness.
Hollander, J.   By the Sound.
Howe, F.   You float inside your water.
Hughes, T.   Man Seeking Experience Enquires His Way of a Drop of Water, The.
Ifowodo, O.   Abundance of Grey, An.
Ishikawa Takuboku.   Tanka: "As if in water."
Issa.   Ducks bobbing on the water.
  Its mother on guard.
  Spring day, The.
Iverem, E.   Peace Be Still.
Jarman, M.   Desire of Water, The.
Jarrell, R.   Well Water.
Jiménez, J.   To the bridge of love.
Jinkag Haesim.   Because of the Rain.
Jordan, J.   October 23, 1983.
Juana Inés de la Cruz.   Since Love is shivering.
Kang Ún'gyo.   Becoming Water.
Kasa.   I shall think of you.
Kassid, A.   Seer, The.
Keats.   Bright Star.
Kenney.   Sailing.
Kikaku.   Single yam leaf, A.
  Sprinkle water wide / For the sparrow.
Kim Ku.   I Spy the Three-Colored Peach Blossom.
Kinzie.   Glinting like water.
Kizer, C.   Muse of Water, A.
Ko Un.   Ripples.
Koch, K.   Boiling Water, The.
Kooser.   Dishwater.
Kruit, J.   Landscape.
  Way of the Water, The.
Kusano Shimpei.   4 Or 5 Tadpoles.
Larkin, P.   Water.
Lawrence, D. H.   Snake.
  Wild Common, The.
Leithauser.   Buried Graves, The.

Levertov.   Laying the Dust.
  Wavering.
Levine, P.   Belief.
Li Yu [or Li Hou-Chu].   One Dream.
Lili'u-o-ka-lani.   Lawn Sprinkler, The.
Livingston, M.   Swimming Pool.
Lorde.   Fishing the White Water.
Lowell, R.   Water.
Loynaz, D. M.   Cloud, The.
  Snow.
"Lucebert.".   I Reel Off.
Lyons, S.   Touching You Underwater.
MacCaig.   Likenesses.
MacDiarmid, H.   Glass of Pure Water, The.
MacLeish.   What Any Lover Learns.
Mahadevi.   It was like a stream.
Major, C.   Water USA.
Mandell, A.   Middle Age.
Martial.   After her wedding-night, the nymph.
Masahide.   When bird passes on.
Mayo, E.   Word of Water, The.
McCord, D.   When I Was Christened.
McGuckian.   Sea or Sky?
McMichael.   Posited.
Meng Hao Jan.   Passing Seven-League Rapids.
Milton.   Forthwith the sounds and seas, each creek and bay.
Mirabai [or Mira Bai].   I was going to the river for water.
Mitchell, K.   Night Rain.
  Tree Stillness.
Montale.   Dora Markus.
Moore, H.   Spuyten Duyvil.
Moore, M.   Like a Bulrush.
Moore, T.   Meeting of the Waters, The.
Morejón.   Poem Fifty.
Morgan, E.   Dowser, The.
Morley, H.   Curve of the Water.
Motsapi, S.   Samaki.
Mouré.   8 Little Theatres of the Cornices.
Mueller, J.   Year.
Mutis.   You Are a Daughter of the Lagides.
Neruda.   Sexual Water.
Nicholson, N.   From a Boat at Coniston.
Niedecker.   Something in the water.
Nietzsche.   Notes.
  Undiscouraged.
Norgate, S.   Water on the Moon.
Norris, L.   Water.
O'Neill, M.   Sound of Water.
Oswald, A.   Sea Sonnet.
Otten, W. J.   Mud-Flat.
  Mud-Flat.
Padilla.   Daily Habits.
Page, P.   Water and Marble.
Paljor, N.   Exhausted by jogging.
Pao Chao.   Splash water on level ground.
Pastan.   Erosion.
  Love Poem.
Paz.   Lake.
  Wind and Water and Stone.
Peacocke.   Soap.
Phillips, C.   In the blood, Winnowing.
Pinchas-Cohen.   Journey of a Doe.
Piper, E.   Big Swimming.
Ponge.   Water.
Pound, E.   Bathtub [or Bath Tub], The.
Rafferty, P.   View from the Bathysphere.
Ramsey, J.   Power Quest, Sooke Park.
Randell.   Jetty, The.
Rexroth, K.   Water is always the same.
Reznikoff.   Aphrodite Vrania.
Richards, Peter.   Away from you the seafloor's longitudinal.
Rizal, J.   Water and Fire.
Rothman, D.   Shape of Water Most Like Love, The.
Roy, L.   Suffering The Sea Change: All My Pretty Ones.
Rumi.   Inside water, a waterwheel turns.
Ryuzan.   Clear in the blue, the moon!
Sarton, M.   Glass of Water, A: "Here is a glass of water from my well."
Seshadri.   Lifeline.
Shcherbina.   They cut off my hot water.
Simms, C.   Lochside silverschistsand disturbed-

to-black-below distributed.
Smelcer.   Bonanza Creek.
Smith, W.   Brooklyn Bridge.
Sorescu, M.   Fountains in the Sea.
Spaulding-Convy, A.   Why Women Become Water.
Su Tung-p'o.   White Crane Hill.
Sy, T.   Cup of Clear Water, A.
Tadic.   Laocoon/Serpent.
Taggard.   To the Powers of Desolation.
Taufer, V. et al.   Mother loves me loves me not.
Taylor, A.   Water.
Thoreau.   Fog.
Tonks.   Hydromaniac.
Traherne.   Shadows in the Water.
Truitt, S.   Kerf, The.
Tsvetayeva [or Tsvetaeva].   To Kiss a Forehead Is to Erase Worry.
Tu Fu [or Du Fu].   Moon, Rain, Riverbank.
Unknown.   Cleared by its flowing, dip the flood water up.
  Inscription in Osmington Church, Dorset.
  Medicine Songs.
  Petelia Tablet, The.
  Song of the Prophet.
  Water Bug and the Shadows, The.
Valentine, J.   Lines in Dejection.
Van Winckel, N.   Back When.
Vasalis.   Idiot in the Bath, The.
Velichansky, A.   Flame's speech is confused, The. The muttering of the water is hollow.
Vigil, A.   Hogarcito de La Madrugada, El.
Villa, D.   It is.
Volkman.   Create Desire.
Warren, R.   Watershed.
Wen Yi-tuo [or Wen I-to].   Dead Water.
West, K.   By Water Divined.
Woods, V.   Asylum is Water, The.
Wright, C.   Wages of Love.
Wright, J.   Journey to the Place of Ghosts.
Yamaguchi Seishi.   Cleaning yellowtail.
Yevtushenko [or Evtushenko].   Siberian Wooing.
Yun Sŏndo.   They say the color of clouds is fine.
Zawacki, Andrew.   From the Book of Divine Consolation.
Zawgee.   Way of the Water-Hyacinth, The.
Zukofsky, L.   To my wash-stand.
  When the crickets.
Xenophanes.

Water Lilies
Barnes, W.   Clote, The.
Black, D.   Water-Lily, The.
Clare, J.   Water-Lilies.
Ferlinghetti, L.   Monet's Lilies Shuddering.
Hughes, T.   To Paint a Water Lily.
Mills, R.   Water Lilies.
Stein, G.   Preciosilla.
Teasdale.   Water-Lilies.
Voigt.   Lotus Flowers, The.
Wakoski.   Light.
Welch, L.   Claude Monet's Water Landscapes.

Waterbeds
Updike.   Insomnia the Gem of the Ocean.

Waterfalls
Ammons.   Enfield Falls.
Basho.   Secluded for a while.
Carrera Andrade.   Your body is bathed eternally.
Ch'ôn Yanghûi.   Entering Chikso Falls.
Dubie.   Buffalo Clouds over the Maestro Hoon.
Everson, W.   Stone Face Falls.
Gaspar de Alba.   5: Rainstorm: The Gorge.
Hardy, T.   Under the Waterfall.
Hartley, M.   West Pitch at the Falls.
Heaney, S.   Waterfall.
Landon.   Scale Force, Cumberland.
Li Po.   Viewing the Waterfall at Mount Lu.
  Waterfall at Lu-shan.
Longley, M.   Waterfall, The.
Merwin.   Hearing.
Muso Soseki.   Poem on Dry Mountain (A Zen Garden).
  Three-Step Waterfall.
Na Hûidôk.   Song of Grass.
Ormond.   Definition of a Waterfall.
Owen, G.   Waterfall.
Ray, H.   At the Cascade.

Southey, R.   Cataract of Lodore, The.
Tremayne.   Falls of Falloch, The.
Vaughan, H.   Waterfall [*or* Water-Fall], The.
Wagoner, D.   By a Waterfall.
Williams, W.   Paterson: The Falls.
Williamson, G.   Waterfall.
Woody.   She-Who-Watches . . . The Names are Prayer.
Young, A.   Falls of Glomach, The.

Waterfowl
Bryant, W.   To a Waterfowl.
Dogen.   Coming, going, the waterfowl.
Niedecker.   My Life by Water.

Watergate
Woddis.   Final Curtain.
See also **Nixon, Richard Milhous**

Waterloo, Battle of (1815)
Byron, G.   Revelry by Night.
  There Was a Sound of Revelry by Night.
Hugo, V.   Waterloo! Waterloo! Waterloo! dismal plain!
Scott, S.   Charge at Waterloo.

Watermelons
Alexander, E.   Overture: Watermelon City.
Barber, D.   Small Hours.
Donovan, K.   Watermelon Man.
Issa.   Now listen, you watermelons.
Levitt, Peter.   Watermelon and Zen students.
Simic.   Watermelons.
Unknown.   O love, round as the watermelon.
Yi Yônju.   Taking a Watermelon as a Paradigm.

Waterwheels
Diego, G.   Perpetual Motion.
Machado Ruiz.   Water Wheel, The.
  Water Wheel, The ("Afternoon arrived, The.").

Watts, Isaac
Carroll, L.   Crocodile, The.
Rodriguez, L.   Speaking with Hands.

Watts, Los Angeles, California
Rivers, C.   Watts.
Rodriguez, L.   Heavy Blue Veins.

Waugh, Evelyn
Connolly, C.   On Himself.

Waves
Agran, R.   Swimming with Seiger.
Barrington, J.   Villanelle VI.
Barrow, Raymond.   There is a Mystic Splendour.
Buson.   Short night, The.
Bynner.   Wave, The.
Cho Chihun.   Spring Day.
Clampitt.   Marine Surface, Low Overcast.
Copus, J.   Cricketer's Retirement Day, The.
Curnow.   You Will Know When You Get There.
D'Aguiar, F.   Dread.
Ficke.   Wave Symphony, The.
Forrester, S.   Writing a haiku.
Goeckel, L.   Wave Falling on the Beach, A.
Graham, J.   Complex Mechanism of the Break, The.
  Gulls.
  Soul Says.
Greer, J.   Rodin's "Gates of Hell".
Gunn, T.   From the Wave.
Hadas, R.   Sentimental Education.
Jarman, M.   Wave.
Kanchev, Nikolai.   Miracle.
Kasa.   I love and fear him.
Kikaku.   Shrine gate / Through morning mist.
Laird, N.   Length of a Wave, The.
Longley, M.   Comber, The.
Lugones.   Gray Waves.
Mac Low.   Waves Broke on the Shore, The.
MacLeish.   Dover Beach—a Note to That Poem.
Martínez, V.   Coastal.
McGuckian.   Sea or Sky?
McNiece, R.   My shadow on waves.
Morrison, L.   Surf.
No Hyangnim.   Ap'ae Island 1—Diving Women.
  Ap'ae Island 45—Once Upon a Time.
Noguchi, R.   His Waves.
Oppen.   Party on Shipboard.
Po Chü-i.   One anchorage of sand appears as another dissolves away.
Robertson, R.   Waves: "I have swum too far."

Rossetti, C.   Horses of the sea, The.
Rothman, D.   When the Wind and Dark Waves Come.
Shakespeare, W.   Sonnet 60: "Like as the waves make toward[s] the pebbled [*or* pibled] shore."
Shokushi.   Guide me on my way.
Skelton, R.   Night Piece.
Southwick.   Waves, The.
Spicer, J.   Lament for the Makers: "No call upon anyone but the timber drifting in the waves."
Stephens, J.   Main-Deep, The.
Swenson, M.   How Everything Happens (Based on a Study of the Wave).
  Wave and the Dune, The.
Taneda Santoka.   Edge of town.
Tantan.   On the rock / Waves can't reach.
Teasdale.   I Would Live in Your Love.
Unknown.   All too soon, I fear.
  Am I to go on.
  Safe, here, now.
Virgil [*or* Vergil].   Wave, The.
Whitman, W.   By that Long Scan of Waves.
  Had I the Choice.
Wilbur, R.   Beacon, The.
Williams, W.   There are no perfect waves.
Zukofsky, L.   I Sent Thee Late.

Wayne, John
Carbó, N.   Little Brown Brother.
Erdrich.   Dear John Wayne.

Wealth
Adams, F.   Rich Man, The.
Alexie.   After the Trial of Hamlet, Chicago.
Anderson, W.   I'm Naebody Noo.
Belloc.   Lord Finchley.
Berlin.   Little Things in Life, The.
  Puttin' on the Ritz (Original Version).
  Puttin' on the Ritz (Revised Version).
Blake, W.   Proverbial Philosophy.
Bock, J.   Little Tin Box.
Borges.   Matthew 25:14–30; "For it will be as when a man".
Brontë, E.   Old Stoic, The.
Brooks, G.   Beverly Hills, Chicago.
Brown, L.   Best Things in Life Are Free, The.
Burke, J.   Ain't It a Shame About Mame.
Cavendish, M.   Her Descending Down.
Chaucer.   Miller's [*or* Milleres] Tale, The.
Clare, J.   Thou far-fled pasture, long evanished scene.
Coleridge, M.   Insincere Wish Addressed to a Beggar, A.
Constantine, D.   Door, The.
Cortez, J.   Global Inequalities.
Coward.   Stately Homes of England, The.
Cox, J.   Nobody Knows You When You're Down and Out.
Crowley, R.   Of unsaciable purchasers.
Daryush.   Children of Wealth.
Davie, D.   Garden Party, The.
Davies, W. H.   No Man's Wood.
de Fréine, C.   Chattels.
DeSylva, B. G.   Best Things in Life Are Free, The.
Dugan, A.   American Variation on How Rilke Loved a Princess and Got to Stay in Her Castle.
Dunbar, P.   Common Things.
  Place Where the Rainbow Ends, The.
Dylan.   Lonesome Death of Hattie Carroll, The.
Emerson, R.   Chartist's Complaint, The.
  Compensation ("Wings of Time are black and white, The.").
Enzensberger, H.   Rich, The.
Feld, Andrew.   Intermission.
Fletcher, P.   Against a Rich Man Despising Poverty.
Frost, R.   In Divés' Dive.
  Lovely Shall Be Choosers, The.
  Luke 16:19–26; "There was a rich man".
Hardy, T.   Ruined Maid, The.
Harnick.   If I Were a Rich Man.
Hart, L.   I've Got Five Dollars.
Henderson, R.   Best Things in Life Are Free, The.
Herndon, C.   Poem: "And I went up to that chandeliered place."

Herrick.   His Grange, or Private Wealth.
Hershon.   Unless You Are a Horse.
Hoagland, T.   America.
Hughes, L.   Advertisement for the Waldorf-Astoria.
Issa.   What's the lord's vast wealth.
  Writing shit about new snow.
Johnson, S.   Short Song of Congratulation, A [*or* To a Young Heir].
Juana Inés de la Cruz.   World! why do you hound me?
Juvenal.   Satire 10.
Kamienska.   Matthew 19:16–24; And behold, one came up to him.
Kennedy, X.   In a Prominent Bar in Secaucus [One Day].
Knott.   Funny Poem.
Komunyakaa, Y.   Seven Deadly Sins.
Landon.   Bonds of Affection.
  Poor, The.
Leapor.   Strephon to Celia. A modern Love-Letter.
Martial.   Agriculture.
  Oh If the Gods Would Make Me Rich.
Mendelssohn, Anna.   On Being Reproached by Saintly Mediators for Bad Budgeting.
Nash, O.   Song of Songs, The.
  Terrible People, The.
North, M.   Ordnance Survey in the Northern Counties.
Orr, T.   Soybeans.
Pao Chao.   Desolate City, The: A Rhapsody.
  Ruined City, The.
Parrott.   More Bagpipe Music.
Peacock, T.   Rich and Poor; or, Saint and Sinner.
Persius.   Satire 6: "Has Sabine winter brought you to your fireside."
Po Chü-i.   Inscription Written by Me in My Small Garden.
Pope, A.   Sir Balaam.
Porter, C.   I've a Shooting Box in Scotland.
  My Heart Belongs to Daddy.
Probyn.   Love in Mayfair.
Rickword.   Luxury.
Robinson, E.   Bewick Finzer.
  Richard Cory.
Rossetti, D.   86: Lost Days.
Schmitz.   Carmel.
Sidney.   Sonnet 37: "My mouth doth water, and my breast doth swell."
Soyinka.   After the Deluge.
Stevenson, R.   To A Gardener.
Tate, J.   Sadness of My Neighbors, The.
Taylor, C.   Renting.
Thompson, P.   Jade.
Tree.   Pity the Slain that Laid Away Their Lives.
Tsvetayeva [*or* Tsvetaeva].   If the Soul was Born with Pinions.
Unknown.   I Know Where I'm Going.
  On Late-acquired Wealth *or* Riches.
  One Little Boy.
  When a Beggar Beholds You.
Wang Wei.   Peerless Lady, The.
Warren, H.   Gold Digger's Song (We're in the Money), The.
Wilbur, R.   Summer Morning, A.
Wylie.   Full Moon.
Yellen, J.   Are You Havin' Any Fun?
Zephaniah.   De Rich Getting Rich.

Weapons
Anyte [*or* Anytes].   Stand there, manslaying spear; no longer drip.
Behn, A.   Song. Love Arm'd [*or* Armed].
Bowman, C.   No Sorry.
Bryll.   Ballad of the Bayonet, A.
Cangiullo.   Detonation.
Césaire, A.   Miraculous Weapons, The.
Char.   Every Life.
Crosby, E.   I am a great inventor, did you but know it.
Elfyn, Menna.   Pins.
Eugenius Vulgarius.   Metrum Parhemiacum Tragicum.
Harrison, T.   History Classes.
Herrera.   Fuselage Installation.
Hofer, J.   Tactics ("Licit tremendous unjust

oxidized fancified notions tremulously.").
Homer. Thus Neptune rous'd these men.
Hughes, T. Crow's Theology.
Knevet. Vote, The.
Koordada, M. You Can't Escape Your Life
Record.
Locklin. Do you remember the scene in *The
Godfather* where James Caan says, "Now
make sure that the gun gets stashed in the rest
room—I don't want my kid brother walking
out of there with nothing but his dick in his
hand"?
Lu Lun. Black moon geese fly high.
Meeks, B. Is Culcha Weapon?
Milton. He sat; and in the assembly next
upstood.
Owen, W. Arms and the Boy.
Reed, H. Naming of Parts.
Ryan, G. If I Had a Gun.
Scannell. Bayonet Training.
Scarfe. Grenade.
Schilpp, M. Under the Scorpion's Heart.
Sivudu. Warrior, Bhaskar!
Spender, S. Ultima Ratio Regum.
Unknown. To your question: why are my
private parts.
Webb, F. Gunner, The.
Weigl. Mines.
Wilkie, B. Virus, The.
Williams, M. First Kill.

Weariness
Aleixandre. In Front of the Mirror.
Apollinaire. Zone.
Basho. Exhausted, / time to find a lodging.
Taking a nap.
Tired.
Baudelaire. Cracked Bell, The.
Beckett, S. Enueg 1.
Enueg 2.
Bouwers. Final Signs, The.
Bradstreet, A. As Weary Pilgrim, Now at Rest.
Breton, N. Wearie thoughts doe waite upon me.
Browning, E. My Heart and I.
Byron, G. So We'll Go No More A-Roving.
Campo. El Curandero.
Codrescu. Work.
Corso. Zizi's Lament.
Coward. (I'm So) Weary of It All.
Why Must the Show Go On?
Crapsey. Trapped.
Dallerès, J. Museum.
De la Mare. Tired Tim.
Delgado, J. Recommitted.
Du Maurier. Music.
Fields, D. It's All Yours.
Fisher, D. Tired.
Galich. Hospital Gypsy Song.
Glück, L. Winged Horse, The.
Grimké, A. Butterflies.
Harburg. Then I'll Be Tired of You.
Hughes, L. Po' Boy Blues.
Weary Blues, The.
Hupfeld, H. Let's Put Out the Lights and Go to
Sleep.
Ishikawa Takuboku. Do Not Get Up.
Issa. Having slept, the cat gets up.
In spring rain.
Jastrun, T. Seed, The.
Ku K'uang. Hard Traveling.
Laird, N. Bearhug, The.
Li Ho. Days of Rain.
Longfellow, H. Broken Oar, The.
Martory, P. Blues.
Masefield. Sorrow of Mydath.
McDonald, R. Incident in Transylvania.
McGinnis, M. Sending Men Back to the Sea.
Mishol, A. Sacred Cow of Hardship, The.
Muso Soseki. To the Emperor's Messenger.
Na Hûidôk. Dirty Nylons.
Women Within Me.
Neruda. Walking Around.
Walking Around.
No Hyangnim. Ap'ae Island 1—Diving
Women.
Nowlan. Day's End.
Nye, N. New Year.

Penna. Life...is remembering waking up.
Pound, E. Greek Epigram.
Radnóti. Clouded Sky.
Rexroth, K. Night is too long to the sleepless,
The.
Rimbaud, A. Decidedly we are out of the
world. No longer any sound.
Roberts, A. Tired.
Rossetti, C. From the Antique.
In Progress.
Sleeping at Last.
Thinking of you, and all that was, and all.
Ryan, G. Orbit.
Schwartz, D. Tired and Unhappy, You Think of
Houses.
Shakespeare, W. Sonnet 27: "Weary with toil, I
haste me to my bed."
Sonnet 50: "How heavy do I journey on the
way."
Shaku Chōkū. Tanka: "Somewhere around."
Teng Yu-pin. Taoist Song: "In white clouds, in
green mountains."
Tucker, M. I am Weary, Mother.
Weariness.
Turner, W. Music of a Tree, The.
Unknown. Don't Be Weary, Traveller.
Lord Randal[l].
Scribe, The: "For Weariness My Hand Writes
Ill".
Vanshenkin. Sunset fades, and from the little
hill, The.
Verlaine. Spleen.
Vogel, D. With gentle fingers.
Wildman, E. Cure, The.
Wylie. Nebuchadnezzar.
Yesenin [*or* Essenin]. Letter to My Mother.

Weasels
Levchev. Weasel.
Unknown. Song of the Weasel.

Weather
Afrika, T. Respite.
Aled, Sion. Weather Forecast.
Ashbery, J. Crazy Weather.
Franchises in Flux.
Bang, M. Crossed-Over, Fiend-Snitched, X-ed
Out.
Becker, R. Near Sheridan.
Berlin. Isn't This a Lovely Day (To Be Caught
in the Rain?).
It's a Lovely Day Today.
I've Got My Love to Keep Me Warm.
Bryant, W. After a Tempest.
Burnside, J. Dundee.
Bynner. Opus 17.
Cherry, K. Forecast.
Coultas, B. Weather Report.
Curbelo. Tourist Weather.
De la Mare. Scarecrow, The.
Denby. Climate, The.
Dickinson, E. Sun and Fog Contested, The.
Dove, R. Turning Thirty, I Contemplate
Students Bicycling Home.
Drummond, W. All Changeth.
Farjeon, E. F is for Forecast.
Forbes, D. Forecast.
France, L. Meteorology.
Fulton, R. Note for Robert Henryson, A.
Gibson, C. There's a straw in the manger and
babies in danger.
Graves, R. Love Story, A.
Weather of Olympus, The.
Hardy, T. Weathers [*or* Weather].
Harvey, M. Definition of Weather.
Heaney, S. Dogger, Rockall, Malin, Irish Sea.
Henley, W. E. At Queensferry.
Hoban. Pedalling Man, The.
Holden, C. Biblical Winnipeg.
Hooper, V. Reading, A.
Hughes, L. Strange Hurt.
Ignatow, D. Cloud Creates, A.
Johnson, M. F. Thunder Storm.
Jones, H. Weather.
Kang Ûn'gyo. Poem's Visit, A.
Sleet.
Katz, E. Weather Seems Different, The.
Khlebnikov, V. Hey...y! Uh...hm!, covered with

sweat.
Kim Sisŭp. Now Shine, Now Rain.
Kirchwey. He Considers the Birds of the Air.
Kirsch, S. Wintery Music.
Koehler, T. Stormy Weather (Keeps Rainin' All
the Time).
Lerner, A. Camelot.
Mayer, B. Max Carries the One.
Mayröcker. Schubert, or: Notes on the Weather,
Vienna.
Merriam, E. Spell of Weather, A.
Weather.
Momaday. Headwaters.
Newman, J. Elements, The.
Orléans, C. Temps a Laissié, Le.
Pastan. Weather.
Robertson, Lisa. Residence at C——— ("My
purpose here is to advance into.").
Wednesday.
Robertson, R. Aberdeen.
Rosemurgy, C. Why God Invented the Cold.
Roubaud. Past, The.
Seale, J. Subtropical.
Shakespeare, W. We are but warriors for the
working-day.
Simonides. As whenever.
Sri Sri. Announcement, An.
Strand. Morning, Noon and Night.
Street, S. Shipping Forecast, Donegal.
Sutter. Hoarfrost and Fog.
Swenson, M. Cat and the Weather.
Weather.
Tomlinson, C. Weather Report.
Tremayne. Mixed Weather.
Trowbridge, W. Stark Weather.
Unknown. Imploration for Clear Weather.
Red sky at night, A.
Rhyme from Lincolnshire, A.
Song to Bring Fair Weather.
Williamson, G. Belvedere Marittimo.
Wright, J. Black Cockatoos.
Wu Wen-ying. Tune: "Rouged Lips" Rain Just
Over on the Night of the Lantern Preview.
Young, K. Degrees.
Zondberg, O. They all but cry out.

Weathervanes
Hine. Riddle: "Invisible, chimerical."
Hoban. Pedalling Man, The.
Yi Hyangji. Acromatic Dawn.

Weaving and Weavers
Branch, A. What witchlike spell weaves here its
deep design.
Bridges, C. Gordian Knot.
Cherry, K. Raiment We Put On, The.
Chester, A. Tapestry Weaver, The.
Coleridge, M. Wilderspin.
Deloney. Weavers Song, The.
Doolittle, H. Archer.
At Ithaca.
Esteves. Weaver.
Hall, H. Maker of Songs.
Heine, H. Silesian Weavers, The.
Sappho. It's no use.
Stoddard, E. Before the Mirror.
Tobrise. Dyeing.
Unknown. Factory Workers' Song.
Poverty Knock.
[Version 1].
[Version 2].
You might easy know a doffer.
Vicuña. Shadow of a Loom, The.
Yeats. Fragments: "Locke sank into a swoon."
Yu Mongin. Poor Woman, A.

Webster, Daniel
Coatsworth. Daniel Webster's Horses.
Whittier. Ichabod[!].

Wedding Songs
Beaumont, F. *et al.* Bridal Song: "Cynthia, to
thy power."
Góngora y Argote. Come Hymen come, for
here to thee we bring.
McFadden, R. Epithalamium: "So you are
married, girl. It makes me sad."
Meleager. Upon a Maid That Died [*or* Dyed]
the Day She Was Married [*or* Marryed].
Mock, Jeff. Epithalamion for Sarah and Tony.

Sidney.   Epithalamium: "Let mother Earth".
Weddings
Adair, V. H.   Cutting the Cake.
Adisa.   Rainbow, The.
Akhmadulina.   Bride, The.
Alcaeus [*or* Alkaios].   Story goes, from evil, The.
Ancient Sumerian Oral Tradition.   Bridegroom, dear to my heart.
Baillie, J.   Song: Woo'd and married and a'.
  Storm-Beat Maid, The.
Bandeira.   Spiritual Wedding.
Barnes, W.   Sister Gone.
Biespiel, D.   After the Wedding.
Bloch, C.   Kiss, The.
  White Petticoats.
Bly, R.   My Father's Wedding.
Bourne, Lesley-Anne.   Out of the Blizzard.
Chapman, G.   New light gives new directions, Fortunes new.
Clanchy, K.   For a Wedding.
Colum, P.   She Moved through the Fair.
Copus, J.   Pulling the Ivy.
Corso.   Marriage.
Cruz, S.   Spiritual Canticle.
Cutler, Y.   Shir Asheydim Ansher.
D'Aquino, A.   Boda, La.
  Wedding, The.
De Cristoforo, Violet Kazue.   Tenth Wedding Anniversary (July 3, 1994): Tsuki Oboro Totsugishi Yoru No Sora Datta.
Donaldson, W.   Because My Baby Don't Mean Maybe Now.
Dove, R.   In the Old Neighborhood.
Dubin, A.   Shuffle Off to Buffalo.
Dubrava.   Miraculous Marriage of Zarife Dominquez.
Dybek.   Cherry.
Foster, A.   No Dice.
Foust, G.   On the Evening of a Wedding.
Gill, K.   Ghazal 5: "My white mare on the Punjabi plains, the stamp of her hooves."
Goetz, E.   For Me and My Gal.
Goodison.   Wedding in Hanover.
Gu Cheng.   Feel of the Wind, The.
Gylys, B.   Balloon Heart.
Heaney, S.   Wedding Day.
Henry, P.   Winter Wedding, The.
Heywood, J.   Egles byrde hath spred his wings, The.
Hill, S.   I Will Be Arriving Next Thursday in My Wedding-Dress.
Hoagland, T.   Kind of Shadow That Calls Out Fate, The.
Hurd, B.   My Son's Wedding, My Daughter's.
Hussein, Nadir.   Wedding, A.
Joseph, A.   Wedding Party.
Kahal, I.   Wedding Bells Are Breaking Up That Old Gang of Mine.
Keckler, W.   Wedding, A.
Killigrew, T.   Epilogue to "The Parson's Wedding".
Krayer, S.   My Mother Dressed for the Wedding.
Lafleur, W.   Wedding Party.
Larkin, P.   Waiting For Breakfast, While She Brushed Her Hair.
  Whitsun Weddings, The.
Laskey, M.   Tightrope Wedding, The.
Leslie, E.   For Me and My Gal.
Levine, M.   Wedding Day.
Lewis, S.   Dinah.
Longley, M.   Pattern, The.
Luterman, S.   Justice of the Peace, The.
Mapanje.   *From* Florrie Abraham Witness, *December 1972.*
Martial.   After her wedding-night, the nymph.
Masters, E.   Wedding Feast, The.
McMorris, M.   Tell me again, Love, what is a wedding?
Molloy, D.   Grands Seigneurs, Les.
Mouré.   Thirteen Years.
Nash, O.   Here Usually Comes the Bride.
Newman, A.   **Fall back.** To give ground; recede; retreat.
Nicholson, N.   Epithalamium for a Niece.

Niedecker.   I rose from marsh mud.
No Hyegyông.   Wedding: "Inside the womb-like darkness."
Norris, K.   Wedding in the Courthouse, The.
O'Hehir, D.   Questions and Answers.
  Wedding Banquet.
Oswald, A.   Wedding.
Ovid.   Iphis and Ianthe.
Pankey.   Reason, The.
Parson-Nesbitt.   Strange Country.
Pelizzon, V.   Wedding Day, The.
Philpot, T.   Louisa's Wedding.
Porter, C.   It's De-Lovely.
Quinn, J.   Strand of Hair, A.
Raskin, W.   Wedding Bells Are Breaking Up That Old Gang of Mine.
Robertson, R.   Wedding the Locksmith's Daughter.
Robinson, E.   Matthew 22:1–14; And again Jesus spoke to them.
Rodgers, Gordon.   White Wedding.
Rohrer, M.   After the Wedding Party.
Rosenberg, L.   Big White Dress, The.
Rossetti, D.   6a: Nuptial Sleep.
Ruefle.   Rain Effect.
St. John, D.   Wedding Preparations in the Country.
Salter.   What Do Women Want?
Sappho.   Raise high the roof.
  Since yes you [were] once a child.
  There a bowl of ambrosia.
  There is no other girl, bridegroom, like this.
  With what, dear bridegroom, can I fairly compare you?
Scott, S.   Lochinvar.
See, P.   Shotgun.
Sexton.   How We Danced.
Shaughnessy, B.   Epithalament.
Spenser, E.   Epithalamion: "Ye learned sisters which have oftentimes."
  Prothalamion.
Steele, P.   Cana.
Stein, G.   Little called Pauline, A.
Storace.   Wedding Song.
Su, A.   Wedding Gifts.
Suckling, S.   Ballad[e] [upon a Wedding], A.
Sullivan, Mary Louise.   Wedding Song: "Where the bridesmaid waits in the vestibule."
Tate, J.   Wedding, A.
Thatcher, C.   Moggy's Wedding.
Thomas, R.   Ensenada Wedding.
Thompson, P.   Tribute to the Bride and Groom, A.
Unknown.   Bridegroom, beloved of my heart.
  Robin Hood and Allen [*or* Allin] -a-Dale.
  Weddings.
Valentine, J.   Bride's Hours, A.
Vando.   Blanca's Red Lips.
Vazirani, R.   Mrs. Biswas Breaks Her Connection with Another Relative.
Whitney, I.   I. W. To her unconstant Lover.
Wright, F.   Wedding, The.
Young, J.   Dinah.
See also **Marriage**
Weeds
Allen, P.   Weed.
Ammons.   Reflective.
Basho.   Fishy smell, A.
Chiun.   Nameless / Weed quickening.
Clark, L.   Ground Elder.
Curry, N.   Dandelion.
Dean, D. K.   Taproot.
Dickey, J.   Weeds.
Dugan, A.   Weeds as Partial Survivors.
Freneau.   And by that light around the dome appear'd.
Hamburger, M.   Weeding.
Hughes, T.   Thistles.
Layzer.   Lawn Roller, The.
Levitt, Peter.   Before falling to the scythe.
Rendra.   Tall Weeds.
Roethke.   Long Live the Weeds.
  Weed Puller.
Shakespeare, W.   Go bind thou up young dangling apricots.
Taggard.   Weed, The.

Weekends
Mercredi, D.   Coffee Table Blues.
Starck, Clemens.   Job No. 75-14.
Trethewey, N.   Secular.
Weeping
Adisa.   No, Women Don't Cry.
Anwar, C.   Twilight at a Little Harbor.
Barnes, D.   Every Man His Own Cross.
Basho.   Tomb, bend / To autum wind—.
Beck, R.   Interlude: "Sing together."
Brown, M.   Calgary Bay.
Chippewa Oral Tradition.   Sioux Women Gather Up Their Wounded, The.
Cho Chihun.   As I Play the Flute.
Cortázar.   Instructions on How to Cry.
Crapsey.   Anguish.
Crozier, L.   Excellence in the Small. Tears Frozen on Your Face.
Đỗ Tấn Xuân.   Twenty Years.
Donne.   I am a little world made cunningly.
Drummond de Andrade.   Boy Crying in the Night.
Du Bellay.   Given all my worries over each day's trivia.
Dumas, H.   Saba.
Ellis, Zoila.   Catalyst.
Ettinger, E.   Believe Me.
García Lorca.   Poet Speaks the Truth, The.
Grin, B.   My Shtetl on the Dnestr.
Hemans.   Bride's Farewell, The.
Herbert, Z.   Rain, The.
Hirschman, J.   Weeping, The.
Hirshfield, J.   Monk Stood Beside a Wheelbarrow, The.
Hô Sugyông.   Weeping Singer, A.
Hugo, V.   At Villequier.
Iofe, Y.   Olsanski Cemetery, The.
Issa.   Don't weep, insects / Lovers, stars, themselves.
Kang Ŭn'gyo.   Azalea.
  Leaves of Grass.
  Sound 8.
Kim Ch'unsu [*or* Chun-soo].   Prelude to a Poem.
Kim Sŭnghŭi.   Wailer.
Kossman.   Cassandra to Agamemnon.
McKay, D.   Waking At The Mouth Of The Willow River.
Nejati.   Those glances rain down arrows on the country.
Pak Chaesam.   Autumn River in Burning Tears.
Parham, Mary Gomez.   Other People's Pain.
Paul, C.   Georgina.
Pitcher, O.   Man, in some lan.
Ramsdell, H.   This is not about her but she is an example in this. At this show of kindness the person begins to cry.
Seferis.   Narration.
Shannon, A.   Returning the Water.
Tennyson, A.   Tears of the widower, when he sees.
Terranova.   Why Your Father Cried.
Unknown.   All too soon, I fear.
Verlaine.   Sky above the roof's, The.
Vietnamese Oral Tradition.   Whisky Lovers.
Villaurrutia.   They and I.
Volkman.   Lady of the lake, what does all our weeping lead to? A pair of keys, paucity of summer—just because.
Wilkinson, A.   On a Bench in a Park.
Yi Kyôngnim.   At the Grave.
  Song: "In the world are many roads I haven't walked, and I have pain."
Zati.   Oh heavens, why do you cry? Is your beloved seen.
See also **Tears**
Weight Lifting
Ackerman, D.   Pumping Iron.
Barresi.   Lifting.
Conway, J.   Weight Belt.
Reid, C.   Baldanders.
Rouse, A.   Uni-Gym, The.
Shepherd, R.   That Man.
Welcome
Cisneros, S.   *Bienvenido* Poem for Sophie.
Herman, J.   Hello, Dolly!

McElroy, C. To Welcome a Changeling.
Motsapi, S. Samaki.
Nims, J. Watching the Planes Come In at La Guardia.
Ozer. For Many Years.
Roberts, L. Poem from Llanybri.
Scott, A. Welcum, illustrat Ladye, and oure Quene!
Tu Fu [or Du Fu]. Guest, A.

Welfare
Castillo, A. Me and Baby.
Lee, D. Lazy.

Wellington, Arthur Wellesley, 1st Duke of
Byron, G. On Wellington.
Hardy, T. Something stands here to peril our advance.
Harpur, C. Wellington.

Wells
Bonnefoy. Well, The.
Buson. At the ancient well.
Camellia, The.
Old well.
Chappell, F. Cleaning the Well.
Chiyojo. In the well-bucket / A morning glory.
Morning glory!, The.
Since morning glories.
Dickinson, E. What mystery pervades a well!
Frost, R. For Once, Then, Something.
Gonzalez, N. Deepest Well in Madras, The.
Heaney, S. Personal Helicon.
Hudgins. In the Well.
Jarrell, R. Well Water.
Kakei. At the break of dawn.
Kim Chiha. Well.
Lovecraft. Well, The.
MacDonald, Hugh. Digging of Deep Wells, The.
Macpherson, J. Well, The.
Penrose, V. Rain Finding Once More, The.
Raymund. Well, The.
Reps, Paul. Well silently overflowing.
Rilke. Departure of the Prodigal Son, The.
Sachdev. Well, The.
Salom. Well, The.
Sexauer, T. Well, The.
Stewart, S. Dark the Star.
Warren, R. Well House, The.
Yi Kyubo. Evening on the Mountain: Song to the Moon in the Well.
Yüan Chên. Pitcher, The.

Welsh Poetry
Lewis, G. Her End.

Welsh, The
Abse. Case History.
Ap Glyn, Ifor. Cucumbers of Wolverhampton, The.
Clarke, G. Translation.
Conran. Elegy for the Welsh Dead, in the Falkland Islands, 1982.
Davies, B. Consideration.
Davies, G. Time's Muteness.
Davies, J. Visitor's Book, 9, The.
Drysdale, A. Language Difficulty.
Evans, D. Wales '99.
Garlick, R. Consider Kyffin.
Gurney, I. First Time In.
Hemans. Meeting of the Bards, The. Written for an Eisteddford, or Meeting of Welsh Bards, Held in London, 22 May 1822.
Hodges, C. Naturalised.
Humphreys, E. Poughkeepsie.
Huws, Meirion MacIntyre. City, The.
Llwyd, Alan. Welsh Language, The.
Morris, B. Dinas Emrys.
Philips, K. On the Welsh Language.
Phillips, E. Ties.
Thomas, G. Welsh-speaking Welsh, The.
Thomas, R. S. Expatriates.
Other.
Welsh History.
Welsh Testament, A.
Welshman at St. James' Park, A.
Unknown. On the Welch.
Williams, H. Old Tongue, The.
Williams, R. Listen. / The rejoicing of waters

fills my ears this evening.
Williams, W. After the Mute Centuries.
Welsh and Wales.
See also **Wales**

Werewolves
Reed, I. Loup Garou Means Change Into.
Schoolcraft. My Brother, my brother.
Swartwout. Gypsy Teaches Her Grandchild Wolfen Ways, The.
Walcott. Le Loupgarou.
Watson, R. Ballad of the Were-Wolf, A.
Wilbur, R. Beasts.

West, Mae
Field, E. Mae West.
McElroy, C. Mae West Chats It Up with Bessie Smith.

West, The, United States
Andrews, B. West West.
Benét, R. et al. Western Wagons.
Benét, S. Western Wagons.
Benét, W. Horse Thief, The.
Bishop, E. Vague Poem.
Bryant, W. Prairies, The.
Cary, A. West Country, The.
Chapman, A. Out Where the West Begins.
Crosby, F. Let Me Die on the Prairie.
On Hearing a Description of a Prairie.
Cunningham, J. I drive Westward. Tumble and loco weed.
Davis, M. Going Out and Coming In.
Fisher, L. Pioneers.
Freneau. On the Emigration to America [and Peopling the Western Country].
Garrigue. Grand Canyon, The.
Ginsberg, A. Green Automobile, The.
Guest, B. Santa Fe Trail.
Harms. After West.
Hollo. Wild West Workshop Poem.
MacLeish. Wildwest.
MacNeice. Western Landscape.
McGrath, C. Wheatfield Under Clouded Sky.
Messer, S. Look.
Michie. Arizona Nature Myth.
Snyder, G. Milton by Firelight.
Stephen, J. On a Rhine Steamer.
Unknown. Home on the Range.
Whitman, W. Promise to California, A.

West Indies
Clampitt. Hispaniola.
Crane, H. O Carib Isle!

West Virginia (state)
Atkins, R. Narrative.
Burgess, F. Trapping Fairies.
Givens, Bettye Hammer. Lonesome Texas.
McKinney, I. Twilight in West Virginia: Six O'Clock Mine Report.
Wright, J. Mad Fight Song for William S. Carpenter, 1966, A.

West Wind
Burns, R. Of A' the Airts [the Wind Can Blaw].
Herrick. To the Western Wind.
Masefield. West Wind, The.
Shelley, P. Ode to the West Wind.
Unknown. Western Wind.
Warren, R. Blow, West Wind.

Westminster Abbey
Beaumont, F. Lines on the Tombs in Westminster.
Betjeman. In Westminster Abbey.
Cope, W. Engineers' Corner.

Whales and Whaling
Bancquart. Portrait of Jonah with woman.
Beachy-Quick, Dan. Halt (Naïve).
Benét, W. Whale.
Berrigan, T. Mid-Friday morn, 10 o'clock, I go to India.
Blight. Death of a Whale.
Davis, C. Murderer, The.
Fishman, C. Whapmagoostui.
Glenday, J. Hydrodamalis Gigas.
Gyodai. Whales / Bellowing dawn.
Helwig. Cape Breton in Autumn.
Hoagland, T. Reading Moby-Dick at 30,000 Feet.
Hoffman, D. Armada of Thirty Whales, An.

Holm, B. Whale Breathing: Bartlett Cove, Alaska.
Hope, Andrew, III. Shagoon 1–4.
Hugo, R. Lady in Kicking Horse Reservoir, The.
Jeffers, R. Ocean's Tribute, The.
Juhász, F. Rainbow-Colored Whale, The.
Kunitz, S. Wellfleet Whale, The.
Lawrence, D. H. Whales Weep Not!
Marcus, M. Whales.
Margolis, G. Kicking and Breathing.
McGinn, M. Big Orange Whale, The.
McSweeney, Joyelle. Still Life w/Influences.
Meinke. Death of the Pilot Whales, The.
Melville, H. Ribs and Terrors, The.
Merwin. For a Coming Extinction.
Leviathan.
Shore, The.
Musgrave. Equinox.
Nickerson. At Auke Bay the whales dance.
Noyes, S. Seascape.
Osborn, J. Whaling Song, A.
Pavlov, Konstantin. Interview from the Belly of a Whale.
Prévert. Whale Hunt, The.
Schmitz. Monstrous Pictures of Whales.
Shapiro, D. In a Blind Garden.
Strand. Shooting Whales.
Takamura Kotaro. Whale Spouting.
Yevtushenko [or Evtushenko]. Cemetery of the Whales, The.
Young, E. Submarine Jaunt, A.

Wharves
Bishop, E. Bight, The.
Bontemps. Nocturne of the Wharves.

Wheat
Alexander, M. Iowa Farmer.
Auden. As I Walked Out One Evening.
Bunting. Autobiography, An.
Devara Dasimayya. Tattered Sack, The.
Field. Wheat-miners.
Gehrke, S. Walking Fields at Night South of Hampton, Iowa.
Gu Cheng. Solar Flare.
Heaney, S. Harvest Bow, The.
Ibn 'Iyad. Grainfield.
Ishihara Yoshiro. Wheat.
Kinsella, J. Drowning in Wheat.
Lindsay, J. Voice of the Wheat, The.
Merrill, J. Upward Look, An.
Merwin. Chaff, The.
Pasolini. John 12:24–25; Truly, truly, I say to you.
Riley, P. 171. 115.
Robinson, E. Sheaves, The.
Rossetti, C. Amen.
Unamuno. Delicately Sloping Neck, The.

Wheatley, Phillis
Hayden, R. Letter from Phillis Wheatley, A.
Jordan, J. Something Like a Sonnet for Phillis Miracle Wheatley.
Shockley, E. Bio / autography (or, 18th-Century Multiculturalism).
Williams, K. From the Spirit of Phillis Wheatley to the Spirit of Thomas Jefferson (A Note 212 Years Later).

Wheelbarrows
Goodell, L. Our Red Wheelbarrow.
Spicer, J. Red Wheelbarrow, The.
Williams, W. Red Wheelbarrow, The.

Wheelchairs
Owen, W. Disabled.
Teasley, L. As Dancers.

Wheels
Armitage, S. Tyre, The.
Bingen, Hildegard von. Song to the Creator.
Buckley, C. Train in the Desert—1916.
Heaney, S. Wheels within Wheels.
Hwang Tonggyu. When I See a Wheel.
Justice, D. Train.
Kinzie. But her arm—damp, small.
Lattimore. Note on the L and N.
Levy, A. March Day in London, A.
Miller, A. Song of the Wheel.
Morrison, L. Surf.

Pinsky. Figured Wheel, The.
Prunty. Ferris Wheel, The.
Sri Sri. Wheels of Jagannatha, The.
Taylor, Kate. Wheel Building.
Wellman, M. All the way clear to Aliquippa.
Wojahn. "Mystery Train" Janis Joplin Leaves Port Arthur for Points West, 1964.

Whippoorwills
Clampitt. Whippoorwill in the Woods, A.
Kenyon, J. Twilight: After Haying.
McLoughland. Whippoorwill Calls, The.

Whiskey
Brecht, B. Alabama Song.
Brown, G. Ballad of John Barleycorn, the Ploughman, and the Furrow, The.
Burns, R. Scotch Drink.
Carruth, H. Scrambled Eggs and Whiskey.
Evans, Mayme. Whiskey-Bomb Battle.
Hughes, L. Bar.
Le Fanu. Drunkard's Address to a Bottle of Whiskey, A.
Pak Inhwan. Rocking Horse and the Lady, The.
Rexroth, K. Proust's Madeleine.

Whistler, James Abbott McNeill
Pound, E. To Whistler, American.
Salmon, A. Painting.
Wilde, O. Impression du Matin.

Whistling and Whistlers
Baxter, J. Twenty Little Engines.
Bishop, E. Behind Stowe.
Ch'eng-kung Sui. Rhapsody on Whistling.
Lover. Whistlin' Thief, The.
Smith, D. Out Whistling.
Zolynas. Whistling Woman.

White (color)
al-Saygh, S. White Sleep.
Aygi, G. House—In the Grove of the World.
Basho. Winter leeks,The.
Behrle. White Album.
Bobyshev. White Peacock, The.
Buson. Makes the eye happy.
Chavez, L. Clean Sheets.
Clark, T. To John Ashbery.
Coleridge, M. White Women, The.
Comer, Carrie St. George. Arbor.
Dadié. I Give You Thanks My God.
Donne. Oh my black[e] soul[e]! now thou art summoned.
Emerson, J. White Flowers.
Field. Cyclamens.
Greenberg, A. Man in the Moon, The.
Groarke, V. Trousseau.
Gyatso, T. White teeth smiling.
Hartley, M. Wingaersheek Beach.
Kitasono Katsue. Collection of White Poems.
Levertov. Wings, The.
Lowry, M. About Ice.
Lugones. White Solitude.
Merwin. Hope for Her.
Nichols, G. White.
Pasternak, B. Don't Touch.
Pulido, A. De la ventana.
Out of the window.
Senghor. Pearls.
Song. Ikebana.
Warsh. To John Ashbery.
Yeryomin. Street lamp. Something missing. Drugstore.

Whitefield, George
Wheatley, P. On the Death of the Rev. Mr. George Whitefield [1770].

Whitman, Walt
Alexie. Defending Walt Whitman.
Andrade, E. Walt Whitman and the Birds.
Barnstone, A. Wild With It.
Barnstone, T. *et al.* Hair of the Field.
Barnstone, W. Jiang Yuying, Famous Professor at Beijing University, Who Daringly Rendered into Chinese the First Complete Walt Whitman.
Bell, M. Whitman's Grass.
Benevento, Joe. May 31, 1989.
Berrigan, T. Whitman in Black.
Bibbins, M. Whitman on the Beach.
Bly, R. This Night: For Walt Whitman.
Two Ramages for Old Masters.

Borges. Camden, 1892.
Matthew XXV:30.
Brown, L. Encyclopedia Botanica.
Browne, M. Your Sister.
Butler, C. E. Other Places, The.
Bynner. Highest Bidder, The.
Byrne, Edward. Early Evening.
Carnevali. Walt Whitman.
Centolella. Small Acts.
Christopher. Walt Whitman at the Reburial of Poe.
Citino. Walt Whitman in New Orleans, 1848.
Cohen, J. Walt Whitman in Ohio.
Conoley, G. Walt Whitman in the Car Lot, Repo or Used.
Cope, David. Labor Day.
Crane, H. Cape Hatteras.
Cutler, B. February 12, 1865.
Dacey, P. Whitman: The Wall.
Dahlberg. Walt Whitman.
Derricotte. Whitman, Come Again to the Cities.
Di Piero. Walt, the Wounded.
Doty, M. Letter to Walt Whitman.
Eberhart, R. Centennial For Whitman.
Emanuel, L. Walt, I Salute You!
Fein, Richard. To Walt Whitman.
Ferlinghetti, L. Poem for Old Walt.
Forbes, C. Reading Walt Whitman.
Freisinger. Walt Whitman at Timber Creek.
Fried, D. Story Having to Do with Walt Whitman, A.
Gannon, Thomas. Meeting the Master.
García Lorca. Ode to Walt Whitman ("Along the East River and the Bronx.").
Gardinier. Memorials: "Walt Whitman I lay on the grass today."
Ginsberg, A. I Love Old Whitman So.
Supermarket in California, A.
Glass, Jesse. Lecturing on Walt Whitman and Emily Dickinson in China.
Goldbarth. Poem of the Praises, The.
Goldberg, B. Whitman's Confession: In the Cleft of Eternity.
Graham, M. Matthew Brady Speaks of Whitman.
Harrison, J. Ghazal 39: "If you laid out all the limbs from the Civil War hospital."
Hass, R. Futures in Lilacs.
Heyen. Bread: "I'm standing in elm shadow."
Hirsch, E. Whitman Leaves the Boardwalk.
Hoffman, D. Crossing Walt Whitman Bridge.
Honig, E. [Walt Whitman]: "W / A / L / WHITMAN."
Hoover, P. Whitman in a Corner.
Hughes, L. Old Walt.
Hummer, T. Walt Whitman in Hell.
Ignatow, D. Walt Whitman in the Civil War Hospitals.
Jacobik, G. Under the Sign of Walt Whitman.
Jiménez, J. Walt Whitman: "But do you really want to see Whitman's house instead of Roosevelt's?"
Jong, E. Testamant (Or, Homage to Walt Whitman).
Komunyakaa, Y. Kosmos [2003].
Kowit. Whitman Portrait, A.
Krapf. Civil War Veteran from Indiana Recalls Visiting with Walt Whitman in a Washington Hospital, A.
Kraushaar, M. Dear Mr. Whitman.
Kushner, B. In the Hairy Arms of Whitman.
Levis. Whitman.
Liu, T. Reading Whitman in a Toilet Stall.
Lux. Walt Whitman's Brain Dropped on Laboratory Floor.
Mason, D. Whit for Whitman, A.
McNiece, R. Letter Left On the Porch of the Kerouac House.
Miranda. Second-Born Son: Lines for Walt Whitman Composed on Nantucket Island.
Mitchell, R. To Walt Whitman on America's Birthday.
Moffett. Reaching Around.
Moss, S. Postcard to Walt Whitman from Siena.
Nelson, H. Reading "Crossing Brooklyn Ferry" on a Summer Morning.

Nemerov. Modern Poet, A.
Neruda. Ode to Walt Whitman.
Olds, S. Nurse Whitman.
Piccione. With Whitman at the Friendship Hotel.
Plumly. Reading with the Poets.
Pound, E. Pact, A.
Rawls, Alex. Song of Myself by Walt Whitman.
Robinson, E. Walt Whitman: "Master-songs are ended, and the man, The."
Rottman. Porter on the Trail, A.
Sadoff. Against Whitman.
Savoie. Reading Whitman's *Democratic Vistas*.
Schevill. Whitman Stock-Taking, Cataloguing.
Seely, Shane. Walt Whitman at the Irish Festival, Syracuse, New York: Four Snapshots.
Shaw, R. Last Days in Camden.
Simpson, L. Walt Whitman at Bear Mountain.
Skloot. Whitman Pinch Hits, 1861.
Smith, D. With Walt Whitman at Fredericksburg.
Smith, George Jay. When Helen Keller Spoke.
Spicer, J. Book of Galahad, The.
Stafford, W. For You, Walt Whitman.
Suermondt, Tim. Briefly Eavesdropping on Walt Whitman, Virginia, 1863.
Symonds. Love and Death: A Symphony.
Thou dost establish—and our hearts receive—.
Tabakow, Phil. Walt Whitman at Pfaff's: A Fantasy.
Taylor, B. Night the Eighth: Camerados.
Torgerson. Apple from Walt Whitman, An.
Wagoner, D. Walt Whitman Bathing.
Waldman, A. On Walt Whitman's Birthday.
Wang Yin. Walt Whitman: "He is simply chopping wood in my front yard."
Weiss, T. Good Grey Poet, The.
White, G. Walt Whitman Encounters the Cosmos with the Cats of New York.
Whitman, W. I celebrate myself, and sing myself.
Now Precedent Songs, Farewell.
Walt Whitman, a kosmos, of Manhattan the son.
York, Jake Adam. Walt Whitman in Alabama.

Whittier, John Greenleaf
Heard, J. To Whittier.
Koch, K. You Were Wearing.

Widows and Widowers
Akhmatova, A. As if with a straw.
Bateman, M. After the Funeral.
Beatty, J. Pittsburgh Poem.
Behlen, Charles. Widow Zebach.
Berggolts [*or* Bergholts]. Don't turn around, don't look back.
Bowering, M. Widow's Winter.
Brecht, B. What Did the Nazi Send His Wife?
Buson. Home for three days.
Clifton, L. She Lived.
Copus, J. Widower.
Coward. Bar on the Piccola Marina, A.
Craik. Douglas, Douglas, Tender and True.
Crawford, R. Downtown Sunday.
Davies, R. Widow.
Drayton. Queen Katherine to Owen Tudor.
Dyer, C. My Dearest Dust: Epitaph on the Monument of Sir William Dyer at Colmworth, 1641.
"Eliza.". To My Husband.
Espaillat. Find Work.
Fields, J. Jolly Fat Widows, The.
Gallagher, T. Widow in Red Shoes.
Gilbert, S. June 15, 1992: Widow's Walk, Harpswell, Maine.
Glück, L. Racer's Widow, The.
Hands, E. Widower's Courtship, The.
Hardy, T. At the Draper's.
Harris, P. Next Malcolm Poem, The.
Hemans. Edith; a Tale of the Woods.
Herarty, T. Cyclus.
Herrick. Widow's Tears [*or* Widdowes Teares]: or, Dirge of Dorcas, The.
Hesketh. Dilemma.
Jarrell, R. Burning the Letters.
Jewell, Terri L. Felled Shadows.
Jewett, S. Widows' House, The.
Kercheval, J. Your Wife, a Widow, Waits for

You.
Kharms. Death of the Wild Warrior.
King, H. Exequy, The.
Kizer, C. Widow in Wintertime, A.
Komunyakaa, Y. Way the Cards Fall, The.
Kooser. Widow, A.
Lloyd, C. On the Death of Priscilla Farmer.
Martial. Agriculture.
Masters, E. Veterans of the Wars.
 Widows.
McGinnis, M. Widow Opening Her Heart, The.
Mei Yao Ch'en. Sad Remembrance.
Milton. On His Deceased Wife.
Montague, J. Dowager.
Moulsworth, M. Memorandum of Martha
 Moulsworth, Widow, The.
Patterson, G. BLS.
Phaedrus. Widow and the Soldier or: The
 Measure of a Woman's Inconstancy and Lust,
 The.
Po Chü-i. To a Young Widow.
Poe. Annabel Lee.
Sagan. Open the Door.
Senryū, K. You're in the prime.
Smith, S. He Told His Life Story to Mrs.
 Courtly.
Sŏ Chŏngju. Great Wave, The.
Southey, R. Soldier's Wife, The.
 Widow, The.
Stafford, W. Widow.
Steele, T. Fae.
Stevenson, A. Musician's Widow.
Su Tung-p'o. Remembering My Wife.
Sze. Moon Is a Diamond, The.
Tennyson, A. Tears of the widower, when he
 sees.
Unknown. Bo-zhou: Like a Lonely Bark.
 Far Away.
Voigt. Exile.
Williams, K. I Watched.
Williams, W. Widow's Lament in Springtime,
 The.
Wilson, R. Rejoicing That Attends the Murder
 of Famous Men, The.
Wordsworth, W. Experiment that Failed, An.
 Ruined Cottage, The.
Wotton, S. Upon the Death of Sir Albert
 Morton's Wife.

Wigs
Hemphill. Homocide.
Rossetti, C. If a pig wore a wig.

Wilde, Oscar
Auden. Oscar Wilde.
Betjeman. Arrest of Oscar Wilde at the
 Cadogan Hotel, The.
Crane, H. C33.
Douglas, L. Dead Poet, The.
Elmslie, K. Venus Preserved.
Hardie, K. Stranger.
O'Connor, U. Oscar Wilde.
Parker, D. Oscar Wilde.

Wilderness
al-Rahim, A. Who?
Atwood. Further Arrivals.
 Journey to the Interior.
Baraka, I. Lefty.
Berry, W. Peace of Wild Things, The.
Birney. Bushed.
Chang K'o-chiu. At Waterfall Temple.
Chen Zi'ang. Meditation on the Past at White
 Emperor City.
Cook, W. Spiritual: "How did you feel when
 you come out the wilderness?".
Davidson, D. Sanctuary.
Dickson, S. Song—Written at the North.
Everson, W. High Embrace, The.
George, F. Wilderness.
Goodtimes. Art of Getting Lost, The.
Graves, R. Rocky Acres.
Greene, Richard. Utopia.
Guillén, J. Nature Alive.
Han-shan. Body Asking Shadow.
Hecht, A. Alceste in the Wilderness.
Hopkins, G. Inversnaid.
Jacobsen, J. Bush.
Kao Shih. North Tower of Golden Fort, The.

Le Pan. Country without a Mythology, A.
 Coureurs de Bois.
Lee, L. Table in the Wilderness, A.
Lewis, A. Grey monkeys gibber, ignorant and
 wise.
Liu Tsung-yüan. From the City-Tower of
 Liuzhou To My Four Fellow-Officials at
 Zhang, Ding, Feng, and Lian Districts.
Milosz, C. Matthew 4:1–11; Then Jesus was led
 up by the spirit.
Mother Goose. Man In the Wilderness Asked
 [of] Me [or said to me], The [or A].
Réda, Jacques. Autumn Distance.
Rutsala. Wilderness.
Sandburg, C. Wilderness.
Schneiders, J. Weight.
Scott, F. Laurentian Shield.
Simmons, J. In the Wilderness.
Smith, A. Lonely Land, The.
Snyder, G. Above Pate Valley.
 Message from Outside.
Stevens, W. Anecdote of the Jar.
Tollet. Winter Song.
Tu Mu. Wilderness, A.
Unknown. Go in the Wilderness.
 I'm Going Home.
Whitman, W. Alone far in the wilds and
 mountains I hunt.
 Italian Music in Dakota.
Wilbur, R. Man Running.

Wildflowers
Kenny, M. Wild Flower.
Krylova, E. Cornflowers.
Mazur. Bluebonnets.
Rossetti, D. Woodspurge, The.
Unknown. My lover prefers well mannered
 garden flowers.
Williams, W. Queen Anne's Lace.

**William III, King of England (William of
 Orange)**
Pugh. King Billy on the Walls.
Watts, I. On the Landing of William III [or A
 Hymn of Praise for Three Great Salvations].

Williams, Theodore Samuel ("Ted")
Corso. Dream of a Baseball Star.

Williams, William Carlos
Berrigan, T. In Joe Brainard's collage its white
 arrow.
 Sonnet LIX: "In Joe Brainard's collage its white
 arrow."
Berryman. 324. Elegy for W. C. W., the Lovely
 Man, An.
Blackburn, P. Phone Call to Rutherford.
Bly, R. Dream of William Carlos Williams, A.
Clements, Brian. Historia.
Creeley. For W. C. W ("Rhyme is after, The.").
Eady. William Carlos Williams.
Enzensberger, H. In Memory of William Carlos
 Williams.
Gambino. This Is Just to Say.
Ginsberg, A. Death News.
 Written in My Dream by W. C. Williams.
Hernández Cruz. Essay on William Carlos
 Williams, An.
Kinnell. To William Carlos Williams.
Koch, K. Variations on a Theme by William
 Carlos Williams.
Kreymborg. To W. C. W. M. D.
Levertov. September 1961.
 Williams: An Essay.
Niedecker. If I Were a Bird.
Scott, J. Typing the Letters.
Spicer, J. Red Wheelbarrow, The.
Stone, J. Getting to Sleep in New Jersey.
Williams, F. Reply (crumped on her desk).
Young, G. Letter to William Carlos Williams,
 A.
Zukofsky, L. William / Carlos / Williams /
 alive!

Willow Herbs
Issa. My spring is just this.
Ray, J. Rose Bay Willow Herb.

Willow Trees
Ammons. White Echo.
Basho. To the willow.

 With a warbler for.
Bell, M. To an Adolescent Weeping Willow.
Bly, R. Hunting Pheasants in a Cornfield.
Buson. Willow leaves fallen, The.
Chiyojo. Bearing no flowers.
Crane, H. Repose of Rivers.
Delmore, E. Willow.
Gladding. Blue Willow.
Gu Cheng. Willow Jar.
Haavikko. Soul against the state, The.
Herrick. To the Willow-Tree.
Hongnang. I send you, my love.
Ikkyu Sojun. Oh green green willow
 wonderfully red flower.
Liu Yin. Miscellaneous Poem on Rural Life.
Lumbreras, E. Overflowing Willow.
 Regresión del sauce.
 Regression of the Willow.
 Sauce desbordado.
MacDiarmid, H. Sauchs in the Reuch Heuch
 Hauch, The.
Pack, R. Thrasher in the Willow by the Lake,
 The.
Quasimodo. From the Willow Branches.
Rossetti, C. Under Willows.
Rossetti, D. 49: Willowwood ("I sat with Love
 upon a woodside well").
 51: Willowwood ("O ye, all ye that walk in
 Willowwood").
Unknown. Do Not Pluck Me.
Wang Chien. Willow.
Williams, W. Willow Poem.
Yen Chen. On the Willow Bank.

Wills
Arghezi. Testament.
Brown, G. Ikey: His Will in Winter Written.
Carruth, H. Testament.
Donne. Will, The.
Du Tû' Lě. What I Leave to My Son.
Fogel, A. Printer's Error, The.
Leapor. Mira's Will.
Lewis, G. Language's Will and Testament, The.
Martial. You gave Bithynicus thousands yearly;
 still.
McGrath, T. Last Will and Testament.
Rossetti, C. Bruised Reed Shall He Not Break,
 A.
San Juan. Owl of Minerva Takes Flight in the
 Evening, The.
Unknown. Lord Randal[l].
Whitney, I. Aucthour Maketh Her Wyll and
 Testament, The.
 I whole in body, and in mind.
 Manner of Her Will and What She Left to
 London and to All Those in It, at Her
 Departing, The.
Winstanley, J. Last Will and Testament, A.

Wilmot, John, 2d Earl of Rochester.
See **Rochester, John Wilmot, 2d Earl of**

Wiltshire, England
Sassoon, S. Prehistoric Burials.

Winchester, England
Betjeman. Hike on the Downs, A.

Wind
al-Musawi, S. Four Beats of the Heart.
Alakoye. Eshu.
Alberti. Warlike Angels, The.
Aleixandre. Closed.
Ammons. Grassy Sound.
 Mansion.
 Small Song.
Armstrong, J. Winds: "Winds moving clouds."
Austin, A. Flocks of the wandering waves I
 hold, The.
Aygi, G. Beginning from the Field.
Bang, M. Crossed-Over, Fiend-Snitched, X-ed
 Out.
Barba-Jacob. Song of the Fleeting Day.
Barnes, W. Wind at the Door, The.
Basho. Autumn wind / Blasting the stones.
 Banana tree, The.
 Blowing stones.
 Tomb, bend / To autumn wind—.
 What voice.
 Winter solitude.

Wintry wind.
You've heard monkeys crying.
Beachy-Quick, Dan.   Flag-Tree.
Beckett, S.   Enueg 1.
Bécquer, G.   As the Breeze that Cools the
   Blood.
   Gentle Breeze with a Whispered Cry, The.
Berrigan, T.   Each tree stands alone in stillness.
Blake, W.   Crystal Cabinet, The.
Bogan, L.   Zone.
Borisov.   What Freedom Said.
Brand, D.   Wind.
Brontë, E.   Night Wind, The.
Brooke, R.   Sonnet: "Oh! Death will find me,
   long before I tire."
Brown, G.   Haddock Fishermen.
Bryant, W.   Summer Wind.
Bryher.   Thessalian.
Burns, R.   Of A' the Airts [the Wind Can Blaw].
   O[h] Wert Thou in the Cauld Blast.
Buson.   Autumn breezes.
   Evening wind.
   Going home.
   Gust of wind, A.
   In a bitter wind.
   Slung over a screen.
   Tub with no bottom, A.
   Wind in the west / Fallen leaves.
   With no underrobes.
Carew, T.   Prayer to the Wind, A.
Chamberlain, K.   Riding the Lion, Riding the
   Lamb.
Ch'i-chi.   Song of the Spring Wind.
Chivers.   Wind, The.
Coleridge, M.   Lord of the winds, I cry to Thee.
Coleridge, S.   Homeric Hexameter, The.
Cox, M.   Sonata.
Crapsey.   Night Winds.
Cucchi, M.   Every season has its dead.
Cummings, E. E.   What If a Much of a Which
   of a Wind.
   Wind has blown the rain away and blown, A.
Dafydd [or David] ap Gwilym.   Wind, The.
   Wind, The.
Daive.   Under the wind.
Damas.   Wind, The: "Wide sea—black night—I
   woke up lovesick."
Davies, W. H.   Villain, The.
Davis, O.   Panic of Birds, The.
Day Lewis.   Stand-To, The.
Deguy.   When the wind.
Desnos.   If, like winds.
Dickinson, E.   There came a Wind like a Bugle.
   Wild Nights—Wild Nights!
   Wind begun to knead the Grass, The.
   Wind's Visit, The.
   Wind—tapped like a tired man, The.
Doolittle, H.   Heat.
   Sea Rose.
Dowson.   Villanelle of Marguerites.
Dugan, A.   On an East Wind from the Wars.
Dybek.   Windy City.
Eady.   Success.
Éluard, P.   Deaf and Blind, The.
Emerson, R.   Snow-Storm [or Snowstorm], The.
Eytan Eytan.   Wind Grinds, The.
Faigao, B.   Balitaw.
Field.   O Wind, thou hast thy kingdom in the
   trees.
Forrester, S.   Autumn wind.
   Backyard sun shower.
   Plum blossom breeze.
   Winter wind.
Freneau.   Rude, from the wide extended
   Chesapeke.
Frost, R.   Aim Was Song, The.
   Bereft.
   Brown's Descent; or, The Willy-Nilly.
   Wind and Window Flower.
Gascoyne.   Yves Tanguy.
Gillespie, H.   Breezin' Along with the Breeze.
Glazer, M.   Box.
Graham, J.   Gulls.
   Of Forced Sightes and Trusty Ferefulness.
Graves, R.   Weather of Olympus, The.
Gu Cheng.   Feel of the Wind, The.

Gunn, T.   Elegy on the Dust.
Gurney, I.   April Gale.
   Possessions.
Hamill, S.   What the Water Knows.
Han Yong'un [or Yongwun].   I Cannot Know.
Harjo, J.   Santa Fe.
Haviaras, Stratis.   Stone-Throw.
Hesiod.   Winter.
Hine.   Riddle: "Invisible, chimerical."
Ho Hsun.   Spring Wind.
Hoban.   Pedalling Man, The.
Howe, F.   Veteran.
Hsüeh T'ao [or Xue Tao].   Wind.
Hughes, T.   Wind.
Hugo, R.   Spinazzola: Quella Cantina Là.
Hwang Tonggyu.   Wind Burial 1.
   Wind Burial 3.
İnce.   Wind, Ant, History.
Inp'yŏng, Prince.   Don't mock a pine.
Issa.   Autumn wind / Mountain's shadow.
   Autumn wind / The beggar looks.
   Before this autumn wind.
   Cool breeze.
   O autumn winds.
   Prostitute's shack, The.
   Windy fall.
Izumi.   Although the wind.
Jaccottet.   Right at the end of night.
Jackson, L.   Wind Suffers [of Blowing], The.
   Wind, the Clock, the We, The.
Jacobsen, R.   Crust on Fresh Snow.
Jeffers, R.   Gale in April.
Jungkwan Ilson.   At Daedun Temple.
Kang [Grossjean], Ok-Ku [or Ok-Koo].   Wind:
   "Like a well-trained soldier."
Kang Ŭn'gyo.   Leaves of Grass.
Kasa.   I shall think of you.
Kawamura Yoichi.   On the Sand Dune.
Kgositsile.   Gods Wrote, The.
Kherdian.   Wind rips through the.
Ki no Tsurayuki.   Wind that scatters, The.
Kim Chiha.   Truth.
Kingsley, C.   Ode to the Northeast Wind.
Koehler, T.   Ill Wind.
Kooser.   Hands in the Wind.
Kreymborg.   Improvisation.
Krolow.   Wind in the Room, The.
La Fontaine.   Phoebus and Boreas.
Lane, P.   Wind Thoughts.
Lawrence, D. H.   Butterfly.
   Suspense.
Le Guin.   Child on the Shore, The.
Levin, D.   Wind.
Lewis, Emyr.   Mad Magnet of a Wild Wind.
Li'aibi, S.   Butterfly frozen in stone, A.
Lisnyanskaya [or Lisnianskaia].   Wind blows
   and makes the light tremble, The.
Liu Pang.   Song of the Great Wind.
Loerke, Oskar (1884-1941).   Winter Evening,
   Berlin.
Loseff [/or Losev].   Petrograd Side, The.
MacCarthy, C.   Island of Miracles.
Macdonald, G.   Wind and the Moon, The.
Machado Ruiz.   Breeze Tells Me, Loved One,
   The.
   Wind, One Brilliant Day, The.
MacLeish.   Cook County.
Magidson, H.   Gone with the Wind.
Mahon.   Window, The.
Markham, M.   Rock in the Garden Allows
   People In, The.
Martinson.   Sea Wind, The.
Masaoka Shiki.   Autumn wind / Gods, Buddha.
Masefield.   Trade Winds.
   West Wind, The.
Meddeb, Abdelwahab.   On Forgotten Tracks.
Merwin.   Utterance.
Meynell, A.   To the Beloved.
   Wind Is Blind, The.
Milova, V.   I've overslept my stop. . .the train
   will spit me out.
Moore, L.   Homeplace, The.
Morikawa Kyoroku.   Even the dumplings / Are
   smaller.
Morley, D.   Politicisation of the North Wind,
   The.

Morris-Jones.   Wind's Lament, The.
Mother Goose.   When the wind is in the east.
Muldoon, P.   Wind and Tree.
No Hyangnim.   Windy Day.
Onitsura.   Autumn wind / Across the fields.
   Cherry blossoms, The.
Ortiz.   Vision Shadows.
Osundare.   Eyeful Glances.
Oswald, A.   Excursion to the Planet Mercury.
Ou-yang Hsiu.   East Wind.
Pak Mogwŏl [or Mokwŏl].   Bare Wind, A.
Pak Nohae.   Wind to the Stones, The.
Pak Sŏwŏn.   Wind God Sends Forth, The.
Pasos, J.   This Is Not Her.
Pasternak, B.   As With Them.
   Wind, The.
Paz.   Wind and Water and Stone.
Perk.   Iris.
Phillips, D.   Hounds are either the work of wind,
   The.
Po Chü-i.   Cranes, The.
Porter, H.   Four Winds.
Probyn.   Rondelet: "Say what you please."
Quasimodo.   Street in Agrigento.
Radcliffe, A.   To the Winds.
Ransetsu.   Single leaf falls, A.
Reese, L.   Wind.
Reznikoff.   [Winter Sketches III].
Ridge, L.   Fifth-Floor Window, The.
   Kerensky.
Rilke.   O you lovers that are so gentle, step
   occasionally.
   Walk, A.
Robertson, R.   Affair of Kites.
Robinson, E.   New England.
Roethke.   Big Wind.
   Child on Top of a Greenhouse.
   Mid-Country Blow.
Roland Holst.   Autumn Wind.
   Beggar Love.
Rose, P.   Wind Debates Asian Immigration, The.
Rosen, M.   From the winter wind.
Rossetti, C.   Who Has Seen the Wind?
   Wind Has Such a Rainy Sound, The.
Rothman, D.   When the Wind and Dark Waves
   Come.
Rubin, L.   North of Amsterdam.
Rumann, Son of Colman.   Storm at Sea.
Salaam.   Our Natures Rise.
Sandburg, C.   Four Preludes on Playthings of
   the Wind.
   Wind Song.
Sanguineti.   Wind shoves my New Year's Day
   sun in my face, The.
Sargent, E.   Sea-Breeze at Matanzas, The.
Segal, J.   Wind in the Willow.
Shakespeare, W.   Amiens's Song.
   Song: "When that I was and a little tiny boy."
Shelley, P.   Dirge, A: "Rough wind, that
   moanest loud."
Shepherd, R.   Maritime.
Shih Shu.   After Shih-te ("I climb these hills as
   if walking on air.").
Shiki.   O autumn winds.
Shokushi.   Guide me on my way.
"Shunzei's Daughter.".   Brought by the breeze.
Simms, C.   Pallid Harrier.
Simonides.   No leaf-shaking blast of winds.
Sŏ Chŏngju.   Like a Wind from Lotus
   Blossoms.
Sogetsuni.   After the Dance for the Dead.
Soloukhin.   Wind, The.
Southern Bushmen Oral Tradition.   Day We Die,
   The.
Stanley, G.   Rupert Winds.
Steele, T.   Library, The.
Stephens, J.   Wind, The.
Stevens, W.   Valley Candle.
Stevenson, A.   Gales.
Strand.   Marriage, The.
Sub-ok.   Spring at Yesan Station.
Sung Yu.   Wind, The.
Supervielle.   Missing France.
Suzuki, M.   Monastery gate.
Tada.   Wind Invites Wind.
Takai Kito.   Contending / Temple bell.

Taylor, A.   Air.
Taylor, H.   At South Fork Cemetery.
Teasdale.   After Love.
Teiga.   In the poor man's house.
Thompson, J.   Turnip Field.
Torres, E.   Breezy Delicious Day.
Tu Fu [or Du Fu].   My Thatched Roof Is Ruined by the Autumn Wind.
   South Wind.
Turner, F.   April Wind.
Tzu Yeh.   I had not fastened my sash over my gown.
U T'ak.   Wind that melted the spring hills, The.
Unknown.   All too soon, I fear.
   Autumn.
   Autumn: "Autumn wind sweeps in through the windows, The."
   Breeze, you who blow from the mountainside where my lover fights.
   I Have a Young Sister.
   Levis Exsurgit Zephirus.
   No weather is ill.
   Riddle: "High as the sky it flies."
   Song of the Trees.
   Two Spring Charms.
   Western Wind.
   Wind Last Night Blew Down.
   Withered, withered, by the wind's omen.
Van Eeden, F.   North Wind, The.
Veiga.   Wind of Liberty.
Velichansky, A.   Trunks of birches, like scrolls.
Verlaine.   Cold wind hurls itself at, A.
Vietnamese Oral Tradition.   Linked Verses.
Virgil [or Vergil].   Aeolus Looses the Winds.
Warren, R.   Blow, West Wind.
Weinberger, E.   Wind: "Wind: what is it? You don't see it but you hear it, and you feel its force."
Wescott.   Poet at Night-Fall, The.
White, M.   Recurrence.
Wilbur, R.   After the Last Bulletins.
   Sleepless at Crown Point.
Williams, W.   Black Winds, The.
   January.
Wilson, Emily.   Wind in bare vines.
Wordsworth, D.   Address to a Child during a Boisterous Winter Evening.
Wu of Han [or Wu Ti or Ou-ty or Liu Ch'e or Liu Ch'u].   Autumn Wind, The.
Yesenin [or Essenin].   Winds, Winds, Winds.
Yu Xuanji.   At Home in the Summer Mountains.
Yusuf, S.   Attention.
Zabolotsky [or Zabolotskii].   Popryshchin.
Zisquit.   There is always a sound.
Zurita, R.   Splendor in the Wind.
See also **North Wind; Tornadoes; West Wind; East Wind**

Windflowers.
See **Anemones**

Windhovers.
See **Falcons**

Windmills
Bergman, A.   Windmills of Your Mind, The.
Bergman, M.   Windmills of Your Mind, The.
Clarke, G.   Windmill.
Goldberg, L.   Song of the Strange Woman.
Huidobro.   So you're a windmill.

Window Washing and Window Washers
Kearns, J.   Moving Furniture.
Thompson, P.   Window Washing.

Windows
Aichinger.   Glimpse from the Past.
Bedregal.   Gestures From My Window.
Bei Dao.   Collection, The.
Bremer, C.   En la ventana.
   In the Window.
Brodsky, J.   I Sit by the Window.
Brooks, G.   Boy Breaking Glass.
Browning, E.   I heard last night a little child go singing.
Cary, A.   Window Just Over the Street, The.
Chŏng Chiyong.   Windowpane I.
Corbet [or Corbett].   Upon Fairford Windows.
Cummings, E. E.   Spring is like a perhaps hand.
Daryush.   Still-Life.

Davis, J.   Zoo, The.
Davis, O.   Panic of Birds, The.
Dickinson, E.   I had been hungry, all the Years.
Dunn, D.   From the Night-Window.
Field.   Nightfall.
Fishman, L.   V's Farmhouse.
Fuertes.   Painted Windows.
Gonzáles Martínez.   Window, The.
Grennan.   Woman at Lit Window.
Grubb, D.   Windows of Sarajevo, The.
Heaney, S.   Skylight, The.
Herbert, G.   Windows, The.
Huws, Meirion MacIntyre.   Window.
Ibáñez, S.   I Cannot.
Jackson, L.   Prisms.
Jiménez, J.   Lavender Windowpanes and White Curtains.
Johnson, K.   Meadow, The.
Lane, P.   Girl at the Window.
Langille.   Sadness of Windows, The.
Larkin, P.   Aubade: "I work all day, and get half-drunk at night."
Levertov.   Crack, The.
Lindsay, V.   Factory Windows Are Always Broken.
Longfellow, H.   Ropewalk, The.
Lysohorsky.   At a Sunlit Window.
Machado Ruiz.   Her Street Is Dark.
Madhubuti.   After Her Man Had Left Her for the Sixth Time That Year (An Uncommon Occurrence).
Mahon.   Window, The.
Mallarmé.   Saint.
Mew.   On the Asylum Road.
Millay, E.   From a Train Window.
Moore, H.   Window at Key West, A.
Nemerov.   Storm Windows.
Nemes Nagy.   Four-Light Window, A.
Paino.   1965.
Palmer, M.   Untitled (February 2000).
Parnok, S.   Through a Window-Light.
Prado, A.   Stained Glass Window.
Raab, L.   Sudden Appearance of a Monster at a Window.
Rankine.   New Windows.
Reed, H.   Door and the Window, The.
Ridge, L.   Fifth-Floor Window, The.
Rossetti, C.   Reflection.
Roubaud.   Meditation of 8/5/85.
Shange.   Tango.
Smith, I.   Old Woman, The.
Spellman, A.   Beautiful day, The V.
Synge.   Dread.
Taggart, J.   Sainte-Chapelle.
Thomas, R. S.   View from the Window, The.
Vitale, M.   Who trusteth in hilarity.
Wallace-Crabbe.   Windows, The.
Whalen, P.   Pet Shop.
Williams, W.   Young Woman at a Window.
Yavuz, Hilmi.   Windy Windows.
Zagajewski.   Moths.

Windsor Castle
Denham.   Cooper's Hill.
Surrey.   Prison in Windsor Castle.

Wine
Al-Bayati, A.   Three Ruba'iyat.
Aldrich, H.   Catch, A.
Archpoet.   His Confession.
Ayres.   Fly, The.
Bhatt, S.   Wine from Bordeaux.
Buson.   Two men drink wine at the only table.
Carruth, H.   Quality of Wine.
Cassells.   From the Theater of Wine.
Ceravolo.   After the Rain.
Clements, A.   Elegy.
Dickinson, E.   Let me not thirst with this Hock at my Lip.
Doolittle, H.   Wine Bowl.
Dubrava.   Miraculous Marriage of Zarife Dominquez.
Emerson, R.   Bacchus.
Faiz.   Before You Came.
Garrett, E.   Moules à la Marinière.
Garza.   Why I Make the Best Barrels.
Goldsmith, O.   Entry of the Villagers.
Ha-Levi, J.   Summer.

Hafiz, K [or Hafez].   As Rich as Solomon (21).
   Fish in Deep Water, The (144).
   Ghazal: Half-Way Through the Night.
   Light of my eyes, there *is* something to be said.
   Night Visit, The (22).
Han Yü.   Discontent.
Herrick.   His Farewell [or Fare-well] to Sack.
   To Live Merrily, and To Trust to Good Verses.
Hô Sugyông.   One at Rest, The.
Hofmannsthal.   Two of Them, The.
Hsin Ch'i-chi.   Tune: "Moon of the Western River".
Huerta, D.   Pathological Beings.
   Seres patológicos.
Hwang Hŭi.   Are chestnuts falling.
Ibn Arfa' Ra'suh.   Singing Lute, The.
Ibn Bājja.   Trail the edge of your robe wherever it pleases, and add more drunkenness to your intoxication.
Ibn Hamdīs, A.   I remember a certain brook that offered the impiety of drunkenness to the topers [sitting] along its course, with [its] cups of golden [wine].
Kooser.   How to Make Rhubarb Wine.
Kuan Han-ch'ing.   Tune: "Four Pieces of Jade".
Lee, N.   Nay, *Clytus*, you that cou'd advise—.
Li Po.   Bring On the Wine.
   Drinking Alone in the Moonlight.
   Drinking Alone in the Moonlight.
   Old Tai's Wine Shop.
   Remembering Our Excursion in the Past.
   Take Wine.
   Wine.
Li Qi.   To Zhang Xu.
Liu Ling.   Hymn to the Virtue of Wine.
Lu Chih.   Tune: "Drunk in the East Wind".
Machado Ruiz.   Poem: "We think to create festivals."
Martial.   You serve the best wines always, my dear sir.
Moiro.   Beneath Aphrodite's golden portico you now lie.
Moore, M.   Camellia Sabina.
Nonnus.   But Dionysos had no healing physic for his comrade fallen, of dancing he thought no more.
Olds, S.   This Hour.
O'Rourke, D.   Wine and Wooing.
Ou-yang Hsiu.   Tune: "Gathering Mulberry Leaves".
Page, G.   In Dante's Hell.
Pankey.   Reason, The.
Po Chü-i.   Lodging with the Old Man of the Stream.
Redi.   Bacchus's Opinion of Wine, and Other Beverages.
Rilke.   John 2:1–12; On the third day there was a marriage.
   On the Marriage at Cana.
Rumi.   That moon which the sky never saw.
Sanguineti.   So it takes very little indeed: a brasserie.
Sapgir.   Dionysus.
Senryū, K.   Even in the time of gods.
Shen Chou.   Taoist Huang Has Died of Alcoholism, The.
Steele, P.   Cana.
Sterling, G.   Ballad of the Grapes.
Su Tung-p'o.   Tune: "Fragrance Fills the Courtyard".
T'ao Ch'ien [or T'ao Yuan-ming].   Two Poems Written While Drunk.
Thomas, D.   This Bread I Break.
Tibullus.   Fill up my glass again! The anodyne.
Tighe.   Wine, I Say! I'll Drink to Madness!
Trần Tế Xu'o'ng.   Women.
Tu Fu [or Du Fu].   Climbing on the Double Ninth Day.
Tu Mu.   Tower by the Yangtze River, A.
Unknown.   Drinking Wine.
   I'm sixty, this autumn.
Wang Han.   Song of Liang-chou.
Wilkinson, J.   Torn Ones, The.
Williams, G.   Winemaking.
Winters, Y.   In Praise of California Wines.
Yen Shu.   Tune: "Treading on Fragrant Grass".

Yi Kyubo.   Sung Impromptu.
Wings
Agustini.   Wings, The.
Andrews, N.   That Cold Summer.
Asim, J.   Memory of Wings.
Barot, R.   Reading Plato.
Beachy-Quick, Dan.   Nightbook.
Bingen, Hildegard von.   Antiphon for Divine
    Wisdom.
Brontë, C.   Like wolf—and black bull or goblin
    hound.
Day Lewis.   Conflict, The.
Dickinson, E.   Bat, The.
Dove, R.   Wingfoot Lake.
Field, E.   Icarus.
Fumi Saito.   With wings that will not ever.
Haslam, M.   01 84.
Herbert, G.   Easter Wings.
Hopkins, G.   God's Grandeur.
Iio Sogi.   Night frost / Pulsing wings.
Ku Sang.   Wings.
Levertov.   Dead Butterfly, The.
    Wings, The.
Masaoka Shiki.   Such silence / Snow tracing
    wings.
Mataka.   Ornithology.
Meyerhoff, J.   Three Ravens.
Newman, A.   Architecture of the Wings, The.
Reid, C.   Fetish.
Robinson, A.   Song: "Oh for the wings of a
    dove."
Rossetti, C.   On the Wing.
Ryan, K.   Paired Things.
Sappho.   Beneath its wings.
    Their souls became cold.
Sewell, L.   Expulsion.
Sexton.   To a Friend Whose Work Has Come to
    Triumph.
Smith, C.   On the Aphorism "L'Amitié est
    l'Amour sans Ailes".
Stewart, S.   Wings.
Unknown.   Wings.
Vlasova, E.   There is a way to sew wings on
    arms.
Warren, R.   Evening Hawk.
Watson, R.   Cage, The.
Yeats.   Mother of God, The.

Winnie-the-Pooh
Behn, R.   Yellow House Writes a Story for the
    Boy, The.

Winter
Acorn.   That Corrugated Look To Water.
Aichinger.   Enumeration.
Akhmatova, A.   Such Days as These.
Alegría.   We Were Three.
Allingham, W.   In Snow.
Ammons.   Looking Way Off.
Anderson, P.   Sestina in Time of Winter.
Annensky.   Capitol, The.
Bachmann.   Land of Fog.
Baillie, J.   Winter's Day, A.
Barclay, A.   Winter.
Barnes, W.   Winter Night, A.
Bartlett, B.   Shuffles.
Basho.   Dried salmon.
    First winter rain.
    I'm a wanderer.
    On New Year's Day.
    On the cow shed.
    When the winter chrysanthemums go.
    Winter garden.
    Winter leeks,The.
    Winter rain.
    Winter seclusion—.
    Winter showers.
    Winter solitude.
    Winter storm, The.
    Winter sun, The.
    Wintry day / On my horse.
Berryman.   Winter Landscape.
Binyon.   Winter Sunrise.
Bishop, E.   Paris, 7 A.M.
Bishop, J.   Aliens.
Bleakney, J.   Winter Solstice.
Blind.   Winter Landscape, A.
Bly, R.   Six Winter Privacy Poems.

When My Dead Father Called.
Borisov.   And when the winter wind rushed
    straight into my heart.
Boyarskikh, E.   Person is reflected by the
    whirlpool, not the face, A.
Bradstreet, A.   Winter: "Cold, moist, young
    phlegmy Winter now doth lie."
Brody.   Winter Nocturne: The Hospital.
Brooks, G.   Cynthia in the Snow.
Brown, L.   Winter Sonnet.
Brown, S.   Virginia Portrait.
Bryant, W.   Death of the Flowers, The.
    Scene on the Banks of the Hudson, A.
    Winter Piece, A.
Bu-er.   Late Indian summer's.
Burlingame.   Late Winter in West Texas.
Burns, R.   Up in the Morning Early.
Busceti, G.   Dissonances.
Buson.   Bamboo hat, straw coat—.
    Blow of an ax.
    By moonlight.
    Cover my head.
    Ferry departs, The.
    Flowers offered to the Buddha.
    Flying squirrel, A.
    Going home.
    Light winter rain.
    My ax sinks in.
    Nobly, the great priest.
    Roots of the camphor tree.
    Sound of a saw.
    That handsaw marks time.
    This cold winter night.
    Winter rain on moss.
    Winter warbler.
Buxton.   Putting the World to Bed.
Bynner.   Wintry Mind, The.
Cahn, S.   Let It Snow! Let It Snow! Let It
    Snow!
Campion, T.   Now Winter Nights Enlarge.
Campo.   Begging for Change in Winter.
Chang Chi.   Maple Bridge Night Mooring.
Char.   Dowry of Maubergeonne, The.
Chia Tao.   Evening View as the Snow Clears.
Chiasson, D.   Song for a Play.
Ch'in Kuan.   Along the Grand Canal.
Chinnov.   Black bird on a black and snowy
    branch, A.
Cho, P.   One Wintry Day.
Cho Sik.   Wearing hemp clothes in the coldest
    winter.
Ch'oe Sûngja.   Do You Remember Ch'ôongp'a
    Street?
Chula, M.   This Winter's Night.
Clare, J.   Winter.
    Winter Winds Cold and Blea.
Clark, L.   Singing in the Streets.
Coleridge, M.   Witch, The.
Collins, Martha.   Epiphany.
Collins, Mortimer.   Winter in Brighton.
Cope, J.   Winter Sky.
Cowper, W.   Just when our drawing-rooms
    begin to blaze.
    Winter Evening, The: A Brown Study.
Cranch.   December.
Crapsey.   Arbutus.
Cristall.   Snow-Fiend, The.
    Song: "Through springtime walks, with flowers
    perfumed."
Crowe, T.   Winter Moon Haiku.
Crozier, L.   Excellence in the Small. Tears
    Frozen on Your Face.
Cummings, E. E.   I was sitting in mcsoreley's.
    outside it was New York and beauti- / fully
    snowing.
Daniel, G.   Robin, The.
Davies, J.   Winter.
Davis, W.   Overnight Winder: Texas.
Davison, P.   Frozen Drought.
Day Lewis.   Winter Night.
De la Mare.   Winter ("Clouded with snow / The
    cold winds blow.").
    Winter ("Green Mistletoe! / Oh, I remember
    now.").
Dickinson, E.   I think the Hemlock likes to
    stand.

There's a certain Slant of light.
    Tree in Winter.
    'Twas here my summer paused.
Dillon, G.   Snow.
Donne.   Nocturnal[l] upon Saint Lucy's [or S.
    Lucy's or S. Lucies] Day, Being the Shortest
    Day, A.
Doolittle, H.   Blue-geese, white-geese, you may
    say.
Dugan, A.   Glad at the Cold (1955).
Eberhart, R.   Spider, The.
Eigner.   Open Air Where.
Eliot, T. S.   Journey of the Magi.
    Little Gidding.
Emperor Ch'ien-wen of Liang.   Getting Up in
    Winter.
Erdrich, H.   Quiet Earth, The.
Evance, S.   To Melancholy.
Fallon, P.   Winter Work.
Farrar, J.   Comparison, A.
Ferguson, G.   Winter Rose, The.
    Winter Sunflowers.
Field, M.   Sullenness.
    To the Winter Aphrodite.
Field, R.   Something Told the Wild Geese.
Finch, B.   Written in a Winter's Morning.
Follain.   Music of Spheres.
Ford, Katie.   Flesh.
Frost, R.   Birches.
    Good Hours.
    Hillside Thaw, A.
    Old Man's Winter Night, An.
    Onset, The.
    Reluctance.
    Stopping by Woods on a Snowy Evening.
Fulton, R.   Note for Robert Henryson, A.
Gerner, K.   House of Breath.
Gibbs, Robert J.   Kind of Wakefulness, A.
Gilbert, J.   White Heart of God, The.
Glück, L.   Illuminations.
Goetsch, D.   Nobody's Hell.
Gorbanevskaya.   Savage cold of Russian
    winters, The.
Grant, Peter.   Winter Resolve.
Graves, R.   Frosty Night, A.
    Star-Talk.
Greenberg, A.   Wintering Over at the End of the
    Century.
Grimké, A.   Winter Twilight, A.
Grumman, Bob.   Mathemaku No. 16.
Guidacci.   Map of the Winter Sky, The.
Guillory, D.   Retinal burn of warm November
    light.
Hall, D.   Her Long Illness.
Hamill, S.   Rising.
Han-shan Te-ch'ing.   Bone-chilling snow on a
    thousand peaks.
    Snow obstructs my brushwood door with me
    inside alone.
    Solitary winter lantern casts a feeble shadow, A.
Hardy, T.   Birds at Winter Nightfall.
    Frozen Greenhouse, The.
    I Need Not Go.
    Neutral Tones.
    Winter in Durnover Field.
Harjo, J.   Skeleton of Winter.
Hauge.   Midwinter. Snow.
Hayden, R.   Those Winter Sundays.
Hayman, R.   To a Worthy Friend, Who Often
    Objects the Coldnesse of the Winter in
    Newfound-Land.
Hayne, P.   On the Occurrence of a Spell of
    Arctic Weather in May, 1858.
Hecht, A.   Sestina d'Inverno.
Henry, P.   Winter Wedding, The.
Henson, L.   I Am Singing the Cold Rain.
Herlin.   Warmth of the wind-break wall, The.
Hesiod.   Beware of the month Lenaion, bad
    days.
    Winter.
Heym.   With the Ships of Passage.
Hierro, José.   Fe de vida.
Hine.   After the Solstice.
Hölderlin.   Winter.
Hollander, J.   Effet de Neige.
Hopes.   Don't think the stars and moon are all.

On the Feast of Saint John the Evangelist.
When the wolf moon howls, when the juncos.
Hopkins, G.   Winter with the Gulf Stream.
Horan.   Soft Swimmer, Winter Swan.
Horsley, K.   Winter Grieving Poem.
Housman.   Night Is Freezing Fast, The.
Huchel.   Landscape Beyond Warsaw.
Hughes, R.   Winter.
Hughes, T.   New Year's [or Year] Song.
Roe-Deer.
Snowdrop.
Hugo, R.   Letter to Hill from St. Ignatius.
Hunter, A.   Winter.
Hunter, C.   Two Thousand and Two.
Iio Sogi.   Life in this world.
Im Yŏngjo.   Winter Tree.
Issa.   Give me a homeland.
No talent.
Vanity of men, The.
Winter fly, The.
Ivanov, V.   Winter Sonnets, The.
Jaimes Freyre.   Sad Voices, The.
Jauss.   Quotations for a Winter Evening.
Jewett, S.   Country Boy in Winter, A.
Jordan, J.   Winter.
Kantaris.   Stocking Up.
Kaplinski, J.   We started home, my son and I.
Keithley.   First Morning.
Kell.   Spring Night.
Kennedy, X.   One Winter Night in August.
Kenny, M.   December.
Kenyon, J.   Depression in Winter.
February: Thinking of Flowers.
Walking Alone in Late WInter.
Killeen, G.   Wishes.
Klink, J.   Porch in Snow.
Knoepfle.   Late Winter in Menard County.
Kopland.   Breughel's Winter.
Lampman.   In November: "Hills and leafless
forests slowly yield, The."
Winter Evening.
Langille.   Scanning an Afternoon in Winter.
Lea, S.   Tempted by the Classical on Returning
from the Store at Twenty Below Zero.
Levertov.   Crack, The.
Levine, P.   On the Birth of Good and Evil
During the Long Winter of '28.
Lewis, G.   Woods: "Midwinter and this beech
wood's mind."
Lewis, J. Patrick.   Stories.
Lewis, Janet.   Winter Garden.
Li Ho.   Cold in the North (After Yueh-Fu).
Liu Tsung-yüan.   River Snow ("These thousand
peaks cut off the flight of birds.").
Snowy River.
Llwyd, M.   Winter, The.
Locke, M.   Sonnet: "I hate the Spring in parti-
coloured vest."
Lombardy, Anthony.   Shall I Compare Thee . . .
?
Longenbach.   What You Find in the Woods.
Longfellow, H.   Afternoon in February.
Fragment: December 18, 1847.
Snow-Flakes.
Longley, M.   Remembering Carrigskeewaun.
Lovelace, R.   Grasshopper, The [To My Noble
Friend Mr Charles Cotton: Ode].
Lowell, R.   Inauguration Day: January 1953.
New Year's Day.
MacCaig.   Sleet.
Macdonald, G.   Sweet Peril.
Machado Ruiz.   Recuerdo Infantil.
MacLaine, Brent.   North Shore Park.
Maeng Sasŏng.   Winter comes to rivers and
lakes.
Majer.   On my winter walk.
Mallarmé.   This virginal long-living lovely day.
Virginal, vibrant, and beautiful dawn, The.
Virginal, Vivid, Beautiful, Will This Be.
Markus, P.   Shooting Crows.
Martinson.   No Name for It.
Matveyeva [or Matveieva].   Eggplants Have
Pins and Needles, The.
Mayor, C.   Driving Away.
Winter Night.
McAuley, J.   Winter Drive.

McGough, R.   Cinders.
McGrath, T.   Black Train, The.
McNiece, R.   Bare birch mountainside.
Merwin.   Dusk in Winter.
Miles, S.   Plumbers.
Miliauskaite.   On Winter Nights.
Millay, E.   Winter Night.
Milligan, Bryce.   Trusting steel.
Mok, J.   Winter Mirror.
Winter Mirror II.
Momaday.   Winter Holding off the Coast of
North America.
Monnier, Pascalle.   Winter.
Montgomery, Judith H.   Ophelia, in Winter.
Morgan, F.   Winter Poem.
Morris, L.   Poem of the Frost and Snow.
Morton, A.   Shortest Day.
Mueller, L.   Another Version.
Murray, A.   Winter Night, Glencoe.
Muso Soseki.   Snow.
Nameroff, R.   California Dreaming.
Nash, O.   Winter Morning.
Neshâtî.   Sky's face has turned dark, don't
believe, The.
Neumann, S.   Winter Night.
Newton, Violette.   Mythology of Snow, A.
Ngo Chi Lan.   Winter.
Nibenegenesabe.   Quiet Until the Thaw.
Niedecker.   Swept snow, Li Po.
No Hyangnim.   Country Where Snow Has Not
Yet Fallen, A.
O'Brien, S.   After Laforgue.
Oliver, M.   Crows.
Foxes in Winter.
Olsen, W.   Winter, Voyeurism.
Opie.   To Winter.
Oppen.   From a Photograph.
Osgood, F.   Winter Fairyland in Vermont.
Owen, G.   Winter Days.
Owen, W.   Exposure.
Parini.   Function of Winter, The.
Pasternak, B.   Winter Night.
Winter Night: "Snow, snow over the whole
land."
Paz.   Solo for Two Voices.
Peake.   Conceit.
Peaux, A.   Old Houses on the Quays.
Pfeiffer, E.   Song of Winter, A.
Philips, A.   Winter-Piece, A.
Plath.   Wintering.
Po Chü-i.   Sitting at Night.
Winter Night.
Potocki, W.   Winter, Before the War.
Pound, E.   Ancient Music.
Quasimodo.   Dead of Winter.
Rakosi.   Fluteplayers from Finmarken.
Ramler.   Yearning for Winter.
Ramsay, A.   Up in the Air.
Reznikoff.   [Winter Sketches I].
Richard, M. C.   Snow: "White moths in crazy
mobs."
Rickword.   Winter Warfare.
Rizdvenko, T.   Frost and sun, as needed.
It was such a pearly, pink season.
Roberson, E.   Blue Horses.
Roberts, S.   Winter Fields, The.
Robinson, M.   January, 1795.
Rochester, J.   Mistress, The: A Song.
Roethke.   Coming of the Cold, The.
Rossetti, C.   Amen.
Christmas Carol, A: "In the bleak mid-winter."
Winter: My Secret.
Rothman, D.   Let It Snow.
Ryan, R.   Lake of the Woods, The.
Winter in Minneapolis.
Ryokan.   Late at night, listening to the winter
rain.
Saarikoski.   Winter solstice.
Samyn, M.   Trompe L'Oeil in Winter.
Sansom, A.   Confinement.
Santos, S.   Augury.
Sarton, M.   On a Winter Night.
Satterfield, J.   Wintering.
Scott-Heron.   Winter in America.
Scupham.   After Ovid, Tristia.
Seward.   December Morning.

While one sere leaf, that parting autumn yields.
Sexton.   Landscape Winter.
Shakespeare, W.   Amiens's Song.
Holla, Approach.
Sonnet 97: "How like a winter hath my absence
been[e]."
Winter: "When icicles hang by the wall."
Shelley, P.   Summer and Winter.
Shiki.   In the winter river.
Shin Kyŏngnim.   On a Winter's Night.
Shumaker.   First Winter: Joy.
Simic.   February: "One who lights the wood
stove, The."
Winter Night.
Simmons, J.   Archæologist, The.
Simonides.   As whenever.
Sirr.   Collector's Marginalia, The.
Smith, C.   Still Winter (Spring).
Smith, Douglas Burnet.   Skull.
Smith, M.   Stopping to Take Notes.
Snyder, G.   Dragonfly.
Sŏ Chŏngju.   Winter Sky.
Solari, R.   December 25, 1991.
Soutar.   Winter Beauty.
Southey, R.   Wrinkled, crabbèd man they picture
thee, A.
Stafford, W.   Shepherd.
Steeves, Andrew.   Winter Marsh.
Stevens, W.   Annual Gaiety.
Course of a Particular, The.
Snow Man, The.
Stevenson, R.   Winter Time [or Winter-Time].
Stroud, J.   Oh Yes.
Stryk, L.   Winter Storm.
Suhl.   Winter: "Now winter's standing at the
door."
Sutter.   Hoarfrost and Fog.
Synge.   Winter.
Tabb.   Winter Twilight, A.
Takai Kito.   Contending / Temple bell.
Tan Taigi.   Temple in / Deep winter grove.
Tate, A.   Seasons of the Soul.
Taylor, A.   Fire.
Taylor, C.   Winterdirge.
Teasdale.   Night.
Thaxter.   Chanticleer.
Thomas, E.   Thaw.
Thompson, P.   Winter Night, A.
Thomson, J.   For, see! where Winter comes,
himself, confest.
Keener tempests come: and fuming dun, The.
Thoreau.   Pray to what earth does this sweet
cold belong.
Winter and Spring Scene, A.
Thrale [later Mrs. Piozzi].   Winter in Wales, A.
Tomlinson, C.   Weather Report.
Trail, C.   Sonnet: "This is for the afternoon we
lay in the leaves."
Trakl.   Winter Night, A.
Triplett, P.   Winter Swim.
Tu Fu [or Du Fu].   Deep in Winter.
Facing the Snow ("Northern snows invade the
city.").
Turner, W.   Song: "Lovely hill-torrents are."
Twichell.   Pine.
Unknown.   Bei-feng: Cold Is the North Wind.
De Ramis Cadunt Folia (Love in Winter).
Hidden-in-winter.
Night Was Growing Cold, The.
Prayer at the Winter Thanksgiving.
Snowy Day, A.
Song of Winter, A.
Wind piercing, hill bare, hard to find shelter.
Winter.
Winter, The.
Winter Wise.
Wynter Wakeneth Al My Care.
Vale, Edmund.   Bowl Over, Wheel.
Valentine, J.   Snow Landscape, in a Glass
Globe.
Valéry.   Helen ("O Light, 'tis I, who from
death's other shores.").
Vallejo.   Our Daily Bread.
Van Walleghen.   Elephant in Winter, The.
Vanshenkin.   Forest in winter, The! From edge
to edge.

Vaughan, H.   I Walked [or Walkt or Walk'd] the Other Day to Spend My Hour.
Verlaine.   Endless sameness.
Very.   Spirit, The.
Winter Rain, The.
Volkman.   I believe there is a song that is stranger than wind, that sips the scald from the telling, toss, toss.
Walcott.   Village Life, A.
Waldman, A.   Icy Rose.
Wanek.   Duluth, Minnesota.
Watson, E.   Natural.
Watts, Enos D.   Crocuses and Crown-of-Thorns.
Weslowski.   Heart.
White, H.   Winter Traveler, The.
Whitman, W.   To a Locomotive in Winter.
Whittier.   Snow-Bound [or Snow-Bound] [A Winter Idyl].
Wilbur, R.   April 5, 1974.
Sonnet: "Winter deepening, the hay all in, The."
Year's End.
Williams, M.   Heading for the Heights.
Williams, W.   These.
Willis, N.   January 1, 1829.
Wingfield.   Winter.
Wolfe, M.   Thaw, The.
Wordsworth, D.   Address to a Child during a Boisterous Winter Evening.
Wright, C.   As Our Bodies Rise, Our Names Turn into Light.
Christmas East of the Blue Ridge.
Winter-Worship.
Wright, D.   Winter at Gurnard's Head.
Wright, F.   Sitting Up Late with My Father, 1977.
Wright, James.   I slouch in bed.
Sparrows in a Hillside Drift.
Wright, Jay.   Boleros #36.
Desire's Persistence.
Wright, Judith.   Sonnet for Christmas.
Wright, R.   On winter mornings.
Wylie.   Puritan Sonnet.
Velvet Shoes.
Xiao Zihui.   Winter Dawn.
Yasui.   Who's that?
Yearsley.   To———: "Lo! dreary Winter, howling o'er the waste."
Yi Yuksa.   Summit, The.
Yoshida Issui.   Swans.
Yu Hsin.   Season of Shadow, The.
Yu Ŭngbu.   Do you say the wind blew last night.
Zanzotto.   Epiphany.
Zenmaro.   Tanka: "All the young men I know."
Zondberg, O.   Cockle-antarctica / has been cast up onto the shore.

Wisconsin (state)
Eberhart, R.   La Crosse at Ninety Miles an Hour.
Finney, Janice.   Lightning and Thunder.
Wallace, R.   Makings of Happiness, The.

Wisdom
Aeschylus.   God, whose law it is that he who learns must suffer.
Arnold, M.   Shakespeare: "Others abide our question. Thou art free."
Atwood.   Procedures for Underground.
Babu, S.   Sex Everywhere.
Berry, W.   Heaviness of His Wisdom, The.
Bingen, Hildegard von.   Antiphon for Divine Wisdom.
Blake, W.   Auguries of Innocence.
What is the price of Experience? Do men buy it for a song.
Bogan, L.   Men Loved Wholly Beyond Wisdom.
Brecht, B.   Three Fragments.
Chénier.   Happy is he given to sage disciplines.
Chimombo.   Messengers, The.
Cowper, W.   Wisdom.
Crane, H.   Praise for an Urn.
Crane, S.   I met a seer.
Crashaw.   Neither Durst Any Man From That Day Ask Him Any More Questions.
Creeley.   En Famille.
Cummings, E. E.   You Shall Above All Things Be Glad and Young.

Davenant [or D'Avenant].   Lover and Philosopher.
Davison, P.   Star Watcher, The.
Dickinson, E.   We learned the Whole of Love.
"Why do I love" You, Sir?
Duggan, L.   Eight xx.
Eclipse.   Cicada.
Emerson, R.   Limits.
Fabian, C.   Prayer of Dedication.
Forrest-Thomson.   Garden of Proserpine, The.
Goedicke.   Meaning of Life, The.
Goethe.   Song from the Coptic, A.
Gottlieb, A.   Meditation on the Feminine Nature of Shekinah, A.
Guiney.   Kings, The.
Hacker, M.   Rune of the Finland Woman.
Hafiz, K [or Hafez].   Ghazal 24: For Years My Heart Asked Me for Jamshid's Cup.
Han-shan.   There's a naked bug at Cold Mountain.
Herbert, G.   Elixir [or Elixer], The.
Hewitt, J.   Once Alien Here.
Hillman, B.   Adult Joy.
Hixon, L.   Who can keep a blazing fire tied in a cotton cloth?
Hölderlin.   In the Days of Socrates.
Ismail.   Donkeys in Anantapur.
Jeffers, R.   Prescription of Painful Ends.
Jiménez, J.   Intelligence, Give Me.
Juan Chi.   As Dew-Drops Freeze.
Learning.
Kim Chŏngnan.   Leafy Plant of Wisdom, A.
Kochanowski, J.   I'd Buy You, Wisdom.
Lal Ded [or Lalla].   On the way to God the difficulties.
Lao Tzu.   Without going out-of-doors.
Lawrence, D. H.   Race and Battle.
Li Po.   For Meng Hao-Jan.
Macdonald, G.   Baby-Sermon, A.
Makeda (Queen of Sheba).   I fell.
Wisdom is / sweeter than honey.
Maybe, E.   Umbilical Cord.
Menicanti.   If.
Merrill, J.   World and the Child, The.
Mirabai [or Mira Bai].   Wild woman of the forests, The.
Montagu, L.   Lover, The; a Ballad.
Morabito, F.   Elefantes nacen viejos, Los.
Elephants are born old.
Moses.   Hands, The.
Muso Soseki.   For Gen the New Head Priest of Erin-ji.
For Ko Who Has Come Back from China.
For Myo's Departure for Anzen-ji.
I wake from my noon nap.
Jewel Cliff.
Old Man at Leisure.
Nesbit, E.   Things That Matter, The.
Nguyen, Hoa.   Dark.
Nijhoff.   Musician, The.
Nossis.   Even from a distance, this picture is known.
"Novalis.".   When geometric diagrams and digits.
Ono.   Mother of the Universe.
Ortiz.   On late-night television, two U.S. scientists talk about why the U.S.
Owen, M.   African Sunday.
Pelizzon, V.   Clever and Poor.
Philips, A.   Wit and Wisdom.
Porter, B.   First Time Going to School All by Myself.
Ransom, J.   Tall Girl, The.
Rexroth, K.   Homer in Basic.
Richardson, J.   Vectors: Forty-five Aphorisms and Ten-second Essays.
Ríos, A.   Advice to a First Cousin.
Robinson, A.   Wise-Woman, The.
Robinson, E.   Master, The.
Rossi, T.   Leaving.
Rothman, D.   Youth.
Ruefle.   Topophilia.
Rumi.   Love and Silence.
Two Kinds of Intelligence.
Rupp.   Sophia.
Santayana.   When I discover that the substance

of the beautiful is a certain rhythm.
Sassoon, S.   Wisdom of the World, The.
Scott, G.   What Was Solomon's Mind?
Shih Shu.   Enlightenment.
Shushtarī, A.   Little shaikh from the land of Meknès sings in the middle of the marketplaces, A.
Sill.   Truth at Last.
Smith, C.   Thirty-eight: Addressed to Mrs H—y.
Smith, S.   Is It Wise?
Sowle, J.   Short Testimony for Anne Whitehead, A.
Stevenson, A.   He Who Loved Beauty.
Swift, J.   Stella's Birthday [1721].
Stella's Birthday ([March 13,] 1727).
Tachibana Akemi.   Pleasure is / when you rarely cook.
Tennyson, A.   I will not shut me from my kind.
Thomas, D.   Should Lanterns Shine.
Thomas, E.   Glory, The.
Tolson, M.   African China.
Tsogyel.   Listen.
Tufts, C.   We Take the New Young Couple Out to Dinner.
Unknown.   Epitaph for Cu Chuimne.
Humble Petition of a Beautiful Young Lady, The.
Lofty trees of the south, The.
Lü-yi: Green Robe.
Voice, A.
Words of the All-Wise, The.
Van Doren.   Slowly, Slowly Wisdom Gathers.
Van Dyke.   Reliance.
Various authors.   His nature being one with Heaven.
Wang An-shih.   Had I been an ox or horse.
Whalen, P.   Sourdough Mountain Lookout.
Whitman, W.   When I Heard the Learn'd Astronomer.
Winner, R.   Segregated Railway Diner—1946.
Winter, M.   In the Beginning.
Wojahn.   Allegory: Attic and Fever.
Wordsworth, W.   Resolution and Independence.
Wright, J.   Gum-trees Stripping.
Yates, D.   Century Plant.
Yeats.   Coming of Wisdom with Time, The.
Yeryomin.   Faceted grains of wisdom.
Yosano Akiko.   And then one morning.
Zabolotsky [or Zabolotskii].   Face of a Horse, The.
See also **Reason**

Wisemen
Doolittle, H.   When in the company of the gods.
Kuan Hsiu.   I came in a dream to a mountain in the sea.
Kuzmin.   Were I a general of olden times.
Segalen.   In Praise of Jade.
See also **Magi**

Wishes
Archilochus.   May he lose his way on the cold sea.
Belli, G.   What Might Have Been.
Bingxin.   Springwater, Part 105.
Bowles, W.   To a Friend.
Chudleigh.   Wish, The.
Clare, J.   Wish, A ("Be where I may when death brings in his bill.").
Coleridge, M.   Insincere Wish Addressed to a Beggar, An.
Cook, W.   Spiritual: "How did you feel when you come out the wilderness?".
Cowley, A.   Wish, The.
Creeley.   In London.
Cruickshank, H.   Wishin' Well, The.
Dante Alighieri.   Love and Poetry.
Darwish, M.   On Wishes.
Du Tū' Lê.   What I Leave to My Son.
Emmens, J.   Lion of Judah, The.
Greenwell, D.   Scherzo, A.
Harburg.   If I Only Had a Brain (If I Only Had a Heart) (If I Only Had the Nerve).
Over the Rainbow.
Harnick.   If I Were a Rich Man.
Heyen.   Wish.
Hipponax.   Still Waiting for My Winter Coat: A Sequence of Fragments.

Housman. If truth in hearts that perish.
Jarrell, R. Man Meets a Woman in the Street, A.
Kahal, I. I Can Dream, Can't I?
Kahn, G. Carolina in the Morning.
When My Ship Comes In.
Kelleher, D. For C. K. at His Christening.
Ki Joon. Elegy for Myself.
Killeen, G. Wishes.
Lamantia. Time Traveler's Potlatch.
Lamb, L. William Lamb's Return from Paris, Asking Me My Wish.
Larkin, P. Born Yesterday.
Lu Yu. To Show to My Sons.
Marston, P. Vain Wish, A.
McGinley. Reflections at Dawn.
Neruda. Ode to the Cat.
Nibenegenesabe. I try to make wishes right.
Padilla. Self-Portrait of the Other.
Paljor, N. Wish of my Amala, The.
Pellicer, C. Wishes.
Pilkington, L. Wish, By a Young Lady, The.
Poe. Stanzas.
Pollard, C. I enjoy dancing.
Porter, A. Five Wishes.
Rimbaud, A. Runt of a Dream, A.
Rogers, S. Wish, A.
Salter. What Do Women Want?
Sandburg, C. Mag.
Shakespeare, W. Blossom, The.
Sissle, N. I'm Craving for That Kind of Love.
Stein, G. Wish, A.
Stewart, S. Dark the Star.
Sutphen, J. Wishbone USA.
Tanikawa, S. Request.
Teasdale. Moods.
Sanctuary, The.
Tzu Yeh. When I started wanting.
Unknown. I wish I was.
Malediction.
Wishing Poem.
Vala. Bridge.
Vasileva, E. I wish I could look.
Weatherly, T. Fishes / theirs fit.
Yeats. He Wishes for the Cloths of Heaven.
Yo Inlŏ. Meditating on the Start of a New Era.

Wisteria
Basho. Exhausted, I sought.
Tired.
Buson. In pale moonlight.
Healy, E. Wisteria.
Masaoka Shiki. Sprays of wisteria.
Sprays of wisteria, The / arranged in a vase.
Muso Soseki. All on my own I'm happy.
Smith, R. Illumination.

Wit
Calverley. Flight.
Carroll, L. Father William.
Cowley, A. Ode: Of Wit.
Martial. Out of an Epigram of Martial.
Pope, A. Impromptu: To Lady Winchelsea Occasioned by Four Satirical Verses on Women Wits, In *The Rape of the Lock.*
Vaughan, H. To the Most Excellently Accomplished Mrs. Katherine Philips.
Winchilsea. Introduction, The: "Did I, my lines intend for public[k] view."

Witchcraft and Witches
Abercrombie. Witchcraft: New Style.
Alvarez, J. Sonnet 1: "Everything that happens to me these days."
Benét, R. *et al.* Cotton Mather.
Benét, S. Cotton Mather.
Bennett, R. Witch of Willowby Wood, The.
Boychuk. Fairy Tale, A.
Burns, R. Tam o' Shanter; A Tale.
Clifton, L. In Salem.
Coleridge, M. Witch, The.
Witches' Wood, The.
Cooley, N. Mary Warren's Sampler.
Mother: Dorcas Good, The.
Publick Fast on Account of the Afflicted: March 31, 1692.
Crapsey. Witch, The.
Cummings, E. E. Hist whist / little ghostthings.
De la Mare. As Lucy Went A-Walking.

Ride-by-Nights, The.
Dizhur. Eve's Monologue.
Frost, R. Witch of Coös, The.
Gertsyk, A. Spring.
Gowar. Annabell and the Witches.
Hogg, J. Witch o' Fife, The.
Witch's Chant, A.
Housman. Her Strong Enchantments Failing.
Issa. Withered fields, The.
Jackson, G. 1691. Tituba of Salem.
Johnson, J. White Witch, The.
Kim Sŭnghŭi. Between Saint and Witch.
Kuskin. Witches' Ride, The.
Leigh, C. Witchcraft.
Li Ho. Magic Strings.
Livingston, M. Lazy Witch.
Mora. Bruja: Witch.
Ovid. Before the Moone should cirlcewise close both hir hornes in one.
Parra, N. Tunnel, The.
Pavlova. Crone, The.
Pfeiffer, E. Witch's Last Ride, The.
Piatt, S. Witch in the Glass, The.
Reed, I. Black Cock, The.
Reznikoff. Beggar Woman.
Robinson, A. Wise-Woman, The.
Ronsard. Invective Against Denise, a Witch.
Rossetti, D. 78: Body's Beauty.
Santal. Witch, The.
Scott, W. Witch's Ballad, The.
Sexton. Her Kind.
Simic. Modern Sorcery.
Speyer. Witch!
Unknown. Queen Nefertiti.
Villanueva, A. Power.
Walker, M. Molly Means.
Whittier. Changeling, The.
Yeats. Song of Wandering Aengus, The.

Wittgenstein, Ludwig Josef Johann
Fox, Skip. I cannot observe myself unobserved.
Mahon. Tractatus.
Mouré. Wittgenstein Letters to Mel Gibson's Braveheart, The.
Olin. Like Beatrix Potter.
Riley, P. 1134. 39.

Wives
Adams, J. There's Nae Luck about the House.
Ai. Mother's Tale, The.
Aleixandre. In Front of the Mirror.
Alvi, M. Backgrounds.
Carrying My Wife.
Fish.
Man Impregnated.
Missing.
Bachinsky, E. ATM.
Baillie, J. Hooly and Fairly.
Bang, M. Crossed-Over, Fiend-Snitched, X-ed Out.
Baraka, I. For Hettie.
Barber, M. Advice to Her Son on Marriage.
Conclusion of a Letter to the Rev. Mr. C——, The.
Barnes, W. Wife a-Lost, The.
Beachy-Quick, Dan. Echo and A.
Berry, W. Marriage.
Bevington, H. Princess and the Pea, The.
Bhatt, S. Written After Hearing About the Soviet Invasion of Afghanistan.
Blamire. O Donald! Ye Are Just the Man.
Bloom, V. Sun-a-shine, Rain-a-fall.
Bottke, A. How to Approach Your Lover's Wife.
Boylan, G. Dames of Washington.
Breton, A. Free Union.
Brontë, C. Pilate's Wife's Dream.
Browning, R. Any Wife to Any Husband.
Carver, R. Bonnard's Nudes.
Cave. Elegy on a Maiden Name, An.
Chudleigh. To the Ladies.
Coleridge, M. Marriage.
Cowper, W. To Mary.
Cunningham, J. Epigram: "Here lies my wife. Eternal peace."
Davies, Lynn. When You Can't Leave Me Anymore.
Day, C. Who Drags the Fiery Artist Down?

Delgado, J. Recommitted.
Donne. Since whom[e] I loved [*or* lov'd *or* lovd] hath paid [*or* payd] her last debt.
Dove, R. Daystar.
Duffy, C. Anne Hathaway.
Dunbar, P. To Alice Dunbar.
Earl of Longford. Careful Husband, The.
Egerton, S. Emulation, The.
Erdrich. Leonard Commits Redeeming Adulteries with All the Women in Town.
Ezekiel. Song to be Shouted Out.
Galanskov. Bird-cherry was my wife, The.
Garry, F. Professor's Wife, The.
George, D. Asenath.
Gioia. Country Wife, The.
Goldsmith, O. Double Transformation, The.
Greene, R. Shepherd's Wife's Song, The.
Harington [*or* Harrington]. To His Wife, for Striking Her Dog.
Hartnett. Retreat of Ita Cagney, The.
Haynes, C. Any Wife or Husband.
Hikmet. Poems from Prison.
Hill, S. Being a Wife.
Hirsch, E. Husband and Wife.
Hồ Xuân Hương. General's Plaque, The.
Holst-Warhaft. Old Men of Athens, The.
Homer. Ulysses Reunited with Penelope.
Ibaragi Noriko. What a Little Girl Had on Her Mind.
Istarú, A. Crescent moon, A.
Jamie, K. Bogey-Wife, The.
Jarrell, R. Next Day.
Kaufman, S. Job's Wife.
Kavanagh, P. Tinker's Wife.
Kendrick, D. Sadie Snuffs a Candle.
Kirby, D. I Think I Am Going to Call My Wife Paraguay.
Korean Oral Tradition. Chŏngsŏn Arirang.
Wretched Married Life (Folk Song from Koch'ang).
Kossman. Pilate's Wife.
Layton. Berry Picking.
Lear, E. Limerick: "There was an Old Man on some rocks."
Leonard, W. That once the gentle mind of my dead wife.
Li K'ai-hsien. Parable, A.
Li Po. Lonely Wife, The.
Song of Ch'ang-Kan (Yueh-Fu), The.
Lim-Wilson. Ringmaster's Wife.
Lindsay, L. Auld Robin Gray.
Lowell, R. Old Flame, The.
Lux. Wife Hits Moose.
Martial. Out of an Epigram of Martial.
Masters, E. Mrs. Benjamin Pantier.
Mrs. Meyers.
McBride, M. Knife-Thrower's Wife, The.
Mei Yao Ch'en. Sad Remembrance.
Millay, E. Witch-Wife.
Milton. On His Deceased Wife.
Monck. Verses Written on Her Death-bed at Bath to Her Husband in London.
Mugo, M. G. Wife of the Husband.
Muhibbi. My very own queen, my everything.
Nash, O. Watchman, What of the First First Lady?
Nesbit, E. Wife of All Ages, The.
Newman, A. Darwin's Unfinished Notes to Emma.
Ó Dálaigh, M. Elegy on Mael Mhedha, his Wife.
Ogiwara Seisensui. I suck at.
Ondaatje. Cinnamon Peeler, The.
Ovid. I have been looking these pages over, my dearest wife.
Not so dear was Lyde to the Clarian poet, not so truly.
Pahmeier, G. Grief Comes in Smallest Ways.
Pastan. Marks.
Self-Portrait.
Pathabhi. Sita.
P'Bitek. Woman with Whom I Share My Husband, The.
Penn, R.E. Hand.
Petronius Arbiter. However, Eumolpus, our champion in time of trouble and the author of

the present harmony.
Prior.　Fable, A: "In Æsop's tales an honest wretch we find."
Probyn.　Mésalliance, A.
Purdy, A.　Alive or Not.
Radnóti.　Letter to My Wife.
Ramanujan.　Love Poem for a Wife, 2.
Reitenauer, Vicki L.　Wife Of.
Rexroth, K.　Andrée Rexroth ("Now once more gray mottled buckeye branches.").
　Andrée Rexroth ("Years have gone, The. It is spring.").
Ríos, A.　Teodoro Luna's Two Kisses.
Roethke.　Wish for a Young Wife.
Rossetti, C.　I caught a little ladybird.
Rungano.　Woman, The.
Sajé, N.　I am peeling four pink grapefruit.
Senryū, K.　Guy, The.
　His wife away from home.
Shiraishi.　Seven Cats Are Happy, The.
Simic.　At the Cookout.
Sims.　Garden Song, A.
Smedley, M.　Contrast, A.
Smith, W.　There Was an Old Woman Named Piper.
Stein, G.　Sacred Emily.
Stoddard, E.　Wife Speaks, The.
Storni.　Lyrical Letter to the Other Woman.
Strong, L.　Brewer's Man, The.
Tallie, M.　Note from a Loving Wife.
Thomas, E.　Forsaken Wife, The.
Tribal Chieftain.　Come here, my love, the crown of my home.
Ts'ao Chih.　In the northwest there is a Weaving-lady.
Unknown.　Annie of Tharaw.
　As I Was A-walking by Yon Green Garden.
　Ballad of the Mulberry Road.
　Grass by the River-Bank, The.
　Green beyond green, the grass along the river.
　He's to the War.
　In *Bath* a wanton wife did dwell.
　Jun-zi yu-yi.
　Old Poem.
　Ru-fen: Along Yew's Banks.
　Shady Grove.
　Song of a Foolish Wife.
　Substituted Poem of Laureate Quynh, The.
　Summer: "She has done with silkworms and the fieldwork."
　Wee Cooper of Fife, The.
　Where is my husband now?
　Wife's Lament, The.
　Woman Who Married a Caterpillar, The.
Velter, André.　My Wife I Sing.
Vietnamese Oral Tradition.　Bare Rocks and Stars.
　Colonial Troops Transport, The.
　Complaining about the Second Wife.
　Concubine, The.
　Husband and Wife.
Viorst.　Honeymoon is Over, The.
Wang Ch'ang-ling.　Complaint from a Lady's Chamber.
Watkyns.　Shrew, The.
Webster, A.　Love's Mourner.
Whur.　First-Rate Wife, The.
Wickham.　Sung in a Graveyard.
Williams, C. K.　Alzheimer's: The Wife.
Williams, W.　Mezzo Forte.
　Young Housewife, The.
Winchilsea.　Letter to Daphnis, A.
Winstanley, J.　Last Will and Testament, A.
Wotton, S.　Upon the Death of Sir Albert Morton's Wife.
Yi Chŏngbo.　When the owl hoots.
Yi Talch'ung.　Neglected Wife, The.
Young, D.　For a Wife in Jizzen.
Zhang Hua.　Emotion.
See also **Marriage**

Wolsey, Thomas, Cardinal
Skelton, J.　Such a prelate, I trow.

Wolverines
Tallmountain.　Brother Wolverine.

Wolves
Adam, H.　Song for a Sea Tower.

Al-Haidari, B.　Death in Four Voices.
Bierds, L.　It.
Blue Cloud.　Wolf.
Borisov.　And when the winter wind rushed straight into my heart.
Brontë, C.　Like wolf—and black bull or goblin hound.
Burnside, J.　Tundra's Edge.
Carson, A.　Wolf God, The.
Di Prima.　If he did not come apart in her hands, he fell.
　Les Americains.
Dragomoschenko.　March Elegy.
Duffy, C.　Little Red-Cap.
Durston.　Wolf, The.
Esquinca, Jorge.　Fable of the Hunter.
Grotz, J.　Wolf, The.
Gunn, T.　Allegory of the Wolf Boy, The.
Harjo, J.　Wolf Warrior.
Hogan, L.　Bear Fat.
Hughes, T.　Amulet.
　Modest Proposal, A.
Ivanov, Binyo.　Tale That's Not a Tale, A.
Kipling, R.　Hunting-Song of the Seeonee Pack.
Klee.　Wolf Speaks, The.
Kramer, L.　Immigrants.
Krasicki, I.　Lamb and the Wolves, The.
La Fontaine.　Wolf and the Stork, The.
MacLean, S.　Dogs and Wolves.
MacNeice.　Wolves.
Marie de France.　Wolf and the Lamb, The.
　Wolf and the Sow, The.
Marquis.　Aesop Revised by Archy.
Matthews, W.　Wolf of Gubbio, The.
McDonald, W.　Hauling Over Wolf Creek Pass in Winter.
More, S.　De Principe Bono et Malo.
　Good Princes and Bad.
Mortimer.　Wolves.
Nemerov.　Wolves in the Zoo.
Noyes, S.　Wolf's Road, The.
Phaedrus.　Wolf and the Lamb, The.
Popa.　Burning Shewolf.
Remizov, Alexei.　Eaten by the Wolf.
Rontsh, Y.　Wolves.
Seshadri.　Wolf Soup.
Tada.　Wind Invites Wind.
Tallmountain.　Last Wolf, The.
Tate, A.　Wolves, The.
Unknown.　Gray She-Wolf, The.
　Song of an Old Gray Wolf.
Walwicz.　Little Red Riding Hood.
Webster, J.　Call for the Robin-Redbreast and the Wren.
Yesenin [*or* Essenin].　Mysterious, Ancient World of Mine.
Zabolotsky [*or* Zabolotskii].　Poem about Rain.

Women
Acam-Oturu.　Arise to the Day's Toil.
Acholonu.　Water Woman.
"Ada.".　Appeal to Women, An.
　Scroll is open, The.
Adcock, F.　Soho Hospital for Women, The.
Addonizio.　Them.
Adisa.　Discover Me.
　No, Women Don't Cry.
Agosin.　Dance, The.
Akhmatova, A.　Sister, I have come to take your place.
Albert-Birot.　Balalaïka.
Alegría.　Accounting.
Alexander, P.　Person of.
Algarin.　Trampling.
Allen, P.　Dear World.
Alvarez, J.　Woman's Work.
Amadiume.　Bloody Masculinity.
　Oya Now.
Amichai, Y.　Ideal Woman, An.
　Ideal Woman, An.
Amis, K.　Sight Unseen.
Andreus.　For Some Future Day.
Angelou, M.　Family Affairs.
　Our Grandmothers.
　Woman Me.
Aristophanes.　How the Women Will Stop War.
Armantrout.　Getting Warm.

Arnold, C.　Disembodied Voices of Women, The.
Arp.　Man, The. The Woman.
Arrillaga.　Dream.
　Like Raquel.
Arteaga, Alfred.　Corrido Blanco.
Arturo, A.　Song of the Silent Night.
Ashur-Nasir-Pal.　Hymn to Ishtar.
Askhari.　Circular Fate.
Atwood.　Daphne and Laura and So Forth.
　Romantic.
　This story was told to me by another traveller.
Azad, R.　Woman: The Eternal.
Balbulus, N.　Hymn to Holy Women, A.
Bancquart.　Curriculum vitae.
　Woman asleep.
Bansode.　Woman.
Barbauld.　Rights of Woman, The.
Barber, M.　Conclusion of a Letter to the Rev. Mr. C——, The.
Barer, M.　Shall We Join the Ladies?
Bartlett, E.　Themes for Women.
Basho.　Now I see her face.
　Wrapping dumplings in.
Baudelaire.　Giantess, The.
Beer, P.　Footbinding.
　Jane Austen.
Behn, A.　To the Fair Clarinda [*or* Clorinda], Who Made Love to Me, Imagin'd [*or* Imagined] More than Woman.
Benn.　Before a Cornfield.
　Night Café.
Bennett, G.　To a Dark Girl.
Bennett, L.　Jamaica Oman.
Benton, S.　Lilith.
　Second Coming, The.
Berezan, J.　Hail Mother full of grace power is with thee.
Berk, İ.　Women: "They stand there and chat near the breakwater."
Berry, J.　Girls Can We Educate We Dads?
Berry, W.　Marriage.
Betham-Edwards.　Urge me no more! nor think, because I seem.
Betjeman.　Business Girls.
Blaser.　Image-Nation 22 (in memoriam).
Bogan, L.　Evening in the Sanitarium.
　Women.
Borson.　Talk.
Borum, Wille ("Memphis Willie B.").　Bad Girl Blues.
Bradstreet, A.　I am obnoxious to each carping tongue.
　In Honour of that High and Mighty Princess Queen Elizabeth of Happy Memory.
　Prologue, The: "To sing of wars, of captain[e]s, and of kings."
Braxton, J.　Conversion.
Breton, A.　Free Union.
　Free Union.
　Free Union.
Brontë, C.　Lonely Lady, The.
Brooks, G.　Mrs. Small.
　Sadie and Maud.
　To Black Women.
Broughton, T.　Shall I Compare Thee?
Broumas, O.　Calypso.
　Rapunzel.
Brown, K.　Lonely Women.
Brown, L.　Magnolia.
　Turn On the Heat.
Brown, M.　Village Woman.
Brown, S.　Feminine Intuition.
Browne, F.　Australian Emigrant, The.
Browning, E.　Lord Walter's Wife.
　To George Sand: A Desire.
　To George Sand: A Recognition.
Buchanan, O.　Walk, The.
Buchanan, R.　Bicycle Song (For Women).
Budapest.　Medea speaks: / This is God, children, listen up well. The.
Bukowski.　Way it is now, The.
Bunina.　Conversation between Me and the Women.
Burke, C.　Motor Oil Queen.
Burke, J.　Personality.

Burns, R. Bonnie Lesley.
Busia, A. Liberation.
Buson. Bats flitting here and there.
  With a woman friend.
Byron, G. She Walks In Beauty.
Cable, G. Belle Layotte.
Cambridge, A. Desire.
Campbell, J. Old Woman, The.
Campion, T. I Care Not for These Ladies.
Canan. Inanna's Chant.
  Mother Dawning.
  Oh Kali.
Caraion. Enveloping Echo, The.
Cardenal. Prayer for Marilyn Monroe.
Cardiff. Combing.
Carew, T. Rapture, A.
  Song[, A]: "Ask[e] me no more where Jove
  bestow[e]s."
Carolan [or O'Carolan]. Mabel Kelly.
  Peggy Browne.
Carruth, H. Sonnet: "To see a woman long
  oppressed by fear."
Carson, A. God's Woman.
Cary, P. Advice Gratis to Certain Women.
Cassells. Women, The.
Castellanos. Meditation on the Threshold.
  You Are Not Poetry.
Castillo, A. Women Are Not Roses.
Cataldi. It's Easy.
  We Could Have Met.
Catullus. Unto no body my woman saith she
  had rather a wife be [or bee].
Cavalli. I don't have any seed to cast about the
  world.
Cavendish, M. Of Many Worlds in This World.
  Woman drest by Age, A.
Cendrars. My Dance.
Ceravolo. Women, The.
Cervantes. Beneath the Shadow of the Freeway.
  Isla Mujeres.
  To We Who Were Saved by the Stars.
Chatterton. There Lackethe Somethynge Stylle.
Chaucer. Ballade: "Hide, Absalom, thy gilte
  tresses clear."
  Wife of Bath's Prologue, The.
  Wife of Bath's Tale, The.
Chipasula. Ritual Girl.
  Those Rainy Mornings.
Chrystos. Old Indian Granny, The.
Chudleigh. To the Ladies.
  Unhappy they, who by their duty led.
Cisneros, A. To a Dead Lady.
Cisneros, S. Loose Women.
Clampitt. Dodona: Asked of the Oracle.
Claus. Woman 12, A.
Cleveland, J. Antiplatonic[k], The.
Clifton, L. Calming Kali.
  Kali.
  Love the Human.
  Song at Midnight.
  Thirty-Eighth Year, The.
  Women You Are Accustomed To, The.
Clinton, M. Warning to Young Bright Sisters /
  White AM. Culture 101A.
Cofer, J. Old Women.
  Spring.
  Why There Are No Unicorns.
  Women Who Love Angels.
Cohen, L. Suzanne [Takes You Down].
Coleridge, M. Clever Woman, A.
  Marriage.
  White Women, The.
Collier, M. Womans Labour, an epistle, The.
Collins, B. Man in Space.
Collins, J. Big World Look Out.
Cook, E. Song of the Ugly Maiden.
Cook, W. Seth Bingham.
Cooley, N. John Winthrop, "Reasons to be
  Considered for...the Intended Plantation in New
  England," 1629.
  Publick Fast on Account of the Afflicted: March
  31, 1692.
Coolidge. My Rights.
Corbett, E. Three Wise Old Women.
Corfield, J. Morse Lesson.
Cortez, J. Grinding Vibrato.

Cott, J. Isis (Lady of Petals).
Cousins, L. Ms. Cousins' Rap.
Couzyn. House of Changes.
  Mystery, The.
  Pain, The.
  Spell to Soften the Hard Heart of a Woman.
Coward. Nina.
Cowley, A. To His Mistress.
Creeley. Air: "The Love of a Woman".
  All That Is Lovely in Men.
  Song: "What I took in my hand."
  Whip, The.
Cristall. Elegy on a Young Lady.
Crompton. Epigram VII: Winifred.
Cross, E. Uma Worshipping Shiva (On a
  Kangra miniature).
Crow, S. They say a man dies.
Crowell, Elizabeth. Portraits of the Ladies.
Cuney. No Images.
Cuthand, B. She Ties Her Bandanna.
Dacre, C. Female Philosopher, The.
  Similie.
Daive. She does not move.
  Woman measures, A.
Daniels, K. Women's Room in Pennsylvania
  Station, The.
Dante Alighieri. Sestina: "I have reached, alas,
  the long shadow."
  To Waning Day, To the Wide Round of Shadow.
Datcher, M. I am open.
De Angelis. There's a Hand that Nails Down.
de Fréine, C. Mother tongue.
De Kok. Small passing.
De Los Santos, M. Women Watching
  Basketball.
DeCarteret, M. Town Clerk, The.
Degenaar. Phenomenon, A.
Denis, J. Women of My Country.
Derricotte. For Black Women Who Are Afraid.
DeSylva, B. G. Magnolia.
  Turn On the Heat.
Dharker. Purdah, 1.
Di Prima. If he did not come apart in her hands,
  he fell.
  Loba as Eve.
  Practice of Magical Evocation, The.
Dickey, J. Weeds.
Dickinson, E. Her breast is fit for pearls.
  Title divine—is mine!
  What Soft—Cherubic Creatures.
DiPalma. Fragment.
DiPrima, C. Her Eyes a Thousand Times Over.
Donaghy, M. Bacchae, The.
Donne. Indifferent, The.
  Love's Alchemy [or Alchemie].
  Love's Progress.
  Song: "Go and catch a falling star."
  Twickenham [or Twicknam] Garden.
  Woman's Constancy.
Donovan, K. Old Women's Summer.
  Underneath Our Skirts.
Dorantes, D. Meter todas las manos en el agua.
  To put all hands into the water.
D'Orleans. Oft in My Thought.
Dorn, E. On the Debt My Mother Owed to
  Sears Roebuck.
Dove, R. Exit.
  Great Palaces of Versailles, The.
  Taking in Wash.
Doyle, R. E. Susu.
Doyle, S. Some Girls.
Drummond, W. Madrigal: "Like the Idalian
  Queen[e]."
Dryden, J. To the Pious Memory of the
  Accomplished [or Accomplisht] Young Lady,
  Mrs. Anne Killigrew, [Excellent in the Two
  Sister-Arts of Poesie and Painting. An Ode].
Dubin, A. Dames.
Dufferin and Clandeboye. Charming Woman,
  The.
Dunbar, P. Made to Order Smile, The.
Dunbar, W. In Prais[e] of Women [or Wemen].
Duncan, R. Bending the Bow.
  Dancing Concerning a Form of Women, A.
  Tribal Memories.
Duncombe, J. Females, Sacred and Profane.

Dunn, C. Margaret/Haskell Indian School.
Dunn, S. Routine Things Around the House,
  The.
Durcan. She Mends an Ancient Wireless.
Eady. I'm a Fool to Love You.
Egerton, S. Blasphemous wretch! How canst
  thou think or say.
  Emulation, The.
  Liberty, The.
Eichner, Maura. Litany for the Living.
El-Dinasouri, O. If I Were a God.
"Eliot.". from Chapter 46.
Éluard, P. She Is Always Unwilling to
  Understand.
  Unknown, She Was My Favorite Shape.
  Woman In Love.
Emperor Ch'ien-wen of Liang. Getting Up in
  Winter.
Erdrich, H. Fat in America.
Erdrich, L. Butcher's Wife, The.
  Fooling God.
Esteves. For Lolita Lebron.
  One Woman.
Evans, M. Black Queen Blues.
Evans, R. Femininity.
Ewart. Great Women Composers, The.
Fabian, C. Liturgy for Lilith.
  Prayer of Dedication.
  Qadesha (Sacred Whore).
Fagin, L. Women.
Fell, A. Women in the Cold War.
Ferré. Message.
Field. Fifty Quatrains.
  To Christina Rossetti.
Fife, C. Dear Webster.
Finch, Anne. For Grizzel McNaught (1709–
  1792).
Finch, Annie. Intellect of Woman, The.
Fingueret, M. Leviticus (Chapter 7, Verse 2-5).
Fisher, D. Put the Blame on Mame.
Fisher, J. Gooseflesh.
Foley, M. Brothers and Sisters.
Follain. Mirror, A.
Foppa. Woman.
Fordham. Coming Woman, The.
Forman, R. You So Woman.
Francis, R. On a Theme by Frost.
Fuertes. Birds Nest.
Gallagher, T. I Stop Writing the Poem.
  On Your Own.
García Lorca. Ballad of Black Grief.
Garrett, E. Womanhood, The.
Garza, E. Why I Make the Best Barrels.
Gaspar de Alba. Making Tortillas.
Gay, J. Would You Have a Young Virgin?
Gerard, M. Flow.
Gershwin, I. Oh, Lady, Be Good!
Gertler, P. Right Thing, The.
Gidlow. Creed for Free Women, A.
Gilbert, S. Ladies' Home Journal, The.
Gilman, C. Anti-Suffragists, The.
  Homes.
  Matriatism.
Gilmore, M. Eve-Song.
Giovanni. Life I Led, The.
Glazer, J. Final Disposition.
Glover, S. Power of the Soul.
Glück, L. Palais des Arts.
Goddess, R. Why I Be a Goddess.
Godfrey. So Let's Look at It Another Way.
Goldsmith, O. When Lovely Woman Stoops to
  Folly.
Goodison. From the Garden of the Women
  Once Fallen.
Goran. Woman and Beauty.
Gorges. Her Face, Her Tongue, Her Wit.
Gottlieb, L. Greeting Shekinah.
Gould, H. Child's Address to the Kentucky
  Mummy, The.
Gould, J. Coyotismo.
Grahn. Grand Grand Mother Is Returning.
Graves, R. White Goddess, The.
Greenhalgh, C. Man in the Valley of Women,
  A.
Greenwell, D. Fidelity Rewarded.
Grennan. Woman at Lit Window.

Greshoff, J. Friendship for a Woman of Grace.
Griffin, S. Ordinary, as Love.
Grimké, A. Caprichosa.
Groves. Heroine.
Guest, B. Farewell Stairway, The.
Guillén, N. Madrigal.
Haavikko. Hades is an even worse place.
Hacker, M. Ballad of Ladies Lost and Found.
Invocation: "This is for Elsa, also known as Liz."
Rune of the Finland Woman.
Year's End.
Hafiz, K [or Hafez]. Lost Daughter, The (19).
Hagedorn, J. Vulva Operetta.
Hall, H. Light Sleep.
Hamby, B. St. Clare's Underwear.
Hammerstein. Last Time I Saw Paris, The.
There Is Nothin' like a Dame.
Hampton. Women who Speak with Steak Knives.
Hardy, J. Computer Aided Design: Creation.
Hardy, T. Epitaph on a Pessimist.
Harjo, J. Woman Hanging from the Thirteenth Floor Window, The.
Harrington, J. Inconstancy.
Harris, J. Sending the Mare to Auction.
Harris, P. Some Songs Women Sing.
Hart, L. Lady Is a Tramp, The.
Hartnett. Sonnet: "I saw magic on a green country road."
Harvor, Elisabeth. Damp Hips of the Women, The.
Hass, R. Elm.
Hawoldar. To Be a Woman.
Woman, The.
You Have Touched My Skin.
Hayden, R. Sphinx.
Hayman, R. To All Those Worthy Women, Who Have Any Desire to Live in Newfound-Land.
Healy, E. Changing the Oil.
Heath. Women.
Hecht, A. Dover Bitch, The.
Heine, H. Song of Songs, The.
Hemans. Grave of a Poetess, The.
Indian Woman's Death-Song, The.
To a Wandering Female Singer.
Woman and Fame.
Hemingway. Lady Poets With Foot Notes, The.
Henderson, R. Magnolia.
Turn On the Heat.
Herrera. Portrait of Woman in Long Black Dress / Aurelia.
Resurrection of the Flesh, The.
Herrick. Request to the Graces, An.
To Meadows [or Meddowes].
Upon the Loss[e] of His Mistresses.
Hildebrandt, Z. Kali.
Persephone.
Hinckley, P. New Our Father, The.
Hirschman, J. Weeping, The.
Hirshfield, J. Picnic.
Hisle, Janeya K. We.
Hồ Xuân Hương. Condition of Women, The.
Hodgson, R. Gipsy Girl, The.
Hollander, J. Lady's-Maid's Song, The.
Hollander, V. Rosh Chodesh Tisheri.
Hoogerhuis. Search, The.
Hoornik. To Love a Woman.
Hope, A. Beyond Phigalia.
Möbius Strip-Tease.
Horne, N. Note to My Liberal Feminist Sister, A.
Horovitz, F. Women.
Hovanessian, D. Two Voices.
Hughes, L. Harlem Sweeties.
Preference.
Hugo, R. Letter to Blessing from Missoula.
To Women.
Huidobro. Canto 2 (excerpts).
Hull, A. Another Rhythm.
Hummell, A. I Never Saw a Goddess Go.
Huntington, C. Virtue: "All the houses are white."
Hupfeld, H. Are You Makin' Any Money?
Hyneman, R. No. 5, Judith.

Woman's Rights.
Hyppolite, M. Woman: "Women carry life."
Ibarbourou. Woman.
Irish Oral Tradition. I Shall Not Die for Thee.
Iskrenko. Another Woman.
Ismaili. Solange.
Issa. Give me a homeland.
In the thicket's shade.
Ivanova, O. To Russian Women.
Jackson, G. Alice.
Jackson, L. Tiger, The.
Jackson, R. 1973.
Jacobik, G. Skirts.
Jacobs, H. On Growing Up the Darker Berry.
Jacobsen, R. Old Women, The.
James, S. Sisters of Saida Manoubia, The.
Jamie, K. St Bride's.
Jarrell, R. Next Day.
Jenyns. For love no time has she, or inclination.
Jin. Judgement.
Johnson, G. Heart of a Woman, The.
Johnson, J. Eclipse.
Johnson, M. F. Village Maid, The.
Johnston, E. Lines to Ellen, the Factory Girl.
Jones, P. Song: "I have so little sorrow."
Jordan, J. Poem About My Rights.
Jordan, N. When A Woman Gets Blue.
Joseph, A. My Father's Heroes ("Not JFK, not MLK.").
Juvenal. Satire 6.
Kabir. Only Woman Awake, The.
Kasdorf. When Our Women Go Crazy.
Katz, J. Women Must Put Off Their Rich Apparel.
Kemble. Sonnet: "What is my lady like? thou fain would'st know."
Kendall, M. Lower Life, The.
Woman's Future.
Kennedy, X. Nude Descending a Staircase.
Keyes, S. Moon is a poor woman, The.
Khalifa, I. No Need to Discourage Dreams.
Killigrew, A. Upon the Saying That My Verses Were Made by Another.
Kim Chôngnan. Women's Language.
Women's Words—Yellow-Green Leaves and Low Sun.
Kim Hyesun. Women.
Women: "Did I write that I'll endure this."
Kim Sŭnghŭi. Mother's Feet.
Na Hyesôk's Complex.
Kinsella, J. Sick Woman.
Kinsella, T. Ancestor.
Kipling, R. Harp Song of the Dane Women.
Ladies, The.
Vampire, The.
Kizer, C. American Beauty, An.
Erotic Philosophers, The.
Fearful Women.
One: "From Sappho to myself, consider the fate of women."
Three.
Two.
Klugman, E. She Who Listens.
Klugman, S. God's Body.
Ko Chônghŭi. It Will Be a New World.
Sisters, Now We Are the Path and the Light.
Koch, K. Energy in Sweden.
Kohler. Vessel.
Konie, G. We Are Equals.
Konishi Raizan. For rice-planting women.
Kopland. Ontology.
Korican, L. City Goddess.
Her Story.
Korinna [or Corinna]. I blame even clear-voiced.
Kowit. In the Morning.
What Chord Did She Pluck.
Kremer. Choice, Inanna and the Galla.
Krysl. Persephone, to Demeter.
Kshetrayya. Courtesan to Her Lover, A.
Kuan Hsiu. Three or four young sylph women.
Kulman. To Diana.
Landon. History of the Lyre, A.
Marriage Vow, The.
Lanier, E. Our Mother Eve, who tasted of the Tree.

To the Queen's Most Excellent Majesty.
Lao Tzu. Valley Spirit never dies, The.
Lars. Sketch of the Frontier Woman.
Laux, D. Laundromat, The.
Lawrence, D. H. To Women, as Far as I'm Concerned.
Le Guin. At the Party.
Le Sueur. Behold This and Always Love It.
Leapor. Essay on Woman, An.
To Artemisia.—'Tis to her we sing.
Lee, A. Confession.
Lee, L. I Ask My Mother to Sing.
Irises.
Leithauser. Old Bachelor Brother.
Leto. Mary Morelle Show, The.
Levertov. Abel's Bride.
Cancion: "When I am the sky."
Hypocrite Women.
In Mind.
Mutes, The.
Stepping Westward.
Woman Alone, A.
Li Yen-nien. Song, A: "In the north there is a lovely woman."
Li'aibi, S. Stone of the Arabian woman, The.
Lihn. Of All Despondencies.
Six Poems of Loneliness.
Lim, S. Pantoun for Chinese Women.
Limburg, J. Inner Bloke.
Lindamichellebaron. I'm the Man.
Lindsay, C. Love or Fame.
Livesay, D. Other.
Unquiet Bed, The.
Livingston, J. Femininity.
Loesser. Adelaide's Lament.
Loftin, E. Black Lady, A.
Weeksville Women.
Logau. Women's Rule.
Logghe. Madonna of the Peaches.
Lorde. Stations.
Women of Dan Dance with Swords in Their Hands to Mark the Time When They Were Warriors, The.
Love, M. Objects of Desire.
Lovelace, R. Gratiana Dancing [or Dauncing] and [or &] Singing.
Løvgreen, G. First Day, The.
Lowell, A. Patterns.
Sisters, The.
Loy. Three Moments in Paris.
Lum. Riding the North Point Ferry.
Lummis, Suzanne. Femme Fatale.
Lydgate. Duplicity of Women, The.
Lyly, J. Serving Men's Song, A.
M–rt–n. Humble Wish, The.
MacDonogh. She Walked Unaware.
Mackey, N. One hand on her hip, one hand.
MacLean, S. Highland Woman, A.
Madgett. Black Woman.
Woman with Flower.
Madhubuti. Magnificent Tomorrows.
Magrelli. I have a brain populated by women.
Like ground that's been walked over, it echoes.
Maiden. Green Side, The.
Major, C. Balance and Beauty.
Giant Red Woman.
Majorino. Hints.
Maksimovic. For the Barren Woman.
Malé. Women Don't Die on the Front Lines.
Mansour, J. Woman Kneeling in the Sorry Jelly, A.
Mapanje. Cheerful Girls at Smiller's Bar, 1971, The.
Marion, G. Ladies Who Sing with a Band, The.
Maroon, B. Neighbor.
Nude Woman Spotted in Cappuccino Cup as Advertising Dollar Co-opts Another Life.
Marston, J. Pigmalion, whose hie love-hating minde.
Martial. My taste in women, Flaccus? Give me one.
Martin, C. Victoria's Secret.
Martinaitis, M. Zuveliskes's Women Mourn Over Kukutis.
Martinez, D. Room itself, The. The women.
The absence of women.

Martínez, V. Into the Next One.
It Is Not.
Max, L. Stone Fruit.
Mayer, B. Easy Puddings.
McCarriston. Wrought Figure.
McDaniel, J. D.
McElroy, C. Illusion.
In My Mother's Room.
McFerrin, B. 23rd Psalm, The: "Lord is my Shepherd, I have all I need, The."
McGinley. Why, Some of My Best Friends Are Women.
Women of Jericho, The.
McGlashan, J. Island of Women, The.
McGuckian. Dream-Language of Fergus, The.
Mr. McGregor's Garden.
Orchid House, The.
Sitting, The.
McKay, C. Wild Goat, The.
McOrlan. Battery Woman.
McVeigh, J. Eve Falling.
Meador, B. Fields Belong to Woman, The.
Meng Chiao. Risks.
Meredith, W. Korean Woman Seated by a Wall, A.
Meynell, A. Father of Women, A [Ad Sororem E. B.].
Letter from a Girl to Her Own Old Age, A.
Michaux. Simplicity.
Milán, E. Marionetas son metáforas perfectas, Las.
Riddle me what marionettes are.
Miliauskaite. These are Lilacs.
Millay, E. I, Being Born A Woman [And Distressed].
Oh, Oh, you will be sorry for that word!
Sonnet: "Women have loved before as I love now."
Miller, J. Crazed Woman, The.
Woman I Know, The.
Mitchell, E. Thoughts After Ruskin.
Mitchell, N. Love Story in Subtitles.
Mitford. On a Beautiful Woman.
Mkangelwa. Women Sing, The.
Monaghan. Persephone's Journey.
Venus of Laussel.
Montagu, L. Lover, The; a Ballad.
Summary of Lord Lyttleton's 'Advice to a Lady', A.
Moore, M. Sojourn in the Whale.
Morgan, Elin Llwyd. Schizo de Picasso.
Mori. Speaking Through White: For My Mother.
Moss, T. Raising a Humid Flag.
Moulds, J. Renoir's Bathers.
When Bad Angels Love Women.
Mphande. Why the Old Woman Limps.
Mueller, L. Naming the Animals.
Nude by Edward Hopper, A.
Muhammad, T. Extremes Ain't My Thing As Salaam Alaikum.
Mullen, H. Anatomy.
Roadmap.
Mun Chônghui. Elderly Woman, An.
Murray, J. Men and Women Have Meaning Only as Man and Woman.
Mutén, B. Demeter's Blessing.
Hesperides, The.
Queen Hera.
Queen Medusa.
Naden. Two Artists, The.
Nance. Frontier Mystery.
Naranjo-Morse. Gia's Song.
Nasrin. Another Life.
At the Back of Progress . . . .
Border.
Character.
Nathan, L. Body Count.
Toast.
Neely, L. Eight Ways of Looking at Pussy.
Nelson, M. Ballad of Aunt Geneva, The.
Nepote, M. A esta mujer la sangre se le fuga.
Blood leaks from this woman, The.
Neruda. Every Day, Matilde.
Ode to a Beautiful Nude.
Nesbit, E. Wife of All Ages, The.

Nezval. Lilac by the Museum on St. Wenceslas Square, The.
Ní Chuilleanáin. Secret, The.
Nichols, G. Tropical Death.
Nikolayeva [or Nikolaeva]. Party on Women's Day, A.
Seven Beginnings.
Noel, L. Understanding Each Other.
Nolla. Manifest, The.
Thoughts on Innocence.
Norris, K. Persephone.
Prayer to Eve, A.
Norte, M. Peeping Tom Tom Girl.
Norton, C. Obscurity of Woman's Worth.
Picture of Sappho, The.
Notley. Back.
Destroy.
How the Dead Women May Operate from Negative Space.
Latticed Culotte and Starry Blouse.
White Peacock, The.
O'Curry, E. Litany to Our Lady.
Ogundipe-Leslie. On Reading an Archeological Article.
O'Hara, F. Female Torso.
Olds, S. Ecstasy.
Ombres. Morning Hours.
Oppen. Morality Play, A: Preface.
Osgood, F. Ah! Woman Still.
Osofisan. She Thinks in Song.
Palladas [or Pallades]. Women all / cause rue.
Pande, M. Two Women Knitting.
Parker, A. No Fool, the God of Salt.
Parker, Dominique. Foxfire.
Parker, Dorothy. General Review of the Sex Situation.
On Being a Woman.
Song of One of the Girls.
Parker, M. Whither away good neighbour.
Parker, P. For Willyce.
Parkes, B. Lilian's Second Letter.
Parnell, P. Apotheosis of Medusa.
Medusa and Perseus III: Lilith.
Sheila the Hat.
Sile Na gCioch.
Partlow, L. Overworked.
Pavlova, K. Crone, The.
Pavlova, V. And God saw.
Pearlberg, G.G. Think Back.
Pegram, A. Mr. White Discoverer.
Peppermint, Heidi. Real Toads.
Peri Rossi. Tired of women.
Perillo, L. Dangerous Life.
Floating Rib, The.
Pfeiffer, E. Peace to the odalisque, whose morning glory.
Philips, K. Answer to Another Persuading a Lady to Marriage, An.
Friendship in Emblem[e], or the Seal[e], to My Dearest Lucasia.
Friendship's Mystery[s], to My Dearest Lucasia.
To My Excellent Lucasia, On Our Friendship.
"Philo-Philippa.". To the Excellent Orinda.
Piatt, S. Pique at Parting, A.
Piercy. Moon Is Always Female, The.
What's That Smell in the Kitchen?
Pierson, J. Thrift Shop Ladies.
Pietri. 9th Untitled Poem.
Pike, M. When Gerty Goes A-Wheeling.
Pilkington, L. Wish, By a Young Lady, The.
Pinchas-Cohen. Her, Me, and Yochanan.
Pinkney, E. Health, A.
Pitter. Old, Childless, Husbandless.
Pizarnik. Fragments to Overcome Silence.
I gave the surge of myself to the dawn.
Plath. Ariel.
Edge.
Poe. Stanzas.
To Helen ("I saw thee once—once only—years ago.").
Poetker-Thiessen, A. Fallen Women.
Poliziano. What song will ever be so sorrowful.
Pollarolo, G. At Breakfast.
Good Marriage, A.
Grocer's Dream, The.
S.L.A.M.

When We Meet Again.
Polwhele. Alas! in every aspiration bold.
Pope, A. Epistle [II,] to a Lady[: Of the Characters of Women].
Impromptu: To Lady Winchelsea Occasioned by four Satirical Verses on Women Wits, in *The Rape of the Lock*.
On a Certain Lady at Court.
Pound, E. Bathtub [or Bath Tub], The.
Tame Cat.
Prado, A. Easter.
Heart's Desire.
Serenade.
Time.
Prescod. Women Are Different.
Prestwich. How to Choose a Mistress.
Probyn. Ballade of Lovers.
Frustrated.
Masquerading.
Procter, A. Woman's Answer, A.
Qabbani. Fortune Teller, The.
Radoev, Ivan. Parable of the Poet's Reward.
Ramke, B. According to Ovid.
Randall, D. Blackberry Sweet.
Randall, M. I Want the Words Back.
Randell. She had the stance of a snowdrop.
Randolph, T. In Praise of Women in General.
Ransom, J. Lady Lost.
Ratushinskaya [or Ratushinskaia]. Thus you lived your life without regret.
Reilly, P. Imagine a woman who honors the face of the Goddess in her own changing face.
Rendon. You See This Body.
Reynolds, S. F. Moon/light quarter/back sack.
Open Letter to All Black Poets, An.
Reznikoff. In the shop, she, her mother, and grandmother.
Rich, A. After Twenty Years.
Cartographies of Silence.
Culture and Anarchy.
Dark lintels, the blue and foreign stones, The.
Every peak is a crater. This is the law of volcanoes.
Floating Poem, Unnumbered, The.
From a Survivor.
From an Old House in America.
Letters in the Family.
No one's fated or doomed to love anyone.
Paula Becker to Clara Westhoff.
Phantasia for Elvira Shatayev.
Phenomenology of Anger, The.
Planetarium.
Rules break like a thermometer, The.
Sleeping, turning in turn like planets.
Snapshots of a Daughter-in-Law.
Suppose you want to write.
That conversation we were always on the edge.
Translations.
Women.
Your small hands, precisely equal to my own.
Roberts, A. Put the Blame on Mame.
Robin, L. Diamonds Are a Girl's Best Friend.
Robinson, A. Wise-Woman, The.
Robinson, M. Modern Female Fashions.
Rochester, J. Song: "Love a woman? You're [or Y'are] an ass."
Rodgers, W. Stormy Night.
Rodriguez, J. About this Woman.
Roethke. I Knew a Woman.
Rohrer, M. Brooklyn Bridge.
Romano, R. So I Lost My Temper.
Romo-Carmona, M. Signs.
Rosenberg, L. Silence of Women, The.
Rossetti, C. From the Antique.
Goblin Market.
Rostopchina. Unfinished Sewing, The.
Rouse, A. Lilies of the Field.
Rowe, E. To Celinda.
Rózewicz. Pigtail.
Rubin, L. Houses of Emily Dickinson, The.
Ruiz, J. Charms of Small Women.
Rukeyser, M. Käthe Kollwitz.
More of a Corpse Than a Woman.
Myth.
Painters.
Rupp. Sophia.

Rushin. Black Back-Ups, The.
Russell, P. Be Careful When You Go Looking for a Madonna Cuz You Just Might Find a Woman.
Sabina. Midnight Velada, The.
Sabines. I Do Not Know It for Sure.
Saïd, A. My Woman's Transparence.
Salter. What Do Women Want?
Sandburg, C. Adelaide Crapsey.
Sanguineti. So it takes very little indeed: a brasserie.
Sappho. Anaktoria.
In the young spring evening.
Prayer to my lady of Paphos.
Sarah, R. Fugue: "Women are on their way."
Sarton, M. My Sisters, O My Sisters.
Sassoon, S. Glory of Women.
Satyamurti. Ourstory.
Satyanarayana, V. Song of Krishna.
Savageau. All Night She Dreams.
Scalise, G. Days pass on that face, The.
Scamell, B. Diaries.
Scammell, W. Retrospective.
Schwartz, D. Sonnet on Famous and Familiar Sonnets and Experiences.
Schwartz, P. Snapshots of the Chameleon Woman.
Sedakova. Female Figure.
Seidel. Men and Women.
Semonides. God in His Wisdom from the start.
Senghor. Before Night Comes.
Serote. This Old Woman.
Sexton. Consorting with Angels.
Her Kind.
In Celebration of My Uterus.
Shakur, Tupac. Why Must U Be Unfaithful (4 Women).
Shange. We Need a God Who Bleeds Now.
Shapiro, K. Buick.
Dome of Sunday, The [or A].
Recognition of Eve, The.
Sharp, S. In the Tradition of Bobbitt.
Tribal Marks.
Shaughnessy, B. Postfeminism.
Shaw, A. Rear Window.
Shcherbina. Stepmother, The.
Shen Manyuan. Parody of the Other Woman.
Sheridan, R. Drinking Song.
Silko. When Sun Came to Riverwoman.
Simon, L. Hattie Went to Market.
Skelton, J. To Mistress [or Maystres] Margaret Hussey.
Smedley, M. Cavour.
Contrast, A.
Smith, I. Herring Girls, The.
Smith, K. Old Women and Love.
Smith, P. Blonde White Women.
Smith, S. Celts, The.
Dear Female Heart.
House of Mercy, A.
Södergran. Vierge Moderne.
Song. Girl Powdering Her Neck.
Mehinaku Girl in Seclusion, A.
Sornberger. When She Laughs.
Sousa, N. Call.
Souza. Women in Dutch Painting.
Spaulding-Convy, A. Why Women Become Water.
Speght. *Disswasion* hearing her assigne my helpe.
Dream[e], The [or A].
Spencer, A. Lady, Lady.
Letter to My Sister.
Spenser, E. Epithalamion: "Ye learned sisters which have oftentimes."
Sonnet 8: "More than most fair [or fayre], full of the living fire [or fyre]."
Sonnet 15: "Ye tradeful merchants that, with weary toil."
Sonnet 54: "Of this world's Theatre in which we stay."
Sonnet 67: "Like a huntsman after weary chase."
Sonnet 70: "Fresh Spring the herald of love's [or loves] mighty king."
Sonnet 81: "Fair [or Fayre] is my love, when

her fair [or fayre] golden heares."
Spires. Bodies, The.
Spofford. Magdalen.
Sruoginis, L. Irish Woman Washing.
Standing. Hopper's Women.
Starhawk. Demeter's Song.
Steele, N. Diminutive.
Stephens, J. Glass of Beer, A.
Stevens, Meic. Sylvia.
Strand. Prediction, The.
Strange. Transits.
Suckling, S. Constant Lover, A [or The].
Woman's Constancy.
Sumangalamata. At last free.
Sun, Phillina. Untitled: "In the living room sit the men."
Supervielle. Voyages.
Sute-Jo, Lady Den. Woman.
Sweet, D. My Mother and I Had a Discussion One Day.
Swenson, M. Women.
Swift, J. Gentle Echo on Woman, A.
Lady's Dressing Room, The.
Swirszczynska [or Swir]. Greatest Love, The.
Szymborska, W. Women of Rubens, The.
Taggard. At Last the Women are Moving.
Everyday Alchemy.
To One Loved Wholly Within Wisdom.
Takagi Kyozo. How To Cook Women.
Tallie, M. Raindrop Women.
Tasso. Who first of Christian warriors now did chance.
Taylor, S. Elena's Song.
Tennyson, A. Hear Icenian, Catieuchlanian, hear Coritanian, Trinobant!
Terrazas. To a Lady.
Thesen. Mean Drunk Poem.
Thomas, L. Electricity of Blossoms.
Hurricane Doris.
Thompson, D. P. Sister Lakin and Lally.
Thomson, D. Herring Girls, The.
Tohe. She Was Telling It This Way.
Torres, A. Eskimo's Woman, The.
Trần Tế Xu'o'ng. Women.
Tremblay, G. Surviving.
Trethewey, N. Cameo.
Trinidad. Answer Song.
Tsang. Street Angel, The.
Tsui. Suzy Wong's Been Dead a Long Time.
Tsujii Takashi. Woman Singing.
Tsvetayeva [or Tsvetaeva]. Fatal Volume, The.
Tu Fu [or Du Fu]. Second Letter to My Nephew Wulang.
Tynes, M. Womanskin.
Uflyand [or Ufliand]. It has for ages been observed.
Ullman. History of Women, The.
Umpierre, L. No Hatchet Job.
Ungar. Groundhog Day.
Unger, B. Photo Taken in Winter, 1944.
Unknown. Army Dance, The.
Ballad of Mulan, The.
Ballad of Mulan, The.
Beautiful Nahid rose up and in her clear voice cried, The.
Chalcan Female Song.
Chu-qi dong-men: At the Great Gate.
Cloe to Artimesa.
Epitaph for Cu Chuimne.
Female Wits, The: A Song by a Lady of Quality.
Fressh lusty beautee joyned wyth gentilesse.
God, do not let any woman die in exile!
Holy Priestess of Heaven, The.
How to Choose a Mistress.
Hymn to Nut.
Lady of the Morning, The.
Lady Who Ascends into the Heavens, The.
Litany to Our Lady.
Maiden, The.
Marrying Maiden, The.
Maxim Revised, A.
May Isis heal me.
Mayden in the moor lay—.
My sisters, tie your veils around like waistbands.
One of the Awl Songs.

Rare sight, a woman lost in the trance.
Song of the Little Miss by the Green Rill.
Those Women.
Twelfth Song of the Thunder.
Woman in exile never stops dying, The.
Woman is by aptitude.
Woman of Three Cows, The.
Woman's Love.
Women as women, me had never charmed.
Valiente. Charge of the Goddess, The.
Vallejo. Down to the Dregs.
Van Haren, E. Stepping Out With Edvard Munch ("When from the virile grave.").
Vaughan, H. To the Most Excellently Accomplished Mrs. Katherine Philips.
Venkatarao, K. Workers in Love.
Verlaine. Beauty of women, their weakness, those pale hands.
Femme et Chatte.
Woman and Cat.
Vicioso. Wo/men.
Vietnamese Oral Tradition. Wicked Women.
Woman's Heart, A.
Villanueva, A. From the Healing Dark.
Planet Earth Speaks, The.
Villon. Gone Ladies.
Vivar. Delivery.
Femmemasochism.
Voigt. Woman Who Weeps.
Volková, B. I am not an Amazon—a warrior.
Vollmer. Wildsisters Bar.
Voznesensky [or Voznesenskii].
Darkmotherscream.
Someone Is Beating a Woman.
Waddington, M. Old Women of Toronto.
Wakoski. Belly Dancer.
Waldman, A. Admonitions of the Boudoir.
Waldrop, R. Lawn of Excluded Middle.
Walker, A. Women.
Wallace, W. Hand That Rocks the Cradle Is the Hand That Rules the World, The.
Waller, E. To a Fair Lady Playing with a Snake.
Waniek. Ballad of Aunt Geneva, The.
Waring, B. When a Beautiful Woman Gets on the Jutiapa Bus.
Washington, N. Woman's Intuition, A.
Watson, R. Ballad of the Bird-Bride.
Weatherford, C. Ladies of Dimbaza, The.
Webster, A. Love's Mourner.
Wechsler, E. Child is Born, A.
Wei Chuang. Green Pond, A.
Wells, C. Poster Girl's Defence, The.
Whitman, R. Bubba Esther, 1888.
Whitman, S. Morning-Glory, The.
Whitman, W. I Sing the Body Electric.
This is the female form.
Woman Waits for Me, A.
Whittemore, R. For the Life of Him and Her.
Whur. Female Friend, The.
Wickham. Creatrix.
Dedication of the Cook.
Friend Cato.
Meditation at Kew.
Wilbur, R. Catch, The.
She.
Wilcox, E. Burdened.
Woman.
Willard, N. Cat's Second Song, The.
Williams, C. K. Dress, The.
Williams, S. She Had Known Brothers.
Straight Talk from Plain Women.
You Were Never Miss Brown to Me.
Williams, W. Marriage.
Portrait of a Lady.
Proletarian Portrait.
Queen Anne's Lace.
To an Old Jaundiced Woman.
To Daphne and Virginia.
Woman Walking.
Wilson, S. Experiments in the Impersonal.
Winchilsea. Answer, The [*To Pope's Impromptu*].
Circuit of Apollo, The.
Friendship Between Ephelia and Ardelia.
On Myself.
Winter, M. In the Beginning.

Wise, S. I Was Very Prolific.
Wither. I Loved a Lass.
  Shall I, Wasting in Despair.
Woody. Girlfriends, The.
Wordsworth, W. She Was a Phantom of
  Delight.
  Solitary Reaper, The.
Wright, C. Everything Good Between Men and
  Women.
Wright, J. Ishtar.
Wyatt. Divers[e] [or Dyvers] doth[e] use, as I
  have heard and kno[w].
  Lover Showeth How He Is Forsaken of Such as
  He Sometime Enjoyed, The.
Yamada. Club, The.
Yau. January 18, 1979.
  Radiant Silhouette II.
Yeats. Crazy Jane Talks with the Bishop.
  Friends.
  Lapis Lazuli.
  No Second Troy.
  On Woman.
  Prayer for My Daughter, A.
Yosano Akiko. Heart of a Thirtyish Woman,
  The.
Young, I. Visit to the Palace of Venus.
Young, K. Almanac, 1939, An.
Young, M. J. Friendship.
Ziyalan, Mustafa. Night Ride On 21.
Zucker, R. Portrait of Unknown.

Women's Suffrage
Cary, P. Advice Gratis to Certain Women.
See also **Voting and Voters**

Wonder
Adcock, F. Unexpected Visit.
Bradley, Leo. Sub Umbra.
Craig, David. Apprentice Is Amazed, The.
Han-shan. Cold Mountain has many hidden
  wonders.
Levertov. This Day.
Parini. Belonging.
Rumi. Love and Silence.
Tokareva, Y. Brief reflection on the greatness of
  God.
Whitman, W. Who Learns My Lesson
  Complete.

Wood
Andrade, O. Babbling.
Armstrong, Tammy. Wood Stove Sunday.
Bartlett, B. Afterlife of Trees, The.
Bernstein, C. Take Then, These.
Bly, R. Old Boards.
Boncho. Piled for burning/ Brushwood.
Brathwaite, E. Ogun.
Carter, M. Bitter Wood.
Cook, Geoffrey. Chopping Wood.
Davis, K. Green Noise of Ohio Hardwoods,
  The.
Dorn, E. Rick of Green Wood, The.
Frost, R. Wood-Pile, The.
García Lorca. Song of the Barren Orange Tree.
Griffiths, B. Fragment 13: "Maple."
Gurney, I. Felling a Tree.
Hardy, T. Workbox, The.
Hart-Smith. Boomerang.
Ikeda, P. Wood.
Kagawa Kageki. Buy it! But it!
Kuong Viet. Wood and Fire.
Marlatt, D. Working Girl.
Nash, O. Termite, The.
Niedecker. New-sawed.
Palmer, H. Woodworker's Ballad.
Ponge. Three Shops, The.
Ramsey, J. Tally Stick, The.
Shinkichi Takahashi. Wood in Sound, A.
Spicer, J. Lament for the Makers: "No call upon
  anyone but the timber drifting in the waves."
Walker, T. Owl.
Waniek. My Grandfather Walks in the Woods.
Warren, R. Gold Glade.
Welch, L. He Thanks His Woodpile.

Woodcocks
Sanger, Peter. Woodcock Feather.

Woodpeckers
Alcosser. Woodpecker.

Basho. But for a woodpecker.
Bullett, G. Woodpecker.
Buson. Thwack of an ax, The.
Cary, P. Legend of the Northland, A.
Clare, J. Green Woodpecker's Nest, The.
Creeley. Like They Say.
Issa. Woodpecker, The.
Meade, G. Great Spotted Woodpecker, The.
Pastan. Hardwood.
Perillo, L. For the Pileated Woodpecker and Its
  Cousin, the Ivory-Billed, Who May or May
  Not Be Extinct.
Roberts, E. Woodpecker, The.
Trethewey, N. Limen.

Woods
Bennett, J. Alexander. Tribute to a Mohogany
  Cutter.
Berry, W. Independence Day.
  1985 III.
  Stay Home.
Bolt, T. I crossed.
Buchanan, O. Walk, The.
Buson. Blow of an ax.
Carpenter, E. Summer Heat.
Carruth, H. Bearer, The.
Clampitt. Green.
Clare, J. Give Me the Gloomy Walk.
  Nightingale's Nest, The.
Cody, James. Big Thicket Words.
Erdrich. Woods, The.
Frost, R. Come In.
Greppi, C. Like a handful of leaves.
Hagiwara Sakutaro. So Terrifyingly
  Melancholy.
Hemans. Edith; a Tale of the Woods.
Hoover, P. Heart's Ease.
Jones, R. Beginning, A.
Kang Ŭn'gyo. Woods: "Tree trembles, A."
Kinnell. That Silent Evening.
Kinsella, T. In the Ringwood.
Kunitz, S. River Road.
Landor, W. Separation.
Lefroy. Idler Listening to Socrates Discussing
  Philosophy with His Boy-Friends, An.
Lewis, G. Hedge, The.
Lewis, J. Indians in the Woods, The.
Li Po. Going to Visit a Taoist Recluse on
  Heaven's Mountain Only to Find Him Gone.
Li Yü [or Li Hou-Chu]. Flowered Woods, The.
Lingche. In Reply to Wei Dan.
Marks, S. November Woods.
Oppen. But So as by Fire.
Pessoa. No One in the Wide Wilderness of the
  Wood.
Petrarch. Woods Are Wild and Were Not Made
  for Man, The.
Remizov, Alexei. Eaten by the Wolf.
Rukeyser, M. Then I Saw What the Calling
  Was.
Shillaber, B. Sagamore, The.
Spenser, E. Ye wastefull woodes bear witness
  of my woe.
Suntsova, E. Beyond is where the passersby
  end.
Thomas, E. Hollow Wood, The.
Tranströmer. Encroaching shadows.
Tu Mu. Mountain Walk, A.
Unknown. In the Woods.
  Summer Sunday.
Unknown, fr. Terezin Concentration Camp.
  Birdsong.
Wang Wei. Answer to Vice-Prefect Chang.
Wilbur, R. In Trackless Woods.
Wordsworth, W. How sweet it is, when mother
  Fancy rocks.
  Nutting.
See also **Forests**

Woodstock, New York
Llwyd, Iwan. El Buen Samaritano keeps
  reappearing.
Sherrill, J. Woodstock.

Wool
Fergusson. Braid Claith.
Jones, T. Thursday.

Woolf, Virginia
Howe, F. Doubt.
Pak Inhwan. Rocking Horse and the Lady, The.
Wright, N. Acrophobia.

Word of God
Laux, D. Dust.
Machado Ruiz. I love Jesus, who said to us.

Words
Agard, J. Poetry Jump-Up.
Algarin. Talking.
Alvarez, J. Bilingual Sestina.
  Sonnet 42: "Sometimes the words are so close I
  am."
Ammons. Triphammer Bridge.
Andrade, E. Silence.
Angeles, C. Words.
Arends, J. I.
Aridjis. Wounded Self-Portrait, A.
Armand. Another Poetics.
Armantrout. Almost.
Atwood. Variations on the Word *Love.*
Bachmann. Verily.
  You Words.
Balaban. Georgi Borisov in Paris.
Baraka, I. A, B, C's, The.
  Ka 'Ba.
Barnstone, T. *et al.* Hair of the Field.
Bartlett, L. What It Means to be Avant-Garde.
Beachy-Quick, Dan. Flag-Tree.
Beadle. Words.
Behn, A. Love's Witness.
Belchenko, N. It's boring looking at the same
  old contents.
Benn. Word, A.
Bermeo, O. Oda para Leticia.
Bernstein, C. Kiwi Bird in the Kiwi Tree, The.
  Virtual Reality.
Berry, W. Meditation in the Spring Rain.
Berryman. To My Father.
Beskin, Lisa. On the Sixth Day the Word Is
  Taken from Me.
Bingxin. Paper Boat—Sent to Mother.
Blackwell, Holley. Message No. 57.
  Message No. 69.
Bobis, M. Word Gifts for an Australian Critic.
Bolton, J. Lights at Newport Beach, The.
Borges. Compass.
  Poem of the Gifts.
Boruch. Think of the Words.
Bradstreet, A. Another ("Anne Bradstreate.").
Branch, A. I say that words are men and when
  we spell.
Brasfield, J. Celan.
Bromige. Lines: "Repressive desublimation."
Broumas, O. Etymology.
Brown Rosellen. Fry says a word.
Brutus. Sometimes a mesh of ideas.
Buffoni, F. Song of Diamond Eyes, The.
Bynner. Horses.
Campo, C. Love, Today My Lip.
Campo, R. Superman Is Dead.
Castillo, S. Letter to Yeni on Peering into Her
  Life.
Cavalli. I don't have any seed to cast about the
  world.
Ceravolo. Data.
Césaire, A. Lagoonal Calendar.
  Macumba Word.
  Nothing ever delivers but the opacity of words.
Char. Dyne.
Coleridge, M. Words.
Collins, M. Lines: "Draw a line. Write a line.
  There."
Coolidge, C. Hand Further, The.
  Leaving Rattle Bar.
  Listene / secting.
  Ounce code orange.
  Tab, The.
  This Garden Being: The Hanging of Books.
Cortez, J. No Simple Explanations.
Creeley. Language, The.
Cross, E. Palabras.
  Words.
Crowe, T. After Reading Han-Shan.
Cullen, C. Incident.
Cummings, E. E. Little joe gould has lost his

teeth and doesn't know where.
Darío, R.   I Seek a Form.
Darling, J.   Too Heavy.
Darragh.   Numb to Number.
   Pie in the Sky: Part 2.
Darwish, M.   Words.
Davidson, J.   Battle.
Davidson, M.   Form of Chiasmus; The
   Chiasmus of Forms, The.
Davies, A.   Outer Layers of Nervousness, The.
De Kok.   Text of necessity.
Deanovich.   My Favorite Monk Is.
Deltoro, A.   Cartografía.
   Cartography.
Deniz, G.   Ignorance.
   Ignorancia.
Desnos.   Like.
Dickey, J.   Basics.
Dickinson, E.   Man may make a Remark, A.
   Word is dead, A.
DiPalma.   Poem for Claude.
Dissanayake.   Freedom.
Doolittle, H.   Strophe.
Dove, R.   Ö.
Dowden, E.   Old Letters.
Drummond de Andrade.   Looking for Poetry.
Du Maurier.   Music.
Duffy, C.   Words, Wide Night.
Duhig, I.   From the Irish.
DuPlessis, R.   Draft 55: Quiptych.
Eady.   Sherbet.
   Song: "Nigger-Lover is a song, spat out."
   Why Do So Few Blacks Study Creative
      Writing?
Ellis, T.   Hush Yo Mouf.
Ezrokhi, Z.   Repetition.
Faiz.   Once Again the Mind.
Fearing.   Twentieth-Century Blues.
Fermini, I.   Statue, The.
   Wistaria-faced Visigoth, The.
Filkova, Fedya.   Under a Wing.
Fischer, N.   I've Changed.
Fisher, C.   Words.
Fisher, J.   There are only so many words.
Flores, I.   Last Visit to Chestnut Middle School.
Follain.   Speech Alone.
   Useful, The.
Forrest-Thomson.   Sonnet: "My love, if I write a
   song for you."
Fortini.   Italy 1942.
Fried, E.   Logos.
Frost, R.   Beyond Words.
   Ends.
Furberg, J.   Nightspell.
Gerber.   Afterwords.
Gilbert, C.   Kite-Flying.
Gilbert, S.   Simplicity.
Gloria.   In Language.
Gomez, M.   Solo Palabras.
Gomringer, E.   Words: "Words are shadows."
Graham, J.   Fission.
   Surface, The.
Graham, W.   Malcolm Mooney's Land.
Graves, R.   In the Beginning Was a Word.
   Tilth.
Greenwald, T.   Privets Come into Season at
   High Tide.
Grenier.   Open the door Oakland.
Grennan.   Journey: "Get the word and go."
Greppi, C.   What words must rush in.
Griffiths, J.   Errata.
   Lost and Found.
Gullar.   In the Body.
   Noise.
Hacker, M.   Squares and Courtyards.
Hadas, R.   Winged Words.
Hamill, S.   Gift of Tongues, The.
Harrison, J.   Swifts at Evening.
Hass, R.   Meditation at Lagunitas.
Hejinian.   Moment yellow, just as four years
   later, when my father returned home from the
   war, The.
   Tree rows in orchards are capable of patterns.
   What, The.
Herlin.   So many traces.
Hoagland, E.   Anti-Semanticist, The.

Puttin' on the Dog.
Hoagland, T.   Dickhead.
Holland, J.   Wavelength.
Hollander, J.   For "Fiddle-De-De".
Holst-Warhaft.   John 1:1 and 14.
Hughes, L.   Songs.
Hyppolite, M.   Speech.
Iijima Koichi.   Imperfect Poetry and
   Meaningless Poetry.
Imbriglio, C.   Rumor.
Inman, P.   Numb to Number.
Irwin, M.   Five Panels.
Jabès.   Book, The.
Jaccottet.   It's easy to talk, and writing words on
   the page.
   Reason.
Jackson, L.   World and I, The.
Jacobsen, R.   Cobalt.
Jandl, E.   My : T.
Jarrell, R.   Islands, The.
Jennings, E.   About These Things.
Jiménez, J.   Intelligence, Give Me.
Jooris.   Village, A.
Kalmar et al.   Three Little Words.
Kaschnitz.   Poem, A: "Poem made of words,
   A."
Kaufman, B.   Crootey Songo.
Kekova.   Ants, The.
   Everything has come true. The punishment fits
      the crime.
   Running water is cold, the river from Eden
      flows east.
Kenjeev.   Gone is the sound of my favorite
      misfortune, which even yesterday.
Kennelly.   Big Words, The.
Kgositsile.   To Mother.
   To My Daughter.
Khlebnikov, V.   Incantation by Laughter.
Klink, J.   Scarcity.
Koch, K.   Permanently.
Komunyakaa, Y.   Jeanne Duval's Confession.
Kruchyonykh [or Kruchionykh or Kruchenykh].
   Declaration of the Word as Such.
Kunin, A.   Sore Throat, The.
Lal Ded [or Lalla].   To learn the scriptures is
   easy.
Landon.   Power of Words, The.
Landor, W.   Idle Words.
Larkin, P.   Talking in Bed.
Lee, L.   Persimmons.
Leonidov, Rumen.   Mouths of the people eating
   their lunch, The.
Levchev, Vladimir.   Four Seekers of the Great
   Metaphor.
Levi, P.   Voices.
Lewis, G.   Last Minutes, The.
   Oxford Booklicker.
Longfellow, H.   Day Is Done, The.
López Colomé, P.   Death of the Kiss.
   Muerte del beso, La.
Lorde.   Coal.
Lowry, M.   Strange Type.
Lu Chi.   Music of Words, The.
MacCaig.   Instrument and Agent.
   No Consolation.
Machado Ruiz.   It's Possible That While We
   Were Dreaming.
Magdeburg, Mechthild von.   Of all that God has
   shown me.
Magrelli.   Before the last curve of the day.
   I prefer to come from silence to talk.
   There are words that coast alongside thought.
Major, C.   Swallow the Lake.
Markham, G.   Orange Tree Glistens, The.
Matthews, J.   Inverse Proportions.
Mayer, B.   Index.
McCarthy, G.   Hooded Legion, The.
McDaniel, J.   Quiet World, The.
McDonald, C.   Cheers.
McDonald, R.   Hollow Thesaurus, The.
McHugh, H.   I Knew I'd Sing.
McLain, P.   Connor in the Wind and Rain with
   His Coat on.
McMorris, M.   Near Speech, The.
Mercer, J.   Too Marvelous for Words.
Meredith, W.   Illiterate, The.

Merriam, E.   How to Eat a Poem.
Merrill, J.   Dedication: "Hans, there are
   moments when the whole mind."
   Processional.
Merwin.   Utterance.
Metodiev, Ivan.   These Things from Words.
Millay, E.   It is the fashion now to wave aside.
Miller, J.   Poetry: "Invited onto the grounds of
   the god."
Mistral, G.   One Word.
Mo Shih-lung.   To the Monk Wu-hsia on the
   Occasion of His Editing the Lotus Sutra.
Montgomery, Vaida Stewart.   Cattle Brands.
Morgan, E.   Opening the Cage.
Morgan, R.   Battery.
Morrissey, S.   If Words.
Muldoon, P.   Quoof.
Mullen, H.   Blah-Blah.
   Momma Sayings.
   Zen Acorn.
Mutis.   Word, A.
Nelson, J.   Just Word Wranglin'.
Nepote, M.   To take up the word again.
   Tomar de nuevo la palabra.
Nester, Daniel.   Third Maisie Poem.
Nichol.   Song for saint ein.
Nisker, Wes "Scoop.".   Whatever.
Noguere.   Scribes, The.
Nooteboom.   Basho 4.
Notley.   Jack Would Speak Through the
   Imperfect Medium of Alice.
Nurkse.   August Horizon.
Nye, N.   Vocabulary of Dearness.
Odio, E.   Prologue to a Time That Is Not Itself.
Ormsby, E.   Origins.
Pacheco, J.   Job 18, 2.
Padgett, R.   Louisiana Perch.
   Who and Each.
Pai, S.   Poem: "Life, A / of collecting pollen."
Palmer, M.   All those words we once used for
   things but have now discarded in order to
   come to know things.
   Notes for Echo Lake 3.
   Sun ("Write this. We have burned all their
      villages.").
   Voice and Address.
Pankey.   Unstrung Lyre, The.
Parkes, B.   For Adelaide.
Patchen.   Moon, Sun, Sleep, Birds, Live.
Peacock, M.   Anger Sweetened.
   Veil of If, The.
Pinchas-Cohen.   My English Teacher.
Piombino.   Pyramids, The.
Plath.   Words.
Po Chü-i.   Laozi.
Polkowski.   World is Only Air, The.
Ponge.   Rhetoric.
Porchia, Antonio.   Voices (an Excerpt).
Prado, A.   In Portuguese.
Prejsnar, Mark.   Assuage Bane.
Pritchard, N.   Junt.
Probyn.   Rondelet: "Say what you please."
"Rachel." [or "Rahel."].   Wrestling.
Ratushinskaya [or Ratushinskaia].   Like
   Mandelstam's swallow.
Redmond.   Love Is Not a Word.
Reed, H.   Naming of Parts.
Reed, I.   Beware: Do Not Read This Poem.
Reese, L.   Reserve.
Rekdal, Paisley.   What Was There to Bring Me
   to Delight But to Love and Be Loved?
Riley, D.   Misremembered Lyric, A.
Robinson, K.   Nesting of Layer Protocols.
Rojas.   And to Be Born Is Here an Unnameable
   Feast.
Rosales.   Root, The.
Rosen, M.   Humpty Dumpty.
Rossetti, C.   City plum is not a plum, A.
Rózewicz.   Voice, A.
Ruby, H.   Three Little Words.
Ruden, S.   Letter.
Rukeyser, M.   Ballad of Orange and Grape.
Rutsala.   Words.
Sagan.   Prayer Flag.
Salamun.   Words.
Sandburg, C.   Languages.

Little Girl, Be Careful What You Say.
Precious Moments.
Sanguineti.   What you're reading (if you're reading me) are the effects.
Satyamurti.   Erdywurble.
Scalise, G.   Days pass on that face, The.
Scannell.   Protest Poem.
Schnackenberg.   Supernatural Love.
Schuyler, J.   Freely Espousing.
Scott, D.   For Norman Nicholson.
Sears, P.   Place for Four-Letter Words.
Seiferle, R.   What We Need Words For.
Shelley, P.   To—: "One word is too often profaned."
Shinkichi Takahashi.   Words: "I don't take your words."
Sia, B.   No Words Empty.
Sidney.   Sonnet 1: "Loving in truth, and fain[e] in verse my love to show."
Singer, B.   Still and All.
Your Words, My Answers.
Sisson.   In Flood.
Smith, Douglas Burnet.   Multiple Choice.
Smith, L.   Into Still Air.
Smith, S.   Pretty.
Snyder, G.   Riprap.
Sŏ Chŏngju.   Sneeze, A.
Solórzano, L.   House Poem.
Poema de casa.
Soutar.   Room, The.
Staff.   Speech.
Steiger.   How do we break the habit of big words.
Stevenson, A.   Minister.
Stewart, B.   Words Is Not Enough.
Stroud, J.   Homage to the *Word-Hoard*.
Su, A.   Four Sonnets About Food.
Surprice, L.   Result of an Observation.
Sylvain, P.   Collective Search.
Taggart, J.   Never Too Late.
Taylor, E.   Meditation. Rom. 9.5. God blessed forever.
Thomas, D.   Especially When the October Wind.
Thomas, L.   Another Poem in English.
Thompson, P.   Erato.
Tikhonov.   Fire and Rope, Bullet and Axe.
Todd, M.   Wire Song.
Tornero, A.   Arden la torcida, entre mis ojos, y la jerarquía intermedia de una imagen esta tarde.
They blaze, between my eyes, the wick-twist and the intermediate hierarchy of an image this afternoon.
Tranströmer.   From March 1979.
Tritica, J.   Not Masterpieces, Planting Astonishments.
Troupe.   And Syllables Grow Wings There.
Turnbull.   There Are Words.
Vaynper, Z.   Word: "So many bright words covered."
Villa, E.   Lend me a battle of unavoidable suggestions.
Ugly season of putrifying buzzards, An.
Vinokurov.   Objects.
Violi.   Rifacimento.
Volkow.   Varas.
Wands.
Wagoner, D.   Words, The.
Waldrop, R.   To explore the nature of rain I opened the door because inside the workings of language clear vision is impossible.
Wallace-Crabbe.   Double Dactyl.
Walters, W.   Meridian Hill Terrace.
Watten.   Radio.
Weaver, A.   Borders.
Weekend Equestrian, The.
Weiner, H.   From *Spoke / Aug 19.*
Remembered Sequel.
Seen Words.
Weiss, T.   Good Grey Poet, The.
White, L.   Station. He.She.You.Me.
Wilbur, R.   Barred Owl, A.
Wilcox, E.   Woman.
Williams, W.   Fragment: "As for him who."
Sort of a Song, A.

Wilson, E.   Nursery Vignette.
Wylie.   Ejaculation.
Yeats.   Song of the Happy Shepherd, The.
Young, D.   Project for Freight Trains, A.
Zamora, D.   Precisely.
Zarin.   Song: "My heart, my dove, my snail, my sail, my."
Zukofsky, L.   Non Ti Fidar.
(Ryokan's scroll).

See also **Language**
Wordsworth, Dorothy
North, C.   For Dorothy Wordsworth.
Wordsworth, William
Arnold, M.   Memorial Verses.
Browning, E.   On a Portrait of Wordsworth by B. R. Haydon.
Browning, R.   Lost Leader, The.
Byron, G.   Dedication: "Bob Southey! You're a poet—poet-laureate."
Carroll, L.   White Knight's Song, The.
Coleridge, H.   He Lived amidst th' Untrodden Ways.
Coleridge, S.   To William Wordsworth [1817 version].
Collins, B.   Lines Composed Over Three Thousand Miles From Tintern Abbey.
Ewart.   William Wordsworth (1770-1850).
Ferlinghetti, L.   I am waiting for my case to come up.
Fried, E.   Wordsworth's Socks.
Grimke, C.   Wordsworth.
Harrison, T.   Remains.
Hemans.   To [*or* the Poet] Wordsworth.
Nicholson, N.   To the River Duddon.
Shelley, P.   To Wordsworth.
Stephen, J.   Sonnet, A: "Two voices are there: one is of the deep."
Voznesensky [*or* Voznesenskii].   For a Portrait of Annette Vallon.
Work and Workers
Abbott, D.   All Day at Work.
Acam-Oturu.   Arise to the Day's Toil.
Achterberg.   Ballad of the Gasfitter.
Ballade van de gasfitter.
Arnold, B.   No Tool or Rope or Pail.
Atkins, R.   Irritable Songs.
Auden.   Taller To-day.
Babcock, M.   Be Strong.
Baratier, D.   American Standard.
Barkan, S.   Italian Masons.
Bass, E.   They're Family Men.
Beecher, J.   Report to the Stockholders.
Bennett, J. Alexander.   Tribute to a Mohogany Cutter.
Berlin.   There's No Business Like Show Business.
Bevington, L.   Morning.
Black, S.   To a War Correspondent.
Boyle, K.   Ode to a Maintenance Man and His Family.
Bradley, Dickie.   Sista.
Brown, S.   Slim Lands a Job?
Brownstein.   Monkey Blues.
Budbill.   This Shining Moment in the Now.
Buson.   Gleaning the rice field.
Springs passed.
Cervantes.   Cannery Town in August.
Chin.   Autumn Leaves.
Chitwood, Michael.   Hard Surface Road.
Hardened Arm, The.
Cleyre, V.   Out of the Darkness.
Codrescu.   Work.
Colby, T.   Boy and the Girl, The.
Coleridge, S.   Work without Hope.
Cornish, S.   Work to Be Done.
Crowe, T.   Occam's Razor.
Tools.
Damacion, K.   Canciones.
Davies, Grahame.   DIY.
Davis, C.   Any Nest I Can't Sleep in Should Be Burned.
Davis, G.   Children in the Arbor.
de Folgar.   Monday.
Dent, A.   Restricting Gate, The.
Dodge, M.   Tinker, Come Bring Your Solder.
Dougherty.   Pantoum of the Working Classes.

Dove, R.   Great Palaces of Versailles, The.
Straw Hat.
Dugan, A.   Prayer: "God, I need a job because I need money."
Swing Shift Blues.
Dunn, D.   Ballad of the Two Left Hands.
Men of Terry Street.
Eich.   Man in the Blue Smock, The.
Emmott, K.   Who Looks after Your Kids?
Espada.   David Leaves the Saints for Paterson.
Espaillat.   Find Work.
Everson, W.   Muscat Pruning.
Fanthorpe.   You Will Be Hearing from Us Shortly.
Faruqi, M.   Return, The: "After washing Paddington loos."
Figueroa, J.   Jelly Bean Policy, The.
Flynn, N.   Workers (attendants).
Forbes, C.   Blue Monday.
French, T.   Pity the Bastards.
Frost, R.   Out, Out—.
Galanskov.   It shames one to look.
Gallaher, C.   Deb at the Ham Slicer.
Gandlevsky, S.   Dear God, allow me to recall my works.
Garrison, D.   Fight Song.
Gershwin, I.   Nice Work If You Can Get It.
Gillespie, H.   That Lucky Old Sun.
Ginsberg, A.   Bricklayer's Lunch Hour, The.
Goodell, L.   I Was Going to Be.
Grin, B.   Man Falls at Work, A.
Grinshpan, Y.   To My Shtetl Years.
Guevara, M.   Hands of the Old Métis, The.
Guillén, J.   Stream with Washerwomen.
Gumilyov [*or* Gumiliov *or* Gumilev].   Worker, The ("Grizzly squab comrade, A.").
Hammerstein.   Gentleman Is a Dope, The.
Han Yü.   Leaves fall turning turning to the ground.
Helfrich, Karen.   Influencing Factors.
Hernandez, D.   Workers.
Hirsch, E.   Second Story Warehouse.
Hood, T.   Literary Reminiscences.
Written in the Workhouse.
Housman.   When smoke stood up from Ludlow.
Howard, B.   Break.
Howe, J.   House of Rest, The.
Hughes, L.   Brass Spittoons.
Florida Road Workers.
Madam and Her Madam.
Necessity.
Share-Croppers.
Song to a Negro Wash-woman, A.
Jamie, K.   St Bride's.
Jensma.   Confidentially Yours.
Joseph, L.   That's All.
Kavulu.   Forces of Production.
Kingston, M.   Restaurant.
Kinsella, J.   Wild Radishes.
Kipling, R.   Sons of Martha, The.
Klassen, S.   Making the Rate (factory journals).
Knight, S.   Double Writing.
Kodama Kagai.   Suicide of an Unemployed Person, The.
Kumin, M.   Chores.
Lawrence, D. H.   Work.
Lee, D.   This all happened before.
Levine, P.   Drum: *Leo's Tool & Die, 1950.*
Every Blessed Day.
Fear and Fame.
Sweet Will.
Travelling Music.
What Work Is.
You Can Have It.
Li Shang-yin.   Without Title (1).
Lima, M.   Shoeshine Boy.
Liu Cheng.   Poem without a Category.
Lojowski, M.   Big Fort Island Buddha.
Longfellow, H.   Village Blacksmith, The.
Ma Chih-yüan.   Tune: "Song of Clear River".
Mabuza.   Tired Lizi Tired.
Masters, E.   "Butch" Weldy.
Mayhall.   Painkiller.
McDaniel, W.   My Room at Aunt Eura's, 1937.
McGrath, C.   At the Freud Hilton.
Melville, H.   My Jacket Old.

Menken. Working and Waiting.
Millar, J. Fiber Optics.
Mirville, E. All the tongues are wagging.
Don't give me food.
Montague, J. Cage, The.
Moore, F. For a Working Woman.
More, H. Hackney Coachman, The; Or, The
Way to Get a Good Fare.
Morley, D. Errand.
Morris, J. Schedule of Benefits, A.
Mr. Social Control. History Never Happened.
Murphy, R. Roof-Tree.
Nash, O. Introspective Reflection.
Newburn, L. Office Geraniums.
North, M. Pheasant Plucker's Son, The.
Poems to My Father.
Novak, H. Freezing Pan, The.
Packing Herring.
O'Callaghan. Managing the Common Herd:
Two Approaches for Senior Management.
O'Driscoll, D. Lads, The.
Oppen. It brightens up into the branches.
Pak Chaesam. Road Back, The.
Pao Chao. Folded Wings.
Patten, B. Job Hunting.
Picková, E. Fear.
Po Chü-i. Lazy Man's Song.
Planting Bamboos.
Porteous. Wrecked Creeves.
Prodromos. To the Emperor.
Ratzlaff, K. Necessity.
Razaf, A. My Handy Man.
Porter's Love Song to a Chambermaid, A.
Regier, G. Where We All Went.
Rimbaud, A. Lovely Morning Thought.
Roland Holst. Visitation.
Rome, H. Chain Store Daisy.
Rouse, A. Her Retirement.
Rumens. Jarrow.
Two Women.
Rungano. Woman, The.
Salinas, L. My Fifty-Plus Years Celebrate
Spring.
Sandburg, C. Blue Island Intersection.
Scovell. Workers in Metal.
Senryū, K. All he does at work.
Guy, The.
Shapiro, D. House (Blown Apart).
Silano, M. Sweet Red Peppers, Sun-Drieds, the
Hearts of Artichokes.
Smith, I. Herring Girls, The.
Soto. Red Palm, A.
Stein, K. World Without End.
Steptoe. O' Yes.
Stevenson, R. To A Gardener.
Stickney, T. Requiescam.
Suárez, C. Workwoman's Death, A.
Suárez, V. Cuban-American Gothic.
Swingler. Drinking Song.
Sze. Moon Is a Diamond, The.
Tafolla. Allí Por La Calle San Luis.
Tkachenko. Like Thousands of Others.
Trethewey, N. Letter Home.
Uflyand [or Ufliand]. Working week comes to
an end, The.
Ulku, A. Spring Forward, Fall Back.
Unknown. Ground-Thumping Song.
Leave the service of your master and be my
loyal follower.
My horse / thickens.
Stanza: "What, my Lord, shall I do with."
Woodcutter on His Way Home, A.
Working on the Railway.
Work's end.
Vallejo. Mule Drivers, The.
Van Jordan, A. My Father's Retirement.
Venkatarao, K. Workers in Love.
Verlaine. Humble life of dull and easy work,
The.
Vertreace, M. Arc Welder.
Vietnamese Oral Tradition. Lullaby: "Little one,
go to sleep. Sleep soundly."
Voss, F. Making America Strong.
Termination.
Wachtel. Workingman's Wife: Who She Is, Who
She Is Not, What She Buys—And Why.

Wainwright, K. Trouble.
Watts, I. How Doth the Little Busy Bee.
Webster, P. Doctor, Lawyer, Indian Chief.
Welish. Textile 13.
Whitman, W. Song for Occupations, A.
Whittier. Dedication: "I would the gift I offer
here."
Wiese, B. Everyone Who Wants to Work Can.
Wilbur, R. Plain Song for Comadre, A.
Summer Morning, A.
Wilkins, Machine. Mobile City.
Williams, C. K. Sanctity, The.
Williams, W. Paterson—the Strike.
Williamson, G. On His Birthday.
Wise, S. 50 Years in the Career of an Aspiring
Thug.
Wise, W. When I Grow Up.
Wojahn. Allegory: Attic and Fever.
Distance.
Wright, C. Yard Work.
Wright, J. Youth.
Yang Shih-ch'i. On the Hall of Precious Virtue.
Yi Sanghûi. Night, Work.
Zenmaro. Tanka: "In sullen silence."
See also Labor and Laborers
World
Basho. Come, see / real flowers.
Bass, F. Home.
Bat-Miriam. Sound of the waves in the silence,
The.
Carman, B. World Voice, The.
Cavendish, M. Of Many Worlds in This World.
Cuetzpaltzin, Ayocuan. Let the earth last.
Dove, R. Testimonial.
Epictetus. Pleasd with thy Place.
Hsüeh T'ao [or Xue Tao]. Crabapple Brook.
Huidobro. Canto 2 (excerpts).
Quiet Spaces.
Inada. Nice Place, A.
Iosifova, Ekaterina. Beneath Winter's Roof.
Issa. World of dew, The.
Kekova. Tsar sits on his throne as if he sat on
bones, The.
Levchev, Vladimir. Blue Pond at Berkovitsa.
Lima, J. Words of Departure.
Lindsay, S. World Truffle.
Lowry, Brigid. In the World.
Mahon. Tractatus.
Masaoka Shiki. Stone / On summer plain.
Nadir, M. Selfwriting.
Pagis, D. Lesson in Observation, A.
Rilke. Initiation.
Ryushu Shutaku. Why bother with the world?
Saisho. On Joshu's Nothingness.
Sen, R. Brother / This world.
Soen. Calm, activity—each has its use. At
times.
Spahr, J. January 28, 2003.
Stevens, W. Indigo Glass in the Grass, The.
Storni. World is Bitter, The.
Taggard. To the Natural World: at 37.
Unknown. Behold.
Gloria mundi est.
Unknown, fr. Terezin Concentration Camp.
Birdsong.
Birdsong 2.
Verwey, A. Beautiful World, The.
Villa, E. It is world of the back hune wone it is.
Vlasova, E. Create me a world.
White, L. World as I Found It, The.
See also Earth
World Trade Center, The
Kraus, S. (We) Promenade.
Lehman. 9/15/01.
World Trade Center, The.
Mercado, N. Going to Work.
World War I
Allen, H. Dragon's Breath.
Apollinaire. Calligram, 15 May 1915.
Little Car, The.
Post Card.
Stanzas Against Forgetting.
Aragon. Embrace, The.
Baker, K. Eagle Youth.
Bard, W. E. Seventh Seal, The.

Bellinger, A. R. Bright as a single poppy in a
field.
Bensko. Last Look in the Sambre Canal, A.
Binyon. For the Fallen.
Bishop, J. In the Dordogne.
Blunden. Concert Party: Busseboom.
Vlamertinghe.
Zonnebeke Road, The.
Bogan, L. To My Brother: Killed: Hammont
Wood: October, 1918.
Brooke, R. Peace.
Soldier, The: "If I should die, think only this of
me."
Buck, H. Mort, Le.
Cannan. Rouen.
Chesterton. Elegy in a Country Churchyard.
Cohan. Over There.
Cowley, M. Chateau de Soupir, 1917.
Crosland. White Feather Legion, The.
Cummings, E. E. Bigness of cannon, The.
Come,gaze with me upon this dome.
My sweet old etcetera.
Denwood. For Whom.
Douglas, K. Soissons.
Dove, R. Alfonzo Prepares to Go Over the Top.
La Chapelle. 92nd Division. Ted.
Passage, The.
Eliot, T. S. 2. A Game of Chess.
Frankau. Deserter, The.
French, T. No Man's Land.
García Lorca. Rundown Church (Ballad of the
First World War).
Gershwin, I. 'Strike Up the Band.
Gibson, W. Golden Room, The.
Graves, R. Escape.
Goliath and David.
Recalling War.
Sergeant-Major Money.
Greer, Hilton Ross. To General Pershing.
Grenfell, J. Into Battle.
Griffith, L. Silver Jubilee.
Gurney, I. After War.
Ballad of the Three Spectres.
Behind the Line.
First Time In.
Laventie.
Silent One, The.
To the Prussians of England.
Towards Lillers.
Hardy, T. Channel Firing.
In Time of "The Breaking of Nations".
Men Who March Away.
Often When Warring.
Heaney, S. In Memoriam Francis Ledwidge.
Hemingway. Riparto d'Assalto.
Hill, G. Violent contrariety of men and days;
calm.
Housman. Epitaph: "Here dead lie we because
we did not choose."
Hughes, T. Walt.
Hugo, R. Yards of Sarajevo, The.
Johnstone, P. High Wood.
Jones, D. Across upon this undulated board of
verdure chequered bright.
But sweet sister death has gone debauched
today and stalks.
So thus he sorrowed till it was day and heard
the foules sing, then somewhat he was
comforted.
Kipling, R. Death-Bed, R.
Epitaphs of the War [1914–1918].
Gethsemane.
Mesopotamia.
Larkin, P. MCMXIV.
Lawrence, D. H. Song of a Man Who Has
Come Through.
Tommies in the Train.
Longley, M. Wounds.
MacLeish. Memorial Rain.
MacSweeney. Seared to the echo.
McCrae, J. In Flanders Fields.
Meynell, A. Summer in England, 1914.
Monroe, H. These Two.
Munro, N. Hey, Jock, Are Ye Glad Ye 'Listed?
O'Hara, G. K-K-K-Katy.
Owen, W. A Terre.

Anthem for Doomed Youth.
Apologia Pro Poemate Meo.
Conscious.
Disabled.
Dulce et Decorum Est.
Exposure.
Futility.
Greater Love.
Parable of the Old Men and the Young, The.
S.I.W.
Send-Off, The.
Show, The.
Strange Meeting.
Palmer, V. Farmer Remembers the Somme, The.
Péret. Hymn of the Patriotic War Veterans.
Little Song of the Maimed.
Pound, E. Coming of War, The; Actaeon.
Read, H. To a Conscript of 1940.
Rickword. Soldier Addresses his Body, The.
Trench Poets.
Winter Warfare.
Rosenberg, I. August 1914.
Break of Day in the Trenches.
Dead Man's Dump.
On Receiving News of the War.
Soldier: Twentieth Century.
Troop ship, The.
Worm Fed on the Heart of Corinth, A.
Rukeyser, M. In adolescence I knew travellers.
Poem: "I lived in the first century of world wars."
"Saki.". Carol: "While shepherds watched their flocks by night."
Sandburg, C. Buttons.
Sassoon, S. Aftermath.
Attack.
Base Details.
Blighters.
Counter-Attack.
Death-Bed, The.
Does It Matter?
Dreamers.
Dug-Out, The.
Everyone Sang.
Fight to a Finish.
General, The.
Glory of Women.
Good-morning, good-morning! the General said.
On Passing the New Menin Gate.
Rear-Guard, The.
Repression of War Experience.
Suicide in the Trenches.
Working Party, A.
Scannell. Great War, The.
Seeger, A. Aisne, The (1914–15).
I Have a Rendezvous with Death.
Service. Only a Boche.
Sorley. Sonnet, A: "When you see millions of the mouthless dead."
Teasdale. There Will Come Soft Rains.
Tennant, E. A Bas la Gloire!
Thomas, E. As the Team's Head-Brass.
In Memoriam (Easter, 1915).
Private, A.
This Is No Case of Petty Right or Wrong.
Trakl. Grodek ("At evening the woods of autumn are full of the sound.").
Grodek ("In the evening the autumn woods ring.").
Grodek (Second Version).
Unknown. I Don't Want to be a Soldier.
Registration of 1918.
We are Fred Karno's army.
We mean to thrash these Prussian Pups.
Vietnamese Oral Tradition. Colonial Troops Transport, The.
West, A. Night Patrol, The.
Wilder, A. Those sultry nights we used to pass outdoors.
Wilson, T. Magpies in Picardy.
Yeats. On Being Asked for a War Poem.
Reprisals.

World War II
"Agyeya.". Hiroshima.
Ai. German Army, Russia, 1943, The.

Aiken, C. Three Star Final.
Akhmatova, A. In 1940.
Aragon. Lilacs and the Roses, The.
Night at Dunkirk.
Richard II Forty.
Waltz of the Twenty-Year-Olds, The.
Auden. September 1, 1939.
Belitt. Spool, The.
Berggolts [or Bergholts]. Blockade Swallow, The.
Berryman. Moon and the Night and the Men, The.
Betjeman. In Westminster Abbey.
Blanding Henriette de Saussure. Aftermath (1945).
Bobrowski. Kaunas 1941.
Borowski. Two Countries.
Bowers, E. Aix-La-Chappelle, 1945.
Stoic, The: For Laura Von Courten.
Brecht, B. War Has Been Given a Bad Name.
Brooks, G. Negro Hero.
Brownjohn. September 1939.
Butler, C. E. Letter to the Survivors.
Caraion. Song from the Occupation Time.
Carruth, H. On a Certain Engagement South of Seoul.
Causley. Conversation in Gibraltar 1943.
Chin. American Rain.
Ciardi, J. Box Comes Home, A.
Elegy Just in Case.
V-J Day.
Coulehan, J. D-Day, 1994.
Coward. Don't Let's Be Beastly to the Germans.
Crow, S. El Alamein.
Cunard. To Eat To-day.
Desnos. Letter to Youki.
Night Watchman of Pont-au-Change, The.
Dickey, J. Firebombing, The.
Doolittle, H. Still the walls do not fall.
Dorsett, T. Survivor, The.
Douglas, K. Aristocrats.
Vergissmeinnicht.
Dove, R. Sightseeing.
Dugan, A. Memorial Service for the Invasion Beach Where the Vacation in the Flesh Is Over.
Stentor and Mourning.
Duncan, A. Martyrdom and Triumph of Sergei Korolev.
Eich. Old Postcards.
Eimers. Another Kimono.
Éluard, P. Nazi Song.
Elytis, O. March toward the Front, The.
Fenton, J. His wife nods, and a secret smile.
Field, E. World War II.
Fitzgerald, R. Pacific.
French, T. Holding the Line.
Garioch. 1941.
Gascoyne. Wartime Dawn, A.
Gonzalez, R. José's Japanese Sword.
Gorbanevskaya. Notes of a Cold War Veteran.
Guthrie, W. Blinding of Isaac Woodard, The.
Hayes, A. City of Beggars, The.
Hecht, A. More Light! More Light!
Henderson, H. Ballad of the D-Day Dodgers.
Ballad of the Taxi Driver's Cap.
First Elegy: End of a Campaign.
Prologue: "Obliterating face and hands."
Herbert, Z. Painter.
Herd. Bombshell.
Holan. Children at Christmas in 1945.
Hongo. O-Bon: Dance for the Dead.
Hottel, J. Shikata ga nai.
Huchel. Landscape Beyond Warsaw.
Roads.
Hughes, L. Beaumont to Detroit: 1943.
World War II.
Hugo, R. Napoli Again.
Spinazzola: Quella Cantina Là.
View from Cortona, A.
Ibaragi Noriko. When I Was Prettiest in My Life.
Igloria, L. Lost Photograph.
Inada. 10. The Legend of the Magic Marbles.
Jarrell, R. Burning the Letters.

Camp in the Prussian Forest, A.
Dead Wingman, The.
Death of the Ball Turret Gunner, The.
Eighth Air Force.
Field Hospital, A.
Front, A.
Losses.
Pilot from the Carrier, A.
Pilots, Man Your Planes.
Prisoners.
Range in the Desert, The.
Second Air Force.
Transient Barracks (1944).
Truth, The.
Jeffers, R. May-June, 1940.
Pearl Harbor.
Justice, D. Voice of Col. Von Stauffenberg Rising from Purgatory, The.
Keesing. Reverie of a Mum.
Keyes, S. Timoshenko.
Kirstein. DP's.
Patton.
Kizer, C. Twelve O'Clock.
Klein, A. Upon the Heavenly Scarp.
Klepfisz. Death Camp.
Perspectives on the Second World War.
Koch, K. To Carelessness.
To World War Two.
Kunitz, S. Last Picnic, The.
Kurihara Sadako. When We Say "Hiroshima".
Laing, A. New Jerusalem, The.
Lewis, A. Peasants, The.
Raiders' Dawn.
Lewis, S. Deluge 1939, The.
Lowell, R. Holy Innocents, The.
On the Eve of the Feast of the Immaculate Conception: 1942.
Maar, Dora. These Tall Constructions.
MacLean, S. Death Valley.
MacNeice. Streets of Laredo, The.
Matthews, G. For Edward Thomas Killed at Arras.
McGrath, T. Blues for Warren.
Remembering That Island.
Meredith, W. Simile: "As when a heavy bomber in the cloud."
Merton. Dark Morning, The.
Merwin. Tide Line Garden.
Millay, E. I Forgot for a Moment.
Milosz, C. Child of Europe.
Dedication: "You whom I could not save."
Poor Christian Looks at the Ghetto, A.
With Her.
Mitchison. Farm Woman, The: 1942.
Mitsui. Photograph of a Child, Japanese-American Evacuation, Bainbridge Island, Washington, March 30, 1942.
Montague, J. Welcoming Party, A.
Moore, M. In Distrust of Merits.
Keeping Their World Large.
Morgan, E. Cinquevalli.
Mura. Argument: on 1942, An.
Blueness of the Day, The.
Narovchatov. In Those Years.
Nekrasov, V. And I Speak of Cosmic Things.
Nemerov. Fable of the War, A.
IFF.
Memory of the War, A.
War in the Air, The.
Nicholson, N. Stalingrad: 1942.
O'Callaghan, C. Coventry.
Olds, S. Leningrad Cemetery, Winter of 1941.
Oppen. Myth of the Blaze.
Osherow. Villanelle from a Sentence in a Poet's Brief Biography.
Osterhaus, J. Gambier.
Otero, B. Children of the Planet.
Pack, R. Fathering the Map.
Pasternak, B. Fresco Come to Life.
Perelman. Broken Mirror, The.
Phillips, E. Ties.
Porter, P. May, 1945.
Quasimodo. Milan, August 1943.
19 January 1944.
Radnóti. Serbian Postcard 1.
Ramke, B. Zoo.

Read, H.   To a Conscript of 1940.
Reed, H.   Chard Whitlow.
Reznikoff.   During the Second World War, I was going home one night.
Rich, A.   History.
  Letters in the Family.
Rickword.   To the Wife of a Non-interventionist Statesman (March 1938).
Root, W.   Sonnet 20: Remembering, from a Nazi Prison, a Teacher Years Before.
Rothenberg, J.   Dos Oysleydikn (The Emptying).
Rukeyser, M.   Poem: "I lived in the first century of world wars."
"Sagittarius.".   Croaked the Eagle: "Nevermore".
St. John, D.   Six/Nine/Forty-Four.
Sakaki.   Sugar Loaf Hill.
Scott, W.   Three American Women and a German Bayonet.
  U.S. Sailor with the Japanese Skull, The.
Scovell.   Child Waking.
Seifert.   Never Again.
Shapcott, T.   Shadow of War, 1941.
Shapiro, H.   Battle Report.
  War Stories.
Shapiro, K.   Full Moon: New Guinea.
  Homecoming: "Lost in the vastness of the void Pacific."
  Troop Train.
Shepherd, R.   Lucky One, The.
Sheppard, R.   Empty Diary 1944.
Simic.   Prodigy.
Simpson, L.   Arm in Arm.
  Battle, The.
  Carentan O Carentan.
  Memories of a Lost War.
  On the Ledge.
  Runner, The.
Sitwell, E.   Still Falls the Rain.
Slessor.   Beach Burial.
Slutsky [or Slutskii].   How Did They Kill My Grandmother?
Smith, S.   I Remember.
Soupault.   You Who Sleep.
Stafford, W.   Explaining the Big One.
Stern, G.   Dancing, The.
Stone, R.   That Winter.
Stryk, L.   Pit, The.
  Return to Hiroshima.
  Sniper.
Swingler.   Day the War Ended, The.
Swirszczynska [or Swir].   Conversation Through the Door, A.
  I Am Afraid of Fire.
  White Wedding Slippers.
Sze.   Spring Smoke.
Takamura Kotaro.   Final Battle for the Ryūkyū Islands, The.
Tate, A.   Ode to Our Young Pro-consuls of the Air.
Tate, J.   Lost Pilot, The.
Taylor, E.   Welcome Eumenides.
Thwaites.   On either side the *Jervis Bay* the convoy was dipping.
Viereck, P.   Kilroy.
  Vale from Carthage.
Waniek.   Lonely Eagles.
  Three Men in a Tent.
  Tuskegee Airfield.
Wilbur, R.   First Snow in Alsace.
Winters, Y.   Night of Battle.
  Summer Noon: 1941.
Wojahn.   Wartime Photos of My Father.
Wong, N.   Can't Tell.
Zavatsky.   Walker Evans in Bridgeport.

Worldliness
Akhmatova, A.   As if with a straw.
Brooks, G.   Mrs. Small.
Chia Tao.   Meng Jung, Gainfully Unemployed.
Donne.   Satire 1 [A London Street].
  Since she whom[e] I loved [or lov'd or lovd] hath paid [or payd] her last debt.
Han-shan.   In a Tangle of Cliffs.
Herbert, Z.   Mr. Cogito Tells about the Temptation of Spinoza.

Herrick.   Temporall Goods.
Killigrew, A.   Farewell to Worldly Joys, A.
K'ung Chih-kuei.   Proclamation on North Mountain.
Machado Ruiz.   I Have Walked Down Many Roads.
Mookam Choinul.   Living at Eunjok Hermitage.
Wordsworth, W.   World Is Too Much with Us, The.
Zukofsky, L.   Song for the Year's End, A.

Worms
Basho.   Autumn moonlight.
Blake, W.   Sick Rose, The.
Doolittle, H.   In me (the worm) clearly.
Francis, R.   Earthworm.
Fuller, R.   Autobiography of a Lungworm.
Gregerson.   Elegant.
Griffiths, J.   Parasites.
Guidacci.   First to feast is love, The. On the scraps of love the fever feasts.
Issa.   Old dog bends his head listening, The.
  Old dog, The.
  Old dog listens, The.
  Under my house.
Lawrence, D. H.   Worm Either Way.
Lux.   Commercial Leech Farming Today.
MacDiarmid, H.   Ex Vermibus.
Martinson.   Earthworm, The.
Marvell.   Mower to the Glowworms [or Glow-Worms or Glo-Worms], The.
McFadden, D.   17. The Inchworm.
Menicanti.   Epigram for a Worm.
Rosen, M.   Christmas Dinner.
Rosenberg, I.   Worm Fed on the Heart of Corinth, A.
Rossetti, C.   Handy Mole who plied no shovel, A.
Stevens, W.   Worms at Heaven's Gate, The.
Tate, J.   Aunt Sophie's Morning.
Toomer.   Face.
Unknown.   Maggot Song.
Van de Woestijne.   I Am the Hazel-Nut.

Wormwood
Lenski, H.   Wormwood has enchanted me completely.

Worry
Akhmatova, A.   Requiem.
Anstett.   Worry.
Balaban.   Georgi Borisov in Paris.
Berlin.   Let's Have Another Cup of Coffee.
Cherches, P.   Where is She?
Chuang Tzu.   Need to Win, The.
Chung-ch'ang T'ung.   Speaking My Mind.
Cope, W.   I Worry.
Davies, W. H.   Leisure.
Dixon, M.   Bye Bye Blackbird.
Evans, R.   Haven't Got a Worry.
Gershwin, I.   Who Cares?
Gillespie, H.   That Lucky Old Sun.
Glickman.   But till that morning, ain't no one gonna harm you.
Goese, M.   Dive, The.
Herman, J.   Tap Your Troubles Away.
Hirshfield, J.   Man Walks through His Life, A.
Hŏ Nansŏrhŏn.   For My Brother Hagok.
Jên Jui.   Midnight.
Jiménez, J.   Black Thought, A.
Jungkwon Kim.   Returning to Dupawon.
Kahn, G.   All God's Chillun Got Rhythm.
Kanik.   Erol Güney's Cat.
Kayacan.   Division of Labor.
Kenyon, J.   Insomnia at the Solstice.
Kim Yuk.   Be sure to invite me.
Lee, L.   Words for Worry.
Livingston, J.   Haven't Got a Worry.
Lomax, M.   Gulf.
Loncar, M.   Insomniac.
Matson.   Worry.
Morris, A.   Worry All the Time.
Muso Soseki.   Green mountains.
Nguyen Binh Khiem.   Worried.
Pak Inhwan.   Fortnight.
Pao Chao.   Water Spilt.
Phillips, R.   Panic Bird, The.
Pozzi, C.   Nyx.
Roberson, E.   Sonnet.

Ruby, H.   Give Me the Simple Life.
Schuyler, J.   Letter to a Friend: Who Is Nancy Daum?
Simic.   Spoons with Realistic Dead Flies on Them.
Thomas, L.   Blues Variations.
Tsvetayeva [or Tsvetaeva].   To Kiss a Forehead Is to Erase Worry.
Tu Fu [or Du Fu].   Hundred Worries, A.
Unknown.   Muiveyo Cow, The.
  Our Little Sister is Worried.
  Song of Ch'ŏngŭp.
Woods, H.   Over My Shoulder.
Wordsworth, W.   Affliction of Margaret, The.
Yang Shih-ch'i.   Night Rain: A Wall Collapses—Sent To My Neighbors.
Yellen, J.   Are You Havin' Any Fun?
Yi Kyŏngnim.   Oh Life.

Worship and Worshipers
Achterberg.   Trinity.
Awoonor.   At the Gates.
Basho.   Forbidden to speak.
Bhattācārya, K.   External rituals mean nothing. What's the fault of the poor mind?
Bible, *O.T.*   Psalm 100.
Carrera Andrade.   Your body is a golden temple.
Catullus.   Accept, O Priapus, the moister.
Clough.   Epi-strauss-ium.
Coleridge, S.   Aeolian [or Eolian] Harp, The.
Crashaw.   O sweet incendiary! shew here thy art.
Cross, E.   Sri Nityananda Mandir (The Temple of Nityananda).
Dās, R.   Now I'll see whether Siva.
Davies, W. H.   Moon, The.
Dickinson, E.   Some keep the Sabbath going to Church.
Dīnrām.   O Baba! Look at this Cadak tree.
  Out of love for You.
Dodge, C.   Wheel Ethics.
Doolittle, H.   Hippolytus Temporizes.
Dybek.   Benediction.
Emerson, R.   Sursum Corda.
Enheduanna.   From The Hymn to Inanna.
Fitzgerald, J.   House Beyond, The.
Gascoigne.   Gascoigne's Good-Morrow.
Gay, J.   Molly Mog [or The Fair Maid of the Inn].
Godolphin.   Hymn: "Lord, when the wise men came from far[r]."
Goode, S.   Lady of Pazardzik.
Han Yü.   Girl of Mount Hua, The.
Hemans.   Despondency and Aspiration.
Henderson, D.   Song of Devotion to the Forest.
Herbert, G.   Altar, The.
  Christmas.
  Praise (2).
  Prayer (1): "Prayer the Church's banquet, Angels' age."
  Temper (1), The.
Hill, A.   Between Worlds.
Hope, M.   Praise the Daughter.
Hopkins, G.   Pied Beauty.
Hudgins.   Gospel.
Hughes, L.   Testimonial.
Hung Hung.   Hymn to Hualien, A.
Inada.   List, The.
Kabir.   Hopeful Spiritual Athlete, The.
  Lamp without Oil, The.
  My First Marriage.
  To Be a Slave of Intensity.
  Why Arrange the Pillows.
Keats.   Fragment of an Ode to Maia Written on May Day, 1818.
Kendall, M.   Education's Martyr.
Kyger.   Every day I burn a stick of incense.
Kyunyŏ, Great Master.   Homage to the buddhas.
  I bow before the buddhas.
Li Po.   Up into the Clouds Music.
Magdeburg, Mechthild von.   True love in every moment praises God.
Mahadevi.   I do not call it his sign.
Mant, R.   Social Worship.
Mirabai [or Mira Bai].   Heat of Midnight Tears, The.
  I was going to the river for water.

Why Mira Can't Go Back to Her Old House.
Mukhopādhyāy, K.   Is there any treasure like the Mother's name?
Murray, L.   Gaelic Long Tunes, The.
Pāthak, G.   I'll worship You with tears, Ma.
Pātunī, N.   Ma, Hara's Beloved, Tara.
Perronet.   All Hail the Power of Jesus' Name.
Procter, A.   Present, The.
Rabi'a al-Adawiyya.   O my Lord.
Rāy, M. R.   Moon flashes in Her blessed face, The.
Rexroth, K.   Wednesday of Holy Week, 1940.
Riach, A.   Sankey Hymns.
Sappho.   In the young spring evening.
Savithri, M.   Black and White.
Sen, R.   Mind, how do you think you'll find Her?
Mind, you're still not rid of your illusions.
Oh my Mind, worship Kali.
So, Mind / You've decided to go on pilgrimage?
Smart, C.   My Cat Jeoffry.
O David, highest in the list.
Southwell.   Child[e] My Choice [or Choyse], A.
Stanley, T.   Paraphrase Upon Part of the CXXXIX Psalm, A.
Unknown.   I Found My Love by the Secret Canal.
Walk Softly.
Wang Wei.   Second Song for the Worship of the Goddess at Yu Mountain: "Bidding the Goddess Farewell".
Watts, I.   Flying Fowl, and Creeping Things, Praise Ye the Lord.
Whittier.   First-Day Thoughts.
Worship.
Winchilsea.   Hymn, The: "To the Almighty on his radiant throne."
Wright, J.   Ishtar.
Yu Xuanji.   At Home in the Summer Mountains.
See also **Churches; Prayer; Religion**

Wrath of God
Addonizio.   Theodicy.
Rosenberg, I.   God.
Spencer, A.   Letter to My Sister.
Weaver, A.   New Nephilim, A.

Wreaths
Shoneyin, T.   Bedside Wreaths.

Wrecks
Bolt, T.   I crossed.
Paterson, D.   Wreck, The.
Smith, D.   Wreck in the Woods.

Wren, Sir Christopher
Bentley, E.   Sir Christopher Wren.

Wrens
Clare, J.   Wren, The.
Conran.   Fledgling.
Davies, W. H.   Jenny Wren.
De la Mare.   Jenny Wren.
Goldberg, B.   Wren.
Issa.   That wren.
Levertov.   Wren, A.
Thompson, P.   Little Wren, A.
Unknown.   Hunting the Wren.
Wee Jenny Wren, The.

Wrestling and Wrestlers
Bevington, L.   Wrestling.
Francis, R.   Two Wrestlers.
Lefroy.   Palaestral Study, A.
Ramanujan.   At Forty.
Rogers, P.   Moving God.
Senryū, K.   Sumo wrestler, The.
Strato [or Straton].   Fitness expert. Big gym-man.
To start with, grapple your opponent 'round.

Wright Brothers (Wilbur and Orville Wright)
Crane, H.   Stars scribble on our eyes the frosty sagas.
Frost, R.   Wrights' Biplane, The.
Moolten, D.   Ode for Orville and Wilbur Wright.
Plumly.   Altitude.

Wright, James
Ai.   More.
Cooper, J.   Hotel de Dream.

Wright, Richard
Madgett.   Images.
Medina, T.   Big House Revisited, The.
Young, A.   One Snapshot I Couldn't Take in France, The.

Writer's Block
Akhmadulina.   To Await Arrival.
Bukowski.   Not So Good Night in the San Pedro of the World, A.
Christensen.   Poem on Death.
Hyde, E.   Explaining.
Radner, Rebecca.   I Want to Write like a Postcard.
Roberts, C.   Poor Zelda.
Rodríguez, A.   Apple.
Strand.   My Life by Somebody Else.

Writing and Writers
Abish, Walter.   What Else (Part 2).
Adamson.   Home, The Spare Room, The.
Agard, J.   Poetry Jump-Up.
Aiken, C.   Prelude II: "Two coffees in the Español, the last."
Aiken, J.   Do It Yourself.
Akhmadulina.   Lines Written During a Sleepless Night in Tbilisi.
Al-Rihani.   It Was All for Him.
Alexie.   How to Write the Great American Indian Novel.
Ali, A.   Homage to Faiz Ahmed Faiz.
Alvarez, J.   Bilingual Sestina.
Sonnet 42: "Sometimes the words are so close I am."
Woman's Work.
Ammons.   Anxiety's Prosody.
Anderson, M.   Sleep Writer, The.
Andrews, T.   Cinema Vérité: The Death of Alfred, Lord Tennyson.
Antin.   David ross called up from syracuse and wanted to know if.
Private Occasion in a Public Place, A.
Arghezi.   Flowers of Mildew.
Aridjis.   Wounded Self-Portrait, A.
Armand.   Another Poetics.
Arnold, M.   Memorial Verses.
Artaud.   All Writing Is Garbage.
Pounding and Gism.
Ten years that the language is gone.
Ashbery, J.   And "Ut Pictura Poesis" Is Her Name.
Auden.   In Memory of W. B. Yeats.
Babu, S.   Sound of Silence, The.
Baca.   It Started.
Bachmann.   No Delicacies.
Bandeira.   Poetics.
Barber, M.   Conclusion of a Letter to the Rev. Mr. C——, The.
Barkova, A.   Few Autobiographical Facts, A.
Barnard, M.   Fable of the Ant and the Word.
Basho.   When the winter chrysanthemums go.
Beer, P.   Jane Austen.
Bell, J.   Poem to Line My Casket with, Ramona.
Bell, M.   Shakespeare's Wages.
Berg, S.   Writing Class.
Berman, D.   Democratic Vistas.
Bernstein, C.   Klupzy Girl, The.
Wait.
Berrigan, T.   Academy of the future is opening its doors, The.
Final Sonnet, A.
It is a human universe: & I.
It is night. You are asleep. And beautiful tears.
It's 8:54 a.m. in Brooklyn it's the 28th [or 26th] of July [and].
On the 15th day of November in the year of the motorcar.
Sonnet LV: "Grace to be born and live as variously as possible."
Words for Love.
Berryman.   Henry's Fate.
Of Suicide.
Winters close, Springs open, no child stirs, The.
Betjeman.   Ballad of George R. Sims, The.
Reproof Deserved; or After the Lecture.
Blagden.   To George Sand on her Interview with Elizabeth Barrett Browning.
Blaser.   Image-Nation 22 (in memoriam).

Bloem, J. C.   Writing on a Tombstone.
Borges.   Matthew XXV:30.
Other Tiger, The.
Poem of the Gifts.
Boyle, K.   Poets.
Bradstreet, A.   Prologue, The: "To sing of wars, of captain[e]s, and of kings."
To My Dear Children.
Brecht, B.   Bad Time for Poetry.
Breytenbach.   Out There.
Bristol.   Crime of the Ages, The.
Brontë, E.   Alone I sat; the summer day.
Aye there it is! It wakes tonight.
Night Wind, The.
Brown, L.   Respond to Me.
Browne, W.   On the Countess Dowager of Pembroke.
Browning, E.   Aurora Leigh.
Curse for a Nation, A.
Fifth Book.
To George Sand: A Desire.
To George Sand: A Recognition.
Bryant, W.   Poet, The.
Buchanan, G.   Lyle Donaghy, Poet, 1902-1949.
Budenz.   Poeta Fui.
Bukowski.   Black Poets, The.
So you want to be a writer?
Bunimovich.   Excuse and Explanation.
Bunting.   What the Chairman Told Tom.
Burgess, F.   Cinq Ans Après.
Burns, R.   Second Epistle to Davie.
Buson.   Remembering how.
Cairns, Scott.   In Praise of Darkness.
Campbell, R.   On Some South African Novelists.
Cano, Luis.   I Light My Lamp.
Carew, T.   Fancy, A.
To Ben Jonson.
Carey, H.   Author's Quietus, The.
Carroll, K.   Short Poem.
Carruth, H.   On Being Asked to Write a Poem Against the War in Vietnam.
Cassian.   Other Life, The.
Cavalli.   Someone told me.
Cavendish, M.   Claspe, The.
Poetresses Petition, The.
Cawein.   Poetry.
Cervantes.   Poem for the Young White Man Who Asked Me How I, An Intelligent, Well-Read Person Could Believe in the War Between Races.
Chapman, G.   Homer and the Brazen Head of Rumour.
Chaucer.   Chaucer's Wordes unto Adam, his Owne Scriveyn.
Cheney-Coker.   Letter to a Tormented Playwright.
On Being a Poet in Sierra Leone.
Cherry, K.   History.
Ch'ŏn Yanghûi.   Every Morning in the Mirror.
Cisneros, A.   Paris Cinquième.
Cisneros, S.   Poet Reflects On Her Solitary Fate, The.
Clanchy, K.   Spell.
Coleridge, H.   He Lived amidst th' Untrodden Ways.
Coleridge, S.   On Donne's Poetry.
Collins, B.   Lines Lost among Trees.
Tuesday, June 4, 1991.
Writing in the Afterlife.
Cook, E.   Lines / Suggested by the Song of a Nightingale.
To the Late William Jerdan.
Coolidge, C.   Noon Point.
On Induction of the Hand.
Cooper, D.   Dreamt Up.
Poem for George Miles.
Cope, W.   Engineers' Corner.
Exchange of Letters.
Serious Concerns.
Triolet.
Corey, S.   Whatever Light.
Cortez, J.   Adupe.
No Simple Explanations.
Cowley, A.   Written in Juice of Lem[m]on.
Cowley, H.   Ode to Della Crusca.

To Della Crusca. The Pen.
Cowper, W. To Mary Unwin.
Crane, S. Many red devils ran from my heart.
Cronin, A. Lines for a Painter.
Cross, D. Let's try something.
Crowe, T. After Reading Han-Shan.
Cuadra, P. Manuscript in a Bottle.
Cucchi, M. Hibernation.
Cullen, C. Yet Do I Marvel.
Cunningham, J. Homer was poor. His scholars live at ease.
Dacre, C. Sappho; or, The Resolve.
Dalton, R. From a Revolutionary to J. L. Borges.
Darío, R. I Pursue a Form.
Darley. Pass of Death, The.
Davenant [or D'Avenant]. There, when they thought they saw in well sought Books.
Davie, D. Epistle. To Enrique Caracciolo Trejo.
Rejoinder to a Critic.
Davies, J. How to Write Anglo-Welsh Poetry.
Davies, Mererid Puw. Computers Are Poets Too.
Day Lewis. Where Are the War Poets?
de Folgar. Protest.
De la Mare. Moonshine.
Scribe, The.
Derricotte. For Black Women Who Are Afraid.
Devi. Invocation.
Di Prima. On Sitting Down to Write, I Decide Instead to Go to Fred Herko's Concert.
Poem on the Limits for My Writing Group: Atlantic Center for the Arts, New Smyrna Beach, Florida.
Dickinson, E. I reckon—when I count at all.
Missing All—prevented Me, The.
Publication—is the Auction.
This Is My Letter to the World.
This was a Poet—It is That.
Dimitrova. Ars Poetica.
Dischell. Tenant at Will, A.
Dobyns. His life was the practice of forming a single.
Donne. Canonization, The.
Sappho to Philaenis.
Triple Fool, The.
Dooley, D. How I Wrote It.
Doolittle, H. Fragment 36 [or Thirty-Six]: "I know not what to do."
Doty, M. My Tattoo.
Douglas, L. Dead Poet, The.
Dove, R. Nexus.
Dransfield. Day at a Time.
Endsight.
Dryden, J. Mac Flecknoe [or, A Satire upon the True-Blue Protestant Poet T. S.].
To the Pious Memory of the Accomplished [or Accomplisht] Young Lady, Mrs. Anne Killigrew, [Excellent in the Two Sister-Arts of Poesie and Painting. An Ode].
Duffy, C. Little Red-Cap.
Dunbar, P. Choice, A.
Poet, The.
Duncan, R. Bending the Bow.
Dancing Concerning a Form of Women, A.
In Blood's Domaine.
Poetry, a Natural Thing.
Duncombe, J. Females, Sacred and Profane.
Dupin. He Breathes before Writing.
There Exists.
When It Is Impossible.
Eady. Nature Poem.
Why Do So Few Blacks Study Creative Writing?
Edwards, K. Art of definition—is this, An.
Provisionally.
Einzig et al. Reading for Pleasure.
Eliot, T. S. So here I am, in the middle way, having had twenty years.
Ellis, T. Sticks.
View of the Library of Congress from Paul Laurence Dunbar High School.
Emerson, R. Poet.
Enright, D. Evil Days, The.
Erb, E. In the Picture.
Ettinger, E. Micrographic Manuscript,

Miniature (1).
Ewart. Black Box, The.
Fathy, S. For Heiner Muller: Poem 2.
Fearing. Literary.
Ferlinghetti, L. Adieu À Charlot.
Constantly Risking Absurdity.
Poem for Old Walt.
21.
Field. To Christina Rossetti.
Finch, A. Dickinson.
Reply From His Coy Mistress, A.
Finney, N. Fishing Among the Learned.
Fisher, R. Occasional Poem 7.1.72.
Fisken, Thomas Scott. Window Box.
Forbes, C. Poet's Shuffle, The.
Forbes, J. Monkey's Pride.
Forché. Ourselves or Nothing.
Fordham. Pen, The.
Frere. I've often wish'd that I could write a book.
Frost, R. It takes all sorts of in- and outdoor schooling.
Fusselman, A. Journal.
Gallagher, T. I Stop Writing the Poem.
Galvin, J. Story of the End of the Story, The.
Garcilaso de la Vega. Your Face Is Written in My Soul.
Gifford, W. Lo, Della Crusca! In his closet pent.
Gilbert, C. And, Yes, Those Spiritual Matters.
Gilbert, W. Ferdinando and Elvira; or, The Gentle Pieman.
Ginsberg, A. Howl.
Gioia. In Chandler Country.
My Confessional Sestina.
Next Poem, The.
Glaser, E. And in the Afternoons I Botanized.
Glück, L. Mountain, The.
Poem: "In the early evening, as now, a man is bending."
Glück, R. Burroughs.
Gorbanevskaya. Curse! Joy! Writing!, A.
What I drink is not hot, not sweet.
Gorham. Empress Receives the Head of a Taiping Rebel, The.
Graham, J. Covenant.
Graham, W. Malcolm Mooney's Land.
Grapes, J. I Like My Own Poems.
Listen.
Graves, R. Laureate, The.
Plea to Boys and Girls, A.
Reader over My Shoulder, The.
Gray, T. Progress of Poesy, The.
Greenberg, S. Etching.
Greenwell, D. To Christina Rossetti.
To Elizabeth Barrett Browning, in 1851.
To Elizabeth Barrett Browning, in 1861.
Gunn, T. J Car, The.
Hacker, M. Boy, The.
Feeling and Form.
Hadas, R. Winged Words.
Hall, D. For an Early Retirement.
To a Waterfowl.
Halliday, M. Get It Again.
Han Yü. Leaves fall turning turning to the ground.
This morning I can't seem to get out of bed.
Hands, E. Poem on the Supposition of the Book Having Been Published and Read, A.
Hardy, T. I Looked up from My Writing.
Harington [or Harrington]. Of honest Theft. To my good friend Master Samuel Daniel.
Harjo, J. Bird.
Strange Fruit.
Harper, M. In Hayden's Collage.
Harrison, T. Heartless Art, The.
On Not Being Milton.
Harte, B. Miss Edith's Modest Request.
Hartnett. I Have Exhausted the Delighted Range.
Man Who Wrote Yeats, the Man Who Wrote Mozart, The.
Harwood, L. Poem for Writers, A.
Hass, R. Churchyard.
Measure.
Hayden, R. Paul Laurence Dunbar.

Heaney, S. Digging.
From the Frontier of Writing.
Hejinian. Can one take captives by writing.
It is the writer's object.
Helle, A. Poem for Natalia Ginzburg.
Hemans. Grave of a Poetess, The.
Hemensley. Poem by John Thorpe, A.
Hemingway. Lady Poets With Foot Notes, The.
Herbert, G. Jordan (2).
Posy [or Posie], The.
Sonnet: "My God, where is that ancient heat towards Thee."
Herbert, Z. Five Men.
Hen.
Knocker, A.
Hernández Cruz. For the Far-Out Experimental Writer.
Today Is a Day of Great Joy.
Hernton, C. Distant Drum, The.
Herrick. Argument of His Book, The.
Departure of the Good Daemon, The.
His Poetry His Pillar.
His Prayer to Ben Jonson.
His Request to Julia.
To God ("Do with me, God! as Thou didst deal with John.").
Upon His Verses.
When He Would Have His Verses Read.
Hewitt, J. I Write For.
Local Poet, A.
Hikmet. All the things I've written about us are untrue.
Hilton, D. In Praise of Bic Pens.
Hirschman, J. Transfiguration.
Hirshfield, J. In Praise of Coldness.
Hoagland, E. Puttin' on the Dog.
Hokushi. Writing / Rubbing it out—.
Hollander, J. Forget How to Remember How to Forget.
Holmes, O. After-Dinner Poem (Terpsichore), An.
At the "Atlantic" Dinner, December 15, 1874.
Holub. Brief Reflection on Brief Reflections.
Hongo. Stomping with Pettit on the Battenkill.
Hood, T. First Attempt in Rhyme, A.
Literary Reminiscences.
Written in the Workhouse.
Hoover, P. Poems We Can Understand.
Horton, G. On Hearing of the Intention of a Gentleman to Purchase the Poet's Freedom.
Housman. Terence, this is stupid stuff.
Howe, F. Goodbye, Post Office Square.
Hudgins. Southern Literature.
Hughes, L. Letter to the Academy.
Theme for English B.
Hughes, T. Thought-Fox, The.
Hugo, R. Letter to Birch from Deer Lodge.
Letter to Goldbarth from Big Fork.
Letter to Haislip from Hot Springs.
Hugo, V. More about God (But with Some Reservations).
Ibáñez, S. Empty Page, The.
Ignatow, D. Witness.
Ismail. Buried Poem, The.
Issa. Writing shit about new snow.
Jaccottet. I Rise with an Effort.
Jackson, L. Poet's Corner, The.
Troubles of a Book, The.
Jackson, M. L. To Afaa Michael S. Weaver.
Urban Renewal 12.
Jackson, R. After the Dance.
1973.
Jacobs, H. It is not Just.
James, C. Book of My Enemy Has Been Remaindered, The.
Jeffers, R. But I Am Growing Old and Indolent.
Love the Wild Swan.
Jiménez, J. Intelligence, Give Me.
Name Drawn from the Names, The.
Johnson, J. O Black and Unknown Bards.
Johnson, S. Prologue Spoken by Mr[.] Garrick at the Opening of the Theatre in Drury Lane, 1747.
Johnston, A. To Robert Baron.
Johnston, E. Address to Nature on its Cruelty, An.

Jonas, S.   Book V.

Jones, R.   What effect has your new son had on your writing life?

Jong, E.   Castration of the Pen.

Jonson, B.   On Playwright ("Playwright convict of public wrongs to men.").

Sonnet to the Noble Lady, the Lady Mary Wroth, A.

To Thomas Palmer [on His Book *The Sprite of Trees and Herbs*].

Juana Inés de la Cruz.   In Acknowledgment of the Praises of European Writers.

Judson, J.   Whitman Again.

Kao Ch'i.   Song of the Man of Green Hill, The.

Kaplinski, J.   To Write More.

Kaufman, B.   Unhistorical Events.

Kavanagh, P.   Sanctity.

Keats.   Ode: "Bards of passion and of mirth."

On Leaving Some Friends at an Early Hour.

Kelly, R.   Rainmakers, The.

Kemble.   Impromptu.

Lines.

Kendall, M.   Failures.

Kendrick, D.   We are the Writing on the Wall.

Keyes, S.   War Poet.

Khalid, A.   Morning Window, A.

Killigrew, A.   Upon the Saying That My Verses Were Made by Another.

Kilmer, J.   Trees.

Kizer, C.   Promising Author.

Three.

Two.

Kleinzahler.   Case in Point, A.

Knight, E.   Black Poet Leaps to His Death, A.

For Black Poets Who Think of Suicide.

Green Grass and Yellow Balloons.

Poem to Galway Kinnell, A.

Koch, K.   Circus, The ("I remember when I wrote The Circus.").

Koertge.   Even Ornaments of Speech Are Forms of Deceit.

Komunyakaa, Y.   My Father's Love Letters [*or* Loveletters].

Kulishova, I.   Till now / I've not been able to imagine.

Kunitz, S.   Round, The.

Lahey, Joy.   Buckles.

Lamb, C.   In My Own Album.

Landon.   Stanzas on the Death of Mrs Hemans.

Landor, W.   Proud word you never spoke, but you will speak.

Lane, P.   Midnight Song.

Lanier, E.   To the Queen's Most Excellent Majesty.

Lanier, S.   Crystal, The.

Larkin, P.   Limerick: "There was an old fellow of Kaber."

Lars.   Recollection of Gabriela Mistral.

Lauterbach.   Novelist Speaks, The.

Lawrence, D. H.   I Am in a Novel.

Layton.   Berry Picking.

Birth of Tragedy, The.

Lazarus, E.   Echoes.

Leapor.   Headache, The.

Lear, E.   How Pleasant to Know Mr. Lear.

Lederer, K.   Sympathy and Envy.

LeFlore, S. B.   This Poem.

Leonard, T.   Fathers and Sons.

Levertov.   Caedmon.

Novel, The.

Secret, The.

Levine, P.   Poem of Chalk, The.

Levy, A.   London Poets.

Lewis, A.   To Edward Thomas.

Li Ho.   My Man Pa Replies.

Livingstone, D.   Giovanni Jacopo meditates.

Loftis, N.   Delirium.

In Memorium: Robert Hayden.

Longfellow, H.   Picture-Writing.

Poets, The.

Longley, M.   Freeze-Up.

López Mills, T.   Carta.

Letter: "Endings always erase the traces of their plot."

Lorde.   Learning to Write.

Lowell, A.   Sisters, The.

Lowell, J.   Emerson.

Lowell, R.   Epilogue: "Those blessèd structures, plot and rhyme."

Lowry, M.   Epitaph: "Malcolm Lowry."

Strange Type.

Lu Chi.   Rhymeprose on Literature.

Riding Crop, The.

Satisfaction, The.

Lumbreras, E.   Colina verde, una colina verde, Una.

Green Hill, a Green Hill, A.

MacBeth [*or* Macbeth].   Orange Poem, The.

MacDiarmid, H.   Caledonian Antisyzygy, The.

Poetry and Science.

To a Friend and Fellow Poet.

MacLeish.   Ars Poetica: "Poem should be palpable and mute, A."

MacNeice.   Elegy for Minor Poets.

Madhubuti.   Gwendolyn Brooks.

Poet: What Ever Happened to Luther?

Magrelli.   I look for a way of writing.

I prefer to come from silence to talk.

Pen slides, The.

Ten poems written in one month.

Mallarmé.   Toast.

Mansour, J.   Of Sweet Rest.

Markotić, N.   Try book-ending punctuation vouchers.

Marston, J.   Fy Satyre fie, shall each mechanick slave.

Martial.   Post-Obits and the Poets.

Why is it modern books are little read.

Marvell.   On Mr Milton's "Paradise Lost".

Masaoka Shiki.   Hands so cold.

Masters, E.   Margaret Fuller Slack.

Margaret Fuller Slack.

Petit, the Poet.

Matthews, W.   Mingus at The Showplace.

Maxton.   Ode.

Mayer, B.   Sonnet: "Beauty of songs your absence I should not show."

McElroy, C.   Learning to Swim at Forty-Five.

McGrath, T.   Ordonnance.

McOrlan.   Modern circus, The.

Meinke.   Poet, Trying to Surprise God, The.

Meng Chiao.   Lament for Lu Yin.

Mengham, Rod.   Smitten.

Menicanti.   To the Readers Who Write to Me.

Meredith, G.   Camelus Saltat.

Meredith, W.   What I Remember the Writers Telling Me When I Was Young.

Merrill, J.   Angel.

Clearing the Title.

From a Notebook.

Merry.   Genius, or Muse, whate'er thou art! whose thrill.

To Anna Matilda.

Merwin.   One of the Lives.

Milán, E.   I mean *you* as though referring to two furies because.

Me refiero a ti como a dos fieras porque.

Miller, E.   Another Love Affair/Another Poem.

Milosz, C.   Preparation.

Milton.   On Shakespear[e].

Moore, E.   To the Right Hon. Henry Pelham.

Moore, H.   Poem for the End.

Moore, M.   Baseball and Writing.

Poetry [1921 version]: "I, too, dislike it: there are things that are important beyond all this fiddle."

Moore, M.   Literature: The God, Its Ritual.

Moore, T.   Announcement of a New Grand Acceleration Company for the Promotion of the Speed of Literature.

Moramarco, F.   Novel.

Morgan, R.   Horace Kephart.

Morris, J.   Reading the Writing.

Morton, J.   Someone Asked the Publisher.

Moxley, Jennifer.   Transom Over Death's Door, A.

Mueller, L.   American Literature.

Muldoon, P.   Briefcase, The.

Lunch with Pancho Villa.

Mura.   Grandfather-in-law.

Murphy, R.   Moonshine.

Mutis.   Word, A.

Myers, J.   Experts, The.

Myrddin ap Dafydd.   Poet's Insurance Risk, The.

Naden.   Moonlight and Gas.

Poet and Botanist.

Nadir, M.   In Pencil.

Nemerov.   Style.

Nemes Nagy.   To a Poet.

Neruda.   Ode to César Vallejo.

Ode to Federico García Lorca.

Ni Dhomhnaill.   Language Issue, The.

Niccolai.   "What's that?" the boy asks his mother, pointing to the flag.

Nicholson, N.   To the River Duddon.

Niedecker.   Element Mother, The.

Who was Mary Shelley?

Noguere.   Scribes, The.

Secret, The.

Norse.   Believing in the Absurd.

Business of Poetry, The.

Norton, C.   Obscurity of Woman's Worth.

Notley.   Jack Would Speak Through the Imperfect Medium of Alice.

O'Grady, D.   Reading the Unpublished Manuscripts of Louis MacNeice at Kinsale Harbour.

O'Hara, F.   Critic, The.

Day Lady Died, The.

Getting Up Ahead of Someone (Sun).

Les Luths.

Memorial Day 1950.

My Heart.

Ode: Salute to the French Negro Poets.

Personal Poem.

Poetry.

Why I Am Not a Painter.

Oldham, J.   One night, as I was pondering of late.

Oliver, M.   Morning.

Ondaatje.   Burning Hills.

King Kong Meets Wallace Stevens.

Oppen.   Silver as / The needle's eye.

Whether, as the intensity of seeing increases, one's distance from Them, the people, does not also increase.

Orlovsky.   Collaboration: Letter to Charlie Chaplin.

Ovid.   Conclusion.

Elegy 1.15: "Envy, why carp'st [*or* carpest] thou my time is spent so ill."

Elegy 3.1: "Old wood stands uncut, of long years' space, An."

Every letter you've read in this whole book was written.

Padgett, R.   Poetic License.

Voice.

Page, G.   Elegist, The.

Jerry's Plains, 1848.

Late Night Radio.

Pak Mogwŏl [*or* Mokwŏl].   Bare Wind, A.

Palmer, M.   Eighth Sky.

Fifth Prose.

Sun ("Write this. We have burned all their villages.").

Word is coming up on the screen, give me a moment, A.

Parker, D.   Danger of Writing Defiant Verse, The.

Fighting Words.

Pig's-Eye View of Literature, A.

Parkes, B.   For Adelaide.

To an Author who Loved Truth More than Fame.

To Elizabeth Barrett Browning.

Parra, N.   I Take Back Everything I've Said.

Pasolini.   Day of My Death, The.

Paz.   Certainty.

Solo for Two Voices.

Writing.

Peake.   I cannot give the reasons.

Pellicer, C.   Wishes.

Perelman, C.   Chronic Meanings.

Let's Say.

Money.

Room.

Things.

Pérez Estrada, R.   Unpublished Man, The.
Perrine.   Janus.
Petersen, P.   I Listen to Alice Walker on a Pocket Radio.
Phillips, C.   As a Blow, from the West.
   Passing.
Pickard, T.   My Pen.
Pietri.   1st Untitled Poem.
Pizarnik.   Deaf Lantern.
   Foundation Stone.
Plath.   Stillborn.
Plumpp.   Poem: "Poems are not places."
Po Chü-i.   Madly Singing in the Mountains.
Polwhele.   Thou, who with all the poet's genuine rage.
Pope, A.   Epistle to Dr. Arbuthnot.
   Epitaph for One Who Would Not Be Buried in Westminster Abbey.
   Essay on Criticism.
   Impromptu: To Lady Winchelsea Occasioned by Four Satirical Verses on Women Wits, In *The Rape of the Lock*.
Popova, O.   What's left for me to say? God.
Porter, P.   On This Day I Complete My Fortieth Year.
Pound, E.   Hugh Selwyn Mauberley.
   Silet.
   Soirée.
   Tea-rose tea-gown, etc., The.
Powell, K.   Mental Terrorism.
Prado, A.   Fluency.
Pratt, M.   Poem for My Sons.
Prior.   In Imitation of Anacreon.
Prismanova.   Brontë Sisters, The.
   Lomonosov.
Prufer, K.   Ars Poetica: "I've written love notes all my life."
Pygge.   Robert Lowell's Notebook.
Quiller-Couch.   Harbour of Fowey, The.
Quillinan.   Hour Glass, The.
Radner, Rebecca.   Like That.
Radnóti.   Unnoticed.
Ralin, Radoi.   Safety Pins (excerpts).
Ransom, J.   Survey of Literature.
Reddy, S.   We Write.
Redmond.   Aerolingual Poet of Prey.
Reese, L.   Lyric on the Lyric, A.
Reeves, J.   W.
Remizov, Alexei.   Without Heat.
Reynolds, S. F.   Open Letter to All Black Poets, An.
Reznikoff.   I had been bothered by a secret weariness.
Ricard, R.   Visions of Arthur.
Rich, A.   I Am in Danger—Sir.
   Upper Broadway.
Rivera, M.   Transfer of Title.
   Traslación de dominio.
Roberts, E.   Primo Levi.
Robinson, E.   Shadrach O'Leary.
   Sonnet: "Master and the slave go hand in hand, The."
   Sonnet: "Oh for a poet—for a beacon bright."
Rome, H.   Don't Wanna Write About the South.
Rossetti, C.   L. E. L.
Rossetti, D.   On the Poet, Arthur O'Shaughnessy—.
Rothenberg, J.   Portrait of Myself with Arshile Gorky and Gertrude Stein.
Roubaud.   In This Tree.
Rowe, E.   Forgo the charming Muses! No, in spite.
Rowlands.   Prologue: "Under the shadow of the gloomy night."
Roy, L.   Bread Man, The.
Rózewicz.   Memory of a Dream From the Year 1963.
   Who Is a Poet.
Ryan, G.   Epilogue: "His money-making properties come back like a beach."
San Juan.   Three for the Road.
Sanchez, S.   To P. J. (2 Yrs Old Who Sed Write a Poem for Me in Portland, Oregon).
Sarton, M.   My Sisters, O My Sisters.
Scalise, G.   Dora Markus and Her Actors.
Scammell, W.   Jean Rhys.

Scannell.   Poem on Bread.
Schorn, B.   Entering Poetic Blindspots.
Schuyler, J.   Dec. 28, 1974.
   Dining Out with Doug and Frank.
Seth.   Week ago, when I had finished, A.
Sexton.   Black Art, The.
Shakespeare, W.   Sonnet 21: "So is it not with me as with that Muse."
   Sonnet 23: "As an unperfect actor on the stage."
   Sonnet 76: "Why is my verse so barren of new pride?"
   Sonnet 78: "So oft have I invok'd thee for my muse."
   Sonnet 80: "O, how I faint when I of you do write."
   Sonnet 86: "Was it the proud full sail[e] of his great verse."
   Sonnet 100: "Where art thou, Muse, that thou forget'st so long."
   Sonnet 106: "When in the chronicle of wasted time."
   Sonnet 108: "What's in the brain[e] that in[c]k may character."
   Sonnet 110: "Alas, 'tis true, I have gone here and there."
Shange.   Oh, I'm 10 Months Pregnant.
   You are Sucha Fool.
Shapiro, D.   Archaic Torsos.
   Realistic Bar and Grill, A.
Shehadeh, Mohammed.   Letters to Childhood.
Shelley, P.   Adonais; An Elegy on the Death of John Keats.
Shockley, E.   Shall become as.
Sidney.   Sonnet 1: "Loving in truth, and fain[e] in verse my love to show."
   Sonnet 3: "Let dainty wits cry on the sisters nine."
   Sonnet 15: "You that do search for every purling spring."
   Sonnet 27: "Because I oft, in dark abstracted guise."
   Sonnet 90: "Stella, think not that I by verse seek fame."
Silano, M.   In Henry Carlile's *Writing 213*.
Simmons, J.   Written, Directed by and Starring.
Sirr.   Beginnings.
Smith, C.   Partial Muse, has from my earliest hours, The.
   To a Friend.
   To Miss C—on Being Desired To Attempt Writing a Comedy.
   To Mr. Hayley, on Receiving Some Elegant Lines from Him.
   To the Naiad of the Arun.
   To the River Arun ("Be the proud Thames of trade the busy mart!").
   To the River Arun ("On thy wild banks, by frequent torrents worn.").
Smith, D.   Spring Poem, The.
Smith, I.   At the Scott Exhibition, Edinburgh Festival.
Smith, P.   Building Nicole's Mama.
Smith, S.   Souvenir de Monsieur Poop.
Snyder, G.   As for Poets.
   Axe Handles.
   How Poetry Comes to Me.
   Riprap.
Solomon ibn Gabirol.   Pen, The.
Spaziani.   Merciful Shore, The.
Spencer, B.   Night-Time: Starting to Write.
Spenser, E.   Sonnet 75: "One day I wrote her name upon the strand."
   Sonnet 80.
Stanton, M.   Space.
Starbuck, G.   Said ("Agatha Christie to.").
Stephen, J.   Sonnet, A: "Two voices are there: one is of the deep."
Stevenson, A.   Making Poetry.
   Re-reading Jane.
Strand.   Eating Poetry.
Suárez.   Poem, The: "If you start to write a poem."
Suckling, S.   Wits, The; A Session[s] of the Poets.
Sutherland, Fraser.   Auden's Face.
Swirszczynska [*or* Swir].   Woman Writer Does

Laundry, A.
Tada.   Poetry Calendar, A.
Taggart, J.   Pen Vine and Scroll.
Tate, A.   Non Omnis Moriar.
Tate, G.   Last Instructions.
Tate, J.   Poem: "Angel kissed my alphabet, The."
   Teaching the Ape to Write Poems.
Thomas, D.   Author's Prologue.
   Especially When the October Wind.
   In My Craft or Sullen Art.
Thomas, L.   Marvelous Land of Indefinitions, The.
Thomas, R.   Salamander.
Thompon, E.   My Study.
Thwaite, A.   Great Foreign Writer Visits Age-Old Temple, Greeted by Venerable Abbess, 1955.
Tipping.   Poet at Work.
Tornero, A.   Lisos al extremo cuando voltearon diurnos.
   Smooth in the extreme when they turned around diurnal.
Torres, E.   Bio-Rodent-Oriole.
Tranströmer.   Signatures.
Troupe.   In Jimmy's Garden.
Tsvetaeva [*or* Tsvetaeva].   I opened my veins. Unstoppably.
Tu Fu [*or* Du Fu].   Snow Storm.
   Spring Vigil in the Imperial Chancellery.
   To Pi Ssu Yao.
   Traveler at Night Writes His Thoughts, A.
Tuckerman, F.   As Sometimes in a Grove.
   But war his overturning trumpet blew.
Turner, F.   On the Pains of Translating Miklós Radnóti.
Twichell.   Quality of Striving, The ("Eye-catching as a dog on a chain.").
   Soul in Space.
Umpierre, L.   No Hatchet Job.
Unknown.   Leaving behind my writing brush and.
   Limerick: "Well, it's partly the shape of the thing."
   Riddle: "Land was white, The."
   Scribe, The: "For Weariness My Hand Writes Ill."
   Writing on an Ink-Stone, A.
Updike.   To Two of My Characters.
Valentine, J.   Waiting.
Van Duyn.   Moose in the Morning, Northern Maine.
   Vision Test, The.
Van Walleghen.   Walking the Baby to the Liquor Store.
Vaughan, H.   To the Most Excellently Accomplished Mrs. Katherine Philips.
Vazirani, R.   E-Mail.
Velichansky, A.   Trunks of birches, like scrolls.
Vilariño.   No.
Villaurrutia.   Poetry.
Voeten.   Sun On My Hand, The ("Sun lights my hand writing, The.").
   Sun On My Hand, The ("Writing with the sun on my hand.").
Voiture.   Rondeau: "Lord, I'm done for: now Margot."
Voznesensky [*or* Voznesenskii].   Autumn Prelude.
   Dogalypse.
   In the Mountains.
   Ironical Elegy, Composed in Those Terribly Sad Moments When I Cannot Write.
   Two Poems.
Wagoner, D.   Words, The.
Wakoski.   Hummingbird Light.
Walcott.   Camps hold [*or* held] their distance—[of] brown chestnuts and grey smoke, The.
   Codicil.
   Hotel Normandie Pool, The.
   Man Who Loved Islands, The.
Waldman, A.   How the Sestina (Yawn) Works.
   Paul Eluard.
Waller, E.   Of English Verse.
Ward, BJ.   Shakespeare as a Waiter.
Warren-Moore.   For Etheridge Knight.

Warren, R.   Flaubert in Egypt.
Warsh.   Dreaming Over a Page.
Watkins, V.   Demands of the Muse.
Watten.   Statistics.
Webb, H.   Synopsis of the Great Welsh Novel.
Weiner, E.   When My Poem Appeared.
Welch, L.   In Answer to a Question From P. W.
   Whenever I Make a New Poem.
Welish.   Blood or Color.
   Kiss Tomorrow Goodbye.
   Textile 12.
Welt.   I stopped writing poetry.
Whalen, P.   Walking beside the Kamogawa,
   Remembering Nansen and Fudo and Gary's
   Poem.
Wheatley, P.   To Maecenas.
Whitman, W.   As I Lay with My Head in Your
   Lap Camerado.
   As I Sit Writing Here.
   Excelsior.
   Had I the Choice.
   Here the Frailest Leaves of Me.
   I Am the Poet.
   Now Precedent Songs, Farewell.
   To a Certain Civilian.
Whittier.   Proem: "I love the old melodious
   lays."
Wieners.   Morgana La Fay.
Wilbur, R.   Beasts.
   Cottage Street, 1953.
   To an American Poet Just Dead.
   Writer, The.
Wilcox, E.   In the Night.
Wilde, L.   Désillusion.
   Poet's Destiny, The.
Williams, C. K.   Critic, The.
Williams, H.   Last Poem.
Williams, W.   Apology.
   Sort of a Song, A.
   There are no perfect waves.
Wilner, E.   Muse, The.
Wilson, E.   Enemies of Promise.
   Past Midnight.
Wilson, T.   Magpies in Picardy.
Winchilsea.   Answer, The [To Pope's
   Impromptu].
   Circuit of Apollo, The.
   Introduction, The: "Did I, my lines intend for
   public[k] view."
Winters, Y.   To a Young Writer.
Wise, S.   Advice.
Wither.   For a Poet.
Wordsworth, W.   London 1802 ("Milton! thou
   shouldst be living at this hour.").
   Scorn Not the Sonnet [Critic, You Have
   Frowned].
Wright, C. D.   Next to Last Draft, The.
Wright, C.   California Dreaming.
   Cicada Blue.
   Quotations.
   Reunion.
Wright, F.   Circle Drawn in Water.
   Lines Written in the Dark Illegible Next Day.
   Publication Date.
Wyat, H.   What makes me write my dearest
   Freind you aske.
Yearsley.   Rural Lyre, The.
Yeats.   Coole Park, 1929.
   On Being Asked for a War Poem.
Yevtushenko [or Evtushenko].   Cemetery of the
   Whales, The.
   From a Talk.
Yi Kyubo.   Burning My Manuscripts.
Yosano Akiko.   In the First Person.
Young, A.   Studio Up Over In Your Ear.
Young, E.   Seascape.
Yüan Hao-wen.   With Chang Hung-lüeh, Court
   Attendant, Discussing Literature.
Yuan Mei.   Writing What I've Seen.
Zephaniah.   According to my Mood.
See also **Handwriting**
Wyatt, Sir Thomas
Amis, K.   Note on Wyatt, A.
Surrey.   Wyatt Resteth Here.

Wyoming (state)
Becker, R.   Dreaming at the Rexall Drug.
Buckley, C.   Early Morning—Ucross, Wyoming.
Jacobik, G.   Dust Storm.
Major, C.   I Was Looking for the University.
Rawlins, C.   Living in at Least Two Worlds.
Rosten.   I am immortal in Cheyenne!
Slicer, D.   Sunflowers, Wyoming.
Wedmore, S.   Why I'm Different in Wyoming.

X

Xenophanes
Emerson, R.   Xenophanes.
X-Rays
Abse.   X-Ray.
Bonset.   X-Rays.
Charach, R.   MRI.
Harwood, G.   Bone Scan.
Shwarts [*or* Shvarts].   Elegy on an X-ray Photo
   of My Skull.
Tatarunis, P.   Chest X-Ray.
Triplett, P.   Studies in Desire.

Y

Yachts
Spencer, B.   Yachts on the Nile.
Williams, W.   Yachts, The.
See also **Boats and Boating; Sailing and Sailors**
Yaks
Belloc.   Yak, The.
Buchanan, O.   Only Yak in Batesville, Virginia,
   The.
Corso.   Mad Yak, The.
Roethke.   Yak, The.
Yangtze River
Daisen.   All things come apart.
Lu Yu.   I Had Occasion to Tell a Visitor about
   an Old Trip I Took.
   Merchant's Joy, The.
Shunoku.   After the spring song, "Vast
   emptiness, no holiness".
Su Tung-p'o.   Tune: "Charming Nien-Nu".
Unknown.   South of the Yangtze.
Yankees
Harper, F.   Learning to Read.
Yankees (New York baseball team)
Moore, M.   Baseball and Writing.
Years
Benét, S.   Song of the Riders.
Chih-Wen, S.   On Old Zhang's Pine Tree.
Coolbrith.   Years, The: "What do I owe the
   years, that I should bring."
Haavikko.   Days become years. Years.
   One who writes us is now doing four plays a
   year, The.
Lister, R.   Toast to 2,000, A.
Longfellow, H.   Poet's Calendar, The.
Lu Chih.   Seventy Years Are Few.
Moore, M.   What Are Years?
Pagis, D.   Wall Calendar.
Pow.   Years, The: "Sometimes to get their own
   back."
Probyn.   Anniversaries.
Smith, D.   2000.
Stowe.   Only a Year.
Tada.   Poetry Calendar, A.
Walders, D.   Anniversary.
Willis, N.   New Year, The.
Yeats, John Butler
Eichner, Maura.   Imagist at Coney Island.
Yeats, William Butler
Auden.   In Memory of W. B. Yeats.
Booth, P.   Relations: Old Light / New Sun /
   Postmistress / Earth / 04421.
Fallon, P.   Yeats at Athenry Perhaps.
French, W.   Queen's After-Dinner Speech, The.
Ginsberg, A.   After Yeats.
Hartnett.   Man Who Wrote Yeats, the Man Who
   Wrote Mozart, The.
Jackson, F.   Elvis Reads The Wild Swans at
   Coole.
Keyes, S.   William Yeats in Limbo.
Muldoon, P.   Wystan.
Wright, K.   Love Song of Tooting, A.
Yellow (color)
Al-Mushafi.   Yellow Its Color.
Buson.   Evening primrose.
Cabico, R.   Afternoon in Pangasinan with No
   Electricity, An.
Collop.   Praise of a Yellow Skin, The, or An
   Elizabeth in Gold.
Harrison, D.   Yellow.
Herrera.   Yellow Room, The.
Hongo.   Yellow Light.
Jacobsen, J.   Yellow.
Jiménez, J.   Yellow Spring.
Senior.   Meditation on Yellow.
Shy, S.   Bringing My Son to the Police Station
   to Be Fingerprinted.
Wilde, O.   La Dame Jaune.
   Symphony in Yellow.
Yellow River [China]
Unknown.   Having not yet crossed the Yellow
   River, my heart is not at peace.
Yellowstone National Park
Beath, M.   Solid Ground.
Kumin, M.   October, Yellowstone Park.
Yesenin, Sergey
Harrison, J.   I am four years older than you but
   scarcely an unwobbling.
   I don't have any medals. I feel their lack.
   I wanted to feel exalted so I picked up.
   It would surely be known for years after as the
   day I shot.
   Lustra. Officially the cold comes from
   Manitoba.
   This matted and glossy photo of Yesenin.
   What if I own more paper clips than I'll ever
   use in this.
Yew Trees
Boker.   Sonnet 25: "Leaden eyelids of wan
   twilight close, The."
Delmore, E.   Yew.
Plath.   Moon and the Yew Tree, The.
Tennyson, A.   Old yew, which graspest at the
   stones.
Thompson, F.   Fallen Yew, A.
Yiddish
Amir, D.   Nightingale of Uncle Yair, The.
Morris, Matt.   Sham Jew.
Osherow.   Yiddish Muses, The.
Pelletiere, M.   Under Her Crib.
Utkin.   Tale of Red-Haired Motele, Mister
   Inspector, Rabbi Isaiah and Commissar Blokh,
   The.
Ying Yao
Wang Wei.   Weeping for Ying Yao.
Yoga and Yogis
Bhattācārya, M.   Screening its face amongst
   lotus stalks.
Dīnrām.   Renunciation's agonies.
Han-shan.   Ever since I left home.
Sen, R.   Kulakundalini, Goddess Full of
   Brahman, Tara.
   Managing the house is a big problem.
   Who is that Syama woman.
Yom Kippur
Ettinger, E.   Glass, The.
Osherow.   Yom Kippur Sonnet, with a Line from
   Lamentations.
Yorkshire, England
Ewart.   Yorkshiremen in Pub Gardens.
Hughes, T.   Heptonstall.
Stroud, J.   Directions.
Young Adult
Aguilar, M.   Sunshine.
Alviso, M.   Barbies, Las.
Anderson, T.   I Think You Got Me Confused.
Angguish, D.   Arrythmia (1–10).
Aragon, F.   Doubletalk.
   Earplugs.
Arroyo, R.   Longing: "It wasn't just about sex,
   but about."
   My Mysterious Body.
B., L.   After School Commute with My Girl.
Bailey, S.   Hide-n-Seek.
Banzon, K.   Here's a Match.

Boden, C.   Sombreo Beach, Vancouver Island, BC.
Brannan, J.   Texas Sunrise, A.
Coccia, M.   We Are Not Vegetarians.
Conway, J.   Odd Years, The.
Costello, R.   Uncertain Geometry.
   When My Sister Was Fifteen.
Dalby, L.   MacArthur High School.
Daugherty, B.   Lilac.
   Nightfire.
de la Parra Jr., J.   Awakening.
   Courage!
De la Tierra.   Butterflying.
Evans, A.   Playing for Love.
   Something More Obvious.
González, R.   Crush.
   Mariposa.
Healey, T.   Bubble.
   Ode to DJ.
Helfand, J.   Girl in the Boy's Dressing Room, The.
Hightower, S.   Cruising a Hungry World.
   Spending the Night.
Holland, W.   Black Water Creek.
Mann, R.   Elegy for the Hurdler.
Martin, D.   Clock.
   If We Were in a Gregg Araki Movie.
Murray, C.   I Got Beat Up A Lot in High School.
   Mickey Mouse.
Pafunda, Danielle.   Saltbox Brothel.
Palmer, R.   Logic of Queerness, The: (Releasing Your Ivy Evening Within).
Pickering, R.   Untitled: "First thought in my head waking up was, oh no."
Rachel, T.   You Can't Go Back to Sleep.
Richard, B.   My Sixth Grade Sex Life: Milne Elementary, New Orleans.
Schneiderman, J.   Last Ditch.
Shakan, J.   Soft.
Shipley, A.   Mama Said.
Simon, O.   Heat.
Stahl, C.   Greyhound.
   Polestar.
Stillpoint, H.   Form a Band, Goddammit.
   This I Whisper.
Trinidad.   Boy, The.
   Slicker.
Wascovich, M.   Serial Toxic Teen.
   Wolf Packet and Rural America.
Wozek, G.   Song to Myself at Seventeen.
Zetter, S.   Misdemeanor.

Young, Lester
Young, A.   Lester Leaps In.
Zimmer.   Sitting with Lester Young.

Youth
Adcock, F.   Kissing.
Addonizio.   Them.
Allen, E.   Rock Me to Sleep[, Mother].
Alpaugh, D.   Young, The.
Anderson, M.   September Song.
Aragon.   Waltz of the Twenty-Year-Olds, The.
Ashbery, J.   Other Tradition, The.
Bandeira.   Evocation of Recife.
Barker, J.   To My Young Lover.
Barnett, C.   Return, 2, The.
Bawer.   Grand Central Station, 20 December 1987.
Becker, R.   Midlife.
Bei Dao.   Résumé.
Berrigan, A.   Four Minute History of Getting It Together in Order to Be Fabulous, Briefly, A.
Bhartrihari.   While His Body's Vigor Is Whole.
Blake, W.   Ah, Sun-Flower [or Ah! Sun-Flower].
   School-Boy, The.
Bloem, J. C.   Sunday.
Bly, R.   For My Son Noah, Ten Years Old.
Bogan, L.   Tale, A.
Bolton, J.   In Memory of the Boys of Dexter, Kentucky.
Brewer, G.   Journals, The.
   Teen Drowns in Rehabilitation Camp Days Before 17th Birthday, Questions Persist.
Brome.   Epithalamy.
Brooke, R.   Sonnet: In Time of Revolt.

Brooks, G.   We Real Cool.
Broumas, O.   Way a Child Might Believe, The.
Browning, R.   Evelyn Hope.
   Rabbi Ben Ezra.
   Youth and Art.
Bryant, W.   Return of Youth, The.
Burke, C.   Lizzie.
Bynner.   Lines to Do with Youth.
Byron, G.   'All Is Vanity, Saith the Preacher'.
   Stanzas Written on the Road between Florence and Pisa.
Camlan.   Education in Wales.
Campion, T.   What Fair[e] Pomp[e].
Carroll, L.   Father William.
Carson, A.   Short Talk on the Youth at Night.
Castro, R.   Feet of Spring Are on the Stair, The.
Cernuda.   Shadow, The.
Cervantes.   Meeting Mescalito at Oak Hill Cemetery.
Chédid Andrée.   Looking at Childhood.
Cherokee Oral Tradition.   Formula to Secure Love.
Ch'i-chi.   Song of the Insolent Air.
Clive.   Old Age.
Cole, W.   William Shakespeare.
Coleridge, H.   First Birthday, The.
Coleridge, M.   Unwelcome.
Coleridge, S.   Youth and Age.
Connolly, G.   Summer I Was Sixteen, The.
Coward.   Poor Little Rich Girl.
Cowley, H.   Departed Youth.
Creeley.   First Love.
Cullen, C.   Uncle Jim.
Cummings, E. E.   You Shall Above All Things Be Glad and Young.
Cunningham, J.   I married in my youth a wife.
Curtis, T.   Pembrokeshire Buzzards.
D'Aguiar, F.   English Sampler, An.
Dalton, R.   Looking for Trouble.
   Memory.
Darr.   At Sixteen.
Davie, D.   Garden Party, The.
Dickey, J.   Leap, The.
Dooley, M.   What Every Woman Should Carry.
Dove, R.   Flash Cards.
Drake, E.   It Was a Very Good Year.
   Just for Today.
Dubin, A.   Young and Healthy.
Duhamel.   Ego.
Dunn, S.   Tenderness.
El-Gabry, M.   Child Hunting Tales, A.
El-Hadi, S.   Drama, The.
Elizabeth I.   When I Was Fair and Young.
Emerson, R.   In an Age of Fops and Toys.
Engvick, W.   While We're Young.
Fanshawe, C.   When Last We Parted.
Felltham [or Feltham].   On a Hopeful Youth.
Ferlinghetti, L.   Pennycandystore beyond the El, The.
Frost, R.   Birches.
Gardner, I.   Milkman, The.
Gelman.   Eyes.
Glück, L.   Garden, The: "I couldn't do it again."
   Unwritten Law.
Goethe.   Mignon Aspiring to Heaven.
Goodman, M.   February Ice Years.
Gordon, M.   You Make Me Feel So Young.
Gray, T.   Ode on a Distant Prospect of Eton College.
Grossman, A.   Enough Rain for Agnes Walquist.
Gruffydd, W.   1914–1918 The Young to the Old.
Hall, D.   X.
Hamer.   Different Strokes Bar, San Francisco, The.
Han-shan.   Graceful handsome youth, A.
HaNagid.   You Mock Me Now in Your Youth.
Harbach, O.   Let's Begin.
   Yesterdays.
Harris, Ken.   You Don't Know What Love Is.
Hart, L.   I Didn't Know What Time It Was.
Haskins, L.   Prodigy, The.
Hayden, R.   Paul Laurence Dunbar.
Heaney, S.   Guttural Muse, The.
Heard, J.   To Youth.
Heine, H.   Young Man Loves a Maiden, A.
Herbert, G.   Answer, The.

Herd.   Bathing Girls, The.
Herrick.   To the Virgins, to Make Much of Time.
Heyman, E.   Blame It on My Youth.
Hine.   Côte de Liesse.
Hinsey, E.   Body in Youth, The.
Hogg, J.   Boy's Song, A.
Holmes, O.   Illustration of a Picture.
Hope, M.   Sixth Grade.
Horace.   Ode 1.25: Ribald Romeos Less and Less Berattle ("Parcius iunctas quatiunt fenestras").
   Ode 4.7: "Snow dissolv'd no more is seen, The."
Housman.   Epitaph: "Here dead lie we because we did not choose."
   Lads in their hundreds to Ludlow come in for the fair, The.
   When I was one-and-twenty.
Hsin Ch'i-chi.   Tune: "Picking Mulberry Seeds" Written on a Wall en route to Po-shan.
Hull, L.   Midnight Reports.
Ibaragi Noriko.   When I Was Prettiest in My Life.
Ifan, W.   Vale of My Youth, The.
Irvine, W.   To be Young, Gifted, and Black.
Ishikawa Takuboku.   After Endless Discussions.
Iskander.   Once a girl, all April-fresh.
Issa.   Even a fleabite.
Jacob, M.   Little Poem.
Jacobsen, J.   Blue-Eyed Exterminator, The.
Jamie, K.   Rooms.
Jarman, M.   Astragaloi.
Jarrell, R.   Face, The.
Jeffers, R.   Age in Prospect.
Johnson, B.   Advice to a Reckless Youth.
Johnson, S.   Short Song of Congratulation, A [or To a Young Heir].
Jones, A.   Communal Living.
Jones, R.   Song of the Old Man.
Jonson, B.   Song. To Celia ("Come my Celia, let us prove.").
Juan Chi.   Elder lives by the side of the river, An.
   In My Youth.
   Weird Dances.
Kerouac.   127th Chorus.
Kingsley, C.   Young and Old.
Kinsella, T.   Chrysalides.
Kinzie.   Glinting like water.
Kipling, R.   R.A.F. (Aged Eighteen).
Kitahara Hakushū.   Summer Mist, A.
Knight, E.   For Freckle-Faced Gerald.
Knott.   Unsubscriber, The.
Koch, K.   To My Twenties.
Külebi, C.   Once Upon a Time: "Every morning you used to play hooky."
Kushner, A.   Memoirs.
Lamb, C.   To Louisa M[artin], Whom I Used to Call "Monkey".
Landesman.   Ballad of the Sad Young Men, The.
Larkin, P.   Sad Steps.
Lawrence, D. H.   Fight! O My Young Men.
   Youth Mowing, A.
Le Pan.   Incident, An.
Leigh, C.   Young at Heart.
Leopardi.   To Sylvia.
Levine, P.   You Can Have It.
Levis.   Poet at Seventeen, The.
Lewis, J.   Girl Help.
Lewis, S.   How 'Ya Gonna Keep 'Em Down on the Farm? (After They've Seen Paree).
Li Po.   River Merchant's Wife, The; A Letter.
Li Shang-yin.   Boasting of My Son.
Lindsay, V.   Leaden-eyed, The.
Llywelyn-Williams.   When I Was Young.
Loesser.   They're Either Too Young or Too Old.
Longfellow, H.   My Lost Youth.
Longley, M.   Flowering, A.
Lukata, B.   Rehearsal.
Mapanje.   On African Writing.
Marbod of Rennes.   This vision of a face, radiant and full of beauty.
Martial.   Epigram: Likeness, The.
   This was the young Camonus; this his face.
Marvell.   Horatian Ode upon Cromwell's Return

from Ireland, An.
McCord, D.   Blessed Lord, What It Is to Be Young.
McDaniel, J.   Logic in the House of Sawed-Off Telescopes.
McGinley.   Ballade of Lost Objects.
Portrait of a Girl with Comic Book.
Village Spa.
Mei Yao Ch'en.   Next Door.
Meireles.   Sketch.
Meredith, W.   Myself, Rousseau, a Few Others.
Merrill, B.   Staying Young.
Merrill, J.   Watching the Dance.
Merwin.   Lament for the Makers.
Meynell, A.   October Redbreast, The.
Miles, J.   Album: "This is a hard life you are living."
Milnes.   Youth, That Pursuest.
Milton.   How soon hath Time the subtle [or suttle] thief [or theef] of youth.
L'Allegro.
Moody, E.   To a Friend, Who Gave the Author a Reading Glass.
Moore, T.   No—Leave My Heart to Rest.
Murphy, R.   Morning Call.
Murray, J.   Epithalamium, An.
Nemerov.   Blue Suburban.
Boy with Book of Knowledge.
Noguchi, R.   From Rooftops, Kenji Takezo Throws Himself.
Really Long Ride, The.
Norton, C.   Recollections: "Do you remember all the sunny places."
Nye, N.   Boy Removes All Traces from His Room, The.
O'Hara, F.   Animals.
Blocks.
Orr, G.   Gray Fox, The.
Orton, B.   Beekeeper.
Sea Monkeys, The.
Ou-yang Chiung.   Offering Congratulations to the Enlightened Reign.
Ovid.   Elegy 3.6: "Either she was foul, or her attire was bad."
Owen, W.   Anthem for Doomed Youth.
Parable of the Old Men and the Young, The.
Sonnet, to a Child.
Parra, N.   Tunnel, The.
Pasolini.   Civil Song.
Pastan.   Death's Blue-Eyed Girl.
Patchen.   Street Corner College.
Perillo, L.   Skin: "Back then it seemed that wherever a girl took off her clothes the police would find her."
Petri.   Christmas 1956.
Petronius Arbiter.   Long may our hearts, Nealce, guard that night.
Philodemus.   I Loved—Who Hasn't?
Pilinszky, J.   On the Back of a Photograph.
Pindar.   Ode on Theoxenos.
Pinkney, E.   Voyager's Song, The.
Pizarnik.   Awakening, The.
Po Chü-i.   At the End of Spring.
Poe.   Lake: To———, The.
Pollard, C.   On the first of January.
Powell, D. A.   Nicholas the ridiculous: you will always be 27 and impossible. No more expectations.
Thicknesses of victor decreased: blanket->sheet->floss. Until no material would do, The.
Praed.   School and Schoolfellows.
Propertius.   Night's best of all. Night brings delight.
Randall, D.   Haymakers.
Ransom, J.   Piazza Piece.
Vision by Sweetwater.
Redgrove, P.   My Father's Trapdoors.
Reid, A.   Daedalus.
Rexroth, K.   For Eli Jacobson.
Rhianos.   To Theodorus et al.
Rich, A.   Middle-Aged, The.
Rilke.   We Must Die Because We Have Known Them.
Rimbaud, A.   Romance.
Robinson, A.   Sibyl, The.

Robinson, R.   Creek, The.
Rochester, J.   Against Constancy.
Roethke.   Wish for a Young Wife.
Ronsard.   Roses.
Rosenthal, G.   Only 20 Years Old.
Rosnay, J.   Piazza San Marco.
Rossetti, C.   Youth gone, and beauty gone if ever there.
Rothman, D.   Youth.
Rowe, V.   Youth.
Sanchez, S.   Ballad: "Forgive me if i laugh."
Sappho.   With what, dear bridegroom, can I fairly compare you?
Satyamurti.   Day Trip.
Schuyler, J.   Can I Tempt You to a Pond Walk?
Schwartz, R. L.   Why I Forgive My Younger Self Her Transgressions.
Scott, W.   Early Aspirations.
Scovell.   Listening to Collared Doves.
Seidman.   Gail.
Seifert.   Candlestick, The.
Shakespeare, W.   O[h] Mistress Mine.
Sonnet 3: "Look in thy glass, and tell the face thou viewest."
Sonnet 126: "O thou, my lovely boy, who in thy power."
Shaoxuan.   Black hair and red cheeks: for how long?
Shurbanov, A.   Attractions.
Sidney.   Sonnet 21: "Your words my friend (right healthful caustics) blame."
Simmons, J.   One of the Boys.
Solon.   Love of Boys, The.
Sorrentino.   Razzmatazz.
Soto.   Dizzy Girls in the Sixties.
Southey, R.   Old Man's Comforts and How He Gained Them, The.
Remembrance.
Stallings.   Dead Language Lesson.
Strato [or Straton].   Twelve-year-old looks fetching in his prime, A.
Strickland, A.   Infant, The.
Suckling, S.   Against Fruition ("Stay here, fond youth, and ask no more.").
Surrey.   Laid in My Quiet Bed.
Symons, A.   Faint Love.
Taylor, B.   Love Returned.
Tennyson, A.   We leave the well-beloved place.
Theocritus.   Idyll 29: ""Truth in the cups" men say, dear youth."
Thompson, D.   Days of Yore, The.
Toomer.   Delivered at the Knighting of Lord Durgling by Great Bruce-Jean.
Trethewey, N.   Cameo.
Troupe.   Reflections on Growing Older.
Tufts, C.   We Take the New Young Couple Out to Dinner.
Turner, C.   Hence with your jeerings, petulant and low.
Unknown.   Little Rose.
Lofty trees of the south, The.
Milla.
Please, Sir Second-born.
Seize the moment!—.
Youth.
Van Duyn.   What the Motorcycle Said.
Velichansky, A.   Infant is white, like down, The.
And the youth dark-complexioned, like shingle.
Verlaine.   In Prison.
Vroomkoning.   Together Again ("I behold her there.").
Walcott.   Glory Trumpeter, The.
Walden, G.   Misguided Angels.
Waller, E.   Of the Last Verses in the Book.
Wang Ch'ang-ling.   Silent at Her Window.
Warren, R.   Red-Tail Hawk and Pyre of Youth.
Watts.   Ten Years Ago.
Wei Chuang.   Tune: "The Bodhisattva Foreigner".
Wever.   In Youth Is Pleasure.
Whitman, W.   We Two Boys Together Clinging.
Wilbur, R.   Star System, The.
Wilkinson, A.   On a Bench in a Park.
Williams, C. K.   Love: Beginnnings.
World's Greatest Tricycle-Rider, The.

Williams, J.   On Reading Aloud My Early Poems.
Winchilsea.   There's No To-Morrow.
Upon My Lord Winchilsea's Converting the Mount in His Garden to a Terrace.
Winters, Y.   Summer Commentary, A.
To a Young Writer.
Witt, S.   Michael Masse.
Wodehouse.   You Never Knew About Me.
Wohlfeld.   That Which Is Fugitive, That Which Is Medicinally Sweet or Alterable to Gold, That Which Is Substantiated by Unscientific Means.
Wordsworth, W.   Our birth is but a sleep and a forgetting.
Wright, J.   Child, The.
Wrigley, R.   For the Last Summer.
Yeats.   Down by the Salley Gardens.
On Hearing That the Students of Our New University Have Joined the Agitation against Immoral Literature.
Politics.
Who Goes with Fergus?
Yesenin [or Essenin].   I Regret Nothing.
Sleigh, The.
Yi Kyubo.   Burning My Manuscripts.
Yi Sanghûi.   Farewell, My Youth.
Young, J.   How 'Ya Gonna Keep 'Em Down on the Farm? (After They've Seen Paree).
Yüan Mei.   Growing Old (2).
Yun Tongju.   Self-portrait.

Yugoslavia
Hampton.   Yugoslav Story.
Harrison, T.   Cycles of Donji Vakuf.
Hugo, R.   Yards of Sarajevo, The.
Teschke, H.   Minutes of Hasiba, The.

Yukon Territory
Ramanujan.   Foundlings in the Yukon.
Service.   Cremation of Sam McGee, The.
Tarn.   Kluane, the Yukon.

Z

Zapata, Emiliano
Herrera.   Mexican World Mural / 5 x 25.

Zebras
Campbell, R.   Zebras, The.
Laurencin, M.   Zebra, The.

Zen Buddhism
Allen, P.   Zen Americana.
Anbun.   Years keeping that in mind.
Andrews, N.   Satori.
Baekoon Kyunghan.   Twelve More Songs for Master Jikong.
Baiho.   On Entering His Coffin.
Basho.   Autumn moon / Tide foams.
Come, let's go / snow-viewing.
Come, see / real flowers.
Cormorant fishing / How stirring.
Crow's / Abandoned nest.
Dozing on horseback / smoke from tea-fires.
Journey's end / Still alive.
June rain / hollyhocks turning.
Melon / In morning dew.
Shrieking plovers / Calling darkness.
Skylark.
Smell of autumn / Heart longs.
Temple bell / A cloud of cherry flowers.
To the willow.
Wintry day / On my horse.
Withered grass / Under piling.
Year's end / All corners.
Year's end / Still in straw hat.
Betsugen.   All night long I think of life's labyrinth.
Bokuo.   For seventy-two years / I've kept the ox well under.
Bun-Etsu.   Sixty-five years.
Bunan.   Moon's the same old moon, The.
When you're both alive and dead.
Chia Tao.   Weeping for the Zen Master Boyan.
Chiao-jan.   I don't like foreign languages; I won't study them.
Chien Chang.   Sent to Zen Master Yun-Shui.

Chifu. No mind, no Buddhas, no live beings.
Chikusen. He's part of all, yet all's transcended.
Chimi Sucho. To a Monk Asking About Zen.
Chitsu. No more head shaving.
Cole, H. Buddha and the Seven Tiger Cubs.
Daegak Euchon. At Chonymyung Temple.
Daichi. Thoughts arise endlessly.
Daichu. Fiery unicorn snapped, The.
Daie-Soko. Life's as we / Find it—death too.
Daigu. Here none think of wealth or fame.
  Who dares approach the lion's.
Daisen. All things come apart.
Daito. At last I've broken Unmon's barrier!
  To slice through Buddhas, Patriarchs.
Dangai. Earth, river, mountain.
Dankyo-Myorin. Coming, I clench my hands.
Di Prima. Dokusan: Visit to Katagiri Roshi.
  For Suzuki Roshi.
  Tassajara, Early 1970's.
Dogen. Coming, going, the waterfowl.
  Western Patriarch's doctrine is transplanted!,
  The.
Eian. Joshu's "Oak in the courtyard".
Eichu. My eyes eavesdrop on their lashes!
Emperor Kōkō. Word at last, The.
Fugai. Only the Zen-man knows tranquillity.
Fumon. Magnificent! Magnificent!
Fuyo-Dokai. Seventy-six: done.
Gasan. Invaluable is the Soto Way.
Gekko-Sojo. How Zenists carry on.
Gekkutsu-Sei. I set down the emerald lamp.
Genko. Unaware of illusion or enlightenment.
Gesshu Soko. Seven seas sucked up together,
  The.
Getsudo. I moved across the Dharma-nature.
Gido. Inscription over His Door.
Gojusan. Seamless.
Greening, T. My Children Visit the Zendo.
Guchu. Men without rank, excrement spatulas.
Hakugai. Last year in a lovely temple in
  Hirosawa.
Hakuin. How lacking in permanence the minds
  of the sentient.
  Past, present, future: unattainable.
  Priceless is one's incantation.
  You no sooner attain the great void.
Hakuyo. Over the peak spreading clouds.
Hamill, S. To Hayden Carruth on His Eightieth
  Birthday.
Han Wo. Letter to a Zen Master.
Han-shan Te-ch'ing. Late at night I sit alone
  and work on deadwood zen.
  Moonlight and the sound of pines are things we
  all know.
Hoge. How long the tree's been barren.
Hoin. On the rocky slope, blossoming.
Homyo. Wino, always stumbling.
Ichigen. Joshu exclaimed, "Dog's no Buddha".
  Seventy-eight awkward years.
Ikkyu Sojun. Form in Void.
  Void in Form.
Ikuo-Joun. This fellow, perfect in men's eyes.
Ikuo-Myotan. Seventy-two years I've hung.
Inada. Picking Up Stones.
Issa. Just by being / I'm here.
Jakushitsu. Refreshing, the wind against the
  waterfall.
Jinkag Haesim. At the Zendo.
  Because of the Rain.
Jinzu. In serving, serve.
Jones, J. Zen Baker.
Juo. Beyond the snatch of time, my daily life.
Kaigen. Old master held up fluff, The.
Kando. It's as if our heads were on fire, the
  way.
Kanemitsu-Kogun. My hands released at last,
  the cliff soars.
Kanzan-Shigyo. Where is the dragon's cave?
Karasumaru-Mitsuhiro. Beware of gnawing the
  ideogram of nothingness.
Keppo. Searching Him took.
Kikaku. May he who brings / Flowers tonight.
Kiko. Mount Sumeru—my fist!
Kishu. Once the goal's reached.
Kodo. Serving the Shogun in the capital.
Kokai. Taking hold, one's astray in nothingness.

Kosen. Blind horse trotting up an icy ledge, A.
Kuchu. Joshu's word—Nothingness.
Kukoku. Riding backwards this wooden horse.
Kyger. Philip Whalen's Hat.
Kyurin-Eki. Eighty-three years—at last.
Levitt, Peter. Watermelon and Zen students.
Liu Ch'ang-ch'ing. Rejoicing that the Zen
  Master Pao Has Arrived from Dragon
  Mountain.
Logue, C. Good Taste.
Maezumi, Taizan. Untransmittable and moving
  eastward.
Makusho, Layman. Loving old priceless things.
Manan. Unfettered at last, a traveling monk.
Manzan. One minute of sitting, one inch of
  Buddha.
Masaoka Shiki. Wicker chair / In pinetree's
  shade.
Moan. Clear, clear—clearest!
Mokusen. On Climbing the Mountain Where
  Buddha Trained.
Monju-Shindo. Joshu's "Oak in the courtyard".
Montag, T. April 30, 2001 (1).
Monk's bowl, The.
Mookam Choinul. For a Zen Seeker.
Mumon Gensen. Life: a cloud crossing the
  peak.
Munom-Ekai. Thunderbolt—eyes wide, A.
Muso Soseki. All worries and troubles.
  Beyond Light.
  Climbing Down the Snowy Mountain.
  Cloud Mountain.
  For Ko Who Has Come Back from China.
  For Myo's Departure for Anzen-ji.
  Many times the mountains have turned from
  green to yellow.
  Patriarch Peaks.
  Reply to Reizan Osho.
  Reply to Suzan Osho's Snow Poem.
  Thanks for Daisen Osho's Visit.
  Toki-no-Ge (Satori Poem).
  Vainly I dug for a perfect sky.
  Withered Zen.
Myoyu. Defying the power of speech, the Law
  Commission on Mount Vulture!
Naito Joso. No need to cling.
Nan-o-myo. Not falling, not ignoring.
Nanei. Splitting the void in half.
Nantembo. On New Year's Day.
Naong. Hyunsong Asks for an Enlightenment
  Song.
Nelson, M. Misunderstanding, A.
Nensho. Only genuine awakening results in
  that.
Pai, S. Circle, triangle, square.
Piper, P. Bowing.
  Christmas Eve, 2003.
  There is no ripple on the world.
Pritchard, N. Love Poem.
Ragain. Don't Expect Anything.
  Hungry Ghost Surrenders His Tackle Box, A.
Rakan-Keinan. Today Rakan, riding an iron
  horse.
Ramanujan. Chicago Zen.
Reid-Marr, David Tokuyu. Zen Mountain
  Center.
Reito. Ox bridle tossed, vows taken.
Reizan. Myriad differences resolved by sitting,
  all doors opened, The.
Ronci, Seido R. Diamond Cutter.
Rosenthal, G. Ghetto Dokusan.
Ryokan. Without a jot of ambition left.
Ryushu Shutaku. For all these years, my certain
  Zen.
  Mind set free in the Dharma-realm.
  Why bother with the world?
Ryuzan. Clear in the blue, the moon!
Saisho. On Joshu's Nothingness.
Seigen-yuiin. How vast karma.
Seiho. Sky's not high, earth not solid.
Seiken-Chiju. Twenty years a pilgrim.
Sekioku-Seikyo. This body won't pollute.
Sekishitsu-Soei. Fifty-three years / This clumsy
  ox has managed.
Seng-ts'an. Believing Mind, The.
Shih Shu. After Shih-te ("Perfumed springs

ripple over skeletal outcrops.").
Shinkichi Takahashi. Flight of the Sparrow.
Shishin-Goshin. Talking: seven steps, eight
  falls.
Shofu. No dust speck anywhere.
Shoichi. All-meaning circle, The.
Shokaku. High wind, cold moon.
Shozan. No mind, no Buddha.
Shunoku. After the spring song, "Vast
  emptiness, no holiness,".
Sŏ Chŏngju. Cuckoo and Skylark.
Soan. Sailing on Men River, I heard.
Sodo. Question clear, the answer deep, The.
Soen. Calm, activity—each has its use. At
  times.
  Master Joshu and the dog.
  On Visiting Shorin Temple, Where
  Bodhidharma Once Lived.
Sotoba, Layman. Mountain—Buddha's body,
  The.
Soyo Taeneung. Deathbed Song.
  To the Old Reverend Monk, Hwasung.
Sozan-Kyonin. Rootless tree, A.
Stryk, L. Awakening.
Suian. Traceless, no more need to hide.
Takuan. Though night after night.
Tan Taigi. Fallen leaves / Raking.
Tanzan. Madness, the way they gallop off to
  foreign shores!
Tarn. First Zen Abbess of America, The.
Tekkan. No mind, no Buddha, no being.
Tendo-Nyojo. Sixty-six years.
Tessho. Finally out of reach.
Tesshu. How heal the phantom body of its
  phantom ill.
  On Visiting Sokei, Where the Sixth Patriarch
  Lived.
Tokuo. Town's aflame with summer heat, The.
Tosui Unkei. Content with chipped bowl and
  tattered robe.
Tozan-Gyoso. Way's not for the blind.
Trigilio. Five Verses for Shariputra Mugged
  Outside His Building.
  Sitting, Wedding Morning.
Tsugen Jakurei. Not a mote in the light above.
Uncho. Forty-nine years / —What a din!
Ungo Kiyo. Whirled by the three passions,
  one's eyes go blind.
Wakuan-Shitai. Iron tree blooms.
Wenger, Michael. Zen Corners.
Whalen, P. Silence in the middle of traffic.
Will, C. Satori in Fauldhouse.
Xuanjian. Zen Sermon.
Yakusai, Layman. Deafening peal, A.
Yoketsu. Nothing longed for.
Yüan Hung-tao. On Receiving My Letter of
  Termination.
Yuishun. Why, it's but the motion of eyes and
  brows!
Zekkai Chushin. Void has collapsed upon the
  earth, The.
Zuian. Sky-piercing sword, gleaming cold.

See also **Buddha and Buddhism**

Zeus
Archilochus. Nothing is unexpected or sworn
  impossible.
  Zeus, Father Zeus, you've power over heaven.
Drummond, R. As Zeus.
Field. Prometheus fashioned man.
Greenwell, D. Demeter and Cora.
Homer. Dardanus...was son of Zeus the Lord of
  the clouds.
  "Here," said the Cloud-gatherer Zeus, "that is a
  journey you may well postpone."
Marlowe. What is't, sweet wag, I should deny
  thy youth?
Meleager. Hot day. Dying of thirst. Slake
  myself.
Moiro. Great Zeus was reared in Krete and no
  one.
Ovid. Zeus and Ganymede.
Sappho. Queen Hera, may your [graceful form].
Theognis. It's a thrill to love a boy: even
  Kronos' son, king of immortals, once longed
  for Ganymede.
Unknown. Zeus as an eagle came to Ganymede.

Yeats. Leda and the Swan.

Zinnias
Worth, V. Zinnias.

Zion
Malachi. Psalm of Silk.
Unknown. Old Ship of Zion, The [Maryland version].
Sabbath Has No End.

Zodiac
Doolittle, H. Splintered the crystal of identity.
Ilkov, Ani. Ram.
Zabolotsky [*or* Zabolotskii]. Signs of the Zodiac are fading, The.
Zawacki, Andrew. Astrelegy.

Zola, Émile
Stéfan, Jude. Emma Zola at Wimbledon Let's Say.

Zoos
Arnold, C. Extravagance of Zoos, The.
Barnett, R. Taxidermist at the Zoo, The.
Belev. Zoo.
Burnham, D. Maintaining the Species.
Butts, A. Belle Isle Men, The.

Clark, P. Zoo.
Cooley. Sleep of Beasts, The.
Davies, J. At the Zoo.
Davis, J. Zoo, The.
Deutsch. Creatures in the Zoo.
Edgar, M. Lion and Albert, The.
Fanning, R. Parable of the Boy and the Polar Bear.
Frost, C. St. Louis Zoo, The.
Hahn, K. Rockhopper, The.
Hartman, J. Shy breathing of the radiator, The. night sighs.
Hughes, T. Jaguar, The.
Jarrell, R. Woman at the Washington Zoo, The.
Kavanagh, P. Goldie Sapiens.
Ku Sang. Shame.
Lopez, B. Desert Reservation.
Mazur. In Houston.
McFadden, D. 7. Elephants.
5. Visit to the Zoo, A.
Michaux. Slices of Knowledge.
Ramanujan. In the Zoo.
Rilke. Panther, The.
Panther, The.

Panther, The.
Sandburg, C. Elephants Are Different to Different People.
Sears, P. One Polar Bear, The.
Tanikawa, S. Zoo.
Thackeray. At the Zoo.
Thế Lữ'. Green Nostalgia.
Tsanev, Stefan. Penguins.

Zukofsky, Louis
Niedecker. Cricket-song.
If I Were a Bird.
Palmer, M. Notes for Echo Lake 3.

Zulus
Adisa. Women at the Crossroad / (May Elegba Forever Guard the Right Doors).
Campbell, R. Zulu Girl, The.
Pfeiffer, E. Fight at Rorke's Drift, The.
Shapiro, H. National Cold Storage Company.

Zuni
Major, C. Lost in the Desert.
Merwin. Gardens of Zuñi, The.
See also **Native Americans**

Zurich, Switzerland
Celan. Zurich, at the Stork.